IUPUI
OCT 3 0 2008
LIBRARY

SCHOLARSHIPS, FELLOWSHIPS AND LOANS

ISSN 1058-5699

SCHOLARSHIPS, FELLOWSHIPS AND LOANS

A GUIDE TO EDUCATION-RELATED FINANCIAL AID PROGRAMS FOR STUDENTS AND PROFESSIONALS

Twenty-Fifth Edition

Detroit • New York • San Francisco • New Haven, Conn • Waterville, Maine • London

Scholarships, Fellowships and Loans, 25th Edition

Project Editor: Bohdan Romaniuk

Editorial Support Services: Wayne Fong

Composition and Electronic Prepress: Gary Leach

Manufacturing: Rita Wimberley

Product Manager: Jenai Mynatt

IUPUI
UNIVERSITY LIBRARY
755 W. MICHIGAN ST
INDIANAPOLIS, IN 46202-5195

© 2009 Gale, Cengage Learning

ALL RIGHTS RESERVED. No part of this work covered by the copyright herein may be reproduced, transmitted, stored, or used in any form or by any means graphic, electronic, or mechanical, including but not limited to photocopying, recording, scanning, digitizing, taping, Web distribution, information networks, or information storage and retrieval systems, except as permitted under Section 107 or 108 of the 1976 United States Copyright Act, without the written permission of the publisher.

This publication is a creative work fully protected by all applicable copyright laws, as well as by misappropriation, trade secret, unfair competition, and other applicable laws. The authors and editors of this work have added value to the underlying factual material herein through one or more of the following: unique and original selection, coordination, expression, arrangement, and classification of the information.

For product information and technology assistance, contact us at
Gale Customer Support, 1-800-877-4253.
For permission to use material from this text or product,
submit all requests online at **www.cengage.com/permissions.**
Further permissions questions can be emailed to
permissionrequest@cengage.com

While every effort has been made to ensure the reliability of the information presented in this publication, Gale, a part of Cengage Learning,does not guarantee the accuracy of the data contained herein. Gale accepts no payment for listing; and inclusion in the publication of any organization, agency, institution, publication, service, or individual does not imply endorsement of the editors or publisher. Errors brought to the attention of the publisher, and verified to the satisfaction of the publisher, will be corrected in future editions.

EDITORIAL DATA PRIVACY POLICY: Does this product contain information about you as an individual? If so, for more information about our editorial data privacy policies, please see our Privacy Statement at www.gale.cengage.com.

Gale
27500 Drake Rd.
Farmington Hills, MI, 48331-3535

ISBN-13: 978-0-7876-9944-4
ISBN-10: 0-7876-9944-6

ISSN 1058-5699

This title is also available as an e-book.
ISBN-13: 978-1-4144-4961-6
ISBN-10: 1-4144-4961-5
Contact your Gale sales representative for ordering information.

Printed in the United States of America
1 2 3 4 5 6 7 12 11 10 09 08

University Library of Columbus
4555 Central Avenue, LC 1600
Columbus, IN 47203-1892
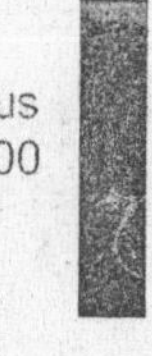

This edition of *Scholarships, Fellowships, and Loans (SFL)* provides access to almost 6,000 sources of education-related financial aid for students and professionals at all levels. *SFL*'s scope ranges from undergraduate and vocational/technical education through post-doctoral and professional studies. Students and others interested in education funding will find comprehensive information on a variety of programs in all educational areas, including:

- Architecture
- Area and Ethnic Studies
- Art
- Business
- Communications
- Computer Science
- Education
- Engineering
- Health Science
- Humanities
- Industrial Arts
- Language
- Law
- Literature
- Liberal Arts
- Library Science
- Life Science
- Medicine
- Mathematics
- Performing Arts
- Philosophy
- Physical Sciences
- Social Sciences
- Theology and Religion

SFL Provides Detailed Information on Awards

SFL provides all the information students need to complete their financial aid search. Entries include: administering organization name and address; purpose of award; qualifications and restrictions; selection criteria; award amount and number of awards granted; application details and deadlines; detailed contact information.

Additionally, look for the section on federal financial aid following the User's Guide for a quick summary of programs sponsored by the U.S. government, as well as information on the AmeriCorps program. We have also added a section that lists higher education agencies by state.

Five Indexes Allow Quick and Easy Access to Awards

Whether you are a high school student looking for basic undergraduate financial aid, a scientist investigating research grants, or a professional attempting to finance additional career training, SFL aids your search by providing access to awards through the following indexes:

Field of Study Index categorizes awards by very specific subject fields.

Legal Resident Index targets awards restricted to applicants from specific geographic locations.

Place of Study Index provides a handy guide to awards granted for study within specific states, provinces, or countries.

Special Recipient Index lists awards that are reserved for candidates who qualify by virtue of their gender, organizational affiliation, minority or ethnic background.

Sponsor and Scholarship Index provides a complete alphabetical listing of all awards and their administering organizations.

Catchwords

This issue of *SFL* includes catchwords of the organization on each corresponding page, to aid the user in finding a particular entry.

As we enter the twenty-first century, there is a growing need for a more highly-trained and educated work force. From political discussions and debates to reports from future-oriented think tanks and other groups, there is agreement that postsecondary education is a key to success. Yet how are students and their families to afford the already high (and constantly rising) cost of higher education? Searching for financial aid can be very tedious and difficult, even though hundreds of millions of dollars in aid reportedly go unclaimed every year.

Scholarships, Fellowships and Loans (SFL), the most comprehensive single directory of education-related financial aid available, can save you time, effort, and money by helping you to focus your search within the largest pool of awards and avoid pursuing aid for which you do not qualify. In most cases, the detailed descriptions contain enough information to allow you to decide if a particular scholarship is right for you to begin the application process. *SFL* lists almost 6,000 major awards available to U.S. and Canadian students for study throughout the world. Included are:

- scholarships, fellowships, and grants, which do not require repayment;
- loans, which require repayment either monetarily or through service;
- scholarship loans, which are scholarships that become loans if the recipient does not comply with the award's terms;
- internships and work study programs, which provide training, work experience, and (usually) monetary compensation; and
- awards and prizes that recognize excellence in a particular field.

Also included are other forms of assistance offered by associations, corporations, religious groups, fraternal organizations, foundations, and other private organizations and companies. *SFL* includes a broad representation of government-funded awards at the national and state levels, as well as a representative sampling of lesser-known and more narrowly focused awards, such as those of a strictly local nature or programs sponsored by small organizations. Financial aid programs administered and funded by individual colleges or universities are not included in *SFL*. Both need- and merit-based awards are included. Competition-based awards and prizes are included when they offer funds that support study or research and are intended to encourage further educational or professional growth.

Students of All Types Can Benefit

Traditional students as well as those returning to school, non- degree learners, those in need of retraining, and established professionals can use the funding sources listed in *SFL* for formal and non-formal programs of study at all levels:

- high school
- vocational
- undergraduate
- graduate
- postgraduate
- doctorate
- postdoctorate
- professional development

Content and Arrangement

Scholarships, Fellowships and Loans is organized into a main section containing descriptive listings of award programs and their administering organizations, and five indexes.

The main section, Sponsors and Their Scholarships, is arranged alphabetically by name of administering organization. Entries for each organization's awards appear immediately following the entry on the organization. Each entry contains detailed contact and descriptive information, often providing users with all the information they need to make a decision about applying.

The indexes provide a variety of specific access points to the information contained within the organization and award listings, allowing users to easily identify awards of interest.

Practical Tips on How to Find Financial Aid

While there are many education-related financial aid programs for students of all types and study levels, the competition for available funds is steadily increasing. You will improve the likelihood of meeting your financial aid goals if you:

- carefully assess your particular needs and preferences;
- consider any special circumstances or conditions that might qualify you for aid; and
- carefully research available aid programs.

The following pages list some general guidelines for making your way through the search and application process.

Start Your Search Early

Any search for financial aid is likely to be more successful if you begin early. If you allow enough time to complete all of the necessary steps, you will be more likely to identify a wide variety of awards for which you qualify with plenty of time to meet their application deadlines. This can increase your chances of obtaining aid.

Some experts recommend that you start this process up to two years before you think you will need financial assistance. While you will probably be able to obtain some support if you allow less time, you might overlook some important opportunities.

Some awards are given on a first-come, first-served basis, and if you do not file your application early enough, the aid will already be distributed. In many cases, if your application is late you will not be considered, even if you have met all of the other criteria.

An early start will also allow you to identify organizations that offer scholarships to members or participants, such as student or professional associations, in time to establish membership or otherwise meet their qualifying criteria.

Assess Your Needs and Goals

The intended recipients for financial aid programs and the purposes for which awards are established can vary greatly. Some programs are open to almost anyone, while others are restricted to very specific categories of recipients. The majority of awards fall somewhere in between. Your first step in seeking financial aid is to establish your basic qualifications as a potential recipient. The following are some general questions to ask yourself to help define your educational and financial needs and goals:

- What kinds of colleges or universities interest me?
- What careers or fields of study interest me?
- Do I plan to earn a degree?
- Am I only interested in financial aid that is a gift, or will I consider a loan or work study?
- In what parts of the country am I willing to live and study?

Leave No Stone Unturned

After you have defined your goals, the next step is to identify any special factors that might make you eligible for aid programs offered only to a restricted group. Examine this area carefully, and remember that even minor or unlikely connections may be worth checking. The most common qualifications and restrictions involve:

- citizenship
- community involvement or volunteer work
- creative or professional accomplishment
- employer
- financial need
- gender
- merit or academic achievement
- military or veteran status
- organization membership (such as a union, association, or fraternal group)
- place of residence
- race or ethnic group
- religious affiliation

With many awards, you may be eligible if your spouse, parents, or guardians meet certain criteria by status or affiliations. You should be aware of your parents' affiliations even if you don't live with one (or both) of them, or if they are deceased. And given enough lead time, it may be possible for you (or your parents) to join a particular organization, or establish necessary residence, in time for you to be eligible for certain funds.

Contact Financial Aid Offices

Most colleges, universities, and other educational institutions offer their own financial aid programs. Their financial aid offices may also have information on privately sponsored awards that are specifically designated for students at those institutions. Contact their respective financial aid offices to request applications and details for all of the aid programs they sponsor and/or administer.

Use *SFL* to Identify Awards Sponsored by Private Organizations and Corporations

Scholarships, Fellowships and Loans (SFL) is the most comprehensive single source of information on major education-related financial aid programs sponsored and administered by private organizations and companies for use by students and professionals. Using *SFL* as a starting point, you can quickly compile a substantial list of financial aid programs for which you may qualify by following these simple steps:

- Compile an initial list of awards offered in your field of study.
- If you have already chosen your field of study, look in the Field of Study Index to find listings of awards grouped by more precise disciplines (such as Accounting or Journalism). If you choose this approach, your initial list is likely to be shorter but more focused. Eliminate awards that cannot be used at your chosen level of study or that do not meet your financial needs. Are you an undergraduate only interested in scholarships? Are you a graduate student willing to participate in an internship or take out a loan? Consult the User's Guide to determine which of the study level categories and award types apply to your particular situation. Both indexes clearly note the study levels at which awards may be used. The Field of Study Index also lists the type of financial aid provided.
- Eliminate awards by citizenship, residence, and other restrictions (minority status, ethnic background, gender, organizational affiliation) that make you ineligible.
- If your list is based on the Field of Study Index, you will need to look under the section for qualifications in each descriptive listing to see what requirements apply.
- Read the descriptive listings for each of the award programs left on your list. The descriptive listings should contain all the information you need to decide if you qualify and should apply for each of the awards on your list.

Expand Your List of Possibilities

If you are willing to take the initiative and do a little extra digging, you should be able to add to your list of institution-related and privately sponsored programs. In most cases, the best possibilities fall into these two areas:

Government Agencies and Programs. The Sponsors and Their Scholarships main section includes a broad representation of award programs sponsored by federal and state governments. Since these listings are not meant to be exhaustive, you should be able to identify additional programs by contacting the government agencies responsible for education-related financial aid programs listed here. On the federal level, contact the U.S. Department of Education at 400 Maryland Ave., SW, Washington, DC 20202, or on their website at http://www.ed.gov, for up-to-date information on U.S. Government award programs. For a broad overview of federal financial aid, consult the Federal Programs section. Similarly, you may contact your state department of education for details on what is offered in your particular state. Please see the State Higher Education Agencies section for state-by-state listings.

Local Sources of Awards. A surprisingly large number of financial aid programs are sponsored by small and/or local organizations. *SFL* contains a representative sampling of such programs to encourage you to seek similar programs in your own geographic area. High school guidance counselors are often aware of local programs as well, and they can usually tell you how to get in touch with the sponsoring or administering organizations. Local newspapers are also rich sources of information on financial aid programs.

Allow Enough Time for the Application Process

The amount of time needed to complete the application process for individual awards will vary, so you should pay close attention to application deadlines. Some awards carry applications deadlines that require you to apply a year or more before your studies will begin. In general, allow plenty of time to:

- Write for official applications. You may not be considered for some awards unless you apply with the correct forms.
- Read all instructions carefully.
- Take note of application deadlines.
- Accurately and completely file all required supporting material, such as essays, school transcripts, and financial records. If you fail to answer certain questions, you may be disqualified even if you are a worthy candidate.
- Give references enough time to submit their recommendations. Teachers in particular get many requests for letters of recommendation and should be given as much advance notice as possible.

Make Sure You Qualify

Finally, don't needlessly submerge yourself in paperwork. If you find you don't qualify for a particular award, don't apply for it. Instead, use your time and energy to find and apply for more likely sources of aid.

Available in Electronic Formats

Licensing. *Scholarships, Fellowships and Loans* is available for licensing. The complete database is provided in a fielded format and is deliverable on such media as disk or CD-ROM. For more information, contact Gale's Business Development group at 1-800-877-GALE, or visit our website at http://gale.cengage.com/bizdev/.

The Directory is also available online as part of the Gale Directory Library. For more information, call 1-800-877-GALE.

Comments and Suggestions Welcome

We welcome reader suggestions regarding new and previously unlisted organizations and awards. Please send your suggestions to:

Scholarships, Fellowships and Loans
Gale, Cengage Learning
27500 Drake Rd.
Farmington Hills, MI 48331-3535
Phone: (248) 699-4253
Toll-free: 800-347-4253
Fax: (248) 699-8070
Email: Bob.Romaniuk@cengage.com

Scholarships, Fellowships and Loans is comprised of a main section containing descriptive listings on award programs and their administering organizations, and five indexes that aid users in identifying relevant information. Each of these sections is described in detail below.

Sponsors and Their Scholarships

SFL contains two types of descriptive listings:

- brief entries on the organizations that sponsor or administer specific award programs
- desriptive entries on the award programs themselves

Entries are arranged alphabetically by administering organization; awards administered by each organization follow that organization's listings. Entries contain detailed contact and descriptive information. Users are strongly encouraged to read the descriptions carefully and pay particular attention to the various eligibility requirements before applying for awards.

The following sample organization and award entries illustrate the kind of information that is or might be included in these entries. Each item of information is preceded by a number, and is explained in the paragraph with the same number on the following pages.

Sample Entry

1 3445
2 Microscopy Society of America
3 4 Barlows Landing Rd., Ste. 8 Woods Hole, MA 02543
4 *Ph:* (508) 563-1155
5 *Fax:* (508) 563-1211
6 *Free:* 800-538-3672
7 *E-mail:* businessofficemsa.microscopy.com
8 *URL:* http://www.msa.microscopy.com
9 3446
10 MSA Presidential Student Awards
11 *(Graduate, Undergraduate/*
12 *Award*

13 Purpose: To recognize outstanding original research by students. **14** Focus: Biological Clinical Sciences—Microscopy, Physical Sciences—Microscopy. **15** Qualif.: Candidate may be of any nationality, but must be enrolled at a recognized college or university in the United States at the time of the MSA annual meeting. **16** Criteria: Selection is done based on the applicant's career objectives, academic record, and financial need. **17** Funds Avail.: Registration and round-trip travel to the MSA annual meeting, plus a stipend to defray lodging and other expenses. **18** Number awarded: 5. **19** To Apply: Write to MSA for application form and guidelines. **20** Deadline: March 15. **21** Remarks: Established in 1979. **22** Contact: Alternate phone number: 800-538-EMSA.

Descriptions of Numbered Elements

1 Organization Entry Number. Administering organizations are listed alphabetically. Each entry is followed by an alphabetical listing of its awards. All entries (organization and award) are numbered in a single sequence. These numbers are used as references in the indexes.

2 Organization Name. The name of the organization administering the awards that follow.

3 Mailing Address. The organization's permanent mailing address is listed when known; in some cases an award address is given.

4 Telephone Number. The general telephone number for the administering organization. Phone numbers pertaining to specific awards are listed under "Contact" in the award description.

5 Fax Number. The facsimile number for the administering organization. Fax numbers pertaining to specific awards are included under "Contact" in the award description.

6 Toll-free Number. The toll-free number for the administering organization. Toll-free numbers pertaining to specific awards are included under "Contact" in the award description.

7 E-mail Address. The electronic mail address for the administering organization. Electronic mail addresses pertaining to specific awards are included under "Contact" in the award description.

8 URL. The web address for the administering organization.

9 Award Entry Number. Awards are listed alphabetically following the entry for their administering organizations. All entries (organization and award) are numbered in a single sequence. These numbers are used as references in the indexes.

10 Award Name. Names of awards are always listed. Organization titles or acronyms have been added to generic award names (for example, MSA Undergraduate Scholarships, Canadian Council Fiction Writing Grant, etc.) to avoid confusion.

▌11▌ Study Level. The level of study for which the award may be used. One or more of the following terms will be listed:

- All: not restricted to a particular level.
- High School: study at the secondary level.
- Vocational: study leading to postsecondary awards, certificates, or diplomas requiring less than two years of study.
- 2 Year: study leading to a bachelor's degree within two years
- 4 Year: study leading to a bachelor's degree within four years
- Undergraduate: study immediately beyond the secondary level, including associate, colleges and universities, junior colleges, technical institutes leading to a bachelor's degree, and vocational technical schools.
- Graduate: study leading to an M.A., M.S., LL.B., LL.M., and other intermediate degrees.
- Master's: study leading specifically to a master's degree, such as a M.A., M.S., or M.B.A.
- Postgraduate: study beyond the graduate level not specifically leading to a degree.
- Doctorate: study leading to a Ph.D., Ed.D., Sc.D., M.D., D.D.S., D.O., J.D., and other terminal degrees.
- Postdoctorate: study beyond the doctorate level; includes awards intended for professional development when candidates must hold a doctoral degree to qualify.
- Professional Development: career development not necessarily restricted by study.

▌12▌ Award Type. The type or category of award. One or more of the following terms will be listed:

- Award: generally includes aid given in recognition and support of excellence, including awards given through music and arts competitions. Non-monetary awards and awards given strictly for recognition are not included.
- Fellowship: awards granted for graduate- or postgraduate- level research or education that do not require repayment.
- Grant: includes support for research, travel, and creative, experimental, or innovative projects.
- Internship: training and work experience programs. Internships that do not include compensation of some type are not included.
- Loan: aid that must be repaid either monetarily or through service. Some loans are interest-free, others are not.
- Prize: funds awarded as the result of a competition or contest. Prizes that are not intended to be used for study or to support professional development are not included.
- Scholarships: support for formal educational programs that does not require repayment.
- Scholarship Loan: a scholarship that becomes a loan if the recipient does not comply with the terms.
- Work Study: combined study and work program for which payment is received.
- Other: anything that does not fit the other categories, such as a travel award.

▌13▌ Purpose. The purpose for which the award is granted is listed here when known.

▌14▌ Focus. The field(s) of study that the recipient must be pursuing.

▌15▌ Qualif. Information regarding applicant eligibility. Some examples of qualification requirements include the following: academic record, citizenship, financial need, organizational affiliation, minority or ethnic background, residency, and gender.

▌16▌ Criteria Information concerning selection criteria.

▌17▌ Funds Avail. The award dollar amounts are included here along with other relevant funding information, such as the time period covered by the award, a breakdown of expenses covered (e.g., stipends, tuition and fees, travel and living allowances, equipment funds, etc.), the amount awarded to the institution, loan repayment schedules, service-in-return-for-funding agreements, and other obligations.

▌18▌ Number awarded. Typical number of awards distributed.

▌19▌ To Apply. Application guidelines, requirements, and other information.

▌20▌ Deadline. Application due dates, notification dates (the date when the applicant will be notified of receipt or denial of award), disbursement dates, and other relevant dates.

▌21▌ Remarks. Any additional information concerning the award.

▌22▌ Contact. When contact information differs from that given for the administering organization, relevant addresses, telephone and fax numbers, and names of specific contact persons are listed here. When the address is that of the administering organization, the entry number for the organization is provided.

Indexes

Field of Study Index classifies awards by one or more of 480 specific subject categories, allowing users to easily target their search by specific area of study. Citations are arranged alphabetically under all appropriate subject terms. Each citation is followed by the study level and award type, which appear in parentheses and can be used to narrow the search even further.

Legal Residence Index lists awards that are restricted by the applicant's residence of legal record. Award citations are arranged alphabetically by country and subarranged by region, state or province (for U.S. and Canada). Each citation is followed by the study level and award type, which appear in parentheses and can be used to eliminate inappropriate awards.

Place of Study Index lists awards that carry restrictions on where study can take place. Award citations are arranged alphabetically under the following geographic headings:

- United States
- United States—by Region
- United States—by State
- Canada
- Canada—by Province
- International
- International—by Region
- International—by Country

Each citation is followed by the study level and award type, which appear in parentheses.

Special Recipient Index lists awards that carry restrictions or special qualifying factors relating to applicant affiliation. This index allows users to quickly identify awards relating to the following categories:

- African American
- Asian American
- Disabled
- Employer
- Ethnic
- Female
- Hispanic American
- Male
- Military
- Minority
- Native American
- Religion

Awards are listed under all appropriate headings. Each citation includes information on study level and award type, which appear in parentheses and can be used to further narrow the search. Users interested in awards restricted to particular minorities should also look under the general Minorities heading, which lists awards targeted for minorities but not restricted to any particular minority group.

Sponsor and Scholarship Index lists, in a single alphabetic sequence, all of the administering organizations, awards, and acronyms included in *SFL*.

Federal aid for college students is available through a variety of programs administered by the U.S. Department of Education. Most colleges and universities participate in federal programs, but there are exceptions. Contact a school's financial aid office to find out if it is a participating institution. If it participates, the student works with financial aid counselors to determine how much aid can be obtained.

Aid for students comes in three forms: grants (gifts to the student), loans (which must be repaid), and work-study jobs (a job for the student while enrolled in which his/her pay is applied to his school account). These types of aid are further explained below. More information can be found at http://www.ed.gov.

Grants

Pell Grants are intended to provide funds for any undergraduate student (who does not already have a degree) who wishes to attend college regardless of family financial background. They are available through the financial aid office at the school. The maximum Pell Grant award for the 2008-2009 award year (July 1, 2008 to June 30, 2009) is $4,731

Federal Supplemental Educational Opportunity Grants (FSEOG) are intended for students with exceptional financial need, these grants are typically for smaller amounts (between $100 and $4,000) than Pell Grants. They are available on a limited basis.

Loans

Student loans are available a variety of ways. Loans may not be taken out for more than the cost of attendance at the school, which is determined by the financial aid administrator. Grants and other forms of aid are taken into consideration when determining the amount a student will be allowed to borrow. Loan amounts may be reduced if a student receives other forms of aid. Loans are divided into two types, subsidized and unsubsidized:

Subsidized loans: the federal government pays the interest on the loan until after schooling is complete.

Unsubsidized loans: the student incurs the interest charges while in school, but payment of the charges may be deferred until schooling is complete. The advantage of unsubsidized loans is that there are usually fewer restrictions against obtaining them. Amounts available through these programs vary depending on academic level. The total debt a student or a student's parents may accumulate for that student is $31,000 for a dependent undergraduate student, $57,000 for an independent undergraduate student (with a limit of $23,000 in subsidized loans), and $138,500 for a graduate or professional student (with a limit of $65,500 in subsidized loans).

Available Funding Programs Direct Loan Program

These low-interest loans bypass lending institutions such as banks. They are a direct arrangement between the government and the student (administered by the school). There are four repayment options for the Direct Loan program: the Income Contingent Repayment Plan, the Extended Repayment Plan, the Graduated Repayment Plan, and the Standard Repayment Plan.

Direct subsidized loans may be taken out for a maximum of $3,500 by incoming freshmen, while juniors and seniors may borrow up to a maximum of $5,500. The amounts for independent undergraduate students range from $9,500 to $12,500 per year. Independent students face some restrictions on the amount of subsidized funds they can receive from the program. At least half of the funds borrowed through the Direct Loan program by independent students must come from unsubsidized loans. Graduate students may borrow up to $20,500 directly, $8,500 of which must be in unsubsidized loans.

Federal Family Education Loans (FFEL)/Stafford Loans This program provides funds to the lending institution(s) of the student's choice. Before borrowing the funds, the student must complete a Free Application for Federal Student Aid (FAFSA) and a Federal Stafford Loan Application (FSLA). Both forms are available at participating schools' financial aid offices and on the Internet at http://www.ed.gov. There are three repayment options for FFEL/Stafford Loans:

Fixed, Graduated, and Income-Sensitive. Any FFEL/Stafford loan must be paid back within ten years.

This program is also divided into subsidized and unsubsidized loans. However, students may not borrow simultaneously from this program and the Direct Loan program. Students may borrow separately subsidized and unsubsidized funds from either program. The maximum amounts that can be borrowed through this program are the same as through the Direct Loan program.

Direct and FFEL/Stafford Program Loans for Parents (PLUS) Parents may borrow for their children's education through the aforementioned Federal Loan programs. They are responsible for the repayment of the loans. The maximum amount to be borrowed is the cost of attending the school minus other forms of aid already obtained. The interest rate on the loans is variable and has a slightly higher ceiling (8.5%) than when students themselves bear the responsibility of repayment (7.9%). Parents who borrow through the FFEL/Stafford program make arrangements with the lender for repayment.

With the Direct PLUS loan, parents fill out a Direct PLUS Loan Application, available at the school's financial aid office. The funds are disbursed to the school. Parents may choose from three repayment plans: Standard, Extended, or Graduated. To obtain funds for their children through the FFEL/Stafford Program, parents make the arrangements with the lending institution. The school is not involved in the application process.

Perkins Loan Program The Perkins Loan program allows students who have unusual financial need to borrow funds not otherwise available from other loan or grant programs. Up to $4,000 is available to undergraduates each year (up to $6,000 for graduate students). These loans have a fixed interest rate of 5%. Perkins Loans must be repaid within ten years.

Federal Work-Study Program Work-study is an arrangement that allows students to work on campus while they are enrolled to help pay their expenses. The federal government pays the majority of the student's wages, although the department where the student works also contributes. The employment must be relevant to the student's field of study and only so much time per semester may be devoted to the job. If the student earns the amount of aid prior to the end of the semester, work is terminated for the duration of the award period.

Other Considerations

Application: Applying for federal student aid is free. All federal aid is obtained by first completing a Free Application for Federal Student Aid (FAFSA). After the application is submitted, it will be processed by the Department of Education. The student then receives a Student Aid Report (SAR), which contains a figure for Expected Family Contribution. This is the amount that the student should plan on providing from non-federal sources in order to attend school.

Dependency: If a student is eligible for independent status, more money may be available in the form of loans. The interest rates and the programs for repayment, however, are the same. Independent status provides more financial aid for students who do not have the benefit of parental financial contributions.

Deadline: The FAFSA online application must be received by June 30 for the following school year. Applicants are encouraged to apply as soon as possible after January 1 of the year they plan to enroll, but no earlier.

Special Circumstances: The financial aid counselor at the school will often listen to extenuating circumstances such as unexpected medical expenses, private education expenses for other family members, or recent unemployment when evaluating requests for assistance.

Contact Information for Federal Financial Aid Programs

Call (800)433-3243 to have questions answered or to request the *Student Guide to Financial Aid*; (319) 337-5665 to find out if your application has been processed; (800) 730-8913 (TDD) if you are hearing impaired; (800) 647-8733 to report fraud, waste, or abuse of federal student aid funds; or visit http://www.ed.gov for application forms, guidelines, and general information.

President Clinton launched this volunteer community service program in September 1993 through the *National and Community Service Trust Act*, aimed at helping college-bound young people pay for their education while serving their communities. AmeriCorps volunteers receive minimum wage, health benefits, and a grant toward college for up to two years.

Funds for the program are distributed by the Federal government in the form of grants to qualifying organizations and community groups with the goal of achieving direct results in addressing the nation's critical education, human services, public safety, and environmental needs at the community level. The program provides meaningful opportunities for Americans to serve their country in organized efforts, fostering citizen responsibility, building community, and providing educational opportunities for those who make a substantial commitment to service.

The AmeriCorps programs are run by not-for-profit organizations or partnerships, institutions of higher learning, local governments, school or police districts, states, Native American tribes, and federal agencies. Examples of participating programs include Habitat for Humanity, the American Red Cross, Boys and Girls Clubs, and local community centers and places of worship. Volunteers have nearly 1,000 different groups from which to choose. The AmeriCorps Pledge: "I will get things done for America to make our people safer, smarter, and healthier. I will bring Americans together to strengthen our communities. Faced with apathy, I will take action. Faced with conflict, I will seek a common ground. Faced with adversity, I will persevere. I will carry this commitment with me this year and beyond. I am an AmeriCorps Member and I am going to get things done."

Eligibility and Selection for Service in AmeriCorps

Citizens and legal resident aliens who are 17 years of age or older are eligible to serve in AmeriCorps before, during, or after post- secondary education. In general, participants must be high school graduates or agree to achieve their GED prior to receiving education awards. Individual programs select service participants on a nondiscriminatory and nonpolitical basis. There are national and state- wide recruiting information systems and a national pool of potential service volunteers.

Term of Service

One full-time term of service is a minimum of 1,700 hours over the course of one year or less; one part-time term of service is at least 900 hours over two years or less. Short-term service (such as a summer program) provides eligibility for reduced part-time status.

Compensation

You will receive a modest living allowance, health insurance, student loan deferment, and training. After you complete your term of service, you will receive an education award to help pay for your education. Serve part-time and you will receive a portion of the full amount. Full-time participants receive an award of $4,725, part-time participants receive $2,362.50, and reduced part-time participants will receive $1,000 or less. Participants may receive up to two awards.

How Can I Use an Award?

These awards may be used to repay qualified existing or future student loans, to pay all or part of the cost of attending a qualified institute of higher education (including some vocational programs), or to pay expenses while participating in an approved school-to-work program. Awards must be used within seven years of completion of service.

Contact

Individuals interested in participating in AmeriCorps national service programs should apply directly. For basic program information, individuals can call the AmeriCorps Information Hotline at 1-800-942- 2677 or visit their Web site at http://www.americorps.org or http://www.learnandserve.org.

State Higher Education Agencies

The following is an alphabetic state-by-state listing of agencies located in the United States. Many of these agencies administer special federal award programs, as well as state-specific awards, such as the Tuition Incentive Program (TIP) offered by the state of Michigan for low-income students to receive free tuition at community colleges. Financial aid seekers should contact the agency in their home state for more information.

ALABAMA

Alabama Comm. on Higher Education
P.O. Box 302000
Montgomery, AL 36130-2000
(334)242-1998
http://www.ache.state.al.us

ALASKA

Alaska Comm. on Postsecondary Education
3030 Vintage Blvd.
Juneau, AK 99801-7100
(907)465-2962
http://www.alaskaadvantage.state.ak.us/

ARIZONA

Arizona Comm. for Postsecondary Education
2020 N. Central Ave., Ste. 550
Phoenix, AZ 85004-4503
(602)258-2435
http://www.azhighered.org

ARKANSAS

Arkansas Dept. of Higher Education
114 E. Capitol Ave.
Little Rock, AR 72201-3818
(501)371-2030
http://www.adhe.arknet.edu

CALIFORNIA

California Student Aid Comm.
PO Box 419026
Rancho Cordova, CA 95741-9026
(916)526-8047
http://www.csac.ca.gov

COLORADO

Colorado Dept. of Higher Education
1560 Broadway, Ste. 1600
Denver, CO 80202
(303)866-2723
http://www.state.co.us/cche_dir/hecche.html

CONNECTICUT

Connecticut Dept. of Higher Education
61 Woodland St.
Hartford, CT 06105-2326
(860)947-1800
http://www.ctdhe.org

DELAWARE

Delaware Higher Education Comm.
820 N. French St., 5th Fl.
Carvel State Office Bldg.
Wilmington, DE 19801
(302)577-3240
http://www.doe.k12.de.us/services/guide/highered.shtml

DISTRICT OF COLUMBIA

District of Columbia Dept. of Human Services
Office of Postsecondary Education, Research, and Assistance
2100 Martin Luther King, Jr. Ave. SE, Ste. 401
Washington, DC 20020
(202)698-2400

FLORIDA

Office of Student Financial Assistance
Dept. of Education
325 W. Gaines St.
Turlington Bldg., Ste. 1514
Tallahassee, FL 32399-0400
(904)487-0049
http://www.floridastudentfinancialaid.org

GEORGIA

Georgia Student Finance Commission
2082 E. Exchange Pl., Ste. 200
Tucker, GA 30084
(770)724-9000
http://www.gsfc.org/gsfcnew/index.cfm

HAWAII

Hawaii State Postsecondary Education Comm.
2444 Dole St., Rm. 209
Honolulu, HI 96822-2302
(808)956-8213

IDAHO

Idaho State Board of Education
PO Box 83720
Boise, ID 83720-0037
(208)334-2270
http://www.boardofed.idaho.gov

ILLINOIS

Illinois Student Assistance Comm.
1755 Lake Cook Rd.
Deerfield, IL 60015-5209
(847)948-8500
http://www.collegezone.com

INDIANA

State Student Assistance Comm. of Indiana
150 W. Market St., Ste. 500
Indianapolis, IN 46204-2811

(317)232-2350
www.in.goc/ssaci/

IOWA

Iowa College Student Aid Comm.
200 10th St., 4th Fl.
Des Moines, IA 50309
(515)281-3501
http://www.iowacollegeaid.org

KANSAS

Kansas Board of Regents
1000 SW Jackson St., Ste. 520
Topeka, KS 66612-1368
(785)296-3421
http://www.kansasregents.org

KENTUCKY

Kentucky Higher Education Assistance Authority
PO Box 798
Frankfurt, KY 40602-0798
(800)928-8926
http://www.kheaa.com

LOUISIANA

Louisian Office of Student Financial Assistance
PO Box 91202
Baton Rouge, LA 70821-9202
(225)922-1012
http://www.osfa.state.la.us

MAINE

Maine Education Assistance Division
Finance Authority of Maine (FAME)
5 Community Dr.
Augusta, ME 04332-0949
(207)623-3263
http://www.famemaine.com

MARYLAND

Maryland Higher Education Comm.
839 Bestgate Rd., Ste. 400
Annapolis, MD 21401
(410)260-4500
http://www.mhec.state.md.us

MASSACHUSETTS

Massachusetts Board of Higher Education
One Ashburton Pl., Rm. 1401
Boston, MA 02108-1696
(617)994-6950
http://www.mass.edu

MICHIGAN

Michigan Higher Education Student Loan Authority
Student Financial Services Bureau
P.O. Box 30047
Lansing, MI 48909-7547
(800)642-5626
http://www.michigan.gov/mistudentaid

MINNESOTA

Minnesota Office of Higher Education
1450 Energy Park Dr., Ste. 350
St. Paul MN 55108-5227
(651)642-0567
http://www.ohe.state.mn.us/index.cfm

MISSISSIPPI

Mississippi Postsecondary Education Financial Assistance Board
3825 Ridgewood Rd.
Jackson, MS 39211
(601)432-6997
http://www.ihl.state.ms.us

MISSOURI

Missouri Dept. of Higher Education
3515 Amazonas Dr.
Jefferson City, MO 65109-5717
(573)751-2361
http://www.dhe.mo.gov/

MONTANA

Montana Board of Regents
Office of Commissioner of Higher Education
Montana University System
46 N. Last Chance Gulch
PO Box 203201
Helena, MT 59620-3201
(406)444-6570
http://www.mus.edu

NEBRASKA

Nebraska Coordinating Comm. for Postsecondary Education
P.O. Box 95005
Lincoln, NE 68509-5005
(402)471-2847
http://www.ccpe.state.ne.us/PublicDoc/CCPE/Default.asp

NEVADA

Nevada Department of Education
700 East Fifth St.
Carson City, NV 89701
(775)687-9200
http://www.nde.state.nv.us

NEW HAMPSHIRE

New Hampshire Postsecondary Education Comm.
3 Barrell Court
Concord, NH 03301
(603)271-2555
http://www.state.nh.us/postsecondary

NEW JERSEY

Higher Education Student Assistance Authority
Quakerbridge Plaza, Bldg. 4
P.O. Box 540
Trenton, NJ 08625-0540
(609)588-3226
http://www.hesaa.org

NEW MEXICO

New Mexico Dept. of Higher Education
1068 Cerillos Rd.
Santa Fe, NM 87505-1650
(505)476-6500
http://www.hed.state.nm.us

NEW YORK

New York State Higher Education Svcs. Corp.
99 Washington Ave.
Albany, NY 12255
(518)473-7087
http://www.hesc.com

NORTH CAROLINA

North Carolina State Education Assistance Authority
PO Box 13663
Research Triangle Park, NC 27709
(919)549-8614
http://www.ncseaa.edu

NORTH DAKOTA

North Dakota University System
North Dakota Student Financial Assistance Program

600 E. Boulevard Ave., Dept. 215
Bismarck, ND 58505-0230
(701)328-2960
http://www.ndus.edu

OHIO

Ohio Board of Regents
State Grants and Scholarships Dept.
P.O. Box 182452
Columbus, OH 43218-2452
(614)466-7420
http://www.regents.ohio.gov/

OKLAHOMA

Oklahoma State Regents for Higher Education
Oklahoma Guaranteed Loan Program
655 Research Pkwy.
Oklahoma City, OK 73104
(405)225-9100
http://www.okhighered.org

OREGON

Oregon Student Assistance Comm.
1500 Valley River Dr., Ste. 100
Eugene, OR 97401
(541)687-7400
http://www.osac.state.or.us

PENNSYLVANIA

Pennsylvania Higher Education Assistance Agency
1200 N. 7th St.
Harrisburg, PA 17102-1444
(717)720-2800
http://www.pheaa.org

RHODE ISLAND

Rhode Island Higher Education Assistance Authority
560 Jefferson Blvd., Ste. 100
Warwick, RI 02886
(401)736-1100
http://www.riheaa.org

SOUTH CAROLINA

South Carolina Comm. on Higher Education
1333 Main St., Ste. 200
Columbia, SC 29201
(803)737-2260
http://www.che400.state.sc.us

SOUTH DAKOTA

South Dakota Education Assistance Corp.
115-1st Ave., SW
Aberdeen, SD 57401
(605)225-6423
http://www2.eac-easci.org/welcome.shtml

TENNESSEE

Tennessee Higher Education Comm.
Parkway Towers
404 James Robertson Pkwy., Ste. 1900
Nashville, TN 37243-0830
(615)741-3605
http://www.state.tn.us/thec

TEXAS

Texas Higher Education Coordinating Board
P.O. Box 12788
Austin, TX 78711
(512)427-6101
http://www.thecb.state.tx.us

UTAH

Utah State Board of Regents
Board of Regents Building, The Gateway
60 South 400 West
Salt Lake City, UT 84101-1284
(801)321-7100
http://www.utahsbr.edu

VERMONT

Vermont Student Assistance Corp.
10 E. Allen St.
P.O. Box 2000
Winooski, VT 05404
(802)655-9602
http://www.vsac.org

VIRGINIA

State Council of Higher Education for Virginia
James Monroe Bldg.
101 N. 14th St., 9th Fl.
Richmond, VA 23219
(804)225-2600
http://www.schev.edu

WASHINGTON

Washington State Higher Education Coordinating Board
917 Lakeridge Way
P.O. Box 43430
Olympia, WA 98504-3430
(360)753-7800
http://www.hecb.wa.gov

WEST VIRGINIA

West Virginia Higher Education Policy Comm.
1018 Kanawha Blvd., E., Ste. 700
Charleston, WV 25301
(304)558-2101
http://www.hepc.wvnet.edu

WISCONSIN

Wisconsin Higher Education Aids Board
131 W. Wilson St., Rm. 902
Madison, WI 53707-7885
(608)267-2206
http://heab.state.wi.us

WYOMING

Wyoming Community College Comm.
2020 Carey Ave., 8th Fl.
Cheyenne, WY 82002
(307)777-7763
http://www.commission.wcc.edu

U.S. State Abbreviations

AK Alaska
AL Alabama
AR Arkansas
AZ Arizona
CA California
CO Colorado
CT Connecticut
DC District of Columbia
DE Delaware
FL Florida
GA Georgia
GU Guam
HI Hawaii
IA Iowa
ID Idaho
IL Illinois
IN Indiana
KS Kansas
KY Kentucky
LA Louisiana
MA Massachusetts
MD Maryland
ME Maine
MI Michigan
MN Minnesota
MO Missouri
MS Mississippi
MT Montana
NC North Carolina
ND North Dakota
NE Nebraska
NH New Hampshire
NJ New Jersey
NM New Mexico
NV Nevada
NY New York
OH Ohio
OK Oklahoma
OR Oregon
PA Pennsylvania
PR Puerto Rico
RI Rhode Island
SC South Carolina
SD South Dakota
TN Tennessee
TX Texas
UT Utah
VA Virginia
VI Virgin Islands
VT Vermont
WA Washington
WI Wisconsin
WV West Virginia
WY Wyoming

Canadian Province Abbreviations

AB Alberta
BC British Columbia
MB Manitoba
NB New Brunswick
NL Newfoundland and Labrador
NS Nova Scotia
NT Northwest Territories
ON Ontario
PE Prince Edward Island
QC Quebec
SK Saskatchewan
YT Yukon Territory

Other Abbreviations

ACT American College Testing Program
B.A. Bachelor of Arts
B.Arch. Bachelor of Architecture
B.F.A. Bachelor of Fine Arts
B.S. Bachelor of Science
B.Sc. Bachelor of Science
CSS College Scholarship Service
D.D.S. Doctor of Dental Science/Surgery
D.O. Doctor of Osteopathy
D.Sc. Doctor of Science
D.S.W. Doctor of Social Work
D.V.M. Doctor of Veterinary Medicine
D.V.M.S. Doctor of Veterinary Medicine and Surgery
D.V.S. Doctor of Veterinary Science
FAFSA Free Application for Federal Student Aid
FWS Federal Work Study
GED General Education Development Certificate
GPA Grade Point Average
GRE Graduate Record Examination
J.D. Doctor of Jurisprudence
LL.B. Bachelor of Law
LL.M. Master of Law
LSAT Law School Admission Test
M.A. Master of Arts
M.Arch. Master of Architecture
M.B.A. Master of Business Administration
M.D. Doctor of Medicine
M.Div. Master of Divinity
M.F.A. Master of Fine Arts
MIA Missing in Action
M.L.S. Master of Library Science
M.N. Master of Nursing
M.S. Master of Science
M.S.W. Master of Social Work
O.D. Doctor of Optometry
Pharm.D. Doctor of Pharmacy
Ph.D. Doctor of Philosophy
POW Prisoner of War
PSAT Preliminary Scholastic Aptitude Test
ROTC Reserve Officers Training Corps
SAR Student Aid Report
SAT Scholastic Aptitude Test
Sc.D. Doctor of Science
TDD Telephone Device for the Deaf
Th.d. Doctor of Theology
U.N. United Nations
U.S. United States

1 ■ 101st Airborne Division Association

PO Box 929
Fort Campbell, KY 42223-0929
Ph: (931)431-0199
E-mail: 101stairbornedivisionassociation@comcast.net
URL: http://www.screamingeagle.org

2 ■ Chappie Hall Scholarship Program *(Graduate, Postgraduate, Undergraduate/Scholarship)*

Purpose: To provide financial assistance to students who have the potential of becoming assets to the nation. **Focus:** General Studies. **Qualif.:** Applicant's parents, grandparents, spouse, living or deceased must be a former or present member of the 101st Airborne Division; must have at least 2.5 GPA; must demonstrate financial need. **Criteria:** Selection is done based on the applicant's career objectives, academic record, financial need and insight gained from the letter requesting consideration, as well as letters of recommendation.

Funds Avail.: $1,000. **Number Awarded:** 11. **To Apply:** Applicant must submit complete application package. **Deadline:** May 31. **Contact:** Executive Secretary-Treasurer, phone: 270-439-0445, email: sambass101@comcast.net.

3 ■ AAUW Legal Advocacy Fund

1111 16th St. NW
Washington, DC 20036
Ph: (202)785-7700
Fax: (202)872-1425
E-mail: helpline@aauw.org
URL: http://www.aauw.org

4 ■ AAUW Legal Advocacy Fund American Fellowships *(Doctorate/Fellowship)*

Purpose: To support women doctoral candidates completing dissertations or scholars seeking funds for postdoctoral research leave from accredited institutions. **Focus:** General studies. **Qualif.:** Applicants for postdoctoral fellowships must be US citizens and must hold a Ph.D., Ed.D., D.B.A., M.F.A., D.M.; Applicants for the summer/short-term must be US citizens and will hold a doctorate or M.F.A. degree; Applicants for dissertation must be US citizens or permanent residents, must be in a program other than an engineering program, must be in or entering the final year of dissertation, must have a dissertation proposal approved by the committee, must have all course work completed and have passed all preliminary exams. **Criteria:** Candidates are evaluated on the basis of scholarly excellence, teaching experience, and active commitment to helping women and girls through service in their communities, professions, or fields of research.

Funds Avail.: $30,000 (postdoctoral research leave fellowship); $20,000 (dissertation fellowship); $6,000 (summer/short-term research publication grant). **To Apply:** Candidates may apply for only one of the awards. A complete application must consist of: application with budget information, narrative autobiography, statement of project (description of project, design, research methodology and excepted contribution to knowledge); clear statement of financial need; name(s) of the university, institution, or other location where study will be carried out; and three recommendations. All documents must be postmarked by the deadline in hard copy format: Transcript(s)/Proof of Doctorate; Institution Certification Form; Institution Letter; and Filing Fee. **Deadline:** November 15. **Contact:** AAUW Educational Foundation Dept. 60, 301 ACT Drive, Iowa City, IA 52243-4030.

5 ■ AAUW Legal Advocacy Fund Career Development Grants *(Professional Development/Grant)*

Purpose: To support women who hold a bachelor's degree and are preparing to advance their careers, change careers, or re-enter the work force. **Focus:** General studies. **Qualif.:** Applicants must be US citizens or permanent residents who hold a bachelor's degree or specialized training in technical or professional fields. **Criteria:** Special consideration is given to AAUW members, women of color, and women pursuing their first advanced degree or credentials in nontraditional fields.

Funds Avail.: $2,000-$12,000. **To Apply:** Questions on the application form must be answered. Applicants must submit all the required components: proposed Budget and narrative; recommendation - to be completed online; and filing fee of $25 for AAUW members and $35 for nonmembers. **Deadline:** December 15. **Contact:** AAUW Educational Foundation Dept. 60, 301 ACT Drive, Iowa City, IA 52243-4030.

6 ■ AAUW Legal Advocacy Fund International Fellowships *(Doctorate, Graduate/Fellowship)*

Purpose: To award full-time study or research in the United States to women who are not United States citizens or permanent residents. **Focus:** General studies. **Qualif.:** Applicants must be citizens in a country other than the United States, or must hold a non-immigrant visa if applicants reside in the United States; must complete an academic degree (either in the US or abroad) equivalent to a US

Awards are arranged alphabetically below their administering organizations

bachelor's degree; must intend to devote herself full time to her proposed academic plan during the fellowship year; must intend to return to her home country to pursue a professional career; and must be proficient in English, unless applicants can verify that their native language is English or that you received you undergraduate degree from or will have completed one semester of full-time study in your discipline at a university in the United States. **Criteria:** Award is given based on academic and professional qualifications; the need of the applicant's country for the specialized knowledge and skills that she plans to acquire; applicant's commitment to the advancement of women and girls in her home country as demonstrated by her previous work and her proposed study or research; documented evidence of prior community or civic service in the home country, particularly activities that contributed to the improvement of the lives of women and girls; quality and feasibility of the proposed plan of study or research and proposed time schedule; planned confirmed place of work after returning to home country; English proficiency; financial need; and country of residence at the time of application (Preference will be given to women who reside in their home country at the time of application).

Funds Avail.: $18,000-$30,000. **To Apply:** Applications must be submitted online. Applications and supporting documents will not be accepted via fax or e-mail. The following requirements must be submitted before the deadline: application form which includes research program/thesis/ course work proposal, three recommendations and filing fee of $30. **Deadline:** December 1. **Contact:** AAUW Educational Foundation Dept. 60, 301 ACT Drive, Iowa City, IA 52243-4030.

7 ■ AAUW Legal Advocacy Fund Selected Professions Fellowships *(Doctorate, Graduate/ Fellowship)*

Purpose: To award women who intend to pursue a full-time course of study at accredited institutions during the fellowship year. **Focus:** Architecture; Computer and Information Sciences; Engineering; Statistics; Business Administration; Law; Medicine. **Qualif.:** Applicants must be US citizens or permanent residents who are full-time students. **Criteria:** Panel of academic and practicing professionals who work in the respective selected professions fields will review and evaluate all fellowship applications for recommendation to the Program Committee of the AAUW Educational Foundation Board. Final fellowship selections are approved by the Foundation Board of Directors.

Funds Avail.: Master's and First Professional Awards-$5,000-$12,000; Engineering Dissertation Awards-$20,000. **To Apply:** Applicants must accomplish complete application package which consist of application; budget information for Administrative and Internal Revenue Service Purposes; narrative autobiography; detailed statement of thesis or special project (applicable to engineering and medical students only); statement of applicant's career plans and professional goals; three letters of recommendation; and dean's letter (applicable to medical students). Applicants must also submit supporting documents such as: official transcripts and a bound set of reproductions of a range of the applicant's design projects. 10 to 12 samples may be submitted in the portfolio, no larger than 8" x 10" in size (applicable to architecture students only). **Deadline:** Master's and First Professional Awards-January 10; Engineering Dissertation Awards-December 15. **Contact:** AAUW Educational Foundation Dept. 60, 301 ACT Drive, Iowa City, IA 52243-4030.

8 ■ Aboriginal Nurse Association of Canada

56 Sparks St., Ste. 502
Ottawa, ON, Canada K1P 5A9
Ph: (613)724-4677
Fax: (613)724-4718
Free: (866)724-3049
URL: http://www.anac.on.ca

9 ■ Baxter Corporation - Jean Goodwill Scholarships *(Postgraduate/Scholarship)*

Purpose: To encourage and help nurses of Aboriginal ancestry to obtain the specialized knowledge they require. **Focus:** Nursing. **Qualif.:** Applicants must be students who are graduating from a registered nurse course and are accepted into one of the following specialized training programs: community health nursing, outpost nursing, midwifery; Applicants who are or will be enrolled in a bachelor level nursing program. **Criteria:** Applicants are selected based on the selection board's review of the application materials. Preference will be given to applicants of aboriginal ancestry who intend to serve in the North.

Funds Avail.: $2,500. **Deadline:** July 1.

Remarks: Candidates may apply for scholarship for each year of study.

10 ■ The Frederick B. Abramson Memorial Foundation

1050 Connecticut Ave. NW, Ste. 200
Washington, DC 20036
Ph: (202)828-6490
Fax: (202)828-6490
E-mail: info@abramsonfoundation.org
URL: http://www.abramsonfoundation.org

11 ■ The Frederick B. Abramson Memorial Foundation Scholarships *(Undergraduate/ Scholarship)*

Purpose: To help defer college expenses at a four-year accredited institution. **Focus:** General studies. **Qualif.:** Applicants must be graduating from a public senior high school located in the District of Columbia; applicants must have demonstrated commitment to community service and social change; applicants must have demonstrated financial need; applicants must have at least 2.75 GPA or better; at least 1000 between math and verbal SATs and at least a score of 3 and above in the essay section; must have a family income of less than $70,000. **Criteria:** Recipients are selected based on financial need, academic standing, and upon the decision of the Foundation Board of Directors.

Funds Avail.: $10,000. **To Apply:** Applicants must submit an application form; essay; two letters of recommendation in which one is from the councilor and one is from the teacher; a copy of College Financial Aid Application or Student Aid Report; official transcript through midterm period of second semester of senior year including the SAT scores; budget for preferred college; letter of acceptance from college of choice; and a financial aid award letter from college of choice. **Deadline:** April 14.

12 ■ The Frederick B. Abramson Public Interest Fellowships Award *(All/Fellowship)*

Purpose: To honor and further the ongoing value of educational attainment; to further the importance of community service and mentoring, especially for minorities and

Awards are arranged alphabetically below their administering organizations

women; to further the legal representation for disadvantaged individuals and the public interest. **Focus:** Law. **Qualif.:** Applicants must be graduating law students, judicial law clerks, or practicing attorneys wishing to work in public interest law. **Criteria:** Recipients are selected based on the determination of the Foundation Board of Directors.

Funds Avail.: $10,000. **To Apply:** Applicants must complete the application form; applicants must submit a resume; two letters of recommendation; confirmation of public interest job; statement of financial responsibilities; statement of interest and career plans. **Deadline:** August 18.

13 ■ Academy of Criminal Justice Science

PO Box 960
Greenbelt, MD 20768-0960
Ph: (301)446-6300
Fax: (301)446-2819
Free: 800-757-2257
E-mail: info@acjs.org
URL: http://www.acjs.org

14 ■ Affirmative Action Mini Grant and Student Scholarships *(All/Grant)*

Purpose: To promote the involvement of all minority groups in the academy. **Focus:** Law. **Qualif.:** Applicants must be members of a group who have experienced historical discrimination (i.e., African American, Asian American, Native American, persons of Hispanic descent); enrolled in criminal justice, criminology or related programs; available for undergraduates, masters, and doctoral students. **Criteria:** Recipients are selected based on the AACJS Affirmative Action Committee panel's review of application materials.

Funds Avail.: $550. **Number Awarded:** 2. **To Apply:** Applicants must submit a completed manuscript (not more than 30 pages in length) examining criminal justice/criminological issue; a 10 pages, double spaced, typed proposals discussing: (a) the nature of the research topic, (b) why the research is important, and where relevant, (c) the methods used, (d) the findings of the research, and (e) the theoretical, methodological, and/or policy implications of the results. **Deadline:** October 15. **Contact:** Florence Ferguson, 6600 Peachtree-Dunwoody, Atlanta, GA 30328.

15 ■ Academy of Medical-Surgical Nurses

E Holly Ave., Box 56
Pitman, NJ 08071-0056
Free: (866)877-2676
E-mail: amsn@ajj.com
URL: http://www.medsurgnurse.org/

16 ■ Career Mobility Scholarship Awards *(Doctorate, Undergraduate/Scholarship)*

Purpose: To provide financial assistance for AMSN members who with to further their education. **Focus:** Nursing; Surgery; Medicine. **Qualif.:** Applicants must be members of AMSN for at least one year. **Criteria:** Applicants will be selected based on the jury's review of application materials and other supporting documents.

Funds Avail.: $500. **Number Awarded:** 1. **To Apply:** Applicants must submit a completed application form; a brief description (one page, double-spaced with size 12 font) discussing how additional education will enhance the care of Adult Medical-Surgical patient; and a self-addressed stamped postcard. Electronic submission is preferred; otherwise applicant must submit additional 9 blinded photocopies of application and of required documentation. **Deadline:** August 1.

Remarks: Fax copies will not be considered.

17 ■ Academy of Model Aeronautics

5161 E Memorial Dr.
Muncie, IN 47302
Ph: (765)287-1256
Fax: (765)289-4248
Free: 800-435-9262
URL: http://www.modelaircraft.org

18 ■ AMA/Charles H. Grant Scholarships *(Undergraduate/Scholarship)*

Purpose: To assist students in their educational pursuits. **Focus:** Aeronautics. **Qualif.:** Applicants must be full members of AMA for 36 months prior to applying; high school graduate; accepted by a college/university offering a degree program. **Criteria:** Applications will be evaluated by the AMA Scholarship Committee.

Funds Avail.: No specific amount. **To Apply:** Applicants must submit a completed application form. **Deadline:** April 30. **Contact:** Scholarship Committee Chairman, Bob Underwood.

19 ■ Sig Memorial Scholarships *(Undergraduate/Scholarship)*

Purpose: To assist students in their educational pursuits. **Focus:** Aeronautics. **Qualif.:** Applicants must be full members of AMA for 36 months prior to applying; high school graduate; accepted by a college/university offering a degree program; and have demonstrated financial need. **Criteria:** Applications will be evaluated by the AMA Scholarship Committee.

Funds Avail.: No specific amount. **To Apply:** Applicants must submit a completed application form together with a 1-page statement about the need of financial support. **Deadline:** April 30. **Contact:** Scholarship Committee Chairman, Bob Underwood.

20 ■ Telford Scholarships *(Undergraduate/Scholarship)*

Purpose: To assist students in their educational pursuits. **Focus:** Aeronautics. **Qualif.:** Applicants must be full members of AMA 36 months prior to applying; high school graduate; accepted by a college/university offering a degree program; and have participated in any of AMA and FAI activities/events. **Criteria:** Applications will be evaluated by the AMA Scholarship Committee. Selection is based on the participation in competition activity by AMA and FAI.

Funds Avail.: No Specific amount. **To Apply:** Applicant must submit a Contest Classification form to list competitions that applicant participated in. **Deadline:** April 30. **Contact:** Scholarship Committee Chairman, Bob Underwood.

21 ■ ACMPE Scholarship Fund

104 Inverness Terr. E
Englewood, CO 80112-5306
Ph: (303)799-1111
Fax: (303)643-4439

Awards are arranged alphabetically below their administering organizations

Free: 877-275-6462
E-mail: acmpe@mgma.com
URL: http://www.mgma.com

22 ■ ACMPE Scholarship Fund Program *(Graduate, Undergraduate/Scholarship)*

Purpose: To support and promote health care leaders' personal and professional growth toward advancement of the profession. **Focus:** Health care services. **Qualif.:** Applicants must be students enrolled in an undergraduate or graduate degree program relevant to medical practice management, including public health, business administration, health care administration and other related areas. **Criteria:** Applicants will be evaluated by the ACMPE Scholarship Fund Program Committee.

Funds Avail.: $1,000 to $5,000. **To Apply:** Applicants must complete the online application and submit a recent unofficial academic transcript; a current resume; two reference letters; and for students recently accepted, documentation indicating acceptance into a graduate or undergraduate college or university. **Deadline:** May 1.

23 ■ Adoptive Families Today

PO Box 1726
Barrington, IL 60011-1726
Ph: (847)382-0858
Fax: (847)382-0831
E-mail: adoptivefamiliestoday@hotmail.com
URL: http://adoptivefamiliestoday.com

24 ■ Adoptive Families Today Commemorative Scholarships *(Undergraduate/Scholarship)*

Purpose: To provide financial assistance to a foster child who is a current year high school graduate or GED recipient who plans to attend a technical/ vocational college, junior college or a four year accredited college or university. **Focus:** General studies. **Qualif.:** Applicant must live in foster care in one of the following Illinois counties: Cook, Lake, Kane, McHenry or DuPage who is graduating high school senior or GED recipient with a maintained GPA of 2.0 or above and demonstrates leadership in one or more of these areas: academics, student government, athletics, high school organizations and clubs, community service and employment. **Criteria:** Applicants will be evaluated based on the criteria designed by The Scholarship Committee.

Funds Avail.: $1,785. **To Apply:** Applicants must submit completed application form (for graduating senior); for GED recipient, test scores from the institution administering the exam; verification of wardship in writing; and reference form should be sent directly to the Scholarship Committee. **Deadline:** May 15.

25 ■ Adult Higher Education Alliance

St. Edward's University
3001 S Congress Ave.
Austin, TX 78704
Ph: (512)428-1333
URL: http://www.ahea.org

26 ■ International Graduate Student Awards *(Graduate/Scholarship)*

Purpose: To assist students in the field of Adult Higher Education. **Focus:** Adult Education. **Qualif.:** Applicants must be undertaking graduate or post graduate studies in the field of adult education and must not receive other financial support. **Criteria:** Selection is based on the application and other materials.

Funds Avail.: $1000. **To Apply:** Send nomination letters electronically to iowolabi@montreat.edu, Subject: Scholarship Submission. Letter must include names, affiliated college/university, role (faculty/administrator/student), and answers to the application questions. **Deadline:** July 31.

Remarks: In memory of the founder of the Alliance. **Contact:** Prof. Isaac Owalabi, Alliance Past President, iowolabi@montreat.edu.

27 ■ Advertising Production Club of New York

428 E State St.
Long Beach, NY 11561
Ph: (212)671-2975
Fax: (718)228-8202
E-mail: admin@apc-ny.org
URL: http://www.apc-ny.org

28 ■ Advertising Production Club Scholarship Awards *(Graduate, Undergraduate/Scholarship)*

Purpose: To provide financial assistance to students pursuing a full-time graphic arts/communications degree. **Focus:** Graphic art and design; Communications. **Qualif.:** Applicant must be a resident of New York City metro area attending a graphic arts/communications degree program full-time in any college in the New York City metro area. **Criteria:** Preference will be given to those individuals who have not previously been awarded a scholarship through the APC.

Funds Avail.: $500. Funds are applied to tuition expenses. **Number Awarded:** 4. **To Apply:** Guidelines and application forms are available from the Advertising Production Club office or can be downloaded from the APC website. Applicants must submit a completed hard copy application with the APC office together with registration receipt for the new semester, college transcript and acceptance letter. **Deadline:** October 15.

29 ■ APC High School Scholarships *(Undergraduate/Scholarship)*

Purpose: To provide financial assistance to those studying graphic arts and communications. **Focus:** Graphic art and design; Communications. **Qualif.:** Applicants must present a positive identification and confirmation by the high school principal; graduate high school with at least a B average; be duly accepted as a full-time, matriculated student in an accredited graphic arts or communications program at a college in the United States. **Criteria:** Preference will be given to those individuals who have not previously been awarded a scholarship through the APC.

Funds Avail.: $250. Funds are applied to tuition expenses. **Number Awarded:** 2. **To Apply:** Guidelines and application forms are available from the Advertising Production Club office or can be downloaded from the APC website. Applicants must submit a completed hard copy application with the APC office together with registration receipt for the new semester, college transcript and acceptance letter. **Deadline:** October 15.

30 ■ APC Tuition-Assist Scholarship Awards *(Graduate, Undergraduate/Scholarship)*

Purpose: To provide assistance to students with financial need. **Focus:** General studies. **Qualif.:** Applicant must be

Awards are arranged alphabetically below their administering organizations

a resident of New York City metro area enrolled as a full-time student in an accredited degree-granting program in any college in the U.S. **Criteria:** Preference will be given to those individuals who have not previously been awarded a scholarship through the APC.

Funds Avail.: No specific amount. **To Apply:** Guidelines and application forms are available from the Advertising Production Club office or can be downloaded from the APC website. Applicants must submit a completed hard copy application with the APC office together with registration receipt for the new semester, college transcript and acceptance letter. **Deadline:** October 15.

31 ■ PGSF-GATF Scholarships *(Graduate, Undergraduate/Scholarship)*

Purpose: To provide financial assistance to students pursuing graphic communications careers. **Focus:** Graphic art and design; Communications. **Qualif.:** Applicant must be a resident of New York City metro area attending a graphic arts/communications degree program full-time in an accredited college in the U.S. **Criteria:** Preference will be given to those individuals who have not previously been awarded a scholarship through the APC.

Funds Avail.: $500. Funds are applied to tuition expenses. **Number Awarded:** 2. **To Apply:** Guidelines and application forms are available from the Advertising Production Club office or can be downloaded from the APC website. Applicants must submit a completed hard copy application with the APC office together with registration receipt for the new semester, college transcript and acceptance letter. **Deadline:** October 15.

32 ■ Advocates for the American Osteopathic Association

142 E Ontario St.
Chicago, IL 60611
Ph: (312)202-8190
E-mail: aaoa@osteopathic.org
URL: http://www.advocates4dos.org

33 ■ AOA Research Fellowships *(Doctorate/ Fellowship)*

Purpose: To advance the philosophy and practice of osteopathic medicine. **Focus:** Osteopathic. **Qualif.:** Applicants must be a postdoctoral osteopathic medical student, possessing an earned D.O. degree awarded by an AOA-accredited institution, and be enrolled in an internship, residency, or Research Fellowship; or, an undergraduate osteopathic medical student enrolled in an AOA-accredited institution. **Criteria:** All initial funding recommendations of the Council are submitted to the Bureau for review and approval of final recommendations, which are then made to the AOA Board of Trustees for final approval at its annual meeting in July.

Funds Avail.: The award is for $5,000, made payable to the Fellow, consisting of a $4,250 stipend and a $750 travel allowance to attend the annual AOA Research Conference during the year of the fellowship. Up to an additional $5,000, made payable to the institution, is available to allow for itemized budgeted costs. **To Apply:** An AOA Fellowship application also requires a research proposal containing the following information: Specific Aims (1 page); Background and Significance (2 pages); Preliminary Studies (should not exceed one page); Experimental Design and Methods (5 pages are recommended); Human Subjects; Vertebrate Animals; Personnel and Consultants; Resources and Funding Support; Literature Cited. **Deadline:** January 30.

34 ■ AOA Research Grants *(Graduate/Grant)*

Purpose: To improve American health care through the promotion of osteopathic medicine. **Focus:** Osteopathic. **Qualif.:** Applicants must be an osteopathic physician, holding a faculty or staff appointment at an AOA accredited, affiliated, or approved osteopathic institution; or a biochemical researcher who demonstrates evidence of professional training and experience as appropriate for his/her individual discipline and who holds a faculty or staff appointment at an AOA accredited, affiliated or approved osteopathic institution; An osteopathic physician, holding a faculty or staff appointment at an academic or health care institution having accreditation, affiliation, or approval as appropriate for that institution's activities. **Criteria:** All awards are subject to final approval by the AOA Board of Trustees.

Funds Avail.: Will not exceed $50,000 per year. **To Apply:** Application forms are available at DO Online, under "Research and Grants" in both a fillable form and PDF format. Applicants are encouraged to review all materials and instructions, and are invited to contact division staff if there are questions about the meaning of a specific provision in the application prior to submission. **Deadline:** December 1.

35 ■ Agricultural Institute of Canada

280 Albert St., Ste. 900
Ottawa, ON, Canada K1P 5G8
Ph: (613)232-9459
Fax: (613)594-5190
Free: 888-277-7980
E-mail: office@aic.ca
URL: http://www.aic.ca

36 ■ Dr. Karl C. Ivarson Scholarships *(Postgraduate/Scholarship)*

Purpose: To support students pursuing studies in soil science. **Focus:** Soil Science. **Qualif.:** Applicants must hold Canadian citizenship or landed immigrant status; must be registered full-time in a master or doctorate program in the area of soil science. **Criteria:** Recipients are selected on the basis of scholastic ability, character, leadership, and potential.

Funds Avail.: $2,000. **Number Awarded:** 2. **To Apply:** Applicants must submit an official transcript. **Deadline:** November 1. **Contact:** Jean Sullivan.

37 ■ Douglas McRorie Memorial Scholarships *(Doctorate, Graduate/Scholarship)*

Purpose: To provide financial support to post-graduate masters or PhD students specializing in agricultural business, economics, finance or trade. **Focus:** Agribusiness; Economics; Finance. **Qualif.:** Applicants must hold Canadian citizenship or landed immigrant status; must be registered full time in a master or PhD program in the area of agricultural business, economics, finance or trade. **Criteria:** Recipients are selected on the basis of academic achievement, areas of study, leadership and career interests.

Funds Avail.: $1,500. **To Apply:** Applicants must submit a completed application form available at the university's website umanitoba.ca. **Deadline:** November 1.

Awards are arranged alphabetically below their administering organizations

38 ■ Agriculture Future of America

PO Box 414838
Kansas City, MO 64141
Ph: (816)472-4232
Fax: (816)472-4239
Free: 888-472-4232
URL: http://www.agfuture.org

39 ■ Agriculture Future of America Community Scholarships *(Undergraduate/Scholarship)*

Purpose: To support local students preparing for a career in the agriculture and food industry. **Focus:** Agricultural economics. **Qualif.:** Applicants must be graduating high school seniors planning to pursue a bachelor's degree in an agriculture-related program. **Criteria:** Recipients are selected based on academic performance and financial need.

Funds Avail.: No specific amount. **To Apply:** Applicants must contact AFA to request an application form.

40 ■ Agriculture Future of America Scholarship Program *(Undergraduate/Scholarship)*

Purpose: To support academic development through partnerships with rural communities, agriculture organizations, colleges and universities. **Focus:** Agricultural economics. **Qualif.:** Applicants must be students who plan to pursue a four year degree in an agriculture-related field. **Criteria:** Recipients are selected based on academic performance.

Funds Avail.: No specific amount. **To Apply:** Applicants must contact AFA to request an application form.

41 ■ Ahepa Buckeye Scholarship Foundation

6437 Tylers Crossing
West Chester, OH 45069
Ph: (513)779-0842
URL: http://www.ahepadistrict11.org

42 ■ Ahepa Buckeye Scholarship Awards *(Undergraduate/Scholarship)*

Purpose: To provide financial assistance to deserving students entering college or in undergraduate school. **Focus:** General studies. **Qualif.:** Applicant must be an active member of the AHEPA, Daughters of Penelope, Sons of Pericles, Maids of Athena, or whose parent(s) have been active members of the Senior Orders for three consecutive years. **Criteria:** Recipient is selected based on scholastic achievement and financial need.

Funds Avail.: No amount mentioned. **To Apply:** Applicant must submit the completed application form along with a letter of recommendation from the counselor, principal, or other appropriate school official.

43 ■ Ahepa District No. 1 Scholarship Foundation

18 Riverdale Dr.
Charleston, SC 29407
Ph: (843)571-4181
URL: http://www.ahepadistrict1.org

44 ■ Ahepa District No. 1 Scholarship Program *(Graduate, Undergraduate/Scholarship)*

Purpose: To promote, encourage, induce and advance education at the college, university and graduate school level. **Focus:** General studies. **Qualif.:** Applicant must be a student in the graduating class of his/her high school and planning to attend full time an accredited college or university during the current calendar year; a high school graduate planning to attend full time an accredited college or university during the calendar year; or attending an accredited college or university and will continue to attend full time during the calendar year. **Criteria:** Recipient is selected based on financial need, scholastic achievement, extra-curricular activities, athletic achievements, work and community service.

Funds Avail.: $500 to $1,500. **To Apply:** Applicant must complete the application form and submit it with the required materials asked in order to apply for the scholarship. **Deadline:** January 10.

45 ■ Air Force Association

1501 Lee Highway
Arlington, VA 22209-1198
Free: 800-727-3337
E-mail: service@afa.org
URL: http://www.afa.org

46 ■ AFROTC Scholarships *(Undergraduate/Scholarship)*

Purpose: To educate the public about the critical role of aerospace power in the defense of the nation. **Focus:** Aerospace. **Qualif.:** Applicants must be current Air Force ROTC cadets in good standing, enrolled full-time as incoming juniors or seniors for the academic year; and must be committed to studying in the fields of science, technology, engineering or math. **Criteria:** Selection of the recipients must be made by a selection board. The selection board must consider a combination of both academic merit and financial need. AFROTC will verify the applicant's financial need. AFROTC may select a prior award winner to receive this scholarship. AFROTC will make arrangement ad at their expense, make the cadets available to receive their scholarship at the Air Force Associations' Air and Space Conference and Technology Exhibition. Cadets must appear in uniform to receive their scholarship.

Funds Avail.: $5,000. **Number Awarded:** 2. **To Apply:** Applicants must submit complete application package to Captain Douglas Huttenlocker. **Contact:** Captain Douglas Huttenlocker; douglas.huttenlocker@maxwell.af.mil.

47 ■ Air Force Association Excellence Scholarships *(Undergraduate/Scholarship)*

Purpose: To educate the public about the critical role of aerospace power in the defense of the nation. **Focus:** Aerospace. **Qualif.:** Applicants must be enrolled or planning to enroll, full-time or part-time in an undergraduate or graduate program of studies leading to an associate's, bachelor's or master's degree at an accredited college or university. **Criteria:** Scholarship is given based on the committee's criteria and applicant's eligibility.

Funds Avail.: $5,000. **Number Awarded:** 5. **To Apply:** Applicants must submit completed scholarship application form and three essays to the Air Force Association. **Deadline:** April 30. **Contact:** Anne Sagle; 800-727-3337 ext. 4869.

48 ■ Air Force Association/Grantham Scholarships *(Undergraduate/Scholarship)*

Purpose: To promote aerospace education, specifically the study of science, mathematics and technology. **Focus:**

Awards are arranged alphabetically below their administering organizations

Aerospace Science. **Qualif.:** Candidates must have a high school diploma or GED and must be members of AFA or their dependents. **Criteria:** Selection will be based on the committee's criteria.

Funds Avail.: $28,000. **To Apply:** Applicants must submit a completed application form; a two-page, double-spaced essay describing your academic and career goals and explaining why you are interested in pursuing your degree via an online degree program. Explain why this is the right time in your life and why you would be committed to continuing your education to get a degree; two letters of recommendation (These should be character references with descriptions of your performance and your potential as a student); and proof of GED completion or high school transcripts (or college transcripts if applicable). College transcript(s) and proof of undergraduate degree are required for the graduate programs. Applicants will be required to provide us with information requested on a feedback form six months after the scholarship is awarded.

49 ■ Air Force Association Spouse Scholarships *(Undergraduate/Scholarship)*

Purpose: To encourage Air Force spouses worldwide to pursue associates/bachelor undergraduate or graduate/postgraduate degrees. **Focus:** Aerospace. **Qualif.:** Applicants must be spouses of Air Force Active Duty, Air National Guard or Air Force Reserve. Spouses who are themselves Air Force members, or in ROTC, are not eligible. **Criteria:** Selection will be based on the committee's criteria and applicant's eligibility.

Funds Avail.: $2,500. **To Apply:** Applicants must include the following in their application: an original or copy of the most recent college/university transcript or a report card from your last semester verifying your minimum 3.5 GPA or higher; proof of acceptance into a regionally accredited community college/ college/ university (this may consist of a short letter on college/university stationery from either the admissions office or the registrar); a two-page double-spaced essay, describing your academic and career goals and the motivation which led you to this decision and describing how Air Force and other local community activities in which you are involved will enhance your goals; two letters of recommendation (should be character references and descriptions of performance and potential as a student, employee or volunteer); a letter of endorsement from the local AFA Chapter would be welcomed and encouraged. (the two letters must be from the different sources). Letters from previous or present professors, employers and volunteer organizations referencing work you have done are encouraged.

50 ■ Jodi Callahan Memorial Scholarships *(Undergraduate/Scholarship)*

Purpose: To provide scholarships for active duty of Air Force, full-time Air National Guard or full-time Air Force Reserve. **Focus:** Aerospace. **Qualif.:** Applicants must be enrolled in the current or upcoming semester with a minimum of 3 credit hours or the equivalent. Proof of acceptance may consist of a short letter on college/university stationery from either the admissions office or the registrar. A minimum Grade Point Average of 3.0 is required. **Criteria:** Selection will be based on the committee's criteria.

Funds Avail.: $1,000. **To Apply:** Applicants must complete both online portion and mail required documents by the deadline to be considered: one letter of recommendation from the Air Force supervisor or commander; proof of acceptance into an accredited college/university; and proof of Grade Point Average. Applicants essay should describe the academic goals and how you expect your degree to enhance your service to the Air Force. The letter of recommendation should include a character reference, a description of your performance and an assessment of your potential as an Air Force leader and volunteer. **Deadline:** June 30. **Contact:** Lynetter Cross 800-727-3337 ext. 4807.

51 ■ Lt. Col. Romeo and Josephine Bass Ferretti Scholarships *(Undergraduate/Scholarship)*

Purpose: To provide educational assistance for graduating high school students. **Focus:** Science; Technology; Engineering. **Qualif.:** Applicants must be in their final year of high school and must be entering an accredited institute of higher learning. Applicants must state an intent to study in the area of science, technology, engineering or math. **Criteria:** Selection will be based on the committee's criteria.

Funds Avail.: $2,500. **Number Awarded:** 2. **To Apply:** Students must submit an application to Douglas J. Huttenlocker, Capt., USAF. **Contact:** Douglas J. Huttenlocker, Capt., USAF; Chief, Operations and Support Branch, HQ AFROTC/DOS; 334-953-6396; douglas.huttenlocker@maxwell.af.mil.

52 ■ Pitsenbarger Awards *(Undergraduate/Scholarship)*

Purpose: To provide a one-time grant to selected top USAF enlisted personnel. **Focus:** Aerospace. **Qualif.:** Applicants must be USAF personnel and graduating from the Community College of the Air Force (CCAF) who plan to pursue a baccalaureate degree. **Criteria:** Recipient selection is determined at the base level by a committee of the Base Education Officer, Senior Enlisted Advisor and a local Air Force Association (AFA) representative. Committee considers job performance, scholastic achievement, educational goals and leadership qualities. Total achievements will be carefully considered by the selection committee.

Funds Avail.: $500. **To Apply:** Applicants may download an application form at AFA web site.

53 ■ Air Force Sergeants Association

5211 Auth Rd.
Suitland, MD 20746
Ph: (301)899-3500
Fax: (301)899-8136
Free: 800-638-0594
E-mail: staff@afsahq.org
URL: http://www.afsahq.org

54 ■ AFSA Scholarship Program *(Undergraduate/Scholarship)*

Purpose: To financially assist the undergraduate studies of eligible, dependent children of the Air Force Sergeants Association. **Focus:** General studies. **Qualif.:** Applicants must be a dependent youth of an AFSA or AFSA Auxiliary members. **Criteria:** Recipients are selected based on the applicant's academic record, character, leadership skills, writing ability, versatility and potential for success.

Funds Avail.: $500-$3,000. **To Apply:** Applicants must submit a completed application form; a copy of proof of sponsor's military status (copy of DD 214, copy of the sponsor's ID and discharge letter); official transcript of grades (high school graduates must include all grades from 9th to 12th grades, college applicants must include cumulative record of grades); a letter of recommendation written

Awards are arranged alphabetically below their administering organizations

on the official school stationary with original signature (for high school graduate, letter must be written by the school principal or counselor; for college student, letter must be written by a college professor); a typed paragraph of the applicant's objectives (double-spaced) answering the question, "What do you plan to do with the education you receive?"; an essay (double-spaced) answering the question, "What is the most urgent problem facing society today?" and a typed, double-spaced two-page essay about a current, controversial issue; two self-addressed, stamped, blank postcards. High school graduate must include a valid record of combined SAT I or ACT scores (must be recorded on an official school transcript). **Deadline:** March 31. **Contact:** AFSA/CMSAF/AMF Scholarship Program, 5211 Auth Rd., Suitland, Maryland 20746.

55 ■ Air Force Sergeants Association-Chapter 155

PO Box 422
Dover, NH 03821
E-mail: redolbec@comcast.net
URL: http://www.afsa155.org

56 ■ AFSA Chapter 155 Division 1 Scholarships - Category 1 *(Undergraduate/Scholarship)*

Purpose: To enhance education opportunities for AFSA members and their families. **Focus:** General studies. **Qualif.:** Applicants must be graduating high school senior entering 1st year college; the parents, grandparents and/or guardians are current members of AFSA/Auxiliary; have a GPA of 3.0. **Criteria:** Recipients are selected based on their submitted applications.

Funds Avail.: $500. **Number Awarded:** 1. **To Apply:** Applicants must submit a completed application form (available at the website) **Deadline:** April. **Contact:** Susan L. Williams, Scholarship Chair, 419 Ocean Rd. Portsmouth, NH 03801-6020.

57 ■ AFSA Chapter 155 Division 1 Scholarships - Category 2 *(Undergraduate/Scholarship)*

Purpose: To enhance education opportunities for AFSA members and their families. **Focus:** General studies. **Qualif.:** Applicants must be 2nd, 3rd and 4th year college student up to 26 years age; the parents, grandparents and/or guardians are current members of AFSA/Auxiliary; have a GPA of 3.0. **Criteria:** Recipients are selected based on their submitted applications.

Funds Avail.: $500. **Number Awarded:** 1. **To Apply:** Applicants must submit a completed application form (available at the website) **Deadline:** April. **Contact:** Susan L. Williams, Scholarship Chair, 419 Ocean Rd. Portsmouth, NH 03801-6020.

58 ■ AFSA Chapter 155 Division 1 Scholarships - Category 3 *(Undergraduate/Scholarship)*

Purpose: To enhance education opportunities for AFSA members and their families. **Focus:** General studies. **Qualif.:** Applicants must be AFSA/Auxiliary members seeking to complete advanced schooling at credited college or trade school. **Criteria:** Recipients are selected based on their submitted applications.

Funds Avail.: $500. **Number Awarded:** 1. **To Apply:** Applicants must submit a completed application form (available at the website) **Deadline:** April. **Contact:** Susan L. Williams, Scholarship Chair, 419 Ocean Rd. Portsmouth, NH 03801-6020.

59 ■ Master Sergeant Neal E. Powers Memorial Scholarships *(Undergraduate/Scholarship)*

Purpose: To enhance education opportunities for AFSA members and their families. **Focus:** General studies. **Qualif.:** Applicants must be members or dependents of members of Chapter 155/A155; accepted and will be entering first post secondary education program. **Criteria:** Recipients are selected based on their submitted applications.

Funds Avail.: $500. **Number Awarded:** 1. **To Apply:** Applicants must submit a completed application form (available at the website). **Deadline:** June 30. **Contact:** Susan L. Williams, Scholarship Chair, 419 Ocean Rd. Portsmouth, NH 03801-6020.

60 ■ Master Sergeant William Sowers Memorial Scholarships *(Undergraduate/Scholarship)*

Purpose: To enhance education opportunities for AFSA members and their families. **Focus:** General studies. **Qualif.:** Applicants must be members or dependents of members of Chapter 155/A155; enrolled in an accredited institution and have completed at least one semester or term. **Criteria:** Recipients are selected based on their submitted applications.

Funds Avail.: $500. **Number Awarded:** 1. **To Apply:** Applicants must submit a completed application form (available at the website). **Deadline:** June 30. **Contact:** Susan L. Williams, Scholarship Chair, 419 Ocean Rd. Portsmouth, NH 03801-6020.

61 ■ Air Traffic Control Association

1101 King St., Ste. 300
Alexandria, VA 22314
Ph: (703)299-2430
Fax: (703)299-2437
E-mail: info@atca.org
URL: http://www.atca.org

62 ■ Air Traffic Control Association Full-time Employee Student Scholarships *(Other/Scholarship)*

Purpose: To provide financial assistance to full-time employees enrolled in advanced study programs that enhance employee's skills in aviation-related position. **Focus:** Traffic management. **Qualif.:** Applicants must have attendance equal to at least half-time (6 semester hours or the equivalent) and a minimum of 30 semester or 45 hours still to be completed before graduation; must be enrolled or accepted in a two-year or greater air traffic control program at an institution approved and/or listed by the Federal Aviation Administration as directly supporting the FAA's college training initiative; must be enrolled or accepted in an accredited college or university and planning to continue the following academic year; must be enrolled in course work related to his/her aviation-related career and leading to a bachelor's degree or greater; must be engaged in full-time employment in an aviation-related field; must be enrolled in course work designed to enhance the applicant's skill in an air traffic control or other aviation-related discipline. **Criteria:** Recipient will be selected by the Scholarship Selection Committee based on set of criteria.

Funds Avail.: No amount mentioned. **To Apply:** Applicants must provide two letters of recommendation (from present or previous teachers, professors, instructors, supervisors, or managers) from within the last 12 months; submit certi-

Awards are arranged alphabetically below their administering organizations

fied transcript of all college coursework. If less than 30 semester or 45 quarter hours of college coursework have been completed, all high school transcripts also are required, work or experience that supports your educational and/or aviation career goals must be addressed in the application and/or essay; financial need must be addressed in your application and/or essay; submit a paper on the subject, "How My Education Efforts Will Enhance My Potential Contribution To Aviation." which should be typed, doubled spaced, 400 words maximum.

63 ■ Air Traffic Control Association Non-employee Student Scholarships *(Undergraduate/Scholarship)*

Purpose: To provide financial assistance to students enrolled in an aviation related program of study leading to a bachelor's degree or greater. **Focus:** Traffic management. **Qualif.:** Applicants must have attendance equal to at least half-time (6 semester hours or the equivalent) and a minimum of 30 semester or 45 hours still to be completed before graduation; must be enrolled or accepted in a two-year or greater air traffic control program at an institution approved and/or listed by the Federal Aviation Administration as directly supporting the FAA's college training initiative; must be enrolled or accepted in an accredited college or university and planning to continue the following academic year; must be enrolled in course work related to his/her aviation-related career and leading to a bachelor's degree or greater; must be engaged in full-time employment in an aviation-related field; must be enrolled in course work designed to enhance the applicant's skill in an air traffic control or other aviation-related discipline. **Criteria:** Recipient will be selected by the Scholarship Selection Committee based on set of criteria.

Funds Avail.: No amount mentioned. **To Apply:** Applicants must provide two letters of recommendation (from present or previous teachers, professors, instructors, supervisors, or managers) from within the last 12 months; submit certified transcript of all college coursework. If less than 30 semester or 45 quarter hours of college coursework have been completed, all high school transcripts also are required, work or experience that supports your educational and/or aviation career goals must be addressed in the application and/or essay; financial need must be addressed in your application and/or essay; submit a paper on the subject, "How My Education Efforts Will Enhance My Potential Contribution To Aviation." which should be typed, doubled spaced, 400 words maximum.

64 ■ Gabe A. Hartl Scholarships *(Undergraduate/Scholarship)*

Purpose: To provide financial assistance to students enrolled in air traffic control curriculum at FAA approved institution. **Focus:** Traffic management. **Qualif.:** Applicants must have attendance equal to at least half-time (6 semester hours or the equivalent) and a minimum of 30 semester or 45 hours still to be completed before graduation; must be enrolled or accepted in a two-year or greater air traffic control program at an institution approved and/or listed by the Federal Aviation Administration as directly supporting the FAA's college training initiative; must be enrolled or accepted in an accredited college or university and planning to continue the following academic year; must be enrolled in course work related to his/her aviation-related career and leading to a bachelor's degree or greater; must be engaged in full-time employment in an aviation-related field; must be enrolled in course work designed to enhance the applicant's skill in an air traffic control or other aviation-related disciplines. **Criteria:** Recipient will be selected by the Scholarship Selection Committee based on this set of criteria.

Funds Avail.: No amount mentioned. **To Apply:** Applicants must provide two letters of recommendation (from present or previous teachers, professors, instructors, supervisors, or managers) from within the last 12 months; submit certified transcript of all college coursework. If less than 30 semester or 45 quarter hours of college coursework have been completed, all high school transcripts also are required, work or experience that supports your educational and/or aviation career goals must be addressed in the application and/or essay; financial need must be addressed in your application and/or essay; submit a paper on the subject, "How My Education Efforts Will Enhance My Potential Contribution To Aviation." which should be typed, doubled spaced, 400 words maximum.

65 ■ Aircraft Electronics Association

4217 S Hocker
Independence, MO 64055
Ph: (816)373-6565
Fax: (816)478-3100
E-mail: info@aea.net
URL: http://www.aea.net

66 ■ Aircraft Owners and Pilots Association Scholarships *(Undergraduate/Scholarship)*

Purpose: To provide support to the individuals intending to pursue their career in aircraft electronics and aviation maintenance industry. **Focus:** Aviation. **Qualif.:** Applicant must be a high school senior and/or college student who plans to or are attending an accredited school in an avionics or aircraft repair program. **Criteria:** Selection of candidates will be based on their application materials.

Funds Avail.: $2,000. **To Apply:** For further information about the scholarship, applicants are advice to contact the foundation at Aircraft Electronics Association, 4217 S Hocker, Independence, MO 64055.

67 ■ David Arver Memorial Scholarships *(Undergraduate/Scholarship)*

Purpose: To provide support for individuals intending to pursue their career in aircraft electronics and aviation maintenance industry. **Focus:** Aviation. **Qualif.:** Applicant must be a high school senior and/or college students planning to or are attending an accredited school in an avionics or aircraft repair program. **Criteria:** Selection of candidates will be based on their application materials.

Funds Avail.: $1,000. **To Apply:** For further information about the scholarship, applicants are advised to contact the foundation at Aircraft Electronics Association, 4217 S Hocker, Independence, MO 64055.

Remarks: Scholarship given by Dutch and Ginger Arver in memory of their son, David. Dutch Arver was a strong supporter of the AEA for many years and served on the board of Directors until his retirement.

68 ■ Dutch and Ginger Arver Scholarships *(Undergraduate/Scholarship)*

Purpose: To provide support to the individuals intending to pursue their career in aircraft electronics and aviation maintenance industry. **Focus:** Aviation. **Qualif.:** Applicant must be a senior and/or college students planning to or are attending an accredited school in an avionics or aircraft repair program. **Criteria:** Selection of candidates will be based on the criteria of the scholarship committee.

Funds Avail.: $1,000. **To Apply:** For further information about the scholarship, applicants are advice to contact the foundation at Aircraft Electronics Association, 4217 S Hocker, Independence, MO 64055.

69 ■ Johnny Davis Memorial Scholarships *(Undergraduate/Scholarship)*

Purpose: To provide support to the individuals who wants to pursue their career in aircraft electronics and aviation maintenance industry. **Focus:** Aviation. **Qualif.:** Applicant must be a high school senior and/or college student who plans to or are attending an accredited school in an avionics or aircraft repair program. **Criteria:** Selection of candidates will be based on their application materials.

Funds Avail.: $1,000. **To Apply:** For further information about the scholarship, applicants are advice to contact the foundation at Aircraft Electronics Association, 4217 S Hocker, Independence, MO 64055.

Remarks: Scholarship is named in memory of Johnny Davis, president of Dallas Avionics, Dallas, Texas, who supported general aviation for over 30 years and served as an AEA Associate Board Member.

70 ■ Duncan Aviation Scholarships *(Undergraduate/Scholarship)*

Purpose: To provide support to the individuals intending to pursue their career in aircraft electronics and aviation maintenance industry. **Focus:** Aviation. **Qualif.:** Applicant must be a high school senior and/or college students who plan to or are attending an accredited school in an avionics or aircraft repair program. **Criteria:** Selection of candidates will be based on the criteria of the scholarship committee.

Funds Avail.: $1,000. **To Apply:** For further information about the scholarship, applicants are advice to contact the foundation at Aircraft Electronics Association, 4217 S Hocker, Independence, MO 64055.

71 ■ Field Aviation Co., Inc. Scholarships *(Undergraduate/Scholarship)*

Purpose: To provide support to the individuals intending to pursue their career in aircraft electronics and aviation maintenance industry. **Focus:** Aviation. **Qualif.:** Applicant must be a high school senior and/or college students planning to or are attending an accredited college/university in an aircraft repair program. **Criteria:** Selection of candidates will be based on the decision of the scholarship committee.

Funds Avail.: $1,000. **To Apply:** For further information about the scholarship, applicants are advice to contact the foundation at Aircraft Electronics Association, 4217 S Hocker, Independence, MO 64055.

72 ■ Garmin Scholarships *(Undergraduate/Scholarship)*

Purpose: To provide support to the individuals intending to pursue their career in aircraft electronics and aviation maintenance industry. **Focus:** Aviation. **Qualif.:** Applicants must be a senior and/or college students who plan to or are attending an accredited school in an avionics or aircraft repair program. **Criteria:** Selection of candidates will be based on their application materials.

Funds Avail.: $2,000. **To Apply:** For further information about the scholarship, applicants are advice to contact the foundation at Aircraft Electronics Association, 4217 S Hocker, Independence, MO 64055.

73 ■ Lowell Gaylor Memorial Scholarships *(Undergraduate/Scholarship)*

Purpose: To provide support to the individuals intending to pursue their career in aircraft electronics and aviation maintenance industry. **Focus:** Aviation. **Qualif.:** Applicant must be a high school senior and/or college students who plan to or are attending an accredited school in an avionics or aircraft repair program. **Criteria:** Selection of candidates will be based on their application materials.

Funds Avail.: $1,000. **To Apply:** For further information about the scholarship, applicants are advice to contact the foundation at Aircraft Electronics Association, 4217 S Hocker, Independence, MO 64055.

Remarks: Scholarship is named in memory of Lowell Gaylor, president of AvEL Co., Dallas, Texas, who supported general aviation and the AEA for over 25 yrs.

74 ■ Bud Glover Memorial Scholarships *(Undergraduate/Scholarship)*

Purpose: To provide support for individuals intending to pursue their career in aircraft electronics and aviation maintenance industry. **Focus:** Aviation. **Qualif.:** Applicant must be a high school senior and/or college students who plan to or are attending an accredited school in an avionics or aircraft repair program. **Criteria:** Selection of candidates will be based on their application materials.

Funds Avail.: $1,000. **To Apply:** For further information about the scholarship, applicants are advised to contact the foundation at Aircraft Electronics Association, 4217 S Hocker, Independence, MO 64055.

Remarks: Scholarship is named in memory of Bud Glover, former vice president of general aviation sales for Bendix/King. Bud was a 25-year contributor to our avionics industry.

75 ■ Leon Harris/Les Nichols Memorial Scholarships to Spartan College of Aeronautics & Technology *(Undergraduate/Scholarship)*

Purpose: To provide support for individuals intending to pursue a career in aircraft electronics and aviation maintenance industry. **Focus:** Aviation. **Qualif.:** Applicant must be a student planning to pursue an Associate's Degree in Applied Science in Aviation Electronics (avionics) at Spartan College of Aeronautics and Technology campus in Tulsa, Oklahoma. **Criteria:** Selection of candidates will be based on their application materials.

Funds Avail.: $35,000. **To Apply:** For further information about the scholarship, applicants are advised to contact the foundation at Aircraft Electronics Association, 4217 S Hocker, Independence, MO 64055.

Remarks: Award will cover all tuition expenses for eight quarters or until the recipient completes an Associate's Degree.

76 ■ Don C. Hawkins Memorial Scholarships *(Undergraduate/Scholarship)*

Purpose: To provide support to the individuals who wants to pursue their career in aircraft electronics and aviation maintenance industry. **Focus:** Aviation. **Qualif.:** Applicant must be a high school senior and/or college students who plan to or are attending an accredited school in an avionics or aircraft repair program. **Criteria:** Selection of candidates

Awards are arranged alphabetically below their administering organizations

will be based on their application materials.

Funds Avail.: $1,000. **To Apply:** For further information about the scholarship, applicants are advice to contact the foundation at Aircraft Electronics Association, 4217 S Hocker, Independence, MO 64055.

Remarks: Scholarship is named in memory of Don C. Hawkins.

77 ■ Honeywell Avionics Scholarships
(Undergraduate/Scholarship)

Purpose: To provide support to the individuals intending to pursue their career in aircraft electronics and aviation maintenance industry. **Focus:** Aviation. **Qualif.:** Applicant must be a high school, college, or vocational/technical school student planning to or are attending an accredited school in an avionics or aircraft repair program. **Criteria:** Selection of candidates will be based on the decision of the scholarship committee.

Funds Avail.: $1,000. **To Apply:** For further information about the scholarship, applicants are advice to contact the foundation at Aircraft Electronics Association, 4217 S Hocker, Independence, MO 64055.

78 ■ L-3 Avionics Systems Scholarships
(Undergraduate/Scholarship)

Purpose: To provide support to the individuals intending to pursue their career in aircraft electronics and aviation maintenance industry. **Focus:** Aviation. **Qualif.:** Applicant must be a high school, college, or vocational/technical school students planning to or are attending an accredited school in an avionics or aircraft repair program. **Criteria:** Selection of candidates will be based on the decision of the scholarship committee.

Funds Avail.: $2,500. **To Apply:** For further information about the scholarship, applicants are advice to contact the foundation at Aircraft Electronics Association, 4217 S Hocker, Independence, MO 64055.

79 ■ Mid-Continent Instrument Scholarships
(Undergraduate/Scholarship)

Purpose: To provide support to the individuals intending to pursue their career in aircraft electronics and aviation maintenance industry. **Focus:** Aviation. **Qualif.:** Applicant must be a high school senior and/or college students planning to or are attending an accredited school in an avionics or aircraft repair program. **Criteria:** Selection of candidates will be based on the criteria of the scholarship committee.

Funds Avail.: $1,000. **To Apply:** For further information about the scholarship, applicants are advice to contact the foundation at Aircraft Electronics Association, 4217 S Hocker, Independence, MO 64055.

80 ■ Monte R. Mitchell Global Scholarships
(Undergraduate/Scholarship)

Purpose: To provide support to the individuals intending to pursue their career in aircraft electronics and aviation maintenance industry. **Focus:** Aviation. **Qualif.:** Applicant must be a European student pursuing a degree in aviation maintenance technology, avionics or aircraft repair at an accredited school located in Europe or the United States. **Criteria:** Selection of candidates will be based on the criteria of the scholarship committee.

Funds Avail.: $1,000. **To Apply:** For further information about the scholarship, applicants are advised to contact the foundation at Aircraft Electronics Association, 4217 S Hocker, Independence, MO 64055.

81 ■ Chuck Peacock Memorial Scholarships
(Undergraduate/Scholarship)

Purpose: To recognize the importance of management skills. **Focus:** Aviation. **Qualif.:** Applicant must be high school seniors and/or college students who plan to or are attending an accredited school in an aviation management program. **Criteria:** Selection of candidates will be based on their application materials.

Funds Avail.: $1,000. **To Apply:** For further information about the scholarship, applicants are advised to contact the foundation at Aircraft Electronics Association, 4217 S Hocker, Independence, MO 64055.

Remarks: Scholarship is given by Wanda Peacock in memory of her late husband Chuck. As the founder of the Aircraft Electronics Association, Chuck credited his aviation and business management skills as the cornerstones for his success in the industry.

82 ■ Plane and Pilot Magazine/Garmin Scholarships *(Undergraduate/Scholarship)*

Purpose: Focus: Qualif.: Applicant must be a high school, college or vocational/ technical school students who plan to or are attending an accredited vocational/technical school in an avionics or aircraft repair program. **Criteria:** Candidates will be selected based on their application materials.

Funds Avail.: $2,000. **To Apply:** For further information about the scholarship, applicants are advised to contact the foundation at Aircraft Electronics Association, 4217 S Hocker, Independence, MO 64055.

83 ■ Rockwell Collins Scholarships
(Undergraduate/Scholarship)

Purpose: To provide support to the individuals intending to pursue their career in aircraft electronics and aviation maintenance industry. **Focus:** Aviation. **Qualif.:** Applicants must be a high school senior and/or college students planning to or are attending an accredited school in an avionics or aircraft repair program. **Criteria:** Selection of candidates will be based on the criteria of the scholarship committee.

Funds Avail.: $1,000. **To Apply:** For further information about the scholarship, applicants are advice to contact the foundation at Aircraft Electronics Association, 4217 S Hocker, Independence, MO 64055.

84 ■ Thomas J. Slocum Memorial Scholarships to Westwood College of Aviation Technology
(Undergraduate/Scholarship)

Purpose: To provide support for individuals intending to pursue their career in aircraft electronics and aviation maintenance industry. **Focus:** Aviation. **Qualif.:** Applicant must be a student who plans to attend Westwood College of Aviation Technology in Broomfield, Colorado, in the avionics program. **Criteria:** Selection of candidates will be based on their application materials.

Funds Avail.: $6,000. **Number Awarded:** 3. **To Apply:** For further information about the scholarship, applicants are advised to contact the foundation at Aircraft Electronics Association, 4217 S Hocker, Independence, MO 64055.

85 ■ Southeast Aerospace Inc. Scholarships
(Undergraduate/Scholarship)

Purpose: Focus: Qualif.: Applicant must be a high school senior and/or college students who plan to or are attending

Awards are arranged alphabetically below their administering organizations

an accredited school in an avionics or aircraft repair program. **Criteria:** Selection of candidates will be based on the criteria of the scholarship committee.

Funds Avail.: $1,000. **To Apply:** For further information about the scholarship, applicants are advice to contact the foundation at Aircraft Electronics Association, 4217 S Hocker, Independence, MO 64055.

86 ■ Sporty's Pilot Shop/Cincinnati Avionics Scholarships *(Undergraduate/Scholarship)*

Purpose: To provide support to the individuals intending to pursue their career in aircraft electronics and aviation maintenance industry. **Focus:** Aviation. **Qualif.:** Applicant must be a high school, college, or vocational/technical school students planning to or are attending an accredited school in an avionics or aircraft repair program. **Criteria:** Selection of candidates will be based on the decision of the scholarship committee.

Funds Avail.: $2,000. **To Apply:** For further information about the scholarship, applicants are advice to contact the foundation at Aircraft Electronics Association, 4217 S Hocker, Independence, MO 64055.

87 ■ Kei Takemoto Memorial Scholarships *(Undergraduate/Scholarship)*

Purpose: To provide support to the individuals intending to pursue their career in aircraft electronics and aviation maintenance industry. **Focus:** Aviation. **Qualif.:** Applicant must be a high school senior and/or college students who plan to or are attending an accredited school in an avionics or aircraft repair program. **Criteria:** Candidates will be selected based on the scholarship criteria.

Funds Avail.: $500. **To Apply:** For further information about the scholarship, applicants are advice to contact the foundation at Aircraft Electronics Association, 4217 S Hocker, Independence, MO 64055.

Remarks: Scholarship is named in memory of Kei Takemoto whose technical expertise, engineering skill and passion for customer service was an inspiration to the avionics industry for many years.

88 ■ Lee Tarbox Memorial Scholarships *(Undergraduate/Scholarship)*

Purpose: To provide support for individuals intending to pursue a career in aircraft electronics and aviation maintenance industry. **Focus:** Aviation. **Qualif.:** Applicant must be a high school senior and/or college students planning to or are attending an accredited school in an avionics or aircraft repair program. **Criteria:** Selection of candidates will be based on their application materials.

Funds Avail.: $2,500. **To Apply:** For further information about the scholarship, applicants are advised to contact the foundation at Aircraft Electronics Association, 4217 S Hocker, Independence, MO 64055.

Remarks: Scholarship is given by Pacific Southwest Instruments.

89 ■ Tom Taylor Memorial Scholarships to Spartan College of Aeronautics and Technology *(Undergraduate/Scholarship)*

Purpose: To encourage young individuals to pursue study in Applied Science or in Aviation Maintenance Technology. **Focus:** Aviation. **Qualif.:** Applicant must be an individual who wants to pursue their Associates Degree in Applied Science or a diploma in Aviation Maintenance Technology at Spartan College of Aeronautics & Technology's campus in Tulsa, Oklahoma. **Criteria:** Selection of applicants will be based on the scholarship criteria.

Funds Avail.: $35,000. **To Apply:** For further information about the scholarship, applicants are advice to contact the foundation at Aircraft Electronics Association, 4217 S Hocker, Independence, MO 64055.

90 ■ Texas State Technical College Scholarships *(Undergraduate/Scholarship)*

Purpose: To provide support to the individuals intending to pursue their career in aircraft electronics and aviation maintenance industry. **Focus:** Aviation. **Qualif.:** Applicant must be students intending to pursue an associate's degree in avionics. **Criteria:** Selection of candidates will be based on the criteria of the scholarship committee.

Funds Avail.: $1,000. **To Apply:** For further information about the scholarship, applicants are advice to contact the foundation at Aircraft Electronics Association, 4217 S Hocker, Independence, MO 64055.

91 ■ Airport Minority Advisory Council Educational and Scholarship Program

Ronald Reagan Washington National Airport
Washington, DC 20001
Ph: (703)417-2622
Fax: (703)417-2620
E-mail: amac.manager@verizon.net
URL: http://amac-org.com

92 ■ AMACESP Student Scholarships *(Undergraduate/Scholarship)*

Purpose: To provide financial assistance for education and outreach to full-time college students interested in pursuing aviation careers. **Focus:** Aviation. **Qualif.:** Applicant must be a U.S. citizen admitted by an accredited school or university for the current school term in which he/she is applying for a scholarship with a cumulative 3.0 GPA and demonstrates involvement in community activities and extracurricular activities and interest and desire to pursue a career in the aviation/airport industry and seeking a degree in aviation, business administration, accounting, architecture, engineering or finance. **Criteria:** Recipient will be selected by the AMACESP Scholarship Selection Committee based on a set of criteria.

Funds Avail.: No amount mentioned. **To Apply:** Applicants must complete current Scholarship Application; enclose transcripts to show proof of 3.0 GPA; and a one-page essay on career goals and why he/she have chosen his/her particular field of study.

93 ■ Airports Council International-North America

1775 K St. NW, Ste. 500
Washington, DC 20006
Ph: (202)293-8500
Fax: (202)331-1362
Free: 888-424-7767
E-mail: nzimini@aci-na.org
URL: http://www.aci-na.org

94 ■ Airports Council International-North America Scholarship *(Graduate, Undergraduate/Scholarship)*

Purpose: To provide educational assistance for students at an accredited educational institution working towards a degree and a career in airport management or airport administration. **Focus:** General studies. **Qualif.:** Applicants must be officially enrolled in an accredited college or university in either an undergraduate program focused on airport management and/or airport operations, or a graduate program focused on research on airport management or airport operations; must reside and attend school in the U.S. or Canada and must maintain a minimum GPA of 3.0 at the time of application. **Criteria:** Applicants are evaluated based on demonstrated academic excellence and leadership and economic need.

Funds Avail.: $2,500. **Number Awarded:** 3. **To Apply:** Applicants must submit scholarship application (Form 101-06); official school transcript; two recent letters of recommendation, with one from a former or current professor/instructor and the other letter from someone other than a professor/instructor that has knowledge of the student's leadership qualities; a 300-500 word personal statement along with the application, with an emphasis on the applicant's interest in airport management or airport operations; and a current resume (maximum of two pages).

95 ■ Akron Bar Association Foundation

7 W Bowery St., Ste. 1100
Akron, OH 44308
Ph: (330)253-5007
E-mail: lindaf@akronbar.org
URL: http://www.akronbar.org

96 ■ Akron Bar Association Foundation Scholarships *(Undergraduate/Scholarship)*

Purpose: To provide scholarships to students enrolled in a law school. **Focus:** Law. **Qualif.:** Applicants must be citizens of the United States and in good academic standing with their respective schools. Applicants should demonstrate financial need, have an affiliation with Summit County, and demonstrate an established history of community involvement. Scholarship recipients are encouraged to become active members in the Akron Bar Association upon joining the legal profession. **Criteria:** Selection will be based on the committee's criteria.

Funds Avail.: No specific amount. **To Apply:** An applicant must submit the following requirements: a formal letter indicating how and why they became a law student, their connections to Summit County, their volunteer and extracurricular involvement and the reasons they deserve the award; a completed application form; a certified or verified transcript from their school; a copy of their Federal Income Tax Return; an updated resume; and two letters of recommendation from people familiar with their character. Application may be downloaded online. **Deadline:** April 14. **Contact:** ABAF at the above address (see entry 95).

97 ■ Alabama Commission on Higher Education

PO Box 302000
Montgomery, AL 36130-2000
Ph: (334)242-1998
Fax: (334)242-0268
URL: http://www.ache.alabama.gov

98 ■ ACHE/American Legion Auxiliary Scholarships *(Undergraduate/Scholarship)*

Purpose: To support the education of Alabama students. **Focus:** General studies. **Qualif.:** Applicants must be either the son, daughter, grandson, granddaughter of veterans of World War I, World War II, Korea, or Vietnam and who are residents of Alabama; and must be attending an institutions having on-campus housing. **Criteria:** Selection is based on the application.

Funds Avail.: No specific amount. **To Apply:** Applications are available from the American Legion Department Headquarters, American Legion Auxiliary, 120 North Jackson Street, Montgomery, AL 36104. **Deadline:** April 1. **Contact:** 334-262-1176.

99 ■ ACHE/American Legion Scholarships *(Undergraduate/Scholarship)*

Purpose: To support the education of Alabama students. **Focus:** General studies. **Qualif.:** Applicants must be either the son, daughter, grandson, granddaughter of veterans of World War I, World War II, Korea, or Vietnam and who are residents of Alabama; and must be attending an institutions having on-campus housing. **Criteria:** Selection is based on the application.

Funds Avail.: No specific amount. **To Apply:** Applications are available from the Department Adjutant, The American Legion, P.O. Box 1069, Montgomery, AL 36192. **Deadline:** May 1. **Contact:** 334-262-6638.

100 ■ ACHE Junior and Community College Athletic Scholarships *(Undergraduate/Scholarship)*

Purpose: To support the education of Alabama students. **Focus:** General studies. **Qualif.:** Applicant must be full-time student enrolled in public junior and community colleges in Alabama. **Criteria:** Selection is based on demonstrated athletic ability determined through try-outs.

Funds Avail.: Not to exceed total tuition and books. **To Apply:** Applicants must contact the coach, athletic director, or financial aid officer at any public junior or community college in Alabama in order to be considered.

101 ■ ACHE Junior and Community College Performing Arts Scholarships *(Undergraduate/Scholarship)*

Purpose: To support the education of Alabama students. **Focus:** Performing arts. **Qualif.:** Applicant must be full-time student enrolled in public junior and community colleges in Alabama. **Criteria:** Selection is based on demonstrated talent determined through competitive auditions.

Funds Avail.: Not to exceed total tuition and books. **To Apply:** Applications must contact the financial aid office at any public junior or community college in Alabama. Competitive auditions will also be scheduled as part of the application process.

102 ■ ACHE Police Officers and Firefighters Survivors' Educational Assistance Programs *(Undergraduate/Scholarship)*

Purpose: To assist the education of the dependents or spouses of police officers or firefighters killed in the line of duty in Alabama. **Focus:** General studies. **Qualif.:** Applicant must be the dependent or the spouse of a police officer or firefighter killed in the line of duty; enrolled in an undergraduate program at a public postsecondary educational institution in Alabama. **Criteria:** Selection is based on the application.

Funds Avail.: Covers tuition, fees, books and supplies. **To Apply:** Application forms may be obtained from the Alabama Commission on Higher Education. **Contact:** 334-242-2273.

Awards are arranged alphabetically below their administering organizations

103 ■ ACHE Senior Adult Scholarships *(Two Year College, Undergraduate/Scholarship)*

Purpose: To support Alabama senior citizens with educational pursuits. **Focus:** General studies. **Qualif.:** Applicant must be a senior citizen (aged 60 and over) who meet the admission requirements and attend public two-year postsecondary institutions in Alabama. **Criteria:** Selection is based on the admission at the public two-year postsecondary educational institution in Alabama.

Funds Avail.: Full-tuition. **To Apply:** Applicants must contact the financial aid office at any public two-year postsecondary educational institution in Alabama in order to be considered.

104 ■ ACHE Two-Year College Academic Scholarships *(Two Year College, Undergraduate/Scholarship)*

Purpose: To support students with educational pursuits. **Focus:** General studies. **Qualif.:** Applicant must be student accepted for enrollment at public two-year postsecondary educational institutions in Alabama. **Criteria:** Selection is based on demonstrated academic merit as determined by the institutional scholarship committee.

Funds Avail.: Not to exceed in-state tuition and books. **To Apply:** Application forms are available at the financial aid office at any public two-year postsecondary educational institution in Alabama.

105 ■ Alabama Gi Dependents Educational Benefit Programs *(Undergraduate/Scholarship)*

Purpose: To support the education of Alabama students. **Focus:** General studies. **Qualif.:** Applicant must be a dependent or spouses of eligible Alabama veterans attending a public postsecondary educational institutions in Alabama; enrolled as an undergraduate student. **Criteria:** Selection is based on the application.

Funds Avail.: Tuition, fees and book assistance. **To Apply:** Application forms may be obtained from the Alabama State Department of Veterans Affairs, PO Box 1509, Montgomery, AL 36102-1509, or from any county veterans service officer. **Contact:** Alabama State Department of Veterans Affairs, at 334-242-5077.

106 ■ Alabama National Guard Educational Assistance Programs *(Undergraduate/Scholarship)*

Purpose: To assist Alabama National Guard members to attend a public postsecondary educational institution in Alabama. **Focus:** General studies. **Qualif.:** Applicants must be a student who is an active member in good standing with a federally recognized unit of the Alabama National Guard. **Criteria:** Selection is based on the application.

Funds Avail.: $500-$1000. **To Apply:** Applications are available from Alabama National Guard units. Forms must be signed by a representative of the Alabama Military Department and the financial aid officer at the college/ university the applicant plans to attend.

107 ■ Alabama Scholarships for Dependents of Blind Parents *(Undergraduate/Scholarship)*

Purpose: To support the education of students from families in which the head of the family is blind and whose family income is insufficient to provide educational benefits. **Focus:** General studies. **Qualif.:** Applicant must be an Alabama resident; having a family in which the head of the family is blind or with family income is insufficient to provide educational benefits for attendance at an Alabama postsecondary institution. **Criteria:** Selection is based on need.

Funds Avail.: Covers instructional fees and tuition. **To Apply:** Applications are available from Debra Culver, Rehab. Specialist, Alabama Department of Rehabilitation Services, 2129 East South Blvd., Montgomery, AL 36116-2455.

Remarks: Students must apply within two years of high school graduation. **Contact:** 800-441-7607, 334-613-2248, or 256-362-0638.

108 ■ Alabama Student Assistance Programs *(Undergraduate/Scholarship)*

Purpose: To support the education of Alabama students. **Focus:** General studies. **Qualif.:** Applicant must be undergraduate student; an Alabama resident attending an eligible Alabama institution. **Criteria:** Selection is based on need.

Funds Avail.: $300-$2500. **To Apply:** Applicants must submit the Free Application for Federal Student Aid available from high school guidance office or the financial aid office at the institution planning to attend.

109 ■ Alabama Student Grant Programs *(Undergraduate/Grant)*

Purpose: To support the education of Alabama students. **Focus:** General studies. **Qualif.:** Applicant must be part-time or full-time undergraduate student; an Alabama resident; and attending Birmingham-Southern College, Concordia College, Faulkner University, Huntingdon College, Judson College, Miles College, Oakwood College, Samford University, Selma University, Southeastern Bible College, Southern Vocational College, Spring Hill College, Stillman College, or the University of Mobile. **Criteria:** Selection is based on the application.

Funds Avail.: Up to $1200. **To Apply:** Applications are available from the financial aid office at the institution the applicant is planning to attend.

110 ■ Alabama Horse Council

PO Box 260
Morris, AL 35116
Free: 800-945-8033
E-mail: info@alabamahorsecouncil.org
URL: http://www.alabamahorsecouncil.org

111 ■ Alabama Horse Council Scholarships *(Undergraduate/Scholarship)*

Purpose: To support the education of an AHC members and their children. **Focus:** Equine studies. **Qualif.:** Applicants or their parents/grandparents must be current members of AHC; must be majoring in a field of study for a career in the equine industry; must have demonstrated record of activity in the equine industry prior to college application. **Criteria:** Recipients are selected based on their submitted applications.

Funds Avail.: $1000. **To Apply:** Applicants must submit 4 copies of: one page-cover form; two letters of references attesting to the applicant's commitment to the equine industry, activity in the industry and character; short (500 word maximum) essay about how horses have shaped the lives and the goals that applicant want to pursue in the horse industry; and a list of activities and honors received. **Deadline:** June 1. **Contact:** Charlotte Collins at the above address (see entry 110).

Awards are arranged alphabetically below their administering organizations

112 ■ Auburn Animal Science Department Graduate Student Scholarships *(Graduate/Scholarship)*

Purpose: To support students studying Animal Science. **Focus:** Animal science and behavior. **Qualif.:** Applicants must be graduate students in Auburn's Department of Animal Science; have strong background in Alabama's livestock industry; and have current research project involving beef or beef cattle. **Criteria:** Selection is based on merit.

Funds Avail.: $1500. **To Apply:** Applicants must submit a completed application form. **Deadline:** December. **Contact:** Martha Davis.

113 ■ Auburn University College of Veterinary Medicine Scholarships *(Undergraduate/Scholarship)*

Purpose: To promote Veterinary Medicine education in Alabama. **Focus:** Veterinary science and medicine. **Qualif.:** Applicants must be currently enrolled at Auburn's College of Veterinary Medicine; must have strong background in Alabama's livestock industry; and intending to pursue a career involving large animal medicine. **Criteria:** Selection is based on merit.

Funds Avail.: $1500. **To Apply:** Applicants must submit a completed application form. **Deadline:** December. **Contact:** Martha Davis.

114 ■ Cecil Lane Family Scholarships *(Undergraduate/Scholarship)*

Purpose: To provide financial assistance and recognition to students with strong ties to the beef cattle industry. **Focus:** Agricultural sciences. **Qualif.:** Applicants must be resident of Alabama; must be incoming freshman at the Auburn University College of Agriculture; and must be children or grandchildren of ACA members for two consecutive years. **Criteria:** Recipients are selected based on their submitted applications.

Funds Avail.: $1750. **To Apply:** Applicants must submit a completed application form. **Deadline:** December. **Contact:** Martha Davis.

115 ■ Ina E. Powell Memorial Scholarships *(Undergraduate/Scholarship)*

Purpose: To provide financial assistance for female students. **Focus:** Agricultural sciences; Forestry; Education—Curricula. **Qualif.:** Applicants must be female students from Alabama; must be high school seniors accepted at the Auburn University; must be planning to pursue agricultural-related courses at the College of Agriculture, School of Forestry and Wildlife sciences, College of Human Sciences or College of Education; must demonstrate leadership abilities; must have GPA of 3.0 or above; and must be children or grandchildren of ACA members for two consecutive years. **Criteria:** Recipients are selected based on their submitted applications.

Funds Avail.: $1500. **To Apply:** Applicants must submit a completed application form. **Deadline:** December. **Contact:** Martha Davis.

116 ■ Tagged for Greatness Scholarships *(Undergraduate/Scholarship)*

Purpose: To support the education of AHC members and their children. **Focus:** General studies. **Qualif.:** Applicants must be high school senior and accepted to a 4-year university; must be children or grandchildren of ASA members for two consecutive years. **Criteria:** Recipients are selected based on academic excellence and leadership skills.

Funds Avail.: $1000-$1500. **To Apply:** Applicants must submit a completed application form. **Deadline:** December. **Remarks:** Funded by the Alabama Cattlemen's Foundation through the sale of the "Cowboy Tag". **Contact:** Martha Davis.

117 ■ Troy University Rodeo Team Scholarships *(Graduate/Scholarship)*

Purpose: To assist Alabama students with their education. **Focus:** General studies. **Qualif.:** Applicants must be current members of the Troy University Rodeo Team; have strong background in Alabama's livestock industry; and must be children or grandchildren of ASA members for two consecutive years. **Criteria:** Recipients are selected based on academic excellence and leadership skills.

Funds Avail.: $1000. **To Apply:** Applicants must submit a completed application form. **Deadline:** December. **Contact:** Martha Davis.

118 ■ University of West Alabama Rodeo Team Scholarships *(Graduate/Scholarship)*

Purpose: To support the education of University of West Alabama Rodeo Team members. **Focus:** General studies. **Qualif.:** Applicants must be current members of the University of West Alabama Rodeo Team; have strong background in Alabama's livestock industry; and must be children or grandchildren of ASA members for two consecutive years. **Criteria:** Recipients are selected based on academic excellence and leadership skills.

Funds Avail.: $1000. **To Apply:** Applicants must submit a completed application form. **Deadline:** December. **Contact:** Martha Davis.

119 ■ Samuel Upchurch Memorial Scholarships *(Undergraduate/Scholarship)*

Purpose: To support the education of AHC members and their children. **Focus:** Agricultural economics; Animal science and behavior. **Qualif.:** Applicants must be children or grandchildren of ACA members for two consecutive years; and must be accepted in Animal Science or Agriculture Economics at Auburn University. **Criteria:** Preference is given to applicants whose parents are members of the Alabama Santa Gertrudis Association.

Funds Avail.: $4000. **To Apply:** Applicants must submit a completed application form. **Deadline:** December. **Contact:** Martha Davis.

120 ■ Ed Wadsworth Memorial Scholarships *(Undergraduate/Scholarship)*

Purpose: To support the education of AHC members and their children. **Focus:** Animal science and behavior. **Qualif.:** Applicants must be resident of Alabama; must be junior or senior in the Animal Sciences Department at Auburn University; involved in beef cattle production; have demonstrated leadership abilities; have a GPA of 3.0 and above; and must be children or grandchildren of ACA members for two consecutive years. **Criteria:** Recipients are selected based on their submitted applications.

Funds Avail.: $1500. **To Apply:** Applicants must submit a completed application form. **Deadline:** December. **Contact:** Martha Davis.

121 ■ The Wax Company Scholarships *(Undergraduate/Scholarship)*

Purpose: To financially support students studying agriculture at the Auburn University. **Focus:** Agricultural sciences.

Awards are arranged alphabetically below their administering organizations

Qualif.: Applicants must be high senior or college students studying agriculture at the Auburn University; and must be children of ACA members. **Criteria:** Recipients are selected based on their submitted applications.

Funds Avail.: $1000. **To Apply:** Applicants must submit a completed application form. **Deadline:** December.

Remarks: Funded through the sale of Marshall and Jackson ryegrass seed. **Contact:** Martha Davis.

122 ■ Alabama Law Foundation

PO Box 671
Montgomery, AL 36101
Ph: (334)269-1515
E-mail: tdaniel@alfinc.org
URL: http://www.alfinc.org

123 ■ Johnston Cabaniss Scholarships

(Undergraduate/Scholarship)

Purpose: To recognize and assist outstanding second-year law students in their academic pursuits. **Focus:** Law. **Qualif.:** Applicants must be resident of Alabama; and must be law students entering second year at any accredited law school in the United States. **Criteria:** Selection will be based on the committee's criteria.

Funds Avail.: $5,000-first place; $1,000-second place. **To Apply:** Applicants may download an application form ALFINC website. Applicants must submit a completed application form with school transcript attached. **Contact:** ALFINC at the above address (see entry 122).

124 ■ Alaska Airmen Association

4200 Floatplane Dr.
Anchorage, AK 99502
Ph: (907)245-1251
Fax: (907)245-1259
Free: 800-464-7030
E-mail: info@alaskaairmen.org
URL: http://www.alaskaairmen.org

125 ■ John P. Culhane Memorial Scholarships

(Undergraduate/Scholarship)

Purpose: To promote development in aviation careers. **Focus:** Aviation. **Qualif.:** Applicants must be enrolled in an aviation-related program at an accredited college, university, trade school or approved training center or be in current training with a certified Flight Instructor or A&P Mechanic; must have completed one year of a commercial aviation training program or at least 25% of the work toward it; must maintain a minimum GPA of 3.0 if enrolled in an accredited college, university or trade school program; must be legal U.S. residents and have no felony convictions. **Criteria:** Recipients are selected based on commitment to aviation goals, interest in both general and commercial aviation in Alaska, evidence of financial need, personal and career goals.

Funds Avail.: $2,500. **To Apply:** Applicants must provide a letter of recommendation from one of their current instructors attesting to the commitment of the applicant to the program; must submit a completed application form; school transcripts; proof of U.S. citizenship. **Deadline:** May 31. **Contact:** Erin Hall Meade, Merrill Lynch, 3601 C. St., Penthouse Anchorage, AK 99503-5996.

126 ■ F. Atlee Dodge Maintenance Scholarships

(Undergraduate/Scholarship)

Purpose: To promote development in aviation careers. **Focus:** Aviation. **Qualif.:** Applicants must be enrolled in an aviation-related program at an accredited college, university, trade school, approved training center or be in current training with a certified Flight Instructor or A&P Mechanic; must have completed one year of a commercial aviation training program or at least 25% of the work; must maintain a minimum GPA of 3.0 if enrolled in an accredited college, university or trade school program; must be legal U.S. residents and have no felony convictions. **Criteria:** Recipients are selected based on commitment to aviation goals, interest in both general and commercial aviation in Alaska, evidence of financial need, personal and career goals.

Funds Avail.: $2,500. **To Apply:** Applicants must provide a letter of recommendation from one of their current instructors attesting to the commitment of the applicant to the program; must submit a completed application form; school transcripts; proof of U.S. citizenship. **Deadline:** May 31. **Contact:** Erin Hall Meade, Merrill Lynch, 3601 C. St., Penthouse Anchorage, AK 99503-5996.

127 ■ Bob Reeve Professional Aviation Management Scholarships *(Undergraduate/Scholarship)*

Purpose: To promote development in aviation careers. **Focus:** Aviation. **Qualif.:** Applicants must be enrolled in an aviation-related program with an accredited college, university, trade school, approved training center or be in current training with a certified Flight Instructor or A&P Mechanic; must have completed one year of a commercial aviation training program or at least 25% of the work; must maintain a minimum GPA of 3.0 if enrolled in an accredited college, university or trade school program; must be legal U.S. residents and have no felony convictions. **Criteria:** Recipients are selected based on commitment to aviation goals, interest in both general and commercial aviation in Alaska, evidence of financial need, personal and career goals.

Funds Avail.: $2,500. **To Apply:** Applicants must provide a letter of recommendation from one of their current instructors attesting to the commitment of the applicant to the program; must submit a completed application form; school transcripts; proof of U.S. citizenship. **Deadline:** May 31. **Contact:** Erin Hall Meade, Merrill Lynch, 3601 C. St., Penthouse Anchorage, AK 99503-5996.

128 ■ Alaska Community Foundation

400 L St., Ste. 100
Anchorage, AK 99501
Ph: (907)334-6700
Fax: (907)334-5780
E-mail: info@alaskacf.org
URL: http://www.alaskacf.org/index.php

129 ■ Nordic Ski Association of Anchorage Scholarships *(Undergraduate/Scholarship)*

Purpose: To encourage scholastic performance, cross-country skiing, and participation in community ski activities. **Focus:** General studies. **Qualif.:** Applicants must be Alaska residents who are high school seniors or currently enrolled college students; must be members of the high school cross-country ski team during their junior and senior years and must have individual or family memberships in the NSAA; and must have a cumulative GPA of at least 2.7 on a 4.0 scale. **Criteria:** Preference will be given to students attending college in Alaska. Applicants will be selected based on their academic performance and application materials.

Awards are arranged alphabetically below their administering organizations

Funds Avail.: $1,500. **To Apply:** Application forms are available at Nordic Skiing Association of Anchorage, 203 W 15th Ave., No. 204, Anchorage, AK 99501. Applicants must have a letter of recommendation, list of personal achievements and honors, a brief statement describing any community service, a maximum 500 word essay on the "benefits you have received from skiing", and a copy of official transcript from all high school or university work. **Deadline:** April 1.

130 ■ Alaska Pulp Scholarship Foundation

PO Box 651
Wrangell, AK 99929
Ph: (907)874-3395
URL: http://www.apc-foundation.com

131 ■ APC Scholarships *(Undergraduate/Scholarship)*

Purpose: To provide financial assistance for furthering education. **Focus:** General studies. **Qualif.:** Applicant must be a senior student in good standing at Wrangell and Sitka High School who plans to pursue post-secondary education. **Criteria:** Recipient will be selected based on outstanding academic achievement and/or special talent.

Funds Avail.: $10,000. **To Apply:** Applicant must submit completed application form along with the biography tackling about his/her career plans, family, special talents, interests and financial need and must include a recent photo, an original transcript, latest SAT and ACT test scores and two letters of recommendation.

132 ■ Alberta 4-H

97 E Lake Ramp NE
Airdrie, AB, Canada T4A 0C3
Ph: (403)948-8510
Fax: (403)948-2069
E-mail: marquerite.stark@gov.ab.ca
URL: http://www.4h.ab.ca

133 ■ Grande Prairie 4-H District Scholarships *(Undergraduate/Scholarship)*

Purpose: To financially support deserving student members of the Organization who seek for continuing education. **Focus:** General studies. **Qualif.:** Applicant must be a Grande Prairie 4-H District member student and a resident of Alberta based on Student Finance Regulations who have minimum year residency in Alberta immediately prior to the application date and enrolled full-time in a post secondary program recognized by Alberta Advanced Education. **Criteria:** Applicants will be evaluated based on their financial need, commitment to living and working in northern Alberta for a specified amount of time upon graduation, and reasonable good prospects for employment in northern Alberta after graduation.

Funds Avail.: $1,500. **Number Awarded:** 2. **To Apply:** Applicants must submit complete Provincial 4-H Scholarship application and NADC scholarship application. **Deadline:** May 5.

Remarks: In partnership with Northern Alberta Development Council (NADC).

134 ■ Provincial and Regional 4-H Scholarships *(Undergraduate/Scholarship)*

Purpose: To financially support deserving student members of the Organization who seek to continuing their education. **Focus:** General studies. **Qualif.:** Applicant must be a past or present member of Alberta 4-H Club and/or a full-time post-secondary student at an officially recognized institution. **Criteria:** Recipients are selected based on a set of criteria designed by the Selection Committee, made up of representatives from Alberta 4-H Council, 4-H Foundation of Alberta, 4-H Branch.

Funds Avail.: $80,000. **Number Awarded:** 100. **To Apply:** Applicants must submit a completed type-written scholarship application form and must include original photo along with the official transcript request for the last year's education. **Deadline:** May 5.

135 ■ Servus Credit Union 4-H Scholarships *(Undergraduate/Scholarship)*

Purpose: To provide financial assistance for Alberta 4-H members to further education. **Focus:** General studies. **Qualif.:** Applicants must be Alberta 4-H members who have been involved for a minimum of three years; entering their first year of study at a postsecondary institution in Alberta within one year of graduation from high school; and reside in the following Servus Credit Union trade areas: Andrew, Devon, Drayton Valley, Elk Point, Entwistle, Fort Saskatchewan, Gibbons, Lamont, Leduc, Legal, Morinville, Mundare, Myrnam, Plamondon, Sangudo, St. Paul, Stony Plain and Wabamun. **Criteria:** Recipients are selected based on their demonstrated outstanding 4-H achievement, leadership skills, community involvement and academic standing.

Funds Avail.: $500. **Number Awarded:** 2. **To Apply:** Applicants must submit application form and the complete materials needed to avail the scholarship. **Deadline:** May 5.

136 ■ Alberta Agricultural Economics Association

University of Alberta
515 General Services Bldg.
Edmonton, AB, Canada T6G 2H1
Ph: (780)492-4562
E-mail: info@aaea.ab.ca
URL: http://www.aaea.ab.ca

137 ■ Alberta Agricultural Economics Association Scholarships *(Graduate/Scholarship)*

Purpose: To recognize the deserving students in Alberta. **Focus:** Agribusiness, Agricultural economics. **Qualif.:** Applicants must be students enrolled in a M.Sc program in Agricultural Economics or Agri-Food Business Management or Natural Resource Economics in the Department of Rural Economy; must have a GPA of 7.5 in their first year of their Masters program. **Criteria:** Selection of applicants will be based on academic achievement, commitment, contribution, initiative and leadership at the University, in the community and in Alberta's agri-business.

Funds Avail.: $1,000. **To Apply:** For further information about the scholarship and requirements, applicants are advice to contact the Association at AAEA, 515 General Services Bldg., University of Alberta, Edmonton, AB T6G 2H1.

138 ■ Alberta Agricultural Economics Association Undergraduate Scholarships *(Undergraduate/Scholarship)*

Purpose: To recognize the deserving students in Alberta. **Focus:** Economics; Agribusiness. **Qualif.:** Applicants must

Awards are arranged alphabetically below their administering organizations

be full-time students enrolled in the third or fourth year of a B.Sc. Applied Economics or Agri-Food Business Management program in the faculty of Agriculture, Forestry and Home Economics; must have a GPA of 7.5 in their most recent academic year. **Criteria:** Selection of applicants will be based on academic achievement, commitment, contribution, initiative and leadership at the University, in the community and in Alberta's agri-business.

Funds Avail.: $500. **To Apply:** For further information about the scholarship and requirements, applicants are advised to contact the Association at AAEA, 515 General Services Bldg., University of Alberta, Edmonton, AB T6G 2H1.

139 ■ Alberta Barley Commission

3601A21 St. NE, No. 200
Calgary, AB, Canada T2E 6T5
Ph: (403)291-9111
Free: 800-265-9111
E-mail: barleyinfo@albertabarley.com
URL: http://www.albertabarley.com

140 ■ Eugene Boyko Scholarships *(Undergraduate/Scholarship)*

Purpose: To provide scholarship opportunity to the students of Alberta, Canada. **Focus:** Agricultural sciences. **Qualif.:** Applicants must be: Canadian citizens or permanent Canadian residents living in Alberta; attending a post-secondary institution in Alberta; enrolled full-time in the second or subsequent year of post-secondary study. **Criteria:** Selection will be based on academic achievement in their previous year of post-secondary studies.

Funds Avail.: $500. **To Apply:** Application forms are available from Alberta Scholarship Programs and from Alberta post-secondary institutions. Mail completed application and an official transcript to: Alberta Scholarship Programs 4th Floor - 9940 106 St. Box 28000 Station Main, Edmonton, AB TGJ 4R4. **Deadline:** August 1. **Contact:** Alberta Scholarship Program, 780-427-8640, scholarships@gov.ab.ca.

141 ■ Alberta Indian Investment Corporation

PO Box 180
Enoch, AB, Canada T7X 3Y3
Ph: (780)470-3600
Fax: (780)470-3605
Free: 888-308-6789
E-mail: info@aiicbusiness.org
URL: http://www.aiicbusiness.org

142 ■ Sam Bull Memorial Scholarships *(Undergraduate/Scholarship)*

Purpose: To provide scholarship assistance to qualified individuals who want to pursue their education. **Focus:** Law; Political science. **Qualif.:** Applicant must be a First Nation native who has resided in Alberta for at least one year; must demonstrate interest in law or political science education. **Criteria:** Recipient will be evaluated by the selection committee based on academic performance, chosen area of study in relation to First Nation community development, and future career aspirations.

Funds Avail.: $1,000. **To Apply:** Applicant must prepare a 100 to 200 word statement of personal and academic objectives, which should emphasize how their proposed course of study will contribute to First Nation community development in Canada. Application forms are available online and must be sent together with other supporting documents to General Manager, PO Box 180, Enoch, AB T7X 3Y3. **Deadline:** February 15.

143 ■ Senator James Gladstone Memorial Scholarships *(Undergraduate/Scholarship)*

Purpose: To provide scholarship assistance to qualified individuals who want to pursue their education. **Focus:** Law; Political science. **Qualif.:** Applicant must be a First Nation native who has resided in Alberta for at least one year; must demonstrate interest in law or political science education. **Criteria:** Recipient will be evaluated by the selection committee based on strong academic performance, chosen area of study in relation to First Nation business/economic development, and future career aspirations.

Funds Avail.: $750-$1,000. **To Apply:** Applicant must submit a transcript of record; must prepare a 100 to 200 word statement of personal and academic objectives which should emphasize how their proposed course of study will contribute to First Nation economic and business development in Canada. Application form and other supporting documents must be sent to General Manager, Alberta Indian Investment Corporation, PO Box 180, Enoch, AB T7X 3Y3. **Deadline:** February 15.

144 ■ Alberta Learning Information Service - Alberta Scholarship Program

Box 28000 Sta. Main
Edmonton, AB, Canada T5J 4R4
Ph: (780)427-8640
Fax: (780)427-1288
E-mail: scholarship@gov.ab.ca
URL: http://www.alis.alberta.ca

145 ■ Alberta Award for the Study of Canadian Human Rights and Multiculturalism *(Doctorate, Graduate/Award/Prize)*

Purpose: To encourage the pursuit of studies in Canadian human rights, cultural diversity, and multiculturalism. **Focus:** Human rights. **Qualif.:** Applicant must be: a Canadian citizen or permanent resident; enrolled or planning to enroll as a full-time graduate student (Master's or Doctoral level) at an Alberta public post-secondary institution; taking a program of study that supports the purpose of this scholarship; planning to do research that is within a Canadian context and will ultimately benefit Albertans. **Criteria:** Selection will be based on the committee's criteria.

Funds Avail.: $10,000. **To Apply:** Applicants may obtain an application form from Graduate and Awards Offices at post-secondary institutions and through Alberta Scholarship Programs. **Deadline:** February 1. **Contact:** Alberta Scholarship Programs at the above address (see entry 144).

146 ■ Alberta Centennial Premier's Scholarships - Alberta *(Undergraduate/Scholarship)*

Purpose: To commemorate the Province of Alberta's Centennial. **Focus:** General studies. **Qualif.:** Applicants must: be Canadian citizens or permanent residents of Canada and Alberta; entering any level of postsecondary study at any university, college, technical institute or apprenticeship program in Canada. **Criteria:** Scholarship

Awards are arranged alphabetically below their administering organizations

recipients are selected from nominations received for the Premier's Citizenship Award. Each high school in Alberta nominates a recipient for the Premier's Citizenship Award and each recipient is considered a nominee for the Alberta Centennial Scholarship. A selection committee will meet and review the nominations and select 25 recipients.

Funds Avail.: No specific amount. **To Apply:** Nominations are submitted by high school counselors. **Deadline:** June 15. **Contact:** Alberta Scholarship Program at the above address (see entry 144).

147 ■ Janet and Horace Allen Scholarship
(Undergraduate/Scholarship)

Purpose: To recognize the academic excellence of a student from Crowsnest Pass high School in the area of the sciences. **Focus:** Science. **Qualif.:** Applicants must be Alberta residents and plan to enroll full-time in a post-secondary program of at least one semester in length. **Criteria:** Recipient will be selected on the basis of achieving the highest average on two of the following Grade 12 courses at the 30 level: Biology, Chemistry, Physics or Science.

Funds Avail.: $1,500. **To Apply:** Applicants may obtain an application form from Alberta Scholarship Programs and Crowsnest Pass High School. **Deadline:** June 1.

148 ■ Art Graduate Scholarships *(Graduate/Scholarship)*

Purpose: To reward outstanding students pursuing full-time study at the masters or equivalent level. **Focus:** Arts. **Qualif.:** Applicants must be residents of Alberta enrolled or planning to enroll full-time either in music, dance, literary arts or visual arts at a Master's level or equivalent level; there is a lifetime maximum of two awards per student. Scholarships are for study at graduate faculties and equivalent institutions anywhere in the world. **Criteria:** Recipients are chosen by a selection committee appointed by the presidents of the universities in Alberta. Applicants are judged on previous academic accomplishments, program of study, appraiser's evaluations, answers to the essay question, and general impressions from the application form.

Funds Avail.: $5,000. **Number Awarded:** 5. **To Apply:** Application form can also be obtained from Alberta Scholarship Programs. **Deadline:** February 1. **Contact:** Alberta Scholarship Program at the above address (see entry 144).

149 ■ Arts for Career Development Scholarships *(Professional Development/Internship)*

Purpose: To assist Alberta artists in furthering their training through non-academic, short-term courses, internship or apprenticeship programs. Funding for full-time masters or equivalent level study is available through the Arts Graduate Scholarships. **Focus:** Creative arts. **Qualif.:** Applicants must be residents of Alberta seeking training in the creative arts and have been employed or practicing in their field for at least three years in Alberta. Fields eligible for this award include: music, drama, dance, literary arts, and the visual arts. Programs eligible for funding are normally of a non-academic nature and may include apprenticeship, internship, mentorship or any studies conducted by a master in the field; full-time study towards a degree or college equivalent will not be considered. **Criteria:** Recipients are chosen by a selection committee representing music, drama, and visual arts; applicants are evaluated on the basis of the number of times the individual received assistance, the type of training proposed and its applicability to their artistic accomplishments, a work record in excess of three years demonstrating their professional merit, comments from appraisers, answer to the essay question and general impressions from the application form.

Funds Avail.: $3,000. **To Apply:** Application forms are also available from Alberta Scholarship Programs. Applicants must apply before starting their course. **Deadline:** March 15 and November 15. **Contact:** Alberta Scholarship Program at the above address (see entry 144).

150 ■ Theodore R. Campbell Scholarship
(Undergraduate/Scholarship)

Purpose: To reward the accomplishments of an aboriginal student from Blue Quills First Nations College. **Focus:** General studies. **Qualif.:** Applicants must be Alberta residents and have completed the first year towards an Education degree at Blue Quills First Nations College. **Criteria:** Selection will be based on the academic achievement during first year of study.

Funds Avail.: $1,500. **To Apply:** Application forms are available from Alberta Scholarship Programs and from the Research and Planning Office at Blue Quills First Nations College. **Deadline:** June 1. **Contact:** Alberta Scholarship Program at the above address (see entry 144).

151 ■ Canada Millennium Bursary
(Undergraduate/Scholarship)

Purpose: To help Alberta's needy students access this bursary and reduce their debt load. **Focus:** General studies. **Qualif.:** Students must be enrolled full-time at a Canadian post-secondary institution attending their second or subsequent year of undergraduate study or any year of a professional program. **Criteria:** Selection will be based on financial need.

Funds Avail.: $2,250-$3,000. **To Apply:** Students do not need to apply for this scholarship separately. Students are automatically considered for Canada Millennium Bursaries when they apply for a student loan. **Contact:** Alberta Scholarship Program at the above address (see entry 144).

152 ■ Carmangay Home and School Association Scholarships *(Undergraduate/Scholarship)*

Purpose: To recognize the accomplishments of students who attended Carmangay School and to commemorate the closing of the school. **Focus:** General studies. **Qualif.:** Applicants must: be Canadian citizens or landed immigrants and residents of Alberta according to Alberta Heritage Scholarship Fund regulations; have attended Carmangay School for at least one complete school year; have achieved a high academic standing in their Grade 12 year at an Alberta high school; and plan on entering full-time studies at a recognized post-secondary institution. **Criteria:** Selection will be based on the academic achievement in Grade 12, demonstrated leadership and community involvement. Applicants must provide proof of attendance at Carmangay School either by reference letter or other documentation.

Funds Avail.: $2,500. **To Apply:** Application forms are available from regional school counselors and from the office of Alberta Scholarship Programs. Applicants must mail their application form to Alberta Scholarship Programs. **Deadline:** August 1. **Contact:** Alberta Scholarship Programs at the above address (see entry 144).

153 ■ Robert C. Carson Memorial Bursary
(Undergraduate/Scholarship)

Purpose: To provide financial assistance to aboriginal students who have successfully completed the first year of

Awards are arranged alphabetically below their administering organizations

a program relating to criminal justice, criminology or law. **Focus:** Criminal justice; Criminology; Law. **Qualif.:** Applicants must be Alberta residents and full-time students enrolled in the second year of either Law Enforcement or Criminal Justice. The qualifying Alberta institutions are: Lethbridge Community College, Mount Royal College, Grant MacEwan College, the University of Calgary or the University of Alberta. **Criteria:** Recipients are nominated by the educational institution they are attending. Preference will be given to non-sponsored aboriginal students.

Funds Avail.: $500. **To Apply:** Application forms are available from the Institution's Student Award Office. **Deadline:** October 1. **Contact:** Alberta Scholarship Program at the above address (see entry 144).

154 ■ Laurence Decore Awards for Student Leadership *(Undergraduate/Scholarship)*

Purpose: To recognize those post-secondary students who have demonstrated outstanding dedication and leadership to fellow students and to their community. **Focus:** General studies. **Qualif.:** Applicants must be Alberta residents who are currently enrolled in a minimum of three courses at a designated Alberta post-secondary institution. **Criteria:** Selection will be based on the committee's criteria.

Funds Avail.: $500. **To Apply:** Applicants do not need to apply. Schools may submit a nomination for this scholarship. **Deadline:** March 1. **Contact:** Alberta Scholarship Programs at the above address (see entry 144).

155 ■ Earl and Countess of Wessex - World Championships in Athletics Scholarships *(Undergraduate/Scholarship)*

Purpose: To recognize the top male and female Alberta students who have excelled in track and field. **Focus:** Athletics. **Qualif.:** Applicants must be Canadian citizens or landed immigrants and residents of Alberta, according to Alberta Scholarship Programs regulations. Applicants must have completed Grade 12 in Alberta in the same year they apply for the scholarship. Student must be planning on continuing their studies at a post-secondary institution in Alberta and participating on that institution's track and field team. **Criteria:** Selection will be based on placement in provincial and national championships, AADP standards, best performances, Mercier scores and recommendations from the applicants' coaches. Academic achievement will also be a consideration.

Funds Avail.: $3,000. **To Apply:** Applicants may obtain an application form from all Alberta high schools and from Alberta Scholarship Programs. **Deadline:** October 1. **Contact:** Alberta Scholarship Program at the above address (see entry 144).

156 ■ Fellowships for Full-time Studies in French *(Undergraduate/Fellowship)*

Purpose: To assist Albertans in pursuing post-secondary studies taught in French. **Focus:** French studies. **Qualif.:** Applicants must be Alberta residents, Canadian citizens or landed immigrants enrolled full-time in a post-secondary program. In addition, applicants must be enrolled in a minimum of three courses per semester which have French as the language of instruction. **Criteria:** Selection will be based on academic achievement.

Funds Avail.: $500-$1,000. **To Apply:** Applicants may obtain an application form from the Students Awards Office at Alberta post-secondary institutions that offer programs taught in French and from Alberta Scholarship Programs. Applicants must include proof of Canadian citizenship: either a photocopy of Canadian birth certificate, passport or immigration papers. College applicants must include a transcript. **Deadline:** November 15. **Contact:** Alberta Scholarship Programs at the above address (see entry 144).

157 ■ Graduate Student Scholarship *(Graduate/Scholarship)*

Purpose: To reward the outstanding academic achievement of students studying at the Masters level. **Focus:** General studies. **Qualif.:** Applicants must be enrolled in the second year of a Masters program. Students must be Canadian citizens or landed immigrants and attending a post-secondary institution in Alberta. **Criteria:** Selection will be based on the committee's criteria.

Funds Avail.: $2,000. **To Apply:** No application required. Students are nominated by the faculty of graduate studies. **Contact:** Alberta Scholarship Programs at the above address (see entry 144).

158 ■ Lois Hole Humanities and Social Sciences Scholarship *(Undergraduate/Scholarship)*

Purpose: To recognize student's leadership and community service. **Focus:** Humanities; Social sciences. **Qualif.:** Applicants must be students enrolled full-time in the second or subsequent year of post-secondary study in the Faculty of Humanities or the Faculty of Social Sciences, at the University of Alberta, the University of Calgary, the University of Lethbridge, or Athabasca University. **Criteria:** Selection will be based on academic merit, demonstrated leadership and community service.

Funds Avail.: $5,000. **To Apply:** Applicants may contact the Student Awards Office at participating educational institutions for other application requirements. **Deadline:** October 15 for University of Alberta and Athabasca University; November 15 for University Lethbridge and the University of Calgary. **Contact:** Alberta Scholarship Programs at the above address (see entry 144).

159 ■ Informatics Circle of Research Excellence Scholarships *(Doctorate, Graduate/Scholarship)*

Purpose: To foster a strong graduate student population and support the development of strong informatics research teams. **Focus:** Computer and information sciences; Engineering. **Qualif.:** Applicants must be graduate students in information science and engineering attending an Alberta university. **Criteria:** Selection will be based on the committee's criteria.

Funds Avail.: $30,000-Masters level; $35,000-Doctoral level. **To Apply:** Applicants may contact the Faculty of Graduate Studies for other requirements. The institution will nominate a students to receive this award. **Contact:** Alberta Scholarship Program at the above address (see entry 144).

160 ■ International Education Awards - Ukraine *(Undergraduate/Scholarship)*

Purpose: To recognize the accomplishments of intern, co-op, practicum, apprenticeship, and research students. **Focus:** General studies. **Qualif.:** Applicant must be a post-secondary student or an apprenticeship student taking a practicum, internship, co-op or apprenticeship program, or may be a student conducting research. **Criteria:** The student will be selected based on demonstrated past accomplishments and potential for improving relations

Awards are arranged alphabetically below their administering organizations

between Ukraine and Alberta.

Funds Avail.: $5,000. **Number Awarded:** 5. **To Apply:** Application forms will also be available from the Alberta Scholarship Programs' office, Alberta Colleges and Universities, the Canadian Embassy in Kyiv, and the Ministry of Education of Ukraine. In total, five copies of the completed application form must be submitted (an original plus four photocopies). This requirement does not apply to academic transcripts and reference letters. **Deadline:** February 1. **Contact:** Alberta Scholarship Program at the above address (see entry 144).

161 ■ Helen and George Kilik Scholarship *(Undergraduate/Scholarship)*

Purpose: To assist student from Olds High School to pursue a post-secondary education. **Focus:** General studies. **Qualif.:** Candidate must be an Alberta resident, have completed all high school studies at Olds High school and intend to pursue post-secondary studies. The selected student must demonstrate financial need, and involvement in extracurricular activities. **Criteria:** Selection will be based on academic achievement particularly in math and science.

Funds Avail.: $1,000. **To Apply:** Applicants may obtain an application from Olds High School or Alberta Scholarship Programs. **Deadline:** June 1. **Contact:** Alberta Scholarship Programs at the above address (see entry 144).

162 ■ Anna and John Kolesay Memorial Scholarship *(Undergraduate/Scholarship)*

Purpose: To recognize and reward the academic excellence of a student entering a Faculty of Education. **Focus:** General studies. **Qualif.:** Applicant must be: a Canadian citizen or permanent resident and an Alberta resident; from a family where neither parent obtained a university degree; enrolling full-time in the first year of a program in a Faculty of Education. **Criteria:** The recipient will be selected on the basis of academic excellence as calculated from the final standings received in three subjects as shown on an Alberta Education transcript.

Funds Avail.: $1,200. **To Apply:** Application form can be obtained from Alberta Scholarship Programs and at Alberta high schools. **Deadline:** July 1. **Contact:** Alberta Scholarship Program at the above address (see entry 144).

163 ■ Jason Lang Scholarship *(Undergraduate/Scholarship)*

Purpose: To reward the outstanding academic achievement of Alberta post-secondary students who are continuing full-time in an undergraduate program in Alberta. **Focus:** Law; Medicine; Pharmacy; Dentistry. **Qualif.:** Nominees must be enrolled full-time in an undergraduate or professional program, such as Law, Medicine, Pharmacy or Dentistry at an eligible Alberta post-secondary institution. These include publicly-funded colleges, technical institutes, universities, private colleges accredited to grant degrees, and the Banff Centre. **Criteria:** Selection will be based on the committee's criteria.

Funds Avail.: $1,000. **To Apply:** Recipients are nominated by the Awards Office at participating Alberta institutions where they have obtained qualifying grades. For information on the nomination process and eligibility, contact the Awards Office. **Deadline:** October 15 and February 15. **Contact:** Alberta Scholarship Programs at the above address (see entry 144).

164 ■ Language Teacher Bursary Program Awards *(Professional Development/Award/Prize)*

Purpose: To assist certified Alberta teachers to take a summer post-secondary program in a language other than English or language pedagogy course at an institution outside of Canada. **Focus:** Languages. **Qualif.:** Applicants must: be Canadian citizens or individuals lawfully admitted to Canada for permanent residence and residents of Alberta; hold a valid Alberta professional teaching certificate; have been teaching in Alberta for a minimum of three years by the end of the current school year; demonstrate a background in language learning or have recently initiated the study of this language; plan to take a summer program of at least four weeks duration in a language/language teaching methodology other than English, or related field at an institution outside of Canada; must have not previously been awarded a Language Teacher Bursary. **Criteria:** Selection will be based on the committee's criteria.

Funds Avail.: $2,500-$5,000. **To Apply:** Application form can be obtained from Alberta Scholarship Programs. Completed application form must be submitted to your local school authority for endorsement. Once endorsement has been given, the school authority will mail your application to Alberta Scholarship Programs. **Deadline:** February 10. **Contact:** Alberta Scholarship Programs at the above address (see entry 144).

165 ■ Languages In Teacher Education Scholarships *(Professional Development/Scholarship)*

Purpose: To reward Alberta students enrolled in a recognized Alberta teacher preparation program taking courses that will allow them to teach languages other than English in Alberta schools. **Focus:** Languages. **Qualif.:** Applicants must be: Canadian citizens or individuals lawfully admitted to Canada for permanent residence in Alberta. Visa students are not eligible for this award. Applicants must be registered full-time in their final two years of a recognized Alberta teacher preparation program at an Alberta faculty of education and intend to teach in Alberta schools upon completion of their program. **Criteria:** Selection will be based on the committee's criteria.

Funds Avail.: $2,500. **Number Awarded:** 13. **To Apply:** No applications required. Students will be nominated by their post-secondary institution. **Contact:** Alberta Scholarship Program at the above address (see entry 144).

166 ■ Sir James Lougheed Awards of Distinction *(Doctorate, Graduate/Award/Prize)*

Purpose: To recognize academic achievement and provide Albertans with the opportunity for advanced study at institutions outside of Alberta. Students studying in Alberta should apply for the Ralph Steinhauer Awards for Distinction. **Focus:** General studies. **Qualif.:** Applicants must be: Canadian citizens or landed immigrants; Alberta residents; enrolled or planning to enroll full-time in a graduate program at an institution outside of Alberta. **Criteria:** Selection will be based on the committee's criteria.

Funds Avail.: $15,000 for Masters level; $20,000 for Doctoral level. **To Apply:** An application form can be obtained from Alberta Scholarship Program, however, applicants cannot send their application electronically. Submit the original and four signed unstapled copies of the completed application form and attachments. This requirement does not apply to academic transcripts and appraisals; these documents must be sent directly to Alberta Scholarship Programs. **Deadline:** February 1. **Contact:** Alberta Scholarship Programs at the above address (see entry 144).

167 ■ Louise McKinney Post-secondary Scholarship *(Undergraduate/Scholarship)*

Purpose: To recognize exceptional academic achievement and encourage outstanding students to continue their stud-

Awards are arranged alphabetically below their administering organizations

ies at the post-secondary level. **Focus:** General studies. **Qualif.:** Applicants must be residents of Alberta and in their second or subsequent year of full-time study. Alberta students studying outside the province because their program of study is not offered in Alberta will be considered for a scholarship if their class standing is in the top two percent of their program. **Criteria:** Selection will be based on the committee's criteria.

Funds Avail.: $2,500. **To Apply:** Students studying in-province are nominated by the Student Awards Office at participating Alberta post-secondary institutions. Other students may contact the Awards Office to determine their eligibility. **Contact:** Alberta Scholarship Programs at the above address (see entry 144).

168 ■ Dr. Ernest and Minnie Mehl Scholarship *(Undergraduate/Scholarship)*

Purpose: To encourage students to pursue a post-secondary education and to recognize and reward exceptional academic at the senior high school level. **Focus:** General studies. **Qualif.:** Applicants must be Canadian citizens or landed immigrants who have completed their Grade 12 in Alberta at a school that follows the Alberta Education Curriculum. Applicants must be continuing their studies at a degree granting post-secondary institution in Canada. University transfer programs are acceptable. **Criteria:** Selection will be based on the committee's criteria.

Funds Avail.: $3,500. **To Apply:** Applicants may obtain an application form from high school counselors and from Alberta Scholarship Programs. **Deadline:** June 1. **Contact:** Alberta Scholarship Programs at the above address (see entry 144).

169 ■ Millennium Alberta Rural Incentive Bursary Award *(Undergraduate/Award/Prize)*

Purpose: To provide financial assistance to rural Albertans attending a designated post-secondary institution in Canada. **Focus:** General studies. **Qualif.:** Applicants must: have attended a rural high school in Alberta; have lived in rural Alberta for a minimum of 12 months immediately prior to starting post-secondary studies; be attending a designated post-secondary institution in Canada; be enrolled in the first or second year of an undergraduate program of at least two years in length; be eligible for a minimum of $1,000 in student loan funding. **Criteria:** Selection will be based on a student's eligibility for student loan funding.

Funds Avail.: $1,000. **To Apply:** Students must complete both an Application for Financial Assistance and the Schedule 3 of the application for financial assistance. **Contact:** Alberta Scholarship Programs at the above address (see entry 144).

170 ■ Charles S. Noble Scholarships for Study at Harvard *(Undergraduate/Scholarship)*

Purpose: To reward academic excellence and provide opportunities for Albertans to pursue studies at Harvard University. **Focus:** General studies. **Qualif.:** Applicants must be Alberta residents who plan to apply or are enrolled full-time in any year of study in an undergraduate program at Harvard. **Criteria:** Selection will be based on the committee's criteria.

Funds Avail.: May 15. **To Apply:** Applicants may obtain an application form from the Office of Admissions at Harvard and from the Alberta Heritage Scholarship Fund. **Deadline:** May 15. **Contact:** Alberta Scholarship Programs at the above address (see entry 144).

171 ■ Northern Alberta Development Council Bursary Award *(Undergraduate/Award/Prize)*

Purpose: To increase the number of trained professionals in Northern Alberta and to encourage students from Northern Alberta to obtain a post-secondary education. **Focus:** General studies. **Qualif.:** Applicants must be residents of Alberta, and planning to enroll in a full-time post-secondary program. Applicants must also be within two years of completion of their post-secondary program. **Criteria:** Selection will be based on the committee's criteria.

Funds Avail.: $1,750. **To Apply:** Applicants may obtain an application form from www.benorth.ca. Application forms for these bursaries are also available from Alberta Scholarship Programs, Student Awards Offices and from the Northern Alberta Development Council. **Deadline:** May 15. **Contact:** Northern Alberta Development Council, 2nd Fl., Provincial Bldg. 9621 - 96 Ave. Postal Bag 900-14 Peace River, AB T8S 1T4; 780-624-6545; nadc.council@gov.ab.ca.

172 ■ Northern Alberta Development Council Bursary for Medical Students *(Undergraduate/Award/Prize)*

Purpose: To increase the number of trained professionals in Northern Alberta and to encourage students from Northern Alberta to obtain a post-secondary education. **Focus:** Medicine. **Qualif.:** Applicants must be residents of Alberta and enrolled in a medical program. Applicants must not be in default of a provincial student loan. **Criteria:** Selection will be based on the committee's criteria.

Funds Avail.: $5,000. **To Apply:** Applicants may obtain an application form from www.benorth.ca. Application forms for these bursaries are also available from Alberta Scholarship Programs, Student Awards Offices and from the Northern Alberta Development Council. **Deadline:** June 1. **Contact:** Northern Alberta Development Council, 2nd Fl., Provincial Bldg. 9621 - 96 Ave. Postal Bag 900-14 Peace River, AB T8S 1T4; 780-624-6545; nadc.council@gov.ab.ca.

173 ■ Northern Alberta Development Council Bursary Partnership Program *(Undergraduate/Award/Prize)*

Purpose: To assist students in pursuing a post-secondary education. **Focus:** General studies. **Qualif.:** Applicants must be residents of Alberta and plan to enroll full-time in a post-secondary program. In addition, applicants must demonstrate financial need and be willing to live and work in northern Alberta after completion of the program. **Criteria:** Selection will be based on the committee's criteria.

Funds Avail.: $1,750. **To Apply:** Applicants may obtain an application form from www.benorth.ca. Application form for these bursaries are also available from Alberta Scholarship Programs, Student Awards Offices and from the Northern Alberta Development Council. **Deadline:** May 15. **Contact:** Northern Alberta Development Council, 2nd Fl., Provincial Bldg. 9621 - 96 Ave. Postal Bag 900-14 Peace River, AB T8S 1T4; 780-624-6545; nadc.council@gov.ab.ca.

174 ■ Northern Alberta Development Council Bursary for Pharmacy Students *(Undergraduate/Scholarship)*

Purpose: To increase the number of trained professionals in Northern Alberta and to encourage students from Northern Alberta to obtain a post-secondary education. **Focus:** Pharmacy. **Qualif.:** Applicants must be: a resident of Alberta based on Students Finance Regulations; enrolled in a four year pharmacy degree program; planning to live

Awards are arranged alphabetically below their administering organizations

and work in northern Alberta upon completion of studies; in good standing with any provincial student loan. **Criteria:** Selection will be based on the committee's criteria.

Funds Avail.: $3,500. **To Apply:** Applicants may obtain an application form from www.benorth.ca. Application forms for these bursaries are also available from Alberta Scholarship Programs, Student Awards Offices and from the Northern Alberta Development Council. **Deadline:** May 15. **Contact:** Northern Alberta Development Council, 2nd Fl., Provincial Bldg. 9621 - 96 Ave. Postal Bag 900-14 Peace River, AB T8S 1T4; 780-624-6545; nadc.council@gov.ab.ca.

175 ■ Northern Student Supplement
(Undergraduate/Award/Prize)

Purpose: To provide incentive for Northern Alberta students with high financial need to enter post-secondary programs. **Focus:** General studies. **Qualif.:** Student must be: first time, first or second year post-secondary students; attending an educational institution participating in the Alberta Opportunities Bursary (AOB) program. Applicants are considered a northern Alberta resident if they have lived in the Northern Alberta Development Council (NADC) area for two consecutive years immediately prior to beginning their present post-secondary program. **Criteria:** Selection will be based on financial need.

Funds Avail.: $500-$1,500. **To Apply:** Students will automatically be assessed for the supplement if they complete and submit the appropriate schedule with their online application for student financial assistance. Students applying on a paper application must complete and attach a separate application for the Northern Student Supplement. **Contact:** Northern Alberta Development Council, 2nd Fl., Provincial Bldg. 9621 - 96 Ave. Postal Bag 900-14 Peace River, AB T8S 1T4; 780-624-6545; nadc.council@gov.ab.ca.

176 ■ Persons Case Scholarships
(Undergraduate/Scholarship)

Purpose: To assist students whose studies will ultimately contribute to the advancement of women, or who are studying in fields where members of their gender are traditionally few in number. **Focus:** General studies. **Qualif.:** Applicants must be residents of Alberta and enrolled full-time at a post-secondary institution in Alberta. In addition, applicants must be enrolled in a program that is either non-traditional for their sex, or a program that will contribute to the advancement of women. Students studying out-of-province may be considered for this award if their program of study is not available in Alberta. **Criteria:** Selection will be based on program of studies, academic achievement and financial need.

Funds Avail.: $5,000. **To Apply:** Applicant must submit the following requirements with their complete application form: official transcript of all-post secondary studies; short essay of two or three pages outlining why the issues they are studying are important to them and how their studies, activities and community contribute to the advancement of women; curriculum vitae/resume outlining academic achievement, volunteer experience, awards won, etc. In total, submit six copies of the completed application form, and six copies of all attachments (the original and five photocopies). **Deadline:** September 30.

Remarks: Established in 1979. **Contact:** Alberta Scholarship Program at the above address (see entry 144).

177 ■ Prairie Baseball Academy Scholarships
(Undergraduate/Scholarship)

Purpose: To reward the athletic and academic excellence of baseball players and to provide an incentive and means for these players to continue with their post-secondary education. **Focus:** General studies. **Qualif.:** Applicants must be Alberta residents and enrolled full-time at a post-secondary institution in Alberta. Applicants must be participants in the Prairie Baseball Academy and must have achieved a minimum GPA of 2.0 on a 4.0 scale in the previous semester. **Criteria:** Selection will be based on academic achievement, community involvement and baseball achievements.

Funds Avail.: $500-$2,500. **To Apply:** Applicant may obtain an application form from Alberta Scholarship Programs, and from the Prairie Baseball Academy. **Deadline:** October 15. **Contact:** Alberta Scholarship Programs at the above address (see entry 144).

178 ■ Queen Elizabeth II Graduate Scholarship Program *(Doctorate, Graduate/Scholarship)*

Purpose: To reward the achievement of students pursuing graduate studies in Alberta. **Focus:** General studies. **Qualif.:** Applicants must be Canadian citizens or landed immigrants and enrolled full-time in a faculty of graduate studies in Alberta. **Criteria:** Selection will be based on the committee's criteria.

Funds Avail.: $9,300-Masters level; $10,500-Doctoral level. **To Apply:** Applicants may contact the faculty of graduate studies at their institution for more information about the nomination process. **Contact:** Alberta Scholarship Program at the above address (see entry 144).

179 ■ Registered Apprenticeship Program (RAP) Scholarships *(Undergraduate/Scholarship)*

Purpose: To recognize the accomplishments of Alberta high school students taking the Registered Apprenticeship Program (RAP) and to encourage recipients to continue their apprenticeship training after completing high school. **Focus:** General studies. **Qualif.:** Applicant must: be a Canadian citizen or landed immigrant, and a resident of Alberta; have completed the requirements for high school graduation in Alberta; be registered as an Alberta apprentice in a trade while still attending high school; have completed a minimum of 250 hours of on-the-job training and work experience in their chosen trade; plan to continue in an approved regular apprenticeship program after completing high school; have not been awarded a RAP Scholarship previously. **Criteria:** Selection will be based on the committee's criteria.

Funds Avail.: $1,000. **To Apply:** Application form can be obtained from Alberta Scholarship Program. Applications must be supported by: one or two paragraph (written or typed) autobiography confirming plans to continue their apprenticeship program and detailing why a career in that trade is a good fit for them; completed employer recommendation form; recommendation letter from a high school teacher or counselor. **Deadline:** July 15. **Contact:** Alberta Scholarship Programs at the above address (see entry 144).

180 ■ Robin Rousseau Memorial Mountain Achievement Scholarship *(Undergraduate/Scholarship)*

Purpose: To recognize excellence in an individual involved in leadership development and safety in the mountain community. **Focus:** General studies. **Qualif.:** Applicants must be Alberta residents and active in the mountain community and plan to study in any recognized Mountain Leadership and Safety program. **Criteria:** Applicants are evaluated based on their previous work and volunteer commitment for the mountain community, their personal goals and their ideas on how to continue to improve safety in the mountains.

Funds Avail.: No specific amount. **To Apply:** Applicants may obtain an application form from Alberta Scholarship Programs. **Deadline:** January 30. **Contact:** Alberta Scholarship Programs at the above address (see entry 144).

181 ■ Rutherford Scholars *(Undergraduate/Scholarship)*

Purpose: To reward the best Alexander Rutherford Scholarship recipients. **Focus:** General studies. **Qualif.:** Applicants must be in the top ten students as determined on the first writing of Diploma Examination. **Criteria:** Recipients are selected on the basis of results obtained on Diploma Examinations in one of: English 30-1, 30-2 or Francais 30, 30-2, Social Studies 30 plus three other subjects. Averages normally are in the 96.0 to 98.8 percent range. Only the first writing of the diploma exam will be considered.

Funds Avail.: $2,500. **To Apply:** No application is required. Recipients are selected from all Alexander Rutherford Scholarship applications received before the deadline. **Deadline:** August 1. **Contact:** Alberta Scholarship Programs at the above address (see entry 144).

182 ■ Alexander Rutherford Scholarships for High School Achievement *(Undergraduate/Scholarship)*

Purpose: To recognize and reward academic achievement at the senior high school level and to encourage students to pursue post-secondary studies. **Focus:** General studies. **Qualif.:** Applicants must be Canadian citizens or permanent residents and Alberta residents and plan to enroll full-time in a post-secondary program or apprenticeship program. Students must have a minimum combined average based on five designated courses in at least one grade: Grade 10, 11 or 12. The minimum average, value of the award, and courses that can be used depend on the student's graduation year. **Criteria:** Selection will be based on the committee's criteria.

Funds Avail.: $2,500. **To Apply:** There is no limit to apply for the scholarship except that the applicant must be planning to pursue post-secondary studies. Students who apply after the application deadline may not be recognized at their high school awards ceremony. High school grades obtained through upgrading at a post-secondary institution are not accepted. Eligible students who complete high school outside of Alberta must submit an official transcript of their high school marks from that province. **Deadline:** May 1. **Contact:** Alberta Scholarship programs at the above address (see entry 144).

183 ■ Dr. Robert Norman Shaw Scholarship *(Undergraduate/Scholarship)*

Purpose: To recognize and reward the exceptional achievement of a student graduating from Sexsmith Secondary School who is entering post-secondary studies in a health-related field. **Focus:** Health sciences. **Qualif.:** Applicants must have completed Grade 12 at Sexsmith Secondary School; be Alberta residents and plan to enroll full-time in a health-related post-secondary program of at least one semester in length. **Criteria:** Selection will be based on the highest average on five 30 level Grade 12 subjects.

Funds Avail.: $1,500. **To Apply:** Applicants may obtain an application form from the Counseling Office at Sexsmith Secondary School and also from Alberta Scholarship Programs. **Deadline:** June 1. **Contact:** Alberta Scholarship Programs at the above address (see entry 144).

184 ■ Dr. Robert and Anna Shaw Scholarships *(Undergraduate/Scholarship)*

Purpose: To recognize and reward the academic and leadership accomplishments of three students graduating from Sexsmith Secondary School who are entering post-secondary studies. **Focus:** Agriculture; Engineering; Art industries and trade; Fine arts. **Qualif.:** Applicants must be Alberta residents and plan to enroll full-time in a post-secondary program related to agriculture, engineering/trades or fine arts. **Criteria:** Selection will be based on academic accomplishments, leadership qualities, community spirit; involvement in extracurricular activities and a student's commitment to place the welfare of others above their own needs.

Funds Avail.: $500. **To Apply:** Applicants may obtain application form from Alberta Scholarship Programs and from the Counseling Office at Sexsmith Secondary School. **Deadline:** June 1. **Contact:** Alberta Scholarship Programs at the above address (see entry 144).

185 ■ Ralph Steinhauer Awards of Distinction *(Doctorate, Graduate/Award/Prize)*

Purpose: To recognize the academic achievement of students studying in Alberta. Students studying outside of Alberta should apply for the Sir James Lougheed Awards of Distinction. **Focus:** General studies. **Qualif.:** Applicants must be Canadian citizens or permanent residents and enrolled or planning to enroll full-time in a graduate program at an institution in Alberta. **Criteria:** Selection will be based on the committee's criteria.

Funds Avail.: $15,000-Masters level; $20,000-Doctoral level. **To Apply:** Application form can be obtained from Alberta Scholarship Programs. Applicants must submit the original and four signed and unstapled copies of the completed application form and attachments. This requirement does not apply to academic transcript and appraisals; these documents should be sent directly to Alberta Scholarship Programs. To verify the completeness of your application, send an email to Alberta Scholarship Programs' office with your name and social insurance number. **Deadline:** February 1. **Contact:** Alberta Scholarship Programs at the above address (see entry 144).

186 ■ Alberta Press Council

PO Box 2576
Medicine Hat, AB, Canada T1A 8G8
Ph: (403)580-4104
Fax: (403)580-4010
Free: 888-580-4104
E-mail: abpress@telus.net
URL: http://www.albertapresscouncil.ca

187 ■ Alberta Press Council Scholarships *(Undergraduate/Scholarship)*

Purpose: To assist high school students in pursuing post-secondary studies. **Focus:** General studies. **Qualif.:** Applicants must be Canadian citizens or permanent residents; must have been residents of Alberta for at least one year prior to time of application; must be students currently attending Grade 12 in a recognized school in Alberta or students who are enrolled full-time in a postsecondary degree or diploma program. Family members of newspaper

Awards are arranged alphabetically below their administering organizations

staff are eligible to apply; relatives of current Press Council Members are not. Scholarship is open to any field of study. Applicants must agree to allow the publishing of their essay on the Alberta Press Council's website and on Newswire Services. **Criteria:** Selection will be based on a 1000-1100 word essay on a pre-determined topic. Essays will be judged based on creativity, style and content.

Funds Avail.: $1,500 for the winning essay. **To Apply:** Essay must be typed, double spaced, 12 point font, 1,000-1,100 words. It is essential that essays be carefully checked/proofread before submission, and neat and tidy word processed on standard size paper (8 1/2 x 11). Six copies of the essay and the application form, with only one cover page, are to be sent to the Selection Committee, Alberta Press Council. Please submit by regular mail or express post, faxed applications will not be accepted. **Deadline:** February 28. **Contact:** Alberta Press council at the above address (see entry 186).

188 ■ Albuquerque Community Foundation

PO Box 36960
Albuquerque, NM 87176-6960
Ph: (505)883-6240
Fax: (505)883-3629
E-mail: foundation@albuquerquefoundation.org
URL: http://www.swcp.com

189 ■ Robby Baker Memorial Scholarships
(Undergraduate/Scholarship)

Purpose: To provide financial support to those deserving students. **Focus:** General Studies. **Qualif.:** Applicants must be coping with dyslexia or other reading disability; must have earned a minimum of 2.5 GPA and must be enrolled as full time students in an accredited college or university. **Criteria:** Preference will be given to those students who meet the criteria.

Funds Avail.: No specific amount. **To Apply:** Applicants must submit a completed application form and two references from teachers or counselors. **Contact:** Albuquerque Community Foundation at the above address (see entry 188).

190 ■ Notah Begay III Scholarship Program
(Undergraduate/Scholarship)

Purpose: To provide financial assistance to those students who are in need. **Focus:** General Studies. **Qualif.:** Applicants must be Native American scholar athletes; must have a minimum GPA 3.0; must attend a community college, 4 year college or university full time. **Criteria:** Preference will be given to those students who meet the criteria.

Funds Avail.: $2,000. **To Apply:** Applicants must submit the following: copy of FAFSA, Student Aid Report or statement of financial aid; proof of tribal enrollment or Certificate of Indian Blood (minimum 25%); one reference from a current academic teacher or counselor; one reference from an athletic coach; include in your personal statement how you plan to give back to your community after college. **Contact:** Albuquerque Community Foundation at the above address (see entry 188).

191 ■ Bryan Cline Memorial Soccer Scholarship Program *(Undergraduate/Scholarship)*

Purpose: To support the education of graduating senior varsity soccer players. **Focus:** General Studies. **Qualif.:** Applicants must attend a college or university full time. **Criteria:** Preference will be given to those students who meet the criteria.

Funds Avail.: No specific amount. **To Apply:** Applicants must submit a completed application form including the name of your varsity soccer team coach and two letters of reference- one from a teacher or counselor and one from a soccer coach.

Remarks: This scholarship is for Eldorado High School students only. **Contact:** Albuquerque Community Foundation at the above address (see entry 188).

192 ■ Excel Staffing Companies Scholarships for Excellence in Continuing Education
(Undergraduate/Scholarship)

Purpose: To assist individuals who demonstrate a commitment towards reaching a career goal. **Focus:** General Studies. **Qualif.:** Applicants must be individuals who are employed full time while attending school part time; must be residents of Albuquerque; must have a minimum of 3.0 GPA; must be working with a minimum of 30 hours per week. **Criteria:** Preference will be given to those students who meet the criteria.

Funds Avail.: $1,000. **To Apply:** Applicants must check the available website for the required materials. **Contact:** Albuquerque Community Foundation at the above address (see entry 188).

193 ■ New Mexico Manufactured Housing Association Scholarship Program *(Undergraduate/Scholarship)*

Purpose: To provide scholarship awards to New Mexico high school graduates residing in a manufactured home. **Focus:** General Studies. **Qualif.:** Applicants must live in a mobile/manufactured home; must have earned a minimum GPA 3.0; must attend a college or university full time. **Criteria:** Preference will be given to those students who meet the criteria.

Funds Avail.: $1,000. **To Apply:** Applicants must submit the following: written statement of financial need; proof of residency in a mobile/manufactured home: a copy of title or rental agreement or retail installment contract or county tax assessment; one reference from a teacher or counselor (1 page, 1 side only). **Contact:** Albuquerque Community Foundation at the above address (see entry 188).

194 ■ Barnes W. Rose, Jr. and Eva Rose Nichol Scholarship Fund *(Undergraduate/Scholarship)*

Purpose: To provide financial assistance to those students who are in need. **Focus:** Engineering. **Qualif.:** Applicants must demonstrate math and/or science interest and skill through SAT/ACF scores and/or strong grades in appropriate high school classes; must have a minimum of 3.6 GPA; must demonstrate financial need; must attend a college or university in pursuit of an engineering degree. **Criteria:** Preference will be given to those students who meet the criteria.

Funds Avail.: No specific amount. **To Apply:** Applicants must submit a completed application form and a minimum of one reference from an Albuquerque High School Math or Science teacher. **Contact:** Albuquerque Community Foundation at the above address (see entry 188).

195 ■ Sussman-Miller Educational Assistance Award Program *(Undergraduate/Scholarship)*

Purpose: To provide financial assistance to address the gap in financial aid packages for both students beginning their college careers and those continuing their undergraduate work. **Focus:** General Studies. **Qualif.:** Applicants must attend a college or university full-time; must be graduating high school seniors or currently enrolled in college/university; must be federal financial aid recipients. **Criteria:** Preference will be given to those students who meet the criteria.

Funds Avail.: No specific amount. **To Apply:** Applicants must check the available website for the required materials. **Deadline:** April 24; July 1. **Contact:** Albuquerque Community Foundation at the above address (see entry 188).

196 ■ Woodcock Family Education Scholarship Program *(Undergraduate/Scholarship)*

Purpose: To support students of exceptional promise in the fields of science and math. **Focus:** Math; Science. **Qualif.:** Applicants must be Albuquerque graduating high school seniors; with strong math and/or science credentials; must attend a college or university full time; must have a minimum GPA of 3.8; **Criteria:** Preference will be given to those students who meet the criteria.

Funds Avail.: $11,000. **To Apply:** Applicants must attach these to their application packet: career goals in personal statement MUST include those in the field of math or science; one reference from a math or science teacher; one or more references from other teachers, internship or work programs, or community services. **Contact:** Albuquerque Community Foundation at the above address (see entry 188).

197 ■ Horatio Alger Association

99 Canal Center Plaza, Ste. 320
Alexandria, VA 22314
Ph: (703)684-9444
Fax: (703)548-3822
URL: http://www.horatioalger.com

198 ■ Horatio Alger Ak-Sar-Ben Scholarships *(Undergraduate/Scholarship)*

Purpose: To provide financial assistance to students in the state of Nebraska and western Iowa. **Focus:** General studies. **Qualif.:** Applicants must be enrolled full time as a high school senior, progressing normally toward graduation, and planning to enter college no later than the fall following graduation; must have a strong commitment to pursue a bachelor's degree at an accredited institution (students may start their studies at a two-year institution and then transfer to a four-year institution); must have critical financial need ($50,000 or less adjusted gross income per family is preferred; if higher, an explanation must be provided); must be involved in co-curricular and community activities; must have a minimum grade point average of 2.0; must be a resident of Nebraska or western Iowa; be a citizen or permanent resident of the United States. **Criteria:** Recipients will be selected based on financial need.

Funds Avail.: $5,000. **Number Awarded:** 50. **To Apply:** Applicants must have one letter of support and must be logged in to the application process at the HAA website. Faxes/emails will not be accepted. Students must download the certification page from the HAA web site, complete it and obtain the proper signatures prior to mailing.

199 ■ Horatio Alger Alabama Scholarships *(Undergraduate/Scholarship)*

Purpose: To provide financial assistance to students in the state of Alabama who exhibited integrity and perseverance in overcoming personal adversity and aspire to pursue higher education. **Focus:** General studies. **Qualif.:** Applicants must be enrolled full time as a high school senior, progressing normally toward graduation, and planning to enter college no later than the fall following graduation; must have a strong commitment to pursue a bachelor's degree at an accredited institution (students may start their studies at a two-year institution and then transfer to a four-year institution); must have critical financial need ($50,000 or less adjusted gross income per family is preferred; if higher, an explanation must be provided); must be involved in co-curricular and community activities; must have a minimum grade point average of 2.0; be a resident of Alabama; and be a citizen or permanent resident of the United States. **Criteria:** Recipients will be selected based on financial need.

Funds Avail.: $5,000. **Number Awarded:** 12. **To Apply:** Applicants must have one letter of support and must be logged in to the application process at the HAA website. Faxes/emails will not be accepted. Students must download the certification page from the HAA web site, complete it and obtain the proper signatures prior to mailing.

200 ■ Horatio Alger California and California Orange County Scholarships *(Undergraduate/Scholarship)*

Purpose: To provide financial assistance to students in the state of California who have exhibited integrity and perseverance in overcoming personal adversity and aspire to pursue higher education. **Focus:** General studies. **Qualif.:** Applicants must be enrolled full time as a high school senior, progressing normally toward graduation, and planning to enter college no later than the fall following graduation; must have a strong commitment to pursue a bachelor's degree at an accredited institution (students may start their studies at a two-year institution and then transfer to a four-year institution); must have critical financial need ($50,000 or less adjusted gross income per family is preferred; if higher, an explanation must be provided); must be involved in co-curricular and community activities; must have a minimum grade point average of 2.0; be a resident of California; and be a citizen or permanent resident of the United States. **Criteria:** Recipients will be selected based on financial need.

Funds Avail.: $5,000 for Orange County residents; $2,500 for California residents outside Orange County. **Number Awarded:** 50-Orange county Residents; 100-California Residents outside Orange County. **To Apply:** Applicants must have one letter of support and must be logged in to the application process at the HAA website. Faxes/emails will not be accepted. Students must download the certification page from the HAA web site, complete it and obtain the proper signatures prior to mailing.

201 ■ Horatio Alger Delaware Scholarships *(Undergraduate/Scholarship)*

Purpose: To provide financial assistance to students in the state of Delaware. **Focus:** General studies. **Qualif.:** Applicants must be enrolled full time as a high school senior, progressing normally toward graduation, and planning to enter college no later than the fall following graduation; must have a strong commitment to pursue a bachelor's degree at an accredited institution (students may start their studies at a two-year institution and then transfer to a four-year institution); must have critical financial need ($50,000 or less adjusted gross income per family is preferred; if higher, an explanation must be provided); must be involved in co-curricular and community activities; must have a

Awards are arranged alphabetically below their administering organizations

minimum grade point average of 2.0; be a resident of Delaware; and be a citizen or permanent resident of the United States. **Criteria:** Recipients will be selected based on financial need.

Funds Avail.: $5,000. **Number Awarded:** 25. **To Apply:** Applicants must have one letter of support and must be logged in to the application process at the HAA website. Faxes/emails will not be accepted. Students must download the certification page from the HAA web site, complete it and obtain the proper signatures prior to mailing.

202 ■ Horatio Alger District of Columbia, Maryland, and Virginia Scholarships
(Undergraduate/Scholarship)

Purpose: To recognize deserving students from the Washington D.C., Metro area in the following counties: District of Columbia, Maryland, Virginia. **Focus:** General studies. **Qualif.:** Applicants must be enrolled full time as a high school senior, progressing normally toward graduation, and planning to enter college no later than the fall following graduation; must have a strong commitment to pursue a bachelor's degree at an accredited institution (students may start their studies at a two-year institution and then transfer to a four-year institution); must have critical financial need ($50,000 or less adjusted gross income per family is preferred; if higher, an explanation must be provided); must be involved in co-curricular and community activities; must have a minimum grade point average of 2.0; and be a citizen or permanent resident of the United States. **Criteria:** Recipients will be selected based on financial need.

Funds Avail.: $2,500. **Number Awarded:** 25. **To Apply:** Applicants must have one letter of support and must be logged in to the application process at the HAA website. Faxes/emails will not be accepted. Students must download the certification page from the HAA web site, complete it and obtain the proper signatures prior to mailing.

203 ■ Horatio Alger Florida Scholarships
(Undergraduate/Scholarship)

Purpose: To provide financial assistance to students in the counties of Broward, Martin, and St. Lucie in the state of Florida. **Focus:** General studies. **Qualif.:** Applicants must be enrolled full time as a high school senior, progressing normally toward graduation, and planning to enter college no later than the fall following graduation; must have a strong commitment to pursue a bachelor's degree at an accredited institution (students may start their studies at a two-year institution and then transfer to a four-year institution); must have critical financial need ($50,000 or less adjusted gross income per family is preferred; if higher, an explanation must be provided); must be involved in co-curricular and community activities; must have a minimum grade point average of 2.0; and be a citizen or permanent resident of the United States. **Criteria:** Recipients will be selected based on financial need.

Funds Avail.: $5,000. **Number Awarded:** 50. **To Apply:** Applicants must have one letter of support and must be logged in to the application process at the HAA website. Faxes/emails will not be accepted. Students must download the certification page from the HAA web site, complete it and obtain the proper signatures prior to mailing.

204 ■ Horatio Alger Franklin Scholarships
(Undergraduate/Scholarship)

Purpose: To provide financial assistance to high school seniors in the state of Pennsylvania. **Focus:** General studies. **Qualif.:** Applicants must reside and attend high school in the state of Pennsylvania; must be enrolled full time as a high school senior, progressing normally toward graduation, and planning to enter college no later than the fall following graduation; must have a strong commitment to pursue a bachelor's degree at an accredited institution (students may start their studies at a two-year institution and then transfer to a four-year institution); must have critical financial need ($50,000 or less adjusted gross income per family is preferred; if higher, an explanation must be provided); must be involved in co-curricular and community activities; must have a minimum grade point average of 2.0; and be a citizen or permanent resident of the United States. **Criteria:** Recipients will be selected based on financial need.

Funds Avail.: $10,000. **Number Awarded:** 25. **To Apply:** Applicants must have one letter of support and must be logged in to the application process at the HAA website. Faxes/emails will not be accepted. Students must download the certification page from the HAA web site, complete it and obtain the proper signatures prior to mailing.

205 ■ Horatio Alger Georgia Scholarships
(Undergraduate/Scholarship)

Purpose: To provide financial assistance to students in the state of Georgia. **Focus:** General studies. **Qualif.:** Applicants must be enrolled full time as a high school senior, progressing normally toward graduation, and planning to enter college no later than the fall following graduation; must have a strong commitment to pursue a bachelor's degree at an accredited institution (students may start their studies at a two-year institution and then transfer to a four-year institution); must have critical financial need ($50,000 or less adjusted gross income per family is preferred; if higher, an explanation must be provided); must be involved in co-curricular and community activities; must have a minimum grade point average of 2.0; and be a citizen or permanent resident of the United States. **Criteria:** Recipients will be selected based on financial need.

Funds Avail.: $5,000. **Number Awarded:** 5. **To Apply:** Applicants must have one letter of support and must be logged in to the application process at the HAA website. Faxes/emails will not be accepted. Students must download the certification page from the HAA web site, complete it and obtain the proper signatures prior to mailing.

206 ■ Horatio Alger Idaho University Scholarships *(Undergraduate/Scholarship)*

Purpose: To provide financial assistance to students entering their final two years of study in the College of Business at Idaho State University. **Focus:** General studies. **Qualif.:** Applicants must attend Idaho State University and be enrolled in the College of Business; must have critical financial need based on the Student Aid Report; must be a resident of the State of Idaho; must have a minimum cumulative grade point average of 2.25 or better. **Criteria:** Recipients will be selected based on the committee's review of all applications.

Funds Avail.: $5,000. **Number Awarded:** 5. **To Apply:** Applicants must have one letter of support and must be logged in to the application process at the HAA website. Faxes/emails will not be accepted. Students must download the certification page from the HAA web site, complete it and obtain the proper signatures prior to mailing. **Deadline:** May 9.

207 ■ Horatio Alger Illinois Scholarships *(Undergraduate/Scholarship)*

Purpose: To provide financial assistance to students in the state of Illinois. **Focus:** General studies. **Qualif.:** Applicants must be enrolled full time as a high school senior, progressing normally toward graduation, and planning to enter college no later than the fall following graduation; must have a strong commitment to pursue a bachelor's degree at an accredited institution (students may start their studies at a two-year institution and then transfer to a four-year institution); must have critical financial need ($50,000 or less adjusted gross income per family is preferred; if higher, an explanation must be provided); must be involved in co-curricular and community activities; must have a minimum grade point average of 2.0; be a resident of Illinois; and be a citizen or permanent resident of the United States. **Criteria:** Recipients will be selected based on financial need.

Funds Avail.: $5,000. **Number Awarded:** 25. **To Apply:** Applicants must have one letter of support and must be logged in to the application process at the HAA website. Faxes/emails will not be accepted. Students must download the certification page from the HAA web site, complete it and obtain the proper signatures prior to mailing.

208 ■ Horatio Alger Indiana Scholarships *(Undergraduate/Scholarship)*

Purpose: To financial assistance to students in the state of Indiana. **Focus:** General studies. **Qualif.:** Applicants must be enrolled full time as a high school senior, progressing normally toward graduation, and planning to enter college no later than the fall following graduation; must have a strong commitment to pursue a bachelor's degree at an accredited institution (students may start their studies at a two-year institution and then transfer to a four-year institution); must have critical financial need ($50,000 or less adjusted gross income per family is preferred; if higher, an explanation must be provided); must be involved in co-curricular and community activities; must have a minimum grade point average of 2.0; be a resident of Indiana; and be a citizen or permanent resident of the United States. **Criteria:** Recipients will be selected based on financial need.

Funds Avail.: $5,000. **Number Awarded:** 8. **To Apply:** Applicants must have one letter of support and must be logged in to the application process at the HAA website. Faxes/emails will not be accepted. Students must download the certification page from the HAA web site, complete it and obtain the proper signatures prior to mailing.

209 ■ Horatio Alger Iowa Scholarships *(Undergraduate/Scholarship)*

Purpose: To provide financial assistance to students in the state of Iowa. **Focus:** General studies. **Qualif.:** Applicants must be enrolled full time as a high school senior, progressing normally toward graduation, and planning to enter college no later than the fall following graduation; must have a strong commitment to pursue a bachelor's degree at an accredited institution (students may start their studies at a two-year institution and then transfer to a four-year institution); must have critical financial need ($50,000 or less adjusted gross income per family is preferred; if higher, an explanation must be provided); must be involved in co-curricular and community activities; must have a minimum grade point average of 2.0; and be a citizen or permanent resident of the United States. **Criteria:** Recipients will be selected based on financial need.

Funds Avail.: $3,000. **Number Awarded:** 100. **To Apply:** Applicants must have one letter of support and must be logged in to the application process at the HAA website. Faxes/emails will not be accepted. Students must download the certification page from the HAA web site, complete it and obtain the proper signatures prior to mailing.

210 ■ Horatio Alger Kentucky Scholarships *(Undergraduate/Scholarship)*

Purpose: To provide financial assistance to students in the state of Kentucky. **Focus:** General studies. **Qualif.:** Applicants must be enrolled full time as a high school senior, progressing normally toward graduation, and planning to enter college no later than the fall following graduation; must have a strong commitment to pursue a bachelor's degree at an accredited institution (students may start their studies at a two-year institution and then transfer to a four-year institution); must have critical financial need ($50,000 or less adjusted gross income per family is preferred; if higher, an explanation must be provided); must be involved in co-curricular and community activities; must have a minimum grade point average of 2.0; be a resident of Kentucky; and be a citizen or permanent resident of the United States. **Criteria:** Recipients will be selected based on financial need.

Funds Avail.: $5,000. **Number Awarded:** 8. **To Apply:** Applicants must have one letter of support and must be logged in to the application process at the HAA website. Faxes/emails will not be accepted. Students must download the certification page from the HAA web site, complete it and obtain the proper signatures prior to mailing.

211 ■ Horatio Alger Lola and Duane Hagadone Idaho Scholarships *(Undergraduate/Scholarship)*

Purpose: To provide scholarships to students in the State of Idaho. **Focus:** General studies. **Qualif.:** Applicants must be enrolled full time as a high school senior, progressing normally toward graduation, and planning to enter college no later than the fall following graduation; must have a strong commitment to pursue a bachelor's degree at an accredited institution (students may start their studies at a two-year institution and then transfer to a four-year institution); must have critical financial need ($50,000 or less adjusted gross income per family is preferred; if higher, an explanation must be provided); must be involved in co-curricular and community activities; must have a minimum grade point average of 2.0; and be a resident of Benewah, Boundary, Bonner, Kootenai, Latah, or Shoshone counties in the State of Idaho. Recipients must pursue a bachelor's degree at the University of Idaho or Lewis-Clark State College. **Criteria:** Recipients will be selected based on the committee's review of all applications.

Funds Avail.: $5,000. **Number Awarded:** 25. **To Apply:** Applicants must have one letter of support and must be logged in to the application process at the HAA website. Faxes/emails will not be accepted. Students must download the certification page from the HAA web site, complete it and obtain the proper signatures prior to mailing.

212 ■ Horatio Alger Louisiana Scholarships *(Undergraduate/Scholarship)*

Purpose: To provide financial assistance to students in the state of Louisiana. **Focus:** General studies. **Qualif.:** Applicants must be enrolled full time as a high school senior, progressing normally toward graduation, and planning to enter college no later than the fall following graduation; must have a strong commitment to pursue a bachelor's degree at an accredited institution (students may start their studies at a two-year institution and then transfer to a four-year institution); must have critical financial need ($50,000 or less adjusted gross income per family is preferred; if higher, an explanation must be provided); must be involved in co-curricular and community activities; must have a minimum grade point average of 2.0; be a citizen or permanent resident of the United States. Students must plan to attend and enroll in one of the following five schools to be awarded the Louisiana Scholarship: Loyola University - New Orleans; McNeese State University; Tulane University; University of New Orleans; Xavier University. **Criteria:** Recipients will be selected based on financial need.

Funds Avail.: $10,500. **Number Awarded:** 50. **To Apply:** Applicants must have one letter of support and must be logged in to the application process at the HAA website. Faxes/emails will not be accepted. Students must download the certification page from the HAA web site, complete it and obtain the proper signatures prior to mailing.

213 ■ Horatio Alger Minnesota Scholarships

(Undergraduate/Scholarship)

Purpose: To provide financial assistance to students in the state of Minnesota. **Focus:** General studies. **Qualif.:** Applicants must be enrolled full time as a high school senior, progressing normally toward graduation, and planning to enter college no later than the fall following graduation; must have a strong commitment to pursue a bachelor's degree at an accredited institution (students may start their studies at a two-year institution and then transfer to a four-year institution); must have critical financial need ($50,000 or less adjusted gross income per family is preferred; if higher, an explanation must be provided); must be involved in co-curricular and community activities; must have a minimum grade point average of 2.0; must be a resident of Anoka, Carver, Dakota, Hennepin, Ramsey, Scott, and Washington counties; and be a citizen or permanent resident of the United States. **Criteria:** Recipients will be selected based on financial need.

Funds Avail.: $4,000. **Number Awarded:** 42. **To Apply:** Applicants must have one letter of support and must be logged in to the application process at the HAA website. Faxes/emails will not be accepted. Students must download the certification page from the HAA web site, complete it and obtain the proper signatures prior to mailing.

214 ■ Horatio Alger Mississippi Scholarships

(Undergraduate/Scholarship)

Purpose: To provide financial assistance to students in the state of Mississippi. **Focus:** General studies. **Qualif.:** Applicants must be enrolled full time as a high school senior, progressing normally toward graduation, and planning to enter college no later than the fall following graduation; must have a strong commitment to pursue a bachelor's degree at an accredited institution (students may start their studies at a two-year institution and then transfer to a four-year institution); must have critical financial need ($50,000 or less adjusted gross income per family is preferred; if higher, an explanation must be provided); must be involved in co-curricular and community activities; must have a minimum grade point average of 2.0; be a resident of Mississippi; and be a citizen or permanent resident of the United States. **Criteria:** Recipients will be selected based on financial need.

Funds Avail.: $5,000. **Number Awarded:** 12. **To Apply:** Applicants must have one letter of support and must be logged in to the application process at the HAA website. Faxes/emails will not be accepted. Students must download the certification page from the HAA web site, complete it and obtain the proper signatures prior to mailing.

215 ■ Horatio Alger Missouri Scholarships

(Undergraduate/Scholarship)

Purpose: To provide financial assistance to students in the state Missouri. **Focus:** General studies. **Qualif.:** Applicants must be enrolled full time as a high school senior, progressing normally toward graduation, and planning to enter college no later than the fall following graduation; must have a strong commitment to pursue a bachelor's degree at an accredited institution (students may start their studies at a two-year institution and then transfer to a four-year institution); must have critical financial need ($50,000 or less adjusted gross income per family is preferred; if higher, an explanation must be provided); must be involved in co-curricular and community activities; must have a minimum grade point average of 2.0; must be a resident of Missouri; and be a citizen or permanent resident of the United States. **Criteria:** Recipients will be selected based on financial need.

Funds Avail.: $5,000. **Number Awarded:** 50. **To Apply:** Applicants must have one letter of support and must be logged in to the application process at the HAA website. Faxes/emails will not be accepted. Students must download the certification page from the HAA web site, complete it and obtain the proper signatures prior to mailing.

216 ■ Horatio Alger Montana Scholarships

(Undergraduate/Scholarship)

Purpose: To provide financial assistance to students in the state of Montana. **Focus:** General studies. **Qualif.:** Applicants must be enrolled full time as a high school senior, progressing normally toward graduation, and planning to enter college no later than the fall following graduation; must have a strong commitment to pursue a bachelor's degree at an accredited institution (students may start their studies at a two-year institution and then transfer to a four-year institution); must have critical financial need ($50,000 or less adjusted gross income per family is preferred; if higher, an explanation must be provided); must be involved in co-curricular and community activities; must have a minimum grade point average of 2.0; must be a resident of Montana; and be a citizen or permanent resident of the United States. Recipients must pursue a bachelor's degree at the University of Montana, The University of Montana-Western, The University of Montana-Missoula College of Technology, Helena College of Technology of The University of Montana, or Montana Tech of The University of The University of Montana. **Criteria:** Recipients will be selected based on financial need.

Funds Avail.: $5,000. **Number Awarded:** 50. **To Apply:** Applicants must have one letter of support and must be logged in to the application process at the HAA website. Faxes/emails will not be accepted. Students must download the certification page from the HAA web site, complete it and obtain the proper signatures prior to mailing.

217 ■ Horatio Alger National Scholarships

(Undergraduate/Scholarship)

Purpose: To assist high school students who have faced and overcome great obstacles in their young lives. **Focus:** General studies. **Qualif.:** Applicants must be enrolled full time as a high school senior, progressing normally toward graduation, and planning to enter college no later than the fall following graduation; must have a strong commitment to pursue a bachelor's degree at an accredited institution

Awards are arranged alphabetically below their administering organizations

(students may start their studies at a two-year institution and then transfer to a four-year institution); must have critical financial need ($50,000 or less adjusted gross income per family is preferred; if higher, an explanation must be provided); must be involved in co-curricular and community activities; must have a minimum grade point average of 2.0; and be a citizen or permanent resident of the United States. **Criteria:** Recipients will be selected based on the committee's review of all applications.

Funds Avail.: $20,000. **To Apply:** Applicants must have one letter of support and must be logged in to the application process at the HAA website. Faxes/emails will not be accepted. Students must download the certification page from the HAA web site, complete it and obtain the proper signatures prior to mailing.

218 ■ Horatio Alger New Jersey Scholarships
(Undergraduate/Scholarship)

Purpose: To provide financial assistance to students in the state of New Jersey. **Focus:** General studies. **Qualif.:** Applicants must be enrolled full time as a high school senior, progressing normally toward graduation, and planning to enter college no later than the fall following graduation; must have a strong commitment to pursue a bachelor's degree at an accredited institution (students may start their studies at a two-year institution and then transfer to a four-year institution); must have critical financial need ($50,000 or less adjusted gross income per family is preferred; if higher, an explanation must be provided); must be involved in co-curricular and community activities; must have a minimum grade point average of 2.0; and be a citizen or permanent resident of the United States. **Criteria:** Recipients will be selected based on financial need.

Funds Avail.: $5,000. **Number Awarded:** 5. **To Apply:** Applicants must have one letter of support and must be logged in to the application process at the HAA website. Faxes/emails will not be accepted. Students must download the certification page from the HAA web site, complete it and obtain the proper signatures prior to mailing.

219 ■ Horatio Alger New York Scholarships
(Undergraduate/Scholarship)

Purpose: To provide financial assistance to students in the state of New York. **Focus:** General studies. **Qualif.:** Applicants must be enrolled full time as a high school senior, progressing normally toward graduation, and planning to enter college no later than the fall following graduation; must have a strong commitment to pursue a bachelor's degree at an accredited institution (students may start their studies at a two-year institution and then transfer to a four-year institution); must have critical financial need ($50,000 or less adjusted gross income per family is preferred; if higher, an explanation must be provided); must be involved in co-curricular and community activities; must have a minimum grade point average of 2.0; and be a citizen or permanent resident of the United States. **Criteria:** Recipients will be selected based on financial need.

Funds Avail.: $5,000. **Number Awarded:** 5. **To Apply:** Applicants must have one letter of support and must be logged in to the application process at the HAA website. Faxes/emails will not be accepted. Students must download the certification page from the HAA web site, complete it and obtain the proper signatures prior to mailing.

220 ■ Horatio Alger North Dakota Scholarships
(Undergraduate/Scholarship)

Purpose: To provide financial assistance to students in the state of North Dakota. **Focus:** General studies. **Qualif.:** Applicants must be enrolled full time as a high school senior, progressing normally toward graduation, and planning to enter college no later than the fall following graduation; must have a strong commitment to pursue a bachelor's degree at an accredited institution (students may start their studies at a two-year institution and then transfer to a four-year institution); must have critical financial need ($50,000 or less adjusted gross income per family is preferred; if higher, an explanation must be provided); must be involved in co-curricular and community activities; must have a minimum grade point average of 2.0; be a resident of North Dakota; and be a citizen or permanent resident of the United States. **Criteria:** Recipients will be selected based on financial need.

Funds Avail.: $5,000. **Number Awarded:** 25. **To Apply:** Applicants must have one letter of support and must be logged in to the application process at the HAA website. Faxes/emails will not be accepted. Students must download the certification page from the HAA web site, complete it and obtain the proper signatures prior to mailing.

221 ■ Horatio Alger Oregon Scholarships
(Undergraduate/Scholarship)

Purpose: To provide financial assistance to students in the state of Oregon. **Focus:** General studies. **Qualif.:** Applicants must be enrolled full time as a high school senior, progressing normally toward graduation, and planning to enter college no later than the fall following graduation; must have a strong commitment to pursue a bachelor's degree at an accredited institution (students may start their studies at a two-year institution and then transfer to a four-year institution); must have critical financial need ($50,000 or less adjusted gross income per family is preferred; if higher, an explanation must be provided); must be involved in co-curricular and community activities; must have a minimum grade point average of 2.0; be a resident of Oregon; and be a citizen or permanent resident of the United States. **Criteria:** Recipients will be selected based on financial need.

Funds Avail.: $5,000. **Number Awarded:** 5. **To Apply:** Applicants must have one letter of support and must be logged in to the application process at the HAA website. Faxes/emails will not be accepted. Students must download the certification page from the HAA web site, complete it and obtain the proper signatures prior to mailing.

222 ■ Horatio Alger Pennsylvania Scholarships
(Undergraduate/Scholarship)

Purpose: To provide financial assistance to students in the State of Pennsylvania. **Focus:** General studies. **Qualif.:** Applicants must be enrolled full time as a high school senior, progressing normally toward graduation, and planning to enter college no later than the fall following graduation; must have a strong commitment to pursue a bachelor's degree at an accredited institution (students may start their studies at a two-year institution and then transfer to a four-year institution); must have critical financial need ($50,000 or less adjusted gross income per family is preferred; if higher, an explanation must be provided); must be involved in co-curricular and community activities; must have a minimum grade point average of 2.0; be a resident of Pennsylvania; and be a citizen or permanent resident of the United States. **Criteria:** Recipients will be selected based on financial need.

Funds Avail.: $5,000. **Number Awarded:** 50. **To Apply:** Applicants must have one letter of support and must be logged in to the application process at the HAA website.

Faxes/emails will not be accepted. Students must download the certification page from the HAA web site, complete it and obtain the proper signatures prior to mailing.

223 ■ Horatio Alger South Dakota Scholarships
(Undergraduate/Scholarship)

Purpose: To provide financial assistance to students in the state of South Dakota. **Focus:** General studies. **Qualif.:** Applicants must be enrolled full time as a high school senior, progressing normally toward graduation, and planning to enter college no later than the fall following graduation; must have a strong commitment to pursue a bachelor's degree at an accredited institution (students may start their studies at a two-year institution and then transfer to a four-year institution); must have critical financial need ($50,000 or less adjusted gross income per family is preferred; if higher, an explanation must be provided); must be involved in co-curricular and community activities; must have a minimum grade point average of 2.0; be a resident of South Dakota; and be a citizen or permanent resident of the United States. **Criteria:** Recipients will be selected based on financial need.

Funds Avail.: $5,000. **Number Awarded:** 25. **To Apply:** Applicants must have one letter of support and must be logged in to the application process at the HAA website. Faxes/emails will not be accepted. Students must download the certification page from the HAA web site, complete it and obtain the proper signatures prior to mailing.

224 ■ Horatio Alger Texas - Fort Worth Scholarships *(Undergraduate/Scholarship)*

Purpose: To provide financial assistance to students from Fort Worth, Texas. **Focus:** General studies. **Qualif.:** Applicants must be enrolled full time as a high school senior, progressing normally toward graduation, and planning to enter college no later than the fall following graduation; must have a strong commitment to pursue a bachelor's degree at an accredited institution (students may start their studies at a two-year institution and then transfer to a four-year institution); must have critical financial need ($50,000 or less adjusted gross income per family is preferred; if higher, an explanation must be provided); must be involved in co-curricular and community activities; must have a minimum grade point average of 2.0; and be a citizen or permanent resident of the United States. **Criteria:** Recipients will be selected based on financial need.

Funds Avail.: $5,000. **Number Awarded:** 12. **To Apply:** Applicants must have one letter of support and must be logged in to the application process at the HAA website. Faxes/emails will not be accepted. Students must download the certification page from the HAA web site, complete it and obtain the proper signatures prior to mailing.

225 ■ Horatio Alger Texas Scholarships
(Undergraduate/Scholarship)

Purpose: To provide financial assistance to students in the state of Texas. **Focus:** General studies. **Qualif.:** Applicants must be enrolled full time as a high school senior, progressing normally toward graduation, and planning to enter college no later than the fall following graduation; must have a strong commitment to pursue a bachelor's degree at an accredited institution (students may start their studies at a two-year institution and then transfer to a four-year institution); must have critical financial need ($50,000 or less adjusted gross income per family is preferred; if higher, an explanation must be provided); must be involved in co-curricular and community activities; must have a minimum grade point average of 2.0; be a resident of Texas; and be a citizen or permanent resident of the United States. **Criteria:** Recipients will be selected based on financial need.

Funds Avail.: $5,000. **Number Awarded:** 28. **To Apply:** Applicants must have one letter of support and must be logged in to the application process at the HAA website. Faxes/emails will not be accepted. Students must download the certification page from the HAA web site, complete it and obtain the proper signatures prior to mailing.

226 ■ Horatio Alger Utah Scholarships
(Undergraduate/Scholarship)

Purpose: To provide financial assistance to students in the state of Utah. **Focus:** General studies. **Qualif.:** Applicants must be enrolled full time as a high school senior, progressing normally toward graduation, and planning to enter college no later than the fall following graduation; must have a strong commitment to pursue a bachelor's degree at an accredited institution (students may start their studies at a two-year institution and then transfer to a four-year institution); must have critical financial need ($50,000 or less adjusted gross income per family is preferred; if higher, an explanation must be provided); must be involved in co-curricular and community activities; must have a minimum grade point average of 2.0; and be a citizen or permanent resident of the United States. **Criteria:** Recipients will be selected based on financial need.

Funds Avail.: $5,000. **Number Awarded:** 25. **To Apply:** Applicants must have one letter of support and must be logged in to the application process at the HAA website. Faxes/emails will not be accepted. Students must download the certification page from the HAA web site, complete it and obtain the proper signatures prior to mailing.

227 ■ Horatio Alger Washington Scholarships
(Undergraduate/Scholarship)

Purpose: To provide financial assistance to students in the state of Washington. **Focus:** General studies. **Qualif.:** Applicants must be enrolled full time as a high school senior, progressing normally toward graduation, and planning to enter college no later than the fall following graduation; must have a strong commitment to pursue a bachelor's degree at an accredited institution (students may start their studies at a two-year institution and then transfer to a four-year institution); must have critical financial need ($50,000 or less adjusted gross income per family is preferred; if higher, an explanation must be provided); must be involved in co-curricular and community activities; must have a minimum grade point average of 2.0; be a resident of Washington; and be a citizen or permanent resident of the United States. **Criteria:** Recipients will be selected based on financial need.

Funds Avail.: $5,000. **Number Awarded:** 5. **To Apply:** Applicants must have one letter of support and must be logged in to the application process at the HAA website. Faxes/emails will not be accepted. Students must download the certification page from the HAA web site, complete it and obtain the proper signatures prior to mailing.

228 ■ Horatio Alger Wyoming Scholarships
(Undergraduate/Scholarship)

Purpose: To provide financial assistance to students in the state of Wyoming. **Focus:** General studies. **Qualif.:** Applicants must be enrolled full time as a high school senior, progressing normally toward graduation, and planning to enter college no later than the fall following graduation; must have a strong commitment to pursue a bachelor's degree at an accredited institution (students may start their studies at a two-year institution and then transfer to a four-year institution); must have critical financial need ($50,000 or less adjusted gross income per family is preferred; if higher, an explanation must be provided); must be involved in co-curricular and community activities; must have a minimum grade point average of 2.0; and be a citizen or permanent resident of the United States. **Criteria:** Recipients will be selected based on financial need.

Funds Avail.: $5,000. **Number Awarded:** 5. **To Apply:** Applicants must have one letter of support and must be logged in to the application process at the HAA website. Faxes/emails will not be accepted. Students must download the certification page from the HAA web site, complete it and obtain the proper signatures prior to mailing.

229 ■ All Star Association

PO Box 911050
Lexington, KY 40591-1050
Ph: (859)255-3644
Fax: (859)255-3647
Free: 800-930-3644
URL: http://www.allstardairy.com

230 ■ John D. Utterback Undergraduate Scholarships *(Undergraduate/Scholarship)*

Purpose: To provide support for dependents of association members. **Focus:** Food science and technology. **Qualif.:** Applicant must be a high school or college student enrolled in food science, marketing, business, nutrition, packaging, or AG education programs. **Criteria:** Applicants will be selected based on their academic performance, courses related to food science, apparent commitment to a career in dairy/beverage/food industry; involvement in extra-curricular activities, and by the evidence of leadership ability, initiative, character, and integrity.

Funds Avail.: $1,000. **Number Awarded:** 5. **To Apply:** Applicants must complete and print the online questionnaire; must have the official transcript from all high schools, colleges, and universities attended; must submit a request letter of recommendation from a faculty member familiar with the applicant's scholastic performance; must have a recent photograph. Application form and other supporting documents must be sent to: All Star Dairy Association, Inc., 1050 Monarch St., Ste. No, 101, Lexington, KY 40513. **Deadline:** April 1.

231 ■ Allen University

1530 Harden St.
Columbia, SC 29204
Ph: (803)376-5700
URL: http://www.allenuniversity.edu

232 ■ Legislative Incentive for Future Excellence (LIFE) Scholarships *(Undergraduate/Scholarship)*

Purpose: To provide educational assistance for honor students. **Focus:** General studies. **Qualif.:** Applicants must be U.S. citizens or legal permanent residents and must be South Carolina residents at the time of high school graduation and at the time of college enrollment. **Criteria:** Applicants should belong to the top 30% (student rank) of the graduating class.

Funds Avail.: No specific amount. **To Apply:** Applicants must have earned a cumulative 3.0 grade point average (GPA) based on the SC Uniform Grading Scale upon high school graduation.

Remarks: Allen University's academic regulations specify the minimum cumulative grade point average a student must earn in order to avoid being placed on academic probation or suspension.

233 ■ Alliance for Choice in Education

1201 E Colfax Ave., Ste. 302
Denver, CO 80218
Ph: (303)573-1603
Fax: (720)266-6798
E-mail: mcooke@acescholarships.org
URL: http://www.acescholarships.org

234 ■ ACE K-12 Scholarships Program *(High School/Scholarship)*

Purpose: To provide financial assistance to deserving students and to increase the access to high quality educational options. **Focus:** General Studies. **Qualif.:** Applicants must be grades K-12; must be Colorado residents. **Criteria:** Preference will be given to those students who meet the criteria.

Funds Avail.: Maximum of $2,000. **To Apply:** Applicants must submit the scholarship application form and must check the available website for more information. **Contact:** Alliance for Choice in Education at the above address (see entry 233).

235 ■ Alliance of Technology and Women

25 Highland Park Vill., No. 100-393
Dallas, TX 75205
Free: 888-895-1566
E-mail: info@atwinternational.org
URL: http://www.atwinternational.org

236 ■ GREAT MINDS Collegiate Scholarship Program *(Undergraduate/Scholarship)*

Purpose: To provide financial assistance to women whose academic and professional goals include work in science, math, engineering or technology. **Focus:** Science; Math; Engineering; Technology. **Qualif.:** Applicants must be first-time students or adult learners returning to school to pursue a new career; must be enrolled in an Associate's or Bachelor's Degree program; may have diverse levels of life experience, academic merit, age, race and religion. **Criteria:** Recipients are chosen on the basis of volunteer service, passion for technology, leadership activities, scholastic grades, letters of recommendation and previous awards. Demonstrated passion and spirit is weighted most heavily in the selection process.

Funds Avail.: No specific amount. **To Apply:** Applicants must submit a completed application form. **Contact:** Alliance of Technology and Women at the above address (see entry 235).

237 ■ Alpha Chi

Harding University Box 12249
900 E Ctr.
Searcy, AR 72149-0001
URL: http://www.harding.edu

238 ■ Benedict Fellowships *(Graduate/Fellowship)*

Purpose: To provide financial support individuals for their first year of graduate study toward the master's, doctorate,

Awards are arranged alphabetically below their administering organizations

or professional degree at any recognized institution. **Focus:** General studies. **Qualif.:** Nominee must be enrolled as an undergraduate or graduate with the baccalaureate degree during the school year in which application is made and must identify the graduate or professional school(s) to which he/she has applied for study the following fall. **Criteria:** Nominee must be enrolled for the following fall semester as a full-time student in graduate or professional study.

Funds Avail.: $2,500. **Number Awarded:** 10. **To Apply:** Nominee must submit the official nomination form completed, signed by the sponsor, and included with the entry; a letter of application from the student outlining his/her plans for study and detailing his/her extracurricular activities, maximum length of two pages, double-spaced; an academic paper or other appropriate work in the student's major field; one letter of recommendation/evaluation from a faculty member in the field represented by the paper or project addressed to the significance of the work; a self-addressed, stamped envelope. **Deadline:** February 22.

239 ■ Gaston Scholarships *(Undergraduate/ Scholarship)*

Purpose: To provide financial support for the education of senior undergraduate students. **Focus:** General studies. **Qualif.:** Nominee must be a senior year undergraduate student. **Criteria:** Nominee must be enrolled for the fall semester as a full-time student in undergraduate study toward the baccalaureate degree.

Funds Avail.: $2,000. **Number Awarded:** 2. **To Apply:** Nominee must submit the official nomination form completed, signed by the sponsor, and included with the entry; a letter of application from the student outlining his/her plans for study and detailing his/her extracurricular activities, maximum length of two pages, double-spaced; an academic paper or other appropriate work in the student's major field; one letter of recommendation/evaluation from a faculty member in the field represented by the paper or project addressed to the significance of the work; a self-addressed, stamped envelope. **Deadline:** February 22.

240 ■ Nolle Scholarships *(Undergraduate/ Scholarship)*

Purpose: To provide financial support for the education of senior undergraduate students. **Focus:** General studies. **Qualif.:** Nominee must be a senior year undergraduate student. **Criteria:** Nominee must be enrolled for the fall semester as a full-time student in undergraduate study toward the baccalaureate degree.

Funds Avail.: $1,500. **Number Awarded:** 10. **To Apply:** Nominee must submit the official nomination form completed, signed by the sponsor, and included with the entry; a letter of application from the student outlining his/her plans for study and detailing his/her extracurricular activities, maximum length of two pages, double-spaced; an academic paper or other appropriate work in the student's major field; one letter of recommendation/evaluation from a faculty member in the field represented by the paper or project addressed to the significance of the work; a self-addressed, stamped envelope. **Deadline:** February 22.

241 ■ Pryor Graduate Fellowships *(Graduate/ Fellowship)*

Purpose: To provide financial assistance individuals for full-time graduate or professional study (beyond the baccalaureate level). **Focus:** General studies. **Qualif.:** Applicant must be an active alumni member and a graduate student member at Alpha Chi institutions at the time of application. **Criteria:** Candidates will be evaluated based on criteria by the Pryor Fellowship Committee.

Funds Avail.: $8,000. **To Apply:** Applicants must submit evidence of outstanding scholarship; 300-500 word essay introducing their academic/professional goals, but not indicating financial need; two letters of recommendation from employers or professors or other persons qualified to give an evaluation; two complete official transcripts sealed by registrar; copy of official results of GRE, LSAT, MCAT or equivalent to applicant's discipline; and completed application form. **Deadline:** February 1.

242 ■ Sledge Fellowships *(Graduate/Fellowship)*

Purpose: To provide financial support for individuals for their first year of graduate study toward the master's, doctorate, or professional degree at any recognized institution. **Focus:** General studies. **Qualif.:** Nominee must be enrolled as an undergraduate or graduate with the baccalaureate degree during the school year in which application is made and must identify the graduate or professional school(s) to which he/she has applied for study the following fall. **Criteria:** Nominee must be enrolled for the following fall semester as a full-time student in graduate or professional study.

Funds Avail.: $3,500. **Number Awarded:** 2. **To Apply:** Nominee must submit the official nomination form completed, signed by the sponsor, and included with the entry; a letter of application from the student outlining his/her plans for study and detailing his/her extracurricular activities, maximum length of two pages, double-spaced; an academic paper or other appropriate work in the student's major field; one letter of recommendation/evaluation from a faculty member in the field represented by the paper or project addressed to the significance of the work; a self-addressed, stamped envelope. **Deadline:** February 22.

243 ■ Alpha Chi Sigma

2141 N Franklin Rd.
Indianapolis, IN 46219
Free: 800-ALC-HEMY
E-mail: foundation@alphachisigma.org
URL: http://alphachisigma.org

244 ■ Alpha Chi Sigma Scholarship Award *(Graduate, Undergraduate/Award/Prize)*

Purpose: To encourage and recognize outstanding scholarship among Collegiate members of Alpha Chi Sigma Fraternity. **Focus:** General studies. **Qualif.:** Nominee must have been a member of Alpha Chi Sigma Fraternity for one year, and enrolled in an institution of higher learning at the time of nomination. Undergraduate nominees must have completed the Junior year at the time of nomination. Graduate nominees may be nominated based upon both their undergraduate and graduate records upon the completion of their first year of graduate study. Graduate students may also be nominated, based upon their graduate records alone, after admission to candidacy for the terminal degree in the field of graduate study. **Criteria:** Nominees will be evaluated by the appointed award committee with established criteria.

Funds Avail.: $1,000. **To Apply:** Application process is done through nomination.

245 ■ Alpha Delta Gamma

946 Sanders Dr.
St. Louis, MO 63126

Awards are arranged alphabetically below their administering organizations

E-mail: topadg@aol.com
URL: http://www.alphadeltagamma.org

246 ■ ADGEF Scholarships *(All/Scholarship)*

Purpose: To support and promote educational opportunities for the members of Alpha Delta Gamma National Fraternity. **Focus:** General studies. **Qualif.:** Applicant must be a member of Alpha Delta Gamma National Fraternity. **Criteria:** Selection is based on the application.

Funds Avail.: No specific amount. **To Apply:** Applicants must submit a completed application form along with the required materials. **Deadline:** June 15.

Remarks: The scholarship is payable to the present school, to be used for tuition, books, or housing, unless otherwise noted in the application. **Contact:** ADGEF President Charlie Johnson toll-free at 708-514-0926.

247 ■ Alpha Kappa Alpha - Educational Advancement Foundation

5656 S Stony Island Ave.
Chicago, IL 60637
Ph: 800-653-6528
Fax: (773)947-0277
E-mail: akaeaf@akaeaf.net
URL: http://www.akaeaf.org

248 ■ Alpha Kappa Alpha - Educational Advancement Foundation Financial Need-Based Scholarships *(Graduate, Undergraduate/ Scholarship)*

Purpose: To provide financial support to undergraduate and graduate students for the advancement of education and to promote life-long learning. **Focus:** General studies. **Qualif.:** Applicants must be full-time undergraduate students, sophomores or beyond, currently enrolled in an accredited campus-based degree-granting institution of higher learning or currently enrolled, full-time graduate students; must have a minimum 2.5 GPA or C+ average. **Criteria:** Recipients are selected based on financial need.

Funds Avail.: $750 to $2,500. **To Apply:** Applicants must submit all the required application information. **Deadline:** April 15 for the undergraduates' applications; August 15 for graduates' applications.

249 ■ Alpha Kappa Alpha - Educational Advancement Foundation Merit Scholarships *(Graduate, Undergraduate/Scholarship)*

Purpose: To provide financial support to undergraduate and graduate students for the advancement of education and to promote life-long learning. **Focus:** General studies. **Qualif.:** Applicants must be full-time and currently enrolled undergraduate students with at least sophomore standing at an accredited campus-based degree-granting institution or full-time and currently enrolled graduate students at an accredited campus-based degree-granting institution. Both must possess a minimum grade point average of 3.0. **Criteria:** Applicants are evaluated based on academic achievement and demonstrated community service and involvement.

Funds Avail.: $1,000 to $2,000. **To Apply:** Applicants must submit all the required application information. **Deadline:** April 15 for undergraduates' applications; August 15 for graduates' applications.

250 ■ Youth Partners Accessing Capital (P.A.C.) *(Graduate, Undergraduate/Scholarship)*

Purpose: To provide financial support to undergraduate and graduate students for the advancement of education and to promote life-long learning. **Focus:** General studies. **Qualif.:** Applicants must be members of the Alpha Kappa Alpha Sorority, Inc.; at least college sophomores who have a minimum 3.0 of GPA. **Criteria:** Applicants are evaluated based on demonstrated exceptional academic achievement; financial need; and leadership or volunteerism in civic or campus activities.

Funds Avail.: $1,000 up to $3,000. **To Apply:** Applicants must submit all the required application information. **Deadline:** April 15.

251 ■ Alpha Phi Sigma

3301 College Ave.
Fort Lauderdale, FL 33314
Ph: (954)262-7004
Fax: (954)262-3646
E-mail: headquarters@alphaphisigma.org
URL: http://www.gannon.edu/resource/other/org/APSDP/index.html

252 ■ Commander James Carr Forensic Science Scholarships *(Undergraduate/Scholarship)*

Purpose: To assist students in their educational pursuits. **Focus:** General studies. **Qualif.:** Applicants must be Alpha Phi Sigma members. **Criteria:** Recipients are selected based on academic achievement, professional recommendations, and extracurricular activities.

Funds Avail.: $1000. **Number Awarded:** 1. **To Apply:** Applicants must submit required materials and documents following the stipulated guidelines. **Deadline:** January 31.

253 ■ V.A. Leonard Scholarships *(Graduate, Undergraduate/Scholarship)*

Purpose: To assist students in their educational pursuits. **Focus:** General studies. **Qualif.:** Applicants must be Alpha Phi Sigma members. **Criteria:** Recipients are selected based on academic achievement, professional recommendations, and extracurricular activities.

Funds Avail.: $1000. **Number Awarded:** 1. **To Apply:** Applicants must submit required materials and documents following the stipulated guidelines. **Deadline:** January 31.

Remarks: Established in 1982 in honor and recognition of Dr. Leonard's leadership and hard work in the field of Criminal Justice.

254 ■ Public Agency Training Council Criminal Justice Scholarships *(Undergraduate/Scholarship)*

Purpose: To assist students in their educational pursuits. **Focus:** General studies. **Qualif.:** Applicants must be Alpha Phi Sigma members. **Criteria:** Recipients are selected based on academic achievement, professional recommendations, and extracurricular activities.

Funds Avail.: $1000. **Number Awarded:** 1. **To Apply:** Applicants must submit required materials and documents following the stipulated guidelines. **Deadline:** January 31.

Remarks: Established in 1987.

255 ■ Detective Cheryl Seiden Memorial Scholarships *(Undergraduate/Scholarship)*

Purpose: To assist students in their educational pursuits. **Focus:** General studies. **Qualif.:** Applicants must be Alpha Phi Sigma members. **Criteria:** Recipients are selected based on academic achievement, professional recom-

Awards are arranged alphabetically below their administering organizations

mendations, and extracurricular activities.

Funds Avail.: $1000. **Number Awarded:** 1. **To Apply:** Applicants must submit required materials and documents following the stipulated guidelines. **Deadline:** January 31.

Remarks: In memory of Metro-Dade Police Detective Cheryl Seiden, killed in the line of duty.

256 ■ Regina B. Shearn Scholarships *(Graduate, Undergraduate/Scholarship)*

Purpose: To assist students in their educational pursuits. **Focus:** General studies. **Qualif.:** Applicants must be Alpha Phi Sigma members. Applicants are not eligible to receive the same scholarship two years in succession. **Criteria:** Selection is based on academic performance, leadership and service, personal statement and evaluation reports.

Funds Avail.: $1000. **Number Awarded:** 1. **To Apply:** Applicants must submit required materials and documents following the stipulated guidelines. **Deadline:** January 31.

Remarks: Established in 2001, named after the first National Executive Director of Alpha Phi Sigma.

257 ■ Ambucs Resource Center

PO Box 5127
High Point, NC 27262
Fax: (336)852-6830
Free: 800-838-1845
E-mail: janiceb@ambucs.org
URL: http://www.ambucs.org

258 ■ AMBUCS Scholarships for Therapists Program *(Graduate, Undergraduate/Scholarship)*

Purpose: To ensure that a new generation of therapists will continue to enhance the lives of people with disabilities. **Focus:** Physical therapy; Occupational therapy; Speech and language pathology/audiology. **Qualif.:** Applicant must be a citizen of the United States; with documented financial need; with good scholastic standing; be accepted at the junior or senior undergraduate, or graduate level in a program which qualifies the applicant for clinical practice in occupational therapy, physical therapy, speech and language pathology and hearing audiology; express an intent to enter clinical practice in chosen field of therapy in the United States upon completion of course of study for which aid is requested. **Criteria:** Applicants are evaluated based on some criteria designed by the Scholarships Selection Committee.

Funds Avail.: $500-$1,500. **To Apply:** Applicants should complete online application and must submit most current IRS form 1040, narrative statement and enrollment certification. **Deadline:** Mid-January until April 15 annually.

259 ■ American Academy of Neurology

1080 Montreal Ave.
St. Paul, MN 55116
Ph: (651)695-2717
Fax: (651)695-2791
Free: 800-879-1960
E-mail: memberservices@aan.com
URL: http://www.aan.com

260 ■ Clinical Research Training Fellowships *(Other/Fellowship)*

Purpose: To support clinical research training in the neurosciences. **Focus:** Neurology. **Qualif.:** Applicants must be neurologists and clinical investigators interested in academic careers in clinical research. **Criteria:** Candidates' applications are evaluated by the Clinical Research Subcommittee of the Science Committee of the AAN based on the applicant's ability and promise as a clinician-scientist based on prior record of achievement and career plan, letters of reference, and curriculum vitae; quality and nature of the training to be provided and the institutional, departmental, and mentor-specific training environment; quality and originality of the research plan.

Funds Avail.: $10,000 up to $55,000. **To Apply:** Applicants must submit one complete copy of the letter of nomination from the chair of the department of neurology, including assurance that clinical service responsibilities will be restricted to no more than 20 percent of the fellow's time; three-page research plan; copy of a current curriculum vitae; two letters of reference supporting applicant's potential for a clinical, academic research career and qualifications for the fellowship; listing of the applicant's and mentor's current and pending for support, other than this fellowship, using NIH format; letter from proposed mentor detailing the support of and commitment to the applicant and the proposed research and training plan; copy of the proposed mentor's NIH Biosketch; and document describing arrangements for formal course work including quantitative clinical epidemiology, biostatistics, study design, data analysis, and ethics.

261 ■ Medical Student Summer Research Scholarships *(Undergraduate/Scholarship)*

Purpose: To provide financial support for projects in either institutional, clinical, or laboratory setting where there are ongoing programs of research, service or training, or a private practice. **Focus:** Neurology. **Qualif.:** Applicants must be second-year medical students who have a supporting preceptor and a project with clearly defined goals, third-year medical students who are on an official summer break will also be considered with accompanying documentation, whose project is conducted through US or Canadian institution of the students' choice and jointly designed by the students and sponsoring institutions. **Criteria:** More than one student from an institution may apply, but only one student will be selected from an institution.

Funds Avail.: $3,000. **To Apply:** Applicant must submit completed application form, 1-2 page project proposal, 1-2 page curriculum vitae, 2 letters of recommendation: one from the project preceptor and one from the SIGN faculty advisor, completed tax form with institution information. **Deadline:** February 15.

262 ■ American Academy of Nurse Practitioners

PO Box 12846
Austin, TX 78711
Ph: (512)442-4262
Fax: (512)442-6469
E-mail: admin@aanp.org
URL: http://www.aanp.org

263 ■ CFIDS Association of America NP Student Scholarships *(Graduate/Scholarship)*

Purpose: To assist an AANP student and members in their education. **Focus:** Nursing. **Qualif.:** Applicants must be an AANP student and full member; an MSN-NP student pursuing a Master's in Nursing with NP specialty; have a minimum MSN-NP study GPA of 3.5. **Criteria:** Recipients are selected based on the Selection Committee's review of the application materials.

Awards are arranged alphabetically below their administering organizations

Funds Avail.: $1,000. **Number Awarded:** 1. **To Apply:** Applicants must request an application at scholarship@aanp.org. **Deadline:** April 28.

Remarks: Post-MS NP, DNP and doctoral students are not qualified. Scholarship is sponsored by the Chronic Fatigue and Immune Dysfunction Syndrome (CFIDS) Association of America.

264 ■ Frank Cole Memorial Emergency NP Student Scholarships *(Graduate/Scholarship)*

Purpose: To assist an AANP student and members in their education. **Focus:** Nursing. **Qualif.:** Applicants must be an AANP student and full member; an MSN-NP student pursuing a Master's in Nursing with NP specialty; have a minimum MSN-NP study GPA of 3.5. **Criteria:** Applicant with an Emergency focus or with ER work history will be given preference.

Funds Avail.: $1,000. **Number Awarded:** 1. **To Apply:** Applicants must request an application form at scholarship@aanp.org. **Deadline:** April 28.

Remarks: Post-MS NP, DNP and doctoral students are not qualified for the scholarship. Scholarship is sponsored by the fellows of the American Academy of Nurse Practitioners (FAANP) in memory of Frank L. Cole, PhD, RN, CEN, FNP, FAAN, FAANP, FAEN (1955-2006).

265 ■ Cranberry Institute NP Student Scholarships *(Graduate/Scholarship)*

Purpose: To assist an AANP student and members in their education. **Focus:** Nursing. **Qualif.:** Applicants must be an AANP student and full member; an MSN-NP student pursuing a Master's in Nursing with NP specialty; have a minimum MSN-NP study GPA of 3.5. **Criteria:** Recipients are selected based on the Selection Committee's review of the application materials.

Funds Avail.: $1,000. **Number Awarded:** 1. **To Apply:** Applicants must request an application form at scholarship@aanp.org. **Deadline:** April 28.

Remarks: Post-MS NP, DNP and doctoral students are not qualified for the scholarship.

266 ■ Daiichi Sankyo Inc. NP Student Scholarships *(Graduate/Scholarship)*

Purpose: To assist an AANP student and members in their education. **Focus:** Nursing. **Qualif.:** Applicants must be an AANP student and full member; an MSN-NP student pursuing a Master's in Nursing with NP specialty; have a minimum MSN-NP study GPA of 3.5. **Criteria:** Recipients are selected based on the Selection Committee's review of the application materials.

Funds Avail.: $1,000. **Number Awarded:** 1. **To Apply:** Applicants must request an application form at scholarship@aanp.org. **Deadline:** April 28.

Remarks: Post-MS NP, DNP and doctoral students are not qualified for the scholarship.

267 ■ Deets-Laine Geriatric NP Student Scholarships *(Doctorate, Graduate/Scholarship)*

Purpose: To assist an AANP student and members in their education. **Focus:** Nursing; Geriatric medicine. **Qualif.:** Applicants must be an AANP student and full member; a MSN-Geriatric NP student pursuing a Master's in Nursing with a Geriatric NP specialty; practicing NP with an MSN pursuing Geriatric NP education in an accredited Post-MS Geriatric NP program; have a Master's in Nursing; and be pursuing Geriatric NP education in an accredited Post-MS Geriatric NP program. For MSN-Geriatric NP students, applicant must have a minimum MSN-GNP study GPA of 3.5 and above and enrolled in a BSN-MSN bridge program or direct entry program. For Post-MS Geriatric NP student, applicant must have a minimum MSN-GNP study GPA of 3.5 and above. For DNP students, applicant must have a DNP study GPA of 3.75 and above. **Criteria:** Recipients are selected based on the Selection Committee's review of the application materials.

Funds Avail.: $1,000. **Number Awarded:** 1. **To Apply:** Applicants must request an application form at scholarship@aanp.org. **Deadline:** April 28.

Remarks: Scholarship is sponsored by Denise Laine, PhD, NP-C, COHN-S, CCM, FAANP.

268 ■ Fitzgerald Health Education Associates NP Student Scholarships *(Graduate/Scholarship)*

Purpose: To assist an AANP student and members in their education. **Focus:** Nursing. **Qualif.:** Applicants must be an AANP student and full member; an MSN-NP student pursuing a Master's in Nursing with NP specialty; have a minimum MSN-NP study GPA of 3.5. **Criteria:** Recipients are selected based on the Selection Committee's review of the application materials.

Funds Avail.: $1,000. **Number Awarded:** 1. **To Apply:** Applicants must request an application form at scholarship@aanp.org. **Deadline:** April 28.

Remarks: Post-MS NP, DNP and doctoral students are not qualified for the scholarship. Scholarship is sponsored by Fitzgerald Health Education Associates.

269 ■ National Heartburn Alliance NP Student Scholarships *(Graduate/Scholarship)*

Purpose: To assist an AANP student and members in their education. **Focus:** Nursing. **Qualif.:** Applicants must be an AANP student and full member; an MSN-NP student pursuing a Master's in Nursing with NP specialty; have a minimum MSN-NP study GPA of 3.5. **Criteria:** Recipients are selected based on the Selection Committee's review of the application materials.

Funds Avail.: $1,000. **Number Awarded:** 1. **To Apply:** Applicants must request an application form at scholarship@aanp.org. **Deadline:** April 28.

Remarks: Post-MS NP, DNP and doctoral students are not qualified for the scholarship.

270 ■ Novartis Pharmaceutical Corporation NP Student Scholarships *(Graduate/Scholarship)*

Purpose: To assist an AANP student and members in their education. **Focus:** Nursing. **Qualif.:** Applicants must be an AANP student and full member; an MSN-NP student pursuing a Master's in Nursing with NP specialty; have a minimum MSN-NP study GPA of 3.5. **Criteria:** Recipients are selected based on the Selection Committee's review of the application materials.

Funds Avail.: $1,000. **Number Awarded:** 1. **To Apply:** Applicants must request an application form at scholarship@aanp.org. **Deadline:** April 28.

Remarks: Post-MS NP, DNP and doctoral students are not qualified. Scholarship is sponsored by Novartis Pharmaceutical Corporation.

271 ■ Novo Nordisk NP Doctoral Education Scholarships *(Doctorate/Scholarship)*

Purpose: To assist an AANP student and members in their education. **Focus:** Medical education; Nursing. **Qualif.:** Ap-

Awards are arranged alphabetically below their administering organizations

plicants must be an AANP student and full member; U.S. citizen; an NP pursuing a Doctoral degree; currently licensed practicing NP in the United States; have a minimum Doctoral study GPA of 3.75 and above. **Criteria:** Recipients are selected based on the Selection Committee's review of the application materials.

Funds Avail.: $2,000. **Number Awarded:** 2. **To Apply:** Applicants must request an application form at scholarship@aanp.org. **Deadline:** April 28.

Remarks: MSN-NP and Post-MS NP students are not qualified for the scholarship.

272 ■ Pfizer Inc. 2007 NP Student Scholarships *(Graduate/Scholarship)*

Purpose: To assist an AANP student and members in their education. **Focus:** Nursing. **Qualif.:** Applicants must be an AANP student and full member; an MSN-NP student pursuing a Master's in Nursing with NP specialty; have a minimum MSN-NP study GPA of 3.5. **Criteria:** Recipients are selected based on the Selection Committee's review of the application materials.

Funds Avail.: $1,000. **Number Awarded:** 1. **To Apply:** Applicants must request an application form at scholarship@aanp.org. **Deadline:** April 28.

Remarks: Post-MS NP, DNP and doctoral students are not qualified. Scholarship is sponsored by Pfizer Inc.

273 ■ Pharmavite LLC NP Doctoral Education Scholarships *(Doctorate/Scholarship)*

Purpose: To assist an AANP student and members in their education. **Focus:** Medical education; Nursing. **Qualif.:** Applicants must be an AANP student and full member; U.S. citizen; an NP pursuing a Doctoral degree; currently licensed practicing NP in the United States; have a minimum Doctoral study GPA of 3.75 and above. **Criteria:** Recipients are selected based on the Selection Committee's review of the application materials.

Funds Avail.: $2,000. **Number Awarded:** 1. **To Apply:** Applicants must request an application form at scholarship@aanp.org. **Deadline:** April 28.

Remarks: MSN-NP and Post-MS NP students are not qualified for the scholarship.

274 ■ UCB, Inc. NP Student Scholarships *(Graduate/Scholarship)*

Purpose: To assist an AANP student and members in their education. **Focus:** Nursing. **Qualif.:** Applicants must be an AANP student and full member; an MSN-NP student pursuing a Master's in Nursing with NP specialty; have a minimum MSN-NP study GPA of 3.5. **Criteria:** Recipients are selected based on the Selection Committee's review of the application materials.

Funds Avail.: $1,000. **Number Awarded:** 1. **To Apply:** Applicants must request an application form at scholarship@aanp.org. **Deadline:** April 28.

Remarks: Post-MS NP, DNP and doctoral students are not qualified. Scholarship is sponsored by the UCB Inc.

275 ■ American Academy of Optometry

6110 Executive Blvd., Ste. 506
Rockville, MD 20852
Ph: (301)984-1441
Fax: (301)984-4737
E-mail: aaoptom@aaoptom.org
URL: http://www.aaopt.org

276 ■ The William C. Ezell Fellowships *(Postgraduate/Fellowship)*

Purpose: To encourage talented persons to pursue full-time careers in optometric research and education. **Focus:** Optometry. **Qualif.:** Applicants must be post-graduate students, continuing a full-time study and training in research that leads to a Masters or PhD degree. **Criteria:** Applicants fellowship applications will be reviewed by the Research Committee of the American Academy of Optometry and recommendations will then be sent to the AOF Board which approves and funds the Ezell Fellowships.

Funds Avail.: $8,000. **To Apply:** Applicants must submit application form together with three letters of recommendation from the persons qualified to comment on his/her educational qualifications, research abilities and potential and current and future teaching capabilities; one-page statement describing the applicant's educational objectives, future research and/or teaching interest and career objectives; and a copy of scientific publications, copies of papers in press must be included. **Deadline:** March 14.

277 ■ Terrance Ingraham Pediatric Optometry Residency Award *(Graduate/Award/Prize)*

Purpose: To promote the practice and development of the field of pediatric optometry by providing incentive and support to talented optometric residents who demonstrate a passion and commitment to practice, research and education in the field of children's vision. **Focus:** Optometry. **Qualif.:** Applicant must be an optometrist continuing a pediatric/vision therapy residency at an accredited school or college of optometry. **Criteria:** Applicants will be evaluated on the basis of their educational background and their ability and potential as teachers, researchers, and practitioners in the field of pediatric optometry.

Funds Avail.: $4,000. **Number Awarded:** 2. **To Apply:** Applicant must submit an application which includes applicant's education, research and teaching experience; a description of the applicant's residency program and his/her plans for the next academic year; a one-page statement of the applicant's career goals; three letters of recommendation from persons qualified to comment on educational qualifications, research abilities and potential. **Deadline:** March 1.

278 ■ VISTAKON George Mertz and Sheldon Wechsler Residency Awards *(All/Award/Prize)*

Purpose: To promote the practice and development of the field of optometry by providing incentive and support to talented optometric residents who demonstrate a passion and commitment to practice, research, and education. **Focus:** Optometry. **Qualif.:** Applicant must be optometrist continuing a contact lens residency program at an accredited school or college of optometry. **Criteria:** Applicants will be evaluated primarily on the basis of their educational background and their ability and potential as teachers, researchers and practitioners in the field of contact lenses.

Funds Avail.: $4,000. **To Apply:** Applicants must submit summary of the their education, research and teaching experience; description of the residency program and plans for the next academic year; one-page statement of the applicant's career goals; and three letters of reference. **Deadline:** March 1.

279 ■ Antoinette M. Molinari Memorial Scholarships *(Doctorate/Scholarship)*

Purpose: To assist an exceptional student who has extraordinary financial needs and would have difficulty

Awards are arranged alphabetically below their administering organizations

meeting the financial requirements of attending an optometry school. **Focus:** Optometry. **Qualif.:** Applicants must be students pursuing a doctorate of optometry through a full-time course of study and who maintain a grade point average of 3.5 (4 point scale) or higher for all course work taken in optometry school. **Criteria:** Recipient will be selected based on academic and leadership potential and financial need.

Funds Avail.: $6,000. **To Apply:** Applicants must submit completed application form together with the requirements. **Deadline:** June 2.

280 ■ VISTAKON Research Grants *(All/Grant)*

Purpose: To encourage talented persons to pursue full-time careers in optometry. **Focus:** Optometry. **Qualif.:** Applicants must be individuals in optometry and vision science. **Criteria:** Applicants will be judged by the VISTAKON Research Grants Selection Committee based on some criteria.

Funds Avail.: $10,000 to $25,000. **To Apply:** Applicant must submit proposal electronically and must contain the following components: introduction; background and significance; specific aims; preliminary studies; and study design and methods. These sections should total no more than five pages. References (maximum of one page) Budget and budget justification (maximum of one page) Biographical sketch(es) of Principal and one co-investigator only (maximum of two pages for each investigator) Education/training; research and professional experience; honors and awards publications (refereed) for the last three years and representative earlier publications. **Deadline:** June 1.

281 ■ VSP Research Grants *(All/Grant)*

Purpose: To support the research into the efficacy of optometric care and optometric medical interventions. **Focus:** Optometry. **Qualif.:** Applicants must be individuals who are research-oriented, including but not limited to individual researchers; corporations; schools and colleges of optometry; schools and colleges of public health; schools and colleges of medicine; professional associations; and private foundations. **Criteria:** Applicants will be evaluated by the American Academy of Optometry's Research Committee.

Funds Avail.: $42,000. **To Apply:** Applicants must submit proposals, electronically, which must contain the following components: introduction; background and significance; specific aims; preliminary studies; and study design and methods. These sections should total no more than five pages. References (maximum of one page) Budget and budget justification (maximum of one page) Biographical sketch(es) of Principal and one co-investigator only (maximum of two pages for each investigator) Education/training; research and professional experience; honors and awards. Publications (refereed) for the last three years and representative earlier. **Deadline:** March 1.

282 ■ American Academy of Periodontology

737 N Michigan Ave., Ste. 800
Chicago, IL 60611
Ph: (312)787-5518
Fax: (312)787-3670
URL: http://www.perio.org

283 ■ American Academy of Periodontology Educator Scholarships *(Postdoctorate/Scholarship)*

Purpose: To provide financial relief to students intending to pursue a career as a full-time teacher at a U.S. periodontal program upon graduation from a U.S. periodontal postdoctoral training program. **Focus:** Dentistry. **Qualif.:** Applicants must be student members of the AAP who have been accepted into or are currently enrolled in a U.S. periodontal postdoctoral training program and who intend to enter full-time teaching in a U.S. program. **Criteria:** Applicants are evaluated based on merit and financial need.

Funds Avail.: $50,000. **To Apply:** Applicants must submit completed application form; dental school transcripts; periodontal program transcripts; curriculum vitae; letter of nomination from the periodontal program director or the designated mentor; two letters of recommendation; and essay of approximately 1,000 words which addresses their commitment to education. **Deadline:** July 1.

284 ■ American Academy of Periodontology Foundation Education Fellowships *(Postdoctorate/Fellowship)*

Purpose: To support research projects focused on the prevention of periodontitis. **Focus:** Dentistry. **Qualif.:** Applicants must be first or second year students of a U.S. periodontal postdoctoral program and must be student members of the American Academy of Periodontology. **Criteria:** Applicants are evaluated based on financial need.

Funds Avail.: $15,000. **To Apply:** Applicants must submit completed application form; proposal for research project focusing on the prevention of periodontitis; dental school and periodontal postdoctoral transcripts; letter of support from the periodontal institution's Program Director; and essay of approximately 750 words in which the applicant discusses their future plans in periodontal education and research. **Deadline:** May 31.

285 ■ American Academy of Periodontology Teaching Fellowships *(Postdoctorate/Fellowship)*

Purpose: To support the young periodontal educators' commitment to a career in academia by providing debt relief to qualified applicants. **Focus:** Dentistry. **Qualif.:** Applicants must be in the first three years of full-time teaching employment, as defined by the institution, at a U.S. periodontal program or have accepted a full-time faculty position at a U.S. periodontal program. **Criteria:** Applicants are judged based on personal attributes.

Funds Avail.: $50,000. **To Apply:** Applicants must submit completed application form; dental school transcripts; periodontal program transcripts; curriculum vitae; letter of nomination from the periodontal chair or other appropriate individual from their employing institution; two letters of recommendation; and essay of approximately 1,000 words which addresses their commitment to education. **Deadline:** July 1.

286 ■ Abram and Sylvia Chasens Teaching and Research Fellowships *(Postdoctorate/Fellowship)*

Purpose: To encourage periodontal students to enter the teaching field. **Focus:** Dentistry. **Qualif.:** Applicants must be periodontal postgraduate students in their third year of a non-military, accredited periodontal post-doctoral training program in the United States who intend to pursue a career in periodontal teaching and research in the United States. **Criteria:** Applicants are evaluated based on demonstrated excellence of character and integrity, record of academic and personal achievements, and aptitude for teaching and research.

Funds Avail.: $15,000. **Number Awarded:** 2. **To Apply:** Applicants must submit completed application form;

Awards are arranged alphabetically below their administering organizations

transcript of grades from dental school and postgraduate work; curriculum vitae; personal statement of 750 words that addresses the special qualities they will bring to education, their philosophy of education, research interests, extracurricular and community activities, financial need and career plans; and three letters of reference. **Deadline:** April 15.

287 ■ Richard J. Lazzara Fellowships in Advanced Implant Surgery *(Postdoctorate/ Fellowship)*

Purpose: To provide educational and clinical experiences that reflect the most current techniques in implant dentistry. **Focus:** Dentistry. **Qualif.:** Applicants must be third year students in an accredited periodontal post-doctoral training program in the United States; must be recommended by the students' periodontal program director. **Criteria:** Applicants are evaluated based on merit.

Funds Avail.: $50,000. **To Apply:** Applicants must submit completed application form; three letters of recommendation, one letter must be from the periodontal program director, another from a periodontist, and the third from a personal reference; transcript of grades from both dental school and postgraduate work; curriculum vitae; and personal essay. **Deadline:** February 1.

288 ■ Bud and Linda Tarrson Fellowships *(Postdoctorate/Fellowship)*

Purpose: To provide financial assistance to the brightest scientific and clinical minds with demonstrated facility for teaching, and to encourage these individuals to pursue an academic career in periodontology. **Focus:** Dentistry. **Qualif.:** Applicants must be either full-time or part-time faculty members at the instructor or assistant level; must be affiliated with a U.S. training institution for 10 years or less; must have the goal of teaching and research in periodontology. **Criteria:** Applicants are evaluated based on financial need.

Funds Avail.: $30,000. **To Apply:** Applicants must submit completed application form; letter of nomination; recommendations; curriculum vitae; and personal statement. **Deadline:** May 1.

289 ■ Tarrson Regeneration Scholarships *(Postdoctorate/Scholarship)*

Purpose: To provide financial assistance to students doing research in regeneration. **Focus:** Medical research. **Qualif.:** Applicants must be students who have been accepted in an accredited U.S. periodontal postdoctoral training program or first-year residents within the first six months of their periodontal postdoctoral training program. **Criteria:** Applicants are evaluated based on merit.

Funds Avail.: $37,000. **To Apply:** Applicants must submit a completed Tarrson Regeneration Scholarship application form; a proposal abstract describing their clinical research project relevant to clinical or translational regeneration studies; dental school transcripts; two letters of reference; personal essay; and curriculum vitae. **Deadline:** July 15.

290 ■ American Advertising Federation-Cleveland

20325 Center Ridge Rd., Ste. 670
Cleveland, OH 44116
Ph: (440)673-0020
Fax: (440)673-0025
E-mail: adassoc@aafcleveland.com
URL: http://clevead.com

291 ■ American Advertising Federation-Cleveland College Scholarships *(Undergraduate/ Scholarship)*

Purpose: To bring advertising, public relations, sales and marketing professionals together to build networks and create business solutions. **Focus:** Advertising. **Qualif.:** Applicants must be Ohio college students majoring in advertising, marketing and communications; must be Ohio residents and enrolled on a full-time basis; must have a current minimum cumulative 3.0 GPA; must be seniors, juniors or in the last semester of the sophomore year. **Criteria:** Recipients are selected on a financial need and merit basis.

Funds Avail.: No specific amount. **To Apply:** Applicants must submit a completed application form, transcript of records, two letters of recommendation from faculty and/or professionals and a one page, double-spaced essay stating their career goals. **Deadline:** October 29.

292 ■ American Advertising Federation-Cleveland High School Scholarships *(Undergraduate/Scholarship)*

Purpose: To provide opportunity for students who plan to pursue careers in advertising, marketing, communication, photography and graphic design. **Focus:** Advertising. **Qualif.:** Applicants must be enrolled in a Cleveland Municipal School District high school; must be planning to enroll in a communication/marketing-related major at an accredited college or university with the goal of pursuing a degree; must carry a full course-load and hold a current minimum cumulative GPA of 2.5 or higher on a 4.0 scale; must be in their senior year. **Criteria:** Recipients are selected on a financial need and merit basis.

Funds Avail.: No specific amount. **To Apply:** Applicants must submit a completed application form, two letters of recommendation from teachers or other professionals and a typed one page, double-spaced essay describing their career goals. **Deadline:** January 22.

293 ■ American Antiquarian Society

185 Salisbury St.
Worcester, MA 01609-1634
Ph: (508)755-5221
Fax: (508)753-3311
E-mail: ladams@mwa.org
URL: http://www.americanantiquarian.org

294 ■ AAS-American Historical Print Collectors Society Fellowships *(Doctorate/Fellowship)*

Purpose: To enable scholars, advanced graduate students and others to spend an uninterrupted block of time doing research in the AAS library. **Focus:** American Studies. **Qualif.:** Applicants must be enrolled in doctoral degree of accredited institutions or universities. **Criteria:** Recipients are selected based on: significance or importance of the project; appropriateness of the proposed study to AAS collections.

Funds Avail.: $1,200-$1,700. **To Apply:** Applicants must fill out the online application form. **Deadline:** January 15. **Contact:** Mr. Paul Erickson, academicfellowships@mwa.org.

295 ■ AAS-American Society for Eighteenth Century Studies Fellowships *(Postdoctorate/ Fellowship)*

Purpose: To enable scholars, advanced graduate students and others to spend an uninterrupted block of time doing

Awards are arranged alphabetically below their administering organizations

research in the AAS library. **Focus:** General Studies. **Qualif.:** Applicants are not necessarily members of ASECS; must be an ABD graduate students or postdoctorals, holding the PhD or equivalent degree at the time of the application. **Criteria:** Recipients are selected based on: significance or importance of the project; appropriateness of the proposed study to the AAS collections.

Funds Avail.: $1,200-$1,700. **To Apply:** Applicants must fill out the online application form. **Deadline:** January 15. **Contact:** Mr. Paul Erickson, academicfellowships@mwa.org.

296 ■ AAS Fellowships for Creative and Performing Artists and Writers *(All/Fellowship)*

Purpose: To improve the ways in which an understanding of history is communicated to the American people. **Focus:** American History; Culture; Performing Arts; Writing; Filmmaking; Journalism. **Qualif.:** Applicants must have work for the general public which produces imaginative, nonformulaic works dealing with pre-twentieth century American history. **Criteria:** Recipients are selected based on the quality of performed task.

Funds Avail.: $1,200. **Number Awarded:** 3. **To Apply:** Applicants must provide a cover sheet; two letters of reference; a current resume including a listing of any awards, scholarship, or grant received; a statement of not more than five-typed, double spaced pages briefly summarizing the applicants educational and professional background and goals, describing the research for the project including readings in primary and secondary sources, and indicating the nature of the research program proposed for the AAS fellowship; ten copies of representative samples of previous works must included for the distribution of the committee. **Deadline:** October 5.

297 ■ AAS National Endowment for the Humanities Long-Term Fellowships *(Postdoctorate/Fellowship)*

Purpose: To enable scholars, advanced graduate students and others to spend an uninterrupted block of time doing research in the AAS library. **Focus:** Humanities. **Qualif.:** Applicants must have completed their formal professional training; maybe foreign nationals who have been residents in the United States for at least three years immediately preceding the application deadline. **Criteria:** Recipients are selected based on: significance or importance of the project; appropriateness of the proposed study to the AAS collections.

Funds Avail.: $40,000. **Number Awarded:** 3. **To Apply:** Applicants must fill out the online application form. **Deadline:** January 15. **Contact:** Mr. Paul Erickson, academicfellowships@mwa.org.

298 ■ AAS-Northeast Modern Language Association Fellowships *(All/Fellowship)*

Purpose: To enable scholars, advanced graduate students and others to spend an uninterrupted block of time doing research in the AAS library. **Focus:** American History. **Qualif.:** Applicants are not necessarily members of NEMLA. **Criteria:** Recipients are selected based on: significance or importance of the project; appropriateness of the proposed study to the AAS collections.

Funds Avail.: $1,200-$1,700. **To Apply:** Applicants must fill out the online application form. **Deadline:** January 15. **Contact:** Mr. Paul Erickson, academicfellowships@mwa.org.

299 ■ ACLS Frederick Burkhardt Fellowships *(Professional Development/Fellowship)*

Purpose: To support an academic year (normally nine months) of residence at any one of the national residential research centers participating in the program. **Focus:** Humanities; Social Sciences. **Qualif.:** Applicants must be recently tenured humanists; must be employed in a tenured position at a degree granting academic institution in the United States. **Criteria:** Recipients are selected based on the quality of the proposal and required qualifications.

Funds Avail.: $75,000. **Number Awarded:** 11. **To Apply:** Applicants must fill out the application form. Applicants must submit no more than ten pages, double-spaced proposal; no more than three pages bibliography; no more than two pages publications list; three reference letters. Applicants must provide an institutional statement. **Deadline:** October 1.

300 ■ Stephen Botein Fellowships *(Doctorate/Fellowship)*

Purpose: To enable scholars, advanced graduate students and others to spend an uninterrupted block of time doing research in the AAS library. **Focus:** American History; Culture. **Qualif.:** Applicants must be enrolled in doctoral degree of accredited institution or universities; must be engaged in scholarly research and writing including doctoral dissertation in any field of American history and culture. **Criteria:** Recipients are selected based on: significance or importance of the project; appropriateness of the proposed study to the AAS collections.

Funds Avail.: $1,200-$1,700. **To Apply:** Applicants must fill out the online application form. **Deadline:** January 15. **Contact:** Mr. Paul Erickson, academicfellowships@mwa.org.

301 ■ The "Drawn to Art" Fellowships *(Doctorate/Fellowship)*

Purpose: To enable scholars, advanced graduate students and others to spend an uninterrupted block of time doing research in the AAS library. **Focus:** Art; Culture. **Qualif.:** Applicants must be enrolled in doctoral degree of accredited institution or universities. **Criteria:** Recipients are selected based on: significance or importance of the project; appropriateness of the proposed study to the AAS collections.

Funds Avail.: $1,200-$1,700. **To Apply:** Applicants must fill out the online application form. **Deadline:** January 15. **Contact:** Mr. Paul Erickson, academicfellowships@mwa.org.

302 ■ The Christoph Daniel Ebeling Fellowships *(Doctorate/Fellowship)*

Purpose: To enable scholars, advanced graduate students and others to spend an uninterrupted block of time doing research in the AAS library. **Focus:** American Studies. **Qualif.:** Applicants must be scholars in American Studies doing dissertation or rehabilitation research at universities in Germany. **Criteria:** Recipients are selected based on: significance or importance of the project; appropriateness of the proposed study to the AAS collections.

Funds Avail.: $1,200-$1,700. **To Apply:** Applicants must fill out the online application form. **Deadline:** January 15. **Contact:** Mr. Paul Erickson, academicfellowships@mwa.org.

303 ■ Hench Post-Dissertation Fellowships *(Postdoctorate/Fellowship)*

Purpose: To provide scholars with time and resources to extend research and/or to revise the dissertation for

Awards are arranged alphabetically below their administering organizations

publication. **Focus:** History; Literature; American Studies; Political Science; Music. **Qualif.:** Applicants must have more than three years beyond receipt of the doctorate. **Criteria:** Recipients are selected based on: appropriateness of the project to the AAS collections and interests; likelihood that the revised dissertation will make a highly significant books.

Funds Avail.: $35,000. **To Apply:** Applicant must fill out the on-line application form. **Deadline:** October 15. **Contact:** perickson@mwa.org.

304 ■ Jay and Deborah Last Fellowships *(Doctorate/Fellowship)*

Purpose: To enable scholars, advanced graduate students and others to spend an uninterrupted block of time doing research in the AAS library. **Focus:** Art; Culture. **Qualif.:** Applicants must be enrolled in doctoral degree of accredited institution or universities. **Criteria:** Recipients are selected based on: significance or importance of the project; appropriateness of the proposed study to the AAS collections.

Funds Avail.: $1,200-$1,700. **To Apply:** Applicants must fill out the online application form. **Deadline:** January 15. **Contact:** Mr. Paul Erickson, academicfellowships@mwa.org.

305 ■ The Legacy Fellowships *(Doctorate/Fellowship)*

Purpose: To enable scholars, advanced graduate students and others to spend an uninterrupted block of time doing research in the AAS library. **Focus:** American History; Culture. **Qualif.:** Applicants must be enrolled in doctoral degree of accredited institution or universities; must be engaged in scholarly research and writing including doctoral dissertation in any field of American history and culture. **Criteria:** Recipients are selected based on: significance or importance of the project; appropriateness of the proposed study to the AAS collections.

Funds Avail.: $1,200-$1,700. **To Apply:** Applicants must fill out the online application form. **Deadline:** January 15. **Contact:** Mr. Paul Erickson, academicfellowships@mwa.org.

306 ■ Kate B. and Hall J. Peterson Fellowships *(Doctorate/Fellowship)*

Purpose: To enable scholars, advanced graduate students and others to spend an uninterrupted block of time doing research in the AAS library. **Focus:** American History; Culture. **Qualif.:** Applicants must be enrolled in doctoral degree of accredited institution or universities; must be engaged in scholarly research and writing including doctoral dissertation in any field of American history and culture. **Criteria:** Recipients are selected based on: significance or importance of the project; appropriateness of the proposed study to the AAS collections.

Funds Avail.: $1,200-$1,700. **To Apply:** Applicants must fill out the online application form. **Deadline:** January 15. **Contact:** Mr. Paul Erickson, academicfellowships@mwa.org.

307 ■ The Reese Fellowships *(Doctorate/Fellowship)*

Purpose: To enable scholars, advanced graduate students and others to spend an uninterrupted block of time doing research in the AAS library. **Focus:** American Studies. **Qualif.:** Applicants must be enrolled in doctoral degree of accredited institution or universities. **Criteria:** Recipients are selected based on: significance or importance of the project; appropriateness of the proposed study to the AAS collections.

Funds Avail.: $1,200-$1,700. **To Apply:** Applicants must fill out the online application form. **Deadline:** January 15. **Contact:** Mr. Paul Erickson, academicfellowships@mwa.org.

308 ■ The Joyce Tracy Fellowships *(Doctorate/Fellowship)*

Purpose: To enable scholars, advanced graduate students and others to spend an uninterrupted block of time doing research in the AAS library. **Focus:** American History; Culture. **Qualif.:** Applicants must be enrolled in doctoral degree of accredited institution or universities; must be engaged in scholarly research and writing including doctoral dissertation in any field of American history and culture. **Criteria:** Recipients are selected based on: significance or importance of the project; appropriateness of the proposed study to the AAS collections.

Funds Avail.: $1,200-$1,700. **To Apply:** Applicants must fill out the online application form. **Deadline:** January 15. **Contact:** Mr. Paul Erickson, academicfellowships@mwa.org.

309 ■ American Architectural Foundation

1799 New York Ave. NW
Washington, DC 20006
Ph: (202)626-7318
Fax: (202)626-7420
E-mail: info@archfoundation.org
URL: http://www.archfoundation.org

310 ■ The RTKL Traveling Fellowships *(Undergraduate/Fellowship)*

Purpose: To encourage and support foreign travel undertaken to further educational goals. **Focus:** Architecture. **Qualif.:** Applicants must be students planning independent foreign travel outside the United States and those who have been selected to participate in established school travel programs. Students must be in the second-to-last year of a BArch or MArch program when applying and complete the travel prior to graduation. Those undertaking independent travel must be accepted in an advanced degree program. **Criteria:** Applicants are selected based on the jury's review of the application materials.

Funds Avail.: $2,500. **Number Awarded:** 1. **To Apply:** Applicants must submit a completed official application form; an 800-word proposal describing the objective for the trip and the relationship to his/her education goals; an official transcript from each college attended; three references in support of the proposal; an itinerary; an estimated budget; a list of previous scholarships and architectural awards. **Deadline:** February 15.

311 ■ American Art Therapy Association

5999 Stevenson Ave.
Alexandria, VA 22304
Fax: (703)212-2238
Free: 888-290-0878
E-mail: info@arttherapy.org
URL: http://www.arttherapy.org

312 ■ AATA Anniversary Scholarships *(Graduate/Scholarship)*

Purpose: To promote education in Art therapy. **Focus:** Art therapy. **Qualif.:** Applicant must be active student members

Awards are arranged alphabetically below their administering organizations

of AATA; accepted or attending an AATA approved graduate art therapy program; have a GPA of 3.25; and demonstrated financial need. **Criteria:** Selection is based on the application.

Funds Avail.: No specific award. **To Apply:** Applicants must submit a completed application form. **Deadline:** July 15.

313 ■ Myra Levick Scholarships *(Graduate/Scholarship)*

Purpose: To promote education in art therapy. **Focus:** Art therapy. **Qualif.:** Applicant must be active student members of AATA; accepted or attending an AATA approved graduate art therapy program; have a GPA of 3.0; and demonstrated financial need. **Criteria:** Selection is based on the application.

Funds Avail.: No specific award. **To Apply:** Applicants must submit a completed application form. **Deadline:** July 15.

314 ■ Rawley Silver Award for Excellence *(Graduate/Scholarship)*

Purpose: To promote education in art therapy. **Focus:** Art therapy. **Qualif.:** Applicant must be active student members of AATA; accepted or attending an AATA approved graduate art therapy program; and have an excellent academic record. **Criteria:** Selection is based on the application.

Funds Avail.: $100 (no financial need); full scholarship (with financial need). **To Apply:** Applicants must submit a completed application form together with official academic transcripts; two academic/work related letters of recommendations; student financial information form; a two-pages essay (biography); and proof of acceptance in an AATA approved graduate art therapy program. Submit the original and four more copies of the complete required application packets. **Deadline:** June 15. **Contact:** July 15.

315 ■ American Association for the Advancement of Science

1200 New York Ave. NW
Washington, DC 20005
Ph: (202)326-6400
E-mail: webmaster@aaas.org
URL: http://www.aaas.org

316 ■ AAAS Mass Media Science and Engineering Fellowships *(Graduate, Postgraduate, Undergraduate/Fellowship)*

Purpose: To increase public understanding of science and technology. **Focus:** Media Art; Science Technologies; Engineering. **Qualif.:** Applicants must be undergraduates in their senior year; must be graduate or post-graduate students. **Criteria:** Recipients are selected based on telephone interview made by the AAAS staff.

Funds Avail.: $450. **To Apply:** Applicants must fill out the application form. Applicants must submit a copy of resume including honors, awards and relevant activities; one brief sample of their writing (two-to-three pages on any subjects written in terms appropriate for the general public); journal articles; three letters of recommendation; transcript of the undergraduate and graduate work. **Deadline:** January 15.

317 ■ AAAS Science and Technology Policy Fellowships *(Postdoctorate/Fellowship)*

Purpose: To provide professional development opportunity to individuals interested in learning about the science-policy interface while applying their scientific and technical knowledge and analytical skills to the federal policy realm. **Focus:** Engineering; Science; Science Technologies. **Qualif.:** Applicants must hold doctoral-level degree in any physical, biological, health/medical or behavioral science, any field of engineering, or any interdisciplinary field; must demonstrate exceptional competence in their specialty appropriate to their career stage; must show an understanding of the opportunities for science and engineering to support a broad range of non-scientific issues, and display commitment to apply their scientific or technical expertise to serve society; must exhibit awareness and sensitivity to the political, economic, and social issues that influence policy; must be articulate communicators, both verbally and writing, to decision-makers and non-scientific audiences; must have the ability to work effectively with the individual and groups outside the scientific community; must demonstrate initiative, problem solving ability, leadership capacity, flexibility and willingness to address policy issues outside their scientific realm; must be U.S. citizens or hold a dual citizenship with the other country. **Criteria:** Recipients are selected based on the scientific/technical background and professional accomplishment, leadership and potential, analytical and problem solving abilities, communication, interpersonal and outreach skills.

Funds Avail.: No stated amount. **Number Awarded:** 2. **To Apply:** Applicants must provide profile indicating the name and contact information; candidates' data; candidates' statement providing the qualifications for the fellowship and career goals; reasons for applying for the fellowship. Applicants must also submit curriculum vitae; extracurricular activities; and references including three recommendation letters. **Deadline:** December 20. **Contact:** fellowships@aaas.org

318 ■ Merck Undergraduate Science Research Scholarships *(Undergraduate/Scholarship)*

Purpose: To enhance undergraduate education through research experience that emphasize the interrelationship between chemistry and biology; to encourage students to pursue graduate education in chemistry and life sciences; to foster undergraduate programs and activities that bridge chemistry and biology; **Focus:** Chemistry; Biology; Life Sciences. **Qualif.:** Applicants must be located in 50 United States; offered American Chemical Society-approved program in Chemistry; confer ten or fewer graduate degrees annually in Biology and Chemistry combined; defined by the U.S. Internal Revenue Service Tax Code as a not-for-profit entity under section 501; must not be current Merck/AAAS USRP Award Recipient. **Criteria:** Recipients are selected based on the scientific merit of the proposed research project.

Funds Avail.: $60,000. **Number Awarded:** 15. **To Apply:** Applicants must submit an application cover page; eligibility form including a copy of the school's 501(c)(3) certification letter from the U.S. Internal Revenue Service. **Deadline:** November 2.

319 ■ American Association of Ambulatory Care Nursing

PO Box 56
Pitman, NJ 08071-0056
Free: 800-262-6877
E-mail: aaacn@ajj.com
URL: http://www.aaacn.org

Awards are arranged alphabetically below their administering organizations

320 ■ AAACN Scholarships *(Undergraduate/Scholarship)*

Purpose: To provide financial support for researches. **Focus:** Nursing. **Qualif.:** Applicants must be members of American Academy of Ambulatory Care Nursing (AAACN) for a minimum of two years; currently enrolled in accredited school of nursing or a program deemed by the committee to advance the profession of nursing; request for payment of tuition, books, academic supplies; proof of acceptance in course; must submit a research abstract and proof of acceptance of research study by academic institution or by Investigational Review Board of employing or sponsoring institution; willing to present research findings at AAACN Annual Conference following receipt of award; willing to publish article in Viewpoint describing research study and outcome. **Criteria:** Recipient will be selected by the AAACN Committee.

Funds Avail.: $100 to $1,000. **To Apply:** Applicants must complete application fully and submit two copies to the AAACN National Office. **Deadline:** January 15.

321 ■ American Association of Attorney-Certified Public Accountants

3921 Old Lee Hwy., Ste. 71A
Fairfax, VA 22030
Ph: 888-288-9272
Fax: 888-272-2889
E-mail: info@attorney-cpa.com
URL: http://www.attorney-cpa.com

322 ■ Attorney-CPA Foundation Scholarships *(Undergraduate/Scholarship)*

Purpose: To promote the study and understanding of the fields of Law and Accounting and other related professions. **Focus:** Law. **Qualif.:** Applicants must be graduating law students who have obtained CPA Certificate. **Criteria:** Recipients must be graduating law school students, must have commitment to the profession of accounting as evidenced by a CPA certificate, must have outstanding academic performance, and must have shown leadership in school and community.

Funds Avail.: $250-$1,000. **To Apply:** Applicants must submit the completed application form. **Deadline:** March 15.

323 ■ American Association of Blacks in Energy

1625 K St. NW, Ste. 405
Washington, DC 20006
Ph: (202)371-9530
Fax: (202)371-9218
E-mail: info@aabe.org
URL: http://www.aabe.org

324 ■ American Association of Blacks in Energy Scholarships *(Undergraduate/Scholarship)*

Purpose: To help increase the number of African Americans and other misrepresented minorities in energy-related fields. **Focus:** Energy-related areas. **Qualif.:** Applicants must have at least an overall "B" academic average and a "B" average in mathematics and science courses; must be graduating high school seniors who have applied to one or more accredited colleges/universities; must be planning to major in engineering, mathematics, or the physical sciences; must demonstrate financial need; and must be members of one of the underrepresented minority groups in the sciences and related areas of technology. **Criteria:** Applicants are evaluated based on criteria designed by the organization's National Scholarship Committee.

Funds Avail.: $1,500. **Number Awarded:** 6. **To Apply:** Applicants must submit completed AABE application form; high school transcript; two letters of reference (one academic, one non-academic); and parent(s) or guardian(s) official verification of income (copy of signed tax return for previous year or W2 or a verified FAFSA form).

325 ■ American Association of Bovine Practitioners

PO Box 3610
Auburn, AL 36831-3610
Ph: (334)821-0442
Fax: (334)821-9532
E-mail: aabphq@aabp.org
URL: http://www.aabp.org

326 ■ AABP Amstutz Scholarships *(Undergraduate/Scholarship)*

Purpose: To enhance the professional lives of its members through relevant continuing education that will improve the well-being of cattle and the economic success of the owners; increase awareness; to promote leadership for issues critical to cattle industries; to improve opportunities for careers in bovine medicine. **Focus:** Veterinary science and medicine. **Qualif.:** Applicant must be student enrolled in college of veterinary medicine in Canada and United States; applicant must be in second year of the veterinarian curriculum at the time of the application. **Criteria:** Applicants will be evaluated for the overall interest of the applicant in bovine practice, involvement in bovine medicine and bovine-related extracurricular activities, ability to express oneself in writing, and insightful answers to the essay questions.

Funds Avail.: $2,000. **To Apply:** Applicants must submit a current cumulative school GPA through December, 2007 and a current class rank; he/she must submit a biographical account that outlines the background of the cattle industry; an applicant must prepare a one-page or less list factors that stimulate the interest and involvement in bovine medicine and extracurricular activities; ten lines or less description of plans following graduation from veterinary school; 30 lines or less answer about the experiences that stimulate in pursuing a career in food/animal/bovine medicine; 30 lines or less answering the question "What is our role today and in the future as a veterinarian in shaping public perception of food animal welfare in U.S. or Canada?"; an essay about the plans in using the money acquired from the award if considered; applicant must submit two letters of recommendation from either veterinarian or faculty members regarding the applicant's worthiness for the award. **Deadline:** March 31.

327 ■ AABP Bovine Veterinary Student Recognition Award *(Undergraduate/Scholarship)*

Purpose: To provide awards to 3rd and/or 4th year veterinary students who are interested in dairy and/or beef veterinary medicine. **Focus:** Veterinary science and medicine. **Qualif.:** Applicant must be a student member of AABP enrolled at Veterinary Colleges and Schools during the 2nd year and/or 3rd year. **Criteria:** Award committee will evaluate student's application based on the interest in

Awards are arranged alphabetically below their administering organizations

bovine medicine, work experience, academic and professional experience, career goals, and recommendation letter.

Funds Avail.: $1,500. **To Apply:** An applicant must fill out the on-line application form which outlines the background, work, and academic experience, primary interests in veterinary medicine, career goals and providing the name of a faculty sponsor. **Deadline:** March 15.

328 ■ AABP Education Grants *(Undergraduate/Grant)*

Purpose: To help expand the skills and knowledge base of the cattle production medicine practitioner. **Focus:** Veterinary science and medicine. **Qualif.:** An applicant must be a member or student member of the AABP. **Criteria:** Recipients will evaluate the application based on the academic award of th applicant.

Funds Avail.: $500. **To Apply:** Applicant must fill out the online application form including the career goal, current job description, prior experience with food animal production medicine, and goals of advanced education program; an applicant must submit a brief course outline, a letter of recommendation, a signed hold harmless agreement release form; and applicant must obtain a completion of the advanced training, and the successful applicants will be required to submit an evaluation from detailing the experience. **Deadline:** April 15.

329 ■ AABP Research Assistantship *(Doctorate/Scholarship)*

Purpose: To enhance the professional lives of its members through continuing relevant education that will improve the well-being of cattle and economic success of the owners; to increase the awareness; to promote leadership for issues critical to cattle industries; to improve opportunities for careers in bovine medicine. **Focus:** Veterinary science and medicine. **Qualif.:** Applicant must be enrolled at an accredited North American veterinary college (school) pursuing a concurrent master's or doctoral degree; applicant must be a student AABP member. **Criteria:** Scholarship Committee will evaluate the student's application based on the academic qualifications and experience; justification and relevance to the concerns of private practice and the cattle industry; clarity of objectives and probability of completing the research; methodology and scientific merit; budget; site suitability for proposed research.

Funds Avail.: $10,000. **To Apply:** Applicants must fill out the online application form; applicant must submit an evaluation criteria and scoring system, and a progress report. **Deadline:** February 1. **Contact:** 334-821-9532.

330 ■ AABP Student Externship Program *(Undergraduate/Scholarship)*

Purpose: To support veterinary students. **Focus:** Veterinary science and medicine. **Qualif.:** Applicant must be admitted to veterinary school and complete an externship of at least two weeks in bovine practice; applicant must be a student and AABP member; applicants must be full-time veterinary students at an American, Canadian, or Caribbean veterinary college or be a newly admitted freshmen at such college. **Criteria:** Scholarship will be given to students who have an interest in food animal practice but who may not have extensive exposure to bovine practice or cattle industry; awards will be given to underclassmen and to externship where the practice provides some tangible support for the student, such as room or board.

Funds Avail.: $500. **To Apply:** An applicant must submit the filled out online application form including dates of expected externship, practice where it is to take place, projected cost support to be provided by the practice and amount of aid requested, and student's career interests, prior experience with food producing animals, and goals for the externship; an applicant must provide a letter from the practice describing what the students will be doing; a letter from a faculty member at the student's veterinary college; he/she must submit a completed release agreement. **Deadline:** May 1-October 31.

331 ■ American Association of Candy Technologists

175 Rock Rd.
Glen Rock, NJ 07452
Ph: (201)652-2655
Free: (201)652-3419
E-mail: aactinfo@gomc.com
URL: http://www.aactcandy.org

332 ■ National Candy Technologist Scholarship Program *(Undergraduate/Scholarship)*

Purpose: To provide support for individuals pursuing their career. **Focus:** Food science and technology, Biological and clinical sciences. **Qualif.:** Applicants must be Sophomore, Junior, or Senior Status; have demonstrated interest in confectionery technology; attend an accredited four-year college or university within North America; be majoring in a food science, chemical science, biological science, or related area; minimum 3.0 GPA required (or equivalent on another scale). **Criteria:** Selection of applicants will be based on the application.

Funds Avail.: $5,000. **To Apply:** Applicants must submit a complete application with short statement of personal and professional goals; must attach the academic activities including those relating to confectionery technology; must have the current copy of college transcript and a recommendation letter. Application must be mailed to: Warrell Corp., 1250 Slate Hill Rd., Camp Hill, PA 17011. **Deadline:** April 18. **Contact:** Mr. Karen Silva at the above address (see entry 331).

333 ■ American Association of Colleges of Nursing

One Dupont Circle NW, Ste. 530
Washington, DC 20036
Ph: (202)463-6930
Fax: (202)785-8320
E-mail: scasey@aacn.nche.edu
URL: http://www.aacn.nche.edu

334 ■ AACN Excellence in Academics Nursing Scholarships *(Undergraduate/Scholarship)*

Purpose: To promote education in nursing. **Focus:** Nursing. **Qualif.:** Applicant must have a GPA of 3.5 or better; enrolled full-time in a baccalaureate program; a junior student pursuing a Bachelor of Science in Nursing (BSN) program. **Criteria:** Selection is based on the application.

Funds Avail.: $2500. **Number Awarded:** 2. **To Apply:** Applicants must submit a completed application form together with the required materials. Send application and materials to Laura Guetter at AACN via email scholarship@aacn.nche.edu, or fax to 202785-8320. **Deadline:** August 1 and November 1.

Awards are arranged alphabetically below their administering organizations

Remarks: In partnership with Lydia's Professional Uniforms, a leading supplier of apparel for health professionals.

335 ■ AACN Minority Nurse Faculty Scholarships *(Graduate/Scholarship)*

Purpose: To diversify the faculty population to the field of nursing education. **Focus:** Nursing. **Qualif.:** Applicant must be enrolled full-time in an accredited graduate nursing program; a U.S. citizen, permanent resident, refugee or qualified immigrant; an underrepresented Minority, (Caucasian/non-Hispanic applicants are not eligible); committed to teach nursing in the United States after successful completion of graduate studies. **Criteria:** Selection is based on merit.

Funds Avail.: $18,000. **Number Awarded:** 5. **To Apply:** Applicants must submit a completed application form together with the required materials. **Deadline:** June 13.

Remarks: Awardees will be required to sign a letter of commitment that they will provide a one-year payback in a teaching role for each year of scholarship support provided. Failure to complete the payback requirement will require that funding be repaid to the program by the recipient. **Contact:** Project Coordinator Debbie Latimer at dlatimer@aacn.nche.edu.

336 ■ AfterCollege/AACN Nursing Scholarships *(Graduate, Undergraduate/Scholarship)*

Purpose: To promote education in nursing. **Focus:** Nursing. **Qualif.:** Applicant must be enrolled at an AACN member institution; seeking baccalaureate, master's or doctoral degree in nursing; and have a GPA of 3.25 or higher. **Criteria:** Consideration is given to students enrolled in a master's or doctoral program and pursuing a nursing faculty career; completing an RN to baccalaureate program (BSN); or enrolled in an accelerated baccalaureate or master's degree nursing program.

Funds Avail.: $2500. **To Apply:** Applicants are advised to visit the website for the application forms. **Deadline:** January 31, April 30, July 31 and October 31.

Remarks: In partnership with AfterCollege, the leading employment website for nursing/allied health care student. **Contact:** scholarship@aacn.nche.edu.

337 ■ The California Endowment and AACN Minority Nurse Faculty Scholarships *(Graduate/Scholarship)*

Purpose: To increase the number of minority faculty teaching in California Nursing schools. **Focus:** Nursing. **Qualif.:** Applicant must be enrolled full-time in an accredited graduate nursing program; a U.S. citizen, permanent resident, refugee or qualified immigrant; resident of the state of California; an underrepresented Minority, (Caucasian/non-Hispanic applicants are not eligible); committed to teach nursing in the United States after successful completion of graduate studies. **Criteria:** Selection is based on the application.

Funds Avail.: $18,000. **To Apply:** Applicants must submit a completed application form together with the required materials. **Deadline:** May 30.

338 ■ American Association of Colleges of Osteopathic Medicine

5550 Friendship Blvd., Ste. 310
Chevy Chase, MD 20815-7231
Ph: (301)968-4100
Fax: (301)968-4101
URL: http://www.aacom.org

339 ■ AACOM Scholar in Residence Program *(Graduate, Undergraduate/Scholarship)*

Purpose: To promote leadership roles in the profession and positions of influence in health policy. **Focus:** Osteopathic medicine. **Qualif.:** Individuals with a professional connection to the osteopathic profession. Applicants must be an undergraduate, graduate or continuing medical education. **Criteria:** Recipients will be selected based on the review of all application materials submitted.

Funds Avail.: $2,225. **To Apply:** Applicants must be nominated by their dean and together with the dean and department chair, develop a proposal for study that will enhance both their college's medical education and provide leadership to the greater osteopathic medical education community. **Deadline:** December 31. **Contact:** Linda Heun 5550 Friendship Blvd., Suite 310 Chevy Chase MD 20815; Phone: 301-968-4143, Fax: 301-968-4101; meded@.aacom.org.

340 ■ American Association of Critical-Care Nurses

101 Columbia
Aliso Viejo, CA 92656-4109
Ph: (949)362-2000
Fax: (949)362-2020
Free: 800-899-2226
E-mail: info@aacn.org
URL: http://www.aacn.org

341 ■ American Association of Critical-Care Nurses BSN Scholarships *(Undergraduate/Scholarship)*

Purpose: To provide financial assistance to AACN members who are registered nurses completing a baccalaureate or graduate degree program in nursing. **Focus:** Nursing. **Qualif.:** Applicant must be a bonafide AACN member; have an active RN license; cumulative GPA of 3.0 or better; currently working in critical care or have worked in critical care for at least one year in the past three years; junior or upper division status for the following fall semester; and currently enrolled in or accepted to a nursing program accredited by the state Board of Nursing for the following fall semester. **Criteria:** Applicants will be evaluated based on comprehensiveness of response; dedication to patient care outcomes; modeling of professional commitment; relation to the AACN vision; and ability to clearly communicate in writing.

Funds Avail.: $1,500. **To Apply:** Applicants must submit application online, completed along with a cover checklist page and supporting documents. **Deadline:** April 1.

342 ■ American Association of Critical-Care Nurses Graduate Scholarships *(Doctorate, Graduate/Scholarship)*

Purpose: To provide financial assistance to AACN members who are registered nurses completing a baccalaureate or graduate degree program in nursing. **Focus:** Nursing. **Qualif.:** Applicant must be a bonafide AACN member; have an active RN license; cumulative GPA of 3.0 or better; currently working in critical care or have worked in critical care for at least one year in the past three years; graduate of a

Awards are arranged alphabetically below their administering organizations

baccalaureate degree program; and currently enrolled or accepted to a nursing program leading to a master's or doctorate degree in nursing. **Criteria:** Applicants will be evaluated based on comprehensiveness of response; dedication to patient care outcomes; modeling of professional commitment; relation to the AACN vision; and ability to clearly communicate in writing.

Funds Avail.: $1,500. **To Apply:** Applicants must submit application online, completed along with a cover checklist page and supporting documents. **Deadline:** April 1.

343 ■ American Association of Equine Practitioners

4075 Iron Works Pkwy.
Lexington, KY 40511
Ph: (859)233-0147
Fax: (859)233-1968
E-mail: aaepoffice@aaep.org
URL: http://www.aaep.org

344 ■ AAEP/ALSIC Scholarships *(Undergraduate/Scholarship)*

Purpose: To advance the health and welfare of horses by promoting the discovery and sharing of new knowledge; to enhance awareness of the need to the targeted research; to educate the public; to expand fundraising opportunities; to facilitate cooperation among funding agencies. **Focus:** Veterinary science and medicine. **Qualif.:** Applicants must be senior veterinary students who have indicated a strong desire to pursue a career in equine medicine at schools nationwide.

Funds Avail.: $2,500. **Number Awarded:** 8. **To Apply:** An applicant must fill out the online application form. **Deadline:** October 1.

345 ■ AAEP Foundation Research Fellowships *(Doctorate/Scholarship)*

Purpose: To emphasize the importance of equine research; to reward a researcher for his or her contributions. **Focus:** Veterinary science and medicine. **Qualif.:** An applicant must be a current doctoral student or resident, or have completed their residency or doctorate within two years. **Criteria:** Scholarship Committee will evaluate application based on the potential for proposed research to contribute to equine veterinary medicine; sincere intent for long-term career in equine veterinary research; experience within horse industry; experience and activity in equine veterinary medicine; experience with equine research; academic performance; and based on the professional accomplishments before and after graduation.

Funds Avail.: $5,000. **To Apply:** An applicant must attach the complete filled out AAEP Research Fellow Cover Sheet; he/she must prepare a maximum one-page cover letter outlining long-term research intent, as well as how it will impact equine veterinary medicine and positively affect horse health; an applicant must include how the scholarship will help in doing the research; a maximum two-page scientific abstract and budget of the intent research project; an applicant must obtain a curriculum vitae, a completed evaluation form, a signed and sealed letter of recommendations; and an applicant must provide a self-addressed, stamped postcard to be returned as confirmation of receipt; an applicant must attend the AAEP Convention; he/she must provide information to AAEP for AAEP Foundation Publications such as biographical sketch, benefits of fellowship, impact of research result, **Deadline:** July 31.

346 ■ American Association of Family and Consumer Sciences

400 N Columbus St., Ste. 202
Alexandria, VA 22314
Ph: (703)706-4600
Fax: (703)706-4663
Free: 800-424-8080
E-mail: staff@aafcs.org
URL: http://www.aafcs.org

347 ■ American Association of Family and Consumer Sciences Scholarships *(Undergraduate/Scholarship)*

Purpose: To encourage undergraduate study in family and consumer sciences and its subspecialties. **Focus:** Sciences. **Qualif.:** Applicants must be citizens or permanent residents of the United States; must be planning to pursue or currently pursuing a degree in family and consumer sciences or its specialties at the undergraduate level on a full-time basis; must be currently enrolled in an undergraduate program that will continue into the coming academic year or have been admitted to an undergraduate program for the coming academic year; must be willing to commit themselves to meet the specific requirements of the scholarship for which they are applying. **Criteria:** Recipients are selected based on ability to pursue undergraduate study, experience in relation to preparation for study in proposed field, special recognition and awards, participation in professional/community organizations and activities, evidence of professional commitment and leadership, significance of proposed area of study to families and individuals, professional goals, written communication and evaluation of applicant's recommendations.

Funds Avail.: $5,000. **To Apply:** Applicants must complete the application form; must have a maximum of three evaluators; must obtain official or unofficial copies of transcript; must mail five hard copies of labeled CDs of the completed application form. **Deadline:** January 7.

348 ■ American Association for Hand Surgery

20 N Michigan Ave., Ste. 700
Chicago, IL 60602
Ph: (312)236-3307
Fax: (312)782-0553
E-mail: contact@handsurgery.org
URL: http://www.handsurgery.org

349 ■ American Association for Hand Surgery Annual Research Awards *(Professional Development/Award/Prize)*

Purpose: To foster creativity and innovation in basic and/or clinical research in all areas pertinent to hand surgery. **Focus:** Surgery. **Qualif.:** Applicant must be a member of AAHS and willing to travel abroad for up two weeks to a chosen host country. **Criteria:** Applicants are selected according to the potential of their research project.

Funds Avail.: $5,000. **Number Awarded:** 3. **To Apply:** Applicants must submit application form plus seven copies of investigators' demographic information, description of research, and curriculum vitae for each researcher. **Deadline:** November 1. **Contact:** at the above address (see entry 348).

Awards are arranged alphabetically below their administering organizations

350 ■ American Association for Health Education

1900 Association Dr.
Reston, VA 20191-1598
Ph: (703)476-3400
Free: 800-213-7193
URL: http://www.aahperd.org/aahe

351 ■ Ruth Abernathy Presidential Scholarships
(Graduate, Undergraduate/Scholarship)

Purpose: To support members with their educational pursuit. **Focus:** Health education; Physical education. **Qualif.:** Applicant must be undergraduate or graduate student members majoring in a field related to one or more of the disciplines represented by AAHPERD and its associations; and have a cumulative GPA of 3.5. **Criteria:** The scholarship committee will review the applications submitted by the districts and select award recipients in early January.

Funds Avail.: $1000-$1500; and a three-year AAHPERD membership. **Number Awarded:** Three undergraduates; Two graduate students. **To Apply:** Applicants must submit a completed application from together with the required materials. Application materials should be submitted by U.S. mail (fax copies will not be accepted). **Deadline:** October 15. **Contact:** Deb Callis at dcallis@aahperd.org.

352 ■ American Association of Healthcare Administrative Management

11240 Waples Mill Rd., Ste. 200
Fairfax, VA 22030
Ph: (703)281-4043
Fax: (703)359-7562
E-mail: moayad@aaham.org
URL: http://www.aaham.org

353 ■ National AAHAM Scholarships
(Undergraduate/Scholarship)

Purpose: To provide educational scholarship to individual AAHAM members and their dependents. **Focus:** General studies. **Qualif.:** Applicants must be individuals who have been National AAHAM members for at least one year and have paid their current dues by March 30 of the year in which applications are submitted. **Criteria:** Applicants are judged based on the established criteria by the review and selection committee comprised of the Chairmen of the Board and the current chairs of the Education and Finance Committees.

Funds Avail.: $2,500. **To Apply:** Applicants must submit all the required application information.

354 ■ American Association for the Improvement of Boxing

86 Fletcher Ave.,
Mount Vernon, NY 10552-3319
Ph: (914)664-4571
Fax: (914)664-3164
E-mail: aaib@verizon.net
URL: http://www.aaib.org

355 ■ AAIB Scholarships *(Undergraduate/Scholarship)*

Purpose: To provide educational opportunities and financial assistance to working students. **Focus:** General Studies. **Qualif.:** Program is open to high school seniors who must be accepted by an accredited college or university; must be nominated by a current paid member. **Criteria:** Recipient is chosen based on scholastic achievement, athletic achievement and community service.

Funds Avail.: No specific amount. **Number Awarded:** 1. **To Apply:** Application form is available in the website. **Deadline:** May 1.

356 ■ American Association for Justice

1050 31 St. NW
Washington, DC 20007
Ph: (202)965-3500
Free: 800-424-2725
E-mail: membership@justice.org
URL: http://www.justice.org

357 ■ AAJ Trial Advocacy Scholarships
(Undergraduate/Scholarship)

Purpose: To assist law students to further their studies. **Focus:** Law. **Qualif.:** Applicants must be second and third year AAJ law student members; must be enrolled in an ABA accredited law school. **Criteria:** Scholarships are given to applicants who: exhibit an interest and proficiency of skills in trial advocacy; express a desire to represent victims; demonstrate a commitment and dedication to AAJ mission through involvement in an AAJ student chapter and minority caucus activities; and show financial need.

Funds Avail.: $2,500. **To Apply:** Applicants must submit resume; 500-word essay on how the applicants will meet the criteria; up to three recommendations from a faculty adviser, trial advocacy professor, Dean, AAJ member, or trial lawyer; and a completed form verifying applicant's student status. **Deadline:** April 30. **Contact:** Natalie Etori at the above address (see entry 356).

358 ■ The Richard D. Hailey AAJ Law Student Scholarships *(Undergraduate/Scholarship)*

Purpose: To assist law students to further their studies. **Focus:** Law. **Qualif.:** Applicants must be incoming first, second or third year African, American, Hispanic Asian American, Native American and bi-racial AAJ law student members; must be enrolled in an ABA accredited law school. **Criteria:** Scholarships are given to applicants who: exhibit an interest and proficiency of skills in trial advocacy; express a desire to represent victims; demonstrate a commitment and dedication to AAJ mission through involvement in an AAJ student chapter and minority caucus activities; and show financial need.

Funds Avail.: $1,000. **Number Awarded:** 6. **To Apply:** Applicants must submit resume; 500-word essay on how the applicants will meet the criteria; up to three recommendations from a faculty adviser, trial advocacy professor, Dean, AAJ member or trial lawyer; and a completed form verifying applicant's student status. **Deadline:** April 30. **Contact:** Natalie Etori at the above address (see entry 356).

359 ■ Alia Herrera Memorial Scholarships
(Undergraduate/Scholarship)

Purpose: To assist law students to further their studies. **Focus:** Law. **Qualif.:** Applicants must be students entering second or third year of law school, or having the equivalent of one year to complete; must be attending law schools in the Philadelphia, PA area; must be members of the law

Awards are arranged alphabetically below their administering organizations

student section of AAJ; must be children of AAJ members. **Criteria:** Recipients are selected based on the Scholarship Committee's review of academic records.

Funds Avail.: $3,000. **To Apply:** Applicants must submit cover letter; resume; transcript; letter of recommendation from a law professor or Dean of law school; 500-word essay on the topic ("Damage Caps": Limiting Damage awards in Civil cases by State and/or federal statutes, compared to juries making damage awards, with judicial review; Who should bare the risk or loss, and why?). **Deadline:** May 1. **Contact:** Cheryl Lange, 1643 Monaco Pkwy. Denver, CO 80220; cheryllange@yahoo.com.

360 ■ The Leesfield/AAJ Law Student Scholarships *(Undergraduate/Scholarship)*

Purpose: To assist law students to further their studies. **Focus:** Law. **Qualif.:** Applicants must be first and second year AAJ law student members. **Criteria:** Recipients are selected based on submitted application materials.

Funds Avail.: $1,500. **To Apply:** Applicants must submit resume; statement of financial need; 500-word written request substantiating the applicant's commitment to preserving the civil justice system; three recommendations from a faculty adviser, trial advocacy professor, dean AAJ member, or trial lawyer; and a completed form verifying applicant's student status. **Deadline:** April 30. **Contact:** Natalie Etori at the above address (see entry 356).

361 ■ American Association of Law Libraries

53 W Jackson, Ste. 940
Chicago, IL 60604
Ph: (312)939-4764
Fax: (312)431-1097
E-mail: aallhq@aall.org
URL: http://www.aallnet.org

362 ■ AALL Scholarships for Continuing Education Classes *(Postgraduate/Scholarship)*

Purpose: To provide financial assistance to individuals who wish to pursue courses related to law librarianship. **Focus:** Library and archival sciences. **Qualif.:** Applicants must be law librarians with a degree from an ALA-accredited library school or an ABA-accredited law school, who are registered in continuing education courses related to law librarianship. Applicants must also be AALL members. **Criteria:** Applicants who are permanent residents of United States and Canada will be given preference.

Funds Avail.: $500. **To Apply:** Applicants must submit a completed application form; course description and registration; personal statement; and letters of recommendation. **Deadline:** April 1. **Contact:** Email: scholarships@aall.org

363 ■ AALL Scholarships for Library School Graduates Seeking a Non-Law Degree *(Postgraduate/Scholarship)*

Purpose: To assist individuals who wish to develop a professional career in law librarianship and who intend to have a career as a law librarian. **Focus:** Library and archival sciences. **Qualif.:** Applicants must be library school graduates who are degree candidates in an area other than law. Scholarship is restricted to members of AALL. **Criteria:** Recipients are selected based on the application packet and financial need.

Funds Avail.: No specific amount. **To Apply:** Applicant must submit an application form; transcript of records; letters of recommendation; and a personal statement. **Deadline:** April 1.

364 ■ AALL & Thomson West - George A. Strait Minority Scholarship Endowment *(Postgraduate/Scholarship)*

Purpose: To support the education of minority students who wish to pursue their career goals in law librarianship. **Focus:** Library and archival sciences. **Qualif.:** Applicants must be college graduates with meaningful law library experience; members of a minority group as defined by current U.S. Government guidelines; degree candidates in an ALA-accredited library school or an ABA-accredited law school; intend to have a career in law librarianship; must have at least one quarter/semester remaining after the scholarship is awarded. **Criteria:** Recipients are selected based on the application materials submitted.

Funds Avail.: Exact scholarship amount is not specified. **To Apply:** Applicants must submit a completed application form; course description and registration; personal statement; and letters of recommendation. **Deadline:** April 1.

365 ■ American Association of Law Libraries Library School Scholarships *(Postgraduate/Scholarship)*

Purpose: To assist individuals in achieving their goal of becoming a law librarian. **Focus:** Library and archival sciences. **Qualif.:** Applicant must be a law school graduate working towards a degree in an accredited library school or a college graduate with meaningful law library experience and a degree candidate in an accredited library school. Applicant must have the intention of having a career as a law librarian. **Criteria:** Applicants who are law school graduates with meaningful library experience or college graduates working for degrees with emphasis on courses in law are given preference.

Funds Avail.: Exact scholarship amount is not specified. **To Apply:** Applicants must submit an application form; transcripts; three letters of recommendation and a personal statement. Evidence of financial need must be submitted. **Deadline:** April 1. **Contact:** scholarships@aall.org.

366 ■ James F. Connolly LexisNexis Academic & Library Solutions Scholarships *(Postgraduate/Scholarship)*

Purpose: To provide financial assistance to individuals who wish to pursue a career related to law librarianship. **Focus:** Library and archival sciences. **Qualif.:** Applicants must be law school graduates with law library experience; pursuing a degree in an accredited law school with the intention of having a career in law librarianship; must have no more than 36 semester (54 quarter) credit hours remaining before qualifying for the degree. **Criteria:** Applicants who have demonstrated an interest in government documents will be given preference.

Funds Avail.: $3,000. **To Apply:** Applicants must submit a completed application; library school transcript; law school letter regarding student status; personal statement; law school transcript; letters of recommendation. **Deadline:** April 1.

367 ■ American Association of Medical Assistants

20 N Wacker Dr., Ste. 1575
Chicago, IL 60606

Ph: (312)899-1500
Fax: (312)899-1259
URL: http://www.aama-ntl.org

368 ■ Maxine Williams Scholarships
(Postdoctorate/Scholarship)

Purpose: To support students in a medical assisting program. **Focus:** Medical assisting. **Qualif.:** Applicant must be currently enrolled, and have completed a minimum of one quarter or a semester at a postsecondary medical assisting program accredited by (CAAHEP); and have a GPA of 3.0 or higher. **Criteria:** Selection is based on academic ability and financial need.

Funds Avail.: $1000, and one-year membership in AAMA. **To Apply:** Applicants must request an application electronically to boardservices@aama-ntl.org, including applicant's name; accreditation code; and program's institution name, city and state. **Deadline:** February 15.

Remarks: Established in 1959, named after the first president and founder of the AAMA, Maxine Williams.

369 ■ American Association of Neurological Surgeons

5550 Meadowbrook Dr.
Rolling Meadows, IL 60008
Ph: (847)378-0500
Fax: (847)378-0600
Free: 888-566-2267
E-mail: info@aans.org
URL: http://www.aans.org

370 ■ AANS Medical Student Summer Research Fellowships (MSSRF) *(Undergraduate/Fellowship)*

Purpose: To provide first or second year medical students the opportunity to participate in neurosurgical research through a summer fellowship within an academic department of neurosurgery in the United States or Canada. **Focus:** Neurology. **Qualif.:** Applicants must be American or Canadian medical students. **Criteria:** Candidates will be judged based upon the scientific merits of the proposed project, the credentials of the applicant, letters of reference, the preceptor statement and the support provided by the sponsoring program/laboratory.

Funds Avail.: $2,500. **Number Awarded:** 15. **To Apply:** Applicants must submit applications through mail (hard-copy format) or electronically to nref@aans.org which must include the curriculum vitae and bio-sketch, a description of future plans, and a statement of why this fellowship is of interest to the applicant and why it would be beneficial to him/her. **Deadline:** February 1.

371 ■ ACS/NREF-AANS Faculty Career Development Award *(Professional Development/Award/Prize)*

Purpose: To support the establishment of a new and independent research program in an area of neurological surgery, co-sponsored by the ACS and the NREF. **Focus:** Neurology. **Qualif.:** Applicants must be surgeons who are members or candidate members of both the ACS and the AANS; have completed specialty training within the preceding five years and have received a full-time faculty appointment at a US or Canadian accredited medical school. **Criteria:** Candidates will be evaluated based on the criteria designed by the Award Committee.

Funds Avail.: $40,000. **To Apply:** Applicants must submit complete application form found in AANS.org website. **Deadline:** November 15.

372 ■ William P. Van Wagenen Fellowships
(Undergraduate/Fellowship)

Purpose: To provide financial support to a post neurosurgical resident for foreign travel for scientific enrichment, prior to beginning an academic career in neurological surgery. **Focus:** Neurology. **Qualif.:** Applicants must be senior neurosurgical residents whose country of study is different from the country of residence in approved neurosurgery residency programs and whose intent is to pursue an academic career in neurological surgery. **Criteria:** Candidates will be evaluated by the Van Wagenen Selection Committee based on the originality and quality of proposal, thoroughness with which the plan for a period abroad has been designed, personal attributes, and the quality of the research environment.

Funds Avail.: $60,000. **To Apply:** Applicants must submit completed application together with the letter of reference. **Deadline:** October 1.

373 ■ American Association of Neuroscience Nurses

4700 W Lake Ave.
Glenview, IL 60025
Ph: (847)375-4733
Fax: (847)375-3430
Free: 888-557-2266
E-mail: info@aann.org
URL: http://www.aann.org

374 ■ Certified Neuroscience Registered Nurse (CNRN) Recertification Grants Program *(Professional Development/Grant)*

Purpose: To award financial assistance to nurses seeking recertification as a CNRN during their 5th year after CNRN certification. **Focus:** Neuroscience; Nursing. **Qualif.:** Open to all CNRNs in their 5th year of certification. The applicants must meet the requirements for recertification as delineated by the ABNN. One letter of recommendation from a supervisor in support of applicant is to accompany the application. **Criteria:** Selection will be based on the committee's criteria.

Funds Avail.: $150. **To Apply:** Applicants must provide one complete original (with Form A) and four blinded (no identifying information, such as name, institution name, city, etc. Use generic terms instead), collated copies of the application (without Form A). The Agreement Statement and letter of recommendation should be included with the complete original application. **Deadline:** June 1. **Contact:** AANN at the above address (see entry 373).

375 ■ Integra Foundation NNF Research Grants Award *(Professional Development/Grant)*

Purpose: To encourage qualified nurses to contribute to the advancement of neuroscience nursing through research. **Focus:** Neuroscience; Nursing. **Qualif.:** Principal investigator must be a registered nurse. Investigators must be ready to start the research project, or are already in the process of conducting the research, which must be congruent with NNF research priorities and must be significant to neuroscience nursing. **Criteria:** Selection will be based on the quality of the proposed research and the NNF research fund budget.

Awards are arranged alphabetically below their administering organizations

Funds Avail.: $10,000. **To Apply:** Applicants must submit the following requirements: Application Form - One copy of the application form with all information included, six copies of the application form with all identifying information removed; Investigator Information Form - One copy of investigator information form (Form A) with all information included (one for each investigator), six copies of each investigator information form (Form B) for use in blind review; Budget Page - Six copies of the budget page; The Proposal - One copy of the proposal which may include names and identifying information, six additional copies of the proposal without names or identifying information; Local Institution Approval Approval from local institutional review board indicating approval of protection of human participants (if Local institutional approval is pending, submit it when obtained). Study must have been submitted to local review committee prior to the time of application. **Deadline:** June 30. **Contact:** American Association of Neuroscience Nurses at the above address (see entry 373).

376 ■ NNF Scholarships Program *(Graduate, Undergraduate/Scholarship)*

Purpose: To promote excellence in neuroscience nursing. **Focus:** Neuroscience; Nursing. **Qualif.:** Applicants must be registered nurses pursuing a career in neuroscience nursing at the undergraduate or graduate level. **Criteria:** Selection will be based on the committee's criteria.

Funds Avail.: $1,500. **To Apply:** Applications must be typed or word-processed. The application is available at the NNF web site, www.aann.org. Complete all information as requested. Incomplete applications will not be considered and will be returned to the applicants. School which the applicant attends, or plans to attend must be accredited. Submit one copy of Form A, four copies of Form B (including personal statement). **Deadline:** January 15. **Contact:** AANN at the above address (see entry 373).

377 ■ American Association of Occupational Health Nurses

2920 Brandywine Rd., Ste. 100
Atlanta, GA 30341
Ph: (770)455-7757
Fax: (770)455-7271
E-mail: don@aaohn.org
URL: http://www.aaohn.org

378 ■ AAOHN Academic Study Scholarships *(Graduate, Undergraduate/Scholarship)*

Purpose: To provide opportunities to further professional education for occupational and environment health professionals. **Focus:** Occupational safety and health. **Qualif.:** Undergraduate candidate must be a registered nurse enrolled full or part time in a nationally accredited school of nursing baccalaureate program and demonstrate an interest in, and commitment to, occupational and environmental health. Graduate candidate must be a registered nurse enrolled full or part time in a graduate program that has application to occupational and environmental health. Applicants must submit documentation of enrollment status. **Criteria:** Selection will be based on the committee's criteria.

Funds Avail.: $2,500-$3,000. **Number Awarded:** 4. **To Apply:** Applicants must submit a 500 word or less narrative (double-spaced with one-inch margins in 12-point font) addressing: professional goals as they pertain to academic activity and the field of occupational and environmental health; impact of education on career. **Deadline:** December 1. **Contact:** Don Bollmer, Dir. of Business Affairs, at the above address (see entry 377).

379 ■ AAOHN Continuing Education Scholarships *(Professional Development/Scholarship)*

Purpose: To support occupational and environmental health professionals in attending and successfully completing continuing education activities. **Focus:** Occupational safety and health. **Qualif.:** Candidates must be employed in the field of occupational and environmental health nursing and demonstrate an interest in, and commitment to, occupational and environmental health. **Criteria:** Selection will be based on the committee's criteria.

Funds Avail.: $1,500. **Number Awarded:** 6. **To Apply:** Applicants must submit a 500 word or less narrative (double-spaced with one-inch margins in 12-point font) addressing: career goals as they pertain to applicant's professional development and continued competence; how continuing education will further applicant's goals; need for financial support; commitment to ongoing continuing education activities. Applicants must also submit a letter of support from their employer/supervisor and copy of continuing education activity brochure or other printed information describing the activity. **Deadline:** December 1. **Contact:** Don Bollmer, Dir. of Business Affairs, at the above address (see entry 377).

380 ■ Leadership Development Scholarships *(Professional Development/Scholarship)*

Purpose: To support volunteer leadership development in occupational and environmental health nursing. **Focus:** Occupational safety and health. **Qualif.:** Candidates must be employed in the field of occupational and environmental health nursing and demonstrate an interest in, and commitment to, occupational and environmental health. **Criteria:** Selection will be based on the committee's criteria.

Funds Avail.: $1,000. **To Apply:** This scholarship is to be applied to leadership development activity/program registration, travel and/or associated travel-related expenses. Types of activities that will be considered for funding include the AAOHN Conference of Leaders, Nurse in Washington Internship Program, mentoring development program, etc. Applicant must submit a 500 word or less narrative (double-spaced with one-inch margins in 12-point font) addressing: why the applicant considers him/herself an emerging leader in volunteer service; leadership skills applicant would develop by participating in the selected leadership development activity/program; how learned skills will be applied serving in a volunteer leadership role within the profession of occupational and environment health nursing; quality/relevance of leadership development activity/program to stated goals. Applicants must also submit a letter of support from employer/supervisor. **Deadline:** August 1. **Contact:** Don Bollmer, Dir. of Business Affairs, at the above address (see entry 377).

381 ■ American Association of People with Disabilities

1629 K St. NW, Ste. 503
Washington, DC 20006
Ph: (202)457-0046
Free: 800-840-8844
E-mail: aapd@aol.com
URL: http://www.aapd.com

382 ■ ABA Legal Scholarships *(Graduate/Scholarship)*

Purpose: To encourage racial and ethnic minority students to apply to law schools and to provide financial assistance to ensure that these students have the opportunity to attend law school for three years. **Focus:** Law. **Qualif.:** Applicant must be an entering first year law student; must have achieved a minimum cumulative grade point average of 2.5 on a 4.0 scale at his/her undergraduate institution; and must be a citizen or permanent resident of the United States of America. **Criteria:** Recipients are selected based on academic standing and financial need.

Funds Avail.: $5,000. **To Apply:** Applicants must complete the application form and submit along with a personal statement, two recommendations, of which one must be submitted from one of the applicant's professors, and a copy of the transcript from his/her undergraduate institution. **Deadline:** March 1. **Contact:** 321 North Clark St., Chicago IL 60610-4714.

383 ■ Actuarial Scholarships for Minority Students *(Undergraduate/Scholarship)*

Purpose: To provide educational assistance for black students at the undergraduate or graduate level pursuing careers in the area of actuarial sciences. **Focus:** Actuarial science. **Qualif.:** Applicants must be students of African descent in the actuarial profession and must be originating from the United States, Canada, Caribbean or African Nations; must have a GPA of at least 3.0 on a 4.0 scale; must have a Math SAT score of at least 600 or an ACT Math score of at least 28; and must be junior, senior or graduate students. **Criteria:** Recipients are selected based on proficient communications skills that should demonstrate clear interest in the actuarial profession; excellent recommendations from mathematics-related instructors; determination and self-motivation; familiarity with actuarial profession demands; and financial need.

Funds Avail.: No specific amount. **To Apply:** Applicants must complete the application form and submit along with two nomination forms; an official, sealed current college transcript; an official sealed record of any educational examination scores taken; a Student Aid Report; and a copy of the page in college or university catalog or an information sheet showing an estimate of tuition, fees, and other expenses. **Deadline:** May 21. **Contact:** iabafdvp@blackactuaries.org.

384 ■ American Association of Physics Teachers

One Physics Ellipse
College Park, MD 20740-3845
Ph: (301)209-3300
Fax: (301)209-0845
E-mail: webmaster@aapt.org
URL: http://www.aapt.org

385 ■ Barbara Lotze Scholarships for Future Teachers *(Undergraduate/Scholarship)*

Purpose: To provide scholarships for future high school physics teachers. **Focus:** Physics. **Qualif.:** Applicants must be U.S. citizens attending U.S. schools. Undergraduate students who are enrolled or planning to enroll in physics teacher preparation curricula or high school seniors entering such programs are eligible to apply. **Criteria:** Recipients are selected based on merit.

Funds Avail.: $2,000. **Number Awarded:** 2. **To Apply:** Application materials are available as a PDF or may be requested from Programs Department, American Association of Physics Teachers at the above address. **Deadline:** December 1.

386 ■ American Association of Plastic Surgeons

900 Cummings Ctr., Ste. 221-U
Beverly, MA 01915
Ph: (978)927-8330
Fax: (978)524-8890
URL: http://www.aaps1921.org

387 ■ American Association of Plastic Surgeons Academic Scholars Program *(Graduate/Grant)*

Purpose: To assist surgeons in establishing a new and independent research program. **Focus:** Plastic surgery. **Qualif.:** Applicants must be plastic and reconstructive surgeons who have: (1) completed the chief residency year within the preceding five years; and (2) received a full-time faculty appointment in a department of surgery/plastic surgery at a medical school accredited by the Liaison Committee on Graduate Medical Education in the United States or by the Committee for Accreditation of Canadian Medical Schools in Canada. **Criteria:** Applicants who are not current recipients of major research grants are given preference.

Funds Avail.: $30,000. **To Apply:** Applicants must complete application online and submit a research plan and supporting letters from the Chair of the Department/Division of Plastic Surgery. **Deadline:** November 1.

388 ■ American Association of Poison Control Centers

515 King St., Ste. 510
Alexandria, VA 22314
Ph: (703)894-1858
Fax: (703)683-2812
E-mail: info@aapcc.org
URL: http://www.aapcc.org

389 ■ Clinical Toxicology Fellowships *(Doctorate/Fellowship)*

Purpose: To train doctors of pharmacy graduates to function in a professional, administrative and research capacity. **Focus:** Toxicology. **Qualif.:** Applicants must possess a Pharm.D. degree from accredited schools or College of Pharmacy. **Criteria:** Selection will be based on the committee's review of application materials.

Funds Avail.: No specific amount. **To Apply:** Applicants must submit letters of reference; and letters of application with curriculum vitae attached. **Contact:** Wendy Klein-Scwartz.

390 ■ American Association of Police Polygraphists

PO Box 657
Waynesville, OH 45068
Ph: (937)728-7827
Fax: (937)488-1046
Free: 888-743-5479
E-mail: nom@policepolygraph.org

Awards are arranged alphabetically below their administering organizations

URL: http://www.policepolygraph.org

391 ■ William "Buddy" Sentner Scholarship Awards *(Undergraduate/Scholarship)*

Purpose: To provide financial assistance for deserving graduating high school senior or student currently attending college. **Focus:** General studies. **Qualif.:** Applicants must be a graduating high school senior or a college student; must be a relative of a full, life, or honorably retired member in good standing with the AAPP. **Criteria:** Recipients are selected based on the Selection Committee's review of the application materials.

Funds Avail.: Scholarship amount not specified. **To Apply:** Applicants must submit a completed application form; a recent official transcript of all courses and grades; and two character reference letters (from current institution's faculty and from a non-relative). Completed application package must be sent to the AAPP's Office. **Deadline:** March 31. **Contact:** aappnom@hughes.net.

392 ■ American Association of Professional Apiculturists

c/o Dept. of Entomology University of Minnesota
219 Hodson Hall
1980 Folwell Ave.
St. Paul, MN 55108-6125
Ph: (612)624-4798
Fax: (612)625-5299
URL: http://entomology.ucdavis.edu/home.cfm

393 ■ AAPA Research Scholarships *(Undergraduate/Award/Prize)*

Purpose: To recognize and promote outstanding research by students in the field of apiculture. **Focus:** Entomology. **Qualif.:** Applicants must be undergraduate or graduate students working in North America with completed research on Apis; must be active AAPA members. **Criteria:** Award Committee will review proposals and rank them to the top three. Ranks will be based on scientific merit, presentation, originality, and the overall value of the work within the field of apiculture.

Funds Avail.: $1,000. **To Apply:** Research proposal package must include a curriculum vitae of the nominee, one letter of recommendation, and a summary of the research problem not exceeding three pages including: objectives, significance, and methods. Nominees may also include: up to three publication reprints, submitted manuscripts or abstracts of theses or dissertations. Four copies of the proposal package should be sent to the Chair of the AAPA Student Award Committee at least one month prior to the annual meeting.

394 ■ American Association of Railroad Superintendents

PO Box 200
LaFox, IL 60147
Ph: (331)643-3369
Fax: (630)762-0755
E-mail: aars@supt.org
URL: http://www.railroadsuperintendents.org

395 ■ Frank J. Richter Scholarships *(Graduate, Undergraduate/Scholarship)*

Purpose: To support the education of students enrolled at an accredited college or university in the U.S. or Canada. **Focus:** Transportation. **Qualif.:** Applicant must be enrolled full-time undergraduate or graduate student at an accredited college or university; demonstrated successful completion of the previous year's study by maintaining at least a 2.75 accumulated GPA on a scale of 1 to 4 with an "A" equal to 4; have accumulate enough credits from accredited schools in time for the Fall Semester to have obtained at least a sophomore level standing at the college or university of enrollment. **Criteria:** Preference will be given to applicants enrolled in the transportation field and all applicants will be considered.

Funds Avail.: $1000. **Number Awarded:** 1. **To Apply:** Applicants must submit a completed application form together with an official transcript from the schools attended; and two letters of recommendation. The application and narrative statement are to be submitted in one envelope. The transcripts and letters of recommendation must be sent directly to AARS from the appropriate person. **Deadline:** June 1.

396 ■ American Association of School Administrators

801 N Quincy St., Ste. 700
Arlington, VA 22203-1730
Ph: (703)528-0700
Fax: (703)841-1543
E-mail: info@aasa.org
URL: http://www.aasa.org

397 ■ Educational Administration Scholarships Award *(Postgraduate/Scholarship)*

Purpose: To provide incentive, honor and financial assistance for outstanding graduate students in school administration intending to make school superintendency a career. **Focus:** General studies. **Qualif.:** Applicants must be recommended by the chair of the school of education in which the applicant is currently enrolled. Only one application may be submitted from each college or university campus. **Criteria:** Recipients are selected based on academic performance.

Funds Avail.: $2,000. **To Apply:** Applicants must submit completed application form available on the website; a declaration of mission consisting of no more than three separate statements (single-spaced, typewritten) addressing the following: an account of how you came to be interested in school administration, what you conceive the job of a school superintendent to be, what aspects of it chiefly appeal to you, what type of contribution you would like to make in this field, the particular kind of further training and experience which you believe most essential to your best performance, and how you would apply a scholarship toward achieving your professional goals; a succinct statement of an administrative problem you have already encountered, a description of how you met it, and what, on reflection, you wish you had done about it. If you have had no administrative experience, select a problem in the field of classroom teaching or of student activities or discipline; no more than two paragraphs in which you describe specific instances in your training and experience which highlight your individual strengths and focus on your successes. These paragraphs should help the reader know you as an administrator; also submit a letter of recommendation (one original and five photocopies) from the dean of the school of education where applicant is currently enrolled; and letters of endorsement. **Deadline:** August 31. **Contact:** awards@aasa.org; 703-875-0762.

Awards are arranged alphabetically below their administering organizations

398 ■ Stop Hunger Scholarships *(Undergraduate/ Scholarship)*

Purpose: To recognize students involved in the fight against hunger in America. **Focus:** General studies. **Qualif.:** Applicants must be enrolled in an accredited education institution (kindergarten through college) in the United States; and must have demonstrated ongoing commitment to their community by performing volunteer services impacting hunger in the United States at least within the last 12 months. **Criteria:** Recipients are selected based on academic performance.

Funds Avail.: $3,000. **To Apply:** Applicants and nominators must supply a valid e-mail address; applicants must submit a completed application form. **Deadline:** January 1-February 29.

399 ■ American Association of State Troopers

1949 Raymond Diehl Rd.
Tallahassee, FL 32308
Ph: (850)385-7904
Free: 800-765-5456
URL: http://www.statetroopers.org

400 ■ American Association of State Troopers Scholarship Foundation First Scholarships *(Undergraduate/Scholarship)*

Purpose: To provide financial assistance for the education of students who are dependents of the members of American Association of State Troopers, Inc. **Focus:** Law enforcement. **Qualif.:** Applicants must be high school or college students who are sons or daughters of a trooper members by natural birth, legal adoption, step child, or legal guardian. **Criteria:** Applicants will be evaluated based on academic performance and financial need.

Funds Avail.: $500. **To Apply:** Applicants must submit an official transcripts indicating a minimum 2.5 GPA (4.0 scale) at an accredited school; for high school students: final four-year high school transcripts; for college students: a current official college transcripts indicating all grades earned through the current year which he or she is applying for; letter of acceptance from an accredited college, state university or community college for the academic year; typed essay of 500 words entitled "How my Education Will Advance My Career Plans"; and a small photo attached to the bottom of the application where indicated. **Deadline:** July 31.

401 ■ American Association of State Troopers Scholarship Foundation Second Scholarships *(Undergraduate/Scholarship)*

Purpose: To provide financial assistance for the education of students who are dependents of the members of American Association of State Troopers, Inc. **Focus:** Law enforcement. **Qualif.:** Applicants must be a high school or college students who are sons or daughters of trooper members by natural birth, legal adoption, step child, or legal guardian. **Criteria:** Applicants will be evaluated based on academic performance and financial need.

Funds Avail.: $1,000. **To Apply:** Applicants must submit an original and official transcript indicating the minimum 3.5 GPA (4.0 scale) maintained during the fall through spring semesters for which the scholarship award was granted; a letter or registration notice as proof of enrollment for the academic year; and a small photo attached to the bottom of the application where indicated. **Deadline:** July 31.

402 ■ V.J. Johnson Memorial Scholarships *(Undergraduate/Scholarship)*

Purpose: To provide financial assistance to a student who intends to use his or her education to pursue a career in law enforcement. **Focus:** Law enforcement. **Qualif.:** Applicants must be high school or college students who are sons or a daughters of trooper members by natural birth, legal adoption, step child, or legal guardian (in Florida only). **Criteria:** Recipients are selected based on academic performance and financial need.

Funds Avail.: $1,500. **Number Awarded:** 1. **To Apply:** Applicants must submit an original and official transcript indicating, a minimum of 3.8 GPA (4.0 scale) was maintained during the fall through spring semesters for which the second scholarship award was granted; a letter or registration notice as proof of enrollment for the academic year; a typed essay of 500 words entitled "How my Education Will Advance My Plans for a Career in Law Enforcement"; and a small photo attached to the bottom of the application where indicated. **Deadline:** July 31.

403 ■ American Association of Stratigraphic Palynologists

University of North Carolina at Pembroke
Geology, Old Main 213
Pembroke, NC 28372
Ph: (910)521-6478
E-mail: mbfarley@sigmaxi.net
URL: http://www.palynology.org

404 ■ American Association of Stratigraphic Palynologists Student Scholarships *(Graduate/ Scholarship)*

Purpose: To support studies in palynology. **Focus:** Earth Sciences; Geology. **Qualif.:** Applicants must be a beginning graduate students or advanced graduate students. **Criteria:** Selection is based on applicant's qualifications and the quality of proposed project.

Funds Avail.: $1500. **Number Awarded:** 2. **To Apply:** Applicants must submit four copies of completed application form (available from the AASP Awards Committee Chair, or can be downloaded at the website). **Deadline:** March 31. **Contact:** Martin Farley, mbfarley@sigmaxi.net.

405 ■ Paleontological Society Student Research Grants *(Graduate, Undergraduate/Grant)*

Purpose: To support research in the field or any aspect related to paleontology. **Focus:** Earth Sciences; Geology. **Qualif.:** Applicant must be undergraduate or graduate student member of the Paleontological Society conducting a research on any aspect of paleontology. **Criteria:** Awards are based upon scholastic ability, potential, professional interest, character, and financial need.

Funds Avail.: $750. **To Apply:** Applicants must submit a completed application form (available at the website) and a letter of support from research advisor (must be sent to michalk@vt.edu). **Deadline:** February 25.

406 ■ American Association for the Surgery of Trauma

633 N Saint Clair St., Ste. 2400
Chicago, IL 60611
Ph: (312)202-5252
Fax: (312)202-5013

Awards are arranged alphabetically below their administering organizations

Free: 800-789-4006
E-mail: squatschy@aast.org
URL: http://www.aast.org

407 ■ AAST/ACS/NIGMS Scholarships *(Professional Development/Scholarship)*

Purpose: To facilitate the career development of individuals pursuing careers in trauma surgery research. **Focus:** Surgery. **Qualif.:** Applicants must be surgeon-scientists working in the early stages of their research careers; must be members in good standing of the ACS and eligible for membership in AAST. **Criteria:** Recipients are selected based on the committee's review of application materials.

Funds Avail.: $75,000. **To Apply:** Applicants must submit K08 or K23 application simultaneously to NIGMS and ACS Scholarship administrators. **Deadline:** October 12. **Contact:** kearly@facs.org

408 ■ AAST/KCI Research Grants *(All/Grant)*

Purpose: To sponsor clinical research in the area of wound care. **Focus:** Surgery. **Qualif.:** Program is open to individuals intending to conduct clinical research in the area of wound care only. **Criteria:** Recipients are selected based on the Scholarship Committee's review of application materials.

Funds Avail.: $50,000. **To Apply:** Applicants must submit a completed application form including curriculum vitae, bibliography and research proposals. Applicants are also required to submit one typed original copy of the application form and four 3-hole punched photocopies. **Deadline:** February 15. **Contact:** Robert C. Mackersie.

409 ■ AAST Medical Student Scholarships *(All/Scholarship)*

Purpose: To sponsor medical research in the fields of burns, trauma and acute care surgery. **Focus:** Surgery. **Qualif.:** Program is open for medical students who attend the AAST annual meeting. **Criteria:** Recipients are selected based on the Scholarship Committee's review of application materials.

Funds Avail.: No stated amount. **To Apply:** Applicants must submit letters of recommendation and curriculum vitae to Robert C. Mackersie. **Deadline:** June 1. **Contact:** Tamara Jenkins.

410 ■ Hemostasis and Resuscitation Research Scholarships *(All/Scholarship)*

Purpose: To support post residency research of surgeons with a major commitment in trauma surgery. **Focus:** Surgery. **Qualif.:** Program is open to individuals intending to conduct clinical research in the areas of hemostasis and resuscitation only. **Criteria:** Recipients are selected based on the Scholarship Committee's review of application materials.

Funds Avail.: $50,000. **To Apply:** Applicants must submit a completed application form including curriculum vitae, bibliography and research proposals. Applicants are also required to submit 1 typed original copy of the application form and 4 3-hole punched photocopies. **Deadline:** February 15. **Contact:** Tamara Jenkin.

411 ■ Local Wound Haemostatics and Hemorrhage Control Scholarships *(All/Scholarship)*

Purpose: To support post residency research of surgeons with a major commitment in trauma surgery. **Focus:** Surgery. **Qualif.:** Program is open for individuals intending to conduct clinical research in the areas of hemostasis and resuscitation only; must have commitment to trauma surgery academic research. **Criteria:** Recipients are selected based on the Scholarship Committee's review of application materials.

Funds Avail.: $40,000. **To Apply:** Applicants must submit a completed application form including curriculum vitae, bibliography and research proposals. Applicants are also required to submit one typed original copy of the application form and 4 3-hole punched photocopies. **Deadline:** February 15. **Contact:** Tamara Jenkins.

412 ■ American Association of Textile Chemists and Colorists

PO Box 12215
Research Triangle Park, NC 27709-2215
Ph: (919)549-8141
Fax: (919)549-8933
URL: http://www.aatcc.org

413 ■ Charles H. Stone Scholarships *(Undergraduate/Scholarship)*

Purpose: To provide financial assistance to junior or senior students who reside in NC, SC, VA or WV and attend North Carolina State University or Clemson University. **Focus:** Textile science. **Qualif.:** Applicants must be U.S. citizens; junior or senior students in an undergraduate program; must have a minimum GPA of 2.85 on a 4.0 scale; must be a Textile Chemistry undergraduate in Dyeing/Fiber Science/Polymers/Color Science; must be Piedmont Section Textile employees. **Criteria:** Recipients are selected based on extracurricular activities; employment experience and financial need.

Funds Avail.: $5,000. **To Apply:** Applicants must submit all the required application information.

414 ■ American Association for Thoracic Surgery

900 Cummings Center, Ste. 221-U
Beverly, MA 01915
Ph: (978)927-8330
Fax: (978)524-8890
URL: http://www.aats.org

415 ■ Advanced Cardiovascular Surgery Fellowships *(Graduate, Postdoctorate/Fellowship)*

Purpose: To provide exposure in the field of advanced cardiovascular surgery. **Focus:** Medicine. **Qualif.:** Applicants must complete either of ABTS requirements or their equivalence in cardiothoracic surgery training abroad. **Criteria:** Priority is given to applicants who passed the United States Medical Licensing Examination (USMLE) or the former Foreign Medical Graduate Exam in the Medical Sciences (FMGEMS) and the ECFMG English examination.

Funds Avail.: No specific amount. **To Apply:** Applicants must submit: completed online application; curriculum vitae; personal statement of professional goals; copy of graduate school and or medical/dental school diploma. Postdoctoral fellowship applications includes: official transcripts; three letters of recommendation from faculty members. Other residency and fellowship program applications includes: dean's letter; official transcripts; official test transcripts for

Awards are arranged alphabetically below their administering organizations

all applicable examinations; valid ECFMG certificate; three original letters of recommendation. **Deadline:** December 31. **Contact:** Carla MacLean.

416 ■ American Association for Thoracic Surgery Clinical Fellowships *(Graduate/Fellowship)*

Purpose: To provide fellows with primary surgical responsibility and opportunity for first hand patient care in the management of esophageal, gastric and pulmonary disease. **Focus:** Medicine. **Qualif.:** Applicants must be first hand patient care in the management of esophageal gastric and pulmonary disease. **Criteria:** Recipients are selected based on the committee's review of application.

Funds Avail.: No specific amount. **To Apply:** Applicants may apply online at AATS website. **Deadline:** May 15. **Contact:** Cheryl Correia.

417 ■ Edward D. Churchill Research Scholarships *(Professional Development/Scholarship)*

Purpose: To provide an opportunity for research, training and experience for North American surgeons committed to pursuing academic career in cardiothoracic surgery. **Focus:** Medicine. **Qualif.:** Applicants must be in the final year of cardiothoracic residency or in their first two years in an academic position. **Criteria:** Recipients are selected based on the submitted research proposals.

Funds Avail.: $80,000. **To Apply:** Applicants must submit a proposal for the research; and a statement of career plans and how the research activity will relate to the applicant's academic career. **Deadline:** July 1.

Remarks: The scholarship will be funded by the Association and administered by the Graham Education and Research Foundation. **Contact:** AATS at the above address (see entry 414).

418 ■ Ryan Hill Thoracoesophageal Fellowships *(Graduate/Fellowship)*

Purpose: To promote unique opportunity for clinical research involving thoracoesophageal surgery and/or interventions endoscopy. **Focus:** Medicine. **Qualif.:** Applicants must be pursuing both clinical research and additional surgical training in esophageal or general thoracic surgery. **Criteria:** Recipients are selected based on the committee's review of application.

Funds Avail.: No specific amount. **To Apply:** Applicants may apply at AATS website. **Deadline:** February 1. **Contact:** Donald Low, gtsdel@vmmc.org.

419 ■ Massachusetts General Hospital Summer Scholars Program *(Undergraduate/Fellowship)*

Purpose: To promote unique opportunity for clinical research involving thoracoesophageal surgery and/or interventions endoscopy. **Focus:** Medicine. **Qualif.:** Applicants must be first or second year medical students. **Criteria:** Selections are based on: applicant's care of patients, time spend in the operating room; and clinical research project.

Funds Avail.: No specific amount. **To Apply:** Applicants must send a letter of interest and curriculum vitae. **Deadline:** March 1. **Contact:** Douglas J. Mathisen.

420 ■ Summer Intern Scholarships in Cardiothoracic Surgery *(Undergraduate/Scholarship)*

Purpose: To introduce the field of cardiothoracic surgery. **Focus:** Medicine. **Qualif.:** Applicants must have the approval of the prospective sponsoring institutions; must be a member of the AATS; must be first or second year medical students. **Criteria:** Recipients are selected based on the committee's review of application materials.

Funds Avail.: $5,000. **To Apply:** Applicants must complete an online application and include a one-page outline of what they hope to accomplish during their eight weeks internship. Applicants must also submit a letter of support from the host sponsor. **Deadline:** January 15. **Contact:** AATS at the above address (see entry 414).

421 ■ American Association of University Women

1111 6th St. NW
Washington, DC 20036
Ph: (202)785-7700
Fax: (202)872-1425
E-mail: helpline@aauw.org
URL: http://www.aauw.org

422 ■ American Association of University Women American Fellowships *(All/Fellowship)*

Purpose: To support female doctoral candidates and scholars completing dissertations and seeking funds for postdoctoral research leave from accredited institutions. **Focus:** Women's studies. **Qualif.:** Applicants must be U.S. citizens or permanent residents. **Criteria:** Candidates are evaluated on the basis of scholarly excellence, teaching experience, and active commitment to helping women and girls through service in their communities, professions, or fields of research.

Funds Avail.: $6,000 up to $30,000. **To Apply:** Applicants must check online for further information about the award. **Deadline:** November 30.

423 ■ American Association of University Women Career Development Grants *(Postdoctorate/Grant)*

Purpose: To support women who hold bachelor's degree preparing to advance their careers, change careers, or reenter the work force. **Focus:** Women's studies. **Qualif.:** Applicants must be U.S. citizens or permanent residents. **Criteria:** Applicants must be AAUW members, women of color, and women pursuing their first advanced degree or credentials in non-traditional fields.

Funds Avail.: $2,000 up to $12,000. **To Apply:** Applicant must check online for further information about the award. **Deadline:** December 15.

424 ■ American Association of University Women Engineering Dissertation Awards *(Professional Development/Award/Prize)*

Purpose: To support women intending to pursue a full-time course of study at an accredited institution. **Focus:** Women's studies. **Qualif.:** Applicants must be U.S. citizens or permanent residents. **Criteria:** Selection of candidates based upon the following programs: Architecture (M.Arch, M.S.Arch), Computer/Information Sciences (M.S.), Engineering (M.E., M.S., Ph.D.), Engineering Dissertation Award also awarded Mathematics/Statistics (M.S.), and fellowships in the following degree programs are restricted to women of color, who have been underrepresented in these fields: Business Administration (M.B.A., E.M.B.A.), Law (J.D.), Medicine (M.D., D.O.).

Awards are arranged alphabetically below their administering organizations

Funds Avail.: $20,000. **To Apply:** Applicant must check online for further information about the award. **Deadline:** January 10.

425 ■ American Association of University Women International Fellowships *(All/Fellowship)*

Purpose: To provide fund for full-time study or research in the United States to women who are not United States citizens or permanent residents. **Focus:** General studies. **Qualif.:** Applicant must be a citizen in a country other than the United States, or must hold a nonimmigrant visa if residing in the United States. **Criteria:** Candidates are selected based on academic and professional qualifications, need for the specialized knowledge and skills of the country where she came from, commitment to the advancement of women and girls in her home country as demonstrated by her previous work and proposed study or research, documented evidence prior to her community service in the home country particularly activities concerning women and girls lives' improvement.

Funds Avail.: $18,000 up to $30,000. **To Apply:** Applicant must check online for further information about the award. **Deadline:** December 1.

426 ■ American Association of University Women Master's and First Professional Awards *(Professional Development/Award/Prize)*

Purpose: To financially support women intending to pursue a full-time course of study at accredited institutions. **Focus:** Women's studies. **Qualif.:** Applicants must be U.S. citizens or permanent residents. **Criteria:** Selected Professions Fellowships are awarded for the following programs: Architecture (M.Arch, M.S.Arch), Computer/Information Sciences (M.S.), Engineering (M.E., M.S., Ph.D.), Engineering Dissertation Award also awarded Mathematics/Statistics (M.S.), and fellowships in the following degree programs are restricted to women of color, who have been underrepresented in these fields: Business Administration (M.B.A., E.M.B.A.), Law (J.D.), Medicine (M.D., D.O.).

Funds Avail.: $5,000 up $12,000. **To Apply:** Applicant must check online for further information about the award. **Deadline:** January 10.

427 ■ American Astronomical Society

2000 Florida Ave. NW, Ste. 400
Washington, DC 20009-1231
Ph: (202)328-2010
Fax: (202)234-2560
E-mail: aas@aas.org
URL: http://www.aas.org

428 ■ American Astronomical Society Small Research Grants *(Doctorate/Grant)*

Purpose: To promote research related to astronomy. **Focus:** Astronomy and astronomical sciences. **Qualif.:** Applicant must be a U.S. citizen or foreign astronomer with Ph.D. or equivalent; and must not be connected to the institution. **Criteria:** Recipients are evaluated based on: scientific merit, student participation, budget, other funds available for the proposed project.

Funds Avail.: $1,000-$7,000. **To Apply:** Applicants must submit the proposal (maximum of four pages); curriculum vitae (maximum of two pages); and a cover letter. Send four copies of the proposal and other materials to: Small Research Grant Committee, American Astronomical Society 2000 Florida Avenue, NW Suite 400 Washington, DC 20009-1231, or mail the proposal in PDF to grier@aas.org (must mail a hardcopy of the cover page). **Deadline:** November 30. **Contact:** Dr. Jennifer Grier, grant administrator at grier@aas.org.

429 ■ Chretien International Research Grants *(Doctorate, Professional Development/Grant)*

Purpose: To promote research or projects related to astronomy. **Focus:** Astronomy and astronomical sciences. **Qualif.:** Applicants must be astronomers with a PhD or equivalent. **Criteria:** Recipients are selected based on the submitted proposals.

Funds Avail.: $20,000. **To Apply:** Applicants must submit a description of research (maximum of three pages); a statement on the applicant's ability to finish the project; a proposed budget; description of other financial resources (if applicable); curriculum vitae and bibliography of recent papers; two reference letters from astronomers who know the applicant's work; other circumstances that might help in the selection process. Applications must be forwarded to: Chretien International Research Grant Committee, American Astronomical Society 2000 Florida Avenue, NW Suite 400 Washington, DC 20009-1231. **Deadline:** April 1.

430 ■ American Bar Association

321 North Clark St.
Chicago, IL 60610
Ph: (312)988-5927
Fax: (312)988-6392
E-mail: dfrankiin3@staff.abanet.org
URL: http://www.abanet.org/fje

431 ■ The Allen E. Broussard Scholarships *(Undergraduate/Scholarship)*

Purpose: To provide law students with financial assistance. **Focus:** Law. **Qualif.:** Applicants must be law students attending California Bay Area law schools. **Criteria:** Recipients are selected based on financial need/economic background.

Funds Avail.: $5,000. **To Apply:** Applicants need to complete single application available at ABA website. **Deadline:** March 1. **Contact:** ABA at the above address (see entry 430).

432 ■ American Bar Foundation

750 North Lake Shore Dr.
Chicago, IL 60611-4403
Ph: (312)988-6500
URL: http://www.abf-sociolegal.org

433 ■ ABF Doctoral Fellowships *(Doctorate, Graduate/Fellowship)*

Purpose: To encourage original and significant research on law, the legal profession, and legal institutions. **Focus:** Law. **Qualif.:** Applicant must be a PhD candidate in social sciences; have completed all doctoral requirements except the dissertation; or students who will complete their dissertation prior to the beginning of the award. Research must be in the general area of socio-legal studies or in social scientific approaches to law. Dissertations must address issues in the field and show major contribution to social scientific understanding of law and legal process. **Criteria:** Selection is based on the submitted dissertation abstract or proposal.

Awards are arranged alphabetically below their administering organizations

Funds Avail.: $25,000. **To Apply:** Applicants must submit a dissertation abstract or proposal; two letters of reference; a curriculum vitae; a transcript of graduate records; and a short sample of written work (optional). Application materials must be sent to Tim Watson, Program Associate. **Deadline:** January 7. **Contact:** Chair of the Appointments Committee, Janice Nadler, jnadler@abfn.org.

434 ■ Law and Social Science Dissertation Fellowship and Mentoring Program *(Doctorate, Graduate/Fellowship)*

Purpose: To promote education in Law and Social Sciences. **Focus:** Law; Social sciences. **Qualif.:** Applicant must be a U.S. citizen and permanent resident; a third year or fourth year graduate student in the field of law and social science; a student in a PhD program in a social science department; or Humanities student pursuing a dissertation with relation to social science. **Criteria:** Selection is based on the application.

Funds Avail.: $25,000 and $1,500 for research and travel expenses. **To Apply:** Applicants must submit a 1-2 page application; a 2-3 page description of research project; a resume or curriculum vitae; a writing sample; three letters of recommendation from faculty members; and undergraduate and graduate transcripts. A complete set of application materials must be sent to Mary McClintock, Law and Society Association, University of Massachusetts, 40 Campus Center Way, Amherst, MA 01003-9244. Another set of complete application materials must be sent to Tom Watson, Program Associate, American Bar Foundation, 750 Lake Shore Drive - 4th Fl., Chicago, IL 60611. **Deadline:** December 1. **Contact:** Laura Beth Nielsen, lnielsen@abfn.org.

435 ■ Summer Research Diversity Fellowships in Law and Social Science *(Undergraduate/Fellowship)*

Purpose: To promoted education in social sciences. **Focus:** Law; Social sciences. **Qualif.:** Applicant must be an American citizen and permanent resident; an African American, Hispanic/Latino, Native American, or Puerto Rican, or individuals who will add diversity to the field of law and social science; a sophomore or junior student who have not yet received a degree; have a GPA of 3.0; and pursuing an academic major in the social sciences. **Criteria:** Selection is based on the application materials.

Funds Avail.: $3600. **To Apply:** Applicants must send the completed application form together with the essay, official transcripts, and a letter of recommendation from a faculty. **Deadline:** February 15.

Remarks: Contact: fellowships@abfn.org.

436 ■ American Birding Association

4945 N 30th St., Ste. 200
Colorado Springs, CO 80919
Ph: (719)578-9703
Fax: (719)578-1480
Free: 800-850-2473
E-mail: member@aba.org
URL: http://www.americanbirding.org

437 ■ ABA Scholarships *(Undergraduate/Scholarship)*

Purpose: To recognize and stimulate interest in birds. To promote the pursuit of educational and other bird-related activities. **Focus:** Animal science and behavior; Animal rights. **Qualif.:** Scholarship is open to American Birding Association active members only. **Criteria:** Scholarship recipients will be selected based on scholastic ability, professional interest, character and financial need.

Funds Avail.: No specific amount. **To Apply:** Applicants must submit a complete application form available from the ABA office and can be downloaded from the website; an essay about the importance of a bird; a letter of recommendation from a teacher, bird club member or mentor. Send complete documents to: Lori L. Fujimoto, Youth Scholarships, American Birding Association, 4945 N 30th St., Ste. 200, Colorado Springs, CO 80919. **Deadline:** April 30.

438 ■ Richard E. Andrews Memorial Scholarships *(Undergraduate/Scholarship)*

Purpose: To provide financial assistance to young birders. **Focus:** Animal science and behavior; Animal rights. **Qualif.:** Scholarship is open to American Birding Association active members. **Criteria:** Scholarship recipients will be selected based on scholastic ability, professional interest, character and financial need.

Funds Avail.: No specific amount. **To Apply:** Applicants must submit a complete application form available from the ABA office and can be downloaded from the website; an essay explaining why he/she deserves the Andrews Scholarships; a letter of recommendation from a teacher, bird club member or mentor. Send complete documents to: Youth Scholarships, American Birding Association, 4945 N 30th St., Ste. 200, Colorado Springs, CO 80919. **Deadline:** April 30.

439 ■ WildBird/Clements Memorial Scholarships *(Undergraduate/Scholarship)*

Purpose: To recognize and stimulate interest in birds by promoting the pursuit of educational and other bird-related activities. **Focus:** Animal science and behavior; Animal rights. **Qualif.:** Scholarship is open to American Birding Association active members only. **Criteria:** Scholarship recipients will be selected based on scholastic ability, professional interest, character and financial need.

Funds Avail.: $500. **To Apply:** Applicants must submit a complete application form available from the ABA office and can be downloaded from the website; an essay explaining why he/she believes that he/she qualifies for the Clements Scholarships; a letter of recommendation from a teacher, bird club member or mentor. Send complete documents to: Youth Scholarships, American Birding Association, 4945 N. 30th St., Ste. 200, Colorado Springs, CO 80919. **Deadline:** April 30.

440 ■ American Board of Funeral Service Education

3432 Ashland Ave., Ste. U
St. Joseph, MO 64506
Ph: (816)233-3747
Fax: (816)233-3793
URL: http://www.abfse.org

441 ■ ABFSE National Scholarship Program *(Undergraduate/Scholarship)*

Purpose: To provide financial awards to students enrolled in funeral service or mortuary science programs to assist them in obtaining their professional education. **Focus:**

Funeral services, Mortuary science. **Qualif.:** Applicant must have at least completed one semester (or quarter) of study in a funeral service or mortuary science education accredited by the American Board of Funeral Service Education; must have one term or semester remaining in his/her program which will commence after the award date in order to be considered for a full award; must be a citizen of the United States. **Criteria:** Selection of scholarship recipients is competitive. Awards are made by the Scholarship Committee of ABFSE.

Funds Avail.: $500 - $2,500. **To Apply:** Application forms are available online. Applicant must have the tax forms, letter of recommendation and transcript of records. Application materials must be sent to: Scholarship Committee, ABFSE, 3432 Ashland Ave., Ste. U, St. Joseph, MO 64506. **Deadline:** March 1 and September 1.

442 ■ American Brain Tumor Association

2720 River Rd.
Des Plaines, IL 60018
Ph: (847)827-9910
Fax: (847)827-2282
Free: 800-886-2282
E-mail: info@abta.org
URL: http://www.abta.org

443 ■ Basic Research Fellowships
(Postdoctorate/Fellowship)

Purpose: To encourage talented scientists early in their careers to enter, or remain in, the field of brain tumor research. **Focus:** Oncology. **Qualif.:** Applicant must be post-doctorate student intending to pursue a career in neuro-oncology. **Criteria:** Candidates will be evaluated based on some criteria by members of the Association's distinguished Scientific Advisory Council which include the caliber of the applicants, training program, and proposed research.

Funds Avail.: $80,000. **To Apply:** Applicants must seek application form from the ABTA office. **Deadline:** January 7.

444 ■ American Bus Association

700 13th St. NW, Ste. 575
Washington, DC 20005-5923
Ph: (202)842-1645
Fax: (202)842-0850
E-mail: abainfo@buses.org
URL: http://www.buses.org

445 ■ ABA Academic Merit Scholarships
(Undergraduate/Scholarship)

Purpose: To financially assist deserving students who has a potential to be future leaders in the transportation, travel, and tourism industry. **Focus:** Transportation; Travel and tourism. **Qualif.:** Applicants must completed first year of studies and majoring or have a course of study relevant to the transportation, travel, and tourism industry at an accredited university; must have a minimum of 3.4 GPA or higher. **Criteria:** Applicants will be selected based on their academic record, personal promise, character and financial need. Applicant affiliated with ABA-member companies will be given priority.

Funds Avail.: $2,500. **Number Awarded:** 2. **To Apply:** Application process is online (please visit the website). Applicants must also submit an essay (500 words) discussing the role they will play in advancing the future of the transportation, motorcoach, travel, and tourism/hospitality industry. **Contact:** James Simon.

446 ■ ABA Diversity Scholarships
(Undergraduate/Scholarship)

Purpose: To promote understanding and to mobilize greater involvement in the transportation industry. **Focus:** Transportation; Travel and tourism. **Qualif.:** Applicants must completed first year of studies and majoring or have a course of study relevant to the transportation, travel, and tourism industry at an accredited university; must have a minimum of 3.0 GPA. **Criteria:** Recipients are selected on the basis of academic merit, character, leadership and financial need.

Funds Avail.: $2,500. **Number Awarded:** 2. **To Apply:** Application process is online (please visit the website). **Contact:** James Simon.

447 ■ ABA Members Scholarships (ABA Bus and Tour Operators Only) *(Undergraduate/Scholarship)*

Purpose: To financially assist deserving students who have potentials to be future leaders in the transportation, travel, and tourism industry. **Focus:** General studies. **Qualif.:** Applicant must be a member or a dependent of ABA bus and tour member companies employed for at least one year; must be entering fist year of college, university, or professional training school by fall; must have a minimum of 3.0 GPA or an average of B. **Criteria:** Applicants will be selected based on their academic merit, community service, extracurricular activities, leadership, and anticipated financial need.

Funds Avail.: $2,500. **Number Awarded:** 13. **To Apply:** Application process is online (please visit the website). **Contact:** James Simon.

448 ■ ABA Members Scholarships (All ABA Member Companies) *(Undergraduate/Scholarship)*

Purpose: To financially assist deserving students who have potentials to be future leaders in the transportation, travel and tourism industry. **Focus:** Transportation; Travel and tourism. **Qualif.:** Applicants must be a member or a dependent of ABA members companies employed for at least one year; must completed first year of studies and majoring or have a course of study relevant to the transportation, travel and tourism industry; must have a minimum of 3.0 GPA or an average of B. **Criteria:** Applicants will be selected based on their academic merit, community service, extracurricular activities, leadership, and anticipated financial need.

Funds Avail.: $2,500. **Number Awarded:** 13. **To Apply:** Application process is online (please visit the website). **Contact:** James Simon.

449 ■ Peter L. Picknelly Honorary Scholarships
(Undergraduate/Scholarship)

Purpose: To honor the contribution of bus drivers, mechanics and maintenance personnel to the motorcoach industry. **Focus:** Transportation; Travel and tourism. **Qualif.:** Applicants must be a bus driver or maintenance personnel, or dependents of ABA operator members; must be in a technical school with two-years or more transportation-related education programs. **Criteria:** Recipients are selected on

Awards are arranged alphabetically below their administering organizations

the basis of academic merit, extra curricular activities and financial need.

Funds Avail.: $2,500. **Number Awarded:** 2. **To Apply:** Application process is online (please visit the website). **Contact:** James Simon.

450 ■ American Business Travel Association

7301 Burnet Rd., Ste. 102
Austin, TX 78757
Ph: (512)356-7154
E-mail: info@austinbta.org
URL: http://www.austinbta.org

451 ■ Educational and Professional Achievement Scholarships *(Undergraduate/Scholarship)*

Purpose: To award scholarship to local high school students applying for higher education support. **Focus:** General studies. **Qualif.:** Applicants must be senior students currently registered and attending classes in the Greater Austin Metropolitan Area, including students in public schools, home-schooled students and students attending private educational institutions; must be planning to further their education or professional development by enrolling in an accredited college or university, a community college, a professional, technical or vocational institute or school. **Criteria:** Selection will be based on the committee's criteria.

Funds Avail.: $1,500. **To Apply:** Applicants may download an application form on-line. Applicants must submit the following requirements: a transcript of grades with a minimum cumulative GPA of 3.0; complete scholarship application form; at least three, but not more than five personal evaluations; a 500-word personal essay titled "Building My Future"; a resume detailing activities at school, work, community service, sports, clubs, etc.; a brief (less than 200 words), creative autobiographical statement. **Deadline:** February 16. **Contact:** Kevin Maguire, Scholarship Committee Chair, Austin Business Travel Association, 512-272-7023, kevin1maguire@yahoo.com.

452 ■ American Ceramic Society

600 N Cleveland Ave., Ste. 210
Westerville, OH 43082
Ph: (866)721-3322
Fax: (301)206-9789
E-mail: customerservice@ceramics.org
URL: http://www.ceramics.org

453 ■ Electronics Division Lewis C. Hoffman Scholarships *(Undergraduate/Scholarship)*

Purpose: To encourage academic interest and excellence among undergraduate students. **Focus:** Materials research/science; Engineering, Materials. **Qualif.:** Applicant must be a junior-year student, or a student who has recently completed his or her junior year; must have acquired a total of 70 or more semester credits or equivalent quarter credits; must have extracurricular activities. **Criteria:** Applicants will be selected based on the application requirements.

Funds Avail.: $2,000. **To Apply:** Applicants must submit a recommendation letter from a faculty member in the department; must have a 500 word essay on the year's topic. Application form and materials must be sent to Dr. Quanxi Jia, MS 763, Materials Physics and Application Division, Los Alamos National Laboratory, Los Alamos, NM 87545. **Deadline:** July 18.

454 ■ American Citizens for Justice

P.O. Box 2735
Southfield, MI 48037
Fax: (313)557-2772
URL: http://www.americancitizensforjustice.org

455 ■ Vincent Chin Memorial Fund Scholarships *(Graduate/Scholarship)*

Purpose: To honor an aspiring leader in the Asian Pacific American community who desires to continue working for the benefit of the community through obtaining a law degree. **Focus:** Law. **Qualif.:** Applicant must be attending law school in the state of Michigan and will be a first-year or second-year law student, either full-time or part-time, during the 2007-2008 academic year; must demonstrate at minimum a previous one-year commitment to working for the Asian Pacific American community; must have an undergraduate GPA of no less than 3.0. **Criteria:** Selection is based on merit.

Funds Avail.: No specific amount. **To Apply:** Applicants must submit completed application, along with transcript, letter of recommendation, and an essay of no more than 5,000 words describing the applicant's desire to contribute to the Asian Pacific American community through the law profession. **Deadline:** March 31.

456 ■ American Clan Gregor Society

238 W 1220 N
American Fork, UT 84003
URL: http://acgs.thecapitalscot.com/

457 ■ Harry and Edith Blunt Scholarships *(Undergraduate/Scholarship)*

Purpose: To provide educational assistance to incoming college students. **Focus:** General studies. **Qualif.:** Applicants must be ACGS members or children of ACGS members. **Criteria:** Priority will be given to children of the members of the society.

Funds Avail.: $ 1,000. **To Apply:** Applicants must submit their transcript of record, college acceptance and personal letter about activities and educational plans. **Deadline:** April 1. **Contact:** Susan Tichy stichy@gmu.edu.

458 ■ Dr. Edward May Magruder Medical Scholarships *(Other/Scholarship)*

Purpose: To provide educational assistance to the students of the University of Virginia School of Medicine. **Focus:** Medicine. **Qualif.:** Applicants who are ACGHS members, children of members, or others who have lineage to the Clan Gregor are welcome to apply. Applicants must also be enrolled at least half-time or full-time for Federal Title VII programs. Those applicants that are in default on a federal loan or owe a refund on a federal grant are disqualified. Registration in Selective Service is also required for the application. **Criteria:** Recipients will be selected based on their satisfactory academic progress and financial information.

Funds Avail.: The amount will depend on the number of the grantees. **Number Awarded:** The number of awards will be based on the selected students. **To Apply:** Applicants must complete both the FAFSA and the UVA

Awards are arranged alphabetically below their administering organizations

School of Medicine Application (refer and download from www.healthsystem.virginia.edu). Previous year U.S Tax Returns is also required for the completion of the requirements. **Deadline:** April 1 for entering students and April 15 for returning students. **Contact:** Ms. Nancy L. Zimmer, nlb3w@virginia.edu or www.healthsystem.virginia.edu.

459 ■ The American Classical League

Miami University
Oxford, OH 45056
Ph: (513)529-7741
Fax: (513)529-7742
E-mail: info@aclclassics.org
URL: http://www.aclclassics.org

460 ■ Glenn Knudsvig Memorial Scholarships
(Graduate, Undergraduate/Scholarship)

Purpose: To encourage teaching profession of classics by providing educational fund for deserving teacher and undergraduate or graduate member of the American Classical League. **Focus:** Classical studies. **Qualif.:** Applicant must be a current JCL sponsor who attended the most recent NJCL convention; teacher of Latin, Greek or Classics with less than five years classroom experience and has never attended an ACL Institute; graduate student who plans to teach K-12 Latin, Greek or Classics; teacher whose students participated in the 2007 National Latin Exam and has never attended an ACL Institute. **Criteria:** Recipient is chosen based on merit.

Funds Avail.: $1,000 covering expenses on registration, room, board on campus and travel for Annual ACL Institute. **To Apply:** Application form and instructions are available at the website. **Deadline:** January 15.

461 ■ Arthur Patch McKinlay Scholarships
(Graduate, Undergraduate/Scholarship)

Purpose: To provide educational fund for deserving teachers, undergraduate or graduate members of the American Classical League as they pursue careers in teaching classics. **Focus:** Classical studies. **Qualif.:** Applicant must be an ACL member for the preceding three years and planning to teach classics at elementary through secondary level for the school year 2008-2009. **Criteria:** Recipient is chosen based on a review of proposed bonafide study program.

Funds Avail.: $1,500 covering expenses on registration, room, board on campus and the cost of transportation. **To Apply:** Application form and instructions are available at the website. **Deadline:** January 15.

462 ■ Ed Phinney Commemorative Scholarships
(Graduate, Undergraduate/Scholarship)

Purpose: To provide educational fund for deserving teachers, undergraduate or graduate members of the American Classical League. **Focus:** Classical studies. **Qualif.:** Applicant must be a current member of The American Classical League; must also have been an ACL member for year prior to applying (if applying to attend ACL Institute for the first time, only current ACL membership required.) **Criteria:** Award is given to an eligible and proficient undergraduate classic major or graduate student of classics intending to teach at the elementary through college level.

Funds Avail.: $1,000 covering expenses on registration, room, board on campus and the cost of transportation. **To Apply:** Application form and instructions are available at the website. **Deadline:** January 15.

463 ■ American College of Chiropractic Orthopedics

1030 Broadway, Ste. 101
El Centro, CA 92243
Ph: (760)370-9106
Fax: (760)352-3966
E-mail: wvalusek@accoweb.org
URL: http://www.accoweb.org

464 ■ F. Maynard Lipe Scholarship Award
(Postdoctorate/Award/Prize)

Purpose: To provide financial assistance to eligible individuals pursuing research in line with chiropractic. **Focus:** Chiropractic. **Qualif.:** Applicants must be doctors enrolled in Post Graduate Orthopedics leading to diplomat status or the masters program in musculoskeletal manipulation and rehabilitation. **Criteria:** Candidates will be evaluated by the ACCO assigned Scholarship Committee.

Funds Avail.: $500. **To Apply:** Applicants must submit application form and their articles.

465 ■ American College of Healthcare Executives

1 N Franklin, Ste. 1700
Chicago, IL 60606-3529
Ph: (312)424-2800
Fax: (312)424-0023
E-mail: geninfo@ache.org
URL: http://www.ache.org

466 ■ Albert W. Dent Graduate Student Scholarships *(Undergraduate/Scholarship)*

Purpose: To help ACHE Student Associates finance their education. **Focus:** Health care services. **Qualif.:** Applicant must be a Student Associate in good standing in the American College of Healthcare Executives; must be enrolled in full-time study for the upcoming term; must demonstrate financial need; must be a U.S or Canadian citizen; must have not been a previous recipient of the scholarship. **Criteria:** Selection of applicants will be based on the Scholarship application criteria.

Funds Avail.: $4,000. **Number Awarded:** 15-25. **To Apply:** Applicants must submit and complete the application form available online; must submit a current curriculum vitae or resume; an official undergraduate and graduate transcript; must provide three current letters of recommendation and essay. **Deadline:** March 31.

Remarks: American College of Healthcare Executives established the scholarship in honor of Foster G. McGaw, the founder of the American Hospital Supply Corporation.

467 ■ Foster G. McGaw Graduate Student Scholarships *(Undergraduate/Scholarship)*

Purpose: To help ACHE Student Associates finance their education. **Focus:** Health care services. **Qualif.:** Applicant must be a Student Associate in good standing in the American College of Healthcare Executives; must be enrolled in full-time study for the upcoming term; must demonstrate financial need; must be a U.S or Canadian citizen; must have not been a previous recipient of the scholarship. **Criteria:** Selection of applicants will be based on the scholarship application criteria.

Funds Avail.: $4,000. **Number Awarded:** 15-25. **To Ap-**

ply: Applicants must submit and complete the application form available online; must submit a current curriculum vitae or resume; an official undergraduate and graduate transcript; must provide three current letters of recommendation and essay. **Deadline:** March 31.

Remarks: Foundation of the American College of Healthcare Executives established the scholarship in honor of Foster G. McGaw, the founder of the American Hospital Supply Corporation.

468 ■ American College of Nurse-Midwives Foundation

8403 Colesville Rd., Ste. 1550
Silver Spring, MD 20910
Ph: (240)485-1800
Fax: (240)485-1818
URL: http://www.midwife.org

469 ■ ACNM Foundation, Inc. Fellowship for Graduate Education *(Doctorate, Postdoctorate/Fellowship)*

Purpose: To provide financial assistance for midwives actively enrolled in doctoral or post-doctoral studies. **Focus:** Midwifery. **Qualif.:** Applicants must be certified nurse-midwives (CNM) or certified midwives (CM); must be current members of the American College of Nurse-Midwives (ACNM); must be actively enrolled in a doctoral or post-doctoral education program; and must be graduate students in good standing as verified by the Academic Program Director. **Criteria:** Applicants are evaluated based on financial need and academic achievement.

Funds Avail.: No specific amount. **To Apply:** Applicants must submit application form; academic/career goals and plans; academic director form; and two academic recommendations. **Deadline:** March 17.

470 ■ Basic Midwifery Student Scholarship Program *(Undergraduate/Scholarship)*

Purpose: To provide assistance to students of nurse-midwifery. **Focus:** Nursing; Midwifery. **Qualif.:** Applicants must be students in good standing in an ACNM DOA accredited basic midwifery education program; must have successfully completed one academic or clinical semester/quarter or clinical module; and must be current members of the American College of Nurse-Midwives (ACNM). **Criteria:** Applicants are judged based on demonstrated academic excellence and financial need.

Funds Avail.: No specific amount. **To Apply:** Applicants must submit application information form; statement of career goals and plans; financial assessment form; statement of financial need; program director form; and the faculty recommendation form. **Deadline:** March 17.

471 ■ Hazel Corbin/Childbirth Connection Grant for Evidence-based Midwifery Care *(Professional Development/Award/Prize)*

Purpose: To support or augment projects that advance understanding of the safety and/or effectiveness of midwifery practices for mothers and newborns. **Focus:** Nursing; Midwifery. **Qualif.:** Applicants must be professionals involved in furthering understanding of the safety and/or effectiveness of midwifery practices for mothers and newborns; may be professionals from midwifery or any other field that may contribute to such objective (for example, nursing, public health, social science); may be affiliated with an academic institution, an advocacy group, a clinical entity, a professional organization (including ACNM), a public agency, a research or consulting organization, or other group that may be concerned with evidence-based midwifery care; and may be based in the United States or in another country. **Criteria:** Applicants will be evaluated based on completed application form which should clearly describe information needed to address the review criteria, including assessment of the project relevance, excellence and impact.

Funds Avail.: $6,000. **To Apply:** Applicants must submit completed application form and all other required application materials and information to: Hazel Corbin/Childbirth Connection Grant, A.C.N.M. Foundation, Inc., 8403 Colesville Road, Suite 1550, Silver Spring, MD 20910. **Deadline:** April 7.

472 ■ American College of Nursing Practitioners

1501 Wilson Blvd., Ste. 509
Arlington, VA 22209
Ph: (703)740-2529
Fax: (703)740-2533
E-mail: acnp@acnpweb.org
URL: http://www.acnpweb.org

473 ■ ACNP Nurse Practitioner Student Scholarship Awards *(Undergraduate/Scholarship)*

Purpose: To recognize an outstanding student in the field of nursing. **Focus:** Nursing. **Qualif.:** Applicants must be a member of ACNP; enrolled in an accredited NP program; have a GPA of 3.4. **Criteria:** Recipients will be selected based on the Award Committee's review of all applications.

Funds Avail.: $1,000. **To Apply:** Applicants must complete the application form and submit with the following supporting documents: proof of Student Membership in ACNP; official transcript of an accredited NP program that indicates a 3.4 GPA; curriculum vitae (not more than 2 pages); two letters from professional colleagues indicating leadership roles and involvement in any organizational policy development; statement of the applicant's goals related to the ACNP Mission (not more than 200 words). **Deadline:** June 30.

474 ■ American College of Radiation Oncology

5272 River Rd., Ste. 630
Bethesda, MD 20816
Ph: (301)718-6515
Fax: (301)656-0989
E-mail: info@acro.org
URL: http://www.acro.org

475 ■ American College of Radiation Oncology Resident Scholarships *(Graduate/Scholarship)*

Purpose: To support subspecialty electives at any qualified institution in North America demonstrating expertise in the desired subspecialty area. **Focus:** Oncology. **Qualif.:** Applicant must be ACRO and ARRO radiation oncology resident members in their second, third, or fourth years of an accredited U.S. residency program; or U.S. citizens attending an accredited residency program in Canada; and have not previously been awarded an ACRO resident scholarship. **Criteria:** Applications are reviewed by the ACRO Resident Scholarship Committee.

Funds Avail.: No specific amount. **To Apply:** Applicants

Awards are arranged alphabetically below their administering organizations

must submit an application. **Deadline:** Fall of each year.

476 ■ American Composites Manufacturers Association

1010 North Glebe Rd., Ste. 450
Arlington, VA 22201
Ph: (703)525-0511
Fax: (703)525-0743
E-mail: info@acmanet.org
URL: http://www.acmanet.org

477 ■ American Composites Manufacturers Association Scholarships *(Undergraduate/Scholarship)*

Purpose: To support individuals involved in the composites industry. **Focus:** General studies. **Qualif.:** Applicants must be graduating high school seniors planning to pursue a degree in accredited four-year colleges or universities. **Criteria:** Recipients are selected based on personal merit and background (merit is demonstrated in academic achievement; leadership in school; civic and other extracurricular activities; and motivations to serve and succeed).

Funds Avail.: $2,000. **To Apply:** Application forms are available at ACMA website (www.acmanet.org).

478 ■ American Composites Manufacturers Association Western Chapter Scholarships *(Undergraduate/Scholarship)*

Purpose: To provide special services and networking opportunities to member companies in the 13 most western states. **Focus:** General Studies. **Qualif.:** Applicants must be employees, spouses, children or grandchildren of individuals who are employed by a company located in the 13 most western states (Alaska, Arizona, California, Colorado, Hawaii, Idaho, Montana, New Mexico, Nevada, Oregon, Utah, Washington, or Wyoming) that is a member of the ACMA; must be registered full-time students (minimum 12 hours) at an accredited college or university. **Criteria:** Recipients are selected based on: scholastic aptitude; career objectives; leadership; and extracurricular activities such as community involvement.

Funds Avail.: $2,000. **To Apply:** Applicants must submit the completed application form; transcript of all college work; statement of educational goals; career intentions and resume of extracurricular activities; work experience; community involvement; and two letters of reference (personal reference and a reference from a professor or teacher). **Deadline:** December 31. **Contact:** ACMA at the above address (see entry 476).

479 ■ Gary B. Multanen/CM Magazine Scholarships *(All/Scholarship)*

Purpose: To encourage students to pursue their career in the composites industry. **Focus:** Engineering; Research. **Qualif.:** Applicants must be registered full-time at an accredited college or university; and must be in good academic standing; must reside in the United States of America; must be pursuing a degree in engineering, research or other composites-based curriculum; open to undergraduate, graduate, and doctoral students. **Criteria:** Selection will be based on the committee's review of application materials.

Funds Avail.: $1,000. **To Apply:** Application forms are available at ACMA website. Applicants must also submit: reference from the professor related to or overseeing research; college transcripts (photocopies are acceptable); and composites-related research in the form of a report or paper (no less than 1,500 words). **Deadline:** August 7. **Contact:** ACMA at the above address (see entry 476).

480 ■ American Congress on Surveying and Mapping

6 Montgomery Village Ave., Ste. 403
Gaithersburg, MD 20879
Ph: (240)632-9716
Fax: (240)632-1321
E-mail: curtis.summer@acsm.net
URL: http://www.acsm.net

481 ■ AAGS Graduate Fellowship Award *(Undergraduate/Fellowship)*

Purpose: CSM Scholarships are designed to encourage, recognize, and support exceptional surveying and mapping students. **Focus:** Surveying. **Qualif.:** Applicants must be enrolled in or accepted to a graduate program in geodetic surveying or geodesy. **Criteria:** Recipients will be selected based on academic record, applicant's statement, letters of recommendation and professional activities.

Funds Avail.: $2,000. **To Apply:** Applicants must complete the application form; applicants must provide a proof of membership in ACSM; a brief yet complete statement indicating educational objectives, future plans of study or research, professional activities and financial need; at least three letters of recommendation (minimum of two from faculty members familiar with the student's work); a complete original official transcript through year prior to when the award will be presented. **Deadline:** October 1. **Contact:** dawn.james@asm.net; American Congress on Surveying and Mapping at the above address (see entry 480).

482 ■ AAGS Joseph F. Dracup Scholarship Award *(Undergraduate/Scholarship)*

Purpose: CSM Scholarships are designed to encourage, recognize, and support exceptional surveying and mapping students. **Focus:** Surveying. **Qualif.:** Applicants must be enrolled in two-year or four-year-surveying (and closely related) degree program, either full or part-time. **Criteria:** Recipients will be selected based on academic record, applicant's statement, letters of recommendation and professional activities.

Funds Avail.: $2,000. **To Apply:** Applicants must complete the application form; applicants must provide a proof of membership in ACSM; a brief yet complete statement indicating educational objectives, future plans of study or research, professional activities and financial need; at least three letters of recommendation (minimum of two from faculty members familiar with the student's work); a complete original official transcript through year prior to when the award will be presented. **Deadline:** October 1. **Contact:** dawn.james@asm.net; American Congress on Surveying and Mapping at the above address (see entry 480).

483 ■ ACSM Fellowship Scholarships *(Undergraduate/Scholarship)*

Purpose: To encourage, recognize, and support exceptional surveying and mapping students. **Focus:** Surveying. **Qualif.:** Applicants must be junior or higher standing in any

Awards are arranged alphabetically below their administering organizations

of the ACSM disciplines. **Criteria:** Recipients will be selected based on academic record, applicant's statement, letters of recommendation and professional activities.

Funds Avail.: $2,000. **To Apply:** Applicants must complete the application form; applicants must provide a proof of membership in ACSM; a brief yet complete statement indicating educational objectives, future plans of study or research, professional activities and financial need; at least three letters of recommendation (minimum of two from faculty members familiar with the student's work); a complete original official transcript through year prior to when the award will be presented. **Deadline:** October 1. **Contact:** dawn.james@asm.net; American Congress on Surveying and Mapping at the above address (see entry 480).

484 ■ The Bernsten International Scholarships in Surveying Technology *(Undergraduate/Scholarship)*

Purpose: To encourage, recognize and support exceptional surveying and mapping students. **Focus:** Surveying. **Qualif.:** Applicant must be enrolled in two-year degree programs in surveying technology. **Criteria:** Recipients will be selected based on academic record, applicant's statement, letters of recommendation and professional activities.

Funds Avail.: $500. **Number Awarded:** October 1. **To Apply:** Applicants must complete the application form; applicants must provide a proof of membership in ACSM; a brief yet complete statement indicating educational objectives, future plans of study or research, professional activities and financial need; at least three letters of recommendation (minimum of two from faculty members familiar with the student's work); a complete original official transcript through year prior to when the award will be presented. **Deadline:** October 1. **Contact:** dawn.james@asm.net; American Congress on Surveying and Mapping at the above address (see entry 480).

485 ■ Nettie Dracup Memorial Scholarships *(Undergraduate/Scholarship)*

Purpose: To provide financial assistance to a United States citizen. **Focus:** Surveying. **Qualif.:** Applicants must be undergraduate student who is enrolled in Geodetic Surveying in an accredited college or university. **Criteria:** Recipients will be selected based on academic record, applicant's statement, letters of recommendation and professional activities.

Funds Avail.: $2,000. **To Apply:** Applicants must complete the application form; applicants must provide a proof of membership in ACSM; a brief yet complete statement indicating educational objectives, future plans of study or research, professional activities and financial need; at least three letters of recommendation (minimum of two from faculty members familiar with the student's work); a complete original official transcript through year prior to when the award will be presented. **Deadline:** October 1. **Contact:** dawn.james@asm.net; American Congress on Surveying and Mapping at the above address (see entry 480).

486 ■ Kris M. Kunze Memorial Scholarships *(Undergraduate/Scholarship)*

Purpose: To encourage, recognize, and support exceptional surveying and mapping students. **Focus:** Surveying. **Qualif.:** Applicants must be licensed Professional Land Surveyors of Certified Photogrammetrists pursuing college level courses in Business Administration or Business Management or applicants must be full-time students enrolled in a two or four-year degree program in Surveying and Mapping pursuing a course of study including Business Administration or Business Management. **Criteria:** Recipients will be selected based on academic record, applicant's statement, letters of recommendation and professional activities.

Funds Avail.: $1,000. **To Apply:** Applicants must complete the application form; applicants must provide a proof of membership in ACSM; a brief yet complete statement indicating educational objectives, future plans of study or research, professional activities and financial need; at least three letters of recommendation (minimum of two from faculty members familiar with the student's work); a complete original official transcript through year prior to when the award will be presented. **Deadline:** October 1. **Contact:** dawn.james@asm.net; American Congress on Surveying and Mapping at the above address (see entry 480).

487 ■ The Lowell H. and Dorothy Loving Undergraduate Scholarships *(Undergraduate/Scholarship)*

Purpose: To encourage, recognize, and support exceptional surveying and mapping students. **Focus:** Surveying. **Qualif.:** Applicants must be junior or senior standing in a four-year program at a university or college in the United States. **Criteria:** Recipients will be selected based on academic record, applicant's statement, letters of recommendation and professional activities.

Funds Avail.: $2,500. **To Apply:** Applicants must complete the application form; applicants must provide a proof of membership in ACSM; a brief yet complete statement indicating educational objectives, future plans of study or research, professional activities and financial need; at least three letters of recommendation (minimum of two from faculty members familiar with the student's work); a complete original official transcript through year prior to when the award will be presented. **Deadline:** October 1. **Contact:** dawn.james@asm.net; American Congress on Surveying and Mapping at the above address (see entry 480).

488 ■ The Cady McDonnell Memorial Scholarships *(Undergraduate/Scholarship)*

Purpose: To encourage, recognize, and support exceptional surveying and mapping students. **Focus:** Surveying. **Qualif.:** Applicants must be a resident of one of the following western states; Montana, Idaho, Washington, Oregon, Wyoming, Colorado, Utah, Nevada, California, Arizona, New Mexico, Alaska, and Hawaii; applicants must be a woman student enrolled in the field of surveying. **Criteria:** Recipients will be selected based on academic record, applicant's statement, letters of recommendation and professional activities.

Funds Avail.: $1,000. **To Apply:** Applicants must complete the application form; applicants must provide a proof of membership in ACSM; a brief yet complete statement indicating educational objectives, future plans of study or research, professional activities and financial need; at least three letters of recommendation (minimum of two from faculty members familiar with the student's work); a complete original official transcript through year prior to when the award will be presented. **Deadline:** October 1. **Contact:** dawn.james@asm.net; American Congress on Surveying and Mapping at the above address (see entry 480).

489 ■ NSPS Board of Governors Scholarships *(Undergraduate/Scholarship)*

Purpose: To encourage, recognize, and support exceptional surveying and mapping students. **Focus:** Surveying. **Qualif.:** Applicants must be enrolled in studies in surveying entering their junior year of study in a four-year degree program of their choice; applicants must maintain a minimum 3.0 grade point average. **Criteria:** Recipients will be selected based on academic record, applicant's statement, letters of recommendation and professional activities.

Funds Avail.: $1,000. **To Apply:** Applicants must complete the application form; applicants must provide a proof of membership in ACSM; a brief yet complete statement indicating educational objectives, future plans of study or research, professional activities and financial need; at least three letters of recommendation (minimum of two from faculty members familiar with the student's work); a complete original official transcript through year prior to when the award will be presented. **Deadline:** October 1. **Contact:** dawn.james@asm.net; American Congress on Surveying and Mapping at the above address (see entry 480).

490 ■ The NSPS Scholarships *(Undergraduate/Scholarship)*

Purpose: To recognize outstanding students enrolled full-time in undergraduate surveying programs. **Focus:** Surveying. **Qualif.:** Applicants must complete the application form; applicants must provide a proof of membership in ACSM; a brief yet complete statement indicating educational objectives, future plans of study or research, professional activities and financial need; at least three letters of recommendation (minimum of two from faculty members familiar with the students work); a complete original official transcript through year prior to when the award. **Criteria:** Recipients will be selected based on academic record, applicant's statement, letters of recommendation and professional activities.

Funds Avail.: $1,000. **To Apply:** Applicants must complete the application form; applicants must provide a proof of membership in ACSM; a brief yet complete statement indicating educational objectives, future plans of study or research, professional activities and financial need; at least three letters of recommendation (minimum of two from faculty members familiar with the student's work); a complete original official transcript through year prior to when the award will be presented. **Deadline:** October 1. **Contact:** dawn.james@asm.net; American Congress on Surveying and Mapping at the above address (see entry 480).

491 ■ The Schonstedt Scholarships in Surveying *(Undergraduate/Scholarship)*

Purpose: ACSM Scholarships are designed to encourage, recognize, and support exceptional surveying and mapping students. **Focus:** Surveying. **Qualif.:** Applicant must be junior or senior student enrolled in a college or university. **Criteria:** Recipients will be selected based on academic record, applicant's statement, letters of recommendation and professional activities.

Funds Avail.: 1,500. **To Apply:** Applicants must complete the application form; applicants must provide a proof of membership in ACSM; a brief yet complete statement indicating educational objectives, future plans of study or research, professional activities and financial need; at least three letters of recommendation (minimum of two from faculty members familiar with the student's work); a complete original official transcript through year prior to when the award will be presented. **Deadline:** October 1.

492 ■ American Conifer Society

175 Charisma Ln.
Lewisville, NC 27023-9611
Ph: (336)945-0483
Fax: (336)945-0484
E-mail: nationaloffice@conifersociety.org
URL: http://conifersociety.org

493 ■ American Conifer Society Scholarships *(Undergraduate/Scholarship)*

Purpose: To provide financial assistance to ACS members to pursue their education. **Focus:** Horticulture. **Qualif.:** Applicant must be a current ACS member. **Criteria:** Selection of applicant is based on merit in the field of agriculture.

Funds Avail.: $1,000. **To Apply:** Application form may be downloaded from The American Conifer Society Web Page; www.conifersociety.org or you may request a form from; The American Conifer Society Scholarship Committee, 900 Winston Rd. N., Rochester, NY 14609. Forms are also available from the National Office. **Deadline:** April 30.

494 ■ American Copy Editors Society

333 W State St.
Milwaukee, WI 53203
URL: http://www.copyblock.com/acesdenver

495 ■ Aubespin Scholarships *(Undergraduate/Scholarship)*

Purpose: To encourage young individuals to continue their career as potential professional copy editors. **Focus:** Editors and editing. **Qualif.:** Applicant must be a junior, senior or graduate student in the fall, graduating student who will take full-time copy editing jobs or internships. **Criteria:** Applications are evaluated by a panel of five people with copy desk experience.

Funds Avail.: $2,500. **To Apply:** Application forms are available on the website. Applicant must send a list of course work relevant to copy editing, list of copy editing experience, including work on student and professional publications; must provide an essay (750 words, double spaced); must have two recommendation letters: one from a faculty member or adviser and one from someone on a college or professional publicaton; must have two copies of five to 10 headlines; must submit a copy of a story that demonstrate the applicant's ability. Application form and other supporting documents must be sent to: ACES Scholarships, Milwaukee Journal Sentinel, 333 W State St., Milwaukee, WI 53203. **Deadline:** November 15.

496 ■ American Council of Engineering Companies of Illinois

5221 S 6th Rd., Ste. 120
Springfield, IL 62703
Ph: (217)529-7430
Fax: (217)529-2742
E-mail: acec-il@acec-il.org
URL: http://www.acec-il.org

497 ■ American Council of Engineering Companies of Illinois Scholarships *(Doctorate, Graduate, Undergraduate/Scholarship)*

Purpose: To assist engineering students of Illinois in reaching their goals of higher education. **Focus:** Engineering.

Awards are arranged alphabetically below their administering organizations

Qualif.: Applicants must be U.S. citizens, specifically, Illinois engineering students currently enrolled and pursuing a bachelor's, master's or PhD degree in an Accreditation Board for Engineering and Technology (ABET)-accredited engineering program or in an accredited land surveying program located in the state of Illinois; may be students entering their junior, senior, fifth, master's or graduate year in the fall. **Criteria:** Applicants are evaluated based on academic merit.

Funds Avail.: $1,500. **Number Awarded:** 13. **To Apply:** Applicants must submit the completed application form along with student's GPA; work experience; extracurricular college activities; recommendation from a professor, consulting engineering or land surveyor; and an essay. **Deadline:** December.

498 ■ American Council on Exercise

4851 Paramount Dr.
San Diego, CA 92123
Ph: (858)279-8227
Fax: (858)279-8064
Free: 888-825-3636
URL: http://www.acefitness.org

499 ■ Joe Q. Bryant American Council on Exercise Educational Scholarships *(Undergraduate/Scholarship)*

Purpose: To provide support to the Penn State students. **Focus:** Health care services. **Qualif.:** Candidates must a student of Penn State; must maintain at least a 3.0 GPA on a 4.0 scale (verified by academic transcript); must meet the eligibility requirements for the ACE Certification Exam; must have perform two (2) hours of community service monthly during any term in which the student is enrolled. **Criteria:** American Council on Exercises will evaluate each application materials.

Funds Avail.: $1,000. **To Apply:** Applicant must submit the following: (1) Applicant information form; (2) An official copy of academic transcript; (3) Two recommendation forms and statements of support: One academic reference and one non-academic reference; (4) Academic/ Leadership/Awards Form; (5) Essay form and 500-word essay.

500 ■ William J. Merriman American Council on Exercise Educational Scholarships *(Undergraduate/Scholarship)*

Purpose: To provide support to the Manhattan College students. **Focus:** Health care services. **Qualif.:** Applicant must be a student of Manhattan College; must have at least a 3.0 GPA on a 4.0 scale (verified by academic transcript); must meet the eligibility requirements for the ACE Certification Exam; must perform two hours of community service monthly during any term in which the student is enrolled. **Criteria:** American Council on Exercises will evaluate each application.

Funds Avail.: $1.000. **To Apply:** Applicant must have the following: (1) Applicant information form; (2) An official copy of academic transcript; (3) Two recommendation forms and statement of support: One academic reference and One non-academic reference; (4) Activities/Leadership/Awards form; (5) Essay form and 500-word essay.

501 ■ William Shannon American Council on Exercise Certification Scholarships *(Professional Development, Undergraduate/Scholarship)*

Purpose: To provide support to the student and employee of Duke University. **Focus:** Health care services. **Qualif.:** Applicant must be a student or employee of Duke University; must meet the requirements for the ACE Certification Exam; must perform two hours of community service monthly during any term in which the student is enrolled. **Criteria:** American Council on Exercises will evaluate each application.

Funds Avail.: $1.000. **To Apply:** Application form must consists of the following: (1) Applicant information form; (2) An official copy academic transcript; (3) Two recommendation forms and statements of support: One academic reference and one non-academic reference; (4) Activities/Leadership/Awards form; (5) Essay form and 500 word essay.

502 ■ The American Council on Germany

14 E 60th St., Ste. 1000
New York, NY 10022
Ph: (212)826-3636
Fax: (212)758-3445
E-mail: info@acgusa.org
URL: http://www.acgusa.org

503 ■ Dr. Guido Goldman Fellowships *(Doctorate, Postdoctorate/Fellowship)*

Purpose: To promote the study of German and European issues by American scholars. **Focus:** European studies; German studies. **Qualif.:** Applicant must be U.S. citizen; postgraduate student; or enrolled in PhD programs and finishing their dissertation. **Criteria:** Selection Committee will select applicants based on the contribution the project will make to an understanding of the economics and foreign relations of Germany, Europe, and North America; the feasibility of the proposed project; the training of the applicant; and the scholarly potential of the applicant.

Funds Avail.: Covers the cost of pre-approved international and domestic travel and a per diem of $150. **To Apply:** Applicants must submit a cover letter, outlining the applicant's professional and personal objectives for the fellowship; a project proposal (two pages); a current CV; and two letters of reference. **Deadline:** July 6.

504 ■ Dr. Richard M. Hunt Fellowships *(Doctorate, Postdoctorate/Fellowship)*

Purpose: To promote the study of German issues by American scholars. **Focus:** German studies. **Qualif.:** Applicant must be U.S. citizen; postgraduate student; or enrolled in PhD programs and finishing their dissertation. **Criteria:** The selection committee will evaluate applications based on the contribution the project will make to a better understanding of German history; the feasibility of the proposed project; the training of the applicant; and the scholarly potential of the applicant.

Funds Avail.: Covers the cost of pre-approved international and domestic travel and a per diem of $150. **To Apply:** Applicants must submit a cover letter, outlining the applicant's professional and personal objectives for the fellowship; a project proposal (two pages); a current CV; and two letters of reference. **Deadline:** July 6.

505 ■ American Council of Independent Laboratories

1629 K St. NW, Ste. 400
Washington, DC 20006-1633
Ph: (202)887-5872

Awards are arranged alphabetically below their administering organizations

Fax: (202)887-0021
E-mail: info@acil.org
URL: http://www.acil.org

506 ■ American Council of Independent Laboratories Scholarships *(Undergraduate/ Scholarship)*

Purpose: To provide financial assistance for helping to ensure future generations of skilled employees for the laboratory testing community. **Focus:** Physical sciences. **Qualif.:** Applicants must be students attending their junior year or higher in a four-year, bachelor degree major in any of the physical sciences practiced by ACIL members: physics, chemistry, engineering, geology, biology, or environmental science in granting institution or graduate program within the United States. **Criteria:** Recipient will be selected based on academic achievement, career goals, leadership, and financial need.

Funds Avail.: $1,000 to 4,000. **To Apply:** Applicant must submit a brief resume or personal statement outlining the activities in college, including field of study and future plans; two letters of recommendation from faculty members of the university currently attending; transcript of grades; and information on any other scholarship or grant aid now receiving. **Deadline:** April 4.

507 ■ American Council of Learned Societies

633 3rd Ave.
New York, NY 10017-6795
Ph: (212)697-1505
Fax: (212)949-8058
E-mail: paulineyu@acls.org
URL: http://www.acls.org

508 ■ American Council of Learned Societies Fellowships *(Postdoctorate/Fellowship)*

Purpose: To help scholars devote six to twelve continuous months to full-time research and writing. **Focus:** General studies. **Qualif.:** Applicants must be PhD degree holders conferred at least two years before the application deadline; must be U.S. citizens or have permanent resident status; must be lapse of at least two years since the last supported research leave. **Criteria:** Recipients are selected based on academic rank.

Funds Avail.: $30,000 for Assistant Professor; $40,000 for Associate Professor; $60,000 for full professor. **Number Awarded:** 3. **To Apply:** Applicants must complete the application form; a double-spaced proposal of not more than five pages; two-page of supporting materials; not more than two-page of bibliography; not more than two page of publication list; and two reference letters. **Deadline:** October 3.

509 ■ Henry Luce Foundation Dissertation Fellowships in American Art *(Doctorate/Fellowship)*

Purpose: To provide support for young scholars who are in the phase of completing their dissertation and to advance research after being awarded the PhD. **Focus:** Art. **Qualif.:** Applicants must be PhD candidates in a department of art history in the United States completing their dissertation focused on a topic in the history of the visual arts of the United States; must be US citizens or have permanent residency. **Criteria:** Recipients are selected based on academic standing and completed requirements.

Funds Avail.: $25,000. **To Apply:** Applicants must complete the application form including statement of all university and external support received during graduate study; double-spaced proposal including a timeline for the expected completion of the dissertation writing and defense (not more than five pages); up to additional three pages of supporting materials; bibliography of not more than two pages; a completed chapter of the dissertation; three reference letters; a letter from the applicant's institution; and official transcript of graduate record. **Deadline:** November 14.

510 ■ Andrew W. Mellon Dissertation Completion Fellowships *(Doctorate/Fellowship)*

Purpose: To provide support for young scholars who are in the phase of completing their dissertation; to advance research after being awarded the PhD. **Focus:** Humanities; Social Sciences. **Qualif.:** Applicants must be PhD candidates in a humanities or social science department in the United States; must have all requirements for the PhD except the dissertation completed before beginning fellowship tenure; must be no more than six years in the degree program. **Criteria:** Recipients are selected based on academic standing and completed requirements.

Funds Avail.: $25,000; $3,000 for research cost; $5,000 for university fees. **To Apply:** Applicants must complete the application form including statement of all university and external support received during graduate study; double-spaced proposal including a timeline for the expected completion of the dissertation writing and defense (not more than five pages); up to additional three pages of supporting materials; not more than two pages bibliography; a completed chapter of the dissertation; two reference letters; and a letter from the applicant's institution. **Deadline:** November 14.

511 ■ Charles A. Ryskamp Research Fellowships *(Doctorate/Fellowship)*

Purpose: To support advanced assistant professors and untenured associate professors in the humanities and related science. **Focus:** Humanities; Science. **Qualif.:** Applicants must be tenured-track assistant professors and untenured associate professors; must hold the PhD or equivalent and be employed in tenure-track positions at degree granting academic institutions in the United States. **Criteria:** Recipients are selected based on academic standing.

Funds Avail.: $64,000; $2,500 for research and travel. **To Apply:** Applicants must submit completed application form; double-spaced proposal (not more than ten pages); bibliography (not more than two pages); publication list (not more than two pages); and four reference letters. **Deadline:** October 3.

512 ■ American Council on Rural Special Education

Montana Center on Disabilities/MSU-Billings
1500 University Dr.
Billings, MT 59101
Ph: (406)657-2312
Fax: (406)657-2313
Free: 888-866-3822
E-mail: inquiries@acres-sped.org
URL: http://www.acres-sped.org

513 ■ ACRES Scholarships *(Postgraduate, Professional Development/Scholarship)*

Purpose: To provide financial assistance to rural teachers for an opportunity to pursue education and training. **Focus:**

Awards are arranged alphabetically below their administering organizations

Education, Special; Special education. **Qualif.:** Applicants must be a U.S. citizen; currently or have been employed by a rural school district as a teacher in regular or special education; working with disabled students or with regular education students and "retooling" for work in a special education setting; pursuing to increase skills in special education or "retooling" from a regular education to a special education career. **Criteria:** Applicants are selected based on the selection committee's review of the application materials.

Funds Avail.: $1,000. **To Apply:** Applicants must submit a completed application form; an essay describing the advantages and disadvantages of rural special education, applicant's need for the scholarship, how the scholarship will be used, and how the applicant will share the gained information with other educators; and two letters of recommendation from persons in a position to judge the applicant's capabilities as a rural special educator. At least one reference must be from an individual actively involved in rural special education. **Deadline:** February 15. **Contact:** Lori Garnes, garnesl@minotstateu.edu.

514 ■ American Counsel Association

150 Fayetteville St. PO Box 2611
Raleigh, NC 27602-2611
Ph: (919)821-1220
E-mail: jdorsett@smithlaw.com
URL: http://www.amcounsel.org

515 ■ American Counsel Association Scholarships *(Undergraduate/Scholarship)*

Purpose: To provide scholarships to academically gifted and financially needy third-year law students. **Focus:** Law. **Qualif.:** Applicants must be enrolled in a law school located within the Seventh Federal Judicial District. **Criteria:** Selection will be based on the committee's criteria.

Funds Avail.: No specific amount. **To Apply:** The law school deans are invited to submit nominations which are reviewed by the Committee.

516 ■ American Counseling Association

5999 Stevenson Ave.
Alexandria, VA 22304
Ph: (703)823-6862
Fax: (703)823-0252
Free: 800-347-6647
E-mail: canfield@sandiego.edu
URL: http://www.counseling.org

517 ■ Ross Trust Graduate Student Scholarships *(Graduate/Scholarship)*

Purpose: To provide support to students preparing for counseling roles in the nation's elementary, middle and secondary schools. **Focus:** Counseling/Guidance. **Qualif.:** Applicants must be currently enrolled in either a master's level or a doctoral level program of studies in preparation to work as a professional counselor at the elementary, middle or secondary education level. **Criteria:** Selection of applicants will be based on the following: (a) Master's-level students must have an outstanding academic performance (based on a minimum of 15 graduate hours completed) and exemplary volunteer activities; (b) Doctoral-level students must have an outstanding academic performance (based on a minimum of 15 graduate hours completed), exemplary volunteer activities in schools and/or community, and scholarly research, writing and presentations.

Funds Avail.: $1,375. **Number Awarded:** 15. **To Apply:** Applicants must have a statement of career goals; must provide a description of volunteer experiences in schools and/or the community. For doctoral level scholarships, applicants must have a statement reflecting research, writing and presentation activities.

518 ■ American Criminal Justice Association

PO Box 601047
Sacramento, CA 95860-1047
Ph: (916)484-6553
E-mail: acjalae@aol.com
URL: http://www.acjalae.org

519 ■ American Criminal Justice Association Scholarships *(Undergraduate/Scholarship)*

Purpose: To provide financial support to members who are upper or lower division students or graduate students enrolled in a course of study in the criminal justice field. **Focus:** Criminal Justice. **Qualif.:** Applicants must be US citizens or eligible non-citizens; must be ACJA/LAE chapter members; must be currently enrolled in a recognized course of study directly or indirectly associated with the criminal justice field; must have achieved a minimum overall GPA of 3.0 on a scale of 4.0; must be currently enrolled with a minimum course of at least two-thirds of full-time loads. **Criteria:** Recipients are selected based on: overall GPA of 3.0 or better on a scale of 4.0; GPA of basic courses completed in criminal justice or related field of study; and statement of career and educational goals.

Funds Avail.: $400; $200; $100. **To Apply:** Applicants must fill out application form. Applicants must submit: five copies of school transcript; five copies of letters of recommendation from chapter officers and faculty advisors; career and educational goal statement. **Deadline:** December 31. **Contact:** Dr. Archie Rainey at the above address (see entry 518).

520 ■ American Culinary Federation

The American Academy of Chefs
180 Center Place Way
St. Augustine, FL 32095
Ph: (904)824-4468
Fax: (904)825-4758
Free: 800-624-9458
E-mail: academy@acfchefs.net
URL: http://www.acfchefs.org

521 ■ American Culinary Federation Chair's Scholarship Grants *(All/Scholarship)*

Purpose: to provide financial assistance to those studying culinary arts. **Focus:** Culinary arts. **Qualif.:** Applicants must be a student hot food team sponsored by an ACF Chapter; have already won their state competition and are ready to go to the regional competition, or have won their regional competition and are ready to go to the national competition; must be ACF Student Members in good standing and have held at least one fundraiser. **Criteria:** Recipient will be selected based on the American Academy of Chefs Scholarship Committee's review of the application materials.

Funds Avail.: No specific amount. **To Apply:** Applicants

Awards are arranged alphabetically below their administering organizations

must submit a completed application form; proof of fundraiser and amount raised; and signed images release to use the team's names and/or photos in ACF publications. **Deadline:** For state teams going to Regionals: the application is due at least 15 days before the regional competition. For Regional teams going to Nationals: the application is due by June 1.

522 ■ American Culinary Federation Educational Scholarship Grants *(All/Scholarship)*

Purpose: to provide financial assistance to those studying culinary arts. **Focus:** Culinary arts. **Qualif.:** Applicants must be a student hot food team sponsored by an ACF Chapter; have already won their state competition and are ready to go to the regional competition, or have won their regional competition and are ready to go to the national competition; must be ACF Student Members in good standing and have held at least one fundraiser. **Criteria:** Recipient will be selected based on the American Academy of Chefs Scholarship Committee's review of the application materials.

Funds Avail.: No specific amount. **To Apply:** Applicants must submit a completed application form; proof of fundraiser and amount raised; and signed images release to use the team's names and/or photos in ACF publications. **Deadline:** For state teams going to Regionals: the application is due at least 15 days before the regional competition. For Regional teams going to Nationals: the application is due by June 1.

523 ■ Balestreri/Cutino Scholarships *(Undergraduate/Scholarship)*

Purpose: to provide financial assistance to those studying culinary arts. **Focus:** Culinary arts. **Qualif.:** Applicants must be an exemplary student currently enrolled in an accredited, post-secondary college, with a major in either culinary or pastry arts, or be an ACF registered apprentice. Applicant must have completed a grading or marking period (trimester, semester or quarter) and must have a career goal of becoming a chef or pastry chef. **Criteria:** Scholarship recipient will be selected based on the American Academy of Chefs Scholarship Committee's review of the application materials.

Funds Avail.: No specific amount. **To Apply:** Applicants must submit a completed application form; two letters of recommendation from industry and/or culinary professionals (may not be related to the applicant in any manner); a Financial Aid Release Form completed by the financial aid office; sealed official transcript showing current GPA; and signed photo and/or photo in ACF publications. **Deadline:** December 31.

524 ■ Chaine des Rotisseurs Scholarships *(Undergraduate/Scholarship)*

Purpose: to provide financial assistance to those studying culinary arts. **Focus:** Culinary arts. **Qualif.:** Applicants must be an exemplary student currently enrolled in an accredited, post-secondary college, with a major in either culinary or pastry arts, or be an ACF registered apprentice. Applicant must have completed a grading or marking period (trimester, semester or quarter) and must have a career goal of becoming a chef or pastry chef. **Criteria:** Scholarship recipient will be selected based on the American Academy of Chefs Scholarship Committee's review of the application materials.

Funds Avail.: No specific amount. **To Apply:** Applicants must submit a completed application form; two letters of recommendation from industry and/or culinary professionals (may not be related to the applicant in any manner); a Financial Aid Release Form completed by the financial aid office; sealed official transcript showing current GPA; and signed photo and/or photo in ACF publications. **Deadline:** December 31.

525 ■ Julia Child Memorial Scholarships *(Undergraduate/Scholarship)*

Purpose: to provide financial assistance to those studying culinary arts. **Focus:** Culinary arts. **Qualif.:** Applicants must be an exemplary student currently enrolled in an accredited, post-secondary college, with a major in either culinary or pastry arts, or be an ACF registered apprentice. Applicant must have completed a grading or marking period (trimester, semester or quarter) and must have a career goal of becoming a chef or pastry chef. **Criteria:** Scholarship recipient will be selected based on the American Academy of Chefs Scholarship Committee's review of the application materials.

Funds Avail.: No specific amount. **To Apply:** Applicants must submit a completed application form; two letters of recommendation from industry and/or culinary professionals (may not be related to the applicant in any manner); a Financial Aid Release Form completed by the financial aid office; sealed official transcript showing current GPA; and signed photo and/or photo in ACF publications. **Deadline:** December 31.

526 ■ Linda Cullen Memorial Scholarships *(High School/Scholarship)*

Purpose: to provide financial assistance to those studying culinary arts. **Focus:** Culinary arts. **Qualif.:** Applicants must be an exemplary senior high school student eligible to graduate the same year as the scholarship is applied for. Applicants must be currently accepted to an accredited, post-secondary college, with a major in either culinary or pastry arts, or must be an ACF registered apprentice; have a career goal of becoming a chef or pastry chef. **Criteria:** Scholarship recipient will be selected based on the American Academy of Chefs Scholarship Committee's review of the application materials.

Funds Avail.: No specific amount. **To Apply:** Applicants must submit a completed application form; two letters of recommendation from industry and/or culinary professionals (may not be related to the applicant in any manner); a Financial Aid Release Form completed by the financial aid office; sealed official high school transcript showing current GPA; and signed photo and/or photo in ACF publications. **Deadline:** March 31.

527 ■ Senior Chef Frank Farello Scholarships *(Professional Development/Scholarship)*

Purpose: To support professional chefs who wish to continue their education or initial certification class. **Focus:** Culinary arts. **Qualif.:** For initial certification, applicants must pass an initial ACF certification class with a "C" grade or better. For continuing education, applicants must be certified by the American Culinary Federation as a Certified Chef d' Cuisine or higher; enrolled in a state accredited educational institution for the purpose of enhancing culinary skills or knowledge; an active member of the American Culinary Federation in good standing for three or more years. **Criteria:** Scholarship recipient will be selected based on the American Academy of Chefs Scholarship Committee's review of the application materials.

Funds Avail.: $750. Funds will be used for approved

Awards are arranged alphabetically below their administering organizations

courses only. **To Apply:** Applicants must submit a completed application form, proof of certification, proof of ACF membership and total cost of class.

528 ■ Stanley "Doc" Jensen Scholarships *(High School/Scholarship)*

Purpose: to provide financial assistance to those studying culinary arts. **Focus:** Culinary arts. **Qualif.:** Applicants must be an exemplary senior high school student eligible to graduate the same year as the scholarship is applied for. Applicants must be currently accepted to an accredited, post-secondary college, with a major in either culinary or pastry arts, or must be an ACF registered apprentice; have a career goal of becoming a chef or pastry chef. **Criteria:** Scholarship recipient will be selected based on the American Academy of Chefs Scholarship Committee's review of the application materials.

Funds Avail.: No specific amount. **To Apply:** Applicants must submit a completed application form; two letters of recommendation from industry and/or culinary professionals (may not be related to the applicant in any manner); a Financial Aid Release Form completed by the financial aid office; sealed official high school transcript showing current GPA; and signed photo and/or photo in ACF publications. **Deadline:** March 31.

529 ■ Andrew Macrina Scholarships *(High School/Scholarship)*

Purpose: to provide financial assistance to those studying culinary arts. **Focus:** Culinary arts. **Qualif.:** Applicants must be an exemplary senior high school student eligible to graduate the same year as the scholarship is applied for. Applicants must be currently accepted to an accredited, post-secondary college, with a major in either culinary or pastry arts, or must be an ACF registered apprentice; have a career goal of becoming a chef or pastry chef. **Criteria:** Scholarship recipient will be selected based on the American Academy of Chefs Scholarship Committee's review of the application materials.

Funds Avail.: No specific amount. **To Apply:** Applicants must submit a completed application form; two letters of recommendation from industry and/or culinary professionals (may not be related to the applicant in any manner); a Financial Aid Release Form completed by the financial aid office; sealed official high school transcript showing current GPA; and signed photo and/or photo in ACF publications. **Deadline:** March 31.

530 ■ Ray and Gertrude Marshall Scholarships *(Undergraduate/Scholarship)*

Purpose: to provide financial assistance to those studying culinary arts. **Focus:** Culinary arts. **Qualif.:** Applicants must be an exemplary student currently enrolled in an accredited, post-secondary college, with a major in either culinary or pastry arts, or be an ACF registered apprentice. Applicant must have completed a grading or marking period (trimester, semester or quarter) and must have a career goal of becoming a chef or pastry chef. **Criteria:** Scholarship recipient will be selected based on the American Academy of Chefs Scholarship Committee's review of the application materials.

Funds Avail.: No specific amount. **To Apply:** Applicants must submit a completed application form; two letters of recommendation from industry and/or culinary professionals (may not be related to the applicant in any manner); a Financial Aid Release Form completed by the financial aid office; sealed official transcript showing current GPA; and signed photo and/or photo in ACF publications. **Deadline:** December 31.

531 ■ Hermann G. Rusch Scholarships *(Professional Development/Scholarship)*

Purpose: To support professional chefs who wished to continue education or initial certification class. **Focus:** Culinary arts. **Qualif.:** For initial certification, applicants must pass an initial ACF certification class with a "C" grade or better. For continuing education, applicants must be certified by the American Culinary Federation as a Certified Chef d' Cuisine or higher; enrolled in a state accredited educational institution for the purpose of enhancing culinary skills or knowledge; an active member of the American Culinary Federation in good standing for three or more years. **Criteria:** Scholarship recipient will be selected based on the American Academy of Chefs Scholarship Committee's review of the application materials.

Funds Avail.: $750 for approved courses only. **To Apply:** Applicants must submit a completed application form, proof of certification, proof of ACF membership and total cost of class.

532 ■ Spice Box Grants *(Professional Development/Grant)*

Purpose: To support professional chefs who wish to continue their education or initial certification class. **Focus:** Culinary arts. **Qualif.:** For initial certification, applicants must pass an initial ACF certification class with a "C" grade or better. For continuing education, applicants must be certified by the American Culinary Federation as a Certified Chef d' Cuisine or higher; enrolled in a state accredited educational institution for the purpose of enhancing culinary skills or knowledge; an active member of the American Culinary Federation in good standing for three or more years. **Criteria:** Scholarship recipient will be selected based on the American Academy of Chefs Scholarship Committee's review of the application materials.

Funds Avail.: $750 for approved courses only. **To Apply:** Applicants must submit a completed application form, proof of certification, proof of ACF membership and total cost of class.

533 ■ Tomato Fest Scholarship Grants *(Undergraduate/Scholarship)*

Purpose: to provide financial assistance to those studying culinary arts. **Focus:** Culinary arts. **Qualif.:** Applicants must be an exemplary student currently enrolled in an accredited, post-secondary college, with a major in either culinary or pastry arts, or be an ACF registered apprentice. Applicant must have completed a grading or marking period (trimester, semester or quarter) and must have a career goal of becoming a chef or pastry chef. **Criteria:** Scholarship recipient will be selected based on the American Academy of Chefs Scholarship Committee's review of the application materials.

Funds Avail.: No specific amount. **To Apply:** Applicants must submit a completed application form; two letters of recommendation from industry and/or culinary professionals (may not be related to the applicant in any manner); a Financial Aid Release Form completed by the financial aid office; sealed official transcript showing current GPA; and signed photo and/or photo in ACF publications. **Deadline:** December 31.

534 ■ American Dental Association

211 E Chicago Ave.
Chicago, IL 60611-2678

Awards are arranged alphabetically below their administering organizations

Ph: (312)440-2500
E-mail: membership@ada.org
URL: http://www.ada.org

535 ▪ American Dental Association Dental Assisting Scholarship Program *(Undergraduate/Scholarship)*

Purpose: To provide financial assistance for furthering education of students in pursuing the field of dentistry. **Focus:** Dentistry. **Qualif.:** Applicants must be a U.S. citizen (permanent resident status does not qualify); entering as student at the time of application and enrolled in a dental assisting program accredited by the Commission on Dental Accreditation of the American Dental Association; enrolled as a full-time student, a minimum of 12 credit hours; demonstrate a minimum financial need of $1,000; have a minimum accumulative grade point average of 3.0 based on a 4.0 scale; and, two reference forms, one from a dentist or dental assisting representative and/or one from a school representative in support of the application must be submitted as part of the application form. **Criteria:** Applicant will be evaluated based on applicants demonstrated financial need, academic achievement, biographical sketch questionaire and two completed reference forms.

Funds Avail.: $1,000. **Number Awarded:** 10. **To Apply:** Applicant must submit an application form that is typed or printed in black ink, completed and signed by school officials; completed application form, including the Academic Achievement Record Form and Financial Needs Assessment Form, which are a part of the application form, and signed by school official; a copy of the school's letter of acceptance, if entering first-year student; two completed reference forms, sealed and signed on the back flap of the envelopes by the referrers (required forms must be used which are a part of the scholarship application form); typed, biographical sketch questionnaire (required form must be used which is a part of the scholarship application form); a self-addressed, stamped postcard, which can be mailed upon receipt of the application (if the applicant wishes to have verification that the application was received). **Deadline:** September 5.

536 ▪ American Dental Association Dental Hygiene Scholarship Program *(Undergraduate/Scholarship)*

Purpose: To provide financial assistance for furthering education of students in pursuing the field of dentistry. **Focus:** Dentistry. **Qualif.:** Applicants must be U.S. citizen (permanent resident status does not qualify); entering final year student at the time of application and currently attending a dental hygiene program accredited by the Commission on Dental Accreditation of the American Dental Association; enrolled as a full-time student, a minimum of 12 credit hours; demonstrate a minimum financial need of $1,000; have a minimum accumulative grade point average of 3.0 based on a 4.0 scale; and two reference forms from two dental hygiene program representatives in support of the application must be submitted as part of the application form. **Criteria:** Applicant will be evaluated based on applicants demonstrated financial need, academic achievement, biographical sketch questionaire and two completed reference forms.

Funds Avail.: $1,000. **Number Awarded:** 15. **To Apply:** Applicant must submit an application form that is typed or printed in black ink, completed and signed by school officials; completed application form, including the Academic Achievement Record Form and Financial Needs Assessment Form, which are a part of the application form, and signed by school official; a copy of the school's letter of acceptance, if entering first-year student; two completed reference forms, sealed and signed on the back flap of the envelopes by the referrers (required forms must be used which are a part of the scholarship application form); typed, biographical sketch questionnaire (required form must be used which is a part of the scholarship application form); a self-addressed, stamped postcard, which can be mailed upon receipt of the application (if the applicant wishes to have verification that the application was received). **Deadline:** June 2.

537 ▪ American Dental Association Dental Laboratory Technology Scholarship Program *(Undergraduate/Scholarship)*

Purpose: To provide financial assistance for students to further their education in the field of dentistry. **Focus:** Dentistry. **Qualif.:** Applicants must be a U.S. citizen (permanent resident status does not qualify); entering final year student at the time of application and currently attending a dental laboratory technology program accredited by the Commission on Dental Accreditation of the American Dental Association; enrolled as a full-time student, a minimum of 12 credit hours; demonstrate a minimum financial need of $1,000; have a minimum accumulative grade point average of 3.0 based on a 4.0 scale; and, must have two reference forms from two dental laboratory technology program representatives in support of the application must be submitted as part of the application form. **Criteria:** Applicant will be evaluated based on applicants demonstrated financial need, academic achievement, biographical sketch questionnaire and two completed reference forms.

Funds Avail.: $1,000. **Number Awarded:** 5. **To Apply:** Applicant must submit an application form that is typed or printed in black ink, completed and signed by school officials; completed application form, including the Academic Achievement Record Form and Financial Needs Assessment Form, which are a part of the application form, and signed by school official; a copy of the school's letter of acceptance, if entering first-year student; two completed reference forms, sealed and signed on the back flap of the envelopes by the referrers (required forms must be used which are a part of the scholarship application form); typed, biographical sketch questionnaire (required form must be used which is a part of the scholarship application form); a self-addressed, stamped postcard, which can be mailed upon receipt of the application (if the applicant wishes to have verification that the application was received). **Deadline:** September 5.

538 ▪ American Dental Association Dental Student Scholarship *(Undergraduate/Scholarship)*

Purpose: To provide financial assistance for furthering education of dental students. **Focus:** Dentistry. **Qualif.:** Applicant must be a U.S. Citizen (permanent resident status does not qualify); entering second year student at the time of application and currently attending or enrolled at a dental school accredited by the Commission on Dental Accreditation of the American Dental Association; enrolled as a full-time student, a minimum of 12 credit hours; must demonstrate a minimum financial need of $2,500; have a minimum accumulative grade point average of 3.0 based on a 4.0 scale; and two reference forms from two dental school representatives. **Criteria:** Applicant will be evaluated based on Applicants demonstrated financial need, academic achievement, biographical sketch questionaire and two completed reference forms.

Awards are arranged alphabetically below their administering organizations

Funds Avail.: $2,500. **Number Awarded:** 25. **To Apply:** Applicant must submit an application form that is typed or printed in black ink, completed and signed by school officials; completed application form, including the Academic Achievement Record Form and Financial Needs Assessment Form, which are a part of the application form, and signed by school official; a copy of the school's letter of acceptance, if entering first-year student; two completed reference forms, sealed and signed on the back flap of the envelopes by the referrers (required forms must be used which are a part of the scholarship application form); typed, biographical sketch questionnaire (required form must be used which is a part of the scholarship application form); a self-addressed, stamped postcard, which can be mailed upon receipt of the application (if the applicant wishes to have verification that the application was received). **Deadline:** June 2.

539 ■ American Dental Association Minority Dental Student Scholarships *(Undergraduate/Scholarship)*

Purpose: To provide financial assistance for furthering education of the minority dental students. **Focus:** Dentistry. **Qualif.:** Applicants must be U.S. Citizen (permanent resident status does not qualify); entering second year student at the time of application and currently attending or enrolled at a dental school accredited by the Commission on Dental Accreditation of the American Dental Association; enrolled as a full-time student, a minimum of 12 credit hours; demonstrate a minimum financial need of $2,500; have a minimum accumulative grade point average of 3.0 based on a 4.0 scale; and two reference forms from two dental school representatives (i.e., professor or academic advisor) in support of the application must be submitted as part of the application form. **Criteria:** Applicant will be evaluated based on applicant's demonstrated financial need, academic achievement, biographical sketch questionaire and two completed reference forms.

Funds Avail.: $2,500. **Number Awarded:** 25. **To Apply:** Applicant must submit an application form that is typed or printed in black ink, completed and signed by school officials; completed application form, including the Academic Achievement Record Form and Financial Needs Assessment Form, which are a part of the application form, and signed by school official; a copy of the school's letter of acceptance, if entering first-year student; two completed reference forms, sealed and signed on the back flap of the envelopes by the referrers (required forms must be used which are a part of the scholarship application form); typed, biographical sketch questionnaire (required form must be used which is a part of the scholarship application form); a self-addressed, stamped postcard, which can be mailed upon receipt of the application (if the applicant wishes to have verification that the application was received). **Deadline:** June 2.

540 ■ American Division Veterans Association

3839 Ols Savannah Dr.
Kalamazoo, MI 49009
Ph: (269)372-2129
E-mail: c146thinf@aol.com
URL: http://www.americal.org

541 ■ American Division Veterans Association Scholarships *(Undergraduate/Scholarship)*

Purpose: To provide college and vocational scholarships to the children and grandchildren, including those by adoption, of current and deceased ADVA members, provided the deceased member held good membership standing at the time of death, and to any child or adopted child of an American Division soldier who was killed or died while on active duty with the division. **Focus:** History, Military. **Qualif.:** An applicant must be a high school graduate and planning to attend college. **Criteria:** Recipients will be selected based on financial need.

Funds Avail.: No specific amount. **To Apply:** Applicant must submit a letter from the sponsor attesting to the applicant's eligibility according to ADVA Scholarship Fund Purpose and By-Laws; a letter of admission from the applicant's college or vocational school of choice; a letter from the applicant's high school principal attesting to the applicant's character if applicant is attending or has graduated from high school; two letters of recommendation from current teachers concerning the applicant's progress in current classes or subjects; a photocopy of the applicant's high school or college transcript; a detailed statement of the applicant's academic accomplishments, extracurricular activities, and community service involvement; an applicant must submit a 200-300 word essay on subjects pertaining to American Division history, national pride, loyalty to the nation, and patriotism. **Contact:** Mr. Bob Short 3839 Old Savannah Drive Kalamazoo MI 49009; 269-372-2192; c146thinf@aol.com

542 ■ American Educational Research Association

1430 K St. NW, Ste. 1200
Washington, DC 20005
Ph: (202)238-3200
Fax: (202)238-3250
URL: http://www.aera.net

543 ■ AERA-AIR Fellows Program *(Postdoctorate/Fellowship)*

Purpose: To support early career scholars by providing intensive research and training opportunities to recent doctoral recipients in the fields and disciplines related to the scientific study of education and education processes; to increase the number of underrepresented minority professionals conducting advanced research or providing technical assistance. **Focus:** Education. **Qualif.:** Applicants must be U.S citizens and permanent residents; must have completed their PhD/EdD degrees within the three years prior to application. **Criteria:** Selection of applicants will be based on their research proposal.

Funds Avail.: $45,000-$50,000. **To Apply:** Applicants must complete the application form available online; must submit a letter of recommendation and transcript of record. Application form and other supporting documents must be sent to AERA-AIR Fellows Program, American Educational Research Association, 1430 K St. NW, Ste. 1200, Washington, DC 20005. **Deadline:** December 17.

544 ■ AERA-ETS Fellowship Program in Measurement *(Postdoctorate/Fellowship)*

Purpose: To increase the involvement of women and underrepresented minority professionals in measurement, psychometrics, assessment, and related fields. **Focus:** Testing, educational/psychological. **Qualif.:** Applicants must be U.S citizens and permanent residents; must have completed their PhD/EdD degrees within the three years prior to application. **Criteria:** Selection of applicants will be based on the scholarship selection criteria.

Funds Avail.: $50,000. **To Apply:** Applicants must complete the application form available online; must submit a letter of recommendation and transcript of record. Application form and other supporting documents must be sent to AERA-AIR Fellows Program, American Educational Research Association, 1430 K St. NW, Ste. 1200, Washington, DC 20005. **Deadline:** December 17.

545 ■ AERA Minority Fellowship Program in Education Research *(Postdoctorate/Fellowship)*

Purpose: To provide support for doctoral dissertation research and to advance education research by outstanding minority graduate students and to improve the quality and diversity of university faculties. **Focus:** Education. **Qualif.:** Applicant must be a U.S citizen and permanent resident; must work full-time on his or her dissertations and course requirements. **Criteria:** Selection of applicants will be based on the application requirements.

Funds Avail.: Stipend of $12,000 and up to $1,000 in travel support to attend the AERA Annual Meeting. **To Apply:** Applicants must complete the application form available online; must submit a letter of recommendation and transcript of record. Application form and other supporting documents must be sent to AERA-AIR Fellows Program, American Educational Research Association, 1430 K St. NW, Ste. 1200, Washington, DC 20005. **Deadline:** December 17.

546 ■ American Federation of Police and Concerned Citizens

6350 Horizon Dr.
Titusville, FL 32780
Ph: (321)264-0911
E-mail: policeinfo@aphf.org
URL: http://www.afp-cc.org

547 ■ American Federation of Police and Concerned Citizen Scholarships *(Undergraduate/Scholarship)*

Purpose: To assist family members and children of officers killed in the line of duty. **Focus:** Law Enforcement. **Qualif.:** Applicants must be high school graduates attending a traditional four year college, university, technical or vocational educational institutions. **Criteria:** Recipients are selected based on financial need.

Funds Avail.: $1,500. **To Apply:** Applicants must submit an application form.

548 ■ American Floral Endowment

1601 Duke St.
Alexandria, VA 22314
Ph: (703)838-5211
Fax: (703)838-5212
E-mail: afe@endowment.org
URL: http://endowment.org

549 ■ American Floral Endowment Scholarships *(Undergraduate/Scholarship)*

Purpose: To further the advancement of education and science in the floriculture and environmental horticulture field by funding research and studies and financing scholarships and other educational activities for individuals interested in the field. **Focus:** Horticulture. **Qualif.:** Applicants must be pursuing a career in a horticulture-related field; must have a minimum of 3.0 GPA; must be residents of the United States or Canada. **Criteria:** Recipients are selected based on academic performance.

Funds Avail.: Maximum of $2,000. **To Apply:** Applicants must send a completed online application form; must submit two letters of recommendations and a transcript of records. **Deadline:** May 1. **Contact:** afe@endowment.org.

550 ■ Ball Horticultural Company Scholarships *(Undergraduate/Scholarship)*

Purpose: To further the advancement of education and science in the floriculture and environmental horticulture field by funding research and studies and financing scholarships and other educational activities for individuals interested in the field. **Focus:** Horticulture. **Qualif.:** Applicants must be students currently enrolled in their third to fifth year of college; must be pursuing a career in commercial floriculture. **Criteria:** Recipients are selected based on academic performance.

Funds Avail.: No specific amount. **To Apply:** Applicants must send a completed online application form; must submit two letters of recommendation and transcript of records.

551 ■ Vic and Margaret Ball Student Intern Scholarships *(Undergraduate/Internship)*

Purpose: To further the advancement of education and science in the floriculture and environmental horticulture field by funding research and studies and financing scholarships and other educational activities for individuals interested in the field; to assure continuance of practical experience opportunities. **Focus:** Horticulture. **Qualif.:** Applicants must be full-time undergraduate students who are currently enrolled in a floriculture/environmental horticulture program at a two or four year college/university within the United States; must be U.S. citizens; must maintain "C" or better GPA with satisfactory progress in a degree or certificate program. **Criteria:** Recipients are selected based on academic performance, financial need and interest in a horticulture career.

Funds Avail.: varies. **To Apply:** Applicants must submit a completed and signed application form, official transcript from all institutions attended, a statement explaining the reasons for applying and future career goals, a letter of recommendation and endorsement by a faculty member. Applicants must submit a 500 word report evaluating the experience within 30 days of completing the program; pictures of the student working at the intern location must be included. Applicants must have permission to interrupt studies for the length of the training period. **Deadline:** March 1 and October 1.

552 ■ Harold Bettinger Scholarships *(Undergraduate/Scholarship)*

Purpose: To further the advancement of education and science in the floriculture and environmental horticulture field by funding research and studies and financing scholarships and other educational activities for individuals interested in the field. **Focus:** Horticulture. **Qualif.:** Applicants must be sophomore or graduate students pursuing a career in business and/or marketing with the intent to apply it to a horticulture-related business. **Criteria:** Recipients are selected based on academic performance.

Funds Avail.: No specific amount. **To Apply:** Applicants must send a completed online application form; must submit two letters of recommendation and transcript of records.

553 ■ Leonard Bettinger Scholarships *(Undergraduate/Scholarship)*

Purpose: To further the advancement of education and science in the floriculture and environmental horticulture field

Awards are arranged alphabetically below their administering organizations

by funding research and studies and financing scholarships and other educational activities for individuals interested in the field. **Focus:** Horticulture. **Qualif.:** Applicants must be vocational students in a one or two-year program who intend to become growers or greenhouse managers. **Criteria:** Recipients are selected based on academic performance.

Funds Avail.: No specific amount. **To Apply:** Applicants must send a completed online application form; must submit two letters of recommendation and transcript of records.

554 ■ James Bridenbaugh Memorial Scholarship *(Undergraduate/Scholarship)*

Purpose: To further the advancement of education and science in the floriculture and environmental horticulture field by funding research and studies and financing scholarships and other educational activities for individuals interested in the field. **Focus:** Horticulture. **Qualif.:** Applicants must be sophomore to fifth-year students pursuing a career in floral design and marketing fresh flowers and plants. **Criteria:** Recipients are selected based on academic performance.

Funds Avail.: No specific amount. **To Apply:** Applicants must send a completed online application form; must submit two letters of recommendation and transcript of records.

555 ■ John Carew Memorial Scholarships *(Undergraduate/Scholarship)*

Purpose: To further the advancement of education and science in the floriculture and environmental horticulture field by funding research and studies and financing scholarships and other educational activities for individuals interested in the field. **Focus:** Horticulture. **Qualif.:** Applicants must be graduate students with an interest in greenhouse crops. **Criteria:** Recipients are selected based on academic performance.

Funds Avail.: No specific amount. **To Apply:** Applicants must send a completed online application form; must submit two letters of recommendation and transcript of records.

556 ■ Earl Deadman Memorial Scholarships *(Undergraduate/Scholarship)*

Purpose: To further the advancement of education and science in the floriculture and environmental horticulture field by funding research and studies and financing scholarships and other educational activities for individuals interested in the field. **Focus:** Horticulture. **Qualif.:** Applicants must be sophomore to fifth-year students who plan to become greenhouse growers; must be from the Northwestern area of the U.S. **Criteria:** Recipients are selected based on academic performance.

Funds Avail.: No specific amount. **To Apply:** Applicants must send a completed online application form; must submit two letters of recommendation and transcript of records.

557 ■ Dosatron International Inc. Scholarships *(Undergraduate/Scholarship)*

Purpose: To further the advancement of education and science in the floriculture and environmental horticulture field by funding research and studies and financing scholarships and other educational activities for individuals interested in the field. **Focus:** Horticulture. **Qualif.:** Applicants must be third to fifth year students who are interested in floriculture production and plan to work in the greenhouse environment. **Criteria:** Recipients are selected based on academic performance.

Funds Avail.: No specific amount. **To Apply:** Applicants must send a completed online application form; must submit two letters of recommendation and transcript of records.

558 ■ Paris Fracasso Production Floriculture Scholarships *(Undergraduate/Scholarship)*

Purpose: To further the advancement of education and science in the floriculture and environmental horticulture field by funding research and studies and financing scholarships and other educational activities for individuals interested in the field. **Focus:** Horticulture. **Qualif.:** Applicants must be third to fifth year students who plan to work in floriculture production. **Criteria:** Recipients are selected based on academic performance.

Funds Avail.: No specific amount. **To Apply:** Applicants must send a completed online application form; must submit two letters of recommendation and transcript of records.

559 ■ John Holden Vocational Scholarships *(Undergraduate/Scholarship)*

Purpose: To further the advancement of education and science in the floriculture and environmental horticulture field by funding research and studies and financing scholarships and other educational activities for individuals interested in the field. **Focus:** Horticulture. **Qualif.:** Applicants must be vocational students in a one or two-year program who intend to become growers or greenhouse managers. **Criteria:** Recipients are selected based on academic performance.

Funds Avail.: No specific amount. **To Apply:** Applicants must send a completed online application form; must submit two letters of recommendation and transcript of records.

560 ■ Ed Markham International Scholarships *(Undergraduate/Scholarship)*

Purpose: To further the advancement of education and science in the floriculture and environmental horticulture field by funding research and studies and financing scholarships and other educational activities for individuals interested in the field. **Focus:** Horticulture. **Qualif.:** Applicants must be sophomore to graduate students pursuing a career in horticulture marketing through international travel. **Criteria:** Recipients are selected based on academic performance.

Funds Avail.: No specific amount. **To Apply:** Applicants must send a completed online application form; must submit two letters of recommendation and transcript of records.

561 ■ Mossmiller Student Intern Scholarships Program *(Undergraduate/Internship)*

Purpose: To provide quality professional training for selected, motivated floriculture and environmental horticulture students. **Focus:** Horticulture. **Qualif.:** Applicants must be full-time undergraduate students who are currently enrolled in a recognized floriculture/environmental horticulture or business program at a two or four year college or university in the U.S.; must maintain a "C" average with satisfactory progress in a degree or certificate program. **Criteria:** Recipients are selected based on outstanding potential and serious interest in a floral industry field.

Funds Avail.: $2,000. **To Apply:** Applicants must submit: completed and signed application form; official transcript from all institutions attended; a statement explaining the reasons for applying and future career goals; a letter of recommendation and endorsement by a faculty member. Applicants must submit a 500 word report evaluating the experience within 30 days of completing the program; pictures of the student working at the intern location must be included. Applicants must have permission to interrupt studies for the length of the training period. **Deadline:** March 1 and October 1.

562 ■ National Greenhouse Manufacturers Association Scholarships *(Undergraduate/Scholarship)*

Purpose: To further the advancement of education and science in the floriculture and environmental horticulture field by funding research and studies and financing scholarships and other educational activities for individuals interested in the field. **Focus:** Horticulture. **Qualif.:** Applicants must be junior, senior or graduate students pursuing a career in horticulture and bio-engineering or the equivalent at a four-year college. **Criteria:** Recipients are selected based on academic performance.

Funds Avail.: No specific amount. **To Apply:** Applicants must send a completed online application form; must submit two letters of recommendation and transcript of records.

563 ■ Mike and Flo Novovesky Scholarships *(Undergraduate/Scholarship)*

Purpose: To further the advancement of education and science in the floriculture and environmental horticulture field by funding research and studies and financing scholarships and other educational activities for individuals interested in the field. **Focus:** Horticulture. **Qualif.:** Applicants must be second year to graduating married students with a GPA of 2.5 or higher. **Criteria:** Recipients are selected based on academic performance.

Funds Avail.: No specific amount. **To Apply:** Applicants must send a completed online application form; must submit two letters of recommendation and transcript of records.

564 ■ Lawrence "Bud" Ohlman Memorial Scholarships *(Undergraduate/Scholarship)*

Purpose: To further the advancement of education and science in the floriculture and environmental horticulture field by funding research and studies and financing scholarships and other educational activities for individuals interested in the field. **Focus:** Horticulture. **Qualif.:** Applicant must be in his or her third to final year in college, with a career goal to become a bedding plant grower for an established business. **Criteria:** Recipients are selected based on academic performance.

Funds Avail.: No specific amount. **To Apply:** Applicants must send a completed online application form; must submit two letters of recommendation and transcript of records.

565 ■ Jim Perry Vocational Scholarships *(Undergraduate/Scholarship)*

Purpose: To further the advancement of education and science in the floriculture and environmental horticulture field by funding research and studies and financing scholarships and other educational activities for individuals interested in the field. **Focus:** Horticulture. **Qualif.:** Applicant must be a vocational student in a one or two-year program with the intent of becoming a grower or greenhouse manager. **Criteria:** Recipients are selected based on academic performance.

Funds Avail.: No specific amount. **To Apply:** Applicants must send a completed online application form; must submit two letters of recommendation and transcript of records.

566 ■ James K. Rathmell Jr. Scholarships *(Undergraduate/Scholarship)*

Purpose: To further the advancement of education and science in the floriculture and environmental horticulture field by funding research and studies and financing scholarships and other educational activities for individuals interested in the field. **Focus:** Horticulture. **Qualif.:** Applicants must be in their third to final year of undergraduate studies or be graduate students; must plan to work or study outside of the United States. **Criteria:** Recipients are selected based on academic performance.

Funds Avail.: No specific amount. **To Apply:** Applicants must send a completed online application form; must submit two letters of recommendation, transcript of records, and specific plan for horticulture work/study outside of the USA.

567 ■ Seed Companies Scholarships *(Undergraduate/Scholarship)*

Purpose: To further the advancement of education and science in the floriculture and environmental horticulture field by funding research and studies and financing scholarships and other educational activities for individuals interested in the field. **Focus:** Horticulture. **Qualif.:** Applicants must be third to final year or graduate students who are pursuing a career in the seed industry in sales, breeding, research or marketing. **Criteria:** Recipients are selected based on academic performance.

Funds Avail.: No specific amount. **To Apply:** Applicants must send a completed online application form; must submit two letters of recommendation and transcript of records.

568 ■ John Tomasovic, Sr. Scholarships *(Undergraduate/Scholarship)*

Purpose: To further the advancement of education and science in the floriculture and environmental horticulture field by funding research and studies and financing scholarships and other educational activities for individuals interested in the field. **Focus:** Horticulture. **Qualif.:** Applicants must be in their second to final year in college and pursuing a career in a horticulture-related field; must have 3.0-3.5 GPA. **Criteria:** Recipients are selected based on financial need and GPA.

Funds Avail.: No specific amount. **To Apply:** Applicants must send a completed online application form; must submit two letters of recommendation and transcript of records.

569 ■ Edward Tuinier Memorial Scholarships *(Undergraduate/Scholarship)*

Purpose: To further the advancement of education and science in the floriculture and environmental horticulture field by funding research and studies and financing scholarships and other educational activities for individuals interested in the field. **Focus:** Horticulture. **Qualif.:** Applicants must be in their second to final year in a floriculture program at Michigan State University. **Criteria:** Recipients are selected based on academic performance.

Funds Avail.: No specific amount. **To Apply:** Applicants must send a completed online application form; must submit two letters of recommendation and transcript of records.

570 ■ Jacob VanNamen-Vans Marketing Scholarships *(Undergraduate/Scholarship)*

Purpose: To further the advancement of education and science in the floriculture and environmental horticulture field by funding research and studies and financing scholarships and other educational activities for individuals interested in the field. **Focus:** Horticulture. **Qualif.:** Applicants must be in their second to final year in college; must be interested in agribusiness marketing and distribution of floral products. **Criteria:** Recipients are selected based on academic performance.

Funds Avail.: No specific amount. **To Apply:** Applicants must send a completed online application form; must submit two letters of recommendation and transcript of records.

571 ■ Western Michigan Greenhouse Association Scholarships *(Undergraduate/Scholarship)*

Purpose: To further the advancement of education and science in the floriculture and environmental horticulture field by funding research and studies and financing scholarships and other educational activities for individuals interested in the field. **Focus:** Horticulture. **Qualif.:** Applicants must be in their second to final year in a Michigan college; must be studying commercial horticulture. **Criteria:** Recipients are selected based on academic performance.

Funds Avail.: No specific amount. **To Apply:** Applicants must send a completed online application form; must submit two letters of recommendation and transcript of records.

572 ■ American Floral Industry Association

PO Box 420244
Dallas, TX 75342-0244
Ph: (214)742-2747
Fax: (214)742-2648
E-mail: afia@afia.net
URL: http://www.afia.net

573 ■ AFIA Scholarships *(Undergraduate/Scholarship)*

Purpose: To provide financial support to graduating high school seniors planning to continue their education in an accredited school. **Focus:** General studies. **Qualif.:** Applicants must be an employee or a dependent of an AFIA member company in good standing; must be high school seniors graduating from an accredited high school; have a minimum of a 3.0 GPA on a 4.0 grading system. **Criteria:** Scholarship recipients will be selected on the basis of academic record, potentiality, leadership, participation in school and community activities, honors, and work experience.

Funds Avail.: $1,000. **Number Awarded:** 2. **To Apply:** Applicants must submit a completed application form; an official high school transcript; two letters of recommendation; and a stated objective. **Deadline:** May 4. **Contact:** rpoling@afia.net.

574 ■ American Foreign Service Association

2101 E St. NW
Washington, DC 20037
Ph: (202)338-4045
Fax: (202)338-6820
Free: 800-704-AFSA
E-mail: member@afsa.org
URL: http://www.afsa.org

575 ■ American Foreign Service Association Scholarship Fund *(Undergraduate/Scholarship)*

Purpose: To provide financial assistance for college education of deserving students who are dependents of the active, retired with pension, deceased or separated US government Foreign Service employees who served or serving at least a year abroad in a foreign affairs agencies. **Focus:** General studies. **Qualif.:** Applicants must be students who attended or will be attending full-time (12 credit hours or more) as an undergraduate at a 2 or 4 year accredited college, university, community college, art school or conservatory (stateside or overseas); have cumulative 2.0 GPA on a 4.0 scale; must complete undergraduate in four years; and must demonstrate financial need. **Criteria:** Applicants will be evaluated on the basis of academic record and financial need.

Funds Avail.: $1,000 to $4,500. **Number Awarded:** 55. **To Apply:** Applicants must submit the Scholarship Application accompanied with a copy of high school/college transcripts; students or parents must complete the CSS PROFILE. **Deadline:** February 6. **Contact:** Lori Dec, Scholarship Director, at the above address (see entry 574).

576 ■ American Foundation for Pharmaceutical Education

One Church St., Ste. 202
Rockville, MD 20850
Ph: (301)738-2160
Fax: (301)738-2161
E-mail: info@afpenet.org
URL: http://www.afpenet.org

577 ■ American Foundation for Pharmaceutical Education Gateway Research Scholarships *(Professional Development/Scholarship)*

Purpose: To increase the number of students who undertake a faculty-mentored research program and decide to enroll in graduate programs leading to a Ph.D. in the basic, clinical, or administrative pharmaceutical sciences. **Focus:** Pharmaceutical sciences. **Qualif.:** Scholar must be selected and nominated by a faculty member; must be enrolled in a Pharm.D. program; must have completed at least two years of college; must be enrolled in at least the first year of the professional pharmacy curriculum; and must be enrolled in a baccalaureate degree program and have completed at least one year of the degree program; must be enrolled for at least one full academic year after initiation of the award; and must be U.S. citizens. **Criteria:** Preference will be given to applications from students who need relevant research experience in order to have the basis to decide whether to pursue the Ph.D. degree in the pharmaceutical sciences.

Funds Avail.: $5,000. **Number Awarded:** 15. **To Apply:** Applicants must complete the application form, in MS Word format, which can be downloaded from the website or requested by letter, telephone, or fax from AFPE. Forms may also be available in the Dean's office at US schools/colleges of pharmacy. The faculty member seeking support and who will be responsible for mentoring the research scholar must provide: a copy of the faculty member's curriculum vitae including education and training, experience in research, and bibliography/publications; official copies of all of the student's college transcripts; a typewritten letter by the student (not more than one page) explaining his/her interest in a pharmaceutical science research experience and his/her potential career goal(s); two fully completed statements of recommendation and evaluation forms from the faculty applicant and a professor who is familiar with both the faculty member and the student's work. **Deadline:** January 25.

578 ■ American Foundation for Pharmaceutical Education Pre-Doctoral Fellowships in the Pharmaceutical Sciences *(Doctorate/Fellowship)*

Purpose: To encourage outstanding African-American/Black pre-doctoral students who have completed at least

Awards are arranged alphabetically below their administering organizations

three semesters of graduate study and have not more than three years remaining to continue their studies and earn their Ph.D. in the pharmaceutical sciences at a U.S. school or college of pharmacy. To identify and support those students who have the potential to become leaders in the pharmaceutical profession. **Focus:** Pharmaceutical sciences. **Qualif.:** Applicants must be Africa-American/Black students who have completed at least three semesters of graduate study toward the Ph.D. and who have no more than three years remaining to obtain the Ph.D. degree in a graduate program in the pharmaceutical sciences administered by, or affiliated with a U.S. school or college of pharmacy. Students enrolled in joint Pharm.D./Ph.D programs are eligible if they have completed the equivalent of three semesters of graduate credit toward Ph.D., and if the Ph.D. degree will be awarded within three additional years. Applicants must be U.S. citizens or permanent residents. **Criteria:** Recipients are selected based on academic achievement as decided by the Board of Grant based on the completed requirements.

Funds Avail.: $6,000. **Number Awarded:** 2. **To Apply:** Applicants must complete the pre-doctoral fellowship form; statements of recommendation and evaluation forms from three college faculty members who are acquainted with applicant's progress in graduate study; and official transcripts of all collegiate grades. **Deadline:** March 3.

579 ■ American Foundation for Pharmaceutical Education Pre-Doctoral Fellowships in the Pharmaceutical Sciences *(Doctorate/Fellowship)*

Purpose: To encourage outstanding pre-doctoral students who have completed at least three semesters of graduate study and have not more than three years remaining to continue their studies and earn a Ph.D. in the pharmaceutical sciences at a U.S. school or college of pharmacy. **Focus:** Pharmaceutical sciences. **Qualif.:** Applicants must have completed at least three semesters of graduate study toward a Ph.D. and have no more than three years remaining to obtain a Ph.D. degree in a graduate program in the pharmaceutical sciences administered by, or affiliated with a U.S. school or college of pharmacy. Students enrolled in joint Pharm.D./Ph.D programs are eligible to apply if they have completed the equivalent of three full semesters of graduate credit toward Ph.D., and if the Ph.D. degree will be awarded within three additional years; Applicants must be U.S. citizens or permanent residents. **Criteria:** Recipients are selected based on merit as decided by the Board of grant based on the completed requirements.

Funds Avail.: $6,000. **Number Awarded:** 60. **To Apply:** Applicants must complete the pre-doctoral fellowship form; statements of recommendation and evaluation forms from three college faculty members who are acquainted with the student's progress in graduate study; and official transcripts of all collegiate grades. **Deadline:** March 3.

580 ■ Clinical Pharmacy Post-Pharm.D. Fellowships in the Biomedical Research Sciences *(Postdoctorate/Fellowship)*

Purpose: To enable a Pharm.D. level clinical pharmacist to obtain advanced education, training, and expertise in relevant areas of the biomedical and related basic sciences in order to become a competent clinical scientist in academia, the pharmaceutical industry, institutional settings, or government, able to create and maintain a prominent peer-reviewed research program and make major contributions to the biomedical and pharmaceutical sciences; to generate skilled clinical scientists capable of conducting and teaching clinically-oriented research, advanced training is required in disciplines beyond those provided in a Pharm.D. program. **Focus:** Biomedical research. **Qualif.:** Applicants must have received the Pharm.D. degree within the past ten years; must have received a postdoctoral clinical residency and/or clinical fellowship program of at least one year duration; must agree to carry out the fellowship on a full-time basis and not engage in any part-time work; must be able to provide evidence of acceptance for the desired postdoctoral training by a suitable mentor at a recognized academic/research institution, which is not necessarily a college of pharmacy; and must be U.S. citizens or permanent residents. **Criteria:** Recipients are selected based on merit.

Funds Avail.: $27,500. **Number Awarded:** 2. **To Apply:** Applicants must submit a description of the fellowship program including course work to be taken and research project to be carried out; description of the mentor's research program; description of the resources and facilities available to the applicant; a curriculum vitae of both applicant and mentor; statement from the applicant outlining career aspirations and expected impact of the fellowship on career goals; agreements concerning progress reports, other financial support, full-time commitment to the program, publications, acknowledgement of AFPE support; letters of recommendation; and letters from Dean and Department Chair assuring that the fellowship recipient will be relieved of all teaching, advisory, service, clinical, and administrative responsibilities during the two-year fellowship. **Deadline:** February 15.

581 ■ Minority Pharmacy Faculty New Investigator Grants *(Professional Development/Grant)*

Purpose: To serve the needs of new minority investigators by providing initial funding for their research programs. **Focus:** Pharmaceutical sciences; Pharmacy. **Qualif.:** Applicants must be African-American/Black students who have earned terminal degrees in their disciplines (Pharm.D., Ph.D.); must have regular full-time faculty appointment at the assistant professor or higher level at a U.S. School or College of Pharmacy. **Criteria:** Recipients are selected based on the proposal review and recommendation for funding.

Funds Avail.: $10,000. **Number Awarded:** 1. **To Apply:** Applicants must submit a proposal including title page, abstract, research narrative, budget, biographical sketch, animal research approval letter, human subjects research approval letter, and other supporting documents. **Deadline:** March 3.

582 ■ Minority Student Gateway to Research Scholarships *(Professional Development/ Scholarship)*

Purpose: To increase the number of African American/ Black Pharm.D. students and baccalaureate science students who graduate and enroll in graduate programs leading to a Ph.D. in the basic, clinical, or administrative pharmaceutical sciences. **Focus:** Pharmacy. **Qualif.:** Scholars must be selected and nominated by a faculty member; must be African American/Black; must be enrolled in a Pharm.D. program; must have completed at least two years of college; must be enrolled in at least the first year of the professional pharmacy curriculum or in a baccalaureate degree program; must have completed at least one year of the degree program; must be U.S. citizens or permanent residents; and must be enrolled for at least one full academic year after initiation of the award. Students enrolled in joint Pharm.D./Ph.D. programs may not apply.

Awards are arranged alphabetically below their administering organizations

The student award recipient must not accept any other concurrent research support (e.g., from AACP, AFAR, ASHP, PhRMA, or any other external organization) during the 1-year scholarship period. In case of multiple source awards, the student must choose only one. **Criteria:** Preference will be given to applications from students who need relevant research experience in order to have a basis to decide whether to pursue the Ph.D. degree in the pharmaceutical sciences.

Funds Avail.: $5,000. **Number Awarded:** 1. **To Apply:** Faculty member seeking support and who will be responsible for mentoring the research scholar must provide: a copy of the faculty/member's curriculum vitae including education and training, experience in research, and bibliography/publications; official copies of all of the student's college transcripts; completed application; a letter written by the student (must be not more than one page and typewritten); and two fully completed statements of recommendation and evaluation forms from the faculty applicant and a professor who is familiar with both the faculty member and the student's work. **Deadline:** January 25.

583 ■ Pharmacy Faculty Fellowships in Community Pharmacy Practice *(Postdoctorate/Fellowship)*

Purpose: To increase the number of full-time faculty at schools/colleges of pharmacy with specific expertise in community pharmacy practice teaching and/or research. To develop pharmacy college teaching faculty and/or researchers capable of making major contributions to curriculum design, experiential education, clinical research, and/or basic research in the area of community pharmacy practice. **Focus:** Pharmacy; Pharmaceutical sciences. **Qualif.:** Applicants must have received the Pharm.D. degree, preferably within the past ten years, and may also hold a B.S. and/or M.S; must have completed post-doctoral work in community pharmacy practice as documented by curriculum development, publications, community pharmacy experiential education activities, and/or basic research; must agree to carry out the fellowship on a full-time basis and not engage in any part-time work; and must be U.S. citizens or permanent residents. **Criteria:** Recipients are selected based on proposals.

Funds Avail.: $25,000. **Number Awarded:** 1. **To Apply:** Applicants must provide a letter with his/her application from his/her Dean or Department Chair assuring that the applicant will be relieved of all teaching or clinical responsibilities during the fellowship period; and evidence of acceptance for the desired fellowship training by a suitable mentor at a recognized academic and/or research institution, which is not necessarily a school/college of pharmacy. **Deadline:** May 30.

584 ■ Pharmacy Faculty Fellowships in Geriatric Pharmacy/Geriatric Pharmaceutical Science *(Postdoctorate/Fellowship)*

Purpose: To increase the number of full-time faculty at schools/colleges of pharmacy with specific expertise in geriatric pharmacy and/or geriatric pharmaceutical sciences; to generate pharmacy college faculty teachers and/or researchers capable of making major contributions to curriculum design, experiential education, clinical research, and basic research in priority areas of geriatric pharmacy and/or geriatric pharmaceutical sciences. **Focus:** Geriatric; Pharmaceutical sciences. **Qualif.:** Applicants must have received the Pharm.D. degree preferably within the past ten years and may also hold a B.S. and/or M.S; must have completed post-doctoral work in geriatric pharmacy and/or geriatric pharmaceutical science as documented by curricula development, publications, geriatric clinical pharmacy service delivery, and/or basic research; must agree to carry out the fellowship on a full-time basis and not engage in any part-time work; and must be U.S. citizens or permanent residents. **Criteria:** Recipients are selected based on proposals.

Funds Avail.: $25,000. **Number Awarded:** 1. **To Apply:** Applicants must provide a letter with his/her application from his/her Dean, or Department Chair assuring that the applicant will be relieved of all teaching or clinical responsibilities; a letter with his/her application form from his/her Dean assuring that the applicant's educational institution will provide a minimum of $25,000 in matching financial support for the applicants during the six-month fellowship period; and evidence of acceptance for the desired fellowship training by a suitable mentor at a recognized academic and/or research institution, not necessarily a school/college of pharmacy. **Deadline:** March 3.

585 ■ Pharmacy Faculty New Investigator Grants Program *(Doctorate/Grant)*

Purpose: To serve the needs of new investigators by providing initial funding for their research programs. **Focus:** Pharmacy. **Qualif.:** Applicants must have earned terminal degrees in their disciplines and have regular full-time faculty appointment at the assistant professor level. **Criteria:** Recipients are selected based on a review of the proposals.

Funds Avail.: $10,000. **Number Awarded:** 15. **To Apply:** Applicants must submit a title page with signatures of department chair and dean; abstract page; research narrative; budget page; biographical sketch; animal research approval letter (if applicable); and other supporting documentation. Successful applicants must submit two copies of a final report and two copies of any reprints of abstract/papers published in referred journals. **Deadline:** May 23.

586 ■ American Foundation for Suicide and Prevention

120 Wall St., 22nd Fl.
New York, NY 10005
Ph: (212)363-3500
Fax: (212)363-6237
E-mail: inquiry@afsp.org
URL: http://www.afsp.org

587 ■ AFSP - Distinguished Investigator Grants *(Postgraduate/Grant)*

Purpose: To support the work of investigators from all disciplines that contribute to the understanding of suicide and suicide prevention. **Focus:** Suicide. **Qualif.:** Investigators from all academic disciplines are eligible to apply, and both basic science and applied research projects will be considered, providing the study has an essential focus on suicide prevention. Applicants must be at the level of associate professor or higher with an established record of research and publication on suicide. **Criteria:** Awards are given based on the research proposals.

Funds Avail.: $100,000. **To Apply:** Applicant may fill-up an application form online. **Deadline:** December 15. **Contact:** Tracy Auster, Research Administrator; 212-363-3500 ext. 15; tauster@afsp.org.

588 ■ AFSP Postdoctoral Research Fellowships *(Postgraduate/Fellowship)*

Purpose: To support the work of investigators from all disciplines that contribute to the understanding of suicide and suicide prevention. **Focus:** Suicide. **Qualif.:** Applicant must have received a Ph.D., M.D., or other doctoral degree within the preceding years and have not had more than three years of fellowship support. **Criteria:** Applicants are chosen based on his/her research proposal.

Funds Avail.: $100,000. Fellows receive a progressive stipend of $42,000 in the first year and $46,000 in the second, with an institutional allowance of $6,000. **To Apply:** Applicants may go online to fill out an application form. **Deadline:** December 15. **Contact:** Tracy Auster, Research Administrator; 212-363-3500 ext. 15; tauster@afsp.org.

589 ■ AFSP Standard Research Grants *(Postgraduate/Grant)*

Purpose: To support the work of investigators from all disciplines that contribute to the understanding of suicide and suicide prevention. **Focus:** Suicide. **Qualif.:** Investigators from all academic disciplines are eligible to apply, and both basic science and applied research projects will be considered, providing the study has an essential focus on suicide prevention. **Criteria:** Awards are given based on the research proposals.

Funds Avail.: $75,000. **To Apply:** Applicant may fill-up an application form online. **Deadline:** December 15. **Contact:** Tracy Auster, Research Administrator; 212-363-3500 ext. 15; tauster@afsp.org.

590 ■ AFSP Young Investigator Grants *(Postgraduate/Grant)*

Purpose: To support the work of investigators from all disciplines that contribute to the understanding of suicide and suicide prevention. **Focus:** Suicide. **Qualif.:** Applicant must be at the level of assistant professor or lower. **Criteria:** Awards is given based on the submitted research proposals.

Funds Avail.: $85,000. Additional $10,000 for an established suicide researcher who will mentor the Young Investigator. **To Apply:** Applicants may apply and fill out the application form online. **Deadline:** December 15. **Contact:** Tracy Auster, Research Administrator; 212-363-3500 ext. 15; tauster@afsp.org.

591 ■ American Foundation for Suicide and Prevention Pilot Grants *(Postgraduate/Grant)*

Purpose: To support the work of investigators from all disciplines that contribute to the understanding of suicide and suicide prevention. **Focus:** Suicide. **Qualif.:** Any investigator at any level. **Criteria:** Grants are given based on the submitted research proposals.

Funds Avail.: $30,000. **To Apply:** Applicant may fill out an application form online. **Deadline:** December 15.

592 ■ American Geographical Society

120 Wall St., Ste. 100
New York, NY 10005-3904
Ph: (212)422-5456
Fax: (212)422-5480
E-mail: ags@amergeog.org
URL: http://www.amergeog.org

593 ■ McColl Family Fellowships *(Professional Development/Fellowship)*

Purpose: To promote the study of geology. **Focus:** Geology. **Qualif.:** Applicants must be geographers. **Criteria:** Recipient will be selected by the selection committee.

Funds Avail.: No specific amount. **To Apply:** Applicants must submit a curriculum vitae; a cover letter (maximum of 3 pages); and a statement of the sum request. **Deadline:** October 15. **Contact:** Mary Lynne Bird, 212-422-5456.

594 ■ American GI Forum of San Jose

765 Story Rd.
San Jose, CA 95122
Ph: (408)288-9470
Fax: (408)288-9473
E-mail: sjgif@sjgif.org
URL: http://www.sjgif.org

595 ■ American GI Forum of San Jose Scholarships *(Undergraduate/Scholarship)*

Purpose: To establish a program of financial assistance for qualified students of Hispanic descent that reside in the County of Santa Clara, California. **Focus:** General Studies. **Qualif.:** Applicants must be graduating from a high school located in Santa Clara County; must be enrolled or plan to enroll in an accredited college or university leading to an associate or bachelor's degree; and must have a minimum grade point average of 2.5. **Criteria:** Recipients are selected based on academic achievement, career goals and aspirations, community school activities and financial need.

Funds Avail.: No specific amount. **To Apply:** Applicants must submit completed application form; wallet size senior picture; official copy of high school transcript; biographical data sheet; an autobiographical essay; and a copy of parent's most recent Federal Income Tax or Student Aid Application for California.

596 ■ American Handel Society

School of Music, University of Maryland
College Park, MD 20742
Ph: (909)607-3568
E-mail: info@americanhandelsociety.org
URL: http://www.americanhandelsociety.org

597 ■ J. Merrill Knapp Research Fellowships *(Undergraduate/Fellowship)*

Purpose: To support work in the area of Handel or other related research. **Focus:** General studies. **Qualif.:** Applicant must be students at North American universities and residents of North America. **Criteria:** Preference will be given to advanced graduate student who has not previously held this fellowship.

Funds Avail.: $2,000. **To Apply:** Applicant must submit a curriculum vitae, a description of the project (not to exceed 750 words), a budget showing how and when the applicant plans to use the funds, and a description of other grants applied for or received for the same project; must have two recommendation letters. Application and other materials must be sent to: School of Music, University of Maryland, College Park **Deadline:** March 15. **Contact:** Richard King.

598 ■ American Head and Neck Society

11300 W Olympic Blvd., Ste. 600
Los Angeles, CA 90064
Ph: (310)437-0559
Fax: (310)437-0585

Awards are arranged alphabetically below their administering organizations

E-mail: admin@ahns.info
URL: http://www.ahns.info

599 ■ AHNS-ACS Career Development Awards *(Professional Development/Grant)*

Purpose: To support clinical, basic science or translational researches in neoplastic disease of the head and neck. **Focus:** Medical research. **Qualif.:** Applicants must be members of both ACS and AHNS. **Criteria:** Applicant who is within five years of completion of training, and is a full-time faculty member will receive the award.

Funds Avail.: $40,000. R Two years.

600 ■ AHNS Pilot Research Grants *(Professional Development/Grant)*

Purpose: To support basic, translational or clinical researches in head and neck oncology. **Focus:** Medical research. **Qualif.:** Applicants must be residents, fellows or junior faculty for pilot research in head and neck related topics; must be a resident of U.S. or Canada, medical students, Ph.D.s or faculty members at the rank of associate professor or below. **Criteria:** Recipient is chosen based on reviewed quality of research project.

Funds Avail.: $10,000. **Deadline:** January 15.

601 ■ AHNS Young Investigator Awards *(Professional Development/Grant)*

Purpose: To support clinical, basic science or translational research in the study of neoplastic disease of the head and neck. **Focus:** Medical research. **Qualif.:** Applicants must be AHNS member (may be a candidate member). Also open to fellows and assistant professors. **Criteria:** Priority is given to investigators with outstanding research.

Funds Avail.: $20,000 per year for up to two years. R Two years.

602 ■ Ballantyne Resident Research Grants *(Professional Development/Grant)*

Purpose: To support basic, translational or clinical researches in head and neck oncology. **Focus:** Medical research. **Qualif.:** Applicants must be residents, fellows or junior faculty for pilot research in head and neck related topics; must be a resident of U.S. or Canada; must be medical students, Ph.D.s or faculty members at the rank of associate professor or below. **Criteria:** Recipient is chosen based on ability to meet mentioned criteria and potential of proposed research.

Funds Avail.: $10,000. **Number Awarded:** 1. **Deadline:** January 15.

603 ■ Surgeon Scientist Career Development Awards *(Professional Development/Grant)*

Purpose: To support research in pathogenesis, pathophysiology, diagnosis, prevention, or treatment of head and neck neoplastic disease. **Focus:** Medical research. **Qualif.:** Award is open to surgeons. **Criteria:** Recipient of the award must be a surgeon starting a clinician-scientist career track supporting research in pathogenesis, pathophysiology, diagnosis, prevention, or treatment of head and neck neoplastic disease.

Funds Avail.: $35,000. **Number Awarded:** 1.

604 ■ American Historical Association

400 A St. SE
Washington, DC 20003-3889
Ph: (202)544-2422
Fax: (202)544-8307
E-mail: info@historians.org
URL: http://www.historians.org

605 ■ Fellowships in Aerospace History *(Doctorate/Fellowship)*

Purpose: To provide funding support for a research project related to aerospace history; to encourage engagement in significant and sustained advanced research in all aspects of the history of aerospace from the earliest human interest in flight to the present including cultural and intellectual history, economic history, history of law and public policy, history of science, engineering, and management. **Focus:** History. **Qualif.:** Applicants must possess a doctorate degree in history or in a closely related field, or be enrolled as a student having completed all coursework in a doctoral degree-granting program. **Criteria:** Recipients are selected based on the significance of the research project.

Funds Avail.: $20,000. **To Apply:** Applicants must complete the application form and submit along with seven copies (each copy should contain one application form, proposal and CV, collated and paperclipped together), and a letter of recommendations sealed in a separate envelope. **Deadline:** March 1.

606 ■ The J. Franklin Jameson Fellowship in American History *(Doctorate/Fellowship)*

Purpose: To support significant scholarly research in the collections of the Library Congress for one semester for scholars who are at an early stage in their careers in history. **Focus:** History. **Qualif.:** Applicants must hold a Ph.D. degree or equivalent; must have received this degree within the past seven years; and must have not published or had accepted for publication a book-length historical work. **Criteria:** Recipients are selected based on academic performance.

Funds Avail.: $5,000. **To Apply:** Applicants must submit an original and six copies of complete application including applicant's vita (not more than three to five pages in length), a statement concerning the proposed project and its relationship to the Library of Congress holdings, a tentative schedule for residence of the fellowship, and three letters of recommendation. **Deadline:** March 15.

607 ■ American Hotel and Lodging Educational Foundation

1201 New York Ave. NW., Ste. 600
Washington, DC 20005-3931
Ph: (202)289-3100
Fax: (202)289-3199
E-mail: chammond@ahlef.org
URL: http://www.ahlef.org

608 ■ The AAA (American Automobile Association) Five Diamond Hospitality Scholarships *(Undergraduate/Scholarship)*

Purpose: To provide educational assistance to hospitality management students. **Focus:** Hotel, institutional, and restaurant management. **Qualif.:** Applicants must be enrolled in at least 12 credit hours for the upcoming Fall and Spring semesters; at least a sophomore at the time of nomination; have a minimum 3.0 GPA; and must be U.S. citizens or permanent U.S. residents. **Criteria:** Recipients are selected based on academic performance, hospitality

Awards are arranged alphabetically below their administering organizations

work experience, financial need, extracurricular/professional attributes and honors, as well as personal attributes as defined in their career goal statement.

Funds Avail.: $5,000. **To Apply:** Applicants must complete all the required sections of the application. **Deadline:** May 1.

609 ■ American Express Professional Development Scholarships *(Professional Development/ Scholarship)*

Purpose: To enhance the skills of hospitality professionals. **Focus:** Hotel, institutional, and restaurant management. **Qualif.:** Applicants must be working a minimum of 35-hours per week at an AH&LA member hotel and with at least 12-months hotel experience. If applying for a certification, applicant must qualify for the certification program. **Criteria:** Applicants are selected based on merits, statements and industry-related work experience.

Funds Avail.: $2,000 for full-time enrollment; $1,000 for part-time. **To Apply:** Applicants must submit an application form and attach the appropriate EI distance learning enrollment form or professional certification form. **Deadline:** January 1, April 1, July 1, and October 1.

Remarks: Founded by American Express in 1994. **Contact:** Email Crystal Hammond, manager of the Foundation's programs at chammond@ahlef.org or call 202-289-3188.

610 ■ The American Express Scholarship Competition *(Undergraduate/Scholarship)*

Purpose: To provide educational assistance for current lodging employees and their dependents. **Focus:** Hotel, institutional, and restaurant management. **Qualif.:** Applicants must be enrolled full-time or part-time; must be working a minimum of 20-hours per week at an AH & LA member hotel and with at least 12 months hotel experience. **Criteria:** Recipients are selected based on academic performance, hospitality work experience, financial need, extracurricular/professional attributes and honors, as well as personal attributes as defined in their career goal statement.

Funds Avail.: Baccalaureate Majors - $2,000 full-time enrollment; or $1,000 part-time; Associate Majors - $1,000 full-time enrollment; or $500 part- time. **To Apply:** Applicants must complete all the required sections of the application. **Deadline:** May 1.

Remarks: Founded by American Express in 1994. **Contact:** Crystal Hammond, manager of the Foundation's programs, at chammond@ahlef.org.

611 ■ The Hyatt Hotels Fund For Minority Lodging Management Students *(Undergraduate/ Scholarship)*

Purpose: To provide financial aid to minority students pursuing a degree in hotel management. **Focus:** Hotel, institutional, and restaurant management. **Qualif.:** Applicant must be enrolled in at least 12 credit hours for the upcoming Fall and Spring semesters, or just the Fall semester if graduating this December; at least a sophomore in a four-year program at the time of application; a minority descent: African-American, Hispanic, American Indian, Alaskan Native, Asian or Pacific Islander; a U.S. citizen or permanent U.S. resident. **Criteria:** Recipients are selected based on academic performance, hospitality work experience, financial need, extracurricular/professional attributes and honors, as well as personal attributes as defined in their career goal statement.

Funds Avail.: $2,000. **Number Awarded:** 18. **To Apply:** Applicants must complete all the required sections of the application. **Deadline:** May 1.

Remarks: Established by Hyatt in 1988.

612 ■ The Steve Hymans Extended Stay Scholarship Program *(Undergraduate/Scholarship)*

Purpose: To provide educational assistance to hospitality management students. **Focus:** Hotel, institutional, and restaurant management. **Qualif.:** Applicant must be enrolled full-time or part-time; have a minimum of 3.0 GPA; be a U.S. citizen or permanent U.S. resident; and have at least some experience either working or interning (paid or unpaid) at a lodging property. **Criteria:** Applicants with experience at an extended stay property will be given preference.

Funds Avail.: Baccalaureate Majors - $2,000 full-time enrollment; or $1,000 part-time. Associate Majors - $1,000 full-time enrollment; or $500 part-time. **To Apply:** Applicants must complete all the required sections of the application. **Deadline:** May 1.

Remarks: Established in honor of Steve Hymans.

613 ■ Lodging Management Program (LMP) Scholarships *(Undergraduate/Scholarship)*

Purpose: To provide educational assistance to students pursuing a degree in hospitality-related degree programs. **Focus:** Hotel, institutional, and restaurant management. **Qualif.:** Applicants must be graduating high school seniors and have completed Year 1 and 2 of the LMP; must have a minimum 2.0 GPA. **Criteria:** Awards are given based on merit.

Funds Avail.: $1,000 per scholarship. **To Apply:** Applications are self nominated which means students do not have to attend a particular school or be nominated by their respective schools. Applicants must complete all sections of the AH&LEF scholarship application form. **Contact:** Email Crystal Hammond, manager of the Foundation's programs, at chammond@ahlef.org.

614 ■ The Arthur J. Packard Memorial Scholarship Competition *(Undergraduate/Scholarship)*

Purpose: To provide educational assistance for lodging management students. **Focus:** Hotel, institutional, and restaurant management. **Qualif.:** Applicants must be enrolled full-time for the upcoming Fall and Spring semesters; have a minimum GPA of 3.5 or higher; and must be U.S. residents. **Criteria:** Recipients are selected based on academic performance, hospitality work experience, financial need, extracurricular/professional attributes and honors, as well as personal attributes as defined in their career goal statement.

Funds Avail.: First-place winner $5,000; Second-place $3,000; Third-place $2,000. **To Apply:** Applicants must complete all the required sections of the application. **Deadline:** May 1.

Remarks: Established in honor of Arthur J. Packard. **Contact:** Crystal Hammond at 202-289-3188 or chammond@ahlef.org.

615 ■ Pepsi Scholarships *(Undergraduate/ Scholarship)*

Purpose: To provide educational assistance to students pursuing a degree in hospitality-related degree programs. **Focus:** Hotel, institutional, and restaurant management.

Awards are arranged alphabetically below their administering organizations

Qualif.: Applicants must be graduates of the Hospitality High School in Washington, D.C.; enrolled in at least 12 credit hours for the upcoming Fall and Spring semesters; worked at least 250 hours in the hotel/hospitality industry; and have a minimum 2.5 GPA. **Criteria:** Recipients are selected based on academic performance, hospitality work experience, financial need, extracurricular/professional attributes and honors, as well as personal attributes as defined in their career goal statement.

Funds Avail.: $500-$3,000 depending upon enrollment. Funds must be used exclusively for tuition, fees and books. **To Apply:** Applicants must complete all the required sections of the application. **Deadline:** May 1.

Remarks: Created by PepsiCo Foundation. **Contact:** 202-312-2007.

616 ■ Rama Scholarships for the American Dream *(Graduate, Undergraduate/Scholarship)*

Purpose: To provide educational assistance to lodging management students. **Focus:** Hotel, institutional, and restaurant management. **Qualif.:** Applicants must be enrolled in at least 9-credit hours for the upcoming Fall and Spring semesters or just the Fall semester if graduating in December; undergraduate or graduate hospitality management majors; have a minimum 2.5 GPA; be U.S. citizens or permanent U.S. residents. **Criteria:** Applicants who are students of Asian-Indian descent and other minority groups, as well as JHM employees and their dependents will be given preference.

Funds Avail.: $1,000-$3,000. **To Apply:** Applicants must complete all the required sections of the application. **Deadline:** May 1.

Remarks: Established by JHM Hotels, Inc. **Contact:** Crystal Hammond at 202-289-3188 or email at chammond@ahlef.org.

617 ■ American Indian College Fund

8333 Greenwood Blvd.
Denver, CO 80221
Ph: (303)426-8900
Fax: (303)426-1200
Free: 800-776-3863
E-mail: info@collegefund.org
URL: http://www.collegefund.org

618 ■ Cartwright Scholarships Program *(Undergraduate/Scholarship)*

Purpose: To provide financial assistance for American Indian students who are pursuing postsecondary education. **Focus:** General studies. **Qualif.:** Applicants must be male students who have at least a 3.0 grade point average; must commit to mentoring other male students and encouraging them to attend college; must be American Indian or Alaskan Native with proof of enrollment or descendancy; must be enrolled full-time at an eligible tribal college; and must have demonstrated exceptional academic achievement and financial need. **Criteria:** Selection will be based on criteria.

Funds Avail.: $2,000. **To Apply:** Applicants must check the available website for the required materials and for the online application process.

Remarks: In 2004, Dorwin "Doc" and Barbara Cartwright's passion for education compelled them to establish an endowment through the American Indian College Fund. **Contact:** American Indian College Fund at the above address (see entry 617).

619 ■ Citi Foundation Scholarships Program *(Undergraduate/Scholarship)*

Purpose: To provide students with exposure to career options, leadership skills and information on the education and commitment necessary to succeed in the business world. **Focus:** General studies. **Qualif.:** Applicants must have at least a 3.0 grade point average; must commit to organizing and participating in a career exploration day; must be American Indian or Alaskan Native with proof of enrollment or descendancy; must be enrolled full-time at an eligible tribal college; and must have demonstrated exceptional academic achievement and financial need. **Criteria:** Preference will be given to those students who meet the criteria.

Funds Avail.: $4,000. **To Apply:** Applicants must check the available website for the required materials and for the application process online. **Contact:** American Indian College Fund at the above address (see entry 617).

620 ■ Coca-Cola First Generation Scholarships *(Undergraduate/Scholarship)*

Purpose: To provide financial assistance for students who are in need. **Focus:** General studies. **Qualif.:** Applicants must have at least a 3.0 grade point average; must be in first or second semester of college; must be the first member of their immediate family to attend college; must be American Indian or Alaskan Native with proof of enrollment or descendancy; must be enrolled full-time at an eligible tribal college; and must have demonstrated exceptional academic achievement and financial need. **Criteria:** Preference will be given to those students who meet the criteria.

Funds Avail.: $5,000. **To Apply:** Applicants must check the available website for the application process online and for the required materials. **Contact:** American Indian College Fund at the above address (see entry 617).

621 ■ Vine Deloria Jr. Memorial Scholarships *(Graduate/Scholarship)*

Purpose: To provide financial support for outstanding American Indian students who are pursuing a graduate degree. **Focus:** General studies. **Qualif.:** Applicants must be pursuing an advanced degree (MA, MS, J.D., Ph.D., MD, other); must be able to demonstrate financial need; and must be American Indian or Alaskan Native with proof of enrollment or descendancy. **Criteria:** Preference will be given to students who meet the criteria.

Funds Avail.: No specific amount. **To Apply:** Applicants must check the available website to download the application form. **Contact:** American Indian College Fund at the above address (see entry 617).

622 ■ General Mills Foundation Scholarships *(Undergraduate/Scholarship)*

Purpose: To provide need-based scholarships for outstanding American Indian students who are currently enrolled at a tribal college in Minnesota or New Mexico. **Focus:** General studies. **Qualif.:** Applicants must have at least a 2.5 grade point average; must be American Indian or Alaskan Native with proof of enrollment or descendancy; must be enrolled full-time at an eligible Minnesota or New Mexico tribal college; and must have demonstrated exceptional academic achievement and financial need. **Cri-**

teria: Preference will be given to those who meet the criteria.

Funds Avail.: $2,000. **To Apply:** Applicants must check the available website for the required materials. **Contact:** American Indian College Fund at the above address (see entry 617).

623 ■ Hilton Tribal College Diversity Scholarships *(Undergraduate/Scholarship)*

Purpose: To award need-based scholarships to outstanding American Indian youth who will be entering freshmen at a tribal college. **Focus:** General studies. **Qualif.:** Applicants must have at least a 3.0 grade point average; must be high school graduates; must be American Indian or Alaskan Native with proof of enrollment or descendancy; must be enrolled full-time at an eligible tribal college; and must have demonstrated exceptional academic achievement and financial need. **Criteria:** Preference will be given to those students who meet the criteria.

Funds Avail.: $2,500. **To Apply:** Applicants must check the available website to fill out the application form online. **Contact:** American Indian College Fund at the above address (see entry 617).

624 ■ Nissan North America, Inc. Scholarships *(Undergraduate/Scholarship)*

Purpose: To award scholarships to outstanding American Indian students who are currently enrolled in tribal colleges. **Focus:** General studies. **Qualif.:** Applicants must have at least a 2.5 grade point average; must be enrolled full-time at an eligible tribal college; must be American Indian or Alaskan Native with proof of enrollment or descendancy; and must have demonstrated exceptional academic achievement. **Criteria:** Preference will be given to students who meet the criteria.

Funds Avail.: $3,000. **To Apply:** Applicants must check the available website to download the application form. **Contact:** American Indian College Fund at the above address (see entry 617).

625 ■ Sovereign Nations Scholarship Fund *(Undergraduate/Scholarship)*

Purpose: To award scholarships to American Indian students who are enrolled in a tribal college. **Focus:** General studies. **Qualif.:** Applicants must have demonstrated exceptional academic achievement by maintaining a 3.0 or higher G.P.A.; must commit to working for their tribe or an Indian organization upon completion of their degree; must be enrolled full-time at an eligible tribal college; and must be American Indian or Alaskan Native with proof of enrollment or descendancy. **Criteria:** Preference will be given to those students who meet the criteria.

Funds Avail.: $2,000. **To Apply:** Applicants must check the available website for the application process online. **Contact:** American Indian College Fund at the above address (see entry 617).

626 ■ Morgan Stanley Tribal Scholars Program *(Undergraduate/Scholarship)*

Purpose: To award scholarships to outstanding American Indian students who are currently enrolled at a tribal college and who have an interest in business or the financial services industry. **Focus:** Business or related field. **Qualif.:** Applicants must have at least a 3.0 grade point average; must have declared a major in business or a related field; must be enrolled full-time at an eligible tribal college; must be American Indian or Alaskan Native with proof of enrollment or descendancy; and must have demonstrated exceptional academic achievement. **Criteria:** Preference will be given to those students who meet the criteria.

Funds Avail.: $2,500. **To Apply:** Applicants must check the available website to download the application form. **Contact:** American Indian College Fund at the above address (see entry 617).

627 ■ Time Warner Tribal Scholars Program *(Undergraduate/Scholarship)*

Purpose: To award scholarships for outstanding American Indian students who are enrolled in a tribal college. **Focus:** General studies. **Qualif.:** Applicants must have at least a 2.5 grade point average; must be enrolled full time at an eligible tribal college; and must be American Indian or Alaskan Native with proof of enrollment or descendancy. **Criteria:** Preference will be given to students who meet the criteria.

Funds Avail.: $2,500. **To Apply:** Applicants must check the available website to download the application form. **Contact:** American Indian College Fund at the above address (see entry 617).

628 ■ Woksape Oyate: "Wisdom of the People" Distinguished Scholars Award *(Undergraduate/Scholarship)*

Purpose: To award a scholarship to the best and the brightest American Indian student attending a tribal college. **Focus:** General studies. **Qualif.:** Program is open to valedictorians or salutatorians of their high school class; must be American Indian or Alaskan Native with proof of enrollment or descendancy; must be enrolled full-time at an eligible tribal college; and must have demonstrated exceptional academic achievement. **Criteria:** Preference will be given to students who meet the criteria.

Funds Avail.: $8,000. **Number Awarded:** 1. **To Apply:** Applicants must check the available website to download the application form. **Contact:** American Indian College Fund at the above address (see entry 617).

629 ■ American Indian Education Foundation

2401 Eglin St.
Rapid City, SD 57703
Ph: (866)866-8642
Fax: (605)342-4113
Free: (866)866-8642
E-mail: info@programs.org
URL: http://www.nrcprograms.org

630 ■ Association on American Indian Affairs Emergency Aid Scholarship *(Undergraduate/Scholarship)*

Purpose: To award scholarship to Native American undergraduates of any major. **Focus:** General studies. **Qualif.:** Applicants must be enrolled members of a federally recognized tribe. **Criteria:** Awards will be given based on financial need and severity of the emergency.

Funds Avail.: $100-$400. **Number Awarded:** 20. **To Apply:** Applicants must: complete AIEF Scholarship Application; provide documentation of tribal enrollment for themselves or their parents; provide transcripts with ACT and GPA scores; attach an essay that outlines the following information: introduction, academics, career plans, service

Awards are arranged alphabetically below their administering organizations

to the Native American community, leadership/community service, financial needs and unique circumstances. **Deadline:** April 4. **Contact:** Association on American Indian Affairs, ENA Scholarship, 966 Hungerford Dr. Ste. 12 B Rockeville, MD 20850. 240-314-7155.

631 ■ Brown Foundation College Scholarship *(Undergraduate/Scholarship)*

Purpose: To award scholarship to the students of Native American ancestry wishing to attend college. **Focus:** Education. **Qualif.:** Applicants must be students wishing to attend college and major in education. **Criteria:** Selection will be based on the committee's criteria.

Funds Avail.: $1,000. **Number Awarded:** 10. **To Apply:** Applicants must: complete AIEF Scholarship Application; provide documentation of tribal enrollment for themselves or their parents; provide transcripts with ACT and GPA scores; attach an essay that outlines the following information: introduction, academics, career plans, service to the Native American community, leadership/community service, financial needs and unique circumstances. **Deadline:** April 4. **Contact:** Brown Foundation Scholarship Program, 1515 SE Monroe, Topeka, KS 66612; Phone: 785-235-3939; brownfoundation@juno.com.

632 ■ Catching the Dream Scholarship *(Graduate, Undergraduate/Scholarship)*

Purpose: To give American Indian students the tools, resources and opportunities to learn and succeed. **Focus:** Education; Business; Science; Engineering. **Qualif.:** Applicants must be enrolled members of a federally recognized tribe; both undergraduate and graduate students may apply. **Criteria:** Selection will be based on the committee's criteria.

Funds Avail.: $500-$5,000. **To Apply:** Applicants may submit an application to the Scholarship Affairs Office of Catching the Dream. **Deadline:** March 15-Summer; April 15-Fall; September 15-spring. **Contact:** Catching the Dream 8200 Mountain Rd. NE Ste. 203 Albuquerque, NM 87110; 505-262-2351 x 116; nscholarsh@aol.com.

633 ■ Daughters of the American Revolution American Indian Scholarships *(Undergraduate/Scholarship)*

Purpose: To give American Indian students the tools, resources and opportunities to learn and succeed. **Focus:** General studies. **Qualif.:** Applicants must be: Native Americans who can show proof of ancestry; undergraduate or graduate students who have a GPA of 2.75 or higher; may be in any major. **Criteria:** Selection will be based on the committee's criteria.

Funds Avail.: $500. **Number Awarded:** 60. **To Apply:** Applicants must submit an application to the American Indian Scholarship, 1776 D St. NW Washington, DC 20006-5303; 202-628-1776; www.dar.org. **Deadline:** April 1.

634 ■ Indian Health Service Scholarship Program *(Undergraduate/Scholarship)*

Purpose: To give American Indian students the tools, resources and opportunities to learn and succeed. **Focus:** Health sciences. **Qualif.:** Applicants must be enrolled members of state or federally recognized tribes; must be undergraduate or graduate students who are majoring in any health-related pre-professional program. **Criteria:** Selection will be based on the committee's criteria.

Funds Avail.: No specific amount. **To Apply:** Applicants may submit their application to the Foundation or to the Indian Health Service Scholarship Program 801 Thompson Ave. Ste. 120 Rockville, MD 20852; 301-443-6197. **Deadline:** February.

635 ■ International Order of the King's Daughters and Sons North American Indian Scholarship Program *(Undergraduate/Scholarship)*

Purpose: To give American Indian students the tools, resources and opportunities to learn and succeed. **Focus:** General studies. **Qualif.:** Applicants must be: Native Americans who have (or whose parents have) a reservation number; undergraduates of any major. **Criteria:** Selection will be based on the committee's criteria.

Funds Avail.: $650. **To Apply:** Applicants must: complete AIEF Scholarship Application; provide documentation of tribal enrollment for themselves or their parents; provide transcripts with ACT and GPA scores; attach an essay that outlines the following information: introduction, academics, career plans, service to the Native American community, leadership/community service, financial needs and unique circumstances. **Deadline:** April 1. **Contact:** International Order of the King's Daughters and Sons. Attn: Director, North American Indian Department PO Box 1040 Chautauqua, NY 14722-1040; 716-357-4951.

636 ■ Native American Education Grants *(Graduate, Undergraduate/Grant)*

Purpose: To give American Indian students the tools, resources and opportunities to learn and succeed. **Focus:** General studies. **Qualif.:** Applicants must be: enrolled members of federally recognized tribes; undergraduate or graduate students of any major. **Criteria:** Selection will be based on the committee's criteria.

Funds Avail.: $200-$3,000. **To Apply:** Applicants must: complete AIEF Scholarship Application; provide documentation of tribal enrollment for themselves or their parents; provide transcripts with ACT and GPA scores; attach an essay that outlines the following information: introduction, academics, career plans, service to the Native American community, leadership/community service, financial needs and unique circumstances. **Deadline:** June 1. **Contact:** Frances Cook, Native American Education Grants, Presbyterian Church-USA, 100 Witherspoon St. Rm M052B, Louisville, KY 40202; 888-728-7228 x 5776.

637 ■ Jackie Robinson Foundation Minority Scholarship *(Undergraduate/Scholarship)*

Purpose: To give American Indian students the tools, resources and opportunities to learn and succeed. **Focus:** General studies. **Qualif.:** Applicants must be high school seniors entering an accredited college or university as freshmen. **Criteria:** Selection will be based on the committee's criteria.

Funds Avail.: $6,000. **To Apply:** Applicants must: complete AIEF Scholarship Application; provide documentation of tribal enrollment for themselves or their parents; provide transcripts with ACT and GPA scores; attach an essay that outlines the following information: introduction, academics, career plans, service to the Native American community, leadership/community service, financial needs and unique circumstances. **Deadline:** April 1. **Contact:** Jackie Robinson Foundation, Attn: Scholarship Coordinator, 3 W 35th St. 11th Fl. New York, NY 10001; 212-290-8600; www.jackierobinson.org.

Awards are arranged alphabetically below their administering organizations

638 ■ U.S. BIA Indian Higher Education Grants *(Undergraduate/Grant)*

Purpose: To give American Indian Students the tools, resources and opportunities to learn and succeed. **Focus:** General studies. **Qualif.:** Applicants must be: Native American undergraduate students of any major; enrolled in a federally recognized tribe. **Criteria:** Awards will be given based on financial need.

Funds Avail.: $300-$900. **To Apply:** Applicants must: complete AIEF Scholarship Application; provide documentation of tribal enrollment for themselves or their parents; provide transcripts with ACT and GPA scores; attach an essay that outlines the following information: introduction, academics, career plans, service to the Native American community, leadership/community service, financial needs and unique circumstances. Applicants may contact their tribe's education office for more information.

639 ■ American Indian Graduate Center Scholars (AIGCS)

4520 Montgomery Blvd., NE, Ste. 1B
Albuquerque, NM 87109
Ph: (505)881-4584
Free: 800-628-1920
URL: http://www.aigc.com

640 ■ Accenture American Indian Scholarship Program *(Graduate, Undergraduate/Scholarship)*

Purpose: To provide financial assistance to undergraduate and graduate American Indians in furthering their education. **Focus:** Technology; Engineering; Medicine; Law; Business. **Qualif.:** Applicants must be American Indians who are incoming freshmen with a cumulative GPA of 3.25 or greater on a 4.0 scale at the end of the seventh semester of high school or graduates/professionals who have attained a cumulative GPA of 3.25 or greater on a 4.0 scale, as measured by undergraduate transcripts; must be enrolled members of a U.S. federally-recognized American Indian tribe or Alaska Native group; must be seeking a degree and career in fields of study including technology, engineering, medicine, law, and business. **Criteria:** Applicants are evaluated on the basis of demonstrated character; personal merit evident through leadership in school, civic and extracurricular activities, academic achievement and motivation to serve and succeed; and commitment to the American Indian Community, locally and/or nationally.

Funds Avail.: No specific amount. **To Apply:** Applicants must submit completed application form; copy of certificate of Indian Blood (CIB); unofficial undergraduate and/or graduate academic transcripts; biographical data and/or resume; essay describing their character, personal merit and commitment to community and heritage; two personal letters of recommendation (one must come from an education professional who is familiar with their academic work and the other one must come from an individual having knowledge of their leadership and community service activities); and financial aid award letter from the institution they will attend. **Deadline:** June 2.

641 ■ AIGC Fellowship for Graduates *(Graduate/Fellowship)*

Purpose: To provide financial assistance to Native Americans and Alaska Native graduates or professional degree-seeking students in furthering their education. **Focus:** General studies. **Qualif.:** Applicants must be pursuing a post-baccalaureate graduate or professional degree as full-time students at an accredited institution in the U.S.; must be enrolled members of a federally-recognized American Indian or Alaska Native group, or provide documentation of descendency; must possess one-fourth federally-recognized Indian blood. **Criteria:** Recipients are selected based on financial need.

Funds Avail.: $1,000 up to $5,000. **To Apply:** Applicants must submit all the required application information including the Tribal Eligibility Certificate and Financial Need Form.

642 ■ BIE-Loan for Service for Graduates *(Graduate/Loan)*

Purpose: To provide financial assistance to eligible American Indians and Alaska Natives seeking graduate and professional degrees. **Focus:** General studies. **Qualif.:** Applicant must be an enrolled member of a United States federally-recognized American Indian tribe or Alaska Native group, or possess one-fourth federally-recognized Indian blood; must have 3.0 grade point average; and must be pursuing a graduate or a professional degree as a full-time student at an accredited institution in the United States. **Criteria:** Applicants are evaluated based on financial need.

Funds Avail.: No specific amount. **To Apply:** Applicants must submit all the required application information. **Deadline:** July 9.

643 ■ Wall-Mart Stores, Inc. Fellowships - Graduate *(Undergraduate/Scholarship)*

Purpose: To provide financial assistance to American Indian tribe or Alaska Native group in furthering their education. **Focus:** Banking; Gaming industry; Management; Accounting; Finance; Information science and technology; Human resource.s **Qualif.:** Applicants must be enrolled members of a United States federally-recognized American Indian tribe or Alaska Native group; pursuing a career and degree in fields relating to banking, resort management, gaming operations, management and administration, including accounting, finance, information technology, and human resources. Full-time graduate students at U.S. accredited colleges or universities with a cumulative GPA of 3.0 on 4.0 scale at the time of application are eligible. **Criteria:** Applicants are evaluated based on financial need.

Funds Avail.: No specific amount. **To Apply:** Applicants must submit all the required application information.

644 ■ Wells Fargo American Indian Scholarship for Graduates *(Graduate/Scholarship)*

Purpose: To provide financial assistance to American Indian graduates in furthering their education. **Focus:** Banking; Gaming industry; Management; Accounting; Finance; Information science and technology. **Qualif.:** Applicants must be enrolled members of a United States federally-recognized American Indian tribe or Alaska Native group; must be pursuing career and degree fields relating to banking, resort management, gaming operations, management and administration, including accounting, finance, information technology and human resources; must be full-time graduate students at a U.S. accredited college or university; and must have a cumulative average GPA of 3.0 on a 4.0 scale at the time of application. **Criteria:** Applicants are evaluated based on financial need.

Funds Avail.: No specific amount. **To Apply:** Applicants must submit all the required application information.

Awards are arranged alphabetically below their administering organizations

645 ■ American Institute of Aeronautics and Astronautics Foundation

1801 Alexander Bell Drive, Ste. 500
Reston, VA 20194-4344
Ph: (703)264-7500
Fax: (703)264-7551
Free: 800-639-AIAA
E-mail: ceciliac@aiaa.org
URL: http://www.aiaa.org

646 ■ AIAA Foundation Scholarship Program *(Undergraduate/Scholarship)*

Purpose: To advance the arts, sciences, and technology of aeronautics and astronautics. **Focus:** Aeronautics; Astronautics. **Qualif.:** Applicant must: have completed at least one academic quarter or semester of full-time college work; have a college GPA of not less than the equivalent of a 3.3 on a 4.0 scale; be enrolled in an accredited college or university. Applicant does not have to be an AIAA student member in good standing to apply, but must become one before receiving a scholarship. Applicant's scholarship plan shall be such as to provide entry into some field of science or engineering encompassed by the technical activities of AIAA. Applicants shall not have, or subsequently receive, any other scholarship/award which, when combined with the AIAA Foundation award covers more than the cost of tuition. Applicant may be students of any nationality, not restricted by the US State Department, in full-time study at any accredited college or university within the United States. **Criteria:** Selection will be based on the committee's criteria.

Funds Avail.: No specific amount. **To Apply:** The completed application must be received on or before the deadline. Students submitting their applications should include the essay and also make arrangements to have their official college transcripts sent directly to AIAA. Sophomore and junior students who have received one of these scholarship awards and wish to be considered for continuation of this award should arrange to have transcripts of their college academic record, and letters of recommendation from their faculty members and others supporting their continuance in the program sent to AIAA. **Deadline:** January 31.

647 ■ American Institute of Architecture Students

1735 New York Ave. NW
Washington, DC 20006
Ph: (202)626-7472
Fax: (202)626-7414
E-mail: mailbox@aias.org
URL: http://www.aias.org

648 ■ AIAS/AIA Trust Scholarships for Emerging Professionals *(Postgraduate/Scholarship)*

Purpose: To assist financially-challenged students in paying their tuition and/or direct educational expenses. **Focus:** Architecture. **Qualif.:** Applicants must be enrolled in a National Architectural Accrediting Board (NAAB) accredited program; must be in the fifth year of an undergraduate professional degree or the first year of a graduate professional degree; must have a minimum GPA of 3.0 on a 4.0 scale or "B" average in the architecture program; must have a full-time status; and must be U.S. citizens or permanent residents. **Criteria:** Recipients are selected based on eligibility, financial need, intent to continue education in architectural studies, intent to seek a career as a licensed architect, and thoroughness and quality of the essay.

Funds Avail.: $750. **Number Awarded:** 6. **To Apply:** Applicants must provide evidence of financial need in the written applicant review; documentation including the result page of the Streamlined Expected Family Contribution and certification from the academic institution that the applicant qualifies for the participation in an educational assistance program; proof of enrollment and year in school; and an essay. **Deadline:** December 14. **Contact:** scholarship@aias.org.

649 ■ American Institute of Baking

PO Box 3999
Manhattan, KS 66505-3999
Ph: (785)537-4750
Fax: (785)537-1493
URL: http://www.aibonline.org

650 ■ American Institute of Baking Scholarships *(Undergraduate/Scholarship)*

Purpose: To support self-sponsored students in attending AIB's 20-week Baking Science and Technology course and/or its 11-week Maintenance Engineering course. **Focus:** Food science and technology. **Qualif.:** Applicants must be company-sponsored or self-sponsored students. **Criteria:** Recipients will be selected by a committee of AIB faculty and staff based on his/her educational background, three submitted letters of recommendation, and work experience relative to the baking and food industries.

Funds Avail.: $500. **To Apply:** Applicant must submit a complete application form and three letters of recommendation.

651 ■ American Institute of Bangladesh Studies

South Asia Center - 820 Williams Hall
36th and Spruce Sts. University of Pennsylvania
Philadelphia, PA 19104-6305
Ph: (215)898-7475
Fax: (215)573-2138
E-mail: gwelbon@ccat.sas.upenn.edu
URL: http://www.aibs.net

652 ■ AIBS Junior Fellowships *(Doctorate/Fellowship)*

Purpose: To financially support a junior research fellowship in Bangladesh. **Focus:** General studies. **Qualif.:** Applicants must be U.S. citizens or permanent residents; must be in the ABD phase of their Ph.D. programs; and must be in the stage of data collection and writing. **Criteria:** Recipients are selected based on the submitted applications and supporting materials.

Funds Avail.: Round trip transportation, $800, and allowances per month. **To Apply:** Applicants must send five copies each of: application form (available on the website); curriculum vitae (maximum of 3 pages); and research proposal (maximum of 10 pages). **Deadline:** February.

653 ■ AIBS Senior Fellowships *(Doctorate, Postdoctorate/Fellowship)*

Purpose: To financially support a senior research fellowship in Bangladesh. **Focus:** General studies. **Qualif.:** Ap-

Awards are arranged alphabetically below their administering organizations

plicants must be U.S. citizens or permanent residents; must have a Ph.D. degree. **Criteria:** Recipients are selected based on the submitted applications and supporting materials.

Funds Avail.: Round trip transportation, $1,000 and allowances per month. **To Apply:** Applicants must send five copies each of: application form (available at the website); curriculum vitae (maximum of 3 pages); and research proposal (maximum of 10 pages). **Deadline:** February.

654 ■ American Institute of Chemical Engineers

3 Park Ave.
New York, NY 10016-5991
Ph: (203)702-7660
Fax: (203)775-5177
Free: 800-242-4363
URL: http://www.aiche.org

655 ■ AIChE/Donald F. and Mildred Topp Othmer National Scholarship Awards *(Undergraduate/Scholarship)*

Purpose: To provide financial assistance for AIChE national student members for their undergraduate education in chemical engineering. **Focus:** Engineering, Chemical. **Qualif.:** Nominees must be AIChE national student members at the time of the nomination. **Criteria:** Recipients are selected based on academic record; participation in AIChE Student Chapter and other professional activities as outlined by the Student Chapter Advisor in their nomination letter; support of the nominee by the Student Chapter Advisor; and nominees' career objectives and plans as outlined in their letter.

Funds Avail.: $15,000. **To Apply:** Nominators must submit completed nomination form; letter of nomination from the AIChE Student Chapter Advisor containing, but not limited to, the following: a) verification of the nominees' GPAs and projected completion date; b) an evaluation of the nominees' academic performance and participation in AIChE Student Chapter and other professional activities; statement from the nominees (not to exceed 300 words) outlining their career plans and objectives in chemical engineering and including, but not limited to, the following: a) immediate plans after graduation and area(s) of chemical engineering of most interest; b) long-range career objectives. **Deadline:** May 16.

656 ■ John J. McKetta Undergraduate Scholarships *(Undergraduate/Scholarship)*

Purpose: To provide financial assistance for chemical engineering undergraduate students planning a career in the chemical engineering process industries. **Focus:** Engineering, Chemical. **Qualif.:** Nominees must be national student members of AIChE attending an ABET accredited schools in the US, Canada or Mexico who are in their junior or senior year of a 4-year program in Chemical Engineering or equivalent for a 5-year co-op program. Nominees must have maintained a minimum of 3.0/4.0 GPA. **Criteria:** Preference is given to nominees from Mexican universities participating in ABET's Equivalent Education Program.

Funds Avail.: $5,000. **To Apply:** Nominees must submit a maximum two-page essay outlining career goals in the chemical engineering process industries (2 single-sided, single-spaced typed pages) and nominations must be accompanied by a minimum of two letters of recommendation, one from AIChE student advisor and the other from either a departmental faculty member or technical work supervisor. **Deadline:** May 30.

657 ■ Minority Scholarship Awards for College Students *(Undergraduate/Scholarship)*

Purpose: To provide educational assistance for chemical engineering undergraduate students. **Focus:** Engineering, Chemical. **Qualif.:** Applicants must be AIChE national student members at the time of application. **Criteria:** Selection of recipients will be based on academic record, participation in AIChE student and professional activities, career objectives and financial need.

Funds Avail.: No specific amount. **Number Awarded:** 10. **To Apply:** Nominations must be submitted containing the following items: from the students: a) a completed application form; b) a career essay not to exceed 300 words outlining the following: immediate plans after graduation and area(s) of chemical engineering of most interest; long-range career objectives; official transcript of college grades. Nominations from the college financial aid office must contain: a letter indicating that the student is eligible for financial aid based on their records; a letter of recommendation from the AIChE student chapter advisor, department chair, or chemical engineering faculty member containing, but not limited to, the following: verification of nominee's GPA and projected completion date; evaluation of the student's academic performance and participation in AIChE and other professional or civic activities. **Deadline:** May 15.

658 ■ Minority Scholarship Awards for Incoming College Freshmen *(Undergraduate/Scholarship)*

Purpose: To provide educational assistance for chemical engineering college freshmen. **Focus:** Engineering, Chemical. **Qualif.:** Applicants must be members of a minority group (i.e. African-American, Hispanic, Native American, or Alaskan Native) that is underrepresented in chemical engineering; must be high school graduates during the previous academic year and plan to enroll during the following academic year in a four-year university offering a science/engineering degree. **Criteria:** Recipients are selected based on academic record, participation in school and work activities, reason for choosing science or engineering, and financial need.

Funds Avail.: $1,000. **Number Awarded:** 10. **To Apply:** Nominations must be submitted containing the following items from the student: a) completed application form; b) career essay not to exceed 300 words outlining the following: (1) college or university chosen to attend, (2) reasons for choosing science/engineering, (3) possible career choices that may be of interest; c) official transcript of high school grades. Nominations must also include documents from the parent/guardian which should contain a letter verifying financial need which includes a list of financial resources for educational support; and a letter of recommendation from the high school counselor, math teacher or science teacher containing, but not limited to, the following: a) verification of student's GPA and graduation date; b) verification of high school senior class average grade (if confidential, high school counselor statement is required); c) confirmation of minority group of student; d) information about the student's school, job and/or other activities. **Deadline:** May 15.

659 ■ American Institute for Conservation of the Historic and Artistic Works

1156 15th St. NW, Ste. 320
Washington, DC 20005-1714

Awards are arranged alphabetically below their administering organizations

Ph: (202)452-9545
Fax: (202)452-9328
E-mail: info@aic-faic.org
URL: http://www.aic.stanford.edu

660 ■ FAIC Latin American and Caribbean Scholars Program *(Professional Development/ Scholarship)*

Purpose: To provide financial support for conservation professionals from Latin America and the Caribbean to participate in the annual meeting. **Focus:** Latin American Studies. **Qualif.:** Applicants must be Latin American. **Criteria:** Recipients are selected based on financial need.

Funds Avail.: No specific amount. **To Apply:** Applicants must complete the application form and submit a curriculum vitae and an essay. **Deadline:** October 15. **Contact:** becas@aic-faic.org.

661 ■ Foundation of American Institute for Conservation Lecture Grants *(Professional Development/Grant)*

Purpose: To provide funds and presentations of public lectures to help advance public awareness of conservation. **Focus:** Latin American Studies. **Qualif.:** Applicants must be Latin American. **Criteria:** Recipients are selected based on the ability of the project to advance public awareness of conservation; number of people reached, other project outcomes; speaker's ability to communicate the proposed topic; and feasibility of project.

Funds Avail.: $500. **To Apply:** Applicants must complete the online application form and are asked to wait for the application packet that will be sent by the award committee. **Deadline:** February 15.

662 ■ American Institute of Iranian Studies

118 Riverside Dr.
New York, NY 10024
E-mail: aiis@nyc.rr.com
URL: http://www.simorgh-aiis.org

663 ■ Persian Language Study in Tehran *(Doctorate, Graduate/Fellowship)*

Purpose: To help graduate students with advanced learning in Persian studies. **Focus:** Humanities; Social sciences. **Qualif.:** Applicants should be U.S. citizens enrolled in a doctoral program in humanities or social sciences; must have an approved research topic that requires use of Persian, and must have completed at least one full academic year of Persian language study. **Criteria:** Mastery of Persian language study is not required but could be prioritized.

Funds Avail.: Covers the cost of international air travel, tuition, board, and lodging. **To Apply:** Applications must include a letter-form curriculum vitae, with the following information: citizenship, research plans, level of Persian study attained, academic affiliation, and status. Recommendation letters mentioning the relevance of Persian study to the dissertation should be sent directly to AIIrS. Applications must be sent to aiis@nyc.rr.com or mailed to Dr. Erica Ehrenberg. **Deadline:** January 10 and 15. **Contact:** Dr. Erica Ehrenberg, executive Director.

664 ■ Research Fellowships in Iranian Studies (Resident Director-Tehran) *(Doctorate, Graduate/ Fellowship)*

Purpose: To help graduate students with advanced learning in Persian studies. **Focus:** Persian studies. **Qualif.:** Applicants should be U.S. citizens, have completed a doctoral program and be proficient in Persian. **Criteria:** Mastery of Persian language study is not required but could be prioritized.

Funds Avail.: No specific amount. **To Apply:** Applicants must submit a detailed description of research plans including the names, addresses, and e-mail addresses of two references, and a curriculum vitae. Applications must be sent to aiis@nyc.rr.com or mailed to Dr. Erica Ehrenberg. **Contact:** Dr. Erica Ehrenberg, executive Director.

665 ■ Short-term senior fellowships in Iranian Studies *(Doctorate, Graduate/Fellowship)*

Purpose: To promote research in the field of Iranian Studies. **Focus:** Humanities; Social sciences; Interracial studies. **Qualif.:** Applicants must be U.S. citizens, scholars, faculty members, or museum staff. **Criteria:** Preference will be given to applicant with knowledge of Persian study and a record of research in the humanities or the social sciences relating to Iran.

Funds Avail.: No specific amount. **To Apply:** Applicants must submit a curriculum vitae; and a detailed letter explaining how the fellowship would benefit the applicant's work, the names and addresses of the relevant contacts in Iran who have provided permission to research, and the names and e-mail addresses of two referees. Applicant must specify preferred dates of travel. Applications must be sent to aiis@nyc.rr.com or mailed to Dr. Erica Ehrenberg. **Contact:** Dr. Erica Ehrenberg, executive Director.

666 ■ American Institute for Maghrib Studies

845 N Park Ave., Marshall Bldg., Rm. 477
PO Box 210158-B
Tucson, AZ 85721-0158
Ph: (520)626-6498
Fax: (520)621-9257
E-mail: aimscmes@u.arizona.edu
URL: http://aimsnorthafrica.org

667 ■ AIMS Long-term Research Grants *(Postdoctorate/Grant)*

Purpose: To render fund for US scholars interested in conducting research on North Africa in any Maghrib country. **Focus:** General studies. **Qualif.:** Applicant must be a U.S. citizen graduate student, independent scholar, and faculty in all disciplines currently enrolled in a M.A. or Ph.D. program. **Criteria:** Applicant must be a member of AIMS at the time of application.

Funds Avail.: $15,000. **Number Awarded:** 1. **To Apply:** Applicant must submit completed grant application, proposal or research design, proposed itinerary with approximate dates, budget, vitae indicating language proficiency and institutional affiliation, letters of recommendation from two referees, including the candidate's dissertation advisor, or in the case of applicants holding a Ph.D., the names of two persons who may be contacted for references, and one page summary of the proposed research in either French or Arabic. **Deadline:** December 31. **Contact:** Kerry Adams at the above address (see entry 666).

668 ■ AIMS Short-term Research Grants *(Postdoctorate/Grant)*

Purpose: To render fund for US scholars interested in conducting research on North Africa in any Maghrib country. **Focus:** General studies. **Qualif.:** Applicant must be a U.S.

Awards are arranged alphabetically below their administering organizations

citizen graduate student, independent scholar, and faculty in all disciplines currently enrolled in a M.A. or Ph.D. program. **Criteria:** Applicant must be a member of AIMS at the time of application.

Funds Avail.: $6,000. **Number Awarded:** 1. **To Apply:** Applicant must submit completed grant application, proposal or research design, proposed itinerary with approximate dates, budget, vitae indicating language proficiency and institutional affiliation, letters of recommendation from two referees, including the candidate's dissertation advisor, or in the case of applicants holding a Ph.D., the names of two persons who may be contacted for references, and one page summary of the proposed research in either French or Arabic. **Deadline:** December 31. **Contact:** Kerry Adams at the above address (see entry 666).

669 ■ American Institute for Paralegal Studies

2777 Finley Rd., Ste. 11
Downers Grove, IL 60515
Fax: (630)916-6694
Free: 800-553-2420
E-mail: info@americanparalegal.edu
URL: http://www.americanparalegal.edu

670 ■ American Institute for Paralegal Studies Alumni Achievement Scholarships *(Undergraduate/Scholarship)*

Purpose: To advance the paralegal profession and to promote a global presence for the paralegal profession and leadership. **Focus:** Paralegal studies. **Qualif.:** Applicants must be students with a bachelor's degree; must have a minimum of 3.0 GPA at the undergraduate or graduate level; and must have three years or more legal work experience. **Criteria:** Recipients are selected based on academic performance and financial need.

Funds Avail.: $2,500. **To Apply:** Applicants must submit completed application form; an official transcript of record; a personal statement; and letters of recommendation from AIPS Alumni.

671 ■ American Institute for Paralegal Studies Alumni Competitive Scholarships *(Undergraduate/Scholarship)*

Purpose: To advance the paralegal profession and to promote a global presence for the paralegal profession and leadership. **Focus:** Paralegal studies. **Qualif.:** Applicants must be students with a bachelor's degree, must have a minimum of 3.0 GPA at the undergraduate or graduate level, and must have a law-related work experience. **Criteria:** Recipients are selected based on academic performance and financial need.

Funds Avail.: No specific amount. **To Apply:** Applicants must submit completed application form; an official transcript of record; a personal statement; two letters of recommendation; and grade for the introductory course, American Jurisprudence.

672 ■ American Institute for Paralegal Studies Merit Scholarships *(Undergraduate/Scholarship)*

Purpose: To advance the paralegal profession and to promote a global presence for the paralegal profession and leadership. **Focus:** Paralegal studies. **Qualif.:** Applicants must be students with a bachelor's degree and must have a minimum of 3.0 GPA at the undergraduate or graduate level. **Criteria:** Recipients are selected based on academic performance and financial need.

Funds Avail.: No specific amount. **To Apply:** Applicants must complete the application form and submit along with an official transcript of record. Applicants are advised to contact admissions for details and availability.

673 ■ American Institute of Polish Culture

1440 79th St. Causeway, Ste. 117
Miami, FL 33141
Ph: (305)864-2349
Fax: (305)865-5150
E-mail: info@ampolinstitute.org
URL: http://www.ampolinstitute.org

674 ■ Harriet Irsay Scholarships *(Graduate, Undergraduate/Scholarship)*

Purpose: To provide financial support American students of Polish descent who wish to continue their education after high school. **Focus:** Communications; Education; Media arts; History; International affairs and relations; Journalism; Liberal arts; Polish studies; Public relations. **Qualif.:** Applicants must be of Polish heritage; an American citizen or permanent resident; full-time graduate or undergraduate students in the field of communication, education, film, history, International Relation, journalism, liberal arts, polish studies, public relations; or graduate student in business programs with a thesis related to Poland, or graduate students with a thesis with Polish subject. **Criteria:** Recipients are selected on the basis of merits.

Funds Avail.: $1,000. **Number Awarded:** 10-15. **To Apply:** Applicants must submit a completed application form; school transcripts; resume; essay (200-400 words) about "Why should I receive the scholarship"; an article about Poland (maximum of 700 words); and 3 signed recommendation letters on a letterhead stationary from teachers or other person knowledgeable about the applicant's academic background. A non-refundable $10 processing fee (check or money order) must also be included. **Deadline:** April 20.

675 ■ American Institute of Steel Construction

1 E Wacker Dr., Ste. 700
Chicago, IL 60601-1802
Ph: (312)670-5408
Fax: (312)670-5403
URL: http://www.aisc.org

676 ■ AISC/Carolina Steel Scholarships *(Undergraduate/Scholarship)*

Purpose: To encourage greater interest in structural steel design. **Focus:** Civil engineering; Architectural engineering. **Qualif.:** Applicants must be full-time civil or architectural engineering students of U.S. Citizenship entering their 3rd or 4th year of study from a university in Alabama, North Carolina, South Carolina and Virginia. **Criteria:** Applicant selection is based on academic merit, faculty recommendation and evaluation of short essay and steel design analysis/designs submitted giving preference to students concentrating in the field of structural steel.

Funds Avail.: $3,000. **Number Awarded:** 1. **To Apply:** Applicants must submit an official transcript; a reference and optional letter of reference; a short essay on overall career objective and an original sample steel design

Awards are arranged alphabetically below their administering organizations

analysis/design solution with calculations. **Deadline:** April 9. **Contact:** Fromy Rosenburg at the above address (see entry 675).

677 ■ AISC/Fred R. Havens Fellowships *(Graduate, Undergraduate/Fellowship)*

Purpose: To provide financial assistance to those studying civil engineering. **Focus:** Civil engineering; Architectural engineering. **Qualif.:** Applicants must be U.S. citizens studying civil or architectural engineering full-time at universities in Missouri, Kansas or at MIT. Applicants must be graduate or undergraduate students who have completed one steel design course. **Criteria:** Undergraduate applicants are selected based on academic merit, faculty recommendation and evaluation of short essay and steel design analysis/designs submitted while graduate students applying are evaluated.

Funds Avail.: $5,000. **Number Awarded:** 1. **To Apply:** Undergraduate applicants must submit an official transcript; a reference and optional letter of reference; a two-page essay on his/her interest in steel structures and an original sample steel design analysis/design solution with calculations. In addition to the mentioned requirements, graduate students applying must submit an official transcript; a reference and optional letter of reference; and a one-page detailed answers to the following: (a) Demonstrate concentration on steel related course work and/or thesis with a strong steel orientation, or (b) Demonstrate proposed course work and proposed thesis concentration in structural steel. **Deadline:** April 9. **Contact:** Fromy Rosenberg at the above address (see entry 675).

678 ■ AISC/Great Lakes Fabricators and Erectors Association Fellowships *(Graduate/Fellowship)*

Purpose: To provide financial assistance to those studying civil engineering. **Focus:** Civil engineering; Architectural engineering. **Qualif.:** Applicants must be full-time civil or architectural engineering students who are currently/or will be doing masters-level work at any graduate school in Michigan. **Criteria:** Applicants will be selected based on academic merit, faculty recommendation and jury's review of application materials.

Funds Avail.: $5,000. **Number Awarded:** 1. **To Apply:** Applicants must submit an official transcript; a reference and optional letter of reference; and a one-page detailed answers to the following: (a) Demonstrate concentration on steel related course work and/or thesis with a strong steel orientation, or (b) Demonstrate proposed course work and proposed thesis concentration in structural steel. **Deadline:** April 9. **Contact:** Fromy Rosenberg at the above address (see entry 675).

679 ■ AISC/Rocky Mountain Steel Construction Association Fellowships *(Graduate/Fellowship)*

Purpose: To provide financial assistance to those studying civil engineering. **Focus:** Civil engineering; Architectural engineering. **Qualif.:** Applicants must be full-time civil or architectural engineering students who are currently/or will be doing masters-level work in either Colorado or Wyoming. Applicants must be U.S. Citizens. **Criteria:** Applicants will be selected based on academic merit, faculty recommendation and jury's review of the application materials.

Funds Avail.: $3,000. **Number Awarded:** 1. **To Apply:** Applicants must submit an official transcript; a reference and optional letter of reference; and a one-page detailed answers to the following: (a) Demonstrate concentration on steel related course work and/or thesis with a strong steel orientation, or (b) Demonstrate proposed course work and proposed thesis concentration in structural steel. **Deadline:** April 9. **Contact:** Fromy Rosenberg at the above address (see entry 675).

680 ■ AISC/Southern Association of Steel Fabricators Fellowships *(Graduate/Fellowship)*

Purpose: To provide financial assistance to those studying civil engineering. **Focus:** Civil engineering; Architectural engineering. **Qualif.:** Applicants must be full-time civil or architectural engineering students who are currently/or will be doing masters-level work at any graduate school in Alabama, Arkansas, Florida, Georgia, Kentucky, Louisiana, Mississippi and Tennessee. Applicants must be U.S. Citizens. **Criteria:** Applicants will be selected based on academic merit, faculty recommendation and jury's review of the application materials.

Funds Avail.: $2,500. **Number Awarded:** 1. **To Apply:** Applicants must submit an official transcript; a reference and optional letter of reference; and one-page detailed answers to the following: (a) Demonstrate concentration on steel related course work and/or thesis with a strong steel orientation, or (b) Demonstrate proposed course work and proposed thesis concentration in structural steel. **Deadline:** April 9. **Contact:** Fromy Rosenberg at the above address (see entry 675).

681 ■ AISC/Southern Association of Steel Fabricators Scholarships *(Undergraduate/Scholarship)*

Purpose: To encourage greater interest in structural steel design. **Focus:** Civil engineering; Architectural engineering. **Qualif.:** Applicants must be full-time civil or architectural engineering students who are U.S. Citizens entering their 3rd or 4th year of study with an interest in structural steel from a university in Alabama, Arkansas, Florida, Georgia, Kentucky, Louisiana, Mississippi and Tennessee. **Criteria:** Applicants are selected based on academic merit and faculty recommendation. Preference will be given to those students who have selected a concentration in structural steel.

Funds Avail.: $2,500. **Number Awarded:** 1. **To Apply:** Applicants must submit an official transcript; a reference and optional letter of reference; and a short essay on overall career objective. **Deadline:** April 9. **Contact:** Fromy Rosenberg at the above address (see entry 675).

682 ■ AISC/Structural Steel Education Council Fellowships *(Graduate/Fellowship)*

Purpose: To provide financial assistance to those studying civil engineering. **Focus:** Civil engineering; Architectural engineering. **Qualif.:** Applicants must be full-time civil or architectural engineering students undertaking masters-level work in a any graduate program from universities in California and Nevada. **Criteria:** Applicants will be selected based on academic merit and faculty recommendation. Preference will be given to applicants who are legal residents from either California or Nevada.

Funds Avail.: $2,500. **Number Awarded:** 3. **To Apply:** Applicants must submit an official transcript; a reference and optional letter of reference; and a one-page detailed answers to the following: (a) Demonstrate concentration on steel related course work and/or thesis with a strong steel orientation, or (b) Demonstrate proposed course work and proposed thesis concentration in structural steel. **Deadline:** April 9. **Contact:** Fromy Rosenberg at the above address (see entry 675).

683 ■ AISC/US Steel Fellowships *(Graduate/Fellowship)*

Purpose: To provide financial assistance to those studying civil engineering. **Focus:** Civil engineering; Architectural engineering. **Qualif.:** Applicants must be full-time civil or architectural engineering students who are currently/will be doing masters-level work at universities in Alaska, Delaware, Hawaii, Iowa, Maryland, Minnesota, Nebraska, Ohio, Texas and Wisconsin. Applicants must be U.S. Citizens. **Criteria:** Applicants will be selected based on academic merit, faculty recommendation and jury's review of the application materials.

Funds Avail.: $2,500. **Number Awarded:** 1. **To Apply:** Applicants must submit an official transcript; a reference and optional letter of reference; and a one-page detailed answers to the following: (a) Demonstrate concentration on steel related course work and/or thesis with a strong steel orientation, or (b) Demonstrate proposed course work and proposed thesis concentration in structural steel. **Deadline:** April 9. **Contact:** Fromy Rosenberg at the above address (see entry 675).

684 ■ American Intellectual Property Law Education Foundation

485 Kinderkamack Rd.
Oradell, NJ 07649
Ph: (201)634-1870
Fax: (201)634-1871
E-mail: admin@aiplef.org
URL: http://www.aiplef.org

685 ■ Sidney B. Williams, Jr. Scholarships *(Undergraduate/Scholarship)*

Purpose: To increase the number of underrepresented minority groups serving as intellectual property law practitioners in law firms and departments of corporations. **Focus:** Law. **Qualif.:** Applicants must be entering or attending law school; **Criteria:** Recipients are selected based on: demonstrated commitment to developing a career in intellectual property law; academic performance during the undergraduate, graduate, and law school levels; financial need; leadership Skills, community activities or special accomplishments.

Funds Avail.: $10,000. **To Apply:** Applicants must submit completed scholarship application form; FAFSA form (or similar form) and other supporting documentation required. Applicants must also submit undergraduate transcript and graduate law transcript(if applicable); two letters of recommendation from, but not limited to former teachers, college administrators, community leaders, or other similar persons concerning the academic ability, character, reputation or professional aptitude of the applicant; evidence of being US citizen; personal or telephonic interview; and recent resume. **Deadline:** February 25. **Contact:** Sophia Rogers Thurgood Marshall College Fund at 80 Maiden Lane, Ste. 2204, New York, NY 10038; srogers@tmcfund.org.

686 ■ American Jersey Cattle Association

6486 E Main St.
Reynoldsburg, OH 43068-2362
Ph: (614)861-3636
Fax: (614)861-8040
URL: http://www.usjersey.com

687 ■ Cedarcrest Farms Scholarships *(Undergraduate/Scholarship)*

Purpose: To financially support secondary students entering college freshmen through graduate school. **Focus:** General studies. **Qualif.:** Applicants must be junior member or lifetime member of the American Jersey Cattle Association. **Criteria:** Applicants must have minimum grade point average of 2.5 on a 4 point scale.

Funds Avail.: $10,000. **To Apply:** Applicants must submit complete scholarship application form and a copy of most recent transcript listing all completed coursework. **Deadline:** July 7.

688 ■ Reuben R. Cowles Youth Awards *(Undergraduate/Award/Prize)*

Purpose: To financially support secondary students entering as college freshmen through graduate school. **Focus:** General studies. **Qualif.:** Applicants must be junior member or lifetime member of the American Jersey Cattle Association. **Criteria:** Applicants must have minimum grade point average of 2.5 on a 4 point scale.

Funds Avail.: $10,000. **To Apply:** Applicants must submit complete scholarship application form and a copy of most recent transcript listing all completed coursework. **Deadline:** July 7.

689 ■ American Kidney Fund

6110 Executive Blvd., Ste. 1010
Rockville, MD 20852
Free: 800-638-8299
E-mail: helpline@kidneyfund.org
URL: http://www.kidneyfund.org

690 ■ American Kidney Fund's Patient Scholarship Program *(Other/Scholarship)*

Purpose: To provide support for people with chronic kidney disease to further their education or vocational training as part of an effort to initiate, maintain or resume employment and independent living. **Focus:** General studies. **Qualif.:** Applicants must be individuals residing in the United States and who have been diagnosed with stage 3, 4, or 5 chronic kidney disease. **Criteria:** Applicants will be evaluated based on financial needs.

Funds Avail.: $3,000. **To Apply:** Applicants must submit application documenting: diagnosis of chronic kidney disease, acceptance by desired program, financial need, funding request including tuition bill; essay describing the effect of kidney disease on their lives; and how the proposed education or training program will enhance their ability to initiate, maintain or resume employment and independent living; reference from nephrology professional caring for the patient with an assessment of the patient's ability to maintain compliance with their treatment regimen while pursuing the educational or vocational program. **Deadline:** June 6.

691 ■ American Lebanese Engineering Society

PO Box 585
Norwood, MA 02062
Ph: (617)642-7185
E-mail: ales@alesonline.org
URL: http://www.alesonline.org

692 ■ American Lebanese Engineering Society Scholarship Program *(Other/Scholarship)*

Purpose: To provide scholarships and educational grants to qualified Lebanese students. **Focus:** Engineering. **Qua-**

Awards are arranged alphabetically below their administering organizations

lif.: Applicants must be undergraduate and graduate students of an ABET accredited university. **Criteria:** Candidate must be of Lebanese descent or Lebanese junior, senior, or graduate student that has a GPA of 3.25 on a 4.00 scale.

Funds Avail.: $1,000. **Number Awarded:** 2. **To Apply:** Applicants must submit completed application form, a copy of most recent academic transcript, two letters of recommendation, a recent clear black or white passport type photo and a one page essay describing academic background, achievements, and goals and the relevance of studies to ALES goals and the reason why should be the recipient of the award.

693 ■ The American Legion

PO Box 1055
Indianapolis, IN 46206
Ph: (317)630-1200
Fax: (317)630-1223
URL: http://www.legion.org

694 ■ The American Legion Legacy Scholarships *(Undergraduate/Scholarship)*

Purpose: To financially support the education of the dependents of active duty United States military and guard and reserve personnel **Focus:** General studies. **Qualif.:** Applicant must be the dependent of active duty United States military and guard and reserve personnel who were federalized and killed on active duty on or after September 11, 2001. **Criteria:** Awards are given based on merit.

Funds Avail.: Varies. **To Apply:** Applicants must submit a completed scholarship application with a photocopy of the deceased veteran's Certificate of Death (DD 1300). **Deadline:** April 15.

695 ■ The American Legion National High School Oratorical Scholarships Contest *(Undergraduate/Scholarship)*

Purpose: To support the education of deserving high school students. **Focus:** General studies. **Qualif.:** Candidate must be a high school student. **Criteria:** Students must win the oratorical contest to acquire the scholarship.

Funds Avail.: 1st place: $18,000; 2nd place: $16,000; 3rd place: $14,000. Each Department (State) winner in the first round will receive a $1,500 scholarship. Each first round winner that does not advance to the Final Round will receive an additional $1,500 scholarship. **Number Awarded:** Varies. **To Apply:** Applicants may contact their Department (State) or the National Organization of the American Legion for more information about the scholarships.

Remarks: The awards may be used to attend any college or university in the United States.

696 ■ Eight and Forty Lung and Respiratory Disease Nursing Scholarships *(Professional Development/Scholarship)*

Purpose: To assist registered nurses (RN) with advanced preparation for positions in supervision, administration or teaching. **Focus:** Nursing, Pediatric. **Qualif.:** Applicant must be a registered nurse with a current state license; must have graduated at a regionally accredited school of nursing or will be graduated by the application deadline; must be a registered nurse pursuing nursing education in the field of pediatric lung and respiratory diseases on a part-time or full-time basis; must be accepted by a regionally accredited school of nursing; must be a U.S. citizen; must have leadership qualities; and must have the ability to pursue full-time employment after school. **Criteria:** Awards are given based on personal and academic qualifications with consideration given to past experience and future employment plans as they relate to pediatric lung and respiratory disease nursing.

Funds Avail.: $3,000 each. **To Apply:** Applicants must submit a completed scholarship application along with a current state Registered Nurse License or registration; three letters of recommendation; transcript of all college credit attempted; and letter of acceptance from an accredited school of nursing. **Deadline:** May 15.

Remarks: In cooperation with Eight and Forty.

697 ■ Samsung American Legion Scholarships *(Undergraduate/Scholarship)*

Purpose: To assist the education of a child, grandchild, great grandchild, etc. or a legally adopted child of a U.S. wartime veteran. **Focus:** General studies. **Qualif.:** Applicant must be a high school junior who participates in either an American Legion Boys State or American Legion Auxiliary Girls State Program and be a direct descendant (child, grandchild, great grandchild, etc. or a legally adopted child) of a U.S. wartime veteran who served on active duty during one or more of the periods of war officially designated as eligibility dates for membership in The American Legion by the United States government. **Criteria:** Awards are given based on merit.

Funds Avail.: In 2007, ten $20,000 scholarships and 88 $1,000 scholarships were awarded. **Number Awarded:** Varies. **To Apply:** Applicants must submit a completed scholarship application along with a photocopy of the veteran's Certification of Release or Discharge from Active Duty (DD-214), to Boys/Girls State program.

Remarks: In cooperation with Samsung.

698 ■ American Library Association

50 E Huron St.
Chicago, IL 60611
Free: 800-545-2433
E-mail: alsc@ala.org
URL: http://www.ala.org

699 ■ Marshall Cavendish Scholarships *(Graduate/Scholarship)*

Purpose: To provide financial assistance for furthering the education of an individual. **Focus:** General studies. **Qualif.:** Applicant must be an American or Canadian or permanent resident attending ALA accredited Master's Program and no more than 12 semester hours towards MLS/MLIS/MIS prior to June 1 of year awarded. **Criteria:** Applicants will be evaluated on the basis of academic excellence, leadership and evidence of commitment to a career in librarianship.

Funds Avail.: $3,000. **To Apply:** Applicants must submit applications and all supporting documents. **Deadline:** March 1.

700 ■ David H. Clift Scholarships *(Graduate/Scholarship)*

Purpose: To provide financial assistance for furthering the education of a deserving individual. **Focus:** General stud-

Awards are arranged alphabetically below their administering organizations

ies. **Qualif.:** Applicant must be a US or Canadian citizen or permanent resident attending an ALA accredited Master's program and no more than 12 semester hours towards MLS/MLIS/MIS prior to June of year awarded. **Criteria:** Applicants will be evaluated based on academic excellence, leadership and evidence of commitment to a career in librarianship.

Funds Avail.: $3,000. **To Apply:** Applicants must submit applications and all supporting documents. **Deadline:** March 1.

701 ■ Christopher Hoy/ERT Scholarships *(Graduate/Scholarship)*

Purpose: To provide financial assistance for furthering the education of a deserving individual. **Focus:** General studies. **Qualif.:** Applicant must be a US or Canadian citizen or permanent resident attending ALA accredited Master's Program and no more than 12 semester hours towards MLS/MLIS/MIS prior to June 1 of year awarded. **Criteria:** Applicants will be evaluated based on academic excellence, leadership and evidence of commitment to a career in librarianship.

Funds Avail.: $5,000. **To Apply:** Applicants must submit applications and all supporting documents. **Deadline:** March 1.

702 ■ American Liver Foundation

75 Maiden Ln., Ste. 603
New York, NY 10038
Ph: (212)668-1000
Fax: (212)483-8179
URL: http://www.liverfoundation.org

703 ■ American Liver Foundation Liver Scholar Awards *(Doctorate/Award/Prize)*

Purpose: To develop the potential of outstanding, young scientists and encouraging research in liver physiology and disease. **Focus:** Medical Research. **Qualif.:** Applicants must hold a M.D., Ph.D., or equivalent. **Criteria:** Awards are made to eligible institutions and are for salary support only for the awardee.

Funds Avail.: $225,000. **To Apply:** Applicants may must download an application form online. Applicants must submit an application which contain the following section: Application Information; Summary and Abstract; Biographical Sketch; Research Plan; Research Facilities; Candidate's Statement; Letters of Commitment; Letters of Recommendation; Institution Review Board; Signatures. Original and eight (8) copies of the completed application must be received at ALF. **Deadline:** October 16. **Contact:** American Liver Foundation Research Department/Liver Scholars 1425 Pompton Avenue, Suite 3 Cedar Grove, NJ 07009

704 ■ American Liver Foundation Special Research Initiatives *(Doctorate/Award/Prize)*

Purpose: To support investigational work relating to liver physiology and disease. **Focus:** Medical Research. **Qualif.:** Applicant can be a faculty member at any level. **Criteria:** Award is made to eligible institutions. There are no restrictions on how the monies are to be used on the research but no indirect costs are provided.

Funds Avail.: $100,000. **To Apply:** Applicants may download an application form online. Applicants must submit an application which contain the following section: Application Information; Summary and Abstract; Biographical Sketch; Research Plan; Research Facilities; Candidate's Statement; Letters of Commitment; Letters of Recommendation; Institution Review Board; Signatures. Original and eight (8) copies of the completed application must be received at ALF. **Deadline:** October 16. **Contact:** American Liver Foundation Research Department Biliary Atresia Special Research Initiative 1425 Pompton Avenue, Suite 3 Cedar Grove, NJ 07009

705 ■ Cystic Fibrosis Cholestatic Liver Disease Liver Scholarships *(Doctorate/Award/Prize)*

Purpose: To develop the potential of outstanding, young scientists and encouraging research in liver physiology and disease. **Focus:** Medical research. **Qualif.:** Applicants must hold a M.D., Ph.D., or equivalent. **Criteria:** Awards are made to eligible institutions and are for salary support only for the awardee.

Funds Avail.: $225,000. **To Apply:** Applicants may must download an application form online. Applicants must submit an application which contain the following section: Application Information; Summary and Abstract; Biographical Sketch; Research Plan; Research Facilities; Candidate's Statement; Letters of Commitment; Letters of Recommendation; Institution Review Board; Signatures. Original and eight (8) copies of the completed application must be received at ALF. **Deadline:** October 16. **Contact:** American Liver Foundation Research Department/Liver Scholars Cystic Fibrosis Cholestatic Liver Scholar 1425 Pompton Avenue, Suite 3 Cedar Grove, NJ 07009.

706 ■ Postdoctoral Research Fellowships *(Doctorate/Award/Prize)*

Purpose: To support investigational work relating to liver physiology and disease. **Focus:** Medical Research. **Qualif.:** Applicants must hold a M.D., Ph.D., or equivalent. **Criteria:** Award is given on the basis of the applicant's eligibility.

Funds Avail.: $12,500. **To Apply:** Applicants may download an application form online. Applicants must submit an application which contain the following section: Application Information; Summary and Abstract; Biographical Sketch; Research Plan; Research Facilities; Candidate's Statement; Letters of Commitment; Letters of Recommendation; Institution Review Board; Signatures. Original and eight (8) copies of the completed application must be received at ALF. **Deadline:** October 16. **Contact:** American Liver Foundation Research Department Postdoctoral Research Fellowship 1425 Pompton Avenue, Suite 3 Cedar Grove, NJ 07009

707 ■ American Marketing Association Foundation

311 S Wacker Dr., Ste. 5800
Chicago, IL 60606
Ph: (312)542-9000
Fax: (312)542-9001
E-mail: lchernick@ama.org
URL: http://www.themarketingfoundation.org

708 ■ Richard A. Hammill Scholarships Fund *(Undergraduate/Scholarship)*

Purpose: To provide an annual scholarship award for students who are enrolled in the Marketing Program. **Focus:** Marketing and distribution. **Qualif.:** Applicants must be students enrolled at Georgia State University. **Criteria:**

Awards are arranged alphabetically below their administering organizations

Selection will be based on the committee's criteria.

Funds Avail.: No specific amount. **To Apply:** Interested applicants may apply online via the AMAF website. **Contact:** AMA Foundation at the above address (see entry 707).

709 ■ Robert J. Lavidge Nonprofit Marketing Research Scholarships *(Professional Development/Scholarship)*

Purpose: To provide scholarship for marketing professionals working in the nonprofit sector to further their marketing research-related education. **Focus:** Marketing and distribution. **Qualif.:** Applicants must be nonprofit marketing professionals with an interest in furthering their marketing research education. **Criteria:** Selection will be based on the committee's criteria.

Funds Avail.: No specific amount. **To Apply:** Interested applicants may apply online via the AMAF website. **Contact:** AMAF at the above address (see entry 707).

710 ■ Valuing Diversity PhD Scholarships *(Doctorate/Scholarship)*

Purpose: To provide scholarship to underrepresented populations in the marketing profession. **Focus:** Marketing and distribution. **Qualif.:** Applicant must be a US citizen or a permanent resident; must be enrolled on campus, in a full-time AACSB-accredited marketing doctoral program, and have successfully completed at least one year; must have not previously received a Valuing Diversity Scholarship; must be African American, Hispanic American, or Native American. **Criteria:** Selection will be based on the committee's criteria.

Funds Avail.: No specific amount. **To Apply:** Applicants must complete the online application found on the AMAF's website. Essays must be in Microsoft Word format. Essays should be two-pages, double-space, in 12 pt. type (approximately 500 words). Sources you mention in your essay should be credited on an additional page and do not count against the two-page maximum. Applicants must also submit two letters of recommendation. **Deadline:** June 9. **Contact:** AMAF at the above address (see entry 707).

711 ■ American Medical Association

515 N State St.
Chicago, IL 60610
Ph: (312)464-4200
Fax: (312)464-4142
Free: 800-621-8335
E-mail: steven.churchill@ama-assn.org
URL: http://www.ama-assn.org

712 ■ AMA Foundation Minority Scholars Award *(Undergraduate/Scholarship)*

Purpose: To advance health care through support of programs in medical education, research, and service. **Focus:** Medical Education. **Qualif.:** Applicant must be a current first or second year student and a permanent resident or citizen of the U.S.; must be African American, American Indian, Native American, Alaska Native, or Hispanic/Latino. **Criteria:** Recipients are selected based on academic standing.

Funds Avail.: $10,000. **Number Awarded:** 10. **To Apply:** Applicants must complete the application form. Detailed requirement will be sent by the AMA Foundation to each medical school's Office of the Dean, Office of the Student Affairs, and Office of Financial Aid. **Deadline:** April 15.

713 ■ AMA Foundation Physicians of Tomorrow Scholarships *(Undergraduate/Scholarship)*

Purpose: To advance health care through support of programs in medical education, research, and service. **Focus:** Medical Education. **Qualif.:** Applicants must be current third year medical students who are entering their fourth year of study. **Criteria:** Recipients are selected based on academic standing and financial need.

Funds Avail.: $10,000. **Number Awarded:** 8. **To Apply:** Applicants must complete the application form. Detailed requirements will be sent by the AMA Foundation to each medical school's Office of the Dean, Office of the Student Affairs, and Office of Financial Aid. **Deadline:** May 30.

714 ■ The Arthur N. Wilson, MD, Scholarships *(Undergraduate/Scholarship)*

Purpose: To advance health care through support of programs in medical education, research, and service. **Focus:** Medical Education. **Qualif.:** Applicants must be medical students who attended high school in Alaska. **Criteria:** Recipients are selected based on academic standing and financial need.

Funds Avail.: $5,000. **To Apply:** Applicants must submit completed application form; a one-page personal statement outlining the career goals in the field of medicine; a curriculum vitae; official transcript from the applicant's high school in Southeast Alaska; official Medical school transcript; and letter of recommendation from a faculty member at the medical school or office of the dean. **Deadline:** June 16. **Contact:** dina.lindenberg@ama-assn.org; 312-464-4193.

715 ■ American Military Retirees Association

5436 Peru St., Ste. 1
Plattsburgh, NY 12901
Ph: (518)563-9479
Fax: (518)324-5204
Free: (180)0424-2969
E-mail: info@amra1973.org
URL: http://www.amra1973.org

716 ■ Sergeant Major Douglas R. Drum Memorial Scholarship Fund *(Undergraduate/Scholarship)*

Purpose: To protect and improve the benefits of the military retirees. **Focus:** General studies. **Qualif.:** Applicants must be a current member of AMRA, his/her dependent, child or grandchild; he/she must pursuing a degree in an accredited college or university. **Criteria:** Scholarship Committee will evaluate the application based on the student's educational achievements, leadership abilities, character, citizenship, and financial need.

Funds Avail.: $1,000; $2,500; $5,000. **Number Awarded:** 24. **To Apply:** Applicants must present the award letter to the college/university and request that AMRA be billed for half the scholarship for the first semester and half the scholarship for the second semester; an applicant must submit a 500 word or less essay telling why an applicant deserve a scholarship from AMRA stating the Educational plans, achievements, leadership abilities, extracurricular and community activities, work experiences, character and citizenship traits, or any other circumstance that assist the committee during the selection process; an applicant must submit a letter of recommendation either from a teacher or professor, non-family member, past or current employer, from a project coordinator or a team leader. **Deadline:** April 4.

717 ■ American Montessori Society

281 Park Ave. S
New York, NY 10010-6102
Ph: (212)358-1250
Fax: (212)358-1256
E-mail: info@amshq.org
URL: http://www.amshq.org

718 ■ AMS Teacher Education Scholarships *(Undergraduate/Scholarship)*

Purpose: To support the growth of Montessori teachers. **Focus:** Education, Teaching. **Qualif.:** Applicant must be accepted or in the process of acceptance by an affiliated AMS teacher education program. **Criteria:** Selection of applicant will not be based on the gender, race, creed, color or national origin, or sexual orientation. Applicants are considered on the basis of financial need, a compelling personal statement, three letters of recommendation, and official verification of acceptance into an AMS Teacher Education Program.

Funds Avail.: $28,000. **To Apply:** Application forms are available on the website. Applicant must have a personal statement and three recommendation letters. Application materials must be sent to: The American Montessori Society, 281 Park Ave., S, New York, NY, 10010. **Deadline:** May 1.

719 ■ American Musicological Society

6010 College Station
Brunswick, ME 04011-8451
Ph: (207)798-4243
Fax: (207)798-4254
Free: 877-679-7648
E-mail: ams@ams-net.org
URL: http://www.ams-net.org

720 ■ Alvin H. Johnson AMS Dissertation Fellowships *(Undergraduate/Fellowship)*

Purpose: To provide financial assistance for full-time studies. **Focus:** Music. **Qualif.:** Applicants must be anyone eligibly registered in good standing for a doctorate at a North American university and must have completed all formal degree requirements except the dissertation at the time of full application. **Criteria:** Recipients will be selected on the basis of academic merit.

Funds Avail.: $19,000. **Number Awarded:** 50. **To Apply:** Applicants can apply and submit applications online via the AMS website. **Deadline:** January 15.

721 ■ Howard Mayer Brown Fellowships *(Postdoctorate/Fellowship)*

Purpose: To increase the presence of minority scholars and teachers in musicology by providing financial aid. **Focus:** Music. **Qualif.:** Applicants must be students who have completed at least one year of graduate work, intend to pursue a Ph.D. and are in good standing at their home institution. **Criteria:** Recipients are selected based on their academic merit.

Funds Avail.: $17,000. **To Apply:** Applicants must use the online submission form. **Deadline:** January 15.

722 ■ American Nuclear Society

555 N Kensington Ave.
La Grange Park, IL 60526
Ph: (708)352-6611
Fax: (708)352-0499
Free: 800-323-3044
URL: http://www.ans.org

723 ■ American Nuclear Society Incoming Freshman Scholarships *(High School/Scholarship)*

Purpose: To assist students complete their post-secondary education and prepare for careers in nuclear science and technology (NS&T). **Focus:** Engineering, Nuclear. **Qualif.:** Applicants must be graduating high school seniors who have the intention to pursue a degree in nuclear engineering. **Criteria:** Applicants are evaluated based on high school academic achievement, freshman college courses enrolled in, quality and content of 500 word essay, letters of recommendation by counselors and/or teachers, and other information.

Funds Avail.: $1,000 for each recipient. **Number Awarded:** 4. **To Apply:** Applicants must submit all the required application information. **Deadline:** April 1.

724 ■ American Nuclear Society Undergraduates Scholarships *(Undergraduate/Scholarship)*

Purpose: To help students complete their post-secondary education and prepare for careers in nuclear science and technology (NS&T). **Focus:** Nuclear science; Engineering, Nuclear. **Qualif.:** Applicants must be students who have completed at least one year in a course of study leading to a degree in nuclear science, nuclear engineering, or a nuclear-related field. **Criteria:** Recipients are selected based on merit and financial need.

Funds Avail.: No specific amount. **To Apply:** Applicants must submit all the required application information.

725 ■ American Occupational Therapy Foundation

4720 Montgomery Ln., PO Box 31220
Bethesda, MD 20824-1220
Ph: (301)652-6611
Fax: (301)656-3620
Free: 800-729-2682
E-mail: aotf@aotf.org
URL: http://www.aotf.org

726 ■ Renee Achter Scholarship Program *(Postgraduate/Scholarship)*

Purpose: To provide financial assistance for AOTF members to promote research and education in the field of occupational therapy. **Focus:** Occupational therapy. **Qualif.:** Applicants must be a member of the AOTF; must demonstrate a need for financial assistance; sustained a record of outstanding scholastic achievement. Post-baccalaureate applicants must be enrolled as a full-time student at the professional level in an accredited or developing occupational therapy educational program. **Criteria:** Recipients are selected based on the application and the materials submitted.

Awards are arranged alphabetically below their administering organizations

Funds Avail.: $1,000. **To Apply:** Applicants must complete the online application (please visit AOTF website); two personal references; curriculum Director's statement; official transcripts; financial statement; and an essay. **Deadline:** February 8.

727 ■ Naida Ackley Scholarship Program
(Postgraduate/Scholarship)

Purpose: To provide financial assistance for AOTF members to promote research and education in the field of occupational therapy. **Focus:** Occupational therapy. **Qualif.:** Applicants must be a member of the AOTF; must demonstrate a need for financial assistance; sustained a record of outstanding scholastic achievement. Post-baccalaureate applicants must be enrolled as a full-time student at the professional level in an accredited or developing occupational therapy educational program. **Criteria:** Recipients are selected based on the application and the materials submitted.

Funds Avail.: $1,000. **To Apply:** Applicants must complete the online application (please visit AOTF website); two personal references; curriculum Director's statement; official transcripts; financial statement; and an essay. **Deadline:** February 8.

728 ■ Diane Blicksilver Aja Memorial Scholarship Program *(Postgraduate/Scholarship)*

Purpose: To provide financial assistance for AOTF members to promote research and education in the field of occupational therapy. **Focus:** Occupational therapy. **Qualif.:** Applicants must be a member of the AOTF; must be focused on injury prevention or ergonomics; must demonstrate a need for financial assistance; sustained a record of outstanding scholastic achievement. Post-baccalaureate applicants must be enrolled full-time student at the professional level in an accredited or developing occupational therapy educational program. **Criteria:** Recipients are selected based on the application and the materials submitted.

Funds Avail.: $1,000. **To Apply:** Applicants must complete the online application, (please visit AOTF website); two personal references; curriculum Director's statement; official transcripts; financial statement; and an essay. **Deadline:** February 8.

729 ■ Ethel Beard Burstein Scholarship Program *(Postgraduate/Scholarship)*

Purpose: To provide financial assistance for AOTF members to promote research and education in the field of occupational therapy. **Focus:** Occupational therapy. **Qualif.:** Applicants must be a member of the AOTF; must demonstrate a need for financial assistance; sustained a record of outstanding scholastic achievement. Post-baccalaureate applicants must be enrolled as a full-time student at the professional level in an accredited or developing occupational therapy educational program. **Criteria:** Priority will be given to applicants who are enrolled at a Philadelphia school.

Funds Avail.: $1,200. **Number Awarded:** 2. **To Apply:** Applicant must complete online application, (please visit AOTF website); must prepare two personal references; curriculum Director's statement; official transcripts; financial statement; and an essay. **Deadline:** February 8.

730 ■ Kappa Delta Phi Scholarship Program
(Postgraduate/Scholarship)

Purpose: To provide financial assistance for AOTF members to promote research and education in the field of occupational therapy. **Focus:** Occupational therapy. **Qualif.:** Applicants must be a member of the AOTF; must demonstrate a need for financial assistance; sustained a record of outstanding scholastic achievement. Post-baccalaureate applicants must be enrolled as a full-time student at the professional level in an accredited or developing occupational therapy educational program. **Criteria:** Recipients are selected based on the application and the materials submitted.

Funds Avail.: $5,000. **Number Awarded:** 2. **To Apply:** Applicants must complete the online application, (please visit AOTF website); must prepare two personal references; curriculum Director's statement; official transcripts; financial statement; and an essay. **Deadline:** February 8. **Contact:** Jane Huntington; jhuntington@aotf.org.

731 ■ Susan Lang Scholarship Program
(Postgraduate/Scholarship)

Purpose: To provide financial assistance for AOTF members to promote research and education in the field of occupational therapy. **Focus:** Occupational therapy. **Qualif.:** Applicants must be a resident of Illinois; must be committed to clinical practice; must be a member of the AOTF; must be focused on injury prevention or ergonomics; must demonstrate a need for financial assistance; and must have a sustained record of outstanding scholastic achievement. Post-baccalaureate applicants must be enrolled as a full-time student at the professional level in an accredited or developing occupational therapy educational program. **Criteria:** Recipients are selected based on the application and the materials submitted.

Funds Avail.: $1,000. **To Apply:** Applicants must complete the online application, (please visit AOTF website); prepare two personal references; curriculum Director's statement; official transcripts; financial statement; and an essay. **Deadline:** February 8.

732 ■ Janice McGraw Memorial Scholarship Program *(Postgraduate/Scholarship)*

Purpose: To provide financial assistance for AOTF members, and to promote research and education in the field of occupational therapy. **Focus:** Occupational therapy. **Qualif.:** Applicants must be a resident of North Carolina; committed to clinical practice; must be a member of the AOTF; must focus on injury prevention or ergonomics; demonstrate a need for financial assistance; and must have a sustained record of outstanding scholastic achievement. Post-baccalaureate applicants must be enrolled as a full-time student at the professional level in an accredited or developing occupational therapy educational program. **Criteria:** Recipients are selected based on the application and the materials submitted.

Funds Avail.: $1,000. **To Apply:** Applicants must complete the online application; prepare two personal references; curriculum Director's statement; official transcripts; financial statement; and an essay. **Deadline:** February 8.

733 ■ Mary Minglen Scholarship Program
(Postgraduate/Scholarship)

Purpose: To provide financial assistance for AOTF members to promote research and education in the field of occupational therapy. **Focus:** Occupational therapy. **Qualif.:** Applicants must be a member of the AOTF; must demonstrate a need for financial assistance; sustained a record of outstanding scholastic achievement. Post-baccalaureate applicants must be enrolled as a full-time student at the professional level in an accredited or developing occupational therapy educational program. **Criteria:** Recipients are selected based on the application and the materials submitted.

Funds Avail.: $1,000. **To Apply:** Applicants must complete the online application, (please visit AOTF website); must prepare two personal references; curriculum Director's statement; official transcripts; financial statement; and an essay. **Deadline:** February 8.

734 ■ NorthCoast Medical Scholarship Program *(Postgraduate/Scholarship)*

Purpose: To provide financial assistance for AOTF members to promote research and education in the field of occupational therapy. **Focus:** Occupational therapy. **Qualif.:** Applicants must be a member of the AOTF; must demonstrate a need for financial assistance; sustain a record of outstanding scholastic achievement. Post-baccalaureate applicants must be enrolled as a full-time student at the professional level in an accredited or developing occupational therapy educational program. **Criteria:** Recipients are selected based on the application and the materials submitted.

Funds Avail.: $5,000. **Number Awarded:** 2. **To Apply:** Applicants must complete the online application, (please visit AOTF website); must prepare two personal references; curriculum Director's statement; official transcripts; financial statement; and an essay. **Deadline:** February 8.

735 ■ Frank Oppenheimer Scholarship Program *(Postgraduate/Scholarship)*

Purpose: To provide financial assistance for AOTF members to promote research and education in the field of occupational therapy. **Focus:** Occupational therapy. **Qualif.:** Applicants must be a member of the AOTF; must demonstrate a need for financial assistance; sustained a record of outstanding scholastic achievement. Post-baccalaureate applicants must be enrolled as a full-time student at the professional level in an accredited or developing occupational therapy educational program. **Criteria:** Recipients are selected based on the application and the materials submitted.

Funds Avail.: $1,000. **To Apply:** Applicants must complete the online application, (please visit AOTF website); must prepare two personal references; curriculum Director's statement; official transcripts; financial statement; and an essay. **Deadline:** February 8.

736 ■ Willard and Spackman Scholarship Program *(Postgraduate/Scholarship)*

Purpose: To provide financial assistance for AOTF members to promote research and education in the field of occupational therapy. **Focus:** Occupational therapy. **Qualif.:** Applicants must be a member of the AOTF; must demonstrate a need for financial assistance; sustained a record of outstanding scholastic achievement. Post-baccalaureate applicants must be enrolled as a full-time student at the professional level in an accredited or developing occupational therapy educational program. **Criteria:** Recipients are selected based on the application and the materials submitted.

Funds Avail.: $2,000. **Number Awarded:** 2. **To Apply:** Applicants must complete the online application, (please visit AOTF website); must prepare two personal references; curriculum Director's statement; official transcripts; financial statement; and an essay. **Deadline:** February 8.

737 ■ Edith Weingarten Scholarship Program *(Postgraduate/Scholarship)*

Purpose: To provide financial assistance for AOTF members to promote research and education in the field of occupational therapy. **Focus:** Occupational therapy. **Qualif.:** Applicants must be a member of the AOTF; must demonstrate a need for financial assistance; sustained a record of outstanding scholastic achievement. Post-baccalaureate applicants must be enrolled as a full-time student at the professional level in an accredited or developing occupational therapy educational program. **Criteria:** Recipients are selected based on the application and the materials submitted.

Funds Avail.: $1,000. **To Apply:** Applicants must complete the online application, (please visit AOTF website); must prepare two personal references; curriculum Director's statement; official transcripts; financial statement; and an essay. **Deadline:** February 8.

738 ■ American Orff-Schulwerk Association

PO Box 391089
Cleveland, OH 44139-8089
Ph: (440)543-5366
Fax: (440)543-2687
E-mail: info@aosa.org
URL: http://www.aosa.org

739 ■ AOSA Research Grants *(All/Grant)*

Purpose: To promote philosophy and encourage research in varied applications of Orff Schulwerk. **Focus:** Music; Education, Music. **Qualif.:** Applicants must be active and expert AOSA members. **Criteria:** Applicants are selected based on merits.

Funds Avail.: $100-$5,000. **To Apply:** Applicants must submit a completed application form and a project proposal and forward it to the AOSA Research Chair. **Deadline:** January 15 or July 15.

Remarks: The proposal (limited to 15 pages double spaced) must include an introduction and problem, related literature, procedure, bibliography and proposed budget.

740 ■ AOSA Research Partnership Grants *(All/Grant)*

Purpose: To encourage joint research by music teachers and researchers. **Focus:** Music. **Qualif.:** Applicants must be groups consisting of one practicing music teacher (must be a member of the AOSA) of grades P-12 in a school setting and one faculty member with substantial research experience at a college or university. **Criteria:** Applicants are selected based on the panel's review of the application materials.

Funds Avail.: $800. **To Apply:** Applicants must submit a completed application form; a proposal indicating the purpose, procedure, budget summary and timeline of the project. **Deadline:** January 15 and July 15.

741 ■ Barbara Potter Scholarships *(All/Scholarship)*

Purpose: To provide financial assistance to members of AOSA who wish to study at the Orff Institute in Salzburg, Austria. **Focus:** General studies. **Qualif.:** Applicants must be a U.S. citizen or must have resided in the U.S. for the past five years; a must be member of AOSA; planning to study at the Orff Institute in Salzburg, Austria; must have

Awards are arranged alphabetically below their administering organizations

completed Level III Orff Schulwerk Training; must demonstrate personal need of financial aid. **Criteria:** Applicants are selected based on the jury's review of application materials.

Funds Avail.: No specific amount. **To Apply:** Applicants must submit a completed application and agreement form; resume; project description and 3 reference letters. Submit all requirements to the Office of the Executive Director. **Deadline:** January 25.

742 ■ Shields-Gillespie Scholarships *(All/Scholarship)*

Purpose: To support special creative projects that are associated with Orff Schulwerk and that will benefit the music education of children. **Focus:** Music. **Qualif.:** Applicants must be a U.S. citizen or must have resided in the U.S. for the past five years; a current member of AOSA and must have been an AOSA member in good standing for one year; must be actively involved in teaching low-income preschool or kindergarten students; must have a strong motivation to study music; and demonstrated financial need. **Criteria:** Applicants are selected based on the jury's review of application materials.

Funds Avail.: No specific amount. **To Apply:** Applicants must submit completed application and agreement form; resume; project description and 3 reference letters. Submit all requirements to the Office of the Executive Director. **Deadline:** January 25.

743 ■ American Oriental Society

Hatcher Graduate Library
University of Michigan
Ann Arbor, MI 48109-1205
Ph: (734)647-4760
URL: http://www.umich.edu/~aos/

744 ■ Louise Wallace Hackney Fellowship for the Study of Chinese Art *(Doctorate/Fellowship)*

Purpose: To permit the study of Chinese art, with special relation to painting and its reflection of Chinese culture, **Focus:** Chinese studies. **Qualif.:** Applicants must have completed three years study of the Chinese language or its equivalent and must be able to demonstrate that they have already committed themselves to the serious study of this important area of oriental art; must be post-doctoral as well as doctoral students. **Criteria:** Applicants are selected by the two committees of specialists in the field.

Funds Avail.: $8,000. **To Apply:** Applicants should submit the following materials in duplicate: (1) transcript of their undergraduate and graduate course work; (2) statement of personal finances; (3)three or four page summary of the proposed project to be undertaken during the year of the fellowship award, appended with a financial statement explaining the expense involved in this study; (4) no less than three letters of recommendation. **Deadline:** March 1.

745 ■ American Orthopedic Foot and Ankle Society

6300 N River Rd., Ste. 510
Rosemont, IL 60018
Ph: 800-235-4855
E-mail: aofasinfo@aofas.org
URL: http://www.aofas.org

746 ■ AOFAS Research Grants Program *(Graduate/Grant)*

Purpose: To assist members and other orthopedists in providing the highest quality foot and ankle care to the public. **Focus:** Orthopedic. **Qualif.:** Eligibility for grant funding is a benefit of membership in AOFAS, and the principle or co-principle project investigator must be an AOFAS active, Candidate or International member. **Criteria:** Investigator will not be awarded more than two grants in any four consecutive years.

Funds Avail.: $10,000. **To Apply:** The grant application form and administrative policies and procedures are available online. **Deadline:** December 1.

747 ■ Orthopedic Foot and Ankle Fellowships *(Graduate/Fellowship)*

Purpose: To assist members and other orthopedists in providing the highest quality foot and ankle care to the public. **Focus:** Orthopedic. **Qualif.:** Applicants must be orthopedic surgeons. **Criteria:** Recipients will be selected based on a consensus by foot and ankle fellowship directors.

Funds Avail.: No specific amount. **To Apply:** Applicants may download an application form online. Upon completion of the requirements, the applicants must submit their application together with curriculum vitae, Personal Vitae, Personal Statement, and check list of programs. **Deadline:** May 7. **Contact:** Ms. Zan Lofgren, AOFAS Executive Director, zlofgren@aofas.org.

748 ■ American Osteopathic Foundation

142 East Ontario St., Ste. 502
Chicago, IL 60611
Ph: (312)202-8234
Fax: (312)202-8216
E-mail: info@aof-foundation.org
URL: http://www.aof-foundation.org

749 ■ William G. Anderson, DO, Minority Scholarship *(Undergraduate/Scholarship)*

Purpose: To provide monetary scholarship to help defer the cost of students' osteopathic medical education. **Focus:** Osteopathic medicine. **Qualif.:** Any osteopathic student who will be entering his or her second- to fourth-year studies at an AOA accredited college/school of osteopathic medicine. **Criteria:** The recipient is chosen based on their outstanding academic achievement, participation in extracurricular activities, strong commitment toward osteopathic medicine, and financial need.

Funds Avail.: $5,000. **To Apply:** Applicant shall meet the following criteria: Strong interest in osteopathic medicine, its philosophy and principles; Excellent academic achievement; Demonstrated leadership efforts in addressing the educational, societal, and health needs of minorities; Demonstrated leadership efforts to eliminate inequities in medical education and health care; Noteworthy accomplishments, awards and honors, clerkship or special projects, and extracurricular activities in which the student has shown leadership abilities; Financial need. **Deadline:** March 28.

750 ■ Russell C. McCaughan, DO, Education Scholarships *(Undergraduate/Scholarship)*

Purpose: To provide monetary scholarship to help defer the cost of students' osteopathic medical education. **Focus:** Osteopathic medicine. **Qualif.:** Any osteopathic medical student who will be entering their second year of studies in an AOA approved college/school of osteopathic medicine is eligible to be nominated for this scholarship. **Criteria:** Recipients shall meet the following criteria: Demonstrated commitment to the osteopathic profession; Outstanding academic achievement during their first year of osteopathic medical education; Participation in extracurricular activities during their first year of osteopathic medical education; Demonstrated financial need to cover the cost of their osteopathic education.

Funds Avail.: $400. **To Apply:** Applicant must submit the following in one packet: Completed, typewritten or computer generated Nomination form; Letter of recommendation from the nominator; Letter from Dean certifying that the applicant is in good academic standing and states the applicant's class ranking; Letter from the Director of Financial Aid verifying the students financial need for educational assistance; Personal statement of one page or less expressing why the nominee believes he or she should receive third scholarship and should emphasize how they meet the eligibility criteria; Official medical school academic transcript. **Deadline:** April 25.

751 ■ Procter and Gamble Complex PE Scholars Grant *(Undergraduate/Award/Prize)*

Purpose: To provide monetary aid to osteopathic medical students to help defray the costs involved of taking COMPLEX-USA Level 2-PE. **Focus:** Osteopathic medicine. **Qualif.:** Any osteopathic student who will be an OMS III or OMS IV during December of the year the grant is offered, and is currently enrolled at an AOA accredited college/ school of osteopathic medicine, is eligible to be nominated for this grant. **Criteria:** Recipients shall meet the following criteria: Strong interest in osteopathic medicine, its philosophy and principle. Excellent academic achievement and successful completion COMPLEX-USA Level 1; Participation in school/community life outside of class requirements, as well as participation in professionally related activities during osteopathic medical school; Serves as an ambassador for the school and the osteopathic profession.

Funds Avail.: $1,000. **To Apply:** The Dean at each COM/ SOM is invited to nominate one student who best meets the eligibility criteria. The following should be sent in own complete packet: Completed, typewritten or computer generated nomination form; Letter of recommendation from the Dean (nominator); One letter of recommendation from someone involved with the nominee's osteopathic education that can speak to the nominee's qualifications for this grant based on the eligibility criteria. **Deadline:** April 4.

752 ■ Savvy Student Traveler Grant Program *(Undergraduate/Grant)*

Purpose: To provide funding for osteopathic medical students. **Focus:** Osteopathic medicine. **Qualif.:** Any osteopathic student who will be entering his or her second- to fourth year of studies at an AOA accredited college/ school of osteopathic medicine. **Criteria:** Grant will be given based on the committee's criteria.

Funds Avail.: $750. **To Apply:** Applicant must submit the following in one packet: Completed, typewritten, or computer generated Nomination form; Letter of recommendation from the nominator; Letter from Dean certifying that the applicant is in good academic standing and states the applicant's class ranking; Personal statement; Official COM/ SOM transcript; Current curriculum vitae or resume. **Deadline:** April 4.

753 ■ Welch Scholars Grants *(Undergraduate/ Grant)*

Purpose: To promote education within the osteopathic profession. **Focus:** Osteopathic medicine. **Qualif.:** Any osteopathic student who will be entering his or her second to fourth year of studies at an AOA accredited college/ school of osteopathic medicine. **Criteria:** The recipient are chosen based on their outstanding academic achievement, participation in extracurricular activities, strong commitment toward osteopathic medicine, and financial need.

Funds Avail.: $2,000. **To Apply:** Applicant must submit the following in one packet: Completed, typewritten or computer generated Nomination form; Letter from Dean certifying that the applicant is in good academic standing and states the applicant's class ranking; Letter from the Director of Financial Aid verifying the student's financial need for educational assistance; Letters of recommendation from two references who can speak to the applicant's qualification for this grant based on the eligibility criteria; Personal statement of not more than two pages; Personal financial need statement of not more than one page. Official medical school academic transcript (may be mailed separately). **Deadline:** April 25.

754 ■ American Paint Horse Foundation

PO Box 961023
Fort Worth, TX 76161-0023
Ph: (817)834-2742
Fax: (817)222-8488
E-mail: rteate@apha.com
URL: http://www.aphfoundation.org

755 ■ American Paint Horse Foundation Scholarships *(Undergraduate/Scholarship)*

Purpose: To promote educational and social growth of young horsemen and women. **Focus:** General studies. **Qualif.:** Applicants must have at least a B average in high school; must pass the college entrance exam; must be APHA members in good standing; must have at least 3.0 cumulative grade point average; and must be enrolled in at least 12 credits hours per semesters. **Criteria:** Recipients are selected based on a review of submitted requirements.

Funds Avail.: No specific amount. **To Apply:** Applicants must provide three letters of reference and an essay explaining their educational plans. **Deadline:** March 1.

756 ■ American Parkinson Disease Association

135 Parkinson Ave.
Staten Island, NY 10305
Ph: (718)981-8001
Fax: (718)981-4399
Free: 800-223-2732
E-mail: apda@apdaparkinson.org
URL: http://www.apdaparkinson.org

757 ■ APDA Postdoctoral Fellowships *(Professional Development/Fellowship)*

Purpose: To support postdoctoral scientists whose research training holds promise into new insights of geriatric psychology, pathophysiology, etiology and treatment of Parkinson's disease. **Focus:** Geriatric Medicine; Parkinson's disease. **Qualif.:** Applicants must have completed their MD, DO, PhD, MD/PhD, DO/PhD or clinical residency program within two (2) years of the onset of the proposed study and must perform the research project at an academic institution within the United States. **Criteria:** Preference will be given to those who meet the criteria.

Funds Avail.: Up to $35,000. **To Apply:** Applicants must

Awards are arranged alphabetically below their administering organizations

submit the application form electronically. One (1) original and two (2) hard copies of the application should be submitted to the attention of Paul Maestrone, DVM, Director of Scientific & Medical Affairs for consideration by the APDA Scientific Advisory Board. **Deadline:** March 1. **Contact:** American Parkinson Disease Association at the above address (see entry 756).

758 ■ APDA Research Grants *(Professional Development/Grant)*

Purpose: To provide financial support for junior investigators intending to pursue research in Parkinson's disease. **Focus:** General studies. **Qualif.:** Applicants must be affiliated with and perform the research project at an academic institution within the United States. **Criteria:** Selection of recipients will be based on merit.

Funds Avail.: $50,000. **To Apply:** Applicant's Research Grant application should be completed and submitted electronically along with one (1) original and two (2) hard copies of the completed application. Application packet must be sent to the attention of Paul Maestrone, DVM, Director of Scientific & Medical Affairs for consideration by the APDA Scientific Advisory Board. **Contact:** American Parkinson Disease Association at the above address (see entry 756).

759 ■ APDA Summer Fellowships *(Doctorate/Fellowship)*

Purpose: To provide a stipend to enable medical students to perform supervised laboratory or clinical research designed to clarify our understanding of Parkinson's disease, its nature, manifestations, etiology or treatment. **Focus:** Medicine. **Qualif.:** Applicant should be a full-time medical student in good academic standing in an approved American medical school. The proposed research project must be performed in an academic medical center or recognized research institute in the United States and be sponsored by a full time faculty member or established institute scientist. The project must be part of the sponsor's ongoing research and be performed under the sponsor's direct supervision. **Criteria:** Preference will be given to those who meet the qualifications.

Funds Avail.: No specific amount. **To Apply:** Applicant's application form must be accompanied by a supporting letter from the sponsor; a letter of reference from another faculty member familiar with the student's previous academic performance and a letter from the Dean's office assuring the student is in good academic standing. Applications which must contain one (1) original and two (2) hard copies of the application should be submitted electronically to the attention of Paul Maestrone, DVM, Director of Scientific & Medical Affairs. **Deadline:** December 31. **Contact:** American Parkinson Disease Association at the above address (see entry 756).

760 ■ George C. Cotzias, MD Memorial Fellowships *(Professional Development/Fellowship)*

Purpose: To assist promising neurologists in establishing careers in research, teaching and clinical services relevant to the problems, causes, prevention, diagnosis and treatment of Parkinson's disease and related neurological movement disorders. **Focus:** Neurology. **Qualif.:** Applicant must be a physician with an MD or DO degree who has completed clinical training in adult neurology, child neurology, neurosurgery, neuropathology or neuroradiology and demonstrates a promising career trajectory as a clinician scientist; should be in the formative years of career development and must not have achieved tenure status or been promoted to Associate Professor; must have an appointment at an academic institution located within the United States that has shown a clear commitment to the career development of the candidate; must be a U.S. citizen or permanent U.S. resident. **Criteria:** Awards will be given to those who meet the qualifications.

Funds Avail.: $80,000 will be awarded each year for three (3) consecutive years to support salary and research expenses. **To Apply:** Applicants must submit the following requirements: an abstract of the proposed study (150 words); a budget for each year; resources provided or to be provided by the sponsoring institution; other sources of funding, to include sponsoring agency, amount and award period (indicate how the other sponsored research complements or supplements the present proposal); two letters of recommendation (one from the applicant's institutional sponsor and one from an academic colleague with knowledge of the applicant's professional performance). **Contact:** American Parkinson Disease Association at the above address (see entry 756).

761 ■ Roger C. Duvoisin, MD Research Grants *(Professional Development/Grant)*

Purpose: To provide support funds for established scientists affiliated with research or academic institutions located within the United States and who presently not working on Parkinson's disease research. **Focus:** Neurology. **Qualif.:** Applicant must be a physician with an MD or DO degree who has completed clinical training in adult neurology, child neurology, neurosurgery, neuropathology or neuroradiology. **Criteria:** Awards will be given to those who meet the qualifications.

Funds Avail.: $80,000 per year for two consecutive years. **To Apply:** Applicants must submit the proposal requirements, (proposal should not exceed three pages); a brief abstract of the proposed study (150 words); NIH BioSketch; and budget (a detailed budget should be submitted for the first year and a continuing budget for the second year). **Deadline:** March 1. **Contact:** American Parkinson Disease Association at the above address (see entry 756).

762 ■ American Pediatric Surgical Nurses Association

PO Box 1605
Lansdale, PA 19446
Ph: (614)722-3926
E-mail: webadmin@apsna.org
URL: http://www.apsna.org

763 ■ APSNA Educational Scholarships *(Professional Development/Scholarship)*

Purpose: To assist APSNA members to further their professional education. **Focus:** Nursing; Pediatric medicine; Surgery. **Qualif.:** Applicants must be an APSNA member in good standing for at least one year; a registered nurse or advanced practice nurse with 2 years experience in pediatric surgical nursing involved in pediatric surgery patient care, education or research; must be active in the development of professional pediatric surgical nursing practices and standards. **Criteria:** Scholarship recipients will be selected based on the Education Committee's review of the application materials.

Funds Avail.: No specific amount. **To Apply:** Applicants must submit a completed application form; a documenta-

Awards are arranged alphabetically below their administering organizations

tion of program conference or educational needs which the scholarship will be used; description of the program course; a current curriculum vitae; a letter of recommendation from a co-worker; a cover letter to the Director at Large stating the applicant's credentials, experience, and involvement in the pediatric surgical nursing practices and standards; and an essay about the importance of the award. **Contact:** Beverly Haynes, beverly.haynes@ccc.uab.edu.

764 ■ American Pet Products Manufacturers Association

255 Glenville Rd.
Greenwich, CT 06831
Ph: (203)532-0000
Fax: (203)532-0551
Free: 800-452-1225
URL: http://www.appma.org

765 ■ APPMA's Jules Schwimmer Scholarship Program *(Undergraduate/Scholarship)*

Purpose: To aid deserving students who are eligible based on their parent's employment with an APPMA member firm. **Focus:** General studies. **Qualif.:** Applicant must be a dependent of a full-time employee of an APPMA member firm. Parent of the applicant must still be an employee of the APPMA member firm by the time the winners are selected. **Criteria:** Applicants will be ranked based on academic merit. Top-ranked applicants will then be further ranked based on financial need.

Funds Avail.: $1,500. **Number Awarded:** 8. **To Apply:** Applicants must obtain and submit online at www.scholarshipadministrators.net and use the ID code "APPMA". **Deadline:** May 4.

766 ■ American Philosophical Society

104 S Fifth St.
Philadelphia, PA 19106-3387
Ph: (215)440-3400
URL: http://www.amphilsoc.org

767 ■ Daland Fellowships in Clinical Investigation *(Doctorate/Fellowship)*

Purpose: To provide financial support in clinical investigation for research in the several branches of clinical medicine, including internal medicine, neurology, pediatrics, psychiatry and surgery. **Focus:** Clinical sciences; Neurology; Pediatric medicine; Surgery; and Psychiatry. **Qualif.:** Candidates must be both U.S. citizen and foreign national; have an MD or MD/PhD degree for fewer than eight years; do not have more than two years of post-doctoral training and research; expecting to perform the research at an institution in the United States. **Criteria:** Fellowship recipients will be selected on the basis of merits.

Funds Avail.: $50,000 for first year and $50,000 for second year. **To Apply:** Applicants must submit a completed application form and letter of support form. Maintain the application format, do not include additional page. Three references are required. **Deadline:** September 1. **Contact:** Linda Musumeci, Research Administrator at lmusumeci@amphilsoc.org, 215-440-3429.

768 ■ John Hope Franklin Dissertation Fellowships *(Doctorate/Fellowship)*

Purpose: To support the doctoral projects of minority students. **Focus:** General studies. **Qualif.:** Applicants must completed all course work and examinations preliminary to the dissertation; devote full-time for twelve months with no teaching obligations-to research on the dissertation. **Criteria:** Fellowship recipient will be selected on the basis of merits.

Funds Avail.: $25,000. **To Apply:** Applicants must submit a completed application form and letter of support form available at the website; must maintain the 3-page format and must not be in 11pt. font smaller. Applications must be submitted as email attachments to applications@amphilsoc.org. References are required, referees must follow the format (must not exceed one page) and must be sent electronically to lettersofsupport@amphilsoc.org. **Deadline:** April 1.

Remarks: The Fellowship is named in honor of a distinguished member of the APS. Recipient of the award is expected to spend a three months in Philadelphia. **Contact:** Linda Musumeci, Research Administrator, lmusumeci@amphilsoc.org or 215-440-3429.

769 ■ Franklin Research Grants *(Doctorate/Grant)*

Purpose: To support research in all areas of knowledge leading to publication. **Focus:** General studies. **Qualif.:** Applicants must have a doctorate or have published work of doctoral character and quality. Pre-doctoral graduate students are not eligible. **Criteria:** Recipients will be selected based on the jury's review of the application materials.

Funds Avail.: Maximum of $6,000. **To Apply:** Applicants must submit a completed application form and letter of support form available at the website; must maintain the 4-page format and must not be in 11pt. font smaller. Two references are required, referees must follow the format (must not exceed one page) and must be sent in a sealed envelope with the proposal or sent electronically to lettersofsupport@amphilsoc.org. **Deadline:** October and December.

Remarks: Recipients of the award may re-apply after two years. **Contact:** Linda Musumeci, Research Administrator at lmusumeci@amphilsoc.org, 215-440-3429.

770 ■ Lewis and Clark Fund for Exploration and Field Research *(Doctorate/Grant)*

Purpose: To provide funds for projects related to the astrobiological field. **Focus:** Biological and clinical sciences. **Qualif.:** Applicant must be a post-doctoral student and a U.S. resident performing research anywhere in the world. Foreign applicants must be based at a U.S. institution or planning to carry out research in the United States. **Criteria:** Grant recipient will be selected on the basis of merits.

Funds Avail.: $5,000. **To Apply:** Applicants must submit a completed application form and letter of support form available at the website; must maintain the 3-page format and must have a font size greater than 11pt. Applicant must also submit two references. Referees must also follow the format (must not exceed one page) and send their letters of support to lettersofsupport@amphilsoc.org. Applications must be submitted as email attachments to applications@amphilsoc.org. **Deadline:** February 15. **Contact:** Linda Musumeci, Research Administrator, lmusumeci@amphilsoc.org or 215-440-3429.

771 ■ Phillips Fund Grant for Native American Research *(Graduate/Grant)*

Purpose: To support research on Native American linguistics, ethnohistory and the history of studies of Native

American in the continental United States and Canada. **Focus:** Native American studies. **Qualif.:** Applicant must be a graduate student for research on masters theses or doctoral dissertations. **Criteria:** Grant recipient will be selected on the basis of merits.

Funds Avail.: $2,500-$3,000. **To Apply:** Applicants must submit a completed application form and letter of support form available at the website; must maintain the 3-page format and must not be in 11pt. font smaller. Two references are required, referees must follow the format (must not exceed one page) and must be sent in a sealed envelope with the proposal or sent electronically to lettersofsupport@amphilsoc.org. Applications must be submitted to: Philips Fund for Native American Research, American Philosophical Society 104 S Fifth St., Philadelphia, PA 19106-3386; or to applications@amphilsoc.org. **Deadline:** March 1. **Contact:** Linda Musumeci, Research Administrator, lmusumeci@amphilsoc.org or 215-440-3429.

772 ■ American Physical Society

One Physics Ellipse
College Park, MD 20740-3844
Ph: (301)209-3200
Fax: (301)209-0865
E-mail: alinger@aps.org
URL: http://www.aps.org

773 ■ American Physical Society Undergraduate Scholarships *(Undergraduate/Scholarship)*

Purpose: To advance and diffuse the knowledge of physics. **Focus:** Physics. **Qualif.:** Applicants must be African American, Hispanic American, or Native American US citizens or permanent residents who are majoring or planning to major in physics; must be high school seniors, college freshmen, or sophomores. **Criteria:** Recipients are selected based on financial need and academic standing.

Funds Avail.: Maximum amount of $2,000. **To Apply:** Applicants must complete an application form and other materials that will be sent by the office after November 30. **Deadline:** February 6.

774 ■ American Planning Association

122 S Michigan Ave., Ste. 1600
Chicago, IL 60603
Ph: (312)431-9100
Fax: (312)431-9985
E-mail: customerservice@planning.org
URL: http://www.planning.org

775 ■ Charles Abrams Scholarship Program *(Graduate/Scholarship)*

Purpose: To aid students who will pursue careers as practicing planners. **Focus:** Urban affairs/design/planning. **Qualif.:** Applicants must be U.S. citizens, and must be accepted into the graduate planning program of one of the following schools: Columbia University, Harvard University, Massachusetts Institute of Technology, New School University and University of Pennsylvania. A nomination by the department chair is required. **Criteria:** Recipients will be selected based on the Selection Committee's review of all applications.

Funds Avail.: $2000. **To Apply:** Applicants must submit a letter of nomination; a one- to two-page statement written by the applicant describing their commitment to complete the planning curriculum of the university and to pursue a career in the planning profession, as well as an outline of the applicants' qualifications, extra-curricular activities, and reasons for believing that a scholarship award is justified; a financial aid application; official transcripts of all previous collegiate and academic work; an official copy of all GRE scores. **Deadline:** April 30. **Contact:** Kriss Blank at the above address (see entry 774).

776 ■ APA Planning Fellowships *(Graduate/Fellowship)*

Purpose: To foster increased minority interest in the study of urban planning at the graduate level. **Focus:** Urban affairs/design/planning. **Qualif.:** Applicants must be first or second year masters degree students; members of one of the following minority groups: African American, Hispanic American or Native American; citizens of the United States; enrolled or officially accepted for enrollment in a graduate planning program accredited by the Planning Accreditation Board. Recipients must intend to work as practicing planners in the public sector. Students must be able to document their financial need. **Criteria:** Recipients will be selected based on academic achievement/improvement, letters of recommendation, financial need, professional presentation and geographic balance of awards during the particular award year.

Funds Avail.: $1000-$5000, depending on the number of fellowships awarded. **To Apply:** Applicants must submit a two- to five-page personal and background statement describing how their graduate education will be applied to career goals and why they chose planning as a career path; a completed and signed APA financial aid application; two letters of recommendation; official transcripts; written verification from the school's financial officer or copies of a school's publication or website indicating the average cost of one academic year; a copy of an acceptance letter from a PAB-accredited graduate planning school (incoming students only); a notarized statement of financial independence signed by the student's parents. **Deadline:** April 30. **Contact:** Kriss Blank at the above address (see entry 774).

777 ■ Robert A. Catlin/David W. Long Memorial Scholarships *(Graduate/Scholarship)*

Purpose: To foster increased interest among African American undergraduates in urban planning as a graduate field of study and as a professional career. **Focus:** Urban affairs/design/planning. **Qualif.:** Applicants must be African Americans who are rising juniors and seniors majoring in urban planning and related fields; must have a minimum GPA of 3.0; and must be full time enrolled students. **Criteria:** Recipients will be selected based on the committee's review of all submitted applications.

Funds Avail.: $2500. **To Apply:** Applicants must submit an application form; a personal statement; two letters of recommendation; one sealed Official Academic Transcript for each college or university attended; self-addressed, stamped postcard for notification of the receipt of a complete application. **Deadline:** October 30. **Contact:** Sigmund Shipp, Ph.D. Vice Chairperson of Policy Planning and the Black Community Division, American Planning Association, Hunter College, 695 Park Avenue, New York, NY 10021.

778 ■ Economic Development Division Graduate Scholarships *(Graduate/Scholarship)*

Purpose: To provide financial assistance to those studying economic development and planning. **Focus:** Urban affairs/

Awards are arranged alphabetically below their administering organizations

design/planning. **Qualif.:** Applicant's must be Master's level students from PAB-accredited planning departments across the United States. **Criteria:** Recipients will be selected based on the merits of the application materials submitted.

Funds Avail.: $1,000. **To Apply:** Applicants must submit a letter of recommendation from a full-time faculty member and an original paper or work having to do with a substantive and relevant topic related to economic development and planning. **Deadline:** February 15. **Contact:** Dr. Heike Mayer, Urban Affairs and Planning-Alexandria Center, 1021 Prince St., Ste. 200, Alexandria, VA 22314, 703-706-8122.

779 ■ Environment, Natural Resource and Energy (ENRE) Division Fellowships *(Graduate/Scholarship)*

Purpose: To provide financial support for students excelling in graduate level studies in planning related to natural resources, energy or the environment. **Focus:** Urban affairs/design/planning; Natural resources; Energy-related areas. **Qualif.:** Applicants must be second year graduate students enrolled in an accredited graduate school planning program focusing on issues related to the environment, natural resources or energy. Candidates must also have a minimum GPA of B or 3.0 on a 4.0 scale, and must be in a program or course of study consistent with ENRE's mission. The ENRE Division's mission is to promote sound environmental, natural resources and energy planning and sound resource use policies among individual members of APA and the general public, and within the planning profession and communities of all scales. **Criteria:** Recipient will be selected based on the quality of application materials and the connection of the student's course of study to ENRE's mission. Priority will be given to ENRE Division members.

Funds Avail.: $2,500. $1,250 for each of the two semesters. **To Apply:** Applicants must submit an application form; recommendation letter from the student's thesis/project faculty advisor; an 800-word description of the student's master's thesis or project, including how it relates to the division's mission; a 600-word essay describing interest in environmental planning, experience and future goals; a resume. **Deadline:** September 10.

780 ■ Judith McManus Price Scholarships *(Graduate, Undergraduate/Scholarship)*

Purpose: To provide partial funding for women and minority students. **Focus:** Urban affairs/design/planning. **Qualif.:** Applicants must be U.S. citizens enrolled in Planning Accreditation Board accredited planning programs. Candidates must also be women members of the following minority groups: African American, Hispanic American or Native American. **Criteria:** Recipients will be selected based on academic achievement, letters of recommendation, financial need, professional presentation and geographic balance of awards for the year.

Funds Avail.: $2000-$4000. **To Apply:** Applicant must submit a two- to fivepage background statement describing how the applicant's graduate education will be applied to career goals and why he/she chose planning as a career path; a completed and signed APA financial aid application; two letters of recommendation; written verification from the school's financial officer indicating the average cost of one academic year; resume; copy of acceptance letter from a PAB-accredited graduate planning school; a notarized statement of financial independence signed by the applicant's parents. **Deadline:** April 30.

Remarks: The award also includes a paid one-year student membership to APA. **Contact:** Kriss Blank at the above address (see entry 774).

781 ■ American Political Science Association

1527 New Hampshire Ave. NW
Washington, DC 20036-1206
Ph: (202)483-2512
Fax: (202)483-2657
E-mail: apsa@apsnet.org
URL: http://www.apsanet.org

782 ■ American Political Science Association Federal Executives Fellowships *(Professional Development/Fellowship)*

Purpose: To give senior-level federal executives an opportunity to learn more about Congress and the legislative process through direct participation. **Focus:** Political Science. **Qualif.:** Applicants must have a minimum grade of GS-13 or equivalent at time of application; must have at least two years of federal service in the executive branch, and a long term career goals relevant to a congressional experience; and must demonstrate a commitment to public service, adaptability to new, diverse working environments, and an interest in the legislative process and public affairs. **Criteria:** Recipients are selected based on the result of the nominations and interviews.

Funds Avail.: No specific amount. **To Apply:** Applicants must submit seven copies of: a detailed resume providing contact information, current grade, work experiences, educational background, languages, and special skills and talents; a statement assessing the nominee's executive potential and need for training by the supervisor(s) or agency Executive Resources Board; and a statement by the nominee presenting a need for training, the relevance of training to career goals, and the utilization of training by agency. **Deadline:** March 31. **Contact:** The American Political Science Association at the above address (see entry 781).

783 ■ American Political Science Association Journalists Fellowships *(Professional Development/Fellowship)*

Purpose: To give early-to mid career journalists an opportunity to learn more about Congress and the legislative process through direct participation. **Focus:** Journalism. **Qualif.:** Applicants must be U.S. citizens or permanent U.S. residents; must demonstrate interest in communications and policy making process; must either be print journalists, or broadcast journalists. Print journalists must have a bachelor's degree and two-ten years of continuous, full-time professional experience in newspaper or magazine at the time of application; Broadcast journalists must have a bachelor's degree and two-ten years of continuous, full-time professional experience in radio or television at the time of the application. They must have a background in reporting, producing, directing, or writing. **Criteria:** Recipients are selected based on the result of the interview.

Funds Avail.: $38,000. **To Apply:** Applicants must submit a detailed resume; around 500-word personal statement explaining how the Congressional Fellowship relates to professional goals; contact information for three professional references who have written letters of recommendation; a sample of the best writing whether published or unpublished for the scholar; seven copies of the five clips of the best writing for print journalist; and seven VHS tapes,

Awards are arranged alphabetically below their administering organizations

CD-ROMS, or DVD's with scripts of the five clips of the best reporting for broadcast journalists. **Deadline:** December 1. **Contact:** American Political Science at the above address (see entry 781).

784 ■ American Political Science Association/ MCI Scholarships *(Postdoctorate/Scholarship)*

Purpose: To give early-to-mid scholars and journalists an opportunity to learn more about Congress and the legislative process through direct participation. **Focus:** Journalism; Political Science. **Qualif.:** Applicants must be U.S. citizens or permanent U.S. residents; must demonstrate an interest in communications and policy making process; must be either scholars, print journalists or broadcast journalists. Scholars must have a Ph.D. completed within the last 15 years or will have defended their dissertation by November of the fellowship year. Print journalists must have a bachelor's degree and two-ten years of continuous, full-time professional experience in newspaper or magazine at the time of application; Broadcast journalists must have a bachelor's degree and two-ten years of continuous, full-time professional experience in radio or television at the time of the application. They must have a background in reporting, producing, directing, or writing. **Criteria:** Recipients are selected based on the result of the interview.

Funds Avail.: No specific amount. **To Apply:** Applicants must submit a detailed resume; around 500-words personal statement explaining how the Congressional Fellowship relates to his/her professional goals; contact information for three professional references who have written letters of recommendation; a sample of the best writing whether it published or unpublished for the scholar; seven copies of the five clips of the best writing for print journalist; and seven VHS tapes, CD-ROMS, or DVDs with scripts of the five clips of the best reporting for broadcast journalists. **Deadline:** December 1. **Contact:** American Political Science at the above address (see entry 781).

785 ■ American Political Science Association Political Scientists Fellowships *(All/Fellowship)*

Purpose: To give early-to-mid career political scientists an opportunity to learn more about Congress and the legislative process through direct participation. **Focus:** Political Science. **Qualif.:** Applicants must be U.S. citizens or permanent U.S. residents; must demonstrate an interest in Congress and policy making process; must have a Ph.D. completed within the last 15 years or a dissertation near completion. **Criteria:** Recipients are selected based on the result of the interview.

Funds Avail.: $38,000. **To Apply:** Applicants must submit a detailed resume; around 500-words personal statement explaining how the Congressional Fellowship relates to your professional goals; contact information for three professional references who have written letters of recommendation; a sample of the best writing whether it published or unpublished manuscript. **Deadline:** December 1. **Contact:** American Political Science at the above address (see entry 781).

786 ■ Health and Aging Policy Fellows *(Professional Development/Fellowship)*

Purpose: To make a positive contribution to the development and implementation of health policies that affect the older Americans. **Focus:** Health Care Services. **Qualif.:** Applicants must be engaged in all career stages; must be U.S. citizens or permanent residents of the U.S. territories who have career plans that anticipate continued work in the U.S. after the fellowship period. **Criteria:** Recipients are selected based on the commitment to health and aging issues and improving the health and well-being of older Americans; potential for leadership in health policy; professional qualifications and achievements; impact of the fellowship experience on the applicant's career; and interpersonal and communication skills.

Funds Avail.: $120,000-salary; $3,500-relocation; $400-health insurance. **Number Awarded:** 6. **To Apply:** Applicants must fill out and submit the application form; an essay stating the reasons why you need the fellowship, description of the experiences or contributions in the health aging field, and plans for continued development of the health policy leadership skills after completing the fellowship; a curriculum vitae; a one-page biographical sketch; and the name and contact information of the institutional references and from two professional references. **Deadline:** May 27. **Contact:** 1051 Riverside Drive, Unit 9, New York, NY 10032; healthandagingpolicy@columbia.edu.

787 ■ The Robert Wood Johnson Health Policy Fellowship Program *(All/Fellowship)*

Purpose: To build and maintain a strong and diverse leadership and workforce in health and health care as well as to develop specific fields. **Focus:** Health Sciences; Health Care Services. **Qualif.:** Applicants must have a background in allied health professions, biomedical sciences, dentistry, economics, or other social sciences, health services and administration, medicine, nursing, public health, or social and behavioral health. **Criteria:** Recipients are selected based on professional achievements; potential for leadership in health policy; potential for future growth and career advancement; and interpersonal and communication skills.

Funds Avail.: $165,000. **Number Awarded:** 10. **To Apply:** Applicants must submit a cover letter including contact information; most recent curriculum vitae; a one-page biographical sketch; names and contact information of three references; a brief essay stating the reasons why you need the RWJF Fellowship; a description of most significant community-related activity or that utilized professional expertise; a sample letter to a congressional representative, plans for continued development of health policy leadership (300-words); and a letter from the sponsoring institution. **Contact:** 500 5th Street, NW, Washington, DC 20001; 202-334-1506; info@healthpolicyfellows.org

788 ■ American Polygraph Association

PO Box 8037
Chattanooga, TN 37414-0037
Ph: (423)892-3992
Fax: (423)894-5435
Free: 800-APA-0037
E-mail: manager@polygraph.org
URL: http://www.polygraph.org

789 ■ William J. Yankee Memorial Scholarships *(Undergraduate/Scholarship)*

Purpose: To provide financial assistance to deserving students. **Focus:** General studies. **Qualif.:** Applicants must have a 4-year degree from an accredited college or university; must attend an APA accredited basic polygraph examiner training course; must qualify for APA membership upon completion of training. **Criteria:** Selection of candidates will be based on academic success and a demonstrated interest in the field of polygraphing.

Funds Avail.: $5,000. **To Apply:** Applicants must submit an essay of up to 1000 words on detection of deception, interviewing, interrogation or related fields; must have at least two letters of recommendation. **Deadline:** June 1.

790 ■ American Psychiatric Association Alliance

c/o Angela Poblocki, Executive Director
PO Box 285
North Boston, NY 14110
Ph: (703)907-7304
E-mail: ang3689@aol.com
URL: http://www.apaalliance.org

791 ■ Elsa Barton Educational Scholarships Fund *(Undergraduate/Scholarship)*

Purpose: To provide financial assistance for post secondary educational needs of a spouse/partner or dependents of impaired, disabled, or deceased physicians unable to provide family income. **Focus:** General Studies. **Qualif.:** Program is open for the spouse, partner, widow, or child of an impaired, disabled or deceased physician who could exhibit a need for additional financial resources in acquiring a post secondary education or vocational training. **Criteria:** Recipient is selected based on financial need.

Funds Avail.: No specific amount. **To Apply:** Applicants must submit completed application form available on the website; a brief statement (300 words or less) on the applicant's professional or vocational goals, explanation of financial situation, amount of funding needed and purpose, and list of financial aid or scholarships applicant receives or will be receiving; verification of financial need: CSS Financial Aid Profile, or FAFSA, and applicant's Federal Income Tax returns for years 2006 and 2007 (If applicant is a child of a physician, also include copies of both parents' Federal Income Tax Returns for years 2006 and 2007); Proof of physician's inability to practice or a death certificate; and the applicant's relevant high school, university, or course of study transcripts. Mail completed application with supporting documents to: Elsa Barton Scholarship, American Psychiatric Association Alliance, P.O. Box 285, N. Boston, NY 14110. **Deadline:** April 15. **Contact:** Angela Poblocki.

792 ■ American Psychiatric Publishing Inc.

1000 Wilson Blvd., Ste. 1825
Arlington, VA 22209-3901
Free: 800-368-5777
E-mail: appi@psych.org
URL: http://pn.psychiatryonline.org

793 ■ Minority Medical Student Fellowships in HIV Psychiatry *(Undergraduate/Fellowship)*

Purpose: To support minority medical students who have primary interest in services related to HIV/AIDS and substance abuse and its relationship to the mental health or psychological well-being of ethnic minorities. **Focus:** Psychology. **Qualif.:** Applicants must be minority medical students. **Criteria:** Preference will be given to those who meet the criteria.

Funds Avail.: No specific amount. **To Apply:** Applicants must submit a completed application form. **Deadline:** March 31. **Contact:** More information is available from Carol Svoboda at 703-907-8642 or csvoboda@psych.org; or Diane Pennessi at 703-907-8668 or dpennessi@psych.org.

794 ■ American Psychological Association of Graduate Students

750 1st St. NE
Washington, DC 20002-4242
Ph: (202)336-6014
E-mail: apags@apa.org
URL: http://www.apa.org/apags

795 ■ APAGS-CLGBTC Grant Program *(Graduate/Grant)*

Purpose: To fund a project that promotes training and educational experiences in Lesbian, Gay, Bisexual and Transgender Concerns practice. **Focus:** Psychology. **Qualif.:** Applicant must be a graduate student member of APAGS; enrolled as a student in good standing at an accredited university; must be in a masters or doctoral program. Undergraduates are not eligible for the scholarships. **Criteria:** Scholarship Selection Committee will review applications based on objective, qualitative and quantitative criteria.

Funds Avail.: $1,000. **To Apply:** Applicants must submit a title page; summary of the proposed project; evaluation; organization profile; appendix. **Deadline:** May. **Contact:** APAGS-CLGBT Grant Program, American Psychological Association of Graduate Students (APAGS), 750 First St. NW, Washington, DC 20002-4242.

796 ■ APAGS' Committee on Ethic Minority Affairs (CEMA) Grant Program *(Graduate/Grant)*

Purpose: To promote education and training opportunities for ethnic minorities and enhance the recruitment and retention efforts for ethnic minority students in psychology. **Focus:** Psychology. **Qualif.:** Applicant must be a graduate student member of APAGS; enrolled as a student in good standing at an accredited university; must be in a masters or doctoral program. Undergraduates are not eligible for the scholarships. **Criteria:** Scholarship Selection Committee will review applications based on objective, qualitative and quantitative criteria.

Funds Avail.: $1,000 for Spring Semester and $1,000 for Fall Semester. **Number Awarded:** 5. **To Apply:** Applicants must submit a title page indicating the name of the program; name and address of the applicant and date submitted; summary of the proposed project; evaluation; organizational profile; appendix. **Deadline:** December 1 and May 16. **Contact:** The Forest and Honaker Master's Scholarship, American Psychological Association of Graduate Students (APAGS), 750 First St. NW, Washington, DC 20002-4242.

797 ■ ASPPB Larry J. Bass Jr., PhD. Memorial Scholarship Awards *(Graduate, Undergraduate/Grant)*

Purpose: To provide funds for research on the regulation of psychology. **Focus:** Psychology. **Qualif.:** Applicants must be psychology graduate students or advanced undergraduate psychology majors. **Criteria:** Scholarship Selection Committee will review applications based on objective, qualitative and quantitative criteria.

Funds Avail.: $1,000. **To Apply:** Applicants must submit a curriculum vitae/resume; a recommendation from a professor or advisor who will mentor the research; a written proposal that includes: outline of the desired area of research, description of the proposed methodology and estimate of project timeline. **Deadline:** May.

Remarks: The Scholarship was named after the former

Awards are arranged alphabetically below their administering organizations

president of the Association of State and Provincial Psychology Boards (ASPPB) Larry J. Bass Jr. PhD (1999-2000). **Contact:** Larry J. Bass, Jr., PhD. Memorial Scholarship Award, c/o The ASPPB Foundation, 7177 Halcyon Summit Dr., Montgomery, AL 36117.

798 ■ Ellin Bloch and Pierre Ritchie Honorary Scholarships *(Doctorate, Graduate/Grant)*

Purpose: To support a proposed research. **Focus:** Psychology. **Qualif.:** Applicant must be a graduate student member of APAGS; enrolled as a student in good standing at an accredited university; must be in a masters or doctoral program. Undergraduates are not eligible for the scholarships. **Criteria:** Scholarship Selection Committee will review applications based on objective, qualitative and quantitative criteria.

Funds Avail.: $1,500. **To Apply:** Applicants must submit a cover letter that indicates the name of the scholarship; a curriculum vitae; a statement (500 words) addressing the applicant's short and long-term goals; a formal proposal; and two letters of recommendation that supports the application. **Deadline:** May 16.

799 ■ Diversity Dissertation Scholarships *(Doctorate/Fellowship)*

Purpose: To encourage and support graduate students in their research in the field of psychology concerning diversity issues. **Focus:** Psychology. **Qualif.:** Applicant must be a graduate student member of APAGS; enrolled as a student in good standing at an accredited university; must be in a doctoral program. **Criteria:** Recipient is selected based on the relevance of the study to diversity.

Funds Avail.: $1,500. Funds must be used to support proposed research. **To Apply:** Applicants must submit a cover letter that indicates the name of the nominee and the scholarship being applied for; graduate school affiliation; dissertation chair, current address, phone number and email address; a letter of recommendation supporting the application; an abbreviated dissertation proposal; and a curriculum vitae. **Deadline:** May.

800 ■ Nancy B. Forest and L. Michael Honaker Master's Scholarships for Research *(Doctorate, Graduate/Scholarship)*

Purpose: To fund a research in the field of Psychology at the Masters level. **Focus:** Psychology. **Qualif.:** Applicant must be a graduate student member of APAGS; enrolled as a student in good standing at an accredited university; must be in a masters or doctoral program. Undergraduates are not eligible for the scholarships. **Criteria:** Scholarship Selection Committee will review applications based on objective, qualitative and quantitative criteria.

Funds Avail.: $1,500. **To Apply:** Applicants must submit a cover letter that indicates the name of the scholarship; a curriculum vitae; a thesis proposal; and two letters of recommendation that supports the application. **Deadline:** May 16.

Remarks: The scholarship is named in honor of APA staff members Nancy B. Forest and L. Michael Honaker, PhD for their support of APAGS over the years.

801 ■ Scott Mesh Honorary Scholarships for Research in Psychology *(Graduate/Fellowship)*

Purpose: To support dissertation research related to the field of psychology. **Focus:** Psychology. **Qualif.:** Applicant must be a graduate student member of APAGS; enrolled as a student in good standing at an accredited university; must be in a masters or doctoral program. Undergraduates are not eligible for the scholarships. **Criteria:** Scholarship Selection Committee will review applications based on objective, qualitative and quantitative criteria.

Funds Avail.: $1,500. **To Apply:** Applicants must submit a cover letter that indicates the name of the scholarship; a curriculum vitae; a dissertation proposal; and two letters of recommendation that supports the application. **Deadline:** May 16.

Remarks: The scholarship is named after Scott Mesh, one of the founding co-chairs of APAGS in 1988.

802 ■ David Pilon Scholarships for Training in Professional Psychology *(Doctorate, Graduate/Scholarship)*

Purpose: To promote training and educational experiences in professional practice. **Focus:** Psychology. **Qualif.:** Applicant must be a graduate student member of APAGS; must be enrolled as a student in good standing at an accredited university; must be in a masters or doctoral program. Undergraduates are not eligible for the scholarships. **Criteria:** Scholarship Selection Committee will review applications based on objective, qualitative and quantitative criteria.

Funds Avail.: $1,500. **To Apply:** Applicants must submit a cover letter that indicates the name of the scholarship; a curriculum vitae; a statement (500 words) addressing the applicant's short and long-term goals; a formal proposal; and two letters of recommendation that supports the application. **Deadline:** May 16.

Remarks: Established in honor of David Pilon, one of the founding co-chairs of APAGS in 1988.

803 ■ American Public Power Association

1875 Connecticut Ave. NW, Ste. 1200
Washington, DC 20009-5715
Ph: (202)467-2900
Fax: (202)467-2910
URL: http://www.appanet.org

804 ■ DEED Student Research Grant/Internships *(Graduate, Undergraduate/Grant)*

Purpose: To promote the involvement of students in studying energy-related disciplines in the public power industry, and to provide host utilities with technical assistance. **Focus:** Energy-related areas. **Qualif.:** Applicants must be graduate or undergraduate students studying in energy-related disciplines from accredited colleges or universities; must be willing to work in a state with at least one sponsor DEED member. **Criteria:** Selection of applicants will be based on the scholarship criteria: (a) Broad applicability of benefits to public power systems; (b) Close involvement of the host utility in project monitoring, sponsorship, and guidance; (c) Major in an academic field related to the electric power or energy service industries; (d) Superior academic performance; (e) Special consideration to utilities who have not previously sponsored a student and to small utilities; (f) Educational and learning opportunities for student(s) in public power and utility field.

Funds Avail.: $4,000. **To Apply:** Applicants must complete the information on the DEED Student Research Grant/Internship application coversheet available online; must submit the original signature of the student, utility authority and school official as well as other information requested in

Awards are arranged alphabetically below their administering organizations

required signature section; must have a single transcript of the student's academic record. Application form and other requirements must be sent to DEED Administrator, American Public Power Association, 1875 Connecticut Ave. NW, Ste. 1200, Washington, DC 20009-5715. **Deadline:** February 15 and October 1.

805 ■ American Public Works Association

2345 Grand Blvd., Ste. 700
Kansas City, MO 64108-2625
Ph: (816)472-6100
Fax: (816)472-1610
Free: 800-848-APWA
E-mail: pking@apwa.net
URL: http://www.apwa.net

806 ■ APWA Engineering Scholarships
(Undergraduate/Scholarship)

Purpose: To provide financial assistance for the students taking up civil engineering. **Focus:** Civil engineering. **Qualif.:** Applicants must be students pursuing a career in civil engineering or a related field within the Antelope Valley, Santa Clarita, and Victor Valley areas. **Criteria:** Applicants are evaluated based on their GPA and financial need.

Funds Avail.: $500-$1,500. **To Apply:** Applicants must submit all the required application information. **Deadline:** March 15. **Contact:** Brian Glidden, 42138 10th St. West, Lancaster, CA 93534.

807 ■ American Public Works Association-Nevada

c/o Leslie R. Henley, Pres.
Clark County Public Works
PO Box 554000
Las Vegas, NV 89155
Ph: (702)455-6065
Fax: (702)455-6113
E-mail: lrh@co.clark.nv.us
URL: http://www.apwa-nv.org

808 ■ Michael Koizumi APWA Scholarships
(Undergraduate/Scholarship)

Purpose: To promote education in the field of public works, public administration or related field. **Focus:** Public administration. **Qualif.:** Applicant must be a Nevada resident; must plan to enroll in a course of study leading to a career in the field of public works, public administration or a related private enterprise (e.g. business, architecture, science, engineering, etc.); and must be an entering their freshman year or currently enrolled in college. **Criteria:** Awards are given based on nominations by APWA members; financial need-income, family size; desire; achievements; grades. Preference is for students attending a Nevada school.

Funds Avail.: $1000 and $2000. **Number Awarded:** 4. **To Apply:** Applicants must submit completed application form together with copy of transcripts, reference, list of experience, a written statement on financial status, and career objectives. **Contact:** Northern Branch (All Counties except Clark, Lincoln and Nye), Peter Gulash, Terracon 1360 Greg St., Stes. 111-112 Sparks, NV 89431, P: 775-351-2400, F: 775-351-2423, or pmgulash@terracon.com. Southern Branch (Clark, Lincoln and Nye Counties), Michael B. Holloway, Poggemeyer Design Group, Inc. 2601 North Tenaya Way Las Vegas, NV 89128-0427, P: 702-255-8100, F: 702-255-8375.

809 ■ Lari Ann Vest Memorial Scholarships
(Undergraduate/Scholarship)

Purpose: To support minority students studying engineering. **Focus:** Engineering. **Qualif.:** Applicant must be a minority student majoring in engineering. **Criteria:** Award is given based on merit.

Funds Avail.: No specific amount. **To Apply:** Applicants may contact APWA-Nevada for more information about the scholarships.

Remarks: Established in memory of Lari Anne Vest. **Contact:** Vanessa Pestka, 702-278-0911, or vanessa@pestilenthen.com. Derek Pendergraft, 702-743-7049, or dereko66@hotmail.com.

810 ■ American Quarter Horse Youth Association

PO Box 200
Amarillo, TX 79168
Ph: (806)376-4811
URL: http://www.aqha.com/youth.html

811 ■ American Quarter Horse Foundation Scholarships *(Undergraduate/Scholarship)*

Purpose: To develop and educate the future professionals. **Focus:** Education; Nursing; Journalism; Veterinary science and medicine. **Qualif.:** An applicant must be enrolled in college specializing degree programs such as education, nursing, journalism, veterinary and racing. **Criteria:** Applicant will be selected based on the financial need, academic merit, equine involvement, and civic activities.

Funds Avail.: No specific amount. **To Apply:** Applicant must fill out the application form and submit proof that he/she is currently enrolled in a college or university. **Deadline:** not stated. **Contact:** 806-378-5000.

812 ■ American Quilt Study Group

1610 L St.
Lincoln, NE 68508-2509
Ph: (402)477-1181
Fax: (402)477-1183
E-mail: AQSG2@windstream.net
URL: http://www.americanquiltstudygroup.org

813 ■ Lucy Hilty Research Grants *(All/Grant)*

Purpose: To provide support for research in the industry of quilting. **Focus:** Art. **Qualif.:** Applicants can be individuals or group affiliated with quilt-related studies. **Criteria:** Grantees will be selected according to the quality and impact of their projects; ability to complete the project; compatibility of the projects for the goal of AQSG; and how the projects will contribute to the quilting industry.

Funds Avail.: $2000. **To Apply:** Application form is available at the website. Proposal should be limited to a cover letter and the application; completed proposal description; must state the qualifications of the researcher; include letters of support from cooperating institutions or individuals; and a line-item budget for the amount of funding required. **Deadline:** February 1.

814 ■ American Radio Relay League (ARRL) Foundation

225 Main St.
Newington, CT 06111

Awards are arranged alphabetically below their administering organizations

Ph: (860)594-0200
Fax: (860)594-0259
E-mail: foundation@arrl.org
URL: http://www.arrlf.org

815 ■ American Radio Relay League Louisiana Memorial Scholarships *(Undergraduate/Scholarship)*

Purpose: To support the education of students holding a valid FCC-granted Amateur Radio license for post-secondary education. **Focus:** Radio and television. **Qualif.:** Applicant must hold an FCC amateur radio license, and be a Louisiana resident or attending a four-year college/university in Louisiana. **Criteria:** Award is given based on the submitted materials.

Funds Avail.: $500. **Number Awarded:** 1. **To Apply:** Applicants must submit a completed scholarship application form along with a recent high school (or equivalent) or college transcript. **Deadline:** February 1.

816 ■ American Radio Relay League Scholarships Honoring Barry Goldwater, K7UGA *(Undergraduate/Scholarship)*

Purpose: To support the education of students holding a valid FCC-granted Amateur Radio license for post-secondary education. **Focus:** Radio and television. **Qualif.:** Applicant must hold an FCC amateur radio license. **Criteria:** Award is given based on the submitted materials.

Funds Avail.: $5,000. **Number Awarded:** 1. **To Apply:** Applicants must submit a completed scholarship application form along with a recent high school (or equivalent) or college transcript. **Deadline:** February 1.

817 ■ Earl I. Anderson Scholarships *(Undergraduate/Scholarship)*

Purpose: To support the education of students holding a valid FCC-granted Amateur Radio license for post-secondary education. **Focus:** Radio and television. **Qualif.:** Applicant must hold an FCC amateur radio license, and be an Illinois, Indiana, Michigan, or Florida resident. **Criteria:** Awards are given based on the submitted materials.

Funds Avail.: $1,250. **Number Awarded:** 3. **To Apply:** Applicants must submit a completed scholarship application form along with a recent high school (or equivalent) or college transcript. **Deadline:** February 1.

818 ■ ARRL Foundation General Fund Scholarships *(Undergraduate/Scholarship)*

Purpose: To support the education of students holding a valid FCC-granted Amateur Radio license for post-secondary education. **Focus:** Radio and television. **Qualif.:** Applicant must hold an FCC amateur radio license. **Criteria:** Awards are given based on the submitted materials.

Funds Avail.: $1,000. **Number Awarded:** Multiple. **To Apply:** Applicants must submit a completed scholarship application form along with a recent high school (or equivalent) or college transcript. **Deadline:** February 1.

819 ■ ARRLF Mississippi Scholarships *(Undergraduate/Scholarship)*

Purpose: To support the education of students holding a valid FCC-granted Amateur Radio license for post-secondary education. **Focus:** Radio and television; Electronics; Communications. **Qualif.:** Applicant must hold an FCC amateur radio license; be a Mississippi resident; be studying in baccalaureate or higher courses of study in electronics, communications or related fields; and be under 30 years of age. **Criteria:** Award is given based on the submitted materials.

Funds Avail.: $500. **Number Awarded:** 1. **To Apply:** Applicants must submit a completed scholarship application form along with a recent high school (or equivalent) or college transcript. **Deadline:** February 1.

820 ■ Richard W. Bendicksen Memorial Scholarships *(Undergraduate/Scholarship)*

Purpose: To support the education of students holding a valid FCC-granted Amateur Radio license for post-secondary education. **Focus:** Radio and television. **Qualif.:** Applicant must hold an FCC amateur radio license, and attending a four-year college/university. **Criteria:** Award is given based on the submitted materials.

Funds Avail.: $1,000. **Number Awarded:** 1. **To Apply:** Applicants must submit a completed scholarship application form along with a recent high school (or equivalent) or college transcript. **Deadline:** February 1.

821 ■ William Bennett W7PHO Memorial Scholarships *(Undergraduate/Scholarship)*

Purpose: To support the education of students holding a valid FCC-granted Amateur Radio license for post-secondary education. **Focus:** Radio and television. **Qualif.:** Applicant must hold an FCC amateur radio license; be a Northwest, Pacific or Southwest Division resident; be enrolled in a four-year college/university; and have a GPA of 3.0 or better for an ongoing course of study. **Criteria:** Award is given based on the submitted materials.

Funds Avail.: $500. **Number Awarded:** 1. **To Apply:** Applicants must submit a completed scholarship application form along with a recent high school (or equivalent) or college transcript. **Deadline:** February 1.

822 ■ Henry Broughton, K2AE Memorial Scholarships *(Undergraduate/Scholarship)*

Purpose: To support the education of students holding a valid FCC-granted Amateur Radio license for post-secondary education. **Focus:** Radio and television; Engineering; Science. **Qualif.:** Applicant must hold an FCC amateur radio license; reside within 70 miles of Schenectady NY; studying in baccalaureate or higher courses of study in engineering, sciences or a similar field in an accredited four-year college/university. **Criteria:** Award is given based on the submitted materials.

Funds Avail.: $1,000. **Number Awarded:** 1. **To Apply:** Applicants must submit a completed scholarship application form along with a recent high school (or equivalent) or college transcript. **Deadline:** February 1.

823 ■ Mary Lou Brown Scholarships *(Undergraduate/Scholarship)*

Purpose: To support the education of students holding a valid FCC-granted Amateur Radio license for post-secondary education. **Focus:** Radio and television. **Qualif.:** Applicant must hold an FCC amateur radio license; be a resident of ARRL Northwest Division (AK, ID, MT, OR, WA); studying baccalaureate or higher courses; and have a GPA of 3.0 or higher. **Criteria:** Awards are given based on the submitted materials.

Funds Avail.: $2,500. **To Apply:** Applicants must submit a completed scholarship application form along with a recent

Awards are arranged alphabetically below their administering organizations

high school (or equivalent) or college transcript. **Deadline:** February 1.

824 ■ L.B. Cebik, W4RNL, and Jean Cebik, N4TZP, Memorial Scholarships *(Undergraduate/ Scholarship)*

Purpose: To support the education of students holding a valid FCC-granted Amateur Radio license for post-secondary education. **Focus:** Radio and television. **Qualif.:** Applicant must hold an FCC amateur radio license, and be attending a four-year college/university. **Criteria:** Award is given based on the submitted materials.

Funds Avail.: $1,000. **Number Awarded:** 1. **To Apply:** Applicants must submit a completed scholarship application form along with a recent high school (or equivalent) or college transcript. **Deadline:** February 1.

825 ■ Central Arizona DX Association Scholarships *(Undergraduate/Scholarship)*

Purpose: To support the education of students holding a valid FCC-granted Amateur Radio license for post-secondary education. **Focus:** Radio and television. **Qualif.:** Applicant must hold an FCC amateur radio license; be a resident of Arizona; and have a GPA of 3.2 or above. **Criteria:** Graduating high school students will be considered before current college students.

Funds Avail.: $500. **Number Awarded:** 1. **To Apply:** Applicants must submit a completed scholarship application form along with a recent high school (or equivalent) or college transcript. **Deadline:** February 1.

826 ■ Challenge Met Scholarships *(Undergraduate/Scholarship)*

Purpose: To support the education of students holding a valid FCC-granted Amateur Radio license for post-secondary education. **Focus:** Radio and television. **Qualif.:** Applicant must hold an FCC amateur radio license, and be attending an accredited two- or four-year college technical school or university. **Criteria:** Preference is given to application with documented learning disability (by physician or school) and indications that the applicant is putting forth substantial effort regardless of resulting academic grades.

Funds Avail.: $500. **To Apply:** Applicants must submit a completed scholarship application form along with a recent high school (or equivalent) or college transcript. **Deadline:** February 1.

827 ■ Chicago FM Club Scholarships *(Undergraduate/Scholarship)*

Purpose: To support the education of students holding a valid FCC-granted Amateur Radio license for post-secondary education. **Focus:** Radio and television. **Qualif.:** Applicant must hold an FCC amateur radio license; residency in FCC Ninth Call district (IN, IL, WI); be attending a post-secondary course of study at an accredited two- or four-year college or trade school; and must be a U.S. citizen or within three months of citizenship. **Criteria:** Awards are given based on the submitted materials.

Funds Avail.: $500. **To Apply:** Applicants must submit a completed scholarship application form along with a recent high school (or equivalent) or college transcript. **Deadline:** February 1.

828 ■ Tom and Judith Comstock Scholarships *(Undergraduate/Scholarship)*

Purpose: To support the education of students holding a valid FCC-granted Amateur Radio license for post-secondary education. **Focus:** Radio and television. **Qualif.:** Applicant must hold an FCC amateur radio license; be a resident of Texas or Oklahoma; and be a high school senior accepted at a twoor four-year college. **Criteria:** Award is given based on the submitted materials.

Funds Avail.: $2,000. **Number Awarded:** 1. **To Apply:** Applicants must submit a completed scholarship application form along with a recent high school (or equivalent) or college transcript. **Deadline:** February 1.

829 ■ Irvine W. Cook WA0CGS Scholarships *(Undergraduate/Scholarship)*

Purpose: To support the education of students holding a valid FCC-granted Amateur Radio license for post-secondary education. **Focus:** Radio and television; Electronics; Communications. **Qualif.:** Applicant must hold an FCC amateur radio license; residency in Kansas; and be studying baccalaureate or higher courses in electronics, communications or a related field. **Criteria:** Award is given based on the submitted materials.

Funds Avail.: $1,000. **Number Awarded:** 1. **To Apply:** Applicants must submit a completed scholarship application form along with a recent high school (or equivalent) or college transcript. **Deadline:** February 1.

830 ■ Charles Clarke Cordle Memorial Scholarships *(Undergraduate/Scholarship)*

Purpose: To support the education of students holding a valid FCC-granted Amateur Radio license for post-secondary education. **Focus:** Radio and television; Electronics; Communications. **Qualif.:** Applicant must hold an FCC amateur radio license; be a resident of Georgia or Alabama; have a GPA of 2.5 or higher; and be attending an institution in Georgia or Alabama. **Criteria:** Preference is given to applicant studying electronics, communications or related field.

Funds Avail.: $1,000. **Number Awarded:** 1. **To Apply:** Applicants must submit a completed scholarship application form along with a recent high school (or equivalent) or college transcript. **Deadline:** February 1.

831 ■ Albuquerque ARC/Toby Cross Scholarships *(Undergraduate/Scholarship)*

Purpose: To support the education of students holding a valid FCC-granted Amateur Radio license for post-secondary education. **Focus:** Radio and television. **Qualif.:** Applicant must hold an FCC amateur radio license, and be a New Mexico resident. **Criteria:** Award is given based on the submitted materials.

Funds Avail.: $500. **Number Awarded:** 1. **To Apply:** Applicants must submit a completed scholarship application form along with a recent high school (or equivalent) or college transcript. **Deadline:** February 1.

832 ■ Dayton Amateur Radio Association Scholarships *(Undergraduate/Scholarship)*

Purpose: To support the education of students holding a valid FCC-granted Amateur Radio license for post-secondary education. **Focus:** Radio and television. **Qualif.:** Applicant must hold an FCC amateur radio license and be attending an accredited four-year college/university. **Criteria:** Awards are given based on the submitted materials.

Funds Avail.: $1,000. **Number Awarded:** 4. **To Apply:** Applicants must submit a completed scholarship application form along with a recent high school (or equivalent) or college transcript. **Deadline:** February 1.

833 ■ Charles N. Fisher Memorial Scholarships *(Undergraduate/Scholarship)*

Purpose: To support the education of students holding a valid FCC-granted Amateur Radio license for post-secondary education. **Focus:** Radio and television; Electronics; Communications. **Qualif.:** Applicant must hold an FCC amateur radio license; must be a resident of ARRL Southwestern Division (AZ, Los Angeles, Orange, San Diego, Santa Barbara); studying in electronics, communications or related fields. **Criteria:** Award is given based on the submitted materials.

Funds Avail.: $1,000. **Number Awarded:** 1. **To Apply:** Applicants must submit a completed scholarship application form along with a recent high school (or equivalent) or college transcript. **Deadline:** February 1.

834 ■ William R. Goldfarb Memorial Scholarships *(Undergraduate/Scholarship)*

Purpose: To support the education of students holding a valid FCC-granted Amateur Radio license for post-secondary education. **Focus:** Radio and television; Business; Computer and information sciences; Medicine; Nursing; Engineering; Science. **Qualif.:** Applicant must hold an FCC amateur radio license; must be studying baccalaureate courses in business-related, computers, medical, nursing, engineering or sciences; be a high school senior; and must demonstrate financial need. **Criteria:** Award is given based on the submitted materials.

Funds Avail.: No specific amount. **Number Awarded:** 1. **To Apply:** Applicants must submit a completed scholarship application form along with a recent high school (or equivalent) or college transcript, and the Free Application for Federal Student Aid (FAFSA) or Student Aid Report (SAR). **Deadline:** February 1.

835 ■ Paul and Helen L. Grauer Scholarships *(Undergraduate/Scholarship)*

Purpose: To support the education of students holding a valid FCC-granted Amateur Radio license for post secondary-education. **Focus:** Radio and television; Electronics; Communications. **Qualif.:** Applicant must hold an FCC amateur radio license; be a resident of ARRL Midwest Division (IA, KS, MO, NE); be studying in baccalaureate or higher courses in electronics, communications or related field; and be attending school in the Midwest Division. **Criteria:** Award is given based on the submitted materials.

Funds Avail.: $1,000. **Number Awarded:** 1. **To Apply:** Applicants must submit a completed scholarship application form along with a recent high school (or equivalent) or college transcript. **Deadline:** February 1.

836 ■ K2TEO Martin J. Green, Sr. Memorial Scholarships *(Undergraduate/Scholarship)*

Purpose: To support the education of students holding a valid FCC-granted Amateur Radio license for post-secondary education. **Focus:** Radio and television. **Qualif.:** Applicant must hold an FCC amateur radio license. **Criteria:** Preference is given to a student from a "ham family".

Funds Avail.: $1,000. **Number Awarded:** 1. **To Apply:** Applicants must submit a completed scholarship application form along with a recent high school (or equivalent) or college transcript. **Deadline:** February 1.

837 ■ Perry F. Hadlock Memorial Scholarships *(Undergraduate/Scholarship)*

Purpose: To support the education of students holding a valid FCC-granted Amateur Radio license for post-secondary education. **Focus:** Radio and television; Technology; Engineering, Electrical. **Qualif.:** Applicant must hold an FCC amateur radio license; must be studying in baccalaureate or higher courses in a technology-related field; preference to electrical and electronics engineering. **Criteria:** Preference is given to applicant studying at Clarkson University, Potsdam NY, or any Atlantic or Hudson Division.

Funds Avail.: $2,000. **Number Awarded:** 1. **To Apply:** Applicants must submit a completed scholarship application form along with a recent high school (or equivalent) or college transcript. **Deadline:** February 1.

838 ■ Albert H. Hix, W8AH Memorial Scholarships *(Undergraduate/Scholarship)*

Purpose: To support the education of students holding a valid FCC-granted Amateur Radio license for post-secondary education. **Focus:** Radio and television. **Qualif.:** Applicant must hold an FCC amateur radio license; be a resident and attending school in the WV Section; and have a GPA of 3.0 or higher. **Criteria:** Award is given based on the submitted materials.

Funds Avail.: $500. **Number Awarded:** 1. **To Apply:** Applicants must submit a completed scholarship application form along with a recent high school (or equivalent) or college transcript. **Deadline:** February 1.

839 ■ Seth Horen, K1LOM Memorial Scholarships *(Undergraduate/Scholarship)*

Purpose: To support the education of students holding a valid FCC-granted Amateur Radio license for post-secondary education. **Focus:** Radio and television. **Qualif.:** Applicant must hold an FCC amateur radio license, and be attending a four-year college/university. **Criteria:** Award is given based on the submitted materials.

Funds Avail.: $500. **Number Awarded:** 1. **To Apply:** Applicants must submit a completed scholarship application form along with a recent high school (or equivalent) or college transcript. **Deadline:** February 1.

840 ■ IRARC Memorial Joseph P. Rubino WA4MMD Scholarships *(Undergraduate/Scholarship)*

Purpose: To support the education of students holding a valid FCC-granted Amateur Radio license for post-secondary education. **Focus:** Radio and television; Electronics. **Qualif.:** Applicant must hold an FCC amateur radio license; have a minimum 2.5 GPA on a 4.0 scale; and be enrolled in an undergraduate degree or electronic technician certification program at an accredited institution. **Criteria:** Preference is given to the residents of Florida (Brevard County).

Funds Avail.: $750. **To Apply:** Applicants must submit a completed scholarship application form along with a recent high school (or equivalent) or college transcript. **Deadline:** February 1.

841 ■ Dr. James L. Lawson Memorial Scholarships *(Undergraduate/Scholarship)*

Purpose: To support the education of students holding a valid FCC-granted Amateur Radio license for post-secondary education. **Focus:** Radio and television Electronics; Communications. **Qualif.:** Applicant must hold an FCC amateur radio license; be a resident of one of the New England states (ME, NH, VT, CT, RI) or New York State; and be studying in baccalaureate or higher courses in

Awards are arranged alphabetically below their administering organizations

electronics, communications or related fields. **Criteria:** Award is given based on the submitted materials.

Funds Avail.: $500. **Number Awarded:** 1. **To Apply:** Applicants must submit a completed scholarship application form along with a recent high school (or equivalent) or college transcript. **Deadline:** February 1.

842 ■ Fred R. McDaniel Memorial Scholarships *(Undergraduate/Scholarship)*

Purpose: To support the education of students holding a valid FCC-granted Amateur Radio license for post-secondary education. **Focus:** Radio and television; Electronics; Communications. **Qualif.:** Applicant must hold an FCC amateur radio license; be a resident of the FCC 5th call district (TX, OK, AR, LA, MS, NM); be studying in baccalaureate or higher courses of study in electronics, communications or related fields. **Criteria:** Preference is given to students with a GPA of 3.0 or higher.

Funds Avail.: $500. **Number Awarded:** 1. **To Apply:** Applicants must submit a completed scholarship application form along with a recent high school (or equivalent) or college transcript. **Deadline:** February 1.

843 ■ Edmond A. Metzger Scholarships *(Undergraduate/Scholarship)*

Purpose: To support the education of students holding a valid FCC-granted Amateur Radio license for post-secondary education. **Focus:** Radio and television; Electrical engineering. **Qualif.:** Applicant must hold an FCC amateur radio license; be a resident of ARRL Central Division (IL, IN, WI); be studying in baccalaureate or higher courses of study in electrical engineering; be an ARRL member; and attending school in the Central Division. **Criteria:** Award is given based on the submitted materials.

Funds Avail.: $500. **Number Awarded:** 1. **To Apply:** Applicants must submit a completed scholarship application form along with a recent high school (or equivalent) or college transcript. **Deadline:** February 1.

844 ■ David W. Misek, N8NPX Memorial Scholarships *(Undergraduate/Scholarship)*

Purpose: To support the education of students holding a valid FCC-granted Amateur Radio license for post-secondary education. **Focus:** Radio and television. **Qualif.:** Applicant must hold an FCC amateur radio license; currently reside in one of nine Ohio counties: Greene, Montgomery, Champaign, Darke, Preble, Miami, Clark, Butler, Warren; and be attending four-year college/university. **Criteria:** Awards are given based on the submitted materials.

Funds Avail.: $1,500. **Number Awarded:** Up to 3. **To Apply:** Applicants must submit a completed scholarship application form along with a recent high school (or equivalent) or college transcript. **Deadline:** February 1.

845 ■ NCDXF Scholarships *(Undergraduate/Scholarship)*

Purpose: To support the education of students holding a valid FCC-granted Amateur Radio license for post-secondary education. **Focus:** Radio and television. **Qualif.:** Applicant must hold an FCC amateur radio license; be attending a junior college, four-year college/university or trade school in the U.S.; and must demonstrate activity and interest in DXing. **Criteria:** Awards are given based on the submitted materials.

Funds Avail.: $1,500. **Number Awarded:** 2. **To Apply:** Applicants must submit a completed scholarship application form along with a recent high school (or equivalent) or college transcript. **Deadline:** February 1.

846 ■ New England FEMARA Scholarships *(Undergraduate/Scholarship)*

Purpose: To support the education of students holding a valid FCC-granted Amateur Radio license for post-secondary education. **Focus:** Radio and television. **Qualif.:** Applicant must hold an FCC amateur radio license, and be a resident of one of the New England states (ME, NH, VT, CT, RI). **Criteria:** Awards are given based on the submitted materials.

Funds Avail.: $1,000. **To Apply:** Applicants must submit a completed scholarship application form along with a recent high school (or equivalent) or college transcript. **Deadline:** February 1.

847 ■ Ray, NORP and Katie, WOKTE Pautz Scholarships *(Undergraduate/Scholarship)*

Purpose: To support the education of students holding a valid FCC-granted Amateur Radio license for post-secondary education. **Focus:** Radio and television; Electronics; Computer and information sciences. **Qualif.:** Applicant must hold an FCC amateur radio license; be a resident of the ARRL Midwest Division (IA, KS, MO, NE); be enrolled in electronics, computer science or related field at an accredited 4-year college/university; and be an ARRL member. **Criteria:** Award is given based on the submitted materials.

Funds Avail.: $500-$1,000. **Number Awarded:** 1. **To Apply:** Applicants must submit a completed scholarship application form along with a recent high school (or equivalent) or college transcript. **Deadline:** February 1.

848 ■ Peoria Area Amateur Radio Club Scholarships *(Undergraduate/Scholarship)*

Purpose: To support the education of students holding a valid FCC-granted Amateur Radio license for post-secondary education. **Focus:** Radio and television. **Qualif.:** Applicant must hold an FCC amateur radio license; be a resident of Central Illinois in one of these counties: Peoria, Tazewell, Woodford, Knox, McLean, Fulton, Logan, Marshall or Stark; and attending an accredited two- or four-year college/university. **Criteria:** Award is given based on the submitted materials.

Funds Avail.: $500. **Number Awarded:** 1. **To Apply:** Applicants must submit a completed scholarship application form along with a recent high school (or equivalent) or college transcript. **Deadline:** February 1.

849 ■ PHD ARA Scholarships *(Undergraduate/Scholarship)*

Purpose: To support the education of students holding a valid FCC-granted Amateur Radio license for post-secondary education. **Focus:** Radio and television; Journalism; Computer and information sciences; Electronics. **Qualif.:** Applicant must hold an FCC amateur radio license; be a resident of ARRL Midwest Division (IA, KS, MO, NE); with course sof study in journalism, computer science or electronic engineering; and be the child of a deceased radio amateur. **Criteria:** Award is given based on the submitted materials.

Funds Avail.: $500. **Number Awarded:** 1. **To Apply:** Applicants must submit a completed scholarship application form along with a recent high school (or equivalent) or col-

Awards are arranged alphabetically below their administering organizations

lege transcript. **Deadline:** February 1.

850 ■ Thomas W. Porter, W8KYZ Scholarships Honoring Michael Daugherty, W8LSE
(Undergraduate/Scholarship)

Purpose: To support the education of students holding a valid FCC-granted Amateur Radio license for post-secondary education. **Focus:** Radio and television. **Qualif.:** Applicant must hold an FCC amateur radio license, and attending an accredited 2- or 4-year college/university or technical school. **Criteria:** Preference is given to the resident of Ohio or West Virginia.

Funds Avail.: $1,000. **Number Awarded:** 1. **To Apply:** Applicants must submit a completed scholarship application form along with a recent high school (or equivalent) or college transcript. **Deadline:** February 1.

851 ■ Donald Riebhoff Memorial Scholarships
(Undergraduate/Scholarship)

Purpose: To support the education of students holding a valid FCC-granted Amateur Radio license for post-secondary education. **Focus:** Radio and television. **Qualif.:** Applicant must hold an FCC amateur radio license; be studying in baccalaureate or higher courses of study in international studies at an accredited post-secondary school; and be an ARRL member. **Criteria:** Award is given based on the submitted materials.

Funds Avail.: $1,000. **Number Awarded:** 1. **To Apply:** Applicants must submit a completed scholarship application form along with a recent high school (or equivalent) or college transcript. **Deadline:** February 1.

852 ■ Bill Salerno, W2ONV, Memorial Scholarships *(Undergraduate/Scholarship)*

Purpose: To support the education of students holding a valid FCC-granted Amateur Radio license for post-secondary education. **Focus:** Radio and television. **Qualif.:** Applicant must hold an FCC amateur radio license; have a high school GPA of 3.7 or higher; have an annual family income not exceeding $100,000; and be enrolled at an accredited 4-year college/university. **Criteria:** Award is given based on the submitted materials.

Funds Avail.: $1,000. **Number Awarded:** 1. **To Apply:** Applicants must submit a completed scholarship application form along with a recent high school (or equivalent) or college transcript. **Deadline:** February 1.

853 ■ Eugene Gene Sallee, W4YFR Memorial Scholarships *(Undergraduate/Scholarship)*

Purpose: To support the education of students holding a valid FCC-granted Amateur Radio license for post-secondary education. **Focus:** Radio and television. **Qualif.:** Applicant must hold an FCC amateur radio license; be a resident of the state of Georgia; and have a GPA of 3.0 or higher. **Criteria:** Award is given based on the submitted materials.

Funds Avail.: $500. **Number Awarded:** 1. **To Apply:** Applicants must submit a completed scholarship application form along with a recent high school (or equivalent) or college transcript. **Deadline:** February 1.

854 ■ Scholarships of the Morris Radio Club of New Jersey *(Undergraduate/Scholarship)*

Purpose: To support the education of students holding a valid FCC-granted Amateur Radio license for post-secondary education. **Focus:** Radio and television. **Qualif.:** Applicant must hold an FCC amateur radio license, and be attending a four-year college/university. **Criteria:** Award is given based on the submitted materials.

Funds Avail.: $1,000. **Number Awarded:** 1. **To Apply:** Applicants must submit a completed scholarship application form along with a recent high school (or equivalent) or college transcript. **Deadline:** February 1.

855 ■ Six Meter Club of Chicago Scholarships
(Undergraduate/Scholarship)

Purpose: To support the education of students holding a valid FCC-granted Amateur Radio license for post-secondary education. **Focus:** Radio and television. **Qualif.:** Applicant must hold an FCC amateur radio license; a resident of Illinois; and be enrolled in a post-secondary course of study leading to undergraduate degree. **Criteria:** Award is given based on the submitted materials.

Funds Avail.: $500. **Number Awarded:** 1. **To Apply:** Applicants must submit a completed scholarship application form along with a recent high school (or equivalent) or college transcript. **Deadline:** February 1.

856 ■ Zachary Taylor Stevens Memorial Scholarships *(Undergraduate/Scholarship)*

Purpose: To support the education of students holding a valid FCC-granted Amateur Radio license for post-secondary education. **Focus:** Radio and television. **Qualif.:** Applicant must hold an FCC amateur radio license, and be enrolled in an accredited two- or four-year college/university or technical school. **Criteria:** Preference is given to the residents of Amateur radio call areas in MI, OH and WV.

Funds Avail.: $750. **Number Awarded:** 1. **To Apply:** Applicants must submit a completed scholarship application form along with a recent high school (or equivalent) or college transcript. **Deadline:** February 1.

857 ■ Carole J. Streeter, KB9JBR Scholarships
(Undergraduate/Scholarship)

Purpose: To support the education of students holding a valid FCC-granted Amateur Radio license for post-secondary education. **Focus:** Radio and television. **Qualif.:** Applicant must hold an FCC amateur radio license, and be enrolled in an accredited college/university studying healing arts. **Criteria:** Preference is given to applicants with basic Morse Code proficiency; healing arts study may include courses at teaching hospitals or local colleges.

Funds Avail.: $750. **Number Awarded:** 1. **To Apply:** Applicants must submit a completed scholarship application form along with a recent high school (or equivalent) or college transcript. **Deadline:** February 1.

858 ■ Norman E. Strohmeier, W2VRS Memorial Scholarships *(Undergraduate/Scholarship)*

Purpose: To support the education of students holding a valid FCC-granted Amateur Radio license for post-secondary education. **Focus:** Radio and television. **Qualif.:** Applicant must hold an FCC amateur radio license; be a resident of Western New York; and have a cumulative GPA of 3.2 or better. **Criteria:** Preference is given to graduating high school seniors.

Funds Avail.: $550. **Number Awarded:** 1. **To Apply:** Applicants must submit a completed scholarship application form along with a recent high school (or equivalent) or college transcript. **Deadline:** February 1.

859 ■ Gary Wagner, K3OMI Scholarships
(Undergraduate/Scholarship)

Purpose: To support the education of students holding a valid FCC-granted Amateur Radio license for post-

Awards are arranged alphabetically below their administering organizations

secondary education. **Focus:** Radio and television; Engineering. **Qualif.:** Applicant must hold an FCC amateur radio license; be a resident of NC, VA, WV, MD or TN; enrolled in an accredited four-year college/university (NC, VA, WV, MD, or TN) working towards a Bachelor's of Science in any field of engineering; and have financial need. **Criteria:** Award is given based on the submitted materials.

Funds Avail.: $1,000. **Number Awarded:** 1. **To Apply:** Applicants must submit a completed scholarship application form along with a recent high school (or equivalent) or college transcript. **Deadline:** February 1.

860 ■ Francis Walton Memorial Scholarships
(Undergraduate/Scholarship)

Purpose: To support the education of students holding a valid FCC-granted Amateur Radio license for post-secondary education. **Focus:** Radio and television. **Qualif.:** Applicant must hold an FCC amateur radio license; be a resident of Illinois or Central Division (IL, IN, WI); and studying baccalaureate or higher degree. **Criteria:** Awards are given based on the submitted materials.

Funds Avail.: $500. **Number Awarded:** 1 or more. **To Apply:** Applicants must submit a completed scholarship application form along with a recent high school (or equivalent) or college transcript. **Deadline:** February 1.

861 ■ L. Phil Wicker Scholarships
(Undergraduate/Scholarship)

Purpose: To support the education of students holding a valid FCC-granted Amateur Radio license for post-secondary education. **Focus:** Radio and television; Electronics; Communications. **Qualif.:** Applicant must hold an FCC amateur radio license; be a resident of ARRL Roanoke Division (NC, SC, VA, WV); enrolled in a baccalaureate or higher course in electronics, communications and related fields. **Criteria:** Award is given based on the submitted materials.

Funds Avail.: $1,000. **Number Awarded:** 1. **To Apply:** Applicants must submit a completed scholarship application form along with a recent high school (or equivalent) or college transcript. **Deadline:** February 1.

862 ■ Yankee Clipper Contest Club, Inc. Youth Scholarships *(Undergraduate/Scholarship)*

Purpose: To support the education of students holding a valid FCC-granted Amateur Radio license for post-secondary education. **Focus:** Radio and television. **Qualif.:** Applicant must hold an FCC amateur radio license; residency or college/university attendance within 175 miles of YCCC Center in Erving MA, including MA, RI, CT, Long Island NY, some of VT, NH, ME, PA, and NJ; and be enrolled in a 2 or 4-year degree program at an accredited college/university. **Criteria:** Award is given based on the submitted materials.

Funds Avail.: $1,000. **Number Awarded:** 1. **To Apply:** Applicants must submit a completed scholarship application form along with a recent high school (or equivalent) or college transcript. **Deadline:** February 1.

863 ■ Yasme Foundation Scholarships
(Undergraduate/Scholarship)

Purpose: To support the education of students holding a valid FCC-granted Amateur Radio license for post-secondary education. **Focus:** Radio and television; Science; Engineering. **Qualif.:** Applicant must hold an FCC amateur radio license, and be enrolled in a science or engineering course at an accredited four-year college/university. **Criteria:** Preference is given to high school applicants ranked in top 5%-10%, or to college students in the top 10%. Participation in local Amateur Radio club and community service is important to selection.

Funds Avail.: $2,000. **Number Awarded:** 5 in 2006. **To Apply:** Applicants must submit a completed scholarship application form along with a recent high school (or equivalent) or college transcript. **Deadline:** February 1.

864 ■ American Railway Engineering and Maintenance-of-Way Association

10003 Derekwood Ln., Ste. 210
Lanham, MD 20706
Ph: (301)459-3200
Fax: (301)459-8077
E-mail: chemely@arema.org
URL: http://www.arema.org

865 ■ AREMA Committee Scholarships 18 - Light Density & Short Line Railways
(Undergraduate/Scholarship)

Purpose: To support the education of an engineering student who has a potential interest in railway engineering careers. **Focus:** Engineering. **Qualif.:** Applicant must be enrolled full-time in a four or five year program leading to a Bachelor's degree in Engineering or Engineering Technology in a curriculum accredited by the Accreditation Board of Engineering and Technology; have completed at least one quarter or semester in college prior to the application; and have a GPA of 2.00. **Criteria:** Selection is based on the submitted materials.

Funds Avail.: $1000. **Number Awarded:** 2. **To Apply:** Applicants must submit completed AREMA data form together with a cover letter (maximum of 350 words); a resume; two letters of recommendation, one from a faculty member, and another from a present employer, AREMA member, or other responsible person; and a transcript from the schools attended, and courses currently enrolled in. **Deadline:** March 14.

Remarks: Staple application materials in the upper left hand corner and do not include any photos.

866 ■ AREMA Committee Scholarships 24 - Education and Training *(Undergraduate/Scholarship)*

Purpose: To support the education of an engineering student who has a potential interest in railway engineering careers. **Focus:** Engineering. **Qualif.:** Applicant must be enrolled full-time in a four or five year program leading to a Bachelor's degree in Engineering or Engineering Technology in a curriculum accredited by the Accreditation Board of Engineering and Technology; have completed at least one quarter or semester in college prior to the application; and have a GPA of 2.00. **Criteria:** Selection is based on the submitted materials.

Funds Avail.: $1000. **Number Awarded:** 1. **To Apply:** Applicants must submit completed AREMA data form together with a cover letter (maximum of 350 words); a resume; two letters of recommendation, one from a faculty member, and another from a present employer, AREMA member, or other responsible person; and a transcript from the schools attended, and courses currently enrolled in. **Deadline:** March 14.

Remarks: Staple application materials in the upper left

Awards are arranged alphabetically below their administering organizations

hand corner and do not include any photos.

867 ■ AREMA Committee Scholarships 33 - Electric Energy Utilization *(Undergraduate/Scholarship)*

Purpose: To support the education of an engineering student who has a potential interest in railway engineering careers. **Focus:** Engineering. **Qualif.:** Applicant must be enrolled full-time in a four or five year program leading to a Bachelor's degree in Engineering or Engineering Technology in a curriculum accredited by the Accreditation Board of Engineering and Technology; have completed at least one quarter or semester in college prior to the application; and have a GPA of 2.00. **Criteria:** Selection is based on the submitted materials.

Funds Avail.: $1000. **Number Awarded:** 1. **To Apply:** Applicants must submit completed AREMA data form together with a cover letter (maximum of 350 words); a resume; two letters of recommendation, one from a faculty member, and another from a present employer, AREMA member, or other responsible person; and a transcript from the schools attended, and courses currently enrolled in. **Deadline:** March 14.

Remarks: Staple application materials in the upper left hand corner and do not include any photos.

868 ■ AREMA Presidential Spouse Scholarships *(Undergraduate/Scholarship)*

Purpose: To support the education of a female engineering student with a potential interest in railway engineering careers. **Focus:** Engineering. **Qualif.:** Applicant must be an enrolled full-time female student in a four or five year program leading to a Bachelor's degree in Engineering or Engineering Technology in a curriculum accredited by the Accreditation Board of Engineering and Technology; have completed at least one quarter or semester prior to the application; and have a minimum GPA of 2.0. **Criteria:** Selection is based on the materials submitted.

Funds Avail.: $1000. **Number Awarded:** 1. **To Apply:** Applicants must submit completed AREMA data form together with a cover letter (maximum of 350 words); a resume; two letters of recommendation, one from a faculty member, and another from a present employer, AREMA member, or other responsible person; and a transcript from the schools attended, and courses currently enrolled in. **Deadline:** March 14.

Remarks: Staple application materials in the upper left hand corner and do not include any photos.

869 ■ AREMA Scholarships *(Undergraduate/Scholarship)*

Purpose: To support the education of undergraduate engineering student who has potential interest in railway engineering careers. **Focus:** Engineering. **Qualif.:** Applicant must be enrolled as a full-time undergraduate student in a four or five year program leading to a Bachelor's degree in Engineering or Engineering Technology in a curriculum accredited by the Accreditation Board of Engineering and Technology; have completed at least one quarter or semester prior to the application; interest in railway engineering; and maintaining a minimum GPA of 2.0. **Criteria:** Selection is based on the materials submitted.

Funds Avail.: $1000. **Number Awarded:** 1. **To Apply:** Applicants must submit completed AREMA data form together with a cover letter (maximum of 350 words); a resume; two letters of recommendation, one from a faculty member, and another from a present employer, AREMA member, or other responsible person; and a transcript from the schools attended, and courses currently enrolled in. **Deadline:** March 14.

Remarks: Staple application materials in the upper left hand corner and do not include any photos.

870 ■ AREMA Staff Scholarships *(Undergraduate/Scholarship)*

Purpose: To support the education of undergraduate engineering student who has potential interest in railway engineering careers. **Focus:** Engineering. **Qualif.:** Applicant must be enrolled full-time undergraduate student in a four or five year program leading to a Bachelor's degree in Engineering or Engineering Technology in a curriculum accredited by the Accreditation Board of Engineering and Technology; have completed at least one quarter or semester prior to the application; interest in railway engineering; and maintaining a minimum GPA of 2.0. **Criteria:** Selection is based on the materials submitted.

Funds Avail.: $1000. **Number Awarded:** 1. **To Apply:** Applicants must submit completed AREMA data form together with a cover letter (maximum of 350 words); a resume; two letters of recommendation, one from a faculty member, and another from a present employer, AREMA member, or other responsible person; and a transcript from the schools attended, and courses currently enrolled in. **Deadline:** March 14.

Remarks: Staple application materials in the upper left hand corner and do not include any photos.

871 ■ Paul I. and Elena H. Cohen Scholarships *(Graduate, Undergraduate/Scholarship)*

Purpose: To support education of railway-engineering students at the University of Illinois in the Engineering Department at Urbana-Champaign. **Focus:** Engineering. **Qualif.:** Applicant must be a student at the University of Illinois at Urbana-Champaign; have at least 2.0 GPA; an undergraduate or graduate student in the Engineering Department; and interested in railwayengineering. **Criteria:** Selection is based on the submitted materials.

Funds Avail.: $2000. **Number Awarded:** 1. **To Apply:** Applicants must submit completed AREMA data form together with a cover letter (maximum of 350 words); a resume; two letters of recommendation, one from a faculty member, and another from a present employer, AREMA member, or other responsible person; and a transcript from the schools attended, and courses currently enrolled in. **Deadline:** March 14.

Remarks: Staple application materials in the upper left hand corner and do not include any photos.

872 ■ Committee 12 - Rail Transit Scholarships *(Undergraduate/Scholarship)*

Purpose: To support the education of a student who is also working full-time in the railway industry. **Focus:** Engineering. **Qualif.:** Applicant must be enrolled as full-time student, or part-time working as full-time in the railway industry, in a four or five year program leading to a Bachelor's degree in Engineering or Engineering Technology in a curriculum accredited by the Accreditation Board of Engineering and Technology; have completed at least one quarter or semester in college prior to the application; and have a GPA of 2.00. **Criteria:** Selection is based on the submitted materials.

Funds Avail.: $1000. **Number Awarded:** 1. **To Apply:** Ap-

plicants must submit completed AREMA data form together with a cover letter (maximum of 350 words); a resume; two letters of recommendation, one from a faculty member, and another from a present employer, AREMA member, or other responsible person; and a transcript from the schools attended, and courses currently enrolled in. **Deadline:** March 14.

Remarks: Staple application materials in the upper left hand corner and do not include any photos.

873 ■ Committee 27 - Maintenance-of-Way Work Equipment Scholarships *(Undergraduate/Scholarship)*

Purpose: To support the education of an engineering student. **Focus:** Engineering. **Qualif.:** Applicant must be enrolled full-time student in a four or five year program leading to a Bachelor's degree in Engineering or Engineering Technology in a curriculum accredited by the Accreditation Board of Engineering and Technology; have completed at least one quarter or semester in college prior to the application; and have a GPA of 2.00. **Criteria:** Priority is given to a Committee 27 family member or a family member of someone in the work equipment industry for railroads.

Funds Avail.: $1000. **Number Awarded:** 1. **To Apply:** Applicants must submit completed AREMA data form together with a cover letter (maximum of 350 words); a resume; two letters of recommendation, one from a faculty member, and another from a present employer, AREMA member, or other responsible person; and a transcript from the schools attended, and courses currently enrolled in. **Deadline:** March 14.

Remarks: Staple application materials in the upper left hand corner and do not include any photos.

874 ■ CSX Scholarships *(Undergraduate/Scholarship)*

Purpose: To support the education of an undergraduate engineering student who has potential interest in railway engineering careers. **Focus:** Engineering. **Qualif.:** Applicant must be enrolled full-time as an undergraduate student in a four or five year program leading to a Bachelor's degree in Engineering or Engineering Technology in a curriculum accredited by the Accreditation Board of Engineering and Technology; have completed at least one quarter or semester prior to the application; interest in railway engineering; and maintaining a minimum GPA of 2.0. **Criteria:** Selection is based on the materials submitted.

Funds Avail.: $2500. **Number Awarded:** 1. **To Apply:** Applicants must submit completed AREMA data form together with a cover letter (maximum of 350 words); a resume; two letters of recommendation, one from a faculty member, and another from a present employer, AREMA member, or other responsible person; and a transcript from the schools attended, and courses currently enrolled in. **Deadline:** March 14.

Remarks: Staple application materials in the upper left hand corner and do not include any photos.

875 ■ John J. Cunningham Memorial Scholarships *(Undergraduate/Scholarship)*

Purpose: To support the education of student in a professional field that has direct applications in the passenger rail sector. **Focus:** Engineering. **Qualif.:** Applicant must be an enrolled full-time Junior or Senior student in a four or five year program leading to an undergraduate degree in a professional field that has direct applications in the passenger rail sector; and have a GPA of 2.00. **Criteria:** Selection is based on the submitted materials.

Funds Avail.: $1000. **Number Awarded:** 1. **To Apply:** Applicants must submit completed AREMA data form together with a cover letter (maximum of 350 words); a resume; two letters of recommendation, one from a faculty member, and another from a present employer, AREMA member, or other responsible person; and a transcript from the schools attended, and courses currently enrolled in. **Deadline:** March 14.

Remarks: Staple application materials in the upper left hand corner and do not include any photos. Sponsored jointly by Committees 11 and 17.

876 ■ Larry L. Etherton Scholarships *(Graduate, Undergraduate/Scholarship)*

Purpose: To support education of railway engineering students at the University of Illinois in the Engineering Department at Urbana-Champaign. **Focus:** Engineering. **Qualif.:** Applicant must be a student at the University of Illinois at Urbana-Champaign; have at least 2.0 GPA; an undergraduate or graduate student in the Engineering Department; and interested in railway engineering. **Criteria:** Selection is based on the submitted materials.

Funds Avail.: $1500. **Number Awarded:** 1. **To Apply:** Applicants must submit completed AREMA data form together with a cover letter (maximum of 350 words); a resume; two letters of recommendation, one from a faculty member, and another from a present employer, AREMA member, or other responsible person; and a transcript from the schools attended, and courses currently enrolled in. **Deadline:** March 14.

Remarks: Staple application materials in the upper left hand corner and do not include any photos.

877 ■ Michael W. and Jean D. Franke Family Foundation Scholarships *(Graduate, Undergraduate/Scholarship)*

Purpose: To support education of railway engineering students at the University of Illinois in the Engineering Department at Urbana-Champaign. **Focus:** Engineering. **Qualif.:** Applicant must be a student at the University of Illinois at Urbana-Champaign; have at least 2.0 GPA; an undergraduate or graduate student in the Engineering Department; and interested in railwayengineering. **Criteria:** Selection is based on the submitted materials.

Funds Avail.: $5000. **Number Awarded:** 1. **To Apply:** Applicants must submit completed AREMA data form together with a cover letter (maximum of 350 words); a resume; two letters of recommendation, one from a faculty member, and another from a present employer, AREMA member, or other responsible person; and a transcript from the schools attended, and courses currently enrolled in. **Deadline:** March 14.

Remarks: Staple application materials in the upper left hand corner and do not include any photos.

878 ■ Belknap Freeman Carnegie Mellon Scholarships *(Undergraduate/Scholarship)*

Purpose: To support education of students pursuing a degree in Electrical Engineering at Carnegie Mellon University. **Focus:** Engineering, Electrical. **Qualif.:** Applicant must be a student of Carnegie Mellon University; pursuing an Electrical Engineering degree; and interested in railway engineering and have a goal of obtaining a "Professional Engineering" license. **Criteria:** Selection is

Awards are arranged alphabetically below their administering organizations

based on the submitted materials and on the interview.

Funds Avail.: $10,000. **Number Awarded:** 1. **To Apply:** Applicants must submit completed AREMA data form together with a cover letter (maximum of 350 words); a resume; and a transcript from the schools attended, and courses currently enrolled in. **Deadline:** March 14.

Remarks: Staple application materials in the upper left hand corner and do not include any photos.

879 ■ Michael and Gina Garcia Rail Engineering Scholarships *(Undergraduate/Scholarship)*

Purpose: To support the education of an engineering student, especially two students already married or supporting a family. **Focus:** Engineering. **Qualif.:** Applicant must be enrolled in a four or five year program leading to a Bachelor's degree in Engineering or Engineering Technology. **Criteria:** Priority is given to a student already married or supporting a family.

Funds Avail.: $2000. **To Apply:** Applicants must submit completed AREMA data form together with a cover letter (maximum of 350 words); a resume; two letters of recommendation, one from a faculty member, and another from a present employer, AREMA member, or other responsible person; and a transcript from the schools attended, and courses currently enrolled in. **Deadline:** March 14.

Remarks: Staple application materials in the upper left hand corner and do not include any photos.

880 ■ Chris Harding Scholarships *(Undergraduate/Scholarship)*

Purpose: To support the education of a railway-engineering student at Clarkson University. **Focus:** Engineering. **Qualif.:** Applicant must be enrolled full-time in a four or five year program leading to a Bachelor's degree in Engineering or Engineering Technology in a curriculum accredited by the Accreditation Board of Engineering and Technology; have completed at least one quarter or semester in college prior to the application; and have a GPA of 2.00. **Criteria:** Selection is based on the submitted materials.

Funds Avail.: $1000. **To Apply:** Applicants must submit completed AREMA data form together with a cover letter (maximum of 350 words); a resume; two letters of recommendation, one from a faculty member, and another from a present employer, AREMA member, or other responsible person; and a transcript from the schools attended, and courses currently enrolled in. **Deadline:** March 14.

Remarks: Staple application materials in the upper left hand corner and do not include any photos.

881 ■ Michigan Tech Alumni Scholarships *(Undergraduate/Scholarship)*

Purpose: To support the education of an engineering student at Michigan Technological University. **Focus:** Engineering. **Qualif.:** Applicant must be an engineering student at Michigan Tech University and interested in railway engineering. **Criteria:** Selection is based on the materials submitted.

Funds Avail.: $1000. **To Apply:** Applicants must submit completed AREMA data form together with a cover letter (maximum of 350 words); a resume; two letters of recommendation, one from a faculty member, and another from a present employer, AREMA member, or other responsible person; and a transcript from the schools attended, and courses currently enrolled in. **Deadline:** March 14.

Remarks: Staple application materials in the upper left hand corner and do not include any photos.

882 ■ Norfolk Southern Foundation Scholarships *(Undergraduate/Scholarship)*

Purpose: To support the education of an engineering student. **Focus:** Engineering. **Qualif.:** Applicant must be enrolled full-time in a four or five year undergraduate program in Engineering or Engineering Technology; institution must be located in Norfolk Southern; service area (22 states, the District of Columbia and Ontario, Canada); have completed at least one quarter or semester in college prior to the application; and have a GPA of 2.00. **Criteria:** Selection is based on the submitted materials.

Funds Avail.: $1000. **Number Awarded:** 1. **To Apply:** Applicants must submit completed AREMA data form together with a cover letter (maximum of 350 words); a resume; two letters of recommendation, one from a faculty member, and another from a present employer, AREMA member, or other responsible person; and a transcript from the schools attended, and courses currently enrolled in. **Deadline:** March 14.

Remarks: Staple application materials in the upper left hand corner and do not include any photos.

883 ■ PB Rail Engineering Scholarships *(Undergraduate/Scholarship)*

Purpose: To support the education of an undergraduate engineering student who have potential interest in railway engineering careers. **Focus:** Engineering. **Qualif.:** Applicant must be enrolled full-time as an undergraduate student in a four or five year program leading to a Bachelor's degree in Engineering or Engineering Technology in a curriculum accredited by the Accreditation Board of Engineering and Technology; have completed at least one quarter or semester prior to the application; interest in railway engineering; and maintaining a minimum GPA of 2.0. **Criteria:** Selection is based on the materials submitted.

Funds Avail.: $2000. **Number Awarded:** 1. **To Apply:** Applicants must submit completed AREMA data form together with a cover letter (maximum of 350 words); a resume; two letters of recommendation, one from a faculty member, and another from a present employer, AREMA member, or other responsible person; and a transcript from the schools attended, and courses currently enrolled in. **Deadline:** March 14.

Remarks: Staple application materials in the upper left hand corner and do not include any photos.

884 ■ REMSA Scholarships *(Undergraduate/Scholarship)*

Purpose: To support the education of an undergraduate engineering student who has potential interest in railway engineering careers. **Focus:** Engineering. **Qualif.:** Applicant must be enrolled full-time as an undergraduate student in a four or five year program leading to a Bachelor's degree in Engineering or Engineering Technology in a curriculum accredited by the Accreditation Board of Engineering and Technology; have completed at least one quarter or semester prior to the application; interest in railway engineering; and maintaining a minimum GPA of 2.0. **Criteria:** Selection is based on the materials submitted.

Funds Avail.: $1000. **Number Awarded:** 1. **To Apply:** Applicants must submit completed AREMA data form together with a cover letter (maximum of 350 words); a resume; two letters of recommendation, one from a faculty member, and another from a present employer, AREMA member, or other

Awards are arranged alphabetically below their administering organizations

responsible person; and a transcript from the schools attended, and courses currently enrolled in. **Deadline:** March 14.

Remarks: Staple application materials in the upper left hand corner and do not include any photos.

885 ■ American Red Cross

2025 E St. NW
Washington, DC 20006
Ph: (703)206-6000
Free: 800-733-2767
E-mail: williamscaro@usa.redcross.org
URL: http://www.redcross.org

886 ■ Jane Delano Society Scholarships
(Undergraduate/Scholarship)

Purpose: To advance nursing as a career option and to promote the involvement of young nurses in the Red Cross. **Focus:** Nursing. **Qualif.:** Applicants must have contributed volunteer service to a Red Cross unit during the past five years; must have current enrollment in an associate degree, diploma, or baccalaureate program preparing students for Registered Nurse licensure, or an RN to BSN completion program; and must have at least one semester, or quarter, left before graduation. **Criteria:** Selection will be based on Scholarship Selection Committee's criteria.

Funds Avail.: $1,000. **Number Awarded:** 2. **To Apply:** Candidates must submit the required documentation including: application which includes a one-page personal statement from student; letter of endorsement from Red Cross Unit (chapter, Blood Services region, or SAF station) leadership; and letter of endorsement from College/School of Nursing saying that the applicant is in good academic standing and verifying that student is enrolled (attach form to application). **Deadline:** April 7.

Remarks: Established in 2001. **Contact:** Carolyn Williams at the above address (see entry 885).

887 ■ American Rental Association Foundation

1900 19th St.
Moline, IL 61265
Fax: (309)764-1533
Free: 800-334-2177
E-mail: arafoundation@ararental.org
URL: http://www.ararental.org/Foundation

888 ■ American Rental Association Foundation Scholarships *(Undergraduate/Scholarship)*

Purpose: To provide scholarships to promising young students looking to enter the rental industry. **Focus:** Industrial education. **Qualif.:** Applicants must be students pursuing a field of study they will use while working in the rental industry or completing a rental-related vocational or certification program. **Criteria:** Selection of applicants will be based on the scholarship application criteria.

Funds Avail.: $37,000. **Number Awarded:** 23. **To Apply:** For further information, applicants are advised to contact the ARA Foundation at 1900 19th St., Moline, IL 61265.

889 ■ Ron Marshall Scholarships
(Undergraduate/Scholarship)

Purpose: To provide scholarships to promising young students looking to enter the rental industry. **Focus:** Industrial education. **Qualif.:** Applicants must be pursuing an education applicable to the rental industry. **Criteria:** Selection of applicants will be based on the scholarship application criteria.

Funds Avail.: $500. **Number Awarded:** 2. **To Apply:** Applicants are advised to contact the ARA Foundation at 1900 19th St., Moline, IL 61265.

Remarks: Ron Marshall was the owner of Reading Rentals in Reading, Pa., until his death in October 1995. He was active in the Keystone Rental Association and ARA's Region Two.

890 ■ Dorothy Wellnitz Canadian Scholarships
(Undergraduate/Scholarship)

Purpose: To provide scholarships to promising young students looking to enter the rental industry. **Focus:** Industrial education. **Qualif.:** Applicants must be pursuing an education program applicable to the rental industry. **Criteria:** Selection of applicants will be based on the scholarship application criteria.

Funds Avail.: $1,000. **To Apply:** For further information, applicants are advised to contact the ARA Foundation at 1900 19th St., Moline, IL 61265.

Remarks: Scholarship is named for Dorothy Wellnitz, former executive director of the Canadian Rental Association and is administered by the ARA Foundation.

891 ■ American Research Institute in Turkey

3260 S St.
Philadelphia, PA 19104-6324
Ph: (215)898-3474
Fax: (215)898-0657
E-mail: leinwand@sas.upenn.edu
URL: http://www.ccat.sas.upenn.edu

892 ■ Critical Language Scholarships for Intensive Summer Institutes *(Graduate, Undergraduate/Scholarship)*

Purpose: To expand the number of Americans studying and mastering critical need foreign languages. **Focus:** Business; Engineering; Science; Social Sciences; Humanities. **Qualif.:** Applicants must be U.S. citizens; must be currently enrolled in a degree-granting program at the undergraduate or graduate level; must have graduated from an undergraduate or graduate program no more than two-years ago; undergraduate students must have completed at least one year of general college course-work by program start date (one year is defined as two semesters or three quarters); or students in all disciplines including business, engineering, science, the social sciences and humanities are encourage to apply. **Criteria:** Recipients are selected base on academic records.

Funds Avail.: no stated amount. **To Apply:** Applicants must submit completed application form; transcript of records; and letters of recommendation. **Deadline:** January 25.

893 ■ Kenan Erim Fellowships for Research at Ancient Aphrodisiacs *(Postdoctorate/Fellowship)*

Purpose: To support excavation and/or research about art history and archeology at Aphrodisias in Turkey during the summer. **Focus:** Art History; Architecture; Archeology. **Qualif.:** Applicants must be advanced graduate students engaged in excavation and research at Aphrodisias. **Criteria:** Recipients are selected base on academic records and financial need.

Awards are arranged alphabetically below their administering organizations

Funds Avail.: $2,375. **To Apply:** Applicants must provide complete application information; three letters of recommendation; 100-word abstract of the project; letters of reference; and a copy of graduate transcript. **Deadline:** November 1.

894 ■ Fellowships in the Humanities and Social Sciences in Turkey *(Postdoctorate/Fellowship)*

Purpose: To promote American and Turkish research and exchange related to Turkey. **Focus:** Ancient; Medieval Studies; Modern Languages; Humanities; Social Sciences. **Qualif.:** Applicants must be advance graduate students engaged in research on ancient, medieval, or modern times in Turkey, in any field of humanities and social sciences; must have fulfilled all requirements for the doctorate except the dissertation by June and before beginning any ARIT-sponsored research. (Non-U.S. applicants are expected to maintain an affiliation with an educational institution in the United States or Canada). **Criteria:** Recipients are selected based on academic records and financial need.

Funds Avail.: No stated amount. **To Apply:** Applicants must provide complete application information; three letters of recommendation; 100-word abstract of the project; letters of reference; and a copy of graduate transcript. **Deadline:** November 1.

895 ■ Fellowships for Intensive Advanced Turkish Language Study in Turkey *(Undergraduate/Fellowship)*

Purpose: To promote American and Turkish research and exchange related to Turkey. **Focus:** General Studies. **Qualif.:** Applicants must be citizens or national/ permanent residents of the United States; must be currently enrolled in an undergraduate or graduate level academic program; must have a minimum B average in studies; must perform at the high-intermediate level on a proficiency-based admission examination. **Criteria:** Recipients are selected base on academic records and financial need.

Funds Avail.: $2,375. **To Apply:** Applicants must submit complete application information; three letters of recommendation; letters of reference; and a copy of graduate transcript. **Deadline:** February 11. **Contact:** Erika H. Gilson at 110 Jones Hall, Princeton University, Princeton, NJ 08544-1008.

896 ■ Getty Research Exchange Fellowship Program for Cultural Heritage Preservation *(Doctorate/Fellowship)*

Purpose: To support advanced regional research and exchanges between research centers in the Mediterranean and Middle East regions. **Focus:** General Studies. **Qualif.:** Applicants must be Turkish citizens who have already obtained PhD; must have professional experience in the study or preservation of cultural heritage; must be willing to undertake specific research project in overseas research centers of another country. **Criteria:** Recipients are selected based on: the significance of the proposal; value of the collaboration proposed; feasibility of the research design; and applicant's research background.

Funds Avail.: $3,000. **To Apply:** Applicants must fill out application form; must submit a project abstract and project description; one letter of recommendation; and three pages curriculum vitae. **Deadline:** February 15. **Contact:** 212-257-8111; 312-427-2222.

897 ■ Ilse and George Hanfmann Fellowships *(Doctorate/Fellowship)*

Purpose: To enable nationals of the Republic of Turkey who are graduate students at or recent PhDs from Turkish universities in archaeology and related fields to study abroad (North America or elsewhere). **Focus:** General studies. **Qualif.:** Applicants must be candidates for M.A. or Ph.D. degrees who have finished all course work and passed all qualifying examinations for the degree before entering the tenure of a Hanfmann Fellowship; must be a scholars who have received their Ph.D. and have not yet reached 45 years of age. **Criteria:** Recipients are selected based on achievement.

Funds Avail.: $15,000-$45,000. **To Apply:** Applicants must submit a curriculum vitae; one-paragraph summary of the project; statement of purpose (no more than five double-spaced pages, and includes description of the project and its importance, a brief summary of the literature, the reasons for wanting to study or conduct research abroad, what institution this work would be conducted, and why such tenure abroad would be professionally advantageous to the present academic career); official transcript of undergraduate and graduate course work; demonstration of proficiency in the language or languages necessary for conducting research abroad; minimum of three letters of recommendation from scholars familiar with the applicant's work. **Deadline:** February 15. **Contact:** 212-257-8111; 212-257-8369.

898 ■ Kress Pre-Doctoral Fellowships in the History of Art and Archeology in Turkey *(Postdoctorate/Fellowship)*

Purpose: To promote American and Turkish research and exchange related to Turkey. **Focus:** Art History; Architecture; Archeology. **Qualif.:** Applicants must be advanced graduate students engaged in research in Turkey; must have fulfilled all preliminary requirements for the doctorate except dissertation by June and before beginning any ARIT-sponsored research; Applicants must be U.S. (Non-U.S. matriculated at U.S. or Canadian institutions). **Criteria:** Recipients are selected base on academic records and financial need.

Funds Avail.: $17,000. **To Apply:** Applicants must provide complete application information; three letters of recommendation; 100-word abstract of the project; letters of reference; and a copy of graduate transcript. **Deadline:** November 1.

899 ■ Mellon Post-Doctoral Fellowships in Turkey for East European Scholars *(Doctorate/Fellowship)*

Purpose: To bring the East-Central European scholars into a broader research community. **Focus:** General Studies. **Qualif.:** Applicants must be scholars from Czech Republic, Hungary, Poland, Bulgaria, Romania, Slovakia, Estonia, Latvia and Lithuania who have completed all requirements for the PhD or who hold a PhD degree or its equivalent; must be citizens and permanent residents of one of the nine included countries. **Criteria:** Recipients are selected base on project statement, academic records, and financial need.

Funds Avail.: $11,500. **Number Awarded:** 3. **To Apply:** Applicants must submit three to five-pages project statement outlining the project and its significance; current curriculum vitae; two letters of reference from scholars in the applicant's field commenting on the value and feasibility of the project. **Deadline:** March 5.

900 ■ National Endowment for the Humanities Advanced Fellowship for Research in Turkey *(Postdoctorate/Fellowship)*

Purpose: To promote American and Turkish research and exchange related to Turkey. **Focus:** Humanities; Social

Awards are arranged alphabetically below their administering organizations

Sciences; History; Art; Archeology; Literature; Linguistics. **Qualif.:** Applicants must complete formal training and have plan to carry out research in Turkey; must be U.S citizens or three year residents of U.S. **Criteria:** Recipients are selected base on academic records and financial need.

Funds Avail.: $13,335-$40,000. **To Apply:** Applicants must provide complete application information; three letters of recommendation; 100-word abstract of the project; letters of reference; and a copy of graduate transcript. **Deadline:** November 1.

901 ■ American Risk and Insurance Association

716 Providence Rd.
Malvern, PA 19355-3402
Ph: (610)640-1997
Fax: (610)725-1007
E-mail: aria@cpcuiia.org
URL: http://www.aria.org

902 ■ Griffith Foundation Scholarships *(Undergraduate/Scholarship)*

Purpose: To advance knowledge in Risk Management and Insurance; To enhance the career development of its members; to provide programs, awards, and services that expand risk management and insurance knowledge; to improve academic instruction and position its members. **Focus:** Management. **Qualif.:** All applicants must be students enrolled in college majoring in actuarial science, business, or non-business making a commitment to take a risk in management and insurance course; he must be a U.S. citizen; must be at least sophomore and enrolled in an insurance, risk management, actuarial science or other related program; have a cumulative point of average of 3.0 above.

Funds Avail.: $2,000. **Number Awarded:** 8. **To Apply:** Applicant must fill out the application form and mail to the above address. **Deadline:** March 10. **Contact:** The Griffith Foundation for Insurance Education 623, High Street Worthington, Ohio 43085; 614-880-9870; 614-880-9872; info@griffithfoundation.org.

903 ■ American Road and Transportation Builders Association

The ARTBA Building
1219 28th St. NW
Washington, DC 20007-3389
Ph: (202)289-4434
E-mail: artbadc@aol.com
URL: http://www.artba.org

904 ■ Highway Worker Memorial Scholarship Program *(Undergraduate/Scholarship)*

Purpose: To provide financial assistance to help the children or legally adopted children of highway workers killed or permanently disabled in the line of duty to pursue post-highschool education. **Focus:** General studies. **Qualif.:** Applicants must be sons, daughters or legally adopted children of highway workers who died or became permanently disabled in roadway construction zone accidents and their parents have been employed by a transportation construction firm or a transportation public agency at the time of his or her death or disabling injury. **Criteria:** Candidates are evaluated on the basis of their submitted application materials.

Funds Avail.: $2000. **Number Awarded:** 1. **To Apply:** Candidates must submit completed and signed award application form; proof of parent's death in line of duty; if parent is permanently disabled, must submit documentation that shows disability work-related; proof of guardianship if not living with surviving parent; an official copy of transcript and grade report from the school currently attended or most recently attended; a brief, typewritten statement explaining reasons for wanting to continue education accompanied by recent photo; completed and signed "Free Application for Federal Student Aid" (FAFSA) forms for the current year; federal tax return copy; copy of acceptance letter from the college, university, technical school where the applicants plan to attend; and two letters of recommendation from teachers in support of their application. **Deadline:** February 29.

905 ■ American Roentgen Ray Society

44211 Slatestone Ct.
Leesburg, VA 20176-5109
Fax: (703)729-4839
Free: 800-438-2777
E-mail: info@arrs.org
URL: http://www.arrs.org

906 ■ American Roentgen Ray Society Scholarships *(Professional Development/Scholarship)*

Purpose: To support study in a field selected by the scholars to attain their professional career goals. **Focus:** Radiology. **Qualif.:** Applicants must have earned MD or DO from an accredited institution; completed all the required residency or fellowship training or equivalent; must be a full-time faculty appointment as a lecturer, instructor, assistant professor or equivalent for no more than five years beyond completion of training; be certified by the American Board of Radiology or equivalent. **Criteria:** Recipients will be selected based on competence and promise of the candidate in research, education or administration related to medical imaging, as indicated by the institution making the nomination and personal qualities of the candidate that indicate that he or she is a true scholar and leader with exceptional potential.

Funds Avail.: $140,000. **Number Awarded:** 2. **To Apply:** Applicants must submit a cover letter stating his or her address, phone and fax numbers and e-mail address, for use by the ARRS administrative office; a curriculum vitae; a three-page summary of the applicant's qualifications, goals and purpose of study; statements from the department and applicant regarding present interests in a specific area related to radiological sciences or education, and long-term scientific and professional objectives or aspirations as they may relate to his or her future career; statement from the Department Chair as to the department's commitment to provide time for the scholar to study, and a commitment ensuring his or her return to the faculty at the completion of the scholarship; and an estimated budget covering the scholar's program over the one- or two-year period. **Deadline:** November 5.

907 ■ ARRS/Leonard Berlin Scholarships in Medical Professionalism *(Professional Development/Scholarship)*

Purpose: To support study and research related to medical ethics, medico-legal principles, patient accountability, sensitivity to patient diversity and/or other topics encompassing medical professionalism. **Focus:** Bioethics. **Qua-**

Awards are arranged alphabetically below their administering organizations

lif.: Applicants must have an MD or DO from an accredited institution, or equivalent; have completed a radiology residency, and fellowship training where appropriate, or the equivalent; must be certified by the American Board of Radiology or equivalent; must be members of the ARRS at the time the application is submitted and for the duration of the award. **Criteria:** Recipients will be selected based on competence and promise of the candidate in research, education or administration related to medical imaging, as indicated by the institution making the nomination and personal qualities of the candidate that indicate that he or she is a true scholar and leader with exceptional potential.

Funds Avail.: $100,000. **Number Awarded:** 1. **To Apply:** Applicants must submit a cover letter from the applicant stating his or her address, phone and fax numbers and e-mail address, for use by the ARRS administrative office; a curriculum vitae including details of any other current or pending salary support; a three-page summary of the applicant's qualifications, goals and purpose of study; a description of course-work that will be undertaken; a listing of mentors, as appropriate to the proposal, and their contributions to the proposal; a letter of nomination from the Department Chair, or when applicable, the Radiology Group Director, and two additional letters of recommendation; and an estimated budget covering the scholar's program over the one- or two-year period. **Deadline:** November 5.

908 ■ American Romanian Orthodox Youth

8033 N Kenton Ave., Apt. 1W
Skokie, IL 60076
Ph: (330)519-6187
E-mail: lnemes@aroy.org
URL: http://www.aroy.org

909 ■ A.R.F.O.R.A. Undergraduate Scholarships for Women *(Undergraduate/Scholarship)*

Purpose: To support the continuing education of student members. **Focus:** General studies. **Qualif.:** Applicant must be a female voting member of a parish of the Romanian Orthodox Episcopate of America; a graduate of a duly accredited university/college; and accepted by a graduate school or a duly accredited university and specify her course of study. **Criteria:** Selection is based on the application materials.

Funds Avail.: $1000. **Number Awarded:** 2. **To Apply:** Applicants must send a request for application to ARFORA/ Martha Gavrila Scholarship c/o 222 Orchard Park Dr New Castle, PA 16105. Three letters of recommendation must be mailed sealed, directly to the attention of the Scholarship Committee. A photo must be included and a formal letter projecting the plans of the applicant. **Deadline:** April 30.

910 ■ A.R.O.Y. Stanitz Scholarships *(Undergraduate/Scholarship)*

Purpose: To support the continuing education of student members. **Focus:** General studies. **Qualif.:** Applicant must be an active AROY member; a high school graduate; and a college student or one who intends to enroll in a school or college of university level. **Criteria:** Selection is based on the application.

Funds Avail.: $1000. **Number Awarded:** 2. **To Apply:** Applicants must submit a biographical history including family; an educational background and grades; list of AROY and church activities; list of extra-curricular interests or achievements; reasons why applying for the scholarship; a photograph; and a letter of recommendation from parish priest or AROY advisors regarding parish and AROY activities. Send all materials to William R Stanitz/AROY Scholarship The Romanian Orthodox Episcopate of America PO Box 309 Grass Lake, MI 49240-0309. **Deadline:** July 1.

Remarks: Established in 1971.

911 ■ Bujea Memorial Scholarships *(Undergraduate/Scholarship)*

Purpose: To support the education of students seeking ordination into priesthood or wish to serve the Church in a professional manner. **Focus:** Religion. **Qualif.:** Applicant must be a Canadian student; and a communicant voting member of The Romanian Orthodox Episcopate of America. **Criteria:** Award is limited to those who either seek ordination into the priesthood or who wish to serve the Church.

Funds Avail.: %500. **Number Awarded:** 1. **To Apply:** Applicants must send a request for application to Bujea Memorial Scholarship Committee PO Box 1341 Regina SK S4P 3B8 Canada. **Deadline:** April 30.

912 ■ A.R.F.O.R.A. Martha Gavrila Scholarships for Women *(Graduate/Scholarship)*

Purpose: To support the student members in post-graduate studies. **Focus:** General studies. **Qualif.:** Applicant must be a female voting member of a parish of the Romanian Orthodox Episcopate of America; a graduate of a duly accredited university/college; and accepted by a graduate school or a duly accredited university and specify her course of study. **Criteria:** Selection is based on the application materials.

Funds Avail.: $1000. **Number Awarded:** 1. **To Apply:** Applicants must send a request for application to ARFORA/ Martha Gavrila Scholarship c/o 222 Orchard Park Dr New Castle, PA 16105. Three letters of recommendation must be mailed sealed, directly to the attention of the Scholarship Committee. A photo must be included and a formal letter projecting the plans of the applicant. **Deadline:** April 30.

913 ■ R.O.E.A. Dumitru Golea Goldy-Gemu Scholarships *(Undergraduate/Scholarship)*

Purpose: To support the continuing education of student members. **Focus:** General studies. **Qualif.:** Applicant must be of Romanian descent and a citizen or permanent resident of the U.S. or Canada. **Criteria:** Selection is based on the application.

Funds Avail.: $1500. **Number Awarded:** 2. **To Apply:** Applicants must submit a completed application form together with a high school administration form/transcript of grades/ letter of acceptance; an essay; and a photograph. Send application materials to Goldy Scholarship Committee PO Box 309 Grass Lake, MI 49240-0309. **Deadline:** May 31.

914 ■ American School Health Association

7263 State Rte. 43
Kent, OH 44240
Ph: (330)678-1601
Fax: (330)678-4526
E-mail: asha@ashaweb.org
URL: http://www.ashaweb.org

915 ■ ASHA Scholarships *(Graduate, Undergraduate/Scholarship)*

Purpose: To provide financial assistance to students concentrating on school health education, school nursing, and pediatric or adolescent medicine or dentistry. **Focus:** Health education; Nursing; Pediatric medicine; Medicine; Dentistry; Nutrition; Counseling/Guidance. **Qualif.:** Applicants must be a junior, senior or graduate student; enrolled full-time at institution of higher education; have 3.0 GPA on a 4.0 scale; have a major related to School Health Education or School Nursing or Pediatric or Adolescent Medicine or Dentistry or other school health specializations (nutrition, counseling, etc.); not a previous recipient of this award. **Criteria:** Awards are given based on academic merit and extra curricular activities.

Funds Avail.: $500 and a complimentary registration to ASHA's annual school health conference and a one-year ASHA membership. **Number Awarded:** 3. **To Apply:** Applicants must send one original and nine copies of the completed application form (application form available online); current resume; transcript; one page personal statement; three letters of recommendation. **Deadline:** April 4. **Contact:** Pamela Dorazio Dean, pdean@ashaweb.org.

916 ■ ASHA Student Research Grants *(Graduate, Undergraduate/Scholarship)*

Purpose: To provide financial assistance for research in areas related to the mission of ASHA. **Focus:** Health education; Nursing; Pediatric medicine; Medicine; Dentistry; Nutrition; Counseling/Guidance. **Qualif.:** Applicants must be student members of ASHA. **Criteria:** Recipients will be selected by the scholarship committee.

Funds Avail.: No specific amount. **To Apply:** Applicants must send one original and five copies of a proposal which includes a cover sheet; a narrative (title-problem, review of related literature, methodology, data analyst, institution IRB protocol documented); and a budget. Proposal should have one inch margins, doubled spaced and a font size not smaller than 12. Forward the original and 5 copies to: ASHA Student Research Grants, PO Box 708, Kent, OH 44240. **Deadline:** April 4. **Contact:** Pamela Dorazio, pdean@ashaweb.org, 330-678-1601.

917 ■ American Small Businesses Association

PO Box 300777
Chicago, IL 60630-0777
Free: 877-906-2722
E-mail: info@asbaonline.org
URL: http://www.asbaonline.org

918 ■ ASBA College Scholarship Program *(Undergraduate/Scholarship)*

Purpose: To provide educational financial aid to members and their grandchildren. **Focus:** General studies. **Qualif.:** Applicant must be a dependent or grandchild of an ASBA member; enrolled at least one year in college or university. **Criteria:** Awards are given based on academic merit and evaluation of the submitted essay.

Funds Avail.: $1,000. **To Apply:** Applicant must submit an application form (please visit the website); an essay; two letters of recommendation; high school/college transcript. **Deadline:** May.

919 ■ American Society of Association Executives

1575 I St. NW
Washington, DC 20005
Ph: (202)371-0940
Fax: (202)371-8315
Free: 888-950-ASAE
E-mail: asaeservice@asaecenter.org
URL: http://www.apaalliance.org

920 ■ Diversity Executive Leadership Program Scholarships *(Professional Development/Scholarship)*

Purpose: To help individuals from underrepresented segments of the association community advance into the ranks of leadership in the association management profession; to encourage leadership roles in association management; to increase diversity within the field of association management by providing educational and networking opportunities to potential leaders form underrepresented populations; to support scholars by providing opportunities to increase their connections and understanding of association management; to match scholars with mentors to provide career guidance and enhance networking opportunities; to demonstrate the long-term benefit of the program to ASAE and The Center, to the association profession, and to the scholars. **Focus:** Leadership, Institutional and community; Management. **Qualif.:** Member of a racial or ethnic minority group, GLBT, or person with a disability; currently employed as a mid-to-senior level association employee with minimum of three years experience in association management or as an association CEO for a minimum of one year; has a professional, volunteer, civic or community leadership experience. **Criteria:** Preference is given to individuals who are members of ASAE & The Center and/or individuals who work with ASAE & The Center members; Recipients are selected on the basis of commitment to attend the DELP orientation, professional education programs and service on an ASAE and The Center or allied society committee or council.

Funds Avail.: No specific amount. **Number Awarded:** 10. **To Apply:** Specific application guidelines are available at the ASAE website. **Deadline:** April 18. **Contact:** Marilu Morada, DELP Staff Liaison, Phone: 202-326-9527, email: mmorada@asaecenter.org.

921 ■ American Society of Brewing Chemists

3340 Pilot Knob Rd.
St. Paul, MN 55121
Ph: (651)454-7250
Fax: (651)454-0766
E-mail: asbc@scisoc.org
URL: http://www.asbcnet.org

922 ■ ASBC Foundation Graduate Scholarships *(Doctorate, Graduate/Scholarship)*

Purpose: To provide financial support to students who are pursuing MS or Ph.D. degrees in brewing science or related areas. **Focus:** Chemistry and Science. **Qualif.:** Candidates must be a current ASBC student member. Candidates must be enrolled in graduate studies by the time the graduate scholarship becomes effective, or be a current graduate student pursuing a course of study leading to an MS or a Ph.D. degree. For full-time graduate study, candidates must be enrolled in an academic schedule that meets the minimum requirements of the university involved. Educational institution in which the recipient is enrolled must be conducting fundamental investigations for the advancement of brewing and malting science. **Criteria:** Scholarship recipients will be selected based on the jury's review of the application materials.

Funds Avail.: $2,500. Scholarship winners will also receive

Awards are arranged alphabetically below their administering organizations

a certificate presented at a local section meeting. **To Apply:** Applicants must submit a completed application form; copies of transcripts; a letter of application describing career plans; and three letters of recommendation. At least two of which are from deans, department heads and/or professors who have supervised the applicant's most recent academic work. These letters should present essential facts regarding scholastic record, capacity for work, extracurricular activities, career potential, ability to cooperate, character and personality and interest and capability in research. **Deadline:** March 1. **Contact:** Beth Elliott.

923 ■ ASBC Foundation Undergraduate Scholarships *(Undergraduate/Scholarship)*

Purpose: To provide financial support to a student who is a daughter or son of an active ASBC member. **Focus:** General studies. **Qualif.:** Candidates must be the daughter or son of an active ASBC member. Candidates must be enrolled as an undergraduate student at a college or university and be actively pursuing a bachelor's degree. For full-time undergraduate students, candidates must be enrolled in an academic schedule that meets the minimum requirements of the attending college or university. **Criteria:** Scholarship recipients will be selected based on the jury's review of the application materials.

Funds Avail.: $1,000. **To Apply:** Applicants must submit a completed application form; copies of transcripts; a letter of application describing career plans; and three letters of recommendation with at least two from the academic adviser and/or faculty members familiar with the applicant's academic record. The confidential letter(s) should include a general appraisal of the scholarship, extracurricular activities and abilities in particular relation to the purposes and eligibility requirements of the scholarships. **Deadline:** March 1. **Contact:** Beth Elliott.

924 ■ American Society of Business Publication Editors

214 North Hale St.
Wheaton, IL 60187
Ph: (630)510-4588
Fax: (630)510-4501
E-mail: info@asbpe.org
URL: http://www.asbpe.org

925 ■ ASBPE Young Leaders Scholarships *(All, Professional Development/Scholarship)*

Purpose: To help young editors in their careers. **Focus:** Business; Editors and editing. **Qualif.:** Applicant must be an editor; 30 years old or younger; worked as an editor in a business magazine for at least two years; must be sponsored by the applicant's chief editor; pursuing career in business press; not a past winner of the ASBPE Young Leaders Scholarship. **Criteria:** Selection is based on the applications.

Funds Avail.: Exact amount is not specified. **Number Awarded:** 5. **To Apply:** Application form is available at the website. Completed application forms may be emailed to: asbpe.info@asbpe.org or faxed to: 630510-4501. **Deadline:** March 3.

926 ■ American Society of Certified Engineering Technicians

PO Box 1536
Brandon, MS 39043
Ph: (601)824-8991
URL: http://www.ascet.org

927 ■ Joseph C. Johnson Memorial Grants *(Undergraduate/Scholarship)*

Purpose: To diminish the cost of tuition, books, and lab fees for students. **Focus:** Engineering. **Qualif.:** Applicant must be an American citizen or a legal resident, a student, certified, regular, registered or associate member of ASCET; full or part-time student in an Engineering Technology program (students in a two year program should apply in the first year to receive the grant for their second year. Students in a four year program who apply in the third year may receive the grant for their fourth year); and qualified for financial aid under the Federal College Work Study Program. Applicant must meet the following grade requirements: 2 points on a 3 point system, 3 points on a 4 point system, 4 points on a 5 point system, or 5 points on a 6 point system. **Criteria:** Priority given to applicants who show financial need, as verified by the Dean or Registrar of Engineering Technology, or the Financial Aid Office at the institution the applicant attends.

Funds Avail.: $750. **To Apply:** Applicants must submit the a fully accomplished printed or typewritten application form available online; a letter of recommendation from a faculty member of the Engineering Technology Department indicating the motivation, progress, achievements, and an evaluation of the applicant's potential in the field of Engineering Technology; letters of recommendation from two personal acquaintances, employers or former employers, outlining association, motivation and potential for success; a copy of transcript of records and be sure to pass all the requirements on time.

928 ■ Joseph M. Parish Memorial Grants *(Undergraduate/Scholarship)*

Purpose: To diminish the cost of tuition, books, and lab fees for students. **Focus:** Engineering. **Qualif.:** Applicants must meet the following minimum grade points average: 2 points on a 3 point system, 3 points on a 4 point system, 4 points on a 5 point system, or 5 points on a 6 point system. Applicant must be an American citizen or a legal resident; a student member of ASCET; a full time student in an Engineering Technology program; qualified for financial aid under the Federal Work Study Program. **Criteria:** Priority given to applicants who show financial need, as verified by the Dean or Registrar of Engineering Technology, or the Financial Aid Office at the institution the applicant is attending.

Funds Avail.: $500. **Number Awarded:** 1. **To Apply:** Applicants must submit a fully accomplished printed or typewritten application form available online; a letter of recommendation from a faculty member of the Engineering Technology Department indicating the motivation, progress, achievements, and an evaluation of the applicant's potential in the field of Engineering Technology; letters of recommendation from two personal acquaintances, employers or former employers, outlining association, motivation and potential for success; a copy of transcript of records and be sure to pass all the requirements on time.

929 ■ Small Cash Grants *(Undergraduate/Scholarship)*

Purpose: To offset the cost of educational expenses as desired. **Focus:** Engineering. **Qualif.:** Applicants must either be a student, certified, regular, registered, or associate member of ASCET; a high school senior in the last five

Awards are arranged alphabetically below their administering organizations

months of the academic year who will be enrolled in an Engineering Technology curriculum no later than six months following selection for award; achieved passing grades in their present curriculum. **Criteria:** Priority given to applicants who show financial need, as verified by the Dean or Registrar of Engineering Technology, or the Financial Aid Office at the institution the applicant is attending.

Funds Avail.: $100. **To Apply:** Applicants must provide a copy of transcript; a letter of recommendation from a personal acquaintance, faculty member, or employer outlining motivation, progress, outstanding achievements, and an evaluation of the applicant's potential in the field of Engineering Technology.

930 ■ American Society for Clinical Laboratory Science

6701 Democracy Blvd., Ste. 300
Bethesda, MD 20817
Ph: (301)657-2768
Fax: (301)657-2909
E-mail: ascls@ascls.org
URL: http://www.ascls.org

931 ■ Alpha Mu Tau Undergraduate Scholarships *(Undergraduate/Scholarship)*

Purpose: To provide financial assistance for professionals who are involved in advancement of clinical laboratory sciences. **Focus:** Clinical Laboratory sciences. **Qualif.:** Applicants must be United States citizens or permanent residents of the United States; accepted into an NAACLS accredited program in Clinical Laboratory Science, to include Clinical Laboratory Science, Medical Technology, Clinical Laboratory Technician/Medical Laboratory Technician, Cytotechnology or Histotechnology; in or entering their last year of study on September 1st. **Criteria:** Candidates will be evaluated by the Scholarship Committee.

Funds Avail.: $15,000. **To Apply:** Applicants must submit the completed application form. **Deadline:** April 1.

932 ■ The AMTF Graduate Scholarships *(Graduate/Scholarship)*

Purpose: To provide financial assistance for professionals who are involved in advancement of clinical laboratory sciences. **Focus:** Clinical Laboratory sciences. **Qualif.:** Applicants must be U.S. citizens or permanent residents of the country; must be accepted into or are in an approved Masters or Doctoral program in areas related to Clinical Laboratory Science including Clinical Laboratory Education or Management Programs. **Criteria:** Candidates will be evaluated by the Scholarship Committee.

Funds Avail.: $1,000 up to $2,000. **To Apply:** Applicants must submit the completed application form. **Deadline:** April 1.

933 ■ Ruth M. French Graduate Scholarships *(Doctorate, Graduate/Scholarship)*

Purpose: To provide financial assistance for professionals who are involved in advancement of clinical laboratory sciences. **Focus:** Clinical Laboratory sciences. **Qualif.:** Applicants must be U.S. citizens or permanent residents of the country; must be accepted into or are in an approved Master's or Doctoral program in areas related to Clinical Laboratory Science including Clinical Laboratory Education or Management Programs; must be accepted into an NAACLS accredited program in Clinical Laboratory Science, to include Clinical Laboratory Science/Medical Technology, Clinical Laboratory Technician/Medical Laboratory Technician, Cytotechnology or Histotechnology; in or entering their last year of study on September 1st. **Criteria:** Candidates will be evaluated by the Scholarship Committee.

Funds Avail.: $3,000. **Number Awarded:** 1. **To Apply:** Applicants must submit the completed application form. **Deadline:** April 1.

934 ■ Dorothy Morrison Undergraduate Scholarships *(Undergraduate/Scholarship)*

Purpose: To provide financial assistance for professionals who are involved in advancement of clinical laboratory sciences. **Focus:** Clinical Laboratory sciences. **Qualif.:** Applicants must be United States citizens or permanent residents of the United States; accepted into an NAACLS accredited program in Clinical Laboratory Science, to include Clinical Laboratory Science/Medical Technology, Clinical Laboratory Technician/Medical Laboratory Technician, Cytotechnology or Histotechnology; in or entering their last year of study on September 1st. **Criteria:** Candidates will be evaluated by the Scholarship Committee.

Funds Avail.: $2,000. **To Apply:** Applicants must submit the completed application form. **Deadline:** April 1.

935 ■ Ida and May Reilly Graduate Scholarships *(Doctorate, Graduate/Scholarship)*

Purpose: To provide financial assistance for professionals who are involved in advancement of clinical laboratory sciences. **Focus:** Clinical Laboratory sciences. **Qualif.:** Applicants must be U.S. citizens or permanent residents of the country; must be accepted into or are in an approved Master's or Doctoral program in areas related to Clinical Laboratory Science including Clinical Laboratory Education or Management Programs; must be accepted into an NAACLS accredited program in Clinical Laboratory Science, to include Clinical Laboratory Science/Medical Technology, Clinical Laboratory Technician/Medical Laboratory Technician, Cytotechnology or Histotechnology; in or entering their last year of study on September 1st. **Criteria:** Candidates will be evaluated by the Scholarship Committee.

Funds Avail.: $2,500. **To Apply:** Applicants must submit the completed application form. **Deadline:** April 1.

936 ■ American Society of Comparative Law

245 Winter St. SE
Salem, OR 97301
Ph: (503)370-6402
Fax: (503)370-6828
E-mail: symeon@willamette.edu
URL: http://www.comparativelaw.org

937 ■ American Society of Comparative Law TransCoop Programs *(All/Fellowship)*

Purpose: To provide funds for cooperative research between German, American and/or Canadian scholars in the fields of humanities, social sciences, law, and economics. **Focus:** Humanities; Social Sciences; Law; Economics. **Qualif.:** Applicants must permanent residents or scholars of United States, Germany, and Canada. **Criteria:** Recipients are selected based on originality of the proposed

Awards are arranged alphabetically below their administering organizations

research work; scholarly qualifications of the applicants; and potential to strengthen transatlantic cooperation.

Funds Avail.: No specific amount. **To Apply:** Applicants must submit completed application form; time and expenses schedule indicating when and for what purpose funds will be required; one confidential reference letter; publication list; proof of matching funds. **Deadline:** April 30. **Contact:** info@avh.de

938 ■ American Society of Composers, Authors and Publishers (ASCAP) Foundation

1 Lincoln Plaza
New York, NY 10023-7142
Ph: (212)621-6219
E-mail: concertmusic@ascap.com
URL: http://www.ascapfoundation.org

939 ■ Louis Armstrong Scholarships *(High School/Scholarship)*

Purpose: To award scholarship to students in their junior year. **Focus:** Music. **Qualif.:** Applicant must be a junior-year student and enrolled full-time at Mt. Vermon High School. **Criteria:** Selection will be based on abilities in music performance and composition.

Funds Avail.: No specific amount. **To Apply:** The ASCAP Foundation does not accept applications for this scholarship. Interested students should consult their financial aid office for application information. **Contact:** Mt. Vermon High School, Guidance and Career Center, 703-619-3244 or ASCAP Foundation at the above address (see entry 938).

940 ■ Charlotte V. Bergen Scholarships *(Undergraduate/Scholarship)*

Purpose: To provide scholarship to young composers, aged 18 or under, to be used for music study at an accredited college or music conservatory. **Focus:** Music. **Qualif.:** Applicants must be citizens or permanent residents of the United States, or enrolled students with Students Visas. **Criteria:** Selection will be based on the committee's criteria.

Funds Avail.: No specific amount. **To Apply:** Applicants must submit a completed application form, one reproduction of a manuscript or score, biographical information including music studies, background and experience and a list of compositions. Completed Application materials must be postmarked on or before the deadline. **Deadline:** March 1.

941 ■ Cherry Lane Foundation/Music Alive! Scholarships *(Undergraduate/Scholarship)*

Purpose: To award scholarships annually to African-American college or university students. **Focus:** Music. **Qualif.:** Applicant must be an African-American college or university student majoring in music. Applicants must demonstrate musical talent and proficiency in the areas of arranging, producing, conducting, performing. **Criteria:** Selection will be based on the committee's criteria.

Funds Avail.: No specific amount. **To Apply:** The ASCAP Foundation does not accept applications for this scholarship. Interested students should consult their school's financial aid office for application information.

942 ■ David Rose Scholarships *(Undergraduate/Scholarship)*

Purpose: To award scholarship to qualified college-level students. **Focus:** Filmmaking; Music. **Qualif.:** Applicant must be a college-level student working toward a career in scoring for film and/or television who is participating in ASCAP's Film and Television Scoring Workshop. **Criteria:** Selection will be based on the committee's criteria.

Funds Avail.: No specific amount. **To Apply:** The ASCAP Foundation does not accept applications for this scholarship. Interested students should consult their school's financial aid office for application information.

943 ■ Fran Morgenstern Davis Scholarships *(Undergraduate/Scholarship)*

Purpose: To provide scholarship to the music composition students at the Manhattan School of Music. **Focus:** Music. **Qualif.:** Applicants must be full-time undergraduate music composition students at the Manhattan School of Music who demonstrate the potential to produce creative and original work and who also demonstrate financial need. **Criteria:** Selection will be based on the Manhattan School of Music faculty's criteria.

Funds Avail.: No specific amount. **Number Awarded:** 2. **To Apply:** Applicants must submit an application together with other required documents to the Manhattan School of Music.

944 ■ John Denver Music Scholarships *(Undergraduate/Scholarship)*

Purpose: To provide young music students with an opportunity to attend a summer music camp which they would otherwise not be able to afford. **Focus:** Music. **Qualif.:** Applicants must be students, aged 10-16, who demonstrate both musical promise and financial need. **Criteria:** Selection will be based on the committee's criteria.

Funds Avail.: No specific amount. **Number Awarded:** 3. **To Apply:** Applicants must submit an application to the Perry-Mansfield School in Steamboat Springs, Colorado. **Contact:** Perry-Mansfield School in Steamboat Springs, Colorado; 800-430-ARTS; p-m@cmn.ne.

945 ■ Louis Dreyfus Warner-Chappell City College Scholarships *(Undergraduate/Scholarship)*

Purpose: To award scholarships to composition students for scores written for dance, film/video or theater. **Focus:** Music. **Qualif.:** Applicants must be students enrolled in either a B.A. or B.F.A. program at the City College/City University of New York. **Criteria:** Selection will be based on the committee's criteria.

Funds Avail.: No specific amount. **To Apply:** The ASCAP Foundation does not accept applications for this scholarship. Interested students should consult their school's financial aid office for application information.

946 ■ Steve Kaplan TV and Film Studies Scholarships *(Professional Development/Scholarship)*

Purpose: To provide financial assistance for an aspiring television and film composer to attend ASCAP's Film Scoring Workshop in Los Angeles. **Focus:** Filmmaking; Music. **Qualif.:** Applicant must be a television and film composer. **Criteria:** Selection will be based on the committee's criteria.

Funds Avail.: No specific amount. **To Apply:** Interested applicants may contact the Foundation for the application information.

947 ■ Leiber and Stoller Music Scholarships *(Undergraduate/Scholarship)*

Purpose: To provide assistance to young aspiring songwriters, musicians and vocalists. **Focus:** Music. **Qualif.:**

Awards are arranged alphabetically below their administering organizations

Applicants must be incoming freshmen at Berklee College of Music. **Criteria:** Selection will be based on the committee's criteria.

Funds Avail.: No specific amount. **Number Awarded:** 2. **To Apply:** Interested students should consult their financial aid office for application information.

948 ■ Rudy Perez Songwriting Scholarships *(Undergraduate/Scholarship)*

Purpose: To present scholarships to aspiring Latino songwriters. **Focus:** Music. **Qualif.:** Applicant must be an aspiring Latino songwriter who demonstrates potential to produce creative and original work and also demonstrates financial need. **Criteria:** Selection will be based on the committee's criteria.

Funds Avail.: No specific amount. **To Apply:** The ASCAP Foundation does not accept applications for this scholarship. Interested students should consult their school's financial aid office for application information.

949 ■ American Society of Echocardiography

1500 Sunday Dr., Ste. 102
Raleigh, NC 27607
Ph: (919)861-5574
Fax: (919)787-4916
E-mail: ase@asecho.org
URL: http://www.asecho.org

950 ■ Cardiac Sonographer Education Development Grants *(Professional Development, Undergraduate/Grant)*

Purpose: To financially support the graduating students in the cardiac sonography program. **Focus:** Cardiology. **Qualif.:** Applicant must be involved in the cardiac sonography programs. **Criteria:** Recipients of the awards are based on ASE guidelines for the award.

Funds Avail.: $50,000. **To Apply:** Applicant must send application form and other supporting documents including lists of participants in the submission process (academic titles and affiliations, participants contribution to the proposal), summary of the proposal not exceeding 400 words (specific aims, how the program will use the money to increase qualified sonographer graduates, how the program will sustain the effort after the grant ended); budget, proposed method, additional supporting material, if any. **Deadline:** April 18.

951 ■ Quality Initiative Grant-in-Aid *(Doctorate, Graduate/Grant)*

Purpose: To support meritorious research focusing on specific issues. **Focus:** General studies. **Qualif.:** Applicants must hold the professional degree of MD, PhD or equivalent or a sonographer; faculty of an institution; open to individuals, teams, firms with appropriate qualifications to implement the project, including a demonstrated track record with similar research projects. **Criteria:** Recipients are selected based on committee's review on proposal.

Funds Avail.: $100,000. **To Apply:** Application form should include the following: Name of the grant applied for; title of the project; summary of the proposal (not to exceed 400 words); listing of all co-investigators, with degrees, titles and affiliation and a paragraph delineating their contribution to the proposed project; abbreviate curriculum vitae or NIH biosketch of all investigators (maximum 2 pages per investigator) or a professional resume; proposed budget including budget justifications; other funding; proposed approach to the problem; full description of the project including reference and any figures should not exceed 7 typewritten pages with 1-inch margins using a minimum of a 10-point font. **Deadline: Contact:** Cathy Kerr.

952 ■ American Society of Electroneurodiagnostic Technologists

6501 E Commerce Ave., Ste. 120
Kansas City, MO 64120
Ph: (816)931-1120
Fax: (816)931-1145
E-mail: info@aset.org
URL: http://www.aset.org

953 ■ ASET Educational Seminars, Courses and Program Scholarships *(All, Professional Development/Scholarship)*

Purpose: To provide conference, seminars, and other educational opportunities to ASET members. **Focus:** Neuroscience. **Qualif.:** Applicant must be an ASET member who wishes to attend an ASET conference, seminar, and other educational opportunities. **Criteria:** Selection is based on the application.

Funds Avail.: No specific amount. **To Apply:** Application form is available at the website. Applicant must include a typed, signed statement and a recommendation letter from a supervisor.

954 ■ ASET Student Education Grants *(All/Grant)*

Purpose: To assist and encourage students to further or continue their interest in selecting the allied health field of electroneurodiagnostic technology as a pending or continued career. **Focus:** Health sciences. **Qualif.:** Applicant must be a student enrolled full-time in a CAAHEP accredited END school; or employees of ASET member companies or individuals. Relatives of the Foundation Selection Committee and the Foundation Board of Directors are not qualified for grants. **Criteria:** Selection Committee will review all submitted applications.

Funds Avail.: $1500. **To Apply:** Applicants must submit an application; copies of transcript; and recommendations and reference letters. **Deadline:** June 1. **Contact:** Shiela R. Navis, CAE Executive Director, sheila@aset.org.

955 ■ American Society for Engineering Education

1818 N St. NW, Ste. 600
Washington, DC 20036-2479
Ph: (202)331-3500
E-mail: aseeexec@asee.org
URL: http://www.asee.org

956 ■ NASA Aeronautics Scholarship Undergraduate Program *(Undergraduate/Scholarship)*

Purpose: To provide financial assistance for rising undergraduate students entering their third year of education at a college or university. **Focus:** Engineering, Mechanical; Engineering, Electrical. **Qualif.:** Applicants must be citizens or nationals of the United States with at least two years of full time study left to complete at an accredited U.S. college

Awards are arranged alphabetically below their administering organizations

or university as of fall. **Criteria:** Applicants are evaluated based on academic performance.

Funds Avail.: $1,500. **Number Awarded:** 20. **To Apply:** Applicants must submit all the required application information electronically at www.asee.org. **Deadline:** March 24.

957 ■ American Society for Enology and Viticulture

PO Box 1855
Davis, CA 95617-1855
Ph: (530)753-3142
Fax: (530)753-3318
URL: http://www.asev.org

958 ■ American Society for Enology and Viticulture Scholarships *(Undergraduate/Scholarship)*

Purpose: To define questions in the wine industry and work towards answers based on the relevant and scientifically rigorous information on selected topics. **Focus:** Viticulture. **Qualif.:** All applicants must be undergraduate and graduate students and enrolled in or accepted into a full-time accredited four year college or university program; applicant should be a minimum of junior status for the upcoming academic year(45/06 quarter units); undergraduate students must have a minimum cumulative grade point average of 3.0; graduate students must have a minimum overall grade point average of 3.2. These averages must be based on a scale maximum of 4.0; applicants must be enrolled in a major or in a graduate group emphasizing enology or viviculture, or in a curriculum emphasizing a science basic to the wine and grape industry. **Criteria:** Undergraduate and graduate students will be rated on a separate basis.

Funds Avail.: No specific amount. **To Apply:** Applicant must download the scholarship application form or contact ASEV office; fill out the application form after receiving the packet; an applicant must send the application, copies of transcript, and two original letters of recommendation to the ASEV office; an applicant must submit a list of planned courses for the upcoming academic year. **Deadline:** March 1.

959 ■ American Society of Genealogists

PO Box 519
Williamstown, MA 01267
E-mail: asg.sec@gmail.com
URL: http://www.fasg.org

960 ■ ASG Scholar Awards *(Professional Development/Scholarship)*

Purpose: To provide financial assistance to a scholar to attend an educational training program. **Focus:** Genealogy. **Qualif.:** Applicants must be a genealogist, genealogical librarians, and researchers working in related fields. **Criteria:** Applicants will be selected by the ASG Scholarship Committee.

Funds Avail.: $500 for tuition expenses. **To Apply:** Applicants must submit three copies of resume; manuscript or published work (maximum of 5000 words); and a 100-150 words statement to Melinde Lutz Sanborn, Chair, ASG Scholarship Committee. **Deadline:** March 15.

Remarks: Created in 1996. **Contact:** Melinde Lutz Sanborn, Chair, ASG Scholarship Committee.

961 ■ American Society of Heating, Refrigerating and Air-Conditioning Engineers

1791 Tullie Circle NE
Atlanta, GA 30329
Ph: (404)636-8400
Fax: (404)321-5478
Free: 800-527-4723
E-mail: ashrae@ashrae.org
URL: http://www.ashrae.org

962 ■ Henry Adams Scholarships *(Undergraduate/Scholarship)*

Purpose: To help reduce the financial burdens of obtaining an engineering education. **Focus:** Engineering. **Qualif.:** Applicants must be full-time undergraduates in ABET-accredited Engineering Technology program leading to Bachelors of Science or Engineering degree; must have cumulative GPA of at least 3.0 on a scale where 4.0 is the highest. **Criteria:** Recipients are selected based on financial need; leadership ability; and character.

Funds Avail.: $3,000. **To Apply:** Applicants must submit an official transcript of college grades; letter of recommendation; and evaluation form from three references including professor or faculty advisor. **Deadline:** December 1.

963 ■ American Society of Heating, Refrigerating, and Air-Conditioning Memorial Scholarships *(Undergraduate/Scholarship)*

Purpose: To help reduce the financial burdens of obtaining an engineering education. **Focus:** Engineering. **Qualif.:** Applicants must be full-time undergraduates in an ABET-accredited Engineering Technology program leading to a Bachelor of Science or Engineering Degree and must have cumulative GPA of at least 3.0 on a 4.0 scale. **Criteria:** Recipients are selected based on the need for financial assistance; leadership ability; and character.

Funds Avail.: $3,000. **To Apply:** Applicants must submit an official transcript of college grades; a letter of recommendation; and an evaluation form from three references including professor or faculty advisor. **Deadline:** December 1.

964 ■ American Society of Heating, Refrigerating, and Air-Conditioning Undergraduate Scholarships *(Undergraduate/Scholarship)*

Purpose: To help reduce the financial burdens of obtaining an engineering education. **Focus:** Engineering. **Qualif.:** Applicants must be full-time undergraduate in an ABET-accredited Engineering Technology program leading to a Bachelor of Science or Engineering Degree and must have cumulative GPA of at least 3.0 on a 4.0 scale. **Criteria:** Recipients are selected based on the need for financial assistance; leadership ability; and character.

Funds Avail.: $3,000. **To Apply:** Applicants must submit an official transcript of college grades; a letter of recommendation; and an evaluation form from three references including professor or faculty advisor. **Deadline:** December 1.

965 ■ Willis H. Carrier Scholarships *(Undergraduate/Scholarship)*

Purpose: To help reduce the financial burdens of obtaining an engineering education. **Focus:** Engineering. **Qualif.:** Applicants must be full-time undergraduates in an ABET-accredited Engineering Technology program leading to a Bachelor of Science or Engineering Degree; must have cumulative GPA of at least 3.0 on a 4.0 scale. **Criteria:** Recipients are selected based on need for financial as-

Awards are arranged alphabetically below their administering organizations

sistance; leadership ability; and character.

Funds Avail.: $10,000. **To Apply:** Applicants must submit an official transcript of college grades; a letter of recommendation; and an evaluation form from three references including professor or faculty advisor. **Deadline:** December 1.

966 ■ Frank M. Coda Scholarships
(Undergraduate/Scholarship)

Purpose: To help reduce the financial burdens of obtaining the engineering education. **Focus:** Engineering. **Qualif.:** Applicants must be full-time undergraduates in an ABET-accredited Engineering Technology program leading to a Bachelor of Science or Engineering Degree and must have cumulative GPA of at least 3.0 on a 4.0 scale. **Criteria:** Recipients are selected based on the need for financial assistance; leadership ability; and character.

Funds Avail.: $5,000. **To Apply:** Applicants must submit an official transcript of college grades; a letter of recommendation and an evaluation form from three references including professor or faculty advisor. **Deadline:** December 1.

967 ■ Duane Hanson Scholarships
(Undergraduate/Scholarship)

Purpose: To help reduce the financial burdens of obtaining an engineering education. **Focus:** Engineering. **Qualif.:** Applicants must be full-time undergraduates in ABET-accredited Engineering Technology program leading to Bachelors of Science or Engineering degree; must have cumulative GPA of at least 3.0 on a scale where 4.0 is the highest. **Criteria:** Recipients are selected based on financial need; leadership ability; and character.

Funds Avail.: $3,000. **To Apply:** Applicants must submit an official transcript of college grades; letter of recommendation; and evaluation form from three references including professor or faculty advisor. **Deadline:** December 1.

968 ■ Alwin B. Newton Scholarships
(Undergraduate/Scholarship)

Purpose: To help reduce the financial burdens of obtaining an engineering education. **Focus:** Engineering. **Qualif.:** Applicants must be full-time undergraduates in an ABET-accredited Engineering Technology program leading to a Bachelors of Science or Engineering degree; must have cumulative GPA of at least 3.0 on a scale of 4.0. **Criteria:** Recipients are selected based on financial need; leadership ability; and character.

Funds Avail.: $3,000. **To Apply:** Applicants must submit official transcripts of college grades; a letter of recommendation; and an evaluation form from three references including a professor or faculty advisor. **Deadline:** December 1.

969 ■ Donald E. Nichols Scholarships
(Undergraduate/Scholarship)

Purpose: To help reduce the financial burdens of obtaining the engineering education. **Focus:** Engineering. **Qualif.:** Applicants must be full-time undergraduates in an ABET-accredited Engineering Technology program leading to a Bachelor of Science or Engineering Degree; must have cumulative GPA of at least 3.0 on a 4.0 scale. **Criteria:** Recipients are selected based on the need for financial assistance; leadership ability; and character.

Funds Avail.: $3,000. **To Apply:** Applicants must submit an official transcript of college grades; a letter of recommendation; and an evaluation form from three references including professor or faculty advisor. **Deadline:** December 1.

970 ■ Reuben Trane Scholarships
(Undergraduate/Scholarship)

Purpose: To help reduce the financial burdens of obtaining the engineering education. **Focus:** Engineering. **Qualif.:** Applicants must be full-time undergraduates in an ABET-accredited Engineering Technology program leading to a Bachelor of Science or Engineering Degree; must have cumulative GPA of at least 3.0 on a 4.0 scale. **Criteria:** Recipients are selected based on the need for financial assistance; leadership ability; and character.

Funds Avail.: $10,000. **To Apply:** Applicants must submit an official transcript of college grades; a letter of recommendation; and an evaluation form from three references including professor or faculty advisor. **Deadline:** December 1.

971 ■ American Society for Horticultural Science

113 SW St., Ste. 200
Alexandria, VA 22314-2851
Ph: (703)836-4606
Fax: (703)836-2024
E-mail: webmaster@ashs.org
URL: http://www.ashs.org

972 ■ American Society for Horticultural Science Student Travel Grants *(Graduate, Undergraduate/Grant)*

Purpose: To provide financial assistance to students in the area of horticulture. **Focus:** General studies. **Qualif.:** Applicants must be enrolled in horticultural science as a major course of study and must have submitted an abstract title or complete abstract for presentation at the ASHS Annual Conference. **Criteria:** Grants will be awarded on the basis of merit and geographical distribution.

Funds Avail.: $500 (domestic graduate and undergraduate students); $750 (international students). **Number Awarded:** Varies. **To Apply:** Applicants must accomplish application and abstract. Application forms and instructions are available at the website. **Deadline:** March 4. **Contact:** ASHS Headquarters, 113 S West St., Ste. 200, Alexandria, VA 22314-2851, phone: 703-836-4606; fax: 703-836-2024.

973 ■ ASHS Industry Division Student Travel Grants *(Graduate, Undergraduate/Grant)*

Purpose: To provide financial assistance to students in the area of horticulture who are attending the ASHS Annual Conference. **Focus:** Horticulture. **Qualif.:** Award is open to all undergraduate and graduate Horticulture students. **Criteria:** Applicants will be selected based on academic achievement (30 points for 4.0 GPA), recommendation (20 points) and essay (50 points).

Funds Avail.: $750. **To Apply:** Applicants must submit transcripts, completed application, letter of recommendation from undergraduate advisor or faculty member, and a 500-word essay outlining interest in horticulture and career goals.

974 ■ ASHS Scholars Awards *(Undergraduate/Scholarship)*

Purpose: To recognize and support scholastic achievement and to encourage career development in horticultural

Awards are arranged alphabetically below their administering organizations

science at the undergraduate level. **Focus:** Horticulture. **Qualif.:** Applicant must be an undergraduate student of any class standing at the time of the application; must be registered as a full-time student (minimum 10 credit hours) and actively pursuing a degree in horticulture. **Criteria:** Recipients are chosen based on excellence in academic and scholastic performance in the major (an area of horticulture) and supporting areas of science; participation in extra curricular, leadership and research activities relating to horticulture; participation in university and community service; demonstrated commitment to the horticulture science profession and related career fields; and related horticultural experiences.

Funds Avail.: $1,500. **Number Awarded:** 2. **To Apply:** Applicants must be nominated by the chair/head of the department in which they are majoring; must submit completed application supported by a 250-500 essay, complete resume, three letters of reference, and official university/college transcripts. Forms and information are available at the website. **Deadline:** February 4. **Contact:** Mary McGuire, email: mmcguire@ashs.org.

975 ■ Miklos Faust International Travel Awards
(Postdoctorate/Fellowship)

Purpose: To promote international cooperation in fruit crops research and education. **Focus:** Horticulture. **Qualif.:** Applicants must be young scientists (less than 40 yrs. old) who are actively involved in fruit science research; must hold or pursuing a doctoral degree. **Criteria:** Applications are reviewed according to evidence of high originality and strong commitment to research in fruit science.

Funds Avail.: No specific amount. **Number Awarded:** 1. **To Apply:** Applicants must submit a completed application form (available at the website). **Deadline:** February 4. **Contact:** Mary McGuire, email: mmcguire@ashs.org.

976 ■ American Society of International Law

2223 Massachusetts Ave. NW
Washington, DC 20008
Ph: (202)939-6000
Fax: (202)797-7133
E-mail: services@asil.org
URL: http://www.asil.org

977 ■ ASIL Helton Fellowship Program *(All/Fellowship)*

Purpose: To contribute in paying for logistics, housing, and living expenses, and other costs related to the fellows fieldwork and research in affiliation with the sponsoring organization. **Focus:** Law. **Qualif.:** Applicants must be students practicing lawyer, human rights professionals, scholars and other individuals seeking assistance in conducting international fieldwork and law-related research. **Criteria:** Recipients are selected based on the performance in conducting research.

Funds Avail.: No specific amount. **To Apply:** Applicants must complete the online application form including description of intended project and career statement; a writing sample; current CV or resume; evidence of law students status and/or date of graduation from a law school; and two letters of recommendation or support. **Deadline:** October 15 February 15. **Contact:** fellowship@asil.org

978 ■ American Society of Landscape Architects

636 Eye St. NW
Washington, DC 20001-3736
Ph: (202)898-2444
Fax: (202)898-1185
Free: 888-999-2752
E-mail: dsaunders@asla.org
URL: http://www.asla.org

979 ■ American Society of Landscape Architects Council of Fellow Scholarships
(Undergraduate/Scholarship)

Purpose: To aid outstanding students who would not otherwise have an opportunity to continue a professional degree program in the area of landscape architecture due to unmet financial need; to increase the interest and participation of economically disadvantaged and underrepresented populations in the study of landscape architecture through a more diverse population; to enrich the profession of landscape architecture through a more diverse population. **Focus:** Landscape architecture and design. **Qualif.:** Applicants must be permanent U.S. citizens or permanent resident aliens who are third, fourth, or fifth year undergraduates at Landscape Architecture Accreditation Board accredited programs of landscape architecture. **Criteria:** Recipients are selected based on financial need.

Funds Avail.: $4,000. **Number Awarded:** 2. **To Apply:** Applicants must submit a 300-word essay about how the applicant envisions himself or herself contributing to the profession of landscape architecture; two letters of recommendation specifically addressing the quality of applicant's performance as a student of landscape architecture and promise as a professional (one letter of recommendation must come from a faculty member and the other one must be sent by a non-academic member); and a student aid report. **Deadline:** February 15.

980 ■ Class Fund Ornamental Horticulture Scholarship Program *(Undergraduate/Scholarship)*

Purpose: To assist undergraduate or graduate students enrolled in programs in landscape architecture and ornamental horticulture in California. **Focus:** Landscape architecture; Horticulture. **Qualif.:** Applicants must be undergraduate or graduate students in financial need who show promise and commitment to the profession; must be continuing their studies in landscape architecture or ornamental horticulture. **Criteria:** Recipients are selected based on financial need.

Funds Avail.: $3,000. **Number Awarded:** 1. **To Apply:** Applicants must submit a 300-word statement on the profession; 100-word statement indicating intended use of funds; two letters of recommendation from the faculty; and one confidential letter of recommendation from the department head. **Deadline:** February 15.

981 ■ The Dangermond Fellowships
(Postgraduate/Fellowship)

Purpose: To promote and facilitate the integration of art, science, method, and technology in the study and profession of landscape architecture; to encourage the use of geographic information systems as a framework for exploring integrated approaches to landscape assessment and intervention. **Focus:** Landscape architecture and design. **Qualif.:** Applicants must be graduate students of landscape architecture. **Criteria:** Recipients are selected based on the creative use of geographic information systems as a framework for exploring integrated approaches to landscape assessment (analysis) and intervention (planning, design and management).

Awards are arranged alphabetically below their administering organizations

Funds Avail.: $10,000. **To Apply:** Applicants must submit a three page-or-less proposal for the work to be undertaken stating an objective, outcome and method, transferability of the proposed work, deliverables, and level of institutional support; a cover letter from the principal faculty advisor indicating his/her faculty position and confirming department approval and adherence to the overall goals of the fellowship; a specific delineation of the roles of each team member and faculty advisor; one-page biographical sketch of the faculty advisor; and two letters of recommendation for individual or team efforts from faculty members not involved in project. **Deadline:** February 15.

982 ■ Edith H. Henderson Scholarships *(Undergraduate/Scholarship)*

Purpose: To recognize an outstanding architect student. **Focus:** Landscape architecture and design. **Qualif.:** Applicants must be students pursuing a program in landscape architecture. **Criteria:** Recipients are selected based on academic achievement.

Funds Avail.: $1,000. **To Apply:** Applicants must submit a typewritten essay review of Mrs. Henderson's book entitled "Edith Henderson's Home Landscape Companion" (200-400 words maximum). **Deadline:** April 1. **Contact:** rfigura@lafoundation.org.

983 ■ LAF/Class Fund AILA/YAMAGAMI/Hope Fellowships *(Postgraduate/Fellowship)*

Purpose: To provide for the middle ground where the designer, landscape contractor and nursery man, as well as those in formal training could meet and discuss common problems and experiences. **Focus:** Landscape architecture and design. **Qualif.:** Applicants must have earned a bachelor's or a mater's degree in landscape architecture; must be landscape architects who have been in practice for a minimum of three years and wish to use the funds for continuing education. **Criteria:** Recipients are selected based on innovative nature of the proposed endeavor; the benefits that may accrue to other members of the profession and the profession in general; the personal goals to be achieved; and qualifications of the applicant.

Funds Avail.: $1,000. **To Apply:** Applicants must submit a summary of the uniqueness of the proposed activity, skills/knowledge to gain, increased proficiency, and opportunity to exist (500-word); a statement of intent (maximum of 100 words) detailing how the funds would be used and a line item budget if applicable; and two letters of recommendation from licensed landscape architects. **Deadline:** August 1.

984 ■ William J. Locklin Scholarships *(Undergraduate/Scholarship)*

Purpose: To recognize an outstanding architect student and to emphasize the importance of 24-hour lighting in landscape designs. **Focus:** Landscape architecture and design. **Qualif.:** Applicants must be students pursuing a program in lighting design or landscape architectural students focusing on lighting design in studio projects. **Criteria:** Recipients are selected based on quality of the design and its effect.

Funds Avail.: $1,000. **To Apply:** Applicants must submit a typed, double-spaced 300-word essay highlighting the design project, the overall effect to be obtained, rationale for choice of lamp and placement of fixture, and anticipated results; visual samples (schematics/renderings/sketchers or other plans) reduced 81/2"X11"; and one letter of recommendation relevant to the proposed project and applicant, preferably from a current professor. **Deadline:** April 1. **Contact:** rfigura@lafoundation.org.

985 ■ Raymond E. Page Scholarships *(Undergraduate/Scholarship)*

Purpose: To give an undergraduate student the opportunity to follow Mr. Page's example of directing profession in the area of landscape architecture and design by answering the challenges of tomorrow. **Focus:** Landscape architecture and design. **Qualif.:** Applicants must be currently enrolled in an institution or university. **Criteria:** Recipients are selected based on academic standing and financial need.

Funds Avail.: $1,000. **To Apply:** Applicants must submit a double-spaced, two-page essay describing the applicant's need for financial assistance and how the award is to be used; a letter of recommendation from a current professor who is familiar with the applicant's character and goals in pursuing an education in landscape architecture; three copies of application; and a cover sheet. **Deadline:** April 1. **Contact:** rfigura@lafoundation.org.

986 ■ Rae L. Price Scholarships *(Undergraduate/Scholarship)*

Purpose: To bring young creative individuals into careers in the area of landscape architecture and design who may not otherwise have the financial ability to cover all the costs of their educational program. **Focus:** Landscape architecture and design. **Qualif.:** Applicants must be U.S. citizens who are undergraduate students in the final two years of study in LAAB accredited schools; must demonstrate financial need; and must have a minimum "B" GPA. **Criteria:** Recipients are selected based on financial need.

Funds Avail.: $5,000. **To Apply:** Applicants must submit a 500-word essay describing the applicant's aspirations, ability to surmount obstacles, high level of drive, and need for financial assistance; two letters of recommendations from current professors familiar with the applicant's character and goals in pursuing an education in landscape architecture. **Deadline:** February 15.

987 ■ Rain Bird Scholarships *(Undergraduate/Scholarship)*

Purpose: To recognize an outstanding architect student. **Focus:** Landscape architecture and design. **Qualif.:** Applicants must be undergraduate students majoring in landscape architecture. **Criteria:** Recipients are selected based on demonstrated commitment to the profession through participation in extracurricular activities and exemplary scholastic achievements.

Funds Avail.: $1,000. **To Apply:** Applicants must submit a typed, double-spaced 300 word-essay stating career goals and explaining how he/she will contribute to the advancement of landscape architecture. **Deadline:** April 1. **Contact:** rfigura@lafoundation.org.

988 ■ Harriet Barnhart Wimmer Scholarships *(Undergraduate/Scholarship)*

Purpose: To recognize an outstanding architect student. **Focus:** Landscape architecture and design. **Qualif.:** Applicants must be females entering their final year of undergraduate landscape studies who have demonstrated excellence in design ability and sensitivity to the environment. **Criteria:** Recipients are selected based on demonstrated excellence in design ability and sensitivity to the environment.

Funds Avail.: $1,000. **To Apply:** Applicants must submit a typed, double-spaced autobiography and statement of personal and professional goals with a maximum of 500-words; one letter of recommendation regarding student's design abilities and attitude from a design instructor; graphic samples of work from three different projects, comprising a total of six 8X10 black and white or color photos; brief written descriptions of design intent for each graphic; and financial aid forms. **Deadline:** April 1. **Contact:** rfigura@lafoundation.org.

989 ■ David T. Woolsey Scholarships *(Undergraduate/Scholarship)*

Purpose: To recognize an outstanding architect student. **Focus:** Landscape architecture and design. **Qualif.:** Applicants must be third, fourth, or fifth year undergraduate or graduate students of landscape architecture who are permanent residents of Hawaii. **Criteria:** Recipients are selected based on academic achievement.

Funds Avail.: $1,000. **To Apply:** Applicants must submit a typed, double-spaced autobiography and statement of personal and professional goals with a maximum of 500-words; a design work; three 8X10 color and/or black and white photographs; two letters of recommendation including one from a design instructor; and proof of Hawaii residency. **Deadline:** April 1. **Contact:** rfigura@lafoundation.org.

990 ■ American Society for Legal History

University of Minnesota School of Law
326 Mondale Hall
229-19th Ave. S
Minneapolis, MN 55455
Fax: (612)625-2011
E-mail: gallanis@umn.edu
URL: http://www.h-net.msu.edu/~law/ASLH/aslh.htm

991 ■ Cromwell Fellowships *(Undergraduate/Fellowship)*

Purpose: To support research and writing in American legal history. **Focus:** American History. **Qualif.:** Applicants must be currently enrolled in an institution, college, or university. **Criteria:** Recipients are selected based on academic standing.

Funds Avail.: $5,000. **Number Awarded:** 3-5. **To Apply:** Applicants must complete the application form.

992 ■ American Society for Mass Spectrometry

2019 Galisteo St. Bldg. I-1
Santa Fe, NM 87505
Ph: (505)989-4517
Fax: (505)989-1073
E-mail: office@asms.org
URL: http://www.asms.org

993 ■ ASMS Research Awards *(Professional Development/Grant)*

Purpose: To promote research done by young scientists in mass spectrometry. **Focus:** Science. **Qualif.:** Applicants must be academic scientists within four years of joining the term track faculty or equivalent in a North American university; have not received awards under this program. **Criteria:** Recipients are selected based on applications and proposals.

Funds Avail.: $25,000. **To Apply:** Applicants must send seven sets of: one-page fiscal proposal and justification; list of current research support; curriculum vitae; two letters of recommendation. **Deadline:** November 30.

994 ■ American Society of Mechanical Engineers

Three Park Ave.
New York, NY 10016-5990
Ph: (212)591-7733
Fax: (212)591-7739
Free: 800-843-2763
E-mail: infocentral@asme.org
URL: http://www.asme.org

995 ■ Auxiliary Undergraduate Scholarships *(Undergraduate/Scholarship)*

Purpose: To provide scholarships and new developments in Mechanical Engineering. To honor students who demonstrate outstanding personal and academic characteristics. **Focus:** Mechanical engineering. **Qualif.:** Applicants must be a full-time students seeking either Mechanical Engineering courses or any related field of study engineering; must be a U.S citizen. **Criteria:** Recipients will be selected based on a review of all applications.

Funds Avail.: $2,000 Cash scholarship used for one academic year. **Number Awarded:** 1. **To Apply:** Applicants must be enrolled in U.S. school in an ABET accredited Mechanical Engineering Department; Applicants must submit letter of recommendation by the Head of The Mechanical Engineering Faculty Advisor; Applicants must file a letter from a non-academic reference; Applicants should have a letter from any other person will not fulfill the requirement; Applicants must prepare letter of recommendation from an instructor, preferably in the Engineering School; Applicants must submit Official transcript with academic record; Applicants should have Completed Application Form; Guidelines and application form are available from the ASME scholarship office or can be downloaded from the ASME website. **Deadline:** March 15. **Contact:** Alverta E. Cover 5425 Caldwell Mill Rd. Birmingham, AL 35242; 205-991-6109 at the above address (see entry 994).

996 ■ Lucy and Charles W.E. Clarke Scholarships *(Undergraduate/Scholarship)*

Purpose: To promote art, science and practice of mechanical and multidisciplinary engineering and allied sciences through educational assistance. **Focus:** Mechanical engineering. **Qualif.:** Scholarship is open to schools accredited by the Accreditation Board for Engineering and Technology or substantially equivalent mechanical engineering technology departments who directly choose incoming freshmen beginning engineering studies in the fall to receive the scholarship. **Criteria:** Recipients are chosen by the departments on the basis of need, academic achievement, community involvement, work experience and recommendations.

Funds Avail.: $6,000 (for the winning schools). **To Apply:** Applications for deserving schools are made by the AMSE Student Section as endorsed by the mechanical engineering technology department; Necessary forms are available in the website also indicating other instructions. **Deadline:** October 20. **Contact:** Marcelle Austin, tel: 212-591-7733, fax: 212-591-7739, email: austinm@asme.org.

Awards are arranged alphabetically below their administering organizations

997 ■ Elizabeth M. and Winchell M. Parson Scholarships *(Doctorate/Scholarship)*

Purpose: To establish education funds for the purpose of assisting worthy students in the study of mechanical engineering or for graduate work. To promote the advancement of the art and science of mechanical engineering and the dissemination to engineers and the general public of advance and new development in mechanical engineering. **Focus:** Mechanical engineering. **Qualif.:** Applicants must be full-time student seeking doctoral degree in mechanical engineering. **Criteria:** Awards are given based on academic merit. Priority is given to students with financial need.

Funds Avail.: $2,000. **To Apply:** Applicants must be U.S. Citizen; Applicants must be enrolled in U.S. school in an ABET accredited Mechanical Engineering Department; Applicants must submit letter of recommendation from the Head of the Mechanical Engineering Department or the Faculty Advisor; Applicants must file a letter from a non-academic reference; and applicants must prepare list scholastic recognition, honors or prizes won, membership in honorary or professional societies; Applicants must present list extra-curricular college or civic activities in which they have participated, and offices held; Applicants must submit official transcript with academic record; Applicants must submit grade and membership number in the American Society of Mechanical Engineers; Applicants should have completed application form; Guidelines and application form are available from the ASME scholarship office or can be downloaded from the ASME website. **Deadline:** March 15. **Contact:** Mrs. Michael Snyder, 216 Churchill Crossing Nicholasville, Kentucky 40356 at the above address (see entry 994).

998 ■ Rice-Cullimore Scholarships *(Graduate/Scholarship)*

Purpose: To honor foreign students demonstrating outstanding personal and academic characteristics and to promote art, science, and practice of mechanical and multidisciplinary engineering and allied sciences. **Focus:** Mechanical Engineering. **Qualif.:** Candidate must be a foreign student intending to do graduate work for a Master's or Doctoral Degree in mechanical engineering in the United States. **Criteria:** Awards are given based on academic record, personal promise, character and financial need; Applicants must demonstrate their commitment to a career in mechanical engineering.

Funds Avail.: $2,000. **To Apply:** Applicant must submit Letter of Recommendation from the Head of the Mechanical Engineering Department or the Faculty Advisor; Letter from a non-academic reference; and profile indicating scholastic recognition, honors or prizes won, membership in honorary or professional societies; extra-curricular college or civic activities in which they have participated, and offices held; official transcript; and completed application form. Guidelines and application form can be obtained from the ASME Scholarship Office or can be downloaded from the ASME website. **Contact:** Robert A. Bennett, email: bennettr@asme.org.

999 ■ Marjorie Roy Rothermel Scholarship *(Graduate/Scholarship)*

Purpose: To honor students who demonstrate outstanding personal and academic characteristics. To promote art, science, and practice of mechanical and multidisciplinary engineering and allied sciences. **Focus:** Mechanical engineering. **Qualif.:** Scholarships and grants are given to students working toward a Master's Degree in Mechanical Engineering. **Criteria:** Awards are given based on academic merit. Selection of applicants is based on academic performance character, need, and ASME participation reviewed and scored by the Scholarship Committee.

Funds Avail.: $2,000. **To Apply:** Applicants must be U.S. Citizen; Applicants must be enrolled in U.S. school in an ABET accredited Mechanical Engineering Department; Applicants must submit letter of recommendation from the Head of The Mechanical Engineering Department or the Faculty Advisor; Applicants must file a letter from a non-academic reference; and applicants must prepare list scholastic recognition, honors or prizes won, membership in honorary or professional societies; Applicants must present list extra-curricular college or civic activities in which they have participated, and offices held; Applicants must submit official transcript with academic record; Applicants should have completed application form; Guidelines and application form are available from the ASME scholarship office or can be downloaded from the ASME website. **Deadline:** March 15. **Contact:** Otto Prochaska, 332 Valencia Street Gulf Breeze, FL 32561.

1000 ■ American Society for Microbiology

1752 N St. NW
Washington, DC 20036-2904
Ph: (202)942-9207
Fax: (202)942-9333
E-mail: chouston@utmb.edu
URL: http://www.asm.org

1001 ■ American Society for Microbiology International Fellowships for Africa *(Postdoctorate/Fellowship)*

Purpose: To promote American/Asian collaborations in microbiological research and training. **Focus:** Microbiology. **Qualif.:** Applicants must be members of ASM or any other national microbiological society; must actively involved in research in the microbiological sciences; must have obtained or be in the process of obtaining masters, Ph.D. or other equivalent academic degree within the last five years; must be nationals of non-developed Asian countries; and must be proficient in the use of the English language. **Criteria:** Recipients are selected based on academic excellence of the applicant; depth of the applicant's research experience; quality and originality of work proposed during the fellowship; and relevance of the work proposed.

Funds Avail.: no stated amount. **To Apply:** Applicants must fill out the application form. **Deadline:** April 15; October 15.

1002 ■ American Society for Microbiology International Fellowships for Asia *(Postdoctorate/Fellowship)*

Purpose: To promote American/Asian collaborations in microbiological research and training. **Focus:** Microbiology. **Qualif.:** Applicants must be members of ASM or any other national microbiological society; must be actively involved in research in the microbiological sciences; must have obtained or be in the process of obtaining masters, Ph.D. or other equivalent academic degree within the last five years; must be nationals of non-developed Asian countries; must be proficient in the use of the English language. **Criteria:** Recipients are selected based on the academic excellence; depth of the applicant's research experience; quality and originality of work proposed during the fellowship; and relevance of the work proposed.

Funds Avail.: No stated amount. **To Apply:** Applicants must fill out the application form. **Deadline:** April 15; October 15.

1003 ■ American Society for Microbiology International Fellowships for Latin America *(Postdoctorate/Fellowship)*

Purpose: To promote American/Latin American collaborations in microbiological research and training. **Focus:** Latin American Studies. **Qualif.:** Applicants must be members of ASM or any other national microbiological society; must be actively involved in research in the microbiological sciences; must have obtained, or be in a process of obtaining masters, Ph.D. or other equivalent academic degree within the last five years; must be nationals of Latin American countries; must be proficient in the use of the English language. **Criteria:** Preference will be given to applicants who can prove three years of membership in ASM or any other national microbiological society; and who have not previously had the opportunity to travel to a facility in another country **Number Awarded:** 5. **To Apply:** Applicants must complete the application form; must submit an updated resume; copy honors and awards received; statement of career plans; potential collaborations and proposed research plans; budget; certificates; and letters of reference from academic advisors and/or supervisors. **Deadline:** April 15.

1004 ■ American Society for Microbiology Undergraduate Research Fellowships *(Undergraduate/Fellowship)*

Purpose: To support programs for education, training, and public information. **Focus:** General Studies. **Qualif.:** Applicants must be enrolled as full-time matriculating undergraduate in an accredited U.S. institution; must be involved in a research project; must have ASM members in their home institutions willing to serve as a mentor; must not have receive any financial support for research. **Criteria:** Recipients are selected based on academic achievement; relevant career objectives; potential contribution to overall project outcome; personal motivation to participate in the program; and achievement in previous research experiences.

Funds Avail.: $4,000; $1,000-travel support. **To Apply:** Applicants must submit a complete application form. **Deadline:** February 1.

1005 ■ ASM/CCID Program in Infectious Disease and Public Health Microbiology *(Postdoctorate/Fellowship)*

Purpose: To support the development of new approaches, methodologies, and knowledge in infectious disease prevention and control in areas within the public health mission of the CDC. **Focus:** Microbiology. **Qualif.:** Applicants must have earned their doctorate degree or completed primary residency within three years from proposed start date; may not have a faculty position or enrolled in a graduate degree program during the fellowship. **Criteria:** Recipients are selected based on scientific merit and training potential of the research proposal; training resources; and have significance with the Centers for Diseases public health mission.

Funds Avail.: $42,188; $3,000-health benefit; $500-$2,000 for professional development. **To Apply:** Applicants must fill out the application form. **Deadline:** January 15.

1006 ■ Congressional Science Fellowships *(Postdoctorate/Fellowship)*

Purpose: To broaden the perspective of both the scientific and governmental communities regarding the value of science-government interaction; to enable more effective use in government of scientific knowledge; and to provide experience to scientists seeking careers involving public use of technical information. **Focus:** Science. **Qualif.:** Applicants must be citizens of the United States; must be members of ASM for at least one year; must have completed their Ph.D. by the time the fellowship begins; must show competence in some aspect of microbiology; must have broad background in science and technology; must have interest and experience in applying scientific knowledge toward the solution of social problems; must be articulate, literate, adaptable, interested in public policy problems; must able to work with a variety of people from diverse professional backgrounds. **Criteria:** Recipients are selected based on the result of the interview.

Funds Avail.: $55,000. **To Apply:** Applicants must submit a letter indicating a desire to apply; three letters of references; and 1,000-word statement about the qualifications and career goals. **Deadline:** February 22.

1007 ■ Microbiology Undergraduate Research Fellowships *(Undergraduate/Fellowship)*

Purpose: To increase the number of underrepresented undergraduate students who have demonstrated the ability to pursue graduate careers in microbiology. **Focus:** Microbiology. **Qualif.:** Applicants must be enrolled as full-time matriculating undergraduate in an accredited U.S. institution; must be either freshmen with college level research experience or sophomores, juniors, or seniors who will not graduate before the completion date of the summer program; must be members of underrepresented group of microbiology; must have taken introductory courses in biology, chemistry and preferably microbiology prior to submission of the application; must have strong interests in obtaining a Ph.D. or M.D/Ph.D. in the microbiological sciences; must have laboratory research experience. **Criteria:** Recipients are selected based on academic achievement; relevant career objectives; potential contribution to overall project outcome; personal motivation to participate in the program; achievement in previous research experiences.

Funds Avail.: $3,500-student; $850-lodging; $500-roundtrip travel; $1,000 travel support. **To Apply:** Applicants must submit a complete application form. **Deadline:** February 1.

1008 ■ Microbiology Undergraduate Teaching Fellowships *(Undergraduate/Fellowship)*

Purpose: To support students who are interested in a career as an elementary or secondary school science teacher. **Focus:** Education. **Qualif.:** Applicants must be enrolled as full-time matriculating undergraduate in an accredited U.S. institution; must be involved in educational outreach project; must be a science major interested in education; must have strong faculty ASM members in their home institutions willing to serve as a co-mentor; must have not receive any financial support for the project during the fellowship. **Criteria:** Recipients are selected based on academic achievement; relevant career objectives; potential contribution to overall project outcome; personal motivation to participate in the program; achievement in previous teaching experience.

Funds Avail.: $2,500-student; $500-supplies and instructional materials; $1,000-travel support. **To Apply:** Applicants must submit six copies of complete application form. **Deadline:** April 1.

1009 ■ Robert D. Watkins Graduate Research Fellowships *(Postdoctorate/Fellowship)*

Purpose: To increase the number of underrepresented groups completing doctoral degrees in the microbiological sciences. **Focus:** Microbiology. **Qualif.:** Applicants must be formally admitted to a doctoral program in the microbiological sciences in an accredited U.S. institution; have successfully completed the first year of the graduate program; have successfully completed all graduate course work requirements for the doctoral degree by the date of activation of the fellowship; must be student members of ASM; must be mentored by ASM members; must be U.S. citizens or permanent residents. **Criteria:** Recipients are selected base on academic achievement; evidence of successful research plan developed in collaboration with research advisor/mentor; relevant career goals in the microbiological sciences; involvement in activities that serve the needs of underrepresented groups.

Funds Avail.: $63,000. **To Apply:** Applicants must submit a three letters of recommendation; and official transcript from all colleges and universities attended. **Deadline:** May 1.

1010 ■ American Society of Military Comptrollers

415 N Alfred
Alexandria, VA 22314
Ph: (703)549-0360
Fax: (703)549-3181
Free: 800-462-5637
E-mail: asmchq@asmconline.org
URL: http://www.asmconline.org

1011 ■ American Society of Military Comptrollers National Scholarship Program *(Undergraduate/Scholarship)*

Purpose: To provide financial assistance to seniors to accomplish their future financial management baccalaureate educational goals. **Focus:** Business Administration, Economics, Public Administration, Accounting, Finance. **Qualif.:** Applicants must be entering a field of study directly related to financial/resource management. **Criteria:** Recipients are selected based on the selection panel's review of applications. The selection panel will make final recommendations to the ASMC National Executive Committee, who will approve the final award winners.

Funds Avail.: $3,000. **Number Awarded:** One. **To Apply:** Applicants must have endorsement letters from ASMC chapters. Applicants must submit completed application form and three letters of recommendation from local ASMC chapter president, high school principal, academic dean, or guidance counselor, and a high school teacher. **Deadline:** March 31. **Contact:** Linda Ryan; 301-227-6341; linda.c.ryan@nga.mil.

1012 ■ American Society of Mining and Reclamation

3134 Montavesta Rd.
Lexington, KY 40502
Ph: (859)351-9032
Fax: (859)335-6529
E-mail: asmr@insightbb.com
URL: http://ces.ca.uky.edu/asmr/

1013 ■ American Society of Mining and Reclamation Memorial Scholarships *(Undergraduate/Scholarship)*

Purpose: To grant deserving undergraduate students from academic institutions. **Focus:** Mining. **Qualif.:** Applicants must have completed at least sophomore year of curriculum in a science discipline directly relating to and leading to a profession in reclamation; must be full time students; and must have an adequate grade point of average, carry the curriculum required hours and participated in other curricular activities. **Criteria:** Recipients are selected based on extracurricular activities; participation; and leadership.

Funds Avail.: $750-undergraduate; $1,000-masters; $1,500-Ph.D. **Number Awarded:** 3. **To Apply:** Applicants must complete the application form found at ASMR website. Applicants must submit a letter containing education and career goals; three reference letters with two academic (one from advisor); college transcripts; and resume with list of awards, honors and extracurricular activities listed. **Deadline:** March 14. **Contact:** Robert W. Naim, UASMR Memorial Scholarship Chair, University of Oklahoma, 202 W. Boyd St., Rm. 334, Norman OK 73019; 405-325-3354; 405-325-4217; naim@ou.edu.

1014 ■ American Society of Naval Engineers

1452 Duke St.
Alexandria, VA 22314-3458
Ph: (703)836-6727
Fax: (703)836-7491
E-mail: asnehq@navalengineers.org
URL: http://www.navalengineers.org

1015 ■ ASNE Scholarships *(Graduate, Undergraduate/Scholarship)*

Purpose: To improve and promote the profession of naval engineering. **Focus:** Naval engineering. **Qualif.:** Applicant must be a U.S. citizen; undergraduate full-time student in the last year of undergraduate program at an accredited college or university; or graduate student on a full graduate program leading to an engineering or physical science degree at an accredited university; be members of ASNE. **Criteria:** Selection is based on academic standing (transcript); work history; extracurricular activities; the recommendations and other character references; financial need (many also be considered); and proven interest and commitment to the naval engineering field.

Funds Avail.: $3,000 for undergraduate students; $4,000 for graduate students. **To Apply:** Applicants must submit a completed application form. **Deadline:** February 15.

Remarks: Inaugurated in 1979.

1016 ■ American Society of Nephrology

1725 I St. NW, Ste. 510
Washington, DC 20006
Ph: (202)659-0599
Fax: (202)659-0709
E-mail: email@asn-online
URL: http://www.asn-online.org

1017 ■ Alaska Kidney Foundation-ASN Research Grants *(Doctorate/Grant)*

Purpose: To provide financial assistance for young faculty to foster evolution towards an independent research career. **Focus:** General studies. **Qualif.:** Applicants must be residents of North America, active member of the ASN and hold an MD or PhD or equivalent degree. **Criteria:** Applicants will be assessed based on his/ her potential and the proposed project for eventual funding by a NIH R01 grant or its equivalent; qualifications with respect to prior training, productivity and independence, as well as the scientific merit of the proposed project; and commitment to the development as an independent investigator.

Funds Avail.: $100,000. **To Apply:** Applicants must submit original and three paper copies of the application (including letter from Department Chair or Division Director), and three letters of reference. **Deadline:** February 1.

1018 ■ Carl W. Gottschalk Research Scholar Grants *(Doctorate/Grant)*

Purpose: To provide financial assistance for young faculty to foster evolution towards an independent research career. **Focus:** General studies. **Qualif.:** Applicants must be residents of North America, active member of the ASN and hold an MD or PhD or equivalent degree. **Criteria:** Applicants will be assessed based on his/ her potential and the proposed project for eventual funding by a NIH R01 grant or its equivalent; qualifications with respect to prior training, productivity and independence, as well as the scientific merit of the proposed project; and commitment to the development as an independent investigator.

Funds Avail.: $100,000. **To Apply:** Applicants must submit original and three paper copies of the application (including letter from Department Chair or Division Director), and three letters of reference. **Deadline:** February 1.

1019 ■ Norman Siegel Research Scholar Grants *(Doctorate/Grant)*

Purpose: To provide financial assistance for young faculty to foster evolution towards an independent research career. **Focus:** General studies. **Qualif.:** Applicants must be residents of North America, active member of the ASN and hold an MD or PhD or equivalent degree. **Criteria:** Applicants will be assessed based on his/ her potential and the proposed project for eventual funding by a NIH R01 grant or its equivalent; qualifications with respect to prior training, productivity and independence, as well as the scientific merit of the proposed project; and commitment to the development as an independent investigator.

Funds Avail.: $100,000. **To Apply:** Applicants must submit original and three paper copies of the application (including letter from Department Chair or Division Director), and three letters of reference. **Deadline:** February 1.

1020 ■ American Society for Nondestructive Testing

PO Box 28518
Columbus, OH 43228-0518
Ph: (614)274-6003
Fax: (614)274-6899
Free: 800-222-2768
URL: http://www.asnt.org

1021 ■ ASNT Fellow Awards *(Postdoctorate/Fellowship)*

Purpose: To honor outstanding and significant contributions of an individual in the advancement of NDT. **Focus:** Engineering. **Qualif.:** Nominees must have 15 years of NDT professional experience and 10 years ASNT membership. **Criteria:** Recipients are selected based on the Selection Committee's review of the application materials.

Funds Avail.: Amount not specified. **Number Awarded:** 15. **To Apply:** Applicants must submit a completed application and nomination forms to ASNT headquarter. **Deadline:** February 1.

Remarks: Nominations shall be made by the candidate's local section chairman, members of the ASNT Board of Directors, or by ASNT Fellow. **Contact:** Carole Chesla, ASNT Executive Assistant.

1022 ■ ASNT Fellowship Awards *(Graduate/Fellowship)*

Purpose: To fund a specific research in nondestructive testing. **Focus:** Materials research/science; Testing, educational/psychological. **Qualif.:** Any institution with a graduate educational research program is eligible to submit a proposal. **Criteria:** Applicant who has the most outstanding proposal about NDT research, investigation or development will be given preference and will be judged based on creativity, content, format, and readability.

Funds Avail.: $15,000. **Number Awarded:** 3. **To Apply:** Applicants must submit a research proposal (maximum of 21 pages) consist of a title page, table of contents, research proposal, program of study, research facilities, budget, research advisor, and background on potential graduate student. An original and eight (8) copies of the proposal shall be forwarded to ASNT. **Deadline:** November. **Contact:** Lynn Anderson, landerson@asnt.org.

1023 ■ Robert B. Oliver ASNT Scholarships *(Undergraduate/Scholarship)*

Purpose: To assist students who have chosen a career in NDT. **Focus:** Materials research/science; Testing, educational/psychological. **Qualif.:** Applicants must be enrolled in a course work related to nondestructive testing (NDT) leading to an undergraduate degree, an associate degree or a post-secondary certificate. **Criteria:** Applicant who has the most outstanding manuscript about NDT research, investigation or development will be given preference. The manuscript is judge based on creativity, content, format, and readability.

Funds Avail.: $2,500. **To Apply:** Applicants must submit one original and 4 copies of student manuscript with original illustrations and photos (maximum of ten). Manuscripts must contain the title, author, complete references and must be limited to 5,000 words. International System of Units or SI is preferred for all measurements. Applicants must also submit a completed application form; student's curriculum; transcript; verification of enrollment letter from an instructor. **Deadline:** February 15. **Contact:** Lynn Anderson, landerson@asnt.org.

1024 ■ American Society for Photogrammetry and Remote Sensing

5410 Grosvenor Ln., Ste. 210
Bethesda, MD 20814-2160
Ph: (301)493-0290
Fax: (301)493-0208
E-mail: asprs@asprs.org
URL: http://www.asprs.org

1025 ■ Robert E. Altenhofen Memorial Scholarships *(Graduate, Undergraduate/Scholarship)*

Purpose: To promote education in the theoretical aspects of photogrammetry. **Focus:** Photogrammetry. **Qualif.:** Applicants must be undergraduate or graduate student members of ASPRS. **Criteria:** Recipients are selected based on the highest overall ranking.

Funds Avail.: $2,000 and a certificate. **To Apply:** Applicants must submit an application form; a statement (2

Awards are arranged alphabetically below their administering organizations

pages) regarding plans for continuing studies in theoretical photogrammetry; evidence of capabilities of the applicant in these fields; and academic transcripts.

Remarks: Funded by the estate of Mrs. Helen Altenhofen as a memorial to her husband and the past president of ASPRS, Robert E. Altenhofen.

1026 ■ Robert N. Colwell Memorial Fellowships *(Doctorate, Graduate/Fellowship)*

Purpose: To promote remote sensing or other related geospatial information technologies to college/university graduate students and to post-doctoral researchers. **Focus:** Remote sensing. **Qualif.:** Applicant must be a graduate student (Masters or PhD level); enrolled or planning to enroll in a college/university in the U.S. or Canada; or recently graduated post-doctoral researcher pursuing a study in remote sensing or related geospatial information technologies. **Criteria:** Recipients are selected based on the applications submitted.

Funds Avail.: $5,000 and a certificate. **To Apply:** Applicants must submit an application form; a listing of courses taken; transcript of all college/university level courses completed; a listing of internships, special projects or work experience; three letters of recommendation; a statement (maximum of 2 pages) detailing the applicant's educational or research goals.

Remarks: Established in memory of Robert N. Colwell.

1027 ■ William A. Fisher Memorial Scholarships *(Graduate/Scholarship)*

Purpose: To facilitate studies and career goals directed towards new and innovative uses of remote sensing data/ techniques. **Focus:** Remote sensing. **Qualif.:** Applicants must be current or prospective graduate student members of ASPRS. **Criteria:** Applicants are selected based on the highest overall ranking.

Funds Avail.: $2,000 and a certificate. **To Apply:** Applicant must submit an application form; a statement (2 pages) detailing educational and career plans for continuing studies in remote sensing applications; transcript of grades. **Deadline:** December 3.

1028 ■ Intergraph Scholarships *(Graduate/ Scholarship)*

Purpose: To support graduate-level studies addressing new and innovative uses of signal processing, image processing techniques and the application of photogrammetry to real-world techniques. **Focus:** Photogrammetry. **Qualif.:** Applicant must be a member of ASPRS; currently pursuing graduate-level studies; or planning to enroll for graduate studies in a college/university in the U.S. or elsewhere. **Criteria:** Applicants are selected based on submitted applications.

Funds Avail.: $2,000. **To Apply:** Applicants must submit an application form; a statement (2 pages) detailing educational and career plans for continuing studies in photogrammetric applications; two reference forms/letters from faculty members who have knowledge of the applicant's capabilities; and evidence materials of the applicant's capabilities in this field. **Deadline:** December 3.

1029 ■ Leica Geosystems Internships *(Graduate/ Internship)*

Purpose: To fund a research or continue an existing Leica Geosystems project. **Focus:** Photogrammetry; Remote sensing. **Qualif.:** Applicant must be a graduate student of photogrammetry and remote sensing; and a student member of ASPRS. **Criteria:** Applicants are selected based on the submitted applications.

Funds Avail.: $2,500. **To Apply:** Applicants must submit an application form; letters of recommendation; official transcripts from each college and university attended; a proposal (maximum of 1000 words) stating the significance of the research, the proposed methodology, the expected results and a schedule. **Deadline:** December 3.

Remarks: Funded by Leica Geosystems GIS and Mapping, LLC.

1030 ■ Ta Liang Memorial Awards *(Graduate/ Grant)*

Purpose: To support research-related travel in remote sensing. **Focus:** Remote sensing. **Qualif.:** Applicant must be a graduate student member of ASPRS. **Criteria:** Applicants are selected based on scholastic record, research travel plan, letters of recommendation and community service activities.

Funds Avail.: $500. **To Apply:** Applicants must submit an application form; a letter of recommendation; a statement (2 pages) detailing the plan for research-related travel; a transcript of all college-level courses completed and grades received; class rank; a description of extracurricular activities (particularly relating to community service). **Deadline:** December 3.

1031 ■ Francis H. Moffitt Memorial Scholarships *(Graduate, Undergraduate/Scholarship)*

Purpose: To promote study in surveying and photogrammetry leading to a career in the geospatial mapping profession. **Focus:** Remote sensing; Photogrammetry. **Qualif.:** Applicants must be students currently enrolled or planning to enroll in a college/university in the United States or Canada; pursuing a program of study in surveying or photogrammetry. **Criteria:** Applicants are selected based on the submitted applications.

Funds Avail.: $2,500. **To Apply:** Applicants must submit an application form; a listing of courses taken and/or those to be taken in surveying and photogrammetry and other related geospatial information technologies; a transcript of all college/university level courses completed; a listing of internships, special projects or work experience; two letters of recommendation or reference form; a statement (maximum of 2 pages) detailing the applicant's educational and research goals. **Deadline:** December 3.

Remarks: Established in memory of Frank Moffitt for his lifetime contributions to the photogrammetric surveying profession.

1032 ■ The Kenneth J. Osborn Memorial Scholarships *(Undergraduate/Scholarship)*

Purpose: To encourage students to enter the profession of surveying, mapping and photogrammetry or geospatial information and technology. **Focus:** Photogrammetry. **Qualif.:** Applicant must be an undergraduate student enrolled or planning to enroll in a college/university in the U.S. **Criteria:** Applicants are selected based on the applications.

Funds Avail.: $1,500. **To Apply:** Applicants must submit an application form; a listing of courses taken in surveying; mapping; photogrammetry and geospatial information and technology and the academic grades received; a transcript of all college or university level courses completed; two letters of recommendation from faculty members or professionals; evidence materials of the applicant's capabilities in

Awards are arranged alphabetically below their administering organizations

this field; a statement of work experience; and a personal statement (maximum of 2 pages).

Remarks: Established as a tribute to Kenneth J. Osborn.

1033 ■ Paul R. Wolf Memorial Scholarships *(Graduate/Scholarship)*

Purpose: To encourage college students to enter the profession of teaching Surveying, Mapping or Photogrammetry. **Focus:** Photogrammetry, Education. **Qualif.:** Applicant must be a graduate student member of ASPRS; enrolled or planning to enroll in a college/university in the U.S.; pursuing a program of study in preparation for entering the teaching profession in the general area of Surveying, Mapping or Photogrammetry. **Criteria:** The committee evaluates each application and will select the applicant who best meets the criteria.

Funds Avail.: $1,500. **To Apply:** Applicants must submit an application form; a listing of courses taken in Surveying, Mapping and Photogrammetry and the academic grades received; a transcript of all college or university level courses; two letters of recommendation from faculty members having knowledge of the applicant's capabilities as an educator in this field; evidence materials of the applicant's capabilities in this field; and a statement of teaching experience. **Deadline:** December 3.

Remarks: Established in memory of Paul R. Wolf.

1034 ■ American Society of Podiatric Medical Assistants

2124 S Austin Blvd.
Cicero, IL 60804
Ph: (708)863-6303
Free: 888-882-7762
E-mail: aspmaex@aol.com
URL: http://www.aspma.org

1035 ■ Zelda Walling Vicha Memorial Scholarships *(Undergraduate/Scholarship)*

Purpose: To improve the profession of Podiatric Medical Assisting by providing educational opportunities for ASPMA members. **Focus:** Podiatry. **Qualif.:** Applicant must be a student entering his/her fourth year of school; must have a high scholastic achievement and a definite financial need. **Criteria:** Trustees of the Zelda Walling Vicha Memorial Scholarship Fund will evaluate the application requirements of the candidates.

Funds Avail.: $2,000. **To Apply:** Application forms are available in the website address. Applicant must submit the proof of financial need provided by the Financial Aid Office; must prepare an essay which describes the applicant's personal background, career, vocational or academic goals. **Deadline:** May 1.

1036 ■ American Society for Quality - Statistic Division

611 E Wisconsin Ave.
PO Box 3005
Milwaukee, WI 53201-3005
E-mail: contact@asqstatdiv.org
URL: http://www.asqstatdiv.org

1037 ■ Ellis R. Ott Scholarships *(Graduate, Undergraduate/Scholarship)*

Purpose: To provide financial assistance to deserving students who are in applied statistics and/or quality management field. **Focus:** Statistics; Quality assurance and control. **Qualif.:** Applicants must be students who are planning to enroll or currently enrolled in a masters degree or higher level US or Canadian program that has concentration in applied statistics and/or quality management. **Criteria:** Recipients are selected on the basis of (a) demonstrated ability, (b) academic achievement, including honors, (c) career objectives, (d) faculty recommendations, (e) involvement in campus activities, including teaching and tutoring, and (f) industrial exposure including part-time work and internships.

Funds Avail.: No specific amount. **Number Awarded:** 3. **To Apply:** Applicants must submit completed application form; resume; undergraduate transcript; graduate transcript, for students who have graduate school experience; essay of no longer than one page, typewritten, no smaller than 10-point type, stating qualifications, career goals, reasons for seeking the scholarship; two letters of recommendation from professors in the current or intended field of study. **Deadline:** April 1.

1038 ■ American Society of Radiologic Technologists

15000 Central Ave. SE
Albuquerque, NM 87123-3909
Ph: (505)298-4500
Fax: (505)298-5063
Free: 800-444-2778
E-mail: customerinfo@asrt.org
URL: http://www.asrt.org

1039 ■ GE Healthcare Management Scholarship Program *(Postgraduate/Scholarship)*

Purpose: To provide resources for healthcare and business administration students sciences. **Focus:** Health services administration. **Qualif.:** Applicants must be students pursuing master's or doctoral degree in the areas of business and healthcare administration. **Criteria:** Recipients are selected based on academic standing and financial need.

Funds Avail.: $5,000. **To Apply:** Applicants must complete the application form and submit along with an essay, summary of financial need and scholastic information documents. **Contact:** foundation@asrt.org.

1040 ■ Jerman-Cahoon Student Scholarship Program *(Undergraduate/Scholarship)*

Purpose: To provide resources for radiologic technologists intending to improve patient care and to support education and research in the radiologic sciences. **Focus:** Radiology. **Qualif.:** Applicants must be students attending an entry-level radiologic sciences program. **Criteria:** Recipients are selected based on academic standing and financial need.

Funds Avail.: $2,500. **To Apply:** Applicants must complete the application form and submit along with an essay, summary of financial need and scholastic information documents. **Contact:** foundation@asrt.org.

1041 ■ Monster Medical Imaging Educators Scholarship Program *(Postdoctorate/Scholarship)*

Purpose: To provide resources for radiologic technologists intending to improve patient care; to support education and research in the radiologic sciences; and to assist educators who are pursuing their baccalaureate, master's, or doctoral

Awards are arranged alphabetically below their administering organizations

degree to enhance their position as a program director, faculty member, clinical coordinator or clinical instructor. **Focus:** Radiology. **Qualif.:** Applicants must be pursuing their baccalaureate master's or doctoral degree in the area of radiologic technology. **Criteria:** Recipients are selected based on academic standing and financial need.

Funds Avail.: $5,000. **To Apply:** Applicants must complete the application form and submit along with an essay, summary of financial need and scholastic information documents. **Contact:** foundation@asrt.org.

1042 ■ Royce-Osborn Minority Scholarship Program *(Undergraduate/Scholarship)*

Purpose: To provide resources for radiologic technologists intending to improve patient care and to support education and research in the radiologic sciences. **Focus:** Radiology. **Qualif.:** Applicants must be minority students attending an entry-level radiologic sciences program. **Criteria:** Recipients are selected based on academic standing and financial need.

Funds Avail.: $4,000. **Number Awarded:** 5. **To Apply:** Applicants must complete the application form and submit along with an essay, summary of financial need and scholastic information documents. **Contact:** foundation@asrt.org.

1043 ■ Siemens Clinical Advancement Scholarship Program *(Postgraduate/Scholarship)*

Purpose: To provide resources for radiologic technologists intending to improve patient care; to support education and research in the radiologic sciences; and to advance the radiologic sciences in promoting the professionalism of technologists. **Focus:** Radiology. **Qualif.:** Applicants must be pursuing their baccalaureate master's degree in radiologic sciences. **Criteria:** Recipients are selected based on academic standing and financial need.

Funds Avail.: $3,000. **To Apply:** Applicants must complete the application form and submit along with an essay, summary of financial need and scholastic information documents. **Contact:** foundation@asrt.org.

1044 ■ Varian Radiation Therapy Scholarship Program *(Postdoctorate/Scholarship)*

Purpose: To provide resources for radiologic technologists intending to improve patient care; to support education and research in the radiologic sciences; and to assist educator therapists pursuing their baccalaureate or doctoral degree to enhance their position as a program director, faculty member, clinical coordinator or clinical instructor. **Focus:** Radiology. **Qualif.:** Applicants must be students pursuing their baccalaureate, master's or doctoral degree in the area of radiation therapy. **Criteria:** Recipients are selected based on academic standing and financial need.

Funds Avail.: $5,000. **To Apply:** Applicants must complete the application form and submit along with an essay, summary of financial need and scholastic information documents. **Contact:** foundation@asrt.org.

1045 ■ American Society of Safety Engineers

1800 E Oakton St.
Des Plaines, IL 60018
Ph: (847)699-2929
Fax: (847)768-3434
E-mail: customerservice@asse.org
URL: http://www.asse.org

1046 ■ America Responds Memorial Scholarships *(Undergraduate/Scholarship)*

Purpose: To provide financial support to deserving students. **Focus:** Occupational safety and health. **Qualif.:** Applicant must be a U.S citizen; must be pursuing an undergraduate degree in occupational safety and health. **Criteria:** Selection of applicants will be based on the scholarship application criteria.

Funds Avail.: $1,000. **To Apply:** Applicants must submit a transcript of record; for further information about the application form and requirements, applicants are advised to contact the ASSE Foundation at 1800 E Oakton St., Des Plaines, IL 60018. **Deadline:** December 1.

1047 ■ ASSE Construction Safety Scholarships *(Undergraduate/Scholarship)*

Purpose: To provide financial support to deserving students. **Focus:** Occupational safety and health; Construction. **Qualif.:** Applicant must be a student pursuing an undergraduate degree in occupational safety and health with an emphasis in construction safety. **Criteria:** Selection of applicants will be based on the scholarship application criteria.

Funds Avail.: $1,000. **To Apply:** Applicants must submit a transcript of record; for further information about the application form and requirements, applicants are advised to contact the ASSE Foundation at 1800 E Oakton St., Des Plaines, IL 60018. **Deadline:** December 1.

1048 ■ ASSE Diversity Committee Scholarships *(Graduate, Undergraduate/Scholarship)*

Purpose: To provide financial support to deserving students. **Focus:** Occupational safety and health. **Qualif.:** Applicant must be a student pursuing an undergraduate or graduate degree in occupational safety & health or a closely related field. **Criteria:** Scholarship is open to any individual regardless of race, ethnicity, gender, religion, personal beliefs, age, sexual orientation, physical challenges, geographic location, university or specific area of study.

Funds Avail.: $1,000. **To Apply:** Applicants must submit a transcript of record; for further information about the application form and requirements, applicants are advised to contact the ASSE Foundation at 1800 E Oakton St., Des Plaines, IL 60018. **Deadline:** December 1.

1049 ■ Bechtel Group Foundation Scholarship for Safety & Health *(Undergraduate/Scholarship)*

Purpose: To provide financial support to deserving students. **Focus:** Occupational safety and health; Construction. **Qualif.:** Applicant must be a student pursuing an undergraduate degree in occupational safety and health with an emphasis in construction safety. **Criteria:** Selection of applicants will be based on the scholarship application criteria.

Funds Avail.: $8,000. **To Apply:** Applicants must submit a transcript of record; for further information about the application form and requirements, applicants are advised to contact the ASSE Foundation at 1800 E Oakton St., Des Plaines, IL 60018. **Deadline:** December 1.

1050 ■ Warren K. Brown Scholarships *(Undergraduate/Scholarship)*

Purpose: To provide financial support to deserving students. **Focus:** Occupational safety and health. **Qualif.:** Applicant must be a student pursuing an undergraduate degree in occupational safety & health or a closely related

Awards are arranged alphabetically below their administering organizations

field at Murray State University in Murray, KY or Indiana State University in Terre Haute, IN. **Criteria:** Selection of applicants will be based on the scholarship application criteria.

Funds Avail.: $1,000. **To Apply:** Applicants must submit a transcript of record; for further information about the application form and requirements, applicants are advised to contact the ASSE Foundation at 1800 E Oakton St., Des Plaines, IL 60018. **Deadline:** December 1.

1051 ▪ Central Indiana ASSE Scholarships *(Graduate, Undergraduate/Scholarship)*

Purpose: To provide financial support to deserving students. **Focus:** Occupational safety and health. **Qualif.:** Applicant must be a student pursuing an undergraduate or graduate degree in occupational safety & health or a closely related field. **Criteria:** Priority will be given to Indiana residents attending school in Indiana or anywhere in the U.S or to non-residents attending an Indiana university.

Funds Avail.: $1,000. **To Apply:** Applicants must submit a transcript of record; for further information about the application form and requirements, applicants are advised to contact the ASSE Foundation at 1800 E Oakton St., Des Plaines, IL 60018. **Deadline:** December 1.

1052 ▪ CNA Foundation Scholarships *(Graduate, Undergraduate/Scholarship)*

Purpose: To provide financial support to deserving students. **Focus:** Occupational safety and health. **Qualif.:** Applicant must be a student pursuing an undergraduate or graduate degree in occupational safety & health or a closely related field. **Criteria:** Selection of applicants will be based on the scholarship application criteria.

Funds Avail.: $4,000. **Number Awarded:** 2. **To Apply:** Applicants must submit a transcript of record; for further information about the application form and requirements, applicants are advised to contact the ASSE Foundation at 1800 E Oakton St., Des Plaines, IL 60018. **Deadline:** December 1.

1053 ▪ Scott Dominguez - Craters of the Moon Chapter Scholarships *(Graduate, Undergraduate/Scholarship)*

Purpose: To provide financial support to deserving students. **Focus:** Occupational safety and health. **Qualif.:** Applicant must be a student pursuing an undergraduate or graduate degree in occupational safety & health or a closely related field. **Criteria:** Priority will be given to students that reside within the Craters of the Moon Chapter, Idaho and the Region II area.

Funds Avail.: $1,000. **To Apply:** Applicants must submit a transcript of record; for further information about the application form and requirements, applicants are advised to contact the ASSE Foundation at 1800 E Oakton St., Des Plaines, IL 60018. **Deadline:** December 1.

1054 ▪ Georgia Chapter of ASSE Annual Scholarships *(Undergraduate/Scholarship)*

Purpose: To provide financial support to deserving students. **Focus:** Occupational safety and health. **Qualif.:** Applicant must be a student pursuing an undergraduate degree in occupational safety & health or a closely related field; must be a Georgia resident. **Criteria:** Selection of applicants will be based on the scholarship application criteria.

Funds Avail.: $1,000. **To Apply:** Applicants must submit a transcript of record; for further information about the application form and requirements, applicants are advised to contact the ASSE Foundation at 1800 E Oakton St., Des Plaines, IL 60018. **Deadline:** December 1.

1055 ▪ Gold Country Section & Region II Scholarships *(Graduate, Undergraduate/Scholarship)*

Purpose: To provide financial support to deserving students. **Focus:** Occupational safety and health. **Qualif.:** Applicant must be a student pursuing an undergraduate or graduate degree in occupational safety & health or a closely related field; must be a student that resides within the Region II (MT, ID, WY, CO, UT, NV, AZ, NM) area. **Criteria:** Selection of applicants will be based on the scholarship application criteria.

Funds Avail.: $1,000. **To Apply:** Applicants must submit a transcript of record; for further information about the application form and requirements, applicants are advised to contact the ASSE Foundation at 1800 E Oakton St., Des Plaines, IL 60018. **Deadline:** December 1.

1056 ▪ Greater Baton Rouge Chapter - Don Jones Excellence in Safety Scholarships *(Undergraduate/Scholarship)*

Purpose: To provide financial support to deserving students. **Focus:** Occupational safety and health. **Qualif.:** Applicant must be a student pursuing a degree in occupational safety & health or a closely related field. **Criteria:** Priority will be given to students attending Southeastern Louisiana University in Hammond, Louisiana, then to those attending any college or university within Louisiana or any within the southeast U.S. region.

Funds Avail.: $1,000. **To Apply:** Applicants must submit a transcript of record; for further information about the application form and requirements, applicants are advised to contact the ASSE Foundation at 1800 E Oakton St., Des Plaines, IL 60018. **Deadline:** December 1.

1057 ▪ Gulf Coast Past President's Scholarships *(Undergraduate/Scholarship)*

Purpose: To provide financial support to deserving students. **Focus:** Occupational safety and health. **Qualif.:** Applicant must be a student pursuing an undergraduate degree in occupational safety and health or a closely related field. **Criteria:** Selection of applicants will be based on the scholarship application criteria.

Funds Avail.: $1,000. **Number Awarded:** 2. **To Apply:** Applicants must submit a transcript of record; for further information about the application form and requirements, applicants are advised to contact the ASSE Foundation at 1800 E Oakton St., Des Plaines, IL 60018. **Deadline:** December 1.

1058 ▪ George Gustafson HSE Memorial Scholarships *(Graduate, Undergraduate/Scholarship)*

Purpose: To provide financial support to deserving students. **Focus:** Occupational safety and health. **Qualif.:** Applicant must be a student pursuing an undergraduate or graduate degree in occupational safety & health or a closely related field. **Criteria:** Priority will be given to students from Texas attending a Texas University.

Funds Avail.: $2,500. **To Apply:** Applicants must submit a transcript of record; for further information about the application form and requirements, applicants are advised to contact the ASSE Foundation at 1800 E Oakton St., Des

Awards are arranged alphabetically below their administering organizations

Plaines, IL 60018. **Deadline:** December 1.

1059 ■ David Iden Memorial Safety Scholarships *(Undergraduate/Scholarship)*

Purpose: To provide financial support to deserving students. **Focus:** Occupational safety and health. **Qualif.:** Applicant must be a student pursuing an undergraduate degree in occupational safety & health or a closely related field. **Criteria:** Selection of applicants will be based on the scholarship application criteria.

Funds Avail.: $4,000. **Number Awarded:** 4. **To Apply:** Applicants must submit a transcript of record; for further information about the application form and requirements, applicants are advised to contact the ASSE Foundation at 1800 E Oakton St., Des Plaines, IL 60018. **Deadline:** December 1.

1060 ■ Karl A. Jacobson Scholarships *(Undergraduate/Scholarship)*

Purpose: To provide financial support to deserving students. **Focus:** Occupational safety and health. **Qualif.:** Applicant must be a student pursuing an undergraduate degree in occupational safety & health or a closely related field. **Criteria:** Selection of applicants will be based on the scholarship application criteria.

Funds Avail.: $2,000. **To Apply:** Applicants must submit a transcript of record; for further information about the application form and requirements; applicants are advised to contact the ASSE Foundation at 1800 E Oakton St., Des Plaines, IL 60018. **Deadline:** December 1.

1061 ■ James P. Kohn Memorial Scholarships *(Graduate/Scholarship)*

Purpose: To provide financial support to deserving students. **Focus:** Occupational safety and health. **Qualif.:** Applicant must be a student pursuing a graduate degree in occupational safety & health or a closely related field. **Criteria:** Selection of applicants will be based on the scholarship application criteria.

Funds Avail.: $2,000. **To Apply:** Applicants must submit a transcript of record; for further information about the application form and requirements, applicants are advised to contact the ASSE Foundation at 1800 E Oakton St., Des Plaines, IL 60018. **Deadline:** December 1.

1062 ■ Liberty Mutual Scholarships *(Undergraduate/Scholarship)*

Purpose: To provide financial support to deserving students. **Focus:** Occupational safety and health. **Qualif.:** Applicant must be a student pursuing an undergraduate degree in occupational safety & health or a closely related field. **Criteria:** Selection of applicants will be based on the scholarship application criteria.

Funds Avail.: $3,000. **Number Awarded:** 2. **To Apply:** Applicants must submit a transcript of record; for further information about the application form and requirements, applicants are advised to contact the ASSE Foundation at 1800 E Oakton St., Des Plaines, IL 60018. **Deadline:** December 1.

1063 ■ Medina Scholarships for Hispanics in Safety *(Graduate, Undergraduate/Scholarship)*

Purpose: To provide financial support to deserving students. **Focus:** Occupational safety and health. **Qualif.:** Applicant must be a student pursuing an undergraduate or graduate degree in occupational safety & health or a closely related field; must be a bilingual student. **Criteria:** Selection of applicants will be based on the scholarship application criteria.

Funds Avail.: $2,000. **Number Awarded:** 2. **To Apply:** Applicants must submit a transcript of record; for further information about the application form and requirements, applicants are advised to contact the ASSE Foundation at 1800 E Oakton St., Des Plaines, IL 60018. **Deadline:** December 1.

1064 ■ North Florida Chapter Safety Education Scholarships *(Graduate, Undergraduate/Scholarship)*

Purpose: To provide financial support to deserving students. **Focus:** Occupational safety and health. **Qualif.:** Applicant must be a student pursuing an undergraduate or graduate degree in occupational safety & health or a closely related field. **Criteria:** Priority will be given to part-time or fulltime students that belong to the North Florida chapter, full-time students that attend any Florida college or university or to full-time students that attend an ASAC/ABET accredited program nationwide.

Funds Avail.: $1,000. **To Apply:** Applicants must submit a transcript of record; for further information about the application form and requirements, applicants are advised to contact the ASSE Foundation at 1800 E Oakton St., Des Plaines, IL 60018. **Deadline:** December 1.

1065 ■ Northeastern Illinois Chapter Scholarships *(Graduate, Undergraduate/Scholarship)*

Purpose: To provide financial support to deserving students. **Focus:** Occupational safety and health. **Qualif.:** Applicant must be a student pursuing an undergraduate or graduate degree in occupational safety & health or a closely related field. **Criteria:** Selection of applicants will be based on the scholarship application criteria.

Funds Avail.: $2,000. **Number Awarded:** 2. **To Apply:** Applicants must submit a transcript of record; for further information about the application form and requirements, applicants are advised to contact the ASSE Foundation at 1800 E Oakton St., Des Plaines, IL 60018. **Deadline:** December 1.

1066 ■ PDC Scholarships *(Undergraduate/Scholarship)*

Purpose: To provide financial support to deserving students. **Focus:** Occupational safety and health. **Qualif.:** Applicant must be a student pursuing a degree in occupational safety & health or a closely related field. **Criteria:** Selection of applicants will be based on the scholarship application criteria.

Funds Avail.: $1,200. **Number Awarded:** 2. **To Apply:** Applicants must submit a transcript of record; for further information about the application form and requirements, applicants are advised to contact the ASSE Foundation at 1800 E Oakton St., Des Plaines, IL 60018. **Deadline:** December 1.

1067 ■ Harold F. Polston Scholarships *(Undergraduate/Scholarship)*

Purpose: To provide financial support to deserving students. **Focus:** Occupational safety and health. **Qualif.:** Applicant must be a student pursuing an undergraduate or graduate degree in occupational safety & health or a closely related field. **Criteria:** Priority will be given to students that belong to the Middle Tennessee Chapter, those attending

Awards are arranged alphabetically below their administering organizations

Middle Tennessee State University in Murfreesboro, TN or Murray State University in Murray, KY and those that live in the Region VII.

Funds Avail.: $2,000. **To Apply:** Applicants must submit a transcript of record; for further information about the application form and requirements, applicants are advised to contact the ASSE Foundation at 1800 E Oakton St., Des Plaines, IL 60018. **Deadline:** December 1.

1068 ■ William C. Ray, CIH, CSP Arizona Scholarships *(Graduate, Undergraduate/Scholarship)*

Purpose: To provide financial support to deserving students. **Focus:** Occupational safety and health. **Qualif.:** Applicant must be a student pursuing an undergraduate or graduate degree in occupational safety & health or a closely related field; must reside in Arizona. **Criteria:** Selection will be based on the requirements.

Funds Avail.: $1,000. **To Apply:** Applicants must submit a transcript of record; for further information about the application form and requirements, applicants are advised to contact the ASSE Foundation at 1800 E Oakton St., Des Plaines, IL 60018. **Deadline:** December 1.

1069 ■ Marsh Risk Consulting Scholarships *(Undergraduate/Scholarship)*

Purpose: To provide financial support to deserving students. **Focus:** Occupational safety and health. **Qualif.:** Applicant must be a student pursuing an undergraduate degree in occupational safety & health or a closely related field. **Criteria:** Selection of applicants will be based on the scholarship application criteria.

Funds Avail.: $1,000. **To Apply:** Applicants must submit a transcript of record; for further information about the application form and requirements, applicants are advised to contact the ASSE Foundation at 1800 E Oakton St., Des Plaines, IL 60018. **Deadline:** December 1.

1070 ■ Southwest Chapter Roy Kinslow Scholarships *(Undergraduate/Scholarship)*

Purpose: To provide financial support to deserving students. **Focus:** Occupational safety and health. **Qualif.:** Applicant must be a student pursuing an undergraduate degree in occupational safety & health or a closely related field at Southeastern Oklahoma State University in Durat, OK or for any student from the Southwest Chapter area attending a school within the Region III boundaries. **Criteria:** Selection of applicants will be based on the scholarship application criteria.

Funds Avail.: $1,000. **To Apply:** Applicants must submit a transcript of record; for further information about the application form and requirements, applicants are advised to contact the ASSE Foundation at 1800 E Oakton St., Des Plaines, IL 60018. **Deadline:** December 1.

1071 ■ Harry Taback 9/11 Memorial Scholarships *(Undergraduate/Scholarship)*

Purpose: To provide financial support to deserving students. **Focus:** Occupational safety and health. **Qualif.:** Applicant must be a student pursuing an undergraduate or graduate degree in occupational safety & health or a closely related field; must be a natural born U.S citizen. **Criteria:** Selection of applicants will be based on the scholarship application criteria.

Funds Avail.: $1,000. **To Apply:** Applicants must submit transcript of record; for further information about the application form and requirements, applicants are advised to contact the ASSE Foundation at 1800 E Oakton St., Des Plaines, IL 60018. **Deadline:** December 1.

1072 ■ Thompson Scholarship for Women in Safety *(Graduate/Scholarship)*

Purpose: To provide financial support to deserving students. **Focus:** Occupational safety and health; Engineering; Medicine; Risk management; Industrial hygiene; Fires and fire prevention; Environmental technology. **Qualif.:** Applicant must be a woman pursuing a degree in safety engineering, safety management, occupational health nursing, occupational medicine, risk management, ergonomics, industrial hygiene, fire safety, environmental safety, environmental health or any other closely related field. **Criteria:** Selection of applicants will be based on the scholarship application criteria.

Funds Avail.: $1,000. **To Apply:** Applicants must submit a transcript of record; for further information about the application form and requirements, applicants are advised to contact the ASSE Foundation at 1800 E Oakton St., Des Plaines, IL 60018. **Deadline:** December 1.

1073 ■ UPS Diversity Scholarships *(Undergraduate/Scholarship)*

Purpose: To provide financial support to deserving students. **Focus:** Occupational safety and health. **Qualif.:** Applicant must be a student pursuing an undergraduate degree in occupational safety & health or a closely relative field; must be of a minority ethnic or racial group and must be a United States citizen. **Criteria:** Selection of applicants will be based on the scholarship application criteria.

Funds Avail.: $5,250. **Number Awarded:** 2. **To Apply:** Applicants must submit a transcript of record; for further information about the application form and requirements, applicants are advised to contact the ASSE Foundation at 1800 E Oakton St., Des Plaines, IL 60018. **Deadline:** December 1.

1074 ■ Washington Group International Safety Scholarships *(Undergraduate/Scholarship)*

Purpose: To provide financial support to deserving students. **Focus:** Occupational safety and health; Construction. **Qualif.:** Applicant must be a student pursuing an undergraduate degree in occupational safety & health with an emphasis in construction safety. **Criteria:** Consideration will be given to students attending an ASAC/ABET accredited program.

Funds Avail.: $1,000. **To Apply:** Applicants must submit a transcript of record; for further information about the application form and requirements, applicants are advised to contact the ASSE Foundation at 1800 E Oakton St., Des Plaines, IL 60018. **Deadline:** December 1.

1075 ■ American Society for Theatre Research

PO Box 1798
Boulder, CO 80306-1798
Ph: (303)530-1838
Fax: (303)530-1839
Free: 888-530-1838
E-mail: info@astr.org
URL: http://www.astr.org

1076 ■ American Society for Theatre Research Dissertation Research Fellowships *(Doctorate/Fellowship)*

Purpose: To financially support PhD candidates with their travel in conducting a research projects connected with

Awards are arranged alphabetically below their administering organizations

their dissertations. **Focus:** Theater arts. **Qualif.:** Applicants must be PhD candidates who have passed their qualifying exams within the last two years and have begun working on their dissertations. **Criteria:** Recipients will be selected based on clarity, originality and critical rigor.

Funds Avail.: A total of $3,000 to be divided equally into three awards. **Number Awarded:** 3. **To Apply:** Applicants must submit a project abstract (100 words); description of the proposed project (500 words, including the nature of the project, research strategy, current status of the project and a rationale for the project); a statement on how the award will be used and how will it help the project; a curriculum vitae; and two letters of recommendation (one from the dissertation advisor, and another from a scholar familiar with the applicant's work). Applications must be in .rtf or .doc format. **Deadline:** March 15. **Contact:** Julie Stone Peters, Department of English and Comparative Literature, Columbia University, 1150 Amsterdam Ave. Rm. 602 New York, NY 10027, jpeters@columbia.edu.

1077 ■ ASTR Research Fellowships *(All/Grant)*

Purpose: To underwrite some of the research expenses of scholars undertaking projects significant to the field of theatre and/or performance studies. **Focus:** Theater arts; Performing arts. **Qualif.:** Applicant must be holding a terminal degree and a member of ASTR for at least three years. **Criteria:** Selection is based on the merit of the project within the field of theatre or performance studies.

Funds Avail.: A total of $4,000 which can be divided among multiple winners. **To Apply:** Applicants must submit a 150-word abstract of the project; a longer narrative description of the project indicating its procedures, goals and significance; a budget; a two-page curriculum vitae; and three letters of support from scholars in the proposed or related fields of study. **Deadline:** March 15. **Contact:** Gretchen Smith email address: gesmith@mail.smu.edu.

1078 ■ American Society of Travel Agents

1101 King St.
Alexandria, VA 22314
E-mail: askasta@asta.org
URL: http://www.asta.org

1079 ■ Alaska Airlines Scholarships
(Undergraduate/Scholarship)

Purpose: To encourage people to go into the travel and tourism business as their profession. **Focus:** Travel and Tourism. **Qualif.:** Applicants must be travel/tourism students in either a four-year college/university or propriety travel school; must have at least 2.5 GPA on a 4.0 scale; must have relevant training in basic statistics or other social research method courses; must have at least basic computer skills; and must be residents, citizens, or legal aliens of the United States or Canada. **Criteria:** Recipients are selected based on academic standing.

Funds Avail.: $2,000. **To Apply:** Applicants must submit proof of enrollment/acceptance at a travel school, community/junior college, college or university; an official school-printed description or listing of the curriculum where they are enrolled; proof of enrollments in travel and tourism courses, or letter from business colleague that can attest to the applicant's desire to pursue a career in the travel and tourism industry; four identical collated copies of applications and required materials (one original and three photocopies); and a 500-word paper on why the applicant is pursuing a career in the travel and tourism industry, which must include at least two career goals.

1080 ■ American Express Travel Scholarships
(Undergraduate/Scholarship)

Purpose: To encourage the pursuit of education and the growth and development of tomorrow's travel/tourism work force. **Focus:** Travel and Tourism. **Qualif.:** Applicants must be travel/tourism students in either a two or four-year college/university or propriety travel school; must have at least 3.0 GPA on a 4.0 scale; must have relevant training in basic statistics or other social research method courses; must have at least basic computer skills; and must be residents, citizens, or legal aliens of the United States or Canada. **Criteria:** Recipients are selected based on academic standing.

Funds Avail.: No specific amount. **To Apply:** Applicants must submit a proof of enrollment/acceptance at a travel school, community/junior college, college or university; an official school-printed description or listing of the curriculum where they enrolled; proof of enrollments in travel and tourism courses, or letter from business colleague that can attest to the applicant's desire to pursue a career in the travel and tourism industry; four identical collated copies of applications and required materials (one original and three photocopies); and a 500-word statement detailing the student's plans in travel and tourism as well as the student's view of the travel industry's future.

1081 ■ American Society of Travel Agents AVIS Scholarships *(Graduate, Professional Development, Undergraduate/Scholarship)*

Purpose: To help future travel professionals meet the need for broader business management skills, beyond those dealing solely with travel and tourism issues. **Focus:** Travel and Tourism. **Qualif.:** Applicants must have a minimum of two years of full-time travel industry experience or an undergraduate degree in travel/tourism; may be currently employed in the travel industry; or may be currently enrolled in a minimum of two courses per semester in an accredited undergraduate or graduate level degree program in business or equivalent degree program. **Criteria:** Recipients are selected based on merit.

Funds Avail.: $2,000. **Number Awarded:** 1. **To Apply:** Applicants must provide a proof of current employment in the travel industry; transcript from last academic term with proof of a GPA of 3.0 on a 4.0 scale, or if the applicant is returning to school after time spent in the workforce, applicant must submit transcript showing a GPA of 3.0 on 4.0 scale; and a brief essay (500-750 words) explaining how the degree program relates to applicant's future career in the travel industry.

1082 ■ Arizona Chapter Gold Scholarships
(Undergraduate/Scholarship)

Purpose: To encourage serious academic study in the field of travel and tourism. **Focus:** Travel and Tourism. **Qualif.:** Applicants must be travel/tourism students in either a two or four-year college/university or propriety travel school; must have at least 2.5 GPA on a 4.0 scale; must have relevant training in basic statistics or other social research method courses; must have at least basic computer skills; and must be residents, citizens, or legal aliens of the United States or Canada. **Criteria:** Recipients are selected based on academic standing.

Funds Avail.: $3,000. **To Apply:** Applicants must submit a proof of enrollment/acceptance at a travel school, community/junior college, college or university; an official

Awards are arranged alphabetically below their administering organizations

school-printed description or listing of the curriculum where they are enrolled; proof of enrollments in travel and tourism courses, or letter from business colleague that can attest to the applicant's desire to pursue a career in the travel and tourism industry; four identical collated copies of applications and required materials (one original and three photocopies); and a 500-word statement detailing the student's plans in travel and tourism as well as the student's view of the travel industry's future.

1083 ■ David J. Hallissey Memorial Scholarships *(Undergraduate/Scholarship)*

Purpose: To encourage academic research in the tourism field. **Focus:** Travel and Tourism. **Qualif.:** Applicants must be travel/tourism students from Washington, DC metro area colleges/universities in undergraduate or graduate travel or tourism programs; must have at least 3.0 GPA on a 4.0 scale; must have relevant training in basic statistics or other social research method courses; must have at least basic computer skills; and must be residents, citizens, or legal aliens of the United States or Canada. **Criteria:** Recipients are selected based on academic standing.

Funds Avail.: No specific amount. **To Apply:** Applicants must submit a proof of enrollment/acceptance at a travel school, community/junior college, college or university; an official school-printed description or listing of the curriculum where he/she is enrolled; proof of enrollments in travel and tourism courses, or letter from a business colleague that can attest to the applicant's desire to pursue a career in the travel and tourism industry. Complete application must consist of four identical collated copies of applications and required materials (one original and three photocopies).

1084 ■ Healy Scholarships *(Undergraduate/Scholarship)*

Purpose: To encourage serious academic study in the field of travel and tourism. **Focus:** Travel and Tourism. **Qualif.:** Applicants must be travel/tourism students in either a four-year college/university or propriety travel school; must have at least 2.5 GPA on a 4.0 scale; must have relevant training in basic statistics or other social research method courses; must have at least basic computer skills; and must be residents, citizens, or legal aliens of the United States or Canada. **Criteria:** Recipients are selected based on academic standing.

Funds Avail.: $2,000. **To Apply:** Applicants must submit a proof of enrollment/acceptance at a travel school, community/junior college, college or university; an official school-printed description or listing of the curriculum where they are enrolled; proof of enrollments in travel and tourism courses, or letter from business colleague that can attest to the applicant's desire to pursue a career in the travel and tourism industry; four identical collated copies of applications and required materials (one original and three photocopies); and a 500-word statement suggesting improvements in the travel industry.

1085 ■ Holland America Line-Westours Research Grants *(Undergraduate/Grant)*

Purpose: To provide funding support for research projects in the travel and tourism field. **Focus:** Travel and Tourism. **Qualif.:** Applicant must be a resident, a citizen, or a legal alien of the United States or Canada and have an, at least, 2.5 grade point of average on a 4.0 scale. **Criteria:** Recipients are selected based on academic standing.

Funds Avail.: No specific amount. **To Apply:** Applicant must submit a proof of enrollment/acceptance at a travel school, community/junior college, or university; an official school-printed description or listing of the curriculum where he/she is enrolled; a proof of enrollment in travel and tourism courses; and a letter of recommendation from a professor, employer, or business colleague that can attest to the applicant's desire to pursue a career in the travel and tourism industry.

1086 ■ Pleasant Hawaiian Holidays Scholarships *(Undergraduate/Scholarship)*

Purpose: To encourage people to go into the travel and tourism business as their profession. **Focus:** Travel and Tourism. **Qualif.:** Applicants must be travel/tourism students in either a four-year college/university or propriety travel school; must have at least 2.5 GPA on a 4.0 scale; must have relevant training in basic statistics or other social research method courses; must have at least basic computer skills; and must be residents, citizens, or legal aliens of the United States or Canada. **Criteria:** Recipients are selected based on academic standing.

Funds Avail.: $2,500. **To Apply:** Applicants must submit a proof of enrollment/acceptance at a travel school, community/junior college, college or university; an official school-printed description or listing of the curriculum where they are enrolled; proof of enrollments in travel and tourism courses, or letter from business colleague that can attest to the applicant's desire to pursue a career in the travel and tourism industry; four identical collated copies of applications and required materials (one original and three photocopies); and a 500-word paper stating the applicant's career goals.

1087 ■ Stan and Leone Pollard Scholarships *(Undergraduate/Scholarship)*

Purpose: To encourage people to go into the travel and tourism business as their profession. **Focus:** Travel and Tourism. **Qualif.:** Applicants must be travel/tourism students in either a two or four-year college/university or propriety travel school; must have at least 2.5 GPA on a 4.0 scale; must have relevant training in basic statistics or other social research method courses; must have at least basic computer skills; must be residents, citizens, or legal aliens of the United States or Canada. **Criteria:** Recipients are selected based on academic standing.

Funds Avail.: $2,000. **Number Awarded:** 2. **To Apply:** Applicants must submit proof of enrollment/acceptance at a travel school, community/junior college, college or university; an official school-printed description or listing of the curriculum where they are enrolled; proof of enrollments in travel and tourism courses, or letter from business colleague that can attest to the applicant's desire to pursue a career in the travel and tourism industry; four identical collated copies of applications and required materials (one original and three photocopies); and a 500-word paper on the student's objectives in the travel and tourism industry.

1088 ■ George Reinke Scholarships *(Undergraduate/Scholarship)*

Purpose: To help educate future travel agents. **Focus:** Travel and Tourism. **Qualif.:** Applicants must be travel/tourism students in either a two or four-year college/university or propriety travel school; must have at least 2.5 GPA on a 4.0 scale; must have a relevant training in basic statistics or other social research method courses; must have at least basic computer skills; and must be residents, citizens, or legal aliens of the United States or Canada. **Criteria:** Recipients are selected based on academic standing.

Funds Avail.: $2,000. **Number Awarded:** 6. **To Apply:** Applicants must submit proof of enrollment/acceptance at a travel school, community/junior college, college or university; an official school-printed description or listing of the curriculum where they are enrolled; proof of enrollments in travel and tourism courses, or letter from business colleague that can attest to the applicant's desire to pursue a career in the travel and tourism industry; four identical collated copies of applications and required materials (one original and three photocopies); and a 500-word paper explaining why applicant needs the scholarship.

1089 ■ Nancy Stewart Scholarships

(Undergraduate/Scholarship)

Purpose: To fund research projects in the travel and tourism field. **Focus:** Travel and Tourism. **Qualif.:** Applicants must have a minimum of three years of full-time travel industry experience; must be pursuing one of the Travel Institute's four certification program: CTC accreditation, Destination Specialist, Travel Career Development, Professional Management. **Criteria:** Recipients are selected based on the academic standing.

Funds Avail.: $400. **Number Awarded:** 4. **To Apply:** Applicants must provide a proof of current employment in the travel industry; transcript from last academic term with proof of a GPA of 3.0 on a 4.0 scale or if the applicant is returning to school after time spent in the workforce, submit a cover letter explaining why applicant is returning to school; a letter of intent to enroll in a Travel Institute course within one year and explaining what benefits they hope to obtain from the Travel Institute program or an application to the ASTA educational program; a letter of recommendation from the official ASTA employer to confirm the employment status; and an original headshot picture. **Contact:** scholarships@asta.org.

1090 ■ American Society of Women Accountants

8405 Greensboro Dr., Ste. 800
McLean, VA 22102
Ph: (703)506-3265
Fax: (703)506-3266
Free: 800-326-2163
E-mail: aswa@aswa.org
URL: http://www.aswa.org

1091 ■ ASWA 2-Year College Scholarships

(Undergraduate/Scholarship)

Purpose: To provide financial assistance to students attending Community, State or 2-year Colleges in accounting or finance degree. **Focus:** Accounting; Finance. **Qualif.:** Applicants must be community college students entering their second year of an Associates Degree Program who have completed 15 semester hours or equivalent; must have a minimum cumulative GPA of 3.0 on a 4.0 scale; and must be majoring in accounting or finance. **Criteria:** Scholarship recipients will be selected on the basis of leadership, character and communication skills, scholastic average and financial need.

Funds Avail.: Scholarship amount not specified. **To Apply:** Applicants must submit a completed application form; seventy-five word essay about the his/her goals and objectives, what impact he/she wants to have on the accounting world and most likes about accounting; three references (two references must be from accounting faculty); and a copy and the original Academic Transcript from school. **Deadline:** April.

1092 ■ ASWA Undergraduate Scholarships

(Undergraduate/Scholarship)

Purpose: To provide financial assistance to students attending Community, State or 2-year Colleges in accounting or finance degree. **Focus:** Accounting; Finance. **Qualif.:** Applicants must be students who have completed their sophomore year of college and are majoring in accounting or finance. **Criteria:** Recipients are selected on the basis of leadership, character and communication skills, scholastic average and financial need.

Funds Avail.: Scholarship amount not specified. **To Apply:** Applicants must submit a completed application form; seventy-five word essay about the his/her goals and objectives, what impact he/she wants to have on the accounting world and most likes about accounting; three references (two references must be from accounting faculty); and a copy and the original Academic Transcript from school. **Deadline:** April.

1093 ■ American Sociological Association

1430 K St. NW, Ste. 600
Washington, DC 20005
Ph: (202)383-9005
Fax: (202)638-0882
E-mail: apap@asanet.org
URL: http://www.asanet.org

1094 ■ ASA Minority Fellowships Program

(Doctorate, Master's/Fellowship)

Purpose: To provide financial assistance for students showing interests in studying mental disorder. **Focus:** Drug Abuse; Mental Health. **Qualif.:** Program is open to individuals who are in M.A. programs who have been accepted into sociology Ph.D. programs, or students in the early stages of a doctoral program. **Criteria:** Selection is based on the evidence of: research relevance; trainee skills and ability; supportive institutional environment; and mentor.

Funds Avail.: No specific amount. **To Apply:** Applicants must check the website for the required materials. **Contact:** American Sociological Association at the above address (see entry 1093).

1095 ■ American Sokol

122 W 22nd St.
Oak Brook, IL 60523-1557
Ph: (630)368-0771
Fax: (630)368-0758
E-mail: aso@american-sokol.org
URL: http://american-sokol.com

1096 ■ American Sokol Merit Awards

(Undergraduate/Scholarship)

Purpose: To help incoming students pursue their studies in college. **Focus:** Physical education; Physical sciences. **Qualif.:** Applicants must be Sokol Youth or Sokol Adult members who are planning a full-time course or program in an accredited college. Applications must be made in advance of the year of study. **Criteria:** Applicants will be selected based on the following: regular attendance in American Sokol classes for at least three years (juniors may be included but must become American Sokol adult

Awards are arranged alphabetically below their administering organizations

members at age 17); successful completion of Sokol Instructor School(s) - Unit, District, or National; teaching or assisting experience in Sokol gym classes; and service American Sokol Units, Districts, and/or National Organization.

Funds Avail.: $500. **Number Awarded:** 2 students per district. **To Apply:** Successful candidates must submit a recommendation proof of the Unit or District Physical Director; a parent or guardian will be required to sign to the condition that if the candidate cannot submit the needed requirements completely, he or she should repaid the whole amount of the award. **Deadline:** June 1.

Remarks: The award was instituted by the XIIth American Sokol Convention to be paid from the American Sokol Future Leaders Fund.

1097 ■ American Speech Language Hearing Foundation

2200 Research Blvd.
Rockville, MD 20850-3289
Ph: (301)296-8700
E-mail: foundation@asha.org
URL: http://www.ashfoundation.org

1098 ■ American Speech Language Hearing Foundation Clinical Research Grants *(Doctorate/Grant)*

Purpose: To support investigations that will advance knowledge of the efficacy of treatment and assessment practices. **Focus:** Disabilities. **Qualif.:** Applicants must have received a Ph.D or equivalent research doctorate within the discipline of communication sciences and disorders or related field and must demonstrate the potential and commitment to conducting independent research with a clear plan for applying for extramural research support. **Criteria:** Recipients are selected based on objectives and significance; experimental design and research method; innovation; facilities and resources; management plan and budget; investigator; mentor and mentoring plan; collaborators and collaboration plan.

Funds Avail.: $50,000-$75,000. **To Apply:** Applicants must submit original application form with all accompanying documents along with a hard copy or electronic version of the proposal. **Deadline:** June 2.

1099 ■ American Speech Language Hearing Foundation Endowed Scholarships *(Postdoctorate/Scholarship)*

Purpose: To support the advancement of knowledge in the area of disabilities and to improve the lives of people with speech, language, or hearing disorders. **Focus:** Disabilities. **Qualif.:** Applicants must be enrolled or accepted in a master's or doctoral in communication sciences and disorders program in the United States; and must be enrolled in full-time study for full academic year. **Criteria:** Recipients are selected based on financial need and academic standing.

Funds Avail.: $5,000. **Number Awarded:** 5. **To Apply:** Applicants must complete the Student Information form; Optional Form; letter of application; accompanying documents including statement of good standing, transcript, GPA, Essay, and Confidential Reference form. **Deadline:** June 6. **Contact:** Emily Diaz at the above address (see entry 1097).

1100 ■ American Speech Language Hearing Foundation General Scholarships *(Postgraduate/Scholarship)*

Purpose: To support the advancement of knowledge in the area of disabilities and to improve the lives of people with speech, language, or hearing disorders. **Focus:** Disabilities. **Qualif.:** Applicants must be enrolled or accepted in a graduate study in communication sciences and disorders program in the United States and must be enrolled in a full-time study for full academic year. **Criteria:** Recipients are selected based on financial need.

Funds Avail.: $5,000. **Number Awarded:** 7. **To Apply:** Applicants must complete the Student Information form; Optional Form; letter of application; accompanying documents including statement of good standing, transcript, GPA, Essay, and Confidential Reference form. **Deadline:** June 6. **Contact:** Emily Diaz at the above address (see entry 1097).

1101 ■ American Speech Language Hearing Foundation Scholarships for International Students *(Graduate/Scholarship)*

Purpose: To support the advancement of knowledge in the area of disabilities and to improve the lives of people with speech, language, or hearing disorders. **Focus:** Disabilities. **Qualif.:** Applicants must be international graduate students studying in the United States. **Criteria:** Recipients are selected based on financial need and academic standing.

Funds Avail.: $4,000. **Number Awarded:** 2. **To Apply:** Applicants must complete the Student Information form and the Optional Form. They must submit letter of application and accompanying documents including statement of good standing, transcript, GPA, Essay, and Confidential Reference form. **Deadline:** June 6. **Contact:** Emily Diaz at the above address (see entry 1097).

1102 ■ American Speech Language Hearing Foundation Scholarships for Students with Disability *(All/Scholarship)*

Purpose: To support the advancement of knowledge in the area of disabilities and to improve the lives of people with speech, language, or hearing disorders. **Focus:** Disabilities. **Qualif.:** Program is open to individuals who have disorders or disabilities. **Criteria:** Recipients are selected based on financial need and academic standing.

Funds Avail.: $4,000. **To Apply:** Applicants must complete the Student Information form; Optional Form; letter of application; accompanying documents including statement of good standing, transcript, GPA, Essay, and Confidential Reference form. **Deadline:** June 6. **Contact:** Emily Diaz at the above address (see entry 1097).

1103 ■ ASHFA Scholarships for Minority Students *(Postgraduate/Scholarship)*

Purpose: To support the advancement of knowledge in the area of disabilities and to improve the lives of people with speech, language, or hearing disorders. **Focus:** Disabilities. **Qualif.:** Applicants must be members of a racial or ethnic minority group and must be U.S. citizens. **Criteria:** Recipients are selected based on financial need and academic standing.

Funds Avail.: $4,000. **Number Awarded:** 2. **To Apply:** Applicants must complete the Student Information form and Optional Form. They must submit letter of application, accompanying documents including statement of good standing, transcript, GPA, Essay, and Confidential Reference

Awards are arranged alphabetically below their administering organizations

form. **Deadline:** June 6. **Contact:** Emily Diaz at the above address (see entry 1097).

1104 ■ New Century Scholars Doctoral Scholarships *(Postdoctorate/Scholarship)*

Purpose: To support strong doctoral candidates who are committed to attaining the research doctoral degree and to working in the higher education academic community in the field of communication sciences and disorders in the United States. **Focus:** Disabilities. **Qualif.:** Applicants must be enrolled in a doctorate study in a communication sciences and disorders program in the United States. **Criteria:** Recipients are selected based on academic standing.

Funds Avail.: No specific amount. **To Apply:** Applicants must fill out the application form.

1105 ■ New Century Scholars Research Grants *(Doctorate/Grant)*

Purpose: To support investigations that will advance knowledge of the efficacy of treatment and assessment practices; to support innovative studies or unmet research. **Focus:** Disabilities. **Qualif.:** Applicants must be scientists with research doctorate within the discipline of communication sciences and disorders or related field; must demonstrate the potential and commitment to conducting independent research with a clear plan for applying for extramural research support. **Criteria:** Recipients are selected based on the objectives and significance; experimental design and research method; innovation; facilities and resources; management plan and budget; investigator; mentor and mentoring plan; collaborators and collaboration plan.

Funds Avail.: $10,000. **To Apply:** Applicants must submit original application form with all accompanying documents along with a hard copy or electronic version of the proposal. **Deadline:** June 2.

1106 ■ Research Grants in Speech Science *(Doctorate/Grant)*

Purpose: To support investigations that will advance knowledge of the efficacy of treatment and assessment practices; to help further research activities of new investigators that have particular relevance to audiology and/or speech language pathology. **Focus:** Audiology. **Qualif.:** Applicants must have received a doctoral degree within the past five years and wish to further research activities in the areas of speech communication. **Criteria:** Recipients are selected based on the clearly stated project aims; significance of the research and its potential impact on the clinical needs relevant to speech-language pathology or audiology; merit of the design for answering the question, including detailed account of the methodology to be used; adequate provision for evaluating the results of the project, explicit statement of how the objectives will be measured; indication of the facilities, resources, personnel and subjects to which the applicant would have access in order to carry out the activities described in the proposal; the perceived ability of the applicant to complete the proposed research within one year period; Management plan that clearly outlines the activities and timeliness.

Funds Avail.: $5,000. **To Apply:** Applicants must submit original application form with all accompanying documents and a hard copy or electronic version of the proposal. **Deadline:** May 9.

1107 ■ Student Research Grants in Audiology *(Doctorate/Grant)*

Purpose: To support investigations that will advance knowledge of the efficacy of treatment and assessment practices. To help further research activities of new investigators that have particular relevance to audiology and/or speech language pathology. **Focus:** Audiology. **Qualif.:** Applicants must have received a master's and doctoral degree in communication sciences and disorders and aim to conduct research. **Criteria:** Recipients are selected based on the clearly stated project aims; the significance of the research and it's potential impact on the clinical needs relevant to speech-language pathology or audiology; the merit of the design for answering the question, including detailed account of the methodology to be used; adequate provision for evaluating the results of the project, explicit statement of how the objectives will be measured; indication of the facilities, resources, personnel and subjects to which the applicant would have access in order to carry out the activities described in the proposal; the perceived ability of the applicant to complete the proposed research within a one year period; and management plan that clearly outlines the activities and timeliness.

Funds Avail.: $2,000. **To Apply:** Applicants must submit original application form with all accompanying documents and a hard copy or electronic version of the proposal. **Deadline:** May 23.

1108 ■ Student Research Grants in Early Childhood Language Development *(Doctorate/Grant)*

Purpose: To support investigations that will advance knowledge of the efficacy of treatment and assessment practices; to help further research activities of new investigators that have particular relevance to audiology and/or speech language pathology. **Focus:** Audiology. **Qualif.:** Applicants must have received a master's and doctoral degree in communication sciences and disorders and aim to conduct research in early childhood language development. **Criteria:** Recipients are selected based on the clearly stated project aims; the significance of the research and its potential impact on the clinical needs relevant to speech-language pathology or audiology; the merit of the design for answering the question, including detailed account of the methodology to be used; adequate provision for evaluating the results of the project, explicit statement of how the objectives will be measured; indication of the facilities, resources, personnel and subjects to which the applicant would have access in order to carry out the activities described in the proposal; the perceived ability of the applicant to complete the proposed research within one year period; and management plan that clearly outlines the activities and timeliness.

Funds Avail.: $2,000. **To Apply:** Applicants must submit original application form with all accompanying documents along with a hard copy or electronic version of the proposal. **Deadline:** May 23.

1109 ■ American Spinal Injury Association

2020 Peachtree Rd. NW
Atlanta, GA 30309
Ph: (404)355-9772
Fax: (404)355-1826
E-mail: asia_office@shepherd.org
URL: http://www.asia-spinalinjury.org

1110 ■ G. Helner Sell Research and Training Grants *(Professional Development/Grant)*

Purpose: To provide support to research by qualified spinal cord injury health care provider. **Focus:** Medicine. **Qualif.:** Applicants must be member of ASIA and an institution and

Awards are arranged alphabetically below their administering organizations

spinal cord injury health care provider. **Criteria:** Recipients are selected based on committee's review of the proposal.

Funds Avail.: $5,000. **To Apply:** Applicants must submit proposal via email at pat_duncan@shepherd.org, and complete the GHS-REF program to Fund Educational Projects application form. For institutional application, signature of authorized official of the applicant organization must be included. **Deadline:** February 1. **Contact:** Patricia Duncan, ASIA/Shepherd Center Inc., 404-350-7591 or pat_duncan@shepherd.org.

1111 ■ American Statistical Association

732 N Washington St.
Alexandria, VA 22314-1943
Ph: (703)684-1221
Fax: (703)684-2037
Free: 888-231-3473
E-mail: asainfo@amstat.org
URL: http://www.amstat.org

1112 ■ ASA/NSF/BLS Fellowships *(Graduate/Fellowship)*

Purpose: To improve the collaboration between government and academics research. **Focus:** Statistics. **Qualif.:** Applicants should have recognized research records and considerable expertise in their areas of proposed research. **Criteria:** Preference will be given to those who meet the criteria.

Funds Avail.: No specific amount. **To Apply:** Applicants must submit the following information via e-mail: a curriculum vitae; names and addresses of three references; a detailed research proposal that includes background information about research topic, significance of expected results; advantages of conducting research at the BLS; and detailed budget estimate (salary, relocation, travel expenses, research support). **Deadline:** December 10. **Contact:** American Statistical Association at the above address (see entry 1111).

1113 ■ Edward C. Bryant Scholarships Trust Fund *(Graduate/Fellowship)*

Purpose: To provide financial assistance for graduate education. **Focus:** Statistics. **Qualif.:** Applicants must have the potential to contribute in survey statistics; must have experience in survey statistics; and must be in a graduate school. **Criteria:** Recipients will be chosen by the ASA Bryant Scholarship Award Committee.

Funds Avail.: $2,500. **To Apply:** Applicants may check the website for the required materials.

Remarks: Westat established the Edward C. Bryant Scholarship Trust Fund in 1995 to honor its co-founder and Chairman Emeritus. Under Dr. Bryant's leadership, Westat, an employee-owned statistical firm established in 1961, has grown into what is now one of the world's leading statistical research corporations serving Federal, state, and local governments, as well as businesses and foundations. **Contact:** American Statistical Association at the above address (see entry 1111).

1114 ■ Gertrude M. Cox Scholarships *(Doctorate, Graduate/Fellowship)*

Purpose: To encourage more women to enter statistically-oriented professions. **Focus:** Statistics. **Qualif.:** Applicants must be female residents of United States or Canada and must be admitted in a graduate statistical program. **Criteria:** Awards will be given based on merit.

Funds Avail.: $2,000. **To Apply:** Applicants must submit the completed application form, academic reference letter and Cox status form. These forms are available at their website. **Contact:** American Statistical Association at the above address (see entry 1111).

1115 ■ Wilks Memorial Awards *(Undergraduate/Award/Prize)*

Purpose: To provide financial assistance for students who are in need; to honor the memory and distinguished career of Sam by honoring contributions (either recent or past) to the advancement of scientific or technical knowledge, ingenious application of existing knowledge, or successful activity in the fostering of cooperative scientific efforts that have been directly involved in matters of national defense or public interest. **Focus:** Statistics. **Qualif.:** Applicants must demonstrate financial need. **Criteria:** Selection of recipients will be based primarily on contributions (either recent or past) to the advancement of scientific or technical knowledge, ingenious application of existing knowledge, or successful activity in fostering of cooperative scientific efforts that have been directly involved in matters of national defense or public interest.

Funds Avail.: No specific amount. **To Apply:** Applicants may check website for scholarship instructions and information. **Contact:** American Statistical Association at the above address (see entry 1111).

1116 ■ American Surgical Association

900 Cummings Ctr., Ste. 221-U
Beverly, MA 01915
Ph: (978)927-8330
Fax: (978)524-8890
URL: http://www.americansurgical.info

1117 ■ ACS/ASA Health Policy and Management Scholarships *(Professional Development/Scholarship)*

Purpose: To subsidize attendance and participation in the Executive Leadership Program in Health Policy and Management at Brandeis University. **Focus:** Health education. **Qualif.:** Applicants must be surgeons; must be members in good standing of both the ACS and ASA; must be between 30-55 years old; and planning to attend the Executive Leadership Program in Health Policy and Management at Brandeis University. **Criteria:** Scholarship recipients will be selected based on the Selection Committee's review of the application materials.

Funds Avail.: $8,000. **To Apply:** Applicants must submit a completed application form, a copy of curriculum vitae and one-page essay that discusses why the applicant needs the scholarship to ASA Scholarships Section. **Deadline:** February 1.

1118 ■ American Swedish Institute

2600 Pk. Ave.
Minneapolis, MN 55407-1090
Ph: (612)871-4907
Fax: (612)871-8682
URL: http://www.americanswedishinst.org

1119 ■ Lilly Lorenzen Scholarships *(Undergraduate/Scholarship)*

Purpose: To promote the study of Swedish heritage. **Focus:** Swedish studies. **Qualif.:** Applicants must be Min-

Awards are arranged alphabetically below their administering organizations

nesota residents and have knowledge of the Swedish language. **Criteria:** Recipients are selected based on the applications and other submitted documents.

Funds Avail.: $2,500. **To Apply:** Applicants must submit a complete application form and a transcript or a statement of professional and community achievement. **Deadline:** May 1.

Remarks: Established in memory of Lilly Lorenzen, an instructor in Swedish University of Minnesota and the American Swedish Institute, and author of the book "Of Swedish Ways".

1120 ■ Malmberg Fellowships *(Undergraduate/Fellowship)*

Purpose: To promote study at the American Swedish Institute. **Focus:** Swedish studies. **Qualif.:** Applicants must be students aged 21 years old and above; Sweden residents are also qualified. For organizational applicants, the project manager is identified as the applicant. **Criteria:** Recipients are selected based on the submitted documents.

Funds Avail.: $4,000. **To Apply:** Applicant must send a study proposal. **Deadline:** November.

1121 ■ Malmberg Scholarships *(Undergraduate/Scholarship)*

Purpose: To provide financial assistance to individuals to study in Sweden. **Focus:** Swedish studies. **Qualif.:** Applicants must be U.S. citizens; enrolled in a degree-granting program in college/university; or in a study or research that requires or can be enhanced by study in Sweden; have knowledge in Swedish language. **Criteria:** Recipients are selected based on the submitted applications.

Funds Avail.: $10,000. **To Apply:** Applicants must submit an application form and a letter of invitation or affiliation from the Swedish institution/organization; a project summary; transcript (optional if out of school for 3 years); resume; and two letters of recommendation. **Deadline:** November 15.

1122 ■ American University - School of Public Affairs

Ward Circle Bldg.
4400 Massachusetts Ave. NW
Washington, DC 20016
Ph: (202)885-2940
Fax: (202)885-2353
E-mail: spagrad@american.edu
URL: http://spa.american.edu

1123 ■ Center for Congressional and Presidential Studies (CPPS) Endowment *(Graduate, Undergraduate/Scholarship)*

Purpose: To support students with financial disabilities. **Focus:** Public administration. **Qualif.:** Applicants must be students attending CPPS programs. **Criteria:** Recipients are selected based on merit and financial need.

Funds Avail.: $2,500. **To Apply:** Applicants must submit resume; 1-2 pages letter to the Director of CPPS (the letter should address academic and professional achievements and future aspirations, with detailed financial need).

Remarks: The Support allocated to any students account will replace a current financial need. The award will not necessarily be available as a cash reimbursement from students account, unless a credit remains on the system after all debts are paid.

1124 ■ Jane R. Glaser Scholarships *(Undergraduate/Scholarship)*

Purpose: To provide financial assistance to School of Public Administration students. **Focus:** Public affairs. **Qualif.:** Applicants should be undergraduate students of School of Public Administration. **Criteria:** Recipients are selected based on a review of applications; interviews and consultation with faculty and staff.

Funds Avail.: $2,500. **To Apply:** Applicants must submit one page formal recommendation from advisor; outline of grade point average; activities; reason for studying at Hebrew University; and statement stating interest in receiving the scholarship and studying abroad. **Deadline:** May 15 and September **Contact:** Jenine Rabine; 202-885-3968; rabin@american.edu

1125 ■ American Urological Association Foundation

1000 Corporate Blvd.
Linthicum, MD 21090
Ph: (410)689-3700
Fax: (410)689-3800
Free: (866)746-4282
E-mail: auafoundation@auafoundation.org
URL: http://www.auafoundation.org

1126 ■ AUA Foundation/Astellas Rising Star in Urology Research Awards *(Postdoctorate/Fellowship)*

Purpose: To encourage a young urology faculty to go into, or continue a research career. **Focus:** Urology. **Qualif.:** Applicants must be Board certified or eligible urologists; must have successfully competed for a career development award within the current federal fiscal year. **Criteria:** Applicants will be selected based on scholarship panel's review of the application materials.

Funds Avail.: No specific amount. **To Apply:** Applicants must complete the online application form. Applicants must also prepare a registration summary form; curriculum vitae; application agreement form with all necessary signatures; letter of support from each mentor; letter from urology department chair; current NIH-style biosketch of each mentor; copy of career development grant award letter; copy of career development grant; copy of career development grant review summary sheets and scores. All materials must be uploaded into a single .pdf file. **Deadline:** November 29.

1127 ■ AUA Foundation Bridge Awards *(Postgraduate/Fellowship)*

Purpose: To support research that will help those who suffer from the effects of urological diseases. **Focus:** Urology. **Qualif.:** Applicants must be a member of AUA; not a previous recipient of the award; must have competed for a peer-reviewed external funding for the project during the current federal fiscal year. **Criteria:** Applicants are selected based on the jury's review of the application materials.

Funds Avail.: $15,000. **To Apply:** Applicants must register online at the AUA Foundation website in order to apply. Applicants must submit the completed the application form; a registration summary form; and an application agreement form. The form must be signed by the applicant, department chair and sponsoring institution representative. **Deadline:** March 31. **Contact:** Rodney Cotten, Research

Coordinator, grants@auafoundation.org.

1128 ■ AUA Foundation M.D./Ph.D. Fellowships *(Postdoctorate, Postgraduate/Fellowship)*

Purpose: To promote research related to the epidemiology of urologic diseases. **Focus:** Urology. **Qualif.:** Applicants must be trained urologists or basic scientists within five years of completing their residency or doctorate. **Criteria:** Fellowship recipients will be selected based on the scholarship committee's review of the application materials.

Funds Avail.: $60,000 ($30,000 from AUA Foundation, $30,000 from the institution). **To Apply:** Applicants must complete the online application form and the application agreement form; must submit two letters of support from individuals other than the mentor; research career goals of the candidate; description of research proposal in layman's terms; research proposal (maximum of 10 pages) which consist of following: specific aims (1-2 pages), background (2 pages), preliminary data (2-3 pages), and methods and procedure (2-4 pages). Applicants must also submit a curriculum vitae (maximum of 5 pages); notification of applications filed to other funding sources. For mentors, requirements are institutional plans; concise statement of reasons that the candidate and mentor should be selected; outline of clinical/research time (M.D. researchers only); mentor's letters of support for applicant; mentor's biosketches; list of mentor's previous fellows current positions. **Deadline:** August 31.

1129 ■ AUA Foundation M.D. Post-resident Fellowships *(Postgraduate/Fellowship)*

Purpose: To promote research related to the epidemiology of urologic diseases. **Focus:** Urology. **Qualif.:** Applicants must be trained urologists within five years of completing residency. Mentors should have experience in health services or policy or in another clinical discipline with formal urologic input. **Criteria:** Fellowship recipients will be selected based on the Scholarship Committee's review of the application materials.

Funds Avail.: $60,000 ($30,000 from AUA Foundation, $30,000 from the institution). **To Apply:** Applicants must complete the online application form; must submit two letters of support from individuals other than the mentor; research career goals of the candidate; description of research proposal in layman's terms; research proposal (maximum of 10 pages) which consist of the following: specific aims (1-2 pages), background (2 pages), preliminary data (2-3 pages), and methods and procedure (2-4 pages). Applicants must also submit a curriculum vitae (maximum of 5 pages); notification of applications filed to other funding sources. For mentors, the requirements are institutional plans; concise statement of reasons that the candidate and mentor should be selected; outline of clinical/research time (M.D. researchers only); mentor's letters of support for the applicant; mentor's biosketches; list of mentor's previous fellows and their current positions. **Deadline:** August 31. **Contact:** Rodney Cotten, Research Coordinator, grants@auafoundation.org.

1130 ■ AUA Foundation - NIDDK/NCI Surgeon-Scientist Awards *(Postgraduate/Fellowship)*

Purpose: To support urology faculty who wish to pursue becoming an independent investigator. **Focus:** Urology. **Qualif.:** Applicants must be Board certified or eligible urologists; must be participating in a training program to obtain a Board Certification in Urology; have successfully competed for NIDDK or NCI career development for the current year. **Criteria:** Award recipients are selected based on the selection committee's review of application materials.

Funds Avail.: $52,000. **To Apply:** Applicants must complete the online application form. Applicants must also prepare a registration summary form; applicant curriculum vitae; application agreement form; letter of support from mentor; letter from urology department chair; current NIH-style biosketch for each mentor; copy of career development grant award letter; copy of career development grant; copy of career development grant review summary sheets and scores. All materials must be uploaded into a single .pdf file. **Deadline:** November.

1131 ■ AUA Foundation Ph.D. Post-Doctoral Fellowships *(Postdoctorate/Fellowship)*

Purpose: To promote research related to epidemiology of urologic diseases. **Focus:** Urology. **Qualif.:** Applicants must be PhDs with less than five years of post-doctoral experience. Mentors should be an established basic science academician in either the basic science or clinical department. Mentors must also have experience with funded grants. **Criteria:** Fellowship recipients will be selected based on the scholarship committee's review of the application materials.

Funds Avail.: $60,000 ($30,000 from AUA Foundation, $30,000 from the institution). **To Apply:** Applicants must complete the online application form and the application agreement form; two letters of support from individuals other than the mentor; research career goals of the candidate; description of research proposal in layman's terms; research proposal (maximum of 10 pages) which consist of the following: specific aims (1-2 pages), background (2 pages), preliminary data (2-3 pages), and methods and procedure (2-4 pages). Applicants must also submit a curriculum vitae (maximum of 5 pages); notification of applications filed to other funding sources. For mentors, requirements are institutional plans; concise statement of reasons that the candidate and mentor should be selected; outline of clinical/research time (M.D. researchers only); mentor's letters of support for applicant; mentor's biosketches; list of mentor's previous fellows and their current positions. **Deadline:** August 31. **Contact:** Rodney Cotten, Research Coordinator, grants@auafoundation.org.

1132 ■ American Veterans

4647 Forbes Blvd.
Lanham, MD 20706-4380
Ph: (301)459-9600
Fax: (301)459-7924
Free: 877-726-8387
E-mail: amvets@amvets.org
URL: http://www.amvets.org

1133 ■ AMVETS National Scholarships - Entering College Freshmen *(Undergraduate/Scholarship)*

Purpose: To assist deserving children and grandchildren of veterans in attaining post-secondary education. **Focus:** General studies. **Qualif.:** Applicant must be a graduating high school senior entering at the college freshmen level; must have a minimum high school GPA of 3.0; must be the child or grandchild of a United States veteran; must be a U.S. citizen; must have demonstrated academic promise and financial need; and must agree to authorize AMVETS to publicize the scholarship award, if selected. **Criteria:** Selection is based on academic promise, financial need and merit.

Funds Avail.: $1,000 each year. **Number Awarded:** 6. **To Apply:** Applicants must submit a copy of the veteran's honorable discharge (Form DD 214). Dependents of current military personnel must submit a letter from the base commander certifying the active duty status of the parent; an official high school transcript (must be in the 4.0 grade scale, or if in a different system, translated to the 4.0 scales); SAT and/or ACT scores; a complete and signed copy of the parent(s)'/guardian(s)' 1040 tax form (applicant's name must appear on the tax form); a copy of the applicant's Free Application For Federal Student Aid (FAFSA); essay (50-100 words); acceptance letter from the accredited school to be attended; proof of college expenses; and a resume detailing extracurricular activities, volunteer activities, community services, and jobs held during the past four years. **Deadline:** April 15. **Contact:** at the above address (see entry 1132).

1134 ■ AMVETS National Scholarships - For Veterans *(Undergraduate/Scholarship)*

Purpose: To financially assist veterans who have exhausted government aid or who might not otherwise have the financial means to further their education. **Focus:** General studies. **Qualif.:** Applicant must be a U.S. veteran; a U.S. citizen; must demonstrate financial need; and must agree to authorize AMVETS to publicize the scholarship award, if selected. **Criteria:** Selection is based on academic promise, financial need and merit.

Funds Avail.: $1,000 each year. **Number Awarded:** 3. **To Apply:** Applicants must submit a copy of the veteran's honorable discharge or a letter certifying current service and eligibility for release from active duty prior to attending school; official college transcripts for all courses attempted and any degrees or certificates awarded (must be in the 4.0 grade scale, or if in a different system, translated to the 4.0 scales); a complete and signed copy of the applicant's 1040 tax form; a copy of the Free Application For Federal Student Aid (FAFSA); an essay (50-100 words); acceptance letter, or a letter stating current student status from an accredited school; proof of college expenses; and a resume detailing military duty and awards, volunteer activities, community services, and jobs held during the past four years. **Deadline:** April 15. **Contact:** at the above address (see entry 1132).

1135 ■ AMVETS National Scholarships - JROTC *(Undergraduate/Scholarship)*

Purpose: To support Junior ROTC cadets in pursuing study at an undergraduate college or university. **Focus:** General studies. **Qualif.:** Applicant must be an active JROTC cadet and currently a high school senior; have a minimum high school GPA of 3.0; be the child or grandchild of a U.S. veteran; a U.S. citizen; have demonstrated academic promise and financial need; and agree to authorize AMVETS to publicize the scholarship award, if selected. **Criteria:** Selection is based on academic promise, financial need and merit.

Funds Avail.: $1,000. **Number Awarded:** 1. **To Apply:** Applicant must submit a copy of the veteran's honorable discharge (Form DD 214). Dependents of current military personnel must submit a letter from the base commander certifying the active duty status of the parent; an official transcript including the first grading period of the current school year (must be in the 4.0 grade scale, or if in a different system, translated to the 4.0 scale); SAT and/or ACT scores; a complete and signed copy of the parent(s)'/guardian(s)'s 1040 tax form; a copy of the Free Application For Federal Student Aid (FAFSA); the essay (50-100 words); acceptance letter from the accredited school to attend; proof of college expenses; a letter from program commander verifying participation in ROTC/JROTC activities; and a resume detailing extracurricular activities, volunteer activities, community services and jobs held during the past four years. **Deadline:** April 15. **Contact:** at the above address (see entry 1132).

1136 ■ Dr. Aurelio M. Caccomo Family Foundation Memorial Scholarships *(Undergraduate/Scholarship)*

Purpose: To provide financial assistance for veterans/guardsmen/reservists who have exhausted government aid, or who might not otherwise have the financial means to further their education. **Focus:** General studies. **Qualif.:** Applicant must be a U.S. veteran or member of the National Guard or Reserves; a U.S. citizen; have demonstrated financial need; have a high school diploma or GED; agree to authorize AMVETS to publicize the scholarship award, if selected; enrolled or accepted for enrollment to an eligible program; must not be in default on a federal student loan; and not convicted under state or federal law of sale or possession of illegal drugs. **Criteria:** Award is given based on the application materials.

Funds Avail.: $3,000. **Number Awarded:** 2. **To Apply:** Applicants must submit a copy of the veteran's honorable discharge or a letter from the commanding officer certifying current Guard or Reserve status; an official college transcript for all courses attempted and any degrees or certificates awarded. (must be in the 4.0 grade scale or if in a different system, translated to the 4.0 scale); a complete and signed copy of the applicant's 1040 tax form; a copy of the Free Application for Federal Student Aid (FAFSA); an Essay (50-100 words); acceptance letter or a letter stating current student status from an accredited program; proof of expenses; and a resume detailing military duty and awards, volunteer activities, community services, and jobs held during the past four years. **Deadline:** April 15. **Contact:** at the above address (see entry 1132).

1137 ■ American Water Resources Association

PO Box 1626
Middleburg, VA 20118
Ph: (540)687-8390
Fax: (540)687-8395
E-mail: info@awra.org
URL: http://www.awra.org

1138 ■ Richard A. Herbert Memorial Scholarships *(Undergraduate/Scholarship)*

Purpose: To enhance the education in water resources. **Focus:** Water Resources. **Qualif.:** Applicant must be a national AWRA member; an applicant must be undergraduate student working toward his/her undergraduate degree enrolled in a program related to water resources; or applicant must be a full-time graduate student enrolled in a program relating to water resources. **Criteria:** AWRA Student activities Committee will evaluate the application based on the academic performance including the cumulative grade point average, relevance of the student's curriculum to water resources, and leadership in extracurricular activities related to water resources; while graduate student applicants will be evaluated based on the research and it's relevance to water resources.

Funds Avail.: $4,000. **Number Awarded:** 2. **To Apply:** Applicant should prepare a title page and two-page sum-

Awards are arranged alphabetically below their administering organizations

mary of their academic interests and their achievements, extracurricular interests, and career goals; he/she must include three-letters of reference(preferably from professors and/or advisors); a transcript of record including full name, permanent mailing address, e-mail address, and a phone number at which applicant may be easily reached. **Deadline:** April 23,2008.

1139 ■ American Water Ski Educational Foundation

1251 Holy Cow Rd.
Polk City, FL 33868-8200
Ph: (863)324-2472
Fax: (863)324-3996
E-mail: info@waterskihalloffame.com
URL: http://www.waterskihalloffame.com

1140 ■ American Water Ski Educational Foundation Scholarships *(Undergraduate/Scholarship)*

Purpose: To preserve the traditions of one America's most popular family recreational activities; to encourage and to educate the safe enjoyment of the challenges of water skiing. **Focus:** General Studies. **Qualif.:** Applicant must be enrolled with a minimum of two year course in the secondary education; he/she must be a U.S. citizen who is a current member of USA Water Ski Foundation. **Criteria:** Applicants will be evaluated based upon the academic qualifications, leadership, extracurricular involvement, recommendations, and financial need.

Funds Avail.: $1,500. **Number Awarded:** 6. **To Apply:** Applicant must fill out the application form; he/she must submit two letters of reference; a 500 word essay on topic "AWSEF has a beautiful new facility"; an official transcript of grades; an official high school transcript. **Deadline:** April 1.

1141 ■ American Water Works Association

666 W Quincy Ave.
Denver, CO 80235
Ph: (303)794-7711
Fax: (303)347-0804
Free: 800-926-7337
URL: http://www.awwa.org

1142 ■ Thomas R. Camp Scholarships *(Graduate/Scholarship)*

Purpose: To support and encourage graduate students conducting applied research in the drinking water field. **Focus:** Water resources; Water supply industry. **Qualif.:** Applicants must be in pursuit of a graduate degree (either masters or doctoral) at an institution of higher education located in Canada, Guam, Puerto Rico, Mexico or the United States. Completion of degree requirements shall be no sooner than December 1 of the application year. **Criteria:** Scholarship recipient will be selected based on academic record and potential to provide leadership in applied research and consulting in the drinking water field.

Funds Avail.: $5,000. **Number Awarded:** 1. **To Apply:** Applicants must submit a completed official application form; a two-page resume that includes educational history; official transcripts of all university education; official GRE Scores (quantitative, verbal and analytical) sent directly from the GRE Testing Center, or a photocopy of the official report; three letters of recommendation (one of which must be from the academic or research advisor); a one-page statement of educational plans and career objectives demonstrating or declaring an interest in the drinking water field; a two to three page proposed plan of research. **Deadline:** January 15.

Remarks: Camp Dresser and McKee, Inc., created the Thomas R. Camp Scholarship in honor of the contributions of Dr. Camp in the drinking water field. **Contact:** Linda Moody at the above address (see entry 1141).

1143 ■ Holly A. Cornell Scholarships *(Graduate/Scholarship)*

Purpose: To encourage and support outstanding female and/or minority masteral students in pursuit of advanced training in the field of water supply and treatment. **Focus:** Engineering; Water resources; Water supply industry. **Qualif.:** Applicants must be female and/or minority U.S. citizens, who are currently masters degree students anticipating completion of the requirements for a Masters degree in engineering no sooner than December 1 of the application year. **Criteria:** Recipients are selected based on academic merit and potential to provide leadership in the field of water supply and treatment.

Funds Avail.: $5,000. **To Apply:** Applicants must submit a completed official application form; a two-page resume that includes educational history; official transcripts of all university education; official GRE Scores (quantitative, verbal, and analytical) sent directly from the GRE Testing Center, or a photocopy of the official report; three letters of recommendation (one of which must be from the academic or research advisor); a proposed curriculum of study; a brief (one to two pages) statement describing the student's career objectives. **Deadline:** January 15.

Remarks: The Holly A. Cornell Scholarship was created by CH2M Hill, Inc. in honor of their co-founder, Holly A. Cornell. **Contact:** Linda Moody at the above address (see entry 1141).

1144 ■ Larson Aquatic Research Support *(Graduate/Scholarship)*

Purpose: To support and encourage outstanding graduate students preparing for careers in the fields of science or engineering. **Focus:** Biochemistry; Water resources; Water supply industry. **Qualif.:** Applicants must be students pursuing a masters or doctoral degree at an institution of higher education located in Canada, Guam, Puerto Rico, Mexico, or the United States. Applicants should anticipate completion of their degree requirements no sooner than December 1 of the application year. **Criteria:** Awards are given based on academic record and candidate's potential to provide leadership in the fields served by Dr. Larson.

Funds Avail.: $5,000 for the Masters student recipient; $7,000 for the Ph.D. student recipient. **Number Awarded:** 2. **To Apply:** Applicants must submit a completed application form; a two-page resume that includes educational history; official transcripts of all university education; official GRE Scores (quantitative, verbal and analytical) sent directly from the GRE Testing Center, or a photocopy of the official report; three letters of recommendation (one of which must be from the academic or research advisor); a proposed curriculum of study; a statement of educational plans and career objectives demonstrating or declaring an interest in an appropriate field of endeavor; a research plan, if applicable (required for Masters students conducting research and all Ph.D. students). **Deadline:** January 15.

Remarks: Larson Aquatic Research Support scholarships

honor the memory of Dr. Thurston E. "Lars" Larson. **Contact:** Linda Moody at the above address (see entry 1141).

1145 ■ Abel Wolman Fellowships *(Doctorate/Fellowship)*

Purpose: To support promising doctoral students in the U.S., Canada and Mexico pursuing advanced training and research in the field of water supply and treatment. **Focus:** Water resources; Water supply industry. **Qualif.:** Candidates must complete the requirements for a Ph.D. within two years of the award and have citizenship or permanent residence in Canada, Mexico or the United States. **Criteria:** Fellowship recipients are selected based on academic record, significance of the proposed research to water supply and treatment and the candidate's potential to do high quality research.

Funds Avail.: $15,000 stipend distributed over 12 months, plus $1,000 for research supplies and equipment and an education allowance of up to $4,000 to cover the cost of tuition and other fees. **To Apply:** Applicants must submit a completed official application form; a two-page resume that includes educational history; official transcripts of all university education; official GRE scores sent directly from the Testing Center or a photocopy of the official report; three letters of recommendation, one of which must be from the dissertation advisor; proposed curriculum of study; a brief description of the dissertation research, including a statement describing how the research will relate specifically to water supply and treatment (two pages of text plus two pages of figures and tables). **Deadline:** January 15.

Remarks: Created in honor of Dr. Abel Wolman, the "Dean of Water Supply." **Contact:** Linda Moody at the above address (see entry 1141).

1146 ■ American Watercolor Society

47 Fifth Ave.
New York, NY 10003-4303
Ph: (212)206-8986
Fax: (212)206-1960
E-mail: awshq@verizon.net
URL: http://www.americanwatercolorsociety.com

1147 ■ American Watercolor Society Scholarship Program for Art Teachers *(Professional Development/Scholarship)*

Purpose: To enhance and improve the capabilities of teachers in watercolor media. **Focus:** Art; Painting. **Qualif.:** Applicant must be a U.S. citizen and an art teacher at a high school or college level institution in the United States. **Criteria:** Grantees are selected based on the application materials.

Funds Avail.: $500. **To Apply:** Application form is available at the website. **Contact:** Gordon West, AWS Chairman, AWS Scholarship Program 2910 Briarcroft St. San Antonio, TX 78217-3801. gojowe@earthlink.net.

1148 ■ American Welding Society

550 NW LeJeune Rd.
Miami, FL 33126
Ph: (305)443-9353
Fax: (305)443-7559
Free: 800-443-9353
E-mail: info@aws.org
URL: http://www.aws.org

1149 ■ Howard E. and Wilma J. Adkins Scholarships *(Undergraduate/Scholarship)*

Purpose: To provide financial assistance to individuals interested in pursuing a career in welding engineering. **Focus:** Welding. **Qualif.:** Applicants must be undergraduate students pursuing a four-year bachelors degree in welding engineering or welding engineering technology; must be 18 years old and above; must have a minimum of 2.5 overall grade point average; must be a citizen of the United States; and must plan to attend an accredited engineering school within the United States. **Criteria:** Recipients are selected based on financial need, career work experience, and extracurricular activities.

Funds Avail.: $2,500. **To Apply:** Applicants must complete the application form and submit it along with a high school diploma and a financial statement. **Deadline:** January 15. **Contact:** found@aws.org

1150 ■ American Welding Society District Scholarships *(Undergraduate/Scholarship)*

Purpose: To provide financial assistance to students preparing for a career in the welding and related joining technologies. **Focus:** Welding. **Qualif.:** Applicants must be high school graduates is planning to enroll in a welding course program; must attend a school located in the U.S. or its territories. **Criteria:** Recipients are selected based on academic standing.

Funds Avail.: No specific amount. **To Apply:** Applicants must submit a financial statement; transcript of records; personal statement; biography and photo. **Deadline:** March 1.

1151 ■ American Welding Society International Scholarships *(Undergraduate/Scholarship)*

Purpose: To provide financial assistance to international students who wish to pursue their education in welding and related joining technologies. **Focus:** Welding. **Qualif.:** Applicants must have completed at least one year of welding or related fields of study at a Baccalaureate degree-granting institution; must be full-time students; and must be U.S. or Canadian citizens. **Criteria:** Recipients are selected based on financial need and academic standing.

Funds Avail.: $2,500. **To Apply:** Applicants must submit a copy of the proposed curriculum; verification of enrollment to the institution; two letters of personal reference; two-page professional goal statement with a brief bibliography; transcript of grades or equivalent from each college; proof of country of citizenship; AWS membership number, if member; and financial information regarding tuition fees from the academic institution. **Contact:** found@aws.org.

1152 ■ American Welding Society National Scholarships *(Undergraduate/Scholarship)*

Purpose: To advance opportunities for students preparing for a career in the welding and related joining technologies. **Focus:** Welding. **Qualif.:** Applicants must be students pursuing a specific degree at an accredited four-year college or university. **Criteria:** Recipients are selected based on academic standing.

Funds Avail.: $2,500. **To Apply:** Applicants must submit a financial statement; transcript of records; personal statement; biography; and photo. **Deadline:** January 15.

1153 ■ American Welding Society Past Presidents Scholarships *(Undergraduate/Scholarship)*

Purpose: To provide financial assistance to individuals interested in pursuing a bachelor's degree in welding

Awards are arranged alphabetically below their administering organizations

engineering, welding engineering technology, or an engineering program with an emphasis in welding. **Focus:** Welding. **Qualif.:** Applicants must be junior, senior, or graduate level students pursuing a degree in Welding Engineering or Welding Engineering Technology. **Criteria:** Recipients will be selected based on financial need.

Funds Avail.: $2,500. **To Apply:** Applicants must complete the application form and submit it along with one or more recommendation letters from community members, local AWS officers, and/or AWS district directors attesting to the applicant's leadership capability; and a 300-500 word essay on the applicant's objectives and aspirations in the field of welding.

1154 ■ American Welding Society Research Fellowships *(Postgraduate/Scholarship)*

Purpose: To advance opportunities for students preparing for a career in the welding and related joining technologies. **Focus:** Welding. **Qualif.:** Applicants must be graduate students who wish to pursue areas of research related to the welding and joining industry. **Criteria:** Recipients are selected based on academic standing.

Funds Avail.: No specific amount. **To Apply:** Applicants must submit a financial statement; transcript of records; personal statement; biography and photo. **Deadline:** March 1.

1155 ■ Arsham Amirikian Engineering Scholarships *(Undergraduate/Scholarship)*

Purpose: To provide financial assistance to individuals interested in pursuing a career in either welding engineering or the application of the art of welding in civil and structural engineering. **Focus:** Welding; Civil Engineering. **Qualif.:** Applicants must be undergraduate students pursuing a bachelors degree in civil engineering or welding related degree at an accredited university; must be 18 years of age or above; must have a minimum of 3.0 grade point average; must be citizens of the United States; and plan to attend an accredited engineering school within the United States. Applicants must have a minimum of 3.0 grade point average throughout the academic year. **Criteria:** Recipients are selected based on financial need.

Funds Avail.: $2,500. **To Apply:** Applicants must submit an application; a high school diploma; and a financial statement. **Deadline:** January 15.

1156 ■ Jerry Baker Scholarships *(Undergraduate/Scholarship)*

Purpose: To provide financial assistance to individuals interested in pursuing a bachelor's degree in welding engineering, welding engineering technology, or an engineering program with an emphasis in welding. **Focus:** Welding. **Qualif.:** Applicants must be undergraduate students pursuing a four-year bachelors degree in welding engineering or welding engineering technology; must be 18 years of age or above; must be full-time students as defined by the academic institution; must have at least a 2.8 overall point average with a 3.0 grade point average in engineering courses; must be citizen of the United States or Canada; and plan to attend an institution located within the United States or Canada. **Criteria:** Recipients are selected based on need.

Funds Avail.: $2,500. **To Apply:** Applicants must submit an application form and a high school diploma. **Deadline:** January 15.

1157 ■ Jack R. Barckhoff Welding Management Scholarships *(Undergraduate/Scholarship)*

Purpose: To provide financial assistance to individuals interested in pursuing a career in welding engineering. **Focus:** Welding. **Qualif.:** Applicants must be college juniors pursuing a four-year bachelors degree in welding engineering at the Ohio State University; must be 18 years old and above; must have a minimum of 2.5 overall grade point average; must be a citizen of the United States and plan to attend an accredited engineering school within the United States; must be enrolled and must complete the two-hour credit course in Total Welding Management at the Ohio State University. **Criteria:** Recipients are selected based on the financial need.

Funds Avail.: $2,500. **To Apply:** Applicants must complete the application form and submit it along with a high school diploma and a financial statement. Applicants must also submit a 300-500 word essay on how they see their role once they have graduated in improving the world of welding and the welding industry in the United States, and how they plan to use their education to improve the US competitive position in welding and manufacturing. **Deadline:** January 15. **Contact:** found@aws.org

1158 ■ Edward J. Brady Memorial Scholarships *(Undergraduate/Scholarship)*

Purpose: To provide financial assistance to individuals interested in pursuing a career in welding engineering. **Focus:** Welding. **Qualif.:** Applicants must be undergraduate students pursuing a four-year bachelors degree in welding engineering or welding engineering technology; must be 18 years old and above; must have a minimum of 2.5 overall grade point average; must be a citizen of the United States; and must plan to attend an accredited engineering school within the United States. **Criteria:** Recipients are selected based on financial need, career work experience, and extracurricular activities.

Funds Avail.: $2,500. **To Apply:** Applicants must complete the application form and submit it along with a high school diploma and a financial statement. **Deadline:** January 15. **Contact:** found@aws.org

1159 ■ William A. and Ann M. Brothers Scholarships *(Undergraduate/Scholarship)*

Purpose: To provide financial assistance to individuals interested in pursuing a bachelor's degree in welding engineering, welding engineering technology, or an engineering program with an emphasis in welding. **Focus:** Welding. **Qualif.:** Applicants must be full-time undergraduate students pursuing a four-year degree in Welding Engineering or Welding Engineering Technology; must have demonstrated leadership abilities; must be 18 years of age or above; must be United States citizens; plan to attend an academic institution within the United States or Canada; and must have at least 2.5 overall grade point average. **Criteria:** Recipients are selected based on financial need.

Funds Avail.: $3,500. **To Apply:** Applicants must submit an application form and a high school diploma. **Deadline:** January 15. **Contact:** found@aws.org

1160 ■ Donald F. Hastings Scholarships *(Undergraduate/Scholarship)*

Purpose: To provide financial assistance to individuals interested in pursuing a career in welding engineering. **Focus:** Welding. **Qualif.:** Applicants must be undergraduate students pursuing a bachelors degree in welding

Awards are arranged alphabetically below their administering organizations

engineering or welding engineering technology; must be 18 years of age or above; must have a minimum of 2.5 overall grade point average; must be United States citizens; and plan to attend an accredited engineering school within the United States. Applicants may be enrolled full or part time. **Criteria:** Recipients are selected based on financial need.

Funds Avail.: $2,500. **To Apply:** Applicants must submit an application; a high school diploma; and a financial statement. **Deadline:** January 15.

1161 ■ Donald and Shirley Hastings Scholarships *(Undergraduate/Scholarship)*

Purpose: To provide financial assistance to individuals interested in pursuing a career in welding engineering. **Focus:** Welding. **Qualif.:** Applicants must be undergraduate students pursuing a bachelors degree in welding engineering or welding engineering technology; must be 18 years of age or above; must have a minimum of 2.5 overall grade point average; must be United States citizens; and plan to attend an accredited engineering school within the United States. Applicants may be enrolled full or part time. **Criteria:** Recipients are selected based on financial need.

Funds Avail.: $2,500. **To Apply:** Applicants must submit an application; a high school diploma; and a financial statement. **Deadline:** January 15. **Contact:** found@aws.org

1162 ■ William B. Howell Scholarships *(Undergraduate/Scholarship)*

Purpose: To provide financial assistance to individuals interested in pursuing a bachelor's degree in welding engineering, welding engineering technology, or an engineering program with an emphasis in welding. **Focus:** Welding. **Qualif.:** Applicants must be full-time undergraduate students pursuing a four-year degree in Welding Engineering or Welding Engineering Technology; must have demonstrated leadership abilities; be 18 years of age or above; must be United States citizens; plan to attend an academic institution within the United States or Canada; and must have at least 2.5 overall grade point average. **Criteria:** Recipients are selected based on financial need.

Funds Avail.: $2,500. **To Apply:** Applicants must submit an application form and a high school diploma. **Deadline:** January 15. **Contact:** found@aws.org

1163 ■ Hypertherm International HyTech Leadership Scholarships *(Postgraduate/Scholarship)*

Purpose: To provide financial assistance to individuals interested in pursuing a career in welding engineering. **Focus:** Welding. **Qualif.:** Applicant must be a graduate student pursuing an advanced degree in engineering management within the welding and cutting industry; must have completed a Bachelor of Science degree or be in the final year and has been accepted for graduate work in engineering management at an accredited graduate school; must have graduated within a minimum overall grade point average of 2.8. **Criteria:** Recipients are selected based on the financial need.

Funds Avail.: $2,500. **To Apply:** Applicants must complete the application form and submit it along with a high school diploma and a financial statement. **Deadline:** January 15. **Contact:** found@aws.org

1164 ■ ITW Welding Companies Scholarships *(Undergraduate/Scholarship)*

Purpose: To provide financial assistance to individuals interested in pursuing a career in welding engineering. **Focus:** Welding. **Qualif.:** Applicant must be a senior, full-time undergraduate student working towards a bachelors degree in welding engineering or welding engineering technology; must be 18 years old and above; must have a minimum of 3.0 overall grade point average; must be a citizen of the United States; and must plan to attend an accredited engineering school within the United States. **Criteria:** Recipients are selected based on financial need.

Funds Avail.: $3,000. **Number Awarded:** 2. **To Apply:** Applicants must complete the application form and submit it along with a high school diploma and a financial statement. **Deadline:** January 15. **Contact:** found@aws.org

1165 ■ Terry Jarvis Memorial Scholarships *(Undergraduate/Scholarship)*

Purpose: To provide financial assistance to individuals interested in pursuing a bachelor's degree in welding engineering, welding engineering technology, or an engineering program with an emphasis in welding. **Focus:** Welding. **Qualif.:** Applicants must be undergraduate students pursuing a four-year bachelors degree in welding engineering or welding engineering technology; must be 18 years of age or above; must be full-time students as defined by the academic institution; must have at least a 2.8 overall point average with a 3.0 grade point average in engineering courses; must be citizen of the United States or Canada; and plan to attend an institution located within the United States or Canada. **Criteria:** Recipients are selected based on need.

Funds Avail.: $2,500. **To Apply:** Applicants must submit an application form and a high school diploma. **Deadline:** January 15.

1166 ■ John C. Lincoln Memorial Scholarships *(Undergraduate/Scholarship)*

Purpose: To provide financial assistance to individuals interested in pursuing a career in welding engineering. **Focus:** Welding. **Qualif.:** Applicants must be undergraduate students pursuing a four-year Bachelors Degree in a welding program at an accredited university; must have a 2.5 overall grade point average; must be 18 years old and above; must be a citizen of the United States and plan to attend an academic institution located within the United States. **Criteria:** Recipients are selected based on financial need.

Funds Avail.: $3,500. **To Apply:** Applicants must complete the application form and submit it along with a high school diploma and a financial statement. **Deadline:** January 15. **Contact:** found@aws.org

1167 ■ Miller Electric International WorldSkills Competition Scholarships *(Undergraduate/Scholarship)*

Purpose: To provide financial assistance to individuals interested in pursuing a bachelor's degree in welding engineering, welding engineering technology, or an engineering program with an emphasis in welding. **Focus:** Welding. **Qualif.:** Applicants must be undergraduate students pursuing a four-year degree program in an accredited university. **Criteria:** Recipients are selected based on financial need.

Funds Avail.: Maximum of $40,000. **To Apply:** Applicants must complete the National Skills USA Competition and complete the application form.

1168 ■ Robert L. Peaslee-Detroit Brazing and Soldiering Division Scholarships *(Undergraduate/Scholarship)*

Purpose: To provide financial assistance to individuals interested in pursuing a bachelor's degree in welding engineering, welding engineering technology, or an engineering program with an emphasis in welding. **Focus:** Welding. **Qualif.:** Applicants must be college junior or senior students pursuing a degree in Welding Engineering or Welding Engineering Technology; must have demonstrated leadership abilities; must be 18 years old and above; must be United States citizens and plan to attend an academic institution within the United States or Canada; must at least have a 3.0 overall grade point average; must express an interest in the resistance welding process; must show emphasis on Brazing and Soldiering application in their coursework. **Criteria:** Recipients are selected based on financial needs.

Funds Avail.: $2,500. **To Apply:** Applicants must submit an application form along with a high school diploma. **Deadline:** January 15. **Contact:** found@aws.org

1169 ■ Ronald C. and Joyce Pierce Scholarships *(Undergraduate/Scholarship)*

Purpose: To provide financial assistance to individuals interested in pursuing a bachelor's degree in welding engineering, welding engineering technology, or an engineering program with an emphasis in welding. **Focus:** Welding. **Qualif.:** Applicants must be college junior or senior students pursuing a degree in Welding Engineering or Welding Engineering Technology. Applicants must have demonstrated leadership abilities; must be 18 years of age or above; must be United States citizens; must plan to attend an academic institution within the United States or Canada; and must have at least 3.0 overall grade point average. Applicants must also express an interest in the resistance welding process and show emphasis on Brazing and Soldiering application in their coursework. **Criteria:** Recipients are selected based on financial need.

Funds Avail.: $2,500. **To Apply:** Applicants must submit an application form; a high school diploma; two letters of reference; personal statement; transcript of records; statement of the unmet financial need; and verification of enrollment. **Deadline:** January 15. **Contact:** found@aws.org

1170 ■ Praxair International Scholarships *(Undergraduate/Scholarship)*

Purpose: To provide financial assistance to individuals interested in pursuing a bachelor's degree in welding engineering, welding engineering technology, or an engineering program with an emphasis in welding. **Focus:** Welding. **Qualif.:** Applicants must be undergraduate students pursuing a degree in Welding Engineering or Welding Engineering Technology; must have demonstrated leadership abilities; must be 18 years old and above; must be a citizen of the United States and plan to attend an academic institution within the United States or Canada. **Criteria:** Recipients are selected based on financial need.

Funds Avail.: $2,500. **To Apply:** Applicants must an application form along with a high school diploma. **Deadline:** January 15.

1171 ■ Resistance Welder Manufacturers' Association Scholarships *(Undergraduate/Scholarship)*

Purpose: To provide financial assistance to individuals interested in pursuing a bachelor's degree in welding engineering, welding engineering technology or an engineering program with an emphasis in welding. **Focus:** Welding. **Qualif.:** Applicants must be college junior students pursuing a degree in Welding Engineering or Welding Engineering Technology; must have demonstrated leadership abilities; must be 18 years old and above; must be United States citizens and plan to attend an academic institution within the United States or Canada; must at least have a 3.0 overall grade point average; must express an interest in the resistance welding process. **Criteria:** Recipients are selected based on financial needs.

Funds Avail.: $2,500. **To Apply:** Applicants must submit an application form along with a high school diploma and an essay of 500 words or less about why the applicant wishes to become involved in the resistance welding industry. **Deadline:** January 15.

1172 ■ Jerry Robinson Inweld Corporation Scholarships *(Undergraduate/Scholarship)*

Purpose: To provide financial assistance to individuals interested in pursuing a career in welding engineering. **Focus:** Welding. **Qualif.:** Applicants must be undergraduate students pursuing a four-year Bachelors Degree in a welding program at an accredited university; must have a 2.5 overall grade point average; must be 18 years old and above; must be a citizen of the United States and plan to attend an academic institution located within the United States. **Criteria:** Recipients are selected based on financial need.

Funds Avail.: $2,500. **To Apply:** Applicants must complete the application form and submit it along with a high school diploma and a financial statement. **Deadline:** January 15. **Contact:** found@aws.org

1173 ■ James A. Turner, Jr. Memorial Scholarships *(Undergraduate/Scholarship)*

Purpose: To provide financial assistance to individuals interested in pursuing a career in welding engineering. **Focus:** Welding. **Qualif.:** Applicants must be full-time students pursuing a four-year Bachelor of Business Degree leading to a management career in welding store operations or a welding distributorship. Applicants must be employed for at least ten hours a week at a welding distributorship at the time of application. Applicants must be 18 years old and above. **Criteria:** Recipients are selected based on financial need.

Funds Avail.: $3,500. **To Apply:** Applicants must complete the application form and submit it along with a high school diploma and a financial statement. **Deadline:** January 15. **Contact:** found@aws.org

1174 ■ Armos and Marilyn Winsand-Detroit Section Named Scholarships *(Undergraduate/Scholarship)*

Purpose: To provide financial assistance to individuals interested in pursuing a career in welding engineering. **Focus:** Welding. **Qualif.:** Applicants must be enrolled in a two or four-year program and must be residents of Michigan or attending a Michigan College. **Criteria:** Recipients are selected based on financial.

Funds Avail.: No specific amount. **To Apply:** Applicants must submit an application form and a high school diploma. **Deadline:** January 15.

1175 ■ Americans for Informed Democracy

701 Cathedral St., Ste. L3
Baltimore, MD 21201

Awards are arranged alphabetically below their administering organizations

Ph: (410)962-8773
E-mail: info@globalscholar.org
URL: http://www.aidemocracy.org

1176 ■ Americans for Informed Democracy Global Scholar Tuition *(Undergraduate/ Scholarship)*

Purpose: To provide financial assistance for students from all different fields, backgrounds and interests who have a strong academic record. **Focus:** General studies. **Qualif.:** Applicants must be junior or senior students who have experienced with honors or advanced placement-level courses. **Criteria:** Applicants will be evaluated based on academic records, extracurricular achievements and essay writing.

Funds Avail.: $2,000. **To Apply:** Applicants must file online application. Applicants must also submit a short essay explaining "what issue in international affairs he/she has most interest, why and how will it fit into his or her future plans?"

1177 ■ Anaheim Police Association

508 N Anaheim Blvd.
Anaheim, CA 92805
Ph: (714)635-0272
Fax: (714)635-3240
E-mail: office@anaheimpoliceassociation.org
URL: http://www.anaheimpoliceassociation.org

1178 ■ Anaheim Police Survivors and Scholarship Fund *(Undergraduate/Scholarship)*

Purpose: To provide financial assistance for family and the children of any Anaheim Police Officers who could lose their life while in the performance of their job through education. **Focus:** General studies. **Qualif.:** Applicants must be entering students or recently high school graduates; continuing students (already enrolled in College Program) or a returning students (entering college after a break in educational experience); children (natural or adopted) of Anaheim Police Officers or Anaheim Reserve Officers enrolled in at least twelve units; must have cumulative GPA of 3.0 or higher. **Criteria:** Recipients are recommended by the American Police Officer's Honorary Association Scholarship Committee and approved by the Board of Trustees of Anaheim Police Survivors and Scholarship Fund.

Funds Avail.: $250 to $1,000. **To Apply:** Applicants must submit completed application form and a short essay of 500 words or less on need for scholarship and goals. **Deadline:** April 1.

1179 ■ The Anderson Group Summer Institute

PO Box 38334
Los Angeles, CA 90038-0334
Ph: (323)469-3050
E-mail: kmoon@uclalumni.net
URL: http://www.harpsociety.org

1180 ■ The Anderson Group Summer Institute Scholarships *(Other/Scholarship)*

Purpose: To provide financial assistance for promising individuals for advanced study of harp at a college or university. **Focus:** Music. **Qualif.:** Applicants must be active members of the American Harp Society with maximum age limit of 40 years old by February 18, 2007. **Criteria:** Recipient will be selected based on financial need and musical promise in the study of harp.

Funds Avail.: $1,000. **Number Awarded:** 2. **To Apply:** Applicants must submit biography including applicant's full name, legal residence, present address, telephone number, email address, proof of age, musical and academic education, personal profile, general analysis of financial need and long-range goals for harp-playing, hand-written statement, CD recording, and letter of reference. **Deadline:** February 18.

1181 ■ Wilbur H. Anderson Memorial Scholarship Foundation, Inc.

2443 Skyland Place, SE
Washington, DC 20020
Ph: (202)678-8830
E-mail: info@whamscholarship.org
URL: http://www.whamscholarship.org

1182 ■ Wilbur H. Anderson Memorial Scholarships *(Undergraduate/Scholarship)*

Purpose: To provide financial assistance to deserving students who want to pursue their studies. **Focus:** General studies. **Qualif.:** Applicant must be living in the greater Metropolitan Washington, DC Area; must have a cumulative GPA of 2.5 or above. **Criteria:** Recipient will be selected based on the scholarship application requirements.

Funds Avail.: $500. **To Apply:** Applicant must complete the application form available online; must submit an official copy of the recent transcript or record; must provide proof of enrollment confirmation from an accredited academic institution; must submit a letter of recommendation from the church pastor and/or church mentor, two copies of FAFSA/SAR, statement of financial need, and recent photograph. Application form and other supporting documents must be sent to The Wilbur H. Anderson, Scholarship Foundation, Inc., c/o Pastor Giles H. Jackson, 2443 Skyland Place SE, Washington, DC 20020. **Deadline:** April 30.

1183 ■ Anxiety Disorders Association of America

8730 Georgia Ave., Ste. 600
Silver Spring, MD 20910
Ph: (240)485-1001
Fax: (240)485-1035
E-mail: information@adaa.org
URL: http://www.adaa.org

1184 ■ Anxiety Disorders Association of America Career Development Travel Awards *(Professional Development/Award/Prize)*

Purpose: To help young professionals with a career interest in fields related to anxiety disorders. To encourage mental health professionals to advance the field of study of disorders, including the causes, prevention, treatment options, and other related issues. **Focus:** Mental health. **Qualif.:** Applicants must be individuals who have completed their master's degree or are training for Ph.D. or M.D. degrees; must be Ph.D level scientists or clinicians who have received doctorates or completed postdoctoral fellow-

Awards are arranged alphabetically below their administering organizations

ships within the past three years; must be a physician-scientists or clinicians who have completed their residencies or research fellowships within the past three years. **Criteria:** Candidates will be judge based on the following criteria: (1) Evidence of commitment to field of anxiety disorders; (2) Strength of current program and training; (3) Quality, extent, and multidisciplinary nature of research; (4) Professional reference and personal statement; (5) Interest in becoming involved with ADAA.

Funds Avail.: Travel and expenses stipend of up to $1,000 to attend the ADAA Annual Conference. **To Apply:** Applicant must submit the application form with the following materials: (1) Essay (with a 200 word abstract for the research poster); (2) Curriculum vitae (including the list of publication if applicable); (3) brief statement (maximum of three pages) describing the applicant's research interest and career goals; (4) Letter of recommendation from the Chair of the Department of Psychiatry or Psychology, training and program director, or the applicant's research mentor/advisor; (5) One reference letter from a mentor, supervisor, department chair, or residency advisor. Application materials must be sent to: Career Development Travel Awards, 8730 George Ave., Ste. 600, Silver Spring, MD 20910. **Deadline:** November 30.

1185 ■ Anxiety Disorders Association of America Junior Faculty Research Grants *(Professional Development/Grant)*

Purpose: To support the junior faculty making the transition to independent investigator. To assist individuals in making the transition from trainee to junior faculty and independent investigator. **Focus:** Mental health. **Qualif.:** Applicant must have completed at least one year of a doctoral fellowship or post-residency research training by the time the research grant is awarded; must have a mentor or senior research collaborator who is an established investigator in anxiety disorders research. Previous ADAA Career Development and Trainee Travel Award winners are eligible to apply. **Criteria:** Special consideration will be given to those applicants whose research with their affiliated institution is dependent on outside funding sources.

Funds Avail.: $1,000 travel grant is awarded to cover expenses. **To Apply:** Applicant must submit a proposal with 250 word abstract and a statement (three-page maximum, single-spaced) from the applicant describing research that will accomplished within the grant period; must have the budget outline stating the amount requested with a brief justification; must have a curriculum vitae of the applicant; must have a research training or career plans with a brief description (two-pages maximum) of the applicant's current research focus or the research training just completed, as well as a short discussion of the applicant's future career plans; must have the curriculum vitae of the applicant's mentor submitted in the NIMH Biographical Sketch format; must have a collaborator letter and mentor letter from an on-site or off-site mentor. Applicant must submit the application online with the other application materials at www.adaa.org **Deadline:** December 14.

1186 ■ Appalachian School of Law

PO Box 2825
Grundy, VA 24614
Ph: (276)935-4349
Fax: (276)935-8261
Free: 800-895-7411
E-mail: aslinfo@asl.edu
URL: http://www.asl.edu

1187 ■ Angela D. Dales Merit Scholarship Program *(Undergraduate/Loan)*

Purpose: To support students financially in the form of credit against tuition charged. **Focus:** Law. **Qualif.:** Applicants must be at least incoming first year law students. **Criteria:** Recipients are selected based on the Law School Admission Test (LSAT) and Undergraduate Grade Point Average (UGPA).

Funds Avail.: No specific amount. **To Apply:** Applicants must complete and submit an online application available at the website; online certification page; two letters of recommendation; and 500 words or less describing professional goals and qualifications.

Remarks: Scholarship is awarded on a first-come, first-served basis.

1188 ■ Appraisal Institute Education Trust

550 W Van Buren St., Ste. 1000
Chicago, IL 60607
Ph: (312)335-4100
Fax: (312)335-4400
E-mail: information@appraisalinstitute.org
URL: http://www.appraisalinstitute.org

1189 ■ Appraisal Institute Education Trust Scholarships *(Graduate, Undergraduate/Scholarship)*

Purpose: To help finance the education endeavors of individuals concentrating in real estate appraisal, land economics, real estate or allied fields. **Focus:** Real estate; Land economics. **Qualif.:** Applicants must be U.S. citizens, enrolled full-time for the academic year beginning August through June in a University or Community College in the U.S. majoring in real estate appraisal, land economics, real estate or allied fields. **Criteria:** Awarded on the basis of academic excellence.

Funds Avail.: $2,000 Undergraduate; $3,000 Graduate. **To Apply:** Applicants must submit a completed application together with letters of recommendation from the college Dean and two individuals, a signed statement regarding general activities and intellectual interests in college, official copies of all collegiate records and proposed student program. Graduate student applicants must have served, or is about to serve, an internship with an appraiser or the appraisal department of a corporation (letter from employer required). **Deadline:** March 15. **Contact:** Olivia Carreon at the above address (see entry 1188).

1190 ■ Arab American Institute

1600 K St. NW, Ste. 601
Washington, DC 20006
Ph: (202)429-9210
Fax: (202)429-9214
E-mail: aai@aaiusa.org
URL: http://www.aaiusa.org

1191 ■ Al Muammar Scholarships for Journalism *(Undergraduate/Scholarship)*

Purpose: To provide scholarship opportunity to the American students who are Arab descent. **Focus:** Journalism. **Qualif.:** Applicants must: be Arab American, college students who are majoring in journalism, as well as college seniors who have been accepted to a graduate journalism

Awards are arranged alphabetically below their administering organizations

school; be a UC citizen or permanent resident of Arab descent; be a full-time student at an accredited college or university in the United States; have current GPA of 3.3 or higher. **Criteria:** Selection will be based on the committee's criteria.

Funds Avail.: $5,000. **To Apply:** Applicant may download an application from the Foundation's website. Applicant must also include an official transcript and letter of recommendation (one letter must be from the professor in the applicant's journalism program and second would be ideally be from a leader in an Arab American community organization with which the applicant has had a relationship). Applicant must send five copies of the following items, collated into five complete packets, each with one copy of each item, in the following order: Completed application form; Unofficial transcript; Resume; Short Essay; Work samples. **Deadline:** March 3. **Contact:** Al Muammar Scholarship Administrator, Arab American Institute Foundation, 1600 K St. NW Ste. 600 Washington, DC 20006.

1192 ■ Barakat Trust and Barakat Foundation Scholarships *(Graduate/Scholarship)*

Purpose: To provide financial support for students and scholars of Islamic culture. **Focus:** General studies. **Qualif.:** Applicants must have completed at least a B.A. degree and have been accepted for graduate study or an apprenticeship at an accredited university or institution. **Criteria:** Selection will be based on the committee's criteria.

Funds Avail.: No specific amount. **To Apply:** Applicant may contact the Barakat Trust and Barakat Foundation for application requirements. **Contact:** Barakat Trust and Barakat Foundation, 2665 Kimball Pomona, CA 91767; rc101@earthlink.net.

1193 ■ Ameen Rihani Scholarship Program *(Undergraduate/Scholarship)*

Purpose: To promote academic excellence and to provide an opportunity for outstanding student to reach their fullest potential. **Focus:** Literature; Philosophy; Political science. **Qualif.:** Individual must: be a Lebanese or other Arab Descent; be a citizen or legal permanent residents of the United States; have attained a cumulative GPA of 3.25 on a 4.0 scale; enter a college or university as a full-time, degree-seeking freshman in the fall of the year; have demonstrated leadership abilities through participation in community service, extracurricular or other activities. **Criteria:** Selection will be based on the committee's criteria.

Funds Avail.: $1,500. **To Apply:** Teachers, counselors, and principals are invited to nominate students with outstanding academic qualifications, particularly those who would promote success in the fields of literature, philosophy, or political science. **Deadline:** May 31. **Contact:** Ameen Rihani Scholarship Program, The Ameen Rihani Organization, 1010 Wayne Ave. Ste 420 Silver Spring, MD 20910.

1194 ■ Archaeological Institute of America

656 Beacon St., 6th Fl.
Boston, MA 02215-2006
Ph: (617)353-9361
Fax: (617)353-6550
E-mail: aia@aia.bu.edu
URL: http://www.archaeological.org

1195 ■ Jane C. Waldbaum Archaeological Field School Scholarships *(Undergraduate/Scholarship)*

Purpose: To help students pay their expenses associated with participation on an archaeological excavation or survey project. **Focus:** Archeology. **Qualif.:** Applicant must be a junior and senior undergraduate student and first-year graduate student currently enrolled at a college or university in the U.S or Canada; must be at least 18 years old and have not previously participated in an archaeological excavation. **Criteria:** Selection of applicant will be based on the application form and other supporting documents.

Funds Avail.: $1,000. **To Apply:** Applicant must complete the online application form; must submit two copies of transcript, brief cover letter (300 words or less) in the applicant's own words, outline of anticipated expenses associated with participation on the project and a statement from the applicant indicating any other financial resources available to help cover expenses and two references for letters of recommendation from professors or academic advisors at the applicant's college or university. **Deadline:** March 15.

1196 ■ Architectural Precast Association

6710 Winkler Rd., Ste. 8
Fort Myers, FL 33919
Ph: (239)454-6989
Fax: (239)454-6787
E-mail: info@archprecast.org
URL: http://www.archprecast.org

1197 ■ Tom Cory Memorial Scholarships *(Undergraduate/Scholarship)*

Purpose: To provide financial assistance to those studying architectural. **Focus:** Architecture. **Qualif.:** Applicants must have a cumulative GPA of 3.0 or higher; must have at least two semesters of school left to complete from date of award; must be involved in activities related to the architectural field. **Criteria:** Recipients are selected based on academic merit and committee's review of the application.

Funds Avail.: $1,500. **To Apply:** Applicants must send a completed application form; transcript of two years college through the last grading period to the date of application; letter of recommendation from a faculty member of the collage; written description of the applicant's career plans after graduation; an essay explaining why the applicant chose the architectural field. **Deadline:** March 1.

1198 ■ Arctic Institute of North America

2500 University Dr., NW
Calgary, AB, Canada T2N 1N4
Ph: (403)220-7515
Fax: (403)282-4609
URL: http://www.arctic.ucalgary.ca

1199 ■ Lorraine Allison Scholarships *(Postgraduate/Scholarship)*

Purpose: To advance the study of the North American and circumpolar Arctic through the natural and social sciences, the arts and humanities and to acquire, preserve and disseminate information on physical, environmental and social conditions in the North. **Focus:** Natural sciences; Social sciences. **Qualif.:** Applicants must be students enrolled at a Canadian university in a program of graduate study related to northern issues. **Criteria:** Candidates will be selected based on the selection committee's review of the application materials.

Funds Avail.: $3,000. **To Apply:** Applicant must provide a

Awards are arranged alphabetically below their administering organizations

two page description of the northern studies program and relevant project(s) being undertaken; must submit three letters of reference from the applicant's current or past professors; complete curriculum vitae with academic transcript and list of the current source and amounts of research funding, including scholarships, grants and bursaries. Send application and supporting documents to: Arctic Institute of North America, 2500 University Dr. NW, Calgary, AB, T2N 1N4. **Deadline:** January 10.

1200 ■ Jim Bourque Scholarships *(Postgraduate/Scholarship)*

Purpose: To support the mature and matriculating students in their studies. **Focus:** Environmental technology; Telecommunications systems. **Qualif.:** Applicants must be students who are enrolled or intend to take, post-secondary education in environmental studies, traditional knowledge or telecommunications. **Criteria:** Scholarships are given based on financial need, relevance of study and achievements.

Funds Avail.: $1,000. **To Apply:** Applicants must submit a description of their intended program of study and the reason for their choice of program (500 words); a copy of the recent high school or college/university transcript; letter of recommendation from a community leader; a statement of financial need; and proof of enrollment to post-secondary institution. Send application and supporting documents to: Arctic Institute of North America, 2500 University Dr. NW, Calgary, AB, T2N 1N4. **Deadline:** July 18.

1201 ■ Arent Fox LLP

1050 Connecticut Ave. NW
Washington, DC 20036-5339
Ph: (202)857-6000
Fax: (202)857-6395
E-mail: charyk.william@arentfox.com
URL: http://www.arentfox.com

1202 ■ Arent Fox Diversity Scholarships *(Undergraduate/Scholarship)*

Purpose: To provide financial assistance for qualified individuals intending to pursue their law career. **Focus:** Law. **Qualif.:** Applicants must be U.S citizens or otherwise authorized to work in the United States; must have an excellent academic performance during college and law school; must have excellent oral and written communication skills; must have leadership qualities and community involvement; must be members of a diverse population that historically has been underrepresented in the legal profession; must agree to join the Arent Fox summer program after the first year of law school; and must be first-year law students. **Criteria:** Selection of applicants will be based on their academic performance and financial need.

Funds Avail.: $15,000. **Number Awarded:** 3. **To Apply:** Applicants must submit a resume with cover letter; must provide a undergraduate transcript and law school grades when available; must have three professional or academic references and Arent Fox essay. Application forms are available online and must be sent to Arent Fox LLP/Diversity Scholarship Program, Washington Office, Ms. Jessica L. Salvaterra, Recruitment and Career Development Manager, 1050 Connecticut Ave., N.W., Washington, D.C. 20036. **Deadline:** January 15.

1203 ■ Arizona Airport Association

4697 S Golden Arrow Dr.
Green Valley, AZ 85622
Ph: (520)398-6287
E-mail: mcovalt@cox.net
URL: http://www.azairports.org

1204 ■ Marty Rosness Student Scholarships *(Undergraduate/Scholarship)*

Purpose: To enhance careers in the aviation industry. **Focus:** Aviation. **Qualif.:** Applicants must be enrolled in bachelor's or master's degree programs in the state of Arizona. **Criteria:** Recipients are selected based on academic performance.

Funds Avail.: $3,000. **To Apply:** Applicants must submit a completed application form; must submit a brief statement of their interest in the scholarship; must write an at least one page brief autobiography of their aviation education, experience and background. **Contact:** 480-312-8475.

1205 ■ Arizona Artist Blacksmith Association

840 E McKellips
Apache Jct., AZ 85219
Ph: (602)254-4976
E-mail: education@az-blacksmiths.org
URL: http://www.az-blacksmiths.org

1206 ■ AABA Read Carlock Memorial Scholarship Fund *(Professional Development/Scholarship)*

Purpose: To provide financial assistance to interested blacksmiths and/or immediate family members of AABA members for skills and abilities development. **Focus:** General studies. **Qualif.:** Applicants must be members of the Arizona Artist Blacksmith Association, as defined by Article 2 sections (a), (b, paragraphs I, II, III, and IV) of the AABA Bylaws, who have been members for at least one year prior to their application, or immediate family of those members. **Criteria:** Applicants are evaluated based on evidence of their strong desire for continued and serious investigation of the craft; quality of work as demonstrated by visual materials submitted with application; level of blacksmithing ability; record of professional activity and achievement; benefit to the Arizona Artist Blacksmith Association and demonstrated involvement with and commitment to AABA.

Funds Avail.: $500. **To Apply:** Applicants must submit all the required application information.

1207 ■ Arizona Association of Student Financial Aid Administrators

PMB No. 123
4939 W Ray Rd., Ste. 4
Chandler, AZ 85226-2099
E-mail: support@aasfaa.org
URL: http://www.aasfaa.org

1208 ■ BIA Higher Education Grants *(Undergraduate/Grant)*

Purpose: To provide quality services to the Hopi people by enhancing a full range of educational opportunities; to maintain efforts to increase the number of employable, degree-holding Hopi professionals; to maintain retention services which will enable students to complete programs. **Focus:** General studies. **Qualif.:** Applicants must be students pursuing an associate, baccalaureate, graduate, or post-graduate degree; must be entering freshmen with a

Awards are arranged alphabetically below their administering organizations

GPA of 2.5 for high school course work or a minimum composite of 50% on the GED exam; must have 2.5 GPA for all college work. **Criteria:** Recipients are selected based on financial need.

Funds Avail.: $2,500. **To Apply:** Applicants must submit an official high school transcript or original GED scores; must submit an official transcript from all post-secondary schools; must submit a Program of Study (POS) or Letter of Acceptance (LOA). **Deadline:** July 1; December 1; April 1. **Contact:** 928-734-3533.

1209 ■ Educational Enrichment Awards *(Undergraduate/Scholarship)*

Purpose: To develop leadership and personal skills and acquire educational or pre-occupational experiences. **Focus:** General studies. **Qualif.:** Applicants must be students in fifth grade through post-secondary level education. **Criteria:** Recipients are selected based on financial need.

Funds Avail.: $500. **To Apply:** Applicants must submit an official high school transcript or original GED scores; must submit an official transcript from all post-secondary schools; must submit a Program of Study (POS) or Letter of Acceptance (LOA). **Deadline:** July 1; December 1; April 1. **Contact:** 928-734-3533.

1210 ■ Hopi Education Awards *(All/Award/Prize)*

Purpose: To provide quality services to the Hopi people by enhancing a full range of educational opportunities; to maintain efforts to increase the number of employable degree-holding Hopi professionals; to maintain retention services which will enable students to complete programs. **Focus:** General studies. **Qualif.:** Applicants must be students pursuing an AA, BA, BS or PhD from an accredited college or university; entering freshmen students must have a GPA 0f 2.5 for high school course work or a minimum composite of 50% on the GED exam while continuing students must have an at least 2.5 GPA for all college work. **Criteria:** Recipients are selected based on financial need.

Funds Avail.: $2,500. **To Apply:** Applicants must submit an official high school transcript or original GED scores; must submit an official transcript from all post-secondary schools; must submit a Program of Study (POS) or Letter of Acceptance (LOA). **Deadline:** July 1; December 1; April 1. **Contact:** 928-734-3533.

1211 ■ Private High School Awards *(Undergraduate/Award/Prize)*

Purpose: To encourage Hopi students to achieve and maintain a high level of academic excellence at an accredited private high school. **Focus:** General studies. **Qualif.:** High school applicants must have an eighth grade education with a GPA of 3.50 while continuing students must have a GPA of 3.25. **Criteria:** Recipients are selected based on financial need.

Funds Avail.: $4,000. **Number Awarded:** 10. **To Apply:** Applicants must submit an official high school transcript or original GED scores; must submit an official transcript from all post-secondary schools; must submit a Program of Study (POS) or Letter of Acceptance (LOA) (if applicable). **Deadline:** July 1; December 1; April 1. **Contact:** 928-734-3533.

1212 ■ Tribal Priority Scholarships *(Undergraduate/Scholarship)*

Purpose: To encourage Hopi college students to obtain degrees in subject areas of priority interest to Hopi Tribal Goals and Objectives. **Focus:** General studies. **Qualif.:** Applicants must be junior and senior undergraduate, graduate, post-graduate and professional students in the areas of priority interest to the Hopi Tribe; must have an at least 3.5 GPA. **Criteria:** Recipients are selected based on academic performance.

Funds Avail.: $1,500. **Number Awarded:** 5. **To Apply:** Applicants must submit an official high school transcript or original GED scores; must submit an official transcript from all post-secondary schools; must submit a Program of Study (POS) or Letter of Acceptance (LOA). **Deadline:** July 1; December 1; April 1. **Contact:** 928-734-3533.

1213 ■ Arizona Christian School Tuition Organization

PO Box 6580
Chandler, AZ 85246
Ph: (480)820-0403
Fax: (480)820-2027
URL: http://www.acsto.org

1214 ■ Arizona Christian School Tuition Organization Scholarships *(Undergraduate/Scholarship)*

Purpose: To support students planning to attend K-12. **Focus:** General studies. **Qualif.:** Student must be planning to attend K-12 in a Christian private school. **Criteria:** Awards are given based on the application.

Funds Avail.: No specific amount. **To Apply:** Students must submit a completed application form. **Deadline:** June, October, February.

Remarks: All scholarships awarded will be sent directly to the student's school to be applied towards tuition.

1215 ■ Arizona City County Management Association

1820 W Washington St.
Phoenix, AZ 85007
Ph: (602)258-5786
Fax: (602)253-3874
E-mail: acma@azmanagement.org
URL: http://www.azmanagement.org

1216 ■ Marvin A. Andrews Scholarships/Internships *(Graduate/Scholarship)*

Purpose: To provide the scholarship recipient the opportunity to intern with a participating Arizona city, town or county. **Focus:** Public Administration. **Qualif.:** Applicants must be full-time students attending either Arizona State University, Northern Arizona University or the University of Arizona who have exhibited strong academic achievement. **Criteria:** Recipients are selected based on demonstrated strong academic achievement.

Funds Avail.: No specific amount. **To Apply:** Applicants must submit: completed application form; resume; two letters of recommendation; an official graduate-level transcript; a letter addressed to Gayle Mabery, ACMA President addressing their interest in local government management, career goals and financial need or plans for using the scholarship. **Contact:** 602-253-3874.

1217 ■ Charles A. Esser Memorial Scholarships *(Graduate/Scholarship)*

Purpose: To honor and financially assist Arizona graduate students in public administration who aspire to a career in local government management. **Focus:** Public administration. **Qualif.:** Applicants must be part-time MPA students attending either Arizona State University, Northern Arizona University or the University of Arizona who are currently working in local government. **Criteria:** Recipients are selected based on demonstrated strong academic achievement.

Funds Avail.: No specific amount. **To Apply:** Applicants must submit: completed application form; resume; two letters of recommendation; an official graduate-level transcript, a letter addressed to Gayle Mabery, ACMA President addressing their interest in local government management, career goals and financial needs or plans for using the scholarship. **Deadline:** December 28. **Contact:** 602-253-3874

1218 ■ Arizona Nursery Association

1430 W. Broadway, Ste. 110
Tempe, AZ 85282
Ph: (480)966-1610
Fax: (480)966-0923
E-mail: info@azna.org
URL: http://www.azna.org

1219 ■ Arizona Nursery Association Scholarships *(Undergraduate/Scholarship)*

Purpose: To promote and advance the nursery industry for its members and the public they serve. **Focus:** Horticulture. **Qualif.:** Applicants must be residents of Arizona currently or planning to be enrolled in a horticultural-related curriculum at a university, community college or continuing education program; must be currently employed in or have an interest in the nursery industry as a career; must have above-average scholastic achievement or at least two years work experience in the industry; must display involvement in extracurricular activities related to industry. **Criteria:** Recipients are selected based on academic performance.

Funds Avail.: $500-$3,000. **To Apply:** Applicants must complete the online application form. **Deadline:** April 15. **Contact:** 480-966-1610.

1220 ■ Arizona Nurses Association

1850 E Southern Ave., Ste. 1
Tempe, AZ 85282
Ph: (480)831-0404
URL: http://www.aznurse.org

1221 ■ Arizona Nurses Foundation Scholarships *(Graduate, Undergraduate/Scholarship)*

Purpose: To enhance the development of Arizona nurses and further the nursing profession in Arizona. **Focus:** Nursing. **Qualif.:** Applicants must be undergraduate and graduate students enrolled in or accepted in an academic education program; must be enrolled part-time or full-time. **Criteria:** Recipients are selected based on potential for leadership in nursing, merit, commitment to professional nursing in Arizona, expressed need for financial assistance, interest in teaching nursing in Arizona.

Funds Avail.: No specific amount. **To Apply:** Applicants must submit: completed application form; evidence of admission such as official or unofficial transcript of records, current courses schedule, copy of letter or certificate of admission or a written statement from an appropriate academic official; a brief statement describing the professional's activities, community service and other activities in the last three years that demonstrate the potential for leadership; a statement describing the need for financial assistance; one confidential reference form from an immediate supervisor, the student's academic advisor or another faculty member. **Deadline:** March 1; October 15. **Contact:** carol@aznurse.org

1222 ■ Arizona Parks and Recreation Association

1422 N 44th St., Ste. 211
Phoenix, AZ 85008
Ph: (602)335-1962
Fax: (602)335-1965
E-mail: apra@azpra.org
URL: http://azpra.affiniscape.com

1223 ■ Arizona Parks and Recreation Educational Scholarship Program *(Graduate, Undergraduate/Scholarship)*

Purpose: To enhance the professional development of individuals in the field. **Focus:** Parks and Recreation. **Qualif.:** Applicants must be full-time undergraduate or graduate students in good standing who are enrolled in a professional degree program in parks and recreation or a related field. **Criteria:** Recipients are selected based on academic performance.

Funds Avail.: $500. **Number Awarded:** 4. **To Apply:** Applicants must submit: completed application form; a professional resume including education and employment history; letter of recommendation from current faculty member; and copy of their most recent transcript. **Deadline:** August 17. **Contact:** Vern Biaett at the above address (see entry 1222).

1224 ■ Michael A. Ramnes Professional Scholarships *(Professional Development/ Scholarship)*

Purpose: To enhance the professional development of individuals in the field. **Focus:** Parks and Recreation. **Qualif.:** Applicants must be professionals in parks and recreation or a related field; must demonstrate evidence of work in the parks and recreation profession; must attend a professional development meeting, training, school or conference; must have respect of his/her peers. **Criteria:** Recipients are selected based on demonstrated evidence of work in the parks and recreation profession.

Funds Avail.: $500. **To Apply:** Applicants must submit a completed application form and write a 500 word statement describing the purpose of the professional development proposal within the context of their goals and achievements. **Deadline:** August 17. **Contact:** 602-543-6617.

1225 ■ Arkansas Environmental Federation

1400 W Markham St., Ste. 302
Little Rock, AR 72201
Ph: (501)374-0263
Fax: (501)374-8752
URL: http://www.environmentark.org

1226 ■ Randall Matthis for Environmental Studies Scholarships *(Graduate, Undergraduate/ Scholarship)*

Purpose: To provide financial assistance for selected students from Arkansas universities. **Focus:** Environmental science; Health education; Natural resources. **Qualif.:** Applicants must be U.S. citizens residing in Arkansas and must be undergraduate or graduate students with at least 2.8 cumulative GPA based on 4.0 system. **Criteria:** Applicants are evaluated based on academic achievement and financial need.

Funds Avail.: $2,500. **To Apply:** Applicants must submit a completed application form along with current official transcript(s) and letters. **Deadline:** April 11.

1227 ■ Larry Wilson for Environmental Studies Scholarships *(Graduate, Undergraduate/ Scholarship)*

Purpose: To provide financial assistance for selected students from Arkansas universities. **Focus:** Environmental science. **Qualif.:** Applicants must be U.S. citizens residing in Arkansas; must be full-time undergraduate or graduate students at the time of application and in the year scholarship is awarded; must have a minimum of 2.8 cumulative grade point average based of 4.0 scale; and must be nominated by a faculty member. **Criteria:** Applicants are evaluated based on scholastic and personal attributes.

Funds Avail.: No specific amount. **To Apply:** Applicants must submit a completed application form along with current official transcript(s) and letters. **Deadline:** April 11.

1228 ■ Larry Wilson Scholarships for Undergraduate Civil Engineering Students *(Undergraduate/Scholarship)*

Purpose: To provide financial assistance for selected students from Arkansas universities. **Focus:** Engineering, Civil. **Qualif.:** Applicants must be U.S. citizens who are residents of Arkansas; must be undergraduate students who have Civil Engineering as a degree goal; must be full-time students at time of application and for year scholarship is awarded; must have a minimum of 2.8 cumulative grade point average based on 4.0 system; and must be nominated by a faculty member. **Criteria:** Applicants are evaluated based on academic achievement and financial need.

Funds Avail.: No specific amount. **To Apply:** Applicants must submit a completed application form along with current official transcript(s) and letters. **Deadline:** April 11.

1229 ■ Arkansas Nurses Association

1123 S University, Ste. 1015
Little Rock, AR 72204
Ph: (501)244-2363
E-mail: arna@arna.org
URL: http://www.arna.org

1230 ■ Arkansas Nursing Foundation - Dorothea Funk Scholarships *(Professional Development/ Scholarship)*

Purpose: To provide financial assistance to nurses throughout the state of Arkansas. **Focus:** Nursing. **Qualif.:** Applicant must: be a registered nurse; give a statement of commitment to community health nursing; be seeking a degree to become an advanced practice nurse; demonstrate need. **Criteria:** Selection will be based on the committee's criteria.

Funds Avail.: No specific amount. **To Apply:** Applicants must complete the application packet and must include the following: completed application form; cover letter stating desire for the scholarship and intended use of funds (including a statement regarding other financial assistance); statement regarding institutional financial assistance toward the planned degree (tuition waivers or reductions); current resume (one page including education, work experience, achievements, and honors, if applicable); two letters of recommendation (with one being from current supervisor or faculty) including information concerning leadership and academic ability of the applicant; official undergraduate and graduate transcript(s) from all nursing programs attended (in sealed envelope with Registrar's signature or stamp on flap); letter of acceptance into degree program accredited by NLNAC or CCNE; and extracurricular activities (achievements, organization memberships, volunteer work). **Deadline:** June 1. **Contact:** Arkansas Nursing Foundation c/o Arkansas Nurses Association at the above address (see entry 1229).

1231 ■ Arkansas Nursing Foundation - Mary Gray Scholarships *(Professional Development/ Scholarship)*

Purpose: To provide financial assistance to nurses throughout the state of Arkansas. **Focus:** Nursing. **Qualif.:** Applicant must be: a registered nurse; seeking an advanced degree in nursing; interested and/or involved in advanced practice nursing (Advance Nurse Practitioner, Clinical Nurse Specialist, Certified Nurse Midwife, and Certified Nurse Anesthetist). **Criteria:** Selection will be based on the committee's criteria.

Funds Avail.: No specific amount. **To Apply:** Applicants must complete the application packet and must include the following: completed application form; cover letter stating desire for the scholarship and intended use of funds (including a statement regarding other financial assistance); statement regarding institutional financial assistance toward the planned degree (tuition waivers or reductions); current resume (one page including education, work experience, achievements, and honors, if applicable); two letters of recommendation (with one being from current supervisor or faculty) including information concerning leadership and academic ability of the applicant; official undergraduate and graduate transcript(s) from all nursing programs attended (in sealed envelope with Registrar's signature or stamp on flap); letter of acceptance into degree program accredited by NLNAC or CCNE; and extracurricular activities (achievements, organization memberships, volunteer work). **Deadline:** June 1. **Contact:** Arkansas Nursing Foundation c/o Arkansas Nurses Association at the above address (see entry 1229).

1232 ■ Arkansas Public Health Association

4815 W Marketing St., Slot 52
Little Rock, AR 72205
Ph: (501)661-2392
E-mail: catherine.tapp@arkansas.gov
URL: http://www.arkpublichealth.org

1233 ■ Arkansas Public Health Association Scholarships *(Undergraduate/Scholarship)*

Purpose: To provide financial support to Arkansas students. **Focus:** Public health. **Qualif.:** Applicants must be an Arkansas resident; must be enrolled, or have plans to enroll, in a field of public health; must be currently classified as at least a sophomore in college, university or approved Vo-Tech; must have at least 2.5 GPA; must demonstrate financial need. **Criteria:** Applicants will be judged based on the following criteria: (a) GPA; (b) Goals in public health; (c) Honors, organizations, volunteering with health-related organizations; (d) Letter from major professor; (e) Personal reference letter; (f) Present or past public health experience; (f) Full-time student; (g) Part-time student; (h) Financial need.

Funds Avail.: $500-$1,000. **To Apply:** Application forms are available online. Applicants must submit official college, university, or Vo-Tech transcripts; must have a letter of recommendation from major professor; must have a letter of personal reference; must have a statement/explanation of financial need; must have an explanation in 150 words or less concerning their goals and plans with the scholarship, their past and present public health experiences. Application form and other requirements must be sent to 447 W Gaines Monticello, AR 71655. **Deadline:** March 16.

1234 ■ Arkansas Society of Professional Sanitarians Scholarships *(Undergraduate/ Scholarship)*

Purpose: To support Arkansas students. **Focus:** Environmental technology. **Qualif.:** Applicant must be Arkansas resident; must be enrolled, or have plans to enroll, in an environmental fieid; must be a sophomore student; must have at least a 2.5 GPA; must demonstrate financial need. **Criteria:** Selection of applicants will be based on the criteria of the ASPS Scholarship Committee.

Funds Avail.: $250-$500. **To Apply:** Application forms are available online. Application form must be sent to Rebecca Wright, Scholarship Chairman, 1195 N Charley's Loop, Camden, AR 71701. **Deadline:** April 11.

1235 ■ Armed Forces Communications and Electronics Association

4400 Fair Lakes Court
Fairfax, VA 22033
Ph: (703)631-6141
Fax: (703)631-4693
Free: 800-336-4583
URL: http://www.afcea.org

1236 ■ AFCEA Distance Learning/Online Scholarships *(Undergraduate/Scholarship)*

Purpose: To provide scholarship for the general public. **Focus:** Engineering; Mathematics; Physics; Communications; Electronics. **Qualif.:** Applicants must be U.S. citizens currently enrolled full time pursuing either a Bachelor of Science or Master's of Science degree through distance learning or online program (only a few second-year students only will be accepted). **Criteria:** Primary consideration will be given for academic excellence.

Funds Avail.: $1,500. **To Apply:** Applicants may apply online at AFFECT website. Applicants must also submit two letters of recommendation printed in school stationery and with signature from field-of-study professors. **Deadline:** June 1. **Contact:** Norma Corrales; 703-631-6149.

1237 ■ AFCEA Fellowships *(Doctorate, Graduate/ Fellowship)*

Purpose: To support the development of engineers and technical personnel. **Focus:** Engineering; Physics; Mathematics; Electronics. **Qualif.:** Candidates must be US citizens with Bachelor of Science and Master of Science degree; must be currently enrolled in a doctoral program at any accredited university in the United States. **Criteria:** Selection will be based on the submitted thesis.

Funds Avail.: No specific amount. **To Apply:** Applicants may apply online at AFCEA website. **Deadline:** February 15. **Contact:** Norma Corrales; 703-631-6149.

1238 ■ AFCEA General John A. Wickham Scholarships *(Undergraduate/Scholarship)*

Purpose: To provide scholarship to the general public. **Focus:** Engineering; Mathematics; Physics; Communications; Electronics. **Qualif.:** Applicants must be US citizens; must have GPA of 3.5 on 4.0 scale. **Criteria:** Recipients are selected based on the committee's criteria.

Funds Avail.: $2,000. **To Apply:** Applicants may apply at AFCEA web site. Applicants must also submit two letters of recommendation printed in school stationery and with signature from field-of-study professors. **Deadline:** May 1. **Contact:** Norma Corrales; 703-631-6149.

1239 ■ AFCEA Math and Science Teachers Scholarships *(Graduate/Scholarship)*

Purpose: To promote science, mathematics or information technology education at the US Secondary School. **Focus:** Science; Mathematics. **Qualif.:** Applicants must be degree seeking candidates; must be enrolled full time in an education curriculum of accredited college or university in the United States; must be U.S. citizens; and must be at least sophomores or juniors at the time of application (only a few second-year students only). For graduating students: at least two classes per semester are required. **Criteria:** Recipients are selected based on committee's review of eligibility and other criteria.

Funds Avail.: No specific amount. **To Apply:** Applicants may apply online. Applicants must also submit transcript issued by the school Registrar's Office; and two letters of recommendation from relevant faculty. If currently employed as a teacher, one additional letter from the school principal. Additional documents may be provided (optional). **Deadline:** June 1. **Contact:** Norma Corrales; 703-631-6149.

1240 ■ AFCEA Scholarship for Working Professionals *(Graduate/Scholarship)*

Purpose: To provide scholarship to those students pursuing an undergraduate or graduate degree while employed. **Focus:** Engineering; Mathematics; Physics; Communications. **Qualif.:** Applicants must be US citizens attending an accredited college or university in the United States as either a traditional or distance learning students, and majoring in electrical, chemical, systems or aerospace engineering; mathematics; physics; technical management; computer information systems; computer science or related fields; and must have an overall GPA of 3.4. For graduates, must have completed at least two postgraduate-level courses and are enrolled in an eligible degree-granting master's degree program. **Criteria:** Recipients are selected based on committee's review of applications.

Funds Avail.: $1,500. **To Apply:** Applicants may apply online at the AFCEA web site. **Deadline:** September 1. **Contact:** Norma Corrales; 703-631-6149.

1241 ■ William E. "Buck" Bragunier Scholarships *(Undergraduate/Scholarship)*

Purpose: To provide scholarship for the general public. **Focus:** Engineering; Mathematics; Physics; Communications; Electronics. **Qualif.:** Applicants must be at least second year college students; must be enrolled full time as sophomores or juniors at the time of application; must have an outstanding record of demonstrated leadership within university or local community. **Criteria:** Primary consideration will be given for academic excellence.

Funds Avail.: $2,000. **To Apply:** Applicants may apply online at AFFECT website. Applicants must also submit two letters of recommendation printed in school stationery and with signature from field-of-study professors. **Deadline:** May 1. **Contact:** Norma Corrales; 703-631-6149.

1242 ■ LT.G. Douglas D. Buchholz Memorial Scholarships *(Undergraduate/Scholarship)*

Purpose: To provide scholarships to students connected to the US Military. **Focus:** Engineering; Mathematics; Physics; Communications. **Qualif.:** Applicants must be currently active enlisted soldiers assigned to Fort Gordon, Georgia; must have completed a minimum of 15 semester hours/25 quarter hours; must be currently enrolled either full or part time in an accredited US college; and must have a minimum GPA of 2.5 on a 4.0 scale. **Criteria:** Recipients are selected based on recommendation of Scholarship Board under the guidance of the Fort Gordon Command Sergeant Major.

Funds Avail.: $2,000. **To Apply:** Students may apply online at the AFCEA web site. **Deadline:** November 15. **Contact:** Mr. Joseph S. Yavorsky, President; president@afcea-augusta.org.

1243 ■ Milton E. Cooper/Young AFCEAN Graduate Scholarships *(Graduate/Scholarship)*

Purpose: To support local chapters and promote education. **Focus:** Electronics; Communication. **Qualif.:** Applicants must be US citizens and young professionals currently employed in a field related to communications, computer science or electronics; must demonstrate strong commitment to the pursuit of advanced college degree (M.S. or Ph.D.) related to communications, computer science, electronics, electrical or systems engineering in preparation for a career in science or engineering; must have GPA of 3.2 or higher; must be currently enrolled in an accredited university or college in the United States. **Criteria:** Recipients are selected based on scholarship committee's review of application materials.

Funds Avail.: $3,000. **To Apply:** Applicants must submit three letters of recommendation with at least one from current employer; and official college transcript reflecting all college-level work. **Deadline:** March 15. **Contact:** Luanne M. Balestrucci; D&S PO Box 7259 Freehold, NJ 07728; lmbalestrucci@dsci-usa.com.

1244 ■ Disabled War Veterans Scholarships *(Undergraduate/Scholarship)*

Purpose: To provide educational incentives, opportunities and assistance for people engaged in information management, communications and intelligence efforts and fostering excellence in education particularly in the "hard science" disciplines related to C4ISR. **Focus:** Engineering; Mathematics; Physics; Communications. **Qualif.:** Applicants must be currently enrolled and attending either a two year or four year in an accredited college or university in the United States; must be enrolled in an accredited distance learning or online degree granting program affiliated with major, accredited two year or four year college or university in the United States. **Criteria:** Recipients are selected based on academic excellence, leadership and financial need.

Funds Avail.: $2,500. **To Apply:** Applicants may apply online at AFFECT website. Applicants must also submit two letters of recommendation printed on school stationery and with signature from field-of-study professors. **Deadline:** November 1. **Contact:** Norma Corrales; 703-631-6149.

1245 ■ Lockheed Martin IT Scholarships *(Undergraduate/Scholarship)*

Purpose: To provide scholarship to the general public. **Focus:** Engineering; Mathematics; Physics; Communications. **Qualif.:** Applicants must be at least second year college students, must be enrolled full time as sophomores or juniors at the time of application. **Criteria:** Recipients are selected based from the qualified General Wickham Scholarship applicants.

Funds Avail.: $3,000. **To Apply:** Applicants may apply online. Applicants must also submit two letters of recommendation printed in school stationery and with signature from field-of-study professors; and official transcript of all college level study. **Deadline:** May 1. **Contact:** Norma Corrales; 703-631-6149.

1246 ■ Lockheed Martin Graduate Scholarships *(Graduate/Scholarship)*

Purpose: To provide scholarships to postgraduate students. **Focus:** Engineering; Mathematics; Physics; Communications. **Qualif.:** Applicants must be US citizens currently enrolled full time in a master's degree program in the following or related fields of electrical, chemical, computer or systems engineering; physics; mathematics; computer science; computer technology; communications technology; communications engineering; technology management; or information management systems. **Criteria:** Recipients are selected based on academic excellence.

Funds Avail.: $3,000. **To Apply:** Applicants may apply online at the AFCEA web site. **Deadline:** January 1. **Contact:** Norma Corrales; 703-631-6149.

1247 ■ AFCEA General Emmett Paige Scholarships *(Undergraduate/Scholarship)*

Purpose: To provide scholarships to students connected to the US Military. **Focus:** Engineering; Mathematics; Physics; Communications. **Qualif.:** Applicants must be US citizens; must have a minimum GPA of 3.0 on 4.0 scale. **Criteria:** Recipients are selected based on committee's review of applications.

Funds Avail.: $2,000. **To Apply:** Applicants may apply online at the AFCEA web site. Applicants must also submit a copy of Certificate of Service, Discharge From DD214, or facsimile of current Department of Defense or Coast Guard Identification Card; and two letters of recommendation printed in school stationery and with signature from field-of-study professors. **Deadline:** March 1. **Contact:** Norma Corrales; 703-631-6149.

1248 ■ Ralph W. Shrader Diversity Scholarships *(Graduate/Scholarship)*

Purpose: To provide educational opportunities for talented individuals pursuing advanced degrees at the master's level. **Focus:** General Studies. **Qualif.:** Applicants must be US citizens currently enrolled full time in a master's degree program in an accredited university in the United States. **Criteria:** Recipients are selected based on academic excellence.

Funds Avail.: $3,000. **To Apply:** Applicants may apply online at the AFCEA web site. **Deadline:** March 1. **Contact:** Norma Corrales; 703-631-6149.

Awards are arranged alphabetically below their administering organizations

1249 ■ Vice Adm. Jerry O. Tuttle, USN (Ret.) and Mrs. Barbara A. Tuttle Science and Technology Scholarships *(Undergraduate/Scholarship)*

Purpose: To support students working full time. **Focus:** Engineering; Computer and Information Sciences. **Qualif.:** Applicants must be U.S. citizens enrolled full time with majoring in technology; and must be sophomores and juniors at the time of application. **Criteria:** Recipients are selected are based on the committee's review of application materials.

Funds Avail.: $2,000. **To Apply:** Applicants may apply online. Applicants must also submit two letters of recommendation printed in school stationery and with signature from field-of-study professors; and official transcript of all college level study. **Deadline:** November 1. **Contact:** Norma Corrales; 703-631-6149.

1250 ■ Veterans of Enduring Freedom (Afghanistan) and Iraqi Freedom Scholarships *(Undergraduate/Scholarship)*

Purpose: To provide scholarships to students connected to the US military. **Focus:** Engineering; Mathematics; Physics; Communications. **Qualif.:** Applicants must be currently enrolled and attending either a two year accredited college or university in the United States. **Criteria:** Recipients are selected based on the committee's review of application.

Funds Avail.: $2,500. **To Apply:** Applicants may apply online at AFCEA web site. **Deadline:** April 1 and November 1.

Remarks: The AFCEA Educational Foundation is pleased to co-sponsor this scholarship opportunity for U.S. War Veterans. **Contact:** Norma Corrales 703-631-6149.

1251 ■ Marine Corps Sgt. Jeannette L. Winters Memorial Scholarships *(Undergraduate/Scholarship)*

Purpose: To provide scholarships to students connected with the US Military. **Focus:** Engineering; Mathematics; Physics; Communications. **Qualif.:** Applicants must be enrolled full time in a Bachelor of Science degree program in accredited colleges or universities in the United States; and must have a minimum GPA of 3.0 on 4.0 scale. Majors directly related to the support of US Intelligence enterprises or national security with relevance to the mission of AFCEA are also eligible. **Criteria:** Recipients are selected based on academic performance.

Funds Avail.: $2,000. **To Apply:** Applicants may apply online at the AFCEA web site. Applicants must also submit two letters of recommendation printed in school stationery and with signature from field-of-study professors. **Deadline:** September 1. **Contact:** Norma Corrales; 703-631-6149.

1252 ■ Armenian Educational Foundation

600 W Broadway, Ste. 130
Glendale, CA 91204
Ph: (818)242-4154
E-mail: aef@aefweb.org
URL: http://www.instantweb.com/a/aef

1253 ■ Richard R. Tufenkian Memorial Scholarships *(Undergraduate/Scholarship)*

Purpose: To provide financial support to qualified students of Armenian parentage. **Focus:** General studies. **Qualif.:** Applicants should have Armenian origin; have a 3.0 GPA; and be an undergraduate student. **Criteria:** Awards are given based on academic merit; financial need.

Funds Avail.: $2000. **Number Awarded:** 5. **To Apply:** Applicants must submit an application form; proof of acceptance to the university or college; first two pages of income return of the applicant and parents of previous year; sealed official transcript; a letter of reference from university or college and from Armenian community service; and an essay. **Deadline:** July 30.

1254 ■ Armenian General Benevolent Union

55 E 59th St.
New York, NY 10022-1112
Ph: (212)319-6383
Fax: (212)319-6507
E-mail: agbuwb@agbu.org
URL: http://www.agbu.org

1255 ■ AGBU Scholarships *(Graduate/Loan)*

Purpose: To support the higher education of students of Armenian descent. **Focus:** Communications; Educational administration; Public administration; International affairs and relations; Armenian studies; Law; Medicine. **Qualif.:** Applicant must be a full-time graduate student of Armenian descent; must be a U.S. resident or citizen; and must be enrolled in a competitive college or university in the United States. **Criteria:** Awards are given based on merit.

Funds Avail.: $2,500-$7,500. **To Apply:** Applicants must submit a completed application form with two letters of recommendation; undergraduate/graduate transcript; copy of acceptance letter from the university; copy of Student Aid Report; copy of Financial Awards Letter or a copy of latest filed Federal Tax Return (Form 1040); resume; copies of published work; and a photograph. **Deadline:** April 1.

Remarks: Students must start repayment of their loans one year after graduating or leaving school.

1256 ■ Armenian Professional Society

PO Box 10306
Glendale, CA 91209
Ph: (818)685-9946
E-mail: apsla@apsla.org
URL: http://www.apsla.org

1257 ■ Armenian Professional Society Scholarship Fund *(Graduate/Scholarship)*

Purpose: To provide financial assistance for the advancement of education. **Focus:** General studies. **Qualif.:** Applicants must be students who have been accepted or enrolled in a graduate school in the United States. **Criteria:** Recipients are selected based on financial need, scholastic achievements, faculty recommendations and involvement in the Armenian Community.

Funds Avail.: No amount mentioned. **To Apply:** Applicants must submit print out of the scholarship application form (in portrait format - neatly typed requested information) along with the official transcripts for the past four years; brief one-page essay about him/her self, his/her involvement in the Armenian community and why he/she thinks he/she should be a scholarship recipient; copies of applicant's and parent's most recent IRS Tax Returns or equivalent financial information; and the obtained two college or university recommendations. **Deadline:** September 1.

1258 ■ Armenian Relief Society - Eastern United States

80 Bigelow Avenue, Ste. 200
Watertown, MA 02472

Awards are arranged alphabetically below their administering organizations

Ph: (617)926-3801
Fax: (617)924-7238
E-mail: arseastus@aol.com
URL: http://www.arseastus.com

1259 ■ ARS Undergraduate Scholarships *(Four Year College, Two Year College, Undergraduate/ Scholarship)*

Purpose: To encourage educational pursuits among undergraduate students of Armenian descent. **Focus:** Law; History; Political science; Journalism; Government; Economics; Business administration; Medicine; Public service. **Qualif.:** Applicants must be of Armenian descent; must be undergraduate students who have completed at least one semester at an accredited four-year college or university in the United States or must be enrolled in a two-year college and are transferring to a four-year college or university as a full-time student in the Fall. **Criteria:** Grants are made on the basis of financial need, merit and involvement in the Armenian community.

Funds Avail.: No specific amount. **To Apply:** Application must include financial aid forms, recent official transcript, two letters of recommendation and tuition costs. Forward materials to: Scholarship Committee, Armenian Relief Society of Eastern USA, Inc., 80 Bigelow Ave., Ste. 200, Watertown, MA 02472. **Deadline:** April 1.

1260 ■ Lazarian Graduate Scholarships *(Graduate/Scholarship)*

Purpose: To encourage educational pursuits among undergraduate students of Armenian descent. **Focus:** General Studies. **Qualif.:** Applicants must be of Armenian descent; must pursue their studies at the graduate level (Master's Degree or Doctorate) in the fields of law, history, political science, international relations, journalism, government, economics, business administration, medicine, and public service. **Criteria:** Grants are made on the basis of financial need, merit and involvement in the Armenian community.

Funds Avail.: No specific amount. **To Apply:** Application package must include official transcript of college grades with raised seal, tuition costs, applicant's most recent Income Tax Return, three letters of recommendation and proof of acceptance into a graduate program. Forward to: Lazarian Scholarship Committee, Armenian Relief Society of Eastern USA, Inc., 80 Bigelow Ave., Ste. 200, Watertown, MA 02472. Application forms and instructions are available at the website. **Deadline:** April 1.

1261 ■ Armenian Scholarship Foundation

14 Sandrick Rd.
Belmont, MA 02478
E-mail: leon@armenianscholarships.org
URL: http://www.armenianscholarships.org

1262 ■ Armenian Scholarship Foundation Scholarships *(Graduate, Undergraduate/ Scholarship)*

Purpose: To support the education of Armenian students in the U.S. **Focus:** General studies. **Qualif.:** Applicant must be an Armenian student living in the U.S. and attending an undergraduate or graduate program in the U.S.; must demonstrate financial need and merit. **Criteria:** Awards are given based on merit and need.

Funds Avail.: $750. **Number Awarded:** 2. **To Apply:** Applicants must submit: completed scholarship application form; high school or college official or unofficial transcript; an essay; and letters of recommendation (must be in a sealed envelope, signed by the recommender, included inside the application packet). **Deadline:** May 15.

1263 ■ Leon and Talin Barsoumian Scholarships *(Graduate, Undergraduate/Scholarship)*

Purpose: To support the education of Armenian students in the U.S. **Focus:** General studies. **Qualif.:** Applicant must be an Armenian student living in the U.S. and attending an undergraduate or graduate program in the U.S. who demonstrates financial need and merit. **Criteria:** Awards are given based on merit and need.

Funds Avail.: $500. **Number Awarded:** 1. **To Apply:** Applicants must submit: completed scholarship application form; high school or college official or unofficial transcript; an essay; and letters of recommendation (must be in a sealed envelope, signed by the recommender, included inside the application packet). **Deadline:** May 15.

Remarks: Named after ASF president and his wife.

1264 ■ Norair M. Kebabjian Memorial Scholarships *(Undergraduate/Scholarship)*

Purpose: To support the education of Armenian students in the U.S. **Focus:** General studies. **Qualif.:** Applicant must be an Armenian student living in the U.S. and attending an undergraduate program in the U.S.; must demonstrate financial need and merit. **Criteria:** Awards are given based on merit and need.

Funds Avail.: $500. **Number Awarded:** 1. **To Apply:** Applicants must submit: completed scholarship application form; high school or college official or unofficial transcript; an essay; and letters of recommendation (must be in a sealed envelope, signed by the recommender, included inside the application packet). **Deadline:** May 15.

1265 ■ Armenian Students' Association of America

333 Atlantic Ave.
Warwick, RI 02888
Ph: (401)461-6114
E-mail: asa@asainc.org
URL: http://www.asainc.org

1266 ■ Armenian American Citizen's League Scholarships *(Undergraduate/Scholarship)*

Purpose: To provide financial assistance to those students who are in need. **Focus:** General Studies. **Qualif.:** Applicants must be permanent residents of the United States who have been living in California for at least two years and are enrolled full-time in an accredited college or university; minimum GPA of 3.0 (B average) is required. **Criteria:** Awards will be based on financial need, academic achievement and involvement in school and community services.

Funds Avail.: $500-$1,500. **To Apply:** Applicants must check the available website for the required materials. **Deadline:** February 1. **Contact:** For more information, contact: Mrs. Dorothy Deradoorian. Co-Chairperson Educational and Scholarship Fund; P.O. Box 14, Moorpark, CA 93020-0014

1267 ■ Armenian American Medical Association Scholarships *(Undergraduate/Scholarship)*

Purpose: To provide financial assistance to those students who are in need. **Focus:** Medicine. **Qualif.:** Applicants must

Awards are arranged alphabetically below their administering organizations

be students enrolled in a U.S. medical school. Award is primarily intended for students residing and studying in a private New England medical school. **Criteria:** Awards granted on the basis of need, merit and involvement in Armenian cultural affairs.

Funds Avail.: $1,000-2,000. **Number Awarded:** 3. **To Apply:** Applicants must check the available website for the required materials. **Deadline:** September 15; October 30. **Contact:** For more information, please contact Dr. Edward Karian, Chairperson; 324 Common St. Watertown, MA 02472-4940

1268 ■ Armenian American Pharmacists' Association Scholarships *(Doctorate, Graduate/Scholarship)*

Purpose: To provide financial support to those students who are pursuing pharmacy. **Focus:** Pharmacy. **Qualif.:** Applicants must be students of Armenian descent, pursuing a baccalaureate of pharmacy, doctor of pharmacy, or graduate degree program at a College of Pharmacy in the commonwealth of Massachusetts, Connecticut or Rhode Island. **Criteria:** Awards will be based on academic excellence and financial need.

Funds Avail.: No specific amount. **To Apply:** Applicants must check the available website for the required materials. **Deadline:** September 15. **Contact:** For inquiries, please contact: Susan A. Krikorian, Chairman of Scholarship Committee; Department of Pharmacy Practice 179 Longwood Avenue, Boston, MA 02115

1269 ■ Armenian General Athletic Union Scholarships *(Undergraduate/Scholarship)*

Purpose: To provide financial assistance to those students who are in need. **Focus:** General Studies. **Qualif.:** Applicants must be high school students entering college; must be permanent U.S residents. **Criteria:** Awards will be based on academic merit and financial need.

Funds Avail.: $1,000. **To Apply:** Applicants must check the available website for the required materials. **Deadline:** May 15. **Contact:** Mrs. Ann Ajemian at 211 Grand Boulevard, Emerson, NJ 07630-1170.

1270 ■ Armenian Relief Society Scholarships *(Graduate, Undergraduate/Scholarship)*

Purpose: To provide financial assistance to those students who are in need. **Focus:** General Studies. **Qualif.:** Applicants must be undergraduate or graduate students in a four-year college or university. **Criteria:** Awards will be based on academic merit, financial need and involvement in Armenian community.

Funds Avail.: No specific amount. **To Apply:** Applicants must check the available website for the required materials. **Contact:** For more information, please contact: Mr. Sonanz Papazian at 617-926-02472.

1271 ■ Michael M. Assarian Scholarships *(Undergraduate/Scholarship)*

Purpose: To provide financial assistance to those students who are in need. **Focus:** General studies. **Qualif.:** Applicants must be full-time students of Armenian descent enrolled at Wayne State University. **Criteria:** Selection of scholars will be based on scholastic achievement, extracurricular activities and financial need.

Funds Avail.: No specific amount. **To Apply:** Applicants must check the available website for the required materials. **Deadline:** April 29. **Contact:** Private Scholarship Coordinator Office of Scholarships and Financial Aid Detroit, MI 48202; Tel: 313-577-4969

1272 ■ John M. Azarian Memorial Armenian Youth Scholarships Fund *(Undergraduate/Scholarship)*

Purpose: To provide financial assistance to those students who are in need. **Focus:** General Studies. **Qualif.:** Applicants must be full time enrolled in an accredited college or university; must be permanent residents of the United States. **Criteria:** Awards will be based on financial need, academic merit and involvement in the Armenian community.

Funds Avail.: $500-$3,000. **To Apply:** Applicants must submit a completed application form and two letters of reference. **Deadline:** May 1. **Contact:** Mr. John M. Azarian, Jr. c/o Azarian Management and Development Company at 6 Prospect Street, Suite 1B, Midland Park, NJ 07432.

1273 ■ Hagop Bogigian Scholarship Fund *(Undergraduate/Scholarship)*

Purpose: To provide financial assistance to those students who are in need. **Focus:** General studies. **Qualif.:** Applicants must be students of Armenian descent who are enrolled in a four-year Bachelor of Arts degree program at Mt. Holyoke College; must maintain over a 3.0 GPA, and demonstrate financial need. **Criteria:** Priority will be given to those students with financial need.

Funds Avail.: No specific amount. **To Apply:** Applicants should apply directly to the financial aid office for financial aid and should indicate on the form that they are of Armenian descent. **Deadline:** March 1. **Contact:** Mt. Holyoke College Financial Aid Office, South Hadley, MA 01075 Tel: 413-538-2457.

1274 ■ Armen H. Bululian Scholarships *(Undergraduate/Scholarship)*

Purpose: To provide financial assistance to those students who are in need. **Focus:** General Studies. **Qualif.:** Applicants must be graduating high school seniors or enrolled full-time undergraduate students in an accredited college or university; must be residents of Monmouth or Ocean Counties in New Jersey. **Criteria:** Awards will be based on academic excellence and involvement in community services.

Funds Avail.: $1,000. **To Apply:** Applicants must check the available website for the required materials. **Deadline:** June 30. **Contact:** For more information, Please contact: Mr. Harout Karakashian at 1184 Ocean Avenue, Elberon, NJ 07740.

1275 ■ Constantinople Armenian Relief Society (C.A.R.S.) Scholarships *(Undergraduate/Scholarship)*

Purpose: To provide financial assistance to those students who are in need. **Focus:** General studies. **Qualif.:** Applicants must be undergraduate students of Armenian descent; must have a minimum of 3.0 GPA; must be attending college in or residing in the NY/NJ area. **Criteria:** Preference will be based on criteria.

Funds Avail.: $400-$600. **Number Awarded:** 20. **To Apply:** Applicants must check the available website for the required materials. **Deadline:** June 30. **Contact:** For inquiries, please contact: Talin Sesetyan CARS Scholarship Committee at PO Box 769 Times Square Station New York, NY 10108 e-mail: talins11@hotmail.com

Awards are arranged alphabetically below their administering organizations

1276 ■ Karekin DerAvedision Memorial Endowment Fund *(Undergraduate/Scholarship)*

Purpose: To provide financial assistance to those who are in need. **Focus:** Armenian Studies. **Qualif.:** Applicants must be graduate students in Armenian Studies who has been accepted for admission to UCLA. **Criteria:** Preference will be given to those students who are in need.

Funds Avail.: Maximum of $8,000. **To Apply:** Applicants must check the available website for the required materials. **Deadline:** December 15. **Contact:** UCLA Graduate Division Special; Fellowship Office 1252 Murphy Hall Box 951419 Los Angeles, CA 90095-1419 Tel: (310) 825-3521

1277 ■ George & Isabelle Elanjian Scholarships *(Undergraduate/Scholarship)*

Purpose: To provide financial assistance to those students who are in need. **Focus:** General Studies. **Qualif.:** Applicants must be incoming freshmen students or enrolled for at least one year at the University of Michigan-Dearborn. **Criteria:** Preference will be given to those who meet the criteria.

Funds Avail.: $700 for tuition to one incoming first year student; $2,000 for one continuing upper-class student. **Number Awarded:** 2. **To Apply:** Applicants must be incoming students and should apply to the UM-D Admissions Office and upperclassmen should apply to the UM-D Financial Aid Office. Applicants must check the available website for the required materials. **Deadline:** February 1. **Contact:** Armenian Students' Association of America at the above address (see entry 1265).

1278 ■ Emmanuel Bible College Scholarships *(Undergraduate/Scholarship)*

Purpose: To provide financial support to those students who are in need. **Focus:** Religious Education. **Qualif.:** Applicants must be willing to pledge to work as a minister, evangelist, missionary, or youth director after graduation; must study in one of the institutions of Emmanuel Bible College. **Criteria:** Awards will be based on merit and good character.

Funds Avail.: No specific amount. **To Apply:** Applicants must check the contact information for inquiries. **Deadline:** June 30. **Contact:** Dr. Yeghia Babikian, Director; 1605 East Elizabeth Street, Pasadena, CA 91104 Fax: 818-398-2424 Tel: 818-791-2575.

1279 ■ Garikian Scholarship Fund *(Undergraduate/Scholarship)*

Purpose: To provide financial assistance to those students who are in need. **Focus:** Armenian Studies; Sociology; Psychology; Political Science; Middle Eastern History; Journalism; Education; Music. **Qualif.:** Applicants must have completed their first academic year in college or university in California; must be pursuing one of the above field of studies. **Criteria:** Preference will be given to those who meet the criteria.

Funds Avail.: $750-$1,000. **To Apply:** Applicants must apply to the Executive Board for application forms and return them, completed, before the deadline. **Deadline:** August 31. **Contact:** Berj S. Baghdoyan c/o Western Prelacy at 4401 Russell Avenue, Los Angeles, CA 90027.

1280 ■ Hai Guin Scholarships Association *(Undergraduate/Scholarship)*

Purpose: To provide financial assistance to those students who are in need. **Focus:** General Studies. **Qualif.:** Applicants must be students of Armenian descent, must reside in and attend school in Massachusetts. **Criteria:** Preference will be granted to a college student who has completed the first semester of freshman year; selection based on scholarship achievement and financial need.

Funds Avail.: $1,000. **To Apply:** Applicants must check the available website for the required materials. **Deadline:** October 25. **Contact:** For inquiries, please contact: Hasmig Maserjian (Scholarship Chairperson) at P.O. Box 509, Belmont, MA 02478.

1281 ■ Calouste Gulbenkian Foundation Scholarships *(Graduate, Undergraduate/Scholarship)*

Purpose: To provide financial assistance to those students who are in need. **Focus:** General Studies. **Qualif.:** Applicants must be sophomores or above who are enrolled full-time in an accredited college or university. **Criteria:** Awards will be based on academic merit and financial need; preference will be given to those applicants whose immediate family has not previously received a scholarship.

Funds Avail.: No specific amount. **To Apply:** Applicants must check the available website for the required materials. **Deadline:** Between February 15 and April 1.

Remarks: Calouste Sarkis Gulbenkian was an Armenian businessman and philanthropist, he played a major role in making the petroleum reserves of the Middle East available to Western development. By the end of his life he had become one of the world's wealthiest individuals and his art acquisitions are considered one of the greatest private collections. **Contact:** Department of Armenian Communities Avenida de Berna 45-A, P-1067 Lisboa Codex, Portugal; Fax: 351-793-4080.

1282 ■ Sophia Hagopian Memorial Fund *(Undergraduate/Scholarship)*

Purpose: To help those students who demonstrate extreme financial need. **Focus:** General Studies. **Qualif.:** Applicants must be students of Armenian descent demonstrating financial need; must provide service to the community by being involved in Armenian organizations and/or activities; and must be full-time students in their junior or senior year of undergraduate studies at an accredited California college or university. **Criteria:** Awards will be given to those who demonstrate financial need.

Funds Avail.: $2,000. **Number Awarded:** 6. **To Apply:** Applicants must check the available website for the required materials. **Deadline:** April 15. **Contact:** 600 West Broadway, Suite 130, Glendale, CA 91204 Tel: 818-242-4154.

1283 ■ Kaspar Hovannisian Memorial Scholarships *(Graduate/Scholarship)*

Purpose: To provide financial assistance to those students who are in need. **Focus:** General Studies. **Qualif.:** Applicants must be graduate students in the field of Armenian Studies. **Criteria:** Preference will be given to those studying Armenian History.

Funds Avail.: Up to $8,000. **To Apply:** Applicants must check the available website for the required materials. **Deadline:** December 15. **Contact:** Armenian Students' Association of America at the above address (see entry 1265).

1284 ■ Hirair and Anna Hovnanian Foundation Presidential Scholarships *(Undergraduate/Scholarship)*

Purpose: To provide financial assistance to those students who are in need. **Focus:** General Studies. **Qualif.:** Ap-

Awards are arranged alphabetically below their administering organizations

plicants must be students of Armenian ethnic origin who demonstrate financial need and outstanding academic achievements; must maintain a minimum 2.75 GPA. **Criteria:** Consideration is given to all students of Armenian descent who apply and meet Villanova University's general admissions requirements.

Funds Avail.: No specific amount. **To Apply:** Applicants must check the available website for the required materials. **Contact:** Villanova University; Office of Student Financial Assistance; 800 Lancaster Avenue, Villanova, PA 19085

1285 ■ Hirair and Anna Hovnanian Foundation Scholarships *(Undergraduate/Scholarship)*

Purpose: To provide financial assistance to those students who are in need. **Focus:** General Studies. **Qualif.:** Applicants must be full-time students enrolled at the Women's College at Georgian Court University, preferably of Armenian descent, who exhibit financial need. **Criteria:** Priority will be given to those who demonstrate financial need and with good academic standing.

Funds Avail.: No specific amount. **To Apply:** Applicants must check the contact information for inquiries. **Contact:** For more information please contact the Financial Aid Office of Georgian Court University at Tel: 908-364-2200, ext. 258

1286 ■ Rev. and Mrs. A.K. Jizmejian Educational Fund *(Undergraduate/Scholarship)*

Purpose: To provide financial assistance to those students who are in need. **Focus:** Theology. **Qualif.:** Applicants must be full-time theological seminary students and fourth-year undergraduate students who intend to continue their education in a theological seminary. **Criteria:** Preference will be given to those who meet the criteria.

Funds Avail.: $500-$1,500. **To Apply:** Applicants must check the available website for more information. **Deadline:** June 30. **Contact:** Armenian Evangelical Church; Mr. Mihran Jizmejian, Chairman 816-60 Pavane Linkway Don Mills, Ontario, M3C 1A2 Canada.

1287 ■ Knights of Vartan, Fresno Lodge No. 9 Scholarships *(Undergraduate/Scholarship)*

Purpose: To provide financial assistance to those students who are in need. **Focus:** Armenian Studies. **Qualif.:** Applicants must be new or continuing full-time students (12 units per semester) at Fresno State and maintain a 3.0 GPA or higher. **Criteria:** Scholarship will be given to those students who meet the criteria.

Funds Avail.: $750, one for an entering freshman and one for a continuing student at C.S.U.F. **Number Awarded:** 2. **To Apply:** Applicants must check the available website for the required materials. **Deadline:** November 1. **Contact:** Ms. Linda Tamura; Scholarship Coordinator; Tel: 209-278-6572

1288 ■ Mangasar M. Mangasarian Scholarship Fund *(Graduate/Scholarship)*

Purpose: To provide financial assistance to those students who are in need. **Focus:** General Studies. **Qualif.:** Applicants must be full-time graduate students of Armenian parentage attending the University of California, Berkley. Scholarship is also offered to international students of Armenian descent. **Criteria:** Preference will be given to those who meet the criteria.

Funds Avail.: $500-$3,000. **To Apply:** Applicants must check the available website for the required materials. **Contact:** Mr. Tony Bernez, Scholarship Director or Ms. Diana Bischey 210 Sproul Hall, Berkeley, CA 94720.

1289 ■ National Association for Armenian Studies and Research Scholarships *(Undergraduate/Scholarship)*

Purpose: To provide financial assistance to those students who are in need. **Focus:** General Studies. **Qualif.:** Applicants must be graduates or post-graduates doing research about Armenian Studies. **Criteria:** Selection will be based on criteria.

Funds Avail.: No specific amount. **To Apply:** Awards will be given to those who meet the criteria. **Contact:** For more information, please contact: Mr. Manoog S. Young, Chairman, Board of Directors; 395 Concord Avenue, Belmont, MA 02478 Fax: 617-484-1759 Tel: 617-489-1610.

1290 ■ St. James Armenian Church Memorial Scholarships *(Undergraduate/Scholarship)*

Purpose: To provide financial assistance to those students who are in need. **Focus:** General Studies. **Qualif.:** Applicants must be affiliated with St. James Armenian Church by being a graduate of the Sunday school, a Sunday school teacher, a church choir member for at least one year, or in some other way acceptable to the scholarship committee. **Criteria:** Scholarships are awarded on the basis of academic achievement, financial need, service to school, community and church and seriousness of purpose.

Funds Avail.: $250-$2,000. **To Apply:** Applicants must check the available website for the required materials. **Deadline:** April 1. **Contact:** Ms. Anita Assarian; 465 Mount Auburn Street, Watertown, MA 02172 Tel: 617-923-8860 Fax: 617-926-5503.

1291 ■ Hazaros Tabakoglu Scholarship Fund *(Undergraduate/Scholarship)*

Purpose: To provide financial assistance to those who are in need. **Focus:** General Studies. **Qualif.:** Applicants must be full-time undergraduates of Armenian descent who are or will be enrolled at colleges in the United States. **Criteria:** Preference will be given to those who meet the criteria.

Funds Avail.: $1,000-$5,000. **To Apply:** Applicants must check the available website for the required materials. **Deadline:** May 1. **Contact:** 2 Park Avenue, New York, NY 1016 Tel: 212-686-0010.

1292 ■ Aram Torossian Memorial Scholarships *(Undergraduate/Scholarship)*

Purpose: To provide financial assistance to those students who are in need. **Focus:** General studies. **Qualif.:** Applicant must be a full-time student of Armenian parentage attending the University of California, Berkley. **Criteria:** Preference will be given to those who meet the criteria.

Funds Avail.: $300-$3,000. **To Apply:** Applicants must check the available website for the required materials. **Contact:** Armenian Students' Association of America at the above address (see entry 1265).

1293 ■ Union of Marash Armenian Scholarships *(Graduate, Undergraduate/Scholarship)*

Purpose: To provide financial assistance to those students who are in need. **Focus:** General Studies. **Qualif.:** Applicants must be matriculated, full-time undergraduate or graduate students accepted at an accredited institution of higher education. Must demonstrate academic excellence; be of good moral character; be in financial need; and show

Awards are arranged alphabetically below their administering organizations

involvement in community; and must be a descendant of a Marashtsi (a part of Armenia/Asia Minor). **Criteria:** Preference will be given to those who meet the criteria.

Funds Avail.: $500-$1,000. **To Apply:** Applicants must check the available website for the required materials. **Contact:** Mrs. Siroon P. Shahinian, Ph.D.; Secretary, The Student Fund; One Sussex Road, Great Neck, NY 11020-1828.

1294 ■ Hurad Van Der Bedrosian Memorial Scholarships *(Graduate/Scholarship)*

Purpose: To provide financial assistance to those students who are in need. **Focus:** General Studies. **Qualif.:** Applicants must be graduate students in Armenian studies at universities with an established chair in the Armenian studies; applicants must be U.S citizens. **Criteria:** Preference will be given to those who meet the criteria.

Funds Avail.: $3,000. **Number Awarded:** 2. **To Apply:** Applicants must submit the following: completed application form; transcript; curriculum vitae; letter from Chairholder. **Deadline:** April 15. **Contact:** 600 West Broadway, Suite 130, Glendale, CA 91204 Tel: 818-242-4154

1295 ■ Harry and Angel Zerigian Scholarships *(Undergraduate/Scholarship)*

Purpose: To provide financial assistance to those students who are in need. **Focus:** Accounting. **Qualif.:** Applicant must be a full-time student with financial need and of Armenian ancestry; must be day-division sophomores majoring in Accounting at Bentley College who have satisfactorily completed all course work through the fall of sophomore year. **Criteria:** Preference is given to those students who attended Haverhill, Lawrence, Waltham or Watertown High Schools.

Funds Avail.: No specific amount. **To Apply:** Applicants must check the available website for the required materials.

1296 ■ Ethel Louise Armstrong Foundation

2450 N Lake Ave., PMB No. 128
Altadena, CA 91001
Ph: (626)398-8840
Fax: (626)398-8843
URL: http://www.ela.org

1297 ■ ELA Foundation Scholarships *(Graduate/Scholarship)*

Purpose: To financially support women with disabilities who are currently pursuing graduate degrees. **Focus:** General studies. **Qualif.:** Applicant must be a woman with a physical disability; currently accepted to a graduate program working towards a Masters degree or above in an accredited college or university in the U.S.; active in a local, state, or national disability organization which is providing services and/or advocacy for people with disabilities; willing, as an ELA Scholar, to network with the ELA Board of Directors and previous ELA Scholarship recipients on our listserv; and willing, as an ELA Scholar, to update the ELA Foundation with an annual letter on September 1st of each year on her progress in her academic and/or working career. **Criteria:** Awards are given based on the application materials.

Funds Avail.: $500-$2000. **To Apply:** Applicants must first submit a completed online application, then submit the completed ELA Scholarship Application form with signed affidavit along with completed ELA Verification of Disability form filled out and signed by Vocational Rehabilitation Counselor or physician; an essay of 1,000 words or less (typewritten in 16-point font, doubled spaced); two typed letters of recommendation from current teachers, faculty members or employers on their letterhead regarding your scholastic aptitude, leadership abilities and personal qualifications; unofficial copy of the college/university transcript, to Deborah Lewis, Executive Director, ELA Foundation. **Deadline:** June 1.

Remarks: All applications have to be typed in order to be considered. **Contact:** Deborah Lewis.

1298 ■ Army Aviation Association of America

755 Main St., Ste. 4D
Monroe, CT 06468-2830
Ph: (203)268-2450
Fax: (203)268-5870
E-mail: aaaa@quad-a.org
URL: http://www.quad-a.org

1299 ■ AAAA Scholarship Program *(Undergraduate/Scholarship)*

Purpose: To provide grants and loans to members who seek further education as well as the member's family who sought college-entry financial aid. **Focus:** General studies. **Qualif.:** Applicants must be a member of AAAA, the spouse of an AAAA member or deceased member, the unmarried son or daughter of an AAAA member or deceased member or the unmarried grandchild of an AAAA member or deceased member. Applicants must be attending an accredited college or university or selected for Fall entry as an undergraduate or graduate. **Criteria:** Scholarship recipients will be selected based on the selection committee's review of the application materials.

Funds Avail.: $1,000-$10,000. **Number Awarded:** Varies. **To Apply:** Applicants must submit the completed application including the applicant's references made by two individuals; school recommendation; teacher's recommendation; academic reporting form; current transcripts of grades; and a photograph. For graduate students, applicants must submit a 250-word essay about the applicant's life experiences, work history and aspirations. **Deadline:** May 1.

1300 ■ Army Nurse Corps Association

PO Box 39235
San Antonio, TX 78218-1235
Ph: (210)650-3534
Fax: (210)650-3494
E-mail: education@e-anca.org
URL: http://e-anca.org

1301 ■ ANCA Scholarships *(Graduate, Undergraduate/Scholarship)*

Purpose: To provide financial assistance to nursing students. **Focus:** Nursing. **Qualif.:** Applicants must be a student in a nursing program approved by an agency acceptable to the United States Secretary of Education; have Internal Revenue Service tax-exempt status; have scholarship fund under the school control; been a supportive of Army Nurse Corps recruitment. **Criteria:** Applicants who are students planning to enter the Army Nurse Corps, Army Reserve or National Guard; previously served in the United States Army, Army Reserve or National Guard; Army Nurse

Awards are arranged alphabetically below their administering organizations

Corps officers enrolled in undergraduate or graduate nursing programs not funded by United States Army, Army Reserve or National Guard; members of Army Medical Department pursuing baccalaureate degree in nursing not funded by United States Army, Army Reserve or National Guard will be given preference.

Funds Avail.: Scholarship amount not specified. **To Apply:** Applicants must submit application template consist of school and location; agency accreditation; internal revenue status; scholarship program; support of army nurse corps recruitment activities; award criteria; application for specific student; and agreement to Education Committee. **Deadline:** May 15.

1302 ■ Army Scholarship Foundation

6412 Brandon Ave., Ste. 201
Springfield, VA 22150
Fax: (703)451-1257
E-mail: contactus@armyscholarshipfoundation.org
URL: http://www.armyscholarshipfoundation.org

1303 ■ First Lieutenant Scott McClean Love Memorial Scholarship - Children of Soldiers

(Undergraduate/Scholarship)

Purpose: To financially assist deserving sons/daughters of current or former United States Army personnel in their pursuit of higher education. **Focus:** General studies. **Qualif.:** Applicant must be the son/daughter of a serving regular active duty, active duty Reserve, or active duty National Guard U.S. Army member in good standing, or the son/daughter of a former U.S. Army member who received an Honorable Discharge or Medical Discharge, or was killed while serving in the U.S. Army. Must be a U.S. citizen not reaching 24th birthday by application deadline; and a high school senior, high school graduate, or registered as an undergraduate student at an accredited college or vocational/technical institution. **Criteria:** Award is given based on the application materials.

Funds Avail.: $500-$2,000. **To Apply:** Applicants must submit a completed scholarship application form along with a Free Application for Federal Student Aid (FAFSA); a signed copy of the appropriate income tax return for the previous year; a certificate of good service or the parent's/spouse's DD 214; a high school transcript and transcripts from all post high school educational institutions (if applicable); an essay; and a photograph. **Deadline:** May 1.

Remarks: In memory of First Lieutenant Scott McClean Love.

1304 ■ First Lieutenant Scott McClean Love Memorial Scholarship - Spouses of Soldiers

(Undergraduate/Scholarship)

Purpose: To financially assist deserving spouses of current or former United States Army personnel in their pursuit of higher education. **Focus:** General studies. **Qualif.:** Applicant must be spouse of a serving enlisted regular active duty, active duty Reserve, or active duty National Guard U. S. Army member in good standing. Must be a U.S. citizen not reaching 30th birthday by application deadline; and a high school senior, high school graduate, or registered as an undergraduate student at an accredited college or vocational/technical institution. **Criteria:** Award is given based on the application materials.

Funds Avail.: $500-$2000. **To Apply:** Applicants must submit a completed scholarship application form along with a Free Application for Federal Student Aid (FAFSA); a signed copy of the appropriate income tax return for the previous year; a certificate of good service or the parent's/spouse's DD 214; a high school transcript and transcripts from all post high school educational institutions (if applicable); an essay; and a photograph. **Deadline:** May 1.

Remarks: In memory of First Lieutenant Scott McClean Love.

1305 ■ Captain Jennifer Shafer Odom Memorial Scholarships - Children of Soldiers

(Undergraduate/Scholarship)

Purpose: To financially assist deserving sons/daughters of current or former United States Army personnel in their pursuit of higher education. **Focus:** General studies. **Qualif.:** Applicant must be the son/daughter of a serving regular active duty, active duty Reserve, or active duty National Guard U.S. Army member in good standing, or the son/daughter of a former U.S. Army member who received an Honorable Discharge or Medical Discharge, or was killed while serving in the U.S. Army. Must be a U.S. citizen not reaching 24th birthday by application deadline; and a high school senior, high school graduate, or registered undergraduate student at an accredited college or vocational/technical institution. **Criteria:** Award is given based on the application materials.

Funds Avail.: $500-$2,000. **To Apply:** Applicants must submit a completed scholarship application form along with a Free Application for Federal Student Aid (FAFSA); a signed copy of the appropriate income tax return for the previous year; a certificate of good service or the parent's/spouse's DD 214; a high school transcript and transcripts from all post-high school educational institutions (if applicable); an essay; and a photograph. **Deadline:** May 1.

Remarks: In memory of Captain Jennifer Shafer Odom.

1306 ■ Captain Jennifer Shafer Odom Memorial Scholarships - Spouses of Soldiers

(Undergraduate/Scholarship)

Purpose: To financially assist deserving spouses of current or former United States Army personnel in their pursuit of higher education. **Focus:** General studies. **Qualif.:** Applicant must be spouse of a serving enlisted regular active duty, active duty Reserve, or active duty National Guard U. S. Army member in good standin. Must be a U.S. citizen not reaching 30th birthday by application deadline; and a high school senior, high school graduate, or registered as an undergraduate student at an accredited college or vocational/technical institution. **Criteria:** Award is given based on the application materials.

Funds Avail.: $500-$2,000. **To Apply:** Applicants must submit a completed scholarship application form along with a Free Application for Federal Student Aid (FAFSA); a signed copy of the appropriate income tax return for the previous year; a certificate of good service or the parent's/spouse's DD 214; a high school transcript and transcripts from all post high school educational institutions (if applicable); an essay; and a photograph. **Deadline:** May 1.

Remarks: In memory of Captain Jennifer Shafer Odom.

1307 ■ Aaron Arnoldsen Memorial Scholarship Fund

1325 Airmotive Way, Ste. 220
Reno, NV 89502
E-mail: info@aamemorial.com
URL: http://aamemorial.com

Awards are arranged alphabetically below their administering organizations

1308 ■ Aaron Edward Arnoldsen Memorial Scholarships *(Undergraduate/Scholarship)*

Purpose: To provide financial support to aid students educational endeavor. **Focus:** General studies. **Qualif.:** Applicant must be a male or a female; junior or senior class standing; graduate of Nevada High School; have 3.0 GPA or below; a full time student at the University of Nevada, Reno; and continuing employment through the forthcoming school-year. **Criteria:** Applicants will be evaluated by Scholarship Selection Committee.

Funds Avail.: $25,000. **To Apply:** Applicants must submit completed application form and the other requirements needed.

1309 ■ Art Institute of Colorado

1200 Lincoln St.
Denver, CO 80203-2172
Ph: (303)837-0825
Free: 800-275-2420
E-mail: aicadm@aii.edu
URL: http://www.artinstitutes.edu/denver

1310 ■ Art Institute of Colorado Scholarships *(Undergraduate/Scholarship)*

Purpose: To provide higher education programs leading to professional opportunities in the fields of art and design, culinary arts, and technology that prepare graduates for job entry and career advancement. **Focus:** Art. **Qualif.:** Applicants must be high school seniors from the Sixth Congressional District who enter their work in The Artistic Discovery Art Program. **Criteria:** Recipients are selected based on financial need and academic standing.

Funds Avail.: $7,000. **Number Awarded:** 1. **To Apply:** Applicants must complete the application form.

1311 ■ Art Institute's Best Teen Chef in America Culinary Scholarships *(Undergraduate/Scholarship)*

Purpose: To provide higher education programs leading to professional opportunities in the fields of art and design, culinary arts, and technology which prepare graduates for job entry and career advancement. **Focus:** Art. **Qualif.:** Applicants must be high school seniors. **Criteria:** Recipients are selected based on financial need and academic standing.

Funds Avail.: Maximum amount of $30,000. **Number Awarded:** 1. **To Apply:** Applicants must complete the application form. Applicants must submit a notebook that includes the menu and detailed recipes and directions from each course. Applicants must submit a paragraph stating their reason for wanting to be a culinary professional; and a current high school transcript. **Deadline:** February 14.

1312 ■ James Beard Foundation/Art Institute of Colorado Scholarships *(Undergraduate/Scholarship)*

Purpose: To provide higher education programs leading to professional opportunities in the fields of art and design, culinary arts, and technology which prepare graduates for job entry and career advancement. **Focus:** Art. **Qualif.:** Applicants must be freshmen high school students. Applicants must have a 3.0 GPA. **Criteria:** Recipients are selected based on academic record and financial need.

Funds Avail.: Maximum amount of $1,500. **Number Awarded:** 2. **To Apply:** Applicants must complete the application form and must submit a transcript of records. **Contact:** 212-675-4984.

1313 ■ Colorado PROSTART/Art Institute of Colorado Art Scholarships for High School Seniors *(Undergraduate/Scholarship)*

Purpose: To provide higher education programs leading to professional opportunities in the fields of art and design, culinary arts, and technology which prepare graduates for job entry and career advancement. **Focus:** Art. **Qualif.:** Applicants must be senior high school students. **Criteria:** Recipients are selected based on high school GPA, recommendation, and commitment to pursuing a career in culinary arts.

Funds Avail.: Maximum amount of $14,490. **To Apply:** Applicants must complete the application form and must submit a transcript of records.

1314 ■ Colorado Springs Pikes Peak Region School District Young Peoples Art Show Scholarships *(Undergraduate/Scholarship)*

Purpose: To provide higher education programs leading to professional opportunities in the fields of art and design, culinary arts, and technology, to prepare graduates for job entry and career advancement. **Focus:** Art. **Qualif.:** Applicants must be high school seniors selected as winners through this art show. **Criteria:** Recipients are selected based on financial need and academic standing.

Funds Avail.: $4,416. **Number Awarded:** 1. **To Apply:** Applicants must complete the application form.

1315 ■ Denver Public School Art Award/Scholarships for High School Seniors *(Undergraduate/Scholarship)*

Purpose: To provide higher education programs leading to professional opportunities in the fields of art and design, culinary arts, and technology which prepare graduates for job entry and career advancement. **Focus:** Art. **Qualif.:** Applicants must be senior high school students in Denver public schools. **Criteria:** Recipients are selected based on high school GPA and artwork.

Funds Avail.: Maximum amount of $13,248. **To Apply:** Applicants must complete the application form and submit a transcript of records.

1316 ■ Douglas County Art Awards Scholarship for High School Seniors *(Undergraduate/Scholarship)*

Purpose: To provide higher education programs leading to professional opportunities in the fields of art and design, culinary arts, and technology which prepare graduates for job entry and career advancement. **Focus:** Art. **Qualif.:** Applicants must be senior high school students in Denver public schools. **Criteria:** Recipients are selected based on high school GPA and artwork.

Funds Avail.: Maximum amount of $13,248. **Number Awarded:** 2. **To Apply:** Applicants must complete the application form and must submit a transcript of record.

1317 ■ Jefferson County Art Awards Scholarship for High school Seniors *(Undergraduate/Scholarship)*

Purpose: To provide higher education programs leading to professional opportunities in the fields of art and design,

Awards are arranged alphabetically below their administering organizations

culinary arts, and technology which prepare graduates for job entry and career advancement. **Focus:** Art. **Qualif.:** Applicants must be high school students. **Criteria:** Recipients are selected based on high school GPA and student artwork.

Funds Avail.: Maximum amount of $13,248. **To Apply:** Applicants must complete the application form and must submit a transcript of records.

1318 ■ Wyoming Art Symposium Scholarships *(Undergraduate/Scholarship)*

Purpose: To provide higher education programs leading to professional opportunities in the fields of art and design, culinary arts, and technology, to prepare graduates for job entry and career advancement. **Focus:** Art. **Qualif.:** Applicants must be high school senior students in Wyoming high schools. **Criteria:** Recipients are selected based on high school GPA and student artwork.

Funds Avail.: Maximum amount of $13,248. **To Apply:** Applicants must complete the application form and must submit a transcript of records.

1319 ■ ASCE San Diego Section

PO Box 1028
El Cajon, CA 92022
Ph: (619)588-0641
Fax: (619)749-2188
E-mail: sdcivil@asce-sd.org
URL: http://www.asce-sd.org

1320 ■ Charles McMahon Memorial Construction Management/Engineering Scholarship Awards *(Undergraduate/Scholarship)*

Purpose: To provide financial assistance for students pursuing Construction Management, Construction Engineering and/or Construction Practices as a career goal. **Focus:** Construction, Engineering. **Qualif.:** Applicant must be a freshman, sophomore, junior or senior level ASCE student member in good standing at one of the local San Diego universities and must have a minimum 2.5 overall grade point average. **Criteria:** Applicants will be evaluated based on appraisal of applicant's needs, educational plans, academic performance, potential for development, leadership, ASCE activities and other student activities.

Funds Avail.: No specific amount. **To Apply:** Applicants must submit application package that must include a filled out scholarship application form and proof of ASCE Student Membership. **Deadline:** March 3.

1321 ■ Charles Smith Memorial Scholarship Awards *(Undergraduate/Scholarship)*

Purpose: To provide financial assistance for student members of ASCE intending to continue their education in college. **Focus:** Engineering, Civil. **Qualif.:** Applicant must be a freshman, sophomore, junior or senior ASCE student member in good standing at one of the local San Diego universities who has a minimum 2.5 overall grade point average. **Criteria:** Applicants will be evaluated based on appraisal of applicant's needs, educational plans, academic performance, potential for development, leadership, ASCE activities and other student activities.

Funds Avail.: No specific amount. **To Apply:** Applicants must submit application package which includes a filled out scholarship application form and proof of ASCE Student Membership. **Deadline:** March 3.

1322 ■ Ashburn Institute

444 North West Capitol St., NW
PO Box 77164
Washington, DC 20013-7164
Ph: (703)728-6482
Fax: (703)753-1910
E-mail: info@ashburninstutute.org
URL: http://www.ashburninstitute.org

1323 ■ Mayme and Herb Frank Scholarship Program *(Graduate, Undergraduate/Scholarship)*

Purpose: To support the study of international integration and federalism at the graduate level. **Focus:** International affairs and relations. **Qualif.:** Applicant must be a graduate student of strong academic standing; must have a thesis or dissertation relating to international integration and/or federalism and coursework that places major weight on international and/or federalism or must have an independent study project relating to international integration and federalism to be conducted as part of a graduate program. **Criteria:** Selection of candidates will be based on the quality of the project, and academic standing. Consideration is made by the Frank Education Fund Committee of the Ashburn Institute.

Funds Avail.: $500-$2,000 depending on relevance of the goals of the fund. **To Apply:** Applicant must complete the FEF Application form and must have the description of any course planned to be completed by the applicant during the period of the proposed grant; must submit the copy of the graduate transcript if currently enrolled in a graduate program, or a copy of the applicant's undergraduate transcript if enrolled in a graduate program but ha not yet started it. Application form and other supporting materials must be submitted to: Association to Unite the Democracies c/o The Ashburn Institute, The Frank Educational Fund, PO Box 77164, Washington, DC, 200137164. **Deadline:** April 1 for Fall term awards and October 1 for Spring term awards.

1324 ■ Asian American Bar Association

PO Box 190517
San Francisco, CA 94119-0571
Ph: (415)623-6433
E-mail: info@aaba-bay.com
URL: http://www.aaba-bay.com

1325 ■ California Bar Foundation Diversity Scholarships *(Undergraduate/Scholarship)*

Purpose: To support newly admitted law students from groups historically underrepresented in the legal profession, who have committed to attend California Law School. **Focus:** Law. **Qualif.:** Applicants must be students of California law school and come from racial or ethnic groups that are underrepresented in the legal profession; must have financial need; and must demonstrate leadership in making a positive impact to the community. **Criteria:** Recipients are selected based on financial need.

Funds Avail.: $7,500. **To Apply:** Applicants must submit two current letters of recommendation; certification and authorization form; evidence of acceptance to law school; resume; one-page between 250-400 words personal statement; undergraduate transcript; evidence of financial need;

Awards are arranged alphabetically below their administering organizations

and optional statement of financial circumstance. **Deadline:** June 18. **Contact:** California Bar Foundation, 180 Howard St., San Francisco, CA 94105.

1326 ■ California Bar Law Foundation Scholarships *(Undergraduate/Scholarship)*

Purpose: To recognize the importance of fostering the growth of law students and to improve the future development of the Asian Pacific American Bar. **Focus:** Law. **Qualif.:** Applicants must be law students who are committed to advocating and improving their communities. **Criteria:** Recipients are selected based on submitted requirements and quality of the personal statement.

Funds Avail.: No stated amount. **To Apply:** Applicants must submit completed application form; resume; personal statement of no more than three pages, double-spaced describing the perception in facing the Asian American community, including the role in advocating or engaging in such issues and experiences in overcoming the economic or other discriminatory barriers. **Deadline:** February 1. **Contact:** amathai-jackson@hansonbridgett.com

1327 ■ Asian American Journalists Association

1182 Market St., Ste. 320
San Francisco, CA 94102
Ph: (415)346-2051
Fax: (415)346-6343
E-mail: national@aaja.org
URL: http://www.aaja.org

1328 ■ AAJA/CNN Scholar Program *(Graduate, Undergraduate/Scholarship)*

Purpose: To provide financial assistance to students majoring in broadcast or online journalism. **Focus:** Journalism; Broadcasting. **Qualif.:** Applicants must be graduating high school senior, undergraduate or graduate student enrolled full time with at least 12 credit units for each semester; must be currently taking or planning to take journalism courses. **Criteria:** Recipients will be selected on the basis of academic achievement; demonstrated journalistic ability; financial need; commitment to the field of journalism.

Funds Avail.: $25,000. **Number Awarded:** 4. **To Apply:** Applicants must submit the completed application form; a resume; an official transcript; two letters of recommendation; a short essay, not exceeding 500 words, on the topic: "Describe any involvement or interest that you have in the Asian American community. If you were awarded an AAJA scholarship, propose how you would contribute to the field of journalism and/or media issues involving the Asian American and Pacific Islander community." **Deadline:** March 28. **Contact:** Nao Vang; AAJA Student Programs Coordinator; 415-346-2051; programs@aaja.org.

1329 ■ AAJA/COX Foundation Scholarships *(Graduate, Undergraduate/Scholarship)*

Purpose: To assist students who are interested in pursuing a career in print, broadcast, or photojournalism. **Focus:** Journalism; Broadcasting; Photography, Journalistic. **Qualif.:** Applicants must be graduating high school senior, undergraduate or graduate student enrolled full time with at least 12 credit units for each semester; must be currently taking or planning to take journalism courses. **Criteria:** Recipients will be selected on the basis of academic achievement; demonstrated journalistic ability; financial need; commitment to the field of journalism.

Funds Avail.: $1,250. **Number Awarded:** 1. **To Apply:** Applicants must submit the completed application form; a resume; an official transcript; two letters of recommendation; a short essay, not exceeding 500 words, on the topic: "Describe any involvement or interest that you have in the Asian American community. If you were awarded an AAJA scholarship, propose how you would contribute to the field of journalism and/or media issues involving the Asian American and Pacific Islander community." **Deadline:** March 28. **Contact:** Nao Vang; AAJA Student Programs Coordinator; 415-346-2051; programs@aaja.org.

1330 ■ AAJA/S.I. Newhouse Foundation Scholarships *(Graduate, Undergraduate/Scholarship)*

Purpose: To provide educational funds to students pursuing a career in print journalism. **Focus:** Journalism. **Qualif.:** Applicants must be graduating high school senior, undergraduate or graduate student enrolled full time with at least 12 credit units for each semester; must be currently taking or planning to take journalism courses. **Criteria:** Recipients will be selected on the basis of academic achievement; demonstrated journalistic ability; financial need; commitment to the field of journalism. This scholarship will also focus on underserved AAPI communities, e.g. Southeast Asians, South Asians and Pacific Islanders.

Funds Avail.: $5,000. **To Apply:** Applicants must submit the completed application form; a resume; an official transcript; two letters of recommendation; a short essay, not exceeding 500 words, on the topic: "Describe any involvement or interest that you have in the Asian American community. If you were awarded an AAJA scholarship, propose how you would contribute to the field of journalism and/or media issues involving the Asian American and Pacific Islander community." **Deadline:** March 28. **Contact:** Nao Vang; AAJA Student Programs Coordinator; 415-346-2051; programs@aaja.org.

1331 ■ Asian American Lawyers Association of Massachusetts

PO Box 6254
Boston, MA 02114
Ph: (617)248-4865
E-mail: ckim@choate.com
URL: http://www.aalam.org

1332 ■ Asian American Lawyers Associations of Massachusetts Scholarships *(Undergraduate/Scholarship)*

Purpose: To promote and enhance the Asian American legal profession by furthering and encouraging professional interaction and the exchange of ideas among its members and with other individuals, groups, and organizations; to improve and facilitate the administration of law and justice through various means. **Focus:** Law. **Qualif.:** Applicants must be enrolled at a law school in the Commonwealth of Massachusetts and must be in good standing. **Criteria:** Recipients are selected based on demonstrated leadership potential, maturity and responsibility, and commitment in making a contribution to the Asian-American community and other indication of excellence whether personal, professional, or academic.

Funds Avail.: $2,500. **Number Awarded:** 1. **To Apply:** Applicants must complete the application form; must submit an official transcript of records; resume; one letter of recommendation written by a person who is not related to the

Awards are arranged alphabetically below their administering organizations

candidate; and a signed certification contained at the end of the scholarship application form. **Deadline:** April 3. **Contact:** 111 Huntington Ave., Boston MA 02199.

1333 ■ Asian American Psychological Association

1600 Holloway Ave.
San Francisco, CA 94132
Ph: (415)338-1690
Fax: (415)338-0594
E-mail: aalvarez@sfsu.edu
URL: http://www.aapaonline.org

1334 ■ APA Minority Fellowships Program
(Postdoctorate/Fellowship)

Purpose: To provide financial support and professional guidance to individuals pursuing predoctoral and postdoctoral training. **Focus:** General Studies. **Qualif.:** Applicants must be individuals who are pursuing predoctoral and postdoctoral training. **Criteria:** Preference will be given to those students who meet the criteria.

Funds Avail.: No specific amount. **To Apply:** Applicants must check the available website for the required materials. **Contact:** Asian American Psychological Association at the above address (see entry 1333).

1335 ■ Asian Pacific American Librarians Association

PO Box 1592
Goleta, CA 93116-1592
Ph: (805)893-8067
E-mail: colmenar@library.ucsb.edu
URL: http://www.apalaweb.org

1336 ■ APALA Scholarship Program *(Doctorate, Graduate/Scholarship)*

Purpose: To provide financial assistance to a student of Asian or Pacific background. **Focus:** Library and archival sciences; Information science and technology. **Qualif.:** Applicant must be of Asian/Pacific Islander heritage; must be a U.S. citizen or permanent resident of the U.S. or Canada; must be admitted full-time or part-time into a master's degree or doctoral program in library or information science at a library school accredited by ALA. **Criteria:** Recipients are selected based on the Scholarship Committee's review of the application materials.

Funds Avail.: $1,000. **Number Awarded:** 1. **To Apply:** Applicant must submit a completed application form available at the website together with a resume; copy of acceptance letter to an ALA accredited library school or library graduate school transcript; two letters of recommendation; and one page essay on one of the following topics: Your vision of a librarian's role in the twenty-first century and what contributions can I make as an APA Librarian? If applicable, number of hours completed towards degree. **Deadline:** April 30. **Contact:** Laura Park, Co-Chair, APALA Scholarship Committee, Pierce County Library, 3005 112th St. E, Tacoma, WA 98446. Fax: 253-537-1809 or lpark@piercecountylibrary.org.

1337 ■ Asian/Pacific Bar Association of Sacramento

PO Box 2215
Sacramento, CA 95812
Ph: (916)492-3170
E-mail: brownd@insurance.ca.gov
URL: http://www.sacasianpacbar.com

1338 ■ Asian/Pacific Bar Association of Sacramento Law Foundation Scholarships
(Undergraduate/Scholarship)

Purpose: To recognize law students and recent law school graduates who possess extraordinary skills, desire and potential to serve and lead the greater Sacramento Asian-Pacific Islander community. **Focus:** Law. **Qualif.:** Applicants must be either currently enrolled and in good standing at a Sacramento area (including U.C. Davis) law school or currently residing in the Sacramento area; have graduated from law school in Spring/Summer 2007 or winter 2007-08. **Criteria:** Recipients are selected based on potential for community service, leadership in the Asian Pacific Islander community, academic achievement, and financial need.

Funds Avail.: $1,000-$4,000. **To Apply:** Applicants must submit evidence of scholarship eligibility (a copy of current law school registration or law school diploma will suffice); a personal statement; a current resume; current law school transcripts; financial information; and two references. **Deadline:** February 29.

1339 ■ Asian and Pacific Islander American Scholarship Fund

1900 L St. NW, Ste. 210
Washington, DC 20036-5002
Ph: (202)986-6892
Fax: (202)530-6843
E-mail: info@apiasf.org
URL: http://www.apiasf.org

1340 ■ APIASF Scholarships *(Undergraduate/Scholarship)*

Purpose: To support and encourage all Asian and Pacific Islander American students to pursue higher education by developing future leaders who will contribute back to their communities. **Focus:** General studies. **Qualif.:** Applicant must be of Asian and/or Pacific Islander ethnicity as defined by 2000 census; a U.S. citizen, U.S. National, legal permanent resident or a citizen of the Federated States of Micronesia, Republic of the Marshall Islands or the Republic of Palau; a first-time, incoming college student; enrolled full-time in a two or four-year program at a U.S. accredited college or university in the U.S., Guam, American Samoa, or the Commonwealth of the Northern Mariana Islands for the coming school year. (In the Freely Associated States, this includes the Community Colleges of the Federated States of Micronesia, the Republic of Marshall Islands and the Republic of Palau.) Applicants must have cumulative, unweighted grade point average (GPA) of 2.7 or higher on a 4.0 scale. **Criteria:** Recipient is selected based on academic record and future plans; community service and leadership; and financial need.

Funds Avail.: $2,500. **Number Awarded:** 200. **To Apply:** Applicants must complete the application form online, available at the website of APIASF, www.apiasf.org/apply. **Deadline:** January 22.

1341 ■ ASIS International

1625 Prince St.
Alexandria, VA 22314-2818

Awards are arranged alphabetically below their administering organizations

Ph: (703)519-6200
Fax: (703)519-6299
E-mail: asis@asisonline.org
URL: http://www.asisonline.org

1342 ■ ASIS Foundation Chapter Matching Scholarships *(Undergraduate/Scholarship)*

Purpose: To provide educational assistance to chapter members, student members or student nonmembers pursuing a security career. **Focus:** General studies. **Qualif.:** Applicants must be part- or full-time students who have completed one year of study at an accredited college, university or community college towards a career in security profession; must be undergraduate students (their chapter will set the grade point average required, for them to be qualified for the scholarship) or graduate students who earned at least a 3.0 GPA on a 4.0 scale. **Criteria:** Applicants are evaluated based on their achievements and abilities.

Funds Avail.: $1,000. **To Apply:** Applicants must submit all the required application information.

1343 ■ Associated General Contractors of America

2300 Wilson Blvd., Ste. 400
Arlington, VA 22201
Ph: (703)548-3118
Fax: (703)548-3119
Free: 800-242-1767
E-mail: info@agc.org
URL: http://www.agc.org

1344 ■ AGC Foundation Outstanding Educator Awards *(Professional Development/Award/Prize)*

Purpose: To provide recognition and encouragement for university teaching faculty members in construction education. **Focus:** Construction. **Qualif.:** Nominees must be a full-time teaching faculty member of a university construction program or a construction-related engineering program or with an institution-approved construction option. Nominees must have at least four years full-time teaching experience. Program must be accredited by either the American Council for Construction Education (ACCE) or the Accreditation Board for Engineering and Technology (ABET). **Criteria:** Award winner is chosen based on the teaching responsibilities and activities with AGC and/or other construction industry organizations.

Funds Avail.: $5,000 cash award and an all-expenses paid trip to the AGC Annual Convention. **To Apply:** Nominees must submit two copies of nomination form and attachments; the joint letter of nomination; the nomination checklist; a maximum of three letters of reference; and a "Notification of Receipt" Postcard. **Deadline:** November 1.

1345 ■ Associated Locksmiths of America

3500 Easy St.
Dallas, TX 75247
Ph: (214)819-9733
Free: 800-532-2562
URL: http://www.aloa.org

1346 ■ ALOA Scholarship Foundation *(Undergraduate/Scholarship)*

Purpose: To provide financial assistance for educational services, programs and materials concerning locksmithing and security devices and procedures. **Focus:** Technical training. **Qualif.:** Applicants must be individuals desirous of entering the locksmithing field or individuals already in the field of locksmithing who wish to improve their professional skills through education. **Criteria:** Applicants will be evaluated based on their financial needs, character, aptitude for the skills necessary in locksmithing, desire for a career in locksmithing, availability to attend the event for which award is given, demonstrated commitment to the locksmith industry, letters of recommendation from locksmith industry reference, and previous scholarship awards.

Funds Avail.: No amount mentioned. **To Apply:** Applicants must complete the application form provided in the website of the Foundation and submit it along with the letters of recommendation from locksmith industry references.

1347 ■ Association for the Advancement of Baltic Studies

14743 Braemar Crescent Way
Darnestown, MD 20878-3911
Ph: (301)977-8491
E-mail: aabs@washington.edu
URL: http://depts.washington.edu/aabs

1348 ■ Association for the Advancement of Baltic Studies Dissertation Grants for Graduate Students *(Doctorate/Grant)*

Purpose: To support doctoral dissertation research and write-up in any field of Baltic Studies. **Focus:** General studies. **Qualif.:** Applicants must be currently enrolled in a PhD program and have completed all requirements for a PhD except the dissertation. **Criteria:** Recipients are selected based on the scholarly potential of the applicant, and quality and scholarly importance of the proposed work, especially to the development of Baltic studies.

Funds Avail.: $2,000. **To Apply:** Applicants must send three copies of a 500-word proposal, a one-page budget specifying expenses, a CV, evidence of current enrollment in a PhD program and a no more than 25-page writing sample. **Deadline:** November 15.

1349 ■ Association for the Advancement of Cost Engineering

209 Prairie Ave., Ste. 100
Morgantown, WV 26501-5934
Ph: (304)296-8444
Fax: (304)291-5728
Free: 800-858-2678
E-mail: president@aacei.org
URL: http://www.aacei.org

1350 ■ AACE International Competitive Scholarships *(Undergraduate/Scholarship)*

Purpose: To advance the study of cost engineering and cost management through the integrative process of total cost management. **Focus:** Engineering. **Qualif.:** Applicants must be full-time students pursuing a related degree in engineering and other related courses. **Criteria:** Recipients are selected based on academic performance, extracurricular activities, and an essay on the value of study of cost engineering or total cost management.

Funds Avail.: $2,000-$8,000. **To Apply:** Applicants must fill out the application form. **Deadline:** February 17. **Con-**

Awards are arranged alphabetically below their administering organizations

tact: AACE International at the above address (see entry 1349).

1351 ■ Association of American Geographers

1710 16th St. NW
Washington, DC 20009-3198
Ph: (202)324-1450
Fax: (202)234-2744
E-mail: aagguide@aag.org
URL: http://www.aag.org

1352 ■ AAG IGIF Graduate Research Awards *(Graduate, Undergraduate/Scholarship)*

Purpose: To support college and university student career development in the academic areas of applied spatial data analysis or geographic information systems (GIS). **Focus:** Geography. **Qualif.:** Applicants must be full-time students who are currently registered in an undergraduate or graduate degree program providing either a degree or explicit specialization in some area of applied spatial data analysis or GIS study at a duly accredited and recognized college, university or other educational institution located within the United States. **Criteria:** Selection of applicants will be based on the following criteria: (a) The problem statement and context of the proposed research within the literature; (b) Originality and relevance of the research; (c) Validity and effectiveness of the methodology to complete the research; (d) Writing clarity and quality; (e) Faculty endorsement.

Funds Avail.: $500. **To Apply:** Applications for an AAG IGIF Graduate Research Award must consist of the following: (a) Abstract of research intent; (b) Statement of problem and relevancy; (c) Context of proposed research in the literature; (d) Methodology/research design; (e) Anticipated results and significance of such results; (e) Schedule of research; (f) Budget; (g) A letter of recommendation from a faculty member. **Deadline:** December 31. **Contact:** Application form and other supporting materials must be sent to Association of American Geographers, Hess Scholarship, 1710 16th Street NW, Washington, DC 20009-3198.

1353 ■ AAG IGIF Student Travel Grants *(Graduate, Undergraduate/Grant)*

Purpose: To support college and university student career development in the academic areas of applied spatial data analysis or geographic information systems (GIS). **Focus:** Geography. **Qualif.:** Applicants must be full-time students who are currently registered in an undergraduate or graduate degree program providing either a degree or explicit specialization in some area of applied spatial data analysis or GIS study at a duly accredited and recognized college, university or other educational institution located within the United States. **Criteria:** Selection of applicants will be based on academic record, letters of reference by the advisor and chair, and the focus and clarity of the applicant's statement related to his/her career goals as determined by the AAG IGIF Student Travel Grant Committee of Reviewers.

Funds Avail.: $500. **To Apply:** Applicants must submit a letter of no more than three pages in length which may be supplemented by no more than two pages of supporting illustrations (letter should specifically address how the grant funds will be used and should indicate the career goals of the student and how these funds will assist in meeting those goals); must provide a letter from the student's faculty advisor including an endorsement from the chairperson of the applicable program; must have a brief curriculum vita and recent transcript of records. Application form and other supporting materials must be sent to Association of American Geographers, Hess Scholarship, 1710 16th Street NW, Washington, DC 200093198. **Deadline:** December 31.

1354 ■ Darrel Hess Community College Geography Scholarships *(Undergraduate/Scholarship)*

Purpose: To provide financial assistance to qualified individuals who want to pursue their education. **Focus:** Geography. **Qualif.:** Applicants must be students currently enrolled at a US community college, junior college, city college, or similar two-year educational institution; must have completed at least two transfer courses in geography and plan to transfer to a four-year institution as a geography major during the coming academic year. **Criteria:** Selection of applicants will be based on the overall quality of the application, scholastic excellence and academic promise. Consideration will be given to those in need of financial support.

Funds Avail.: $1,000. **Number Awarded:** 2. **To Apply:** Applicants must complete the scholarship application available online at www.aag.org/grantsawards/hessform.rtf; must submit a two page personal statement describing the applicant's academic and personal background, as well as the applicant's academic goals and interest in pursuing geography as a major at a baccalaureate institution; must have two letters of recommendation from college instructors; must have a copy of the applicant's current unofficial transcripts. Application form and other supporting materials must be sent to Association of American Geographers, Hess Scholarship, 1710 16th St. NW, Washington, DC 20009-3198. **Deadline:** December 31.

1355 ■ Association on American Indian Affairs

966 Hungerford Dr., Ste. 12-B
Rockville, MD 20850
Ph: (240)314-7155
Fax: (240)314-7159
E-mail: general.aaia@verizon.net
URL: http://indian-affairs.org

1356 ■ Elizabeth and Sherman Asche Memorial Scholarship Fund *(Graduate, Undergraduate/Scholarship)*

Purpose: To provide financial assistance for helping native people for higher education. **Focus:** Public health, Science. **Qualif.:** Applicants must be graduate and undergraduate students pursuing a degree in public health or science. **Criteria:** Applicants will be judged by the Scholarship Committee.

Funds Avail.: $1,500. **To Apply:** Students are eligible to apply on a yearly basis. **Deadline:** July 1.

1357 ■ Allogan Slagle Memorial Scholarships *(Graduate/Scholarship)*

Purpose: To provide financial assistance for helping native people for higher education. **Focus:** American Indian studies. **Qualif.:** Applicants must be Graduate students. **Criteria:** Applicants must be students from tribes that are not federally recognized.

Funds Avail.: $1,500. **To Apply:** Students are eligible to apply on a yearly basis. **Deadline:** July 1.

Awards are arranged alphabetically below their administering organizations

1358 ■ Adolph Van Pelt Special Fund for Indians Scholarships *(Undergraduate/Scholarship)*

Purpose: To provide financial assistance for helping native people for higher education. **Focus:** American Indian studies. **Qualif.:** Applicants must be students from any curriculum. **Criteria:** Applicants must be undergraduate students.

Funds Avail.: $1,500. **To Apply:** Students are eligible to apply on a yearly basis. **Deadline:** July 1.

1359 ■ Association of American Indian Physicians

1225 Sovereign Row, Ste. 103
Oklahoma City, OK 73108
Ph: (405)946-7072
Fax: (405)946-7651
URL: http://www.aaip.org

1360 ■ Association of American Indian Physicians Scholarships *(Graduate, Undergraduate/Scholarship)*

Purpose: To provide a framework for undergraduate and graduate students in the application process to a health professional school. **Focus:** Health Education. **Qualif.:** Applicants must be undergraduate and graduate medical students; must be American Indian and Alaska Native Students. **Criteria:** Preference will be given to those students who meet the criteria.

Funds Avail.: No specific amount. **To Apply:** Applicants must submit the completed application form; AAIP Student Primary Data Sheet Scholarship Application; Recent College and/or University Transcripts; one letter of recommendation from a professor or academic advisor; copy of Certificate of Degree of Indian Blood or Tribal Identification Card; recent photograph for identification and publication purposes; one page personal statement answering: Why they are seeking a professional career in the health professions? What influenced them and the experience(s) they have had to support this decision? Their career goals and where they plan to work. The physician and medical students will use this in their mock interview. **Deadline:** June 27.

1361 ■ Association of American Medical Colleges

2450 N St. NW
Washington, DC 20037-1126
Ph: (202)828-0400
Fax: (202)828-1125
E-mail: amcas@aamc.org
URL: http://www.aamc.org

1362 ■ Herbert W. Nickens Medical Student Scholarships *(Undergraduate/Scholarship)*

Purpose: To eliminate inequities in medical education and health care and demonstrated leadership efforts in addressing educational, societal, and health care needs of minorities in United States. **Focus:** Medicinal Education. **Qualif.:** Applicants must be US citizens or permanent residents; must be entering third year of study in an accredited US medical school. **Criteria:** Recipients are selected based on academic standing.

Funds Avail.: $5,000. **To Apply:** Applicants must submit one original and nine photocopies of nomination letter from the medical school's dean or the dean's designate discussing the leadership, academic achievement, awards and honors; letters of recommendation from the medical school and faculty member; personal statement (does not exceed 250 words) discussing motivation for pursuing medical career; curriculum vitae; and official medical school academic transcript. **Deadline:** May 2. **Contact:** nickensawards@aamc.org

1363 ■ Association for Applied and Therapeutic Humor

65 Enterprise
Aliso Viejo, CA 92656
Ph: (949)715-2284
Fax: (949)715-6931
E-mail: staff@aath.org
URL: http://www.aath.org

1364 ■ The Dave Family "Humor Studies" Scholarships *(Undergraduate/Scholarship)*

Purpose: To help cultivate the next generation of AATH members. **Focus:** Therapy. **Qualif.:** Applicants must be college students pursuing humor/laughter studies with an interest in entering the field of applied or therapeutic humor. **Criteria:** Priority is given to applicants entering colleges and universities in the United States.

Funds Avail.: $500. **To Apply:** Applicants must submit three essays (up to 250 words each) answering these questions: How do you plan to apply our Humor/Laughter education in the field after college?; Why do you feel you are most deserving of this conference scholarship?; How has humor/laughter helped you in a difficult situation? **Deadline:** October 15. **Contact:** Association for Applied Therapeutic Humor; email at staff@aath.org.

1365 ■ Ed Dunkelblau Scholarships *(All/Scholarship)*

Purpose: To honor the work, dedication, commitment and contribution to AATH and the field of therapeutic humor. **Focus:** Therapy. **Qualif.:** Applicants must be practitioners of color or researchers interested in the cultural applications of therapeutic humor. **Criteria:** Selection will be based on the applicant's awareness of AATH mission.

Funds Avail.: No specific amount. **To Apply:** Applicants are required to submit an application demonstrating interest, statement of work and awareness to the AATH mission. **Deadline:** October 15. **Contact:** AATH at the above address (see entry 1363).

1366 ■ Margie Klein "Paper Plate" Scholarships *(All/Scholarship)*

Purpose: To honor the work, dedication, commitment and contribution to AATH and in the field of therapeutic humor. **Focus:** Therapy. **Qualif.:** Applicants must show interest in therapeutic humor. **Criteria:** Recipients are selected based on submitted essay.

Funds Avail.: No specific amount. **To Apply:** Applicants must submit an essay (not to exceed 250 words) describing how humor helped them in work-related situations. **Deadline:** October 15. **Contact:** AATH at the above address (see entry 1363).

1367 ■ Lenny Ravich "Shalom" Scholarships *(All/Scholarship)*

Purpose: To help cultivate the next generation of AATH members. **Focus:** Therapy. **Qualif.:** Program is open to

Awards are arranged alphabetically below their administering organizations

individuals whose works in humor and laughter clearly and tangibly demonstrate commitment to world peace. **Criteria:** Selection will be based on the impact of the applicant's essay.

Funds Avail.: No specific amount. **To Apply:** Applicants must submit three essays (up to 250 words each) answering these questions: How do you presently apply (or plan to apply) you knowledge and experience in humor and laughter to advance world peace?; How has your mission and purpose in life brought you to this moment?; Why do you feel that you are deserving of this scholarship? **Deadline:** October 15. **Contact:** Association for Applied Therapeutic Humor; staff@aath.org.

1368 ■ Patty Wooten Scholarships
(Undergraduate/Scholarship)

Purpose: To honor the work, dedication, commitment and contribution to AATH and the field of therapeutic humor. **Focus:** Therapy. **Qualif.:** Program is open to nurses (R.N., L.P.N., L.V.N. or C.N.A). **Criteria:** Recipients are selected based on submitted essay.

Funds Avail.: No amount specified. **To Apply:** Applicants must submit an essay (not to exceed 250 words) describing how humor helped them in work-related situations. **Deadline:** October 15.

1369 ■ Association for Asian Studies

1021 E Huron St.
Ann Arbor, MI 48104
Ph: (734)665-2490
Fax: (734)665-3801
URL: http://www.aasianst.org

1370 ■ AAS CIAC Small Grants *(Graduate, Other/Grant)*

Purpose: To support funding requests for indirect costs of research. **Focus:** General studies. **Qualif.:** Applicant must be an AAS member, junior and independent scholar, adjunct faculty, and dissertation-level graduate student. **Criteria:** Applicants must express sincere interest in research, particularly in Chinese or Inner Asia studies.

Funds Avail.: $2,000. **To Apply:** Applicants need not fill out an application form; however, they must submit a 250-word abstract of the project, a detailed budget of anticipated expenses, including other sources of funding; a two-page (maximum) curriculum vitae of the director and the principal participants; in the case of graduate students, a letter of support from their dissertation advisor, without which the application will not be considered. **Deadline:** February 1.

1371 ■ AAS Korean Studies Scholarship Program *(Doctorate, Graduate/Scholarship)*

Purpose: To provide scholarship to graduate students majoring in Korean studies in North America for their coursework and/or research. **Focus:** General studies. **Qualif.:** Applicants must be M.A. or Ph.D. students majoring in Korean studies in any university in North America. **Criteria:** Applicants must exhibit sufficient ability to use Korean-language sources in their research and study.

Funds Avail.: $15,000. **To Apply:** Applicants must complete a Foundation Application Form, a three-page proposal outlining research interests and academic progress of the student, with a separate one-page bibliography; grade transcripts of coursework; and three letters of recommendation, one of which must be from someone able to attest to the applicant's language ability. **Deadline:** January 31.

1372 ■ Association of Black Women Physicians

4712 Admiralty Way, Ste. No. 175
Marina Del Rey, CA 90292
Ph: (310)364-1438
URL: http://www.blackwomenphysicians.org

1373 ■ Rebecca Lee, M.D. Scholarships
(Undergraduate/Scholarship)

Purpose: To provide educational assistance for female medical students who are permanent residents of Southern California or enrolled in Southern California medical schools. **Focus:** Medicine. **Qualif.:** Applicants must be permanent residents of Southern California at any medical school, or students at a Southern California medical school, who are in good academic standing. **Criteria:** Applicants are evaluated based on academic performance and financial need.

Funds Avail.: $1,000-$5,000. **To Apply:** Applicants must submit academic and financial aid transcripts, medical school acceptance letter or medical school dean's letter of good standing, three letters of recommendation, curriculum vitae and typed personal statement. **Deadline:** September 5.

1374 ■ Association of California Water Agencies

910 K St., Ste. 100
Sacramento, CA 95814-3577
Ph: (916)441-4545
Fax: (916)325-4849
Free: 888-666-2292
E-mail: acwabox@acwa.com
URL: http://www.acwa.com

1375 ■ ACWA Water Law and Policy Scholarships *(Graduate/Scholarship)*

Purpose: To promote study focusing on water resources. **Focus:** Water resources. **Qualif.:** Applicant must be attending a public or private school located in the United States of America; have completed undergraduate work and at the time of the award be either a part-time or full-time student in graduate studies; and must be carrying at least 8 units per term. **Criteria:** The award will be based not only on scholastic achievement, but also on the individual's commitment and motivation to their chosen vocation. Financial need will be considered.

Funds Avail.: $7,000. **To Apply:** Applicants must submit a completed scholarship application form along with the essay. **Deadline:** April 1. **Contact:** ACWA at acwabox@acwa.com, or 916-441-4545.

1376 ■ Association of California Water Agencies Scholarships *(Undergraduate/Scholarship)*

Purpose: To promote study focusing on water resources. **Focus:** Water resources. **Qualif.:** Applicant must be a resident of California attending one of the selected California schools full-time as a junior or senior during the current academic year. **Criteria:** The award will be based not only on scholastic achievement but also on the individual's commitment and motivation to their chosen vocation. Financial need will be considered.

Funds Avail.: $3,000. **Number Awarded:** 2. **To Apply:**

Applicants must submit a completed scholarship application form along with an essay. **Deadline:** April 1. **Contact:** ACWA at acwabox@acwa.com, or 916-441-4545.

1377 ■ Clair A. Hill Scholarships *(Undergraduate/Scholarship)*

Purpose: To promote study focusing on water resources. **Focus:** Water resources. **Qualif.:** Applicant must be a resident of California attending one of the selected California schools full-time as a sophomore, junior or senior during the current academic year. **Criteria:** The award will be based not only on scholastic achievement but also on the individual's commitment and motivation to their chosen vocation. Financial need will be considered.

Funds Avail.: $5,000. **To Apply:** Applicants must submit a completed scholarship application. **Deadline:** February 1. **Contact:** Meggan Reed, Rancho California Water District, at 951-396-6922, or e-mail at reedm@ranchowater.com, or by fax at 951-296-6922.

1378 ■ Association of College Unions International

One City Center, Ste. 200
120 W 7th St.
Bloomington, IN 47404
Ph: (812)245-2284
Fax: (812)245-6710
E-mail: acui@acui.org
URL: http://www.acui.org

1379 ■ Gretchen Laatsch Scholarships *(Undergraduate/Scholarship)*

Purpose: To encourage graduate students to submit professional quality articles in the field of college unions and students activities. **Focus:** General studies. **Qualif.:** Applicants must be recognized by an institution as students in pursuit of graduate degrees in any academic area. **Criteria:** Consideration will be given to students either currently in the field of college union and student activities or those intending to enter the profession.

Funds Avail.: $500. **To Apply:** Applicants must submit an article containing a minimum of 500 words; must have a letter of recommendation from a college union or student activities professional. Application form and requirements must be sent to Association of College Unions International, Gretchen Laatsch Scholarship, One City Center, Ste. 200, 120 W 7th St., Bloomington, IN 47404.

Remarks: Scholarship was established by former ACUI President Gretchen Laatsch from the University of Akron and her husband, Jim Switzer.

1380 ■ Association of College and University Auditors

342 N Main St., Ste. 301
West Hartford, CT 06117
Ph: (860)586-7561
Fax: (860)586-7550
E-mail: info@acua.org
URL: http://www.acua.org

1381 ■ ACUA Scholarships *(Graduate, Undergraduate/Scholarship)*

Purpose: To assist students in their education leading to careers in accounting, auditing, finance, or higher education administration. **Focus:** Accounting; Finance; Educational administration. **Qualif.:** Applicants must be a undergraduate or graduate student in a degree program leading to careers in accounting, auditing, finance, or higher education administration. **Criteria:** Selection is based on merits.

Funds Avail.: $500. **Number Awarded:** 2. **To Apply:** Applicants must submit a completed application form together with a single page essay; written recommendation; and a copy of transcript. **Deadline:** May 31. **Contact:** Larry Mandel, ACUA Scholarship Chair, lmandel@calstate.edu.

1382 ■ Association for College and University Clubs

1733 King St.
Alexandria, VA 22314-2720
Ph: (703)299-2630
Fax: (703)299-0925
E-mail: acuc@acuclubs.org
URL: http://www.acuclubs.org

1383 ■ Association for College And University Clubs Scholarships *(Other/Scholarship)*

Purpose: To promote reciprocal privileges, management education, and resource sharing among university clubs; to assist the education of a club employee through academic courses work, seminars or other practicum activities. **Focus:** Writing. **Qualif.:** Any employee of an ACUC member. **Criteria:** Recipients are selected base on the presented ideas that is evaluated by the sponsors.

Funds Avail.: $150. **To Apply:** A member should submit a written nominations from the Club's Manager and Board President along with the employees own statement of career goals; planned use for the scholarship; brief bibliography; official application form; **Deadline:** December 31.

1384 ■ Association for Compensatory Educators of Texas

PO Box 4987
Whitefish, MT 59937
Ph: (406)862-3275
Fax: (406)862-3276
E-mail: wburroughs@bresnan.net
URL: http://acetx.org

1385 ■ Association for Compensatory Educators of Texas Paraprofessionals Scholarships *(Undergraduate/Scholarship)*

Purpose: To provide financial assistance for deserving students. **Focus:** General studies. **Qualif.:** Applicants must be paraprofessionals who wish to return to school to pursue a degree and teacher certification. They must be currently working with a school district in a compensatory program. **Criteria:** Preference will be given to those students who meet the criteria.

Funds Avail.: No specific amount. **Number Awarded:** 4. **To Apply:** Applicants must submit proof of a high school diploma or GED and must check the available website to download the scholarship application, information letter, scoring rubric and scoring grid. **Deadline:** March 10. **Contact:** Applications must be submitted in one envelope as one complete document to: Jeanne Walker 1302 Oak Creek Dr. Ennis, TX 75119.

1386 ■ Association for Compensatory Educators of Texas Scholarships *(Undergraduate/Scholarship)*

Purpose: To provide remedial assistance and support for students who have failed TAKS or are at-risk of dropping out of school. **Focus:** General studies. **Qualif.:** Applicants must be students who historically have more difficult time in school due to language, economic and other barriers. **Criteria:** Selection will be made by the committee.

Funds Avail.: $1,000. **Number Awarded:** 20. **To Apply:** Applicants must submit a completed application form. **Deadline:** March 10. **Contact:** Applications must be submitted in one envelope as one complete document to: Jeanne Walker 1302 Oak Creek Dr. Ennis, TX 75119.

1387 ■ Association of Desk and Derrick Clubs

5153 E 51st St., Ste. 107
Tulsa, OK 74135
Ph: (918)622-1749
Fax: (918)622-1675
E-mail: adotulsa@swbell.net
URL: http://www.addc.org

1388 ■ Association of Desk and Derrick Clubs Education Trust Scholarships *(Undergraduate/Scholarship)*

Purpose: To provide financial assistance to college students planning a career in the petroleum energy or allied industries. **Focus:** Geology; Geophysics; Engineering, Petroleum; Engineering, Nuclear; Engineering, Mechanical; Energy-related areas. **Qualif.:** Applicant must have completed at least two years or be currently enrolled in the second year of undergraduate study at an accredited college or university; be a U.S. or Canadian citizen; maintain a GPA of 3.2 or above on a 4.0 scale; be pursuing a career in the field of petroleum, energy or allied industry. **Criteria:** Preference will be given to applicants with financial need.

Funds Avail.: $1,500. **To Apply:** Applicants must submit a completed application form to Desk and Derrick Educational Trust, 5153 E 51st St., Ste. 107, Tulsa, OK 74135. **Deadline:** April 1.

1389 ■ Association for Education and Rehabilitation of the Blind and Visually Impaired

1703 N Beauregard St., Ste. 440
Alexandria, VA 22311
Ph: (703)671-4500
Fax: (703)671-6391
Free: 877-492-2708
E-mail: aer@aerbvi.org
URL: http://www.aerbvi.org

1390 ■ William and Dorothy Ferrell Scholarship Program *(Undergraduate/Scholarship)*

Purpose: To support the education of selected students who are blind. **Focus:** Visual impairment. **Qualif.:** Applicant must be legally blind; must be studying at the post-secondary level for a career in the field of services to persons who are blind or visually impaired. **Criteria:** Applicants are selected based on the submitted applications and supporting materials.

Funds Avail.: $500. **Number Awarded:** 2. **To Apply:** Applicants must submit an application form (available at the website) to scholarships@aerbvi.org; a signed certification of visual status; and original letters of recommendation at the above address. **Deadline:** February 15.

1391 ■ Association of Electronic Journalists

4121 Plank Rd., Ste. 512
Fredericksburg, VA 22407
Ph: (202)659-6510
Fax: (202)223-4007
E-mail: barbarac@rtnda.org
URL: http://www.rtnda.org

1392 ■ Association of Electronic Journalists President's Scholarships *(Undergraduate/Scholarship)*

Purpose: To help RTNDF members embody and uphold the standards of ethical journalism. To promote leadership in the newsroom. **Focus:** Journalism. **Qualif.:** Applicants must be currently enrolled as college sophomores, juniors, and seniors in good standing. **Criteria:** Recipients are selected based on academic standing and financial need.

Funds Avail.: $2,500. **Number Awarded:** 2. **To Apply:** Applicant must complete the application form and provide evidence proving that he/she is currently enrolled. Applicants must submit one to three examples showing journalistic skills, totaling 15 minutes of editing and producing, and a list of colleagues; a one-page statement explaining why applicant seeks a career in electronic journalism; and a letter of reference from the dean or faculty sponsor. **Contact:** stacey@rtnda.org; 202-467-5205.

1393 ■ N.S. Beinstock Fellowships *(Undergraduate/Fellowship)*

Purpose: To recognize a promising minority journalist in radio or television news. **Focus:** Journalism. **Qualif.:** Applicants must be journalism students or senior broadcast news and mid-career professionals. **Criteria:** Recipients are selected based on the completed application form and completed requirements.

Funds Avail.: $2,500. **To Apply:** Applicants must complete the application form. Applicants must submit a resume; a cover letter with the reasons for seeking a fellowship and how the award will be used; a letter of recommendation from the news manager; a sample of the best work relevant to the fellowship, not exceeding 15 minutes on audio (cassette or CD) or video (VHS or DVD), and accompanied by scripts. International applications must include a full English translation. **Deadline:** May 12. **Contact:** 202-467-5205; staceys@rtnda.org.

1394 ■ Ed Bradley Scholarships *(Undergraduate/Scholarship)*

Purpose: To help RTNDF members embody and uphold the standards of ethical journalism; to promote leadership in the newsroom. **Focus:** Journalism. **Qualif.:** Applicants must be enrolled in radio and television news. Applicants must be full-time college students with at least one full year of college remaining whose career objective is to enter into the electronic journalism field. **Criteria:** Recipients are selected based on academic standing.

Funds Avail.: $10,000. **To Apply:** Applicant must complete the application form and provide evidence proving that he/she is currently enrolled. Applicants must submit one to three examples showing their journalistic skills, totaling 15 minutes of editing and producing, and a list of colleagues;

a one-page statement explaining why they seek a career in electronic journalism; a letter of reference from the dean or faculty sponsor. **Contact:** stacey@rtnda.org; 202-467-5205.

1395 ■ Broadcast News Management Fellowships *(Undergraduate/Scholarship)*

Purpose: To send journalists of color to leadership and management training programs. **Focus:** Journalism. **Qualif.:** Applicants must be senior broadcast news and mid-career professionals. **Criteria:** Recipients are selected based on academic standing.

Funds Avail.: No specific amount. **To Apply:** Applicants must submit an application form. Applicant must submit a letter of recommendation from his or her supervisor. **Contact:** melaniel@rtnda.org; 202-467-5218.

1396 ■ Michelle Clark Fellowships *(Undergraduate/Fellowship)*

Purpose: To honor women journalists in television news. **Focus:** Journalism. **Qualif.:** Applicants must be journalism students or senior broadcast news and midcareer professionals. **Criteria:** Recipients are selected based on the completed application form and completed requirements.

Funds Avail.: $1,000. **To Apply:** Applicants must complete the application form. Applicants must submit a resume; a cover letter with the reasons for seeking a fellowship and how the award will be used; a letter of recommendation from the news manager; a sample of the best work relevant to the fellowship, not exceeding 15 minutes on audio (cassette or CD) or video (VHS or DVD) and accompanied by scripts. International applications must include a full English translation. **Deadline:** May 12. **Contact:** 202-467-5205; staceys@rtnda.org.

1397 ■ George Foreman Tribute to Lyndon B. Johnson Scholarships *(Undergraduate/Scholarship)*

Purpose: To help RTNDF members embody and uphold the standards of ethical journalism. To promote leadership in the newsroom. **Focus:** Journalism. **Qualif.:** Applicants must be journalism students at the University of Texas-Austin. **Criteria:** Recipients are selected based on academic standing, and financial need.

Funds Avail.: $6,000. **To Apply:** Applicant must complete the application form and provide evidence proving that he/she is currently enrolled. Applicants must submit a copy of their FAFSA Student Aid Report (SAR). Applicants must submit one to three examples showing journalistic skills, totaling 15 minutes of editing and producing, and a list of colleagues; a one-page statement explaining why applicant seeks a career in electronic journalism; and a letter of reference from the dean or faculty sponsor. **Contact:** stacey@rtnda.org; 202-467-5205.

1398 ■ Ken Kashiwara Scholarships *(Undergraduate/Scholarship)*

Purpose: To help RTNDF members embody and uphold the standards of ethical journalism. To promote leadership in the newsroom. **Focus:** Journalism. **Qualif.:** Applicants must be enrolled in radio and television news. Applicants must be full-time college students whose career objective is to enter the electronic journalism field. Applicants must have at least one full year of college remaining. **Criteria:** Recipients are selected based on academic standing.

Funds Avail.: $2,500. **To Apply:** Applicant must complete the application form and provide evidence proving that he/she is currently enrolled. Applicants must submit one to three examples showing journalistic skills, totaling 15 minutes of editing and producing, and a list of colleagues; a one-page statement explaining why applicant seeks a career in electronic journalism; a letter of reference from the dean or faculty sponsor . **Contact:** stacey@rtnda.org; 202-467-5205.

1399 ■ Jacque I. Minnotte Health Reporting Fellowships *(Undergraduate/Fellowship)*

Purpose: To recognize excellence in health or medical television and radio reporting. **Focus:** Journalism. **Qualif.:** Applicants must be journalism students or senior broadcast news and mid-career professionals. **Criteria:** Recipients are selected based on the completed application form and completed requirements.

Funds Avail.: $2,000. **To Apply:** Applicants must complete the application form. Applicants must submit a resume; a cover letter with the reasons for seeking a fellowship and how the award will be used; a letter of recommendation from the news manager; a sample of the best work relevant to the fellowship, not exceeding 15 minutes on audio (cassette or CD) or video (VHS or DVD) and accompanied by scripts. International applications must include a full English translation. **Deadline:** May 12. **Contact:** 202-467-5205; staceys@rtnda.org.

1400 ■ Lou and Carole Prato Sports Reporting Scholarships *(Undergraduate/Scholarship)*

Purpose: To help RTNDF members embody and uphold the standards of ethical journalism. To promote leadership in the newsroom. **Focus:** Journalism. **Qualif.:** Applicants must be students pursuing a career as a sports reporter in television or radio. **Criteria:** Recipients are selected based on academic standing and strong writing skills.

Funds Avail.: $1,000. **To Apply:** Applicant must complete the application form and provide evidence proving that he/she is currently enrolled. Applicants must submit one to three examples showing journalistic skills, totaling 15 minutes of editing and producing, and a list of colleagues; a one-page statement explaining why applicant seeks a career in electronic journalism; and a letter of reference from the dean or faculty sponsor. **Contact:** stacey@rtnda.org; 202-467-5205.

1401 ■ Nike Reynolds Journalism Scholarships *(Undergraduate/Scholarship)*

Purpose: To help RTNDF members embody and uphold the standards of ethical journalism. To promote leadership in the newsroom. **Focus:** Journalism. **Qualif.:** Applicants must be currently enrolled in journalism school and have good writing abilities, excellent grades, and a dedication to the news business. Applicants must have strong interest in pursuing electronic journalism. Applicants must have demonstrated financial need. **Criteria:** Recipients are selected based on academic standing and financial need.

Funds Avail.: $1,000. **To Apply:** Applicant must complete the application form and provide evidence proving that he/she is currently enrolled. Applicants must submit a copy of their FAFSA Student Aid Report (SAR). Applicants must submit one to three examples showing journalistic skills, totaling 15 minutes of editing and producing, and a list of colleagues; a one-page statement explaining why applicant seeks a career in electronic journalism; and a letter of reference from the dean or faculty sponsor. **Contact:** stacey@rtnda.org; 202-467-5205.

1402 ■ Abe Schecter Graduate Scholarships
(Postgraduate/Scholarship)

Purpose: To help RTNDF members embody and uphold the standards of ethical journalism. To promote leadership in the newsroom. **Focus:** Journalism. **Qualif.:** Applicants must be pursuing careers in radio and television news. Applicants must be full-time college students whose career objective is to enter the electronic journalism field. Applicants must be enrolled in college and in good standing. **Criteria:** Recipients are selected based on academic standing and financial need.

Funds Avail.: $2,000. **To Apply:** Applicant must complete the application form and provide evidence proving that he/she is currently enrolled. Applicants must submit a copy of their FAFSA Student Aid Report (SAR). Applicants must submit one example showing journalistic skills, totaling 15 minutes of editing and producing, and a list of colleagues; a one-page statement explaining why applicant seeks a career in electronic journalism; and a letter of reference from the dean or faculty sponsor. **Contact:** stacey@rtnda.org; 202-467-5205.

1403 ■ Carole Simpson Scholarships
(Undergraduate/Scholarship)

Purpose: To help RTNDF members embody and uphold the standards of ethical journalism. To promote leadership in the newsroom. To encourage and help minority students overcome hurdles along their career path. **Focus:** Journalism. **Qualif.:** Applicants must be enrolled in radio and television news; applicants must be full-time college students whose career objective is to enter the electronic journalism field and who have at least one full year of college remaining. **Criteria:** Recipients are selected based on academic standing.

Funds Avail.: $2,000. **To Apply:** Applicant must complete the application form and provide evidence proving that he/she is currently enrolled. Applicants must submit one to three examples showing journalistic skills, totaling 15 minutes of editing and producing, and a list of colleagues; a one-page statement explaining why applicant seeks a career in electronic journalism; and a letter of reference from the dean or faculty sponsor. **Contact:** stacey@rtnda.org; 202-467-5205.

1404 ■ Pete Wilson Graduate Scholarships
(Postgraduate/Scholarship)

Purpose: To help RTNDF members embody and uphold the standards of ethical journalism. To promote leadership in the newsroom. **Focus:** Journalism. **Qualif.:** Applicant must be pursuing a career in radio and television news. Applicant must be a graduate or undergraduate student in the San Francisco Bay area, whose career objective is to enter the electronic journalism field. Applicant must be enrolled in college and be in good standing. **Criteria:** Recipients are selected based on academic standing and financial need.

Funds Avail.: $4,000. **To Apply:** Applicant must complete the application form and provide evidence proving that he/she is currently enrolled. Applicants must submit a copy of their FAFSA Student Aid Report (SAR). Applicants must submit one example showing their journalistic skills, totaling 15 minutes of editing and producing, and a list of colleagues; a one-page statement explaining why the applicant seeks a career in electronic journalism; and a letter of reference from the dean or faculty sponsor explaining applicant is a good candidate for an award. **Contact:** stacey@rtnda.org; 202-467-5205.

1405 ■ Pete Wilson Journalism Scholarships
(Undergraduate/Scholarship)

Purpose: To help RTNDF members embody and uphold the standards of ethical journalism. To promote leadership in the newsroom. **Focus:** Journalism. **Qualif.:** Applicants must be full-time undergraduate or graduate students who plan to work in the electronic journalism field in the San Francisco Bay area. **Criteria:** Recipients are selected based on academic standing.

Funds Avail.: $4,000. **To Apply:** Applicant must complete the application form and provide evidence proving that he/she is currently enrolled. Applicants must submit one to three examples showing journalistic skills, totaling 15 minutes of editing and producing, and a list of colleagues; a one-page statement explaining why applicant seeks a career in electronic journalism; and a letter of reference from the dean or faculty sponsor. **Contact:** stacey@rtnda.org; 202-467-5205.

1406 ■ Association of Energy Engineers Foundation

4025 Pleasantdale Rd., Ste. 420
Atlanta, GA 30340
Ph: (770)447-5083
Fax: (770)446-3969
E-mail: maryelise@aeecenter.org
URL: http://www.aeecenter.org

1407 ■ Association of Energy Engineers Foundation Scholarship Program *(Graduate, Undergraduate/Scholarship)*

Purpose: To encourage qualified practitioners in energy engineering and energy management by awarding scholarships to further education in the field. **Focus:** Energy-related areas. **Qualif.:** Applicants must be undergraduate and graduate degree candidates who are enrolled in engineering or management programs at accredited colleges or universities. **Criteria:** Applicants are evaluated based on the criteria designed by the Scholarship Selection Committee.

Funds Avail.: No specific amount. **To Apply:** Applicants must submit all the required application information. **Deadline:** May 1.

1408 ■ Association of Environmental and Engineering Geologists

PO Box 460518
Denver, CO 80246
Ph: (303)757-2926
Fax: (303)757-2969
E-mail: aeg@aegweb.org
URL: http://www.aegweb.org

1409 ■ Marliave Scholarship Fund
(Undergraduate/Scholarship)

Purpose: To provide scholarships to those outstanding students in the field of geological engineering. **Focus:** Geological Engineering. **Qualif.:** Applicants must be outstanding students in geological engineering. **Criteria:** Awards will be given to those students who meet the criteria.

Funds Avail.: No specific amount. **To Apply:** Applicants must submit a completed application form.

Remarks: The Marliave Scholarship Fund was established in 1968 by the Association of Environmental & Engineering Geologists (AEG). The fund name honors an eminent family of engineering geologists: Chester E. Marliave (1888-1958), and his sons Elmer C. Marliave (1910-1967) and Burton H. Marliave (1917-199), who were pioneers in the profession. **Contact:** Association of Environmental and Engineering Geologists at the above address (see entry 1408).

1410 ■ Martin L. Stout Scholarships
(Undergraduate/Scholarship)

Purpose: To provide financial support to those students who are in need. **Focus:** Geological Engineering. **Qualif.:** Applicants must be students who are pursuing geological engineering; must be in good academic standing; must have financial need. **Criteria:** Selection will be based on scholastic record.

Funds Avail.: No specific amount. **To Apply:** Applicants must submit a completed application form. **Contact:** Association of Environmental and Engineering Geologists at the above address (see entry 1408).

1411 ■ Association of Family Practice Physician Assistants

1905 Woodstock Rd., Ste. 2150
Roswell, GA 30075
Ph: (770)640-7605
Fax: (770)640-1095
Free: 877-890-0181
URL: http://www.afppa.org

1412 ■ AFPPA Student Scholarships
(Undergraduate/Scholarship)

Purpose: To financially assist first and second year physician students. **Focus:** Medicine. **Qualif.:** Applicants must be PA students attending an accredited PA program for more than 12 months or students with 12 months or less of PA education. **Criteria:** Applicants who are AFPPA student members who are in good academic standing and demonstrate interest in family practice medicine are given priority.

Funds Avail.: $500 for first year students and $1,000 for second year students. **Number Awarded:** 2. **To Apply:** Applicants must submit an essay (maximum of 750 words or less) describing the commitment to family practice medicine and how the current and past community involvement demonstrates this commitment. **Deadline:** September 1.

1413 ■ Association for Federal Information Resources Management

PO Box 2848
Alexandria, VA 22301
Ph: (703)549-1160
Fax: (703)995-4890
E-mail: info@affirm.org
URL: http://www.affirm.org

1414 ■ AFFIRM University Scholarships
(Undergraduate/Scholarship)

Purpose: To provide scholarships for undergraduate students to achieve a degree in Information Technology. **Focus:** Information science and technology; Technology. **Qualif.:** Applicant must be a full-time student (12 credits or more); must be a junior or above; have a minimum of 3.0 cumulative GPA; majoring in some aspect of information technology or related field. **Criteria:** U.S. Citizens are given preference.

Funds Avail.: No specific amount is given. **To Apply:** Scholarship applications will be provided by the universities; applicants must prepare a letter of reference from a professor.

1415 ■ Lisa Winkler Memorial Scholarships
(Undergraduate/Scholarship)

Purpose: To provide educational assistance for graduates of Edison High School who wish to continue their education in Information Technology. **Focus:** Information science and technology; Technology. **Qualif.:** Applicant must be a graduating senior who completed two full-years at Edison High School; accepted at an accredited four-year college/university; have a minimum of 3.0 cumulative GPA by the end of the first semester (senior year). **Criteria:** Applicants who are members of honor societies will be given consideration.

Funds Avail.: No specific amount. **To Apply:** Applicant must prepare an essay (maximum of 200) on "Why I would like to pursue a career in information technology in the Federal Government".

Remarks: In memory of Lisa Winkler, for her devotion to support of IT education.

1416 ■ Association for Financial Technology

34 N High St.
New Albany, OH 43054
Ph: (614)895-1208
Fax: (614)895-3466
URL: http://www.aftweb.com

1417 ■ James E. Stoner Memorial Scholarships
(Undergraduate/Scholarship)

Purpose: To provide educational support for members and members' dependents. **Focus:** General studies. **Qualif.:** Applicants are the employees and their dependents. **Criteria:** Selection is based on a scoring point system. Applicant with the most points will receive the award.

Funds Avail.: $3000. **To Apply:** Applicants must submit a completed application form available at the website. **Deadline:** July 2.

1418 ■ Association of Flight Attendants

501 3rd St., NW
Washington, DC 20001
Ph: (202)434-1300
E-mail: afatalk@afanet.org
URL: http://www.afanet.org

1419 ■ Association of Flight Attendants Scholarship Fund *(Undergraduate/Scholarship)*

Purpose: To further the education of promising young men and women who are dependents of AFA members in good standing to have the opportunity for higher education. **Focus:** Aviation. **Qualif.:** Applicants must be dependent of AFA members in good standing seeking to further education at an accredited college or university. **Criteria:** Candidates should: be ranked in the top 15% of their high school class; have excellent scores in SAT or ACT; have demonstrated financial need.

Awards are arranged alphabetically below their administering organizations

Funds Avail.: $5,000 for the cost of tuition, room, board and book expenses. **Number Awarded:** 1. **To Apply:** Applicants must submit a completed application form (available at the website), 300-word essay, three references and transcript, if applicable. **Deadline:** April 10.

1420 ■ Association of Food and Drug Officials

2550 Kingston Rd., Ste. 311
York, PA 17402
Ph: (717)757-2888
Fax: (717)755-8089
E-mail: afdo@afdo.org
URL: http://www.afdo.org

1421 ■ George M. Burditt Scholarships
(Undergraduate/Scholarship)

Purpose: To provide financial assistance for students to further their education. **Focus:** General studies. **Qualif.:** Applicants must be sophomores preparing to enter junior year or juniors preparing to enter senior year. **Criteria:** Applicants must demonstrate a desire to serve in a career of research, regulatory work, quality control, or teaching in an area related to some aspect of foods, drugs or consumer product safety; potential to be a leader; and must have at least 3.0 GPA during the first two years of undergraduate study on a 4.0 scale.

Funds Avail.: $1,500. **To Apply:** Applicant must submit completed application form; official and complete college transcript, and two letters of recommendation from faculty members. **Deadline:** February 1.

1422 ■ Betsy B. Woodward Scholarships
(Undergraduate/Scholarship)

Purpose: To provide financial assistance for students to further their education. **Focus:** General studies. **Qualif.:** Applicants must be sophomores preparing to enter junior year or juniors preparing to enter senior year. **Criteria:** Applicants must demonstrate a desire to serve in a career of research, regulatory work, quality control, or teaching in an area related to some aspect of foods, drugs or consumer product safety; potential to be a leader; and must have at least 3.0 GPA during the first two years of undergraduate study on a 4.0 scale.

Funds Avail.: $1,500. **To Apply:** Applicants must submit completed application form, official and complete college transcript; and two letters of recommendation from faculty members. **Deadline:** February 1.

1423 ■ Association of Former Intelligence Officers

6723 Whittier Ave., Ste. 303A
McLean, VA 22101-4533
Ph: (703)790-0320
Fax: (703)991-1278
E-mail: afio@afio.com
URL: http://www.afio.com

1424 ■ David L. Boren Undergraduate Scholarships *(Graduate, Undergraduate/Scholarship)*

Purpose: To provide funding for graduate and undergraduate study in a number of targeted countries and fields. **Focus:** General studies. **Qualif.:** Applicants must be students currently enrolled in undergraduate study or graduates planning to attend graduate school; and must have desire to study foreign languages in addition to any major-related study. **Criteria:** Preferences are given for those students who are interested in studying critical languages or fields related to security interest.

Funds Avail.: $10,000 up to $20,000. **To Apply:** Applicants must complete official application form which can be obtained from the Loyola College faculty representative. Applicants must also submit application forms online together with the 3 letters of recommendation, and 4 semesters' worth of transcripts. **Deadline:** February 10.

1425 ■ CIA Undergraduate Scholarships
(Undergraduate/Scholarship)

Purpose: To assist minority, disabled and non-disabled deserving students to increase knowledge and academic skills. **Focus:** General studies. **Qualif.:** Applicants must be high school seniors planning to enroll in a 4- or 5-year college program, or college sophomores enrolled in a 4- or 5-year college program. **Criteria:** Applicants must demonstrate financial need.

Funds Avail.: $18,000. **To Apply:** Applicants must apply online and must successfully complete medical and psychological exam, polygraph interview and extensive background investigation.

1426 ■ Association General Contractors of America, New York State Chapter

10 Airline Dr., Ste. 203
Albany, NY 12205
Ph: (518)456-1134
Fax: (518)456-1198
E-mail: agcadmin@agcnys.org
URL: http://www.agcnys.org

1427 ■ AGC New York State Chapter Scholarship Program *(Undergraduate/Scholarship)*

Purpose: To provide financial assistance to college students working toward a degree in Civil Engineering or Construction Technology at a college or university. **Focus:** Civil engineering. **Qualif.:** Applicant must be entering the 2nd, 3rd or 4th year of a two or four-year college; seriously intent upon a career in the highway construction industry. Applicant must pursue a Bachelor or Associate degree in construction or civil engineering and have at least a 2.50 GPA. **Criteria:** Applicants will be evaluated by the Selection Committee of the New York State Chapter, Inc., Associated General Contractors.

Funds Avail.: $2,500. **To Apply:** Applicant must submit a signed, completed five-page application; three evaluation forms: one completed by a college faculty advisor, and two completed by adults not related to the applicant and preferably in the industry; and, official transcript of all college grades. **Deadline:** May 15.

1428 ■ Association of Independent Colleges and Universities of Pennsylvania

101 N Front St.
Harrisburg, PA 17101-1405
Ph: (717)232-8649
Fax: (717)233-8574
E-mail: duck@aicup.org
URL: http://www.aicup.org

Awards are arranged alphabetically below their administering organizations

1429 ■ Air Products and Chemicals, Inc. Scholarships *(Undergraduate/Scholarship)*

Purpose: To promote the engineering and information technology profession to individuals from groups historically underrepresented in engineering. **Focus:** Chemical engineering; Mechanical, Engineering; Computer and information sciences. **Qualif.:** Applicants must: be full-time undergraduate students majoring only in Chemical engineering, Mechanical engineering, Information technology (computer science, management information systems, IST); be enrolled as a junior in fall; have a minimum GPA of 3.0; be women and/or members of the following minority groups: American Indian or Alaska Native, Asian, Black or African American, Hispanic or Latino, Native Hawaiian or other Pacific Islander. Student must be accepted at, or currently attending, one of 84 member colleges and universities of the Association of Independent Colleges and Universities of Pennsylvania. **Criteria:** Selection will be based on the committee's criteria.

Funds Avail.: $7,500. **To Apply:** Application forms are available at the Financial Aid office; applicant must submit complete application materials to Mary Maronic, Foundation Associate, Association of Independent Colleges and Universities of Pennsylvania. A complete application consists of a completed, signed application form, a copy of the student's transcript, a resume and an essay; the candidate may submit a letter of recommendation. **Deadline:** April 29. **Contact:** Mary Maronic, 717-232-8649 ext. 232; maronic@aicup.org.

1430 ■ Michael Baker Corporation Scholarship Program *(Undergraduate/Scholarship)*

Purpose: To promote the engineering and information technology profession to individuals from groups historically underrepresented in engineering. **Focus:** Civil engineering; Architectural engineering. **Qualif.:** Applicant must be: full-time undergraduate students majoring in Civil, Environmental or Architectural Engineering only; enrolled as juniors in the fall; maintaining a minimum GPA of 3.0; women and/or members of the following minority groups: American Indians or Alaska Natives, Asians, Black or African Americans, Hispanics or Latinos, Native Hawaiians or Other Pacific Islanders. Student must be accepted at, or currently attending, one of 84 member colleges and universities of the Association of Independent Colleges and Universities of Pennsylvania. **Criteria:** Selection will be based on the committee's criteria.

Funds Avail.: $2,500. **Number Awarded:** 1. **To Apply:** Application forms are available at the Financial Aid office. Applicant must submit complete application to Mary Maronic, Foundation Associate, Association of Independent Colleges and Universities of Pennsylvania. A complete application consists of a completed, signed application form, a copy of the student's transcript, a resume and an essay; the candidate may submit a letter of recommendation. **Deadline:** April 29. **Contact:** Mary Maronic, 717-232-8649 ext. 232; maronic@aicup.org.

1431 ■ Commonwealth "Good Citizen" Scholarships *(Undergraduate/Scholarship)*

Purpose: To provide scholarship to the students who have shown an extraordinary commitment to community service and who have demonstrated creativity in shaping their volunteer activities. **Focus:** General studies. **Qualif.:** Applicant must be a full-time undergraduate student with an extraordinary commitment to community service and who has demonstrated creativity in shaping his/her volunteer activities. **Criteria:** Selection will be based on the committee's criteria.

Funds Avail.: $1,000. **Number Awarded:** 7. **To Apply:** Applicants must write a brief essay describing their college experience, and focusing upon the answers to the following: what volunteer/extracurricular activities do they participate in, either on or off campus; how do their community service activities relate to their major and what leadership roles have they taken; what are their career/academic goals upon graduation; how will they remain involved in their community upon graduation. Applicants should include any additional information that they feel will be helpful in choosing them as a recipients of the Commonwealth "Good Citizen" Scholarship; must limit essay to two double-spaced pages (essay must have 1-inch margins) with a font that is easily readable and set no smaller than 11. Completed applications should be returned to applicants' Financial Aid Office. **Contact:** Mary Maronic, 717-232-8649 ext. 232; maronic@aicup.org.

1432 ■ HDR Engineering, Inc. Scholarship for Diversity in Engineering *(Undergraduate/Scholarship)*

Purpose: To promote the engineering and information technology profession to individuals from groups historically underrepresented in engineering. **Focus:** Civil engineering; Architectural engineering; Engineering, Geological. **Qualif.:** Applicants must: be full-time undergraduate students majoring only in civil engineering, structural engineering or geotechnical engineering; be enrolled as juniors in fall; have a minimum GPA of 3.0; be women and/or members of one of the following minority groups: American Indian or Alaska Native, Asian, Black or African American, Hispanic or Latino, Native Hawaiian or Other Pacific Islander. Applicants must be accepted at, or currently attending, one of 84 member colleges and universities of the Association of Independent Colleges and Universities of Pennsylvania. **Criteria:** Selection will be based on the committee's criteria.

Funds Avail.: $2,500. **To Apply:** Application forms are available at the Financial Aid office. Applicant must submit complete application materials to Mary Maronic, Foundation Associate, Association of Independent Colleges and Universities of Pennsylvania. A complete application consists of a completed, signed application form, a copy of the student's transcript, a resume and an essay; the candidate may submit a letter of recommendation. **Deadline:** April 29. **Contact:** Mary Maronic, 717-232-8649 ext. 232; maronic@aicup.org.

1433 ■ McLean Scholarships *(Undergraduate/Scholarship)*

Purpose: To help full-time undergraduate students who are enrolled in a Nursing or Physician's Assistant program. **Focus:** Nursing. **Qualif.:** Applicant must be a full-time undergraduate student enrolled in a Nursing or Physician Assistant program at one of the Association of Independent Colleges and Universities of Pennsylvania's member institutions, and have at least a 3.0 GPA. Ideal candidates are campus leaders and community volunteers. **Criteria:** Selection will be based on the committee's criteria.

Funds Avail.: $2,500. **Number Awarded:** 7. **To Apply:** Application forms are available at the Financial Aid office. Along with the completed applications, students may submit a copy of their transcript, a letter of recommendation, and any other materials that they feel will be helpful to the committee in making their decision. Students must also submit a brief essay describing their college experience, including the following information: why they chose their major; What steps they are taking to ensure that they succeed in their major; what they plan to do upon graduating and their academic/career goals. Applicants should also describe the primary volunteer/extracurricular activities in which they participate; how these activities relate to their major and what leadership roles they have taken. Completed applications should be returned to the applicants' Financial Aid office, which will then select one application to submit to AICUP. **Deadline:** April 29. **Contact:** Mary Maronic, 717-232-8649 ext. 232; maronic@aicup.org.

1434 ■ Association for International Training

10400 Little Patuxent Parkway, Ste. 250
Columbia, MD 21044-3519
Ph: (410)992-3924
Fax: (410)992-3924
E-mail: aipt@aipt.org
URL: http://www.aipt.org

1435 ■ IAESTE United States Scholarships

(Undergraduate/Scholarship)

Purpose: To help defray some of the costs associated with relocating overseas. **Focus:** General studies. **Qualif.:** An applicant must be of IAESTE United States at the time of internship. **Criteria:** Recipient will be based on the choice of destination which enables a student to leave the familiar and thereby grow professionally, culturally, and personally; a drive to use the international experience as a springboard to further develop the skills and competencies needed to fulfill a successful career of lifelong learning; choice of a region that directly relates to a student's academic, personal, and cultural interests.

Funds Avail.: No specific amount. **Number Awarded:** 3. **To Apply:** Applicant must submit a scholarship application form; a photo of the internship experience; a 500 word essay explaining the meaning and value of IAESTE internship. **Deadline:** December 1. **Contact:** outbound@aipt.org.

1436 ■ Jessica King Scholarships

(Undergraduate/Scholarship)

Purpose: to help defray some of the costs associating with relocating overseas. **Focus:** Hospitals-Administration. **Qualif.:** All applicants must be 18 years old and not older than 35; he/she must have been participating in an AIPT-sponsored program; must have been approved for the work permit to take up that position; must have been offered an overseas position; must have a degree in the hospitality industry; he/she must be currently employed for at least one year in hospitality industry; must be a U.S. citizen only. **Criteria:** Committee will evaluate the application based upon the merit, and not on the financial need.

Funds Avail.: No specific amount. **To Apply:** An applicant must complete and submit a filled out application form. **Contact:** aipt@aipt.org

1437 ■ Association for Iron and Steel Technology

186 Thorn Hill Rd.
Warrendale, PA 15086-7528
Ph: (724)776-6040
Fax: (724)776-1880
E-mail: info@aist.org
URL: http://www.aist.org

1438 ■ AIST Baltimore Chapter Scholarships

(Undergraduate/Scholarship)

Purpose: To enhance education and careers in engineering or metallurgy. **Focus:** Engineering; Metallurgy. **Qualif.:** Applicant must be a dependent or a spouse of a commendable member of the AIST Baltimore Chapter Scholarship; must be attending an eligible, full-time course in the field of engineering at an institution; demonstrate interest towards a career in the field of iron and steel industry. **Criteria:** Recipients are selected by the Scholarship Award Committee.

Funds Avail.: $1,500. **Number Awarded:** 1. **To Apply:** Applicants must submit an application form available at the website; a resume; a copy of SAT/ACT scores; copy of transcripts; two essays about the applicant's accomplishments, and the applicant's interest/involvement in the steel and iron industry. Send all documents to: AIST Baltimore Chapter Scholarships, Thomas J. Russo, 1430 Sparrows Point Blvd. Sparrows Point, MD 21219-1014. **Deadline:** April 30. **Contact:** Thomas J. Russo, 410-388-4337, tom.russo@mittalsteel.com.

1439 ■ AIST Detroit Chapter Scholarships

(Undergraduate/Scholarship)

Purpose: To enhance education and careers in the iron and steel-related industry. **Focus:** Engineering; Metallurgy. **Qualif.:** Applicant must be a dependent of an AIST Detroit Chapter member in good standing for two or more consecutive years; have a minimum cumulative GPA of 3.0 on a 4.0 scale; must be enrolled full-time as an undergraduate student majoring in engineering, metallurgy or materials science program at an accredited North American university; demonstrate interest towards a career in the field of iron and steel industry. **Criteria:** Recipients are selected by the Scholarship Award Committee.

Funds Avail.: $2,500. **Number Awarded:** 2. **To Apply:** Applicant must submit an application form available at the website; a resume; three letters of recommendation (addressing character, academic status, leadership potential and career commitment) from a high school counselor or college academic advisor, teacher/professor or a previous employer; copy of SAT/ACT scores; copy of current transcripts; an essay (maximum of 2 pages) about the applicant's professional goals, interest in a career in the iron and steel industry, and how the applicant's skills could be applied to enhance the industry. Requirements must be sent to: AIST Detroit Member Chapter Scholarships, c/o Judith A. Quinn, Chapter Secretary 41158 Savage Road Belleville, MI 48111. **Deadline:** April 30. **Contact:** Judith Quinn, 313-319-2815, judieqn@aol.com.

1440 ■ AIST Northwest Chapter Scholarships

(Undergraduate/Scholarship)

Purpose: To enhance education and careers in the field of engineering. **Focus:** Engineering. **Qualif.:** Applicant must be a relative of a member of the AIST Northwest Member Chapter; must be a Pacific Northwest student; must demonstrate great interest in the iron and steel profession. Chemistry, metallurgy, mathematics, engineering and physics students are also qualified for the scholarships. **Criteria:** Priority will be given to engineering students. Academic achievements in chemistry, mathematics and physics are a major basis for the selection. Extra-curricular activities and student statements are also considered.

Funds Avail.: $1,000. **Number Awarded:** 2. **To Apply:** Applicants must submit an application form available at the website; a resume; a recommendation/evaluation from a

Awards are arranged alphabetically below their administering organizations

counselor, teacher or professor; copy of SAT/ACT scores; copy of transcripts; and an essay (maximum of 2 pages) with one of the topics: Purpose in going to college; beneficial experience during the last two summers; most significant experiences and effect on future plans; accomplishments providing the greatest satisfaction; reason why the applicant should be chosen as the recipient of the award. Requirements must be sent to: Gerardo L. Giraldo, Quality Assurance Manager Nucor Steel Seattle, Inc. Washington Steel Division 2424 SW Andover St., Seattle, Washington 98106-1100. **Deadline:** April 30. **Contact:** Gerardo L. Giraldo at gerry.giraldo@nucor-seattle.com 206-933-2245.

1441 ■ AIST Ronald E. Lincoln Memorial Scholarships *(Undergraduate/Scholarship)*

Purpose: To enhance education and careers iron and steel-related industries. **Focus:** Engineering; Metallurgy. **Qualif.:** Applicant must be enrolled full-time in an engineering, metallurgy or materials science program at an accredited North American university; have a minimum cumulative GPA of 3.0 on a 4.0 scale; demonstrate interest toward a career in the field of iron and steel industry. **Criteria:** Recipients are selected based on the application materials submitted.

Funds Avail.: $3,000. **Number Awarded:** 2. **To Apply:** Applicants must submit an application form available at the website; a resume; three letters of recommendation (addressing character, academic status, leadership potential and career commitment) from a college academic advisor, professor and previous employer; transcripts; an essay (maximum of 2 pages) about the applicant's professional goals, interest in a career in the iron and steel industry, and how the applicant's skills could be applied to enhance the industry. **Deadline:** March 2.

Remarks: Established by Chaparral Steel. **Contact:** Lori Wharrey lwharrey@aist.org or 724-776-6040 ext.621.

1442 ■ AIST San Francisco Chapter Scholarships *(Undergraduate/Scholarship)*

Purpose: To provide financial assistance to students who are planning to enter an accredited North American school. **Focus:** General studies. **Qualif.:** Applicant must be related to a San Francisco Chapter member; must be planning to attend or currently enrolled at an accredited university or college (full-time course only). **Criteria:** Recipients are selected by the Scholarship Award Committee.

Funds Avail.: $1,500. **Number Awarded:** 1. **To Apply:** Applicants must submit an application form available at the website; resume; a recommendation/evaluation from a counselor, teacher or professor; copy of SAT/ACT scores; copy of transcripts; an essay (not more than 250 words) that answers the question, "Why are you motivated to attend college and how do you hope to utilize your degree after you graduate?". All requirements must be sent to: Frank Martucci Department Manager - Project Development USS-POSCO Industries 900 Loveridge Rd. Pittsburg, CA 94565. **Deadline:** April 30. **Contact:** Frank Martucci at 925-439-6708 fmartucci@ussposco.com.

1443 ■ AIST William E. Schwabe Memorial Scholarships *(Undergraduate/Scholarship)*

Purpose: To enhance education and careers in iron and steel-related industries. **Focus:** Engineering; Metallurgy. **Qualif.:** Applicant must be enrolled full-time in an engineering, metallurgy or materials science program at an accredited North American university; have a minimum cumulative GPA of 3.0 on a 4.0 scale; demonstrate interest in a career in the iron and steel industry. **Criteria:** Recipient will be selected based on the application materials submitted.

Funds Avail.: $3,000. **Number Awarded:** 1. **To Apply:** Applicants must submit an application form available at the website; a resume; three letters of recommendation (addressing character, academic status, leadership potential and career commitment) from a college academic advisor, professor and previous employer; transcripts; an essay (maximum of 2 pages) about the applicant's professional goals, interest in a career in the iron and steel industry, and how the applicant's skills could be applied to enhance the industry. **Deadline:** March 2.

Remarks: Established in 2005 by the Steel Manufacturers Association (SMA). **Contact:** Lori Wharrey at lwharrey@aist.org or 724-776-6040, ext. 621.

1444 ■ AIST Willy Korf Memorial Fund *(Undergraduate/Scholarship)*

Purpose: To enhance education and careers in iron and steel-related industry. **Focus:** Engineering; Metallurgy. **Qualif.:** Applicant must be enrolled full-time in an engineering, metallurgy or materials science program at an accredited North American university; have a minimum cumulative GPA of 3.0 on a 4.0 scale; demonstrate interest in a career in the iron and steel industry. **Criteria:** Recipients are selected based on the application materials submitted.

Funds Avail.: $3,000. **Number Awarded:** 3. **To Apply:** Applicants must submit an application form available at the website; a resume; three letters of recommendation which address the applicant's character, academic status, leadership potential and career commitment from a college academic advisor, professor and previous employer; transcripts; and an essay (maximum of 2 pages) about the applicant's professional goals, interest in a career in the iron and steel industry, and how the applicant's skills could be applied to enhance the industry. **Deadline:** March 2.

Remarks: Established by Korf Lurgi Steeltec, Inc. **Contact:** Lori Wharrey lwharrey@aist.org or 724-776-6040, ext. 621.

1445 ■ AIST Benjamin F. Fairless Scholarships (AIME) *(Undergraduate/Scholarship)*

Purpose: To enhance education and careers in the iron and steel-related industries. **Focus:** Engineering; Metallurgy. **Qualif.:** Applicant must be enrolled full-time in an engineering, metallurgy or materials science program at an accredited North American university; have a minimum GPA of 3.0 on a 4.0 scale; demonstrate interest toward a career in the field of iron and steel industry. **Criteria:** Recipient is selected based on the application and other documents.

Funds Avail.: $2,000. **Number Awarded:** 11. **To Apply:** Applicant must submit an application form available at the website; a resume; an essay (maximum of 2 pages) about the applicant's professional goals, interest in a career in the steel industry, and how the applicant's skills could be applied to enhance the industry; three letters of recommendation (addressing the character, academic status, leadership potential and career commitment) from a college academic advisor, professor and previous employer; and transcripts. **Deadline:** March 2.

Remarks: Established in 1954. **Contact:** Lori Wharrey at lwharrey@aist.org or 724-776-6040 ext. 621.

1446 ■ Midwest Chapter Scholarships - Jack Gill *(Undergraduate/Scholarship)*

Purpose: To provide educational assistance to engineering students. **Focus:** Engineering. **Qualif.:** Applicant must be a

Awards are arranged alphabetically below their administering organizations

graduating high school student or a full-time freshman, sophomore or junior student in good academic standing from an accredited institution. **Criteria:** Recipient will be selected according to merit.

Funds Avail.: $3,000. **Number Awarded:** 1. **To Apply:** Applicants must submit an application form available at the website; a resume; a recommendation/evaluation from a counselor, teacher or professor; copy of SAT/ACT scores; copy of transcripts; and an essay (maximum of 2 pages) describing the applicant's objectives for college and career. Requirements should be sent to: AIST Midwest Member Chapter Scholarships c/o Barry Felton 250 W US Highway 12 Burns Harbor, IN 46304. **Deadline:** March 15. **Contact:** Barry Felton barry.felton@arcelormittal, 219-787-4280.

1447 ■ Globe-Trotters Chapter Scholarships *(Undergraduate/Scholarship)*

Purpose: To enhance education and careers in the iron and steel-related industry. **Focus:** Metallurgy. **Qualif.:** Applicant must be a dependent of a member (Globe-Trotters member must also be a current member of AIST); be currently enrolled in an accredited college or university. Postgraduate students are also qualified for the scholarships. **Criteria:** Recipients are selected based on the submitted essay, academic and extracurricular activities.

Funds Avail.: $2,500. **Number Awarded:** 5. **To Apply:** Applicants must submit an application form available at the website; resume; copy of SAT/ACT scores; a copy of transcripts; an essay (maximum of 300 words) about the reason the applicant has selected the particular field of study, and an explanation on how the scholarship will be applied, such as tuition, books, etc. All required documents, together with the application, must be sent to: Globe-Trotter Scholarships Dennis Foster Day Melter Nucor Steel Texas PO Box 126 Jewett, TX 75846. **Deadline:** April 30. **Contact:** Dennis Foster at dennis.foster@nstexas.com, Phone: 903-626-4461 ext. 606, Fax: 903-626-6295.

1448 ■ Midwest Chapter Scholarships - Betty McKern *(Undergraduate/Scholarship)*

Purpose: To provide educational assistance to engineering students. **Focus:** Engineering. **Qualif.:** Applicant must be a graduating female high school student or a full-time freshman, sophomore or junior student in good academic standing from an accredited institution. **Criteria:** Recipient will be selected according to merits.

Funds Avail.: $3,000. **Number Awarded:** 1. **To Apply:** Applicants must submit an application form available at the website; a resume; a recommendation/evaluation from a counselor, teacher or professor; copy of SAT/ACT scores; transcripts; and an essay (maximum of 2 pages) describing the applicant's objectives for college and career. Requirements should be sent to: AIST Midwest Member Chapter Scholarships c/o Barry Felton 250 W US Highway 12 Burns Harbor, IN 46304. **Deadline:** March 15. **Contact:** Barry Felton barry.felton@arcelormittal, 219-787-4280.

1449 ■ Midwest Chapter Scholarships - Don Nelson *(Undergraduate/Scholarship)*

Purpose: To provide educational assistance to engineering students. **Focus:** Engineering. **Qualif.:** Applicant must be a graduating high school student or a full-time freshman, sophomore or junior student in good academic standing from an accredited institution. **Criteria:** Grantee will be selected according to merit.

Funds Avail.: $3,000. **Number Awarded:** 1. **To Apply:** Applicants must submit an application form available at the website; a resume; a recommendation/evaluation from a counselor, teacher or professor; copy of SAT/ACT scores; copy of transcripts; and an essay (maximum of 2 pages) describing the applicant's objectives for college and career. Requirements should be sent to: AIST Midwest Member Chapter Scholarships c/o Barry Felton 250 W US Highway 12 Burns Harbor, IN 46304. **Deadline:** March 15. **Contact:** Barry Felton barry.felton@arcelormittal, 219-787-4280.

1450 ■ Midwest Chapter Scholarships - Engineering *(Undergraduate/Scholarship)*

Purpose: To provide educational assistance to engineering students. **Focus:** Engineering. **Qualif.:** Applicant must be a graduating high school student or a full-time freshman, sophomore or junior student in good academic standing from an accredited institution. **Criteria:** Recipients will be selected according to merit.

Funds Avail.: $1,500. **Number Awarded:** 2. **To Apply:** Applicants must submit an application form available at the website; a resume; a recommendation/evaluation from a counselor, teacher or professor; copy of SAT/ACT scores; a copy of transcripts; and an essay (maximum of 2 pages) describing the applicant's objectives for college and career. Requirements should be sent to: AIST Midwest Member Chapter Scholarships c/o Barry Felton 250 W US Highway 12 Burns Harbor, IN 46304. **Deadline:** March 15. **Contact:** Barry Felton barry.felton@arcelormittal, 219-787-4280.

1451 ■ Midwest Chapter Scholarships - Mel Nickel *(Undergraduate/Scholarship)*

Purpose: To provide educational assistance to engineering students. **Focus:** Engineering. **Qualif.:** Applicant must be a graduating high school student or a full-time freshman, sophomore or junior student in good academic standing from an accredited institution. **Criteria:** Recipients will be selected according to merit.

Funds Avail.: $3,000. **Number Awarded:** 1. **To Apply:** Applicants must submit an application form available at the website; a resume; a recommendation/evaluation from a counselor, teacher or professor; copy of SAT/ACT scores; copy of transcripts; and an essay (maximum of 2 pages) describing the applicant's objectives for college and career. Requirements should be sent to: AIST Midwest Member Chapter Scholarships c/o Barry Felton 250 W US Highway 12 Burns Harbor, IN 46304. **Deadline:** March 15. **Contact:** Barry Felton barry.felton@arcelormittal, 219-787-4280.

1452 ■ Midwest Chapter Scholarships - Non-Engineering *(Undergraduate/Scholarship)*

Purpose: To provide educational assistance to non-engineering students. **Focus:** General studies. **Qualif.:** Applicant must be a graduating high school student or a full-time freshman, sophomore or junior student in good academic standing from an accredited institution. **Criteria:** Beneficiary will be selected according to merit.

Funds Avail.: $1,500. **Number Awarded:** 1. **To Apply:** Applicants must submit an application form available at the website; a resume; a recommendation/evaluation from a Counselor, Teacher or Professor; copy of SAT/ACT scores; a copy of transcripts; and an essay (maximum of 2 pages) describing the applicant's objectives for college and career. Requirements should be sent to: AIST Midwest Member Chapter Scholarships c/o Barry Felton 250 W US Highway 12 Burns Harbor, IN 46304. **Deadline:** March 15. **Contact:** Barry Felton barry.felton@arcelormittal, 219-787-4280.

1453 ■ Midwest Chapter Scholarships - Western States Award *(Undergraduate/Scholarship)*

Purpose: To provide educational assistance to both engineering and non-engineering students. **Focus:** General studies. **Qualif.:** Applicant must be a graduating high school student or a full-time freshman, sophomore or junior in good academic standing from an accredited institution. **Criteria:** Recipients will be selected according to merit.

Funds Avail.: $3,000. **Number Awarded:** 1. **To Apply:** Applicants must submit an application form available at the website; a resume; a recommendation/evaluation from a counselor, teacher or professor; copy of SAT/ACT scores; copy of transcripts; and an essay (maximum of 2 pages) describing the applicant's objectives for college and career. Requirements should be sent to: AIST Midwest Member Chapter Scholarships c/o Barry Felton 250 W US Highway 12 Burns Harbor, IN 46304. **Deadline:** March 15. **Contact:** Barry Felton barry.felton@arcelormittal, 219-787-4280.

1454 ■ Northeastern Ohio Chapter Scholarships - Alfred B. Glossbrenner and John Klusch Scholarships *(Undergraduate/Scholarship)*

Purpose: To provide educational assistance to students who wish to pursue their education and career in engineering and metallurgy. **Focus:** Engineering; Metallurgy. **Qualif.:** Applicant must be a dependent of an at least two-year member of the Association for Iron and Steel Technology, which must be a U.S. citizen or a U.S landed immigrant. Applicant should also be a full-time student from an accredited North American University; pursuing education in the field of engineering or metallurgy. Chemistry, geology, mathematics or physics students are also qualified for the scholarships. **Criteria:** Recipient is selected based on academic achievements in science (i.e. chemistry, mathematics and physics); extra-curricular activities and student statements will also be considered.

Funds Avail.: $2,000. **Number Awarded:** 1. **To Apply:** Applicants must submit an application form available at the website; a resume; a recommendation/evaluation from a counselor, teacher or professor; copy of SAT/ACT scores; copy of transcripts; and an essay (maximum of 2 pages) with one of the topics: Purpose in going to college; beneficial experience during the last two summers; most significant experiences and effect on future plans; accomplishments providing the greatest satisfaction; reason why the applicant should be chosen as the recipient of the award. All documents and application should be sent to: Richard J. Kurz, Chapter Secretary AIST Northeastern Ohio Chapter 22831 East State Street, Rte. 62 Alliance, Ohio 44601. **Deadline:** April 30. **Contact:** Richard J. Kurz at rkurz@eohiomach.com, 330-821-7198 ext.109.

1455 ■ Ohio Valley Chapter Scholarships *(Undergraduate/Scholarship)*

Purpose: To enhance education and careers in engineering, metallurgy, physical science, computer technology or an engineering technology field. **Focus:** Engineering; Metallurgy; Physical sciences. **Qualif.:** Applicant must be a dependent or member of Ohio Valley Chapter of the AIST; planning to attend or currently enrolled full-time curriculum at an accredited university or college; pursuing a degree in Mechanical Engineering, Electrical Engineering, Engineering/Engineering Technology, Environmental Engineering/Sciences, Metallurgy, Physical Sciences, Computer Technology, Computer Programming, Information Systems Technology, Chemistry, Biology/Microbiology, Physics, other engineering-related fields, or other related fields approved by the committee. **Criteria:** Recipient is selected based on academic performance and achievements in mathematics and science, extracurricular activities and essays.

Funds Avail.: $1,000. **Number Awarded:** 2. **To Apply:** Applicants must submit an application form available at the website; a resume; a recommendation/evaluation from a counselor and teacher or professor; copy of SAT/ACT scores; copy of transcripts; an essay (maximum of 2 pages) with either one of the topics: purpose in going to college; beneficial experience during the last two summers; most significant experiences and effect on future plans; accomplishments providing the greatest satisfaction; reasons why he/she should be chosen as the recipient of the award. All requirements must be sent to: Jeff McKain, 11451 Reading Road Cincinnati, OH 45241. Or thru email, Attn: AIST Scholarship, E-mail subject: AIST Scholarship to jeff.mckain@xtek.com. **Deadline:** March 31. **Contact:** Jeff Mckain 513-200-3000.

1456 ■ AIST David H. Samson Scholarships *(Undergraduate/Scholarship)*

Purpose: To provide financial support for Canadian students who are pursuing a career in engineering. **Focus:** Engineering. **Qualif.:** Applicant must be a dependent of a Canadian citizen or an immigrant who is a commendable member of the Association for Iron and Steel Technology; must be attending full-time engineering course at an accredited Canadian university or college. Chemistry, geology, mathematics or physics students are also welcome for the scholarships. **Criteria:** Priority will be given to engineering students.

Funds Avail.: $2,000. **Number Awarded:** 1. **To Apply:** Applicant must submit an application form available at the website; a resume; a recommendation/evaluation (from a counselor, teacher or professor); a copy of SAT/ACT scores; a copy of current transcripts; an essay (1-2 pages) with either one of the topics: purpose in going to college; beneficial experience during the last two summers, most significant experiences and effect on future plans; accomplishments providing the greatest satisfaction; reasons why he/she should be chosen as the recipient of the award. All requirements should be sent to: Robert Kneale, AIST Northern Member Chapter, David H. Samson Canadian Scholarship PO Box 1734 Cambridge, ON NIR7G8 Canada. **Deadline:** June 30.

Remarks: Managed by the AIST Northern Member Chapter. **Contact:** Robert Kneale at 519-740-2488, bkneale@gerdauameristeel.com.

1457 ■ Southeast Member Chapter Scholarships *(Undergraduate/Scholarship)*

Purpose: To provide educational assistance to students who are planning a career in Engineering or the sciences. **Focus:** Engineering. **Qualif.:** Applicant must be a Southeast Chapter student; planning to take up courses in engineering, sciences or other majors related to iron and steel production. **Criteria:** Recipient will be selected based on the SAT or ACT scores for college applicants and on the applicant's GPA from an accredited college or institution (non-first year student). Extra-curricular activities and student's written essays are also considered.

Funds Avail.: $1,500. **Number Awarded:** 1. **To Apply:** Applicants must submit an application form available at the website; a resume; a recommendation/evaluation from a counselor, teacher or professor; copy of SAT/ACT scores; copy of transcripts; and an essay (maximum of 250 words)

Awards are arranged alphabetically below their administering organizations

discussing the applicant's involvement in high school and the reason why the applicant deserves the scholarship. All documents together with the application should be sent to: AIST Southeast Chapter Mike Hutson, Secretary 803 Floyd St., Kings Mountain, NC, 29086. **Deadline:** April 30. **Contact:** Mike Hutson at mike@johnhutsoncompany.com.

1458 ■ Association of Jewish Libraries

PO Box 1118
Teaneck, NJ 07666
Ph: (212)725-5359
Free: 877-395-9257
E-mail: ajlibs@osu.edu
URL: http://www.jewishlibraries.org

1459 ■ AJL Convention Travel Grants *(All/Grant)*

Purpose: To provide financial assistance to members with financial need. **Focus:** General studies. **Qualif.:** Applicants must be current members of AJL at the time of application. Members in the local area are not eligible to apply. **Criteria:** Applicants are selected based on the committee's review of the application materials.

Funds Avail.: No specific amount. **To Apply:** Applicants must complete the application form available online and send it via e-mail, fax, or regular mail to: Ronda Rose, Past President AJL 11257 Dona Lisa Dr., Studio City, CA 91604, frose@sbcglobal.net, Fax: 323650-8414. **Deadline:** April 1.

Remarks: Grantees must submit an article describing the applicant's convention experience to the AJL Newsletter a year after receiving the award. **Contact:** Ronda Rose, 323-654-3652/323-650-8414, frose@sbcglobal.net.

1460 ■ AJL Scholarship Program *(Undergraduate/Scholarship)*

Purpose: To encourage students to train for, and enter, the field of Judaica librarianship. **Focus:** Archival science. **Qualif.:** Applicants must be attending an ALA-accredited library school or equivalent; should have an interest in, and demonstrate a potential for, pursuing a career in Judaica librarianship. **Criteria:** Selection is based on the application.

Funds Avail.: $500. **To Apply:** Applicants must complete and submit the application form available online and a brief statement about the involvement in Judaic activities. Submit requirements via e-mail, fax, or regular mail to: Lynn Feinman, 92nd St. Y 1395 Lexington Ave. New York, NY 10128, lfainman@92Y.org, fax: 212427-6119. **Deadline:** March 15.

1461 ■ Lucius Littauer Foundation Travel Grants *(All/Grant)*

Purpose: To provide financial assistance to members with financial need. **Focus:** General studies. **Qualif.:** Applicants must be current members of AJL at the time of application. **Criteria:** Applicants are selected based on the committee's review of the application materials.

Funds Avail.: No specific amount. **To Apply:** Applicants must complete the application form available online and send it via e-mail, fax, or regular mail to: Laurel Wolfson, AJL VP/Pres.-Elect, Klau Library, Hebrew Union College-Jewish Institute of Religion, 3101 Clifton Ave., Cincinnati, OH 45220-2488, lwolfson@huc.edu, Fax: 513221-0519. **Deadline:** April 1. **Contact:** Laurel Wolfson, Phone: 513-487-3274, Fax: 513-221-0519, lwolfson@huc.edu.

1462 ■ Doris Orenstein Memorial Convention Travel Grants *(All/Grant)*

Purpose: To provide financial assistance to members with financial need. **Focus:** General studies. **Qualif.:** Applicants must be members of the AJL and first time to attend the convention. **Criteria:** Applicants are selected based on the committee's review of the application materials.

Funds Avail.: No specific amount. **To Apply:** Applicants must complete the application form available online and send it via e-mail, fax, or regular mail to: Yelena Luckert, Doris Orenstein Memorial Fund Chairperson, McKeldin Library University of Maryland, College Park, MD 20742-7011, yluckert@umd.edu, Fax: 301-314-2795. **Deadline:** April 1. **Contact:** Yelena Luckert, yluckert@atsumd.edu, Phone: 301-405-9365, Fax: 301-314-2795.

1463 ■ Association for Library Service to Children

50 E Huron St.
Chicago, IL 60611
Free: 800-545-2433 x2163
E-mail: alsc@ala.org
URL: http://www.ala.org/alsc

1464 ■ Bound to Stay Bound Books (BTSB) Scholarships *(Graduate/Scholarship)*

Purpose: To provide financial assistance for individuals pursuing a master's or advanced degree in children's librarianship. **Focus:** Library and archival sciences. **Qualif.:** Applicants must be U.S. or Canadian citizens pursuing a master or advanced degree in children's librarianship. **Criteria:** Applicants will be selected on the basis of academic excellence, leadership qualities and the desire to work with children in any type of library.

Funds Avail.: $6,500. **Number Awarded:** 4. **To Apply:** Applicants must submit a completed application form; a personal statement describing career interests and goals; a commitment to library service to children; and three references (must be completed online). **Deadline:** March 1.

Remarks: The scholarship is sponsored by the Bound to Stay Bound Books, Inc.

1465 ■ Frederic G. Melcher Scholarships *(Graduate/Scholarship)*

Purpose: To provide financial assistance for individuals pursuing a master's or advanced degree in children's librarianship. **Focus:** Library and archival sciences. **Qualif.:** Applicants must be U.S. or Canadian citizens pursuing a master or advanced degree in children's librarianship. **Criteria:** Applicants will be selected on the basis of academic excellence, leadership qualities and the desire to work with children in any type of library.

Funds Avail.: $6,000. **Number Awarded:** 2. **To Apply:** Applicants must submit a completed application form; a personal statement describing career interests and goals; a commitment to library service to children; and three references (must be completed online). **Deadline:** March 1.

Remarks: The scholarship was established as a tribute to Frederic G. Melcher, a great leader in promoting better books for children. **Contact:** lmays@ala.org.

1466 ■ Association of Moving Image Archivists

1313 N Vine St.
Hollywood, CA 90028
Ph: (323)463-1500
Fax: (323)463-1506
E-mail: amia@amianet.org
URL: http://www.amianet.org

Awards are arranged alphabetically below their administering organizations

1467 ■ CFI Sid Solow Scholarships *(Graduate/Scholarship)*

Purpose: To provide financial assistance to deserving students who want to pursue a career in the field of moving image archiving. **Focus:** Library and archival sciences; Museum science. **Qualif.:** Applicant must be enrolled full time in a graduate-level or other advanced program in moving image studies or production, library or information services, archival administration, museum studies or a related discipline; must have a GPA of at least 3.0 in his/her current or most recently completed academic program. **Criteria:** Recipient will be selected based on the scholarship application criteria.

Funds Avail.: $4,000. **To Apply:** Applicant must complete the application form available online; must have the official transcript from the applicant's most recent academic program; must provide an essay of no more than 1,000 words describing applicant's major field of study, interest in moving image archiving, relevant experience and/or education, and career goals; must submit two letters of recommendation. **Deadline:** May 15.

1468 ■ Rick Chace Foundation Scholarships *(Graduate/Scholarship)*

Purpose: To provide financial assistance to deserving students who want to pursue a career in the field of moving image archiving. **Focus:** Library and archival sciences; Museum science. **Qualif.:** Applicant must be enrolled full-time in a graduate-level or other advanced program in moving image studies or production, library or information services, archival administration, museum studies or a related discipline; must have a GPA of at least 3.0. **Criteria:** Recipient will be selected based on the scholarship application criteria.

Funds Avail.: $4,000. **To Apply:** Applicant must complete the application form available online; must have the official transcript from the applicant's most recent academic program; must provide an essay of no more than 1,000 words describing their major field of study, interest in moving image archiving, relevant experience and/or education, and career goals; must submit two letters of recommendation. **Deadline:** May 15.

1469 ■ Kodak Fellowships in Film Preservation *(Graduate/Scholarship)*

Purpose: To provide financial assistance to deserving students who want to pursue a career in the field of moving image archiving. **Focus:** Library and archival sciences; Museum science. **Qualif.:** Applicant must be enrolled full-time in a graduate-level or other advanced program in moving image studies or production, library or information services, archival administration, museum studies or a related discipline; must be accepted into such a program for the next academic year; must have a GPA of at least 3.0; must have strong organizational and interpersonal skills and demonstrate an interest in pursuing a career in the moving image archival field; must be at least 21 years of age and must possess a valid driver's license; must be a US citizen or have a US work visa. **Criteria:** Recipient will be selected based on the following criteria: (1) Commitment to pursuing a career in moving image archiving; (2) Academic record; (3) Program of study as it applies to moving image archiving.

Funds Avail.: $4,000. **To Apply:** Applicant must complete the application form, available online; must submit an official transcript from the applicant's current or most recently completed academic program; must have an essay of no more than 1,000 words describing the applicant's interest and involvement in moving image archiving; must have two letters of recommendation. Application form and other supporting documents must be sent to 1313 North Vine St., Hollywood, CA 90028. **Deadline:** May 1.

1470 ■ Mary Pickford Scholarships *(Graduate/Scholarship)*

Purpose: To provide financial assistance to deserving students who want to pursue a career in the field of moving image archiving. **Focus:** Library and archival sciences; Museum science. **Qualif.:** Applicant must be enrolled full-time in a graduate-level or other advanced program in moving image studies or production, library or information services, archival administration, museum studies or a related discipline; must have a GPA of at least 3.0. **Criteria:** Recipient will be selected based on the scholarship application criteria.

Funds Avail.: $4,000. **To Apply:** Applicant must complete the application form available online; must have the official transcript from the applicant's most recent academic program; must provide an essay of no more than 1,000 words describing applicant's major field of study, interest in moving image archiving, relevant experience and/or education, and career goals; must submit two letters of recommendation. **Deadline:** May 15.

1471 ■ Sony Pictures Scholarships *(Graduate/Scholarship)*

Purpose: To provide financial assistance to deserving students who want to pursue a career in the field of moving image archiving. **Focus:** Library and archival sciences; Museum science. **Qualif.:** Applicant must be enrolled full-time in a graduate-level or other advanced program in moving image studies or production, library or information services, archival administration, museum studies or a related discipline; must have a GPA of at least 3.0. **Criteria:** Recipient will be selected based on the scholarship application criteria.

Funds Avail.: $4,000. **To Apply:** Applicant must complete the application form available online; must have the official transcript from the applicant's most recent academic program; must provide an essay of no more than 1,000 words describing applicant's major field of study, interest in moving image archiving, relevant experience and/or education, and career goals; must submit two letters of recommendation. **Deadline:** May 15.

1472 ■ Universal Studios Preservation Scholarships *(Graduate/Scholarship)*

Purpose: To provide financial assistance to deserving students who want to pursue their career in the field of moving image archiving. **Focus:** Library and archival sciences; Museum science. **Qualif.:** Applicant must be enrolled full-time in a graduate-level or other advanced program in moving image studies or production, library or information services, archival administration, museum studies or a related discipline; must have a GPA of at least 3.0. **Criteria:** Recipient will be selected based on the scholarship application criteria.

Funds Avail.: $4,000. **To Apply:** Applicant must complete the application form available online; must have the official transcript from the applicant's most recent academic program; must provide an essay of no more than 1,000 words describing their major field of study, interest in moving image archiving, relevant experience and/or education, and career goals; must submit two letters of recommendation. **Deadline:** May 15.

1473 ■ Association of Occupational Health Professionals in Healthcare

109 VIP Dr., Ste. 220
Wexford, PA 15090
Fax: (724)935-1560
Free: 800-362-4347
E-mail: info@aohp.org
URL: http://www.aohp.org

1474 ■ Sandra Bobbitt Continuing Education Scholarships *(Undergraduate/Scholarship)*

Purpose: To provide annual education scholarships to subsidize the educational efforts of members. **Focus:** General studies. **Qualif.:** Applicant must be an AOHP active member in good standing. **Criteria:** Applicants will be evaluated by the Scholarship Selection Committee.

Funds Avail.: $2,000. **To Apply:** Applicants must submit essay typewritten, double-spaced, and limited to 1,000 words. Provide a formal title for the project. State the one category from the following list that best describes the area the research project will address: employment examinations, medical surveillance, immunizations, infectious diseases, employee health records, work injuries, administration, marketing occupational health services, or other healthcare-related topics. Briefly describe the impact/ significance of the research project to the occupational health professional in a healthcare setting. List the objectives and goal of the research project. Describe the activities that will be implemented to achieve the goals of the project, e.g., questionnaire. As appropriate, describe the target population, e.g., clinical (nursing, etc.) nonclinical employees. **Deadline:** July 15.

1475 ■ Julie Schmid Research Scholarships *(All/ Scholarship)*

Purpose: To encourage, promote, and strengthen the knowledge base and expertise of the occupational health professional in healthcare. **Focus:** Occupational safety and health. **Qualif.:** Applicants must have proposals for an original research project on current and/or anticipated issues in healthcare-related occupational health. **Criteria:** Recipient will be selected based on merit in accordance with the evaluation tool; completed proposals shall be submitted according to the format outlined below; please include a cover letter with your name and address; do not include your name or any personal identification data on the proposal itself; address completed proposals and correspondence to the AOHP executive secretary, Research Scholarship Committee chairperson.

Funds Avail.: $2,000. **To Apply:** Applicants must submit a formal title for the project; state the one category from the following list that best describes the area the research project will address: employment examinations, medical surveillance, immunizations, infectious diseases, employee health records, work injuries, administration, marketing occupational health services, or other healthcare-related topics; briefly describe the impact/ significance of the research project to the occupational health professional in a healthcare setting; list the objectives and goal of the research project; describe the activities that will be implemented to achieve the goals of the project, e.g., questionnaire. As appropriate, describe the target population, e.g., clinical (nursing, etc.) nonclinical employees. **Deadline:** July 15.

1476 ■ Association of PeriOperative Registered Nurses

2170 S Parker Rd., Ste. 300
Denver, CO 80231
Ph: (303)755-6304
Free: 800-755-2676
URL: http://www.aorn.org

1477 ■ AORN Foundation Scholarship Program *(Undergraduate/Scholarship)*

Purpose: To provide financial assistance to students enrolled in nursing schools and to perioperative nurses pursuing bachelors, masters, or doctoral degrees. **Focus:** Nursing. **Qualif.:** Nursing students must be enrolled in an accredited program as a nursing major for the 2008-2009 academic year; must be a program leading to licensure as an RN. Current nurses must have a commitment to perioperative nursing; must be enrolled in an accredited master's degree program in nursing or in an accredited master's degree program in another discipline for the 2008-2009 academic year. **Criteria:** Recipient is selected based on academics, essay and accurate completion of the scholarship application.

Funds Avail.: $1,000 up to $5,000. **To Apply:** Applicant must submit all the required application information. **Deadline:** June 15.

1478 ■ Association of Physician Assistants in Cardiovascular Surgery

PO Box 4834
Englewood, CO 80155
Ph: (303)221-5651
Fax: (303)771-2550
Free: 877-221-5651
E-mail: admin@apacvs.org
URL: http://www.apacvs.org

1479 ■ APACVS Scholarships *(Professional Development/Scholarship)*

Purpose: To support individuals for the continuous medical education in the field of cardiovascular and thoracic surgery. **Focus:** Cardiology. **Qualif.:** Applicant must be a P.A. surgical resident, student member of the APACVS who are planning on going into cardiovascular and thoracic surgery. **Criteria:** Candidate will be evaluated by the Scholarship Committee.

Funds Avail.: No amount mentioned. **Deadline:** October 30.

1480 ■ Association for Psychological Science

1133 15th St. NW, Ste. 1000
Washington, DC 20005
Ph: (202)293-9300
Fax: (202)293-9350
URL: http://www.psychologicalscience.org

1481 ■ APS Student Grants *(Graduate, Undergraduate/Grant)*

Purpose: To provide financial support for APS students for their research currently in early development. **Focus:** Psychology. **Qualif.:** Applicant must be an APS undergraduate or graduate student. **Criteria:** Recipients are selected based on committee's review of the proposal.

Funds Avail.: $500 per graduate student and $300 per undergraduate student. **Number Awarded:** 3 for graduate student and 2 for undergraduate student. **To Apply:** Applicant must submit a cover letter; project summary; and review board approval. Submit through E-mail at grad.advocate@gmail.com, with a subject, APSSC Student Grant Submission except the Review Board Approval, or mail to Ewa J. Szymanska Department of Psychology University of Pennsylvania 3720 Walnut Street, Solomon Lab Bldg. Philadelphia, PA 19104. **Deadline:** November 1. **Contact:** Ewa J. Szymanska grad.advocate@gmail.com.

1482 ■ Association of Public Treasurers of the United States and Canada

962 Wayne Ave., Ste. 910
Silver Spring, MD 20910
Ph: (301)495-5560
Fax: (301)495-5561
E-mail: info@aptusc.org
URL: http://www.aptusc.org

1483 ■ APT US&C Scholarships *(All/Scholarship)*

Purpose: To encourage continuing of education for all active members. **Focus:** General studies. **Qualif.:** Applicant must be an active member in good standing. **Criteria:** Selection is based on total cost of the conference or institute being attended; the financial condition of the Scholarship Fund; maximum number of awards to any one person is two; and on the letter from the applicants' city, town, county, etc.

Funds Avail.: $250-$500. **To Apply:** Applicants must submit a completed APT US & C Scholarship application form together with a letter from the applicants' city, town, county, etc. **Deadline:** 60 days prior to the conference or institute.

1484 ■ Association of Rehabilitation Nurses

4700 W Lake Ave.
Glenview, IL 60025-1485
Ph: (847)375-4710
Fax: (847)375-6481
Free: 800-229-7530
E-mail: info@rehabnurse.org
URL: http://www.rehabnurse.org

1485 ■ Association of Rehabilitation Nurses Scholarship Program *(Undergraduate/Scholarship)*

Purpose: To provide financial assistance to rehabilitation nurses working toward a Bachelor of Science in Nursing (BSN) degree. **Focus:** Nursing. **Qualif.:** Applicants must be a member of ARN currently enrolled in a BSN degree program, in good standing, completed at least one course and practices rehabilitation nursing at present, a minimum of two years. **Criteria:** The recipient will be selected by ARN based on the application materials provided.

Funds Avail.: $1,000. **To Apply:** Applicants must submit completed form; transcript documenting enrollment in a BSN program; typed 1-3 page summary of professional and educational goals and achievements, which includes, involvement in ARN at the national and local levels, continuing education participation in the past three to five years, professional publications or presentations, community involvement, particularly related to advocating for individuals with disabilities, efforts made to improve rehabilitation nursing practice and the delivery of care in your work setting. **Deadline:** June 2. **Contact:** ARN Scholarship Program; Fax: 888/458-0456; email: nwallace@connect2amc.com.

1486 ■ Mary Ann Mikulic Scholarships *(Undergraduate/Scholarship)*

Purpose: To provide financial assistance covering full tuition of the Professional Rehabilitation Nursing course. **Focus:** Nursing. **Qualif.:** Applicants must be registered nurses with current license currently practicing in the specialty of rehabilitation nursing and able to meet all other financial responsibilities incurred by participating in the course. **Criteria:** Applicants will be evaluated by the Scholarship committee based on the application provided.

Funds Avail.: No amount specified. **To Apply:** Applicants must submit the completed application and supporting materials to ARN. **Deadline:** June 2. **Contact:** Nicole Wallace; ARN; Email: nwallace@connect2amc.com; Fax: 888/458-0456.

1487 ■ Association of School Business Officials of Maryland and the District of Columbia

PO Box 943
Rockville, MD 20848-0943
Ph: (301)318-4969
E-mail: asbomddc@comcast.net
URL: http://www.asbo.org

1488 ■ Dwight P. Jacobus Scholarships *(Undergraduate/Scholarship)*

Purpose: To assist individuals who need financial assistance for college education. **Focus:** General studies. **Qualif.:** Applicants must be residents of Maryland or District of Columbia for at least one year preceding the date of the award; must be accepted for admission as a full-time student; must demonstrate financial need; and must have a minimum 3.0 overall GPA. **Criteria:** Recipients are selected based on scholastic achievement; financial need; SAT and ACT scores; and quality of extra-curricular achievements.

Funds Avail.: $1000. **Number Awarded:** 4. **To Apply:** Applicants must submit a completed application form and other supporting documents. **Deadline:** March 1.

1489 ■ Association of Science-Technology Centers

1025 Vermont Ave. NW, Ste. 500
Washington, DC 20005-6310
Ph: (202)783-7200
Fax: (202)783-7207
E-mail: info@astc.org
URL: http://www.astc.org

1490 ■ Lee Kimche McGrath Worldwide Fellowships *(Professional Development/Fellowship)*

Purpose: To foster greater understanding among international colleagues and encourage global participation in ASTC. To support professionals who have genuine need for financial assistance in order to attend conference. **Focus:** Museum science. **Qualif.:** Applicant must be an individual from a science center or museum (open or in development) outside the United States; must be an institution that can't afford to send a representative to an ASTC conference; must be willing to participate in a conference

Awards are arranged alphabetically below their administering organizations

session. **Criteria:** Applicants are reviewed and selected by the ASTC International Advisory Board.

Funds Avail.: $1,500 (travel and accommodation). **To Apply:** Application forms are available in the website and must be sent to: Association of ScienceTechnology Centers, 1025 Vermont Ave., NW, Ste. 500, Washington, DC 20005. **Deadline:** June 29.

1491 ■ Association of Seventh-Day Adventist Librarians

James White Library, Andrews University
Berrien Springs, MI 49104-1400
E-mail: helmsc@andrews.edu
URL: http://www.asdal.org

1492 ■ ALPFA Scholarship Programs
(Postgraduate, Undergraduate/Scholarship)

Purpose: To financially support Hispanic students pursuing studies in accounting, finance, IT or related field. **Focus:** Business; Finance; Accounting. **Qualif.:** Applicants must be full-time Hispanic students or of Hispanic descent; U.S. citizens or permanent residents of the United States or Puerto Rico; attending an accredited university; have a cumulative grade point average of 3.0 and above on a 4.0 scale; must demonstrate financial need; and pursuing an undergraduate or master's degree in business, finance and accounting. **Criteria:** Recipients are selected based on the selection committee's review of all applications.

Funds Avail.: $1,250-$1,500. **To Apply:** Applicants must register first in order to apply online (please visit the website). Applicants must submit an official transcript; proof of family income and citizen status; an essay; letter of recommendation; resume; and The Financial Aid Verification (for semi-finalist only). **Deadline:** March 15. **Contact:** Hispanic College Fund, HCF-info@hispanicfund.org.

1493 ■ D. Glenn Hilts Scholarships Program
(Graduate, Undergraduate/Scholarship)

Purpose: To encourage employment of potential leaders in a Seventh-day Adventist Library while upholding excellence in scholarship. **Focus:** General studies; Library and archival sciences. **Qualif.:** Applicant must be a Seventh-Day Adventist in good standing; be accepted in an American Library Association accredited library school; and must be a full-time student. **Criteria:** Priority is given to applicants with complete application packages.

Funds Avail.: $1,200. **To Apply:** Applicant must submit completed application form available at the website; submit a copy of the acceptance letter from the ALA-accredited library; GRE scores; an essay (maximum of three pages); high school and college transcripts; three letters of reference (there must be one from the applicant's Seventh-day Adventist pastor). **Deadline:** June 15. **Contact:** Cynthia Mae Helms, Scholarship and Awards Committee at the above address (see entry 1491).

1494 ■ Association for the Social Scientific Study of Jewry

201 Mullica Hill Rd.
Glassboro, NJ 08028
Ph: (856)256-4500
Fax: (856)256-5610
E-mail: hartman@rowan.edu
URL: http://www.assj.org

1495 ■ Association for the Social Scientific Study of Jewry Travel Grant *(Graduate/Grant)*

Purpose: To provide travel grant for interested students. **Focus:** Social sciences. **Qualif.:** Applicants must be ASSJ graduate student members. **Criteria:** Applicants are eligible to apply if they have research on social scientific study of Jews.

Funds Avail.: No specific amount. **To Apply:** Applicants must submit the following: a brief curriculum vitae (2 pages); the title and 500-word abstract of the paper proposal; a copy of the letter of acceptance from the AJS; and a proposed budget (including other sources of financial support for attending the conference). **Deadline:** September 15th. **Contact:** ASSJ c/o Harriet Hartman, Ph.D. Professor of Sociology Rowan University at the above address (see entry 1494).

1496 ■ Association of State Dam Safety Officials

450 Old Vine St.
Lexington, KY 40507
Ph: (859)257-5140
Fax: (859)323-1958
E-mail: info@damsafety.org
URL: http://www.damsafety.org

1497 ■ ASDSO Undergraduate Scholarships
(Undergraduate/Scholarship)

Purpose: To promote the study of civil engineering and related fields as a career. **Focus:** Engineering, Civil. **Qualif.:** Applicant must be a U.S. citizen; enrolled in a civil engineering program and in their senior year; pursuing a career in hydraulics, hydrology or geotechnical disciplines or related to design, construction and operation of dams; have 2.5 GPA for the first three years in college and recommended by advisor. **Criteria:** Awards are given based on academic merit; financial need; work experience and essay.

Funds Avail.: A maximum of $10,000. **To Apply:** Applicant must send application form; transcript; three letters of recommendation; essay about what is ASDSO and why is dam safety important and include proposed curriculum study. **Deadline:** March29.

1498 ■ Association of Surgical Technologists

6 W Dry Creek Cir., Ste. 200
Littleton, CO 80120-8031
Ph: (303)694-9130
Fax: (303)694-9169
Free: 800-637-7433
E-mail: bteutsch@ast.org
URL: http://www.ast.org

1499 ■ AST National Honor Society Student Scholarships *(Graduate/Scholarship)*

Purpose: To reward members of the AST National Honor Society who are continuing their education by attending a CAAHEP-accredited surgical assisting program. **Focus:** Surgery. **Qualif.:** Applicants must be a member of the AST National Honor Society; must be in the process of completing a CAAHEP-accredited surgical assisting program or must begin classes within one year of receipt of scholarship; must maintain a 3.0 GPA (based on a 4.0 scale); and must remain in good standing within the institution and

Awards are arranged alphabetically below their administering organizations

must document current AST membership. **Criteria:** Recipients will be selected based on the quality of the application materials submitted.

Funds Avail.: $1,000. **To Apply:** Applicant must submit a completed application form with a professional resume attached. **Deadline:** April 1.

1500 ■ Thomson Delmar Learning Surgical Technology Scholarships *(Graduate/Scholarship)*

Purpose: To reward an individual who is striving to further his/her personal and educational goals by completing a surgical technology program. **Focus:** Surgery. **Qualif.:** Applicants must be enrolled in a CAAHEP-accredited program, or accepted to begin the program. Recipients must maintain a minimum GPA of 2.5. **Criteria:** Recipients are selected based on academic achievement and progress.

Funds Avail.: $1,000. **Number Awarded:** 1. **To Apply:** Applicants must submit a short report of 500 words or less stating the following: professional goals, strengths as a student, and reasons for wanting to enter the surgical technology profession. Applicants must also submit the completed application form. **Deadline:** April 1.

1501 ■ Foundation for Surgical Technology Advanced Education/Medical Mission Scholarships *(Graduate/Scholarship)*

Purpose: To provide financial assistance to current AST members who are pursuing advanced education related to the practice or who are seeking to perform medical mission work. **Focus:** Surgery. **Qualif.:** Applicant must be a current AST member. **Criteria:** Recipients will be selected based on the committee's review of all applications submitted.

Funds Avail.: No specific amount. **To Apply:** Applicants must provide a description of their membership history; an official documentation of the educational program that they are entering; and two letters of recommendation. All educational programs must include an official course outline, program fees and transcript. **Deadline:** There is no deadline for applications. Applications are accepted throughout the year and are reviewed individually by the national AST Foundation Committee.

1502 ■ Foundation for Surgical Technology Scholarships *(Graduate/Scholarship)*

Purpose: To encourage and reward educational excellence as well as to respond to the financial need demonstrated by the surgical technology student and offer assistance to those who seek a career in surgical technology. **Focus:** Surgery. **Qualif.:** Applicants must be currently enrolled in an accredited surgical technology program and eligible to sit for the NBSTSA national surgical technologist certifying examination; must demonstrate superior academic ability; and must have a need for financial assistance. **Criteria:** Recipient selection is based on academic excellence and financial need.

Funds Avail.: No specific amount. **To Apply:** Applicants must complete the four parts of the application form: Student Responsibility; Official Transcript; Instructor Section; and Preceptor Section. **Deadline:** April 1.

1503 ■ Association of Universities and Colleges of Canada

350 Albert St., Ste. 600
Ottawa, ON, Canada K1R 1B1
Ph: (613)563-1236
Fax: (613)563-9745
E-mail: info@aucc.ca
URL: http://www.aucc.ca

1504 ■ Association of Universities and Colleges of Canada Public Scholarships *(Undergraduate/Scholarship)*

Purpose: To foster and promote the interest of higher education. **Focus:** General studies. **Qualif.:** Applicants must be interested in pursuing their postsecondary studies in Canada or abroad and must be Canadian citizens or permanent residents of Canada. **Criteria:** Recipients are selected based on completeness of the application form, requirements, and academic performance.

Funds Avail.: No specific amount. **To Apply:** Applicants must complete the application form and submit along with an official, sealed or stamped and signed transcript; letters of reference; essays; and community service. **Contact:** 613-563-9745.

1505 ■ Association for Women in Architecture

22815 Frampton Ave.
Torrance, CA 90501-5034
Ph: (310)534-8466
Fax: (310)257-6885
E-mail: president@awa-la.org
URL: http://www.awa-la.org

1506 ■ Association for Women in Architecture Scholarships *(Undergraduate/Scholarship)*

Purpose: To advance and support the positions of women in architecture and allied fields. **Focus:** Architecture. **Qualif.:** Applicants must be residents of California or attending a California school; must be enrolled in one of the qualifying majors for the current school term; must have completed a minimum of 18 units in their major by the application due date. **Criteria:** Recipients are selected based on merit as evidenced by grades, personal statement, letter of recommendation and quality of student work.

Funds Avail.: $1,000. **Number Awarded:** 5. **To Apply:** Applicants must complete the application form; must submit an official transcript of records from each college and university attended, two sealed letters of recommendation with signature over the seal from an instructor who has taught in their major; must submit a typewritten personal statement stating the reasons for studying the chosen field and career objectives; must submit a portfolio in "11x17" format showing one-to-three projects from their school work and self-addressed stamped envelope, standard business size. **Deadline:** April 15.

1507 ■ Association for Women Geoscientists

PO Box 30645
Lincoln, NE 68503-0645
Ph: (402)470-3110
Fax: (402)470-3110
E-mail: office@awg.org
URL: http://www.awg.org

1508 ■ AWG Maria Luisa Crawford Field Camp Scholarships *(Undergraduate/Scholarship)*

Purpose: To support students with their educational pursuits. **Focus:** Geosciences. **Qualif.:** Applicant must be a full-time undergraduate student pursuing a degree in geo-

Awards are arranged alphabetically below their administering organizations

sciences and must have a GPA of 3.0. **Criteria:** selection is based on merits.

Funds Avail.: $500. **Number Awarded:** 2. **To Apply:** Applicants must submit a completed application form together with an essay; two letters of recommendations; and college transcripts. **Deadline:** February 16. **Contact:** Alice L. Hoersch, PhD, hoersch@lasalle.edu.

1509 ■ AWG Minority Scholarships
(Undergraduate/Scholarship)

Purpose: To support students with their educational pursuits. **Focus:** Geosciences. **Qualif.:** Applicant must be a woman who is African-American, Hispanic, or Native American; full-time student pursuing an undergraduate degree in the geosciences at an accredited college or university (high school students who will enter one of these fields during their freshman year may also apply). **Criteria:** Selection is based on merits.

Funds Avail.: $5000. **Number Awarded:** 1. **To Apply:** Applicants must submit a completed application form together with a statement of academic career goals; two letters of recommendation; transcript; and SAT/ACT scores. **Deadline:** June 30. **Contact:** Christina Tapia, awgscholarship@yahoo.com.

1510 ■ Chrysalis Scholarships *(Graduate/Grant)*

Purpose: To support a geoscience graduate student with their thesis/ dissertation. **Focus:** Geosciences. **Qualif.:** Applicant must be a female geoscience graduate student. **Criteria:** Selection is based on the application materials.

Funds Avail.: $2000. **Number Awarded:** 2. **To Apply:** Applicants must submit a letter of application and a reference letter electronically to chrysalis@awg.org, with a subject line: Chrysalis Scholarship. **Deadline:** March 15.

1511 ■ Penelope Hanshaw Scholarships *(Graduate, Undergraduate/Scholarship)*

Purpose: To support students with their educational pursuit. **Focus:** Geosciences. **Qualif.:** Applicant must be enrolled full-time graduate or undergraduate geosciences major; and have a GPA of 3.0. **Criteria:** Selection is based on merit.

Funds Avail.: $500. **To Apply:** Applicant must submit a nomination letter from a geoscience professor; a recommendation letter from a geoscience faculty; a letter of application; and academic transcripts. Send materials to Laurel M. Bybell, US Geological Survey 926 National Center Reston, VA 20192. **Deadline:** April 30.

Remarks: Sponsored by AWG Potomac Area Chapter. **Contact:** Laurel M. Bybell.

1512 ■ Puget Sound Chapter Scholarships
(Undergraduate/Scholarship)

Purpose: To encourage women to study geoscience. **Focus:** Geosciences. **Qualif.:** Applicant must be an undergraduate woman committed to completing a Bachelor's Degree; pursuing a career or graduate work in the geosciences; a sophomore, junior, or senior woman enrolled in a university or two year college in Washington state west of the Columbia and Okanogan Rivers; have a minimum of 3.2 GPA (or equivalent academic achievement). **Criteria:** Applicants will be judged based on their potential for professional success, academic achievement and financial need.

Funds Avail.: $1000. **To Apply:** Applicants must submit their name, address, phone number, and email (if available); One paragraph each describing your (1) financial needs, (2) current resources, and (3) academic achievements; One-page essay summarizing your commitment to a career in the geosciences; Copies of all college transcripts (photocopies accepted); Three letters of reference; provide names, affiliations, phone numbers. **Deadline:** November 3.

Remarks: Sponsored by AWG Puget Sound Chapter.

1513 ■ William Rucker Greenwood Scholarships
(Graduate, Undergraduate/Scholarship)

Purpose: To support students with educational pursuits. **Focus:** Geosciences. **Qualif.:** Applicant must be a minority woman; enrolled full-time graduate or undergraduate geosciences major. **Criteria:** Selection is based on merit.

Funds Avail.: $1000. **To Apply:** Applicants must submit a letter of recommendation from a geoscience professor or chairperson, and another from a geoscience faculty or employer; and a letter of application. Send materials to Laurel M. Bybell, US Geological Survey 926 National Center Reston, VA 20192. **Deadline:** April 30.

Remarks: Sponsored by AWG Potomac Area Chapter. **Contact:** Laurel M. Bybell.

1514 ■ Association for Women in Mathematics

11240 Waples Mill Rd., Ste. 200
Fairfax, VA 22030
Ph: (703)934-0163
Fax: (703)359-7562
E-mail: awm@awm-math.org
URL: http://www.awm-math.org

1515 ■ Mentoring Travel Grants for Women
(Postdoctorate/Scholarship)

Purpose: To help young women to develop a long-term working and mentoring relationship with senior mathematicians. **Focus:** Mathematics and mathematical sciences. **Qualif.:** Applicants must be women holding a doctorate degree or equivalent with a work address in the United States; must be in a field supported by the Division of the Mathematical Sciences of the National Science Foundation. **Criteria:** Awards will be determined on a competitive basis by a selection panel consisting of distinguished mathematicians appointed by the AWM.

Funds Avail.: $5,000. **Number Awarded:** 7. **To Apply:** Applicants must have a curriculum vitae; must provide a research proposal which specifies why the proposed travel would be particularly beneficial; must submit a supporting letter from the proposed mentor with the curriculum vitae of the proposed mentor; must have a proposed budget and information about other sources of funding available. **Deadline:** February 8.

1516 ■ Travel Grants for Women Researchers
(Postdoctorate/Scholarship)

Purpose: To enable women to attend research conferences in their fields and to provide valuable opportunities for them to advance their research activities and their visibility in the research community. **Focus:** Mathematics and mathematical sciences. **Qualif.:** Applicants must be women holding a doctorate degree and with a work address in the USA. **Criteria:** Awards will be determined on a competitive basis by a selection panel consisting of distinguished mathematicians appointed by the AWM.

Funds Avail.: $1,500 for domestic travel and $2,000 for

Awards are arranged alphabetically below their administering organizations

foreign travel. **Number Awarded:** 3. **To Apply:** Application requirements and a complete step-by-step process are available online; application must be submitted online. **Deadline:** May 8.

1517 ■ Association for Women in Science

1200 New York Ave. NW, Ste. 650
Washington, DC 20005
Ph: (202)326-8940
Fax: (202)326-8960
E-mail: awis@awis.org
URL: http://www.awis.org

1518 ■ Association for Preservation Technology International Student Scholarships *(All/ Scholarship)*

Purpose: To promote research or projects on preservation technology. **Focus:** Historic preservation. **Qualif.:** Applicants must be enrolled in a trade, undergraduate or graduate program which is affiliated with a trade school, college or university. **Criteria:** Recipients are selected based on the quality of a submitted abstract and a personal statement.

Funds Avail.: No amount specified. **Number Awarded:** 15. **To Apply:** Applicants are required to submit their personal as well as their professor's contact information; a 250-word abstract describing the scope of the project/ research and summarizing its relationship to an aspect of preservation technology and/or heritage conservation that relates to the conference theme and/or paper tracks; and 250-word personal statement stating why the conference would be of value to them. Applicants are also required to create an electronic presentation and give an oral presentation during the conference.

Remarks: Established in 2000.

1519 ■ AWIS College Scholarships *(Undergraduate/Scholarship)*

Purpose: To promote education in science. **Focus:** Astronomy and astronomical sciences; Geosciences; Biology; Mathematics and mathematical sciences; Chemistry; Physics; Computer and information sciences; Engineering; Psychology. **Qualif.:** Applicant must be a female high school senior; U.S. citizen or permanent resident; have at least 3.75 GPA; at least 1200 score in SAT or a composite score of 25 in ACT; planning to study in any field of Astronomy, Geoscience, Biology, Mathematics, Chemistry, Physics, Computer and Information Science, Engineering, Psychology; planning to become a researcher or teacher. **Criteria:** Recipients are selected based on submitted applications.

Funds Avail.: No specific amount. **Number Awarded:** 2-5. **To Apply:** Applicants must send five copies of: summary form; essay describing research experience; resume; two recommendation letters from science or research teachers; high school transcript and score of standardized test if available. **Deadline:** January 17.

1520 ■ Association for Women in Sports Media

3899 N Front St.
Harrisburg, PA 17110
Ph: (717)903-3086
E-mail: president@awsmonline.org
URL: http://www.awsmonline.org

1521 ■ Association for Women in Sports Media Internship Program *(Graduate, Undergraduate/ Internship)*

Purpose: To assist female college students interested in sports media careers through paid internships with employers. **Focus:** Media arts. **Qualif.:** Applicants must be full-time female students seeking an undergraduate or graduate degree. **Criteria:** Applications will be evaluated by the AWSM board members and appropriate media professionals.

Funds Avail.: $1,000. **To Apply:** Applicants must submit the completed application form or a typewritten page containing the information required on the form; one-page essay of 750 words or less, describing the most memorable experience in sports and sports media; one-page resume highlighting journalism experience; three references with contact information; one letter of recommendation from a professor, advisor, editor, producer or other supervisor who is familiar with their work; maximum of five samples of their work: clips, editing examples, headlines, layout, press releases, video or audio tapes. Limit recordings to 10 minutes or less. $15 application fee must be paid by check or money order.

1522 ■ Association for Women Veterinarians

PO Box 7200
Denver, PA 17517
Ph: (717)336-4921
Fax: (717)336-5344
E-mail: stacy.pritt@covance.com
URL: http://www.vet.ksu.edu/AWV/index.htm

1523 ■ Association for Women Veterinarians Foundation Scholarships Program *(Graduate/ Scholarship)*

Purpose: To provide financial assistance to veterinary medical students. **Focus:** Medicine, Veterinary. **Qualif.:** Applicants must be second or third year veterinary medical students; must be attending a College/School of Veterinary Medicine in U.S. or Canada. **Criteria:** Scholarship recipients will be selected based on the Selection Committee's review of the application materials.

Funds Avail.: $1,500. **Number Awarded:** 4. **To Apply:** Applicants must submit (in a Word or PDF file) full name, address, school's address, present year of attendance in veterinary medical school (2nd or 3rd Year); a resume or curriculum vitae; letter of recommendation from a faculty member; and an essay (maximum of 500 words) on the applicant's purpose for applying for the scholarship and why the association should award the scholarship to the applicant. **Deadline:** January 31.

1524 ■ Association of Zoo Veterinary Technicians (AZVT)

903 10th St. SW
Albuquerque, NM 87102
Ph: (505)764-6264
Fax: (505)764-6275
E-mail: gdragoo@cabq.gov
URL: http://www.azvt.org

1525 ■ Laurie Page-Peck Scholarships Fund *(Undergraduate/Scholarship)*

Purpose: To provide educational assistance for veterinary or medical technology students. **Focus:** Veterinary science

Awards are arranged alphabetically below their administering organizations

and medicine. **Qualif.:** Applicant must be a veterinary or medical technology student interested in zoo veterinary technology. **Criteria:** Grantees will be selected based on the content, format and grammar of the submitted paper.

Funds Avail.: $1,000. **To Apply:** The applicant must submit a paper about zoo veterinary technology. **Deadline:** Deadline for receipt of abstracts- March 10; Deadline for first- draft paper submission- April 28; Deadline for final draft of paper July 7. **Contact:** Gwen A. Dragoo, B.S., R.V.T. Head Veterinary Technician Albuquerque Biological Park 903 10th Street SW Albuquerque, NM 87102.

1526 ■ Astronaut Scholarship Foundation

6225 Vectorspace Blvd.
Titusville, FL 32780
Fax: (321)264-9176
URL: http://www.astronautscholarship.org

1527 ■ Astronaut Scholarship Foundation Scholarships *(Undergraduate/Scholarship)*

Purpose: To support the promising students who want to pursue their masters in the fields of science and engineering. **Focus:** Science; Engineering; Applied mathematics. **Qualif.:** Applicants must be nominated by faculty members; must be U.S citizens; must be engineering or natural or applied science majors, or mathematics students intending to pursue research or advance their field upon completion of their final degree; must be junior, senior or master's students; must have shown initiative, creativity, and excellence in their chosen field. **Criteria:** Recipients will be selected by the ASF Scholarship Committee.

Funds Avail.: No specific amount. **To Apply:** For further information, applicants are advised to contact the Astronaut Scholarship Foundation, 6225 Vectorspace Blvd., Titusville, FL 32780.

1528 ■ Athenaeum of Philadelphia

219 S Sixth St.
Philadelphia, PA 19106-3794
Ph: (215)925-2688
Fax: (215)925-3755
E-mail: sltatman@philaathanaeum.org
URL: http://www.philaathenaeum.org

1529 ■ Charles E. Peterson Research Senior Fellowships *(Professional Development/Fellowship)*

Purpose: To support individuals with their education. **Focus:** General studies. **Qualif.:** Applicant must hold a terminal degree and possess a distinguished record of accomplishment. **Criteria:** Applications are reviewed by a committee of architects, architectural historians, and educators appointed by the Athenaeum board of directors.

Funds Avail.: $5000. **To Apply:** Applications should be in a single-page letter with a brief statement of the project, with attached budget, schedule for completion, and professional resume, two letters of reference and submitted directly to the committee. Must not be submitted by fax or electronic mail. **Deadline:** January 1 and March 1.

1530 ■ Athletic Equipment Managers Association

460 Hunt Hill Rd.
Freeville, NY 13068
Ph: (607)539-6300
Fax: (607)539-6340
E-mail: aema@frontiernet.net
URL: http://www.aema1.com

1531 ■ Athletic Equipment Managers Association College Scholarships *(Undergraduate/Scholarship)*

Purpose: To develop further the professional ability of each of its members. **Focus:** General studies. **Qualif.:** Applicant must be full-time college student with one year of collegiate athletic equipment management experience; displays an interest in the field of Athletic Equipment Management. **Criteria:** Selection is based on academic achievement, community involvement, displayed interest in Athletic Equipment Management, completion of an essay and letters of recommendation.

Funds Avail.: $500. **Number Awarded:** 6. **To Apply:** Applicants must submit a completed application form along with the required materials. **Deadline:**.

Remarks: March 15. **Contact:** Dorothy Cutting.

1532 ■ Atlantic Provinces Library Association

166 Bedford Hwy.
Halifax, NS, Canada B3M 2J6
Ph: (902)457-6108
E-mail: Donna.Bourne-Tyson@msvu.ca
URL: http://www.apla.ca

1533 ■ Atlantic Provinces Library Association Memorial Awards *(Professional Development/Scholarship)*

Purpose: To provide financial assistance for students who are in need. **Focus:** General studies. **Qualif.:** Applicants must have a degree and must be currently doing research. **Criteria:** Priority will be given to those students with financial need.

Funds Avail.: No specific amount. **To Apply:** Applicants must send a letter outlining proposed research and estimated costs along with a copy of your curriculum vitae. **Deadline:** March 31. **Contact:** Nominations should be submitted to: Tanja Harrison, Librarian Vaughan Memorial Library Acadia University PO Box 4 Wolfville NS B4P 2R6 with Tel: (902) 585-1378 Fax: (902) 585-1748 Email: tanja.harrison@acadiau.ca.

1534 ■ Carin Alma E. Somers Scholarship Trust *(Undergraduate/Scholarship)*

Purpose: To support the education of Canadian students with financial need. **Focus:** Library and Information Studies. **Qualif.:** Applicants must be Canadian citizens; must be residents of Atlantic Provinces; and must have demonstrated financial need. **Criteria:** Selection of recipients will be recommended by a committee of the four Provincial Vice Presidents and the President-Elect to the Executive Committee.

Funds Avail.: $2,000. **To Apply:** Applicants must submit a completed application form.

Remarks: Successful applicants will have been accepted in a School of Graduate Studies as candidates for a Master's degree in Library and Information Studies accredited by the American Library Association. The award will normally be announced at the Annual Atlantic Provinces Library Association Spring Conference. **Contact:** Atlantic

Provinces Library Association at the above address (see entry 1532).

1535 ■ Atlantic Salmon Federation
PO Box 5200
St. Andrews, NB, Canada E5B 3S8
Ph: (506)529-1033
Fax: (506)529-4438
E-mail: savesalmon@asf.ca
URL: http://www.asf.ca

1536 ■ Atlantic Salmon Federation Olin Fellowships *(All/Fellowship)*

Purpose: To improve knowledge or skills in advanced fields while looking for solutions to current problems in Atlantic salmon biology, management and conservation. **Focus:** Marine biology. **Qualif.:** Applicants need not be enrolled in any degree program. Applicants must be legal residents of the United States or Canada; must be enrolled in any accredited university, research laboratory or active management program. **Criteria:** Recipients are selected based on the committee's review of all applications.

Funds Avail.: $1,000-$3,000. **To Apply:** Application forms may be obtained from the Atlantic Salmon Federation Office in Canada or in USA. **Deadline:** March 15.

1537 ■ Audio Engineering Society
60 E 42nd St., Ste. 2520
New York, NY 10165
Ph: (212)661-8528
Fax: (212)682-0477
E-mail: hq@aes.org
URL: http://www.aes.org

1538 ■ Audio Engineering Society Educational Foundation Scholarships *(Undergraduate/Grant)*

Purpose: To encourage entry of talented students into the profession of audio engineering and related fields. **Focus:** Engineering. **Qualif.:** Applicants must have successfully completed an undergraduate degree program (typically four years) at a recognized college or university; a demonstrated commitment to audio engineering or related fields as a career choice; acceptance or a pending application for graduate studies leading to a masters or higher degree, or an internationally recognized equivalent. **Criteria:** Recipients are selected based on the submitted application requirements.

Funds Avail.: No specific amount. **To Apply:** Applicants must submit two current letters of recommendation (one must be from major professor or academic advisors); a cover page; essays on past achievements and future plans; and list of references. **Deadline:** March 15.

1539 ■ Autism Society of America
7910 Woodmont Ave., Ste. 300
Bethesda, MD 20814-3067
Ph: (301)657-0881
Free: 800-328-8476
URL: http://www.autism-society.org

1540 ■ CVS/All Kids Can Scholars Program *(Undergraduate/Scholarship)*

Purpose: To assist individuals with autism intending to pursue education. **Focus:** Mental health. **Qualif.:** Candidate must be an individual with autism completing post-secondary educational or vocational program. **Criteria:** Priority is given to applicants with complete application packages.

Funds Avail.: $1,000. **Number Awarded:** 5. **To Apply:** Applicant must submit the documentation of status as an individual with autism; secondary school transcripts; documentation of acceptance into an accredited, post-secondary educational or vocational program of study; two recommendation letters; and a personal statement (maximum of 500 words) outlining the applicant's qualifications and proposed plan of study.

1541 ■ Automotive Aftermarket Industry Association
7101 Wisconsin Ave., Ste. 1300
Bethesda, MD 20814-3415
Ph: (301)654-6664
Fax: (301)654-3299
E-mail: aaia@aftermarket.org
URL: http://www.aftermarket.org

1542 ■ APSAIL's Ralph Silverman Memorial Scholarships *(Undergraduate/Scholarship)*

Purpose: To further promote quality and high standards through education within the automotive aftermarket industry. **Focus:** Automotive technology. **Qualif.:** Applicants must be students who intend to pursue a career in the automotive aftermarket industry. **Criteria:** Recipients are selected based on academic performance and demonstrated interest in the automotive industry.

Funds Avail.: $500. **Number Awarded:** 6. **To Apply:** Applicants must submit a complete application form. **Deadline:** June 30.

1543 ■ AVI Scholarships *(Undergraduate/Scholarship)*

Purpose: To develop quality technicians, managers, and shop owners. **Focus:** Automotive technology. **Qualif.:** Applicants must be 21 years of age; must have a minimum of two years work experience in the mechanical repair industry; must demonstrate an interest in self-improvement through education and training. If an applicant is not a business owner, he/she must be recommended by a business owner. **Criteria:** Recipients are selected based on academic performance and demonstrated interest in automotive industry.

Funds Avail.: $1,000. **To Apply:** Applicants must submit a complete application form. **Deadline:** August 17.

1544 ■ Tom Babcox Memorial Scholarships *(All/Scholarship)*

Purpose: To support continuing education tailored specifically for the business needs of the automotive service industry. **Focus:** Automotive technology. **Qualif.:** Applicants must work in mechanical repair industry; must demonstrate an interest in self-improvement through management education; must own or work for a business that as an ASA Collision division member in good standing. If an applicant is not a business owner, he/she must be recommended by a business owner. **Criteria:** Recipients are selected based on academic performance and demonstrated interest in automotive industry.

Funds Avail.: $1,000. **To Apply:** Applicants must submit a complete application form. **Deadline:** August 17.

1545 ■ Richard Cossette/Gale Memorial Scholarships *(All/Scholarship)*

Purpose: To provide and promote practical business management service. **Focus:** Automotive technology. **Qualif.:** Applicants must work in the collision repair industry; must demonstrate an interest in self-improvement through management education; must own or work for a business that as an ASA Collision division member in good standing. If an applicant is not a business owner, he or she must be recommended by a business owner. **Criteria:** Recipients are selected based on academic performance and demonstrated interest in automotive industry.

Funds Avail.: $1,000. **To Apply:** Applicants must submit a complete application form.

1546 ■ Florida Automotive Industry Scholarships *(Undergraduate/Scholarship)*

Purpose: To provide and promote practical business management service. **Focus:** Automotive technology. **Qualif.:** Applicants must be high school seniors, or high school graduates, or persons possessing a GED. **Criteria:** Recipients are selected based on the academic achievement, merit, and need.

Funds Avail.: No specific amount. **To Apply:** Applicants must submit a complete application form. **Contact:** 813-962-4445.

1547 ■ Sloan Northwood Heavy-Duty Scholarships *(Undergraduate/Scholarship)*

Purpose: To provide and promote practical business management service. **Focus:** Automotive technology. **Qualif.:** Applicants must be enrolled in the university's Automotive Aftermarket Management curriculum, Heavy Duty Management program or the Heavy Duty Vehicle Technology program; must be U.S. citizens and maintain a 2.5 cumulative grade point average. **Criteria:** Recipients are selected based on financial need and demonstrated career interest.

Funds Avail.: No specific amount. **To Apply:** Applicants must submit a complete application form. **Contact:** 616-395-5620.

1548 ■ Automotive Hall of Fame

21400 Oakwood Blvd.
Dearborn, MI 48124
Ph: (313)240-4000
Fax: (313)240-8641
URL: http://www.automotivehalloffame.org

1549 ■ Larry H. Averill Memorial Scholarships *(Undergraduate/Scholarship)*

Purpose: To financially support students pursuing education in an automotive related career. **Focus:** Automotive technology; Engineering, Automotive. **Qualif.:** Applicant must be an upper level undergraduate; interested in careers in automotive; have a 3.0 GPA; enrolled full-time at an accredited college or university; and have demonstrated financial need. **Criteria:** Applicants are selected based on the application.

Funds Avail.: No specific amount. **To Apply:** Application form is available at the website or send a letter of request with a self-addressed stamped envelope. Applicants must submit a completed application form; an official transcript; two recommendation letters; and a letter of acceptance for an associate, bachelor or masters program. Send all materials to: Automotive Hall of Fame, Scholarship Programs 21400 Oakwood Blvd. Dearborn, MI 48124. **Deadline:** May 30.

1550 ■ Harold Dieckmann Draper, Sr. Scholarships *(Undergraduate/Scholarship)*

Purpose: To financially support students pursuing education in an automotive related career. **Focus:** Automotive technology; Engineering, Automotive. **Qualif.:** Applicant must be an upper level undergraduate; interested in careers in automotive; have a 3.4 GPA; enrolled full-time at an accredited college or university; and have demonstrated financial need. **Criteria:** Applicants are selected based on the application.

Funds Avail.: No specific amount. **To Apply:** Application form is available at the website or send a letter of request with a self-addressed stamped envelope. Applicants must submit a completed application form; an official transcript; two recommendation letters; and a letter of acceptance for an associate, bachelor or masters program. Send all materials to: Automotive Hall of Fame, Scholarship Programs 21400 Oakwood Blvd. Dearborn, MI 48124. **Deadline:** May 30.

1551 ■ John E. Echlin Memorial Scholarships *(Undergraduate/Scholarship)*

Purpose: To financially support students pursuing education in an automotive related career. **Focus:** Automotive technology; Engineering, Automotive. **Qualif.:** Applicant must be an upper level undergraduate; interested in careers in automotive; have a 3.0 GPA; enrolled full-time at an accredited college or university; and have demonstrated financial need. **Criteria:** Applicants are selected based on the application.

Funds Avail.: No specific amount. **To Apply:** Application form is available at the website or send a letter of request with a self-addressed stamped envelope. Applicants must submit a completed application form; an official transcript; two recommendation letters; and a letter of acceptance for an associate, bachelor or masters program. Send all materials to: Automotive Hall of Fame, Scholarship Programs 21400 Oakwood Blvd. Dearborn, MI 48124. **Deadline:** May 30.

1552 ■ Carlyle Fraser/Wilton Looney Scholarships *(Undergraduate/Scholarship)*

Purpose: To financially support students pursuing education in an automotive related career. **Focus:** Automotive technology; Engineering, Automotive. **Qualif.:** Applicant must be an upper level undergraduate; interested in careers in automotive; have a 3.4 GPA; enrolled full-time at an accredited college or university; and have demonstrated financial need. **Criteria:** Preference is given to applicants attending Northwood University.

Funds Avail.: No specific amount. **To Apply:** Application form is available at the website or send a letter of request with a self-addressed stamped envelope. Applicants must submit a completed application form; an official transcript; two recommendation letters; and a letter of acceptance for an associate, bachelor or masters program. Send all materials to: Automotive Hall of Fame, Scholarship Programs 21400 Oakwood Blvd. Dearborn, MI 48124. **Deadline:** May 30.

Awards are arranged alphabetically below their administering organizations

1553 ■ John Goerlich Memorial Scholarships *(Undergraduate/Scholarship)*

Purpose: To financially support students pursuing education in an automotive related career. **Focus:** Automotive technology; Engineering, Automotive. **Qualif.:** Applicant must be an upper level undergraduate; interested in careers in automotive; have a 3.4 GPA; enrolled full-time at an accredited college or university; and have demonstrated financial need. **Criteria:** Applicants are selected based on the application.

Funds Avail.: No specific amount. **To Apply:** Application form is available at the website or send a letter of request with a self-addressed stamped envelope. Applicants must submit a completed application form; an official transcript; two recommendation letters; and a letter of acceptance for an associate, bachelor or masters program. Send all materials to: Automotive Hall of Fame, Scholarship Programs 21400 Oakwood Blvd. Dearborn, MI 48124. **Deadline:** May 30.

1554 ■ Charles V. Hagler Scholarships *(Undergraduate/Scholarship)*

Purpose: To financially support students pursuing education in an automotive related career. **Focus:** Automotive technology; Engineering, Automotive. **Qualif.:** Applicant must be an interested in careers in automotive; have a 3.0 GPA; enrolled full-time at an accredited college or university; and have demonstrated financial need. **Criteria:** Applicants are selected based on the application.

Funds Avail.: No specific amount. **To Apply:** Application form is available at the website or send a letter of request with a self-addressed stamped envelope. Applicants must submit a completed application form; an official transcript; two recommendation letters; and a letter of acceptance for an associate, bachelor or masters program. Send all materials to: Automotive Hall of Fame, Scholarship Programs 21400 Oakwood Blvd. Dearborn, MI 48124. **Deadline:** May 30.

1555 ■ Zenon C.R. Hansen Memorial Scholarships *(Undergraduate/Scholarship)*

Purpose: To financially support students pursuing education in an automotive related career. **Focus:** Automotive technology; Engineering, Automotive. **Qualif.:** Applicant must be an upper level undergraduate; interested in careers in automotive/trucking; have a 3.4 GPA; enrolled full-time at an accredited college or university; and have demonstrated financial need. **Criteria:** Applicants are selected based on the application.

Funds Avail.: No specific amount. **To Apply:** Application form is available at the website or send a letter of request with a self-addressed stamped envelope. Applicants must submit a completed application form; an official transcript; two recommendation letters; and a letter of acceptance for an associate, bachelor or masters program. Send all materials to: Automotive Hall of Fame, Scholarship Programs 21400 Oakwood Blvd. Dearborn, MI 48124. **Deadline:** May 30.

1556 ■ John W. Koons, Sr. Memorial Scholarships *(Undergraduate/Scholarship)*

Purpose: To financially support students pursuing education in an automotive related career. **Focus:** Automotive technology; Engineering, Automotive. **Qualif.:** Applicant must be an upper level undergraduate; interested in careers in automotive; have a 3.4 GPA; enrolled full-time at an accredited college or university; and have demonstrated financial need. **Criteria:** Applicants are selected based on the application.

Funds Avail.: No specific amount. **To Apply:** Application form is available at the website or send a letter of request with a self-addressed stamped envelope. Applicants must submit a completed application form; an official transcript; two recommendation letters; and a letter of acceptance for an associate, bachelor or masters program. Send all materials to: Automotive Hall of Fame, Scholarship Programs 21400 Oakwood Blvd. Dearborn, MI 48124. **Deadline:** May 30.

1557 ■ Ken Krum/Bud Kouts Memorial Scholarships *(Undergraduate/Scholarship)*

Purpose: To financially support students pursuing education in an automotive related career. **Focus:** Automotive technology; Engineering, Automotive. **Qualif.:** Applicant must be an upper level undergraduate; interested in careers in automotive; have a 3.0 GPA; enrolled full-time at an accredited college or university; and have demonstrated financial need. **Criteria:** Applicants are selected based on the application.

Funds Avail.: No specific amount. **To Apply:** Application form is available at the website or send a letter of request with a self-addressed stamped envelope. Applicants must submit a completed application form; an official transcript; two recommendation letters; and a letter of acceptance for an associate, bachelor or masters program. Send all materials to: Automotive Hall of Fame, Scholarship Programs 21400 Oakwood Blvd. Dearborn, MI 48124. **Deadline:** May 30.

1558 ■ Brouwer D. McIntyre Memorial Scholarships *(Undergraduate/Scholarship)*

Purpose: To financially support students pursuing education in an automotive related career. **Focus:** Automotive technology; Engineering, Automotive. **Qualif.:** Applicant must be an upper level undergraduate; interested in careers in automotive replacement parts industry; have a 3.0 GPA; enrolled full-time at Northwood University; and have demonstrated financial need. **Criteria:** Applicants are selected based on the application.

Funds Avail.: No specific amount. **To Apply:** Application form is available at the website or send a letter of request with a self-addressed stamped envelope. Applicants must submit a completed application form; an official transcript; two recommendation letters; and a letter of acceptance for an associate, bachelor or masters program. Send all materials to: Automotive Hall of Fame, Scholarship Programs 21400 Oakwood Blvd. Dearborn, MI 48124. **Deadline:** May 30.

1559 ■ Jim Moran Scholarships *(Undergraduate/Scholarship)*

Purpose: To financially support students pursuing education in an automotive related career. **Focus:** Automotive technology; Engineering, Automotive. **Qualif.:** Applicant must have a 2.7 GPA; enrolled full-time at Northwood University majoring in Automotive Marketing or Automotive Aftermarket; and have demonstrated financial need. **Criteria:** Preference is given to previous winners.

Funds Avail.: No specific amount. **To Apply:** Application form is available at the website or send a letter of request with a self-addressed stamped envelope. Applicants must submit a completed application form; an official transcript;

two recommendation letters; and a letter of acceptance for an associate, bachelor or masters program. Send all materials to: Automotive Hall of Fame, Scholarship Programs 21400 Oakwood Blvd. Dearborn, MI 48124. **Deadline:** May 30.

1560 ■ Dorothy M. Ross Memorial Scholarships *(Undergraduate/Scholarship)*

Purpose: To financially support students pursuing education in an automotive related career. **Focus:** Automotive technology; Engineering, Automotive. **Qualif.:** Applicant must be an undergraduate student; interested in careers in automotive; have a 3.0 GPA; and enrolled full-time at an accredited college or university. **Criteria:** Applicants are selected based on the application.

Funds Avail.: No specific amount. **To Apply:** Application form is available at the website or send a letter of request with a self-addressed stamped envelope. Applicants must submit a completed application form; an official transcript; two recommendation letters; and a letter of acceptance for an associate, bachelor or masters program. Send all materials to: Automotive Hall of Fame, Scholarship Programs 21400 Oakwood Blvd. Dearborn, MI 48124. **Deadline:** May 30.

1561 ■ Stuart H. Snyder Memorial Scholarships *(Undergraduate/Scholarship)*

Purpose: To financially support students pursuing education in an automotive related career. **Focus:** Automotive technology; Engineering, Automotive. **Qualif.:** Applicant must be an undergraduate student; interested in careers in automotive/trucking; have a 3.0 GPA; enrolled full-time at an accredited college/university; and have demonstrated financial need. **Criteria:** Applicants are selected based on the application.

Funds Avail.: No specific amount. **To Apply:** Application form is available at the website or send a letter of request with a self-addressed stamped envelope. Applicants must submit a completed application form; an official transcript; two recommendation letters; and a letter of acceptance for an associate, bachelor or masters program. Send all materials to: Automotive Hall of Fame, Scholarship Programs 21400 Oakwood Blvd. Dearborn, MI 48124. **Deadline:** May 30.

1562 ■ Society of Automotive Analyst Scholarships *(Undergraduate/Scholarship)*

Purpose: To financially support students pursuing education in an automotive related career. **Focus:** Automotive technology; Engineering, Automotive; Economics; Finance; Business administration; Marketing and distribution. **Qualif.:** Applicant must be an undergraduate student; interested in careers in automotive analysis; have a 3.0 GPA; and enrolled full-time at an accredited college or university majoring in economics, finance, business administration, or marketing management. **Criteria:** Applicants are selected based on the application.

Funds Avail.: No specific amount. **To Apply:** Application form is available at the website or send a letter of request with a self-addressed stamped envelope. Applicants must submit a completed application form; an official transcript; two recommendation letters; and a letter of acceptance for an associate, bachelor or masters program. Send all materials to: Automotive Hall of Fame, Scholarship Programs 21400 Oakwood Blvd. Dearborn, MI 48124. **Deadline:** May 30.

1563 ■ Walter W. Stillman Scholarships *(Undergraduate/Scholarship)*

Purpose: To financially support students pursuing education in an automotive related career. **Focus:** Automotive technology; Engineering, Automotive. **Qualif.:** Applicant must be an upper level undergraduate; interested in careers in automotive; have a 3.0 GPA; enrolled full-time at Northwood University; and have demonstrated financial need. **Criteria:** Preference is given applicants from New Jersey.

Funds Avail.: No specific amount. **To Apply:** Application form is available at the website or send a letter of request with a self-addressed stamped envelope. Applicants must submit a completed application form; an official transcript; two recommendation letters; and a letter of acceptance for an associate, bachelor or masters program. Send all materials to: Automotive Hall of Fame, Scholarship Programs 21400 Oakwood Blvd. Dearborn, MI 48124. **Deadline:** May 30.

1564 ■ TRW Foundation Scholarships *(Undergraduate/Scholarship)*

Purpose: To financially support students pursuing education in an automotive related career. **Focus:** Automotive technology; Engineering, Automotive. **Qualif.:** Applicant must be an undergraduate student; interested in careers in automotive; have a 3.0 GPA; enrolled full-time at an accredited college or university; a U.S. citizen; and have demonstrated financial need. **Criteria:** Preference is given to applicant attending the University of Michigan.

Funds Avail.: No specific amount. **To Apply:** Application form is available at the website or send a letter of request with a self-addressed stamped envelope. Applicants must submit a completed application form; an official transcript; two recommendation letters; and a letter of acceptance for an associate, bachelor or masters program. Send all materials to: Automotive Hall of Fame, Scholarship Programs 21400 Oakwood Blvd. Dearborn, MI 48124. **Deadline:** May 30.

1565 ■ Universal Underwriters Scholarships *(Undergraduate/Scholarship)*

Purpose: To financially support students pursuing education in an automotive related career. **Focus:** Automotive technology; Engineering, Automotive. **Qualif.:** Applicant must be an upper level undergraduate; interested in careers in automotive; have a 3.0 GPA; enrolled full-time Northwood University; and have demonstrated financial need. **Criteria:** Applicants are selected based on the application.

Funds Avail.: No specific amount. **To Apply:** Application form is available at the website or send a letter of request with a self-addressed stamped envelope. Applicants must submit a completed application form; an official transcript; two recommendation letters; and a letter of acceptance for an associate, bachelor or masters program. Send all materials to: Automotive Hall of Fame, Scholarship Programs 21400 Oakwood Blvd. Dearborn, MI 48124. **Deadline:** May 30.

1566 ■ J. Irving Whalley Memorial Scholarships *(Undergraduate/Scholarship)*

Purpose: To financially support students pursuing education in an automotive related career. **Focus:** Automotive technology; Engineering, Automotive. **Qualif.:** Applicant must be an upper level undergraduate; interested in careers in automotive; have a 3.0 GPA; enrolled full-time Northwood University; and have demonstrated financial need.

Awards are arranged alphabetically below their administering organizations

Criteria: Applicants are selected based on the application.

Funds Avail.: No specific amount. **To Apply:** Application form is available at the website or send a letter of request with a self-addressed stamped envelope. Applicants must submit a completed application form; an official transcript; two recommendation letters; and a letter of acceptance for an associate, bachelor or masters program. Send all materials to: Automotive Hall of Fame, Scholarship Programs 21400 Oakwood Blvd. Dearborn, MI 48124. **Deadline:** May 30.

1567 ■ M.H. Yager Memorial Scholarships *(Undergraduate/Scholarship)*

Purpose: To financially support students pursuing education in an automotive related career. **Focus:** Automotive technology; Engineering, Automotive. **Qualif.:** Applicant must be an upper level undergraduate; interested in careers in automotive; have a 3.4 GPA; enrolled full-time at an accredited college or university; and have demonstrated financial need. **Criteria:** Applicants are selected based on the application.

Funds Avail.: No specific amount. **To Apply:** Application form is available at the website or send a letter of request with a self-addressed stamped envelope. Applicants must submit a completed application form; an official transcript; two recommendation letters; and a letter of acceptance for an associate, bachelor or masters program. Send all materials to: Automotive Hall of Fame, Scholarship Programs 21400 Oakwood Blvd. Dearborn, MI 48124. **Deadline:** May 30.

1568 ■ Automotive Industries Association of Canada

1272 Wellington St. W
Ottawa, ON, Canada K1Y 3A7
Ph: 800-808-2920
Fax: (613)728-6021
E-mail: info.aia@aiacanada.com
URL: http://www.aiacanada.com

1569 ■ AIA and the Global Automotive Aftermarket Symposium Scholarships *(Undergraduate/Scholarship)*

Purpose: To financially support deserving secondary, college and university students intending to pursue a career in automotive aftermarket. **Focus:** Automotive technology. **Qualif.:** Applicants must be graduating high school senior or have graduated from high school within the past two years; must be enrolled in a college-level program, university or an accredited automotive technical program through either a CAMPE college or a CARS-approved institute; must be attending a full-time program in Canada or the United States. **Criteria:** Applicants will be selected based on their academic merit.

Funds Avail.: $1,000. **To Apply:** Application forms are available at the website. Applicants must prepare a copy of the current school transcript with official school seal; must submit an essay (at least 250 words in length, no longer than one page, double-spaced); letter of recommendation (from a non-family member, preferably an employer, teacher or someone other than a family friend). **Deadline:** June 15.

1570 ■ Hans McCorriston Motive Power Machinist Grant Programs *(Postgraduate/Scholarship)*

Purpose: To support students pursuing careers as motive power machinists. **Focus:** Automotive technology. **Qualif.:** Applicants must be enrolled in the AIA Motive Power Machinist Training Program or a college-level machinist training program within Canada. **Criteria:** Applications and other supporting documents are reviewed by the Scholarship Committee.

Funds Avail.: $500,000. **To Apply:** Applicant must fill up the application form available at the website. **Deadline:** October 15.

Remarks: Grant is named after Hans McCorriston, in honor of his contributions to the motive power industry. **Contact:** Patty Kettles at the above address (see entry 1568).

1571 ■ Arthur Paulin Automotive Aftermarket Scholarship Awards *(Postgraduate/Scholarship)*

Purpose: To provide monetary assistance to deserving students in the automotive field. **Focus:** Automotive technology. **Qualif.:** Applicants must be enrolled in an automotive aftermarket industry-related program or curriculum at a Canadian college or university. **Criteria:** Recipients are selected based on the Scholarship Committee's review of applications and other supporting documents.

Funds Avail.: $700,000. **To Apply:** Application form is available at the website. Applicants must submit a letter stating his/her long-term automotive goals; and a letter from his/her automotive instructor; recent academic achievements, as well as achievements in the automotive sector. **Deadline:** October 31.

Remarks: Scholarship award was named after long-time AIA volunteer Arthur Paulin, who served on the AIA board of directors for more than nine years.

1572 ■ Marion Roberts Memorial Scholarships *(Postgraduate/Scholarship)*

Purpose: To provide financial assistance and encouragement enabling students to further their education at the post-secondary school level. **Focus:** General studies. **Qualif.:** Applicant must be a dependent child or spouse of a full-time employee in an active ad AIA member company; confirmation of the parent's/spouse employment must be provided by the member company. Applicant must be enrolled in a full-time post-secondary program leading to a degree, certificate or diploma at an accredited university, college, technical school or C.E.G.E.P. **Criteria:** Recipients are selected based on the Scholarship Committee's review of applications.

Funds Avail.: Amount not specified. **To Apply:** Applicants must fill up the application form available at the website; must prepare a letter that demonstrates leadership ability in school, social or other activities; must have a transcript indicating academic achievement, with an official seal or photocopy of the seal of the school; recent passport-sized photo. **Deadline:** July 15.

Remarks: Funds established in honor of Marion Roberts, a long-time staff member of the association's head office in Ottawa.

1573 ■ SEMA Memorial Scholarships *(Graduate/Scholarship)*

Purpose: To support educational goals for students pursuing careers in the automotive aftermarkets. **Focus:** Automotive technology. **Qualif.:** Applicants must be graduate-level students at an accredited university or college; four-year accredited university or college; three-year accredited university or community college; or vocational/technical school. **Criteria:** Applications are reviewed and scored by

Awards are arranged alphabetically below their administering organizations

an independent panel comprised of business professionals.

Funds Avail.: $1,000-$4,000, depending on the category. **To Apply:** Applicants must submit an official transcript; two letters of recommendation from (a non-family member) employer, career counselors or professor on company letterhead; current photographs (head shot) for publication and promotional use.

1574 ■ Automotive Recyclers Association

3975 Fair Ridge Dr., Ste. 20-N
Fairfax, VA 22033
Ph: (703)385-1001
Fax: (703)385-1494
Free: 888-385-1005
E-mail: kelly@a-r-a.org
URL: http://www.a-r-a.org

1575 ■ ARA Scholarship Awards *(Undergraduate/Scholarship)*

Purpose: To assist outstanding students to pursue their educational goal. **Focus:** Business; Trades training; Technical training. **Qualif.:** Applicants must be children of an employee of a direct ARA member company; must be a high school senior or pursuing a full-time post high school program in an institution providing trade, business, or technical programs; have at least 3.0 GPA or equivalent. **Criteria:** Applicants will be selected based on their academic achievement.

Funds Avail.: Scholarship amount not specified. **To Apply:** Applicants must submit a completed application form and profile sheet. Transcript of academic record must be sent by the applicant's school/college directly to the ARA Scholarship Advisor. Applicants must obtain a certification and letter of verification from the parents' employer who is a direct member of ARA (should include current employment and the hiring date). Send all requirements to the ARA Scholarship Foundation Advisor. **Deadline:** March 15. **Contact:** ARA Scholarship Advisor, arascholar@sbcglobal.net.

1576 ■ Automotive Women's Alliance Foundation

PO Box 4305
Troy, MI 48099
Ph: (248)643-6590
Fax: (248)643-9685
URL: http://www.automotivewomensalliance.com

1577 ■ Automotive Women's Alliance Foundation Scholarships *(Undergraduate/Scholarship)*

Purpose: To support the advancement of automotive professionals and motivate current and future students studying an automotive related field. **Focus:** Automotive technology. **Qualif.:** Candidates must be high school seniors preparing to enter college, current college students, those starting postgraduate work, or women in the workforce looking to enhance their current positions through additional education. **Criteria:** Scholarships are given based on academic merit.

Funds Avail.: $2,000. **To Apply:** Candidates must submit complete application letter.

1578 ■ Aviation Distributors and Manufacturers Association

100 N 20th St., 4th Fl.
Philadelphia, PA 19103-1443
Ph: (215)564-3484
Fax: (215)963-9784
E-mail: adma@fernley.com
URL: http://www.adma.org

1579 ■ Aviation Distributors and Manufacturers Association Scholarship Fund *(All/Scholarship)*

Purpose: To provide assistance to students pursuing careers in the aviation field. **Focus:** Aviation. **Qualif.:** Applicants must be enrolled in an accredited Aviation program and possess a minimum of 3.0 grade point average. **Criteria:** Recipients are selected based on academic performance, financial need, recommendations, extracurricular activities and leadership contributions.

Funds Avail.: No specific amount. **Number Awarded:** 2. **To Apply:** Applicants must submit two letters of reference and a 500-word essay describing their desire to pursue a career in the aviation field. **Deadline:** March 28.

1580 ■ AVS Science and Technology Society

120 Wall St., 32nd Fl.
New York, NY 10005
Ph: (212)248-0200
Fax: (212)248-0245
URL: http://www.avs.org

1581 ■ IUVSTA Welch Scholarships *(Professional Development/Scholarship)*

Purpose: To give promising scholars an opportunity to work for one year in a country in which they have not previously studied. **Focus:** Vacuum science and technology. **Qualif.:** Applicants must take arrangements for the proposed research program with a laboratory outside the applicant's native country and the research must be on a topic of vacuum science, technique or application. **Criteria:** Candidates for the scholarship should have at least a Bachelors degree and a Doctoral degree is preferred.

Funds Avail.: $15,000. **Number Awarded:** 1. **Deadline:** April 15.

1582 ■ Charles Babbage Institute

222-21st Ave. S
Minneapolis, MN 55455
Ph: (612)624-5050
Fax: (612)625-8054
E-mail: cbi@umn.edu
URL: http://www.cbi.umn.edu

1583 ■ Arthur L. Norberg Travel Grants *(All/Grant)*

Purpose: To provide short-term grants to help scholars offset travel expenses needed to use archival collections at the Charles Babbage Institute. **Focus:** Information Science and Technology. **Qualif.:** Applicants must be scholars intending to use CBI collections for research projects. To be eligible, scholars must reside outside the Twin Cities metropolitan region. **Criteria:** Recipients are selected based on eligibility.

Funds Avail.: $750. **Number Awarded:** 2. **To Apply:** Applicants must submit a two-page CV as well as a 500-word project description that describes the overall research project, identifies the importance of specific CBI collections, and discusses the projected outcome (journal article, book chapter, museum exhibit, etc.). Materials must be submitted by email at cbi@umn.edu or mailed at: Charles Babbage Institute: Norberg Travel Fund, 211 Andersen Library, University of Minnesota, 222 - 21st Avenue South, Minneapolis, MN 55455. **Deadline:** February 15.

1584 ■ The Adelle and Erwin Tomash Fellowships *(Doctorate/Fellowship)*

Purpose: To administer research projects in the history of information technology and inspire engagement in original research that is disseminated through scholarly publications and conference presentations. **Focus:** Information Science and Technology. **Qualif.:** Applicants must be graduating students of doctoral dissertation research in the history of computing. **Criteria:** Recipients are selected based on the need of the CBI materials, research plans and willingness to make a brief presentation of the research findings.

Funds Avail.: $14,000. **To Apply:** Applicants must submit a curriculum vitae; a five-page, single-spaced statement and justification of the research program including a discussion of methods, research materials, evidence of faculty support for the project, and bibliography. **Deadline:** January 15.

1585 ■ The Bailey Family Foundation

912 W Platt St.
Tampa, FL 33606
Ph: (813)549-6140
Fax: (813)549-6141
E-mail: bailey@bailey-family.org
URL: http://www.bailey-family.org

1586 ■ The Bailey Family Foundation College Scholarship Program *(Undergraduate/Scholarship)*

Purpose: To financially assist students in continuing their education. **Focus:** General studies. **Qualif.:** Applicants must possess a minimum cumulative GPA of 2.5; must demonstrate financial need; must be enrolled or accepted to one of the participating schools listed on the scholarship application; and must be pursuing an undergraduate degree. **Criteria:** Applicants will be evaluated based on academic achievement and financial need.

Funds Avail.: No specific amount. **To Apply:** Applicants must submit the completed scholarship application form and an essay of no more than 300 words.

1587 ■ The Bailey Family Foundation High School Scholarship Program *(Undergraduate/Scholarship)*

Purpose: To provide financial assistance for high school seniors intending to continue their post-secondary education. **Focus:** General studies. **Qualif.:** Applicant must possess a minimum cumulative GPA of 2.5; must demonstrate financial need; must be a graduating senior from a participating high school; and must be pursuing an undergraduate degree. **Criteria:** Applicants will be evaluated based on academic achievement and financial need.

Funds Avail.: No specific amount. **To Apply:** Applicants must submit the completed scholarship application form and an essay of no more than 300 words.

1588 ■ Howard Baker Foundation

12313 County Rd. 10
Ranburne, AL 36273
Ph: (313)268-0636
Fax: (256)568-5714
URL: http://www.howardbakerfoundation.org

1589 ■ Howard Baker Foundation Scholarships *(Undergraduate/Scholarship)*

Purpose: To provide assistance to City of Detroit residents in financing their education at Wayne State University, to encourage continued progress towards a degree and to recognize scholastic achievement. **Focus:** Nursing. **Qualif.:** Applicants must be undergraduate minority students of Wayne State University or from minority students accepted for full-time study at Wayne State University; must be majoring nursing or in a natural science curriculum; must be Detroit (public, private or parochial) high school graduates, residents of the City of Detroit and United States citizens; must have a minimum of 2.5 cumulative Grade Point Average (GPA) at the time of the selection. **Criteria:** Recipients are selected on the basis of financial need.

Funds Avail.: No specific amount. **To Apply:** Applicants must submit all required application information.

1590 ■ Baltimore City College

600 E Lombard St., Rm. 206
Baltimore, MD 21202
Ph: (410)986-5518
Fax: (410)986-5510
URL: http://www.bccc.edu

1591 ■ BCCC Foundation Scholarships *(Undergraduate/Scholarship)*

Purpose: To provide financial assistance to individuals who have the desire and commitment to pursue their educational goals. **Focus:** General studies. **Qualif.:** Applicants must be graduating high school students with at least 6 credits at BCCC with 2.5 GPA. **Criteria:** Recipients are selected based on academic achievement and financial need.

Funds Avail.: No specific amount. **To Apply:** Applicants must submit completed scholarship application along with personal statement and copy of unofficial transcript.

1592 ■ BCCC Foundation Workforce Scholarships *(Undergraduate/Scholarship)*

Purpose: To provide financial assistance to those who have the desire and commitment to pursue their educational goals. **Focus:** General studies. **Qualif.:** Applicants must be US citizens and residents of Maryland working at least 20 hours a week; must have a 2.5 GPA enrolled in at least three credits per semester if pursuing credit courses; and must demonstrate financial need through submission of FAFSA. **Criteria:** Recipients are selected based on academic achievement and financial need.

Funds Avail.: No specific amount. **To Apply:** Applicants must submit completed scholarship application along with 300-500 word essay and a copy of transcript.

1593 ■ Banner & Witcoff, Ltd.

10 S Wacker Dr., Ste. 3000
Chicago, IL 60606-7407
Ph: (312)463-5000
Fax: (312)463-5001
E-mail: info@bannerwitcoff.com
URL: http://www.bannerwitcoff.com

1594 ■ Donald W. Banner Diversity Scholarship for Law Students *(Undergraduate/Scholarship)*

Purpose: To foster the development of intellectual property lawyers from diverse backgrounds. **Focus:** Law. **Qualif.:**

Applicants must be law students who have entered into a JD program at an ABA-accredited law school in the United States. **Criteria:** Scholarship recipients will be selected by the Donald W. Banner Diversity Scholarship review board based on the following criteria: (1) academic merit (undergraduate, graduate and law school); (2) commitment to the pursuit of a career in IP law; (3) member of a historically underrepresented group in IP law; (3) written communication skills; (4) oral communication skills determined through an interview; and (5) leadership qualities and community involvement.

Funds Avail.: $5,000. **To Apply:** Applicants must complete the Donald W. Banner Diversity Scholarship application form, available online; must submit a resume, academic transcripts (law, undergraduate/graduate school), a writing sample (5-10 pages), three references including contact information, and a one-page statement describing how diversity has impacted the candidate. **Deadline:** October 1.

1595 ■ Bar Association of San Francisco

301 Battery St., 3rd Fl.
San Francisco, CA 94111
Ph: (415)982-1600
Fax: (415)477-2388
URL: http://www.sfbar.org

1596 ■ Bay Area Minority Law Student Scholarships *(Graduate, Undergraduate/Scholarship)*

Purpose: To reaffirm a commitment to diversity in legal education and the legal profession. **Focus:** Law. **Qualif.:** Applicants must be students from minority groups who are underrepresented in Bay Area law schools; and must have received a "letter of admission" from one of the eight Northern California law schools. **Criteria:** Recipients are selected on the submitted application materials.

Funds Avail.: $10,000. **To Apply:** Applicants must submit a completed application with official undergraduate or graduate transcript; 500-word personal statement; copies of current IRS tax forms; statement of economic need (optional); copies of "letters of admissions" from any ABA accredited law school in Northern California. **Deadline:** May 30. **Contact:** Jayne Salinger at 415-782-9000 x8710, or email at jsalinger@sfbar.org.

1597 ■ Barrientos Scholarship Foundation

PO Box 7173
Omaha, NE 68107
Ph: (402)215-5106
E-mail: info@barrientosscholarship.org
URL: http://www.barrientosscholarship.org

1598 ■ Artistic Scholarship Awards *(Undergraduate/Scholarship)*

Purpose: To provide financial assistance to qualified students who want to pursue their studies. **Focus:** Music; Visual arts; Theater arts; Dance. **Qualif.:** Applicants must be students pursuing higher education and career goals that focus on one or more of the arts - music, visual arts, theater, or dance; must be of Latino heritage; must be high school graduating seniors, currently enrolled in college, or adults ready to pursue college; must plan to enroll in at least two classes and attend an accredited community college, university, or technical or vocational school in the state of Nebraska or surrounding greater Omaha Metropolitan area; must have a minimum of 2.5 GPA. **Criteria:** Selection of applicants will be based on the criteria of the Scholarship Selection Committee.

Funds Avail.: $250-$500. **Number Awarded:** No specific amount. **To Apply:** Applicants must complete the application form available online; must have a personal essay with a minimum of two pages; must submit letters of recommendation and official high school or college transcript. Application form and requirements must be sent to Barrientos Scholarship Foundation, P.O Box 7173, Omaha, NE 68107. **Deadline:** May 15.

1599 ■ General Scholarship Awards *(Undergraduate/Scholarship)*

Purpose: To provide financial assistance to qualified students who want to pursue their studies. **Focus:** Interdisciplinary studies. **Qualif.:** Applicants must be students pursuing higher education and career goals that focus on disciplines other than arts; must be of Latino Heritage; must be high school graduating seniors, currently enrolled in college, or adults ready to pursue college; must plan to enroll in at least two classes and attend an accredited community college, university, or technical or vocational school in the State of Nebraska or surrounding greater Omaha Metropolitan area; must have a minimum of a 2.5 cumulative GPA. **Criteria:** Selection of applicants will be based on the criteria of the Scholarship Selection Committee.

Funds Avail.: $250-$500. **Number Awarded:** No specific amount. **To Apply:** Applicants must have the application form available online; must have a personal essay with a minimum of two pages; must submit a letter of recommendation and official high school or college transcript. Application form and requirements must be sent to Barrientos Scholarship Foundation, P.O Box 7173, Omaha, NE 68107. **Deadline:** May 15.

1600 ■ Bat Conservation International

PO Box 162603
Austin, TX 78716
Ph: (512)327-9721
Fax: (512)327-9724
Free: 800-538-2287
E-mail: bathouses@batcon.org
URL: http://www.batcon.org

1601 ■ Bat Conservation International Student Research Scholarships *(Undergraduate/Scholarship)*

Purpose: To teach people the value of bats; to protect and conserve critical bat habitats; to advance scientific knowledge through research. **Focus:** Environmental conservation. **Qualif.:** Applicant must be enrolled in any college or university. **Criteria:** Committee will consider the application if projects meet the conservation goals of the program; sufficient materials were received prior to the deadline; materials meet the submission requirements; applicant meets eligibility requirements; and significant changes were submitted before the deadline.

Funds Avail.: $1,000-$5,000. **Number Awarded:** 1. **To Apply:** Applicant must apply online or send documents as attachments to grant@batcon.org; he/she must submit a proposal, budget, and curriculum vitae. **Deadline:** December15. **Contact:** grant@batcon.org.

1602 ■ John Bayliss Broadcast Foundation

PO Box 51126
Pacific Grove, CA 93950

Awards are arranged alphabetically below their administering organizations

Ph: (831)655-5229
Fax: (831)655-5228
E-mail: cbutrum@baylissfoundation.org
URL: http://www.baylissfoundation.org

1603 ■ John Bayliss Broadcast Foundation Internship Programs *(Undergraduate/Internship)*

Purpose: To enhance students' education at Bayliss Schools across the nation. To provide practical skills that will prepare them for a rewarding future. **Focus:** Broadcasting. **Qualif.:** Applicants must be studying for a career in the radio industry and have taken basic journalism courses as well as specialized courses in the radio communication fields. Applicants must have previous radio-related experience. Applicants must be enrolled in a degree program and entering their junior or senior year in college; must have a GPA of 3.0 or better; must be at least 18 years of age. **Criteria:** Recipients are selected based on financial need and academic record.

Funds Avail.: No specific amount. **To Apply:** Applicants must submit a resume and complete the application form.

1604 ■ John Bayliss Broadcast Foundation Scholarships *(Undergraduate/Scholarship)*

Purpose: To support broadcasting students. **Focus:** Broadcasting. **Qualif.:** Applicants must be entering thier junior or senior year at an institution in the United States. Applicants must be preparing for a career in the radio industry, preferably commercial radio. Applicants must maintain a 3.0 GPA or better. **Criteria:** Recipients are selected based on financial need, merit, history of radio-related activities, and based the demonstrated degree of integrity and a personal sense of responsibility.

Funds Avail.: $5,000. **Number Awarded:** 15. **To Apply:** Applicants must provide a typewritten resume; an official transcript; three letters of recommendation written by people other than relatives. Applicant must submit a two-page typewritten essay describing his/her broadcasting goals as they relate to radio and the ways in which they hope to achieve their goals. **Deadline:** March.

1605 ■ BDPA Education Technology Foundation

4423 Lehigh Rd., No. 277
College Park, MD 20740
Ph: (513)362-2703
Fax: (202)318-2194
E-mail: info@betf.org
URL: http://www.betf.org

1606 ■ Black Data Processing Associates Scholarships *(High School/Scholarship)*

Purpose: To provide outstanding minority students financial assistance in pursuing an information technology-related degree at an accredited two or four-year college or university of their choice. **Focus:** Information science and technology. **Qualif.:** Applicants must be U.S. citizens or permanent U.S. residents and graduating high school seniors at the time of their application; must be pursuing an information technology-related degree at an accredited two or four-year college or university; must be student members of BDPA and participate in computer training activities. **Criteria:** Applicants are evaluated based on academic excellence; exceptional leadership potential; and impact through service to their communities.

Funds Avail.: $2,500. **Number Awarded:** 6. **To Apply:** Applicants must submit the completed application form; high school transcript; two 500-word essays explaining why information technology is important and the importance of personal commitment in giving back to your community; and two letters of recommendation. **Deadline:** May 28.

1607 ■ Beacon of Hope Scholarship Foundation

7230 Medical Center Dr., Ste. 300
West Hills, CA 91307
Ph: (818)716-7003
URL: http://www.beaconhope.org

1608 ■ Beacon of Hope Scholarships *(Undergraduate/Scholarship)*

Purpose: To provide financial assistance to qualified, underprivileged, college-bound African American high school students. **Focus:** General studies. **Qualif.:** Applicants must be African American graduating high school students; must be residents of Mississippi and/or Los Angeles, California; must have at least a "B" average and verification of acceptance and attendance at a four-year college or university in the United States, must participate in any scholarship-related public relations activities. **Criteria:** Recipients are selected based on academic achievement and financial need.

Funds Avail.: $1,000. **To Apply:** Applicants must submit the completed application form along with one certified copy of high school academic transcript; one original photograph; and a hard copy of an essay of at least 1,000 words entitled "Why I am Deserving of the Beacon of Hope Scholarship".

1609 ■ BECA Foundation

830 E Grand Ave., Ste. B
Escondido, CA 92025
Ph: (760)741-8246
E-mail: sdbeca@sbcglobal.net
URL: http://www.becafoundation.org

1610 ■ BECA Foundation-CUSM Scholarships *(Undergraduate/Scholarship)*

Purpose: To seek promising students and provide them with the necessary financial assistance, moral support and guidance to complete their education, thereby promoting higher educational and leadership standards within the Hispanic community. **Focus:** General studies. **Qualif.:** Applicants must be Latino students enrolled at CSU San Marcos. **Criteria:** Recipients are selected based on financial need, scholastic determination and community and cultural awareness.

Funds Avail.: $1,000. **To Apply:** Applicants must complete the application form. **Deadline:** March 3. **Contact:** sdbeca@sbcglobal.net; 760-741-8246.

1611 ■ BECA Foundation General Scholarships Fund *(Undergraduate/Scholarship)*

Purpose: To seek promising students and provide them with the necessary financial assistance, moral support and guidance to complete their education, thereby promoting higher educational and leadership standards within the Hispanic community. **Focus:** General studies. **Qualif.:** Applicant must be a San Diego County High School graduate who is entering college. **Criteria:** Recipients are selected based on financial need, scholastic determination, com-

Awards are arranged alphabetically below their administering organizations

munity and cultural awareness.

Funds Avail.: $1,000. **To Apply:** Applicants must complete the application form. **Deadline:** March 3. **Contact:** sdbeca@sbcglobal.net; 760-741-8246.

1612 ■ Alice Newell Joslyn Medical Fund
(Undergraduate/Scholarship)

Purpose: To seek promising students and provide them with the necessary financial assistance, moral support and guidance to complete their education, thereby promoting higher educational and leadership standards within the Hispanic community. **Focus:** Medical Education. **Qualif.:** Applicants must be entering medical/health care professions. **Criteria:** Recipients are selected based on financial need, scholastic determination, community and cultural awareness.

Funds Avail.: $1,000. **To Apply:** Applicants must complete the application form. **Deadline:** March 3. **Contact:** sdbeca@sbcglobal.net; 760-741-8246.

1613 ■ Alexander Graham Bell Association for the Deaf and Hard of Hearing

3417 Volta Pl. NW
Washington, DC 20007
Ph: (202)337-5220
Fax: (202)337-8314
E-mail: info@agbell.org
URL: http://www.agbell.org

1614 ■ College Scholarship Awards
(Undergraduate/Scholarship)

Purpose: To promote communication for people with hearing loss. **Focus:** Hearing and Deafness. **Qualif.:** Must be enrolled in or applied to a mainstream and accredited college/university as a full-time student. **Criteria:** Award will be given to applicant who has been diagnosed with a moderate to profound hearing loss prior to acquiring a spoken language (pre-lingual hearing loss); Applicants hearing loss must be bilateral and in the moderate to profound range; Spoken communication must be the student's primary mode of communication.

Funds Avail.: $5,000. **Number Awarded:** Varies. **To Apply:** Applicants must submit an application, with pages in numbered order; For children who use hearing aids, an unaided Audiogram performed within the last twelve (12) months or for those with cochlear implants, the most recent mapping report (first page only); Verification of the student's application, acceptance or enrollment to a mainstream and accredited university/college; Official transcripts for the most recent two years completed of high school or college; Student essay; Recommendation from a hearing health professional (maximum of two single-sided pages); Recommendation from a current AG Bell member (Maximum of two singe-sided pages). If you do not know an AG Bell member, please provide a recommendation from an educational or therapeutic professional; Recommendation from a non-relative who is familiar with the family's financial need (maximum of two single-sided pages). **Deadline:** February 15.

1615 ■ George H. Nofer Scholarships for Law and Public Policy *(Doctorate, Graduate/ Scholarship)*

Purpose: To promote communication for people with hearing loss. **Focus:** Hearing and Deafness. **Qualif.:** Applicant must be accepted at or recently enrolled in an accredited law school or masters/doctoral program in public policy or public administration as a full-time first year rising graduate student. **Criteria:** Award will be given to those applicant who has been diagnosed with a moderate to profound hearing loss prior to acquiring spoken language (pre-lingual hearing loss); Applicants hearing loss must be bilateral and in the moderate to profound range; Must have an unaided Pure-Tone Average of 60dB or greater in the better hearing ear in the speech frequencies of 500, 1000 and 2000 Hz. Applicants with cochlear implants meet this eligibility requirement. Unilateral (one-sided) hearing loss does not qualify; Applicants uses spoken language as the primary mode of communication.

Funds Avail.: $5000. **Number Awarded:** Varies. **To Apply:** Applicants must submit an application, with pages in numbered order; For students who use hearing aids, an unaided Audiogram performed within the last twelve months or for those with cochlear implants, the most recent mapping report (first page only); Official transcripts for the most recent two completed years of college. For third year applicants, a transcript of your previous year of study will suffice. Verification of the student's application, acceptance or enrollment to a mainstream and accredited university/college (a readable photocopy of a letter, tuition notice, or other correspondence is acceptable); Student essay (as indicated in the application); Recommendation from a hearing health professional (maximum of two single-sided pages); Recommendation from a current AG Bell member (Maximum of two singe-sided pages). If you do not know an AG Bell member, please provide a recommendation from an educational or therapeutic professional; Recommendation from a non-relative who is familiar with the family's financial need (maximum of two single-sided pages). **Deadline:** May 1.

1616 ■ School Age Financial Aid Program
(Undergraduate/Scholarship)

Purpose: To promote communication for people with hearing loss. **Focus:** Hearing and Deafness. **Qualif.:** Applicants must be a resident of the United States (including territories) or Canada, and must be enrolled or registered for enrollment on a full-time basis in a parochial, independent or private school in which the child participates in a mainstream setting. **Criteria:** Awards will be given to those hearing loss has been diagnosed prior to acquiring spoken language (pre-lingual hearing loss); Hearing loss must be in the moderate to profound range: Spoken communication must be the child's primary mode of communication; The child must be at least six years of age and no older than twenty-one (21) years of age on December 31, 2008; Parents/guardians must demonstrate financial need.

Funds Avail.: No specific amount. **Number Awarded:** Varies. **To Apply:** Applicants must submit an application, with pages in numbered order; For children who use hearing aids, an unaided Audiogram performed within the last twelve months or for those with cochlear implants, the most recent mapping report (first page only); Verification of the child's enrollment, and a narrative from a teacher or principal on the child's progress on school letterhead; Recommendation from a hearing health professional (maximum of two single-sided pages); Recommendation from a current AG Bell member (Maximum of two singe-sided pages). If you do not know an AG Bell member, please provide a recommendation from an educational or therapeutic professional; Recommendation from a non-relative who is familiar with the family's financial need (maximum of two single-sided pages). **Deadline:** April 1.

Awards are arranged alphabetically below their administering organizations

1617 ■ March and Ruti Bell Foundation

6800 Broken Sound Parkway
Boca Raton, FL 33487
Ph: (561)988-1700
Fax: (561)988-1738
URL: http://bellfamily.org

1618 ■ March and Ruti Bell Foundation Scholarships *(Undergraduate/Scholarship)*

Purpose: To encourage undergraduates in the College of Arts and Science to choose careers in public service. **Focus:** Public service. **Qualif.:** Applicants must be junior and senior high school students who have declared their majors in the field of public service; must have a strong sense of their career goals. **Criteria:** Selection will be based on the following criteria: an excellent academic record; unmet financial need (which would otherwise be covered by a burdensome loan); commitment to entering a public interest profession, as demonstrated in a personal statement, as well as by a track record of community service and (in some cases) a relevant course of study; an interview (for those who survive a preliminary cut on the basis of the three other criteria mentioned here).

Funds Avail.: No specific amount. **To Apply:** Students may submit an application letter together with other requirements. **Deadline:** April 1. **Contact:** Matthew S. Santirocco, Dean, College of Arts and Science, New York University, 100 Washington Square E. New York, NY 10003-6688. 212-998-8100.

1619 ■ Ben Meadows

PO Box 5277
Janesville, WI 53547-5277
Fax: (608)743-8007
Free: 800-241-6401
E-mail: mail@benmeadows.com
URL: http://www.benmeadows.com

1620 ■ Ben Meadows Natural Resource Scholarships - Academic Achievement Scholarships *(Undergraduate/Scholarship)*

Purpose: To provide fund for students enrolled in a natural resource program. **Focus:** Forestry; Environmental science; Natural resources; Wildlife conservation, management, and science; Fisheries sciences/management. **Qualif.:** Applicant must be a junior or senior student enrolled in a natural resource program working toward a bachelor of arts or science degree, which includes, but not limited to, agro forestry, urban forestry, environmental studies, natural resource management, natural resource recreation, wildlife management, wood science and fisheries management. Student must have a GPA of 3.2 or higher on a 4.0 scale. **Criteria:** Award is given based on the application.

Funds Avail.: $2,500. **Number Awarded:** 1. **To Apply:** Applicants must complete the online scholarship application and must provide a letter of recommendation from educational superior (professor, teacher, advisor), and attach official copies of transcripts reflecting the GPA. **Deadline:** June 30.

1621 ■ Ben Meadows Natural Resource Scholarships - Leadership Scholarships *(Undergraduate/Scholarship)*

Purpose: To provide fund for students enrolled in a natural resource program. **Focus:** Forestry; Environmental science; Natural resources; Wildlife conservation, management, and science; Fisheries sciences/management. **Qualif.:** Applicant must be a junior or senior student enrolled in a natural resource program working toward a bachelor of arts or science degree, which includes, but not limited to, agro forestry, urban forestry, environmental studies, natural resource management, natural resource recreation, wildlife management, wood science and fisheries management. Student must have a GPA of 2.5 or higher on a 4.0 scale. **Criteria:** Award is given based on the application.

Funds Avail.: $2,500. **Number Awarded:** 1. **To Apply:** Applicants must complete the online scholarship application and must provide a letter of recommendation from educational superior (professor, teacher, advisor), and attach official copies of transcripts reflecting the GPA. **Deadline:** June 30.

1622 ■ Benign Essential Blepharospasm Research Foundation

PO Box 12468
Beaumont, TX 77726-2468
Ph: (409)832-0788
Fax: (409)832-0890
E-mail: bebrf@blepharospasm.org
URL: http://www.blepharospasm.org

1623 ■ Benign Essential Blepharospasm Research Foundation Research Grant *(Postdoctorate/Grant)*

Purpose: To encourage researches on cranial dystonia (blepharospasm and Meige's Syndrome) by providing financial support. **Focus:** Medicine. **Qualif.:** Principal investigator must hold M.D. or Ph.D. and intend to conduct researches that relate specifically to benign essential blepharospasm and Meige covering new treatments, pathophysiology and genetics, photophobia and dry eye; non-US citizens working at institutions abroad are eligible to apply. **Criteria:** Recipients are selected based on committee's review of the proposal.

Funds Avail.: $150,000. **To Apply:** Applicants must send curriculum vitae and eight copies of proposals with consent form and necessary signatures. Specific grant guidelines and forms are available on the website. **Deadline:** July 1.

1624 ■ Benton County Foundation

PO Box 911
Corvallis, OR 97339
Ph: (541)753-1603
URL: http://www.bentoncountyfoundation.org

1625 ■ Margaret Dowell-Gravatt, M.D. Scholarship *(Undergraduate/Scholarship)*

Purpose: To encourage and support ethnic minority undergraduate women enrolled in the College of Science. **Focus:** Zoology; Microbiology; Medical technology; Medicine; Nursing; Physical therapy; Occupational therapy. **Qualif.:** Applicant must: be pursuing a degree in Zoology or Microbiology or one of the following pre-health programs: Medical Technology, Medicine, Nursing, Physical and/or Occupational therapy. Applicant must: be enrolled full-time at the sophomore, junior, or senior level; have a GPA of 2.5 overall and 3.0 in science courses required in their major field or pre-health curriculum; qualify for financial assistance as defined by the Financial Aid Office of OSU. **Criteria:**

Awards are arranged alphabetically below their administering organizations

Selection will be based on the committee's criteria.

Funds Avail.: No specific amount. **To Apply:** Applicant may contact the Foundation for application form and other requirements. **Contact:** Benton County Foundation at the above address (see entry 1624).

1626 ■ Joel R. Friend Scholarship *(Undergraduate/Scholarship)*

Purpose: To provide scholarship opportunity to the students from OSU. **Focus:** General studies. **Qualif.:** Applicants must be foreign students from Thailand, Taiwan (Republic of China) in attendance at OSU in any field of study; must qualify for financial assistance as defined by the Financial Aid Office of OSU. **Criteria:** Selection will be based on the committee's criteria.

Funds Avail.: No specific amount. **To Apply:** Applicant may contact the Foundation for application form and other requirements. **Contact:** Benton County Foundation at the above address (see entry 1624).

1627 ■ William Harrison Gill Education Fund *(Undergraduate/Scholarship)*

Purpose: To provide scholarship to the students of Oregon State University. **Focus:** General studies. **Qualif.:** Applicant must: be of Native American descent and must be an American citizen with a permanent or guardian residence in one of the following states: Arizona, California, Colorado, Idaho, Montana, Nevada, New Mexico, Oregon, Utah, Washington or Wyoming. **Criteria:** Selection will be based on the committee's criteria.

Funds Avail.: No specific amount. **To Apply:** Applicant may contact the Foundation for application process and other requirements.

1628 ■ Lucy Hsu Ho Scholarship *(Undergraduate/Scholarship)*

Purpose: To award scholarship to the foreign students of ethnic Chinese descent. **Focus:** General studies. **Qualif.:** Applicants must be foreign students of ethnic Chinese descent; pimary preference in awarding the scholarship shall be given to those candidates who have demonstrated leadership in student and/or community activities and organizations, as well as the desire to serve others in the candidate's future chosen field of work. Secondary preference shall be determined by level of financial need; must re-apply for this scholarship each year; must qualify for financial assistance as defined by the Financial Aid Office of OSU. **Criteria:** Selection will be based on the committee's criteria.

Funds Avail.: No specific amount. **To Apply:** Applicant may contact the Foundation for application form and other requirements. **Contact:** Benton County Foundation at the above address (see entry 1624).

1629 ■ Kilbuck Family Native American Scholarship *(Undergraduate/Scholarship)*

Purpose: To provide scholarship opportunity to the students enrolled at Oregon State University. **Focus:** General studies. **Qualif.:** Applicant must have a cumulative GPA of 3.0 or above; have at least 1/16 enrolled or documented tribal affiliation; must be a graduate of Oregon or Alaska high schools. Scholarship is renewable for up to 12 terms if a 3.0 cumulative GPA is maintained. **Criteria:** Selection will be based on the committee's criteria.

Funds Avail.: No specific amount. **To Apply:** Applicant may contact the Foundation for application process and other requirements.

1630 ■ David W. Schacht Native American Student Scholarship *(Undergraduate/Scholarship)*

Purpose: To provide scholarship to the students of Oregon State University. **Focus:** General studies. **Qualif.:** Applicants must: be students of Native American descent, defined as self-identified individuals with tribal affiliation; have demonstrated ability and scholarship during high school or during previous college years; must qualify for financial assistance as defined by the Financial Aid Office of OSU. **Criteria:** Selection will be based on the committee's criteria.

Funds Avail.: No specific amount. **To Apply:** Applicant may contact the Foundation for application form and other requirements.

1631 ■ Helen J. and Harold Gilman Smith Scholarship *(Graduate, Undergraduate/Scholarship)*

Purpose: To provide scholarship to the students pursuing their first baccalaureate or graduate degree in any field of study. **Focus:** General study. **Qualif.:** Applicant must: be a Native American student; have a minimum GPA of 2.75 for their undergraduate freshman year. Graduate students must maintain the minimum GPA level required by their college graduate degree program. Preference is given to students graduating from an American Indian high school. Applicant must qualify for financial assistance as defined by the Financial Aid Office of OSU. **Criteria:** Selection will be based on the committee's criteria.

Funds Avail.: No specific amount. **To Apply:** Applicant may contact the Foundation for application form and other requirements. **Contact:** Benton County Foundation at the above address (see entry 1624).

1632 ■ Hugh and Helen Wood Nepales Scholarship *(Undergraduate/Scholarship)*

Purpose: To provide scholarship to the students who are current citizens of Nepal. **Focus:** General studies. **Qualif.:** Applicants must be current students who are citizens of Nepal; primary preference in awarding the scholarship shall be given to those candidates who agree to become a public servant in Nepal for at least five years following graduation. Other requirements include: a 3.5 GPA; a minimum TOEFL score of 550 or other language competency score satisfactory to the university: and all preparatory work completed in Nepal. Secondary consideration will be given to African American students if no Nepalese students meet the requirements. **Criteria:** Selection will be based on the committee's criteria.

Funds Avail.: No specific amount. **To Apply:** Applicant may contact the Foundation for application form and other requirements. **Contact:** Benton County Foundation at the above address (see entry 1624).

1633 ■ Berks County Bar Foundation

PO Box 1058
544 Court St.
Reading, PA 19603
Ph: (610)375-4591
Fax: (610)373-0256
E-mail: info@berksbarfoundation.org
URL: http://www.berksbarfoundation.org

Awards are arranged alphabetically below their administering organizations

1634 ■ Howard Fox Memorial Law Scholarship *(Undergraduate/Scholarship)*

Purpose: To provide financial assistance for the education of Berks County residents planning to take up law courses. **Focus:** Law. **Qualif.:** Applicants must be Berks County residents entering their second year at an accredited law school who demonstrate financial need, without discrimination to color, race, national origin or religion. **Criteria:** Recipients are selected based on financial need.

Funds Avail.: $3,000. **To Apply:** Applicant must submit the completed application form with two letters of reference from people who are not related to him or her; copy of law school transcript; and a written recommendation from a professor at the law school he or she is attending. **Deadline:** April 1.

1635 ■ Beta Phi Mu

PO Box 3062100
Tallahassee, FL 32306-2100
Ph: (850)645-7145
E-mail: ckoontz@ci.fsu.edu
URL: http://www.beta-phi-mu.org

1636 ■ Eugene Garfield Doctoral Dissertation Fellowships *(Doctorate, Graduate/Fellowship)*

Purpose: To support library and information science doctoral students working with their dissertation. **Focus:** Library and archival sciences. **Qualif.:** Applicant must be a doctoral student in library and information science; has advanced candidacy with all requirements for degree completed except writing and defense of dissertation. **Criteria:** The Scholarship Committee meets during May, and the recipients are announced at the annual meeting in June.

Funds Avail.: $3000. **Number Awarded:** 6. **To Apply:** Applicants must submit a completed application form together with the abstract of the dissertation (maximum of 300 words); Letter of approval from the Dean or Director; personal statement (maximum of 500 words) on post-dissertation plans; and three letters of reference sent to the address on the application. Mail application to Beta Phi Mu, School of Information Studies, Florida State University, Tallahassee, FL 32306-2100. **Deadline:** March 15.

1637 ■ Sarah Rebecca Reed Scholarships *(Graduate/Scholarship)*

Purpose: To support students with their educational pursuits. **Focus:** Library and archival sciences. **Qualif.:** Applicant must be admitted to a graduate program in library and information studies accredited by the American Library Association and have not completed more than 12 hours by the Fall semester following to the application deadline. **Criteria:** The Scholarship Committee meets during May, and the recipients are announced at the annual meeting in June. Applicants are judged on several factors but the autobiographical note is the prime importance.

Funds Avail.: $2000. **Number Awarded:** 1. **To Apply:** Applicants must submit a completed application form together with a one-page typed autobiography; current transcripts from all institutions of higher learning; and five letters of recommendation. Mail application to Beta Phi Mu, College of Information Studies, Florida State University, 101 Louis Shores Building, Tallahassee, FL 32306-2100. **Deadline:** March 15.

1638 ■ Frank B. Sessa Scholarships for Continuing Professional Education *(Professional Development/Scholarship)*

Purpose: To support librarians in increasing their professional skills through additional study or attendance at a formal program or workshop. **Focus:** Library and archival sciences. **Qualif.:** Applicant must be librarian pursuing to attend a formal program or workshop, or activities that will increase their professional skills. **Criteria:** Scholarship will be awarded based on the plan of study; usefulness of the planned study to the applicants present job; or usefulness of the planned study to the applicants future professional endeavors. The Scholarship gives low priority to applicants pursuing a formal degree program.

Funds Avail.: $1250. **To Apply:** Applicants must submit a current vita and a 1-2 page typed description of plans for study and their relevance to the present job and plans for the future. Send materials to Beta Phi Mu, School of Information Studies, Florida State University, Tallahassee, FL 32306-2100. **Deadline:** March 15.

1639 ■ Blance E. Woolls Scholarships *(Graduate/Scholarship)*

Purpose: To support students with their educational pursuits. **Focus:** Library and archival sciences. **Qualif.:** Applicant must be admitted to a graduate program in library and information studies accredited by the American Library Association and have not completed more than 12 hours by the Fall semester following to the application deadline. **Criteria:** The Scholarship Committee meets during May, and the recipients are announced at the annual meeting in June. Applicants are judged on several factors but the autobiographical note is the prime importance.

Funds Avail.: $1500. **To Apply:** Applicants must submit a completed application form together with a one-page typed autobiography; current transcripts from all institutions of higher learning; and five letters of recommendation. Mail application to Beta Phi Mu, College of Information Studies, Florida State University, 101 Louis Shores Building, Tallahassee, FL 32306-2100. **Deadline:** March 15.

1640 ■ Beta Theta Pi

PO Box 6277
Oxford, OH 45056
Ph: (513)523-7591
Free: 800-800-BETA
E-mail: beta@betathetapi.org
URL: http://www.betathetapi.org

1641 ■ William H. Bates Oxford Cup Scholarships *(Graduate, Undergraduate/Scholarship)*

Purpose: To financially assist students in their pursuit of academic achievement. **Focus:** General Studies. **Qualif.:** Applicant must be undergraduate or graduate student; a member of Beta Theta Pi enrolled as full-time student. Previous recipients are not qualified. **Criteria:** Scholarships are awarded based on final scores from a three judge panel.

Funds Avail.: $1475. **Number Awarded:** 1. **To Apply:** Applicants must submit a completed standard application form along with transcript of grades and a passport type photo (head and shoulders, wallet size, in coat and tie). **Deadline:** April 1.

1642 ■ Stephen D. Bechtel Oxford Cup Scholarships *(Graduate, Undergraduate/Scholarship)*

Purpose: To financially assist students in their pursuit of academic achievement. **Focus:** General Studies. **Qualif.:**

Awards are arranged alphabetically below their administering organizations

Applicant must be undergraduate or graduate student; a member of Beta Theta Pi enrolled as full-time student. Previous recipients are not qualified. **Criteria:** Scholarships are awarded based on final scores from a three judge panel.

Funds Avail.: $700. **Number Awarded:** 1. **To Apply:** Applicants must submit a completed standard application form along with transcript of grades and a passport type photo (head and shoulders, wallet size, in coat and tie). **Deadline:** April 1. **Contact:** Laura Lednik, at laura.lednik@betathetapi.org.

1643 ■ Bertram W. Bennett Memorial Scholarships *(Graduate, Undergraduate/Scholarship)*

Purpose: To financially assist students in their pursuit of academic achievement. **Focus:** General Studies. **Qualif.:** Applicant must be undergraduate or graduate student; a member of Beta Theta Pi enrolled as full-time student. Previous recipients are not qualified. **Criteria:** Scholarships are awarded based on final scores from a three judge panel.

Funds Avail.: $1050. **Number Awarded:** 2. **To Apply:** Applicants must submit a completed standard application form along with transcript of grades and a passport type photo (head and shoulders, wallet size, in coat and tie). **Deadline:** April 1.

1644 ■ Seth R. and Corrine H. Brooks Memorial Scholarships *(Graduate, Undergraduate/Scholarship)*

Purpose: To financially assist students in their pursuit of academic achievement. **Focus:** General Studies. **Qualif.:** Applicant must be undergraduate or graduate student; a member of Beta Theta Pi enrolled as full-time student; and a son or daughter of a Beta alumnus. Previous recipients are not qualified. **Criteria:** Scholarships are awarded based on final scores from a three judge panel.

Funds Avail.: $1350. **Number Awarded:** 2. **To Apply:** Applicants must submit a completed standard application form along with transcript of grades and a passport type photo (head and shoulders, wallet size, in coat and tie). **Deadline:** April 1. **Contact:** Laura Lednik, at laura.lednik@betathetapi.org.

1645 ■ Edward M. Brown Oxford Cup Memorial Scholarships *(Graduate, Undergraduate/Scholarship)*

Purpose: To financially assist students in their pursuit of academic achievement. **Focus:** General Studies. **Qualif.:** Applicant must be undergraduate or graduate student; a member of Beta Theta Pi enrolled as full-time student. Previous recipients are not qualified. **Criteria:** Scholarships are awarded based on final scores from a three judge panel. Preference is given to Alpha chapter at Miami.

Funds Avail.: $1050. **Number Awarded:** 2. **To Apply:** Applicants must submit a completed standard application form along with transcript of grades and a passport type photo (head and shoulders, wallet size, in coat and tie). **Deadline:** April 1.

1646 ■ Adam S. Burford Memorial Scholarships *(Graduate, Undergraduate/Scholarship)*

Purpose: To financially assist students in their pursuit of academic achievement. **Focus:** General Studies. **Qualif.:** Applicant must be undergraduate or graduate student; a member of Beta Theta Pi enrolled as full-time student. Previous recipients are not qualified. **Criteria:** Scholarships are awarded based on final scores from a three judge panel. Preference is given to West Virginia chapter.

Funds Avail.: $400. **Number Awarded:** 1. **To Apply:** Applicants must submit a completed standard application form along with transcript of grades and a passport type photo (head and shoulders, wallet size, in coat and tie). **Deadline:** April 1. **Contact:** Laura Lednik, at laura.lednik@betathetapi.org.

1647 ■ Thad Byrne Memorial Scholarships *(Graduate, Undergraduate/Scholarship)*

Purpose: To financially assist students in their pursuit of academic achievement. **Focus:** General Studies. **Qualif.:** Applicant must be undergraduate or graduate student; a member of Beta Theta Pi enrolled as full-time student. Previous recipients are not qualified. **Criteria:** Scholarships are awarded based on final scores from a three judge panel.

Funds Avail.: $1475. **Number Awarded:** 1. **To Apply:** Applicants must submit a completed standard application form along with transcript of grades and a passport type photo (head and shoulders, wallet size, in coat and tie). **Deadline:** April 1. **Contact:** Laura Lednik, at laura.lednik@betathetapi.org.

1648 ■ Thomas D. and Karen Cassady Scholarships *(Graduate, Undergraduate/Scholarship)*

Purpose: To financially assist students in their pursuit of academic achievement. **Focus:** General Studies. **Qualif.:** Applicant must be undergraduate or graduate student; a member of Beta Theta Pi enrolled as full-time student. Previous recipients are not qualified. **Criteria:** Scholarships are awarded based on final scores from a three judge panel. Preference is given to Beta Nu chapter at Cincinnati.

Funds Avail.: $1000. **Number Awarded:** 1. **To Apply:** Applicants must submit a completed standard application form along with transcript of grades and a passport type photo (head and shoulders, wallet size, in coat and tie). **Deadline:** April 1. **Contact:** Laura Lednik, at laura.lednik@betathetapi.org.

1649 ■ Oscar Chapman Memorial Scholarships *(Graduate, Undergraduate/Scholarship)*

Purpose: To financially assist students in their pursuit of academic achievement. **Focus:** General Studies. **Qualif.:** Applicant must be undergraduate or graduate student; a member of Beta Theta Pi enrolled as full-time student. Previous recipients are not qualified. **Criteria:** Scholarships are awarded based on final scores from a three judge panel. Preference is given to Delta chapter at DePauw.

Funds Avail.: $1200. **Number Awarded:** 1. **To Apply:** Applicants must submit a completed standard application form along with transcript of grades and a passport type photo (head and shoulders, wallet size, in coat and tie). **Deadline:** April 1. **Contact:** Laura Lednik, at laura.lednik@betathetapi.org.

1650 ■ Cleveland Alumni Association Scholarships *(Graduate, Undergraduate/Scholarship)*

Purpose: To financially assist students in their pursuit of academic achievement. **Focus:** General Studies. **Qualif.:** Applicant must be undergraduate or graduate student; a member of Beta Theta Pi enrolled as full-time student. Previous recipients are not qualified. **Criteria:** Scholarships are awarded based on final scores from a three judge panel.

Funds Avail.: $1050. **Number Awarded:** 4. **To Apply:** Applicants must submit a completed standard application form along with transcript of grades and a passport type photo (head and shoulders, wallet size, in coat and tie). **Deadline:** April 1.

1651 ■ L. Robert Clough Memorial Scholarships
(Graduate, Undergraduate/Scholarship)

Purpose: To financially assist students in their pursuit of academic achievement. **Focus:** General Studies. **Qualif.:** Applicant must be undergraduate or graduate student; a member of Beta Theta Pi enrolled as full-time student; a Gamma Alpha at South Dakota. Previous recipients are not qualified. **Criteria:** Scholarships are awarded based on final scores from a three judge panel.

Funds Avail.: $1000. **Number Awarded:** 1. **To Apply:** Applicants must submit a completed standard application form along with transcript of grades and a passport type photo (head and shoulders, wallet size, in coat and tie). **Deadline:** April 1.

1652 ■ William W. Dawson Memorial Scholarships *(Graduate, Undergraduate/Scholarship)*

Purpose: To financially assist students in their pursuit of academic achievement. **Focus:** General Studies. **Qualif.:** Applicant must be undergraduate or graduate student; a member of Beta Theta Pi enrolled as full-time student. Previous recipients are not qualified. **Criteria:** Scholarships are awarded based on final scores from a three judge panel.

Funds Avail.: $1000. **Number Awarded:** 2. **To Apply:** Applicants must submit a completed standard application form along with transcript of grades and a passport type photo (head and shoulders, wallet size, in coat and tie). **Deadline:** April 1. **Contact:** Laura Lednik, at laura.lednik@betathetapi.org.

1653 ■ Delta Tau Chapter Scholarships *(Graduate, Undergraduate/Scholarship)*

Purpose: To financially assist students in their pursuit of academic achievement. **Focus:** General Studies. **Qualif.:** Applicant must be undergraduate or graduate student; a member of Beta Theta Pi enrolled as full-time student. Previous recipients are not qualified. **Criteria:** Scholarships are awarded based on final scores from a three judge panel.

Funds Avail.: $725. **Number Awarded:** 1. **To Apply:** Applicants must submit a completed standard application form along with transcript of grades and a passport type photo (head and shoulders, wallet size, in coat and tie). **Deadline:** April 1. **Contact:** Laura Lednik, at laura.lednik@betathetapi.org.

1654 ■ John Holt Duncan Memorial Scholarships *(Graduate, Undergraduate/Scholarship)*

Purpose: To financially assist students in their pursuit of academic achievement. **Focus:** General Studies. **Qualif.:** Applicant must be undergraduate or graduate student; a member of Beta Theta Pi enrolled as full-time student. Previous recipients are not qualified. **Criteria:** Scholarships are awarded based on final scores from a three judge panel.

Funds Avail.: $2375. **Number Awarded:** 1. **To Apply:** Applicants must submit a completed standard application form along with transcript of grades and a passport type photo (head and shoulders, wallet size, in coat and tie). **Deadline:** April 1.

Remarks: Funded by the estate of Robert C. Lafferty, Ohio Wesleyan '28. **Contact:** Laura Lednik, at laura.lednik@betathetapi.org.

1655 ■ Todd Elias Memorial Scholarships
(Graduate, Undergraduate/Scholarship)

Purpose: To financially assist students in their pursuit of academic achievement. **Focus:** General Studies. **Qualif.:** Applicant must be undergraduate or graduate student; a member of Beta Theta Pi enrolled as full-time student. Previous recipients are not qualified. **Criteria:** Scholarships are awarded based on final scores from a three judge panel. Preference is given for an Alpha Tau chapter at Nebraska.

Funds Avail.: $1625. **Number Awarded:** 1. **To Apply:** Applicants must submit a completed standard application form along with transcript of grades and a passport type photo (head and shoulders, wallet size, in coat and tie). **Deadline:** April 1.

1656 ■ James L. Gavin Memorial Scholarships
(Graduate, Undergraduate/Scholarship)

Purpose: To financially assist students in their pursuit of academic achievement. **Focus:** General Studies. **Qualif.:** Applicant must be undergraduate or graduate student; a member of Beta Theta Pi enrolled as full-time student. Previous recipients are not qualified. **Criteria:** Scholarships are awarded based on final scores from a three judge panel.

Funds Avail.: $1125. **Number Awarded:** 3. **To Apply:** Applicants must submit a completed standard application form along with transcript of grades and a passport type photo (head and shoulders, wallet size, in coat and tie). **Deadline:** April 1. **Contact:** Laura Lednik, at laura.lednik@betathetapi.org.

1657 ■ Burton L. Gerber Scholarships *(Graduate, Undergraduate/Scholarship)*

Purpose: To financially assist students in their pursuit of academic achievement. **Focus:** Military science and education; International affairs and relations. **Qualif.:** Applicant must be undergraduate or graduate student; a member of Beta Theta Pi enrolled as full-time student; and a senior pursuing a career in military or international affairs. Previous recipients are not qualified. **Criteria:** Scholarships are awarded based on final scores from a three judge panel.

Funds Avail.: $1025. **Number Awarded:** 1. **To Apply:** Applicants must submit a completed standard application form along with transcript of grades and a passport type photo (head and shoulders, wallet size, in coat and tie). **Deadline:** April 1.

1658 ■ Thomas Boston Gordon Memorial Scholarships *(Graduate, Undergraduate/Scholarship)*

Purpose: To financially assist students in their pursuit of academic achievement. **Focus:** General Studies. **Qualif.:** Applicant must be undergraduate or graduate student; a member of Beta Theta Pi enrolled as full-time student. Previous recipients are not qualified. **Criteria:** Scholarships are awarded based on final scores from a three judge panel.

Funds Avail.: $2375. **Number Awarded:** 1. **To Apply:** Applicants must submit a completed standard application form along with transcript of grades and a passport type photo (head and shoulders, wallet size, in coat and tie). **Deadline:** April 1.

Awards are arranged alphabetically below their administering organizations

Remarks: Funded by the estate of Robert C. Lafferty, Ohio Wesleyan '28. **Contact:** Laura Lednik, at laura.lednik@betathetapi.org.

1659 ■ Charles Henry Hardin Memorial Scholarships *(Graduate, Undergraduate/Scholarship)*

Purpose: To financially assist students in their pursuit of academic achievement. **Focus:** General Studies. **Qualif.:** Applicant must be undergraduate or graduate student; a member of Beta Theta Pi enrolled as full-time student. Previous recipients are not qualified. **Criteria:** Scholarships are awarded based on final scores from a three judge panel.

Funds Avail.: $2375. **Number Awarded:** 1. **To Apply:** Applicants must submit a completed standard application form along with transcript of grades and a passport type photo (head and shoulders, wallet size, in coat and tie). **Deadline:** April 1.

Remarks: Funded by the estate of Robert C. Lafferty, Ohio Wesleyan '28. **Contact:** Laura Lednik, at laura.lednik@betathetapi.org.

1660 ■ Ronald, Randall and Roger Helman Scholarships *(Graduate, Undergraduate/Scholarship)*

Purpose: To financially assist students in their pursuit of academic achievement. **Focus:** General Studies. **Qualif.:** Applicant must be undergraduate or graduate student; a member of Beta Theta Pi enrolled as full-time student. Previous recipients are not qualified. **Criteria:** Scholarships are awarded based on final scores from a three judge panel. Preference is given to Miami, Central Michigan and Michigan chapters.

Funds Avail.: $850. **Number Awarded:** 1. **To Apply:** Applicants must submit a completed standard application form along with transcript of grades and a passport type photo (head and shoulders, wallet size, in coat and tie). **Deadline:** April 1. **Contact:** Laura Lednik, at laura.lednik@betathetapi.org.

1661 ■ Douglas W. Hill, Jr. Memorial Scholarships *(Graduate, Undergraduate/Scholarship)*

Purpose: To financially assist students in their pursuit of academic achievement. **Focus:** General Studies. **Qualif.:** Applicant must be undergraduate or graduate student; a member of Beta Theta Pi enrolled as full-time student. Previous recipients are not qualified. **Criteria:** Scholarships are awarded based on final scores from a three judge panel. Preference is given to Gamma Psi chapter at Michigan State.

Funds Avail.: $1250. **Number Awarded:** 2. **To Apply:** Applicants must submit a completed standard application form along with transcript of grades and a passport type photo (head and shoulders, wallet size, in coat and tie). **Deadline:** April 1. **Contact:** Laura Lednik, at laura.lednik@betathetapi.org.

1662 ■ John A. Hill Memorial Scholarships *(Graduate, Undergraduate/Scholarship)*

Purpose: To financially assist students in their pursuit of academic achievement. **Focus:** General Studies. **Qualif.:** Applicant must be undergraduate or graduate student; a member of Beta Theta Pi enrolled as full-time student; and a member of Alpha Zeta at Denver. Previous recipients are not qualified. **Criteria:** Scholarships are awarded based on final scores from a three judge panel.

Funds Avail.: $1100. **Number Awarded:** 1. **To Apply:** Applicants must submit a completed standard application form along with transcript of grades and a passport type photo (head and shoulders, wallet size, in coat and tie). **Deadline:** April 1.

1663 ■ James P. Kirkgasser Memorial Scholarships *(Graduate, Undergraduate/Scholarship)*

Purpose: To financially assist students in their pursuit of academic achievement. **Focus:** General Studies. **Qualif.:** Applicant must be undergraduate or graduate student; a member of Beta Theta Pi enrolled as full-time student; and a Beta from District IV schools. Previous recipients are not qualified. **Criteria:** Scholarships are awarded based on final scores from a three judge panel. Preference is given to Syracuse shapters.

Funds Avail.: $625. **Number Awarded:** 1. **To Apply:** Applicants must submit a completed standard application form along with transcript of grades and a passport type photo (head and shoulders, wallet size, in coat and tie). **Deadline:** April 1. **Contact:** Laura Lednik, at laura.lednik@betathetapi.org.

1664 ■ John Reily Knox Memorial Scholarships *(Graduate, Undergraduate/Scholarship)*

Purpose: To financially assist students in their pursuit of academic achievement. **Focus:** General Studies. **Qualif.:** Applicant must be undergraduate or graduate student; a member of Beta Theta Pi enrolled as full-time student. Previous recipients are not qualified. **Criteria:** Scholarships are awarded based on final scores from a three judge panel.

Funds Avail.: $2375. **Number Awarded:** 1. **To Apply:** Applicants must submit a completed standard application form along with transcript of grades and a passport type photo (head and shoulders, wallet size, in coat and tie). **Deadline:** April 1.

Remarks: Funded by the estate of Robert C. Lafferty, Ohio Wesleyan '28.

1665 ■ Carl A. Kroch Oxford Cup Memorial Scholarships *(Graduate, Undergraduate/Scholarship)*

Purpose: To financially assist students in their pursuit of academic achievement. **Focus:** General Studies. **Qualif.:** Applicant must be undergraduate or graduate student; a member of Beta Theta Pi enrolled as full-time student. Previous recipients are not qualified. **Criteria:** Scholarships are awarded based on final scores from a three judge panel.

Funds Avail.: $1200. **Number Awarded:** 2. **To Apply:** Applicants must submit a completed standard application form along with transcript of grades and a passport type photo (head and shoulders, wallet size, in coat and tie). **Deadline:** April 1. **Contact:** Laura Lednik, at laura.lednik@betathetapi.org.

1666 ■ Otho E. Lane Memorial Scholarships *(Graduate, Undergraduate/Scholarship)*

Purpose: To financially assist students in their pursuit of academic achievement. **Focus:** General Studies. **Qualif.:** Applicant must be undergraduate or graduate student; a member of Beta Theta Pi enrolled as full-time student. Previous recipients are not qualified. **Criteria:** Scholarships are awarded based on final scores from a three judge panel. Preference is given to Alpha chapter in Miami.

Awards are arranged alphabetically below their administering organizations

Funds Avail.: $1400. **Number Awarded:** 1. **To Apply:** Applicants must submit a completed standard application form along with transcript of grades and a passport type photo (head and shoulders, wallet size, in coat and tie). **Deadline:** April 1. **Contact:** Laura Lednik, at laura.lednik@betathetapi.org.

1667 ■ David Linton Memorial Scholarships
(Graduate, Undergraduate/Scholarship)

Purpose: To financially assist students in their pursuit of academic achievement. **Focus:** General Studies. **Qualif.:** Applicant must be undergraduate or graduate student; a member of Beta Theta Pi enrolled as full-time student. Previous recipients are not qualified. **Criteria:** Scholarships are awarded based on final scores from a three judge panel.

Funds Avail.: $2375. **Number Awarded:** 1. **To Apply:** Applicants must submit a completed standard application form along with transcript of grades and a passport type photo (head and shoulders, wallet size, in coat and tie). **Deadline:** April 1.

Remarks: Funded by the estate of Robert C. Lafferty, Ohio Wesleyan '28.

1668 ■ Horace G. Lozier Memorial Scholarships
(Graduate, Undergraduate/Scholarship)

Purpose: To financially assist students in their pursuit of academic achievement. **Focus:** General Studies. **Qualif.:** Applicant must be undergraduate or graduate student; a member of Beta Theta Pi enrolled as full-time student. Previous recipients are not qualified. **Criteria:** Scholarships are awarded based on final scores from a three judge panel.

Funds Avail.: $1800. **Number Awarded:** 1. **To Apply:** Applicants must submit a completed standard application form along with transcript of grades and a passport type photo (head and shoulders, wallet size, in coat and tie). **Deadline:** April 1.

1669 ■ Samuel Taylor Marshall Memorial Scholarships *(Graduate, Undergraduate/Scholarship)*

Purpose: To financially assist students in their pursuit of academic achievement. **Focus:** General Studies. **Qualif.:** Applicant must be undergraduate or graduate student; a member of Beta Theta Pi enrolled as full-time student. Previous recipients are not qualified. **Criteria:** Scholarships are awarded based on final scores from a three judge panel.

Funds Avail.: $2375. **Number Awarded:** 1. **To Apply:** Applicants must submit a completed standard application form along with transcript of grades and a passport type photo (head and shoulders, wallet size, in coat and tie). **Deadline:** April 1.

Remarks: Funded by the estate of Robert C. Lafferty, Ohio Wesleyan '28. **Contact:** Laura Lednik, at laura.lednik@betathetapi.org.

1670 ■ Steven Craig Merrill Memorial Scholarships *(Graduate, Undergraduate/Scholarship)*

Purpose: To financially assist students in their pursuit of academic achievement. **Focus:** General Studies. **Qualif.:** Applicant must be undergraduate or graduate student; a member of Beta Theta Pi enrolled as full-time student; and a member of Omicron at Virginia. Previous recipients are not qualified. **Criteria:** Scholarships are awarded based on final scores from a three judge panel.

Funds Avail.: $1050. **Number Awarded:** 1. **To Apply:** Applicants must submit a completed standard application form along with transcript of grades and a passport type photo (head and shoulders, wallet size, in coat and tie). **Deadline:** April 1. **Contact:** Laura Lednik, at laura.lednik@betathetapi.org.

1671 ■ Edith Cantor Morrison Memorial Scholarships *(Graduate, Undergraduate/Scholarship)*

Purpose: To financially assist students in their pursuit of academic achievement. **Focus:** Education—Curricula. **Qualif.:** Applicant must be undergraduate or graduate student; a member of Beta Theta Pi enrolled as full-time student; and a Beta majoring in education. Previous recipients are not qualified. **Criteria:** Scholarships are awarded based on final scores from a three judge panel.

Funds Avail.: $600. **Number Awarded:** 1. **To Apply:** Applicants must submit a completed standard application form along with transcript of grades and a passport type photo (head and shoulders, wallet size, in coat and tie). **Deadline:** April 1. **Contact:** Laura Lednik, at laura.lednik@betathetapi.org.

1672 ■ Douglas J. Neeley Memorial Scholarships *(Graduate, Undergraduate/Scholarship)*

Purpose: To financially assist students in their pursuit of academic achievement. **Focus:** General Studies. **Qualif.:** Applicant must be undergraduate or graduate student; a member of Beta Theta Pi at Kenyon and enrolled as full-time student. Previous recipients are not qualified. **Criteria:** Scholarships are awarded based on final scores from a three judge panel.

Funds Avail.: $1125. **Number Awarded:** 2. **To Apply:** Applicants must submit a completed standard application form along with transcript of grades and a passport type photo (head and shoulders, wallet size, in coat and tie). **Deadline:** April 1. **Contact:** Laura Lednik, at laura.lednik@betathetapi.org.

1673 ■ E. William Palmer Memorial Scholarships
(Graduate, Undergraduate/Scholarship)

Purpose: To financially assist students in their pursuit of academic achievement. **Focus:** General Studies. **Qualif.:** Applicant must be undergraduate or graduate student; a member of Beta Theta Pi enrolled as full-time student. Previous recipients are not qualified. **Criteria:** Scholarships are awarded based on final scores from a three judge panel. Preference is given to Beta Chi chapter at Lehigh.

Funds Avail.: $1300. **Number Awarded:** 1. **To Apply:** Applicants must submit a completed standard application form along with transcript of grades and a passport type photo (head and shoulders, wallet size, in coat and tie). **Deadline:** April 1. **Contact:** Laura Lednik, at laura.lednik@betathetapi.org.

1674 ■ John J. and Elizabeth Rhodes Scholarships *(Graduate, Undergraduate/Scholarship)*

Purpose: To financially assist students in their pursuit of academic achievement. **Focus:** General Studies. **Qualif.:** Applicant must be undergraduate or graduate student; a member of Beta Theta Pi enrolled as full-time student. Previous recipients are not qualified. **Criteria:** Scholarships are awarded based on final scores from a three judge panel. Preference is given to students from Kansas State, Kansas, and Arizona.

Funds Avail.: $1625. **Number Awarded:** 1. **To Apply:** Applicants must submit a completed standard application form along with transcript of grades and a passport type photo (head and shoulders, wallet size, in coat and tie). **Deadline:** April 1.

1675 ■ Ben C. Rich Memorial Scholarships
(Graduate, Undergraduate/Scholarship)

Purpose: To financially assist students in their pursuit of academic achievement. **Focus:** General Studies. **Qualif.:** Applicant must be undergraduate or graduate student; a member of Beta Theta Pi enrolled as full-time student. Previous recipients are not qualified. **Criteria:** Scholarships are awarded based on final scores from a three judge panel.

Funds Avail.: $1000. **Number Awarded:** 2. **To Apply:** Applicants must submit a completed standard application form along with transcript of grades and a passport type photo (head and shoulders, wallet size, in coat and tie). **Deadline:** April 1. **Contact:** Laura Lednik, at laura.lednik@betathetapi.org.

1676 ■ Michael Clarkson Ryan Memorial Scholarships *(Graduate, Undergraduate/Scholarship)*

Purpose: To financially assist students in their pursuit of academic achievement. **Focus:** General Studies. **Qualif.:** Applicant must be undergraduate or graduate student; a member of Beta Theta Pi enrolled as full-time student. Previous recipients are not qualified. **Criteria:** Scholarships are awarded based on final scores from a three judge panel.

Funds Avail.: $2375. **Number Awarded:** 1. **To Apply:** Applicants must submit a completed standard application form along with transcript of grades and a passport type photo (head and shoulders, wallet size, in coat and tie). **Deadline:** April 1.

Remarks: Funded by the estate of Robert C. Lafferty, Ohio Wesleyan '28. **Contact:** Laura Lednik, at laura.lednik@betathetapi.org.

1677 ■ William C. Scheetz Family Scholarships
(Graduate, Undergraduate/Scholarship)

Purpose: To financially assist students in their pursuit of academic achievement. **Focus:** General Studies. **Qualif.:** Applicant must be undergraduate or graduate student; a member of Beta Theta Pi enrolled as full-time student. Previous recipients are not qualified. **Criteria:** Scholarships are awarded based on final scores from a three judge panel. Preference is given to resident of state of Pennsylvania.

Funds Avail.: $1325. **Number Awarded:** 2. **To Apply:** Applicants must submit a completed standard application form along with transcript of grades and a passport type photo (head and shoulders, wallet size, in coat and tie). **Deadline:** April 1. **Contact:** Laura Lednik, at laura.lednik@betathetapi.org.

1678 ■ Fred A. Seaton Memorial Scholarships
(Graduate, Undergraduate/Scholarship)

Purpose: To financially assist students in their pursuit of academic achievement. **Focus:** General Studies. **Qualif.:** Applicant must be undergraduate or graduate student; a member of Beta Theta Pi enrolled as full-time student. Previous recipients are not qualified. **Criteria:** Scholarships are awarded based on final scores from a three judge panel.

Funds Avail.: $1000. **Number Awarded:** 3. **To Apply:** Applicants must submit a completed standard application form along with transcript of grades and a passport type photo (head and shoulders, wallet size, in coat and tie). **Deadline:** April 1. **Contact:** Laura Lednik, at laura.lednik@betathetapi.org.

1679 ■ Misty and Sally Shoop Scholarships
(Graduate, Undergraduate/Scholarship)

Purpose: To financially assist students in their pursuit of academic achievement. **Focus:** General Studies. **Qualif.:** Applicant must be undergraduate or graduate student; a member of Beta Theta Pi enrolled as full-time student. Previous recipients are not qualified. **Criteria:** Scholarships are awarded based on final scores from a three judge panel.

Funds Avail.: $825. **Number Awarded:** 1. **To Apply:** Applicants must submit a completed standard application form along with transcript of grades and a passport type photo (head and shoulders, wallet size, in coat and tie). **Deadline:** April 1. **Contact:** Laura Lednik, at laura.lednik@betathetapi.org.

1680 ■ John R. Simpson Memorial Scholarships
(Graduate, Undergraduate/Scholarship)

Purpose: To financially assist students in their pursuit of academic achievement. **Focus:** General Studies. **Qualif.:** Applicant must be undergraduate or graduate student; a member of Beta Theta Pi enrolled as full-time student. Previous recipients are not qualified. **Criteria:** Scholarships are awarded based on final scores from a three judge panel. Preference is given for Alpha chapter at Miami.

Funds Avail.: $1050. **Number Awarded:** 8. **To Apply:** Applicants must submit a completed standard application form along with transcript of grades and a passport type photo (head and shoulders, wallet size, in coat and tie). **Deadline:** April 1. **Contact:** Laura Lednik, at laura.lednik@betathetapi.org.

1681 ■ James George Smith Memorial Scholarships *(Graduate, Undergraduate/Scholarship)*

Purpose: To financially assist students in their pursuit of academic achievement. **Focus:** General Studies. **Qualif.:** Applicant must be undergraduate or graduate student; a member of Beta Theta Pi enrolled as full-time student. Previous recipients are not qualified. **Criteria:** Scholarships are awarded based on final scores from a three judge panel.

Funds Avail.: $2375. **Number Awarded:** 1. **To Apply:** Applicants must submit a completed standard application form along with transcript of grades and a passport type photo (head and shoulders, wallet size, in coat and tie). **Deadline:** April 1.

Remarks: Funded by the estate of Robert C. Lafferty, Ohio Wesleyan '28. **Contact:** Laura Lednik, at laura.lednik@betathetapi.org.

1682 ■ H. Hiram Stephenson Oxford Cup Scholarships *(Graduate, Undergraduate/Scholarship)*

Purpose: To financially assist students in their pursuit of academic achievement. **Focus:** General Studies. **Qualif.:** Applicant must be undergraduate or graduate student; a member of Beta Theta Pi enrolled as full-time student. Previous recipients are not qualified. **Criteria:** Scholarships are awarded based on final scores from a three judge panel.

Funds Avail.: $500. **Number Awarded:** 1. **To Apply:** Applicants must submit a completed standard application form along with transcript of grades and a passport type photo (head and shoulders, wallet size, in coat and tie). **Deadline:** April 1. **Contact:** Laura Lednik, at laura.lednik@betathetapi.org.

1683 ■ Hugh E. Stephenson Oxford Cup Scholarships *(Graduate, Undergraduate/Scholarship)*

Purpose: To financially assist students in their pursuit of academic achievement. **Focus:** General Studies. **Qualif.:** Applicant must be undergraduate or graduate student; a member of Beta Theta Pi enrolled as full-time student. Previous recipients are not qualified. **Criteria:** Scholarships are awarded based on final scores from a three judge panel.

Funds Avail.: $550. **Number Awarded:** 1. **To Apply:** Applicants must submit a completed standard application form along with transcript of grades and a passport type photo (head and shoulders, wallet size, in coat and tie). **Deadline:** April 1. **Contact:** Laura Lednik, at laura.lednik@betathetapi.org.

1684 ■ Michael W. Toennis Scholarships *(Graduate, Undergraduate/Scholarship)*

Purpose: To financially assist students in their pursuit of academic achievement. **Focus:** General Studies. **Qualif.:** Applicant must be undergraduate or graduate student; a member of Beta Theta Pi enrolled as full-time student. Previous recipients are not qualified. **Criteria:** Scholarships are awarded based on final scores from a three judge panel. Preference is given to Houston chapter.

Funds Avail.: $650. **Number Awarded:** 1. **To Apply:** Applicants must submit a completed standard application form along with transcript of grades and a passport type photo (head and shoulders, wallet size, in coat and tie). **Deadline:** April 1.

1685 ■ Gupton A. Vogt Oxford Cup Memorial Scholarships *(Graduate, Undergraduate/Scholarship)*

Purpose: To financially assist students in their pursuit of academic achievement. **Focus:** General Studies. **Qualif.:** Applicant must be undergraduate or graduate student; a member of Beta Theta Pi enrolled as full-time student. Previous recipients are not qualified. **Criteria:** Scholarships are awarded based on final scores from a three judge panel.

Funds Avail.: $875. **Number Awarded:** 1. **To Apply:** Applicants must submit a completed standard application form along with transcript of grades and a passport type photo (head and shoulders, wallet size, in coat and tie). **Deadline:** April 1. **Contact:** Laura Lednik, at laura.lednik@betathetapi.org.

1686 ■ Bethesda Lutheran Homes and Services

600 Hoffmann Dr.
Watertown, WI 53094
Free: 800-369-4636
E-mail: dwinter@blhs.org
URL: http://www.blhs.org

1687 ■ Scholarships for Lutheran College Students *(Undergraduate/Scholarship)*

Purpose: To financially support Lutheran students pursuing degrees in any area of service to people with developmental disabilities. **Focus:** Mental health. **Qualif.:** Applicant must be active communicant member of a Lutheran church; have achieved sophomore status or higher at a college or university; have a 3.0 overall GPA; and have an interest in a career in the field of developmental disabilities. **Criteria:** Selection is based on the application.

Funds Avail.: $1500. **Number Awarded:** 3. **To Apply:** Applicants must submit a completed application form together with an essay (1-2 pages, double-spaced) on planned career in the field of developmental disabilities; four letters of recommendations; an official college transcript; an autobiography (1 page, double-spaced); a documentation of service to people who are developmentally disabled (minimum of 100 hrs); and other materials helpful from the application. **Deadline:** April 15. **Contact:** ncrc@blhs.org.

1688 ■ Scholarships for Lutheran Nursing Students *(Undergraduate/Scholarship)*

Purpose: To financially support Lutheran students pursuing degrees in nursing and planning to serve people with developmental disabilities. **Focus:** Mental health; Nursing. **Qualif.:** Applicant must be an active communicant member of a Lutheran church; achieved sophomore status or higher at a college or university, or completed one year of a two-year ADN program; have a 3.0 overall GPA; and have an interest in working as a nurse in the field of developmental disabilities. **Criteria:** Selection is based on the application.

Funds Avail.: $1500. **Number Awarded:** 2. **To Apply:** Applicants must submit a completed application form together with an essay (1-2 pages, double-spaced) on planned career in the field of developmental disabilities; four letters of recommendations; an official college transcript; an autobiography (1 page, double-spaced); a documentation of service to people who are developmentally disabled (minimum of 100 hrs); and other materials helpful from the application. **Deadline:** April 15.

1689 ■ Bethune-Cookman University

640 Dr. Mary McLeod Bethune Blvd.
Daytona Beach, FL 32114
Ph: (386)481-2000
URL: http://www.cookman.edu

1690 ■ Bethune-Cookman University Excelsior Scholarships *(Undergraduate/Scholarship)*

Purpose: To provide financial assistance for students intending to pursue their education. **Focus:** General studies. **Qualif.:** Applicants must be completing high school in spring; must be incoming freshmen at a university; and must maintain a 3.4 cumulative GPA. **Criteria:** Selection is based on merit.

Funds Avail.: Funds may cover the cost of full-time tuition that is not covered by federal or state financial aid and other non-institutional scholarships. **To Apply:** Applicants must apply for admission to be considered. **Deadline:** February 1.

1691 ■ Bethune-Cookman University Presidential Scholarships *(Undergraduate/Scholarship)*

Purpose: To provide financial assistance to students intending to pursue their education. **Focus:** General studies. **Qualif.:** Applicants must be completing high school in spring; must incoming freshmen at any university; and must maintain a 3.5 cumulative GPA. **Criteria:** Selection is based on merit.

Awards are arranged alphabetically below their administering organizations

Funds Avail.: Fund may be used for full-time tuition, room, boarding fees, and a $500 per semester book voucher only. **To Apply:** Applicants must apply for admission to be considered. **Deadline:** February 1.

1692 ■ Noorali Bharwani Professional Corporation

821A 5th St. SW
Medicine Hat, AB, Canada T1A 4H7
Ph: (403)527-0099
E-mail: nb786@shaw.ca
URL: http://nbharwani.com

1693 ■ Dr. Noorali & Sabiya Bharwani Endowment *(Undergraduate/Scholarship)*

Purpose: To provide financial assistance to qualified individuals who want to pursue their studies. **Focus:** Nursing. **Qualif.:** Applicants must be first year nursing students with a minimum GPA of B, equivalent of 3.0. **Criteria:** Preference will be given to students with financial need.

Funds Avail.: No specific amount. **To Apply:** For further information about the scholarship and application form, applicants are advice to contact Noorali Bharwani Professional Corporation, 821A 5th St. SW, Medicine Hat, AB T1A 4H7.

1694 ■ Hussein Jina Bharwani Memorial Endowment *(Undergraduate/Scholarship)*

Purpose: To provide financial assistance to qualified individuals who wants to pursue their studies. **Focus:** Nursing. **Qualif.:** Applicants must be nursing students having completed the second year of the nursing program; must have maintained a GPA of 3.0 or better; must have demonstrated a keen interest in the nursing patient; must demonstrate strong clinical skills including good organization and assessment skills and have the ability to establish a positive and constructive rapport with patients, their families and co-workers. **Criteria:** Recipients will be selected based on the committee's review of the application materials.

Funds Avail.: No specific amount. **Number Awarded:** 2. **To Apply:** For further information about the scholarship and application form, applicants are advice to contact Noorali Bharwani Professional Corporation, 821A 5th St. SW, Medicine Hat, AB T1A 4H7.

1695 ■ Bibliographical Society of America

PO Box 1537
New York, NY 10021
Ph: (212)452-2710
Fax: (212)452-2710
URL: http://www.bibsocamer.org

1696 ■ Katharine Pantzer Senior Fellowships in the British Book Trades *(Professional Development/Fellowship)*

Purpose: To support sustained research in topics relating to book production history in Britain and other related aspects. **Focus:** Library and archival sciences; Printing—History. **Qualif.:** Program is open to individuals conducting research on topics relating to book production and distribution in Britain during the hand-press period as well as studies of authorship, reading and collecting based on the examination of British books published in that period. **Criteria:** Awards are given based on merit.

Funds Avail.: up to $2,000. **To Apply:** Application instructions and forms are available at the website. **Deadline:** December 1. **Contact:** BSA Executive Secretary, bsa@bibsocamer.org.

1697 ■ Bibliographical Society of Canada

PO Box 575, Postal Sta. P
Toronto, ON, Canada M5S 2T1
E-mail: gretagolick@rogers.com
URL: http://www.library.utoronto.ca/bsc/bschomeeng.html

1698 ■ Bernard Amtmann Fellowships *(Postgraduate/Grant)*

Purpose: To support the work of a scholar engaged in some area of bibliographical research, including textual studies and publishing history and with a particular emphasis on Canada. **Focus:** General studies. **Qualif.:** Applicants must be members of the Bibliographical Society of Canada. **Criteria:** Scholarship recipient will be selected based on scholastic ability. Preference is given to applicants who display great interest in research work.

Funds Avail.: $1,500. **To Apply:** Application forms are available at the website. Application and attachments must be sent to: Bibliographical Society of Canada PO Box 575, Postal Sta. P, Toronto, ON M5S 2T1. **Deadline:** February 28.

Remarks: Established in 1992, established in memory of Bernard Amtmann, the bookseller and specialist in Canadiana.

1699 ■ Marie Tremaine Fellowships *(Postgraduate/Grant)*

Purpose: To support the work of a scholar engaged in some area of bibliographical research, including textual studies and publishing history and with a particular emphasis on Canada. **Focus:** General studies. **Qualif.:** Applicants must be members of the Bibliographical Society of Canada. **Criteria:** Scholarship recipient will be selected based on scholastic ability. Preference is given to applicants who display great interest in research work.

Funds Avail.: $2,000. **To Apply:** Application forms are available at the website. Application and attachments must be sent to: Bibliographical Society of Canada PO Box 575, Postal Sta. P, Toronto, ON M5S 2T1. **Deadline:** February 28.

Remarks: Established in 1987 in memory of and through the generosity of Marie Tremaine, the doyenne of Canadian bibliographers.

1700 ■ Big Sandy Community and Technical College

1 Bert T. Combs Dr.
Prestonsburg, KY 41653
Ph: (606)886-3863
Free: 888-641-4132
URL: http://www.bigsandy.kctcs.edu

1701 ■ Early Childhood Development Scholarships *(Undergraduate/Scholarship)*

Purpose: To provide a seamless system to upgrade the professional development of child-care workers and trainers by providing financial assistance for qualified Kentucky

Awards are arranged alphabetically below their administering organizations

students intending to pursue a childhood development degree. **Focus:** Early childhood education. **Qualif.:** Applicants must be residents of Kentucky; must be U.S. citizens, national, or permanent residents; must be enrolled in no more than 9 credit hours per academic term in the scholarship program curriculum at a participating Kentucky institution and must be pursuing at least one of the approved credentials and maintaining satisfactory academic progress; must be employed at least 20 hours weekly in a participating early childhood facility or must be providing training in early childhood development at least 12 times per year for an organization approved to offer training by the Office of Inspector General of the Cabinet for Health Services or must be employed as a preschool associate teacher in a state-funded preschool program; must have no unpaid financial obligation to the Kentucky Higher Education Assistance Authority or in default on any other Title IV program; and must be agreeable to a service commitment based on the credential pursued. **Criteria:** Selection of applicant will be based on the eligibility and application requirements.

Funds Avail.: $1,800. **To Apply:** Applicants must submit completed application package which include the Free Application for Federal Student Aid which can be obtained up to three copies by calling the Federal Student Aid Information Center toll free at 800433-3243.

1702 ■ Kentucky Educational Excellence Scholarships *(Graduate, Undergraduate/Scholarship)*

Purpose: To provide financial support for deserving Kentucky high school students and GED recipients intending to pursue their education. **Focus:** General studies. **Qualif.:** Applicants be high school students; must be U.S. citizens, national or permanent residents; must be residents of Kentucky; must have earned at least a 2.5 GPA in any year of high school while meeting the KEES curriculum requirements; must attend and graduate from a certified Kentucky high school or other approved high school; and must not be a convicted felon. High school graduates applying for a KEES bonus award must have at least an ACT composite score of 15 or a score of 710 or higher on the SAT and must have earned at least a 2.5 GPA in any year of high school while meeting the KEES curriculum requirements. Home school graduates applying for a KEES bonus award must have an ACT composite score of 15 or better on a national exam; must be U.S citizens, national or permanent residents; must be residents of Kentucky; must be enrolled in a participating college; and must not be a convicted felon. GED graduate applicants must have an ACT composite score of 15 or better on a national exam; must have earned a GED in Kentucky within five years of turning 18 years old; must be U.S citizens, national or permanent residents; must be residents of Kentucky; must be enrolled in a participating college within five years of receiving a GED; and must not be a convicted felon. **Criteria:** Selection will be based on merit.

Funds Avail.: Varies. **To Apply:** Applicants are advised to contact KEES for scholarship information and instructions at kees@kheaa.com.

1703 ■ Kentucky Tuition Grants *(Undergraduate/Grant)*

Purpose: To help students offset the high tuition charges at independent colleges. **Focus:** General studies. **Qualif.:** Applicants must be residents of Kentucky who are enrolled in the Commonwealth's independent colleges. Institutions must be accredited by a regional accrediting association recognized by U.S Department of Education and must not be comprised solely of religious instruction; must be full-time undergraduates enrolled in an associate or baccalaureate degree program and must have no past due financial obligations to KHEAA to any Title IV program. **Criteria:** Selection will be based on the application requirements and eligibility.

Funds Avail.: $2,000-$3,000. **To Apply:** Applicants must complete the Application for Federal Student Aid form. Applicants are advised to contact the Federal Student Aid Information Center at 800-433-3243 for further information.

1704 ■ KHEAA Teacher Scholarships *(Undergraduate/Scholarship)*

Purpose: To provide financial aid for highly qualified Kentucky students intending to pursue initial teacher certification at participating Kentucky institutions. **Focus:** Teaching. **Qualif.:** Applicants must be residents of Kentucky who are enrolled full-time in a teacher certification program; must demonstrate financial need; and must meet their institution's educational program GPA requirements. **Criteria:** Priority is given to financially incapable applicants.

Funds Avail.: $2,500 for each semester and $1,250 for summer awarded to juniors, seniors, post-baccalaureate or graduate students; $625 each semester and $325 for summer awarded to freshmen and sophomore recipients. **To Apply:** Applicants must complete application package which include the Free Application for Federal Student Aid and a Teacher Scholarship application. Applicants are advised to contact the Federal Student Aid Information Center at 800433-3243 for further information and instructions. **Deadline:** May 1.

1705 ■ Mary Jo Young Scholarships *(Undergraduate/Scholarship)*

Purpose: To improve educational opportunities for Kentuckians. **Focus:** General studies. **Qualif.:** Program is open to high school students in grades 9 thru 12 enrolled in dual credit classes at any college or university or to students taking Advanced Placement courses through the Kentucky Virtual High School. **Criteria:** Priority is given to low-income students, minority students and first-generation college attendees.

Funds Avail.: No specific amount. **To Apply:** Applicants must send completed application to: KHEAA Mary Jo Young Scholarship Program, PO Box 798, Frankfort, KY 40602-0798. **Deadline:** May 1.

1706 ■ BioCommunications Association

220 Southwind Ln.
Hillsborough, NC 27278
Ph: (919)245-0906
E-mail: office@bca.org
URL: http://www.bca.org

1707 ■ Endowment Fund for Education Grants *(Undergraduate/Grant)*

Purpose: To promote and assist study and research in the field of biological communication. **Focus:** Biological and clinical sciences. **Qualif.:** High school students and students currently enrolled in their freshman year at a university or college are not eligible for grant funds. Applicants who are currently enrolled in sophomore, junior and senior years must present documentary evidence to demonstrate that they are in good academic standing for

Awards are arranged alphabetically below their administering organizations

all courses directly related to their major. **Criteria:** Fund Committee will evaluate the complete applications. Selection of applicants will be based on the merit and availability of funds.

Funds Avail.: $500 or less. **To Apply:** Applicants must submit the following documentation: (1) Current curriculum vitae; (2) A full and complete statement of what the applicant/ applicants intend(s) to accomplish within the field of biological photography; (3) Time frame for the project; (4) Details of how the project will benefit biomedical communications and biocommunicators as a whole, and of how this will be measured; (5) An agreement to provide the EFFE Committee with a final report describing the results of the project and its impact on biocommunication; (6) Description of plan to share the resulting educational benefits with the BCA membership; (7) An agreement that the BioCommunications Association, Inc., shall have the right of first publication on any results from project funded wholly or partially from the Endowment Fund for Education. **Deadline:** April 25.

1708 ■ Endowment Fund for Education (Loan) *(Undergraduate/Loan)*

Purpose: To promote and assist study and research in the field of biological communication. **Focus:** Biological and clinical sciences. **Qualif.:** Applicants must be high school students or students currently enrolled in their freshman year at a university or college; must present documentary evidence to demonstrate that they are in good academic standing for all courses directly related to their major (for sophomore, junior and senior years of high school). **Criteria:** Fund Committee will evaluate the complete applications. Selection of applicants will be based on the merit and availability of funds.

Funds Avail.: $500 or less. **To Apply:** Applicants must submit the following documentation: (1) Current curriculum vitae; (2) A financial statement; (3) High school graduates applying for a loan to be used as tuition for the freshman year must present documentation to assure the EFFE Committee that they are in good academic standing for their full senior year. Application forms are available online. **Deadline:** April 25.

1709 ■ Endowment Fund for Education (Loan/ Grants for Equipment) *(Undergraduate/Grant)*

Purpose: To promote and assist study and research in the field of biological communication. **Focus:** Biological and clinical sciences. **Qualif.:** High school students and students currently enrolled in their freshman year at a university or college are not eligible for grant funds. Applicants who are currently enrolled in sophomore, junior and senior years must present documentary evidence to demonstrate that they are in good academic standing for all courses directly related to their major. **Criteria:** Fund Committee will evaluate the complete applications. Selection of applicants will be based on the merit and availability of funds.

Funds Avail.: $500 or less. **To Apply:** Applicants must submit the following documentation: (1) A complete description of each piece of equipment; (2) The life expectancy of each piece of equipment; (3) The role each piece of equipment will play in the education of biocommunicators; (4) The number of students who can be expected to benefit from the equipment; (5) The total cost of the equipment; (6) The intended supplier of the equipment; (7) An agreement to provide the EFFE Committee with reports at six and twelve months after installation stating how the equipment has been used to benefit the education of biophotography students. **Deadline:** April 25.

1710 ■ Endowment Fund for Education (Loans/ Grants for Educational Materials) *(Undergraduate/ Grant)*

Purpose: To promote and assist study and research in the field of biological communication. **Focus:** Biological and clinical sciences. **Qualif.:** High school students and students currently enrolled in their freshman year at a university or college are not eligible for grant funds. Applicants who are currently enrolled in sophomore, junior and senior years must present documentary evidence to demonstrate that they are in good academic standing for all courses directly related to their major. **Criteria:** Fund Committee will evaluate the complete applications. Selection of applicants will be based on the merit and availability of funds.

Funds Avail.: $500 or less. **To Apply:** Applicants must submit the following materials: (1) A complete description of the materials to be purchased; (2) Information about where the materials will be housed and who is to be responsible for their security; (3) Details on how the materials will be made available to the students; (4) The life expectancy of the materials; (5) The relevance of the material to biophotography; (6) The number of students who will use the materials; (7) The total cost and supplier of the materials. **Deadline:** April 25.

1711 ■ Biomagnetic Therapy Association

PO Box 394
Lyons, CO 80540
Ph: (303)823-0307
E-mail: info@biomagnetic.org
URL: http://www.biomagnetic.org

1712 ■ William Philpott Scholarships *(All/ Scholarship)*

Purpose: To encourage educational pursuits among Biomagnetic Therapy Association members who are pursuing certification as a Biomagnetic Specialist at the Biomagnetic Institute. **Focus:** Therapy. **Qualif.:** Applicants must be enrolled at a post-secondary institution and must be pursuing certification as a Biomagnetic Specialist at the Biomagnetic Institute. **Criteria:** Selection is based on ability to complete the program successfully as well as on the applicants' ability to share Biomagnetic Therapy with their communities.

Funds Avail.: Varies. **To Apply:** Applicants must submit a copy of their personal information through e-mail indicating their names, e-mails, addresses and phone numbers and their answers to the question: "Why should you be honored with the scholarship". **Contact:** BTA at the above address (see entry 1711).

1713 ■ Biophysical Society

9650 Rockville Pike
Bethesda, MD 20814
Ph: (301)634-7114
Fax: (301)634-7133
E-mail: society@biophysics.org
URL: http://www.biophysics.org

1714 ■ Fulbright New Century Scholars Program *(Professional Development/Scholarship)*

Purpose: To provide supporting fund for researches on various academic and professional fields conducted

Awards are arranged alphabetically below their administering organizations

abroad. **Focus:** General studies. **Qualif.:** Applicants must be conducting current research relevant to the program's theme and objectives, be open to exploring and incorporating comparative, interdisciplinary approaches in their investigations, and interested in developing collaborative activities with other NCS Scholars. **Criteria:** Selection criteria include professional qualifications, lecturing activity, research activity, and language proficiency report. Preference is given to candidates who do not have substantial recent experience abroad in the country to which they are applying; preference will also be given to candidates who have not previously been awarded a Fulbright award.

Funds Avail.: No specific amount. **Number Awarded:** 2. **To Apply:** Application instructions and forms are available at the website. **Deadline:** August 1.

1715 ■ Long-Term Postdoctoral Fellowships for Biomedical and Behavioral Research in Japan
(Professional Development/Fellowship)

Purpose: To support meritorious biomedical and behavioral research projects undertaken in NIH laboratories by young Japanese postdoctoral researchers who intend to hold research positions at Japanese universities or other academic institutions or public institutions in Japan in the future. **Focus:** Biomedical research. **Qualif.:** Applicants must possess either nationality, permanent residence or citizenship of the nominating country; must hold a doctorate degree when the fellowship goes into effect; and have arranged in advance a research plan with their Japanese host. Individuals who have previously been awarded a fellowship of 12 months or longer under the JSPS Postdoctoral Fellowship Program or the STA Fellowship Program are not eligible. **Criteria:** Awards are given based on merit.

Funds Avail.: 392,000 yen (monthly maintenance allowance); 200,000 yen (settling-in allowance); 58,500 yen (domestic research travel allowance); and round-trip air ticket. **To Apply:** Application requirements and instructions are available at the website. **Deadline:** May 31. **Contact:** JSPS Foreign Fellowship Office Division of International Training and Research, jsps@nih.gov.

1716 ■ Birmingham Public School

550 W Merrill St.
Birmingham, MI 48009
Ph: (248)203-3000
E-mail: webmaster-main@birmingham.k12.mi.us
URL: http://www.birmingham.k12.mi.us

1717 ■ Birmingham Student Scholarship Fund Association *(Undergraduate/Scholarship)*

Purpose: To provide college financial assistance for students who reside within the boundaries of the Birmingham School District upon high school graduation. **Focus:** General studies. **Qualif.:** Applicants must have their primary residence within the boundaries of the Birmingham Public School or private school district during that year. **Criteria:** Scholarship grants are based on a variety of factors including family financial need, student's academic performance, school or community activities, employment experience, educational goals, and enrollment at a Michigan college, as well as counselor recommendations and other student and family circumstances. In addition, some of the scholarship grants may consider other factors prescribed by a benefactor, including student gender, performance in a particular field of study or a student's school attendance area.

Funds Avail.: $750-$2,000. **Number Awarded:** Varies **To Apply:** Applicants must submit completed application to the student's high school counselor prior to the filing date set by the Scholar Board each year. The application must be signed by both the student and one parent certifying the truth of the application. The application requires student's and parents' current income tax information, as well as information regarding family housing, Unless there is independent written verification of an established pattern of non-support by a parent; scholarship grants will be reduced by 50 percent if information is not received from both parents. The application and instructions can be printed from the web page. **Deadline:** March 1. **Contact:** BPS at the above address (see entry 1716).

1718 ■ Mary E. Bivins Foundation

301 S Polk Ste. 860
PO Box 1727
Amarillo, TX 79105-1727
Ph: (806)379-9400
Fax: (806)379-9404
E-mail: info@bivinsfoundation.org
URL: http://www.bivinsfoundations.org

1719 ■ Mary E. Bivins Foundation Religious Scholarship Program *(Graduate, Undergraduate/Scholarship)*

Purpose: To educate ministers to preach the Christian religion. **Focus:** Religious Education. **Qualif.:** Applicants must be dedicated to seeking an undergraduate or graduate education leading to a Bachelors or Masters Degree in a field that prepares the students to preach the Christian religion; must have the intent to serve as pulpit pastors; must be committed to studies and maintain a cumulative undergraduate GPA of 2.75 or above or a cumulative graduate GPA of 3.0 or above; must be permanent residents of one of the 26 counties of the Texas Panhandle; must enroll and pass a minimum of 12 hours each semester at the undergraduate level or 9 hours each semester at the graduate level; must enroll in an accredited college or university. **Criteria:** Preference will be given to those students who meet the criteria.

Funds Avail.: $1,000 per semester for those students classified as freshmen or sophomores, $2,000 per semester for those students classified as a juniors or seniors and $3,000 per semester for graduate students to be used for tuition, books, fees, and other expenses as necessary for college/university attendance. **To Apply:** Applicants must check the available website for the required materials.

Remarks: Scholarships are awarded on an annual basis, and the students are required to continue to meet all award criteria each semester and to complete an application annually. **Contact:** Mary E. Bivins Foundation at the above address (see entry 1718).

1720 ■ Black Alliance for Educational Options

888 16th St. NW, Ste. 800
Washington, DC 20006
Ph: (202)429-2236
Fax: (202)349-9879
URL: http://www.baeo.org

1721 ■ BAEO Children's Scholarship Fund *(High School/Scholarship)*

Purpose: To provide partial tuition assistance for low-income families to send their children to private schools.

Focus: General Studies. **Qualif.:** Applicants must be: 5 years of age or older; from low-income families; students from kindergarten-8th grade. **Criteria:** Preference will be given to those students who meet the criteria.

Funds Avail.: No specific amount. **To Apply:** Applicants must check the available website for the required materials. **Contact:** Black Alliance for Educational Options at the above address (see entry 1720).

1722 ■ Black Student Fund *(High School/ Scholarship)*

Purpose: To provide financial assistance and support services to Washington DC metropolitan area African-American students. **Focus:** General Studies. **Qualif.:** Applicants must be African American students; must be in grades pre-kindergarten to 12; must be residents in Greater Washington area. **Criteria:** Preference will be given to students who meet the criteria.

Funds Avail.: No specific amount. **To Apply:** Applicants must check the available website for more information. **Contact:** For more information, contact Gwen Thompson, Director, at 202-387-1414 or mail@blackstudentfund.org.

1723 ■ Black Business and Professional Association

675 King St. W, Ste. 210
Toronto, ON, Canada M5V 1M9
Ph: (416)504-4097
Fax: (416)504-7343
E-mail: bbpa@bellnet.ca
URL: http://www.bbpa.org

1724 ■ Hon. Lincoln Alexander Scholarships *(Undergraduate/Scholarship)*

Purpose: To provide support for Black Canadian students. **Focus:** General studies. **Qualif.:** Applicant must be a Canadian citizen or a permanent resident; must be 17 to 30 years of age; and must be enrolled in a full-time degree (graduate or undergraduate), diploma or certificate program at a Canadian college or university for the academic year. **Criteria:** Selection of applicants will be based on academic achievement, financial need, and recognized contribution to the Black community.

Funds Avail.: $2,000. **To Apply:** Applicants must submit completed application form; a letter describing the reasons why they would be worthy recipients of a BBPA National Scholarship; a completed financial information schedule stating their budget for the coming year including information on their expected sources of funding, family income and related information; and a letter of reference from the two individuals named in their application (must be a teacher from their high school, college or university, and an individual who is familiar with their community service). Application form and requirements must be sent to The Board of Trustees, BBPA National Scholarship Fund, 675 King St., W, Ste. 210, Toronto, ON M5V 1M9. **Deadline:** May 30.

1725 ■ Louise Bennett-Coverley Scholarships *(Undergraduate/Scholarship)*

Purpose: To provide support to Black Canadian students. **Focus:** General studies. **Qualif.:** Applicant must be a Canadian citizen or a permanent resident; must be 17 to 30 years of age; must be enrolled in a full time degree (graduate or undergraduate), diploma or certificate program at a Canadian college or university for the academic year. **Criteria:** Selection of applicants will be based on academic achievement, financial need, and recognized contribution to the Black community.

Funds Avail.: $2,000. **To Apply:** Applicants must complete the application form, submit a letter describing the reasons why they would be a worthy recipient of a BBPA National Scholarship; must provide the completed financial information schedule stating their budget for the coming year including information on their expected sources of funding, family income and related information; must have a letter of reference from the two individuals named in their application (must be a teacher from their high school, college or university, and an individual who is familiar with their community service). Application form and requirements must be sent to The Board of Trustees, BBPA National Scholarship Fund, 675 King St., W, Ste. 210, Toronto, ON M5V 1M9. **Deadline:** May 30.

1726 ■ BMO Financial Group Scholarships *(Undergraduate/Scholarship)*

Purpose: To provide support for Black Canadian students. **Focus:** General studies. **Qualif.:** Applicants must be students with academic achievements who have demonstrated social responsibility; must be Canadian citizens or permanent residents; must be 17 to 30 years of age; and must be enrolled in a full-time degree (graduate or undergraduate), diploma or certificate program at a Canadian college or university for the academic year. **Criteria:** Selection of applicants will be based on academic achievement, financial need, and recognized contribution to the Black community.

Funds Avail.: $5,000. **Number Awarded:** 2. **To Apply:** Applicants must complete the application form and submit along with a letter describing the reasons why they would be a worthy recipient of a BBPA National Scholarship; a completed financial information schedule stating their budget for the coming year including information on their expected sources of funding, family income and related information; and a letter of reference from the two individuals named in their application (must be a teacher from their high school, college or university, and an individual who is familiar with their community service). Application form and requirements must be sent to The Board of Trustees, BBPA National Scholarship Fund, 675 King St., W, Ste. 210, Toronto, ON M5V 1M9. **Deadline:** May 30.

1727 ■ Herb Carnegie Scholarships *(Undergraduate/Scholarship)*

Purpose: To provide support to Black Canadian students. **Focus:** General studies. **Qualif.:** Applicants must be a Canadian citizen or a permanent resident; must be 17 to 30 years of age; must be enrolled in a full time degree (graduate or undergraduate), diploma or certificate program at a Canadian college or university for the academic year. **Criteria:** Selection of applicants will be based on academic achievement, financial need, and recognized contribution to the Black community.

Funds Avail.: $2,000. **To Apply:** Applicants must complete the application form, submit a letter describing the reasons why they would be a worthy recipient of a BBPA National Scholarship; must provide the completed financial information schedule stating their budget for the coming year including information on their expected sources of funding, family income and related information; must have a letter of reference from the two individuals named in their application (must be a teacher from their high school, college or

Awards are arranged alphabetically below their administering organizations

university, and an individual who is familiar with their community service). Application form and requirements must be sent to The Board of Trustees, BBPA National Scholarship Fund, 675 King St., W, Ste. 210, Toronto, ON M5V 1M9. **Deadline:** May 30.

1728 ■ Fraser Milner Casgrain LLP Scholarships *(Undergraduate/Scholarship)*

Purpose: To provide support for Black Canadian students. **Focus:** General studies. **Qualif.:** Applicants must be Canadian citizens or permanent residents; must be 17 to 30 years of age; and must be enrolled in a full time degree (graduate or undergraduate), diploma or certificate program at a Canadian college or university for the academic year. **Criteria:** Selection of applicants will be based on academic achievement, financial need, and recognized contribution to the Black community.

Funds Avail.: $5,000. **To Apply:** Applicants must complete the application form and submit along with a letter describing the reasons why they would be worthy recipients of a BBPA National Scholarship; a completed financial information schedule stating their budget for the coming year including information on their expected sources of funding, family income and related information; and a letter of reference from the two individuals named in their application (must be a teacher from their high school, college or university, and an individual who is familiar with their community service). Application form and requirements must be sent to The Board of Trustees, BBPA National Scholarship Fund, 675 King St., W, Ste. 210, Toronto, ON M5V 1M9. **Deadline:** May 30.

1729 ■ CIBC Scholarships *(Undergraduate/Scholarship)*

Purpose: To provide support for Black Canadian students. **Focus:** General studies. **Qualif.:** Applicants must be students attending college or university who have shown academic achievement, leadership potential and a commitment to helping in the community; must be Canadian citizens or permanent residents; must be 17 to 30 years of age; and must be enrolled in a full-time degree (graduate or undergraduate), diploma or certificate program at a Canadian college or university for the academic year. **Criteria:** Selection of applicants will be based on academic achievement, financial need, and recognized contribution to the Black community.

Funds Avail.: $5,000. **To Apply:** Applicants must complete the application form and submit along with a letter describing the reasons why they would be a worthy recipient of a BBPA National Scholarship; a completed financial information schedule stating their budget for the coming year including information on their expected sources of funding, family income and related information; and a letter of reference from the two individuals named in their application (must be a teacher from their high school, college or university, and an individual who is familiar with their community service). Application form and requirements must be sent to The Board of Trustees, BBPA National Scholarship Fund, 675 King St., W, Ste. 210, Toronto, ON M5V 1M9. **Deadline:** May 30.

1730 ■ Erma Collins Scholarships *(Undergraduate/Scholarship)*

Purpose: To provide support for Black Canadian students. **Focus:** General studies. **Qualif.:** Applicants must be students attending community college; must be Canadian citizens or permanent residents; must be 17 to 30 years of age; and must be enrolled in a full time degree (graduate or undergraduate), diploma or certificate program at a Canadian college or university for the academic year. **Criteria:** Selection of applicants will be based on academic achievement, financial need, and recognized contribution to the Black community.

Funds Avail.: $1,000. **To Apply:** Applicants must complete the application form and submit along with a letter describing the reasons why they would be worthy recipients of a BBPA National Scholarship; a completed financial information schedule stating their budget for the coming year including information on their expected sources of funding, family income and related information; and a letter of reference from the two individuals named in their application (must be a teacher from their high school, college or university, and an individual who is familiar with their community service). Application form and requirements must be sent to The Board of Trustees, BBPA National Scholarship Fund, 675 King St., W, Ste. 210, Toronto, ON M5V 1M9. **Deadline:** May 30.

1731 ■ Harry Gairey Scholarships *(Undergraduate/Scholarship)*

Purpose: To provide support for Black Canadian students. **Focus:** General studies. **Qualif.:** Applicant must be a Canadian citizen or a permanent resident; must be 17 to 30 years of age; must be enrolled in a full time degree (graduate or undergraduate), diploma or certificate program at a Canadian college or university for the academic year. **Criteria:** Selection of applicants will be based on academic achievement, financial need, and recognized contribution to the Black community.

Funds Avail.: $2,000. **Number Awarded:** 2. **To Apply:** Applicants must complete the application form, letter describing the reasons why they would be worthy recipients of a BBPA National Scholarship; a completed financial information schedule stating their budget for the coming year including information on their expected sources of funding, family income and related information; and a letter of reference from the two individuals named in their application (must be a teacher from their high school, college or university, and an individual who is familiar with their community service). Application form and requirements must be sent to The Board of Trustees, BBPA National Scholarship Fund, 675 King St., W, Ste. 210, Toronto, ON M5V 1M9. **Deadline:** May 30.

1732 ■ Lucille May Gopie Scholarships *(Undergraduate/Scholarship)*

Purpose: To provide support for Black Canadian students. **Focus:** General studies. **Qualif.:** Applicant must be a person who has been encouraged by a single parent to pursue higher education; must be a Canadian citizen or a permanent resident; must be 17 to 30 years of age; and must be enrolled in a full-time degree (graduate or undergraduate), diploma or certificate program at a Canadian college or university for the academic year. **Criteria:** Selection of applicants will be based on academic achievement, financial need, and recognized contribution to the Black community.

Funds Avail.: $2,000. **To Apply:** Applicants must complete the application form and submit along with a letter describing the reasons why they would be a worthy recipient of a BBPA National Scholarship; a completed financial information schedule stating their budget for the coming year including information on their expected sources of funding, family income and related information; and a letter of refer-

Awards are arranged alphabetically below their administering organizations

ence from the two individuals named in their application (must be a teacher from their high school, college or university, and an individual who is familiar with their community service). Application form and requirements must be sent to The Board of Trustees, BBPA National Scholarship Fund, 675 King St., W, Ste. 210, Toronto, ON M5V 1M9. **Deadline:** May 30.

1733 ■ Guntley-Lorimer Science and Arts Scholarships *(Undergraduate/Scholarship)*

Purpose: To provide support for Black Canadian students. **Focus:** Science; Art. **Qualif.:** Applicant must be a Canadian citizen or a permanent resident; must be 17 to 30 years of age; and must be enrolled in a full-time degree (graduate or undergraduate), diploma or certificate program at a Canadian college or university for the academic year. **Criteria:** Selection of applicants will be based on academic achievement, financial need, and recognized contribution to the Black community.

Funds Avail.: $2,000-$3,000. **Number Awarded:** 4. **To Apply:** Applicants must complete the application form and submit along with a letter describing the reasons why they would be worthy recipients of a BBPA National Scholarship; a completed financial information schedule stating their budget for the coming year including information on their expected sources of funding, family income and related information; and a letter of reference from the two individuals named in their application (must be a teacher from their high school, college or university, and an individual who is familiar with their community service). Application form and requirements must be sent to The Board of Trustees, BBPA National Scholarship Fund, 675 King St., W, Ste. 210, Toronto, ON M5V 1M9. **Deadline:** May 30.

1734 ■ Al Hamilton Scholarships *(Undergraduate/Scholarship)*

Purpose: To provide support for Black Canadian students. **Focus:** General studies. **Qualif.:** Applicants must be a Canadian citizen or a permanent resident; must be 17 to 30 years of age; must be enrolled in a full time degree (graduate or undergraduate), diploma or certificate program at a Canadian college or university for the academic year. **Criteria:** Selection of applicants will be based on academic achievement, financial need, and recognized contribution to the Black community.

Funds Avail.: $2,000. **To Apply:** Applicants must submit a completed application form, a letter describing the reasons why they would be worthy recipients of a BBPA National Scholarship; a completed financial information schedule stating their budget for the coming year including information on their expected sources of funding, family income and related information; and a letter of reference from the two individuals named in their application (must be a teacher from their high school, college or university, and an individual who is familiar with their community service). Application form and requirements must be sent to The Board of Trustees, BBPA National Scholarship Fund, 675 King St., W, Ste. 210, Toronto, ON M5V 1M9. **Deadline:** May 30.

1735 ■ William Peyton Hubbard Scholarships *(Undergraduate/Scholarship)*

Purpose: To provide support for Black Canadian students. **Focus:** General studies. **Qualif.:** Applicant must be a Canadian citizen or a permanent resident; must be 17 to 30 years of age; and must be enrolled in a full-time degree (graduate or undergraduate), diploma or certificate program at a Canadian college or university for the academic year. **Criteria:** Selection of applicants will be based on academic achievement, financial need, and recognized contribution to the Black community.

Funds Avail.: $2,000. **To Apply:** Applicants must complete the application form and submit along with a letter describing the reasons why they would be a worthy recipient of a BBPA National Scholarship; a completed financial information schedule stating their budget for the coming year including information on their expected sources of funding, family income and related information; and a letter of reference from the two individuals named in their application (must be a teacher from their high school, college or university, and an individual who is familiar with their community service). Application form and requirements must be sent to The Board of Trustees, BBPA National Scholarship Fund, 675 King St., W, Ste. 210, Toronto, ON M5V 1M9. **Deadline:** May 30.

1736 ■ Right Hon. Michaelle Jean Scholarships *(Undergraduate/Scholarship)*

Purpose: To provide support for Black Canadian students. **Focus:** General studies. **Qualif.:** Applicant must be a Canadian citizen or a permanent resident; must be 17 to 30 years of age; and must be enrolled in a full-time degree (graduate or undergraduate), diploma or certificate program at a Canadian college or university for the academic year. **Criteria:** Selection of applicants will be based on academic achievement, financial need, and recognized contribution to the Black community.

Funds Avail.: $2,000. **To Apply:** Applicants must complete the application form and submit along with a letter describing the reasons why they would be worthy recipients of a BBPA National Scholarship; a completed financial information schedule stating their budget for the coming year including information on their expected sources of funding, family income and related information; and a letter of reference from the two individuals named in their application (must be a teacher from their high school, college or university, and an individual who is familiar with their community service). Application form and requirements must be sent to The Board of Trustees, BBPA National Scholarship Fund, 675 King St., W, Ste. 210, Toronto, ON M5V 1M9. **Deadline:** May 30.

1737 ■ Harry Jerome Scholarships *(Undergraduate/Scholarship)*

Purpose: To provide support for Black Canadian students. **Focus:** General studies. **Qualif.:** Applicant must be a Canadian citizen or a permanent resident; must be 17 to 30 years of age; and must be enrolled in a full-time degree (graduate or undergraduate), diploma or certificate program at a Canadian college or university for the academic year. **Criteria:** Selection of applicants will be based on academic achievement, financial need, and recognized contribution to the Black community.

Funds Avail.: $5,000. **To Apply:** Applicants must complete the application form and submit along with a letter describing the reasons why they would be worthy recipients of a BBPA National Scholarship; a completed financial information schedule stating their budget for the coming year including information on their expected sources of funding, family income and related information; and a letter of reference from the two individuals named in their application (must be a teacher from their high school, college or university, and an individual who is familiar with their community service). Application form and requirements must be sent to The Board of Trustees, BBPA National Scholarship Fund, 675 King St., W, Ste. 210, Toronto, ON M5V 1M9. **Deadline:** May 30.

1738 ■ Beverly Mascoll Scholarships *(Undergraduate/Scholarship)*

Purpose: To provide support for Black Canadian students. **Focus:** General studies. **Qualif.:** Applicant must be a Canadian citizen or a permanent resident; must be 17 to 30 years of age; and must be enrolled in a full-time degree (graduate or undergraduate), diploma or certificate program at a Canadian college or university for the academic year. **Criteria:** Selection of applicants will be based on academic achievement, financial need, and recognized contribution to the Black community.

Funds Avail.: $2,000. **To Apply:** Applicants must complete the application form and submit along with a letter describing the reasons why they would be worthy recipients of a BBPA National Scholarship; a completed financial information schedule stating their budget for the coming year including information on their expected sources of funding, family income and related information; and a letter of reference from the two individuals named in their application (must be a teacher from their high school, college or university, and an individual who is familiar with their community service). Application form and requirements must be sent to The Board of Trustees, BBPA National Scholarship Fund, 675 King St., W, Ste. 210, Toronto, ON M5V 1M9. **Deadline:** May 30.

1739 ■ Minerva Scholarships *(Undergraduate/Scholarship)*

Purpose: To provide support for Black Canadian students. **Focus:** General studies. **Qualif.:** Applicant must be a Canadian citizen or a permanent resident; must be 17 to 30 years of age; and must be enrolled in a full-time degree (graduate or undergraduate), diploma or certificate program at a Canadian college or university for the academic year. **Criteria:** Selection of applicants will be based on academic achievement, financial need, and recognized contribution to the Black community.

Funds Avail.: $2,000-$4,000. **Number Awarded:** 2-4. **To Apply:** Applicants must complete the application form and submit along with a letter describing the reasons why they would be a worthy recipient of a BBPA National Scholarship; a completed financial information schedule stating their budget for the coming year including information on their expected sources of funding, family income and related information; and a letter of reference from the two individuals named in their application (must be a teacher from their high school, college or university, and an individual who is familiar with their community service). Application form and requirements must be sent to The Board of Trustees, BBPA National Scholarship Fund, 675 King St., W, Ste. 210, Toronto, ON M5V 1M9. **Deadline:** May 30.

1740 ■ RBC Financial Group Scholarships *(Graduate/Scholarship)*

Purpose: To provide support for Black Canadian students. **Focus:** Business administration. **Qualif.:** Applicants must be students enrolled in a course of study leading to a bachelor's or master's degree in Business Administration or a related program; must be a Canadian citizen or a permanent resident; must be 17 to 30 years of age; and must be enrolled in a full-time degree (graduate or undergraduate), diploma or certificate program at a Canadian college or university for the academic year. **Criteria:** Selection of applicants will be based on academic achievement, financial need, and recognized contribution to the Black community.

Funds Avail.: $4,000. **Number Awarded:** 2. **To Apply:** Applicants must complete the application form and submit along with a letter describing the reasons why they would be worthy recipients of a BBPA National Scholarship; a completed financial information schedule stating their budget for the coming year including information on their expected sources of funding, family income and related information; and a letter of reference from the two individuals named in their application (must be a teacher from their high school, college or university, and an individual who is familiar with their community service). Application form and requirements must be sent to The Board of Trustees, BBPA National Scholarship Fund, 675 King St., W, Ste. 210, Toronto, ON M5V 1M9. **Deadline:** May 30.

1741 ■ Scotiabank Scholarships *(Graduate/Scholarship)*

Purpose: To provide support for Black Canadian students. **Focus:** General studies. **Qualif.:** Applicant must be a student who has demonstrated high academic achievement as well as leadership skills and a commitment to helping in the community; must be a Canadian citizen or a permanent resident; must be 17 to 30 years of age; and must be enrolled in a full-time degree (graduate or undergraduate), diploma or certificate program at a Canadian college or university for the academic year. **Criteria:** Selection of applicants will be based on academic achievement, financial need, and recognized contribution to the Black community.

Funds Avail.: $5,000. **Number Awarded:** 2. **To Apply:** Applicants must complete the application form and submit along with a letter describing the reasons why they would be worthy recipients of a BBPA National Scholarship; a completed financial information schedule stating their budget for the coming year including information on their expected sources of funding, family income and related information; and a letter of reference from the two individuals named in their application (must be a teacher from their high school, college or university, and an individual who is familiar with their community service). Application form and requirements must be sent to The Board of Trustees, BBPA National Scholarship Fund, 675 King St., W, Ste. 210, Toronto, ON M5V 1M9. **Deadline:** May 30.

1742 ■ Julia Viola Simms Science Scholarships *(Postgraduate/Scholarship)*

Purpose: To provide support for Black Canadian students. **Focus:** Mathematics and mathematical sciences; Physics; Chemistry; Biology; Medicine. **Qualif.:** Applicant must be a female student who has been accepted into a postsecondary degree program in one of the sciences such as mathematics, physics, chemistry, biology or medicine; must be a Canadian citizen or a permanent resident; must be 17 to 30 years of age; and must be enrolled in a full-time degree (graduate or undergraduate), diploma or certificate program at a Canadian college or university for the academic year. **Criteria:** Selection of applicants will be based on academic achievement, financial need, and recognized contribution to the Black community.

Funds Avail.: $3,000. **To Apply:** Applicants must complete the application form and submit along with a letter describing the reasons why they would be worthy recipients of a BBPA National Scholarship; a completed financial information schedule stating their budget for the coming year

Awards are arranged alphabetically below their administering organizations

including information on their expected sources of funding, family income and related information; and a letter of reference from the two individuals named in their application (must be a teacher from their high school, college or university, and an individual who is familiar with their community service). Application form and requirements must be sent to The Board of Trustees, BBPA National Scholarship Fund, 675 King St., W, Ste. 210, Toronto, ON M5V 1M9. **Deadline:** May 30.

1743 ■ Tropicana Community Services - Robert K. Brown Scholarships *(Undergraduate/ Scholarship)*

Purpose: To provide support for Black Canadian students. **Focus:** Social work. **Qualif.:** Applicant must be enrolled in a course of study in the field of social services; must be a Canadian citizen or a permanent resident; must be 17 to 30 years of age; and must be enrolled in a full-time degree (graduate or undergraduate), diploma or certificate program at a Canadian college or university for the academic year. **Criteria:** Selection of applicants will be based on academic achievement, financial need, and recognized contribution to the Black community.

Funds Avail.: $1,500. **To Apply:** Applicants must complete the application form and submit along with a letter describing the reasons why they would be worthy recipients of a BBPA National Scholarship; a completed financial information schedule stating their budget for the coming year including information on their expected sources of funding, family income and related information; and a letter of reference from the two individuals named in their application (must be a teacher from their high school, college or university, and an individual who is familiar with their community service). Application form and requirements must be sent to The Board of Trustees, BBPA National Scholarship Fund, 675 King St., W, Ste. 210, Toronto, ON M5V 1M9. **Deadline:** May 30.

1744 ■ Urban Financial Services Coalition Scholarships *(Undergraduate/Scholarship)*

Purpose: To provide support for Black Canadian students. **Focus:** Business, Economics, Finance, Information science and technology. **Qualif.:** Applicant must be a student pursuing studies in business, economics, finance or information technology; must be a Canadian citizen or a permanent resident; must be 17 to 30 years of age; and must be enrolled in a full-time degree (graduate or undergraduate), diploma or certificate program at a Canadian college or university for the academic year. **Criteria:** Selection of applicants will be based on academic achievement, financial need, and recognized contribution to the Black community.

Funds Avail.: $2,000. **Number Awarded:** 2. **To Apply:** Applicants must complete the application form and submit along with a letter describing the reasons why they would be worthy recipients of a BBPA National Scholarship; a completed financial information schedule stating their budget for the coming year including information on their expected sources of funding, family income and related information; and a letter of reference from the two individuals named in their application (must be a teacher from their high school, college or university, and an individual who is familiar with their community service). Application form and requirements must be sent to The Board of Trustees, BBPA National Scholarship Fund, 675 King St., W, Ste. 210, Toronto, ON M5V 1M9. **Deadline:** May 30.

1745 ■ Portia White Scholarships *(Undergraduate/Scholarship)*

Purpose: To provide support for Black Canadian students. **Focus:** General studies. **Qualif.:** Applicant must be a Canadian citizen or a permanent resident; must be 17 to 30 years of age; and must be enrolled in a full-time degree (graduate or undergraduate), diploma or certificate program at a Canadian college or university for the academic year. **Criteria:** Selection of applicants will be based on academic achievement, financial need, and recognized contribution to the Black community.

Funds Avail.: $2,000. **To Apply:** Applicants must complete the application form and submit along with a letter describing the reasons why they would be worthy recipients of a BBPA National Scholarship; a completed financial information schedule stating their budget for the coming year including information on their expected sources of funding, family income and related information; and a letter of reference from the two individuals named in their application (must be a teacher from their high school, college or university, and an individual who is familiar with their community service). Application form and requirements must be sent to The Board of Trustees, BBPA National Scholarship Fund, 675 King St., W, Ste. 210, Toronto, ON M5V 1M9. **Deadline:** May 30.

1746 ■ Dwight Whylie Scholarships *(Undergraduate/Scholarship)*

Purpose: To provide support for Black Canadian students. **Focus:** General studies. **Qualif.:** Applicant must be a Canadian citizen or a permanent resident; must be 17 to 30 years of age; and must be enrolled in a full-time degree (graduate or undergraduate), diploma or certificate program at a Canadian college or university for the academic year. **Criteria:** Selection of applicants will be based on academic achievement, financial need, and recognized contribution to the Black community.

Funds Avail.: $2,000. **To Apply:** Applicants must submit completed application form; a letter describing the reasons why they would be worthy recipients of a BBPA National Scholarship; a completed financial information schedule stating their budget for the coming year including information on their expected sources of funding, family income and related information; and a letter of reference from the two individuals named in their application (must be a teacher from their high school, college or university, and an individual who is familiar with their community service). Application form and requirements must be sent to The Board of Trustees, BBPA National Scholarship Fund, 675 King St., W, Ste. 210, Toronto, ON M5V 1M9. **Deadline:** May 30.

1747 ■ Black Coaches and Administrators

Pan American Plaza, 201 S Capitol Ave., Ste. 495
Indianapolis, IN 46225
Ph: (317)829-5600
Fax: (317)829-5601
URL: http://www.bcasports.cstv.com

1748 ■ BCA Ethnic Minority Postgraduate Scholarships for Careers in Athletics *(Undergraduate/Scholarship)*

Purpose: To support and encourage minorities who wish to pursue a career in athletics. **Focus:** Sports studies. **Qualif.:** Applicants must be seeking admission or have been

Awards are arranged alphabetically below their administering organizations

accepted into a sports-administration or related program that will assist the applicant in obtaining a career in athletics. **Criteria:** Selection of recipient is based on merit.

Funds Avail.: $2,500. **To Apply:** Program application is available at the website. **Deadline:** May 1. **Contact:** Lauren Peterson, Director of Operations and Administration at 317-829-5619.

1749 ■ Black Nurses Association of Greater Washington

PO Box 55285
Washington, DC 20040
Ph: (202)291-8866
E-mail: contactus@bnaofgwdca.org
URL: http://www.bnaofgwdca.org

1750 ■ Dr. Johnella Banks Memorial Scholarships *(Undergraduate/Scholarship)*

Purpose: To empower the community through education, service and caring. **Focus:** Nursing. **Qualif.:** Applicants must be sophomore, junior or first-semester senior nursing students in a registered nursing or practical nursing program; must be currently enrolled in a National League for Nursing accredited program and be in good academic standing with a cumulative grade point average of at least 2.8. **Criteria:** Recipients are selected based on financial need.

Funds Avail.: No specific amount. **To Apply:** Applicants must submit a current official transcript from their nursing program, two letters of recommendation from which one must come from current faculty member and one must come from the Nursing Faculty Advisor or Designee; must submit a written essay that describes the applicant's objectives and need-based reasons for scholarship application; documented evidence to add support for the applicant's desirability that includes participation in student and nursing activities, community service in the Greater Washington area, awards, letters and certificates; must provide a proof of United States citizenship and evidence of financial need. **Deadline:** December 31. **Contact:** 202-291-8866.

1751 ■ Margaret Pemberton Scholarships *(Undergraduate/Scholarship)*

Purpose: To empower the community through education, service and caring. **Focus:** Nursing. **Qualif.:** Applicants must be graduating high school senior students who have been accepted into an accredited National League for Nursing baccalaureate program at a college or university in the United States; must be currently enrolled in a District of Columbia High School in good academic standing with a cumulative GPA of at least 2.8. **Criteria:** Recipients are selected based on financial need.

Funds Avail.: $2,000. **To Apply:** Applicants must submit an at least one-page long written essay describing personal and educational goals, contributions to the community and reasons they should be selected; must submit documented evidence for support, including participation in activities and organizations, awards, certificates, and/or letters of commendation; must submit an official high school transcript, copy of letter of acceptance to a Baccalaureate Nursing Program in a college or university in the United States of America; must submit two letters of recommendation, from which one must come from a high school counselor or designee and the other one must come from non-related adult who has knowledge of the applicant's potential for success. **Deadline:** April 15. **Contact:** 202-291-8866.

1752 ■ Black Theatre Network

2609 Douglas Road SE, Ste. 109
Washington, DC 20020-6540
Ph: (202)274-5667
E-mail: lreese@udc.edu
URL: http://www.blacktheatrenetwork.org

1753 ■ S. Randolph Edmonds Young Scholars Competition *(Graduate, Undergraduate/Scholarship)*

Purpose: To encourage research and scholarship in black theatre. **Focus:** Theatre arts. **Qualif.:** Applicant must be a college/university undergraduate or graduate working on a paper concerned with an aspect of the Black Theatre in either the United States or throughout the world. **Criteria:** Selection will be based on the criteria of the panel of judges.

Funds Avail.: $250. **To Apply:** Applicants must submit their papers. Papers must typed double-spaced, and in MLA format with a works cited page. If applicable, also include endnotes that demonstrate awareness of formal methods of documentation. Papers should be approximately 10 pages in length, not including endnotes. **Deadline:** May 12. **Contact:** Koritha Mitchell; mitchell.717@osu.edu; 543 Denney Hall, 164 West 17th Avenue, Columbus, Ohio 43210.

1754 ■ Black Women Lawyers' Association of Greater Chicago

321 S Plymouth Ct., Ste. 600
Chicago, IL 60604
Ph: (312)554-2088
Fax: (708)201-9342
E-mail: administrator@bwla.org
URL: http://www.bwla.org

1755 ■ DRI Law Student Diversity Scholarships *(Undergraduate/Scholarship)*

Purpose: To provide financial assistance to deserving law students from ABA accredited law schools. **Focus:** Law. **Qualif.:** Applicants must be second-year African American, Hispanic, Asian, Pan Asian or Native American students; or second-year female law students, regardless of race or ethnicity. **Criteria:** Applicants will be evaluated based on demonstrated academic excellence; and service to the profession, community and the cause of diversity.

Funds Avail.: $10,000. **Number Awarded:** 2. **To Apply:** Applicants must submit three recommendations, one each from the following individuals: a) the dean of the student's law school, b) a current or past law professor, and c) an individual who is personally acquainted with the applicant, but who is not related by blood line or adoption; and a cover letter which identifies their academic, personal and/or professional accomplishments and how those accomplishments qualify him or her for DRI's Law Student Diversity Scholarship Award.

1756 ■ Black Women Lawyers Association of Los Angeles

PO Box 8179
Los Angeles, CA 90008

Awards are arranged alphabetically below their administering organizations

Ph: (213)538-0137
URL: http://www.blackwomenlawyersla.org

1757 ■ Black Women Lawyers Association of Los Angeles Scholarships *(Undergraduate/ Scholarship)*

Purpose: To encourage careers and increase interest in the field of law. **Focus:** Law. **Qualif.:** Program is open to second or third year full-time law students as well as to fourth year law students enrolled in night programs intending to practice law in California. **Criteria:** Recipients are selected on the basis of financial need, community service, academic achievement and legal writing ability.

Funds Avail.: No specific amount. **To Apply:** Applicants must return completed application along with other required documents. Applications should be either typed or handwritten in black or dark blue ink. Applicants must submit the following attachments: current official school transcript, including school grading scale; letter from law school verifying the current academic status; and resume. Application forms are available at the website. **Deadline:** March 31. **Contact:** Mika M. Hilaire, 15233 Ventura Blvd., Suite 420, Sherman Oaks, CA 91403; mika@ahblegal.com.

1758 ■ Black Women in Sisterhood for Action

PO Box 1529
Washington, DC 20013
Ph: (202)543-5719
Fax: (202)543-5719
E-mail: info@bisa-hq.org
URL: http://www.bisa-hq.org

1759 ■ BISA's Scholarship Assistance Program *(Undergraduate/Scholarship)*

Purpose: To provide financial assistance for prospective college students who have been accepted for admission to a college or university and who are in need of financial assistance. **Focus:** General studies. **Qualif.:** Black female high school graduates (currently graduating from high school in the year of application) are eligible to apply. **Criteria:** Recipients will be selected based on academic achievement, leadership potential, financial need, honors, potential for academic growth and leadership development.

Funds Avail.: $1,000. **To Apply:** Applicants must submit transcript of records and SAT or ACT Scores; parent's Income Tax Submission to IRS (with W-2 Statement); Financial Aid Award Letter; and two typed double-spaced pages or one single-spaced page highlighting where you expect to be in your career development in ten years. **Deadline:** April 6.

1760 ■ Black Women in Sisterhood for Action

PO Box 1592
Washington, DC 20013
Ph: (202)543-6013
Fax: (202)543-5719
E-mail: info@bisa-hq.org
URL: http://www.bisa-hq.org

1761 ■ BISA's Scholarships Assistance Program *(High School/Scholarship)*

Purpose: To provide financial assistance to college students who have been accepted for admission to a college or university and need financial assistance. **Focus:** General studies. **Qualif.:** Applicants must be black females; must be graduates or graduating high school seniors. **Criteria:** Recipients are selected based on academic achievement, leadership potential, financial need, honors and potential for academic growth and leadership development.

Funds Avail.: $1,000. **To Apply:** Applicants must submit completed application form; transcript; SAT or ACT scores; parents' income tax submission to IRS (with W-2 Statement); financial aid award letter; and written self-portrait (two typed double spaced pages or one single spaced page) highlighting where they expect to be in their career development in 10 years. **Deadline:** April 6.

1762 ■ Richard Gregory Freeland, II Educational Scholarships *(High School/Scholarship)*

Purpose: To provide financial assistance to offset the cost of education for qualified students who have been accepted by an accredited college or university. **Focus:** Computer and information sciences; Engineering; Telecommunications systems; Business administration. **Qualif.:** Applicants must be graduating high school students of African American ethnicity; reside in Maryland, Washington, DC or the Northern Virginia area; hold a grade point average of 2.5 or above; be pursuing a degree in the areas of computer science, information management, engineering, telecommunications, business management/administration or another technology-related field. **Criteria:** Recipients are selected based on academic achievement, leadership potential, financial need, community service and honors.

Funds Avail.: $500 to $2,500. **To Apply:** Applicants must submit all the required application information. **Deadline:** May 5.

1763 ■ Blair Chiropractic Society

8603 34th St. N
Lake Elmo, MN 55042
Ph: (651)748-5731
URL: http://www.blairchiropractic.com

1764 ■ Beatrice K. Blair Scholarships *(Undergraduate/Scholarship)*

Purpose: To enhance the educational opportunities of chiropractic students with an interest in specific upper cervical Blair technique by providing financial assistance to eligible students attending chiropractic schools. **Focus:** Chiropractic. **Qualif.:** The applicant must be a student in good standing at an accredited chiropractic college and a member of a student Blair club if available at their school. **Criteria:** The recipient will be selected based on his or her GPA of at least 2.5 out of 4.0 (C+), and he or she must have completed at least one Primary Blair Seminar.

Funds Avail.: 1,000. **Deadline:** June 30. **Contact:** Dr. Alfred Tomp, Blair Scholarship Committee, 22421 Gilberto No. F, Rancho Santa Margarita, CA 92688.

1765 ■ Blood Assurance Foundation

705 E 4th St.
Chattanooga, TN 37403-1916
Ph: (423)756-0966
Fax: (423)752-8460
Free: 800-962-0628
E-mail: wlf@bloodassurance.org
URL: http://www.bloodassurance.org

Awards are arranged alphabetically below their administering organizations

1766 ■ The Crystal Green Blood Assurance Scholarships *(Undergraduate/Scholarship)*

Purpose: To encourage educational pursuits by providing financial assistance. **Focus:** General studies. **Qualif.:** Applicants must be high school senior students planning to enter an accredited two or four-year college or university; and must have an, at least, "B" average and score at least 20 on the ACT or 1100 on the SAT cumulative. **Criteria:** Recipients are selected based on the written application, high school transcript, school and community service, letters of recommendation, and a marketing plan for a blood drive.

Funds Avail.: $1,500. **Number Awarded:** 12. **To Apply:** Applicants must submit a detailed marketing plan for a new drive promotion; applicants must secure two letters of recommendation and obtain an official high school transcript which includes the first semester senior grades and ACT/SAT test scores.

1767 ■ Blues Heaven Foundation

2120 S Michigan Ave.
Chicago, IL 60616
Ph: (312)808-1286
Fax: (312)808-0273
E-mail: info@bluesheaven.com
URL: http://www.bluesheaven.com

1768 ■ Muddy Waters Scholarships *(Undergraduate/Scholarship)*

Purpose: To provide financial assistance to students in Chicago. **Focus:** Music education, music, African-American studies, folklore, performing arts, journalism, radio and television. **Qualif.:** Applicant must have a full-time enrollment status in a Chicago area college or university; must be in at least their first year of undergraduate studies or graduate program. **Criteria:** Awards are given based on academic achievement, concentration of studies and financial need.

Funds Avail.: NO specific amount. **To Apply:** Application form are available in the website address; must be sent to: Blues Heaven Foundation Inc., 2120 S Michigan Ave., Chicago, IL 60616. **Deadline:** April 30.

1769 ■ Bowling Writers Association of America

8501 N Manor Ln.
Fox Point, WI 53217
Ph: (414)351-6085
E-mail: sjames2652@wi.rr.com
URL: http://www.bowlingwriters.com

1770 ■ Chuck Pezzano Scholarships *(Undergraduate/Scholarship)*

Purpose: To provide financial support for students pursuing a career in communications that involve the sport of bowling. **Focus:** Communication; Sports writing. **Qualif.:** Applicants must have a minimum of 2.5 GPA; must be a high school or vocational school senior or college student. **Criteria:** Awards are given based on academic merit, civic and bowling participation.

Funds Avail.: $1000. **To Apply:** Applicant must send application form (available at the website); transcript; at least one reference letter; and any other information to support your application. **Deadline:** May 15.

Remarks: Established in honor of Chuck Pezzano a BWAA, American Bowling Congress and Professional Bowlers Association Hall of Fame journalist. **Contact:** Steve James, Executive Director

1771 ■ Boys and Girls Club of Ottawa

2825 Dumaurier Ave.
Ottawa, ON, Canada K2B 7W3
Ph: (613)232-0925
E-mail: sbradford@bgcottawa.org
URL: http://www.bgcottawa.org

1772 ■ Ottawa Police 150th Anniversary Scholarships *(Undergraduate/Scholarship)*

Purpose: To promote, encourage and sponsor promising individuals who would otherwise experience extreme hardships in pursuing a post-secondary education. **Focus:** Criminal justice. **Qualif.:** Applicants must be students pursuing a career in policing or a related criminal justice field. **Criteria:** Recipients are selected based on financial need, academic achievement and community involvement.

Funds Avail.: $5,000. **To Apply:** Applicants must submit: a completed application form; completed expenses and income form; up-to-date resume; two letters of recommendation; copy of most recent school transcript; proof of citizenship status; copy of letter of acceptance to an accredited post-secondary school; professional quality color photo; and a 300-1,000 word essay discussing their community involvement, financial need, accomplishment and academics. **Deadline:** March 30.

1773 ■ Brian Smith Scholarship *(Undergraduate/Scholarship)*

Purpose: To promote, encourage and sponsor promising individuals who would otherwise experience extreme hardships in pursuing a post-secondary education. **Focus:** General studies. **Qualif.:** Applicants must be graduating students from a high school in the Ottawa area planning to attend any university or college in the city of Ottawa. **Criteria:** Recipients are selected based on financial need and demonstrated participation as a community volunteer.

Funds Avail.: $2,500-$5,000. **Number Awarded:** 2. **To Apply:** Applicants must submit: a completed application form; completed expenses and income form; up-to-date resume; two letters of recommendation; copy of most recent school transcript; proof of citizenship status; copy of letter of acceptance to an accredited post-secondary school; professional quality color photo; and a 300-1,000 word essay discussing their community involvement, financial need, accomplishment and academics. **Deadline:** March 30.

1774 ■ Brain Tumor Foundation for Children

6065 Roswell Rd. NE, Ste. 505
Atlanta, GA 30328
Ph: (404)252-4107
Fax: (404)252-4108
E-mail: info@braintumorkids.org
URL: http://www.braintumorkids.org

1775 ■ Larry Dean Davis Scholarships Program *(Undergraduate/Scholarship)*

Purpose: To encourage educational pursuits among survivors of a pediatric brain or spinal cord tumor by providing financial support. **Focus:** General Studies. **Qualif.:**

Awards are arranged alphabetically below their administering organizations

Candidates must be survivors of pediatric brain or spinal cord tumor who are residents of the state of Georgia; must be entering or currently enrolled in an advanced educational program at a college, university, vocational school, or other setting; must demonstrate a need for financial assistance. **Criteria:** Recipients are chosen based on combined merit and need.

Funds Avail.: 2,500. **Number Awarded:** 2. Varies. **To Apply:** Applicants must submit completed application available on the website, along with two qualified recommendations to: Brain Tumor Foundation for Children, Inc., 6065 Roswell Road, Suite 505; Atlanta, GA 30328-4015; Applicants may call the foundation for further information or to request an application. **Deadline:** April 15. **Contact:** Brain Tumor Foundation for Children, Inc., tel: 404-252-4107.

1776 ■ Bretzlaff Foundation

1550 N Milford Rd.
Milford, MI 48381
Ph: (248)684-3408
Fax: (248)684-2648
URL: http://www.hebf.org

1777 ■ Hilda E. Bretzlaff Foundation Scholarships *(Undergraduate/Grant)*

Purpose: To provide scholarships that will be a credit to American Society. **Focus:** General studies. **Qualif.:** Applicants must have a 2.0 cumulative grade point average or better. **Criteria:** Recipients will be selected based on financial need.

Funds Avail.: No specific amount. **To Apply:** All applications are by invitation only. Interested students my contact the OPBEA office for more information.

1778 ■ British American Foundation of Texas

PO Box 421234
Houston, TX 77242
Ph: (713)587-9900
Fax: (713)784-7712
E-mail: info@baftx.org
URL: http://baftx.org

1779 ■ BAFTX Early Starters Awards *(Undergraduate/Scholarship)*

Purpose: To assist the students seeking financial resources for their education. **Focus:** General studies. **Qualif.:** Applicants must be permanent residents of Texas; enrolled in full-time education; between 11 and 14 years old and must maintain a competitive GPA and hold an excellent school attendance record. **Criteria:** Applicants are evaluated based on financial need.

Funds Avail.: $500 up to $1,000. **To Apply:** Applicants must submit the completed application form; essay between 300 and 500 words regarding a British person (past or present) whom they admire; current transcript signed by a member of their teaching staff; letter of recommendation which must come from a teacher in whose class they were enrolled within the past year, or from a guidance counselor at their school (letter must be on school letterhead paper); and a recent photograph.

1780 ■ BAFTX Graduate Awards *(Undergraduate/Scholarship)*

Purpose: To provide financial assistance to aspiring individuals from Great Britain or Texas, USA that are intent on furthering their education in their chosen field. **Focus:** General studies. **Qualif.:** Applicants must be permanent residents of Texas; enrolled in full time education; between 21 and 25 years old; must hold an undergraduate degree with a GPA of 3.5 or above for U.S. applicants and 2:1 (65+) for U.K. applicants. **Criteria:** Applicants are evaluated based on academic achievement and financial need.

Funds Avail.: No specific amount. **To Apply:** Applicants must submit completed application form; essay, not less than 1,000 words, on one of the topics from the application form found at the website of BAFTX; current transcript of academic performance signed by a member of the teaching staff; letter of recommendation from a graduate or undergraduate professor in whose class they were enrolled or from a guidance counselor at their university (letter must be on university letterhead paper); financial statement declaring their eligibility for the program; budget outline stating the sum being requested for tuition fees and other costs associated with graduate tuition; and a recent photograph.

1781 ■ BAFTX Junior Achievers Awards *(Undergraduate/Scholarship)*

Purpose: To provide a summer study program for academically adept students from low-income families in the Houston area. **Focus:** General studies. **Qualif.:** Applicants must be permanent residents of Texas; enrolled in full-time education; between 16 and 17 years old; and must maintain a competitive GPA and excellent school attendance record. **Criteria:** Applicants are evaluated based on financial need.

Funds Avail.: No specific amount. **To Apply:** Applicants must submit completed application form; an essay between 500 and 750 words regarding a British person (past or present) whom they admire; current transcript of academic performance signed by a member of the teaching staff; letter of recommendation which must come from a teacher in whose class they were enrolled within the past year or from a guidance counselor at their school (letter must be on school letterhead); and a recent photograph.

1782 ■ BAFTX Undergraduate Awards *(Undergraduate/Scholarship)*

Purpose: To alleviate the financial burden of college fees. **Focus:** General studies. **Qualif.:** Applicants must be permanent residents of Texas; enrolled in full time education; between 18 and 22 years old; and must maintain a GPA of 3.5. **Criteria:** Applicants are evaluated based on merit and financial need.

Funds Avail.: No specific amount. **To Apply:** Applicants must submit an essay, not less than 1,000 words, on one of the topics given in the application form found at the website of BAFTX; a letter of recommendation which must come from a teacher in whose class they were enrolled within the past year or from a guidance counselor at their university (letter must be on university letterhead paper); current transcript of their academic performance signed by a member of the teaching staff; financial statement declaring their eligibility for the program; budget outline stating the sum being requested for tuition fees and other costs associated with their education for one semester; and a recent photograph.

1783 ■ Broadcast Education Association

1771 N St., NW
Washington, DC 20036-2891
Ph: (202)429-3935
Free: 888-380-7222

Awards are arranged alphabetically below their administering organizations

E-mail: beamemberservices@nab.org
URL: http://www.beaweb.org

1784 ■ Harold E. Fellows Scholarships *(All/Scholarship)*

Purpose: To provide a broad range of services to academic and professional members to keep them abreast with the latest electronic media developments in radio, television, news technologies, management, sales, news reporting, production, research, communication, law, policy and international systems. **Focus:** Broadcasting. **Qualif.:** Applicants must be professors, industry professionals and students involved in teaching and research related to radio, television and electronic media; must be juniors, seniors and graduate students at BEA Member institutions. **Criteria:** Recipients are selected based on academic performance and potential as professionals.

Funds Avail.: $1,750. **Number Awarded:** 4. **To Apply:** Applicants must submit an official application form from the campus faculty; must submit transcript of records, broadcast and other experiences; written statement of goals and supportive statement from three references. **Deadline:** September 29 for application form; October 10 for supporting materials. **Contact:** beamemberservices@nab.org.

1785 ■ Walter S. Patterson Scholarships *(All/Scholarship)*

Purpose: To provide a broad range of services to academic and professional members to keep them abreast with the latest electronic media developments in radio, television, news technologies, management, sales, news reporting, production, research, communication, law, policy and international systems. **Focus:** Broadcasting. **Qualif.:** Applicants must be professors, industry professionals and students involved in teaching and research related to radio, television and electronic media; must be juniors, seniors and graduate students at BEA Member institutions. **Criteria:** Recipients are selected based on academic performance and potential as professionals.

Funds Avail.: $1,750. **Number Awarded:** 2. **To Apply:** Applicants must submit official application form from the campus faculty; must submit transcript of records, broadcast and other experiences; written statement of goals and supportive statement from three references. **Deadline:** September 29 for application form; October 10 for supporting materials. **Contact:** beamemberservices@nab.org.

1786 ■ Helen J. Sioussat/Fay Wells Scholarships *(All/Scholarship)*

Purpose: To provide a broad range of services to its academic and professional members to keep them abreast with the latest electronic media developments in radio, television, news technologies, management, sales, news reporting, production, research, communication, law, policy and international systems. **Focus:** Broadcasting. **Qualif.:** Applicants must be professors, industry professionals and students involved in teaching and research related to radio, television and electronic media; must be juniors, seniors and graduate students at BEA Member institutions. **Criteria:** Recipients are selected based on academic performance and potential as professionals.

Funds Avail.: $1,250. **Number Awarded:** 2. **To Apply:** Applicants must submit an official application form from the campus faculty; must submit transcript of records, broadcast and other experiences; written statement of goals and supportive statement from three references. **Deadline:** September 29 for application form; October 10 for supporting materials. **Contact:** beamemberservices@nab.org.

1787 ■ Alexander M. Tanger Scholarships *(All/Scholarship)*

Purpose: To provide a broad range of services to academic and professional members to keep them abreast with the latest electronic media developments in radio, television, news technologies, management, sales, news reporting, production, research, communication, law, policy and international systems. **Focus:** Broadcasting. **Qualif.:** Applicants must be professors, industry professionals and students involved in teaching and research related to radio, television and electronic media; must be juniors, seniors and graduate students at BEA Member institutions. **Criteria:** Recipients are selected based on academic performance and potential as professionals.

Funds Avail.: $5,000. **Number Awarded:** 1. **To Apply:** Applicants must submit official application form from the campus faculty; must submit transcript of records, broadcast and other experiences; written statement of goals and supportive statement from three references. **Deadline:** September 29 for application form; October 10 for supporting materials. **Contact:** beamemberservices@nab.org.

1788 ■ Two Year/Community Broadcast Education Association Scholarships Award *(All/Scholarship)*

Purpose: To provide a broad range of services to academic and professional members to keep them abreast with the latest electronic media developments in radio, television, news technologies, management, sales, news reporting, production, research, communication, law, policy and international systems. **Focus:** Broadcasting. **Qualif.:** Applicants must be professors, industry professionals and students involved in teaching and research related to radio, television and electronic media; must be juniors, seniors and graduate students at BEA Member institutions. **Criteria:** Recipients are selected based on academic performance and potential as professionals.

Funds Avail.: $1,500. **Number Awarded:** 2. **To Apply:** Applicants must submit official application form from the campus faculty; must submit transcript of records, broadcast and other experiences; written statement of goals and supportive statement from three references. **Deadline:** September 29 for application form; October 10 for supporting materials. **Contact:** beamemberservices@nab.org.

1789 ■ Abe Voron Scholarships *(All/Scholarship)*

Purpose: To provide a broad range of services to academic and professional members to keep them abreast with the latest electronic media developments in radio, television, news technologies, management, sales, news reporting, production, research, communication, law, policy and international systems. **Focus:** Broadcasting. **Qualif.:** Applicants must be professors, industry professionals and students involved in teaching and research related to radio, television and electronic media; must be juniors, seniors and graduate students at BEA Member institutions. **Criteria:** Recipients are selected based on academic performance and potential as professionals.

Funds Avail.: $5,000. **Number Awarded:** 2. **To Apply:** Applicants must submit official application form from the campus faculty; must submit transcript of records, broadcast and other experiences; written statement of goals and supportive statement from three references. **Deadline:** September 29 for application form; October 10 for supporting materials. **Contact:** beamemberservices@nab.org.

1790 ■ Vincent T. Wasilewski Scholarships *(All/ Scholarship)*

Purpose: To provide a broad range of services to academic and professional members to keep them abreast with the latest electronic media developments in radio, television, news technologies, management, sales, news reporting, production, research, communication, law, policy and international systems. **Focus:** Broadcasting. **Qualif.:** Applicants must be professors, industry professionals and students involved in teaching and research related to radio, television and electronic media; must be juniors, seniors and graduate students at BEA Member institutions. **Criteria:** Recipients are selected based on academic performance and potential as professionals.

Funds Avail.: $5,000. **Number Awarded:** 1. **To Apply:** Applicants must submit official application forms from the campus faculty; must submit transcript of records, broadcast and other experiences; written statement of goals and supportive statement from three references. **Deadline:** September 29 for application form; October 10 for supporting materials. **Contact:** beamemberservices@nab.org.

1791 ■ Bronx County Bar Association

New York State Supreme Court Bldg.
851 Grand Concourse
Bronx, NY 10451-2937
Ph: (718)293-2227
Fax: (718)681-0098
E-mail: info@bronxbar.com
URL: http://www.bronxbar.com

1792 ■ Peggy Bernheim Memorial Scholarships *(Undergraduate/Scholarship)*

Purpose: To provide financial assistance for the education of law school students who are domiciled in Bronx County. **Focus:** Law. **Qualif.:** Applicants must be first, second, or third year law students who are graduating in May or June; must be enrolled at an A.B.A. accredited school; may also be first year students who have completed one semester of study. **Criteria:** Applicants will be evaluated based on academics, financial need, writing sample, personal interview, and law school transcript.

Funds Avail.: $2,500. **To Apply:** Applicants must submit general application. **Deadline:** February 29.

1793 ■ Alexander A. DelleCese Memorial Scholarships *(Undergraduate/Scholarship)*

Purpose: To provide financial assistance for the education of law school students who are domiciled in Bronx County. **Focus:** Law. **Qualif.:** Applicants must be first, second, or third year law students who are graduating in May or June; must be enrolled at an A.B.A. accredited school; may also be first year students who have completed one semester of study. **Criteria:** Applicants will be evaluated based on academics, financial need, writing sample, personal interview, and law school transcript.

Funds Avail.: $2,500. **To Apply:** Applicants must submit general application. **Deadline:** February 29.

1794 ■ Craig Lensch Memorial Scholarships *(Undergraduate/Scholarship)*

Purpose: To provide financial assistance for the education of law school students who are domiciled in Bronx County. **Focus:** Law. **Qualif.:** Applicants must be first, second, or third year law students who are graduating in May or June; must be enrolled at an A.B.A. accredited school; may also be first year students who have completed one semester of study. **Criteria:** Applicants will be evaluated based on academics, financial need, writing sample, personal interview, and law school transcript.

Funds Avail.: $2,500. **To Apply:** Applicants must submit general application. **Deadline:** February 29.

1795 ■ Brown Foundation

1515 SE Monroe St.
Topeka, KS 66612
Ph: (785)235-3939
E-mail: brownfound@juno.com
URL: http://brownvboard.org

1796 ■ Brown Foundation Academic Scholarships *(Undergraduate/Scholarship)*

Purpose: To assist qualified minority students to pursue a career in education by providing financial support. **Focus:** Education. **Qualif.:** Applicants must be minority students entering their junior year of college; must be admitted to a teacher education program; must be enrolled at an institution of higher education with an accredited program in teacher education for at least half-time as defined by the higher education institution of attendance; must have minimum 3.0 grade point average on a 4.0 scale. **Criteria:** Applicants are evaluated based on academic achievement and financial need.

Funds Avail.: $1,000. **To Apply:** Applicants must submit all the required application information.

1797 ■ Ron Brown Scholar Program

1160 Pepsi Place Ste. 206
Charlottesville, VA 22901
Ph: (434)964-1588
Fax: (434)964-1589
URL: http://www.ronbrown.org

1798 ■ Ron Brown Scholars Program *(High School/Scholarship)*

Purpose: To identify African-American high school seniors who will make significant contributions to society; to provide financial support to those who are in need. **Focus:** General Studies. **Qualif.:** Applicants must be senior high school students; must excel academically; exhibit exceptional leadership potential; participate in community service activities and demonstrate financial need; must be US a citizen or hold a permanent resident visa card. **Criteria:** Preference will be given to those who meet the criteria.

Funds Avail.: $10,000 annually. **To Apply:** Applicants must mail the application materials in one packet. Transcripts and letters of recommendation should not be sent under separate cover; incomplete, e-mailed or faxed applications will not be considered. **Deadline:** November 1. **Contact:** CAP Charitable Foundation at the above address (see entry 1797).

1799 ■ Susan Thompson Buffett Foundation

222 Kiewit Plz.
Omaha, NE 68131
Ph: (402)943-1300

Awards are arranged alphabetically below their administering organizations

URL: http://www.buffettscholarships.org

1800 ■ Susan Thompson Buffett Foundation Scholarships *(Undergraduate/Scholarship)*

Purpose: To provide financial assistance to qualified individuals. **Focus:** General studies. **Qualif.:** Applicants must be residents of the State of Nebraska; must be graduating high school seniors or undergraduate students who have not already earned a bachelor's degree; must be attending or applying to a Nebraska state public school; must be in need of financial assistance; must have maintained at least a 2.5 GPA throughout high school; must have applied for federal financial aid and have already received back the Student Aid Report that contains their Expected Family Contribution. **Criteria:** Recipients will be selected based on financial need.

Funds Avail.: $3,200 plus a textbook allowance of $400. **To Apply:** Applicants must complete the application form available online; must submit a high school or college transcript; two letters of reference from teachers, employers or clergy members; must have a copy of the Information Summary of their financial aid; must provide one-page handwritten background and personal information. **Deadline:** March 1.

1801 ■ Building Owners and Managers Association of Greater New York

11 Penn Plz., 22nd Fl., Ste. 2201
New York, NY 10001
Ph: (212)239-3662
Fax: (212)268-7441
E-mail: mary@bomany.com
URL: http://www.bomany.org

1802 ■ BOMA/NY Scholarships *(Undergraduate/Scholarship)*

Purpose: To financially assist students to further their professional education. **Focus:** General studies. **Qualif.:** Applicants must be currently enrolled RPA, FMA, SMA, or SMT students, taking home study, classroom study or accelerated courses; must be employed by a BOMA/NY member firm and working within the 5 Boroughs of New York. **Criteria:** Applicants are evaluated on the basis of merit and demonstrated financial need.

Funds Avail.: No specific amount. **To Apply:** Applicants must submit completed application form along with a one page essay and letter of recommendation from current employer. **Deadline:** June 22.

1803 ■ Bulletin of the Atomic Scientists

77 W Washington St., Ste. 2120
Chicago, IL 60602
Ph: (312)364-9715
Fax: (312)364-9715
E-mail: kbenedict@thebulletin.org
URL: http://www.thebulletin.org/index.htm

1804 ■ Rieser Fellowships *(Undergraduate/Fellowship)*

Purpose: To provide financial support to undergraduate students pursuing a project relating to interaction of science, global security, and public policy. **Focus:** Peace studies; National security. **Qualif.:** Applicant must be undergraduate student at a U.S. college/university. **Criteria:** Awards are given based on academic interests, extracurricular activities and career aspiration.

Funds Avail.: $2500 $5000. **Number Awarded:** 3-5. **To Apply:** Applicant must send an application form (available at the website); resume; proposal (800-1000 words); official letters confirming internships, acceptance to conference; an essay (one-page, single-spaced) explaining how the fellowship would be benefit to the applicant; project budget; and two letters of recommendation. **Deadline:** December. **Contact:** Rieser Fellowship rieser@thebulletin.org.

1805 ■ Business and Professional Women's Foundation

1900 M St. NW, Ste. 310
Washington, DC 20036
Ph: (202)293-1100
Fax: (202)861-0298
E-mail: foundation@bpwfoundation.org
URL: http://www.bpwusa.org

1806 ■ Career Advancement Scholarships *(Undergraduate/Scholarship)*

Purpose: To provide financial assistance to disadvantaged women seeking to further their education. **Focus:** General studies. **Qualif.:** Applicant must be a female at least 25 years of age; must be a U.S citizen or U.S national; must demonstrate critical financial need; must have an expected family contribution (EFC) of $2,500 or less; must be officially accepted into an accredited U.S college or university, including those in American Samoa, Puerto Rico, and the Virgin Islands; must demonstrate clear career plans; must not be earning a doctoral-level or terminal degree. **Criteria:** Applications will be reviewed by the scholarship committee.

Funds Avail.: No specific amount. **To Apply:** Scholarship application and other supporting documents must be sent to BPW foundation. **Deadline:** April 15.

Remarks: The Business and Professional Women's Foundation established the Career Advancement Scholarship Program in 1969 to provide scholarships, grants and loans to women seeking to improve their lives.

1807 ■ Business Professionals of America

5454 Cleveland Ave.
Columbus, OH 43231-4021
Ph: (614)895-7277
Fax: (614)895-1165
Free: 800-334-2007
URL: http://www.bpanet.org

1808 ■ National Honor Roll Scholarships *(Undergraduate/Scholarship)*

Purpose: To assist outstanding seniors of Business Professionals of America in the Secondary Division. **Focus:** Business. **Qualif.:** Applicants must be members of Business Professionals of America who are graduating high school seniors with minimum grade point average of 3.0. **Criteria:** Applicants are evaluated based on academic success and involvement within the organization.

Funds Avail.: $2,000. **To Apply:** Applicants must submit completed application form along with the school grade transcript or letter form school principal verifying GPA; one page, typed resume of activities involving both Business

Awards are arranged alphabetically below their administering organizations

Professionals of America and other school and community activities; three signed recommendation letters on official letterhead from local advisor and two individuals of their choice; one page, double spaced, typed essay on topic "Where I see myself professionally in ten years." **Deadline:** April 15.

1809 ■ Calhoun Community College

PO Box 2216
Decatur, AL 35609
Ph: (256)306-2500
Free: 800-626-3628
URL: http://www.calhoun.edu

1810 ■ Calhoun Scholarships *(Undergraduate/Scholarship)*

Purpose: To provide educational assistance for Calhoun students. **Focus:** General studies. **Qualif.:** Applicants must be enrolled at the Calhoun College. **Criteria:** Selection is based on the application materials.

Funds Avail.: $1,500 for full-tuition. **To Apply:** Applicants must complete a FAFSA (Free Application for Federal Student Aid) by March 1 in order to be considered. Applicants must also complete the online scholarship application and submit along with other required materials and information. **Deadline:** March 1. **Contact:** Student Financial Services, 256-306-2624.

1811 ■ California Association of Pest Control Advisers

1143 Market Blvd., Ste. 7
Sacramento, CA 95834
Ph: (916)928-1625
Fax: (916)928-0705
URL: http://www.capca.com

1812 ■ Stanley W. Strew Educational Fund Scholarship *(Undergraduate/Scholarship)*

Purpose: To support and promote agricultural pest control advisers or professional production consultants who serve California agricultural and horticultural producers. **Focus:** Agricultural economics. **Qualif.:** Applicants must be currently attending, entering or returning to college in agricultural or horticultural fields; must plan to pursue a career in pest management; must have a 2.5 GPA or better. **Criteria:** Recipients are selected based on financial need.

Funds Avail.: $3,000; $2,000. **Number Awarded:** 2. **To Apply:** Applicants must submit a completed application form; must include a current official transcript of records; must submit at least two letters of recommendation. **Deadline:** May 15. **Contact:** 916-928-1625.

1813 ■ California Association of Private Postsecondary Schools

400 Capitol Mall, Ste. 1560
Sacramento, CA 95814
Ph: (916)447-5500
Fax: (916)440-8970
Free: 888-92-CAPPS
E-mail: info@cappsonline.org
URL: http://www.cappsonline.org

1814 ■ California Association of Private Postsecondary Schools Scholarships *(Undergraduate/Scholarship)*

Purpose: To ensure that the needs of the entire sector, from small registered schools to large institutions are met from an educational, policy and business perspective. **Focus:** Cosmetology. **Qualif.:** Applicants must be enrolled in a cosmetology, massage, aesthetics, or allied health program at a CAPP's member School; must be U.S. citizens and residents of California; and must have a high school diploma. **Criteria:** Recipients are selected based on academic performance.

Funds Avail.: $5,000. **Number Awarded:** 4. **To Apply:** Applicants must submit one to two-page essay along with the completed application form, transcript and three letters of recommendation. **Deadline:** June 1. **Contact:** info@cappsonline.com.

1815 ■ California Bar Association

180 Howard St.
San Francisco, CA 94105-1939
Ph: (415)856-0780
Fax: (415)856-0788
URL: http://www.calbarfoundation.org

1816 ■ Public Interest Scholarships *(Undergraduate/Scholarship)*

Purpose: To help offset high cost of law school education. **Focus:** Law. **Qualif.:** Candidates must be enrolled in a California law school or must have completed at least one year of study at a California law school (the candidates' law school must certify good ethical standing of the candidate while attending law school and must also attest to the candidate's financial need); must maintain at least a 2.5 or equivalent on a 4.0 scale (or provide an explanation of extenuating circumstances if GPA is lower than 2.5). **Criteria:** Selection will be based on the committee's criteria.

Funds Avail.: No specific amount. **To Apply:** Applicants must accomplish complete application package which includes: application; certification and authorization form (which includes certification of non-relationship, authorization t use information, name and likeness and consent and authorization to obtain information); resume; personal statement describing the candidate's commitment to and plans for a legal career in public service (not to exceed 400 words); three letters of recommendation; law school transcript; certification of financial need; certification of ethical standing and statement of nomination; and optional statement of financial circumstances. Candidate's name must appear in the upper right-hand corner of each page of every document submitted. **Deadline:** March 19. **Contact:** California Bar Foundation at the above address (see entry 1815).

1817 ■ Rosenthal Bar Exam Scholarships *(Undergraduate/Scholarship)*

Purpose: To provide financial support for outstanding graduating California law students who are embarking on careers in public service law. **Focus:** Law. **Qualif.:** Candidates must be graduating or have graduated from a California law school; must be taking the California Bar Exam for the first time; and must maintain at least a 2.5 GPA or equivalent on a 4.0 scale (or provide an explanation of extenuating circumstances if GPA is lower than 2.5). **Criteria:** Selection will be based on the committee's criteria.

Funds Avail.: $1,000. **To Apply:** Candidates must be nominated by their law school. **Deadline:** February 14. **Contact:** CBF at the above address (see entry 1815).

1818 ■ California Grocers Association

1415 L St., Ste. 450
Sacramento, CA 95814-3910

Ph: (916)448-3545
Fax: (916)448-2793
URL: http://www.cagrocers.com

1819 ■ Lou Amen Legacy Scholarship *(Undergraduate/Scholarship)*

Purpose: To provide proactive leadership, education, advocacy and information. **Focus:** General studies. **Qualif.:** Applicants must be full-time college students at an accredited, non-profit college or university in the United States. **Criteria:** Recipients are selected based on academic merit, evidence of outstanding character and leadership potential.

Funds Avail.: $1,000. **To Apply:** Applicants must submit a completed application form.

1820 ■ Don C. Beaver Memorial Scholarship *(Undergraduate/Scholarship)*

Purpose: To provide proactive leadership, education, advocacy and information. **Focus:** General studies. **Qualif.:** Applicants must be full-time college students at an accredited, non-profit college or university in the United States. **Criteria:** Recipients are selected based on academic merit, evidence of outstanding character and leadership potential.

Funds Avail.: $2,000. **To Apply:** Applicants must submit a completed application form.

1821 ■ Jack H. Brown Scholarship *(Undergraduate/Scholarship)*

Purpose: To provide proactive leadership, education, advocacy and information. **Focus:** General studies. **Qualif.:** Applicants must be full-time college students at an accredited, non-profit college or university in the United States. **Criteria:** Recipients are selected based on academic merit, evidence of outstanding character and leadership potential.

Funds Avail.: $1,000. **To Apply:** Applicants must submit a completed application form.

1822 ■ California Shopping Cart Retrieval Corporation Inc. Scholarships *(Undergraduate/Scholarship)*

Purpose: To provide proactive leadership, education, advocacy and information. **Focus:** General studies. **Qualif.:** Applicants must be full-time college students at an accredited, non-profit college or university in the United States. **Criteria:** Recipients are selected based on academic merit, evidence of outstanding character and leadership potential.

Funds Avail.: $2,500. **Number Awarded:** 1. **To Apply:** Applicants must submit a completed application form.

1823 ■ Classic Wines of California Scholarships *(Undergraduate/Scholarship)*

Purpose: To provide proactive leadership, education, advocacy and information. **Focus:** General studies. **Qualif.:** Applicants must be full-time college students at an accredited, non-profit college or university in the United States. **Criteria:** Recipients are selected based on academic merit, evidence of outstanding character and leadership potential.

Funds Avail.: $2,000. **Number Awarded:** 2. **To Apply:** Applicants must submit a completed application form.

1824 ■ Joey and Florence Franco Legacy Scholarship *(Undergraduate/Scholarship)*

Purpose: To provide proactive leadership, education, advocacy and information. **Focus:** General studies. **Qualif.:** Applicants must be full-time college students at an accredited, non-profit college or university in the United States. **Criteria:** Recipients are selected based on academic merit, evidence of outstanding character and leadership potential.

Funds Avail.: $1,000. **To Apply:** Applicants must submit a completed application form.

1825 ■ Hall of Achievement Scholarships *(Undergraduate/Scholarship)*

Purpose: To provide proactive leadership, education, advocacy and information. **Focus:** General studies. **Qualif.:** Applicants must be full-time college students at an accredited, non-profit college or university in the United States. **Criteria:** Recipients are selected based on academic merit, evidence of outstanding character and leadership potential.

Funds Avail.: $2,000. **To Apply:** Applicants must submit a completed application form.

1826 ■ Roger K. Hughes Legacy Scholarship *(Undergraduate/Scholarship)*

Purpose: To provide proactive leadership, education, advocacy and information. **Focus:** General studies. **Qualif.:** Applicants must be full-time college students at an accredited, non-profit college or university in the United States. **Criteria:** Recipients are selected based on academic merit, evidence of outstanding character and leadership potential.

Funds Avail.: $1,000. **To Apply:** Applicants must submit a completed application form.

1827 ■ Paul A. Hughes Memorial Scholarship *(Undergraduate/Scholarship)*

Purpose: To provide proactive leadership, education, advocacy and information. **Focus:** General studies. **Qualif.:** Applicants must be full-time college students at an accredited, non-profit college or university in the United States. **Criteria:** Recipients are selected based on academic merit, evidence of outstanding character and leadership potential.

Funds Avail.: $1,000. **Number Awarded:** 1. **To Apply:** Applicants must submit a completed application form.

1828 ■ Illuminator Educational Foundation Scholarships *(Undergraduate/Scholarship)*

Purpose: To provide proactive leadership, education, advocacy and information. **Focus:** General studies. **Qualif.:** Applicants must be full-time college students at an accredited, non-profit college or university in the United States. **Criteria:** Recipients are selected based on academic merit, evidence of outstanding character and leadership potential.

Funds Avail.: $1,000. **Number Awarded:** 10. **To Apply:** Applicants must submit a completed application form.

1829 ■ Don Kaplan Legacy Scholarship *(Undergraduate/Scholarship)*

Purpose: To provide proactive leadership, education, advocacy and information. **Focus:** General studies. **Qualif.:** Applicants must be full-time college students at an accredited, non-profit college or university in the United States. **Criteria:** Recipients are selected based on academic merit, evidence of outstanding character and leadership potential.

Funds Avail.: $1,000. **To Apply:** Applicants must submit a completed application form.

1830 ■ Peter and Jody Larkin Legacy Scholarship *(Undergraduate/Scholarship)*

Purpose: To provide proactive leadership, education, advocacy and information. **Focus:** General studies. **Qualif.:** Applicants must be full-time college students at an accredited, non-profit college or university in the United States. **Criteria:** Recipients are selected based on academic merit, evidence of outstanding character and leadership potential.

Funds Avail.: $1,000. **To Apply:** Applicants must submit a completed application form.

1831 ■ Bill MacAloney Legacy Scholarship *(Undergraduate/Scholarship)*

Purpose: To provide proactive leadership, education, advocacy and information. **Focus:** General studies. **Qualif.:** Applicants must be full-time college students at an accredited, non-profit college or university in the United States. **Criteria:** Recipients are selected based on academic merit, evidence of outstanding character and leadership potential.

Funds Avail.: $1,000. **To Apply:** Applicants must submit a completed application form.

1832 ■ Al Plamann Legacy Scholarship *(Undergraduate/Scholarship)*

Purpose: To provide proactive leadership, education, advocacy and information. **Focus:** General studies. **Qualif.:** Applicants must be full-time college students at an accredited, non-profit college or university in the United States. **Criteria:** Recipients are selected based on academic merit, evidence of outstanding character and leadership potential.

Funds Avail.: $1,000. **To Apply:** Applicants must submit a completed application form.

1833 ■ Save Mart Legacy Scholarships *(Undergraduate/Scholarship)*

Purpose: To provide proactive leadership, education, advocacy and information. **Focus:** General studies. **Qualif.:** Applicants must be full-time college students at an accredited, non-profit college or university in the United States. **Criteria:** Recipients are selected based on academic merit, evidence of outstanding character and leadership potential.

Funds Avail.: $1,000. **To Apply:** Applicants must submit a completed application form.

1834 ■ Trelut Family Legacy Scholarships *(Undergraduate/Scholarship)*

Purpose: To provide proactive leadership, education, advocacy and information. **Focus:** General studies. **Qualif.:** Applicants must be full-time college students at an accredited, non-profit college or university in the United States. **Criteria:** Recipients are selected based on academic merit, evidence of outstanding character and leadership potential.

Funds Avail.: $1,000. **To Apply:** Applicants must submit a completed application form.

1835 ■ Bob Wilson Legacy Scholarship *(Undergraduate/Scholarship)*

Purpose: To provide proactive leadership, education, advocacy and information. **Focus:** General studies. **Qualif.:** Applicants must be full-time college students at an accredited, non-profit college or university in the United States. **Criteria:** Recipients are selected based on academic merit, evidence of outstanding character and leadership potential.

Funds Avail.: $1,000. **To Apply:** Applicants must submit a completed application form.

1836 ■ California Groundwater Association

PO Box 14369
Santa Rosa, CA 95402-6369
Ph: (707)578-4408
Fax: (707)546-4906
E-mail: wellguy@groundh2o.org
URL: http://www.groundh2o.org

1837 ■ California Groundwater Association Scholarships *(Undergraduate/Scholarship)*

Purpose: To provide financial assistance to those students who are in need. **Focus:** General Studies. **Qualif.:** Applicants must be California residents; must demonstrate an interest in some facet of groundwater technology. **Criteria:** Preference will be given to those who meet the criteria.

Funds Avail.: $1,000. **To Apply:** Applicants must obtain a CGA sponsor and provide a 500 word essay about their interest in the groundwater field or their chosen field of study. Applicants must check the available website for the additional requirements. **Contact:** Please call at 707-578-4408 for details.

1838 ■ California Landscape Contractors Association

1491 River Park Dr., Ste. 100
Sacramento, CA 95815
Ph: (916)830-2780
Fax: (916)830-2788
E-mail: web_admin@clca.org
URL: http://www.clca.org

1839 ■ California Landscape Contractors Association Scholarships *(Undergraduate/Scholarship)*

Purpose: To serve and protect the interest of members, promote professionalism and advance public awareness of the landscape industry. **Focus:** Landscape architecture and design. **Qualif.:** Applicants must be students attending an accredited California community college or state university, majoring in ornamental horticulture and taking a minimum of six units. **Criteria:** Recipients are selected based on academic performance and financial need.

Funds Avail.: No specific amount. **To Apply:** Applicants must submit typed, printed and completed application form, personal reference letters and resume. **Deadline:** April 1.

1840 ■ California Library Association

717 20th St., Ste. 200
Sacramento, CA 95811
Ph: (916)447-8541

Awards are arranged alphabetically below their administering organizations

Fax: (916)447-8394
E-mail: info@cla-net.org
URL: http://www.cla-net.org

1841 ■ Emerging Leaders Scholarships
(Undergraduate/Scholarship)

Purpose: To enable more than 100 new librarians to get on the fast track to ALA and professional leadership. **Focus:** General studies. **Qualif.:** Applicant must be under 35 years of age or be a new librarian of any age with fewer than five years post-MLS experience; must have recent MLS degree from an ALA or NCATE accredited or be in an MLS program; must attend both ALA conferences and work virtually in between each; must be prepared to commit to serve on an ALA, divisions, chapter, or round table committee, taskforce or workgroup upon completion of the program; must be an ALA member or join upon selection if not already a member. **Criteria:** Recipients are selected based on demonstrated interest to be an ALA member and academic performance.

Funds Avail.: $1,500. **To Apply:** Applicants must submit a completed application form. **Deadline:** June 20.

1842 ■ California Police Youth Charities
3800 Watt Ave., Ste. 125
Sacramento, CA 95821
Ph: (916)482-4245
Fax: (916)482-4246
E-mail: cbuzzeaton@sbcglobal.net
URL: http://www.calpyc.com

1843 ■ Herbie Morici Memorial Scholarships
(Undergraduate/Scholarship)

Purpose: To provide spirit lifting opportunities to critically ill children with the purpose of enhancing their quality of life while allowing them to experience something unique and important also to their families. **Focus:** General studies. **Qualif.:** Applicants must be high school seniors in each California's 58 counties. **Criteria:** Recipients are selected based on test scores in the least amount of time.

Funds Avail.: $500. **To Apply:** Applicants must submit a completed application form.

1844 ■ Youth Leadership Scholarships
(Undergraduate/Scholarship)

Purpose: To recognize twelfth grade students who have engaged in meaningful leadership and citizenship volunteer activities during the past year. **Focus:** General studies. **Qualif.:** Applicants must be high school seniors who wish to pursue their studies in college; must be residents of California, sons, daughters or wards of an active or retired California Peace Officer. **Criteria:** Recipients are selected based on the content, grammar, format creativity and structure of essay, demonstrated importance of good citizenship in their essay, demonstrated leadership, volunteerism, student's work in school and community and number of hours the students volunteered.

Funds Avail.: $1,000. **Number Awarded:** 20. **To Apply:** Applicants must submit a completed application form and essay. **Deadline:** May 1. **Contact:** cbuzzeaton@msn.com.

1845 ■ California School Library Association
1300 Baker St.
Bakersfield, CA 93305
Ph: (661)631-4808
E-mail: yoons@bcsd.com
URL: http://www.csla.net

1846 ■ Above and Beyond Scholarships
(Graduate/Scholarship)

Purpose: To encourage practicing Teacher Librarians to pursue either a Master's or Doctorate degree in librarianship or in a related field. **Focus:** Library and archival sciences. **Qualif.:** Applicants must be a professional member of the California School Library Association; must be a resident of California with plans to continue working in the school library profession in California upon completion of the graduate program. **Criteria:** Selection of applicants will be judged based on the criteria of the scholarship selection committee.

Funds Avail.: $1,000. **To Apply:** Application forms are available online. Applicants must present college transcripts and proof of enrollment in a master's or doctoral program, or proof of pursuing National Board Certification; must submit 500 words describing their professional goals; must provide three letters of recommendation. Application form and requirements must be sent to Above and Beyond Scholarship Committee, California School Library Association, 1001 26th St., Sacramento, CA 95816. **Deadline:** April 30.

1847 ■ John Blanchard Memorial Scholarships
(Graduate/Scholarship)

Purpose: To assist a school library paraprofessional in obtaining the preparation needed to qualify and serve as a school library media teacher. **Focus:** Library and archival sciences. **Qualif.:** Applicants must be working or have worked within the last three years in a classified position in the library media field either in a school or at a district or county office; must be enrolled in a college or university working towards a BA, BS, or advanced degree in preparation to become a school library media teacher; must be a resident of California; must be a member of the California School Library Association. **Criteria:** Selection of applicants will be based on the criteria of the Scholarship committee.

Funds Avail.: $1,000. **To Apply:** Applicants must provide three letters of recommendation. Application forms are available online and must be sent to John Blanchard Memorial Scholarship, California School Library Association, 1001 26th St., Sacramento, CA 95816. **Deadline:** April 30. **Remarks:** Mook and Blanchard, in collaboration with CSLA, have established the John Blanchard, Jr. Memorial Scholarships.

1848 ■ Jewels Gardiner Scholarships
(Undergraduate/Scholarship)

Purpose: To assist Northern California students. **Focus:** Library and archival sciences. **Qualif.:** Applicants must be enrolled in a Library Media Teacher Credential program. **Criteria:** Preference will be given to first-time recipients, current CSLA/NS members, and to applicants with teaching experience.

Funds Avail.: $1,000. **Number Awarded:** 2. **To Apply:** Application forms are available online. Applicants must submit a letter of recommendation. Application form and requirements must be sent to Chair, Jewel Gardiner Memorial Fund, California School Library Association, 1001 26th St., Sacramento, CA 95816. **Deadline:** August 1 and November 1.

Awards are arranged alphabetically below their administering organizations

1849 ■ Library Media Teacher Scholarships *(Graduate/Scholarship)*

Purpose: To assist individuals seeking preparation leading toward a degree or certification which will qualify the individual to work as a professional in the library media field in a school setting. **Focus:** Library and archival sciences. **Qualif.:** Applicants must be enrolled in a professional school library media teacher credentialing program or a master's degree program; must be a resident of the area served by the CSLA Southern Section; must be a member of the California School Library Association. **Criteria:** Selection of applicants will be based on the criteria of the selection committee.

Funds Avail.: $1,000. **To Apply:** Applicants must provide three letters of recommendation: (a) must be from a CSLA member; (b) must be from a professor in the library media teacher; (c) must be from a former or current supervisor or a fellow teacher. Application form and requirements must be sent to Pam Oehlman, Southern Section President-Elect, 2033 Volk Ave., Long Beach, CA 90815. **Deadline:** February 15.

1850 ■ School Library Paraprofessional Scholarships *(Graduate/Scholarship)*

Purpose: To assist school library paraprofessionals in completing a school library technician/paraprofessional certificate program. **Focus:** Library and archival sciences. **Qualif.:** Applicants must be working in a classified position in the library media field, either in a school, district, or County Office of Education; must be enrolled in a two-year paraprofessional program with the goal of becoming a qualified library technician or in a teacher credential program with the ultimate goal of pursuing a Library Media Teacher Services Credential; must be a resident of the area served by the CSLA Southern Section; must be a member of the California School Library Association. **Criteria:** Selection of applicants will be based on the criteria of the selection committee.

Funds Avail.: $500. **To Apply:** Application forms are available online. Applicants must provide three letters of recommendation: (a) must be from a professor of the school in which the applicant is enrolled; (b) must be from a CSLA Southern Section member; (c) must be from a former or current supervisor. Application form and requirements must be sent to Pam Oehlman, Southern Section President-Elect, 2033 Volk Ave., Long Beach, CA 90815. **Deadline:** February 15.

1851 ■ California Scottish Rite Foundation

855 Elm Ave.
Long Beach, CA 90813
URL: http://www.scottishritecalifornia.org

1852 ■ California Scottish Rite Foundation Scholarships *(Undergraduate/Scholarship)*

Purpose: To provide financial assistance to young men and women who want to pursue their education at university and graduate level. **Focus:** General studies. **Qualif.:** Applicants must be undergraduate students who are residents of California state with ages ranging from 17 to 25 years old; must have a grade point average of 3.0 or better. **Criteria:** Applicants are evaluated based on demonstrated high ideals and ability; high grades in school; financial need and part-time employment.

Funds Avail.: $1,500. **To Apply:** Applicants must submit completed application form along with certified transcript of grades for previous semester; typed letter with handwritten signature by student of their employment, planned courses in the coming quarter/semester and current mailing address. **Deadline:** March 14.

1853 ■ California Society of Radiologic Technologists

PO Box 14502
Torrance, CA 90503
Ph: (310)782-0927
Fax: (310)787-0478
URL: http://www.csrt.org

1854 ■ Anna Ames Clinical Excellence Student Grants *(Undergraduate/Grant)*

Purpose: To provide financial assistance to radiologic science students enrolled in JRCERT-approved California schools. **Focus:** Radiology. **Qualif.:** Applicants must be CSRT members or apply for membership at the time of application; must be enrolled full-time in California Department of Health Services approved and Joint Review Committee for Education in Radiologic Technology (JRCERT) accredited education program of Radiologic Sciences; must be enrolled in the program for at least 6 months at the time of receipt of the award; and, must possess exceptional skills in the clinical environment. **Criteria:** Applicants are evaluated based on academic merit.

Funds Avail.: $500. **To Apply:** Applicants must submit the completed application form and all other required materials for the Grant. **Deadline:** September 30.

1855 ■ Ruth McMillan Student Grants *(Undergraduate/Grant)*

Purpose: To provide financial assistance to radiologic science students enrolled in approved California schools. **Focus:** Radiology. **Qualif.:** Applicants must be CSRT members enrolled full-time in a California Department of Health Services approved and CSRT-recognized education program of Radiologic Sciences (at least 6 months enrolled in the program at the time of receipt of the award); must possess a minimum grade point average of 2.5 in all college courses. **Criteria:** Applicants are evaluated based on academic merit.

Funds Avail.: $500. **To Apply:** Applicants must submit completed application form obtained from the CSRT office and other required materials for the Grant. **Deadline:** September 30.

1856 ■ Superior District Legislative Mentoring Student Grants *(Undergraduate/Grant)*

Purpose: To provide an opportunity to radiologic science students enrolled in approved California schools, through financial assistance, in order for them to participate in the legislative process. **Focus:** Radiology. **Qualif.:** Applicants must be CSRT members enrolled full-time in a California Department of Health Services-approved and CSRT-recognized education program of Radiologic Sciences for at least 6 months at the time of receipt of the award; and, must possess exceptional interest in leadership and the legislative process. **Criteria:** Applicants are evaluated based on personal merit and attributes.

Funds Avail.: $250. **Number Awarded:** 4. **To Apply:** Applicants must submit the completed application form obtained from the CSRT office and the all other required

Awards are arranged alphabetically below their administering organizations

application information materials. **Deadline:** May 15.

1857 ■ Superior District Legislative Mentoring Student Grants RT to DC *(Undergraduate/Grant)*

Purpose: To provide an opportunity to radiologic science students enrolled in approved California schools, through financial assistance, in order for them to participate in the legislative process. **Focus:** Radiology. **Qualif.:** Applicants must be CSRT members enrolled full-time in a California Department of Health Services approved and CSRT-recognized education program of Radiologic Sciences for at least 6 months at the time of receipt of the award; must possess exceptional interest in leadership and the legislative process. **Criteria:** Recipients are selected based on academic merit and financial need.

Funds Avail.: $1,300. **Number Awarded:** 2. **To Apply:** Applicants must submit the completed application form obtained from the CSRT office and the other required materials for the award. **Deadline:** February 1.

1858 ■ California State University San Macros Alumni Association

Cal State San Macros
333 S Twin Oaks Valley Rd.
San Marcos, CA 92096
Ph: (760)750-4405
E-mail: alumni@csusm.edu
URL: http://www.csusmalumni.org

1859 ■ Cal State San Macros Alumna Scholarships *(Undergraduate/Scholarship)*

Purpose: To support fellow and future alumni in furthering their education. **Focus:** General studies. **Qualif.:** Applicant must be admitted to a degree or certificate program and enrolled in at least six units. **Criteria:** Selection is based on academic merit, commitment to the community, leadership potential, and diverse interest.

Funds Avail.: $500. **Number Awarded:** 1. **To Apply:** Applicant must submit an application to the Financial Aid and Scholarship Office. **Contact:** Financial Aid and Scholarship Office, 760-750-4850.

1860 ■ Cost-of-Books Relief Scholarships *(Undergraduate/Scholarship)*

Purpose: To support fellow and future alumni in furthering their education. **Focus:** General studies. **Qualif.:** Applicant must be a student with financial need, enrolled in at least 6 units and have a GPA of 3.0. **Criteria:** Selection is based on creativity and writing ability.

Funds Avail.: $500. **Number Awarded:** 1. **To Apply:** Applicant must submit an application and a 250-500 word essay to the Financial Aid and Scholarship Office. **Contact:** Financial Aid and Scholarship Office, 760-750-4850.

1861 ■ California Waterfowl Association

4630 Northgate Blvd., Ste. 150
Sacramento, CA 95834
Ph: (916)648-1406
Fax: (916)648-1665
E-mail: cwa@calwaterfowl.org
URL: http://www.calwaterfowl.org

1862 ■ Dennis Raveling Scholarships *(Undergraduate/Scholarship)*

Purpose: To provide field experience a training in the tools, methods, concepts of waterfowl, wetlands research and management. **Focus:** Wildlife conservation, management and sciences; Zoology; Botany; Ecology. **Qualif.:** Applicants must be students with a desire to pursue a career in waterfowl or wetlands ecology. **Criteria:** Recipients are selected based on candidates resolve, high academic achievement and project merit.

Funds Avail.: $2,000 for first place; $1,000 for 2nd place. **Number Awarded:** 2. **To Apply:** Applicants must submit a "one-page" proposal summary description on an original research or management project; must submit a detailed proposal if required or "one-page" statement explaining the course of study for which they need to support. **Deadline:** October 31. **Contact:** Nocole Berset at the above address (see entry 1861).

1863 ■ Calista Corporation

301 Calista Ct., Ste. A
Anchorage, AK 99518-3028
Ph: (907)279-5516
Fax: (907)272-5060
E-mail: calista@calistacorp.com
URL: http://www.calistacorp.com

1864 ■ Calista Scholarships *(Undergraduate/Scholarship)*

Purpose: To provide financial assistance to Alaska Natives to enable them to participate in continuing educational activities, formal programs of study and programs to improve their status. **Focus:** General studies. **Qualif.:** Applicant must be accepted to an accredited school and enrolling on a full-time basis; must be a high school graduate or have earned a GED and be in good academic standing with an at least 2.0 GPA; must be employees of Calista Corporation or their descendants. **Criteria:** Recipient will be selected based on the scholarship application requirements.

Funds Avail.: $500-$1,000. **To Apply:** Applicant must complete the application form available online; must have the official transcript of record; must have a copy of birth certificate or Certificate of Indian Blood; must have a letter of acceptance from their college, university or vocational school; must provide an essay (up to 500 words) describing their educational and career goals, their reasons for attending school and what they hope to accomplish in the future using the knowledge gained from their educational experience. Application form and other supporting documents must be sent to Calista Scholarship Fund, 301 Calista Ct., Ste. A, Anchorage, AK 99518-3028. **Deadline:** June 30.

1865 ■ Calvin Alumni Association

3201 Burton St. SE
Grand Rapids, MI 49546
Ph: (616)526-6000
Fax: (616)526-8551
Free: 800-688-0122
E-mail: alumni@calvin.edu
URL: http://www.calvin.edu

1866 ■ Calvin Alumni Association Arizona Central Chapter Scholarships *(Undergraduate/Scholarship)*

Purpose: To build community among Calvin College alumni and friends; to provide opportunities for service and aspiring alumni to answer God's call in life and vocation. **Focus:** General studies. **Qualif.:** Applicants must be high school seniors who have applied to Calvin and live in central Arizona. **Criteria:** Recipients are selected based on academic performance and financial need.

Funds Avail.: $1,000. **To Apply:** Applicants must answer all questions on the application; must submit a transcript that shows the two most recent years of education; must attach a written references. **Deadline:** March 1. **Contact:** 480-785-9852.

1867 ■ Calvin Alumni Association-Black Alumni Chapter Scholarships *(Undergraduate/Scholarship)*

Purpose: To build community among Calvin College alumni and friends; to provide opportunities for service and aspiring alumni to answer God's call in life and vocation. **Focus:** General studies. **Qualif.:** Applicants must be current Calvin College black students who have completed two semesters; must be in good standing; must be enrolled in a full-time status. **Criteria:** Recipients are selected based on academic performance and financial need.

Funds Avail.: No specific amount. **To Apply:** Applicants must submit a completed application form. **Deadline:** April 15.

1868 ■ Calvin Alumni Association British Columbia Scholarships *(Undergraduate/ Scholarship)*

Purpose: To build community among Calvin College alumni and friends; to provide opportunities for service and aspiring alumni to answer God's call in life and vocation. **Focus:** General studies. **Qualif.:** Applicants must be enrolled as freshmen students. **Criteria:** Recipients are selected based on Christian character and personal involvement in the life of their community, desire for a Christian higher education, evidence of leadership, volunteerism and service to the Community.

Funds Avail.: $500. **To Apply:** Applicants must submit a completed application form.

1869 ■ Calvin Alumni Association California-Bay Area Scholarships *(Undergraduate/ Scholarship)*

Purpose: To build community among Calvin College alumni and friends; to provide opportunities for service and aspiring alumni to answer God's call in life and vocation. **Focus:** General studies. **Qualif.:** Applicants must be current high school seniors; must live in the LA/Inland Empire Chapter area; must have a minimum GPA of 3.0. **Criteria:** Recipients are selected based on academic performance and financial need.

Funds Avail.: No specific amount. **To Apply:** Applicants must submit a completed application form. **Deadline:** April 15. **Contact:** 526-461-1489.

1870 ■ Calvin Alumni Association Colorado Chapter Scholarships *(Undergraduate/Scholarship)*

Purpose: To build community among Calvin College alumni and friends; to provide opportunities for service and aspiring alumni to answer God's call in life and vocation. **Focus:** General studies. **Qualif.:** Applicants must be students who are in good standing, leader in the church community and will continue attributes at Calvin College. **Criteria:** Recipients are selected based on the academic standing.

Funds Avail.: $1,000. **Number Awarded:** 7. **To Apply:** Applicants must submit a completed application form; must submit a typed essay, completed evaluation/Letter from Youth Pastor/Minister; completed evaluation/Letter from High School Teacher/Counselor High School Transcript and signature of applicant. **Deadline:** March 14.

1871 ■ Calvin Alumni Association Florida-Gulf Coast Scholarships *(Undergraduate/Scholarship)*

Purpose: To build community among Calvin College alumni and friends; to provide opportunities for service and inspiring alumni to answer God's call in life and vocation. **Focus:** General studies. **Qualif.:** Applicants must be first year students from the Gulf Coast Florida; must live within the Gulf Coast Chapter area. **Criteria:** Recipients are selected based on academic performance and community involvement.

Funds Avail.: No stated amount. **To Apply:** Applicants must submit a completed application form. **Deadline:** March 14. **Contact:** 941-794-3016.

1872 ■ Calvin Alumni Association-Illinois Scholarships *(Undergraduate/Scholarship)*

Purpose: To build community among Calvin College alumni and friends; to provide opportunities for service and inspiring alumni to answer God's call in life and vocation. **Focus:** General studies. **Qualif.:** Applicants must be first year students from the Chicagoland Areas. **Criteria:** Recipients are selected based on scholastic achievement, commitment in the areas of leadership, volunteerism and service to the community.

Funds Avail.: $1,000. **To Apply:** Applicants must submit a completed application form; two completed recommendation forms; must submit a completed recommendation from their school Principal or Counselor; must submit an official high school transcript. **Deadline:** April 4. **Contact:** 630-462-0406.

1873 ■ Calvin Alumni Association-Iowa/Pella Scholarships *(Undergraduate/Scholarship)*

Purpose: To build community among Calvin College alumni and friends; to provide opportunities for service and inspiring alumni to answer God's call in life and vocation. **Focus:** General studies. **Qualif.:** Applicants must be first year students entering Calvin College and students living within the Pella Chapter area are eligible to apply. **Criteria:** Recipients are selected based on GPA, financial need, recommendations and questions about goals and character.

Funds Avail.: No stated amount. **To Apply:** Applicants must submit a completed application form, academic recommendation form and character recommendation form. **Deadline:** April 1. **Contact:** jkuy05@iowatelecom.net.

1874 ■ Calvin Alumni Association-Maryland/ Baltimore Scholarships *(Undergraduate/ Scholarship)*

Purpose: To build community among Calvin College alumni and friends; to provide opportunities for service and inspiring alumni to answer God's call in life and vocation. **Focus:** General studies. **Qualif.:** Applicants must be first year students entering Calvin College; must have at least 2.5 GPA; must attend a high school in Kent County. **Criteria:** Recipients are selected based on the record of volunteer activity or service in church, community, school or elsewhere.

Funds Avail.: $2,500. **Number Awarded:** 9. **To Apply:** Applicants must submit a completed application form and three recommendation from non-relatives. **Deadline:** January 30. **Contact:** alumnievents@calvin.edu.

1875 ■ Calvin Alumni Association-Michigan Lakeshore Scholarships *(Undergraduate/Scholarship)*

Purpose: To build a community among Calvin College alumni and friends; to provide opportunities for service and inspiring alumni to answer God's call in life and vocation. **Focus:** General studies. **Qualif.:** Applicants must be first year students entering Calvin College; must attend a high school on Ottawa, Muskegon or Allegan Counties. **Criteria:** Recipients are selected based on the faith commitment in the areas of leadership, volunteerism and service to the community.

Funds Avail.: $1,000. **To Apply:** Applicants must submit a completed application form, short essay, transcript of records and two reference letter. **Deadline:** March 21. **Contact:** 231-557-1311.

1876 ■ Calvin Alumni Association-Michigan, Lansing Scholarships *(Undergraduate/Scholarship)*

Purpose: To build community among Calvin College alumni and friends; to provide opportunities for service and inspiring alumni to answer God's call in life and vocation. **Focus:** General studies. **Qualif.:** Applicants must be first year students entering Calvin College; must have at least 2.5 GPA or better; must live in Mid-Michigan Chapter area. **Criteria:** Recipients are selected based on academic performance.

Funds Avail.: $1,000. **To Apply:** Applicants must submit a completed application form and two written references. **Deadline:** February 1. **Contact:** 517-487-6326.

1877 ■ Calvin Alumni Association-New Jersey Scholarships *(Undergraduate/Scholarship)*

Purpose: To build community among Calvin College alumni and friends; to provide opportunities for service and inspiring alumni to answer God's call in life and vocation. **Focus:** General studies. **Qualif.:** Applicants must be students planning to attend Calvin for the first time; must be from local area (New Jersey or New York City metro area). **Criteria:** Recipients are selected based on academic performance and not yet receiving other academic scholarships from Calvin or other sources.

Funds Avail.: $1,000. **To Apply:** Applicants must submit a completed application and recommendation form. **Deadline:** March 31. **Contact:** 201-444-0844.

1878 ■ Calvin Alumni Association-New York, Rochester Scholarships *(Undergraduate/Scholarship)*

Purpose: To build community among Calvin College alumni and friends; to provide opportunities for service and inspiring alumni to answer God's call in life and vocation. **Focus:** General studies. **Qualif.:** Applicants must be first year Calvin students; must live in Rochester area. **Criteria:** Recipients are selected based on academic performance, christian character and service and curricular activities.

Funds Avail.: $750. **To Apply:** Applicants must submit a completed application form, completed references from Pastor/Youth Leader and Teacher/Counselor and transcript of grades. **Deadline:** March 14. **Contact:** 585-671-8735.

1879 ■ Calvin Alumni Association-South Florida Scholarships *(Undergraduate/Scholarship)*

Purpose: To build community among Calvin College alumni and friends; to provide opportunities for service and inspiring alumni to answer God's call in life and vocation. **Focus:** General studies. **Qualif.:** Applicants must be first year students entering Calvin college; students from Palm Beach and surrounding counties are eligible. **Criteria:** Recipients are selected based on GPA, Christian commitment, character, participation in extracurricular school activities, participation in church and community activities.

Funds Avail.: No stated amount. **To Apply:** Applicants must submit a completed application form. **Deadline:** February 15. **Contact:** wierengap@bellsouth.net.

1880 ■ Calvin Alumni Association-South Florida Sophomore Scholarships *(Undergraduate/Scholarship)*

Purpose: To build community among Calvin College alumni and friends; to provide opportunities for service and inspiring alumni to answer God's call in life and vocation. **Focus:** General studies. **Qualif.:** Applicants must be students from Palm Beach and surrounding counties who will be sophomores at Calvin; must have an accumulated GPA of at least 2.0. **Criteria:** Recipients are selected based on academic performance.

Funds Avail.: $500. **To Apply:** Applicants must submit a completed application form; must write a brief letter of application including name, local Florida address, majors and a copy of the most current Calvin transcript. **Deadline:** February 14. **Contact:** wierenap@bellsouth.net.

1881 ■ Calvin Alumni Association-Southeast Michigan Scholarships *(Undergraduate/Scholarship)*

Purpose: To build community among Calvin College alumni and friends; to provide opportunities for service and inspiring alumni to answer God's call in life and vocation. **Focus:** General studies. **Qualif.:** Applicants must be first year students entering Calvin College; must living in Southeast Michigan Chapter area. **Criteria:** Recipients are selected based on academic performance.

Funds Avail.: $1,000. **To Apply:** Applicants must submit a completed application form and two written references. **Deadline:** March 1. **Contact:** 734-945-0683.

1882 ■ Calvin Alumni Association-Southeastern Wisconsin Scholarships *(Undergraduate/Scholarship)*

Purpose: To build community among Calvin College alumni and friends; to provide opportunities for service and inspiring alumni to answer God's call in life and vocation. **Focus:** General studies. **Qualif.:** Applicants must be undergraduate college students who have completed at least two years of undergraduate education; must be residents of Dodge, Jefferson, Kenosha, Milwaukee, Ozaukee, Racine, Walworth, Washington, or Waukesha County, Wisconsin who attended a church in one of those counties; must intend to attend Calvin College during the next academic year. **Criteria:** Recipients are selected based on academic performance and demonstrated faith in church.

Funds Avail.: No stated amount. **To Apply:** Applicants must submit a complete application form, a complete "Statement of Ways and Means" and a certified copy of transcript from each of the colleges attended. **Deadline:** March 31. **Contact:** alumni@calvin.edu.

1883 ■ Calvin Alumni Association Southern California Chapter Scholarships *(Undergraduate/Scholarship)*

Purpose: To build community among Calvin College alumni and friends; to provide opportunities for service and aspir-

Awards are arranged alphabetically below their administering organizations

ing alumni to answer God's call in life and vocation. **Focus:** General studies. **Qualif.:** Applicants must be current high school senior students; must live within the Southern California Chapter area; must have a GPA of 3.0. **Criteria:** Recipients are selected based on the consistent pattern of volunteer service, character and scholastic ability.

Funds Avail.: $1,000. **Number Awarded:** 1. **To Apply:** Applicants must submit a completed application form. **Deadline:** March 14. **Contact:** trena@boonstras.com.

1884 ■ Calvin Alumni Association-Southwest Michigan, Kalamazoo Scholarships *(Undergraduate/Scholarship)*

Purpose: To build community among Calvin College alumni and friends; to provide opportunities for service and inspiring alumni to answer God's call in life and vocation. **Focus:** General studies. **Qualif.:** Applicants must be high school senior students who live in Southwest Michigan Chapter area. **Criteria:** Recipients are selected based on answers to application questions and involvement in extra-curricular activities.

Funds Avail.: No stated amount. **To Apply:** Applicants must submit a completed application form including activities and awards. **Deadline:** April 14. **Contact:** 269-388-8052.

1885 ■ Calvin Alumni Association-Washington, D.C. Scholarships *(Undergraduate/Scholarship)*

Purpose: To build community among Calvin College alumni and friends; to provide opportunities for service and inspiring alumni to answer God's call in life and vocation. **Focus:** General studies. **Qualif.:** Applicants must be incoming first year or transfer Calvin students in the greater D.C./Baltimore area who will be entering Calvin. **Criteria:** Recipients are selected based on Christian commitment, scholastic achievement, personal character and professional promise.

Funds Avail.: No stated amount. **To Apply:** Applicants must complete the application form and three copies of recommendation form. **Deadline:** March 14. **Contact:** 209-401-3331.

1886 ■ Calvin Alumni Association-Washington, Lynden Scholarships *(Undergraduate/Scholarship)*

Purpose: To build community among Calvin College alumni and friends; to provide opportunities for service and inspiring alumni to answer God's call in life and vocation. **Focus:** General studies. **Qualif.:** Applicants must be students living within the lynden Chapter area; must be high school seniors entering Calvin College with a minimum GPA of 2.50. **Criteria:** Recipients are selected based on demonstrated faith commitment in areas of leadership, volunteerism and service to the church, school and community.

Funds Avail.: $500. **To Apply:** Applicants must complete the application form. **Deadline:** March 15. **Contact:** matterdj@msn.com.

1887 ■ Calvin Alumni Association-Washington-Seattle/Tacoma Scholarships *(Undergraduate/Scholarship)*

Purpose: To build community among Calvin College alumni and friends; to provide opportunities for service and inspiring alumni to answer God's call in life and vocation. **Focus:** General studies. **Qualif.:** Applicants must be first year students including transferee entering Calvin and must living within the Seattle/Tacoma Chapter. **Criteria:** Recipients are selected based on academic performance, not yet receiving other academic scholarships from Calvin, financial need, demonstrated Christian service, personal character and professional promise.

Funds Avail.: No stated amount. **To Apply:** Applicants must submit a completed application form. **Deadline:** April 25. **Contact:** b_wolt@yahoo.com.

1888 ■ Camden County College

200 N Broadway
Camden, NJ 08102-1185
Ph: (856)338-1817
URL: http://www.camdencc.edu

1889 ■ Diane Basilone-Engle Memorial Scholarships *(Undergraduate/Scholarship)*

Purpose: To provide opportunity to qualified students to pursue an education at CCC. **Focus:** Theater arts; Secretarial sciences; Veterinary science and medicine; Education. **Qualif.:** Applicants must be students who want to continue their degree or certificate in theater, secretariat science, veterinary science or education. **Criteria:** Recipients are chosen by the College's Scholarship Selection Committee and/or recommendation by department faculty.

Funds Avail.: No specific amount. **To Apply:** Applicants must submit one recommendation from a faculty member or administrator at Camden County College. Application forms are available online and must be sent to Camden County College Foundation, PO Box 200, College Dr., Blackwood, NJ 08012. **Deadline:** February 18.

1890 ■ Scott Bonners Memorial Scholarships *(Undergraduate/Scholarship)*

Purpose: To provide financial assistance to individuals who want to continue their studies at CCC. **Focus:** General studies. **Qualif.:** Applicant must be full time, single parent with financial need; must have a minimum of GPA 3.0. **Criteria:** Recipients are selected based on financial need and academic standing.

Funds Avail.: No specific amount. **To Apply:** Applicants must submit one recommendation from a faculty member or administrator at Camden County College. Application forms are available online and must be sent to Camden County College Foundation, PO Box 200, College Dr., Blackwood, NJ 08012. **Deadline:** February 18.

1891 ■ Camden County College Employee Memorial Scholarships *(Undergraduate/Scholarship)*

Purpose: To provide support to qualified individuals who want to pursue an education at CCC. **Focus:** General studies. **Qualif.:** Applicants must have a cumulative GPA of 3.0. **Criteria:** Recipients are chosen by the College's Scholarship Selection Committee and/or recommendation by department faculty.

Funds Avail.: No specific amount. **To Apply:** Applicants must submit one recommendation from a faculty member or administrator at Camden County College. Application forms are available online and must be sent to Camden County College Foundation, PO Box 200, College Dr., Blackwood, NJ 08012. **Deadline:** February 18.

1892 ■ Camden County College Foundation Scholarships *(Undergraduate/Scholarship)*

Purpose: To provide support to the outstanding individuals who want to pursue higher education and career goals at

CCC. **Focus:** General studies. **Qualif.:** Applicants must be full-time or part-time students returning to CCC; must have a minimum of 3.0 GPA; must have completed a 12 college credits. **Criteria:** Recipients are chosen by the College's Scholarship Selection Committee and/ or by recommendation from department faculty.

Funds Avail.: No specific amount. **Number Awarded:** 2. **To Apply:** Applicants must submit one recommendation from a faculty member or administrator at Camden County College. Application forms are available online and must be sent to Camden County College Foundation, PO Box 200, College Dr., Blackwood, NJ 08012. **Deadline:** February 18.

1893 ■ Camden County Retired Educators Association Scholarships *(Undergraduate/Scholarship)*

Purpose: To provide financial assistance to qualified individuals who wants to pursue an education at CCC. **Focus:** General studies. **Qualif.:** Applicants must be a full time education students returning to CCC. **Criteria:** Recipients are chosen by the College's Scholarship Selection Committee and/or recommendation by department faculty.

Funds Avail.: No specific amount. **Number Awarded:** 2. **To Apply:** Applicants must submit one recommendation from a faculty member or administrator at Camden County College. Application forms are available online and must be sent to Camden County College Foundation, PO Box 200, College Dr., Blackwood, NJ 08012. **Deadline:** February 18.

1894 ■ James & Maryetta Cook Scholarships *(Undergraduate/Scholarship)*

Purpose: To encourage a widowed or divorced non-traditional students to continue their studies at CCC. **Focus:** General studies. **Qualif.:** Applicants must be widowed or divorced non-traditional students and returning to CCC; must demonstrates a motivation to succeed despite personal pr professional obstacles; must have a minimum GPA of 3.0. **Criteria:** Recipients are chosen by the College's Scholarship Selection Committee and/or recommendation by department faculty.

Funds Avail.: No specific amount. **To Apply:** Applicants must submit one recommendation from a faculty member or administrator at Camden County College. Application forms are available online and must be sent to Camden County College Foundation, PO Box 200, College Dr., Blackwood, NJ 08012. **Deadline:** February 18.

1895 ■ Garden State Rotary Club of Cherry Hill Scholarships *(Undergraduate/Scholarship)*

Purpose: To provide financial support to qualified individuals who wants to pursue their studies. **Focus:** General studies. **Qualif.:** Applicants must have a minimum GPA of 3.0. **Criteria:** Recipients are chosen by the College's Scholarship Selection Committee and/or recommendation by department faculty.

Funds Avail.: No specific amount. **To Apply:** Applicants must submit one recommendation from a faculty member or administrator at Camden County College. Application forms are available online and must be sent to Camden County College Foundation, PO Box 200, College Dr., Blackwood, NJ 08012. **Deadline:** February 18.

1896 ■ Dr. Martin Luther King & Coretta Scott King Student Leadership Scholarships *(Undergraduate/Scholarship)*

Purpose: To provide financial assistance to qualified individuals who want to pursue their career. **Focus:** General studies. **Qualif.:** Applicants must have completed a minimum of 12 college credits; must have a cumulative GPA of 3.0. **Criteria:** Recipients are chosen by the College's Scholarship Selection Committee and/or recommendation by department faculty.

Funds Avail.: No specific amount. **To Apply:** Applicants must submit one recommendation from a faculty member or administrator at Camden County College. Application forms are available online and must be sent to Camden County College Foundation, PO Box 200, College Dr., Blackwood, NJ 08012. **Deadline:** February 18.

1897 ■ Carolyn Murray Memorial Scholarships *(Undergraduate/Scholarship)*

Purpose: To encourage individuals to pursue an education at CCC. **Focus:** General studies. **Qualif.:** Applicants must be students returning to CCC; must have a minimum GPA of 3.0. **Criteria:** Recipients are chosen by the College's Scholarship Selection Committee and/or recommendation by department faculty.

Funds Avail.: No specific amount. **To Apply:** Applicants must submit one recommendation from a faculty member or administrator at Camden County College. Application forms are available online and must be sent to Camden County College Foundation, PO Box 200, College Dr., Blackwood, NJ 08012. **Deadline:** February 18.

1898 ■ H.N. Neal Memorial Scholarships *(Undergraduate/Scholarship)*

Purpose: To provide financial support to male students who wants to pursue an education at CCC. **Focus:** General studies. **Qualif.:** Applicants must be male students with a minimum cumulative GPA of 3.0. **Criteria:** Preference will be given to male students who are attending classes at the Camden Campus, or residents of Camden.

Funds Avail.: No specific amount. **To Apply:** Applicants must submit one recommendation from a faculty member or administrator at Camden County College. Application forms are available online and must be sent to Camden County College Foundation, PO Box 200, College Dr., Blackwood, NJ 08012. **Deadline:** February 18.

1899 ■ Jerrothia Allenfonzo Riggs & Anna & Dorothy Mae Barnes Scholarships *(Undergraduate/Scholarship)*

Purpose: To encourage African-American students to pursue their education. **Focus:** General studies. **Qualif.:** Applicants must be an African-American female; must be a first-generation high school graduate and resident of Camden City; must have a minimum GPA of 3.0. **Criteria:** Preference will be given to an adoptee and/or foster child.

Funds Avail.: No specific amount. **To Apply:** Applicants must submit one recommendation from a faculty member or administrator at Camden County College. Application forms are available online and must be sent to Camden County College Foundation, PO Box 200, College Dr., Blackwood, NJ 08012. **Deadline:** February 18.

1900 ■ Madlyn D. Thompson Memorial Scholarships *(Undergraduate/Scholarship)*

Purpose: To provide financial assistance to qualified individuals who want to continue their studies at CCC. **Focus:** General studies. **Qualif.:** Applicants must be a single female parent returning to CCC; must have completed at least 30 credits toward degree and be residents of Camden; must have a minimum GPA of 3.0. **Criteria:**

Preference is given to a single, female parent.

Funds Avail.: No specific amount. **To Apply:** Applicants must submit one recommendation from a faculty member or administrator at Camden County College. Application forms are available online and must be sent to Camden County College Foundation, PO Box 200, College Dr., Blackwood, NJ 08012. **Deadline:** February 18.

1901 ■ Mercedes Laurie Wade Scholarships *(Undergraduate/Scholarship)*

Purpose: To provide financial assistance to qualified individuals. **Focus:** General studies. **Qualif.:** Applicants must be female athletes, must be currently enrolled full time and with financial need; must have a minimum GPA of 2.5. **Criteria:** Applicants are selected based on application and financial need.

Funds Avail.: No specific amount. **To Apply:** Applicants must submit one recommendation from a faculty member or administrator at Camden County College. Application forms are available online and must be sent to Camden County College Foundation, PO Box 200, College Dr., Blackwood, NJ 08012. **Deadline:** February 18.

1902 ■ Watsontown Volunteer Fire Company Scholarships *(Undergraduate/Scholarship)*

Purpose: To provide financial assistance to individuals who want to pursue an education at CCC. **Focus:** General studies. **Qualif.:** Applicants must be students who want to return to CCC; must have a minimum cumulative GPA 3.0. **Criteria:** Recipients are selected based on financial need and academic standing.

Funds Avail.: No specific amount. **To Apply:** Applicants must submit one recommendation from a faculty member or administrator at Camden County College. Application forms are available online and must be sent to Camden County College Foundation, PO Box 200, College Dr., Blackwood, NJ 08012. **Deadline:** February 18.

1903 ■ Cameco Corporation

2121-11th St. W
Saskatoon, SK, Canada S7M 1J3
Ph: (306)956-6290
Fax: (306)956-6201
URL: http://www.cameco.com

1904 ■ Cameco Corporation Scholarships in the Geological Sciences - Continuing Students *(Undergraduate/Scholarship)*

Purpose: To support the students who want to pursue their career in geological sciences. **Focus:** Geology. **Qualif.:** Applicants must be full-time students who are Canadian citizens entering their second year of university study and pursuing Bachelor of Science degrees; must have declared majors in the geological sciences; must be registered in 200 level courses related to their majors; must have a sessional weighted average of at least 70% for all credit units attempted in the last regular session. **Criteria:** Recipient will be selected based on the scholarship application form and requirements.

Funds Avail.: No specific amount. **Number Awarded:** 2. **To Apply:** Application form can be obtained from: Continuing Students, Student Central, University of Saskatchewan, 105 Administration Place, Saskatoon, SK S7N 5A2. **Deadline:** June 1.

1905 ■ Cameco Corporation Scholarships in the Geological Sciences - Entering Students *(Undergraduate/Scholarship)*

Purpose: To support the students who want to pursue their career in geological sciences. **Focus:** Geology. **Qualif.:** Applicants must be full-time students who are Canadian citizens pursuing Bachelor of Science degrees and are entering their first year of university study and are registered in specified courses as outlined in guidelines. **Criteria:** Recipient will be selected based on the scholarship application form and requirements.

Funds Avail.: No specific amount. **Number Awarded:** 2. **To Apply:** Application form can be obtained from: Entering Students, Recruitment and Admissions, University of Saskatchewan, 105 Administration Place, Saskatoon, SK S7N 5A2. **Deadline:** February 15.

1906 ■ Cameco Northern Scholarships - Technical Institute *(Undergraduate/Scholarship)*

Purpose: To provide financial assistance to deserving individuals in northern Saskatchewan who want to pursue their education. **Focus:** General studies. **Qualif.:** Applicant must be a resident of northern Saskatchewan and must have lived in the north for a minimum of five years; must be enrolled as a full-time student in a program of study leading to certification from a recognized technical institute located in Saskatchewan. **Criteria:** Scholarship application will be reviewed by the selection committee which recommends candidates to Cameco.

Funds Avail.: $5,000. **To Apply:** Applicant must complete the scholarship application available online; must submit a letter that includes the following: (1) a statement regarding the applicant's academic plans; (2) a list of the courses the applicant plans to take; (3) the name of the institution at which the applicant plans to enroll (or is enrolled); (4) the applicant's career objectives; (5) reference to the applicant's academic, social and athletic interests; (6) the applicant's goals for the future. Application form and other supporting documents must be sent to Cameco Corporation, Northern Affairs Office, PO Box 1049, La Ronge, SK SOJ 1LO. **Deadline:** June 30.

1907 ■ Cameco Northern Scholarships - University *(Undergraduate/Scholarship)*

Purpose: To provide financial assistance to deserving individuals in north Saskatchewan who want to pursue their education. **Focus:** General studies. **Qualif.:** Applicant must be a resident of northern Saskatchewan and must have lived in the north for a minimum of five years; must be enrolled as a full-time student in a program of study leading to a degree from a Saskatchewan university, or from another Canadian university in situations where the student's program of study is not available in Saskatchewan. **Criteria:** Scholarship application will be reviewed by the selection committee which recommends candidates to Cameco.

Funds Avail.: $750. **To Apply:** Applicant must complete the scholarship application available online; must submit a letter that includes the following: (1) a statement regarding the applicant's academic plans; (2) a list of the courses the applicant plans to take; (3) the name of the institution at which the applicant plans to enroll (or is enrolled); (4) the applicant's career objectives; (5) reference to the applicant's academic, social and athletic interests; (6) the applicant's goals for the future. Application form and other supporting documents must be sent to Cameco Corporation, Northern Affairs Office, PO Box 1049, La Ronge, SK

SOJ 1LO. **Deadline:** June 30.

1908 ■ Bernard Michel Scholarships
(Undergraduate/Scholarship)

Purpose: To provide financial support to a Saskatchewan aboriginal student who wants to pursue their studies. **Focus:** Engineering; Liberal arts. **Qualif.:** Applicant must be a Saskatchewan aboriginal student entering his or her first or second year of study within the Colleges of Engineering, Commerce, or Arts and Science at the University of Saskatchewan. **Criteria:** Recipient will be selected based on the scholarship application form and requirements.

Funds Avail.: $20,000. **To Apply:** Applicant must complete the application form available online and must be sent to University of Saskatchewan, 105 Administration Place, Saskatoon, SK S7N 5A2. **Deadline:** June 1.

1909 ■ Canada Millennium Scholarship Foundation

1000 Sherboke St. W, Ste. 800
Montreal, QC, Canada H3A 3R2
Ph: (514)985-0026
Fax: (514)985-5987
Free: 877-786-3999
E-mail: millennium.foundation@bm-ms.org
URL: http://www.millenniumscholarships.ca

1910 ■ Canada Millennium Scholarship Foundation Millennium Bursary Award *(Undergraduate/Award/Prize)*

Purpose: To complement provincial and territorial student assistance programs. **Focus:** General studies. **Qualif.:** Applicants must be post-secondary students who demonstrate merit and financial need. **Criteria:** Preference is given to applicants with the greatest financial need as reviewed according to the foundation's merit criteria.

Funds Avail.: $1,000. **To Apply:** Applicants may apply for the student financial assistance from their province or territory of residence. In some cases, students must indicate on their student assistance application that they wish to be considered for a millennium bursars. In most cases, students do not need to apply; their names are automatically considered when they apply from their home province or territorial governments which then provide the foundation with the names of eligible students. **Contact:** CMSF at the above address (see entry 1909).

1911 ■ Canadian Anesthesiologists' Society

1 Eglinton Ave. E, Ste. 208
Toronto, ON, Canada M4P 3A1
Ph: (416)480-0602
Fax: (416)480-0320
E-mail: director@cas.ca
URL: http://www.cas.ca

1912 ■ Baxter Corporation Canadian Research Awards in Anesthesia *(Professional Development/Award/Prize)*

Purpose: To support anesthesia-related research in Canada. **Focus:** Anesthesiology. **Qualif.:** Applicants must be associate/active members of CAS who propose to carry out an original project and are eligible for the New Investigator Awards. **Criteria:** Award winner is chosen based on the scientific merit, importance, and feasibility of the project.

Funds Avail.: $20,000. **To Apply:** Application forms are available online. Applicants must submit documentation of institutional approval of human and/or animal experimentation. **Deadline:** February 1.

1913 ■ Canadian Anesthesiologists' Society Research Awards *(Professional Development/Award/Prize)*

Purpose: To support anesthesia-related research in Canada. **Focus:** Anesthesiology. **Qualif.:** Applicants must be associate/active members of CAS who propose to carry out an original project and are eligible for the New Investigator Awards. **Criteria:** Award winner is chosen based on the scientific merit, importance, and feasibility of the project.

Funds Avail.: $30,000. **To Apply:** Application forms are available online. Applicants must submit documentation of institutional approval of human and/or animal experimentation. **Deadline:** February 1.

1914 ■ CAS/GE Healthcare Canada Inc. Research Awards *(Professional Development/Award/Prize)*

Purpose: To provide support for infrastructure costs related to a specific research project or program. **Focus:** Medical research. **Qualif.:** Nominees must be associate or active members of the society who are eligible for an award in the field of perioperative imaging related to anesthesia and/or critical care. **Criteria:** Award winner is chosen based on the scientific merit, importance, and feasibility of the project.

Funds Avail.: $40,000. **To Apply:** Application forms are available online. Applicants must submit documentation of institutional approval of human and or animal experimentation. **Deadline:** February 1.

1915 ■ CAS/Vitaid-LMA Residents' Research Grant Competition *(Professional Development/Award/Prize)*

Purpose: To support anesthesia-related research performed by a resident in Canada. **Focus:** Anesthesiology. **Qualif.:** Nominees must be resident physicians who are in good standing at a Canadian university department of anesthesia. Nominees must be members of the CAS and must propose to carry out an original project within Canada. **Criteria:** Award winner is chosen based on the scientific merit, importance, and feasibility of the project.

Funds Avail.: $5,000. **To Apply:** Application forms are available online. Applicants must submit documentation of institutional approval of human and/or animal experimentation. **Deadline:** February 1.

1916 ■ Frank Newman Leadership Awards
(Undergraduate/Scholarship)

Purpose: To provide financial support to students pursuing college. **Focus:** General studies. **Qualif.:** Applicants must be undergraduate students at Campus Compact member colleges and universities. **Criteria:** Awards are given based on financial need and leadership.

Funds Avail.: $5,000. **Number Awarded:** 2. **To Apply:** Applicants must complete the online application form. Prepare a student-written essay; letter of nomination from applicant's president/chancellor; mentoring plan; and a recent head-and-shoulder photo. **Contact:** awards2008@compact.org.

Awards are arranged alphabetically below their administering organizations

1917 ■ Novo Nordisk Canada-CAS Research Awards *(Professional Development/Award/Prize)*

Purpose: To support infrastructure costs related to a specific research project or program. **Focus:** Medical research. **Qualif.:** Nominee must be an associate or an active member of the society who is eligible for an award in the field of perioperative hemorrhage, hemostasis, and/or transfusion medicine. **Criteria:** Award winner is chosen based on the scientific merit, importance, and feasibility of the project.

Funds Avail.: $40,000. **To Apply:** Applicants must fill up the application forms available online. Applicants must submit documentation of institutional approval of human and or animal experimentation. **Deadline:** February 1.

1918 ■ David S. Sheridan Canadian Research Awards *(Professional Development/Award/Prize)*

Purpose: To support anesthesia-related research in Canada. **Focus:** Anesthesiology. **Qualif.:** Applicants must be associate/active members of CAS who propose to carry out an original project and are eligible for the New Investigator Awards. **Criteria:** Award winner is chosen based on the scientific merit, importance, and feasibility of the project.

Funds Avail.: $10,000. **To Apply:** Applicants must fill up the application forms available online. Applicants must submit documentation of institutional approval of human and/or animal experimentation. **Deadline:** February 1.

1919 ■ Smiths Medical Canada Ltd. Research Awards *(Professional Development/Award/Prize)*

Purpose: To support pain and regional anesthesia-related research in Canada. **Focus:** Anesthesiology. **Qualif.:** Applicants must be associate or active members of the society who are eligible for a subspecialty award. **Criteria:** Award winner is chosen based on the scientific merit, importance, and feasibility of the research.

Funds Avail.: $10,000. **To Apply:** Applicants must fill up the application forms available online. Applicants must submit documentation of institutional approval of human and/or animal experimentation. **Deadline:** February 1.

1920 ■ Canadian Association of Broadcasters

PO Box 627, Sta. B
Ottawa, ON, Canada K1P 1A4
Ph: (613)233-4035
Fax: (613)233-6961
E-mail: cab@cab-acr.ca
URL: http://www.cab-acr.ca

1921 ■ Jim Allard Broadcast Journalism Scholarships *(Undergraduate/Scholarship)*

Purpose: To provide financial assistance to deserving students enrolled in a broadcast journalism course. **Focus:** Journalism. **Qualif.:** Applicants must be aspiring broadcasters enrolled in broadcast journalism courses at a Canadian college or university. **Criteria:** Recipient will be judged based on academic standing and natural talent.

Funds Avail.: $2,500. **To Apply:** Applicant must provide a 500-word essay outlining why they are interested in broadcast journalism, career goals, and how the scholarship can help them to attain their goal; must submit a signed recommendation from the course director. **Deadline:** June 30.

Remarks: Established in 1963 by the Canadian Association of Broadcasters, in memory of T.J. Allard, its long-time executive vicepresident.

1922 ■ BBM Canada Scholarships *(Undergraduate/Scholarship)*

Purpose: To provide support to qualified individuals who want to pursue their career in broadcasting. **Focus:** Broadcasting. **Qualif.:** Applicant must be enrolled in a graduate studies program, or be in the final year of an honors degree with the intention of entering a graduate program, anywhere in Canada. **Criteria:** Recipient will be selected based on the demonstrated achievement in and knowledge of statistical and/or quantitative research methodology in a course of study at a Canadian university or post-secondary institution.

Funds Avail.: $4,000. **To Apply:** Applicant must submit a 250-word essay outlining their interest in and thoughts on audience research; must provide a recommendation from their course director. Application forms are available online and must be sent together with the application requirements to BBM Canada Scholarship, c/o The Canadian Association of Broadcasters, PO Box 627, Sta. B, Ottawa, ON K1P 5S2. **Deadline:** June 30.

1923 ■ Ruth Hancock Scholarships *(Undergraduate/Scholarship)*

Purpose: To provide support to qualified individuals who want to pursue their career in broadcasting or broadcast sales/marketing. **Focus:** Broadcasting. **Qualif.:** Applicant must be a student enrolled in a recognized communication or marketing course in Canada; must have strong character and leadership qualities; must have a willingness to assist others; must have a genuine interest in pursuing a broadcasting career, as reflected in extracurricular activities related to broadcasting or broadcast sales/marketing, and/or self-initiated undertakings; must have community involvement and/ or volunteer work. **Criteria:** Recipient will be selected based on the criteria of the Scholarship Selection Committee.

Funds Avail.: $1,500. **To Apply:** Applicant must provide 500-word outline and a signed recommendation from their course director. Application forms are available online and must be sent with the other supporting documents to Ruth Hancock Memorial Scholarships, c/o Canadian Association of Broadcasters, PO Box 627 Sta. B, Ottawa, K1P 5S2. **Deadline:** June 30.

1924 ■ Canadian Association of Chiefs of Police

582 Somerset St. W
Ottawa, ON, Canada K1R 5K2
Ph: (613)233-1106
Fax: (613)233-6960
E-mail: membership@cacp.ca
URL: http://www.cacp.ca

1925 ■ Jack Ackroyd Scholarships *(Professional Development/Scholarship)*

Purpose: To encourage members of police forces across Canada to further their education with a view of promoting professionalism and excellence throughout the policing community. **Focus:** Law enforcement. **Qualif.:** Applicants must be all uniform and civilian members of police forces, who have completed a degree or certificate program in police studies, criminology, law, or other programs related

Awards are arranged alphabetically below their administering organizations

to law enforcement in an accredited Canadian university or community college. **Criteria:** Applicants who have demonstrated academic excellence in police related studies will be given preference.

Funds Avail.: $100. **Number Awarded:** 5. **To Apply:** Applicants must submit documents pertaining to their personal information, police service of employment, date of graduation, official transcripts of courses and grades, and any other information which may be considered relevant including any letter of support from the police service of which they are members. **Deadline:** October 15.

1926 ■ Canadian Association on Gerontology

222 College St., Ste. 106
Toronto, ON, Canada M5T 3J1
Ph: (416)978-7977
Fax: (416)978-4771
E-mail: contact@cagacg.ca
URL: http://www.cagacg.ca

1927 ■ CAG Donald Menzies Bursary Awards *(Postgraduate/Award/Prize)*

Purpose: To support post-baccalaureate students registered in a program of study focused on aging or the aged. **Focus:** Gerontology. **Qualif.:** Applicant must be a CAG member; must be registered, or formally accepted as a full-time student in a post-baccalaureate program at a recognized Canadian university at the time the application is submitted; must be a Canadian citizen or have permanent resident status. **Criteria:** Recipient will be selected by the Awards Committee based on academic merit among students demonstrating financial need.

Funds Avail.: $1,500. **To Apply:** Applicant must submit the application form with the university transcript; proof of registration, or acceptance in university program; a letter of support from the faculty supervisor; and an approved thesis/ research project proposal (if applicable). Applicant must submit a photo and a short biographical profile for the CAG Newsletter. **Deadline:** April 15.

1928 ■ CAG Margery Boyce Bursary Awards *(Postgraduate/Award/Prize)*

Purpose: To support post-baccalaureate students who have made a significant contribution to their community through volunteer activities and who are registered in a program of study focused on aging or the aged. **Focus:** Gerontology. **Qualif.:** Applicant must be a CAG member; must be registered, or formally accepted at a recognized Canadian university at the time the application is submitted; must be a Canadian citizen or have permanent resident status. **Criteria:** Recipient will be recommended by the Awards Committee based on his/her contribution to the community through volunteer activities and based on his/ her academic performance. Preference will be given to persons returning to university after an absence from formal study.

Funds Avail.: $500. **To Apply:** Applicants must submit an application form with transcripts; proof of registration or acceptance in a university program; letter of support from the faculty supervisor or program Chair which addresses the criteria for the bursary and the letter of support from any community organization that can address the amount and quality of the applicant's volunteer activities as related to the criteria; Applicant must submit a photo and a short biographical profile for the CAG Newsletter. **Deadline:** April 15.

1929 ■ Canadian Association of Law Libraries

PO Box 1570
Kingston, ON, Canada K7L 5C8
Ph: (613)531-9338
Fax: (613)531-0626
E-mail: office@callacbd.ca
URL: http://www.callacbd.ca

1930 ■ CALL/ACBD Education Reserve Fund Grants *(Graduate/Grant)*

Purpose: To provide funding support for members of CALL/ ACBD intending to further their education in pursuits that do not fit the guidelines of the association's already established scholarships. **Focus:** Law. **Qualif.:** Members of the Canadian Association of Law Libraries/Association canadienne des bibliotheques de droit who have been in good standing for a minimum of 12 months are invited to apply. Applicants' pursuits must be relevant to their career in law libraries or law librarianship. **Criteria:** Selection will be based on merit.

Funds Avail.: No specific amount. **To Apply:** Application form is available online. Applicants must submit completed application form along with a resume and a letter of support from your employer. **Contact:** Janet Moss CALL/ACBD Scholarships and Awards Committee, Head Law Librarian, Gerard V. La Forest Law Library, University of New Brunswick, Bag Service 44999 41 Dineen Dr. Fredericton, NB E3B 6C9; jmoss@unb.ca.

1931 ■ Canadian Association of Law Libraries CALL Research Grants *(Graduate/Grant)*

Purpose: To provide financial assistance for members working in law libraries intending to do research in various areas of interest. **Focus:** Law. **Qualif.:** Program is open to members of CALL/ACBD; must be intending to do research projects that promote an understanding of legal information sources or law librarianship. **Criteria:** Selection will be based on the recommendation of the committee to promote proposed research.

Funds Avail.: Up to $4,900. **To Apply:** Applicants may apply individually or in partnership with another member of CALL/ACBD; Applicants must submit completed application available in the website outlining the proposed project, the amount of money requested and a brief budget setting out how funds will be spent. Applicants should be prepared to demonstrate that they have completed a preliminary investigation as to the feasibility of their proposed project. **Deadline:** March 1 or October 15 of every year. **Contact:** Marianne Rogers; 416-736-2100x33934; rogers@yorku.ca.

1932 ■ James D. Lang Memorial Scholarships *(Graduate/Scholarship)*

Purpose: To support attendance at a continuing education program, be it a workshop, certificate program or other similar activity deemed appropriate by the CALL/ACBD Scholarships and Awards Committee. **Focus:** Law. **Qualif.:** Members of CALL/ACBD who have been in good standing for a minimum of 12 months are invited to apply. **Criteria:** Scholarship is given based on merit.

Funds Avail.: $2,500. **To Apply:** Application form is available online. Applicants must submit the completed application form along with resume and a letter of support from their employer. **Deadline:** March 15; June 15; September 15. **Contact:** Janet Moss CALL/ACBD Scholarships and Awards Committee, Head Law Librarian, Gerard V. la Forest Law Library, University of New Brunswick, Bag Service

44999 41 Dineen Dr. Fredericton, NB E3B 6C9; jmoss@unb.ca.

1933 ■ Diana M. Priestly Memorial Scholarships *(Undergraduate/Scholarship)*

Purpose: To encourage and support professional development in the area of law librarianship. **Focus:** Law. **Qualif.:** Program is open to Canadian citizens or landed immigrants; must have previous law library experience and will be enrolled in an accredited Canadian Library School during the next academic term or year; must have a degree from or are currently enrolled in an accredited Canadian Library School and will be enrolled in an approved Canadian Law School during the next academic term or year; or who have a degree from or are currently enrolled in an approved Canadian law School and will be enrolled in an accredited Canadian Library school during the next academic term/year; or who will be concurrently enrolled in an approved Canadian Law School and an accredited Canadian Library School during the next academic term/year. **Criteria:** Recipients are chosen based on the applicant's work experience, letter of application and letters of reference. Preference will be given to members of the Canadian Association of Law Libraries/Association canadienne des bibliotheques de droit.

Funds Avail.: $2,500. **To Apply:** Applicants must submit the completed application form available on the website along with resume; written statement from applicant; transcripts; and references. **Deadline:** February 15. **Contact:** Janet Moss, Chair; CALL/ACBD Scholarships and Awards Committee, Head Law Librarian, Gerard V. La Forest Law Library, University of New Brunswick, Bag Service 44999 41 Dineen Dr. Fredericton, NB E3B 6C9; jmoss@unb.ca.

1934 ■ Canadian Bar Association

500-865 Carling Ave.
Ottawa, ON, Canada K1S 5S8
Ph: (613)237-8860
Fax: (613)237-0185
Free: 800-267-8860
E-mail: info@acba.org
URL: http://www.cba.org

1935 ■ The Viscount Bennett Fellowships *(Graduate/Fellowship)*

Purpose: To improve the law and it's administration; to promote equal access to justice; to promote the equality in legal profession and the justice system; to enhance the knowledge, ethical standards and well-being of members of the legal profession; to safeguard the interest of legal profession; and to encourage the high standards of legal education, training, and ethics. **Focus:** Law. **Qualif.:** Applicants must be Canadian citizens who have graduated from the approved law school in Canada. **Criteria:** Recipients are selected based on the result of the conducted interview.

Funds Avail.: $40,000. **To Apply:** Applicants must submit a photocopy of birth certificate; one certified copy of the law transcripts; academic distinctions; curriculum vitae; one-page synopsis of the extra-curricular interests as well as activities during the post-secondary studies; one-page statement outlining the course of study to be pursued; and three letters of reference. **Deadline:** November 15. **Contact:** Stephen Hanaon at the above address (see entry 1934).

1936 ■ Canadian Cartographic Association

PO Box 3050
Victoria, BC, Canada V8W 3P5
URL: http://www.cca-acc.org

1937 ■ Norman Nicholson Scholarships *(Undergraduate/Scholarship)*

Purpose: To recognize and encourage exceptional student achievement and ability in any aspect of cartography. **Focus:** Cartography. **Qualif.:** Applicant must be a full-time student in a recognized college or university program; must be a Canadian citizen or landed immigrant. **Criteria:** Applicants are selected based on the committee's review of the application materials.

Funds Avail.: $5,000. **To Apply:** Applicants must submit an official transcript of all college or university courses complete with grades received; letters of recommendation from two faculty members who are familiar with the student's works and capabilities; one-page statement from the student regarding plans for continuing education in cartography. Application and attachments must be sent to: Canadian Cartographic Association 66 Meredith Dr., PO Box 225, Ilderton, ON N0M 2A0. **Deadline:** March 15. **Contact:** Alberta Auringer Wood.

1938 ■ Canadian Council for Aboriginal Business

250 The Esplanade, Ste. 204
Toronto, ON, Canada M5A 1J2
Ph: (416)961-8663
Fax: (416)961-3995
E-mail: info@ccab.com
URL: http://www.ccab.com

1939 ■ Foundation for the Advancement of Aboriginal Youth Bursary Program *(Undergraduate/Scholarship)*

Purpose: To provide scholarship assistance to qualified individuals who want to pursue their post-secondary education. **Focus:** General studies. **Qualif.:** Applicant must be a Canadian resident, of First Nation, Metis or Inuit heritage and attending either a high school or a post-secondary institute full-time within Canada. **Criteria:** Recipient will be selected based on financial need, academic and career commitment, contribution to family and community, and leadership and role model qualities.

Funds Avail.: $750. **To Apply:** Applicant must complete the application form available online; must be provide proof of First Nations, Inuit or Metis ancestry; must have two signed, original letters of support; must provide a copy of the most recent official school transcripts and report card; must include a letter of acceptance; must provide a recent color photo. Application form and other supporting documents must be sent to the Foundation for the Advancement of Aboriginal Youth, c/o Canadian Council for Aboriginal Business, 250 The Esplanade, Ste. 204, Toronto, ON M5A 1J2. **Deadline:** October 15.

1940 ■ Foundation for the Advancement of Aboriginal Youth Scholarships *(Undergraduate/Scholarship)*

Purpose: To provide scholarship assistance to qualified individuals who want to pursue their post-secondary education. **Focus:** General studies. **Qualif.:** Applicant must be a

Awards are arranged alphabetically below their administering organizations

Canadian resident, of First Nation, Metis or Inuit heritage and attending either high school or a post-secondary institute full-time within Canada. **Criteria:** Recipient will be selected based on financial need, academic and career commitment, contribution to family and community, and leadership and role model qualities.

Funds Avail.: $2,500. **To Apply:** Applicant must complete the application form available online; must provide proof of First Nation, Inuit or Metis ancestry; must have two signed, original letters of support; must provide a copy of the most recent official school transcripts and report card; must include a letter of acceptance; must provide a recent color photo. Application form and other supporting documents must be sent to Foundation for the Advancement of Aboriginal Youth, c/o Canadian Council for Aboriginal Business, 250 The Esplanade, Ste. 204, Toronto, ON M5A 1J2. **Deadline:** October 15.

1941 ■ Canadian Council on International Law

215-236, rue Metcalfe St.
Ottawa, ON, Canada K2P 1R3
Ph: (613)235-0442
Fax: (613)230-5978
E-mail: info@ccil-ccdi.ca
URL: http://www.ccil-ccdi.ca

1942 ■ John Peter Humphrey Student Fellowships *(Graduate/Fellowship)*

Purpose: To inspire educational achievement by providing support for outstanding students pursuing graduate studies at leading graduate institutions in Canada or worldwide. **Focus:** Political science; Law. **Qualif.:** Applicants must be students of Canadian law and political science (or their equivalent) faculties. **Criteria:** Selection committee appointed by the President of the CCIL will review the applications and base its determination on the applicant's academic accomplishments, proposed program of study, letter of reference, and other information contained in the application.

Funds Avail.: CDN$25,000 for tuition plus a stipend of CDN$10,000 for living expenses. **To Apply:** Applicants must submit the official transcript from each post-secondary academic institution, three letters of reference which speak both of the candidate's academic strengths and weaknesses and his/her likelihood of success in a programme of graduate studies. Complete application package must be submitted to: John Peters Humphrey Fellowship, c/o Canadian Council on International Law, 215-236 Metcalfe St., Ottawa, ON, K2P 1R3. **Deadline:** November 15.

1943 ■ Dick Martin Scholarships *(Postgraduate/Scholarship)*

Purpose: To encourage students to continue their career in occupational health and safety. **Focus:** Occupational safety and health. **Qualif.:** Applicants must be students who are enrolled, either full-time or part-time, in an occupational health and safety related course or program. **Criteria:** Recipients will be selected based on knowledge of the subject matter, understanding of the principles and values of Dick Martin, and understanding of the role of CCOHS.

Funds Avail.: $3,000. **To Apply:** Applicants must contact CCOHS at 800263-8466 for further information. **Deadline:** January 31.

1944 ■ Canadian Council of Technicians and Technologists

295 - 1101 Prince of Wales Dr.
Ottawa, ON, Canada K2C 3W7
Ph: (613)238-8123
Fax: (613)238-8822
Free: 800-891-1140
E-mail: ccttadm@cctt.ca
URL: http://www.cctt.ca

1945 ■ Scholarships for Technology Students *(Postgraduate/Scholarship)*

Purpose: To assist the students with expenses incurred to undertake studies leading to a technician or technologist diploma in a recognized program of study in engineering or applied science technology. **Focus:** Science technologies, Engineering. **Qualif.:** Applicant must be a son or daughter of an individual member of a Constituent member (CM) of CCTT. **Criteria:** Recipients are selected based on the committee's review of the application materials.

Funds Avail.: $1,000. **To Apply:** Applicant must secure a letter from a Constituent member of the council, attesting to the fact that his or her parents are members in good standing; must confirm by official transcripts that he/she is a graduate from grade 12 secondary school program with second-class, or better, standing and prove by official letter that she/he is enrolled as a full-time student in an Engineering or Applied Science Technology Program in Canada. Send application to: Canadian Council of Technicians and Technologists, 295-1101 Prince of Wales Dr., Ottawa, ON K2C 3W7. **Deadline:** October 1.

1946 ■ Canadian Engineering Memorial Foundation

PO Box 370
Renfrew, ON, Canada K7V 4A6
Fax: (613)432-6840
Free: (866)883-2363
E-mail: info@cemf.ca
URL: http://www.cemf.ca

1947 ■ AMEC Aboriginal Undergraduate Scholarships *(Undergraduate/Scholarship)*

Purpose: To provide financial assistance to qualified individuals who want to pursue their studies. **Focus:** Engineering. **Qualif.:** Applicants must be women who are pursuing their studies in an accredited university engineering program. **Criteria:** Selection of applicants will be based on the scholarship application requirements.

Funds Avail.: $5,000. **To Apply:** For further information and requirements about the scholarship, applicants are advised to contact the Canadian Engineering Memorial Foundation at PO Box 370, Refrew, ON K7V 4A6.

1948 ■ AMEC Masters Scholarships *(Graduate/Scholarship)*

Purpose: To provide financial assistance to qualified individuals who want to pursue their studies. **Focus:** Engineering. **Qualif.:** Applicants must be women in Canada who are pursuing their studies in engineering at the Masters level. **Criteria:** Selection of applicants will be based on the scholarship application requirements.

Funds Avail.: $10,000. **To Apply:** For further information and requirements about the scholarship, applicants are advised to contact the Canadian Engineering Memorial Foundation at PO Box 370, Refrew, ON K7V 4A6.

1949 ■ CEMF Undergraduate Engineering Scholarships *(Undergraduate/Scholarship)*

Purpose: To provide financial assistance to qualified individuals who want to pursue their studies. **Focus:**

Awards are arranged alphabetically below their administering organizations

Engineering. **Qualif.:** Applicants must be Canadian women in engineering in either their 1st, 2nd, or 3rd year of study in an accredited program in Canada. **Criteria:** Selection of applicants will be based on the scholarship application requirements.

Funds Avail.: $5,000. **To Apply:** For further information and requirements about the scholarship, applicants are advised to contact the Canadian Engineering Memorial Foundation at PO Box 370, Refrew, ON K7V 4A6.

1950 ■ Hewlett-Packard Undergraduate Scholarships *(Undergraduate/Scholarship)*

Purpose: To provide financial assistance to qualified individuals who want to pursue their studies. **Focus:** Engineering. **Qualif.:** Applicants must be women in Canada who are pursuing their studies in engineering. **Criteria:** Selection of applicants will be based on the scholarship application requirements.

Funds Avail.: $2,500. **To Apply:** For further information and requirements about the scholarship, applicants are advised to contact the Canadian Engineering Memorial Foundation at PO Box 370, Refrew, ON K7V 4A6.

1951 ■ IBM Canada Undergraduate Scholarships *(Undergraduate/Scholarship)*

Purpose: To provide financial assistance to qualified individuals who want to pursue their studies. **Focus:** Electrical engineering; Engineering, Computer. **Qualif.:** Applicants must be Canadian women who are pursuing their undergraduate engineering studies in either electrical or computer engineering. **Criteria:** Selection of applicants will be based on the scholarship application requirements.

Funds Avail.: $2,500. **To Apply:** For further information and requirements about the scholarship, applicants are advised to contact the Canadian Engineering Memorial Foundation at PO Box 370, Refrew, ON K7V 4A6.

1952 ■ Vale Inco Limited Masters Scholarships *(Graduate/Scholarship)*

Purpose: To provide financial assistance to qualified individuals who want to pursue their studies. **Focus:** Engineering. **Qualif.:** Applicants must be women in Canada who are pursuing their studies in engineering at the Masters level. **Criteria:** Selection of applicants will be based on the scholarship application requirements.

Funds Avail.: $10,000. **Number Awarded:** 4. **To Apply:** For further information and requirements about the scholarship, applicants are advice to contact the Canadian Engineering Memorial Foundation at PO Box 370, Refrew, ON K7V 4A6.

1953 ■ Canadian Federation of Independent Grocers

2235 Sheppard Ave. E, Ste. 902
Willowdale, ON, Canada M2J 5B5
Ph: (416)492-2311
Fax: (416)492-2347
Free: 800-661-2344
E-mail: info@cfig.ca
URL: http://www.cfig.ca

1954 ■ CFIG National Scholarships *(Undergraduate/Scholarship)*

Purpose: To provide financial assistance to residents and students of Canada for their further educational enrichment. **Focus:** General studies. **Qualif.:** Applicants must be Canadian residents studying in Canada; enrolled or expecting to be enrolled in a postsecondary program of at least 2 years. High school applicants must be in their last year of secondary studies; college or university applicants must be enrolled in at least one more full year of study as of spring. **Criteria:** Applicants are evaluated based on merit.

Funds Avail.: $8,000. **To Apply:** Applicants must submit a 1,000-word essay on topic given by the scholarship committee; list of academic achievements, awards, and extracurricular activities; official grade transcript of the last completed year; and the completed application form with all pertinent information properly filled in.

1955 ■ Canadian Federation for Sexual Health

1 Nicholas St., Ste. 430
Ottawa, ON, Canada K1N 7B7
Ph: (613)241-4474
Fax: (613)241-7550
E-mail: admin@cfsh.ca
URL: http://www.cfsh.ca

1956 ■ Phyllis P. Harris Scholarships *(Postgraduate/Award/Prize)*

Purpose: To provide educational assistance to a volunteer or individual to pursue studies in the general field of human sexuality, family planning or population. **Focus:** Human relations; Family planning; Population studies. **Qualif.:** Applicant must be a full-time junior or senior at a Canadian university; must be a Canadian citizen or landed immigrant; must have a previous work or volunteer experience in the general field of human sexuality with the intent to pursue a degree in the field of family planning or population issues. **Criteria:** Applicants will be selected based on the evaluation of the submitted essays. Scholarship winners will be selected by a review committee constituted by the Canadian Federation for Sexual Health.

Funds Avail.: $2,500-$3,000. **To Apply:** Applicants must submit a recent academic transcript; a 500-word typewritten essay outlining their relevant background education, objective and plans for the future. Application and other documents must be submitted to: Canadian Federation for Sexual Health, 1 Nicholas St., Ste. 430, Ottawa, ON, K1N 7B7. **Deadline:** April 30.

1957 ■ John and Lois Lamont Graduate Scholarships *(Postgraduate/Award/Prize)*

Purpose: To provide educational assistance to medical students enrolled in full-time graduate studies in a Canadian University. **Focus:** Medical education. **Qualif.:** Applicants must be Canadian citizens or landed immigrants who are graduates of any recognized university; possess an honour degree or its equivalent and intend to pursue a higher degree in the field of sexual and reproductive health. **Criteria:** Applicants will be selected based on the evaluation of the candidate's essay. Scholarship winners will be selected by a review committee constituted by the Canadian Federation for Sexual Health.

Funds Avail.: $2,600. **To Apply:** Applicants must submit a typewritten essay of 500-700 words, outlining their education, background in sex and reproductive health and/or women's issues, aspiration, and plans to access abortion provider training as an elective; must include the curriculum vitae and a full list of publications; and must submit a letter of recommendation. Application and other documents must

Awards are arranged alphabetically below their administering organizations

be submitted to: Canadian Federation for Sexual Health 1 Nicholas St., Ste. 430, Ottawa, ON, L1N 7B7. **Deadline:** April 30.

1958 ■ Dr. Henry Morgentaler Future Choice Scholarships *(Postgraduate/Award/Prize)*

Purpose: To provide financial assistance to medical students to access abortion provider training as an elective. **Focus:** Family planning. **Qualif.:** Applicants must be their 2nd, 3rd or 4th year of medical school at a recognized Canadian university; must have demonstrated a commitment to pro-choice and sex-positive sexual and reproductive health care and can demonstrate an intent to promote sexual and reproductive health and rights in Canada. **Criteria:** Recipients are selected based on the evidence of commitment to right-based pro-choice sexual/reproductive health care and in community-based pro-choice volunteer activities; based on the evaluation of the candidate's essay and demonstration of potential as a pro-choice champion in Canada. Scholarship winners will be selected by a review committee constituted by the Canadian Federation for Sexual Health.

Funds Avail.: $1,000. **Number Awarded:** 5. **To Apply:** Applicants must submit a typewritten essay of 500-700 words, outlining their education, background in sex and reproductive health and/or women's issues, aspiration, and plans to access abortion provider training as an elective; must include the curriculum vitae and a full list of publications; and must submit a letter of recommendation. Application and other documents must be submitted to: Canadian Federation for Sexual Health 1 Nicholas St., Ste. 430, Ottawa, ON, L1N 7B7. **Deadline:** May 31.

1959 ■ Canadian Federation of University Women

251 Bank St., Ste. 305
Ottawa, ON, Canada K2P 1X3
Ph: (613)234-8252
Fax: (613)234-8221
URL: http://www.cfuw.org

1960 ■ JAUW Fellowship Awards *(Postgraduate/Fellowship)*

Purpose: To assist in developing a sound concept of educational values and in maintaining high standards of public education in Canada. To encourage advanced study and research by women university graduates. To foster a sense of responsibility and encourage women university graduates to place their educational and professional training at the service of the community in local, national and international fields. **Focus:** Japanese studies. **Qualif.:** Applicants must have Academic degree equivalent to the bachelor's degree; must have been accepted in a Japanese institution at which they propose to undertake their work; must be members of national federation affiliated to IFUW. **Criteria:** Recipients are selected based on academic degree and committee's reviewed on the application and other supporting documents.

Funds Avail.: 500 yen; 1,000 yen. **To Apply:** Application form and other required documents and materials should be enclosed on one envelope and should be sent to: International Fellowship Committee, Japanese Association of University Women. **Deadline:** April 20.

1961 ■ Canadian Fire Safety Association

2175 Sheppard Ave., E, Ste. 310
North York, ON, Canada M2J 1W8
Ph: (416)492-9417
Fax: (416)491-1670
E-mail: cfsa@taylorenterprises.com
URL: http://www.canadianfiresafety.com/HOME/default.asp

1962 ■ Randall Brown and Associates Awards *(Postgraduate/Award/Prize)*

Purpose: To inspire pursuits on fire safety awareness by providing financial support to students attending an approved Fire Safety Technology Course in a post-secondary school in Canada. **Focus:** Fires and fire prevention. **Qualif.:** Applicants must be enrolled in a Fire Protection Technology course at a Canadian college or university; must have exceptional overall skills in Codes/Standard Technology; have an academic proficiency of 3.25/4.00; and must be students entering the second and subsequent years of an approved course. **Criteria:** Applicants will be evaluated based on academic achievement and letter of application as required by the association.

Funds Avail.: $850. **To Apply:** Applicants must submit their academic grades accompanied by completed application form to: School of Fire Protection Technology, Senera College, 150 Finch Ave., E, Toronto, ON M2J 2X5. **Deadline:** March 15. **Contact:** Mr. Anthony Van Odyk at the above address (see entry 1961).

1963 ■ Fire Safety Awards *(Postgraduate/Award/Prize)*

Purpose: To expand fire safety awareness by providing financial assistance to individuals attending an approved Fire Safety Technology Course in a post-secondary school in Canada. **Focus:** Fires and fire prevention. **Qualif.:** Applicants must be enrolled in a Fire Protection Technology course at a Canadian college or university; must have excelled with outstanding leadership, motivation and technical skills and an overall academic proficiency; must be students entering the second and subsequent years of an approved course. **Criteria:** Applicants will be evaluated based on academic achievement and letter of application as required by the association.

Funds Avail.: $850. **To Apply:** Applicants must submit their academic grades together with completed application form to: School of Fire Protection Technology, Senera College, 150 Finch Ave., E, Toronto, ON M2J 2X5. **Deadline:** March 15. **Contact:** Mr. Anthony Van Odyk at the above address (see entry 1961).

1964 ■ Leber Rubes Inc. Awards *(Postgraduate/Award/Prize)*

Purpose: To inspire pursuits on fire safety awareness by providing financial support to students attending an approved Fire Safety Technology Course in a post-secondary school in Canada. **Focus:** Fires and fire prevention. **Qualif.:** Applicants must be enrolled in a Fire Protection Technology course at a Canadian college or university; must have exceptional overall skills in Fire Alarm System Technology; have an academic proficiency of 3.25/4.00; and must be students entering the second and subsequent years of an approved course. **Criteria:** Applicants will be evaluated based on academic achievement and letter of application as required by the association.

Funds Avail.: $850. **To Apply:** Applicants must submit their academic grades together with completed application form to: School of Fire Protection Technology, Senera College, 150 Finch Ave., E, Toronto, ON M2J 2X5. **Deadline:** March 15. **Contact:** Mr. Anthony Van Odyk at the above address (see entry 1961).

1965 ■ Nadine International Inc. Awards *(Postgraduate/Award/Prize)*

Purpose: To expand pursuits on fire safety awareness by providing financial assistance to students enrolled in an approved Fire Safety Technology Course in a post-secondary school in Canada. **Focus:** Fires and fire prevention. **Qualif.:** Applicants must be enrolled in a Fire Protection Technology course at a Canadian college or university; must have exceptional overall skills in Fire Suppression Technology; must have an academic proficiency of 3.25/4.00; must be students entering the second and subsequent years of an approved course. **Criteria:** Applicants will be evaluated based on academic achievement and letter of application as required by the association.

Funds Avail.: $850. **To Apply:** Applicants must submit completed application form accompanied by copy of academic grades to: School of Fire Protection Technology, Senera College, 150 Finch Ave., E, Toronto, ON M2J 2X5. **Deadline:** March 15. **Contact:** Mr. Anthony Van Odyk at the above address (see entry 1961).

1966 ■ Underwriters' Laboratories of Canada Awards *(Postgraduate/Award/Prize)*

Purpose: To inspire pursuits on fire safety awareness by providing financial assistance to students attending an approved Fire Safety Technology Course in a post-secondary school in Canada. **Focus:** Fires and fire prevention. **Qualif.:** Applicants must be enrolled in a Fire Protection Technology course at a Canadian college or university; must have exceptional academic skills in Codes and Standards; must have an overall proficiency of 3.25/4.00; and must be students entering the second and subsequent years of an approved course. **Criteria:** Applicants will be evaluated based on academic achievement and letter of application as required by the association.

Funds Avail.: $500. **To Apply:** Applicants must submit their academic grades and completed application form to: School of Fire Protection Technology, Senera College, 150 Finch Ave. E, Toronto, ON M2J 2X5. **Deadline:** March 15. **Contact:** Mr. Anthony Van Odyk at the above address (see entry 1961).

1967 ■ Canadian Hard of Hearing Association

2415 Holly Ln., Ste. 205
Ottawa, ON, Canada K1V 7P2
Ph: (613)526-1584
Fax: (613)526-4718
Free: 800-263-8068
E-mail: chhanational@chha.ca
URL: http://www.chha.ca

1968 ■ Canadian Hard of Hearing Association Scholarships *(Undergraduate/Scholarship)*

Purpose: To offer financial assistance and recognition to hard of hearing and deafened students. **Focus:** General studies. **Qualif.:** Applicants must be students registered in a full-time program at a recognized Canadian college or university, with a goal of obtaining a diploma or degree; must be either hard of hearing, deafened or orally deaf. **Criteria:** Selection of applicants will be judged by a number of criteria including academic achievement, determination to cope with hearing loss, and community involvement.

Funds Avail.: $1,000. **To Apply:** Application forms are available online. Applicants must submit a copy of the most recent school transcript; must have a personal statement, and two letters of reference. **Deadline:** January 31. **Remarks:** Established in 2002.

1969 ■ Canadian Hemophilia Society

625 Pres. Kennedy Ave., Ste. 505
Montreal, QC, Canada H3A 1K2
Ph: (514)848-0503
Fax: (514)848-9661
Free: 800-668-2686
E-mail: chs@hemophilia.ca
URL: http://www.hemophilia.ca

1970 ■ CHS - Bursary Program Scholarships *(Undergraduate/Scholarship)*

Purpose: To bring young volunteers into the CHS while recognizing the importance of education. **Focus:** General studies. **Qualif.:** Applicants must possess academic proficiency; must have experience in community service at volunteer level; and must possess leadership qualities. **Criteria:** Priority is given to those who have financial needs.

Funds Avail.: $4,000. **To Apply:** Applicant must provide three letters of reference with the application stating the abilities and suitability of the candidate; must provide a letter from his/her physician or any medical authority confirming his/her medical status; must submit an original essay (500 words) to emphasize the logical thinking and adequate writing skills of the applicant; and must submit the original transcript of grades for the last year in secondary school. Application forms are available from the website. **Deadline:** April 30.

1971 ■ CHS - Mature Student Bursary Program Scholarships *(Professional Development/ Scholarship)*

Purpose: To encourage educational pursuits of students with hemophilia. **Focus:** General studies. **Qualif.:** Applicant must be at least 30 years of age. **Criteria:** Recipients are selected based on application materials and financial need as reviewed by a committee of academics and lay persons.

Funds Avail.: $4,000. **To Apply:** Applicants must submit a detailed budget showing their source of income and their projected expenses for a year of study at the institution of their choice; must submit an essay of intent describing past employment and assessment of new career; must provide three letters of reference with their application, none of which may be from a relative (such letters should attest to the abilities and suitability of the candidate for the program being applied for as well as act as a character reference for the candidate); must provide a separate letter from their physician or some medical authority confirming their medical status regarding eligibility to this program. **Deadline:** April 30.

1972 ■ CHS Scholarships *(Undergraduate/ Scholarship)*

Purpose: To bring young volunteers into the CHS while recognizing the importance of education. **Focus:** General studies. **Qualif.:** Applicants must possess academic proficiency (GPA of 3.0 on a 4.0 scale); must have experience in community service at a volunteer level; and must possess leadership qualities. **Criteria:** Priority is given to those who might not be able to succeed in a vocational course requiring strenuous physical labor.

Funds Avail.: $4,000. **To Apply:** Applicant must provide three letters of reference with the application stating the abilities and suitability of the candidate; must provide a letter from his/her physician or any medical authority confirming his/her medical status; must submit an original essay (500 words) to emphasize the logical thinking and adequate writing skills of the applicant; and must submit the original transcript of grades for the last year in secondary school. Application forms are available from the website. **Deadline:** April 30.

1973 ■ Peter Stainsby Awards *(Postgraduate/Award/Prize)*

Purpose: To encourage fire safety awareness by providing financial assistance to students attending an approved Fire Safety Technology Course in a post-secondary school in Canada. **Focus:** Fires and fire prevention. **Qualif.:** Applicants must be enrolled in a Fire Protection Technology course at a Canadian college or university; must have excelled with outstanding leadership, motivation and technical skills and an overall academic proficiency; must be students entering the second and subsequent years of an approved course. **Criteria:** Applicants will be evaluated based on academic achievement and letter of application as required by the association.

Funds Avail.: $1,000. **To Apply:** Applicants must submit their academic grades together with completed application form to: School of Fire Protection Technology, Senera College, 150 Finch Ave., E Toronto, ON M2J 2X5. **Deadline:** March 15. **Contact:** Mr. Anthony Van Odyk at the above address (see entry 1969).

1974 ■ Canadian Hospitality Foundation

300 Adelaide St. E, No. 399
Toronto, ON, Canada M5A 1N1
Ph: (416)363-3401
Fax: (416)363-3403
E-mail: chf@theohi.ca
URL: http://www.chfscholarships.com

1975 ■ Applied Hospitality Degree Scholarships *(Undergraduate/Scholarship)*

Purpose: To provide scholarship to the students enrolled in the first or second year of a community college. **Focus:** Hotel, institutional, and restaurant management; Travel and tourism. **Qualif.:** Applicants must be college students currently enrolled in the first or second year of a community college. Applicants must be Canadian citizens or permanent residents. **Criteria:** Selection will be based on work experience, scholastic record, leadership and ability to get along with others, professional promise, essay and discretionary points.

Funds Avail.: $2,500. **To Apply:** Applicants must complete the application form on-line. In addition, students must submit hard copies of the following documents (please note that missing or incomplete documents may be grounds for elimination): Most current official transcripts of your complete academic history at the college you are enrolled in at this time; one or more letters of recommendation from an instructor and/or administrator form your college; One letters of recommendation from past or present employers; Resume; An essay on one of the topics listed on application form (600 words). Employer and school letters must include telephone numbers and, where possible, e-mail addresses. **Deadline:** April 30. **Contact:** CHF at the above address (see entry 1974).

1976 ■ Canadian Hospitality Foundation College Entrance Scholarships *(Undergraduate/Scholarship)*

Purpose: To provide scholarship to the High School students in their final year of school. **Focus:** Culinary arts; Hotel, institutional, and restaurant management; Travel and tourism. **Qualif.:** Applicants must be high school students in their final year of school and who are enrolling in a minimum two-year college program in one of the following areas of training or study: Accommodation; Chef; Cook; Culinary; Events; Food and Beverages; Golf Club; Hospitality; Hotel; Resort; Restaurant; Tourism; Applicants must be Canadian citizens or permanent residents. **Criteria:** Selection will be based on work experience, scholastic record, leadership and ability to get along with others, professional promise and discretionary points.

Funds Avail.: $3,000. **To Apply:** Applicants must complete the application form on-line. In addition, students must submit hard copies of the following documents (please note that missing or incomplete documents may be grounds for elimination): Final-year official transcripts from your previous academic year and report card from your current academic year (first semester/first term); Letter/s of recommendation from your school principal, teacher or guidance counselor; Letter/s of recommendation form past or present employers. School and employer letters must include telephone numbers and, where possible, e-mail addresses. **Deadline:** April 30. **Contact:** CHF at the above address (see entry 1974).

1977 ■ Canadian Hospitality Foundation University Entrance Scholarships *(Undergraduate/Scholarship)*

Purpose: To provide scholarships to High School students in their final year of school. **Focus:** Hotel, institutional, and restaurant management; Travel and tourism. **Qualif.:** Applicants must be high school students in their final year of school who are enrolling in a university degree program in one of the following areas of training or study: Hospitality; Hotel; Tourism. Applicants must be Canadian citizens or permanent residents. **Criteria:** Selection will be based on the following criteria: Work experience; Scholastic record; Leadership and ability to get along with others; Professional promise; Discretionary points.

Funds Avail.: $3,500. **To Apply:** Applicants must complete the application form on-line; in addition, students must submit hard copies of the following documents (please note that missing or incomplete documents may be grounds for elimination): Final-year official transcripts from your previous academic year and report card from your current academic year (first semester/first term); Letter/s of recommendation from your school principal, teacher or guidance counselor; Letter/s of recommendation form past or present employers. School and employer letters must include telephone numbers and, where possible, e-mail addresses. **Deadline:** April 30. **Contact:** CHF at the above address (see entry 1974).

1978 ■ Culinary (1-Year Program) Scholarships *(Undergraduate/Scholarship)*

Purpose: To provide scholarship to the students enrolled in a one-year culinary program. **Focus:** Culinary arts. **Qualif.:** Applicants must: be college students currently enrolled in a one-year (minimum ten months) culinary certificate program; not have received any other Canadian Hospitality Foundation scholarships; be Canadian citizens or permanent residents. **Criteria:** Selection will be based on work

Awards are arranged alphabetically below their administering organizations

experience, scholastic record, leadership and ability to get along with others, professional promise and discretionary points. Application selected by the judges are ranked and the scholarships awarded in order of their dollar value.

Funds Avail.: $1,500. **To Apply:** Applicants must complete the application form on-line. In addition, students must submit hard copies of the following documents (please note that missing or incomplete documents may be grounds for elimination): Final-year official transcripts from your previous academic year and report card from your current academic year (first semester/first term); Letter/s of recommendation from your school principal, teacher or guidance counselor; Letter/s of recommendation form past or present employers. School and employer letters must include telephone numbers and, where possible, e-mail addresses. **Deadline:** April 30. **Contact:** CHF at the above address (see entry 1974).

1979 ■ Canadian Institute of Planners

116 Albert St., Ste. 801
Ottawa, ON, Canada K1P 5G3
Ph: (613)237-7526
Fax: (613)237-7045
Free: 800-207-2138
E-mail: general@cip-icu.ca
URL: http://www.cip-icu.ca

1980 ■ CIP Fellow's Travel Scholarships
(Postgraduate/Scholarship)

Purpose: To inspire future planners by allowing them to travel, observe and study innovative planning projects first hand. **Focus:** General studies. **Qualif.:** Applicant must be a student member enrolled in a planning program recognized by the Canadian Institute of Planners. **Criteria:** Recipients will be selected based on demonstrated leadership and commitment to their chosen profession and professional association; academic achievement; and a proposal to travel and explore a leading-edge, innovative or new planning initiative or project that will contribute to the depth and breadth of the student's educational experience, as reviewed by a jury consisting of three members of the College of Fellows and the Vice President of the Student Scholarship Trust Fund.

Funds Avail.: $4,000. **To Apply:** Applicants must provide contact information, university and program enrollment information, official transcript, recommendation letter from the department head and from someone who is familiar with the applicant's commitment to community service, a list of accomplishments and a travel proposal (not more than 4-5 pages in length). Application and attachments must be sent to: Planning Students Trust Fund, Canadian Institute of Planners, 116 Albert St., Ste. 801. **Deadline:** February 29.

1981 ■ Canadian Institute of Ukrainian Studies

4-50 Athabasca Hall
Edmonton, AB, Canada T6G 2E8
Ph: (780)492-2972
Fax: (780)492-4967
E-mail: cius@ualberta.ca
URL: http://www.ualberta.ca/CIUS

1982 ■ Leo J. Krysa Family Undergraduate Scholarships *(Undergraduate/Scholarship)*

Purpose: To help students pursue their final year of study in the faculty of Arts or Education. **Focus:** Ukrainian studies. **Qualif.:** Candidates must be Canadian citizens or permanent residents of Canada at the time of application; must be students in the faculty of Arts and Education about to enter their final year of study in pursuit of an undergraduate degree. **Criteria:** Applications will be judged on a points system that emphasizes academic achievement, performance in Ukrainian-content course, writing sample (paper or essay), and community involvement.

Funds Avail.: $3,500. **To Apply:** Applicants must submit an official transcript of records. Application form is available from the Canadian Institute of Ukrainian Studies, 450 Athabasca Hall, University of Alberta, Edmonton, AB, CAN T6G 2E8. **Deadline:** March 1.

1983 ■ Ukrainian Canadian Professional and Business Club Scholarships in Education
(Undergraduate/Scholarship)

Purpose: To support students who wish to pursue their final year of study in the faculty of Education. **Focus:** Ukrainian studies. **Qualif.:** Applicant must be a full-time undergraduate student completing the third or fourth year in the faculty of Education at the University of Alberta; must have taken one course in language acquisition or teaching and one senior course in Ukrainian language or literature; must have both academic standing and demonstrated involvement in the Ukrainian community. **Criteria:** Application will be judged on a points system that emphasizes academic achievement, performance in Ukrainian-content course, writing sample (paper or essay), and community involvement.

Funds Avail.: $800. **To Apply:** Applicants must submit an official transcript of records. Application form is available from the Canadian Institute of Ukrainian Studies, 450 Athabasca Hall, University of Alberta, Edmonton, AB, CAN T6G 2E8. **Deadline:** March 1.

1984 ■ Canadian Library Association

328 Frank St.
Ottawa, ON, Canada K2P 0X8
Ph: (613)232-9625
Fax: (613)563-9895
E-mail: info@cla.ca
URL: http://www.cla.ca

1985 ■ CLA/ACB Dafoe Scholarships *(Graduate/Scholarship)*

Purpose: To encourage individuals to pursue their masters degree in library and information studies. **Focus:** Library and archival sciences. **Qualif.:** Candidates must be Canadian citizens or landed immigrants; must have professional library/information science degrees at an ALA-accredited institution. **Criteria:** Applicants are selected based on academic achievement, leadership potential and expressed interest in the profession.

Funds Avail.: $5,000. **To Apply:** Application and scholarship reference forms are available from the website. **Deadline:** May 1.

1986 ■ H.W. Wilson Scholarships *(Graduate/Scholarship)*

Purpose: To encourage individuals to pursue their masters degree in library and information studies. **Focus:** Library and archival sciences. **Qualif.:** Candidates must be Canadian citizens or with landed immigrant status; must have professional library degrees at an ALA-accredited institution. **Criteria:** Scholarship applications are reviewed by the committee of members of the Canadian Library Association.

Funds Avail.: $2,000. **To Apply:** Application and scholarship reference forms are available at the website. **Deadline:** May 1.

1987 ■ World Book Graduate Scholarships in Library and Information Science *(Graduate/Scholarship)*

Purpose: To support individuals who wish to pursue a PhD degree in library and information studies. **Focus:** Library and archival sciences. **Qualif.:** Applicant must be an individual who holds a MLS/MLIS degree, and is pursuing a PhD degree in library and information studies in either Canada or the United States; must be a Canadian citizen or landed immigrant. **Criteria:** Recipients are selected based on the application and other supporting documents.

Funds Avail.: $2,500. **To Apply:** Application form is available at the website; applicants are advised to visit the Scholarships Committee, c/o CLA/ACB Memver Service Department, 328 Frank St., Ottawa, ON K2P 0X8. **Deadline:** May 1.

1988 ■ Canadian National Institute for the Blind

1929 Bayview Ave.
Toronto, ON, Canada M4G 3E8
Fax: (416)480-7700
Free: 800-563-2642
E-mail: info@cnib.ca
URL: http://www.cnib.ca/en

1989 ■ Scholarship Award of The Aliant Pioneer Volunteers *(Postgraduate/Scholarship)*

Purpose: To provide financial assistance to a person with vision lost while attending a post-secondary educational program. **Focus:** General studies. **Qualif.:** Candidates must be aged 25 years or under; must have acuity of 20/70 or less with correction; must be a Canadian citizen residing in Nova Scotia or Prince Edward Island; must be graduating from grade 12 during the application year (or be a high school graduate) and registered in a postsecondary educational program. Candidates may also be presently employed but returning to an educational program; must have a reasonable level of achievement and a genuine need for financial assistance. **Criteria:** Candidates will be selected based on the Selection Committee's review of the application materials. Priority is given to candidates with financial need.

Funds Avail.: $2,000. **To Apply:** Applicants must submit a completed application form (available at the website); must submit two letters of reference: (1) educational letter of recommendation, and (2) personal or community letter of recommendation including contact information (address, telephone, fax and e-mail); letter of acceptance from post-secondary education institution; must provide a documentation about the candidate's visual acuity. Application form and other supporting documents must be sent to: Selection Committee, Scholarship Award of the Aliant Pioneer Volunteers, 6136 Almon St., Halifax, NS B3K 1T8. **Deadline:** May 15.

1990 ■ Canadian Nurses Foundation

50 Driveway St.
Ottawa, ON, Canada K2P 1E2
Ph: (613)237-2159
Fax: (613)237-3520
Free: 800-361-8404
E-mail: info@cnf-fiic.ca
URL: http://www.canadiannursesfoundation.com/overview.htm

1991 ■ Aplastic, Anemia and Myelosdysplasia Scholarships *(Graduate/Scholarship)*

Purpose: To support students who want to pursue their education. **Focus:** Hematology; Oncology. **Qualif.:** Applicants must be nurses who will be focusing their research in the field of hematology or oncology; must be willing to increase awareness of Aplastic, Anemia and Myelodysplasia issues by presenting to colleagues or sitting on the Board of the Association; must be a Canadian citizen or permanent resident status; must be studying in Canada; must be RNs enrolled in a Masters program in a health related field; must be non-nurses who hold a degree in a health-related field and are in a nursing-related program, which will qualify them as RNs at the Master's level; must be full-time or part-time students, but part-time students must be taking a minimum of 2 courses each semester. **Criteria:** Preference will be given to CANO members.

Funds Avail.: No specific amount. **To Apply:** Applicants must complete and print the application form available online. For further information, applicants are advised to contact, Jacqueline Solis, Foundation Coordinator at 613237-2159. **Deadline:** MArch 31.

1992 ■ Astra Zeneca RURAL Scholarships *(Doctorate/Scholarship)*

Purpose: To support students who want to pursue their education. **Focus:** Nursing. **Qualif.:** Applicant must be a student doing research that will impact front line nursing care delivery to under serviced or marginalized populations in rural setting; must be a Canadian citizen or permanent resident status; must be studying in Canada; must be an RNs full-time or part-time students, but part-time students must be taking a minimum of 2 courses each semester or doing thesis work; must not receive other awards or scholarships during the Scholar Year of the application. **Criteria:** Selection of applicants will be based on the Scholarship application criteria.

Funds Avail.: No specific amount. **To Apply:** Applicants must complete and print the application form available online. For further information, applicants are advised to contact, Jacqueline Solis, Foundation Coordinator at 613237- 2159. **Deadline:** March 31.

1993 ■ Ann Beckingham Scholarships *(Doctorate/Scholarship)*

Purpose: To support students who want to pursue their education. **Focus:** Nursing. **Qualif.:** Applicant must be a Canadian citizen or permanent resident status; must be studying in Canada; must be an RNs full-time or part-time students, but part-time students must be taking a minimum of 2 courses each semester or doing thesis work; must not receive other awards or scholarships during the Scholar Year of the application. **Criteria:** Selection of applicants will be based on the Scholarship application criteria.

Funds Avail.: No specific amount. **To Apply:** Applicants must complete and print the application form available online; for further information, applicants are advice to contact, Jacqueline Solis, Foundation Coordinator at 613237-2159. **Deadline:** March 31.

Awards are arranged alphabetically below their administering organizations

1994 ■ Birks Family Foundation Scholarships *(Undergraduate/Scholarship)*

Purpose: To support students who want to pursue their education. **Focus:** Nursing. **Qualif.:** Applicant must be a Canadian citizen or permanent resident status; must be studying in Canada; must be entering at least year 2 as a full-time student of a baccalaureate-nursing program. **Criteria:** Selection of applicants will be based on the Scholarship application criteria.

Funds Avail.: No specific amount. **To Apply:** Applicants must complete and print the application form available online. For further information, applicants are advice to contact, Jacqueline Solis, Foundation Coordinator at 613237-2159. **Deadline:** March 31.

Remarks: Scholarship was established by the Birks Family Foundation out of an interest in contributing to a higher standard of living and quality of life by supporting higher education, the hospital sector, and health organizations.

1995 ■ Canadian Nurses Foundation - Baxter Corporation Scholarships *(Graduate/Scholarship)*

Purpose: To support students who want to pursue their education. **Focus:** Nursing. **Qualif.:** Applicants must be students in Nursing Sciences program; must be Canadian citizens or permanent resident status; must be studying in Canada; must be RNs enrolled in a Masters program in a health related field; must be non-nurses who hold a degree in a health-related field and are in a nursing-related program, which will qualify them as RNs at the Master's level; must be full-time or part-time students, but part-time students must be taking a minimum of 2 courses each semester. **Criteria:** Selection of applicants will be based on the Scholarship application criteria.

Funds Avail.: No specific amount. **To Apply:** Applicants must complete and print the application form available online. For further information, applicants are advised to contact, Jacqueline Solis, Foundation Coordinator at 613237-2159. **Deadline:** March 31.

1996 ■ Canadian Nurses Foundation Northern Scholarships *(Undergraduate/Scholarship)*

Purpose: To support students who want to pursue their education. **Focus:** Nursing. **Qualif.:** Applicant must be a student intending to work in Canada's North. **Criteria:** Preference will be given to aboriginal origin or nurses who have worked in the north for at least 2 years.

Funds Avail.: No specific amount. **To Apply:** Applicants must complete and print the application form available online. For further information, applicants are advised to contact, Jacqueline Solis, Foundation Coordinator at 613237-2159. **Deadline:** March 31.

1997 ■ Canadian Nurses Foundation Scholarships *(Undergraduate/Scholarship)*

Purpose: To support students who want to pursue their education. **Focus:** Nursing. **Qualif.:** Applicants must be Canadian citizens or permanent residents status; must be studying in Canada; must be entering at least year 2 as a full-time student of a baccalaureate-nursing program. **Criteria:** Selection of applicants will be based on the Scholarship application criteria.

Funds Avail.: No specific amount. **To Apply:** Applicants must complete and print the application form available online. For further information, applicants are advice to contact, Jacqueline Solis, Foundation Coordinator at 613237-2159. **Deadline:** MArch 31.

1998 ■ Extendicare Scholarships *(Graduate/Scholarship)*

Purpose: To support students who want to pursue their education. **Focus:** Gerontology. **Qualif.:** Applicants must be nurses who intend to practice, teach or do research in gerontology/long term care; must be Canadian citizens or permanent residents status; must be studying in Canada; must be RNs enrolled in a Masters program in a health related field; must be non-nurses who hold a degree in a health-related field and are in a nursing-related program, which will qualify them as RNs at the Master's level; must be full-time or part-time students, but part-time students must be taking a minimum of 2 courses each semester. **Criteria:** Selection of applicants will be based on the scholarship application criteria.

Funds Avail.: No specific amount. **To Apply:** Applicants must complete and print the application form available online; for further information, applicants are advised to contact, Jacqueline Solis, Foundation Coordinator at 613237-2159. **Deadline:** March 31.

1999 ■ Helen Glass Scholarships *(Doctorate/Scholarship)*

Purpose: To support students who want to pursue their education. **Focus:** Nursing. **Qualif.:** Applicants must be Nurses from Manitoba who are studying in community health nursing, primary health care, health nursing and studies which focus on "at risk population"; must be registered nurses who are undertaking graduate studies in nursing; must be willing to practice in Canada for a period of not less than 6-12 months after the Scholarship has been received; must be a Canadian citizen or permanent resident status; must be studying in Canada; must be an RNs full-time or part-time students, but part-time students must be taking a minimum of 2 courses each semester or doing thesis work. **Criteria:** Selection of applicants will be based on the Scholarship application criteria.

Funds Avail.: No specific amount. **To Apply:** Applicants must complete and print the application form available online. For further information, applicants are advice to contact, Jacqueline Solis, Foundation Coordinator at 613237-2159. **Deadline:** March 31

2000 ■ Judy Hill Scholarships *(Undergraduate/Scholarship)*

Purpose: To support students who want to pursue their education. **Focus:** Nursing. **Qualif.:** Applicant must be a student who has worked in the north and must sign a statement that they will practice nursing in the north for a period of 12 months; must be Canadian citizen or permanent resident status; must be studying in Canada; must be entering at least year 2 as a full-time student of a baccalaureate-nursing program. **Criteria:** Selection of applicants will be based on the Scholarship application criteria.

Funds Avail.: No specific amount. **To Apply:** Applicants must complete and print the application form available online; for further information, applicants are advised to contact, Jacqueline Solis, Foundation Coordinator at 6132372159. **Deadline:** March 31.

2001 ■ Hoffman-Laroche Scholarships *(Graduate/Scholarship)*

Purpose: To support students who want to pursue their education. **Focus:** Nursing. **Qualif.:** Applicants must be pursuing a Nurse Practitioner or Advanced Nurse Practitioner master or nursing degree with an emphasis on Hepatitis

Awards are arranged alphabetically below their administering organizations

C; must be Canadian citizens or permanent residents status; must be studying in Canada; must be RNs enrolled in a Masters program in a health related field; must be non-nurses who hold a degree in a health-related field and are in a nursing-related program, which will qualify them as RNs at the Master's level; must be full-time or part-time students, but part-time students must be taking a minimum of 2 courses each semester. **Criteria:** Selection of applicants will be based on the Scholarship application criteria.

Funds Avail.: No specific amount. **To Apply:** Applicants must complete and print the application form available online. For further information, applicants are advised to contact, Jacqueline Solis, Foundation Coordinator at 613237-2159. **Deadline:** March 31.

2002 ■ Johnson & Johnson Scholarships *(Undergraduate/Scholarship)*

Purpose: To support students who want to pursue their education. **Focus:** Nursing. **Qualif.:** Applicant must be a student who plans to practice nursing in an operating room or a critical care area; must be a Canadian citizen or permanent resident status; must be studying in Canada; must be entering at least year 2 as a full-time student of a baccalaureate-nursing program. **Criteria:** Selection of applicants will be based on the Scholarship application criteria.

Funds Avail.: No specific amount. **To Apply:** Applicants must complete and print the application form available online. For further information, applicants are advised to contact, Jacqueline Solis, Foundation Coordinator at 613237-2159. **Deadline:** March 31.

2003 ■ Dorothy Kergin Scholarships *(Doctorate/Scholarship)*

Purpose: To support students who want to pursue their education. **Focus:** Nursing. **Qualif.:** Applicant must be a Canadian citizen or permanent resident status; must be studying in Canada; must be an RNs full-time or part-time students, but part-time students must be taking a minimum of 2 courses each semester or doing thesis work; must be a student at the doctoral level. **Criteria:** Selection of applicants will be based on the Scholarship application criteria.

Funds Avail.: No specific amount. **To Apply:** Applicants must complete and print the application form available online. For further information, applicants are advised to contact, Jacqueline Solis, Foundation Coordinator at 613237-2159. **Deadline:** March 31.

Remarks: Established by Dr. Kergin, a distinguished nurse, who was Professor and Associate Dean of Health Sciences at McMaster University and later Professor and Director of the School of Nursing at the University of Victoria.

2004 ■ Tecla Lin & Nelia Laroza Memorial Scholarships *(Undergraduate/Scholarship)*

Purpose: To support students who want to pursue their education. **Focus:** Nursing. **Qualif.:** Applicant must be a foreign educated nurse working towards baccalaureate degree; must be a Canadian citizen or permanent resident status; must be studying in Canada; must be entering at least year 2 as a full-time student of a baccalaureate-nursing program. **Criteria:** Selection of applicants will be based on the Scholarship application criteria.

Funds Avail.: No specific amount. **To Apply:** Applicants must complete and print the application form available online. For further information, applicants are advised to contact, Jacqueline Solis, Foundation Coordinator at 613237-2159. **Deadline:** March 31.

2005 ■ Eleanor Martin Scholarships *(Graduate/Scholarship)*

Purpose: To support students who want to pursue their education. **Focus:** Nursing. **Qualif.:** Applicants must be students interested in studying either Neurosurgical or Cancer nursing fields; must be Canadian citizens or permanent resident status; must be studying in Canada; must be RNs enrolled in a Masters program in a health related field; must be non-nurses who hold a degree in a health-related field and are in a nursing-related program, which will qualify them as RNs at the Master's level; must be full-time or part-time students, but part-time students must be taking a minimum of 2 courses each semester. **Criteria:** Selection of applicants will be based on the Scholarship application criteria.

Funds Avail.: No specific amount. **To Apply:** Applicants must complete and print the application form available online. For further information, applicants are advised to contact, Jacqueline Solis, Foundation Coordinator at 613237-2159. **Deadline:** March 31.

2006 ■ Meloche-Monnex Scholarships *(Doctorate/Scholarship)*

Purpose: To support students who want to pursue their education. **Focus:** Nursing. **Qualif.:** Applicant must be a Canadian citizen or permanent resident status; must be studying in Canada; must be an RNs full-time or part-time students, but part-time students must be taking a minimum of 2 courses each semester or doing thesis work; must be a student at the doctoral level. **Criteria:** Selection of applicants will be based on the Scholarship application criteria.

Funds Avail.: No specific amount. **To Apply:** Applicants must complete and print the application form available online. For further information, applicants are advised to contact, Jacqueline Solis, Foundation Coordinator at 613237-2159. **Deadline:** March 31.

Remarks: Established by TD Meloche Monnex, Canada's leading provider of insurance and added-value financial services, known for its exceptional quality of customer service.

2007 ■ Military Nurses Association Scholarships *(Graduate/Scholarship)*

Purpose: To support students who want to pursue their education. **Focus:** Nursing. **Qualif.:** Applicants must be students at master level; must be Canadian citizens or permanent residents status; must be studying in Canada; must be RNs enrolled in a Masters program in a health related field; must be non-nurses who hold a degree in a health-related field and are in a nursing-related program, which will qualify them as RNs at the Master's level; must be full-time or part-time students, but part-time students must be taking a minimum of 2 courses each semester. **Criteria:** Preference will be given to military nurses, or former military.

Funds Avail.: No specific amount. **To Apply:** Applicants must complete and print the application form available online. For further information, applicants are advised to contact, Jacqueline Solis, Foundation Coordinator at 613237-2159. **Deadline:** March 31.

Awards are arranged alphabetically below their administering organizations

2008 ■ Margaret Munro Scholarships *(Undergraduate/Scholarship)*

Purpose: To support students who want to pursue their education. **Focus:** Nursing. **Qualif.:** Applicant must be a student form Prince Edward Island; must be a Canadian citizen or permanent resident status; must be studying in Canada; must be entering at least year 2 as a full-time student of a baccalaureate-nursing program. **Criteria:** Selection of applicants will be based on the Scholarship application criteria.

Funds Avail.: No specific amount. **To Apply:** Applicants must complete and print the application form available online. For further information, applicants are advised to contact, Jacqueline Solis, Foundation Coordinator at 613237-2159. **Deadline:** March 31.

2009 ■ Helen Mussallem Scholarships *(Graduate/Scholarship)*

Purpose: To support students who want to pursue their education. **Focus:** Nursing. **Qualif.:** Applicants must be students at master level; must be Canadian citizens or permanent residents status; must be studying in Canada; must be RNs enrolled in a Masters program in a health related field; must be non-nurses who hold a degree in a health-related field and are in a nursing-related program, which will qualify them as RNs at the Master's level; must be full-time or part-time students, but part-time students must be taking a minimum of 2 courses each semester. **Criteria:** Selection of applicants will be based on the Scholarship application criteria.

Funds Avail.: No specific amount. **To Apply:** Applicants must complete and print the application form available online. For further information, applicants are advice to contact, Jacqueline Solis, Foundation Coordinator at 613237-2159. **Deadline:** March 31.

2010 ■ New Brunswick Nurses Association Scholarships *(Graduate/Scholarship)*

Purpose: To support students who want to pursue their education. **Focus:** Nursing. **Qualif.:** Applicants must be students from New Brunswick; must be Canadian citizens or permanent resident status; must be studying in Canada; must be RNs enrolled in a Masters program in a health related field; must be non-nurses who hold a degree in a health-related field and are in a nursing-related program, which will qualify them as RNs at the Master's level; must be full-time or part-time students, but part-time students must be taking a minimum of 2 courses each semester. **Criteria:** Selection of applicants will be based on the Scholarship application criteria.

Funds Avail.: No specific amount. **To Apply:** Applicants must complete and print the application form available online. For further information, applicants are advice to contact, Jacqueline Solis, Foundation Coordinator at 613237-2159. **Deadline:** March 31.

2011 ■ Sharon Nield Memorial Scholarships *(Undergraduate/Scholarship)*

Purpose: To support students who want to pursue their education. **Focus:** Nursing. **Qualif.:** Applicants must be registered nurses returning to school; must be Canadian citizens or permanent residents status; must be studying in Canada; must be entering at least year 2 as full-time students of a baccalaureate-nursing program. **Criteria:** Selection of applicants will be based on the Scholarship application criteria.

Funds Avail.: No specific amount. **To Apply:** Applicants must complete and print the application form available online; for further information, applicants are advised to contact, Jacqueline Solis, Foundation Coordinator at 613237-2159. **Deadline:** March 31.

2012 ■ Senator Norman Paterson Fellowship Scholarships *(Doctorate/Scholarship)*

Purpose: To support students who want to pursue their education. **Focus:** Nursing. **Qualif.:** Applicant must be a Canadian citizen or permanent resident status; must be studying in Canada; must be an RNs full-time or part-time students, but part-time students must be taking a minimum of 2 courses each semester or doing thesis work; must be a student at the doctoral level. **Criteria:** Selection of applicants will be based on the Scholarship application criteria.

Funds Avail.: No specific amount. **To Apply:** Applicants must complete and print the application form available online. For further information, applicants are advised to contact, Jacqueline Solis, Foundation Coordinator at 613237-2159. **Deadline:** March 31.

Remarks: Established to honour the memory of Mr. Norman M. Paterson, who served as President of the Victorian Order of Nurses in Canada.

2013 ■ Sanofi Pasteur Scholarships *(Graduate/Scholarship)*

Purpose: To support students who want to pursue their education. **Focus:** Nursing. **Qualif.:** Applicants must be Canadian citizens or permanent residents status; must be studying in Canada; must be RNs enrolled in a Masters program in a health related field; must be non-nurses who hold a degree in a health-related field and are in a nursing-related program, which will qualify them as RNs at the Master's level; must be full-time or part-time students, but part-time students must be taking a minimum of 2 courses each semester. **Criteria:** Selection of applicants will be based on the Scholarship application criteria.

Funds Avail.: No specific amount. **To Apply:** Applicants must complete and print the application form available online. For further information, applicants are advised to contact, Jacqueline Solis, Foundation Coordinator at 613237-2159. **Deadline:** March 31.

Remarks: Established in 1990 by Sanofi Pasteur Ltd. the largest vaccine company in Canada.

2014 ■ Sigma Theta Tau International Scholarships *(Doctorate/Scholarship)*

Purpose: To support students who want to pursue their education. **Focus:** Nursing. **Qualif.:** Applicants must be nurses who are working on their PhD dissertation; must be a Canadian citizen or permanent resident status; must be studying in Canada; must be an RNs full-time or part-time students, but part-time students must be taking a minimum of 2 courses each semester or doing thesis work. **Criteria:** Selection of applicants will be based on the Scholarship application criteria.

Funds Avail.: No specific amount. **To Apply:** Applicants must complete and print the application form available online. For further information, applicants are advised to contact, Jacqueline Solis, Foundation Coordinator at 613237-2159. **Deadline:** March 31.

2015 ■ John Vanderlee Scholarships *(Undergraduate/Scholarship)*

Purpose: To support students who want to pursue their education. **Focus:** Nursing. **Qualif.:** Applicant must be a male student entering at least year 2 as a full-time student of a baccalaureate-nursing program; must be a Canadian citizen or permanent resident status; must be studying in Canada. **Criteria:** Selection of applicants will be based on the Scholarship application criteria.

Funds Avail.: No specific amount. **To Apply:** Applicants must complete and print the application form available online; for further information, applicants are advised to contact, Jacqueline Solis, Foundation Coordinator at 613237-2159. **Deadline:** March 31.

2016 ■ Canadian Occupational Therapy Foundation

1125 Colonel By Dr., Ste. No. 3401
Ottawa, ON, Canada K1S 5R1
Ph: (613)523-2268
Fax: (613)523-2552
Free: 800-434-2268
E-mail: skamble@cotfcanada.org
URL: http://www.cotfcanada.org

2017 ■ Canadian Occupational Therapy Foundation Graduate Scholarships *(Graduate/ Scholarship)*

Purpose: To support CAOT student members. **Focus:** Occupational therapy. **Qualif.:** Applicants must be life or student members of CAOT enrolled full-time or part-time in a master's or doctoral program related to occupational therapy research. **Criteria:** Selection of applicants will be based on scholarship reviewer criteria.

Funds Avail.: $3,000 for doctoral and $1,500 for masters. **To Apply:** Applicants must provide ten collated and completed copies of the application form and ten collated and completed copies of all materials listed: (a) Proof of program enrollment for the period of the award; (b) One original and ten copies of postsecondary transcripts; (c) A letter of intent that gives a description of, and rationale for, the proposed or ongoing thesis research; must provide a curriculum vitae; must have two references that will provide statements of support for academic objectives and appraisal of candidate's ability to do graduate work; (d) A photocopy of CAOT membership card. **Deadline:** September 30.

2018 ■ Canadian Occupational Therapy Foundation Invacare Master's Scholarships *(Graduate/ Scholarship)*

Purpose: To support CAOT student members. **Focus:** Occupational therapy **Qualif.:** Applicants must be a student member of CAOT enrolled full-time or part-time in a master's program related to occupational therapy. **Criteria:** Selection of applicants will be based on scholarship reviewer criteria.

Funds Avail.: $2,000. **To Apply:** Applicants must provide ten collated and completed copies of the application form and ten collated and completed copies of all materials listed: (a) Proof of program enrollment for the period of the award; (b) One original and ten copies of postsecondary transcripts; (c) A letter of intent that gives a description of, and rationale for, the proposed or ongoing thesis research; must provide a curriculum vitae; must have two references that will provide statements of support for academic objectives and appraisal of candidate's ability to do graduate work; (d) A photocopy of CAOT membership card. **Deadline:** September 30.

2019 ■ Thelma Cardwell Scholarships *(Graduate/ Scholarship)*

Purpose: To support CAOT student members. **Focus:** Occupational therapy. **Qualif.:** Applicants must be a student member of CAOT enrolled full-time in a master's or doctoral level program who has demonstrated an outstanding contribution to occupational therapy; must be a CAOT individual, life or student member in good standing. Applicants enrolled in a university program outside Canada should indicate their intention to return to practice and/or take up an academic appointment in Canada. **Criteria:** Selection of applicants will be based on scholarship reviewer criteria.

Funds Avail.: $2,000. **To Apply:** Applicants must provide ten collated and completed copies of the application form and ten collated and completed copies of all materials listed: (a) Proof of program enrollment for the period of the award; (b) One original and ten copies of postsecondary transcripts; (c) A letter of intent that gives a description of, and rationale for, the proposed or ongoing thesis research; must provide a curriculum vitae; must have two references that will provide statements of support for academic objectives and appraisal of candidate's ability to do graduate work; (d) A photocopy of CAOT membership card. **Deadline:** September 30.

2020 ■ Goldwin Howland Scholarships *(Graduate/Scholarship)*

Purpose: To provide financial support to CAOT students. **Focus:** Occupational therapy. **Qualif.:** Applicants must be enrolled in graduate study related to occupational therapy in Canada; must be a CAOT individual, life or student member in good standing. Applicants enrolled in a university program outside Canada should indicate their intention to return to practice and/or to take up an academic appointment in Canada. **Criteria:** Selection of applicants will be based on scholarship reviewer criteria.

Funds Avail.: $2,000. **To Apply:** Applicants must provide ten collated and completed copies of the application form and ten collated and completed copies of all materials listed: (a) Proof of program enrollment for the period of the award; (b) One original and ten copies of postsecondary transcripts; (c) A letter of intent that gives a description of, and rationale for, the proposed or ongoing thesis research; must provide a curriculum vitae; must have two references that will provide statements of support for academic objectives and appraisal of candidate's ability to do graduate work; (d) A photocopy of CAOT membership card. **Deadline:** September 30.

2021 ■ Canadian Organic Growers

323 Chapel St.
Ottawa, ON, Canada K1N 7Z2
Ph: (613)216-0741
Fax: (613)236-0743
Free: 888-375-7383
E-mail: office@cog.ca
URL: http://www.cog.ca

2022 ■ Mary Pelmutter Scholarships *(Postgraduate/Award/Prize)*

Purpose: To encourage researches on the benefits of organic growers through financial assistance. **Focus:** Botany. **Qualif.:** Applicants must be a Canadian citizens or landed immigrants; must have obtained satisfactory results

Awards are arranged alphabetically below their administering organizations

in undergraduate studies in a recognized Canadian college or university; and must have been admitted to the faculty of their choice. **Criteria:** Recipients are selected based on transcripts, the relevant benefit of the proposed research on organic growers, and reference letters. Selection of winners is made by the COG MPS Committee.

Funds Avail.: $4,000. **To Apply:** Application forms and letter of support forms are available from the website. Applicants must submit academic transcripts and research proposals to the selection committee. **Deadline:** June 30.

Remarks: The scholarship is named after COG past president and long-time organic grower Mary Perlmutter. **Contact:** Achim Mohssen-Beyk.

2023 ■ Canadian Paraplegic Association

1101 Prince of Wales Dr., Ste. 230
Ottawa, ON, Canada K2C 3W7
Ph: (613)723-1033
Fax: (613)723-1060
E-mail: info@canparaplegic.org
URL: http://www.canparaplegic.org/en

2024 ■ Copnick/Hilliard Scholarships *(Professional Development/Scholarship)*

Purpose: To assist and support students with permanent severe mobility impairment such as spinal cord injury to continue their post-secondary education. **Focus:** General studies. **Qualif.:** Applicants must have a spinal cord injury or other physical disability; must be volunteers or staff members of the Canadian Paraplegic Association; must be Canadian citizens or landed immigrants; must demonstrate outstanding initiative and scholastic achievement in a recognized post-secondary institution in Canada. **Criteria:** Recipients will be selected based on academic standing, merit and financial needs.

Funds Avail.: $500. **To Apply:** Applicants must submit a letter of reference and transcripts of the last two years of study. Application and attachments must be sent to: 1101 Prince of Wales Dr., Ste. 230, Ottawa, ON K2C 3W7. **Deadline:** August 31. **Contact:** Freddy Martinez.

2025 ■ Sun Life Financial Peer Support Scholarships *(Professional Development/Scholarship)*

Purpose: To assist peer volunteers and participants with an SCI or other physical disability to advance their post-secondary education in the disability fields. **Focus:** General studies. **Qualif.:** Applicants must have been diagnosed with a spinal cord injury or other physical disability; must be volunteers or staff members of the Canadian Paraplegic Association; must be Canadian citizens or landed immigrants; must be attending, or will be attending, a recognized post-secondary institution in Canada. **Criteria:** Recipients will be selected based on academic standing, merit and financial needs.

Funds Avail.: $1,500. **To Apply:** Application forms are available from the website. Applicants must provide a copy of their most recent transcripts. Application and attachments must be sent to: 1101 Prince of Wales Dr., Ste. 230, Ottawa, ON K2C 3W7. **Deadline:** August 31. **Contact:** Freddie Martinez, fmartinez@canparaplegic.org.

2026 ■ Canadian Parking Association

350-2255 St. Laurent Blvd.
Ottawa, ON, Canada K1G 4K3
Ph: (613)727-0700
Fax: (613)727-3183
E-mail: info@canadianparking.ca
URL: http://www.canadianparking.ca

2027 ■ Canadian Parking Association Scholarships *(Undergraduate/Scholarship)*

Purpose: To provide financial assistance to students in their pursuit of academic excellence and to encourage post-secondary study that enhances the parking industry in Canada. **Focus:** General studies. **Qualif.:** Applicants must be registered CPA members whose job function is 50% related to parking, their spouses and dependents, members' employees whose job function is 50% related to parking, their spouses and dependents with a minimum average of 70% in the last three semesters of studies (non-academic courses such as career or personal development related courses will not be considered). **Criteria:** Applicants will be evaluated based on academic performance; extracurricular activities or volunteer/community involvement, excluding those which are included in the high school curriculum; and quality of reference letters (one from a teacher and one from a person familiar with extracurricular activities or community involvement, excluding family members).

Funds Avail.: $2,000. **Number Awarded:** 10. **To Apply:** Applicants must submit the completed application form; official transcript of the last three semesters of available marks; description of extracurricular activities or volunteer/community involvement; two signed letters of reference; and the parental consent form. **Deadline:** May 15.

2028 ■ Canadian Sanitation Supply Association

910 Dundas St., W
PO Box 10009
Whitby, ON, Canada L1P 1P7
Ph: (905)430-7267
Fax: (905)430-6418
URL: http://cssa.com

2029 ■ Canadian Sanitation Supply Association Scholarships *(Undergraduate/Scholarship)*

Purpose: To provide scholarship assistance to qualified Canadian students who will be attending college or university in Canada. **Focus:** General studies. **Qualif.:** Applicant must be a student who will be graduating high school; must be an individual who is already enrolled in a college or university in Canada; must be a young Canadian who has achieved a high level of academic and leadership standards. **Criteria:** Applicant will be judged based on the following criteria: (1) Applicant's ability to read and fully comprehend the terms and conditions of the application procedure; (2) Applicant's ability to ensure that all components of the application-the Applicant Information Form, the 2"x3" photo, the essay, the transcripts, the evaluation form and the typed resume-are received by the CSSA Scholarship Foundation office; (3) Applicant's academic achievements as well as school/college activities, volunteerism and social achievements; (4) Quality of the essay - originality, clarity, grammar and presentation.

Funds Avail.: $2,000 offered in each of the six regions: Atlantic Canada, Quebec, Ontario, Manitoba & Saskatchewan, Alberta, British Columbia. **Number Awarded:** 6. **To Apply:** Applicant must complete the application form available online; must have a photograph, and official high school or college transcript; must provide

Awards are arranged alphabetically below their administering organizations

an essay on: "What does your school custodian or facilities manager think about the Green cleaning Movement?"; must have a typed resume with name, planned occupation or profession, high school information, college or university information, employment history, activity and leadership record, and applicant evaluation form completed by a counselor or teacher. **Deadline:** June 1.

2030 ■ International Sanitary Supply Association Foundation Scholarships *(High School/Scholarship)*

Purpose: To provide scholarship assistance to qualified Canadian students who will be attending college or university in Canada. **Focus:** General studies. **Qualif.:** Applicant must be a student who will be graduating high school; must be an individual who is already enrolled in a college or university in Canada; must be a young Canadian who has achieved a high level of academic and leadership standards. **Criteria:** Applicant will be judged based on the following criteria: (1) Applicant's ability to read and fully comprehend the terms and conditions of the application procedure; (2) Applicant's ability to ensure that all components of the application - the Applicant Information Form, the 2x3 photo, the essay, the transcripts, the evaluation form and the typed resume - are received by the CSSA Scholarship Foundation office; (3) Applicant's academic achievements as well as school/college activities, volunteerism and social achievements; (4) Quality of the essay - originality, clarity, grammar and presentation.

Funds Avail.: $2,000. **To Apply:** Applicant must complete the application form available online; must have a photograph, and official high school or college transcript; must provide an essay on: "What does your school custodian or facilities manager think about the Green cleaning Movement?"; must have a typed resume with name, planned occupation or profession, high school information, college or university information, employment history, activity and leadership record, and applicant evaluation form completed by a counselor or teacher. **Deadline:** June 1.

2031 ■ Sam Tughan Scholarships *(Undergraduate/Scholarship)*

Purpose: To provide scholarship assistance to qualified Canadian students who will be attending college or university in Canada. **Focus:** Medicine. **Qualif.:** Applicant must be a student who will be graduating high school; must be an individual who is already enrolled in a college or university in Canada; must be a young Canadian who has achieved a high level of academic and leadership standards. **Criteria:** Applicant will be judged based on the following criteria: (1) Applicant's ability to read and fully comprehend the terms and conditions of the application procedure; (2) Applicant's ability to ensure that all components of the application - the Applicant Information Form, the 2"x3" photo, the essay, the transcripts, the evaluation form and the typed resume - are received by the CSSA Scholarship Foundation office; (3) Applicant's academic achievements as well as school/college activities, volunteerism and social achievements; (4) Quality of the essay - originality, clarity, grammar and presentation.

Funds Avail.: $2,000. **To Apply:** Applicant must complete the application form available online; must have a photograph, and official high school or college transcript; must provide an essay on: "What does your school custodian or facilities manager think about the Green cleaning Movement?"; must have a typed resume with name, planned occupation or profession, high school information, college or university information, employment history, activity and leadership record, and applicant evaluation form completed by a counselor or teacher. **Deadline:** June 1.

2032 ■ Geoffrey H. Wood Scholarships *(Undergraduate/Scholarship)*

Purpose: To provide scholarship assistance to qualified Canadian students who will be attending college or university in Canada. **Focus:** Education. **Qualif.:** Applicant must be a student who will be graduating high school; must be an individual who is already enrolled in a college or university in Canada; must be a young Canadian who has achieved a high level of academic and leadership standards. **Criteria:** Applicant will be judged based on the following criteria: (1) Applicant's ability to read and fully comprehend the terms and conditions of the application procedure; (2) Applicant's ability to ensure that all components of the application-the Applicant Information Form, the 2"x3" photo, the essay, the transcripts, the evaluation form and the typed resume-are received by the CSSA Scholarship Foundation office; (3) Applicant's academic achievements as well as school/college activities, volunteerism and social achievements; (4) Quality of the essay-originality, clarity, grammar and presentation.

Funds Avail.: $2,000. **To Apply:** Applicant must complete the application form available online; must have a photograph and official high school or college transcript; must provide an essay on: "What does your school custodian or facilities manager think about the Green cleaning Movement?"; must have a typed resume with name, planned occupation or profession, high school information, college or university information, employment history, activity and leadership record, and applicant evaluation form completed by a counselor or teacher. **Deadline:** June 1.

2033 ■ Canadian Simmental Association

No. 13-4101-19th St. NE
Calgary, AB, Canada T2E 7C4
Ph: (403)250-7979
Fax: (403)250-5121
Free: (866)860-6051
E-mail: cansim@simmental.com
URL: http://www.simmental.com

2034 ■ Dr. Allan A. Dixon Memorial Scholarships *(Postgraduate/Scholarship)*

Purpose: To support members of the Canadian Simmental Association and their children. **Focus:** General studies. **Qualif.:** Applicants must be members of the Canadian Simmental Association or children of members, for one year or more by the date of registration. Applicants must have past/present involvement with Simmental cattle; must be Canadian citizens. **Criteria:** Preference is given to applicants who are active members of the Canadian Simmental Association.

Funds Avail.: No specific amount. **To Apply:** Application forms are available from the Canadian Simmental Association. Application and other documents must be submitted to: Canadian Simmental Association Scholarship Committee, No. 13, 4101-19th St. NE, Calgary, AB T2E 7C4. **Deadline:** October 1.

Remarks: The scholarship is in the memory of Dr. Allan A. Dixon.

2035 ■ Canadian Society of Club Managers

2943-B Bloor St., W
Etobicoke, ON, Canada M8X 1B3

Awards are arranged alphabetically below their administering organizations

Ph: (416)979-0640
Fax: (416)979-1144
Free: 877-376-CSCM
E-mail: national@cscm.org
URL: http://www.cscm.org

2036 ■ Val Mason Scholarships *(Postgraduate/Scholarship)*

Purpose: To provide financial assistance to individuals pursuing a career in club management. **Focus:** Management. **Qualif.:** Applicants must be nominated by a member of the society presently enrolled in a school, college or university and must intend to pursue a career in the Private Club Industry; must be employed or have been recently employed at a member club of the society; and must have shown a keen interest in pursuing a career in club management. **Criteria:** Applications and proposals will be reviewed and judged by the society's Scholarship Subcommittee.

Funds Avail.: $1,000. **To Apply:** Applicants must submit a letter of recommendation from the nominating member; transcript of records; a 500-word essay explaining their interests in the Private Club Industry; and must indicate how their education is presently funded. Complete application package must be submitted to: Canadian Society of Club Managers 2 Carlton St., Ste. 1304 Toronto, ON M5B 1J3. **Deadline:** August 4.

2037 ■ Canadian Society of Exploration Geophysicists

No. 600,640-8th Ave., SW
Calgary, AB, Canada T2P 1G7
Ph: (403)262-0015
Fax: (403)262-7383
E-mail: csegoffice@shaw.ca
URL: http://www.cseg.ca

2038 ■ CSEG Scholarship Trust Fund *(Postgraduate/Scholarship)*

Purpose: To provide financial support for promising graduate students pursuing careers in the field of exploration geophysics. **Focus:** Geophysics. **Qualif.:** Applicants must be undergraduates with above average standing or graduate students enrolled in an academic program directed toward an exploration geophysics career at any Canadian university. **Criteria:** Applicants are selected based on academic performance, financial need, interest in geophysics and extra-curricular activities.

Funds Avail.: No specific amount. **To Apply:** Applicants must provide a transcript of post-secondary education accompanied by a list of courses currently in progress; must submit recommendation letters from two faculty members or a past or current employer mailed directly to the Committee by the author. Application forms and supporting documents must be submitted to: CSEG Scholarship Committee, 600,640-8th Ave. SW, Calgary, AB T2P 1P7. **Deadline:** June 15.

2039 ■ Canadian Society for Medical Laboratory Science

PO Box 2830, LCD 1
Hamilton, ON, Canada L8N 3N8
Ph: (905)528-8642
Fax: (905)528-4968
E-mail: alison@csmls.org
URL: http://www.csmls.org

2040 ■ Dade Behring Student Scholarship Awards *(Postgraduate/Scholarship)*

Purpose: To cultivate and nurture future leaders in the field of medical laboratory science. **Focus:** Medical laboratory technology. **Qualif.:** Applicants must be current members of CSMLS and enrolled in the final year of a full-time Canadian training program in general medical laboratory technology, diagnostic cytology, and clinical genetics; must be Canadian citizens or permanent residents. **Criteria:** Applicants will be evaluated based on academic achievement, leadership and volunteer service, and financial need. Scholarship applications will be reviewed by the CSMLS Grants and Scholarships Committee.

Funds Avail.: $2,500. **To Apply:** Applicants must submit the application forms together with the official transcript of records, description of leadership abilities and professional goals, two letters of recommendation and a self-addressed, stamped return envelope to: Dade Behring Student Scholarship Award c/o CSMLS, P.O. Box 2830 LCD 1, Hamilton, ON L8N 3N8. **Deadline:** November 1.

2041 ■ Canadian Society of Petroleum Geologists

600-640 8th Ave. SW
Calgary, AB, Canada T2P 1G7
Ph: (403)264-5610
Fax: (403)264-5898
E-mail: tim.howard@cspg.org
URL: http://www.cspg.org

2042 ■ Canadian Aboriginal Science and Technology Society Scholarships *(Undergraduate/Scholarship)*

Purpose: To encourage educational pursuits among aboriginal students involved in the earth sciences. **Focus:** Geosciences. **Qualif.:** Applicants must be aboriginal students pursuing academic programs in the earth sciences. The program of study must be at least two years in length and the student must have completed the first year of his/her studies. **Criteria:** Selection is based on on merit.

Funds Avail.: $1,250. **To Apply:** Applicants must submit the following: high school transcript; university transcript (second semester midterm results accepted if received under separate cover and signed by department head); recommendation by department head and another teaching faculty member of the department. **Contact:** Shawna Christensen; 403-218-1625; Schristensen@petrelrob.com.

2043 ■ Canadian Society of Petroleum Geologists Regional Graduate Scholarships *(Doctorate, Graduate/Scholarship)*

Purpose: To promote advanced education and research in fields of geology that are applicable to the petroleum industry. **Focus:** Geology. **Qualif.:** Program is open to M.Sc. or Ph.D. students attending Canadian universities who are progressing to their second or subsequent year(s) of study in petroleum geology-related disciplines. Candidates must hold Canadian citizenship or landed immigrant status and must be accepted into their second year as full-time graduate student at a Canadian University. **Criteria:** Applicants will be evaluated on the basis of academic standing.

Funds Avail.: $1,500. **To Apply:** Applicants must com-

Awards are arranged alphabetically below their administering organizations

pleted application containing background information; academic program; appraisal by academic supervisor and one other academic member of the department; and undergraduate and graduate transcripts. **Deadline:** May 31. **Contact:** Shawna Christensen; 403-218-1625; Schristensen@petrelrob.com.

2044 ■ Canadian Society of Petroleum Geologists Regional Undergraduate Scholarships
(Undergraduate/Scholarship)

Purpose: To encourage educational pursuits in the field of geology. **Focus:** Earth Sciences. **Qualif.:** Program is open to all undergraduates enrolled in an accredited Earth Science program of a Canadian University who are in their second or third year. Candidates must hold Canadian citizenship or landed immigrants status. **Criteria:** Applicants will be evaluated on the basis of academic standing.

Funds Avail.: $1,250. **To Apply:** Applicants must submit the following: high school transcript; university transcript (second semester midterm results accepted if received under separate cover and signed by department head); recommendation by department head and another teaching faculty member of the department. **Contact:** Shawna Christensen; 403-218-1625; Schristensen@petrelrob.com.

2045 ■ Glen Ruby Memorial Scholarships
(Undergraduate/Scholarship)

Purpose: To promote excellence in petroleum geology and geophysics by assisting in the development of future geoscientists. **Focus:** Geoscience. **Qualif.:** Applicants must be students in their second, third or fourth year of studies in areas related to petroleum geology and geophysics. **Criteria:** Selection will be based on merit.

Funds Avail.: $2,000-$4,000. **To Apply:** Applicants must submit the completed application form together with copy of transcripts. Application forms are available online. **Deadline:** October 31.

Remarks: Scholarships will be administered through the CSPG Trust Fund. **Contact:** June Hamm, Conoco Philips Canada; PO Box 130, 401-9th Avenue S.W., Calgary, AB, T2P 2H7.

2046 ■ Canadian Water Resources Association

280 Albert St., Ste. 900
Ottawa, ON, Canada K1P 5G8
Ph: (613)237-9363
Fax: (613)594-5190
E-mail: services@aic.ca
URL: http://www.cwra.org

2047 ■ Canadian Water Resources Association Scholarships *(All/Scholarship)*

Purpose: To raise awareness of the value of water; to promote responsible and effective water resource management in Canada. **Focus:** Water resources. **Qualif.:** Applicants must be members of the Canada Water Resources Association. **Criteria:** Recipients are selected based on academic excellence and project relevance to water management.

Funds Avail.: $1,500. **Number Awarded:** 3. **To Apply:** Applicants must provide a statement from the chairman/director of the department which verifies that the application is reflective of the project; a 500-word statement which outlines the applicant's research project and its relevance to sustainable water resources; official transcript of records; two references to be sent directly to the Scholarship Committee by the referees or appropriate official of the university or college; a statement from the program chairman or director endorsing the application from that program, including confirmation of the applicant's full-time registration; and completed application form. **Deadline:** February 29.

2048 ■ Ken Thomson Scholarships
(Undergraduate/Scholarship)

Purpose: To raise awareness of the value of water; to promote responsible and effective water resource management in Canada. **Focus:** Water resources. **Qualif.:** Applicant must be the second-highest ranked graduate student whose program of study focuses upon applied, natural or social science aspects of water resources; must be Canadian citizen or landed immigrant attending a Canadian University or college; must be enrolled in full-time graduate studies in any discipline. **Criteria:** Recipients are selected based on academic excellence and project relevance to water management and development.

Funds Avail.: $2,000. **To Apply:** Applicants must provide a statement from the chairman/director of the department which verifies that the application is reflective of the project; a 500-word statement which outlines the applicant's research project and its relevance to sustainable water resources; official transcript of records; two references to be sent directly to the Scholarship Committee by the referees or appropriate official of the university or college; a statement from the program chairman or director endorsing the application from that program, including confirmation of the applicant's full-time registration; and completed application form. **Deadline:** February 29.

2049 ■ Canadian Water and Wastewater Association

1010 Polytek St., Unit 11
Ottawa, ON, Canada K1J 9H9
Ph: (613)747-0524
Fax: (613)747-0523
E-mail: admin@cwwa.ca
URL: http://www.cwwa.ca

2050 ■ Steve Bonk Scholarships *(Postgraduate/Scholarship)*

Purpose: To provide educational assistance to those embarking on careers associated with municipal water supply or wastewater. **Focus:** General studies. **Qualif.:** Applicants must be Canadian citizen or permanent residents of Canada; must be resident of current CWWA municipal members, or attend college or university in a municipal or CWWA Academic members; must have completed successfully one year of post secondary education; must be registered as a full-time student in further studies; must intend to pursue a career related to the municipal water or wastewater industry. **Criteria:** Candidates will be selected based on the academic achievement, statement/essay, and work experience/extracurricular activities.

Funds Avail.: $500. **To Apply:** Applicants must have a copy of the post-secondary course transcripts completed to date; must have a description/list of planned further studies; must provide a statement or essay (500 words) of the applicant's interest, knowledge and future goals in the water/wastewater industry together with applicable work experience or extracurricular activities. Application and other supporting documents must be sent to: CWWA - Steve Bonk Scholarship, 11-1010 Polytek Rd., Ottawa, ON K1J 9H9. **Deadline:** May 30.

Awards are arranged alphabetically below their administering organizations

2051 ■ Cancer Survivors Fund

PO Box 792
Missouri City, TX 77459
Ph: (281)437-7142
Fax: (281)437-9568
E-mail: csf@cancersurvivorsfund.org
URL: http://www.cancersurvivorsfund.org

2052 ■ Cancer Survivors' Fund Scholarships *(Undergraduate/Scholarship)*

Purpose: To augment the expenses associated with the college education of young cancer survivors. **Focus:** General Studies. **Qualif.:** Applicants must be cancer survivors or currently diagnosed with cancer; must be enrolled in or accepted for enrollment in an undergraduate school. **Criteria:** Recipients are selected by a committee based on applicants' personal hardship and financial need.

Funds Avail.: No specific amount. **To Apply:** Applicants must complete the online scholarship application; must submit two letters of recommendation from two different academic teachers addressing why they should receive the scholarship; a letter from your attending physician verifying your medical history and current medical situation; must agree to do volunteer work to use their cancer experience to help other young cancer patients and survivors coping with a life threatening or life-altering event; Must submit an essay discussing the following question. HOW HAS MY EXPERIENCE WITH CANCER IMPACTED MY LIFE VALUES AND CAREER GOALS? Essays must be a minimum of 500 words and a maximum of 1200 words.

Remarks: The applicants and their parents if they are minors, must sign a release, that they agree to have their name and photo published in the news media or any CSF publication as a recipient of Cancer Survivors' Fund scholarship and that they agree to have their name, photo and success story to be published on this website or in any CSF publication. **Contact:** Cancer Survivors' Fund at the above address (see entry 2051).

2053 ■ Cape Coral Community Foundation

4729 Vincennes Blvd.
Cape Coral, FL 33904
Ph: (239)542-5594
E-mail: cccf@capecoralcf.org
URL: http://capecoralcf.planyourlegacy.org

2054 ■ The Helen and Edward Brancati Teacher Development Scholarships *(Professional Development/Scholarship)*

Purpose: To assist teachers employed by an accredited school in the United States who wish to continue their education. **Focus:** General studies. **Qualif.:** Applicants must be teachers employed by an accredited school in the United States who are seeking post-graduate education or need funds to continue their education classes, workshops, conferences or certification courses; must be U.S. citizens. **Criteria:** Recipients are selected based on demonstrated ability to create an atmosphere of learning for students across the broad spectrum of a mainstream classroom, complete application, letter of recommendation, essay and other materials.

Funds Avail.: Maximum amount of $1,000. **To Apply:** Applicants must show proof of employment; must provide a copy of teaching certificate, written evaluations from their school principal; must outline a plan for how these funds will be used to increase their professional development or enhance their classroom; must provide a 500 word original essay discussing their reasons for becoming a teacher and how this scholarship will be beneficial; must submit a proof of enrollment or most recent transcript. **Deadline:** September 1; October 31.

2055 ■ The Rotary Club of Cape Coral Goldcoast Scholarships Fund *(Undergraduate/Scholarship)*

Purpose: To assist eligible high school seniors to further their education by attending college. **Focus:** General Studies. **Qualif.:** Applicants must be graduating seniors of any high school in Lee County; must have a 3.2 GPA or better; must be accepted to at least one accredited junior college, college or university; must be residents of Cape Coral; must be U.S. citizens and active in school and community. **Criteria:** Recipients are selected based on academic standing, academic history, school and community involvement, career and academic goals and three letters of recommendation.

Funds Avail.: $4,000. **Number Awarded:** 3. **To Apply:** Applicants must submit a completed application form. **Deadline:** April 1.

2056 ■ Cape Fear Community College Foundation

411 N Front St.
Wilmington, NC 28401
Ph: (910)362-7207
URL: http://cfcc.edu/foundation

2057 ■ Cape Fear Community College Merit Scholarships *(Undergraduate/Scholarship)*

Purpose: To assist the local high school students of North Carolina throughout the course of their studies. **Focus:** General studies. **Qualif.:** Applicants must be U.S. citizen high school senior students who have applied for or been approved to enroll in Cape Fear Community College in a curriculum program and possess academic potential as shown by high school grades, rank in class. **Criteria:** Applicants are judged based on academic achievement and financial need.

Funds Avail.: $1,800. **Number Awarded:** 10. **To Apply:** Applicants must submit all required application information including the letter of recommendation from high school principal, guidance counselor or high school teacher. **Deadline:** April 1.

2058 ■ Caribbean Hotel Association

2655 Le Juene Rd., Ste. 910
Coral Gables, FL 33134
Ph: (305)443-3040
Fax: (305)443-3005
E-mail: executive@caribbeanhotelassociation.com
URL: http://www.caribbeanhotelassociation.com

2059 ■ Caribbean Hotel Association Academic Scholarships *(Undergraduate/Scholarship)*

Purpose: To provide people throughout the Caribbean region with an awareness of the industry's varied career opportunities a well as technical and professional development. **Focus:** Hotel, Institutional, and Restaurant Management. **Qualif.:** Applicants must be full-time or must be secondary school graduates pursuing a diploma or degree in hotel and restaurant management or culinary arts in a two-year or four-year program at an affiliated CHA institution; or either be full-time students who are currently pursuing a diploma or degree in hotel and restaurant management, culinary arts in a two-year, four-year, or a graduate program at an affiliated CHA institution and who has completed first semester of the program; must be born in the Caribbean and registered as a Caribbean National. **Criteria:** Recipients are selected based on potential for success in the hotel industry, and financial need.

Funds Avail.: No stated amount. **To Apply:** Applicants must complete the application form; must submit a copy of certificates or awards; must include a current photo; must submit a references or recommendation. **Deadline:** March 15.

2060 ■ The John Carter Brown Library

PO Box 1894
Providence, RI 02912
Ph: (401)863-2725
E-mail: jcbl_publications@brown.edu
URL: http://www.brown.edu

2061 ■ The John Carter Brown Library Long-Term Fellowships *(All/Fellowship)*

Purpose: To give scholars from the U.S. and abroad an opportunity to pursue their work in proximity to a distinguished collection of primary sources. **Focus:** General studies. **Qualif.:** Applicants must be American citizens or have been residents in the United States for three years. **Criteria:** Recipients are selected based on academic standing and financial need.

Funds Avail.: $4,000. **To Apply:** Applicants must complete the application form. **Deadline:** January 10.

2062 ■ The John Carter Brown Library Short-Term Fellowships *(Doctorate, Postdoctorate/ Fellowship)*

Purpose: To give scholars from the U.S. and abroad an opportunity to pursue their work in proximity to a distinguished collection of primary sources. **Focus:** General studies. **Qualif.:** Applicants must be Americans and foreign nationals who are engaged in pre- or post-doctoral, or independent research. **Criteria:** Recipients are selected based on the academic standing and financial need.

Funds Avail.: $2,000. **To Apply:** Applicants must complete the application form. **Deadline:** January 10.

2063 ■ Cascade Blues Association

PO Box 14493
Portland, OR 97293-0493
Ph: (503)223-1850
Fax: (503)223-1850
E-mail: cbastaff@cascadeblues.org
URL: http://www.cascadeblues.org

2064 ■ Christopher Mesi Music Scholarships *(Undergraduate/Scholarship)*

Purpose: To encourage anyone to pursue an undergraduate degree at a local college. **Focus:** Music. **Qualif.:** Applicants must be high school senior or college music students; must have a GPA of 2.5 or better. **Criteria:** Recipients are selected based on demonstrated achievement through his or her involvement in school or community activities.

Funds Avail.: $500. **To Apply:** Applicants must submit a transcript of records, two letters of recommendation from which one must come from music teacher and one must come from a counselor, employer or teacher. **Deadline:** July 15.

2065 ■ Catching the Dream

8200 Mountain Rd. NE., Ste. 203
Albuquerque, NM 87110
Ph: (505)262-2351
E-mail: nscholarships@aol.com
URL: http://www.catchingthedream.org

2066 ■ Sergeant Douglas and Charlotte De-Horse Scholarships *(Undergraduate/Scholarship)*

Purpose: To support American Indian students in their education. **Focus:** Military science and education. **Qualif.:** Applicants must be American Indian students who have completed one year of any Army, Navy, or Air Force Junior Reserve Officer Training program; enrolled in an Army, Navy, or Air Force Reserve Officer Training Program; a veteran of the United States Army, Navy, Air Force, Merchant Marine or Coast Guard; and enrolled in undergraduate or graduate program of study. **Criteria:** Applicants are selected based on criteria.

Funds Avail.: No specific amount. **To Apply:** Applicants must submit a completed application; letters of recommendation; personal essay; and high school transcripts. **Deadline:** April and September 15.

Remarks: The First Sergeant Douglas and Charlotte De-Horse Scholarship was established in 2007 to honor the American Indian veterans.

2067 ■ MESBEC Scholarships *(Undergraduate/ Scholarship)*

Purpose: To support the education of Native Schools. **Focus:** Mathematics and mathematical sciences; Engineering; Science; Business; Education; Computer and information sciences. **Qualif.:** Applicants must be 1/4 or more degree Native American; an enrolled member of a "U.S. tribe"; attending or planning to attend a college/university within the U.S. on a full-time basis that is fully accredited; studying in the field of business, finance, management, economics, banking, hotel management, and related field; have excellent grades; high ACT or SAT scores; and have a strong commitment to their Native American community. **Criteria:** Scholarships are awarded based on merit.

Funds Avail.: $500-$5000. **To Apply:** Applicants must submit a completed application form (available at the website); financial need analysis; a copy of the IRS 1040 Federal Tax Return for the previous year; Certificate of Native American Blood; an essay explaining career goals; three letters of recommendation; official transcripts; a copy of standardized test scores; copy of letter of admission from an accredited college or university or graduate school and degree program in the US; and a photograph (2X3) of head and shoulders. **Deadline:** March 15, April 15, and September 15.

2068 ■ Native American Leadership Education (NALE) Scholarships *(Postdoctorate, Undergraduate/Scholarship)*

Purpose: To support paraprofessionals native students in Native American Schools planning to complete their degree

Awards are arranged alphabetically below their administering organizations

in education, counseling, or school administration. **Focus:** Education; Counseling/Guidance; Educational administration. **Qualif.:** Applicants must be 1/4 or more degree Native American; an enrolled member of a "U.S. tribe"; attending or planning to attend a college/university within the U.S. on a full-time basis that is fully accredited (college level and can range from bachelor's degrees to postdoctoral study); have excellent grades; high ACT or SAT scores; and have a strong commitment to their Native American community. **Criteria:** Scholarships are awarded based on merit.

Funds Avail.: $500-$5000. **To Apply:** Applicants must submit a completed application form (available at the website); financial need analysis; a copy of the IRS 1040 Federal Tax Return for the previous year; Certificate of Native American Blood; an essay explaining career goals; three letters of recommendation; official transcripts; a copy of standardized test scores; copy of letter of admission from an accredited college/university or graduate school and degree program in the US; and a photograph (2X3) of head and shoulders. **Deadline:** March 15, April 15, and September 15.

2069 ■ Tribal Business Management Program (TBM) Scholarships *(Undergraduate/Scholarship)*

Purpose: To support students planning to work in economic development for tribes. **Focus:** Business; Finance; Management; Economics; Banking; Hotel, institutional, and restaurant management. **Qualif.:** Applicants must be 1/4 or more degree Native American; an enrolled member of a "U.S. tribe"; attending or planning to attend a college/university within the U.S. on a full-time basis that is fully accredited; studying in the field of business, finance, management, economics, banking, hotel management, and related field; have excellent grades; high ACT or SAT scores; and have a strong commitment to their Native American community. **Criteria:** Scholarships are awarded based on merit.

Funds Avail.: $500-$5000. **To Apply:** Applicants must submit a completed application form (available at the website); financial need analysis; a copy of the IRS 1040 Federal Tax Return for the previous year; Certificate of Native American Blood; an essay explaining career goals; three letters of recommendation; official transcripts; a copy of standardized test scores; copy of letter of admission from an accredited college or university or graduate school and degree program in the US; and a photograph (2X3) of head and shoulders. **Deadline:** March 15, April 15, and September 15.

2070 ■ Catholic Biblical Association of America

Catholic University of America
433 Caldwell Hall
Washington, DC 20064
Ph: (202)319-5519
Fax: (202)319-4799
E-mail: cua-cathbib@cua.edu
URL: http://cba.cua.edu

2071 ■ Catholic Biblical Association of America Scholarships *(Undergraduate/Scholarship)*

Purpose: To provide support to students who want to pursue their biblical studies. **Focus:** Bible studies. **Qualif.:** Applicant must be a full-time student in doctoral programs on biblical studies at four institutions: (a) Catholic University of America; (b) Graduate Theological Union at Barkeley; (c) University of Notre Dame. **Criteria:** Applicants will be selected based on the following criteria: (1) Doctoral programs in both Old Testament and New Testament, which include a theological component; (2) Quality programs, as judge on faculty and on course requirements, including biblical language requirements resembling those of the Pontifical Biblical Institute for the S.S.L., including both Hebrew and Greek.

Funds Avail.: Full tuition fee and a stipend of $12,500. **To Apply:** For further information, applicants are advised to contact the Association at Catholic University of America, 433 Caldwell Hall, Washington, DC 20064.

2072 ■ Catholic Library Association

100 N. St., Ste. 224
Pittsfield, MA 01201-5109
Ph: (413)443-2252
Fax: (413)442-2252
E-mail: cla@cathla.org
URL: http://www.cathla.org

2073 ■ Rev. Andrew L. Bouwhuis Memorial Scholarship Program *(Graduate/Scholarship)*

Purpose: To promote education and career in the field of Library Science. **Focus:** Library and archival sciences; Science. **Qualif.:** Applicant must be attending a graduate library school; and in need of financial assistance. **Criteria:** Recipient is selected based on collegiate record, evidence of need for financial help, and acceptance in a graduate school program.

Funds Avail.: $1,500. **To Apply:** Applicant must prepare a copy of an acceptance letter at a graduate library school; resume; personal statement on the applicant's interest in librarianship; statement of financial need; reference letter (from a librarian, employer or college instructor); and official transcript. Application materials must be forwarded to the Scholarship Committee. **Deadline:** February 1.

Remarks: In memory of Reverend Andrew L. Bouwhuis.

2074 ■ CDC Foundation

55 Park Place, Ste. 400
Atlanta, GA 30303
Ph: (404)653-0790
Fax: (404)653-0330
Free: 888-880-4CDC
URL: http://www.cdcfoundation.org

2075 ■ CDC Foundation Scholarships *(Undergraduate/Scholarship)*

Purpose: To provide an opportunity for third and fourth-year medical and veterinary students to gain public health experience in an international setting. **Focus:** Medicine; Veterinary science and medicine. **Qualif.:** Applicants must be attending an LCME-accredited medical school or an AVMA-accredited veterinary school; must be current or incoming third or fourth-year students; must be either U.S. citizens or valid greencard holders. **Criteria:** Applicants are evaluated based on financial need.

Funds Avail.: $3,000. **To Apply:** Applicants must submit all application materials on 8 1/2" x 11" white paper, in triplicate, which includes three copies of the application form; two (2) letters of recommendation; current curriculum vitae; one personal statement; and signed insurance coverage statement.

2076 ■ CEDAM International

1 Fox Rd.
Croton-on-Hudson, NY 10520

Awards are arranged alphabetically below their administering organizations

E-mail: cedam@bestweb.net
URL: http://www.cedam.org

2077 ■ Lloyd Bridges Scholarships *(Graduate/Scholarship)*

Purpose: To enable a qualified educator to participate at no cost in a CEDAM sponsored or sanctioned expedition. **Focus:** Aquaculture. **Qualif.:** Applicant must be a certified scuba diver, a teacher (elementary or secondary level), or actively engaged in an education program at an institution or environmental organization, such as an aquarium, science center, or relevant non-profit organization. **Criteria:** Scholarship will be awarded based on the applicants merit and financial need.

Funds Avail.: CEDAM International will cover the recipient's airfare and REEF Field Survey expenses (excluding incidentals and personal expenses). **To Apply:** Applicant must complete the application form available on the website; must submit a 500 word essay and two recommendation letters. **Deadline:** April 1.

2078 ■ Center for Austrian Studies

314 Social Sciences Building
267 19th Ave. S
Minneapolis, MN 55455
Ph: (612)624-9811
Fax: (612)626-9004
E-mail: casahy@umn.edu
URL: http://www.cas.umn.edu

2079 ■ Leo Baeck Fellowships Program *(Doctorate, Postdoctorate/Fellowship)*

Purpose: To foster research on the history and culture of German-speaking Jewry in Central Europe and in exile. **Focus:** History; Culture; European Studies. **Qualif.:** Applicants must hold either PhD or PsD and must have obtained university degrees in not more than three years from the date of application, seeking support to pursue researches focusing on the history and culture of German-speaking Jewry in Central Europe and in exile. **Criteria:** Grantees will be selected according to merits.

Funds Avail.: PHD grantees shall receive EUR 1,000 per month in Europe, EUR 1,200 in the UK and in Israel, EUR 1,400 in the US. Postdoctoral grantees shall receive EUR 1,500, EUR 1,800 (UK, IL), EUR 2,100 (US). All fellows will receive a travel grant of EUR 1,000. **Number Awarded:** 10 PhD scholarships and 2 postdoctoral scholarships. **To Apply:** Applicants must submit (three copies each): application form (available in CAS's website); a statement of purpose; a resume; a copy of the university degree or degrees; an outline of the research project, maximum 5 pages; a time schedule for the academic year 2008/9, including prospective research visits; a reference from the dissertation supervisor (does not apply for postdoctoral applicants); and a second reference by a university teacher or scholar. **Deadline:** February 1. **Contact:** Studienstiftung des deutschen Volkes Dr. Roland Hain, Johannes Sabel Ahrstr. 41, 53175 Bonn, Tel. +49 (0)228 82096-285 leobaeck@studienstiftung.de www.studienstiftung.de/leobaeck.htm

2080 ■ Center for the Education of Women

330 E Liberty St.
Ann Arbor, MI 48103
Ph: (734)764-6005
Fax: (734)998-6203
E-mail: contactCEW@umich.edu
URL: http://www.umich.edu/~cew

2081 ■ CEW Scholarships *(All/Scholarship)*

Purpose: To honor the academic performance of women students at the University of Michigan. **Focus:** General studies. **Qualif.:** Applicants must be undergraduate, graduate, and full-time or part-time students attending the University of Michigan (Ann Arbor, Flint, Dearborn Campuses); must have experienced a lapse of at least 48 consecutive months and 50 non-consecutive months any time after graduation from high school; and have not received a scholarship. **Criteria:** Awards are given based on academic merit.

Funds Avail.: $1,000-$8,000. **Number Awarded:** 40. **To Apply:** Contact the scholarship committee for the application forms and for information about the program. **Contact:** Roxann Keating 734-764-7271.

2082 ■ Robert Krembil Scholarships of Merit *(Postgraduate/Scholarship)*

Purpose: To recognize an incoming MBA student who has demonstrated the highest academic standing. **Focus:** General studies. **Qualif.:** Applicants must be female MBA students who are currently enrolled in the second year of study; must demonstrate academic excellence; must have a working experience of no less than four years; must have excellent communication skills and leadership ability. **Criteria:** Applicants are evaluated based on academic excellence and financial need.

Funds Avail.: $30,000. **To Apply:** Applicants are advised to visit the organization for the application procedure. **Deadline:** February 1.

2083 ■ Student Research Grants *(Undergraduate/Grant)*

Purpose: To promote every woman's career, leadership, education, growth and development, healing and wellbeing. **Focus:** Women's studies. **Qualif.:** Applicants must be undergraduate students. **Criteria:** Recipients are selected based on the submitted proposals.

Funds Avail.: $750. **To Apply:** Applicants must send an applications which includes the applicant's name, address, contact number, email address, and student ID number; proposal (2 pages) accompanied with project budget; a statement of support from an advisor; a curriculum vitae; and proof of IRB approval for the project (if relevant). Submit application packets to: Dr. Jean Waltman, Center for the Education of Women 330 E Liberty St., Ann Arbor, MI 48104-2289. **Contact:** Jean Waltman, jwaltman@umich.edu.

2084 ■ Center for Lesbian and Gay Studies

City University of New York; 365 Fifth Ave
New York, NY 10016
Ph: (212)817-1955
E-mail: clags@gc.cuny.edu
URL: http://web.gc.cuny.edu/clags

2085 ■ CLAGS Fellowships *(Graduate/Fellowship)*

Purpose: To provide fund to support research, travel or writing. **Focus:** Homosexuality. **Qualif.:** Applicants must be graduate students, academic or independent scholars who work on dissertation. **Criteria:** Applicants will be selected

Awards are arranged alphabetically below their administering organizations

by the fellowships committee of the Center for Lesbian and Gay Studies based on the review of the application materials.

Funds Avail.: $3,500. **To Apply:** Applicants must submit a cover letter with contact information; proposal of 5-10 pages; a curriculum vitae; and two letters of recommendation. **Deadline:** November.

2086 ■ Martin Duberman Fellowships *(Professional Development/Fellowship)*

Purpose: To award a senior scholar from any country doing scholarly research on the lesbian, gay, bisexual, transgender, and queer experience. **Focus:** Homosexuality. **Qualif.:** Applicant must be a tenured university professor; advanced independent scholar; must be able to show a prior contribution to the field of LGBTQ. **Criteria:** Applicants will be selected based on the fellowships committee's review of the application materials.

Funds Avail.: $7,500. **To Apply:** Applicants must submit a completed application form; a cover letter with contact information; a proposal of 5-10 pages; curriculum vitae; and two letters of recommendation.

2087 ■ Joan Heller-Diane Bernard Fellowships *(Graduate, Undergraduate/Fellowship)*

Purpose: To supports research into the impact of lesbians and/or gay men on U.S. society and culture. **Focus:** Homosexuality. **Qualif.:** Applicants must be junior scholars, graduate students, untenured professors, independent researchers, or senior scholars. **Criteria:** Applicants will be selected based on the fellowships committee's review of the application materials.

Funds Avail.: $5,000. **Number Awarded:** 2. **To Apply:** Applicants must submit a cover letter with contact information; a proposal of 5-10 pages; evidence of contribution to the field of LGTBQ studies; curriculum vitae; and two letters of recommendation. **Deadline:** November.

2088 ■ Center for Plant Conservation

PO Box 299
St. Louis, MO 63166-0299
Ph: (314)577-9450
E-mail: cpc@mobot.org
URL: http://www.centerforplantconservation.org

2089 ■ Catherine H. Beattie Fellowships *(Graduate/Fellowship)*

Purpose: To enable a graduate student in biology, horticulture, or a related field to conduct research on a rare or endangered U.S. plant. **Focus:** Biology, Horticulture. **Qualif.:** Applicant must be a graduate student in biology or horticulture. **Criteria:** Preference will be given to students focusing on endangered flora of the Carolinas or the southeastern United States.

Funds Avail.: $1,000-$4,000 and will serve as compensation for work done by a graduate student. **To Apply:** Applications should be submitted to the Center for Plant Conservation and must include the following: (a) a 2-3 page proposal, which includes a description of the research project, and how it relates to the student's academic and professional development; (b) an itemized budget for the funds requested; (c) a current resume; (d) a letter of endorsement by an academic advisor from the institution where the student is pursuing graduate studies; (e) the names of three additional persons qualified to describe the student's character and ability; (f) official transcripts for both undergraduate and graduate academic records. **Deadline:** December 31.

2090 ■ Center for Women in Government and Civil Society

University at Albany
135 Western Ave.
Draper Hall, Rm. 302
Albany, NY 12222
Ph: (518)442-3900
Fax: (518)442-3877
E-mail: cwig@csc.albany.edu
URL: http://www.cwig.albany.edu

2091 ■ Center for Women in Government and Civil Society Fellowships *(Postgraduate/Fellowship)*

Purpose: To encourage graduate students to pursue careers in public policy while increasing the capacity of the New York State Government. **Focus:** Government. **Qualif.:** Applicant must be a graduate student at any accredited college or university in New York State; applicant must have completed 12 graduate credits before applying, with degree completion scheduled after fellowships. **Criteria:** Recipients are selected based on the demonstrated interest in public policy and the issue of underrepresented populations, candidate's curriculum vitae, transcript, letters of recommendation, and conducted interviews.

Funds Avail.: $9,000. **To Apply:** Applicants must submit curriculum vitae; transcript of record; letters of reference.

2092 ■ Center for Wooden Boats

1010 Valley St.
Seattle, WA 98109-4468
Ph: (206)382-2628
Fax: (206)382-2699
URL: http://www.cwb.org

2093 ■ Ed Monk Scholarships *(Professional Development/Scholarship)*

Purpose: To provide educational opportunities for professionals working in traditional maritime trades and to further maritime professionals' knowledge of traditional marine trades in other cultures. **Focus:** Maritime studies. **Qualif.:** Study and research may include current and historical methods of boat construction. Applicants must have background in traditional maritime trades. **Criteria:** Recipients will be selected on the basis of merit.

Funds Avail.: $4,000. **To Apply:** Applicants should explain how the project will enrich their existing knowledge and how the funds would be used. Applicants must provide background in traditional marine trades and a list of references. **Deadline:** June 1. **Contact:** Dick Wagner, 206-382-2628.

2094 ■ Central Ohio Diabetes Association

1100 Dennison Ave.
Columbus, OH 43201
Ph: (614)884-4400
Fax: (614)884-4484
URL: http://www.diabetesohio.org

2095 ■ The Youth Scholarship Program *(Undergraduate/Scholarship)*

Purpose: To provide scholarships to those students with diabetes. **Focus:** Diabetes. **Qualif.:** Applicants must be

Awards are arranged alphabetically below their administering organizations

full-time undergraduate students with diabetes in the Central Ohio area; must demonstrate exemplary adjustment to living with diabetes; show financial need; and demonstrate involvement in extracurricular activities which help others and foster personal growth. **Criteria:** Preference will be given to those students who will meet the criteria.

Funds Avail.: No specific amount. **To Apply:** Applicants must submit a completed application form. **Deadline:** February. **Contact:** Central Ohio Diabetes Association at the above address (see entry 2094).

2096 ■ Central Texas Bluegrass Association

PO Box 9816
Austin, TX 78766-9816
Ph: (512)261-9440
E-mail: ctba@centraltexasbluegrass.org
URL: http://www.centraltexasbluegrass.org

2097 ■ Willa Beach-Porter Music Scholarships *(Undergraduate/Scholarship)*

Purpose: To further the enjoyment of bluegrass music through teaching, sharing and playing; to promote bluegrass music in Central Texas. **Focus:** Music. **Qualif.:** Applicants must be 12 years of age or over. **Criteria:** Recipients are selected based on financial need.

Funds Avail.: No specific amount. **To Apply:** Applicants must complete an application form. **Deadline:** May 15. **Contact:** 512-261-9440.

2098 ■ CentraState Healthcare Foundation

916 Rte. 33, Ste. 6
Freehold, NJ 07728
Ph: (732)294-7030
URL: http://www.centrastatefoundation.org

2099 ■ CentraState Associated Auxiliaries Scholarships *(Undergraduate/Scholarship)*

Purpose: To provide scholarship assistance to a deserving student who wants to pursue the health care field. **Focus:** Health care services. **Qualif.:** Applicant must be a student or adult who lives and volunteers in the CentraState service area; must be pursuing a career in the health care field. **Criteria:** Recipient will be selected based on the criteria of the Scholarship Selection Committee.

Funds Avail.: $500. **Number Awarded:** 3. **To Apply:** Applicant must submit the application form along with transcript, two letters of recommendation, and complete essay requirements to Mrs. Valerie MacPhee, PO Box 32, Perrineville, NJ 08535. **Deadline:** April 25.

2100 ■ CentraState Band Aid Open Committee Scholarships *(Undergraduate/Scholarship)*

Purpose: To provide scholarship assistance to a graduating high school senior who attends the Freehold Regional High School District's Medical Science Program. **Focus:** Health sciences. **Qualif.:** Applicant must be planning to pursue a career in the health profession; must be a student enrolled in the Medical Sciences Program in the Freehold Regional High School District. **Criteria:** Recipient will be selected based on the criteria of the CentraState Healthcare Foundation Scholarship Committee.

Funds Avail.: $2,000. **To Apply:** Applicant must submit a current transcript, letters of recommendation from two teachers and/or counselors and the completed essay requirements. Scholarship application form may be obtained from Dr. Nicholas Mennuti at the school or from CentraState Healthcare Foundation Office by calling 732-294-7030. Application form and requirements must be sent to CentraState Healthcare Foundation, 916 Rte. 33, Ste. 6, Freehold, NJ 07728. **Deadline:** March 30.

2101 ■ CentraState Healthcare Foundation Health Professional Scholarships *(Undergraduate/Scholarship)*

Purpose: To provide scholarship assistance to a deserving student who wants to pursue the healthcare field. **Focus:** Health care services. **Qualif.:** Applicant must be a graduating student who has chosen to pursue a career in the health profession. **Criteria:** The Scholarship Selection Committee will review scholarship application.

Funds Avail.: $1,000. **Number Awarded:** 3. **To Apply:** Applicant must submit the appropriate form along with transcript, two letters of recommendation, and the complete essay requirements. **Deadline:** April 30. **Contact:** Alicia Zicha at the above address (see entry 2098).

2102 ■ DCH Freehold Toyota Scholarships *(Undergraduate/Scholarship)*

Purpose: To provide scholarship assistance to a graduating high school senior who attends the Freehold Regional High School District's Medical Science Program. **Focus:** Health sciences. **Qualif.:** Applicant must be planning to pursue a career in the health profession; must be a student enrolled in the Medical Sciences Program in the Freehold Regional High School District. **Criteria:** Recipient will be selected based on the criteria of the CentraState Healthcare Foundation Scholarship Committee.

Funds Avail.: $1,000. **To Apply:** Applicant must submit a current transcript, letters of recommendation from two teachers and/or counselors and the completed essay requirements. Scholarship application form may be obtained from Dr. Nicholas Mennuti at the school or from CentraState Healthcare Foundation Office by calling 732-294-7030. Application form and requirements must be sent to CentraState Healthcare Foundation, 916 Rte. 33, Ste. 6, Freehold, NJ 07728. **Deadline:** March 30.

2103 ■ Norkus Charitable Foundation Scholarships *(Undergraduate/Scholarship)*

Purpose: To provide scholarship assistance to a graduating high school senior who attends the Freehold Regional High School District's Medical Science Program. **Focus:** Health sciences. **Qualif.:** Applicant must be planning to pursue a career in the health profession; must be a student enrolled in the Medical Sciences Program in the Freehold Regional High School District. **Criteria:** Recipient will be selected based on the criteria of the CentraState Healthcare Foundation Scholarship Committee.

Funds Avail.: $1,000. **To Apply:** Applicant must submit a current transcript, letters of recommendation from two teachers and/or counselors and the completed essay requirements. Scholarship application form may be obtained from Dr. Nicholas Mennuti at the school or from CentraState Healthcare Foundation Office by calling 732-294-7030. Application form and requirements must be sent to CentraState Healthcare Foundation, 916 Rte. 33, Ste. 6, Freehold, NJ 07728. **Deadline:** March 30.

Awards are arranged alphabetically below their administering organizations

2104 ■ Star and Barry Tobias Scholarships *(Undergraduate/Scholarship)*

Purpose: To provide scholarship assistance to a graduating high school senior who attends the Freehold Regional High School District's Medical Science Program. **Focus:** Health sciences. **Qualif.:** Applicant must be planning to pursue a career in the health profession; must be a student enrolled in the Medical Sciences Program in the Freehold Regional High School District. **Criteria:** Recipient will be selected based on the criteria of the CentraState Healthcare Foundation Scholarship Committee.

Funds Avail.: $2,500. **To Apply:** Applicant must submit a current transcript, letters of recommendation from two teachers and/or counselors and the completed essay requirements. Scholarship application form may be obtained from Dr. Nicholas Mennuti at the school or from CentraState Healthcare Foundation Office by calling 732-294-7030. Application form and requirements must be sent to CentraState Healthcare Foundation, 916 Rte. 33, Ste. 6, Freehold, NJ 07728. **Deadline:** March 30.

2105 ■ Chemical Heritage Foundation

315 Chestnut St.
Philadelphia, PA 19106
Ph: (215)925-2222
Fax: (215)925-1954
E-mail: info@chemheritage.org
URL: http://www.chemheritage.org

2106 ■ Robert W. Allington Fellowships *(Doctorate, Postdoctorate/Fellowship)*

Purpose: To promote research about history of chemical and molecular sciences, technologies, and industries. **Focus:** Biology, Molecular; Chemistry. **Qualif.:** Applicant must be Ph.D. or a doctoral candidate at the dissertation stage with research regarding history of chemical and molecular sciences, technologies and industries. **Criteria:** Recipients are selected based on committee's reviewed the proposal.

Funds Avail.: Funds provide for travel allowance and $43,000. **To Apply:** Applicant must send a cover sheet indicating the type of fellowship applying for, number of months of support, contact and personal information; a research proposal not more than 1000 words; curriculum vitae not more than three pages; two letters of recommendation sent directly to fellowships coordinator. Send materials electronically to fellowships@chemheritage.org, while letters of recommendations must be mailed to the Fellowship Coordinator. **Deadline:** February 15.

Remarks: Awards was created with donation from the estate of Robert W. Allington.

2107 ■ Gordon Cain Fellowships in Technology, Policy, and Entrepreneurship *(Doctorate, Postdoctorate/Fellowship)*

Purpose: To promote research about the historical development of chemical industries. **Focus:** Chemistry. **Qualif.:** Applicant must be Ph.D. or a doctoral candidate at the dissertation stage with research about development of chemical industries. **Criteria:** Recipients are selected based on committee's review of the proposal.

Funds Avail.: Funds provide for travel allowance and $43,000. **To Apply:** Applicant must send a cover sheet indicating the type of fellowship applying for, number of months of support, contact and personal information; a research proposal not more than 1000 words; curriculum vitae not more than three pages; two letters of recommendation sent directly to fellowships coordinator. Send materials electronically to fellowships@chemheritage.org, while letters of recommendations must be mailed to the Fellowship Coordinator. **Deadline:** February 15.

2108 ■ CHF Travel Grants *(All/Grant)*

Purpose: To promote research about history of chemical and molecular sciences, technologies and industries. **Focus:** Chemistry. **Qualif.:** Applicants must be researchers residing more than 75 miles from Philadelphia. **Criteria:** Recipients are selected based on committee's review of the research.

Funds Avail.: $750 per week. **Number Awarded:** 1. **To Apply:** Applicant must send a one-page statement of research project; curriculum vitae less than three pages; budget estimate; and a letter of reference which must be submitted to travelgrants@chemheritage.org.

2109 ■ Sidney M. Edelstein Fellowships *(Doctorate, Postdoctorate/Fellowship)*

Purpose: To promote research about history of chemical and molecular sciences, technologies and industries. **Focus:** Chemistry. **Qualif.:** Applicant must be Ph.D. or a doctoral candidate at the dissertation stage with research regarding history of chemical and molecular sciences, technologies and industries. **Criteria:** Recipients are selected based on committee's review of the proposal.

Funds Avail.: Funds provide for travel allowance and $43,000. **To Apply:** Applicant must send a cover sheet indicating the type of fellowship applying for, number of months of support, contact and personal information; a research proposal not more than 1000 words; curriculum vitae not more than three pages; two letters of recommendation sent directly to fellowships coordinator. Send materials electronically to fellowships@chemheritage.org, while letters of recommendations must be mailed to the Fellowship Coordinator. **Deadline:** February 15.

Remarks: Awards was created with generosity of the Sidney and Mildred Edelstein Foundation.

2110 ■ Robert W. Gore Fellowships in Materials Innovation *(Doctorate, Postdoctorate/Fellowship)*

Purpose: To assist fellows to pursue their own research and academic interest while at CHF. **Focus:** Chemistry. **Qualif.:** Applicant must be Ph.D. or a doctoral candidate at the dissertation stage with experience in conducting historical case studies of chemical and molecular sciences, technologies and industries. **Criteria:** Recipients are selected based on committee's reviewed the proposal.

Funds Avail.: $35,000. **To Apply:** Applicant must send a cover sheet indicating the type of fellowship applying for, number of months of support, contact and personal information; a research proposal not more than 1000 words; curriculum vitae not more than three pages; two letters of recommendation sent directly to fellowships coordinator. Send materials electronically to fellowships@chemheritage.org, while letters of recommendations must be mailed to the Fellowship Coordinator. **Deadline:** February 15.

2111 ■ John C. Haas Fellowships in the History of Chemical Industries *(Doctorate, Postdoctorate/Fellowship)*

Purpose: To promote research that will improve public understanding of chemical industries in relation to environ-

Awards are arranged alphabetically below their administering organizations

mental, societal, health, and safety issues. **Focus:** Chemistry. **Qualif.:** Applicant must be Ph.D. or a doctoral candidate at the dissertation stage with project to increase public understanding of chemical industries in relation to environmental, societal, health, and safety issues. **Criteria:** Recipients are selected based on committee's reviewed the proposal.

Funds Avail.: $43,000. **Number Awarded:** 2. **To Apply:** Applicant must send a cover sheet indicating the type of fellowship applying for, number of months of support, contact and personal information; a research proposal not more than 1000 words; curriculum vitae not more than three pages; two letters of recommendation sent directly to fellowships coordinator. Send materials electronically to fellowships@chemheritage.org, while letters of recommendations must be mailed to the Fellowship Coordinator. **Deadline:** February 15.

Remarks: Awards was created with generosity of Mr. John C. Haas.

2112 ■ Roy G. Neville Fellowships *(Doctorate, Postdoctorate/Fellowship)*

Purpose: To promote research about history of chemical and molecular sciences, technologies and industries. **Focus:** Chemistry. **Qualif.:** Applicant must be a historians of science, technology, and allied fields, book historians and print culture, bibliographers and librarians; Ph.D., Ph.D. candidates, or equivalent preferred but not required. **Criteria:** Recipients are selected based on committee's review of the proposal.

Funds Avail.: $3000 per month. **To Apply:** Applicant must send a cover sheet indicating the type of fellowship applying for, number of months of support, contact and personal information; a research proposal not more than 1000 words; curriculum vitae not more than three pages; two letters of recommendation sent directly to fellowships coordinator. Send materials electronically to fellowships@chemheritage.org, while letters of recommendations must be mailed to the Fellowship Coordinator. **Deadline:** February 15.

2113 ■ Charles C. Price Fellowships in Polymer History *(Doctorate, Postdoctorate/Fellowship)*

Purpose: To promote research about history of chemical sciences and technologies. **Focus:** Chemistry. **Qualif.:** Applicant must be Ph.D. or a doctoral candidate at the dissertation stage with research on history of polymers. **Criteria:** Recipients are selected based on committee's reviewed the proposal.

Funds Avail.: $20,000. **To Apply:** Applicant must send a cover sheet indicating the type of fellowship applying for, number of months of support, contact and personal information; a research proposal not more than 1000 words; curriculum vitae not more than three pages; two letters of recommendation sent directly to fellowships coordinator. Send materials electronically to fellowships@chemheritage.org, while letters of recommendations must be mailed to the Fellowship Coordinator. **Deadline:** February 15.

Remarks: Awards was created by friends and admirers of Professor Price.

2114 ■ Chi Eta Phi Sorority

3029 13th St. NW
Washington, DC 20009
Ph: (202)232-3858
Fax: (202)232-3460
URL: http://www.chietaphi.com

2115 ■ The Mabel Keaton Staupers National Scholarship Award *(Doctorate, Graduate, Undergraduate/Scholarship)*

Purpose: To recognize the life long commitment made by Soror Staupers to America's struggle for complete equality for all people. **Focus:** Nursing. **Qualif.:** Applicants must be current members of Chi Eta Phi Sorority, Inc. and the American Nurses Association and must be enrolled in a program of study leading to the Baccalaureate, masters or doctoral degree in a nationally accredited school of nursing. **Criteria:** Recipient are selected based upon their demonstrated leadership, contributed to the recruitment and retention of minorities into nursing and for the advancement of minority nurses in education and nursing.

Funds Avail.: $50,000. **To Apply:** Applicants must submit completed applications to the Chi Eta Phi, Inc.

2116 ■ Chi Phi Fraternity

1160 Satellite Blvd.
Suwanee, GA 30024
Ph: (404)231-1824
Fax: (404)237-5090
E-mail: chiphi@chiphi.org
URL: http://www.chiphi.org

2117 ■ Chi Phi Educational Trust *(Undergraduate/Scholarship)*

Purpose: To encourage the Chi Phi members to pursue their education. **Focus:** General studies. **Qualif.:** Applicants must be Chi Phi members. **Criteria:** Selection of candidates will be based on the scholarship criteria.

Funds Avail.: Over $80,000. **To Apply:** Applicant must provide a cover letter, summarize the applicant's qualifications and provide a description of his future aspirations and goals; must have the current academic transcript and recommendation letter from one faculty member and from the chapter Alpha. **Deadline:** May 1.

2118 ■ Chicago Bar Foundation

21 S Plymouth Ct., Ste. 3B
Chicago, IL 60604
Ph: (312)554-1204
Fax: (312)554-1203
E-mail: khamilton@chicagobar.org
URL: http://www.chicagobarfoundation.org

2119 ■ Abraham Lincoln Marovitz Public Interest Law Scholarships *(Undergraduate/Scholarship)*

Purpose: To support a needy law student who is deeply committed to public interest work so that upon graduation financial need will not prevent the student from pursuing a public interest legal career. **Focus:** Law. **Qualif.:** Applicants must be students attending one of the nine Illinois law schools (Chicago-Kent College of Law, University of Chicago Law School, DePaul University College of Law, University of Illinois College of Law, John Marshall Law School, Loyola University School of Law, Northern Illinois University Law School, Northwestern University School of Law and Southern Illinois University School of Law). **Criteria:** Recipients are selected based on committee's review of application materials.

Awards are arranged alphabetically below their administering organizations

Funds Avail.: $10,000 in the first year. **To Apply:** Applicants must submit cover letter with attached application form; resume; official transcript from undergraduate institution and graduate institution; two letters of reference about commitment to public interest work; brief essay (no more than three pages, explaining commitment to pursue a career in public interest law). **Deadline:** April 15.

2120 ■ Chicana/Latina Foundation

1419 Burlingame Ave. Ste. N
Burlingame, CA 94010
Ph: (650)373-1083
Fax: (650)373-1090
E-mail: olga@chicanalatina.org
URL: http://www.chicanalatina.org

2121 ■ Chicana Latina Scholarship Fund *(Graduate, Undergraduate/Scholarship)*

Purpose: To assist Latina students in completing their undergraduate and graduate college education. **Focus:** General Studies. **Qualif.:** Applicants must be Chicana/Latina women of the Northern California counties; must be enrolled in accredited colleges, universities and community colleges in one of the listed Northern California counties; must have been residents for at least two years in one of the listed Northern California counties; must be enrolled as full-time college students, have completed a minimum of 15 college semester units after high school graduation, and have at least a 2.5 GPA; must have demonstrated leadership and civic/community involvement. **Criteria:** Preference will be given to those who meet the criteria.

Funds Avail.: No specific amount. **To Apply:** Applicants must check the available website to download the application form. **Contact:** Chicana Latina Foundation at the above address (see entry 2120).

2122 ■ Childhood Cancer Foundation

1300 Yonge St., Ste. No. 405
Toronto, ON, Canada M4T 1X3
Ph: (416)489-6440
Fax: (416)489-9812
Free: 800-363-1062
E-mail: info@childhoodcancer.ca
URL: http://www.candlelighters.ca

2123 ■ Childhood Cancer Foundation Scholarships *(Undergraduate/Scholarship)*

Purpose: To provide scholarships to young Canadians who are in treatment or who have survived childhood care. **Focus:** Cancer. **Qualif.:** Applicant must be a Canadian citizen or landed immigrant; must be between the ages of 17-25 years and be either treated for some form of childhood cancer or still be on treatment. **Criteria:** Scholarship is based on financial need.

Funds Avail.: $300-$1,000, depending on the availability of funds. **Number Awarded:** 51 in 2007. **To Apply:** Applicant must write a 300-500 word letter describing their future academic goals and reasons for applying for the scholarship; must provide a letter of acceptance; a statement from their doctor, pediatrician or oncologist stating that they have had some form of childhood cancer; must print and complete the application form available online. Application form and requirements must be sent to Scholarship Program, Childhood Cancer Foundation, 1300 Yonge St., Ste. 405, Toronto, ON M4T 1X3. **Deadline:** June 30.

2124 ■ Childhood Cancer Foundation Candlelighters Canada

1300 Yonge St., Ste. 405
Toronto, ON, Canada M4T 1X3
Ph: (416)489-6440
Fax: (416)489-9812
Free: 800-363-1062
E-mail: info@childhoodcancer.ca
URL: http://www.candlelighters.ca

2125 ■ Childhood Cancer Foundation Candlelighters Canada Scholarships *(All/Scholarship)*

Purpose: To support young Canadians and assist them financially with their first year of post-secondary school education. **Focus:** Cancer. **Qualif.:** Applicants must be young Canadians who are childhood cancer survivors; must be Canadian citizens or landed immigrants between the ages of 17-25 years. **Criteria:** Recipients are selected based on financial need.

Funds Avail.: $1,000. **To Apply:** Applicants must write a 300-500 word letter describing their future academic goals and highlighting their reasons fpr applying for this scholarship; must provide a copy of the letter of acceptance to a university, college or any post-secondary educational program and a copy of their most recent transcript, if not first year students; must provide a statement from a doctor/pediatrician and oncologist stating that they had some form of childhood cancer; must complete the application form. **Deadline:** June 30. **Contact:** 416-489-9812.

2126 ■ Children's Hospital of Philadelphia

34th St. and Civic Center Blvd.
Philadelphia, PA 19104-4399
Ph: (215)590-1000
Free: 800-879-2467
E-mail: fordg@email.edu
URL: http://www.chop.edu

2127 ■ Eagles Fly for Leukemia Scholarships *(Undergraduate/Scholarship)*

Purpose: To abolish childhood cancers and enhance the lives of children and families in their communities. **Focus:** Health care services. **Qualif.:** Applicants must be survivors of childhood cancer. **Criteria:** Recipients are selected based on the financial need.

Funds Avail.: $1,500. **Number Awarded:** 3. **To Apply:** Applicants must submit a complete application form. **Contact:** efleukemia@aol.com.

2128 ■ Barbara Palo Foster Memorial Scholarships *(Undergraduate/Scholarship)*

Purpose: To support the financial needs of young adults who have lost a parent/guardian to cancer or have a parent/guardian with cancer and are seeking higher education in the field of nursing. **Focus:** Nursing. **Qualif.:** Applicant must be 35 years or younger at the time of the application; must be a young adult who has lost a parent/guardian to cancer or has a parent/guardian with cancer; must be currently attending, or planning to attend a two- to four-year college or university or training program, and seeking a degree in the field of nursing (including graduate and professional schools); and must demonstrate an interest in furthering patient education, focusing on persons from medically underserved communities and/or women's health issues. **Criteria:** Selection is based on merit and income criteria.

Funds Avail.: Varies. **To Apply:** Applicants must complete application.

2129 ■ Tim and Tom Gullikson Foundation Scholarships *(Undergraduate/Scholarship)*

Purpose: To advance healthcare for children by integrating patient care, innovative research and quality professional education into all programs. **Focus:** General studies. **Qualif.:** Program is open to individuals with brain tumor; patients/survivors and/or children of brain tumor patients/ survivors who intend to pursue programs at an accredited four-year college, university,vocational-technical school or other institution of higher learning. **Criteria:** Recipients are selected based on financial need.

Funds Avail.: $20,000. **To Apply:** Applicants must submit a complete application form. **Deadline:** May 1.

2130 ■ Michael A. Hunter Memorial Scholarships *(Undergraduate/Scholarship)*

Purpose: To help improve the quality of life for those affected by leukemia. **Focus:** General Studies. **Qualif.:** Applicants must be graduating high school seniors, community college and four-year university students who are leukemia patients and/or children of non-surviving leukemia patients; must be enrolled full-time; and must have a minimum GPA of 3.0 or "B" average. **Criteria:** Recipients are selected based on financial need.

Funds Avail.: $5,000. **Number Awarded:** 2. **To Apply:** Applicants must submit a complete application form. **Deadline:** May 1.

2131 ■ Matt Stauffer Memorial Scholarships *(Undergraduate/Scholarship)*

Purpose: To support the financial needs of young adults who have been affected by cancer and intend to pursue higher education. **Focus:** Health care services. **Qualif.:** Applicants must be 35 years or younger at the time of application; must be young adult cancer survivor/patients diagnosed between the ages of 15 and 35; must be currently attending or accepted at a two- to four-year college, university or vocational program including graduate and professional schools; and must be degree-seeking. **Criteria:** Recipients are selected based on the demonstrated leadership abilities and commitment to their community.

Funds Avail.: varies. **To Apply:** Applicants must submit a complete application form.

2132 ■ Marilyn Yetso Memorial Scholarships *(Undergraduate/Scholarship)*

Purpose: To support the financial needs of young adults who have lost a parent/guardian to cancer or have a parent/ guardian with cancer and are seeking higher education. **Focus:** Health care services. **Qualif.:** Applicants must be 35 years at younger time of application; must be young adults who have lost a parent/guardian to cancer or have a parent/guardian with cancer or the parent/guardian experienced a cancer diagnosis between the ages of 15 and 35; must be currently attending or accepted to a two- to four-year college, university or vocational program including graduate and professional schools; and must be degree-seeking. **Criteria:** Recipients are selected based on their demonstrated leadership abilities and commitment to their community.

Funds Avail.: Varies. **To Apply:** Applicants must submit a completed application form.

2133 ■ Vera Yip Memorial Scholarships *(Undergraduate/Scholarship)*

Purpose: To support the financial needs of young adults who are impacted by cancer and seeking higher education. **Focus:** General Studies. **Qualif.:** Applicant must be 35 years or younger at the time of application; must be young adult who has lost a parent/guardian to cancer or has a parent/guardian with cancer or the parent/guardian has experienced a cancer diagnosis between the ages of 15 and 35; must be currently attending or planning to attend a four-year college, university or vocational program and seeking a bachelor's degree or higher; and must have demonstrated leadership abilities and commitment to their community. **Criteria:** Recipients are selected based on merit.

Funds Avail.: Varies. **To Apply:** Applicants must accomplish complete application.

2134 ■ Chinese American Medical Society

281 Edgewood Ave.
New York, NY 10013
Ph: (212)965-0723
URL: http://www.camsociety.org

2135 ■ Chinese American Medical Society Summer Research Outreach Programs *(Undergraduate/Grant)*

Purpose: To support clinical and basic science research among Chinese American, medical and dental students. **Focus:** Medical technology; Dental laboratory technology. **Qualif.:** Applicant must be a current student in an accredited medical or dental school in the United States; working on a project in the basic science or clinical research. **Criteria:** Special consideration will be given to projects involving Chinese American health issues.

Funds Avail.: $400 per week. **To Apply:** The Applicants must submit completed CAMS Summer Research Fellowship Application; Project description; personal statement; curriculum vitae; a two letter from a supervising investigator supporting the research project and from the Dean verifying good standing. Send all materials to: Jerry Huo, MD, Chairman of CAMS Scholarship Committee 32 Aspen Road Scardale, NY 10583, jerryhuomd@gmail.com. **Deadline:** March 31. **Contact:** Jerry Huo, MD, Chairman of CAMS Scholarship Committee, (718)670-0066, or jerryhuomd@gmail.com.

2136 ■ Esther Lim Memorial Scholarships *(Undergraduate/Scholarship)*

Purpose: To provide educational assistance to medical, dental students, and scientists. **Focus:** Medical technology; Dental laboratory technology. **Qualif.:** Applicant must be a medical or dental student or scientist matriculated in a medical or dental school. **Criteria:** Selection is based on merit.

Funds Avail.: No specific amount. **Number Awarded:** 3-5. **To Apply:** Application form is available at the website. Applicants must submit completed application form along with a letter from the Dean of Students verifying good standing; two letters of recommendation; a personal statement; and a current vitae. Send all materials to: Jerry Huo MD, Chairman, CAMS Scholarship Committee 32 Aspen Road, Scarsdale NY 10583, jerryhuomd@gmail.com. **Deadline:** March 31.

Remarks: Established as a result of a bequest by Dr. Lim, a late member of the society, and her family. **Contact:** Jerry Huo MD, Chairman of the CAMS Scholarship Committee, (718)670-0066, or jerryhuomd@gmail.com.

2137 ■ Ruth Liu Memorial Scholarships
(Undergraduate/Scholarship)

Purpose: To provide educational assistance to medical, dental students, and scientists. **Focus:** Medical technology; Dental laboratory technology. **Qualif.:** Applicant must be a medical or dental student or scientist matriculated in a medical or dental school. **Criteria:** Selection is based on merit.

Funds Avail.: No specific amount. **Number Awarded:** 3-5. **To Apply:** Application form is available at the website. Applicants must submit completed application form along with a letter from the Dean of Students verifying good standing; two letters of recommendation; a personal statement; and a current vitae. Send all materials to: Jerry Huo MD, Chairman, CAMS Scholarship Committee 32 Aspen Road, Scarsdale NY 10583, jerryhuomd@gmail.com. **Deadline:** March 31.

Remarks: Established in 1996 by her husband Dr. George Liu and friends. **Contact:** Jerry Huo MD, Chairman of the CAMS Scholarship Committee, (718)670-0066, or jerryhuomd@gmail.com.

2138 ■ Chopin Foundation of the United States

1440 79th St. Causeway, Ste. 117
Miami, FL 33141
Ph: (305)868-0624
Fax: (305)865-5150
E-mail: info@chopin.org
URL: http://www.chopin.org

2139 ■ Chopin Foundation of the United States Scholarships *(Undergraduate/Scholarship)*

Purpose: To support pianists studying music. **Focus:** Music, Piano. **Qualif.:** Applicant must be American pianists (citizens or legal residents); not younger than 14 and not older than 17 years; studying in the field of music, majoring in piano, and enrolled at the secondary or undergraduate school level as a full-time student. **Criteria:** Applicants are selected based on the criteria.

Funds Avail.: No specific amount. **To Apply:** Applicants must submit a statement of career goals; a minimum of two references from piano teachers or performers; a video tape of 20-30 minutes of Chopin's works and registration fee of $25. **Deadline:** February.

2140 ■ Choristers Guild

2834 W Kingsley Rd.
Garland, TX 75041-2498
Ph: (972)271-1521
Fax: (972)840-3113
Free: 800-246-7478
E-mail: membership@mailcg.org
URL: http://www.choristerguild

2141 ■ Ruth K. Jacobs Memorial Scholarship Fund *(Graduate, Undergraduate/Scholarship)*

Purpose: To provide financial aid to full time students preparing for church music ministry. **Focus:** Music. **Qualif.:** Applicant must be a junior, senior or graduate student majoring in music, who holds choral music with children and youth as a primary interest; have an official transcript sent from all past and current institutions in which enrolled; demonstrate talent and leadership ability and demonstrate promise of future usefulness in church music; and show the need for financial aid. **Criteria:** Recipient is selected on the basis of academic merit, interest in church music, ministry of church music as a vocation, and financial need.

Funds Avail.: No amount mentioned. **To Apply:** Applicant must submit applications for the Ruth Jacobs Memorial Scholarship must be submitted prior to February 1 of each year; recipients will be notified by June 1; scholarship funding will be payable to the school and will be dispensed upon receipt of verification of enrollment, full-time status and chosen major; applicant may reapply using application provided for renewal request. Renewing scholarship funding amounts may vary from stated scholarship at the discretion of the Memorial Scholarship Committee. **Deadline:** March 1.

2142 ■ Christian Pharmacists Fellowship International

Palm Beach Atlantic University
PO Box 24708
West Palm Beach, FL 33416-4708
Ph: (561)803-2737
Fax: (561)803-2738
Free: 888-253-6885
E-mail: info@cpfi.org
URL: http://www.cpfi.org

2143 ■ Christian Pharmacist Fellowship International Scholarships *(Professional Development/Fellowship)*

Purpose: To assist Christian students in pursuing a career of pharmacy. **Focus:** Pharmacy. **Qualif.:** Applicant must be a national CPFI member; enrolled in an accredited pharmacy college/university or training program. **Criteria:** Awards are given based on the merit of the application and the Christian relevance of the project.

Funds Avail.: $250 - $1000. **To Apply:** Applicant must send completed application form; description of the plan or project; an email support from the Dean and from an instructor/mentor; and a resume. **Deadline:** October 1, March 1, and June 1. **Contact:** Scholarship Committee Chairman, Daniel Sparado, 501-686-6491 or sparadodanielc@uams.edu.

2144 ■ Christian Record Services

PO Box 6097
Lincoln, NE 68506-0097
Ph: (402)488-0981
Fax: (402)488-7582
E-mail: info@christianrecord.org
URL: http://www.christianrecord.org

2145 ■ CRS Scholarships *(Undergraduate/Scholarship)*

Purpose: To assist blind young people who wish to pursue their college education. **Focus:** General studies. **Qualif.:** Applicants must be legally blind; planning to attend college as a full-time student on the undergraduate level. **Criteria:** Scholarship recipients will be selected based on the Selec-

Awards are arranged alphabetically below their administering organizations

tion Committee's review of the application materials.

Funds Avail.: $500. **To Apply:** Applicants must submit a completed Scholarship application and character reference forms. **Deadline:** April 1. **Contact:** Shelly Kittleson.

2146 ■ Winston Churchill Foundation

600 Madison Ave., 16th Fl.
New York, NY 10022-1615
Ph: (212)752-3200
Fax: (212)246-8330
E-mail: info@winstonchurchillfoundation.org
URL: http://www.winstonchurchillfoundation.org

2147 ■ The Churchill Scholarships
(Postgraduate/Scholarship)

Purpose: To pursue graduate studies in engineering, mathematics, or the sciences at the Cambridge. **Focus:** Engineering; Mathematics and mathematical science. **Qualif.:** Applicants must be citizens of the United States and must be enrolled in one of the institutions participating in the scholarship program competition or students who have recently graduated from one of those institutions. **Criteria:** Recipients are selected based on the academic achievement in all disciplines; the capacity to contribute to the advancement of knowledge in the sciences, engineering or mathematics by pursuing original, creative work at advanced levels as demonstrated by awards and prizes as reference.

Funds Avail.: Total amount of $50,000. **To Apply:** Applicants must complete the application form; four letters of reference; proposed program of the study; personal statement. **Deadline:** November 12. **Contact:** 212-984-5442.

2148 ■ Cincinnati Scholarship Foundation

652 Main St.
Cincinnati, OH 45202
Ph: (513)345-6701
Fax: (513)345-6705
URL: http://www.cincinnatischolarshipfoundation.org

2149 ■ Cincinnati High School Scholarships
(High School/Scholarship)

Purpose: To encourage students to achieve their highest academic potential. **Focus:** General studies. **Qualif.:** Applicant must attend a Cincinnati Public School in grades 7-12; meet the Federal Poverty Income Guidelines; maintains a minimum 2.50 GPA with no "Fs", "Xs" or "Is" in any subject; and be referred by a designated counselor or school representative. **Criteria:** Award is given based on the application.

Funds Avail.: A monthly stipend based on GPA. **To Apply:** Applications are only available from the representative at the student's school. The CSF representatives provide applications to students they recommend for the program.

Remarks: Started in 1918. The program works only for students attending Cincinnati Public Schools.

2150 ■ Cincinnati Scholarship Foundation CFT/ ACPSOP Scholarships *(Undergraduate/ Scholarship)*

Purpose: To help students from Greater Cincinnati area to achieve their dream of a college education. **Focus:** General studies. **Qualif.:** Applicant must be a resident of Greater Cincinnati, and attending college as a full-time student. **Criteria:** Awards are given based on need.

Funds Avail.: No specific amount. **To Apply:** Applicants must submit a completed scholarship application form along with a copy of recent transcript; expected Family Contribution (EFC) from Student Aid Report (SAR), which comes as a result of filing the FAFSA; and a copy of Financial Aid Award Letter from the chosen college to be attended. **Deadline:** April 30.

Remarks: Faxed applications will not be considered.

2151 ■ CSF Ach Family Scholarships
(Undergraduate/Scholarship)

Purpose: To help students from Greater Cincinnati area to achieve the dream of a college education. **Focus:** General studies. **Qualif.:** Applicant must be a resident of Greater Cincinnati, and attending college as a full-time student. **Criteria:** Awards are given based on need.

Funds Avail.: No specific amount. **To Apply:** Applicants must submit a completed scholarship application form along with a copy of recent transcript; expected Family Contribution (EFC) from Student Aid Report (SAR), which comes as a result of filing the FAFSA; and a copy of Financial Aid Award Letter from the chosen college to be attended. **Deadline:** April 30.

Remarks: Faxed applications will not be considered.

2152 ■ CSF Barr Foundation Scholarships
(Undergraduate/Scholarship)

Purpose: To help students from Greater Cincinnati area to achieve the dream of a college education. **Focus:** General studies. **Qualif.:** Applicant must be a resident of Greater Cincinnati, and attending college as a full-time student. **Criteria:** Awards are given based on need.

Funds Avail.: No specific amount. **To Apply:** Applicants must submit a completed scholarship application form along with a copy of recent transcript; expected Family Contribution (EFC) from Student Aid Report (SAR), which comes as a result of filing the FAFSA; and a copy of Financial Aid Award Letter from the chosen college to be attended. **Deadline:** April 30.

Remarks: Faxed applications will not be considered.

2153 ■ CSF Barrett Family Scholarships
(Undergraduate/Scholarship)

Purpose: To help students from Greater Cincinnati area to achieve the dream of a college education. **Focus:** General studies. **Qualif.:** Applicant must be a resident of Greater Cincinnati, and attending college as a full-time student. **Criteria:** Awards are given based on need.

Funds Avail.: No specific amount. **To Apply:** Applicants must submit a completed scholarship application form along with a copy of recent transcript; expected Family Contribution (EFC) from Student Aid Report (SAR), which comes as a result of filing the FAFSA; and a copy of Financial Aid Award Letter from the chosen college to be attended. **Deadline:** April 30.

Remarks: Faxed applications will not be considered.

2154 ■ CSF Bigg's/Curtis Breeden Scholarships
(Undergraduate/Scholarship)

Purpose: To help students from Greater Cincinnati area to achieve the dream of a college education. **Focus:** General studies. **Qualif.:** Applicant must be a resident of Greater Cincinnati, and attending college as a full-time student.

Criteria: Awards are given based on need.

Funds Avail.: No specific amount. **To Apply:** Applicants must submit a completed scholarship application form along with a copy of recent transcript; expected Family Contribution (EFC) from Student Aid Report (SAR), which comes as a result of filing the FAFSA; and a copy of Financial Aid Award Letter from the chosen college to be attended. **Deadline:** April 30.

Remarks: Faxed applications will not be considered.

2155 ■ CSF Bob and Linda Kohlhepp Scholarships *(Undergraduate/Scholarship)*

Purpose: To help students from Greater Cincinnati area to achieve the dream of a college education. **Focus:** General studies. **Qualif.:** Applicant must be a resident of Greater Cincinnati, and attending college as a full-time student. **Criteria:** Awards are given based on need.

Funds Avail.: No specific amount. **To Apply:** Applicants must submit a completed scholarship application form along with a copy of recent transcript; expected Family Contribution (EFC) from Student Aid Report (SAR), which comes as a result of filing the FAFSA; and a copy of Financial Aid Award Letter from the chosen college to be attended. **Deadline:** April 30.

Remarks: Faxed applications will not be considered.

2156 ■ CSF Borden Inc. Scholarships *(Undergraduate/Scholarship)*

Purpose: To help students from Greater Cincinnati area to achieve the dream of a college education. **Focus:** General studies. **Qualif.:** Applicant must be a resident of Greater Cincinnati, and attending college as a full-time student. **Criteria:** Awards are given based on need.

Funds Avail.: No specific amount. **To Apply:** Applicants must submit a completed scholarship application form along with a copy of recent transcript; expected Family Contribution (EFC) from Student Aid Report (SAR), which comes as a result of filing the FAFSA; and a copy of Financial Aid Award Letter from the chosen college to be attended. **Deadline:** April 30.

Remarks: Faxed applications will not be considered.

2157 ■ CSF Carl H. Linder Family Scholarships *(Undergraduate/Scholarship)*

Purpose: To help students from Greater Cincinnati area to achieve the dream of a college education. **Focus:** General studies. **Qualif.:** Applicant must be a resident of Greater Cincinnati, and attending college as a full-time student. **Criteria:** Awards are given based on need.

Funds Avail.: No specific amount. **To Apply:** Applicants must submit a completed scholarship application form along with a copy of recent transcript; expected Family Contribution (EFC) from Student Aid Report (SAR), which comes as a result of filing the FAFSA; and a copy of Financial Aid Award Letter from the chosen college to be attended. **Deadline:** April 30.

Remarks: Faxed applications will not be considered.

2158 ■ CSF Castellini Foundation Scholarships *(Undergraduate/Scholarship)*

Purpose: To help students from Greater Cincinnati area to achieve the dream of a college education. **Focus:** General studies. **Qualif.:** Applicant must be a resident of Greater Cincinnati, and attending college as a full-time student. **Criteria:** Awards are given based on need.

Funds Avail.: No specific amount. **To Apply:** Applicants must submit a completed scholarship application form along with a copy of recent transcript; expected Family Contribution (EFC) from Student Aid Report (SAR), which comes as a result of filing the FAFSA; and a copy of Financial Aid Award Letter from the chosen college to be attended. **Deadline:** April 30.

Remarks: Faxed applications will not be considered.

2159 ■ CSF Charles and Claire Phillips Scholarships *(Undergraduate/Scholarship)*

Purpose: To help students from Greater Cincinnati area to achieve their dream of a college education. **Focus:** General studies. **Qualif.:** Applicant must be a resident of Greater Cincinnati, and attending college as a full-time student. **Criteria:** Awards are given based on need.

Funds Avail.: No specific amount. **To Apply:** Applicants must submit a completed scholarship application form along with a copy of recent transcript; expected Family Contribution (EFC) from Student Aid Report (SAR), which comes as a result of filing the FAFSA; and a copy of Financial Aid Award Letter from the chosen college to be attended. **Deadline:** April 30.

Remarks: Faxed applications will not be considered.

2160 ■ CSF Charlotte R. Schmidlapp Scholarships *(Undergraduate/Scholarship)*

Purpose: To help students from Greater Cincinnati area to achieve their dream of a college education. **Focus:** General studies. **Qualif.:** Applicant must be a resident of Greater Cincinnati, and attending college as a full-time student. **Criteria:** Awards are given based on need.

Funds Avail.: No specific amount. **To Apply:** Applicants must submit a completed scholarship application form along with a copy of recent transcript; expected Family Contribution (EFC) from Student Aid Report (SAR), which comes as a result of filing the FAFSA; and a copy of Financial Aid Award Letter from the chosen college to be attended. **Deadline:** April 30.

Remarks: Faxed applications will not be considered.

2161 ■ CSF Christopher Todd Grant Memorial Scholarships *(Undergraduate/Scholarship)*

Purpose: To help students from Greater Cincinnati area to achieve the dream of a college education. **Focus:** General studies. **Qualif.:** Applicant must be a resident of Greater Cincinnati, and attending college as a full-time student. **Criteria:** Awards are given based on need.

Funds Avail.: No specific amount. **To Apply:** Applicants must submit a completed scholarship application form along with a copy of recent transcript; expected Family Contribution (EFC) from Student Aid Report (SAR), which comes as a result of filing the FAFSA; and a copy of Financial Aid Award Letter from the chosen college to be attended. **Deadline:** April 30.

Remarks: Faxed applications will not be considered.

2162 ■ CSF Cincinnati Bell Scholarships *(Undergraduate/Scholarship)*

Purpose: To help students from Greater Cincinnati area to achieve the dream of a college education. **Focus:** General studies. **Qualif.:** Applicant must be a resident of Greater Cincinnati, and attending college as a full-time student. **Criteria:** Awards are given based on need.

Funds Avail.: No specific amount. **To Apply:** Applicants

Awards are arranged alphabetically below their administering organizations

must submit a completed scholarship application form along with a copy of recent transcript; expected Family Contribution (EFC) from Student Aid Report (SAR), which comes as a result of filing the FAFSA; and a copy of Financial Aid Award Letter from the chosen college to be attended. **Deadline:** April 30.

Remarks: Faxed applications will not be considered.

2163 ■ CSF Cincinnati Financial Corporation Scholarships *(Undergraduate/Scholarship)*

Purpose: To help students from Greater Cincinnati area to achieve the dream of a college education. **Focus:** General studies. **Qualif.:** Applicant must be a resident of Greater Cincinnati, and attending college as a full-time student. **Criteria:** Awards are given based on need.

Funds Avail.: No specific amount. **To Apply:** Applicants must submit a completed scholarship application form along with a copy of recent transcript; expected Family Contribution (EFC) from Student Aid Report (SAR), which comes as a result of filing the FAFSA; and a copy of Financial Aid Award Letter from the chosen college to be attended. **Deadline:** April 30.

Remarks: Faxed applications will not be considered.

2164 ■ CSF Cincinnati Milacron Scholarships *(Undergraduate/Scholarship)*

Purpose: To help students from Greater Cincinnati area to achieve the dream of a college education. **Focus:** General studies. **Qualif.:** Applicant must be a resident of Greater Cincinnati, and attending college as a full-time student. **Criteria:** Awards are given based on need.

Funds Avail.: No specific amount. **To Apply:** Applicants must submit a completed scholarship application form along with a copy of recent transcript; expected Family Contribution (EFC) from Student Aid Report (SAR), which comes as a result of filing the FAFSA; and a copy of Financial Aid Award Letter from the chosen college to be attended. **Deadline:** April 30.

Remarks: Faxed applications will not be considered.

2165 ■ CSF Corwin Nixon Scholarships *(Undergraduate/Scholarship)*

Purpose: To help students from Greater Cincinnati area to achieve the dream of a college education. **Focus:** General studies. **Qualif.:** Applicant must be a resident of Greater Cincinnati, and attending college as a full-time student. **Criteria:** Awards are given based on need.

Funds Avail.: No specific amount. **To Apply:** Applicants must submit a completed scholarship application form along with a copy of recent transcript; expected Family Contribution (EFC) from Student Aid Report (SAR), which comes as a result of filing the FAFSA; and a copy of Financial Aid Award Letter from the chosen college to be attended. **Deadline:** April 30.

Remarks: Faxed applications will not be considered.

2166 ■ CSF Crosset Family Scholarships *(Undergraduate/Scholarship)*

Purpose: To help students from Greater Cincinnati area to achieve the dream of a college education. **Focus:** General studies. **Qualif.:** Applicant must be a resident of Greater Cincinnati, and attending college as a full-time student. **Criteria:** Awards are given based on need.

Funds Avail.: No specific amount. **To Apply:** Applicants must submit a completed scholarship application form along with a copy of recent transcript; expected Family Contribution (EFC) from Student Aid Report (SAR), which comes as a result of filing the FAFSA; and a copy of Financial Aid Award Letter from the chosen college to be attended. **Deadline:** April 30.

Remarks: Faxed applications will not be considered.

2167 ■ CSF Dater Foundation Scholarships *(Undergraduate/Scholarship)*

Purpose: To help students from Greater Cincinnati area to achieve the dream of a college education. **Focus:** General studies. **Qualif.:** Applicant must be a resident of Greater Cincinnati, and attending college as a full-time student. **Criteria:** Awards are given based on need.

Funds Avail.: No specific amount. **To Apply:** Applicants must submit a completed scholarship application form along with a copy of recent transcript; expected Family Contribution (EFC) from Student Aid Report (SAR), which comes as a result of filing the FAFSA; and a copy of Financial Aid Award Letter from the chosen college to be attended. **Deadline:** April 30.

Remarks: Faxed applications will not be considered.

2168 ■ CSF David J. Joseph Company Scholarships *(Undergraduate/Scholarship)*

Purpose: To help students from Greater Cincinnati area to achieve the dream of a college education. **Focus:** General studies. **Qualif.:** Applicant must be a resident of Greater Cincinnati, and attending college as a full-time student. **Criteria:** Awards are given based on need.

Funds Avail.: No specific amount. **To Apply:** Applicants must submit a completed scholarship application form along with a copy of recent transcript; expected Family Contribution (EFC) from Student Aid Report (SAR), which comes as a result of filing the FAFSA; and a copy of Financial Aid Award Letter from the chosen college to be attended. **Deadline:** April 30.

Remarks: Faxed applications will not be considered.

2169 ■ CSF Dee Wacksman Memorial Scholarships *(Undergraduate/Scholarship)*

Purpose: To help students from Greater Cincinnati area to achieve the dream of a college education. **Focus:** General studies. **Qualif.:** Applicant must be a resident of Greater Cincinnati, and attending college as a full-time student. **Criteria:** Awards are given based on need.

Funds Avail.: No specific amount. **To Apply:** Applicants must submit a completed scholarship application form along with a copy of recent transcript; expected Family Contribution (EFC) from Student Aid Report (SAR), which comes as a result of filing the FAFSA; and a copy of Financial Aid Award Letter from the chosen college to be attended. **Deadline:** April 30.

Remarks: Faxed applications will not be considered.

2170 ■ CSF Duke Energy Scholarships *(Undergraduate/Scholarship)*

Purpose: To help students from Greater Cincinnati area to achieve the dream of a college education. **Focus:** General studies. **Qualif.:** Applicant must be a resident of Greater Cincinnati, and attending college as a full-time student. **Criteria:** Awards are given based on need.

Funds Avail.: No specific amount. **To Apply:** Applicants must submit a completed scholarship application form along with a copy of recent transcript; expected Family Contribution (EFC) from Student Aid Report (SAR), which comes as a result of filing the FAFSA; and a copy of Financial Aid Award Letter from the chosen college to be attended. **Deadline:** April 30.

Remarks: Faxed applications will not be considered.

2171 ■ CSF Dwight Hibbard Scholarships *(Undergraduate/Scholarship)*

Purpose: To help students from Greater Cincinnati area to achieve the dream of a college education. **Focus:** General studies. **Qualif.:** Applicant must be a resident of Greater Cincinnati, and attending college as a full-time student. **Criteria:** Awards are given based on need.

Funds Avail.: No specific amount. **To Apply:** Applicants must submit a completed scholarship application form along with a copy of recent transcript; expected Family Contribution (EFC) from Student Aid Report (SAR), which comes as a result of filing the FAFSA; and a copy of Financial Aid Award Letter from the chosen college to be attended. **Deadline:** April 30.

Remarks: Faxed applications will not be considered.

2172 ■ CSF Ella Wilson Johnson Scholarships *(Undergraduate/Scholarship)*

Purpose: To help students from Greater Cincinnati area to achieve the dream of a college education. **Focus:** General studies. **Qualif.:** Applicant must be a resident of Greater Cincinnati, and attending college as a full-time student. **Criteria:** Awards are given based on need.

Funds Avail.: No specific amount. **To Apply:** Applicants must submit a completed scholarship application form along with a copy of recent transcript; expected Family Contribution (EFC) from Student Aid Report (SAR), which comes as a result of filing the FAFSA; and a copy of Financial Aid Award Letter from the chosen college to be attended. **Deadline:** April 30.

Remarks: Faxed applications will not be considered.

2173 ■ CSF Estelle Davis Memorial Scholarships *(Undergraduate/Scholarship)*

Purpose: To help students from Greater Cincinnati area to achieve the dream of a college education. **Focus:** General studies. **Qualif.:** Applicant must be a resident of Greater Cincinnati, and attending college as a full-time student. **Criteria:** Awards are given based on need.

Funds Avail.: No specific amount. **To Apply:** Applicants must submit a completed scholarship application form along with a copy of recent transcript; expected Family Contribution (EFC) from Student Aid Report (SAR), which comes as a result of filing the FAFSA; and a copy of Financial Aid Award Letter from the chosen college to be attended. **Deadline:** April 30.

Remarks: Faxed applications will not be considered.

2174 ■ CSF Eugene Carroll Scholarships *(Undergraduate/Scholarship)*

Purpose: To help students from Greater Cincinnati area to achieve the dream of a college education. **Focus:** General studies. **Qualif.:** Applicant must be a resident of Greater Cincinnati, and attending college as a full-time student. **Criteria:** Awards are given based on need.

Funds Avail.: No specific amount. **To Apply:** Applicants must submit a completed scholarship application form along with a copy of recent transcript; expected Family Contribution (EFC) from Student Aid Report (SAR), which comes as a result of filing the FAFSA; and a copy of Financial Aid Award Letter from the chosen college to be attended. **Deadline:** April 30.

Remarks: Faxed applications will not be considered.

2175 ■ CSF E.W. Scripps Scholarships *(Undergraduate/Scholarship)*

Purpose: To help students from Greater Cincinnati area to achieve the dream of a college education. **Focus:** General studies. **Qualif.:** Applicant must be a resident of Greater Cincinnati, and attending college as a full-time student. **Criteria:** Awards are given based on need.

Funds Avail.: No specific amount. **To Apply:** Applicants must submit a completed scholarship application form along with a copy of recent transcript; expected Family Contribution (EFC) from Student Aid Report (SAR), which comes as a result of filing the FAFSA; and a copy of Financial Aid Award Letter from the chosen college to be attended. **Deadline:** April 30.

Remarks: Faxed applications will not be considered.

2176 ■ CSF Farmer Family Foundation Scholarships *(Undergraduate/Scholarship)*

Purpose: To help students from Greater Cincinnati area to achieve the dream of a college education. **Focus:** General studies. **Qualif.:** Applicant must be a resident of Greater Cincinnati, and attending college as a full-time student. **Criteria:** Awards are given based on need.

Funds Avail.: No specific amount. **To Apply:** Applicants must submit a completed scholarship application form along with a copy of recent transcript; expected Family Contribution (EFC) from Student Aid Report (SAR), which comes as a result of filing the FAFSA; and a copy of Financial Aid Award Letter from the chosen college to be attended. **Deadline:** April 30.

Remarks: Faxed applications will not be considered.

2177 ■ CSF Fifth Third Bank Combined Scholarships *(Undergraduate/Scholarship)*

Purpose: To help students from Greater Cincinnati area to achieve the dream of a college education. **Focus:** General studies. **Qualif.:** Applicant must be a resident of Greater Cincinnati, and attending college as a full-time student. **Criteria:** Awards are given based on need.

Funds Avail.: No specific amount. **To Apply:** Applicants must submit a completed scholarship application form along with a copy of recent transcript; expected Family Contribution (EFC) from Student Aid Report (SAR), which comes as a result of filing the FAFSA; and a copy of Financial Aid Award Letter from the chosen college to be attended. **Deadline:** April 30.

Remarks: Faxed applications will not be considered.

2178 ■ CSF Fletemeyer Family Scholarships *(Undergraduate/Scholarship)*

Purpose: To help students from Greater Cincinnati area to achieve the dream of a college education. **Focus:** General studies. **Qualif.:** Applicant must be a resident of Greater Cincinnati, and attending college as a full-time student. **Criteria:** Awards are given based on need.

Funds Avail.: No specific amount. **To Apply:** Applicants must submit a completed scholarship application form along with a copy of recent transcript; expected Family Contribution (EFC) from Student Aid Report (SAR), which comes as a result of filing the FAFSA; and a copy of Financial Aid

Award Letter from the chosen college to be attended. **Deadline:** April 30.

Remarks: Faxed applications will not be considered.

2179 ■ CSF Florette B. Hoffheimer Scholarships *(Undergraduate/Scholarship)*

Purpose: To help students from Greater Cincinnati area to achieve the dream of a college education. **Focus:** General studies. **Qualif.:** Applicant must be a resident of Greater Cincinnati, and attending college as a full-time student. **Criteria:** Awards are given based on need.

Funds Avail.: No specific amount. **To Apply:** Applicants must submit a completed scholarship application form along with a copy of recent transcript; expected Family Contribution (EFC) from Student Aid Report (SAR), which comes as a result of filing the FAFSA; and a copy of Financial Aid Award Letter from the chosen college to be attended. **Deadline:** April 30.

Remarks: Faxed applications will not be considered.

2180 ■ CSF Frank Foster Skillman Scholarships *(Undergraduate/Scholarship)*

Purpose: To help students from Greater Cincinnati area to achieve the dream of a college education. **Focus:** General studies. **Qualif.:** Applicant must be a resident of Greater Cincinnati, and attending college as a full-time student. **Criteria:** Awards are given based on need.

Funds Avail.: No specific amount. **To Apply:** Applicants must submit a completed scholarship application form along with a copy of recent transcript; expected Family Contribution (EFC) from Student Aid Report (SAR), which comes as a result of filing the FAFSA; and a copy of Financial Aid Award Letter from the chosen college to be attended. **Deadline:** April 30.

Remarks: Faxed applications will not be considered.

2181 ■ CSF Gardner Foundation Scholarships *(Undergraduate/Scholarship)*

Purpose: To help students from Greater Cincinnati area to achieve the dream of a college education. **Focus:** General studies. **Qualif.:** Applicant must be a resident of Greater Cincinnati, and attending college as a full-time student. **Criteria:** Awards are given based on need.

Funds Avail.: No specific amount. **To Apply:** Applicants must submit a completed scholarship application form along with a copy of recent transcript; expected Family Contribution (EFC) from Student Aid Report (SAR), which comes as a result of filing the FAFSA; and a copy of Financial Aid Award Letter from the chosen college to be attended. **Deadline:** April 30.

Remarks: Faxed applications will not be considered.

2182 ■ CSF G.E. Aircraft Engines Scholarships *(Undergraduate/Scholarship)*

Purpose: To help students from Greater Cincinnati area to achieve the dream of a college education. **Focus:** General studies. **Qualif.:** Applicant must be a resident of Greater Cincinnati, and attending college as a full-time student. **Criteria:** Awards are given based on need.

Funds Avail.: No specific amount. **To Apply:** Applicants must submit a completed scholarship application form along with a copy of recent transcript; expected Family Contribution (EFC) from Student Aid Report (SAR), which comes as a result of filing the FAFSA; and a copy of Financial Aid Award Letter from the chosen college to be attended. **Deadline:** April 30.

Remarks: Faxed applications will not be considered.

2183 ■ CSF George and Amy Polley Scholarships *(Undergraduate/Scholarship)*

Purpose: To help students from Greater Cincinnati area to achieve the dream of a college education. **Focus:** General studies. **Qualif.:** Applicant must be a resident of Greater Cincinnati, and attending college as a full-time student. **Criteria:** Awards are given based on need.

Funds Avail.: No specific amount. **To Apply:** Applicants must submit a completed scholarship application form along with a copy of recent transcript; expected Family Contribution (EFC) from Student Aid Report (SAR), which comes as a result of filing the FAFSA; and a copy of Financial Aid Award Letter from the chosen college to be attended. **Deadline:** April 30.

Remarks: Faxed applications will not be considered.

2184 ■ CSF Goldman, Sachs and Company Scholarships *(Undergraduate/Scholarship)*

Purpose: To help students from Greater Cincinnati area to achieve the dream of a college education. **Focus:** General studies. **Qualif.:** Applicant must be a resident of Greater Cincinnati, and attending college as a full-time student. **Criteria:** Awards are given based on need.

Funds Avail.: No specific amount. **To Apply:** Applicants must submit a completed scholarship application form along with a copy of recent transcript; expected Family Contribution (EFC) from Student Aid Report (SAR), which comes as a result of filing the FAFSA; and a copy of Financial Aid Award Letter from the chosen college to be attended. **Deadline:** April 30.

Remarks: Faxed applications will not be considered.

2185 ■ CSF Greater Cincinnati Scholarships Association *(Undergraduate/Scholarship)*

Purpose: To help students from Greater Cincinnati area to achieve the dream of a college education. **Focus:** General studies. **Qualif.:** Applicant must be a resident of Greater Cincinnati, and attending college as a full-time student. **Criteria:** Awards are given based on need.

Funds Avail.: No specific amount. **To Apply:** Applicants must submit a completed scholarship application form along with a copy of recent transcript; expected Family Contribution (EFC) from Student Aid Report (SAR), which comes as a result of filing the FAFSA; and a copy of Financial Aid Award Letter from the chosen college to be attended. **Deadline:** April 30.

Remarks: Faxed applications will not be considered.

2186 ■ CSF H.C. Schott Foundation Scholarships *(Undergraduate/Scholarship)*

Purpose: To help students from Greater Cincinnati area to achieve the dream of a college education. **Focus:** General studies. **Qualif.:** Applicant must be a resident of Greater Cincinnati, and attending college as a full-time student. **Criteria:** Awards are given based on need.

Funds Avail.: No specific amount. **To Apply:** Applicants must submit a completed scholarship application form along with a copy of recent transcript; expected Family Contribution (EFC) from Student Aid Report (SAR), which comes as a result of filing the FAFSA; and a copy of Financial Aid

Award Letter from the chosen college to be attended. **Deadline:** April 30.

Remarks: Faxed applications will not be considered.

2187 ■ CSF HCRTA/Glen O. and Wyllabeth Wise Scholarships *(Undergraduate/Scholarship)*

Purpose: To help students from Greater Cincinnati area to achieve the dream of a college education. **Focus:** General studies. **Qualif.:** Applicant must be a resident of Greater Cincinnati, and attending college as a full-time student. **Criteria:** Awards are given based on need.

Funds Avail.: No specific amount. **To Apply:** Applicants must submit a completed scholarship application form along with a copy of recent transcript; expected Family Contribution (EFC) from Student Aid Report (SAR), which comes as a result of filing the FAFSA; and a copy of Financial Aid Award Letter from the chosen college to be attended. **Deadline:** April 30.

Remarks: Faxed applications will not be considered.

2188 ■ CSF Heidelberg Distributing Co. Scholarships *(Undergraduate/Scholarship)*

Purpose: To help students from Greater Cincinnati area to achieve the dream of a college education. **Focus:** General studies. **Qualif.:** Applicant must be a resident of Greater Cincinnati, and attending college as a full-time student. **Criteria:** Awards are given based on need.

Funds Avail.: No specific amount. **To Apply:** Applicants must submit a completed scholarship application form along with a copy of recent transcript; expected Family Contribution (EFC) from Student Aid Report (SAR), which comes as a result of filing the FAFSA; and a copy of Financial Aid Award Letter from the chosen college to be attended. **Deadline:** April 30.

Remarks: Faxed applications will not be considered.

2189 ■ CSF Heinz Pet Products Scholarships *(Undergraduate/Scholarship)*

Purpose: To help students from Greater Cincinnati area to achieve the dream of a college education. **Focus:** General studies. **Qualif.:** Applicant must be a resident of Greater Cincinnati, and attending college as a full-time student. **Criteria:** Awards are given based on need.

Funds Avail.: No specific amount. **To Apply:** Applicants must submit a completed scholarship application form along with a copy of recent transcript; expected Family Contribution (EFC) from Student Aid Report (SAR), which comes as a result of filing the FAFSA; and a copy of Financial Aid Award Letter from the chosen college to be attended. **Deadline:** April 30.

Remarks: Faxed applications will not be considered.

2190 ■ CSF Helen Steiner Rice Scholarships *(Undergraduate/Scholarship)*

Purpose: To help students from Greater Cincinnati area to achieve the dream of a college education. **Focus:** General studies. **Qualif.:** Applicant must be a resident of Greater Cincinnati, and attending college as a full-time student. **Criteria:** Awards are given based on need.

Funds Avail.: No specific amount. **To Apply:** Applicants must submit a completed scholarship application form along with a copy of recent transcript; expected Family Contribution (EFC) from Student Aid Report (SAR), which comes as a result of filing the FAFSA; and a copy of Financial Aid Award Letter from the chosen college to be attended. **Deadline:** April 30.

Remarks: Faxed applications will not be considered.

2191 ■ CSF Johnny Bench Scholarships *(Undergraduate/Scholarship)*

Purpose: To help students from Greater Cincinnati area to achieve the dream of a college education. **Focus:** General studies. **Qualif.:** Applicant must be a resident of Greater Cincinnati, and attending college as a full-time student. **Criteria:** Awards are given based on need.

Funds Avail.: No specific amount. **To Apply:** Applicants must submit a completed scholarship application form along with a copy of recent transcript; expected Family Contribution (EFC) from Student Aid Report (SAR), which comes as a result of filing the FAFSA; and a copy of Financial Aid Award Letter from the chosen college to be attended. **Deadline:** April 30.

Remarks: Faxed applications will not be considered.

2192 ■ CSF Joseph S. Stern, Jr. Scholarships *(Undergraduate/Scholarship)*

Purpose: To help students from Greater Cincinnati area to achieve the dream of a college education. **Focus:** General studies. **Qualif.:** Applicant must be a resident of Greater Cincinnati, and attending college as a full-time student. **Criteria:** Awards are given based on need.

Funds Avail.: No specific amount. **To Apply:** Applicants must submit a completed scholarship application form along with a copy of recent transcript; expected Family Contribution (EFC) from Student Aid Report (SAR), which comes as a result of filing the FAFSA; and a copy of Financial Aid Award Letter from the chosen college to be attended. **Deadline:** April 30.

Remarks: Faxed applications will not be considered.

2193 ■ CSF Judge Benjamin Schwartz Scholarships *(Undergraduate/Scholarship)*

Purpose: To help students from Greater Cincinnati area to achieve the dream of a college education. **Focus:** General studies. **Qualif.:** Applicant must be a resident of Greater Cincinnati, and attending college as a full-time student. **Criteria:** Awards are given based on need.

Funds Avail.: No specific amount. **To Apply:** Applicants must submit a completed scholarship application form along with a copy of recent transcript; expected Family Contribution (EFC) from Student Aid Report (SAR), which comes as a result of filing the FAFSA; and a copy of Financial Aid Award Letter from the chosen college to be attended. **Deadline:** April 30.

Remarks: Faxed applications will not be considered.

2194 ■ CSF Juilfs Foundation Scholarships *(Undergraduate/Scholarship)*

Purpose: To help students from Greater Cincinnati area to achieve the dream of a college education. **Focus:** General studies. **Qualif.:** Applicant must be a resident of Greater Cincinnati, and attending college as a full-time student. **Criteria:** Awards are given based on need.

Funds Avail.: No specific amount. **To Apply:** Applicants must submit a completed scholarship application form along with a copy of recent transcript; expected Family Contribution (EFC) from Student Aid Report (SAR), which comes as a result of filing the FAFSA; and a copy of Financial Aid

Award Letter from the chosen college to be attended. **Deadline:** April 30.

Remarks: Faxed applications will not be considered.

2195 ■ CSF Kroger Cincinnati/Dayton Scholarships *(Undergraduate/Scholarship)*

Purpose: To help students from Greater Cincinnati area to achieve the dream of a college education. **Focus:** General studies. **Qualif.:** Applicant must be a resident of Greater Cincinnati, and attending college as a full-time student. **Criteria:** Awards are given based on need.

Funds Avail.: No specific amount. **To Apply:** Applicants must submit a completed scholarship application form along with a copy of recent transcript; expected Family Contribution (EFC) from Student Aid Report (SAR), which comes as a result of filing the FAFSA; and a copy of Financial Aid Award Letter from the chosen college to be attended. **Deadline:** April 30.

Remarks: Faxed applications will not be considered.

2196 ■ CSF L and T Woolfolk Memorial Scholarships *(Undergraduate/Scholarship)*

Purpose: To help students from Greater Cincinnati area to achieve the dream of a college education. **Focus:** General studies. **Qualif.:** Applicant must be a resident of Greater Cincinnati, and attending college as a full-time student. **Criteria:** Awards are given based on need.

Funds Avail.: No specific amount. **To Apply:** Applicants must submit a completed scholarship application form along with a copy of recent transcript; expected Family Contribution (EFC) from Student Aid Report (SAR), which comes as a result of filing the FAFSA; and a copy of Financial Aid Award Letter from the chosen college to be attended. **Deadline:** April 30.

Remarks: Faxed applications will not be considered.

2197 ■ CSF Lazarus/Federated Scholarships *(Undergraduate/Scholarship)*

Purpose: To help students from Greater Cincinnati area to achieve the dream of a college education. **Focus:** General studies. **Qualif.:** Applicant must be a resident of Greater Cincinnati, and attending college as a full-time student. **Criteria:** Awards are given based on need.

Funds Avail.: No specific amount. **To Apply:** Applicants must submit a completed scholarship application form along with a copy of recent transcript; expected Family Contribution (EFC) from Student Aid Report (SAR), which comes as a result of filing the FAFSA; and a copy of Financial Aid Award Letter from the chosen college to be attended. **Deadline:** April 30.

Remarks: Faxed applications will not be considered.

2198 ■ CSF L.B. Zapoleon Scholarships *(Undergraduate/Scholarship)*

Purpose: To help students from Greater Cincinnati area to achieve the dream of a college education. **Focus:** General studies. **Qualif.:** Applicant must be a resident of Greater Cincinnati, and attending college as a full-time student. **Criteria:** Awards are given based on need.

Funds Avail.: No specific amount. **To Apply:** Applicants must submit a completed scholarship application form along with a copy of recent transcript; expected Family Contribution (EFC) from Student Aid Report (SAR), which comes as a result of filing the FAFSA; and a copy of Financial Aid Award Letter from the chosen college to be attended. **Deadline:** April 30.

Remarks: Faxed applications will not be considered.

2199 ■ CSF Lowe Simpson Scholarships *(Undergraduate/Scholarship)*

Purpose: To help students from Greater Cincinnati area to achieve the dream of a college education. **Focus:** General studies. **Qualif.:** Applicant must be a resident of Greater Cincinnati, and attending college as a full-time student. **Criteria:** Awards are given based on need.

Funds Avail.: No specific amount. **To Apply:** Applicants must submit a completed scholarship application form along with a copy of recent transcript; expected Family Contribution (EFC) from Student Aid Report (SAR), which comes as a result of filing the FAFSA; and a copy of Financial Aid Award Letter from the chosen college to be attended. **Deadline:** April 30.

Remarks: Faxed applications will not be considered.

2200 ■ CSF Lyle and Arlene Everingham Scholarships *(Undergraduate/Scholarship)*

Purpose: To help students from Greater Cincinnati area to achieve the dream of a college education. **Focus:** General studies. **Qualif.:** Applicant must be a resident of Greater Cincinnati, and attending college as a full-time student. **Criteria:** Awards are given based on need.

Funds Avail.: No specific amount. **To Apply:** Applicants must submit a completed scholarship application form along with a copy of recent transcript; expected Family Contribution (EFC) from Student Aid Report (SAR), which comes as a result of filing the FAFSA; and a copy of Financial Aid Award Letter from the chosen college to be attended. **Deadline:** April 30.

Remarks: Faxed applications will not be considered.

2201 ■ CSF Lyle Everingham Scholarships *(Undergraduate/Scholarship)*

Purpose: To help students from Greater Cincinnati area to achieve the dream of a college education. **Focus:** General studies. **Qualif.:** Applicant must be a resident of Greater Cincinnati, and attending college as a full-time student. **Criteria:** Awards are given based on need.

Funds Avail.: No specific amount. **To Apply:** Applicants must submit a completed scholarship application form along with a copy of recent transcript; expected Family Contribution (EFC) from Student Aid Report (SAR), which comes as a result of filing the FAFSA; and a copy of Financial Aid Award Letter from the chosen college to be attended. **Deadline:** April 30.

Remarks: Faxed applications will not be considered.

2202 ■ CSF M and E Brown Scholarships *(Undergraduate/Scholarship)*

Purpose: To help students from Greater Cincinnati area to achieve the dream of a college education. **Focus:** General studies. **Qualif.:** Applicant must be a resident of Greater Cincinnati, and attending college as a full-time student. **Criteria:** Awards are given based on need.

Funds Avail.: No specific amount. **To Apply:** Applicants must submit a completed scholarship application form along with a copy of recent transcript; expected Family Contribution (EFC) from Student Aid Report (SAR), which comes as a result of filing the FAFSA; and a copy of Financial Aid

Award Letter from the chosen college to be attended. **Deadline:** April 30.

Remarks: Faxed applications will not be considered.

2203 ■ CSF M. Kantor and Brothers Scholarships *(Undergraduate/Scholarship)*

Purpose: To help students from Greater Cincinnati area to achieve the dream of a college education. **Focus:** General studies. **Qualif.:** Applicant must be a resident of Greater Cincinnati, and attending college as a full-time student. **Criteria:** Awards are given based on need.

Funds Avail.: No specific amount. **To Apply:** Applicants must submit a completed scholarship application form along with a copy of recent transcript; expected Family Contribution (EFC) from Student Aid Report (SAR), which comes as a result of filing the FAFSA; and a copy of Financial Aid Award Letter from the chosen college to be attended. **Deadline:** April 30.

Remarks: Faxed applications will not be considered.

2204 ■ CSF Martha W. Tanner Memorial Scholarships *(Undergraduate/Scholarship)*

Purpose: To help students from Greater Cincinnati area to achieve the dream of a college education. **Focus:** General studies. **Qualif.:** Applicant must be a resident of Greater Cincinnati, and attending college as a full-time student. **Criteria:** Awards are given based on need.

Funds Avail.: No specific amount. **To Apply:** Applicants must submit a completed scholarship application form along with a copy of recent transcript; expected Family Contribution (EFC) from Student Aid Report (SAR), which comes as a result of filing the FAFSA; and a copy of Financial Aid Award Letter from the chosen college to be attended. **Deadline:** April 30.

Remarks: Faxed applications will not be considered.

2205 ■ CSF Marvin Rammelsberg Memorial Scholarships *(Undergraduate/Scholarship)*

Purpose: To help students from Greater Cincinnati area to achieve the dream of a college education. **Focus:** General studies. **Qualif.:** Applicant must be a resident of Greater Cincinnati, and attending college as a full-time student. **Criteria:** Awards are given based on need.

Funds Avail.: No specific amount. **To Apply:** Applicants must submit a completed scholarship application form along with a copy of recent transcript; expected Family Contribution (EFC) from Student Aid Report (SAR), which comes as a result of filing the FAFSA; and a copy of Financial Aid Award Letter from the chosen college to be attended. **Deadline:** April 30.

Remarks: Faxed applications will not be considered.

2206 ■ CSF Mary Roberts Scholarships *(Undergraduate/Scholarship)*

Purpose: To help students from Greater Cincinnati area to achieve the dream of a college education. **Focus:** General studies. **Qualif.:** Applicant must be a resident of Greater Cincinnati, and attending college as a full-time student. **Criteria:** Awards are given based on need.

Funds Avail.: No specific amount. **To Apply:** Applicants must submit a completed scholarship application form along with a copy of recent transcript; expected Family Contribution (EFC) from Student Aid Report (SAR), which comes as a result of filing the FAFSA; and a copy of Financial Aid Award Letter from the chosen college to be attended. **Deadline:** April 30.

Remarks: Faxed applications will not be considered.

2207 ■ CSF McCall Educational Scholarships *(Undergraduate/Scholarship)*

Purpose: To help students from Greater Cincinnati area to achieve the dream of a college education. **Focus:** General studies. **Qualif.:** Applicant must be a resident of Greater Cincinnati, and attending college as a full-time student. **Criteria:** Awards are given based on need.

Funds Avail.: No specific amount. **To Apply:** Applicants must submit a completed scholarship application form along with a copy of recent transcript; expected Family Contribution (EFC) from Student Aid Report (SAR), which comes as a result of filing the FAFSA; and a copy of Financial Aid Award Letter from the chosen college to be attended. **Deadline:** April 30.

Remarks: Faxed applications will not be considered.

2208 ■ CSF Michael Bany Memorial Scholarships *(Undergraduate/Scholarship)*

Purpose: To help students from Greater Cincinnati area to achieve the dream of a college education. **Focus:** General studies. **Qualif.:** Applicant must be a resident of Greater Cincinnati, and attending college as a full-time student. **Criteria:** Awards are given based on need.

Funds Avail.: No specific amount. **To Apply:** Applicants must submit a completed scholarship application form along with a copy of recent transcript; expected Family Contribution (EFC) from Student Aid Report (SAR), which comes as a result of filing the FAFSA; and a copy of Financial Aid Award Letter from the chosen college to be attended. **Deadline:** April 30.

Remarks: Faxed applications will not be considered.

2209 ■ CSF Midland Company Scholarships *(Undergraduate/Scholarship)*

Purpose: To help students from Greater Cincinnati area to achieve the dream of a college education. **Focus:** General studies. **Qualif.:** Applicant must be a resident of Greater Cincinnati, and attending college as a full-time student. **Criteria:** Awards are given based on need.

Funds Avail.: No specific amount. **To Apply:** Applicants must submit a completed scholarship application form along with a copy of recent transcript; expected Family Contribution (EFC) from Student Aid Report (SAR), which comes as a result of filing the FAFSA; and a copy of Financial Aid Award Letter from the chosen college to be attended. **Deadline:** April 30.

Remarks: Faxed applications will not be considered.

2210 ■ CSF Nelson Schwab Jr. Family Scholarships *(Undergraduate/Scholarship)*

Purpose: To help students from Greater Cincinnati area to achieve the dream of a college education. **Focus:** General studies. **Qualif.:** Applicant must be a resident of Greater Cincinnati, and attending college as a full-time student. **Criteria:** Awards are given based on need.

Funds Avail.: No specific amount. **To Apply:** Applicants must submit a completed scholarship application form along with a copy of recent transcript; expected Family Contribution (EFC) from Student Aid Report (SAR), which comes as a result of filing the FAFSA; and a copy of Financial Aid

Award Letter from the chosen college to be attended. **Deadline:** April 30.

Remarks: Faxed applications will not be considered.

2211 ■ CSF Nethercott Family Scholarships *(Undergraduate/Scholarship)*

Purpose: To help students from Greater Cincinnati area to achieve the dream of a college education. **Focus:** General studies. **Qualif.:** Applicant must be a resident of Greater Cincinnati, and attending college as a full-time student. **Criteria:** Awards are given based on need.

Funds Avail.: No specific amount. **To Apply:** Applicants must submit a completed scholarship application form along with a copy of recent transcript; expected Family Contribution (EFC) from Student Aid Report (SAR), which comes as a result of filing the FAFSA; and a copy of Financial Aid Award Letter from the chosen college to be attended. **Deadline:** April 30.

Remarks: Faxed applications will not be considered.

2212 ■ CSF Ohio National Foundation Scholarships *(Undergraduate/Scholarship)*

Purpose: To help students from Greater Cincinnati area to achieve the dream of a college education. **Focus:** General studies. **Qualif.:** Applicant must be a resident of Greater Cincinnati, and attending college as a full-time student. **Criteria:** Awards are given based on need.

Funds Avail.: No specific amount. **To Apply:** Applicants must submit a completed scholarship application form along with a copy of recent transcript; expected Family Contribution (EFC) from Student Aid Report (SAR), which comes as a result of filing the FAFSA; and a copy of Financial Aid Award Letter from the chosen college to be attended. **Deadline:** April 30.

Remarks: Faxed applications will not be considered.

2213 ■ CSF Pepper Family Scholarships *(Undergraduate/Scholarship)*

Purpose: To help students from Greater Cincinnati area to achieve the dream of a college education. **Focus:** General studies. **Qualif.:** Applicant must be a resident of Greater Cincinnati, and attending college as a full-time student. **Criteria:** Awards are given based on need.

Funds Avail.: No specific amount. **To Apply:** Applicants must submit a completed scholarship application form along with a copy of recent transcript; expected Family Contribution (EFC) from Student Aid Report (SAR), which comes as a result of filing the FAFSA; and a copy of Financial Aid Award Letter from the chosen college to be attended. **Deadline:** April 30.

Remarks: Faxed applications will not be considered.

2214 ■ CSF Pichler Family Scholarships *(Undergraduate/Scholarship)*

Purpose: To help students from Greater Cincinnati area to achieve the dream of a college education. **Focus:** General studies. **Qualif.:** Applicant must be a resident of Greater Cincinnati, and attending college as a full-time student. **Criteria:** Awards are given based on need.

Funds Avail.: No specific amount. **To Apply:** Applicants must submit a completed scholarship application form along with a copy of recent transcript; expected Family Contribution (EFC) from Student Aid Report (SAR), which comes as a result of filing the FAFSA; and a copy of Financial Aid Award Letter from the chosen college to be attended. **Deadline:** April 30.

Remarks: Faxed applications will not be considered.

2215 ■ CSF PNC Bank Scholarships *(Undergraduate/Scholarship)*

Purpose: To help students from Greater Cincinnati area to achieve the dream of a college education. **Focus:** General studies. **Qualif.:** Applicant must be a resident of Greater Cincinnati, and attending college as a full-time student. **Criteria:** Awards are given based on need.

Funds Avail.: No specific amount. **To Apply:** Applicants must submit a completed scholarship application form along with a copy of recent transcript; expected Family Contribution (EFC) from Student Aid Report (SAR), which comes as a result of filing the FAFSA; and a copy of Financial Aid Award Letter from the chosen college to be attended. **Deadline:** April 30.

Remarks: Faxed applications will not be considered.

2216 ■ CSF Priscilla Gamble Scholarships *(Undergraduate/Scholarship)*

Purpose: To help students from Greater Cincinnati area to achieve the dream of a college education. **Focus:** General studies. **Qualif.:** Applicant must be a resident of Greater Cincinnati, and attending college as a full-time student. **Criteria:** Awards are given based on need.

Funds Avail.: No specific amount. **To Apply:** Applicants must submit a completed scholarship application form along with a copy of recent transcript; expected Family Contribution (EFC) from Student Aid Report (SAR), which comes as a result of filing the FAFSA; and a copy of Financial Aid Award Letter from the chosen college to be attended. **Deadline:** April 30.

Remarks: Faxed applications will not be considered.

2217 ■ CSF Procter and Gamble Scholarships *(Undergraduate/Scholarship)*

Purpose: To help students from Greater Cincinnati area to achieve the dream of a college education. **Focus:** General studies. **Qualif.:** Applicant must be a resident of Greater Cincinnati, and attending college as a full-time student. **Criteria:** Awards are given based on need.

Funds Avail.: No specific amount. **To Apply:** Applicants must submit a completed scholarship application form along with a copy of recent transcript; expected Family Contribution (EFC) from Student Aid Report (SAR), which comes as a result of filing the FAFSA; and a copy of Financial Aid Award Letter from the chosen college to be attended. **Deadline:** April 30.

Remarks: Faxed applications will not be considered.

2218 ■ CSF Raymond and Augusta Klink Scholarships *(Undergraduate/Scholarship)*

Purpose: To help students from Greater Cincinnati area to achieve the dream of a college education. **Focus:** General studies. **Qualif.:** Applicant must be a resident of Greater Cincinnati, and attending college as a full-time student. **Criteria:** Awards are given based on need.

Funds Avail.: No specific amount. **To Apply:** Applicants must submit a completed scholarship application form along with a copy of recent transcript; expected Family Contribution (EFC) from Student Aid Report (SAR), which comes as a result of filing the FAFSA; and a copy of Financial Aid

Award Letter from the chosen college to be attended. **Deadline:** April 30.

Remarks: Faxed applications will not be considered.

2219 ■ CSF Richard Heekin Scholarships *(Undergraduate/Scholarship)*

Purpose: To help students from Greater Cincinnati area to achieve the dream of a college education. **Focus:** General studies. **Qualif.:** Applicant must be a resident of Greater Cincinnati, and attending college as a full-time student. **Criteria:** Awards are given based on need.

Funds Avail.: No specific amount. **To Apply:** Applicants must submit a completed scholarship application form along with a copy of recent transcript; expected Family Contribution (EFC) from Student Aid Report (SAR), which comes as a result of filing the FAFSA; and a copy of Financial Aid Award Letter from the chosen college to be attended. **Deadline:** April 30.

Remarks: Faxed applications will not be considered.

2220 ■ CSF Robert H. Reakirt Foundation Scholarships *(Undergraduate/Scholarship)*

Purpose: To help students from Greater Cincinnati area to achieve the dream of a college education. **Focus:** General studies. **Qualif.:** Applicant must be a resident of Greater Cincinnati, and attending college as a full-time student. **Criteria:** Awards are given based on need.

Funds Avail.: No specific amount. **To Apply:** Applicants must submit a completed scholarship application form along with a copy of recent transcript; expected Family Contribution (EFC) from Student Aid Report (SAR), which comes as a result of filing the FAFSA; and a copy of Financial Aid Award Letter from the chosen college to be attended. **Deadline:** April 30.

Remarks: Faxed applications will not be considered.

2221 ■ CSF Roger and Joyce Howe Family Scholarships *(Undergraduate/Scholarship)*

Purpose: To help students from Greater Cincinnati area to achieve the dream of a college education. **Focus:** General studies. **Qualif.:** Applicant must be a resident of Greater Cincinnati, and attending college as a full-time student. **Criteria:** Awards are given based on need.

Funds Avail.: No specific amount. **To Apply:** Applicants must submit a completed scholarship application form along with a copy of recent transcript; expected Family Contribution (EFC) from Student Aid Report (SAR), which comes as a result of filing the FAFSA; and a copy of Financial Aid Award Letter from the chosen college to be attended. **Deadline:** April 30.

Remarks: Faxed applications will not be considered.

2222 ■ CSF S. David Shor Scholarships *(Undergraduate/Scholarship)*

Purpose: To help students from Greater Cincinnati area to achieve the dream of a college education. **Focus:** General studies. **Qualif.:** Applicant must be a resident of Greater Cincinnati, and attending college as a full-time student. **Criteria:** Awards are given based on need.

Funds Avail.: No specific amount. **To Apply:** Applicants must submit a completed scholarship application form along with a copy of recent transcript; expected Family Contribution (EFC) from Student Aid Report (SAR), which comes as a result of filing the FAFSA; and a copy of Financial Aid Award Letter from the chosen college to be attended. **Deadline:** April 30.

Remarks: Faxed applications will not be considered.

2223 ■ CSF SC Johnson, A Family Company Scholarships *(Undergraduate/Scholarship)*

Purpose: To help students from Greater Cincinnati area to achieve the dream of a college education. **Focus:** General studies. **Qualif.:** Applicant must be a resident of Greater Cincinnati, and attending college as a full-time student. **Criteria:** Awards are given based on need.

Funds Avail.: No specific amount. **To Apply:** Applicants must submit a completed scholarship application form along with a copy of recent transcript; expected Family Contribution (EFC) from Student Aid Report (SAR), which comes as a result of filing the FAFSA; and a copy of Financial Aid Award Letter from the chosen college to be attended. **Deadline:** April 30.

Remarks: Faxed applications will not be considered.

2224 ■ CSF Scripps Headliners Scholarships *(Undergraduate/Scholarship)*

Purpose: To help students from Greater Cincinnati area to achieve the dream of a college education. **Focus:** General studies. **Qualif.:** Applicant must be a resident of Greater Cincinnati, and attending college as a full-time student. **Criteria:** Awards are given based on need.

Funds Avail.: No specific amount. **To Apply:** Applicants must submit a completed scholarship application form along with a copy of recent transcript; expected Family Contribution (EFC) from Student Aid Report (SAR), which comes as a result of filing the FAFSA; and a copy of Financial Aid Award Letter from the chosen college to be attended. **Deadline:** April 30.

Remarks: Faxed applications will not be considered.

2225 ■ CSF Semple Foundation Scholarships *(Undergraduate/Scholarship)*

Purpose: To help students from Greater Cincinnati area to achieve the dream of a college education. **Focus:** General studies. **Qualif.:** Applicant must be a resident of Greater Cincinnati, and attending college as a full-time student. **Criteria:** Awards are given based on need.

Funds Avail.: No specific amount. **To Apply:** Applicants must submit a completed scholarship application form along with a copy of recent transcript; expected Family Contribution (EFC) from Student Aid Report (SAR), which comes as a result of filing the FAFSA; and a copy of Financial Aid Award Letter from the chosen college to be attended. **Deadline:** April 30.

Remarks: Faxed applications will not be considered.

2226 ■ CSF Thomas J. Emery Memorial Scholarships *(Undergraduate/Scholarship)*

Purpose: To help students from Greater Cincinnati area to achieve the dream of a college education. **Focus:** General studies. **Qualif.:** Applicant must be a resident of Greater Cincinnati, and attending college as a full-time student. **Criteria:** Awards are given based on need.

Funds Avail.: No specific amount. **To Apply:** Applicants must submit a completed scholarship application form along with a copy of recent transcript; expected Family Contribution (EFC) from Student Aid Report (SAR), which comes as a result of filing the FAFSA; and a copy of Financial Aid

Award Letter from the chosen college to be attended. **Deadline:** April 30.

Remarks: Faxed applications will not be considered.

2227 ■ CSF T.L. Conlan Memorial Scholarships *(Undergraduate/Scholarship)*

Purpose: To help students from Greater Cincinnati area to achieve the dream of a college education. **Focus:** General studies. **Qualif.:** Applicant must be a resident of Greater Cincinnati, and attending college as a full-time student. **Criteria:** Awards are given based on need.

Funds Avail.: No specific amount. **To Apply:** Applicants must submit a completed scholarship application form along with a copy of recent transcript; expected Family Contribution (EFC) from Student Aid Report (SAR), which comes as a result of filing the FAFSA; and a copy of Financial Aid Award Letter from the chosen college to be attended. **Deadline:** April 30.

Remarks: Faxed applications will not be considered.

2228 ■ CSF Union Central 135th Anniversary Scholarships *(Undergraduate/Scholarship)*

Purpose: To help students from Greater Cincinnati area to achieve the dream of a college education. **Focus:** General studies. **Qualif.:** Applicant must be a resident of Greater Cincinnati, and attending college as a full-time student. **Criteria:** Awards are given based on need.

Funds Avail.: No specific amount. **To Apply:** Applicants must submit a completed scholarship application form along with a copy of recent transcript; expected Family Contribution (EFC) from Student Aid Report (SAR), which comes as a result of filing the FAFSA; and a copy of Financial Aid Award Letter from the chosen college to be attended. **Deadline:** April 30.

Remarks: Faxed applications will not be considered.

2229 ■ CSF U.S. Bank N.A. Scholarships *(Undergraduate/Scholarship)*

Purpose: To help students from Greater Cincinnati area to achieve the dream of a college education. **Focus:** General studies. **Qualif.:** Applicant must be a resident of Greater Cincinnati, and attending college as a full-time student. **Criteria:** Awards are given based on need.

Funds Avail.: No specific amount. **To Apply:** Applicants must submit a completed scholarship application form along with a copy of recent transcript; expected Family Contribution (EFC) from Student Aid Report (SAR), which comes as a result of filing the FAFSA; and a copy of Financial Aid Award Letter from the chosen college to be attended. **Deadline:** April 30.

Remarks: Faxed applications will not be considered.

2230 ■ CSF Walter and Marilyn Bartlett Scholarships *(Undergraduate/Scholarship)*

Purpose: To help students from Greater Cincinnati area to achieve the dream of a college education. **Focus:** General studies. **Qualif.:** Applicant must be a resident of Greater Cincinnati, and attending college as a full-time student. **Criteria:** Awards are given based on need.

Funds Avail.: No specific amount. **To Apply:** Applicants must submit a completed scholarship application form along with a copy of recent transcript; expected Family Contribution (EFC) from Student Aid Report (SAR), which comes as a result of filing the FAFSA; and a copy of Financial Aid Award Letter from the chosen college to be attended. **Deadline:** April 30.

Remarks: Faxed applications will not be considered.

2231 ■ CSF Western-Southern Foundation Scholarships *(Undergraduate/Scholarship)*

Purpose: To help students from Greater Cincinnati area to achieve the dream of a college education. **Focus:** General studies. **Qualif.:** Applicant must be a resident of Greater Cincinnati, and attending college as a full-time student. **Criteria:** Awards are given based on need.

Funds Avail.: No specific amount. **To Apply:** Applicants must submit a completed scholarship application form along with a copy of recent transcript; expected Family Contribution (EFC) from Student Aid Report (SAR), which comes as a result of filing the FAFSA; and a copy of Financial Aid Award Letter from the chosen college to be attended. **Deadline:** April 30.

Remarks: Faxed applications will not be considered.

2232 ■ CSF William A. Friedlander Scholarships *(Undergraduate/Scholarship)*

Purpose: To help students from Greater Cincinnati area to achieve the dream of a college education. **Focus:** General studies. **Qualif.:** Applicant must be a resident of Greater Cincinnati, and attending college as a full-time student. **Criteria:** Awards are given based on need.

Funds Avail.: No specific amount. **To Apply:** Applicants must submit a completed scholarship application form along with a copy of recent transcript; expected Family Contribution (EFC) from Student Aid Report (SAR), which comes as a result of filing the FAFSA; and a copy of Financial Aid Award Letter from the chosen college to be attended. **Deadline:** April 30.

Remarks: Faxed applications will not be considered.

2233 ■ CSF Wm. J. Rielly/MCURC Scholarships *(Undergraduate/Scholarship)*

Purpose: To help students from Greater Cincinnati area to achieve the dream of a college education. **Focus:** General studies. **Qualif.:** Applicant must be a resident of Greater Cincinnati, and attending college as a full-time student. **Criteria:** Awards are given based on need.

Funds Avail.: No specific amount. **To Apply:** Applicants must submit a completed scholarship application form along with a copy of recent transcript; expected Family Contribution (EFC) from Student Aid Report (SAR), which comes as a result of filing the FAFSA; and a copy of Financial Aid Award Letter from the chosen college to be attended. **Deadline:** April 30.

Remarks: Faxed applications will not be considered.

2234 ■ CSF Woodward Trustees Scholarships *(Undergraduate/Scholarship)*

Purpose: To help students from Greater Cincinnati area to achieve the dream of a college education. **Focus:** General studies. **Qualif.:** Applicant must be a resident of Greater Cincinnati, and attending college as a full-time student. **Criteria:** Awards are given based on need.

Funds Avail.: No specific amount. **To Apply:** Applicants must submit a completed scholarship application form along with a copy of recent transcript; expected Family Contribution (EFC) from Student Aid Report (SAR), which comes as a result of filing the FAFSA; and a copy of Financial Aid

Award Letter from the chosen college to be attended. **Deadline:** April 30.

Remarks: Faxed applications will not be considered.

2235 ■ CSF Wynne Family Memorial Scholarships *(Undergraduate/Scholarship)*

Purpose: To help students from Greater Cincinnati area to achieve the dream of a college education. **Focus:** General studies. **Qualif.:** Applicant must be a resident of Greater Cincinnati, and attending college as a full-time student. **Criteria:** Awards are given based on need.

Funds Avail.: No specific amount. **To Apply:** Applicants must submit a completed scholarship application form along with a copy of recent transcript; expected Family Contribution (EFC) from Student Aid Report (SAR), which comes as a result of filing the FAFSA; and a copy of Financial Aid Award Letter from the chosen college to be attended. **Deadline:** April 30.

Remarks: Faxed applications will not be considered.

2236 ■ Civic Music Association of Milwaukee

3195 S Superior St., Ste. 209
Milwaukee, WI 53207
Ph: (414)483-3223
Fax: (414)483-3356
E-mail: info@civicmusicmilwaukee.org
URL: http://www.civicmusicmilwaukee.org

2237 ■ John D. Anello Sr. and Albert A. Silverman Memorial Scholarships *(Undergraduate/Scholarship)*

Purpose: To provide music education and performance opportunities with an emphasis on youth in the greater Milwaukee area. **Focus:** Music, vocal. **Qualif.:** Applicants must be full-time high school or college Wisconsin music students, ages 14-22 and must have one Italian parent or grandparent. **Criteria:** Recipients are selected based on the performance.

Funds Avail.: $1,000; $500. **Number Awarded:** 3. **To Apply:** Applicants must submit a complete application form; must pass the audition process; must attach a 250-word brief description including the musical study they plan to focus on and why and a brief biography that includes school involvement, honors, awards, and any other accomplishments. **Deadline:** December 15. **Contact:** 3195 S. Superior St., Ste. 209 Milwaukee, WI 53207.

2238 ■ Norbert J. Beihoff Scholarships *(Undergraduate/Scholarship)*

Purpose: To encourage one or more students who have demonstrated exceptional musical potential but are not presently taking private lessons. **Focus:** Music. **Qualif.:** Applicants must be fourth to seventh grade band and orchestra students who have not yet had the opportunity for private study. **Criteria:** Recipients are selected based on the quality of the audition, musical ability, potential, attitude and reliability, parent's statement describing their commitment and support for the lessons and home practice, and student's essay about his/her musical experiences and participation in school music activities.

Funds Avail.: No specific amount. **To Apply:** Applicants must undergo an audition and must prepare an essay about his or her experiences in school music activities. **Deadline:** December 15. **Contact:** civicmusiccma@aol.com

2239 ■ Elizabeth W. Boyce Scholarships *(Undergraduate/Scholarship)*

Purpose: To provide music education and performance opportunities with an emphasis on youth in the greater Milwaukee area. **Focus:** Music, vocal. **Qualif.:** Applicants must be high school sophomores, juniors, and seniors in Milwaukee Metropolitan Area High School in Milwaukee. **Criteria:** Recipients are selected based on the performance.

Funds Avail.: $2,000. **To Apply:** Applicants must submit a completed application form; 250-words including the musical study they to focus on and why and a brief biography that includes school involvement, honors, awards, and other accomplishments. **Deadline:** December 15. **Contact:** 3195 S. Superior St., Ste. 209 Milwaukee, WI 53207.

2240 ■ Harold A. Levin Scholarships *(Undergraduate/Scholarship)*

Purpose: To provide music education and performance opportunities with an emphasis on youth in the greater Milwaukee area. **Focus:** Music. **Qualif.:** Applicants must be college students majoring in music who graduated from a Milwaukee area high school or who currently attend a Milwaukee area college, who are under 30 years of age. **Criteria:** Recipients are selected based on the quality of the taped performances.

Funds Avail.: Varies. **To Apply:** Applicants must submit three copies of a CD, or high quality cassette tape containing not more than 15 minutes of music, including at least two contrasting periods and styles, and recorded within the last 12 months. **Deadline:** October 1. **Contact:** civicmusiccma@aol.com.

2241 ■ Donald and Idabelle Mohr Scholarships *(Undergraduate/Scholarship)*

Purpose: To provide music education and performance opportunities with an emphasis on youth in the greater Milwaukee area. **Focus:** Music education. **Qualif.:** Applicants must be graduating seniors pursuing further education in a musical field, including music education, music therapy, theory-composition, performance and musicology. **Criteria:** Recipients are selected based on the performance.

Funds Avail.: $500. **To Apply:** Applicants must submit a completed application form; must pass the audition process; must attach a 250-word brief description including the musical study they plan to focus on and why and a brief biography that includes school involvement, honors, awards, and any other accomplishments. **Deadline:** December 15. **Contact:** 3195 S. Superior St., Ste. 209 Milwaukee, WI 53207.

2242 ■ Civitan International

PO Box 130744
Birmingham, AL 35213-0744
Ph: (205)591-8910
Free: 800-CIV-ITAN
E-mail: civitan@civitan.org
URL: http://www.civitan.com

2243 ■ Civitan Shropshire Scholarships *(Undergraduate/Scholarship)*

Purpose: To provide financial assistance to students enrolled in undergraduate or graduate studies. **Focus:** General studies. **Qualif.:** Applicants must be Civitans (or

Awards are arranged alphabetically below their administering organizations

Civitans' children or grandchildren) and must have been Civitan for at least two years and/or must be or have been Junior Civitans for no less than two years; must be students pursuing careers which help further the ideals and purposes of Civitan International as embodied in its Creed; must be enrolled in a degreed or certificate program at an accredited community college, vocational school, four-year college or graduate school. **Criteria:** Recipients are selected based on academic record; professional objectives; civitan involvement; community-service activities; financial need.

Funds Avail.: $2,000. **To Apply:** Applicants must submit all required application information. **Deadline:** January 31.

2244 ■ Clan Ross Association of the United States

1867 Via Acorde
Camarillo, CA 93010
Ph: (805)389-4338
URL: http://www.clanrossassociation.org/USA.htm

2245 ■ Clan Ross Foundation Scholarships
(Undergraduate/Scholarship)

Purpose: To enhance the knowledge of the youth about Scottish culture. **Focus:** Scottish studies. **Qualif.:** Applicants must be current members of Clan Ross Association of the United States, Inc. for at least a year. Applicants who are also related with the current members of the Association are also welcome to apply. Families or members of the Clan Ross Scholarship Committee are disqualified for the scholarships. **Criteria:** Recipients will be selected based on their keen interests and dedications in studying Scottish culture.

Funds Avail.: $ 1,000 each. **Number Awarded:** 2. **To Apply:** Applicants must write or call the Clan Ross Association for complete information of the Clan Ross Association of the United States, Inc. **Deadline:** March 1. **Contact:** Virgil Bumann.

2246 ■ Clinical Laboratory Management Association

989 Old Eagle School Rd., Ste. 815
Wayne, PA 19087-1704
Ph: (610)995-9580
Fax: (610)995-9568
URL: http://www.meclma.com

2247 ■ Clinical Laboratory Management Association High School Senior Scholarships *(High School/Scholarship)*

Purpose: To financially assist talented people pursuing education in the field of laboratory medicine. **Focus:** Medicine. **Qualif.:** Applicants must be undergraduate students who are Maine residents and who wish to become Medical Technologists (Clinical Laboratory Scientists), Medical Laboratory Technicians, Histotechnologists, or Cytologists. **Criteria:** Recipients are selected based on academic performance, character, commitment to laboratory medicine and financial need.

Funds Avail.: $500. **To Apply:** Applicants must submit completed application form; printed essay; transcript of high school grades; two letters of recommendation (at least one must come from an academic source, e.g. teacher, guidance counselor, or principal). **Deadline:** May 17. **Contact:** Sonia E. Russell MT (ASCP); DCPA; 417 State Street, Webber W. Suite 541, Bangor, Maine 04401; 207-561-2413.

2248 ■ Clinical Laboratory Management Association Undergraduate Scholarships
(Undergraduate/Scholarship)

Purpose: To financially assist talented people pursuing education in the field of laboratory medicine. **Focus:** Medicine. **Qualif.:** Applicant must be a clinical laboratory scientist working towards an advanced degree or a student who is a Maine resident and wishes to become a Medical Technologist, a Medical Laboratory Technician, a Histotechnologist or a Cytologist. **Criteria:** Recipient will be selected based on academic performance, character, commitment to laboratory medicine and financial need.

Funds Avail.: $1,000. **Number Awarded:** 3. **To Apply:** Applicants must submit completed application form; printed essay, completed as described on the application; transcript of college grades; and two letters of recommendation from teachers or employers. **Deadline:** May 3.

2249 ■ Club Managers Association of America

1733 King St.
Alexandria, VA 22314
Ph: (703)739-9500
Fax: (703)739-0124
E-mail: cmaa@cmaa.org
URL: http://www.cmaa.org

2250 ■ Club Managers Association of America (CMAA) Research Grants *(All/Grant)*

Purpose: To support research that is significant to the club management industry. **Focus:** Management. **Qualif.:** Applicants must submit a completed application; a detailed project description; a project budget narrative; and appendixes. **Criteria:** Candidates are evaluated by The Club Foundation Allocation Committee (CFAC) using the following criteria: a) problem conceptualization; b) research technique; c) contribution to the field; d) clarity and thoroughness; e) project budget.

Funds Avail.: $2,500. **Number Awarded:** 2-4. **To Apply:** Applicants must download application form from the CMAA website; the application, narrative and other required attachments must be typed using 12-point font and one-inch margins. **Deadline:** June 1. **Contact:** Mr. Seth Gregg; Email at clubfoundation@clubfoundation.org.

2251 ■ CMAA Student Conference Travel Grants
(All/Grant)

Purpose: To help student chapters offset the costs associated with attending the CMAA World Conference on Club Management. **Focus:** General studies. **Qualif.:** Applicants must be student chapters of CMAA. **Criteria:** Recipients will be selected based on the quality of application material submitted.

Funds Avail.: $500. Funds must be used for expenditures related to the CMAA Annual Conference. **To Apply:** Applicant student chapters must hold a fundraising event; submit a president's annual report; submit the current chapter budget; submit an application for the grant; and submit a grantee form stipulating that funds will be used for its intended purpose. **Deadline:** May 1.

Remarks: Started in 1988. The grant is supported by contributions from E-Z-GO Textron, Inc. **Contact:** clubfoundation@clubfoundation.org.

Awards are arranged alphabetically below their administering organizations

2252 ■ Willmoore H. Kendall Scholarships
(Postgraduate/Scholarship)

Purpose: To provide tuition support to assist club managers interested in pursuing the Certified Club Manager (CCM) designation. **Focus:** Management. **Qualif.:** Candidate must be a CMAA member; an assistant manager; currently pursuing the CMMA designation; have at least one remaining BMI course to complete; must be nominated by their chapter. **Criteria:** Applicants who are recommended by The Club Foundation Allocation Committee and approved by The Club Foundation Board of Governors will be given preference.

Funds Avail.: No specific amount. **To Apply:** Applicants must submit an official application form; a letter provided by the applicant's chapter supporting his/her application and must be signed by a chapter officer; a letter of recommendation from a member and the general manager of the applicant's club; a resume; an essay (500-1000 words) addressing the following components: a) Describe in detail your career objectives and goals; b) Detail the reason(s) you wish to pursue your CCM designation; c) What are your specific interests within the private club management field?; d) Select one characteristic of Mr. Kendall's with which you identify and explain why. **Deadline:** November 3.

Remarks: Established in 2001 in memory of CMAA Past President Mr. Bill Kendall. **Contact:** clubfoundation@clubfoundation.org.

2253 ■ Joe Perdue Scholarships *(Undergraduate/Scholarship)*

Purpose: To financially support the professional development of club managers through education, training and research initiatives. **Focus:** Management. **Qualif.:** Candidates must be pursuing managerial careers in the private club industry; must have completed freshman year of college and be enrolled for the full academic year in an accredited four-year institution; must have achieved and maintained a grade point average of at least 2.5 on a 4.0 scale, or 4.5 on a 6.0 scale. **Criteria:** Applicants who are CMAA student chapter members are given additional points.

Funds Avail.: No specific amount. **To Apply:** Candidates must submit an official application available from the website; a sealed copy of official college transcripts; a recommendation form and recommendation letter from a faculty advisor/professor and a private club industry professional; a resume; an essay (500-1000 words) addressing the following components: 1) your career objectives and goals; 2) the characteristics you possess that will enable you to succeed as a club manager; 3) your perception of CMAA and the private club industry; 4) your specific interests within the private club management field; 5) why you feel that you should be a Club Foundation Scholarship recipient. **Deadline:** May 1. **Contact:** joeperduescholarship@clubfoundation.org.

2254 ■ COACH - Canada's Health Informatics Association

250 Consumers Rd., Ste. 301
Toronto, ON, Canada M2J 4V6
Ph: (416)494-9324
Fax: (416)495-8723
Free: 888-253-8554
E-mail: info@coachorg.com
URL: http://www.coachorg.com

2255 ■ Steven Huesing Scholarships
(Undergraduate/Scholarship)

Purpose: To encourage health education by providing financial assistance for post-secondary education. **Focus:** Health education. **Qualif.:** Applicants must be enrolled in a health informatics or related program at an accredited post-secondary institution; and must demonstrate active involvement and achievement in health informatics. **Criteria:** Recipient will be selected based on academic standing and potential of the recipient's work in contributing advancements to Health Informatics.

Funds Avail.: $500. **To Apply:** Applicants must submit a transcript of records and an assessment by an academic advisor; must have proof of enrollment in a recognized Canadian post-secondary institution and current attendance in a health informatics and related program; must prepare a description (500 words) of their involvement and achievements in health informatics. Application forms and other supporting documents must be sent to: COACH, 301-250 Consumer Rd., Toronto, On M2J 4V6. **Deadline:** September 17.

Remarks: Established in 1999 in recognition of Founding President Steven Huesing's contribution to COACH.

2256 ■ Coalition of Higher Education Assistance Organizations

1101 Vermont Ave. NW, Ste. 400
Washington, DC 20005-3586
Ph: (202)289-3910
Fax: (202)371-0197
URL: http://www.coheao.org

2257 ■ COHEAO Scholarships *(Undergraduate/Scholarship)*

Purpose: To provide financial assistance to those students who are in need. **Focus:** General Studies. **Qualif.:** Applicants must be U.S citizens; must attend a COHEAO member school; must have a minimum GPA of 3.75 on a 4.0 scale. Only undergraduate students who are entering their sophomore, junior or senior year are eligible to apply; freshmen and graduate students are not eligible. **Criteria:** Preference will be given to those students who meet the criteria.

Funds Avail.: No specific amount. **To Apply:** Applicants must check the available website for the application process online. **Contact:** Coalition of Higher Education Assistance Organizations at the above address (see entry 2256).

2258 ■ Coastal Bend Community Foundation

600 Leopard St., Ste. 1716
Corpus Christi, TX 78473
Ph: (361)882-9745
Fax: (361)882-2865
URL: http://www.cbcfoundation.org

2259 ■ Alejandro "Alex" Abecia Reaching High Scholarships *(Undergraduate/Scholarship)*

Purpose: To provide resources for educational opportunities including vocational schools and two and four-year universities. **Focus:** General studies. **Qualif.:** Applicants must be senior members of the Mary Caroll High School Band or graduating senior members of the Mary Caroll High School soccer team; must be members of the A/B

Awards are arranged alphabetically below their administering organizations

Honor Roll; must have taken honor classes in high school and maintained a courseload of at least 12 hours per semester. **Criteria:** Applicants are evaluated based on merit.

Funds Avail.: $100. **Number Awarded:** 4. **To Apply:** Applicants must download the applications from the website of the Foundation. **Deadline:** March 14.

2260 ■ Chris Nance Adler Scholarship Fund *(High School/Scholarship)*

Purpose: To provide financial assistance to graduating seniors at W.B. Ray High School to attend college. **Focus:** General studies. **Qualif.:** Applicants must be graduating seniors at W.B. Ray High School and chosen by the Hall of Honor Selection Committee from the students named to the permanent honor roll. **Criteria:** Applicants are evaluated based on financial need.

Funds Avail.: $500. **Number Awarded:** 2. **To Apply:** Applicants must obtain applications from the Ray High School counselor's Office. **Deadline:** April 20.

2261 ■ Allen - Marty Allen Scholarships *(High School, Undergraduate/Scholarship)*

Purpose: To provide resources for educational opportunities including vocational schools and two and four-year universities. **Focus:** General studies. **Qualif.:** Applicants must be graduating seniors of a Coastal Bend high school or college students who attended a Coastal Bend high school; must be majoring in music; must maintain GPA of 2.5 and course load of at least 12 college credits per semester. **Criteria:** Applicants who are jazz musicians will be given preference.

Funds Avail.: $200. **Number Awarded:** 1. **To Apply:** Applicants must submit all the required application information. **Deadline:** March 14.

2262 ■ Zachary Barriger Memorial Scholarships *(High School/Scholarship)*

Purpose: To provide financial assistance to high school seniors who are planning to pursue a career in computer/electrical engineering. **Focus:** Engineering, Computer; Engineering, Electrical. **Qualif.:** Applicants must be seniors at Tuloso-Midway High School; must be attending an accredited two or four-year college in Texas; must demonstrate interest in pursuing studies in the field of engineering or medicine; and must excel academically with A/B Honor Roll status and honor classes. **Criteria:** Applicants are evaluated based on merit.

Funds Avail.: $500. **Number Awarded:** 1. **To Apply:** Applicants must submit all the required application information. **Deadline:** March 14.

2263 ■ O.J. Beck, Jr. Memorial Scholarships *(Undergraduate/Scholarship)*

Purpose: To provide educational assistance to students seeking a bachelor's degree in building construction. **Focus:** Construction. **Qualif.:** Applicants must be students at Texas A&M University - College Station who are seeking a bachelor's degree in building construction; must have maintained residency in the area served by the South Texas Chapter of Associated General Contractors. **Criteria:** Recipients are selected based on financial need.

Funds Avail.: $2,000. **Number Awarded:** 1. **To Apply:** Applicants must obtain application form from the Associated General Contractors office located at 518 S Enterprise Pkwy., Corpus Christi, TX 78405; Phone number: 361-289-0996.

2264 ■ Beecroft Family Scholarships *(High School/Scholarship)*

Purpose: To provide financial assistance to students who are determined to succeed and planning to attend college. **Focus:** General studies. **Qualif.:** Applicants must be graduating high school seniors in Nueces or San Patricio County, recipients of a GED certificate or currently attending college; must maintain at least 12 credit hours per semester at Del Mar College or Texas A&M-Corpus Christi. **Criteria:** Applicants who are students who live at home while attending college will be given preference.

Funds Avail.: $1,500. **Number Awarded:** 2. **To Apply:** Applicants must download applications from the website of the Foundation. **Deadline:** March 14.

2265 ■ Reverend E.F. Bennett Scholarships *(High School/Scholarship)*

Purpose: To provide financial support to graduating seniors from a Coastal Bend high school. **Focus:** General studies. **Qualif.:** Applicants must be: graduating seniors from a Coastal Bend high school; in the top 10% of their graduating class; attending Del Mar College, Texas A&M University-Corpus Christi or Texas A&M University-Kingsville. **Criteria:** Applicants are evaluated based on financial need.

Funds Avail.: $300. **Number Awarded:** 1. **To Apply:** Applicants must download the application form from the website of the Foundation or obtain it by calling the Foundation office at 361-882-9745. **Deadline:** March 15.

2266 ■ Marion Luna Brem/Pat McNeil Teen Parent Scholarships *(Undergraduate/Scholarship)*

Purpose: To provide financial assistance to teenage parents in Coastal Bend to pursue a college education while raising and supporting their children. **Focus:** General studies. **Qualif.:** Applicants must be: teenage parents who have attended high school in Coastal Bend; pursuing college education while raising and supporting a child; recipients of a high school diploma or GED certification; must attend Coastal Bend College, Del Mar College, Texas A&M University-Corpus Christi or Texas A&M University-Kingsville; must maintain a 2.0 GPA on a 4.0 scale and a minimum of 9 credit hours per semester. **Criteria:** Applicants are evaluated based on academic achievement and financial need.

Funds Avail.: $1,000. **Number Awarded:** 2. **To Apply:** Applicants must submit all the required application information. **Deadline:** March 14.

2267 ■ Cecil E. Burney Scholarships *(High School, Undergraduate/Scholarship)*

Purpose: To provide financial assistance to high school seniors or graduates of a Coastal Bend high school in furthering their college education. **Focus:** Liberal arts; History; Political science; Music; Education. **Qualif.:** Applicants must be high school seniors or graduates of a Coastal Bend high school pursuing a liberal arts degree majoring in history, political science, music or education; have a high school GPA of 90 percent or higher; maintain a college 3.0 GPA or higher and at least 12 hours per semester. **Criteria:** Applicants are evaluated based on academic performance.

Funds Avail.: $2,000. **To Apply:** Applicants must submit all the required application information. **Deadline:** March 14.

2268 ■ C.C.H.R.M.A. Scholarships *(High School, Undergraduate/Scholarship)*

Purpose: To assist students majoring in business with an interest in human resources. **Focus:** Business; Personnel administration/human resources. **Qualif.:** Applicants must: be high school seniors or undergraduate college students majoring in business; be enrolled as full-time students in the Coastal Bend seven-county service area; maintain a 3.0 GPA on a 4.0 scale (85% on 100% scale if high school students). **Criteria:** Applicants are evaluated based on academic achievement and financial need.

Funds Avail.: $500. **Number Awarded:** 1. **To Apply:** Applicants must download application form from the website of the Foundation or obtain it by calling the Foundation at 361-882-9745. **Deadline:** March 15.

2269 ■ Justin Forrest Cox "Beat the Odds" Memorial Scholarships *(Undergraduate/Scholarship)*

Purpose: To provide educational support for students who graduated from a Victoria ISD high school. **Focus:** General studies. **Qualif.:** Applicants must be students who graduated from a Victoria ISD high School; have a "C" average or better; be pursuing a four-year baccalaureate degree; complete at least 12 credit hours per semester; have overcome a significant difficulty in graduating from high school and have maintained a 2.5 GPA. **Criteria:** Applicants are evaluated based on academic achievement and financial need.

Funds Avail.: $2,500. **Number Awarded:** 1. **To Apply:** Applicants must obtain application form from Making the Grade-Victoria, 1908 Laurent Tower, Ste. 290 (PO Box 105), Victoria, TX 77902; Phone or Fax: 361-578-0270. **Deadline:** February 24.

Remarks: Scholarship is to be used for books and tuition only.

2270 ■ D.C. and Virginia Brown Scholarships *(High School, Undergraduate/Scholarship)*

Purpose: To provide financial assistance to graduates of Mathis High School and current Mathis High School students to further their education in college. **Focus:** General studies. **Qualif.:** Applicants must be graduates or current students of Mathis High School who have earned their GED certificate and who have good potential and character; must maintain a course load of 12 semester hours and a 2.5 GPA on a 4.0 scale. **Criteria:** Applicants are evaluated based on academic merit and personal attributes.

Funds Avail.: $4,000. **Number Awarded:** 4. **To Apply:** Applicants must download application form from the website of the Foundation or obtain it from Mathis High School counseling office. **Deadline:** March 15.

2271 ■ Derek Lee Dean Soccer Scholarships *(High School/Scholarship)*

Purpose: To assist outstanding high school students of W.B. Ray High School who have a passion for soccer. **Focus:** General studies. **Qualif.:** Applicants must be outstanding W.B. Ray High School students and members of the soccer team who exhibit love for soccer, teamwork and sportsmanship. **Criteria:** Applicants are evaluated based on academic achievement and personal involvement in the sport.

Funds Avail.: $500. **To Apply:** Applicants must download the application form from the website of the Foundation or obtain it from the W.B. Ray High School counselor's office. **Deadline:** April 1.

2272 ■ Doraine Pursuit of Educational Excellence Scholarships *(High School/Scholarship)*

Purpose: To promote educational excellence in Coastal Bend. **Focus:** General studies. **Qualif.:** Applicants must be graduating high school seniors in the Coastal Bend; must be in the top 10% of the graduating class; and have maintained a GPA of 3.0 and enrolled in at least 12 hours per semester. **Criteria:** Applicants are evaluated based on academic performance and merit.

Funds Avail.: $2,000. **Number Awarded:** 1. **To Apply:** Applicants must download applications found at the website of the Foundation. **Deadline:** March 14.

2273 ■ Jay Downes Memorial Scholarships *(High School/Scholarship)*

Purpose: To provide financial assistance to graduating Alice High School senior students in pursuing college. **Focus:** General studies. **Qualif.:** Applicants must be graduating Alice High School seniors who lettered in UIL-sanctioned golf for at least two years; have an overall high school GPA of "B" or better; participated in extracurricular activities other than athletics; have high ideals, and spirit of good conduct and sportsmanship benefiting the "Fighting Alice Coyote"; must attend a four-year college or university, register for at least 12 hours of classes and maintain a minimum college GPA of 2.5 on 4.0 scale. **Criteria:** Applicants are evaluated based on academic achievement and financial need.

Funds Avail.: $1,000. **Number Awarded:** 1. **To Apply:** Applicants must be nominated by the athletic director and head golf coach at Alice High School.

2274 ■ John R. Eidson Jr., Scholarships *(Undergraduate/Scholarship)*

Purpose: To provide financial assistance to Coastal Bend students who intend to study engineering in college. **Focus:** Engineering. **Qualif.:** Applicants must be students who are in good standing with the Engineering Department; must be sophomores or higher; must exhibit academic potential; must have participated in professional and social societies; and maintained full-time status and a GPA of 3.0 higher. **Criteria:** Recipients are selected based on financial need.

Funds Avail.: $1,000. **Number Awarded:** 1. **To Apply:** Applicants must obtain application form from the financial aid office at Texas A&M University in College Station.

2275 ■ Barney Flynn Memorial Scholarships *(High School/Scholarship)*

Purpose: To provide financial assistance to graduating seniors of Corpus Christi, Flour Bluff or Tuloso-Midway ISD high schools in furthering their education. **Focus:** General studies. **Qualif.:** Applicants must be graduating seniors of Corpus Christi, Flour Bluff or Tuloso-Midway ISD high schools; must be members of the high school band with a high performance level in band. **Criteria:** Applicants are evaluated based on merit.

Funds Avail.: $1,000. **Number Awarded:** 1. **To Apply:** Applicants must submit all the required application information. **Deadline:** March 14.

2276 ■ Food for Thought Scholarships *(High School/Scholarship)*

Purpose: To financially assist students in completing high school and attending college. **Focus:** General studies. **Qua-**

Awards are arranged alphabetically below their administering organizations

lif.: Applicants must be ninth-grade, at-risk high school students in Coastal Bend or graduates from high school. **Criteria:** Applicants are evaluated based on academic achievement and financial need.

Funds Avail.: $1,250. **Number Awarded:** 1. **To Apply:** Applicants must obtain applications by contacting Dee Haven at 361-884-5802.

2277 ■ Melissa Guerra Scholarships
(Undergraduate/Scholarship)

Purpose: To provide educational assistance to senior students of Mary Caroll High School. **Focus:** General studies. **Qualif.:** Applicants must be Mary Carroll High School seniors; must attend a publicly funded college or university in Texas; and maintain a minimum of a 3.0 GPA and 12 credit hours per semester. **Criteria:** Applicants are evaluated based on academic performance.

Funds Avail.: $1,000. **To Apply:** Applicants must submit all the required application information. **Deadline:** March 14.

2278 ■ Manuel Hernandez, Jr. Foundation Scholarships *(High School/Scholarship)*

Purpose: To provide the high school graduating senior students of Roy Miller High School financial assistance for their college education. **Focus:** General studies. **Qualif.:** Applicants must be graduating seniors of Roy Miller High School; must have been accepted at a college, university, trade or vocational institution. **Criteria:** Applicants are evaluated based on financial need.

Funds Avail.: $500. **Number Awarded:** 4. **To Apply:** Applicants must submit all the required application information. **Deadline:** March 14.

2279 ■ Casey Laine Armed Forces Scholarships
(High School/Scholarship)

Purpose: To assist high school students who are seeking financial resources to further their college education. **Focus:** General studies. **Qualif.:** Applicants must graduate in top 50% of high school class; maintain a GPA of 2.5 and enrolled in at least 12 hours per semester; must be graduating seniors or current graduates from a Coastal Bend high school, or members or honorably discharged veterans of the armed services, or R.O.T.C. members (high school seniors must agree to join an R.O.T.C. program upon entering college). **Criteria:** Applicants are evaluated based on academic performance.

Funds Avail.: $200. **Number Awarded:** 1. **To Apply:** Applicants must submit all the required application information. **Deadline:** March 14.

2280 ■ Sue Kay Lay Memorial Scholarships
(High School/Scholarship)

Purpose: To assist high school seniors seeking financial resources to further their education. **Focus:** General studies. **Qualif.:** Applicants must be high school seniors graduating at the end of the spring semester; must be enrolled in college full-time (12 hours or more); must have high school GPA of 3.5; have graduated from a high school in Coastal Bend; and maintain a permanent residence in the Coastal Bend. **Criteria:** Applicants are evaluated based on financial need.

Funds Avail.: $1,500. **Number Awarded:** 5. **To Apply:** Applicants must submit all the required application information. **Deadline:** March 14.

2281 ■ Brian and Colleen Miller Scholarships
(High School/Scholarship)

Purpose: To assist high school juniors or seniors attending a Coastal Bend high school. **Focus:** General studies. **Qualif.:** Applicants must be high school juniors or seniors attending a Coastal Bend high school; must attend any accredited four-year college or university. **Criteria:** Applicants are evaluated based on financial need.

Funds Avail.: $500. **Number Awarded:** 1. **To Apply:** Applicants must submit completed application form along with the documentation of participation and/or awards in the areas of mathematics and/or science. **Deadline:** March 14.

2282 ■ Puedo Scholarships - Joseph Huerta
(High School/Scholarship)

Purpose: To provide financial assistance to students in continuing their education in college. **Focus:** General studies. **Qualif.:** Applicants must have graduated from a CCISD high school and have a high school GPA of at least 90 percent on a 100-point scale; must be enrolled as full-time college students (at least 12 semester credits) at a four-year accredited college or university; and must maintain a course load of at least 12 college credits per semester and a GPA of 3.0 or higher. **Criteria:** Applicants are evaluated based on academic achievement and financial need.

Funds Avail.: $1,000 to $5,000. **Number Awarded:** 10. **To Apply:** Applicants must submit all the required application information. Application form can be downloaded at the website of the Foundation, www.cbcfoundation.org. **Deadline:** March 14.

2283 ■ J.J. Rains Memorial Scholarships *(High School/Scholarship)*

Purpose: To provide graduating CCISD high school seniors financial assistance for their college education. **Focus:** General studies. **Qualif.:** Applicants must be graduating CCISD high school seniors with preference for students who have participated in speech or debate; have a cumulative high school GPA of 2.5; must maintain a cumulative college GPA of 2.5 on a 4.0 scale and enroll in a minimum of 12 semester hours. **Criteria:** Applicants are evaluated based on academic achievement and financial need.

Funds Avail.: $1,000. **Number Awarded:** 1. **To Apply:** Applicants must submit all the required application information. **Deadline:** March 14.

2284 ■ W.B. Ray HS Class of '56 Averill Johnson Scholarships *(High School/Scholarship)*

Purpose: To provide financial assistance for graduating seniors of W.B. Ray High School. **Focus:** General studies. **Qualif.:** Applicants must be W.B. Ray high school seniors in the top 10% of their graduating class; enrolled as full-time (12 semester hours) students in an accredited college or university in the United States in the fall semester following graduation. **Criteria:** Recipients are selected based on academic achievement and financial need.

Funds Avail.: $500. **Number Awarded:** 1. **To Apply:** Applicants must submit all the required application information. **Deadline:** March 14.

2285 ■ Rotary Club of Corpus Christi Scholarships *(High School/Scholarship)*

Purpose: To advance higher education in the immediate Corpus Christi area. **Focus:** General studies. **Qualif.:** Applicants must be graduating seniors from the following: all CCISD high schools, Tuloso-Midway, Calallen, West Oso

Awards are arranged alphabetically below their administering organizations

or Flour Bluff high schools, Incarnate Word Academy, Corpus Christi Academy or Annapolis Christian Academy; must attend Texas A&M Corpus Christi or Del Mar College; must maintain a minimum GPA of 2.0 on a 4.0 scale and courseload of at least 12 hours per semester. **Criteria:** Applicants are evaluated based on financial need.

Funds Avail.: $2,500 to $3,000. **Number Awarded:** 2. **To Apply:** Applicants must submit all the required application information and application form can be downloaded from the website of the Foundation. **Deadline:** March 14.

2286 ■ Seaman Family Scholarships *(High School/Scholarship)*

Purpose: To provide financial assistance for Coastal Bend students who are home-schooled and need financial aid. **Focus:** General studies. **Qualif.:** Applicant must be a Coastal Bend or Calhoun County home-schooled student who demonstrates financial need; must be accepted at an accredited college or university; and must maintain a courseload of 12 semester hours. **Criteria:** Applicants are judged on the basis of academic performance and financial need.

Funds Avail.: $500. **To Apply:** Applicants must submit completed application form; essay of 500 words about the topic "Freedom." **Deadline:** March 14.

2287 ■ Judge Terry Shamsie Scholarships *(High School/Scholarship)*

Purpose: To assist graduating high school senior students in Coastal Bend, financially, to continue their education. **Focus:** General studies. **Qualif.:** Applicants must be graduating high school seniors in the Coastal Bend (Arkansas, Bee Jim Wells, Kleberg, Nueces, Refugio, San Patricio). **Criteria:** Applicants are evaluated based on academic achievement and financial need.

Funds Avail.: $1,000. **Number Awarded:** 4. **To Apply:** Applicants must submit completed applications which can be downloaded from the website of the Foundation. **Deadline:** March 14.

2288 ■ South Texas Lighthouse for the Blind Scholarships *(Undergraduate/Scholarship)*

Purpose: To provide financial assistance to further the education of eligible students in Coastal Bend. **Focus:** General studies. **Qualif.:** Applicants must be graduating seniors from a Coastal Bend high school or employees or immediate family members of employees of the South Texas Lighthouse for the Blind; must have high school GPA of at least 80% on a 100% scale; must be enrolled in an accredited college or university of the United States; and must maintain a courseload of 12 college credits per semester and cumulative college GPA of at least 3.0 on a 4.0 scale. **Criteria:** Recipients are selected based on academic achievement and financial need.

Funds Avail.: $5,000. **To Apply:** Applicant must submit a completed application form that can be downloaded from the website of the Foundation. **Deadline:** March 14.

2289 ■ Jim Springer Memorial Scholarships *(Undergraduate/Scholarship)*

Purpose: To provide financial assistance to further the education of deserving students in Coastal Bend. **Focus:** Public relations; Marketing and distribution; Advertising; Communications. **Qualif.:** Applicants must be Coastal Bend residents; full-time college sophomore, junior or senior students with grade point average of 2.5; majoring in public relations, marketing, advertising or communications. **Criteria:** Applicants are evaluated based on academic performance and financial need.

Funds Avail.: $500. **Number Awarded:** 1. **To Apply:** Applicants must submit all the required application information. **Deadline:** March 14.

2290 ■ Stewart Title Firefighters Scholarships *(High School, Undergraduate/Scholarship)*

Purpose: To provide financial assistance to high school seniors and college students who are descendants of volunteer firefighters in Coastal Bend. **Focus:** General studies. **Qualif.:** Applicants must be high school seniors or college students in Coastal Bend; must be children of uniformed and volunteer firefighters for a fire department located in Coastal Bend; and must have maintained a 3.0 GPA and complete at least 12 credit hours per semester. **Criteria:** Applicants are evaluated based on academic performance and financial need.

Funds Avail.: $1,000. **Number Awarded:** 2. **To Apply:** Applicants must submit all the required application information. **Deadline:** March 14.

2291 ■ Talbert Family Memorial Accounting Scholarships *(Undergraduate/Scholarship)*

Purpose: To provide financial assistance to deserving accounting students of Texas for furthering their education in the field. **Focus:** Accounting. **Qualif.:** Applicants must be full-time college juniors majoring in accounting at a Texas college with 3.25 grade point average; must have graduated from a Coastal Bend high school and permanently reside in Coastal Bend. **Criteria:** Applicants must submit all the required application information.

Funds Avail.: $2,000. **To Apply:** Applicants must submit all the required application information. **Deadline:** March 14.

2292 ■ Faye and Rendell Webb Scholarships *(High School, Undergraduate/Scholarship)*

Purpose: To help needy students in financing their college education. **Focus:** General studies. **Qualif.:** Applicants must be students graduated from Miller or Moody high schools, with preference for students who attended Los Encinos, Lamar or Lozano elementary schools for at least one year; must be education majors who are attending college in the state of Texas; must be students who have an average of 85 percent or better or maintain 3.0 GPA on 4.0 scale and complete at least 12 credits per semester. **Criteria:** Applicants are evaluated based on academic achievement and financial need.

Funds Avail.: $1,000. **Number Awarded:** 2. **To Apply:** Applicants must download application form from the website of CBC Foundation or obtain it from Miller and Moody high school counselor's offices. **Deadline:** March 14.

2293 ■ Wheelchair Success Foundation Scholarships *(Undergraduate/Scholarship)*

Purpose: To provide an opportunity for people permanently confined to a wheelchair to attend college or technical school. **Focus:** General school. **Qualif.:** Applicants must be graduates or GED certificate holders who attended a Coastal Bend high school; permanently confined to a wheelchair; must maintain nine credit hours per semester with GPA of 2.5 while attending an accredited university, college or technical school. **Criteria:** Applicants are evaluated based on scholastic performance and financial need.

Awards are arranged alphabetically below their administering organizations

Funds Avail.: $500. **Number Awarded:** 1. **To Apply:** Applicants must download application form from the website of CBC Foundation or inquire through telephone call to the Foundation. **Deadline:** March 14.

2294 ■ Dr. Dana Williams Scholarships *(High School, Undergraduate/Scholarship)*

Purpose: To provide educational assistance to students planning to become teachers or public school administrators. **Focus:** Education. **Qualif.:** Applicants must be: high school seniors graduating at the end of the spring semester; planning to become teachers or public school administrators; enrolled as full-time students in college (12 hours or more). Applicants must have a cumulative high school GPA of 90 percent or more; must be graduates from a high school in the Corpus Christi Independent School District and must be permanent residents of Corpus Christi. **Criteria:** Applicants are judged based on financial need.

Funds Avail.: $4,000. **Number Awarded:** 1. **To Apply:** Applicants must download application form from the website of the CBC Foundation or obtain it by calling 361-882-9745. **Deadline:** March 14.

2295 ■ Coca-Cola Scholars Foundation

PO Box 442
Atlanta, GA 30301-0442
Fax: (404)733-5439
Free: 800-306-2653
E-mail: scholars@na.ko.com
URL: http://www.coca-colascholars.org

2296 ■ Coca-Cola Scholars Foundation Four-Year Award for Seniors *(Undergraduate/Scholarship)*

Purpose: To provide scholarships to high school seniors. **Focus:** General studies. **Qualif.:** Applicants must be high school seniors attending school in the US; must be U.S. citizens; must be seniors anticipating completion of a high school diploma during the academic year in which application is made; must be seniors planning to pursue a degree at an accredited U.S. postsecondary institution; and must be carrying a minimum 3.0 GPA at the end of their junior year of high school. **Criteria:** Selection will be based on the committee's criteria.

Funds Avail.: $10,000-$20,000. **Number Awarded:** 50-200. **To Apply:** Applicants may apply online. They must complete all parts of the application process. **Deadline:** October 31. **Contact:** Coca-Cola at the above address (see entry 2295).

2297 ■ College of Healthcare Information Management Executives

3300 Washtenaw Ave., Ste. 225
Ann Arbor, MI 48104-4250
Ph: (734)665-0000
Fax: (734)665-4922
E-mail: staff@cio-chime.org
URL: http://www.cio-chime.org

2298 ■ John Glaser Scholarships *(Undergraduate/Scholarship)*

Purpose: To acknowledge IT staff members who show potential for advancement to a CIO and who are dedicated to professional development. **Focus:** Health care services. **Qualif.:** Candidates must be employed and nominated by a current CHIME member. **Criteria:** Recipients are selected based on the committee's review of the CIO potential and dedication to professional development.

Funds Avail.: $3,000. **Number Awarded:** 2. **To Apply:** Candidates may visit the website to apply online, or download the application form and mail to: John Glaser, Scholarship Committee c/o CHIME 3300 Washtenaw Ave., Ste. 225 Ann Arbor, MI 48104. **Deadline:** August 15.

2299 ■ College Student Educators International

One Dupont Circle NW, Ste. 300
Washington, DC 20036-1188
Ph: (202)835-2272
Fax: (202)296-3286
E-mail: info@acpa.nche.edu
URL: http://www.acpa.nche.edu

2300 ■ Educational Leadership Foundation Grants *(Undergraduate/Grant)*

Purpose: To enhance the student affairs profession; to generate and disseminate knowledge about college students. **Focus:** General studies. **Qualif.:** Applicants must be currently enrolled in a college, university and institution. **Criteria:** Recipients are selected based on the submitted project proposal.

Funds Avail.: $60,000. **To Apply:** Applicants must complete the online application form including the name and contact information. **Deadline:** February 1. **Contact:** lwillett@coastal.edu.

2301 ■ Collegiate Soaring Association

4671 Kipling St., No. 68
Wheat Ridge, CO 80033
Ph: (303)432-2137
E-mail: president.jhpc@hotmail.com
URL: http://www.coloradosoaring.org

2302 ■ Gogos Scholarships *(Undergraduate/Scholarship)*

Purpose: To support young people in school, primarily college students, from first flight through advanced soaring. **Focus:** Aviation. **Qualif.:** Applicant must be a U.S. citizen or permanent resident student, age 14-25 nominated by an FAI soaring badge holder within a sponsoring Soaring Club or Operator. **Criteria:** Candidates are judged based on criteria like the applicants' desire to soar, plans to help promote the amateur sport of soaring among young people in school, and financial need.

Funds Avail.: $2,000. **Number Awarded:** 1. **To Apply:** Applicants must submit complete application form. **Deadline:** March 31.

2303 ■ Colorado Christian University Alumni Association

8787 W Alameda Ave.
Lakewood, CO 80226
Ph: (303)963-3330
Fax: (303)963-3331
Free: 800-44-FAITH
E-mail: ccualumni@ccu.edu

Awards are arranged alphabetically below their administering organizations

URL: http://www.ccu.edu/alumni

2304 ■ CCU Alumni Endowed Scholarships
(Undergraduate/Scholarship)

Purpose: To assist students with the cost of post-secondary education. **Focus:** General studies. **Qualif.:** Applicant must be pursuing a baccalaureate degree; completed at least 85 credits, with a minimum of 24 credits earned at CCU; have a GPA of 3.3 or above; demonstrated the need of financial assistance; shows local church or community involvement; and have an alumni sponsor. **Criteria:** Selection is based on merits.

Funds Avail.: No specific amount. **To Apply:** Contact the Alumni Relations for more details on the scholarship.

Remarks: Funds was established by the CCU Alumni Association.

2305 ■ Colorado Hotel and Lodging Association
730 17th St., Ste. 920
Denver, CO 80202
Ph: (303)297-8335
Fax: (303)297-8104
E-mail: info@chla.com
URL: http://www.coloradolodging.com

2306 ■ Karl Mehlmann Scholarships
(Undergraduate/Scholarship)

Purpose: To offer college students an opportunity to apply for this scholarship to overcome financial need. **Focus:** Culinary Arts. **Qualif.:** Applicants must be enrolled in an accredited four-year university or college and be majoring in hotel and/or restaurant management; must also be enrolled in the final year at the Culinary Institute of America; must be freshmen, sophomores, juniors, or seniors who are going to graduate school; must carry a minimum workload of 12 hours per quarter or semester; must have maintain a minimum overall GPA of 3.0 on a 4.0 scale; must be U.S. citizens. **Criteria:** Recipients are selected based on the grammar and spelling of the essay.

Funds Avail.: No specific amount. **To Apply:** Applicants must submit one official transcript from current school, or most recent if not currently attending school; must submit a brief autobiography; one-page, typewritten essay answering why you've the selected the hospitality industry for your career and what definition of hospitality is; must submit a type, signed and on letterhead recommendation letter from College or University; signature from Director/Dean. **Deadline:** April 25. **Contact:** stephanie@chla.com

2307 ■ Colorado Nurses Foundation
7831 Lewis Court
Arvada, CO 80005
Ph: (303)758-4291
E-mail: conursesfoundation@comcast.net
URL: http://www.coloradonursesfoundation.org

2308 ■ Roy Anderson Memorial Scholarships
(Graduate, Undergraduate/Scholarship)

Purpose: To provide scholarships for qualified nursing students from both rural and urban settings. **Focus:** Nursing. **Qualif.:** Applicant must be a Colorado resident committed to practicing nursing in Colorado; must be a student in an approved Colorado Nursing Program; must have a minimum of 3.25 GPA (for undergraduate applicants) or 3.5 GPA (for graduate applicants); and must have one of the following student statuses: (1) Junior or senior level BSN undergraduate student; (2) RN enrolled in a baccalaureate or higher degree nursing program in a school of nursing; (3) Student in second year of nursing studies in an associate degree in nursing program; (4) RN with master's degree in nursing, currently practicing in Colorado and enrolled in a doctoral program; (5) Student in second or third year of a Doctorate Nursing Practice (DNP) program. **Criteria:** Scholarship application will be rated based on the following: (1) Professional philosophy and goals; (2) Dedication to the improvement of patient care in Colorado; (3) Demonstrated commitment to nursing, critical thinking skills, and potential for leadership; (4) Involvement in community and professional organizations; (5) GPA-minimum of 3.25 undergraduate, 3.5 graduate; (6) Financial need; (7) Recommendation of one faculty member, and (8) Employer/Supervisor recommendation.

Funds Avail.: $2,000. **To Apply:** Applicants are advised to contact the foundation at Colorado Nurses Foundation, 7831 Lewis Court, Arvada, CO 80005 for further information.

2309 ■ Banner Health System - McKee Medical Center, Loveland: Nightingale Scholarships
(Graduate, Undergraduate/Scholarship)

Purpose: To provide scholarships for qualified nursing students from both rural and urban settings. **Focus:** Nursing. **Qualif.:** Applicants must be Colorado residents committed to practicing nursing in Colorado; must be students in an approved Colorado Nursing Program; must have a minimum of 3.25 GPA (undergraduate) and 3.5 GPA (graduate); and must have one of the following student statuses: (1) Junior or senior level BSN undergraduate student; (2) RN enrolled in a baccalaureate or higher degree nursing program in a school of nursing; (3) Student in second year of nursing studies in an associate degree in nursing program; (4) RN with master's degree in nursing, currently practicing in Colorado and enrolled in a doctoral program; (5) Student in second or third year of a Doctorate Nursing Practice (DNP) program. **Criteria:** Scholarship application will be rated based on the following: (1) Professional philosophy and goals; (2) Dedication to the improvement of patient care in Colorado; (3) Demonstrated commitment to nursing, critical thinking skills, and potential for leadership; (4) Involvement in community and professional organizations; (5) GPA-minimum of 3.25 undergraduate, 3.5 graduate; (6) Financial need; (7) Recommendation of one faculty member, and (8) Employer/Supervisor recommendation.

Funds Avail.: $1,000. R One year. Applicants are advised to contact the foundation at Colorado Nurses Foundation, 7831 Lewis Court, Arvada, CO 80005 for further information.

2310 ■ Banner Health System - North Colorado Medical Center, Greeley: Nightingale Scholarships *(Graduate, Undergraduate/Scholarship)*

Purpose: To provide scholarships for qualified nursing students from both rural and urban settings. **Focus:** Nursing. **Qualif.:** Applicant must be a Colorado resident committed to practicing nursing in Colorado; must be a student in an approved Colorado Nursing Program; must have a minimum of 3.25 GPA undergraduate and 3.5 GPA graduate; and must have one of the following student statuses: (1) Junior or senior level BSN undergraduate student; (2) RN enrolled in a baccalaureate or higher degree nursing

Awards are arranged alphabetically below their administering organizations

program in a school of nursing; (3) Student in second year of nursing studies in an associate degree in nursing program; (4) RN with master's degree in nursing, currently practicing in Colorado and enrolled in a doctoral program; (5) Student in second or third year of a Doctorate Nursing Practice (DNP) program. **Criteria:** Scholarship application will be rated based on the following: (1) Professional philosophy and goals; (2) Dedication to the improvement of patient care in Colorado; (3) Demonstrated commitment to nursing, critical thinking skills, and potential for leadership; (4) Involvement in community and professional organizations; (5) GPA-minimum of 3.25 undergraduate, 3.5 graduate; (6) Financial need; (7) Recommendation of one faculty member, and (8) Employer/Supervisor recommendation.

Funds Avail.: $1,000. **To Apply:** Applicants are advised to contact the foundation at Colorado Nurses Foundation, 7831 Lewis Court, Arvada, CO 80005 for further information.

2311 ■ Marcy and Bruce Benson: Nightingale Scholarships *(Graduate, Undergraduate/Scholarship)*

Purpose: To provide scholarships for qualified nursing students from both rural and urban settings. **Focus:** Nursing. **Qualif.:** Applicant must be a Colorado resident committed to practicing nursing in Colorado; must be a student in an approved Colorado Nursing Program; must have a minimum of 3.25 GPA undergraduate and 3.5 GPA graduate; and must have one of the following student statuses: (1) Junior or senior level BSN undergraduate student; (2) RN enrolled in a baccalaureate or higher degree nursing program in a school of nursing; (3) Student in second year of nursing studies in an associate degree in nursing program; (4) RN with master's degree in nursing, currently practicing in Colorado and enrolled in a doctoral program; (5) Student in second or third year of a Doctorate Nursing Practice (DNP) program. **Criteria:** Scholarship application will be rated based on the following: (1) Professional philosophy and goals; (2) Dedication to the improvement of patient care in Colorado; (3) Demonstrated commitment to nursing, critical thinking skills, and potential for leadership; (4) Involvement in community and professional organizations; (5) GPA-minimum of 3.25 undergraduate, 3.5 graduate; (6) Financial need; (7) Recommendation of one faculty member, and (8) Employer/Supervisor recommendation.

Funds Avail.: $1,000. **To Apply:** Applicants are advised to contact the foundation at Colorado Nurses Foundation, 7831 Lewis Court, Arvada, CO 80005 for further information.

2312 ■ Colorado Nurses Association: Nightingale Scholarships *(Graduate, Undergraduate/Scholarship)*

Purpose: To provide scholarships for qualified nursing students from both rural and urban settings. **Focus:** Nursing. **Qualif.:** Applicant must be a Colorado resident committed to practicing nursing in Colorado; must be a student in an approved Colorado Nursing Program; must have a minimum of 3.25 GPA undergraduate and 3.5 GPA graduate; and must have one of the following student statuses: (1) Junior or senior level BSN undergraduate student; (2) RN enrolled in a baccalaureate or higher degree nursing program in a school of nursing; (3) Student in second year of nursing studies in an associate degree in nursing program; (4) RN with master's degree in nursing, currently practicing in Colorado and enrolled in a doctoral program; (5) Student in second or third year of a Doctorate Nursing Practice (DNP) program. **Criteria:** Scholarship application will be rated based on the following: (1) Professional philosophy and goals; (2) Dedication to the improvement of patient care in Colorado; (3) Demonstrated commitment to nursing, critical thinking skills, and potential for leadership; (4) Involvement in community and professional organizations; (5) GPA-minimum of 3.25 undergraduate, 3.5 graduate; (6) Financial need; (7) Recommendation of one faculty member, and (8) Employer/Supervisor recommendation.

Funds Avail.: $1,000. **To Apply:** Applicants are advised to contact the foundation at Colorado Nurses Foundation, 7831 Lewis Court, Arvada, CO 80005 for further information.

2313 ■ Colorado Nurses Association: Virginia Paulson Memorial Scholarships *(Graduate, Undergraduate/Scholarship)*

Purpose: To provide scholarships for qualified nursing students from both rural and urban settings. **Focus:** Nursing. **Qualif.:** Applicant must be a Colorado resident committed to practicing nursing in Colorado; must be a student in an approved Colorado Nursing Program; must have a minimum of 3.25 GPA (for undergraduate applicants) or 3.5 GPA (for graduate applicants); and must have one of the following student statuses: (1) Junior or senior level BSN undergraduate student; (2) RN enrolled in a baccalaureate or higher degree nursing program in a school of nursing; (3) Student in second year of nursing studies in an associate degree in nursing program; (4) RN with master's degree in nursing, currently practicing in Colorado and enrolled in a doctoral program; (5) Student in second or third year of a Doctorate Nursing Practice (DNP) program. **Criteria:** Scholarship application will be rated based on the following: (1) Professional philosophy and goals; (2) Dedication to the improvement of patient care in Colorado; (3) Demonstrated commitment to nursing, critical thinking skills, and potential for leadership; (4) Involvement in community and professional organizations; (5) GPA-minimum of 3.25 undergraduate, 3.5 graduate; (6) Financial need; (7) Recommendation of one faculty member, and (8) Employer/Supervisor recommendation.

Funds Avail.: $2,000. **To Apply:** Applicants are advised to contact the foundation at Colorado Nurses Foundation, 7831 Lewis Court, Arvada, CO 80005 for further information.

2314 ■ Colorado Nurses Foundation Nightingale Scholarships *(Graduate, Undergraduate/Scholarship)*

Purpose: To provide scholarships for qualified nursing students from both rural and urban settings. **Focus:** Nursing. **Qualif.:** Applicant must be a Colorado resident committed to practicing nursing in Colorado; must be a student in an approved Colorado Nursing Program; must have a minimum of 3.25 GPA (for undergraduate applicants) or 3.5 GPA (for graduate applicants); and must have one of the following student statuses: (1) Junior or senior level BSN undergraduate student; (2) RN enrolled in a baccalaureate or higher degree nursing program in a school of nursing; (3) Student in second year of nursing studies in an associate degree in nursing program; (4) RN with master's degree in nursing, currently practicing in Colorado and enrolled in a doctoral program; (5) Student in second or third year of a Doctorate Nursing Practice (DNP) program. **Criteria:** Scholarship application will be rated based on the following: (1) Professional philosophy and goals; (2) Dedication to the improvement of patient care in Colorado; (3)

Demonstrated commitment to nursing, critical thinking skills, and potential for leadership; (4) Involvement in community and professional organizations; (5) GPA-minimum of 3.25 undergraduate, 3.5 graduate; (6) Financial need; (7) Recommendation of one faculty member, and (8) Employer/ Supervisor recommendation.

Funds Avail.: $1,000. **Number Awarded:** 10. **To Apply:** Applicants are advised to contact the foundation at Colorado Nurses Foundation, 7831 Lewis Court, Arvada, CO 80005 for further information.

2315 ■ Colorado Organization of Nursing Leaders Scholarships *(Graduate, Undergraduate/ Scholarship)*

Purpose: To provide scholarships for qualified nursing students from both rural and urban settings. **Focus:** Nursing. **Qualif.:** Applicant must be a Colorado resident committed to practicing nursing in Colorado; must be a student in an approved Colorado Nursing Program; must have a minimum of 3.25 GPA (for undergraduate applicants) or 3.5 GPA (for graduate applicants); and must have one of the following student statuses: (1) Junior or senior level BSN undergraduate student; (2) RN enrolled in a baccalaureate or higher degree nursing program in a school of nursing; (3) Student in second year of nursing studies in an associate degree in nursing program; (4) RN with master's degree in nursing, currently practicing in Colorado and enrolled in a doctoral program; (5) Student in second or third year of a Doctorate Nursing Practice (DNP) program. **Criteria:** Scholarship application will be rated based on the following: (1) Professional philosophy and goals; (2) Dedication to the improvement of patient care in Colorado; (3) Demonstrated commitment to nursing, critical thinking skills, and potential for leadership; (4) Involvement in community and professional organizations; (5) GPA-minimum of 3.25 undergraduate, 3.5 graduate; (6) Financial need; (7) Recommendation of one faculty member, and (8) Employer/ Supervisor recommendation.

Funds Avail.: $1,000. **To Apply:** Applicants are advised to contact the foundation at Colorado Nurses Foundation, 7831 Lewis Court, Arvada, CO 80005 for further information.

2316 ■ Arthur L. Davis Publishing Agency Scholarships *(Graduate, Undergraduate/ Scholarship)*

Purpose: To provide scholarships for qualified nursing students from both rural and urban settings. **Focus:** Nursing. **Qualif.:** Applicant must be a Colorado resident committed to practicing nursing in Colorado; must be a student in an approved Colorado Nursing Program; must have a minimum of 3.25 GPA (for undergraduate applicants) or 3.5 GPA (for graduate applicants); and must have one of the following student statuses: (1) Junior or senior level BSN undergraduate student; (2) RN enrolled in a baccalaureate or higher degree nursing program in a school of nursing; (3) Student in second year of nursing studies in an associate degree in nursing program; (4) RN with master's degree in nursing, currently practicing in Colorado and enrolled in a doctoral program; (5) Student in second or third year of a Doctorate Nursing Practice (DNP) program. **Criteria:** Scholarship application will be rated based on the following: (1) Professional philosophy and goals; (2) Dedication to the improvement of patient care in Colorado; (3) Demonstrated commitment to nursing, critical thinking skills, and potential for leadership; (4) Involvement in community and professional organizations; (5) GPA-minimum of 3.25 undergraduate, 3.5 graduate; (6) Financial need; (7) Recommendation of one faculty member, and (8) Employer/ Supervisor recommendation.

Funds Avail.: $1,000. **To Apply:** Applicants are advised to contact the foundation at Colorado Nurses Foundation, 7831 Lewis Court, Arvada, CO 80005 for further information.

2317 ■ Red and Lola Fehr: Nightingale Scholarships *(Graduate, Undergraduate/Scholarship)*

Purpose: To provide scholarships for qualified nursing students from both rural and urban settings. **Focus:** Nursing. **Qualif.:** Applicant must be a Colorado resident committed to practicing nursing in Colorado; must be a student in an approved Colorado Nursing Program; must have a minimum of 3.25 GPA (for undergraduate applicants) or 3.5 GPA (for graduate applicants); and must have one of the following student statuses: (1) Junior or senior level BSN undergraduate student; (2) RN enrolled in a baccalaureate or higher degree nursing program in a school of nursing; (3) Student in second year of nursing studies in an associate degree in nursing program; (4) RN with master's degree in nursing, currently practicing in Colorado and enrolled in a doctoral program; (5) Student in second or third year of a Doctorate Nursing Practice (DNP) program. **Criteria:** Scholarship application will be rated based on the following: (1) Professional philosophy and goals; (2) Dedication to the improvement of patient care in Colorado; (3) Demonstrated commitment to nursing, critical thinking skills, and potential for leadership; (4) Involvement in community and professional organizations; (5) GPA-minimum of 3.25 undergraduate, 3.5 graduate; (6) Financial need; (7) Recommendation of one faculty member, and (8) Employer/ Supervisor recommendation.

Funds Avail.: $1,000. **To Apply:** Applicants are advised to contact the foundation at Colorado Nurses Foundation, 7831 Lewis Court, Arvada, CO 80005 for further information.

2318 ■ Amy and Horace Hagedorn Trust: Nightingale Scholarships *(Graduate, Undergraduate/Scholarship)*

Purpose: To provide scholarships for qualified nursing students from both rural and urban settings. **Focus:** Nursing. **Qualif.:** Applicants must be Colorado residents committed to practicing nursing in Colorado; must be students in an approved Colorado Nursing Program; must have a minimum of 3.25 undergraduate GPA and 3.5 graduate GPA; and must have one of the following student statuses: (1) Junior or senior level BSN undergraduate student; (2) RN enrolled in a baccalaureate or higher degree nursing program in a school of nursing; (3) Student in second year of nursing studies in an associate degree in nursing program; (4) RN with master's degree in nursing, currently practicing in Colorado and enrolled in a doctoral program; (5) Student in second or third year of a Doctorate Nursing Practice (DNP) program. **Criteria:** Scholarship application will be rated based on the following: (1) Professional philosophy and goals; (2) Dedication to the improvement of patient care in Colorado; (3) Demonstrated commitment to nursing, critical thinking skills, and potential for leadership; (4) Involvement in community and professional organizations; (5) GPA-minimum 3.25 undergraduate, 3.5 graduate; (6) Financial need; (7) Recommendation of one faculty member, and (8) Employer/Supervisor recommendation.

Funds Avail.: $1,000. **To Apply:** Applicants are advised to contact the foundation at Colorado Nurses Foundation,

Awards are arranged alphabetically below their administering organizations

7831 Lewis Court, Arvada, CO 80005 for application.

2319 ■ Johnson and Johnson: Nightingale Scholarships *(Graduate, Undergraduate/Scholarship)*

Purpose: To provide scholarships for qualified nursing students from both rural and urban settings. **Focus:** Nursing. **Qualif.:** Applicant must be a Colorado resident committed to practicing nursing in Colorado; must be a student in an approved Colorado Nursing Program; must have a minimum of 3.25 GPA (for undergraduate applicants) or 3.5 GPA (for graduate applicants); and must have one of the following student statuses: (1) Junior or senior level BSN undergraduate student; (2) RN enrolled in a baccalaureate or higher degree nursing program in a school of nursing; (3) Student in second year of nursing studies in an associate degree in nursing program; (4) RN with master's degree in nursing, currently practicing in Colorado and enrolled in a doctoral program; (5) Student in second or third year of a Doctorate Nursing Practice (DNP) program. **Criteria:** Scholarship application will be rated based on the following: (1) Professional philosophy and goals; (2) Dedication to the improvement of patient care in Colorado; (3) Demonstrated commitment to nursing, critical thinking skills, and potential for leadership; (4) Involvement in community and professional organizations; (5) GPA-minimum of 3.25 undergraduate, 3.5 graduate; (6) Financial need; (7) Recommendation of one faculty member, and (8) Employer/Supervisor recommendation.

Funds Avail.: $1,000. **To Apply:** Applicants are advised to contact the foundation at Colorado Nurses Foundation, 7831 Lewis Court, Arvada, CO 80005 for further information.

2320 ■ Kaiser Permanente: Nightingale Scholarships *(Graduate, Undergraduate/Scholarship)*

Purpose: To provide scholarships for qualified nursing students from both rural and urban settings. **Focus:** Nursing. **Qualif.:** Applicant must be a Colorado resident committed to practicing nursing in Colorado; must be a student in an approved Colorado Nursing Program; must have a minimum of 3.25 GPA (for undergraduate applicants) or 3.5 GPA (for graduate applicants); and must have one of the following student statuses: (1) Junior or senior level BSN undergraduate student; (2) RN enrolled in a baccalaureate or higher degree nursing program in a school of nursing; (3) Student in second year of nursing studies in an associate degree in nursing program; (4) RN with master's degree in nursing, currently practicing in Colorado and enrolled in a doctoral program; (5) Student in second or third year of a Doctorate Nursing Practice (DNP) program. **Criteria:** Scholarship application will be rated based on the following: (1) Professional philosophy and goals; (2) Dedication to the improvement of patient care in Colorado; (3) Demonstrated commitment to nursing, critical thinking skills, and potential for leadership; (4) Involvement in community and professional organizations; (5) GPA-minimum of 3.25 undergraduate, 3.5 graduate; (6) Financial need; (7) Recommendation of one faculty member, and (8) Employer/Supervisor recommendation.

Funds Avail.: $1,000. **To Apply:** Applicants are advised to contact the foundation at Colorado Nurses Foundation, 7831 Lewis Court, Arvada, CO 80005 for further information.

2321 ■ Metropolitan State College of Denver, President's Office: Nightingale Scholarships *(Graduate, Undergraduate/Scholarship)*

Purpose: To provide scholarships for qualified nursing students from both rural and urban settings. **Focus:** Nursing. **Qualif.:** Applicant must be a Colorado resident committed to practicing nursing in Colorado; must be a student in an approved Colorado Nursing Program; must have a minimum of 3.25 GPA (for undergraduate applicants) or 3.5 GPA (for graduate applicants); and must have one of the following student statuses: (1) Junior or senior level BSN undergraduate student; (2) RN enrolled in a baccalaureate or higher degree nursing program in a school of nursing; (3) Student in second year of nursing studies in an associate degree in nursing program; (4) RN with master's degree in nursing, currently practicing in Colorado and enrolled in a doctoral program; (5) Student in second or third year of a Doctorate Nursing Practice (DNP) program. **Criteria:** Scholarship application will be rated based on the following: (1) Professional philosophy and goals; (2) Dedication to the improvement of patient care in Colorado; (3) Demonstrated commitment to nursing, critical thinking skills, and potential for leadership; (4) Involvement in community and professional organizations; (5) GPA-minimum of 3.25 undergraduate, 3.5 graduate; (6) Financial need; (7) Recommendation of one faculty member, and (8) Employer/Supervisor recommendation.

Funds Avail.: $1,000. **To Apply:** Applicants are advised to contact the foundation at Colorado Nurses Foundation, 7831 Lewis Court, Arvada, CO 80005 for further information.

2322 ■ H.M. Muffly Memorial Scholarships *(Graduate, Undergraduate/Scholarship)*

Purpose: To provide scholarships for qualified nursing students from both rural and urban settings. **Focus:** Nursing. **Qualif.:** Applicant must be a Colorado resident committed to practicing nursing in Colorado; must be a student in an approved Colorado Nursing Program; must have a minimum of 3.25 GPA (for undergraduate applicants) or 3.5 GPA (for graduate applicants); and must have one of the following student statuses: (1) Junior or senior level BSN undergraduate student; (2) RN enrolled in a baccalaureate or higher degree nursing program in a school of nursing; (3) Student in second year of nursing studies in an associate degree in nursing program; (4) RN with master's degree in nursing, currently practicing in Colorado and enrolled in a doctoral program; (5) Student in second or third year of a Doctorate Nursing Practice (DNP) program. **Criteria:** Scholarship application will be rated based on the following: (1) Professional philosophy and goals; (2) Dedication to the improvement of patient care in Colorado; (3) Demonstrated commitment to nursing, critical thinking skills, and potential for leadership; (4) Involvement in community and professional organizations; (5) GPA-minimum of 3.25 undergraduate, 3.5 graduate; (6) Financial need; (7) Recommendation of one faculty member, and (8) Employer/Supervisor recommendation.

Funds Avail.: $1,000. **To Apply:** Applicants are advised to contact the foundation at Colorado Nurses Foundation, 7831 Lewis Court, Arvada, CO 80005 for further information.

2323 ■ Poudre Valley Health System, Fort Collins: Nightingale Scholarships *(Graduate, Undergraduate/Scholarship)*

Purpose: To provide scholarships for qualified nursing students from both rural and urban settings. **Focus:** Nursing. **Qualif.:** Applicant must be a Colorado resident committed to practicing nursing in Colorado; must be a student in an approved Colorado Nursing Program; must have a minimum of 3.25 GPA (for undergraduate applicants) or 3.5 GPA (for graduate applicants); and must have one of the following student statuses: (1) Junior or senior level BSN undergraduate student; (2) RN enrolled in a baccalaureate or higher degree nursing program in a school of nursing; (3) Student in second year of nursing studies in an associate degree in nursing program; (4) RN with master's degree in nursing, currently practicing in Colorado and enrolled in a doctoral program; (5) Student in second or third year of a Doctorate Nursing Practice (DNP) program. **Criteria:** Scholarship application will be rated based on the following: (1) Professional philosophy and goals; (2) Dedication to the improvement of patient care in Colorado; (3) Demonstrated commitment to nursing, critical thinking skills, and potential for leadership; (4) Involvement in community and professional organizations; (5) GPA-minimum of 3.25 undergraduate, 3.5 graduate; (6) Financial need; (7) Recommendation of one faculty member, and (8) Employer/ Supervisor recommendation.

Funds Avail.: $1,000. **To Apply:** Applicants are advised to contact the foundation at Colorado Nurses Foundation, 7831 Lewis Court, Arvada, CO 80005 for further information.

2324 ■ Rocky Mountain Region of Wound Ostomy Continence Nurses Society Scholarships *(Graduate, Undergraduate/Scholarship)*

Purpose: To provide scholarships for qualified nursing students from both rural and urban settings. **Focus:** Nursing. **Qualif.:** Applicant must be a Colorado resident committed to practicing nursing in Colorado; must be a student in an approved Colorado Nursing Program; must have a minimum of 3.25 GPA (for undergraduate applicants) or 3.5 GPA (for graduate applicants); and must have one of the following student statuses: (1) Junior or senior level BSN undergraduate student; (2) RN enrolled in a baccalaureate or higher degree nursing program in a school of nursing; (3) Student in second year of nursing studies in an associate degree in nursing program; (4) RN with master's degree in nursing, currently practicing in Colorado and enrolled in a doctoral program; (5) Student in second or third year of a Doctorate Nursing Practice (DNP) program. **Criteria:** Scholarship application will be rated based on the following: (1) Professional philosophy and goals; (2) Dedication to the improvement of patient care in Colorado; (3) Demonstrated commitment to nursing, critical thinking skills, and potential for leadership; (4) Involvement in community and professional organizations; (5) GPA-minimum of 3.25 undergraduate, 3.5 graduate; (6) Financial need; (7) Recommendation of one faculty member, and (8) Employer/ Supervisor recommendation.

Funds Avail.: $1,500. **To Apply:** Applicants are advised to contact the foundation at Colorado Nurses Foundation, 7831 Lewis Court, Arvada, CO 80005 for further information.

2325 ■ Rose Medical Center, Denver: Nightingale Scholarships *(Graduate, Undergraduate/Scholarship)*

Purpose: To provide scholarships for qualified nursing students from both rural and urban settings. **Focus:** Nursing. **Qualif.:** Applicant must be a Colorado resident committed to practicing nursing in Colorado; must be a student in an approved Colorado Nursing Program; must have a minimum of 3.25 GPA (for undergraduate applicants) or 3.5 GPA (for graduate applicants); and must have one of the following student statuses: (1) Junior or senior level BSN undergraduate student; (2) RN enrolled in a baccalaureate or higher degree nursing program in a school of nursing; (3) Student in second year of nursing studies in an associate degree in nursing program; (4) RN with master's degree in nursing, currently practicing in Colorado and enrolled in a doctoral program; (5) Student in second or third year of a Doctorate Nursing Practice (DNP) program. **Criteria:** Scholarship application will be rated based on the following: (1) Professional philosophy and goals; (2) Dedication to the improvement of patient care in Colorado; (3) Demonstrated commitment to nursing, critical thinking skills, and potential for leadership; (4) Involvement in community and professional organizations; (5) GPA-minimum of 3.25 undergraduate, 3.5 graduate; (6) Financial need; (7) Recommendation of one faculty member, and (8) Employer/ Supervisor recommendation.

Funds Avail.: $1,000. **To Apply:** Applicants are advised to contact the foundation at Colorado Nurses Foundation, 7831 Lewis Court, Arvada, CO 80005 for further information.

2326 ■ St. Anthony's Hospitals, Denver: Nightingale Scholarships *(Graduate, Undergraduate/Scholarship)*

Purpose: To provide scholarships for qualified nursing students from both rural and urban settings. **Focus:** Nursing. **Qualif.:** Applicant must be a Colorado resident committed to practicing nursing in Colorado; must be a student in an approved Colorado Nursing Program; must have a minimum of 3.25 GPA (for undergraduate applicants) or 3.5 GPA (for graduate applicants); and must have one of the following student statuses: (1) Junior or senior level BSN undergraduate student; (2) RN enrolled in a baccalaureate or higher degree nursing program in a school of nursing; (3) Student in second year of nursing studies in an associate degree in nursing program; (4) RN with master's degree in nursing, currently practicing in Colorado and enrolled in a doctoral program; (5) Student in second or third year of a Doctorate Nursing Practice (DNP) program. **Criteria:** Scholarship application will be rated based on the following: (1) Professional philosophy and goals; (2) Dedication to the improvement of patient care in Colorado; (3) Demonstrated commitment to nursing, critical thinking skills, and potential for leadership; (4) Involvement in community and professional organizations; (5) GPA-minimum of 3.25 undergraduate, 3.5 graduate; (6) Financial need; (7) Recommendation of one faculty member, and (8) Employer/ Supervisor recommendation.

Funds Avail.: $1,000. **Number Awarded:** 2. **To Apply:** Applicants are advised to contact the foundation at Colorado Nurses Foundation, 7831 Lewis Court, Arvada, CO 80005 for further information.

2327 ■ St. Mary's Hospital and Medical Center, Grand Junction: Nightingale Scholarships *(Graduate, Undergraduate/Scholarship)*

Purpose: To provide scholarships for qualified nursing students from both rural and urban settings. **Focus:** Nursing. **Qualif.:** Applicant must be a Colorado resident committed to practicing nursing in Colorado; must be a student in an approved Colorado Nursing Program; must have a minimum of 3.25 GPA (for undergraduate applicants) or 3.5 GPA (for graduate applicants); and must have one of the following student statuses: (1) Junior or senior level BSN

Awards are arranged alphabetically below their administering organizations

undergraduate student; (2) RN enrolled in a baccalaureate or higher degree nursing program in a school of nursing; (3) Student in second year of nursing studies in an associate degree in nursing program; (4) RN with master's degree in nursing, currently practicing in Colorado and enrolled in a doctoral program; (5) Student in second or third year of a Doctorate Nursing Practice (DNP) program. **Criteria:** Scholarship application will be rated based on the following: (1) Professional philosophy and goals; (2) Dedication to the improvement of patient care in Colorado; (3) Demonstrated commitment to nursing, critical thinking skills, and potential for leadership; (4) Involvement in community and professional organizations; (5) GPA-minimum of 3.25 undergraduate, 3.5 graduate; (6) Financial need; (7) Recommendation of one faculty member, and (8) Employer/ Supervisor recommendation.

Funds Avail.: $1,000. **Number Awarded:** 2. **To Apply:** Applicants are advised to contact the foundation at Colorado Nurses Foundation, 7831 Lewis Court, Arvada, CO 80005 for further information.

2328 ■ Seedworks Fund: Nightingale Scholarships *(Graduate, Undergraduate/Scholarship)*

Purpose: To provide scholarships for qualified nursing students from both rural and urban settings. **Focus:** Nursing. **Qualif.:** Applicant must be a Colorado resident committed to practicing nursing in Colorado; must be a student in an approved Colorado Nursing Program; must have a minimum of 3.25 GPA (for undergraduate applicants) or 3.5 GPA (for graduate applicants); and must have one of the following student statuses: (1) Junior or senior level BSN undergraduate student; (2) RN enrolled in a baccalaureate or higher degree nursing program in a school of nursing; (3) Student in second year of nursing studies in an associate degree in nursing program; (4) RN with master's degree in nursing, currently practicing in Colorado and enrolled in a doctoral program; (5) Student in second or third year of a Doctorate Nursing Practice (DNP) program. **Criteria:** Scholarship application will be rated based on the following: (1) Professional philosophy and goals; (2) Dedication to the improvement of patient care in Colorado; (3) Demonstrated commitment to nursing, critical thinking skills, and potential for leadership; (4) Involvement in community and professional organizations; (5) GPA-minimum of 3.25 undergraduate, 3.5 graduate; (6) Financial need; (7) Recommendation of one faculty member, and (8) Employer/ Supervisor recommendation.

Funds Avail.: $1,000. **To Apply:** Applicants are advised to contact the foundation at Colorado Nurses Foundation, 7831 Lewis Court, Arvada, CO 80005 for further information.

2329 ■ Patty Walter Memorial Scholarships *(Graduate, Undergraduate/Scholarship)*

Purpose: To provide scholarships for qualified nursing students from both rural and urban settings. **Focus:** Nursing. **Qualif.:** Applicant must be a Colorado resident committed to practicing nursing in Colorado; must be a student in an approved Colorado Nursing Program; must have a minimum of 3.25 GPA (for undergraduate applicants) or 3.5 GPA (for graduate applicants); and must have one of the following student statuses: (1) Junior or senior level BSN undergraduate student; (2) RN enrolled in a baccalaureate or higher degree nursing program in a school of nursing; (3) Student in second year of nursing studies in an associate degree in nursing program; (4) RN with master's degree in nursing, currently practicing in Colorado and enrolled in a doctoral program; (5) Student in second or third year of a Doctorate Nursing Practice (DNP) program. **Criteria:** Scholarship application will be rated based on the following: (1) Professional philosophy and goals; (2) Dedication to the improvement of patient care in Colorado; (3) Demonstrated commitment to nursing, critical thinking skills, and potential for leadership; (4) Involvement in community and professional organizations; (5) GPA-minimum of 3.25 undergraduate, 3.5 graduate; (6) Financial need; (7) Recommendation of one faculty member, and (8) Employer/ Supervisor recommendation.

Funds Avail.: $1,000. **To Apply:** Applicants are advised to contact the foundation at Colorado Nurses Foundation, 7831 Lewis Court, Arvada, CO 80005 for further information.

2330 ■ Columbian Lawyers Association of Westchester County

800 Westchester Ave., Ste. S608
Rye Brook, NY 10573
Ph: (914)253-6533
E-mail: awcornachio3@westcla.org
URL: http://www.westcla.org

2331 ■ Columbian Lawyers Association of Westchester County Scholarships *(Undergraduate/Scholarship)*

Purpose: To develop a program for Italian-American law students to give them an opportunity to serve as legal interns with judges who are associations members and to assist Italian-American educators and community members with their efforts to continue the teaching of the Italian language at several involving law, government, social, historical and contemporary issues. **Focus:** Law. **Qualif.:** Applicants must be residents of Westchester County who are enrolled in any law school; must not be children of CLAW member; and should be ranked in the upper half of their class. **Criteria:** Recipients are selected based on financial need.

Funds Avail.: No specific amount. **To Apply:** Applicants must submit a complete application form and a resume; a letter to scholarship committee demonstrating the Italian descent, academic achievement, financial need, aspirations and goals; and a firm adherence to the ideals championed by the association. **Deadline:** October.

2332 ■ PACE/Columbian Lawyers Association of Westchester County Endowed Scholarships *(Undergraduate/Scholarship)*

Purpose: To develop a program for Italian-American law students to give them an opportunity to serve as legal interns with judges who are associations members and to assist Italian-American educators and community members with their efforts to continue the teaching of the Italian language at several involving law, government, social, historical and contemporary issues. **Focus:** Law. **Qualif.:** Applicants must be Pace Law School students; should be of an Italian-American heritage; and must maintain an overall minimum academic 3.0 GPA. **Criteria:** Recipients are selected based on financial need.

Funds Avail.: $5,000. **To Apply:** Applicants must submit completed application form.

2333 ■ Columbus Citizens Foundation

8 E 69th St.
New York, NY 10021

Awards are arranged alphabetically below their administering organizations

Ph: (212)249-9923
Fax: (212)737-4413
E-mail: ccf@columbuscitizens.org
URL: http://www.columbuscitizensfd.org

2334 ■ Columbus Citizens Foundation College Scholarships *(Undergraduate/Scholarship)*

Purpose: To provide financial assistance to underwrite the cost of Italian descent students' college tuition. **Focus:** General studies. **Qualif.:** Applicants must be students who are of Italian descent and who are from households where the total gross income does not exceed $30,000 per capita; must have a minimum grade average of 85% or a 3.0 GPA; and must be residents of one of the following states: NY, NJ, DE, DC, MD, PA, VT, RI, ME, MA, NH, or CT. **Criteria:** Applicants are evaluated based on existence of Italian-American ancestry; financial need; academic excellence; and service to school and community.

Funds Avail.: No specific amount. **To Apply:** Application is available for download in .pfd format and must be sent to the Private School Aid Service. **Deadline:** February 1.

2335 ■ Columbus Citizens Foundation High School Scholarships *(High School/Scholarship)*

Purpose: To provide educational assistance for students of Italian descent. **Focus:** General studies. **Qualif.:** Applicants must be students of Italian descent and must come from households where the total gross income does not exceed $25,000 per capita. Applicants must maintain a 3.0 GPA and demonstrate that they have performed community service activities. **Criteria:** Applicants are evaluated based on existence of Italian-American ancestry; academic achievement and school/community service; financial need.

Funds Avail.: No specific amount. **To Apply:** Application is available for download in .pdf format and must be sent to the Private School Aid Service **Deadline:** March 14.

2336 ■ The Committee of 200

980 North Michigan Ave., Ste. 1575
Chicago, IL 60611-7540
Ph: (312)255-0296
Fax: (312)255-0789
E-mail: info@c200.org
URL: http://www.c200.org

2337 ■ C200 Scholar Awards *(All/Scholarship)*

Purpose: To provide scholarship to outstanding MBA women students. **Focus:** Business. **Qualif.:** Applicants must be enrolled in business school hosting a C200 Outreach Seminar. **Criteria:** Selections are based on work experience, GPA, recommendations, and essays.

Funds Avail.: 25,000; an internship at a C200 member's company; and an opportunity to attend C200's Annual Conference. **To Apply:** Applicant must submit recommendations and essays.

2338 ■ Communal Studies Association

PO Box 122
Amana, IA 52203
Ph: (319)622-6446
Fax: (319)622-6446
E-mail: csa@netins.net
URL: http://www.communalstudies.info

2339 ■ Communal Studies Association Research Fellowships *(Graduate/Grant)*

Purpose: To provide financial support for qualified CSA members. **Focus:** General studies. **Qualif.:** Applicant must be a CSA member in good standing at the time of application and at presentation of the research. **Criteria:** Awards will be given to those who meet the qualifications.

Funds Avail.: $1200. **To Apply:** Applicant should provide: a curriculum vita or resume and letters from two relevant references; a two-page description of the overall project, how he/she plans to accomplish such research, its goals, a timeline and how it will be presented at the CSA conference (paper, panel, A/V presentation, performance, exhibition, etc.); a bibliography of intended resources to be consulted during the grant project and a statement that these resources are open to the applicant; and a detailed budget (specify if funds other than this grant are to be used and their sources). **Deadline:** March 1. **Contact:** Communal Studies Association at the above address (see entry 2338).

2340 ■ Communications Workers of America

7B-1050 Baxter Rd.
Ottawa, ON, Canada K2C 3P1
Ph: (613)820-9777
Fax: (613)820-8188
Free: 877-486-4292
E-mail: info@cwa-scacanada.ca
URL: http://www.cwa-scacanada.ca

2341 ■ Communications Workers of America Scholarships *(Undergraduate/Scholarship)*

Purpose: To raise professional standards and promote ethical business and journalistic practices. **Focus:** General studies. **Qualif.:** Applicants must be full-time students at an accredited college, university, community college, technical or trade school. **Criteria:** Recipients are selected based on academic performance.

Funds Avail.: $1,000. **To Apply:** Applicants must complete the application form. **Deadline:** October 31.

2342 ■ Community Forestry and Environmental Research Partnerships

101 Giannini Hall 3100
Berkeley, CA 94720
Ph: (510)642-3431
E-mail: cffellow@nature.berkeley.edu
URL: http://www.cnr.berkeley.edu

2343 ■ CFERP Masters Fellowships *(Graduate/Fellowship)*

Purpose: To provide financial support to deserving students. **Focus:** General studies. **Qualif.:** Applicants must be graduate students. **Criteria:** Preference will be given to those who meet the criteria.

Funds Avail.: $7,000 for Masters research - Eligible expenditures include living expenses in the field and transportation, communication and other research-related expenses. **To Apply:** Applicants must check the available website for more information regarding this fellowship. **Contact:** Community Forestry and Environmental Research Partnerships at the above address (see entry 2342).

2344 ■ Community-based Natural Resource Management Assistantships *(All/Internship)*

Purpose: To provide financial assistance to those students who are in need. **Focus:** General studies. **Qualif.:** Ap-

plicants must be faculty or students at any U.S. college or university, in any department. **Criteria:** Priority will be given to those who meet the criteria.

Funds Avail.: $6,200. **To Apply:** Applicants must check the available website for more information. **Deadline:** April 14. **Contact:** Community Forestry and Environmental Research Partnerships at the above address (see entry 2342).

2345 ■ Community Foundation of Calhoun County

PO Box 1826
Anniston, AL 36202-1826
Ph: (256)231-5160
Fax: (256)231-5161
E-mail: info@yourcommunityfirst.org
URL: http://www.yourcommunityfirst.org

2346 ■ Joe Bynum/Raymond James Investment Services Technical Excellence Scholarships Fund *(Undergraduate/Scholarship)*

Purpose: To help young men and women secure a college education. **Focus:** General studies. **Qualif.:** Applicants must be graduates of Oxford High School in Calhoun County; must have a 2.5 average on a 4.0 scale; must be enrolled as part- or full-time students. **Criteria:** Recipients are selected based on financial need, academic ability and good character.

Funds Avail.: $2,500. **To Apply:** Applicants must submit a completed application form and an essay describing their personal aspirations, educational or career goals and how this scholarship will help in achieving their career goals. **Deadline:** February 1.

2347 ■ Calhoun County Auduburn University Scholarships *(Undergraduate/Scholarship)*

Purpose: To provide financial resources enabling local students to pursue higher education at Auduburn University. **Focus:** General studies. **Qualif.:** Applicants must be graduates of any accredited public or private high school within Calhoun County; must have maintained 2.5 GPA on a 4.0 scale. **Criteria:** Recipients are selected based on financial need.

Funds Avail.: No specific amount. **To Apply:** Applicants must submit a completed application form and an essay describing their personal aspirations, educational and career goals. **Deadline:** February 1. **Contact:** info@yourcommunityfirst.org.

2348 ■ Melanie and Todd Edmonson Memorial Scholarship *(Undergraduate/Scholarship)*

Purpose: To encourage young people to follow their dreams and to help lessen some of life's challenges. **Focus:** General studies. **Qualif.:** Applicants must be graduates of Oxford High School or its successor; must have 3.0 or "B" average; must be actively involved in their community, school and religious activities; must be full or part-time enrolled students at an accredited institution of higher learning in the United States; may be pursuing any field of academic study or technical training. **Criteria:** Recipients are selected based on financial need and academic performance.

Funds Avail.: No specific amount. **To Apply:** Applicants must submit a completed application form, transcript of records, an essay describing their personal aspirations, educational or career goals and how this scholarship will help in achieving their career goals. **Deadline:** February 1. **Contact:** info@yourcommunityfirst.org.

2349 ■ Gadsden State/McClellan Campus Nursing Scholarships Award *(Undergraduate/Scholarship)*

Purpose: To promote and celebrate the nursing profession. **Focus:** Nursing. **Qualif.:** Applicants must be graduates of an accredited public or private high school within Calhoun County currently attending Gadsden State/McClellan Campus; must be enrolled in LPN Nursing Program. **Criteria:** Recipients are selected based on character, academic ability, school/community service and financial need.

Funds Avail.: $2,500. **To Apply:** Applicants must submit a completed application form and an essay describing their personal aspirations and contributions to nursing profession. **Deadline:** February 1. **Contact:** info@yourcommunityfirst.org.

2350 ■ Farley Moody Galbraith Scholarship Fund *(Undergraduate/Scholarship)*

Purpose: To encourage high school seniors to attain a four-year college degree. **Focus:** General studies. **Qualif.:** Applicants must be graduating seniors from any public or private high school including home school; must have 3.0 average on a 4.0 scale; must be enrolled as part- or full-time students. **Criteria:** Recipients are selected based on financial need, academic ability and good character.

Funds Avail.: $2,500. **To Apply:** Applicants must submit a completed application form and an essay describing their personal aspirations, educational or career goals and how this scholarship will help in achieving their career goals. **Deadline:** February 1.

2351 ■ Whitney Laine Gallahar Memorial Scholarship Fund *(Undergraduate/Scholarship)*

Purpose: To provide supplement funding for full- or part-time enrolled students at an accredited state college or university within Alabama. **Focus:** General studies. **Qualif.:** Applicants must be graduating seniors of Ohatchee High school or its successor institution; must have 2.5 GPA; must be enrolled as part- or full-time. **Criteria:** Recipients are selected based on financial need, academic ability and good character.

Funds Avail.: $1,000. **To Apply:** Applicants must submit a completed application form and an essay describing their personal aspirations, educational or career goals and how this scholarship will help in achieving their career goals. **Deadline:** February 1.

2352 ■ Guin-Stanford Scholarships *(Professional Development/Scholarship)*

Purpose: To enhance the quality of life in Calhoun County, Alabama. **Focus:** General studies. **Qualif.:** Applicants must have earned a bachelor's degree from an accredited college or university; must hold a current Teaching Certificate from the State of Alabama. **Criteria:** Recipients are selected based on financial need and character.

Funds Avail.: No specific amount. **To Apply:** Applicants must submit a completed application form, letter of enrollment and two letters of recommendation. **Contact:** info@yourcommunityfirst.org.

2353 ■ Cleve Holloway Memorial Scholarship Fund *(Undergraduate/Scholarship)*

Purpose: To provide full or supplemental funding for full-time enrolled students at an accredited state college or

Awards are arranged alphabetically below their administering organizations

university within Alabama. **Focus:** General studies. **Qualif.:** Applicants must be graduating seniors of Anniston High School or its successor institution; must maintain high personal standards and moral character; must have a minimum of 2.5 or "C" average on a 4.0 scale; must be enrolled full-time. **Criteria:** Recipients are selected based on financial need, academic ability and good character.

Funds Avail.: No specific amount. **To Apply:** Applicants must submit a completed application form, transcript of records and an essay describing their personal aspirations, educational or career goals and how this scholarship will help in achieving their career goals. **Contact:** info@yourcommunityfirst.org.

2354 ■ Edyie G. Kirby Nursing Scholarships Award *(Undergraduate/Scholarship)*

Purpose: To promote and celebrate the nursing profession. **Focus:** Nursing. **Qualif.:** Applicants must be graduates of an accredited public or private high school within Calhoun County. **Criteria:** Recipients are selected based on character, academic ability, school/community service and financial need.

Funds Avail.: $2,500. **To Apply:** Applicants must submit a completed application form and an essay describing their personal aspirations and contributions to nursing profession. **Deadline:** February 1. **Contact:** info@yourcommunityfirst.org.

2355 ■ E.C. Lloyd and J.C.U. Johnson Scholarships Fund *(Undergraduate/Scholarship)*

Purpose: To provide supplement funding for full or part-time enrolled students at any accredited two-or-four-year college or university within the United States. **Focus:** General studies. **Qualif.:** Applicants must be graduating seniors from any public or private high school including home schools; must have 2.5 or "C" average on a 4.0 scale; must be enrolled as part- or full-time students. **Criteria:** Recipients are selected based on financial need, academic ability and good character.

Funds Avail.: $2,500. **To Apply:** Applicants must submit a completed application form and an essay describing their personal aspirations, educational or career goals and how this scholarship will help in achieving the career goal. **Deadline:** February 1.

2356 ■ Gertie S. Lowe Nursing Scholarships Award *(Undergraduate/Scholarship)*

Purpose: To promote and celebrate the nursing profession. **Focus:** Nursing. **Qualif.:** Applicants must be full- or part-time students in the LPN or RN program at Gadsten State Community College; must be graduates of any accredited public or private high school within Calhoun County currently attending Gadsden State Community College. **Criteria:** Recipients are selected based on character, academic ability, school/community service and financial need.

Funds Avail.: $2,500. **To Apply:** Applicants must submit a completed application form and an essay describing their personal aspirations and contributions to nursing profession. **Contact:** info@yourcommunityfirst.org.

2357 ■ Jerry Medforth Nursing Scholarships Award *(Undergraduate/Scholarship)*

Purpose: To promote and celebrate the nursing profession. **Focus:** Nursing. **Qualif.:** Applicants must be graduates of any accredited public or private high school within Calhoun County possessing an unencumbered Registered Nurse License; must be full-time students enrolled at the Jacksonville State University Lurleen B. Wallace College of Nursing and Health Sciences RN to BSN Strategic Teaching for Enhanced Professional Preparation program. **Criteria:** Recipients are selected based on character, academic ability, school/community service and financial need.

Funds Avail.: $2,500. **To Apply:** Applicants must submit a completed application form and an essay describing their personal aspirations and contributions to nursing profession. **Contact:** info@yourcommunityfirst.org.

2358 ■ Reverend John S. Nettled Scholarship *(Undergraduate/Scholarship)*

Purpose: To foster hope, self-confidence and ambition in the graduates of Anniston High School. **Focus:** General studies. **Qualif.:** Applicants must be graduating seniors from Anniston high School; must have 2.5 GPA or above on a 4.0 scale. **Criteria:** Recipients are selected based on character, academic ability, school, church and community service and financial need.

Funds Avail.: No specific amount. **To Apply:** Applicants must submit a completed application form and an essay describing the personal aspirations, educational and career goals. **Deadline:** February 1. **Contact:** info@yourcommunityfirst.org.

2359 ■ The Nightingale Scholarships Award *(Undergraduate/Scholarship)*

Purpose: To promote and celebrate the nursing profession. **Focus:** Nursing. **Qualif.:** Applicants must be full-time students attending an accredited four-year college or university within the United States in pursuit of a bachelor's degree in nursing; must be graduates of an accredited public or private high school within Calhoun County; must have a 3.0 overall high school GPA on a 4.0 scale. **Criteria:** Recipients are selected based on financial need.

Funds Avail.: $20,000. **To Apply:** Applicants must submit a completed application form and an essay describing the person or experience that has been the greatest influence in their life. **Deadline:** February 1. **Contact:** info@yourcommunityfirst.org.

2360 ■ Gerald Powell Scholarship *(Undergraduate/Scholarship)*

Purpose: To support tuition assistance for students attending Sacred Heart of Jesus Catholic School in Anniston, Alabama. **Focus:** General studies. **Qualif.:** Applicants must be enrolled on a full-time basis at Sacred Heart of Jesus Catholic School either in elementary or high school levels; must maintain a GPA of 2.5 or "C" on a 4.0 scale. **Criteria:** Recipients are selected based on background, financial need and clarity and completeness of application.

Funds Avail.: No specific amount. **To Apply:** Applicants must submit a completed application form. **Deadline:** May 1.

2361 ■ Joseph and Amelia Saks Scholarship Fund *(Undergraduate/Scholarship)*

Purpose: To foster educational opportunities for graduates of Saks High School; to provide full or supplemental funding for full-time enrolled students over a four-year period at an accredited college or university within the United States. **Focus:** General studies. **Qualif.:** Applicants must be graduating senior students of Saks High School or it's successor institution; must have maintained high personal standards and moral character; must have a minimum of

Awards are arranged alphabetically below their administering organizations

2.5 or "C" average on a 4.0 scale; must be full-time students completing academics aligned with their specific major or degree. **Criteria:** Recipients are selected based on financial need and academic performance.

Funds Avail.: No specific amount. **To Apply:** Applicants must submit: a completed application form; an essay describing their personal aspirations, educational or career goals and how this scholarship will help in achieving their career goals; a signed letter of acceptance; certified proof of enrollment from an institution and confirmation that the recipient is enrolled; and an official college or university transcript at the end of academic term. **Deadline:** February 1. **Contact:** info@yourcommunityfirst.org.

2362 ■ Mark Dauglas Sawyer Memorial Scholarship *(High School/Scholarship)*

Purpose: To provide tuition assistance for students attending Sacred Heart of Jesus Catholic School in Anniston, Alabama. **Focus:** General studies. **Qualif.:** Applicants must be enrolled on a full-time basis at the School of Sacred Heart of Jesus Catholic School either at the elementary or high school level; must have a "C" or 2.5 average on a 4.0 scale. **Criteria:** Recipients are selected based on financial need.

Funds Avail.: No specific amount. **To Apply:** Applicants must submit a completed application form. **Deadline:** May 1.

2363 ■ Leslie and Mary Ella Scales Memorial Scholarship *(Undergraduate/Scholarship)*

Purpose: To recognize the value of higher education and provide support for graduates of Anniston High School. **Focus:** General studies. **Qualif.:** Applicants must be full-time or part-time students attending any accredited institution of higher learning in United States; may pursue any field of academic study or technical training. **Criteria:** Recipients are selected based on financial need.

Funds Avail.: No specific amount. **To Apply:** Applicants must submit a completed application form. **Contact:** info@yourcommunityfirst.org.

2364 ■ Nathan Sparks Memorial Scholarship *(Undergraduate/Scholarship)*

Purpose: To provide supplemental funding for full or part-time enrolled students at an accredited college, university or technical institution within United States. **Focus:** General studies. **Qualif.:** Applicants must be graduating seniors of Saks High School or its successor institution. **Criteria:** Recipients are selected based on financial need.

Funds Avail.: $1,000. **To Apply:** Applicants must submit a completed application form, an essay describing their personal character and two letters of recommendation. **Contact:** info@yourcommunityfirst.org.

2365 ■ H.T. and Terrell Stanford Scholarship *(Undergraduate/Scholarship)*

Purpose: To supplement tuition at the baccalaureate level. **Focus:** General studies. **Qualif.:** Applicants must be graduating senior students from Oxford High School; must maintain a GPA of 2.5 and have strong moral character as attested to by recommendations; must be recognized for school and community service. **Criteria:** Recipients are selected based on financial need.

Funds Avail.: No specific amount. **To Apply:** Applicants must submit a completed application form and other documents are available at the guidance office of Oxford High School. **Deadline:** February 1. **Contact:** info@yourcommunityfirst.org.

2366 ■ Mary Katherine "Kathy" Williamson Scholarship Fund *(Undergraduate/Scholarship)*

Purpose: To enhance the quality of life in Calhoun County, Alabama. **Focus:** General studies. **Qualif.:** Applicants must be individuals who have a diploma from any accredited public or private high school or who have earned the General Education Development (GED) certificate; must be residents of Calhoun County; must have a 2.5 overall GPA or better on a 4.0 scale. **Criteria:** Recipients are selected based on financial need, passion to serve the needs of others and community service.

Funds Avail.: No specific amount. **To Apply:** Applicants must submit a completed application form, transcript of records, and an essay describing their personal aspirations, educational or career goals and how this scholarship will help in achieving their career goals. **Deadline:** February 1. **Contact:** info@yourcommunityfirst.org.

2367 ■ Community Foundation of the Eastern Shore

1324 Belmont Ave.
Salisbury, MD 21804
Ph: (410)742-9911
Fax: (410)742-6638
E-mail: info@cfes.org
URL: http://www.cfes.org

2368 ■ William R. Bowen Scholarship *(Undergraduate/Scholarship)*

Purpose: To empower donors to make a profound difference in the quality of life in Maryland's Lower Eastern Shore; to provide community leadership through grants, non-profit support programs, charitable partnerships and local initiatives in Somerset, Wicomico and Worcester counties. **Focus:** General studies. **Qualif.:** Applicants must be graduating seniors of Snow Hill High School. **Criteria:** Recipients are selected based on academic performance and financial need.

Funds Avail.: $1,000. **To Apply:** Applicants must submit a completed application form.

2369 ■ William T. Burbage Family Memorial Scholarship *(Undergraduate/Scholarship)*

Purpose: To empower donors to make a profound difference in the quality of life in Maryland's Lower Eastern Shore; to provide community leadership through grants, non-profit support programs, charitable partnerships and local initiatives in Somerset, Wicomico and Worcester counties. **Focus:** General studies. **Qualif.:** Applicants must be graduating seniors of Stephen Decatur High School who have selected their college and have been accepted for admission as full-time students; must have 3.0 GPA. **Criteria:** Recipients are selected based on leadership potential.

Funds Avail.: $1,000. **To Apply:** Applicants must submit a completed application form; an official high school transcript of grades; letter of acceptance from college or university; two letters of recommendation from non-family members; a detailed listing by high school year of activities and an essay explaining how growing up on the Eastern Shore has contributed the individual leadership style. **Deadline:** April 15.

Awards are arranged alphabetically below their administering organizations

2370 ■ Irene Culver Collins and Louis Franklin Collins Scholarship *(Undergraduate/Scholarship)*

Purpose: To empower donors to make a profound difference in the quality of life in Maryland's Lower Eastern Shore; to provide community leadership through grants, non-profit support programs, charitable partnerships and local initiatives in Somerset, Wicomico and Worcester counties. **Focus:** General studies. **Qualif.:** Applicants must be post-graduates or current 12th grade students of Parkside High School, Wicomico County, Maryland who have been accepted for admission as full-time college students; must have successfully completed a minimum of three advanced placement social studies during the enrollment at Parkside High School. **Criteria:** Recipients are selected based on academic performance and financial need.

Funds Avail.: $5,000. **To Apply:** Applicants must submit a completed application form; an official high school transcript of grades; letter of acceptance from college or university; an essay describing the personal character and two letters of recommendation from non-family members. **Deadline:** April 15.

2371 ■ Eastern Shore Builder's Association Scholarships *(Undergraduate/Scholarship)*

Purpose: To empower donors to make a profound difference in the quality of life in Maryland's Lower Eastern Shore; to provide community leadership through grants, non-profit support programs, charitable partnerships and local initiatives in Somerset, Wicomico and Worcester counties. **Focus:** General studies. **Qualif.:** Applicants must be current 12th grade students of high schools in Eastern Shore of Maryland counties of Kent, Queen Anne's, Caroline, Talbot, Dorchester, Somerset and Worcester who have been accepted for admission as full-time students; must have a minimum of 2.5 GPA on a 4.0 scale; must be participated in some extracurricular activities. **Criteria:** Recipients are selected based on academic performance, financial need and extracurricular activities.

Funds Avail.: $500. **To Apply:** Applicants must submit a completed application form; an official high school transcript of grades; letter of acceptance from college or university; must submit an essay describing the reasons of choosing the career path and two letters of recommendation from non-family members. **Deadline:** April 1.

2372 ■ Federalsburg Rotary Club Scholarships *(Undergraduate/Scholarship)*

Purpose: To empower donors to make a profound difference in the quality of life in Maryland's Lower Eastern Shore; to provide community leadership through grants, non-profit support programs, charitable partnerships and local initiatives in Somerset, Wicomico and Worcester counties. **Focus:** General studies. **Qualif.:** Applicants must be graduating seniors of Colonel Richardson High School who have selected their college and have been accepted for admission as full-time students; must have 2.5 GPA. **Criteria:** Recipients are selected based on financial need.

Funds Avail.: $500. **To Apply:** Applicants must submit a completed application form; an official high school transcript of grades and letter of acceptance from college or university.

2373 ■ Herb Fincher Memorial Scholarship *(Undergraduate/Scholarship)*

Purpose: To empower donors to make a profound difference in the quality of life in Maryland's Lower Eastern Shore; to provide community leadership through grants, non-profit support programs, charitable partnerships and local initiatives in Somerset, Wicomico and Worcester counties. **Focus:** Engineering. **Qualif.:** Applicants must be graduates of the four public high schools in Wicomico County, Maryland who have been accepted into a course of study for either math or engineering; must have a reputation of good character and be well-rounded young citizens who participated in extra-curricular school or community activities. **Criteria:** Recipients are selected based on demonstrated maturity and commitment to succeed in college level courses of study.

Funds Avail.: $6,000. **To Apply:** Applicants must submit a completed application form, an official high school transcript of grades, letter of acceptance from college or university and two letters of recommendation from non-family members. **Deadline:** April 1.

2374 ■ Green Hill Yacht and Country Club Scholarships *(Undergraduate/Scholarship)*

Purpose: To empower donors to make a profound difference in the quality of life in Maryland's Lower Eastern Shore; to provide community leadership through grants, non-profit support programs, charitable partnerships and local initiatives in Somerset, Wicomico and Worcester counties. **Focus:** General studies. **Qualif.:** Applicants must be graduating seniors of any Wicomico, Somerset or Worcester County School; must be past graduates or current 12th grade students who have been accepted for admission as full-time students in an accredited four-year college or university or accredited two-year educational/vocational institution. **Criteria:** Recipients are selected based on academic achievement and financial need.

Funds Avail.: $1,000. **To Apply:** Applicants must submit a completed application form, an official high school transcript of grades and two letters of recommendation from non-family member. **Deadline:** April 15.

2375 ■ Gruwell Scholarships *(Undergraduate/Scholarship)*

Purpose: To empower donors to make a profound difference in the quality of life in Maryland's Lower Eastern Shore; to provide community leadership through grants, non-profit support programs, charitable partnerships and local initiatives in Somerset, Wicomico and Worcester counties. **Focus:** General studies. **Qualif.:** Applicants must be residents of Lake Forest School District, Kent County, Delaware who have selected their college and have been accepted for admission as full-time students. **Criteria:** Recipients are selected based on financial need, community involvement, academic achievement and extracurricular activities.

Funds Avail.: $1,000. **To Apply:** Applicants must submit a completed application form, an official high school transcript of grades and letter of acceptance from college or university; must submit a copy of parent/guardian and student's most recent income tax return and two letters of recommendation from non-family members.

2376 ■ Hancock Family Snow Hill High School Scholarships *(Undergraduate/Scholarship)*

Purpose: To empower donors to make a profound difference in the quality of life in Maryland's Lower Eastern Shore; to provide community leadership through grants, non-profit support programs, charitable partnerships and local initiatives in Somerset, Wicomico and Worcester counties. **Focus:** General studies. **Qualif.:** Applicants must be graduating seniors at Snow Hill High School who have been

Awards are arranged alphabetically below their administering organizations

accepted by an Accredited academic college program; must have 2.5 GPA in appropriate course work indicating the students are able to be successful at the college level; must have three or more year residents of Snow Hill area; must be active in school activity, church, community and youth clubs; must have good moral character. **Criteria:** Recipients are selected based on academic performance, financial need and participation in extracurricular activities.

Funds Avail.: $2,000. **To Apply:** Applicants must submit a completed application form; an official high school transcript of grades; letter of acceptance from college or university; a copy of parent/guardian and student's most recent income tax return and two letters of recommendation from non-family members. **Deadline:** April 21.

2377 ■ Dick and Pat Hazel Minority Scholarships *(Professional Development/Scholarship)*

Purpose: To empower donors to make a profound difference in the quality of life in Maryland's Lower Eastern Shore; to provide community leadership through grants, non-profit support programs, charitable partnerships and local initiatives in Somerset, Wicomico and Worcester counties. **Focus:** Education. **Qualif.:** Applicants must be members of a minority group and must commit teaching for two years within the public education systems of Somerset, Wicomico or Worcester counties; must be minority residents of Wicomico, Somerset or Worcester County, Maryland who have selected their college and have been accepted for admission as full-time students whose pursuit must be education/teaching. **Criteria:** Recipients are selected based on financial need, community involvement, academic achievement and extracurricular activities.

Funds Avail.: $3,000. **To Apply:** Applicants must submit a completed application form; "one-page" describing the reasons of wanting to teach; an official high school transcript of grades; letter of acceptance from college or university and summary of financial assistance from college/university financial aid and office; must also submit a copy of parent/guardian and student's most recent income tax return and two letters of recommendation from non-family members. **Deadline:** May 1.

2378 ■ Martin S. Kane Memorial Community Service Award Scholarships *(Undergraduate/Scholarship)*

Purpose: To empower donors to make a profound difference in the quality of life in Maryland's Lower Eastern Shore; to provide community leadership through grants, non-profit support programs, charitable partnerships and local initiatives in Somerset, Wicomico and Worcester counties. **Focus:** General studies. **Qualif.:** Applicants must be from Wicomico High School. **Criteria:** Recipients are selected based on financial need.

Funds Avail.: $600. **To Apply:** Applicants must submit a completed application form.

2379 ■ TFC Edward A. Plank, Jr. Memorial Scholarship *(Undergraduate/Scholarship)*

Purpose: To empower donors to make a profound difference in the quality of life in Maryland's Lower Eastern Shore; to provide community leadership through grants, non-profit support programs, charitable partnerships and local initiatives in Somerset, Wicomico and Worcester counties. **Focus:** General studies. **Qualif.:** Applicants must be graduating seniors of any Wicomico, Somerset or Worcester County School; must have 3.0 overall GPA; must be accepted in a full-time basis at an accredited two-to-four-year college. **Criteria:** Recipients are selected based on academic achievement and financial need.

Funds Avail.: $1,000. **To Apply:** Applicants must submit a completed application form, a "500-word" essay on how crimes and/or drug abuse have been affected today's society and personal letters of recommendation from two responsible adults other than relatives. **Deadline:** March 31.

2380 ■ Progress Lane Scholarships
(Undergraduate/Scholarship)

Purpose: To empower donors to make a profound difference in the quality of life in Maryland's Lower Eastern Shore; to provide community leadership through grants, non-profit support programs, charitable partnerships and local initiatives in Somerset, Wicomico and Worcester counties. **Focus:** General studies. **Qualif.:** Applicants must be current graduating 12th grade students of Washington High School, Princess Anne, Maryland who are financially advantaged and have been accepted for admission as students with a minimum of six credit hours in a course of study that will serve the educational requirements for their chosen career. **Criteria:** Recipients are selected based on academic performance and financial need.

Funds Avail.: $500. **To Apply:** Applicants must submit a completed application form; an official high school transcript of grades; a letter of acceptance from college; university or training institute and "250-word" essay describing the reasons of wanting to attend college. **Deadline:** April 1.

2381 ■ Duane V. Puerde Memorial Scholarship
(Undergraduate/Scholarship)

Purpose: To empower donors to make a profound difference in the quality of life in Maryland's Lower Eastern Shore; to provide community leadership through grants, non-profit support programs, charitable partnerships and local initiatives in Somerset, Wicomico and Worcester counties. **Focus:** General studies. **Qualif.:** Applicants must be past graduates or current 12th grade students of Parkside High school who are residents of rural Eastern Wicomico County, Maryland including but not exclusive to the communities of Parsonburg, Pittsville, Powellville, Williards or Melson who have been accepted for admission as full-time college students or vocational school. **Criteria:** Recipients are selected based on academic performance and participation in extracurricular activities.

Funds Avail.: $500. **To Apply:** Applicants must submit a completed application form, an official high school transcript of grades and two letters of recommendation from non-family members.

2382 ■ Elizabeth Pusey Scholarship
(Undergraduate/Scholarship)

Purpose: To empower donors to make a profound difference in the quality of life in Maryland's Lower Eastern Shore; to provide community leadership through grants, non-profit support programs, charitable partnerships and local initiatives in Somerset, Wicomico and Worcester counties. **Focus:** General studies. **Qualif.:** Applicants must be graduating seniors at any Wicomico County high school who have selected their college and have been accepted from admission as full-time students; must be in the top 10% of their class. **Criteria:** Recipients are selected based on financial need.

Funds Avail.: $1,000. **To Apply:** Applicants must submit a completed application form, an official transcript of grades ad letter of acceptance from college or university. **Deadline:** April 1.

2383 ■ Lana K. Rinehart Scholarship
(Undergraduate/Scholarship)

Purpose: To empower donors to make a profound difference in the quality of life in Maryland's Lower Eastern Shore; to provide community leadership through grants, non-profit support programs, charitable partnerships and local initiatives in Somerset, Wicomico and Worcester counties. **Focus:** General studies. **Qualif.:** Applicants must be graduating senior students at Parkside High School. **Criteria:** Recipients are selected based on academic performance and financial need.

Funds Avail.: $1,000. **To Apply:** Applicants must submit a completed application form.

2384 ■ Drew Smith Memorial Scholarship
(Undergraduate/Scholarship)

Purpose: To empower donors to make a profound difference in the quality of life in Maryland's Lower Eastern Shore; to provide community leadership through grants, non-profit support programs, charitable partnerships and local initiatives in Somerset, Wicomico and Worcester counties. **Focus:** General studies. **Qualif.:** Applicants must be adults or graduating public or private high school seniors who are pursuing a degree in golf turf management from an accredited college or university and must be domiciled residents of the Eastern Shore Counties of Maryland and Virginia or the State of Delaware; must be enrolled in college for a minimum of six credit hours per scholastic year. **Criteria:** Recipients are selected based on academic record, financial need, extracurricular activities or community service.

Funds Avail.: $1,000. **To Apply:** Applicants must submit a completed application form. **Deadline:** July 14.

2385 ■ Esther M. Smith Scholarship
(Undergraduate/Scholarship)

Purpose: To empower donors to make a profound difference in the quality of life in Maryland's Lower Eastern Shore; to provide community leadership through grants, non-profit support programs, charitable partnerships and local initiatives in Somerset, Wicomico and Worcester counties. **Focus:** General studies. **Qualif.:** Applicants must be graduating seniors with a disability as accepted defined by the Americans with Disabilities Act (ADA) who attended in Wicomico County; must be nominated by their school principal, guidance counselor or teacher; must have a minimum GPA of 2.0 and have been accepted for admission as full-time students at an accredited four-year college or university or a two-year education or career training institution. **Criteria:** Recipients are selected based on academic performance and financial need.

Funds Avail.: $2,000. **To Apply:** Applicants must submit completed application form; an official high school transcript of grades and letter of recommendation from non-family members. **Deadline:** April 1.

2386 ■ Wicomico High School Class of '55 Scholarships *(Undergraduate/Scholarship)*

Purpose: To empower donors to make a profound difference in the quality of life in Maryland's Lower Eastern Shore; to provide community leadership through grants, non-profit support programs, charitable partnerships and local initiatives in Somerset, Wicomico and Worcester counties. **Focus:** General studies. **Qualif.:** Applicants must be graduating senior students of Wicomico High School who have spent at least their junior and senior years in that school's program; must have selected their college and have been accepted for admission as full-time students; must have 3.0 cumulative GPA. **Criteria:** Recipients are selected based on community involvement, academic achievement and extracurricular activities.

Funds Avail.: $1,000. **To Apply:** Applicants must submit a completed application form; an official high school transcript of grades; letter of acceptance from college or university; three letters of recommendation from non-family members and "250-word" essay on "How they can make a difference". **Deadline:** April 15.

2387 ■ M. William and Frances J. Tilghman Scholarship *(Undergraduate/Scholarship)*

Purpose: To empower donors to make a profound difference in the quality of life in Maryland's Lower Eastern Shore; to provide community leadership through grants, non-profit support programs, charitable partnerships and local initiatives in Somerset, Wicomico and Worcester counties. **Focus:** General studies. **Qualif.:** Applicants must be graduating high school senior students of Somerset County. **Criteria:** Recipients are selected based on academic achievement, extracurricular activities and financial need.

Funds Avail.: $1,500. **To Apply:** Applicants must submit a completed application form; an official high school transcript of grades; letter of acceptance from a college or university and two letters of recommendation from non-family members. **Deadline:** April 15.

2388 ■ Community Foundation of the Fox River Valley

111 W Downer Place, Ste. 312
Aurora, IL 60506-6106
E-mail: info@communityfoundationfrv.org
URL: http://www.communityfoundationfrv.org

2389 ■ Community Foundation of the Fox River Valley Scholarships *(Undergraduate/Scholarship)*

Purpose: To enhance and support the quality of life in the Fox River Valley of Illinois. **Focus:** General studies. **Qualif.:** Applicants must be students who will attend an accredited institution of higher learning on a full-time basis and whose permanent residence is within the Foundation's service area. **Criteria:** Recipients are selected based on academic ability and financial need.

Funds Avail.: No specific amount. **To Apply:** Applicants must submit a completed application form. **Contact:** 630-896-7800.

2390 ■ Community Foundation for Greater New Haven

70 Audubon St.
New Haven, CT 06510-9755
Ph: (203)777-2386
Fax: (203)787-6584
E-mail: contactus@cfgnh.org
URL: http://www.cfgnh.org

2391 ■ Bambey Bailey Scholarships
(Undergraduate/Scholarship)

Purpose: To create positive and sustainable change in Greater New Haven by increasing the amount of and

Awards are arranged alphabetically below their administering organizations

enhancing the impact of community philanthropy and to provide college scholarships based on financial need. **Focus:** General studies. **Qualif.:** Applicants must be students from New Haven who may not consider college as an option; must demonstrate an interest and ability in writing; must attend or plan to attend Wellesley College. **Criteria:** Recipients are selected based on financial need.

Funds Avail.: No specific amount. **To Apply:** Applicants must complete the application form and attach a personal essay; academic verification; letter of recommendation; and Parent/Guardian IRS Form. **Deadline:** March 21. **Contact:** 203-777-7097; 203-787-6584.

2392 ■ George J. Bysiewicz Scholarship Fund *(Undergraduate/Scholarship)*

Purpose: To create positive and sustainable change in Greater New Haven by increasing the amount of and enhancing the impact of community philanthropy. **Focus:** General studies. **Qualif.:** Applicants must be students from New Haven, Catholic School planning to attend Sacred Heart Academy and Notre Dame High School. **Criteria:** Recipients are selected based on financial need.

Funds Avail.: No specific amount. **To Apply:** Applicants must complete the application form and attach a personal essay; academic verification; letter of recommendation; and Parent/Guardian IRS Form. **Deadline:** March 21. **Contact:** 203-777-7097; 203-787-6584.

2393 ■ Murtha Cullina Scholarships *(Undergraduate/Scholarship)*

Purpose: To create positive and sustainable change in Greater New Haven by increasing the amount of and enhancing the impact of community philanthropy. **Focus:** General Studies. **Qualif.:** Applicants must be students from the greater New Haven area planning to attend a college or university. **Criteria:** Recipients are selected based on financial need.

Funds Avail.: No specific amount. **To Apply:** Applicants must complete the application form and attach a personal essay; academic verification; letter of recommendation; and Parent/Guardian IRS Form. **Deadline:** March 21. **Contact:** 203-777-7097; 203-787-6584.

2394 ■ John S. Martinez and Family Scholarships Fund *(Undergraduate/Scholarship)*

Purpose: To create positive and sustainable change in Greater New Haven by increasing the amount of and enhancing the impact of community philanthropy. **Focus:** General studies. **Qualif.:** Applicants must be students in an institution or university. **Criteria:** Recipients are selected based on financial need.

Funds Avail.: No specific amount. **To Apply:** Applicants must complete the application form and must attach a personal essay; academic verification; letter of recommendation; and Parent/Guardian IRS Form. **Deadline:** March 21. **Contact:** 203-777-7097; 203-787-6584.

2395 ■ Curtis M. Saulsbury Scholarship Fund *(Undergraduate/Scholarship)*

Purpose: To create positive and sustainable change in Greater New Haven by increasing the amount of and enhancing the impact of community philanthropy. **Focus:** Music. **Qualif.:** Applicants must be graduating from secondary school in the region serviced by the community foundation. **Criteria:** Recipients are selected based on financial need.

Funds Avail.: No specific amount. **To Apply:** Applicants must complete the application form and attach a personal essay; academic verification; letter of recommendation; and Parent/Guardian IRS Form. **Deadline:** March 21. **Contact:** 203-777-7097; 203-787-6584.

2396 ■ Charles L. Terrell/New Haven Savings Bank Scholarship Fund *(Undergraduate/Scholarship)*

Purpose: To create positive and sustainable change in Greater New Haven by increasing the amount of and enhancing the impact of community philanthropy. **Focus:** General studies. **Qualif.:** Applicants must be high school students with financial need who have demonstrated a commitment to community service. **Criteria:** Recipients are selected based on financial need and demonstrated commitment to community service.

Funds Avail.: No specific amount. **To Apply:** Applicants must complete the application form and attach a personal essay; academic verification; letter of recommendation; and parent/Guardian IRS Form. **Deadline:** March 21. **Contact:** 203-777-7097; 203-787-6584.

2397 ■ Ruth and Sherman Zudekoff Scholarships *(Undergraduate/Scholarship)*

Purpose: To create positive and sustainable change in Greater New Haven by increasing the amount of and enhancing the impact of community philanthropy. **Focus:** General studies. **Qualif.:** Applicants must be students graduating from secondary school in regions served by the foundation. **Criteria:** Recipients are selected based on financial need.

Funds Avail.: No specific amount. **To Apply:** Applicants must complete the application form and attach a personal essay; academic verification; letter of recommendation; and Parent/Guardian IRS Form. **Deadline:** March 21. **Contact:** 203-777-7097; 203-787-6584.

2398 ■ Community Foundation of Greene County

PO Box 768
Waynesburg, PA 15370
Ph: (724)627-2010
Fax: (724)627-2011
E-mail: cfgcpa@gmail.com
URL: http://www.cfgcpa.org

2399 ■ The William H. Davis, Jr. Scholarship Fund *(Undergraduate/Scholarship)*

Purpose: To maintain and enhance the educational, social, cultural, health and civic resources of the community through support of qualified non-profit organizations. **Focus:** General studies. **Qualif.:** Applicants must be graduating seniors of Southeastern Greene School District or its equivalent; must be accepted students at Westmoreland County Community College as full-time students or registered for a minimum of 12 credit hours; must be qualified for no more than three-quarters financial aid. **Criteria:** Recipients are selected based on financial need.

Funds Avail.: $500. **Number Awarded:** 2. **To Apply:** Applicants must submit five copies of their FAFSA, Special Condition Form, verification of GPA from the guidance counselor, copy of acceptance letter from WCCC and attendance record.

Awards are arranged alphabetically below their administering organizations

2400 ■ The Thelma S. Hoge Memorial Scholarship Fund *(Undergraduate/Scholarship)*

Purpose: To maintain and enhance the educational, social, cultural, health and civic resources of the community through support of qualified non-profit organizations. **Focus:** General studies. **Qualif.:** Applicants must be graduating seniors from West Greene; must be accepted at a post-secondary or four-year college degree program; must have a minimum GPA of 3.0. **Criteria:** Recipients are selected based on essay, results of an interview and completed application.

Funds Avail.: $1,000. **To Apply:** Applicants must provide a brief essay about themselves; copy of high school transcript and two character references.

2401 ■ The Renardo A. Matteucci Scholarship Fund *(Undergraduate/Scholarship)*

Purpose: To provide an annual need-based scholarship to the Jefferson-Morgan High School. **Focus:** General studies. **Qualif.:** Applicants must be graduating students from Jefferson-Morgan High School; must be planning to pursue a Bachelor Degree, an Associate Degree or a Diploma from a trade school; must have a minimum GPA of 2.75. **Criteria:** Recipients are selected based on financial need.

Funds Avail.: $1,000. **To Apply:** Applicants must submit five copies of their FAFSA, Special Condition Form, verification of their GPA from guidance counselor, an official attendance record and post-secondary acceptance letter. **Deadline:** April 15.

2402 ■ The Walter Samek III Memorial Scholarship Fund *(Undergraduate/Scholarship)*

Purpose: To assist graduating senior class members of Carmichaels High School to continue post-secondary education. **Focus:** General studies. **Qualif.:** Applicants must be Carmichaels senior boys or girls who are enrolled in an approved post-secondary college/university; must have a 3.5 GPA. **Criteria:** Recipients are selected based on financial need and community service.

Funds Avail.: No specific amount. **To Apply:** Applicants must submit a completed application form. **Deadline:** April 15.

2403 ■ The Community Foundation of Middle Tennessee

3833 Cleghorn Ave., Ste. 400
Nashville, TN 37215-2519
Ph: (615)321-4939
Free: 888-540-5200
E-mail: mail@cfmt.org
URL: http://www.cfmt.org

2404 ■ Lt. Holly Adams Memorial Scholarship *(Undergraduate/Scholarship)*

Purpose: To help students in planning their postsecondary education. **Focus:** General studies. **Qualif.:** Applicants must be students from the Page High School area in Williamson County who not only achieve, but also possess the integrity, courage, and caring spirit to help others achieve. **Criteria:** Recipients are selected based on financial need.

Funds Avail.: No specific amount. **To Apply:** Applicants must complete the application form. Applicants must submit two applicant appraisals; transcript of grades; student essay describing educational plans and how these will help in career goals. Applicants must submit one recent photograph. **Deadline:** March 15. **Contact:** pcole@cfmt.org

2405 ■ Kathy D. and Stephen J. Anderson Scholarships *(Undergraduate/Scholarship)*

Purpose: To help students in planning their postsecondary education. **Focus:** General studies. **Qualif.:** Applicants must be graduate students from the Page High School area in Williamson County, who have attended for a minimum of three years. Applicants must be in good standing as citizens in the school and community. Applicants must have a 3.2 or better GPA and minimum ACT score of 22 or SAT of 1100. Applicants must be involved in at least one extracurricular activity. **Criteria:** Recipients are selected based on financial need.

Funds Avail.: Maximum amount of $10,000. **To Apply:** Applicants must complete the application form. Applicants must submit two applicant appraisals; transcript of grades; student essay describing educational plans and how these will help in career goals. Applicants must submit one recent photograph. **Deadline:** March 15. **Contact:** pcole@cfmt.org

2406 ■ Belmont University Commercial Music Scholarships *(Undergraduate/Scholarship)*

Purpose: To help students in planning their postsecondary education. **Focus:** Music. **Qualif.:** Applicants must be high school seniors, college freshmen, sophomores, or juniors accepted to or attending Belmont University in Nashville, Tennessee as commercial music majors. **Criteria:** Recipients are selected based on financial need.

Funds Avail.: No specific amount. **To Apply:** Applicants must complete the application form. Applicants must submit two applicant appraisals; transcript of grades; student essay describing their educational plans and how these will help in career goals. Applicants must submit one recent photograph. **Deadline:** March 15. **Contact:** pcole@cfmt.org

2407 ■ George Oliver Benton Memorial Scholarships *(Undergraduate/Scholarship)*

Purpose: To help students in planning their postsecondary education. **Focus:** General studies. **Qualif.:** Applicants must be students who attend an accredited fouryear college/university in the state of Tennessee. Applicants must be residents of Tennessee. **Criteria:** Recipients are selected based on financial need.

Funds Avail.: No specific amount. **To Apply:** Applicants must complete the application form. Applicants must submit two applicant appraisals; transcript of grades; student essay describing educational plans and how these will help in career goals. Applicants must submit one recent photograph. **Deadline:** March 15. **Contact:** pcole@cfmt.org

2408 ■ Dody Boyd Scholarships *(Undergraduate/Scholarship)*

Purpose: To help students in planning their postsecondary education. **Focus:** General studies. **Qualif.:** Applicants must be seniors graduating from Cheatham County Central High School and wishing to attend a two-year community college/technical school or four-year university. Applicants must have a GPA of at least 2.5 or better and an ACT score of 20 or better. **Criteria:** Recipients are selected based on financial need.

Funds Avail.: No specific amount. **To Apply:** Applicants must complete the application form. Applicants must submit two applicant appraisals; transcript of grades; student essay describing educational plans and how these will help in

Awards are arranged alphabetically below their administering organizations

career goals. Applicants must submit one recent photograph. **Deadline:** March 15. **Contact:** pcole@cfmt.org

2409 ■ JoAhn Brown-Nash Memorial Scholarships *(Undergraduate/Scholarship)*

Purpose: To help students in planning their postsecondary education. **Focus:** General studies. **Qualif.:** Applicants must be female students at Fisk University, entering their junior year, who exemplify outstanding leadership skills, with a GPA of 3.2 or above. **Criteria:** Recipients are selected based on the financial need.

Funds Avail.: No specific amount. **To Apply:** Applicants must complete the application form. Applicants must submit two applicant appraisals; transcript of grades; student essay describing educational plans and how these will help in career goals. Applicants must submit one recent photograph. **Deadline:** March 15. **Contact:** pcole@cfmt.org

2410 ■ William and Clara Bryan Scholarships *(Undergraduate/Scholarship)*

Purpose: To help students in planning their postsecondary education. **Focus:** General studies. **Qualif.:** Applicants must be high school seniors, or college freshmen, sophomores or juniors who are from Giles County, Tennessee and have lived there for the majority of their pre-college schooling. **Criteria:** Recipients are selected based on merit and financial need.

Funds Avail.: No specific amount. **To Apply:** Applicants must complete the application form. Applicants must submit two applicant appraisals; transcript of grades; student essay describing educational plans and how these will help in career goals. Applicants must submit one recent photograph. **Deadline:** March 15. **Contact:** pcole@cfmt.org

2411 ■ Leigh Carter Scholarships *(Undergraduate/Scholarship)*

Purpose: To help students in planning their postsecondary education. **Focus:** Health care services. **Qualif.:** Applicants must be full-time students attending one of the nation's accredited chiropractic colleges or universities. **Criteria:** Recipients are selected based on the financial need, interest in health care delivery, extracurricular and civic participation.

Funds Avail.: No specific amount. **To Apply:** Applicants must complete the application form. Applicants must submit two applicant appraisals; transcript of grades; student essay describing educational plans and how these will help in career goals. Applicants must submit one recent photograph. **Deadline:** March 15. **Contact:** pcole@cfmt.org

2412 ■ Cheatham County Scholarships *(Undergraduate/Scholarship)*

Purpose: To help students in planning their postsecondary education. **Focus:** General Studies. **Qualif.:** Applicants must be Cheatham County, Tennessee residents for a minimum period of one year. Applicants must have a high school diploma or GED with a GPA of 2.0 or better. Applicants must attend an accredited college, university, or technical school and maintain a grade point average of 2.0 or better. **Criteria:** Recipients are selected based on financial need, extracurricular and civic participation.

Funds Avail.: No specific amount. **To Apply:** Applicants must complete the application form. Applicants must submit two applicant appraisals; transcript of grades; student essay describing educational plans and how these will help in career goals. Applicants must submit one recent photograph. **Deadline:** March 15. **Contact:** pcole@cfmt.org

2413 ■ Choose Your Future Scholarships *(Undergraduate/Scholarship)*

Purpose: To help students in planning their postsecondary education. **Focus:** General studies. **Qualif.:** Applicants must be graduates of the Metropolitan Nashville Public School of Davidson County with a minimum GPA of 2.5 and a score of 21 on the ACT. Applicants must be attending a college or university in the United States. **Criteria:** Recipients are selected based on financial need, extracurricular and civic participation.

Funds Avail.: No specific amount. **To Apply:** Applicants must complete the application form. Applicants must submit two applicant appraisals; transcript of grades; student essay describing educational plans and how these will help in career goals. Applicants must submit one recent photograph. **Deadline:** March 15. **Contact:** pcole@cfmt.org

2414 ■ Howard A. Clark Horticulture Scholarships *(Undergraduate/Scholarship)*

Purpose: To help students in planning their postsecondary education. **Focus:** Horticulture. **Qualif.:** Applicants must be graduating seniors from Avery County High School, North Carolina, attending a two or four-year college to study horticulture or agriculture. Applicants must have at least a 2.5 GPA in high school. **Criteria:** Recipients are selected based on financial need, extracurricular and civic participation.

Funds Avail.: No specific amount. **To Apply:** Applicants must complete the application form. Applicants must submit two applicant appraisals; transcript of grades; student essay describing educational plans and how these will help in career goals. Applicants must submit one recent photograph. **Deadline:** March 15. **Contact:** pcole@cfmt.org

2415 ■ The Community Foundation DBI Scholarships *(Undergraduate/Scholarship)*

Purpose: To help students in planning their postsecondary education. **Focus:** General studies. **Qualif.:** Applicants must be graduating high school seniors, undergraduates and graduates enrolling or enrolled at an accredited college/university, junior college or technical/vocational school on a full-time basis, maintaining a B average or better. **Criteria:** Recipients are selected based on financial need, extracurricular and civic participation.

Funds Avail.: No specific amount. **To Apply:** Applicants must complete the application form. Applicants must submit two applicant appraisals; transcript of grades; student essay describing educational plans and how these will help in career goals. Applicants must submit one recent photograph. **Deadline:** March 15. **Contact:** pcole@cfmt.org

2416 ■ The Community Foundation Student Education Loans *(Undergraduate/Loan)*

Purpose: To help students in planning their postsecondary education. **Focus:** General studies. **Qualif.:** Applicants must be young men or women whose parents have discontinued financial support for their education because they are gay or lesbian. **Criteria:** Recipients are selected based on financial need, extracurricular and civic participation.

Funds Avail.: No specific amount. **To Apply:** Applicants must complete the application form. Applicants must submit two applicant appraisals; transcript of grades; student essay describing the educational plans and how these will

Awards are arranged alphabetically below their administering organizations

help in career goals. Applicants must submit one recent photograph. **Deadline:** March 15. **Contact:** pcole@cfmt.org

2417 ■ Colonel Richard M. Dawson Scholarships *(Undergraduate/Scholarship)*

Purpose: To help students in planning their postsecondary education. **Focus:** Criminal justice. **Qualif.:** Applicants must be children of employees of the Tennessee Highway Patrol who serve in uniform, undercover, or plainclothes. Applicants must be rising sophomores, juniors, or seniors in college who demonstrate a commitment to a career in criminal justice through their course of study. **Criteria:** Recipients are selected based on financial need, extracurricular and civic participation.

Funds Avail.: No specific amount. **To Apply:** Applicants must complete the application form. Applicants must submit two applicant appraisals; transcript of grades; student essay describing educational plans and how these will help in career goals. Applicants must submit one recent photograph. **Deadline:** March 15. **Contact:** pcole@cfmt.org

2418 ■ B.J. Dean Scholarships *(Undergraduate/Scholarship)*

Purpose: To help students in planning their postsecondary education. **Focus:** General studies. **Qualif.:** Applicants must be a female preparing for full-time ministry, but scholarship is not limited to those seeking ordination or serving in any particular denomination. Applicant must be a resident of Tennessee or Texas or be enrolled in Yale Dignity School. **Criteria:** Recipients are selected based on financial need, extracurricular and civic participation.

Funds Avail.: No specific amount. **To Apply:** Applicants must complete the application form. Applicants must submit two applicant appraisals; transcript of grades; student essay describing educational plans and how these will help in career goals. Applicants must submit one recent photograph. **Deadline:** March 15. **Contact:** pcole@cfmt.org

2419 ■ Jimmy Edwards Scholarships *(Undergraduate/Scholarship)*

Purpose: To help students in planning their postsecondary education. **Focus:** General studies. **Qualif.:** Applicants must be past students or graduates of Donelson High School, and descendents of alumni of Donelson High School. **Criteria:** Recipients are selected based on financial need, extracurricular and civic participation.

Funds Avail.: No specific amount. **To Apply:** Applicants must complete the application form. Applicants must submit two applicant appraisals; transcript of grades; student essay describing educational plans and how these will help in career goals. Applicants must submit one recent photograph. **Deadline:** March 15. **Contact:** pcole@cfmt.org

2420 ■ Fine Arts and Music Scholarships *(Undergraduate/Scholarship)*

Purpose: To help students in planning their postsecondary education. **Focus:** Fine arts; Music. **Qualif.:** Applicants must be rising sophomores, juniors and seniors in college, and graduate students at an accredited college, university, or institute full-time or part-time (6 or more credits). **Criteria:** Recipients are selected based on financial need, extracurricular and civic participation.

Funds Avail.: No specific amount. **To Apply:** Applicants must complete the application form. Applicants must submit two applicant appraisals; transcript of grades; student essay describing educational plans and how these will help in career goals. Applicants must submit one recent photograph. **Deadline:** March 15. **Contact:** pcole@cfmt.org

2421 ■ Pauline LaFon Gore Scholarships *(Undergraduate/Scholarship)*

Purpose: To help students in planning their postsecondary education. **Focus:** General studies. **Qualif.:** Applicants must be high school seniors and current college underclassmen who are from Smith County, Tennessee and have lived there for the majority of their pre-college schooling. **Criteria:** Recipients are selected based on financial need, extracurricular and civic participation.

Funds Avail.: No specific amount. **To Apply:** Applicants must complete the application form. Applicants must submit two applicant appraisals; transcript of grades; student essay describing educational plans and how these will help in career goals. Applicants must submit one recent photograph. **Deadline:** March 15. **Contact:** pcole@cfmt.org

2422 ■ Frank and Charlene Harris Scholarships *(Undergraduate/Scholarship)*

Purpose: To help students in planning their postsecondary education. **Focus:** General studies. **Qualif.:** Applicants must be seniors of Cumberland Gap High School in Claiborne County, TN. Applicants should have a GPA of 3.0 or higher at the time of the application. **Criteria:** Recipients are selected based on financial need, extracurricular and civic participation.

Funds Avail.: No specific amount. **To Apply:** Applicants must complete the application form. Applicants must submit two applicant appraisals; transcript of grades; student essay describing educational plans and how these will help in career goals. Applicants must submit one recent photograph. **Deadline:** March 15. **Contact:** pcole@cfmt.org

2423 ■ Regina Higdon Scholarships *(Undergraduate/Scholarship)*

Purpose: To help students in planning their postsecondary education. To help graduates of Christ the King School of Nashville, Tennessee who have a desire to attend either Father Ryan High School or St. Cecilia Academy, both in Nashville, Tennessee. **Focus:** Art. **Qualif.:** Applicants must be graduating eighth graders of Christ the King School and/or former graduates of Christ the King School attending Father Ryan High School or St. Cecilia Academy. Applicants must have at least a 2.5 GPA or equivalent. Applicants must exhibit a love for the arts. **Criteria:** Recipients are selected based on financial need, extracurricular and civic participation.

Funds Avail.: No specific amount. **To Apply:** Applicants must complete the application form. Applicants must submit two applicant appraisals; transcript of grades; student essay describing educational plans and how these will help in career goals. Applicants must submit one recent photograph. **Deadline:** March 15. **Contact:** pcole@cfmt.org

2424 ■ Jennifer Ingrum Scholarships *(Undergraduate/Scholarship)*

Purpose: To help students in planning their postsecondary education. **Focus:** General studies. **Qualif.:** Applicants must be students who qualify academically for college but need financial assistance. **Criteria:** Recipients are selected based on financial need, extracurricular and civic participation.

Funds Avail.: $2,000. **Number Awarded:** 2. **To Apply:** Applicants must complete the application form. Applicants

Awards are arranged alphabetically below their administering organizations

must submit two applicant appraisals; transcript of grades; student essay describing educational plans and how these will help in career goals. Applicants must submit one recent photograph. **Deadline:** March 15. **Contact:** pcole@cfmt.org

2425 ■ Maude Keisling/Cumberland County Extension Homemakers Scholarships
(Undergraduate/Scholarship)

Purpose: To help students in planning their postsecondary education. **Focus:** Ecology; Education; Social work. **Qualif.:** Applicants must be residents of Cumberland County, Tennessee for a period of four years or more. Applicants must be graduating high school seniors, GED graduates, or current college undergraduates with a GPA of 2.5 or better. Applicants must pursue a field of study such as, but not limited to, human ecology, family and consumer science, education, and social services. **Criteria:** Recipients are selected based on financial need, extracurricular and civic participation.

Funds Avail.: No specific amount. **To Apply:** Applicants must complete the application form. Applicants must submit two applicant appraisals; transcript of grades; student essay describing educational plans and how these will help in career goals. Applicants must submit one recent photograph. **Deadline:** March 15. **Contact:** pcole@cfmt.org

2426 ■ Knox-Hume Scholarships
(Undergraduate/Scholarship)

Purpose: To help students in planning their postsecondary education. **Focus:** General studies. **Qualif.:** Applicants must be graduates of Hume-Fogg High School who exhibit academic merit and financial need. **Criteria:** Recipients are selected based on financial need, extracurricular and civic participation.

Funds Avail.: No specific amount. **To Apply:** Applicants must complete the application form. Applicants must submit two applicant appraisals; transcript of grades; student essay describing educational plans and how these will help in career goals. Applicants must submit one recent photograph. **Deadline:** March 15. **Contact:** pcole@cfmt.org

2427 ■ Senator Carl O. Koella, Jr. Memorial Scholarships *(Undergraduate/Scholarship)*

Purpose: To help students in planning their postsecondary education. **Focus:** Law. **Qualif.:** Applicants must be legislative interns, either public or private, currently enrolled or planning to enroll in a four-year college the year of the application. **Criteria:** Recipients are selected based on financial need, extracurricular and civic participation.

Funds Avail.: No specific amount. **To Apply:** Applicants must complete the application form. Applicants must submit two applicant appraisals; transcript of grades; student essay describing educational plans and how these will help in career goals. Applicants must submit one recent photograph. **Deadline:** March 15. **Contact:** pcole@cfmt.org

2428 ■ Michael B. Kruse Scholarships
(Undergraduate/Scholarship)

Purpose: To help students in planning their postsecondary education. **Focus:** Accounting. **Qualif.:** Applicants must be rising juniors, seniors, and graduate students majoring in accounting. Applicants must be residents of Tennessee and attend an accredited college/university in the State of Tennessee. Applicants must maintain a minimum GPA of 3.2 or better. **Criteria:** Recipients are selected based on financial need, extracurricular and civic participation.

Funds Avail.: No specific amount. **To Apply:** Applicants must complete the application form. Applicants must submit two applicant appraisals; transcript of grades; student essay describing educational plans and how these will help in career goals. Applicants must submit one recent photograph. **Deadline:** March 15. **Contact:** pcole@cfmt.org

2429 ■ Heloise Werthan Kuhn Scholarships
(Undergraduate/Scholarship)

Purpose: To help students in planning their postsecondary education. **Focus:** General studies. **Qualif.:** Applicants must be pregnant or parenting teens. Applicants must be enrolled or planning to enroll in postsecondary education at an accredited college, university, junior college, technical school, or job training program as a way to increase their job skills and become more employable. **Criteria:** Recipients are selected based on financial need, extracurricular and civic participation.

Funds Avail.: No specific amount. **To Apply:** Applicants must complete the application form. Applicants must submit two applicant appraisals; transcript of grades; student essay describing the educational plans and how these will help in career goals. Applicants must submit one recent photograph. **Deadline:** March 15. **Contact:** pcole@cfmt.org

2430 ■ Diane G. Lowe and John Gomez, IV Scholarships *(Undergraduate/Scholarship)*

Purpose: To help students in planning their postsecondary education. To provide financial assistance to students who would be otherwise unable to take qualifying entrance exams to institutions of higher learning and to provide gifted students financial assistance to attend academic programs that offer intellecutally-accelerated content. **Focus:** General studies. **Qualif.:** Applicants must be students with financial need in Grades 6-12 who reside in Rutherford, Cannon, Dekalb, or Wilson Counties. **Criteria:** Recipients are selected based on financial need, extracurricular and civic participation.

Funds Avail.: No specific amount. **To Apply:** Applicants must complete the application form. Applicants must submit two applicant appraisals; transcript of grades; student essay describing educational plans and how these will help in career goals. Applicants must submit one recent photograph. **Deadline:** March 15. **Contact:** pcole@cfmt.org

2431 ■ Dr. Mac Scholarships *(Undergraduate/Scholarship)*

Purpose: To help students in planning their postsecondary education. **Focus:** Dentistry. **Qualif.:** Applicants must be enrolled at the University of Tennessee at Memphis School of Dentistry and entering their third year of school with a minimum of 2.7 GPA. **Criteria:** Recipients are selected based on financial need, extracurricular and civic participation.

Funds Avail.: No specific amount. **To Apply:** Applicants must complete the application form. Applicants must submit two applicant appraisals; transcript of grades; student essay describing educational plans and how these will help in career goals. Applicants must submit one recent photograph. **Deadline:** March 15. **Contact:** pcole@cfmt.org

2432 ■ Edna Martin Scholarships
(Undergraduate/Scholarship)

Purpose: To help students in planning their postsecondary education. **Focus:** Education. **Qualif.:** Applicants must be high school seniors, or individuals who previously gradu-

Awards are arranged alphabetically below their administering organizations

ated from the Davidson County-Metropolitan Nashville Public School System, who have a desire to pursue a career in teaching in elementary, middle, or high school. **Criteria:** Recipients are selected based on financial need, extracurricular and civic participation.

Funds Avail.: No specific amount. **To Apply:** Applicants must complete the application form. Applicants must submit two applicant appraisals; transcript of grades; student essay describing educational plans and how these will help in career goals. Applicants must submit one recent photograph. **Deadline:** March 15. **Contact:** pcole@cfmt.org

2433 ■ Juliann and Joseph Maxwell Scholarships *(Undergraduate/Scholarship)*

Purpose: To help students in planning their postsecondary education. **Focus:** General studies. **Qualif.:** Applicants must be high school seniors, college freshmen, sophomores, and juniors who are dependent children, including adopted and stepchildren of employees, or full-time or part-time employees of the Tractor Supply Company. **Criteria:** Recipients are selected based on financial need, extracurricular and civic participation.

Funds Avail.: No specific amount. **To Apply:** Applicants must complete the application form. Applicants must submit two applicant appraisals; transcript of grades; student essay describing their educational plans and how these will help in career goals. Applicants must submit one recent photograph. **Deadline:** March 15. **Contact:** pcole@cfmt.org

2434 ■ Juliann King Maxwell Scholarships for Students in White County, Arkansas *(Undergraduate/Scholarship)*

Purpose: To help students in planning their postsecondary education. **Focus:** General studies. **Qualif.:** Applicants must be graduating seniors from Riverview High School or prior recipients of this scholarship. **Criteria:** Recipients are selected based on financial need, extracurricular and civic participation.

Funds Avail.: No specific amount. **To Apply:** Applicants must complete the application form. Applicants must submit two applicant appraisals; transcript of grades; student essay describing educational plans and how these will help in career goals. Applicants must submit one recent photograph. **Deadline:** March 15. **Contact:** pcole@cfmt.org

2435 ■ John E. Mayfield ABLE Scholarships *(Undergraduate/Scholarship)*

Purpose: To help students in planning their postsecondary education. **Focus:** General studies. **Qualif.:** Applicants must be graduating seniors and be participants of the ABLE program. **Criteria:** Recipients are selected based on financial need, extracurricular and civic participation.

Funds Avail.: No specific amount. **To Apply:** Applicants must complete the application form. Applicants must submit two applicant appraisals; transcript of grades; student essay describing educational plans and how these will help in career goals. Applicants must submit one recent photograph. **Deadline:** March 15. **Contact:** pcole@cfmt.org

2436 ■ John E. Mayfield Scholarships for Cheatham County Central High School *(Undergraduate/Scholarship)*

Purpose: To help students in planning their postsecondary education. **Focus:** General studies. **Qualif.:** Applicants must be alumni and/or graduating seniors of Cheatham County Central High School in Cheatham County, Tennessee; Applicants must be residents of Cheatham County and have a grade point average of 2.0 or better. **Criteria:** Recipients are selected based on financial need, extracurricular and civic participation.

Funds Avail.: No specific amount. **To Apply:** Applicants must complete the application form. Applicants must submit two applicant appraisals; transcript of grades; student essay describing educational plans and how these will help in career goals. Applicants must submit one recent photograph. **Deadline:** March 15. **Contact:** pcole@cfmt.org

2437 ■ John E. Mayfield Scholarships for Harpeth High School *(Undergraduate/Scholarship)*

Purpose: To help students in planning their postsecondary education. **Focus:** General studies. **Qualif.:** Applicants must be alumni and/or graduating seniors of Harpeth High School in Cheatham County, Tennessee. Applicants must be residents of Cheatham County and have a GPA of 2.0 or better. **Criteria:** Recipients are selected based on financial need, extracurricular and civic participation.

Funds Avail.: No specific amount. **To Apply:** Applicants must complete the application form. Applicants must submit two applicant appraisals; transcript of grades; student essay describing educational plans and how these will help in career goals. Applicants must submit one recent photograph. **Deadline:** March 15. **Contact:** pcole@cfmt.org

2438 ■ John E. Mayfield Scholarships Pleasant View Christian School *(Undergraduate/Scholarship)*

Purpose: To help students in planning their postsecondary education. **Focus:** General studies. **Qualif.:** Applicants must be alumni and/or graduating seniors of Pleasant View Christian School in Cheatham County, Tennessee. Applicants must be residents of Cheatham County and have a GPA of 2.0 or better. **Criteria:** Recipients are selected based on financial need, extracurricular and civic participation.

Funds Avail.: No specific amount. **To Apply:** Applicants must complete the application form. Applicants must submit two applicant appraisals; transcript of grades; student essay describing educational plans and how these will help in career goals. Applicants must submit one recent photograph. **Deadline:** March 15. **Contact:** pcole@cfmt.org

2439 ■ John E. Mayfield Scholarships for Sycamore High School *(Undergraduate/Scholarship)*

Purpose: To help students in planning their postsecondary education. **Focus:** General studies. **Qualif.:** Applicants must be alumni and/or graduating seniors of Sycamore High School in Cheatham County, Tennessee. Applicants must be residents of Cheatham County and have a GPA of 2.0 or better. **Criteria:** Recipients are selected based on financial need, extracurricular and civic participation.

Funds Avail.: No specific amount. **To Apply:** Applicants must complete the application form. Applicants must submit two applicant appraisals; transcript of grades; student essay describing educational plans and how these will help in career goals. Applicants must submit one recent photograph. **Deadline:** March 15. **Contact:** pcole@cfmt.org

2440 ■ Archie Hartwell Nash Memorial Scholarships *(Undergraduate/Scholarship)*

Purpose: To help students in planning their postsecondary education. **Focus:** General studies. **Qualif.:** Applicants must be Middle Tennessee State University sophomores or above including graduate students who are working at a minimum of 20 hours and have a GPA of 2.0 or better. **Criteria:** Recipients are selected based on financial need, extracurricular and civic participation.

Funds Avail.: No specific amount. **To Apply:** Applicants must complete the application form. Applicants must submit two applicant appraisals; transcript of grades; student essay describing educational plans and how these will help in career goals. Applicants must submit one recent photograph. **Deadline:** March 15. **Contact:** pcole@cfmt.org

2441 ■ Jerry Newson Scholarships
(Undergraduate/Scholarship)

Purpose: To help students in planning their postsecondary education. **Focus:** General studies. **Qualif.:** Applicants must currently reside in Davidson County, Tennessee. High school graduates and adults are encouraged to apply. Applicants must be pursuing a degree in the social sciences or areas where they will be helping and giving back to their community. **Criteria:** Recipients are selected based on financial need, extracurricular and civic participation.

Funds Avail.: No specific amount. **To Apply:** Applicants must complete the application form. Applicants must submit two applicant appraisals; transcript of grades; student essay describing educational plans and how these will help in career goals. Applicants must submit one recent photograph. **Deadline:** March 15. **Contact:** pcole@cfmt.org

2442 ■ Eloise Pitts O'More Scholarships
(Undergraduate/Scholarship)

Purpose: To help students in planning their postsecondary education. **Focus:** Interior Design. **Qualif.:** Applicants must be interior design students who are currently pursuing a degree in interior design at O'More College of Design. Applicants must be classified as juniors or higher and have a GPA of 3.0 or higher at the time of application. Applicants must be actively participating members of either the American Society of Interior Design and/or International Design Association's student chapters. **Criteria:** Recipients are selected based on financial need, extracurricular and civic participation.

Funds Avail.: No specific amount. **To Apply:** Applicants must complete the application form. Applicants must submit two applicant appraisals; transcript of grades; student essay describing educational plans and how these will help in career goals. Applicants must submit one recent photograph. **Deadline:** March 15. **Contact:** pcole@cfmt.org

2443 ■ Buster Pool Memorial Scholarships
(Undergraduate/Scholarship)

Purpose: To help students in planning their postsecondary education. **Focus:** General studies. **Qualif.:** Applicants must be graduating seniors of Meridian High School in Meridian, Mississippi and/or previous recipients of this scholarship. Applicants must have a GPA of 2.5 or higher at the time of application. **Criteria:** Recipients are selected based on financial need, extracurricular and civic participation.

Funds Avail.: No specific amount. **To Apply:** Applicants must complete the application form. Applicants must submit two applicant appraisals; transcript of grades; student essay describing educational plans and how these will help in career goals. Applicants must submit one recent photograph. **Deadline:** March 15. **Contact:** pcole@cfmt.org

2444 ■ Barbara Hagan Richards Scholarships
(Undergraduate/Scholarship)

Purpose: To help students in planning their postsecondary education. **Focus:** General studies. **Qualif.:** Applicants must be graduating seniors, undergraduates, and/or graduate students currently enrolled in a college/university and/or alumni of any high school located and serving Giles County, Tennessee. Applicants must have a GPA of 3.0. **Criteria:** Recipients are selected based on financial need, extracurricular and civic participation.

Funds Avail.: No specific amount. **To Apply:** Applicants must complete the application form. Applicants must submit two applicant appraisals; transcript of grades; student essay describing educational plans and how these will help in career goals. Applicants must submit one recent photograph. **Deadline:** March 15. **Contact:** pcole@cfmt.org

2445 ■ James Edward "Bill" Richards Scholarships *(Undergraduate/Scholarship)*

Purpose: To help students in planning their postsecondary education. **Focus:** General studies. **Qualif.:** Applicants must be graduating seniors, undergraduates, and/or alumni of East High School in Nashville, Tennessee. Applicants must have a GPA of at least 3.0. **Criteria:** Recipients are selected based on financial need, extracurricular and civic participation.

Funds Avail.: No specific amount. **To Apply:** Applicants must complete the application form. Applicants must submit two applicant appraisals; transcript of grades; student essay describing educational plans and how these will help in career goals. Applicants must submit one recent photograph. **Deadline:** March 15. **Contact:** pcole@cfmt.org

2446 ■ Meyer and Dorothy Silverman Scholarships *(Undergraduate/Scholarship)*

Purpose: To help students in planning their postsecondary education. **Focus:** General studies. **Qualif.:** Applicants must be students in Grade 7 to 12 in Oak Ridge Public Schools who are committed to developing their talents as string instrument players but who, otherwise, would be financially unable to take private string instruction. **Criteria:** Recipients are selected based on financial need, extracurricular and civic participation.

Funds Avail.: No specific amount. **To Apply:** Applicants must complete the application form. Applicants must submit two applicant appraisals; transcript of grades; student essay describing educational plans and how these will help in career goals. Applicants must submit one recent photograph. **Deadline:** March 15. **Contact:** pcole@cfmt.org

2447 ■ Drue Smith/Society of Professional Journalists Scholarships *(Undergraduate/Scholarship)*

Purpose: To help students in planning their postsecondary education. **Focus:** Journalism. **Qualif.:** Applicants must be college juniors, seniors or graduate students who have graduated from high school in Middle Tennessee and have chosen journalism or broadcast news for a career, or mid-career working journalists who seek training to develop professionally or further their careers. **Criteria:** Recipients are selected based on financial need, extracurricular and civic participation.

Funds Avail.: No specific amount. **To Apply:** Applicants must complete the application form. Applicants must submit two applicant appraisals; transcript of grades; student essay describing educational plans and how these will help in career goals. Applicants must submit one recent photograph. **Deadline:** March 15. **Contact:** pcole@cfmt.org

2448 ■ Richie Stevenson Scholarships
(Undergraduate/Scholarship)

Purpose: To help students in planning their postsecondary education. **Focus:** General studies. **Qualif.:** Applicants must be graduates of Benton Hall School who wish to attend a technical school, vocational school, community college, junior or four-year college or university. **Criteria:** Recipients are selected based on the financial need, extracurricular and civic participation.

Funds Avail.: No specific amount. **To Apply:** Applicants must complete the application form. Applicants must submit two applicant appraisals; transcript of grades; student essay describing educational plans and how these will help in career goals. Applicants must submit one recent photograph. **Deadline:** March 15. **Contact:** pcole@cfmt.org

2449 ■ Tennessee Trucking Association Scholarships *(Undergraduate/Scholarship)*

Purpose: To help students in planning their postsecondary education. **Focus:** General studies. **Qualif.:** Applicants must be Tennessee residents who are dependent children, spouses or employees who are members in good standing of the Tennessee Trucking Association. Applicants must be entering their junior or senior years at accredited colleges or universities located in the State of Tennessee. **Criteria:** Recipients are selected based on financial need, extracurricular and civic participation.

Funds Avail.: No specific amount. **To Apply:** Applicants must complete the application form. Applicants must submit two applicant appraisals; transcript of grades; student essay describing the educational plans and how these will help in career goals. Applicants must submit one recent photograph. **Deadline:** March 15. **Contact:** pcole@cfmt.org

2450 ■ Emmett H. Turner Scholarships *(Undergraduate/Scholarship)*

Purpose: To help students in planning their postsecondary education. **Focus:** Criminal justice. **Qualif.:** Applicants must be students enrolling or currently enrolled at Tennessee University in the Criminal Justice program. **Criteria:** Recipients are selected based on financial need, extracurricular and civic participation.

Funds Avail.: No specific amount. **To Apply:** Applicants must complete the application form. Applicants must submit two applicant appraisals; transcript of grades; student essay describing educational plans and how these will help in career goals. Applicants must submit one recent photograph. **Deadline:** March 15. **Contact:** pcole@cfmt.org

2451 ■ Teddy Wilburn Scholarships *(Undergraduate/Scholarship)*

Purpose: To help students in planning their postsecondary education. **Focus:** General studies. **Qualif.:** Applicants must be students enrolling or currently enrolled at Tennessee State University or Vanderbilt University; Applicants must have at least a B grade average overall during the last two years of high school; must have attended high school within the 40 counties of Middle Tennessee for the majority of high school. **Criteria:** Recipients are selected based on financial need, extracurricular and civic participation.

Funds Avail.: No specific amount. **To Apply:** Applicants must complete the application form. Applicants must submit two applicant appraisals; transcript of grades; student essay describing educational plans and how these will help in career goals. Applicants must submit one recent photograph. **Deadline:** March 15. **Contact:** pcole@cfmt.org

2452 ■ The Woman's Club of Nashville Scholarships *(Undergraduate/Scholarship)*

Purpose: To help students in planning their postsecondary education. **Focus:** General studies. **Qualif.:** Applicants must be women residing in Davidson County, Tennessee. Applicants must be graduating high school seniors or high school graduates with a GPA of 3.0 or higher. **Criteria:** Recipients are selected based on financial need, extracurricular and civic participation.

Funds Avail.: No specific amount. **To Apply:** Applicants must complete the application form. Applicants must submit two applicant appraisals; transcript of grades; student essay describing educational plans and how these will help in career goals. Applicants must submit one recent photograph. **Deadline:** March 15. **Contact:** pcole@cfmt.org

2453 ■ John W. Work III Memorial Foundation Scholarships *(Undergraduate/Scholarship)*

Purpose: To help students in planning their postsecondary education. **Focus:** Music. **Qualif.:** Applicants must be undergraduate juniors, seniors, or graduate students pursuing a degree in music at an accredited university, college or institute. Applicants must have a B average and demonstrate potential for excellence in music. Special preference will be given to African Americans. **Criteria:** Recipients are selected based on financial need, extracurricular and civic participation.

Funds Avail.: No specific amount. **To Apply:** Applicants must complete the application form. Applicants must submit two applicant appraisals; transcript of grades; student essay describing educational plans and how these will help in career goals. Applicants must submit one recent photograph. **Deadline:** March 15. **Contact:** pcole@cfmt.org

2454 ■ Community Foundation of Northern Illinois

946 N 2nd St.
Rockford, IL 61107
Ph: (815)962-2110
Fax: (815)962-2116
URL: http://www.cfnil.org

2455 ■ Charles Lee Anderson Memorial Scholarship *(Undergraduate/Scholarship)*

Purpose: To serve the four county area (Boone, Ogle, Stephenson and Winnebago) through philanthropy; to provide leadership in meeting charitable needs. **Focus:** Education. **Qualif.:** Applicants must be Rock Valley or Sycamore High School graduating seniors who will enter a college or university to pursue a degree in education. **Criteria:** Recipients are selected based on demonstrated optimism, determination and love of neighbor.

Funds Avail.: No specific amount. **To Apply:** Applicants must submit a completed application form, verification form, an official college transcript in a sealed envelope and two completed recommendation forms. **Deadline:** March 1. **Contact:** jpatterson@cfnil.org.

2456 ■ Richard L. Bernardi Memorial Scholarship *(Undergraduate/Scholarship)*

Purpose: To serve the four county area (Boone, Ogle, Stephenson and Winnebago) through philanthropy; to provide leadership in meeting charitable needs and to be a responsible steward to the Foundation's donors and of the Foundation's endowment. **Focus:** General studies. **Qualif.:** Applicants must be attending or planning to attend Rock Valley College; must be committed to completing a bachelor's degree; must have an at least 2.0 GPA. **Criteria:** Recipients are selected based on demonstrated enthusiasm and leadership.

Awards are arranged alphabetically below their administering organizations

Funds Avail.: No specific amount. **To Apply:** Applicants must submit a completed application form, verification form, an official college transcript in a sealed envelope and two completed recommendation forms. **Deadline:** March 1. **Contact:** jpatterson@cfnil.org.

2457 ■ Lindsay Buster Memorial Scholarship *(Undergraduate/Scholarship)*

Purpose: To serve the four county area (Boone, Ogle, Stephenson and Winnebago) through philanthropy; to provide leadership in meeting charitable needs and to be a responsible steward to the Foundation's donors and of the Foundation's endowment. **Focus:** General studies. **Qualif.:** Applicants must be graduating senior athletes from Jefferson High school who have participated in high school sports for a minimum of three years including their senior year; must have 2.5 or higher cumulative GPA; must have plans to attend a two-or-four year college or university. **Criteria:** Recipients are selected based on financial need.

Funds Avail.: No specific amount. **To Apply:** Applicants must submit a completed application form, verification form, an official transcript in a sealed envelope and two letters of recommendation. **Deadline:** March 1. **Contact:** jpatterson@cfnil.org.

2458 ■ Joe Carnes Scholarship *(Undergraduate/Scholarship)*

Purpose: To serve the four county area (Boone, Ogle, Stephenson and Winnebago) through philanthropy; to provide leadership in meeting charitable needs and to be a responsible steward to the Foundation's donors and of the Foundation's endowment. **Focus:** General studies. **Qualif.:** Applicants must be graduating senior students at Crystal Lake South High School with a GPA of at least 3.0. **Criteria:** Recipients are selected based on financial need and involvement in school, community and/or church activities.

Funds Avail.: No specific amount. **To Apply:** Applicants must submit a completed application form, verification form, an official transcript in a sealed envelope, two letters of recommendation and a copy of their FAFSA. **Deadline:** March 1. **Contact:** jpatterson@cfnil.org.

2459 ■ May Cassioppi Scholarship *(Undergraduate/Scholarship)*

Purpose: To serve the four county area (Boone, Ogle, Stephenson and Winnebago) through philanthropy; to provide leadership in meeting charitable needs and to be a responsible steward to the Foundation's donors and of the Foundation's endowment. **Focus:** General studies. **Qualif.:** Applicants must be former Guilford High school swimmers and/or divers; must exhibit character traits of strength, discipline, leadership, teamwork and loyalty. **Criteria:** Recipients are selected based on financial need.

Funds Avail.: No specific amount. **To Apply:** Applicants must submit a completed application form, verification form, an official transcript in a sealed envelope, two letters of recommendation and a copy of their FAFSA. **Deadline:** March 1. **Contact:** jpatterson@cfnil.org.

2460 ■ Harry H. and Floy B. Chapin Scholarship *(Undergraduate/Scholarship)*

Purpose: To serve the four county area (Boone, Ogle, Stephenson and Winnebago) through philanthropy; to provide leadership in meeting charitable needs and to be a responsible steward to the Foundation's donors and of the Foundation's endowment. **Focus:** General studies. **Qualif.:** Applicants must be graduating senior students from Durand, Dakota or Pecatonica High school; must rank in top 15% of graduating class; must plan to attend a recognized college or university. **Criteria:** Recipients are selected based on financial need and involvement in school, community and/or church activities.

Funds Avail.: No specific amount. **To Apply:** Applicants must submit a completed application form, verification form, an official transcript in a sealed envelope and two letters of recommendation. **Deadline:** March 1. **Contact:** jpatterson@cfnil.org.

2461 ■ Community Foundation Scholarships *(Undergraduate/Scholarship)*

Purpose: To serve the four county area (Boone, Ogle, Stephenson and Winnebago) through philanthropy; to provide leadership in meeting charitable needs and to be a responsible steward to the Foundation's donors and of the Foundation's endowment. **Focus:** General studies. **Qualif.:** Applicants must be graduating senior students and residents of Winnebago county; must have an at least 2.75 or higher GPA and have plans to attend a college, university or trade school. **Criteria:** Recipients are selected based on financial need.

Funds Avail.: No specific amount. **To Apply:** Applicants must submit a completed application form, verification form, an official transcript in a sealed envelope, two letters of recommendation and a copy of their FAFSA. **Deadline:** March 1. **Contact:** jpatterson@cfnil.org.

2462 ■ Margaret T. Craig Community Service Scholarship *(Undergraduate/Scholarship)*

Purpose: To serve the four county area (Boone, Ogle, Stephenson and Winnebago) through philanthropy; to provide leadership in meeting charitable needs and to be a responsible steward to the Foundation's donors and of the Foundation's endowment. **Focus:** General studies. **Qualif.:** Applicants must be high school graduates under the age of 23 or graduating seniors with a permanent address in Winnebago County; must have a plan to pursue a two or four-year degree at an accredited college, university or trade school; must have a minimum of 2.75 GPA. **Criteria:** Recipients are selected based on financial need, community involvement and strong commitment to improving the quality of life for people in their school, community and country.

Funds Avail.: No specific amount. **To Apply:** Applicants must submit a completed application form, verification form, an official transcript in a sealed envelope and two letters of recommendation. **Deadline:** March 1. **Contact:** jpatterson@cfnil.org.

2463 ■ William R. Durham/Theater Scholarship *(Undergraduate/Scholarship)*

Purpose: To serve the four county area (Boone, Ogle, Stephenson and Winnebago) through philanthropy; to provide leadership in meeting charitable needs and to be a responsible steward to the Foundation's donors and of the Foundation's endowment. **Focus:** Theater Arts. **Qualif.:** Applicants must be high school graduates or graduating seniors with a permanent address within Winnebago or Boone county with a GPA of at least 3.0 on a 4.0 scale; must plan to attend an accredited four-year college or university to obtain an M.A. or B.A.; must intend to teach theater or work professionally as a performer or technician in theater. **Criteria:** Recipients are selected based on financial need.

Awards are arranged alphabetically below their administering organizations

Funds Avail.: No specific amount. **To Apply:** Applicants must submit a completed application form, verification form, an official transcript in a sealed envelope and two letters of recommendation. **Deadline:** March 1. **Contact:** jpatterson@cfnil.org.

2464 ■ Helen R. Finley-Loescher Scholarships *(Undergraduate/Scholarship)*

Purpose: To serve the four county area (Boone, Ogle, Stephenson and Winnebago) through philanthropy; to provide leadership in meeting charitable needs and to be a responsible steward to the Foundation's donors and of the Foundation's endowment. **Focus:** Arts. **Qualif.:** Applicants must be Freeport High School students demonstrating academic achievement, self-motivation and an interest in the arts; must have exhibited artistic talent through participation in the high school arts curriculum; must have plans to pursue education in fine arts. **Criteria:** Recipients are selected based on financial need and demonstrated active involvement in social studies organizations, clubs and classes such as student government, political campaigns, social service and community service.

Funds Avail.: No specific amount. **To Apply:** Applicants must contact a Freeport High school Art Department Instructor for an application form. **Deadline:** March 1. **Contact:** jpatterson@cfnil.org.

2465 ■ John Flynn Memorial Scholarship *(Undergraduate/Scholarship)*

Purpose: To serve the four county area (Boone, Ogle, Stephenson and Winnebago) through philanthropy; to provide leadership in meeting charitable needs and to be a responsible steward to the Foundation's donors and of the Foundation's endowment; to provide educational resources to Pecatonica High School senior students who are pursuing higher education. **Focus:** General studies. **Qualif.:** Applicants must be graduating Pecatonica High School senior students who are pursuing higher education; must have at least a 2.0 GPA on a 4.0 scale and have been involved in community service. **Criteria:** Recipients are selected based on financial need.

Funds Avail.: No specific amount. **To Apply:** Applicants must submit a completed application form, verification form, an official transcript in a sealed envelope and two letters of recommendation. **Deadline:** March 1. **Contact:** jpatterson@cfnil.org.

2466 ■ Louise J. Franchini Rockford Police Department Scholarships *(Undergraduate/Scholarship)*

Purpose: To serve the four county area (Boone, Ogle, Stephenson and Winnebago) through philanthropy; to provide leadership in meeting charitable needs and to be a responsible steward to the Foundation's donors and of the Foundation's endowment. **Focus:** Law Enforcement. **Qualif.:** Applicants must be high school graduates currently enrolled in an accredited law enforcement program or high school seniors who are planning to pursue a career in law enforcement; must reside in Winnebago County. **Criteria:** Recipients are selected based on financial need.

Funds Avail.: No specific amount. **To Apply:** Applicants must submit a completed application form, verification form, an official transcript in a sealed envelope and two letters of recommendation. **Deadline:** March 1. **Contact:** jpatterson@cfnil.org.

2467 ■ Susan Kay Munson Gilmore Memorial Scholarship *(Undergraduate/Scholarship)*

Purpose: To serve the four county area (Boone, Ogle, Stephenson and Winnebago) through philanthropy; to provide leadership in meeting charitable needs and to be a responsible steward to the Foundation's donors and of the Foundation's endowment. **Focus:** General studies. **Qualif.:** Applicants must be graduating senior students or former graduates of a Guilford or Mendota Township high school; must have "C" or better average; and must be pursuing a vocational career. **Criteria:** Recipients are selected based on financial need.

Funds Avail.: No specific amount. **To Apply:** Applicants must submit a completed application form, verification form, an official transcript in a sealed envelope, two letters of recommendation and a copy of their FAFSA. **Deadline:** March 1. **Contact:** jpatterson@cfnil.org.

2468 ■ Nettie and Jesse Gorov Scholarship *(Undergraduate/Scholarship)*

Purpose: To serve the four county area (Boone, Ogle, Stephenson and Winnebago) through philanthropy; to provide leadership in meeting charitable needs and to be a responsible steward to the Foundation's donors and of the Foundation's endowment; to provide educational resources to graduating seniors, current college students or non-traditional students. **Qualif.:** Applicants must plan to attend an accredited two or four-year school. **Criteria:** Recipients are selected based on financial need, character and academic achievement.

Funds Avail.: No specific amount. **To Apply:** Applicants must submit a completed application form, verification form, an official transcript in a sealed envelope, two letters of recommendation and a copy of their FAFSA. **Deadline:** March 1. **Contact:** jpatterson@cfnil.org.

2469 ■ Karen Harter Recruitment Scholarship Grant *(Undergraduate/Scholarship)*

Purpose: To serve the four county area (Boone, Ogle, Stephenson and Winnebago) through philanthropy; to provide leadership in meeting charitable needs and to be a responsible steward to the Foundation's donors and of the Foundation's endowment. **Focus:** Education. **Qualif.:** Applicants must be female Rockford College or Northern Illinois University sophomore or junior students who are pursuing a career in secondary math or science education. **Criteria:** Recipients are selected based on financial need.

Funds Avail.: No specific amount. **To Apply:** Applicants must submit a completed application form, verification form, an official transcript in a sealed envelope and two letters of recommendation. **Deadline:** March 1. **Contact:** jpatterson@cfnil.org.

2470 ■ Karen Harter Recruitment Scholarship Grant *(Undergraduate/Scholarship)*

Purpose: To serve the four county area (Boone, Ogle, Stephenson and Winnebago) through philanthropy; to provide leadership in meeting charitable needs and to be a responsible steward to the Foundation's donors and of the Foundation's endowment; to provide educational resources to students pursuing a career in education. **Focus:** Education. **Qualif.:** Applicants must be female Rockford College or Northern Illinois University sophomore or junior students who are pursuing a career in secondary math or science education. **Criteria:** Recipients are selected based on financial need.

Funds Avail.: No specific amount. **To Apply:** Applicants must submit a completed application form, verification form, an official transcript in a sealed envelope and two letters of recommendation. **Deadline:** March 1. **Contact:** jpatterson@cfnil.org.

2471 ■ Amber Huber Memorial Scholarship *(Undergraduate/Scholarship)*

Purpose: To serve the four county area (Boone, Ogle, Stephenson and Winnebago) through philanthropy; to provide leadership in meeting charitable needs and to be a responsible steward to the Foundation's donors and of the Foundation's endowment. **Focus:** General studies. **Qualif.:** Applicants must be graduating senior females from Byron High School who have participated in the Byron High School girls track program and/or Byron High School Cheerleading program for at least three seasons including their senior year; must have a minimum GPA of 5 on an 11 point scale or "C" average. **Criteria:** Recipients are selected based on financial need.

Funds Avail.: No specific amount. **To Apply:** Applicants must submit a completed application form, verification form, an official transcript in a sealed envelope and two letters of recommendation. **Deadline:** March 31. **Contact:** jpatterson@cfnil.org.

2472 ■ International Management Council (IMC) Scholarships *(Undergraduate/Scholarship)*

Purpose: To serve the four county area (Boone, Ogle, Stephenson and Winnebago) through philanthropy; to provide leadership in meeting charitable needs and to be a responsible steward to the Foundation's donors and of the Foundation's endowment; to provide educational resources to Winnebago County high school graduating seniors to pursue a degree in business. **Focus:** Business. **Qualif.:** Applicants must be graduating seniors residing in Winnebago County who are pursuing a degree in business; must have a GPA of at least 3.0 on a 4.0 scale and have been active in community service. **Criteria:** Recipients are selected based on financial need.

Funds Avail.: No specific amount. **To Apply:** Applicants must submit a completed application form, verification form, an official transcript in a sealed envelope and two letters of recommendation. **Deadline:** March 1. **Contact:** jpatterson@cfnil.org.

2473 ■ Ashley E. Ketcher Memorial Scholarships *(Undergraduate/Scholarship)*

Purpose: To serve the four county area (Boone, Ogle, Stephenson and Winnebago) through philanthropy; to provide leadership in meeting charitable needs and to be a responsible steward to the Foundation's donors and of the Foundation's endowment; to provide educational funds to support Auburn High school CAPA students planning to attend an accredited college or university. **Focus:** General studies. **Qualif.:** Applicants must be graduating Auburn High School seniors in the CAPA program who have an interest in and prior experience in the performing arts; must have a cumulative GPA of at least 2.5. **Criteria:** Recipients are selected based on financial need.

Funds Avail.: No specific amount. **To Apply:** Applicants must submit a completed application form, verification form, an official transcript in a sealed envelope, two letters of recommendation and a copy of FAFSA. **Deadline:** March 1. **Contact:** jpatterson@cfnil.org.

2474 ■ La Voz Latina Scholarships *(Undergraduate/Scholarship)*

Purpose: To serve the four county area (Boone, Ogle, Stephenson and Winnebago) through philanthropy; to provide leadership in meeting charitable needs and to be a responsible steward to the Foundation's donors and of the Foundation's endowment. **Focus:** Education. **Qualif.:** Applicants must be high school graduates of Hispanic origin who reside in Winnebago County; must be enrolled in a post-secondary education program. **Criteria:** Recipients are selected based on financial need.

Funds Avail.: No specific amount. **To Apply:** Applicants must submit a completed application form. **Deadline:** March 14. **Contact:** 815-965-5784.

2475 ■ Leopold Education Project Scholarships *(Undergraduate/Scholarship)*

Purpose: To serve the four county area (Boone, Ogle, Stephenson and Winnebago) through philanthropy; to provide leadership in meeting charitable needs and to be a responsible steward to the Foundation's donors and of the Foundation's endowment. **Focus:** General studies. **Qualif.:** Applicants must be graduating high school seniors or high school graduates who are enrolled or planning to enroll in a full-time course of study at an accredited four-year college or university in a natural resources filed. **Criteria:** Recipients are selected based on financial need.

Funds Avail.: No specific amount. **To Apply:** Applicants must contact Jackie Falkenstein for more information. **Contact:** 815-544-2677.

2476 ■ Keith Miffioli Scholarship *(Undergraduate/Scholarship)*

Purpose: To serve the four county area (Boone, Ogle, Stephenson and Winnebago) through philanthropy; to provide leadership in meeting charitable needs and to be a responsible steward to the Foundation's donors and of the Foundation's endowment; to provide awards to worthy scholars who otherwise might not receive a college or university education. **Focus:** General studies. **Qualif.:** Applicants must be graduating senior students from a Boone, Stephenson, Ogle or Winnebago County School who have a cumulative GPA of 3.0 or higher. **Criteria:** Recipients are selected based on financial need.

Funds Avail.: No specific amount. **To Apply:** Applicants must submit a completed application form, verification form, an official transcript in a sealed envelope, two letters of recommendation and a copy of their FAFSA. **Deadline:** March 1. **Contact:** jpatterson@cfnil.org.

2477 ■ Paul and Ruth Neidhold Business Scholarship *(Undergraduate/Scholarship)*

Purpose: To serve the four county area (Boone, Ogle, Stephenson and Winnebago) through philanthropy; to provide leadership in meeting charitable needs and to be a responsible steward to the Foundation's donors and of the Foundation's endowment. **Focus:** Business. **Qualif.:** Applicants must be Harvard High School seniors with a minimum GPA of 2.0 ; must have plans to pursue an education or training in a business field. **Criteria:** Recipients are selected based on financial need.

Funds Avail.: No specific amount. **To Apply:** Applicants must submit a completed application form, verification form, an official transcript in a sealed envelope, two letters of recommendation and a copy of their FAFSA. **Deadline:** March 1. **Contact:** jpatterson@cfnil.org.

Awards are arranged alphabetically below their administering organizations

2478 ■ Northwest Community Center Scholarships *(Undergraduate/Scholarship)*

Purpose: To serve the four county area (Boone, Ogle, Stephenson and Winnebago) through philanthropy; to provide leadership in meeting charitable needs and to be a responsible steward to the Foundation's donors and of the Foundation's endowment. **Focus:** General studies. **Qualif.:** Applicants must be graduating senior students or graduates from a Rockford high school who have a GPA of at least 2.0; must have plans to attend a college, university or trade school; must be residents of northwest Rockford or have a history of involvement at the Northwest Community Center as either a volunteer or participant. **Criteria:** Recipients are selected based on financial need.

Funds Avail.: No specific amount. **To Apply:** Applicants must submit a completed application form, verification form, an official transcript in a sealed envelope, two letters of recommendation and a copy of their FAFSA. **Deadline:** March 1. **Contact:** jpatterson@cfnil.org.

2479 ■ Katharine H. Obye Scholarship Award *(Undergraduate/Scholarship)*

Purpose: To serve the four county area (Boone, Ogle, Stephenson and Winnebago) through philanthropy; to provide leadership in meeting charitable needs and to be a responsible steward to the Foundation's donors and of the Foundation's endowment. **Focus:** General studies. **Qualif.:** Applicants must be female students who are graduating from a public high school within Boone or Winnebago county who have plans to teach at any level or in any field; must have done outstanding work on a high school publication staff such as newspaper or yearbook. **Criteria:** Recipients are selected based on financial need.

Funds Avail.: No specific amount. **To Apply:** Applicants must submit a completed application form, verification form, an official transcript in a sealed envelope, two letters of recommendation and a copy of their FAFSA. **Deadline:** March 1. **Contact:** jpatterson@cfnil.org.

2480 ■ William Pigott Memorial Scholarship *(Undergraduate/Scholarship)*

Purpose: To serve the four county area (Boone, Ogle, Stephenson and Winnebago) through philanthropy; to provide leadership in meeting charitable needs and to be a responsible steward to the Foundation's donors and of the Foundation's endowment. **Focus:** Engineering. **Qualif.:** Applicants must be graduating senior students from McHenry, Boone or Winnebago county majoring in engineering. **Criteria:** Recipients are selected based on financial need.

Funds Avail.: No specific amount. **To Apply:** Applicants must submit a completed application form, verification form, an official transcript in a sealed envelope and two letters of recommendation. **Deadline:** March 1. **Contact:** jpatterson@cfnil.org.

2481 ■ Mark A. Reid Memorial Scholarship Grant *(Undergraduate/Scholarship)*

Purpose: To serve the four county area (Boone, Ogle, Stephenson and Winnebago) through philanthropy; to provide leadership in meeting charitable needs and to be a responsible steward to the Foundation's donors and of the Foundation's endowment; to encourage and support other students who are actively involved in extracurricular activities. **Focus:** Drama. **Qualif.:** Applicants must be graduating seniors at Oregon High School who actively participate in music or drama. **Criteria:** Recipients are selected based on demonstrated leadership.

Funds Avail.: No specific amount. **To Apply:** Applicants must contact Mitch Lauer for more information. **Contact:** 732-6241.

2482 ■ Rockford Area Habitat for Humanity College Scholarships *(Undergraduate/Scholarship)*

Purpose: To serve the four county area (Boone, Ogle, Stephenson and Winnebago) through philanthropy; to provide leadership in meeting charitable needs and to be a responsible steward to the Foundation's donors and of the Foundation's endowment. **Focus:** General studies. **Qualif.:** Applicants must have plans to attend an accredited junior college or university; must be current homeowner residents or dependents of homeowner residents of a home built by Rockford Area Habitat for Humanity; must be residing in that home at time of scholarship application. **Criteria:** Recipients are selected based on financial need.

Funds Avail.: No specific amount. **To Apply:** Applicants must submit a completed application form, verification form, an official transcript in a sealed envelope, two letters of recommendation and a copy of FAFSA. **Deadline:** March 1. **Contact:** jpatterson@cfnil.org.

2483 ■ Rockford Chapter Daughters of the American Revolution Memorial Scholarships *(Undergraduate/Scholarship)*

Purpose: To serve the four county area (Boone, Ogle, Stephenson and Winnebago) through philanthropy; to provide leadership in meeting charitable needs and to be a responsible steward to the Foundation's donors and of the Foundation's endowment. **Focus:** General studies. **Qualif.:** Applicants must be graduating seniors from Winnebago or Boone County pursuing a two or four year degree. **Criteria:** Recipients are selected based on academic achievement and financial need.

Funds Avail.: No specific amount. **To Apply:** Applicants must contact Audrey Johnson for more information.

2484 ■ Deborah Jean Rydberg Memorial Scholarship *(Undergraduate/Scholarship)*

Purpose: To serve the four county area (Boone, Ogle, Stephenson and Winnebago) through philanthropy; to provide leadership in meeting charitable needs and to be a responsible steward to the Foundation's donors and of the Foundation's endowment. **Focus:** General studies. **Qualif.:** Applicants must be graduating female senior athletes at Guilford High school who have at least a "C" or better average and have plans to attend college. **Criteria:** Recipients are selected based on financial need.

Funds Avail.: No specific amount. **To Apply:** Applicants must submit a completed application form, verification form, an official transcript in a sealed envelope and two letters of recommendation. **Deadline:** March 1. **Contact:** jpatterson@cfnil.org.

2485 ■ Richard J. Schnell Memorial Scholarship *(Postdoctorate/Scholarship)*

Purpose: To serve the four county area (Boone, Ogle, Stephenson and Winnebago) through philanthropy; to provide leadership in meeting charitable needs and to be a responsible steward to the Foundation's donors and of the Foundation's endowment. **Focus:** General studies. **Qualif.:** Applicants must have been accepted into or enrolled in an American Dental Association accredited dental or dental

Awards are arranged alphabetically below their administering organizations

hygiene program or a graduate post-doctoral program in United States. **Criteria:** Recipients are selected based on financial need.

Funds Avail.: No specific amount. **To Apply:** Applicants must submit a completed application form, verification form, an official transcript in a sealed envelope, two letters of recommendation and a copy of their FAFSA. **Deadline:** March 1. **Contact:** jpatterson@cfnil.org.

2486 ■ Bonnie Sorenson Scudder Scholarship *(Undergraduate/Scholarship)*

Purpose: To serve the four county area (Boone, Ogle, Stephenson and Winnebago) through philanthropy; to provide leadership in meeting charitable needs and to be a responsible steward to the Foundation's donors and of the Foundation's endowment. **Focus:** Physical education. **Qualif.:** Applicants must be female senior students at Harvard High School who have exhibited an interest in women's physical education and who wish to pursue a degree in women's physical education. **Criteria:** Recipients are selected based on financial need.

Funds Avail.: No specific amount. **To Apply:** Applicants must submit a completed application form and must contact Melissa Laffey for more information. **Contact:** 1103 N Jefferson, Harvard, IL 60033.

2487 ■ Elisabeth Seegmiller Recruitment Scholarship Grant *(Undergraduate/Scholarship)*

Purpose: To serve the four county area (Boone, Ogle, Stephenson and Winnebago) through philanthropy; to provide leadership in meeting charitable needs and to be a responsible steward to the Foundation's donors and of the Foundation's endowment. **Focus:** General studies. **Qualif.:** Applicants must be female Rockford College sophomore or junior students who are pursuing a degree in education. **Criteria:** Recipients are selected based on financial need.

Funds Avail.: No specific amount. **To Apply:** Applicants must submit a completed application form, verification form, an official transcript in a sealed envelope and two letters of recommendation. **Deadline:** March 1. **Contact:** jpatterson@cfnil.org.

2488 ■ Senior Memorial Scholarships *(Undergraduate/Scholarship)*

Purpose: To serve the four county area (Boone, Ogle, Stephenson and Winnebago) through philanthropy; to provide leadership in meeting charitable needs and to be a responsible steward to the Foundation's donors and of the Foundation's endowment. **Focus:** General studies. **Qualif.:** Applicants must be graduating senior students from a Rockford School District No. 205 high school; must plan to attend a college, university or higher institution of learning. **Criteria:** Recipients are selected based on academic potential and financial need.

Funds Avail.: No specific Amount. **To Apply:** Applicants must submit a completed application form. **Deadline:** March 1.

2489 ■ Ernest and Charlene Stachowiak Memorial Scholarship *(Undergraduate/Scholarship)*

Purpose: To serve the four county area (Boone, Ogle, Stephenson and Winnebago) through philanthropy; to provide leadership in meeting charitable needs and to be a responsible steward to the Foundation's donors and of the Foundation's endowment; to provide educational resources for residents in the four counties of Boone, Ogle, Stephenson and Winnebago. **Focus:** General studies. **Qualif.:** Applicants must be graduating seniors or college students with a permanent address within Boone, Ogle, Stephenson or Winnebago county; must have a GPA of at least 2.5 on 4.0 sale. **Criteria:** Recipients are selected based on financial need.

Funds Avail.: No specific amount. **To Apply:** Applicants must submit a completed application form, verification form, an official transcript in a sealed envelope, two letters of recommendation and a copy of their FAFSA. **Deadline:** March 1. **Contact:** jpatterson@cfnil.org.

2490 ■ Gary S. Wilmer RAMI Music Scholarship *(Undergraduate/Scholarship)*

Purpose: To serve the four county area (Boone, Ogle, Stephenson and Winnebago) through philanthropy; to provide leadership in meeting charitable needs and to be a responsible steward to the Foundation's donors and of the Foundation's endowment. **Focus:** Music. **Qualif.:** Applicants must be graduating senior students from Boone or Winnebago County who have a GPA of at least 2.5; must have plans to pursue a degree in music performance, education or composition and be actively involved in school or community musical groups; must be nominated by a music teacher. **Criteria:** Recipients are selected based on financial need.

Funds Avail.: No specific amount. **To Apply:** Applicants must submit a completed application form, verification form, an official transcript in a sealed envelope, two letters of recommendation and a five minute or less performance tape or C.D. **Deadline:** March 1. **Contact:** jpatterson@cfnil.org.

2491 ■ Women of Today's Manufacturing Scholarships *(Undergraduate/Scholarship)*

Purpose: To serve the four county area (Boone, Ogle, Stephenson and Winnebago) through philanthropy; to provide leadership in meeting charitable needs and to be a responsible steward to the Foundation's donors and of the Foundation's endowment. **Focus:** Manufacturing. **Qualif.:** Applicants must be male or female residents of Ogle, Winnebago, Boone, Stephenson or Rock County who are attending or plan to attend a college, university or trade/technical school; must demonstrate how their course work will impact manufacturing technology in the region. **Criteria:** Recipients are selected based on financial need.

Funds Avail.: No specific amount. **To Apply:** Applicants must submit a completed application form, verification form, an official transcript in a sealed envelope and two letters of recommendation. **Deadline:** March 1. **Contact:** jpatterson@cfnil.org.

2492 ■ Carolyn Wones Recruitment Scholarships Grant *(Undergraduate/Scholarship)*

Purpose: To serve the four county area (Boone, Ogle, Stephenson and Winnebago) through philanthropy; to provide leadership in meeting charitable needs and to be a responsible steward to the Foundation's donors and of the Foundation's endowment. **Focus:** General studies. **Qualif.:** Applicants must be females who graduated from a public high school within Boone or Winnebago county; must have plans to pursue a degree in secondary teaching; must exhibit academic potential and have participated in a number of high school activities. **Criteria:** Recipients are selected based on financial need.

Funds Avail.: No specific amount. **To Apply:** Applicants

must submit a completed application form, verification form, an official transcript in a sealed envelope and two letters of recommendation. **Deadline:** March 1. **Contact:** jpatterson@cfnil.org.

2493 ■ Margaret Wyeth Scholarship *(Undergraduate/Scholarship)*

Purpose: To serve the four county area (Boone, Ogle, Stephenson and Winnebago) through philanthropy; to provide leadership in meeting charitable needs and to be a responsible steward to the Foundation's donors and of the Foundation's endowment. **Focus:** General studies. **Qualif.:** Applicants must be graduating public high school senior students and residing in Boone, Ogle or Winnebago County; must plan to attend a college or university. **Criteria:** Recipients are selected based on financial need and demonstrated active involvement in social studies organizations, clubs and classes such as student government, political campaigns, social service and community service.

Funds Avail.: No specific amount. **To Apply:** Applicants must submit a completed application form, verification form, an official transcript in a sealed envelope, two letters of recommendation and a copy of their FAFSA. **Deadline:** March 1. **Contact:** jpatterson@cfnil.org.

2494 ■ Zeta Chapter Memorial Scholarships Award *(Undergraduate/Scholarship)*

Purpose: To serve the four county area (Boone, Ogle, Stephenson and Winnebago) through philanthropy; to provide leadership in meeting charitable needs and to be a responsible steward to the Foundation's donors and of the Foundation's endowment. **Focus:** General studies. **Qualif.:** Applicants must be females who are graduating from a public high school within Boone or Winnebago county; must have plans to teach at any level; must exhibit academic potential and have participated in a number of high school activities. **Criteria:** Recipients are selected based on financial need and demonstrated active involvement in social studies organizations, clubs and classes such as student government, political campaigns, social service and community service.

Funds Avail.: No specific amount. **To Apply:** Applicants must submit a completed application form, verification form, an official transcript in a sealed envelope and two letters of recommendation. **Deadline:** March 1. **Contact:** jpatterson@cfnil.org.

2495 ■ Community Foundation of Prince Edward Island

119-121 Quenn St., Ste. 105
Charlottetown, PE, Canada C1A 1Z4
Ph: (902)892-3440
Fax: (902)892-0880
Free: 800-566-7307
E-mail: foundation@cfpei.ca
URL: http://www.cfpei.ca

2496 ■ Architects Association of PEI Scholarships *(Undergraduate/Scholarship)*

Purpose: To provide financial assistance to qualified individuals who want to pursue their education. **Focus:** Architecture. **Qualif.:** Applicant must be a Prince Edward Island student who graduated from a PEI High School and has been accepted into a recognized architectural program. **Criteria:** Recipient will be selected based on the scholarship application requirements.

Funds Avail.: No specific amount. **To Apply:** Applicant must complete the application form available online; must submit an official transcript of marks, copy of letter of acceptance from the university, an essay, two reference letters, and portfolio of work. Application form and other supporting documents must be sent to Community Foundation of Prince Edward Island, 119-121 Queen St. Ste. 105, Charlottetown, PE C1A 4B3. **Deadline:** May 30.

2497 ■ Joan Auld Scholarships *(Undergraduate/Scholarship)*

Purpose: To provide financial assistance to qualified individuals who want to pursue their education. **Focus:** Art; Crafts; Design. **Qualif.:** Applicant must be a Canadian citizen; must have been a resident of P.E.I for at least the 6 months prior to application; must be undertaking full-time studies in a craft-related field at a recognized institution of applied art, craft and design; must demonstrate high school graduation or equivalence. **Criteria:** Recipient will be selected based on the scholarship application criteria.

Funds Avail.: $200. **To Apply:** Applicants must complete the application form available online; must provide an outline of the proposed course of study and the name of the institution where they will attend the class; must submit a essay about their background, interest, aims, and ambitions; must submit a letter of reference and portfolio demonstrating previous work, samples of craft-related work, sketches, video or pictures; must include written verification of acceptance. Application form and other supporting documents must be sent to Joan Auld Scholarship Fund c/o The Community Foundation of Prince Edward Island, 119- 121 Queen St. Charlottetown, PE C1A 4B3. **Deadline:** May 30.

2498 ■ Lorne and Ruby Bonnell Scholarships *(Undergraduate/Scholarship)*

Purpose: To provide scholarship assistance to qualified individuals who want to pursue their studies. **Focus:** General studies. **Qualif.:** Applicant must be a graduate of a Prince Edward Island high school; must be a graduate of the University of Prince Edward Island with high academic standing; must be accepted into graduate studies in the sciences at a Canadian university. **Criteria:** Recipient will be selected by the selection committee following the guidelines of conditions of eligibility.

Funds Avail.: $1,000. **To Apply:** Applicant must complete the application form available online; must submit an official letter of acceptance from a Canadian graduate school. Application form and other supporting documents must be sent to Lorne and Ruby Bonnell Scholarship Fund c/o The Community Foundation of Prince Edward Island, 119-121 Queen St. Ste. 105, Charlottetown, PE C1A 4B3. **Deadline:** May 30.

Remarks: Scholarship Fund was established on December 14, 2000 by the Honorable M. Lorne Bonnell, a prominent Prince Edward Island medical doctor, past Cabinet Minister of the Provincial Legislature, and Senator.

2499 ■ Orin Carver Scholarships *(Undergraduate/Scholarship)*

Purpose: To provide financial assistance to qualified individuals who want to pursue their education. **Focus:** General studies. **Qualif.:** Applicants must be high school graduates in the top 25% of their class; must exhibit excellence and leadership in either athletics, arts and/or community service; must be accepted into a post-secondary

Awards are arranged alphabetically below their administering organizations

program at UPEI or Holland College. **Criteria:** Recipient will be selected based on the scholarship application requirements.

Funds Avail.: No specific amount. **To Apply:** Applicants must complete the application form available online; must have a formal statement of academic standing and official academic transcript for most recent academic year, as verified by educational institute attended; must have two letters of reference (one from the educational institution and one from a community member); must provide a 500 word essay or portfolio of their excellent works. Application form and other supporting documents must be sent to Orin Carver Scholarship Selection Committee, c/o Community Foundation of PEI, 119-121 Queen St. Ste. 105, Charlottetown, PE C1A 4b3. **Deadline:** May 30.

2500 ■ Phillips Scholarships *(Undergraduate/Scholarship)*

Purpose: To provide financial assistance to qualified individuals who want to pursue their education. **Focus:** General studies. **Qualif.:** Applicant must be a high school graduate from the Western School District with a physical disability; must be a resident of Prince County; must have financial need; must have been accepted at a recognized post-secondary institution. **Criteria:** Recipient will be selected based on the scholarship application criteria.

Funds Avail.: No specific amount. **To Apply:** Applicant must complete the application form available online; must submit a copy of their final grades; must have a brief description of their physical disability and what they hope to gain from their studies; must have a letter of acceptance for the next year's study. Application form and other supporting documents must be sent to Lowell Phillips Scholarship Award c/o Community Foundation of Prince Edward Island, 119-121 Queen St. Ste. 105, Charlottetown, PEI C1A 4B3. **Deadline:** May 30.

2501 ■ Summerside-Natick Hockey Scholarships *(Undergraduate/Scholarship)*

Purpose: To provide financial assistance to qualified individuals who want to pursue their education. **Focus:** General studies. **Qualif.:** Applicant must be a high school graduate of Prince Edward Island; must be accepted at a post-secondary institution; must be entering the first year of study; must have played in the Summerside Area Minor Hockey Association. **Criteria:** Recipient will be selected based on the scholarship application criteria.

Funds Avail.: No specific amount. **To Apply:** Applicant must complete the application form available online; must include a letter detailing how he/she meets the selection criteria; must have an official letter of acceptance from a recognized post-secondary institution; must submit two letters of reference; and most recent transcript. Application form and other supporting documents must be sent to The Summerside-Natick International Friendship Fund c/o The Community Foundation of Prince Edward Island, 119-121 Queen St. Ste. 105, Queen Square Place, Charlottetown, PE C1A 4B3. **Deadline:** May 30.

Remarks: Founding members of the International Friendship Hockey Series Committee established the Summerside-Natick International Friendship Hockey Fund.

2502 ■ Community Foundation of Sarasota County

PO Box 49587
Sarasota, FL 34237
Ph: (941)955-3000
Fax: (941)952-1951
E-mail: stewart@cfsarasota.org
URL: http://www.cfsarasota.org

2503 ■ American Business Women's Association Sarasota Chapter Scholarships *(Undergraduate/Scholarship)*

Purpose: To encourage and enable caring individuals to easily and effectively support the charitable causes that they care about. **Focus:** Business. **Qualif.:** Applicants must be female students with 3.0 unweighted high school GPA and must be of good character and have a career goal related to their college or university studies. **Criteria:** Recipients are selected based on financial need.

Funds Avail.: No specific amount. **To Apply:** Applicants must complete the application form; must submit a parent or guardian's most recent 1040 federal tax form; must provide two letters of reference from people who know the applicant well; official acceptance letter from college or vocational school; and a copy of SAT and ACT scores.

2504 ■ byourself Scholarship Fund *(Undergraduate/Scholarship)*

Purpose: To encourage and enable caring individuals to easily and effectively support the charitable causes that they care about. **Focus:** Nursing. **Qualif.:** Applicants must be non-traditional students, males or females in Sarasota County pursuing RN, LPN, or CNA; must be accepted into the nursing programs at Manatee Community College or Sarasota County Technical Institute; and must maintain a 2.8 GPA to retain scholarship. **Criteria:** Recipients are selected based on financial need.

Funds Avail.: No specific amount. **To Apply:** Applicants must complete the application form; must submit a parent or guardian's most recent 1040 federal tax form; and must provide two letters of reference from people who know the applicant well; official acceptance letter from college or vocational school; and a copy of SAT and ACT scores.

2505 ■ Community Foundation of Sarasota County Adult Learner Scholarships *(Undergraduate/Scholarship)*

Purpose: To encourage and enable caring individuals to easily and effectively support the charitable causes that they care about. **Focus:** General studies. **Qualif.:** Applicants must be adult learners who are returning to vocational school or college after having been out of high school for a number of years. **Criteria:** Recipients are selected based on the objective and competitive academic and non-academic factors plus demonstrated financial need.

Funds Avail.: No specific amount. **To Apply:** Applicants must complete the application form; must submit a parent or guardian's most recent 1040 federal tax form; and must provide two letters of reference from people who know the applicant well. **Deadline:** September 15.

2506 ■ Davis Educational Scholarship Fund *(Undergraduate/Scholarship)*

Purpose: To encourage and enable caring individuals to easily and effectively support the charitable causes that they care about; to help students obtain a college degree or vocational training to pursue a career in nursing or the medical field. **Focus:** Medical education. **Qualif.:** Applicants must be accepted into a health related program.

Awards are arranged alphabetically below their administering organizations

Criteria: Recipients are selected based on financial need and on their educational objectives that will lead to a career in the health care field.

Funds Avail.: No specific amount. **To Apply:** Applicants must complete the application form; must submit a parent or guardian's most recent 1040 federal tax form; must provide two letters of reference from people who know the applicant well; official acceptance letter from college or vocational school; and a copy of SAT and ACT scores.

2507 ■ Father Connie Dougherty Scholarships
(Undergraduate/Scholarship)

Purpose: To further education at a college, university, or institution of higher learning including education in advanced vocational training. **Focus:** General studies. **Qualif.:** Applicants must be graduates of Sarasota County public and private school. **Criteria:** Recipients are selected based on academic performance and financial need.

Funds Avail.: $5,000. **To Apply:** Applicants must submit a completed application form; an official transcript; SAT or ACT scores; copy of Student Aid Report; and three letters of recommendation (one must come from a teacher and one from a community member who is not a teacher or relative). **Deadline:** April 1. **Contact:** mimi@sarasota.org

2508 ■ James Franklin and Dorothy J. Warnell Scholarship Fund *(Undergraduate/Scholarship)*

Purpose: To encourage and enable caring individuals to easily and effectively support the charitable causes that they care about and to provide scholarships for adult learners in Sarasota County to pursue a professional certificate in hairdressing. **Focus:** General studies. **Qualif.:** Applicants must be residents of Sarasota County and post high school students. **Criteria:** Recipients are selected based on financial need and on their educational objectives.

Funds Avail.: No specific amount. **To Apply:** Applicants must submit completed application form; a parent or guardian's most recent 1040 federal tax form; two letters of reference from people who know the applicant well; official transcript of record; official acceptance letter from college or vocational school; and a copy of SAT and ACT scores.

2509 ■ Helen F. "Jerri" Rand Memorial Scholarships *(Undergraduate/Scholarship)*

Purpose: To encourage and enable caring individuals to easily and effectively support the charitable causes that they care about and to provide scholarships for adult learners in Sarasota County to pursue a professional certificate in hairdressing. **Focus:** Cosmetology. **Qualif.:** Applicants must be adult learners who are accepted to any accredited beauty school in Sarasota County. **Criteria:** Recipients are selected based on financial need and on their educational objectives that will lead to a career.

Funds Avail.: No specific amount. **To Apply:** Applicants must complete the application form; must submit a parent or guardian's most recent 1040 federal tax form; must provide two letters of reference from people who know the applicant well; must provide official transcript of record, official acceptance letter from college or vocational school; and must submit a copy of SAT and ACT scores.

2510 ■ Traditional Student Scholarships
(Undergraduate/Scholarship)

Purpose: To encourage and enable caring individuals to easily and effectively support the charitable causes that they care about. **Focus:** General studies. **Qualif.:** Applicants must be high school seniors, or those who are 25 years old or younger who are currently attending college. **Criteria:** Recipients are selected based on financial need, leadership potential, academic performance, work experience, and commitment to school and community through volunteerism.

Funds Avail.: No specific amount. **To Apply:** Applicants must complete the application form; must submit a parent or guardian's most recent 1040 federal tax form; and must provide two letters of reference from people who know the applicant well. **Deadline:** March 1. **Contact:** rebekah@cfsarasota.org.

2511 ■ Community Foundation for Southeast Michigan

333 West Fort St., Ste. 2010
Detroit, MI 48226-3134
Ph: (313)961-6675
Fax: (313)961-2886
E-mail: cfsem@cfsem.org
URL: http://www.cfsem.org

2512 ■ Dick Depaolis Memorial Scholarships
(Undergraduate/Scholarship)

Purpose: To provide financial assistance to graduating seniors from North Farmington High School who demonstrate leadership, good grades and male varsity athlete who will enter college majoring liberal studies, especially History and English. **Focus:** History; English language and literature. **Qualif.:** Applicants must be members of the graduating class at North Farmington High School; must demonstrate exemplary desire, ability and have a GPA of 3.0 or higher; must be male athletes demonstrating leadership, academic discipline and good sportsmanship on and off the field; must be playing varsity sports (football preferred); have applied or been accepted as full-time students in an accredited educational institution in the United States with a major in liberal studies, especially History and English. **Criteria:** Recipients are evaluated based on academic records, recommendations, and the statement of goals.

Funds Avail.: $500. **To Apply:** Applicants must use a computer, typewriter or print neatly in blue or black ink in completing the application form. **Deadline:** April 2.

2513 ■ Detroit Economic Club Scholarships
(Undergraduate/Scholarship)

Purpose: To provide financial assistance to students of Southeast Michigan region for their education. **Focus:** General studies. **Qualif.:** Applicants must be high school seniors in public or private high school in Wayne, Oakland or Macomb counties. **Criteria:** Recipients are selected based on scholastic, social and financial need.

Funds Avail.: $2,000. **Number Awarded:** 2. **To Apply:** Applicants must first be nominated by his or her counselor and then invited to apply, for scholarship consideration. **Deadline:** April 1.

2514 ■ Detroit Tigers Willie Horton Scholarships
(Undergraduate/Scholarship)

Purpose: To provide financial assistance to students of Southeast Michigan region for education. **Focus:** General studies. **Qualif.:** Applicants must be graduating seniors at Northwestern High School in Detroit; must show leadership and character through extra curricular activities, volunteer involvement and work experience in school and in the community; have applied or have been accepted as full time students in an accredited educational institution in the United States. **Criteria:** Applicants are evaluated based on scholastic, personal attributes and experience in school or community.

Funds Avail.: $5,000. **Number Awarded:** 1. **To Apply:** Applicants must use a computer, typewriter or print neatly in blue or black ink all appropriate forms. **Deadline:** April 1.

2515 ■ Robert Holmes Scholarships
(Undergraduate/Scholarship)

Purpose: To provide financial assistance to students of Southeast Michigan region for their education. **Focus:** General studies. **Qualif.:** Applicants must be dependents of eligible Michigan Teamsters and high school seniors who will attend a Michigan College or University as full time students. **Criteria:** Applicants are evaluated based on criteria designed by the Scholarship Selection Committee.

Funds Avail.: $1,000. **Number Awarded:** 6. **To Apply:** Applicants must submit the completed application form and other required documents. **Deadline:** April 1.

2516 ■ Chris Kurzweil Scholarships
(Undergraduate/Scholarship)

Purpose: To provide financial assistance to students in the Southeast Michigan region for their education. **Focus:** General studies. **Qualif.:** Applicants must be dependents of members of the Intertape Polymer Group, formerly American Tape; and must be high school seniors. **Criteria:** Applicants are evaluated based on academic records, recommendations, and their statement of goals.

Funds Avail.: $1,500. **Number Awarded:** 2. **To Apply:** Applicants must use a computer, typewriter or print neatly in blue or black ink all appropriate forms. **Deadline:** April 1.

2517 ■ Imelda and Ralph LeMar Scholarship Program *(Undergraduate/Scholarship)*

Purpose: To provide educational assistance to students who are graduates from public high schools in Fowlerville. **Focus:** General studies. **Qualif.:** Applicants must be members of a graduating class in a public high school in Fowlerville, Michigan; must demonstrates exemplary desire, ability and good grades; must show leadership and character through extra curricular activities, volunteer involvement and work experience in school and in the community; have applied or been accepted as full-time students in an accredited educational institution in the United States; must be planning to study chemistry, physics or electrical or mechanical engineering in college. **Criteria:** Applicants are evaluated based on academic records, recommendations and the student's statement of goals.

Funds Avail.: $900. **To Apply:** Applicants must use a computer, typewriter or print neatly in blue or black ink all appropriate forms. **Deadline:** April 1.

2518 ■ Virgil K. Lobring Scholarships
(Undergraduate/Scholarship)

Purpose: To provide financial assistance to students of Southeast Michigan region for their education. **Focus:** General studies. **Qualif.:** Applicants must be members of the graduating class at Southwestern High School in Detroit, Michigan; must demonstrate exemplary desire, ability and good grades; demonstrate leadership and character through extra curricular activities, volunteer involvement and work experience in school and in the community; have applied or been accepted as full-time students in an accredited educational institution in the United States; must be students who have demonstrated the greatest improvement from the time during freshman year in high school as determined by the Lobring Scholarship committee; must demonstrate financial need. **Criteria:** Applicants are evaluated based on academic records, recommendations and statement of goals.

Funds Avail.: $1,500. **To Apply:** Applicants must submit the application containing scholarship guidelines and deadlines, student application, essay question, recommendation forms from counselor, teacher and community service forms; and transcripts release form. **Deadline:** April 1.

2519 ■ Cary Moore Memorial Scholarship Fund
(Undergraduate/Scholarship)

Purpose: To provide financial assistance to the male varsity athlete from North Farmington High School student who best personifies school spirit and good sportsmanship. **Focus:** General studies. **Qualif.:** Applicants must be members of the graduating class at North Farmington High School who demonstrates exemplary desire, ability and good grades; must be male athletes who show leadership, character and sportsmanship by participation in varsity athletics at North Farmington High School and Raiders Pride; have applied or been accepted as a full-time students in an accredited educational institution in the United States. **Criteria:** Applicants are evaluated based on academic records, recommendations, and the statement of goals.

Funds Avail.: $1,500. **Number Awarded:** 1. **To Apply:** Applicants must use a computer, typewriter or print neatly in blue or black ink all appropriate forms. **Deadline:** April 2.

2520 ■ Jean and Tom Rosenthal Scholarship Program *(Undergraduate/Scholarship)*

Purpose: To provide financial assistance to students of Southeast Michigan region for their education. **Focus:** General studies. **Qualif.:** Applicants must be members of the graduating class at Pontiac Northern High School or Pontiac Central High School demonstrating exemplary desire, ability and good grades of at least 2.5 or higher; must show leadership and character through extracurricular activities, volunteer involvement and work experience in school and in the community; have applied or been accepted as full-time students in an accredited educational institution in the United States. **Criteria:** Applicant will be evaluated based on academic records, recommendations and the student's essay on personal commitment of service to others.

Funds Avail.: $1,000. **Number Awarded:** 2. **To Apply:** Applicants must submit the application containing scholarship guidelines and deadlines, student application, essay question, recommendation forms from counselor, teacher and community service forms; and transcripts release form. **Deadline:** April 1.

2521 ■ Jeptha Wade Schureman Scholarship Program *(Undergraduate/Scholarship)*

Purpose: To provide financial assistance to students of Southeast Michigan region for their education. **Focus:** Law; Nursing; Medicine; Dentistry. **Qualif.:** Applicants must be residents of Wayne, Oakland, Macomb, Lenawee, Monroe, Livingston, Washtenaw, or St. Clair counties at the time of high school graduation; must be fatherless either through death or through termination of parental rights; must be pursuing, or planning to pursue, a degree in the fields of law, nursing, medicine or dentistry. **Criteria:** Applicants are evaluated based on academic records, recommendations and statement of goals.

Funds Avail.: $7,500. **To Apply:** Applicants must submit the completed application form and other required documents. **Deadline:** June 2.

2522 ■ Community Foundation of Western Massachusetts

PO Box 15769
Springfield, MA 01115
Ph: (413)732-2858
Fax: (413)733-8565
URL: http://www.communityfoundation.org

2523 ■ Community Foundation of Western Massachusetts Community Scholarship Program *(Undergraduate/Scholarship)*

Purpose: To help bring higher education within reach of residents in Massachusetts who might not otherwise be able to afford it. **Focus:** General studies. **Qualif.:** Applicants must be residents from Franklin, Hampden, Hampshire or combination or city/town; must be freshmen, sophomores, juniors, graduating seniors or graduates of specific high school. **Criteria:** Applicants are evaluated based on the criteria designed by the Scholarship Selection Committee.

Funds Avail.: $10,000. **Number Awarded:** 2. **To Apply:** Applicants must submit all the required application information.

2524 ■ Composite Panel Association

19465 Deerfield Ave., Ste. 306
Leesburg, VA 20176
Ph: (703)724-1128
Fax: (703)724-1588
URL: http://www.pbmdf.com

2525 ■ Robert E. Dougherty Scholarships *(Undergraduate/Scholarship)*

Purpose: To provide financial assistance to students pursuing a career in the composite panel and affiliated industries. **Focus:** Forestry; Chemistry; Engineering. **Qualif.:** Applicant must be North American citizen; and nominated by a member of the Robert E. Dougherty Education Foundation. **Criteria:** Member companies are permitted to nominate one or more individuals for scholarship consideration.

Funds Avail.: 5,000. **Number Awarded:** 8. **To Apply:** Scholarship Application forms can be downloaded at the website and must be filled out and returned to the Foundation. **Deadline:** March 21.

2526 ■ Conference of State Bank Supervisors

1155 Connecticut Ave. NW, 5th Fl.
Washington, DC 20036-4306
Ph: (202)296-2840
Fax: (202)296-1928
URL: http://www.csbs.org

2527 ■ Conference of State Bank Supervisors Graduate School Scholarships *(Graduate/Award/Prize)*

Purpose: To encourage and assist qualified bank and trust examiners to prepare themselves for expanded duties and responsibilities in their banking departments; broaden the examiner's understanding of banking or trust operations; encourage excellence in bank and trust examination; provide the opportunity for State Bank Supervisors to recognize their outstanding examiners; and raise the level of proficiency of state banking departments. **Focus:** Banking. **Qualif.:** Program is open to outstanding and deserving examiners who demonstrate excellence in their work by supporting their attendance at the graduate banking or graduate trust school of their choice. Nominees must have 3 years of experience in bank or trust supervision as examiners-in charge or 3 years of experience as bank or trust examiners plus 2 years of experience in a bank or trust company; must have a degree from an accredited college and must have successfully completed the CSBS Senior School; must have demonstrated fully to the State Bank that they have the potential to assume senior level responsibilities; must continue to be employed by a state banking department. **Criteria:** Recipients are selected based on experience, education, promotion potential and other requirements set by the schools and the banking departments.

Funds Avail.: $3,000. **To Apply:** State Bank Supervisors must nominate candidates using nomination forms provided by the Foundation. **Contact:** Roger Stromberg, Senior VP - Education, Conference of State Bank Supervisors; 1155 Connecticut Ave., Ste. 500, Washington, DC 20036-4306; 800-886-2727 ext. 714 Toll Free; 202-728-5714 Direct; FAX 202-296-1928; rstromberg@csbs.org.

2528 ■ Connecticut Association of Land Surveyors

78 Beaver Rd.
Wethersfield, CT 06109
Ph: (860)563-1990
Fax: (860)529-9700
E-mail: kathy@ctsurveyor.com
URL: http://www.ctsurveyor.com

2529 ■ Connecticut Association of Land Surveyors Memorial Scholarships *(Undergraduate/Scholarship)*

Purpose: To provide information about land surveying in Connecticut to the growing global surveying/internet community. **Focus:** Surveying. **Qualif.:** Applicants must be residents of Connecticut; must be enrolled in a program leading to a degree in surveying or related fields; must be accepted to attend the program and could be a freshman; must show an interest or work history in being a part of the surveying profession. **Criteria:** Recipients are selected based on academic performance and interest in surveying profession.

Funds Avail.: No stated amount. **To Apply:** Applicants must submit a statement outlining qualifications, transcript, resume and other pertinent information. **Deadline:** June 1. **Contact:** 49 Arlington St., West Haven, CT 06516.

2530 ■ Connecticut Construction Industries Association

912 Silas Deane Hwy.
Wethersfield, CT 06109
Ph: (860)529-6855
Fax: (860)563-0616
E-mail: ccia-info@ctconstruction.org
URL: http://www.ctconstruction.org

Awards are arranged alphabetically below their administering organizations

2531 ■ Associated General Contractors of Connecticut Scholarships *(Undergraduate/Scholarship)*

Purpose: To provide constant resource of information services and educational seminars; to maintain strong working relationships with federal and state agencies; to utilize lobbying efforts focused on removing unnecessary regulatory inefficiencies and costly restrictions that hinder progress and stifle the economy. **Focus:** Construction. **Qualif.:** Applicants must be graduating high school seniors entering college as freshmen or entering a two-year technical school with a construction course of study with the intent of entering a four-year college upon completion of the technical school; must desire a career in construction; must pursue a B.S. degree in construction technology or construction civil engineering; must be U.S. citizen or documented resident of the United States. **Criteria:** Recipients are selected based on academic performance and interest in the field of construction.

Funds Avail.: $2,500. **To Apply:** Applicants must complete the "four-page" signed application; must submit one faculty evaluation form completed by high school faculty member with scholastic achievement and school history, two personal evaluation forms and official transcript of records. **Deadline:** March 30.

2532 ■ John Costello Memorial Scholarships *(Undergraduate/Scholarship)*

Purpose: To assist students studying in the field of construction management including civil engineering at an accredited college in Connecticut. **Focus:** Construction. **Qualif.:** Applicants must be graduating senior high school students with a GPA of 2.5. **Criteria:** Recipients are selected based on academic performance and financial need.

Funds Avail.: $2,000. **To Apply:** Applicants must submit a completed application form.

2533 ■ Construction Financial Management Association

29 Emmons Dr., Ste. F-50
Princeton, NJ 08540
Ph: (609)452-8000
Fax: (609)452-0474
URL: http://www.cfma.org

2534 ■ Cindy P. Dennis Scholarship Fund *(Undergraduate/Scholarship)*

Purpose: To provide resources to meet challenges of construction financial professionals. To support the qualified individual who want to pursue a degree in business or construction management. **Focus:** Business, Construction. **Qualif.:** Applicant must be a resident of Atascosa, Bandera, Bexar, Comal, Guadalupe, Kendall, Medina, or Wilson County; must be a candidate for a degree in business or construction management at any accredited college or university, taking a minimum of 12 hours; must have a high school scholastic B average at the end of fall semester of senior year or have a minimum 3.0 cumulative GPA, if already in college. **Criteria:** Applicants will be selected based on scholarship criteria and by the scholarship application materials.

Funds Avail.: $500. **To Apply:** Applicant must submit the following: name, address, and telephone numbers; must have the high school transcript through fall semester of senior year or cumulative college transcripts for classes taken to date; must prepare an essay (not to exceed 500 words); must have a letter of recommendation from a non-family member; must have a summary of extracurricular and outside activities. Application and other supporting documents must be sent to: CFMA - San Antonio Chapter Scholarship Committee, 100 NE Loop 410, Ste. 1100, San Antonio, TX 78216. **Deadline:** April 15.

2535 ■ Consultant Dietitians in Health Care Facilities

2219 Cardinal Dr.
Waterloo, IA 50701
Ph: (319)235-0991
Fax: (319)235-7224
E-mail: fewalker@stellarnet.com
URL: http://www.cdhcf.org

2536 ■ CD-HCF Chair's Scholarships *(Professional Development/Scholarship)*

Purpose: To provide new learning experiences and endorse leadership within the organization. **Focus:** Health care services. **Qualif.:** Applicants must be members or student members of the American Dietetic Association and CD-HCF. **Criteria:** Recipients are selected based on the submitted applications.

Funds Avail.: $1,500. **To Apply:** Applicants must send an application form (available at the website) and return it electronically to Maria Carlson at carslsonmom@mchsi.com. **Deadline:** December.

2537 ■ Gaynold Jensen Education Stipends *(Postdoctorate, Professional Development/Scholarship)*

Purpose: To provide learning programs to improve the contributions of consultant dietitians to health care. **Focus:** Health care services. **Qualif.:** Applicants must be American Dietetic Association members; must be at least a two-year member in Consultant Dietitians in Health Care Facilities; a registered dietitian; currently practicing as a consultant dietitian; planning to expand knowledge in the consultant role. **Criteria:** Recipients are selected based on the committee's review of how and why the program will improve the applicant's contributions as a consultant dietitian in health care.

Funds Avail.: $500. **To Apply:** Applicants must send the application forms (available at the website) to: Manager, Scholarships and Grants, American Dietetic Association Foundation 120 South Riverside Pl., Ste. 2000 Chicago, IL 60606-6995.

2538 ■ Cooley's Anemia Foundation

129-09 26th Ave., No. 203
Flushing, NY 11354
Ph: (718)321-2873
Fax: (718)321-3340
E-mail: info@cooleysanemia.org
URL: http://www.cooleysanemia.org

2539 ■ Cooley's Anemia Foundation Research Fellowships *(Doctorate/Fellowship)*

Purpose: To serve people afflicted with various forms of thalassemia. **Focus:** Cooley's anemia. **Qualif.:** Applicants must be a post doctoral or junior faculty member interested in clinical or basic research related to thalassemia.

Funds Avail.: $40,000. **Deadline:** March 3.

2540 ■ Copper and Brass Service Center Association Inc.

994 Old Eagle School Rd., Ste. 1019
Wayne, PA 19087-1802
Ph: (610)971-4850
Fax: (610)971-4859
E-mail: diana@cbsa.copper-brass.org
URL: http://www.cbsa.copper-brass.org

2541 ■ Copper and Brass Service Center Inc. Scholarship Program *(Undergraduate/Scholarship)*

Purpose: To provide financial educational assistance to employees of CBSA's service center or associate member companies. **Focus:** Education-Curricula. **Qualif.:** Applicants must be dependents of an individual employed in CBSA's service center or any associate member company; must be college students entering Sophomore, Junior, or Senior year in the fall. **Criteria:** Scholarships will be granted only to children of CBSA's service center or associate member companies.

Funds Avail.: No specific amount. **Number Awarded:** 5. **To Apply:** Applicants are advised to visit the website to apply online.

2542 ■ Corporation for Public Broadcasting

401 9th St. NW
Washington, DC 20004-2129
Ph: (202)879-9600
Free: 800-272-2190
E-mail: nstaples@cpb.org
URL: http://www.cpb.org

2543 ■ Producers Academy Scholarships *(All/Scholarship)*

Purpose: To facilitate the development of and ensure universal access to non-commercial high quality programming and telecommunications services. **Focus:** Broadcasting. **Qualif.:** Applicants must have an interest in broadcasting. **Criteria:** Recipients are selected based on the research proposal.

Funds Avail.: No specific amount. **Number Awarded:** 20. **To Apply:** Applicants must complete the application form.

2544 ■ Small Station Training Scholarships *(Professional Development/Scholarship)*

Purpose: To support and extend training beyond a public television station's normal training capacity; to enable station management and staff to access more training and professional development opportunities than the stations training budget would normally support. **Focus:** Media. **Qualif.:** Applicants must be individuals who have an interest in radio or television broadcasting. **Criteria:** Recipients are selected based on the quality of the training and whether the training is directly connected to the stated individual and station goals, and the likelihood that the training will garner the desired, anticipated and stated outcomes.

Funds Avail.: Maximum amount of $2,000. **Number Awarded:** 2. **To Apply:** Applicants must complete the application form and submit 1-2 page proposals. **Contact:** nstaples@cpb.org.

2545 ■ Correctional Education Association

8182 Lark Brown Rd., Ste. 202
Elkridge, MD 21075
Ph: (443)459-3080
Fax: (443)459-3088
Free: 800-783-1232
URL: http://www.ceanational.org

2546 ■ Correctional Education Association Scholarships *(Graduate, Undergraduate/Scholarship)*

Purpose: To encourage students to continue a course of study in correctional education. **Focus:** Criminal justice. **Qualif.:** Applicant must be a graduate or undergraduate student in correctional education; must be a voting member of the Correctional Education Association and have been a member for a minimum of two years prior to application. **Criteria:** Application materials (quality of the application will be taken into consideration) will be evaluated by the Scholarship Committee. Priority will be given to first time applicants.

Funds Avail.: $500. **Number Awarded:** Scholarship Committee will determine the number of scholarships to be awarded. **To Apply:** Application forms are available in the website (application format must be completed in full in order to be considered by the Committee). Application materials must be sent to: Correctional Educational Association, Scholarship Committee, 8182 Lark Brown Rd., Ste. 202, Elkridge, MD 21075.

2547 ■ Council for the Advancement of Science Writing

PO Box 910
Hedgesville, WV 25427
Ph: (304)754-5077
URL: http://www.casw.org

2548 ■ Taylor/Blakeslee University Fellowships *(Undergraduate/Fellowship)*

Purpose: To provide financial support to students who want to pursue a career in science writing. **Focus:** Journalism. **Qualif.:** Applicant must be a enrolled in U.S graduate-level science writing program; must be a U.S citizen. **Criteria:** Scholarship application will be evaluated by CASW selection committee based on CASW criteria. Journalists with at least two years of mass-media experience will receive preferential treatment in the selection process.

Funds Avail.: $2,000. **To Apply:** Applicant must complete the application form and must have resume, samples of writing, and a statement (not to exceed 500 words). Application form and other supporting materials must be sent to: CASW Rennie Taylor/Alton Blakeslee Fellowship Program at PO Box 910, Hedgesville, WV 25427. **Deadline:** July 1.

2549 ■ Council on Library and Information Resources

1755 Massachusetts Ave. NW, Ste. 500
Washington, DC 20036
Ph: (202)939-4750

Awards are arranged alphabetically below their administering organizations

Fax: (202)939-4765
URL: http://www.clir.org

2550 ■ Mellon Fellowships *(Doctorate, Graduate/Fellowship)*

Purpose: To help junior scholars in the humanities and related social-science fields gain skill and creativity in developing knowledge from original sources. **Focus:** Humanities; Social sciences. **Qualif.:** Applicant must be enrolled in a doctoral program in a graduate school in the United States; have completed all doctoral requirements except the dissertation; planning to do dissertation research primarily in original source material in the holdings of archives, libraries, historical societies, museums, related repositories, or a combination. Candidates for the Ed.D, J.D., or D.D. degrees are not eligible. **Criteria:** A special committee of senior scholars in the humanities, archivists, and special-collections librarians will select recipients.

Funds Avail.: $1600 per month. **Number Awarded:** Varies. **To Apply:** Applicants must complete and submit the online application form; official transcripts; a letter from the appropriate dean, department head, or dissertation advisor certifying that the candidate has completed or will complete all doctoral work except the dissertation; and three letters of reference. All documents must be submitted in triplicate by mail. **Deadline:** November.

2551 ■ A.R. Zipf Fellowships *(Graduate/Fellowship)*

Purpose: To support students in graduate school in early stages of study. **Focus:** General studies. **Qualif.:** Applicants must be citizens or permanent residents of the United States. **Criteria:** Selection is based on the application.

Funds Avail.: $10,000. **To Apply:** Applicants must complete and submit the online application form; four letters of reference; undergraduate and graduate school transcripts; and scores of Graduate Record Examinations (if taken). All supporting documents must be sent to A. R. Zipf Fellowship Council on Library and Information Resources 1755 Massachusetts Avenue, NW, Suite 500 Washington, DC 20036-2124 USA. **Deadline:** April 18.

2552 ■ Council on Social Work Education

1725 Duke St., Ste. 500
Alexandria, VA 22314-3457
Ph: (703)683-8080
Fax: (703)683-8099
E-mail: info@cswe.org
URL: http://www.cswe.org

2553 ■ Council on Social Work Education Minority Fellowship Programs *(Postdoctorate/Fellowship)*

Purpose: To educate ethnic minority social work professionals to prepare them for leadership roles in mental health research and in the delivery of mental health services. **Focus:** General studies. **Qualif.:** Applicants must be currently enrolled in a doctoral program in a school of social work. **Criteria:** Recipients are selected based on the academic standing and letters of recommendation.

Funds Avail.: No specific amount. **To Apply:** Applicants must submit an application instruction sheet. All permanent residents must provide the following: photocopy of Permanent Resident Card signed by the notary public; official transcript of records; GRE and MAT scores; letter of admission; resume; financial list of information including the resources applied for, personal financial costs and anticipated income. **Deadline:** February 28.

2554 ■ Council on Social Work Education Scholars Program *(Postdoctorate/Scholarship)*

Purpose: To provide opportunities for senior and junior scholars to work on research projects or programmatic initiatives of their choosing that is in line with the priorities of CSWE. **Focus:** General studies. **Qualif.:** Program is open to senior scholars, faculty members and junior scholars such as doctoral students or individuals recently completing their doctoral dissertation. **Criteria:** Selection is based on proposed research.

Funds Avail.: No specific amount. **To Apply:** Applicants must submit completed application together with project proposal; budget; task list; and curriculum vitae. **Contact:** jholmes@cswe.org; 703-519-2062.

2555 ■ Carl A. Scott Book Scholarships *(Undergraduate/Scholarship)*

Purpose: To promote equity and social justice in social work. **Focus:** General Studies. **Qualif.:** Applicants must be in the last year of study for a social work degree in a baccalaureate or master's degree program accredited by the Council on Social Work Education; must be African American, American Indian, Asian American, Mexican American or Puerto Rican; must have a cumulative GPA of at least 3.0 on a 4.0 scale; and must be enrolled in 12 credit hours. **Criteria:** Recipients are selected based on the demonstrated commitment in promoting equity and social justice.

Funds Avail.: $500. **Number Awarded:** 2. **To Apply:** Applicants must submit a two-three page, double-spaced, typewritten statement that include professional interests, and experiences; two letters of recommendation preferably from a professor, a field instructor, or a community-based leader; an official letter from the school's registrar verifying that you are enrolled and in good standing with the university or college; and an official academic transcript from university/college. **Deadline:** May 5.

2556 ■ Creative Glass Center of America

1501 Glasstown Rd.
Millville, NJ 08332-1566
Fax: (856)825-2410
Free: 800-998-4552
E-mail: cgca@wheatons.org
URL: http://www.wheatonarts.org/creativeglasscenteramerica

2557 ■ Creative Glass Center of America Fellowships *(All/Fellowship)*

Purpose: To provide focused, self-directed artists with three-month and six-week fellowships. **Focus:** General studies. **Qualif.:** Applicants must be artists with young families, artists whose professional commitments do not afford them the option of a three-month residency, and for teams of artists wishing to collaborate on a particular project. **Criteria:** Applicants will be evaluated by the Fellowship Selection Committee based on their designed criteria.

Funds Avail.: No amount mentioned. **To Apply:** Applicants must submit completed application form; two letters of

Awards are arranged alphabetically below their administering organizations

recommendation; CDrom containing ten images of the applicant's work, image information sheet, one paragraph biography, statement of intent, and current resume/CV. **Deadline:** August 25.

2558 ■ Crohn's and Colitis Foundation of America

386 Park Ave. S, 17th Fl.
New York, NY 10016
Free: 800-932-2423
E-mail: info@ccfa.org
URL: http://www.ccfa.org

2559 ■ CCFA Career Development Awards *(Doctorate, Graduate/Grant)*

Purpose: To support a research that will help prepare for a career of independent basic or clinical investigation in the area of inflammatory bowel disease. **Focus:** Medicine. **Qualif.:** Applicants must be employed in an institution; engaged in heath care or health related research within the United States; have MD, PhD or equivalent; must not be in excess of ten years beyond the attainment of the doctoral degree; and have at least two years of documented post-doctoral research relevant to IBD. Proposals must be relevant to inflammatory bowel disease (Crohn's Disease or ulcerative colitis). **Criteria:** Applicants will be selected on the basis of intellectual background; mentor's record; number of important techniques to be learned; importance of the research area; relevance of BID; and applicant's career objectives.

Funds Avail.: $90,000. **To Apply:** Applicants must download, complete and submit the application form, CDA Letter of Intent and CDA forms available at the website. **Deadline:** January or July.

2560 ■ CCFA Research Fellowship Awards *(Doctorate, Graduate/Fellowship)*

Purpose: To support a research that will help prepare for a career of independent basic or clinical investigation in the area of Crohn's disease and ulcerative colitis. **Focus:** Medicine. **Qualif.:** Applicants must be employed in an institution; engaged in heath care or health related research within the United States; have MD, PhD or equivalent. Applicants with MD degrees must have at least two years of post doctoral experience. Proposals must be relevant to inflammatory bowel disease (Crohn's Disease or ulcerative colitis). **Criteria:** Applicants will be selected on the basis of intellectual background; research experience; mentor's track record; number of important techniques to be learned; importance of the research area; relevance of IBD; and career objectives.

Funds Avail.: $58,250. **To Apply:** Applicants must download, complete and submit the application form, RFA Letter of Intent and RFA forms available at the website. **Deadline:** May and October.

2561 ■ CCFA Student Research Fellowship Awards *(Graduate, Undergraduate/Grant)*

Purpose: To fund a research on topics relevant to inflammatory bowel disease. **Focus:** Medicine. **Qualif.:** Applicants must be undergraduates, medical, or graduate students in an accredited institution in the United States. **Criteria:** Applicants will be judged based on novelty, feasibility, and significance of the proposal.

Funds Avail.: $2,500. **Number Awarded:** 16. **To Apply:** Applicants must download, complete and submit the application form and SRFA forms available at the website. **Deadline:** March 15.

2562 ■ Crohn's and Colitis Foundation of America Senior Research Awards *(Doctorate, Graduate/Grant)*

Purpose: To provide funds for research relevant to Crohn's Disease. **Focus:** Medicine. **Qualif.:** Applicants must have an MD, PhD or equivalent degree; must be employed in an institution or engaged in health care or health related research; must have attained independence from their mentors. Proposals must be relevant to inflammatory bowel disease (Crohn's Disease or ulcerative colitis). **Criteria:** Awards will be given on the basis of scientific merit; relevance to IBD; excellence of investigator and research environment.

Funds Avail.: Maximum of $140,000. **To Apply:** Applicants must download, complete and submit the application form, SRA Letter of Intent and SRA forms available at the website. **Deadline:** January or July.

2563 ■ CSA Fraternal Life

122 W 22nd St.
Oak Brook, IL 60523
Ph: (630)472-0500
Fax: (630)472-1100
Free: 800-543-3272
URL: http://www.csafraternallife.org

2564 ■ CSA Fraternal Life Scholarships *(Undergraduate/Scholarship)*

Purpose: To help students on their financial needs for studying in college. **Focus:** Education. **Qualif.:** Applicants must be student-members with satisfactory class standing no less than a "B" or Better or 3.0 in average (minimum of two years); have at least $5,000 face value in permanent life insurance or $1,000 in a CSA annuity at the time of application. **Criteria:** Selection will be made based on class rank, grade point average, college placement test scores, extracurricular activities including CSA activities, and essay made.

Funds Avail.: $1,250. **Number Awarded:** Varies. **To Apply:** Applicants must submit a completed application form to the Fraternal Department; a complete official transcript to be sent to CSA; submit a photo for publication in the Journal to be attached to the first page of the application over the cap and diploma and a 400-600 words essay about the applicant's interests. **Deadline:** March 9.

2565 ■ Culinary and Hospitality Foundation of San Benito County

PO Box 1153
Tres Pinos, CA 95075
Ph: (831)628-3320
E-mail: info@chfsbc.com
URL: http://chfsbc.com

2566 ■ Culinary and Hospitality Foundation of San Benito County Scholarships *(Undergraduate/Scholarship)*

Purpose: To encourage professional development within the culinary, hospitality, tourism or related industry. **Focus:** Culinary Arts. **Qualif.:** Applicants must be high school

Awards are arranged alphabetically below their administering organizations

senior students who are permanent residents of San Benito County and are graduating from an accredited high school; must plan to seek a career in the culinary, hospitality or tourism related industry; and must have a high school GPA of 2.0 or above. **Criteria:** Recipients are selected based on financial need.

Funds Avail.: $1,000. **Number Awarded:** 2. **To Apply:** Applicants must submit a completed application form; two letters of recommendation; official high school transcript; and a personal essay. **Deadline:** April 15. **Contact:** PO Box 1153, Tres Pinos, CA 95075.

2567 ■ The Culinary Trust

PO Box 273
New York, NY 10013
Ph: (646)224-6989
Free: 888-345-4666
E-mail: info@theculinarytrust.com
URL: http://www.theculinarytrust.com

2568 ■ L'Academie de Cuisine Culinary Arts Scholarships *(All, Professional Development/ Scholarship)*

Purpose: To assist individuals who wish to advance their knowledge in the culinary arts. **Focus:** Culinary arts. **Qualif.:** Applicant must be a new student toward the 12-month Culinary Arts Certificate Program; have a GPA of 3.0 or higher (for applicants who have been students during the five years prior to the application). **Criteria:** Recipients are selected based on merit, work experience, culinary goals and skills and references.

Funds Avail.: No specific amount. **Number Awarded:** 1. **To Apply:** Applicants must submit a completed Culinary Trust Scholarship application form; a project proposal (two pages, double-spaced) illustrating their culinary goals; two letters of reference on business or personal letterhead; a current academic transcript; a non-refundable application fee of $25. **Deadline:** December 15.

Remarks: For information about L'Academie de Cuisine visit www.lacademie.com. **Contact:** scholarships@theculinarytrust.com.

2569 ■ Harry A. Bell Travel Grants *(All/Grant)*

Purpose: Provides financial support for travel and research to food writers during the time in which a proposal is being written. **Focus:** Culinary arts. **Qualif.:** Applicants must write a proposal that demonstrates contribution to knowledge about food. **Criteria:** Applicants are evaluated by a committee of culinary professionals.

Funds Avail.: $3,000-4,000. **To Apply:** Applicants must download a Harry A. Bell Grant application form; submit a project description (three pages, double-spaced) that includes: steps had led to this project, relevance of the project, contribution to the knowledge about food, intended audience; a brief description of projected budget; two references written on business or professional letterhead with complete contact information (professional references that will provide an opinion on the applicant and the applicant's work). **Deadline:** May 31.

Remarks: In memory of Harry A. Bell.

2570 ■ Cuisinart Culinary Study Scholarships *(All, Professional Development/Scholarship)*

Purpose: To assist individuals who wish to advance their knowledge in the culinary arts. **Focus:** Culinary arts. **Qualif.:** Applicant must be a new student or currently enrolled student working toward any Culinary Arts degree or certificate program at any accredited national culinary school; have a GPA of 3.0 or higher (for applicants who have been students during the five years prior to the application). **Criteria:** Recipient is selected based on merit, work experience, culinary goals and skills, and references.

Funds Avail.: $1,500. **Number Awarded:** 1. **To Apply:** Applicants must submit a completed Culinary Trust Scholarship application form; a project proposal (two-pages, double-spaced) illustrating their culinary goals; two letters of reference on business or personal letterhead; a current academic transcript; a non-refundable application fee of $25. **Deadline:** December 15.

Remarks: For information about Cuisinart visit www.cuisinart.com. **Contact:** scholarships@theculinarytrust.com.

2571 ■ The Culinary Trust's Memorial Journalism Scholarships *(Professional Development/ Grant)*

Purpose: To assist career journalists who wish to conduct an independent study and research on an original and innovative culinary topic. **Focus:** Culinary arts. **Qualif.:** Applicant must be a writer whose work is focused on food, wine or other aspect of gastronomy and culinary arts; have a minimum of two years experience in food service/industry related. **Criteria:** Recipients are selected based on merit, work experience, culinary goals and skills, and references.

Funds Avail.: $3,000. **Number Awarded:** 1. **To Apply:** Applicants must submit a completed Culinary Trust Scholarship application form; a project proposal that demonstrates true literary merit in both promise and achievement at writing (not just knowledge about food); two letters of reference on business or personal letterhead; an itemized budget detailing the use of the award; a tentative travel schedule with dates and locations; a resume; a non-refundable application fee of $25. **Deadline:** December 15.

2572 ■ The eGullet Society for Culinary Arts and Letters Brian and Thelma Moore Memorial Culinary Journalist Independent Study Scholarships *(Professional Development/Grant)*

Purpose: To assist career journalists who wish to conduct an independent study and research on an original and innovative culinary topic. **Focus:** Culinary arts. **Qualif.:** Applicant must be a writer whose work is focused on food, wine or other aspect of gastronomy and culinary arts; must have a minimum of two years experience in food service/ industry related. **Criteria:** Recipients are selected based on merit, work experience, culinary goals and skills, and references.

Funds Avail.: $5,000. **Number Awarded:** 1. **To Apply:** Applicants must submit a completed Culinary Trust Scholarship application form; a project proposal that demonstrates true literary merit in both promise and achievement at writing (not just knowledge about food); two letters of reference on business or personal letterhead; an itemized budget detailing the use of the award; a tentative travel schedule with dates and locations; a resume; a non-refundable application fee of $25. **Deadline:** December 15.

Remarks: Funded by Marlene and Don Newell in memory of their brother Brian Moore and mother Thelma Moore.

Awards are arranged alphabetically below their administering organizations

2573 ■ The eGullet Society for Culinary Arts and Letters Culinary Journalist Independent Study Scholarships *(Professional Development/ Grant)*

Purpose: To assist career journalists who wish to conduct an independent study and research on an original and innovative culinary topic. **Focus:** Culinary arts. **Qualif.:** Applicant must be a writer whose work is focused on food, wine or other aspect of gastronomy and culinary arts; have a minimum of two years experience in the food service industry. **Criteria:** Recipients are selected based on merit, work experience, culinary goals and skills, and references.

Funds Avail.: $5,000. **Number Awarded:** 1. **To Apply:** Applicants must submit a completed Culinary Trust Scholarship application form; a project proposal that demonstrates true literary merit in both promise and achievement at writing (not just knowledge about food); two letters of reference on business or personal letterhead; an itemized budget detailing the use of the award; a tentative travel schedule with dates and locations; a resume; a non-refundable application fee of $25. **Deadline:** December 15.

2574 ■ The eGullet Society for Culinary Arts and Letters Matthew X. Hassett Memorial Culinary Arts Scholarships *(All, Professional Development/Scholarship)*

Purpose: To assist individuals who wish to advance their knowledge in the culinary arts. **Focus:** Culinary arts. **Qualif.:** Applicant must be a new student, currently enrolled student or career professional toward a culinary degree or certificate program at any accredited domestic or foreign institution; have a GPA of 3.0 or higher (for applicants who have been students during the five years prior to the application). **Criteria:** Recipients are selected based on merit, work experience, culinary goals and skills, and references.

Funds Avail.: $5,000. **Number Awarded:** 1. **To Apply:** Applicants must submit a completed Culinary Trust Scholarship application form; a project proposal (two-pages, double-spaced) illustrating their culinary goals; two letters of reference on business or personal letterhead; a current academic transcript; a non-refundable application fee of $25. **Deadline:** December 15.

Remarks: Funded by James and Dora Hassett in memory of eGullet Society member Matthew X. Hassett.

2575 ■ The eGullet Society for Culinary Arts and Letters Professional Chef Independent Study Scholarships *(Other, Professional Development/Grant)*

Purpose: To assist professional culinary or pastry chefs who wish to conduct an independent study to advance their skills as a chef or pastry chef. **Focus:** Culinary arts. **Qualif.:** Applicant must be a professional chef with a minimum of two years experience in the food service industry. **Criteria:** Recipients are selected based on merit, work experience, culinary goals and skills, and references.

Funds Avail.: $5,000. **Number Awarded:** 1. **To Apply:** Applicants must submit a completed Culinary Trust Scholarship application form; a project proposal that demonstrates the utilization of skills obtained during the study; two letters of reference on business or personal letterhead; an itemized budget detailing the use of the award; a tentative travel schedule with dates and locations; a resume; a non-refundable application fee of $25. **Deadline:** December 15.

Remarks: For information on The eGullet Society for Culinary Arts and Letters visit www.egullet.org. **Contact:** scholarships@theculinarytrust.com.

2576 ■ The French Culinary Institute Classic Pastry Arts Scholarships *(All, Professional Development/Scholarship)*

Purpose: To assist individuals who wish to advance their knowledge in the culinary arts. **Focus:** Culinary arts. **Qualif.:** Applicant must be a new student or career professional toward the 9-months Classic Pastry Arts Diploma Program; have a GPA of 3.0 or higher (for applicants who have been students during the five years prior to the application). **Criteria:** Recipients are selected based on merit, work experience, culinary goals and skills, and references.

Funds Avail.: $5,000. **Number Awarded:** 1. **To Apply:** Applicants must submit a completed Culinary Trust Scholarship application form; a project proposal (two pages, double-spaced) illustrating their culinary goals; two letters of reference on business or personal letterhead; a current academic transcript; a non-refundable application fee of $25. **Deadline:** December 15.

2577 ■ The French Culinary Institute Culinary Arts Scholarships *(All, Professional Development/ Scholarship)*

Purpose: To assist individuals who wish to advance their knowledge in the culinary arts. **Focus:** Culinary arts. **Qualif.:** Applicant must be a new student or career professional toward the 9-months Classic Culinary Arts Diploma Program; have a GPA of 3.0 or higher (for applicants who have been students during the five years prior to the application). **Criteria:** Recipients are selected based on merit, work experience, culinary goals and skills, and references.

Funds Avail.: $5,000. **Number Awarded:** 1. **To Apply:** Applicants must submit a completed Culinary Trust Scholarship application form; a project proposal (two pages, double-spaced) illustrating their culinary goals; two letters of reference on business or personal letterhead; a current academic transcript; a non-refundable application fee of $25. **Deadline:** December 15. **Contact:** scholarships@theculinarytrust.com.

2578 ■ The French Culinary Institute's Food and Technology Scholarships - Magic Potions Transglutaminase *(Professional Development/ Scholarship)*

Purpose: To assist individuals who wish to advance their knowledge in the culinary arts. **Focus:** Culinary arts. **Qualif.:** Applicant must be a career professional toward Magic Potions: Transglutaminase at the French Culinary Institute; have a minimum of two years experience in food service/ industry related. **Criteria:** Recipients are selected based on merit, work experience, culinary goals and skills, and references.

Funds Avail.: No specific amount. **Number Awarded:** 1. **To Apply:** Applicants must submit a completed Culinary Trust Scholarship application form; a project proposal (three pages, double-spaced) illustrating their culinary goals; two letters of reference on business or personal letterhead; an essay with a budget and tentative travel dates; a current academic transcript; a non-refundable application fee of $25. **Deadline:** December 15.

Remarks: The Magic Potions: Transglutaminase is taught through lecture and hands-on use of transglutaminase.

Awards are arranged alphabetically below their administering organizations

2579 ■ Kendall College Bachelor of Arts in Culinary Arts Scholarships *(Undergraduate/ Scholarship)*

Purpose: To assist freshmen students pursuing a bachelor's degree in Culinary Arts at Kendall College. **Focus:** Culinary arts. **Qualif.:** Applicant must be a freshman student pursuing a degree in Culinary Arts; have a GPA of 3.0 or higher. **Criteria:** Recipients are selected based on merit, work experience, culinary goals and skills, and references.

Funds Avail.: $500. **Number Awarded:** 1. **To Apply:** Applicants must submit a completed Culinary Trust Scholarship application form; a project proposal (two pages, double-spaced) illustrating their culinary goals; two letters of reference on business or personal letterhead; a current academic transcript; a non-refundable application fee of $25. **Deadline:** December 15.

Remarks: For information about Kendall College visit www.kendall.edu. **Contact:** scholarships@theculinarytrust.com.

2580 ■ Le Cordon Bleu Ottawa Culinary Arts Institute Basic Cuisine Certificate Scholarships *(All, Professional Development/Scholarship)*

Purpose: To assist individuals who wish to advance their knowledge in the culinary arts. **Focus:** Culinary arts. **Qualif.:** Applicant must be a new student, currently enrolled student or career professional toward the 11-week Basic Cuisine Certificate Program; have a GPA of 3.0 or higher (for applicants who have been students during the five years prior to the application). **Criteria:** Recipients are selected based on merit, work experience, culinary goals and skills, and references.

Funds Avail.: Covers tuition fees. Uniforms, equipment, airfares, accommodations or living expenses are not included. **Number Awarded:** 1. **To Apply:** Applicants must submit a completed Culinary Trust Scholarship application form; a project proposal (two pages, double-spaced) illustrating their culinary goals; two letters of reference on business or personal letterhead; a current academic transcript; a non-refundable application fee of $25. **Deadline:** December 15.

Remarks: For information about Le Cordon Bleu Ottawa Culinary Arts Institute visit www.lcbottawa.com. **Contact:** scholarships@theculinarytrust.com.

2581 ■ New England Culinary Institute Scholarships *(All/Scholarship)*

Purpose: To assist individuals who wish to advance their knowledge in the culinary arts. **Focus:** Culinary arts; Hotel, institutional, and restaurant management. **Qualif.:** Applicant must be a new student working in a degree program in: Bachelor's Degree in Culinary Arts, Associate's Degree in Culinary Arts, Associate's Degree in Baking and Pastry Arts, Associate's Degree in Hospitality and Restaurant Management or Bachelor's Degree in Hospitality and Restaurant Management; must have a GPA of 3.0 or higher (for applicants who have been students during the five years prior to the application). **Criteria:** Recipient is selected based on merit, work experience, culinary goals and skills, and references.

Funds Avail.: $5,000. **Number Awarded:** 2. **To Apply:** Applicants must submit a completed Culinary Trust Scholarship application form; a project proposal (two-page, double-spaced) illustrating their culinary goals; two letters of reference on business or personal letterhead; a current academic transcript; a non-refundable application fee of $25. **Deadline:** December 15.

Remarks: Scholarships are based on space availability. **Contact:** scholarships@theculinarytrust.com.

2582 ■ Charlie Trotters's Culinary Education Foundation Culinary Study Scholarships *(All, Professional Development/Scholarship)*

Purpose: Provides financial assistance to individuals pursuing their career in the culinary arts. **Focus:** Culinary arts. **Qualif.:** Applicants must reside in Illinois; be a new student currently enrolled or a career professional interested in any Culinary Arts degree or certificate program at any accredited national culinary school; have a GPA of 3.0 or higher (for applicants who have been students during the five years prior to the application). **Criteria:** Recipient is selected based on merit, work experience, culinary goals and skills and references.

Funds Avail.: $5,000. **Number Awarded:** 1. **To Apply:** Applicants must submit a completed Culinary Trust Scholarship application form; a project proposal (two-page, double-spaced) illustrating their culinary goals; two letters of reference on business or personal letterhead; a current academic transcript; a non-refundable application fee of $25. **Deadline:** December 15.

Remarks: For information about Charlie Trotter's Culinary Education Foundation visit www.charlietrotters.com. **Contact:** scholarships@theculinarytrust.com.

2583 ■ Zwilling, J.A. Henckels Culinary Arts Scholarships *(All, Professional Development/ Scholarship)*

Purpose: To assist individuals who wish to advance their knowledge in the culinary arts. **Focus:** Culinary arts. **Qualif.:** Applicant must be a new student currently enrolled or a career professional working toward a Culinary Arts degree or certificate program at any accredited national culinary institution; must have a GPA of 3.0 or higher (for applicants who have been students during the five years prior to the application). **Criteria:** Recipient is selected based on merit, work experience, culinary goals and skills and references.

Funds Avail.: $5,000. For tuition only. **Number Awarded:** 1. **To Apply:** Applicants must submit a completed Culinary Trust Scholarship application form; a project proposal (two-page, double-spaced) illustrating their culinary goals; two letters of reference on business or personal letterhead; an essay with a budget and tentative travel dates; a current academic transcript; a non-refundable application fee of $25. **Deadline:** December 15.

Remarks: For information about Zwilling J.A. Henckels, Inc., visit www.jahenckels.com. **Contact:** scholarships@theculinarytrust.com.

2584 ■ Cystic Fibrosis Foundation

6931 Arlington Rd.
Bethesda, MD 20814
Ph: (301)951-4422
Free: 800-344-4823
E-mail: info@cff.org
URL: http://www.cff.org

2585 ■ Cystic Fibrosis Foundation Scholarships *(Undergraduate/Scholarship)*

Purpose: To provide financial assistance to individuals with Cystic Fibrosis intending to pursue studies in undergraduate or vocational schools. **Focus:** General studies. **Qualif.:** Applicants may either be individuals entering college or vocational school or those who have already completed two semesters of college or vocational school. **Criteria:** Scholarships are awarded based on a combination of financial need, academic achievement, and leadership.

Funds Avail.: $1,000. **To Apply:** Application forms and instructions are available in the website. **Deadline:** March 21. **Contact:** Cystic Fibrosis Scholarship Foundation, 1555 Sherman Avenue, 116 Evanston, IL 60201.

2586 ■ Cystic Fibrosis Worldwide

210 Park Ave., No. 267
Worcester, MA 01609
Ph: (508)733-6120
E-mail: information@cfww.org
URL: http://www.cfww.org

2587 ■ Boomer Esiason Foundation Scholarship Program *(All/Scholarship)*

Purpose: To provide educational assistance for students with cystic fibrosis. **Focus:** General studies. **Qualif.:** Applicants must be proven to have been diagnosed with cystic fibrosis. **Criteria:** Grantees will be selected based on scholastic merits and type of lifestyle.

Funds Avail.: $500-$2000. **Number Awarded:** 10-15. **To Apply:** Applicants must submit an application form available at the website. The application form and other required materials must be forwarded to: Boomer Esiason Foundation, Attn: Scholarship Program, 52 Vanderbilt Ave., 15th Fl., New York, NY 10017. **Deadline:** Scholarships are granted quarterly: March 15, June 15, September 15 and December 15. **Contact:** jcahill@esiason.org.

2588 ■ Exercise For Life Athletic Scholarships Program *(Undergraduate/Scholarship)*

Purpose: To provide educational assistance to student athletes with cystic fibrosis. **Focus:** General studies. **Qualif.:** Applicants must be high school senior athletes pursuing undergraduate degrees. **Criteria:** Grantees will be selected according to financial need, academic accomplishment and athletic ability.

Funds Avail.: $10,000. **Number Awarded:** 2. **To Apply:** Applicants must submit an application form (available at the website); EFL training log (print from website); an essay (one-page, single-spaced) on the importance of exercise and compliance; recent photo; letter from physician (on letterhead) confirming CF diagnosis and therapy routine; recent W2 form verification for both parents; high school transcript; letter of acceptance from a college institution; and signed waiver. Requirements must be mailed to: Boomer Esiason Foundation, Attn: Scholarship Program, 52 Vanderbilt Ave., 15th Fl., New York, NY 10017. **Deadline:** June 27. **Contact:** jcahillbef@aol.com.

2589 ■ Sacks For CF Scholarships *(All/Scholarship)*

Purpose: To provide educational assistance for students with cystic fibrosis. **Focus:** General studies. **Qualif.:** Applicants must be proven to have been diagnosed with cystic fibrosis. **Criteria:** Grantees will be selected based on scholastic merits and type of lifestyle.

Funds Avail.: $1,000. **To Apply:** Applicants must submit an application form (downloaded from the website); recent photo; letter from a doctor confirming diagnosis of cystic fibrosis and list of daily medication routine; 2-part essay; an official/unofficial high school/college transcript; tuition breakdown; and W2 form for verification for both parents. Completed application form and other requirements must be mailed to: Boomer Esiason Foundation, Attn: Scholarship Program, 52 Vanderbilt Ave., 15th Fl., New York, NY 10017. **Deadline:** January 11.

Remarks: A joint program by Novartis and Boomer Esiason Foundation.

2590 ■ Scholarships of the Arts *(Graduate, Undergraduate/Scholarship)*

Purpose: To provide educational assistance to students engaged in arts. **Focus:** General studies. **Qualif.:** Applicants must be artists with cystic fibrosis (CF). **Criteria:** Grantees will be selected according to credits.

Funds Avail.: No specific amount. **To Apply:** Applicants must submit an application form (available at the website); a recent photo; letter from the doctor confirming diagnosis of cystic fibrosis and list of daily medication routine; 2-part essay; an official/unofficial high school/college transcript; tuition breakdown; W2 form for verification for both parents and picture of the art entry. Applications and other requirements must be mailed to: Boomer Esiason Foundation, Attn: Scholarship Program, 52 Vanderbilt Ave. 15th Fl., New York, NY 10017. **Deadline:** May 23.

2591 ■ Bonnie Strangio Education Scholarships *(Graduate, Undergraduate/Scholarship)*

Purpose: To provide educational assistance to students with cystic fibrosis. **Focus:** General studies. **Qualif.:** Applicants must be undergraduate or graduate students who have cystic fibrosis. **Criteria:** Grantees will be selected by a majority vote.

Funds Avail.: $2,500. **To Apply:** Applicants must submit an application form (available at the website); an essay on post-graduation goals; a recent photo; a letter from a physician confirming CF diagnosis; most recent W2 form verification for both parents; transcript (high school, college, or graduate); and letter of acceptance from an academic institution. All requirements must be mailed to: Boomer Esiason Foundation, Attn: Scholarship Program, 52 Vanderbilt Ave., 15th Fl., New York, New York, 10017. **Deadline:** June 13. **Contact:** jcahillbef@aol.com.

2592 ■ University of Phoenix Touchdown Mondays Scholarship Program *(All/Scholarship)*

Purpose: To provide educational assistance to students with cystic fibrosis. **Focus:** General studies. **Qualif.:** Applicants must be proven to have been diagnosed with cystic fibrosis. **Criteria:** Grantees will be selected according to credentials.

Funds Avail.: No specific amount. **Number Awarded:** 26. **To Apply:** Applicants must submit an application form (downloaded from the website); a recent photo; letter from the doctor confirming diagnosis of cystic fibrosis and list of daily medication routine; 2-part essay; an official/unofficial high school/college transcript; and W2 form for verification for both parents. Completed application form and other requirements must be mailed to: Boomer Esiason Foundation, Attn: Scholarship Program, 52 Vanderbilt Ave., 15th Fl., New York, NY 10017. **Deadline:** March 28.

Remarks: University of Phoenix contributed 26 full-tuition scholarships to the Boomer Esiason Foundation.

2593 ■ Dade Community Foundation, Inc.

200 S Biscayne Blvd., Ste. 505
Miami, FL 33131-2343

Awards are arranged alphabetically below their administering organizations

Ph: (305)371-2711
Fax: (305)371-5342
URL: http://www.dadecommunityfoundation.org

2594 ■ Judge Sidney M. Aronovitz Memorial Scholarships *(High School/Scholarship)*

Purpose: To provide financial assistance to Miami-Dade County minority students planning to continue their education at the university level and pursue a career in South Florida. **Focus:** General studies. **Qualif.:** Applicants must be minority high school seniors or GED recipients no older than 19 years of age attending a Miami Dade County public school with a minimum high school grade point average of 3.0. **Criteria:** Recipients are selected based on personal statement/goals; recommendations; academic achievement; financial need; and, volunteer/work experience.

Funds Avail.: $500. **Number Awarded:** 1. **To Apply:** Applicants must submit the completed application form and enclose all proper attachments. **Deadline:** March 19.

2595 ■ Jennet Colliflower Nursing Scholarships *(Undergraduate/Scholarship)*

Purpose: To provide financial assistance to students in their junior or senior year of undergraduate nursing degree, who are Florida residents and enrolled full-time in a Florida public or private university. **Focus:** Nursing. **Qualif.:** Applicants must be entering junior or senior year undergraduate studies; must be full-time students (minimum of 12 credits hours per semester) in a public or private four-year Florida university or college; and, must be seeking an undergraduate degree in Nursing. **Criteria:** Recipients are selected based on the volunteer experience, work experience and school activities; academic achievement; financial need; and, personal aspirations/career goals and relationship with nursing.

Funds Avail.: $1,000. **Number Awarded:** 2. **To Apply:** Applicants must submit the completed application form along with the required materials. **Deadline:** May 7.

2596 ■ The Continental Group Scholarship Fund *(High School/Scholarship)*

Purpose: To provide educational opportunities for the children of current, full-time employees of The Continental Group, Inc and its subsidiaries. **Focus:** General studies. **Qualif.:** Applicants must be high school seniors graduating in 2008 with a minimum 3.0 grade point average and have a parent who is a fulltime employee of The Continental Group, Inc. or one of its Subsidiaries for at least one year. **Criteria:** Applicants are evaluated based on financial need.

Funds Avail.: $1,000. **Number Awarded:** 4. **To Apply:** Applicants must submit all the required application information. **Deadline:** March 27.

2597 ■ Alan R. Epstein "Reach for the Stars" Scholarships *(Undergraduate/Scholarship)*

Purpose: To provide financial assistance to deserving students in Dade County who have successfully dealt with life's obstacles. **Focus:** General studies. **Qualif.:** Applicants must be high school seniors graduating in June. **Criteria:** Applicants are evaluated based on financial need.

Funds Avail.: $10,000. **To Apply:** Applicants must submit completed application form; high school official transcript; college acceptance letter(s); two letters of recommendation; volunteer/work experience and school activities; personal statement; one or two paragraphs describing the importance of scholarship. **Deadline:** April 11.

2598 ■ Randy Green Memorial Scholarship Fund *(High School/Scholarship)*

Purpose: To provide financial assistance to students at Miami Springs Senior High School who are enrolled in a college program related to public education, political science, history or social work. **Focus:** Political science; economics; Social work. **Qualif.:** Applicants must be permanent residents or citizens of the U.S. and domiciled in South Florida; must have minimum high school grade point average of 3.0; must be Miami Springs high-school seniors demonstrating merit and financial need; must be accepted into accredited university and plan to be enrolled in two year or four year university programs concentrating in public education, political science, history, social work, or other major related to community service. **Criteria:** Recipients are selected based on academic achievement; personal statement/career goals; volunteer/work experience and school activities; recommendations; and financial need.

Funds Avail.: $1,000. **Number Awarded:** 2. **To Apply:** Applicants must submit the completed application form and all other required application information. **Deadline:** June 3.

2599 ■ Dr. Felix H. Reyler Memorial Scholarships *(Undergraduate/Scholarship)*

Purpose: To provide financial assistance to business students entering their junior/senior year of undergraduate studies. **Focus:** Business; Finance. **Qualif.:** Applicants must be permanent residents or citizens of the U.S. and domiciled in Florida; must be business students entering their junior/senior year of undergraduate studies; must be students graduating from the Academy for International Business and Finance at Miami Jackson Senior High and the children of FIBA members; must be currently or enrolling as full-time students in four-year Florida college/ university and seeking for a degree in Business. **Criteria:** Recipients are selected based on financial need; academic achievement; personal aspirations/career goals and interests within Business and Finance; volunteer/work experience; and, school activities.

Funds Avail.: $2,500. **Number Awarded:** 2. **To Apply:** Applicants must submit completed application form; personal statement; official transcript; original recommendation letter on school letterhead; and, one photocopy of the entire completed application. **Deadline:** April 25.

2600 ■ Samalot - Sebastian Scholarship Fund *(High School/Scholarship)*

Purpose: To support minority high school students in need of financial assistance. **Focus:** General studies. **Qualif.:** Applicants must be permanent residents or citizens of the U.S. and domiciled in South Florida; must have minimum high school grade point average of 3.5; must be enrolling as full-time students (minimum of 12 credit hours per semester) in a four-year college/university. **Criteria:** Recipients are selected based on merit and financial need.

Funds Avail.: $2,000. **Number Awarded:** 3. **To Apply:** Applicants must submit all the required application information. **Deadline:** April 4.

2601 ■ Leo Suarez Journalism Scholarships *(Undergraduate/Scholarship)*

Purpose: To help talented South Florida students for aspiring a career in journalism, broadcast or mass communications. **Focus:** Journalism; Broadcasting; Communications.

Qualif.: Applicants must be high school seniors in Miami-Dade or Broward public school; must have minimum of 3.0 grade point average; must intend to major in journalism, broadcast or mass communications in undergraduate studies at four year university and/or two year college. **Criteria:** Applicants are evaluated based on career goals; writing samples; teacher recommendation; and academic achievement.

Funds Avail.: $1,000. **To Apply:** Applicants must submit the completed application form together with the three writing samples that have been published and letter of recommendation from the journalism sponsor or English professor at their high school. **Deadline:** March 21.

2602 ■ The Rodney Thaxton Justice Fund *(Undergraduate/Scholarship)*

Purpose: To assist students pursuing career in the insurance industry and business. **Focus:** Business; Insurance and insurance-related fields. **Qualif.:** Applicants must be high school seniors with minimum high school grade point average of 3.0 who have interest in pursuing career in business or the insurance industry. **Criteria:** Applicants are evaluated based on personal statement/goals, essay on ethics; academic achievement; volunteer/work experience.

Funds Avail.: $1,500. **Number Awarded:** 2. **To Apply:** Applicants must submit completed application form and all required application materials and information. **Deadline:** March 9.

2603 ■ Jacki Tuckfield Memorial Graduate Business Scholarship Fund *(Undergraduate/Scholarship)*

Purpose: To provide financial assistance to African-American students to pursue their professional careers. **Focus:** Business. **Qualif.:** Applicants must be African American United States citizen, resident of South Florida, enrolled in a graduate business degree program (master's or doctoral), at Florida University during the Fall, Winter, Spring or Summer term of the 2008-2009 academic year; must be planning to pursue professional career in South Florida. **Criteria:** Recipients are selected based on merit.

Funds Avail.: $1,000. **To Apply:** Applicants must submit the completed application form; essay; transcripts; color passport photo; letter of recommendation; and resume. **Deadline:** May 25.

2604 ■ Seitlin Franklin E. Wheeler Scholarship Fund *(Undergraduate/Scholarship)*

Purpose: To assist students pursuing careers in the insurance industry and business. **Focus:** Insurance and insurance-related fields; Business. **Qualif.:** Applicants must be high school seniors with minimum high school grade point average of 3.0 and demonstrate interest in pursuing career in business or the insurance industry. **Criteria:** Recipients are selected on the basis of personal statement/goals, essay on ethics; academic achievement; and, volunteer/work experience.

Funds Avail.: $1,500. **Number Awarded:** 2. **To Apply:** Applicants must submit all the required application information. **Deadline:** May 9.

2605 ■ Daedalian Foundation

PO Box 249
Randolph AFB, TX 78148-0249
Ph: (210)945-2113
Fax: (210)945-2112
E-mail: foundationchairman@daedalians.org
URL: http://www.daedalians.org

2606 ■ Descendant Scholarships *(Undergraduate/Scholarship)*

Purpose: To encourage the youth to become military pilots. **Focus:** Aerospace sciences. **Qualif.:** Applicants must be direct-line descendants of Daedalians. **Criteria:** Selection is based on the application.

Funds Avail.: No specific amount. **To Apply:** Applicants must submit a completed application form together with a 3" x 5" photograph and a letter stating the rank, name and number of their sponsoring Daeldalian to the Chairman, Daedalian Foundation, PO Box 249 Randolph AFB, TX 78148-0249.

2607 ■ John and Alice Egan Multi-Year Mentioning Scholarships *(Undergraduate/Scholarship)*

Purpose: To encourage the youth to become military pilots. **Focus:** Aerospace sciences. **Qualif.:** Applicants must be a college/university student pursuing a career as a military aviator. Freshmen are not qualified. **Criteria:** Selection is based on the application.

Funds Avail.: $2000. **To Apply:** Applicants must submit a completed application form together with a 3" x 5" photograph; complete transcripts (sent directly by the educational institution); a copy of FAA medical certificate and annotated copy of the Flight Physical Standards Questionnaire to the Chairman, Daedalian Foundation, PO Box 249 Randolph AFB, TX 78148-0249. **Deadline:** August 1. **Remarks:** The scholarship is not tied to the Matching Program, students may apply for both programs.

2608 ■ Matching Scholarships Program *(Undergraduate/Scholarship)*

Purpose: To encourage the youth to become military pilots. **Focus:** Aerospace sciences. **Qualif.:** Applicants must be a college/university student pursuing a career as a military aviator. **Criteria:** Selection is based on the application.

Funds Avail.: No specific amount. **To Apply:** Applicants must submit a completed application form together with a 3" x 5" photograph to the Chairman, Daedalian Foundation, PO Box 249 Randolph AFB, TX 78148-0249.

2609 ■ Navy, Army or Air Force ROTC Scholarship Program *(Undergraduate/Scholarship)*

Purpose: To encourage the youth to become military pilots. **Focus:** Aerospace sciences. **Qualif.:** Applicants must be a college/university student pursuing a career as a military aviator. **Criteria:** Selection is made by various ROTC headquarters.

Funds Avail.: No specific amount. **To Apply:** Candidates must be nominated by their local commanders.

2610 ■ Dallas Hispanic Bar Association

2101 Ross Ave.
Dallas, TX 75201
Ph: (214)924-3176
Fax: (214)634-9991
E-mail: mail@dallashispanicbar.com
URL: http://www.dallashispanicbar.com

2611 ■ Dallas Hispanic Bar Association Scholarships *(Undergraduate/Scholarship)*

Purpose: To provide financial assistance for Texas law school students. **Focus:** Law. **Qualif.:** Applicants must

Awards are arranged alphabetically below their administering organizations

have high academic performance and demonstrated leadership and must be enrolled in a Texas law school. **Criteria:** Selection of recipients will be based on financial need and academic standing.

Funds Avail.: $1,000-$2,000. **Number Awarded:** 5. **To Apply:** Applicants must complete the application form available online and must send it to Martinez Ramirez Siewcynski LLC, 6318 Gaston Ave., Ste. 201, Dallas, TX 75214. **Deadline:** August 22. **Contact:** Maricela Siewczynski, at the above address (see entry 2610).

2612 ■ Danish America Heritage Society

4105 Stone Brooke Rd.
Ames, IA 50010
Ph: (515)232-7479
E-mail: iversenji@qwest.net
URL: http://www.danishamericanheritagesociety.org

2613 ■ Edith and Arnold N. Bodtker Grant *(All/Grant)*

Purpose: To provide stipends for students interested in studying and performing research in the area of Danish immigration to North America. **Focus:** General studies. **Qualif.:** Applicants must be currently enrolled in or graduated from a university-level institution. **Criteria:** Candidates must have a well-defined research or internship project that makes a stay in the USA (for Danish or North American students) or in Denmark (for North American students).

Funds Avail.: $5,000. **Number Awarded:** Varies. **To Apply:** Applicants planned projects must be for a three to four-month period of residence in the USA or in Denmark, during the next calendar year. Proposals for residence in June-August will also be considered. **Deadline:** October 1.

Remarks: Established in 1998.

2614 ■ Datatel

4375 Fair Lakes Ct.
Fairfax, VA 22033
Ph: (703)968-9000
Free: 800-DAT-ATEL
URL: http://www.datatel.com

2615 ■ Datatel Angelfire Scholarships *(Graduate, Undergraduate/Scholarship)*

Purpose: To support students who served the U.S. military and are attending an eligible Datatel client institution. **Focus:** General studies. **Qualif.:** Applicant must be an outstanding student currently attending an eligible Datatel client institution, who served the U.S. military in the Asian theater (Vietnam, Cambodia, or Laos during the 1964-1975 time-frame), or in Operation Desert Storm, Operation Enduring Freedom and/or Operation Iraqi Freedom; or a spouse or child of a Vietnam Veteran, or a refugee from Vietnam, Cambodia, or Laos. **Criteria:** Award is given based on the application materials.

Funds Avail.: $1700. **To Apply:** Applicants must complete and submit an online application together with the essay. **Deadline:** January 31. **Contact:** Jane H. Roth, Executive Director at scholars@datatel.com.

2616 ■ Datatel Scholarships *(Graduate, Undergraduate/Scholarship)*

Purpose: To help deserving students meet education goals. **Focus:** General studies. **Qualif.:** Applicant must be a student currently attending an eligible Datatel client institution; enrolled as full-time or part-time (taking at least six credit hours) undergraduate or graduate student. **Criteria:** Award is given based on the application.

Funds Avail.: $1000, $1600, and $2400. **Number Awarded:** 180 in 2008-2009 academic year. **To Apply:** Applicants must complete and submit an online application by the deadline; all applications and letters of recommendation are to be submitted electronically. **Deadline:** January 31. **Contact:** Jane H. Roth, Executive Director at scholars@datatel.com.

2617 ■ Russ Griffith Memorial Scholarships *(Graduate, Undergraduate/Scholarship)*

Purpose: To support returning students with their education. **Focus:** General studies. **Qualif.:** Applicant must be an outstanding student attending an eligible Datatel client institution who has returned to school after an absence of five years or longer; full- and part-time, taking at least six credit hours, undergraduate or graduate student. **Criteria:** Awards are given based on the application materials.

Funds Avail.: $2000. **Number Awarded:** 50. **To Apply:** Applicants must complete and submit an on-line application together with the essay. **Deadline:** January 31.

Remarks: Formerly called as Returning Student Scholarship. **Contact:** Jane H. Roth, Executive Director at scholars@datatel.com.

2618 ■ Rebecca Davis Dance Company

PO Box 40892
Philadelphia, PA 19107
Ph: (215)840-3890
E-mail: davis@rebeccadavisdance.com
URL: http://www.rebeccadavisdance.com

2619 ■ Rebecca Davis Scholarships *(Professional Development/Scholarship)*

Purpose: To support dedicated, high-potential artists in pursuit of a career in professional dance. **Focus:** Dance. **Qualif.:** Applicants must be 12 to 18 years of age; have successfully completed the audition for entrance into a Pre-Professional Training Program (PPT); must be registered for a full year of study in the Pre-Professional Training Program. **Criteria:** Awards are given based on merit, in-person audition, and financial need.

Funds Avail.: No specific amount. **To Apply:** Applicants should complete the attached application for the scholarship prior to the audition. **Contact:** Jennifer at jgonserkevis@grgrp.com

2620 ■ Davis Memorial Foundation

1098 Foster City Blvd., No. 204
Foster City, CA 94404-2300
Ph: (650)570-5446
Fax: (650)570-5460
E-mail: dmf@wsrca.com
URL: http://www.davisfoundation.org

2621 ■ Davis Memorial Foundation Scholarship Award Program *(Graduate, Undergraduate/Scholarship)*

Purpose: To develop qualified professionals through education and to award those who have the desire to

Awards are arranged alphabetically below their administering organizations

continue to improve their quality of life. **Focus:** General studies. **Qualif.:** Applicants must be high school students, undergraduate or graduate students or technical trade school students who are provisionally accepted as students into undergraduate or graduate degree programs for the coming academic year by accredited colleges or universities; must be WSRCA members in good standing, their employees or their respective immediate family (spouse or child). The child may be natural, legally adopted or a step child. **Criteria:** Applicants are evaluated based on academic performance.

Funds Avail.: $3,000. **Number Awarded:** 5. **To Apply:** Applicants must submit 6 copies of each: official application form; official transcript of all high school and college records; letter from college, university or technical trade school where the undergraduate or graduate work will be undertaken, indicating provisional acceptance of the proposed course of study; and current picture. **Deadline:** April 1.

2622 ■ Davis Wright Tremaine LLP

701 W Eighth Ave.
Anchorage, AK 99501-3468
Ph: (907)257-5300
Fax: (907)257-5399
Free: 877-398-8416
E-mail: info@dwt.com
URL: http://www.dwt.com

2623 ■ Davis Wright Tremaine 1L Diversity Scholarships *(Undergraduate/Scholarship)*

Purpose: To provide financial assistance for qualified students intending to pursue their law degree. **Focus:** Law. **Qualif.:** Applicants must be first-year law students; must have a record of academic achievement in both undergraduate school and the first year of law school; must demonstrate promise for a successful career in law; must be committed to civic involvement that promotes diversity; be willing to continue that commitment upon entering the legal profession; and must commit to become a Summer Associate in DWT's Seattle Office between the student's first and second years of law school. **Criteria:** Applicants will be selected based on their academic performance and commitment to a successful career in law.

Funds Avail.: $7,500 for the student's second year tuition and expenses. **To Apply:** Applicants must submit a current resume; a complete undergraduate transcript; a grade from the first semester of law school; a short, personal essay indicating the applicant's eligibility for and interest in the scholarship, and a legal writing sample; and two or three references (one of whom should be a person qualified to comment on the applicant's law school work). Application materials must be sent to Davis Wright Tremaine LLP, IL Diversity Scholarship Program, 2600 Century Square, 1501 Fourth Ave., Seattle, WA 98101-1688. **Deadline:** February 3.

2624 ■ Deafness Research Foundation

641 Lexington Ave.
New York, NY 10022
Ph: (212)328-9480
Fax: (212)328-9484
Free: (866)454-3924
E-mail: info@drf.org
URL: http://www.drf.org

2625 ■ Deafness Research Foundation Research Grants *(Doctorate/Grant)*

Purpose: To promote hearing health possible for all people through research and education. **Focus:** Medical Research. **Qualif.:** Applicant should hold the M.D., Ph.D., or equivalent degrees as well as a faculty or post-doctoral appointment. **Criteria:** Priority is given to new investigators in the field of hearing and balance and to projects that are likely to open new lines of inquiry.

Funds Avail.: $25,000 per year. **Number Awarded:** Varies. **To Apply:** For first year application, application must be clear and legible, with a minimum font size of 11 points. Figures, charts, tables, legends, and footnotes may be smaller in size but must be legible. For second year applications, applicant must submit a letter of intent to apply for second year funding to DRF. **Deadline:** December 1. **Contact:** Deafness Research Foundation Grants Management, 1055 Thomas Jefferson St., NW Washington, DC 20007. 202-944-5296. grants@drf.org.

2626 ■ Death Valley '49ers

10 Paseo de Pino
Rancho Palos Verdes, CA 90275-6383
Ph: (310)544-1207
Fax: (310)544-2178
E-mail: lcbaker@cox.net
URL: http://www.deathvalley49ers.org

2627 ■ Death Valley '49ers Scholarships *(Undergraduate/Scholarship)*

Purpose: To assist high school graduates living in the Death Valley Unified School District. **Focus:** Historic preservation. **Qualif.:** Applicants must be residents of the Death Valley Unified School District and/or Death Valley National Park for a minimum of two years and/or parent(s) are employed within the boundaries of Death Valley National Park and/or attended Death Valley Elementary School for a minimum of two years. Completes all the required subjects for high school graduation in their junior and senior academic years at Beatty, Pahrump, or Shoshone High Schools. **Criteria:** Scholarships are awarded based on a four-year program and will be renewed each year based on the academic progress of the student. The scholarship committee will review academic progress at the end of each semester.

Funds Avail.: $4,000. **To Apply:** Applicants must submit a Death Valley '49ers Scholarship Application to the Scholarship Committee by the application deadline in the senior year of high school. **Deadline:** March.

2628 ■ Michael E. DeBakey International Surgical Society

One Baylor Plaza
Houston, TX 77030
Ph: (713)798-4557
Fax: (713)796-9605
E-mail: mediss04@aol.com
URL: http://www.mediss.org

2629 ■ DeBakey International Society Fellowship Awards *(Professional Development/Award/Prize)*

Purpose: To support individuals for training in Houston at Baylor College of Medicine affiliated Hospitals for medi-

Awards are arranged alphabetically below their administering organizations

cine's surgical program. **Focus:** Cardiology. **Qualif.:** Applicants must have completed a general surgical residency and must have passed the ECFMG or any other certifying examinations necessary to obtain a temporary license to practice medicine in Texas. **Criteria:** Candidates will be evaluated based on criteria by the committee of the society.

Funds Avail.: $25,000. **To Apply:** Applicants must submit a letter of support from his/her program director, documents confirming applicant's eligibility for an institutional or temporary Texas license to practice medicine and a current photograph of the applicant should be submitted to the Office of the Secretary. Following receipt of these documents, the secretary will send a formal application to the applicant. **Contact:** Kenneth L. Mattox, M.D. at the above address (see entry 2628).

2630 ■ Decorative Arts Trust

106 Bainbridge St.
Philadelphia, PA 19147
Ph: (215)627-2859
Fax: (215)925-1144
URL: http://www.decorativeartstrust.org

2631 ■ Dewey Lee Curtis Scholarship Fund
(Doctorate, Graduate/Scholarship)

Purpose: To support the individual actively working in the field of American decorative arts with their education. **Focus:** Art. **Qualif.:** Applicant must be working on a Master's thesis or Ph.D dissertation. **Criteria:** Candidates will be selected based on their application form and proposed studies.

Funds Avail.: $500. **To Apply:** Applicant must submit 500-600 word article reviewing the research for the trust newsletter. Application forms are available in the website address; must send to the trust@decorativeartstrust.org. **Deadline:** April 30.

2632 ■ Delaware Community Foundation

PO Box 1636
Wilmington, DE 19899
Ph: (302)571-8004
Fax: (302)571-1553
E-mail: info@delcf.org
URL: http://www.delcf.org

2633 ■ Chrysler Technical Scholarships Fund
(Undergraduate/Scholarship)

Purpose: To provide college scholarship assistance to those worthy students based on demonstrated academic ability, leadership traits and financial need. **Focus:** General Studies. **Qualif.:** Applicants must be residents of Delaware; must have an at least 2.75 GPA and provide evidence of a commitment to leadership in the community; must plan to obtain a degree or certificate from a community college, trade school or university in a technical field related to the design, engineering, manufacturing or repair of automotive products, including but not limited to, automotive repair, skilled trades, and engineering. **Criteria:** Preference will be given to the students who meet the criteria.

Funds Avail.: $1,000 per academic year. **To Apply:** Applicants must download and fill out the application form at the Delaware Community Foundation website. **Deadline:** July 31.

2634 ■ Delta Delta Delta

PO Box 5987
Arlington, TX 76005-5987
Ph: (817)633-8001
Fax: (817)652-0212
E-mail: info@trideltaeo.org
URL: http://www.tridelta.org

2635 ■ Nancy Ashley Adams/Ashley Adams Koetje Scholarships *(Undergraduate/Scholarship)*

Purpose: To provide financial assistance to qualified undergraduate students. **Focus:** General studies. **Qualif.:** Applicant must be a Alpha Eta chapter member in Florida State University; must be an initiated sophomore or junior member. **Criteria:** Preference is given to officer or members from out-of-state. Applicants will be evaluated based on their academic achievement, chapter and campus activities, and financial need.

Funds Avail.: $500-$1,500. **To Apply:** Application forms are available on the website. Applicant must provide a personal statement about their educational and vocational goals; must have a recommendation letter from a faculty member; must have an official transcript from each undergraduate institution. Application materials must be sent to: Delta Delta Delta, PO Box 5987, Arlington, TX 76005. **Deadline:** March 15.

2636 ■ Adams Family Scholarships
(Undergraduate/Scholarship)

Purpose: To provide financial assistance to qualified undergraduate students. **Focus:** General studies. **Qualif.:** Applicant must be a Chi member at the University of Mississippi chapter; must be an initiated sophomore or junior member. **Criteria:** Applicants will be judge based on academic achievement, campus and community involvement, and financial need.

Funds Avail.: $500-$1,500. **To Apply:** Application forms are available in the website. Applicant must provide a personal statement about educational and vocational goals; must have a recommendation letter from a faculty member; must have an official transcript from each undergraduate institutions. Application materials must be sent to: Delta Delta Delta, PO Box 5987, Arlington, TX 76005. **Deadline:** March 15.

2637 ■ Margaret M. Alkek Scholarship
(Undergraduate/Scholarship)

Purpose: To provide financial assistance to qualified undergraduate students. **Focus:** Education, Music, Theater arts. **Qualif.:** Applicant must be a Theta Xi chapter member at the University of Southern California; must have academic achievement at the collegiate level; must be an initiated sophomore or junior members. **Criteria:** Preference should be give to those majoring in education, music or theater.

Funds Avail.: $500-$1,500. **To Apply:** Application forms are available on the website. Applicant must provide a personal statement about their educational and vocational goals; must have a recommendation letter from a faculty member; must have an official transcript from each undergraduate institution. Application materials must be sent to: Delta Delta Delta, PO Box 5987, Arlington, TX 76005. **Deadline:** March 15.

2638 ■ Alpha Eta Scholarships *(Undergraduate/Scholarship)*

Purpose: To provide financial assistance to qualified undergraduate students. **Focus:** General studies. **Qualif.:** Applicant must be a member of Alpha Eta chapter member

Awards are arranged alphabetically below their administering organizations

at Florida State University; must be an initiated sophomore or junior member. **Criteria:** Applicants are judged based on academic standing, chapter and campus activities, and financial need.

Funds Avail.: $500-$1,500. **To Apply:** Application forms are available on the website. Applicant must provide a personal statement about their educational and vocational goals; must have a recommendation letter from a faculty member; must have an official transcript from each undergraduate institution. Application materials must be sent to: Delta Delta Delta, PO Box 5987, Arlington, TX 76005. **Deadline:** March 15.

2639 ■ Alpha Rho Leadership Scholarships *(Undergraduate/Scholarship)*

Purpose: To provide financial assistance to qualified undergraduate students. **Focus:** General studies. **Qualif.:** Applicant must be a Alpha Rho chapter member at the University of Georgia; must be an initiated sophomore or junior member. **Criteria:** Applicants are judge based on academic standing, chapter and campus activities, and financial need.

Funds Avail.: $500-$1,500. **To Apply:** Application forms are available on the website. Applicant must provide a personal statement about their educational and vocational goals; must have a recommendation letter from a faculty member; must have an official transcript from each undergraduate institution. Application materials must be sent to: Delta Delta Delta, PO Box 5987, Arlington, TX 76005. **Deadline:** March 15.

2640 ■ Jane E. Anderson Scholarships *(Undergraduate/Scholarship)*

Purpose: To provide financial assistance to qualified undergraduate students. **Focus:** General studies. **Qualif.:** Applicant must be a Kappa chapter member at the University of Nebraska; must have academic achievement at the collegiate level; must be "without favor or prejudice"; must be an initiated sophomore or junior member. **Criteria:** Applicants will be judged based on their academic achievement, campus and community involvement, and financial need.

Funds Avail.: $500-$1,500. **To Apply:** Application forms are available on the website. Applicant must provide a personal statement about educational and vocational goals; must have a recommendation letter from a faculty member; must have an official transcript from each undergraduate institution. Application materials must be sent to: Delta Delta Delta, PO Box 5987, Arlington, TX 76005. **Deadline:** March 15.

2641 ■ Atlanta Alumnae Achievement Scholarships *(Undergraduate/Scholarship)*

Purpose: To provide financial assistance to qualified undergraduate students. **Focus:** General studies. **Qualif.:** Applicant must be currently enrolled in an undergraduate Tri Delta member in good standing at any public or private college or university; must be a collegiate member who graduated from a Georgia high school in one of the following four counties: Fulton, Dekalb, Cobb or Gwinnett; must be a junior during the application year. **Criteria:** Selection of applicant will be based on the following criteria: (1) Must have a minimum GPA of 3.3 on a 4.0 scale - 50%; (2) Collegiate Chapter Service (must have served or be serving at an elected or appointed position(s)) - 30%; (3) Leadership or community service on campus - 20%.

Funds Avail.: $500-$1,500. **To Apply:** Application forms are available on the website. Applicant must provide a personal statement about educational and vocational goals; must have a recommendation letter from a faculty member; must have an official transcript from each undergraduate institution. Application materials must be sent to: Delta Delta Delta, PO Box 5987, Arlington, TX 76005. **Deadline:** March 15.

2642 ■ Avery Bayle Barth Scholarships *(Undergraduate/Scholarship)*

Purpose: To provide financial assistance to qualified undergraduate students. **Focus:** Education. **Qualif.:** Applicant must be a Theta Xi chapter member at the University of Southern California; must have an academic achievement at the collegiate level; must be an initiated sophomore and junior members. **Criteria:** Preference will be given to those majoring in education.

Funds Avail.: $500-$1,500. **To Apply:** Application forms are available on the website. Applicant must provide a personal statement about educational and vocational goals; must have a recommendation letter from a faculty member; must have an official transcript from each undergraduate institution. Application materials must be sent to: Delta Delta Delta, PO Box 5987, Arlington, TX 76005. **Deadline:** March 15.

2643 ■ Beta Gamma Memorial Scholarship Fund *(Undergraduate/Scholarship)*

Purpose: To provide financial assistance to qualified undergraduate students. **Focus:** General studies. **Qualif.:** Applicant must be a Beta Gamma chapter member at Jacksonville University; must be a full time undergraduate at Jacksonville University; must have a minimum GPA of 2.5; must be a member who has overcome personal hardship or life struggle. **Criteria:** Applicants are judged based on academic standing, chapter and campus activities, and financial need.

Funds Avail.: $500-$1,500. **To Apply:** Application forms are available on the website. Applicant must provide a personal statement about their educational and vocational goals; must have a recommendation letter from a faculty member; must have an official transcript from each undergraduate institution. Application materials must be sent to: Delta Delta Delta, PO Box 5987, Arlington, TX 76005. **Deadline:** March 15.

2644 ■ Chi Chapter Undergraduate Scholarships *(Undergraduate/Scholarship)*

Purpose: To provide financial assistance to a qualified undergraduate students. **Focus:** General studies. **Qualif.:** Applicant must be Chi member at the University of Mississippi chapter; must be an initiated sophomore or junior member. **Criteria:** Applicants will be judged based on academic achievement, campus and community involvement, and financial need.

Funds Avail.: $500-$1,500. **To Apply:** Application forms are available on the website. Applicant must provide a personal statement about their educational and vocational goals; must have a recommendation letter from a faculty member; must have an official transcript from each undergraduate institutions. Application materials must be sent to: Delta Delta Delta, PO Box 5987, Arlington, TX 76005. **Deadline:** March 15.

2645 ■ Durning Sisters Scholarships *(Graduate/Scholarship)*

Purpose: To provide financial assistance to graduate students. **Focus:** General studies. **Qualif.:** Applicant must be a Tri Delta member who has completed 12 hours of graduate study and is unmarried. **Criteria:** Applicants will be evaluated based on academic merit, chapter and campus or community activities.

Funds Avail.: $3,000. **To Apply:** Applicant must complete the application form available on the website; must have a personal statement about educational and vocational goals; must have two letters of academic recommendation and one Tri Delta recommendation letter; must provide a transcript and financial information. Application documents must be sent to: Delta Delta Delta at PO Box 5987, Arlington, TX 76005. **Deadline:** March 15.

2646 ■ Harriet Erich Graduate Fellowships *(Graduate/Scholarship)*

Purpose: To provide financial assistance to graduate students. **Focus:** General studies. **Qualif.:** Applicant must be a Tri Delta member enrolled in an accredited graduate program at the University of Alabama. **Criteria:** Applicants are judged based on academic merit as well as chapter and campus or community activities.

Funds Avail.: $3,000. **To Apply:** Applicant must complete the application form available on the website; must have a personal statement about educational and vocational goals; must have two letters of academic recommendation and one Tri Delta recommendation letter; must provide a transcript and financial information. Application documents must be sent to: Delta Delta Delta at PO Box 5987, Arlington, TX 76005. **Deadline:** March 15.

2647 ■ Louise Bales Gallagher Scholarships *(Undergraduate/Scholarship)*

Purpose: To provide financial assistance to qualified undergraduate students. **Focus:** General studies. **Qualif.:** Applicant must be a Delta Epsilon chapter member at Millikin University; must be an initiated sophomore or junior members. **Criteria:** Scholarship application will be based on the following criteria: (1) Financial need - 50%; (2) Academic achievement - 25%; (3) Chapter and campus involvement - 25%.

Funds Avail.: $500-$1,500. **To Apply:** Application forms are available on the website. Applicant must provide a personal statement about educational and vocational goals; must have a recommendation letter from a faculty member; must have an official transcript from each undergraduate institutions. Application materials must be sent to: Delta Delta Delta, PO Box 5987, Arlington, TX 76005. **Deadline:** March 15.

2648 ■ Peg Hart Harrison Memorial Scholarships *(Undergraduate/Scholarship)*

Purpose: To provide financial assistance to qualified undergraduate students. **Focus:** General studies. **Qualif.:** Applicant must be a Beta Lambda chapter member at the University of Central Florida; must be a member who has overcome insurmountable odds; must be an initiated sophomore or junior member. **Criteria:** Applicants are judge based on academic standing, chapter and campus activities, and financial need.

Funds Avail.: $500-$1,500. **To Apply:** Application forms are available in the website. Applicant must provide a personal statement about their educational and vocational goals; must have a recommendation letter from a faculty member; must have an official transcript from each undergraduate institution. Application materials must be sent to: Delta Delta Delta, PO Box 5987, Arlington, TX 76005. **Deadline:** March 15.

2649 ■ Erin Kumelos Heard Memorial Scholarships *(Undergraduate/Scholarship)*

Purpose: To provide financial assistance to qualified undergraduate students. **Focus:** General studies. **Qualif.:** Applicant must be a member of the Beta Pi chapter at California/Davis; must be an initiated sophomore or junior member in good standing with the foundation; must be a full-time student and active member. **Criteria:** Application will be evaluated by Rae Ann and her committee.

Funds Avail.: $500-$1,500. **To Apply:** Application forms are available in the website. Applicant must provide a personal statement about educational and vocational goals; must have a recommendation letter from a faculty member; must have an official transcript from each undergraduate institutions. Application materials must be sent to: Delta Delta Delta, PO Box 5987, Arlington, TX 76005. **Deadline:** March 15.

2650 ■ Houston Alumnae Chapter Graduate Fellowships *(Graduate/Fellowship)*

Purpose: To provide financial assistance to graduate students. **Focus:** General studies. **Qualif.:** Applicant must be a Tri Delta member enrolled in an accredited graduate program full-time whose permanent residence is in Houston, Texas. **Criteria:** Candidates will be selected based on academic merit as well as chapter and campus or community activities.

Funds Avail.: $3,000. **To Apply:** Applicant must complete the application form available on the website; must have a personal statement about educational and vocational goals; must have two letters of academic recommendation and one Tri Delta recommendation letter; must provide a transcript and financial information. Application documents must be sent to: Delta Delta Delta at PO Box 5987, Arlington, TX 76005. **Deadline:** March 15.

2651 ■ Houston Alumnae Undergraduate Tri Delta Scholarships *(Undergraduate/Scholarship)*

Purpose: To provide financial assistance to qualified undergraduate students. **Focus:** General studies. **Qualif.:** Applicant must be a collegiate member from the Houston Alumnae chapter zip-code area; must be an initiated sophomore or junior member. **Criteria:** Consideration will be given to those who need financial assistance. Consideration also given to: (1) Summer and school year earnings; (2) History of chapter involvement relative to other candidates applying for the award; (3) Academic history/stability/goals; (4) Community service/extracurricular activities.

Funds Avail.: $500-$1,500. **To Apply:** Application forms are available on the website. Applicant must provide a personal statement about educational and vocational goals; must have a recommendation letter from a faculty member; must have an official transcript from each undergraduate institution. Application materials must be sent to: Delta Delta Delta, PO Box 5987, Arlington, TX 76005. **Deadline:** March 15.

2652 ■ Hazel D. Isbell Fellowships *(Graduate/Fellowship)*

Purpose: To provide financial assistance to graduate students. **Focus:** General studies. **Qualif.:** Applicant must be a Tri Delta member pursuing a graduate study. **Criteria:** Preference will be given to Theta Delta alumnae attending the University of Oregon, Theta Mu chapter members.

Funds Avail.: $3,000. **To Apply:** Applicant must complete the application form available on the website; must have a personal statement about educational and vocational goals; must have two letters of academic recommendation and one Tri Delta recommendation letter; must provide a transcript and financial information. Application documents must be sent to: Delta Delta Delta at PO Box 5987, Arlington, TX 76005. **Deadline:** March 15.

2653 ■ Kappa Chapter Centennial Scholarships *(Undergraduate/Scholarship)*

Purpose: To provide financial assistance to qualified undergraduate students. **Focus:** General studies. **Qualif.:** Applicant must be a Kappa chapter member at the University of Nebraska; must be an initiated sophomore or junior member. **Criteria:** Applicants will be judged based on academic achievement, campus and community involvement, and financial need.

Funds Avail.: $500-$1,500. **To Apply:** Application forms are available on the website. Applicant must provide a personal statement about educational and vocational goals; must have a recommendation letter from a faculty member; must have an official transcript from each undergraduate institution. Application materials must be sent to: Delta Delta Delta, PO Box 5987, Arlington, TX 76005. **Deadline:** March 15.

2654 ■ Luella Akins Key Scholarships *(Undergraduate/Scholarship)*

Purpose: To provide financial assistance to qualified undergraduate students. **Focus:** General studies. **Qualif.:** Applicant must be an initiated sophomore or junior member in good standing of Delta Delta; must be a full-time student and active member. **Criteria:** Applicants are judged based on academic standing, chapter and campus activities, and financial need.

Funds Avail.: $500-$1,500. **To Apply:** Application forms are available on the website. Applicant must provide a personal statement about educational and vocational goals; must have a recommendation letter from a faculty member; must have an official transcript from each undergraduate institution. Application materials must be sent to: Delta Delta Delta, PO Box 5987, Arlington, TX 76005. **Deadline:** March 15.

2655 ■ Sarah Shinn Marshall Scholarships *(Undergraduate/Scholarship)*

Purpose: To provide financial assistance to qualified undergraduate students. **Focus:** General studies. **Qualif.:** Applicant must be an initiated sophomore or junior member in good standing of Delta Delta; must be a full-time student and active member. **Criteria:** Applicants are judge based on academic standing, chapter and campus activities, and financial need.

Funds Avail.: $500-$1,500. **To Apply:** Application forms are available on the website. Applicant must provide a personal statement about educational and vocational goals; must have a recommendation letter from a faculty member; must have an official transcript from each undergraduate institution. Application materials must be sent to: Delta Delta Delta, PO Box 5987, Arlington, TX 76005. **Deadline:** March 15.

2656 ■ Martin Sisters Scholarships *(Undergraduate/Scholarship)*

Purpose: To provide financial assistance to qualified undergraduate students. **Focus:** General studies. **Qualif.:** Applicant must be an initiated sophomore or junior members in good standing of Delta Delta; must be a full-time student and active member. **Criteria:** Applicants are judged based on academic standing, chapter and campus activities, and financial need.

Funds Avail.: $500-$1,500. **To Apply:** Application forms are available in the website. Applicant must provide a personal statement about educational and vocational goals; must have a recommendation letter from a faculty member; must have an official transcript from each undergraduate institutions. Application materials must be sent to: Delta Delta Delta, PO Box 5987, Arlington, TX 76005. **Deadline:** March 15.

2657 ■ McKinney Sisters Undergraduate Scholarships *(Undergraduate/Scholarship)*

Purpose: To provide financial assistance to qualified undergraduate students. **Focus:** General studies. **Qualif.:** Applicant must be a graduate from high school in San Antonio, TX or has permanent residence in San Antonio; must be an initiated sophomore or junior member. **Criteria:** Applicants will be judged based on academic achievement, campus and community involvement, and financial need.

Funds Avail.: $500-$1,500. **To Apply:** Application forms are available on the website. Applicant must provide a personal statement about educational and vocational goals; must have a recommendation letter from a faculty member; must have an official transcript from each undergraduate institution. Application materials must be sent to: Delta Delta Delta, PO Box 5987, Arlington, TX 76005. **Deadline:** March 15.

2658 ■ Virginia Nicklas Scholarships *(Undergraduate/Scholarship)*

Purpose: To provide financial assistance to qualified undergraduate students. **Focus:** Literature, Science, Arts. **Qualif.:** Applicant must be an Iota chapter member at the University of Michigan; must be a permanent resident outside of Michigan; must live in Iota chapter house; must be currently enrolled in Literature, Science, and Arts. **Criteria:** Applicants will be judged based on academic achievement, campus and community involvement, and financial need.

Funds Avail.: $500-$1,500. **To Apply:** Application forms are available on the website. Applicant must provide a personal statement about educational and vocational goals; must have a recommendation letter from a faculty member; must have an official transcript from each undergraduate institution. Application materials must be sent to: Delta Delta Delta, PO Box 5987, Arlington, TX 76005. **Deadline:** March 15.

2659 ■ Northern Virginia Alumnae Chapter Scholarships *(Undergraduate/Scholarship)*

Purpose: To provide financial assistance to qualified undergraduate students. **Focus:** General studies. **Qualif.:** Applicant must have academic achievement of 3.0 or better GPA; must have a financial need; must be an initiated sophomore or junior member. **Criteria:** Priority is given to a member from a Virginia Tri Delta chapter, then a member of any Tri Delta chapter with a permanent residence in Northern Virginia.

Funds Avail.: $500-$1,500. **To Apply:** Application forms are available on the website. Applicant must provide a personal statement about educational and vocational goals; must have a recommendation letter from a faculty member; must have an official transcript from each undergraduate institution. Application materials must be sent to: Delta Delta Delta, PO Box 5987, Arlington, TX 76005. **Deadline:** March 15.

2660 ■ Cissy McDaniel Parker Scholarships *(Undergraduate/Scholarship)*

Purpose: To provide financial assistance to qualified undergraduate students. **Focus:** General studies. **Qualif.:** Applicant must be a Theta Zeta chapter member at the University of Texas; must have an academic achievement of 3.0 or better GPA; must be an initiated sophomore or junior members. **Criteria:** Applicants will be judged based on academic achievement, campus and community involvement, and financial need.

Funds Avail.: $500-$1,500. **To Apply:** Application forms are available on the website. Applicant must provide a personal statement about educational and vocational goals; must have a recommendation letter from a faculty member; must have an official transcript from each undergraduate institution. Application materials must be sent to: Delta Delta Delta, PO Box 5987, Arlington, TX 76005. **Deadline:** March 15.

2661 ■ Zoe Gore Perrin Scholarships *(Undergraduate/Scholarship)*

Purpose: To provide financial assistance to qualified undergraduate students. **Focus:** General studies. **Qualif.:** Applicant must be an initiated sophomore and junior member in good standing of Delta Delta; must be a full-time student and active member. **Criteria:** Applicants are judged based on academic standing, chapter and campus activities, and financial need.

Funds Avail.: $500-$1,500. **To Apply:** Application forms are available on the website. Applicant must provide a personal statement about their educational and vocational goals; must have a recommendation letter from a faculty member; must have an official transcript from each undergraduate institution. Application materials must be sent to: Delta Delta Delta, PO Box 5987, Arlington, TX 76005. **Deadline:** March 15.

2662 ■ Cheryl White Pryor Memorial Scholarships *(Undergraduate/Scholarship)*

Purpose: To provide financial assistance to qualified undergraduate students. **Focus:** General studies. **Qualif.:** Applicant must be a member of Delta Sigma chapter member at Tennessee; must be an initiated sophomore or junior members. **Criteria:** Scholarship selection committee shall determine the number of recipients and amounts of each scholarship. Applicants will be evaluated based on the following criteria: (1) Past and present service to the Delta Sigma chapter at the University of Tennessee - 60%; (2) Academic achievement - 30%; (3) Financial need - 10%.

Funds Avail.: $500. **To Apply:** Application forms are available on the website. Applicant must provide a personal statement about educational and vocational goals; must have a recommendation letter from a faculty member; must have an official transcript from each undergraduate institution. Application materials must be sent to: Delta Delta Delta, PO Box 5987, Arlington, TX 76005. **Deadline:** March 15.

2663 ■ Susan E. Riley Scholarships *(Undergraduate/Scholarship)*

Purpose: To provide financial assistance to a qualified undergraduate student. **Focus:** General studies. **Qualif.:** Applicant must be a Theta Mu chapter member at Oregon State University; must be currently a Tri Delta member in good standing; must show academic achievements at the collegiate level; must participate in community service; must be an initiated sophomore or junior member. **Criteria:** Applicants will be judged based on academic achievement, campus and community involvement, and financial need.

Funds Avail.: $500-$1,500. **To Apply:** Application forms are available on the website. Applicant must provide a personal statement about their educational and vocational goals; must have a recommendation letter from a faculty member; must have an official transcript from each undergraduate institution. Application materials must be sent to: Delta Delta Delta, PO Box 5987, Arlington, TX 76005. **Deadline:** March 15.

2664 ■ Jean Wiggin Roach Scholarships *(Undergraduate/Scholarship)*

Purpose: To provide financial assistance to qualified undergraduate students. **Focus:** General studies. **Qualif.:** Applicant must be a Phi Lambda chapter member at Texas Christian University; must have academic achievement at the collegiate level; must be an initiated sophomore and junior members. **Criteria:** Applicants will be judged based on academic achievement, campus and community involvement, and financial need.

Funds Avail.: $500-$1,500. **To Apply:** Application forms are available on the website. Applicant must provide a personal statement about educational and vocational goals; must have a recommendation letter from a faculty member; must have an official transcript from each undergraduate institution. Application materials must be sent to: Delta Delta Delta, PO Box 5987, Arlington, TX 76005. **Deadline:** March 15.

2665 ■ Jeanne Graves Ryland Scholarships *(Undergraduate/Scholarship)*

Purpose: To provide financial assistance to qualified undergraduate students. **Focus:** General studies. **Qualif.:** Applicant must be a Phi Theta chapter member at Auburn University; must be an initiated sophomore or junior member. **Criteria:** Applicants will be judged based on academic achievement, campus and community involvement, and financial need.

Funds Avail.: $500-$1,500. **To Apply:** Application forms are available on the website. Applicant must provide a personal statement about educational and vocational goals; must have a recommendation letter from a faculty member; must have an official transcript from each undergraduate institution. Application materials must be sent to: Delta Delta Delta, PO Box 5987, Arlington, TX 76005. **Deadline:** March 15.

2666 ■ Julie Anne Sadlier Memorial Scholarships *(Undergraduate/Scholarship)*

Purpose: To provide financial assistance to qualified undergraduate students. **Focus:** General studies. **Qualif.:** Applicant must be a Theta Pi chapter member at UCLA; must have overcome a personal hardship or life struggle; must be an initiated sophomore or junior members. **Criteria:** Applicants will be judged based on academic achievement, campus and community involvement, and financial need.

Funds Avail.: $500-$1,500. **To Apply:** Application forms are available on the website. Applicant must provide a personal statement about educational and vocational goals; must have a recommendation letter from a faculty member;

Awards are arranged alphabetically below their administering organizations

must have an official transcript from each undergraduate institution. Application materials must be sent to: Delta Delta Delta, PO Box 5987, Arlington, TX 76005. **Deadline:** March 15.

2667 ■ Virginia Hartford Saharov Memorial Scholarships *(Undergraduate/Scholarship)*

Purpose: To provide financial assistance to qualified undergraduate students. **Focus:** General studies. **Qualif.:** Applicant must be a Delta Pi chapter member at Illinois; must be an initiated sophomore or junior member. **Criteria:** Applicants will be judged based on academic achievement, campus and community involvement, and financial need.

Funds Avail.: $500-$1,500. **To Apply:** Application forms are available on the website. Applicant must provide a personal statement about educational and vocational goals; must have a recommendation letter from a faculty member; must have an official transcript from each undergraduate institution. Application materials must be sent to: Delta Delta Delta, PO Box 5987, Arlington, TX 76005. **Deadline:** March 15.

2668 ■ Edith Scandlyn/Sammie Lynn Scandlyn Puett Memorial Scholarships *(Undergraduate/Scholarship)*

Purpose: To provide financial assistance to a qualified undergraduate students. **Focus:** General studies. **Qualif.:** Applicant must be a Delta Sigma chapter member at the University of Tennessee; must be an initiated sophomore or junior members. **Criteria:** Preference will be given to: (a) Applicants with strong academic records (3.5+); (b) Applicants who rely on the financial support of a single parent (mother) to go to college.

Funds Avail.: $500-$1,500. **To Apply:** Application forms are available on the website. Applicant must provide a personal statement about educational and vocational goals; must have a recommendation letter from a faculty member; must have an official transcript from each undergraduate institution. Application materials must be sent to: Delta Delta Delta, PO Box 5987, Arlington, TX 76005. **Deadline:** March 15.

2669 ■ Teri Wenglein-Callender Undergraduate Scholarships *(Undergraduate/Scholarship)*

Purpose: To provide financial assistance to qualified undergraduate students. **Focus:** General studies. **Qualif.:** Applicant must be a Theta Zeta chapter member at the University of Texas; must be an initiated sophomore or junior member. **Criteria:** Applicants will be judged based on academic achievement, campus and community involvement, and financial need.

Funds Avail.: $500-$1,500. **To Apply:** Application forms are available on the website. Applicant must provide a personal statement about educational and vocational goals; must have a recommendation letter from a faculty member; must have an official transcript from each undergraduate institution. Application materials must be sent to: Delta Delta Delta, PO Box 5987, Arlington, TX 76005. **Deadline:** March 15.

2670 ■ Donna Axum Whitworth Scholarships *(Undergraduate/Scholarship)*

Purpose: To provide financial assistance to qualified undergraduate students. **Focus:** General studies. **Qualif.:** Applicant must be a Delta Iota member at Arkansas; must be an initiated sophomore or junior member. **Criteria:** Applicants will be judge based on academic achievement, campus and community involvement, and financial need.

Funds Avail.: $500-$1,500. **To Apply:** Application forms are available on the website. Applicant must provide a personal statement about educational and vocational goals; must have a recommendation letter from a faculty member; must have an official transcript from each undergraduate institutions. Application materials must be sent to: Delta Delta Delta, PO Box 5987, Arlington, TX 76005. **Deadline:** March 15.

2671 ■ Delta Epsilon Sigma

11300 NE 2nd Ave.
Miami, FL 33161
URL: http://www.deltaepsilonsigma.org

2672 ■ Fitzgerald Fellowships *(Undergraduate/Fellowship)*

Purpose: To provide financial support for the education of member students. **Focus:** General studies. **Qualif.:** Applicants must be junior year members. **Criteria:** Candidates will be judged by the Scholarship Committee based on scholastic achievement, leadership and service activities.

Funds Avail.: $1,000. **To Apply:** Applicants must submit typed application accompanied by three letters of recommendation including one from the Chapter Advisor and official transcripts of all college work through the current fall semester. **Deadline:** April 1.

2673 ■ Fitzgerald Scholarships *(Undergraduate/Scholarship)*

Purpose: To provide financial support for the education of member students. **Focus:** General studies. **Qualif.:** Applicants must be junior year members. **Criteria:** Candidates will be judged by the Scholarship Committee based on scholastic achievement, leadership and service activities.

Funds Avail.: $1,000. **To Apply:** Applicants must submit typed application accompanied by three letters of recommendation including one from the Chapter Advisor and official transcripts of all college work through the current fall semester. **Deadline:** April 1.

2674 ■ Delta Gamma

PO Box 21397
Columbus, OH 43221
Ph: (614)481-8149
Fax: (614)481-0133
URL: http://www.deltagamma.org

2675 ■ Delta Gamma Scholarships *(Undergraduate/Scholarship)*

Purpose: To encourage the Delta Gammas to pursue a career in Science. **Focus:** Science. **Qualif.:** Candidates must have a 3.0 or higher GPA; must be participants in chapter, campus and community leadership activities; must have completed at least three semester or four quarter of college work. **Criteria:** Grants awarded on a competitive basis.

Funds Avail.: No specific amount. **To Apply:** For more information on Delta Gamma scholarship, applicants are advised to contact the Director of Scholarships and Fellowships, Betty Plaggemier Guthrie (at FNScholarFellow@deltagamma.org), or contact Executive Offices at 3250

Awards are arranged alphabetically below their administering organizations

Riverside Drive, PO Box 21397, Columbus OH 43221-0397. **Deadline:** February 15.

2676 ■ Delta Nu Alpha Transportation Fraternity

435 Pennsylvannia Ave. 102
Glen Ellyn, IL 60137
Ph: (630)653-3622
Fax: (630)653-3632
E-mail: admin@deltanualpha.org
URL: http://www.deltanualpha.org

2677 ■ Delta Nu Alpha Foundation Scholarships *(Undergraduate/Scholarship)*

Purpose: To emphasize financial assistance and mentoring for students, excellent continuing education opportunities for the work force, and vigilance in communicating changes in regulations. **Focus:** Transportation; Logistics. **Qualif.:** Program is open to all students studying in the field of Transportation, Logistics and Supply Chain Management. Students pursuing associate and bachelor degrees are encouraged to apply. **Criteria:** Recipients are selected based on scholastic achievement, overall career goals and related interest in their field of study and recommendations.

Funds Avail.: No specific amount. **To Apply:** Applicants must submit completed application form along with transcripts of all college/university level work completed and two letters of recommendation (one should be from the transportation, logistics or supply chain management instructor). **Deadline:** May 31. **Contact:** Tom Bock DNA Foundation Scholarship Chair, 4123 Apple blossom Rd. Lutz, FL 33558.

2678 ■ Delta Phi Epsilon

251 S Camc St.
Philadelphia, PA 19107
Ph: (215)732-5901
E-mail: info@dphie.org
URL: http://www.dphie.org

2679 ■ Delta Phi Epsilon Educational Foundation Scholarships *(Undergraduate/Scholarship)*

Purpose: To develop a social conscience and a willingness to think in terms of the common good in order to assure for its members continuous development and achievement in the collegiate and fraternity world. **Focus:** General studies. **Qualif.:** Applicants must be members of Delta Phi Epsilon or the sons or daughters of members; must be enrolled in undergraduate studies during the academic year. **Criteria:** Scholarship are based on three criteria: service and involvement, academics, and need.

Funds Avail.: No specific amount. **To Apply:** Application forms are available on the website. Applicant must submit an official transcript of grades, letter of introduction and need for scholarship, typed autobiographical sketch (1,000 word max), two recent photos suitable for publication, letter of recommendation from (must provide at least 2): (1) Chapter President; (2) Chapter Advisor; (3) College Professor or Administrator; (4) High School Teacher/Principal; (5) Alumna; (6) Employer. Applicant must provide a name and address of financial aid director for the school. Application materials must be mailed to: Delta Phi Epsilon Educational Foundation, 251 S Camac St., Philadelphia, PA 19107. **Deadline:** April 15.

2680 ■ Delta Tau Lambda Sorority

PO Box 7714
Ann Arbor, MI 48107
E-mail: dtl-info@deltataulambda.org
URL: http://www.deltataulambda.org

2681 ■ Lydia Cruz and Sandra Maria Ramos Scholarships *(Undergraduate/Scholarship)*

Purpose: To assist young Latinas in reaching goals using education as their tool. **Focus:** General studies. **Qualif.:** Applicants must be current Latina high school seniors who are entering their first year of college at a two or four year higher learning institution. **Criteria:** Selection of applicant will be based on academic excellence and community service.

Funds Avail.: No specific amount. **To Apply:** Applicant must complete the application form available on the website; must provide the official high school transcript and a copy of University/College Acceptance Latter. Scholarship application materials must be sent to: Delta Tau Lambda Sorority, Inc., PO Box 7714, Ann Arbor, MI 48107. **Deadline:** For more information on requirements and deadlines contact the foundation at DTL-info@deltataulambda.org.

2682 ■ Delta Zeta Sorority

202 E Church St.
Oxford, OH 45056
Ph: (513)523-7597
URL: http://www.deltazeta.org

2683 ■ Sandra Sebrell Bailey Scholarships *(Undergraduate/Scholarship)*

Purpose: To provide financial assistance to all qualified undergraduate students. **Focus:** General studies. **Qualif.:** Applicant must be a junior or senior woman who has been an initiated member at least one year and is in good standing. **Criteria:** Applicants will be evaluated based on academic achievements, financial need, campus leadership and activities, and services to Delta Zeta. Preference will be given to those members entering the field of education.

Funds Avail.: $1,000-$2,500. **To Apply:** Scholarship applications are available on the website and must be completed properly. Applicant must have the FAFSA reply form. **Deadline:** February 15.

2684 ■ Charline Chilson Scholarships *(Undergraduate/Scholarship)*

Purpose: To provide financial assistance for qualified graduate students. **Focus:** Science. **Qualif.:** Applicant must be a Delta Zeta member in good standing; must be in their junior or senior year or as graduate students; must have a high grade point in their major; must show financial need; must have a history of active leadership and participation in Delta Zeta activities; and must have a commitment to a degree in science. **Criteria:** Applicants will be selected based on academic achievements and financial need.

Funds Avail.: $1,000-$2,500. **To Apply:** Scholarship applications are available on the website and must be completed properly. Applicant must have the FAFSA reply form. **Deadline:** February 15.

2685 ■ Arlene Davis Scholarships *(Undergraduate/Scholarship)*

Purpose: To provide financial assistance to all qualified undergraduate students. **Focus:** Aviation. **Qualif.:** Applicant must be an initiated, active, continuing member entering her sophomore or junior year, who is enrolled in courses showing an interest in aviation; must have a 3.0 grade average. **Criteria:** Candidates will be selected based on academic standing and financial need.

Funds Avail.: $1,000-$2,500. **To Apply:** Scholarship applications are available on the website and must be completed properly. Applicant must have the FAFSA reply form. **Deadline:** February 15.

2686 ■ Delta Zeta Undergraduate Scholarships *(Undergraduate/Scholarship)*

Purpose: To provide financial assistance to all qualified undergraduate students. **Focus:** General studies. **Qualif.:** Applicant must be an initiated, active, continuing member of Delta Zeta entering junior or senior year; must be outstanding in campus and chapter activities, and have maintained at least a B average (3.0). **Criteria:** Scholarship applications will be reviewed and evaluated by the committee. Recommendation for scholarship recipients will be made by the scholarship committees to the Foundation Board of Trustees for final selection.

Funds Avail.: $1,000-$2,500. **To Apply:** Scholarship applications are available on the website and must be completed properly. Applicant must have the FAFSA reply form. **Deadline:** February 15.

2687 ■ Elizabeth M. Gruber Scholarships *(Graduate/Scholarship)*

Purpose: To provide financial assistance to all qualified undergraduate student. **Focus:** Liberal arts. **Qualif.:** Applicant must be a Delta Zeta graduate student working toward a degree in a liberal arts area. **Criteria:** Preference will be given to an Alpha Beta Chapter member or to a Delta Zeta attending a university in the Midwest.

Funds Avail.: $1,000-$15,000. **To Apply:** Applicant must provide a transcript of record; must submit a statement indicating their special service to Delta Zeta, activities and/or community involvement, academic honors and/or honor societies, and personal statement about their need and desire to get the award; must have a list of employment records and at least two recommendation letter from a Delta Zeta (Alumnae Chapter President, College Chapter Director, and/or Regional Collegiate Coordinator), and one from Academic Graduate Advisor and/or Employer. **Deadline:** February 15.

2688 ■ Edith Head Scholarships *(Undergraduate/Scholarship)*

Purpose: To provide financial assistance to all qualified undergraduate students. **Focus:** Fashion design. **Qualif.:** Applicant must be an initiated, active, continuing member of Delta Zeta pursuing a course study leading to a career in design, production, and merchandising of textile and apparel products, and/or costume design; must be a junior or senior student, graduate level, or a professional school which offers fashion merchandising, textiles, and clothing or costume design; must have at least a 3.0 average. **Criteria:** Candidates will be selected based on their academic standing and financial need.

Funds Avail.: $1,000-$2,500. **To Apply:** Scholarship applications are available on the website and must be completed properly. Applicant must have the FAFSA reply form. **Deadline:** February 15.

2689 ■ Lavonne Heghinian Scholarships *(Undergraduate/Scholarship)*

Purpose: To provide financial assistance to all qualified undergraduate students. **Focus:** General studies. **Qualif.:** Applicant must be an initiated, active, continuing member of Delta Zeta in need of financial assistance; must have a 3.0 average. **Criteria:** Application will be evaluated based on the sorority service, campus involvement and employment. Preference will be given to Southern California applicants in accordance with Mrs. Heghinian's will.

Funds Avail.: $1,000-$2,500. **To Apply:** Scholarship applications are available on the website and must be completed properly. Applicant must have the FAFSA reply form. **Deadline:** February 15.

2690 ■ Houston/Nancy Holliman Scholarships *(Undergraduate/Scholarship)*

Purpose: To provide financial assistance to all qualified undergraduate students. **Focus:** Speech and language pathology/audiology; Hearing and deafness; Allied health. **Qualif.:** Applicant must be a junior or senior active, continuing member majoring in hearing and speech, audiology or an allied field; must have an academic achievements (maintaining a 3.0 average), campus honors and activities, and service to Delta Zeta. **Criteria:** Candidates will be selected based on academic standing, honors, and financial need.

Funds Avail.: $1,000-$2,500. **To Apply:** Scholarship applications are available on the website and must be completed properly. Applicant must have the FAFSA reply form. **Deadline:** February 15.

2691 ■ Sarah Jane Houston Scholarships *(Undergraduate/Scholarship)*

Purpose: To provide financial assistance to all qualified undergraduate students. **Focus:** Education, English as a second language. **Qualif.:** Applicant must be an undergraduate Delta Zeta member in good standing with 3.0 or higher grade point average; must have a major field in English or in related fields such as speech, debate, drama, theater, or education. **Criteria:** Applicants from Delta Zeta chapters in Illinois will be given preferences if all other qualifications are equal. Applicants will be evaluated based on academic achievements and campus activities.

Funds Avail.: $1,000-$2,500. **To Apply:** Scholarship applications are available in the website and must be completed properly. Applicant must have the FAFSA reply form. **Deadline:** February 15.

2692 ■ Huenefeld/Denton Scholarships *(Undergraduate/Scholarship)*

Purpose: To provide financial assistance to all qualified undergraduate students. **Focus:** Child development, Education, Library and archival sciences. **Qualif.:** Applicant must be a junior or senior initiated, active continuing members in need of financial help, seeking an undergraduate degree in child development/primary education or library science. **Criteria:** Applicants will be evaluated based on their academic achievements, campus activities, and service to Delta Zeta.

Funds Avail.: $1,000-$2,500. **To Apply:** Scholarship applications are available on the website and must be completed properly. Applicant must have the FAFSA reply form. **Deadline:** February 15.

2693 ■ Betsy B. and Garold A. Leach Scholarship for Museum Studies *(Undergraduate/Scholarship)*

Purpose: To provide financial assistance to all qualified undergraduate students. **Focus:** Museum science. **Qualif.:**

Applicant must be an initiated, continuing member of Delta Zeta pursuing a course of study that could lead to a career in museum work; must be entering his/her junior or senior year or graduate level; must have a financial need and have at least 3.0 average. **Criteria:** Selection of candidates will be based on academic achievements, and campus activities.

Funds Avail.: $1,000-$2,500. **To Apply:** Scholarship applications are available on the website and must be completed properly. Applicant must have the FAFSA reply form. **Deadline:** February 15.

2694 ■ Elsa Ludeke Graduate Scholarships *(Graduate/Scholarship)*

Purpose: To provide financial assistance to all qualified graduate students. **Focus:** General studies. **Qualif.:** Applicant must be an initiated member in need of financial assistance; must have at least a B average (3.0); must be outstanding in undergraduate campus activities and in special service and leadership to Delta Zeta chapter. **Criteria:** Selection of applicant will be based on financial need and academic achievements.

Funds Avail.: $1,000-$15,000. **To Apply:** Applicant must provide a transcript of record; must submit a statement indicating special service to Delta Zeta, activities and/or community involvement, academic honors and/or honor societies, and personal statement about their need and desire to get the award; must have a list of employment records and at least two recommendation letters from a Delta Zeta (Alumnae Chapter President, College Chapter Director, and/or Regional Collegiate Coordinator), and one from Academic Graduate Advisor and/or Employer. **Deadline:** February 15.

2695 ■ John L. and Eleanore I. Mckinley Scholarships *(Undergraduate/Scholarship)*

Purpose: To provide financial assistance to all qualified undergraduate students. **Focus:** General studies. **Qualif.:** Applicant must be a junior or senior Delta Zeta member in good standing; must have earned a B or better average at the conclusion of their sophomore year; must have achieved a high level of service to the Delta Zeta Sorority and her college community. **Criteria:** Financial need is considered.

Funds Avail.: $1,000-$2,500. **To Apply:** Scholarship applications are available on the website and must be completed properly. Applicant must have the FAFSA reply form. **Deadline:** February 15.

2696 ■ Helen Woodruff Nolop Scholarship in Audiology and Allied Fields *(Graduate/Scholarship)*

Purpose: To assist qualified female students in pursuing an education. **Focus:** Speech and language pathology/audiology; Allied health. **Qualif.:** Applicant must be a graduate student in audiology or in allied field; must be an initiated continuing member in good standing in a collegiate chapter with 3.0 cumulative grade average. **Criteria:** Selection of applicant will be based on academic achievement and financial need.

Funds Avail.: $1,000-$15,000. **To Apply:** Applicant must provide a transcript of record; must submit a statement indicating special service to Delta Zeta, activities and/or community involvement, academic honors and/or honor societies, and personal statement about need and desire to get the award; must have a list of employment records and at least two recommendation letters from a Delta Zeta (Alumnae Chapter President, College Chapter Director, and/or Regional Collegiate Coordinator), and one from Academic Graduate Advisor and/or Employer. **Deadline:** February 15.

2697 ■ Gail Patrick Charitable Trust Scholarships *(Undergraduate/Scholarship)*

Purpose: To provide financial assistance to all qualified undergraduate student. **Focus:** General studies. **Qualif.:** Applicant must be an initiated, active, continuing Delta Zeta member in need of financial assistance; must be entering her junior or senior year. **Criteria:** Applicant will be evaluated based on academic achievements and campus activities.

Funds Avail.: $2,500. **To Apply:** Scholarship applications are available on the website and must be completed properly. Applicant must have the FAFSA reply form. **Deadline:** February 15.

2698 ■ Dorothy Worden Ronken Scholarships *(Graduate/Scholarship)*

Purpose: To provide financial assistance to all qualified graduate students. **Focus:** Education, Business. **Qualif.:** Applicant must be a Delta Zeta graduate student working on a degree in education or business; must be a initiated continuing member in good standing in a collegiate chapter with 3.0 cumulative grade average. **Criteria:** Preference will be given to applicants from the Alpha Alpha chapter of Northwestern University.

Funds Avail.: Amount of the awards may vary depending upon the fund earnings. **To Apply:** Applicant must provide a transcript of record; must submit a statement indicating their special service to Delta Zeta, activities and/or community involvement, academic honors and/or honor societies, and personal statement about need and desire to get the award; must have a list of employment records and at least two recommendation letters from a Delta Zeta (Alumnae Chapter President, College Chapter Director, and/or Regional Collegiate Coordinator), and one from Academic Graduate Advisor and/or employer. **Deadline:** February 15.

2699 ■ Elizabeth Coulter Stephenson Scholarships *(Undergraduate/Scholarship)*

Purpose: To provide financial assistance to all qualified undergraduate students. **Focus:** General studies. **Qualif.:** Applicant must be outstanding in campus and chapter activities; must have held, or must currently hold, an executive board position; must have at least 3.0 average; must have been adversely affected, or parents have been adversely affected by a disaster. **Criteria:** Preference will be given to initiated, active, continuing members of Delta Zeta in their junior or senior year who need a financial assistant.

Funds Avail.: $500. **To Apply:** Application forms are available in the website. Applicant must provide the official transcript; must have statement about special service to Delta Zeta, campus activities and/or community involvement, and academic honors; must have the list of employment record; must submit a recommendation letter from the college chapter director (CCD) and if chapter has no CCD, a letter from RCC will suffice. Application materials must be sent to: Delta Zeta Foundation, 202 E Church St., Oxford, OH 45056. **Deadline:** February 15.

Awards are arranged alphabetically below their administering organizations

2700 ■ Thornberg/Havens Scholarships *(Undergraduate/Scholarship)*

Purpose: To provide financial assistance to all qualified undergraduate students. **Focus:** General studies. **Qualif.:** Applicant must be an undergraduate and/or graduate Delta Zeta in good standing; must be an initiated member in need of financial assistance who has shown outstanding campus and chapter activities; must have at least 3.0 undergraduate average. **Criteria:** Candidates will be selected based on their academic standing and financial need.

Funds Avail.: $1,000-$2,500. **To Apply:** Scholarship applications are available on the website and must be completed properly. Applicant must have the FAFSA reply form. **Deadline:** February 15.

2701 ■ DeMolay International

10200 NW Ambassador Dr.
Kansas City, MO 64153
Ph: (816)891-8333
Fax: (816)891-9062
Free: 800-336-6529
E-mail: demolay@demolay.org
URL: http://www.demolay.org

2702 ■ Frank S. Land Scholarships *(Undergraduate/Scholarship)*

Purpose: To provide financial assistance for eligible members of Demolay. **Focus:** General studies. **Qualif.:** Applicants must be active members of DeMolay who have not yet reached their majority or 21st birthday. **Criteria:** Applicants are evaluated based on personal attributes.

Funds Avail.: $800. **Number Awarded:** 1. **To Apply:** Applicants may download the scholarship application form from the Foundation's website. **Deadline:** April 1.

2703 ■ York Rite Grand Chapter Royal Arch Masons Scholarships *(Undergraduate/Scholarship)*

Purpose: To support the post-baccalaureate education of the members of Demolay. **Focus:** General studies. **Qualif.:** Applicants must be active senior DeMolay members. **Criteria:** Applicants are evaluated based on merit.

Funds Avail.: $1,000. **To Apply:** Applicants may download scholarship application form from the foundation's website. **Deadline:** April 1.

2704 ■ Denver Scholarship Foundation

303 E 17th Ave., Ste. 200
Denver, CO 80203
Ph: (303)951-4140
Fax: (303)951-4143
E-mail: info@denverscholarship.org
URL: http://www.denverscholarship.org

2705 ■ Denver Scholarship Foundation Scholarships *(Undergraduate/Scholarship)*

Purpose: To inspire and empower Denver Public School (DPS) students to achieve their post-secondary goals. **Focus:** General studies. **Qualif.:** Applicant must be a DPS graduate, enrolled and included in the State Census (October 1st Count) at a participating DPS school for at least one year immediately preceding graduation; and eligible to receive federal student financial aid (must be U.S. citizen, permanent resident or other eligible non-citizen). **Criteria:** Awards are given based on merit and need.

Funds Avail.: No specific amount. **To Apply:** Applicants must complete and submit the DSF Scholarship Application online. **Deadline:** March 31.

Remarks: All mailings, fax coversheets, or e-mail messages must include the student's full name, student ID number, phone number, and e-mail address.

2706 ■ Development Fund for Black Students in Science and Technology

2705 Bladensburg Rd. NE
Washington, DC 20018
Ph: (202)635-3604
E-mail: dfbsst_info@dlhjr.com
URL: http://www.dfbsst.dlhjr.com

2707 ■ Development Fund for Black Students in Science and Technology Scholarship *(Undergraduate/Scholarship)*

Purpose: To provide scholarships to African American undergraduate students. **Focus:** Scientific or Technical fields. **Qualif.:** Applicants must meet the following criteria: African-American heritage; undergraduate students majoring (or intending to major) in a technical field of study (i.e., engineering, math, science, etc.); enrollment at one of the predominantly Black colleges or universities; U.S. citizenship or permanent residency. **Criteria:** Awards will be based on academic achievement, personal essay describing career goals, current and past relevant extracurricular activities, recommendations from teachers and guidance counselors and financial need.

Funds Avail.: No specific amount. **To Apply:** Applicants must submit a completed application form. **Contact:** Development Fund for Black Students in Science and Technology at the above address (see entry 2706).

2708 ■ Dickey Rural Networks

9628 Hwy. 281
PO Box 69
Ellendale, ND 58436
Free: 877-559-4692
URL: http://www.drtel.net

2709 ■ Dickey Rural Networks College Scholarship Program *(Undergraduate/Scholarship)*

Purpose: To provide financial assistance for rural high school seniors to further their college education. **Focus:** Telecommunications systems. **Qualif.:** Applicants must be graduating high school seniors; must receive local telecommunications service from a current NTCA member (except for students sponsored by an associate member company); must be accepted by an accredited two or four-year college, university or vocational-technical school; must have at least a C grade point average (GPA); must have academic credentials within an average to above-average range; must express an interest to return to a rural community following graduation; and must be sponsored by a contributor to, or supporter of, the Foundation for Rural Service. **Criteria:** Applicants are evaluated based on academic credentials and financial need.

Funds Avail.: $2,500. **Number Awarded:** 30. **To Apply:** Applicants must complete and print the DRN/FRS Scholar-

Awards are arranged alphabetically below their administering organizations

ship Application online, which is also available from the school counselor, with the complete instructions and checklist of items to be considered. **Deadline:** February 15.

2710 ■ Bill Dickey Scholarship Association

1140 E Washington St. Ste. 103
Phoenix, AZ 85034
Ph: (602)258-7851
Fax: (602)258-3412
E-mail: andrea@bdscholar.org
URL: http://www.nmjgsa.org

2711 ■ Bill Dickey Scholarship Association Scholarships *(Undergraduate/Scholarship)*

Purpose: To provide financial support to deserving undergraduate students. **Focus:** General studies. **Qualif.:** Applicants must be high school seniors who are already in BDSA database as well as undergraduate students that previously received a scholarship as freshmen are eligible to apply. **Criteria:** Selection will be based on academic achievement, entrance exam scores, financial need, references, evidence of community service and golfing ability.

Funds Avail.: Maximum award amount: $6,000. **To Apply:** Applicants must check the available website to enter their database profile and to gain information regarding this award. **Contact:** Bill Dickey Scholarship Association at the above address (see entry 2710).

2712 ■ Direct Marketing Fundraisers Association

PO Box 1038
New York, NY 10028
Ph: (646)675-7314
Fax: (646)417-6493
URL: http://www.dmfa.org

2713 ■ Sanky Perlowin Memorial Scholarships *(Undergraduate/Scholarship)*

Purpose: To enhance the skills a new member in direct marketing fundraising. **Focus:** Marketing and distribution. **Qualif.:** Nominees must be involved or interested in fundraising by direct mail and related techniques. **Criteria:** Recipients are selected based on the on information submitted in writing by current DMFA members.

Funds Avail.: $500. **To Apply:** Applicants must fill up the and complete the nomination form.

Remarks: Mrs. Sanky Perlowin was the head of Sanky Perlowin Associates, a direct mail fundraising consulting firm.

2714 ■ Directed Energy Professional Society

2600 Yale Blvd. SE, Ste. 139
Albuquerque, NM 87106
Ph: (505)998-4910
Fax: (505)998-4917
E-mail: office@deps.org
URL: http://www.deps.org

2715 ■ DEPS Graduate Scholarship Program *(Graduate/Scholarship)*

Purpose: To foster research and development of DE technology for national defense and civil applications through professional communication and education. **Focus:** Physics; Engineering, Electrical; Engineering, Chemical; Chemistry; Materials research/science; Optical engineering; Engineering, Aerospace/Aeronautical/Astronautical; Engineering, Optical. **Qualif.:** Applicants must be U.S. citizens or individuals who have demonstrated interest in American citizenship; must be full-time graduate students at a U.S. school; must be pursuing or currently studying DE technology areas of HEL or HPM with scopes similar to those researches published in the Journal of Directed Energy. **Criteria:** Applicants are selected based on the reviews conducted by the DEPS Board of Scientific and Engineering Advisors' (BSEA) review of all applications.

Funds Avail.: $10,000. **To Apply:** Applicants must submit completed application form available at the website; official transcripts of undergraduate and graduate studies sent directly from the school; letter of interest in DE technology and statement of proposed research; and a reference letter from a potential or current research advisor including an assessment of the applicant's potential and description of facilities to be employed for the research. All materials must be forwarded to: DEPS Scholarship Program, Directed Energy Professional Society, 2600 Yale Blvd. SE, Ste. 139 Albuquerque, NM 87106. **Deadline:** April 1.

2716 ■ Directors of Health Promotion and Education

1015 18th St. NW, 3rd Fl.
Washington, DC 20036
Ph: (202)659-2230
Fax: (202)659-2339
URL: http://www.dhpe.org

2717 ■ Scholarships for Leadership Training and Coaching *(Professional Development/Scholarship)*

Purpose: To provide financial assistance for individuals intending to enroll in leadership-related courses. **Focus:** Leadership, Institutional and community; Public health. **Qualif.:** Program is open to DHPE dues-paid members seeking professional development through leadership-related courses or leadership coaching. **Criteria:** Applicant will be assessed based on the application form submitted describing the leadership training opportunity in sufficient detail to evaluate its credentials and content (for training awards), goals and outcomes of coaching (for coaching awards), commitment by the supervisor to allow participation in the training and amount requested.

Funds Avail.: $500 up to $2,000. **To Apply:** Applicants must submit the completed application form provided by the scholarship committee.

2718 ■ Dirksen Cogressional Center

2815 Broadway
Pekin, IL 61554
Ph: (309)347-7113
Fax: (309)347-6432
E-mail: info@dirkcenter.org
URL: http://www.dirkcenter.org

2719 ■ Congressional Research Awards *(Graduate/Award/Prize)*

Purpose: To fund research on congressional leadership and related studies about the U.S. Congress. **Focus:**

Awards are arranged alphabetically below their administering organizations

Government. **Qualif.:** Applicants must have a serious interest in studying the Congress; must be political scientists, historians, biographers, scholars of public administration or American studies, and journalists; must be graduate students who have successfully defended their dissertation prospectus to apply and awards a significant portion of the funds for dissertation research; must be U.S. citizens who reside in the United States. **Criteria:** Recipients are selected based on the project design; plan of work; dissemination; applicant's qualifications; relationship of the project to the Centers Program goals and to current work in the field; and appropriateness of the project request for the requirements.

Funds Avail.: $30,000. **To Apply:** Applicants must submit five copies of application summary sheet listing the name and contact information not exceeding 100-words; a description of the project goals, methods, and intended results, demonstrating clearly its importance to the award program priorities; A vitae including a list of publications; Original and five copies of a letter of reference from the person directing their dissertation work; a proposal letter from the responsible official stipulating that no indirect or overhead costs will be charged against the grant. **Deadline:** February 1. **Contact:** fmackaman@dirksencenter.org. Frank H. Mackaman at the above address (see entry 2718).

2720 ■ Ray and Kathy LaHood Scholarships for the Study of American Government *(Undergraduate/Scholarship)*

Purpose: To provide financial support for Bradley University juniors who are majoring in a discipline related to The Dirksen Center's purpose and interest or in subjects related to the study of Federal Government. **Focus:** Government. **Qualif.:** Applicants must be juniors in good standing entering their senior year of study in a field related to the study of the U.S. government; must be attending Bradley University; must have a grade point average (on a four-point scale) of at least 3.0 overall and 3.75 in their major; must agree to write a 250-word evaluation of the impact of their scholarship before the end of their senior year; and must agree to meet with Ray or Kathy LaHood during the second semester of their senior year. **Criteria:** Recipients are selected based on scholastic records.

Funds Avail.: $2,000-$3,500. **To Apply:** Applicants must fill out the required scholarship form. **Contact:** Brad McMillan, executive Director at 408 Jobs Hall, Bradley University, 1501 W. Bradley Peoria, IL 61625; 309-677-4408; bmcmillan@bradley.edu.

2721 ■ Disabled American Veterans

PO Box 14301
Cincinnati, OH 45250-0301
Ph: (859)441-7300
Free: 877-426-2838
URL: http://www.dav.org

2722 ■ Jesse Brown Memorial Youth Scholarship Program *(Undergraduate/Scholarship)*

Purpose: To provide financial assistance to young volunteers who play active roles in the Department of Veterans Affairs Voluntary Service programs to continue their education. **Focus:** General studies. **Qualif.:** Applicants must be any volunteers who are at the age of 21 or younger and have volunteered for a minimum of 100 hours at a VA medical center during the previous year; immediate family members of the DAV national organization are also eligible. **Criteria:** Applicants will be evaluated based on criteria designed by the Scholarship Selection Committee.

Funds Avail.: No specific amount. **To Apply:** Nominations must be submitted by the Voluntary Service Program Manager at the VA medical center, DAV Department Commander, or the student must submit a self-nomination form, which is available online, including an essay and any supporting documentation.

2723 ■ Distinguished Flying Cross Society

PO Box 530250
San Diego, CA 92153
Free: (866)332-6332
URL: http://www.dfcsociety.org

2724 ■ Distinguished Flying Cross Society Scholarship *(Undergraduate/Scholarship)*

Purpose: To support dependents of DFC Society members in the pursuit of continuing higher education. **Focus:** Aviation. **Qualif.:** Applicants must be descendants (or legally adopted children) of a DFC Society member. **Criteria:** Applicants must be attending the 2009 Spring Semester at an accredited institution of higher education in the pursuit of an undergraduate degree.

Funds Avail.: No amount mentioned. **To Apply:** Applicants must provide 500-word essay on why they deserve a DFCS Scholarship, SAT/SCAT scores, official high school transcript, and a letter from DFCS member attesting that he/she is a descendant of a DFCS member. **Deadline:** November 15.

2725 ■ Dolphin Scholarship Foundation

5040 Virginia Beach Blvd., Ste. 104A
Virginia Beach, VA 23462
Ph: (757)671-3200
Fax: (757)671-3330
E-mail: info@dolphinscholarship.org
URL: http://www.dolphinscholarship.org

2726 ■ Dolphin Scholarships *(Undergraduate/Scholarship)*

Purpose: To support the education of children/stepchildren of members or former members of the Submarine Force or who have served in the Submarine Force. **Focus:** General studies. **Qualif.:** Applicant must be a high school senior or college student; child or stepchild of a member or former member of the U.S. Navy Submarine Force; unmarried; under age 24; must attend a four-year accredited college or university and intend to work toward a BS or BA degree. **Criteria:** Scholarships are awarded based on academic proficiency, financial need, and commitment to and excellence in school and community activities.

Funds Avail.: Varies. **Number Awarded:** Varies. **To Apply:** Applicants must submit a completed scholarship application form.

2727 ■ Douglas-Coldwell Foundation

300-279 Laurier Ave. W
Ottawa, ON, Canada K1P 5J9
Ph: (613)232-1918
Fax: (613)230-9950
E-mail: info@dcf.ca
URL: http://www.dcf.ca

Awards are arranged alphabetically below their administering organizations

2728 ■ Beverlee Bell Scholarships in Human Rights and Democracy *(Graduate/Scholarship)*

Purpose: To provide support to qualified students who want to pursue their education. **Focus:** Human rights. **Qualif.:** Applicants must be graduate students making a significant contribution to human rights and democracy in developing countries. **Criteria:** Applicants are selected based on the committee's review of the application materials.

Funds Avail.: $1,000. **To Apply:** Applicants are advised to contact the Carleton University, Academic Department, 1125 Colonel By Dr., Ottawa, ON for further information about the scholarship application form and requirements. **Deadline:** January.

Remarks: Established in 2002 to honor the memory of NDP activist Beverlee Bell, by her family and the Douglas-Coldwell Foundation.

2729 ■ Douglas-Coldwell Foundation Scholarships in Social Affairs *(Graduate/Scholarship)*

Purpose: To support deserving student who wants to pursue their study. **Focus:** Education, English as a second language; History; Political science; Social work; Sociology. **Qualif.:** Applicants must be fully-qualified graduate students preparing a thesis on a topic involving some aspect of Canadian social theory or history. **Criteria:** Applicants are selected based on the Scholarship Committee's review of the application materials.

Funds Avail.: $3,000. **To Apply:** Scholarship application form and requirements are available at University of Regina, Graduate Studies and Research. **Deadline:** October 31.

2730 ■ Kalmen Kaplansky Scholarships in Economic and Social Rights *(Graduate/Scholarship)*

Purpose: To provide support to qualified students who want to pursue their education. **Focus:** Economics; Civil rights. **Qualif.:** Applicants must be graduate students researching economic and social rights in a School or Department in the Faculty of Public Affairs and Management at Carleton University. **Criteria:** Recipients will be selected based on their research work.

Funds Avail.: $1,000. **To Apply:** Applicants are advised to contact the Carleton University, Academic Unit, 1125 Colonel By Dr., Ottawa, ON for further information about the scholarship application form and other requirements. **Deadline:** February 1.

Remarks: Scholarship was established in 1998 by the Douglas-Coldwell Foundation in honor of the lifetime achievement of Dr. Kalmen Kaplansky, labor and human rights advocate, in the field of economic and social rights.

2731 ■ Drake University Law School

2621 Carpenter Ave.
Des Moines, IA 50311
Ph: (515)271-2824
Free: 800-44-DRAKE
E-mail: lawadmit@drake.edu
URL: http://www.law.drake.edu

2732 ■ William Stone Ayres Scholarships *(Undergraduate/Scholarship)*

Purpose: To support the education of law students. **Focus:** Law. **Qualif.:** Applicants must be students of Drake University law school. **Criteria:** Recipients are selected based on academic record and financial need.

Funds Avail.: No specific amount. **To Apply:** Applicants must file FAFSA and application form.

Remarks: Established by a bequest from Gladys L. Ayres in memory of her husband, a 1894 Law School graduate. **Contact:** Office of Admission and Financial Aid at 515-271-2782.

2733 ■ Beverly Estate Scholarships *(Undergraduate/Scholarship)*

Purpose: To support the education of law students. **Focus:** Law. **Qualif.:** Applicants must be students of Drake University law school. **Criteria:** Recipients are selected based on academic record and financial need.

Funds Avail.: No specific amount. **To Apply:** Applicants must file FAFSA and application form.

Remarks: Awards are made possible by bequests from Francis Cecile Beverly, LW'15, and Adda Brown Beverly, ED'14. **Contact:** Office of Admission and Financial Aid at 515-271-2782.

2734 ■ George and Mary Brammer Scholarships *(Undergraduate/Scholarship)*

Purpose: To support the education of law students. **Focus:** Law. **Qualif.:** Applicants must be students of Drake University law school. **Criteria:** Recipients are selected based on academic record and financial need.

Funds Avail.: No specific amount. **To Apply:** Applicants must file FAFSA and application form.

Remarks: Established by Mary and John Harper as a memorial to Mary's parents, 1908 and 1907 graduates of the Law School. **Contact:** Office of Admission and Financial Aid at 515-271-2782.

2735 ■ Gregory Brunk Scholarships *(Undergraduate/Scholarship)*

Purpose: To support the education of law students. **Focus:** Law. **Qualif.:** Applicants must be students of Drake University law school. **Criteria:** Recipients are selected based on academic record and financial need.

Funds Avail.: No specific amount. **To Apply:** Applicants must file the FAFSA and application form.

Remarks: The scholarship was made available by the late Gregory Brunk, LW'19. **Contact:** Office of Admission and Financial Aid at 515-271-2782.

2736 ■ Donald C. and Doris K. Byers Scholarships *(Undergraduate/Scholarship)*

Purpose: To support the education of law students. **Focus:** Law. **Qualif.:** Applicants must be entering first year students. **Criteria:** Recipients are selected based on merit and financial need. Preferences are given to residents of Newton, Iowa and the surrounding area of Jasper County, Iowa.

Funds Avail.: No specific amount. **To Apply:** Applicants must submit a completed application form.

Remarks: Sponsored by Donald C. and Doris K. Byers. **Contact:** Office of Admission and Financial Aid at 515-271-2782.

2737 ■ Raymond DiPaglia Endowment Scholarships *(Undergraduate/Scholarship)*

Purpose: To support the education of law students. **Focus:** Law. **Qualif.:** Applicants must be returning law students in good standing at the Drake University law school. **Criteria:** Recipients are selected based on academic record and financial need.

Funds Avail.: No specific amount. **To Apply:** Applicants must file FAFSA and application form. **Contact:** Office of Admission and Financial Aid at 515-271-2782.

2738 ■ Grace O. Doane Scholarships
(Undergraduate/Scholarship)

Purpose: To support the education of law students. **Focus:** Law. **Qualif.:** Applicants must be second year Iowa residents who rank in the top one-half of their class. **Criteria:** Recipients are selected based on academic record and financial need.

Funds Avail.: No specific amount. **To Apply:** Applicants must file FAFSA and an application form. **Contact:** Office of Admission and Financial Aid at 515-271-2782.

2739 ■ Joseph M. Dorgan Scholarships
(Undergraduate/Scholarship)

Purpose: To support the education of law students. **Focus:** Law. **Qualif.:** Applicants must be African American law students. **Criteria:** Recipients are selected based on academic record and financial need.

Funds Avail.: No specific amount. **To Apply:** Applicants must file FAFSA and application form. **Contact:** Office of Admission and Financial Aid at 515-271-2782.

2740 ■ Drake University Law School Law Opportunity Scholarships - Disadvantage
(Undergraduate/Scholarship)

Purpose: To support the education of disadvantaged law students. **Focus:** Law. **Qualif.:** Applicants must have been admitted to the Law School and must demonstrate financial need as determined by the Free Application for Federal Student Aid. **Criteria:** Preferences are given to students whose enrollment will significantly contribute to the diversity of the Drake Law School student body, or to those who have overcome economic, educational or other significant disadvantages.

Funds Avail.: One-quarter tuition to full-tuition awards. **To Apply:** Applicants must submit completed application form.

Remarks: Disadvantaged student is "one who, despite facing significant obstacles, has prepared himself or herself for a college education". **Contact:** Office of Admission and Financial Aid at 515-271-2782.

2741 ■ Drake University Law School Law Opportunity Scholarships - Diversity
(Undergraduate/Scholarship)

Purpose: To promote the diversity of students in Drake University. **Focus:** Law. **Qualif.:** Applicants must have been admitted to the law school and must demonstrate financial need as determined by the Free Application for Federal Student Aid. **Criteria:** Preferences are given to students whose enrollment will significantly contribute to the diversity of the Drake University law school student body, or to those who have overcome economic, educational or other significant disadvantages.

Funds Avail.: One-quarter tuition to full-tuition awards. **To Apply:** Applicants must submit completed application form. **Contact:** Office of Admission and Financial Aid at 515-271-2782.

2742 ■ Drake University Law School Public Service Scholarships *(Undergraduate/Scholarship)*

Purpose: To support the education of law students. **Focus:** Law. **Qualif.:** Applicants must exhibit an extraordinary history of public service work and plan to continue that commitment during and after law school. **Criteria:** Recipients are selected based on merit and need.

Funds Avail.: Full-tuition. **To Apply:** Applicants must submit completed application form along with essay, a short description of past work experiences/activities, letters of recommendation, relevant academic curriculum and statement of reasons for award. **Deadline:** March 1. **Contact:** Office of Admission and Financial Aid at 515-271-2782.

2743 ■ Robert E. Early Memorial Scholarships
(Undergraduate/Scholarship)

Purpose: To support the education of law students. **Focus:** Law. **Qualif.:** Applicants must be second or third year full time students who are in need of financial assistance. **Criteria:** Recipients are selected based on academic records and financial need.

Funds Avail.: No specific amount. **To Apply:** Applicants must file FAFSA and application form.

Remarks: Sponsored by Margaret M. Early in memory of her husband, LW'41. **Contact:** Office of Admission and Financial Aid at 515-271-2782.

2744 ■ Electric Cooperative Pioneer Trust Fund Scholarships *(Undergraduate/Scholarship)*

Purpose: To support the education of law students. **Focus:** Law. **Qualif.:** Applicant must be second or third year law students interested in agricultural law. **Criteria:** Recipients are selected based on merit. Preference is given to students planning to practice in Iowa.

Funds Avail.: No specific amount. **To Apply:** Applicants may contact Office of Admission and Financial Aid for more information. **Contact:** Office of Admission and Financial Aid at 515-271-2782.

2745 ■ Herman E. Elgar Memorial Scholarships
(Undergraduate/Scholarship)

Purpose: To support the education of law students. **Focus:** Law. **Qualif.:** Applicants must be third year law students. **Criteria:** Recipients are selected based on academic record and financial need.

Funds Avail.: No specific amount. **To Apply:** Applicants must file FAFSA and application form.

Remarks: Established in memory of Mr. Elgar, LW'11, by his wife and children, John, LW'50, and Alanson, LW'51. **Contact:** Office of Admission and Financial Aid at 515-271-2782.

2746 ■ D.J. Fairgrave Education Trust
(Undergraduate/Scholarship)

Purpose: To support the education of law students. **Focus:** Law. **Qualif.:** Applicants must be students of Drake University law school. **Criteria:** Recipient are selected based on financial need, character, academic record, personal achievements, future goals and anticipated contributions to the profession.

Funds Avail.: No specific amount. **To Apply:** Applicants must file FAFSA and application form.

Remarks: Established by Denio John Fairgrave. **Contact:** Office of Admission and Financial Aid at 515-271-2782.

2747 ■ Leland Stanford Forrest Scholarships
(Undergraduate/Scholarship)

Purpose: To support the education of law students. **Focus:** Law. **Qualif.:** Applicants must be accepted as first year

Awards are arranged alphabetically below their administering organizations

students at Drake law school. **Criteria:** Recipients are selected from among entering students who are graduates of Iowa high schools or colleges.

Funds Avail.: No specific amount. **To Apply:** Applicants must fill up the General Information Form of Scholarship.

Remarks: Scholarship was established through the bequest of Leland Stanford Forrest, former dean of the law school.

2748 ■ Lex and Scott Hawkins Endowed Scholarships *(Undergraduate/Scholarship)*

Purpose: To support the education of law students. **Focus:** Law. **Qualif.:** Applicants must be the president of the Law School's Moot Court Board. **Criteria:** Recipients are selected based on merit.

Funds Avail.: No specific amount. **To Apply:** Applicants may contact Office of Admission and Financial Aid for more information.

Remarks: Established by Lex Hawkins, LW'51, and Scott Hawkins, LW'81. **Contact:** Office of Admission and Financial Aid at 515-271-2782.

2749 ■ Edward and Cora Hayes Scholarships *(Undergraduate/Scholarship)*

Purpose: To support the education of law students. **Focus:** Law. **Qualif.:** Applicants must be accepted as first year students at Drake University law school and not a graduate of Iowa high schools or colleges. **Criteria:** Recipients are selected based on merit.

Funds Avail.: No specific amount. **To Apply:** Applicants must fill up the General Information Form of Scholarship.

Remarks: Established by former associate dean Edward Hayes and his wife.

2750 ■ Annamae Heaps Law Scholarships *(Undergraduate/Scholarship)*

Purpose: To support the education of law students. **Focus:** Law. **Qualif.:** Applicants must be a second year students demonstrating financial need. **Criteria:** Recipients are selected based on academic record and financial need.

Funds Avail.: No specific amount. **To Apply:** Applicants must file FAFSA and application form. **Contact:** Office of Admission and Financial Aid at 515-271-2782.

2751 ■ John M. Helmick Law Scholarships *(Undergraduate/Scholarship)*

Purpose: To support the education of law students. **Focus:** Law. **Qualif.:** Applicants must be students of Iowa backgrounds planning to enter the legal or educational professions in Iowa. **Criteria:** Recipients are selected based on academic record and financial need.

Funds Avail.: No specific amount. **To Apply:** Applicants must file FAFSA and application form.

Remarks: Sponsored by Robert H. Helmick, LW'60, in memory of his grandfather, John Miller Helmick. **Contact:** Office of Admission and Financial Aid at 515-271-2782.

2752 ■ James P. Irish Scholarships *(Undergraduate/Scholarship)*

Purpose: To support the education of law students. **Focus:** Law. **Qualif.:** Applicants must be from Southeast Polk High School or members of the Law Review Board of Editor. **Criteria:** Recipients are selected based on merit.

Funds Avail.: No specific amount. **To Apply:** Applicants may contact Office of Admission and Financial Aid for more information.

Remarks: Established by Edwin Skinner and Donald Beattie in honor of their associate and law partner, James P. Irish, LW'31. **Contact:** Office of Admission and Financial Aid at 515-271-2782.

2753 ■ Edward H. Jones Scholarships *(Undergraduate/Scholarship)*

Purpose: To support the education of law students. **Focus:** Law. **Qualif.:** Applicants must be second year law students. **Criteria:** Recipients are selected based on merit.

Funds Avail.: $2000. **To Apply:** Applicants must submit a completed scholarship application form.

Remarks: Established in honor of the late Edward H. Jones, former executive director of the Iowa State Bar Association. **Contact:** Office of Admission and Financial Aid at 515-271-2782.

2754 ■ Martin Luther King Law Scholarships *(Undergraduate/Scholarship)*

Purpose: To support the education of law students. **Focus:** Law. **Qualif.:** Applicants must be female African-American law students who embodies the spirit and values of Martin Luther King and who have demonstrated financial need. **Criteria:** Recipients are selected based on academic record and financial need.

Funds Avail.: No specific amount. **To Apply:** Applicants must file FAFSA and application form.

Remarks: Established by Naomi Mercer, LW'68. **Contact:** Office of Admission and Financial Aid at 515-271-2782.

2755 ■ Forest A. King Scholarships *(Undergraduate/Scholarship)*

Purpose: To support the education of law students. **Focus:** Law. **Qualif.:** Applicants must be students of Drake University law school. **Criteria:** Recipients are selected based on academic record and financial need.

Funds Avail.: No specific amount. **To Apply:** Applicants must file FAFSA and application form.

Remarks: Established in memory of Mr. King, LW'25, by his wife, Nonnie. **Contact:** Office of Admission and Financial Aid at 515-271-2782.

2756 ■ Verne Lawyer Scholarships *(Undergraduate/Scholarship)*

Purpose: To support the education of law students. **Focus:** Law. **Qualif.:** Applicants must be students of Drake University Law School. **Criteria:** Recipients are selected based on academic record and financial need.

Funds Avail.: No specific amount. **To Apply:** Applicants must file FAFSA and application form.

Remarks: Established in 1992 in honor of D. Verne Lawyer, a 1949 graduate of the Law School. **Contact:** Office of Admission and Financial Aid at 515-271-2782.

2757 ■ League of Attorneys' Wives Scholarships *(Undergraduate/Scholarship)*

Purpose: To support the education of law students. **Focus:** Law. **Qualif.:** Applicants must be second year or third year female law students planning a career in public interest law. **Criteria:** Recipients are selected based on academic record and financial need.

Funds Avail.: No specific amount. **To Apply:** Applicants

Awards are arranged alphabetically below their administering organizations

must file FAFSA and application form. **Contact:** Office of Admission and Financial Aid at 515-271-2782.

2758 ■ Legal Research Service Scholarships *(Undergraduate/Scholarship)*

Purpose: To support the education of law students. **Focus:** Law. **Qualif.:** Applicants must be the presidents of the Student Legal Research Service. **Criteria:** Recipients are selected based on merit.

Funds Avail.: No specific amount. **To Apply:** Applicants may contact Office of Admission and Financial Aid for more information. **Contact:** Office of Admission and Financial Aid at 515-271-2782.

2759 ■ Frederick D. Lewis Jr. Scholarships *(Undergraduate/Scholarship)*

Purpose: To support the education of law students. **Focus:** Law. **Qualif.:** Applicants must be students of Drake University law school. **Criteria:** Recipients are selected based on academic record and financial need.

Funds Avail.: No specific amount. **To Apply:** Applicants must file FAFSA and application form.

Remarks: Established by Patrick D. Kelly, LW'53, in memory of Frederick D. Lewis Jr., a professor at Drake Law School from 1949 to 1959. **Contact:** Office of Admission and Financial Aid at 515-271-2782.

2760 ■ Gordon and Delores Madson Scholarships *(Undergraduate/Scholarship)*

Purpose: To support the education of law students. **Focus:** Law. **Qualif.:** Applicants must be students of Drake University law school. **Criteria:** Recipients are selected based on academic record and financial need.

Funds Avail.: No specific amount. **To Apply:** Applicants must file FAFSA and application form.

Remarks: Established by Gordon Madson, LW'57, and his wife, Delores. **Contact:** Office of Admission and Financial Aid at 515-271-2782.

2761 ■ Jake S. More Scholarships *(Undergraduate/Scholarship)*

Purpose: To support the education of law students. **Focus:** Law. **Qualif.:** Applicants must be students of Drake University law school. **Criteria:** Recipients are selected based on academic record and financial need.

Funds Avail.: No specific amount. **To Apply:** Applicants must file FAFSA and scholarship application form.

Remarks: Established by Jake S. More, LW'28. **Contact:** Office of Admission and Financial Aid at 515-271-2782.

2762 ■ Dwight D. Opperman Scholarships *(Undergraduate/Scholarship)*

Purpose: To support the education of law students. **Focus:** Law. **Qualif.:** Applicants must be accepted as first year students at Drake Law School; must show evidence of superior academic record and potential; must have a high score in law entrance exam; and demonstrate significant community and extracurricular experiences. **Criteria:** Recipients are selected based on achievement and potential.

Funds Avail.: Full-tuition plus $10,000. **Number Awarded:** 5. **To Apply:** Applicants must complete the application packet.

2763 ■ Jerome S. Petz, S.J., Scholarships *(Undergraduate/Scholarship)*

Purpose: To support the education of law students. **Focus:** Law. **Qualif.:** Applicants must be students of Drake University law school. **Criteria:** Recipients are selected based on academic record and financial need.

Funds Avail.: No specific amount. **To Apply:** Applicants must file FAFSA and application form.

Remarks: Established by the faculty as a memorial in honor of Father Jerome Petz, who taught at the Law School from 1971 to 1979. **Contact:** Office of Admission and Financial Aid at 515-271-2782.

2764 ■ Janet Reynoldson Memorial Scholarships *(Undergraduate/Scholarship)*

Purpose: To support the education of law students. **Focus:** Law. **Qualif.:** Applicants must be students of Drake University law school. **Criteria:** Recipients are selected based on student's contributions to community and family, academic achievement, need and significant change in career.

Funds Avail.: No specific amount. **To Apply:** Applicants must file FAFSA and application form.

Remarks: Established by the family of Janet Reynoldson, LW'65. **Contact:** Office of Admission and Financial Aid at 515-271-2782.

2765 ■ Isador M. Robinson Endowment Scholarships *(Undergraduate/Scholarship)*

Purpose: To support the education of law students. **Focus:** Law. **Qualif.:** Applicants must be second or third year law students of Drake University law school. **Criteria:** Recipients are selected based on leadership and academic achievement.

Funds Avail.: No specific amount. **To Apply:** Applicants must file FAFSA and application form. **Contact:** Office of Admission and Financial Aid at 515-271-2782.

2766 ■ Walter and Rita Selvy Scholarships *(Undergraduate/Scholarship)*

Purpose: To support the education of law students. **Focus:** Law. **Qualif.:** Applicants must be students of Drake University law school. **Criteria:** Recipients are selected based on academic record and financial need.

Funds Avail.: No specific amount. **To Apply:** Applicants must file FAFSA and application form.

Remarks: Established by Walter, LW'28, and his late wife, Rita Selvy. **Contact:** Office of Admission and Financial Aid at 515-271-2782.

2767 ■ Charles "Buck" and Dora Taylor Endowed Law Scholarships *(Undergraduate/Scholarship)*

Purpose: To support the education of law students. **Focus:** Law. **Qualif.:** Applicants must be students with financial need and have demonstrated a history of academic success while participating in sports at the undergraduate school level. **Criteria:** Recipients are selected based on merit and need.

Funds Avail.: No specific amount. **To Apply:** Applicants must submit the General Information Form for Scholarships along with the application for admission.

Remarks: Established in honor of 1933 Drake Law School graduate Charles Taylor. **Contact:** Office of Admission and

Awards are arranged alphabetically below their administering organizations

Financial Aid at 515-271-2782.

2768 ■ Haemer Wheatcraft Scholarships *(Undergraduate/Scholarship)*

Purpose: To support the education of law students. **Focus:** Law. **Qualif.:** Applicants must be students of Drake University law school. **Criteria:** Recipients are selected based on academic record and financial need.

Funds Avail.: No specific amount. **To Apply:** Applicants must file the FAFSA and the scholarship application.

Remarks: Established by friends and associates in honor of Haemer Wheatcraft, LW'33. **Contact:** Office of Admission and Financial Aid at 515-271-2782.

2769 ■ Zarley, McKee, Thomte, Voorhees, Sease Law Scholarships *(Undergraduate/Scholarship)*

Purpose: To support the education of law students. **Focus:** Law. **Qualif.:** Applicants must be students interested in intellectual property law. **Criteria:** Recipients are selected based on academic record and financial need.

Funds Avail.: No specific amount. **To Apply:** Applicants must file FAFSA and application form.

Remarks: Established by Donald H. Zarley, LW'54; Bruce W. McKee; Dennis L. Thomte; Michael G. Voorhees, LW'68; Edmund J. Sease, LW'67; and John Beehner. **Contact:** Office of Admission and Financial Aid at 515-271-2782.

2770 ■ Duluth Superior Area Community Foundation

324 W Superior St., Ste. 212
Duluth, MN 55802
Ph: (218)726-0232
Fax: (218)726-0257
E-mail: info@communityfoundation.com
URL: http://www.dsacommunityfoundation.com

2771 ■ Darrell and Palchie Asselin Scholarships *(Undergraduate/Scholarship)*

Purpose: To provide financial assistance to the non-traditional, older students in financial resources for their education. **Focus:** General studies. **Qualif.:** Applicants must be students over the age of 22 who are the primary care givers to one or more children under the age of 18; must have a grade point average of 2.5 (based on a 4.0 system) or higher for a completed of at least 50% of the course of instruction at the time of the award. **Criteria:** Applicants are evaluated based on academic achievement and financial need.

Funds Avail.: $2,000. **To Apply:** Applicants must complete the application form, available online and must submit one recommendation from a teacher, advisor, counselor or administrator; a current transcript indicating the success in completing the course of study; and Federal 1040 form. **Deadline:** January 15.

2772 ■ William E. Barto Scholarships *(Undergraduate/Scholarship)*

Purpose: To provide financial assistance for art students. **Focus:** Arts; Visual arts. **Qualif.:** Applicants must be graduating seniors of public and private high schools in Duluth and Superior; must be planning to major in arts or visual arts; must rank in the upper 25% of their class. **Criteria:** Applicants are evaluated based on financial need; academic record; written recommendations; and, seriousness of purpose.

Funds Avail.: $2,000. **Number Awarded:** 1. **To Apply:** Applicants must submit all the required application information. **Deadline:** January 15.

Remarks: Scholarship may be accepted in addition to other awards, provided that the combined amount does not exceed the full amount of tuition, books, fees and room and board charges.

2773 ■ Bernard and Mary Brusin Scholarships *(Undergraduate/Scholarship)*

Purpose: To provide assistance to Jewish and Roman Catholic students who are in need financial of aid for their college education. **Focus:** General studies. **Qualif.:** Applicants must be either Jewish or Roman Catholic graduating seniors from St. Louis County public or private high schools who are in the top 25% of their high school. **Criteria:** Applicants are evaluated based on financial need; academic record; written recommendations (one of which must be from a clergy) and seriousness of purpose.

Funds Avail.: $4,500. **To Apply:** Applicants must submit all the required application information. **Deadline:** January 15.

Remarks: The award is co-payable to the institution and the recipient.

2774 ■ Duluth Building and Construction Trades Council Scholarships *(Undergraduate/Scholarship)*

Purpose: To provide financial assistance to students entering/attending any post secondary vocational college, community college or other college or university. **Focus:** General studies. **Qualif.:** Applicants must be graduating high school seniors, whose parent/guardian is a member of one of the 17 unions affiliated with the Duluth Building Trades Council; must have grade point average of 2.75, based on 4.0 scale, or higher. **Criteria:** Applicants are evaluated based on academic record (including GPA, class rank, and test scores when relevant); written recommendations; and, seriousness of purpose.

Funds Avail.: $2,500. **Number Awarded:** 2. **To Apply:** Applicants must submit all the required application information. **Deadline:** January 15.

Remarks: The award is co-payable to the institution and the recipient.

2775 ■ Duluth Central HS Alumni Scholarships *(Undergraduate/Scholarship)*

Purpose: To assist the worthy student who customarily would be eliminated from scholarship consideration on the basis of level achievement attained in class work. **Focus:** General studies. **Qualif.:** Applicants must be graduating seniors from Duluth Central High School who will attend the College of St. Scholastica, University of Minnesota-Duluth, University of Wisconsin-Superior, Lake Superior College, or Wisconsin Indianhead Technical College. **Criteria:** Applicants are evaluated based on academic record; financial need; written recommendations; and, seriousness of purpose.

Funds Avail.: $1,000. **Number Awarded:** 1. **To Apply:** Applicants must submit all the required application information. **Deadline:** January 15.

Remarks: The Award is co-payable to the institution and the recipient.

2776 ■ Peter M. Gargano Scholarship Fund *(Undergraduate/Scholarship)*

Purpose: To provide financial assistance for post-secondary education to the children of employees of Ulland

Awards are arranged alphabetically below their administering organizations

school. **Focus:** Law. **Qualif.:** Applicants must be Dutchess County residents who completed at least one year of law school. **Criteria:** Applicants will be evaluated based on financial need.

Funds Avail.: $1,000. **To Apply:** Applicants must submit application; copy of law school transcript; essay of approximately 500 words describing interest in the law and career aspirations; letter of recommendation; and resume. **Deadline:** April 1.

2799 ■ Dystonia Medical Research Foundation

One E Wacker Dr., Ste. 2810
Chicago, IL 60601-1905
Ph: (312)755-0198
Fax: (312)803-0138
Free: 800-377-3978
E-mail: dystonia@dystonia-foundation.org
URL: http://www.dystonia-foundation.org

2800 ■ Dystonia Medical Research Foundation Fellowships *(Postdoctorate/Fellowship)*

Purpose: To assist post-doctoral fellows establish careers in research relevant to dystonia. **Focus:** Muscular dystrophy. **Qualif.:** Applicants must be in their post-doctoral degree. **Criteria:** Applicant will be selected based on their proposal.

Funds Avail.: $50,000 per year for two years. **To Apply:** Applicants may submit application to www.dystoniagrants.org. For new user, they must register on site to access the application. **Deadline:** January 21.

2801 ■ Ear Foundation

PO Box 330867
Nashville, TN 37203
Ph: (615)627-2724
Fax: (615)627-2728
Free: 800-545-HEAR
E-mail: info@earfoundation.org
URL: http://www.earfoundation.org

2802 ■ Minnie Pearl Scholarship Program *(Undergraduate/Scholarship)*

Purpose: To provide educational fund to an impaired person. **Focus:** General Studies. **Qualif.:** Applicant must be a current high school senior with at least a 3.0 cumulative GPA; intending to attend a junior college, university or technical school on a full-time basis (12 hours per quarter or semester); have significant (severe to profound) bilateral hearing loss; must be a mainstreamed hearing-impaired student; and must be a United States citizen. **Criteria:** Recipient is chosen based on merit.

Funds Avail.: $2,500. **To Apply:** Applicant must be submit completed application, copy of audiology report for both ears performed within the last 12 months; certified high school transcript (may be sent separately); two letters of recommendation from teachers; one letter of recommendation from a non-family member; and a recent photo. Submit collated documents to: Minnie Pearl Scholarship Program, The EAR Foundation, PO Box 330867, Nashville, TN 37203. **Deadline:** February 15.

3 ■ Earthquake Engineering Research itute

4th St., Ste. 320
nd, CA 94612-1934
Ph: (510)451-0905
Fax: (510)451-5411
E-mail: eeri@eeri.org
URL: http://www.eeri.org

2804 ■ Earthquake Engineering Research Institute/Fema Graduate Fellowships *(Graduate/Scholarship)*

Purpose: To support study and research that may contribute to the science and practice of earthquake hazard mitigation. **Focus:** Earth sciences. **Qualif.:** Applicant must be enrolled in a graduate degree program at an accredited U.S. college/university and must hold U.S. citizenship or permanent resident status. **Criteria:** Selection is based on the submitted application and materials.

Funds Avail.: $12,000 and $8000 for tuition, fees, and research expenses. **Number Awarded:** 1. **To Apply:** Applicants must submit a completed application form along with the letter of nomination by faculty sponsor; academic transcript; a statement (maximum of 300 words) of educational and career goals; and a resume (maximum of 2 pages). In addition, two letters of recommendation must be sent by the author directly to EERI. **Deadline:** May 16.

2805 ■ East Tennessee Foundation

625 Market St., Ste. 1400
Knoxville, TN 37902
Ph: (865)524-1223
Fax: (865)637-6039
Free: 877-524-1223
URL: http://www.easttennesseefoundation.org

2806 ■ B&W Y-12 Scholarship Fund *(Undergraduate/Scholarship)*

Purpose: To benefit graduating high school seniors wishing to pursue careers in science, math or pre-engineering related fields. **Focus:** Science; math; Engineering. **Qualif.:** Applicants must be enrolled as full-time students at either Roane State Community College or Pellissippi State Technical College; must be U.S citizens; must have a minimum GPA of at least 3.0. **Criteria:** A selection committee will be pre-selected and approved by ETF's board of Directors. The committee's primary function shall be the one to select the scholarship recipient, not only by considering the applicants' qualifications under criteria established above but also in consideration of the following factors: Scholastic and academic achievements; general aptitude for advanced educational work and seriousness of purpose; Qualities of citizenship in school and in community such as volunteer work and employment history; Participation in extracurricular activities at school or in the community; Demonstrated financial need.

Funds Avail.: $1,500. **Number Awarded:** 1. **To Apply:** Applicants must check the application process online. **Deadline:** March 14. **Contact:** East Tennessee Foundation at the above address (see entry 2805).

2807 ■ Ruby A. Brown Memorial Scholarships *(Undergraduate/Scholarship)*

Purpose: To benefit health nurses seeking to continue their nursing education. **Focus:** Nursing. **Qualif.:** Applicant must be currently employed as a public health nurse. Applicant must be a resident in one of 15 counties (Anderson, Blount, Campbell, Claiborne, Cocke, Grainger, Hamblen, Jefferson, Loudon, Monroe, Morgan, Roane, Scott, Sevier or Union).

are arranged alphabetically below their administering organizations

Brothers. **Focus:** General studies. **Qualif.:** Applicants must be children of Ulland Brothers employees who have been employed with the company for a minimum of two years (for salaried employees) or for a minimum of two seasons (for seasonal employees); must be students who are unmarried child under age 25 who is not self-supporting and who are full-time high school seniors or post-secondary students; must have a grade point average of 3.0 (based on 4.0 system) or higher. **Criteria:** Applicants are evaluated based on academic record (including GPA, class rank, and test scores when relevant); financial need; written recommendations; and, seriousness of purpose.

Funds Avail.: $2,000. **Number Awarded:** 1. **To Apply:** Applicants must submit completed application form and recently completed Student Aid Report (SAR) from the Free Application for Federal Student Aid (FAFSA). **Deadline:** January 15.

Remarks: The award is co-payable to the institution and the recipient.

2777 ■ Patricia S. Gustafson '56 Memorial Scholarships *(Undergraduate/Scholarship)*

Purpose: To provide financial assistance to graduating female seniors from Denfeld High School or the Marshall School who exemplifies the characteristics and life exhibited by Patricia Gustafson. **Focus:** General studies. **Qualif.:** Applicants must be young women who will graduate from Denfeld High School or Marshall High School; must plan to attend either the University of Minnesota Duluth, Lake Superior College or the College of St. Scholastica; must have a high school grade point average of 3.4 or higher; must be active participants or leaders in school activities; must have some measure of financial need. **Criteria:** Recipients are selected based on ability to live a full life following the example of Patricia Gustafson; contributions to their schools; high academic achievement; potential and intention to make contributions in the field of education; high level of moral character; and, level of financial need.

Funds Avail.: $800. **To Apply:** Applicants must submit a completed application form and a personal statement answering the question "Considering what you know of Patricia Gustafson, why do you think you would be a worthy recipient of a scholarship honoring her memory?".

Remarks: The award is co-payable to the institution and the recipient.

2778 ■ Jeanne H. Hemmingway Scholarships *(Undergraduate/Scholarship)*

Purpose: To provide assistance to students with financial need. **Focus:** General studies. **Qualif.:** Applicants must be graduate seniors of public or private high schools in St. Louis, Lake and Cook counties who are planning to attend UMD; must be in the top 15% of their high school. **Criteria:** Applicants are evaluated based on financial need; academic record; written recommendations; and, seriousness of purpose.

Funds Avail.: $2,250. **To Apply:** Applicants must submit a completed application form and a recently completed Student Aid Report (SAR) from the Free Application for Federal Student Aid (FAFSA). **Deadline:** $2,250.

Remarks: The award is co-payable to the institution and the recipient.

2779 ■ Gus and Henrietta Hill Scholarships *(Graduate/Scholarship)*

Purpose: To provide financial assistance to graduates of Duluth East High School. **Focus:** General studies. **Qualif.:** Applicants must be graduating seniors from Duluth East High School who are active in the sport of pole vaulting and/or music activities; must be on top third of their high school class. **Criteria:** Applicants will be evaluated based on participation in pole vaulting and/or music activities; financial need; academic record; written recommendations; and, seriousness of purpose.

Funds Avail.: $4,500. **To Apply:** Applicants must submit a completed application form and a recently completed Student Aid Report (SAR) from the Free Application for Federal Student Aid (FAFSA). **Deadline:** January 15.

Remarks: The Award is co-payable to the institution and the recipient.

2780 ■ John Hoffbauer Memorial Scholarships *(Undergraduate/Scholarship)*

Purpose: To provide financial assistance for students who plan to major in education or early childhood education. **Focus:** Early childhood education. **Qualif.:** Applicants must be graduating seniors from Proctor Senior High School and all Duluth public high schools who are planning to be teachers; must be in the top 25% of their high school class. **Criteria:** Applicants are evaluated based on financial need; academic record; written recommendations; and, involvement in community and church activities.

Funds Avail.: $1,000. **Number Awarded:** 1. **To Apply:** Applicants must submit a completed application form and a recently completed Student Aid Report (SAR) from the Free Application for Federal Student Aid (FAFSA). **Deadline:** January 15.

Remarks: The Award is co-payable to the institution and the recipient.

2781 ■ Max and Julia Houghton Duluth Central Scholarships *(Undergraduate/Scholarship)*

Purpose: To provide financial assistance for students of all backgrounds to enable them to pursue higher education. **Focus:** General studies. **Qualif.:** Applicants must be graduating seniors from Duluth Central High School who are in the top 25% of their high school class. **Criteria:** Applicants are evaluated based on financial need; academic performance; and, involvement in community and/or school activities.

Funds Avail.: $2,500. **Number Awarded:** 3. **To Apply:** Applicants must submit all the required application information. **Deadline:** January 15.

Remarks: The award is co-payable to the institution and the recipient.

2782 ■ Greg Irons Student Scholarships *(Undergraduate/Scholarship)*

Purpose: To provide opportunities to students who are seeking for financial resources for their education in college. **Focus:** General studies. **Qualif.:** Applicants must be graduating seniors from Denfeld, East, Central and Unity high schools who are planning to attend an accredited college or university. **Criteria:** Applicants are evaluated based on all submitted materials and an interview with the nominees.

Funds Avail.: $1,000. **Number Awarded:** 2. **To Apply:** Application forms are available on the Foundation's website and from the Duluth Public School Offices. **Deadline:** January 15.

Remarks: The award is co-payable to the institution and the recipient.

Awards are arranged alphabetically below their administering organizations

2783 ■ The Jackson Club Scholarships *(Undergraduate/Scholarship)*

Purpose: To provide financial assistance to the residents of Hermantown and graduates of Hermantown High School. **Focus:** General studies. **Qualif.:** Applicants must be residents of Hermantown and graduates of Hermantown High School planning to attend any accredited post-secondary institution on a full-time basis; must have a 2.3 grade point average. **Criteria:** Applicants are evaluated based on academic record; written recommendation; and, involvement in community activities.

Funds Avail.: $500. **Number Awarded:** 5. **To Apply:** Applicants must submit all the required application information. **Deadline:** January 15.

Remarks: The award is co-payable to the institution and the recipient.

2784 ■ Cory Jam Awards *(Undergraduate/Scholarship)*

Purpose: To provide financial assistance to students who intend to pursue further education or training at any accredited university, college or technical school. **Focus:** General studies. **Qualif.:** Applicants must be graduating seniors from Duluth East High School who attended Congdon Park Elementary School, Homecroft Elementary School or Lowell Elementary School; must have participated in at least two extracurricular activities sponsored by Duluth East High School and at least one community based activity during their high school enrollment years; must intend to pursue education or training at any accredited university, college or technical school; must possess a 3.5 grade point average or higher based on 4.0 system. **Criteria:** Applicants are evaluated based on academic record, written recommendations; and, involvement in community and church activities.

Funds Avail.: $800-$1,000. **Number Awarded:** 1. **To Apply:** Applicants must submit all the required application information. **Deadline:** January 15.

Remarks: The payment is co-payable to the institution and recipient.

2785 ■ Minnesota Power Community Involvement Scholarships *(Undergraduate/Scholarship)*

Purpose: To provide financial assistance to high school seniors residing within Minnesota Power's service territory. **Focus:** General studies. **Qualif.:** Applicants must be high school seniors residing within Minnesota Power's service territory; must be full-time high school students who have a 2.5 GPA (on a 4.0 scale) or above. **Criteria:** Applicants are evaluated based on community involvement and financial need.

Funds Avail.: $2,000. **Number Awarded:** 25. **To Apply:** Applicants must submit application information. **Deadline:** January 15.

Remarks: The award is co-payable to the institution and the recipient.

2786 ■ Modern Woodmen of America Scholarships *(Undergraduate/Scholarship)*

Purpose: To provide financial assistance to students with their educational needs. **Focus:** General studies. **Qualif.:** Applicants must be single parents who are the primary care-givers to one or more children; must have completed at least 50 percent of their course of instruction at the time of the award. **Criteria:** Applicants are evaluated based on academic record; written recommendations; and, involvement in community and church activities.

Funds Avail.: $1,000. **Number Awarded:** 1. **To Apply:** Applicants must submit all the required application information. **Deadline:** January 15.

Remarks: The award is co-payable to the institution and the recipient.

2787 ■ Hubert A. Nelson Scholarships *(Undergraduate/Scholarship)*

Purpose: To provide financial assistance for students studying business and accounting. **Focus:** Business; Accounting. **Qualif.:** Applicants must be graduating seniors of public or private high schools in Duluth and Superior; must be planning to major in business/accounting at the University of Minnesota-Duluth or the University of Wisconsin-Superior; must be in the top 25% of their high school. **Criteria:** Applicants are evaluated based on academic record; financial need; written recommendations; involvement in community; and, extra-curricular activities.

Funds Avail.: $1,400. **To Apply:** Applicants must submit all the required application information. **Deadline:** January 15.

Remarks: The award is co-payable to the institution and the recipient.

2788 ■ Amelia and Emanuel Nessell Scholarships *(Undergraduate/Scholarship)*

Purpose: To provide educational opportunities for students who are in financial need. **Focus:** General studies. **Qualif.:** Applicants must be graduating seniors of Duluth public or private high schools; must be Jewish students who are planning to pursue a post-secondary education, including community colleges and four-year colleges and universities; must be in the top 25% of their high school class. **Criteria:** Applicants are evaluated based on academic record; financial need; written recommendations (one of which must come from a clergy); involvement in community and extra-curricular activities.

Funds Avail.: $500. **To Apply:** Applicants must submit a completed DSACF Common Scholarship Application form along with a recently completed Student Aid Report (SAR) from the Free Application for Federal Student Aid (FAFSA). **Deadline:** January 15.

Remarks: The award is co-payable to the institution and the recipient.

2789 ■ Anderson Niskanen Scholarships *(Undergraduate/Scholarship)*

Purpose: To provide financial assistance for students to achieve higher education. **Focus:** General studies. **Qualif.:** Applicants must be graduating seniors from Duluth public high schools who will attend either the University of Minnesota-Duluth or the University of Minnesota-Twin Cities. **Criteria:** Applicants are evaluated based on financial need; academic achievement; written recommendations and seriousness of purpose.

Funds Avail.: $2,000. **Number Awarded:** 3. **To Apply:** Applicants must submit all the required application information. **Deadline:** January 15.

2790 ■ Dr. Mark Rathke Family Scholarships *(Undergraduate/Scholarship)*

Purpose: To help future generations of Marshall School students to pursue their educational goals. **Focus:** General studies. **Qualif.:** Applicants must be graduating seniors of the Marshall School who will be attending a college or university as full-time students; must have a grade point average of 2.75 (on a 4.0 scale) or higher. **Criteria:** Applicants are evaluated based on academic record, hard-working behavior, good citizenship, leadership qualities, serious commitment to college education, written recommendations and involvement in community and extra-curricular activities.

Funds Avail.: $1,000. **Number Awarded:** 1. **To Apply:** Applicants must submit all the required application information. **Deadline:** January 15.

2791 ■ Lawrence E. & Mabel Jackson Rudberg Scholarships *(Undergraduate/Scholarship)*

Purpose: To provide financial assistance to students pursuing a college degree. **Focus:** General studies. **Qualif.:** Applicants must be graduating seniors from Duluth public and Two Harbors Senior High; must intend to pursue post-secondary education at an accredited four-year public or private college or university. **Criteria:** Applicants are evaluated based on academic record; financial need; written recommendations; involvement in community and extra-curricular activities.

Funds Avail.: $5,000. **To Apply:** Applicants must submit a completed DSACF Common Scholarship Application form along with a recently completed Student Aid Report (SAR) from the Free Application for Federal Student Aid (FAFSA). **Deadline:** January 15.

Remarks: The award is co-payable to the institution and the recipient.

2792 ■ Marie V. Saltwick Scholarships *(Undergraduate/Scholarship)*

Purpose: To provide financial assistance to graduates of Duluth Denfeld High School. **Focus:** General studies. **Qualif.:** Applicants must graduating seniors from Denfeld High School who are intending to pursue post-secondary education at a vocational college, community college, or other college or university on a full-time basis; must have achieved a 2.8 or higher cumulative GPA (on a 4.0 scale) in high school. **Criteria:** Applicants are evaluated based on good character; academic record; and, written recommendations.

Funds Avail.: $2,000. **To Apply:** Applicants must submit a completed DSACF Common Scholarship Application form along with a recently completed Student Aid Report (SAR) from the Free Application for Federal Student Aid (FAFSA). **Deadline:** January 15.

Remarks: The award is co-payable to the institution and the recipient.

2793 ■ Phil Shykes Memorial Scholarships *(Undergraduate/Scholarship)*

Purpose: To provide financial assistance to those in need to pursue trade or career. **Focus:** General studies. **Qualif.:** Applicants must be graduating seniors from Hermantown High School who are intending to pursue post-secondary education at a vocational college, community college, or other college or university on a full-time basis; must have achieved a 2.8 or higher cumulative GPA (on a 4.0 scale) in high school. **Criteria:** Applicants are evaluated based on good character; academic record; and, written recommendation.

Funds Avail.: $1,000. **To Apply:** Applicants must submit a completed DSACF Common Scholarship Application form along with a recently completed Student Aid Report (SAR) from the Free Application for Federal Student Aid (FAFSA). **Deadline:** January 15.

Remarks: The award is co-payable to the institution and the recipient.

2794 ■ Dale and Betty George Sola Scholarships *(Undergraduate/Scholarship)*

Purpose: To provide financial assistance for graduating high school seniors living in or attending school in the central areas of Duluth. **Focus:** General studies. **Qualif.:** Applicants must be students of Duluth Central High School, the Marshall School, and alternative schools (including Unity School, and the Harbor City International School) in the central areas of Duluth; or, graduates residing within the Central Hillside or Park Point areas who have a grade point average of 2.75 (on a 4.0 scale) or higher. **Criteria:** Recipients are selected based on financial need and academic achievement.

Funds Avail.: $2,000. **To Apply:** Applicants must complete the DSACF Common Scholarship Application available from the Guidance Offices and must submit a recently completed Student Aid Report (SAR) from the Free Application for Federal Student Aid (FAFSA). **Deadline:** January 15.

2795 ■ John A. Sullivan Scholarships *(Undergraduate/Scholarship)*

Purpose: To provide financial assistance for students majoring in education who are in financial need. **Focus:** Education. **Qualif.:** Applicants must be graduates of Senior High in Superior, Wisconsin, who will attend their junior and senior years at the University of Wisconsin-Superior with a major in education. **Criteria:** Recipients will be selected based on financial need; academic record; written recommendations; and, seriousness of purpose.

Funds Avail.: $500. **Number Awarded:** 1. **To Apply:** Applicants must complete the Scholarship application and must submit a recently completed Student Aid Report (SAR) from the Free Application for Federal Student Aid (FAFSA). **Deadline:** January 15.

2796 ■ Robert B. and Sophia Whiteside Scholarships *(Undergraduate/Scholarship)*

Purpose: To provide financial assistance to students who are going to attend college. **Focus:** General studies. **Qualif.:** Applicants must be high school seniors graduating from schools, including home schools, in Duluth and seek admission to any fully-accredited, degree granting college or university. **Criteria:** Applicants are evaluated based on academic achievement.

Funds Avail.: $6,000. **To Apply:** Applicants must sub all the completed required application information. **D line:** January 15.

2797 ■ Dutchess County Bar Associatio

PO Box 4865
Poughkeepsie, NY 12602
Ph: (845)473-2488
Fax: (845)485-1484
E-mail: janna@dutchesscountybar.org
URL: http://www.dutchesscountybar.or

2798 ■ Joseph H. Gellert/Dutc Association Scholarships *(Un Scholarship)*

Purpose: To provide financial of Dutchess County intendin

280 Inst 499 Oakla Awards 356

Criteria: Selection of recipient and alternate will be based upon current level of education, additional training being pursued, length of employment, current county of employment, financial need and GPA.

Funds Avail.: $3,250. **To Apply:** Applicant must check the application process online as well as the required materials. **Deadline:** April 25. **Contact:** East Tennessee Foundation at the above address (see entry 2805).

2808 ■ Gordon W. and Agnes P. Cobb Scholarships *(Undergraduate/Scholarship)*

Purpose: To benefit graduates of high schools in Blount, Loudon, and Knox counties in Tennessee who wish to pursue or who are pursuing college education in a health care or medical-related field. **Focus:** Health Sciences. **Qualif.:** Applicants must show proof of maintaining full-time enrollment and a 3.0 or better academic standing in a health care or medical related curriculum each year through the submission of academic transcripts to the foundation at the end of each semester. **Criteria:** Selection will be based on the following criteria: Academic promise and achievement; enrolled in a health care or medical-related curriculum; desire to pursue advanced education in a health care or medical-related field; evidence of a strong work or volunteer history; must demonstrate financial need.

Funds Avail.: $10,000 per year. **To Apply:** Applicants must check the application process online. **Deadline:** April 4.

Remarks: Applicants from single-parent families will be given special consideration. **Contact:** East Tennessee Foundation at the above address (see entry 2805).

2809 ■ Steven L. Coffey Memorial Scholarships *(Undergraduate/Scholarship)*

Purpose: To assist students who possess the potential for excellence but may require some additional support in achieving their educational goals. **Focus:** General Studies. **Qualif.:** Applicants must either be Anderson County residents and graduates of Anderson County High School, Clinton Senior High School or Oak Ridge High School. **Criteria:** Grants are awarded based on academic excellence; must have financial need; must also present an evidence of a 2.5 GPA or better; And the desire to pursue a post secondary education.

Funds Avail.: $1,200 Annually. **To Apply:** Applicants must check the application online for the required materials. **Deadline:** April 18. **Contact:** East Tennessee Foundation at the above address (see entry 2805).

2810 ■ R.G Crossno Memorial Scholarships *(Undergraduate/Scholarship)*

Purpose: To benefit graduating seniors of Anderson County High School who wish to pursue an advanced degree. **Focus:** General studies. **Qualif.:** Applicants must be enrolled as full-time students in an accredited public or private not-for-profit university or community college. **Criteria:** Selection of scholars will be based on applicants' demonstrated financial need, career motivation, academic promise and evidence of strong work experience.

Funds Avail.: $1,400. **To Apply:** Applicants must check the application process online as well as the required materials. **Deadline:** April 11.

Remarks: Mr. R.G. Crossno, past mayor of Norris, Tennessee and 21-year member of the Anderson County School Board dedicated his life to promoting better education throughout the state of Tennessee. **Contact:** East Tennessee Foundation at the above address (see entry 2805).

2811 ■ Michael D. Curtin Renaissance Student Memorial Scholarships *(Undergraduate/Scholarship)*

Purpose: To recognize and benefit students who demonstrate leadership or achievement in a balanced array of activities, including the arts, athletics, citizenship, community/religious service and academics. **Focus:** General Studies. **Qualif.:** Applicants must be enrolled as full time students in an accredited public or private not-for-profit university. **Criteria:** Selection of scholars will be selected by the scholarship committee consisting of five faculty members from Anderson County High School; they will review all applications, conduct interviews and make funding recommendations to East Tennessee Foundation Board of Directors.

Funds Avail.: Up to $1,000. **To Apply:** Applicants must check the application process online. **Deadline:** March 14.

2812 ■ Easter Seals Ontario

1 Concorde Gate, Ste. 700
Toronto, ON, Canada M3C 3N6
Ph: (416)421-8377
Fax: (416)696-1035
Free: 800-668-6252
URL: http://www.easterseals.org

2813 ■ The Leaders of Tomorrow Scholarships *(Undergraduate/Scholarship)*

Purpose: To assist young adults with physical disabilities with the cost of post-secondary education or vocational training. **Focus:** Education, Vocational-technical. **Qualif.:** Applicants must be seeking for post-secondary education; demonstrated consistent level of scholastic achievement throughout their secondary school curriculum; participated as a spokesperson for The Easter Seal Society; must served as models and inspirations to fellow students; and have applied for alternate financial assistance and still require assistance. **Criteria:** Applicants are evaluated based on financial need.

Funds Avail.: No specific amount. **To Apply:** Applicants must submit the completed application form along with typed, one-page letter outlining the qualifications for the award, including scholastic achievement, motivation, initiative and extra-curricular activities; copy of secondary and, if applicable, post-secondary transcripts; any interim marks that are available before the deadline; and, proof of application to applicable alternate sources of financial assistance. **Deadline:** May 15.

2814 ■ Beatrice Drinnan Spence Scholarships *(Undergraduate/Scholarship)*

Purpose: To assist young adults with physical disabilities with the cost of post-secondary education or vocational training. **Focus:** Education, Vocational-technical. **Qualif.:** Applicants must be resident students of Ontario with disabilities who are currently applying to or enrolled in a post-secondary educational facility like university or community college. **Criteria:** Applicants are evaluated based on personal attributes and financial need.

Funds Avail.: $5,000. **To Apply:** Applicants must submit the completed application form along with a one-page letter outlining qualifications for the award including scholastic achievement, motivation, initiative and extra-curricular activities; copy of secondary and, if applicable, post-secondary transcripts; any interim marks that are available

Awards are arranged alphabetically below their administering organizations

before the deadline; and, proof of application to applicable alternate sources of financial assistance. **Deadline:** May 16.

2815 ■ Ecological Society of America

1990 M St. NW, Ste. 700
Washington, DC 20036
Ph: (202)833-8773
Fax: (202)833-8775
E-mail: esahq@esa.org
URL: http://www.esa.org

2816 ■ Jasper Ridge Restoration Fellowships Jasper Ridge Biological Preserve *(Graduate, Postdoctorate/Fellowship)*

Purpose: To provide financial support to deserving students. **Focus:** General studies. **Qualif.:** Applicants must be post-doctoral students up to senior faculty. **Criteria:** Applications will be assessed based on an individual's past accomplishments and on potential to take full advantage of the ecosystems and past research at Jasper Ridge, as well as the intellectual community at Stanford.

Funds Avail.: $45,000/yr. for Postdocs, plus eligible expenses up to $30,000; $25,000/yr. for Graduate Fellows, plus eligible expenses up to $19,500. **To Apply:** Applicants must submit a CV, a 3-page description of their proposed program, and contact information for 3 references. **Deadline:** June 6. **Contact:** For additional information or to submit an application, please contact: Dr. Philippe Cohen at philippe.cohen@stanford.edu. Administrative Director, Jasper Ridge Biological Preserve, 4001 Sand Hill Road, Woodside, CA 94062. Applications should be submitted as email attachments.

2817 ■ Economic History Association

500 El Camino Real
Santa Clara University
Santa Clara, CA 95053-0385
Ph: (408)554-4348
Fax: (408)554-2331
E-mail: afield@scu.edu
URL: http://www.eh.net/EHA

2818 ■ Arthur H. Cole Grants in Aid *(Doctorate/Grant)*

Purpose: To support research in economic history, regardless of time period or geographic area. **Focus:** Economic history. **Qualif.:** Applicant must be a member of the association; and must hold a Ph.D. degree. **Criteria:** Applicants with recent PhD degrees are given preference.

Funds Avail.: $2,500. **To Apply:** Applicants must email required information: name, home address, institutional affiliation and contact information; submit a five-page single spaced proposal, inclusive of any footnotes, tables, and bibliography; a curriculum vitae; a project budget. **Deadline:** April 1. **Contact:** Committee on Research in Economic History Chair Prof. Joyce Burnette burnettj@wabash.edu.

2819 ■ Exploratory Travel and Data Grants *(Doctorate/Grant)*

Purpose: To provide funding for doctoral students intending to write a dissertation in economic history. **Focus:** Economic history. **Qualif.:** Applicants must be doctoral students and current association members. **Criteria:** Recipients will be selected based on the committee's review of the application materials submitted.

Funds Avail.: $2,500. **To Apply:** Applicants must e-mail required information: name, home address, institutional affiliation, contact information and the name of the chair of the dissertation committee; submit a copy of current curriculum vitae; a one-page itemized budget; a three-page single spaced proposal (inclusive of any footnotes, tables, and bibliography) that describe the topic, how the fellowship will help to complete the thesis, describe the work to date, time-table of completion and a brief bibliography. **Deadline:** January 15. **Contact:** Committee on Research in Economic History Chair Prof. Joyce Burnette burnettj@wabash.edu.

2820 ■ Graduate Dissertation Fellowships *(Doctorate/Fellowship)*

Purpose: To support students whose thesis topics have been approved and who have made some progress towards writing their dissertation. **Focus:** Economic history. **Qualif.:** Applicants must be current association members. **Criteria:** Recipients will be selected based on the committee's review of the application materials submitted.

Funds Avail.: $10,000. **To Apply:** Applicants must e-mail required information: name, home address, institutional affiliation, contact information and two reference letters (one from the chair of the thesis committee); submit a copy of current curriculum vitae; a five-page single spaced proposal (inclusive of any footnotes, tables, and bibliography) that describe the topic, how the fellowship will help to complete the thesis, describe the work to date, time-table of completion and a brief bibliography; and a draft of a completed thesis chapter. **Deadline:** January 25. **Contact:** Committee on Research in Economic History Chair Prof. Joyce Burnette burnettj@wabash.edu.

2821 ■ EDiS Company

PO Box 2697
Wilmington, DE 19805
Ph: (302)421-5700
Fax: (302)421-5715
URL: http://www.ediscompany.com

2822 ■ Gen III Scholarships *(Undergraduate/Scholarship)*

Purpose: To recognize members of the community who played a part in the growth of EDiS. **Focus:** Architecture; Engineering; Business. **Qualif.:** Applicant must be a resident within the community in which EDiS is currently working; must not be any employee of an EDiS Company or a relative of an employee of an EDiS Company; must be pursuing either an Associate's degree or Bachelor's degree; field of study is limited to business or construction-related degrees; and must have a cumulative GPA of 2.5 or greater for renewal. **Criteria:** Awards are given based on academic achievement, financial aid, and field of study.

Funds Avail.: $1,000 renewable. **Number Awarded:** 2. **To Apply:** Applicants must submit a completed scholarship application together with official transcript (from current institution), and a copy of best SAT score. **Deadline:** May 2. **Contact:** Ms. Cyndi Slothour.

2823 ■ Edmonton Epilepsy Association

11007-124 St.
Edmonton, AB, Canada T5M 0J5

Awards are arranged alphabetically below their administering organizations

Ph: (780)488-9600
Fax: (780)447-5486
Free: (866)374-5377
E-mail: info@edmontonepilepsy.org
URL: http://www.edmontonepilepsy.org

2824 ■ Edmonton Epilepsy Continuing Education Scholarships *(Undergraduate/Scholarship)*

Purpose: To open doors for incoming or continuing Canadian college students who are under epilepsy care. **Focus:** General studies. **Qualif.:** Applicants must be Greater-Edmonton area students aged 17-29 years of age who are Canadian Citizens or who have Landed Immigrant status and who are currently under a Canadian physician's care for epilepsy. Visa students are not eligible for this award. **Criteria:** Recipients will be selected based on the committee's review of all applications and supporting documents.

Funds Avail.: $1,000. **To Apply:** Applicants must submit a completed application form available from the website; a short essay (600-1,200 words) on "How Can I Personally Help Increase Epilepsy Education in my Community?"; three letters of recommendation of which one must come from someone from academia; copy of immigration papers (if landed immigrant); an unofficial copy of the current academic transcript; and a copy of university, college, or graduate school application(s)/acceptance letter, or confirmation of enrollment. Complete application package must be submitted to: Scholarship Awards, Edmonton Epilepsy Association, 11007-124 St., Edmonton, AB T5M 0J5. **Deadline:** March 1.

2825 ■ Edon Farmers Cooperative Association

PO Box 308
Edon, OH 43518
Ph: (419)272-2121
Fax: (419)272-2304
Free: 800-878-4093
E-mail: efcrdunbar@williams-net.com
URL: http://edonfarmerscoop.com

2826 ■ Edon Farmers Cooperative Scholarships *(Undergraduate/Scholarship)*

Purpose: To provide financial assistance for high school seniors to further their education as full-time students in any post high school institution. **Focus:** Agricultural sciences. **Qualif.:** Applicants must be dependents of a stockholder going into any field of study or any students going into an agricultural field. **Criteria:** Recipients are selected based on demonstrated scholarship potential, spirit of hard work, leadership ability and interest in extracurricular activities and, commitment to reach personal goals.

Funds Avail.: $1,000. **To Apply:** Applicants must submit all the required application information. **Deadline:** April 1.

2827 ■ Educational Audiology Association

3030 W 81st Ave.
Westminster, CO 80031-4111
Ph: 800-460-7322
E-mail: eaa@imigroup.org
URL: http://www.edaud.org

2828 ■ Fred Berg Awards *(All/Award/Prize)*

Purpose: To promote educational audiology. **Focus:** Speech and language pathology/audiology. **Qualif.:** Its not required that the nominee be a member of EAA. **Criteria:** Awards will be given based on committee's criteria. The Nominations and Awards Committee reviews the nominations and makes recommendations to the EAA Executive Committee for approval.

Funds Avail.: No specific amount. **Number Awarded:** Varies. **To Apply:** Nominator must submit a letter of nomination stating the nominee's specific qualifications for the award; two additional letters of support for the nominee; and the nominee's vitae.

2829 ■ Educational Audiology Association Doctoral Scholarships *(Doctorate/Scholarship)*

Purpose: To promote the educational audiology. **Focus:** Speech and language pathology/audiology. **Qualif.:** Applicant must be a member of EAA; practicing as an educational audiologists; Be matriculated in an official doctoral program. **Criteria:** Recipient is awarded based on committee's review of their application.

Funds Avail.: $500. **Number Awarded:** One. **To Apply:** Applicants must submit all supporting documentation. **Deadline:** Rolling submissions will be accepted all year.

2830 ■ Noel D. Matkin Awards *(Undergraduate/Award/Prize)*

Purpose: To promote educational audiology. **Focus:** Speech and language pathology/audiology. **Qualif.:** Applicant must be a member of EAA. **Criteria:** Award will be given practitioner students.

Funds Avail.: **Number Awarded:** Varies. **To Apply:** Members are encouraged to submit proposals for these awards. The proposals should be typed, double spaced, and should include the requested information on the pdf rule. The proposals should include section headings in your proposal and number pages. **Deadline:** February 1. **Contact:** EAA Headquarters, 11166 Huron Street, Suite 27, Denver, Colorado 870234.

2831 ■ Educational Foundation for Women in Accounting

PO Box 1925
Southeastern, PA 19399-1925
Ph: (610)407-9229
Fax: (610)644-3713
E-mail: info@efwa.org
URL: http://www.efwa.org

2832 ■ Michele L. McDonald Scholarships *(Undergraduate/Scholarship)*

Purpose: To provide financial assistance to female reentry students who wish to pursue a degree in accounting. **Focus:** Accounting. **Qualif.:** Applicants must be women returning to college from the work force or after raising children. **Criteria:** Scholarship recipients will be selected based on accounting capabilities. Preference will be given to those individuals who have demonstrated financial need.

Funds Avail.: $1,000. **To Apply:** Applicants must submit a completed application with all attachments (scholastic record; employment record; volunteer activities; professional activities; honors; career goals; personal goals; financial need; tax returns; references; and complete school contact information) to Educational Foundation for Women in Accounting. **Deadline:** April 15.

Remarks: Established by the Albuquerque chapter of the

Awards are arranged alphabetically below their administering organizations

American Society of Women Accountants in memory of one of their members and was transferred to EFWA in 2006.

2833 ■ Rowling, Dold and Associates LLP Scholarships *(Undergraduate/Scholarship)*

Purpose: To provide financial assistance to female reentry students who wish to pursue a degree in accounting. **Focus:** Accounting. **Qualif.:** Applicants must be women returning to school with undergraduate status; incoming, current, or reentry junior or seniors; or minority women. **Criteria:** Scholarship recipients will be selected based on accounting capabilities. Preference will be given to those individuals who have demonstrated financial need.

Funds Avail.: $1,000. **To Apply:** Applicants must submit a completed application with all attachments (scholastic record; employment record; volunteer activities; professional activities; honors; career goals; personal goals; financial need; tax returns; references; and complete school contact information) to Educational Foundation for Women in Accounting. **Deadline:** April 15.

2834 ■ Seattle Chapter ASWA Scholarships *(All/Scholarship)*

Purpose: To provide financial assistance for students pursuing a degree in accounting. **Focus:** Accounting. **Qualif.:** Applicants must be women who are enrolled in an accounting program at an accredited school in the State of Washington. **Criteria:** Scholarship recipients will be selected based on the applicant's accounting capabilities. Preference will be given to those individuals who have demonstrated financial need.

Funds Avail.: $2,000. **To Apply:** Applicants must submit a completed application with all attachments (scholastic record; employment record; volunteer activities; professional activities; honors; career goals; personal goals; financial need; tax returns; references; and complete school contact information) to Educational Foundation for Women in Accounting. **Deadline:** April 15. **Contact:** Cynthia Hires.

2835 ■ Women In Need Scholarships *(Undergraduate/Scholarship)*

Purpose: To provide financial assistance to female reentry students who wish to pursue a degree in accounting. **Focus:** Accounting. **Qualif.:** Applicants should be incoming, current, or reentry juniors or seniors. **Criteria:** Scholarship recipients will be selected based on accounting capabilities. Preference will be given to those individuals who have demonstrated financial need.

Funds Avail.: $2,000. **Number Awarded:** 1. **To Apply:** Applicants must submit a completed application with all attachments (scholastic record; employment record; volunteer activities; professional activities; honors; career goals; personal goals; financial need; tax returns; references; and complete school contact information) to Educational Foundation for Women in Accounting. **Deadline:** April 15.

Remarks: Created by the Board of Trustees in 2000.

2836 ■ Women In Transition Scholarships *(Undergraduate/Scholarship)*

Purpose: To provide financial assistance to female reentry students who wish to pursue a degree in accounting. **Focus:** Accounting. **Qualif.:** Applicants should be incoming or current freshmen and women returning to school with a freshman status. **Criteria:** Scholarship recipients will be selected based on accounting capabilities. Preference will be given to those individuals who have demonstrated financial need.

Funds Avail.: Up to $4,000. **Number Awarded:** 1. **To Apply:** Applicants must submit a completed application with all attachments (scholastic record; employment record; volunteer activities; professional activities; honors; career goals; personal goals; financial need; tax returns; references; and complete school contact information) to Educational Foundation for Women in Accounting. **Deadline:** April 15.

Remarks: Established in 1990 to commemorate the 25th Anniversary of the Educational Foundation. **Contact:** Cynthia Hires.

2837 ■ Educational Portal of the Americas

1889 F St. NW
Washington, DC 20006
Ph: (202)458-6166
E-mail: portal@oas.org
URL: http://www.educoas.org

2838 ■ Educational Portal of the Americas Graduate Scholarships *(Postgraduate/Scholarship)*

Purpose: To award a person to undertake undergraduate or graduate studies that lead to a degree and/or graduate research at a university or higher learning institution of member state. **Focus:** General Studies. **Qualif.:** Applicants must be enrolled in a Master's or Doctorate's degree. **Criteria:** Recipients are selected based on merit and financial need.

Funds Avail.: $30,000. **Number Awarded:** 2. **To Apply:** Applicants must present a complete application form. **Contact:** scholarships@oas.org.

2839 ■ Educational Portal of the Americas Undergraduate Scholarships *(Undergraduate/Scholarship)*

Purpose: To award a person to undertake undergraduate or graduate studies that lead to a degree and/or graduate research in a university or higher learning institution of member state. **Focus:** General Studies. **Qualif.:** Applicants must be accepted into the university where he/she plans to study for the last two years of undergraduate degree. **Criteria:** Recipients are selected based on the available financing and using the ranked.

Funds Avail.: $30,000. **To Apply:** Applicants must present complete application form. **Contact:** scholarships@oas.org.

2840 ■ Eisenhower Institute

915 15th St. NW, 8th Fl.
Washington, DC 20005
Ph: (202)628-4444
Fax: (202)628-4445
E-mail: ei@eisenhowerinstitute.org
URL: http://www.eisenhowerinstitute.org

2841 ■ Conrad N. Hilton Scholarships *(Undergraduate/Scholarship)*

Purpose: To help American students study abroad. **Focus:** Social sciences. **Qualif.:** Applicant must be a Gettysburg College senior or junior undergraduate student planning to study abroad; have at least a 3.0 cumulative GPA(can be waived for applicants with strong needs or qualifications); and must be social science or interdisciplinary majors. **Criteria:** Selection is based on merit.

Awards are arranged alphabetically below their administering organizations

Funds Avail.: $10,000. **Number Awarded:** 1. **To Apply:** Applicant must submit academic transcript; a resume; a statement of career aspirations (maximum of 1,000 words); a letter of recommendation from the candidate's faculty advisor or department chair; and a copy of a 10-15 page paper (within the last four months) from a course in the applicant's major field of study. Submit it at Gettysburg College. **Deadline:** First day of Spring semester.

2842 ■ Clifford Roberts Graduate Fellowships *(Doctorate/Fellowship)*

Purpose: To support study and education dealing with the role of government in a free society, the relationship between international and domestic issues, and improved understanding of world affairs. **Focus:** Public affairs. **Qualif.:** Applicant must be at an advanced stage of their doctoral candidacies, preferably preparing a dissertation. **Criteria:** Selection is based on merit.

Funds Avail.: $7000-$10,000. **To Apply:** Applicants must submit a curriculum vitae; a statement describing the nature and scope of the dissertation; a writing sample (10-15 pages) on a topic related to the dissertation; a 1,000 word statement of career aspirations; two letters of recommendation; and other required materials by the university. Submit materials at the participating universities. **Deadline:** February 28.

Remarks: The program is available only at the participating universities. **Contact:** Jane Kratovil at 202-628-4444, or jkratovil@eisenhowerinstitute.org.

2843 ■ Ann Cook Whitman Scholarships for Perry High School *(Undergraduate/Scholarship)*

Purpose: To help students obtain undergraduate degrees in furtherance of education and leadership skills. **Focus:** General studies. **Qualif.:** Applicant must be a high school senior student at Perry High School planning to receive an undergraduate education; and have an average of B and above (can be waived for applicants with strong needs or qualifications). **Criteria:** Selection is based on need and merit.

Funds Avail.: $4000 each year for four years. **Number Awarded:** 2. **To Apply:** Applicants must submit an academic transcript; a resume; a statement of career aspirations (maximum of 1,000 words); a letter of recommendation from the candidate's faculty advisor or guidance counselor; another letter of recommendation from a member of the Perry, Ohio community, other than a family member; and documentation from Perry High School on its needs-based assessment procedures for its nominees. Submit materials at the Perry High School. **Deadline:** March 1.

2844 ■ Ann Cook Whitman Washington, DC Scholarships *(Undergraduate/Scholarship)*

Purpose: To assist graduating African-American seniors from the District of Columbia public education system in obtaining an undergraduate degree in furtherance of their education and leadership skills. **Focus:** General studies. **Qualif.:** Applicant must be an African-American senior student from any of four eligible high schools (Spingarn, H.D. Woodson, Ballou, and Eastern) pursuing an undergraduate education; and have an average of B and above (can be waived for applicants with strong needs or qualifications). **Criteria:** Selection is based on need and merit.

Funds Avail.: $4000 each year for four years. **Number Awarded:** 2. **To Apply:** Applicants must submit a completed application form; academic transcript; a statement of career aspirations (maximum of 500 words); identification of colleges/universities applied to; a letter of recommendation from a faculty member or the guidance counselor; and another letter of recommendation from a member of the Washington, DC community, other than a family member. Submit materials at the applicant's respective high school. **Deadline:** March 1.

2845 ■ Electronic Document Systems Foundation

1845 Precinct Ln. Rd., Ste. 212
Hurst, TX 76054
Ph: (817)849-1145
Fax: (817)849-1185
E-mail: info@edsf.org
URL: http://www.edsf.org

2846 ■ Electronic Document Systems Foundation Scholarships *(Undergraduate/Scholarship)*

Purpose: To recognize and support the next generation of professionals for the document management and communication companies worldwide. **Focus:** Computer and information sciences; engineering; Communications technologies. **Qualif.:** Applicants must be full-time students who are committed to pursuing careers in document management and communications marketplace which include computer science and engineering, graphic and media communications and those students interested in Business in the document management and communications industry; must have a minimum GPA of 3.0 or a 'B' average; must be technical, trade school, community college, undergraduate and advanced-degree students in the U.S. and/or diploma or tertiary students outside of the U.S. may be considered for scholarships; must be students who are attending full-time, an accredited college or university. **Criteria:** Applicants are evaluated based on any one or a combination of the following: Scholastic achievement, application essay, participation in school activities, community service, honors and organizational affiliations, and education objectives.

Funds Avail.: No specific amount. **To Apply:** Applicants must submit all the required application information.

2847 ■ Elks National Foundation

2750 N Lakeview Ave.
Chicago, IL 60614-2256
Ph: (773)755-4728
Fax: (773)755-4729
E-mail: enf@elks.org
URL: http://www.elks.org

2848 ■ Elks National Foundation Scholarships *(Undergraduate/Scholarship)*

Purpose: To build stronger communities. **Focus:** General studies. **Qualif.:** Applicants must be undergraduates in an institution, college, or university. **Criteria:** Recipients are selected based on financial need and scholastic standing.

Funds Avail.: Maximum amount of $15,000. **To Apply:** Applicants must complete the application form. **Contact:** scholarship@elks.org

2849 ■ Emergency Nurses Association

915 Lee St.
Des Plaines, IL 60016-6569

Ph: (847)460-4123
Fax: (847)460-4001
E-mail: education@ena.org
URL: http://www.ena.org

2850 ■ BCEN Undergraduate Scholarships *(Undergraduate/Scholarship)*

Purpose: To promote education or research on emergency care. **Focus:** Nursing. **Qualif.:** Applicants must be attending a NLN or AACN accredited school; must be an ENA member for at least one year. **Criteria:** Applicants will be evaluated by ENA Foundation review panel.

Funds Avail.: $2,000. **Number Awarded:** 1. **To Apply:** Applicants must provide a letter verifying the school's current accreditation with the application (visit the website for the application). If not a member, applicant must provide a letter of reference from an ENA member. **Deadline:** June 1.

Remarks: Do not staple materials, use paper clips or binder clips. Faxed materials will be disqualified. **Contact:** ENA Foundation Office, 800-900-9658 x-4100, foundation@ena.org.

2851 ■ Emergency Nurses Association Undergraduate Scholarships *(Undergraduate/Scholarship)*

Purpose: To promote education or research on emergency care. **Focus:** Nursing. **Qualif.:** Applicants must be attending a NLN or AACN accredited school; must be an ENA member for at least one year. **Criteria:** Applicants will be evaluated by the ENA Foundation review panel.

Funds Avail.: $3,000 for the highest scoring applicant and $2,500 for the two next highest scoring. **Number Awarded:** 3. **To Apply:** Applicants must provide a letter verifying the school's current accreditation together with the application form. If not a member, applicant must provide a letter of reference from an ENA member. **Deadline:** June 1.

Remarks: Do not staple materials, use paper clips or binder clips. Faxed materials will be disqualified.

2852 ■ ENA Foundation Advanced Practice Scholarships *(Undergraduate/Scholarship)*

Purpose: To promote education or research on emergency care. **Focus:** Nursing. **Qualif.:** Applicants must be attending a NLN or AACN accredited school; must be an ENA member for at least one year applicants; working on a dissertation related to emergency nursing. **Criteria:** Applicants will be evaluated by ENA Foundation review panel.

Funds Avail.: $4,000. **Number Awarded:** 4. **To Apply:** Applicants must provide a letter verifying the school's current accreditation with the application (visit the website for the application). If not a member, applicant must provide a letter of reference from an ENA member. **Deadline:** June 1.

Remarks: Do not staple materials, use paper clips or binder clips. Faxed materials will be disqualified. **Contact:** ENA Foundation Office, 800-900-9658 x-4100, foundation@ena.org.

2853 ■ Faculty Doctoral Scholarships *(Doctorate/Scholarship)*

Purpose: To promote education or research on emergency care. **Focus:** Nursing. **Qualif.:** Applicants must be attending a NLN or AACN accredited school; must be an ENA member for at least one year applicants; working on a dissertation related to emergency nursing. **Criteria:** Applicants will be evaluated by ENA Foundation review panel.

Funds Avail.: $10,000 and $5,000. **Number Awarded:** 2. **To Apply:** Applicants must provide a letter verifying the school's current accreditation with the applications (visit the website for the application); proof of acceptance in an accredited doctoral program in nursing; and a statement about the applicant's career intent. **Deadline:** June 1.

Remarks: Do not staple materials, use paper clips or binder clips. Faxed materials will be disqualified. **Contact:** ENA Foundation Office, 800-900-9658 x-4100, foundation@ena.org.

2854 ■ Energy and Mineral Law Foundation

340 S Broadway, Ste. 101
Lexington, KY 40508
Ph: (859)231-0271
Fax: (859)226-0485
E-mail: eml@aol.com
URL: http://www.blairchiropractic.com

2855 ■ EMLF Law Student Scholarships *(Undergraduate/Scholarship)*

Purpose: To provide educational assistance to encourage the study of energy, environmental, natural resources, and mineral law. **Focus:** Environmental science, Natural resources, Mineralogy, Energy-related areas. **Qualif.:** Applicants must be law school students for the current academic year and must demonstrate an interest in the study of natural resources, energy or mineral law. **Criteria:** Recipient will be selected based on some criteria: a) potential to make a significant contribution in the field of energy, mineral and natural resources law; b) academic ability; c) leadership ability; and d) financial need.

Funds Avail.: $1,000-$3,000. **Deadline:** April 11.

2856 ■ Enlisted Association of National Guard of the United States

3133 Mount Vernon Ave.
Alexandria, VA 22305-2640
Ph: (703)519-3846
Fax: (703)519-3849
Free: 800-234-3264
E-mail: eangus@eangus.org
URL: http://www.eangus.org

2857 ■ CSM Virgil R. Williams Scholarships *(Undergraduate/Scholarship)*

Purpose: To support the education of EANGUS members, their spouses and their unmarried children. **Focus:** General studies. **Qualif.:** Applicant must be EANGUS Auxiliary members; must be unmarried, dependent sons and daughters of EANGUS Auxiliary members; must be spouses of EANGUS Auxiliary members. **Criteria:** Awards will be made based on the applicants character, leadership and financial need.

Funds Avail.: $2,000. **Number Awarded:** 2. **To Apply:** Applicant must submit a transcript of high school credits and/or a transcript of college credits for applicants already in an institution of higher learning; must have a letter from the applicant with personal, specific facts as to his/ her desire to continue his/her educationand why financial assistance is required; must have three letters of academic recommendation verifying the application and giving moral, personal and leadership traits. Application form and other documents must be submitted electronically via the internet to the Chairman of the Scholarship Committee except the school transcript. **Deadline:** July 1.

2858 ■ Entertainment Software Association

575 7th St. NW, Ste. 300
Washington, DC 20004
Ph: (202)223-2400
E-mail: esa@theesa.com
URL: http://www.theesa.com

2859 ■ ESA Foundation Computer and Video Game Scholarship Program *(Undergraduate/ Scholarship)*

Purpose: To assist women and minority students who plan to continue their education in fields supporting Video Game Development. **Focus:** Graphic Arts and Design; Computer and Information Sciences. **Qualif.:** Applicants must be enrolled full time study in an accredited four year colleges and universities. **Criteria:** Recipients are selected based on academic standing.

Funds Avail.: $3,000. **Number Awarded:** 15. **To Apply:** Applicants must complete online application form. Applicants must provide proof that he/she is currently enrolled in a college, university, or institution. **Deadline:** April 15.

2860 ■ Entomological Society of America

10001 Derekwood Ln., Ste. 100
Lanham, MD 20706-4876
Ph: (301)731-4535
Fax: (301)731-4538
E-mail: esa@entsoc.org
URL: http://www.entsoc.org

2861 ■ Stan Beck Fellowships *(Undergraduate/ Fellowship)*

Purpose: To provide educational assistance for needy students at the graduate or undergraduate level of their education in entomology and related disciplines at a college or university in the United States, Mexico, or Canada. **Focus:** Biology. **Qualif.:** Applicants must be graduate or undergraduate students in entomology or related disciplines at colleges or universities in the United States, Mexico, or Canada. **Criteria:** Recipients are selected based on physical limitation, economic, minority, or environmental condition; recommendation of the professors and advisors; enthusiasm, interest and achievement in entomology or related disciplines; notable academic plans; and impact of need.

Funds Avail.: No specific amount. **To Apply:** Applicants must submit a letter of nomination; description of applicant's academic studies including academic plan; a statement of the applicant's need or challenge (not more than 2 pages); letter of recommendation from the applicant's academic advisor; and two letters of support demonstrating the applicant's need or challenge. **Deadline:** July 1. **Contact:** Entomological Foundation, 9331 Annapolis Rd. Ste. 210, Lanham, MD 20706.

2862 ■ BioQuip Scholarships *(Undergraduate/ Scholarship)*

Purpose: To help students achieve their goal of obtaining a degree in entomology or pursuing a career as an entomologist. **Focus:** Biology. **Qualif.:** Applicants must be enrolled as undergraduate students in entomology in any college or university in the United States, Mexico, and Canada. **Criteria:** Recipients are selected based on committee's review of application materials.

Funds Avail.: No stated amount. **To Apply:** Applicants must fill out an application form. Applicants must submit letter of nomination; statement not exceeding two-pages in length stating interest in entomology, career goals, financial need, and other pertinent factors which illustrate qualifications for the scholarship; three statements from school officials or other knowledgeable individuals attesting to entomological interests, character, aptitude and financial need; and current official transcript of college grades. **Deadline:** July 1. **Contact:** Entomological Foundation, 9332 Annapolis Rd. Ste. 210, Lanham MD 20706.

2863 ■ Pioneer Hi-Bred International Graduate Student Fellowships *(Graduate/Fellowship)*

Purpose: To recognize and encourage innovative research and graduate education in the area of entomology with a focus on key insects or complexes of insects that effect corn, soybeans, canola, alfalfa, or other significant commodity crops. **Focus:** Biology. **Qualif.:** Applicants must be graduate students; must have a GPA of 3.5 or higher; must attend college/university in the United States; must have demonstrated excellence in the study of entomology or a related discipline. **Criteria:** Recipients are selected based on the demonstrated excellence in the study of entomology or related discipline.

Funds Avail.: no stated amount. **To Apply:** Applicants must complete the application form. Applicants must submit an official transcript of college grades; three letters of recommendation; description of the student's completed and proposed program of academic studies including brief statement of the goals, rationale and justification for the proposed project; short essay on why the student is interested in the study of insects impacting crops including significant commodity crops; statement of long range career goals and description of how the graduate program will help the student to attain the goals; up to three letters of endorsement from professional colleagues and clientele. **Deadline:** July 1. **Contact:** Entomological Foundation, 9332 Annapolis Rd. Ste. 210, Lanham, MD 20706.

2864 ■ Environmental Research and Education Foundation

901 N Pitt St., Ste. 270
Alexandria, VA 22314
Ph: (703)299-5139
Fax: (703)299-5145
E-mail: mjcagney@erefdn.org
URL: http://www.erefdn.org

2865 ■ Environmental Research and Education Foundation Scholarships *(Postdoctorate/ Scholarship)*

Purpose: To recognize excellence in master's, doctoral or post-doctoral waste management research and education. **Focus:** Waste Management. **Qualif.:** Applicant must be a full-time master's student, doctoral, or post-doctoral researcher; applicant must have demonstrated interest in waste management research. **Criteria:** Recipients are selected based on academics; professional performance; relevance of one's work to the advancement of solid waste management; potential for success.

Awards are arranged alphabetically below their administering organizations

Funds Avail.: $12,000 for doctoral and post-doctoral; $5,000 for master's degree. **To Apply:** Applicants must complete an application form. Applicants must submit an official college transcript; admission test scores; three recommendations; applicants must submit an essay of not more than 500 words that includes an autobiographical statement and discussion of research topic. Essay should be typewritten, double-spaced, unbound and unstapled. **Deadline:** April 30. **Contact:** Dr. Edward W. Repaat the above address (see entry 2864).

2866 ■ Epilepsy Foundation

8301 Professional Place
Landover, MD 20785
Free: 800-332-1000
URL: http://www.epilepsyfoundation.org

2867 ■ Behavioral Sciences Post-Doctoral Fellowships *(Postdoctorate/Fellowship)*

Purpose: To finance behavioral researches on the appropriate psychosocial intervention techniques. **Focus:** Social sciences; Behavioral Sciences; Epilepsy. **Qualif.:** Applicants must be individuals who will receive their doctoral degrees in the field of social sciences by the time the fellowship commences. **Criteria:** Applications are evaluated based on the quality of the proposed project.

Funds Avail.: $40,000. **To Apply:** Applicants may visit the website or contact Epilepsy Foundation for more details. **Deadline:** March 2.

2868 ■ Behavioral Sciences Student Fellowships *(Graduate, Undergraduate/Fellowship)*

Purpose: To encourage individuals to pursue careers in epilepsy in either the research or practice setting. **Focus:** Behavioral sciences; Epilepsy. **Qualif.:** Applicants must be in an appropriate undergraduate or graduate program in the behavioral sciences and must have a defined epilepsy-related study or research plan. **Criteria:** Applications are evaluated based on the quality of the proposed project.

Funds Avail.: $3,000. **To Apply:** Applicants may visit the website or contact Epilepsy Foundation for more details. **Deadline:** March 2.

2869 ■ Epilepsy Foundation Post-doctoral Research Fellowships *(Postdoctorate, Professional Development/Grant)*

Purpose: To develop academic physicians and scientists committed to research related to epilepsy. **Focus:** Epilepsy; Neuroscience. **Qualif.:** Applicants must be physicians or PhD neuroscientists. **Criteria:** Applications are evaluated based on the quality of the proposed project.

Funds Avail.: $40,000. **To Apply:** Applicants may visit the website or contact Epilepsy Foundation for more details. **Deadline:** August 29.

2870 ■ Epilepsy Foundation Pre-doctoral Research Training Fellowships *(Graduate/Grant)*

Purpose: To support in dissertation research related to epilepsy. **Focus:** Epilepsy; Neuroscience; Physiology; Pharmacology; Psychology; Biochemistry; Genetics; Nursing; Pharmacy. **Qualif.:** Applicants must be graduate students enrolled in a full-time doctoral (PhD) program with academic focus on Neuroscience, Physiology, Pharmacology, Psychology, Biochemistry, Genetics, Nursing, or Pharmacy. **Criteria:** Applications are evaluated based on the quality of the proposed project.

Funds Avail.: $20,000. **To Apply:** Applicants may visit the website or contact Epilepsy Foundation for more details. **Deadline:** August 29.

2871 ■ Epilepsy Foundation Research Grants *(All/Grant)*

Purpose: To stimulate epilepsy research by providing funds for biological or behavioral researches by young clinical investigators. **Focus:** Behavioral sciences; Epilepsy. **Qualif.:** Applicants must be conducting a biological or behavioral research that may advance the treatment, understanding and prevention of epilepsy. **Criteria:** Applications are evaluated based on the quality of the proposed project.

Funds Avail.: $50,000. **To Apply:** Applicants may visit the website or contact Epilepsy Foundation for more details. **Deadline:** August 29.

2872 ■ Epilepsy Foundation Research and Training Fellowships for Clinicians *(Doctorate, Professional Development/Grant)*

Purpose: To provide support for study and research by clinically trained professionals. **Focus:** Epilepsy; Neurology; Internal medicine; Psychiatry. **Qualif.:** Applicants must be clinically trained professionals (PharmD, Doctor of Nursing); or have an MD or DO and have completed residency training in neurology, neurosurgery, pediatrics, internal medicine, or psychiatry by the time the fellowship commences. **Criteria:** Applications are evaluated based on the quality of the proposed project.

Funds Avail.: $50,000. **To Apply:** Applicants may visit the website or contact Epilepsy Foundation for more details. **Deadline:** October 1.

2873 ■ Health Sciences Student Fellowships *(Doctorate, Graduate/Fellowship)*

Purpose: To stimulate individuals to pursue careers in epilepsy in either research or practice settings. **Focus:** Health sciences; Epilepsy. **Qualif.:** Applicants must be pre-doctoral training students in Health Sciences. **Criteria:** Applications are evaluated based on the quality of the proposed project; relevance of the proposed work to epilepsy; and the applicant's interest in the field of epilepsy.

Funds Avail.: $3,000. **To Apply:** Applicants may visit the website or contact Epilepsy Foundation for more details. **Deadline:** March 2.

2874 ■ Partnership for Pediatric Epilepsy Research *(Doctorate/Grant)*

Purpose: To support innovative investigator-initiated studies on epilepsies that begin in infancy and childhood. **Focus:** Epilepsy. **Qualif.:** Applicants must hold a relevant advanced degree (MD or PhD); must have completed all research training; and must be based at corporations and academic/university settings. **Criteria:** Applications are evaluated based on the quality of the proposed project.

Funds Avail.: $100,000. **To Apply:** Applicants may visit the website or contact Epilepsy Foundation for more details. **Deadline:** August 29.

2875 ■ Targeted Research Initiative for Health Outcomes *(Doctorate/Grant)*

Purpose: To support research that generates initial data leading to more extensive projects that will generate knowledge that will ultimately improve the healthcare of persons with epilepsy. **Focus:** Behavioral sciences; Epilepsy. **Qualif.:** Applicants must hold a relevant advanced degree; have completed all research training; and must be based at corporations as well as academic/university settings. **Criteria:** Applications are evaluated based on the quality of the proposed project.

Funds Avail.: $100,000. **To Apply:** Applicants may visit the website or contact Epilepsy Foundation for more details. **Deadline:** March 2.

2876 ■ Targeted Research Initiative for Mood Disorders *(Doctorate/Grant)*

Purpose: To provide financial support for behavioral researches leading to new insights in the treatment and understanding of epilepsy and mood disorders. **Focus:** Behavioral sciences; Epilepsy. **Qualif.:** Applicants must hold a relevant advanced degree (MD or PhD); must have completed all research training appropriate to the project proposed; and must be based at corporations as well as academic/university settings. **Criteria:** Applications are evaluated based on the quality of the proposed project.

Funds Avail.: $100,000. **To Apply:** Applicants may visit the website or contact Epilepsy Foundation for more details. **Deadline:** March 2.

2877 ■ Targeted Research Initiative for Seniors *(Doctorate/Grant)*

Purpose: To encourage a breakthrough in behavioral science by funding a pilot research in the fundamental knowledge of aging and epilepsy. **Focus:** Behavioral sciences; Epilepsy. **Qualif.:** Applicants must hold a relevant advanced degree (MD or PhD); and must have completed all research trainings appropriate to the project proposed. **Criteria:** Applications are evaluated based on the scientific quality of the research plan.

Funds Avail.: $100,000. **To Apply:** Applicants may visit the website or contact Epilepsy Foundation for more details. **Deadline:** March 2.

2878 ■ Epilepsy Newfoundland and Labrador

26 O'Leary Ave.
St. John's, NL, Canada A1B 2C7
Ph: (709)722-0502
Fax: (709)722-0999
E-mail: info@epilepsynl.com
URL: http://www.epilepsynl.com

2879 ■ Jim Hierlihy Memorial Scholarships *(Undergraduate/Scholarship)*

Purpose: To widen horizons of ENL student members by providing financial support as they pursue college or university studies. **Focus:** General studies. **Qualif.:** Applicants must be diagnosed with epilepsy and be members in good standing of Epilepsy Newfoundland and Labrador at the time of scholarship application. Scholarship is not open to current ENL board and staff members. Former board or staff members and/or their family members may apply for scholarships if they have been out of the service of Epilepsy Newfoundland and Labrador for two years. **Criteria:** Recipient is chosen based on grades, extracurricular activities and financial need.

Funds Avail.: $1,000. **Number Awarded:** 1. **To Apply:** Applicants must submit the completed application form available from the website along with a copy of the most recent academic transcript to: Epilepsy Newfoundland and Labrador, 26 O'Leary Ave., St. John's, NF A1B 2C7. **Deadline:** November 1.

2880 ■ Mature Student Scholarships *(Undergraduate/Scholarship)*

Purpose: To widen horizons of ENL student members by providing financial support as they pursue college or university studies. **Focus:** General studies. **Qualif.:** Applicants must be 21 years or older; must be diagnosed with epilepsy; and be a member in good standing of Epilepsy Newfoundland and Labrador at the time of the scholarship application. Scholarship is not open to current ENL board and staff members. Former board or staff members and/or their family members can apply for scholarships if they have been out of the service of Epilepsy Newfoundland and Labrador for two years. **Criteria:** Selection is based on the review of application records.

Funds Avail.: $1,000. **Number Awarded:** 1. **To Apply:** Applicants must complete application form available at the website and submit it along with a copy of the most recent academic transcript to: Epilepsy Newfoundland and Labrador, 26 O'Leary Ave., St. John's, NF A1B 2C7. **Deadline:** November 1.

2881 ■ Equal Justice Works

2120 L St., NW, Ste. 450
Washington, DC 20037-1541
Ph: (202)466-3686
Fax: (202)429-9766
E-mail: info@equaljusticeworks.org
URL: http://www.equaljusticeworks.org

2882 ■ Equal Justice Works Fellowship Program *(Graduate, Undergraduate/Fellowship)*

Purpose: To address the shortage of attorneys working on behalf of traditionally under-served populations and causes in the United States and its territories while encouraging partnerships between law firms, corporations and public interest organizations to fund fellowships. **Focus:** Law. **Qualif.:** Applicants must be third year law students or graduates from an EJW law school who are committed to public interest. **Criteria:** Applications will be granted based on the evaluation of submitted materials by EJW staff and/or sponsors.

Funds Avail.: $37,500. **To Apply:** Applicants must provide a completed application, including a project proposal, a fellowship candidate to carry out the project, and a nonprofit public interest organization identified to host the project; Applicants must also submit a certification form and two hard copies of letters of recommendation; and must attend a scheduled interview if evaluated successfully. **Deadline:** September.

2883 ■ Equity Foundation

P.O Box 5696
Portland, OR 97228
Ph: (503)231-5759
E-mail: info@equityfoundation.org
URL: http://www.equityfoundation.org

2884 ■ Gregori Jakovina Endowment Scholarships *(Undergraduate/Scholarship)*

Purpose: To encourage and facilitate post-secondary education in the arts for people who are gay, lesbian,

Awards are arranged alphabetically below their administering organizations

bisexual or transgender (GLBT). **Focus:** Arts. **Qualif.:** Applicants must be Oregon or Clark County Washington residents who demonstrate financial need. **Criteria:** Preference will be given to those who meet the criteria.

Funds Avail.: No specific amount. **To Apply:** Applicants must check the application process online. **Deadline:** August 31. **Contact:** Equity Foundation at the above address (see entry 2883).

2885 ■ Just Out Scholarship Fund *(Undergraduate/Scholarship)*

Purpose: To provide financial assistance to those post secondary LGBT students. **Focus:** General Studies. **Qualif.:** Applicants must be members of the gay, lesbian, bisexual or transgendered communities. **Criteria:** Preference will be given to people outside the Portland area.

Funds Avail.: No specific amount. **To Apply:** Applicants must check the available website for the required materials. **Deadline:** June 30. **Contact:** Equity Foundation at the above address (see entry 2883).

2886 ■ Kaiser Permanente Northwest Pride Scholarships *(Undergraduate/Scholarship)*

Purpose: To provide financial assistance and to encourage members of the gay, lesbian, bisexual and transgender communities and their children, in Northwest Oregon and Southwest Washington to pursue careers in healthcare. **Focus:** Healthcare. **Qualif.:** Applicants must be members of the LGBT communities. **Criteria:** Preference will be given to those who meet the criteria.

Funds Avail.: No specific amount. **To Apply:** Applicants must check the available website for the required materials. **Deadline:** June 30. **Contact:** Equity Foundation at the above address (see entry 2883).

2887 ■ Armistead Maupin Creative Writing Scholarship Fund *(Undergraduate/Scholarship)*

Purpose: To encourage students whom, regardless of sexual orientation or gender identity, have authored material based, in large part, on GLBT themes, to develop their creative writing skills. **Focus:** Creative Writing; Liberal Arts. **Qualif.:** Applicants must be entering or pursuing post-secondary education in the liberal arts, literary arts or creative writing, at accredited colleges and universities in the Northwest of the continental United States (Oregon, Washington, Idaho), who are in need of financial assistance. **Criteria:** Preference will be given to those who meet the criteria.

Funds Avail.: No specific amount. **To Apply:** Applicants must check the application process online. **Deadline:** June 30. **Contact:** Equity Foundation at the above address (see entry 2883).

2888 ■ Larry McDonald Scholarships *(Undergraduate/Scholarship)*

Purpose: To provide financial assistance to those who are in need. **Focus:** Arts; Humanities. **Qualif.:** Applicants must be adults in mid-life who are gay, lesbian, bisexual, or transgender who seek to make a significant change in their lives or vocations by taking classes in the arts or humanities. **Criteria:** Preference will be given to those students who meet the criteria.

Funds Avail.: No specific amount. **To Apply:** Applicants must check the application process online. **Deadline:** August 31. **Contact:** Equity Foundation at the above address (see entry 2883).

2889 ■ Orchard-Hoyman Fund for GLBT Student Scholarships *(Undergraduate/Scholarship)*

Purpose: To provide financial assistance to those students who are in need. **Focus:** General Studies. **Qualif.:** Applicants must be GLBT students ages 20 and under, who reside in Lane County, Oregon and need financial assistance to attain their post secondary educational goals. **Criteria:** Preference will be given to those who meet the criteria.

Funds Avail.: $1,000. **Number Awarded:** 2. **To Apply:** Applicants must check the application process online. **Deadline:** August 31. **Contact:** Equity Foundation at the above address (see entry 2883).

2890 ■ Portland Area Business Association Scholarships *(Undergraduate/Scholarship)*

Purpose: To provide financial assistance to those post secondary LGBT students. **Focus:** General Studies. **Qualif.:** Applicants must be members of the gay, lesbian, bisexual or transgendered communities. **Criteria:** Preference will be given to those who meet the criteria.

Funds Avail.: No specific amount. **To Apply:** Applicants must check the available website for the required materials. **Deadline:** June 30. **Contact:** Equity Foundation at the above address (see entry 2883).

2891 ■ Pride of the Rose Scholarships Fund *(Undergraduate/Scholarship)*

Purpose: To provide financial assistance to those students who are in need. **Focus:** General studies. **Qualif.:** Applicants must be post-secondary education to members of the gay, lesbian, bisexual, and transgender communities and their children residing in the Quad-county area of Portland, OR and Clark County, WA. **Criteria:** Preference will be given to those who meet the criteria.

Funds Avail.: No specific amount. **To Apply:** Applicants must check the application process online. **Deadline:** July 31. **Contact:** Equity Foundation at the above address (see entry 2883).

2892 ■ Bill and Ann Sheperd Legal Scholarships Fund *(Undergraduate/Scholarship)*

Purpose: To provide financial support to those who are in need. **Focus:** Law. **Qualif.:** Applicants must be third year law students dedicated to keeping Oregon a hate-free state. **Criteria:** Preference will be given to those who meet the criteria.

Funds Avail.: No specific amount. **To Apply:** Applicants must check the available website for the required materials. **Deadline:** June 30. **Contact:** Equity Foundation at the above address (see entry 2883).

2893 ■ Executive Women International

515 S 700 E, Ste. 2A
Salt Lake City, UT 84102
Ph: (801)355-2800
Fax: (801)355-2852
Free: 877-4394-669
E-mail: ewi@executivewomen.org
URL: http://www.executivewomen.org

2894 ■ Adults Students in Scholastic Transition (ASIST) *(All/Scholarship)*

Purpose: To provide financial support to adult students in a variety of transitional situations. To enable recipients to

Awards are arranged alphabetically below their administering organizations

improve their self-esteem and to have a positive impact on the recipient's personal life, employment, family, and community. **Focus:** General studies. **Qualif.:** Applicants must be 18 years old and above; must have clearly defined career goals and objectives; must be residing in boundaries of the EWI Chapter to which application is submitted. **Criteria:** Applicants will be selected based on: financial need; socially, physically and economically challenged adults; responsibility for small children.

Funds Avail.: $2,500. **Number Awarded:** 12. **To Apply:** Applicants must submit a completed application form available at the website; a copy of recent federal or state tax return and W-2 Form; an official transcript of grades or ACT scores; two letters of recommendation.

2895 ■ Executive Women International Fellows Program *(Graduate/Fellowship)*

Purpose: To provide financial assistance to EWI members admitted to an accredited baccalaureate, graduate or post graduate programs. **Focus:** General studies. **Qualif.:** Applicant must be an active EWI member for three or more consecutive years; have participated in Chapter activities; have a minimum of five full-time work experience; have demonstrated financial need. **Criteria:** Recipients will be selected based on the selection committee's review of the application materials.

Funds Avail.: $1,000 for Undergraduate Awards; $2,000 for Graduate/Post Graduate Awards; $5,000 for Deborah A. Taylor Scholarship. **Number Awarded:** 9. **To Apply:** Applicants must submit a completed application form; record of participation and accomplishments; two letters of recommendations; resume form/media release; income/financial form; enrollment verification; college transcript (original transcript with the seal of the school, delivered by the school in a sealed envelope); a non-refundable application fee of $25. **Deadline:** April 30.

Remarks: The Deborah A. Taylor Scholarship is awarded to the applicant with the highest point in the undergraduate category.

2896 ■ Executive Women International Scholarship Program (EWISP) *(High School/Scholarship)*

Purpose: To financially help qualified applicants to achieve their academic goals. **Focus:** General studies. **Qualif.:** Applicant must be a high school junior expecting to graduate from high school; and pursuing a degree in an accredited post-secondary institution. **Criteria:** Applicants will be selected based on character, personal merit and background.

Funds Avail.: $10,000. **To Apply:** Applicants must submit a completed application form available at the website; two letters of recommendation (use the Personal Recommendation Form) and official transcript of grades. Applications are to be submitted to the EWI chapter near the applicant's residency.

2897 ■ Fabricators and Manufacturers Association Foundation

833 Featherstone Rd.
Rockford, IL 61107-6302
Ph: (815)399-8700
Free: 888-394-4362
E-mail: foundation@fmanet.org
URL: http://www.fmafoundation.com

2898 ■ College and Trade/Technical School Scholarships *(Undergraduate/Scholarship)*

Purpose: To award scholarships to students in courses of study that may lead to careers in manufacturing. **Focus:** Manufacturing; Engineering. **Qualif.:** Applicant must be a full-time with a minimum cumulative 3.0 GPA for a college scholarship or cumulative 2.0 GPA for a trade/technical school scholarship, and enrolled in a manufacturing-related course of study, or a trade or technical program, that may lead to a career in manufacturing. Applicant must be a member or a non-member of the Association, students must plan to major in an engineering, trade school or manufacturing-related program that may lead to a career in manufacturing and must be accepted in an institution of higher learning college/university/technical school for the fall semester as a full-time student, FMA Foundation will verify acceptance before the award is made. **Criteria:** Selection will be based on the committees. criteria.

Funds Avail.: College Scholarships $2,500 for non-members; $5,000 for members. **To Apply:** Applicants may apply online. The Association will investigate any possible misuse of funds and may withhold disbursement of scholarship awards and seek recovery of disbursement funds if misuse of funds is discovered. Recovered funds will be dedicated for charitable purposes. **Deadline:** April 4. **Contact:** Fabricators and Manufacturers Association Foundation at the above address (see entry 2897).

2899 ■ Faegre & Benson LLP

2200 Wells Fargo Center
90 S 7th St.
Minneapolis, MN 55402-3901
Ph: (612)766-7000
Fax: (612)766-1600
Free: 800-328-4393
E-mail: info@faegre.com
URL: http://www.faegre.com

2900 ■ Faegre & Benson Diversity Scholarships *(Undergraduate/Scholarship)*

Purpose: To encourage and support individuals intending to pursue their legal profession. **Focus:** Law. **Qualif.:** Applicants must be enrolled full-time at an accredited law school in the United States. **Criteria:** Applicants will be selected based on a short essay that explores how diversity has influenced their lives and how it affects the legal profession.

Funds Avail.: $12,000. **Number Awarded:** 2. **To Apply:** Applicants must complete the application form, available online; must submit a resume and cover letter; must provide a personal statement explaining their interest in the scholarship program and how diversity has influenced their life and how it impacts the legal profession; must have an undergraduate transcript(s), legal writing sample and two professional recommendations, one of which must be from a law school professor. Application form and other supporting documents must be sent to Faegre & Benson LLP, 2200 Wells Fargo Center, 90 S 7th St., Minneapolis, MN 55402. **Deadline:** January 3. **Contact:** Dana Gray, Manager of Legal Personnel Services.

2901 ■ Families of Freedom Scholarship Fund

PO Box 297
St. Peter, MN 56082
Fax: (507)931-8924

Awards are arranged alphabetically below their administering organizations

Free: 877-862-0136
E-mail: familiesoffreedom@scholarshipamerica.org
URL: http://www.familiesoffreedom.org

2902 ■ Families of Freedom Scholarship Fund - America Scholarships *(Undergraduate/Scholarship)*

Purpose: To provide education assistance for post-secondary study to dependents - children and spouses - of those killed of permanently disabled as a result of terrorist attacks on September 11, 2001 and during the rescue activities to those attacks. **Focus:** General studies. **Qualif.:** Applicants must be dependents of those killed or permanently disabled as a result of the terrorist attacks on September 11, 2001, and during the rescue activities relating to those attacks. Specifically, families of Freedom benefits children and spouses of the victims, including airplane crew and passengers, World Trade Center and Pentagon workers and visitors, and relief workers, including firefighters and emergency medical personnel and law enforcement personnel. Participants must enroll in a course of study at an accredited two- or four-year college, university or vocational-technical school based in the United States. **Criteria:** Recipients are selected based on merit.

Funds Avail.: $1,000. **To Apply:** Applicants must submit all the required application information.

2903 ■ Farella Braun Martel LLP

235 Montgomery St., 17th Fl.
Russ Bldg.
San Francisco, CA 94104
Ph: (415)954-4400
Fax: (415)954-4480
E-mail: cloof@fbm.com
URL: http://www.fbm.com

2904 ■ Farella Braun Martel LLP Diversity Scholarships *(Undergraduate/Scholarship)*

Purpose: To support outstanding, diverse Bay Area law students. **Focus:** Law. **Qualif.:** Applicants must be current first-year, full or part-time law students who are students of color or from underrepresented backgrounds, who currently attend one of the following local law schools: University of California, Berkeley (Boalt Hall); University of California, Davis (King Hall); University of California, Hastings College of the Law; Golden Gate University; Stanford University; Santa Clara University; or the University of San Francisco. **Criteria:** Recipients will be selected based on a combination of merit and financial need. Preference will be given to applicants who demonstrate a commitment to working and living in the Bay Area.

Funds Avail.: A total of $25,000 is available. **To Apply:** Applicants must submit the completed application form. **Deadline:** March 14.

2905 ■ Federal Circuit Bar Association

1620 St. NW, Ste. 900
Washington, DC 20006
Ph: (202)466-3923
Fax: (202)833-1061
URL: http://www.fedcirbar.org

2906 ■ Howard T. Markey Memorial Scholarships *(Undergraduate/Scholarship)*

Purpose: To provide financial support for qualified individuals intending to pursue their studies. **Focus:** Law. **Qualif.:** Applicants must be law students showing financial need, demonstrated academic promise, and service, either in undergraduate or in law school. **Criteria:** Awards will be given based on a written submission of no more than one page setting out the applicant's financial need, any interests in particular areas of the law, and any qualifications for the awards considered relevant by the applicant. Application materials will be considered, and prior academic performance will not be the primary criteria for selection.

Funds Avail.: $10,000. **To Apply:** Applicants must submit a college and law school transcript and a one-page curriculum vitae. **Deadline:** April 30.

2907 ■ Helen W. Nies Scholarships *(Undergraduate/Scholarship)*

Purpose: To provide financial support for qualified individuals intending to pursue their studies. **Focus:** Law. **Qualif.:** Applicants must be women law students showing financial need, demonstrated academic promise, and service, either in undergraduate or in law school. **Criteria:** Award is given based on a written submission of no more than one page setting out the applicant's financial need, any interests in particular areas of the law, and any qualifications for the awards considered relevant by the applicant. Application materials will be considered and prior academic performance will not be the primary criteria for selection.

Funds Avail.: $10,000. **To Apply:** Applicants must submit a college and law school transcript and a one-page curriculum vitae. **Deadline:** April 30.

2908 ■ Federal Communication Bar Association Foundation

1020 19th St. NW, Ste. 325
Washington, DC 20036-6101
Ph: (202)293-4000
Fax: (202)293-4317
E-mail: fcba@fcba.org
URL: http://www.fcba.org

2909 ■ FCBA Foundation Scholarships *(Undergraduate/Scholarship)*

Purpose: To provide financial assistance for local high school students intending to pursue college studies. **Focus:** General studies. **Qualif.:** Applicants must be high school students attending in any of the 8 high schools located in the District of Columbia. **Criteria:** Scholarship is given based on academic achievement and honors, communication/presentation skills, financial need, motivation, attendance record, service to school, service to community and interest in communications or information technology (not required but will be considered if applicable).

Funds Avail.: No specific amount. **To Apply:** Applicants must complete the application. Please make sure that you have completed and attached all information required by the application. If an applicant does not have certain information specified, that applicant should so note, and provide a brief explanation. Please note that applicants are required to certify that he or she is a legal resident of the United States or must explain, in detail, their residency status in order to be considered for an FCBA Foundation scholarship. Applicants must attach copies of any essays, awards, letters of recommendation or appreciation (in addition to the recommendations specified in the application), or any other documentation or representation of excellence

Awards are arranged alphabetically below their administering organizations

or achievement that demonstrates their future potential or would provide additional insight to the foundation as it reviews the written applications according to the criteria. **Deadline:** March 3. **Contact:** Kerry Loughney, FCBA Foundation; kerry@fcba.org

2910 ■ Federal Court Clerks Association

Philip Burton US Courthouse-Box 36060
450 Golden Gate Ave.
San Francisco, CA 94102-3489
Ph: (415)522-2003
Fax: (415)522-2176
E-mail: ian_keye@cand.uscourts.gov
URL: http://www.fcca.ws

2911 ■ Carol C. Fitzgerald Scholarship Program *(Professional Development/Scholarship)*

Purpose: To assist deserving, qualified individuals to continue their education. **Focus:** General studies. **Qualif.:** Applicant must be a member in good standing of FCCA for a minimum of two consecutive years and must be a deputy clerk, employed by the U.S. Courts. **Criteria:** Committee will review all applications and award scholarships to deserving individuals who meet the qualifications, within the financial limitations of the program. Committee may consider the years of membership, economic need, FCCA contributions, and the applicant's interest in continuing education.

Funds Avail.: Amount awarded per individual scholarship may vary, as determined by the committee. **To Apply:** applicant must submit a complete application forms to: U.S District Court, Northern District of California, 450 Golden Gate Ave., San Francisco, CA 94102-3489. **Deadline:** April 15.

2912 ■ Federal Employee Education and Assistance Fund

8441 W Bowles Ave., Ste. 200
Littleton, CO 80123-9501
Ph: (303)933-7580
Fax: (303)933-7587
Free: 800-323-4140
URL: http://www.feea.org

2913 ■ Federal Employee Education and Assistance Fund Scholarships *(Other/Scholarship)*

Purpose: To provide financial assistance to civilian employees of the US Federal Government. **Focus:** General studies. **Qualif.:** Applicants must be civilian federal and postal employees with at least three years of federal service and their dependent family members (children and spouses) are eligible to apply during their senior year in high school; employee (may be part-time students; dependent must be full-time); enrolled or plan to enroll in an accredited post secondary school in a course of study that will lead to a two-year, four-year or graduate degree; and must have a GPA of 3.0 on a 4.0 scale. **Criteria:** Recipient will be selected based on academic merit.

Funds Avail.: $500 to 2,500. **To Apply:** Applicants must submit complete academic record, including fall semester grades, recommendation (character reference), list of extracurricular and community service activities, and essay. **Deadline:** March 28.

2914 ■ FEEA Scholarship Program *(Other/Scholarship)*

Purpose: To provide financial assistance to civilian employees of the US Federal Government. **Focus:** General studies. **Qualif.:** Applicants must be current civilian federal employees and their dependent family members (spouse/child); adult children and other relatives are eligible if claimed on the sponsoring employee's tax return; active duty military members and their dependents are eligible only through a sponsoring civilian employee spouse; military retirees and dependents are eligible if the retiree (or retiree's spouse) is a current civilian federal employee; must have at least three (3) years of civilian federal service by August 31, 2008; must be at least a college freshman by the fall 2008 semester; must have at least a 3.0 cumulative grade point average (CGPA) unweighted on a 4.0 scale; current college freshmen must have a minimum 3.0 GPA for the fall 2007 semester; must be current high school seniors or college students working toward an accredited degree and enrolled in a two or four year undergraduate, graduate or postgraduate program; dependents must be full-time students; and federal employees may be part-time students. **Criteria:** Applicants will be judged by Scholarship Committee.

Funds Avail.: $5,000. **Number Awarded:** 6. **To Apply:** Applicants must submit FEEA Scholarship Application Form; essay; written recommendation/character reference, transcript, list and briefly describe awards, extracurricular and community service activities, copy of ACT, SAT or other examination scores, copy of most recent standard form 50 "notice of personnel action", and two self-addressed, stamped, No. 10 business-size envelopes with first class postage properly affixed. **Deadline:** March 28.

2915 ■ Federal Law Enforcement Officers Association

PO Box 326
Lewisberry, PA 17339
Ph: (717)938-2300
Fax: (717)932-2262
E-mail: fleoa@fleoa.org
URL: http://www.fleoa.org

2916 ■ FLEOA Foundation Scholarship Program *(Undergraduate/Scholarship)*

Purpose: To provide educational assistance for the children of current, retired or deceased Federal Law Enforcement Officers. **Focus:** General studies. **Qualif.:** Applicants must be high school graduates; dependents of a current, retired or deceased Federal Law Enforcement Officer. **Criteria:** Scholarship will be awarded to the applicant with the highest cumulative ranking as independently reviewed by FLEAO Foundation Scholarship Committee; special consideration will be given to those applicants who are the children of federal law enforcement officers killed or disabled in the line of duty.

Funds Avail.: $1,000. **Number Awarded:** 15. **To Apply:** Applicants must submit completed application form available from the website; transcript of records (with class ranking, SAT scores); and an acceptance letter from a college or university. Submit applications with a self addressed stamped envelope to: FLEOA Foundation PO Box 1306 Grand Central Station New York, NY 10163. **Deadline:** August.

2917 ■ Federal Managers Association

1641 Prince St.
Alexandria, VA 22314-2818
Ph: (703)683-8700
Fax: (703)683-8707
E-mail: info@fedmanagers.org
URL: http://www.fedmanagers.org

2918 ■ FMA-FEEA Scholarship Program *(Undergraduate/Scholarship)*

Purpose: To provide financial assistance for the educational pursuits of current civilian employees and retirees who are FMA members and their dependent family members. **Focus:** General studies. **Qualif.:** Applicants must be at least college freshmen by the fall of 2008 semester; must have a 3.0 cumulative grade point average on 4.0 scale; must be current high school seniors or college students working toward an accredited degree and enrolled in two- or four-year post-secondary, graduate or postgraduate program; full-time students (if dependents); and part-time students (if federal employees). **Criteria:** Candidates will be evaluated based on academic performance.

Funds Avail.: No specific amount. **To Apply:** Applicants must submit complete application package containing the FMA-FEEA Scholarship Application Form; essay; written recommendation/character reference; transcript of scholastic record; brief description of awards, extracurricular and community service activities; copy of ACT, SAT or other examination scores; copy of most recent standard Form 50 "Notice of Personnel Action"; and two self-addressed, stamped, No. 10 business-size envelopes with first class postage properly affixed. **Deadline:** March 28.

2919 ■ Federation of American Consumers and Travelers

318 Hillsboro Ave.
PO Box 104
Edwardsville, IL 62025
Ph: (618)656-5369
E-mail: cservice@usafact.org
URL: http://ww.usafact.org

2920 ■ FACT Graduating Senior Scholarship Program *(Undergraduate/Scholarship)*

Purpose: To assure the continuation of FACT's selfless intents and purposes; to maintain high level of professionalism at the director level; to prevent any special-interest groups or self-serving individuals from assuming control of FACT for their own gain. **Focus:** General studies. **Qualif.:** Program is open to FACT members. Applicants must be graduating from an accredited public, private or parochial high school or equivalent during the 2007-2008 school year; must maintain a "C" grade point average to remain in the funds (if considered). Applicants may be students currently enrolled in 2- or 4-year education in accredited colleges or universities. **Criteria:** Applicants will be evaluated by the Scholarship Committee based on academic records and quality of the essay submitted.

Funds Avail.: $10,000 and $2,500. **Number Awarded:** 4. **To Apply:** Applicants must submit completed application form; Release Authorization and Membership Verification Form; Certification Form; Official Copy of High School Transcript signed by the applicant's high school principal or academic advisor; and a two-page, double-spaced essay. **Deadline:** January 15. **Contact:** FACT Membership Office at the above address (see entry 2919).

2921 ■ Federation of Diocesan Liturgical Commissions

415 Michigan Ave. NE, Ste. 70
Washington, DC 20017
Ph: (202)635-6990
Fax: (202)529-2452
E-mail: nationaloffice@fdlc.org
URL: http://www.fdlc.org

2922 ■ The Tabat Scholarship Fund *(Graduate/Scholarship)*

Purpose: To support graduate students in liturgical studies by providing assistance with the payment of tuition, the purchase of books, or the continuation of research. **Focus:** General studies. **Qualif.:** Applicant must be student pursuing a graduate degree in a program of liturgical studies to prepare for service in the Church of the United States in an academic, diocesan, or parish setting. **Criteria:** Candidates will be evaluated by the Scholarship Committee.

Funds Avail.: $1,000. **To Apply:** Applicants must submit a curriculum vitae, a short description of how the grant will be used, and two letters of recommendation, in a sealed envelope, from professors or from someone knowledgeable about the person's work. **Deadline:** June 30.

2923 ■ Federation of Societies for Coatings Technology

492 Norristown Rd.
Blue Bell, PA 19422-2350
Ph: (610)940-0777
Fax: (610)940-0292
E-mail: fsct@coatingstech.org
URL: http://www.coatingstech.org

2924 ■ Joseph A. Vasta Memorial Scholarships *(Undergraduate/Scholarship)*

Purpose: To pursue educational opportunities for coatings career-oriented students. **Focus:** Technology. **Qualif.:** Applicants must be an outstanding junior or senior college selected by their respected schools. **Criteria:** Priority is given to students with exemplary personal, academic, and community contribution.

Funds Avail.: $2500. **To Apply:** Fund is awarded to the educational institution on a rotating basis. The schools will select deserving students.

Remarks: Established in 1988. **Contact:** George M. Schmitz, CIEF President.

2925 ■ FEI Company

5350 NE Dawson Creek Dr.
Hillsboro, OR 97124
Ph: (503)726-7500
Fax: (503)726-2615
Free: (866)693-3426
URL: http://www.fei.com

2926 ■ Casey Bennett Scholarships *(Undergraduate/Scholarship)*

Purpose: To assist high school seniors who plan careers in the fields of Physical Sciences or Materials Sciences. **Fo-**

Awards are arranged alphabetically below their administering organizations

cus: Physical sciences. **Qualif.:** Applicant must be a high school senior (from either the Beaverton or Hillsboro School Districts); planning to pursue a career in Physical Sciences or Materials Sciences; and must have a 3.5 GPA or above. **Criteria:** Awards are given based on the application.

Funds Avail.: $1,000. **Number Awarded:** 2. **To Apply:** Applicants must complete the online scholarship application; submit a brief essay (approximately 1/2-1 page) explaining why they should receive the award and an explanation of education/career "roadmap"; a letter of recommendation from a science-related faculty member; and high school transcript (copy or scan). Applications are to be submitted online to scholarships@fei.com (include your name in the subject line of the email). **Deadline:** April 30.

2927 ■ Film Arts Foundation

145 9th St., No. 101
San Francisco, CA 94103
Ph: (415)552-8760
Fax: (415)552-0882
E-mail: infoa@filmarts.org
URL: http://www.filmarts.org

2928 ■ Film Arts Foundation Development Grants *(All/Grant)*

Purpose: To provide support for individuals working on non-profit film/video projects or events in soliciting funding from government, foundation, individual and other philanthropic sources. **Focus:** General studies. **Qualif.:** Applicants must be Film Arts members at the Filmmaker level or higher and must reside in San Francisco County. **Criteria:** Proposals are selected based on innovation, originality and artistic merit.

Funds Avail.: $3,000. **To Apply:** Applicants must submit a proposal reflecting a realistic, proper, and detailed budget and timeline completion. **Deadline:** May 7.

2929 ■ Film Studies Association of Canada

York University, Department of Film, CFT 223, 4700 Keele St.
Toronto, ON, Canada M3J 1P3
Ph: (416)736-2100
Fax: (416)736-5710
E-mail: johnmccu@yorku.ca
URL: http://www.filmstudies.ca

2930 ■ Gerald Pratley Awards *(Doctorate, Graduate/Award/Prize)*

Purpose: To inspire Quebec or Canadian cinema development by providing financial support for graduate students doing cinema researches. **Focus:** Cinema. **Qualif.:** Applicants must be students entering or completing a graduate program in Film Studies (or any related discipline) in any recognized post-secondary institution in or outside Canada. Applicants need not be Canadian citizens. **Criteria:** Selection is based on the student's previous academic performance and his or her intentions for a specific paper or body of research on Canadian/Quebec cinema.

Funds Avail.: $1,000. **To Apply:** Applicants must prepare a brief research proposal (500 words) including bibliography; two letters of recommendation; one sample of previous work (3000 to 5000 words); and official university transcripts. Application package must be addressed to: Kay Armatage, Associate Professor, University of Toronto, Women's Studies and Cinema Studies, Innis College 2 Sussex Ave., Toronto, ON M5S 2L8. **Deadline:** June 15.

Remarks: Established in 1991.

2931 ■ Fine Arts Association

38660 mentor Ave.
Willoughby, OH 44094
Ph: (440)951-7500
Fax: (440)975-4590
E-mail: jflemming-gifford@fineartsassociation.org
URL: http://www.fineartsassociation.org

2932 ■ Fine Arts Association Minority Scholarships *(Undergraduate/Scholarship)*

Purpose: To ensure that the opportunity for art education is available to all who deserve it and to create customized educational arts experiences in music, dance, drama, visual arts and music therapy. **Focus:** Fine arts. **Qualif.:** Students applying must be residents of Lake County who are members of a minority population as defined by the Ohio Arts Council. **Criteria:** Recipients are selected based on financial need.

Funds Avail.: No specific amount. **To Apply:** Applicants must complete the application form with parents/guardians if they are dependents. Forms are available at the FAA Customer Service Center and are also available for download at the website. First time applicants must include a copy of the first page of their most recent IRS 1040 form. **Contact:** Peter Grossetti, Director of Development at 440-951-7500.

2933 ■ Fine Arts Association United Way Scholarships *(Undergraduate/Scholarship)*

Purpose: To ensure that the opportunity for art education is available to all who deserve it and to create customized educational arts experiences in music, dance, drama, visual arts and music therapy. **Focus:** Fine Arts. **Qualif.:** Applicants must be students residing in Lake County and must have total family income not exceeding $18,400 annually, unless there are extenuating financial circumstances. **Criteria:** Recipients are selected based on financial need.

Funds Avail.: No specific amount. **To Apply:** Applicants must complete the application form with parents/guardians if they are dependents. Forms are available at the FAA Customer Service Center and are also available for download at the website. First time applicants must include a copy of the first page of their most recent IRS 1040 form. **Contact:** Peter Grossetti, Director of Development at 440-951-7500.

2934 ■ Gwen Yarnell Theatre Scholarships *(Undergraduate/Scholarship)*

Purpose: To ensure that the opportunity for art education is available to all who deserve it and to create customized educational arts experiences in music, dance, drama, visual arts and music therapy. **Focus:** Fine arts; Theater arts. **Qualif.:** Program is open to new and returning Fine Arts students intending to study theatre. **Criteria:** Recipients are selected based on merit.

Funds Avail.: No specific amount. **To Apply:** Forms can be requested by calling the association's Customer Service Center. **Contact:** Peter Grossetti, Director of Development at 440-951-7500.

2935 ■ Finnegan, Henderson, Farabow, Garrett & Dunner LLP

901 New York Ave. NW
Washington, DC 20001
Ph: (202)408-4000
Fax: (202)408-4400
E-mail: info@finnegan.com
URL: http://www.finnegan.com

2936 ■ Finnegan, Henderson, Farabow, Garrett & Dunner, LLP Diversity Scholarships *(Undergraduate/Scholarship)*

Purpose: To develop diversity in the workplace and in the field of intellectual property law. **Focus:** Law. **Qualif.:** Applicant must be enrolled in an American Bar Association accredited law school either as a first year full-time student or second-year part-time student. **Criteria:** Recipients must have demonstrated a commitment to pursuing a career in intellectual property law; exceptional academic performance at the undergraduate, graduate (if applicable), and law school level; a degree in the life sciences, engineering, computer science, or substantial prior trademark experience; and relevant work experience, community service, leadership skills and special accomplishment.

Funds Avail.: $15,000. **To Apply:** Applicants must submit current resume; completed scholarship application; undergraduate and, if applicable, graduate transcripts; law school transcripts; a legal writing sample (10 pages); and one to three letters of recommendation. **Deadline:** February 29.

2937 ■ First Community Foundation of Pennsylvania, Williamsport-Lycoming

330 Pine St., Suite 401
Williamsport, PA 17701
Ph: (570)321-1500
Fax: (570)321-6434
Free: (866)901-2372
E-mail: fcfpa@fcfpa.org
URL: http://www.wlfoundation.org

2938 ■ Ken and Pat Ackerman Family Scholarship Fund *(Undergraduate/Scholarship)*

Purpose: To provide scholarship for Danville Area High School seniors who have been accepted or will attend an accredited 4-year college, full-time. **Focus:** General studies. **Qualif.:** Applicants must have been a varsity wrestler and/or varsity football player and have the highest cumulative 4-year average in English. **Criteria:** Selection will be based on the committee's criteria.

Funds Avail.: No specific amount. **To Apply:** Applicants may request an application from the guidance counselor of Danville Area School District. **Contact:** Gary Grozier, Guidance Counselor of Danville Area School District, 600 Walnut St., Danville, PA 17821; 570-271-3268 ext. 2006; ggrozier@danville.k12.pa.us.

2939 ■ Ruth D. Adams Fund *(Undergraduate/Scholarship)*

Purpose: To provide financial assistance for Montoursville Area High School seniors who are seeking higher education beyond graduation from high school (full-time) and who represent the top 10% GPA of graduating seniors. **Focus:** General studies. **Qualif.:** Applicants shall be approved for full-time admission to any accredited two or four-year college or university of their choice and be enrolled in a course of study of their choice which leads to a degree. **Criteria:** Selection will be based on the committee's criteria.

Funds Avail.: No specific amount. **To Apply:** Applicants may contact and request an application from the Montoursville Area High School. **Contact:** Ronda Albert, Montoursville Area High School, 100 N Arch St, Montoursville, PA 17754; 570-368-3509; ralbert@montoursville.k12.pa.us.

2940 ■ Anne L. Alexander and Blaise Robert Alexander Memorial Scholarships *(Undergraduate/Scholarship)*

Purpose: To provide scholarship for graduating seniors from Mount Carmel Area High School and Montoursville Area High School respectively, who have been accepted into a full-time undergraduate, business or technical program at an accredited institution of higher education. **Focus:** General studies. **Qualif.:** Applicants must have exhibited good citizenship and community involvement; must be a leader with a sense of humor; must be grounded; must show tolerance to others; must be honest; must have integrity; and must make a difference in the school community. **Criteria:** Selection will be based on the committee's criteria.

Funds Avail.: No specific amount. **To Apply:** Applicants may contact and request an application from the Montoursville Area High School. **Contact:** Ronda Albert, Montoursville Area High School, 100 N Arch St, Montoursville, PA 17754; 570-368-3509; ralbert@montoursville.k12.pa.us.

2941 ■ B-Brave McMahon/Stratton Scholarship Fund *(Undergraduate/Scholarship)*

Purpose: To provide financial assistance for graduates who have been in the foster care system or have legal adopted status and who have shown remarkable achievement despite the obstacles in their life. **Focus:** General studies. **Qualif.:** Applicant must be a graduating senior from a Lycoming County High School or Clinton County High School that has believed in herself/himself; must have been accepted into a full-time continuing education program, preferably in Pennsylvania; must have exhibited good citizenship and have no known drug or alcohol record or juvenile offenses; have an unmet financial need; and must show evidence that they have a current minimum GPA of 2.8. **Criteria:** Selection will be based on the committee's criteria.

Funds Avail.: No specific amount. **To Apply:** Candidates must complete the application and submit it along with any requested additional information to the Williamsport-Lycoming Community Foundation. **Deadline:** April 1. **Contact:** Candy Bower, Manager of Program and Scholarship Services candyb@fcfpa.org.

2942 ■ Gina L. Barnhart Memorial Scholarship Fund *(Undergraduate/Scholarship)*

Purpose: To provide financial assistance for Milton Area High school seniors planning to pursue a major in elementary education. **Focus:** Education, Elementary. **Qualif.:** Candidates must be seniors in good standing and members of the cheerleading squad; must have been accepted by a qualified institution of higher education and plan to major in elementary education. Applicants who are planning to major in secondary education may be considered if there are no candidates that are planning to major in elementary education. Preference will be given to applicants with educational and/or career objectives focused on working with children or community service. **Criteria:** Selection will be based on the committee's criteria.

Awards are arranged alphabetically below their administering organizations

Funds Avail.: No specific amount. **To Apply:** Candidates must submit of a 200-word short essay on the following topic: "How has my participating in cheerleading and sports helped to prepare me for a career in elementary education or other work on behalf of children?" **Contact:** Leslie Robinson, Milton Senior High School, 700 Mahoning St., Milton, PA 17847, 570-742-7611.

2943 ■ Bloch-Selinger Education Fund
(Undergraduate/Scholarship)

Purpose: To provide financial assistance for honor students from the Danville Area High School. **Focus:** General studies. **Qualif.:** Applicants must be attending a full-time accredited school or university and be in good standing. **Criteria:** Selection will be based on the committee's criteria.

Funds Avail.: No specific amount. **To Apply:** Applicants may request an application from the guidance counselor of Danville Area School District. **Contact:** Gary Grozier, Guidance Counselor of Danville Area School District, 600 Walnut St., Danville, PA 17821; 570-271-3268 ext. 2006; ggrozier@danville.k12.pa.us.

2944 ■ Diane Booth Memorial Scholarships
(Undergraduate/Scholarship)

Purpose: To provide scholarship to the Danville Area High School seniors. **Focus:** General studies. **Qualif.:** Applicants must be accepted into a full-time undergraduate, associate or technical program in an institution of higher education; have exhibited good citizenship and community involvement; and a strong potential for success. **Criteria:** Selection will be based on the committee's criteria.

Funds Avail.: No specific amount. **To Apply:** Applicants may request an application from the Danville Area School District. **Contact:** Gary Grozier, Guidance Counselor, Danville Area School District, 570-271-3268, ggrozier@danville.k12.pa.us.

2945 ■ Eleanor McWilliams Burke Fund
(Undergraduate/Scholarship)

Purpose: To provide academic support for Danville Area High School seniors who have been accepted into a full-time undergraduate program at an accredited institution of higher education and who are entering a health-related field. **Focus:** Medicine; Nursing; Nutrition; Pharmacy; or Physical therapy. **Qualif.:** Applicants must be entering a health related field. **Criteria:** Selection is based on character, academic performance, career goals and participation in school and/or community activities.

Funds Avail.: No specific amount. **To Apply:** Applicants may request an application from the Guidance Counselor of Danville Area School District. **Contact:** Gary Grozier, Guidance Counselor of Danville Area School District, 600 Walnut St., Danvilled, PA 17821; 570-271-3268 ext. 2006; ggrozier@danville.k12.pa.us.

2946 ■ Joseph R. Calder, Jr., MD Scholarship Fund *(Undergraduate/Scholarship)*

Purpose: To support the education of current and/or aspiring Lycoming County medical professionals who plan to dedicate their lives to helping others. **Focus:** Medicine; Nursing; Pharmacy; Allied health. **Qualif.:** Applicants must be accepted into a full-time or part-time medical or any other related specialty at an accredited institution of higher education. Applicants should be residents of Lycoming County. **Criteria:** Selection will be based on merit.

Funds Avail.: No specific amount. **To Apply:** Applicant must submit an essay not to exceed one page outlining why he/she is pursuing a career in the medical field and summarizing his/her ultimate career objectives. Applicants may download an application form the Foundation's web site. **Contact:** Candy Bower, 570-321-1500; candyb@fcfpa.org

2947 ■ Warren E. "Whitey" Cole American Society of Highway Engineers Scholarships
(Undergraduate/Scholarship)

Purpose: To provide scholarship awards for students enrolled in a Civil Engineering curriculum. **Focus:** Civil engineering. **Qualif.:** Applicants must be enrolled in a civil engineering, civil engineering technology or civil technology curriculum; have completed at least the sophomore year of a four-year curriculum or the freshman year of a two-year curriculum; be either enrolled at Pennsylvania State University, Bucknell University or Pennsylvania College of Technology or have residence in the counties of Bradford, Columbia, Lycoming, Montour, Northumberland, Snyder, Sullivan, Tioga or Union and attend another college. **Criteria:** Selection will be based on the committee's criteria.

Funds Avail.: No specific amount. **To Apply:** Candidates must complete the application and submit it along with any requested additional information to the Williamsport-Lycoming Community Foundation. **Contact:** Ken Klingerman, American Society of Highway Engineers, 570-368-4231.

2948 ■ Cotner Family Scholarships
(Undergraduate/Scholarship)

Purpose: To provide scholarship for Danville Area High School seniors who will attend an accredited 2 or 4-year college. **Focus:** Agricultural economics. **Qualif.:** Applicants must be high school seniors attending an accredited 2 or 4-year college and must be pursuing studies in agriculture or agricultural related fields on a full-time basis. **Criteria:** Selection will be based on the committee's criteria.

Funds Avail.: No specific amount. **To Apply:** Applicants may request an application from the Guidance Counselor of Danville Area School District. **Contact:** Gary Grozier, Guidance Counselor of Danville Area School District, 600 Walnut St., Danvilled, PA 17821; 570-271-3268 ext. 2006; ggrozier@danville.k12.pa.us.

2949 ■ Danville Education Association Scholarship Fund *(Undergraduate/Scholarship)*

Purpose: To provide financial assistance for Danville Area High School seniors who have been accepted into a full-time undergraduate program at an accredited institution of higher education, preferably in Pennsylvania. **Focus:** General studies. **Qualif.:** Applicants must have exhibited good citizenship and community involvement; must have unmet financial need; and must have not been the recipient of other major scholarship awards. **Criteria:** Selection will be based on the committee's criteria.

Funds Avail.: No specific amount. **To Apply:** Applicants may request an application from the Guidance Counselor of Danville Area School District. **Contact:** Gary Grozier, Guidance Counselor of Danville Area School District, 600 Walnut St., Danvilled, PA 17821; 570-271-3268 ext. 2006; ggrozier@danville.k12.pa.us.

2950 ■ Danville High School Class of 1963 Scholarship Fund *(Undergraduate/Scholarship)*

Purpose: To provide financial assistance for Danville Area High School seniors who have been accepted and will be pursuing a Bachelor of Arts or Sciences degree in an accredited institution of higher education. **Focus:** General studies. **Qualif.:** Applicants must have exhibited good citizenship and community involvement. The recipients must have experience with community service and volunteering. **Criteria:** Selection will be based on financial need.

Funds Avail.: No specific amount. **To Apply:** Applicants may request application form from the Guidance Counselor of Danville Area School District. **Contact:** Gary Grozier, Guidance Counselor of Danville Area School District, 600 Walnut St., Danvilled, PA 17821; 570-271-3268 ext. 2006; ggrozier@danville.k12.pa.us.

2951 ■ Danville Rotary Scholarships
(Undergraduate/Scholarship)

Purpose: To provide financial assistance for Danville Area High School seniors who have been accepted and will attend an accredited 2 or 4-year college as full-time students. **Focus:** General studies. **Qualif.:** Applicants must have exhibited good citizenship, honesty, integrity, and volunteerism in the community and/or charity that demonstrate the Rotary's motto. **Criteria:** Selection will be based on the committee's criteria.

Funds Avail.: No specific amount. **To Apply:** Applicants may request an application from the Guidance Counselor of Danville Area School District. **Contact:** Gary Grozier, Guidance Counselor of Danville Area School District, 600 Walnut St., Danvilled, PA 17821; 570-271-3268 ext. 2006; ggrozier@danville.k12.pa.us.

2952 ■ Marian Jones Donaldson Scholarship Fund *(Undergraduate/Scholarship)*

Purpose: To provide financial assistance for Canton Area High School seniors intending to pursue a course of study in elementary or secondary education. **Focus:** Education, Elementary; Education, Secondary. **Qualif.:** Applicants shall have a four-year overall minimum grade average of 85%. **Criteria:** Selection will be based on involvement in community service, extra-curricular activities, and financial need.

Funds Avail.: No specific amount. **Number Awarded:** 1. **To Apply:** Candidate must complete and submit an application, a 500-word or less essay describing why he or she wants to enter the field of education, and three letters of reference. **Deadline:** April 1. **Contact:** Jamie May, Guidance Counselor, Canton Area High School, 570-673-5134, jmay@canton.k12.pa.us.

2953 ■ Lindsay M. Entz Memorial Scholarships
(Undergraduate/Scholarship)

Purpose: To provide financial assistance for the Jersey Shore High School seniors intending to pursue a course of study in elementary education, preferably with an emphasis on education of special-needs children. **Focus:** Education, elementary. **Qualif.:** Candidates must plan to pursue a course of study in elementary education, preferably with an emphasis on education of special-needs children; must have exhibited good citizenship and community involvement; must be a leader with a sense of humor; must be grounded; must show tolerance to others; must be honest; must have integrity; and must make a difference in the school community. **Criteria:** Selection will be based on the committee's criteria.

Funds Avail.: $1,000. **Number Awarded:** 1. **To Apply:** Candidate must complete an application; attach a cover letter (not to exceed two pages) outlining why he or she is applying for the scholarship and summarizing his/her ultimate career objectives; must provide proof that he or she has been accepted to an accredited two-/four-year college/ university; and must provide at least one letter of reference. **Deadline:** April 15. **Contact:** Jeannie Rombach, Guidance Counselor, Jersey Shore Area Senior High School, 570-398-7174 ext. 1009, jrombach@jsasd.k12.pa.us.

2954 ■ Nolan W. Feeser Scholarship Fund
(Undergraduate/Scholarship)

Purpose: To provide financial assistance for South Williamsport Area High School seniors who are pursuing a higher education degree at an accredited college or university. **Focus:** General studies. **Qualif.:** Applicants must have displayed academic achievements; must have unmet financial need; and must be planning to enroll at or pursuing a degree at Lycoming College, Gettysburg College or Pennsylvania College of Technology. **Criteria:** Selection will be based on the committee's criteria.

Funds Avail.: No specific amount. **Number Awarded:** 2. **To Apply:** Applicants may contact and request an application from the South Williamsport Area High School. **Contact:** Verna Correll, Guidance Counselor, South Williamsport Jr./Sr. High School, 700 Percy St., S Williamsport, PA 17702; 570-326-2684; vcorrell@mounties.k12.pa.us.

2955 ■ Daniel G. and Helen I. Fultz Scholarship Fund *(Undergraduate/Scholarship)*

Purpose: To encourage educational pursuits by providing scholarship for Indian Valley High School seniors. **Focus:** General studies. **Qualif.:** Program is open to Indian Valley High School seniors who have been accepted into a full-time undergraduate program at Lycoming College, Williamsport, PA. If there are no applicants from Indian Valley High School, then applicants may be chosen from Lewistown High School in Mifflin County, again, who have been accepted into a full-time undergraduate degree program at Lycoming College, Williamsport, PA. Applicants must have good citizenship and community involvement; be a leader with a sense of humor; be grounded; must show tolerance of others; be honest; have integrity; and make a difference in the school community. Unmet financial need is also considered. **Criteria:** Selection will be based on the committee's criteria.

Funds Avail.: No specific amount. **To Apply:** Applicants may contact and request an application from the Indian Valley High School. **Deadline:** April 15. **Contact:** Jane A. Floor, Guidance Counselor, Indian Valley High School, 717-248-5444, jaf53@mcsdk12.org; Frank A. Zook, Guidance Counselor, Lewistown High School, 717-242-1401, faz42@mcsdk12.org.

2956 ■ Adam Hampton Memorial Scholarship Fund *(Undergraduate/Scholarship)*

Purpose: To provide scholarship for Danville Area High School seniors who have been accepted into a full-time undergraduate program. **Focus:** General studies. **Qualif.:** Applicants must have good citizenship and community involvement; must be a leader with a sense of humor; must be grounded; must show tolerance of others; must be honest; must have integrity; and must make a difference in the school community. Applicants must also have an unmet financial need and must hold a "B" average or above. **Criteria:** Selection will be based on the committee's criteria.

Funds Avail.: No specific amount. **To Apply:** Applicants may request an application from the Guidance Counselor

Awards are arranged alphabetically below their administering organizations

of Danville Area School District. **Contact:** Gary Grozier, Guidance Counselor of Danville Area School District, 600 Walnut St., Danville, PA 17821; 570-271-3268 ext. 2006; ggrozier@danville.k12.pa.us.

2957 ■ Morton Harrison Scholarship Fund *(Undergraduate/Scholarship)*

Purpose: To provide financial assistance for Lycoming County young adults who demonstrate the potential to succeed in pursuing higher education goals. **Focus:** General studies. **Qualif.:** Candidates shall be young adults who, as a result of legal offenses as juveniles or young adults, have come to the attention of Lycoming County's Probation Department; must demonstrate a strong willingness to make positive changes in their lives and pursue educational and/or job training goals that will enable them to fulfill their human potential; and plan to attend a qualified institution of higher education, including but not limited to a 2- or 4-year college or university, a technical college, trade school, or other approved education or training program. **Criteria:** Selection will be based on the committee's criteria.

Funds Avail.: No specific amount. **To Apply:** Candidates must complete the application and submit it along with any requested additional information to the Williamsport-Lycoming Community Foundation. **Contact:** Candy Bower, Manager of Program and Scholarship Services candyb@fcfpa.org.

2958 ■ Mollie Harter Memorial Fund *(Undergraduate/Scholarship)*

Purpose: To provide financial assistance for Danville Area High School seniors intending to pursue higher education goals, preferably in the field of secondary education. **Focus:** Education, Secondary. **Qualif.:** Applicants must be planning to pursue a Bachelor of Arts or Sciences degree from a qualified institution of higher education. Applicants' experience with community service and volunteering, as well as their interest in working with children and the potential to succeed in pursuing their goals may be considered. Preference will be given to applicants interested in a career in education, ideally secondary education, and then to other careers working with children. **Criteria:** Selection will be based on the committee's criteria.

Funds Avail.: No specific amount. **To Apply:** Applicants may request an application from the Guidance Counselor of Danville Area School District. **Contact:** Gary Grozier, Guidance Counselor of Danville Area School District, 600 Walnut St., Danvilled, PA 17821; 570-271-3268 ext. 2006; ggrozier@danville.k12.pa.us.

2959 ■ Jane Hood Memorial Fund *(Undergraduate/Scholarship)*

Purpose: To provide financial assistance for Danville Area High School seniors who have been accepted into a full-time undergraduate program. **Focus:** Visual arts; Mathematics and mathematical science; Science; Engineering. **Qualif.:** Applicants must be accepted in a full-time undergraduate program at an institution of higher education to study graphic-visual arts, math and/or science (including engineering). Applicants must have exhibited good citizenship and community involvement. **Criteria:** Selection will be based on the committee's criteria.

Funds Avail.: No specific amount. **To Apply:** Applicants may request an application to the Guidance Counselor of Danville Area School District. **Contact:** Gary Grozier, Guidance Counselor of Danville Area School District, 600 Walnut St., Danville, PA 17821; 570-271-3268 ext. 2006; ggrozier@danville.k12.pa.us.

2960 ■ ISCALC International Scholarship Fund *(Undergraduate/Scholarship)*

Purpose: To provide financial assistance for Lycoming County high school seniors who have demonstrated an interest in furthering their education in international studies. **Focus:** International affairs and relations; Foreign languages. **Qualif.:** Applicant must be a high school senior within Lycoming county who will be attending an accredited institution of higher education and who plans to pursue major coursework in the area of international studies, including but not limited to international affairs, foreign languages, overseas exchange programs, multicultural studies, and related areas. **Criteria:** Selection will be based on the committee's criteria.

Funds Avail.: $250-$400. **Number Awarded:** 2-4. **To Apply:** Candidates must complete the application and submit it along with any requested additional information to the Williamsport-Lycoming Community Foundation. **Contact:** Candy Bower, Manager of Program and Scholarship Services, candyb@fcfpa.org.

2961 ■ Carl and Lucille Jarrett Scholarship Fund *(Graduate, Undergraduate/Scholarship)*

Purpose: To provide scholarship for Montgomery Area High School seniors and/or graduated alumni who have been accepted and will attend an accredited 2 or 4-year college or university, full-time or part-time. **Focus:** General studies. **Qualif.:** The applicants must exhibit good citizenship; must be honest; must have integrity; must have shown through job or volunteer history his/her ability to succeed; must be self-motivated; and must have strong ethics. **Criteria:** Selection will be based on the committee's criteria.

Funds Avail.: $1,000. **To Apply:** Applicants must complete the application. Applicants may request an application by contacting the Guidance Counselors of Montgomery Area High School or download it through the Foundation's web site. **Deadline:** May 1. **Contact:** Tara Bozella or Stacey Roman, Guidance Counselors, Montgomery Area High School, 570-547-1608 ext. 116; tbozella@montasd.org; sroman@montasd.org.

2962 ■ Gerald J. Levandoski Memorial Scholarship Fund *(Undergraduate/Scholarship)*

Purpose: To provide financial support for Danville Area High School seniors who are pursuing their studies in the field of engineering or science. **Focus:** Engineering. **Qualif.:** Applicants must have exhibited good citizenship and community involvement. **Criteria:** Selection will be based on the committee's criteria.

Funds Avail.: No specific amount. **To Apply:** Applicants may request an application from the guidance counselor of Danville Area School District. **Contact:** Gary Grozier, Guidance Counselor of Danville Area School District, 600 Walnut St., Danville, PA 17821; 570-271-3268 ext. 2006; ggrozier@danville.k12.pa.us.

2963 ■ Carl J. Marrara Memorial Scholarship Fund *(Undergraduate/Scholarship)*

Purpose: To provide financial assistance for Danville Area High School seniors who have been accepted into a full-time undergraduate program at an accredited institution of higher education, preferably in Pennsylvania. **Focus:** General studies. **Qualif.:** Applicants must have exhibited good citizenship and community involvement; must be a leader with a sense of humor; must be grounded; must show tolerance of others; must be honest; must have

Awards are arranged alphabetically below their administering organizations

integrity and make a difference in the school community; and must have an unmet financial need. **Criteria:** Selection will be based on the committee's criteria.

Funds Avail.: No specific amount. **To Apply:** Applicants may request an application from the guidance counselor of Danville Area School District. **Contact:** Gary Grozier, Guidance Counselor of Danville Area School District, 600 Walnut St., Danville, PA 17821; 570-271-3268 ext. 2006; ggrozier@danville.k12.pa.us.

2964 ■ Walter A. and Nan C. McCloskey Memorial Scholarships *(Undergraduate/Scholarship)*

Purpose: To provide financial assistance for Danville Area High School seniors who have been accepted into a full-time undergraduate program at an accredited institution of higher education, preferably in Pennsylvania. **Focus:** General studies. **Qualif.:** Applicants must have attained a Boys or Girls letter in basketball (or football or baseball in the event basketball is discontinued at Danville High School). The award recipient shall be a good school and community citizen in addition to his/her scholastic and athletic qualities. **Criteria:** Selection will be based on the committee's criteria.

Funds Avail.: No specific amount. **To Apply:** Applicants may request an application from the guidance counselor of Danville Area School District. **Contact:** Gary Grozier, Guidance Counselor of Danville Area School District, 600 Walnut St., Danville, PA 17821; 570-271-3268 ext. 2006; ggrozier@danville.k12.pa.us.

2965 ■ Joseph and Catherine Missigman Memorial Nursing Scholarships *(Undergraduate/Scholarship)*

Purpose: To provide financial assistance for Bloomsburg University students who are pursuing a career in nursing. **Focus:** Nursing. **Qualif.:** Candidates must be Bloomsburg University students who have identified nursing as their major; must be completing their second or third year's curricula in the University's nursing education program; have a GPA of 2.5 or greater for all nursing coursework; and have a demonstrated financial need as determined by Bloomsburg University's methods and practices for assessing its student's financial capacities. **Criteria:** Selection will be based on the committee's criteria.

Funds Avail.: No specific amount. **To Apply:** Candidates must have completed and filed an application for the scholarship and must include a one-page cover letter describing his/her rational for applying for the scholarship as well as his/her interest in the nursing field. **Contact:** Margie Eckroth-Bucher, Associate Professor Department of Nursing, Bloomsburg University, 570-389-4607, mekroth@bloomu.edu.

2966 ■ Missigman Scholarship Fund *(Undergraduate/Scholarship)*

Purpose: To provide financial assistance for Sullivan County High School seniors who have been accepted into a full-time undergraduate program at an accredited institution of higher education, preferably in Pennsylvania. **Focus:** General studies. **Qualif.:** Candidate must be a graduating senior at Sullivan County High School and must demonstrate a strong potential to succeed in pursuing their higher education objectives. **Criteria:** Selection will be based on the committee's criteria.

Funds Avail.: No specific amount. **To Apply:** Applicants may request an application from the Sullivan County High School or from the First Community Foundation of Pennsylvania. **Contact:** Jill Sysock, Guidance Office, Sullivan County High School, Beech and South St., Laporte, PA 18626, 570-947-7001, sysojill@sulcosd.k12.pa.us.

2967 ■ Robert E. and Judy More Scholarship Fund *(Undergraduate/Scholarship)*

Purpose: To provide financial assistance for Montgomery Area High School students intending to pursue higher education in finance, engineering, business or science. **Focus:** Finance; Engineering; Business; Science. **Qualif.:** Candidates must exhibit leadership qualities, academic excellence and a cooperative spirit. **Criteria:** Selection will be based on the committee's criteria.

Funds Avail.: No specific amount. **To Apply:** Candidates must complete and submit the application. Scholarship application can be requested from Montgomery Area High School or may be downloaded from the Foundation's web site. **Deadline:** April 15. **Contact:** Tara Bozella, Guidance Counselor, Montgomery Area High School, 120 Penn Street, Montgomery, PA 17752, 570-547-1608 ext. 116, tbozella@montasd.org.

2968 ■ Muncy Rotary Club Scholarship Fund *(Undergraduate/Scholarship)*

Purpose: To provide financial assistance for Muncy High School seniors who have been accepted into a full-time continuing education program. **Focus:** General studies. **Qualif.:** Applicants must have exhibited community involvement. Other than a strong potential for success, such factors as class rank and GPA will not be criteria in making a selection unless, in the judgment of the Muncy Rotary Club Scholarship Committee, such factors are needed to distinguish between multiple potential candidates. **Criteria:** Financial need will be a considering factor.

Funds Avail.: No specific amount. **To Apply:** Applicants may request an application from Erik Berthold of Muncy High School. **Deadline:** April 1. **Contact:** Erik Berthold, Guidance Counselor, Muncy High School, 200 West Penn St., Muncy, PA 17756, 570-546-3127 ext. 3260, eberthold@muncysd.org.

2969 ■ Muncy Scholars Award Fund *(Undergraduate/Award/Prize)*

Purpose: To provide financial assistance for graduating seniors in the Muncy Area School District who have completed grades 9, 10, and 11 at the Muncy High School and who have been accepted and will attend a 4-year college, full-time. **Focus:** General studies. **Qualif.:** Applicants must have exhibited continued growth in his/her citizenship; must be a leader; must be honest; must have integrity; and must be determined to succeed. **Criteria:** Selection will be based on the committee's criteria.

Funds Avail.: No specific amount. **To Apply:** Applicants will be selected from the top 10 academic performers and must have attained at least one varsity letter (either n sports or band). **Contact:** Erik Berthold, guidance counselor, Muncy High School, 200 W Penn St., Muncy, PA 17756; 570-546-3127 ext. 3260; eberthold@muncysd.org.

2970 ■ Albert and Alice Nacinovich Music Scholarships *(Undergraduate/Scholarship)*

Purpose: To provide financial assistance for Lycoming County high school seniors graduating from public or private schools with a demonstrated interest in music who plan to attend a qualified institution of higher education in a music-related field of study. **Focus:** Music. **Qualif.:** Applicants must be graduating high school seniors from any Lycoming County high school, public or private (secular or Christian), or as part of a qualified home-schooling arrangement within Lycoming County; must have been accepted to a qualified institution of higher education with the intention of pursuing further education or a career in music in a degree-granting program in music education or a music-related field of study; and must have a demonstrated interest in music, which may include participation in band, chorus, music theory and composition, and performance service at school, church, or community. **Criteria:** Selection will be based on the committee's criteria.

Funds Avail.: $1,000. **To Apply:** Applicants will be required to complete an application, provide copies of transcripts, and attach a 500-word of essay or less outlining his or her interest in music and how a scholarship award will help to advance his or her goals within a musical field or discipline. A recording of the applicant's work must also be submitted with completed application and essay. **Deadline:** May 1. **Contact:** Candy Bower, Manager of Program and Scholarship Services, candyb@fcfpa.org.

2971 ■ Rechsteiner Family Scholarship Fund *(Undergraduate/Scholarship)*

Purpose: To provide financial assistance for Danville Area High School graduating seniors who have been accepted into a full-time undergraduate program at an institution of higher education to study education or science. **Focus:** Education; Science. **Qualif.:** Applicants must be students studying education or science and who maintain a GPA of 2.7 on a 4.0 scale after the end of their freshman year and for the rest of their undergraduate education. **Criteria:** Selection will be based on the committee's criteria.

Funds Avail.: No specific amount. **To Apply:** Applicants may request an application from the Guidance Counselor of Danville Area School District. **Contact:** Gary Grozier, Guidance Counselor of Danville Area School District, 600 Walnut St., Danville, PA 17821; 570-271-3268 ext. 2006; ggrozier@danville.k12.pa.us.

2972 ■ Kimberly Marie Rogers Memorial Scholarship Fund *(Undergraduate/Scholarship)*

Purpose: To provide scholarship for Montoursville Area High School seniors who are planning to attend a vocational/technical college or a two or four-year accredited college. **Focus:** General studies. **Qualif.:** Applicants must be Montoursville Area High School seniors who are planning to attend a vocational/technical college or a two or four-year accredited college. Their major should fall under the vocational/technical field. **Criteria:** Selection will be based on financial need but with equal emphasis on academics. The recipient must have a GPA of 3.0 or higher.

Funds Avail.: No specific amount. **To Apply:** Applicants may contact and request an application from the Montoursville Area High School. **Contact:** Ronda Albert, Montoursville Area High School, 100 N Arch St, Montoursville, PA 17754; 570-368-3509; ralbert@montoursville.k12.pa.us.

2973 ■ Dr. Wayne F. Rose Scholarship Fund *(Undergraduate/Scholarship)*

Purpose: To provide financial assistance for Loyalsock High School seniors intending to attend a qualified institution of higher education in pursuit of a career in education who have a demonstrated interest in working with children and who exhibit an appreciation of the arts. **Focus:** General studies. **Qualif.:** Applicants must demonstrate family financial need; must demonstrate active involvement working or volunteering with children outside of their own school and typical class responsibilities; must demonstrate participation in the arts while in school and/or through extracurricular activities; and must be in good academic standing with potential for success. **Criteria:** Selection will be based on the committee's criteria.

Funds Avail.: No specific amount. **To Apply:** Applicants may request an application to the Loyalsock Township High School. Applicants must have a recommendation of at least one teacher. **Contact:** Diane Stanzione, Loyalsock Township High School, 1801 Loyalsock Drive, Williamsport, PA 17701, 570-326-3581 ext. 1307, dstanzio@ltsd.k12.pa.us.

2974 ■ Jane Salanky-Onzik Scholarship Fund *(Undergraduate/Scholarship)*

Purpose: To provide financial assistance for South Williamsport Area High School seniors. **Focus:** Spanish studies. **Qualif.:** Applicants must be high school seniors who have been accepted into a full-time undergraduate program at an institution of higher education (preferably in Pennsylvania) to study secondary education (preferably to teach Spanish) or to study Spanish in preparation for a career that would utilize the Spanish language. Applicants must have exhibited good citizenship and community involvement, must have unmet financial need and must not have been the recipient of other major scholarship awards. **Criteria:** Selection will be based on the committee's criteria.

Funds Avail.: No specific amount. **To Apply:** Applicant must submit an application to the Guidance Counselor's office. **Contact:** Verna Correll, Guidance Counselor, s Williamsport Jr./Sr. High School, 700 Percy St., S Williamsport, PA 17702; 570-326-2684; vcorrell@mounties.k12.pa.us.

2975 ■ John A. Savoy Scholarship Fund *(Undergraduate/Scholarship)*

Purpose: To provide financial assistance for South Williamsport Area High School seniors who have been accepted into a full-time undergraduate program at an accredited institution of higher education, preferably in Pennsylvania. **Focus:** General studies. **Qualif.:** Applicants must have exhibited good citizenship and community involvement; have unmet financial need; and must not have been the recipient of other major scholarship awards. **Criteria:** Selection will be based on committee's criteria.

Funds Avail.: $500. **To Apply:** Scholarship is renewable as long as the recipient remains in good standing at an accredited college or university but shall not exceed a maximum of 4 years. Applicant must submit an application to the Guidance Counselor's Office; must include a cover letter (not to exceed two pages) outlining why he or she is applying for the scholarship and summarizing his/her ultimate career objectives; must provide at least one letter of reference; and must provide proof that he or she has been accepted to a qualified two or four-year college/university. **Deadline:** May 1. **Contact:** Verna Correll, Guidance Counselor, South Williamsport Jr./Sr. High School, 700 Percy St., S Williamsport, PA 17702; 570-326-2684; vcorrell@mounties.k12.pa.us.

2976 ■ Ralph and Josephine Smith Scholarship Fund *(Undergraduate/Scholarship)*

Purpose: To defray all or a portion of the costs of attending college or other undergraduate institutions of higher learning beyond the secondary level for Warrior Run High School seniors. **Focus:** General studies. **Qualif.:** Candidate must maintain a GPA of 2.5. Candidate's financial needs shall

Awards are arranged alphabetically below their administering organizations

always be a primary consideration. Extra-curricular activities will not be considered in the selection process. **Criteria:** Selection will be based on the committee's criteria.

Funds Avail.: $625. **Number Awarded:** 4. **To Apply:** Applicants may request an application from the Guidance Office of Warrior Run High School. **Contact:** Jenna Brown or Jim Houser, Guidance Office, Warrior Run High School, 4800 Susquehanna Trail, Turbotville, PA 17772, 570-649-5166 ext. 105, jbrown@wrsd.org or jhouser@wrsd.org.

2977 ■ Margaret E. Waldron Scholarship Fund *(Undergraduate/Scholarship)*

Purpose: To provide financial assistance for Muncy High School seniors who are pursuing higher education. **Focus:** General studies. **Qualif.:** Candidates must have completed grades 10, 11, 12 at Muncy High School and have graduated from academic courses at Muncy High School; must rank in upper 1/5 of the class during junior and senior years; must present letter of acceptance from a postsecondary institution of higher learning. **Criteria:** Selection will be based on the committee's criteria.

Funds Avail.: $3,000 - freshman and sophomore years; $4,000 - junior and senior years. **To Apply:** Applicants may contact Guidance Office of Muncy High School to request an application or download the application from the Foundation's web site. Applicant must submit a copy of his/her parents' current U.S. Individual Income Tax Return and a copy of his or her school transcript through the third marking period of his or her senior year. **Deadline:** April 1. **Contact:** Erik Berthold, Guidance Counselor, Muncy High School, 200 W Penn St., Muncy, PA 17756, 570-546-3127 ext. 3260, eberthold@muncysd.org.

2978 ■ Monica M. Weaver Memorial Fund *(Undergraduate/Scholarship)*

Purpose: To provide scholarship for Montoursville Area High School seniors of high scholastic standing who are enrolled at a college or other educational institution pursuing a major in physical therapy. **Focus:** Physical therapy. **Qualif.:** Students must have resided in the Montoursville Area School District for a minimum of three years prior to graduation. **Criteria:** Selection will be based on the committee's criteria.

Funds Avail.: No specific amount. **To Apply:** Applicants may contact and request an application from the Montoursville Area High School. **Contact:** Ronda Albert, Montoursville Area High School, 100 N Arch St, Montoursville, PA 17754; 570-368-3509; ralbert@montoursville.k12.pa.us.

2979 ■ Williamsport High School Class of 1970 Scholarship Fund *(Undergraduate/Scholarship)*

Purpose: To provide financial assistance for Williamsport Area High School seniors intending to attend a college, university, or vocational school that offers an at least two-year degree or certification program. **Focus:** General studies. **Qualif.:** Candidates must be in need of financial assistance and shall not have received any other scholarship totaling more than $250. Preference is given to applicant who is not necessarily the most outstanding scholar nor the most sensational athlete; but rather, the student who has worked diligently to master his/her selection of academic courses, has earned the respect of his/her teachers and fellow students because he/she possesses unquestionable integrity and who consistently displays compassion or kindness to others. **Criteria:** Selection will be based on the committee's criteria.

Funds Avail.: No specific amount. **To Apply:** Applicants may request an application from the Head Principal of Williamsport Area High School. **Contact:** Head Principal, Williamsport Area High School, 2990 WFourth St., Williamsport, PA 17701, 5703238411.

2980 ■ Williamsport-Lycoming Community Foundation - Benjamin Franklin Scholarships *(Undergraduate/Scholarship)*

Purpose: To provide academic support for students who are attending Pennsylvania College and have graduated from Bradford County, Clinton County, Lycoming County, Potter County, Sullivan County or Tioga County. **Focus:** General studies. **Qualif.:** Applicants must be enrolled at the Pennsylvania College of Technology; must be enrolled in an approved Tech prep high school program and subsequently enroll in a Certificate, Associate or Bachelor's Degree program at the Pennsylvania College of Technology. In schools without approved Tech Prep programs, students must enroll in a high school vocational-technical program and subsequently enroll in a Certificate, Associate, or Bachelor's Degree program at the Pennsylvanian College of Technology. Applicants must have a GPA of "B" or higher and must be enrolled full-time. Preference will be given to continuing students in subsequent years if a cumulative GPA of 2.80 is maintained in the program. **Criteria:** Selection will be based on the committee's criteria.

Funds Avail.: No specific amount. **To Apply:** Applicants must submit a writing sample as defined by the Pennsylvania College of Technology Prep office. **Contact:** Joan Kay, Executive Director, Pennsylvania College of Technology Foundation, Inc., One College Ave., Williamsport, PA 17701-5799; 570-320-8020; jkay@pct.edu.

2981 ■ Eleanor M. Wolfson Memorial Scholarship Fund *(Undergraduate/Scholarship)*

Purpose: To provide scholarship for Montoursville Area High School seniors who will be attending Yale College. **Focus:** Creative writing. **Qualif.:** Students must be graduating seniors at Montoursville Area High School. If there are no graduating students planning to attend Yale College, a graduating student with an outstanding academic record and a demonstrated talent in creative writing will be considered. **Criteria:** Selection will be based on academic merit and potential.

Funds Avail.: No specific amount. **To Apply:** Applicants may contact and request an application from the Montoursville Area High School. **Contact:** Ronda Albert, Montoursville Area High School, 100 N Arch St, Montoursville, PA 17754; 570-368-3509; ralbert@montoursville.k12.pa.us.

2982 ■ Wendy Y. Wolfson Memorial Scholarship Fund *(Undergraduate/Scholarship)*

Purpose: To provide scholarship for Montoursville Area High School seniors who will be attending Yale College. **Focus:** Music; Drama criticism. **Qualif.:** Students must be graduating seniors of Montoursville Area High School. If there are no graduating students planning to attend Yale College, graduating students with an outstanding academic record and a demonstrated talent in music or drama will be considered. **Criteria:** Selection will be based on academic merit and potential.

Funds Avail.: No specific amount. **To Apply:** Applicants may contact and request an application from the Montoursville Area High School. **Contact:** Ronda Albert, Montoursville Area High School, 100 N Arch St, Montoursville, PA 17754; 570-368-3509; ralbert@montoursville.k12.pa.us.

Awards are arranged alphabetically below their administering organizations

2983 ■ Allison E. Fisher Memorial Fund

PO Box 43402
Baltimore, MD 21236
Ph: (410)679-0595
E-mail: fishers@verizon.net
URL: http://www.allisonfisherfund.org

2984 ■ Allison E. Fisher Scholarships *(Undergraduate/Scholarship)*

Purpose: To provide financial assistance to students who are attending an accredited four-year university. **Focus:** Journalism; Photography; Radio and television. **Qualif.:** Applicants must be any foreign or U.S. students who are majoring in journalism-print, photography or radio and television or planning a career in one of those fields; must be currently attending accredited four-year university; must have cumulative grade point average of 3.0 and be enrolled in undergraduate or graduate school during the award year. **Criteria:** Applicants are evaluated based on academic and financial need.

Funds Avail.: $2,500. **To Apply:** Applicants must submit all the required application information.

2985 ■ St. Stephen A.M.E. Allison E. Fisher Book Awards *(Undergraduate/Scholarship)*

Purpose: To provide financial assistance to graduating senior students who have been accepted to a two-year community college or four-year college or university. **Focus:** General studies. **Qualif.:** Applicants must be graduating senior students who attended St. Stephen A.M.E. and who have been accepted to a two-year community college or four-year college or university. **Criteria:** Recipients are selected based on the criteria designed by the Scholarship Selection Committee.

Funds Avail.: $300. **To Apply:** Applicants must submit all the required application information.

2986 ■ Spirit of Allison Graduation Award *(High School/Award/Prize)*

Purpose: To provide financial assistance and recognize graduating seniors at Perry Hall High School. **Focus:** General studies. **Qualif.:** Applicants must be graduating seniors at Perry Hall High School. **Criteria:** Applicants are judged based on materials submitted.

Funds Avail.: $500. **To Apply:** Applicants must submit all the application information.

2987 ■ The Flexible Packaging Association

971 Corporate Blvd., Ste. 403
Linthicum, MD 21090
Ph: (410)694-0800
Fax: (410)694-0900
E-mail: fpa@flexpack.org
URL: http://www.flexpack.org

2988 ■ Flexible Packaging Academic Scholarships & Summer Internship Program *(Undergraduate/Internship)*

Purpose: To provide a learning experience on the flexible packaging industry. **Focus:** Industrial design; Industrial education. **Qualif.:** Applicants must be enrolled in an AA, BA, BS or MS degree program; have a 2.7 GPA; have 24 credit hours, 9 credits of which are in packaging, printing or other areas in the converting industry. **Criteria:** Recipient is selected based on the submitted application and supporting materials.

Funds Avail.: $3,000. **To Apply:** Applicants are advised to visit the website for the online application system. Prepare a recommendation letter from a faculty member; and an essay (maximum of 500 words). Send all materials to: Flexible Packaging Association, Attn: Lauren Kinard, 971 Corporate Blvd., Ste. 403, Linthicum, MD 21090, email to: fpa@flexpack.org.

Remarks: Introduced in 2005.

2989 ■ Florida Association Directors of Nursing Administration

200 Butler St., Ste. 305
West Palm Beach, FL 33407
Ph: (561)659-2167
Fax: (561)659-1291
E-mail: fadona@fadona.org
URL: http://www.fadona.org

2990 ■ Florida Association District of Nursing Administration Scholarships *(Undergraduate/Scholarship)*

Purpose: To provide financial assistance to individuals in nursing looking to continue their education in the LTC setting. **Focus:** Nursing. **Qualif.:** Applicants must be currently licensed registered nurses, LPN or certified nursing assistants; must be currently enrolled or accepted in a RN, LPN or undergraduate health care program; or be currently accepted or enrolled in a baccalaureate or master's program in nursing or gerontology program; must have at least two years employment history in long-term care. **Criteria:** Recipients are selected based on academic performance and experience in a health care program.

Funds Avail.: $500. **To Apply:** Applicants must submit a completed application form; must submit a list of employers and dates of employment.

2991 ■ Imogene Ward Nursing Scholarships *(Undergraduate/Scholarship)*

Purpose: To provide financial assistance to individuals in nursing looking to continue their education in the LTC setting. **Focus:** Nursing. **Qualif.:** Applicants must be pursuing education to become registered nurses; must be enrolled in an accredited Florida Nursing program; must be willing to pledge a minimum of two years, working full-time in long-term care in the state of Florida. **Criteria:** Recipients are selected based on demonstrated determination to overcome personal and/or professional obstacles to pursue nursing education, track record of excellence and the potential for future leadership in long-term care.

Funds Avail.: No specific amount. **To Apply:** Applicants must submit a completed application form including name and full contact information; must submit a 300-word or less narrative essay which outlines what it takes to be an exceptional nurse and also expresses reasons they should be considered for the Imogene Ward Nursing Scholarship Award.

2992 ■ Florida Association for Media in Education

2563 Capital Medical Blvd.
Tallahassee, FL 32308
Ph: (850)531-8351

Awards are arranged alphabetically below their administering organizations

Fax: (850)531-8344
E-mail: info@floridamedia.org
URL: http://www.floridamedia.org

2993 ■ Sandy Ulm Scholarships *(Undergraduate/Scholarship)*

Purpose: To help every student in Florida be involved in and have open access to a quality school library media program, administered by a highly competent, certified library media specialist. **Focus:** Media Arts. **Qualif.:** Applicants must be students studying to be school library media specialists. **Criteria:** Recipients are selected based on academic performance.

Funds Avail.: $1,000. **To Apply:** Applicants must submit a completed application form and submit a copy of the transcript of all college credits for the graduate program in which they are currently enrolled, two letters of recommendation (one must come from a professor) and a notarized statement (found in application).

2994 ■ Florida Atlantic Planning Society

777 Galdes Rd.
Boca Raton, FL 33431
Ph: (561)297-3000
E-mail: marketing@fau.edu
URL: http://www.fau.edu

2995 ■ Delores A. Auzenne Fellowship *(Postgraduate/Fellowship)*

Purpose: To encourage minority students to pursue graduate degree in areas where they are historically underrepresented at Florida Atlantic University. **Focus:** Engineering; mathematics and mathematical sciences; Computer and information science; Psychology. **Qualif.:** Applicants must be pursuing graduate degrees in a discipline in which minority students are underrepresented; must be citizens or permanent residents of the United States. **Criteria:** Recipients are selected based on academic performance and financial need.

Funds Avail.: $5,000. **To Apply:** Applicants must submit a transcript from all institutions attended; one-two page statement on how fellowship will assist in the achievement of their career goals and three current letters of recommendation from which one must come from a professor who is familiar with their academic work. **Deadline:** May 11.

2996 ■ The Robert A Catlin/David W. Long Memorial Scholarship *(Undergraduate/Scholarship)*

Purpose: To foster increased interest among African-American undergraduates in urban planning as a graduate field of study and as a professional career. **Focus:** Environmental science. **Qualif.:** Applicants must be African-Americans who are entering juniors or seniors; must be majoring in urban planning or related fields; must have a minimum of 3.0 GPA and must be full-time enrolled students. **Criteria:** Recipients are selected based on academic performance and financial need.

Funds Avail.: $2,500. **To Apply:** Applicants must submit a completed application form, personal statement, two letters of recommendation, one sealed official academic transcript for each college or university attended and a self-addressed, stamped postcard for notification of the receipt of a complete application form. **Deadline:** October 30.

2997 ■ Florida Atlantic Planning Society Graduate Fellowships for Academic Excellence *(Postgraduate/Fellowship)*

Purpose: To provide financial assistance in the form of a fellowship to outstanding graduate students. **Focus:** General studies. **Qualif.:** Applicants must be degree-seeking students with a minimum GPA of 3.5; must have completed a minimum of one semester in a FAU graduate program. **Criteria:** Recipients are selected based on academic performance and financial need.

Funds Avail.: $5,000. **To Apply:** Applicants must submit two letters of recommendation from FAU Faculty, unofficial transcript of all graduate works attempted by the nominee and application form. **Deadline:** May 11.

2998 ■ Royal Palm Audobon Society Environmental Fellowships *(Postgraduate/Fellowship)*

Purpose: To provide funds to graduate students preparing for a career in the promotion of environmentalism, environmental preservation or environmental protection. **Focus:** Environmental science. **Qualif.:** Applicants must be graduate students conducting research towards increasing public understanding of environmental problems and solutions. **Criteria:** Recipients are selected based on academic performance and financial need.

Funds Avail.: $1,500. **To Apply:** Applicant must submit a one-two page description of academic background, interest and research project and one letter of recommendation from a faculty member who is familiar with the student and his or her research. **Deadline:** April 27.

2999 ■ Florida Engineering Society

PO Box 750
Tallahassee, FL 32302-0750
Ph: (850)224-7121
Fax: (850)222-4349
E-mail: fes@fleng.org
URL: http://www.fleng.org

3000 ■ Cesar A. Calas/FES Miami Chapter Scholarships *(Undergraduate/Scholarship)*

Purpose: To encourage and assist students in pursuing engineering careers; to educate the public about engineering; and to promote and enhance engineering education in Florida in order to position ther state as a technological leader in global economy. **Focus:** Engineering. **Qualif.:** Applicants must be attending an accredited college of higher learning and enrolled in an engineering program approved by the Florida Engineering Society Scholarship Committee; must have at least 3.0 GPA; must maintain 12 credit hours per semester; and must be permanent residents of Miami-Dade or Monroe County. **Criteria:** Recipients are selected based on academic performance and financial need.

Funds Avail.: $1,000. **To Apply:** Applicants must submit completed application form; an official transcript; and letter of recommendation from any appropriate source.

3001 ■ Fecon Scholarships *(Undergraduate/Scholarship)*

Purpose: To encourage and assist students in pursuing engineering careers; to educate the public about engineering; and to promote and enhance engineering education in Florida in order to position the state as a technological

Awards are arranged alphabetically below their administering organizations

leader in global economy. **Focus:** Engineering. **Qualif.:** Applicant must be currently enrolled or accepted into a Florida university engineering program; must be in or entering his/her junior or senior year; must have at least 3.0 average on a 4.0 scale; must be recommended by an engineering faculty member; and must be interested in pursuing a career in the field of construction. **Criteria:** Recipients are selected based on academic performance and financial need.

Funds Avail.: $1,000. **To Apply:** Applicants must submit a complete application form and an official transcript. **Deadline:** February 15. **Contact:** 850-224-7121.

3002 ■ FICE Scholarships *(Undergraduate/Scholarship)*

Purpose: To encourage and assist students in pursuing engineering careers; to educate the public about engineering; and to promote and enhance engineering education in Florida in order to position the state as a technological leader in global economy. **Focus:** Engineering. **Qualif.:** Applicants must be U.S. citizens pursuing a bachelor's degree in an Accreditation Board Engineering and Technology (ABET) program and must be entering their junior, senior, or fifth year of college. **Criteria:** Recipients are selected based on academic performance and financial need.

Funds Avail.: $5,000. **To Apply:** Applicants must submit completed application form and an official transcript. **Deadline:** February 1.

3003 ■ Florida Engineering Society Junior College Scholarships *(Undergraduate/Scholarship)*

Purpose: To encourage and assist students in pursuing engineering careers; to educate the public about engineering; and to promote and enhance engineering education in Florida in order to position the state as a technological leader in global economy. **Focus:** Engineering. **Qualif.:** Applicants must be enrolled in the final year of a pre-engineering program in a Florida Junior Community College; must have at least 3.0 grade point average on a 4.0 scale; must be recommended by an engineering faculty member; and must be United States citizen or resident of Florida. **Criteria:** Recipients are selected based on academic performance and financial need, work experience, activities, honors, letters of recommendation along with the evidence of leadership, motivation, character and self-reliance.

Funds Avail.: $1,000. **To Apply:** Applicants must submit a completed application form; an official transcript; and letter of recommendation from any appropriate source.

3004 ■ Florida Engineering Society University Scholarships *(Undergraduate/Scholarship)*

Purpose: To encourage and assist students in pursuing engineering careers; to educate the public about engineering; and to promote and enhance engineering education in Florida in order to position the state as a technological leader in global economy. **Focus:** Engineering. **Qualif.:** Applicant must be entering his or her junior or senior year in the Florida University Engineering Program; must have at least 3.0 grade point average on a 4.0 scale; must be recommended by an engineering faculty member; and must be a U.S. citizen or resident of Florida. **Criteria:** Recipients are selected based on academic performance and financial need.

Funds Avail.: $30,000. **To Apply:** Applicants must submit a completed application form; an official transcript; and letter of recommendation from an engineering faculty member.

3005 ■ David F. Ludovici Scholarships *(Undergraduate/Scholarship)*

Purpose: To encourage and assist students in pursuing engineering careers; to educate the public about engineering; and to promote and enhance engineering education in Florida in order to position the state as a technological leader in global economy. **Focus:** Engineering. **Qualif.:** Applicants must be enrolled in an ABET accredited Florida engineering school and must be interested in civil, structural, or consulting engineering. **Criteria:** Recipients are selected based on academic performance and financial need.

Funds Avail.: $1,000. **To Apply:** Applicants must submit completed application form; an official transcript; and letter of recommendation from any appropriate source.

3006 ■ Raymond W. Miller, PE and Alice E. Miller Scholarships *(Undergraduate/Scholarship)*

Purpose: To encourage and assist students in pursuing engineering careers; to educate the public about engineering; and to promote and enhance engineering education in Florida in order to position the state as a technological leader in global economy. **Focus:** Engineering. **Qualif.:** Applicants must be enrolled in an ABET accredited Florida engineering school and must plan to attend the University of Florida. **Criteria:** Recipients are selected based on academic performance and financial need.

Funds Avail.: $1,000. **To Apply:** Applicants must submit completed application form; an official transcript; and letter of recommendation from any appropriate source.

3007 ■ Raymond W. Miller, PE Scholarships *(Undergraduate/Scholarship)*

Purpose: To encourage and assist students in pursuing engineering careers; to educate the public about engineering; and to promote and enhance engineering education in Florida in order to position the state as a technological leader in global economy. **Focus:** Engineering. **Qualif.:** Applicants must be enrolled in an ABET accredited Florida engineering school and must plan to attend the University of Florida. **Criteria:** Recipients are selected based on academic performance and financial need.

Funds Avail.: $2,500. **To Apply:** Applicants must submit a complete application form; an official transcript; and letter of recommendation from any appropriate source.

3008 ■ Eric Primavera Memorial Scholarships *(Undergraduate/Scholarship)*

Purpose: To encourage and assist students in pursuing engineering careers; to educate the public about engineering; and to promote and enhance engineering education in Florida in order to position the state as a technological leader in global economy. **Focus:** Engineering. **Qualif.:** Applicants must be enrolled in an ABET accredited Florida engineering school and plan to attend the Florida Institute of Technology. **Criteria:** Recipients are selected based on academic performance and financial need.

Funds Avail.: $1,000. **To Apply:** Applicants must submit completed application form; an official transcript; and letter of recommendation from any appropriate source.

3009 ■ Florida Fertilizer and Agrichemical Association

58 4th St. NW, Ste 200
Winter Haven, FL 33881

Awards are arranged alphabetically below their administering organizations

Ph: (863)293-4827
Fax: (863)294-8626
E-mail: mhartney@ffaa.org
URL: http://www.ffaa.org

3010 ■ Florida Fertilizer and Agrichemical Association Scholarships *(Undergraduate/Scholarship)*

Purpose: To promote the study of agriculture in higher education and to encourage students pursuing agriculture studies. **Focus:** Agricultural sciences. **Qualif.:** Applicants must be agriculture junior, senior, or graduate students at the University of Florida, Florida A&M or Florida Southern; must plan to enroll for the semester immediately following the fall semester; must have a minimum GPA of 3.0 on a 4.0 scale. **Criteria:** Recipients are selected based on academic performance and financial need.

Funds Avail.: No specific amount. **To Apply:** Applicants must submit a completed application form. **Contact:** 863-293-4827.

3011 ■ Florida Nursery, Growers, and Landscape Association

1533 Park Center Dr.
Orlando, FL 32835-5705
Ph: (407)295-7994
Fax: (407)295-1619
Free: 800-375-3642
E-mail: info@fngla.org
URL: http://www.fngla.org

3012 ■ James H. Davis Scholarships *(Undergraduate/Scholarship)*

Purpose: To encourage students to pursue careers in Florida's horticulture industry and related pursuits by providing financial assistance for undergraduate, post-graduate, or other advanced education programs in Florida. **Focus:** Horticulture. **Qualif.:** Applicants must be incoming college freshmen, sophomores, juniors, seniors and/or graduate students planning to attend a community college, college or university in the state of Florida; must be full-time students in horticulture program or related field with the intent to graduate in the field; must have a 2.0 or above GPA. **Criteria:** Recipients are selected based on financial need and students' ability to maintain a 2.0 grade point average.

Funds Avail.: No specific amount. **To Apply:** Applicants must complete the application form; must submit a high school or college transcript; an essay and two letters of recommendation.

3013 ■ Florida Nurses Association

1235 E Concord St.
Orlando, FL 32803
Ph: (407)896-3261
Fax: (407)896-9042
E-mail: info@floridanurse.org
URL: http://www.floridanurse.org

3014 ■ Florida Nurses Association Scholarships *(Professional Development/Scholarship)*

Purpose: To serve and support all registered nurses through professional development, advocacy and the promotion of excellence at every level of professional nursing practice. **Focus:** Nursing. **Qualif.:** Applicants must be enrolled in a nationally accredited nursing program; must be students including those in associate, baccalaureate, and master's degree nursing programs or doctoral programs; and must have a minimum GPA of 2.5 for undergraduate and 3.0 GPA for graduate students. **Criteria:** Recipients are selected based on academic performance and potential contribution to the Nursing Professionals Society.

Funds Avail.: No specific amount. **To Apply:** Applicants must submit a completed application form. **Deadline:** June 2.

3015 ■ Florida Outdoor Writers Association

24 NW, 33rd Court, Ste. A
Gainesville, FL 32607
Ph: (352)392-2801
E-mail: info@fowa.org
URL: http://www.fowa.org

3016 ■ Florida Outdoor Writers Association Scholarships *(Undergraduate/Scholarship)*

Purpose: To motivate and encourage young people to enter outdoor communications career fields. **Focus:** Communications; Journalism. **Qualif.:** Applicants must be students at Florida Colleges and universities, or must be students whose applications are endorsed by a FOWA member or a faculty advisor. **Criteria:** Recipients are selected based on the essay, endorsement of the faculty advisor or FOWA member, scholastic merit and extracurricular activities as indicated in the applicant's resume or supporting materials submitted.

Funds Avail.: $500-$1,000. **To Apply:** Applicants must submit a completed application form; must submit an essay, 500-1,000-words, that expresses their appreciation for the outdoor experience; an up-to-date resume; a letter of endorsement from a FOWA member or faculty advisor. **Deadline:** August 31.

3017 ■ Florida Police Chiefs Association

924 N Gadsden St.
Tallahassee, FL 32303
Ph: (850)219-3631
Fax: (850)219-3640
Free: 800-332-8117
E-mail: amercer@fpca.com
URL: http://www.fpca.org

3018 ■ Police Explorer Scholarships Program *(Undergraduate/Scholarship)*

Purpose: To promote public safety legislation. **Focus:** Government. **Qualif.:** Applicants must have been involved in a police explorer post, and have been a member of the post for a minimum of one year by the time of award presentation; must maintain a minimum of a 2.0 overall grade point average and should be completing their senior year in high school, already enrolled in college or planning to attend college. **Criteria:** Recipients are selected based on the information they submit to the foundation.

Funds Avail.: $1,000. **To Apply:** Applicants must submit a completed application form; must submit a 4x5 glossy, black and white or colored headshot photo, in uniform, if possible. **Deadline:** April 15.

3019 ■ Fluid Power Distributor Association

PO Box 1420
Cherry Hill, NJ 08034-0054

Awards are arranged alphabetically below their administering organizations

Ph: (856)424-8998
Fax: (856)424-9248
E-mail: kdemarco@fpda.org
URL: http://www.fpda.org

3020 ■ Tom D. Ralls Memorial Scholarships *(Professional Development/Scholarship)*

Purpose: To promote the ongoing professional development of industry executives. **Focus:** Engineering, Industrial. **Qualif.:** Applicants must be an employee an FPDA Regular (Distributor) Member organization and a member of FPDA Young Executives. **Criteria:** Applications will be reviewed and evaluated by FPDA Executive Committee.

Funds Avail.: Full tuition. **Number Awarded:** 1. **To Apply:** Applicant must provide a letter of recommendation from the company and submit application form and an essay about the applicant's interest to attend the University Industrial Distribution program. **Deadline:** November.

Remarks: Established in memory of Tom D. Ralls, former FPDA President and Chairman. **Contact:** Kathy DeMarco kdemarco@fpda.org.

3021 ■ FMA Foundation

833 Featherstone Rd.
Rockford, IL 61107-6302
Ph: (815)399-8700
Free: 888-394-4362
E-mail: foundation@fmanet.org
URL: http://www.fmafoundation.com

3022 ■ FMA Foundation Scholarships *(Undergraduate/Scholarship)*

Purpose: To provide financial support to students in courses of study that may lead to careers in manufacturing. **Focus:** Engineering; manufacturing. **Qualif.:** Applicants must be full-time students with a minimum 3.0 GPA (for a college scholarship) or a 2.0 GPA (for a trade/technical school scholarship), enrolled in an engineering or manufacturing-related course of study, or a trade or technical program, that may lead to a career in manufacturing; or a member of FMA, TPA, or OPC the employee of a member company; or the child of a member; or the child of a member company's employee. **Criteria:** Applicants are evaluated based on academic achievement.

Funds Avail.: $2,500 up to $5,000. **To Apply:** Applicants must submit completed online application form and other materials by the application deadline. **Deadline:** April 4.

3023 ■ Food Processing Suppliers Association

1451 Dolley Madison Blvd., Ste. 200
McLean, VA 22101
Ph: (703)761-2600
E-mail: info@fpsa.org
URL: http://www.fpsa.org

3024 ■ Food Engineering Scholarships *(Postdoctorate, Postgraduate/Scholarship)*

Purpose: To attract and retain qualified personnel for the food processing industry. **Focus:** Food science and technology; service food careers. **Qualif.:** Applicants must be current outstanding employees of FPSA and juniors or sophomores in engineering in an educational institution in the U.S. or Canada having an approved degree program or option, be scholastically outstanding, have a well-rounded personality and have an intention to pursue a career in the food industry. **Criteria:** Priority is given to applicants with satisfactory contributions to developments and applications in the food and processing industry.

Funds Avail.: $2,500 for enrollment in a food engineering curriculum and $500 travel grant to attend FPSA Expo. **Number Awarded:** 2. **To Apply:** Candidates must submit one original and seven copies of all application materials in order: application form with certification of Department Head; supporting materials (course details, and entire proof of academic performance); official transcript; letter of recommendation to the FPSA office. **Deadline:** March 30.

Remarks: Established in 1983 as a memorial to food industry leaders Paul K. Girton and Gordon A. Houran. **Contact:** Robyn Roche at rroche@fpsa.org.

3025 ■ V. Duane Rath Graduate Research Fellowships *(Doctorate, Graduate, Postdoctorate/Fellowship)*

Purpose: To financially assist undergraduate and graduate students in researches. **Focus:** Food science and technology; service food careers. **Qualif.:** Candidates must be Masters or PhD candidates in the dairy or food sciences, attending a North American university. **Criteria:** Successful nominees will be selected on the basis of academic performance, commitment to a career in dairy or food industries, evidence of leadership ability and initiative, character and integrity, research proposal; and, for students currently conducting research, a progress report.

Funds Avail.: $10,000 an expense-paid trip to the FPSA Annual Conference to accept the award. **Number Awarded:** 2. **To Apply:** Candidates must submit one original and seven copies of all application materials in order: application form with certification of Department Head; supporting materials (course details, and entire proof of academic performance); official transcript; letter of recommendation to the FPSA office. **Deadline:** December 1.

Remarks: Established by the contributions of V. Duane Rath, Chairman of the Rath Manufacturing Company in coordination with FPSA. **Contact:** Robyn Roche, rroche@fpsa.org.

3026 ■ Thomas B. Fordman Foundation

1016 16th NW 8th Fl.
Washington, DC 20036
Ph: (202)223-5452
Fax: (202)223-9226
E-mail: letters@edexcellence.net
URL: http://www.edexcellence.net

3027 ■ Fordham Fellowships *(Undergraduate/Fellowship)*

Purpose: To support more bright and ambitious people into the world of education policy. **Focus:** Education. **Qualif.:** Applicants must have undergraduate degree; have spent several years in the working; have keen interest in public policy. **Criteria:** Applicants will be selected by admissions committee based on the strength of their written application, recommendations and references.

Funds Avail.: $25,000. **To Apply:** Applicants must submit a resume; cover letter; contact information of three references. **Deadline:** April. **Contact:** Liam Julian; Program Coordinator; ljulian@edexcellence.net.

3028 ■ Fordham Scholarships *(Doctorate/ Scholarship)*

Purpose: To provide educational assistance for junior researchers working on key issues in American Education. **Focus:** Education. **Qualif.:** Applicants must be advanced doctoral students and junior faculty members especially those in economics, law, political science and public policy. **Criteria:** Applicants must be selected based on the application review by a team of scholars, policymakers and Institute personnel.

Funds Avail.: $15,000. **Number Awarded:** varies. **To Apply:** Applicants must submit resume or curriculum vitae; names of three professional references; proposed research project. **Deadline:** February. **Contact:** Liam Julian; ljulian@edexcellence.net.

3029 ■ Forest History Society

701 William Vickers Ave.
Durham, NC 27701-3162
Ph: (919)682-9319
Fax: (919)682-2349
E-mail: recluce2@duke.edu
URL: http://www.foresthistory.org

3030 ■ Alfred D. Bell Travel Grants *(All/Grant)*

Purpose: To provide financial assistance to researchers conducting in-depth studies using resources in the society's archive and library. **Focus:** General studies. **Qualif.:** Candidates must be researchers conducting in-depth studies who use FHS research resources to support their work. **Criteria:** Preference is given to persons whose research topics are well covered in the FHS library and archives. Preference is also given to young scholars per the wishes of the Bell family.

Funds Avail.: Support travel and lodging expenses of up to $950. **To Apply:** Applicants must submit a completed hard copy of the application form at the FHS office.

Remarks: The grant is given in honor of Alfred D. Bell, Jr., former VP of Forest History Society (FHS). **Contact:** Cheryl Oakes.

3031 ■ Frederick K. Weyerhaeuser Forest History Fellowships *(Graduate/Fellowship)*

Purpose: To support FHS programs and to strengthen the society's affiliation with Duke University. **Focus:** Forestry, Environmental conservation and History. **Qualif.:** Applicants must be Duke University graduate students pursuing research in the fields of forest, conservation or environmental history. **Criteria:** Fellowship recipient is selected on the basis of merit. Proposals are judged in terms of overall significance and quality of presentation.

Funds Avail.: The fellowship consists of an $11,000 stipend, distributed quarterly. **To Apply:** Applicants must submit a narrative description of research (up to eight pages), including significance of topic, research approach, author's background, research and writing schedule and budget. Attachments are not necessary but may include previous publications, written chapters and basic bibliography; curriculum vitae and 2-3 letters of recommendation from persons knowledgeable of the applicant's research. Letters of recommendation should address the author's qualifications and may describe the significance of the topic to forest and conservation history; five hard copies of the proposal and an electronic copy of the proposal without supporting documents. Applicants must provide a cover letter that states the title of the proposed research, a one-paragraph summary of the significance of the project and a description of the historical nature of the project. **Deadline:** January 31.

Remarks: The fellowship was established in 1986 to honor the memory of Frederick K. Weyerhaeuser. **Contact:** Andrea Anderson at the above address (see entry 3029).

3032 ■ Forward Face

317 E 34th St., Ste. 901A
New York, NY 10016
Ph: (212)684-5860
Fax: (212)684-5864
E-mail: info@forwardface.org
URL: http://www.forwardface.org

3033 ■ Forward Face Scholarships *(Professional Development/Scholarship)*

Purpose: To support children and young adults with craniofacial conditions. **Focus:** General studies. **Qualif.:** Applicant must be a child or young adult with craniofacial conditions (age 12-13 years old). **Criteria:** Application will be evaluated by the Scholarship Committee.

Funds Avail.: $500-$1,000. **To Apply:** Applicants are advised to visit Forward Face for the application requirements and instructions at info@forwardface.org.

Remarks: Awards are specifically targeted to school or college fees and are paid directly to a specified institution.

3034 ■ Foundation for the Carolinas

217 S Tryon St.
Charlotte, NC 28202
Ph: (704)973-4500
Free: 800-973-7244
URL: http://www.fftc.org

3035 ■ Henry S. and Carolyn Adams Scholarship Fund *(Undergraduate/Scholarship)*

Purpose: To provide educational assistance for deserving students with financial need who are residents of Union County, NC. **Focus:** General studies. **Qualif.:** Applicants must have a minimum cumulative grade point average of 3.0 (on a 4.0 scale); must be legal residents of Union County, NC; must be nominated by the principal of their high school; and must demonstrate a substantial need for financial assistance. **Criteria:** Recipients are selected based on academic achievement; school and community involvement and personal achievements.

Funds Avail.: $4,000. **To Apply:** Applicants must submit completed application form; official copy of high school transcript(s), including SAT/ACT scores; one to two-paged typed statement expressing qualifications for the scholarship, educational goals and financial need for scholarship assistance; two completed recommendation forms including at least one from a current teacher; and a copy of SAR from FAFSA. **Deadline:** March 15.

3036 ■ Herb Adrian Memorial Scholarship Fund *(Undergraduate/Scholarship)*

Purpose: To provide financial assistance for students at the University of North Carolina at Charlotte who have expressed an interest in the multi-family housing field.

Awards are arranged alphabetically below their administering organizations

Focus: Finance; Construction; Management. **Qualif.:** Applicants must be rising UNC Charlotte juniors or seniors; must have interest in the multi-housing industry, including but not limited to finance, construction and management; and must demonstrate financial need. **Criteria:** Recipients are selected based on financial need.

Funds Avail.: No specific amount. **To Apply:** Applicants must contact the UNC Charlotte Student Financial Aid Office at 704687-2461 for application.

3037 ■ African American Network - Carolinas Scholarship Fund *(Undergraduate/Scholarship)*

Purpose: To provide scholarships for college-bound students from North and South Carolina who are pursuing a major in engineering, math, science, computer science, accounting, finance or business administration. **Focus:** Engineering; Mathematics and mathematical sciences; Science; Computer and information sciences; Accounting; Finance; Business administration. **Qualif.:** Applicants must be graduating seniors at a North or South Carolina high school; must attend a four-year college or university located in North or South Carolina; must plan to major in engineering, computer science, the sciences, accounting, finance or business administration. **Criteria:** Applicants are judged based on grade point average; residence; leadership skills and financial need.

Funds Avail.: No specific amount. **Number Awarded:** 2. **To Apply:** Applicants must submit all the required application information.

3038 ■ William Tasse Alexander Scholarship Fund *(Undergraduate/Scholarship)*

Purpose: To provide financial assistance for undergraduate students from Mecklenburg County, NC, primarily in the field of education. **Focus:** Education. **Qualif.:** Applicants must be legal residents of Mecklenburg County, NC who are matriculating full-time juniors or seniors in college; must have a minimum cumulative grade point average of 3.0 on a 4.0 scale; and must be majoring in the field of education or taking courses leading to a career in teaching. **Criteria:** Applicants are evaluated based on academic performance; school and community involvement and personal achievements; and demonstrated potential for a career as an educator.

Funds Avail.: $1,000 to $3,500. **To Apply:** Applicants must submit completed application form; official transcript(s) of academic coursework and grades for at least the last two years; copy of applicants' NTE/Praxis Series scores, if available; three recommendation forms (two from instructors or other campus administrators and one from an employer or other non-related individual); one to two pages typewritten statement expressing reasons for applying for scholarship, qualifications, and educational/career goals; and a copy of the estimated expense budget for tuition, room and board, books, etc. at the school they attended. **Deadline:** March 1.

3039 ■ Andersen Nontraditional Scholarship for Women's Education and Retraining *(Undergraduate/Scholarship)*

Purpose: To provide financial support and encouragement for adult women age 25 and older who are raising school-age children (grades K-12) and hope to earn a two-year nursing degree or a four-year undergraduate degree in the field of their choice. **Focus:** General studies. **Qualif.:** Applicants must be nontraditional female students age 25 or older at the time of the application deadline; legal residents of Mecklenburg County, NC or contiguous county in North Carolina or South Carolina; enrolled or planning to enroll as full-time, degree-seeking students at an accredited institution in North Carolina or South Carolina. **Criteria:** Applicants who are single parents are given preference, with the following basis criteria: financial need as determined by the costs of college attendance compared with an applicants' household income and other financial factors; demonstrated potential for academic success.

Funds Avail.: No specific amount. **To Apply:** Applicants must submit a completed application form; copy of the Student Aid Report from FAFSA; official transcripts of grades for the applicant's most recently completed coursework; three recommendation forms from non-related adults such as instructors or other campus administrators, employers, mentors, etc.; updated, typed resume; one to two-page typed personal statement expressing why the applicant is applying for the scholarship and the applicant's educational and career goals; and copy of the applicant's federal tax return for the preceding year showing dependents and adjusted gross income. **Deadline:** April 2.

3040 ■ Bank of America Junior Achievement Scholarship Fund *(Undergraduate/Scholarship)*

Purpose: To provide financial support for undergraduate students who have expressed an interest in business through their service to Junior Achievement in Atlanta, GA. **Focus:** Business; Technology. **Qualif.:** Applicants must be graduating high school seniors with a minimum cumulative GPA of 3.0 on a 4.0 scale and who have actively participated in Junior Achievement of Georgia and are planning to major in business or computer technology. **Criteria:** Applicants are evaluated based on academic merit and financial need.

Funds Avail.: No specific amount. **To Apply:** Applicants must submit all the required application information.

3041 ■ Pete and Ellen Bensley Memorial Scholarship Fund *(Undergraduate/Scholarship)*

Purpose: To assist graduating seniors at East Mecklenburg High School in Charlotte, NC who demonstrate interest in foreign languages and/or journalism. **Focus:** Foreign languages; Journalism. **Qualif.:** Applicants must be legal residents of Mecklenburg County and graduating seniors at East Mecklenburg High School who are planning to major in foreign languages and/or journalism. **Criteria:** Applicants are selected based on the criteria designed by the Scholarship Selection Committee.

Funds Avail.: Amount not specified. **To Apply:** Applicants must submit all the required materials and complete application information. **Contact:** The Scholarship Coordinator at East Mecklenburg High School, 980-343-6430.

3042 ■ Donald H. Bernstein/John B. Talbert, Jr. Scholarship Fund *(Undergraduate/Scholarship)*

Purpose: To provide financial support for children of the employees of Hanes Companies, Inc., USA. **Focus:** General studies. **Qualif.:** Applicants must be graduating high school seniors who have a minimum cumulative grade point average of 3.0 (on a 4.0 scale). Parents or legal guardians of applicants must be employees who have completed at least two years (24 months) of full-time service with Hanes Companies, Inc. USA prior to the application deadline. Children of employees shall be defined to include natural-born or legally-adopted dependent children and stepchildren and wards of employees. **Criteria:** Applicants are evaluated based on academic/personal

Awards are arranged alphabetically below their administering organizations

achievement; financial need; school and community involvement.

Funds Avail.: $1,000 to $2,500. **To Apply:** Applicants must submit completed application form; copy of high school transcript(s), including SAT/ACT scores; three recommendation forms (two from teachers or other school personnel and one from an employer or other non-related adult); one to two-paged typed statement expressing the reason for applying for the scholarship, qualifications, and educational/career goals; and letter from an official of Hanes Companies, Inc. USA where parent or legally-appointed guardians are employed.

3043 ■ T. Frank Booth Memorial Scholarship Fund *(Undergraduate/Scholarship)*

Purpose: To provide financial assistance for accounting students at East Carolina University. **Focus:** Accounting. **Qualif.:** Applicants must be legal residents of North Carolina who are juniors or seniors with a 3.0 minimum cumulative grade point average (on 4.0 scale) who have declared major in accounting. **Criteria:** Applicants are evaluated based on merit and financial need.

Funds Avail.: No specific amount. **To Apply:** Applicants must submit all the required application information. **Contact:** East Carolina University Department of Accounting, 252-328-6055.

3044 ■ Cadmus Communications Corporation Graphics Scholarship Endowment Fund *(Undergraduate/Scholarship)*

Purpose: To assist students who are enrolled in the associate degree in Graphic Arts Management Program at Central Piedmont Community College. **Focus:** Graphic art and design. **Qualif.:** Applicants must have completed at least two semesters of the CPCC Graphic Arts and Imaging Technology Program with 3.0 minimum cumulative grade point average on 4.0 scale. **Criteria:** Applicants are evaluated based on criteria designed by the Scholarship Selection Committee.

Funds Avail.: No specific amount. **To Apply:** Applicants must submit all the required application information and materials. **Contact:** CPCC Graphic Arts and Imaging Technology Program; 704-330-4437.

3045 ■ Kasie Ford Capling Memorial Scholarship Endowment Fund *(Undergraduate/Scholarship)*

Purpose: To provide financial assistance for high school seniors graduating from Charlotte-Mecklenburg high schools (public or private) who have experienced the death of one or both parents. **Focus:** General studies. **Qualif.:** Applicants must be graduating high school seniors from a high school located in Mecklenburg County, NC (public or private) planning to enter a four-year degree program at an accredited institution; must be legal residents of Mecklenburg County, NC; and must have experienced the death of one or both parents. **Criteria:** Applicants are evaluated based on the criteria designed by the Scholarship Selection Committee.

Funds Avail.: No specific amount. **To Apply:** Applicants must submit all the required application information.

3046 ■ Julian E. Carnes Scholarship Fund *(Undergraduate/Scholarship)*

Purpose: To provide financial assistance for students at Clemson University and the University of North Carolina at Charlotte who are preparing for a career in a technological field appropriate to meet the requirements of the U.S. Patent Office as a patent agent or attorney. **Focus:** Engineering; Chemistry; Physics; Biology; Computer and information sciences. **Qualif.:** Applicants must be legal residents of North or South Carolina; must be rising juniors or seniors at Clemson University or UNC Charlotte whose academic major is appropriate to meet the requirements of the U.S. Patent Office for admission as a patent agent or attorney (including but not limited to engineering, chemistry, physics, biology and computer science); and must have at least a 3.0 cumulative grade point average (on a 4.0 scale). **Criteria:** Applicants are evaluated based on merit.

Funds Avail.: No specific amount. **To Apply:** Applicants must submit all the required application information. **Contact:** Clemson University Office of Student Financial Aid, 864-656-2280 or the UNC Charlotte Student Financial Aid Office, 704-687-2461.

3047 ■ Carolina Panthers Scholarship Fund *(Graduate/Scholarship)*

Purpose: To provide graduate level scholarships for athletes in North and South Carolina. **Focus:** General studies. **Qualif.:** Applicants must have earned an intercollegiate varsity letter in college; must be graduating senior athletes at an accredited North or South Carolina college or university; have minimum cumulative grade point average of 3.0 on a 4.0 scale; must receive a nomination for scholarship consideration from their current Athletic Director. **Criteria:** Applicants are evaluated based on academic performance; record of leadership and citizenship; school and community involvement and personal achievements.

Funds Avail.: $10,000. **To Apply:** Applicants must submit completed application form; official transcript; copy of score report from the Graduate Record Exam (GRE), Law School Admissions Test (LSAT), Medical College Admissions Test (MCAT) or other appropriate graduate admission test scores, if available; three recommendation forms which include one from a faculty member in major course of study, one from a member of the Athletic Department and one from another school official or other non-related individual familiar with the applicants' extracurricular and leadership involvement; and a typed double-spaced personal statement not to exceed 1,000 words expressing the reason for applying for the scholarship, involvement in athletics, and educational/career goals. **Deadline:** March 30.

3048 ■ Carolinas-Virginias Retail Hardware Scholarship Fund *(Undergraduate/Scholarship)*

Purpose: To support the children of employees of member firms of the Carolinas-Virginias Region of the National Retail Hardware Association. **Focus:** General studies. **Qualif.:** Applicants must have a minimum cumulative grade point average of 2.5 on a 4.0 scale; whose parents or legally-appointed guardians are employees who have completed at least two years of full-time service with a member firm of the Carolinas-Virginias Region of the National Retail Hardware Association; children of employees shall be defined to include natural-born or legally-adopted dependent children and stepchildren and wards of employees. **Criteria:** Applicants are evaluated based on academic achievement including grade point average and performance on tests designed to measure preparation and ability for postsecondary study; school and community involvement and personal achievements; work experience particularly in retail hardware.

Funds Avail.: $500 up to $2,000. **To Apply:** Applicants must submit completed application form; copy of the Student Aid Report (SAR) from FAFSA; official transcript(s) of high school and/or college coursework and grades for at least the last two years, including SAT/ACT scores if taken; three recommendation forms, two from teachers or other school personnel and one from an employer or other non-related adult; one to two-page typed statement expressing the reason on why applicant is applying for the scholarship, qualifications and educational and career goals; a letter from an official of the member firm of the Carolinas-Virginias Region of the National Retail Hardware Association where parent or legally-appointed guardian is employed. **Deadline:** February 15.

3049 ■ Charlotte Housing Authority Scholarship Fund (CHASF) *(Undergraduate/Scholarship)*

Purpose: To provide educational assistance for young residents of housing owned or managed by the Charlotte Housing Authority. **Focus:** General studies. **Qualif.:** Applicants must be residents of public housing owned or managed by the Charlotte Housing Authority. Applicants attending college, vocational or technical school for the first time must not be over 21 years of age as of September 1 of the school year for which the scholarship award is to be made; those who have previously attended a college, vocational or technical school must not be over 24 years of age as of September 1 of the school year for which the scholarship award is to be made. **Criteria:** Applicants are evaluated based on financial need; academic performance; personal achievements; school and community involvement; and commitment to and demonstrated potential for success in college, technical or vocational school.

Funds Avail.: $500 up to $3,400. **To Apply:** Applicants must submit completed application form; official transcript(s) of coursework and grades for at least the first two years, including SAT/ACT scores if taken; three recommendation forms (one from an adult in the housing community where the applicant lives, one from a teacher, counselor or other school administrator, and one from an employer, minister, community leader or other non-related adult); one to two pages typed personal statement expressing the applicant's educational and career goals and financial need for scholarship assistance; and copy of the applicant's FAFSA or student aid report. **Deadline:** March 1.

3050 ■ Charlotte-Mecklenburg Schools Scholarship Incentive Program *(Undergraduate/Scholarship)*

Purpose: To provide motivation and encouragement for Charlotte-Mecklenburg public high school students with financial need to stay in school, graduate and pursue post-secondary education. **Focus:** General studies. **Qualif.:** Applicants must be graduating seniors at a Charlotte-Mecklenburg public high school; must be participants in the Communities In Schools ThinkCOLLEGE Program or the Charlotte-Mecklenburg Schools AVID Program; must be legal residents of Mecklenburg County, NC; and must have 2.5 minimum cumulative grade point average on a 4.0 scale. **Criteria:** Applicants will be evaluated based on financial need; academic/personal achievement; and school/community involvement.

Funds Avail.: $800 to $1,500. **To Apply:** Applicants must submit completed application form; official copy of high school transcript(s), including SAT/ACT scores; two recommendation forms from a teacher, counselor or other school administrator, and the other one from an employer, community leader or non-related adult; one to two pages typed personal statement; and copy of SAR from FAFSA. **Deadline:** March 1.

3051 ■ Children's Scholarship Fund of Charlotte *(High School/Scholarship)*

Purpose: To assist children in grades K-8 intending to attend tuition-based schools which their families could not otherwise afford. **Focus:** General studies. **Qualif.:** Applicants must be legal resident children of Mecklenburg County, NC in grades K-8 attending or planning to attend a tuition-based school in the Charlotte-Mecklenburg region. **Criteria:** Recipients are selected based on financial need.

Funds Avail.: No specific amount. **To Apply:** Applicants must submit all the required application information. **Deadline:** October 1.

3052 ■ Lula Faye Clegg Memorial Scholarship Fund *(Undergraduate/Scholarship)*

Purpose: To provide financial assistance for students majoring in education at the University of North Carolina at Charlotte. **Focus:** Education. **Qualif.:** Applicants must be graduates of a high school in the Charlotte-Mecklenburg public school system; must rank in the top 10% of graduating high school class; and must have strong interest and commitment to a career in teaching. **Criteria:** Applicants are evaluated based on the criteria designed by the Scholarship Selection Committee.

Funds Avail.: No specific amount. **To Apply:** Applicants must submit all the required application information. **Contact:** UNC Charlotte Student Financial Aid Office, 704-687-2461.

3053 ■ Cole Foundation Undergraduate Scholarship Program *(Undergraduate/Scholarship)*

Purpose: To increase the number of high school graduates from Richmond County, NC pursuing post-secondary education. **Focus:** General studies. **Qualif.:** Applicants must be legal residents of Richmond County, NC; must be high school seniors scheduled to graduate in the spring of the current school year. Students applying for four-year scholarships must have a minimum cumulative grade point average of 3.0 (on 4.0 scale). Students applying for two-year scholarships must have a minimum cumulative grade point average of 2.5 (on a 4.0 scale). **Criteria:** Preference is given to applicants whose parents do not have a college degree and will be evaluated based on financial need; academic achievement; school and community involvement; and personal achievements.

Funds Avail.: $2,000 for two-year scholarship; $4,000 for four-year scholarships. **Number Awarded:** 2. **To Apply:** Applicants must submit completed application form; copy of SAR from FAFSA; official copy of the applicant's high school transcript(s), including SAT/ACT scores if taken; type-written statement expressing educational and career goals, reasons for applying for the scholarship and why they deserve the scholarship; and copy of both parents' federal tax return(s) for the preceding year showing dependents and adjusted gross income. **Deadline:** March 1.

3054 ■ Sally Cole Visual Arts Scholarship Fund *(Undergraduate/Scholarship)*

Purpose: To provide financial assistance for Richmond County, NC students with demonstrated talent and career interests in the visual arts. **Focus:** Visual arts. **Qualif.:** Applicants must be planning to attend an accredited two-year or four-year postsecondary institution with a degree program in visual arts; must be high school seniors in good academic standing scheduled to graduate in the spring of the current school year; must have an expressed and demonstrated interest in the visual and/or studio arts which primarily includes, but are not limited to, painting, drawing, sculpture, illustration and ceramics; must be legal residents of Richmond County, NC. **Criteria:** Applicants are evaluated based on academic achievement; school and community involvement and personal achievements; and demonstrated aptitude and career potential in the visual arts.

Funds Avail.: $7,500. **To Apply:** Applicants must submit completed application form; official copy of high school transcript(s), including SAT/ACT scores if taken; three recommendation forms, two of which must come from individuals able to evaluate the applicants' aptitude and career potential in the visual arts; one to two pages typewritten statement expressing a) applicants' reasons for applying for the scholarship, b) applicants' interest in the arts, c) applicants' educational and career goals in the field of visual arts; and samples (3-5 labeled color slides) of applicants' original artwork. **Deadline:** March 1.

3055 ■ Judy Crocker Memorial Scholarship Fund *(Undergraduate/Scholarship)*

Purpose: To provide financial assistance for Winthrop University students with an interest in Education, Human Services and related majors. **Focus:** Education. **Qualif.:** Applicants must be legal residents of York County, SC who are rising juniors or seniors at Winthrop University, located in Rock Hill, SC, majoring in education, human services or a related field with 2.9 minimum cumulative grade point average (on a 4.0 scale) and who demonstrate financial need. **Criteria:** Recipients are selected based on financial need.

Funds Avail.: No specific amount. **To Apply:** Applicants must submit all the required application information. **Contact:** Winthrop University Office of Financial Aid, 803-323-2189.

3056 ■ Crowder Scholarship Fund *(Undergraduate/Scholarship)*

Purpose: To provide financial assistance for children of employees of general contracting companies headquartered in Mecklenburg County, NC. **Focus:** General studies. **Qualif.:** Children of employees are defined as natural-born or legally-adopted dependent children and stepchildren and wards of employees. Parents or legally-appointed guardians of applicants must have worked for their respective general contracting company for at least three years prior to the application deadline. A minimum cumulative grade point average of 2.0 (on a 4.0 scale) is required. **Criteria:** Applicants are evaluated based on academic achievement; financial need; school and community involvement; and personal achievements. Preference will be given to children of employees of Crowder Construction Company.

Funds Avail.: $1,000. **To Apply:** Applicants must submit completed application form; copy of SAR from FAFSA; official transcript(s) of high school and/or college coursework and grades for at least the last two years, including SAT/ACT scores if taken; three recommendation forms; a one to two-paged typed statement expressing why the applicant is applying for the scholarship, applicant's qualifications and the applicant's educational and career goals; a letter from an official of the general contracting company where the applicant's parent is employed, certifying that the parent is an employee and stating the employee's position and length of service; and a copy of both parents' federal tax return for the preceding year showing dependents and adjusted gross income. **Deadline:** February 15.

3057 ■ The E.R. and Lilian B. Dimmette Scholarship Fund *(Undergraduate/Scholarship)*

Purpose: To provide financial assistance for undergraduate students who "fall between the cracks" of financial aid and/or scholarship programs. **Focus:** General studies. **Qualif.:** Applicants must be nominated by the Superintendent of Schools in their county; must have a minimum cumulative grade point average of 2.5 (on a 4.0 scale); and must be legal residents of Gaston, Iredell, Mecklenburg, Rowan or Wilkes County, North Carolina. **Criteria:** Applicants are evaluated based on demonstrated substantial need for financial assistance.

Funds Avail.: $1,000 to $4,000. **To Apply:** Applicants must submit completed application form; copy of the SAR from FAFSA; official copy of high school transcript(s), including SAT/ACT scores; three recommendation forms (two from teachers or other school personnel and one from an employer or other non-related adult); one to two-paged typed statement expressing qualifications for the scholarship, educational goals and financial need for scholarship assistance; copy of both parents' federal tax return for the preceding year showing dependents and adjusted gross income; and copy of estimated expense budget for tuition, fees, room, board, books, etc. for the school planning to attend. **Deadline:** February 15.

3058 ■ Laura M. Fleming Scholarship Fund *(Undergraduate/Scholarship)*

Purpose: To provide financial assistance for children of Founders Federal Credit Union members intending to attend an accredited college, vocational or technical school of their choice. **Focus:** General studies. **Qualif.:** Applicants must be children of Founders Federal Credit Union members defined as natural born or legally adopted children and stepchildren and wards of employees; must be high school seniors graduating in the spring of the current school year; must have a minimum 3.5 cumulative grade point average (on a 4.0 scale). Applicant's parents or legally appointed guardians must be Founders Credit Union members in good standing for a minimum of two years (24 months) prior to the application deadline. **Criteria:** Applicants are evaluated based on financial need; record of good citizenship evidenced by school and community involvement; and academic achievement.

Funds Avail.: $1,000 up to $2,500. **To Apply:** Applicants must submit completed application form; official copy of most recent high school transcript; three recommendation forms (two from current teachers or other school personnel and one from an employer or other non-relative); two typed essays of 400 words or less on topics provided in the application form; documentation of school and community involvement; and a copy of Student Air Report (SAR) from FAFSA. **Deadline:** March 1.

3059 ■ Foundation for the Carolinas Rotary Scholarship Fund *(Undergraduate/Scholarship)*

Purpose: To provide financial assistance for students intending to pursue college but who are not capable of paying the school expenses. **Focus:** General studies. **Qualif.:** Applicants must be at least college juniors or seniors at a four-year institution enrolling as full-time students; must have a minimum 3.0 cumulative grade point average (on a 4.0 scale); and must demonstrate financial need. **Criteria:** Recipients are selected based on academic merit, financial need and community service.

Funds Avail.: $1,000 to $2,000. **To Apply:** Applicants must submit completed application form; copy of Student Aid Report (SAR) from Free Application for Federal Student Aid; official transcript(s) of academic coursework and grades for at least the last two years; three recommendation forms (two from instructors or other campus administrators and one from an employer or other non-related individual in Charlotte-Mecklenburg area); one to two-paged typed statement expressing reasons for applying for the scholarship; and a copy of the estimated expense budget for tuition, room and board, books, etc. **Deadline:** April 2.

3060 ■ Richard Goolsby Scholarship Fund *(Undergraduate/Scholarship)*

Purpose: To provide financial assistance for undergraduate students who have shown a career interest or demonstrate practical experiences in the plastics industry. **Focus:** General studies. **Qualif.:** Applicants must be full-time rising college sophomore, junior or senior students at a four-year college or two-year technical school, who are in good academic standing and majoring in or taking courses that would be suited to a career in the plastics industry. **Criteria:** Applicants are evaluated on the basis of academic performance; demonstrated interest in plastics industry; financial need; school and community involvement; and personal achievements.

Funds Avail.: $4,000. **To Apply:** Applicants must submit completed application form; copy of the Student Aid Report (SAR) from Free Application for Federal Student Aid; official transcript(s) of academic coursework and grades for at least the last two years; three recommendation forms (two from teachers or other school administrators and one from an employer or other non-related individual); and a personal statement expressing reasons for applying for the scholarship, qualifications, educational and career goals in plastics industry. **Deadline:** February 15.

3061 ■ Howard B. Higgins South Carolina Dental Scholarships *(Undergraduate/Scholarship)*

Purpose: To provide financial assistance for students attending the College of Dental Medicine at the Medical University of South Carolina. **Focus:** Dentistry. **Qualif.:** Applicants must be students at the College of Dental Medicine at the Medical University of South Carolina; must have at least a 3.0 cumulative grade point average (on a 4.0 scale); and must be legal residents of South Carolina. **Criteria:** Applicants are evaluated based on the criteria designed by the Scholarship Selection Committee.

Funds Avail.: No specific amount. **To Apply:** Applicants must submit all the required application information. **Contact:** College of Dental Medicine Office of Academic and Student Affairs; 843-792-2344.

3062 ■ Wilbert L. and Zora F. Holmes Scholarship Endowment Fund *(Undergraduate/Scholarship)*

Purpose: To provide financial assistance for graduating seniors from South Carolina's York School District One intending to attend an accredited college or technical school of their choice. **Focus:** Vocational-technical education. **Qualif.:** Applicants must be graduating seniors at York Comprehensive High School (currently the only high school in the York School District One) and must have been students at York Comprehensive High School for a minimum of two years as of the application deadline; must be legal residents of York County, South Carolina; and must have a minimum of 3.0 cumulative grade point average (on 4.0 scale) at the end of the first semester of senior year. **Criteria:** Recipients are selected based on academic achievement and financial need.

Funds Avail.: No specific amount. **To Apply:** Applicants must submit all the required application information. **Contact:** Guidance Office at York Comprehensive High School at 803-684-2336.

3063 ■ James V. Johnson Scholarship Fund *(Undergraduate/Scholarship)*

Purpose: To provide financial assistance for students at Pfeiffer University in Misenheimer, NC and Mitchell Community College in Statesville, NC. **Focus:** General studies. **Qualif.:** Applicants must be legal residents of Iredell or Alexander County in North Carolina who are incoming freshmen at Pfeiffer University in Misenheimer, NC or first-year students at Mitchell Community College in Statesville, NC. **Criteria:** Applicants are evaluated based on criteria designed by the Scholarship Selection Committee.

Funds Avail.: No specific amount. **To Apply:** Applicants must submit all the required application information. **Contact:** Pfeiffer University Office Admissions and Financial Aid, 704-463-1360 or the Mitchell Community College Office of Financial Aid, 704-878-3200.

3064 ■ Annabel Lambeth Jones Scholarship Fund *(Undergraduate/Scholarship)*

Purpose: To provide undergraduate scholarships for students of Queens University of Charlotte in Charlotte, NC and Brevard College in Brevard, NC. **Focus:** General studies. **Qualif.:** Applicants must be incoming freshmen; must have high academic merit; and must have demonstrated leadership potential. **Criteria:** Applicants are evaluated based on personal attributes.

Funds Avail.: No specific amount. **To Apply:** Applicants must submit all the required application information.

3065 ■ Mary and Millard Kiker Scholarship Fund *(Undergraduate/Scholarship)*

Purpose: To support deserving students with financial need who are residents of Anson or Union Countries in North Carolina. **Focus:** General studies. **Qualif.:** Applicants must be legal residents of Anson or Union County, NC who are nominated by the Superintendent of Schools in their county with a minimum cumulative grade point average of 2.5 (on a 4.0 scale) and must demonstrate substantial need for financial assistance. **Criteria:** Applicants are evaluated based on financial need.

Funds Avail.: $1,000 to $4,000. **To Apply:** Applicants must submit completed application form; copy of the Student Aid Report from FAFSA; official copy of high school transcript(s), including SAT/ACT scores; three recommendation forms (two from teachers or other school personnel and one from an employer or other non-related adult); one to two-paged typed statement expressing qualifications for the scholarship, educational goals and financial need for scholarship assistance; and a copy of both parents' federal tax return for the preceding year showing dependents and adjusted gross income. **Deadline:** April 2.

3066 ■ Law Enforcement Memorial Scholarship Fund *(Undergraduate/Scholarship)*

Purpose: To provide financial support for students studying law enforcement at Central Piedmont Community College and the University of North Carolina at Charlotte. **Focus:** Law enforcement. **Qualif.:** Applicants must be students at

Awards are arranged alphabetically below their administering organizations

Central Piedmont Community College or the University of North Carolina at Charlotte who have a 2.5 minimum cumulative grade point average (on a 4.0 scale) and are majoring in a law enforcement field. **Criteria:** Applicants are judged based on academic merit.

Funds Avail.: No specific amount. **To Apply:** Applicants must submit all the required application information. **Contact:** CPCC Financial Aid Office, 704-330-6942 or the UNC Charlotte Student Financial Aid Office, 704-687-2461.

3067 ■ George T. Lewis, Jr. Academic Scholarship Fund *(Undergraduate/Scholarship)*

Purpose: To provide motivation and encouragement to George T. Lewis, Jr. Academic Center graduates intending to pursue postsecondary education or training. **Focus:** General studies. **Qualif.:** Applicants must meet or exceed the benchmark goals for attendance set for the George T. Lewis, Jr. Academic Center during their senior year; must have earned a minimum 2.0 cumulative grade point average (on a 4.0 scale) at the end of the first semester of senior year; and must be graduating seniors at the George T. Lewis, Jr. Academic Center and must have at least one full academic year of enrollment and participation in the ThinkCOLLEGE Program (upon graduation). **Criteria:** Applicants are evaluated based on academic achievement; school involvement and personal achievements and financial need.

Funds Avail.: $1,500. **To Apply:** Applicants must submit completed application form; copy of the SAR from FAFSA; official copy of high school transcript(s), including SAT/ACT scores; two recommendation forms (one from a teacher, counselor or other school administrator and one from employer, community leader or other non-related adult); a one to two-paged typed personal statement on one of the following topics: (1) Discuss who or what has been the biggest influence on your decisions to attend college and why or (2) Present and explain the 'personal mission' or 'personal vision' you have adopted for yourself and discuss why you think these goals are important; and a copy of the applicant's completed FAFSA. **Deadline:** March 1.

3068 ■ Albert and Eloise Midyette Memorial Scholarship Fund *(Undergraduate/Scholarship)*

Purpose: To provide undergraduate scholarships for students attending Limestone College in Gaffney, South Carolina. **Focus:** Nursing; Education, Medical. **Qualif.:** Applicants must be full-time U.S. citizen students at Limestone College; must be majoring in the fields of religious and ministry studies, nursing or other medical academic fields; and must have a cumulative unweighted grade point average of at least 2.5 (on a 4.0 scale). **Criteria:** Applicants are evaluated on the basis of academic achievement and financial need.

Funds Avail.: No specific amount. **To Apply:** Applicants must submit all the required application information and materials.

3069 ■ Carolina Panthers Players Sam Mills Memorial Scholarship Fund *(Undergraduate/Scholarship)*

Purpose: To assist high school athletes from Mecklenburg County, NC and Spartanburg County, SC who wish to pursue a four-year undergraduate degree. **Focus:** General studies. **Qualif.:** Applicants must be graduate senior athletes at high schools (public or private) located in Mecklenburg County, NC or Spartanburg County, SC; have earned a varsity letter in high school; with 3.0 minimum cumulative unweighted grade point average on a 4.0 scale; and demonstrated outstanding leadership and citizenship. **Criteria:** Applicants are evaluated based on academic achievement; school and community involvement; evidence of leadership and citizenship.

Funds Avail.: $5,100. **Number Awarded:** 2. **To Apply:** Applicants must submit completed application form; copy of the Student Aid Report (SAR) from Free Application for FAFSA; official copy of high school transcript, including SAT/ACT scores; three recommendation forms, one from a faculty member/school official and one from a member of the coaching staff of the sport in which the athletes participate; a one to two-page statement expressing the reason why applicant is applying for the scholarship, their involvement in athletics, and educational and career goals. **Deadline:** April 30.

3070 ■ North Carolina League for Nursing Academic Scholarship Fund *(Graduate/Scholarship)*

Purpose: To provide financial assistance for graduate students pursuing either a master's degree in nursing or a doctoral degree in nursing or a related discipline. **Focus:** Nursing. **Qualif.:** Applicants must be legal residents of North Carolina; must have completed a minimum of six semester hours of course work in their graduate program of study by the application deadline; and must be granted unconditional admission to a master's degree program in nursing or doctoral degree program in nursing or a related discipline and be classified as a graduate degree student by the college or university. **Criteria:** Applicants are evaluated based on academic performance and financial need.

Funds Avail.: $1,000 to $2,000. **To Apply:** Applicants must submit a completed application form; copy of the Student Aid Report from Free Application for Federal Student Aid; official transcripts; two recommendation forms (one from a faculty member familiar with the applicant's progress in the program and one from any other non-related individual); a one to two-paged typed statement expressing qualifications for the scholarship; and commitment to full-time employment in North Carolina either in nursing practice or in teaching in a nursing education program. **Deadline:** March 15.

3071 ■ North Mecklenburg Teachers' Memorial Scholarships *(Undergraduate/Scholarship)*

Purpose: To provide financial assistance for North Mecklenburg High School students intending to pursue a degree in education. **Focus:** Education. **Qualif.:** Applicants must be graduating seniors with a grade point average of 3.0 on a 4.0 scale at North Mecklenburg High School; must be planning to attend a four-year college or university; and must be majoring in education. **Criteria:** Applicants are evaluated based on academic achievement; extracurricular and community involvement; statement of personal aspirations and educational goals; and financial need.

Funds Avail.: $1,000. **To Apply:** Applicants must submit a completed application form; copy of the Student Aid Report (SAR) from Free Application for Federal Student Aid; official transcript of academic coursework and grades; and a typewritten statement expressing the applicants' educational and career goals and reasons for applying for the scholarship. **Deadline:** February 15.

3072 ■ Ted H. Ousley Scholarship Fund *(Undergraduate/Scholarship)*

Purpose: To provide undergraduate scholarships for graduating seniors at North Mecklenburg High School in

Awards are arranged alphabetically below their administering organizations

Huntersville, NC. **Focus:** General studies. **Qualif.:** Applicants must be graduating seniors at North Mecklenburg High School; must have a minimum cumulative grade point average of 2.5 (on a 4.0 scale); and must be planning to attend a postsecondary institution in North Carolina. **Criteria:** Applicants are evaluated based on criteria designed by the Scholarship Selection Committee.

Funds Avail.: No specific amount. **To Apply:** Applicants must submit all the required application information. **Contact:** Scholarship Coordinator at North Mecklenburg High School, 980-343-3840.

3073 ■ Henry DeWitt Plyler Scholarship Fund *(Undergraduate/Scholarship)*

Purpose: To provide financial support for students from Lancaster County, SC intending to attend Winthrop University. **Focus:** General studies. **Qualif.:** Applicants must be graduating seniors or graduates of Lancaster County public high schools; must have a 3.0 minimum cumulative grade point average (on a 4.0 scale); and must be legal residents of Lancaster County, SC. **Criteria:** Applicants are evaluated based on financial need as determined by the costs of college attendance compared with an applicants' household income and other financial factors; academic performance and achievement; and school and community involvement.

Funds Avail.: $500 to $1,000. **To Apply:** Applicants must submit completed application form; copy of the SAR from FAFSA; official transcript(s) of high school and/or college coursework and grades for at least the last two years, including SAT/ACT scores if taken; three recommendation forms (two from teachers or other school personnel and one from employer or other non-related adult); one to two-paged typed statement expressing reason for applying for the scholarship, qualifications and the educational and career goals. **Deadline:** February 1.

3074 ■ Ben Robinette Scholarship Endowment Fund *(Undergraduate/Scholarship)*

Purpose: To assist graduates of high schools in Charlotte-Mecklenburg (public or private schools) to attend the University of North Carolina at Chapel Hill. **Focus:** General studies. **Qualif.:** Applicants must be graduating seniors at public or private high school in Charlotte-Mecklenburg with minimum of 3.0 grade point average on 4.0 scale. **Criteria:** Preference will be given to competitive runners who have been members of their high school track or cross country teams.

Funds Avail.: No specific amount. **To Apply:** Applicants must submit all the required application information. **Contact:** UNC Chapel Hill Office of Scholarships and Student Aid, 919-962-8396.

3075 ■ Rotary Public Safety Scholarship Fund *(Undergraduate/Scholarship)*

Purpose: To provide financial assistance for the children of Charlotte area public safety personnel. **Focus:** Public service. **Qualif.:** Applicants must be high school seniors intending to enter a two-year or four-year degree program with a minimum of 2.5 cumulative grade point average (on a 4.0 scale), whose mother or father are full time employees of the Charlotte Fire Department, Charlotte-Mecklenburg Police Department, Mecklenburg County Sheriff's Office or MEDIC with minimum of one year of service. **Criteria:** Recipients are selected based on academic performance; financial need; and record of good citizenship as evidenced by school and community involvement beyond required activities.

Funds Avail.: $1,000. **To Apply:** Applicants must submit completed application form; copy of SAR from FAFSA; official transcripts of academic coursework and grades for at least the last two years; four recommendation forms (two from instructors or other school administrators and two from employers or other non-related individuals in the Charlotte-Mecklenburg area); one to two-paged typed statement expressing reasons for applying for the scholarship, qualifications, and educational and career goals; and a copy of estimated expense budget for tuition, room and board, books, etc. at the school the applicant wants to attend. **Deadline:** April 1.

3076 ■ Tacy Ana Smith Memorial Scholarship Fund *(Undergraduate/Scholarship)*

Purpose: To provide financial support for graduating seniors at Providence High School in Charlotte, NC. **Focus:** General studies. **Qualif.:** Applicants must be graduating seniors at Providence High School with a 2.5 minimum cumulative grade point average (on a 4.0 scale), planning to attend a four-year college or university. **Criteria:** Applicants are evaluated based on criteria designed by the Scholarship Committee.

Funds Avail.: No specific amount. **To Apply:** Applicants must submit all the required application information. **Contact:** Scholarship Coordinator at Providence High School, 980-343-5390.

3077 ■ The Spirit Square Center for Arts and Education Scholarship Fund *(Undergraduate/Scholarship)*

Purpose: To provide financial assistance for undergraduate students who demonstrate aptitude and career potential in arts. **Focus:** General studies. **Qualif.:** Applicants must be rising college junior or senior students in good academic standing who have demonstrated talent and a declared major that indicates potential for a significant career contribution to arts. **Criteria:** Recipients are selected based on academic performance; school and community involvement and personal achievements; and commitment to and demonstrated potential for a career in arts.

Funds Avail.: $4,000. **To Apply:** Applicants must submit completed application form; official transcript(s) of academic coursework and grades for at least the last two years; three recommendation forms, two of which must come from individuals who are able to evaluate the applicants' aptitude and career potential in arts; one to two pages typed statement expressing 1) reasons for applying for the scholarship, 2) interest in arts, 3) educational and career goals in arts; and 4) a copy of the estimated expense budget for tuition, room and board, books, etc. **Deadline:** March 1.

3078 ■ Mary Stewart and William T. Covington, Jr. Scholarship Fund *(Undergraduate/Scholarship)*

Purpose: To provide financial support for students who graduate from a public high school located in Hoke County, NC. **Focus:** General studies. **Qualif.:** Applicants must be legal residents of Hoke county, NC who are graduating seniors at Hoke County High School; must have 2.75 minimum cumulative grade point average (on a 4.0 scale); and must attend a four-year college or university. **Criteria:** Applicants are evaluated based on the criteria designed by the Scholarship Selection Committee.

Funds Avail.: No specific amount. **To Apply:** Applicants must submit all the required application information and materials. **Contact:** Scholarship Coordinator at Hoke County High School, 910-875-2156.

3079 ■ Jack Tate/ThinkCOLLEGE Scholarship Fund *(Undergraduate/Scholarship)*

Purpose: To provide scholarship assistance for ThinkCOLLEGE Program participants planning to attend Central Piedmont Community College. **Focus:** General studies. **Qualif.:** Applicants must achieve 90% of the benchmark goal for attendance set for their high school during their senior year (Charlotte-Mecklenburg School System sets individual school goals each year for attendance, academics and behavior, copies are available in the school offices); must have earned a minimum 2.5 cumulative grade point average (on a 4.0 scale) at the end of the first semester of senior year; must be graduating seniors at a Communities In Schools site; and must have at least one full academic year of enrollment and participation in the ThinkCOLLEGE Program (upon graduation). **Criteria:** Recipients are selected based on financial need; academic achievement; school and community involvement; and personal achievements.

Funds Avail.: $800. **To Apply:** Applicants must submit completed application form; official copy of high school transcript(s), including SAT/ACT scores; two recommendation forms (one from a teacher, counselor or other school administrator and one from an employer, community leader or other non-related adult); one to two-paged typed personal statement; and a copy of Student Aid Report from Free Application for Federal Student Aid (FAFSA). **Deadline:** March 1.

3080 ■ Turner Family Scholarship Fund *(Undergraduate/Scholarship)*

Purpose: To provide financial assistance for graduating high school seniors in Mecklenburg County intending to attend an accredited college or vocational school in Mecklenburg County. **Focus:** Vocational-technical education. **Qualif.:** Applicants must be graduating high school seniors who have a minimum cumulative grade point average of 2.5 (on a 4.0 scale) and whose parents or legally appointed guardians are full-time employees who worked for National Welders Supply Company, Inc. for at least two years. Children of employees shall be defined to include natural born or legally adopted dependent children and stepchildren and wards of employees (in the case of stepchildren and wards, the applicant must live in the home with the eligible employee). **Criteria:** Applicants are evaluated based on academic achievement including grade point average and performance on tests designed to measure preparation and ability for postsecondary study; involvement in extracurricular activities and leadership roles held; and record of community service and other personal achievements.

Funds Avail.: $1,000 to 4,000. **To Apply:** Applicants must submit completed application form; copy of the Student Aid Report (SAR) from Free Application for Federal Student Aid (FAFSA); three recommendation forms (two from teachers or other school personnel and one from an employer or other non-related adult); one to two pages typed statement expressing reasons for applying for the scholarship, qualifications and educational/career goals; and a letter from an official of National Welders Supply Company, Inc. where the applicants' parents or legally appointed guardians are employed. **Deadline:** February 15.

3081 ■ The Sibyl Jennings Vorheis Memorial Scholarship Program *(Undergraduate/Scholarship)*

Purpose: To assist North Iredell High School graduates in obtaining a degree in physical therapy, medicine or nursing from a post-secondary accredited institution. **Focus:** Physical therapy; Medicine; Nursing. **Qualif.:** Applicants must have graduated from North Iredell High School with a minimum cumulative grade point average of 3.0 (on 4.0 scale). **Criteria:** Recipients are selected on the basis of academic achievement; school and community involvement; and personal achievements.

Funds Avail.: $3,000. **To Apply:** Applicants must submit completed application form; verification of acceptance into the accredited graduate program; official copy of college transcript; two recommendation forms and letters of recommendation; and a typewritten application statement of eligibility expressing applicant's educational and career goals, reasons for applying for the scholarship, and why the applicant feels they are a good candidate for the scholarship. **Deadline:** April 1.

3082 ■ Laramie Walden Memorial Fund *(Undergraduate/Scholarship)*

Purpose: To provide financial assistance for children of Charlotte, NC firefighters. **Focus:** General studies. **Qualif.:** Applicants must be seniors scheduled to graduate in the spring of the academic year; must have 3.5 minimum cumulative weighted grade point average (on a 4.0 scale) whose parent(s) are full-time employees of the Charlotte Fire Department with at least one year of service; and must participate in state-sanctioned school sport. **Criteria:** Applicants are evaluated based on academic merit and extracurricular involvement.

Funds Avail.: $500. **To Apply:** Applicants must submit completed application form; official transcript(s) of academic coursework and grades for at least the last two years; three recommendation forms (two from instructor or other school administrator and one from a non-related adult in the Charlotte-Mecklenburg area such as an employer, coach, scout leader, etc.); and a one-paged typed statement expressing the reason for applying for the scholarship, qualifications, and educational and career goals.

3083 ■ Fred C. Wikoff, Jr. Scholarship Fund *(Undergraduate/Scholarship)*

Purpose: To provide undergraduate college and/or vocational scholarships for children of employees of Wikoff Color Corporation and its subsidiaries. **Focus:** General studies. **Qualif.:** Applicants must be children of employees (defined to include natural-born or legally-adopted dependent children and stepchildren and wards of employees). Parents or legally-appointed guardians of applicants must be full-time employees who have worked for Wikoff Color Corporation for at least two years prior to the application deadline. Applicants enrolled in high school at the time of application must have a minimum cumulative grade point average 2.5 (on a 4.0 scale). Applicants enrolled in college at the time of application must have a minimum cumulative grade point average of 2.0 (on a 4.0 scale). Applicant's age must not be over 25 as of the application deadline but a student over the age of 25 will be considered on a case to case basis if the student is permanently disabled or has some other special circumstance that requires him or her to be financially dependent upon their parents. **Criteria:** Applicants are evaluated based on academic achievement; school and community involvement and personal achievements; and financial need.

Funds Avail.: $500 to $2,000. **To Apply:** Applicants must submit completed application form; copy of SAR from FAFSA; official transcript(s) of high school and/or college coursework and grades for at least the last two years, including SAT/ACT scores if taken; three recommendation

Awards are arranged alphabetically below their administering organizations

forms (two from teachers or other school personnel and one from an employer or other non-related adult); one to two-page typed statement expressing the reason for applying for the scholarship, qualifications and educational and career goals; and a letter from an official of Wikoff Color Corporation where parents or legally appointed guardians are employed. **Deadline:** February 15.

3084 ■ The Wilmore Scholarship Fund
(Undergraduate/Scholarship)

Purpose: To provide financial assistance for residents of the Wilmore neighborhood in Charlotte, NC intending to attend college or vocational school. **Focus:** Vocational-technical education. **Qualif.:** Applicants must be residents of the Wilmore Neighborhood which is defined by Summit Avenue on the north, Interstate 77 on the west, South Tryon Street on the east and Wilmore Drive on the south; must have lived in Wilmore Neighborhood for at least one year (12 months) prior to the application deadline; and must have a minimum cumulative grade point average of 2.0 (on a 4.0 scale) for the last completed years of education. **Criteria:** Applicants are judged based on academic achievement; financial need; and leadership potential evidenced by school and/or community involvement.

Funds Avail.: $500 to $2,000. **To Apply:** Applicants must submit completed application form; official transcript(s) of high school and/or college coursework and grades for at least the last two years attended, including SAT/ACT score reports if taken; one recommendation form from a teacher, other school personnel or employer; one to two page personal statement expressing the applicants' educational and career goals and financial need for scholarship assistance; and a copy of the Student Aid Report (SAR) from Free Application for Federal Student Aid (FAFSA). **Deadline:** April 1.

3085 ■ Mary and Elliot Wood Foundation Graduate Scholarship Fund *(Graduate/Scholarship)*

Purpose: To provide merit-based graduate scholarships for North Carolina students, primarily in Guilford, Moore and Randolph Counties. **Focus:** Humanities; Environmental science; Ecology; Nutrition; Economics; Peace Studies; Government; Education. **Qualif.:** Candidates must have received or been a candidate for a Mary and Elliott Wood undergraduate or graduate scholarship; must pursue fields of study most appropriate to the purpose of the Mary and Elliot Wood Foundation; and must have expressed their intention of professional pursuit in such fields as The Cultural Arts, Humanities and the Study of Civilizations, Conservation, City and Community Planning, Environmental Studies and Ecology, Environmentally Sensitive Energies, Organic Gardening and Nutrition, Economics, Peace and Prosperity, Political Science and Government and Education. **Criteria:** Applicants are evaluated on the basis of academic achievement, extracurricular activities and statement of personal goals and references.

Funds Avail.: No specific amount. **To Apply:** Applicants must submit all the required application information. **Deadline:** April 1.

3086 ■ Mary and Elliot Wood Foundation Undergraduate Scholarship Fund *(Undergraduate/Scholarship)*

Purpose: To provide financial support for the most gifted future leaders who have the capability, desire, energy, enthusiasm and determination to improve our civilization and to enhance the quality of all life cultural, civic, and ecological. **Focus:** General studies. **Qualif.:** Applicants must be students graduating from high schools in the districts in Guilford County, Davidson County, Randolph County, Moore County. **Criteria:** Applicants are evaluated based on personal character; leadership potential; and scholastic achievement.

Funds Avail.: No specific amount. **To Apply:** Applicants must submit completed application form and all other required materials for the scholarship. **Deadline:** January 15.

3087 ■ Foundation for Community Association Research

225 Reinekers Ln., Ste. 300
Alexandria, VA 22314
Ph: (703)548-8600
Fax: (703)684-1581
Free: 888-224-4321
E-mail: foundation@caionline.org
URL: http://www.cairf.org

3088 ■ Byron Hanke Fellowships
(Undergraduate/Fellowship)

Purpose: To promote positive charge for all stakeholders who live in homeowner associations by discovering future trends and opportunities; to support and conduct research; to facilitate and promote cooperation among industry partners and provide resources that help educate the public. **Focus:** General studies. **Qualif.:** Applicants must be enrolled in an accredited master's, doctoral or law program in United the States of America or Canada. **Criteria:** Recipients are selected based on academic achievements, faculty recommendations, research and writing ability, and the nature of the proposed topic and its benefit to the study and understanding of community associations.

Funds Avail.: Maximum amount of $4,000. **To Apply:** Applicants must submit a completed application form and research proposal.

3089 ■ Foundation for Enhancing Communities

200 N Third St., PO Box 678
Harrisburg, PA 17108-0678
Ph: (717)236-5040
Fax: (717)231-4463
E-mail: dawn@tfec.org
URL: http://www.ghf.org

3090 ■ G. Thomas Balsbaugh Memorial Scholarship Fund *(Undergraduate/Scholarship)*

Purpose: To provide financial assistance for a Dauphin County high school senior planning to attend a four-year college or university. **Focus:** General studies. **Qualif.:** Applicants must have high academic standing and achievement; must exemplify good character; must exhibit a variety of interests and activities in both academic and personal life; and must demonstrate financial need. **Criteria:** Selection will be based on the committee's criteria.

Funds Avail.: $1,000. **To Apply:** Application for the scholarship should include: official academic transcript issued by school; completed personal information; completed financial statement; and personal statement describing current interests and activities as well as future goals and ambitions. **Deadline:** March 31. **Contact:** Dawn Morris,

Awards are arranged alphabetically below their administering organizations

Program Officer; 717-236-5040; dawn@tfec.org.

3091 ■ Robbie Baron Memorial Scholarships *(Undergraduate/Scholarship)*

Purpose: To provide financial support for a graduating senior of Cedar Cliff High School who attended Hillside Elementary School. **Focus:** General studies. **Qualif.:** Applicant must be a graduating senior at Cedar Cliff High School and have attended Hillside Elementary. **Criteria:** Scholarship will be given based on the following: academic achievement; extracurricular activities; services to the community; an essay which identifies the applicant's opinion on values and youth leadership.

Funds Avail.: No specific amount. **To Apply:** Applicants may download the application at the TFEC web site. Applicants must submit the following required attachments: completed student application; high school transcript; completed student essay (question attached); and one personal reference letter. Applicants may return their completed application to the High School Guidance Office. **Deadline:** April 30. **Contact:** Dawn Morris, Program Officer; 717-236-5040; dawn@tfec.org.

3092 ■ Chambersburg/Fannett-Metal School District Scholarship Fund *(Undergraduate/Scholarship)*

Purpose: To provide educational assistance for students of Chambersburg High School and Fannett-Metal High School. **Focus:** Engineering, computer; Computer and information sciences. **Qualif.:** Applicants must have a desire to pursue a career in computer engineering or computer science and must have an academic achievement of a cumulative GPA of 2.0 or higher on a 4.0 scale. **Criteria:** Selection will be based on financial need, submitted essay, academic achievement, extracurricular activities, and personal interview.

Funds Avail.: No specific amount. **To Apply:** Applicants must have the following required attachments: completed student background sheet; official high school transcript with raised school seal; 1st and 2nd page of parent's and student's IRS 1040 and/or 1040 A forms; completed student essay (not to exceed 300 words); two personal letters (one letter should be from a teacher and the other letter should be from an employer or a supervisor of a community service volunteer agency). Letters of reference may not be from a family member. Students must return their completed application to their high school guidance counselor. **Deadline:** March 22.

Remarks: Established in 1999. **Contact:** Dawn Morris, Program Officer; 717-236-5040; dawn@tfec.org.

3093 ■ CODY Foundation Fund *(Undergraduate/Scholarship)*

Purpose: To promote Christian initiatives through education and athletics. **Focus:** General studies. **Qualif.:** Applicants must be graduating high school senior students from Greenwood High School, Susquenita High School, West Perry High School or Newport High School. **Criteria:** Selection will be based on the following: GPA (academic achievements); community involvement; recommendation letters (one from a teacher, the other from an employer, supervisor, or community advisor); completed essay; high moral character (must attend and/or be involved in church activities); and financial need.

Funds Avail.: $250. **Number Awarded:** 1. **To Apply:** Applicants must complete the required attachments: completed application; official high school transcript; FAFSA student aid report; completed student essay; and two personal reference letters. **Contact:** Dawn Morris, Program Officer; 717-236-5040; dawn@tfec.org.

3094 ■ Jan DiMartino Delany Memorial Scholarship Fund *(Undergraduate/Scholarship)*

Purpose: To assist students with their college tuition expenses. **Focus:** General studies. **Qualif.:** Applicant must be a graduating senior of Cumberland Valley High School who will attend a two or four-year institution of higher learning. **Criteria:** Selection will be based on the committee's criteria.

Funds Avail.: $2,000. **To Apply:** Applicants must complete and submit the application to the Cumberland Valley High School Guidance Office. Include an official transcript of complete high school record, including GPA, through the first half of final year, on which the raised school seal is imprinted. On a separate sheet of paper, list your most significant extracurricular or nonacademic activities, noting work experience and community service with the dates of these activities. Attach an essay answering the question: "What are some of the obstacles that you have overcome or challenges that you have met in your life and how do they impact your future goals?" The essay should be titled, typewritten, double-spaced and must not exceed 300 words. Return the completed application and attachments to the CVHS Guidance Department. **Deadline:** April 4. **Contact:** Dawn Morris, Program Officer; 717-236-5040; dawn@tfec.org.

3095 ■ Lou Drane Fund *(Undergraduate/Scholarship)*

Purpose: To provide educational assistance for deserving music students in the areas of classical music composition, teaching, and/or performance. **Focus:** Classical music. **Qualif.:** Applicant must have a serious interest in classical music and display unusual ability and/or creativity; must apply for financial aid from the school he/she plans to attend; must attend an accredited post-secondary institution of higher learning or have been accepted and plan to attend same; be a citizen of the United States and must maintain a permanent residence on one of the following counties in central Pennsylvania: Adams, Cumberland; Dauphin, Franklin, Fulton, Juniata, Lancaster, Lebanon, Montour, Northumberland, Perry, Snyder or York. **Criteria:** Selection will be based on the committee's criteria.

Funds Avail.: No specific amount. **To Apply:** Applicants must attach FAFSA Student Aid Report and a letter detailing applicant's financial need. Applicants must submit, along with the application, an example of their ability, in one of the following fields: Composition or composition-teaching - a CD not to exceed 20 minutes in length - and a written music score - of two separate works of you own composition. Identify yourself, your instrument and title at the beginning of the tape. Label the recording with this information also. Audition recordings of original compositions must be of live performances. MIDI and other electronic performances are not accepted; For applications in Performance or performance-teaching submit a CD, not to exceed 20 minutes in length, of two separate works reflecting a variety of style. Identify yourself, your instrument and title at the beginning of the recording. Label the tape with this information also. All instruments with the exception of piano and classical guitar must be accompanied, but avoid lengthy introductions by accompaniment. **Deadline:** January 31. **Contact:** Dawn Morris, Program Officer; 717-236-5040; dawn@tfec.org.

Awards are arranged alphabetically below their administering organizations

3096 ■ Sue and Ken Dyer Foundation Travel Scholarship Award *(Undergraduate/Scholarship)*

Purpose: To assist students with travel expenses for educational or service trips. **Focus:** Travel and tourism. **Qualif.:** Applicants must be junior or senior students enrolled at one of the following schools: Cedar Cliff, Camp Hill, Mechanicsburg, Trinity or the Harrisburg Academy. **Criteria:** Selection will be based on the committee's criteria.

Funds Avail.: $2,000. **To Apply:** Applicants must complete and return the application and required attachments to the Foundation. Required attachments include: scholastic record and extracurricular activities; an essay on the topic: "The purpose of my proposed trip and what I expect to gain from this experience"; two reference letters from individuals who can speak to the quality of your character, your academic prowess and/or your likelihood of utilizing the proposed travel experience as a tool for personal growth; also include financial information. **Deadline:** April 14. **Contact:** Dawn Morris, Program Officer; 717-236-5040; dawn@tfec.org.

3097 ■ Educational Opportunity Fund *(Undergraduate/Scholarship)*

Purpose: To award scholarship to a graduating senior of Harrisburg High School. **Focus:** General studies. **Qualif.:** Applicant must be a graduating senior of Harrisburg High School who will attend a four-year college or university. Scholarship is renewable for up to eight semesters total, providing the student maintains a minimum GPA of 2.5 on a 4.0 scale. **Criteria:** Selection will be based on the committee's criteria.

Funds Avail.: $1,250. **To Apply:** Applicants must complete and return the application and required attachments to the guidance counselor at Harrisburg High School. Required attachments include: scholastic record and extracurricular activities; an essay on the topic: "How I am Preparing for My Life Goals"; and a FAFSA Student Aid Report. **Deadline:** April 5. **Contact:** Dawn Morris, Program Officer; 717-236-5040; dawn@tfec.org.

3098 ■ Family and Children's Services of Lebanon County Fund *(Undergraduate/Scholarship)*

Purpose: To provide financial assistance for Lebanon County residents pursuing higher education degrees. **Focus:** Medicine; Nursing, Social work, Mental health. **Qualif.:** Applicants must be enrolled full-time in schools of advanced education in the fields of medicine, nursing, social work, mental health and other specialized therapies in the treatment of physical and mental disabilities; must demonstrate financial need, academic aptitude and achievement, and commitment to a career in human services; and must be residents of Lebanon County. **Criteria:** Selection will be based on the committee's criteria. Applicants are considered without regard to race, creed, color, sex or national origin.

Funds Avail.: No specific amount. **To Apply:** Applicants may obtain the application online. Applicants must provide the most recent, either a certified high school transcript or a certified college transcript. **Contact:** Dawn Morris, Program Officer; 717-236-5040; dawn@tfec.org.

3099 ■ Adrienne Zoe Fedok Art and Music Scholarships *(Undergraduate/Scholarship)*

Purpose: To award scholarship to a student from either Central Dauphin High School or Central Dauphin East High School. **Focus:** Art; Music. **Qualif.:** Applicant must be from either Central Dauphin High School or Central Dauphin East High School entering his or her freshman year in post-secondary education in the field of Art and Music. **Criteria:** Selection will be based on the following criteria: interest in art and/or music education; financial need; SAT scores; GPA; demonstrated leadership and community service; and personal essay on the applicant's educational and career goals.

Funds Avail.: $1,000. **To Apply:** The application and the required attachments must be completed and postmarked on or before the deadline. Required attachments include: completed application; high school transcript including GPA; SAT scores; FAFSA Student Aid Report Form (Financial Aid Form); two letters of recommendation (one from a faculty member in the art or music department); a list of extra-curricular activities demonstrating leadership and community service; and personal essay on the applicant's educational and career goals. **Deadline:** April 3. **Contact:** Dawn Morris, Program Officer; 717-236-5040; dawn@tfec.org.

3100 ■ Friends of Megan Bolton Memorial Fund *(Undergraduate/Scholarship)*

Purpose: To assist students with their college expenses. **Focus:** General studies. **Qualif.:** Program is open to graduating high school seniors. **Criteria:** Selection will be based on: financial need; high academic standing and achievement; leadership; and character.

Funds Avail.: No specific amount. **To Apply:** Application form can be obtained online. Applicants must submit an official school transcript of their complete high school record, including GPA, through the first half of final year, on which the raised school seal is imprinted. Students should indicate evidence of meaningful leadership and positive character traits, volunteer work or involvement in community or church activities/charities that contribute to the betterment of that community or organization. Submit a resume if available, though not required, and a reference letter written by one of the contacts from the resume. Students are also asked to submit an essay (300 words or less) describing his or her idea of friendship and the significance of having close friends in their lives. **Deadline:** April 16. **Contact:** Dawn Morris, Program Officer; 717-236-5040; dawn@tfec.org.

3101 ■ Friendship Scholarship Fund *(Undergraduate/Scholarship)*

Purpose: To assist students with tuition expenses. **Focus:** General studies. **Qualif.:** Applicants must be graduating seniors of Harrisburg High School who will attend a four-year college or university or will further their vocational training at an accredited institution. **Criteria:** Selection will be based on scholastic ability, career goals, financial need and community service.

Funds Avail.: No specific amount. **To Apply:** Applicants must complete and submit the application and attachments on or before the deadline. **Deadline:** March 31. **Contact:** Dawn Morris, Program Officer; 717-236-5040; dawn@tfec.org.

3102 ■ Norma Gotwalt Scholarship Fund *(Undergraduate/Scholarship)*

Purpose: To assist students with their college tuition expenses. **Focus:** Education, Elementary. **Qualif.:** Applicants must be female junior or senior students studying Elementary Education at the Penn State Capital College

Awards are arranged alphabetically below their administering organizations

and who have maintained a minimum of 3.0 cumulative GPA while at Capital College. **Criteria:** Selection will be based on the committee's criteria.

Funds Avail.: $3,000. **To Apply:** Applicants must complete and submit the application and attachments on or before the deadline. **Deadline:** February 28. **Contact:** Dawn Morris, Program Officer; 717-236-5040; dawn@tfec.org.

3103 ■ Henry and Janet Guareillo Scholarship Fund *(Undergraduate/Scholarship)*

Purpose: To assist students with their college tuition expenses. **Focus:** Music; Theater arts. **Qualif.:** Program is open to graduating seniors who have studied at Cumberland Valley School of Music for four consecutive years; must have been accepted into a college or conservatory to pursue a degree in music or the theater arts; must have demonstrated ability to become successful candidates in their chosen field; and must demonstrate financial need. Other factors will include performance history, teacher recommendations, if the candidate studied more than one instrument at CVSM or was a Merit Scholarship Award winner. **Criteria:** Selection will be based on the committee's criteria.

Funds Avail.: No specific amount. **To Apply:** Applicants must complete and submit the application and the attachments on or before the deadline. Application can be obtained online. **Deadline:** April 20. **Contact:** Dawn Morris, Program Officer; 717-236-5040; dawn@tfec.org.

3104 ■ Gordon B. and Josephine Hewlet Memorial Fund *(Undergraduate/Scholarship)*

Purpose: To assist students from Franklin County with their nursing studies at a college or university of their choice. **Focus:** Nursing. **Qualif.:** Applicants must be nursing undergraduate students, however if there are no qualified undergraduate student applicants, scholarships may be given to graduate students. **Criteria:** Selection will be based on the following criteria: desire to pursue a career in nursing; academic achievement of a cumulative GPA of 2.5 or higher on a 4.0 scale; extracurricular activities (sports, organizations, clubs); services to the community (volunteering); an essay which identifies the applicant's interest in nursing (not to exceed 300 words); financial need; and residence in Franklin county.

Funds Avail.: No specific amount. **To Apply:** The application and the required attachments must be completed and postmarked on or before the deadline. Required attachments include: completed student background sheet (attached); official high school transcript with raised school seal; 1st and 2nd page of parents and students IRS 1040 and/or 1040 A form(s); completed student essay (question attached); and two personal reference letters (one letter should be from a teacher and the other letter should be from an employer or a supervisor of community service volunteer agency). Letters of reference may not be from a family member. Application form can be obtained online. **Deadline:** March 28. **Contact:** Dawn Morris, Program Officer at the above address (see entry 3089).

3105 ■ Roberta L. Houpt Scholarship Fund *(Undergraduate/Scholarship)*

Purpose: To assist students from Cumberland, Dauphin and Perry Counties studying nursing at a college or university of their choice. **Focus:** Nursing. **Qualif.:** Applicants must be nursing undergraduate students and residents of Dauphin, Cumberland or Perry Counties. **Criteria:** Selection will be based on the following criteria: desire to pursue a career in nursing; academic achievement; extracurricular activities; services to the community; an essay which identifies the applicant's interest in nursing; and financial need.

Funds Avail.: $2,000. **To Apply:** Application and the required attachments must be completed and postmarked on or before the deadline. Required attachments include: completed student background sheet; high school transcript or college transcript; letter of acceptance in nursing program or college transcript showing enrollment in program; FAFSA student aid report form (financial aid form); completed essay (question attached); and two personal reference letters (one letter should be from a science teacher and the other letter should be from an individual who can speak to applicant's ability to successfully complete studies), such as a teacher, employer, or mentor. Application form can be obtained online. **Deadline:** March 31.

Remarks: Established in 1998. **Contact:** Dawn Morris, Program Officer at the above address (see entry 3089).

3106 ■ Carol Hoy Scholarship fund *(Undergraduate/Scholarship)*

Purpose: To assist students from Mechanicsburg Area High School planning to pursue a career in elementary or early childhood education. **Focus:** Elementary Education; early childhood education. **Qualif.:** Applicants must be graduating seniors from Mechanicsburg Area High School. **Criteria:** Selection will be based on the following criteria: academic achievements; leadership and community service; one or two paragraph essay; personal interview; and financial need.

Funds Avail.: No specific amount. **To Apply:** Application and the required attachments must be completed and postmarked on or before the deadline. The required attachments include: completed student background sheet; high school transcript; FAFSA student aid report form (financial aid form); completed student essay; resume including leadership and community service; and two personal reference letters. One letter should be from a teacher and the other letter should be from an individual who can speak to applicant's ability to successfully complete studies, such as a teacher, employer, or mentor. Application form can be obtained online. **Deadline:** April 10.

Remarks: Established in 2006. **Contact:** Dawn Morris, Program Officer at the above address (see entry 3089).

3107 ■ Erin L. Jenkins Memorial Scholarship Fund *(Undergraduate/Scholarship)*

Purpose: To award scholarships for deserving students attending Cumberland Valley High School. **Focus:** General studies. **Qualif.:** Students must reside in the area defined by the Cumberland Valley School District or its successor. **Criteria:** Selection will be based on the committee's criteria.

Funds Avail.: No specific amount. **To Apply:** Students must complete and return the application and attachments to the Foundation. Students must also submit the following: official school transcript; two recommendations; and a list of most memorable community services. (Please write an essay on what meant most to you.) Application form can be obtained online. **Deadline:** April 18. **Contact:** Dawn Morris, Program Officer at the above address (see entry 3089).

3108 ■ Ken and Romaine Kauffman Scholarship Fund *(Undergraduate/Scholarship)*

Purpose: To assist students with college tuition expenses. **Focus:** Automotive technology. **Qualif.:** Students must be residents of Cumberland Perry Counties pursuing a degree in the mechanical or technical field. **Criteria:** Selection will be based on the committee's criteria.

Funds Avail.: No specific amount. **To Apply:** Students must complete and return the application and attachments to the Foundation before the deadline. Application form can be obtained online. **Deadline:** April 14. **Contact:** Dawn Morris, Program Officer at the above address (see entry 3089).

3109 ■ Leon I. Lock and Barbara R. Lock Scholarship Fund *(Undergraduate/Scholarship)*

Purpose: To assist students with their college tuition expenses. **Focus:** Automotive technology. **Qualif.:** Applicants must be graduating seniors of a high school in the Harrisburg School District (including Bishop McDevitt High School) who will attend Harrisburg Area Community College, or Penn State, or students who have graduated from one of the two high schools in no more than five years before the year of application. **Criteria:** Selection will be based on the following: a GPA of 2.5 minimum, financial need, demonstration of good study and work ethic from an employer or volunteer group and an essay which explains the choice of the course of study to be undertaken and why the student is pursuing it.

Funds Avail.: No specific amount. **To Apply:** Students must complete and return the application and attachments to the Foundation before the deadline. Application form can be obtained online. **Deadline:** April 3. **Contact:** Dawn Morris, Program Officer at the above address (see entry 3089).

3110 ■ Carie and George Lyter Scholarship Fund *(Undergraduate/Scholarship)*

Purpose: To provide educational assistance for students attending Greenwood High School, Newport High School, Susquenita High School and West Perry High School. **Focus:** Education, Elementary; Science; Mathematics and mathematical sciences. **Qualif.:** Applicants must have a desire to pursue a career in elementary or middle school education with emphasis in science or mathematics; an academic achievement of a cumulative GPA of 2.5 to 3.0 on a 4.0 scale in their junior/senior year; demonstrated talent for leadership; a high moral character (must have attended and be involved in church activities); and must demonstrate financial need. **Criteria:** Selection will be based on the committee's criteria.

Funds Avail.: No specific amount. **To Apply:** Applicants must submit the following required attachments: completed student background sheet; official high school transcript with raised school seal; FAFSA student aid report; completed student 300-word essay identifying their interest in Elementary or Middle School Education with an emphasis in science and mathematics (include professional goals); and two personal reference letters. One letter should be from a teacher and the other letter should be from an employer or a supervisor of a community service volunteer agency. Letters of reference may not be from a family member. **Deadline:** April 24. **Contact:** Dawn Morris, Program Officer at the above address (see entry 3089).

3111 ■ Sam Mizrahi Memorial Scholarships *(Undergraduate/Scholarship)*

Purpose: To assist students with their college tuition expenses. **Focus:** General studies. **Qualif.:** Applicants must demonstrate financial need; must have a minimum 2.5 GPA; and must have a high moral character. **Criteria:** Selection will be based on the committee's criteria.

Funds Avail.: No specific amount. **To Apply:** Applicants must complete the attached form and any other requested supporting documents and return on or before the deadline to the guidance counselor at Northern York High School. Applicants must include an official transcript of complete high school record, including GPA, through first half of final year, on which the raised school seal is imprinted. On a separate sheet of paper, list the most significant extracurricular or nonacademic activities, noting work experience and community service with the dates of these activities. Applicants must also write a one to two-page essay on the subject "My biggest life challenge and what I learned from the experience". **Deadline:** April 1. **Contact:** Dawn Morris, Program Officer at the above address (see entry 3089).

3112 ■ Leo F. Moro Baseball Memorial Scholarships *(Undergraduate/Scholarship)*

Purpose: To assist students with their college tuition expenses. **Focus:** General studies. **Qualif.:** Applicants must demonstrate financial need, sportsmanship and leadership; must demonstrate academic achievement based on GPA and SAT scores; and must have a potential for success in the sport of baseball. **Criteria:** Selection will be based on the committee's criteria.

Funds Avail.: No specific amount. **To Apply:** Applicants must complete and return the attached form and other requested supporting documents to the foundation. Applicants must include an official transcript of complete high school record, including GPA, through the first half of final year, on which the raised school seal is imprinted. On a separate sheet of paper, list the most significant extracurricular or nonacademic activities, noting work experience and community service with the dates of these activities. Please include a photocopy of your FAFSA with your completed scholarship application. Application form can be obtained online. **Deadline:** April 27. **Contact:** Dawn Morris, Program Officer at the above address (see entry 3089).

3113 ■ Pathways to Success Scholarships *(Undergraduate/Scholarship)*

Purpose: To provide high school students a meaningful, educational and highly-involved look at law and law-related career opportunities. **Focus:** Law; Paralegal studies. **Qualif.:** Applicants must be minority students accepted by (in the case of high school students) or enrolled in an accredited institution of higher learning at its main campus or a branch campus located in Central Pennsylvania. **Criteria:** Selection will be based on the committee's criteria.

Funds Avail.: No specific amount. **To Apply:** Application form can be obtained online. Applicants must provide a copy of high school or college transcript, certified as true and accurate by your guidance counselor, Registrar's Office or equivalent. Applicants must respond to the essay question (maximum of 500 words and typed). If you are in high school, attach a copy of your letter of acceptance to your application. Applicants pursuing post-secondary education should attach a copy of a certification of good standing from the educational institution which they are attending. Submit two letters of recommendation endorsing your candidacy for the Pathways to Success scholarship with your application. Letters of recommendation from teachers, administrators, or community members may be submitted and must reference at least one example of personal interaction with the applicant to underscore the applicant's academic/leadership and/or contribution to community. Applicants must attach a copy of your FAFSA Student Aid Report. With your FAFSA Student Aid Report, please make sure to include the cover letter of the report, which will indicate your EFC (Estimated Family Contribution). **Deadline:** March 1. **Contact:** Central PA Chapter, Association of Corporate Counsel, c/o Frank Miles, Esq., 27 West Chocolate Ave., Hershey, PA 17033.

3114 ■ Dr. Harry V. Pfautz Memorial Scholarship Fund *(Undergraduate/Scholarship)*

Purpose: To assist Susquenita High School students with their college expenses in the field of Forestry and/or Agriculture with an emphasis in forestry. **Focus:** Forestry. **Qualif.:** Applicants must be graduating senior students of Susquenita High School who have a GPA of 2.5 on a 4.0 point scale. **Criteria:** Selection will be based on financial need, community involvement and work ethic, scholastic performance and student essay.

Funds Avail.: No specific amount. **To Apply:** Applicants must complete the attached form and requested supporting documents and send to the foundation. The supporting documents include: official transcript of the complete high school record, including GPA, through the first half of final year, on which the raised school seal is imprinted; list of extracurricular or non-academic activities; and reference letter. **Deadline:** April 10. **Contact:** Dawn Morris, Program Officer at the above address (see entry 3089).

3115 ■ Ruth Cook Pfautz Memorial Scholarship Fund *(Undergraduate/Scholarship)*

Purpose: To assist Susquenita High School students with their college expenses in the field of Elementary Education. **Focus:** Education, Elementary. **Qualif.:** Applicants must be graduating senior students of Susquenita High School who have a GPA of 2.5 on a 4.0 point scale. **Criteria:** Selection will be based on financial need, community service, leadership qualities and career plans.

Funds Avail.: No specific amount. **To Apply:** Application form can be obtained online. Applicants must complete the attached form and requested supporting documents and send to the Foundation. The supporting documents include: official transcript of the complete high school record, including GPA, through the first half of final year, on which the raised school seal is imprinted; list of extracurricular or non-academic activities; reference letter; and a 300-word student essay explaining why they have chosen Elementary Education as a career path and describing their educational plans to achieve their career goal. **Deadline:** April 10. **Contact:** Dawn Morris, Program Officer at the above address (see entry 3089).

3116 ■ Bertha and Byron L. Reppert Scholarship Fund *(Undergraduate/Scholarship)*

Purpose: To encourage and recognize two senior students from the Mechanicsburg Area School District who demonstrate good citizenship. **Focus:** Political science; Horticulture. **Qualif.:** Applicants must have an interest in political science or horticulture; must be in the top one-third of the graduating class; must be accepted to an accredited college or university; must demonstrate good citizenship within the school and local community; and must complete an essay explaining how they meet the criteria. **Criteria:** Selection will be based on the committee's criteria.

Funds Avail.: No specific amount. **To Apply:** Application form can be obtained online. Applicants must attach the following documents: official transcript of the complete high school/college record, including GPA, through the first half of the present year, with the raised school seal imprinted; list of extracurricular or non-academic activities; FAFSA Student Aid Report; and an essay describing how they meet the eligibility criteria of this scholarship. **Deadline:** March 1. **Contact:** Dawn Morris, Program Officer at the above address (see entry 3089).

3117 ■ Ollie Rosenberg Educational Trust *(Undergraduate/Scholarship)*

Purpose: To assist students with business, technical or trade school tuition expenses. **Focus:** General studies. **Qualif.:** Students must attend a state supported school in Pennsylvania; must have a job; must have a Pennsylvania student loan; and must demonstrate financial need. **Criteria:** Selection will be based on the committee's criteria.

Funds Avail.: $2,000. **To Apply:** Applicants must complete and submit the application and required documents to the Foundation. Required documents include official transcript of the complete high school record, including GPA, through first half of final year, on which the raised school seal is imprinted, and a 300-word essay explaining how applicant has overcome the challenges in life and how he or she will apply these lessons to his or her vocation. Applicants must list their most significant extracurricular or nonacademic activities, emphasizing work experience and community volunteer service. **Deadline:** April 6. **Contact:** Dawn Morris, Program Officer at the above address (see entry 3089).

3118 ■ Ollie Rosenberg Scholarship Travel Fund *(Undergraduate/Scholarship)*

Purpose: To assist students with business, technical or trade school tuition expenses. **Focus:** Travel and tourism. **Qualif.:** Applicants must be graduating seniors who wish to travel to Israel to study traditional Jewish customs and culture. **Criteria:** Selection will be based on the committee's criteria.

Funds Avail.: No specific amount. **To Apply:** Applicants must complete the following required attachments: completed student background sheet, verification of family income, completed student essay and two personal reference letters. One letter should be from your Guidance Counselor and the other letter should be from an individual who can speak to your ability to successfully complete your studies, such as a teacher, employer, or mentor. Your letter of reference should not be from a family member. **Deadline:** April 11. **Contact:** Dawn Morris, Program Officer at the above address (see entry 3089).

3119 ■ J. Ward Sleichter and Frances F. Sleichter Memorial Scholarship Fund *(Undergraduate/Scholarship)*

Purpose: To provide aid for needy and deserving students who otherwise would not have the financial means to obtain a four-year college education. **Focus:** General studies. **Qualif.:** Applicants must be full-time students who maintain a B average or equivalent. Students must reside in the area defined by the Shippensburg Area School District, or its successor. **Criteria:** Selection will be based on the committee's criteria.

Funds Avail.: No specific amount. **To Apply:** Applicants must complete the following required attachments: application; official school transcript; two recommendations (one from the student's guidance counselor and one from a teacher who can discuss the student's personal characteristics such as motivation, character, ability, and potential); and FAFSA Student Aid Report (make sure to include the cover letter of the report, which will indicate the student's Estimated Family contribution). **Deadline:** April 6. **Contact:** Erica Frontino, Guidance Counselor, Shippensburg Area High School, 317 N. Morris St., Shippensburg, PA 17257.

Awards are arranged alphabetically below their administering organizations

3120 ■ Soroptimist International of Chambersburg Scholarship Fund *(Undergraduate/Scholarship)*

Purpose: To provide assistance for female seniors of Chambersburg Area Senior High School. **Focus:** General studies. **Qualif.:** Recipients must be accepted at an accredited college or university at the time the awards are made. **Criteria:** Selection will be based on academic performance, citizenship, interest and aptitude, leadership qualities, responsibility, enthusiasm, motivation to learn and improve, citizenship, attitude and cooperative spirit, dependability, financial need, and recommendations from a teacher and also a counselor.

Funds Avail.: $500. **To Apply:** Applicants must complete the required attachments. Required attachments include: application; two letters of recommendation (one from your guidance counselor, containing your GPA, course of study and general character assessment and the other from one of your teacher containing a general character assessment of you as a person and a student); FAFSA Student Aid Report; a paragraph of approximately 150 words answering the question "Why I Have Chosen to Continue My Education". **Deadline:** April 18. **Contact:** Chris Butler, Guidance Counselor, Chambersburg Area Senior High School, 511 S Sixth High School, Chambersburg, PA 17201.

3121 ■ Joseph L. and Vivian E. Steele Music Scholarship Fund *(Undergraduate/Scholarship)*

Purpose: To assist needy students of classical music in the fields of composition, teaching and performance. **Focus:** Music. **Qualif.:** Applicant must have a serious interest in classical music and display unusual ability and/or creativity; must apply for financial aid from the school he/she plans to attend; must attend an accredited post-secondary institution of higher learning or have been accepted and plan to attend same; must be a citizen of the United States and must maintain permanent residence in one of the following counties in central Pennsylvania: Adams, Cumberland, Dauphin, Franklin, Fulton, Juniata, Lancaster, Lebanon, Montour, Northurberland, Perry, Snyder or York. **Criteria:** Selection will be based on the committee's criteria.

Funds Avail.: No specific amount. **To Apply:** Each applicant is required to submit the attached application on or before the deadline. Submit, along with the application, an example of your ability, in one of the following fields: Composition or composition-teaching - a CD not to exceed 20 minutes in length and a written music score for two separate works of your own composition. Identify yourself, your instrument and title at the beginning of the tape. Label the tape with this information also; Performance or performance-teaching - a CD, not to exceed 20 minutes in length, of two separate works reflecting a variety of style. identify yourself, your instrument and title at the beginning of the recording. **Deadline:** January 31. **Contact:** Dawn Morris, Program Officer at the above address (see entry 3089).

3122 ■ Anil and Neema Thakrar Family Fund *(Undergraduate/Scholarship)*

Purpose: To encourage educational pursuits by providing financial assistance. **Focus:** Mathematics and mathematical science; Science; Engineering. **Qualif.:** Program is open to students, intending to study Math, Science and Engineering, from the City of Harrisburg School District and Sci-Tech High School, or to high school students in Dauphin, Cumberland and Perry Counties intending to study in a medical-related discipline. Applicants must have a minimum of 2.5 GPA on a 4.0 scale. **Criteria:** Selection will be based on leadership/community service; character; and financial need.

Funds Avail.: No specific amount. **Number Awarded:** 2. **To Apply:** Applicants must complete and submit the application and other required attachments on or before the deadline. Applicants must provide the following attachments: official transcript of complete high school/college record, including GPA, through the first half of the present year, with the raised school seal imprinted; list of most significant extracurricular or nonacademic activities, emphasizing work experience and community service. Attach a 300-word essay on the following statement: "What was my biggest life challenge and what did I learn form the experience." **Deadline:** March 31. **Contact:** Dawn Morris, Program Officer at the above address (see entry 3089).

3123 ■ Jack and Edna May Yost Scholarship Fund *(Undergraduate/Scholarship)*

Purpose: To assist students with their college tuition expenses. **Focus:** General studies. **Qualif.:** Applicants must be graduating seniors of a Dauphin or Cumberland County High School who will attend a two or four-year accredited college; must have a minimum SAT score of 1,000; must have an overall average between C+ and B-; must be full-time students planning to attend a two or four-year accredited college; must be graduates of any Dauphin or Cumberland County high school; and must be able to demonstrate past or current community service and willingness to work to attain future goals. **Criteria:** Selection will be based on the committee's criteria.

Funds Avail.: No specific amount. **To Apply:** Applicants must complete and submit the following attachments: official transcript of complete high school record, including GPA, through the first half of final year, on which the raised school seal is imprinted; a FAFSA Student Aid Report; and list of most significant extracurricular activities, noting work experience and community service with the dates of these activities. **Deadline:** April 14. **Contact:** Dawn Morris, Program Officer at the above address (see entry 3089).

3124 ■ Foundation of the Federal Bar Association

1220 N Fillmore St., Ste. 444
Arlington, VA 22201
Ph: (571)481-9100
URL: http://www.fedbar.org

3125 ■ Foundation of the Federal Bar Association Public Service Scholarships *(Undergraduate/Scholarship)*

Purpose: To provide financial assistance for high school students continuing higher education. **Focus:** General studies. **Qualif.:** Applicants must be graduating high school seniors planning to attend a four-year college or university; must be students currently enrolled full-time at a four-year college or university; or graduate students enrolled full-time in a graduate or professional degree program. At least one of the applicant's parents or guardians must be a current federal government attorney or federal judge and member of the Federal Bar Association. **Criteria:** Applicants are evaluated based on academic record, leadership recognition, school and community activities and service, and compelling essay response - exhibiting both substance and written communication skills.

Funds Avail.: $5,000. **To Apply:** Applicants must submit

Awards are arranged alphabetically below their administering organizations

completed application along with most recent transcripts (official copy); letter of acceptance from their college, university or graduate/professional school for new enrollees; and an essay. **Deadline:** March 3.

3126 ■ Foundation of the Hospitality Sales and Marketing Association International

1760 Old Meadow Rd., Ste. 500
McLean, VA 22102
Ph: (703)506-3280
Fax: (703)506-3266
E-mail: info@hsmai.org
URL: http://www.hsmai.org

3127 ■ FHSMAI Scholarship Program *(Graduate/Scholarship)*

Purpose: To provide financial assistance to students pursuing associate, baccalaureate and graduate degrees in Hospitality Management or related fields. **Focus:** Hotel, institutional, and restaurant management. **Qualif.:** Applicant must be enrolled as a student in a hospitality management or related curriculum; pursuing a degree; must have hospitality work experience; must demonstrate an interest in a career in hospitality sales and marketing; must be in good academic standing. **Criteria:** Recipients are evaluated based on academic achievement and financial need.

Funds Avail.: No specific amount. **Number Awarded:** 4. **To Apply:** Applicants must submit completed typed application form; transcript from current college or university; two recommendation forms; current resume; and three personal essays. **Deadline:** June 15.

3128 ■ Foundation of the National Student Nurses Association

45 Main St., Ste. 606
Brooklyn, NY 11201
Ph: (718)210-0705
Fax: (718)210-0710
E-mail: nsna@nsna.org
URL: http://www.nsna.org

3129 ■ Breakthrough to Nursing Scholarships *(Undergraduate/Scholarship)*

Purpose: To provide financial support to qualified nursing students. **Focus:** Nursing. **Qualif.:** Applicant must be a student committed to providing quality health care services to underserved population; must possess the necessary leadership skills to influence the delivery of quality care; must be a U.S citizen or Alien with U.S permanent resident status/Alien Registration Number; must establish academic achievement; must have an involvement in student nursing organizations and community health activities; must be attending classes and taking no less than six credits per semester. **Criteria:** Selection of applicants will be based on academic achievement, financial need, and involvement in student nursing organizations and community health activities. Selection committee of faculty and students from various nursing programs is appointed to select recipients.

Funds Avail.: $1,000-$5,000. **To Apply:** Applicants must submit and complete the application form available online; must submit an official transcript of records. Application form and other supporting documents must be sent to Foundation of the National Nurses' Association, 45 Main St., Ste. 606, Brooklyn, NY 11201. **Deadline:** June 16.

3130 ■ Career Mobility Scholarships *(Graduate, Undergraduate/Scholarship)*

Purpose: To provide financial support to qualified nursing students. **Focus:** Nursing. **Qualif.:** Applicants must be nursing or pre-nursing students who are registered nurses (RNs) enrolled in RN and BSN and RN to MSN completion programs or a licensed practical/vocational nurses enrolled in programs leading to RN licensure; must be U.S. citizens or Alien with U.S. permanent residents status/Alien Registration Number; must have established academic achievement; must have an involvement in student nursing organizations and community health activities; must be attending classes and taking no less than six credits per semester. **Criteria:** Selection of Scholarships recipients will be based on academic achievement, financial need, and involvement in student nursing organizations and community health activities.

Funds Avail.: $1,000-$5,000. **To Apply:** Applicants must submit and complete the application form available online; must submit an official transcript of records; application form and other supporting documents must be sent to Foundation of the National Nurses' Association, 45 Main St., Ste. 606, Brooklyn, NY 11201. **Deadline:** June 16.

3131 ■ McKesson Scholarships *(Undergraduate/Scholarship)*

Purpose: To provide financial support to qualified nursing students. **Focus:** Nursing. **Qualif.:** Applicants must be pre-nursing students taking courses to prepare for matriculation into a nursing program; must be U.S citizens or Alien with U.S permanent residents status/Alien Registration Number; must establish academic achievement; must have an involvement in student nursing organizations and community health activities; must be attending classes and taking no less than six credits per semester. **Criteria:** Selection of applicants will be based on academic achievement, financial need, and involvement in student nursing organizations and community health activities. Selection committee of faculty and students from various nursing programs is appointed to select recipients.

Funds Avail.: $1,000-$5,000. **To Apply:** Applicants must submit and complete the application form available online; must submit an official transcript of records. Application form and other supporting documents must be sent to Foundation of the National Nurses' Association, 45 Main St., Ste. 606, Brooklyn, NY 11201. **Deadline:** June 16.

3132 ■ Specialty Nursing Scholarships *(Undergraduate/Scholarship)*

Purpose: To provide financial support to qualified nursing students. **Focus:** Nursing. **Qualif.:** Applicant must be a student interested in pursuing specialized areas of nursing practice; must be a U.S citizen or Alien with U.S permanent resident status/Alien Registration Number; must establish academic achievement; must have an involvement in student nursing organizations and community health activities; must be attending classes and taking no less than six credits per semester. **Criteria:** Selection of applicants will be based on academic achievement, financial need, and involvement in student nursing organizations and community health activities. Selection committee of faculty and students from various nursing programs is appointed to select recipients.

Funds Avail.: $1,000-$5,000. **To Apply:** Applicants must submit and complete the application form available online; must submit an official transcript of records. Application form and other supporting documents must be sent to

Foundation of the National Nurses' Association, 45 Main St., Ste. 606, Brooklyn, NY 11201. **Deadline:** June 16.

3133 ■ Foundation of the Pennsylvania Medical Society

777 E Park Dr.
PO Box 8820
Harrisburg, PA 17105-8820
Ph: (717)558-7750
Fax: (717)558-7818
Free: 800-228-7823
E-mail: foundation@pamedsoc.org
URL: http://www.foundationpamedsoc.org

3134 ■ Allegheny County Medical Society (ACMS) Medical Student Scholarship *(Undergraduate/Scholarship)*

Purpose: To assist local students with the cost of attending a Pennsylvania medical school. **Focus:** Medicine. **Qualif.:** Applicants must be Pennsylvania residents from one of the following counties: Allegheny, Armstrong, Beaver, Butler, Washington, or Westmoreland. **Criteria:** Applicants are evaluated based on financial need.

Funds Avail.: $2,000. **Number Awarded:** 2. **To Apply:** Applicant must submit: completed scholarship application form; two reference letters, from persons other than family members, documenting integrity, interpersonal skills, and potential as a future physician (one must come from either a medical school professor or a physician); letter, on school letterhead, from the applicant's medical school verifying that he/she enrolled full time as a third or fourth-year medical student at that institution; and a typed, one-page essay addressing the following: Where do you see yourself in 10 years? How do you plan to give back to the community? **Deadline:** September 30.

3135 ■ Alliance Medical Education Scholarship Fund (AMES) *(Undergraduate/Scholarship)*

Purpose: To financially assist a deserving medical student enrolled in a Pennsylvania medical school. **Focus:** Medicine. **Qualif.:** Applicants must be residents of Pennsylvania who are enrolled in a Pennsylvania medical school as full-time second- or third-year medical students. **Criteria:** Applicants are evaluated based on financial need, merit, leadership and service.

Funds Avail.: $2,500. **To Apply:** Applicants must submit: the completed application form; two reference letters from persons who know them well (other than their families); letter from their medical school verifying that they are enrolled full-time and currently second or third-year medical students; and a typed statement of one page describing their vision for the future of Pennsylvania Medicine. **Deadline:** January 15.

3136 ■ Scott A. Gunder, MD, DCMS Presidential Scholarships *(Undergraduate/Scholarship)*

Purpose: To financially assist deserving second-year medical students at Penn State College of Medicine. **Focus:** Medicine. **Qualif.:** Applicants must have been residents of Pennsylvania for at least 12 months before registering as medical students; must be second-year medical students; must be enrolled full-time at Penn State College of Medicine; and must be members of Pennsylvania Medical Society and their county medical society. **Criteria:** Applicants are evaluated based on financial need.

Funds Avail.: $1,500. **To Apply:** Applicants must submit: completed application form; two reference letters, from persons other than family members, documenting the applicants' integrity, interpersonal skills, and potential as future physicians; letter, on school letterhead, from Penn State College of Medicine verifying that they are enrolled full-time and second-year medical students; one-page typed essay describing the person or event that most influenced them to become physicians and how they see themselves leading others into medicine; and completed Pennsylvania Medical Society membership applications if students are not current members. **Deadline:** April 15.

3137 ■ Lycoming County Medical Society (LCMS) Scholarships *(Undergraduate/Scholarship)*

Purpose: To provide financial assistance for medical students who are residents of Lycoming County. **Focus:** Medicine. **Qualif.:** Applicants must be residents of Lycoming County in the state of Pennsylvania; must be enrolled full-time in an accredited allopathic or osteopathic medical school within the United States. **Criteria:** Applicants are evaluated based on financial need.

Funds Avail.: $2,000. **To Apply:** Applicants must submit: completed application form; two reference letters, from persons other than family members, documenting the applicants' integrity, interpersonal skills, and potential as future physicians; letter, on school letterhead, from applicants' medical school verifying that they are enrolled full-time as medical students at their respective institutions; and, one-page, typed essay specifically describing why they chose to become physicians and what contributions they expect to make to the health profession. **Deadline:** September 30.

3138 ■ Montgomery County Medical Society (MCMS) Scholarships *(Undergraduate/Scholarship)*

Purpose: To provide financial assistance for medical students who are residents of Montgomery County. **Focus:** Medicine. **Qualif.:** Applicants must be residents of Montgomery County in the state of Pennsylvania; must have been Pennsylvania residents for at least 12 months prior to registering as medical students; must be enrolled full-time in an accredited United States medical school; must be enrolled or entering their first year of medical school. **Criteria:** Applicants are evaluated based on financial need.

Funds Avail.: $1,000. **To Apply:** Applicants must submit completed application form; two reference letters, from persons other than family members, documenting the applicants' integrity, interpersonal skills, and potential as physicians; letter, on school letterhead, from their medical schools verifying that they are enrolled full time as first-year medical students at that institution; one-page, typed essay addressing the reasons for pursuing medical career, personal goals, and plans for future within the profession. **Deadline:** September 30.

3139 ■ Myrtle Siegfried, MD and Michael Vigilante, MD Scholarships *(Undergraduate/Scholarship)*

Purpose: To provide financial assistance to qualified first-year medical students residing in Berks, Lehigh, or Northampton County. **Focus:** Medicine. **Qualif.:** Applicants must be residents of Berks, Lehigh, or Northampton County; must be entering first year of medical school; must be enrolled full-time in an accredited United States medical school. **Criteria:** Applicants are evaluated based on financial need.

Funds Avail.: No specific amount. **To Apply:** Applicants

Awards are arranged alphabetically below their administering organizations

must submit completed application form; two reference letters documenting the applicants' integrity, interpersonal skills, and potential as future physicians (letters must come from persons who know the applicants well but are not family members); letter, on school letterhead, from their medical school verifying that they are enrolled full-time at that institution and first-year medical students; one-page, typed essay specifically describing why they chose to become physicians and what contributions they expect to make to the health profession. **Deadline:** June 1.

3140 ■ Joe Francis Haircare Scholarship Foundation

PO Box 50625
Minneapolis, MN 55405
Ph: (651)769-1757
E-mail: mklarson@qwest.net
URL: http://www.joefrancis.com/jfh

3141 ■ Joe Francis Haircare Scholarships
(Undergraduate/Scholarship)

Purpose: To provide support to deserving students who want to pursue their professional training in hairstyling. **Focus:** Cosmetology. **Qualif.:** Applicant must be actively enrolled in cosmetology school, or planning to enroll in school. **Criteria:** Recipient will be selected by the independent committee composed of individuals drawn from the professional beauty industry. Selection is based on their potential, financial need, and commitment to a long-term career in cosmetology.

Funds Avail.: $1,000. **To Apply:** Applicant must complete the application form available online; must have a letter of recommendation from an employer, instructor, counselor, or someone qualified to offer testimony of his/her character. Application form and other supporting documents must be sent to Joe Francis Haircare Scholarship Foundation Program, PO Box 50625, Minneapolis, MN 55405. **Deadline:** June 1.

3142 ■ Freedom Alliance

22570 Market Court, Ste. 240
Dulles, VA 20166
Ph: (703)444-7940
Fax: (703)444-9893
Free: 800-475-6620
URL: http://www.freedomalliance.org

3143 ■ Freedom Alliance Scholarships
(Undergraduate/Scholarship)

Purpose: To support the children of American heroes. **Focus:** General studies. **Qualif.:** Applicant must be a dependent child of an active service member killed or disabled as the result of an operational mission/training accident; a senior high school, high school graduate or enrolled in an institution of higher learning; and must be 26 years old and below. **Criteria:** Applicants are selected based on the committee's review of the application materials.

Funds Avail.: No specific amount. **To Apply:** Applicants must complete online application and forward a copy of Government Issued Photo Identification (drivers License, ID Card); must submit a certificate of death or rating letter from the Veterans Administration disability; an essay; scholastic record; and a photo (photo of parents are optional).

Remarks: Freedom of Alliance will mail scholarship check to the school.

3144 ■ Friends of the Jose Carreras International Leukemia Foundation

1100 Fairview Ave. N, D5-100
PO Box 19024
Seattle, WA 98109-1024
Ph: (206)667-7108
Fax: (206)667-6498
E-mail: friendsjc@carrerasfoundation.org
URL: http://www.carrerasfoundation.org

3145 ■ E.D. Thomas Post Doctoral Fellowships
(Postdoctorate/Fellowship)

Purpose: To support research of diagnosis, prevention and cure of leukemia and related hematologic malignancies. **Focus:** Leukemia; Medical research; Oncology. **Qualif.:** Applicants must be M.D. or Ph.D. degree holder and have completed at least three years postdoctoral training but must be less than ten years, of any nationalities but application will be considered from each sponsoring institution, committed to foundation research goals, and able to devote at least 80% of time to the project with the sponsoring institution in academic environment to provide support for the proposed project. **Criteria:** Candidates' applications will be reviewed by the recognized leaders in the field of leukemic research, the Scientific Advisory Committee of the Foundation.

Funds Avail.: $50,000. **Number Awarded:** 1. **To Apply:** Applicants must submit type-written, single-spaced, in English application following the format specified in the application packet. **Deadline:** November. **Contact:** Fundacion Internacional Jose Carreras, Muntaner, 383, 08021 Barcelona, Spain Fax: 34 93 201 0588, e-mail: fundacio@fcarreras.es.

3146 ■ The Fund for American Studies

1706 New Hampshire Ave.
Washington, DC 20009
Ph: (202)986-0384
Fax: (202)986-0390
Free: 800-741-6964
E-mail: info@tfas.org
URL: http://www.tfas.org

3147 ■ Congressional Scholarships Award
(Undergraduate/Scholarship)

Purpose: To provide financial support for students who wish to attend the Institute on Business and Government Affairs (IBGA) at Georgetown University. **Focus:** Business; Local government. **Qualif.:** Applicant must be an undergraduate student. **Criteria:** Selection will be based on leadership skills, academics, campus and community involvement.

Funds Avail.: No specific amount. **To Apply:** Applicants can contact Kristy Khachigian for the scholarship information and application.

Remarks: Established in 1990. **Contact:** Kristy Khachigian Tel. No. 202-986-0384.

3148 ■ Eben Tisdale Fellowships *(Graduate, Undergraduate/Fellowship)*

Purpose: To make public policy professionals more competent in both policy advocacy and senior management. **Focus:** Technology. **Qualif.:** Applicant must be a junior or senior student interested in public policy and the high-tech industry, or in a graduate program. **Criteria:** The Advisory Committee will evaluate submitted materials.

Funds Avail.: $5000. **Number Awarded:** 1. **To Apply:** Applicants must submit a completed application form; official academic transcripts; evaluation forms from two academic references (in a sealed envelope, author's signature must be across the seal); a 500-word statement on reasons of wanting to be a Tisdale fellow. **Deadline:** February 15.

Remarks: Established after the death of Eben Tisdale, general manager of government affairs for the Hewlett-Packard Company. **Contact:** Jonathan Tilley, 202-986-0384, jtilley@tfas.org.

3149 ■ Funeral Service Foundation

13625 Bishop's Dr.
Brookfield, WI 53005
Ph: 877-402-5900
Fax: (262)789-6977
E-mail: info@funeralservicefoundation.org
URL: http://www.funeralservicefoundation.org

3150 ■ Joseph E. Hagan Memorial Scholarships
(Undergraduate/Scholarship)

Purpose: To provide financial assistance for mortuary science school students. **Focus:** Mortuary science. **Qualif.:** Applicants must be full-time students who will be enrolled or have been accepted for enrollment in the Fall semester in programs accredited by the American Board of Funeral Service Education. **Criteria:** Applicants are evaluated by the judges from the FSF Board of Trustees based on essay submitted by them.

Funds Avail.: $1,000. **Number Awarded:** 2. **To Apply:** Applicants must submit all the required application information.

3151 ■ Key Memories Scholarships
(Undergraduate/Scholarship)

Purpose: To provide financial assistance for top-scoring mortuary science students via the Key Memories scholarship essay contest. **Focus:** Mortuary science. **Qualif.:** Applicants must be students who are enrolled or accepted for enrollment in a mortuary science school accredited by the American Board of Funeral Service Education. **Criteria:** Applicants are judged by members of the Keystone Advisory Board and a Funeral Service Foundation representative.

Funds Avail.: $1,000. **Number Awarded:** 5. **To Apply:** Applicants must submit an essay and must complete application.

3152 ■ NFDA Professional Women's Conference Scholarships *(Undergraduate/Scholarship)*

Purpose: To provide financial assistance for tuition and travel stipend for selected individuals who attended the National Funeral Directors Association Professional Women's Conference. **Focus:** Funeral service; Mortuary science. **Qualif.:** Applicants must be verifiably employed in funeral service or a related occupation or mortuary science school students enrolled in school accredited by the American Board of Funeral Service Education. **Criteria:** Applicants are evaluated based on answers to essay.

Funds Avail.: $400. **To Apply:** Applicants must submit all the required application information.

3153 ■ Fur Takers of America

853 E 1000 N Rd.
Onarga, IL 60955
Ph: (217)394-2577
E-mail: krumui@illicom.net
URL: http://www.furtakersofamerica.com

3154 ■ Charles Dobbins FTA Scholarships
(Undergraduate/Scholarship)

Purpose: To promote interest in the accumulation and dissemination of knowledge concerning the trapping of fur bearing animals among persons interested therein. **Focus:** Agricultural Science; Biology; Wildlife Conservation and management. **Qualif.:** Applicants must be members of FTA or their immediate relatives; must be majoring in agriculture, biology, wildlife management or related courses in an accredited two-year or four-year college, university, or vocational/technical school. **Criteria:** Recipients are selected based on academic records and quality of the essay submitted.

Funds Avail.: $250. **To Apply:** Applicants must provide proof of high school graduation or pending graduation; official documents indicating that they have been accepted in an institution as first year students, or registration of classes if applicants are already in school. Applicants must also submit an essay that discusses career goals and how the scholarship would help to achieve these goals. **Deadline:** June 1. **Contact:** Carol Krumwiede at the above address (see entry 3153).

3155 ■ Gamewarden of Vietnam Association

PO Box 701786
San Antonio, TX 78270
Free: (186)6220-7477
E-mail: jwoody@texas.net
URL: http://www.tf116.org

3156 ■ Gamewarden Scholarship program *(High School, Undergraduate/Scholarship)*

Purpose: To discuss military history, military news, and othe rtopics of concern or interest about Vietnam. **Focus:** Vietnamese studies. **Qualif.:** Applicant must be 16-21 years old, full-time student; high school student may be considered; must be U.S. citizen; must be needing the assistance; must be the son, daughter or grandchild of a member of Game wardens; an applicant must be receiving an education from a four year or two year college, university, or vocational school. **Criteria:** Committee will consider the application based on the need of the applicant.

Funds Avail.: $500. **Number Awarded:** 3. **To Apply:** an applicant must fill out the application form and send to Game warden of Vietnam Association Office. **Deadline:** April 1.

3157 ■ Garden Club of America

14 East 60th St., 3rd Fl.
New York, NY 10022
Ph: (212)753-8287
Fax: (212)753-0134
URL: http://www.gcamerica.org

3158 ■ GCA Awards in Tropical Botany
(Doctorate/Award/Prize)

Purpose: To assist doctoral candidates enrolled in a U.S. PhD program to undertake field work in the tropics. **Focus:**

Awards are arranged alphabetically below their administering organizations

Botany. **Qualif.:** Applicants must be completing the requirements for a PhD in Botany within two years and are enrolled in a United States university. **Criteria:** Applicants must already be PhD candidates. Applicants are selected based on the committee's review of the application materials.

Funds Avail.: $5,500. **Number Awarded:** varies. **To Apply:** Applicants must submit a curriculum vitae; a two-page of statement of proposed research; personal letter describing plans for the future and commitment to tropical conservation; letter of recommendation from the student's graduate advisor. **Contact:** Andrea Santy; Senior Program Officer; 202-822-3447; andrea.santy@wwfus.org.

3159 ■ Katherine M. Grosscup Scholarships *(Graduate, Undergraduate/Scholarship)*

Purpose: To provide financial assistance to students who wish to pursue study of horticulture and related field. **Focus:** Horticulture. **Qualif.:** Applicants must be current college sophomores, juniors, seniors or master's degree candidates majoring in horticulture. **Criteria:** Applicants will be selected based on the committee's review of the application materials and personal interview.

Funds Avail.: $3,000. **Number Awarded:** varies. **To Apply:** Applicants must submit a completed application form; one letter of recommendation; transcript of college record. **Deadline:** January.

3160 ■ Garden Conservancy

PO Box 219
Cold Spring, NY 10516
Ph: (845)265-2029
Fax: (845)265-9620
E-mail: info@gardenconservancy.org
URL: http://www.gardenconservancy.org

3161 ■ Marco Polo Stufano Garden Conservancy Fellowships *(Professional Development/Fellowship)*

Purpose: To acquire the skills necessary to manage an exceptional garden and develop it for public education and enjoyment. **Focus:** Horticulture. **Qualif.:** Applicants should possess strong horticultural skills and aesthetic judgment, and a sensitivity to the vision and motives behind the creation of exceptional gardens as well as to the needs of new audiences; must have elevated the level of maintenance and horticultural distinction of these exceptional gardens and each of them has completed a special project such as a management plan, garden documentation or plant inventory. **Criteria:** Applicant will be selected based on their skill and educational background.

Funds Avail.: No specific amount. **To Apply:** For more information about the fellowship, applicants are advised to call the Preservation Projects office at 845265-9396.

3162 ■ Bill and Melinda Gates Foundation

PO Box 23350
Seattle, WA 98102
Ph: (206)709-3100
E-mail: info@gatesfoundation.org
URL: http://www.gatesfoundation.org

3163 ■ William H. Gates Public Service Law Scholarships *(Undergraduate/Scholarship)*

Purpose: To recognize the critical role played by lawyers in establishing and preserving a civil society and their calling in the spirit of public service. **Focus:** Law. **Qualif.:** Applicants must be incoming first year students in the University of Washington Law School. **Criteria:** Recipients are selected based on a competitive review process and a commitment on the part of the recipients to work in public service for five years following graduation.

Funds Avail.: No specific amount. **To Apply:** Applicants must submit a cover letter; an essay, not to exceed 750 words, discussing the factors that have shaped the applicants vision and influenced his/her public service commitment; two recommendations related to commitment to potential contributions to public service; Gates PSL Scholarship recommendation form; resume with details of public service experience; and signed application form. **Deadline:** January 15. **Contact:** PO Box 353020 Seattle, WA 98195; gatespsl@u.washington.edu.

3164 ■ Gay Asian Pacific Alliance

PO Box 421884
San Francisco, CA 94142-1884
E-mail: info@gapa.org
URL: http://www.gapa.org

3165 ■ GAPA Scholarships *(Undergraduate/Scholarship)*

Purpose: To provide financial assistance to lesbian, gay, bisexual and transgender Asian and Pacific Islanders in educational pursuits. **Focus:** Homosexuality. **Qualif.:** Applicant must be an Asian/Pacific Islander; applying or attending school in one of the nine-Bay Area counties; and have a minimum GPA of 2.75. **Criteria:** Priority is given to those self-identified as lesbian, gay, bisexual or transgender, or involved in the l/g/b/t community.

Funds Avail.: $1000. **To Apply:** Applicants must submit a completed horizons Foundation's scholarship application form together with a transcript; letter of recommendation; and an essay of 500 words. Send materials to Horizons Foundation, 870 Market St., Suite 728, San Francisco, CA 94102. **Deadline:** July 31.

Remarks: In memory of George Choy. The scholarship is administered by the Horizons Foundation. **Contact:** Hao Thai, hao@gapa.org.

3166 ■ Gay and Lesbian Business Association of Santa Barbara

PO Box 90907
Santa Barbara, CA 93190
E-mail: glba@prideguide.net
URL: http://www.glbasb.com

3167 ■ Carl Joseph Adelhardt Memorial Scholarships *(Undergraduate/Scholarship)*

Purpose: To provide financial assistance to those students who are in need. **Focus:** General Studies. **Qualif.:** Applicants must have the contribution to the Santa Barbara gay and lesbian community, career goals and financial need. **Criteria:** Preference will be given to those who meet the criteria.

Funds Avail.: No specific amount. **To Apply:** Applicants must submit the following: completion of an application, including statements of community involvement and financial need; an autobiography/personal statement; a copy of current college and/or high school transcript of records; two letters of recommendation: one from a com-

Awards are arranged alphabetically below their administering organizations

munity member and the other from a teacher or faculty member at your institution. **Deadline:** July 30. **Contact:** GLBA Santa Barbara at the above address (see entry 3166).

3168 ■ Raffin Gathercole Scholarships
(Undergraduate/Scholarship)

Purpose: To provide exceptional and ongoing support to those GLBA students. **Focus:** General Studies. **Qualif.:** Applicants must have the contribution to the Santa Barbara gay and lesbian community, career goals and financial need. **Criteria:** Preference will be given to those who meet the criteria.

Funds Avail.: No specific amount. **To Apply:** Applicants must submit the following: completion of an application, including statements of community involvement and financial need; an autobiography/personal statement; a copy of current college and/or high school transcript of records; two letters of recommendation: one from a community member and the other from a teacher or faculty member at your institution. **Deadline:** July 30. **Contact:** GLBA Santa Barbara at the above address (see entry 3166).

3169 ■ Stephen Logan Memorial Scholarships
(Undergraduate/Scholarship)

Purpose: To provide financial assistance to students who are in need. **Focus:** General studies. **Qualif.:** Applicants must have the contribution to the Santa Barbara gay and lesbian community, career goals and financial need. **Criteria:** Preference will be given to those who meet the criteria.

Funds Avail.: No specific amount. **To Apply:** Applicants must submit the following: completion of an application, including statements of community involvement and financial need; an autobiography/personal statement; a copy of current college and/or high school transcript of records; two letters of recommendation: one from a community member and the other from a teacher or faculty member at your institution. **Deadline:** July 30. **Contact:** GLBA Santa Barbara at the above address (see entry 3166).

3170 ■ Gemological Institute of America

The Robert Mouawad Campus
5345 Amada Dr.
Carlsbad, CA 92008
Ph: (760)603-4031
Free: 800-421-7250
E-mail: financialaid@gia.edu
URL: http://www.gia.edu

3171 ■ Jack Abelson Scholarships *(Graduate/Scholarship)*

Purpose: To promote education in Gemology. **Focus:** Gemology. **Qualif.:** Applicant must be U.S. citizen and permanent resident; at least 17 years old; have a high school diploma or GED equivalency; currently employed or planning to enter in the jewelry industry; applying for School of Gemology On Campus Graduate Gemologist (GG) program; past recipient of GIA scholarship within last five years are not eligible. **Criteria:** Applications will be reviewed by the GIA scholarship committee.

Funds Avail.: Full tuition. **Number Awarded:** 1. **To Apply:** Applicant must complete the GIA Scholarship application (available at the website), with a letter of recommendation from a person in the jewelry industry. Send application and supporting documents to: Gemological Institute of America, Office of Student Financial Assistance, MS 7 The Robert Mouawad Campus 5345 Armada Drive Carlsbad, CA 92008. **Deadline:** June 15 - October 15. **Contact:** Financial aid representative, 800-421-7250 x-4175, financialaid@gia.edu.

3172 ■ William Argo Scholarships
(Undergraduate/Scholarship)

Purpose: To promote education in Gemology. **Focus:** Gemology. **Qualif.:** Applicant must be U.S. citizen and permanent resident; at least 17 years old; have a high school diploma or GED equivalency; currently employed or planning to enter in the jewelry industry; applying for On Campus or Distance Education School of Gemology course or program; past recipient of GIA scholarship within last five years are not eligible. **Criteria:** Applications will be reviewed by the GIA scholarship committee.

Funds Avail.: $500. **Number Awarded:** 1. **To Apply:** Applicant must complete the GIA Scholarship application (available at the website), with a letter of recommendation from a person in the jewelry industry. Send application and supporting documents to: Gemological Institute of America, Office of Student Financial Assistance, MS 7 The Robert Mouawad Campus 5345 Armada Drive Carlsbad, CA 92008. **Deadline:** June 15 October 15. **Contact:** Financial aid representative, 800-421-7250 x-4175, financialaid@gia.edu.

3173 ■ Michael Beaudry Scholarships *(Graduate/Scholarship)*

Purpose: To promote education in Gemology. **Focus:** Gemology; Art industries and trade. **Qualif.:** Applicant must be U.S. citizen and permanent resident; at least 17 years old; have a high school diploma or GED equivalency; currently employed or planning to enter in the jewelry industry; applying for On Campus School of Gemology Graduate Gemologist (GG) and the Jewelry Manufacturing Arts Applied Jewelry Arts (AJA) programs; past recipient of GIA scholarship within last five years are not eligible. **Criteria:** Applications will be reviewed by the GIA scholarship committee.

Funds Avail.: $29,390. **Number Awarded:** 1. **To Apply:** Applicant must complete the GIA Scholarship application (available at the website), with a letter of recommendation from a person in the jewelry industry. Send application and supporting documents to: Gemological Institute of America, Office of Student Financial Assistance, MS 7 The Robert Mouawad Campus 5345 Armada Drive Carlsbad, CA 92008. **Deadline:** June 15 October 15. **Contact:** Financial aid representative, 800-421-7250 x-4175, financialaid@gia.edu.

3174 ■ ColorMasters Scholarships
(Undergraduate/Scholarship)

Purpose: To promote education in Gemology. **Focus:** Gemology. **Qualif.:** Applicant must be U.S. citizen and permanent resident; at least 17 years old; have a high school diploma or GED equivalency; currently employed or planning to enter in the jewelry industry (ColorMasters products); applying for Distance Education School of Gemology Accredited Jewelry Professionals (AJP) diploma program; past recipient of GIA scholarship within last five years are not eligible. **Criteria:** Applications will be reviewed by the GIA scholarship committee.

Funds Avail.: $390. **Number Awarded:** 8. **To Apply:** Ap-

plicant must complete the GIA Scholarship application (available at the website), with a letter of recommendation from a person in the jewelry industry. Send application and supporting documents to: Gemological Institute of America, Office of Student Financial Assistance, MS 7 The Robert Mouawad Campus 5345 Armada Drive Carlsbad, CA 92008. **Deadline:** June 15 - October 15. **Contact:** Financial aid representative, 800-421-7250 x-4175, financialaid@gia.edu.

3175 ■ Dennis Foltz Scholarships *(Graduate/Scholarship)*

Purpose: To promote education in Gemology. **Focus:** Gemology. **Qualif.:** Applicant must be U.S. citizen and permanent resident; at least 17 years old; have a high school diploma or GED equivalency; currently employed or planning to enter in the jewelry industry; applying for On Campus School of Gemology Graduate Gemologist (GG) courses; past recipient of GIA scholarship within last five years are not eligible. **Criteria:** Applications will be reviewed by the GIA scholarship committee.

Funds Avail.: Full tuition. **Number Awarded:** 1. **To Apply:** Applicant must complete the GIA Scholarship application (available at the website), with a letter of recommendation from a person in the jewelry industry. Send application and supporting documents to: Gemological Institute of America, Office of Student Financial Assistance, MS 7 The Robert Mouawad Campus 5345 Armada Drive Carlsbad, CA 92008. **Deadline:** June 15 - October 15. **Contact:** Financial aid representative, 800-421-7250 x-4175, financialaid@gia.edu.

3176 ■ Eye On Jewels Scholarships *(Undergraduate/Scholarship)*

Purpose: To promote education in Gemology. **Focus:** Gemology. **Qualif.:** Applicant must be U.S. citizen and permanent resident; at least 17 years old; have a high school diploma or GED equivalency; currently employed or planning to enter in the jewelry industry; applying for Distance Education School of Gemology Accredited Jewelry Professionals (AJP) diploma program; past recipient of GIA scholarship within last five years are not eligible. **Criteria:** Applications will be reviewed by the GIA scholarship committee.

Funds Avail.: $395 **Number Awarded:** 2. **To Apply:** Applicant must complete the GIA Scholarship application (available at the website), with a letter of recommendation from a person in the jewelry industry. Send application and supporting documents to: Gemological Institute of America, Office of Student Financial Assistance, MS 7 The Robert Mouawad Campus 5345 Armada Drive Carlsbad, CA 92008. **Deadline:** June 15 October 15. **Contact:** Financial aid representative, 800-421-7250 x-4175, financialaid@gia.edu.

3177 ■ GIA Endowment Scholarships - Distance Education *(Graduate/Scholarship)*

Purpose: To promote education in Gemology. **Focus:** Gemology. **Qualif.:** Applicant must be U.S. citizen and permanent resident; at least 17 years old; have a high school diploma or GED equivalency; currently employed or planning to enter in the jewelry industry; applying for On Campus School of Gemology Graduate Gemologist (GG) program; past recipient of GIA scholarship within last five years are not eligible. **Criteria:** Applications will be reviewed by the GIA scholarship committee.

Funds Avail.: Full tuition. **Number Awarded:** 1. **To Apply:** Applicant must complete the GIA Scholarship application (available at the website), with a letter of recommendation from a person in the jewelry industry. Send application and supporting documents to: Gemological Institute of America, Office of Student Financial Assistance, MS 7 The Robert Mouawad Campus 5345 Armada Drive Carlsbad, CA 92008. **Deadline:** June 15 - October 15. **Contact:** Financial aid representative, 800-421-7250 x-4175, financialaid@gia.edu.

3178 ■ GIA Endowment Scholarships - On Campus *(Graduate/Scholarship)*

Purpose: To promote education in Gemology. **Focus:** Gemology. **Qualif.:** Applicant must be U.S. citizen and permanent resident; at least 17 years old; have a high school diploma or GED equivalency; currently employed or planning to enter in the jewelry industry; applying for On Campus School of Gemology Graduate Gemologist (GG) program, School of Jewelry Manufacturing Arts Applied Jewelry Arts (AJA) or Graduate Jeweler (GJ) program; past recipient of GIA scholarship within last five years are not eligible. **Criteria:** Applications will be reviewed by the GIA scholarship committee.

Funds Avail.: Full tuition. **Number Awarded:** 4. **To Apply:** Applicant must complete the GIA Scholarship application (available at the website), with a letter of recommendation from a person in the jewelry industry. Send application and supporting documents to: Gemological Institute of America, Office of Student Financial Assistance, MS 7 The Robert Mouawad Campus 5345 Armada Drive Carlsbad, CA 92008. **Deadline:** June 15 October 15. **Contact:** Financial aid representative, 800-421-7250 x-4175, financialaid@gia.edu.

3179 ■ GIA Endowment Scholarships - School of Business *(Undergraduate/Scholarship)*

Purpose: To promote education in Gemology. **Focus:** Gemology; Business. **Qualif.:** Applicant must be U.S. citizen and permanent resident; at least 17 years old; have a high school diploma or GED equivalency; currently employed or planning to enter in the jewelry industry; applying for On Campus and Distance Education courses at the School of Business; past recipient of GIA scholarship within last five years are not eligible. **Criteria:** Applications will be reviewed by the GIA scholarship committee.

Funds Avail.: Varies. **To Apply:** Applicant must complete the GIA Scholarship application (available at the website), with a letter of recommendation from a person in the jewelry industry. Send application and supporting documents to: Gemological Institute of America, Office of Student Financial Assistance, MS 7 The Robert Mouawad Campus 5345 Armada Drive Carlsbad, CA 92008. **Deadline:** June 15 October 15. **Contact:** Financial aid representative, 800-421-7250 x-4175, financialaid@gia.edu.

3180 ■ Ray Glynn Scholarships *(Undergraduate/Scholarship)*

Purpose: To promote education in Gemology. **Focus:** Gemology. **Qualif.:** Applicant must be U.S. citizen and legal resident of the state of Alaska, Idaho, Oregon, Montana, or Washington; at least 17 years old; have a high school diploma or GED equivalency; currently employed or planning to enter in the jewelry industry; applying for Distance Education School of Gemology course for Diamonds, Colored Stones, or Gem Identification; past recipient of GIA scholarship within last five years are not eligible. **Criteria:** Applications will be reviewed by the GIA scholarship committee.

Funds Avail.: $500. **Number Awarded:** 1. **To Apply:** Applicant must complete the GIA Scholarship application (available at the website), with a letter of recommendation from a person in the jewelry industry. Send application and supporting documents to: Gemological Institute of America, Office of Student Financial Assistance, MS 7 The Robert Mouawad Campus 5345 Armada Drive Carlsbad, CA 92008. **Deadline:** June 15 October 15. **Contact:** Financial aid representative, 800-421-7250 x-4175, financialaid@gia.edu.

3181 ■ Marion H. Halfacre Scholarships *(Graduate/Scholarship)*

Purpose: To promote education in Gemology. **Focus:** Gemology. **Qualif.:** Applicant must be U.S. citizen and permanent resident; at least 17 years old; have a high school diploma or GED equivalency; currently employed or planning to enter in the jewelry industry; applying for On Campus School of Gemology Graduate Gemologist (GG) program; past recipient of GIA scholarship within last five years are not eligible. **Criteria:** Applications will be reviewed by the GIA scholarship committee.

Funds Avail.: Full tuition. **Number Awarded:** 1. **To Apply:** Applicant must complete the GIA Scholarship application (available at the website), with a letter of recommendation from a person in the jewelry industry. Send application and supporting documents to: Gemological Institute of America, Office of Student Financial Assistance, MS 7 The Robert Mouawad Campus 5345 Armada Drive Carlsbad, CA 92008. **Deadline:** June 15 - October 15. **Contact:** Financial aid representative, 800-421-7250 x-4175, financialaid@gia.edu.

3182 ■ Morris Hanauer Scholarships *(Undergraduate/Scholarship)*

Purpose: To promote education in Gemology. **Focus:** Gemology. **Qualif.:** Applicant must be U.S. citizen and permanent resident; at least 17 years old; have a high school diploma or GED equivalency; currently employed or planning to enter in the jewelry industry; applying for Distance Education School of Gemology course or program; past recipient of GIA scholarship within last five years are not eligible. **Criteria:** Applications will be reviewed by the GIA scholarship committee.

Funds Avail.: $600. **Number Awarded:** 1. **To Apply:** Applicant must complete the GIA Scholarship application (available at the website), with a letter of recommendation from a person in the jewelry industry. Send application and supporting documents to: Gemological Institute of America, Office of Student Financial Assistance, MS 7 The Robert Mouawad Campus 5345 Armada Drive Carlsbad, CA 92008. **Deadline:** June 15 - October 15. **Contact:** Financial aid representative, 800-421-7250 x-4175, financialaid@gia.edu.

3183 ■ Peter Hess Scholarships *(Undergraduate/Scholarship)*

Purpose: To provide educational assistance to students. **Focus:** General studies. **Qualif.:** Applicant must be U.S. citizen and permanent resident; at least 17 years old; must be a member, related to a member or planning to join California Jewelers Association; have a high school diploma or GED equivalency; currently employed or planning to enter in the jewelry industry; applying for any On Campus or Distance Education course or program; past recipient of GIA scholarship within last five years are not eligible. **Criteria:** Applications will be reviewed by the GIA scholarship committee.

Funds Avail.: $1000. **Number Awarded:** 1. **To Apply:** Applicant must complete the GIA Scholarship application (available at the website), with a letter of recommendation from a person in the jewelry industry. Send application and supporting documents to: Gemological Institute of America, Office of Student Financial Assistance, MS 7 The Robert Mouawad Campus 5345 Armada Drive Carlsbad, CA 92008. **Deadline:** June 15 - October 15. **Contact:** Financial aid representative, 800-421-7250 x-4175, financialaid@gia.edu.

3184 ■ The Jhaveri Scholarships *(Graduate/Scholarship)*

Purpose: To promote education in Gemology. **Focus:** Gemology; Business. **Qualif.:** Applicant must be U.S. citizen and permanent resident; at least 17 years old; have a high school diploma or GED equivalency; currently employed or planning to enter in the jewelry industry; applying for On Campus School of Business Jewelry Business Management (JBM) program; past recipient of GIA scholarship within last five years are not eligible. **Criteria:** Applications will be reviewed by the GIA scholarship committee.

Funds Avail.: $5000. **Number Awarded:** 1. **To Apply:** Applicant must complete the GIA Scholarship application (available at the website), with a letter of recommendation from a person in the jewelry industry. Send application and supporting documents to: Gemological Institute of America, Office of Student Financial Assistance, MS 7 The Robert Mouawad Campus 5345 Armada Drive Carlsbad, CA 92008. **Deadline:** June 15 October 15. **Contact:** Financial aid representative, 800-421-7250 x-4175, financialaid@gia.edu.

3185 ■ George W. Juno Memorial Scholarships *(Graduate/Scholarship)*

Purpose: To promote education in Gemology. **Focus:** Gemology. **Qualif.:** Applicant must be U.S. citizens and permanent resident; at least 17 years old; have a high school diploma or GED equivalency; currently employed or planning to enter in the jewelry industry; applying for On Campus School of Gemology Graduate Gemologist (GG) courses; past recipient of GIA scholarship within last five years are not eligible. **Criteria:** Applications will be reviewed by the GIA scholarship committee.

Funds Avail.: $1000. **Number Awarded:** 2. **To Apply:** Applicant must complete the GIA Scholarship application (available at the website), with a letter of recommendation from a person in the jewelry industry. Send application and supporting documents to: Gemological Institute of America, Office of Student Financial Assistance, MS 7 The Robert Mouawad Campus 5345 Armada Drive Carlsbad, CA 92008. **Deadline:** June 15 - October 15. **Contact:** Financial aid representative, 800-421-7250 x-4175, financialaid@gia.edu.

3186 ■ Robert Kammerling Scholarships *(Graduate/Scholarship)*

Purpose: To promote education in Gemology. **Focus:** Gemology. **Qualif.:** Applicant must be U.S. citizen and permanent resident; at least 17 years old; have a high school diploma or GED equivalency; currently employed or planning to enter in the jewelry industry; applying for On Campus of Gemology Graduate Gemologist (GG) program; past recipient of GIA scholarship within last five years are not eligible. **Criteria:** Applications will be reviewed by the GIA scholarship committee.

Funds Avail.: Full tuition. **Number Awarded:** 1. **To Apply:** Applicant must complete the GIA Scholarship application (available at the website), with a letter of recommendation from a person in the jewelry industry. Send application and supporting documents to: Gemological Institute of America, Office of Student Financial Assistance, MS 7 The Robert Mouawad Campus 5345 Armada Drive Carlsbad, CA 92008. **Deadline:** June 15 - October 15. **Contact:** Financial aid representative, 800-421-7250 x-4175, financialaid@gia.edu.

3187 ■ Kazanjian Scholarships *(Undergraduate/Scholarship)*

Purpose: To promote education in Gemology. **Focus:** Gemology. **Qualif.:** Applicant must be U.S. citizen and permanent resident; at least 17 years old; have a high school diploma or GED equivalency; currently employed or planning to enter in the jewelry industry; applying for any School of Gemology course or program; past recipient of GIA scholarship within last five years are not eligible. **Criteria:** Applications will be reviewed by the GIA scholarship committee. Priority is given to applicant with no relatives in the jewelry business.

Funds Avail.: $10,000. **Number Awarded:** 2. **To Apply:** Applicant must complete the GIA Scholarship application (available at the website), with a letter of recommendation from a person in the jewelry industry. Send application and supporting documents to: Gemological Institute of America, Office of Student Financial Assistance, MS 7 The Robert Mouawad Campus 5345 Armada Drive Carlsbad, CA 92008. **Deadline:** June 15 - October 15. **Contact:** Financial aid representative, 800-421-7250 x-4175, financialaid@gia.edu.

3188 ■ Richard Kern Scholarships *(Undergraduate/Scholarship)*

Purpose: To promote education in Gemology. **Focus:** Gemology. **Qualif.:** Applicant must be U.S. citizen and permanent resident; at least 17 years old; have a high school diploma or GED equivalency; currently employed or planning to enter in the jewelry industry; applying for On Campus or Distance Education School of Gemology course or program; past recipient of GIA scholarship within last five years are not eligible. **Criteria:** Applications will be reviewed by the GIA scholarship committee.

Funds Avail.: $500. **Number Awarded:** 1. **To Apply:** Applicant must complete the GIA Scholarship application (available at the website), with a letter of recommendation from a person in the jewelry industry. Send application and supporting documents to: Gemological Institute of America, Office of Student Financial Assistance, MS 7 The Robert Mouawad Campus 5345 Armada Drive Carlsbad, CA 92008. **Deadline:** June 15 October 15. **Contact:** Financial aid representative, 800-421-7250 x-4175, financialaid@gia.edu.

3189 ■ Richard T. Liddicoat Scholarships *(Graduate/Scholarship)*

Purpose: To promote education in Gemology. **Focus:** Gemology. **Qualif.:** Applicant must be U.S. citizen and permanent resident; at least 17 years old; have a high school diploma or GED equivalency; currently employed or planning to enter in the jewelry industry; applying for On Campus and Distance Education School of Gemology Graduate Gemologist (GG) program (includes 3 Lab classes of Diamond Grading, Colored Stone Grading, and Gem Identification); past recipient of GIA scholarship within last five years are not eligible. **Criteria:** Applications will be reviewed by the GIA scholarship committee.

Funds Avail.: $600. **Number Awarded:** 1. **To Apply:** Applicant must complete the GIA Scholarship application (available at the website), with a letter of recommendation from a person in the jewelry industry. Send application and supporting documents to: Gemological Institute of America, Office of Student Financial Assistance, MS 7 The Robert Mouawad Campus 5345 Armada Drive Carlsbad, CA 92008. **Deadline:** June 15 - October 15. **Contact:** Financial aid representative, 800-421-7250 x.4175, financialaid@gia.edu.

3190 ■ Lone Star GIA Associate and Alumni Scholarships *(Undergraduate/Scholarship)*

Purpose: To provide educational assistance to students. **Focus:** General studies. **Qualif.:** Applicant must be U.S. citizen and permanent resident; at least 17 years old; have a high school diploma or GED equivalency; currently employed or planning to enter in the jewelry industry; applying for any On Campus, Distance Education, or Lab course or program; past recipient of GIA scholarship within last five years are not eligible. **Criteria:** Applications will be reviewed by the GIA scholarship committee. Preference will be given to applicants residing in Texas, Oklahoma, Louisiana, New Mexico and Arkansas.

Funds Avail.: $500. **Number Awarded:** 1. **To Apply:** Applicant must complete the GIA Scholarship application (available at the website), with a letter of recommendation from a person in the jewelry industry. Send application and supporting documents to: Gemological Institute of America, Office of Student Financial Assistance, MS 7 The Robert Mouawad Campus 5345 Armada Drive Carlsbad, CA 92008. **Deadline:** June 15 - October 15. **Contact:** Financial aid representative, 800-421-7250 x-4175, financialaid@gia.edu.

3191 ■ James R. Lucey Scholarships *(Graduate/Scholarship)*

Purpose: To promote education in Gemology. **Focus:** Gemology. **Qualif.:** Applicant must be U.S. citizen and permanent resident; at least 17 years old; have a high school diploma or GED equivalency; currently employed or planning to enter in the jewelry industry; applying for On Campus School of Gemology Graduate Gemologist (GG) program; past recipient of GIA scholarship within last five years are not eligible. **Criteria:** Applications will be reviewed by the GIA scholarship committee.

Funds Avail.: Full tuition. **Number Awarded:** 1. **To Apply:** Applicant must complete the GIA Scholarship application (available at the website), with a letter of recommendation from a person in the jewelry industry. Send application and supporting documents to: Gemological Institute of America, Office of Student Financial Assistance, MS 7 The Robert Mouawad Campus 5345 Armada Drive Carlsbad, CA 92008. **Deadline:** June 15 - October 15. **Contact:** Financial aid representative, 800-421-7250 x-4175, financialaid@gia.edu.

3192 ■ Irene Mack Scholarships *(Undergraduate/Scholarship)*

Purpose: To promote education in Gemology. **Focus:** Gemology. **Qualif.:** Applicant must be U.S. citizen and permanent resident; at least 17 years old; have a high school diploma or GED equivalency; currently employed or planning to enter in the jewelry industry; applying for Distance Education School of Gemology course or program;

Awards are arranged alphabetically below their administering organizations

past recipient of GIA scholarship within last five years are not eligible. **Criteria:** Applications will be reviewed by the GIA scholarship committee.

Funds Avail.: $500. **Number Awarded:** 2. **To Apply:** Applicant must complete the GIA Scholarship application (available at the website), with a letter of recommendation from a person in the jewelry industry. Send application and supporting documents to: Gemological Institute of America, Office of Student Financial Assistance, MS 7 The Robert Mouawad Campus 5345 Armada Drive Carlsbad, CA 92008. **Deadline:** June 15 - October 15. **Contact:** Financial aid representative, 800-421-7250 x-4175, financialaid@gia.edu.

3193 ■ Vincent Manson Scholarships *(Graduate/Scholarship)*

Purpose: To promote education in Gemology. **Focus:** Gemology. **Qualif.:** Applicant must be U.S. citizen and permanent resident; at least 17 years old; have a high school diploma or GED equivalency; currently employed or planning to enter in the jewelry industry; applying for On Campus of Gemology Graduate Gemologist (GG) program; past recipient of GIA scholarship within last five years are not eligible. **Criteria:** Applications will be reviewed by the GIA scholarship committee.

Funds Avail.: Full tuition. **Number Awarded:** 1. **To Apply:** Applicant must complete the GIA Scholarship application (available at the website), with a letter of recommendation from a person in the jewelry industry. Send application and supporting documents to: Gemological Institute of America, Office of Student Financial Assistance, MS 7 The Robert Mouawad Campus 5345 Armada Drive Carlsbad, CA 92008. **Deadline:** June 15 - October 15. **Contact:** Financial aid representative, 800-421-7250 x-4175, financialaid@gia.edu.

3194 ■ Mikimoto Scholarships *(Graduate/Scholarship)*

Purpose: To promote education in Gemology. **Focus:** Gemology. **Qualif.:** Applicant must be U.S. citizen and permanent resident; at least 17 years old; have a high school diploma or GED equivalency; currently employed or planning to enter in the jewelry industry; applying for Distance Education School of Gemology Graduate Pearls diploma program; past recipient of GIA scholarship within last five years are not eligible. **Criteria:** Applications will be reviewed by the GIA scholarship committee.

Funds Avail.: $690. **Number Awarded:** 8. **To Apply:** Applicant must complete the GIA Scholarship application (available at the website), with a letter of recommendation from a person in the jewelry industry. Send application and supporting documents to: Gemological Institute of America, Office of Student Financial Assistance, MS 7 The Robert Mouawad Campus 5345 Armada Drive Carlsbad, CA 92008. **Deadline:** June 15 October 15. **Contact:** Financial aid representative, 800-421-7250 x-4175, financialaid@gia.edu.

3195 ■ Eunice Miles Scholarships *(Undergraduate/Scholarship)*

Purpose: To provide educational assistance to students. **Focus:** General studies. **Qualif.:** Applicant must be U.S. citizen and permanent resident; at least 17 years old; have a high school diploma or GED equivalency; currently employed or planning to enter in the jewelry industry; applying for any On Campus School or Distance Education course or program; past recipient of GIA scholarship within last five years are not eligible. **Criteria:** Applications will be reviewed by the GIA scholarship committee.

Funds Avail.: $500. **Number Awarded:** 2. **To Apply:** Applicant must complete the GIA Scholarship application (available at the website), with a letter of recommendation from a person in the jewelry industry. Send application and supporting documents to: Gemological Institute of America, Office of Student Financial Assistance, MS 7 The Robert Mouawad Campus 5345 Armada Drive Carlsbad, CA 92008. **Deadline:** June 15 October 15. **Contact:** Financial aid representative, 800-421-7250 x-4175, financialaid@gia.edu.

3196 ■ North Texas GIA Alumni Association Scholarships *(Undergraduate/Scholarship)*

Purpose: To provide educational assistance to students. **Focus:** General studies. **Qualif.:** Applicant must be U.S. citizen and a resident of Texas; at least 17 years old; have a high school diploma or GED equivalency; currently employed or planning to enter in the jewelry industry; applying for any On Campus, Distance Education, or Lab course or program; past recipient of GIA scholarship within last five years are not eligible. **Criteria:** Applications will be reviewed by the GIA scholarship committee. Preference will be given to applicants residing in Texas with zip codes ending in 750xx-757xx, 760xx-769xx, and 790xx-797xx.

Funds Avail.: $1500. **Number Awarded:** 1. **To Apply:** Applicant must complete the GIA Scholarship application (available at the website), with a letter of recommendation from a person in the jewelry industry. Send application and supporting documents to: Gemological Institute of America, Office of Student Financial Assistance, MS 7 The Robert Mouawad Campus 5345 Armada Drive Carlsbad, CA 92008. **Deadline:** June 15 October 15. **Contact:** Financial aid representative, 800-421-7250 x-4175, financialaid@gia.edu.

3197 ■ Matthew A. Runci, MJSA Scholarships *(Undergraduate/Scholarship)*

Purpose: To promote education in Gemology. **Focus:** Gemology; Art industries and trade. **Qualif.:** Applicant must be U.S. citizen and permanent resident; at least 17 years old; have a high school diploma or GED equivalency; currently employed or planning to enter in the jewelry industry; applying for On Campus School of Jewelry Manufacturing Arts courses; past recipient of GIA scholarship within last five years are not eligible. **Criteria:** Applications will be reviewed by the GIA scholarship committee.

Funds Avail.: $500. **Number Awarded:** 1. **To Apply:** Applicant must complete the GIA Scholarship application (available at the website), with a letter of recommendation from a person in the jewelry industry. Send application and supporting documents to: Gemological Institute of America, Office of Student Financial Assistance, MS 7 The Robert Mouawad Campus 5345 Armada Drive Carlsbad, CA 92008. **Deadline:** June 15 - October 15. **Contact:** Financial aid representative, 800-421-7250 x-4175, financialaid@gia.edu.

3198 ■ S.H. Silver Scholarships *(Graduate/Scholarship)*

Purpose: To promote education in Gemology. **Focus:** Gemology; Art industries and trade. **Qualif.:** Applicant must be U.S. citizen and permanent resident; at least 17 years old; have a high school diploma or GED equivalency; currently employed or planning to enter in the jewelry industry; applying for On Campus School of Jewelry Manufacturing

Awards are arranged alphabetically below their administering organizations

Arts Jewelry Design courses; past recipient of GIA scholarship within last five years are not eligible. **Criteria:** Applications will be reviewed by the GIA scholarship committee.

Funds Avail.: $2500. **Number Awarded:** 1. **To Apply:** Applicant must complete the GIA Scholarship application (available at the website), with a letter of recommendation from a person in the jewelry industry. Send application and supporting documents to: Gemological Institute of America, Office of Student Financial Assistance, MS 7 The Robert Mouawad Campus 5345 Armada Drive Carlsbad, CA 92008. **Deadline:** June 15 - October 15. **Contact:** Financial aid representative, 800-421-7250 x-4175, financialaid@gia.edu.

3199 ■ Daniel Swarovski and Company Scholarships *(Graduate/Scholarship)*

Purpose: To promote education in Gemology. **Focus:** Gemology. **Qualif.:** Applicant must be U.S. citizen and permanent resident; at least 17 years old; have a high school diploma or GED equivalency; have 2-3 years work experience in jewelry industry; applying for On Campus School of Gemology Graduate Gemologist (GG) courses; past recipient of GIA scholarship within last five years are not eligible. **Criteria:** Applications will be reviewed by the GIA scholarship committee.

Funds Avail.: No specific amount. **To Apply:** Applicant must complete the GIA Scholarship application (available at the website), with three letters of recommendation, two of which must be from a person in the jewelry industry. Send application and supporting documents to: Gemological Institute of America, Office of Student Financial Assistance, MS 7 The Robert Mouawad Campus 5345 Armada Drive Carlsbad, CA 92008. **Deadline:** June 15 - October 15. **Contact:** Financial aid representative, 800-421-7250 x-4175, financialaid@gia.edu.

3200 ■ Trillion Diamond Company Scholarships *(Undergraduate/Scholarship)*

Purpose: To promote education in Gemology. **Focus:** Gemology. **Qualif.:** Applicant must be U.S. citizen and residing in the state of New York, New Jersey, or Connecticut; at least 17 years old; have a high school diploma or GED equivalency; currently employed or planning to enter in the jewelry industry; applying for Distance Education School of Gemology courses; past recipient of GIA scholarship within last five years are not eligible. **Criteria:** Applications will be reviewed by the GIA scholarship committee.

Funds Avail.: $500. **Number Awarded:** 2. **To Apply:** Applicant must complete the GIA Scholarship application (available at the website), with a letter of recommendation from a person in the jewelry industry. Send application and supporting documents to: Gemological Institute of America, Office of Student Financial Assistance, MS 7 The Robert Mouawad Campus 5345 Armada Drive Carlsbad, CA 92008. **Deadline:** June 15 - October 15. **Contact:** Financial aid representative, 800-421-7250 x-4175, financialaid@gia.edu.

3201 ■ Kurt Wayne Scholarships *(Graduate/Scholarship)*

Purpose: To promote education in Gemology. **Focus:** Gemology; Art industries and trade. **Qualif.:** Applicant must be U.S. citizen and permanent resident; at least 17 years old; have a high school diploma or GED equivalency; currently employed or planning to enter in the jewelry industry; applying for On Campus School of Jewelry Manufacturing Arts Graduate Jeweler (GJ) program courses; past recipient of GIA scholarship within last five years are not eligible. **Criteria:** Applications will be reviewed by the GIA scholarship committee.

Funds Avail.: $1000. **Number Awarded:** 1. **To Apply:** Applicant must complete the GIA Scholarship application (available at the website), with a letter of recommendation from a person in the jewelry industry. Send application and supporting documents to: Gemological Institute of America, Office of Student Financial Assistance, MS 7 The Robert Mouawad Campus 5345 Armada Drive Carlsbad, CA 92008. **Deadline:** June 15 - October 15. **Contact:** Financial aid representative, 800-421-7250 x-4175, financialaid@gia.edu.

3202 ■ Robert B. Westover Scholarships *(Undergraduate/Scholarship)*

Purpose: To provide educational assistance to students. **Focus:** General studies. **Qualif.:** Applicant must be U.S. citizen and permanent resident; at least 17 years old; must be a member, related to a member or planning to join California Jewelers Association; have a high school diploma or GED equivalency; currently employed or planning to enter in the jewelry industry; applying for any On Campus or Distance Education course or program; past recipient of GIA scholarship within last five years are not eligible. **Criteria:** Applications will be reviewed by the GIA scholarship committee.

Funds Avail.: $1000. **Number Awarded:** 1. **To Apply:** Applicant must complete the GIA Scholarship application (available at the website), with a letter of recommendation from a person in the jewelry industry. Send application and supporting documents to: Gemological Institute of America, Office of Student Financial Assistance, MS 7 The Robert Mouawad Campus 5345 Armada Drive Carlsbad, CA 92008. **Deadline:** June 15 - October 15. **Contact:** Financial aid representative, 800-421-7250 x-4175, financialaid@gia.edu.

3203 ■ William Goldberg Diamond Corp. Scholarships *(Undergraduate/Scholarship)*

Purpose: To promote education in Gemology. **Focus:** Gemology. **Qualif.:** Applicant must be U.S. citizen and permanent resident; at least 17 years old; have a high school diploma or GED equivalency; currently employed or planning to enter in the jewelry industry; applying for any School of Gemology course or program; past recipient of GIA scholarship within last five years are not eligible. **Criteria:** Applications will be reviewed by the GIA scholarship committee.

Funds Avail.: $10,000. **Number Awarded:** 1. **To Apply:** Applicant must complete the GIA Scholarship application (available at the website), with a letter of recommendation from a person in the jewelry industry. Send application and supporting documents to: Gemological Institute of America, Office of Student Financial Assistance, MS 7 The Robert Mouawad Campus 5345 Armada Drive Carlsbad, CA 92008. **Deadline:** June 15 - October 15. **Contact:** Financial aid representative, 800-421-7250 x-4175, financialaid@gia.edu.

3204 ■ Milton Wolf Scholarships *(Undergraduate/Scholarship)*

Purpose: To provide educational assistance to students. **Focus:** General studies. **Qualif.:** Applicant must be U.S. citizen and a legal resident of California; at least 17 years old; have a high school diploma or GED equivalency; currently employed or planning to enter in the jewelry industry; applying for any On Campus educational course or program taken at the GIA Carlsbad campus; past recipient of GIA scholarship within last five years are not eligible. **Criteria:** Applications will be reviewed by the GIA scholarship committee.

Funds Avail.: $500. **Number Awarded:** 1. **To Apply:** Applicant must complete the GIA Scholarship application (available at the website), with a letter of recommendation from a person in the jewelry industry. Send application and supporting documents to: Gemological Institute of America, Office of Student Financial Assistance, MS 7 The Robert Mouawad Campus 5345 Armada Drive Carlsbad, CA 92008. **Deadline:** June 15 - October 15. **Contact:** Financial aid representative, 800-421-7250 x-4175, financialaid@gia.edu.

3205 ■ Zale Corporation Scholarships
(Undergraduate/Scholarship)

Purpose: To provide educational assistance to students. **Focus:** General studies. **Qualif.:** Applicant must be U.S. citizen and permanent resident; at least 17 years old; have a high school diploma or GED equivalency; currently employed or planning to enter in the jewelry industry; applying for any On Campus or Distance Education course or program; past recipient of GIA scholarship within last five years are not eligible. **Criteria:** Applications will be reviewed by the GIA scholarship committee.

Funds Avail.: $5000. **Number Awarded:** 1. **To Apply:** Applicant must complete the GIA Scholarship application (available at the website), with a letter of recommendation from a person in the jewelry industry. Send application and supporting documents to: Gemological Institute of America, Office of Student Financial Assistance, MS 7 The Robert Mouawad Campus 5345 Armada Drive Carlsbad, CA 92008. **Deadline:** June 15 October 15. **Contact:** Financial aid representative, 800-421-7250 x-4175, financialaid@gia.edu.

3206 ■ General Aviation Manufacturers Association

1400 K St. NW, Ste. 801
Washington, DC 20005
Ph: (202)393-1500
Fax: (202)842-4063
E-mail: webmaster@gama.aero
URL: http://www.gama.aero

3207 ■ Dr. Harold S. Wood Award for Excellence
(Undergraduate/Award/Prize)

Purpose: To support a college student attending a National Intercollegiate Flying Association member college or university program. **Focus:** Aviation. **Qualif.:** Candidate for the award must be an enrolled college student and have completed a semester at a NIFA participating institution with GPA of 3.0 on a 4.0 scale or better and must have rendered service to NIFA, aviation clubs or aviation-related activities or non-aviation extra-curricular service and contribution to school and community. **Criteria:** The applicant must be nominated and will be judged on the basis of GPA, community and school activities and aviation-related contributions.

Funds Avail.: $1,000. **Number Awarded:** 1. **To Apply:** Applicants must submit transcript and letters of recommendation with the application. **Deadline:** March 21.

3208 ■ Geological Society of America

PO Box 9140
Boulder, CO 80301-9140
Ph: (303)357-1000
Fax: (303)257-1070
Free: 888-443-4472
E-mail: gsaservice@geosociety.org
URL: http://www.geosociety.org

3209 ■ Farouk El-Baz Student Research Grants
(Doctorate, Graduate, Undergraduate/Grant)

Purpose: To encourage and support desert studies by students in their senior year of undergraduate studies, or at the master's or Ph.D. level. **Focus:** Geology. **Qualif.:** Applicants must be a GSA member; applicants must be in their senior year of their undergraduate studies, or at the master's or Ph.D. level. **Criteria:** Recipients are selected based on the significance of the project proposal.

Funds Avail.: No specified amount. **To Apply:** Applicants must submit a one-page description of proposed research under title; letter of recommendation by university research advisor. **Deadline:** June 1. **Contact:** awards@geosociety.org;

3210 ■ Geological Society of America Graduate Student Research Grants *(Doctorate, Graduate/Grant)*

Purpose: To provide partial support of master's and doctoral thesis research in geological science for graduate students enrolled in universities in the United States, Canada, Mexico, and Central America. **Focus:** Geology. **Qualif.:** Applicants must be GSA members currently enrolled in a U.S., Canadian, Mexican, or Central American university or college in an earth science degree program with geologic component. **Criteria:** Recipients are selected based on the qualifications of the candidate and his/her academic standing.

Funds Avail.: No specified amount. **Number Awarded:** 3. **To Apply:** Applicants must fill out the online application form. **Deadline:** February 1.

3211 ■ Georgia Engineering Foundation

233 Peachtree St. Harris Tower, Ste. 700
Atlanta, GA 30303
Ph: (404)521-2324
Fax: (404)521-0283
URL: http://www.gefinc.org

3212 ■ Georgia Engineering Foundation Scholarships *(Undergraduate/Scholarship)*

Purpose: To provide financial assistance to those students who are in need. **Focus:** Engineering. **Qualif.:** Applicants must be Georgia students who are preparing for a career in engineering or engineering technology; must be U.S citizens; must be enrolled in an engineering or engineering technology ABET-accredited program leading to a B.S or graduate degree. **Criteria:** Preference will be given to students who meet the criteria.

Funds Avail.: Ranging from $1,000-$5,000. **To Apply:** Applicants must check the available website for the required materials. **Deadline:** August 29. **Contact:** Georgia Engineering Foundation at the above address (see entry 3211).

3213 ■ Georgia Press Educational Foundation

3066 Mercer University Dr., Ste. 200
Atlanta, GA 30341-4137

Awards are arranged alphabetically below their administering organizations

Ph: (770)454-6776
Fax: (770)454-6778
E-mail: mail@gapress.org
URL: http://www.gapress.org

3214 ■ Durwood McAlister Scholarships
(Undergraduate/Scholarship)

Purpose: To provide scholarship for outstanding students majoring in print journalism at a Georgia college or university. **Focus:** Journalism. **Qualif.:** Applicants must be enrolled full-time taking up journalism. **Criteria:** Selection will be based on the committee's criteria.

Funds Avail.: No specific amount. **To Apply:** Scholarship application can be obtained from the GPEF website. The following documents must be enclosed in your application: most recent grade transcript; anticipated budget; school photograph; copy of SAT scores; parents'/your tax return; and recommendations of high school counselor, principal, college professor, or Georgia Press Association member. **Deadline:** February 1.

Remarks: The McAlister Scholarship is named in honor of Durwood McAlister, former editor of The Atlanta Journal. **Contact:** Georgia Press Educational Foundation at the above address (see entry 3213).

3215 ■ Morris Newspaper Corp. Scholarships
(Undergraduate/Scholarship)

Purpose: To provide scholarships for outstanding print journalism students. **Focus:** Journalism. **Qualif.:** Applicants must be enrolled full-time taking up journalism. **Criteria:** Selection will be based on the committee's criteria.

Funds Avail.: No specific amount. **To Apply:** Applications are submitted through newspapers in the Morris Newspaper Corporation chain. **Deadline:** February 1.

Remarks: Established in 1987 by Charles Morris. **Contact:** Georgia Press Educational Foundation at the above address (see entry 3213).

3216 ■ William C. Rogers Scholarships
(Undergraduate/Scholarship)

Purpose: To award scholarships to Georgia residents attending Georgia colleges and universities. **Focus:** Journalism. **Qualif.:** Applicant must be a junior or senior majoring in the news-editorial sequence at the Grady College of Journalism and Mass Communication at the University of Georgia. **Criteria:** Recipient is selected from nominations made by the University of Georgia.

Funds Avail.: No specific amount. **To Apply:** Scholarship application can be obtained from the GPEF website. The following documents must be enclosed in your application: most recent grade transcript; anticipated budget; school photograph; copy of SAT scores; parents'/your tax return; and recommendations of high school counselor, principal, college professor, or Georgia Press Association member. **Deadline:** February 1.

Remarks: The Rogers Scholarship is named in honor of William C. Rogers, Publisher of The Blade, Sawinsboro, and a past president of the Georgia Press Association. **Contact:** Georgia Press Educational Foundation at the above address (see entry 3213).

3217 ■ Kirk Sutlive Scholarships
(Undergraduate/Scholarship)

Purpose: To award scholarships to Georgia residents attending Georgia colleges and universities. **Focus:** Journalism. **Qualif.:** Applicant must be a junior or senior majoring in either the news-editorial or public relations sequence at the Henry W. Grady College of Journalism and Mass Communication at the University of Georgia. **Criteria:** The recipient is selected from three nominations submitted by the University of Georgia.

Funds Avail.: No specific amount. **To Apply:** Scholarship application can be obtained from the GPEF website. The following documents must be enclosed in your application: most recent grade transcript; anticipated budget; school photograph; copy of SAT scores; parents'/your tax return; and recommendations of high school counselor, principal, college professor, or Georgia Press Association member. **Deadline:** February 1. **Contact:** Georgia Press Educational Foundation at the above address (see entry 3213).

3218 ■ Gerber Foundation

4747 W 48th St., Ste. 153
Fremont, MI 49412-8119
Ph: (231)924-3175
Fax: (231)924-7906
E-mail: tgf@ncresa.org
URL: http://www.gerberfoundation.org

3219 ■ Gerber Foundation Merit Scholarships
(Undergraduate/Scholarship)

Purpose: To assist graduating students from one of the five school districts in Newaygo County, Michigan. **Focus:** General studies. **Qualif.:** Students must have a GPA of 3.70 or below. **Criteria:** Selection will be based on merit.

Funds Avail.: $2,000. **To Apply:** Applications may be submitted online or by sending the application forms to the Foundation. Application forms can be obtained from the high school counselor's office or from the Foundation office. Applicants must also submit the following: educational report from Counselor (Form S-1); high school transcript; 1st Recommendation (Form S-2 or letter); 2nd Recommendation (Form S-2 or letter); personal information and financial summary (Form S-3); and personal essay (typed, 500-1000 word essay). **Deadline:** February 28. **Contact:** Gerber Foundation at the above address (see entry 3218).

3220 ■ Daniel Gerber, Sr. Medallion Scholarships *(Undergraduate/Scholarship)*

Purpose: To assist graduating students from one of the five school districts in Newaygo County, Michigan. **Focus:** General studies. **Qualif.:** Students must have a GPA of 3.71 or higher. **Criteria:** Selection will be based on the committee's criteria.

Funds Avail.: $8,000. **To Apply:** Applications may be submitted online or by sending the application forms to the Foundation. Application forms can be obtained from the high school counselor's office or from the Foundation office. Applicants must also submit the following: educational report from Counselor (Form S-1); high school transcript; 1st Recommendation (Form S-2 or letter); 2nd Recommendation (Form S-2 or letter); personal information and financial summary (Form S-3); and personal essay (typed, 500-1000 word essay). **Deadline:** July 1. **Contact:** Gerber foundation at the above address (see entry 3218).

3221 ■ German Academic Exchange Service

871 United Nations Plz.
New York, NY 10017
Ph: (212)758-3223

Awards are arranged alphabetically below their administering organizations

Fax: (212)755-5780
E-mail: daadny@daad.org
URL: http://www.daad.org

3222 ■ Leo Baeck Institute - DAAD Fellowship *(Doctorate/Fellowship)*

Purpose: To provide financial assistance to students for dissertation research work and to academics for writing a scholarly essay or book. **Focus:** German studies. **Qualif.:** Applicants must be U.S. citizens and PhD candidates or recent PhDs (degree awarded within the last two years). **Criteria:** Selection of applicants will be based on the application and other supporting documents.

Funds Avail.: $2000. **To Apply:** Applicants must submit the following: completed application form, curriculum vitae, a full description of the research project; for doctoral students, send official transcripts for graduate and undergraduate work, evidence of enrollment in a Ph.D program, one letter of recommendation by their doctoral advisor and one by another scholar familiar with their work; for Ph.Ds, evidence of their degree (transcripts not required) and; two letters of recommendation from two colleagues familiar with their research. **Deadline:** November 15.

3223 ■ DAAD Study Scholarship Awards *(Graduate/Scholarship)*

Purpose: To provide the opportunity to study in Germany, or complete a Master's degree course and obtain a degree from a German higher education institution. **Focus:** Dentistry, Medicine, Pharmacy, Veterinary medicine. **Qualif.:** Applicants must be graduating seniors (fourth or final year of undergraduate studies) or those with undergraduate degree in all academic fields; must be enrolled full-time at any North American University; citizens of US or Canada but foreigners should have studied at any accredited US or Canadian university for two years; requested to have a study project to make a stay in Germany essential. **Criteria:** Preference will be given to applicants who have been invited by a faculty member at a German university to study at a particular university department.

Funds Avail.: No specific amount. **To Apply:** Applicant must submit the application form with the supplemental form (for music, fine arts, dance only), CV/Resume, study proposal, two letter of recommendation, evidence of contact with German Institution, DAAD Language evaluation form and transcript of record. **Deadline:** November 15.

3224 ■ DAAD Undergraduate Scholarship Program *(Undergraduate/Scholarship)*

Purpose: To support undergraduate US and Canadian students interested in studying, doing research, or completing an internship in Germany. **Focus:** General studies. **Qualif.:** Applicant must currently be a second or third year student. Students are eligible with outstanding academic records and personal integrity, as evinced by both their grades and letters of recommendation; must be a U.S. or Canadian citizen or permanent residents; has interest in contemporary German and European affairs; full-time students in an undergraduate degree-granting program at an accredited North American college or university; younger than 32 before the grant starts. **Criteria:** Preference will be given to students whose projects or programs are based at an organized by a German university.

Funds Avail.: No specific amount. **To Apply:** Applicants must submit: the DAAD language evaluation form with signature, supplemental documents and materials, 3 copies; resume; Project Proposal (approximately 3 pages); recommendation letter from major professors; any of: Acceptance into Study Abroad Program, Exchange Program, letter by mentor or invitation from a German university; transcripts; Language Evaluation Certificate. Application and other supporting document must be sent to: German Academic Exchange Service/DAAD New York, 871 United Nations Plaza, New York, NY 10017-USA. **Deadline:** January 31.

3225 ■ Faculty Research Visit Grant *(Doctorate/Grant)*

Purpose: To pursue research at universities, libraries, archives, institutes or laboratories in Germany. **Focus:** General studies. **Qualif.:** Applicants must be Scholars at American or Canadian universities or research institutions holding a Ph.D. (or equivalent) and have been working in research or teaching full time for at least two years after receipt of the doctorate; U.S. or Canadian citizens (German nationals must have been working in a U.S. or Canadian institution for six consecutive years); should possess adequate knowledge of the German language; applicants may not hold a DAAD grant and a grant from another German or German-American organization concurrently for the same project and previous grantees can only be qualified after three years. **Criteria:** Scholarship decisions are made by an independent academic selection committee based on an outstanding academic record and potential, an evaluation of the validity and feasibility of the proposed project, and of the necessity to carry it out in Germany.

Funds Avail.: 2,240 Euros. **To Apply:** Applicant must submit a completed DAAD application form entitled "Research Visit for Faculty"; curriculum vitae not to exceed five pages, complete list of publications; a detailed description of the research project, up to five pages in length which includes a literature review and information on significance methodology, availability or quality of data, and the need for carrying out research in Germany; letter(s) of invitation from the German institution(s) where the applicant plans to undertake research activities; request an itinerary and an approximate time table if more than one institution will be visited. **Deadline:** January 15 and August 1.

3226 ■ German Studies Research Grant *(Undergraduate/Grant)*

Purpose: To encourage research and promote the study of cultural, political, historical, economic, and social aspects of modern and contemporary German affairs from an inter and multidisciplinary perspective. **Focus:** German studies. **Qualif.:** Applicant must be a undergraduates with at least junior standing pursuing a German Studies track or minor may be nominated for the grant by their department and/or program chair; must be citizens of the U.S. enrolled full time at the university that nominates them; must be younger than 32 at the start of the grant period. **Criteria:** Selection of applicant will be based on the application and other supporting documents.

Funds Avail.: $1,500-$2,500. **To Apply:** Applicant must submit a completed DAAD application form, resume, detailed description of the research project or the pre dissertation proposal, including a research plan and itinerary, budget statement, list of German language and German Studies courses taken, two letters of recommendation, including one from the professor supervising the German Studies curriculum or the research project, DAAD language evaluation form signed by a German Department faculty member, official transcript of records. **Deadline:** May 1 and November 1.

Awards are arranged alphabetically below their administering organizations

3227 ■ Intensive Language Course Grants *(Doctorate/Grant)*

Purpose: To enhance language proficiency in Germany. **Focus:** German studies. **Qualif.:** Applicants must be a student currently enrolled full-time in a graduate program in all fields of study except English, German, or any other modern language or literature; must have completed three semesters of college German or have achieved an equivalent level of language proficiency; foreign nationals other than U.S. and Canada must be full-time graduate at a U.S. or Canadian university for at least one academic year; must have completed three semesters of college German or equivalent level of language proficiency; no previous grantee for the past three years; must be no older than 32. **Criteria:** Applicants will be assessed based on academic record and statements of projected academic and professional future.

Funds Avail.: 2,650 Euros. **To Apply:** A complete DAAD application form; a detailed statement (in English) of approximately 500 words explaining why the applicant wants to attend the intensive language course; resume; a recommendation letter from a professor in the applicant's major field of study; complete transcript of records; DAAD language evaluation form (Sprachzeugnis); list of German language courses taken. Application must be sent to: DAAD New York office. **Deadline:** January 31.

3228 ■ InternXchange *(Undergraduate/Internship)*

Purpose: To place strong emphasis on intercultural exchange and the transmission of cultural values; to provide outstanding young journalism students the opportunity to immerse themselves in the society, culture, values, and political attitudes in Germany. **Focus:** Journalism. **Qualif.:** Applicants should be journalism or majoring journalism-related field student in the U.S.; undergraduate, graduate, and graduating seniors; must have German language proficiency at least equal to the advanced intermediate level; has interest in Germany and Germany affairs. **Criteria:** A total of 40 applicants will be invited to a selection interview in New York City. A selection committee of American and German experts will then select up to 20 participants/ scholarship recipients.

Funds Avail.: 600 Euros. **To Apply:** Applicant must Complete the online form with signature with two copies; submit resume in English, statement of motivation in English, two pages, double spaced, one-page journalistic writing sample or broadcast transcript, two letters of recommendation from professors in major field of study, official academic transcripts, DAAD German Language Evaluation Certificate **Deadline:** February 15. **Contact:** Laura Montgomery at montgomery@daad.org.

3229 ■ Learn German in Germany *(Doctorate/Grant)*

Purpose: TO encourage DAAD faculty members to attend intensive language courses at Goethe-Instituts in Germany. **Focus:** German studies. **Qualif.:** Applicants must be faculty members in all academic fields except modern languages and literatures which is working in research or teaching full-time at a U.S. university or research institution for at least two years after receipt of the doctorate; U.S. citizens; no teaching experience in the fields of English, German or any modern languages or literatures accepted. **Criteria:** Preference will be given to applicants in the social sciences, the natural sciences, engineering and professional schools, who are in mid-career and are under 46 years of age; must have a basic knowledge of German; should not have previously studied in a German-speaking country for more than two months and/or received a grant to attend a German language course from DAAD or any other organization within the last three years.

Funds Avail.: 1,700 Euros. **Number Awarded:** 2. **To Apply:** Submit a completed DAAD application form; curriculum vitae not to exceed five pages; a detailed statement explaining why the applicant wants to attend a Goethe Institute language course in Germany; accomplish the language evaluation (self-test form enclosed with application); must have the list of publications and a list of courses taught during the previous academic year. **Deadline:** January 31.

3230 ■ Study Scholarships for Artists or Musicians *(Graduate/Scholarship)*

Purpose: To provide the opportunity to study in Germany, or complete a postgraduate degree course and obtain a degree from a German higher education institution. **Focus:** Fine arts, Architecture, Music, Dance. **Qualif.:** Applicants in the fields of Fine Arts, Architecture, Music and Dance, other academic fields are welcome to apply for the regular Study Scholarship; graduating seniors must be full-time at an accredited university for two years; U.S. or Canadian citizens. **Criteria:** Preference will be given to applicants who have been invited by a faculty member at a German university to study at a particular university department.

Funds Avail.: 750 Euros. **To Apply:** Applicant must complete the online application form available in the website and must have the following: Supplemental materials, CV/Resume, Study proposal, two letter of recommendation, evidence of contact with German Institution and transcript of records. **Deadline:** November 1.

3231 ■ University Summer Course Grants *(Undergraduate/Grant)*

Purpose: To attend a broad range of summer courses at German universities which focus mainly on literary, cultural, political and economic aspects of modern and contemporary Germany. **Focus:** German studies. **Qualif.:** Applicant must be a full-time student in a Canadian or US colleges or universities in any field of study; must at least reached Junior standing or third year (10 full-course credits for Canadians) at the time of application; must be younger than 32 at the start of the grant period. **Criteria:** Applicants will be assessed on the basis of their academic and professional future.

Funds Avail.: 770 Euros. **To Apply:** Applicant must submit a completed DAAD application form, autobiographical essay in German, a detailed statement (in English) of approximately 500 words explaining why the applicant wants to attend a university summer course, recommendation letter written by a professor in the applicant's major field of study but the recommendation should not be from the same professor who evaluates the language proficiency, complete, official transcripts of all post-secondary studies, DAAD language evaluation form (Sprachzeugnis) signed by any member of German Department at the applicant's institution or by an official of a Goethe Institute, **Deadline:** January 31.

3232 ■ German Historical Institute

1607 New Hampshire Ave. NW
Washington, DC 20009-2562
Ph: (202)387-3355
Fax: (202)483-3430
E-mail: info@ghi-dc.org

Awards are arranged alphabetically below their administering organizations

URL: http://www.ghi-dc.org

3233 ■ Doctoral and Postdoctoral Fellowships
(Doctorate, Postgraduate/Fellowship)

Purpose: To provide financial assistance for German and American doctoral students and post-doctoral scholars in the fields of German history, the history of German-American relations, and the history of the role of Germany and the USA in international relations. **Focus:** German studies; History, American. **Qualif.:** Applicants must be German and American doctoral students and post-doctoral scholars in the fields of German history, the history of German-American relations, and the history of the role of Germany and the USA in international relations. **Criteria:** Scholarship recipient will be selected based on the jury's review of the application materials.

Funds Avail.: 1,600 Euro for doctoral students; 2,800 Euro for post-doctoral scholars. **To Apply:** Applicants must submit two copies of: a cover letter; curriculum vitae; transcripts; project descriptions (in 3,000 words); research schedule; letter of reference. **Deadline:** May 20 and October 15.

3234 ■ GHI Fellowships at the Horner Library
(Doctorate/Fellowship)

Purpose: To provide travel subsidy and allowance to PhD and MA students for their research at the Joseph Horner Memorial Library in Philadelphia. **Focus:** General studies. **Qualif.:** Applicants must be PhD or MA students. **Criteria:** Scholarship recipient will be selected based on the Selection Committee's review of the application materials.

Funds Avail.: $1,000-$3,500 and a travel subsidy. **Number Awarded:** 2-4. **To Apply:** Applicants must submit a two-page project description; a curriculum vitae, copies of transcripts; and the name of the reference. Applications (in English or German) should be made electronically to the GHI. **Deadline:** March 1.

3235 ■ Kade-Heideking Fellowships *(Doctorate/Fellowship)*

Purpose: To provide financial assistance for German doctoral students. **Focus:** German studies; History, American; European studies. **Qualif.:** Applicants must be German doctoral students working in the areas of: American history and German-American relations; international history; and German and European history. **Criteria:** Scholarship recipient will be selected based on the Selection Committee's review of the application materials.

Funds Avail.: $30,000. **Number Awarded:** 1. **To Apply:** Applicants must submit a cover letter; curriculum vitae; proof of academic degree; 8-10 pages of project description; research schedule; two confidential reference letters.

Remarks: The fellowship is funded by the Annette Kade Charitable Trust.

3236 ■ Thyssen-Heideking Fellowships
(Postdoctorate/Fellowship)

Purpose: To provide financial assistance for American scholars. **Focus:** German studies; History, American; European studies. **Qualif.:** Applicants must an American scholars working in the areas of: American history and German-American relations; international history; and German and European history. **Criteria:** Scholarship recipient will be selected based on the Selection Committee's review of the application materials.

Funds Avail.: 25,000 Euro. **Number Awarded:** 1. **To Apply:** Applicants must submit a cover letter; curriculum vitae; proof of academic degree; 8-10 pages project description; research schedule; two confidential reference letters. **Deadline:** November 15.

3237 ■ The German Society of Pennsylvania

611 Spring Garden St.
Philadelphia, PA 19123
Ph: (215)627-2332
Fax: (215)627-5297
E-mail: info@germansociety.org
URL: http://www.germansociety.org

3238 ■ German Society Scholarships
(Undergraduate/Scholarship)

Purpose: To provide financial assistance for undergraduate students majoring in German language and literature. **Focus:** Foreign languages; German studies. **Qualif.:** Applicant must be a resident of the Greater Delaware Valley; and a high school senior intending to major in German, or a German major (Double majors are also eligible). **Criteria:** Awards are based on the student's achievement and promise. Financial need may also be considered.

Funds Avail.: $2500. **To Apply:** Applicants must submit a completed application form; a German writing sample (up to one typewritten page); recent transcript; and two letters of reference. **Deadline:** March 17.

3239 ■ Keith Gilmore Foundation

5160 Skyline Way NE
Calgary, AB, Canada T2E 6V1
Ph: (403)274-1734
E-mail: kgf@keithgilmorefoundation.com
URL: http://www.keithgilmorefoundation.com

3240 ■ Keith Gilmore Foundation - Diploma Scholarships *(Professional Development/Scholarship)*

Purpose: To provide scholarships for deserving individuals. **Focus:** Agriculture, Economic aspects; Journalism; Communications. **Qualif.:** Applicants must be individuals enrolled in a recognized diploma program in agriculture, journalism and/or communications, leading to a career in the field of agriculture. **Criteria:** Selection of recipients is based on academic merit, contribution to school and/or community and indication of academic promise.

Funds Avail.: $1,000. **Number Awarded:** 4. **To Apply:** Application forms are available online at www.keithgilmorefoundation.com. Completed application must be sent to Keith Gilmore Foundation, 5160 Skyline Way NE, Calgary, AB T2E 6V1. **Deadline:** July 1.

3241 ■ Keith Gilmore Foundation - Postgraduate Scholarships *(Postgraduate/Scholarship)*

Purpose: To provide scholarships for deserving individuals. **Focus:** Agriculture, Economic aspects; Medicine, Veterinary; Journalism; Communications. **Qualif.:** Applicant must be an individual enrolled in a postgraduate degree program in agriculture, veterinary medicine, journalism and/or communications at a recognized university, leading to a career in the field of agriculture. **Criteria:** Selection of recipients is based on academic merit, contribution to school and/or community and indication of academic promise.

Funds Avail.: $2,000. **Number Awarded:** 2. **To Apply:** Application forms are available online at www.keithgilmorefoundation.com. Completed application must be sent to Keith Gilmore Foundation, 5160 Skyline Way NE, Calgary, AB T2E 6V1. **Deadline:** July 1.

3242 ■ Keith Gilmore Foundation - Undergraduate Scholarships *(Undergraduate/Scholarship)*

Purpose: To provide scholarships for deserving individuals. **Focus:** Agriculture, Economic aspects; Medicine, Veterinary; Journalism; Communications. **Qualif.:** Applicant must be an individual enrolled in an undergraduate degree program in agriculture, veterinary medicine, journalism and/or communications at a recognized university, leading to a career in the field of agriculture. **Criteria:** Selection of recipients is based on academic merit, contribution to school and/or community and indication of academic promise.

Funds Avail.: $1,500. **Number Awarded:** 4. **To Apply:** Application forms are available online at www.keithgilmorefoundation.com. Completed application must be sent to Keith Gilmore Foundation, 5160 Skyline Way NE, Calgary, AB T2E 6V1. **Deadline:** July 1.

3243 ■ Gleaner Life Insurance Association

5200 West Us Hwy. 223
Adrian, MI 49221-7984
Ph: 800-992-1894
Fax: (517)265-6191
E-mail: membercare@gleanerlife.org
URL: http://www.gleanerlife.org

3244 ■ Gleaner Life Insurance Scholarship Foundation *(Undergraduate/Scholarship)*

Purpose: To strengthen the brotherhood. **Focus:** General studies. **Qualif.:** An applicant must be senior high school student or graduate; he or she is planning to attend the college of education; an applicant must be full time which requires ten or more credit hours. **Criteria:** Applicants are scored based on the completion of the application; leadership; quality of activities; letters of recommendation; applicant's personal statement; and overall quality of the application.

Funds Avail.: No specific amount. **Number Awarded:** 1. **To Apply:** Applicant must fill out the application form and present any information and/or reasons for applying; applicant should attach an official transcript of high school records (applicants already graduated from high school are also required to submit high school transcript or attach an official transcript of college record if applicable); applicant must submit a list of scholastic awards won (local, county, district, state or national); result of an aptitude test at junior or senior level; evaluation of student (leadership, perseverance, prediction of post-high school success). **Deadline:** April 1.

3245 ■ Godparents for Tanzania

PO Box 20221
Roanoke, VA 24018
E-mail: tellmemore@godparents4tz.org
URL: http://www.agpsf.org

3246 ■ Godparents for Tanzania Scholarships *(Undergraduate/Scholarship)*

Purpose: To provide financial assistance for projects that are intended to help educate young people. **Focus:** General studies. **Qualif.:** Applicants must be Tanzanian citizens from the Kilimanjaro or Karatu areas of Tanzania; must demonstrate a satisfactory academic record at current level of education; must be attending school in Tanzania; must be studying on the secondary or first degree university level; and must agree to work in Tanzania for five years following graduation. **Criteria:** Recipients are selected based on multiple criteria including academic ability, family circumstances and financial need.

Funds Avail.: No specific amount. **To Apply:** Applicants must submit completed application along with a letter of reference from a non-related adult, preferably an educator or clergy person.

3247 ■ Goethe Society of North America

University of Pittsburgh
1409 Cathedral of Learning
Pittsburgh, PA 15260
URL: http://www.goethesociety.org

3248 ■ Gloria Flaherty Scholarships *(Graduate/Scholarship)*

Purpose: To provide financial aid to worthy undergraduate or graduate students who wish to further their education in areas related to the interests promoted by the society. **Focus:** General studies. **Qualif.:** Applicant must be a graduate student working on Goethe and/or the Age of Goethe; must be a student who will either deliver a paper or complete a research project before receiving a doctoral degree are eligible. **Criteria:** Candidates will be selected based on their research proposal.

Funds Avail.: $500. **Number Awarded:** 2. **To Apply:** Application and other supporting documents must be submitted to: Department of Germanic Languages and Literatures, 745 Williams Hall, University of Pennsylvania, PA 19104-6305. **Deadline:** March 31.

3249 ■ Golden Key International Honour Society

621 Noeth Ave. NE., Ste. C-100
Atlanta, GA 30308
Ph: (404)377-2400
Fax: (678)420-6757
Free: 800-377-2401
E-mail: memberservices@goldenkey.org
URL: http://www.goldenkey.org

3250 ■ Boeing Business Scholarships *(Undergraduate/Scholarship)*

Purpose: To financially assist students studying business. **Focus:** Business. **Qualif.:** Applicant must be a U.S. undergraduate member currently enrolled in classes in a degree-granting program. **Criteria:** Selection is based on academic achievement, and demonstrated leadership qualities.

Funds Avail.: $1000. **Number Awarded:** 1. **To Apply:** Applicants must submit a letter of recommendation from a professor in the discipline; and a current, comprehensive official academic transcript. Submit materials to awards@goldenkey.org. **Deadline:** May 15.

Remarks: Applicants can apply more than one scholarships. **Contact:** awards@goldenkey.org.

3251 ■ Boeing Engineering Scholarships *(Undergraduate/Scholarship)*

Purpose: To financially assist students studying engineering. **Focus:** Engineering. **Qualif.:** Applicant must be a U.S.

undergraduate member currently enrolled in classes at a degree-granting program. **Criteria:** Selection is based on academic achievement, and demonstrated leadership qualities.

Funds Avail.: $10000. **Number Awarded:** 4. **To Apply:** Applicants must submit a letter of recommendation from a professor in the discipline; and a current, comprehensive official academic transcript. Submit materials to awards@goldenkey.org. **Deadline:** May 15.

Remarks: Applicants can apply for more than one scholarship.

3252 ■ Golden Key International Honour Society New Graduate Member Scholarships
(Undergraduate/Scholarship)

Purpose: To support a Golden Key new member with their education. **Focus:** General studies. **Qualif.:** Applicant must be a new U.S. Golden Key graduate student members; have accepted Golden Key membership during the 2007-2008 academic year; and enrolled in classes in a degree-granting program. **Criteria:** Selection is based on the application.

Funds Avail.: $1000. **Number Awarded:** 5. **To Apply:** Applicants must complete the online application form. **Deadline:** May 15 and December 14.

Remarks: A Golden Key Member ID is required to complete the application. **Contact:** awards@goldenkey.org.

3253 ■ Golden Key International Honour Society Study Abroad Scholarships *(Undergraduate/Scholarship)*

Purpose: To assist members who participate in a study abroad program. **Focus:** General studies. **Qualif.:** Applicants must be undergraduate members currently enrolled in a study abroad program; or will be enrolled the academic year immediately following the granting of the award. **Criteria:** Selection committee will review applicants based on academic achievement and relevance of study abroad program to major field of study.

Funds Avail.: $1000. **Number Awarded:** 10. **To Apply:** Applicants must register scholarship application online. Print the cover page from the online registration and use it as a cover for the entire application and attach a description of the planned academic program (maximum of 5 pages), a one-page statement signed by a professor, and a current comprehensive official academic transcript. **Deadline:** April 15. **Contact:** awards@goldenkey.org.

3254 ■ Golden Key International Honour Society Undergraduate Research Grants *(Undergraduate/Grant)*

Purpose: To assist members with their thesis research or presenting their research at professional conferences or student research symposia. **Focus:** General studies. **Qualif.:** Applicants must be undergraduate student members. **Criteria:** Selection committee will review applicants based on academic achievement and quality of research or presentation.

Funds Avail.: $500. **Number Awarded:** 10. **To Apply:** Applicants must register scholarship applications online. Print the cover page from the online registration and use it as a cover for the entire application and attach a description of the proposed research presentation, a summarized budget of overall cost of attending the conference, and a current comprehensive official academic transcript. **Deadline:** April 15 and October 15. **Contact:** awards@goldenkey.org.

3255 ■ Golden Key Math Scholarships
(Undergraduate/Scholarship)

Purpose: To financially assist students studying math. **Focus:** Mathematics and mathematical sciences. **Qualif.:** Applicant must be undergraduate member majoring in math and currently enrolled in classes at a degree-granting program. **Criteria:** Selection is based on academic achievement in field and the quality of paper submitted.

Funds Avail.: $10000. **Number Awarded:** 2. **To Apply:** Applicants must register their scholarship application online. Print the cover page from the online registration and use it as a cover for the entire application and attach a math related paper/report (maximum of 10 pages), an essay (maximum of 500 words), a letter of recommendation, and a current comprehensive official academic transcript. **Deadline:** April 15.

Remarks: Applicants can apply for more than one scholarship. **Contact:** awards@goldenkey.org.

3256 ■ ProWorld Study Abroad Scholarships
(Undergraduate/Scholarship)

Purpose: To provide opportunities for members to explore some of the most beautiful natural and cultural environments in the world. **Focus:** General studies. **Qualif.:** Applicant must be a member in the Australia, Canada or the United States; currently enrolled in a full-time or part-time undergraduate course of study at an accredited four year college or university; and accepted to a ProWorld semester long program. **Criteria:** Selection is based on the application.

Funds Avail.: $1000. **Number Awarded:** 3. **To Apply:** Applicants must submit a ProWorld Scholarship Application to scholarships@myproworld.org. **Deadline:** April 30.

3257 ■ Gonja Association of North America
PO Box 403
Lithonia, GA 30058
URL: http://www.geocities.com/mumuni/index.htm

3258 ■ GANA Scholarship Program
(Undergraduate/Scholarship)

Purpose: To assist Gonjaland to reach its fullest potential by utilizing its vast fertile land in the field of Agriculture, and Industry. To assist the people of Gonjaland to participate in educational, political, social and economic well-being of the traditional area and the nation in general. **Focus:** General studies. **Qualif.:** Applicant must be the first generation (example illiterate parenthood) Jr./Snr. High School including sixth form; must maintain an overall average grade of 80% and above; must originate from Gonjaland; must exhibit financial need. **Criteria:** Awards will be reviewed by the committee based on application and financial need.

Funds Avail.: $100,00. **Number Awarded:** Six. **To Apply:** Applicant must complete the application form available on the website address; must sent a short essay and recommendation letter from the current/last teacher. Application and other materials must be sent to: GANA, Po Box 403, Lithonia, GA, 30058.

3259 ■ Gonzaga University School of Law
PO Box 3528
Spokane, WA 99220
Ph: (509)323-3700

Awards are arranged alphabetically below their administering organizations

E-mail: sharmon@lawschool.gonzaga.edu
URL: http://www.law.gonzaga.edu

3260 ■ Thomas More Scholarships
(Undergraduate/Scholarship)

Purpose: To help individuals in the pursuit of their educational goals. **Focus:** Law. **Qualif.:** Applicants must be US or Canadian citizens who are entering law school for the first time as first year students. **Criteria:** Recipients are selected based on their motivation, academic achievement and commitment to public service through the practice of law.

Funds Avail.: No specific amount. **To Apply:** Applicants must submit their completed application and two letters of recommendation. **Deadline:** March 1.

3261 ■ Goodman and Company, LLP

One Commercial Pl., Ste. 800
Norfolk, VA 23510
Ph: (757)624-5100
Fax: (757)624-5233
Free: (866)455-3261
URL: http://www.goodmanco.com

3262 ■ Goodman and Company, LLP Annual Scholarships *(Undergraduate/Scholarship)*

Purpose: To help promising students pursue public accounting as a profession. **Focus:** Accounting. **Qualif.:** Applicant must be a U.S. citizen; a junior or senior accounting major; currently enrolled in an accredited Virginia college or university with the intent to take the CPA Exam; and have a minimum overall and accounting GPA of 3.0 or higher. **Criteria:** Award is given based on the merit of the application.

Funds Avail.: $2,500. **Number Awarded:** 1. **To Apply:** Applicants must submit a completed scholarship application together with the essay; letter of recommendation from a faculty member; a current resume; and recent official transcript reflecting GPA; application must be typed or printed. **Deadline:** January 10.

3263 ■ Government Finance Officers Association of United States and Canada

203 N LaSalle St., Ste. 2700
Chicago, IL 60601-1210
Ph: (312)977-9700
Fax: (312)977-4806
URL: http://www.gfoa.org

3264 ■ Daniel B. Goldberg Scholarships *(Other/Scholarship)*

Purpose: To recognize outstanding performance in graduate programs by students preparing for a career in state and local government finance. **Focus:** Finance. **Qualif.:** Applicants must be current, full-time students in a graduate program that prepares students for careers in state and local government finance and are expecting to be enrolled in the spring 2008 semester in a baccalaureate degree or its equivalent; must be citizens or permanent residents of the United States or Canada; and must have not been a winner of scholarship program administered by the GFOA of the US and Canada. **Criteria:** Candidates will be assessed on the basis of plans to pursue a career in state or local government finance; strength of past coursework and present plan of study; letters of recommendation from academic advisor, the dean of the graduate program and others; and undergraduate and graduate grade point averages.

Funds Avail.: $10,000. **To Apply:** Applicants must submit completed application form; statement of proposed career plan in state and local government finance; undergraduate and graduate transcript of grades; resume; academic advisor's or dean's letter of recommendation; and other graduate program faculty letters of recommendation. **Deadline:** February 29.

3265 ■ Frank L. Greathouse Government Accounting Scholarships *(Other/Scholarship)*

Purpose: To recognize outstanding performance in accounting studies by students preparing for a career in state and local government finance. **Focus:** Finance. **Qualif.:** Applicants must be current full-time students in an accounting program preparing for a career in state and local government finance (both advanced undergraduate and graduate students); must be citizens or permanent residents of the United States or Canada; must be recommended by the academic advisor or the accounting program chair; and must have not been past winners of a scholarship program administered by the Government Finance Officers Association of the US and Canada. **Criteria:** Applicants will be selected based on the statement of proposed career plan in state and local government finance or proposed plan of graduate studies in government accounting or public administration; strength of past coursework and present plan of study; letters of recommendation by academic advisor, chair of the accounting program and others; and undergraduate/graduate grade point averages.

Funds Avail.: $3,500. **To Apply:** Applicants must submit completed application form; statement of proposed career plan in state and local government finance; plan of graduate study (if applicable); undergraduate and graduate grade transcripts; resume; academic advisor's or department chair's letter of recommendation; and other letters of recommendation (optional). **Deadline:** February 29.

3266 ■ Minorities in Government Finance Scholarships *(Graduate, Undergraduate/Scholarship)*

Purpose: To recognize outstanding performance by minority students preparing for careers in state and local government finance. **Focus:** Finance. **Qualif.:** Applicants must be current full- or part-time upper-division undergraduate or graduate students in public administration, accounting, finance, political science, economics or business administration (with a specific focus on government or nonprofit management); must belong to one of the following groups (as defined by the U.S. Census Bureau): Black or African American, American Indian or Alaska Native, Asian, Native Hawaiian or other Pacific islander, Hispanic or Latino; must be citizens or permanent residents of the United States or Canada; must be recommended by academic advisor, the dean of the graduate program (graduate students) or department chair (undergraduate students); must be students who have not received scholarships administered by the Government Finance Officers Association of the United States and Canada. **Criteria:** Recipients will be selected on the basis of plans to pursue a career in state and local government finance; past academic record and work experience; strength of past coursework and present plan of study; and undergraduate and graduate grade point averages.

Funds Avail.: $5,000. **To Apply:** Applicants must submit application form; statement of proposed state and local government finance career plan and if applicable, plan of graduate study; undergraduate and graduate grade transcripts; resume; and academic advisor's, department chair's or dean's letter of recommendation; and other letters of recommendation (optional). **Deadline:** February 29.

3267 ■ George A. Nielsen Public Investor Scholarships *(Graduate, Undergraduate/ Scholarship)*

Purpose: To inspire careers and interest in the efficient and productive investment of public funds. **Focus:** Public administration; Finance; Business administration. **Qualif.:** Program is open to employees of a local government or other public entity who are enrolled or plan to enroll in an undergraduate or graduate program in public administration, finance, business administration, or related field. Applicants must be employed at least one year by a state, local government, or special district with significant responsibilities for cash management or treasury activities including a specific focus on the investing of available cash; must be a citizen or permanent resident of the United States or Canada; must have a recommendation by employer; must be enrolled in a graduate or undergraduate program in public administration, finance or business administration before fund is awarded; must be a student who has not been a past winner of a scholarship program administered by the Government Finance Officers Association of the United States and Canada. **Criteria:** Candidate will be selected based on plans to pursue a career with a state, local government or other special purpose government entity; past work experience; present plan of study as it relates to a career in the public sector; letters of recommendation from employer; and undergraduate and graduate grade point averages.

Funds Avail.: $5,000 (may be two awards of $2,500 each). **To Apply:** Applicants must submit an application form; statement describing experience working for a state, local government or other special purpose government entity, proposed plan of study and how it will help career in the public sector; undergraduate and graduate grade transcripts; resume; employer's letter of recommendation; and other letters of recommendation (optional). **Deadline:** February 29.

3268 ■ Public Employee Retirement Research and Administration Scholarships *(Graduate/ Scholarship)*

Purpose: To encourage graduate students to pursue research and careers in the area of public-sector retirement benefits. **Focus:** Finance. **Qualif.:** Applicants must be current full- or part-time students in a graduate program in public administration, finance, business administration or social sciences; must have a baccalaureate degree or its equivalent; must be citizens or permanent residents of the United States or Canada; must be recommended by academic advisor or dean of the graduate program; must be students who have not become recipients of scholarships administered by the Government Finance Officers Association of the United States and Canada. **Criteria:** Candidates will be evaluated based on the plan to pursue a career in state or local government with a focus on public-sector retirement benefits; past academic records and relevant work experiences, including research in public-sector retirement benefits; strength of past graduate coursework and present plan of study; letters of recommendation from the academic advisor, dean of the graduate program and others; and undergraduate and graduate grade point average.

Funds Avail.: $4,000. **To Apply:** Applicants must submit application form; statement of proposed plan of graduate study and state and local government career plans; undergraduate and graduate grade transcripts; resume; academic advisor's or dean's letter of recommendation; other letters of recommendation (optional); information on pension-related research (optional). **Deadline:** February 29.

3269 ■ Grand Haven Area Community Foundation

1 S. Harbor Dr.
Grand Haven, MI 49417
Ph: (616)842-6378
Fax: (616)842-9518
E-mail: bpost@ghacf.org
URL: http://www.ghacf.org

3270 ■ Charles A. Bassett Endowed Memorial Scholarship Fund *(Undergraduate/Scholarship)*

Purpose: To improve and enhance the quality of life in the Tri-Cities area by serving as a leader, catalyst and resource for philanthropy; to strive for community improvement through strategic grantmaking in such fields as arts, education, health, environment, youth, social services and other human needs. **Focus:** General studies. **Qualif.:** Applicants must be graduating seniors who have played on the tennis team. **Criteria:** Recipients are selected based on values of positive thought, strong personal convictions and outstanding character.

Funds Avail.: No specific amount. **To Apply:** Applicants must submit: completed application form; current high school or college transcript; Student Aid Report (SAR) from the Free Application for Federal Student Aid (FAFSA); and letter of recommendation. **Deadline:** March 7. **Contact:** 616-842-6378.

3271 ■ James W. Jr.and Jane T. Brown Scholarship Fund *(Undergraduate/Scholarship)*

Purpose: To assist men and women in the Tri-Cities in returning to school to further their education after a period of working. **Focus:** General studies. **Qualif.:** Applicants must be over the age of 21. **Criteria:** Recipients are selected based on financial need.

Funds Avail.: No specific amount. **To Apply:** Applicants must submit: completed application form; current high school or college transcript; Student Aid Report (SAR) from the Free Application for Federal Student Aid (FAFSA), unless applying for scholarships that do not consider financial need; and letter of recommendation. **Deadline:** March 7. **Contact:** 616-842-6378.

3272 ■ Geri Coccodrilli Culinary Scholarship Fund *(Undergraduate/Scholarship)*

Purpose: To improve and enhance the quality of life in the Tri-Cities area by serving as a leader, catalyst and resource for philanthropy; to strive for community improvement through strategic grantmaking in such fields as arts, education, health, environment, youth, social services and other human needs. **Focus:** Culinary Arts. **Qualif.:** Applicants must be graduating high school seniors from the Tri-Cities area and Fruitport High School who wish to pursue studies in the Culinary Arts. **Criteria:** Recipients are selected based

Awards are arranged alphabetically below their administering organizations

on leadership ability, community involvement and academic achievement.

Funds Avail.: No specific amount. **To Apply:** Applicants must submit: completed application form; current high school or college transcript; Student Aid Report (SAR) from the Free Application for Federal Student Aid (FAFSA); and letter of recommendation. **Deadline:** March 7. **Contact:** 616-842-6378.

3273 ■ Dake Community Manufacturing Scholarships *(Undergraduate/Scholarship)*

Purpose: To provide encouragement and support to a student who wants to further his/her manufacturing education. **Focus:** Manufacturing. **Qualif.:** Applicants must be from Northwest Ottawa County, Muskegon County or Oceana County; must be high school graduating seniors, current college students or adult students. **Criteria:** Recipients are selected based on financial need.

Funds Avail.: No specific amount. **To Apply:** Applicants must submit: completed application form; current high school or college transcript; Student Aid Report (SAR) from the Free Application for Federal Student Aid (FAFSA), unless applying for scholarships that do not consider financial need; and letter of recommendation. **Deadline:** March 7. **Contact:** 616-842-6378.

3274 ■ E.V. Erickson Field of Interest Education Scholarships Fund *(Undergraduate/Scholarship)*

Purpose: To improve and enhance the quality of life in the Tri-Cities area by serving as a leader, catalyst and resource for philanthropy; to strive for community improvement through strategic grantmaking in such fields as arts, education, health, environment, youth, social services and other human needs. **Focus:** Education. **Qualif.:** Applicants must be graduating high school seniors who have excelled not only academically but also demonstrate leadership qualities; must have a 3.8 GPA or better on a 4.0 scale. **Criteria:** Recipients are selected based on academic performance, leadership qualities and an outstanding record of community involvement.

Funds Avail.: No specific amount. **To Apply:** Applicants must submit: completed application form; current high school or college transcript; Student Aid Report (SAR) from the Free Application for Federal Student Aid (FAFSA), unless applying for scholarships that do not consider financial need; and letter of recommendation. **Deadline:** March 7. **Contact:** 616-842-6378.

3275 ■ Kevin Ernst Memorial Scholarship Fund *(Undergraduate/Scholarship)*

Purpose: To improve and enhance the quality of life in the Tri-Cities area by serving as a leader, catalyst and resource for philanthropy; to strive for community improvement through strategic grantmaking in such fields as the arts, education, health, environment, youth, social services and other human needs. **Focus:** Mathematics and mathematical sciences. **Qualif.:** Applicants must be students in the Foundation's service area who wish to continue their education in the field of mathematics. **Criteria:** Recipients are selected based on financial need.

Funds Avail.: No specific amount. **To Apply:** Applicants must submit: completed application form; current high school or college transcript; Student Aid Report (SAR) from the Free Application for Federal Student Aid (FAFSA), unless applying for scholarships that do not consider financial need; and letter of recommendation. **Deadline:** March 7. **Contact:** 616-842-6378.

3276 ■ Bertha M. Fase Memorial Scholarship Fund *(Undergraduate/Scholarship)*

Purpose: To improve and enhance the quality of life in the Tri-Cities area by serving as a leader, catalyst and resource for philanthropy; to strive for community improvement through strategic grantmaking in such fields as arts, education, health, environment, youth, social services and other human needs. **Focus:** Education. **Qualif.:** Applicants must be Grand Haven High School graduating seniors with a 3.5 GPA or better; must plan to pursue studies in the field of Education. **Criteria:** Recipients are selected based on financial need, academic excellence, interest in youth through volunteer mentoring; applicants who are members of St. Paul United Church of Christ will be given preference.

Funds Avail.: No specific amount. **To Apply:** Applicants must submit: completed application form; current high school or college transcript; Student Aid Report (SAR) from the Free Application for Federal Student Aid (FAFSA), unless applying for scholarships that do not consider financial need; and letter of recommendation. **Deadline:** March 7. **Contact:** 616-842-6378.

3277 ■ Scott A. Flahive Memorial Scholarship Fund *(Undergraduate/Scholarship)*

Purpose: To improve and enhance the quality of life in the Tri-Cities area by serving as a leader, catalyst and resource for philanthropy; to strive for community improvement through strategic grantmaking in such fields as arts, education, health, environment, youth, social services and other human needs. **Focus:** Criminal justice. **Qualif.:** Applicants must be students pursuing career in the field of law enforcement and/or criminal justice. **Criteria:** Recipients are selected based on demonstrated academic excellence and financial need.

Funds Avail.: No specific amount. **To Apply:** Applicants must submit: completed application form; current high school or college transcript; Student Aid Report (SAR) from the Free Application for Federal Student Aid (FAFSA), unless applying for scholarships that do not consider financial need; and letter of recommendation. **Deadline:** March 7. **Contact:** 616-842-6378.

3278 ■ Floto-Peel Family Scholarships Fund *(Undergraduate/Scholarship)*

Purpose: To improve and enhance the quality of life in the Tri-Cities area by serving as a leader, catalyst and resource for philanthropy; to strive for community improvement through strategic grantmaking in such fields as arts, education, health, environment, youth, social services and other human needs. **Focus:** Nursing; Business. **Qualif.:** Applicants must be Tri-Cities area residents planning to attend a two-to-four year college, university or vocational school; must plan to study in the field of nursing or business; must have 2.5 GPA. **Criteria:** Recipients are selected based on financial need.

Funds Avail.: No specific amount. **To Apply:** Applicants must submit: completed application form; current high school or college transcript; Student Aid Report (SAR) from the Free Application for Federal Student Aid (FAFSA), unless applying for scholarships that do not consider financial need; and letter of recommendation. **Deadline:** March 7. **Contact:** 616-842-6378.

3279 ■ John and Victory E. Frantz Scholarship Fund *(Undergraduate/Scholarship)*

Purpose: To improve and enhance the quality of life in the Tri-Cities area by serving as a leader, catalyst and resource

for philanthropy; to strive for community improvement through strategic grantmaking in such fields as arts, education, health, environment, youth, social services and other human needs; to assist high school graduating seniors of northwest Ottawa County to pursue a college education. **Focus:** General studies. **Qualif.:** Applicants must be high school graduating seniors of northwest Ottawa County. **Criteria:** Recipients are selected based on demonstrated academic excellence and financial need.

Funds Avail.: No specific amount. **To Apply:** Applicants must submit: completed application form; current high school or college transcript; Student Aid Report (SAR) from the Free Application for Federal Student Aid (FAFSA), unless applying for scholarships that do not consider financial need; and letter of recommendation. **Deadline:** March 7. **Contact:** 616-842-6378.

3280 ■ Friends of Loutit District Library Scholarships Fund *(Undergraduate/Scholarship)*

Purpose: To provide educational assistance to a student planning to pursue an advanced degree in Library science. **Focus:** Library science. **Qualif.:** Applicants must be enrolled in an ALA-accredited graduate program in Library Science. **Criteria:** Recipients are selected based on academic achievements, extracurricular activities, educational goals and personal aspirations.

Funds Avail.: No specific amount. **To Apply:** Applicants must submit: completed application form; current high school or college transcript; Student Aid Report (SAR) from the Free Application for Federal Student Aid (FAFSA), unless applying for scholarships that do not consider financial need; and letter of recommendation. **Deadline:** March 7. **Contact:** 616-842-6378.

3281 ■ Gautier Family Scholarships Fund *(Undergraduate/Scholarship)*

Purpose: To improve and enhance the quality of life in the Tri-Cities area by serving as a leader, catalyst and resource for philanthropy; to strive for community improvement through strategic grantmaking in such fields as the arts, education, health, environment, youth, social services and other human needs. **Focus:** Engineering. **Qualif.:** Applicants must be high school students from the Tri-Cities area who wish to pursue studies in mechanical or electrical engineering at Michigan Technical Institute. **Criteria:** Recipients are selected based on demonstrated academic excellence and financial need.

Funds Avail.: No specific amount. **To Apply:** Applicants must submit: completed application form; current high school or college transcript; Student Aid Report (SAR) from the Free Application for Federal Student Ald (FAFSA), unless applying for scholarships that do not consider financial need; and letter of recommendation. **Deadline:** March 7. **Contact:** 616-842-6378.

3282 ■ Tim Gifford Scholarship Fund *(Undergraduate/Scholarship)*

Purpose: To improve and enhance the quality of life in the Tri-Cities area by serving as a leader, catalyst and resource for philanthropy; to strive for community improvement through strategic grantmaking in such fields as arts, education, health, environment, youth, social services and other human needs. **Focus:** General studies. **Qualif.:** Applicants must be graduates of Spring Lake High School; must have been SLHS students for three semesters immediately prior to graduation and must have attended for at least three years; must plan to attend Amherest College within 30 months of high school graduation. **Criteria:** Recipients are selected based on demonstrated academic excellence and financial need.

Funds Avail.: No specific amount. **To Apply:** Applicants must submit: completed application form; current high school or college transcript; Student Aid Report (SAR) from the Free Application for Federal Student Aid (FAFSA), unless applying for scholarships that do not consider financial need; and letter of recommendation. **Deadline:** March 7. **Contact:** 616-842-6378.

3283 ■ Grand Haven Offshore Challenge Scholarships Fund *(Undergraduate/Scholarship)*

Purpose: To improve and enhance the quality of life in the Tri-Cities area by serving as a leader, catalyst and resource for philanthropy; to strive for community improvement through strategic grantmaking in such fields as arts, education, health, environment, youth, social services and other human needs. **Focus:** Natural resources. **Qualif.:** Applicants must be graduating high school seniors from the Tri-Cities area who plan to pursue a career in natural resources such as fisheries, wildlife and environmental water quality at any public or private college or university. **Criteria:** Recipients are selected based on demonstrated academic excellence and financial need.

Funds Avail.: No specific amount. **To Apply:** Applicants must submit: completed application form; current high school or college transcript; Student Aid Report (SAR) from the Free Application for Federal Student Aid (FAFSA), unless applying for scholarships that do not consider financial need; and letter of recommendation. **Deadline:** March 7. **Contact:** 616-842-6378.

3284 ■ Barbara and Nicole Heicox Foreign Travel and Study Scholarships Fund *(Undergraduate/Scholarship)*

Purpose: To improve and enhance the quality of life in the Tri-Cities area by serving as a leader, catalyst and resource for philanthropy; to strive for community improvement through strategic grantmaking in such fields as arts, education, health, environment, youth, social services and other human needs. **Focus:** Travel and tourism. **Qualif.:** Applicants must be junior, high school and/or college students wishing to pursue educational opportunities in foreign countries. **Criteria:** Recipients are selected based on financial need.

Funds Avail.: No specific amount. **To Apply:** Applicants must submit: completed application form; current high school or college transcript; Student Aid Report (SAR) from the Free Application for Federal Student Aid (FAFSA), unless applying for scholarships that do not consider financial need; and letter of recommendation. **Deadline:** March 7. **Contact:** 616-842-6378.

3285 ■ Marjorie M. Hendricks Environmental Education Scholarships Fund *(Undergraduate/Scholarship)*

Purpose: To assist an upperclassman or graduate student majoring in environmental science field. **Focus:** Environmental science. **Qualif.:** Applicants must be upperclassmen or graduate students majoring in an environmental science field who plan to attend Aquinas College or Grand Valley State University. **Criteria:** Recipients are selected based on financial need.

Funds Avail.: No specific amount. **To Apply:** Applicants must submit: completed application form; current high school or college transcript; Student Aid Report (SAR) from the Free Application for Federal Student Aid (FAFSA), unless applying for scholarships that do not consider financial need; and letter of recommendation. **Deadline:** March 7. **Contact:** 616-842-6378.

3286 ■ Michael Herman Memorial Scholarship Fund *(Undergraduate/Scholarship)*

Purpose: To improve and enhance the quality of life in the Tri-Cities area by serving as a leader, catalyst and resource for philanthropy; to strive for community improvement through strategic grantmaking in such fields as arts, education, health, environment, youth, social services and other human needs. **Focus:** General studies. **Qualif.:** Applicants must be soccer players and coaches of younger students who are interested in learning soccer; must be current high school graduates of any Tri-Cities area public or private high school intending to pursue degree or certification at any two-or four-year accredited college, university, vocational or technical school; first consideration shall be given to students who played on a soccer team and wish to continue playing in college on an intramural, club or college team. **Criteria:** Recipients are selected based on demonstrated interest in soccer.

Funds Avail.: No specific amount. **To Apply:** Applicants must submit: completed application form; current high school or college transcript; Student Aid Report (SAR) from the Free Application for Federal Student Aid (FAFSA), unless applying for scholarships that do not consider financial need; and letter of recommendation. **Deadline:** March 7. **Contact:** 616-842-6378.

3287 ■ Hierholzer-Fojtik Scholarship Fund *(Undergraduate/Scholarship)*

Purpose: To improve and enhance the quality of life in the Tri-Cities area by serving as a leader, catalyst and resource for philanthropy; to strive for community improvement through strategic grantmaking in such fields as the arts, education, health, environment, youth, social services and other human needs. **Focus:** Law. **Qualif.:** Applicants must be Grand Haven High School graduates planning to pursue law as a career. **Criteria:** Recipients are selected based on financial need.

Funds Avail.: No specific amount. **To Apply:** Applicants must submit: completed application form; current high school or college transcript; Student Aid Report (SAR) from the Free Application for Federal Student Aid (FAFSA), unless applying for scholarships that do not consider financial need; and letter of recommendation. **Deadline:** March 7. **Contact:** 616-842-6378.

3288 ■ Hoffman Family Scholarships Fund *(Undergraduate/Scholarship)*

Purpose: To improve and enhance the quality of life in the Tri-Cities area by serving as a leader, catalyst and resource for philanthropy; to strive for community improvement through strategic grantmaking in such fields as arts, education, health, environment, youth, social services and other human needs. **Focus:** General studies. **Qualif.:** Applicants must be graduating high school seniors at Grand Haven, Spring Lake or Fruitport high schools; must have a 3.0 GPA; special consideration will be given to an individual who is a member of the first generation in their family to attend college. **Criteria:** Recipients are selected based on demonstrated academic excellence and financial need.

Funds Avail.: No specific amount. **To Apply:** Applicants must submit: completed application form; current high school or college transcript; Student Aid Report (SAR) from the Free Application for Federal Student Aid (FAFSA), unless applying for scholarships that do not consider financial need; and letter of recommendation. **Deadline:** March 7. **Contact:** 616-842-6378.

3289 ■ Seth Koehler Central High School Scholarship Fund *(Undergraduate/Scholarship)*

Purpose: To provide educational financial assistance to a graduating senior from Central High School. **Focus:** General studies. **Qualif.:** Applicants must be graduating seniors from Central High School; must plan to attend any two-to-four year college, university, vocational or technical school. **Criteria:** Recipients are selected based on financial need.

Funds Avail.: No specific amount. **To Apply:** Applicants must submit: completed application form; current high school or college transcript; Student Aid Report (SAR) from the Free Application for Federal Student Aid (FAFSA), unless applying for scholarships that do not consider financial need; and letter of recommendation. **Deadline:** March 7. **Contact:** 616-842-6378.

3290 ■ Paul J. Laninga Memorial Scholarship Fund *(Undergraduate/Scholarship)*

Purpose: To improve and enhance the quality of life in the Tri-Cities area by serving as a leader, catalyst and resource for philanthropy; to strive for community improvement through strategic grantmaking in such fields as arts, education, health, environment, youth, social services and other human needs. **Focus:** Business; Accounting. **Qualif.:** Applicants must be graduating seniors of Northwest Ottawa County who plan to attend a public university; must be pursuing education and long-term careers in the areas of business and/or accounting. **Criteria:** Recipients are selected based on financial need and academic excellence.

Funds Avail.: No specific amount. **To Apply:** Applicants must submit: completed application form; current high school or college transcript; Student Aid Report (SAR) from the Free Application for Federal Student Aid (FAFSA), unless applying for scholarships that do not consider financial need; and letter of recommendation. **Deadline:** March 7. **Contact:** 616-842-6378.

3291 ■ Rick and Beverly Lattin Education Scholarships Fund *(Undergraduate/Scholarship)*

Purpose: To provide financial assistance to graduates of Spring Lake or Grand Haven High school who demonstrate financial need. **Focus:** Business. **Qualif.:** Applicants must be graduates of Spring Lake or Grand Haven High School; must have 2.0 to 3.0 GPA and wish to continue their education; must be pursuing skills in the area of business or technical training. **Criteria:** Recipients are selected based on financial need.

Funds Avail.: No specific amount. **To Apply:** Applicants must submit completed application form; current high school or college transcript; Student Aid Report (SAR) from the Free Application for Federal Student Aid (FAFSA), unless applying for scholarships that do not consider financial need; and letter of recommendation. **Deadline:** March 7. **Contact:** 616-842-6378.

3292 ■ Jack W. Leatherman Family Scholarship Fund *(Undergraduate/Scholarship)*

Purpose: To improve and enhance the quality of life in the Tri-Cities area by serving as a leader, catalyst and resource

for philanthropy; to strive for community improvement through strategic grantmaking in such fields as arts, education, health, environment, youth, social services and other human needs. **Focus:** General studies. **Qualif.:** Applicants must be Grand Haven area public school graduates. **Criteria:** Recipients are selected based on financial need.

Funds Avail.: No specific amount. **To Apply:** Applicants must submit: completed application form; current high school or college transcript; Student Aid Report (SAR) from the Free Application for Federal Student Aid (FAFSA), unless applying for scholarships that do not consider financial need; and letter of recommendation. **Deadline:** March 7. **Contact:** 616-842-6378.

3293 ■ Pat and John MacTavish Scholarship Fund *(Undergraduate/Scholarship)*

Purpose: To improve and enhance the quality of life in the Tri-Cities area by serving as a leader, catalyst and resource for philanthropy; to strive for community improvement through strategic grantmaking in such fields as arts, education, health, environment, youth, social services and other human needs. **Focus:** Science. **Qualif.:** Applicants must be high school or college students seeking to pursue any of the following areas of study: math, chemistry, geology, technical writing, physics or computer science. **Criteria:** Recipients are selected based on demonstrated academic excellence and financial need.

Funds Avail.: No specific amount. **To Apply:** Applicants must submit: completed application form; current high school or college transcript; Student Aid Report (SAR) from the Free Application for Federal Student Aid (FAFSA), unless applying for scholarships that do not consider financial need; and letter of recommendation. **Deadline:** March 7. **Contact:** 616-842-6378.

3294 ■ Kyle Moreland Memorial Endowment Scholarships Fund *(Undergraduate/Scholarship)*

Purpose: To provide assistance to a Grand Haven High School graduating senior student. **Focus:** General studies. **Qualif.:** Applicants must be Grand Haven High School graduating seniors planning to attend a two or four-year college degree program; must be active in their Christian faith community; must have participated on the high school golf or tennis team; must have a 3.0 GPA or above. Scholarship is also open to current graduates of Spring Lake High School and/or Western Christian Michigan High School. **Criteria:** Recipients are selected based on academic performance.

Funds Avail.: No specific amount. **To Apply:** Applicants must submit: completed application form; current high school or college transcript; Student Aid Report (SAR) from the Free Application for Federal Student Aid (FAFSA), unless applying for scholarships that do not consider financial need; and letter of recommendation. **Deadline:** March 7. **Contact:** 616-842-6378.

3295 ■ North Ottawa Hospital Auxiliary Scholarships Fund *(Undergraduate/Scholarship)*

Purpose: To improve and enhance the quality of life in the Tri-Cities area by serving as a leader, catalyst and resource for philanthropy; to strive for community improvement through strategic grantmaking in such fields as arts, education, health, environment, youth, social services and other human needs. **Focus:** Nursing. **Qualif.:** Applicants must be from the Tri-Cities area; currently enrolled as college students who have taken their core requirements and been accepted into their health-care related program of study. **Criteria:** Recipients are selected based on financial need, academic achievement, extracurricular activities, work history, educational goals and personal aspirations.

Funds Avail.: No specific amount. **To Apply:** Applicants must submit: completed application form; current high school or college transcript; Student Aid Report (SAR) from the Free Application for Federal Student Aid (FAFSA), unless applying for scholarships that do not consider financial need; and letter of recommendation. **Deadline:** March 7. **Contact:** 616-842-6378.

3296 ■ Marvin R. and Pearl E. Patterson Family Scholarships Fund *(Undergraduate/Scholarship)*

Purpose: To improve and enhance the quality of life in the Tri-Cities area by serving as a leader, catalyst and resource for philanthropy; to strive for community improvement through strategic grantmaking in such fields as arts, education, health, environment, youth, social services and other human needs. **Focus:** Fine Arts. **Qualif.:** Applicants must be students who will be graduating or graduated from a Tri-Cities area public high school; must have at least 3.0 GPA and plan to attend any two-year or four-year college or university to study graphic arts or fine arts. **Criteria:** Recipients are selected based on leadership ability, community involvement and academic achievement.

Funds Avail.: No specific amount. **To Apply:** Applicants must submit: completed application form; current high school or college transcript; Student Aid Report (SAR) from the Free Application for Federal Student Aid (FAFSA), unless applying for scholarships that do not consider financial need; and letter of recommendation. **Deadline:** March 7. **Contact:** 616-842-6378.

3297 ■ P.E.O. Chapter Scholarship Fund *(Undergraduate/Scholarship)*

Purpose: To improve and enhance the quality of life in the Tri-Cities area by serving as a leader, catalyst and resource for philanthropy; to strive for community improvement through strategic grantmaking in such fields as arts, education, health, environment, youth, social services and other human needs. **Focus:** General studies. **Qualif.:** Applicants must be graduating female students or non-traditional students who graduated from any Tri-Cities area public or private high school; must plan to pursue a degree or certification at any two or four-year accredited college, university, vocational or technical school. **Criteria:** Recipients are selected based on academic performance.

Funds Avail.: No specific amount. **To Apply:** Applicants must submit: completed application form; current high school or college transcript; Student Aid Report (SAR) from the Free Application for Federal Student Aid (FAFSA), unless applying for scholarships that do not consider financial need; and letter of recommendation. **Deadline:** March 7. **Contact:** 616-842-6378.

3298 ■ Terry Linda Potter Scholarship Fund *(Undergraduate/Scholarship)*

Purpose: To improve and enhance the quality of life in the Tri-Cities area by serving as a leader, catalyst and resource for philanthropy; to strive for community improvement through strategic grantmaking in such fields as arts, education, health, environment, youth, social services and other human needs. **Focus:** Health education. **Qualif.:** Applicants must be graduating high school seniors planning to pursue a health-related field at an accredited two-to-four year college. **Criteria:** Recipients are selected based on financial need and scholastic ability.

Awards are arranged alphabetically below their administering organizations

Funds Avail.: No specific amount. **To Apply:** Applicants must submit: completed application form; current high school or college transcript; Student Aid Report (SAR) from the Free Application for Federal Student Aid (FAFSA), unless applying for scholarships that do not consider financial need; and letter of recommendation. **Deadline:** March 7. **Contact:** 616-842-6378.

3299 ■ Jacob L. Reinecke Memorial Scholarship Fund *(Undergraduate/Scholarship)*

Purpose: To provide scholarship assistance to a Grand Haven High School student. **Focus:** General studies. **Qualif.:** Applicants must be Grand Haven High School graduating seniors planning to attend a two-to-four year college, university or trade school; consideration will be given to male students who participated in high school athletics, specifically basketball or baseball; must have a 3.0 GPA or above. **Criteria:** Recipients are selected based on hard-working attitude and strong motivation to succeed.

Funds Avail.: No specific amount. **To Apply:** Applicants must submit: completed application form; current high school or college transcript; Student Aid Report (SAR) from the Free Application for Federal Student Aid (FAFSA), unless applying for scholarships that do not consider financial need; and letter of recommendation. **Deadline:** March 7. **Contact:** 616-842-6378.

3300 ■ Daniel L. Reiss Memorial Scholarship Fund *(Undergraduate/Scholarship)*

Purpose: To improve and enhance the quality of life in the Tri-Cities area by serving as a leader, catalyst and resource for philanthropy; to strive for community improvement through strategic grantmaking in such fields as arts, education, health, environment, youth, social services and other human needs. **Focus:** General studies. **Qualif.:** Applicants must be graduating Grand Haven High School students who have at least a 3.8 GPA; must plan to pursue studies at Grand Valley State University or Western Michigan University. **Criteria:** Recipients are selected based on demonstrated academic excellence and financial need.

Funds Avail.: No specific amount. **To Apply:** Applicants must submit: completed application form; current high school or college transcript; Student Aid Report (SAR) from the Free Application for Federal Student Aid (FAFSA), unless applying for scholarships that do not consider financial need; and letter of recommendation. **Deadline:** March 7. **Contact:** 616-842-6378.

3301 ■ Harold and Eleonor Ringelberg Scholarship Fund *(Undergraduate/Scholarship)*

Purpose: To improve and enhance the quality of life in the Tri-Cities area by serving as a leader, catalyst and resource for philanthropy; to strive for community improvement through strategic grantmaking in such fields as arts, education, health, environment, youth, social services and other human needs. **Focus:** General studies. **Qualif.:** Applicants must be Grand Haven High School graduating seniors with a minimum 3.8 GPA; must plan to pursue a college degree at Michigan State University; must have attended Grand Haven Christian School prior to high school. **Criteria:** Recipients are selected based on financial need.

Funds Avail.: No specific amount. **To Apply:** Applicants must submit: completed application form; current high school or college transcript; Student Aid Report (SAR) from the Free Application for Federal Student Aid (FAFSA), unless applying for scholarships that do not consider financial need; and letter of recommendation. **Deadline:** March 7. **Contact:** 616-842-6378.

3302 ■ Charles and Eleonor Rycenga Education Scholarships Fund *(Undergraduate/Scholarship)*

Purpose: To improve and enhance the quality of life in the Tri-Cities area by serving as a leader, catalyst and resource for philanthropy; to strive for community improvement through strategic grantmaking in such fields as arts, education, health, environment, youth, social services and other human needs. **Focus:** General studies. **Qualif.:** Applicants must be graduating seniors of Grand Haven, Spring Lake or Western Christian High School; must have the desire to continue their education at an accredited four-year college, junior college, trade school or apprenticeship, preferably in Michigan. **Criteria:** Recipients are selected based on financial need.

Funds Avail.: No specific amount. **To Apply:** Applicants must submit: completed application form; current high school or college transcript; Student Aid Report (SAR) from the Free Application for Federal Student Aid (FAFSA), unless applying for scholarships that do not consider financial need; and letter of recommendation. **Deadline:** March 7. **Contact:** 616-842-6378.

3303 ■ Millicent M. Schaffner Endowed Memorial Scholarship *(Undergraduate/Scholarship)*

Purpose: To improve and enhance the quality of life in the Tri-Cities area by serving as a leader, catalyst and resource for philanthropy; to strive for community improvement through strategic grantmaking in such fields as the arts, education, health, environment, youth, social services and other human needs. **Focus:** General studies. **Qualif.:** Applicants must be female students who have a strong motivation to continue their education at an accredited four-year college. **Criteria:** Recipients are selected based on financial need.

Funds Avail.: No specific amount. **To Apply:** Applicants must submit: completed application form; current high school or college transcript; Student Aid Report (SAR) from the Free Application for Federal Student Aid (FAFSA), unless applying for scholarships that do not consider financial need; and letter of recommendation. **Deadline:** March 7. **Contact:** 616-842-6378.

3304 ■ David and Ginny Schultz Family Scholarship Fund *(Undergraduate/Scholarship)*

Purpose: To improve and enhance the quality of life in the Tri-Cities area by serving as a leader, catalyst and resource for philanthropy; to strive for community improvement through strategic grantmaking in such fields as arts, education, health, environment, youth, social services and other human needs. **Focus:** General studies. **Qualif.:** Applicants must be graduating seniors who wish to continue their education at a four-year college, junior college, trade school or apprenticeship. **Criteria:** Recipients are selected based on demonstrated academic excellence and financial need.

Funds Avail.: No specific amount. **To Apply:** Applicants must submit: completed application form; current high school or college transcript; Student Aid Report (SAR) from the Free Application for Federal Student Aid (FAFSA), unless applying for scholarships that do not consider financial need; and letter of recommendation. **Deadline:** March 7. **Contact:** 616-842-6378.

3305 ■ David and Sharon Seaver Family Scholarship Fund *(Undergraduate/Scholarship)*

Purpose: To improve and enhance the quality of life in the Tri-Cities area by serving as a leader, catalyst and resource

for philanthropy; to strive for community improvement through strategic grantmaking in such fields as arts, education, health, environment, youth, social services and other human needs. **Focus:** Business. **Qualif.:** Applicants must be graduating seniors who plan to pursue a career in Business. **Criteria:** Recipients are selected based on financial need.

Funds Avail.: No specific amount. **To Apply:** Applicants must submit: completed application form; current high school or college transcript; Student Aid Report (SAR) from the Free Application for Federal Student Aid (FAFSA), unless applying for scholarships that do not consider financial need; and letter of recommendation. **Deadline:** March 7. **Contact:** 616-842-6378.

3306 ■ Ken and Sandy Sharkey Family Scholarship Fund *(Undergraduate/Scholarship)*

Purpose: To improve and enhance the quality of life in the Tri-Cities area by serving as a leader, catalyst and resource for philanthropy; to strive for community improvement through strategic grantmaking in such fields as arts, education, health, environment, youth, social services and other human needs. **Focus:** General studies. **Qualif.:** Applicants must be graduating seniors from Grand Haven High School who demonstrate civic responsibility and plan to be involved in improving their community in the future. **Criteria:** Recipients are selected based on academic performance.

Funds Avail.: No specific amount. **To Apply:** Applicants must submit: completed application form; current high school or college transcript; Student Aid Report (SAR) from the Free Application for Federal Student Aid (FAFSA), unless applying for scholarships that do not consider financial need; and letter of recommendation. **Deadline:** March 7. **Contact:** 616-842-6378.

3307 ■ Marion A. And Ruth Sherwood Family Fund Education Scholarships *(Undergraduate/Scholarship)*

Purpose: To improve and enhance the quality of life in the Tri-Cities area by serving as a leader, catalyst and resource for philanthropy; to strive for community improvement through strategic grantmaking in such fields as arts, education, health, environment, youth, social services and other human needs. **Focus:** Education. **Qualif.:** Applicants must be planning to pursue a career in the field of Education. **Criteria:** Recipients are selected based on academic excellence and financial need.

Funds Avail.: No specific amount. **To Apply:** Applicants must submit: completed application form; current high school or college transcript; Student Aid Report (SAR) from the Free Application for Federal Student Aid (FAFSA), unless applying for scholarships that do not consider financial need; and letter of recommendation. **Deadline:** March 7. **Contact:** 616-842-6378.

3308 ■ Marion A. and Ruth K. Sherwood Family Fund Engineering Scholarships *(Undergraduate/Scholarship)*

Purpose: To improve and enhance the quality of life in the Tri-Cities area by serving as a leader, catalyst and resource for philanthropy; to strive for community improvement through strategic grantmaking in such fields as the arts, education, health, environment, youth, social services and other human needs. **Focus:** Engineering. **Qualif.:** Applicants must be students planning to pursue a career in the field of engineering. **Criteria:** Recipients are selected based on academic excellence and financial need.

Funds Avail.: No specific amount. **To Apply:** Applicants must submit: completed application form; current high school or college transcript; Student Aid Report (SAR) from the Free Application for Federal Student AId (FAFSA), unless applying for scholarships that do not consider financial need; and letter of recommendation. **Deadline:** March 7. **Contact:** 616-842-6378.

3309 ■ Miller G. Sherwood Family Scholarship Fund *(Undergraduate/Scholarship)*

Purpose: To improve and enhance the quality of life in the Tri-Cities area by serving as a leader, catalyst and resource for philanthropy; to strive for community improvement through strategic grantmaking in such fields as arts, education, health, environment, youth, social services and other human needs. **Focus:** Environmental science. **Qualif.:** Applicants must be graduating seniors of Grand Haven or Spring Lake High School who plan to pursue an education in the areas of environment or social services. **Criteria:** Recipients are selected based on financial need and motivation; do not necessarily possess an excellent academic grade point average.

Funds Avail.: No specific amount. **To Apply:** Applicants must submit: completed application form; current high school or college transcript, Student Aid Report (SAR) from the Free Application for Federal Student Aid (FAFSA), unless applying for scholarships that do not consider financial need; and letter of recommendation. **Deadline:** March 7. **Contact:** 616-842-6378.

3310 ■ Edward P. Suchecki Family Scholarship Fund *(Undergraduate/Scholarship)*

Purpose: To improve and enhance the quality of life in the Tri-Cities area by serving as a leader, catalyst and resource for philanthropy; to strive for community improvement through strategic grantmaking in such fields as arts, education, health, environment, youth, social services and other human needs. **Focus:** Business. **Qualif.:** Applicants must be high school senior athletes from Grand Haven High School, preferably planning to pursue a career in business. **Criteria:** Recipients are selected based on financial need.

Funds Avail.: No specific amount. **To Apply:** Applicants must submit: completed application form; current high school or college transcript; Student Aid Report (SAR) from the Free Application for Federal Student AId (FAFSA), unless applying for scholarships that do not consider financial need; and letter of recommendation. **Deadline:** March. **Contact:** 616-842-6378.

3311 ■ Henry D. and Ruth G. Swartz Family Scholarship Fund *(Undergraduate/Scholarship)*

Purpose: To improve and enhance the quality of life in the Tri-Cities area by serving as a leader, catalyst and resource for philanthropy; to strive for community improvement through strategic grantmaking in such fields as arts, education, health, environment, youth, social services and other human needs. **Focus:** Computer and Information Sciences. **Qualif.:** Applicants must be graduating high school seniors from Grand Haven High School, Spring Lake High School, Holland Christian High School or Western Michigan Christian High School in North Ottawa County; must be pursuing a career in engineering, computer science, prelaw or medicine. **Criteria:** Recipients are selected based on leadership ability, community involvement and academic achievement.

Funds Avail.: No specific amount. **To Apply:** Applicants

Awards are arranged alphabetically below their administering organizations

must submit: completed application form; current high school or college transcript; Student Aid Report (SAR) from the Free Application for Federal Student Aid (FAFSA); and letter of recommendation. **Deadline:** March 7. **Contact:** 616-842-6378.

3312 ■ H. Wayne Van Agtmael Cosmetology Scholarship Fund *(Undergraduate/Scholarship)*

Purpose: To improve and enhance the quality of life in the Tri-Cities area by serving as a leader, catalyst and resource for philanthropy; to strive for community improvement through strategic grantmaking in such fields as arts, education, health, environment, youth, social services and other human needs. **Focus:** Cosmetology. **Qualif.:** Applicants must be students planning to attend a Cosmetology School. **Criteria:** Recipients are selected based on academic excellence and financial need.

Funds Avail.: No specific amount. **To Apply:** Applicants must submit: completed application form; current high school or college transcript; Student Aid Report (SAR) from the Free Application for Federal Student Aid (FAFSA), unless applying for scholarships that do not consider financial need; and letter of recommendation. **Deadline:** March 7. **Contact:** 616-842-6378.

3313 ■ West Michigan Nursery and Landscape Association Scholarships Fund *(Undergraduate/Scholarship)*

Purpose: To assist graduating high school seniors and currently enrolled college students to pursue a horticulture or green industry career. **Focus:** Horticulture. **Qualif.:** Applicants must be graduating high school seniors or currently enrolled college students planning to pursue a horticulture or green industry career at a two-or-four-year college or university; must be residents of Ottawa, Oceana, Newaygo, Muskegon or Allegan Counties. **Criteria:** Recipients are selected based on demonstrated academic excellence and financial need.

Funds Avail.: No specific amount. **To Apply:** Applicants must submit: completed application form; current high school or college transcript; Student Aid Report (SAR) from the Free Application for Federal Student Aid (FAFSA), unless applying for scholarships that do not consider financial need; and letter of recommendation. **Deadline:** March 7. **Contact:** 616-842-6378.

3314 ■ Louise Wachter Wichman Scholarship Fund *(Undergraduate/Scholarship)*

Purpose: To assist local graduating high school seniors interested in obtaining a college degree in elementary education. **Focus:** Education. **Qualif.:** Applicants must be graduating high school seniors interested in obtaining a college degree in elementary education; must have a good (but not necessarily perfect) academic record. **Criteria:** Recipients are selected based on academic performance and financial need.

Funds Avail.: No specific amount. **To Apply:** Applicants must submit: completed application form; current high school or college transcript; Student Aid Report (SAR) from the Free Application for Federal Student Aid (FAFSA), unless applying for scholarships that do not consider financial need; and letter of recommendation. **Deadline:** March 7. **Contact:** 616-842-6378.

3315 ■ Woman's Club of Grand Haven Scholarships Fund *(Undergraduate/Scholarship)*

Purpose: To improve and enhance the quality of life in the Tri-Cities area by serving as a leader, catalyst and resource for philanthropy; to strive for community improvement through strategic grantmaking in such fields as the arts, education, health, environment, youth, social services and other human needs. **Focus:** General studies. **Qualif.:** Applicants may be traditional and non-traditional students. Traditional students must be graduating from a Tri-Cities area high school with a minimum 2.5 GPA; non-traditional must be female, ages 21 or older. **Criteria:** Recipients are selected based on financial need, academic achievement, community service and college plans.

Funds Avail.: No specific amount. **To Apply:** Applicants must submit: completed application form; current high school or college transcript; Student Aid Report (SAR) from the Free Application for Federal Student Aid (FAFSA), unless applying for scholarships that do not consider financial need; and letter of recommendation. **Deadline:** March 7. **Contact:** 616-842-6378.

3316 ■ Zenko Family Scholarship Fund *(Undergraduate/Scholarship)*

Purpose: To provide assistance to students to further their education. **Qualif.:** Applicants must be graduates of Spring Lake, Grand Haven or Fruitport High School. **Criteria:** Recipients are selected based on financial need.

Funds Avail.: No specific amount. **To Apply:** Applicants must submit: completed application form; current high school or college transcript; Student Aid Report (SAR) from the Free Application for Federal Student Aid (FAFSA), unless applying for scholarships that do not consider financial need; and letter of recommendation. **Deadline:** March 7. **Contact:** 616-842-6378.

3317 ■ Leo Zupin Memorial Scholarship Fund *(Undergraduate/Scholarship)*

Purpose: To improve and enhance the quality of life in the Tri-Cities area by serving as a leader, catalyst and resource for philanthropy; to strive for community improvement through strategic grantmaking in such fields as arts, education, health, environment, youth, social services and other human needs. **Focus:** Mathematics and mathematical sciences. **Qualif.:** Applicants must plan to attend any Michigan two-to-four year accredited public college, university, vocational or technology training and/or certification institution; must be students wishing to pursue a degree in mathematics. **Criteria:** Recipients are selected based on financial need, motivation, desire to achieve and academic performance.

Funds Avail.: No specific amount. **To Apply:** Applicants must submit: completed application form; current high school or college transcript; Student Aid Report (SAR) from the Free Application for Federal Student Aid (FAFSA), unless applying for scholarships that do not consider financial need; and letter of recommendation. **Deadline:** March 7. **Contact:** 616-842-6378.

3318 ■ Grand Rapids Community Foundation

161 Ottawa Ave. NW
Ste. 209-C Waters Bldg.
Grand Rapids, MI 49503
Ph: (616)454-1751
Fax: (616)454-6455
E-mail: grfound@grfoundation.org
URL: http://www.grfoundation.org

3319 ■ Altrusa International of Grand Rapids Scholarships *(Undergraduate/Scholarship)*

Purpose: To provide financial support to those students who are in need. **Focus:** General Studies. **Qualif.:** Ap-

Awards are arranged alphabetically below their administering organizations

plicants must be students from Kent, Allegan, Iona, Ottawa, Montcalm or Muskegon counties. Applicants must be entering or returning to college after sitting out of school for two years. Applicants must demonstrate financial need. **Criteria:** Priority will be given to those students with financial need.

Funds Avail.: No specific amount. **To Apply:** Applicants must check the available website for the required materials. **Contact:** Grand Rapids Community Foundation at the above address (see entry 3318).

3320 ■ Dr. Noyes L. Avery, Jr. & Ann E. Avery Scholarships *(Undergraduate/Scholarship)*

Purpose: To provide financial assistance to those students who are in need. **Focus:** Medicine. **Qualif.:** Applicants must be full-time students from Kent County who are attending the University of Michigan for a medical doctor degree. Applicants must have a minimum of 3.0 GPA. Applicants must have financial need. **Criteria:** Preference will be given to those students who meet the criteria.

Funds Avail.: No specific amount. **To Apply:** Applicants must check the available website for the required materials. **Contact:** Grand Rapids Community Foundation at the above address (see entry 3318).

3321 ■ Geraldine Geistert Boss Scholarships *(Undergraduate/Scholarship)*

Purpose: To provide financial support to those students who are in need. **Focus:** General Studies. **Qualif.:** Applicants must be full-time students with financial need residing in Kent County (5 year minimum) and pursuing an undergraduate degree at an accredited college in Michigan. Applicants must have a minimum of 3.0 GPA. **Criteria:** Preference will be given to those students who meet the criteria.

Funds Avail.: No specific amount. **To Apply:** Applicants must check the available website for the required materials. **Contact:** Grand Rapids Community Foundation at the above address (see entry 3318).

3322 ■ Orrie & Dorothy Cassada Scholarships *(Undergraduate/Scholarship)*

Purpose: To provide financial assistance to those students who are in need. **Focus:** General Studies. **Qualif.:** Applicants must be residents of Kent County who will be attending Aquinas, Calvin, Cornerstone, Davenport, GRCC, GVSU or Kendall. Applicants must have financial need and a 3.0 minimum GPA. **Criteria:** Preference will be given to those students who meet the criteria.

Funds Avail.: No specific amount. **To Apply:** Applicants must check the available website for more information. **Contact:** Grand Rapids Community Foundation at the above address (see entry 3318).

3323 ■ Llewellyn L. Cayvan String Instrument Scholarships *(Undergraduate/Scholarship)*

Purpose: To recognize those students with talent in musical instruments by supporting them financially. **Focus:** Music. **Qualif.:** Applicants must be undergraduate or graduate level students studying the violin, viola, violoncello, or the bass violin. No residency or financial need requirements. **Criteria:** Preference will be based on talent.

Funds Avail.: No specific amount. **To Apply:** Applicants must check the available website for the application process and other requirements. **Contact:** Grand Rapids Community Foundation at the above address (see entry 3318).

3324 ■ Thomas D. Coffield Scholarships *(Undergraduate/Scholarship)*

Purpose: To provide financial assistance to those students who are in need. **Focus:** General Studies. **Qualif.:** Applicants must be senior students at Central High School who will be entering a two or four-year accredited college or university; must have a 2.5 minimum GPA; must have demonstrated financial need. **Criteria:** Preference will be given to those who meet the criteria.

Funds Avail.: No specific amount. **To Apply:** Applicants must check the available website for more information. **Contact:** Grand Rapids Community Foundation at the above address (see entry 3318).

3325 ■ Paul Collins Scholarships *(Undergraduate/Scholarship)*

Purpose: To provide financial assistance to deserving students. **Focus:** Applied Arts; Fine Arts. **Qualif.:** Applicants must be undergraduate level students studying Fine or Applied Arts at Aquinas, Calvin, GVSU, GRCC or Kendall. Applicants must be residents of Kent County. Applicants must have a minimum of 2.5 GPA, financial need and demonstrate artistic talent. **Criteria:** Selection will be based on criteria.

Funds Avail.: No specific amount. **To Apply:** Applicants must check the available website for more information. **Contact:** Grand Rapids Community Foundation at the above address (see entry 3318).

3326 ■ Achille & Irene Despres, William & Andre Scholarships *(Undergraduate/Scholarship)*

Purpose: To provide financial assistance to those students who are in need. **Focus:** General Studies. **Qualif.:** Applicants must be of Mexican heritage; must be Kent or Ottawa residents; must be enrolled in an accredited college or university; must have demonstrated financial need; must have a cumulative GPA of at least 2.75. **Criteria:** Priority will be given to those students with financial need.

Funds Avail.: No specific amount. **To Apply:** Applicants must check the available website for the required materials. **Contact:** Grand Rapids Community Foundation at the above address (see entry 3318).

3327 ■ Virginia Valk Fehsenfeld Scholarships *(Undergraduate/Scholarship)*

Purpose: To provide financial support to those students who are in need. **Focus:** General Studies. **Qualif.:** Applicants must be full-time undergraduate students pursuing a degree in Dietetics, Nutrition, Education or General Human Services. Applicants must be residents of Kent County, must have financial need and a 3.4 GPA is required. **Criteria:** Preference will be given to those who meet the criteria.

Funds Avail.: No specific amount. **To Apply:** Applicants must check the available website for the required materials. **Contact:** Grand Rapids Community Foundation at the above address (see entry 3318).

3328 ■ Melbourne & Alice E. Frontjes Scholarships *(Undergraduate/Scholarship)*

Purpose: To provide financial assistance to those students who are in need. **Focus:** General Studies. **Qualif.:** Applicants must be Kent County residents who are pursuing an undergraduate degree at Central Michigan University, Western Michigan University , GRCC, University of Michigan or Michigan State University. Applicants must have demonstrated financial need and have a minimum of 2.75 GPA. **Criteria:** Preference will be given to those students who meet the criteria.

Funds Avail.: No specific amount. **To Apply:** Applicants must check the available website for the required materials. **Contact:** Grand Rapids Community Foundation at the above address (see entry 3318).

3329 ■ Carolyn Gallmeyer Scholarships *(Undergraduate/Scholarship)*

Purpose: To provide financial support to those students who are in need. **Focus:** General Studies. **Qualif.:** Applicants must be Kent County residents who are pursuing an undergraduate degree at any U.S college. **Criteria:** Preference will be given to those students who meet the criteria.

Funds Avail.: No specific amount. **To Apply:** Applicants must check the available website for the required materials. **Contact:** Grand Rapids Community Foundation at the above address (see entry 3318).

3330 ■ Mathilda & Carolyn Gallmeyer Scholarships *(Undergraduate/Scholarship)*

Purpose: To provide financial assistance to those students who are in need. **Focus:** Fine Arts. **Qualif.:** Applicants must be Kent County residents. Applicants must be pursuing Painting or Fine arts. Applicants must demonstrate artistic talent, financial need and a minimum of 2.75 GPA. **Criteria:** Preference will be given to those students who meet the criteria.

Funds Avail.: No specific amount. **To Apply:** Applicants must check the available website for the required materials. **Contact:** Grand Rapids Community Foundation at the above address (see entry 3318).

3331 ■ Grand Rapids Scholarship Association *(Undergraduate/Scholarship)*

Purpose: To provide financial assistance to those students who are in need. **Focus:** General Studies. **Qualif.:** Applicants must be Kent County residents who will be attending Aquinas, Calvin, Cornerstone, Davenport, GRCC, GVSU or Kendall. Applicants must have financial need and must have a 3.0 minimum GPA. **Criteria:** Preference will be given to those students who meet the criteria.

Funds Avail.: No specific amount. **To Apply:** Applicants must check the available website for the required materials. **Contact:** Grand Rapids Community Foundation at the above address (see entry 3318).

3332 ■ Guy D. & Mary Edith Halladay Graduate Scholarships *(Undergraduate/Scholarship)*

Purpose: To provide financial support to those students who are in need. **Focus:** General Studies. **Qualif.:** Applicants must be residents of Kent County and must be graduate level students at a Michigan college. Applicants must have demonstrated financial need and must have a minimum of 3.0 GPA. **Criteria:** Preference will be given to those who meet the criteria.

Funds Avail.: No specific amount. **To Apply:** Applicants must check the available website for more information. **Contact:** Grand Rapids Community Foundation at the above address (see entry 3318).

3333 ■ Guy D. & Mary Edith Halladay Music Scholarships *(Graduate, Undergraduate/Scholarship)*

Purpose: To provide financial assistance to deserving students. **Focus:** Music. **Qualif.:** Applicants must be residents of Kent County who are majoring in Music at any college or university in the U.S. Applicants must have financial need. Applicants must have a cumulative GPA of 3.0. **Criteria:** Priority will be given to those students with high financial need.

Funds Avail.: No specific amount. **To Apply:** Applicants must check the available website for the required materials. **Contact:** Grand Rapids Community Foundation at the above address (see entry 3318).

3334 ■ Harry and Lucille Brown Scholarships *(Undergraduate/Scholarship)*

Purpose: To provide financial support to those students who are in need. **Focus:** General Studies. **Qualif.:** Applicants must be residents of Kent County; must have financial need; must be pursuing an undergraduate degree at any accredited college in the U.S; must have a minimum of 3.3 GPA. **Criteria:** Preference will be given to those students who meet the criteria.

Funds Avail.: No specific amount. **To Apply:** Applicants must check the available website for the required materials. **Contact:** Grand Rapids Community Foundation at the above address (see entry 3318).

3335 ■ Donald & Florence Hunting Scholarships *(Undergraduate/Scholarship)*

Purpose: To provide financial assistance to those students who are in need. **Focus:** General Studies. **Qualif.:** Applicants must be senior students at Rockford High School who will be entering college in the fall. Applicants must have demonstrated financial need. **Criteria:** Priority will be given to those students with financial need.

Funds Avail.: No specific amount. **To Apply:** Applicants must check the available website for more information. **Contact:** Grand Rapids Community Foundation at the above address (see entry 3318).

3336 ■ Jack Family Scholarships *(Undergraduate/Scholarship)*

Purpose: To provide financial assistance to those students who are in need. **Focus:** General Studies. **Qualif.:** Applicants must be undergraduate students residing in Kent County who demonstrate financial need. Applicants must have a minimum of 3.3 GPA. **Criteria:** Preference will be given to those students who meet the criteria.

Funds Avail.: No specific amount. **To Apply:** Applicants must check the available website for more information. **Contact:** Grand Rapids Community Foundation at the above address (see entry 3318).

3337 ■ Camilla C. Johnson Scholarships *(Undergraduate/Scholarship)*

Purpose: To provide financial support to those deserving students. **Focus:** General Studies. **Qualif.:** Applicants must be senior students at Union High School entering college full-time in the fall. Applicants must have financial need. Applicants must have a cumulative of 2.6 GPA. **Criteria:** Preference will be given to those students who meet the criteria.

Funds Avail.: No specific amount. **To Apply:** Applicants must check the available website for the required materials. **Contact:** Grand Rapids Community Foundation at the above address (see entry 3318).

3338 ■ Lavina Laible Scholarships *(Undergraduate/Scholarship)*

Purpose: To provide financial assistance to those students who are in need. **Focus:** General Studies. **Qualif.:** Ap-

plicants must be female students in their third year or above of undergraduate studies at the University of Michigan. Applicants must be Kent County residents. Applicants must have financial need. Applicants must have a minimum of 3.0 GPA. **Criteria:** Preference will be given to those students who meet the criteria.

Funds Avail.: No specific amount. **To Apply:** Applicants must check the available website for the required materials. **Contact:** Grand Rapids Community Foundation at the above address (see entry 3318).

3339 ■ Stephen Lankester Scholarships *(Undergraduate/Scholarship)*

Purpose: To provide financial assistance to those students who are in need. **Focus:** General Studies. **Qualif.:** Applicants must be Kent County residents; must be attending an undergraduate program at a Michigan college; must have financial need; must have a minimum of 3.0 GPA. **Criteria:** Preference will be given to those who meet the criteria.

Funds Avail.: No specific amount. **To Apply:** Applicants must check the available website for more information. **Contact:** Grand Rapids Community Foundation at the above address (see entry 3318).

3340 ■ Shepard L. & Mabel C. Lepard Scholarships *(Undergraduate/Scholarship)*

Purpose: To provide financial assistance to deserving students. **Focus:** General Studies. **Qualif.:** Applicants must be pursuing an undergraduate degree at any accredited college or university in the U.S; must be Kent County residents; must have demonstrated financial need; must have a minimum of 3.3 GPA. **Criteria:** Preference will be given to those students who meet the criteria.

Funds Avail.: No specific amount. **To Apply:** Applicants must check the available website for the required materials. **Contact:** Grand Rapids Community Foundation at the above address (see entry 3318).

3341 ■ John T. & Frances Maghielse Scholarships *(Undergraduate/Scholarship)*

Purpose: To provide financial assistance to students who are in need. **Focus:** General Studies. **Qualif.:** Applicants must be graduates of Grand Rapids Public High School; must be Kent County residents; must be currently pursuing a full-time undergraduate degree in the field of Education at any Michigan public or private college/ university. Applicants must have financial need and must have a minimum of 3.0 GPA. **Criteria:** Preference will be given to those students who meet the criteria.

Funds Avail.: No specific amount. **To Apply:** Applicants must check the available website for the required materials. **Contact:** Grand Rapids Community Foundation at the above address (see entry 3318).

3342 ■ Joshua Esch Mitchell Aviation Scholarships *(Undergraduate/Scholarship)*

Purpose: To provide financial support to those students who study flight science. **Focus:** Aviation. **Qualif.:** Applicants must be U.S citizens. Must be enrolled full or part-time at a college or university in the United States providing an accredited flight science curriculum. Applicants must be second year students or above with a minimum of 2.75 GPA; must be pursuing studies in the field of professional piloting with an emphasis in General Aviation, Aviation Management, or Aviation Safety. **Criteria:** Selection will be based on criteria.

Funds Avail.: No specific amount. **To Apply:** Applicants must check the available website for the required materials. **Contact:** Grand Rapids Community Foundation at the above address (see entry 3318).

3343 ■ Robert L. & Hilda Treasure Mitchell Scholarships *(Undergraduate/Scholarship)*

Purpose: To provide financial assistance to deserving students. **Focus:** General Studies. **Qualif.:** Applicants must be pursuing an undergraduate degree at any accredited college or university in the U.S; must be Kent County residents; must demonstrate financial need; must have a minimum of 3.3 GPA. **Criteria:** Preference will be given to those students who meet the criteria.

Funds Avail.: No specific amount. **To Apply:** Applicants must check the available website for the required materials. **Contact:** Grand Rapids Community Foundation at the above address (see entry 3318).

3344 ■ Peggy (Kommer) Novosad Scholarships *(Graduate, Postgraduate/Scholarship)*

Purpose: To provide financial support to those students who are in need. **Focus:** Business; Law. **Qualif.:** Applicants must be residents of Kent County who are currently completing or possess an undergraduate degree from GVSU or MSU and will be pursuing a full-time graduate or post-graduate degree in business or law at any accredited university in Michigan. Applicants must have financial need and a minimum of 3.5 GPA. **Criteria:** Preference will be given to those who meet the criteria.

Funds Avail.: No specific amount. **To Apply:** Applicants must check the available website for the required materials. **Contact:** Grand Rapids Community Foundation at the above address (see entry 3318).

3345 ■ Patricia & Armen Oumedian Scholarships *(Undergraduate/Scholarship)*

Purpose: To provide financial support to those students who are in need. **Focus:** Engineering. **Qualif.:** Applicants must be second year or above full-time engineering students at Kettering or transferring from GRCC to Kettering. Applicants must be residents of Kent, Ottawa, or Muskegon County. Applicants must have demonstrated financial need and must have a minimum of 3.0 GPA. **Criteria:** Preference will be given to those students who meet the criteria.

Funds Avail.: No specific amount. **To Apply:** Applicants must check the available website for the required materials. **Contact:** Grand Rapids Community Foundation at the above address (see entry 3318).

3346 ■ Josephine Ringold Scholarships *(Undergraduate/Scholarship)*

Purpose: To provide financial support to those students who are in need. **Focus:** General Studies. **Qualif.:** Applicants must be Kent County residents who will be attending Aquinas, Calvin, Cornerstone, Davenport, GRCC, GVSU or Kendall. Applicants must have financial need and a 3.0 minimum GPA is required. **Criteria:** Preference will be given to those students who meet the criteria.

Funds Avail.: No specific amount. **To Apply:** Applicants must check the available website for more information. **Contact:** Grand Rapids Community Foundation at the above address (see entry 3318).

3347 ■ Margery J. Seeger Scholarships *(Undergraduate/Scholarship)*

Purpose: To provide financial assistance to those students who are in need. **Focus:** General Studies. **Qualif.:** Ap-

plicants must be Kent County residents who are pursuing an undergraduate degree at any accredited college in the U.S. Applicants must have financial need. Applicants must have a minimum of 3.3 GPA. **Criteria:** Preference will be given to those students who meet the criteria.

Funds Avail.: No specific amount. **To Apply:** Applicants must check the available website for the required materials. **Contact:** Grand Rapids Community Foundation at the above address (see entry 3318).

3348 ■ Gladys Snauble Scholarships *(Undergraduate/Scholarship)*

Purpose: To provide financial support to those students who are in need. **Focus:** General Studies. **Qualif.:** Applicants must be senior students at Cedar Springs High School who will be entering college in the fall. Applicants must have financial need. **Criteria:** Priority will be given to those students with financial need.

Funds Avail.: No specific amount. **To Apply:** Applicants must check the available website for the required materials. **Contact:** Grand Rapids Community Foundation at the above address (see entry 3318).

3349 ■ Christine Soper Scholarships *(Undergraduate/Scholarship)*

Purpose: To provide financial support to those students who are in need. **Focus:** General Studies. **Qualif.:** Applicants must be Kent County residents who will be attending Aquinas, Calvin, Cornerstone, Davenport, GRCC, GVSU or Kendall. Applicants must have financial need. Applicants must have a cumulative of 3.0 GPA. **Criteria:** Priority will be given to those students who meet the criteria.

Funds Avail.: No specific amount. **To Apply:** Applicants must check the available website for the required materials. **Contact:** Grand Rapids Community Foundation at the above address (see entry 3318).

3350 ■ Dr. William E. & Norma Sprague Scholarships *(Undergraduate/Scholarship)*

Purpose: To provide financial assistance to those students who are in need. **Focus:** Medicine. **Qualif.:** Applicants must be full-time students and permanent residents in the Michigan counties of Kent, Allegan, Barry, Ionia, Montcalm, Muskegon, Newaygo or Athens County, Ohio, who are pursuing a full-time undergraduate or graduate degree in medicine at Ohio University. Applicants must have financial need. Applicants must have a minimum of 3.0 GPA. **Criteria:** Preference will be given to those students who meet the criteria.

Funds Avail.: No specific amount. **To Apply:** Applicants must check the available website for the required materials. **Contact:** Grand Rapids Community Foundation at the above address (see entry 3318).

3351 ■ Dorothy B. & Charles E. Thomas Scholarships *(Undergraduate/Scholarship)*

Purpose: To provide financial assistance to those students who are in need. **Focus:** General Studies. **Qualif.:** Applicants must be Kent County residents who will be attending Aquinas, Calvin, Cornerstone, Davenport, GRCC, GVSU or Kendall. Applicants must have a minimum of 3.0 GPA. Applicants must have financial need. **Criteria:** Priority will be given to those students with financial need.

Funds Avail.: No specific amount. **To Apply:** Applicants must check the available website for the application process and for the required materials. **Contact:** Grand Rapids Community Foundation at the above address (see entry 3318).

3352 ■ Dorothy J. Thurston Graduate Scholarships *(Undergraduate/Scholarship)*

Purpose: To provide financial assistance to those students who are in need. **Focus:** General Studies. **Qualif.:** Applicants must be Kent County residents who are pursuing full or part-time study at any accredited school in Michigan. Applicants must have financial need. Applicants must have a minimum of 3.0 GPA. **Criteria:** Preference will be given to those students who meet the criteria.

Funds Avail.: No specific amount. **To Apply:** Applicants must check the available website for more information. **Contact:** Grand Rapids Community Foundation at the above address (see entry 3318).

3353 ■ Mildred E. Troske Music Scholarships *(Undergraduate/Scholarship)*

Purpose: To provide financial support to those students who are in need. **Focus:** General Studies. **Qualif.:** Applicants must be residents of Kent County who are studying music at a camp or are undergraduate music majors. Applicants must have demonstrated financial need. Applicants must have a minimum of 3.0 GPA. **Criteria:** Preference will be given to those students who meet the criteria.

Funds Avail.: No specific amount. **To Apply:** Applicants must check the available website for the required materials. **Contact:** Grand Rapids Community Foundation at the above address (see entry 3318).

3354 ■ Keith C. Vanderhyde Scholarships *(Undergraduate/Scholarship)*

Purpose: To provide financial assistance to those students who are in need. **Focus:** General Studies. **Qualif.:** Applicants must be senior students or graduates of Ottawa Hills High School who are pursuing a full-time undergraduate degree. Applicants must demonstrate financial need. Applicants must have a minimum of 3.0 GPA. **Criteria:** Priority will be given to those students with financial need.

Funds Avail.: No specific amount. **To Apply:** Applicants must check the available website for the required materials. **Contact:** Grand Rapids Community Foundation at the above address (see entry 3318).

3355 ■ Jacob R. & Mary M. VanLoo & Lenore K. VanLoo Scholarships *(Undergraduate/Scholarship)*

Purpose: To provide financial assistance to those students who are in need. **Focus:** General Studies. **Qualif.:** Applicants must be Kent County residents who will be attending Aquinas, Calvin, Cornerstone, Davenport, GRCC, GVSU or Kendall. Applicants must have financial need. Applicants must have a minimum of 3.0 GPA. **Criteria:** Preference will be given to those students who meet the criteria.

Funds Avail.: No specific amount. **To Apply:** Applicants must check the available website for the required materials. **Contact:** Grand Rapids Community Foundation at the above address (see entry 3318).

3356 ■ Donald M. Wells Scholarships *(Undergraduate/Scholarship)*

Purpose: To provide financial assistance to those students who are in need. **Focus:** General Studies. **Qualif.:** Applicants must be senior students or graduates of Central High School who are pursuing undergraduate studies at GRCC, University of Chicago or University of Michigan. Applicants must have financial need and must have a minimum of 2.5 GPA. **Criteria:** Preference will be given to those students who meet the criteria.

Funds Avail.: No specific amount. **To Apply:** Applicants must check the available website for more information regarding this award. **Contact:** Grand Rapids Community Foundation at the above address (see entry 3318).

3357 ■ Elmo Wierenga Alumni Scholarships *(Undergraduate/Scholarship)*

Purpose: To provide financial support to those students who are in need. **Focus:** General Studies. **Qualif.:** Applicants must be senior students at Ottawa Hills High School pursuing full-time undergraduate studies at any 2 or 4-year accredited school in the U.S. Applicants must have financial need and a minimum of 2.5 GPA. **Criteria:** Priority will be given to those students with financial need.

Funds Avail.: No specific amount. **To Apply:** Applicants must check the available website for the required materials. **Contact:** Grand Rapids Community Foundation at the above address (see entry 3318).

3358 ■ Audrey L. Wright Scholarships *(Undergraduate/Scholarship)*

Purpose: To provide financial support to deserving students. **Focus:** Foreign Language; Education. **Qualif.:** Applicants must be residents of Kent County; must be pursuing an undergraduate degree in Foreign Language or Education; must have financial need; must have a minimum of 3.0 GPA. **Criteria:** Preference will be given to those students who meet the criteria.

Funds Avail.: No specific amount. **To Apply:** Applicants must check the available website for the application process and for the required materials. **Contact:** Grand Rapids Community Foundation at the above address (see entry 3318).

3359 ■ Grandmothers for Peace International

PO Box 580788
Elk Grove, CA 95758
Ph: (916)730-6476
E-mail: lorraine@grandmothersforpeace.org
URL: http://www.grandmothersforpeace.org

3360 ■ Barbara Wiedner and Dorothy Vandercook Memorial Peace Scholarships *(Undergraduate/Scholarship)*

Purpose: To provide financial assistance to students across the United States, Africa, Kyrgzstan, Canada, Norway and the Ukraine. **Focus:** General studies. **Qualif.:** Applicant must be a high school senior or in first year of college. **Criteria:** Recipients will be evaluated by the Scholarship Selection Committee based on some criteria.

Funds Avail.: $250. **To Apply:** Applicants must submit completed application form; brief autobiography of activities relating to peace and social justice, nuclear disarmament issues, or conflict resolution; two letters of recommendation; and must describe how will they contribute to a peaceful and just society in the future. **Deadline:** March 1.

3361 ■ Granger Business Association

PO Box 427
Granger, IN 46530
E-mail: info@grangertoday.com
URL: http://www.grangertoday.com

3362 ■ Granger Business Association College Scholarships *(Undergraduate/Scholarship)*

Purpose: To award scholarships to area students to help defray college expenses. **Focus:** General Studies. **Qualif.:** Applicants must reside in the 46530 zip code and demonstrate financial need. **Criteria:** Preference will be based on academic standing, extra curricular activities, volunteer work and personal narratives.

Funds Avail.: $1,000. **Number Awarded:** 10. **To Apply:** Applicants must check the application process online. **Contact:** Granger Business Association at the above address (see entry 3361).

3363 ■ Great Lakes Commission

2805 S Industrial Hwy., Ste. 100
Ann Arbor, MI 48104-6791
Ph: (734)971-9135
Fax: (734)971-9150
E-mail: eschmidt@glc.org
URL: http://www.glc.org

3364 ■ Great Lakes Commission Sea Grant Fellowships *(Graduate/Scholarship)*

Purpose: To provide fund to work and advance the environmental quality and sustainable economic development goals. **Focus:** Natural resources, Public health. **Qualif.:** Applicants must be a students who are in a graduate or professional degree program in public policy, public health, natural resources, aquatic sciences or other related field at a U.S accredited institution of higher education in the United States. **Criteria:** Selection team will evaluate each candidate by the criteria.

Funds Avail.: $41,000. **To Apply:** Applicant must complete the required documents; personal and academic resume or curriculum vitae (not exceed two pages); education and career goal statement (1,000 words or less); two letters of recommendation with at least one from the student's major professor, a letter of endorsement from the sponsoring sea grant director; a copy of undergraduate and graduate student transcripts. Must be sent to the Great Lakes Commission. **Deadline:** February 29. **Contact:** Tim Eder.

3365 ■ Carol A. Ratza Memorial Scholarships *(Undergraduate/Scholarship)*

Purpose: To recognize outstanding achievement and vision in electronic communications technology. **Focus:** Electronics, Communications technologies. **Qualif.:** Applicant must be enrolled full-time at a college or university in the Great Lakes states or Canadian provinces; must have a career interest in electronic communication technologies; must have a demonstrated interest in the environmental or economic applications of electronic communications technology, exhibit academic excellence and have a sincere appreciation for the Great Lakes and their protection. **Criteria:** Selection of applicant will be based on their demonstrated interest in the environmental or economic applications of electronic communications technology, exhibit academic excellence and their a sincere appreciation for the Great Lakes and their protection.

Funds Avail.: $1,000. **To Apply:** Application must be submitted along with essay/original web page; resume; letter of intent; grade transcripts and two letters of recommendation. **Deadline:** March 31. **Contact:** Christine Manninen.

Awards are arranged alphabetically below their administering organizations

3366 ■ Great Seattle Business Association

400 E Pine St., Ste. 322
Seattle, WA 98122
Ph: (206)363-9188
Fax: (206)568-3123
E-mail: office@thegsba.org
URL: http://www.thegsba.org

3367 ■ Greater Seattle Business Association Scholarships *(Undergraduate/Scholarship)*

Purpose: To support undergraduate students by providing financial resources to pursue their educational goals. **Focus:** General studies. **Qualif.:** Applicant must be a current resident of Washington pursuing an undergraduate degree at any college in the US. **Criteria:** Applicants will be evaluated based on leadership potential; academic strength/ special skills and talents; and diversity.

Funds Avail.: $3,000 up to $10,000. **To Apply:** Applicants must complete and return scholarship application, letters of reference and transcripts by application deadline. **Deadline:** October.

3368 ■ Greater Dayton IT Alliance

900 Kettering Tower
Dayton, OH 45423
Ph: (937)229-0054
E-mail: ahickey@gdita.org
URL: http://www.daytonitalliance.org

3369 ■ Robert V. McKenna Scholarships *(Undergraduate/Scholarship)*

Purpose: To provide financial support to those deserving students. **Focus:** Information science and technology. **Qualif.:** Applicant must have at least sophomore standing (30 semester hours or 45 quarter hours) at his/her respective university or college and currently be enrolled as an undergraduate student as defined by the applicant's institution; must be able to prove that his/her major's relation to the information technology field; must have a minimum cumulative GPA of 2.5 and a minimum major GPA of 3.0 on a 4.0 scale at the date of submission; must have a strong interest in pursuing a career in the Miami Valley IT field; must be a permanent resident of or attend an accredited IT degree-granting college within the 11 county Miami Valley region: Champaign, Clark, Darke, Greene, Logan, Miami, Montgomery, Northern Warren, Northern Butler, Northern Clinton, and Shelby. **Criteria:** Preference will be based on criteria.

Funds Avail.: No specific amount. **To Apply:** Applicants must submit a completed application form. **Deadline:** March 14. **Contact:** Greater Dayton IT Alliance at the above address (see entry 3368).

3370 ■ Greater Philadelphia Law Library Association

PO Box 335
Philadelphia, PA 19105
Ph: (215)977-2779
E-mail: malmendarez@wolfblock.com
URL: http://www.gplla.org

3371 ■ Greater Philadelphia Law Library Association Scholarships *(Undergraduate/Scholarship)*

Purpose: To fulfill the educational mission of GPLLA; to support the recruitment of law librarians to the profession as a whole and to GPLLA in particular. **Focus:** Law. **Qualif.:** Applicants must be students interested in pursuing a career in law librarianship; must be students accepted and/or registered at an ALA-accredited library school (minimum of half-time status) who will continue as a student for another semester or quarter; must reside within the geographic area covered by GPLLA. **Criteria:** Recipients are selected based on the genuine interest in the profession of law librarianship as a career evidenced by; personal statement, letters of recommendation, relevant work or internship experience, relevant course work, relevant volunteer work, relevant professional activity; must also demonstrate financial need.

Funds Avail.: $1,000. **To Apply:** Applicants must submit a certified copy of the graduate library school transcript; must submit a completed application for the student scholarship; must submit a resume; two letters of recommendation from teachers and/or employers with application; must submit a personal statement that indicates a genuine interest in the profession of law librarianship with the application. **Deadline:** May 16.

3372 ■ The Greater Tacoma Community Foundation

PO Box 1995
Tacoma, WA 98401
Ph: (253)383-5622
URL: http://www.tacomafoundation.org

3373 ■ Ruth Murphy Evans Scholarship *(Undergraduate/Scholarship)*

Purpose: To foster generosity by connecting people who care with causes that matter. **Focus:** Nursing. **Qualif.:** Applicants must be students in a nursing program at Highline Community College, Olympic College, South Puget Sound Community College or Tacoma Community College. **Criteria:** Recipients are selected based on financial need.

Funds Avail.: No specific amount. **To Apply:** Applicants must request an application form at their guidance office.

3374 ■ Dayton E. Finnigan Scholarship *(Undergraduate/Scholarship)*

Purpose: To foster generosity by connecting people who care with causes that matter. **Focus:** Metallurgy. **Qualif.:** Applicants must be students enrolled in the sheet metal program at Bates Technical College. **Criteria:** Recipients are selected based on financial need.

Funds Avail.: No specific amount. **To Apply:** Applicants must request an application form at the guidance office of Bates Technical College.

3375 ■ Fuchs-Harden Educational Scholarships Fund *(Undergraduate/Scholarship)*

Purpose: To foster generosity by connecting people who care with causes that matter. **Focus:** Engineering; Business Administration; Social sciences. **Qualif.:** Applicant must be an African American residing in the legal limits of the city of Tacoma, Washington; must be enrolled in and maintain a satisfactory GPA at a college or university in the courses for Business Administration, Engineering, Applied Physics, Dentistry, Medicine, Law, Sociology, Journalism or Home Economics. **Criteria:** Recipients are selected based on financial need.

Funds Avail.: No specific amount. **To Apply:** Applicants must submit a completed application form available through

Awards are arranged alphabetically below their administering organizations

R. Merle Palmer Minority Scholarship Fund. **Contact:** PO Box 7119, Tacoma, WA 98406-0119.

3376 ■ Clay Huntington Sports Communications Scholarships *(Undergraduate/Scholarship)*

Purpose: To benefit students from Pierce County high schools and help tomorrow's leaders reach their goals and fulfill their dreams. **Focus:** General studies. **Qualif.:** Applicants must be graduating seniors at Pierce County High School; must intend to declare a major in radio/television production and/or broadcast editorial journalism or a similar communications-related field. **Criteria:** Recipients are selected based on financial need.

Funds Avail.: No specific amount. **To Apply:** Applicants must request an application form at Tacoma Athletic Commission. **Contact:** PO Box 11304, Tacoma, WA 98411.

3377 ■ The Master Gardeners of Pierce County Scholarships *(Undergraduate/Scholarship)*

Purpose: To foster generosity by connecting people who care with causes that matter; to benefit Washington State University Puyallup Research and Extension Center graduates, undergraduate students or a Pierce County high school student. **Focus:** Horticulture. **Qualif.:** Applicants must plan to study horticulture or the environment. **Criteria:** Recipients are selected based on financial need.

Funds Avail.: No specific amount. **To Apply:** Applicants must contact W.S.U. Puyallup Research and Extension Center Scholarship Committee for application form. **Contact:** 7612 Pioneer Way E Puyallup, WA 98371-4998 or 253-445-4500.

3378 ■ Anna M. Rundguist Memorial Scholarship *(Undergraduate/Scholarship)*

Purpose: To provide assistance for students. **Focus:** General studies. **Qualif.:** Applicants must be graduating students from Highline Community College, Olympic College, South Puget Sound Community College or Tacoma Community College; must be enrolled at a four-year college or university to pursue a nursing career. **Criteria:** Recipients are selected based on academic performance and financial need.

Funds Avail.: No specific amount. **To Apply:** Applicants must submit a completed application form available at the guidance office.

3379 ■ The Tacoma Athletic Commission Scholarships *(Undergraduate/Scholarship)*

Purpose: To foster generosity by connecting people who care with causes that matter. **Focus:** Athletics. **Qualif.:** Applicants must be current graduating senior students at Pierce County High School; must be enrolled at a vocational school or a two or four-year college. **Criteria:** Recipients are selected based on financial need.

Funds Avail.: No specific amount. **To Apply:** Applicants must request an application form at Tacoma Athletic Commission. **Contact:** PO Box 11304, Tacoma, WA 98411.

3380 ■ Green Knight Economic Development Corporation

PO Box 4
Pen Argyl, PA 18072
E-mail: gkedc@gkedc.com
URL: http://www.gkedc.com

3381 ■ Green Knight Economic Development Corporation (GKEDC) Scholarships *(Undergraduate/Scholarship)*

Purpose: To financially support a student living in the Pen Argyl School District who wishes to continue higher education. **Focus:** General studies. **Qualif.:** Applicant must be a graduating high school senior who lives in the Pen Argyl School District and will be continuing his/her education in a college program; must take at least 24 credits per year and must maintain, at a minimum, a cumulative GPA of 2.5. **Criteria:** Award is given based on the application materials.

Funds Avail.: $4,000 each year. **To Apply:** Applicants must submit a completed scholarship application form together with a one-page essay. **Contact:** Community Relations Committee at comm@gkedc.com.

3382 ■ Griffin Foundation

303 W Prospect Rd.
Fort Collins, CO 80526
Ph: (970)482-3030
Fax: (970)484-6648
E-mail: carol.wood@thegriffinfoundation.org
URL: http://www.thegriffinfoundation.org

3383 ■ Griffin Foundation Scholarships *(Undergraduate/Scholarship)*

Purpose: To award scholarship to qualified applicants who have an associate degree from a junior or community college. **Focus:** General studies. **Qualif.:** Applicants must have an associate degree or at least 60 hours from a junior or community college and are seeking to complete a baccalaureate degree. **Criteria:** Scholarships will be awarded on a competitive basis by ranking applicants in the following areas for their activities since graduation from high school: Scholarship; Leadership and service; Personal traits; and Financial need.

Funds Avail.: $5,000. **To Apply:** Application form can be downloaded from the Griffin Foundation website. Applicants must type or print their application legibly; applicants must attach three letters of recommendation, at least one of which is from a college faculty member, counselor or administrator who can comment on applicant qualifications (be sure recommendations are signed). Applicants must attach an official copy of grade transcript(s) from each college attended. Scholarship can only be used at Colorado State University (Fort Collins Campus), the University of Northern Colorado, or the University of Wyoming (Larimie Campus). **Deadline:** March 1. **Contact:** Carol Wood, Program Dir. at the above address (see entry 3382).

3384 ■ Harry Frank Guggenheim Foundation

25 W 53rd Ste.
New York, NY 10019-5401
Ph: (646)428-0971
Fax: (646)428-0981
E-mail: info@hfg.org
URL: http://www.hfg.org

3385 ■ Harry Frank Guggenheim Fellowships *(Doctorate/Fellowship)*

Purpose: To increase of the causes, manifestations, and control of violence, aggression, and dominance in the modern world. **Focus:** Social sciences; Humanities. **Qua-**

Awards are arranged alphabetically below their administering organizations

lif.: Applicants must be citizens of any country and studying as doctoral candidates in colleges and universities in any country. **Criteria:** Recipients are selected based on the comparison of the candidates' theses.

Funds Avail.: $15,000. **To Apply:** Applicants must submit three copies of typewritten title page; abstract; advisors letter; applicant's background; a research plan; protection of subjects. **Deadline:** February 1.

3386 ■ Harry Frank Guggenheim Foundation Grants *(All/Grant)*

Purpose: To increase understanding of the causes, manifestations, and control violence, aggression, and dominance. **Focus:** Social sciences; Humanities. **Qualif.:** Applicants must have a project proposal in the field of natural sciences and humanities. **Criteria:** Recipients are selected based on the project proposal.

Funds Avail.: $15,000-$30,000. **To Apply:** Applicants must submit three copies of typewritten title page; abstract; personnel; budget; budget justification; research plan; protection of subjects; tax exempt status; referees' comments. **Deadline:** August 1.

3387 ■ Gulf and Caribbean Fisheries Institute

Marine Research Institute
2796 Overseas Hwy., Ste. 119
Marathon, FL 33050
Ph: (305)289-2330
Fax: (305)289-2334
URL: http://www.gcfi.org

3388 ■ Ronald L. Schmied Scholarships *(Professional Development, Undergraduate/Grant)*

Purpose: To encourage students with interest in marine recreational fisheries. **Focus:** Fisheries sciences/management; Marine biology. **Qualif.:** Applicant must be enrolled at a college/university degree program in the wider Caribbean or in one of Gulf of Mexico states (Mexico and the United States); or a student engaged in a research project in the Gulf of Mexico and wider Caribbean region. **Criteria:** Applicants will be selected based on the following: involvement with recreational fisheries issues, level of achievement, innovation, and financial need.

Funds Avail.: $1,500 (covers airfare, lodging, and research-related expenses). **To Apply:** Applicants must submit electronically an application letter (includes name, address, contact numbers, educational institution department, degree level, description of current marine research, career goals, and reasons for the needing financial assistance); an endorsement letter from a faculty; and a vita. **Deadline:** August 1. **Contact:** Scholarship Committee, Robert B. Ditton, r-ditton@tamu.edu.

3389 ■ Hamilton Industrial Environmental Association

PO Box 35545
Hamilton, ON, Canada L8H 7S6
Ph: (905)561-4432
E-mail: info@hiea.org
URL: http://www.hiea.org

3390 ■ Hamilton Industrial Environmental Association Bursaries-Mohawk College *(Undergraduate/Scholarship)*

Purpose: To provide financial assistance to those students who are in need. **Focus:** Engineering Technology; Environmental Technology. **Qualif.:** Applicants must be 2nd year students in their final semester; must have been raised in Hamilton or graduated from Hamilton High School. **Criteria:** Applications will be considered based on their year's work in an internship for a Hamilton employer and a written essay on area of study and career goals.

Funds Avail.: No specific amount. **To Apply:** Applicants must check the available website for more information. **Contact:** Hamilton Industrial Environmental Association at the above address (see entry 3389).

3391 ■ George and Mary Josephine Hamman Foundation

3336 Richmond, Ste. 310
Houston, TX 77098
Ph: (713)522-9891
Fax: (713)522-9693
E-mail: hammanfdn@aol.com
URL: http://www.hammanfoundation.org

3392 ■ George and Mary Josephine Hamman Foundation Scholarships *(High School/Scholarship)*

Purpose: To provide undergraduate scholarships for Houston area high school seniors. **Focus:** General studies. **Qualif.:** Applicants must be Houston area high school seniors who attend schools or are homeschooled in the following eight counties: Brazoria, Chambers, Fort Bend, Galveston, Harris, Liberty, Montgomery or Waller; must be US citizens. **Criteria:** Applicants are evaluated based on scholastic ability and financial need.

Funds Avail.: No specific amount. **To Apply:** Applicants must write for the one-page scholarship application and the two-page financial qualification statement or it may be downloaded from the website. Completed scholarship applications must be submitted with these documents (in the following order): (1) Financial Qualification Statement, (2) complete, legible, signed copy of parents'/guardians' and student's most recent federal income tax return (including all schedules) plus, if applicable, corporate or partnership returns, (3) proof of ACT and/or SAT results, and (4) high school transcript (unofficial is okay). Mail to: George and Mary Josephine Hamman Foundation, 3336 Richmond, Suite 310, Houston, TX 77098. **Deadline:** February 29.

3393 ■ Handweavers Guild of America

1255 Boford Hwy., Ste. 211
Suwanee, GA 30024
Ph: (678)730-0010
Fax: (678)730-0836
E-mail: hga@weavespindye.org
URL: http://www.weavespindye.org

3394 ■ Convergence Assistantship Grants *(Undergraduate/Grant)*

Purpose: To provide students in fiber arts programs the opportunity to assist internationally known instructors and to participate in the Convergence experience. **Focus:** Art. **Qualif.:** Applicant must be currently enrolled in an accredited academic program and available to attend a Training Class Saturday at the Convention Center. **Criteria:** Selection of applicants will be based on their application materials.

Funds Avail.: No specific amount. **To Apply:** Awardee

must submit a Letter of Nomination from the Professor; must provide the Convergence complete registration form and personal statement. Application documents must be sent to: HGA, 1255 Boford Hwy., Ste. 211, Suwanee, GA 30024. **Deadline:** April 3.

3395 ■ Mearl K. Gable II Memorial Grants
(Professional Development/Grant)

Purpose: To provide funds for HGA members to study in non-accredited programs for any skill level. **Focus:** Art. **Qualif.:** Recipients must be HGA members. **Criteria:** Selection of applicants will be based on their application materials.

Funds Avail.: $100. **To Apply:** Application form must be printed and must have the following: Name of school or provider of instruction, title and short description of course (attach brochure). Applicant must provide a resume of the background, current activities, and future goals of the applicant in the fiber field. Application must be mailed to: Gable Grant Administrator, Handweavers Guild of America, Inc., 1255 Buford Hwy., Ste. 211, Suwanee, GA 30024. **Deadline:** February 1.

3396 ■ HGA and Dendel Scholarships
(Undergraduate/Scholarship)

Purpose: To further the education in the field of fiber arts, including training for research, textile history, and conservation. **Focus:** Art. **Qualif.:** Applicant must be enrolled in accredited undergraduate or graduate programs in the United States and Canada. **Criteria:** Applications will be evaluated by the Scholarship Committee.

Funds Avail.: Amounts of the awards are based on income from the scholarship funds. **To Apply:** Application forms are available on the website. Applicant must have the following: Transcript (a copy of the transcript must accompany the application), and slide description sheet. Application and other required materials must be sent to: HGA Scholarship Chair, Handweavers Guild of America, Inc., 1255 Buford Hwy., Ste. 211 Suwanee, GA 30024. **Deadline:** March 15.

3397 ■ Silvio and Eugenio Petrini Grants
(Professional Development/Grant)

Purpose: To provide educational opportunity to HGA members and to increase the awareness of and appreciation for the fiber arts. **Focus:** Art. **Qualif.:** Recipients must be a HGA members. **Criteria:** Selection of applicants will be based on application materials.

Funds Avail.: $300. **To Apply:** Application forms are available on the website and must be mailed to: Petrini Grant Administrator Scholarship Committee, Handweavers Guild of America, Inc., 1255 Buford Hwy., Ste. 211, Suwanee, GA 30024. **Deadline:** February 1.

3398 ■ Hardanger Fiddle Association of America

HFAA Scholarship Committee
PO Box 23046
Minneapolis, MN 55423-0046
E-mail: info@hfaa.org
URL: http://www.hfaa.org

3399 ■ Bernt Balchen, Jr. Hardingfele Scholarships *(All, Professional Development/Scholarship)*

Purpose: To assist Hardingfele (Hardanger fiddle) players for the HFAA Annual Workshops. **Focus:** Music. **Qualif.:** Applicants must have an experience in playing a string instrument in either classical or folk tradition. **Criteria:** Scholarship will be given to the applicants who best meet the requirements.

Funds Avail.: No specific amount. **To Apply:** Applicants must submit a completed application form (available at the website www.hfaa.org); a personal statement; a letter of reference from a person not related to the applicant, preferably an instructor or a fellow musician; three copies of a 3-5 minute cassette tape or CD recording on the applicant's string instrument playing ability in classical or folk tradition. Send the complete applications to: HFAA Scholarship Committee PO Box 23046, Minneapolis, MN 55423-0046 USA. **Deadline:** May 15. **Contact:** scholarships@hfaa.org.

3400 ■ Bryce Harlow Foundation

1701 Pennsylvania Ave. NW, Ste. 400
Washington, DC 20006
Ph: (202)654-7812
Fax: (202)638-5178
E-mail: info@bryceharlow.org
URL: http://www.bryceharlow.org

3401 ■ Bryce Harlow Fellowship Program
(Undergraduate/Fellowship)

Purpose: To provide financial assistance to students who are pursuing a career in professional advocacy through public affairs, government relations or lobbying. **Focus:** Public affairs; Government. **Qualif.:** Applicants must be students who have been accepted for admission to a graduate program at a participating university; planning to enroll in part-time graduate studies for credit at the participating university for at least two semesters of the next academic year; demonstrate an interest and strong ability for a career in public affairs, government relations or lobbying; and U.S. citizens. **Criteria:** Applicants are evaluated based on demonstrated strong interest in public affairs, government relations or lobbying; professional achievement and leadership potential; academic achievement and potential; and financial need.

Funds Avail.: $6,000. **To Apply:** Applicants must download and complete the application and recommendation request form(s). Submit it along with two letters of recommendation from persons familiar with the applicants; and official transcripts from all undergraduate universities. **Deadline:** April 18.

3402 ■ Harness Horse Youth Foundation

16575 Carey Rd.
Westfield, IN 46074
Ph: (317)867-5877
Fax: (317)867-5896
E-mail: ellen@hhyf.org
URL: http://www.hhyf.org

3403 ■ Charles Bradley Memorial Scholarships
(Undergraduate/Scholarship)

Purpose: To provide financial assistance to the children or relatives of racing officials who were members of the North American Judges and Stewards and licensed pari-mutuel officials. **Focus:** General studies. **Qualif.:** Applicants must be at least in high school and children or relatives of racing officials who were members of the North American Judges and Stewards Association and/or licensed USTA pari-

Awards are arranged alphabetically below their administering organizations

mutuel officials in the following categories: presiding judges, associate judges, paddock judges, and starters. **Criteria:** Candidates will be assessed based on scholastic achievement, grade point average, financial need, completeness of application and quality of essay.

Funds Avail.: No amount mentioned. **To Apply:** Applicants must complete and submit application form. **Deadline:** April 30.

3404 ■ Gallo Blue Chip Scholarships *(Undergraduate/Scholarship)*

Purpose: To provide financial assistance to the eligible children of harness horse trainers or licensed caretakers. **Focus:** General studies. **Qualif.:** Applicant must be at least a senior high school student and a child of harness horse trainer or caretaker licensed in New York and/or New Jersey raised and/or reside in the two-state region. **Criteria:** Candidates will be evaluated based on demonstrated scholastic achievement, including but not limited to the applicant's GPA, financial need, and quality of essay.

Funds Avail.: No specific amount. **To Apply:** Applicants must submit complete application form. **Deadline:** April 30.

3405 ■ Curt Greene Memorial Scholarships *(Undergraduate/Scholarship)*

Purpose: To provide financial support for senior high school students who may or may not be pursuing harness racing but demonstrates passion for the sport. **Focus:** General studies. **Qualif.:** Applicant must be at least a high school senior. **Criteria:** Candidates will be assessed based on scholastic achievement, grade point average, financial need, completeness of application and quality of essay.

Funds Avail.: No amount mentioned. **To Apply:** Applicants must complete and submit application form. **Deadline:** April 30.

3406 ■ Harness Tracks of America

4640 E Sunrise, Ste. 200
Tucson, AZ 85718
Ph: (520)529-2525
Free: (520)529-3235
E-mail: info@harnesstracks.com
URL: http://www.harnesstracks.com

3407 ■ Harness Tracks of America Scholarship Fund *(Undergraduate/Scholarship)*

Purpose: To provide financial assistance to students for post-secondary education. **Focus:** General studies. **Qualif.:** Applicants must be sons or daughters of licensed drivers, trainers, caretakers, management or young people actively engaged in the harness racing industry. **Criteria:** Recipients will be selected based on his or her academic merit, financial need and active harness racing involvement.

Funds Avail.: $5,000. **Number Awarded:** 5. **To Apply:** Applicants must submit complete application form. **Deadline:** June 15.

3408 ■ Hartfield Coalition

PO Box 4742
Morgantown, WV 26504-4742
E-mail: hfcoalition@email.com
URL: http://www.hartfieldcoalition.org

3409 ■ Scholarship Challenge Flight *(Undergraduate/Scholarship)*

Purpose: To create aviation education and training scholarship opportunities to benefit the youth in Appalachia. **Focus:** Aviation. **Qualif.:** Applicants must be youth from Appalachia. **Criteria:** Preference will be given to deserving applicants.

Funds Avail.: No specific amount. **To Apply:** Applicants must check the available website for the required materials. **Contact:** Hartfield Coalition at the above address (see entry 3408).

3410 ■ Hartford Foundation for Public Giving

10 Columbus Blvd., 8th Flr.
Hartford, CT 06106
Ph: (860)548-1888
Fax: (860)524-8346
E-mail: hfpg@hfpg.org
URL: http://www.hfpg.org

3411 ■ Frederick G. Adams Scholarships *(Undergraduate/Scholarship)*

Purpose: To provide scholarship for graduating high school seniors of Greater Hartford area. **Focus:** General studies. **Qualif.:** Applicants must be graduating seniors who live in or are attending school in Greater Hartford; must be entering a four-year college or university (full-time enrollment); must have a financial need; must be on a top third of the class or a good academic record; and must be active volunteer in school, community, or other extracurricular activities. **Criteria:** Selection will be based on the committee's criteria.

Funds Avail.: $3,000. **To Apply:** Applicants must download and fill out the online application and attach the following requirements: letter of recommendation from your guidance counselor or a teacher; official high school transcript, including SAT or ACT scores; copy of the essay you submitted with your college application (if you did not have to submit one, write a brief essay, no more than 2 pages, regarding your future goals); copy of pages 1 and 2 of your parents' 2006 or most recent completed federal tax form 1040; and mail everything to Hartford Foundation College Scholarship Program. **Deadline:** February 6. **Contact:** Hartford Foundation College Scholarship Program, Scholarship Management Services, Scholarship America, One Scholarship Way, PO Box 297, St. Peter, MN 56082. 800-537-4180.

3412 ■ Alliance for Academic Achievement Program Scholarships *(Undergraduate/Scholarship)*

Purpose: To provide scholarships for graduating seniors from a public high school in Hartford. **Focus:** General studies. **Qualif.:** Applicants must be Hartford residents; must be entering Howard University, Trinity College or University of Connecticut; must have academic excellence and financial need (FAFSA required). **Criteria:** Selection will be based on the committee's criteria.

Funds Avail.: $5,000. **Number Awarded:** 15. **To Apply:** Applicants must complete the General Scholarship Application Form and include a brief personal statement indicating what you intend to study in college and why. **Deadline:** February 29. **Contact:** Ruth E. Torres, The Alliance Program, College Relations, One Hartford Plaza (HO-1-06), Hartford, CT 06155, 860-757-1538, ruth.torres@thehartford.com.

3413 ■ Alliance Francaise of Hartford Harpin/Rohinsky Scholarships *(Undergraduate/Scholarship)*

Purpose: To provide educational assistance for graduating high school seniors who live in or are attending school in

Awards are arranged alphabetically below their administering organizations

Greater Hartford. **Focus:** French studies. **Qualif.:** Applicants must be entering a four-year college or university (full-time enrollment); must pursue French studies in college; must have a financial need; must rank top third of their class; and must be active volunteers in school, community, or other extracurricular activities. **Criteria:** Selection will be based on the committee's criteria.

Funds Avail.: $3,000. **Number Awarded:** 1. **To Apply:** Applicants must download and fill out the online application and attach the following requirements: letter of recommendation from your guidance counselor or a from your teacher; official high school transcript, including SAT or ACT scores; copy of the essay you submitted with your college application (if you did not have to submit one, write a brief essay (no more than 2 pages) regarding your future goals); copy of pages 1 and 2 of your parents' most recent completed federal tax form 1040; and mail everything to Hartford Foundation College Scholarship Program. **Deadline:** February 6. **Contact:** Hartford Foundation College Scholarship Program, Scholarship Management Services, Scholarship America, One Scholarship Way, PO Box 297, St. Peter, MN 56082.800-537-4180.

3414 ■ American Fire Sprinkler Association Scholarships *(Undergraduate/Scholarship)*

Purpose: To award scholarships for graduating high school seniors. **Focus:** General studies. **Qualif.:** Applicants must be Connecticut residents who are entering a four-year college or university. **Criteria:** Selection will be based on the committee's criteria.

Funds Avail.: $1,000. **Number Awarded:** 2. **To Apply:** Applicants must complete and submit an application and essay to the association. Applicants may obtain application materials from the American Fire Sprinkler Association, CT Chapter. **Deadline:** March 22. **Contact:** David K. Thompson, American fire Sprinkler Association, Connecticut Chapter, PO Box 2350, Hartford, CT 06146. 860-246-7711. dave@thesprink.com.

3415 ■ American Marketing Association-Connecticut Chapter, Anna C. Klune Memorial Scholarships *(Graduate/Scholarship)*

Purpose: To award scholarship to a second-year MBA student at any university. **Focus:** Marketing and distribution. **Qualif.:** Applicants must: be a Connecticut resident, may or may not be studying in Connecticut; be a second-year MBA students; be a Marketing or related major; demonstrated leadership record; have entrepreneurial/ innovative spirit. **Criteria:** Selection will be based on the committee's criteria.

Funds Avail.: $1,000-$1,500. **Number Awarded:** 1. **To Apply:** Applicants may obtain application materials from the AMA-CT website at www.amact.org. **Deadline:** January 31. **Contact:** Dr. Subroto Roy, Vice President of Collegiate Relations/Scholarship, 18 Colonial Court Cheshire, CT 06410. 203-271-8051; dr.subrotoroy@gmail.com.

3416 ■ American Savings Foundation Scholarships *(Undergraduate/Scholarship)*

Purpose: To award scholarships for students who demonstrate financial need. **Focus:** General science. **Qualif.:** Applicants must have a 2.5 minimum GPA or top 1/3 of class; must have academic potential and community service; must live in one of the 64 towns served by the American Savings Foundation, including Avon, Andover, Bloomfield, Bolton, Burlington, Canton, East Hartford, Farmington, Glastonbury, Granby, Hebron, Manchester, Marlborough, Newington, New Britain, Simsbury, Tolland, West Hartford, Wethersfield (partial list). **Criteria:** Selection will be based on the committee's criteria.

Funds Avail.: $1,000-$2,000. **To Apply:** Applicants may apply online at www.asfdn.org or call Senior Program Officer of American Savings Foundation. **Deadline:** March 31. **Contact:** Maria Falvo, Senior Program Officer, Scholarships, American Savings Foundation 185 Main St., New Britain, CT 06051. 860-827-2572. mfalvo@asfdn.org.

3417 ■ Amherst College Connecticut Alumni Scholarships *(Undergraduate/Scholarship)*

Purpose: To award educational assistance for students enrolled as undergraduate at Amherst College. **Focus:** General studies. **Qualif.:** Applicants must be residents of Connecticut; must demonstrate financial need; and must demonstrate academic excellence. **Criteria:** Selection will be based on the committee's criteria.

Funds Avail.: $1,000. **To Apply:** Applicants may obtain an application to the Scholarship Chairman of Gordon Muir and Foley, LLP. **Deadline:** December 31. **Contact:** Robert J. O'Brien, scholarship Chairman, Gordon Muir and Foley, LLP. 10 Columbus Blvd., Hartford, CT 06106. 860-525-4849.

3418 ■ ARTC Glenn Moon Scholarships *(Undergraduate/Scholarship)*

Purpose: To provide scholarship for graduating seniors from any public or private high school in Connecticut. **Focus:** Education. **Qualif.:** Applicants must be entering a four-year college or university and must demonstrate financial need and academic excellence. **Criteria:** Selection will be based on the committee's criteria.

Funds Avail.: $1,500 - one-time award; $2,000 renewable. **Number Awarded:** 4. **To Apply:** Applicants may obtain application materials from their high school guidance counselor or online at the www.artcinc.org. **Deadline:** March 31. **Contact:** ARTC Inc. 203-639-9628.

3419 ■ Officer Brian A. Aselton Memorial Scholarships *(Undergraduate/Scholarship)*

Purpose: To provide educational assistance for students entering or enrolled as undergraduate students at Manchester Community College. **Focus:** Criminal Justice. **Qualif.:** Applicants must be Connecticut residents, majoring in Criminal Justice and planning a career in law enforcement. **Criteria:** Selection will be based on the committee's criteria.

Funds Avail.: $500-$1,000. **Number Awarded:** 1. **To Apply:** Applicants may obtain the application materials from the Manchester Community College. **Deadline:** March 1. **Contact:** Donna Nicholson, Coordinator, Criminal Justice Program, Manchester Community College, 60 Bidwell St., Manchester, CT 06040.

3420 ■ Malcolm Baldridge Scholarships *(Undergraduate/Scholarship)*

Purpose: To provide educational assistance for undergraduate students enrolled in a college or university in Connecticut. **Focus:** Manufacturing; International trade. **Qualif.:** Applicant must be an International trade and manufacturing related major; must demonstrate academic excellence; must be studying foreign language, if majoring in International Business; and must be a resident of Connecticut. **Criteria:** Selection will be based on the committee's criteria.

Funds Avail.: 4,000. **Number Awarded:** 1-3. **To Apply:**

Awards are arranged alphabetically below their administering organizations

Applicants may obtain the application materials from the website at www.conncf.org. **Deadline:** March 1. **Contact:** Connecticut Community Foundation. Tallitha Richardson-Selby, Program/Scholarship Associate, 43 Field St. Waterbury, CT 06702. info@conncf.org. fax: 203-756-3054.

3421 ■ John Bell and Lawrence Thornton Scholarship Fund *(Undergraduate/Scholarship)*

Purpose: To provide educational assistance for students presently enrolled at Hampton University. **Focus:** General studies. **Qualif.:** Applicant must be a Greater Hartford resident; must demonstrate academic excellence, financial need, extra curricular activities and community service; must have a GPA of 3.0 and above; and must be rising sophomore and rising junior status. **Criteria:** Selection will be based on the committee's criteria.

Funds Avail.: No specific amount. **Number Awarded:** Varies. **To Apply:** Applicants may obtain application materials from Connecticut River Valley Chapter National Hampton University Alumni Association, Inc. Scholarship Committee, PO Box 2734 Hartford, CT 06146-2734. **Deadline:** march 23. **Contact:** hamptonalumnict@yahoo.com.

3422 ■ Mary Elizabeth Lockwood Beneventi MBA Scholarships *(Graduate/Scholarship)*

Purpose: To provide scholarships for students attending an accredited graduate school. **Focus:** Business administration. **Qualif.:** Applicants must be attending full-time in an accredited graduate school majoring in business administration with a minimum of 3.25 GPA. **Criteria:** Selection will be based on the committee's criteria.

Funds Avail.: %2,000. **Number Awarded:** 1. **To Apply:** Application materials (for Connecticut residents) may be obtained by sending a self-addressed stamped envelope to NSDAR Scholarship Committee 215 Loomis Rd. N Granby, CT 06060. **Deadline:** April 15. **Contact:** Mrs. Michael L. Stewart, CT State Chairperson. 860-653-4203. L2stew@yahoo.com.

3423 ■ Dr. Francis Anthony Beneventi Medical Scholarships *(Undergraduate/Scholarship)*

Purpose: To provide educational assistance for students entering or enrolled in an accredited medical school at a college or university. **Focus:** General studies. **Qualif.:** Applicants must have a minimum of 3.25 GPA. **Criteria:** Selection will be based on the committee's criteria.

Funds Avail.: $5,000. **Number Awarded:** 1. **To Apply:** Application materials (for Connecticut residents) may be obtained by sending a self-addressed stamped envelope to NSDAR Scholarship Committee, 215 Loomis Rd. N Granby, CT 06060. **Deadline:** April 15. **Contact:** Mrs. Michael L. Stewart, CT State Chairperson. 860-653-4203. L2stew@yahoo.com.

3424 ■ Lebbeus F. Bissell Scholarships *(Undergraduate/Scholarship)*

Purpose: To provide educational assistance for graduating high school seniors from Rockville, Tolland or Ellington High Schools. **Focus:** General studies. **Qualif.:** Applicants must demonstrate academic excellence, financial need, extracurricular activities and community service. **Criteria:** Selection will be based on the committee's criteria.

Funds Avail.: $4,000. **Number Awarded:** 3. **To Apply:** Applicants may obtain application materials from Guidance Departments of Rockville, Tolland or Ellington High Schools or from Lebbeus F. Bissel Scholarship Advisory Committee, 183 Reservoir Rd. Vermon, CT 06066. **Deadline:** March 20. **Contact:** Thomas Mason, Chairman. 860-875-0527 or 860-548-1888.

3425 ■ Maria Borrero Scholarships *(Undergraduate/Scholarship)*

Purpose: To provide scholarships for graduating Hispanic students from a public high school in the City of Hartford. **Focus:** Health care services. **Qualif.:** Applicants must be entering a four-year college or university (full-time enrollment) pursuing a health-related field; must demonstrate financial need; must be top third with good academic record; and must be active volunteers in school, community, or other extracurricular activities. **Criteria:** Selection will be based on the committee's criteria.

Funds Avail.: $3,000. **Number Awarded:** 1. **To Apply:** Application form can be downloaded online. Applicants must complete the scholarship application. Applicants must also attach the following requirements: letter of recommendation from your guidance counselor or a teacher; official high school transcript (including SAT or ACT scores); copy of the essay you submitted with your college application (If you did not have to submit one, write a brief (no more than two pages) essay regarding your future goals); and copy of pages 1 and 2 of your parents' 2006 or most recent completed federal tax form 1040. Mail everything to Hartford Foundation College Scholarship Program. **Deadline:** February 6. **Contact:** Hartford Foundation College Scholarship Program, Scholarship Management Services, Scholarship America, One Scholarship Way, PO Box 297, St. Peter, MN 56082. 800-537-4180.

3426 ■ Boy Scouts of America General Scholarships *(Undergraduate/Scholarship)*

Purpose: To provide scholarship for graduating high school seniors. **Focus:** General studies. **Qualif.:** Applicants must be participating in Boy Scout program; must be an Eagle Scout; and must demonstrate financial need and community service. **Criteria:** Selection will be based on the committee's criteria.

Funds Avail.: No specific amount. **To Apply:** Applicants may obtain application materials from www.nesa.org or contact the Program Director of Connecticut Rivers Council, BSA. **Deadline:** January 31. **Contact:** Connecticut Rivers Council, BSA PO Box 280098 60 Darlin St. E Hartford, CT 06128. 860-290-8860.

3427 ■ W. Philip Braender and Nancy Coleman Braender Scholarships *(Undergraduate/Scholarship)*

Purpose: To provide scholarship for graduating high school senior who lives in or attends school in Greater Hartford. **Focus:** General studies. **Qualif.:** Applicants must be entering a four-year college or university (full-time enrollment); must demonstrate financial need; must be in the top third with good academic record; and must be active volunteer in school, community, or other extracurricular activities. **Criteria:** Selection will be based on the committee's criteria.

Funds Avail.: $3,000. **Number Awarded:** 1. **To Apply:** Application form can be downloaded on-line. Applicants must complete the scholarship application. Applicants must also attach the following requirements: letter of recommendation from your guidance counselor or a teacher; official high school transcript. Including SAT or ACT scores; copy of the essay you submitted with your college application. If you did not have to submit one, write a brief (no more than two pages) essay regarding your future goals;

copy of pages 1 and 2 of your parents' 2006 or most recent completed federal tax form 1040. Mail everything to Hartford Foundation College Scholarship Program. **Deadline:** February 6. **Contact:** Hartford Foundation College Scholarship Program, Scholarship Management Services, Scholarship America, One Scholarship Way, PO Box 297, St. Peter, MN 56082. 800-537-4180.

3428 ■ Nellie Love Butcher Scholarships *(Undergraduate/Scholarship)*

Purpose: To provide scholarship for students currently attending Duke Ellington School of Performing Arts in Washington, DC. **Focus:** Music, Piano. **Qualif.:** Applicants must be studying piano or voice with a minimum 3.0 GPA. **Criteria:** Selection will be based on the committee's criteria.

Funds Avail.: No specific amount. **Number Awarded:** 1. **To Apply:** Application materials (for Connecticut residents) may be obtained by sending a self-addressed stamped envelope to NSDAR Scholarship Committee, 215 Loomis Rd. N Granby, CT 06060. **Deadline:** April 15. **Contact:** Mrs. Michael L. Stewart, CT State Chairperson. 860-653-4203. L2stew@yahoo.com.

3429 ■ Rhea Sourifman Caplin Memorial Scholarships *(Undergraduate/Scholarship)*

Purpose: To provide scholarship to the Jewish high school senior or college students. **Focus:** Nursing; Health care services. **Qualif.:** Applicants must: be a Greater Hartford resident; be pursuing nursing or health care profession; have a minimum B average in sciences; have a good citizenship and active involvement in the community. **Criteria:** Selection will be based on the committee's criteria.

Funds Avail.: $1,000-$2,000. **Number Awarded:** 1-2. **To Apply:** Applicants may obtain application materials from Jewish Community Foundation of Greater Hartford, 333 Bloomfield Ave. Ste. D West Hartford, CT 06117. **Deadline:** April 15. **Contact:** Michael Elfenbaum, Phone: 860-523-7460; Fax: 860-231-0576; melfenbaum@jcfhartford.org.

3430 ■ Casabella Family Memorial Scholarships *(Undergraduate/Scholarship)*

Purpose: To provide scholarship for graduating high school seniors from Windsor High School (all cluster). **Focus:** General studies. **Qualif.:** Applicants must be accepted to a two or four-year college, university or an accredited professional or technical school and must demonstrate financial need, academic or technical ability and athletic achievement. **Criteria:** Selection will be based on the committee's criteria.

Funds Avail.: $3,000. **Number Awarded:** 3-6. **To Apply:** Applicants may obtain the Casabella Family Scholarship Brochure at the Windsor High School guidance office. Applicants must complete the General Scholarship Application and include: Portfolio of relevant work with 500-word written description of projects; additional copy of letter of acceptance to educational institution and submit to Casabella Family Scholarship Windsor High School Guidance Office, 50 Sage Park Rd. Windsor, CT 06095. **Deadline:** May 1. **Contact:** aford@windsorct.org; fax: 860-687-2029; phone: 860-687-2020 ext. 371.

3431 ■ Emily Chaison Gold Award Scholarships *(Undergraduate/Scholarship)*

Purpose: To provide scholarship to the graduating high school senior who has earned the Gold award. **Focus:** General studies. **Qualif.:** Applicants must be a registered in Girl Scouts and be a Connecticut resident. **Criteria:** Selection will be based on the committee's criteria.

Funds Avail.: $750. **Number Awarded:** 1. **To Apply:** Applicants may obtain application materials from Girl Scouts of Connecticut 340 Washington St. Hartford, CT 06106. www.gsofct.org. **Deadline:** April 15. **Contact:** Girl Scout of Connecticut, 860-522-0163.

3432 ■ College of Agriculture and Natural Resources Scholarships *(Undergraduate/Scholarship)*

Purpose: To provide scholarship for freshman students of College of Agriculture and Natural Resources at University of Connecticut or Raddcliffe Hicks School. **Focus:** Allied health; Agricultural sciences. **Qualif.:** Applicants must be freshman students interested in Allied Health Sciences, Animal Science, Cytotechnology, Diagnostic Genetic Sciences, Dietetics, Environmental Sciences, Health Promotion Sciences, Horticulture, Landscape Architecture, Medical Technology, Natural Resources, Nutritional Sciences, Pathobiology, Pre-veterinary Science, Resource Economics, Turfgrass and Soil Science, Allied Science; must attend College of Agriculture and Natural Resources at University of Connecticut or Radcliffe Hicks School; and must demonstrate academic excellence. **Criteria:** Selection will be based on the committee's criteria.

Funds Avail.: $500-$2,000. **To Apply:** Applicants may obtain application materials from University of Connecticut College of Agricultural and Natural Resources, Associate Dean, 1376 Storrs Rd. Unit 4090 Storrs, CT 06269-4090. Phone: 860486-2919. acadprog@canr.uconn.edu.

3433 ■ The College Club of Hartford Scholarships *(Undergraduate/Scholarship)*

Purpose: To provide scholarship for graduating high school students. **Focus:** General studies. **Qualif.:** Applicants must be graduating public high school seniors residing in Avon, Bloomfield, Canton, East Hartford, Farmington, Glastonbury, Hartford, Manchester, Newington, Rocky Hill, Simsbury, West Hartford, Wethersfield or Windsor; must be attending in an accredited twoor four-year school; must demonstrate financial need and community service; must be on a class rank upper 10% (Applicant's grades through 2nd quarter of senior year are required); and must be students who attend Trinity College or St. Joseph College in Connecticut. **Criteria:** Selection will be based on the committee's criteria.

Funds Avail.: $1,000. **To Apply:** Applicants may obtain application materials from their high school guidance office and submit it to Scholarship Committee, Mrs. Carolyn Holgerson, Chairman, 391 Robbins Ave. Newington, CT 06111. 860666-9586. **Deadline:** March 15.

3434 ■ Connecticut Association of Latinos in Higher Education Scholarships *(Undergraduate/Scholarship)*

Purpose: To award scholarship to the students entering or enrolled as undergraduate in an accredited college or university. **Focus:** General studies. **Qualif.:** Applicants must be residents of Connecticut; must be of Latino background; must have financial need and community service; and must have an academic excellence ("B" average). **Criteria:** Selection will be based on the committee's criteria.

Funds Avail.: $1,000. **Number Awarded:** 10. **To Apply:** Applicants must complete the General Scholarship Application and include the following requirements: a copy of your

Student Aid Report; a two-page typed, double-space essay on "How you feel education is going to impact your ability to continue assisting others to pursue an education." **Deadline:** April 18. **Contact:** CALAHE Scholarship Chair c/o Office of Dean of Students, Dr. Wilson Luna, Gateway Community College, 60 Sargent Drive New Haven, CT 06511. 203-285-2210. wilsonluna@aol.com.

3435 ■ Connecticut Association of Women Police Scholarships *(Undergraduate/Scholarship)*

Purpose: To provide scholarship for graduating high school seniors. **Focus:** Criminal Justice. **Qualif.:** Applicants must be residents of Connecticut; must be graduating high school senior entering a four-year college or university; must be majoring in criminal justice; and must demonstrate financial need. **Criteria:** Selection will be based on the committee's criteria.

Funds Avail.: No specific amount. **Number Awarded:** 1-4. **To Apply:** Applicants may obtain application materials from their high school guidance counselor or download online at www.cawp.net. **Deadline:** April 30. **Contact:** gmcdonnell@coventryct.org.

3436 ■ Connecticut Building Congress Scholarships *(Undergraduate/Scholarship)*

Purpose: To provide scholarship for graduating high school seniors, undergraduate, or graduate students. **Focus:** Engineering; Architecture. **Qualif.:** Applicants must be attending two or four-year college or university; must demonstrate financial need, academic excellence and community service; must be residents of Connecticut. **Criteria:** Selection will be based on the committee's criteria.

Funds Avail.: $500-$2,000. **To Apply:** Applicants may obtain application materials from Connecticut Bldg. Congress Scholarship Fund, Inc. 10 Westgate Rd. Columbia, CT 06237. Phone: 2032281387; Fax: 203228-2296. info@cbc-ct.org. **Deadline:** March 15.

3437 ■ Connecticut Capitol Scholarship Program *(Undergraduate/Scholarship)*

Purpose: To provide scholarship for graduating high school seniors. **Focus:** General studies. **Qualif.:** Applicants must be residents of Connecticut entering in a Connecticut college or a college located in one of the following states: District of Columbia, Maine, Massachusetts, New Hampshire, Pennsylvania, Rhode Island, or Vermont; must demonstrate academic excellence being on a class rank of top 20% or SAT above 1800. **Criteria:** Selection will be based on the committee's criteria.

Funds Avail.: $300-$3,000. **To Apply:** Applicants may obtain application materials from high school guidance counselor or from Connecticut Department of Higher Education. **Deadline:** February 15. **Contact:** Connecticut Department of Higher Education, 61 Woodland St. Hartford, CT 06105; Phone: 860-947-1855; Fax: 860-947-1313; csp@ctdhe.org.

3438 ■ Connecticut League of Nursing Scholarships *(Undergraduate/Scholarship)*

Purpose: To provide educational assistance for senior nursing students or graduate students attending a Connecticut nursing school. **Focus:** Nursing. **Qualif.:** Applicants must have completed a minimum of 18 credits in a Nursing Program and must demonstrate financial need and academic excellence. **Criteria:** Selection will be based on the committee's criteria.

Funds Avail.: $1,000. **Number Awarded:** 2. **To Apply:** Applicants may obtain application materials from Connecticut League for Nursing, PO Box 365 Wallingford, CT 06492. **Deadline:** October 15. **Contact:** Marcia Proto, Executive Dir. education@ctleaguefornursing.org; Fax: 203-265-5311.

3439 ■ Connecticut Mortgage Bankers Scholarships-Social Affairs Committee *(Undergraduate/Scholarship)*

Purpose: To provide scholarship for graduating high school seniors who live in or are attending school in Greater Hartford. **Focus:** Business; Real estate. **Qualif.:** Applicants must be entering a four-year college or university (full-time enrollment) pursuing a career in business, mortgage or real estate; must have a financial need; must be on a class rank - top third with good academic record; and must be active volunteers in school, community, or other extracurricular activities. **Criteria:** Selection will be based on the committee's criteria.

Funds Avail.: $3,000. **Number Awarded:** 1. **To Apply:** Application form can be downloaded on-line. Applicants must complete the scholarship application. Applicants must also attach the following requirements: letter of recommendation from your guidance counselor or a teacher; official high school transcript. Including SAT or ACT scores; copy of the essay you submitted with your college application. If you did not have to submit one, write a brief (no more than two pages) essay regarding your future goals; copy of pages 1 and 2 of your parents' most recent completed federal tax form 1040. Mail everything to Hartford Foundation College Scholarship Program. **Deadline:** February 6. **Contact:** Hartford Foundation College Scholarship Program, Scholarship Management Services, Scholarship America, One Scholarship Way, PO Box 297, St. Peter, MN 56082. 800-537-4180.

3440 ■ Connecticut Nurserymen's Foundation Scholarships *(Undergraduate/Scholarship)*

Purpose: To provide scholarship for graduating high school seniors or college students enrolled in a Horticulture degree program. **Focus:** Horticulture. **Qualif.:** Applicants must be Connecticut residents entering a two or four-year college program in Horticulture; must demonstrate financial need and academic excellence; must have a work experience and Future Farmers of American membership helpful, but not necessary. **Criteria:** Selection will be based on the committee's criteria.

Funds Avail.: $5,000. **Number Awarded:** 1. **To Apply:** Applicants may obtain the application materials from their high school guidance counselor or from Connecticut Nurserymen's Foundation. **Deadline:** March 14. **Contact:** Judy Mattson, Scholarship Committee Chairman, 131 Hollister St. Manchester, CT 06042, Phone: 860-643-8363; Fax: 860-643-2778; jmattson.negs@sbcglobal.net.

3441 ■ Brian Cummins Memorial Scholarships *(Undergraduate/Scholarship)*

Purpose: To provide scholarship for college junior or senior or graduate students enrolled in a full-time program to teach blind and visually impaired students in Connecticut. **Focus:** General studies. **Qualif.:** Applicants must demonstrate financial need, community service, and academic excellence. **Criteria:** Selection will be based on the committee's criteria.

Funds Avail.: $5,000. **Number Awarded:** 1. **To Apply:** Applicants may obtain scholarship materials from National

Awards are arranged alphabetically below their administering organizations

Federation of the Blind of Connecticut 477 Connecticut Blvd. Ste. 217 E Hartford, CT 06108. **Deadline:** October 15. **Contact:** National Federation of the Blind of Connecticut, Phone: 860-298-1971; Fax: 860-291-2795; info@nfbct.org.

3442 ■ Delta Sigma Theta Hartford Alumnae Scholarships *(Undergraduate/Scholarship)*

Purpose: To provide scholarship to the graduating students from A.I. Prince Technical, Bloomfield, Bulkeley, Hartford Public, Windsor, or Weaver High School. **Focus:** General studies. **Qualif.:** Applicants must be Black/African American female high school senior planning to attend a four-year college or university. Applicants must have a leadership abilities, academic excellence, top 25th percentile and community service. **Criteria:** Selection will be based on the committee's criteria.

Funds Avail.: $2,000. **To Apply:** Applicants may obtain scholarship materials from their high school guidance counselor and submit to the Delta Sigma Theta Sorority, Inc., Hartford Alumnae Chapter. **Deadline:** March 1. **Contact:** Mrs. Shirley Harrison, Scholarship Chairperson, PO Box 2163 Hartford, CT 06145-2163. Phone: 860-985-5501; Fax: 860-833-8804.

3443 ■ C. Rodney Demarest Memorial Scholarships *(Undergraduate/Scholarship)*

Purpose: To provide scholarship for students who are legally blind. **Focus:** General studies. **Qualif.:** Applicants must be graduating high school seniors or college students residing or attending school full-time in Connecticut. Applicants must demonstrate financial need, community service and academic excellence. **Criteria:** Selection will be based on the committee's criteria.

Funds Avail.: $3,000. **Number Awarded:** 1. **To Apply:** Applicants may obtain application materials from National Federation of the Blind of CT, 477 Connecticut Blvd. Ste. 217 E Hartford, CT 06108. 860289-1971. info@nfbct.org. www.nfbct.org. **Deadline:** September 15.

3444 ■ Albert and Jane Dewey Scholarships *(Undergraduate/Scholarship)*

Purpose: To provide scholarship to the graduating senior. **Focus:** General studies. **Qualif.:** Applicants must be residents of Manchester who demonstrate financial need. Preference will be given to minority student. **Criteria:** Selection will be based on the committee's criteria.

Funds Avail.: $1,000-$4,000. **To Apply:** Applicants may obtain application materials from Manchester Scholarship Foundation Inc., 20 Hartford Rd. Manchester, CT 06040. Phone: 860645-1673; Fax; 860432-9136; www.manchesterscholarship.org. **Deadline:** Mid-April.

3445 ■ Harry A. Donn Scholarships *(Undergraduate/Scholarship)*

Purpose: To provide scholarship to a high school senior who lives in or attends school in the Greater Hartford area. **Focus:** General studies. **Qualif.:** Applicants must: be entering a four-year college or university (full-time enrollment); demonstrate financial need; be on a class rank - top third with good academic record; be active volunteer in school, community, or other extracurricular activities. **Criteria:** Selection will be based on the committee's criteria.

Funds Avail.: $3,000. **Number Awarded:** 1. **To Apply:** Application form can be downloaded online. Applicants must complete the scholarship application. Applicants must also attach the following requirements: letter of recommendation from your guidance counselor or a teacher; official high school transcript. Including SAT or ACT scores; copy of the essay you submitted with your college application. If you did not have to submit one, write a brief (no more than two pages) essay regarding your future goals; copy of pages 1 and 2 of your parents' most recent completed federal tax form 1040. Mail everything to Hartford Foundation College Scholarship Program. **Deadline:** February 6. **Contact:** Hartford Foundation College Scholarship Program, Scholarship Management Services, Scholarship America, 1505 Riverview Rd., PO Box 297, St. Peter, MN 56082. 800-537-4180.

3446 ■ Charles Dubose Scholarships *(Undergraduate/Scholarship)*

Purpose: To provide scholarship to the students attending five-year accredited colleges or universities offering Architecture. **Focus:** Architecture. **Qualif.:** Applicants must: completed a two years of Bachelor in Architecture Program; be a Connecticut connection; demonstrated financial need and academic excellence. **Criteria:** Selection will be based on the committee's criteria.

Funds Avail.: $5,000-$10,000. **Number Awarded:** 1-2. **To Apply:** Applicants may obtain application materials from Connecticut Architecture Foundation, 87 Willow St., New Haven, CT 06511. Phone: 203865-2195; Fax: 203562-5378. www.aiact.org. **Deadline:** April 15.

3447 ■ Priscilla Maxwell Endicott Scholarships *(Undergraduate/Scholarship)*

Purpose: To provide scholarship to the students entering or enrolled in a four-year college or university. **Focus:** General studies. **Qualif.:** Applicants must: be a resident of Connecticut; be a female; be active junior golfer with golf handicap; demonstrate financial need and academic excellence. **Criteria:** Selection will be based on the committee's criteria.

Funds Avail.: $3,000. **Number Awarded:** 4. **To Apply:** Applicants may download an application form from www.cwga.org. **Deadline:** April 20. **Contact:** Deborah Boynton, Scholarship Chairwoman, 52 Mountain Spring Rd., Farmington, CT 06032. 860-826-4008. deb@creedmonarch.com.

3448 ■ Farmington UNICO Scholarships *(Undergraduate/Scholarship)*

Purpose: To provide scholarship to the students who will be attending a four-year college or university. **Focus:** General studies. **Qualif.:** Applicants must: be a Farmington or West Hartford resident; be a graduating high school senior; demonstrated financial need and academic excellence. **Criteria:** Selection will be based on the committee's criteria.

Funds Avail.: $1,500. **Number Awarded:** 4. **To Apply:** Applicants may obtain application materials from their high school guidance office or Farmington Chapter of UNICO National, Scholarship Committee, 11 Parkview Rd. West Hartford, CT 06110. **Deadline:** March 15. **Contact:** Jim Kane. Phone: 860-229-0301; Fax: 860-826-1997.

3449 ■ Symee Ruth Feinburg Memorial Scholarships *(Undergraduate/Scholarship)*

Purpose: To provide scholarship to the graduating high school senior who lives in or attends school in Greater Hartford. **Focus:** Human relations. **Qualif.:** Applicants

Awards are arranged alphabetically below their administering organizations

must: be entering a four-year college or university; pursuing a career in human services; be in a class rank- top third with good academic record; be an active volunteer in school. community, or other extracurricular activities. **Criteria:** Selection will be based on the committee's criteria.

Funds Avail.: $3,000. **Number Awarded:** 1. **To Apply:** Application form can be downloaded online. Applicants must complete the scholarship application. Applicants must also attach the following requirements: letter of recommendation from your guidance counselor or a teacher; official high school transcript. Including SAT or ACT scores; copy of the essay you submitted with your college application. If you did not have to submit one, write a brief (no more than two pages) essay regarding your future goals; copy of pages 1 and 2 of your parents' 2006 or most recent completed federal tax form 1040. Mail everything to Hartford Foundation College Scholarship Program. **Deadline:** February 6. **Contact:** Hartford Foundation College Scholarship Program, Scholarship Management Services, Scholarship America, 1505 Riverview Rd., PO Box 297, St. Peter, MN 56082. 800-537-4180.

3450 ■ First Church of Christ in Wethersfield - Metcalf Scholarships *(Undergraduate/Scholarship)*

Purpose: To provide scholarship to the graduating seniors from any public high school in the City of Hartford. **Focus:** General studies. **Qualif.:** Applicants must demonstrate financial need; extracurricular activities; have a potential for completing a four-year undergraduate program; have an interview with selection committee members. **Criteria:** Selection will be based on the committee's criteria.

Funds Avail.: $625. **To Apply:** Applicants may obtain application materials from their high school guidance office or contact First Church of Christ in Wethersfield, Metcalf Scholarship Chairperson 250 Main St., Wethersfield, CT 06109. Phone 860529-1575 ext. 212; Fax: 860721-7861. **Deadline:** March 1.

3451 ■ Jacob and Lewis Fox Scholarships *(Undergraduate/Scholarship)*

Purpose: To provide scholarship to the graduating high school senior. **Focus:** General studies. **Qualif.:** Applicants must: be a graduating high school senior; be a students attend Bulkeley, Hartford Public, or Weaver High School; entering a four-year college or university; have leadership abilities, financial need, spirit of reverence and academic excellence. **Criteria:** Selection will be based on the committee's criteria.

Funds Avail.: $3,000. **Number Awarded:** 18. **To Apply:** Applicants may obtain application materials from their high school guidance office. No direct application sent from Foundation. **Deadline:** December 15. **Contact:** Jacob and Lewis Fox Foundation, 860-633-1429.

3452 ■ Gail Burns-Smith "Dare to Dream" Fund *(Undergraduate/Scholarship)*

Purpose: To provide scholarship to the resident of Connecticut or student attending a Connecticut high school or college/university. **Focus:** Aggression and violence. **Qualif.:** Applicants be paid or volunteer work experience in the field women's issues or sexual violence prevention/advocacy and planned commitment to continuing work in the field of sexual violence prevention/advocacy. **Criteria:** Selection will be based on the committee's criteria.

Funds Avail.: $1,000. **Number Awarded:** 1. **To Apply:** Applicants must complete the application form provided by CONNSACS together with the following requirements: two written essays in response to questions listed on application; two character references, submitted as letters of recommendation on behalf of applicant. Applicants may obtain application from address below and submit to CONNSACS, Inc. **Deadline:** March 1. **Contact:** Tara Martin, Dir. of Resource Development, 96 Pitkin St. E Hartford, CT 06108. Fax: 860-291-9335; Phone: 860-282-9881. tara@connsacs.org.

3453 ■ Marcus Garvey Scholarships *(Undergraduate/Scholarship)*

Purpose: To provide scholarship to the graduating high school senior. **Focus:** General studies. **Qualif.:** Applicants must: be of West Indian parentage; demonstrate financial need, community service and academic excellence. **Criteria:** Selection will be based on the committee's criteria.

Funds Avail.: $1,000. **Number Awarded:** 1. **To Apply:** Applicants must submit a complete application and an essay on "The significance of the life of Marcus Garvey" to the Foundation. **Deadline:** June 30. **Contact:** West Indian Foundation, Inc. Scholarship Committee, PO Box 320394 Hartford, CT 06132. 860-241-0379. westindian@snet.net.

3454 ■ James L. and Genevieve H. Goodwin Scholarships *(Undergraduate/Scholarship)*

Purpose: To award scholarship to the students of Connecticut. **Focus:** Forestry. **Qualif.:** Applicants must be enrolled in an undergraduate or graduate curriculum in silviculture or forest resource management. **Criteria:** Selection will be based on the committee's criteria.

Funds Avail.: $1,000-$5,000. **Number Awarded:** 5-10. **To Apply:** Applicants may complete the General Scholarship Application and include a personal statement indicating why you are interested in Forest Management and submit to Connecticut forest and Park Association, Inc. **Deadline:** March 20. **Contact:** Adam Moore, Executive Dir., 16 Meriden Rd. Rockfall, CT 06481. Phone: 860-346-2372; Fax: 860-347-7463; info@ctwoodlands.org.

3455 ■ William G. and Mayme J. Green Scholarships *(Undergraduate/Scholarship)*

Purpose: To award scholarship to a graduating high school senior from Newington or Hartford Public High School. **Focus:** Nursing. **Qualif.:** Applicants must: be entering a four-year college or university (full-time enrollment) pursuing a degree in Nursing; must demonstrate financial need; be on the class rank - top third with a good academic record; be an active volunteer in school, community, or other extracurricular activities. **Criteria:** Selection will be based on the committee's criteria.

Funds Avail.: $2,500. **Number Awarded:** 1. **To Apply:** Application form can be downloaded online. Applicants must complete the scholarship application. Applicants must also attach the following requirements: letter of recommendation from your guidance counselor or a teacher; official high school transcript. Including SAT or ACT scores; copy of the essay you submitted with your college application. If you did not have to submit one, write a brief (no more than two pages) essay regarding your future goals; copy of pages 1 and 2 of your parents' most recent completed federal tax form 1040. Mail everything to Hartford Foundation College Scholarship Program. **Deadline:** February 13. **Contact:** Hartford Foundation College Scholarship Program, Scholarship Management Services, Scholarship America, One Scholarship Way, PO Box 297, St. Peter, MN 56082. 800-537-4180.

3456 ■ Ida L. Hartenberg Charitable Scholarships *(Undergraduate/Scholarship)*

Purpose: To provide scholarship to the graduating high school senior who lives in or attends school in Greater Hartford. **Focus:** Teaching. **Qualif.:** Applicants must: be entering a four-year college or university (full-time enrollment); be pursuing a career in teaching; demonstrate financial need; be on a class rank - top third with good academic record; be an active volunteer in school, community, or other extracurricular activities. **Criteria:** Selection will be based on the committee's criteria.

Funds Avail.: $3,000. **Number Awarded:** 1. **To Apply:** Application form can be downloaded online. Applicants must complete the scholarship application. Applicants must also attach the following requirements: letter of recommendation from your guidance counselor or a teacher; official high school transcript. Including SAT or ACT scores; copy of the essay you submitted with your college application. If you did not have to submit one, write a brief (no more than two pages) essay regarding your future goals; copy of pages 1 and 2 of your parents' 2006 or most recent completed federal tax form 1040. Mail everything to Hartford Foundation College Scholarship Program. **Deadline:** February 13. **Contact:** Hartford Foundation College Scholarship Program, Scholarship Management Services, Scholarship America, One Scholarship Way, PO Box 297, St. Peter, MN 56082. 800-537-4180.

3457 ■ Hartford County Retired Teachers Association Scholarships *(Undergraduate/Scholarship)*

Purpose: To provide scholarship to the graduating senior residing and attending high school in Hartford County. **Focus:** Teaching. **Qualif.:** Applicants must: be entering a four-year college or university; be a teaching major; demonstrate financial need, community service, leadership abilities and good character; have work experience and school and community participation. **Criteria:** Selection will be based on the committee's criteria.

Funds Avail.: $1,500. **Number Awarded:** 2. **To Apply:** Applicants may obtain application materials from their high school guidance counselor and submit to Hartford County Retired Teachers Association Scholarship Committee. **Deadline:** March 15. **Contact:** Mrs. Roberta Parlin, Chairperson. 35 Ledgecrest Drive, Newington, CT 06111; 860-666-5709.

3458 ■ Hartford Foundation College Scholarship Program *(Undergraduate/Scholarship)*

Purpose: To provide scholarship to the graduating high school senior who lives in or attends school in Greater Hartford. **Focus:** General studies. **Qualif.:** Applicants must: be entering a four-year college or university (full-time enrollment); demonstrate financial need; be on the class rank - top third with good academic record; be an active volunteer in school, community, or other extracurricular activities. **Criteria:** Selection will be based on the committee's criteria.

Funds Avail.: $3,000. **Number Awarded:** 30-40. **To Apply:** Application form can be downloaded on-line. Applicants must complete the scholarship application. Applicants must also attach the following requirements: letter of recommendation from your guidance counselor or a teacher; official high school transcript. Including SAT or ACT scores; copy of the essay you submitted with your college application. If you did not have to submit one, write a brief (no more than two pages) essay regarding your future goals; copy of pages 1 and 2 of your parents' most recent completed federal tax form 1040. Mail everything to Hartford Foundation College Scholarship Program. **Deadline:** February 6. **Contact:** Hartford Foundation College Scholarship Program, Scholarship Management Services, Scholarship America, One Scholarship Way, PO Box 297, St. Peter, MN 56082. 800-537-4180.

3459 ■ Hartford Foundation for Public Giving Occupational Therapy Scholarships *(Undergraduate/Scholarship)*

Purpose: To provide scholarship to the students enrolled in an accredited school of Occupational or Physical Therapy. **Focus:** Art therapy; Music therapy; Physical therapy. **Qualif.:** Applicants must: be a US citizen; be enrolled in an Occupational (including art and music) or Physical Therapy; have a letter of sponsorship form local DAR chapter. **Criteria:** Selection will be based on the committee's criteria.

Funds Avail.: $500. **To Apply:** For Connecticut residents, to obtain application materials, send a self-addressed stamped envelope to: National Society Daughters of American Revolution, 215 Loomis St., North Granby, CT 06060. **Deadline:** February 15 or August 15. **Contact:** Mrs. Michael L. Stewart, CT State Chairperson, NSDAR Scholarship Committee. L2stew@yahoo.com; 860-653-4203.

3460 ■ Hartford Grammar School Scholarships *(Undergraduate/Scholarship)*

Purpose: To award scholarship to a graduating high school senior form a public high school in the City of Hartford. **Focus:** General studies. **Qualif.:** Applicants must be entering a four-year college or university (full-time enrollment); demonstrate financial need; be on class rank with good academic record; be an active volunteer in school, community, or other extracurricular activities. **Criteria:** Selection will be based on the committee's criteria.

Funds Avail.: $3,000. **Number Awarded:** 1-3. **To Apply:** Application form can be downloaded on-line. Applicants must complete the scholarship application. Applicants must also attach the following requirements: letter of recommendation from your guidance counselor or a teacher; official high school transcript. Including SAT or ACT scores; copy of the essay you submitted with your college application. If you did not have to submit one, write a brief (no more than two pages) essay regarding your future goals; copy of pages 1 and 2 of your parents' 2006 or most recent completed federal tax form 1040. Mail everything to Hartford Foundation College Scholarship Program. **Deadline:** February 13. **Contact:** Hartford Foundation College Scholarship Program, Scholarship Management Services, Scholarship America, One Scholarship Way, PO Box 297, St. Peter, MN 56082. 800-537-4180.

3461 ■ Hartford Jazz Society Scholarships *(Undergraduate/Scholarship)*

Purpose: To provide scholarship to the graduating high school senior. **Focus:** Music, Jazz. **Qualif.:** Applicants must: be a Connecticut Capitol Region resident; be attending a four-year college or university; be a Music major with interest in jazz. **Criteria:** Selection will be based on the panel's criteria.

Funds Avail.: $3,000. **Number Awarded:** 2-3. **To Apply:** Applicants must complete the General Scholarship Application and include the following requirements: a cassette tape of applicant both reading and improvising; two letters of reference, at least one form a music teacher or school music director and submit to Hartford Jazz Society, Inc., Chairperson, Scholarship Committee, 116 Cottage Grove

Rd., Bloomfield, CT 06002. Phone: 860242-6688; Fax: 860243-8871. hartjazzsocinc@aol.com. **Deadline:** May 1.

3462 ■ Hartford Whalers Booster Club Scholarships *(Undergraduate/Scholarship)*

Purpose: To provide scholarship to the students entering or enrolled in a four-year college or university. **Focus:** General studies. **Qualif.:** Applicants must: intend to play collegiate hockey; have an outstanding hockey abilities; be a Connecticut resident; have an academic excellence. **Criteria:** Selection will be based on the committee's criteria.

Funds Avail.: $1,000. **Number Awarded:** 1. **To Apply:** Applicants must complete the General Scholarship Application and include a letter of recommendation from your hockey coach outlining your hockey performance and submit to Hartford Whalers Booster Club. **Deadline:** March 20. **Contact:** Heather Turner Scholarship Coordinator, PO Box 273 Hartford, CT 06141. Phone: 860-643-0842. hartfordwhalersboosterclub@hotmail.com.

3463 ■ Hebrew Ladies Sheltering Home Scholarships *(Undergraduate/Scholarship)*

Purpose: To provide scholarship to the Jewish high school senior or college student. **Focus:** Jewish studies. **Qualif.:** Applicants must: be a resident of Greater Hartford; pursuing Jewish studies; have a requisite academic ability. **Criteria:** Selection will be based on the committee's criteria.

Funds Avail.: $1,000-$3,000. **Number Awarded:** 1-3. **To Apply:** Applicants may obtain application from Jewish Community Foundation of Greater Hartford. **Deadline:** April 15. **Contact:** Michael Elfenbaum, 333 Bloomfield Ave. Ste. D, West Hartford, CT06117. Phone: 860-523-7460; Fax: 860-231-0576; melbenbaum@jchartford.org.

3464 ■ Doris E. Higley Memorial Scholarships *(Undergraduate/Scholarship)*

Purpose: To provide scholarship students who are legally blind. **Focus:** General studies. **Qualif.:** Applicants must: be a graduating high school senior or college student residing or attending school full-time in Connecticut; be legally blind; demonstrate financial need. **Criteria:** Selection will be based on the committee's criteria.

Funds Avail.: $8,000. **Number Awarded:** 1. **To Apply:** Applicants may obtain application materials from National Federation of the Blind of Connecticut 477 Connecticut Blvd. Ste. 217, East Hartford, CT 06108; www.nfbct.org; info@nfbct.org; Fax: 860291-2795; Phone: 860289-1971. **Deadline:** September 15.

3465 ■ Cecilia Hillman Scholarships *(Undergraduate/Scholarship)*

Purpose: To provide scholarship to a graduating high school senior. **Focus:** General studies. **Qualif.:** Applicants must: be a Greater Hartford resident; be a Jewish student; be a middle third of graduating class. **Criteria:** Selection will be based on the committee's criteria.

Funds Avail.: $1,000-$2,000. **Number Awarded:** 1-2. **To Apply:** Applicants may obtain application materials from Jewish Community Foundation of Greater Hartford. **Deadline:** April 15. **Contact:** Michael Elfenbaum, 333 Bloomfield Ave. Ste. D, West Hartford, CT 06117; Phone: 860-523-7460; Fax: 860-231-0576; melfenbaum@jcfhartford.org.

3466 ■ Ernest and Charlotte Hirst Family Scholarships *(Undergraduate/Scholarship)*

Purpose: To provide scholarship to a graduating Jewish female high school senior. **Focus:** General studies. **Qualif.:** Applicants must: be attending a four-year college or university; be a Greater Hartford resident; have a minimum B average; be an active involvement in the Jewish community. **Criteria:** Selection will be based on the committee's criteria.

Funds Avail.: $3,000-$10,000. **Number Awarded:** 1-2. **To Apply:** Applicants may obtain application materials from Jewish Community Foundation of Greater Hartford. **Deadline:** April 15. **Contact:** Michael Elfenbaum, 333 Bloomfield Ave. Ste. D, West Hartford, CT 06117; Phone: 860-523-7460; Fax: 860-231-0576; melfenbaum@jcfhartford.org.

3467 ■ Caroline Holt Nursing Scholarships *(Undergraduate/Scholarship)*

Purpose: To award scholarship to the undergraduate student enrolled in a Nursing Program. **Focus:** Nursing. **Qualif.:** Applicants must: be a US citizen; be attending an accredited School of Nursing; demonstrate financial need; have a letter of sponsorship from local DAR chapter. **Criteria:** Selection will be based on the committee's criteria.

Funds Avail.: $500. **To Apply:** For Connecticut residents to obtain materials, send a self-addressed stamped envelope to National Society Daughters of the American Revolution, 215 Loomis Rd. North Granby, CT 06060. **Deadline:** February 15 or August 15. **Contact:** Mrs. Michael L. Stewart, CT State Chairperson. 860-653-4203. L2stew@yahoo.com.

3468 ■ Doc Hurley Scholarships *(Undergraduate/Scholarship)*

Purpose: To award scholarship to the graduating senior from eligible Greater Hartford area high school. **Focus:** General studies. **Qualif.:** Student must be entering college in the fall semester after graduation. Eligible school can be found on www.docscholar.org. Students demonstrate financial need, academic excellence and community service. **Criteria:** Selection will be based on the committee's criteria.

Funds Avail.: $2,000-$10,000. **To Apply:** Applicants may obtain application materials from eligible high school guidance office. Applications will not be mailed to students. Valid applications must include: Student Air Report (SAR) from FAFSA showing Estimated Family Contribution (EFC); Three letter of recommendation (teacher, guidance counselor, and non-educational person); typed essay (no more than 1 1/2 pages); High School Transcript; SAT or ACT scores. All materials must be submitted to Doc Hurley Scholarship Foundation, Inc. **Deadline:** March. **Contact:** Muriel Hurley - Carter, Executive Dir. PO Box 4008 Hartford, CT 06147. Phone: 860-549-5012; Fax: 860-549-5955; dhsf@docscholar.org.

3469 ■ Interracial Scholarship Fund of Greater Hartford *(Undergraduate/Scholarship)*

Purpose: To provide scholarships to students entering a four-year college or university. **Focus:** General studies. **Qualif.:** Applicants must: be graduating high school senior who lives in or attends school in Greater Hartford; be on a class rank - top third with good academic record; be active volunteer in school, community, or other extracurricular activities; be involved in community service. **Criteria:** Selection will be based on the committee's criteria.

Funds Avail.: $3,000. **Number Awarded:** 1. **To Apply:** Application form can be downloaded online. Applicants must complete the scholarship application. Applicants must also attach the following requirements: letter of recommendation from your guidance counselor or a teacher; official high school transcript. Including SAT or ACT scores; copy of the essay you submitted with your college application. If you did not have to submit one, write a brief (no more than two pages) essay regarding your future goals; copy of pages 1 and 2 of your parents' most recent completed federal tax form 1040. Mail everything to Hartford Foundation College Scholarship Program. **Deadline:** February 13. **Contact:** Hartford Foundation College Scholarship Program, Scholarship Management Services, Scholarship America, One Scholarship Way, PO Box 297, St. Peter, MN 56082. 800-537-4180.

3470 ■ J and K Foundation Scholarships
(Undergraduate/Scholarship)

Purpose: To provide scholarship for graduating high school seniors. **Focus:** General studies. **Qualif.:** Applicants must be residents of Hartford or East Hartford; must be attending a four-year college or university; must demonstrate financial need; and must be on class rank in top quarter. **Criteria:** Selection will be based on the committee's criteria.

Funds Avail.: $1,000-$5,000. **Number Awarded:** 1-3. **To Apply:** Applicants must complete the General Scholarship Application and include College acceptance letter and Financial aid award letter. Submit all requirements to J and K Thomas Foundation 74 Boysenberry Court, Suffield, CT 06078; JandKschol@cox.net. **Deadline:** April 29.

3471 ■ Juvenile Arthritis Scholarships
(Undergraduate/Scholarship)

Purpose: To award scholarship to the graduating high school who have arthritis or rheumatic disease. **Focus:** General studies. **Qualif.:** Applicants must; be a graduating Connecticut, Maine, New Hampshire, Rhode Island or Vermont high school senior or college undergraduate; must have arthritis or rheumatic disease; have a school or community volunteer service. **Criteria:** Selection will be based on the committee's criteria.

Funds Avail.: $1,000. **Number Awarded:** 3-4. **To Apply:** Applicants may obtain application materials from Arthritis Foundation, Northern and Southern New England Chapter, 35 Cold Spring Rd., Rocky Hill, CT 06067; Phone: 860563-1177 ext. 102; Fax: 860563-6018; info.sne@arthritis.org. **Deadline:** March 30.

3472 ■ Walter Kapala Scholarships
(Undergraduate/Scholarship)

Purpose: To award scholarship to the graduating high school senior from a public high school of Hartford, West Hartford, or Plainfield. **Focus:** General studies. **Qualif.:** Applicants must be entering a four-year college or university in the fall after high school graduation; demonstrate financial need and have an academic excellence. **Criteria:** Selection will be based on the committee's criteria.

Funds Avail.: No specific amount. **To Apply:** Applicants must complete the General Scholarship Application and mail to Merrill Lynch Trust Company, Walter Kapala Scholarship, Hopewell Charitable Trust Center, 1300 Merill Lynch Drive, Pennington, NJ 08534. **Deadline:** May 1. **Contact:** Merill Lynch Trust Company, 800-513-0742.

3473 ■ Dr. Leizon and Barbara Kessel Scholarships *(Undergraduate/Scholarship)*

Purpose: To provide scholarship to the eligible high school senior or college students. **Focus:** General studies. **Qualif.:** Applicants must: be a Jewish high school senior or college student; a resident of Greater Hartford; demonstrate financial need. **Criteria:** Selection will be based on the committee's criteria.

Funds Avail.: $1,000-$5,000. **Number Awarded:** 1-15. **To Apply:** Applicants may obtain an application materials from Jewish Community Foundation of Greater Hartford. **Deadline:** April 15. **Contact:** Michael Elfenbaum, 333 Bloomfield Ave. Ste. D, West Hartford, CT06117. Phone: 860-523-7460; Fax: 860-231-0576; melbenbaum@jchartford.org.

3474 ■ Herman P. Kopplemann Scholarships
(Undergraduate/Scholarship)

Purpose: To award scholarship to a graduating high school senior who lives in or attends school in Greater Hartford. **Focus:** General studies. **Qualif.:** Applicants must: be entering a four-year college or university; demonstrate financial need; be on a top third with good academic record; be an active volunteer in school, community, or other extracurricular activities; has been a newspaper carrier in Hartford County. **Criteria:** Selection will be based on the committee's criteria.

Funds Avail.: $3,000. **Number Awarded:** 1-4. **To Apply:** Application form can be downloaded on-line. Applicants must complete the scholarship application. Applicants must also attach the following requirements: letter of recommendation from your guidance counselor or a teacher; official high school transcript. Including SAT or ACT scores; copy of the essay you submitted with your college application. If you did not have to submit one, write a brief (no more than two pages) essay regarding your future goals; copy of pages 1 and 2 of your parents' 2006 or most recent completed federal tax form 1040. Mail everything to Scholarship America, Hartford Foundation College Scholarship Program, Scholarship Management Services, 1505 Riverview Rd, PO Box 297, St. Peter, MN 56082. 800537-4180. **Deadline:** February 6.

3475 ■ Lazarus Foundation Scholarships
(Undergraduate/Scholarship)

Purpose: To award scholarship to the graduating high school senior from Greater Hartford region. **Focus:** General studies. **Qualif.:** Applicants must: be a current undergraduate student; have a GPA of 2.23; have 100 hours of demonstrated community service activities. **Criteria:** Selection will be based on the committee's criteria.

Funds Avail.: $3,000. **Number Awarded:** 2. **To Apply:** Applicants must complete the General Scholarship Application and submit it to West Indian Foundation, Inc., Scholarship Committee, 1229 Albany Ave. PO Box 320394 Hartford, CT 06132-0394. **Deadline:** June 30. **Contact:** West Indian Foundation, Inc. westindian@snet.net; 860-241-0379.

3476 ■ H.B. Paul Lowenberg Lions Scholarships
(Undergraduate/Scholarship)

Purpose: To provide scholarship to the graduating senior residing in Hartford, East Hartford, Windsor, Bloomfield, Newington, West Hartford, or Wethersfield. **Focus:** General studies. **Qualif.:** Applicants must: be entering or enrolled in a two- or four-year college or university; demonstrate financial need and academic excellence. Preference is given to entering college students with an interest in music and the arts. **Criteria:** Selection will be based on the committee's criteria.

Funds Avail.: $500-$750. **Number Awarded:** 3. **To Apply:** Applicants must complete the General Scholarship Applica-

Awards are arranged alphabetically below their administering organizations

tion and submit it together with your Student Aid Report (SAR) to Hartford Host Lions Club. **Deadline:** April 30. **Contact:** Atty. Bruce Bergman, Lions Scholarship Chairperson. 63 Imlay St. Hartford, CT 06105. Phone: 860-522-1436; Fax: 860-522-9077.

3477 ■ Irene and Daisy MacGregor Memorial Scholarships *(Graduate/Scholarship)*

Purpose: To provide scholarship to the students enrolled in an accredited School of Medicine. **Focus:** Medicine; Nursing, Psychiatric. **Qualif.:** Applicants must: be a US citizen; be on a graduate level, major in Medicine or Psychiatric Nursing; be enrolled in an accredited School of Medicine; have a letter of sponsorship from local DAR chapter. **Criteria:** Selection will be based on the committee's criteria.

Funds Avail.: $5,000. **To Apply:** For Connecticut residents to obtain materials, send a self-addressed stamped envelope to National Society Daughters of the American Revolution, 215 Loomis Rd. North Granby, CT 06060. **Deadline:** April 15. **Contact:** Mrs. Michael L. Stewart, CT State Chairperson. 860-653-4203. L2stew@yahoo.com.

3478 ■ Mary Main Memorial Scholarships *(Undergraduate/Scholarship)*

Purpose: To provide scholarship to the graduating senior or college student residing or attending school full-time in Connecticut. **Focus:** General studies. **Qualif.:** Applicants must be legally blind and demonstrate financial need, community service, and academic excellence. **Criteria:** Selection will be based on the committee's criteria.

Funds Avail.: $3,000. **Number Awarded:** 1. **To Apply:** Applicants may obtain application materials from National Federation of the Blind of Connecticut 477 Connecticut Blvd. Ste. 217, East Hartford, CT 06108; www.nfbct.org; info@nfbct.org; Fax: 860291-2795; Phone: 860289-1971. **Deadline:** September 15.

3479 ■ Manchester Scholarship Foundation Scholarships *(Undergraduate/Scholarship)*

Purpose: To award scholarship to the graduating senior residing in Manchester. **Focus:** General studies. **Qualif.:** Applicants must: demonstrate financial need; have an academic excellence; be involved in community and school activities. **Criteria:** Selection will be based on the committee's criteria.

Funds Avail.: %500-$4,000. **Number Awarded:** 80. **To Apply:** Mid-April. **Deadline:** Students may obtain application materials from their Guidance Office or from Manchester Scholarship Foundation, Inc. 20 Hartford Rd. Manchester, CT 06040. **Contact:** Manchester Scholarship Foundation, Inc., Phone: 860-645-1673; Fax: 860-432-9136.

3480 ■ Dr. Frank and Florence Marino Scholarships *(Undergraduate/Scholarship)*

Purpose: To provide scholarship to the students entering or enrolled in Medical school. **Focus:** Medicine. **Qualif.:** Applicants must: have attended Connecticut school for at least 8 years (K-12) and graduated from Connecticut public or parochial high school; demonstrate financial need; have academic excellence. **Criteria:** Selection will be based on the committee's criteria.

Funds Avail.: $1,000. **To Apply:** Applicants may contact Mrs. Rita Fry to obtain application materials. **Deadline:** March 20. **Contact:** Scholarship Fund c/o Mrs. Rita Fry, PO Box 75 Brookfield, CT 06804. 203-775-3114; rfry@charter.net.

3481 ■ Katherine Portnoy Mattleson Scholarships *(Undergraduate/Scholarship)*

Purpose: To provide financial support to the graduating high school senior. **Focus:** Nursing. **Qualif.:** Applicants must: be enrolled in a School of Nursing; be a Jewish faith; have an academic excellence; be involved in community service. **Criteria:** Selection will be based on the committee's criteria.

Funds Avail.: $500. **Number Awarded:** 1. **To Apply:** Applicants may obtain an application from Nona Dorman, Scholarship Chairperson, 31 Woodland St., 6L Hartford, CT 06105. 860724-2323. **Deadline:** April 10.

3482 ■ Dr. Cladwell McCoy, Jr. Memorial Scholarships *(Undergraduate/Scholarship)*

Purpose: To provide scholarship to the students entering or enrolled in a four-year college or university. **Focus:** Engineering, Mathematics and mathematical sciences; Science. **Qualif.:** Applicants must be graduating high school senior attending Bloomfield, Bulkeley, Hartford Public, Weaver, or Windsor High School. **Criteria:** Selection will be based on the committee's criteria.

Funds Avail.: $1,000. **Number Awarded:** 5. **To Apply:** Applicants must complete the General Scholarship Application and submit to Dr. Caldwell Mccoy, Jr. Foundation, Inc. **Deadline:** May 15. **Contact:** Mr. Calvin C. Cole, Chairman and CEO, 19 Durnham St. Hartford, CT 06112. 860-243-8004.

3483 ■ Michael Jewelers Foundation Scholarships for Athletes *(Undergraduate/Scholarship)*

Purpose: To provide scholarship to students entering or enrolled in a four-year program at the University of Connecticut. **Focus:** Business. **Qualif.:** Applicants must: be a graduating high school senior residing in Connecticut; be a Business major; participate in intercollegiate athletics. **Criteria:** Selection will be based on the committee's criteria.

Funds Avail.: $2,000. **Number Awarded:** 8. **To Apply:** Applicants may obtain application materials from University of Connecticut Athletic Department. www.michaelsjewelers.com. **Deadline:** March 1. **Contact:** Michael Jewelers Foundation, 203-597-4905. gems@michaelsjewelers.com.

3484 ■ Michaels Jewelers Foundation General Scholarships *(Undergraduate/Scholarship)*

Purpose: To provide scholarship to the students attending the University of Connecticut. **Focus:** General studies. **Qualif.:** Applicants must: be a graduating senior from Avon, Amity, Bristol Central, Ridgefield, Brookfield, Guilford, Laurelton Hall, Masuk, Nonnewaug, Simsbury, or Torrington high school; demonstrate financial need; have at least "C" GPA, making a maximum academic effort. **Criteria:** Selection will be based on the committee's criteria.

Funds Avail.: $500. **Number Awarded:** 9. **To Apply:** Applicants may obtain application materials from their high school guidance counselor at the selected school. **Deadline:** March 1. **Contact:** Michael Jewelers Foundation, 203-597-4905. gems@michaelsjewelers.com.

3485 ■ O'Meara Foundation Scholarships *(Undergraduate/Scholarship)*

Purpose: To award scholarship to the students attending a two- or four-year college or university. **Focus:** General studies. **Qualif.:** Applicants must: be a graduating high school senior; be a resident of Hartford County; demon-

Awards are arranged alphabetically below their administering organizations

strate financial need. **Criteria:** Selection will be based on the committee's criteria.

Funds Avail.: $500-$3,000. **Number Awarded:** 100. **To Apply:** Applicants may obtain application materials from O'Meara Foundation, Inc. Claude-Evalyne Odiaka, 1900 Berlin Turnpike Wethersfield, CT 06109. **Deadline:** June 1. **Contact:** O'Meara Foundation, Inc. Phone: 860-563-2918; Fax: 860-563-9300; bpiincmax@aol.com.

3486 ■ Fitzroy and Mildred Parkinson Memorial Scholarships *(Undergraduate/Scholarship)*

Purpose: To provide scholarship to the graduating high school senior. **Focus:** General studies. **Qualif.:** Applicants must be of West Indian Heritage and demonstrate community service. **Criteria:** Selection will be based on the committee's criteria.

Funds Avail.: No specific amount. **To Apply:** Applicants must complete the General Scholarship Application and submit it to West Indian Foundation, Inc. 1229 Albany Ave. PO Box 320394 Harford, CT 0132-0394. westindian@snet.net. 860241-0379. **Deadline:** June 30.

3487 ■ Sylvia Parkinson Scholarships *(Undergraduate/Scholarship)*

Purpose: To provide scholarship to the students attending the University of Connecticut School of Medicine. **Focus:** Medicine. **Qualif.:** Applicants must: be a Capitol Region resident; demonstrate financial need; have an academic excellence; intend to practice in the Greater Hartford area. **Criteria:** Selection will be based on the committee's criteria.

Funds Avail.: $1,500-$3,000. **To Apply:** Applicants may obtain application materials from University of Connecticut School of Medicine. 263 Farmington Ave. MC 1827 Farmington, CT 06030. **Deadline:** March 20. **Contact:** Andrea Deveraux, Director of Financial Aid, Phone: 860-679-3574; Fax: 860-679-1902; devereux@uchc.edu.

3488 ■ Dorothy E. Hofmann Pembroke Scholarships *(Undergraduate/Scholarship)*

Purpose: To award scholarship to students accepted at and plan to attend Brown University. **Focus:** General studies. **Qualif.:** Applicants must: be a graduating female senior from Hartford Public, Bulkeley, Weaver high school, or any female graduating senior who is a resident of Hartford; have an academic excellence; have extracurricular activities. **Criteria:** Selection will be based on the committee's criteria.

Funds Avail.: $5,000-$7,000. **To Apply:** Applicants may obtain application materials from Bank of America, 777 Main St. Hartford, CT 06115. **Deadline:** April 15. **Contact:** Brenda Betancourt, Trust Assistant, CT2-102-22-02; 860-952-7387; brenda.l.betancourt@bankofamerica.com

3489 ■ Nicholas J. Piergrossi Scholarships *(Undergraduate/Scholarship)*

Purpose: To award scholarship to a first-year student attending the University of Connecticut School of Dental Medicine. **Focus:** Dentistry. **Qualif.:** Applicants must be a resident of Connecticut who demonstrates financial need and academic excellence. **Criteria:** Selection will be based on the committee's criteria.

Funds Avail.: $1,000. **Number Awarded:** 1. **To Apply:** Applicants may obtain application materials from University of Connecticut School of Dental Medicine. 263 Farmington Ave., MC 1827 Farmington, CT 06030. **Deadline:** March 20. **Contact:** Andrea Deveraux, Director of Financial Aid, Phone: 860-679-3574; Fax: 860-679-1902; devereux@uchc.edu.

3490 ■ Day Pitney LLP Scholarships *(Undergraduate/Scholarship)*

Purpose: To provide scholarship to the graduating high school senior in the City of Hartford. **Focus:** General studies. **Qualif.:** Applicants must: be entering a four-year college or university (full-time enrollment); demonstrate financial need; be on the class rank - top third with good academic record; be active volunteer in school, community, or other extracurricular activities. **Criteria:** Selection will be based on the committee's criteria.

Funds Avail.: $3,000. **Number Awarded:** 1. **To Apply:** Application form can be downloaded on-line. Applicants must complete the scholarship application. Applicants must also attach the following requirements: letter of recommendation from your guidance counselor or a teacher; official high school transcript. Including SAT or ACT scores; copy of the essay you submitted with your college application. If you did not have to submit one, write a brief (no more than two pages) essay regarding your future goals; copy of pages 1 and 2 of your parents' 2006 or most recent completed federal tax form 1040. Mail everything to Hartford Foundation College Scholarship Program. **Deadline:** February 6. **Contact:** Hartford Foundation College Scholarship Program, Scholarship Management Services, Scholarship America, 1505 Riverview Rd., PO Box 297, St. Peter, MN 56082. 800-537-4180.

3491 ■ Dr. Sidney Rafal Memorial Scholarships *(Undergraduate/Scholarship)*

Purpose: To award scholarship to students attending the University of Connecticut School of Dental Medicine. **Focus:** Dentistry; Dental hygiene. **Qualif.:** Applicants must demonstrate financial need and academic excellence. **Criteria:** Selection will be based on the committee's criteria.

Funds Avail.: $1,200. **Number Awarded:** 1. **To Apply:** Applicants may obtain application materials from University of Connecticut School of Dental Medicine. 263 Farmington Ave., MC 1827 Farmington, CT 06030. **Deadline:** March 20. **Contact:** Andrea Deveraux, Director of Financial Aid, Phone: 860-679-3574; Fax: 860-679-1902; devereux@uchc.edu.

3492 ■ Ratcliffe Hicks School of Agriculture Heritage Scholarships *(Undergraduate/Scholarship)*

Purpose: To provide scholarship to students attending the University of Connecticut. **Focus:** Animal science and behavior; Horticulture; Turfgrass management. **Qualif.:** Applicants must be graduating seniors planning to attend the University of Connecticut, Ratcliffe Hicks School of Agriculture majoring in Animal Science, Ornamental Horticulture and Turfgrass management. **Criteria:** Selection will be based on the committee's criteria.

Funds Avail.: $1,200. **Number Awarded:** 20. **To Apply:** Applicants may obtain application materials from the University of Connecticut Ratcliffe Hicks School of Agriculture (RHSA). 1376 Storrs Rd., Unit 4090, Storrs, CT 06269-4090. Phone: 860486-2919; Fax: 860486-4643, acadprog@canr.uconn.edu.

3493 ■ Mary C. Rawlins Scholarships *(Undergraduate/Scholarship)*

Purpose: To award financial support to the graduating high school senior. **Focus:** General studies. **Qualif.:** Applicants

Awards are arranged alphabetically below their administering organizations

must: be a resident of Connecticut; graduating high school senior; be entering a two- or four-year college or university; have a GPA of 2.5 or higher at end of Fall semester. **Criteria:** Selection will be based on the committee's criteria.

Funds Avail.: $500. **Number Awarded:** 1. **To Apply:** Applicants may obtain application materials from Division of Criminal Justice, The CTAAAP Scholarship Committee, 300 Corporate Place Rocky Hill, CT 06067. **Deadline:** April 30. **Contact:** Patricia Alston-Tyson, 860-258-5800; patricia.alston-tyson@po.state.ct.us.

3494 ■ Alice W. Rooke Scholarships
(Undergraduate/Scholarship)

Purpose: To provide financial assistance to students accepted by an accredited medical school. **Focus:** Medicine. **Qualif.:** Applicants must be pursuing a course of study in medicine, not pre-med; must be a US citizen; have a letter of sponsorship from local DAR chapter. **Criteria:** Selection will be based on the committee's criteria.

Funds Avail.: $5,000. **To Apply:** For Connecticut residents, to obtain application materials, send a self-addressed stamped envelope to: National Society Daughters of American Revolution, 215 Loomis St., North Granby, CT 06060. **Deadline:** April 15. **Contact:** Mrs. Michael L. Stewart, CT State Chairperson, NSDAR Scholarship Committee. L2stew@yahoo.com; 860-653-4203.

3495 ■ Deedee Segel - Hartford Courant Internships *(Undergraduate/Internship)*

Purpose: To provide financial assistance to students planning a career in Journalism. **Focus:** Journalism; Communication. **Qualif.:** Applicants must be college students majoring in Journalism or Communication. **Criteria:** Selection will be based on the committee's criteria.

Funds Avail.: No specific amount. **To Apply:** Applicants may obtain application materials from The Hartford Courant and include the following requirements: resume with cover letter; application; eight published writings samples; reporting experience; college grades; references. **Deadline:** January 1. **Contact:** Lynne DeLucia, Asst. Managing Ed., State/Metro, 285 Broad St., Hartford, CT 06115.

3496 ■ Tadeusz Sendzimir Scholarships
(Undergraduate/Scholarship)

Purpose: To provide financial assistance to students entering or enrolled as undergraduate or graduate at a four-year college or university or summer program in Poland. **Focus:** Polish studies; American history. **Qualif.:** Applicants must be Connecticut residents; studying Polish/Slavic Language, history or culture in the US or Poland. Preference to students of Polish descent. **Criteria:** Selection will be based on the committee's criteria.

Funds Avail.: $1,000-$5,000. **Number Awarded:** 1-5. **To Apply:** Applicants may obtain application materials from Connecticut Community Foundation, 43 Field St., Waterburry, CT 06702. **Deadline:** March 1. **Contact:** Tallitha Richardson-Selby, Program/Scholarship Associate; 203-756-3054; info@conncf.org.

3497 ■ Bro. Dr. Frank T. Simpson
(Undergraduate/Scholarship)

Purpose: To provide scholarship to the graduating high school seniors attending public or private schools in Hartford County. **Focus:** General studies. **Qualif.:** Applicants must: students who will be enrolled in a two- or four-year college or university; have an academic excellence, class rank with a minimum of 3.0 GPA; have documentation of community service and other extracurricular activities within the community and school. **Criteria:** Selection will be based on the committee's criteria.

Funds Avail.: $1,500. **Number Awarded:** 1-4. **To Apply:** Applicants may obtain application materials from their high school guidance counselor, or download from the website at www.hartfordalphas.com. Applicants must submit all requirements to Scholarship Committee Chairman BSL Educational Foundation, Inc. Alpha Phi Fraternity, Inc. PO Box 335 Hartford, CT 06141-0330. www.hartford.ocm **Deadline:** March 31.

3498 ■ Peter T. Steinwedell Scholarships
(Undergraduate/Scholarship)

Purpose: To provide scholarship for students attending graduate education program at Saint Joseph College, or the University of Connecticut, Hartford campus, or the University of Hartford. **Focus:** Education. **Qualif.:** Applicant must be an Education major with strong preference given to applicants pursuing teaching career; must demonstrate financial need and academic excellence. **Criteria:** Selection will be based on the committee's criteria.

Funds Avail.: $1,250. **Number Awarded:** 1. **To Apply:** Applicants may obtain an application by contacting either: Dr. Kathleen Butler, Chair, Department of Education St. Joseph College, 860231-5322, kbutler@sjc.edu; Monica Gat, Dean's Office Teacher Certification Program for College Graduates UConn Greater Hartford Campus, 860570-9283; Dr. H. Frederick Sweitzer, Associate Dean College of Education, Nursing and Health Professions University of Hartford, 860768-4279, sweitzer@hartford.edu. **Deadline:** March 24.

3499 ■ Town and County Club Scholarships
(Undergraduate/Scholarship)

Purpose: To award scholarship to the female adult learner - age 24 or older. **Focus:** General studies. **Qualif.:** Applicant must be a resident of Greater Hartford region; must be enrolled full or part-time in an accredited community undergraduate college or university in the Greater Hartford region; must have a completion of 15 semester hours or the equivalent of academic work with a 2.5 GPA; and must demonstrate financial need. **Criteria:** Selection will be based on the committee's criteria.

Funds Avail.: $2,000. **To Apply:** Students may contact the Town and County Club or access the website www-.towncounty.com for application form. **Deadline:** March 3. **Contact:** Town and County Club, Scholarship Committee, 22 Woodland St. Hartford, CT 06105. Phone: 860-522-1109; Fax: 860-728-0758; office@towncounty.com.

3500 ■ Tunxis Community College Foundation Scholarships *(Undergraduate/Scholarship)*

Purpose: To provide scholarship for entering freshmen or enrolled sophomores of Tunxis Community College. **Focus:** General studies. **Qualif.:** Applicants must demonstrate financial need, community service and academic excellence. **Criteria:** Selection will be based on the committee's criteria.

Funds Avail.: No specific amount. **To Apply:** Applicants may obtain application materials from Tunxis Community College, 271 Scott Swamp Rd. Farmington, CT 06032. **Deadline:** August 1. **Contact:** David Welsh, Phone: 860-255-3513; Fax: 860-676-8906; dwelsh@txcc.commnet.edu.

3501 ■ West Indian Migrant Farm Workers Memorial Scholarships *(Undergraduate/Scholarship)*

Purpose: To provide scholarship for graduating high school seniors. **Focus:** General studies. **Qualif.:** Applicants must be of West Indian Heritage and must demonstrate academic excellence and financial need. **Criteria:** Selection will be based on the committee's criteria.

Funds Avail.: $3,000. **To Apply:** Applicants may obtain application materials from West Indian Foundation, Inc. Scholarship Committee, PO Box 320394 Hartford, CT 06132-0394. westindian@snet.net; www.westindianfoundation.org; Fax: 860241-0379. **Deadline:** June 30.

3502 ■ Elmer Cooke Young - Taylor Young Scholarships *(Undergraduate/Scholarship)*

Purpose: To award scholarship to students entering a four-year college or university. **Focus:** General studies. **Qualif.:** Students must be graduating seniors from Glastonbury or Windsor High School; must demonstrate financial need; must be on a class rank - top third with good academic record; and must be active volunteers in school, community, or other extracurricular activities. **Criteria:** Selection will be based on the committee's criteria.

Funds Avail.: $3,000. **Number Awarded:** 6. **To Apply:** Application forms can be downloaded on-line. Applicants must complete the scholarship application. Applicants must also attach the following requirements: letter of recommendation from your guidance counselor or a teacher; official high school transcript (including SAT or ACT scores); copy of the essay you submitted with your college application (If you did not have to submit one, write a brief essay of no more than two pages regarding your future goals); copy of pages 1 and 2 of your parents' 2006 or most recent completed federal tax form 1040. Mail everything to Hartford Foundation College Scholarship Program. **Deadline:** February 6. **Contact:** Hartford Foundation College Scholarship Program, Scholarship Management Services, Scholarship America, One Scholarship Way, PO Box 297, St. Peter, MN 56082. 800-537-4180.

3503 ■ Harvard Law School

1563 Massachusetts Ave.
Cambridge, MA 02138
Ph: (617)496-8214
Fax: (617)496-9179
E-mail: qpquery@law.harvard.edu
URL: http://www.law.harvard.edu

3504 ■ Henigson Human Rights Fellowships *(Undergraduate/Fellowship)*

Purpose: To encourage the HLS students to build human rights work and to expand their interest in working in the field. **Focus:** Human rights. **Qualif.:** Applicants must be current and former J.D. students: 3Ls expecting to receive the J.D. degree, as well as J.D graduates who currently clerk for a judge; must be engaged in full-time public interest work; must be active in human rights or public interest work while students at HLS; must be LL.M. students who expect to receive the LL.M. degree and who come from and will return to a country other than the United States. **Criteria:** Selection of recipients will be based on the application materials.

Funds Avail.: $27,000. **To Apply:** Applicants must submit a curriculum vitae, including information about classes, work and extracurricular activities in public interest and human rights inside and outside of Harvard Law School; a personal statement (500 words maximum) about the applicant's relevant experience, interest, and future aspirations with respect to public interest and human rights work; a project description; a letter and supporting materials from sponsoring organization detailing their purpose, function, and particular interest in the work of the applicant; two or three letters of recommendation including at least one from an HLS professor; and an HLS transcript. **Deadline:** March 7.

3505 ■ HRP Global Human Rights Fellowships *(Graduate/Fellowship)*

Purpose: To support the graduating 3Ls, LL.M.s, or recent HLS graduates with a demonstrated commitment to human rights. **Focus:** Human rights. **Qualif.:** Applicants must be Harvard Law School J.D. students: must be 3Ls expecting to receive the J.D. degree, as well as recent J.D. graduates; must be Harvard Law School LL.M. students who expect to receive the LL.M. degree. **Criteria:** Selection of recipients will be based on the application materials.

Funds Avail.: $40,000 plus medical and other benefits. **To Apply:** Applicants must submit a curriculum vitae, including information about classes, work and extracurricular activities in public interest and human rights inside and outside of Harvard Law School; a personal statement (500 words maximum) about the applicant's relevant experience, interest, and future aspirations with respect to public interest and human rights work; a project description; a letter and supporting materials from sponsoring organization detailing their purpose, function, and particular interest in the work of the applicant; two or three letters of recommendation, including at least one from an HLS professor; and an HLS transcript. **Deadline:** March 7.

3506 ■ Satter Human Rights Fellowships *(Graduate/Fellowship)*

Purpose: To enable students to make a significant contribution to addressing human rights violations involving mass atrocities and similar situations during the year of the fellowship and to help students develop careers in human rights. **Focus:** Human rights. **Qualif.:** Applicants must be Harvard Law School J.D. students: 3Ls expecting to receive the J.D. degree, as well as recent J.D. graduates; must be Harvard Law School LL.M. students who expect to receive the LL.M. degree. **Criteria:** Selection of recipients will be based on the application materials.

Funds Avail.: $27,000. **To Apply:** Applicants must submit a curriculum vitae, including information about classes, work and extracurricular activities in public interest and human rights inside and outside of Harvard Law School; a personal statement (500 words maximum) about the applicant's relevant experience, interest, and future aspirations with respect to public interest and human rights work; a project description; a letter and supporting materials from sponsoring organization detailing their purpose, function, and particular interest in the work of the applicant; two or three letters of recommendation including at least one from an HLS professor; and an HLS transcript. **Deadline:** March 7.

3507 ■ Hawaii Hotel and Lodging Association

2270 Kalakaua Ave., Ste. 1506
Honolulu, HI 96815-2552
Ph: (808)923-0407
Fax: (808)924-3843

Awards are arranged alphabetically below their administering organizations

E-mail: hhla@hawaiihotels.org
URL: http://www.hawaiihotels.org

3508 ■ R.W. "Bob" Holden Scholarships
(Undergraduate/Scholarship)

Purpose: To provide support to students with dedication and leadership potential to work toward the standard of excellence. **Focus:** Hotel, institutional, and restaurant management. **Qualif.:** Applicant must be a resident of Hawaii and a U.S citizen; must be a junior or senior attending an accredited university or college and accepted in a hotel management program; must have a minimum of 3.0 grade. **Criteria:** Selection of applicants will be based on the citizenship and leadership as demonstrated through activities and college performance.

Funds Avail.: No specific amount. **To Apply:** Applicants must submit a current transcript, letter of recommendation from a college professor, counselor or dean; must provide an autobiography, photograph, and career goals essay. Application form and other supporting documents must be sent to R.W. Bob Holden Scholarship Committee, Hawaii Hotel Industry Foundation, 2270 Kalakaua Ave., Ste. 1506, Honolulu, HI 96815. **Deadline:** June 30.

3509 ■ Clem Judd Jr. Memorial Scholarships
(Undergraduate/Scholarship)

Purpose: To provide support to students with dedication and leadership potential to work toward the standard of excellence. **Focus:** Hotel, institutional, and restaurant management. **Qualif.:** Applicant must provide proof of Hawaiian ancestry; must be a resident of Hawaii; must be a junior or senior attending an accredited university or college and accepted in a hotel management program; must maintain a minimum 2.8 grade point average. **Criteria:** Selection of applicants will be based on the citizenship and leadership as demonstrated through activities and college performance.

Funds Avail.: No specific amount. **To Apply:** Applicants must have a proof of residency, proof of U.S. citizenship, and proof of Hawaiian ancestry; must have a current transcript of record; must have an autobiography and photograph; must provide a career goals essay; must have a letter of recommendation from a college professor, counselor or dean. Application forms and other supporting documents must be sent to Clem Judd Jr. Memorial Scholarship Committee, Hawaii Hotel Industry Foundation, 2270 Kalakaua Ave., Ste. 1506, Honolulu, HI 96815. **Deadline:** July 1.

3510 ■ Native Hawaiian Scholarships
(Undergraduate/Scholarship)

Purpose: To provide support to undergraduate students who wants to pursue their education. **Focus:** Hotel, institutional, and restaurant management. **Qualif.:** Applicant must provide a proof of Native Hawaiian ancestry; must be a resident of Hawaii; must be a graduating senior accepted an accredited university or college; must maintain a minimum 2.8 grade point average. **Criteria:** Selection of applicants will be based on the citizenship and leadership as demonstrated through activities and college performance.

Funds Avail.: No specific amount. **To Apply:** Applicants must provide a proof of residency, proof of U.S. citizenship, and proof of Native Hawaii ancestry; must have a current high school report card or current college transcript (if transferring from 2 year to 4 year college); must have a autobiography, and photograph; must provide a letter of recommendation from a teacher, counselor or principal, and a career goal essay (500 words or less). Application form and other supporting documents must be sent to Native Hawaiian Scholarships Committee, Hawaii Hotel Industry Foundation, 2270 Kalakaua Ave., Ste. 1506, Honolulu, HI 96815. **Deadline:** June 30.

3511 ■ Health Resources and Services Administration - Bureau of Health Professions

5600 Fishers Ln.
Rockville, MD 20857
Ph: (301)443-2194
Free: 800-221-9393
E-mail: callcenter@hrsa.gov
URL: http://bhpr.hrsa.gov

3512 ■ Nursing Scholarship Program
(Undergraduate/Scholarship)

Purpose: To award scholarships to individuals for attendance at schools of nursing. **Focus:** Nursing. **Qualif.:** Applicants must be US citizens or nationals (permanent residents are not eligible); must be enrolled or accepted for enrollment as full-time or part-time students in an accredited school of nursing in a professional registered nurse program; must begin classes for the fall term on or after July 1 and no later than September 30; must be free from any Federal judgment liens; must be free from existing service commitments; and must not be delinquent on a federal debt. **Criteria:** Preference is given to qualified applicants with the greatest financial need who are enrolled full-time in an undergraduate nursing program.

Funds Avail.: $1,233. **To Apply:** All applicants (regardless of funding preference) must submit an electronic application. Required supporting documentation is available within the online application and includes: a verification of Acceptance/Good Standing Report and Data Collection for Tuition and Fees; an Authorization to Release Information; Form W-4; Standard form 1199A (EG) Direct Deposit Sign Up Form; and a Signed Contract. **Deadline:** June 6. **Contact:** HRSA at the above address (see entry 3511).

3513 ■ Scholarships for Disadvantaged Students *(Undergraduate/Scholarship)*

Purpose: To provide scholarships for full-time, financially needy students from disadvantaged backgrounds who are enrolled in health professions and nursing programs. **Focus:** Health sciences. **Qualif.:** Applicant must be an individual from a disadvantaged background as defined by the US Department of Health and Human Services and must come from an environment that has inhibited the individual from obtaining the knowledge, skill, and abilities required to enroll in and graduate from a health professions school, or from a program providing education or training in an allied health profession; or must come from a family with an annual income below low income thresholds according to family size published by the US Bureau of Census, adjusted annually for changes in the Consumer Price Index, and adjusted by the Secretary, HHS, for use in health professions and nursing programs; must be a citizen, national, or a lawful permanent resident of the United States. **Criteria:** Schools are responsible for selecting scholarship recipients, making reasonable determinations of need, and providing scholarships that do not exceed the cost of attendance (tuition, reasonable educational expenses and reasonable living expenses).

Funds Avail.: No specific amount. **To Apply:** All applicants must submit an electronic application. Required supporting documentation is available within the online application and includes: A verification of Acceptance/Good Standing Report and Data Collection for Tuition and Fees; an Authorization to Re lease Information; Form W-4; Standard form 1199A (EG) Direct Deposit Sign Up Form; and a Signed Contract. **Contact:** HRSA at the above address (see entry 3511).

3514 ■ Healthcare Information and Management Systems Society

230 E Ohio St., Ste. 500
Chicago, IL 60611-3170
Ph: (312)664-4467
Fax: (312)664-6143
URL: http://www.himss.org

3515 ■ Dvora Brodie Scholarships *(Other/Scholarship)*

Purpose: To provide financial support to HIMSS student member who exhibits excellence and future leadership potential in the healthcare information and management system industry. **Focus:** Healthcare services. **Qualif.:** Applicant must be a member in good standing of HIMSS attending a school in New England, or originally be from the New England area; and the primary occupation of the applicant at the time the scholarship is awarded must be that of a student in an accredited undergraduate, Masters, or PhD program related to the healthcare information management systems field. **Criteria:** Recipient will be selected according to merit, financial need, and other factors.

Funds Avail.: $5,000. **To Apply:** Applicants must submit complete application form.

3516 ■ Richard P. Covert, Ph.D./FHIMSS Scholarships for Management Systems *(Other/Scholarship)*

Purpose: To provide financial assistance to students pursuing a degree in Management Engineering. **Focus:** Engineering. **Qualif.:** Applicant must be a member in good standing of HIMSS and the primary occupation of the applicant at the time the scholarship is awarded must be that of student in an accredited undergraduate, Masters or PhD program related to the healthcare information management systems field. **Criteria:** Recipient will be selected according to merit, financial need, and other factors.

Funds Avail.: $5,000. **To Apply:** Applicants must submit complete application form.

3517 ■ Healthcare Information Management Systems Scholarships *(Other/Scholarship)*

Purpose: To provide financial assistance to students in healthcare and IT-related fields. **Focus:** Healthcare services. **Qualif.:** Applicant must be a member in good standing of HIMSS and a student in an accredited undergraduate, Master's or PhD program related to the healthcare information or management systems field. **Criteria:** Recipient will be selected according to merit, financial need, and other factors.

Funds Avail.: $5,000. **To Apply:** Applicants must submit complete application form.

3518 ■ Northern California Chapter of HIMSS Scholarships *(Other/Scholarship)*

Purpose: To provide financial assistance for student in healthcare informatics who exhibits academic excellence and future leadership potential in the healthcare information and management systems industry. **Focus:** Healthcare services. **Qualif.:** Applicant must be a member in good standing of HIMSS or member of National HIMSS and the Northern California Chapter attending a school in the Northern California area and the primary occupation of the applicant at the time the scholarship is awarded must be that of student in an accredited undergraduate, Master's or PhD program related to the healthcare information management systems field. **Criteria:** Recipient will be selected according to merit, financial need, and other factors.

Funds Avail.: $5,000. **To Apply:** Applicants must submit complete application form.

3519 ■ Helicopter Foundation International

1635 Prince St.
Alexandria, VA 22314
Ph: (703)360-1521
E-mail: libby.meade@rotor.com
URL: http://www.helicopterfoundation.org

3520 ■ Helicopter Foundation International Commercial Helicopter Rating Scholarships *(All/Scholarship)*

Purpose: To assist private helicopter pilot candidates who wish to obtain their commercial helicopter ratings. **Focus:** Aviation. **Qualif.:** Applicants must hold a current private helicopter pilot license. **Criteria:** Recipients are selected based on financial need.

Funds Avail.: $4,000. **Number Awarded:** 4. **To Apply:** Applicants must submit a clear copy of any and all FAA or international equivalent certificates; must submit a completed application form, current resume, proof of enrollment in helicopter training program at a qualified school, three current letters of recommendation from individual such as employers, flight instructors, HAI members or members of similar aviation organizations who can attest to candidate's background, training and experiences as it relates to the helicopter industry and international applicants must provide proof of foreign citizenship. **Deadline:** July 15.

3521 ■ Helicopter Foundation International Maintenance Technician Certificate Scholarships *(Professional Development/Scholarship)*

Purpose: To assist candidates who wish to obtain an A, P or A and A and P certificate. **Focus:** Aviation. **Qualif.:** Applicants must hold a current private helicopter pilot license. **Criteria:** Recipients are selected based on financial need.

Funds Avail.: $2,500. **Number Awarded:** 6. **To Apply:** Applicants must submit a completed HFI application for a Maintenance Technician Scholarship, current resume, proof of enrollment in helicopter training program at a qualified school, three current letters of recommendation from individual such as employers, flight instructors, HAI members or members of similar aviation organizations who can attest to candidate's background, training and experiences as it relates to the helicopter industry and international applicants must provide proof of foreign citizenship. **Deadline:** June 27.

3522 ■ Michelle North Scholarships for Safety *(Professional Development/Scholarship)*

Purpose: To assist private helicopter pilot candidates who wish to obtain their commercial helicopter ratings. **Focus:** Aviation. **Qualif.:** Applicants must be employed in the

Awards are arranged alphabetically below their administering organizations

helicopter industry either in the Safety of Safety Management field, preparing to enter or if in a position other than the Safety Management field. **Criteria:** Recipients are selected based on the demonstrated interest in the field of aviation.

Funds Avail.: $3,000. **Number Awarded:** 1. **To Apply:** Applicants must submit a completed application form; must submit a current resume, summary of career plans, two letters of recommendation from employer or other helicopter professional; must submit a clear copy of any and all FAA or international equivalent certificates, a "350-500-word" summary statement attesting how candidate would benefit from the Safety Management course and how would use the knowledge gained to enhance safety at candidate's organization. **Deadline:** July 15-October 1.

3523 ■ Bill Sanderson Aviation Maintenance Technician Scholarship *(Professional Development/Scholarship)*

Purpose: To assist private helicopter pilot candidates who wish to obtain their commercial helicopter ratings. **Focus:** Aviation. **Qualif.:** Applicant must be about to graduate from an FAA approved Part 147 AMT school or be a recent recipient within the last two years of an Airframe and Powerplant Certificate. **Criteria:** Recipients are selected based on demonstrated interest in the field of aviation.

Funds Avail.: No specific amount. **Number Awarded:** 5. **To Apply:** Applicants must submit a completed application form; must submit a clear copies of any and all FAA international equivalent certificate. **Deadline:** November 15. **Contact:** harold.summers@rotor.com

3524 ■ Hellenic News of America

26 W Chester Pike
Havertown, PA 19083
Ph: (610)446-1463
Fax: (610)446-3189
E-mail: info@hellenicnews.com
URL: http://www.hellenicnews.com

3525 ■ The PanHellenic Scholarships *(Undergraduate/Scholarship)*

Purpose: To encourage and support the educational aspirations of gifted high school graduates and university students of Hellenic descent and to recognize students of high scholastic achievement, and provide support for those who have financial need. **Focus:** General studies. **Qualif.:** Applicants must be high school students or currently enrolled in any university. Applicant who is a high school graduate must have completed a state-certified high school, or equivalent and be registered to attend a university or educational institution of similar standing in the USA; Applicants who are currently enrolled in a university must have completed at least one year of full-time study at an accredited university in the USA. **Criteria:** Recipients are selected based on academic excellence and financial need.

Funds Avail.: Maximum amount of $250,000. **To Apply:** Applicants must submit an essay that addresses the connections between Hellenic contributions to the world and America today. Applicants must complete the application form. **Deadline:** August 31.

3526 ■ Hellenic University Club of Philadelphia

PO Box 42199
Philadelphia, PA 19101-2199
Ph: (215)483-7440
E-mail: hucphila@yahoo.com
URL: http://www.hucphila.org

3527 ■ Andrew G. Chressanthis Memorial Scholarships *(Undergraduate/Scholarship)*

Purpose: To provide scholarships for students with outstanding academic qualifications and financial need. **Focus:** General studies. **Qualif.:** Applicants must be of Greek descent; must be U.S. citizens; and must be undergraduate students who have declared majors in Greek studies. **Criteria:** Selection will be based on merit and financial need.

Funds Avail.: $2,000. **To Apply:** Application form can be obtained from the HUCPhila website. Applicants must complete the application form and mail to the attention of the Scholarship Chairman. Applicants must also provide one letter of recommendation and scholastic transcripts. **Deadline:** April 21. **Contact:** Scholarship Chairman at the above address (see entry 3526).

3528 ■ Christopher Demetris Scholarships *(Undergraduate/Scholarship)*

Purpose: To provide scholarships for students with outstanding academic qualifications and financial need. **Focus:** General studies. **Qualif.:** Applicant must be a student who is a Greek Orthodox and a U.S. citizen. **Criteria:** Selection will be based on merit and financial need.

Funds Avail.: $1,200. **To Apply:** Application form can be obtained from the HUCPhila website. Applicants must complete the application form and mail to Scholarship Chairman. Applicants must also provide one letter of recommendation and scholastic transcripts. **Deadline:** April 21.

Remarks: Funded by Jack and Olga Demetris in memory of their infant son. **Contact:** Scholarship Chairman at the above address (see entry 3526).

3529 ■ Dorizas Memorial Scholarships *(Undergraduate/Scholarship)*

Purpose: To provide scholarship for students with outstanding academic qualifications and financial need. **Focus:** General studies. **Qualif.:** Applicants must be enrolled full-time in a degree program at an accredited four-year college or university. High school seniors accepted for enrollment in such a degree program may also apply. **Criteria:** Selection will be based on academic merit and financial need.

Funds Avail.: $3,000. **To Apply:** Application form can be obtained from the HUCPhila website. Applicants must complete the application form and mail to Scholarship Chairman. Applicants must also provide one letter of recommendation and scholastic transcripts. **Deadline:** April 21.

Remarks: Established in honor of the late Dr. Michael Dorizas, a widely respected Philadelphia educator and athlete. **Contact:** Scholarship Chairman at the above address (see entry 3526).

3530 ■ Hellenic University Club of Philadelphia Founders Scholarships *(Undergraduate/Scholarship)*

Purpose: To provide scholarships for students with outstanding academic qualifications and financial need. **Focus:** Greek studies. **Qualif.:** Applicants must be of Greek descent; must be U.S. citizens; and must be undergraduate students who have declared majors in Greek studies. **Criteria:** Award is given based on merit.

Funds Avail.: $3,000. **To Apply:** Application form can be obtained from the HUCPhila website. Applicants must complete the application form and mail to Scholarship Chairman. Applicants must also provide one letter of recommendation and scholastic transcripts. **Deadline:** April 21. **Contact:** Scholarship Chairman at the above address (see entry 3526).

3531 ■ Nicholas S. Hetos, DDS, Memorial Graduate Scholarships *(Graduate/Scholarship)*

Purpose: To provide scholarships for students with outstanding academic qualifications and financial need. **Focus:** Dentistry. **Qualif.:** Applicants must be senior undergraduate or graduate students with financial need pursuing studies leading to a Doctoral of Dental Medicine (D.M.D.) or Doctoral of Dental Surgery (D.D.S.) Degree. **Criteria:** Selection will be based on merits and financial need.

Funds Avail.: $2,000. **To Apply:** Application form can be obtained from the HUCPhila website. Applicants must send their name and address to Scholarship Chairman. Applicants must also provide one letter of recommendation and scholastic transcripts. **Deadline:** April 21.

Remarks: Funded by the Hetos family. **Contact:** Scholarship Chairman at the above address (see entry 3526).

3532 ■ George C. Liacouras Memorial Scholarships *(Undergraduate/Scholarship)*

Purpose: To provide scholarships for students pursuing undergraduate education at the Wharton School of the University of Pennsylvania. **Focus:** General studies. **Qualif.:** Applicants must be of Greek descent; must be U.S. citizens; and must be enrolled full-time at the Wharton School of the University of Pennsylvania. **Criteria:** Selection will be based on merit and financial need.

Funds Avail.: $5,000. **To Apply:** Application form can be obtained from the HUCPhila website. Applicants must complete the application form and mail to Scholarship Chairman. Applicants must also provide one letter of recommendation and scholastic transcripts. **Deadline:** April 21.

Remarks: Established by Mrs. Effie Liacouras. **Contact:** Scholarship Chairman at the above address (see entry 3526).

3533 ■ Dr. Nicholas Padis Memorial Graduate Scholarships *(Graduate/Scholarship)*

Purpose: To provide scholarship for qualified senior undergraduate or graduate students. **Focus:** General studies. **Qualif.:** Applicant must be a full-time senior undergraduate or a graduate student at an accredited university or professional school. **Criteria:** Selection will be based on merits and financial need.

Funds Avail.: $5,000. **To Apply:** Application form can be obtained from the HUCPhila website. Applicants must send their name and address to Scholarship Chairman. Applicants must also provide one letter of recommendation and scholastic transcripts. **Deadline:** April 21.

Remarks: Established in 1986. **Contact:** Scholarship Chairman.

3534 ■ Peter George Pitsakis Memorial Scholarships *(Undergraduate/Scholarship)*

Purpose: To provide scholarships for students with outstanding academic qualifications and financial need. **Focus:** General studies. **Qualif.:** Applicants must be of Greek descent; must be U.S. citizens; and must be undergraduate students who have declared majors in Greek studies. **Criteria:** Selection will be based on educational merit and financial need.

Funds Avail.: $2,500. **To Apply:** Application form can be obtained from the HUCPhila website. Applicants must complete the application form and mail to Scholarship Chairman. Applicants must also provide one letter of recommendation and scholastic transcripts. **Deadline:** April 21.

Remarks: Established in accordance with the request of and in memory of Peter G. Pitsakis, a past president of the Hellenic University Club. **Contact:** Scholarship Chairman at the above address (see entry 3526).

3535 ■ Dr. Peter A. Theodos Memorial Graduate Scholarships *(Graduate/Scholarship)*

Purpose: To provide scholarship for students with outstanding academic qualifications and financial need. **Focus:** Medicine. **Qualif.:** Applicants must be senior undergraduate or graduate students with financial need pursuing studies leading to a Doctor of Medicine (M.D.) Degree. **Criteria:** Selection will be based on academic merit and financial need.

Funds Avail.: $2,500. **To Apply:** Application form can be obtained from the HUCPhila website. Applicants must send their name and address to the Scholarship Chairman and provide one letter of recommendation and scholastic transcripts. **Deadline:** April 21.

Remarks: Established in 1988. **Contact:** Scholarship Chairman at the above address (see entry 3526).

3536 ■ Dimitri J. Ververelli Memorial Scholarships *(Undergraduate/Scholarship)*

Purpose: To provide financial assistance for qualified students pursuing a degree in the fields of Architecture and/or Engineering. **Focus:** Architecture; Engineering. **Qualif.:** Applicants must be of Greek descent; must be U.S. citizens; and must be pursuing a degree in the fields of Architecture and/or Engineering. **Criteria:** Selection will be based on merits and financial need.

Funds Avail.: $2,000. **To Apply:** Application form can be obtained from the HUCPhila website. Applicants must complete the application form and mail to Scholarship Chairman. Applicants must also provide one letter of recommendation and scholastic transcripts. **Deadline:** April 21. **Contact:** Scholarship Chairman at the above address (see entry 3526).

3537 ■ Hemingway Foundation and Society

14 Terhune Dr.
Phippsburg, ME 04562
Ph: (207)389-2939
Fax: (207)389-2939
URL: http://www.hemingwaysociety.org

3538 ■ Ernest Hemingway Research Grants *(Professional Development/Grant)*

Purpose: To provide funds for scholars and students who are doing research in the Ernest Hemingway Collection. **Focus:** General studies. **Qualif.:** Applicant must be a scholar and student interested or doing research in Ernest Hemingway Collection. **Criteria:** Grant applications are evaluated on the basis of expected utilization of the Hemingway Collection. Preference is given to dissertation research by Ph.D candidates working in newly opened or relatively unused portions of the collection, but all proposals are welcome and will receive careful consideration.

Funds Avail.: $200-1,000. **To Apply:** Application forms are available at the website; must be accompanied by a brief proposal (three to four pages) in the form of a letter or more describing the planned research, its significance; must submit two letters of recommendation from academic or other appropriate references; must have a sample of your writing, a project budget, and a vitae. Application forms and other supporting materials must be send to: Grant and Fellowship Coordinator, John F. Kennedy Presidential Library and Museum, Columbia Point, Boston, MA 02125. **Deadline:** November 1.

3539 ■ Jim & Nancy Hinkle Travel Grants *(Postdoctorate/Grant)*

Purpose: To defray travel expenses for graduate students who wants to attend the biennial international conferences. **Focus:** General studies. **Qualif.:** Recipients must be members in good standing of the Hemingway Society; must currently be enrolled in a graduate degree program, and must be planning to present a paper at the conference. **Criteria:** Applications are selected by the Hickle Travel Grant Committee and evaluated by the following criteria: clarity, originality, and value in furthering Hemingway scholarship, criticism, or instruction. Application from previous Hinkle winners are welcome, applications from students who have not won before will be given priority.

Funds Avail.: Travel expenses for the biennial international conference. **To Apply:** Application must include the following information: (1) Full name of applicant, (2) address, phone, email, (3) Social Security Number, (4) Paper title & abstract, (5) Degree program and school, (6) Letter of recommendation. Applications should be sent to Hinkle Selection Committee Chair: Gail Sinclair, Rollins College, Box 2752, 1000 Holt Ave., Winter Park, FL. 32789. **Deadline:** March 1.

3540 ■ Smith-Reynolds Founder Fellowships *(Graduate/Fellowship)*

Purpose: To support the students in their research on Ernest Hemingway. **Focus:** General studies. **Qualif.:** Applicant must be a graduate student, independent scholar, or post-doctoral up through the rank of assistant professor. **Criteria:** Applications are ranked by the committee based on the following criteria: clarity, originality, and feasibility, criticism, or instruction; and the likelihood of its publication.

Funds Avail.: $2,000. **To Apply:** Applicant must submit as a Microsoft word attachment or send by mail the following information and agreements: (1) Full name and Social Security Number, (2) Addresses, phone numbers and email address (including summer and between session), (3) Degree program and school, (4) Verification of graduate enrollment status or awarded degree (if appropriate); must have the description of Hemingway Project (200-word limit). Must be sent to: Prof. Carl P. Eby, Chair, Smith-Reynolds Founders Fellowship Committee, at carlpeby@gwm.sc.edu. **Deadline:** April 1.

3541 ■ Hemophilia Federation of America

1405 W Pinhook Rd., Ste. 101
Lafayette, LA 70503
Ph: (337)261-9787
Fax: (337)261-1787
Free: 800-230-9797
E-mail: info@hemophiliafed.org
URL: http://www.hemophiliafed.org

3542 ■ Hemophilia Federation of America Educational Scholarships *(Undergraduate/Scholarship)*

Purpose: To assists and advocates for the bleeding disorders community. **Focus:** Hemophilia. **Qualif.:** Applicants must have hemophilia or von Willlebrand (VWD) and must be seeking a post-secondary education from a college, university, or trade school. The applicant must also be able to demonstrate a commitment to improving quality of life by pursuing his/her goals with determination. **Criteria:** Selection will be based on the scholarship committee of HFA.

Funds Avail.: $1,500. **To Apply:** Applicants must submit a complete application; essay; proof of academic standing; statement of financial need and parents previous year's tax return (if applicant is a dependent, otherwise the applicant's tax return); proof of enrollment; two letters of reference (one professional reference the other from the HTC or physician) **Deadline:** April 30.

3543 ■ The Herb Society of America

9019 Kirtland Chardon Rd.
Kirtland, OH 44094
Ph: (440)256-0514
Fax: (440)256-0541
E-mail: herbs@herbsociety.org
URL: http://herbsociety.org

3544 ■ Nashville Unit Scholarships *(Undergraduate/Scholarship)*

Purpose: To educate its members and the public on the cultivation of herbs and the study of their history and uses. **Focus:** Horticulture. **Qualif.:** Applicants must be permanent residents of Tennessee; must be current college freshman, sophomore or junior students who are American citizens. **Criteria:** Recipients are selected based on financial need and academic performance.

Funds Avail.: $2,500. **To Apply:** Applicants must submit a completed application form and two letters of reference. **Deadline:** April 1.

3545 ■ Pennsylvania Heartland Unit Scholarships *(Undergraduate/Scholarship)*

Purpose: To educate its members and the public on the cultivation of herbs and the study of their history and uses. **Focus:** Horticulture. **Qualif.:** Applicants must be third or fourth year students of an associate degree program within the study of horticulture; must be residents of Berks, Montgomery, York, Lancaster or Schuylkill county. **Criteria:** Recipients are selected based on financial need and academic performance.

Funds Avail.: $1,500. **To Apply:** Applicants must submit: a completed application form; two letters of reference from which one must come from an advisor or professor and one from a reference of the student's choice; must submit an official school transcript; and an essay stating their reasons for choosing the field of horticulture and future plans. **Deadline:** April 1. **Contact:** jetlan1@aol.com.

3546 ■ South Texas Unit Scholarships *(Undergraduate/Scholarship)*

Purpose: To educate its members and the public on the cultivation of herbs and the study of their history and uses.

Focus: Horticulture. **Qualif.:** Applicants must be students who are studying agronomy, horticulture, botany or a closely-related discipline at an accredited four-year college or university; must be either permanent residents of Texas or attending an accredited college or university in Texas; must have completed two full years of college and be entering their junior or senior year of studies. **Criteria:** Recipients are selected based on academic performance and financial need.

Funds Avail.: $1,000. **To Apply:** Applicants must submit a completed application form and recommendation from professor or guidance counselor. **Deadline:** May 1. **Contact:** 713-513-7808.

3547 ■ Western Reserve Herb Society Scholarships *(Undergraduate/Scholarship)*

Purpose: To educate its members and the public on the cultivation of herbs and the study of their history and uses. **Focus:** Horticulture. **Qualif.:** Applicants must be: undergraduate students; Ohio residents; studying horticulture or a related field such as landscape architecture or horticultural therapy; planning a career involving teaching/research or work in the public sector; entering their second to fifth year of an undergraduate program at an accredited college or university. **Criteria:** Recipients are selected based on academic performance and financial need.

Funds Avail.: $4,000. **To Apply:** Applicants must submit a completed application form.

3548 ■ Francis Sylvia Zverina Scholarship *(Undergraduate/Scholarship)*

Purpose: To educate its members and the public on the cultivation of herbs and the study of their history and uses. **Focus:** Horticulture. **Qualif.:** Applicants must be students in good scholastic standing who are studying horticulture or related fields such as landscape architecture or horticultural therapy; must have horticultural career goals involving teaching/research or work in the public sector; must be U.S. citizens; must have completed their second or third year of undergraduate school at an accredited college or university anywhere in United States. **Criteria:** Recipients are selected based on academic records and financial need.

Funds Avail.: $5,000. **To Apply:** Applicants must submit a completed application form.

3549 ■ Hereditary Disease Foundation

3960 Broadway, 6th Fl.
New York, NY 10032
Ph: (212)928-2121
Fax: (212)928-2172
E-mail: cures@hdfoundation.org
URL: http://www.hdfoundation.org

3550 ■ Hereditary Disease Foundation Research Grants *(Postdoctorate/Grant)*

Purpose: To support for research focusing on Huntington's disease. **Focus:** Huntington's disease. **Qualif.:** Applicants must be post-graduate level. **Criteria:** Applicants are reviewed by a triangle group. Consideration is relevance to treatments and cures for Huntington's disease. Selected applicants will receive an application form for a full proposal.

Funds Avail.: $50,000. **To Apply:** Applicants must complete the one page letter of intent (available at the website) consisting of contact information and summary of the proposed research (maximum of 500 words). Selected proposals are to receive an application form. Application requires an administrative contact, project summary, budgets, other current and pending support, biographical sketch, protection of human subjects, protection of animal subjects, and study proposal. Send application thru email in PDF at carljohnson@hdfoundation.org, and five copies sent to: Hereditary Disease Foundation, Attn: Carl D. Johnson, PhD 3960 Broadway, 6th Fl. New York, NY 10032 USA. **Deadline:** For application, February, June and October 15. **Contact:** Executive Director of Science, Carl D. Johnson, PhD. at carljohnson@hdfoundation.org.

3551 ■ John J. Wasmuth Postdoctoral Fellowships *(Postdoctorate/Fellowship)*

Purpose: To support for research focusing on Huntington's disease. **Focus:** Huntington's disease. **Qualif.:** Applicants must be post-graduate level. **Criteria:** Recipients are given based on the applications.

Funds Avail.: $40,500 - $56,000. **To Apply:** Applicants must complete the one page letter of intent (available at the website); applicant's curriculum vitae and research sponsor; and two recommendation letters (one from the applicant's sponsor). Send application thru email in PDF at carljohnson@hdfoundation.org, and five copies sent to: Hereditary Disease Foundation, Attn: Carl D. Johnson, PhD 3960 Broadway, 6th Fl. New York, NY 10032 USA. **Deadline:** February, June and October 15.

Remarks: Established in honor John J. Wasmuth, a member of the Huntington's Disease Collaborative Research. **Contact:** Executive Director of Science, Carl D. Johnson, PhD. at carljohnson@hdfoundation.org.

3552 ■ Hillel Montreal

3460 Stanley St.
Montreal, QC, Canada H3A 1R8
Ph: (514)845-9171
Fax: (514)345-6418
E-mail: romy@hillel.ca
URL: http://montreal.hillel.ca

3553 ■ Therese and David Bohbot Scholarship *(Undergraduate/Scholarship)*

Purpose: To award annually the needy university students who require an additional assistance for living expenses. **Focus:** General studies. **Qualif.:** Applicants must be currently enrolled in a university. **Criteria:** Recipients are selected based on financial need.

Funds Avail.: No specific amount. **To Apply:** Applicants must submit a letter explaining goals/reasons for request; proof of Quebec residency; transcript of records; acceptance letter to University; two letters of reference and Social Insurance Number. **Deadline:** May 30.

3554 ■ Marlene Brand Memorial Scholarship *(Undergraduate/Scholarship)*

Purpose: To improve the quality and diversity of Hillel Montreal. **Focus:** General studies. **Qualif.:** Applicants must be students living and studying in Montreal. **Criteria:** Recipients are selected based on financial need, academic excellence and involvement in the Montreal Jewish community.

Funds Avail.: $2,500. **To Apply:** Applicants must submit a letter stating the objectives and reasons for request, history of community involvement, proof of Quebec residency, letter of University acceptance, transcript of grades, two letters of recommendation from teachers or employers, Social Insurance number and Montreal address and telephone number. **Deadline:** May 30.

3555 ■ Bernic and Gordon Brown Scholarship *(All/Scholarship)*

Purpose: To improve the quality and diversity of Hillel Montreal. **Focus:** General studies. **Qualif.:** Applicants must be permanent residents of Montreal who have demonstrated academic excellence and community involvement, who have not been to Israel; must have a plan to return to Montreal to participate in Jewish community. **Criteria:** Recipients are selected based on academic performance and financial need.

Funds Avail.: $5,000. **To Apply:** Applicants must submit a completed application form; brief letter outlining the reasons for wishing to attend university in Israel and career goals; record of involvement in Jewish community; letter of acceptance from an Israeli university; transcript of grades; a minimum of two letters of recommendation from professors and Social Insurance Number.

3556 ■ Hadar J. Chemtob Scholarship *(Undergraduate/Scholarship)*

Purpose: To improve the quality and diversity of Hillel Montreal. **Focus:** Fashion design. **Qualif.:** Applicants must be Jewish students pursuing a career in fashion. **Criteria:** Recipients are selected based on financial need and academic merit.

Funds Avail.: No specific amount. **To Apply:** Applicants must submit a letter stating the objectives and reasons for request; proof of Quebec residency; letter of acceptance for fashion studies program; transcript of grades; two letters of recommendation from teachers and Social Insurance Number. **Deadline:** May 30.

3557 ■ Dr. Mark Cohen Scholarship *(Undergraduate/Scholarship)*

Purpose: To provide scholarship through Hillel Montreal as recognition of the financial assistance received by Dr. Cohen as a medical student through the Levitt Family Foundation and Hillel Montreal. **Focus:** Medicine. **Qualif.:** Applicants must be students enrolled in the Faculty of Medicine or the Faculty of Dentistry at McGill University or University de Montreal. **Criteria:** Recipients are selected based in financial need.

Funds Avail.: $5,000. **To Apply:** Applicants must submit a letter stating goals and reasons for request, transcript of grades, curriculum vitae, one academic recommendation, proof of Quebec residency, and Social Insurance Number. **Deadline:** May 30. **Contact:** 514-842-6405.

3558 ■ Leila Klinger Kurtzman Mamorial Scholarship Fund *(Undergraduate/Scholarship)*

Purpose: To improve the quality and diversity of Hillel Montreal. **Focus:** Education. **Qualif.:** Applicants must be students entering the first year of a certified university. **Criteria:** Recipients are selected based on academic performance.

Funds Avail.: $500. **To Apply:** Applicants must submit a letter stating the goals and reasons for request; proof of Quebec residency; transcript of records; acceptance letter from Montreal University; two letters of recommendation and Social Insurance Number.

3559 ■ Karen E. Latt Memorial Scholarship *(Undergraduate/Scholarship)*

Purpose: To improve the quality and diversity of Hillel Montreal. **Focus:** Medical education. **Qualif.:** Applicants must be female graduates entering medical school. **Criteria:** Recipients are selected based on financial need.

Funds Avail.: No specific amount. **To Apply:** Applicants must submit a letter stating the objectives and reasons for request; letter of acceptance to medical school for the coming academic year; transcript of grades; two letters of recommendation from professors and Social Insurance Number. **Deadline:** May 30.

3560 ■ Irene Brand Lieberman Scholarship *(Postgraduate/Scholarship)*

Purpose: To improve the quality and diversity of Hillel Montreal. **Focus:** Early childhood education. **Qualif.:** Applicants must be university students enrolled in a course of study related to children. **Criteria:** Recipients are selected based on financial need and academic merit.

Funds Avail.: No specific amount. **To Apply:** Applicants must submit a letter of acceptance to graduate or postgraduate studies in Montreal; letter of application outlining the reasons for request and goals; transcript of grades and proof of Quebec residency; must also submit two letters of recommendation from professors and Social Insurance Number. **Deadline:** May 30.

3561 ■ Dr. Oskar and Sally Schickler Scholarship *(Undergraduate/Scholarship)*

Purpose: To improve the quality and diversity of Hillel Montreal. **Focus:** General studies. **Qualif.:** Applicants must be first year of CEGEP study. **Criteria:** Recipients are selected based on financial need.

Funds Avail.: $1,000. **To Apply:** Applicants must submit a letter stating the goals; reasons for request; proof of Quebec residency; high school transcript of records; acceptance letter; two letters of recommendation from professors and Social Insurance Number. **Deadline:** May 30.

3562 ■ Mireille and Murray Steinberg Scholarship *(Postgraduate/Scholarship)*

Purpose: To improve the quality and diversity of Hillel Montreal. **Focus:** General studies. **Qualif.:** Applicants must be post-graduate degree students at a Quebec-based institution of higher learning. **Criteria:** Recipients are selected based on financial need and academic merit.

Funds Avail.: $5,000. **To Apply:** Applicants must submit a proof of Quebec residency; letter of acceptance from University; transcript of records; proof of age; must submit a letter explaining the reasons or need for application; two references from Professors and Social Insurance Number. **Deadline:** May 30.

3563 ■ Emanuel Weiner Scholarship *(Postgraduate/Scholarship)*

Purpose: To improve the quality and diversity of Hillel Montreal. **Focus:** Social work. **Qualif.:** Applicants must be students enrolled in a master's program focusing in social policy. **Criteria:** Recipients are selected based on financial need.

Funds Avail.: $2,500. **To Apply:** Applicants must submit a completed application form.

3564 ■ Hispanic Association of Colleges and Universities

8415 Datapoint Dr., Ste. 400
San Antonio, TX 78229

Awards are arranged alphabetically below their administering organizations

Ph: (210)698-3805
Fax: (210)692-0823
E-mail: hacu@hacu.net
URL: http://www.hacu.net

3565 ■ Daimler Chrysler Scholarships Award *(Undergraduate/Scholarship)*

Purpose: To promote the development of member colleges and universities; to improve access to and the quality of post-secondary educational opportunities for Hispanic students; and to meet the needs of business, industry and government through the development and sharing of resources, information and expertise. **Focus:** General studies. **Qualif.:** Applicants must be full-time undergraduate students attending 2-to-4 year institutions; must possess a minimum cumulative GPA of 3.0. **Criteria:** Recipients are selected based on the demonstrated financial need and ability to meet the specified criteria for the scholarship to which they are applying.

Funds Avail.: $1,000. **To Apply:** Applicants must fill out the application form and must provide any documents showing that they are currently enrolled or accepted by a college, university, or institution. **Deadline:** May 23.

3566 ■ GAP, Inc. Scholarships Award *(Undergraduate/Scholarship)*

Purpose: To promote the development of member colleges and universities; to improve access to and the quality of post-secondary educational opportunities for Hispanic students; and to meet the needs of business, industry and government through the development and sharing of resources, information and expertise. **Focus:** Management; Fashion Design. **Qualif.:** Applicants must be full-time or part-time, undergraduate and graduate students attending four year institutions; must possess a minimum cumulative GPA of 3.0. **Criteria:** Recipients are selected based on the demonstrated financial need and ability to meet the specified criteria for the scholarship to which they are applying.

Funds Avail.: $1,000. **To Apply:** Applicants must fill out the application form and must provide any documents showing that they are currently enrolled or accepted by a college, university, or institution. **Deadline:** May 23.

3567 ■ HACU/Wal-Mart Achievers Scholarships *(Undergraduate/Scholarship)*

Purpose: To promote the development of member colleges and universities; to improve access to and the quality of post-secondary educational opportunities for Hispanic students; and to meet the needs of business, industry and government through the development and sharing of resources, information and expertise. **Focus:** Business Administration; Management. **Qualif.:** Applicants must be full-time undergraduate students attending two or four year institutions and must possess a minimum cumulative GPA of 3.0. **Criteria:** Recipients are selected based on the demonstrated financial need and ability to meet the specified criteria for the scholarship to which they are applying.

Funds Avail.: $1,000. **To Apply:** Applicants must fill out the application form and must provide any documents showing that they are currently enrolled or accepted by a college, university, or institution. **Deadline:** May 23.

3568 ■ Hispanic Association of Colleges and Universities Scholarships *(Undergraduate/Scholarship)*

Purpose: To promote the development of member colleges and universities; to improve access to and the quality of post-secondary educational opportunities for Hispanic students; and to meet the needs of business, industry and government through the development and sharing of resources, information and expertise. **Focus:** General studies. **Qualif.:** Applicants must be Hispanic Association of Colleges and Universities member institutions; must be attending a HACU-member institution at the time applications are completed and scholarships are made. **Criteria:** Recipients are selected based on the demonstrated financial need and ability to meet the specified criteria for the scholarship to which they are applying.

Funds Avail.: No specific amount. **To Apply:** Applicants must fill out the application form and must provide any documents showing that they are currently enrolled or accepted by a college, university, or institution. **Deadline:** May 23.

3569 ■ Office Depot Scholarships *(Undergraduate/Scholarship)*

Purpose: To promote the development of member colleges and universities; to improve access to and the quality of post-secondary educational opportunities for Hispanic students; and to meet the needs of business, industry and government through the development and sharing of resources, information and expertise. **Focus:** Business; Marketing and Distribution; Information Science and Technology. **Qualif.:** Applicants must be undergraduate students attending four year institutions and must possess a minimum cumulative GPA of 3.0. **Criteria:** Recipients are selected based on the demonstrated financial need and ability to meet the specified criteria for the scholarship to which they are applying.

Funds Avail.: $1,000. **To Apply:** Applicants must fill out the application form and must provide any documents showing that they are currently enrolled or accepted by a college, university, or institution. **Deadline:** May 23.

3570 ■ Wendell Scott Awards *(Graduate, Undergraduate/Scholarship)*

Purpose: To promote the development of member colleges and universities; to improve access to and the quality of post-secondary educational opportunities for Hispanic students; and to meet the needs of business, industry and government through the development and sharing of resources, information and expertise. **Focus:** Business; Engineering; Public Relation; Technology; Management. **Qualif.:** Applicants must be full-time or part-time, undergraduate and graduate students attending four year institutions; must possess a minimum cumulative GPA of 3.0. Applying graduate students must be attending school at least on a part-time basis and must possess a minimum cumulative GPA of 3.0. **Criteria:** Recipients are selected based on the demonstrated financial need and ability to meet the specified criteria for the scholarship to which they are applying.

Funds Avail.: $1,500-undergraduate; $2,000-graduate. **To Apply:** Applicants must fill out the application form and must provide any documents showing that they are currently enrolled or accepted by a college, university, or institution. **Deadline:** May 23.

3571 ■ Wachovia Scholarship Awards *(Undergraduate/Scholarship)*

Purpose: To promote the development of member colleges and universities; to improve access to and the quality of post-secondary educational opportunities for Hispanic students; and to meet the needs of business, industry and government through the development and sharing of resources, information and expertise. **Focus:** Finance; Accounting; Business Administration. **Qualif.:** Applicants must be full-time undergraduate students attending two or four year institutions and must posses a minimum cumulative GPA of 3.0. **Criteria:** Recipients are selected based on the demonstrated financial need and ability to meet the specified criteria for the scholarship to which they are applying.

Funds Avail.: $1,000. **To Apply:** Applicants must fill out the application form and must provide any documents showing that they are currently enrolled or accepted by a college, university, or institution. **Deadline:** May 23.

3572 ■ Hispanic Association on Corporate Responsibility

1444 I St. NW, Ste. 850
Washington, DC 20005
Ph: (202)682-4012
Fax: (202)682-0086
E-mail: hacr@hacr.org
URL: http://www.hacr.org

3573 ■ Hispanic Association on Corporate Responsibility Scholarship Program
(Undergraduate/Scholarship)

Purpose: To provide financial educational assistance to help the next generation of youth reach their full potential. **Focus:** General studies. **Qualif.:** Applicants must be member students of Hispanic Association of Colleges and Universities; must be full-time undergraduate students with minimum of 3.0 GPA at four-year HACU member higher education institutions who have completed at least 12 undergraduate units of any major with an interest in the entertainment, news, media, and telecommunications industries. **Criteria:** Recipients are evaluated based on academic performance and financial need.

Funds Avail.: $300,000. **To Apply:** Applicants must submit all the required application information.

3574 ■ Vern W. Reeder Memorial Scholarships
(Undergraduate/Scholarship)

Purpose: To provide opportunities for students to achieve a higher education. **Focus:** General studies. **Qualif.:** Applicants must be accepted as full-time undergraduate or post-graduate students at a fully-accredited, non-profit vocational school, technical school, community college, college or university. **Criteria:** Recipients are selected based on merit and financial need.

Funds Avail.: $5,000. **To Apply:** Applicants must submit all the required application information.

3575 ■ Hispanic Faculty Staff Association

1 University Station, D5000
Austin, TX 78712
Ph: (512)471-1511
Fax: (512)471-0239
E-mail: alba.ortiz@mail.utexas.edu
URL: http://www.utexas.edu

3576 ■ Jamail/Long Challenge Grant Scholarships *(Graduate, Undergraduate/Scholarship)*

Purpose: To promote communication and to support networking; to serve as a voice for university, educational, professional and cultural Hispanic issues; to promote career growth, development and initial employment; and to provide opportunities for social and cultural interaction for Hispanic professionals. **Focus:** General studies. **Qualif.:** Applicants must be Hispanic students enrolled as full-time undergraduate, graduate or transfer students at the University of Texas, Austin; must maintain satisfactory progress toward completion of their degree requirements as determined by the regular procedures of the Texas Exes. **Criteria:** Recipients are selected based on academic performance.

Funds Avail.: $1,000. **To Apply:** Applicants must complete the online Continuing & Transfer Scholarship Application provided by the Office of Student Financial Services. Applicants must select "Texas Exes Scholarships" on the "Scholarship Choices" page of the application and then enter the correct scholarship code, ESA-HISPANIC, in the space provided. **Deadline:** March 1.

3577 ■ Hispanic Lawyers Association of Illinois

321 South Plymouth Court, Ste. 600
Chicago, IL 60604
Ph: (312)345-9200
E-mail: hlai-cs@att.net
URL: http://www.hlai.org

3578 ■ Barbri Scholarships for Bar Preparation
(Undergraduate/Scholarship)

Purpose: To help increase excellence among individuals pursuing careers in the legal field. **Focus:** Law. **Qualif.:** Program is open to post-graduation law students that secure legal or related employment with a government agency, a non-profit organization, or public interest agency intending to apply in a BARBRI preparation course. **Criteria:** Scholarship is given based on merit.

Funds Avail.: $500-$1,000. **To Apply:** Applicants may download application form at HLAI website. Complete and submit the application form (including the two short essays about the applicant's commitment to public interest law and to serving the legal and social needs of the Hispanic community). Applicants must also provide a copy of law school transcript. **Deadline:** April 7. **Contact:** Christina Lopez-Nutzman; Wessels and Pautsch, P.C. 35 West Monroe, Suite 1120 Chicago, IL 60603; 312-629-9300 chlopez@chgo.w-p.com.

3579 ■ Hispanic Lawyers Association of Illinois Public Interest Fellowships *(Undergraduate/Scholarship)*

Purpose: To help increase excellence among individuals pursuing careers in the legal field. **Focus:** Law. **Qualif.:** Program is open to law students in need of a summer stipend and have secured legal or related employment with a government agency, a non-profit organization, or public interest agency. **Criteria:** Recipients will be selected based on a review of all application materials submitted.

Funds Avail.: $2,500. **To Apply:** Applicants may download an application form at HLAI website. Complete and submit the application form (including the submission of two short essays about your commitment to public interest law and to serving the legal and social needs of the Hispanic community). Applicants must also provide a copy of law school transcript. **Deadline:** April 7. **Contact:** Christina Lopez-Nutzman; Wessels and Pautsch, P.C. 35 West Monroe, Suite 1120 Chicago, IL 60603; 312-629-9300 chlopez@chgo.w-p.com.

Awards are arranged alphabetically below their administering organizations

3580 ■ Kaplan Scholarships *(Undergraduate/ Scholarship)*

Purpose: To help increase excellence among individuals pursuing careers in the legal field. **Focus:** Law. **Qualif.:** Program is open to law students that demonstrate a genuine interest in pursuing a legal career. **Criteria:** Scholarship is given based on merit.

Funds Avail.: No specific amount. **To Apply:** Applicants must submit completed application (available at the website) and submit along with two short essays about your commitment to public interest law and to serving the legal and social needs of the Hispanic community. Applicants must also provide a copy of law school transcript. **Deadline:** April 7. **Contact:** Christina Lopez-Nutzman; Wessels and Pautsch, P.C. 35 West Monroe, Suite 1120 Chicago, IL 60603; 312-629-9300 chlopez@chgo.w-p.com.

3581 ■ Hispanic National Bar Association

1111 Pennysylvania Ave. NW
Washington, DC 20004
Ph: (202)223-4777
URL: http://www.hnba.com

3582 ■ ABA Legal Opportunity Scholarship Funds *(Undergraduate/Scholarship)*

Purpose: To promote diversity in the legal profession by providing financial assistance to law students attending an ABA-accredited law school. **Focus:** Law. **Qualif.:** Applicants must be students entering their first year in law school; must have achieved a minimum cumulative grade point average of 2.5 on a 4.0 grading scale at their undergraduate degree at the time the application is submitted; must be citizens or permanent residents of the USA. **Criteria:** Committee of ABA members will select the recipients based on their application and financial need.

Funds Avail.: $5,000 renewable up to $15,000. **To Apply:** Applicants must complete the attached application form and must have the following documents: personal statement, recommendation, transcript, and personal, family and educational background. **Deadline:** March 1.

3583 ■ Hispanic College Fund Scholarship Programs *(Undergraduate/Scholarship)*

Purpose: To support and help the nation's top college students to pursue their careers. **Focus:** Business, Finance, Engineering, Science. **Qualif.:** Applicant must be of Hispanic descent and a U.S. citizen or a permanent resident; must be studying at an accredited university in the U.S. or Puerto Rico; must be enrolled full-time as an undergraduate student for the upcoming academic year; must have earned and maintain a grade point of no less than 3.0 on a 4.0 scale; must demonstrate financial need. **Criteria:** Selection of candidates will be based on the academic and financial status.

Funds Avail.: $500-$5,000. **To Apply:** Applicants must submit an official transcript, proof of family income, proof of citizenship status, essay, resume, and financial verification (if chosen as semi finalist only). **Deadline:** March 22.

3584 ■ HNBF Princeton Review Duard Bradshaw Memorial Scholarships *(Undergraduate/ Scholarship)*

Purpose: To provide financial support to the nest generation of Hispanic leaders. **Focus:** Law. **Qualif.:** Applicants must be of Hispanic or Latino heritage; must be U.S. citizens or legal permanent residents; must be juniors enrolled at least part-time in an accredited U.S. college or university; must have a minimum cumulative grade point average of 2.75 on a 4.00 scale; must demonstrate active participation and leadership in an undergraduate student Hispanic/Latino organization. **Criteria:** Selection of candidates will be based on the academic and financial status.

Funds Avail.: $1,000. **To Apply:** Applicants must submit an information sheet, cover letter and resume, personal essay and a recommendation letter from a professor (sealed and mailed in with application packet). Application materials must be mailed in one envelope to: Hispanic National Bar Foundation, 1900 K St. NW, Ste. 100, Washington, DC 20006. **Deadline:** June 1.

3585 ■ Justicia En Diversidad Scholarships *(Undergraduate/Scholarship)*

Purpose: To assist graduating high school students who are interested in the law to attend college. **Focus:** Law. **Qualif.:** Applicants must be high school students interested in law; must have a 2.5 grade point average on a 4.0 scale; must be attending a U.S. school and must be planning to attend law school; must attend an accredited two or four-year U.S. college on a full time basis during the academic year. **Criteria:** Selection of candidates will be based on the application materials and academic records.

Funds Avail.: 1,500. **To Apply:** Candidates must attach the current transcript of record, two recommendation letters (should discuss any or all of the following: academic and extracurricular achievements, community involvement, motivation, and leadership), personal statement, honors, paid and volunteer work, and extracurricular activities, and financial information. Application form is available at the website; send completed application to: La Alianza, Justicia en Diversidad Foundation, c/o Alexander A. Boni-Saenz, Harvard Law School, Cambridge, MA 02138. **Deadline:** February 1.

3586 ■ La Unidad Latina Foundation Scholarships *(Graduate, Undergraduate/Scholarship)*

Purpose: To support and assist the Hispanic students on their education. **Focus:** General studies. **Qualif.:** Applicants must be Hispanic; must have a grade point average between 2.80-3.60 out of a 4.0 GPA scale; must be enrolled in an eligible bachelor's or master's degree program at an accredited four-year college or university; must have at least one full-time year of study for undergraduate applicants, and at least one full-time semester of study for graduate applicants; must be residing in United States. **Criteria:** Scholarships are awarded on a competitive basis.

Funds Avail.: $250-$1,000. **To Apply:** Applicants must submit the official university-issued academic transcript. Graduate students are required to submit graduate and undergraduate transcript. Applicants must have a letter of recommendation from university administrator/faculty or community leader demonstrating student leadership and commitment to civic service (200-350 words). Application form is available at the website. **Deadline:** February 15 and October 15.

3587 ■ MALDEF Law School Scholarships *(Undergraduate/Scholarship)*

Purpose: To provide financial assistance to qualified individuals in pursuit of higher education. **Focus:** Law. **Qualif.:** Applicants must be students entering their first, second or third year in law school; must have an outstanding academic records, including in their participation and leadership in extracurricular activities; must be enrolled as a full time student. **Criteria:** Scholarships are awarded to Latino students based on the following criteria: (1) demonstrated involvement with and commitment to serve the Latino community through their profession; (2) by financial need; (3) by their academic achievement indicating the potential for successful completion of a graduate or law degree.

Funds Avail.: $1,000-$4,000. **To Apply:** Applicants must complete and sign MALDEF scholarship application form; must submit a current resume; must provide a typed personal statement of 750 words or less; must have the official undergraduate transcript or photocopy of an official transcript; have a letter of recommendation describing their involvement in the Latino community from a person familiar with that involvement; have a letter of recommendation from a college, or law school professor; and a complete financial statement from the school they are or will be attending that indicates both the financial assistance. **Deadline:** October 1.

3588 ■ Hispanic Scholarship Fund

55 Second St., Ste. 1500
San Francisco, CA 94105
Fax: (415)808-2302
Free: 877-473-4636
E-mail: info@hsf.net
URL: http://www.hsf.net

3589 ■ Ford Motor Company Scholarship Program *(Undergraduate/Scholarship)*

Purpose: To assist graduating high school seniors of Hispanic heritage obtain a bachelor's degree. **Focus:** General studies. **Qualif.:** Applicant must be of Hispanic heritage; U.S. citizen or legal permanent resident with a valid permanent resident card or passport stamped I-551; graduating from high school in 2008; have a minimum GPA of 3.0 on a 4.0 scale or equivalent; enrolling full-time in a degree-seeking program at a four-year U.S. accredited institution in the U.S., Puerto Rico, U.S. Virgin Islands or Guam; must apply for federal financing aid using the Free Application for Federal Student Aid (FAFSA) at www.fafsa.ed.gov. **Criteria:** Applicants who participated in the Ford PAS program will be given preference.

Funds Avail.: $2,500. **To Apply:** Applications must be submitted using the HSF online application system. **Deadline:** March 15.

Remarks: In partnership with Ford Motor Company Fund. **Contact:** highschool@hsf.net.

3590 ■ The Gates Millennium Scholars *(Undergraduate/Scholarship)*

Purpose: To promote academic excellence and to provide an opportunity for outstanding students with significant financial need to reach their fullest potential. **Focus:** Mathematics and mathematical sciences; Science; Engineering; Education; Public health; Library and archival sciences. **Qualif.:** Applicants must be African American, American Indian/Alaska Native, Asian pacific Islander American and Hispanic American heritage; a U.S. citizen or legal permanent resident; have a minimum 3.3 GPA on a 4.0 scale; must demonstrate leadership skills; must demonstrate financial need. **Criteria:** Recipients will be selected based on the merits of the application.

Funds Avail.: No specific amount. **To Apply:** Applicants must complete all three required forms available at the award site www.gmsp.org. American Indian/Alaska Natives must submit proof of tribal enrollment or a certificate of descent if selected as finalists. **Deadline:** December 31 (paper applications), January 11 (online applications).

Remarks: Established in 1999 and funded by a grant from the Bill and Melinda Gates Foundation. **Contact:** gmsinfo@hsf.nett.

3591 ■ Hispanic Scholarship Fund (HSF) College Scholarship Program *(Graduate, Undergraduate/Scholarship)*

Purpose: To assist students of Hispanic heritage obtain a college degree. **Focus:** General studies. **Qualif.:** Applicant must be of Hispanic heritage; U.S. citizen or legal permanent resident with a valid permanent resident card or passport stamped I-551; have a minimum 3.0 GPA on a 4.0 scale or the equivalent; must apply for federal financing aid using the Free Application for Federal Student Aid (FAFSA) at www.fafsa.ed.gov; must be pursuing his/her first undergraduate of graduate degree; must have plans to enroll full-time in a degree seeking program at a two-year or four-year U.S. accredited institution in the U.S., Puerto Rico, U.S. Virgin Islands or Guam. **Criteria:** Recipients will be selected based on the merits of the application.

Funds Avail.: $1,000-$5,000. **To Apply:** Applications must be submitted using the HSF online application system. **Deadline:** March 15. **Contact:** cctransfer@hsf.net.

3592 ■ HSBC-North America Scholarship Program *(Undergraduate/Scholarship)*

Purpose: For sophomore students who will be transferring to a four-year college. **Focus:** Accounting; Actuarial science; Advertising; Public relations; Business; Engineering, Computer; Computer and information sciences; Economics; Finance; International trade; Marketing and distribution; Management. **Qualif.:** Applicant must be of Hispanic heritage; U.S. citizen or legal permanent resident with a valid permanent resident card or passport stamped I-551; be a current sophomore or community college student transferring to a four-year college/university and will be a junior status for the upcoming academic year; be enrolled full-time in a degree-seeking program at an accredited institution in the U.S., Puerto Rico, U.S. Virgin Islands or Guam; have a minimum 3.0 GPA on a 4.0 scale or 4.00 on a 5.00 scale; must be majoring in one of the following: Accounting, Actuarial Science, Advertising, Public Relations, Business, Computer Engineering, Computer Information Systems (CIS), Computer Science, Economics, Finance, International Business, Marketing or Management; must submit a resume; have applied for Federal Financial Aid; must be a resident of: Los Angeles, CA (LA, Orange, Riverside, San Bernardino, Ventura); Monterey/Salinas, CA (Salinas); San Diego, CA (San Diego); Tampa, FL (Hernando, Hillsborough, Pasco, Pinella); Jacksonville, FL (Nassau, Duval, Clay, St. Johns); Chicago, IL (Cook, DuPage, Grundy, Kane, Kankakee, Kendall, Lake, LaSalle, Will, McHenry); New York, NY (Bronx, Kings, New York, Queens, Richmond); Las Vegas, NV (Clark); Phoenix, AZ (Phoenix-Mesa); Wilmington, DC (New Castle); Bridgewater, NJ (Sussex); or Chesapeake, VA. Applicants must also submit a resume; must have applied for federal financial aid and must be pursuing his/her first undergraduate degree. **Criteria:** Recipients will be selected based on the submitted requirements.

Funds Avail.: $2,500. **To Apply:** Applicants must use the HSF online application system. **Deadline:** November 1.

Awards are arranged alphabetically below their administering organizations

Remarks: In partnership with HSBC. **Contact:** scholar1@hsf.net.

3593 ■ HSF/Atrisco Heritage Foundation Scholarship Program *(Graduate, Undergraduate/Scholarship)*

Purpose: To assist outstanding Latinos who are heirs of the Atrisco Land Grant of New Mexico. **Focus:** General studies. **Qualif.:** Applicant must be of Hispanic heritage; U.S. citizen or legal permanent resident with a valid permanent resident card or passport stamped I-551; have a minimum 2.0 GPA on a 4.0 scale or the equivalent; must apply for federal financing aid using the Free Application for Federal Student Aid (FAFSA) at www.fafsa.ed.gov; must be pursuing his/her first undergraduate of graduate degree; have plans to enroll full-time in a degree seeking program at a two or four year U.S. accredited institution in the U.S., Puerto Rico, U.S. Virgin Islands or Guam. **Criteria:** Recipients will be selected based on the merits of the application.

Funds Avail.: $2,000. **To Apply:** Applications must be submitted using the HSF online application system. **Deadline:** March 15. **Contact:** cctransfer@hsf.net.

3594 ■ HSF/Citi Fellows Program *(Undergraduate/Scholarship)*

Purpose: To provide financial assistance for Hispanic junior and senior students. **Focus:** Business administration; Economics; Finance. **Qualif.:** Applicant must be of Hispanic heritage; U.S. citizen or legal permanent resident with a valid permanent resident card or passport stamped I-551; a sophomore enrolled full-time at a four-year accredited college/university in the U.S. (must be enrolled as junior in the following academic year); be pursuing a Business Administration, Economics or Finance degree; have a minimum 3.0 GPA on a 4.0 scale or the equivalent; must be a resident or attending college in: New York City metropolitan area; Miami/Fort Lauderdale area; Tampa, Florida; Dallas, Texas; Austin, Texas; Los Angeles, California; San Francisco Bay Area, California. Or must attend college at: Columbia University, Cornell University, Dartmouth College, Duke University, Georgetown University, Harvard University, New York University, Northwestern University, Princeton University, Rutgers University, Stanford University, University of California - Los Angeles, University of Chicago, University of Pennsylvania, University of Virginia, University of Texas at Austin, or Yale University. **Criteria:** Recipients will be selected based on the merits of the.

Funds Avail.: $10,000. **To Apply:** Applicants must use the HSF online application system. **Deadline:** March 15.

Remarks: Fellows will be paired with a Citi employee as a professional mentor and offer career guidance. **Contact:** scholar1@hsf.net.

3595 ■ HSF/General Motors Scholarship Program *(Undergraduate/Scholarship)*

Purpose: To provide financial resources to outstanding Latinos pursuing degrees in engineering and business. **Focus:** Electrical engineering; Engineering, Industrial; Manufacturing; Mechanical engineering; Accounting; Business administration; Economics; Finance; Personnel administration/human resources. **Qualif.:** Applicants must be of Hispanic heritage; U.S. citizens or legal permanent residents with a valid permanent resident card or passport stamped I-551; enrolled full-time in a degree-seeking program at any four-year U.S. accredited institution in the U.S., Puerto Rico, U.S. Virgin Islands or Guam; have a minimum 3.0 GPA on a 4.0 scale or the equivalent; pursue degrees in Engineering, Business or Human Resources; must apply for federal financing aid using the Free Application for Federal Student Aid (FAFSA) at www.fafsa.ed.gov. For semi-finalists, applicants must complete the GM Online Assessment. **Criteria:** Applicants who best meet the requirements will be given preference.

Funds Avail.: $2,500. **To Apply:** Applicants must use the HSF online application system. **Deadline:** June 30.

Remarks: Given in partnership with General Motors (GM). **Contact:** scholar1@hsf.net.

3596 ■ HSF/Hewlett Packard (HP) Diversity in Education Scholarship Program *(Undergraduate/Scholarship)*

Purpose: To provide financial assistance to minority students. **Focus:** Computer and information sciences; Engineering, Computer; Engineering, Electrical. **Qualif.:** Applicants must be graduating high school seniors enrolling as a fulltime first-year student or a community college student transferring into University of California, Los Angeles, North Carolina AT&T, Morgan State University or University of Washington; plan to major in computer engineering, computer science or electrical engineering; must be African American, Latino or American Indian; be able to legally work full time in the United States at the time of application. **Criteria:** Applicants will be evaluated based on academic achievement, financial need, family's educational history, letters of recommendation, personal statement, demonstrated academic achievement and interest in math, science and engineering, connections to HP philanthropy partnerships, intended major and willingness to work in major HP locations.

Funds Avail.: $3,000 per year. **To Apply:** Applicants must download application forms from the award site website www.hp.com/scholars. **Deadline:** March 15.

Remarks: In partnership with HP Development Company. **Contact:** highschool@hsf.net.

3597 ■ HSF/IDT Hope High School Scholarship Program *(Undergraduate/Scholarship)*

Purpose: To assist graduating Hispanic high school seniors in obtaining a bachelor's degree. **Focus:** General studies. **Qualif.:** Applicant must be of Hispanic heritage; US citizen or legal permanent resident with a valid permanent resident card or passport stamped I-551; graduating high school from New York City Metropolitan (Bergen, Essex, Hudson, Hunterdon, Middlesex, Passaic, and Somerset); have a minimum GPA of 3.0 on a 4.0 scale; enrolling full-time in a degree-seeking program at a four-year U.S. accredited institution in the U.S., Puerto Rico, U.S. Virgin Islands or Guam; must apply for federal financing aid using the Free Application for Federal Student Aid (FAFSA) at www.fafsa.ed.gov. **Criteria:** Applicants who best meet the requirements will be given preference.

Funds Avail.: $10,600. **To Apply:** Applicants must submit application using the HSF online application system. **Deadline:** March 15. **Contact:** highschool@hsf.net.

3598 ■ HSF/Nissan Community College Transfer Scholarship Program *(Undergraduate/Scholarship)*

Purpose: To support outstanding Community College Transfer Students. **Focus:** Business; Engineering; Communications; Media arts. **Qualif.:** Applicant must be of Hispanic heritage; U.S. citizen or legal permanent resident

Awards are arranged alphabetically below their administering organizations

with a valid permanent resident card or passport stamped I-551; currently enrolled part-time or full-time at a community college; planning to transfer and enroll full-time in a degree-seeking program at a four-year U.S. accredited institution; must reside or transfer to a four-year institution in Atlanta, Georgia; Chicago Illinois; Greater Dallas/Forth Worth, Texas; Jackson/Canton, Mississippi; Los Angeles, California; Nashville, Tennessee; Northern California; New York City/New Jersey; be pursuing a degree in Business, Engineering, Communications or Media Arts; have a minimum GPA of 3.0 on a 4.0 scale; must apply for federal financing aid using the Free Application for Federal Student Aid (FAFSA) at www.fafsa.ed.gov. **Criteria:** Preference will be given to applicants who will best meet the requirements.

Funds Avail.: $2,500. **To Apply:** Applications must be submitted using the HSF online application system. **Deadline:** March 15.

Remarks: In partnership with Nissan North America, Inc. **Contact:** cctransfer@hsf.net.

3599 ■ HSF/Wal-Mart Stores Inc. Scholarship Program *(Graduate, Undergraduate/Scholarship)*

Purpose: To provide financial assistance to students of Hispanic heritage. **Focus:** Marketing and distribution; Accounting; Business; Finance; Management; Computer and information sciences; Information science and technology; Civil engineering; Construction; Electrical engineering; Geology; Engineering, Industrial; Fashion design; Law; **Qualif.:** Applicant must be of Hispanic heritage; U.S. citizen or legal permanent resident with a valid permanent resident card or passport stamped I-551; enrolled as sophomore, junior, senior undergraduate or First or Second year Master student in a full-time degree-seeking program at an accredited U.S. institution in the U.S., Puerto Rico, U.S. Virgin Islands or Guam; have a minimum 3.0 GPA on a 4.0 scale or 4.00 on a 5.00 scale; must apply for Federal Financing Aid; pursuing his/her first undergraduate or graduate degree. Undergraduate students must be majoring in: Marketing, Accounting, Business, Finance, Management, Computer Science, Computer Programming, Information Technology (IT), Civil Engineering, Construction, Electrical Engineering, Environmental/Geological Engineering, Industrial Engineering, and Fashion. Master's students must be majoring in: Business, Finance, Marketing, Civil Engineering, Construction, Electrical Engineering, Environmental/Geological Engineering and Law. **Criteria:** Applicants who best meet the requirements will be given to the preference.

Funds Avail.: $2,500. **To Apply:** Applications must be submitted using the HSF online application system. **Deadline:** March 15.

Remarks: In partnership with Wal-Mart Stores, Inc. **Contact:** scholar1@hsf.net.

3600 ■ Marathon Oil Corporation College Scholarship Program *(Graduate, Undergraduate/Scholarship)*

Purpose: To provide financial assistance to those who are studying engineering. **Focus:** Chemical engineering; Civil engineering; Electrical engineering; Mechanical engineering; Petroleum engineering; Geology; Geophysics; Accounting; Marketing and distribution; Land management; Transportation; Logistics; Engineering, Petroleum **Qualif.:** Applicant must be of Hispanic American, African American, Asian Pacific Islander American or American Indian/Alaskan Native heritage; U.S. citizen or legal permanent resident with a valid Social Security Number and a permanent resident card or passport stamped I-551; have a minimum 3.0 GPA on a 4.0 scale; a sophomore majoring in chemical engineering, civil engineering, electrical engineering, mechanical engineering, petroleum engineering, geology, geophysics, accounting, marketing, global procurement or supply chain management, environmental health & safety, energy management or petroleum land management, transportation & logistics or geotechnical engineering; or a senior pursuing a Masters degree in geology or geophysics; must participate in a possible paid summer internship opportunity in Marathon Oil Corporation; must apply for federal financing aid using the Free Application for Federal Student Aid (FAFSA) at www.fafsa.ed.gov. **Criteria:** Preference will be given to the applicants who best meet the requirements.

Funds Avail.: $20,000. **To Apply:** Applications must be submitted using the HSF online application system. **Deadline:** November 1.

Remarks: Scholars will be paired with a Marathon Oil Corporation employee as a professional mentor. **Contact:** scholar1@hsf.net.

3601 ■ McNamara Family Creative Arts Project Grants *(Graduate, Undergraduate/Grant)*

Purpose: To provide financial assistance to creative arts-related undergraduate and graduate students beginning or completing an art project. **Focus:** Art; Media arts; Broadcasting; Filmmaking; Performing arts; Communications; Writing. **Qualif.:** Applicant must be of Hispanic heritage; U.S. citizen or legal permanent resident with a valid permanent resident card or passport stamped I-551; enrolled full-time undergraduate or graduate student in a degree-seeking program at a U.S. accredited institution in the U.S., Puerto Rico or U.S. Virgin Islands in the upcoming academic year; pursuing a major in Arts, including but not limited to media, film, performing arts, communications or writing; have a minimum 3.0 GPA on a 4.0 scale; must apply for federal financing aid using the Free Application for Federal Student Aid (FAFSA) at www.fafsa.ed.gov. **Criteria:** Grants will be given to applicants who best meet the requirements.

Funds Avail.: $5,000-$20,000. **To Apply:** Applications must be submitted using the HSF online application system. **Deadline:** March 15.

Remarks: In partnership with the McNamara Family Foundation. **Contact:** scholar1@hsf.net.

3602 ■ Peierls Rising Star Scholarship Program *(Undergraduate/Scholarship)*

Purpose: To provide financial assistance to current high school seniors from Colorado and Texas. **Focus:** General studies. **Qualif.:** Applicant must be of Hispanic heritage; U.S. citizen or legal permanent resident with a valid permanent resident card or passport stamped I-551; have a minimum GPA of 2.50 and maximum of 2.99 on a 4.0 scale; enrolling full-time in a degree-seeking program at a four-year U.S. accredited institution in the U.S., Puerto Rico, U.S. Virgin Islands or Guam; must apply for federal financing aid using the Free Application for Federal Student Aid (FAFSA) at www.fafsa.ed.gov; reside in Colorado or Texas. Applicants must have participated in of the pre-collegiate programs: Colorado UpLift; CU-Denver Pre-Collegiate Program; College Summit Peer Leaders; Colorado "I Have A Dream"; Denver Scholarship Foundation; Big Brothers/Big Sisters of South Texas; CAMP; Communities in Schools; HSF Peer Counseling Program; UTSA Early Outreach Program; UTSA G-Force Student Mentor-

Awards are arranged alphabetically below their administering organizations

ship; UTSA Talent Search; UTSA Upward Bound. **Criteria:** Scholarships will be given to applicants who will best meet the requirements.

Funds Avail.: $5,000. **To Apply:** Applicants must apply online. Download and mail the HSF Recommender Form to Hispanic Scholarship Fund: Peierls Rising Star Scholarship Program 55 Second St., Ste. 1500 San Francisco, CA 94105. **Deadline:** February 15. **Contact:** Email: highschool@hsf.net.

3603 ▪ Toyota High School Scholarship Program *(Undergraduate/Scholarship)*

Purpose: To provide financial resources to assist outstanding Latino high school graduates. **Focus:** Accounting; Actuarial science; Advertising; Architecture; Automotive technology; Bioengineering; Business; Chemical engineering; Civil engineering; Engineering, Computer; Electronics; Computer and information sciences; Construction; Drafting; Economics; Education; Education, Bilingual and cross-cultural; Education, Early childhood; Education, Special; Counseling/Guidance; Electrical engineering; Engineering; Environmental design; Environmental science; Geology; Educational administration; Education-Curricula; Personnel administration/human resources; Industrial design; Engineering, Industrial; Information science and technology; Management; Marketing and distribution; International trade; Manufacturing; Mechanical engineering; Engineering, Nuclear; Public administration; Public relations; Transportation. **Qualif.:** Applicant must be of Hispanic heritage; U.S. citizen or legal permanent resident with a valid permanent resident card or passport stamped I-551; have a minimum GPA of 3.0 on a 4.0 scale or equivalent; must apply for federal financing aid using the Free Application for Federal Student Aid (FAFSA) at www.fafsa.ed.gov; enrolling as full-time freshman at: Arizona State University; Central Missouri University; Colorado State University, Pueblo; Cornell University; Ferris State; Florida International University; Harvard University; Indiana University; Massachusetts Institute of Technology; New York University; Northwestern University; Pennsylvania Tech College; Pittsburg State University; Southern Illinois University; Stanford University; Texas A&M University; University of Arizona; University of California, Berkeley; University of California, Davis; University of California, Los Angeles; University of California, San Diego; University of Florida; University of Houston; University of Illinois at Chicago; University of Illinois at Urbana-Champaign; University of Michigan; University of New Mexico; University of Pennsylvania; University of Southern California; University of Texas at Austin; University of Texas at El Paso; University of Texas at San Antonio; University of Texas, Pan American; or Weber State University. Applicants must pursue a degree in: Accounting; Actuarial Science; Advertising; Architecture; Automotive Technology; Bio-Engineering; Business; Chemical Engineering; Civil Engineering; Computer Electronics; Computer Engineering; Computer Information Systems (CIS); Computer Programming; Computer Science; Construction; Drafting/CAD; Economics; Education Admin./ Leadership; Education/Teaching; Education: Bilingual; Education: Early Childhood/ Elementary; Education: Special; Educational Counseling; Electrical Engineering; Engineering; Environmental Design/Landscaping; Environmental Management/Science; Environmental/Geological Engineering; Human Resource Management; Industrial Design; Industrial Engineering; Information Technology (IT); International Business; Management; Management Information Systems (MIS); Manufacturing Engineering; Marketing; Materials/ Manufacturing; Mechanical Engineering; Network Administration; Non-Profit Management; Nuclear Engineering; Office Administration; Public Administration; Public Relations; Supply Chain Management; or Transportation. **Criteria:** Preference will be given to the applicants who best meet the requirements.

Funds Avail.: $5,000. **To Apply:** Applications must be submitted using the HSF online application system. **Deadline:** July 16.

Remarks: In partnership with Toyota Motor Sales, USA. **Contact:** highschool@hsf.net.

3604 ▪ TU@UT HSF College Scholarship Program *(Undergraduate/Scholarship)*

Purpose: To provide financial assistance to high school seniors entering The University of Texas at Austin. **Focus:** General studies. **Qualif.:** Applicant must be of Hispanic heritage; U.S. citizen or legal permanent resident with a valid permanent resident card or passport stamped I-551; must apply by March 1 for federal financing aid using the Free Application for Federal Student Aid (FAFSA) at www-.fafsa.ed.gov; have demonstrated financial need; plan to enroll full-time at the University of Texas at Austin; be a graduate of one of the following high schools: Harlingen, Harlingen South, Rio Hondo, San Benito, Los Fresnos, Gladys Porter, Simon Rivera, James Pace, Homer Hanna, Lopez, John H. Reagan, Sidney Lanier, William B. Travis **Criteria:** Applicants who are Pell grant eligible and those who have unmet needs are given priority.

Funds Avail.: $2,500. **To Apply:** Applications must be submitted using the HSF online application system. **Deadline:** February 15. **Contact:** scholar1@hsf.net.

3605 ▪ University Alliance HSF/UGA College Scholarship Program *(Undergraduate/Scholarship)*

Purpose: To provide financial assistance to students who are classified as Georgia residents. **Focus:** General studies. **Qualif.:** Applicant must be of Hispanic heritage; U.S. citizen or legal permanent resident with a valid permanent resident card or passport stamped I-551; must apply by March 1 for federal financing aid using the Free Application for Federal Student Aid (FAFSA) at www.fafsa.ed.gov; must demonstrate financial need; have a minimum 3.0 GPA on a 4.0 scale; plan to enroll full-time at the University of Georgia. **Criteria:** Applicants who are Pell grant eligible and have demonstrated financial need are given priority.

Funds Avail.: $2,500. **To Apply:** Applicants must use the HSF online application system in applying for the scholarship. **Deadline:** March 15.

Remarks: Students planning to enroll at University of Georgia must be continuing graduates or transfer students. **Contact:** scholar1@hsf.net.

3606 ▪ Valley Alliance of Mentors for Opportunities and Scholarship (VAMOS) Program *(Undergraduate/Scholarship)*

Purpose: To assist high school seniors of Hispanic heritage from Hidalgo County in Texas obtain a bachelor's degree. **Focus:** General studies. **Qualif.:** Applicants must be of Hispanic heritage; U.S. citizen or legal permanent resident with a valid permanent resident card or passport stamped I-551; graduating high school from Hidalgo County, Texas; belong to the top 25% of high school graduating class; have a minimum GPA of 3.0 on a 4.0 scale or equivalent; plan to enroll full-time in a degree-seeking program at a four-year U.S. accredited institution in the U.S., Puerto Rico, U.S. Virgin Islands or Guam; apply for federal financing aid using the Free Application for Federal Student Aid

(FAFSA) at www.fafsa.ed.gov. **Criteria:** Applicants who best meet the requirements will be given preference.

Funds Avail.: $5,000 per year. **To Apply:** Applications must be submitted using the HSF online application system. **Deadline:** February 29. **Contact:** highschool@hsf.net.

3607 ■ Verizon Scholarship Program
(Undergraduate/Scholarship)

Purpose: To provide financial assistance to college students of Hispanic heritage. **Focus:** Accounting; Business; Economics; Finance; Personnel administration/ human resources; Marketing and distribution; Engineering, Computer; Information science and technology; Computer and information sciences; Civil engineering; Electrical engineering; Engineering, Industrial; Engineering, Mechanical. **Qualif.:** Applicant must be of Hispanic heritage; U.S. citizen or legal permanent resident with a valid permanent resident card or passport stamped I-551; enrolled as sophomore, junior or senior in a full-time degree-seeking program at an accredited U.S. institution in the U.S., Puerto Rico, U.S. Virgin Islands or Guam; have a minimum 3.0 GPA on a 4.0 scale or 4.00 on a 5.00 scale; must apply for federal financing aid using the Free Application for Federal Student Aid (FAFSA) at www.fafsa.ed.gov; must submit a resume with application; must be pursuing his/her first undergraduate degree; must be majoring in: Accounting, Business, Economics, Finance, Human Resource Management, Marketing, Computer Science, Computer Engineering, Computer Programming, Computer Electronics, Information Technology (IT), Management Information Systems (MIS), Network Administration, Computer Information Systems (CIS), Civil, Electrical, Industrial, or Mechanical Engineering; must be a resident of: (NY counties) Bronx, Kings, New York, Queens, and Richmond; (NJ) Town of Basking Ridge in Somerset County; (PA Counties) Bucks, Montgomery, Chester, Delaware, Philadelphia; (FL counties) Hernando, Hillsborough, Pasco, and Pinella; (MA counties) Essex, Middlesex, Plymouth, Suffolk; (TX counties) Collin, Dallas, Denton, Dexar, Dorris, Ellis, Henderson, Hood, Hunt, Johnson, Kaufman, Parker, Rockwall, and Tarrant; (VA county) Arlington, Loudoun; (DC) Washington; (Southern CA counties) Los Angeles, Orange, Riverside, San Bernardino, Ventura; Maine, New Hampshire, Washington State. **Criteria:** Preference will be given to the applicants who will best meet the requirements.

Funds Avail.: $5,000. **To Apply:** Applications must be submitted using the HSF online application system. **Deadline:** March 15.

Remarks: In partnership with Verizon. **Contact:** scholar1@hsf.net.

3608 ■ Wells Fargo Scholarship Program
(Graduate, Undergraduate/Scholarship)

Purpose: To assist college students who are interested in financial and banking based careers. **Focus:** Banking; Finance. **Qualif.:** Applicants must be of Hispanic heritage; U.S. citizen or legal permanent resident with a valid permanent resident card or passport stamped I-551; a sophomore enrolled full-time at a four-year accredited college/university in the U.S. (must be enrolled as a junior in the following academic year); pursuing a degree in Business, Economics, Finance, Accounting or IT, including CIS, MIS and Computer Engineering; have a minimum 3.0 GPA on a 4.0 scale or the equivalent; must apply for Federal Financing Aid. **Criteria:** Priority will be given to students from the following universities: Arizona State University, California State University - Fresno, California State University - Fullerton, California State University - San Francisco, Columbia University, Iowa State University, San Jose State University, Santa Clara University, Stanford University, Texas A&M University, University of Arizona, University of California - Berkeley, University of California - Davis, University of California - Los Angeles, University of California - San Diego, University of Minnesota, University of Southern California, University of Texas at Austin, University of Washington. Priority will also be given to residents of: Alaska, Arizona, California, Colorado, Iowa, Idaho, Illinois, Indiana, Michigan, Minnesota, Montana, Nebraska, Nevada, New Mexico, North Dakota, Ohio, Oregon, South Dakota, Texas, Utah, Washington, Wisconsin, Wyoming.

Funds Avail.: $2,000. **To Apply:** Applicants must use the HSF online application system, and visit website www.hsf-.net. **Deadline:** March 15.

Remarks: In partnership with Wells Fargo. **Contact:** scholar1@hsf.net.

3609 ■ Western Governors University Scholarship Program *(Undergraduate/Scholarship)*

Purpose: To provide financial assistance to new students of Western Governors University. **Focus:** General studies. **Qualif.:** Applicants must be of Hispanic heritage; U.S. citizen or legal permanent resident with a valid permanent resident card or passport stamped I-551; have a minimum 3.0 GPA on a 4.0 scale or the equivalent; must apply for federal financing aid using the Free Application for Federal Student Aid (FAFSA) at www.fafsa.ed.gov; be enrolled at Western Governors University. **Criteria:** Applicants who best meet the requirements will be given priority.

Funds Avail.: $1,200. **To Apply:** Applicants must use the HSF online application system. **Deadline:** 30th of each month. **Contact:** scholar1@hsf.net.

3610 ■ Holocaust and Human Rights Center of Maine

University of Maine at Augusta
46 University Dr.
Augusta, ME 04330-1644
Ph: (207)621-3530
E-mail: infohhrc@maine.edu
URL: http://www.hhrc.uma.edu

3611 ■ Lawrence Alan Spiegel Remembrance Scholarships *(Undergraduate/Scholarship)*

Purpose: To provide financial assistance for high school students residing in Maine. **Focus:** General studies. **Qualif.:** Applicants must be high school seniors or homeschoolers who are residents of Maine and who have been accepted at any accredited and Title IV eligible college, university or technical school. **Criteria:** Applicants are evaluated by a panel of judges based on submitted essay.

Funds Avail.: $1,000. **To Apply:** Applicants must write an essay on "Why is it important that the remembrance, history and lessons of the Holocaust be passed to a new generation?" The essay is not to exceed four typed, double-spaced pages. The essay must be accompanied by a self-addressed, stamped envelope and a completed application. Applications may be downloaded from the website or may be requested by mail at: Holocaust and Human Rights Center of Maine, Michael Klahr Center, Lawrence Alan Spiegel Remembrance Scholarship, University of Maine at Augusta, 46 University Drive, Augusta, ME 04330. (When

Awards are arranged alphabetically below their administering organizations

writing for an application, please include a stamped, self addressed envelope). **Deadline:** March 31.

3612 ■ Herbert Hoover Presidential Library Association

PO Box 696
West Branch, IA 52358
Ph: (319)643-5327
Fax: (319)634-2391
Free: 800-828-0475
E-mail: info@hooverassociation.org
URL: http://www.hooverassociation.org

3613 ■ Herbert Hoover Uncommon Student Awards *(Undergraduate/Scholarship)*

Purpose: To encourage academic excellence and innovativeness among young students of Iowa by providing educational assistance. **Focus:** General Studies. **Qualif.:** Applicant must be a senior in an Iowa high school or a home schooled program in the fall of 2008; program is not open to the child or grandchild of a staff member or trustee of the Hoover Library Association, Library-Museum or National Historic Site. **Criteria:** Recipients are selected from the 15 Iowa high school students who have presented their projects during their junior years on the basis of their projects and recommendations (Grades, test score, essays and financial need are not evaluated).

Funds Avail.: $5,000. **Number Awarded:** 3. **To Apply:** Applicant must submit completed application available in the website, along with project proposal and two letters of recommendation (recommendation forms are available at the website and must be sent separately) to: Hoover Library Association, P.O. Box 696, West Branch, IA 52358. **Deadline:** March 31. **Contact:** Patricia Hand, Mgr. of Academic Programs, Tel: 319-643-5327 or 800-828-0475, email: scholarship@hooverassociation.org.

3614 ■ Hormel Foods Corporation

Hormel Pl.
Austin, MN 55912
Ph: (507)437-5345
Free: 800-523-4635
E-mail: media@hormel.com
URL: http://www.hormelfoods.com

3615 ■ Hormel Foods Charitable Trust Scholarships *(Undergraduate/Scholarship)*

Purpose: To help academically-talented students to obtain college scholarships. **Focus:** General studies. **Qualif.:** Applicants must be high school senior students who will enter an accredited college. **Criteria:** Recipients are selected based on financial need, scholastic abilities, involvement in school or community activities and leadership qualities.

Funds Avail.: Maximum amount of $3,000. **To Apply:** Applicants must submit a complete application form and Preliminary Scholastic Aptitude Test Scores.

3616 ■ Hospitality Association of South Carolina

PO Box 7577
Columbia, SC 29201
Ph: (803)765-9000
Fax: (803)252-7136
Free: 800-803-4272
E-mail: tom@schospitality.org
URL: http://www.schospitality.org

3617 ■ Prostart National Certificate of Achievement Scholarships *(Undergraduate/Scholarship)*

Purpose: To encourage educational pursuits by providing financial assistance. **Focus:** Culinary Arts. **Qualif.:** Applicants must be students who earned a Prostart National Certificate of Achievement; must be citizens or permanent residents of the United States of America; and must be graduating high school seniors or juniors who will study culinary arts and food service management at accredited culinary schools, colleges or universities. **Criteria:** Recipients are selected based on presentation, case study and GPA.

Funds Avail.: $2,000. **To Apply:** Applicants must have a signed hard copy of the online application, signed by the parents or guardian if under 18; must submit typed case-study; a copy of current high school transcript of records; if you are graduating senior, transcript must include grades of senior year and a letter of acceptance from the culinary school, college or university; must include a letter of intent stating the plan to enroll in an accredited restaurant or food service program for a minimum of nine credits for high school juniors. **Deadline:** August 15. **Contact:** 175 West Jackson Blvd., Ste. 1500 Chicago, IL 60604-2702.

3618 ■ South Carolina Tourism and Hospitality Educational Foundation Scholarships *(Undergraduate/Scholarship)*

Purpose: To provide educational assistance for students who demonstrate an interest in and commitment to the hospitality (restaurant, lodging tourism) industry. **Focus:** Travel and tourism. **Qualif.:** Applicants must be currently employed in the hospitality industry and/or enrolled in an industry-related educational program at an accredited institution. **Criteria:** Recipients are selected based on presentation of application, strength of letters of recommendation, a well-written and within word count essay, industry-related work experience and GPA.

Funds Avail.: No specific amount. **To Apply:** Applicants must submit a completed application form; three letters of reference; three completed Character Reference Forms; current official transcript; and a double-spaced essay (minimum of 500 words and maximum of 1,000 words). **Deadline:** April 11. **Contact:** PO Box 7577 Columbia, SC 29202.

3619 ■ South Carolina Undergraduate Scholarships *(Undergraduate/Scholarship)*

Purpose: To encourage educational pursuits by providing financial assistance. **Focus:** Culinary arts. **Qualif.:** Applicants must be enrolled in a post-secondary restaurant/hospitality program and must be attending an accredited post college or university in South Carolina. **Criteria:** Recipients are selected based on financial need and academic performance.

Funds Avail.: No specific amount. **To Apply:** Applicants must submit a completed application form along with a one-to-two-page essay outlining their career goals and dreams. **Contact:** monica@schospitality.org.

3620 ■ Houghton Mifflin Company

222 Berkeley St.
Boston, MA 02116

Awards are arranged alphabetically below their administering organizations

Ph: (617)351-5000
URL: http://www.hmco.com

3621 ■ Gerda and Kurt Klein Scholarships *(High School/Scholarship)*

Purpose: To provide financial assistance to high school student working to affect change in the community. **Focus:** General studies. **Qualif.:** Applicant must be a high school student who works to affect change in the community by fostering ethnic and religious tolerance and acting against bigotry and hatred. **Criteria:** Award is given based on the submitted application materials.

Funds Avail.: $10,000. **Number Awarded:** 1. **To Apply:** Applicants must submit a completed scholarship application form, 500-word essay, letter of recommendation and official high school transcript in one envelope to Gerda and Kurt Klein Scholarships, c/o Houghton Mifflin Harcourt Scholarships 6277 Sea Harbor Drive Orlando, FL 32887. **Deadline:** August 30.

3622 ■ Houtan Scholarship Foundation

300 Central Ave.
Egg Harbor Township, NJ 08234
Ph: (609)653-9317
Fax: (609)926-2020
E-mail: info@houtan.org
URL: http://www.houtan.org

3623 ■ Houtan Scholarships *(Graduate/Scholarship)*

Purpose: To promote Iranian studies. **Focus:** Area and ethnic studies. **Qualif.:** Applicants should have a working knowledge of Farsi and should demonstrate an active interest in Iranian culture, heritage and literature; must be attending or anticipate attending an accredited graduate school; must have superior academic performance or a significant increase of academic performance over the course of the academic career; and may have financial need. **Criteria:** Recipient is selected based on submitted documents, financial need, and the interview.

Funds Avail.: $2,500. **Number Awarded:** 1. **To Apply:** Applicants must submit a completed application form along with two letters of recommendation, college transcript, and goals and aspirations essay. **Deadline:** June 1 and October 1. **Contact:** at the above address (see entry 3622).

3624 ■ Human Race Theatre Company

126 N Main St., Ste. 300
Dayton, OH 45402-1710
Ph: (937)461-3823
Fax: (937)461-7223
E-mail: contact@humanracetheatre.org
URL: http://www.humanracetheatre.org

3625 ■ Stephen Schwartz Musical Theatre Scholarships *(Undergraduate/Scholarship)*

Purpose: To support singers/actors in the greater Dayton area who are training for a career in musical theatre. **Focus:** Theater arts. **Qualif.:** Applicants must have a permanent address in Montgomery County or one of seven contiguous counties (Preble, Darke, Miami, Clark, Greene, Warren or Butler); must be currently enrolled at a college in one of the eight counties previously listed. High school senior applicants must be currently applying or accepted into a college program and have plans to train in musical theatre. College student must be currently training for a career in musical theatre. **Criteria:** Awards are given based on the auditions and applications.

Funds Avail.: $1,500 for high school senior; $3,500 for a college student. **Number Awarded:** 2. **To Apply:** Applicants may contact the Executive Director of The Human Race Theatre Company for more information about the scholarship.

Remarks: Established in honor of musical theatre legend Stephen Schwartz. **Contact:** Kevin Moore, Executive Director, at 937-461-3823 x3115, or email kevin@humanracetheatre.org.

3626 ■ Human Resources Research Management

66 Canal Center Plz., Ste. 400
Alexandria, VA 22314
Ph: (703)549-3611
Fax: (703)549-9025
URL: http://www.humrro.org

3627 ■ Meredith P. Crawford Fellowship in I/O Psychology *(Undergraduate/Fellowship)*

Purpose: To provide financial support while the student completes his/her dissertation in the field of Industrial-Organizational (I-O) Psychology, or in a field congruent with the objectives of the Society for Industrial Psychology, Inc. (SIOP). **Focus:** Psychology. **Qualif.:** Applicants must be doctoral candidates whose dissertation topic has been proposed and approved by his/ her graduate faculty in Industrial-Organizational (I-O) Psychology, Inc. **Criteria:** Applicants will be evaluated on the basis of their merit, research promise, academic achievement, and professional productivity.

Funds Avail.: $12,000. **Number Awarded:** 1. **To Apply:** Applicants must provide a completed application form, a personal statement, three completed recommendation forms, and an official transcript from each institution attended for graduate academic work. **Deadline:** March 14.

3628 ■ Hungarian American Coalition

1120 Connecticut Ave. NW, Ste. 280
Washington, DC 20036
Ph: (202)296-9505
Fax: (202)775-5175
E-mail: hac@hacusa.org
URL: http://www.hacusa.org

3629 ■ Dr. Elemer and Eva Kiss Scholarships Fund *(Undergraduate/Scholarship)*

Purpose: To provide partial annual scholarships for Hungarian students who will be admitted at any U.S. college or university. **Focus:** General studies. **Qualif.:** Applicant must be a citizen of Hungary or a member of an ethnic Hungarian community in Slovakia, Romania, Voivodina, Serbia, or Ukraine; must have gained admission as a full-time student to a U.S. college or university. **Criteria:** Preference will be given to deserving students.

Funds Avail.: $1,000. **Number Awarded:** 2-4. **To Apply:** Applicants must provide proof of scholarship and other sources of financial support; record of excellent academic

Awards are arranged alphabetically below their administering organizations

standing; and two letters of recommendation regarding the applicant's personal and academic achievements.

Remarks: Scholarship recipients are asked to provide a copy of their registration form and are expected to keep the Coalition informed of their academic progress. **Contact:** Hungarian American Coalition at the above address (see entry 3628).

3630 ■ Huntington's Disease Society of America

505 8th Ave., Ste. 902
New York, NY 10018
Ph: (212)242-1968
Fax: (212)239-3430
Free: 800-345-4372
E-mail: hdsainfo@hdsa.org
URL: http://www.hdsa.org

3631 ■ HDSA Research Fellowships *(Postdoctorate/Fellowship)*

Purpose: To help promising postdoctoral investigators in the early stages of their careers. **Focus:** Huntington's disease. **Qualif.:** Applicants must be investigators who want to enter the field of HD research. **Criteria:** Recipients are selected according to the potential of their research.

Funds Avail.: $40,000. **Number Awarded:** 3.

3632 ■ HDSA Research Grants *(Other/Grant)*

Purpose: To provide seed funding for new or innovative research projects. **Focus:** Huntington's disease. **Qualif.:** Applicants must be principal investigators. **Criteria:** Recipients are selected based on the potential of their research.

Funds Avail.: $50,000. **Number Awarded:** 1.

3633 ■ Don King Student Fellowships *(Undergraduate/Fellowship)*

Purpose: To sponsor HD investigations that can be conducted over a 10-week period. **Focus:** Huntington's disease. **Qualif.:** Applicants must be matriculated undergraduate life sciences students, pre-medical students, and first-year medical students who are currently attending accredited institutions in the United States where HDSA sponsors ongoing HD research. **Criteria:** Recipient will be selected based on the academic credentials, scientific merit of the proposed project and the relevance of the proposal to HD.

Funds Avail.: $3,000. **Deadline:** May 1.

3634 ■ Hydrocephalus Association

870 Market St., Ste. 705
San Francisco, CA 94102
Ph: (415)732-7040
Fax: (415)732-7044
Free: 888-598-3789
E-mail: info@hydroassoc.org
URL: http://www.hydroassoc.org

3635 ■ Anthony Abbene Scholarships *(Undergraduate/Scholarship)*

Purpose: To offer scholarships to young adults with hydrocephalus. **Focus:** General studies. **Qualif.:** Applicants must be between 17 and 30 years old and have hydrocephalus. **Criteria:** Priority will be given to those students who meet the criteria.

Funds Avail.: $500. **To Apply:** Applicants must check the available website for details. **Deadline:** April 1.

Remarks: This fund was established in 2002 by Anthony Abbene's extended family. Anthony is a teenager with hydrocephalus. This fund awards two scholarships in honor of Anthony and to help others with hydrocephalus with their education. **Contact:** Hydrocephalus Association at the above address (see entry 3634).

3636 ■ Justin Scot Alston Memorial Scholarships *(Undergraduate/Scholarship)*

Purpose: To offer scholarships to young adults with hydrocephalus. **Focus:** General studies. **Qualif.:** Applicants must be between 17 and 30 years old and have hydrocephalus. **Criteria:** Priority will be given to those students who meet the criteria.

Funds Avail.: $500. **To Apply:** Applicants must check the available website for details. **Deadline:** April 1.

Remarks: Gloria M. Alston established this scholarship in loving memory of her son, Justin Scot Alston, who died in 2004. Justin received a Hydrocephalus Association scholarship in 2002 and will be remembered for his tremendous upbeat attitude and for all that he accomplished during his short life. **Contact:** Hydrocephalus Association at the above address (see entry 3634).

3637 ■ Laura Beckley Barsotti Memorial Scholarships *(Undergraduate/Scholarship)*

Purpose: To offer scholarships to young adults with hydrocephalus. **Focus:** General studies. **Qualif.:** Applicants must be between 17 and 30 years old and have hydrocephalus. **Criteria:** Priority will be given to those students who meet the criteria.

Funds Avail.: $500. **To Apply:** Applicants must check the available website for details. **Deadline:** April 1.

Remarks: The Beckley-Clark family established this scholarship in 2008 in loving memory of Laura Beckley Barsotti. Of particular interest are candidates who express an interest in education or social work. **Contact:** Hydrocephalus Association at the above address (see entry 3634).

3638 ■ Gerard Swartz Fudge Memorial Scholarships *(Undergraduate/Scholarship)*

Purpose: To offer scholarships to young adults with hydrocephalus. **Focus:** General studies. **Qualif.:** Applicants must be between 17 and 30 years old and have hydrocephalus. **Criteria:** Priority will be given to those students who meet the criteria.

Funds Avail.: $500. **To Apply:** Applicants must check the available website for details. **Deadline:** April 1.

Remarks: This fund was established in 1994 by the Fudge family. Their son, Gerard, had hydrocephalus and died in 1992 at the age of 22 in the midst of his college experience. **Contact:** Hydrocephalus Association at the above address (see entry 3634).

3639 ■ Mario J. Tocco Hydrocephalus Foundation Scholarships *(Undergraduate/Scholarship)*

Purpose: To offer scholarships to young adults with hydrocephalus. **Focus:** General studies. **Qualif.:** Applicants must be between 17 and 30 years old and have hydrocephalus.

Awards are arranged alphabetically below their administering organizations

Criteria: Priority will be given to those students who meet the criteria.

Funds Avail.: $500. **To Apply:** Applicants must check the available website for details. **Deadline:** April 1.

Remarks: Greg and Georgana Tocco and their families established this scholarship in 2007 in loving memory of Greg's grandfather, Mario, and in honor of the Hydrocephalus Foundation, Inc of Saugus, MA. **Contact:** Hydrocephalus Association at the above address (see entry 3634).

3640 ■ Morris and Rebecca Ziskind Memorial Scholarships *(Undergraduate/Scholarship)*

Purpose: To offer scholarships to young adults with hydrocephalus. **Focus:** General studies. **Qualif.:** Applicants must be between 17 and 30 years old and have hydrocephalus. **Criteria:** Priority will be given to those students who meet the criteria.

Funds Avail.: $500. **To Apply:** Applicants must check the available website for details. **Deadline:** April 1.

Remarks: This fund was established in 2001 by Rebecca Ziskind and her family in memory of her husband, Dr. Morris Ziskind, who had NPH. After Rebecca Ziskind's death in 2005, their three surviving children and their spouses-Carrie and Dee Norton, Jerome and Rosemary Ziskind, and Janet and Charles Tarino-graciously funded one more scholarship in loving memory of their parents, so that two scholarships are now awarded from this fund. **Contact:** Hydrocephalus Association at the above address (see entry 3634).

3641 ■ Ice Skating Institute of America

17120 N Dallas Pkwy., Ste. 140
Dallas, TX 75248-1187
Ph: (972)735-8800
Fax: (972)735-8815
E-mail: isiaef@skateisi.org
URL: http://www.skateisi.com

3642 ■ Ice Skating Institute of America Education Foundation *(Undergraduate/Scholarship)*

Purpose: To promote the intellectual growth of ISI member skaters. **Focus:** General studies. **Qualif.:** Applicants must have completed at least three years of high school or equivalent, with a minimum 3.0 grade point average (based on a 4.0 system) during the last two years; must be a current individual or professional member of the Ice Skating Institute and have been for a minimum of four years; must have participated in the ISI Recreational Skater Program at an ISI Administrative member (rink or club) program for a minimum of four years; must have participated in ISI group classes or ISI Endorsed Competitions within the last two years. Must have completed 120 hours of volunteer service, of which at least 60 hours must be in association with an ISI member facility; must enroll and carry the minimum number of credit hours necessary to be a full time undergraduate student. Teachers or instructors must be a current Professional Member of the Ice Skating Institute, teaching the ISI program at an ISI Administrative Member (rink or club). Instructor status must be verified by the ISI Administrative Member. **Criteria:** Final selection will be made by the Trustees of the ISIA Education Foundation.

Funds Avail.: $4,000. **Number Awarded:** Varies. **To Apply:** Applicants must submit completed application form, two evaluation forms (one from the supervisor at the site where a majority of the volunteer service took place and the second from an adult not associated with ice skating and not a relative of the applicant) and a statement of 500 words or less, typed or printed explaining "Why I should receive an ISIA Education Foundation Scholarship." **Deadline:** March 1.

3643 ■ Idaho Community Foundation

210 W State St.
Boise, ID 83702
Ph: (208)342-3535
Fax: (208)342-3577
Free: 800-657-5357
E-mail: info@idcomfdn.org
URL: http://www.idcomfdn.org

3644 ■ Mike Crapo Math and Science Scholarship Fund *(Undergraduate/Scholarship)*

Purpose: To assist Idaho students who are interested in pursuing math and science degrees at Idaho college and universities. **Focus:** Mathematics and mathematical sciences. **Qualif.:** Applicants must be students pursuing math and science degrees at Idaho colleges and universities. **Criteria:** Recipients are selected based on financial need and academic performance.

Funds Avail.: No specific amount. **To Apply:** Applicants must submit a "300-word or less" original essay discussing the value of math and science to an individual and society as a whole; most recent certified transcript from high school and higher education institution; two letters of reference from teacher/professor of math or science and from two members of the community who are not relatives and ACT/SAT Assessment Report. **Deadline:** April 30.

3645 ■ Goldmann Scholarships Fund *(Undergraduate/Scholarship)*

Purpose: To promote greater understanding of the Holocaust among high school students in Idaho. **Focus:** General studies. **Qualif.:** Applicants must be senior students in an accredited high school or home school in Idaho; must have plans to attend an accredited Idaho Institution of higher learning during the academic year. **Criteria:** Recipients are selected based on originality of an essay or research paper.

Funds Avail.: $1,200. **To Apply:** Applicants must submit a formal research paper, bibliography and references. **Deadline:** April 15.

3646 ■ Idaho Nursing Scholarships *(Undergraduate/Scholarship)*

Purpose: To assist recipients with educational expenses at any Idaho accredited nursing program. **Focus:** Nursing. **Qualif.:** Applicants must be students that have been accepted by an accredited Idaho nursing program or be in the top third of the academic ranking of the class. **Criteria:** Recipients are selected based on financial need.

Funds Avail.: No specific amount. **To Apply:** Applicants must send three copies of signed and completed application form. **Deadline:** April 30.

3647 ■ Idaho Society of CPA's Scholarships *(Undergraduate/Scholarship)*

Purpose: To attract the best and brightest students to the profession pursuing an accounting degree at an Idaho school. **Focus:** Accounting. **Qualif.:** Applicants must be

Awards are arranged alphabetically below their administering organizations

residents of Idaho; must be enrolled as full-time students at the junior or senior level of public or private college or university in the state of Idaho majoring in accounting; must have a cumulative GPA of 2.75 or above for all class work prior to the application. **Criteria:** Recipients are selected based on GPA or academic standing, individual achievement as evidenced through participation in outside and activities, leadership roles, work experience and sincere desire for further education or training.

Funds Avail.: $1,000. **To Apply:** Applicants must submit a completed application form. **Deadline:** April 16.

3648 ■ Jim Poore Memorial Scholarship *(Undergraduate/Scholarship)*

Purpose: To encourage and promote the attainment of higher education goals for students who have demonstrated an aptitude for and an interest in writing. **Focus:** Writing. **Qualif.:** Applicants must be graduating seniors from public or private school of Ada, Adams, Boise, Canyon, Elmore, Gem, Payette, Valley, Washington or a high school serving the Marsing, Homedale, Bruneau or Riggins communities. **Criteria:** Recipients are selected based on general school record, community activities, writing sample and an oral interview in Boise by Committee Members.

Funds Avail.: $1,000. **To Apply:** Applicants must submit a completed application form. **Deadline:** April 15.

3649 ■ Roger C. Sathre Memorial Scholarship Fund *(Undergraduate/Scholarship)*

Purpose: To recognize and encourage outstanding Idaho students pursuing first certificates or degree in professional-technical education or professional-technical teacher education at Idaho Schools. **Focus:** General studies. **Qualif.:** Applicants must be residents of Idaho; must have graduated from an accredited public or private high school in Idaho or equivalent; must have maintained a cumulative GPA of 2.5 or better during the previous two years of school at an accredited high school or post-secondary school; must be enrolled as full-time students as defined by the school in a professional-technical or professional-technical teacher education program at an accredited college or university in Idaho; must be pursuing an undergraduate course of consecutive attendance and leading to a first degree, technical certificate or other approved award. **Criteria:** Recipients are selected based on financial need.

Funds Avail.: $500. **To Apply:** Applicants must submit a completed application form; must write an essay identifying the reasons for wanting to pursue the chosen field; must obtain two letters of recommendation, report documenting financial need and portfolio of academic and technical achievement. **Deadline:** February 1.

3650 ■ W.L. Shattuck Scholarship *(Undergraduate/Scholarship)*

Purpose: To further the education of students at an accredited college, university or technical college. **Focus:** General studies. **Qualif.:** Applicants must be students who are high school graduates of Idaho Falls School District 91 or Bonneville School District 93 not younger than 16 or older than 26 years old; must be accepted and enrolled at an accredited higher education or technical education program. **Criteria:** Recipients are selected based on financial need.

Funds Avail.: $1,000. **To Apply:** Applicants must submit a completed application form; an official high school transcript; two letters of recommendation; resume and short statement of educational goals; must also submit the names and addresses of higher education or technical education programs to be attended and three copies of an original completed application form. **Deadline:** April 24. **Contact:** 208-525-7500 ext. 274.

3651 ■ Idaho Nursery and Landscape Association

PO Box 2065
Idaho Falls, ID 83403
Ph: (208)522-7307
Fax: (208)529-0832
Free: 800-462-4769
E-mail: abates@inlagrow.org
URL: http://www.inlagrow.org

3652 ■ Idaho Nursery and Landscape Association Scholarships *(Undergraduate/Scholarship)*

Purpose: To encourage the study of Horticulture, Floriculture, Plant Pathology, Landscape Design, Turfgrass Management, Botany and allied subjects that pertain to the Green Industry. **Focus:** Horticulture. **Qualif.:** Applicants must be students in an accredited two or four-year program in the State of Idaho pursuing studies in the Green Industry. **Criteria:** Recipients are selected based on scholastic record and student's ability and sincerity in pursuing employment in the Green Industry.

Funds Avail.: $750. **To Apply:** Applicants must submit "one-page, typed" essay stating their reasons for interest in this particular field of endeavor, future plans and goals; must submit a letter of recommendation from someone in the community who will evaluate citizenship; must submit school transcript and letter of recommendation from a professor in the applicant's major field of study. **Contact:** Ann Bates at the above address (see entry 3651).

3653 ■ Illinois Association of Chamber of Commerce Executives

215 E. Adams
Springfield, IL 62701
Ph: (217)522-5512
Fax: (217)522-5518
E-mail: info@iacce.org
URL: http://www.iacce.org

3654 ■ Illinois Association of Chamber of Commerce Executives Scholarships *(Postdoctorate/Scholarship)*

Purpose: To become an accessible and valued resource for the professional development of Chamber of Commerce Executives and staff members in Illinois. **Focus:** General studies. **Qualif.:** Applicants must be students enrolled in a Master's degree program. **Criteria:** Recipients are selected based on rating scale which include the thoroughness of comments, information, verification and explanation, presentation of materials and financial need.

Funds Avail.: No specific amount. **To Apply:** Applicants must complete the application form.

3655 ■ Illinois Landscape Contractors Association

2625 Buterfield Rd., Ste. 204 W
Oak Brook, IL 60523

Awards are arranged alphabetically below their administering organizations

Ph: (630)472-2851
Fax: (630)472-3150
E-mail: sgrams@ilca.net
URL: http://www.ilca.net

3656 ■ Illinois Landscape Contractors Association Scholarships *(Undergraduate/Scholarship)*

Purpose: To enhance the professionalism and capabilities of members by providing leadership, education and valued services while promoting environmental awareness within the landscape industry. **Focus:** Horticulture. **Qualif.:** Applicants must be residents of Illinois and enrolled full-time in an accredited two or four-year college horticultural program in Illinois or a bordering state. **Criteria:** Recipients are selected based on academic performance and financial need.

Funds Avail.: Varies. **To Apply:** Applicants must submit a completed application form; a letter describing their goals and aspirations in the field of horticulture, a transcript of record; must attach evaluation/letters from employers, internships, work study or any horticulture/landscape experience. **Deadline:** February 28. **Contact:** 630-472-2851.

3657 ■ Illinois Society of Professional Engineers

600 S 2nd St., Ste. 403
Springfield, IL 62704
Ph: (217)544-7424
Fax: (217)528-6545
E-mail: info@illinoisengineer.com
URL: http://www.illinoisengineer.com

3658 ■ ISPE/M.E. Amstutz Memorial Award *(Undergraduate/Scholarship)*

Purpose: To provide financial assistance for the education of students for the advancement and betterment of human welfare and the engineering profession. **Focus:** Engineering. **Qualif.:** Applicants must be enrolled in an ABETaccredited engineering program, be at least a junior maintaining a B average or better, and demonstrate financial need. **Criteria:** Recipients are judged based on financial need, extracurricular activities, interest in engineering and the applicants' essays.

Funds Avail.: $1,500. **To Apply:** Applicants must submit official transcripts of all college and university work; two letters of reference from the department chair or department faculty member; from past employer or other character reference; and a typewritten essay in 200 words or less discussing why they want to become a professional engineer. **Deadline:** January 31.

3659 ■ ISPE Advantage Award/Foundation Scholarships *(Undergraduate/Scholarship)*

Purpose: To provide financial assistance for the education of students who are sons or daughters of ISPE members; for the advancement and betterment of human welfare and the engineering profession. **Focus:** Engineering. **Qualif.:** Applicants must be attending an Illinois university; enrolled in an engineering program accredited by the Accreditation Board of Engineering and Technology (ABET); have at least junior standing; a B average or better in courses which are credited toward the engineering degree. **Criteria:** Recipients are judged based on financial need, extracurricular activities, interest in engineering and the applicants' essays.

Funds Avail.: $1,200. **To Apply:** Applicants must submit official transcripts of all college and university work; two letters of reference from the department chair or department faculty member; from past employer or other character reference; and typewritten essay in 200 words or less discussing why they want to become a professional engineer. **Deadline:** January 31.

3660 ■ Illinois Student Assistance Commission

1755 Lake Cook Rd.
Deerfield, IL 60015-5209
Ph: 800-899-4722
E-mail: collegezone@isac.org
URL: http://www.collegezone.com

3661 ■ Allied Health Care Professional Scholarships *(Undergraduate/Scholarship)*

Purpose: To increase the number of nurse practitioners, physician assistants and certified nurse midwives practicing in areas of Illinois. To provide financial support to a qualified allied health care professional students. **Focus:** Allied health. **Qualif.:** Applicant must be nurse practitioner, physician assistant or certified nurse midwife student must be accepted or enrolled in a school located in Illinois and accredited in its field; must be fulltime or part-time students, although part-time students must be enrolled for at least one-third of the number of hours required per term by the school for its full-time students; must demonstrate financial need and must apply to their school's financial aid department on or before the school's designated application deadline date. **Criteria:** Preference will be given to applicants who demonstrated: (1) Previous experience with medically underserved populations; (2) Greatest financial need; and (3) Academic capabilities.

Funds Avail.: $7,500. **To Apply:** Applicant must complete the application forms available online; must have the financial aid award information; must have the proof of enrollment or letter of acceptance into the program. Application form must be sent to: Allied Health Care Professional Scholarship Program, Illinois Department of Public Health, Center for Rural Health, 535 W Jefferson St., Springfield, IL 62761. **Deadline:** June 30.

3662 ■ Robert C. Byrd Honors Scholarships *(Undergraduate/Scholarship)*

Purpose: To provide financial support to deserving individuals who have outstanding academic achievements. **Focus:** General studies. **Qualif.:** Applicant must be a U.S citizen or an eligible non-citizen; must be an Illinois resident; must be an Illinois high school graduate; must be enrolled, or accepted for enrollment on a full-time basis, as an undergraduate student at a U.S Department of Education-approved college in the United States. **Criteria:** Selection of awardees within each Illinois geographic district will be based on their academic performance data reported by the high school at the end of the third semester prior to graduation and by the ACT, SAT, or Prairie State Achievement Exam scores reported by the end of the third semester before high school graduation.

Funds Avail.: $1,500. **To Apply:** Applicant must complete the eligibility certification form and must be sent to ISAC, 775 Lake Cook Rd., Deerfield, IL 60015-5209. **Deadline:** July 15.

3663 ■ Illinois Future Teacher Corps Scholarships *(Undergraduate/Scholarship)*

Purpose: To provide financial support to deserving individuals intending to pursue their careers as teachers. **Focus:**

Awards are arranged alphabetically below their administering organizations

Teaching. **Qualif.:** Applicant must be a U.S citizen or an eligible non-citizen; must be a resident of Illinois; must be a high school graduate or person who has received a General Education Development certificate; must be enrolled, or accepted for enrollment as a junior or above, on at least a half-time basis in a Teacher Education Program at an eligible Illinois public or private college, seeking initial teacher certification; must be pursuing additional coursework needed to gain Illinois State Board of Education approval to teach, including alternative teacher certification; must maintain a cumulative grade point average of 2.5 on a 4.0 scale; must maintain satisfactory academic progress as determined by the college. **Criteria:** Selection will be based on academic performance and eligibility requirements. Priority is given to individuals intending to pursue a teacher shortage discipline and/or making a commitment to teach at a hard-to-staff school and minority students.

Funds Avail.: $5,000 or $10,000 depending on the teaching commitment made. **To Apply:** Applicant must complete the application for Teacher Education Scholarship Programs; must sign the application's Teaching Agreement/ Promissory Note promising to fulfill the teaching commitment or repay funds received, plus interest. **Deadline:** March 1.

3664 ■ Illinois Special Education Teacher Tuition Waiver Scholarships *(Undergraduate/ Scholarship)*

Purpose: To provide support to deserving individuals intending to pursue their career in special education programs. **Focus:** Special education. **Qualif.:** Applicant must be a U.S. citizen or an eligible non-citizen; must be an Illinois resident; must have graduated from an approved high school in the academic year in the upper half of their graduating class according to performance-based academic data provided by the high school; or graduated from an approved high school prior to the academic year in which the award is made, and must hold a valid teaching certificate that is not in the discipline of special education; must be enrolled, or accepted for enrollment, at one of the eligible public four-year colleges in Illinois as an undergraduate or graduate student seeking initial certification in any area of special education; must be enrolled in a program of special education within ten days after the beginning of the term for which the waiver was initially awarded; must comply with federal Selective Service registration requirements. **Criteria:** Candidates will be selected based on their academic standing and eligibility requirements.

Funds Avail.: Full tuition and mandatory fees. **To Apply:** Application forms are available online at the College Zone. **Deadline:** March 1.

3665 ■ Illinois Student Assistance Commission Medical Student Scholarships *(Graduate/ Scholarship)*

Purpose: To financially support the qualified medical students. **Focus:** Osteopathic medicine, Medical technology. **Qualif.:** Applicant must be an approved allopathic or osteopathic medical school in Illinois; must agree to work in an identified physician-shortage area in Illinois; must be an Illinois resident; must demonstrate financial need, and be committed to primary care; must be a student waiting for confirmation of acceptance to medical school. **Criteria:** Preference will be given to applicants who demonstrate: (1) A commitment to primary health care; (2) Financial need; and (3) Prior experience with populations whose health care needs are underserved.

Funds Avail.: $950. **To Apply:** Applicant must complete the application form available online; must provide a autobiographical profile; must have one of the following: (1) For students entering medical school for the first year-a copy of AMCAS application or AACOMAS applicant profile; (2) For all other medical students-a transcript or verification from the college of the GPA or academic standing. **Deadline:** May 15.

3666 ■ Illinois Student Assistance Commission Merit Recognition Scholarships *(Undergraduate/ Scholarship)*

Purpose: To provide financial support to qualified individuals intending to pursue their education. **Focus:** General studies. **Qualif.:** Applicant must be a U.S citizen or an eligible non-citizen; must be a resident of Illinois; must be in the top five percent of their high school class; must take the ACT, SAT or Prairie State Achievement Exam; must attend an approved, Illinois postsecondary institution as an undergraduate on at least a half-time basis, or attend one of the nation's four approved Military Science Academies; must comply with federal Selective Service registration requirements. **Criteria:** Applicant will be selected based on the eligibility requirements.

Funds Avail.: $1,000. **To Apply:** Scholarship application and application documents must be sent to ISAC, 1775 Lake Cook Rd., Deerfield, IL 60015-5209. **Deadline:** June 15.

3667 ■ Illinois Student Assistance Commission Nurse Educator Scholarships *(Undergraduate/ Scholarship)*

Purpose: To provide financial support to a qualified individual intending to pursue a career in professional or practical nursing education in Illinois. **Focus:** Practical nursing. **Qualif.:** Applicant must be a U.S citizen or an eligible non-citizen; must be an Illinois resident; must be a recipient of at least a bachelor's degree; must be enrolled, or accepted for enrollment, on at least a half-time basis in an approved program of practical nursing education at the graduate level at an eligible Illinois college; must have a satisfactory academic progress as determined by the college; must comply with federal Selective Service registration requirements. **Criteria:** Selection of candidates will be based on the following criteria: (1) Cumulative GPA (converted to a 4.0 scale) are prioritized from highest to lowest; (2) EFCs are prioritized from lowest to highest; (3) Renewal applicants receive priority consideration provided that they: maintain their qualified applicant status by continuing to meet all criteria listed under the eligibility section that appears earlier on this page, and submit the renewal application on a timely basis. Priority consideration is given to the qualified applicant who submits a complete application on the earliest date.

Funds Avail.: $10,000 to cover the cost of attendance, including living expenses. **To Apply:** Application forms are available to download and print from College Zone. **Deadline:** March 1.

3668 ■ Illinois Student Assistance Commission Nursing Education Scholarships *(Undergraduate/ Scholarship)*

Purpose: To provide financial assistance to qualified individuals pursuing an associate degree in nursing, an associate degree in applied sciences in nursing, a hospital based diploma in nursing, a baccalaureate degree in nursing, a graduate degree in nursing or a certificate in practical nursing. **Focus:** Nursing. **Qualif.:** Applicant must be a resident of Illinois for at least one year prior to application, and be a citizen or lawful permanent resident alien of the United States; must be enrolled in or accepted for admission to a nursing program in Illinois that is approved by the Illinois Department of Financial and Professional Regulation, Division of Professional Regulation; must be in need of financial assistance based on applicant's Student Aid Report. **Criteria:** Recipients will be selected based on the following criteria: (1) Renewal recipients will receive preference; (2) If the number of qualified applicants exceeds the number of scholarships to be awarded, priority in awarding scholarships will be given to students who: (a) Have the greatest financial need per the Student Aid Report; (b) Are full-time or closest to full-time students; (c) Have the fewest number of credit hours remaining to complete their nursing degree; (c) Already have an associate degree or hospital-based diploma in nursing or a certificate in practical nursing and are pursuing a higher degree; (d) Have the highest cumulative grade point average as documented on an official transcript or other official school form.; (3) When all criteria are equal, a lottery may be used to determine scholarships.

Funds Avail.: $1,603-$5,943. **To Apply:** Applicant must submit a completed, signed and dated application form prior to the deadline; must have a copy of his/her Illinois registered professional nurse license or Illinois practical nurse license; must include a current copy of an official transcript or other current official school form that indicates a cumulative grade point average; must include a copy of a current Student Aid Report (SAR) that indicates an estimated financial contribution. A current SAR is required, even if you are not eligible for or have not applied for other financial assistance. **Deadline:** May 31.

3669 ■ Illinois Student Assistance Commission Podiatric Scholarship Program *(Undergraduate/Scholarship)*

Purpose: To increase the number of podiatric physicians practicing in underserved areas of Illinois. **Focus:** Podiatry. **Qualif.:** Applicant must be a podiatric medicine student; must be an Illinois resident at the time of application and must be accepted or enrolled in a school located in Illinois and accredited in its field; must demonstrate financial need and must apply to their school's financial aid department on or before the school's designated application deadline date. **Criteria:** Preference will be given to the applicants who demonstrate (1) Previous experience with medically underserved populations; (2) financial need; and (3) commitment to practicing in a designated underserved area of Illinois.

Funds Avail.: Awards provides full tuition, matriculation fees and a living stipend. **To Apply:** Applicant must complete the application form available online; must have the financial aid award information; must provide the proof of enrollment or letter of acceptance into the program. Application materials must be sent to: Illinois Podiatric Scholarship Program, Illinois Department of Public Health, Center for Rural Health, 535 W Jefferson St., Springfield, IL 62761. **Deadline:** June 30.

3670 ■ Minority Teachers of Illinois Scholarships *(Undergraduate/Scholarship)*

Purpose: To provide financial support to the qualified individuals intending to pursue their careers as a preschool, elementary or secondary school teacher. **Focus:** Teaching. **Qualif.:** Applicant must be a U.S citizen or an eligible noncitizen; must be a resident of Illinois; must be either a African American/ Black, Hispanic American, Asian American or Native American origin; must be a high school graduate, or hold a General Educational Development certificate; must be enrolled at least a hal-time basis as an undergraduate or graduate student; must be enrolled or accepted for enrollment at a qualified Illinois institutions of higher education in a course of study which, upon completion, qualifies to be certified as a preschool, elementary or secondary school teacher by the Illinois State Board of Education, including alternative teacher certification; must maintain a cumulative grade point average of 2.5 on a 4.0 scale; must maintain a satisfactory academic progress as determined by the college; must comply with federal Selective Service registration requirements. **Criteria:** Applicants will be selected based on the academic standing and eligibility requirements.

Funds Avail.: $5,000. **To Apply:** Applicant must submit the complete application form for the Teacher Education Scholarship Programs (available online); must sign the application's Teaching Agreement or Promissory Note promising to fulfill the teaching commitment or repay funds received plus interest. **Deadline:** March 1.

3671 ■ Imagine America Foundation

1101 Connecticut Ave. NW, Ste. 901
Washington, DC 20036
Ph: (202)336-6800
Fax: (202)408-8102
E-mail: bobm@imagine-america.org
URL: http://www.imagine-america.org

3672 ■ Career Colleges Scholarships *(Undergraduate/Scholarship)*

Purpose: To help high school seniors attend college. **Focus:** Education. **Qualif.:** Applicants must be high school graduates who are pursuing postsecondary career education at participating career colleges across the United States. **Criteria:** Recipients are selected based on financial need.

Funds Avail.: $1,000. **To Apply:** Applicants must complete the online application form including name and contact information.

3673 ■ High School Councilors Scholarships *(Undergraduate/Scholarship)*

Purpose: To help high school seniors attend college. **Focus:** Education. **Qualif.:** Applicants must be high school graduates who are pursuing postsecondary career education at participating career colleges across the United States; Applicants must have a high school grade point average of 2.5 or greater. **Criteria:** Recipients are selected based on financial need.

Funds Avail.: $1,000. **Number Awarded:** 3. **To Apply:** Applicants must complete the online application form including name and contact information.

3674 ■ Imagine America Online Scholarships *(Undergraduate/Scholarship)*

Purpose: To help high school seniors attend college. **Focus:** General studies. **Qualif.:** Applicants must be enrolled in an online/distance learning experience at a participating career in college. **Criteria:** Recipients are selected based on financial need.

Funds Avail.: $1,000. **To Apply:** Applicants must complete the online application form.

Awards are arranged alphabetically below their administering organizations

3675 ■ Imagine America Scholarships *(Undergraduate/Scholarship)*

Purpose: To support and promote the benefits of career colleges to the general public. **Focus:** General studies. **Qualif.:** Applicants must be graduating high school students planning to attend a career college; selected winners usually have a grade point average of 2.5 or greater. **Criteria:** Recipients are selected based on financial need and demonstrated voluntary community service during senior year.

Funds Avail.: $1,000. **Number Awarded:** 3. **To Apply:** Applicants must complete the application form.

3676 ■ Parents Scholarships *(Undergraduate/Scholarship)*

Purpose: To help high school seniors attend college. **Focus:** Education. **Qualif.:** Applicants must be high school graduates who are pursuing postsecondary career education at participating career colleges across the United States. **Criteria:** Recipients are selected based on financial need.

Funds Avail.: $1,000. **To Apply:** Applicants must complete the online application form including name and contact information.

3677 ■ Immune Deficiency Foundation

40 W Chesapeake Ave., Ste. 308
Towson, MD 21204
Ph: (410)321-6647
Fax: (410)321-9165
Free: 800-296-4433
E-mail: idf@primaryimmune.org
URL: http://www.primaryimmune.org

3678 ■ The Eric Marder Scholarships *(Undergraduate/Scholarship)*

Purpose: To improve the diagnosis and treatment of patients with primary immune deficiency diseases through research, education, and advocacy. **Focus:** Disabilities. **Qualif.:** Applicants must be undergraduate students living with primary immune deficiency diseases planning to complete their secondary education. **Criteria:** Recipients are selected based on financial need.

Funds Avail.: No specific amount. **To Apply:** Applicants must complete the application form.

3679 ■ Independent Lubricant Manufacturers Association

400 N Columbus St., Ste. 201
Alexandria, VA 22314
Ph: (703)684-5574
Fax: (703)836-8503
URL: http://hwww.ilma.org

3680 ■ Independent Lubricant Manufacturers Association Scholarships *(Undergraduate/Scholarship)*

Purpose: To provide financial assistance to deserving students. **Focus:** General studies. **Qualif.:** Applicant must be a citizen in a North American country; must attend or be enrolled in a college or university in North America; must be registered as a full-time student (12 credit hours or more per semester, 9 credit hours per trimester or more); must have a minimum of 3.0 cumulative GPA. **Criteria:** Selection of applicants will be based on financial need and GPS. Preference will be given to those with major in Math, Science and Engineering.

Funds Avail.: $1,000. **To Apply:** Applicant must have a letter of recommendation from teacher or advisor. Application forms are available online. **Deadline:** June 30.

3681 ■ Independent Order of Foresters

789 Don Mills Rd.
Toronto, ON, Canada M3C 1T9
Ph: (416)429-3000
Fax: (416)429-3896
Free: 800-828-1540
E-mail: service@forester.com
URL: http://www.foresters.com

3682 ■ Foresters Scholarships *(Undergraduate/Scholarship)*

Purpose: To provide opportunity for Foresters members to pursue higher learning through financial support. **Focus:** General Studies. **Qualif.:** Applicants must be Foresters members or their biological or legally-adopted dependents or children, aged 25 years or under; Foresters members and/or their spouse, aged 25 years or under; Foresters member and/or their spouse who are mature students who are currently enrolled in full-time post-secondary studies. Applicants must have performed a minimum of forty hours of community service in the 2 years prior to application. **Criteria:** Scholarship recipients will be selected based on completed application and academic performance.

Funds Avail.: Up to $8,000 to cover related to post-secondary education. **To Apply:** Applicant must have the Forester life, Foresters annuity, Social Fraternal membership and a registered non-voting member; must submit the application form together with official transcript, community service achievement list, two letters of reference and a member consent form. **Deadline:** September-November.

3683 ■ Independent Organic Inspectors Association

PO Box 6
Broadus, MT 59317
Ph: (406)436-2031
E-mail: ioia@ioia.net
URL: http://www.ioia.net

3684 ■ IOIA Andrew Rutherford Scholarships *(Professional Development/Scholarship)*

Purpose: To provide full tuition for an IOIA Inspector Training Course. **Focus:** Technical training. **Qualif.:** Applicants must come from outside of the US or Canada; be both prospective and experienced inspectors are eligible to apply for the Scholarship. **Criteria:** Recipient will be selected on the basis of his/her potential and financial need.

Funds Avail.: No amount mentioned. **To Apply:** Applicants must submit completed application form, cover letter, current resume, and list of references. **Deadline:** October 1.

3685 ■ IOIA Organic Community Initiative Scholarship *(Other/Scholarship)*

Purpose: To provide full tuition for an IOIA Basic Inspector Training Course. **Focus:** Technical training. **Qualif.:** Ap-

Awards are arranged alphabetically below their administering organizations

plicants must be individuals residing outside of the United States and Canada. **Criteria:** Recipient will be selected based on their potential to effect change in their organic community and financial need.

Funds Avail.: No amount mentioned. **To Apply:** Applicant must submit a completed application form, cover letter, current resume, and list of three references. **Deadline:** October 1. **Contact:** Margaret Scoles, IOIA Executive Director at the above address (see entry 3683).

3686 ■ Independent Professional Seed Association

PO Box 241312
Omaha, NE 68124-5312
Ph: (402)991-3550
Fax: (402)489-2394
E-mail: IPSAGreg@aol.com
URL: http://www.ipsaweb.com

3687 ■ Myron Asplin Foundation Scholarships *(Undergraduate/Scholarship)*

Purpose: To promote education in the field of agriculture. **Focus:** Agricultural sciences. **Qualif.:** Applicants must be active students continuing their education in an agriculture-related field of study. **Criteria:** Applicants are selected based on a combination of academic achievement, community and agricultural involvement.

Funds Avail.: $750. **Number Awarded:** 1. **To Apply:** Applicants must submit application form (available at the website) with high school transcript; list of courses taken and grades received during senior year (if not included in transcript); recent photo (name printed at the back). **Deadline:** May 15. **Contact:** Greg Ruehle at the above address (see entry 3686). IPSAGreg@aol.com. 402-483-2571.

3688 ■ IPSA Student Recognition Awards *(Undergraduate/Scholarship)*

Purpose: To promote education in the field of agriculture. **Focus:** Agriculture. **Qualif.:** Applicants must be an active student entering junior/senior year or graduate students studying agriculture or related field. **Criteria:** Preference is given to the dependents of an IPSA member and associates.

Funds Avail.: $700. **To Apply:** Application form is available at the website. Applicants must attach student transcript; two recommendation letters from professors; a statement about personal and professional goals and objectives; work experience for the last two years; and recommendation from the nominator along with any relationship to IPSA member or Associate member company. **Deadline:** May 15.

Remarks: The Award was created in 1997 with donations from Independent Corn Breeders Association. **Contact:** 402-486-2571.

3689 ■ Indiana Broadcasters Association

3003 E 98th St., Ste 161
Indianapolis, IN 46280
Ph: (317)573-0119
Fax: (317)573-0895
Free: 800-342-6276
E-mail: indba@aol.com
URL: http://www.indianabroadcasters.org

3690 ■ Indiana Broadcasters Association for College Scholarship Program *(Undergraduate/Scholarship)*

Purpose: To promote cooperation and understanding among broadcasters, both radio and television as well as among businesses and other organizations associated with the broadcast industry; to foster and promote the development of the art of broadcasting; to encourage and promote customs and practices which will be in the best interests of the public and the broadcasting industry; to protect members in every lawful and proper manner from injuries and unjust actions; and to act as a contact with other broadcast associations. **Focus:** Broadcasting. **Qualif.:** Applicants must have an overall 3.0 GPA on a 4.0 scale; must be residents of Indiana; must be second semester seniors at an Indiana High school planning to attend an Indiana post-secondary school; must be actively participating in a high school broadcast facility while attending an Indiana high school; and must have received credit in a High School Broadcasting, Telecommunications or Broadcast Journalism course. **Criteria:** Recipients are selected based on academic performance.

Funds Avail.: No specific amount. **To Apply:** Applicants must complete the Transcript Request Form and application form and send them to the College Records Office. **Deadline:** March 3.

3691 ■ Indiana Broadcasters Association High School Scholarship Program *(Undergraduate/Scholarship)*

Purpose: To promote cooperation and understanding among broadcasters, both radio and television as well as among businesses and other organizations associated with the broadcast industry; to foster and promote the development of the art of broadcasting; to encourage and promote customs and practices which will be in the best interests of the public and the broadcasting industry; to protect members in every lawful and proper manner from injuries and unjust actions; and to act as a contact with other broadcast associations. **Focus:** Broadcasting. **Qualif.:** Applicants must have an overall 3.0 GPA on a 4.0 scale; must be residents of Indiana; must be second-semester seniors at an Indiana High school planning to attend an Indiana post-secondary school; must be actively participating in a high school broadcast facility while attending an Indiana high school; and must have received credit in a High School Broadcasting, Telecommunications or Broadcast Journalism course. **Criteria:** Recipients are selected based on academic performance.

Funds Avail.: No specific amount. **To Apply:** Applicants must complete the application form and the High School Transcript Request Form and send them to the high school records office. **Deadline:** March 3. **Contact:** 317-573-0119.

3692 ■ Indiana Library Federation

941 E 86th St., Ste. 260
Indianapolis, IN 46240
Ph: (317)257-2040
Fax: (317)257-1389
E-mail: lkolb@ilfonline.org
URL: http://www.ilfonline.org

3693 ■ Indiana Library Federation AIME Scholarships *(Undergraduate/Scholarship)*

Purpose: To provide funds for at least one scholarship applicant entering or currently enrolled in a program to receive educational certification in the field of School Library Media Services. **Focus:** Library and archival sciences. **Qualif.:** Applicants must be currently enrolled in an undergraduate or graduate certification program for School Library Media Services; must meet the current criteria as set by the Indiana Professional Standards Board. **Criteria:** Recipients are selected based on academic performance.

Funds Avail.: $500. **To Apply:** Applicants must submit three letters of recommendation from which one must come from librarian. Masters candidates must submit (a) transcript or copy of official grade report for any library science courses already completed, (b) transcripts of all undergraduate education and (c) transcripts from other graduate work (may be included, but are not required). Public library certification candidates must submit (a) a copy of the approved public library certification program, (b) transcripts from undergraduate education and/or high school and (c) transcript or copy of official grade report for any course already taken toward library certification. School library media candidates must submit (a) a transcript for any education and/or library science courses already completed, (b) a transcript for all undergraduate or graduate work completed and (c) transcripts from high school may be included by candidates that have not yet completed any graduate or undergraduate work. **Contact:** 317-257-2040.

3694 ■ Esther Schlundt Memorial Scholarships
(Undergraduate/Scholarship)

Purpose: To foster the professional growth of its members and the promotion of all libraries in Indiana. **Focus:** General studies. **Qualif.:** Applicants must be entering or currently enrolled in an ALA-accredited graduate degree program in library and information science; or must be entering or currently enrolled in an Indiana State Library-approved library certification program. **Criteria:** Recipients are selected based on academic performance.

Funds Avail.: $1,000. **To Apply:** Applicants must submit three letters of recommendation from which one must come from a librarian; must submit transcript or copy of official grade report for any library science courses already completed for masters candidates, all undergraduate transcripts and/or high school and transcripts and a copy of official grade report for any course already taken toward library certification. School library media candidates must submit transcripts for any education and/or library science courses already completed. **Contact:** 317-257-2040

3695 ■ Sue Marsh Weller Memorial Scholarships
(Graduate, Postgraduate, Undergraduate/ Scholarship)

Purpose: To foster the professional growth of its members and the promotion of all libraries in Indiana. **Focus:** Library and archival sciences. **Qualif.:** Applicants must be entering or currently enrolled in an ALA-accredited program of graduate study specializing in children librarianship. **Criteria:** Recipients are selected based on interest in librarianship as a profession, personality and character, academic record, economic need and references and/or a personal interview.

Funds Avail.: No specific amount. **To Apply:** Applicants must submit three letters of recommendation from which one must come from a librarian. Masters candidates must submit (a) transcript or copy of official grade report for any library science courses already completed, (b) transcripts of all undergraduate education and (c) transcripts from other graduate work (may be included, but are not required). Public library certification candidates must submit (a) a copy of the approved public library certification program, (b) transcripts from undergraduate education and/or high school and (c) transcript or copy of official grade report for any course already taken toward library certification. School library media candidates must submit (a) official grade report for any education and/or library science courses already completed (undergraduate and/or high school), (b) a transcript for all undergraduate or graduate work completed and (c) transcripts from high school may be included by candidates that have not yet completed any graduate or undergraduate work. **Contact:** 317-257-2040.

3696 ■ Indiana State Alumni Association

200 N 7th St.
Terre Haute, IN 47809-9989
Free: 800-GO-TO-ISU
URL: http://www.indstate.edu/alum/alum_assoc.htm

3697 ■ Academic Promise Scholarships
(Undergraduate/Scholarship)

Purpose: To support educational pursuit of students. **Focus:** Art; Science. **Qualif.:** Applicant must hold an associate of arts, science, or applied science at any Ivy Tech campus or at Vincennes University; have a minimum GPA of 3.0. **Criteria:** Selection is based on merit.

Funds Avail.: $2000. **To Apply:** Student must indicate in the admission application the specific Ivy Tech campus attended. **Deadline:** Must be admitted before June 1 (fall semester) or December 1 (spring semester). **Contact:** admissions@indstate.edu.

3698 ■ Warren M. Anderson Scholarships
(Undergraduate/Scholarship)

Purpose: To support educational pursuit of students. **Focus:** General studies. **Qualif.:** Applicant must be entering college as freshmen at the Indiana State University; belongs to the top 30 percent of the high school; or have a GPA of 3.0. **Criteria:** Selection is based on academic and personal accomplishments.

Funds Avail.: $1200. **To Apply:** Applicant must submit an a list of high school/community accomplishments/activities, and a letter of recommendation from a high school councilor, civic leader, principal, or minister. **Deadline:** Must be admitted before March 1. **Contact:** admissions@indstate.edu.

3699 ■ Child of Alumni Book Voucher Awards
(Undergraduate/Scholarship)

Purpose: To support educational pursuit of a dependent of an alumni. **Focus:** General studies. **Qualif.:** Applicant must be entering college as freshmen at the Indiana State University and a dependent of an alumni. **Criteria:** Selection is based on high school class rank, GPA, rigor of curriculum, academic achievement, and extra curricular activities.

Funds Avail.: $500 ($250 in fall and another in spring). **To Apply:** Student must state that he/she is a dependent of an alumni in the admission application. **Deadline:** Must be admitted before March 1. **Contact:** admissions@indstate.edu.

3700 ■ Gongaware Scholarships College of Business *(Undergraduate/Scholarship)*

Purpose: To support educational pursuit of students. **Focus:** Insurance and insurance-related; Risk management.

Qualif.: Applicant must have a competitive GPA, class rank, SAT/ACT; majoring in insurance and risk management; and entering college as freshmen at the Indiana State University. **Criteria:** Selection is based on academic and personal accomplishments.

Funds Avail.: $2500, notebook computer, and professionals development account. **To Apply:** For application, call 812237-8633. **Deadline:** Must be admitted before December 1.

Remarks: Scholar will participate in two summer internship, be assigned an industry mentor, participate in an international experience, and be offered opportunities in developing leadership skills. Scholarship is funded by Don and Patricia Gongaware. **Contact:** admissions@indstate.edu.

3701 ■ Indiana State Alumni Association Creative and Performing Arts Award
(Undergraduate/Scholarship)

Purpose: To support educational pursuit of students. **Focus:** Art; Music; English language and literature; Theater arts. **Qualif.:** Applicant must be entering college as freshmen at the Indiana State University; majoring or have a minor in Art, Music, English, Physical Education (Dance), Theater. **Criteria:** Selection is based on academic and personal accomplishments.

Funds Avail.: $2000. **To Apply:** Applicant must submit an application form; portfolio review; must audition at the departments; and will be interview. Contact the department where the applicant is majoring. **Deadline:** Must be admitted before February 1. **Contact:** Art: 812-237-3697; Music: 812-237-27771; English: 812-237-3163; Physical Education: 812-237-2520; Theater: 812-237-3331.

3702 ■ Indiana State Alumni Association Dean's Scholarships *(Undergraduate/Scholarship)*

Purpose: To support educational pursuit of students. **Focus:** General studies. **Qualif.:** Applicant must rank in the top 25 percent of the high school class; or have a GPA of 3.5; accepted at the Indiana State University campus as a freshmen. **Criteria:** selection is based on academic achievement.

Funds Avail.: $2000. **To Apply:** Student must be admitted to the Indiana State University and will be automatically qualified for the scholarship. **Deadline:** Must be admitted before February 1.

Remarks: No additional application required. **Contact:** admissions@indstate.edu.

3703 ■ Indiana State Alumni Association Incentive Scholarships *(Undergraduate/Scholarship)*

Purpose: To support educational pursuit of students. **Focus:** General studies. **Qualif.:** Applicant must be an out-of-state freshman; have a 3.0 GPA; has a competitive SAT/ACT scores and class rank. **Criteria:** Selection is based on merit.

Funds Avail.: $4000 (out-of-state tuition). **To Apply:** Student must be admitted to the Indiana State University and will be automatically qualified for the scholarship. **Deadline:** Must be admitted before June 1.

Remarks: No additional application required. Students eligible for the Southern Illinois Free Waiver and reside in the 20 Illinois counties and not eligible for the award. **Contact:** admissions@indstate.edu.

3704 ■ Indiana State Alumni Association President's Academic Excellence Scholarships
(Undergraduate/Scholarship)

Purpose: To support educational pursuit of students. **Focus:** General studies. **Qualif.:** Student must belong to the top ten percent of the high school class; have a GPA of 3.7; a high school graduate entering freshmen; studying 12 or more credit hours per semester; and accepted at the Indiana State University campus. **Criteria:** Selection is based on academic and personal accomplishments.

Funds Avail.: Full tuition. **To Apply:** Student must be admitted to the Indiana State University and will be automatically qualified for the scholarship. **Deadline:** Must be admitted before December 1.

Remarks: No additional application required. **Contact:** admissions@indstate.edu.

3705 ■ Indiana State Alumni Association President's Scholarships *(Undergraduate/Scholarship)*

Purpose: To support educational pursuit of students. **Focus:** General studies. **Qualif.:** Student must belong to the top ten percent of the high school class; have a GPA of 3.7; a high school graduate entering freshmen; studying 12 or more credit hours per semester; and accepted at the Indiana State University campus. **Criteria:** Selection is based on academic and personal accomplishments.

Funds Avail.: Full tuition, room and board, books and supplies, personal laptop computer. **To Apply:** Student must be admitted to the Indiana State University and will be automatically qualified for the scholarship. **Deadline:** Must be admitted before December 1.

Remarks: No additional application required. **Contact:** admissions@indstate.edu.

3706 ■ Indiana State Alumni Association Rural Health Scholarships *(Undergraduate/Scholarship)*

Purpose: To prepare and support student from rural Indiana to return in their hometown as a primary care physician. **Focus:** Physiology. **Qualif.:** Applicant must have a GPA of 3.5; scoring a combined 1200 in Critical Reading (CR) and Mathematics (M) sections of the SAT or 27 on the ACT; and resides in rural Indiana. **Criteria:** Selection is based on academic and personal accomplishments.

Funds Avail.: Full tuition. **To Apply:** For application, call 812237-8633.

Remarks: To complete the program, scholar must maintain an average GPA of 3.5. **Contact:** admissions@indstate.edu.

3707 ■ Indiana State Alumni Association Transfer Student Scholarships *(Undergraduate/Scholarship)*

Purpose: To support educational pursuit of students. **Focus:** General studies. **Qualif.:** Applicant must have a 3.0 GPA with a minimum of 32 transferable semester hours. **Criteria:** Selection is based on merit.

Funds Avail.: $1500. **To Apply:** Student must be admitted to the Indiana State University and will be automatically qualified for the scholarship. The application for admission serves as the scholarship application. **Deadline:** Must be admitted before June 1 (fall semester) or December 1 (spring semester).

Remarks: No additional application required. **Contact:** admissions@indstate.edu.

Awards are arranged alphabetically below their administering organizations

3708 ■ Indiana Top Scholar Award *(Undergraduate/Scholarship)*

Purpose: To support educational pursuit of students. **Focus:** General studies. **Qualif.:** Applicant must be entering college as freshmen at the Indiana State University; ranking first to fifth in their senior class; have a GPA of 3.0; and have academic honors diplomas. **Criteria:** Qualified students are guaranteed for the scholarship.

Funds Avail.: $4000. **To Apply:** Student must be admitted to the Indiana State University and will be automatically qualified for the scholarship. **Deadline:** Must be admitted before March 1.

Remarks: No additional application required. **Contact:** admissions@indstate.edu.

3709 ■ Lilly Fellow Scholarships *(Undergraduate/Fellowship)*

Purpose: To provide students unique opportunities in experimental learning. **Focus:** General studies. **Qualif.:** Applicant must have a GPA of 3.0 with 32 transferable credit hours. **Criteria:** Selection is based on academic excellence and community leadership.

Funds Avail.: $5000. **To Apply:** Applicants must submit an essay on their interest of being a Lilly Fellow; a letter of recommendation; and a resume.

Remarks: A fellow will be working with a faculty mentor on research, community service, outreach and Lilly Fellow activities. **Contact:** University Center for Public Service and Community Engagement, 812-237-7900.

3710 ■ Networks Scholarships College of Business *(Undergraduate/Scholarship)*

Purpose: To support educational pursuit of students. **Focus:** Finance. **Qualif.:** Applicant must be entering college as freshmen at the Indiana State University. **Criteria:** Selection is based on academic and personal accomplishments.

Funds Avail.: Full tuition, notebook computer, and professional development account. **To Apply:** For application, call 812237-8633. **Deadline:** Must be admitted before December 1.

Remarks: Scholar will participate in a paid internship, attend leadership-development activities, have an international experience, and will be mentored. **Contact:** admissions@indstate.edu.

3711 ■ Noyce Scholarships for Secondary Math and Science Education *(Undergraduate/Scholarship)*

Purpose: To support educational pursuit of students. **Focus:** Education, Secondary; Science; Mathematics and mathematical sciences. **Qualif.:** Applicant must be a transfer student with a GPA of 2.75 in all science and mathematics work. **Criteria:** Selection is based on merits.

Funds Avail.: $10,000. **To Apply:** Applicants must submit a signed urban teaching commitment and a scholarship application checklist. **Contact:** Dr. Jay D. Gatrell, project director, 812-237-2785 or jgatrell@indstate.edu.

3712 ■ Phi Theta Kappa Scholarships *(Undergraduate/Scholarship)*

Purpose: To support educational pursuit of students. **Focus:** Art; Science. **Qualif.:** Applicant must hold an associate of arts, science, or applied science; have a minimum GPA of 3.5; and a member of Phi Theta Kappa National Honor Society. **Criteria:** Selection is based on merit.

Funds Avail.: $4000. **To Apply:** Student must be admitted to the Indiana State University and will be automatically qualified for the scholarship. In addition, student must provide a documentation of honor society membership and a letter of recommendation together with the admission application. **Deadline:** Must be admitted before June 1 (fall semester) or December 1 (spring semester). **Contact:** admissions@indstate.edu.

3713 ■ Sycamore Scholar Awards *(Undergraduate/Scholarship)*

Purpose: To support educational pursuit of students. **Focus:** General studies. **Qualif.:** Applicant must be entering college as freshmen at the Indiana State University; belongs to the top ten percent of their graduating class; have a minimum of 3.0 GPA; and have completed academic honors diploma. **Criteria:** Qualified students are guaranteed for the scholarship.

Funds Avail.: Half the cost of in-state tuition. **To Apply:** Student must be admitted to the Indiana State University and will be automatically qualified for the scholarship. **Deadline:** Must be admitted before March 1.

Remarks: No additional application required. Recipients will be disqualified for the Indiana Top Scholar Award. **Contact:** admissions@indstate.edu.

3714 ■ Indigenous Bar Association

9785-152B St., No. 9
Surrey, BC, Canada V3R 9W2
Ph: (604)951-8807
Fax: (604)951-8806
E-mail: glangan@indigenousbar.ca
URL: http://www.indigenousbar.ca

3715 ■ IBA Law Student Scholarships Foundation *(Undergraduate/Scholarship)*

Purpose: To provide assistance to qualified individuals who want to pursue their education. **Focus:** Law. **Qualif.:** Applicant must be an Indigenous law student currently enrolled in law school who, at a minimum, has substantially completed their first year of legal studies; must have demonstrated interest in serving the Indigenous community and the creator with honor and integrity. **Criteria:** Recipient will be selected based on financial need, academic merit and commitment to Indigenous legal matters.

Funds Avail.: $2,000. **To Apply:** Applicant must complete the application form available online; must submit a short personal essay describing why they should receive the scholarship, including financial need, community involvement, as well as his/her goals and career aspirations; must enclose two letters of recommendations. Application form and other supporting documents must be sent to Germaine Langan, No. 9, 9785-152B St., Surrey, BC V3R 9W2. **Deadline:** June 1.

3716 ■ Industrial Supply Association

100 N 20th St., 4th Fl.
Philadelphia, PA 19103
Ph: (215)320-3862
Fax: (215)564-2175
Free: (866)460-2360
E-mail: info@isapartners.org
URL: http://www.isapartners.org

Awards are arranged alphabetically below their administering organizations

3717 ■ Gary L. Buffington Memorial Scholarships *(Undergraduate/Scholarship)*

Purpose: To recognize members who embody the values postered by Gary L. Buffington while performing his duty for the industry. **Focus:** Industrial. **Qualif.:** Applicant must be a rising senior in an established college or university industrial distribution channel. **Criteria:** Recipient will be selected based on criteria of high educational performance, leadership, and community service.

Funds Avail.: $10,000. **To Apply:** Applicants must submit complete application.

3718 ■ Information Technology Industry Alliance of Nova Scotia

PO Box 9410 Sta. A
Halifax, NS, Canada B3K 5S3
Ph: (902)423-5332
Fax: (902)484-5094
E-mail: info@itans.ns.ca
URL: http://www.itans.ns.ca

3719 ■ Dr. Stan Heaps Memorial Scholarships *(Undergraduate/Scholarship)*

Purpose: To provide financial assistance for qualified individuals. **Focus:** Computer and information sciences. **Qualif.:** Applicant must be a student about to enter his or her junior or senior year at a 4-year Nova Scotia university program leading to a degree with specialization in computer studies; must have achieved a minimum overall GPA of 2.67; must be a Canadian citizen or landed immigrant. **Criteria:** Selection of recipients is based on academic merit with an emphasis on courses most relevant to computer science. Consideration will be given to students with extracurricular, leadership and community involvement activities.

Funds Avail.: $2,000. **Number Awarded:** 2. **To Apply:** applicants must complete and submit the scholarship application form available at the CIPS Bluenose website and must also submit any additional information supporting their application. **Deadline:** May 30.

3720 ■ Infusion Nurses Society

315 Norwood Pk. S
Norwood, MA 02062
Ph: (781)440-9408
Fax: (781)440-9409
Free: 800-694-0298
E-mail: ins@ins1.org
URL: http://www.ins1.org

3721 ■ Leslie Baranowski Scholarships for Professional Excellence *(All/Scholarship)*

Purpose: To support and recognize commitment in improving and enhancing the quality of infusion care. **Focus:** Nursing; Health care services. **Qualif.:** Applicants must be a member of INS. **Criteria:** Applicants are selected based on the Scholarship Committee's review of the application materials.

Funds Avail.: $2,500. **Number Awarded:** 2. **To Apply:** Applicants must submit a completed application form; a summary (two-page, double-spaced) on how he/she will use the scholarship award to demonstrate/facilitate leadership in the community of infusion. **Deadline:** February 1.

Remarks: Do not include applicant's name and the affiliated institution in the summary.

3722 ■ Gardner Foundation INS Education Scholarship *(All/Scholarship)*

Purpose: To support and recognize a commitment to continuing education. **Focus:** Nursing; Health care services. **Qualif.:** Applicants must be a member of INS. **Criteria:** Applicants are selected based on the Scholarship Committees' review on the application materials.

Funds Avail.: $1,000. **Number Awarded:** 2. **To Apply:** Applicants must submit a completed application form available at the website; an evidence of acceptance into a collegiate program; and a summary (two-page, double-spaced) of professional goals and how continuing education (collegiate, post-collegiate) will enhance his/her practice. **Deadline:** February 1.

Remarks: Do not include applicant's name and the affiliated institution in the summary.

3723 ■ Institute of Food Technologists

525 W Van Buren, Ste. 1000
Chicago, IL 60607
Ph: (312)782-8424
Fax: (312)782-8348
Free: 800-438-3663
E-mail: info@ift.org
URL: http://www.ift.org

3724 ■ Institute of Food Technologists Graduate Scholarships *(Graduate/Scholarship)*

Purpose: To support and encourage outstanding research and education in food science and technology. **Focus:** Food Technology. **Qualif.:** Applicants must possess a minimum of a 3.0 GPA and an exemplary interest in food science and research together with demonstrated scientific aptitude. Applicants' research must be in such disciplines as genetics, horticulture, nutrition, microbiology, biochemistry, engineering, chemistry, etc. Program is also open to students who are enrolled in graduate studies leading to an M.S. or PhD at the time the scholarship becomes effective. **Criteria:** Recipients are selected based on scholastic standing, leadership ability, and demonstrated diversity in the food industry.

Funds Avail.: $50,000 in total. **Number Awarded:** Varies. **To Apply:** Applicants must submit an application stating his/her name and contact information; degrees held; date received; department and institution where degrees were received; degree; department and institution where study will be conducted; statement outlining student's career objectives; list of extracurricular activities and hobbies; list of awards, honors, and scholarship received; detailed information regarding publications and presentations; summary of work experience; and a typewritten outline of proposed field of research. Applicants must also submit an official transcript of record. **Deadline:** February 1. **Contact:** 312-782-8424; Elizabeth Plumber at the above address (see entry 3723).

3725 ■ Institute of Food Technologists Junior/ Senior Scholarships *(Undergraduate/Scholarship)*

Purpose: To encourage and support undergraduate students intending to pursue a career in the field of food science/technology and in other related areas. **Focus:** Food Technology. **Qualif.:** Program is open to sophomores,

Awards are arranged alphabetically below their administering organizations

juniors or seniors with a 3.0 GPA or above, pursuing a curriculum in food science or food technology in an educational institution having an IFT approved degree program. **Criteria:** Recipients are selected based on scholastic standing, leadership ability and demonstrated diversity in food industry.

Funds Avail.: Varies. **To Apply:** Applicants must submit an application form including name and contact information, degree and department where the study will be conducted; Statement outlining students career objectives; List of extracurricular activities and hobbies; List of awards, honors and scholarship received; Summary of work experience; Applicants must submit an official transcript of all college courses completed; Applicants must submit a letter of recommendation from a faculty member who is familiar with the applicant. **Deadline:** February 1. **Contact:** Institute of Food Technologists at the above address (see entry 3723).

3726 ■ Institute of Food Technologists Sophomore Scholarships *(Undergraduate/ Scholarship)*

Purpose: To inspire careers in the field of food science/ technology. **Focus:** Food Science and Technology. **Qualif.:** Applicants must be freshmen students intending to enroll in an approved food science/technology program and who have maintained at least 3.0 GPA for the first term of study and are recommended by the department head. **Criteria:** Recipients are selected based on scholastic eligibility.

Funds Avail.: $1,000. **Number Awarded:** 15. **To Apply:** Applicants must complete the application form; must submit an official transcript of record; letter of recommendation from a faculty member in the food science/food technology department who is familiar with the applicant's eligibility; a one-page essay stating why they desire to continue their studies in food science and/or food technology. **Deadline:** March 1. **Contact:** Institute of Food Technologists at the above address (see entry 3723).

3727 ■ Institute for Humane Studies

3301 N Fairfax Dr., Ste. 440
Arlington, VA 22201
Ph: (703)993-4880
Fax: (703)993-4890
Free: 800-697-8799
URL: http://www.theihs.org

3728 ■ Humane Studies Fellowships *(Graduate/ Fellowship)*

Purpose: To provide financial assistance to support the work of outstanding students interested in exploring the principles, practices, and institutions necessary for a free society through their academic work. **Focus:** General studies. **Qualif.:** Applicants must be full-time graduate students or undergraduate juniors or seniors during 2008-2009 academic year and who have a clearly demonstrate research interest in the intellectual and institutional foundations of a free society. **Criteria:** Candidates will be evaluated based on academic or professional performance, potential for success in chosen field and relevance of work to the advancement of a free society.

Funds Avail.: $2,000 up to $12,000. **To Apply:** Applicants must submit applications online which include completed application form, college transcripts, admission test scores, two recommendation, essays, writing sample, dissertation proposal, and a non-refundable $25.00 application fee. **Deadline:** December 31.

3729 ■ Institute of Industrial Engineers

3577 Parkway Ln., Ste. 200
Norcross, GA 30092
Ph: (770)449-0460
Fax: (770)441-3295
Free: 800-494-0460
E-mail: cs@iienet.org
URL: http://www.iienet2.org

3730 ■ John S.W. Fargher Scholarships *(Graduate/Scholarship)*

Purpose: To recognize industrial engineering students for academic excellence and campus leadership. **Focus:** Engineering, Industrial. **Qualif.:** Applicants must be graduate students enrolled in any school in the United States and its territories, provided that the school's engineering program or equivalent is accredited by an accrediting agency recognized by IIE and the student is pursuing a course of study in industrial engineering or engineering management. Candidates must be nominated by a faculty advisor or department head; must be active in a student IIE chapter; must have demonstrated leadership and promoted IIE involvement on campus; and have a minimum grade point average of 3.00 on a scale of 0-4.00. **Criteria:** Candidates will be selected based on GPA, IIE student chapter involvement and nomination letter.

Funds Avail.: $1,000. **Number Awarded:** 1. **To Apply:** Candidates must submit a nomination letter, along with an official transcript to IIE. **Deadline:** August 31. **Contact:** Bonnie Cameron at the above address (see entry 3729).

3731 ■ Dwight D. Gardner Scholarships *(Undergraduate/Scholarship)*

Purpose: To recognize undergraduate industrial engineering students for academic excellence and campus leadership. **Focus:** Engineering, Industrial. **Qualif.:** Candidates must be undergraduate students enrolled in any school in the United States and its territories, Canada and Mexico, provided that the school's engineering program or equivalent is accredited by an agency or organization recognized by IIE and the student is pursuing a course of study in industrial engineering. Candidates must be active Institute members and have an overall average of 3.40 on a scale of 0-4.00. **Criteria:** Scholarship recipient will be selected based on scholastic ability, character, leadership, potential service to the industrial engineering profession and need for financial assistance. Preference will be given to applicants who have demonstrated an interest in management consulting.

Funds Avail.: $1,000. **Number Awarded:** 2. **To Apply:** Candidates must be nominated by IE department heads and mailed to the Institute headquarters by November 15. After the review of nominations, eligible candidates will receive an application package that must be completed and sent back to IIE. **Deadline:** February 1.

3732 ■ Gilbreth Memorial Fellowships *(Graduate/ Scholarship)*

Purpose: To recognize graduate industrial engineering students for academic excellence and campus leadership. **Focus:** Engineering, Industrial. **Qualif.:** Candidates must be graduate students enrolled in any school in the United

Awards are arranged alphabetically below their administering organizations

States and its territories, Canada and Mexico, pursuing and advanced degree in industrial engineering or equivalent. Candidates must be active Institute members and have an overall average of 3.40 on a scale of 0-4.00. **Criteria:** Scholarship recipient will be selected based on scholastic ability, character, leadership, potential service to the industrial engineering profession and need for financial assistance. Preference will be given to applicants who have demonstrated an interest in management consulting.

Funds Avail.: $1,000. **Number Awarded:** 2. **To Apply:** Candidates must be nominated by IE department heads and mailed to the Institute headquarters by November 15. After review of nominations, eligible candidates will receive an application package that must be completed and sent back to IIE. **Deadline:** February 1.

3733 ■ IIE Council of Fellows Undergraduate Scholarships *(Undergraduate/Scholarship)*

Purpose: To recognize outstanding academic scholarship and leadership at the undergraduate level. **Focus:** Engineering, Industrial. **Qualif.:** Candidates must be undergraduate students enrolled in any school in the United States and its territories, Canada and Mexico, provided that the school's industrial engineering program or equivalent is accredited by an agency or organization recognized by IIE and the student is pursuing a course of study in industrial engineering. **Criteria:** Recipients will be selected based on scholastic ability, character, leadership, potential service to the industrial engineering profession and need for financial assistance.

Funds Avail.: $1,000 each. **Number Awarded:** 2. **To Apply:** Candidates must request an application packet from the scholarship coordinator and submit the completed form to IIE headquarters. **Deadline:** February 1. **Contact:** Bonnie Cameron at the above address (see entry 3729).

3734 ■ John L. Imhoff Scholarships *(Graduate, Undergraduate/Scholarship)*

Purpose: To recognize industrial engineering students for academic excellence and campus leadership. **Focus:** Engineering, Industrial. **Qualif.:** Candidates must be pursuing a BS in an accredited IE program, or have a BS in IE and pursuing a master's or doctorate degree in an accredited IE program. **Criteria:** Candidates will be selected based on GPA, IIE student chapter involvement and nomination letter.

Funds Avail.: $1,000. **Number Awarded:** 1. **To Apply:** Candidates must submit a completed application form; a written essay describing candidate's international contributions to, or experience in, industrial engineering; and three references reinforcing applicant's contributions to the industrial engineering profession through international understanding. **Deadline:** August 31. **Contact:** Bonnie Cameron at the above address (see entry 3729).

3735 ■ Harold and Inge Marcus Scholarships *(Undergraduate/Scholarship)*

Purpose: To recognize undergraduate industrial engineering students for academic excellence and noteworthy contribution to the development of the industrial engineering profession. **Focus:** Engineering, Industrial. **Qualif.:** Candidates must be undergraduate students enrolled in any school in the United States, provided that the school's engineering program is accredited by an agency recognized by IIE and the student is pursuing a course of study in industrial engineering. Candidates must be active Institute members and have an overall average of 3.40 on a scale of 0-4.00. **Criteria:** Scholarship recipients will be selected based on scholastic ability, character, leadership, potential service to the industrial engineering profession and need for financial assistance.

Funds Avail.: $1,000. **Number Awarded:** 1. **To Apply:** Candidates must be nominated by IE department heads. Nominations must be mailed to the Institute headquarters by November 15. Candidates must submit a completed application package to IIE. **Deadline:** February 1.

3736 ■ Marvin Mundel Memorial Scholarships *(Undergraduate/Scholarship)*

Purpose: To recognize undergraduate industrial engineering students for academic excellence and campus leadership. **Focus:** Engineering, Industrial. **Qualif.:** Candidates must be undergraduate students enrolled in any school in the United States and its territories, Canada and Mexico, provided that the school's industrial engineering program or its equivalent is accredited by an agency or organization recognized by IIE and the student is pursuing a course of study in industrial engineering. **Criteria:** Scholarship recipients will be selected based on scholastic ability, character, leadership, potential service to the industrial engineering profession and need for financial assistance. Preference will be given to students who have demonstrated an interest in work measurement and methods engineering.

Funds Avail.: $600. **Number Awarded:** 1. **To Apply:** Candidates must be nominated by IE department heads. Nominations must be mailed to the Institute headquarters by November 15. Candidates must submit a completed application package to IIE. **Deadline:** February 1.

3737 ■ Presidents Scholarships *(Undergraduate/Scholarship)*

Purpose: To recognize excellence in scholarly activities and leadership of the industrial engineering profession. **Focus:** Engineering, Industrial. **Qualif.:** Candidates must be undergraduate students pursuing a course of study in industrial engineering. Candidates must be active Institute members and have an overall average of 3.40 on a scale of 0-4.00. **Criteria:** Scholarship recipient will be selected based on scholastic ability, character, leadership, potential service to the industrial engineering profession and need for financial assistance. Preference will be given to applicants who have demonstrated an interest in management consulting.

Funds Avail.: To be determined. **To Apply:** Candidates must be nominated by IE department heads and mailed to the Institute headquarters by November 15. After review of nominations, eligible candidates will receive an application package that must be completed and sent back to IIE. **Deadline:** February 1.

3738 ■ A.O. Putnam Memorial Scholarships *(Undergraduate/Scholarship)*

Purpose: To recognize undergraduate industrial engineering students for academic excellence and campus leadership. **Focus:** Engineering, Industrial. **Qualif.:** Candidates must be undergraduate students enrolled in any school in the United States and its territories, Canada and Mexico, provided that the school's industrial engineering program or equivalent is accredited by an agency or organization recognized by IIE and the student is pursuing a course of study in industrial engineering. Candidates must be active Institute members and have an overall average of 3.40 on a scale of 0-4.00. **Criteria:** Scholarship recipient will be

Awards are arranged alphabetically below their administering organizations

selected based on scholastic ability, character, leadership, potential service to the industrial engineering profession and need for financial assistance. Preference will be given to applicants who have demonstrated an interest in management consulting.

Funds Avail.: $600. **Number Awarded:** 1. **To Apply:** Candidates must be nominated by IE department heads and mailed to the Institute headquarters by November 15. After the review of nominations, eligible candidates will receive an application package that must be completed and sent back to IIE. **Deadline:** February 1.

3739 ■ E.J. Sierleja Memorial Fellowships *(Graduate/Fellowship)*

Purpose: To recognize graduate students for academic excellence and campus leadership. **Focus:** Transportation. **Qualif.:** Candidates must be graduate students pursuing advanced studies in the area of transportation. **Criteria:** Preference will be given to students pursuing advanced studies on rail transportation.

Funds Avail.: $600. **Number Awarded:** 1. **To Apply:** Candidates must be nominated by IE department heads. Nominations must be mailed to the Institute headquarters by November 15. Candidates must submit a completed application package to IIE. **Deadline:** February 1. **Contact:** Bonnie Cameron at the above address (see entry 3729).

3740 ■ United Parcel Service Scholarship for Female Students *(Undergraduate/Scholarship)*

Purpose: To recognize undergraduate industrial engineering students for academic excellence and campus leadership. **Focus:** Engineering, Industrial. **Qualif.:** Candidates must be undergraduate students enrolled in any school in the United States and its territories, Canada and Mexico, provided that the school's industrial engineering program or its equivalent is accredited by an agency or organization recognized by IIE and the student is pursuing a course of study in industrial engineering. **Criteria:** Scholarship recipient will be selected based on scholastic ability, character, leadership, potential service to the industrial engineering profession and need for financial assistance.

Funds Avail.: $4,000. **Number Awarded:** 1. **To Apply:** Candidates must be nominated by IE department heads. Nominations must be mailed to the Institute headquarters by November 15. Candidates must submit a completed application package to IIE. **Deadline:** February 1.

3741 ■ United Parcel Service Scholarship for Minority Students *(Undergraduate/Scholarship)*

Purpose: To recognize undergraduate industrial engineering students for academic excellence and campus leadership. **Focus:** Engineering, Industrial. **Qualif.:** Candidates must be undergraduate students enrolled in any school in the United States and its territories, Canada and Mexico, provided that the school's industrial engineering program or its equivalent is accredited by an agency or organization recognized by IIE and the student is pursuing a course of study in industrial engineering. **Criteria:** Scholarship recipient will be selected based on scholastic ability, character, leadership, potential service to the industrial engineering profession and need for financial assistance.

Funds Avail.: $4,000. **Number Awarded:** 1. **To Apply:** Candidates must be nominated by IE department heads. Nominations must be mailed to the Institute headquarters by November 15. Candidates must submit a completed application package to IIE. **Deadline:** February 1.

3742 ■ Lisa Zaken Award For Excellence *(Graduate, Undergraduate/Award/Prize)*

Purpose: To recognize excellence in scholarly activities and leadership related to the industrial engineering profession on campus. **Focus:** Engineering, Industrial. **Qualif.:** Candidates must be undergraduate and graduate students enrolled in any school, and pursuing a course of study in industrial engineering. Candidates must be active in a student chapter, must have demonstrated leadership and promoted IIE involvement on campus. Candidates must have an overall grade point average of 3.00 on a scale of 0-4.00. **Criteria:** Candidates will be selected based on GPA, IIE student chapter involvement and nomination letter.

Funds Avail.: $600. **Number Awarded:** 1. **To Apply:** Candidates must submit a nomination letter, along with an official transcript to IIE. **Deadline:** August 31. **Contact:** Bonnie Cameron at the above address (see entry 3729).

3743 ■ Institute of Management Accountants

10 Paragon Dr.
Montvale, NJ 07645-1718
Ph: (201)573-9000
Fax: (201)474-1600
Free: 800-638-4427
E-mail: ima@imanet.org
URL: http://www.imanet.org

3744 ■ Stuart Cameron and Margaret McLeod Memorial Scholarships (SCMS) *(Graduate, Undergraduate/Scholarship/Forgivable Loan)*

Purpose: To help student members of IMA offset the high cost of education and pursue further studies in preparation for careers in accounting, management and finance. **Focus:** Accounting; Management; Finance. **Qualif.:** Applicants must be IMA student members (membership number must be indicated in the application); may either be a full or part-time student with strictly 12 credits per semester; must be physically located in the United States or Puerto Rico studying at regionally accredited institutions; have a minimum GPA of 3.0 throughout undergraduate/graduate academic career; pursuing a career in management accounting, financial management, or information. **Criteria:** Selection is based on academic merit, IMA participation, quality of applicant's presentation and other materials provided.

Funds Avail.: $5,000 and lodging, transportation and registrations costs for the Annual Conference in June and the Student Conference in November. **Number Awarded:** 2. **To Apply:** Applicants must submit a one-page resume; official university transcripts with school seal and enclosed in a sealed envelope; two recommendations (from a current or past employer, a current or past professor or an IMA member) submitted on the attached form and sealed in an envelope with the reference's signature across the seal; two-page written statement indicating the applicant's reason for applying for the scholarship, reasons why she/he deserves the award, specific contributions to IMA and ideas on how he/she will promote awareness and increase membership and certification within IMA. **Deadline:** February 15.

Remarks: Scholarship has two categories, undergraduate and graduate student category. **Contact:** Jodi Ryan at (800)638-4427, ext. 1556 or jryan@imanet.org.

Awards are arranged alphabetically below their administering organizations

3745 ■ IMA FAR Doctoral Student Grant Program *(Doctorate/Grant)*

Purpose: To provide assistance in securing funding for research activities of accounting doctoral students in observance of their mission to develop and disseminate timely management accounting and financial management research findings that can be applied to current and emerging business issues. **Focus:** Accounting. **Qualif.:** Applicant must be an accounting doctoral student; pursuing a research that may contribute to the management accounting profession. **Criteria:** Proposals will be reviewed and evaluated by the FAR Board of Trustees and Directors.

Funds Avail.: No specific amount. **To Apply:** Applicants must prepare a research plan; two letters (one from dissertation chair or faculty advisor and the other from the applicant). Materials should be submitted electronically and in a .pdf format. **Contact:** Tara Barker, FAR Administrator, 800-638-4427, ext.1535, research@imanet.org. Raef Lawson, Research Director 800-638-4427, ext. 1532, rlawson@imanet.org.

3746 ■ IMA Memorial Education Fund Scholarships (MEF) *(Graduate, Undergraduate/Scholarship/Forgivable Loan)*

Purpose: To help student members of IMA offset the high cost of education and pursue further studies in preparation for careers in accounting, management and finance. **Focus:** Accounting; Management; Finance. **Qualif.:** Applicants must be IMA student members (membership number must be indicated in the application); must be physically located in the United States or Puerto Rico and is currently studying at regionally accredited institutions; must have a minimum GPA of 3.0 throughout undergraduate/graduate academic career; pursuing a career in management accounting, financial management, or information. **Criteria:** Selection is based on academic merit, IMA participation, quality of applicant's presentation and other materials provided.

Funds Avail.: $1,000-$2,500. **Number Awarded:** 2. **To Apply:** Applicants must submit a one-page resume; official university transcripts with school seal and enclosed in a sealed envelope; two letters of recommendations (from a current or past employer, a current or past professor or an IMA member) submitted on the attached form and sealed in an envelope with the reference's signature across the seal; two-page written statement indicating the applicant's reason for applying for the scholarship, statements why the applicant deserves the award, specific contributions to IMA, and suggestions on promoting awareness and increase membership and certification within IMA. **Deadline:** February 15.

Remarks: Scholarship has two categories, undergraduate and graduate student category. **Contact:** Jodi Ryan at (800)638-4427, ext. 1556 or jryan@imanet.org.

3747 ■ Institute of Real Estate Management

430 N Michigan Ave.
Chicago, IL 60611
Ph: 800-837-0706
Fax: 800-338-4736
E-mail: custserv@irem.org
URL: http://www.irem.org

3748 ■ George M. Brooker Collegiate Scholarships for Minorities *(Graduate, Postgraduate, Undergraduate/Scholarship)*

Purpose: To facilitate increased minority participation in the real estate management industry by providing educational assistance. **Focus:** Real Estate; Management. **Qualif.:** Applicant must be a member of a minority (non-Caucasian) group; must be a citizen of the United States; must be beginning junior or senior year of undergraduate work or pursuing graduate or post-graduate studies; has declared a major in real estate or a related field; have a minimum GPA of 3.0 on a 4.0 scale within his or her major; and has completed two courses in real estate or indicate intent to complete such courses. **Criteria:** Recipients are chosen based on merit.

Funds Avail.: $1,000 (undergraduate); $2,500 (graduate). **Number Awarded:** 2 (undergraduate); 1 (graduate). **To Apply:** Applicant must submit complete application (available in the website), three letters of recommendation of which one must come from the college dean, written essay (not to exceed 500 words) explaining the applicant's interest in the industry, and a letter of recommendation from local IREM chapter president or officer. Forward materials to: IREM Foundation Administrator, Attn: Furbush Scholarship: CPM, 430 N. Michigan Ave., Chicago, IL 60611-4090. **Deadline:** March 31.

3749 ■ Donald M. Furbush Scholarships *(Professional Development/Scholarship)*

Purpose: To provide funding for individuals to follow the institute's entire curriculum required to qualify for the CPM designation, ARM certification and Accredited Commercial Manager certification, thus promoting professional development. **Focus:** Real Estate; Management. **Qualif.:** Nominees must be of legal age in the country in which the nominee resides; and must be actively employed in the real estate management industry. **Criteria:** Selection is based on commitment to professional excellence, financial need, strength of recommendation and personal commitment to gaining CPM designation.

Funds Avail.: up to $5,000. **To Apply:** Applicant must submit complete application (available in the website) to: IREM Foundation Administrator, Attn: Furbush Scholarship: CPM, 430 N. Michigan Ave., Chicago, IL 60611-4090. **Deadline:** March 31.

3750 ■ IREM Foundation Minority Outreach Scholarships *(Professional Development/Scholarship)*

Purpose: To encourage professional development among under-represented minorities by providing financial assistance. **Focus:** Real Estate; Management. **Qualif.:** Nominees must be a citizen of the United States or Canada; must be of legal age in the state or country in which the nominee resides; must be an ethnic minority; must be a current CPM candidate or have already submitted application for CPM candidacy; and has not received other scholarships or similar awards from IREM. **Criteria:** Award is given to applicant who is qualified for CPM candidacy; who has demonstrated commitment to the industry as evidenced by years in the property management profession; and has demonstrated commitment to IREM through ARM participation or previous course attendance.

Funds Avail.: up to $5,000. **To Apply:** Applicant must submit complete application (available in the website), along with a brief statement explaining why he or she feels

Awards are arranged alphabetically below their administering organizations

deserving of this scholarship and an official completed recommendation form from the local chapter to: IREM Foundation Administrator, Attn: Furbush Scholarship: CPM, 430 N. Michigan Ave., Chicago, IL 60611-4090. **Deadline:** Any time.

3751 ■ Paul H. Rittle Sr. Memorial Scholarships *(Professional Development/Scholarship)*

Purpose: To provide opportunity worthy individuals who are financially incapable the to attend IREM's courses, either in a classroom setting, online, or home study formats. **Focus:** Real Estate; Management. **Qualif.:** Applicants must be of legal age and currently employed in some aspect of the real estate field. **Criteria:** Recipients are selected on the basis of financial need; commitment to real estate management as a career; and character as demonstrated by community involvement.

Funds Avail.: $2,000 (for CPM designation or Accredited Commercial Manager certification); $1,000 (for ARM certification). **Number Awarded:** Varies. **To Apply:** Applicant must submit official application form, employer affidavit and financial status form; a personal letter describing the objectives and information of the applicant; for U.S. citizen: a letter support from the local president or officer supporting your application; a copy of applicant's signed federal income tax return and Form W-2 for previous year; for international applicants: letter from employee or client if self-employed and total income indicated in Annual Income Statement for the previous year (if married include your spouse). **Deadline:** Anytime.

3752 ■ Institute of Turkish Studies

Intercultural Center - Box 571033
Georgetown University
Washington, DC 20057-1033
Ph: (202)687-0295
Fax: (202)687-3780
URL: http://www.turkishstudies.org

3753 ■ Institute of Turkish Studies Dissertation Writing Grants *(Doctorate/Grant)*

Purpose: To promote training, research, and teaching in the field of Ottoman and modern Turkish Studies. **Focus:** Turkish studies. **Qualif.:** Applicants must be a U.S. citizen or permanent resident; enrolled in a PhD degree; and expecting to finish all requirements except dissertation. **Criteria:** Recipients are selected by on the expert panels.

Funds Avail.: $5000-$10,000. **To Apply:** Applicant must send two-page grant application cover sheet (available at the website); project proposal (maximum of 6 pages, double-space); budget; three letters of recommendation; curriculum vitae; and an academic transcript send by university registrar. Applications must be sent electronically in MAS Word or PDF format to dcc@turkishstudies.org and the supporting documents by regular mail. **Deadline:** March. **Contact:** dcc@turkishstudies.org.

3754 ■ Institute of Turkish Studies Sabbatical Research Grants *(Professional Development/Grant)*

Purpose: To support faculty research during the course of their sabbaticals. **Focus:** Turkish studies. **Qualif.:** Applicant must be faculty member in the field of social sciences and/or humanities; U.S. citizen or permanent resident. **Criteria:** Recipients are selected by the expert panels.

Funds Avail.: $25,000. **To Apply:** Applicant must send two-page grant application cover sheet (available at the website); a project proposal (maximum of 6 pages, double-spaced); and a curriculum vitae. Applications must be sent electronically in MAS Word or PDF format to dcc@turkishstudies.org and the supporting documents by regular mail. **Deadline:** March. **Contact:** dcc@turkishstudies.org.

3755 ■ Institute of Turkish Studies Undergraduate Study Grants *(Undergraduate/Grant)*

Purpose: To honor competent student to study in Turkey. **Focus:** General studies. **Qualif.:** Applicant must be a U.S. citizen; enrolled in college or university in United States. **Criteria:** Recipients are selected by on the expert panels.

Funds Avail.: $10,000. **To Apply:** Applicant must send grant application cover sheet (available at the website); a project proposal (maximum of 3 pages, double-spaced); and a budget. Applications must be sent electronically in MAS Word or PDF format to dcc@turkishstudies.org and the supporting documents by regular mail. **Deadline:** March. **Contact:** dcc@turkishstudies.org.

3756 ■ Post-Doctoral Summer Travel-Research Grants *(Doctorate/Grant)*

Purpose: To provide partial support to those who hold PhD with their travel and research to Turkey. **Focus:** Turkish studies; Humanities; Social science. **Qualif.:** Applicant must be a U.S. citizen or permanent resident; a PhD in social science or humanities. **Criteria:** Recipients are selected by on the expert panels.

Funds Avail.: No specific amount. **To Apply:** Applicant must send two-pages grant application cover sheet (available at the website); a project proposal (maximum of 5 pages, double-spaced); budget; three letters of recommendation; and a curriculum vitae. Applications must be sent electronically in MAS Word or PDF format to dcc@turkishstudies.org and the supporting documents by regular mail. **Deadline:** March. **Contact:** dcc@turkishstudies.org.

3757 ■ Research Grants in Comparative Studies of Modern Turkey *(Graduate, Postdoctorate/Grant)*

Purpose: To provide information about political entity in Turkish Republic and other parts of the world. **Focus:** Turkish studies. **Qualif.:** Applicant must be U.S. citizen or permanent resident; a graduate student at the dissertation stage; or a post doctoral scholars studying the aspect of Republic of Turkey (post-1922) in a comparative context; enrolled in a university in the U.S. **Criteria:** Recipients are selected by on the expert panels.

Funds Avail.: Maximum of $10,000. **To Apply:** Applicant must send two-page grant application cover sheet (available at the website); project proposal (maximum of 5 pages, double-space); budget; three letters of recommendation; curriculum vitae; and an academic transcript send by university registrar. Applications must be sent electronically in MAS Word or PDF format to dcc@turkishstudies.org or and the supporting documents by regular mail. **Deadline:** March. **Contact:** dcc@turkishstudies.org.

3758 ■ Summer Language Study Grants in Turkey *(Graduate/Grant)*

Purpose: To provide summer travel to Turkey in preparation for graduate research in language study. **Focus:** Turkish studies; Humanities; Social science. **Qualif.:** Applicant must be U.S. citizen or permanent resident; a graduate student in the field of social science or humanities; enrolled in a university of United States. **Criteria:** Recipients are

Awards are arranged alphabetically below their administering organizations

selected by on the expert panels.

Funds Avail.: $1000-$2000. **To Apply:** Applicant must send two-page grant application cover sheet (available at the website); a project proposal (maximum of 3 pages, double-spaced); budget; three letters of recommendation; curriculum vitae; academic transcript send by university registrar. Applications must be sent electronically in MAS Word or PDF format to dcc@turkishstudies.org and the supporting documents by regular mail. **Deadline:** March. **Contact:** dcc@turkishstudies.org.

3759 ■ Summer Research Grants in Turkey *(Graduate/Grant)*

Purpose: To provide summer travel to Turkey to complete projects. **Focus:** Turkish studies; Humanities; Social science. **Qualif.:** Applicant must be U.S. citizen or permanent resident; a graduate student in any field of social science or humanities; enrolled in university of United States; and not occupied in a dissertation writing. **Criteria:** Recipients are selected by on the expert panels.

Funds Avail.: $1000-$3000. **To Apply:** Applicant must send two-page grant application cover sheet (available at the website); a project proposal (maximum of 3 pages, double-spaced); budget; three letters of recommendation; curriculum vitae; academic transcript send by university registrar. Applications must be sent electronically in MAS Word or PDF format to dcc@turkishstudies.org and the supporting documents by regular mail. **Deadline:** March. **Contact:** dcc@turkishstudies.org.

3760 ■ Insurance Scholarship Foundation of America

PO Box 866
Hendersonville, NC 28793-0866
Ph: (828)890-3328
Fax: (828)891-2997
Free: (866)379-4732
E-mail: foundation@inssfa.org
URL: http://www.inssfa.org

3761 ■ CPCU Laman Educational Foundation Scholarships *(Professional Development/ Scholarship)*

Purpose: To recognize professional scholarship applicants who demonstrate the desire to enhance their career by becoming a CPCU. **Focus:** Insurance and insurance-related fields. **Qualif.:** Applicants must have a minimum of two years employment in the insurance industry; must be studying the CPCU program; and must not receive full reimbursement for the course, books, etc. from their employer or any other outside source. **Criteria:** Recipients are selected based on academic performance.

Funds Avail.: $50-$1,000. **To Apply:** Applicants must submit a completed application form.

3762 ■ Founders Circle Professional Scholarships *(Professional Development/Scholarship)*

Purpose: To recognize exceptional commitment to the insurance industry. **Focus:** Insurance and insurance-related fields. **Qualif.:** Applicants must have at least five years continuous insurance industry employment; must have demonstrated excellence in educational and career endeavors; and must engage in a course of study designed to improve knowledge and skills in performing employment responsibilities. **Criteria:** Recipients are selected based on academic performance.

Funds Avail.: $1,000-$2,000. **To Apply:** Applicants must submit a completed application form.

3763 ■ Insurance Scholarship Foundation of America College Scholarships *(Undergraduate/ Scholarship)*

Purpose: To promote excellence in the insurance industry by underwriting the education of current and future employees. **Focus:** Insurance and insurance-related fields. **Qualif.:** Applicants must be candidates for a bachelor's or higher degree with a major in insurance, risk management, or actuarial science; must be currently attending a college or university and be completing or have completed the second year of college; must have successfully completed two insurance, risk management, or actuarial science courses having a minimum of three credit hours each; and must have achieved at least 3.0 grade point average on a 4.0 scale. **Criteria:** Recipients are selected based on academic performance.

Funds Avail.: $500-$5,000. **To Apply:** Applicants must submit a completed application form.

3764 ■ Insurance Scholarship Foundation of America Professional Scholarships *(Professional Development/Scholarship)*

Purpose: To promote excellence in the insurance industry by underwriting the education of current and future employees. **Focus:** Insurance and insurance related fields. **Qualif.:** Applicants must have at least two years of insurance industry employment; must be engaged in a course of study to improve knowledge and skills in performing employment responsibilities; must not be receiving full reimbursement for the expenses of tuition, books etc. from an employer or from any other outside source; and must have a background that indicates the applicant's motivation. **Criteria:** Recipients are selected based on academic performance.

Funds Avail.: $50-$1,000. **To Apply:** Applicants must submit a completed application form.

3765 ■ Marsh College Scholarships *(Undergraduate/Scholarship)*

Purpose: To promote excellence in the insurance industry by underwriting the education of current and future employees. **Focus:** Insurance and insurance-related fields. **Qualif.:** Applicants must be candidates for a bachelor's or higher degree with a major in insurance, risk management or actuarial science; must be currently attending a college or university and be completing or have completed the second year of college; must have successfully completed two insurance, risk management, or actuarial science courses having a minimum of three credit hours each; and must have achieved at least 3.0 grade point of average on a 4.0 scale. **Criteria:** Recipients are selected based on academic performance.

Funds Avail.: $500-$5,000. **To Apply:** Applicants must submit a completed application form.

3766 ■ Insurance Women of Portland

8603 SE Powell Blvd.
Portland, OR 97266
Ph: (503)777-0027
Fax: (503)777-3220
E-mail: insuranceladythe@aol.com
URL: http://www.iwop.us

Awards are arranged alphabetically below their administering organizations

3767 ■ Insurance Women of Portland Scholarships *(Graduate/Scholarship)*

Purpose: To provide financial assistance for deserving individuals intending to attend colleges or universities in Oregon. **Focus:** Business; Insurance and insurance-related fields; Education. **Qualif.:** Applicants must be working toward a degree in business, insurance, or education; must be pursuing a professional designation; must either be full-time students (12 hours minimum registration), or be enrolled for at least three hours of college courses if applicants are employed in the insurance industry. **Criteria:** Applicants working in the insurance industry, or dependents of industry-employed individuals are given preference and are judged based on academic records, school and outside activities, career and education goals, and financial need.

Funds Avail.: $200-$500. **To Apply:** Applicants must submit all the required application information. **Deadline:** May 25. **Contact:** Roxane Russell, Farmers Insurance, 8603 SE Powell Blvd., Portland, OR, 97266.

3768 ■ Intellectual Property Owners Association

1255 23rd St. NW, Ste. 200
Washington, DC 20037
Ph: (202)466-2396
Fax: (202)466-2893
E-mail: info@ipo.org
URL: http://www.ipo.org

3769 ■ Donald W. Banner Corporate Intern Scholarships *(Undergraduate/Scholarship)*

Purpose: To improve knowledge and education in intellectual property rights and to recognize outstanding achievement in the fields of invention, creativity, and IP rights. **Focus:** Law. **Qualif.:** Applicants must be law students who have completed an internship in a corporate intellectual property law department and are intending to pursue a career in intellectual property law. **Criteria:** Recipients are selected based on scholastic standing.

Funds Avail.: $10,000. **To Apply:** Applicants must complete the scholarship application form. **Contact:** 202-466-2396.

3770 ■ Inter American Press Association

Jules Dubois Bldg.
1801 SW 3rd Ave.
Miami, FL 33129
Ph: (305)634-2465
Fax: (305)635-2272
E-mail: info@sipiapa.org
URL: http://www.sipiapa.com

3771 ■ Inter American Press Association Scholarships *(Undergraduate/Scholarship)*

Purpose: To defend and promote the right of the peoples of the Americas to be fully and freely informed through an independent press. **Focus:** Journalism. **Qualif.:** Applicants must be journalists or journalism seniors or graduates between 21 to 35 years of age with a good command of the language they are to use; must have completed their degree before beginning the scholarship year; must take a minimum of three university courses; and must participate in the Scholarship Fund's Reporting Program. **Criteria:** Recipients are selected based on academic achievement and financial need.

Funds Avail.: $20,000. **To Apply:** Applicants must complete the application form and submit along with an autobiography; transcripts of the university studies; three letters of recommendation; and proof of certification. **Deadline:** December 31. **Contact:** zchirinos@sipiapa.org

3772 ■ Intercollegiate Studies Institute

PO Box 4431
Wilmington, DE 19807-0431
Ph: (302)652-4600
Fax: (302)652-1760
Free: 800-526-7022
E-mail: info@isi.org
URL: http://www.isi.org

3773 ■ Savatori Fellowships *(Graduate/Fellowship)*

Purpose: To improve the ability of the American people to understand their heritage, to distinguish its principles, and to choose well so that, through self-governance, they may protect their nation and preserve their liberties for themselves and the generations to come. **Focus:** American studies. **Qualif.:** Applicant must be a U.S. citizen and member of the Intercollegiate Studies Institute; must be a college senior or graduate student; must engage in graduate studies for the purpose of teaching at the college level. **Criteria:** Applicant must meet the requirements specific to the fellowship.

Funds Avail.: $10,000. **Number Awarded:** 2. **To Apply:** Application form are available at the website. Applicant must submit the following: (1) Four brief statement; (2) Three essays; (3) Three letters of academic recommendation; (4) College transcript; (5) 2x3 photo or headshot. Application and other documents must be sent to: Graduate Fellowship Program, ISI, 3901 Centerville Rd., PO Box 4431, Wilmington, DE, 19807-0431. **Deadline:** February 15.

3774 ■ Richard M. Weaver Fellowships *(Graduate/Fellowship)*

Purpose: To assist motivated future teachers, similar to Professor Weaver, by the need to integrate the idea of liberal education with their teaching efforts, and, in so doing, to restore to university studies their distinction and worth. **Focus:** Education. **Qualif.:** Applicant must be a U.S. citizen and member of the Intercollegiate Studies Institute; must be a college senior or graduate student; must engage in graduate studies for the purpose of teaching at the college level. **Criteria:** Applicant must meet the requirements specific to the fellowship.

Funds Avail.: Stipend of $5,000 and awards $1,000 in ISI Books. **To Apply:** Application form is available at the website address. Applicant must submit the following: (1) Four brief statements; (2) Three essays; (3) Three letters of academic recommendation; (4) College transcript; (5) 2x3 photo or headshot. Application and other documents must be sent to: Graduate Fellowship Program, ISI, 3901 Centerville Rd., PO Box 4431, Wilmington, DE, 19807-0431. **Deadline:** February 15.

3775 ■ Western Civilization Fellowships *(Graduate/Fellowship)*

Purpose: To support students in the graduate level in the study of the institutions, values, and history of the West. **Focus:** Western European studies. **Qualif.:** Applicant must be a U.S citizen and member of the Intercollegiate Studies Institute; must be a college senior or graduate student; must engage in graduate studies for the purpose of teaching at the college level. **Criteria:** Applicant must meet the requirements specific to the fellowship.

Funds Avail.: $20,000. **Number Awarded:** 2. **To Apply:** Application form are available at the website address. Applicant must submit the following: (1) Four brief statement; (2) Three essays; (3) Three letters of academic recommendation; (4) College transcript; (5) 2x3 photo or headshot. Application and other documents must be sent to: Graduate Fellowship Program, ISI, 3901 Centerville Rd., PO Box 4431, Wilmington, DE, 19807-0431. **Deadline:** February 15.

3776 ■ Intermediaries and Reinsurance Underwriters Association

971 Rte. 202 N
Branchburg, NJ 08876
Ph: (908)203-0211
Fax: (908)203-0213
E-mail: info@irua.com
URL: http://www.irua.com

3777 ■ Intermediaries and Reinsurance Underwriters Association Scholarships
(Undergraduate/Internship)

Purpose: To provide an opportunity for college juniors and seniors to learn about the reinsurance industry and gain practical experience in its operation. **Focus:** Insurance and insurance-related fields. **Qualif.:** Applicants must be full-time students enrolled in an undergraduate program at an accredited four-year college or university; have at least one term remaining following completion of the intern program; have an overall GPA of at least 3.0 and two recommendations from faculty advisor, dean or department chairman; must be enrolled in degree program with a major in insurance, economics, business or a related field; and must be U.S. citizens of at least 18 years of age. **Criteria:** Applicants will be evaluated by the Internship Selection Committee.

Funds Avail.: $400. **To Apply:** Applicants must submit all required application information.

3778 ■ International Alumni Association of Shri Mahavir Jain Vidyalaya

1119 Flanders St.
Garner, NC 27529
Ph: (919)772-8473
URL: http://www.iaamjv.org

3779 ■ College Education Loan Scholarships For U.S. Resident Students *(Undergraduate/Loan)*

Purpose: To promote the cause of college education in the Jain community. **Focus:** General studies. **Qualif.:** Applicant must be born in Jain Family or actively practicing Jainism; graduating U.S. High School senior; have a minimum GPA of 3.0 on 4.0 scale; or a minimum SAT score of 1500 out of max. 2400; or Minimum ACT score of 20; enrolled full-time Undergraduate student in U.S.; a U.S. permanent resident or U.S. Citizen; and in need for financial assistance. **Criteria:** Selection is based on the application.

Funds Avail.: $2,000 for the first year and $1,000 annually for next three years of undergraduate studies. **Number Awarded:** 10. **To Apply:** Applicants must submit a completed application form. **Deadline:** June 30.

Remarks: This is an interest-free loan scholarship. **Contact:** Dr. Dinesh M. Shah Chairman, College Education Loan Committee 2034 Via Del Rey South Pasadena, CA 91030-4146.

3780 ■ Graduate Education Loan Scholarships
(Graduate/Loan)

Purpose: To assist a Jain student for further studies. **Focus:** General studies. **Qualif.:** Applicant must be an Indian student pursuing higher education in USA. **Criteria:** Selection is based on the submitted applications and materials.

Funds Avail.: $2000. **To Apply:** Applicants must submit a completed Loan Application form along with required documents. **Deadline:** September 1 and February 1.

Remarks: This is an interest-free loan scholarships. **Contact:** Mr. Keyur Gandhi, Chairperson Scholarship Committee, IAAMJV, Inc. 44 Normandy Village, No. 16, Naunet, NY 10954, Phone: 845-249-2116, Email: kgandhi@iaamjv.org or keyur_gandhi@hotmail.com.

3781 ■ International Association of Administrative Professionals

PO Box 20404
Kansas City, MO 64195-0404
Ph: (816)891-6600
Fax: (816)891-9118
URL: http://www.iaap-wings.org

3782 ■ IAAP Wings Chapter Scholarships
(Undergraduate/Scholarship)

Purpose: To provide financial assistance for qualified individuals from the Greater Miami Valley area who are pursuing careers as office professionals. **Focus:** Business. **Qualif.:** Applicants must have applied and have been accepted or be currently attending an accredited university, college, junior college, community college, or technical or vocational school. **Criteria:** Applicants are evaluated based on academic merit.

Funds Avail.: No specific amount. **To Apply:** Applicants must submit all the required application information. **Deadline:** February 29.

3783 ■ International Association of Arson Investigators

2151 Priest Bridge Dr., Ste. 25
Crofton, MD 21114
Ph: (410)451-3473
Fax: (410)451-9049
E-mail: aclark@gmrc.com
URL: http://www.firearson.com

3784 ■ John Charles Wilson Scholarships
(Undergraduate/Scholarship)

Purpose: To foster, support and promote fire prevention and arson awareness through education and training. **Focus:** Fires and fire prevention. **Qualif.:** Applicants must be enrolled in a two or four-year accredited college or university that offers courses in police or fire science including fire investigation and related subjects. **Criteria:** Recipients are selected based on academic performance, financial need, and recommendation.

Funds Avail.: Varies. **To Apply:** Applicants must submit completed application form. **Deadline:** February 15.

3785 ■ International Association of Black Actuaries

19 S LaSalle St., Ste. 1400
Chicago, IL 60603
Ph: (215)392-4598
Fax: (215)395-6400
E-mail: iaba_ed@blackactuaries.org
URL: http://www.blackactuaries.org

3786 ■ International Association of Black Actuaries Scholarships *(Undergraduate/ Scholarship)*

Purpose: To provide scholarships among undergraduates or graduate level for qualified black students who are interested in pursuing actuarial careers. **Focus:** Actuarial science. **Qualif.:** Applicants must be permanent residents or U.S./Canadian citizens; must be admitted to college or university which offers either a program in actuarial science or courses that will serve to prepare the students for actuarial career; must have demonstrated mathematical ability an interest in an actuarial career; must have at least 3.0 GPA on a 4.0 scale, a Math SAT score of at least 600 or an ACT Math score of at least 28; must have completed the calculus and probability courses; must be junior, senior or graduate students attempting or already passed the exam; must have completed or completing the validation by educational experience(VEE) requirements; must have determination, self-motivation, excellent recommendations from mathematics-related instructors and familiarity with an actuarial profession demands. **Criteria:** Recipients are selected based on broader math background, high GPA and Math SAT/ACT scores, merit and financial need.

Funds Avail.: No specific amount. **To Apply:** Applicants must submit a completed online application form, two nomination forms completed by instructors and/or advisors at educational institution, an official, sealed record of any educational examination scores, Student Aid Report (SAR) showing the financial date and a copy of college or university catalog or information sheet showing an estimated expenses. **Deadline:** May 21. **Contact:** iabafdvp@blackactuaries.org.

3787 ■ International Association of Defense Counsel

One North Franklin, Ste. 1205
Chicago, IL 60606
Ph: (312)368-1494
Fax: (312)368-1854
E-mail: info@iadclaw.org
URL: http://www.iadclaw.org

3788 ■ Gary Walker Memorial Scholarships *(Professional Development/Scholarship)*

Purpose: To advance the future of the defense and corporate bar by providing tuition reimbursement to deserving IADC Trial Academy students. **Focus:** Law. **Qualif.:** Applicants must be attorneys who have some level of actual trial experience; must have been in trial practice for between 2 and 10 years; and must demonstrate commitment to the advancement of the defense trial bar. **Criteria:** Preference is given to minority and women students as well as those demonstrating financial need.

Funds Avail.: Fund includes the registration fee of $3,300 and the housing and meal package of $1,400 to attend the Trial Academy. **To Apply:** Applicants must submit completed application form available in the website along with a statement of the applicant's actual trial experience (indicating number of trials, nature of the litigation, nature of role in defense team, etc.); copy of resume; list of any professional, civic or volunteer activities that may demonstrate a commitment to the legal profession and the defense bar; description of additional factors supporting scholarship application; and two letters of recommendation from attorneys who have supervised applicant's work. Mail to: Gary Walker Scholarship (c/o Kate Keating Edsey), The Foundation of the IADC, One North Franklin Street, Suite 1205, Chicago, IL 60606 USA. **Deadline:** May 23. **Contact:** International Association Defense Counsel at the above address (see entry 3787).

3789 ■ International Association for Dental Research

1619 Duke St.
Alexandria, VA 22314-3406
Ph: (703)548-1883
Fax: (703)548-0066
E-mail: cfox@iadr.org
URL: http://www.iadr.com

3790 ■ IADR David B. Scott Fellowships *(Undergraduate/Fellowship)*

Purpose: To improve knowledge on oral health by advancing and supporting research projects; to support and represent the oral health research community; and to facilitate the communication and application of research findings. **Focus:** Dental Hygiene. **Qualif.:** Program is open to students who are training to become dentists; must be registered in an accredited or acceptable dental school; and must be sponsored by a dental researcher with the approval of their school's dean. Candidates may not have received their dental degree nor should they be due to receive their degree in the year of the award; may have a college or advanced degree in a discipline other than the industry; and must be IADR members. **Criteria:** Recipients are selected based on the submitted project proposal as reviewed by the IADR Board of Directors.

Funds Avail.: $2,500. **To Apply:** Applicants and their sponsors must submit a research project proposal to the division not exceeding 8 pages (including references), typed and double-spaced. Proposal should include aims, objectives, and significance of the proposal; rationale and background to the study; materials and methods; statistical treatment of data; facilities and equipment; and budget. **Deadline:** October 15. **Contact:** Central Office of IADR at the above address (see entry 3789).

3791 ■ IADR John Clarkson Fellowships *(Postdoctorate/Fellowship)*

Purpose: To allow investigators in the field of public dental health to obtain training and experience at a center of excellence. **Focus:** Dentistry. **Qualif.:** Applicants must hold a degree in dentistry or in a scientific discipline (dental, masters, or PhD degrees); must be members of IADR; and must be actively engaged in research in public dental health. **Criteria:** Recipients are selected based on merit.

Funds Avail.: Up to $15,000 covering accommodation,

Awards are arranged alphabetically below their administering organizations

subsistence and travel. **To Apply:** Applications should be made individually and should include the following details: name, address, current place of work, and position; IADR Division/Section membership; full curriculum vitae and reprints of three relevant publications; references from two recognized scientists and the principal Dean/Chair of the institution where the applicant is employed; and an outline by the applicant describing how his/her experience and interests qualify him/her as a candidate for the Fellowship (no more than 3 single-spaced pages), including: detailed description of the subject areas to be covered in the training program; practical use to which the training acquired would be put, proposed duration and dates of the fellowship; institutes and country it is proposed to visit; reasons for selection of particular institutes(s); previous Fellowships/awards; and detailed budget for program. Applications are sent electronically to Sheri S. Herren, Awards, Fellowships & Grants Manager at sherren@iadr.org. **Contact:** Sheri S. Herren, email at sherren@iadr.org

3792 ■ IADR John Gray Fellowships *(Professional Development/Fellowship)*

Purpose: To allow dental or postgraduate students to obtain training and experience in dental or related research. **Focus:** Dentistry. **Qualif.:** Applicants must be registered student in an accredited or acceptable dental school or in a recognized formal postgraduate program; must be in a training program in the division in which the fellowship is awarded; must be sponsored by their faculty advisor/direct supervisor or the Dean of the School; and must be IADR members. **Criteria:** Recipients are selected based on merit.

Funds Avail.: $10,000. **To Apply:** Applicants must submit a proposal to the division secretary outlining: the precise title of the subject to be studied; detailed description of the subjects to be covered in the training program; practical use to which the training acquired would be put; proposed duration and dates of the fellowship; institute(s) and country it is proposed to visit; reasons for particular institute(s); previous fellowships or awards; and budget for program. The division officers will select the fellowship recipient and will then send the candidate's name to the Central Office (via Sheri S. Herren, Awards, Fellowships & Grants Manager, sherren@iadr.org) for presentation to the IADR Board of Directors for approval. **Contact:** Sheri S. Herren at sherren@iadr.org.

3793 ■ IADR Norton Ross Fellowships *(Professional Development/Fellowship)*

Purpose: To allow dental or postgraduate students to obtain training and experience in dental or related research. **Focus:** Dentistry. **Qualif.:** Applicants must be registered in an accredited or acceptable dental school or in a recognized formal postgraduate program; must be sponsored by their faculty advisor, direct supervisor, or the Dean of the school; may have a college or advanced degree in a discipline other than dentistry; and must be IADR members. **Criteria:** Recipients are selected based on merit.

Funds Avail.: $2,800. **To Apply:** Applicants must submit a proposal directly to their division outlining: the precise title of the subject to be studied; detailed description of the subjects to be covered in the training program; practical use to which the training acquired would be put; proposed duration and dates of the fellowship; institute(s) and country it is proposed to visit; reasons for particular institute(s); previous fellowships or awards; and budget for program. **Contact:** Sheri S. Herren at sherren@iadr.org.

3794 ■ IADR Toshio Nakao Fellowships *(Professional Development/Fellowship)*

Purpose: To allow young investigators in the area of dental materials science to obtain training and experience at a center of excellence. **Focus:** Dentistry. **Qualif.:** Applicants must hold a degree in dentistry or in a scientific discipline; must be within 5 years of obtaining their dental or scientific degree on or at the fellowship proposal deadline; and must be members of IADR and are actively engaged in research. **Criteria:** Recipients are selected based on merit as evaluated by the IADR Fellowships Committee.

Funds Avail.: $15,000. **To Apply:** Applications should be made individually and should include the following details (in English): name, address, date of birth, current place of work, and position; IADR Division/Section membership; full curriculum vitae with list and reprints of three relevant publications; references from two recognized scientists one of whom should be from the principal (Dean/Chair) of the institution where the applicant is employed; and an outline by the applicant of how his/her experience and interests qualify him/her as a candidate for the fellowship (no more than 3 single spaced pages), including: detailed description of the subject areas to be covered in the training program; practical use to which the training acquired would be put; proposed duration and dates of the fellowship; institutes and/or country it is proposed to visit; reasons for particular institutes(s); previous fellowships/awards; and budget for program. Submit proposals electronically to Sheri S. Herren, Awards, Fellowships & Grants Manager at sherren@iadr.org. **Deadline:** October 15. **Contact:** Sheri S. Herren at sherren@iadr.org

3795 ■ International Association of Emergency Managers

201 Park Washington Court
Falls Church, VA 22046-4527
Ph: (703)538-1795
Fax: (703)241-5603
E-mail: shiley@iaem.com
URL: http://www.iaem.com

3796 ■ International Association of Emergency Managers Scholarships *(Undergraduate/Scholarship)*

Purpose: To further education on emergency management by developing students that possess the intellect and technical skills to advance and enhance the profession. **Focus:** Emergency and disaster Services. **Qualif.:** Applicants must be full-time students pursuing an associate or diploma baccalaureate or graduate degree in emergency management or a closely related field. **Criteria:** Selection is based on merit.

Funds Avail.: No specific amount. **To Apply:** Applicants must submit the following: original transcript with official seal (may be sent by the registrar or included in the application package); a verification that they are enrolled as full-time students based on the standards set by their study program (full-time student verification must be provided by the registrar and is deemed a separate document from the applicant's transcript); three references (at least one reference must be from a faculty member); description of applicant's major/program and course description (may be supplied by sending a school catalog, providing printed copies from a Web site, or submitting information sheets provided by the department). **Deadline:** May 16. **Contact:**

Dawn M. Shiley-Danziesen; 703-538-3542; shiley@iaem.com.

3797 ■ International Association of Foundation Drilling

Pacific Center 1
14180 Dallas Pkwy., Ste.510
Dallas, TX 75254
Ph: (214)343-2091
Fax: (214)343-2384
E-mail: adsc@adsc-iafd.com
URL: http://www.adsc-iafd.com

3798 ■ International Association of Foundation Drilling Scholarships for Civil Engineering Students *(Postgraduate/Scholarship)*

Purpose: To protect, promote, foster and advance the interests of persons, firms or corporations engaged in design, construction, equipment manufacture and distribution for the drilled shaft, anchored earth retention and corresponding industries. **Focus:** Engineering. **Qualif.:** Applicants must be full-time graduate students who are enrolled in less than 12 credit hours; must be willing to work on a full and part-time basis; must be U.S. or Canadian citizens; must be currently enrolled in an ABET or CEAB accredited engineering program or be graduates from such program; must have plans to enter or continue graduate school during the academic year. **Criteria:** Recipients are selected based on academic performance and financial need.

Funds Avail.: $3,000. **Number Awarded:** 14. **To Apply:** Applicants must submit a completed application form; current, official transcript of academic records and two letters of reference from persons familiar with their academic or professional experience.

3799 ■ International Association of Foundation Drilling Scholarships for Part-time Civil Engineering Graduate School Students *(Postgraduate/Scholarship)*

Purpose: To protect, promote, foster and advance the interests of persons, firms or corporations engaged in design, construction, equipment manufacture or distribution for the drilled shaft, anchored earth retention and corresponding industries. **Focus:** Civil engineering. **Qualif.:** Applicants must be U.S. or Canadian citizens; must be part-time graduate students majoring in geotechnical or structural engineering; must be currently enrolled in an ABET or CEAB accredited engineering program or be graduates from such program; must have plans to enter or continue graduate school during the academic year and be willing to work on a full or part-time basis. **Criteria:** Recipients are selected based on academic performance and financial need.

Funds Avail.: $3,000. **To Apply:** Applicants must submit a completed application form; current, official transcript of academic record; and two letters of reference from persons familiar with the academic or professional experience. **Deadline:** April 15.

3800 ■ International Association of Healthcare Central Service Materiel Management

213 W Institute Pl., Ste. 307
Chicago, IL 60610
Ph: (312)440-0078
Fax: (312)440-9474
Free: 800-962-8274
E-mail: betty@iahcsmm.org
URL: http://www.iahcsmm.com

3801 ■ IAHCSMM - Purdue University Scholarship Awards *(Professional Development/ Scholarship)*

Purpose: To financially support individuals in pursuing their educational and individual growth. **Focus:** General studies. **Qualif.:** Applicants must be employed in the Steering Processing profession in a non-management position for a minimum of one year. **Criteria:** Applicants will be evaluated based on financial need; interest in pursuing educational and individual growth goals; participation in activities (association, hospital department, community); and years of service in Central Service.

Funds Avail.: Exact scholarship amount is not specified. **Number Awarded:** 1 in each category: Central Service Technicians; Central Service Managers/Supervisors; Healthcare Material Managers. **To Apply:** Applicants must complete the application form available at the website with a reference letter and personal essay attached. **Deadline:** March 1. **Contact:** Carol Brunty, Manager Continuing Education, IAHCSMM-Purdue Scholarship Awards, Purdue University 128 Memorial Mall, 116 Stewart Center West Lafayette, IN 47907-2034.

3802 ■ SPSmedical CS Scholarships *(Other/ Scholarship)*

Purpose: To promote the certification of sterile processing professionals. **Focus:** Medical technology. **Qualif.:** Applicants must be employed in the CS profession for at least of 6 months. **Criteria:** Scholarships will be awarded to applicants who will fulfill the requirements.

Funds Avail.: No specific amount. **Number Awarded:** 3. **To Apply:** Applicants must complete the application form available at the website with a letter of recommendation from the supervisor/manager attached. Mail to: SPSmedical Supply Corp. Attn: Education Department 6789 W Henrietta Road Rush, NY 14543, toll-free: 800722-1529, fax: 585359-0167, email info@spsmedical.com.

3803 ■ International Association of Law Enforcement Intelligence Analysts

PO Box 13857
Richmond, VA 23225
Ph: (804)565-2059
Fax: (804)565-2059
E-mail: admin@ialeia.org
URL: http://www.ialeia.org

3804 ■ Jorge Espejal Contreras Memorial Scholarships *(Graduate, Undergraduate/ Scholarship)*

Purpose: To strive for professionalism in the intelligence field by promoting career development and continued education. **Focus:** Intelligence Service; Statistics; Criminal Justice. **Qualif.:** Program is open to active IALEIA members or immediate family members enrolled in an intelligence, analysis, criminal justice, or other related undergraduate or graduate program at an accredited academic institution; must be based on full-time or part-time enrollment in an ac-

Awards are arranged alphabetically below their administering organizations

credited college/university and can be on campus or via distance-learning. **Criteria:** Recipients are selected based on the eligibility status evaluated through the quality of the essay (minimum of 1,000 words), its originality and its complete response to addressing the required topic, complete check for grammar, punctuation, and spelling.

Funds Avail.: $1,000. **Number Awarded:** 2. **To Apply:** Applicants should download application from the IALEIA website and submit to the IALEIA Training, Education, and Career Development Committee. Eligible submissions must be provided in English. Applicants must submit their work electronically to the attention of the TE&CD Director and a signed original copy to be mailed. Application must include a mandatory 1,000-1,500 word essay on: The Future of Law Enforcement Intelligence as a Profession. Mail application package to: IALEIA Scholarship Program, Attn: IALEIA TE&CD, 705 Somerset Drive, El Paso, Texas 79912, USA. **Deadline:** May 16.

3805 ■ The Henley Putnam University Scholarships *(Professional Development/Scholarship)*

Purpose: To promote career development and continued education in the intelligence field by providing educational assistance. **Focus:** Intelligence service. **Qualif.:** Applicants must be active IALEIA members or their immediate family members. **Criteria:** Applicants will be evaluated by the IALEIA Director of Training, Education and Career Development and TE&CD committee members.

Funds Avail.: $1,000. **To Apply:** Applicants should download and submit an application from the IALEIA website to the Training, Education and Career Development Committee along with the 1,000-1,500 word essay on "The Future of Online Distance Learning in Law Enforcement". **Deadline:** May 15.

3806 ■ International Association of Law Libraries

PO Box 5709
Washington, DC 20016-1309
E-mail: julesw@sas.ac.uk
URL: http://www.iall.org

3807 ■ International Association of Law Libraries Scholarship Program *(Professional Development/Scholarship)*

Purpose: To enable law librarians who are normally unable to benefit from the association's activities to attend the Annual Course in International Law Librarianship that forms the annual conference of the association. **Focus:** Law. **Qualif.:** Applicants must be in current employment in librarianship with significant legal context to their work; applicants need not to be members of the association. **Criteria:** Recipients are selected based on demonstrated promise to make a significant contribution to the profession of law librarianship. Preference is given to applicants who cannot otherwise attend the conference without the scholarship; who have not yet received in IALL bursary or scholarship in the past years of the program; and who have not attended a conference outside their own country. Program is not open to officers or members of the Board of the Association.

Funds Avail.: $1,500. **To Apply:** Applicants must submit a full resume including name and qualifications; full contact details; details of present job; present and past employers; membership in professional associations; attendance of conferences. They must also provide an essay stating the reasons for wanting to attend the conference, the expected benefits and how you intend to disseminate those benefits, along with a letter of reference from the employer including permission to attend the conference. **Deadline:** May 15. **Contact:** halvor.kongshavn@ub.uib.no

3808 ■ International Association of Lighting Designers

The Merchandise Mart, Ste. 9-104
Chicago, IL 60654
Ph: (312)527-3677
Fax: (312)527-3680
E-mail: iald@iald.org
URL: http://www.iald.org

3809 ■ IALD Scholarship Programs *(Graduate, Undergraduate/Scholarship)*

Purpose: To promote education in architectural lighting design. **Focus:** Architecture; Lighting science. **Qualif.:** Applicant must be a graduate or undergraduate student studying in the field of architectural lighting design. **Criteria:** Applicant will be judged based on grades, extra curricular activities, portfolio of work and personal recommendations.

Funds Avail.: $500 $5000. **Number Awarded:** One year. **To Apply:** Applicants must complete an application form (available at the website) attach a copy of official transcript; resume; two letters of recommendation; statement of personal experience with lighting, reasons for studying lighting or why deserve the scholarship (maximum of 2 pages); and examples of work in 8.5x11 format (maximum of 10 images). Send the application and attachments to: Scholarship Chairman, International Association of lighting Designers, Merchandise Mart, Suite 9-104 200 World Trade Center Chicago, IL 60654. **Deadline:** February 15.

3810 ■ International Association of Women Police

777 Memorial Ave.
Orillia, ON, Canada L3V 7V3
Ph: (705)329-7585
Fax: (705)329-7596
E-mail: amy.ramsay@ontario.ca
URL: http://www.iawp.org

3811 ■ IAWP International Recognition and Scholarship Award *(Professional Development/Scholarship)*

Purpose: To increase the understanding about the roles of women officers in various countries; to encourage participation in the International Association of Women Police by all countries of the world; to promote membership through the recipient of this award within the region; to increase the understanding and awareness of women in law enforcement and the International Association of Women Police; and to recognize the accomplishments of a women officer from outside North America. **Focus:** Law enforcement. **Qualif.:** Applicants must be women and members of the police organization. **Criteria:** Recipients are selected based on the pre-selected criteria including completeness of application, evidence of policing skills, interest in increasing awareness and understanding of the role of women in law enforcement, willingness to network, and ability to communicate with other conference attendees.

Funds Avail.: No specific amount. **To Apply:** Applicants

Awards are arranged alphabetically below their administering organizations

must submit personal information including the name, rank, assignment, police organization, and contact information; biography including education, employment history, and interest; a letter of support from the applicant's senior officer or administrator indicating how long they have known the applicant and the basis of the recommendation; and a letter of application written by the applicant showing why they feel they can be a good candidate to receive the scholarship award. **Deadline:** April 30. **Contact:** International Association of Women Police at the above address (see entry 3810).

3812 ■ International Association of Workforce Professionals

1801 Louisville Rd.
Frankfort, KY 40601
Ph: (502)223-4459
Fax: (502)223-4127
Free: 888-898-9960
E-mail: iawp@iawponline.org
URL: http://www.iawponline.org

3813 ■ W. Scott Boyd Group Grants *(All/Grant)*

Purpose: To provide financial assistance for IAWP chapters and subchapters, as well as chapters working with their agencies for the presentation of group educational and training programs. **Focus:** General studies. **Qualif.:** Applicants must be IAWP full members. **Criteria:** Recipients are selected on a first-come-first-serve basis.

Funds Avail.: $250; $500; $750. **Number Awarded:** 5-15. **To Apply:** Applicants must complete the application form and attach a brief explanation of how this course relates to their work or promotional chances. **Contact:** International Association of Workforce Professionals at the above address (see entry 3812).

3814 ■ Logan S. Chambers Individual Scholarships *(Professional Development/Scholarship)*

Purpose: To provide financial assistance for IAWP full members who wish to increase their knowledge, skills, and abilities in a course of study that pertains to employment and training work, or toward a degree program that relates to job performance and/or promotional possibilities. **Focus:** General Studies. **Qualif.:** Applicants must be IAWP full members. **Criteria:** Recipients are selected on a first-come-first-serve basis.

Funds Avail.: $150; $300; $500. **Number Awarded:** 3. **To Apply:** Applicants must complete the application form and attach a brief explanation of how this course relates to their work or promotional chances. **Contact:** International Association of Workforce Professionals at the above address (see entry 3812).

3815 ■ Freddy L. Jacobs Scholarships *(Undergraduate/Scholarship)*

Purpose: To provide financial assistance for IAWP student members or dependents of IAWP full members who wish to increase their knowledge, skills, and abilities in the area of leadership or workforce development. **Focus:** General Studies. **Qualif.:** Applicants must be pursuing an associate, undergraduate degree or other certification who are required to complete an extracurricular educational or training to program to obtain high school diploma. **Criteria:** Recipients are selected based on a first-come-first-serve basis.

Funds Avail.: $75; $150; $250. **To Apply:** Applicants must complete the scholarship application form and attach a brief explanation of how this course will increase their knowledge, skills and abilities in the area of leadership or workforce development. **Contact:** International Association of Workforce professionals at the above address (see entry 3812).

3816 ■ International Beverage Packing Association

One Ocean Spray Dr.
Middleboro, MA 02349
Ph: (508)946-1000
E-mail: info@ibpa.org
URL: http://www.ibpa.org

3817 ■ Richard F. Heaney Memorial Scholarship Fund *(Graduate, Undergraduate/Scholarship)*

Purpose: To encourage educational pursuits among students involved in packaging curriculum. **Focus:** Packaging. **Qualif.:** Scholarship is open to juniors, seniors, and graduate students in packaging curriculums; must be citizens of the United States or Canada. **Criteria:** Selection is based on grade point average overall and in packaging courses, financial need, extra curricular activities and the completed essay.

Funds Avail.: $500-2,000. **To Apply:** Applicants should send an e-mail to the IBPA representatives to request an application form. **Deadline:** October 6.

3818 ■ International Brotherhood of Electrical Workers

263 Ward St.
East Windsor, NJ 08520
Ph: (609)443-4100
Fax: (609)448-8690
URL: http://www.local827.org

3819 ■ Local 827 Peter J. Casey Scholarships *(Undergraduate/Scholarship)*

Purpose: To provide educational support for children of IBEW members. **Focus:** General studies. **Qualif.:** Applicants must be dependents of an IBEW member and must be in their senior year of high school. **Criteria:** Selections are made by the Office of University Undergraduate Admissions Committee.

Funds Avail.: $1,000. **To Apply:** Applicants must submit a completed application form. **Deadline:** January 31.

3820 ■ International Catacomb Society

50 Cross St.
Winchester, MA 01890
Ph: (781)729-1150
URL: http://www.catacombsociety.org

3821 ■ Estelle Shohet Brettman Fellowship *(Postdoctorate/Fellowship)*

Purpose: To promote the preservation, restoration, and documentation of the catacombs in Rome and elsewhere that contain paintings, epigraphy, and artifacts depicting the cultures and customs of early religions under the Roman Empire. **Focus:** Roman art. **Qualif.:** Applicants must be:

Awards are arranged alphabetically below their administering organizations

scholars of all institutional affiliations who are US citizens and possess a doctoral degree or equivalent; at early post-doctoral or launching stage of their careers; independent, unaffiliated scholars without doctoral credentials but equivalent in experience, competence and accomplishments to outstanding early postdoctoral candidates. **Criteria:** Applicants must identify a monitor, someone with sufficient expertise in the proposed research area like a senior faculty member or official of the applicant's institution who can vouch for the feasibility of the proposal, including the likelihood that needed institutional support.

Funds Avail.: $10,000 up to $30,000. **To Apply:** Applicants must submit the completed applications, supporting documents and communications with the Sholet Scholars Program must be in English. **Deadline:** October 15.

3822 ■ International Center for Not-for-Profit Law

1126 16th St. NW, Ste. 400
Washington, DC 20036
Ph: (202)452-8600
Fax: (202)452-8555
E-mail: andrea@ecnl.org.hu
URL: http://www.icnl.org

3823 ■ Fellowships to Promote Research on the Legal Framework for Civil Society in Latin America, Africa and Asia *(All/Fellowship)*

Purpose: To provide opportunities to engage practitioners and scholars to advance the legal environment for civil society by providing them with the support and expertise of ICNL's international staff; access to extensive library of NGO legal materials; and meetings with NGO representatives, academics and others in Washington, DC. **Focus:** Law. **Qualif.:** Applicants must be residents from Latin America (Bolivia, Ecuador, Guatemala, Nicaragua, Peru, Venezuela), Africa (Angola, Burundi, DR Congo, Ethiopia, Guinea, Kenya, Liberia, Madagascar, Mali, Nigeria, Rwanda, Sierra Leone, Somalia, Sudan, Uganda, Zimbabwe) and Asia (Thailand, Vietnam). **Criteria:** Entries will be evaluated based on compliance with eligibility requirements and application procedures and on demonstrated interest and experience relating to the legal environment for civil society.

Funds Avail.: No amount mentioned. **To Apply:** Applicants must accomplish all required documents in English: application coversheet; proposal; resume, curriculum vitae, or other statement of work history and education. **Deadline:** May 30.

3824 ■ Internships in International Civil Society Law *(Undergraduate/Internship)*

Purpose: To provide financial assistance to develop projects that reflect student interests and skills and to assist with the student's career development. **Focus:** Law. **Qualif.:** Applicants should be enrolled in an accredited law school. Good research, writing and analytical skills and foreign language is a plus eligibility. **Criteria:** Applicants are evaluated based on some criteria designed by the Selection Committee.

Funds Avail.: No specific amount. **Number Awarded:** 1. **To Apply:** Applicants must submit resume, writing sample, and a cover letter. **Deadline:** April 30. **Contact:** Human Resources at hr@icnl.org.

3825 ■ Spring Internship in International NGO Law *(Undergraduate/Internship)*

Purpose: To provide financial assistance to students seeking a unique opportunity to be involved in the promotion of an enabling legal environment for civil society, freedom of association and public participation around the world. **Focus:** Law. **Qualif.:** Applicants must come from Washington, DC; must be enrolled in an accredited law school; must possess good research, writing and analytical skills; and must have demonstrable individual initiative and ability to work as part of a team. **Criteria:** Applicants are evaluated based on criteria designed by the Internship Selection Committee.

Funds Avail.: No specific amount. **To Apply:** Applicants must submit a cover letter, resume and writing samples (not longer than 5 pages). **Deadline:** February 1.

3826 ■ International Code Council Foundation

500 New Jersey Ave. NW, 6th Fl.
Washington, DC 20001-2070
Ph: 888-422-7233
E-mail: leslie@flash.org
URL: http://www.icc-foundation.org

3827 ■ C.D. Howard Scholarships *(Undergraduate/Scholarship)*

Purpose: To provide financial assistance for children of ICC governmental members. **Focus:** General studies. **Qualif.:** Applicants must be children of code enforcement agency personnel. The jurisdiction authority must be an active Governmental Member of the International Code Council. Children must be dependents as defined by the Internal Revenue Service. **Criteria:** Recipient selection will be based on merit.

Funds Avail.: $1,000. **Number Awarded:** 1. **To Apply:** Applicants must demonstrate financial need. Financial information will be required along with details of any other financial assistance the applicant is receiving. Applicants must also provide evidence of satisfactory scholastic achievement including grades, test scores and teacher recommendations. Applicants must complete the scholarship application. A one-page narrative on why the applicant should be awarded the scholarship is also required. **Deadline:** June 30. **Contact:** International Code Council Foundation, Attn: Scholarships c/o: COO 900 Montclair Road Birmingham, AL 35213-1206; scholarships@iccsafe.org

3828 ■ International Code Council Foundation General Scholarship Fund *(Undergraduate/Scholarship)*

Purpose: To provide financial assistance for children of ICC governmental members. **Focus:** Architectural Engineering. **Qualif.:** Applicants must be children of code enforcement agency personnel. The jurisdiction authority must be an active Governmental Member of the International Code Council; Children must be dependents as defined by the Internal Revenue Service. Typically, this includes birth children, stepchildren, legally adopted children, or a legal ward financially supported by the employee. **Criteria:** Scholarship is given to those who are pursuing educational opportunities beyond the high school level at a recognized and/or accredited institution. Selection is done on the basis of satisfactory scholastic achievement.

Funds Avail.: $2,500. **Number Awarded:** 2. **To Apply:** Applications and instructions are available in the ICC and ICCF websites. **Deadline:** June 30. **Contact:** International Code Council Foundation, Attn: Scholarships c/o: COO 900 Montclair Road Birmingham, AL 35213-1206; scholarships@iccsafe.org.

3829 ■ J.W. "Bill" Neese Scholarships
(Undergraduate/Scholarship)

Purpose: To provide financial assistance for children of ICC governmental members. **Focus:** Architectural Engineering. **Qualif.:** Applicants must be children of code enforcement agency personnel. The jurisdiction authority must be an active governmental member of the International Code Council. Children must be dependents as defined by the Internal Revenue Service. Typically, this includes birth children, stepchildren, legally adopted children, or a legal ward financially supported by the employee. **Criteria:** Scholarship is given to those who are pursuing educational opportunities beyond the high school level at a recognized and/or accredited institution. Selection is done on the basis of satisfactory scholastic achievement.

Funds Avail.: $1,000. **Number Awarded:** 1. **To Apply:** Applications and instructions are available at the ICC and ICCF websites. **Deadline:** June 30. **Contact:** International Code Council Foundation, Attn: Scholarships c/o: COO 900 Montclair Road Birmingham, AL 35213-1206; scholarships@iccsafe.org.

3830 ■ Charlie O'Meilia Scholarships
(Undergraduate/Scholarship)

Purpose: To provide financial assistance for children of ICC Governmental Members. **Focus:** General studies. **Qualif.:** Applicants must be children of code enforcement agency personnel. The jurisdiction authority must be an active Governmental Member of the International Code Council; children must be dependents as defined by the Internal Revenue Service. Typically, this includes birth children, stepchildren, legally adopted children, or a legal ward financially supported by the employee. **Criteria:** Recipient will be selected by a committee of volunteers and will be notified by the office of the COO on behalf of the Palm Beach County Chapter.

Funds Avail.: $1,000. **Number Awarded:** 1. **To Apply:** Applications and instructions are available in the ICC and ICCF websites. Applicants must provide evidence of satisfactory scholastic achievement including grades, test scores and teacher recommendations. Applicants must complete the scholarship application. A one-page narrative on why the applicant should be awarded the scholarship is also required. **Deadline:** June 30.

Remarks: The Charlie O'meilia Scholarship is awarded by the Palm Beach County chapter in honor of long-time member Charlie O'Meilia. **Contact:** International Code Council Foundation, Attn: Scholarships c/o: COO 900 Montclair Road Birmingham, AL 35213-1206; scholarships@iccsafe.org

3831 ■ William J. Tangye Scholarships
(Undergraduate/Scholarship)

Purpose: To provide financial assistance for children of ICC members intending to pursue higher education. **Focus:** Architectural Engineering. **Qualif.:** Applicants must be children of code enforcement agency personnel. The jurisdiction authority must be an active Governmental Member of the International Code Council; Children must be dependents as defined by the Internal Revenue Service. Typically, this includes birth children, stepchildren, legally adopted children, or a legal ward financially supported by the employee. Applicants must be enrolled in engineering, architecture or construction technology programs in a recognized and/or accredited school such as a university, trade school, business college or other institutions as approved by the ICC prior to distribution of the award. **Criteria:** Scholarship is given based on merit.

Funds Avail.: $2,500. **Number Awarded:** 1. **To Apply:** Applications and instructions are available at the ICC and ICCF websites. **Deadline:** June 30. **Contact:** International Code Council Foundation, Attn: Scholarships c/o: COO 900 Montclair Road Birmingham, AL 35213-1206; scholarships@iccsafe.org.

3832 ■ International Council for Canadian Studies

250 City Centre Ave., Ste. 303
Ottawa, ON, Canada K1R 6K7
Ph: (613)789-7834
Fax: (613)789-7830
URL: http://www.iccs-ciec.ca

3833 ■ Graduate Student Scholarships
(Postgraduate/Scholarship)

Purpose: To facilitate the renewal of the community of Canadianists by supporting the work of young scholars. **Focus:** Canadian studies. **Qualif.:** Applicant must be a student in the social sciences or humanities who are in the process of preparing a graduate thesis or doctoral dissertation in Canada; must obtained the support of a faculty member at a Canadian university who has agreed to act as the student's academic sponsor. **Criteria:** Applicants will be evaluated based on the clarity of the proposal and its methodology, the proposal's potential contribution to knowledge in its field; must demonstrate the need for the research to be carried out in Canada and by the strength of the letter of support. Nominations will be evaluated and ranked by the adjudication committee appointed by the International Council for Canadian Studies.

Funds Avail.: $3,500. **Number Awarded:** 12. **To Apply:** Applicants must submit a two-page proposal outlining the thesis/dissertation project; must have the official university transcript, letter of support from the student's member in a Canadian university indicating his/her willingness to act as the student's academic sponsor. Application must be submitted to the ICCS, 250 City Centre Ave., Ste. 303, Ottawa, ON K1R 6K7. **Deadline:** December 31.

3834 ■ International Dairy-Deli-Bakery Association

PO Box 5528
Madison, WI 53705-0528
Ph: (608)310-5000
Fax: (608)238-6330
URL: http://www.iddba.org

3835 ■ International Dairy-Deli-Bakery Association Undergraduate Scholarships *(Graduate, Undergraduate/Scholarship)*

Purpose: To support employees of IDDBA-member companies. **Focus:** Culinary arts; Food service careers; Business. **Qualif.:** Applicants must have an academic field of study in a food-related field such as culinary arts, baking/

Awards are arranged alphabetically below their administering organizations

pastry arts or food science, business or marketing program. Applicants must also have a 2.5 grade-point average on a 4.0 scale, or equivalent which may be waived for first-time returning adult students. **Criteria:** If financial resources run low, priority will be given to supermarket dairy, deli and bakery employees.

Funds Avail.: $1,000. May be prorated among applicants. **To Apply:** Applicants must submit a completed application form together with at least one letter of reference on letterhead from a department/store manager and/or professional academic contact. Incomplete or illegible applications will not be considered. **Deadline:** January 1, April 1, July 1, October 1. **Contact:** Karen Peckham at the above address (see entry 3834).

3836 ■ International Desalination Association

PO Box 387
Topsfield, MA 01983
Ph: (978)887-0410
Fax: (978)887-0411
E-mail: info@idadesal.org
URL: http://www.idadesal.org

3837 ■ Channabasappa Memorial Scholarships *(Graduate, Professional Development/Scholarship)*

Purpose: To provide assistance for graduate students to further their education in subjects related to desalination. **Focus:** Science; Engineering; Engineering, Hydraulic; Water resources. **Qualif.:** Applicants must be a graduate of an accredited university; must be from the top 10% of the class in science or engineering; must prove admission to a graduate program in desalination/water re-use; must demonstrate leadership and achievement potential. **Criteria:** Applicants will be selected based on the undergraduate transcript, references and motivation for a career in desalination.

Funds Avail.: $10,000 maximum per student. **To Apply:** Applicants must submit a completed application form available at the website; a transcript of undergraduate academic record indicating grade point average or rank in the class; four letters of recommendation, one from a director or a distinguished IDA member; a description of the applicant's objectives and plans for graduate study; an evidence of other sources of funding to complete the applicant's degree objective; proof of acceptance to a graduate program at an accredited university; a faculty sponsor statement indicating the nature and scope of the research. **Deadline:** June 1. **Contact:** Patricia Burke, paburke@idadesal.org.

3838 ■ IDA Fellowship Award *(Professional Development/Fellowship)*

Purpose: To promote development in the desalination and water reuse industry. **Focus:** Science; Engineering; Engineering, Hydraulic; Water resources. **Qualif.:** Applicants must be an IDA member; have 8-10 years working experience in the field of desalination or water reuse. **Criteria:** Applicants will be selected based on the following: high professional achievements; relevance of the experience; responsible career goals for advancement in the chosen field; potential to make a contribution and water reuse; benefits of the attachment to the applicants; assurance that the applicant will remain connected to the desalination water-reuse industry through future work.

Funds Avail.: $10,000. **To Apply:** Applicants must submit a completed application form; a single copy of resume/curriculum vitae; a fellow's proposal (single copy, maximum of five pages, double-spaced); two letters of recommendations from either of the advisors, instructors or individuals who know the applicant's work and personal character. Letters should be sealed in an envelope, signed across by the recommender. Finalists will be interviewed by the selection Committee. **Deadline:** April 1. **Contact:** Patricia Burke, paburke@idadesal.org.

3839 ■ International Door Association

PO Box 246
West Milton, OH 45383-0246
Ph: (937)698-8042
Fax: (937)698-6153
Free: 800-355-4432
E-mail: info@longmgt.com
URL: http://www.doors.org

3840 ■ International Door Association Scholarship Awards *(Undergraduate/Scholarship)*

Purpose: To support advanced educational opportunities for scholastically eligible students. **Focus:** General studies. **Qualif.:** Applicants must be a high school with senior standing, community college, an associate degree program, vocational school or similar certification/diploma program, undergraduate college or university; have a cumulative grade point average equal to or greater than 3.0 on a 4.0 scale (or equivalent); must be an immediate family member, an employee, or an immediate family member of an employee of an IDA Installing/Servicing Dealer Member or an IDA Primary Industry Manufacturer/Vendor Member in good standing. **Criteria:** Applicants will be selected based on their grades, community and school involvement, recommendations and character determined through narrative.

Funds Avail.: $2,000 for full-time; for part-time, award amount is to be determined by semester hours or equivalent taken, and not to exceed $1,000. **To Apply:** Applicants must submit a completed scholarship application, official transcript, personal statement and three letters of recommendation. **Deadline:** July 15.

Remarks: Scholarship has two criteria: Primary Full-Time and Secondary Part-Time. **Contact:** Peggy Sanders, Scholarship Administration, psanders@longmgt.com.

3841 ■ International Executive House Keepers Association

1001 Eastwind Dr., Ste. 301
Westerville, OH 43081-3361
Ph: (614)895-7166
Fax: (614)895-1248
Free: 800-200-6342
E-mail: excel@ieha.org
URL: http://www.ieha.org

3842 ■ IEHA Education Foundation Scholarship Awards *(Undergraduate/Scholarship)*

Purpose: To provide educational assistance to IEHA members. **Focus:** General studies. **Qualif.:** Applicants must be an IEHA member enrolled in an undergraduate or associate degree or IEHA approved certification program. **Criteria:** Scholarship will be awarded to the student(s) submitting the best original manuscript on housekeeping within any industry segment.

Awards are arranged alphabetically below their administering organizations

Funds Avail.: $800. **To Apply:** Applicants must submit a completed application form; a manuscript, transcript of grades; curriculum of student showing classroom hours of coursework; and a letter from the school official or instructor verifying the enrollment of the applicant. **Deadline:** January 10.

3843 ■ Spartan Scholarship Awards
(Undergraduate/Scholarship)

Purpose: To provide educational assistance to the IEHA members and their immediate families. **Focus:** General studies. **Qualif.:** Applicants must be an IEHA member or an immediate family of an IEHA member. **Criteria:** Scholarship recipient will be selected based on the IEHA Education Committee's review of the application materials.

Funds Avail.: $1,500. **To Apply:** Applicants must submit a completed application form and a letter stating the reasons for applying the funds, the use of the award, and explanation of career goals. **Deadline:** September.

3844 ■ International Flight Services Association

1100 Johnson Ferry Rd., Ste. 300
Atlanta, GA 30342
Ph: (404)252-3663
Fax: (404)252-0774
E-mail: ifsa@kellencompany.com
URL: http://www.ifsanet.com

3845 ■ Harvey and Laura Alpert Scholarship Award *(Undergraduate/Scholarship)*

Purpose: To support students preparing for careers in the industry as well as opportunities for established professionals to further their career in onboard food services. **Focus:** Service food careers. **Qualif.:** Applicants must be currently enrolled at or transferring to Michigan State University ultimately receiving a degree from that institution; must have completed a minimum of 32 credit hours or in sophomore level of course study in a post-secondary, hospitality management program and must be in good standing. **Criteria:** Recipients are selected based on scholastic merit, dedications in pursuing a career in onboard services operations and leadership potentials.

Funds Avail.: $5,000. **To Apply:** Applicants must submit a completed application form; must provide three letters of recommendation preferably from high school counselors, college professors or employers and transcript for all high school and post-secondary studies. **Deadline:** May 15. **Contact:** Olena Eaton at the above address (see entry 3844).

3846 ■ Lois Campbell Scholarship Award
(Undergraduate/Scholarship).

Purpose: To provide opportunities for students involved in hospitality programs to further their education. **Focus:** General studies. **Qualif.:** Applicants must have completed a minimum of 20 hours of course study in a post-secondary, hospitality management program; must be in a "good" academic standing and exhibit high leadership potential in the hospitality industry; must able to pursue the chosen course of study beginning with the academic year following the recipient's acceptance of the award. **Criteria:** Recipients are selected based on scholastic merit and dedication in pursuing a career in the hospitality industry.

Funds Avail.: $2,250. **To Apply:** Applicants must provide an official transcript of records for all high school and post-secondary studies at an accredited institution; must provide three letters of recommendation preferably from college professors, clergy and employers; must provide official documentation noting cancer history or loss of a family member due to cancer. **Deadline:** May 15. **Contact:** Olena Eaton at the above address (see entry 3844).

3847 ■ Delta Daily Food (Canada) Inc. Scholarships *(Undergraduate/Scholarship)*

Purpose: To provide opportunity for students involved in food science programs at the University of Guelph and Laval to further their education. **Focus:** Food science and technology. **Qualif.:** Applicants must be currently enrolled as full-time students in food science program; must have completed a minimum of three semesters of course study in food science program; must have a "good" academic standing with an average of 75% or better. **Criteria:** Recipients are selected based on scholastic merit; dedication in pursuing a career in food processing industry; and, financial need.

Funds Avail.: $2,250. **To Apply:** Applicants must submit a completed application form and official transcript for all post-secondary, college and university studies at an accredited institution. **Deadline:** May 15. **Contact:** Olena Eaton at the above address (see entry 3844).

3848 ■ Tommy Depaola Scholarship Award
(Undergraduate/Scholarship)

Purpose: To provide opportunities for students involved in hospitality programs to further their education. **Focus:** General studies. **Qualif.:** Applicants must have completed a minimum of 20 hours of course study in a post-secondary, hospitality management program; must be in a "good" academic standing and exhibit high leadership potential in the hospitality industry; must able to pursue the chosen course of study beginning with the academic year following the recipient's acceptance of the award. **Criteria:** Recipients are selected based on scholastic merit and dedication in pursuing a career in the hospitality industry.

Funds Avail.: $2,250. **To Apply:** Applicants must provide an official transcript of records for all high school and post-secondary studies at an accredited institution; must provide three letters of recommendation preferably from college professors, clergy and employers; must provide official documentation noting cancer history or loss of a family member due to cancer. **Deadline:** May 15. **Contact:** Olena Eaton at the above address (see entry 3844).

3849 ■ International Food Service Executives Association

2609 Surfwood Dr.
Las Vegas, NV 89128
Ph: (702)430-9217
Fax: (702)430-9223
Free: 800-893-5499
URL: http://www.ifsea.com

3850 ■ IFSEA Worthy Goal Scholarships *(Four Year College, Two Year College/Scholarship)*

Purpose: To provide assistance to deserving individuals intending to receive food service management or vocational training beyond the high school level. **Focus:** Food service careers. **Qualif.:** Applicant must be enrolled or accepted as a full time student in a Food Service-related major at a 2 or 4 year college or university for the fall term following the award. **Criteria:** Recipient is chosen based on merit as reviewed by the IFSEA Scholarship Committee.

Funds Avail.: $100,000 (total scholarships). **To Apply:** Applicant must provide a summary of projected 1-year expenses and income/ fundraising beginning with the fall semester or a summary of financial statement; a statement (maximum of 500 words) on personal background focusing on aspects regarding food service and future goals; documentation of work experience, student organizations, transcript of grades, three letters of recommendation, and a statement (maximum of 250 words) on how receiving the scholarship would help you in reaching the goals you have set for yourself. Forward complete application package to: Worthy Goal Scholarship Application, c/o Local IFSEA Branch or IFSEA HQ, 2609 Surfwood Drive, Las Vegas, NV 89128. Applicants may visit website for further information and instructions. **Deadline:** Feb 1.

3851 ■ International Foodservice Editorial Council

PO Box 491
Hyde Park, NY 12538
Ph: (845)229-6973
Fax: (845)229-6993
E-mail: info@ifeconline.com
URL: http://www.ifec-is-us.com

3852 ■ International Foodservice Editorial Council Scholarships *(Graduate, Undergraduate/ Scholarship)*

Purpose: To increase awareness and understanding of the career opportunities available in the field of food service communications and to encourage entry of qualified professionals in the field. **Focus:** Culinary arts; Communications; Food service careers; Food science and technology; Photography; Hotel, institutional, and restaurant management; Nutrition; Dietetics; Journalism; Public relations; Graphic art and design. **Qualif.:** Applicants must be full-time students in a U.S. accredited post-secondary educational institution working towards an associate's, bachelor's or master's degree. **Criteria:** Recipients are selected based on the committee's review of the applicant's portfolio.

Funds Avail.: $3,750. **Number Awarded:** Varies. **To Apply:** Applicants must submit a complete application together with academic transcript and two letters of recommendation. Application requirements must be typewritten and submitted using U.S. Postal Service's Return Receipt Service. **Deadline:** March 15.

3853 ■ International Foundation for Ethical Research

53 W Jackson Blvd., Ste. 1552
Chicago, IL 60604
Ph: (312)427-6025
Fax: (312)427-6524
E-mail: ifer@navs.org
URL: http://www.ifer.org

3854 ■ Graduate Fellowships in Alternatives in Scientific Research *(Doctorate, Graduate/ Fellowship)*

Purpose: To provide monetary assistance to graduate students. **Focus:** Science technologies. **Qualif.:** Applicant must be a student enrolled in Master's and Ph.D programs in the sciences, humanities, psychology, and journalism. **Criteria:** Selection of applicant will be based on the application form and other supporting documents.

Funds Avail.: Fellowships provide up to $12,500 annually in stipendiary support and up to $2,500 for supplies per year. **To Apply:** Application forms are available in the website address; must be sent to: Graduate Fellowships, IFER, 53 W Jackson Blvd., Ste. 1552, Chicago, IL 60604. **Deadline:** March 15.

Remarks: Fellowships are renewable annually for up to three years.

3855 ■ International Franchise Association

1501 K St. NW, Ste. 350
Washington, DC 20005
Ph: (202)628-8000
Fax: (202)628-0812
URL: http://www.franchise.org

3856 ■ Don Debolt Franchising Scholarship Program *(Undergraduate/Scholarship)*

Purpose: To provide financial support to those students who are in need. **Focus:** General Studies. **Qualif.:** Applicants must be graduating high school seniors who have an expressed interest in pursuing a degree in entrepreneurship and franchising. **Criteria:** Preferences will be given to those students who meet the criteria.

Funds Avail.: $2,500. **Number Awarded:** 2. **To Apply:** Applicants must submit completed application form.

Remarks: The Don DeBolt Franchising Scholarship Program, named in honor of IFA's recently-retired president who served from 1995 to 2004, is being conducted in cooperation with DECA and Delta Epsilon. **Contact:** International Franchise Association at the above address (see entry 3855).

3857 ■ Franchise Law Diversity Scholarship Awards *(Undergraduate/Scholarship)*

Purpose: To recognize and support academic achievement among diverse law students. **Focus:** Law. **Qualif.:** Applicants must be enrolled in an ABA-accredited law schools. Applicants must have 2L or 3L status during the period of the scholarship, and they must be enrolled in at least one course oriented towards franchise law (e.g., Torts, Unfair Trade Practices, Trade Secrets, Antitrust, Trademarks, Contracts, Agency, Securities). Applicants must be considered members of diverse groups (African American, American Indian, Hispanic American, Asian American, or Gay/Lesbian). **Criteria:** Preferences will be given to those students who are in need.

Funds Avail.: $4,000. **To Apply:** Applicants must submit completed application form. **Deadline:** February 15. **Contact:** Miriam L. Brewer, Director of Diversity, IFA Educational Foundation, 1501 K Street, N.W., Suite 350 Washington, D.C. 20005.

3858 ■ International Furnishings and Design Association

150 S Warner Rd., Ste. 156
King of Prussia, PA 19406
Ph: (610)535-6422
Fax: (610)535-6423
E-mail: info@ifda.com
URL: http://www.ifdaef.org

3859 ■ IFDA Educational Foundation
(Undergraduate/Scholarship)

Purpose: To foster educational and philanthropic activities which will benefit individuals and institutions; to promote, develop or enhance the furnishings and design industries and the practice of the professions. **Focus:** Architectural Lighting Design. **Qualif.:** Applicant must be attending the college education majoring in lighting designs. **Criteria:** Committee will review the application based on the uniqueness and creativity of work.

Funds Avail.: No. 1500. **To Apply:** An applicant must submit an official transcript of records verifying an students enrollment and GPA; a letter of recommendation from a design educator; four copies of an essay describing personal long and short term goals, award and achievements in no more than 300-400 words; four copies of two digital photos of students own original work preferably in color or in one page; Ruth Clark Furniture design Scholarship requires five different original furniture designs; and recommendation from IFDA member. **Deadline:** March 31.

3860 ■ IFDA Part-time Student Scholarships
(Undergraduate/Scholarship)

Purpose: to promote, develop, or enhance the furnishings and design industries and the practice of these professions. **Focus:** Part-time students. **Qualif.:** All applicants must have completed four courses in interior design or related field; he/she must be enrolled as a part-time student and be currently enrolled in at least two courses. **Criteria:**.

Funds Avail.: Number Awarded: To Apply: Applicant must submit a certified, sealed transcript of course work that verifies enrollment with GPA. It may be sent by the school or college; a separate letter of recommendation from a professor or instructor on official school stationery; four copies of 300-400 word essay explaining long and short-term goals, achievements, awards or accomplishments; four digital copies of two photos of the student's original work preferably on one-page and in color; four copies of completed application form. **Deadline:** March 31. **Contact:** Earline Clark feldman tapis2@bellsouth.org

3861 ■ Charles D. Mayo Student Scholarships
(Undergraduate/Scholarship)

Purpose: To promote, develop, or enhance the furnishings and design industries and the practice of these professions. **Focus:** Interior design. **Qualif.:** All applicants must completed their four design courses in post secondary education at the time of application and must be majoring in interior design or a closely related field. **Criteria:** Committee will evaluate the application based on the uniqueness and creativity of work.

Funds Avail.: $1,000. **Number Awarded:** 1. **To Apply:** All applicants must have completed four design courses in post secondary education at the time of application and are majoring in interior design or a closely related field; an applicant must submit a certified, sealed transcript of course work that verifies full-time status with GPA. It may be sent by the school or college; a separate letter of recommendation from a professor or instructor on official school stationery; four copies of a 300-400 word essay explaining long and short-term goals, achievements, awards and accomplishments; four copies of two digital photos of student's original work preferably on one-page and in color; four copies of the completed application form. **Deadline:** March 31. **Contact:** Earline Clark Feldman 080403tapis2@bellsouth.net

3862 ■ International Grenfell Association
66 Birmingham St.
St. John, NL, Canada A1E 5M8
Ph: (709)745-6162
Fax: (709)745-6163
E-mail: iga@nfld.net
URL: http://www.iga.nf.net

3863 ■ International Grenfell Association Bursary *(Undergraduate/Scholarship)*

Purpose: To support the education of students with financial need who have been accepted into or are currently attending a post-secondary education institution. **Focus:** General studies. **Qualif.:** Applicant must be a Canadian citizen in the IGA region (must have graduated from a high school within the region); must not already possess a post-secondary degree; and must complete at least four courses per semester. **Criteria:** Selection will be based on the committee's criteria.

Funds Avail.: Varies. **To Apply:** Application forms and information can be obtained from the Grenfell Scholarship Committee or may be obtained online. Applications must be completed by the student and returned to the committee on or before the deadline. **Deadline:** May 15. **Contact:** Mr. Paul Canning at the above address (see entry 3862).

3864 ■ International Grenfell Association Secondary/High School Scholarships
(Undergraduate/Scholarship)

Purpose: To support the education of high achievers who are planning to pursue college education. **Focus:** General studies. **Qualif.:** Applicants must be Canadian citizens residing in the IGA region; must be in regular attendance at high schools in the IGA region; must have achieved superior results in the previous year's final exams and the current year's midterms; must complete Level III examinations achieving grades consistent with previous attainment; must be eligible for entrance to a university; and must have taken a full course load (normally a minimum of 5 courses per semester). **Criteria:** Selection will be based on the committee's criteria.

Funds Avail.: $6,000. **To Apply:** Applications must be completed by the student and returned to the principal on or before the deadline. Application form can be downloaded online. **Deadline:** February 15. **Contact:** Mr. Paul Canning at the above address (see entry 3862).

3865 ■ International Grenfell Association University/College Scholarships *(Undergraduate/Scholarship)*

Purpose: To support the education of high achievers and/or those with financial need who have completed one or more years of post-secondary education with one renewable scholarship. **Focus:** General studies. **Qualif.:** Applicant must be a Canadian citizen residing in the IGA region (must have graduated from a high school within the region); have completed one or more years of post-secondary education in a program leading to an undergraduate degree from a recognized university or diploma from a minimum of a three-year program at a recognized college; must achieve superior results in the current fall and winter semesters; must not already possess a post-secondary degree; and must undertake a full course load (minimum of 5 courses per semester). **Criteria:** Selection will be based on the committee's criteria.

Funds Avail.: $6,000. **To Apply:** Application forms and

Awards are arranged alphabetically below their administering organizations

information can be obtained from the Grenfell Scholarship Committee or may be obtained online. The application must be completed by the student and returned to the committee on or before the deadline. **Deadline:** May 15. **Contact:** Mr. Paul Canning at the above address (see entry 3862).

3866 ■ International Harvester Collectors

18324 Monroa Rd. 1073
Madison, MO 65263
Ph: (660)291-8742
E-mail: IHCCLUB@aol.com
URL: http://www.nationalihcollectors.com

3867 ■ International Harvester Collectors Scholarships *(Undergraduate/Scholarship)*

Purpose: To provide a worldwide collector's network for the preservation of history, products, literature and memorabilia of the International Harvester Company. **Focus:** General studies. **Qualif.:** All applicants must be members, children of members, or grandchildren of members of the International Harvester Collectors Inc., Club; must be enrolled or accepted for enrollment in an accredited college, university, junior college, trade, or technical school, or other similar post-high school educational institution; must be graduating high school seniors on the year of the application. **Criteria:** Award is given based on a review of properly submitted essays done by the Board of Directors of the International Harvester Collectors Inc., Club.

Funds Avail.: $1,000-first place; $750-second place. **Number Awarded:** 2. **To Apply:** Applicants are required to submit an essay of not less than 1,000 not more than 2,000 words discussing the historical significance of any aspect of the International Harvester Company. The topic shall be "The evolution of the Farmall"; Each applicant shall include separately information regarding the educational institution. This information shall include the complete mailing address and telephone number of that educational institution's financial aid office; an annotated bibliography that lists the sources of information for the essay; a cover letter stating the institution the applicant will be attending, how the scholarship will be used in achieving the student's goals, and the process by which the applicant acquired the information for the essay. **Deadline:** May 15. **Contact:** Darell Darst; 18324 Country road 1073, Madison, MO 65263; Farmall130@socket.net.

3868 ■ International Horn Society

PO Box 630158
Lanai City, HI 96763-0158
Ph: (808)565-7273
Fax: (808)565-7273
E-mail: exec-secretary@hornsociety.org
URL: http://www.hornsociety.org

3869 ■ Paul Mansur Scholarships *(Undergraduate/Scholarship)*

Purpose: To provide opportunities for full-time students attending the IHS international symposium to receive a lesson from a world renowned artist or teacher. **Focus:** Music. **Qualif.:** Applicants must be full-time students 18 years or younger and 19-26 years old at the time of the symposium. **Criteria:** Candidates essays will be evaluated for both content and grammar by the appointed committee of the IHS President.

Funds Avail.: No amount mentioned. **Number Awarded:** 2. **To Apply:** Applicants must submit applications to the IHS Executive Secretary, either on paper or by email; proof of full-time public or private school, conservatory, or university enrollment; and essay on the subject of how attending and receiving a lesson during the symposium will enhance his/her education. **Deadline:** May 1. **Contact:** Heidi Vogel, IHS Executive Secretary at the above address (see entry 3868).

3870 ■ Barry Tuckwell Scholarships *(All/Scholarship)*

Purpose: To encourage and support worthy horn students to pursue education and performance by attending and participating in masterclasses and workshops throughout the world. **Focus:** Music. **Qualif.:** Applicants must be age 18 or older and not yet have reached age 25. **Criteria:** Recipient will be selected by the appointed committee of IHS Scholarship Chairs based on combination of ability, character, motivation, goals and opportunities available at the selected venue.

Funds Avail.: $500. **To Apply:** Applicants must submit a completed Tuckwell Scholarship application, available online or from the executive secretary; three copies of two brief essays, outlining the applicant's experience and plan to study and perform at a specific event; three copies of a CD-format recording of one movement of a concerto or sonata (with piano), one etude, and two orchestral excerpts; and two letters of recommendation including an assessment of need. **Deadline:** April 1. **Contact:** Heidi Vogel at the above address (see entry 3868).

3871 ■ International Institute for Municipal Clerks

8331 Utica Ave., Ste. 200
Rancho Cucamonga, CA 91730
Ph: (909)944-4162
Fax: (909)944-8545
Free: 800-251-1639
E-mail: Hq@iimc.com
URL: http://www.iimc.com

3872 ■ Certified Municipal Clerk Scholarships (CMC) *(Professional Development/Scholarship)*

Purpose: To encourage professionalism among municipal clerks and deputy clerks (or related titles) for those whose municipality cannot fully pay the costs of participation in an accredited International Institute of Municipal Clerks (IIMC). **Focus:** General studies. **Qualif.:** Applicants must be IIMC members in good standing who are municipal clerks or deputy clerks (or related titles) on the date of application. **Criteria:** Applications are evaluated by the scholarship selection committee based on their designed criteria.

Funds Avail.: $300. **To Apply:** Applicants must submit all the required application information. **Deadline:** January 4.

3873 ■ Master Municipal Clerks Academy Scholarships *(Professional Development/Scholarship)*

Purpose: To assist municipal clerks and deputy clerks (or related titles) for the improvement of their professional performance by providing them with financial support to enroll in an accredited International Institute of Municipal Clerks (IIMC) Academy Program. **Focus:** General studies. **Qualif.:** Applicants must be members in good standing of

IIMC who are Certified Municipal Clerks or Deputy Clerks (or related titles) on the date of application. **Criteria:** Applicants are evaluated based on the criteria designed by the scholarship selection committee.

Funds Avail.: $100. **To Apply:** Applicants must submit all the required application information. **Deadline:** January 4. **Contact:** IIMC's Education Associate, Jennifer Ward at 909-944-4162; email: jward@iimc.com.

3874 ■ International Military Community Executives Association

1530 Dunwoody Village Pkwy., Ste. 203
Atlanta, GA 30338
Ph: (770)396-2101
Fax: (770)396-2198
E-mail: imcea@imcea.com
URL: http://www.imcea.com

3875 ■ The Robert W. Brunsman Memorial Scholarships *(Graduate, Undergraduate/Scholarship)*

Purpose: To assist MWR professionals in continuing their education. **Focus:** General studies. **Qualif.:** Applicant must be a current IMCEA member enrolled in a college or university working towards an Associates Degree, Bachelors Degree or higher. **Criteria:** Recipient selection is based on the committee's review of applications.

Funds Avail.: No specific amount. **To Apply:** Applicants must mail the application form, with a two-page essay regarding, "What is the most important issue society is facing today?", a letter of acceptance to the college or university that the applicant is planning to attend, or a transcript from the college or university currently attended. **Deadline:** February 15.

3876 ■ Roy C. and Dorothy Jean Olson Memorial Scholarships *(Undergraduate/Scholarship)*

Purpose: To assist young men and women in furthering their education beyond the high school level. **Focus:** General studies. **Qualif.:** Applicant must be a son or daughter of a current Regular or Position IMCEA member, graduating from high school in the school year of application submission or to be currently enrolled in a college or university working toward an Associates Degree, Bachelors Degree or higher. **Criteria:** Recipient selection is based on the committee's review of applications.

Funds Avail.: No specific amount. **To Apply:** Applicants must mail the application form, with a two-page essay regarding, "What is the most important issue society is facing today?", a letter of acceptance to the college or university that the applicant is planning to attend, or a transcript from the college or university currently attended. **Deadline:** February 15.

3877 ■ International Municipal Lawyers Association

7910 Woodmont Ave., Ste. 1440
Bethesda, MD 20814
Ph: (202)466-5424
Fax: (202)785-0152
E-mail: info@imla.org
URL: http://www.imla.org

3878 ■ International Municipal Lawyers Association Canadian Scholarships *(Professional Development/Scholarship)*

Purpose: To provide opportunities for the improvement of law practice by supporting young Canadian lawyers intending to attend an IMLA Conference. **Focus:** Law. **Qualif.:** Eligibility is limited to lawyers in Canada, a significant component of whose practice in the last 12 months has been municipal law, and who are under 40 years of age as of December 31, 2008. Eligibility is not restricted to IMLA members. **Criteria:** Selection will be based on the committee's criteria.

Funds Avail.: Fund covers most of the usual IMLA Conference expenses: event registration, hotel and airfare. **To Apply:** Interested applicants may apply by writing to IMLA. Applications must include the following information: name, address, e-mail address, fax number and telephone number; details of the applicant's municipal law experience including approximate percentage of the applicant's practice spent on municipal law; a proposal of not less than 300 words describing the applicant's topic/presentation on Canadian municipal law; a statement certifying that the applicant is under 40 years of age within set date; and a brief sample of the applicant's written work. Complete application package must be faxed and e-mailed in to fax number 202785-0152, email sstadnyk@imla.org. **Deadline:** June 23. **Contact:** Sophia Stadnyk 202-466-5424 ext. 108; sstadnyk@imla.org.

3879 ■ International Narcotics Interdiction Association

11683 La Colina Rd.
San Diego, CA 92131
Ph: (858)271-4407
Fax: (858)271-4407
Free: (866)780-4642
E-mail: info@inia.org
URL: http://www.inia.org

3880 ■ INIA Scholarship Program *(All/Scholarship)*

Purpose: To support a given charity or other non-profit agencies and events. **Focus:** General studies. **Qualif.:** Applicants must be children of INIA members who will be in their senior year of high school; the parent INIA member must be current in his/her membership, or deceased. **Criteria:** Entries will be reviewed and winners will be selected by the scholarship committee.

Funds Avail.: $2,000. **To Apply:** Applicants must submit to INIA completed application form along with an essay not exceeding 500 words on the topic described on the application form. **Deadline:** May 15.

3881 ■ International Order of the King's Daughters and Sons

PO Box 1017
Chautauqua, NY 14722-1017
Ph: (716)357-4951
Fax: (716)357-3762
E-mail: iokds5@windstream.net
URL: http://www.iokds.org

3882 ■ Chautauqua Scholarship Program *(All/Scholarship)*

Purpose: To strengthen faith, build confidence and increase leadership skills. **Focus:** Art. **Qualif.:** Applicants

Awards are arranged alphabetically below their administering organizations

must be Christians between 19-25 years old who have at least two years of college or university and who have an interest in learning and the arts. **Criteria:** Recipients are selected based on the applicant's Christian beliefs and practice; an inquiring mind; energy and enthusiasm; and respect and responsibility.

Funds Avail.: No specific amount. **To Apply:** Applicants must submit a letter of recommendation from the pastor; copy of completed application form. Applicants must also pass the telephone interview with the Director of Chautauqua Department.

3883 ■ International Paralegal Management Association

PO Box 659
Avondale Estates, GA 30002-0659
Ph: (404)292-4762
Fax: (404)292-2931
E-mail: info@paralegalmanagement.org
URL: http://www.paralegalmanagement.org

3884 ■ Therese A. Cannon Educational Scholarships *(Professional Development/Scholarship)*

Purpose: To assist members in continuing their education through advanced formal training. **Focus:** Paralegal studies. **Qualif.:** Applicants must be any regular, associate, life or emeritus IPMA member. **Criteria:** Committee will select applicants based on Content, Writing Skills and Persuasiveness.

Funds Avail.: $1000. **Number Awarded:** 1. **To Apply:** Applicant must complete the application form (available at the website) and submit it along with a one page essay. **Deadline:** August 10.

Remarks: The scholarship was created to honor Teri Cannon's dedicated service to the IPMA and to recognize her commitment to the education of paralegal and paralegal management. **Contact:** awards@paralegalmanagement.org

3885 ■ International Radio and Television Society Foundation

420 Lexington Ave., Ste. 1601
New York, NY 10170
Ph: (212)867-6650
Fax: (212)867-6653
URL: http://www.irts.org

3886 ■ IRTS Foundation Summer Fellowship Program *(Graduate, Undergraduate/Fellowship)*

Purpose: To financially assist students with their educational pursuit. **Focus:** General studies. **Qualif.:** Program is open to college juniors, seniors or graduate students at the time of application; must complete their junior year at the time of the Fellowship (June 2008); college seniors and graduate students cannot graduate prior to May 2008. **Criteria:** Recipient is given based on merit.

Funds Avail.: No specific amount. **To Apply:** Applicants must complete the application form available at the website and send it via email attachment with the subject line format SFPO8.Last Name.First Name to: apply@irts.org. **Deadline:** December 2.

3887 ■ International Reading Association

PO Box 8139
Newark, DE 19714-8139
Ph: (302)731-1600
Fax: (302)731-1057
Free: 800-336-7323
E-mail: customerservice@reading.org
URL: http://www.reading.org

3888 ■ Jeanne S. Chall Research Fellowships *(Doctorate, Graduate/Grant)*

Purpose: To fund research on reading and literacy. **Focus:** Reading. **Qualif.:** Applicant must be a member of the International Reading Association; a doctoral student planning or beginning dissertations; or a university based graduate student embarking on independent research studies. **Criteria:** Applications and proposals will be reviewed by the members of the International Reading Association Studies and Research based on: significance of research question; rationale for the research; adequacy of methods and data treatment; significance of project impact; clarity and specificity.

Funds Avail.: $6,000. **To Apply:** Applicants are advised to visit the website for the online application process. **Deadline:** January 15.

Remarks: The program is established in honor of Dr. Jeanne S. Chall. **Contact:** Marcella Moore at research@reading.org.

3889 ■ Elva Knight Research Grants *(All/Grant)*

Purpose: To fund a research on reading and literacy. **Focus:** Reading. **Qualif.:** Applicant must be a member of the International Reading Association. **Criteria:** Applications and proposals will be reviewed by the members of the International Reading Association Studies and Research based on: significance of research question; rationale for the research; adequacy of methods and data treatment; significance of project impact; clarity and specificity.

Funds Avail.: $10,000. **Number Awarded:** 4. **To Apply:** Applicants are must visit the website for the online application process. **Deadline:** January 15.

Remarks: Applicants can apply for more than one research grant, but limited to one research award per year. **Contact:** Marcella Moore at research@reading.org.

3890 ■ Helen M. Robinson Grants *(Doctorate/Grant)*

Purpose: To assist dissertation research in the area of reading and literacy. **Focus:** Reading. **Qualif.:** Applicant must be a member of the International Reading Association; a doctoral student in the early stages of the dissertation research in areas of reading and literacy. **Criteria:** Applications and proposals will be reviewed by the members of the International Reading Association Studies and Research based on: significance of research question; rationale for the research; adequacy of methods and data treatment; significance of project impact; clarity and specificity.

Funds Avail.: $1,500. **To Apply:** Applicants are advised to visit the website for the online application process. **Deadline:** January 15.

Remarks: The grant is established in memory of Helen M. Robinson. **Contact:** Marcella Moore at research@reading.org.

3891 ■ Nila Banton Smith Research Dissemination Support Grants *(All/Grant)*

Purpose: To facilitate the dissemination of literacy research to the educational community. **Focus:** Reading. **Qualif.:**

Awards are arranged alphabetically below their administering organizations

Applicant must be a member of the International Reading Association. **Criteria:** Applications and proposals will be reviewed by the members of the International Reading Association Studies and Research based on: significance of research question; rationale for the research; adequacy of methods and data treatment; significance of project impact; clarity and specificity.

Funds Avail.: $5,000. **To Apply:** Applicants are advised to visit the website for the online application process. **Deadline:** January 15.

Remarks: The program is funded by the Nila Banton Smith Endowment. **Contact:** Marcella Moore at research@reading.org.

3892 ■ Steven A. Stahl Research Grants
(Graduate/Grant)

Purpose: To fund a classroom research on reading. **Focus:** Reading. **Qualif.:** Applicant must be a member of the International Reading Association; a graduate student who has at least three years of pre-K-12 teaching experience. **Criteria:** Applicant's application will be reviewed by the members of International Reading Association Steven A. Stahl Research Grant Committee.

Funds Avail.: $1,000. **To Apply:** Applicants are advised to visit the website for the online application process. **Deadline:** January 15.

Remarks: The award is established in memory of Steven A. Stahl. **Contact:** Marcella Moore at research@reading.org.

3893 ■ International Research and Exchanges Board

2121 K St., NW Ste. 700
Washington, DC 20037
Ph: (202)628-8188
Fax: (202)628-8189
E-mail: irex@irex.org
URL: http://www.irex.org

3894 ■ ECA Alumni Small Grants Program
(Professional Development/Grant)

Purpose: To enhance the skills and performance of ECA alumni. **Focus:** European studies. **Qualif.:** Applicants must be alumni of the Edmund S. Muskie Graduate Fellowship Program (MUSKIE) or the Eurasian Undergraduate Program (UGRAD). **Criteria:** Selection is based on the applications.

Funds Avail.: $3000. **To Apply:** Applicants must contact their local IREX office for application details. **Contact:** asgp@irex.org.

3895 ■ Individual Advanced Research Opportunities Program (IARO) For Master's Student
(Graduate/Grant)

Purpose: To promote in-depth field research in policy-relevant subjects related to Southeast Europe and Eurasia. **Focus:** European studies. **Qualif.:** Applicants must be currently enrolled in a Master's program. **Criteria:** Grantees will be selected in terms of academic performance and achievements.

Funds Avail.: International coach class round-trip transportation; a monthly allowance for housing and living expenses; travel visas; and evacuation insurance. **To Apply:** Applicants are advised to visit the IREX website for application details. **Contact:** iaro@irex.org.

3896 ■ Individual Advanced Research Opportunities Program (IARO) For Pre-doctoral Students *(Postgraduate/Grant)*

Purpose: To promote in-depth field research in policy-relevant subjects related to Southeast Europe and Eurasia. **Focus:** European studies. **Qualif.:** Applicants must be currently enrolled in a Ph.D. program. **Criteria:** Grantees will be selected in terms of academic performance and achievements.

Funds Avail.: International coach class round-trip transportation; a monthly allowance for housing and living expenses; travel visas; and evacuation insurance. **To Apply:** Applicants are advised to visit the IREX website for the application process. **Contact:** iaro@irex.org.

3897 ■ Individual Advanced Research Opportunities Program (IARO) For Professionals
(Professional Development/Grant)

Purpose: To promote in-depth field research in policy-relevant subjects related to Southeast Europe and Eurasia. **Focus:** European studies. **Qualif.:** Applicants must not currently be enrolled as a student; have a degree in MA, MS, MFA, MBA, MPA, MLIS, MPH, JD, or MD. **Criteria:** Grantees will be selected in terms of academic performance and achievements.

Funds Avail.: No specific amount. **To Apply:** Applicants are advised to visit the IREX website for application details. **Contact:** iaro@irex.org.

3898 ■ Individual Advanced Research Opportunities Program (IARO) for Postdoctoral Scholars *(Postdoctorate/Grant)*

Purpose: To promote in-depth field research in policy-relevant subjects related to Southeast Europe and Eurasia. **Focus:** European studies. **Qualif.:** Applicants must be a Ph.D. holder. **Criteria:** Grantees will be selected in terms of academic performance and achievements.

Funds Avail.: No specific amount. **To Apply:** Applicants are advised to visit the IREX website for application details. **Contact:** iaro@irex.org.

3899 ■ International Safety Equipment Association

1901 N Moore St.
Arlington, VA 22209-1762
Ph: (703)525-1695
Free: (703)528-2148
E-mail: isea@safetyequipment.org
URL: http://www.safetyequipment.org

3900 ■ Lincoln C. Bailey Memorial Scholarship Fund *(Undergraduate/Scholarship)*

Purpose: To Provide financial assistance to the promising dependant of its members in the final year in college or universities. **Focus:** General studies. **Qualif.:** Applicants must be in the first year or second year in college; a dependant of ISEA members. **Criteria:** Scholarship winner is selected by an independent panel, based on academic achievement, extracurricular activity and financial need.

Funds Avail.: $2,500. **To Apply:** Applicants must submit transcript and financial information. **Deadline:** March 25.

3901 ■ International Society of Air Safety Investigators

107 E Holly Ave., Ste. 11
Sterling, VA 20164

Awards are arranged alphabetically below their administering organizations

Ph: (703)430-9668
Fax: (703)430-4970
E-mail: isasi@erols.com
URL: http://www.isasi.org

3902 ■ The ISASI Rudolf Kapustin Memorial Scholarships *(Undergraduate/Scholarship)*

Purpose: To encourage and assist college-level students interested in the field of aviation safety and aircraft occurrence investigation. **Focus:** Aviation. **Qualif.:** Applicant must be a member of ISASI enrolled as full-time student in a recognized education program, which includes courses in aircraft engineering and/or operations, aviation psychology, aviation safety or aircraft occurrence investigation, etc., with major or minor subjects that focus on aviation safety/investigation. **Criteria:** Scholarship Fund Committee will review submitted materials.

Funds Avail.: $1500. **To Apply:** Applicants must submit a the application form and a 1000 word paper in English addressing "the challenges for air safety investigators". Paper must be countersigned by applicant's tutor/academic supervisor as authentic, original work.

3903 ■ International Society for Human Ethology

175 King St.
Charleston, SC 29401
Fax: (843)577-9645
E-mail: fssalter@aol.com
URL: http://www.ishe.org

3904 ■ Owen F. Aldis Scholarship Fund *(Graduate/Scholarship)*

Purpose: To support scholarly works that contribute to the advancement of knowledge and learning in human ethology. **Focus:** Behavioral sciences. **Qualif.:** Applicants must be graduate (pre-doctoral) students, in any academic discipline related to human ethology, who are in good standing as certified by their academic advisor or director at a recognized educational or scientific institution. Research must be ethological in nature; the research should include, when possible, comparisons between individuals, populations, species, sexes, since ethology thrives on comparisons; the research should address problems of adaptation, function, reproduction and other concepts relevant to evolutionary theory. **Criteria:** Scholarship recipients will be selected based on the review of the study and application materials.

Funds Avail.: Stipend is not to exceed $5,000 and is to be applied to documented, legitimate research costs, plus a travel stipend not to exceed $1,000 to attend the next biennial ISHE congress. **To Apply:** Applications must be submitted in English. Applications should consist of the title of the study, the applicant's name and institutional affiliation; a letter from the applicant's institution giving permission for the applicant to conduct the proposed research at that institution; short c.v.s of the applicant and his/her mentor (with publications); an outline of the planned study, of maximum length 12 double-spaced pages, with the following sections: aims, concentrating on innovative aspects; theoretical background; methodological issues and procedure; schedule. **Deadline:** July 31. **Contact:** Frank Salter.

3905 ■ International Society for Humor Studies

Holy Names University
Oakland, CA 94619
Ph: (510)436-1532
E-mail: ishs@hnu.edu
URL: http://www.hnu.edu

3906 ■ International Society for Humor Studies Graduate Student Awards (GSA) *(Graduate/Award/Prize)*

Purpose: To recognize outstanding scholars and promising graduate students conducting research in humor studies with either a Scholarly Contribution or a Graduate Student Award. **Focus:** Humanities. **Qualif.:** Applicants must be graduate students working toward master's or doctorate degrees and doing noteworthy research within humor studies and/or all ISHS graduate student members planning to attend the Society's annual conference. **Criteria:** Candidate will be evaluated by ISHS Awards Committee based on merit.

Funds Avail.: No specific amount. **To Apply:** Applicant must submit a letter of intent to compete for a GSA, a description of their research program within humor studies, a presentation proposal, and all required registration materials and fees.

3907 ■ International Society for Humor Studies Scholarly Contribution Awards (SCA) *(Graduate/Award/Prize)*

Purpose: To recognize outstanding scholars and promising graduate students conducting research in humor studies with either a Scholarly Contribution or a Graduate Student Award. **Focus:** Humanities. **Qualif.:** Applicants must be researchers doing important work but lacking international recognition due to limited opportunities to travel or to publish outside of their region of the world and scholars involved in humor research through high quality publications, conference presentations, and other scholarly activities. **Criteria:** Candidates will be evaluated by the ISHS Awards Committee.

Funds Avail.: No amount mentioned. **To Apply:** Applicants must submit complete application form.

3908 ■ International Society of Offshore and Polar Engineers

495 N Whisman Rd., Ste. 300
Mountain View, CA 94043-5711
Ph: (650)254-1871
Fax: (650)254-2038
E-mail: info@isope.org
URL: http://www.isope.org

3909 ■ ISOPE Offshore Mechanics Scholarships for Outstanding Students *(Graduate/Scholarship)*

Purpose: To promote education and research in the field of offshore mechanics. **Focus:** Mechanics and repairs. **Qualif.:** Applicants must be a graduate student; or admitted to a graduate program and will be a graduate student (verified by the Department Chairman or the supervising professor); must have demonstrated scholastic achievement; must be a person of integrity, good character and strict morals. **Criteria:** Preference is given to applicants whose papers are accepted at the council-supported technical meetings.

Funds Avail.: $700. **To Apply:** Applicants must fill up the application form available at the website and submit a hard copy of the application form at the ISOPE Office together with official college academic transcripts; a statement of

Awards are arranged alphabetically below their administering organizations

personal professional objectives; and a recommendation letter from the supervising professor. **Deadline:** April 3.

3910 ■ International Technology Education Association
1914 Association Dr., Ste. 201
Reston, VA 20191-1539
Ph: (703)860-2100
Fax: (703)860-0353
E-mail: itea@iteaconnect.org
URL: http://www.iteaconnect.org

3911 ■ Litherland/FTE Scholarships
(Undergraduate/Scholarship)

Purpose: To recognize and encourage the integration of a quality technology education program within the school curriculum. **Focus:** Technology. **Qualif.:** Applicant must be a member of ITEA; Applicant must not be a senior by application deadline; Applicant must be a current, full-time undergraduate majoring in technology education teacher preparation. **Criteria:** The award is given based on the committee's criteria.

Funds Avail.: $1,000. **To Apply:** Applicants must send an application package that consists of four-sets of the following requirements: Letter of application that includes statement about personal interest in teaching technology and applicant's address with day and night telephone numbers. Applicant's resume; A photocopy of applicant's college transcript. A grade point average of 2.5 or more; Three faculty recommendations. Applicants must show support for application by having his/her professors and/or advisor provide letters of recommendations. **Deadline:** December 1. **Contact:** ITEA at the above address (see entry 3910).

3912 ■ Litherland/FTE Scholarships
(Undergraduate/Scholarship)

Purpose: To recognize and encourage the integration of a quality technology education program within the school curriculum. **Focus:** Technology. **Qualif.:** Applicant must be a member of ITEA; Applicant must not be a senior by application deadline; Applicant must be a current, full-time undergraduate majoring in technology education teacher preparation. **Criteria:** The award is given based upon interest in acting, academic ability, need, and faculty recommendation.

Funds Avail.: $1,000. **To Apply:** Applicants must submit the following requirements: Letter of application that includes statement about personal interest in teaching technology and applicant's address with day and night telephone numbers; Applicant's resume; A photocopy of applicant's college transcript. A grade point average of 2.5 or more is required; Three faculty recommendations. **Deadline:** December 1. **Contact:** ITEA at the above address (see entry 3910).

3913 ■ Maley/FTE Teacher Scholarships
(Graduate/Scholarship)

Purpose: To recognize and encourage the integration of a quality technology education program within the school curriculum. **Focus:** Technology. **Qualif.:** Applicant must be a member of ITEA; Applicant must not be a technology teacher at any grade level who is beginning or continuing graduate study. **Criteria:** Scholarship is given based on the committee's criteria.

Funds Avail.: $1,000. **To Apply:** Applicant must submit the following requirements: **Deadline:** December 1. **Contact:** ITEA at the above address (see entry 3910).

3914 ■ International Thomas Merton Society
Bellarmine University
2001 Newburg Rd.
Louisville, KY 40205
E-mail: merton@bellarmine.edu
URL: http://www.merton.org/ITMS/

3915 ■ Daggy Youth/Student Scholarships
(Professional Development/Scholarship)

Purpose: To enable young people to participate in an International Thomas Merton Society Conference. **Focus:** General studies. **Qualif.:** Applicants must be young individuals (ages 14-29) who are interested in learning about Thomas Merton. **Criteria:** Scholarships will be awarded to qualified candidates based on their personal statement.

Funds Avail.: Covering all the cost (except transportation) of attendance at the Eleventh Conference of the ITMS. **To Apply:** Applicants must submit a statement explaining why they are interested in learning more about Thomas Merton and how they think they would benefit from attending the ITMS Conference; must have the recommendation from a youth minister, campus minister, pastor, teacher, or other qualified adult. Complete application, including the recommendation must be submitted to: scholarship committee chair, Dr. Virginia Ratigan Religious Studies Department, Rosemont College, 1400 Montgomery Ave., Rosemont, PA 19010. **Deadline:** March 15.

Remarks: Scholarships honor the late Robert E. Daggy, founding member and second President of the ITMS.

3916 ■ William H. Shannon Fellowships *(Professional Development/Fellowship)*

Purpose: To enable qualified researchers to visit the Thomas Merton Center archives. **Focus:** General studies. **Qualif.:** Applicants must be researchers without academic affiliation, and students and younger scholars, including those engaged in research for theses and dissertation; must be members of the ITMS. **Criteria:** Awards will be based on (1) the quality of the proposal submitted and on (2) the need for consulting archival materials at the site proposed.

Funds Avail.: $750. **Number Awarded:** 5. **To Apply:** Applicants must submit a detailed proposal of 500-750 words explaining the subject and goals of the applicant's research and the rationale for consulting primary sources at the Merton collection selected by the applicant; must have a letter of recommendation from a scholar familiar with the applicant's qualifications and research interest; must have a proposed expense budget. **Deadline:** March 15.

Remarks: Awards are named in honor of William H. Shannon, founding President of the International Thomas Merton Society.

3917 ■ International Transplant Nurses Society
1739 E Carson St. Box 351
Pittsburgh, PA 15203
Ph: (412)343-4867
E-mail: itns@msn.com
URL: http://www.itns.org

3918 ■ ITNS Research Grants *(Professional Development/Grant)*

Purpose: To encourage qualified transplant health care providers to contribute to the advancement of transplanta-

Awards are arranged alphabetically below their administering organizations

tion through research by providing financial aid. **Focus:** Medical research. **Qualif.:** Investigators must be members of ITNS; have submitted a complete research application package; are ready to begin the research project immediately upon obtaining funding; and have signed an ITNS research agreement. **Criteria:** Preference is given to studies that address scholarly work such as clinical outcomes and quality improvement; program evaluation projects are encouraged.

Funds Avail.: No specific amount. **To Apply:** Applicants must send application form; four copies of the proposal contains title page, abstract, proposal narrative maximum of 5 singled-spaced pages, appendices, budget and biographical sketch maximum of two pages. Send electronically to russellc@health.missouri.edu. Scholarship information and instructions are available in the website. **Deadline:** July 1.

3919 ■ International Transportation Management Association

PO Box 924146
Houston, TX 77292-4146
Ph: (281)885-7135
Fax: (281)885-7026
E-mail: elizabeth.golden@hlag.com
URL: http://www.itma-houston.org

3920 ■ James Costello Memorial Scholarships
(Undergraduate/Scholarship)

Purpose: To provide educational assistance for qualified graduating high school seniors intending to pursue their studies. **Focus:** Logistics. **Qualif.:** Applicants must be graduating high school seniors and university students majoring in a logistics-related curriculum. **Criteria:** Selection will be based on academic performance.

Funds Avail.: $500-$1,000. **To Apply:** Applicants must complete and submit the electronic scholarship application form. An ITMA scholarship will not be considered unless all three of the following supporting documents are received by the commission deadline: a certified copy of college/ university transcript or high school transcript; two letters of recommendation; and a 200-word essay. Both the completed scholarship application and the required three supporting documents must reach ITMA for the application to be processed and considered. **Deadline:** April 25.

3921 ■ International Union of Bricklayers and Allied Craftworkers

620 F St. NW
Washington, DC 20004
Ph: (202)783-3788
Free: 888-880-8222
E-mail: askbac@bacweb.org
URL: http://www.bacweb.org

3922 ■ Union Plus Scholarship Program
(Undergraduate/Scholarship)

Purpose: To assist students pursuing their post-secondary education. **Focus:** General studies. **Qualif.:** Applicant must be a current or retired members of unions participating in any Union Plus program, their spouses and their dependent children (including foster children, step children, and any other child for whom the individual member provides greater than 50% of his or her support) can apply for a Union Plus Scholarship; must be accepted into an accredited college or university, community college or recognized technical or trade school. **Criteria:** Applicants for scholarships are evaluated according to academic ability, social awareness, financial need and appreciation of labor. Scholarship applications are judged by a committee of impartial post secondary educators.

Funds Avail.: $500-4,000. **To Apply:** Application forms are in the website. **Deadline:** January 31.

3923 ■ U.S. Bates Scholarship Program
(Undergraduate/Scholarship)

Purpose: To assist the children of BAC members in pursuing a college education. **Focus:** General studies. **Qualif.:** Applicant must be a son or daughter of U.S BAC members (in good standing) of U.S. BAC locals who will be juniors in high school; must take or plan to take the standardized PSAT exam in the fall of their junior year. **Criteria:** Selection of recipients is administered through the National Merit Scholarship Corporation.

Funds Avail.: $2,500. **Number Awarded:** 3-4. **To Apply:** Applicant must apply during their junior year in high school. For further information, applicants are advised to contact BAC's Educational Department at askbac@bacweb.org or call 888880-8BAC.

3924 ■ International Women's Fishing Association

PO Box 21066
Fort Lauderdale, FL 33335-1066
E-mail: darlawalker@hotmail.com
URL: http://www.iwfa.org

3925 ■ IWFA Scholarships *(Graduate/Scholarship)*

Purpose: To support students in attaining graduate degrees in marine science. **Focus:** Marine biology. **Qualif.:** Applicants must be matriculated at a recognized University; pursuing a study leading to a graduate degree in marine sciences. **Criteria:** Selection is based on character, academic accomplishments, ability and the need for the award.

Funds Avail.: $2,000. **To Apply:** Applicants must submit a completed application form. **Deadline:** March 1.

Remarks: Established in 1965. **Contact:** IWFA Scholarship trustees, kelleykeys@aol.com.

3926 ■ Interplast

857 Maude Ave.
Mountain View, CA 94043
Ph: (650)962-0123
Free: 888-467-5278
E-mail: info@interplast.org
URL: http://www.interplast.org

3927 ■ Jerome P. Webster Fellowships *(Professional Development/Fellowship)*

Purpose: To provide training for promising health care providers from developing countries to improve medical access and healthcare worldwide. **Focus:** Medical education. **Qualif.:** Applicant must be recently trained in plastic and reconstructive surgery and be judge proficient by his/her mentors in a wide range of reconstructive surgical techniques; must be either eligible or certified by the American

Awards are arranged alphabetically below their administering organizations

Board of Plastic Surgery; must hold either U.S. or Canadian citizenship or possess the appropriate U.S visa; must be free to travel for up to ten months per year. **Criteria:** Selection of applicant will be based on merit and experience in medical programs.

Funds Avail.: No specific amount. **To Apply:** For application requirements and instruction, applicants are advise contact Fran Cunniffe, Medical Education and outreach coordinator, at fran@interplast.org. **Deadline:** September 1.

3928 ■ Iowa Court Reporters Association

8345 University Blvd., Ste. F-1
Des Moines, IA 50325
Ph: (515)225-2323
E-mail: sylvia.kreamalmyer@jb.state.ia.us
URL: http://www.iacra.org

3929 ■ Mary L. Brown Scholarships *(Undergraduate/Scholarship)*

Purpose: To promote and advance the interest of individuals engaged in the profession of shorthand reporting throughout the state of Iowa; to develop greater awareness and appreciation for the profession through public education and to promote the shorthand reporting industry. **Focus:** Broadcasting. **Qualif.:** Applicant must be enrolled as a Realtime Reporting major in either Judicial or Captioning/ CART service; must attend AIB College of Business; and must be a graduate of an Iowa high school. **Criteria:** Recipients are selected based on grades, community, and school activities.

Funds Avail.: $750. **To Apply:** Applicants must submit a completed application form along with two letters of recommendation and a 250-word essay. **Deadline:** April 1. **Contact:** icra@assoc-serv.com

3930 ■ Iowa Library Association

3636 Westown Pkwy., Ste. 202
West Des Moines, IA 50266
Ph: (515)273-5322
Fax: (515)309-4576
Free: 800-452-5507
URL: http://www.iowalibraryassociation.org

3931 ■ Iowa Library Association Foundation Scholarships *(Graduate/Scholarship)*

Purpose: To assist outstanding students who are pursuing a graduate degree in school library studies at the University of Northern Iowa. **Focus:** Library Sciences; Information Science and Technology. **Qualif.:** Applicants must have been fully admitted into the graduate program in school library studies at the University of Northern Iowa and enrolled continuously for three semesters of study. Applicants must have at least a 3.25 grade point average (on a 4.0 scale) for their undergraduate program of study or previous graduate studies of at least 8 credit hours. **Criteria:** Recipients will be chosen based on demonstrated academic excellence, potential to become a successful librarian, evidence of the ability to work well with others, and demonstrated communication skills. Selection shall be made solely on the basis of stated criteria without regard to sex, creed, race, national origin.

Funds Avail.: $1,000 in 2008. **To Apply:** Applicants must accomplish proper completion and filing of the application form (available online) and submit along with three letters of recommendation from persons working in the library science/information science field. **Deadline:** September 12. **Contact:** Iowa Library Association at the above address (see entry 3930).

3932 ■ Jack E. Tillson Scholarships *(Graduate/ Scholarship)*

Purpose: To assist outstanding students who are pursuing a graduate degree in Library Science or Information Science at the University of Iowa. **Focus:** Library Sciences; Information Science and Technology. **Qualif.:** Applicants must have been admitted as regular students in the graduate program in library science/information science and be enrolled at least half-time in that program at the University of Iowa. Applicants must have at least a 3.25 grade point average (on a scale of 4.0) for their undergraduate program of study or previous graduate work of at least 8 credit hours. **Criteria:** Applicants will be evaluated based on academic excellence, potential to become a successful librarian, ability to work well with others, and demonstrated communication skills. Selection shall be made solely on the basis of stated criteria without regard to sex, creed, race, national origin.

Funds Avail.: $1,000 in 2008. **To Apply:** Applicants must accomplish proper completion and filing of the application form (available online) and submit along with three letters of recommendation from persons working in the library science/information science field. **Deadline:** September 12. **Contact:** Iowa Library Association at the above address (see entry 3930).

3933 ■ Iowa Newspaper Association

319 E. 5th St.
Des Moines, IA 50309
Ph: (515)244-2145
Fax: (515)244-4855
E-mail: ina@inanews.com
URL: http://www.inanews.com

3934 ■ INF Scholarships *(Undergraduate/ Scholarship)*

Purpose: To champion the quality and future of Iowa's newspaper enterprises and the communities they serve. **Focus:** Journalism. **Qualif.:** Applicants must be Iowa college students preparing for a career in the newspaper industry. High school seniors and students currently enrolled at a college or university are encouraged to apply. **Criteria:** Recipients are selected based on academic records, financial need, demonstrated talent and desire to work for an Iowa newspaper.

Funds Avail.: $1,000. **Number Awarded:** 2. **To Apply:** Applicants must attach two letters of reference including one from a teacher or guidance counselor; must attach a one-page statement about self, educational and career goals; two samples of writing or other examples of works which attest to the applicant's abilities. Samples should be printed on or affixed to 8.5" x 11" sheets of white copy paper. **Contact:** info@inanews.com.

3935 ■ Iowa Journalism Institute Scholarships *(Undergraduate/Scholarship)*

Purpose: To champion the quality and future of Iowa's newspaper enterprises and the communities they serve. **Focus:** Journalism; Communication. **Qualif.:** Applicants must be students studying journalism, communications, mass communications, photojournalism, graphic design, marketing or public relations at a college or university in Iowa, Illinois, or Wisconsin. **Criteria:** Recipients are selected based on academic records, financial need, demonstrated talent and desire to work for an Iowa newspaper.

Funds Avail.: No specific amount. **To Apply:** Applicants must attach two letters of reference including one from a teacher or guidance counselor; must attach a one-page statement about self, educational and career goals; two samples of writings or other examples of work which attest to the abilities of applicants in their intended career field. These samples should be printed on or affixed to 8.5" x 11" sheets of white copy paper. **Contact:** info@inanews.com.

3936 ■ Carter Pitts Scholarships *(Undergraduate/Scholarship)*

Purpose: To champion the quality and future of Iowa's newspaper enterprises and the communities they serve. **Focus:** Journalism. **Qualif.:** Applicants must be Iowa college students preparing for a career in the newspaper industry. High school seniors and students currently enrolled at a college or university are encouraged to apply. **Criteria:** Recipients are selected based on academic records, financial need, demonstrated talent and desire to work for an Iowa newspaper.

Funds Avail.: $500. **To Apply:** Applicants must attach two letters of reference including one from teacher or guidance counselor; must attach a one-page statement about self, educational and career goals; two samples of writings or other examples of work that attest to their abilities in the journalism field. Samples should be printed on or affixed to 8.5" x 11" sheets of white copy paper. **Contact:** info@inanews.com.

3937 ■ Iranian American Bar Association

1025 Connecticut Ave. NW, Ste. 1012
Washington, DC 20036
E-mail: iaba@iaba.us
URL: http://www.iaba.us

3938 ■ Iranian American Bar Association Scholarships *(Undergraduate/Scholarship)*

Purpose: To recognize the commitment of law students to the advancement of the Iranian American community. **Focus:** Law. **Qualif.:** Applicants must be of Iranian heritage or committed to the advancement of the Iranian American community and IABA's mission; must be enrolled in an accredited law school in US; must be in the position to accept the scholarship in the school year for which it is being awarded; and must be full-time students. **Criteria:** Recipients will be selected by the Scholarship Committee.

Funds Avail.: $2,000. **To Apply:** Applicants must submit a duly completed National Scholarship Application Form; a detailed resume; a statement or essay written by the applicant (no more than one single-sided 1.5 spaced typewritten page); and official law school and college transcripts. **Deadline:** June.

3939 ■ ISA (Instrumentation, Systems, and Automation)

67 Alexander Dr.
Research Triangle Park, NC 27709
Ph: (919)549-8411
Fax: (919)549-8288
E-mail: info@isa.org
URL: http://www.isa.org

3940 ■ ISA Aerospace Industries Division - William H. Atkinson Scholarships *(Graduate, Undergraduate/Scholarship)*

Purpose: To promote education in an instrumentation, systems, or automation discipline. **Focus:** Systems engineering; Automotive technology. **Qualif.:** Applicant must be currently enrolled in a graduate or undergraduate program in an instrumentation, systems, or automation discipline (2-year program or 4-year baccalaureate program or its equivalent). Two-year program applicants must have completed at least one academic semester or its equivalent. Four-year degree program applicants must be in sophomore year or higher at the time of application. Applicants must be full-time students in an educational institution and have at least an overall GPA of 3.0 on a 4.0 scale. **Criteria:** Preference is given to students who are enrolled in a degree program in instrumentation, systems, and automation or other closely related field.

Funds Avail.: Varies. **To Apply:** Applicants must submit completed application (with Department Head Signature); two reference letters; original transcript (with raised seal); list of awards and honors; extracurricular activities; employment history; and an essay. Mail the original and ten copies of the complete application with attachments unfolded in an envelope. **Deadline:** February 15. **Contact:** Randy Buchanan at randy.buchanan@usm.edu.

3941 ■ Norman E. Huston Scholarships *(Graduate, Undergraduate/Scholarship)*

Purpose: To promote education in an instrumentation, systems, or automation discipline. **Focus:** Systems engineering; Automotive technology. **Qualif.:** Applicant must be currently enrolled in a graduate or undergraduate program in an instrumentation, systems, or automation discipline (2-year program or 4-year baccalaureate program or its equivalent). Two-year program applicants must have completed at least one academic semester or its equivalent. Four-year degree program applicants must be in sophomore year or higher at the time of application. Applicants must be full-time students in an educational institution who have at least an overall GPA of 3.0 on a 4.0 scale. **Criteria:** Preference is given to students who are enrolled in a degree program in instrumentation, systems, and automation or other closely related field.

Funds Avail.: Varies. **To Apply:** Applicants must submit a completed application (with Department Head Signature); two reference letters; original transcript (with raised seal); list of awards and honors; extracurricular activities; employment history; and an essay. Mail the original and ten copies of the complete application with attachments unfolded in an envelope. **Deadline:** February 15.

Remarks: Funds were provided by the family of Norman E. Huston.

3942 ■ ISA Educational Foundation Scholarships *(Graduate, Undergraduate/Scholarship)*

Purpose: To promote education in an instrumentation, systems, or automation discipline. **Focus:** Systems engineering; Automotive technology. **Qualif.:** Applicant must be a full-time college/university student in either a graduate, undergraduate, or 2-year degree program; must have an overall GPA of at least 3.0 on a 4.0 scale; and

Awards are arranged alphabetically below their administering organizations

must be enrolled in a program in automation and control or a closely related field. **Criteria:** Preference is given to students who are enrolled in a degree program in instrumentation, systems, and automation or other closely related field.

Funds Avail.: No specific amount. **To Apply:** Applicants must submit completed application (with Department Head Signature); two reference letters; original transcript (with raised seal); list of awards and honors and extracurricular activities; employment history; and an essay. Mail the original and ten copies of the complete application with attachments unfolded in an envelope. **Deadline:** February 15.

3943 ■ ISA Executive Board Scholarships *(Graduate, Undergraduate/Scholarship)*

Purpose: To promote education in an instrumentation, systems, or automation discipline. **Focus:** Systems engineering; Automotive technology. **Qualif.:** Applicant must be currently enrolled in a graduate or undergraduate program in an instrumentation, systems, or automation discipline (2-year program or 4 year baccalaureate program or its equivalent). Two-year program applicants must have completed at least one academic semester. Four-year degree program applicants must be in sophomore year or higher at the time of application. Applicant must be a full-time student in an educational institution who have at least an overall GPA of 3.0 on a 4.0 scale. **Criteria:** Preference is given to applicants with demonstrated leadership capabilities.

Funds Avail.: Varies. **To Apply:** Applicants must submit a completed application (with Department Head Signature); two reference letters; original transcript (with raised seal); list of awards and honors; extracurricular activities; employment history; and an essay. Mail the original and ten copies of the complete application with attachments unfolded in an envelope. **Deadline:** February 15.

Remarks: Funds were provided by past and present members of ISA's Executive Board.

3944 ■ ISA Section and District Scholarships - Birmingham *(Graduate, Undergraduate/Scholarship)*

Purpose: To promote education in an instrumentation, systems, or automation discipline. **Focus:** Systems engineering; Automotive technology. **Qualif.:** Applicant must be currently enrolled in a graduate or undergraduate program in an instrumentation, systems, or automation discipline (2-year program or 4-year baccalaureate program or its equivalent). Two-year program applicants must have completed at least one academic semester or its equivalent. Four-year degree program applicants must be in sophomore year or higher at the time of application. Applicants must be full-time students in an educational institution and have at least an overall GPA of 3.0 on a 4.0 scale. **Criteria:** Preference is given to students who are enrolled in a degree program in instrumentation, systems, and automation or other closely related field.

Funds Avail.: Varies. **To Apply:** Applicants must submit completed application (with Department Head Signature); two reference letters; original transcript (with raised seal); list of awards and honors; extracurricular activities; employment history; and an essay. Mail the original and ten copies of the complete application with attachments unfolded in an envelope. **Deadline:** February 15. **Contact:** Catherine Anrews at candrews@hilealabama.com.

3945 ■ ISA Section and District Scholarships - Houston *(Graduate, Undergraduate/Scholarship)*

Purpose: To promote education in an instrumentation, systems, or automation discipline. **Focus:** Systems engineering; Automotive technology. **Qualif.:** Applicant must be currently enrolled in a graduate or undergraduate program in an instrumentation, systems, or automation discipline (2-year program or 4-year baccalaureate program or its equivalent). Two-year program applicants must have completed at least one academic semester or its equivalent. Four-year degree program applicants must be in sophomore year or higher at the time of application. Applicants must be full-time students in an educational institution and have at least an overall GPA of 3.0 on a 4.0 scale. **Criteria:** Preference is given to students who are enrolled in a degree program in instrumentation, systems, and automation or other closely related field.

Funds Avail.: Varies. **To Apply:** Applicants must submit completed application (with Department Head Signature); two reference letters; original transcript (with raised seal); list of awards and honors; extracurricular activities; employment history; and an essay. Mail the original and ten copies of the complete application with attachments unfolded in an envelope. **Deadline:** February 15. **Contact:** Chan Miller at cmiller@technip.com.

3946 ■ ISA Section and District Scholarships - Lehigh Valley *(Graduate, Undergraduate/Scholarship)*

Purpose: To promote education in an instrumentation, systems, or automation discipline. **Focus:** Systems engineering; Automotive technology. **Qualif.:** Applicant must be currently enrolled in a graduate or undergraduate program in an instrumentation, systems, or automation discipline (2-year program or 4-year baccalaureate program or its equivalent). Two-year program applicants must have completed at least one academic semester or its equivalent. Four-year degree program applicants must be in sophomore year or higher at the time of application. Applicants must be full-time students in an educational institution and have at least an overall GPA of 3.0 on a 4.0 scale. **Criteria:** Preference is given to students who are enrolled in a degree program in instrumentation, systems, and automation or other closely related field.

Funds Avail.: Varies. **To Apply:** Applicants must submit completed application (with Department Head Signature); two reference letters; original transcript (with raised seal); list of awards and honors; extracurricular activities; employment history; and an essay. Mail the original and ten copies of the complete application with attachments unfolded in an envelope. **Deadline:** February 15. **Contact:** Ronald Christman at christr2@apci.com.

3947 ■ ISA Section and District Scholarships - New Jersey *(Graduate, Undergraduate/Scholarship)*

Purpose: To promote education in an instrumentation, systems, or automation discipline. **Focus:** Systems engineering; Automotive technology. **Qualif.:** Applicant must be currently enrolled in a graduate or undergraduate program in an instrumentation, systems, or automation discipline (2-year program or 4-year baccalaureate program or its equivalent). Two-year program applicants must have completed at least one academic semester or its equivalent. Four-year degree program applicants must be in sophomore year or higher at the time of application. Applicants must be full-time students in an educational institution and have at least an overall GPA of 3.0 on a 4.0 scale. **Criteria:**

Awards are arranged alphabetically below their administering organizations

Preference is given to students who are enrolled in a degree program in instrumentation, systems, and automation or other closely related field.

Funds Avail.: Varies. **To Apply:** Applicants must submit completed application (with Department Head Signature); two reference letters; original transcript (with raised seal); list of awards and honors; extracurricular activities; employment history; and an essay. Mail the original and ten copies of the complete application with attachments unfolded in an envelope. **Deadline:** February 15. **Contact:** Bob Linder at boblindner@aol.com.

3948 ■ ISA Section and District Scholarships - Niagara Frontier *(Graduate, Undergraduate/ Scholarship)*

Purpose: To promote education in an instrumentation, systems, or automation discipline. **Focus:** Systems engineering; Automotive technology. **Qualif.:** Applicant must be currently enrolled in a graduate or undergraduate program in an instrumentation, systems, or automation discipline (2-year program or 4-year baccalaureate program or its equivalent). Two-year program applicants must have completed at least one academic semester or its equivalent. Four-year degree program applicants must be in sophomore year or higher at the time of application. Applicants must be full-time students in an educational institution and have at least an overall GPA of 3.0 on a 4.0 scale. **Criteria:** Preference is given to students who are enrolled in a degree program in instrumentation, systems, and automation or other closely related field.

Funds Avail.: Varies. **To Apply:** Applicants must submit completed application (with Department Head Signature); two reference letters; original transcript (with raised seal); list of awards and honors; extracurricular activities; employment history; and an essay. Mail the original and ten copies of the complete application with attachments unfolded in an envelope. **Deadline:** February 15. **Contact:** Maxwell Bennett at maxwell33@adelphia.net.

3949 ■ ISA Section and District Scholarships - Northern California *(Graduate, Undergraduate/ Scholarship)*

Purpose: To promote education in an instrumentation, systems, or automation discipline. **Focus:** Systems engineering; Automotive technology. **Qualif.:** Applicant must be currently enrolled in a graduate or undergraduate program in an instrumentation, systems, or automation discipline (2-year program or 4-year baccalaureate program or its equivalent). Two-year program applicants must have completed at least one academic semester or its equivalent. Four-year degree program applicants must be in sophomore year or higher or its equivalent at the time of application. Applicants must be full-time students in an educational institution and have at least an overall GPA of 3.0 on a 4.0 scale. **Criteria:** Preference is given to students who are enrolled in a degree program in instrumentation, systems, and automation or other closely related field.

Funds Avail.: Varies. **To Apply:** Applicants must submit completed application (with Department Head Signature); two reference letters; original transcript (with raised seal); list of awards and honors; extracurricular activities; employment history; and an essay. Mail the original and ten copies of the complete application with attachments unfolded in an envelope. **Deadline:** February 15. **Contact:** Terry Molloy at tvmolloy@cmes.net.

3950 ■ ISA Section and District Scholarships - Richmond (Hopewell) *(Graduate, Undergraduate/ Scholarship)*

Purpose: To promote education in an instrumentation, systems, or automation discipline. **Focus:** Systems engineering; Automotive technology. **Qualif.:** Applicant must be currently enrolled in a graduate or undergraduate program in an instrumentation, systems, or automation discipline (2-year program or 4-year baccalaureate program or its equivalent). Two-year program applicants must have completed at least one academic semester or its equivalent. Four-year degree program applicants must be in sophomore year or higher at the time of application. Applicants must be full-time students in an educational institution and have at least an overall GPA of 3.0 on a 4.0 scale. **Criteria:** Preference is given to students who are enrolled in a degree program in instrumentation, systems, and automation or other closely related field.

Funds Avail.: Varies. **To Apply:** Applicants must submit completed application (with Department Head Signature); two reference letters; original transcript (with raised seal); list of awards and honors; extracurricular activities; employment history; and an essay. Mail the original and ten copies of the complete application with attachments unfolded in an envelope. **Deadline:** February 15. **Contact:** Bill Sneddon at bill.sneddon@qimonda.com.

3951 ■ ISA Section and District Scholarships - Savannah River *(Graduate, Undergraduate/ Scholarship)*

Purpose: To promote education in an instrumentation, systems, or automation discipline. **Focus:** Systems engineering; Automotive technology. **Qualif.:** Applicant must be currently enrolled in a graduate or undergraduate program in an instrumentation, systems, or automation discipline (2-year program or 4-year baccalaureate program or its equivalent). Two-year program applicants must have completed at least one academic semester or its equivalent. Four-year degree program applicants must be in sophomore year or higher at the time of application. Applicants must be full-time students in an educational institution and have at least an overall GPA of 3.0 on a 4.0 scale. **Criteria:** Preference is given to students who are enrolled in a degree program in instrumentation, systems, and automation or other closely related field.

Funds Avail.: Varies. **To Apply:** Applicants must submit completed application (with Department Head Signature); two reference letters; original transcript (with raised seal); list of awards and honors; extracurricular activities; employment history; and an essay. Mail the original and ten copies of the complete application with attachments unfolded in an envelope. **Deadline:** February 15. **Contact:** Lance Brown at ltbrown1@comcast.net.

3952 ■ ISA Section and District Scholarships - Southwestern Wyoming *(Graduate, Undergraduate/Scholarship)*

Purpose: To promote education in an instrumentation, systems, or automation discipline. **Focus:** Systems engineering; Automotive technology. **Qualif.:** Applicant must be currently enrolled in a graduate or undergraduate program in an instrumentation, systems, or automation discipline (2-year program or 4-year baccalaureate program or its equivalent). Two-year program applicants must have completed at least one academic semester or its equivalent. Four-year degree program applicants must be in sophomore year or higher at the time of application. Applicants

Awards are arranged alphabetically below their administering organizations

must be full-time students in an educational institution and have at least an overall GPA of 3.0 on a 4.0 scale. **Criteria:** Preference is given to students who are enrolled in a degree program in instrumentation, systems, and automation or other closely related field.

Funds Avail.: Varies. **To Apply:** Applicants must submit completed application (with Department Head Signature); two reference letters; original transcript (with raised seal); list of awards and honors; extracurricular activities; employment history; and an essay. Mail the original and ten copies of the complete application with attachments unfolded in an envelope. **Deadline:** February 15. **Contact:** Tom Kottenstette at swwyoisa@hotmail.com.

3953 ■ ISA Section and District Scholarships - Texas, Louisiana and Mississippi *(Graduate, Undergraduate/Scholarship)*

Purpose: To promote education in an instrumentation, systems, or automation discipline. **Focus:** Systems engineering; Automotive technology. **Qualif.:** Applicant must be currently enrolled in a graduate or undergraduate program in an instrumentation, systems, or automation discipline (2 year program or 4 year baccalaureate program or its equivalent). Two-year program applicants must have completed at least one academic semester or its equivalent. Four-year degree program applicants must be in sophomore year or higher at the time of application. Applicants must be full-time students in an educational institution who have at least an overall GPA of 3.0 on a 4.0 scale. **Criteria:** Preference is given to students who are enrolled in a degree program in instrumentation, systems, and automation or other closely related field.

Funds Avail.: Varies. **To Apply:** Applicants must submit a completed application (with Department Head Signature); two reference letters; original transcript (with raised seal); list of awards and honors; extracurricular activities; employment history; and an essay. Mail the original and ten copies of the complete application with attachments unfolded in an envelope. **Deadline:** February 15. **Contact:** Victor Carbajal at viccarba@aol.com.

3954 ■ ISA Section and District Scholarships - Wilmington *(Graduate, Undergraduate/Scholarship)*

Purpose: To promote education in an instrumentation, systems, or automation discipline. **Focus:** Systems engineering; Automotive technology. **Qualif.:** Applicant must be currently enrolled in a graduate or undergraduate program in an instrumentation, systems, or automation discipline (2-year program or 4-year baccalaureate program or its equivalent). Two-year program applicants must have completed at least one academic semester or its equivalent. Four-year degree program applicants must be in sophomore year or higher at the time of application. Applicants must be full-time students in an educational institution and have at least an overall GPA of 3.0 on a 4.0 scale. **Criteria:** Preference is given to students who are enrolled in a degree program in instrumentation, systems, and automation or other closely related field.

Funds Avail.: Varies. **To Apply:** Applicants must submit completed application (with Department Head Signature); two reference letters; original transcript (with raised seal); list of awards and honors; extracurricular activities; employment history; and an essay. Mail the original and ten copies of the complete application with attachments unfolded in an envelope. **Deadline:** February 15. **Contact:** Bill Balascio at w_balascio@carewassoc.com, or George Bentinck at george.c.bentinck-2@usa.dupont.com.

3955 ■ ISA Technical Division Scholarships - Analysis Division *(Graduate, Undergraduate/ Scholarship)*

Purpose: To promote education in an instrumentation, systems, or automation discipline. **Focus:** Systems engineering; Automotive technology. **Qualif.:** Applicant must be currently enrolled in a graduate or undergraduate program in an instrumentation, systems, or automation discipline (2-year program or 4-year baccalaureate program or its equivalent). Two-year program applicants must have completed at least one academic semester or its equivalent. Four-year degree program applicants must be in sophomore year or higher at the time of application. Applicants must be full-time students in an educational institution who have at least an overall GPA of 3.0 on a 4.0 scale. **Criteria:** Preference is given to students who are enrolled in a degree program in instrumentation, systems, and automation or other closely related field.

Funds Avail.: Varies. **To Apply:** Applicants must submit completed application (with Department Head Signature); two reference letters; original transcript (with raised seal); list of awards and honors; extracurricular activities; employment history; and an essay. Mail the original and ten copies of the complete application with attachments unfolded in an envelope. **Deadline:** February 15. **Contact:** Mike Chaney at mwchaney@msn.com, or Don Nettles at dnettles@chevron.com.

3956 ■ ISA Technical Division Scholarships - Chemical and Petroleum Industries Division *(Graduate, Undergraduate/Scholarship)*

Purpose: To promote education in an instrumentation, systems, or automation discipline. **Focus:** Systems engineering; Automotive technology. **Qualif.:** Applicant must be currently enrolled in a graduate or undergraduate program in an instrumentation, systems, or automation discipline (2-year program or 4-year baccalaureate program or its equivalent). Two-year program applicants must have completed at least one academic semester or its equivalent. Four-year degree program applicants must be in sophomore year or higher at the time of application. Applicants must be full-time students in an educational institution who have at least an overall GPA of 3.0 on a 4.0 scale. **Criteria:** Preference is given to students who are enrolled in a degree program in instrumentation, systems, and automation or other closely related field.

Funds Avail.: Varies. **To Apply:** Applicants must submit completed application (with Department Head Signature); two reference letters; original transcript (with raised seal); list of awards and honors; extracurricular activities; employment history; and an essay. Mail the original and ten copies of the complete application with attachments unfolded in an envelope. **Deadline:** February 15. **Contact:** at the above address (see entry 3939).

3957 ■ ISA Technical Division Scholarships - Computer Technology Division *(Graduate, Undergraduate/Scholarship)*

Purpose: To promote education in an instrumentation, systems, or automation discipline. **Focus:** Systems engineering; Automotive technology. **Qualif.:** Applicant must be currently enrolled in a graduate or undergraduate program in an instrumentation, systems, or automation discipline (2-year program or 4-year baccalaureate program or its equivalent). Two-year program applicants must have completed at least one academic semester or its equivalent. Four-year degree program applicants must be in sophomore year or higher at the time of application. Applicants must be full-time students in an educational institution who have at least an overall GPA of 3.0 on a 4.0 scale. **Criteria:** Preference is given to students who are enrolled in a degree program in instrumentation, systems, and automation or other closely related field.

Funds Avail.: Varies. **To Apply:** Applicants must submit completed application (with Department Head Signature); two reference letters; original transcript (with raised seal); list of awards and honors; extracurricular activities; employment history; and an essay. Mail the original and ten copies of the complete application with attachments unfolded in an envelope. **Deadline:** February 15. **Contact:** F. Mike Johnson at mike.johnson@veco.com.

3958 ■ ISA Technical Division Scholarships - Food and Pharmaceutical Industries Division *(Graduate, Undergraduate/Scholarship)*

Purpose: To promote education in an instrumentation, systems, or automation discipline. **Focus:** Systems engineering; Automotive technology. **Qualif.:** Applicant must be currently enrolled in a graduate or undergraduate program in an instrumentation, systems, or automation discipline (2-year program or 4-year baccalaureate program or its equivalent). Two-year program applicants must have completed at least one academic semester or 12 semester hours or its equivalent. Four-year degree program applicants must be in sophomore year or higher at the time of application. Applicants must be full-time students in an educational institution and have an at least 3.0 GPA on a 4.0 scale. **Criteria:** Preference is given to students who are enrolled in a degree program in instrumentation, systems, and automation or other closely related field.

Funds Avail.: Varies. **To Apply:** Applicants must submit completed application (with Department Head Signature); two reference letters; original transcript (with raised seal); list of awards and honors; extracurricular activities; employment history; and an essay. Mail the original and ten copies of the complete application with attachments unfolded in an envelope. **Deadline:** February 15. **Contact:** James Bouchard at jboucha@cpcca.jnj.com.

3959 ■ ISA Technical Division Scholarships - Power Industry Division *(Graduate, Undergraduate/Scholarship)*

Purpose: To promote education in an instrumentation, systems, or automation discipline. **Focus:** Systems engineering; Automotive technology. **Qualif.:** Applicant must be currently enrolled in a graduate or undergraduate program in an instrumentation, systems, or automation discipline (2-year program or 4-year baccalaureate program or its equivalent). Two-year program applicants must have completed at least one academic semester or 12 semester hours or its equivalent. Four-year degree program applicants must be in sophomore year or higher at the time of application. Applicants must be full-time students in an educational institution who have an overall GPA of 3.0 on a 4.0 scale. **Criteria:** Preference is given to students who are enrolled in a degree program in instrumentation, systems, and automation or other closely related field.

Funds Avail.: Varies. **To Apply:** Applicants must submit completed application (with Department Head Signature); two reference letters; original transcript (with raised seal); list of awards and honors; extracurricular activities; employment history; and an essay. Mail the original and ten copies of the complete application with attachments unfolded in an envelope. **Deadline:** February 15. **Contact:** Mike Skoncey at mskoncey@firstenergy.corp.com.

3960 ■ ISA Technical Division Scholarships - Process Measurement and Control Division *(Graduate, Undergraduate/Scholarship)*

Purpose: To promote education in an instrumentation, systems, or automation discipline. **Focus:** Systems engineering; Automotive technology. **Qualif.:** Applicant must be currently enrolled in a graduate or undergraduate program in an instrumentation, systems, or automation discipline (2-year program or 4-year baccalaureate program or its equivalent). Two-year program applicants must have completed at least one academic semester or 12 semester hours or its equivalent. Four-year degree program applicants must be in sophomore year or higher at the time of application. Applicants must be full-time students in an educational institution who have at least an overall GPA of 3.0 on a 4.0 scale. **Criteria:** Preference is given to students who are enrolled in a degree program in instrumentation, systems, and automation or other closely related field.

Funds Avail.: Varies. **To Apply:** Applicants must submit completed application (with Department Head Signature); two reference letters; original transcript (with raised seal); list of awards and honors; extracurricular activities; employment history; and an essay. Mail the original and ten copies of the complete application with attachments unfolded in an envelope. **Deadline:** February 15. **Contact:** Robert Carrell at bcarrell@hofferflow.com.

3961 ■ ISA Technical Division Scholarships - Pulp and Paper Industry Division *(Graduate, Undergraduate/Scholarship)*

Purpose: To promote education in an instrumentation, systems, or automation discipline. **Focus:** Systems engineering; Automotive technology. **Qualif.:** Applicant must be currently enrolled in a graduate or undergraduate program in an instrumentation, systems, or automation discipline (2-year program or 4-year baccalaureate program or its equivalent). Two-year program applicants must have completed at least one academic semester, or 12 semester hours, or its equivalent. Four-year degree program applicants must be in sophomore year or higher at the time of application. Applicants must be full-time students in an educational institution who have an overall GPA of 3.0 on a 4.0 scale. **Criteria:** Preference is given to students who are enrolled in a degree program in instrumentation, systems, and automation or other closely related field.

Funds Avail.: Varies. **To Apply:** Applicants must submit completed application (with Department Head Signature); two reference letters; original transcript (with raised seal); list of awards and honors; extracurricular activities; employment history; and an essay. Mail the original and ten copies of the complete application with attachments unfolded in an envelope. **Deadline:** February 15. **Contact:** Brad Carlberg at brad.carlberg@bsc-engineering.com.

3962 ■ ISA Technical Division Scholarships - Test Measurement Division *(Graduate, Undergraduate/Scholarship)*

Purpose: To promote education in an instrumentation, systems, or automation discipline. **Focus:** Systems engineering; Automotive technology. **Qualif.:** Applicant must be currently enrolled in a graduate or undergraduate program in an instrumentation, systems, or automation discipline (2-year program or 4-year baccalaureate program or its equivalent). Two-year program applicants must have completed at least one academic semester, or 12 semester hours, or its equivalent. Four-year degree program applicants must be in sophomore year or higher at the time of application. Applicants must be full-time students in an educational institution and have at least an overall GPA of 3.0 on a 4.0 scale. **Criteria:** Preference is given to students who are enrolled in a degree program in instrumentation, systems, and automation or other closely related fields.

Funds Avail.: Varies. **To Apply:** Applicants must submit completed application (with Department Head Signature); two reference letters; original transcript (with raised seal); list of awards and honors; extracurricular activities; employment history; and an essay. Mail the original and ten copies of the complete application with attachments unfolded in an envelope. **Deadline:** February 15. **Contact:** Susan Reel at reelsj@y12.doe.gov.

3963 ■ ISA Technical Division Scholarships - Water and Wastewater Industries Division *(Graduate, Undergraduate/Scholarship)*

Purpose: To promote education in an instrumentation, systems, or automation discipline. **Focus:** Systems engineering; Automotive technology. **Qualif.:** Applicant must be currently enrolled in a graduate or undergraduate program in an instrumentation, systems, or automation discipline (2-year program or 4-year baccalaureate program or its equivalent). Two-year program applicants must have completed at least one academic semester, or 12 semester hours, or its equivalent. Four-year degree program applicants must be in sophomore year or higher at the time of application. Applicants must be full-time students in an educational institution and have at least an overall GPA of 3.0 on a 4.0 scale. **Criteria:** Preference is given to students who are enrolled in a degree program in instrumentation, systems, and automation or other closely related field.

Funds Avail.: Varies. **To Apply:** Applicants must submit completed application (with Department Head Signature); two reference letters; original transcript (with raised seal); list of awards and honors; extracurricular activities; employment history; and an essay. Mail the original and ten copies of the complete application with attachments unfolded in an envelope. **Deadline:** February 15. **Contact:** Steve Valdez at stevenvaldez@member.isa.org.

3964 ■ Bob and Mary Ives Scholarships *(Graduate, Undergraduate/Scholarship)*

Purpose: To promote education in an instrumentation, systems, or automation discipline. **Focus:** Systems engineering; Automotive technology. **Qualif.:** Applicant must be currently enrolled in a graduate or undergraduate program in an instrumentation, systems, or automation discipline (2 year program or 4 year baccalaureate program or its equivalent). Two-year program applicants must have completed at least one academic semester or its equivalent. Four-year degree program applicants must be in sophomore year or higher at the time of application. Applicants must be full-time students in an educational institution who have at least an overall GPA of 3.0 on a 4.0 scale. **Criteria:** Preference is given to students who are enrolled in a degree program in instrumentation, systems, and automation or other closely related field.

Funds Avail.: Varies. **To Apply:** Applicants must submit a completed application (with Department Head Signature); two reference letters; original transcript (with raised seal); list of awards and honors; extracurricular activities; employment history; and an essay. Mail the original and ten copies of the complete application with attachments unfolded in an envelope. **Deadline:** February 15.

Remarks: Funds provided by Executive Board action in honor of Robert P. Ives, President of ISA in 2003.

3965 ■ Island Resources Foundation

1718 "P" St. NW, Ste. T-4
Washington, DC 20036
Ph: (202)265-9712
Fax: (202)232-0748
E-mail: bpotter@irf.org
URL: http://www.irf.org

3966 ■ Judith A. Towle Environmental Studies Fund *(Undergraduate/Fellowship)*

Purpose: To support studies and activities that address environmental concerns that transcend the boundaries of any single island or island state. **Focus:** Environmental science. **Qualif.:** Applicant must be a graduate student or resident of, or a not-for-profit institution based in, the U.S. or British Virgin Islands or in the Federation of St. Kitts and Nevis. **Criteria:** Candidates will be evaluated based on criteria.

Funds Avail.: $70,000. **To Apply:** Applicants must submit complete application form.

3967 ■ Italian American Lawyers Association

155 South El Molino Ave., Ste. 202
Pasadena, CA 91101
Ph: (626)793-7788
Fax: (626)793-1013
E-mail: jcapeloto@capelotolaw.com
URL: http://www.iala.lawzone.com

3968 ■ Italian American Lawyers Association Annual Scholarships *(Undergraduate/Scholarship)*

Purpose: To inspire excellence in the practice of law by rendering financial aid and assistance for individuals intending to pursue legal education. **Focus:** Law. **Qualif.:** Program is open to individuals pursuing legal education. **Criteria:** Award is given based on academic achievement, potential contribution to the Italian-American Community and financial need. The selection will be made based upon the quality of applicants received each year.

Funds Avail.: $2,500. **To Apply:** Applicants must submit completed application available in the website and must provide a copy of their transcript. In some cases, applicants may also be asked to attend a personal interview. **Deadline:** September 30. **Contact:** IALA.

3969 ■ Jack and Jill of America Foundation

1930 17th St. NW
Washington, DC 20009
Ph: (202)232-5290
Fax: (202)232-1747
E-mail: administration@jackandjillfoundation.org
URL: http://www.jackandjillfoundation.org

3970 ■ National College Scholarship Award *(Undergraduate/Scholarship)*

Purpose: To provide financial assistance to African American students in preparing them to reach their fullest potential through higher education. **Focus:** General education. **Qualif.:** Applicants must be African American high

Awards are arranged alphabetically below their administering organizations

school seniors with a minimum GPA of 3.0 who will be pursuing a bachelor's degree at any accredited postsecondary institution in the United States. **Criteria:** Applicants will be evaluated based on scholastic performance and active community service.

Funds Avail.: $1,500 to $2,500. **To Apply:** Applicants must submit an essay, resume, academic transcript, letters of recommendation and confirmation of 60 hours or more of active community service. **Deadline:** March 14.

Remarks: Applicants who are alumni of Jack and Jill of America, Inc. are ineligible to apply for the scholarship. **Contact:** United Negro College Fund, Inc., 8260 Willow Oaks Corporate Dr., Fairfax, VA 22031.

3971 ■ Jackson County Community Foundation

One Jackson Square, 100 E Michigan Ave., Ste. 308
Jackson, MI 49201-1406
Ph: (517)787-1321
Fax: (517)787-4333
E-mail: jcf@jacksoncf.org
URL: http://www.jacksoncf.org

3972 ■ Bernice Barabash Sports Scholarship
(Undergraduate/Scholarship)

Purpose: To participate in the sport while maintaining high academic standards in preparation for future educational enrichment. **Focus:** Athletics. **Qualif.:** Applicants must be students in grades seven to twelve who hold a minimum of 3.0 GPA; must play hockey during the school year; must be residing in Jackson County or surrounding communities that do not have ice arenas in the area; must plan to attend an accredited college or university program or vocational/ technical institute. **Criteria:** Recipients are selected based on lottery draw of qualified applicants.

Funds Avail.: $1,000. **Number Awarded:** 2. **To Apply:** Applicants must submit a completed application form and a copy of report card or transcript from the 2nd semester. **Contact:** 517-787-1321.

3973 ■ Dennis J. Beck Memorial Scholarship
(Undergraduate/Scholarship)

Purpose: To assist all citizens of greater Jackson in improving the quality of their lives; to support its work as a community grantmaker and community leader. **Focus:** General studies. **Qualif.:** Applicants must be Ethnic minorities pursuing any field of study with special consideration given to those pursuing a degree in Manufacturing. **Criteria:** Recipients are selected based on demonstrated personal responsibility through work, community or family activities.

Funds Avail.: $1,000. **To Apply:** Applicants must submit a completed application form and must provide a proof of acceptance at an accredited college, university, vocational or technical school.

3974 ■ Dorothy and Dick Burgess Scholarship
(Undergraduate/Scholarship)

Purpose: To provide deserving young students who might otherwise be unable to afford the opportunity to attend a smaller Michigan college. **Focus:** Engineering. **Qualif.:** Applicants must have plan to pursue a course of study that leads to a degree in earth science, engineering, premedical or Christian ministry; must have plan to complete a baccalaureate within four consecutive years; must have a cumulative GPA of 3.0 or above; must have demonstrated good citizenship, high moral character and potential for leadership and academic success. **Criteria:** Recipients are selected based on financial need.

Funds Avail.: $4,000. **To Apply:** Applicants must submit a completed application form and must provide a proof of financial need.

3975 ■ June Danby and Pat Pearse Education Scholarship *(Undergraduate/Scholarship)*

Purpose: To assist all citizens of greater Jackson in improving the quality of their lives; to support its work as a community grantmaker and community leader. **Focus:** Education. **Qualif.:** Applicants must be Jackson High School graduating senior students with cumulative GPA of 3.25 or higher; must be full or part-time students in an accredited college or university majoring in the field of education. **Criteria:** Recipients are selected based on participation in school, community service or volunteer activities, academic performance and financial need.

Funds Avail.: $1,000. **To Apply:** Applicants must submit a completed application form.

3976 ■ Antonia Dellas Memorial Scholarship
(Undergraduate/Scholarship)

Purpose: To assist all citizens of greater Jackson in improving the quality of their lives; to support its work as a community grantmaker and community leader. **Focus:** Education. **Qualif.:** Applicants must be high school senior students with a minimum of 3.35 or above GPA; must be accepted or attending an accredited Michigan college or university; must intend to enroll or are already enrolled in a school of education. **Criteria:** Recipients are selected based on financial need and participation in school, community or volunteer activity.

Funds Avail.: $2,000. **To Apply:** Applicants must submit a completed application form and must provide a proof of financial need.

3977 ■ The Eleonor A. Ernest Scholarship
(Undergraduate/Scholarship)

Purpose: To assist all citizens of greater Jackson in improving the quality of their lives; to support its work as a community grantmaker and community leader. **Focus:** General studies. **Qualif.:** Applicants must be valedictorian, salutatorian or students with highest GPA from a smaller Jackson County High School; must have a cumulative GPA of 3.0 or higher who participates in school activities and/or sports; must have a good citizenship, leadership and outside activities including work experience. **Criteria:** Recipients are selected based on academic performance.

Funds Avail.: $1,000. **To Apply:** Applicants must submit a completed application form.

3978 ■ Melissa Eleonor Ernest Scholarship
(Undergraduate/Scholarship)

Purpose: To assist all citizens of greater Jackson in improving the quality of their lives; to support its work as a community grantmaker and community leader. **Focus:** Cosmetology. **Qualif.:** Applicants must be Jackson County residents; must be adult returning to school, graduating high school senior students already enrolled in an accredited institution of Cosmetology; must be full- or part-time students with a cumulative 2.0 GPA or higher. **Criteria:** Recipients are selected based on financial need.

Funds Avail.: $1,000. **To Apply:** Applicants must submit a completed application form.

3979 ■ Robert P. Ernest Scholarship
(Undergraduate/Scholarship)

Purpose: To assist all citizens of greater Jackson in improving the quality of their lives; to support its work as a community grantmaker and community leader. **Focus:** General studies. **Qualif.:** Applicants must be valedictorian, salutatorian or students with highest GPA from a smaller Jackson County High School; must have a cumulative GPA of 3.0 or higher who participates in school activities and/or sports; must have a good citizenship, leadership and outside activities including work experience. **Criteria:** Recipients are selected based on academic performance.

Funds Avail.: $1,000. **To Apply:** Applicants must submit a completed application form.

3980 ■ Hanover-Horton High School Youth of Promise Scholarships *(Undergraduate/Scholarship)*

Purpose: To recognize a Hanover-Horton students for overall achievement and scholastic excellence. **Focus:** General studies. **Qualif.:** Applicants must be graduating Hanover-Horton High School senior students who hold a GPA of 3.0; must have attended the school for at least one full academic year and demonstrate good character with focused goals; must have the plan to be full-time students and carry a minimum of 12 credit hours or equivalent; must also have the plan to attend an accredited Michigan college or university. **Criteria:** Recipients are selected based on academic performance and financial need.

Funds Avail.: $1,000. **To Apply:** Applicants must submit a completed application form.

3981 ■ Martha and Oliver Hansen Memorial Scholarship *(Undergraduate/Scholarship)*

Purpose: To recognize and encourage those who desire to enter the field of education within the intention of teaching in the classroom. **Focus:** Education. **Qualif.:** Applicants must be incoming college junior or senior majoring in Education with the intention of teaching in the classroom; must attend an accredited Michigan college or university who holds 2.5 GPA or above. **Criteria:** Recipients are selected based on financial need.

Funds Avail.: $1,000. **To Apply:** Applicants must submit a completed application form.

3982 ■ Bob and Dawn Hardy Automotive Scholarship *(Undergraduate/Scholarship)*

Purpose: To help students who desire to make the automobile business their career. **Focus:** Automotive technology. **Qualif.:** Applicants must be currently enrolled full- or part-time at Jackson Community College in Automotive Service Technology, Toyota Technical Education Network, Ford Maintenance and Light Repair Associate in Applied Science program or Automotive Service Technology; must have 2.0 GPA or higher. **Criteria:** Recipients are selected based on financial need and result of an interview.

Funds Avail.: $1,500. **To Apply:** Applicants must submit a completed application form.

3983 ■ William and Beatrice Kavanaugh Scholarship *(Undergraduate/Scholarship)*

Purpose: To assist all citizens of greater Jackson in improving the quality of their lives; to support its work as a community grantmaker and community leader. **Focus:** General studies. **Qualif.:** Applicants must be graduating students of Grass Lake High school seniors who attended the school for the full academic year; must have a cumulative GPA of 2.8 or higher; must have plan to be full-time students and carry at least 12 credit hours or equivalent; must be accepted at an accredited college or university and demonstrated a good citizenship qualities in school and/or community. **Criteria:** Recipients are selected based on academic performance and financial need.

Funds Avail.: $1,000. **To Apply:** Applicants must submit a completed application form.

3984 ■ The Otis and Florence Lapham Memorial Scholarship *(Undergraduate/Scholarship)*

Purpose: To further the education of the students; to assist all citizens of greater Jackson in improving the quality of their lives; to support it's work as a community grantmaker and community leader. **Focus:** General studies. **Qualif.:** Applicants must be senior graduating students of Hanover-Horton High School who hold a minimum of 2.5 GPA; must demonstrate a good work history and participated in both school and extracurricular activities. **Criteria:** Recipients are selected based on financial need.

Funds Avail.: $1,000. **To Apply:** Applicants must submit a completed application form.

3985 ■ Lucile E. McGee Scholarship
(Undergraduate/Scholarship)

Purpose: To further the education of the students; to assist all citizens of greater Jackson in improving the quality of their lives; to support its work as a community grantmaker and community leader. **Focus:** General studies. **Qualif.:** Applicants must be senior graduating students of Hanover-Horton High School who hold a minimum of 2.5 GPA; must demonstrate a good work history and participated in both school and extracurricular activities. **Criteria:** Recipients are selected based on financial need.

Funds Avail.: $1,000. **To Apply:** Applicants must submit a completed application form.

3986 ■ Philip Guy Richardson Memorial Scholarship *(Undergraduate/Scholarship)*

Purpose: To recognize exceptional high school and college achievement in academics, citizenship and extracurricular activity. **Focus:** General studies. **Qualif.:** Applicants must be Napoleon High school candidates for graduation with a minimum GPA of 3.0 or higher; must participated in school activities and/or sports. **Criteria:** Recipients are selected based on academic performance, leadership and outside activities including work experience.

Funds Avail.: $2,000. **To Apply:** Applicants must submit a completed application form.

3987 ■ The John and Marion Selby Engineering Scholarship *(Undergraduate/Scholarship)*

Purpose: To assist all citizens of greater Jackson in improving the quality of their lives; to support its work as a community grantmaker and community leader. **Focus:** Engineering. **Qualif.:** Applicants must intend to pursue an engineering degree in an accredited (ABET) program at a Michigan College or university; must be accepted by a college or university with a GPA of 3.0 or higher. **Criteria:** Recipients are selected based on demonstrated qualifications of high merit in the areas of academics and citizenship, leadership and outside activities including work experience.

Funds Avail.: $3,500. **To Apply:** Applicants must submit a completed application form.

Awards are arranged alphabetically below their administering organizations

3988 ■ The Eileen J. Smith, R.N. Memorial Scholarship *(Undergraduate/Scholarship)*

Purpose: To assist all citizens of greater Jackson in improving the quality of their lives; to support its work as a community grantmaker and community leader. **Focus:** Health care services. **Qualif.:** Applicants must be enrolled in an accredited college or university with a major in a medical profession; must be part or full-time students with cumulative 3.0 GPA or higher. **Criteria:** Recipients are selected based on academic performance and financial need.

Funds Avail.: $1,000. **To Apply:** Applicants must submit a completed application form.

3989 ■ Faith Speckhard Scholarships *(Undergraduate/Scholarship)*

Purpose: To recognize students who demonstrate motivation in their pursuit of higher education, actively involved in their community and have financial need. **Focus:** General studies. **Qualif.:** Applicants must be Jackson High School graduating seniors who are African-Americans or a women of any race; must have a minimum of 2.4 GPA and must be full or part-time students in an accredited college or university. **Criteria:** Recipients are selected based on academic performance, financial need and participation in community activities, leadership and service.

Funds Avail.: $5,000. **To Apply:** Applicants must submit a completed application form and proof of acceptance in an accredited college, university, vocational or technical institute.

3990 ■ Paul Tejada Memorial Scholarship *(Undergraduate/Scholarship)*

Purpose: To assist all citizens of greater Jackson in improving the quality of their lives; to support its work as a community grantmaker and community leader. **Focus:** Health care services. **Qualif.:** Applicants must have plans to pursue a course of study leading to a degree in health services administration, nursing or human medicine; must be full or part-time students who maintain a minimum of 12 credit hours with a minimum of 3.0 GPA. **Criteria:** Recipients are selected based on demonstrated good citizenship, high moral character and potential leadership.

Funds Avail.: $1,500. **To Apply:** Applicants must submit a completed application form.

3991 ■ Barbara and Howard Thompson Scholarship *(Undergraduate/Scholarship)*

Purpose: To assist all citizens of greater Jackson in improving the quality of their lives; to support its work as a community grantmaker and community leader. **Focus:** General studies. **Qualif.:** Applicants must be Jackson High School graduating seniors or previous recipients who have plan to pursue a degree in History and/or political science; must be accepted at an accredited two or four-year college or university; must have 3.0 GPA. **Criteria:** Recipients are selected based on academic performance, financial need, demonstrated good citizenship, leadership qualities and participation in school and/or sports.

Funds Avail.: $5,000. **To Apply:** Applicants must submit a completed application form.

3992 ■ Sue Walicki Nursing Scholarship *(Undergraduate/Scholarship)*

Purpose: To assist all citizens of greater Jackson in improving the quality of their lives; to support its work as a community grantmaker and community leader. **Focus:** Nursing. **Qualif.:** Applicants must be Jackson County residents or current employees of a Jackson county health care facility; must be full or part-time students at an accredited Michigan college or university; must have plans to start, continue or advance education in the field of nursing-related field. **Criteria:** Recipients are selected based on financial need.

Funds Avail.: $5,000. **To Apply:** Applicants must submit a proof of acceptance in an accredited Nursing Program and proof of financial need.

3993 ■ Jamaican Canadian Association

995 Arrow Rd.
Toronto, ON, Canada M9M 2Z5
Ph: (416)746-5772
Fax: (416)746-7035
E-mail: info@jcassoc.org
URL: http://www.jcassoc.org

3994 ■ Anne-Marie Bonner Scholarships *(Undergraduate/Scholarship)*

Purpose: To provide financial assistance to students from the Caribbean/ African community, who are pursuing post-secondary studies in Ontario universities/colleges. **Focus:** Art. **Qualif.:** Applicants must be in the first year of study in an arts or Caribbean studies program; must be Canadian citizens or landed immigrants of Caribbean/African background; must be enrolled as full-time first-year students at an Ontario university/college or other postsecondary institution; must demonstrate remarkable academic performance or progress in high school; must demonstrate involvement and leadership in campus and/or community activities; must demonstrate financial need. **Criteria:** Selection of applicants will be based on the criteria of the JCA Scholarship Selection Committee: (a) Demonstrated scholastic ability; (b) Applicant's response to the essay questions; (c) Involvement and leadership in community/campus activities; (d) Significant personal achievements beyond scholastic ability; (e) References; (f) Commitment to career goals.

Funds Avail.: $1,000. **To Apply:** Application forms are available online and must be sent to The Jamaican Canadian Association Center, 995 Arrow Rd., Toronto M9M 2Z5. **Deadline:** July 25.

Remarks: Scholarship is sponsored by Anne-Marie Bonner, Jamaica's Consular General to Toronto.

3995 ■ Brown Dental Scholarships *(Undergraduate/Scholarship)*

Purpose: To provide financial assistance to students from the Caribbean/ African community, who are pursuing post-secondary studies in Ontario universities/colleges. **Focus:** General studies. **Qualif.:** Applicants must be Canadian citizens or landed immigrants of Caribbean/African background; must be enrolled as full-time first-year students at an Ontario university/ college or other postsecondary institution; must demonstrate remarkable academic performance or progress in high school; must demonstrate involvement and leadership in campus and/or community activities; must demonstrate financial need. **Criteria:** Selection of applicants will be based on the criteria of the JCA Scholarship Selection Committee: (a) Demonstrated scholastic ability; (b) Applicant's response to the essay questions; (c) Involvement and leadership in community/ campus activities; (d) Significant personal achievements beyond scholastic ability; (e) References; (f) Commitment to career goals. Preference will be given to a high school, college or university student demonstrating exceptional aptitude in the health sciences, as well as a natural ability to draw, paint or sculpt.

Funds Avail.: $1,000. **To Apply:** Application forms are available online and must be sent to The Jamaican Canadian Association Center, 995 Arrow Rd., Toronto M9M 2Z5. **Deadline:** July 25.

Remarks: Scholarship is donated by Dr. Lancelot A. Brown, who was born in Montreal to Jamaican parents.

3996 ■ Mary Anne Chambers Scholarships
(Undergraduate/Scholarship)

Purpose: To provide financial assistance to students from the Caribbean/ African community, who are pursuing post-secondary studies in Ontario universities/colleges. **Focus:** General studies. **Qualif.:** Applicant must be a Canadian citizen or landed immigrant of Caribbean/African background; must be enrolled as a full-time first-year student at an Ontario university/ college or other postsecondary institution; must demonstrate remarkable academic performance or progress in high school; must demonstrate involvement and leadership in campus and/or community activities; must demonstrate financial need. **Criteria:** Selection of applicants will be based on the criteria of the JCA Scholarship Selection Committee: (a) Demonstrated scholastic ability; (b) Applicant's response to the essay questions; (c) Involvement and leadership in community/ campus activities; (d) Significant personal achievements beyond scholastic ability; (e) References; (f) Commitment to career goals.

Funds Avail.: $1,200. **To Apply:** Application forms are available online and must be sent to The Jamaican Canadian Association Center, 995 Arrow Rd., Toronto M9M 2Z5. **Deadline:** July 25.

Remarks: Sponsored by the Hon. Mary Ann Chambers, Minister of Training Colleges and Universities.

3997 ■ Marcus Mosiah Garvey Scholarships
(Undergraduate/Scholarship)

Purpose: To provide financial assistance to students from the Caribbean/ African community, who are pursuing post-secondary studies in Ontario universities/colleges. **Focus:** General studies. **Qualif.:** Applicant must be a Canadian citizen or landed immigrant of Caribbean/African background; must be enrolled as a full-time first-year student at an Ontario university/ college or other postsecondary institution; must demonstrate remarkable academic performance or progress in high school; must demonstrate involvement and leadership in campus and/or community activities; must demonstrate financial need. **Criteria:** Selection of applicants will be based on the criteria of the JCA Scholarship Selection Committee: (a) Demonstrated scholastic ability; (b) Applicant's response to the essay questions; (c) Involvement and leadership in community/ campus activities; (d) Significant personal achievements beyond scholastic ability; (e) References; (f) Commitment to career goals.

Funds Avail.: $1,000. **Number Awarded:** 2. **To Apply:** Applicants must submit a two-page essay on The Life and Times of Marcus Garvey. Application forms are available online and must be sent to The Jamaican Canadian Association Center, 995 Arrow Rd., Toronto M9M 2Z5. **Deadline:** July 25.

Remarks: Sponsored by Professor Erma Collins.

3998 ■ Humber College Institute of Technology and Advanced Learning Scholarships
(Undergraduate/Scholarship)

Purpose: To provide financial assistance to students from the Caribbean/ African community, who are pursuing post-secondary studies in Ontario universities/colleges. **Focus:** General studies. **Qualif.:** Applicant must be a Canadian citizen or landed immigrant of Caribbean/African background; must be enrolled as a full-time first-year student at an Ontario university/ college or other postsecondary institution; must demonstrate remarkable academic performance or progress in high school; must demonstrate involvement and leadership in campus and/or community activities; must demonstrate financial need. **Criteria:** Selection of applicants will be based on the criteria of the JCA Scholarship Selection Committee: (a) Demonstrated scholastic ability; (b) Applicant's response to the essay questions; (c) Involvement and leadership in community/ campus activities; (d) Significant personal achievements beyond scholastic ability; (e) References; (f) Commitment to career goals.

Funds Avail.: $1,000. **To Apply:** Application forms are available online and must be sent to The Jamaican Canadian Association Center, 995 Arrow Rd., Toronto M9M 2Z5. **Deadline:** July 25.

Remarks: Sponsored by Humber College for a first-year student attending that institution.

3999 ■ I Have a Dream Scholarships
(Undergraduate/Scholarship)

Purpose: To assist students with significant personal achievements beyond scholastic ability. **Focus:** General studies. **Qualif.:** Applicant must be a Canadian citizen or landed immigrant of Caribbean/African background; must be enrolled as a full-time first-year student at an Ontario university/ college or other postsecondary institution; must demonstrate remarkable academic performance or progress in high school; must demonstrate involvement and leadership in campus and/or community activities; must demonstrate financial need. **Criteria:** Selection of applicants will be based on the criteria of the JCA Scholarship Selection Committee: (a) Demonstrated scholastic ability; (b) Applicant's response to the essay questions; (c) Involvement and leadership in community/campus activities; (d) Significant personal achievements beyond scholastic ability; (e) References; (f) Commitment to career goals.

Funds Avail.: $1,000. **Number Awarded:** 2. **To Apply:** Application forms are available online and must be sent to The Jamaican Canadian Association Center, 995 Arrow Rd., Toronto M9M 2Z5. **Deadline:** July 25.

4000 ■ Jamaica Day Basil Duncan Memorial Scholarships *(Undergraduate/Scholarship)*

Purpose: To provide financial assistance to students from the Caribbean/ African community, who are pursuing post-secondary studies in Ontario universities/colleges. **Focus:** General studies. **Qualif.:** Applicant must be a Canadian citizen or landed immigrant of Caribbean/African background; must be enrolled as a full-time first-year student at an Ontario university/ college or other postsecondary institution; must demonstrate remarkable academic performance or progress in high school; must demonstrate involvement and leadership in campus and/or community activities; must demonstrate financial need. **Criteria:** Selection of applicants will be based on the criteria of the JCA Scholarship Selection Committee: (a) Demonstrated scholastic ability; (b) Applicant's response to the essay questions; (c) Involvement and leadership in community/campus activities; (d) Significant personal achievements beyond scholastic ability; (e) References; (f) Commitment to career goals.

Funds Avail.: $1,500. **To Apply:** Application forms are available online and must be sent to The Jamaican Canadian Association Center, 995 Arrow Rd., Toronto M9M 2Z5. **Deadline:** July 25.

Remarks: Scholarship is donated by the Jamaica Day Event Board of Directors in honor of the late Basil Duncan, who was a member of that Board.

4001 ■ Jamaica National Building Society Scholarships *(Undergraduate/Scholarship)*

Purpose: To provide financial assistance to students from the Caribbean/ African community, who are pursuing post-secondary studies in Ontario universities/colleges. **Focus:** Business; Law; Science; Technology; Nursing. **Qualif.:** Applicant must be a Canadian citizen or landed immigrant of Caribbean or African background; must be enrolled as a full-time first-year student at an Ontario university/college or other postsecondary institution; must demonstrate remarkable academic performance or progress in high school; must demonstrate involvement and leadership in campus and/or community activities; must demonstrate financial need. **Criteria:** Selection of applicants will be based on the criteria of the JCA Scholarship Selection Committee: (a) Demonstrated scholastic ability; (b) Applicant's response to the essay questions; (c) Involvement and leadership in community/campus activities; (d) Significant personal achievements beyond scholastic ability; (e) References; (f) Commitment to career goals.

Funds Avail.: $1,000. **Number Awarded:** 2. **To Apply:** Application forms are available online and must be sent to The Jamaican Canadian Association Center, 995 Arrow Rd., Toronto M9M 2Z5. **Deadline:** July 25.

Remarks: Scholarship is donated by the Jamaica National Building Society, a financial institution that facilitates money transfers from Canada.

4002 ■ Dr. Ezra Nesbeth Scholarships *(Undergraduate/Scholarship)*

Purpose: To provide financial assistance to students from the Caribbean or African community, who are pursuing post-secondary studies in Ontario universities/colleges. **Focus:** Business; Technology; Computer and information sciences; Health sciences. **Qualif.:** Applicants must be college or university students studying business, technology, computer science or health science; must have a high academic standing; must demonstrate leadership; must have completed at least one year of college or university in Canada; must demonstrate strong oral and written communication skills; must have an involvement in extracurricular activities within the university, AfroCanadian community, or wider Canadian community; must have landed immigrant or Canadian citizenship; must not be receiving more than one other award of equal or greater value in the receiving year; must have a good understanding of the importance of economic self-sufficiency and entrepreneurship to the success of African Canadians in the Greater Toronto Area and elsewhere in Canada. **Criteria:** Selection of applicants will be based on the criteria of the JCA Scholarship Selection Committee: (a) Demonstrate scholastic ability; (b) Applicant's response to the essay questions; (c) Involvement and leadership in community/campus activities; (d) Significant personal achievements beyond scholastic ability; which may include personal accomplishment; (e) References; (f) Commitment to career goals.

Funds Avail.: $2,000. **To Apply:** Application forms are available online and must be sent to The Jamaican Canadian Association Center, 995 Arrow Rd., Toronto M9M 2Z5. **Deadline:** July 25.

Remarks: Sponsored by Dr. Ezra Nesbeth, a graduate of the University of Waterloo and the University of Toronto with varied and extensive experience in community and health programs.

4003 ■ Ryerson Scholarships *(Undergraduate/Scholarship)*

Purpose: To provide financial assistance to students from the Caribbean/ African community, who are pursuing post-secondary studies in Ontario universities/colleges. **Focus:** General studies. **Qualif.:** Applicant must be a Canadian citizen or landed immigrant of Caribbean/African background; must be enrolled as a full-time first-year student at an Ontario university/ college or other postsecondary institution; must demonstrate remarkable academic performance or progress in high school; must demonstrate involvement and leadership in campus and/or community activities; must demonstrate financial need. **Criteria:** Selection of applicants will be based on the criteria of the JCA Scholarship Selection Committee: (a) Demonstrated scholastic ability; (b) Applicant's response to the essay questions; (c) Involvement and leadership in community/campus activities; (d) Significant personal achievements beyond scholastic ability; (e) References; (f) Commitment to career goals.

Funds Avail.: $1,000. **Number Awarded:** 2. **To Apply:** Application forms are available online and must be sent to The Jamaican Canadian Association Center, 995 Arrow Rd., Toronto M9M 2Z5. **Deadline:** July 25.

Remarks: Sponsored by Ryerson University for one male and one female first-year student attending that university.

4004 ■ Eva Smith Bursary *(Undergraduate/Scholarship)*

Purpose: To provide support to African-Canadian youth who are pursuing a postsecondary education. **Focus:** General studies. **Qualif.:** Applicant must be a Canadian citizen or landed immigrant of Caribbean/African background; must be enrolled as a full-time first-year student at an Ontario university/ college or other postsecondary institution; must demonstrate remarkable academic performance or progress in high school; must demonstrate involvement and leadership in campus and/or community activities; must demonstrate financial need. **Criteria:** Selection of applicants will be based on the criteria of the JCA Scholarship Selection Committee: (a) Demonstrated scholastic ability; (b) Applicant's response to the essay questions; (c) Involvement and leadership in community/campus activities; (d) Significant personal achievements beyond scholastic ability; (e) References; (f) Commitment to career goals.

Funds Avail.: $750. **To Apply:** Application forms are available online and must be sent to The Jamaican Canadian Association Center, 995 Arrow Rd., Toronto M9M 2Z5. **Deadline:** July 25.

Remarks: Bursary is named in honor of the late Eva Smith, a tireless community worker who dedicated her life to youth concerns, women's rights, immigration issues, education and community empowerment.

Awards are arranged alphabetically below their administering organizations

4005 ■ Barbara Thomas Bursary *(Undergraduate/Scholarship)*

Purpose: To provide financial assistance to students from the Caribbean/ African community, who are pursuing post-secondary studies in Ontario universities/colleges. **Focus:** General studies. **Qualif.:** Applicants must be a Canadian citizens or landed immigrants of Caribbean/African background; must be enrolled as full-time first-year students at an Ontario university/ college or other postsecondary institution; must demonstrate remarkable academic performance or progress in high school; must demonstrate involvement and leadership in campus and/or community activities; must demonstrate financial need. **Criteria:** Selection of applicants will be based on the criteria of the JCA Scholarship Selection Committee: (a) Demonstrated scholastic ability; (b) Applicant's response to the essay questions; (c) Involvement and leadership in community/ campus activities; (d) Significant personal achievement beyond scholastic ability; ; (e) References; (f) Commitment to career goals.

Funds Avail.: $500. **To Apply:** Application forms are available online and must be sent to The Jamaican Canadian Association Center, 995 Arrow Rd., Toronto M9M 2Z5. **Deadline:** July 25.

4006 ■ York Regional Police Scholarships *(Undergraduate/Scholarship)*

Purpose: To provide financial assistance to students from the Caribbean/ African community who are pursuing post-secondary studies in Ontario universities/colleges. **Focus:** General studies. **Qualif.:** Applicants must be Canadian citizens or landed immigrants of Caribbean/African background; must be enrolled as full-time first-year students at an Ontario university/ college or other postsecondary institution; must demonstrate remarkable academic performance or progress in high school; must demonstrate involvement and leadership in campus and/or community activities; must demonstrate financial need. **Criteria:** Selection of applicants will be based on the criteria of the JCA Scholarship Selection Committee: (a) Demonstrated scholastic ability; (b) Applicant's response to the essay questions; (c) Involvement and leadership in community/ campus activities; (d) Significant personal achievements beyond scholastic ability; (e) References; (f) Commitment to career goals.

Funds Avail.: $1,000. **To Apply:** Application forms are available online and must be sent to The Jamaican Canadian Association Center, 995 Arrow Rd., Toronto M9M 2Z5. **Deadline:** July 25.

4007 ■ Youth Affairs Committee Rising Star Scholarships *(Undergraduate/Scholarship)*

Purpose: To provide financial assistance to students from the Caribbean/ African community, who are pursuing post-secondary studies in Ontario universities/colleges. **Focus:** General studies. **Qualif.:** Applicant must be a Canadian citizen or landed immigrant of Caribbean/African background; must be enrolled as a full-time first-year student at an Ontario university/ college or other postsecondary institution; must demonstrate remarkable academic performance or progress in high school; must demonstrate involvement and leadership in campus and/or community activities; must demonstrate financial need. **Criteria:** Selection of applicants will be based on the criteria of the JCA Scholarship Selection Committee: (a) Demonstrated scholastic ability; (b) Applicant's response to the essay questions; (c) Involvement and leadership in community/ campus activities; (d) Significant personal achievements beyond scholastic ability; (e) References; (f) Commitment to career goals.

Funds Avail.: $1,000. **To Apply:** Applicants must produce a 500-word essay on either one of following topics: (a) The Maroon In Jamaica; (b) The Haitian Revolution; (c) The Importance of Civic Engagement as a Youth; (d) The Importance of Youth Cultural Education. Application forms are available online and must be sent to The Jamaican Canadian Association Center, 995 Arrow Rd., Toronto M9M 2Z5. **Deadline:** July 25.

4008 ■ Japan Foundation, New York

152 W 7th St., 17th Fl.
New York, NY 10019
Ph: (212)489-0299
Fax: (212)489-0409
E-mail: info@jfny.org
URL: http://www.jfny.org

4009 ■ Japan Foundation, New York Doctoral Fellowship Program *(Doctorate/Fellowship)*

Purpose: To promote Japanese Studies overseas by supporting outstanding scholars in Japanese Studies conducting research in Japan. **Focus:** Japanese studies. **Qualif.:** Applicants must have completed all academic requirements except the dissertation when they begin the fellowship and are expected to have sufficient proficiency in the Japanese language to pursue their research in Japan; must be residing in the United States (if not U.S citizens); must have achieved ABD status by the time the fellowship begins. Scholar and researcher must hold a Ph.D and have substantial experience in research, teaching and writing in the fields of the humanities and social sciences; must be in good health; must be proficient in either Japanese or English; must be able to stay continuously in Japan for the term of fellowship. **Criteria:** Selection of applicant will be based on the criteria given: (1) Project quality, (2) Training academic history, academic rank or position, professional reputation, and accomplishments, (3) Former Japan Foundation fellows who have been awarded two or more Foundation fellowships will be put under particularly rigorous examination. Higher priority will be given to those who are expected to submit their dissertation thesis shortly after the completion of the fellowship; preference will normally be given to doctoral candidates under 35 years of age.

Funds Avail.: No specific amount. **To Apply:** Applicants must have completed all academic requirements except the dissertation when they begin the fellowship and are expected to have sufficient proficiency in the Japanese language to pursue their research in Japan. Higher priority will be given to applicants who expect to submit their dissertation shortly after the completion of their fellowship. Three letters of reference, an evaluation of Japanese-language ability, and academic transcripts must accompany all applications. Other guidelines and procedures are available in the JFNY website. **Deadline:** November 1.

4010 ■ Japan Foundation, New York Research Fellowship Program *(Undergraduate/Fellowship)*

Purpose: To provide opportunities for outstanding scholars in Japanese Studies to conduct research in Japan. **Focus:** Japanese studies. **Qualif.:** Applicants must be scholars/ researchers from the U.S. holding academic positions in a research institution and must have substantial experience in research, teaching, and writing in their respective fields

Awards are arranged alphabetically below their administering organizations

of study. **Criteria:** Priority will be given to relatively junior scholars and researchers, and to those with less research experience in Japan.

Funds Avail.: No specific amount. **To Apply:** Applicants who have U.S. citizenship or permanent residency should complete the application materials and submit them to the Japan Foundation New York Office. Applications should be sent directly (by mail only) to the JFNY office. U.S. citizenship holders should use a different form, which is available in the nearest Japan Foundation office or Japanese diplomatic mission. Multiple applications will make all applications invalid. Other guidelines and procedures are available in the JFNY website. **Deadline:** November 1.

4011 ■ Japan Foundation, New York Short-Term Fellowship Program *(Doctorate/Fellowship)*

Purpose: To provide opportunities for outstanding scholars in Japanese Studies to conduct research in Japan. **Focus:** Japanese studies. **Qualif.:** Applicants must be established scholars, researchers and professionals; must hold a PhD and have substantial experience in research, teaching and writing in the fields of the humanities and social sciences; must be American citizens temporarily residing abroad (if not a U.S. citizen or permanent resident, use a different form); must be good in health; must be proficient in either Japanese or English; must be able to stay continuously in Japan for the duration of the fellowship. **Criteria:** Priority will be given to relatively experienced scholars and researchers who are expected to publish their research results shortly after the completion of their fellowship.

Funds Avail.: No specific amount. **To Apply:** Applicants who have U.S. citizenship or permanent residency should complete the application materials and submit them to the Japan Foundation New York Office. Applications and other supporting documents should be sent directly (by mail only) to the JFNY office. Other guidelines and procedures are available in the JFNY website. **Deadline:** November 1.

4012 ■ Japanese American Bar Association

PO Box 86812
Los Angeles, CA 90086
Ph: (213)738-6746
E-mail: dyokoyama@swlaw.edu
URL: http://www.jabaonline.org

4013 ■ Japanese American Bar Association Scholarships *(Undergraduate/Scholarship)*

Purpose: To encourage pursuits in legal education among law students with ethnic backgrounds. **Focus:** Law. **Qualif.:** Applicants must be law students of various ethnic backgrounds. **Criteria:** Scholarship is given based on academic achievement, financial need, overcoming adversity, and desire to practice law in the Southern California.

Funds Avail.: $1,500. **To Apply:** Applicants must submit completed application along with their most recent law school transcript, current resume; and a personal statement of no more than 500 words. **Deadline:** January 14. **Contact:** JABA Educational Foundation at the above address (see entry 4012).

4014 ■ Japanese American Citizens League

1765 Sutter St.
San Francisco, CA 94115
Ph: (415)921-5225
Fax: (415)921-4671
E-mail: jacl@jacl.org
URL: http://www.jacl.org

4015 ■ Kyutaro & Yasuo Abiko Memorial Scholarships *(Undergraduate/Scholarship)*

Purpose: To provide financial assistance for qualified individuals. **Focus:** Journalism; Agricultural economics. **Qualif.:** Applicant must be an active National JACL member at either an individual or student/youth level; must be planning to attend full-time at a college, university, trade school, business school, or any other institution of higher learning within the United States at the undergraduate or graduate school level. Entering freshman applicant must be a high school senior. **Criteria:** Preference will be given to a student studying journalism or agriculture.

Funds Avail.: $60,000. **To Apply:** Application forms are available online at www.jacl.org/join.html. **Deadline:** March 1 (entering freshman) and April 1 (all applications excluding entering freshman).

4016 ■ Alice Yuriko Endo Memorial Scholarships *(Undergraduate/Scholarship)*

Purpose: To provide financial assistance for qualified individuals. **Focus:** Public service. **Qualif.:** Applicant must be an active National JACL member at either an individual or student/youth level; must be planning to attend full-time at a college, university, trade school, business school, or any other institution of higher learning within the United States at the undergraduate or graduate school level. Entering freshman applicant must be a high school senior. **Criteria:** Preference for this scholarship will be given to a student residing in the Eastern District Council and/or a student with an interest in public and social service.

Funds Avail.: $60,000. **To Apply:** Application forms are available online at www.jacl.org/join.html. **Deadline:** March 1 (entering freshman) and April 1 (all applications excluding entering freshman).

4017 ■ Thomas T. Hayashi Memorial Scholarships *(Graduate, Undergraduate/Scholarship)*

Purpose: To encourage individuals to pursue their legal profession. **Focus:** Law. **Qualif.:** Applicants must be active National JACL members at either an individual or student/youth level; must be planning to attend full-time at a college, university, trade school, business school, or any other institution of higher learning within the United States at the undergraduate or graduate school level. Entering freshman applicant must be a high school senior. **Criteria:** Recipients will be selected based on their application requirements.

Funds Avail.: $60,000. **To Apply:** Application forms are available online at www.jacl.org/join.html. **Deadline:** March 1 (entering freshman) and April 1 (all applications excluding entering freshman).

4018 ■ Magoichi & Shizuko Kato Memorial Scholarships *(Graduate/Scholarship)*

Purpose: To provide financial assistance for qualified individuals. **Focus:** Medicine; Ministry. **Qualif.:** Applicant must be an active National JACL member at either an individual or student/youth level; must be planning to attend full-time at a college, university, trade school, business school, or any other institution of higher learning within the United States at the undergraduate or graduate school level. Entering freshman applicant must be a high school senior. **Criteria:** Preference will be given to a student planning a career in medicine or ministry.

Awards are arranged alphabetically below their administering organizations

Funds Avail.: $60,000. **To Apply:** Application forms are available online at www.jacl.org/join.html. **Deadline:** March 1 (entering freshman) and April 1 (all applications excluding entering freshman).

4019 ■ Sam S. Kuwahara Memorial Scholarships *(Undergraduate/Scholarship)*

Purpose: To provide financial support for qualified students intending to pursue their education. **Focus:** Agricultural economics. **Qualif.:** Applicant must be an active National JACL member at either an individual or Student/Youth level; must be planning to attend full-time at a college, university, trade school, business school, or any other institution of higher learning within the United States at the undergraduate or graduate school level. Entering freshman applicants must be a high school senior. **Criteria:** Preference for this scholarship will be given to students with an interest in agriculture or related field.

Funds Avail.: $60,000. **To Apply:** Application forms are available online at www.jacl.org/join.html. **Deadline:** March 1 (entering freshman) and April 1 (all applications excluding entering freshman).

4020 ■ Gongoro Nakamura Memorial Scholarships *(Undergraduate/Scholarship)*

Purpose: To provide financial assistance for deserving students intending to pursue their studies. **Focus:** Speech, Debate, and Forensics. **Qualif.:** Applicant must be an active National JACL member at either an individual or Student/ Youth level; must be planning to attend full-time at a college, university, trade school, business school, or any other institution of higher learning within the United States at the undergraduate or graduate school level. Entering freshman applicants must be a high school senior. **Criteria:** Preference for this scholarship will be given to a student with an interest in public speaking or debate.

Funds Avail.: $60,000. **To Apply:** Application forms are available online at www.jacl.org/join.html. **Deadline:** March 1 (entering freshman) and April 1 (all applications excluding entering freshman).

4021 ■ Dr. Kiyoshi Sonoda Memorial Scholarships *(Graduate/Scholarship)*

Purpose: To provide financial assistance for qualified individuals. **Focus:** Dentistry. **Qualif.:** Program is open to students studying in the field of dentistry; must be active National JACL members at either an individual or student/ youth level; must be planning to attend full-time at a college, university, trade school, business school, or any other institution of higher learning within the United States at the undergraduate or graduate school level. Entering freshman applicant must be a high school senior. **Criteria:** Applicants will be selected based on the application requirements.

Funds Avail.: $60,000. **To Apply:** Application forms are available online at www.jacl.org/join.html. **Deadline:** March 1 (entering freshman) and April 1 (all applications excluding entering freshman).

4022 ■ Minoru Yasui Memorial Scholarship *(Graduate/Scholarship)*

Purpose: To provide financial assistance for qualified individuals. **Focus:** Human rights; Civil rights; Sociology; Law; Education. **Qualif.:** Applicant must be an active National JACL member at either an individual or student/ youth level; must be planning to attend full-time at a college, university, trade school, business school, or any other institution of higher learning within the United States at the undergraduate or graduate school level. Entering freshman applicant must be a high school senior. **Criteria:** Preference will be given to students with a strong interest in human rights and civil rights.

Funds Avail.: $60,000. **To Apply:** Application forms are available online at www.jacl.org/join.html. **Deadline:** March 1 (entering freshman) and April 1 (all applications excluding entering freshman).

4023 ■ Jewish Foundation for Education of Women

135 E 64th St.
New York, NY 10065
Ph: (212)288-3931
Fax: (212)288-5798
E-mail: info@jfew.org
URL: http://www.jfew.org

4024 ■ JFEW/UJA-Federation Rose Biller Scholarships *(Undergraduate/Scholarship)*

Purpose: To provide financial assistance for Jewish students through a joint program with the Rose Biller Fund of UJA-Federation of New York. **Focus:** General studies. **Qualif.:** Applicants must be Jewish students, permanent residents of and attending colleges or graduate or professional schools in New York City or the countries of Nassau, Suffolk or Westchester. **Criteria:** Recipients are selected based on financial need.

Funds Avail.: $5,000. **To Apply:** Applicants must complete the application online with all required information. **Deadline:** June 16.

4025 ■ Scholarships for Emigres in the Health Sciences *(Undergraduate/Scholarship)*

Purpose: To provide financial support for emigres from the former Soviet Union to train in medicine, dentistry, dental hygiene, nursing, pharmacy, occupational and physical therapy, physician assistant, CVT, and sonography programs. **Focus:** Medicine; Dentistry; Nursing; Pharmacy; Physical therapy; Physiology. **Qualif.:** Applicants must be students from the former Soviet Union; must be residents of New York City or the counties of Nassau, Suffolk or Westchester; must already be enrolled in or about to enroll in a health science program within that geographic area; and must be enrolled full-time, in good standing, and demonstrate financial need. **Criteria:** Recipients are selected based on financial need.

Funds Avail.: $5,000. **To Apply:** Applicants must submit all the required application information.

4026 ■ Jewish Guild for the Blind

15 W 65th St.
New York, NY 10023
Ph: (212)769-6200
Fax: (212)769-6266
Free: 800-284-4422
E-mail: info@jgb.org
URL: http://www.jgb.org

4027 ■ GuildScholar Awards *(Undergraduate/ Scholarship)*

Purpose: To assist blind high school students to pursue college. **Focus:** General studies. **Qualif.:** Applicants must

Awards are arranged alphabetically below their administering organizations

be legally blind high school student and a U.S citizen. **Criteria:** Scholarship recipient will be selected based on the Selection Committee's review of the application materials.

Funds Avail.: $15,000. **Number Awarded:** 12-15. **To Apply:** Applicants must provide (in tif, jpeg or pdf format) proof of legal blindness; proof of U.S. citizenship; documentation of academic achievement; three letters of recommendations and two personal statements. Applicants are required to apply online. **Deadline:** July 1.

Remarks: Applicants must choose a college that is accredited by a body recognized by the Council of Higher Education Accreditation. **Contact:** Gordon Rovins, 212-769-7801 or guildscholar@jgb.org.

4028 ■ Jewish Vocational Service

216 W Jackson Blvd., Ste. 700
Chicago, IL 60606
Ph: (312)673-3400
Fax: (312)553-5544
E-mail: jvs@jvschicago.org
URL: http://www.jvschicago.org

4029 ■ Jewish Federation Academic Scholarships *(Graduate, Undergraduate/Scholarship)*

Purpose: To support the education of a Jewish college or graduate student. **Focus:** Medicine; Education; Social work; Arts; Public health; Urban affairs/design/planning; Law. **Qualif.:** Applicant must be Jewish; be born or raised in either: Cook County, Chicago metropolitan area, or Northwest Indiana; or have one continuous year of full-time employment in Cook County or Chicago metropolitan area prior to starting professional education; must intend to remain in the Chicago metropolitan area after completing school; must be entering as a full-time student in an accredited professional graduate program or entering as junior or senior undergraduate student at an accredited professional education program; and must be demonstrating career promise in a helping profession. **Criteria:** Award is given based on need.

Funds Avail.: More than $500,000 each year. **To Apply:** Applicants must submit a completed Application Data Form; Career Statement Form; Budget Worksheet; and Academic Budget form as an attachment to jvsscholarship@jvschicago.org. In addition, applicants must send by mail a Legal Domicility Form; two letter of reference form; IRS Forms; parents' or spouse's IRS; documentation of tuition cost; Release of Information form; and official transcripts. **Deadline:** February 15. **Contact:** 312-673-3457.

4030 ■ Jewish War Veterans of the United States of America

1811 R St. NW
Washington, DC 20009
Ph: (202)265-6280
Fax: (202)234-5662
E-mail: jwv@jwv.org
URL: http://www.jwv.org

4031 ■ Bernard Rotberg Memorial Scholarships *(Undergraduate/Scholarship)*

Purpose: To provide financial support for the education of descendants of members of the Jewish War Veterans of the United States of America. **Focus:** General studies. **Qualif.:** Applicant must be a direct descendant (child, grandchild, great grandchild) of members in good standing of the Jewish War Veterans of the United States of America. If applicant's relative is deceased, member must have been in good standing at the time of his/her death. Applicant must be a high school senior accepted as a freshman entering in the fall semester by an accredited four-year college or university or a three-year hospital school of nursing; must be in the upper 25% of their high school graduating class; and must demonstrate involvement and leadership in extracurricular activities, in their Jewish community and the community at large. **Criteria:** Recipients are selected based on College Entrance Examination scores including SAT and/or ACT composite scores and three SAT Achievement (SAT II) scores (one of which should be English).

Funds Avail.: $1,000. **To Apply:** Applicants must complete all sections of Part I of the Application Form which must be signed by the JWV member related to the applicant and the JWV member's Post Commander. After the signatures are obtained, the applicant should forward Part I and II of the application form to school officials along with a stamped envelope addressed to the appropriate Department Commander. The applicant's school must complete Part II of the application form. **Deadline:** May 2.

4032 ■ Journalism Education Association

103 Kedzie Hall
Kansas State University
Manhattan, KS 66506-1505
Ph: (785)532-5532
Fax: (785)532-5563
Free: (866)532-5532
E-mail: jea@spub.ksu.edu
URL: http://www.jea.org

4033 ■ Sister Rita Jeanne Scholarships *(Undergraduate/Scholarship)*

Purpose: To recognize some of the top high school journalists in the country. **Focus:** Journalism. **Qualif.:** Applicants must be graduating high school seniors who plan to study journalism or mass communications in college and pursue a journalism or mass communications career; must have at least a 3.0 GPA on a 4.0 scale with at least two years in high school journalism; must be a student of a JEA member adviser. **Criteria:** Selection is based on skills, variety of journalistic experiences, and quality of work with the school media.

Funds Avail.: $5,000. **Number Awarded:** 7. **To Apply:** Applicants must submit a portfolio which includes: an official entry form; a self-analytical evaluation of "journalistic life" using the most creative form; photo of the applicant that shows journalism (for example: interviewing, taking a photograph, etc.); official copy of transcript; 3 or 4 letters of recommendation from an adviser, people who see the applicant's leadership and journalistic abilities, and practitioners that the applicants have worked with. Applicants must also include samples of their work. **Deadline:** February 15.

4034 ■ Journyx

9011 Mountain Ridge Dr., Ste. 200
Austin, TX 78759
Ph: (512)834-8888
Fax: (512)834-8858
Free: 800-755-9878
URL: http://www.journyx.com

4035 ■ Journyx Scholarships *(Graduate, Undergraduate/Scholarship)*

Purpose: To improve the philosophy and the technology of project accounting. **Focus:** Accounting. **Qualif.:** Applicant must be over 18 years old; a resident of the United States; currently enrolled as a full-time graduate or undergraduate at a university in the United States. **Criteria:** Award is given based on the submitted essay.

Funds Avail.: $500. **Number Awarded:** 1. **To Apply:** Students must submit their entries (an essay of 1000 words or less), along with an official academic transcript containing the student's spring semester grades for the academic year in progress and a copy of student's resume that includes e-mail address, campus address and phone number, student ID number, permanent address and phone number, major and expected graduation date. Submit materials via e-mail. **Deadline:** June 1. **Contact:** scholarship@journyx.com.

4036 ■ Junior Achievement

One Education Way
Colorado Springs, CO 80906
Ph: (719)540-8000
Fax: (719)540-6299
Free: 888-4JA-ALUM
E-mail: newmedia@ja.org
URL: http://www.ja.org

4037 ■ Walt Disney Company Foundation Scholarships *(Undergraduate/Scholarship)*

Purpose: To allow educational advancements by providing financial assistance. **Focus:** Business administration; Fine arts. **Qualif.:** Program is open to exceptional high school seniors who are graduating before June 30. Applicants must have excellent academic and extra-curricular credentials; and must be pursuing a major in either business administration or fine arts. **Criteria:** Selection is based on merit.

Funds Avail.: Covers full-tuition plus $200 cash per year for incidental fees. **Number Awarded:** 1. **To Apply:** Applicants must submit a completed application form along with other supporting materials. **Deadline:** February 1.

Remarks: The scholarship is sponsored by The Walt Disney Company Foundation. **Contact:** scholarships@ja.org.

4038 ■ Joe Francomano Scholarships *(Undergraduate/Scholarship)*

Purpose: To allow educational advancements by providing financial assistance. **Focus:** General studies. **Qualif.:** Applicants must be high school seniors graduating before June 30; must have a minimum GPA of 3.0; must have demonstrated leadership and excellent extracurricular and community activities; and must have financial need. **Criteria:** Selection is based on the merit.

Funds Avail.: $5,000 per year. **Number Awarded:** 1. **To Apply:** Applicants must submit a completed application form along with other supporting materials. **Deadline:** February 1.

Remarks: In memory of Joseph Francomano, past president of JA. **Contact:** scholarships@ja.org.

4039 ■ Johnson and Wales University Scholarships *(Undergraduate/Scholarship)*

Purpose: To allow educational advancements by providing financial assistance. **Focus:** Business; Culinary arts; Technology; Teaching. **Qualif.:** Program is open to individuals who are majoring in the field of business, culinary arts, hospitality, technology or teacher education. **Criteria:** Selection is based on merit.

Funds Avail.: $500 to cover full tuition. **Number Awarded:** Varies. **To Apply:** Applicants must submit a completed application form together with other supporting materials. Mail all materials to Johnson and Wales University, 8 Abbott Park Place, Providence, RI 02903. **Deadline:** February 1. **Contact:** National Student Organizations Office at Johnson and Wales University, 8 Abbott Park Place, Providence, RI 02903, at 800DIAL-JWU x-2345, or nso@jwu.edu.

4040 ■ Hugh B. Sweeny Scholarships *(Undergraduate/Scholarship)*

Purpose: To allow educational advancements by providing financial assistance. **Focus:** General studies. **Qualif.:** Applicants must be high school seniors graduating before June 30; must have a minimum GPA of 3.0; and must exemplify achievement, citizenship, creativity, leadership, motivation, and financial need. **Criteria:** Selection is based on merit.

Funds Avail.: $5,000. **Number Awarded:** 1. **To Apply:** Applicants must submit a completed application form along with other supporting materials. **Deadline:** February 1. **Contact:** scholarships@ja.org.

4041 ■ Kappa Gamma Pi

10215 Chardon Rd.
Chardon, OH 44024-9700
Ph: (440)286-3764
Fax: (440)286-4379
E-mail: kgpnews@aol.com
URL: http://www.kappagammapi.org

4042 ■ Cornaro Scholarships for Graduate Studies *(Graduate/Scholarship)*

Purpose: To provide financial support to individuals as needed for graduate expenses at any accredited college or university. **Focus:** General studies. **Qualif.:** Applicant must be a member of the Kappa Gamma Pi. **Criteria:** Applicant must be already accepted into an accredited graduate or professional program.

Funds Avail.: $3,000. **To Apply:** Applicants be elected by a Kappa affiliated college or university. **Deadline:** April 21.

4043 ■ Kappa Kappa Gamma

PO Box 38
Columbus, OH 43216-0038
Ph: (614)228-6515
Fax: (614)228-7809
Free: (866)554-1870
E-mail: kkghq@kappa.org
URL: http://www.kappakappagamma.org

4044 ■ Kappa Kappa Gamma Graduate Scholarships *(Graduate/Scholarship)*

Purpose: To deliver educational and leadership training, preserve the Fraternity's heritage from an historical perspective, and to provide financial assistance to members in need. **Focus:** General studies. **Qualif.:** Applicants must be members of KappaKappa Fraternity who have a grade average of B or above and who were in good standing as

Awards are arranged alphabetically below their administering organizations

undergraduates. **Criteria:** Scholarship will be evaluated based on the application materials.

Funds Avail.: Scholarships are for full-time study and must be used for educational expenses. **To Apply:** Applicant must submit a personal essay or letter stating educational and career goals and financial need; must have official transcripts from all colleges or universities attended; two recommendation letters, one academic (professor, adviser, dean) and one chapter (President, Vice President-Standards or Chapter Council Adviser). Application materials must be sent to: Kappa Kappa Gamma Foundation, PO Box 38, Columbus, OH 43216-0038. **Deadline:** February 1.

4045 ■ Kappa Kappa Gamma Undergraduate Scholarships *(Undergraduate/Scholarship)*

Purpose: To deliver educational and leadership training, preserve the Fraternity's heritage from an historical perspective, and to provide financial assistance to members in need. **Focus:** General studies. **Qualif.:** Applicant must be a member of KappaKappa Gamma Fraternity who has a grade average of B or above (3.0 on 4.0 scale) and is in good standing. **Criteria:** Scholarship will be evaluated based on the application materials.

Funds Avail.: No specific amount. **To Apply:** Applicant must submit a personal essay or letter stating educational and career goals and financial need; must have official transcripts from all colleges or universities attended; two recommendation letters, one academic (professor, adviser, dean) and one chapter (President, Vice President-Standards or Chapter Council Adviser). Application materials must be sent to: Kappa Kappa Gamma Foundation, PO Box 38, Columbus, OH 43216-0038. **Deadline:** February 1.

4046 ■ Kappa Omicron Nu

4990 Northwind Dr., Ste. 140
East Lansing, MI 48823-5031
Ph: (517)351-8335
Fax: (517)351-8336
E-mail: dmitstifer@kon.org
URL: http://www.kon.org

4047 ■ Kappa Omicron Nu National Alumni Fellowships *(Graduate/Fellowship)*

Purpose: To support members with studies and research in family and consumer sciences. **Focus:** Home Economics. **Qualif.:** Applicant must be an active Kappa Omicron Nu member; enrolled in a master's program in home economics or one of the specializations. **Criteria:** Selection is based on applicant's potential for professional leadership and relevance of study or research to significant concerns related to home and family.

Funds Avail.: $2000. **To Apply:** Applicants must submit a completed application form together with three letters of recommendations. **Deadline:** April 1.

Remarks: Awarded by the National Alumni Chapter.

4048 ■ Kappa Omicron Nu Undergraduate Scholarships *(Undergraduate/Scholarship)*

Purpose: To provide opportunity for its member to attend The LeaderShape Institute. **Focus:** Leadership, Institutional and community. **Qualif.:** Applicant must be undergraduate student member with at least one more year in the undergraduate program of studies. **Criteria:** Applications are accepted on a first-come first-serve basis.

Funds Avail.: $1000. **Number Awarded:** 1. **To Apply:** Applicants must submit a short statement of commitment to leadership on campus during 2008-2009 academic year, and a short description of academic status. Send materials electronically to dmitstifer@kon.org. **Deadline:** February 15.

4049 ■ Eileen C. Maddex Fellowships *(Graduate/Fellowship)*

Purpose: To support members with studies and research in family and consumer sciences. **Focus:** Home Economics. **Qualif.:** Applicant must be an active Kappa Omicron Nu member; enrolled in a master's program in home economics or one of the specializations. **Criteria:** Selection is based on applicant's potential for professional leadership and relevance of study or research to significant concerns related to home and family.

Funds Avail.: $2000. **To Apply:** Applicants must submit a completed application form together with three letters of recommendations. **Deadline:** April 1.

4050 ■ Kappa Omicron Nu Honor Society

4990 Northwind Dr., Ste. 140
East Lansing, MI 48823-5031
Ph: (517)351-8335
Fax: (517)351-8336
E-mail: dmitstifer@kon.org
URL: http://www.kon.org

4051 ■ Hettie M. Anthony Fellowships *(Postdoctorate/Fellowship)*

Purpose: To provide funding support for a study and research in family and consumer sciences or one of its specializations at colleges or universities with strong research programs and supporting disciplines for the chosen major topic. **Focus:** Science; Home Economics. **Qualif.:** Applicants must have demonstrated interest in research; must be enrolled in a master's program in home economics or one of the specializations in a university that has strong research program with supporting disciplines in the area of research interest. **Criteria:** Recipients are selected based on the demonstrated interest in research; relevance of study and/or research to significant concerns related to home and family; potential for professional leadership; demonstrated scholarship; enrollment in a master's program in home economics or one of the specializations in a university that has a strong research program with supporting disciplines in the area of research interest; and current active membership in Kappa Omicron Nu.

Funds Avail.: $2,000. **To Apply:** Applicants must submit five copies of the application form, type or printed along with three letters of recommendations from persons that can represent the applicant's scholarship, research, and potential for professional leadership. **Deadline:** April 15.

4052 ■ Marjorie M. Brown Fellowships Program *(Postdoctorate/Fellowship)*

Purpose: To support research projects intending to continue Brown's Philosophical work using critical social theory, demonstrating understanding of Brown's Philosophical Studies and other recent pieces of work and their ongoing significance for the FCS/Human Sciences profession. **Focus:** General studies. **Qualif.:** Applicants must be Ph.D. or D.Ed. students seeking doctoral degrees from accredited

Awards are arranged alphabetically below their administering organizations

U.S. institutions of higher education; tenure track professors seeking support for a research agenda using critical social theory; or associate professors or professors seeking support for the design and implementation of a graduate course that teaches a critical science research approach. **Criteria:** Recipients are selected based on the evaluation of the Award Committee.

Funds Avail.: Total amount of $10,000. **To Apply:** Applicants must submit a cover page; 100 words or less abstract; introduction of the research including background, need for the study, and statement of the objectives; Review of literature; method including research design, plan of work, approach to analysis; literature citations and supplementary materials; and Applicants' five copies of the application form. **Deadline:** January 15.

4053 ■ Kappa Omicron Nu Honor Society Scholars Program Grants *(Undergraduate/Grant)*

Purpose: To recognize and encourage excellence in scholarship, research, and leadership at the local level. **Focus:** General studies. **Qualif.:** Applicants must be individuals who maintain good standing in the society and must be conducting undergraduate and/or graduate research. **Criteria:** Recipients are selected based on the research; service learning including reflection about the impact on professional development; excellence in communication both oral and written; leadership of a campus or unit change project; and overall record of achievement.

Funds Avail.: varies. **To Apply:** Applicants must complete the application form and submit to National Kappa Omicron Nu. **Contact:** dmitstifer@kon.org; 517-351-8335.

4054 ■ Omicron Nu Research Fellowships *(Postdoctorate/Fellowship)*

Purpose: To provide funding support for a study and research in family and consumer sciences or one of its specializations at colleges or universities with strong research programs and supporting disciplines for the chosen major topic. **Focus:** Science; Home Economics. **Qualif.:** Applicants must have demonstrated interest in research; must be enrolled in a master's program in home economics or one of the specializations in a university that has strong research program with supporting disciplines in the area of research interest. **Criteria:** Recipients are selected based on the demonstrated interest in research; relevance of study and/or research to significant concerns related to home and family; potential for professional leadership; demonstrated scholarship; enrollment in a master's program in home economics or one of the specializations in a university that has a strong research program with supporting disciplines in the area of research interest; and current active membership in Kappa Omicron Nu.

Funds Avail.: $2,000. **To Apply:** Applicants must submit five copies of the application form, type or printed along with three letters of recommendations from persons that can represent the applicant's scholarship, research, and potential for professional leadership. **Deadline:** April 15.

4055 ■ Keats-Shelley Association of America

Rm. 226, The New York Public Library
476 5th Ave.
New York, NY 10018-2788
E-mail: rhartley@optonline.net
URL: http://www.rc.umd.edu/ksaa/index.html

Awards are arranged alphabetically below their administering organizations

4056 ■ Beginning Freshmen Awards *(Undergraduate/Scholarship)*

Purpose: To support students who have demonstrated potential and interest in pursuing an undergraduate degree in engineering. **Focus:** Engineering. **Qualif.:** Applicants must be African American, Latino, and American Indian students who have been approved for admission as engineering majors. Applicants must also have a minimum cumulative grade point average of 2.70-4.00 and minimum cumulative scores on either the ACT/SAT college entrance examination of 25-1000. Students must attend a NAMEPA member institution. **Criteria:** Applicants will be selected based on the coursework in high school and interest in participating in-campus Multi-Cultural Engineering Programs (MEP) initiatives.

Funds Avail.: $1,000. **To Apply:** Applicants must submit the following: an official copy of high school transcript and test scores; a one-page essay expressing their reasons for choosing engineering, why they think they should be selected, and an overview of their future aspirations as an engineer; resume; and a completed recommendation form. The application and recommendation forms are available from the website. **Deadline:** May 15.

4057 ■ Carl H. Pforzheimer, Jr., Research Grants *(Graduate/Grant)*

Purpose: To support research in the field of British Romanticism. To provide funding for expenses related to research in the field of British Romanticism and literary culture between 1789 and 1832. **Focus:** British studies. **Qualif.:** Applicants must be advanced graduate students, independent scholars, and untenured faculties. **Criteria:** Awards are given based on their research proposal and application.

Funds Avail.: $2,500. **Number Awarded:** 2. **To Apply:** Application form is available at the website. Applicants must submit a curriculum vitae; description of the project, not exceed three pages; must have one page bibliography of publications that treat the topic; must have two letters of reference from people who know the applicants work well and can judge its value. Application form must be print out and must be send together with the other application materials to: Chair, Grant Committee, Keats_Shelley Association of America, Inc., Rm. 226, The New York Public Library, 476 5th Ave., New York, NY 10018-2788. **Deadline:** November 1.

Remarks: The awards honor the late Carl H. Pforzheimer, Jr., a past President of the Association and among its most vigorous advocates. He also headed The Carl and Lily Pforzheimer Foundation, Inc., long distinguished for funding scholarship centered on early nineteenth-century English literature.

4058 ■ Transfer Engineering Student Awards *(Undergraduate/Scholarship)*

Purpose: For students who have demonstrated potential and interest in pursuing an undergraduate degree in engineering. **Focus:** Engineering. **Qualif.:** Applicants must be African American, Latino, and American Indian students admitted as transfer students from either a junior college, community college or three/two dual-degree program; must have a minimum grade point average of 2.70-4.00. **Criteria:** High consideration will be given to applicants who demonstrate genuine interest in participating in-campus Multi-Cultural Engineering Programs (MEP) initiatives.

Funds Avail.: $1,000. **To Apply:** Applicants must submit a complete application package including a completed application and recommendation form available from the website; an official copy of college transcripts; a one-page essay expressing their reasons for choosing engineering, why they think they should be selected, and an overview of their future aspirations as an engineer; and a resume. **Deadline:** May 15.

4059 ■ Donald Keene Center of Japanese Culture

Columbia University
507 Kent Hall, MC 3920
New York, NY 10027
Ph: (212)854-5036
Fax: (212)854-4019
URL: http://www.donaldkeenecenter.org

4060 ■ The Shincho Graduate Fellowships for Study in Japan *(Graduate/Fellowship)*

Purpose: To provide financial assistance to cover all expenses of the fellow, including air travel, tuition, research expenses, living expenses, insurance and other kind of expenses. **Focus:** Japanese studies. **Qualif.:** Applicant must be a degree candidate in a graduate program at Columbia University in field of Japanese cultural studies and must have been accepted as a research student in a graduate level program at a Japanese public or private university. **Criteria:** Applicants will be evaluated under the direction of the Donald Keene Center Selection Committee and the Center Director.

Funds Avail.: No specific amount. **To Apply:** Applicant must notify the Foundation in writing of his/her address in Japan and report on his/her program of study or research, which must have been approved in advance by the Selection Committee of the Donald Keene Center. Any change in address or program of study must be reported to the Foundation and the Center; must submit a summary report of his/her study in both Japanese and English to the Selection Committee of Donald Keene Center one month before the completion of the fellowship. A Japanese version of that summary must be submitted to the Foundation by the same deadline. **Deadline:** February 1.

4061 ■ Kegler, Brown, Hill and Ritter

Capitol Sq., Ste. 1800
65 E State St.
Columbus, OH 43215-4294
Ph: (614)462-5400
Fax: (614)464-2634
E-mail: info@keglerbrown.com
URL: http://www.keglerbrown.com

4062 ■ Kegler Brown Minority Merit Scholarships *(Undergraduate/Scholarship)*

Purpose: To assist minority students financially with their legal education. **Focus:** Law. **Qualif.:** Applicant must be a minority student studying law. **Criteria:** Award is given based on academic performance, accomplishments, activities and potential contributions to the legal community.

Funds Avail.: No specific amount. **Number Awarded:** 1. **To Apply:** Students may contact the office for more information about the scholarship.

Remarks: Contact: Jeff Dennis at 614-462-5430, or jdennis@keglerbrown.com.

4063 ■ Kellogg Community College Foundation

450 N Ave.
Battle Creek, MI 49017
Ph: (269)965-3931
URL: http://www.kellogg.edu

4064 ■ Foundation Scholarships *(Undergraduate/Scholarship)*

Purpose: To generate and encourage philanthropic giving and manage funds to enhance the quality of education while building stronger communities. **Focus:** General studies. **Qualif.:** Applicants must have a cumulative GPA of 2.5 and be working towards their first college degree. **Criteria:** Recipients are selected based on financial need, demonstrated academic achievements, number of credit hours and/or special circumstances.

Funds Avail.: No specific amount. **To Apply:** Applicants must submit a 150 word personal statement detailing their goals and achievements, a copy of transcript of records and three letters of recommendation from high school or college instructors, counselors or employers. **Deadline:** March 10.

4065 ■ Gold Key Scholarships *(Undergraduate/Scholarship)*

Purpose: To generate and encourage philanthropic giving and manage funds to enhance the quality of education while building stronger communities. **Focus:** General studies. **Qualif.:** Applicants must be students within the KCC district; must have completed no more than 24 credit hours of college; must have 3.2 cumulative GPA and ACT of 20 or higher. **Criteria:** Recipients are selected based on leadership experience.

Funds Avail.: $6,000. **To Apply:** Applicants must submit: a completed application form; an official high school and/or college transcript; three written letters of recommendation; ACT scores; 150 word written essay discussing achievements and future goals; and resume or employment information including activities, leadership, volunteer or school-related positions. **Deadline:** February 1.

4066 ■ Walter and Lucille Harper Scholarship *(Undergraduate/Scholarship)*

Purpose: To generate and encourage philanthropic giving and manage= funds to enhance the quality of education while building stronger communities. **Focus:** General studies. **Qualif.:** Applicants must be second year KCC students graduating with an associate's degree; must have a minimum of 3.0 GPA; must be citizens of the United States. **Criteria:** Recipients are selected based on academic performance and financial need.

Funds Avail.: No specific amount. **To Apply:** Applicants must submit: a completed application form; a copy of transcript of records; 150 word personal statement detailing their future aspirations; and three written letters of recommendation from teachers, counselors and employers. **Deadline:** March 10.

4067 ■ Kellogg Company Career Scholarships *(Undergraduate/Scholarship)*

Purpose: To generate and encourage philanthropic giving and manage funds to enhance the quality of education while building stronger communities. **Focus:** General studies. **Qualif.:** Applicants must be citizens, legal permanent residents or nationals of the United States; must be residents of the greater Battle Creek area; must have a

Awards are arranged alphabetically below their administering organizations

cumulative GPA of 2.5 on a 4.0 scale; must be entering or have been admitted as full-time degree seeking students at Kellogg Community College; must have demonstrated leadership abilities through participation in community service, extracurricular or other activities; must be pursuing and completing an associate's degree in accounting or business management; must have fewer than 24 credit hours of college credit completed. **Criteria:** Recipients are selected based on academic achievement and leadership potential.

Funds Avail.: $6,000. **To Apply:** Applicants must submit: a completed application form; a transcript of grades; a minimum of 250 word personal statement detailing their future aspirations; and three written recommendations. **Deadline:** April 10.

4068 ■ Trustee Scholarships *(Undergraduate/ Scholarship)*

Purpose: To generate and encourage philanthropic giving and manage funds to enhance the quality of education while building stronger communities. **Focus:** General studies. **Qualif.:** Applicants must be graduating high school seniors within the KCC district; must be in the top 20% of graduating class and have at least a 3.0 GPA. **Criteria:** Recipients are selected based on academic performance and financial need.

Funds Avail.: No specific amount. **To Apply:** Applicants must submit a completed application form.

4069 ■ Kentucky Fried Chicken Foundation

PO Box 725489
Atlanta, GA 31139
Free: 800-225-5532
URL: http://www.kfcscholars.org

4070 ■ KFC Colonel's Scholars Program *(Undergraduate/Scholarship)*

Purpose: To provide funding for tuition, fees, books, room and board for eligible individuals to complete a bachelor's degree. **Focus:** General studies. **Qualif.:** Applicants must be graduates from high school in academic year between December 1, 2007 and August 31, 2008; must have earned a minimum cumulative high school GPA of 2.75; must be planning to pursue a bachelor's degree at a public, in-state college or university; must be U.S. citizens. **Criteria:** Recipients are selected based on financial need.

Funds Avail.: $5,000. **To Apply:** Applicants must submit all the required application information.

4071 ■ Kentucky Paralegal Association

PO Box 2675
Louisville, KY 40201-2675
E-mail: kentuckyparalegal@insightbb.com
URL: http://www.kypa.org

4072 ■ Kentucky Paralegal Association Student Scholarships *(Undergraduate/Scholarship)*

Purpose: To provide financial assistance to those students who are in need. **Focus:** Paralegal studies. **Qualif.:** Applicants must be enrolled in a paralegal program within the Commonwealth of Kentucky; must have at least 12 credit hours of paralegal course work completed with a GPA in those courses of 3.50 or higher and an overall GPA of 3.25 or higher. **Criteria:** Preference will be given to those students who meet the criteria.

Funds Avail.: $1,000. **To Apply:** Applicants must submit the following: application form (typed); 2 letters of recommendation and forms; one writing sample; an essay and Official transcript. **Deadline:** June 30. **Contact:** Kentucky Paralegal Association at the above address (see entry 4071).

4073 ■ Alden Kindred of America

PO Box 2754
Duxbury, MA 02331-2754
Ph: (781)934-9092
Fax: (781)934-9149
URL: http://www.alden.org

4074 ■ Donnell B. Young Scholarships *(Undergraduate/Scholarship)*

Purpose: To provide educational assistance to incoming college students. **Focus:** General studies. **Qualif.:** Applicants must be graduating high school students who are lineage members of the Alden Kindred of America, Inc. **Criteria:** Recipient will be selected based on the submitted research paper.

Funds Avail.: $ 1,000. **Number Awarded:** 1. **To Apply:** Applicants must submit their high school transcripts (mailed directly by their school). A typewritten research paper of 750-1,000 words is a strict requirement. The topic must be extracted from the Early American Period (1620-1750). The preface of the research paper should contain a short paragraph about the reason of the application for the scholarship. Footnotes and bibliography of references should be included. Volunteer work and personal information including hobbies and interests must also be provided. All application forms must have two references (one personal and one from the school). **Deadline:** March 1.

4075 ■ The Esther A. and Joseph Klingenstein Fund

787 Seventh Ave., 6th Fl.
New York, NY 10019-6016
Ph: (212)492-6181
E-mail: kathleen.pomerantz@klingenstein.com
URL: http://www.klingfund.org

4076 ■ Klingenstein Fellowships in the Neurosciences *(Doctorate, Professional Development/ Fellowship)*

Purpose: To support young investigators engaged in basic or clinical research that may lead to a better understanding of epilepsy. **Focus:** Neuroscience. **Qualif.:** Applicant must hold a PhD or M.D. degrees; have completed all research training, including post-doctoral training; must be a permanent resident of the U.S.; must be conducting research which will be carried out in a U.S. institution; and an independent investigator, holding a tenure track academic rank (but not yet tenured) in a university or medical school, or the equivalent standing in a research institute or medical center. **Criteria:** Applications will be reviewed and selections will be made by an Advisory Committee of distinguished neuroscientists.

Funds Avail.: No specific amount. **Number Awarded:** 10. **To Apply:** Applicants must submit one original and ten copies of completed application form, and three letters of recommendation. **Deadline:** December 7.

Awards are arranged alphabetically below their administering organizations

4077 ■ Klingenstein Third Generation Foundation

787 7th Ave., 6th Fl.
New York, NY 10019-6016
URL: http://www.ktgf.org

4078 ■ Depression and ADHD Fellowships
(Professional Development/Fellowship)

Purpose: To support graduates who have demonstrated outstanding promise and are eager to continue in an academic research career. **Focus:** General studies. **Qualif.:** Candidates should be planning a career in research related to child and adolescent ADHD, and should have demonstrated skills for independent research and expected to supply evidence of their credentials and commitment to the field in the form of preliminary publications, invited presentations or other scientific recognition. **Criteria:** Candidates must be sponsored by a their mentors who nominated them.

Funds Avail.: $30,000. **To Apply:** Candidates are nominated. **Deadline:** January. **Contact:** Sally Klingenstein Martell at the above address (see entry 4077).

4079 ■ Susan G. Komen Breast Cancer Foundation

5005 LBJ Freeway, Ste. 250
Dallas, TX 75244
Free: 877-465-6636
URL: http://www.komen.org

4080 ■ Susan G. Komen Breast Cancer Foundation College Scholarship Awards *(Undergraduate/Award/Prize)*

Purpose: To assist young adults in their academic pursuits. **Focus:** General studies. **Qualif.:** Applicants must be U.S. citizens, high school or college graduate students who have lost a parent to breast cancer and planning to attend state-supported college or university in their state where they permanently reside and were never subjected to disciplinary action by any institution. **Criteria:** Applicants will be evaluated by the Awards committee.

Funds Avail.: $10,000. **To Apply:** Applicants must send an email to Susan G. Komen Breast Cancer Foundation to apply for the application.

4081 ■ The Korea Society

950 3rd Ave., 8th Fl.
New York, NY 10022
Ph: (212)759-7525
Fax: (212)759-7530
URL: http://www.koreasociety.org

4082 ■ Fall Fellowships in Korean Studies
(Professional Development/Fellowship)

Purpose: To provide a general overview of Korea's past and present by covering all the expenses of the participants including round-trip international airfare, accommodations and meals. **Focus:** Korean studies. **Qualif.:** Applicant must be an American educator who is professionally engaged as a textbook writer and editor or an East Asia specialist in higher education who would like to include Korea in his/her teaching, research or writing. **Criteria:** Priority is given to applicants who are planning to author textbooks on world history or Asian history and are intending to contribute articles to reference works and who will be editors of such works.

Funds Avail.: No specific amount. **To Apply:** Applicant must submit a completed application packet including the application form and supporting documentation. **Deadline:** May 5.

4083 ■ Korean Language Study Awards
(Graduate/Scholarship)

Purpose: To provide financial assistance for Korean language study at a university in Korea. **Focus:** Korean studies. **Qualif.:** Applicants must be a U.S. citizen or permanent resident, graduate students, enrolled in degree programs, recent college graduates or young professionals with a clearly defined interest in Korea. **Criteria:** Recipient will be selected based on criteria designed by the Scholarship Committee.

Funds Avail.: No amount mentioned. **To Apply:** Applicant must submit application form; resume; official college transcripts; and two letters of reference. **Deadline:** April 1.

4084 ■ Korean American Scholarship Foundation

1952 Gallows Rd., Ste. 340 B
Vienna, VA 22182
Ph: (703)748-5935
Fax: (703)748-1874
E-mail: national@kasf.org
URL: http://www.kasf.org

4085 ■ KASF Chair Scholarships *(Graduate, Undergraduate/Scholarship)*

Purpose: To help meet the financial needs of Korean-American students seeking higher education. **Focus:** General studies. **Qualif.:** Applicant must be a Korean-American student currently enrolled in a full-time undergraduate or graduate program. **Criteria:** Recipient is selected based on financial need, academic achievement, school activities, and community service.

Funds Avail.: An annual $1000 scholarship. **To Apply:** Applicants must submit a completed scholarship application to the respective KASF region (each region is designated by the state where school is located). **Deadline:** Varies with the region.

4086 ■ KASF Designated Scholarships *(Graduate, Undergraduate/Scholarship)*

Purpose: To help meet the financial needs of Korean-American students seeking higher education in a specific field. **Focus:** General studies. **Qualif.:** Applicant must be a Korean-American student currently enrolled in a full-time undergraduate or graduate program in a specific field. **Criteria:** Recipient is selected based on financial need, academic achievement, school activities, and community services.

Funds Avail.: $1000 or more. **To Apply:** Applicants must submit a completed scholarship application to the respective KASF region (each region is designated by the state where school is located). **Deadline:** Varies with the region.

4087 ■ KASF General Scholarships *(Graduate, Undergraduate/Scholarship)*

Purpose: To help meet the financial needs of Korean-American students seeking higher education in various

Awards are arranged alphabetically below their administering organizations

academic fields. **Focus:** General studies. **Qualif.:** Applicant must be a Korean-American student currently enrolled in a full-time undergraduate or graduate program in one of various academic fields. **Criteria:** Recipient is selected based on financial need, academic achievement, school activities, and community services.

Funds Avail.: $1000 or more. **To Apply:** Applicants must submit a completed scholarship application to the respective KASF region (each region is designated by the state where school is located). **Deadline:** Varies with the region.

4088 ■ Kosciuszko Foundation

15 E 65th St.
New York, NY 10065
Ph: (212)734-2130
Fax: (212)628-4552
E-mail: info@thekf.org
URL: http://www.kosciuszkofoundation.org

4089 ■ Kosciuszko Foundation Graduate Study and Research in Poland Scholarships *(Graduate/Scholarship)*

Purpose: To support the graduate level research at universities in Poland by American graduate students and university faculty members. **Focus:** Polish studies. **Qualif.:** Applicants must be a United States citizens with permanent residency status in the U.S. who are graduate level students; must possess proficiency in the Polish language. **Criteria:** Selection is based on academic excellence, motivation and need to pursue research in Poland, and a clear and a well-defined research proposal. The host institution must fall under the jurisdiction of the Polish Ministry of Education and Sports.

Funds Avail.: Scholarship provides a stipend for dormitory housing and living expenses. **To Apply:** Applicant must complete the Polish Ministry of National Education application entitled Bureau for Academic Recognition and International Exchange; must provide an abstract of the project proposal; must attach copies of study certificates such as the level of language proficiency; must have two letters of recommendation from professor; must submit a letter of invitation from the University/Institute in Poland where research is conducted; must have two passport-size photos with printed name on the reverse. **Deadline:** January 15.

4090 ■ Kosciuszko Foundation Tuition Scholarships *(Undergraduate/Scholarship)*

Purpose: To support American students of Polish descent for full-time graduate studies in the United States. **Focus:** Polish studies. **Qualif.:** Applicant must be a United States citizen or permanent resident of Polish descent who are beginning or continuing graduate studies in the academic year; must have a minimum GPA of 3.0 **Criteria:** Selection is based on academic excellence, applicants academic achievements, interests and motivation, applicants interest in polish subjects or involvement in the Polish American community. Financial need is taken into consideration.

Funds Avail.: $1,000 to $7,000. **To Apply:** Applicant must complete the Tuition Scholarship application form and Financial Information page (application may be obtained from the Kosciuszko Foundation); must submit a personal statement about their academic goals, career goals, and the major they are pursuing and area of specialization; must have two passport photos for publication purposes; must have the official transcript; must prepare two confidential letters of academic reference from professors/teachers submitted on letterhead; must provide proof of Polish ancestry. **Deadline:** January 15.

4091 ■ Kosciuszko Foundation Year Abroad Scholarships *(Undergraduate/Scholarship)*

Purpose: To support the deserving students to continue their Polish language studies. **Focus:** Polish studies. **Qualif.:** Applicant must be a United States citizen and permanent resident of Polish descent who are undergraduate sophomore, junior, senior or graduate student; must have a minimum GPA of 3.0. **Criteria:** Selection is based on academic excellence, motivation for pursuing Polish studies, interest in Polish subjects and involvement in the Polish American community.

Funds Avail.: Scholarship includes acceptance to the program, a tuition waiver and a stipend for housing and living expenses. **To Apply:** Applicant must complete the Polish Ministry of National Education application entitled Bureau for Academic Recognition and International Exchange; must attach copies of transcripts of records; must submit two letters of recommendation from professors and must have two passport size photos with printed name on the reverse. **Deadline:** January 15.

4092 ■ Massachusetts Federation of Polish Women's Clubs Scholarships *(Undergraduate/Scholarship)*

Purpose: To support the qualified residents of Massachusetts to pursue their education. **Focus:** Polish studies. **Qualif.:** Applicant must be a United States citizen of Polish descent or Polish citizens with permanent residency status in the United States residing in Massachusetts who will engage in second, third or fourth year of undergraduate studies during academic year; must have a minimum GPA of 3.0. **Criteria:** Selection is based on academic excellence, the applicant's academic achievements, interests, motivation, interest in Polish subjects and involvement in the Polish American community. Financial need is taken into consideration.

Funds Avail.: $1,250. **To Apply:** Applicant must complete the scholarship application form and financial information page; must submit a personal statement about their academic goals, career goals and specialization; must have a two passport size photos for publication purposes; must submit a official transcripts; must have two confidential letters of academic reference from professor and teachers; must provide proof of Polish ancestry. **Deadline:** January 15.

4093 ■ Polish American Club of North Jersey Scholarships *(Undergraduate/Scholarship)*

Purpose: To provide financial assistance to qualified students in the United States. **Focus:** Polish studies. **Qualif.:** Applicant must be a United States citizen of Polish descent or Polish citizens with permanent residency status in the U.S who are active members of the Polish American Club of North Jersey; must have a minimum GPA of 3.0; must be children or grandchildren of club members. **Criteria:** Selection is based on academic excellence, the applicant's academic achievements, interests, motivation, interest in Polish subjects and involvement in the Polish American community. Financial need is taken into consideration.

Funds Avail.: $500-$2,000. **To Apply:** Applicant must complete the scholarship application form and financial information page; must have a personal statement about their academic goals, career goals and specialization; must have two passport photos for publication purposes; must submit an official transcript; must prepare a two confidential letters of academic reference from professor and teachers; must provide a proof of Polish ancestry. **Deadline:** January 15.

4094 ■ Polish National Alliance of Brooklyn, USA Scholarships *(Undergraduate/Scholarship)*

Purpose: To provide financial assistance to all qualified students wanting to pursue their studies in United States. **Focus:** Polish studies. **Qualif.:** Applicants must be a United States citizen of Polish descent or Polish citizens with permanent residency status in the U.S. who are members in good standing of the Polish National Alliance of Brooklyn, USA and the Polish National Alliance of the United States of North America; must have a minimum GPA of 3.0. **Criteria:** Selection is based on academic excellence, the applicant's academic achievements, interests, motivation, interest in Polish subjects and involvement in the Polish American community. Financial need is taken into consideration.

Funds Avail.: $2,000. **To Apply:** Applicant must complete the scholarship application form and financial information page; must submit a personal statement about their academic goals, career goals and the major expect to pursue; must have a two passport photos for publication purposes; must have two confidential letters of academic reference; must have a official transcript of record; must have two letters of academic reference from professor and teachers; must provide a proof of Polish ancestry. **Deadline:** January 15.

4095 ■ Dr. Marie E. Zakrzewski Medical Scholarships *(Undergraduate/Scholarship)*

Purpose: To support the young women of Polish ancestry in their education. **Focus:** Polish studies. **Qualif.:** Applicant must be a U.S. citizen of Polish descent or Polish citizens with permanent residency status in United States who are entering first, second or third year of M.D. studies in academic year; must have a minimum GPA of 3.0; must be a female **Criteria:** Selection is based on academic excellence, applicants academic achievements, interest, motivation, interest in Polish subjects and involvement in the Polish American Community. Financial need is taken into consideration and preference is given to residents of the state of Massachusetts.

Funds Avail.: $3,500. **To Apply:** Applicant must submit a personal statement about the academic goals, career goals and area of specialization; must have a two passport sized photos for publication purposes; must have an official transcript and two confidential letters of academic reference from professors and teachers; must provide a proof of Polish ancestry. **Deadline:** January 15.

4096 ■ KPMG Foundation

3 Chestnut Ridge Rd.
Montvale, NJ 07645
E-mail: us-kpmgfoundation@kpmg.com
URL: http://www.kpmgfoundation.org

4097 ■ KPMG Foundation Minority Accounting Doctoral Scholarships *(Postdoctorate/Scholarship)*

Purpose: To provide financial assistance for students to meet the escalating costs of higher education. **Focus:** Accounting. **Qualif.:** Applicants must be African-American, Hispanic-American or Native American doctoral students. **Criteria:** Applicants are evaluated based on financial need.

Funds Avail.: $10,000. **To Apply:** Applicants must submit all the required application information.

4098 ■ Samuel H. Kress Foundation

174 E 80th St.
New York, NY 10075
Ph: (212)861-4993
Fax: (212)628-3146
E-mail: info.request@kressfoundation.org
URL: http://www.kressfoundation.org

4099 ■ Kress Conservation Fellowships *(Graduate/Fellowship)*

Purpose: To encourage qualified individuals to prepare for careers as conservators in museums of art. **Focus:** Art conservation. **Qualif.:** Applicant must be an individual who has completed an M.A degree in art conservation; must be a U.S citizen. **Criteria:** Selection of applicant will be based on the fellowship criteria.

Funds Avail.: $25,000 as a fellowship stipend, and $5,000 toward administrative costs. **To Apply:** Application must be made by the museum or conservation research facility at which the internship will be based. Applicant must have a brief description of the internship, curriculum vitae of the individual nominated; must have three letters of recommendation. **Deadline:** March 1.

4100 ■ Kress Curatorial Fellowships *(Doctorate/Fellowship)*

Purpose: To encourage qualified individuals to prepare for careers as curators in museums of art. **Focus:** European studies. **Qualif.:** Applicant must be an individual who has completed a Ph.D. in the history of European art. **Criteria:** Selection of applicant will be based on the fellowship criteria.

Funds Avail.: $25,000 as a fellowship stipend, and $5,000 toward administrative costs, benefits for the Fellow, and other direct costs of the Fellowship. **To Apply:** Application must be made at which the fellowship will be based. Applicant must have a brief description of the internship, curriculum vitae of the individual nominated; must have three letters of recommendation. **Deadline:** January 5.

4101 ■ Kress Fellowships in Art History at Foreign Institutions *(Doctorate/Fellowship)*

Purpose: To permit promising art historians to complete the final phases of dissertation research. **Focus:** European studies. **Qualif.:** Applicant must be a pre-doctoral candidate in the history of art; must be a U.S. citizen or individual matriculated at an American university. **Criteria:** Selection of applicant will be based on the fellowship criteria.

Funds Avail.: $22,500. **To Apply:** Application forms are available online and candidates must be nominated by the art history department. Application form and other relevant documents must be sent to: Samuel H. Kress Foundation, 174 E 80th St., New York, NY 10021. **Deadline:** November 30.

4102 ■ Kress Travel Fellowships in the History of Art *(Doctorate/Fellowship)*

Purpose: To permit promising art historians to complete the final phases of dissertation research. **Focus:** European

Awards are arranged alphabetically below their administering organizations

studies. **Qualif.:** Applicant must be a predoctoral candidates in the history of art; must be a U.S citizens or individuals matriculated at an American university. **Criteria:** Selection of applicant will be based on the fellowship criteria.

Funds Avail.: $3500 to $10,000. **To Apply:** Application forms are available online. Application form and other relevant documents must be sent to: Samuel H. Kress Foundation, 174 E 80th St., New York, NY 10021. **Deadline:** November 30.

4103 ■ The Lagrant Foundation

626 Wilshire Blvd., Ste. 700
Los Angeles, CA 90017-2920
Ph: (323)469-8680
Fax: (323)469-8683
URL: http://www.lagrantfoundation.org

4104 ■ The Lagrant Foundation - Graduate Students Scholarships *(Graduate/Scholarship)*

Purpose: To provide financial support for the education of graduate students who belong to one of the following ethnic groups: African American, Asian Pacific American, Hispanic or Native American or Alaska Native. **Focus:** Public relations; Marketing; Advertising. **Qualif.:** Applicants must be U.S. citizens and full-time students at a college or university that is accredited by a regional accrediting association; have a minimum of 3.2 GPA; major in a field of study that has an emphasis in public relations, marketing or advertising; have a minimum of two academic semesters left to complete his/her master's degree. **Criteria:** Applicants are evaluated based on scholastic performance.

Funds Avail.: No specific amount. **To Apply:** Applicants must submit a one- to two-page typewritten essay outlining their career goals and why they feel it is important to increase ethnic representation in the fields of advertising, marketing and public relations; must define the role of an advertising, marketing or public relations practitioner (depending on emphasis), including accomplishments relevant to increasing awareness about diversity in their community; brief paragraph explaining graduate school and/or community activities in which they are involved and describing any honors and awards that they have received; and a letter of reference from a professor or internship advisor; resume which should reflect what they would present to a prospective employer, with the career objective clearly stated; official transcripts from college/university; and proof of acceptance to graduate school (if not currently enrolled).

4105 ■ The Lagrant Foundation - Undergraduate Students Scholarship *(Undergraduate/Scholarship)*

Purpose: To provide financial support for the education of undergraduate students who belong to ethnic groups: African American, Asian Pacific American, Hispanic or Native American or Alaska Native. **Focus:** Public relations; Marketing and distribution; Advertising. **Qualif.:** Applicants must be U.S. citizens and full-time students at a four-year, accredited institution, carrying a total of 12 units or more per semester/quarter; must have a minimum of 2.75 GPA; and must major in a field of study that has an emphasis on public relations, marketing or advertising or must minor in communications with desire to pursue a career in public relations, marketing or advertising. **Criteria:** Applicants will be evaluated based on academic performance.

Funds Avail.: No amount specified. **To Apply:** Applicants must submit a one- to two-page typewritten essay outlining their career goals and what steps they will take to increase the lack of ethnic representation in the fields of advertising, marketing and public relations (must define the role of advertising, marketing or public relations practitioner depending on emphasis); accomplishments relevant to increasing awareness about diversity in their community; brief paragraph describing any honors and awards that they have received (must put the particular dates); a letter of reference from a college professor or internship advisor. **Deadline:** February 29.

Remarks: If chosen, the applicant must attend the Lagrant Foundation's career development workshop and awards reception to receive the scholarship.

4106 ■ Lakselaget

c/o Ingeborg Sorensen
1235 Yale Place, No. 1305
Minneapolis, MN 55403
E-mail: president@lakselaget.org
URL: http://www.lakselaget.org

4107 ■ Lakselaget Foundation Scholarships *(Graduate, Undergraduate/Scholarship)*

Purpose: To promote the international connections between Norway and Minnesota, and learn, teach and share knowledge that will benefit women in their complex roles in today's society. **Focus:** Biology; Mathematics and mathematical sciences; Science. **Qualif.:** Applicant must be female; an American citizen residing in Minnesota, enrolled in undergraduate or graduate studies at an accredited Minnesota college or university or at the University of North Dakota, Grand Forks and wish to study in Norway; or must be a Norwegian citizen attending undergraduate or graduate studies at an accredited Norwegian college or university, who wishes to study at a Minnesota college or university or at the University of North Dakota, Grand Forks. Study areas may include, but are not limited to, non-traditional women's studies such as biotechnology, mathematics, and the sciences. Applicants must be full-time undergraduates who have completed at least one year or full-time graduate students. American students should have a GPA of 3.0 or better, Norwegians the equivalent. **Criteria:** Award is given to applicant who best exemplifies the organization's motto.

Funds Avail.: $1,000. **Number Awarded:** Varies. **To Apply:** Applicant must submit a completed application form with official transcripts, two letters or recommendation, a letter from an individual who can assess the applicant's Norwegian language skills (if an American), and a 1000-word essay. **Deadline:** March 15. **Contact:** scholarships@lakselaget.org.

4108 ■ Lam Research Corporation

4650 Cushing Pkwy.
Fremont, CA 94538
Ph: (510)572-0200
E-mail: ehshelpdesk@lamresearch.com
URL: http://www.lamresearch.com

4109 ■ Carl A. Kountz Engineering Scholarships *(Undergraduate/Scholarship)*

Purpose: To further the education of students who exemplify the core values of the company. **Focus:** Engineering. **Qualif.:** Applicants must students pursuing study in the area of engineering. **Criteria:** Awards are given to students who will best exemplify the core values of the company.

Funds Avail.: $2,500. **Number Awarded:** 2. **To Apply:** Applicants may contact the Community Affairs department for more information about the scholarship.

Remarks: Lam Research Corporation Core Values: Achievement; Honesty and integrity; Innovation and continuous improvement; Mutual trust and respect; Open communication; Ownership and accountability; and Teamwork. **Contact:** communityaffairs@lamrc.com.

4110 ■ Lam Research Corporation Core Value and Performance Scholarships for Interns *(Undergraduate/Scholarship)*

Purpose: To further the education of students who exemplify the core values of the company. **Focus:** General studies. **Qualif.:** Applicants must be intern students at Lam. **Criteria:** Awards are given to students who will best exemplify Lam's Core Values and perform at a high level during their internship at Lam.

Funds Avail.: $2,500. **Number Awarded:** 2. **To Apply:** Applicants may contact the Community Affairs department for more information about the scholarship.

Remarks: Lam Research Corporation Core Values: Achievement; Honesty and integrity; Innovation and continuous improvement; Mutual trust and respect; Open communication; Ownership and accountability; and Teamwork. **Contact:** communityaffairs@lamrc.com.

4111 ■ Lam Research Corporation Core Values Scholarships *(Undergraduate/Scholarship)*

Purpose: To further the education of students who exemplify the core values of the company. **Focus:** General studies. **Qualif.:** Applicants must be graduating seniors from each of the six high schools in Fremont, CA who best exemplifies Lam's Core Values. **Criteria:** Awards are given to students who will best exemplify the core values of the company.

Funds Avail.: $10,000. **Number Awarded:** 6. **To Apply:** Applicants may contact the Community Affairs department for more information about the scholarship.

Remarks: Lam Research Corporation Core Values: Achievement; Honesty and integrity; Innovation and continuous improvement; Mutual trust and respect; Open communication; Ownership and accountability; and Teamwork. **Contact:** communityaffairs@lamrc.com.

4112 ■ Lam Research Corporation - San Jose State University Scholarships *(Undergraduate/Scholarship)*

Purpose: To further the education of students who exemplify the core values of the company. **Focus:** Engineering. **Qualif.:** Applicants must be students pursuing study in the area of engineering. **Criteria:** Awards are given to students who will best exemplify the core values of the company.

Funds Avail.: No specific amount. **Number Awarded:** 4. **To Apply:** Applicants may contact the Community Affairs department for more information about the scholarship.

Remarks: Lam Research Corporation Core Values: Achievement; Honesty and integrity; Innovation and continuous improvement; Mutual trust and respect; Open communication; Ownership and accountability; and Teamwork. **Contact:** communityaffairs@lamrc.com.

4113 ■ Lamaze International

2025 M St. NW, Ste. 800
Washington, DC 20036-3309
Ph: (202)367-1128
Fax: (202)367-2128
Free: 800-368-4404
URL: http://www.lamaze.org

4114 ■ Childbirth Educator Program Scholarships *(Other/Scholarship)*

Purpose: To provide financial support to cover the cost of enrolling in a Lamaze Accredited Childbirth Educator Program. **Focus:** Motherhood. **Qualif.:** Applicants must be currently enrolled or planning to enroll in a Lamaze Childbirth Educator Program; current members of Lamaze International, in good standing; in need of financial assistance. **Criteria:** Scholarship recipients are selected by lottery from a pool of applications that meet the eligibility requirements.

Funds Avail.: $500. **To Apply:** Applicants must submit a completed Childbirth Educator Program Scholarship application and must include the following information in the statement: Circumstances of need, e.g., employment or self-employment status and anticipated gross yearly income (spouse information needed if they file a joint tax return or the equivalent); special medical, educational or unemployment related circumstances (including disabilities and worker's compensation claims), include number of dependents, students they support in college, and special needs family members; other sources of income (savings, bonds stocks, scholarships, etc); and how they will finance the remaining fees, lodging, travel, meals and away-from-home expenses, if they receive a scholarship; letter describing how they plan to promote the Lamaze International Philosophy of Birth. **Deadline:** June 30.

4115 ■ Lambda Iota Tau

Ball State University
Muncie, IN 47306-0460
Ph: (765)285-8370
Fax: (765)285-3765
E-mail: ktaylor@bsu.edu
URL: http://www.bsu.edu/shapps/english/undergraduate/lit

4116 ■ LIT Scholarships *(Graduate, Undergraduate/Scholarship)*

Purpose: To financially support student members with their education. **Focus:** General studies. **Qualif.:** Applicant must be undergraduate in the top 35% of their class and have a B average in at least 12 semester hours; or graduate students who have completed at least one semester or term with an A- average. Candidates must be nominated by a chapter sponsor. **Criteria:** Applications will be reviewed and evaluated by the committee based on scholarship, leadership, character, as well as service.

Funds Avail.: $1000. **Number Awarded:** 2. **To Apply:** Candidates must submit the nomination letter from the sponsor; an essay or piece of creative writing; and another essay of 1000 words or less on career goals and objectives. All materials must be received at the LIT Headquarters, c/o Professor Bruce W. Hozeski. **Deadline:** May 31.

4117 ■ Landscape Architecture Foundation

818 18th St. NW, Ste. 810
Washington, DC 20006

Awards are arranged alphabetically below their administering organizations

Ph: (202)331-7070
Fax: (202)331-7079
E-mail: scholarships@lafoundation.org
URL: http://www.lafoundation.org

4118 ■ ASLA Council of Fellows Scholarships *(Undergraduate/Scholarship)*

Purpose: To aid outstanding students who would not otherwise have an opportunity to continue a professional degree program due to unmet financial need, to increase the interest and participation of economically disadvantaged and under-represented populations in the study of landscape architecture and to enrich the profession of landscape architecture. **Focus:** Landscape architecture and design. **Qualif.:** Applicants must be permanent U.S. citizens or permanent resident aliens who are third-, fourth-, or fifth-year undergraduates at Landscape Architecture Accreditation Board (LAAB) accredited programs of landscape architecture. Applicants seeking special consideration for the diversity scholarship should indicate and identify their association with a specific ethnic or cultural group. **Criteria:** Scholarship recipients will be selected based on the review of application materials.

Funds Avail.: $4,000. **Number Awarded:** 2. **To Apply:** Applicants must submit an entry form, a photo (head shot with a plain background; 300 ppi, size 4 x 6 inches in .jpg format) and a personal profile (two page maximum including education, extracurricular activities and financial information); a 300-word essay about how the applicant envisions herself/himself contributing to the profession of landscape architecture; two letters of recommendation addressing the quality of performance as a student of landscape architecture and the promise as a professional. One letter of recommendation must come from a faculty member; the other letter may be sent by a non-academic member of ASLA or another faculty member; a Student Aid Report (SAR) as proof of unmet financial need. All application materials (with the exception of reference letters) must be sent through email as a single document. Each document must be formatted as follows: create one-inch minimum margins; include page number and surname/document name/award name on all pages of all documents prepared by applicant. **Deadline:** February 15.

Remarks: Established by the ASLA Council of Fellows in 2004.

4119 ■ CLASS Fund Irrigation Scholarship Program *(Graduate, Undergraduate/Scholarship)*

Purpose: To assist undergraduate or graduate students enrolled in programs in landscape architecture and ornamental horticulture in California. **Focus:** Landscape architecture and design. **Qualif.:** Applicants must be undergraduate or graduate students with financial need. Applicants must be continuing their studies in landscape architecture or ornamental horticulture. Student must be enrolled in the irrigation curriculum at Cal Poly Pomona. **Criteria:** Scholarship recipients will be selected based on financial need.

Funds Avail.: $1,500. **Number Awarded:** 1. **To Apply:** Applicants must submit a 300-word (maximum) statement on the profession; a 100-word (maximum) statement indicating intended use of funds; two letters of recommendation from the faculty; and one confidential letter of recommendation from the department head. **Deadline:** February 15.

Remarks: Students applying for multiple CLASS (California Landscape Architectural Student Scholarship) Fund Scholarships must submit a separate application for each scholarship.

4120 ■ CLASS Fund Landscape Architecture Scholarship Program *(Graduate, Undergraduate/Scholarship)*

Purpose: To assist undergraduate or graduate students enrolled in programs in landscape architecture and ornamental horticulture in California. **Focus:** Landscape architecture and design. **Qualif.:** Applicants must be continuing their studies in landscape architecture or ornamental horticulture. Applicants must be enrolled at the University of California-Berkeley, or University of California-Los Angeles. **Criteria:** Preference will be given to applicants who have demonstrated financial need.

Funds Avail.: $1,000. **Number Awarded:** 4. **To Apply:** Applicants must submit a 300-word statement on the profession; a 100-word statement indicating intended use of funds; two letters of recommendation from the faculty; and one confidential letter of recommendation from the department head. **Deadline:** February 15.

Remarks: Students applying for multiple CLASS (California Landscape Architectural Student Scholarship) Fund Scholarships must submit a separate application for each scholarship.

4121 ■ CLASS Fund University Scholarship Program *(Graduate, Undergraduate/Scholarship)*

Purpose: To assist undergraduate or graduate students enrolled in programs in landscape architecture and ornamental horticulture in California. **Focus:** Landscape architecture and design. **Qualif.:** Applicants must be undergraduate or graduate students in financial need who show promise and commitment to the profession. Applicants must be continuing their studies in landscape architecture or ornamental horticulture. **Criteria:** Preference will be given to applicants who have demonstrated financial need.

Funds Avail.: $2,000. **Number Awarded:** maximum of two (2) students at Cal Poly Pomona; one (1) student at Cal Poly San Luis Obispo; one (1) student at Cal Poly (faculty decision); maximum of two (2) students at the University of California, Davis. **To Apply:** Applicants must submit a 300-word (maximum) statement on the profession; a 100-word (maximum) statement indicating intended use of funds; two letters of recommendation from the faculty; and one confidential letter of recommendation from the department head. **Deadline:** February 15.

Remarks: Students applying for multiple CLASS (California Landscape Architectural Student Scholarship) Fund Scholarships must submit a separate application for each scholarship.

4122 ■ Hawaii Chapter/David T. Woolsey Scholarships *(Graduate, Undergraduate/Scholarship)*

Purpose: To provide funds for educational or professional development purposes. **Focus:** Landscape architecture and design. **Qualif.:** Applicants must be third-, fourth-, or fifth-year undergraduate or graduate students of landscape architecture at Landscape Architecture Accreditation Board (LAAB) accredited programs. Applicants must also be permanent residents of Hawaii. **Criteria:** Recipients will be selected based on juries' review of application materials.

Funds Avail.: $2,000. **Number Awarded:** 1. **To Apply:**

Awards are arranged alphabetically below their administering organizations

Applicants must submit an entry form, a photo (head shot with a plain background; 300 ppi, size 4 x 6 inches in extracurricular activities and financial information); a typed, 500-word maximum double-spaced autobiography and statement of personal and professional goals; three 8 1/2 x 11 work samples in either design instructor and proof of Hawaii residency. All application materials (with the exception of reference letters) must be sent through email as a single document. Each document must be formatted as follows: create one-inch minimum margins; include page number and surname/document name/award name on all pages of all documents prepared by applicant. **Deadline:** February 15.

4123 ■ Steven G. King Play Environments Scholarships *(Undergraduate/Scholarship)*

Purpose: To recognize a student who has high potential in the design of play environments. **Focus:** Landscape architecture and design. **Qualif.:** Applicants must be landscape architecture students with an interest and aptitude in the design of play environments. Candidates must be enrolled in graduate or the final two years of undergraduate study in LAAB accredited schools. **Criteria:** Scholarship recipients will be selected on the basis of creativity, openness to innovation and a demonstrated interest in park and playground planning.

Funds Avail.: $5,000. **Number Awarded:** 1. **To Apply:** Applicants must submit an entry form, a photo (head shot with a plain background; 300 ppi, size 4 x 6 inches in extracurricular activities and financial information); a 300 to 500-word essay describing the applicant's views of the significant social and educational value of play and the value of integrating playgrounds into play and recreation environments; a plan and details of a play environment of the applicant's design in either .jpg or PDF format; two letters of recommendation from current professors familiar with the applicant's demonstrated interest in park and playground planning, creativity and openness to innovation. All application materials (with the exception of reference letters) must be sent through email as a single document. Each document must be formatted as follows: create one-inch minimum margins; include page number and surname/document name/award name on all pages of all documents prepared by applicant. **Deadline:** February 15.

4124 ■ Landscape Forms Design for People Scholarships *(Undergraduate/Scholarship)*

Purpose: To honor excellence in design for people. **Focus:** Landscape architecture and design. **Qualif.:** Applicants must be landscape architecture students who will be starting their final year of full-time undergraduate study in an LAAB-accredited program. Applicants must show a proven contribution to the design of public spaces that integrates landscape design and the use of amenities to promote social interaction. **Criteria:** Scholarship recipients will be selected on the basis of academic accomplishment and creative ability.

Funds Avail.: $3,000. **Number Awarded:** 1. **To Apply:** Applicants must submit an entry form, a photo (head shot with a plain background; 300 ppi, size 4 x 6 inches in .jpg format) and a personal profile (two-page maximum including education, extracurricular activities and financial information); a 300-word maximum essay describing the qualities essential to the creation of great and successful public spaces; three 8 1/2 x 11 academic or internship work samples in either .jpg or PDF format; two letters of recommendation from current professors and/or internship employers. All application materials (with the exception of reference letters) must be sent through email as a single document. Each document must be formatted as follows: create one-inch minimum margins; include page number and surname/document name/award name on all pages of all documents prepared by applicant. **Deadline:** February 15.

4125 ■ Courtland Paul Scholarships *(Undergraduate/Scholarship)*

Purpose: To assist students with outstanding academic record and unmet financial need. **Focus:** Landscape architecture and design. **Qualif.:** Applicants must be United States citizens who are undergraduate students in the final two years of study in Landscape Architecture Accreditation Board accredited schools. Applicants must demonstrate financial need and have a minimum grade point average of C. **Criteria:** Recipients will be selected based on the juries' review of application materials.

Funds Avail.: $5,000. Funds must be used for tuition and books within the school year of the award. **Number Awarded:** 1. **To Apply:** Applicants must submit an entry form, a photo (head shot with a plain background; 300 ppi, size 4 x 6 inches in .jpg format) and a personal profile (two page maximum including education, extracurricular activities and financial information); 500-word maximum essay describing the applicant's aspirations, ability to surmount obstacles, high level of drive and need for financial assistance; two letters of recommendation from current professors familiar with the applicant's character and goals in pursuing an education in landscape architecture. All application materials (with the exception of reference letters) must be sent through email as a single document. Each document must be formatted as follows: create one-inch minimum margins; include page number and surname/document name/ award name on all pages of all documents prepared by applicant. **Deadline:** February 15.

Remarks: The scholarship is given in honor of Courtland P. Paul.

4126 ■ Peridian International, Inc./Rae L. Price, FASLA Scholarships *(Undergraduate/Scholarship)*

Purpose: To assist individuals into may not otherwise have the financial ability to cover all the costs of their educational program. **Focus:** Landscape architecture and design. **Qualif.:** Applicants must be United States citizens; students in the final two years of study in Landscape Architecture at the University of California at Los Angeles Extension Program, or in the case of UCLA's termination of the program, other California accredited schools of programs in Landscape Architecture. Applicants must demonstrate financial need and a minimum grade point average of B. **Criteria:** Scholarship recipients will be selected based on the review of application materials.

Funds Avail.: $5,000. Use of funds is restricted to tuition, books and program required supplies within the school year of the award. **Number Awarded:** 1. **To Apply:** Applicants must submit an entry form, a photo (head shot with a plain background; 300 ppi, size 4 x 6 inches in .jpg format) and a personal profile (two pages including education, extracurricular activities and financial information); a 500-word essay describing the applicant's aspirations, ability to surmount obstacles, high level of drive and need for financial assistance; two letters of recommendation from current professors familiar with the applicant's character and goals in pursuing an education in landscape architecture. All application materials (with the exception of reference letters) must be sent through email as a single document. Each document must be formatted as follows: create one-inch minimum margins; include page number and surname/document name/award name on all pages of all documents prepared by applicant. **Deadline:** February 15.

Remarks: The use of funds is restricted to tuition, books and program required supplies within the school year of the award.

4127 ■ Rain Bird Intelligent Use of Water Scholarships *(Undergraduate/Scholarship)*

Purpose: To recognize an outstanding landscape architecture, horticulture or irrigation science student. **Focus:** Landscape architecture and design; Horticulture. **Qualif.:** Applicants must be students in the final two years of undergraduate study (third-, fourth-, or fifth-year students) who have demonstrated commitment to these professions through participation in extracurricular activities and exemplary scholastic achievements. **Criteria:** Scholarship recipient will be selected based on the review of application materials.

Funds Avail.: $2,500. **Number Awarded:** 1. **To Apply:** Applicants must submit an entry form, a photo (head shot with a plain background; 300 ppi, size 4 x 6 inches in extracurricular activities and financial information); a cover letter; a typed, double-spaced 300-word essay stating career goals and explaining how the applicant will contribute to the advancement of the profession of landscape architecture, horticulture or irrigation science. All application materials (with the exception of reference letters) must be sent through email as a single document. Each document must be formatted as follows: create one-inch minimum margins; include page number and surname/document name/award name on all pages of all documents prepared by applicant. **Deadline:** February 15.

4128 ■ Douglas Dockery Thomas Fellowships *(Graduate/Fellowship)*

Purpose: To assist graduate students with study and research at an American institution. **Focus:** Landscape architecture and design. **Qualif.:** Applicants must be studying at an American institution. **Criteria:** Fellowship recipient will be selected based on the degree to which the proposed fellowship work addresses GCA objectives: to stimulate the knowledge and love of gardening and to restore, improve and protect the quality of the environment through educational programs and action in the fields of conservation and civic improvement. Preference will also be given to the student with an excellent academic record.

Funds Avail.: $4,000. **Number Awarded:** 1. **To Apply:** Applicants must submit an entry form, a photo (head shot with a plain background; 300 ppi, size 4 x 6 inches in .jpg format) and a personal profile (two-page maximum including education, extracurricular activities and financial information); a cover letter; a written proposal for the work to be undertaken (four-page maximum; proposal must contain an objective, outcome and method); a one-page budget for the proposed work; a current resume; a letter of endorsement from applicant's faculty advisor, which also certifies enrollment; and two additional recommendations. All application materials (with the exception of reference letters) must be sent through email as a single document. Each document must be formatted as follows: create one-inch minimum margins; include page number and surname/document name/award name on all pages of all documents prepared by applicant. **Deadline:** January 15.

Remarks: Sponsored by the Garden Club of America (GCA); established in 2000 by Mr. and Mrs. Wilmer J. Thomas.

4129 ■ Lane Powell PC

1420 5th Ave., Ste. 4100
Seattle, WA 98101
Ph: (206)223-7000
Fax: (206)223-7107
E-mail: infoatslanepowell.com
URL: http://www.lanepowell.com

4130 ■ George V. Powell Diversity Scholarships *(Undergraduate/Scholarship)*

Purpose: To support the education of a minority law student. **Focus:** Law. **Qualif.:** Applicants must be second year students in good standing at an ABA accredited law school. Students in four-year joint degree programs will be considered after third year. **Criteria:** Award is given to candidates who will contribute meaningfully to the diversity of the legal community, and who have demonstrated desire to work, live and eventually practice law in Seattle or Portland.

Funds Avail.: $6,000. **To Apply:** Applicants must submit a cover letter including a statement indicating eligibility to participate in the program; a resume; current copy of law school transcript; legal writing sample; and a list of two or three professional or academic references. **Contact:** Len Roden, Manager of Attorney Recruiting at 206-223-6123, or redenl@lanepowell.com.

4131 ■ Lanier Technical College

2990 Landrum Educational Dr.
Oakwood, GA 30566
Ph: (770)531-6300
Fax: (770)631-6328
E-mail: info@laniertech.edu
URL: http://www.laniertech.edu

4132 ■ Kenneth H. Breeden Scholarships *(Undergraduate/Scholarship)*

Purpose: To provide financial support to deserving students intending to pursue completion of their programs of study. **Focus:** General studies. **Qualif.:** Applicants must have a previous approved for HOPE grant or HOPE Scholarship funding; must be in good academic standing in accordance with college guidelines. **Criteria:** Awards will be made on a first come, first serve bases. The Lanier Technical College Foundation Scholarship Committee will award the scholarship based upon their normal review procedure, evaluation of the Kenneth H. Breeden Scholarship criteria, and the applicant's academic record if applicable.

Funds Avail.: $500. **To Apply:** Applicants must submit a Kenneth H. Breeden Scholarship application (available online) along with a letter of recommendation from an advisor or instructor. Application documents must be sent to the Financial Aid Office three weeks prior to registration for the quarter aid is requested.

4133 ■ Forsyth County United Way Scholarships *(Undergraduate/Scholarship)*

Purpose: To help students offset their educational costs, specifically with books and supplies and to assist the students who are residents of Forsyth County. **Focus:** General studies. **Qualif.:** Applicants must be in good academic standing in accordance with college and Financial Aid guidelines and must be residents of Forsyth County. **Criteria:** Awards are given on a first come, first serve basis.

The United Way Scholarship Committee will award the scholarship based on the evaluation of the United Way Scholarship criteria which include the applicant's academic record and letters of recommendation.

Funds Avail.: $250. **To Apply:** Applicant must submit a completed United Way Scholarship Application along with a letter of recommendation from an advisor, instructor or a responsible member of the community capable of reporting applicants' work record, leadership and notable skills. Application and other documentations must be submitted to the Financial Aid Office two weeks prior to registration for the quarter aid is requested.

4134 ■ Lanier Merit Scholarships
(Undergraduate/Scholarship)

Purpose: To encourage educational pursuits by providing financial assistance. **Focus:** General studies. **Qualif.:** Applicants must be able to demonstrate outstanding achievement. **Criteria:** Selection will be based on the student achievement in a particular field or overall.

Funds Avail.: No specific amount. **To Apply:** Applicants must submit a completed scholarship application (available online); a letter of endorsement from instructor or community member; and a copy of high school transcript, GED scores and/or work record.

4135 ■ Lanier Need-Based Scholarships
(Undergraduate/Scholarship)

Purpose: To encourage educational pursuits by providing financial assistance. **Focus:** General studies. **Qualif.:** Program is open to individuals with financial need. **Criteria:** Candidates will be selected based on their financial need, instructor or community recommendation, academic progress and attendance.

Funds Avail.: No specific amount. The Lanier Technical College Scholarship Committee will determine selection of the scholarship recipient. **To Apply:** Applicants must complete the scholarship application form and submit along with an endorsement letter from instructor or community member and a letter of applicant explaining the need for financial assistance.

4136 ■ Edna A. Noblin Dawsonville Lions Club Scholarships *(Undergraduate/Scholarship)*

Purpose: To provide financial assistance for deserving students who are residents of Dawson or Lumpkin Counties. **Focus:** General studies. **Qualif.:** Applicants must be residents of Dawson County or Lumpkin County. **Criteria:** Award is given based on the eligibility requirements.

Funds Avail.: No specific amount. **To Apply:** Applicants must submit a completed scholarship application form; a short letter from applicant explaining the need for financial assistance; a list of specific costs for which the applicants require assistance; and a recommendation letter from faculty member or responsible member of the community capable of reporting applicant's work record, leadership, and notable skills.

4137 ■ Lapper County Community Foundation

220 W Nepressing St., Ste. 202
Lapeer, MI 48446
Ph: (810)664-0691
E-mail: lccf@charterinternet.com
URL: http://www.lapeercountycommunityfoundation.org

4138 ■ The Clarke B. Adams Memorial Foundation Lapeer County Community Foundation Fund
(Undergraduate/Scholarship)

Purpose: To attract and manage permanently endowed funds serving a wide range of charitable purposes in order to strengthen the quality of life in Lapeer County. **Focus:** General studies. **Qualif.:** Applicants must be graduating at the end of the current school year from Lapeer East or Lapeer West High School; must be accepted and planning to enroll in an accredited post-secondary college, university or trade school; must have 2.5 or better GPA based on a 4.0 scale. **Criteria:** Recipients are selected based on academic achievement and financial need.

Funds Avail.: No specific amount. **To Apply:** Applicants must submit a completed application form, transcript, resume, an essay and letter of recommendation from a teacher or community leader stating the personal qualities. **Deadline:** April 21.

4139 ■ Ross P. Broesamle Educational Scholarships Fund *(Undergraduate/Scholarship)*

Purpose: To support educational assistance to students from Almont Township or the Village of Almont and the Township of Dryden of the Village of Dryden. **Focus:** General studies. **Qualif.:** Applicants must reside in geographic areas stated and be accepted or enrolled in an accredited state approved degree granting institution. **Criteria:** Recipients are selected based on financial need.

Funds Avail.: No specific amount. **To Apply:** Applicants must be prepared to participate in a brief interview; must submit a transcript of records, test scores, photos and federal tax return for self or family. **Deadline:** April 15.

4140 ■ Irma Gelhausen Scholarship Fund
(Undergraduate/Scholarship)

Purpose: To advance the values of community education through the development and encouragement of teachers who best emulate the qualities of commitment to well-rounded education and social values at the elementary level. **Focus:** General studies. **Qualif.:** Applicants must be in the third or more year of college/university studies; must have a GPA of 3.0 or higher for post-secondary studies and must be residents of Lapeer County. **Criteria:** Recipients are selected based on financial need.

Funds Avail.: No specific amount. **To Apply:** Applicants must submit a completed application form, a "200-word" essay discussing the expectations to achieve as an educator; must attach the most recent transcript of records, verification of current GPA and standardized test scores, IRS federal tax return and current photo to be used for publicity purposes. **Deadline:** August 30. **Contact:** Debbie Cady at the above address (see entry 4137).

4141 ■ Wayne Hildebrant Police Scholarships Fund *(Undergraduate/Scholarship)*

Purpose: To support education in the law enforcement fields. **Focus:** Law enforcement. **Qualif.:** Applicants must be residents of Lapeer County and accepted into an accredited police academy of college/university law enforcement program; must have a cumulative GPA of 3.0 or higher. **Criteria:** Recipients are selected based on financial need.

Funds Avail.: $500. **To Apply:** Applicants must be prepared to participate in a brief interview; must submit a transcript of records, test scores, photos and federal tax return for self or family. **Deadline:** April 15.

Awards are arranged alphabetically below their administering organizations

4142 ■ Lapeer County Medical Scholarships Fund *(Undergraduate/Scholarship)*

Purpose: To promote various medical related purposes. **Focus:** Medical education. **Qualif.:** Applicants must be residents of Lapeer County; must be accepted into and enrolled in an accredited medical program and maintain a GPA of 3.2. **Criteria:** Recipients are selected based on financial need.

Funds Avail.: No specific amount. **To Apply:** Applicants must be prepared to participate in a brief interview; must submit a transcript of records, test scores, photos and federal tax return for self or family. **Deadline:** April 15.

4143 ■ Hazel Simms Nursing Scholarship *(Professional Development/Scholarship)*

Purpose: To promote and foster education of person's accepted by registered nursing programs and registered nurses accepted into Bachelor of Science in nursing programs in Michigan. **Focus:** Nursing. **Qualif.:** Applicants must be accepted into a Michigan registered nursing program approved by the Michigan Board of Nursing; must be registered nurses who are pursuing a Bachelor of Science Degree in Nursing; must have completed one year or more in college; must be residents within 90 days or longer in Almont, Dryden, Imlay, Lakeville, Lapeer and North Branch. **Criteria:** Recipients are selected based on financial need, scholastic record of the applicant and recommendations from college faculty and official of the college.

Funds Avail.: No specific amount. **To Apply:** Applicants must submit a completed application form, statement of applicant, copy of applicant's most recent household federal tax, statement by the Director/Faculty Member of Nursing Program, transcript of courses completed at all colleges and current photo. **Deadline:** April 30.

4144 ■ Latin American Educational Foundation

561 Santa Fe Dr.
Denver, CO 80204
Ph: (303)446-0526
E-mail: info@laef.org
URL: http://www.laef.org

4145 ■ Latin American Educational Foundation Scholarships *(Undergraduate/Scholarship)*

Purpose: To award funds to qualified students who have demonstrated a commitment to the Hispanic community. **Focus:** Hispanic American studies. **Qualif.:** Applicants must be Colorado residents with Hispanic heritage and/or are actively involved in the Hispanic community; must be accepted in an accredited college, university or vocational school; must at least have a 3.0 cumulative grade point average. Recipients will be required to fulfill 10 hours of community service during the year of funding. **Criteria:** Award is given based on the following: academic achievement; financial need; community involvement; letters of recommendation; personal essay; and personal interview of finalists.

Funds Avail.: No specific amount. **To Apply:** Applicants must submit completed application form available in the LAEF website; most recent federal income tax returns; a list of community service and extracurricular activities for the previous 2 years including leadership positions held; a one-page essay to include the applicant's interests and career goals; how you anticipate achieving your goals and what has motivated you to pursue higher education; two letters of recommendation on official letterhead (the first letter must come from an educator and the other must come from a community service organization, employer, clergy or coach). Letters should discuss your academic achievements and community service as well as your potential for future success. Qualities such as maturity, motivation, self-confidence, leadership and commitment should be addressed. **Deadline:** March 1.

4146 ■ Law Foundation of British Columbia

1340-605 Robson St.
Vancouver, BC, Canada V6B 5J3
Ph: (604)688-2337
Fax: (604)688-4586
E-mail: lfbc@tlfbc.org
URL: http://www.lawfoundationbc.org

4147 ■ Law Foundation of British Columbia Graduate Fellowships *(Undergraduate/Fellowship)*

Purpose: To provide financial assistance to qualified individuals who want to pursue their law career. **Focus:** Law. **Qualif.:** Applicants must be either residents of British Columbia, graduates of British Columbia law school, or members of the British Columbia Bar; must devote themselves primarily to full-time graduate studies in law or a law related area. **Criteria:** Recipients will be selected based on academic achievements, leadership qualities, involvement in community activities, and proposed course of study.

Funds Avail.: $13,750. **Number Awarded:** 5. **To Apply:** Applicants must complete the application form available online; must have transcript of records, and three letters of reference. Application form and other supporting documents must be sent to Law Foundation of British Columbia, 1340-605 Robson St., Vancouver, BC V6B 5J3. **Deadline:** January 4.

4148 ■ Law Society of Prince Edward Island

PO Box 128
49 Water St.
Charlottetown, PE, Canada C1A 7K2
Ph: (902)566-1666
Fax: (902)368-7557
E-mail: lawsociety@lspei.pe.ca
URL: http://www.lspei.pe.ca

4149 ■ Prince Edward Island Law Student Scholarships *(Undergraduate/Scholarship)*

Purpose: To provide scholarship assistance to deserving students who want to pursue their studies. **Focus:** Law. **Qualif.:** Applicant must be a student enrolled or accepted for enrollment as a full-time law student at an accredited university law school for the academic year; must be a resident of Prince Edward Island; must demonstrate scholastic achievement in his or her last year of academic study; and must demonstrate financial need. **Criteria:** Recipient will be selected by the Council of Law Society of Prince Edward Island.

Funds Avail.: $1,000. **To Apply:** Applicant must complete the application form available online; must submit an official transcript of record and curriculum vitae. Application form and other supporting documents must be sent to The Law Society of PEI Scholarship Committee, 49 Water St., PO Box 128, Charlottetown, PE C1A 7K2. **Deadline:** July 31.

4150 ■ League of Latin American Citizens

2000 L St. NW, Ste. 610
Washington, DC 20036
Ph: (202)833-6310
Fax: (202)833-6135
E-mail: RosaRosales@LULAC.org
URL: http://www.lulac.org

4151 ■ LULAC GE Scholarships *(Undergraduate/ Scholarship)*

Purpose: To provide high quality educational opportunities to the Hispanic community. **Focus:** Hispanic American Studies. **Qualif.:** Applicant must be a U.S. citizen or legal resident; Must have applied to or be enrolled in a college, university, or graduate school, including 2-year colleges, or vocational schools that lead to an associate's degree; must not be related to a scholarship committee member, the Council President, or an individual contributor to the local funds of the Council. **Criteria:** Recipients are chosen through a very rigorous selection process my members of LULAC's scholarship committee.

Funds Avail.: $2,500. **To Apply:** Applicants should mail their application directly to the nearest LULAC Council.

4152 ■ LULAC GM Scholarships *(Graduate, High School, Undergraduate/Award/Prize)*

Purpose: To provide high quality educational opportunities to the Hispanic community. **Focus:** Hispanic American Studies. **Qualif.:** Applicant must be an American citizen or legal resident; Must have applied to or be enrolled in a college, university, or graduate school, including 2-year colleges, or vocational schools that lead to an associate's degree; must not be related to a scholarship committee member, the Council President, or an individual contributor to the local funds of the Council. **Criteria:** Recipients are chosen through a very rigorous selection process by members of LNESC's scholarship committee.

Funds Avail.: No specific amount. **To Apply:** Applicants should be mailed directly their application to the nearest LULAC Council. **Deadline:** December 14.

Remarks: LULAC GM Scholarship is managed by the LULAC national Educational Service Centers. General Motors Corporation founded in 1908, is best known as the world' largest full-vehicle manufacturer. **Contact:** LULAC at the above address (see entry 4150).

4153 ■ LULAC National Scholarship Fund *(Graduate, High School, Undergraduate/ Scholarship)*

Purpose: To provide high quality educational opportunities to the Hispanic community. **Focus:** Hispanic American Studies. **Qualif.:** Applicant must be a US citizen or legal resident; Must have applied to or be enrolled in a college, university, or graduate school, including 2-year colleges, or vocational schools that lead to an associate's degree; must not be related to a scholarship committee member, the Council President, or an individual contributor to the local funds of the Council. **Criteria:** Recipients are chosen through a very rigorous selection process my members of LNESC's scholarship committee.

Funds Avail.: No specific amount. **To Apply:** Applicants should be mailed directly their application to the nearest LULAC Council. **Deadline:** January 15. **Contact:** LULAC at the above address (see entry 4150).

4154 ■ Pepsi Escribe tu Futuro Scholarships *(Undergraduate/Scholarship)*

Purpose: To provide high quality educational opportunities to the students. **Focus:** Hispanic American studies. **Qualif.:** Applicants must be a U.S. citizen; Must have applied to or be enrolled in a college, university, including 2-year colleges, or vocational schools that lead to an associate's degree. **Criteria:** Recipients of this scholarship are selected on the basis of academic achievement, participation in community service and/or extra-curricular activities, and financial need.

Funds Avail.: $500-$2,000. **To Apply:** Applications are available on the LNESC website and from participating LULAC Council; Students must complete the entire application. It should be mailed with a current complete official high school or college transcript of grade to the LULAC National Educational Service Centers (LNESC) national office. **Deadline:** February 28.

Remarks: The Pepsi Escribe tu Futuro Scholarship is funded by the Pepsi-Cola Company, to help young Latinos in their pursuit towards a college education to help improve their future and career opportunities. **Contact:** www.yourworldyourpepsi.com.

4155 ■ Learning Disabilities Association of Ottawa-Carleton

160 Percy St., Rm. No. 2
Ottawa, ON, Canada K1R 6E5
Ph: (613)567-5864
Fax: (613)567-5979
E-mail: ldaoc@rogers.com
URL: http://ldao-c.ncf.ca

4156 ■ Canada Study Grant for the Accommodation of Students with Permanent Disabilities *(Undergraduate/Grant)*

Purpose: To accommodate and support students with permanent disabilities. **Focus:** General studies. **Qualif.:** Applicants must have appropriate medical documentation; and a need for exceptional education. **Criteria:** Recipients are selected based on the committee's review of the application materials.

Funds Avail.: $8,000. **To Apply:** Applicants must qualify for full-time or part-time Canada Student Loan assistance and then complete a separate application form. **Contact:** LDAO-C at the above address (see entry 4155).

4157 ■ Lentz Peace Research Association

University of Missouri-St. Louis, One University Boulevard
St. Louis, MO 63121-4400
Ph: (314)516-5000
E-mail: web_office@umsl.edu
URL: http://www.umsl.edu

4158 ■ Post-Doctoral or Sabbatical Fellowships *(Doctorate/Fellowship)*

Purpose: To support scholarly research on peace and conflict resolution and violence. **Focus:** Peace Studies. **Qualif.:** Applicants must be a Ph.D.; Graduate of university programs in peace studies and conflict resolution. Graduates of political science, international relations, and other social science programs who specialized in peace and conflict resolution.

Awards are arranged alphabetically below their administering organizations

Funds Avail.: $23,400 for the academic year; $1,000 allowance for research travel and expenses. **To Apply:** Applicant should provide a curriculum vitae, evidence of completion of the Ph.D.; three letters of recommendation; and a research proposal for approximately 750 words. **Deadline:** April 16. **Contact:** Dr. Joel Glassman, Director Center for International Studies; Phone: 314-516-5753 Fax: 314-516-6757; jglassman@umsl.edu.

4159 ■ Lewis-Clark State College

500 8th Ave.
Lewiston, ID 83501
Ph: (208)792-5272
URL: http://www.lcsc.edu

4160 ■ The "21" Endowed Scholarships
(Undergraduate/Scholarship)

Purpose: To offset the educationally-related expenses of a Lewis-Clark State College student from the Culdesac-Lapwai area. **Focus:** General studies. **Qualif.:** Applicants must be entering first year students who have a cumulative GPA of at least 2.5. **Criteria:** Recipients will be selected based on financial need.

Funds Avail.: No specific amount. **To Apply:** Applicants must submit a general application. **Deadline:** March 1.

4161 ■ Mamie Adams Memorial Awards
(Undergraduate/Scholarship)

Purpose: To provide educational assistance for students who demonstrate consistency and improvement in their scholastic records. **Focus:** General studies. **Qualif.:** Applicants must be high school seniors who are planning to attend college in the fall or undergraduate college students enrolled at a 2- or 4-year institution with at least a 2.5 GPA. **Criteria:** Preference is given to demonstrated consistency and improvement in academic records.

Funds Avail.: No specific amount. **To Apply:** Applicants must accomplish a general application available at the website.

4162 ■ American Legion Boys/Girls State Scholarships *(Undergraduate/Scholarship)*

Purpose: To acknowledge outstanding Idaho high school seniors who have participated in The American Legion of Idaho Boys and Girls State competition and who have selected Lewis-Clark State College as their school of choice. **Focus:** General studies. **Qualif.:** Applicants must be outstanding senior students of Idaho High School who are currently enrolled in LCSC. **Criteria:** Awards are given based on academic merit.

Funds Avail.: $200. **To Apply:** Applicants must accomplish a general application available at the website.

4163 ■ Avista Corporation Minds in Motion Scholarships *(Undergraduate/Scholarship)*

Purpose: To provide financial assistance to students who are majoring in these fields: Accounting, Biology, Business, Communications, Computer Science, Economics, Environmental Science, Engineering, Mathematics, Natural Resources, Political Science, Statistics. **Focus:** Accounting; Biology; Business; Communications; Computer and Information Sciences; Economics; Environmental Science; Engineering; Mathematics; Natural Resources; Political Science; Statistics. **Qualif.:** Applicants must be full-time students attending LCSC and must have a cumulative GPA of 2.5. **Criteria:** Recipients will be selected based on financial need.

Funds Avail.: No specific Amount. **Number Awarded:** 2. **To Apply:** Applicants must submit general application. **Deadline:** March 1.

4164 ■ Banner Bank Business Scholarships
(Undergraduate/Scholarship)

Purpose: To provide financial assistance for outstanding junior or senior students in the Business Division. **Focus:** Business. **Qualif.:** Program is open to students pursuing a degree in business and entering their junior or senior year. Applicants must demonstrate financial need as determined by the FAFSA form. **Criteria:** Award is given based on merit.

Funds Avail.: $1,000. **To Apply:** Applicants must accomplish the required general application available in the website. **Deadline:** March 1.

4165 ■ Diana Brown Endowed Scholarships
(Undergraduate/Scholarship)

Purpose: To benefit a non-traditional student that is a cancer survivor, is currently battling cancer, or who has had to deal with cancer in their immediate family. **Focus:** General studies. **Qualif.:** Applicants must be cancer survivors or are currently battling cancer and are registered degree-seeking, full-time students. **Criteria:** Recipients will be selected based on financial need.

Funds Avail.: No specific amount. **To Apply:** Applicants must submit general application. **Deadline:** March 1.

4166 ■ Glen and Babs Carlson Endowed Scholarships *(Undergraduate/Scholarship)*

Purpose: To offset the educationally-related expenses of Lewis-Clark State College students. **Focus:** General studies. **Qualif.:** Applicants must be students at Lewis-Clark State College with a cumulative GPA consistent with the minimum required for admission. **Criteria:** Recipients are evaluated based on financial need.

Funds Avail.: No specific amount. **To Apply:** Applicants must submit a general application. **Deadline:** March 1.

4167 ■ Walter & Elsie Carr Endowed Scholarships *(Undergraduate/Scholarship)*

Purpose: To provide financial assistance for the graduates of Emmett High School. **Focus:** General studies. **Qualif.:** Applicants must be enrolled for at least 12 credits. **Criteria:** Recipients are selected based on financial need.

Funds Avail.: No specific amount. **To Apply:** Applicants must submit a general application. **Deadline:** March 1.

4168 ■ Caterpillar Scholarships in Diesel Mechanics *(Undergraduate/Scholarship)*

Purpose: To provide educational assistance for students enrolled in the Diesel Mechanic program at Lewis-Clark State College. **Focus:** Mechanics and repairs. **Qualif.:** Applicants must register for 12 or more credits; must be students of LCSC majoring in Diesel mechanic. **Criteria:** Recipients will be selected based on financial need.

Funds Avail.: No specific amount. **To Apply:** Applicants must accomplish a general application available in the website. **Deadline:** December 21.

4169 ■ Church Family Scholarships
(Undergraduate/Scholarship)

Purpose: To provide financial assistance for students from Idaho High School. **Focus:** General studies. **Qualif.:** Applicants must be first year students from an Idaho high school with a cumulative high school GPA of at least 3.0.; must be enrolled full-time (12 credits) at Lewis-Clark State College; must have at least a 2.5 semester GPA at the end of their first semester at LCSC; and must maintain at least a 3.0 cumulative GPA by the end of the first year at LCSC and thereafter. **Criteria:** Recipient will be selected based on financial need.

Funds Avail.: No specific amount. **To Apply:** Applicant must submit general application. **Deadline:** March 1.

4170 ■ Fisher Clark Memorial Endowed Scholarships *(Undergraduate/Scholarship)*

Purpose: To offset the educational expenses of Lewis-Clark State College students. **Focus:** General studies. **Qualif.:** Applicants must be female students and must have a cumulative grade point average consistent with the minimum required for admission and for progress toward her major. **Criteria:** Recipient is selected based on financial need.

Funds Avail.: No specific amount. **To Apply:** Applicants must submit a general application. **Deadline:** March 1.

4171 ■ Coeur d'Alene Alumni Scholarships *(Undergraduate/Scholarship)*

Purpose: To inspire educational pursuits among less capable individuals by providing financial assistance. **Focus:** General studies. **Qualif.:** Applicants must be attending the LCSC Couer d'Alene campus; must be currently enrolled in a minimum of six semester credits through the Coeur d'Alene program which includes credits from LCSC and NIC; must have completed at least one semester of course work through LCSC; and must have a minimum GPA of 3.0. **Criteria:** Preference will be given to students who demonstrate financial need as determined by the Financial Aid Office.

Funds Avail.: No specific amount. **To Apply:** Applicants must accomplish a general application available at the website. **Deadline:** March 1.

4172 ■ Rob Copeland Memorial Scholarships *(Undergraduate/Scholarship)*

Purpose: To provide financial assistance for individuals intending to pursue educational goals. **Focus:** Automotive technology. **Qualif.:** Applicants must be full-time students who are majoring in Auto Mechanics Technology. **Criteria:** Preference will be given to students who demonstrate financial need.

Funds Avail.: No specific amount. **To Apply:** Applicants must accomplish a general application available in the website. **Deadline:** March 1.

4173 ■ The Rick Crane Group Real Estate Scholarships Fund *(Undergraduate/Scholarship)*

Purpose: To offset the educationally-related expenses of Lewis-Clark State College students intending to pursue a career in the field of real estate. **Focus:** Real Estate; Business Administration. **Qualif.:** Program is open to individuals seeking a Bachelor's degree in Business, or an Associate of Applied Science degree in Business Management. Applicants must be serious about becoming a real estate agent or otherwise working in the field of real estate, have a grade point average of at least 3.5 with strong potential for academic achievement, and must be full-time students taking 12 or more credits. **Criteria:** Preference will be given to students who are gainfully employed.

Funds Avail.: $100. **To Apply:** Applicants must accomplish the required general application available in the website. **Deadline:** March 1.

4174 ■ Laura Moore Cunningham Foundation General Scholarships *(Undergraduate/Scholarship)*

Purpose: To provide financial assistance for the Idaho youth. **Focus:** General studies. **Qualif.:** Applicants must be classified as full-time students who are carrying 12 or more credits per semester and who have a minimum cumulative GPA of 3.0. and must also be Idaho residents. **Criteria:** Recipient will be selected based on financial need.

Funds Avail.: No specific amount. **To Apply:** Applicants must submit a general application. **Deadline:** March 1.

4175 ■ Kenneth and Kathleen Davis Endowed Scholarships *(Undergraduate/Scholarship)*

Purpose: To provide financial assistance for individuals intending to pursue an education. **Focus:** General studies. **Qualif.:** Applicants must be classified as full-time students, carrying 12 or more credits per semester and must have a minimum cumulative GPA of 3.5. **Criteria:** Applicants will be evaluated based on financial need.

Funds Avail.: $1500. **Number Awarded:** 1. **To Apply:** Applicants must submit general application. **Deadline:** March 1.

4176 ■ Gretchen Dimico Memorial Scholarships *(Undergraduate/Scholarship)*

Purpose: To inspire educational pursuits among less capable individuals by providing financial assistance. **Focus:** Nursing. **Qualif.:** Applicants must be full or part-time students at the LCSC Coeur d'Alene Center; must have a cumulative GPA of 2.75; and must be current or former members of Professional Nursing Organization. **Criteria:** Recipients will be selected based on academic achievements.

Funds Avail.: No specific amount. **To Apply:** Applicants must accomplish a general application available at the website. **Deadline:** March 1.

4177 ■ Bus and Mary Ellen Durant Timberline High School Endowed Scholarships *(Undergraduate/Scholarship)*

Purpose: To encourage promising students from Timberline High School, Clearwater County to continue their education. **Focus:** Nursing; Technical; Industrial. **Qualif.:** Applicants must be alumni of Timberline High School or their successor in Clearwater County, Idaho; must be enrolled full-time who majoring in any other discipline offered at LCSC. **Criteria:** Preference will be given to students who are full-time and are majoring in any program in Technical or Industrial Division.

Funds Avail.: No specific amount. **To Apply:** Applicants must accomplish a general application available in the website. **Deadline:** March 1.

4178 ■ First Security Foundation Business Scholarships *(Undergraduate/Scholarship)*

Purpose: To assist students pursuing a degree in business at Lewis-Clark State College. **Focus:** Business. **Qualif.:** Applicants must be students at Lewis-Clark State College and must have a cumulative GPA of 3.0. **Criteria:** Recipients will be selected based on financial need.

Funds Avail.: $1,500. **Number Awarded:** 2. **To Apply:**

Applicants must submit a general application. **Deadline:** March 1.

4179 ■ Dean A. Froehlich Endowed Scholarships *(Undergraduate/Scholarship)*

Purpose: To provide financial assistance for students and single parents who are in need and are intending to pursue higher education. **Focus:** General studies. **Qualif.:** Applicants must be enrolled for at least 12 credits and have a minimum 2.5 GPA. **Criteria:** Preference is given to students who demonstrate financial need as determined by the Financial Aid Office and to non-traditional, single parents who are returning to higher education and are planning to stay in Idaho.

Funds Avail.: No specific amount. **To Apply:** Applicants must submit a general application. **Deadline:** March 1.

4180 ■ Irene Carlson Gnaedinger Memorial Scholarships *(Undergraduate/Scholarship)*

Purpose: To provide educational assistance for students from Lapwai High School. **Focus:** General studies. **Qualif.:** Applicants must be graduates of Lapwai High School; must demonstrate a minimum cumulative GPA of 2.5; and are enrolled for a minimum of 12 credits in a baccalaureate degree program. **Criteria:** Recipients will be selected based on financial need.

Funds Avail.: No specific amount. **To Apply:** Applicants must submit a general application. **Deadline:** March 1.

4181 ■ Jack & Mary Lou Gruber Scholarships *(Undergraduate/Scholarship)*

Purpose: To provide financial assistance to people who cannot afford college education. **Focus:** General studies. **Qualif.:** Applicants must have a minimum of 3.0 GPA and are enrolled for a minimum of 12 credits. **Criteria:** Recipient will be selected based on financial need and active campus and/or community service.

Funds Avail.: No specific amount. **To Apply:** Applicants must submit a general application. **Deadline:** March 1.

4182 ■ Jimmy Guild Memorial Scholarships *(Undergraduate/Scholarship)*

Purpose: To provide educational assistance for students intending to pursue a career in the area of Computer Science. **Focus:** Mathematics and Mathematical Sciences; Computer and Information Sciences. **Qualif.:** Applicants must be full-time students who are majoring in mathematics; must have interest in Computer science; and must have a cumulative GPA of 3.0. **Criteria:** Selection is based on merit.

Funds Avail.: $1,000. **Number Awarded:** 1. **To Apply:** Preference will be given to graduating students from local high schools who are affiliated with a member of the United Paperworkers International Union. **Deadline:** May 19.

4183 ■ Henderson Memorial Endowed Scholarships *(Undergraduate/Scholarship)*

Purpose: To offset the educationally-related expenses of Lewis-Clark State College students. **Focus:** General studies. **Qualif.:** Applicants must have completed at least one semester at LCSC and must have a cumulative GPA of at least 3.0. **Criteria:** Priority is given to students who are in financial need.

Funds Avail.: No specific amount. **To Apply:** Applicants must submit general application. **Deadline:** March 1.

4184 ■ Hinman-Jensen Endowed Scholarships *(Undergraduate/Scholarship)*

Purpose: To provide educational assistance for students pursuing either the Bachelor of Arts in Applied Technology or the Bachelor of Arts in Applied Science. **Focus:** Science; Technology. **Qualif.:** Applicants must be classified as full-time students with a cumulative GPA that is consistent with the minimum required for admission and for progress toward their major. **Criteria:** Priority is given to applicants with financial need.

Funds Avail.: No specific amount. **To Apply:** Applicants must accomplish a general application available at the website. **Deadline:** March 1.

4185 ■ Frank and Gladys Hopkins Endowed Scholarships *(Undergraduate/Scholarship)*

Purpose: To support varsity players who are also good in academics. **Focus:** General studies. **Qualif.:** Applicants must be classified as full-time students who are participating on the LCSC baseball team. Applicants must also have a cumulative GPA consistent with the minimum required for admission and for progress toward their selected major. **Criteria:** Selection is based on merit.

Funds Avail.: $1,000. **To Apply:** Applicants must accomplish the required general application available at the website. **Deadline:** March 1.

4186 ■ Idaho Attorney General Scholarships *(Undergraduate/Scholarship)*

Purpose: To provide financial assistance to students who are in need. **Focus:** General studies. **Qualif.:** Applicants must be freshmen and have had three years involvement in either Idaho FFA or 4-H. **Criteria:** Recipients will be selected by the Lewis-Clark State College Foundation Selection Committee based on financial need.

Funds Avail.: $750. **Number Awarded:** 2. **To Apply:** Applicants must accomplish general application available in the website. **Deadline:** March 1.

4187 ■ Idaho Promise Category B Scholarships *(Undergraduate/Scholarship)*

Purpose: To inspire educational pursuits among less capable individuals by providing financial assistance. **Focus:** General studies. **Qualif.:** Applicants must graduate from an Idaho High School or its equivalent; must have a 3.0 or better cumulative high school GPA or ACT score of 20 or better; must be under the age of 22; and must be intending to attend as full-time students. **Criteria:** Recipients will be selected based on academic achievements.

Funds Avail.: No specific amount. **To Apply:** Applicants must accomplish a general application available in the website.

4188 ■ Margaret G. Johnson and Marge J. Stout Scholarships *(Undergraduate/Scholarship)*

Purpose: To provide financial assistance to students who are currently enrolled in a vocational program. **Focus:** Vocational; Business. **Qualif.:** Applicants must have completed at least 12 credits; must be residents of Idaho; must be enrolled in a two year vocational-technical program at LCSC; and must demonstrate a minimum GPA of 3.0. **Criteria:** Recipients will be selected based on academic achievement.

Funds Avail.: No specific amount. **To Apply:** Applicants must accomplish a general application available at the website. **Deadline:** March 1.

4189 ■ Lewiston Clarkston Kiwanis Club Scholarships *(Undergraduate/Scholarship)*

Purpose: To provide financial assistance for the benefit of students from Lewiston, Idaho, Clarkston and Washington attending Lewis-Clark State College during the beginning stage of their college experience. **Focus:** General studies. **Qualif.:** Applicants must have completed at least one semester at LCSC and must have a minimum cumulative 2.5 GPA. **Criteria:** Applicants must show evidence of a definite financial need.

Funds Avail.: $100. **To Apply:** Applicants must complete general application available at the website. **Deadline:** March 1.

4190 ■ LCSC Welding Club Scholarships *(Undergraduate/Scholarship)*

Purpose: To offset educationally-related expenses of Lewis-Clark State College Welding Technology students. **Focus:** Welding. **Qualif.:** Applicants must have completed at least one semester as full-time students enrolled in the Welding Technology program; must be classified as full-time students with a declared major in Welding Technology; and must have a cumulative GPA of at least 3.0. **Criteria:** Recipients will be selected based on financial need.

Funds Avail.: No specific amount. **To Apply:** Applicants must accomplish a general application available at the website. **Deadline:** March 1.

4191 ■ Lewis-Clark Coin Club Endowed Scholarships *(Undergraduate/Scholarship)*

Purpose: To offset the educationally-related expenses of Lewis-Clark State College students. **Focus:** General studies. **Qualif.:** Applicants must be classified as full-time students carrying 12 or more credits per semester with a minimum cumulative GPA of 2.5. **Criteria:** Priority is given to applicants with demonstrated financial need.

Funds Avail.: No specific amount. **Deadline:** March 1.

Remarks: Annual awards are variable and are awarded in alternate award cycles to an academic and a professional technical student and may be renewed to students who continue to meet the above criteria.

4192 ■ Lewis-Clark State College/American Chemical Society Scholars Program *(Undergraduate/Scholarship)*

Purpose: To encourage African-American, Hispanic, and American Indian students to pursue undergraduate college degrees in the chemical sciences and chemical technology. **Focus:** Chemistry; Science Technologies; Chemical Engineering. **Qualif.:** Applicants must be students who want to enter the fields of chemistry, biochemistry, or chemical engineering, and students seeking a two-year degree in chemical technology; high school seniors planning a science preparatory program of study and college students who are currently from freshmen to juniors who are committed to the study of chemistry, biochemistry, chemical engineering or other chemically related fields such as environmental science, materials science or toxicology and are interested in pursuing careers in one of these fields; students who have strong academic records and show an interest in and potential for careers in the chemical sciences. **Criteria:** Recipients are selected on the basis of merit and financial need.

Funds Avail.: $3,000. **To Apply:** Applicants must accomplish general application available at the website.

4193 ■ Lewis-Clark State College Foundation Scholars Scholarships *(Undergraduate/Scholarship)*

Purpose: To recognize students who have shown consistency and improvement in their scholastic records. **Focus:** General studies. **Qualif.:** Applicants must have exceptional academic achievement, community involvement and leadership ability; must be outstanding Idaho and Asotin County, Washington high school seniors with a cumulative GPA of 3.5. **Criteria:** Awards are given based on academic merit.

Funds Avail.: $2,500. **To Apply:** Applicants must accomplish a general application available at the website. **Deadline:** March 1.

4194 ■ Lewis-Clark State College Freshman Scholarships *(Undergraduate/Scholarship)*

Purpose: To inspire educational pursuits among less capable individuals by providing financial assistance. **Focus:** General studies. **Qualif.:** Applicants must be Idaho High School seniors planning to attend LCSC in their freshman year and must have a high school cumulative GPA of at least 3.5. **Criteria:** Priority is given to applicants with financial need.

Funds Avail.: $500. **To Apply:** Students must be at least tentatively admitted to the college and have their 7th semester high school transcript on file with the Office of Admission prior to the Deadline. **Deadline:** March 1.

4195 ■ Lewis-Clark State College Governor's Cup Scholarships *(Undergraduate/Scholarship)*

Purpose: To provide 12 awards to Idaho high school seniors planning to attend an Idaho college or university. **Focus:** Public service. **Qualif.:** Applicants must be residents of Idaho; must be graduating seniors of an Idaho high school; must be enrolled as full-time students in an academic or technical program at an Idaho college or university; must have a cumulative GPA of 2.8 or above; and must have documentation of volunteer work, leadership and public service. **Criteria:** Recipients are selected based on demonstrated commitment to public service.

Funds Avail.: No specific amount. **To Apply:** Applicants must accomplish a general application available at the website.

4196 ■ Lewis-Clark State College/Idaho Society of CPAs Scholarships Fund *(Undergraduate/Scholarship)*

Purpose: To benefit junior and senior students of Idaho colleges and universities. **Focus:** Accounting. **Qualif.:** Applicants must be residents of Idaho and must have a cumulative grade point average of 2.75 or above for all class work prior to the application; must maintain the stated grade point for each semester. **Criteria:** Applicants will be evaluated based on financial need.

Funds Avail.: $1000. **To Apply:** Applicants must submit a general application. **Deadline:** April 14. **Contact:** Melissa R. Nelson; 250 Bobwhite Court, Ste. 240 Boise, ID 83706; Fax 208-344-8984.

4197 ■ Lewis-Clark State College Non-Traditional Student Scholarships *(Undergraduate/Scholarship)*

Purpose: To assist non-traditional students who have been out of high school for at least 5 years at the time of their

Awards are arranged alphabetically below their administering organizations

initial enrollment at Lewis-Clark State College. **Focus:** General studies. **Qualif.:** Program is open to full-time, degree seeking students who meet the non-traditional requirement. **Criteria:** Priority is given to students with financial need.

Funds Avail.: $500. **To Apply:** Applicants must accomplish a general application available in the website.

4198 ■ Lewis-Clark State College Presidential Out-of-State Scholarships *(Undergraduate/Scholarship)*

Purpose: To provide financial assistance for students who have shown improvement in their academic records. **Focus:** General studies. **Qualif.:** Program is open to promising new non-resident students with at least a high school or transfer cumulative GPA of 3.0; must maintain a 2.5 semester GPA, completing at least 12 credits per semester and registering for classes during advanced registration each semester. **Criteria:** Awards are given based on academic merit.

Funds Avail.: No specific amount. **To Apply:** Applicants must accomplish a general application available at the website. **Deadline:** March 1 for Fall enrollment or November 1 for Spring enrollment.

4199 ■ Lewis-Clark State College Presidential Technical Out-of-State Scholarships *(Undergraduate/Scholarship)*

Purpose: To inspire educational pursuits among less capable individuals by providing financial assistance. **Focus:** Chemistry; Computer Science; Engineering; Information Systems Analysis; Industrial Electronics; Biology; Earth Information Systems; Radiology; Heating/Air Conditioning; Automated Manufacturing Technology; Mathematics; Printing Technology; Graphic Arts or Web Development. **Qualif.:** Applicants must be new non-resident high school or transfer students who have at least 14 transferable semester credits. **Criteria:** Awards are given based on academic merit.

Funds Avail.: No specific amount. **To Apply:** Applicants must accomplish a general application available in the website. **Deadline:** March 1 for Fall enrollment or November 1 for Spring enrollment.

4200 ■ Lewis-Clark State College Provost Scholarships *(Undergraduate/Scholarship)*

Purpose: To recognize promising Idaho High School seniors by providing educational assistance. **Focus:** General studies. **Qualif.:** Applicants must have a cumulative GPA of 3.0-3.49; must maintain a 3.0 semester GPA while completing at least 12 credits each semester; and must be at least tentatively admitted to the college and have their 7th semester high school transcripts on file with the Office of Admission. **Criteria:** Recipients will be selected based on academic merit.

Funds Avail.: $500. **To Apply:** Applicants must accomplish general application available in the website. **Deadline:** March 1. **Contact:** Financial Aid Office, LCSC, 500 8th Avenue, Lewiston, ID 83501, 800-933-5272 or 208-792-2224.

4201 ■ Lewis-Clark State College Transfer Scholarships *(Undergraduate/Scholarship)*

Purpose: To assist transfer students intending to complete a bachelor's degree at Lewis-Clark State College. **Focus:** General studies. **Qualif.:** Program is open to students who transfer from the following colleges: North Idaho College, Community Colleges in the Spokane area, College of Southern Idaho, Walla Walla Community College, and Treasure Valley Community College. Students must also be full-time, degree seeking students with a cumulative G.P.A. of 3.0 or higher. **Criteria:** Recipients will be selected based on financial need.

Funds Avail.: $500. **To Apply:** Applicants must submit a general application.

4202 ■ Lewis-Clark State College Valley Scholarships *(Undergraduate/Scholarship)*

Purpose: To encourage educational pursuits among less capable students by providing educational assistance. **Focus:** General studies. **Qualif.:** Program is open to promising Lewiston, Clarkston and Asotin High School seniors with a cumulative GPA of 3.0 and are planning to attend LCSC. **Criteria:** Priority is given to applicants with financial need.

Funds Avail.: No specific amount. **To Apply:** Applicants must submit a completed Application for Admission form, 7th semester transcripts and ACT/SAT scores. **Contact:** Financial Aid Office, LCSC, 500 8th Avenue, Lewiston, ID 83501. 800-933-5272 or 208-792-2224.

4203 ■ Lewiston Service League Memorial Scholarships *(Undergraduate/Scholarship)*

Purpose: To encourage educational pursuits by providing financial assistance. **Focus:** General studies. **Qualif.:** Applicants must be full-time students with at least 12 credit hours; must show academic promise or ability to satisfactorily complete college work with a minimum grade point average of 3.0. **Criteria:** Recipient will be selected based on financial need.

Funds Avail.: No specific amount. **To Apply:** Applicants must accomplish general application available at the website. **Contact:** Lewiston Service League, P.O. Box 1811, Lewiston, ID 83501.

4204 ■ Kaia Lynn Markwalter Endowed Scholarships *(Undergraduate/Scholarship)*

Purpose: To encourage educational pursuits among individuals who have experienced congenital heart defects. **Focus:** Business. **Qualif.:** Applicants must be students at Lewis-Clark State College who have been directly impacted by congenital heart defects. The applicant must also have a 3.0 cumulative G.P.A. and be enrolled in 12 credits each semester. **Criteria:** Recipients will be selected based on financial need.

Funds Avail.: No specific amount. **To Apply:** Applicants must submit a general application. **Deadline:** March 1.

4205 ■ Elizabeth McKissick Memorial Scholarships *(Undergraduate/Scholarship)*

Purpose: To provide educational support for young people who, for personal, financial, or other reasons discontinued their education, and for those who are in need of retraining who wish to return to school. **Focus:** General Studies. **Qualif.:** Applicants must be individuals who have graduated from or who attended Lewiston High School. Recipients of this scholarship must be at least 22 years of age at the time of application and must be classified as at least part-time students (taking 6 or more credits per semester). **Criteria:** Recipients will be selected based on financial need.

Funds Avail.: No specific amount. **To Apply:** Applicants

must accomplish a general application available in the website. **Deadline:** March 1.

4206 ■ Military Order of the Perpetual Heart Foundation Scholarships *(Undergraduate/Scholarship)*

Purpose: To provide educational assistance for students intending to pursue a career in Special Education. **Focus:** Special education. **Qualif.:** Program is open to students committed to pursue a teaching career in special education; must be accepted to the Teacher Education Program; must be enrolled for 12 credits; and must have a GPA of 3.25. **Criteria:** Recipients will be selected based on academic achievement.

Funds Avail.: $1,500. **To Apply:** Applicants must accomplish a general application available at the website. **Deadline:** March 1.

4207 ■ Robbie Miller Memorial Scholarships *(Undergraduate/Scholarship)*

Purpose: To encourage educational pursuits among non-traditional students. **Focus:** General studies. **Qualif.:** Program is open to non-traditional students who demonstrate a 2.5 cumulative GPA and must have a current standing of sophomore or above. **Criteria:** Priority is given to students with financial need.

Funds Avail.: No specific amount. **To Apply:** Applicants must accomplish a general application available in the website. **Deadline:** March 1.

4208 ■ Eugene Northrup Scholarships *(Undergraduate/Scholarship)*

Purpose: To provide financial assistance for individuals intending to pursue their educational goals. **Focus:** General studies. **Qualif.:** Program is open to graduating seniors of an area high school and who have a GPA of 3.0. **Criteria:** Recipients will be selected based on financial need.

Funds Avail.: $500. **Number Awarded:** 2. **To Apply:** Applicants must write a 500-word essay on Unionism. **Deadline:** March 1.

4209 ■ Odd Fellows Lodge No. 8 Endowed Scholarships *(Undergraduate/Scholarship)*

Purpose: To provide financial assistance for individuals intending to pursue their educational goals. **Focus:** General studies. **Qualif.:** Applicants must be full-time students carrying 12 or more credits per semester; must have a minimum cumulative GPA of 3.0. **Criteria:** Recipients will be selected based on financial need.

Funds Avail.: $250. **To Apply:** Applicants must accomplish a general application available at the website. **Deadline:** March 1.

4210 ■ Oregon Logging Conference Scholarships *(Undergraduate/Scholarship)*

Purpose: To provide financial assistance for worthy community college and university students in timber-related fields. **Focus:** General studies. **Qualif.:** Applicants must be students in timber-related fields who are enrolled in a community college or university. **Criteria:** Awards are given based on academic merit.

Funds Avail.: No specific amount. **To Apply:** Applicants must accomplish a general application available at the website.

4211 ■ Laura Ann Peck Memorial Endowed Scholarships *(Undergraduate/Scholarship)*

Purpose: To assist Lewis-Clark State College students who are majoring in mathematics. **Focus:** Natural Science. **Qualif.:** Applicants must have successfully completed three semesters of calculus; must have at least a 2.5 cumulative GPA; and must be registered as degree-seeking, full-time (12 credits) students. **Criteria:** Awards are given based on academic merit.

Funds Avail.: No specific amount. **To Apply:** Applicants must submit a general application.

4212 ■ Eleanor Perry Memorial Endowed Scholarships *(Undergraduate/Scholarship)*

Purpose: To offset the educationally-related expenses of Lewis-Clark State College students. **Focus:** General studies. **Qualif.:** Applicants must be full-time students; must have a minimum cumulative GPA of at least a 3.0. **Criteria:** Recipients will be selected based on financial need.

Funds Avail.: No specific amount. **To Apply:** Applicants must accomplish a general application available at the website. **Deadline:** March 1.

4213 ■ Kenneth Rogers Memorial Scholarships *(Undergraduate/Scholarship)*

Purpose: To provide educational assistance for eligible students who are enrolled full-time in the Auto Body Repair Program at LCSC. **Focus:** Automotive Technology. **Qualif.:** Applicants must have a GPA consistent with the minimum required for Admission and for progress toward completion of the Associates degree or certificate and must be enrolled full-time in the Auto Body Repair Program at LCSC. **Criteria:** Applicants will be evaluated based on financial need as determined by the Financial Aid.

Funds Avail.: No specific amount. **To Apply:** Applicants must accomplish a general application available at the website. **Deadline:** March 1.

4214 ■ Bill Sawyer Memorial Scholarships *(Undergraduate/Scholarship)*

Purpose: To offset the educationally-related expenses of Lewis-Clark State College students. **Focus:** Technical. **Qualif.:** Applicants must have a cumulative GPA consistent with the minimum required for admission and for progress toward their selected major. **Criteria:** Applicants will be given preference for their special needs such as physical handicap and learning disability.

Funds Avail.: No specific amount. **To Apply:** Applicants must accomplish a general application available at the website. **Deadline:** March 1.

4215 ■ Susan P. Schroeder Memorial Scholarships *(Undergraduate/Scholarship)*

Purpose: To inspire educational pursuits among less capable individuals by providing financial assistance. **Focus:** Natural Sciences; English Language and Literature. **Qualif.:** Applicants must be graduates of Idaho high school; must be majoring in Natural Sciences or English; and must have a cumulative 3.0 GPA. **Criteria:** Preference will be given to graduates from Nez Perce County.

Funds Avail.: No specific amount. **To Apply:** Applicants must accomplish a general application available at the website. **Deadline:** March 1.

4216 ■ Ethel Shinn Alumni-Vocational Scholarships *(Undergraduate/Scholarship)*

Purpose: To offset the educationally-related expenses of Lewis-Clark State College students. **Focus:** Technical. **Qualif.:** Applicants must be professional/technical students;

Awards are arranged alphabetically below their administering organizations

must have 12 or more credits per semester; and must have completed at least one full semester at LCSC with a cumulative GPA of at least 2.5. **Criteria:** Recipients will be selected based on financial need as determined by the Financial Aid Office.

Funds Avail.: No specific amount. **To Apply:** Applicants must accomplish a general application available at the website. **Deadline:** March 1.

4217 ■ State of Idaho Scholarships Category A *(Undergraduate/Scholarship)*

Purpose: To encourage educational pursuits among less capable students by providing educational assistance. **Focus:** General studies. **Qualif.:** Applicants must be outstanding Idaho High School graduates as evaluated through their rank in graduating class, ACT scores, and recommendations from high school officials. They must also intend to enroll in academic or vocational programs at eligible Idaho postsecondary educational institutions. **Criteria:** Awards are given based on academic merit.

Funds Avail.: $3,000. **To Apply:** Application instructions are available in the website. **Deadline:** January 15.

4218 ■ John Streiff Memorial Scholarships *(Undergraduate/Scholarship)*

Purpose: To provide funding for outstanding students who are majoring in social or political science at LCSC. **Focus:** Political science; Social Sciences. **Qualif.:** Program is open to senior or junior students who have a cumulative GPA of 3.0 and are actively involved in both campus and community. **Criteria:** Priority is given to students with financial need.

Funds Avail.: No specific amount. **To Apply:** Applicants must accomplish a general application available at the website. **Deadline:** March 1.

4219 ■ Tschudy Family Scholarships *(Undergraduate/Scholarship)*

Purpose: To encourage educational pursuits among less capable students by providing educational assistance. **Focus:** General studies. **Qualif.:** Applicants must be residents of Idaho; must be graduating Emmett High School seniors or have graduated within the last seven years from Emmett High School; and must be full-time academic students (at least 14 credit hours) at BSU, ISU, LCSC or UI. **Criteria:** Selection is based on academic merit and financial need.

Funds Avail.: $2,500. **To Apply:** Applicants must accomplish a general application available at the website.

4220 ■ Washington Reciprocity Out-of-State Scholarships *(Undergraduate/Scholarship)*

Purpose: To provide financial assistance for promising students in Washington. **Focus:** General studies. **Qualif.:** Applicants must maintain a 2.5 semester GPA, completing at least 12 credits per semester and registering for classes during advanced registration each semester. **Criteria:** Students who have at least a high school or transfer cumulative GPA of 3.0 will receive first consideration.

Funds Avail.: No specific amount. **To Apply:** Applicants must accomplish a general application available at the website.

4221 ■ Marvin Lewis Community Fund

Longworth Hall
700 W Pete Rose Way, Unit 37
Cincinnati, OH 45203
Ph: (513)381-5437
Fax: (513)381-5439
URL: http://www.marvinlewis.org

4222 ■ Marvin Lewis Scholarships *(Undergraduate/Scholarship)*

Purpose: To recognize and honor outstanding male and female student athletes. **Focus:** General studies. **Qualif.:** Applicant must be a resident of Greater Cincinnati, and attending college as a full-time student. **Criteria:** Awards are given based on merit.

Funds Avail.: No specific amount. **To Apply:** Applicants must submit a completed scholarship application form along with a copy of recent transcript; Expected Family Contribution (EFC) from Student Aid Report (SAR) in the FAFSA; a copy of Financial Aid Award Letter from their chosen college; a 1000-word essay; and evidence of a varsity letter. Faxed applications will not be considered. **Deadline:** April 30.

Remarks: In partnership with The Cincinnati Scholarship Foundation.

4223 ■ Lexington Community Foundation

607 Washington St.
PO Box 422
Lexington, NE 68850
Ph: (308)324-6704
E-mail: lexfoundation@alltel.net
URL: http://www.lexfoundation.org

4224 ■ Lexington Alumni Scholarships *(Undergraduate/Scholarship)*

Purpose: To promote community philanthropy by working with individuals, families and organizations to develop tailored giving plans that effectively meet the charitable goals and financial circumstances. **Focus:** General studies. **Qualif.:** Applicants must be graduating senior students who rank in the upper 1/2 of their class. **Criteria:** Recipients are selected based on qualities of good character and leadership, academic achievement, financial need and participation in extracurriculars and community service.

Funds Avail.: $750. **To Apply:** Applicants must submit a completed application form; must provide three letters of recommendation and must attach a recent photo.

4225 ■ Lexington Community Foundation Annual Scholarships *(Undergraduate/Scholarship)*

Purpose: To promote community philanthropy by working with individuals, families and organizations to develop tailored giving plans that effectively meet the charitable goals and financial circumstances. **Focus:** General studies. **Qualif.:** Applicants must be graduating senior students who rank in the upper 1/3 of their class. **Criteria:** Recipients are selected based on qualities of good character and leadership, academic achievement, financial need and participation in extracurriculars and community service.

Funds Avail.: $2,000. **To Apply:** Applicants must submit a completed application form; must provide three letters of recommendation and must attach a recent photo.

4226 ■ Lexington Community Foundation/CCC Scholarships *(Undergraduate/Scholarship)*

Purpose: To promote community philanthropy by working with individuals, families and organizations to develop

Awards are arranged alphabetically below their administering organizations

tailored giving plans that effectively meet the charitable goals and financial circumstances. **Focus:** General studies. **Qualif.:** Applicants must be graduating senior students who rank in the upper 1/2 of their class. **Criteria:** Recipients are selected based on qualities of good character and leadership, academic achievement, financial need and participation in extracurriculars and community service.

Funds Avail.: $600. **To Apply:** Applicants must submit a completed application form; must provide three letters of recommendation and must attach a recent photo.

4227 ■ Lexington Teacher Appreciation Scholarships *(Professional Development/Scholarship)*

Purpose: To promote community philanthropy by working with individuals, families and organizations to develop tailored giving plans that effectively meet the charitable goals and financial circumstances. **Focus:** General studies. **Qualif.:** Applicants must be Lexington Public High School professionals planning to attend an accredited college for continuing education and have signed a contract for the upcoming school year. **Criteria:** Recipients are selected based on qualities of good character and leadership, academic achievement, financial need and participation in extracurriculars and community service.

Funds Avail.: $250. **To Apply:** Applicants must submit a completed application form. **Deadline:** May 15. **Contact:** PO Box 422, Lexington, NE 68850.

4228 ■ Edsel Newman Scholarship *(Undergraduate/Scholarship)*

Purpose: To promote community philanthropy by working with individuals, families and organizations to develop tailored giving plans that effectively meet the charitable goals and financial circumstances. **Focus:** Engineering; Computer and information sciences. **Qualif.:** Applicants must be graduating seniors who are planning to pursue a career in the field of engineering an/or computer science; must have ranked in the upper 1/3 of their class and must be U.S. citizens. **Criteria:** Recipients are selected based on qualities of good character and leadership, academic achievement, financial need and participation in extracurriculars and community service.

Funds Avail.: $2,000. **To Apply:** Applicants must submit a completed application form; must provide three letters of recommendation and must attach a recent photo.

4229 ■ Norall Scholarships Trust *(Undergraduate/Scholarship)*

Purpose: To promote community philanthropy by working with individuals, families and organizations to develop tailored giving plans that effectively meet the charitable goals and financial circumstances. **Focus:** General studies. **Qualif.:** Applicants must be past graduates of high school in Dawson who are enrolled in a US. college. **Criteria:** Recipients are selected based on goal commitment, academic success, recommendations, financial need and programs of study.

Funds Avail.: No specific amount. **To Apply:** Applicants must complete the application form, a copy of Dawson County High School transcript for first-time applicant, academic transcript for post-secondary education and three personal references. **Deadline:** March 1. **Contact:** PO Box 890 Lexington, NE 68850.

4230 ■ Francelene Skinner Memorial Scholarship *(Undergraduate/Scholarship)*

Purpose: To promote community philanthropy by working with individuals, families and organizations to develop tailored giving plans that effectively meet the charitable goals and financial circumstances. **Focus:** General studies. **Qualif.:** Applicants must be graduating seniors who rank in the upper 1/3 of their class and must be U.S. citizens. **Criteria:** Recipients are selected based on qualities of good character and leadership, academic achievement, financial need and participation in extracurriculars and community service.

Funds Avail.: $500. **To Apply:** Applicants must submit a completed application form; must provide three letters of recommendation and must attach a recent photo.

4231 ■ Mark and Vera Turner Memorial Scholarship *(Undergraduate/Scholarship)*

Purpose: To promote community philanthropy by working with individuals, families and organizations to develop tailored giving plans that effectively meet the charitable goals and financial circumstances. **Focus:** General studies. **Qualif.:** Applicants must be graduating senior students who rank in the upper 1/2 of the class; must be graduating Lexington High School seniors who enroll in a university, college, community college or trade school within the state of Nebraska. **Criteria:** Recipients are selected based on qualities of good character and leadership, academic achievement, financial need and participation in extracurriculars and community service.

Funds Avail.: $1,000. **To Apply:** Applicants must submit a completed application form; must provide three letters of recommendation and must attach a recent photo.

4232 ■ Robert R. Wade Scholarship *(Undergraduate/Scholarship)*

Purpose: To promote community philanthropy by working with individuals, families and organizations to develop tailored giving plans that effectively meet the charitable goals and financial circumstances. **Focus:** General studies. **Qualif.:** Applicants must be graduating senior students who rank in the upper 1/2 of the class; must be U.S. citizens and must be graduating Lexington High School seniors who enroll in a public university, college, community college or trade school within the state of Nebraska. **Criteria:** Recipients are selected based on qualities of good character and leadership, academic achievement, financial need and participation in extracurriculars and community service.

Funds Avail.: $1,000. **To Apply:** Applicants must submit a completed application form; must provide three letters of recommendation and must attach a recent photo.

4233 ■ The Liberace Museum and Foundation

1775 E Tropicana Ave.
Las Vegas, NV 89119-6529
Ph: (702)798-5595
E-mail: info@liberace.org
URL: http://www.liberace.org

4234 ■ Liberace Scholarship Fund *(Undergraduate/Scholarship)*

Purpose: To help talented students pursue careers in the arts by providing financial assistance for them. **Focus:** Arts. **Qualif.:** Applicants must be from accredited institutions of higher learning offering degrees in either the creative or performing arts and local arts organizations. **Criteria:** Preference will be given to leading programs and their disciplines; institutions matching the Liberace Foundation

Awards are arranged alphabetically below their administering organizations

grant; institutions applying with a continuing "Liberace Scholar"; institutions with ensembles bearing the Liberace name.

Funds Avail.: No specific amount. **To Apply:** Applicants must use and sign the official foundation application form; must answer all application questions; supplemental sheets to the application must be attached; and attach a copy of school year calendar for next year.

4235 ■ Library and Information Technology Association

50 E Huron St.
Chicago, IL 60611-2795
Ph: (312)280-4267
Fax: (312)280-3257
Free: 800-545-2433
E-mail: lita@ala.org
URL: http://www.lita.org

4236 ■ Christian Larew Memorial Scholarships
(Graduate/Scholarship)

Purpose: To encourage the entry of qualified persons into the library and information technology field. **Focus:** Information science and technology; Library and archival sciences. **Qualif.:** Candidates must not have earned more than 12 hours towards a Master of Library Science degree from an American Library Association (ALA) Accredited MLS program. **Criteria:** When all other criteria are equal, recipients will be selected based on financial need.

Funds Avail.: $3,000. **Number Awarded:** 1. **To Apply:** Applicants must submit an application form; a statement indicating the nature of their library experience; letters of reference; transcripts. **Deadline:** March 1.

4237 ■ LITA and LSSI Minority Scholarships
(Graduate/Scholarship)

Purpose: To encourage the entry of qualified persons into the library and automation field. **Focus:** Library and archival sciences. **Qualif.:** Applicants must be U.S. or Canadian citizens and must be members of the following minority groups: American Indian or Alaskan Native, Asian or Pacific Islander, African-American or Hispanic. Candidates must not have earned more than 12 hours towards a Master of Library Science degree from an American Library Association MLS program. **Criteria:** When all other criteria are equal, recipients will be selected based on financial need.

Funds Avail.: $2,500. **Number Awarded:** 1. **To Apply:** Applicants must submit an application form; a statement indicating the nature of their library experience; letters of reference; transcripts. **Deadline:** March 1.

4238 ■ LITA/OCLC Minority Scholarships
(Graduate/Scholarship)

Purpose: To encourage the entry of qualified persons into the library and automation field. **Focus:** Library and archival sciences. **Qualif.:** Applicants must be U.S. or Canadian citizens and must be members of the following minority groups: American Indian or Alaskan Native, Asian or Pacific Islander, African-American or Hispanic. Candidates must not have earned more than 12 hours towards a Master of Library Science degree from an American Library Association MLS program. **Criteria:** When all other criteria are equal, recipients will be selected based on financial need.

Funds Avail.: $3,000. **Number Awarded:** 1. **To Apply:** Applicants must submit an application form; a statement indicating the nature of their library experience; letters of reference; transcripts. **Deadline:** March 1.

4239 ■ Life and Health Insurance Foundation for Education

1655 N Fort Myer Dr., Ste. 610
Arlington, VA 22209
Fax: (202)464-5011
Free: 888-LIF-E777
E-mail: info@lifehappens.org
URL: http://www.lifehappens.org

4240 ■ LIFE Lessons Scholarships Program
(Undergraduate/Scholarship)

Purpose: To help deserving young people realize their dream of achieving a college education. **Focus:** General Studies. **Qualif.:** Applicants must be: college students and college-bound high school seniors; legal residents of the fifty United States and the District of Columbia; between 17 and 24 years of age. Applicant must have experienced the death of a parent or legal guardian and be currently enrolled in or accepted to a college, university or trade school within the fifty United States or District of Columbia. A minor should have a parent's or legal guardian's permission to enter. **Criteria:** Selection will be based on criteria.

Funds Avail.: $25,000. **To Apply:** Applicants who qualify must submit essays or videos about how the death of a parent or guardian impacted their lives. **Deadline:** March. **Contact:** Life and Health Insurance Foundation for Education at the above address (see entry 4239).

4241 ■ Lighthouse International

111 E 59th St.
New York, NY 10022-1202
Ph: (212)821-9200
Fax: (212)821-9707
Free: 800-829-0500
E-mail: info@lighthouse.org
URL: http://www.lighthouse.org

4242 ■ Christine H. Eide Memorial Scholarships
(Graduate, Undergraduate/Scholarship)

Purpose: To provide educational support to visually impaired students. **Focus:** General studies. **Qualif.:** Applicant must be a full-time undergraduate or graduate college student in an accredited college/university; and must be impaired visually. **Criteria:** Awards are given based on academic merit and other achievements.

Funds Avail.: A maximum of $1,000. **To Apply:** Application form is available at the website. Applicants must complete and send the application to: Dr. Cynthia Stuen, Senior Vice President, Policy and Professional Affairs, New York Lighthouse Vision Rehabilitation Services 111 East 59th Street New York, NY 10022-1202. **Deadline:** September for the fall semester and January for the spring semester. **Contact:** Gina Obando, gobando@lighthouse.org.

4243 ■ Lighthouse International Scholarships - College-bound Awards *(High School/Scholarship)*

Purpose: To provide support to visually impaired students to continue their education to college. **Focus:** General studies. **Qualif.:** Applicant must be a senior or high school

Awards are arranged alphabetically below their administering organizations

graduate; legally blind; a U.S. citizen; not related to any Lighthouse employees and not a previous winners of program. **Criteria:** Awards are given based on academic merit and other achievements.

Funds Avail.: $5,000. **To Apply:** Applicant must send an application form (can be downloaded at the website); an essay; proof of the applicant's visual condition; transcripts; and two letters of recommendation. All materials must send thru email at sca@lighthouse.org. **Deadline:** February. **Contact:** sca@lighthouse.org.

4244 ■ Lighthouse International Scholarships - Graduate Awards *(Graduate/Scholarship)*

Purpose: To provide support to visually impaired who wants to pursue a graduate -level program. **Focus:** General studies. **Qualif.:** Applicant must be a college senior or college graduate; must be legally blind; a U.S. citizen; not related to any Lighthouse employees and not a previous winner of the program. **Criteria:** Awards are given based on academic merit and other achievements.

Funds Avail.: $5,000. **To Apply:** Applicant must send an application form (can be downloaded at the website); an essay; proof of the applicant's visual condition; transcripts; and two letters of recommendation. All materials must send thru email at sca@lighthouse.org. **Deadline:** February.

4245 ■ Lighthouse International Scholarships - Undergraduate Awards *(Undergraduate/Scholarship)*

Purpose: To provide support to visually impaired students to continue their education. **Focus:** General studies. **Qualif.:** Applicant must be a college student; legally blind; a U.S. citizen; not related to Lighthouse employees and not a previous winner of the program. **Criteria:** Awards are given based on academic merit and other achievements.

Funds Avail.: $5,000. **To Apply:** Applicant must send an application form (can be downloaded at the website); an essay; proof of the applicant's visual condition; transcripts; and two letters of recommendation. **Deadline:** February.

4246 ■ LIN Television Corporation

300 Wavy St.
Portsmouth, VA 23704
Ph: (757)673-5314
Fax: (757)673-5300
E-mail: rosetta.rolan@lintv.com
URL: http://www.lintv.com

4247 ■ LIN Television Corporation Minority Scholarships and Training Program *(Undergraduate/Scholarship)*

Purpose: To help educate and train outstanding minority candidates who seek to enter the television broadcast field. **Focus:** Broadcasting; Journalism. **Qualif.:** Applicants must be citizens of the United States and of non-white origin; must be sophomores or have completed sufficient semester hours or similar educational units to be within two years of receiving an undergraduate bachelor's degree; must have a minimum of 3.0 cumulative GPA and with declared major in journalism, broadcast journalism, business or marketing at an accredited university or college. **Criteria:** Applicants are evaluated based on academic performance and personal attributes.

Funds Avail.: $20,000. **To Apply:** Applicants must submit completed application form; list of organizations and activities in which they have held leadership position where nature of involvement must be briefly described; three references, up to two faculty members (university or secondary) and one or two other references that will recommend their work; list of personal achievements and honors; description of career goals in 50 words or less; and, short essay about themselves (up to 500 words, double-spaced). **Deadline:** March 15.

4248 ■ Lloydminster Region Health Foundation

218 5704-44 St.
Lloydminster, AB, Canada T9V 2A1
Ph: (306)820-6161
Fax: (780)875-9172
URL: http://www.lrhf.ca

4249 ■ Goodfellow Nursing Scholarships *(Undergraduate/Scholarship)*

Purpose: To support nursing students to complete their studies and to assist the future staffing needs of nursing professionals in Lloydminster. **Focus:** Nursing. **Qualif.:** Applicant must be an individual studying Nursing at a Canadian recognized university or post-secondary institution; must be willing to work in Lloydminster at a facility or program run by the Prairie North Health Region; must be a permanent resident in the Lloydminster region; must have good academic ability; must demonstrate community leadership and volunteering. **Criteria:** Scholarship is awarded through a selection committee appointed by the Board of Directors.

Funds Avail.: $2,000. **Number Awarded:** 5. **To Apply:** Applicant must submit a letter of reference from an accredited instructor together with the application form to Lloydminster Region Health Foundation, 3820-43 Ave., Lloydminster, SK S9V 1Y5. **Deadline:** July 31.

Remarks: Scholarship was established in memory of Miss Kitty Goodfellow, a long-time resident of Lloydminster.

4250 ■ Goodfellow Professional Development Fund *(Professional Development/Scholarship)*

Purpose: To support continuing education to advance job knowledge, skills and qualification by funding a major course of study. **Focus:** Nursing. **Qualif.:** Applicant must be a nursing full-time or permanent part-time staff member employed at Lloydminster Hospital or an affiliated program. **Criteria:** Scholarship is awarded through a selection committee made up of one member of the Board of Directors and up to four nurses. Priority will be given to employees that demonstrate a definite course of study.

Funds Avail.: $10,000. **To Apply:** Applicant must submit a letter of reference from an accredited instructor together with the application form to Lloydminster Region Health Foundation, 3820-43 Ave., Lloydminster, SK S9V 1Y5. **Deadline:** July 31.

Remarks: Scholarship was established in memory of Miss Kitty Goodfellow, a long-time resident of Lloydminster.

4251 ■ George Phillips Scholarships *(Undergraduate/Scholarship)*

Purpose: To provide financial assistant to qualified individuals who want to pursue their education. **Focus:** Health care services. **Qualif.:** Applicant must be an individual studying full-time in a healthcare field at an accredited college or university; must demonstrate commitment and dedication to his/her work/education; must be a permanent resident in the Llyodminster area; must have good academic ability **Criteria:** Priority will be given to healthcare professionals that will benefit the hospital and healthcare providers within the region and to students in the second half of their program.

Funds Avail.: $1,000. **Number Awarded:** 1. **To Apply:** Applicant must submit a letter of reference from an accredited instructor together with the application form to Lloydminster Region Health Foundation, 3820-43 Ave., Lloydminster, SK S9V 1Y5. **Deadline:** July 31.

Remarks: Scholarship was created to honor George's remarkable leadership, loyalty, and forward-thinking contributions while serving on the Board of Directors.

4252 ■ Pat Redden Memorial Scholarships
(Undergraduate/Scholarship)

Purpose: To support nursing students to complete their studies and to assist in meeting future staffing needs of Lloydminster. **Focus:** Nursing. **Qualif.:** Applicant must be a Nursing student at a Canadian recognized university or post-secondary institution; must be enrolled and have successfully completed 50% of a minimum two-year fully-accredited program in nursing leading to a RN designation. Applicant must be a permanent resident in the Lloydminster region; must have good academic ability; must demonstrate community leadership and volunteering. **Criteria:** Priority will be given to students willing to work in Lloydminster at a facility or program run by Prairie North Health Region.

Funds Avail.: $5,000. **To Apply:** Applicant must submit a letter of reference from an accredited instructor together with the application to Lloydminster Region Health Foundation, 3820-43 Ave., Lloydminster, SK S9V 1Y5. **Deadline:** July 31.

Remarks: Pat Redden was a pillar for both Hillmond and Lloydminster communities and served for many years as a registered nurse at the Lloydminster Hospital.

4253 ■ Ken Stanley Memorial Scholarships
(Undergraduate/Scholarship)

Purpose: To provide financial assistant to qualified individual who wants to pursue their education. **Focus:** Health care services. **Qualif.:** Applicant must be an individual studying full-time in a healthcare field at an accredited college or university; must demonstrate commitment and dedication to his/her work/education; must be a permanent resident in the Llyodminster area; must have good academic ability **Criteria:** Priority will be given to healthcare occupations that will benefit the hospital and healthcare providers within the region and to students in the second half of their program.

Funds Avail.: $1,000. **Number Awarded:** 1. **To Apply:** Applicant must submit a letter of reference from an accredited instructor together with the application form to Lloydminster Region Health Foundation, 3820-43 Ave., Lloydminster, SK S9V 1Y5. **Deadline:** July 31.

Remarks: Scholarship was established in honor of Ken Stanley a long-time board member of the Lloydminster Hospital and the Hospital Region Health Foundation.

4254 ■ LogiCore Corporation

1015 Henderson Rd. NW
Huntsville, AL 35816
Ph: (256)533-5789
Fax: (256)533-5785
E-mail: hr@logicorehsv.com
URL: http://www.logicorehsv.com

4255 ■ Miranda Bouldin General Scholarships
(Undergraduate/Scholarship)

Purpose: To assist deserving young people of Madison County, Madison City, Huntsville City, Lawrence County and Limestone County. **Focus:** General studies. **Qualif.:** Applicants must be U.S. citizens; graduating seniors from Madison County schools, Madison City schools, Huntsville City schools, Lawrence County schools, or Limestone County schools; have made a 4-year commitment to attend college or university in Alabama; and have cumulative GPA of 3.00 or higher and scored at least 21 on the ACT or 990 on the SAT. **Criteria:** Awards are given based on submitted essay.

Funds Avail.: $1,500. **Number Awarded:** 4. **To Apply:** Applicants must write an essay; must submit application form, and three letters of recommendation. A copy of transcript must be mailed directly from the application's school. **Deadline:** April 20.

Remarks: Founded in 2006 by Miranda Bouldin, President and CEO of LogiCore Corporation.

4256 ■ Louisiana Environmental Health Association

PO Box 2661
Baton Rouge, LA 70821
Ph: (225)219-3242
Fax: (225)219-3310
E-mail: james.miller@la.gov
URL: http://www.leha.net

4257 ■ Frank L. Dautriel Memorial Scholarships (Graduate) *(Graduate/Scholarship)*

Purpose: To encourage an outstanding graduate student to pursue their education. **Focus:** Environmental science; Environmental technology; Public health. **Qualif.:** Applicant must be enrolled as a full-time student in an environmental health, environmental science, environmental engineering, public health, or related degree program; must be a Louisiana resident; must have maintained a GPA of 2.75 or higher on a 4.0 point rating system and have a record of good conduct supported by official transcript; must demonstrate a need for the scholarships. **Criteria:** Application form and requirements will be reviewed by the LEHA Awards Committee.

Funds Avail.: $1,000. **To Apply:** Application forms are available online and must be sent to Louisiana Environmental Health Association, PO Box 2661, Baton Rouge, LA 70821. **Deadline:** October 31.

4258 ■ Frank L. Dautriel Memorial Scholarships (Undergraduate) *(Undergraduate/Scholarship)*

Purpose: To encourage an outstanding undergraduate student to pursue their education. **Focus:** Environmental science; Environmental technology; Public health. **Qualif.:** Applicant must be enrolled as a full-time student in an environmental health, environmental science, environmental engineering, or public health related degree program at an accredited university; must be a Louisiana resident; must have maintained an overall 2.75 or higher on a 4.0 point rating system and have a record of good conduct supported by official transcript; must demonstrate a need for a scholarship. **Criteria:** Selection of applicants will be

Awards are arranged alphabetically below their administering organizations

based on the criteria of LEHA awards Committee.

Funds Avail.: $1,000. **To Apply:** Application forms are available online and must be sent to Louisiana Environmental Health Association, PO Box 2661, Baton Rouge, LA 70821. **Deadline:** October 31.

4259 ■ Luso-American Education Foundation

PO Box 2967
Dublin, CA 94568
Ph: (925)828-3883
Fax: (925)828-3883
E-mail: odom@luso-american.org

4260 ■ John L. Avila Memorial Scholarships
(Professional Development/Scholarship)

Purpose: To provide financial assistance to qualified individuals pursuing continuing education. **Focus:** General studies. **Qualif.:** Applicant must be a Luso-American Fraternal Federation - Luso-American Insurance Society's 20-30s associates member in good standing; 18-39 years old; enrolled in an accredited educational program and a policy holder. **Criteria:** Scholarship recipients will be selected based on the jury's review of the application materials.

Funds Avail.: $1,500. **Number Awarded:** 1. **To Apply:** Applicants must request for the application form available on the Foundation's office. Submit the completed application form together with an official transcript and three letters of recommendation to the Foundation's office. **Deadline:** March 1.

4261 ■ Luso-American Education Foundation C-1 General Scholarships *(Undergraduate/ Scholarship)*

Purpose: To provide financial assistance to qualified students to further their education. **Focus:** Business. **Qualif.:** Applicant must be a California resident; enrolled in trade business school, junior or four-year college/university; have minimum of 3.5 GPA; a Portuguese descent; or currently taking Portuguese language classes with 3.0 GPA. **Criteria:** Scholarship recipients will be selected based on the jury's review of the application materials.

Funds Avail.: $1,500. **To Apply:** Applicants must submit a completed application form; an official transcript; SAT or ACT scores; and two letters of recommendation. **Deadline:** March 1.

4262 ■ Luso-American Education Foundation G-1 Grants *(Professional Development/Grant)*

Purpose: To promote the Portuguese language and culture. **Focus:** Portuguese studies. **Qualif.:** Applicants must be a California resident. **Criteria:** Recipient will be selected based on the Grant Committee's review of the application materials.

Funds Avail.: $500. **Number Awarded:** 1. **To Apply:** Applicants must submit a statement of background and need; description of the research project (if applicable); official transcripts; and three letters of recommendation. **Deadline:** March 1.

4263 ■ Luso-American Education Foundation G-2 Grants *(Professional Development/Grant)*

Purpose: To promote the Portuguese language and culture. **Focus:** Portuguese studies. **Qualif.:** Applicants must be California residents; must be of Portuguese descent or working in an educational setting with Portuguese adults or children; enrolled in a college or university not offering Portuguese language or literature; have a desire to study the language/culture of Portuguese. **Criteria:** Recipient will be selected based on the Grant Committee's review of the application materials.

Funds Avail.: $750. **Number Awarded:** 1. **To Apply:** Applicants must submit statement of background and need; an essay (written in English and Portuguese) on Portuguese history or literature or both; official transcript; list of past teaching experiences and three letters of recommendation. **Deadline:** March 1.

4264 ■ Luso-American Education Foundation G-3 Grants *(Postgraduate/Grant)*

Purpose: To provide support to improve the professional career of Portuguese teachers. **Focus:** Portuguese studies. **Qualif.:** Applicants must be California residents; be teachers of Portuguese in grades K-12; have B.A. or higher degree in Portuguese studies. **Criteria:** Recipient will be selected based on the Grant Committee's review of the application materials.

Funds Avail.: $1,500. **Number Awarded:** 1. **To Apply:** Applicants must submit a statement of background and need (written in English and Portuguese); an essay (minimum of 2 pages) about Portuguese history; transcript; list of past teaching experiences and three letters of recommendation. **Deadline:** March 1.

4265 ■ Luso-American Fraternal Federation B-2 Scholarships *(Postgraduate/Scholarship)*

Purpose: To provide financial assistance to qualified individuals pursuing continuing education. **Focus:** General studies. **Qualif.:** Applicant must be a Luso-American Fraternal Federation Luso-American Insurance Society's 20-30s associates member in good standing; 18-39 years old; in need of financial aid to continue or re-enter a postgraduate program. **Criteria:** Scholarship recipients will be selected based on the jury's review of the application materials.

Funds Avail.: $800. **Number Awarded:** 1. **To Apply:** Applicants must request for the application form available on the Foundation's office. Submit the completed application form together with an official transcript and three letters of recommendation to the Foundation's office. **Deadline:** March 1.

4266 ■ Luso-American Fraternal Federation B-3 Scholarships *(All/Scholarship)*

Purpose: To provide financial assistance to qualified individuals pursuing continuing education. **Focus:** General studies. **Qualif.:** Applicant must be a Luso-American Fraternal Federation Luso-American Insurance Society's 20-30s associates member in good standing; 18-39 years old; in need of financial assistance to attend a vocational school program or a specialty job training program. **Criteria:** Scholarship recipients will be selected based on the jury's review of the application materials.

Funds Avail.: $500. **Number Awarded:** 1. **To Apply:** Applicants must request for the application form available on the Foundation's office. Submit the completed application form together with an official transcript and three letters of recommendation to the Foundation's office. **Deadline:** March 1.

4267 ■ Luso-American Fraternal Federation B-4 Scholarships *(All/Scholarship)*

Purpose: To provide financial assistance to qualified individuals pursuing continuing education. **Focus:** General studies. **Qualif.:** Applicant must be a Luso-American Fraternal Federation Luso-American Insurance Society's 20-30s associates member in good standing; 18-39 years old; in need of financial assistance to make a career change. **Criteria:** Scholarship recipients will be selected based on the jury's review of the application materials.

Funds Avail.: $500. **Number Awarded:** 1. **To Apply:** Applicants must request for the application form available at the Foundation's office. Submit the completed application form together with an official transcript and three letters of recommendation to the Foundation's office. **Deadline:** March 1.

4268 ■ Antonio Mattos Memorial Scholarships *(Undergraduate/Scholarship)*

Purpose: To provide financial assistance to qualified students to further their education. **Focus:** General studies. **Qualif.:** Applicants must be a high school graduating senior or enrolled in a four-year college or university; must have a GPA of 3.5 or higher; a Sacramento or East Bay area (CA) resident; member of the Luso-American Fraternal Federation - Luso-American Life Insurance Society and policy holder in good standing for a minimum of 2 years; excel in a sport during the 4 high school years; and active in the Fraternal Community. **Criteria:** Scholarship recipients will be selected based on the jury's review of the application materials.

Funds Avail.: $1,000. **Number Awarded:** 1. **To Apply:** Applicants must request for the application form available on the Foundation's office. Submit the completed application form together with an official transcript and three letters of recommendation to the Foundation's office. **Deadline:** March 1.

4269 ■ Joaquin Pereira Memorial Scholarships *(Undergraduate/Scholarship)*

Purpose: To provide financial assistance to qualified students to further their education. **Focus:** General studies. **Qualif.:** Applicant must be a high school graduating senior or enrolled in a four-year college or university; must have a GPA of 3.5 or higher; a member of the Luso-American Fraternal Federation - Luso-American Life Insurance Society and policy holder in good standing for a minimum of 2 years. **Criteria:** Scholarship recipients will be selected based on the jury's review of the application materials.

Funds Avail.: $1,000. **Number Awarded:** 1. **To Apply:** Applicants must request for the application form available on the Foundation's office. Submit the completed application form together with an official transcript and three letters of recommendation to the Foundation's office. **Deadline:** March 1.

4270 ■ Ryan "Munchie" Taylor Memorial Scholarships *(Undergraduate/Scholarship)*

Purpose: To provide financial assistance to qualified students who wish to further their education. **Focus:** General studies. **Qualif.:** Applicants must be a high school graduating senior or enrolled in a four-year college or university; must have a GPA of 3.5 or higher; must have held local or state youth office; a Stanislaus County (CA) resident; member of the Luso-American Fraternal Federation - Luso-American Life Insurance Society and policy holder in good standing for a minimum of 2 years; must participated in Fraternal Youth activities for 2 or more years or performed at State Conventions. **Criteria:** Scholarship recipients will be selected based on the jury's review of the application materials.

Funds Avail.: $1,000. **Number Awarded:** 1. **To Apply:** Applicants must request for the application form available on the Foundation's office. Submit the completed application form together with an official transcript and three letters of recommendation to the Foundation's office. **Deadline:** March 1.

4271 ■ Macomb County Bar Foundation

40 N Main St., Ste. 435
Mount Clemens, MI 48043
Ph: (586)468-2940
Fax: (586)468-6926
E-mail: mcba@macombbar.org
URL: http://www.macombbar.org

4272 ■ Philip F. Greco Memorial Scholarships *(Undergraduate/Scholarship)*

Purpose: To provide financial assistance for second or third year law students enrolled in evening classes at the University of Detroit Mercy Law School. **Focus:** Law. **Qualif.:** Applicants must be enrolled as law degree candidates in evening classes at the University of Detroit Marcy Law School. They must demonstrate a need for financial assistance, good academic standing (2.5 GPA or above), and the ability to achieve success as a lawyer. **Criteria:** Selection will be based on the committee's criteria.

Funds Avail.: $3,000. **To Apply:** Applications can be downloaded online. The application packet must include: completed application; candidates most recent law school transcript; resume; three letters of recommendation; a personal statement in which the candidate discusses his/her inertness in law, reason for applying for scholarship, career goals and any other pertinent information he/she would like the Scholarship Committee to know. **Deadline:** January 25. **Contact:** Macomb County Bar Foundation at the above address (see entry 4271).

4273 ■ Trustees College Scholarships *(Undergraduate/Scholarship)*

Purpose: To award scholarships for students enrolled in Macomb County Community College who have been affected by Michigan's economic circumstances. **Focus:** Law. **Qualif.:** Applicants for the Macomb County Bar Foundation Trustees Scholarship must be enrolled or accepted for enrollment at Macomb Community College at least part-time (six credit hours). **Criteria:** Preference is given to students who are returning to school due to job loss resulting from downsizing, restructuring, lay-off or corporate buyout. Preference is also given to students who seek to adjust skills by enrolling in a law-related education program.

Funds Avail.: $2,500 (Award is for tuition, fees and other educational expenses.) **To Apply:** Applicants may download application online. The application packet must include: completed application; brief summary of applicant's educational and career goals; resume; three letters of recommendation; a personal statement in which the candidate discuss their interest in law, reason for applying for scholarship, career goals and any other pertinent information he/she would like the Scholarship Committee to know about. **Deadline:** January 25. **Contact:** Macomb

Awards are arranged alphabetically below their administering organizations

County Bar Foundation at the above address (see entry 4271).

4274 ■ Trustees Law School Scholarships
(Undergraduate/Scholarship)

Purpose: To award scholarships for pursuits in the study of law. **Focus:** Law. **Qualif.:** Applicants must be second or third year law students who demonstrate a commitment to serve or contribute to the Macomb County legal community; must demonstrate a need for financial assistance; and must have high scholastic achievement. Applicants must be enrolled as a law degree candidate at one of the following Michigan Law Schools: Thomas M. Cooley, Michigan State University, University of Michigan, University of Detroit Mercy, Wayne State University. **Criteria:** Selection will be based on the committee's criteria.

Funds Avail.: $3,000. **To Apply:** Applicants may download application online. The application packet must include: complete application; candidate's undergraduate college transcript; candidate's most recent law school transcript; resume; three letters of recommendation; a personal statement in which the candidate discusses his/her interest in law, reason for applying for scholarship, career goals and any other pertinent information he/she would like the Scholarship Committee to know about. **Deadline:** January 25. **Contact:** Macomb County Bar Foundation at the above address (see entry 4271).

4275 ■ Maine Chapter of the International Association of Arson Investigators

PO Box 1101
Auburn, ME 04211-1101
E-mail: rshepar1@maine.rr.com
URL: http://www.maineiaai.com

4276 ■ Joseph C. Menezes Scholarships
(Undergraduate/Scholarship)

Purpose: To provide financial support for individuals pursuing studies in the field of Fire Science Degree programs. **Focus:** Fires and fire prevention. **Qualif.:** Applicants must be student enrolled in Fire Science Degree programs and must desire becoming involved in fire investigation. **Criteria:** Selection is based on merit.

Funds Avail.: No specific amount. **To Apply:** Applicants must submit a completed application form along with the supporting documents. **Contact:** Rick Shepard.

4277 ■ Manufacturing Jewelers and Association of America

45 Royal Little Dr.
Providence, RI 02904
Ph: (401)274-3840
Fax: (401)274-0265
Free: 800-444-6572
E-mail: info@mjsa.org
URL: http://www.mjsa.org

4278 ■ MJSA Education Foundation Scholarship Fund *(Undergraduate/Scholarship)*

Purpose: To financially support students enrolled in jewelry-related field. **Focus:** Design. **Qualif.:** Applicant must be a U.S. citizen; must be enrolled in a jewelry program; pursuing a career in the jewelry industry; and with demonstrated financial need. **Criteria:** Applicants are assessed based on the course of study, academics, career plans, recommendations, and industry experience.

Funds Avail.: $250-$2,000. **To Apply:** Applicant must complete the application form available at the website; must submit a copy of financial aid award letter; official transcript; an essay; and a letter of recommendation. Forward completed application and supporting documents in one envelope to: Libby Monahan MJSA Scholarship The Rhode Island Foundation One Union Station Providence, RI 02903. **Deadline:** June 1.

4279 ■ Stephen T. Marchello Scholarship Foundation

1170 E Long Pl.
Centennial, CO 80122
Ph: (303)886-5018
E-mail: fmarchello@earthlink.net
URL: http://www.stmfoundation.org

4280 ■ Stephen T. Marchello Scholarships
(Undergraduate/Scholarship)

Purpose: To support the education of students who have a history of childhood cancer. **Focus:** General studies. **Qualif.:** Applicant must be a high school graduate in the states of AZ, CA, CO, and MT; must have survived childhood cancer. **Criteria:** Awards are given based on the application materials.

Funds Avail.: No specific amount. **To Apply:** Applicants must submit a completed scholarship application along with a copy of transcript (with GPA); SAT or ACT test scores; a confirmation of the treatment by the doctor or by the hospital or clinic; and a reference letter (from someone other than a family member). **Deadline:** March 15.

4281 ■ Marine Biological Laboratory

7 MBL St.
Woods Hole, MA 02543
Ph: (508)548-3705
E-mail: mdonovan@mbl.edu
URL: http://www.mbl.edu

4282 ■ Bruce and Betty Alberts Endowed Scholarships in Physiology *(Undergraduate/Scholarship)*

Purpose: To provide support for Physiology students. **Focus:** Physiology. **Qualif.:** Applicants must be attending a Marine Biological Laboratory summer course. **Criteria:** Recipients are selected based on academic standing and financial need.

Funds Avail.: No specific amount. **To Apply:** Applicants must complete the application form.

4283 ■ John and Elisabeth Buck Endowed Scholarships *(Undergraduate/Scholarship)*

Purpose: To provide support for a graduate or post-doctoral student taking a summer course in fundamental biological science. **Focus:** Biology. **Qualif.:** Applicants must be attending a summer course at Marine Biological Laboratory. **Criteria:** Recipients are selected based on academic standing and financial need.

Funds Avail.: No specific amount. **To Apply:** Applicants must complete the application form.

4284 ■ C. Lalor Burdick Scholarships
(Undergraduate/Scholarship)

Purpose: To provide support for students attending the Embryology and Frontiers in Reproduction courses. **Focus:**

Awards are arranged alphabetically below their administering organizations

Biology. **Qualif.:** Applicants must be attending a summer course at Marine Biological Laboratory. **Criteria:** Recipients are selected based on academic standing and financial need.

Funds Avail.: No specific amount. **To Apply:** Applicants must complete the application form.

4285 ■ Max M. Burger Endowed Scholarships in Embryology *(Undergraduate/Scholarship)*

Purpose: To provide support for students attending the Embryology course. **Focus:** Biology. **Qualif.:** Applicants must be attending a summer course at Marine Biological Laboratory. **Criteria:** Recipients are selected based on academic standing and financial need.

Funds Avail.: No specific amount. **To Apply:** Applicants must complete the application form.

4286 ■ Robertson Lola Ellis Scholarships *(Undergraduate/Scholarship)*

Purpose: To provide support for students studying at the Marine Biological Laboratory. **Focus:** Biology. **Qualif.:** Applicants must be attending a summer course at Marine Biological Laboratory. **Criteria:** Recipients are selected based on academic standing and financial need.

Funds Avail.: No specific amount. **To Apply:** Applicants must complete the application form.

4287 ■ Thomas B. Grave and Elizabeth F. Grave Scholarships *(Undergraduate/Scholarship)*

Purpose: To provide support for students studying in any Marine Biological Laboratory summer courses. **Focus:** Biology. **Qualif.:** Applicants must be attending a summer course at Marine Biological Laboratory. **Criteria:** Recipients are selected based on academic standing and financial need.

Funds Avail.: No specific amount. **To Apply:** Applicants must complete the application form.

4288 ■ Caswell Grave Scholarships *(Undergraduate/Scholarship)*

Purpose: To provide support for students studying in any Marine Biological Laboratory summer courses. **Focus:** Biology. **Qualif.:** Applicants must be attending a summer course at Marine Biological Laboratory. **Criteria:** Recipients are selected based on academic standing and financial need.

Funds Avail.: No specific amount. **To Apply:** Applicants must complete the application form.

4289 ■ William Randolph Hearst Educational Endowments *(Undergraduate/Scholarship)*

Purpose: To provide support for students studying in any Marine Biological Laboratory summer courses. **Focus:** Biology. **Qualif.:** Applicants must be attending a summer course at Marine Biological Laboratory. **Criteria:** Recipients are selected based on academic standing and financial need.

Funds Avail.: No specific amount. **To Apply:** Applicants must complete the application form.

4290 ■ Benjamin Kaminer Endowed Scholarships in Physiology *(Undergraduate/Scholarship)*

Purpose: To provide support for students studying in any Marine Biological Laboratory summer courses in Physiology. **Focus:** Physiology. **Qualif.:** Applicants must be attending a summer course at Marine Biological Laboratory. **Criteria:** Recipients are selected based on academic standing and financial need.

Funds Avail.: No specific amount. **To Apply:** Applicants must complete the application form.

4291 ■ Arthur Klorfein Scholarships and Fellowship Funds *(Undergraduate/Scholarship)*

Purpose: To provide support for students in their courses and for research fellows working independently in laboratories. **Focus:** Biology. **Qualif.:** Applicants must be attending a summer course at Marine Biological Laboratory. **Criteria:** Recipients are selected based on academic standing and financial need.

Funds Avail.: No specific amount. **To Apply:** Applicants must complete the application form.

4292 ■ Frank R. Lillie Fellowships and Scholarships *(Undergraduate/Scholarship)*

Purpose: To provide support for students in their courses and for research fellows working independently in laboratories. **Focus:** Biology. **Qualif.:** Applicants must be attending a Marine Biological Laboratory summer course. **Criteria:** Recipients are selected based on academic standing and financial need.

Funds Avail.: No specific amount. **To Apply:** Applicants must complete the application form.

4293 ■ Marine Biological Laboratory Pioneers Fund *(Undergraduate/Scholarship)*

Purpose: To provide support for students attending a Marine Biological Laboratory. **Focus:** Biology. **Qualif.:** Applicants must be attending a Marine Biological Laboratory summer course. **Criteria:** Recipients are selected based on academic standing and financial need.

Funds Avail.: No specific amount. **To Apply:** Applicants must complete the application form.

4294 ■ S.O. Mast Founder's Scholarships *(Undergraduate/Scholarship)*

Purpose: To provide support for students attending a Marine Biological Laboratory. **Focus:** Biology. **Qualif.:** Applicants must be attending a Marine Biological Laboratory summer course. **Criteria:** Recipients are selected based on academic standing and financial need.

Funds Avail.: No specific amount. **To Apply:** Applicants must complete the application form.

4295 ■ Frank Morrell Endowed Memorial Scholarships *(Undergraduate/Scholarship)*

Purpose: To provide support for students attending a neurobiology course. **Focus:** Biology. **Qualif.:** Applicants must be attending a Marine Biological Laboratory summer course. **Criteria:** Recipients are selected based on academic standing and financial need.

Funds Avail.: No specific amount. **To Apply:** Applicants must complete the application form.

4296 ■ Mountain Memorial Scholarships *(Undergraduate/Scholarship)*

Purpose: To provide support for students who are accepted in the physiology course. **Focus:** Physiology. **Qualif.:** Applicants must be attending a summer course at Marine Biological Laboratory. **Criteria:** Recipients are selected based on academic standing and financial need.

Awards are arranged alphabetically below their administering organizations

Funds Avail.: No specific amount. **To Apply:** Applicants must complete the application form.

4297 ■ Pfizer Inc. Endowed Scholarships *(Undergraduate/Scholarship)*

Purpose: To provide support for students who studying at the Marine Biological Laboratory. **Focus:** Biology. **Qualif.:** Applicants must be attending a summer course at Marine Biological Laboratory. **Criteria:** Recipients are selected based on academic standing and financial need.

Funds Avail.: No specific amount. **To Apply:** Applicants must complete the application form.

4298 ■ Herbert W. Rand Fellowships and Scholarships *(Undergraduate/Scholarship)*

Purpose: To provide support for students in their courses and for research fellows working independently in laboratories. **Focus:** Biology. **Qualif.:** Applicants must be attending a summer course at Marine Biological Laboratory. **Criteria:** Recipients are selected based on academic standing and financial need.

Funds Avail.: No specific amount. **To Apply:** Applicants must complete the application form.

4299 ■ Florence C. Rose and S. Meryl Rose Scholarships *(Undergraduate/Scholarship)*

Purpose: To provide support for students from Dartmouth studying at the Marine Biological Laboratory. **Focus:** Biology. **Qualif.:** Applicants must be attending a summer course at Marine Biological Laboratory. **Criteria:** Recipients are selected based on academic standing and financial need.

Funds Avail.: No specific amount. **To Apply:** Applicants must complete the application form.

4300 ■ Ruth Sager Scholarships *(Undergraduate/Scholarship)*

Purpose: To provide support for women students studying at the Marine Biological Laboratory. **Focus:** Biology. **Qualif.:** Applicants must be attending a summer course at Marine Biological Laboratory. **Criteria:** Recipients are selected based on academic standing and financial need.

Funds Avail.: No specific amount. **To Apply:** Applicants must complete the application form.

4301 ■ Milton L. Shifman Endowed Scholarships *(Undergraduate/Scholarship)*

Purpose: To provide support for students from Dartmouth College studying at the Marine Biological Laboratory. **Focus:** Biology. **Qualif.:** Applicants must be attending a summer course at Marine Biological Laboratory. **Criteria:** Recipients are selected based on academic standing and financial need.

Funds Avail.: No specific amount. **To Apply:** Applicants must complete the application form.

4302 ■ Horace W. Stunkard Scholarships *(Undergraduate/Scholarship)*

Purpose: To provide support for students studying at the Marine Biological Laboratory. **Focus:** Biology. **Qualif.:** Applicants must be attending a summer course at Marine Biological Laboratory. **Criteria:** Recipients are selected based on academic standing and financial need.

Funds Avail.: No specific amount. **To Apply:** Applicants must complete the application form.

4303 ■ J.P. Madeline Trinkaus Endowed Scholarships in Embryology *(Undergraduate/Scholarship)*

Purpose: To provide support for students studying at the Marine Biological Laboratory in the embryology course. **Focus:** Biology. **Qualif.:** Applicants must be attending a summer course at Marine Biological Laboratory. **Criteria:** Recipients are selected based on academic standing and financial need.

Funds Avail.: No specific amount. **To Apply:** Applicants must complete the application form.

4304 ■ Selma A. Waksman Endowed Scholarships in Microbial Diversity *(Undergraduate/Scholarship)*

Purpose: To provide support for students participating in the microbial diversity course. **Focus:** Microbiology. **Qualif.:** Applicants must be attending a summer course at Marine Biological Laboratory. **Criteria:** Recipients are selected based on academic standing and financial need.

Funds Avail.: No specific amount. **To Apply:** Applicants must complete the application form.

4305 ■ Marine Corps Engineer Association

PO Box 322
Ashville, NY 14710
Ph: (716)763-5655
E-mail: frantzkd@alltel.net
URL: http://www.marcorengasn.org

4306 ■ Marine Corps Engineer Association Assistance Fund *(Graduate, High School, Undergraduate/Scholarship)*

Purpose: To provide financial assistance for the education of the members of the United States Marine Corp's engineer and explosive ordinance disposal communities and their families or for members of the United States Armed Forces who have served with or been attached to Marine Corps Air Ground Task Force engineer or EOD units. **Focus:** Engineering. **Qualif.:** Program is open to citizens of the United States over the age of 18 years old seeking for financial assistance to further education beyond high school at an accredited college, university or higher technical trade school up to a maximum of four years. They can also be individuals who are already enrolled in a post-secondary curriculum. Neither graduate study request nor applications at the high school or prep school level are acceptable. **Criteria:** Applications will be evaluated by the Scholarship Selection Committee.

Funds Avail.: No specified amount. **To Apply:** Applicants must complete and submit the application form and enclose all items requested in the application; name and address; and have the application and attachment notarized. **Deadline:** June 30.

4307 ■ Marine Corps League Foundation

PO Box 3070
Merrifield, VA 22116-3070
Ph: (972)272-6384
E-mail: corpsma@aol.com
URL: http://www.mclfoundation.org

4308 ■ Marine Corps League National Scholarships *(Undergraduate/Scholarship)*

Purpose: To grant scholarship to qualified applicants pursuing full-time undergraduate or technical training at a

Awards are arranged alphabetically below their administering organizations

recognized institution. **Focus:** General studies. **Qualif.:** Applicant must be the spouse, child, grandchild, great grandchild or step child of a Marine Corps League or Auxiliary member in good standing; or the child of a Marine who died in the line of duty; or a member of the Marine Corps League or Auxiliary in good standing or honorably discharged Marines in need of rehabilitation training not provided by government programs. Sponsors must be a member in good standing of the Marine Corps League or Auxiliary. **Criteria:** Award is given based on the application materials.

Funds Avail.: No specific amount. **To Apply:** Applicants must submit a completed application form in which the sponsor has completely filled out their section. **Deadline:** July 1.

Remarks: Do not staple any document to the application.

4309 ■ Marine Technology Society

5565 Sterrett Pl., Ste. 108
Columbia, MD 21044
Ph: (410)884-5330
Fax: (410)884-9060
E-mail: membership@mtsociety.org
URL: http://www.mtsociety.org

4310 ■ Marine Technology Society ROV Scholarships *(Undergraduate/Scholarship)*

Purpose: To help students achieve success. **Focus:** Marine. **Qualif.:** Applicants must be students interested in remotely operated vehicles (ROVs) or underwater work that furthers the use of ROVs. Applicants must be graduate, undergraduate or high school students. **Criteria:** Recipients are selected based on academic standing.

Funds Avail.: $2,000. **To Apply:** Applicants must submit a written recommendation from a current teacher or counselor in a marine-related field; a written letter of reference from someone who is not a teacher or counselor; an official sealed transcript. For high school seniors, proof of acceptance to a two-year or four-year academic program must be submitted. Applicants must submit a biographical sketch including academic, personal and professional goals.

4311 ■ Marine Technology Society Scholarships for Graduate and Undergraduate Students *(Undergraduate/Scholarship)*

Purpose: To help students achieve success. **Focus:** Marine. **Qualif.:** Applicants must be a graduate or undergraduate student, enrolled full-time in a marine-related field. **Criteria:** Recipients are selected based on academic standing.

Funds Avail.: $2,000. **To Apply:** Applicants must submit a written recommendation from a current teacher or counselor in a marine-related field; a written letter of reference from someone who is not a teacher or counselor; an official sealed transcript. For high school seniors, proof of acceptance to a two-year or four-year academic program must be submitted. **Contact:** scholarships@mtsociety.org.

4312 ■ Marine Technology Society Student Scholarships for Graduating High School Seniors *(Undergraduate/Scholarship)*

Purpose: To help students achieve success. **Focus:** Marine. **Qualif.:** Applicants must be high school seniors who have been accepted into a full-time undergraduate program. **Criteria:** Recipients are selected based on academic standing.

Funds Avail.: $2,000. **To Apply:** Applicants must submit a written recommendation from a current teacher or counselor in a marine-related field; a written letter of reference from someone who is not a teacher or counselor; an official sealed transcript; proof of acceptance to a two-year or four-year academic program. **Contact:** scholarships@mtsociety.org.

4313 ■ Marine Technology Society Student Scholarships for Two-year Technical, Engineering and Community College Students *(Undergraduate/Scholarship)*

Purpose: To help students achieve success. **Focus:** Marine; Marine Engineering. **Qualif.:** Applicants must be enrolled in a two-year technical, engineering or community college in a marine-related field. **Criteria:** Recipients are selected based on academic standing.

Funds Avail.: $2,000. **To Apply:** Applicants must submit a written recommendation from a current teacher or counselor in a marine-related field; a written letter of reference from someone who is not a teacher or counselor; an official sealed transcript. For high school seniors, proof of acceptance to a two-year or four-year academic program must be submitted. **Contact:** scholarships@mtsociety.org.

4314 ■ The Paros-Digiquartz Scholarships *(Undergraduate/Scholarship)*

Purpose: To help students achieve success. **Focus:** Marine. **Qualif.:** Applicants must be high school seniors who have been accepted into a full-time undergraduate program, or undergraduate or graduate students. Applicants must have an interest in marine instrumentation. **Criteria:** Recipients are selected based on academic standing.

Funds Avail.: $2,000. **To Apply:** Applicants must submit a written recommendation from a current teacher or counselor in a marine-related field; a written letter of reference from someone who is not a teacher or counselor; an official sealed transcript. For high school seniors, proof of acceptance to a two-year or four-year academic program must be submitted. **Contact:** scholarships@mtsociety.org.

4315 ■ Thurgood Marshall College Fund

80 Maiden Ln., Ste. 2204
New York, NY 10038
Ph: (212)573-8888
Fax: (212)573-8497
Free: 877-690-8673
URL: http://thurgoodmarshallfund.org

4316 ■ TMCF Scholarships *(Undergraduate/Scholarship)*

Purpose: To support schools or specific areas of interest of a student. **Focus:** General studies. **Qualif.:** The applicant must be a full-time U.S. citizen student pursuing a degree in any discipline at one of the 47 TMCF member schools who demonstrates commitment to academic excellence and community service with a high school GPA of not less than 3.0; a combined verbal/math score of 1650 or more on the Scholastic Aptitude Test (SAT) or a score of 25 or higher on the American College Testing (ACT) examination, recommended by his high school as academically exceptional or outstanding in the creative and performing arts, and has financial need. **Criteria:** Candidates will be evalu-

Awards are arranged alphabetically below their administering organizations

ated based on their merit and financial need.

Funds Avail.: $2,200. **To Apply:** Applicants must submit general information form, enrollment/certification of academic standing, acceptance form, financial aid information together with high school transcript (for incoming freshman), undergraduate transcript (for graduate and law school), resume and/or personal information form recommendation letters, essay head shot or personal photograph.

4317 ■ George C. Marshall Foundation

PO Box 1600
Lexington, VA 24450-1600
Ph: (540)463-7103
Fax: (540)464-5229
E-mail: marshallfoundation@marshallfoundation.org
URL: http://www.marshallfoundation.org

4318 ■ Marshall-Baruch Fellowships *(Doctorate/Fellowship)*

Purpose: To encourage doctoral or postdoctoral research in US military or diplomatic history and related fields. **Focus:** Military history, United States studies. **Qualif.:** Applicant must be currently enrolled in an accredited academic program leading to a doctoral degree; must be engaged in postdoctoral research; must be an independent scholar who has already received a Ph.D. **Criteria:** Selection of applicant will be based on the application and other supporting documents.

Funds Avail.: $7,500. **To Apply:** Applicant must submit a recommendation letter. Application instruction and forms are available in the website. **Deadline:** October 29.

4319 ■ Marshall Undergraduate Scholars Programs *(Undergraduate/Award/Prize)*

Purpose: To promote primary research and study as the cornerstone of the library, archives, and educational programs. **Focus:** General studies. **Qualif.:** Applicant must be an undergraduate student at selected Virginia and Mid Atlantic colleges. **Criteria:** Scholars are nominated by their home institutions and work under the direction of a departmental professor who will determine appropriate course credit.

Funds Avail.: $250 cash award plus travel expenses up to $300 for students from distant institutions. **To Apply:** Applicants must complete the requirements on or before the deadline. **Deadline:** May 12.

4320 ■ Maryland Hospitality Education Foundation

6301 Hillside Ct.
Columbia, MD 21046
Ph: (410)290-6800
Fax: (410)290-6882
Free: 800-874-1313
E-mail: webmaster@mhef.org
URL: http://www.mhef.org

4321 ■ Leticia B. Carter Scholarships *(All/Scholarship)*

Purpose: To support students in the restaurant and food service industry. **Focus:** Service food careers. **Qualif.:** Applicants must be Maryland residents; high school, college, corporate instructor/teacher, or hospitality industry professionals. Applicants must be pursuing hospitality-related coursework; applicants must have applied to an MHEF-recognized professional development program in hospitality or enrolled in a MHEFrecognized food service/hospitality program. **Criteria:** Recipients are selected based on the applicants' GPA; industry-related work experience; essay answers; completed application.

Funds Avail.: No specific amount. **To Apply:** Applicants must submit a typewritten application. High school or college students must submit a photocopy of college curriculum vitae; official, sealed transcript from current high school or college; pay stub from most recent/current employer providing industry-related work experience and record of additional work-related experience, supervisor's letter of recommendation, teacher's letter of recommendation. Applicants for instructor or teacher must submit letter of support and employment from employer; two letters of recommendation; pay stub from employer documenting 1,500 hours of industry experience. Applicants for industry must submit pay stub from employer documenting 1,500 hours of industry experience, letter of support and employment from immediate supervisor or owner, two letters of recommendation. **Deadline:** April 11.

4322 ■ Marcia S. Harris Legacy Fund Scholarships *(Undergraduate/Scholarship)*

Purpose: To support students in the restaurant and food service industry. **Focus:** Service food careers. **Qualif.:** Applicants must be high school or college students, or high school or postsecondary instructors who teach culinary arts or hospitality management courses. Applicants must be enrolled in a postsecondary or professional development course; applicants must be pursuing hospitality-related coursework in culinary arts, hospitality management, or bartending academy programs. **Criteria:** Recipients are selected based on the completed application; financial need; strength of teacher and employer recommendation; strength of essay questions; food service work experience; activities; interviews with scholarship committee.

Funds Avail.: No specific amount. **To Apply:** High school or college students must submit a photocopy of college curriculum vitae; supervisor's or employer's letter of recommendation; teacher's letter of recommendation. Applicants for industry must submit pay stub from employer documenting 2,000 hours or two years of industry experience; letter of support and employment from immediate supervisor or owner; two letters of recommendation. **Deadline:** March 14.

4323 ■ The Erika A. Hayes Scholarships *(Undergraduate/Scholarship)*

Purpose: To support students in the restaurant and food service industry. **Focus:** Service food careers. **Qualif.:** Applicants must be high school or college students; enrolled in postsecondary or professional development courses; pursuing hospitality-related coursework in culinary arts, hospitality managements, or a bartending academy program. **Criteria:** Recipients are selected based on the completed application; financial need; strength of teacher and employer recommendation; strength of essay answers.

Funds Avail.: No specific amount. **To Apply:** High school or college students must submit a photocopy of college curriculum vitae; supervisor's or employer's letter of recommendation; teacher's letter of recommendation. Applicants for industry must submit pay stub from employer documenting 2,000 hours or two years of industry experience; letter of support and employment from immediate supervisor or owner; two letters of recommendation. **Deadline:** March 14.

4324 ■ Maryland Hospitality Education Foundation Co-Branded Scholarships *(Undergraduate/Scholarship)*

Purpose: To support students in the restaurant and food service industry. **Focus:** Service food careers. **Qualif.:** Applicants must be high school seniors having an average GPA of 2.75 on a 4.0 scale or equivalent, verified by a transcript from each high school attended. Applicants must have a minimum of 250 hours of restaurant or food service-related work experience, verified by copies of paycheck stubs or letters from employers stipulating numbers of hours worked. **Criteria:** Recipients are selected based on the presentation of application; essay answers; industry-related work experience; strength of letters of recommendation; GPA.

Funds Avail.: No specific amount. **To Apply:** Applicants must complete the application form. Applicants must submit a transcript of records; essays; signed letters of recommendation from current or previous employers; copy of college acceptance letter. **Deadline:** April 11.

4325 ■ Massachusetts Association of Land Surveyors and Civil Engineers

50 Depot St.
Dalton, MA 01226-1806
Ph: (413)684-0925
Fax: (413)684-0267
E-mail: mcorcoran@hillengineers.com
URL: http://www.malsce.org

4326 ■ MALSE Scholarships *(Undergraduate/Scholarship)*

Purpose: To provide support for qualified individuals intending to pursue their studies. **Focus:** Surveying; Civil engineering. **Qualif.:** Applicants must be enrolled full-time in a college, university, junior college, technical institute or community college; must be residents of Massachusetts or attending an out-of-state school; and must be majoring in surveying, civil or environmental engineering. **Criteria:** Selection of applicants will be based on the scholarship application criteria.

Funds Avail.: No specific amount. **To Apply:** Applicants must write/call the chairman for an application; must complete the application form available online; must have a letter of recommendation; and must submit a transcript of grades. Application form and other supporting materials must be sent to MALSE Scholarship Chair, 50 Depot St., Dalton, MA 01226-1806. **Deadline:** July. **Contact:** Mary Ann Corcoran at the above address (see entry 4325).

4327 ■ Massachusetts Association of Women Lawyers

c/o Annette Hines, Esq.
20 Main St. Ste. No. 206A
Natick, MA 01760
E-mail: info@mawi.org
URL: http://www.mawi.org

4328 ■ Carol DiMaiti Scholarship Awards *(Undergraduate/Scholarship)*

Purpose: To award scholarships to law students in Massachusetts. **Focus:** Law. **Qualif.:** Applicants must be entering their second or third year of law school; must be in good academic standing; must have demonstrated high financial need. **Criteria:** Selection of scholars will be based on financial need and academic achievement.

Funds Avail.: $1,000. **To Apply:** Applicants must submit a completed application form and must check the available website for details.

Remarks: This particular fund is maintained solely through voluntary contributions made throughout the year and fundraising events. **Contact:** Massachusetts Association of Women Lawyers at the above address (see entry 4327).

4329 ■ Massachusetts Chapter of the International Association of Arson Investigators (IAAI)

PO Box 237
Southbridge, MA 01550-0237
Ph: (978)567-3300
E-mail: miloseek@aol.com
URL: http://www.maiaai.com

4330 ■ Sgt. Michael F. Cherven Memorial Scholarships *(Undergraduate/Scholarship)*

Purpose: To support the education of a member or an immediate family member or grandchild of a Massachusetts IAAI Chapter member. **Focus:** General studies. **Qualif.:** Applicant must be members, immediate family members or grandchildren of a Massachusetts IAAI Chapter member in good standing; and must be graduating high school seniors or entering/currently enrolled at a college/university. **Criteria:** Selection is based on a demonstrated commitment to public service or a desire to enter public service.

Funds Avail.: $500. **Number Awarded:** 2. **To Apply:** Applicants must submit a completed application form with the required supporting documents. **Deadline:** June 4.

4331 ■ Massachusetts Office of Student Financial Assistance

454 Broadway, Ste. 200
Revere, MA 02151
Ph: (617)727-9420
Fax: (617)727-0667
E-mail: osfa@osfa.mass.edu
URL: http://www.osfa.mass.edu

4332 ■ Early Childhood Educators Scholarship Program *(Undergraduate/Scholarship)*

Purpose: To provide financial assistance for currently employed early childhood educators and providers who enroll in an associate or bachelor degree program in early childhood education or related program. **Focus:** Child care. **Qualif.:** Applicants must be permanent legal residents of Massachusetts; United States citizens or eligible non-citizens; eligible under Title IV Regulations and not in default of a state or federal education loan or grant; enrolled, as matriculated students without a bachelor's degree, in an undergraduate degree program (full- or part-time) in early childhood education or a related field (i.e., elementary education, sociology, psychology); employed as early childhood educators or licensed family child care providers in Massachusetts for at least one year; and must continue employment while enrolled in the required degree program. **Criteria:** Applicants are evaluated based on

Awards are arranged alphabetically below their administering organizations

academic achievement and financial need.

Funds Avail.: No specific amount. **To Apply:** Applicants must submit all the required application information.

4333 ■ Massachusetts State Automobile Dealers Association

59 Temple Pl., Ste. 505
Boston, MA 02111
Ph: (617)451-1051
Fax: (617)451-9309
E-mail: spoikail@msada.org
URL: http://www.msada.org

4334 ■ Automotive Technician Scholarship Program *(Undergraduate/Scholarship)*

Purpose: To enrich the lives of auto tech students through scholarships. **Focus:** Automotive technology. **Qualif.:** Applicants must be retraining for a career change or a recent high school graduate. Applicants must be enrolled in an automotive program at an accredited college. **Criteria:** Recipients are selected based on academic standing and financial need.

Funds Avail.: $6,000. **Number Awarded:** 17. **To Apply:** Applicants must submit a curriculum vitae; the complete application form; a three-page applicant's appraisal; and complete transcript of record. **Contact:** 617-451-9309.

4335 ■ Master Brewers Association of the Americas

3340 Pilot Knob Rd.
St. Paul, MN 55121-2097
Ph: (651)454-7250
Fax: (651)454-0766
E-mail: mbaa@mbaa.com
URL: http://www.mbaa.com

4336 ■ William A. Hipp Scholarships *(All/Scholarship)*

Purpose: To provide funds for MBAA members who wish to further their education at either the MBAA Brewing and Malting Science Course or the MBAA Brewery Packaging Technology Course. **Focus:** Food science and technology. **Qualif.:** Applicants must be members of the MBAA and possess a minimum of five years of service in the brewing or malting industry. **Criteria:** Recipients are selected based on the application materials submitted.

Funds Avail.: No specific amount. **To Apply:** Application forms must be completed and signed by two professional members of the MBAA. **Deadline:** January 15 for the Brewery Packaging Technology Course and August 1 for the Brewing and Malting Science Course. **Contact:** Beth Elliott, belliott@scisoc.org.

4337 ■ Matanuska-Susitna College

PO Box 2889
Palmer, AK 99645
Ph: (907)745-9774
Fax: (907)745-9711
E-mail: info@matsu.alaska.edu
URL: http://www.matsu.alaska.edu

4338 ■ Alaska Aerospace Development Corporation Scholarships *(Undergraduate/Scholarship)*

Purpose: To provide support to deserving students in Alaska who want to pursue an education in any campus of the University of Alaska. **Focus:** Applied mathematics; Physics; Engineering; Business; Technical communications. **Qualif.:** Applicant must be a freshman student majoring in mathematics, physics, engineering, business, or a technical science field such as computer science who has graduated from the Kodiak Island Borough School District; must be a full-time student enrolled in 14 credits and in good academic standing. **Criteria:** Candidates will be selected based on their academic standing and application documents.

Funds Avail.: $5,000. **To Apply:** Applicants must submit a written statement verifying that he/she has not been convicted of a crime other than a minor traffic violation; must complete the application forms available at the website; must attach a personal essay, two letters of recommendation, and current transcripts. **Deadline:** February 15.

4339 ■ Alaska Native Medical Center Auxiliary Scholarships *(Undergraduate/Scholarship)*

Purpose: To provide support to deserving students in Alaska who want to pursue an education in any campus of the University of Alaska. **Focus:** General studies. **Qualif.:** Applicant must have graduated from a rural Alaska high school that is off the highway system in Alaska; must be a full-time student and in good academic standing with a minimum cumulative GPA of 2.0. **Criteria:** Preference will be given to Alaska Natives and/or individuals of Native American descent.

Funds Avail.: $1,000. **To Apply:** Applicant must complete the application forms available at the website; must attach a personal essay, two letters of recommendation, and current transcripts. **Deadline:** February 15.

4340 ■ Alaska Press Club Scholarships *(Undergraduate/Scholarship)*

Purpose: To provide support to deserving students in Alaska who want to pursue an education in any campus of the University of Alaska. **Focus:** Journalism. **Qualif.:** Applicant must be a junior, senior or graduate journalism student with a minimum GPA of 2.0. **Criteria:** Preference will be given to applicants from Rural Alaska communities.

Funds Avail.: $500. **To Apply:** Applicant must complete the application forms available at the website; must attach a personal essay, two letters of recommendation, and current transcripts. **Deadline:** February 15.

4341 ■ Alaska Support Industry Alliance Scholarships *(Undergraduate/Scholarship)*

Purpose: To provide financial support for deserving students in Alaska intending to pursue an education in any campus of the University of Alaska. **Focus:** Resource management, Biology, Wildlife conservation, management, and science, Petroleum engineering. **Qualif.:** Applicants must be full-time students and Alaska residents who have at least 3.0 GPA majoring in a field that will support the industry growth in Alaska and at the same time showing concern for the environment and how industry is developed. **Criteria:** Preference will be given to students who are sons or daughters of employees of companies that belong to the Alaska Support Industry Alliance.

Funds Avail.: $500. **To Apply:** Applicants must complete the application forms available in the website; must attach a personal essay, two letters of recommendation, and their current transcripts. **Deadline:** February 15.

4342 ■ Alaska Visitors Association/Gomar Scholarships *(Undergraduate/Scholarship)*

Purpose: To provide support for deserving students in Alaska intending to pursue an education in any campus of

Awards are arranged alphabetically below their administering organizations

the University of Alaska. **Focus:** Travel and tourism. **Qualif.:** Applicants must be enrolled in programs of study emphasizing travel and tourism. **Criteria:** Preference will be given to students of Latin American descent.

Funds Avail.: $500. **To Apply:** Applicants must complete the application forms available in the website; must attach a personal essay, two letters of recommendation, and their current transcripts. **Deadline:** February 15.

4343 ■ Alaska Yukon Pioneer Memorial Scholarships *(Undergraduate/Scholarship)*

Purpose: To provide support for deserving students in Alaska intending to pursue an education in any campus of the University of Alaska. **Focus:** General studies. **Qualif.:** Applicants must be full-time students and residents of Alaska or the Yukon Territory and must have graduated from high school either in Alaska or the Yukon Territory. **Criteria:** Preference will be given to students who plan to remain in Alaska or the Yukon Territory.

Funds Avail.: $500. **To Apply:** Applicants must complete the application forms available on the website; must attach a personal essay, two letters of recommendation, and their current transcripts. **Deadline:** February 15.

4344 ■ Amos Joe Alter ASCE Section Alaska Section Scholarships *(Undergraduate/Scholarship)*

Purpose: To provide support to deserving students in Alaska who want to pursue an education in any campus of the University of Alaska. **Focus:** Civil engineering. **Qualif.:** Applicant must be a full-time student attending the University of Alaska at Anchorage or the University of Alaska at Fairbanks, and must be a civil engineering major. **Criteria:** Preference will be given to college seniors with a minimum GPA of 3.0.

Funds Avail.: $1,000. **To Apply:** Applicant must complete the application forms available at the website; must attach a personal essay, two letters of recommendation, and current transcripts. **Deadline:** February 15.

4345 ■ Mike Ardaw Scholarships *(Undergraduate/Scholarship)*

Purpose: To provide support to deserving students in Alaska who want to pursue an education in any campus of the University of Alaska. **Focus:** Science; Education; Engineering. **Qualif.:** Applicant must be a full-time student and have a minimum GPA of 2.5. **Criteria:** Preference will be given to students studying science, education or engineering and to students who have been Alaska residents for at least one year and are from the Navy Lake area.

Funds Avail.: $1,000. **To Apply:** Applicant must complete the application forms available at the website; must attach a personal essay, two letters of recommendation, and current transcripts. **Deadline:** February 15.

4346 ■ Lawrence Bayer Business Administration Scholarships *(Undergraduate/Scholarship)*

Purpose: To provide support to deserving students in Alaska who want to pursue an education in any campus of the University of Alaska. **Focus:** Business administration. **Qualif.:** Applicant must be full-time students attending the University of Alaska at Fairbanks or the University of Alaska at Anchorage and have a minimum GPA of 3.0; must be a business administration major active in clubs and/or sports. **Criteria:** Preference will be given to applicants with financial need.

Funds Avail.: $500. **To Apply:** Applicant must complete the application forms available at the website; must attach a personal essay, two letters of recommendation, and current transcripts. **Deadline:** February 15.

4347 ■ Charles E. Behlke Engineering Memorial Scholarships *(Undergraduate/Scholarship)*

Purpose: To provide support to deserving students in Alaska who want to pursue an education in any campus of the University of Alaska. **Focus:** Engineering. **Qualif.:** Applicants must be full-time students entering their sophomore, junior, or senior year; must be engineering majors; must be in good academic standing with a minimum GPA of 2.5. **Criteria:** Selection of applicant will be based on their academic standing and application requirements.

Funds Avail.: $1,000. **To Apply:** Applicant must complete the application forms available at the website; must attach a personal essay, two letters of recommendation, and current transcripts. **Deadline:** February 15.

4348 ■ Bill & Nell Biggs Scholarships *(Undergraduate/Scholarship)*

Purpose: To provide support to deserving students in Alaska who want to pursue an education in any campus of the University of Alaska. **Focus:** Accounting; Business administration; Engineering; Science; Mathematics and mathematical sciences. **Qualif.:** Applicants must be graduates of Juneau-Douglas High School or Juneau residents who have completed a high school equivalency program. **Criteria:** Preference will be given to applicants majoring in accounting, business administration, engineering, science and mathematics, related science subjects or foreign languages areas such as Spanish, German or French.

Funds Avail.: $500. **To Apply:** Applicant must complete the application forms available at the website; must attach a personal essay, two letters of recommendation, and current transcripts. **Deadline:** February 15.

4349 ■ Bolick Foreign Student Scholarships *(Undergraduate/Scholarship)*

Purpose: To provide support to deserving students in Alaska who want to pursue an education in any campus of the University of Alaska. **Focus:** General studies. **Qualif.:** Applicant must be a full-time student holding exclusive citizenship in another country and attending the university on a student visa. **Criteria:** Preference will be given to Swedish citizens.

Funds Avail.: $1,000. **To Apply:** Applicant must complete the application forms available at the website; must attach a personal essay, two letters of recommendation, and current transcripts. **Deadline:** February 15.

4350 ■ Dr. Betty J. Boyd-Beu & Edwin G. Beu, Jr. Scholarships *(Undergraduate/Scholarship)*

Purpose: To provide financial assistance for tuition and other educational expenses to non-traditional students who are seeking degree completion or retraining at the Matanuska-Susitna College. **Focus:** General studies. **Qualif.:** Applicant must be a non-traditional student and have graduated from high school; must have worked prior to enrolling or returning to college, thus re-entering college to complete a degree or enrolling to retrain for another position in the workplace; must be in good academic standing with a minimum cumulative GPA of 3.0; must be formally admitted to a degreeseeking program; must be enrolled in the semester(s) for which the award is made. **Criteria:**

Awards are arranged alphabetically below their administering organizations

Selection will be based on their academic performance and application documents.

Funds Avail.: $2,500. **To Apply:** Applicants must complete the MSC scholarship application; must attach a list of activities/community service in which they have participated; must attach a resume of their work experience over the past four years; must attach a personal essay; must attach two letters of recommendation and transcripts. Application forms must be submitted to: Dr. Betty Boyd-Beu & Edwin G. Beu Jr. Scholarship, Matanuska-Susitna College, Student Services, FSM 102, PO Box 2889, Palmer, AK 99645. **Deadline:** May 31.

4351 ■ Charles E. Bunnell Scholarships *(Undergraduate/Scholarship)*

Purpose: To provide support to deserving students in Alaska who want to pursue an education in any campus of the University of Alaska. **Focus:** General studies. **Qualif.:** Applicants must be full-time students entering his/her junior or senior year with a declared major in an accredited field and have a minimum GPA of 3.2. **Criteria:** Preference will be given to applicants who graduated from an Alaska high school and have lived in Alaska for 3 or more years.

Funds Avail.: $1,000. **To Apply:** Applicant must submit an additional paragraph describing how they emulate the ideals of persistence, vision, selfsacrifice, concern for others and love of the North. Applicant must complete the application forms available at the website; must attach a personal essay, two letters of recommendation, and current transcripts. **Deadline:** February 15.

Remarks: Named after Charles E. Bunnell, the first president of the University of Alaska.

4352 ■ Loyal D. Burkett Memorial Scholarships *(Undergraduate/Scholarship)*

Purpose: To provide support to deserving students in Alaska who want to pursue an education in any campus of the University of Alaska. **Focus:** General studies. **Qualif.:** Applicant must be a full-time student in good academic standing and demonstrate motivation, academic and leadership potential. **Criteria:** Applicants will be selected based on their application and academic standing.

Funds Avail.: $500. **To Apply:** Applicant must complete the application forms available at the website; must attach a personal essay, two letters of recommendation, and current transcripts. **Deadline:** February 15.

4353 ■ Lyle Carlson Wildlife Management Scholarships *(Undergraduate/Scholarship)*

Purpose: To provide support to deserving students in Alaska who want to pursue an education in any campus of the University of Alaska. **Focus:** Wildlife conservation, management, and science. **Qualif.:** Applicant must be a student majoring in wildlife management, wildlife biology or another closely related major and have a minimum GPA of 3.0. **Criteria:** Applicants will be selected based on their academic standing.

Funds Avail.: $500. **To Apply:** Applicant must complete the application forms available at the website; must attach a personal essay, two letters of recommendation, and current transcripts. **Deadline:** February 15.

4354 ■ Mable B. Crawford Memorial Scholarships *(Undergraduate/Scholarship)*

Purpose: To provide support to deserving students in Alaska who want to pursue an education in any campus of the University of Alaska. **Focus:** Accounting; Economics; Law; Business. **Qualif.:** Applicants must be students who have been residents of Alaska for at least two years. **Criteria:** Awarded on the basis of both scholastic ability and need. Preference is given to applicants majoring in accounting, economics, law or business.

Funds Avail.: $500. **To Apply:** Applicant must complete the application forms available at the website; must attach a personal essay, two letters of recommendation, and current transcripts. **Deadline:** February 15.

4355 ■ Patricia Ann Hughes Eastaugh Memorial Teaching Scholarships *(Undergraduate/Scholarship)*

Purpose: To provide support to deserving students in Alaska who want to pursue an education in any campus of the University of Alaska. **Focus:** Teaching. **Qualif.:** Applicants must be first-time incoming freshman students enrolled in a baccalaureate degree program; must intend to become an elementary or secondary school teacher in Alaska and be enrolled in academic programs leading toward that end; must be an Alaska resident and a graduate of a public or private school in Alaska. **Criteria:** Preference will be given to student who shows a desire to teach and is in the top 25% of their class.

Funds Avail.: $8,000. **To Apply:** Applicant must attach an additional statement of 1,000 words or less entitled "Why I Want to become a Teacher of Children in Alaska." Candidates should also briefly express their opinion of Alaska's educational system(s) and their thoughts on changes they would embrace therein. Applicant must complete the application forms available in the website; must attach a personal essay, two letters of recommendation, and current transcripts. **Deadline:** February 15.

4356 ■ Excellence in Geographic Information Systems Scholarships *(Undergraduate/Scholarship)*

Purpose: To provide support to deserving students in Alaska who want to pursue an education in any campus of the University of Alaska. **Focus:** Geography. **Qualif.:** Applicant must be a full-time junior, senior, or graduate student in good standing with a minimum overall cumulative GPA of 2.88 or a major GPA of 3.2; must have declared interest in Geographic Information Systems or Mapping Science and be engaged in a directed or undirected project or class involving Geographic Information Systems during the award period . **Criteria:** Applicants will be selected based on their academic standing.

Funds Avail.: $500. **To Apply:** Applicant must complete the application forms available at the website; must attach a personal essay, two letters of recommendation, and current transcripts. **Deadline:** February 15.

4357 ■ Lydia Fohn-Hansen/Lola Hill Memorial Scholarships *(Undergraduate/Scholarship)*

Purpose: To provide support to deserving students in Alaska who want to pursue an education in any campus of the University of Alaska. **Focus:** Family planning; Consumer affairs. **Qualif.:** Applicant must be full-time undergraduate or degree-seeking graduate students majoring in Family and Consumer Sciences or a related field; must have a minimum GPA of 3.0 and must be a resident of Alaska. **Criteria:** Selection of applicants will be based on their academic performance.

Funds Avail.: $1,000. **To Apply:** Applicant must complete the application forms available at the website; must attach a personal essay, two letters of recommendation, and current transcripts. **Deadline:** February 15.

4358 ■ Johnny and Sarah Frank Scholarships *(Undergraduate/Scholarship)*

Purpose: To provide support to deserving students in Alaska who want to pursue an education in any campus of the University of Alaska. **Focus:** General studies. **Qualif.:** Applicants must be of Gwich in Athabaskan descent; must have a minimum 2.5 GPA and must enroll for at least six credit hours. **Criteria:** Preference will be to students from Arctic Village or Venetie and students from Ft. Yukon, Chalkyitsik, Birch Creek, Circle, Beaver or Eagle.

Funds Avail.: $500. **To Apply:** Applicant must complete the application forms available at the website; must attach a personal essay, two letters of recommendation, and current transcripts. **Deadline:** February 15.

4359 ■ Charles F. Gould Endowment Scholarships *(Undergraduate/Scholarship)*

Purpose: To provide support to deserving students in Alaska who want to pursue an education in any campus of the University of Alaska. **Focus:** General studies. **Qualif.:** Applicant must be a full-time Alaska Native student, preferably Eskimo, with a minimum GPA of 2.0. **Criteria:** Applicants will be selected based on their academic standing.

Funds Avail.: $1,000. **To Apply:** Applicant must complete the application forms available at the website; must attach a personal essay, two letters of recommendation, and their current transcripts. **Deadline:** February 15.

4360 ■ Patty Hamilton Early Childhood Development Scholarships *(Undergraduate/Scholarship)*

Purpose: To provide support to deserving students in Alaska who want to pursue an education in any campus of the University of Alaska. **Focus:** Early childhood education. **Qualif.:** Applicants must be Alaska residents entering their junior or senior year and majoring in early childhood development/ education. **Criteria:** Preference will be given to students who are working with or volunteering for young children.

Funds Avail.: $2,500. **To Apply:** Applicant must complete the application forms available at the website; must attach a personal essay, two letters of recommendation, and current transcripts. **Deadline:** February 15.

4361 ■ John B. Henderson Scholarships *(Undergraduate/Scholarship)*

Purpose: To provide support to deserving students in Alaska who want to pursue an education in any campus of the University of Alaska. **Focus:** General studies. **Qualif.:** Applicants must be full-time students attending any campus of the University of Alaska. **Criteria:** Applicants will be selected based on their application requirements.

Funds Avail.: $500. **To Apply:** Applicant must complete the application forms available at the website; must attach a personal essay, two letters of recommendation, and current transcripts. **Deadline:** February 15.

4362 ■ Donald Wills Jacobs Scholarships *(Undergraduate/Scholarship)*

Purpose: To provide support to deserving students in Alaska who want to pursue an education in any campus of the University of Alaska. **Focus:** Fine arts. **Qualif.:** Applicant must be a full-time junior or senior student enrolled in a Bachelor of Fine Arts program at the University of Alaska. **Criteria:** Applicants will be selected based on their academic performance and application documents.

Funds Avail.: $500. **To Apply:** Applicant must complete the application forms available at the website; must attach a personal essay, two letters of recommendation, and current transcripts. **Deadline:** February 15.

4363 ■ Iver & Cora Knapstad Scholarships *(Undergraduate/Scholarship)*

Purpose: To provide support to deserving students in Alaska who want to pursue an education in any campus of the University of Alaska. **Focus:** General studies. **Qualif.:** Applicants must be full-time students attending any University of Alaska campus. **Criteria:** Applicants will be selected based on their academic standing.

Funds Avail.: $1,000. **To Apply:** Applicant must complete the application forms available at the website; must attach a personal essay, two letters of recommendation, and current transcripts. **Deadline:** February 15.

4364 ■ Robert Wade Korn Endowed Scholarships *(Undergraduate/Scholarship)*

Purpose: To provide support to deserving students in Alaska who want to pursue an education in any campus of the University of Alaska. **Focus:** General studies. **Qualif.:** Applicants must be graduates of Cordova Alaska High School with a minimum of 2.0 average. **Criteria:** Selection of applicants must be based on their academic standing.

Funds Avail.: $1,000. **To Apply:** Applicant must complete the application forms available at the website; must attach a personal essay, two letters of recommendation, and current transcripts. **Deadline:** February 15.

4365 ■ Austin E. Lathrop Scholarships *(Undergraduate/Scholarship)*

Purpose: To provide support to deserving students in Alaska who want to pursue an education in any campus of the University of Alaska. **Focus:** General studies. **Qualif.:** Applicants must be full-time students attending any campus of the University of Alaska. **Criteria:** Preference will be given to students who show a need for financial assistance.

Funds Avail.: $1,000. **To Apply:** Applicant must complete the application forms available at the website; must attach a personal essay, two letters of recommendation, and their current transcripts. **Deadline:** February 15.

4366 ■ Franklin M. Leach Scholarships *(Undergraduate/Scholarship)*

Purpose: To provide support to deserving students in Alaska who want to pursue an education in any campus of the University of Alaska. **Focus:** General studies. **Qualif.:** Applicants must be full-time students seeking a degree in Aviation and have a minimum cumulative GPA of 2.0. **Criteria:** Selection of applicants will be selected based on their academic standing.

Funds Avail.: $1,000. **To Apply:** Applicant must complete the application forms available at the website; must attach a personal essay, two letters of recommendation, and current transcripts. **Deadline:** February 15.

4367 ■ Mat-Su Health Foundation Scholarships *(Undergraduate/Scholarship)*

Purpose: To provide financial support to qualified individuals. **Focus:** Health care services. **Qualif.:** Applicant must

Awards are arranged alphabetically below their administering organizations

be a Matanuske-Susitna Borough resident enrolling or currently enrolled in higher education in any health care field. **Criteria:** Selection of applicants will be based on their application materials.

Funds Avail.: $2,500-$5000. **To Apply:** Scholarship application forms are available at: Mat-Su Regional Outpatient Center in Wasilla, 950 E Bogard, Ste. 218, online at www-.matsuhealthfoundation.org. **Deadline:** April 4.

4368 ■ Matanuska-Susitna College Regent's Scholarships *(Undergraduate/Scholarship)*

Purpose: To provide support to deserving students in Alaska who want to pursue an education in any campus of the University of Alaska. **Focus:** General studies. **Qualif.:** Applicant must be junior, senior or graduate students in good academic standing whose application reflects demonstrated commitment and involvement in leadership and civic or professional service activities and recognized academic achievement. **Criteria:** Applicants will be selected based on their academic standing and application documents.

Funds Avail.: $5,000. **To Apply:** Applicant must complete the application forms available at the website; must attach a personal essay, two letters of recommendation, and current transcripts. **Deadline:** February 15.

4369 ■ Dave McCloud Aviation Memorial Scholarships *(Undergraduate/Scholarship)*

Purpose: To provide support to deserving students in Alaska who want to pursue an education in any campus of the University of Alaska. **Focus:** General studies. **Qualif.:** Applicants must be full-time students seeking a degree in Aviation and have a minimum cumulative GPA of 2.0; must be a resident of Alaska. **Criteria:** Preference will be given to students who are affiliated with the military.

Funds Avail.: $500. **To Apply:** Applicant must complete the application forms available at the website; must attach a personal essay, two letters of recommendation, and current transcripts. **Deadline:** February 15.

4370 ■ Richard Mellon Endowment Scholarships *(Undergraduate/Scholarship)*

Purpose: To provide support to deserving students in Alaska who want to pursue an education in any campus of the University of Alaska. **Focus:** General studies. **Qualif.:** Applicants must be full-time students. **Criteria:** Preference will be given to students who demonstrate a need for financial assistance.

Funds Avail.: $1,500. **To Apply:** Applicant must complete the application forms available at the website; must attach a personal essay, two letters of recommendation, and current transcripts. **Deadline:** February 15.

4371 ■ Molly Ann Mishler Memorial Scholarships *(Undergraduate/Scholarship)*

Purpose: To provide financial assistance for tuition and other educational expenses to students who are enrolled in Early Childhood Development courses at Matanuska-Susitna College. **Focus:** Early childhood education. **Qualif.:** Applicant must demonstrate motivation, academic and leadership potential; must have a good academic standing with a minimum cumulative GPA of 2.0; must be formally admitted to a degree-seeking program at the University of Alaska at Anchorage or Matanuska-Susitna College; must plan on enrolling at least part-time (3 credits) at Matanuska-Susitna College; must be an incoming or continuing student at Matanuska-Susitna College; must be a U.S. citizen, non-U.S. citizen, Alaska resident, or out-of-state resident; must be enrolled in the semester(s) for which the award is offered; must be enrolled in at least three credits for Early Childhood Development courses. **Criteria:** Preference will be given to applicants formally admitted into the Early Childhood Development program.

Funds Avail.: $500. **To Apply:** Applicant must complete the MSC scholarship application form; must attach a list of activities/community service in which they have participated; must attach a resume of their work experience they have held over the past four years; must attach a personal essay (not more than 500 words); must have two letters of recommendation and transcripts. Application documents must be submitted to Molly Ann Mishler Memorial Scholarships, Matanuska-Susitna College, Student Services, FSM 102, PO Box 2889, Palmer, AK 99645. **Deadline:** May 31.

4372 ■ NAPMW Mat-Su Valley Alaska Scholarships *(Undergraduate/Scholarship)*

Purpose: To provide financial assistance for tuition and other educational expenses to students who are formally admitted to a business degreeseeking program and attending the Matanuska-Susitna College. **Focus:** Business. **Qualif.:** Applicant must be in good academic standing with a minimum cumulative GPA of 2.5; must be formally admitted to an undergraduate business degreeseeking program at the University of Alaska Anchorage; must plan to attend at least half-time (6 credits) at the Matanuska-Susitna College; must be an incoming or continuing student. **Criteria:** Preference will be given to students who demonstrate the desire to work in the mortgage field and to applicants who plan on residing and working in Mat-Su after graduation.

Funds Avail.: $2,000. **To Apply:** Applicant must complete the MSC scholarship application form; must attach a list of activities/community service in which they have participated; must attach a resume of their work experience over the past four years; must attach a personal essay (not more than 500 words); must have two letters of recommendation and transcript. **Deadline:** May 31.

4373 ■ Andrew Nerland Endowment Scholarships *(Undergraduate/Scholarship)*

Purpose: To provide support to deserving students in Alaska who want to pursue an education in any campus of the University of Alaska. **Focus:** General studies. **Qualif.:** Applicants must be full-time student. **Criteria:** Preference will be given to students who demonstrate a need for financial assistance.

Funds Avail.: $1,000. **To Apply:** Applicant must complete the application forms available at the website; must attach a personal essay, two letters of recommendation, and current transcripts. **Deadline:** February 15.

4374 ■ Maureen E. Nolan-Cahill Memorial Scholarships *(Undergraduate/Scholarship)*

Purpose: To provide support to deserving students in Alaska who want to pursue an education in any campus of the University of Alaska. **Focus:** Science. **Qualif.:** Applicants must be a female students majoring in science with a GPA of at least 3.0; must demonstrate financial need. **Criteria:** Preference will be given first to applicants who are residents of Southern Alaska and next to graduates of Alaska high schools.

Funds Avail.: $500. **To Apply:** Applicant must complete the application forms available at the website; must attach a personal essay, two letters of recommendation, and current transcripts. **Deadline:** February 15.

4375 ■ Don & Jan O'Dowd/SWAA Scholarships *(Undergraduate/Scholarship)*

Purpose: To provide support to deserving students in Alaska who want to pursue an education in any campus of the University of Alaska. **Focus:** General studies. **Qualif.:** Applicants must be full-time incoming freshmen students with a minimum GPA of 3.0; must be Alaska residents and graduates of an Alaska high school. **Criteria:** Applicants will be selected based on their academic standing.

Funds Avail.: $500. **To Apply:** Applicant must complete the application forms available at the website; must attach a personal essay, two letters of recommendation, and current transcripts. **Deadline:** February 15.

4376 ■ Alvin G. Ott Fish and Wildlife Scholarships *(Undergraduate/Scholarship)*

Purpose: To provide support to deserving students in Alaska who want to pursue an education in any campus of the University of Alaska. **Focus:** General studies. **Qualif.:** Applicants must be full-time students with a minimum GPA of 3.0 and majoring in a field related to fish and wildlife. **Criteria:** Applicants will be selected based on their academic standing.

Funds Avail.: $500. **To Apply:** Applicant must complete the application forms available at the website; must attach a personal essay, two letters of recommendation, and current transcripts. **Deadline:** February 15.

4377 ■ Point Lay Memorial Scholarships *(Undergraduate/Scholarship)*

Purpose: To provide support to deserving students in Alaska who want to pursue an education in any campus of the University of Alaska. **Focus:** General studies. **Qualif.:** Applicants must be full-time students and current or former residents of Pt. Lay, Alaska. **Criteria:** Preference for applicants is given in the following order: (1) Resident or former resident of Pt. Lay, Alaska; (2) Alaska resident of one quarter or more Native ancestry who resides north of the Arctic Circle; (3) Alaska resident of one quarter or more Native ancestry; (4) Alaska resident; (5) undergraduate student.

Funds Avail.: $3,000. **To Apply:** Applicant must complete the application forms available at the website; must attach a personal essay, two letters of recommendation, and current transcripts. **Deadline:** February 15.

4378 ■ A.D. 'Al' Robertson Memorial Scholarships *(Undergraduate/Scholarship)*

Purpose: To provide support to deserving students in Alaska who want to pursue an education in any campus of the University of Alaska. **Focus:** General studies. **Qualif.:** Applicants must be full-time students and a member of the graduating class of Ketchikan High School in the year the scholarship is awarded; must have a minimum GPA of 2.5. **Criteria:** Selection of applicants will be based on their academic standing and application documents.

Funds Avail.: $500. **To Apply:** Applicant must complete the application forms available at the website; must attach a personal essay, two letters of recommendation, and current transcripts. **Deadline:** February 15.

4379 ■ Pat and Cliff Rogers Nursing Scholarships *(Undergraduate/Scholarship)*

Purpose: To provide support to deserving students in Alaska who want to pursue an education in any campus of the University of Alaska. **Focus:** General studies. **Qualif.:** Applicants must be full-time students in his/her junior or senior year of a nursing program at any institution within the U.S. **Criteria:** Applicants will be selected based on their application requirements.

Funds Avail.: $500. **To Apply:** Applicant must complete the application forms available in the website; must attach a personal essay, two letters of recommendation, and current transcripts. **Deadline:** February 15.

4380 ■ Dr. Orrin J. Rongstad Wildlife Management Scholarships *(Undergraduate/Scholarship)*

Purpose: To provide support to deserving students in Alaska who want to pursue an education in any campus of the University of Alaska. **Focus:** Wildlife conservation, management, and science. **Qualif.:** Applicants must be full-time students majoring in wildlife management and be in good academic standing. **Criteria:** Applicants will be selected based on their academic standing and application documents.

Funds Avail.: $500. **To Apply:** Applicant must complete the application forms available at the website; must attach a personal essay, two letters of recommendation, and current transcripts. **Deadline:** February 15.

4381 ■ Russian/Central Asian Student Scholarships *(Undergraduate/Scholarship)*

Purpose: To provide support to deserving students in Alaska who want to pursue an education in any campus of the University of Alaska. **Focus:** General studies. **Qualif.:** Applicants must be residents of Russia, Central Asia or the former Soviet Union, Kazakhstan, Uzbekistan, Turkmenistan, or Kyrgyzstan. **Criteria:** Preference will be given to residents of the Russian Far East.

Funds Avail.: $500. **To Apply:** Applicant must complete the application forms available at the website; must attach a personal essay, two letters of recommendation, and current transcripts. **Deadline:** February 15.

4382 ■ Clair Shirey Scholarships *(Undergraduate/Scholarship)*

Purpose: To provide support to deserving students in Alaska who want to pursue an education in any campus of the University of Alaska. **Focus:** Classical studies. **Qualif.:** Applicants must be music majors with a demonstrated interest or emphasis in classical/liturgical organ. **Criteria:** Preference will be given to students who are residents of the following geographical areas: Anchorage Archdiocese, Alaska and Pacific Northwest.

Funds Avail.: $500. **To Apply:** Applicant must complete the application forms available at the website; must attach a personal essay, two letters of recommendation, and current transcripts. **Deadline:** February 15.

4383 ■ Ward Sims Memorial Scholarships *(Undergraduate/Scholarship)*

Purpose: To provide support to deserving students in Alaska who want to pursue an education in any campus of the University of Alaska. **Focus:** Journalism. **Qualif.:** Applicants must be full-time junior or senior students enrolled in the Journalism program with a minimum GPA of 2.0. **Criteria:** Applicants will be selected based on their academic performance and application materials.

Funds Avail.: $1,000. **To Apply:** Applicant must complete the application forms available at the website; must attach a personal essay, two letters of recommendation, and current transcripts. **Deadline:** February 15.

4384 ■ Snodgrass Scholarships *(Undergraduate/Scholarship)*

Purpose: To provide an incentive for Alaska's middle and high school students to achieve academic excellence, and to encourage the top high school graduates from every community in Alaska to attend the University of Alaska. **Focus:** Accounting; Engineering, Architectural; Computer and information sciences; Fires and fire prevention; Heating, air conditioning, and refrigeration; Business administration; Telecommunications systems. **Qualif.:** Applicant must be admitted to the given Matanuska-Susitna College degree programs; must be a continuing student at Matanuska-Susitna College who has earned at least 20 credit hours; must have a cumulative GPA of 3.0 or higher; must exhibit good moral character and conduct; must be registered for eight or more credit hours. **Criteria:** Candidates will be selected based on their academic achievements and scholarship committee criteria.

Funds Avail.: $500-$2,000. **To Apply:** Applicants must complete the MSC scholarship application and attach a resume showing their work experience; must compose an essay of 500 words or less describing their educational and career goals and how they plan to attain them; must have two letters of recommendation, written within the last two years. Application form and other supporting documents must be sent to Snodgrass Scholarships, Matanuska-Susitna College, Student Service, FSM 102, Palmer, AK 99645. **Deadline:** May 31.

4385 ■ Sourdough Reunion Memorial Scholarships *(Undergraduate/Scholarship)*

Purpose: To provide support to deserving students in Alaska who want to pursue an education in any campus of the University of Alaska. **Focus:** General studies. **Qualif.:** Applicants must be full-time students entering his/her junior or senior year with a minimum GPA of 3.0 and be residents of Alaska or the Yukon Territory; must have graduated from a high school in Alaska or the Yukon Territory. **Criteria:** Selection of recipients will be based on academic performance and application materials.

Funds Avail.: $500. **To Apply:** Applicant must complete the application forms available at the website; must attach a personal essay, two letters of recommendation, and current transcripts. **Deadline:** February 15.

4386 ■ Togiak Village Scholarships *(Undergraduate/Scholarship)*

Purpose: To provide support to deserving students in Alaska who want to pursue an education in any campus of the University of Alaska. **Focus:** General studies. **Qualif.:** Applicants must be full-time students who are residents of Togiak Village seeking a college education. **Criteria:** Selection of applicants will be based on their application materials.

Funds Avail.: $500. **To Apply:** Applicant must complete the application forms available at the website; must attach a personal essay, two letters of recommendation, and current transcripts. **Deadline:** February 15.

4387 ■ Umialik Scholarships *(Undergraduate/Scholarship)*

Purpose: To provide support to deserving students in Alaska who want to pursue an education in any campus of the University of Alaska. **Focus:** General studies. **Qualif.:** Applicants must be full-time students attending any campus of the University of Alaska and be in good academic standing. **Criteria:** Preference will be given to Alaska Natives.

Funds Avail.: $5,000. **To Apply:** Applicant must complete the application forms available at the website; must attach a personal essay, two letters of recommendation, and current transcripts. **Deadline:** February 15.

4388 ■ University of Alaska Scholars Program *(Undergraduate/Scholarship)*

Purpose: To provide an incentive for Alaska's middle and high school students intending to achieve academic excellence; to nourish efforts of schools to provide high quality education; and to encourage the top high school graduates from every community in Alaska to attend the University of Alaska. **Focus:** General studies. **Qualif.:** Applicants must be US citizens or aliens lawfully admitted for permanent residence in the United States; must have successfully earned a high school diploma from a qualified Alaska high school; must be admitted into a certificate or degree program; must be enrolled as full-time, undergraduate students for the first fall semester following the graduation date of the class with which he or she designated and continuously thereafter; and must participate in or attend any mandatory orientation or program as may be required by the campus. **Criteria:** Selection of recipients will be based on their academic standing at the end of their junior year.

Funds Avail.: $1,375. **To Apply:** Applicants must submit the application form at the UA Scholars Program, University of Alaska, Butrovich Bldg., Ste. 207, Fairbanks, AK 99775. **Deadline:** May 1.

4389 ■ William S. Wilson Memorial Scholarships *(Undergraduate/Scholarship)*

Purpose: To provide support to deserving students in Alaska who want to pursue an education in any campus of the University of Alaska. **Focus:** Science. **Qualif.:** Applicants must be full-time students majoring in science. **Criteria:** Preference will be given to undergraduate students, but graduate students will be considered.

Funds Avail.: $5,000. **To Apply:** Applicant must complete the application forms available at the website; must attach a personal essay, two letters of recommendation, and current transcripts. **Deadline:** February 15.

4390 ■ Guy A. Woodings Scholarships *(Undergraduate/Scholarship)*

Purpose: To provide support to deserving students in Alaska who want to pursue an education in any campus of the University of Alaska. **Focus:** Natural resources. **Qualif.:** Applicants must be majoring in Natural Resource Management; must have been enrolled at least 2 years pursuing a 4-year degree. **Criteria:** Preference will be given to: (1) a Mat-Su Borough resident attending a Mat-Su College; (2) a Mat-Su Borough resident attending any UA campus; (3) a resident of Alaska attending a campus of the UA system; (4) a student having an emphasis on Planning and Land Use within the field of Natural Resource Management.

Funds Avail.: $500. **To Apply:** Applicant must complete the application forms available at the website; must attach a personal essay, two letters of recommendation, and current transcripts. **Deadline:** February 15.

4391 ■ Ralph Yetka Memorial Scholarships *(Undergraduate/Scholarship)*

Purpose: To provide support to deserving students in Alaska who want to pursue an education in any campus of the University of Alaska. **Focus:** Engineering; Education, Elementary; Education, Secondary; Computer and information sciences. **Qualif.:** Applicants must be full-time students and graduates of Ketchikan or Revilla High School with a minimum GPA of 2.5; must be majoring in engineering, elementary or secondary education, computer science or aviation. **Criteria:** Applicants will be selected based on their application materials and academic standing.

Funds Avail.: $750. **To Apply:** Applicant must complete the application forms available at the website; must attach a personal essay, two letters of recommendation, and current transcripts. **Deadline:** February 15.

4392 ■ Joan C. Yoder Memorial Nursing Scholarships *(Undergraduate/Scholarship)*

Purpose: To provide support to deserving students in Alaska who want to pursue an education in any campus of the University of Alaska. **Focus:** Nursing. **Qualif.:** Applicants must be full-time students majoring in nursing who have completed one clinical nursing course and is in good academic standing. **Criteria:** Selection of applicants will be based on their academic standing and application materials.

Funds Avail.: $500. **To Apply:** Applicant must complete the application forms available at the website; must attach a personal essay, two letters of recommendation, and current transcripts. **Deadline:** February 15.

4393 ■ Yukon Delta Fisheries Development Association Scholarships *(Undergraduate/Scholarship)*

Purpose: To provide support to deserving students in Alaska who want to pursue an education in any campus of the University of Alaska. **Focus:** General studies. **Qualif.:** Applicants must be undergraduate or graduate students from Alakanuk, Emmonak, Grayling, Kotlik, Mountain Village, Nunam Iqua, Pitka's Point, St. Mary's, Pilot Station, Marshall, Russian Mission, Holy Cross, Anvik and Shageluk; must demonstrate a subsistence and/or commercial fishing relationship to the lower Yukon Delta region and maintain a minimum cumulative GPA of 2.5 or higher. **Criteria:** Applicants will be selected based on their application materials and academic standing.

Funds Avail.: $500. **To Apply:** Applicant must complete the application forms available at the website; must attach a personal essay, two letters of recommendation, and current transcripts. **Deadline:** February 15.

4394 ■ Material Handling Institute of America

8720 Red Oak Blvd., Ste. 201
Charlotte, NC 28217-3992
Ph: (704)676-1190
Fax: (704)676-1199
URL: http://www.mhia.org

4395 ■ Material Handling Institute of America Scholarships *(Graduate, Undergraduate/Scholarship)*

Purpose: To promote the study of material handling and to expose as many students as possible to the material handling industry, including the vast array of equipment, systems and technologies represented by the industry; the role material handling in a productive enterprise; and the many career paths available within the supplier, distributor and end-user (applications) sides of the industry. **Focus:** Industrial. **Qualif.:** Applicants must be enrolled, or intending to enroll, in either an undergraduate, four (4) year baccalaureate program or a post graduate program leading to a masters or Ph.D. degree at a pre-qualified institution. Undergraduates must have completed a minimum of two (2) years of their undergraduate education. Students from junior and community colleges or other two (2) year post secondary institutions are also encouraged to apply if they have been accepted as a transfer student to a four (4) year program; have maintained a "B" overall grade point average and be full-time students; enrolled with courses like Civil, Electrical, Industrial, and Mechanical Engineering (and Engineering Technology); computer engineering; computer science; and business administration with an emphasis in production management, industrial distribution and/or logistics and in an accredited and pre-qualified program of study with the resources and means to support the study of material handling and material handling related subjects either through formal course work, independent study, summer work or coop experience, industry internships or some combination of same. **Criteria:** Candidates will be evaluated based on criteria.

Funds Avail.: No amount mentioned. **To Apply:** Applicants must name a primary faculty contact willing to assist in the preparation and submission of the scholarship application; must sent three letters of recommendation; official transcripts of all academic work completed beyond high school; and completed scholarship application. **Deadline:** March 1.

4396 ■ Materials Information Society

9639 Kinsman Rd.
Novelty, OH 44073
Ph: (440)338-5151
Fax: (440)338-4634
Free: 800-966-4867
E-mail: customerservice@asminternational.org
URL: http://asmcommunity.asminternational.org

4397 ■ Edward J. Dulis Scholarships *(Undergraduate/Scholarship)*

Purpose: To encourage and support capable students with interest and potential in the field of metallurgy/materials engineering and related careers. **Focus:** Metallurgy. **Qualif.:** Applicants must be material advantage members. Applicants must have an intended major in metallurgy or material science engineering. Applicants must have completed at least one year of college. **Criteria:** Recipients are selected based on academic achievement, interest in the field, and personal qualities.

Funds Avail.: $1,500. **To Apply:** Applicants must complete the application form. Applicants must write a personal statement (maximum of two pages). Applicants must submit a resume; a copy of the current academic transcript; a completed undergraduate scholarship recommendation form. Applicants must include a photograph for publication. Applicants must complete the personal statement with a financial officer contact. **Deadline:** May 1. **Contact:** asmif@asmiinternational.org

4398 ■ Nicholas J. Grant Scholarships *(Undergraduate/Scholarship)*

Purpose: To encourage and support capable students with interest and potential in the field of metallurgy/materials engineering and related careers. **Focus:** Metallurgy. **Qualif.:** Applicants must be material advantage members. Applicants must have an intended major in metallurgy or mate-

Awards are arranged alphabetically below their administering organizations

rial science engineering. Applicants must have completed at least one year of college. **Criteria:** Recipients are selected based on academic achievement, interest in the field, and personal qualities.

Funds Avail.: No specific amount. **To Apply:** Applicants must complete the application form. Applicants must write a personal statement (maximum of two pages). Applicants must submit a resume; a copy of the current academic transcript; a completed undergraduate scholarship recommendation form. Applicants must include a photograph for publication. Applicants must complete the personal statement with a financial officer contact. **Deadline:** May 1. **Contact:** asmif@asmiinternational.org

4399 ■ John M. Haniak Scholarships
(Undergraduate/Scholarship)

Purpose: To encourage and support capable students with interest and potential in the field of metallurgy/materials engineering and related careers. **Focus:** Metallurgy. **Qualif.:** Applicants must be material advantage members. Applicants must have an intended major in metallurgy or material science engineering. Applicants must have completed at least one year of college. **Criteria:** Recipients are selected based on academic achievement, interest in the field, and personal qualities.

Funds Avail.: $1,500. **Number Awarded:** 1. **To Apply:** Applicants must complete the application form. Applicants must write a personal statement (maximum of two pages). Applicants must submit a resume; a copy of the current academic transcript; a completed undergraduate scholarship recommendation form. Applicants must include a photograph for publication. Applicants must complete the personal statement with a financial officer contact. **Deadline:** May 1. **Contact:** asmif@asmiinternational.org

4400 ■ Materials Information Society National Merit Scholarships *(Undergraduate/Scholarship)*

Purpose: To encourage and support capable students with interest and potential in the field of metallurgy/materials engineering and related careers. **Focus:** Metallurgy. **Qualif.:** Applicants must be material advantage members. Applicants must have an intended major in metallurgy or material science engineering. Applicants must have completed at least one year of college. **Criteria:** Recipients are selected based on academic achievement, interest in the field, and personal qualities.

Funds Avail.: $1,000. **To Apply:** Applicants must complete the application form. Applicants must write a personal statement, maximum of two pagesn Applicants must submit a resume; a copy of the current academic transcript; a completed undergraduate scholarship recommendation form. Applicants must include a photograph for publication. Applicants must complete the personal statement with a financial officer contact. **Deadline:** May 1. **Contact:** asmif@asmiinternational.org

4401 ■ William Park Woodside Founder's Scholarships *(Undergraduate/Scholarship)*

Purpose: To encourage and support capable students with interest and potential in the field of metallurgy/materials engineering and related careers. **Focus:** Metallurgy. **Qualif.:** Applicants must be material advantage members. Applicants must have an intended major in metallurgy or material science engineering. Applicants must have completed at least one year of college. **Criteria:** Recipients are selected based on academic achievement, interest in the field, and personal qualities.

Funds Avail.: Maximum amount of $10,000. **To Apply:** Applicants must complete the application form. Applicants must write a two-page personal statement. Applicants must submit a resume; a copy of the current academic transcript; a completed undergraduate scholarship recommendation form. Applicants must include a photograph for publication. Applicants must complete the personal statement with a financial officer contact. **Deadline:** May 1. **Contact:** asmif@asmiinternational.org

4402 ■ George A. Roberts Scholarships
(Undergraduate/Scholarship)

Purpose: To encourage and support capable students with interest and potential in the field of metallurgy/materials engineering and related careers. **Focus:** Metallurgy. **Qualif.:** Applicants must be material advantage members. Applicants must have an intended major in metallurgy or material science engineering. Applicants must have completed at least one year of college. **Criteria:** Recipients are selected based on academic achievement, interest in the field, and personal qualities.

Funds Avail.: $6,000. **Number Awarded:** 7. **To Apply:** Applicants must complete the application form. Applicants must write a two-page personal statement. Applicants must submit a resume; a copy of the current academic transcript; a completed undergraduate scholarship recommendation form. Applicants must include a photograph for publication. Applicants must complete the personal statement with a financial officer contact. **Deadline:** May 1. **Contact:** asmif@asmiinternational.org

4403 ■ Lucille and Charles A. Wert Scholarships
(Undergraduate/Scholarship)

Purpose: To encourage and support capable students with interest and potential in the field of metallurgy/materials engineering and related careers. **Focus:** Metallurgy. **Qualif.:** Applicants must be material advantage members. Applicants must have an intended major in metallurgy or material science engineering. Applicants must have completed at least one year of college. **Criteria:** Recipients are selected based on academic achievement, interest in the field, and personal qualities.

Funds Avail.: $10,000. **To Apply:** Applicants must complete the application form. Applicants must write a personal statement (maximum of two pages). Applicants must submit a resume; a copy of the current academic transcript; a completed undergraduate scholarship recommendation form. Applicants must include a photograph for publication. Applicants must complete the personal statement with a financial officer contact. **Deadline:** May 1. **Contact:** asmif@asmiinternational.org

4404 ■ Edmund F. Maxwell Foundation

PO. Box 22537
Seattle, WA 98122-0537
E-mail: admin@maxwell.org
URL: http://www.maxwell.org

4405 ■ Edmund F. Maxwell Scholarships
(Undergraduate/Scholarship)

Purpose: To provide assistance to those who have demonstrated financial need and have shown ability, aptitude and a promise of useful citizenship. **Focus:** General studies. **Qualif.:** Applicant must be planning to attend an accredited independent college/university as freshman; a resident of Western Washington; and have a

Awards are arranged alphabetically below their administering organizations

combined math and reading SAT score of over 1200. **Criteria:** Award is given based on merit.

Funds Avail.: Up to $5000. **To Apply:** Applicants must submit a completed scholarship application along with the 500-word essay; official, certified high school transcript; Certification of SAT/ACT scores; and Financial Aid Worksheet (to be completed by each College/University); applicants must also submit a Free Application For Student Aid form (FAFSA) to the institution that he/she is planning to attend. **Deadline:** April 30.

4406 ■ Ronald McDonald House Charities

One Kroc Dr.
Oak Brook, IL 60523
Ph: (630)623-7048
Fax: (630)623-7488
E-mail: info@rmhc.org
URL: http://www.rmhc.org

4407 ■ Ronald McDonald House Charities African American Future Achievers Scholarships *(Undergraduate/Scholarship)*

Purpose: To help high school seniors attend college. **Focus:** General studies. **Qualif.:** Applicants must be high school seniors; must be younger than 21 years old; must be eligible to attend a two- or four-year college or university with a full course of study; must be legal residents of the United States; must be living in a participating local RMHS Chapter's geographic area; and must have at least one parent of African American or Black Caribbean heritage. **Criteria:** Recipients are selected based on academic performance.

Funds Avail.: No specific amount. **To Apply:** Applicants must complete the application form.

4408 ■ Ronald McDonald House Charities of Hispanic Heritage *(Undergraduate/Scholarship)*

Purpose: To help high school seniors to attend college. **Focus:** General studies. **Qualif.:** Applicants must be high school seniors; must be younger than 21 years old; must be eligible to attend a two- or four-year college or university with a full course of study; must be legal residents of the United States; must be living in a participating local RMHS Chapter's geographic area; and must have at least one parent of Hispanic heritage. **Criteria:** Recipients are selected based on academic performance.

Funds Avail.: No specific amount. **To Apply:** Applicants must complete the application form.

4409 ■ Ronald McDonald House Charities Scholarships *(Undergraduate/Scholarship)*

Purpose: To help high school seniors pursue educational goals. **Focus:** General studies. **Qualif.:** Applicants must be high school students. All students can apply regardless of race, color, creed, religion, sexual orientation, gender, disability or national origin. **Criteria:** Recipients are selected based on academic performance.

Funds Avail.: No specific amount. **To Apply:** Applicants must complete the application form.

4410 ■ Ronald McDonald House Charities Scholarships in Asia *(Undergraduate/Scholarship)*

Purpose: To help high school seniors to attend college. **Focus:** General studies. **Qualif.:** Applicants must be high school seniors; must be younger than 21 years old; must be eligible to attend a two- or four-year college or university with a full course of study; must be legal residents of the United States; must be living in a participating local RMHS Chapter's geographic area; and must have at least one parent of Asian/Pacific Islander heritage. **Criteria:** Recipients are selected based on academic performance.

Funds Avail.: No specific amount. **To Apply:** Applicants must complete the application form.

4411 ■ McDonald's Corporation

2111 McDonald's Dr.
Oak Brook, IL 60523
Free: 800-244-6227
URL: http://www.mcdonalds.com

4412 ■ McDonald's USA National Employee Scholarship Program *(Undergraduate/Scholarship)*

Purpose: To recognize and support the McDonald's USA student-employees for their education. **Focus:** General studies. **Qualif.:** Applicants must be currently employed at a McDonald's restaurant and have at least four months continuous employment at the time of application; must work a minimum of 15 hours per week; must be high school seniors or college students planning to attend an accredited institution offering postsecondary education and/or career training and instruction in the fall; must be employed by McDonald's or a McDonald's owner/operator at the time the scholarship awards are announced. **Criteria:** Recipients are selected based on documented academic achievement, community involvement and job performance.

Funds Avail.: $1,000. **To Apply:** Applicants must complete most of the application online and print out the rest. **Deadline:** March 1.

4413 ■ Richard D. McDonough Golf Scholarship Foundation

c/o Robert A. Provencher
243 Campbell St.
Manchester, NH 03104
Ph: (603)232-2345
E-mail: nhga@usga.org
URL: http://mcdonough.nhgolf.com

4414 ■ Dr. George T. Bottomley Scholarships *(Undergraduate/Scholarship)*

Purpose: To support outstanding young men and women employed at New Hampshire golf courses in pursuing higher education. **Focus:** General studies. **Qualif.:** Applicant must have a minimum of 2 summers of successful work at a NH golf course as a caddie, in the Pro Shop, on the grounds crew, or in the clubhouse; must be a high school graduate at an accredited school; have a minimum GPA of 2.5 on a 4.0 scale; demonstrate promise of academic success; must be from the Seacoast area; and have financial need. **Criteria:** Award is given based on the submitted scholarship application.

Funds Avail.: No specific amount. **To Apply:** Applicants must be recommended by the golf club where they have been employed for a minimum of two seasons. Applicants must submit a completed scholarship application; official copy of high school transcript; a copy of acceptance letter; a copy of FAFSA form. **Deadline:** May 23.

Remarks: Endowed in memory of Dr. George T. Bottomley

by the Fuller Foundation. **Contact:** Mitchell B. Jean, Chairman McDonough Scholarship Committee.

4415 ■ Dr. Robert Elliott Memorial Scholarships *(Undergraduate/Scholarship)*

Purpose: To support outstanding young men and women employed at New Hampshire golf courses in pursuing higher education. **Focus:** General studies. **Qualif.:** Applicant must have a minimum of 2 summers of successful work at a NH golf course as a caddie, in the Pro Shop, on the grounds crew, or in the clubhouse; must be a high school graduate at an accredited school; have a minimum GPA of 2.5 on a 4.0 scale; demonstrate promise of academic success; and have financial need. **Criteria:** Award is given to student with the highest cumulative GPA in their college work.

Funds Avail.: No specific amount. **To Apply:** Applicants must be recommended by the golf club where they have been employed for a minimum of two seasons. Applicants must submit a completed scholarship application; an official copy of high school transcript; a copy of acceptance letter; and a copy of FAFSA form. **Deadline:** May 23.

Remarks: Endowed in memory of Dr. Robert Elliott, president of The McDonough Foundation from 1960-1963. **Contact:** Mitchell B. Jean, Chairman McDonough Scholarship Committee.

4416 ■ Pauline Elliott Scholarships *(Undergraduate/Scholarship)*

Purpose: To support outstanding young men and women employed at New Hampshire golf courses in pursuing higher education. **Focus:** General studies. **Qualif.:** Applicant must have a minimum of 2 summers of successful work at a NH golf course as a caddie, in the Pro Shop, on the grounds crew, or in the clubhouse; must be a high school graduate from an accredited school; have a minimum GPA of 2.5 on a 4.0 scale; demonstrate promise of academic success; and have financial need. **Criteria:** Award is given based on the submitted scholarship application.

Funds Avail.: No specific amount. **To Apply:** Applicants must be recommended by the golf club where they have been employed for a minimum of two seasons. Applicants must submit a completed scholarship application; an official copy of high school transcript; a copy of acceptance letter; a copy of FAFSA form. **Deadline:** May 23.

Remarks: Endowed by the Manchester Country Club membership in honor of Mr. Lencki's 50 years of service to MCC. **Contact:** Mitchell B. Jean, Chairman McDonough Scholarship Committee.

4417 ■ Robert C. Erb Sr. Scholarships *(Undergraduate/Scholarship)*

Purpose: To support outstanding young men and women employed at New Hampshire golf courses in pursuing higher education. **Focus:** General studies. **Qualif.:** Applicant must have a minimum of 2 summers of successful work at a NH golf course as a caddie, in the Pro Shop, on the grounds crew, or in the clubhouse; must be a high school graduate at an accredited school; have a minimum GPA of 2.5 on a 4.0 scale; demonstrate promise of academic success; and have financial need. **Criteria:** Award is given based on the submitted scholarship application.

Funds Avail.: No specific amount. **To Apply:** Applicants must be recommended by the golf club where they have been employed for a minimum of two seasons. Applicants must submit a completed scholarship application; an official copy of high school transcript; a copy of acceptance letter; and a copy of FAFSA form. **Deadline:** May 23.

Remarks: Endowed in memory of Robert C. Erb Sr by his wife, Elizabeth P. Erb, and son, Bob Erb Jr. **Contact:** Mitchell B. Jean, Chairman McDonough Scholarship Committee.

4418 ■ Phil Friel Scholarships *(Undergraduate/Scholarship)*

Purpose: To support outstanding young men and women, employed at New Hampshire golf courses in pursuing higher education. **Focus:** General studies. **Qualif.:** Applicant must have a minimum of 2 summers of successful work at a NH golf course as a caddie, in the Pro Shop, on the grounds crew, or in the clubhouse; must be a high school graduate from an accredited school; have a minimum GPA of 2.5 on a 4.0 scale; demonstrate promise of academic success; must be pursuing a career in the golf industry; and have financial need. **Criteria:** Award is given based on the submitted scholarship application.

Funds Avail.: No specific amount. **To Apply:** Applicants must be recommended by the golf club where they have been employed for a minimum of two seasons. Applicants must submit a completed scholarship application; an official copy of high school transcript; a copy of acceptance letter; and a copy of FAFSA form. **Deadline:** May 23. **Contact:** Mitchell B. Jean, Chairman McDonough Scholarship Committee.

4419 ■ Alex Gissler Memorial Scholarships *(Undergraduate/Scholarship)*

Purpose: To support outstanding young men and women employed at 45 New Hampshire golf courses in pursuing higher education. **Focus:** General studies. **Qualif.:** Applicant must have a minimum of 2 summers of successful work at a NH golf course as a caddie, in the Pro Shop, on the grounds crew, or in the clubhouse; must be a high school graduate at an accredited school; have a minimum GPA of 2.5 on a 4.0 scale; demonstrate promise of academic success; work at Baker Hill Golf Club; and have financial need. **Criteria:** Award is given based on the submitted scholarship application.

Funds Avail.: No specific amount. **To Apply:** Applicants must be recommended by the golf club where they have been employed for a minimum of two seasons. Applicants must submit a completed scholarship application; an official copy of high school transcript; a copy of acceptance letter; and a copy of FAFSA form. **Deadline:** May 23.

Remarks: Endowed by Baker Hill Golf Club membership in memory of Alex Gissler. **Contact:** Mitchell B. Jean, Chairman McDonough Scholarship Committee.

4420 ■ Stan Lencki Scholarships *(Undergraduate/Scholarship)*

Purpose: To support outstanding young men and women employed at New Hampshire golf courses in pursuing higher education. **Focus:** General studies. **Qualif.:** Applicant must have a minimum of 2 summers of successful work at a NH golf course as a caddie, in the Pro Shop, on the grounds crew, or in the clubhouse; must be a high school graduate at an accredited school; have a minimum GPA of 2.5 on a 4.0 scale; demonstrate promise of academic success; and have financial need. **Criteria:** Award is given based on the submitted scholarship application.

Funds Avail.: No specific amount. **To Apply:** Applicants must be recommended by the golf club where they have been employed for a minimum of two seasons. Applicants must submit a completed scholarship application; an official copy of high school transcript; a copy of acceptance letter; and a copy of FAFSA form. **Deadline:** May 23.

Remarks: Endowed by the Manchester Country Club membership in honor of Mr. Lencki's 50 years of service to MCC. **Contact:** Mitchell B. Jean, Chairman McDonough Scholarship Committee.

4421 ■ Rick Mahoney Scholarships
(Undergraduate/Scholarship)

Purpose: To support outstanding young men and women employed at New Hampshire golf courses in pursuing higher education. **Focus:** General studies. **Qualif.:** Applicant must have a minimum of 2 summers of successful work at a NH golf course as a caddie, in the Pro Shop, on the grounds crew, or in the clubhouse; must be a high school graduate at an accredited school; have a minimum GPA of 2.5 on a 4.0 scale; demonstrate promise of academic success; be resident of Nashua, NH; and have financial need. **Criteria:** Award is given based on the submitted scholarship application.

Funds Avail.: No specific amount. **To Apply:** Applicants must be recommended by the golf club where they have been employed for a minimum of two seasons. Applicants must submit a completed scholarship application; an official copy of high school transcript; a copy of acceptance letter; and a copy of FAFSA form. **Deadline:** May 23.

Remarks: Endowed by the McDonough Foundation is honor of Mr. Mahoney. **Contact:** Mitchell B. Jean, Chairman McDonough Scholarship Committee.

4422 ■ NHPGA Apprentice Scholarships
(Undergraduate/Scholarship)

Purpose: To support outstanding young men and women employed at New Hampshire golf courses in pursuing higher education. **Focus:** General studies. **Qualif.:** Applicant must have a minimum of 2 summers of successful work at a NH golf course as a caddie, in the Pro Shop, on the grounds crew, or in the clubhouse; must be a high school graduate at an accredited school; have a minimum GPA of 2.5 on a 4.0 scale; demonstrate promise of academic success; and have financial need. **Criteria:** Award is given based on the submitted scholarship application.

Funds Avail.: No specific amount. **To Apply:** Applicants must be recommended by the golf club where they have been employed for a minimum of two seasons. Applicants must submit a completed scholarship application; an official copy of high school transcript; a copy of acceptance letter; and a copy of FAFSA form. **Deadline:** May 23.

Remarks: Endowed by the New Hampshire Chapter of the New England PGA. **Contact:** Mitchell B. Jean, Chairman McDonough Scholarship Committee.

4423 ■ Walter T. Philippy Scholarships
(Undergraduate/Scholarship)

Purpose: To support outstanding young men and women employed at New Hampshire golf courses in pursuing higher education. **Focus:** General studies. **Qualif.:** Applicant must have a minimum of 2 summers of successful work at a NH golf course as a caddie, in the Pro Shop, on the grounds crew, or in the clubhouse; must be a high school graduate at an accredited school; have a minimum GPA of 2.5 on a 4.0 scale; demonstrate promise of academic success; must be employed at Derryfield Country Club or a Manchester, NH, golf course; and must have financial need. **Criteria:** Award is given based on the submitted scholarship application.

Funds Avail.: No specific amount. **To Apply:** Applicants must be recommended by the golf club where they have been employed for a minimum of two seasons. Applicants must submit a completed scholarship application; an official copy of high school transcript; a copy of acceptance letter; and a copy of FAFSA form. **Deadline:** May 23.

Remarks: Endowed by Matilda Philippy and her family in memory of Walter T. Philippy. **Contact:** Mitchell B. Jean, Chairman McDonough Scholarship Committee.

4424 ■ David J. Pollini Scholarships
(Undergraduate/Scholarship)

Purpose: To support outstanding young men and women employed at New Hampshire golf courses in pursuing higher education. **Focus:** General studies. **Qualif.:** Applicant must have a minimum of 2 summers of successful work at a NH golf course as a caddie, in the Pro Shop, on the grounds crew, or in the clubhouse; must be a high school graduate at an accredited school; have a minimum GPA of 2.5 on a 4.0 scale; demonstrate promise of academic success; must be an employee of Kingswood Golf Club or Lakes Region golf course; and have financial need. **Criteria:** Award is given based on the submitted scholarship application.

Funds Avail.: No specific amount. **To Apply:** Applicants must be recommended by the golf club where they have been employed for a minimum of two seasons. Applicants must submit a completed scholarship application; an official copy of high school transcript; a copy of acceptance letter; and a copy of FAFSA form. **Deadline:** May 23.

Remarks: Endowed by the Kingswood Golf Club membership and friends of Dave. **Contact:** Mitchell B. Jean, Chairman McDonough Scholarship Committee.

4425 ■ Pope Scholarships Award
(Undergraduate/Scholarship)

Purpose: To support outstanding young men and women employed at New Hampshire golf courses in pursuing higher education. **Focus:** General studies. **Qualif.:** Applicant must have a minimum of 2 summers of successful work at a NH golf course as a caddie, in the Pro Shop, on the grounds crew, or in the clubhouse; must be a high school graduate at an accredited school; have a minimum GPA of 2.5 on a 4.0 scale; demonstrate promise of academic success; and have financial need. **Criteria:** Award is given based on the submitted scholarship application.

Funds Avail.: No specific amount. **To Apply:** Applicants must be recommended by the golf club where they have been employed for a minimum of two seasons. Applicants must submit a completed scholarship application; an official copy of high school transcript; a copy of acceptance letter; and a copy of FAFSA form. **Deadline:** May 23.

Remarks: Funded by the Foundation, together with the membership of Concord Country Club, in memory of the former University of New Hampshire golf coach and Concord Country Club member, Ken Pope. **Contact:** Mitchell B. Jean, Chairman McDonough Scholarship Committee.

4426 ■ Jim Sheerin Scholarships
(Undergraduate/Scholarship)

Purpose: To support outstanding young men and women employed at New Hampshire golf courses in pursuing higher education. **Focus:** General studies. **Qualif.:** Applicant must have a minimum of 2 summers of successful work at a NH golf course as a caddie, in the Pro Shop, on the grounds crew, or in the clubhouse; must be a high school graduate from an accredited school; have a minimum GPA of 2.5 on a 4.0 scale; demonstrate promise of academic success; must be employed at Abenaqui Country Club or at a Seacoast-area golf course; and have financial need. **Criteria:** Award is given based on the submitted scholarship application.

Funds Avail.: No specific amount. **To Apply:** Applicants must be recommended by the golf club where they have been employed for a minimum of two seasons. Applicants must submit a completed scholarship application; copy of high school transcript; copy of acceptance; a copy of FAFSA form. **Deadline:** May 23.

Remarks: Endowed by Abenaqui Country Club membership and friends of Jim in honor of his many years of service as head golf professional and director of golf. **Contact:** Mitchell B. Jean, Chairman McDonough Scholarship Committee.

4427 ■ McGill University

4th Flr., James Administration Bldg.
845 Sherbrooke St. W
Montreal, QC, Canada H3A 2T5
Ph: (514)398-3990
Fax: (514)398-1626
URL: http://www.mcgill.ca

4428 ■ Mackenzie King Open Scholarships *(Graduate/Scholarship)*

Purpose: To provide support for graduating students to pursue their education. **Focus:** General studies. **Qualif.:** Applicant must be a graduate of any Canadian university for full-time postgraduate studies in Canada; must be an undergraduate applicants with first Class Honours Standing (CGPA of 3.7 or higher - 3.5 for Law), a graduate applicants must have a "straight A" records. **Criteria:** Awards will be based on high academic achievements, personal qualities, and demonstrated aptitudes. Consideration will also be given to the applicant's proposed program of study.

Funds Avail.: $9,000. **To Apply:** Applicant must complete the application form available in the website at www.mkingscholarships.ca; must have a three letter of reference from persons who have an initiate knowledge of the record and ability and are able to give a critical evaluation of their plans for graduate study; must have the official transcript of record and other academic records from each university they have attended. **Deadline:** February 1.

4429 ■ Mackenzie King Travelling Scholarships *(Graduate/Scholarship)*

Purpose: To provide support for deserving students intending to pursue their studies in the United States or the United Kingdom in the areas of international relations and industrial relations. **Focus:** International affairs and relations, Industrial and labor relations. **Qualif.:** Applicant must be a graduate of any Canadian university who wants to pursue graduate study in the United States or the United Kingdom in international or industrial relation. **Criteria:** Awards are based on academic achievement, personal qualities and demonstrated aptitudes, as well as proposed program of study. Consideration will be given to a undergraduate applicants with First Class Honours Standing (CGPA of 3.7 or higher - 3.5 for Law) and graduate applicants with cumulative "straight A" records.

Funds Avail.: $10,000. **To Apply:** Applicant must complete the application form available in the website at www.mkingscholarships.ca; must have a three letter of reference from persons who have an initiate knowledge of the record and ability and are able to give a critical evaluation of their plans for graduate study; must have the official transcript of record and other academic records from each university they have attended. **Deadline:** February 1.

4430 ■ McGill University Alma Mater Student Travel Grants *(Graduate/Grant)*

Purpose: To award the McGill graduate students in any discipline for their achievements in attending a scholarly meeting or conference where they will be presenting a paper relating to their graduate research. **Focus:** General studies. **Qualif.:** Applicant must be registered as full-time graduate students in a Master's or doctoral program at McGill; must have been accepted to present and have presented a paper or poster at a scholarly meeting or conference that falls within the specific time period of the competition. **Criteria:** Preference will be given to applicants who did not receive an award in the previous competition.

Funds Avail.: $750. **To Apply:** Applicant must submit one copy of the application form, including the required department signatures; must have an abstract or precis of the paper to be presented (1 page maximum); must provide an evidence of acceptance to present a paper or poster (copy of letter of acceptance or the conference program); must submit the payment request form, personal data form, direct deposit form, and proof of participation in the scholarly meeting or conference as defined on the payment request form. **Deadline:** September 15, January 15, and May 15.

4431 ■ McGill University Scholarships for Research Trips to Europe *(Graduate/Scholarship)*

Purpose: To support research trips to Europe that are necessary for completion of a MA or doctoral thesis. **Focus:** European studies. **Qualif.:** Applicant must be registered in full-time graduate studies at McGill University; must be preparing an MA or doctoral thesis that will make a contribution to knowledge about the political, legal, economic, or social system of the European Union or the history of European integration. **Criteria:** Selection of applicant will be based on their research proposal.

Funds Avail.: $600-$5,000. **To Apply:** For further information and for application form, applicants are advice to contact the foundation at www.centreurope-montreal.ca. **Deadline:** April 4.

4432 ■ Philip F. Vineberg Travelling Fellowship in the Humanities *(Graduate/Scholarship)*

Purpose: To provide financial support to a qualified individuals who wants to pursue their education. **Focus:** Law, Art, Education, Library and archival sciences, Music, Religious education, Social work. **Qualif.:** Applicant must be a registered student at McGill in a degree program in Arts, Education, Law, Library Science, Music, Religious Studies or Social Work. **Criteria:** Selection of applicant will be based on their academic achievements and personal qualities.

Funds Avail.: $14,500. **To Apply:** Application forms are available online at www.mkingscholarships.ca. Applicant must have a three letter of reference from persons who have an initiate knowledge of the record and ability and are able to give a critical evaluation of their plans for graduate study; must have the official transcript of record and other academic records from each university they have attended. **Deadline:** February 1.

4433 ■ McKelvey Foundation

200 Park Ave., 44th Fl.
New York, NY 10166
Ph: (212)847-7236
Fax: (212)847-7240
Free: 877-625-3583
E-mail: info@mckelveyfoundation.org
URL: http://www.mckelveyfoundation.org

4434 ■ McKelvey Foundation Entrepreneurial Scholarships *(Undergraduate/Scholarship)*

Purpose: To assist the education of young entrepreneurs. **Focus:** General studies. **Qualif.:** Applicant must be a graduating senior of a U.S. high school or home-school program; plan to attend an accredited four-year college or university in the U.S.; have owned and operated a business for at least one year with at least one paid employee (excluding the applicant); and have generated sales revenue (unless non-profit). **Criteria:** Awards are given based on the application and telephone interview (for finalists).

Funds Avail.: Up to $10,000 per year. **Number Awarded:** 150. **To Apply:** Applicants must submit a completed online scholarship application. **Deadline:** January 25.

4435 ■ McKelvey Scholarships *(Undergraduate/Scholarship)*

Purpose: To financially support the education of a student who is first in the family to pursue a college education. **Focus:** General studies. **Qualif.:** Applicant must attend a partnering high school in the states of NY, PA or WV; be the first generation to attend college (neither mother nor father went to college); have financial need; show involvement in work and/or extracurricular activities; and plan to attend a four-year college within home state. **Criteria:** Awards are given based on need.

Funds Avail.: $3,000 each year. **Number Awarded:** 150. **To Apply:** Applicants must submit a completed online scholarship application. **Deadline:** December 1.

4436 ■ MCRD Museum Historical Society

PO Box 400085 Bldg. 26
San Diego, CA 92140-0085
Ph: (619)524-4426
URL: http://mcrdmuseumhistoricalsociety.org

4437 ■ Colonel Nate Smith Memorial Scholarships *(Graduate, Undergraduate/Scholarship)*

Purpose: To provide educational assistance for MCRD San Diego enlisted marines or sailors, and their dependents, who are enrolled in an accredited graduate or undergraduate college program. **Focus:** Military science and education. **Qualif.:** Applicants must be enlisted active duty marines or sailors currently assigned to MCRD San Diego/Western Recruiting Region or their dependents; must be high school graduates and must provide proof of enrollment in a postsecondary program, or have previously attended college. **Criteria:** Applicants are evaluated based on academic merit.

Funds Avail.: No specific amount. **Number Awarded:** 3. **To Apply:** Applicants must submit all the required application information. **Deadline:** July 3.

4438 ■ Media Action Network for Asian Americans

PO Box 11105
Burbank, CA 91510
Ph: (213)486-4433
Free: 888-90-MANAA
E-mail: manaaletters@yahoo.com
URL: http://www.manaa.org

4439 ■ MANAA Media Scholarships *(Graduate, Undergraduate/Scholarship)*

Purpose: To promote education in filmmaking and in television production. **Focus:** Filmmaking; Television. **Qualif.:** Applicants must be graduate or undergraduate students pursuing careers as filmmakers and in television production (not broadcast journalism). **Criteria:** Selected on the basis of their academic and personal merit, with the desire to uplift the image of Asian Americans in film and television.

Funds Avail.: $1000. **Number Awarded:** 1. **To Apply:** Applicants must submit a copy of all official transcripts; copy of completed financial aid documents; two letters of recommendation; a double-spaced essay (maximum of 1,000 words); and a work sample consisting of a short film or screenplay (optional). Send applications to MANAA Scholarship, P.O. Box 11105, Burbank, CA 91510. Do not send applications via certified or registered mail. **Deadline:** May 9.

Remarks: The scholarship was formed in 1992.

4440 ■ Medical Library Association

65 E Wacker Place, Ste. 1900
Chicago, IL 60601-7246
Ph: (312)419-9094
Fax: (312)419-8950
E-mail: info@mlahq.org
URL: http://www.mlanet.org

4441 ■ Continuing Education Awards *(Graduate/Grant)*

Purpose: To assist MLA members in developing their knowledge of the theoretical, administrative, or technical aspects of librarianship. **Focus:** Library and archival sciences. **Qualif.:** Applicant must have a graduate degree in library science; must be a practicing health science librarian with at least two years of professional experience; a member of the MLA; a U.S. or Canadian citizen or have permanent residence status; must clearly identify a continuing education program within the U.S. or Canada. **Criteria:** Applicants with library experience and their professional activities are given consideration.

Funds Avail.: $100-$500. **To Apply:** Application forms are available at the website. Applicants must complete 7 copies of the application form and three names of references not related to the applicant. Nine copies of the completed application form and all related documents should be submitted to: Medical Library Association, Professional Development Department, 65 E Wacker Place, Ste. 1900, Chicago, IL 60601-7246, email: mlapd2@mlahq.org. **Deadline:** December 1. **Contact:** mlapd2@mlahq.org.

4442 ■ HLS/MLA Professional Development Grants *(Doctorate/Grant)*

Purpose: To support librarians working in hospitals and similar clinical settings with their educational or research activities. **Focus:** Library and archival sciences; Health sciences. **Qualif.:** Applicant must have been employed as a health sciences librarian within the last year in either a hospital or other clinical care institution; must not have previously received an HLS/MLA Professional Development Award or any MLA grant, scholarship, or other award within the past year; must be a member of the Hospital Libraries Sections/MLA. **Criteria:** Selection is based on the submitted application and supporting documents.

Funds Avail.: $800. **To Apply:** Application form is available at the website. Applicants must return nine copies of the completed application and nine copies of other documents to: Medical Library Association, Professional Development Department, 65 E. Wacker Place, Ste. 1900, Chicago, IL 60601-7246, email: mlapd2@mlahq.org. **Deadline:** February 1 or August 1. **Contact:** mlapd2@mlahq.org.

4443 ■ David A. Kronick Travelling Fellowships *(Doctorate/Fellowship)*

Purpose: To promote the education on health information management. **Focus:** Health care services; Management. **Qualif.:** Applicant must be a U.S. or Canadian citizen or have permanent residence status; member of the Medical Library Association; must have a graduate degree in library science; must be a practicing health sciences librarian with at least five years of professional experience. **Criteria:** Applicants and proposals will be selected based on merits and quality of materials submitted including originality and relevance.

Funds Avail.: $2,000. **To Apply:** Application forms are available at the website. Applicant must prepare a resume/CV; names of three references not related to the applicant; and a proposal containing: title, goals, objectives, methodology, significance, and budget of project. Nine copies of completed application and documents must be sent to: Medical Library Association, Professional Development Department, 65 E. Wacker Place, Ste. 1900, Chicago, IL 60601-7246, email: mlapd2@mlahq.org. **Deadline:** December 1. **Contact:** mlapd2@mlahq.org.

4444 ■ Donald A. B. Lindberg Research Fellowships *(Doctorate, Graduate/Fellowship)*

Purpose: To fund a research aimed at expanding the knowledge base used by librarians in improving health care and advances in biomedical research. **Focus:** Biomedical research; Health care services. **Qualif.:** Applicants must be sponsored by an institution or an organization; must be citizens of the United States or Canada; must have a bachelor's, master's, or doctor's degree or is enrolled in a degree program; must be committed to the health sciences. **Criteria:** Applications will be reviewed based on academic, scientific and technical specifications.

Funds Avail.: $8,100. **To Apply:** Applicants must submit an application electronically together with a curriculum vitae or biographical sketch; research proposal (5-10 pages) including background and rationale, research aims, budget, research design and methodology, timeline, and plans for disseminating the results; letters of support from the applicant's home institution or from sponsoring institutions or organizations. **Deadline:** November 15. **Contact:** mlapd2@mlahq.org

4445 ■ MLA/NLM Spectrum Scholarship Program *(Graduate/Scholarship)*

Purpose: To promote health information management education. **Focus:** Health sciences. **Qualif.:** Applicant must be of African American, Hispanic, Asian, Native American, or Pacific Islander heritage attending an ALA-accredited library school. **Criteria:** Recipient is selected based on merit.

Funds Avail.: $6,500. **To Apply:** Applicants must contact ALA Spectrum program for scholarship information. **Deadline:** March 1.

Remarks: The award is jointly sponsored by the MLA and National library of Medicine (NLM) through the American Library Association (ALA) Spectrum Initiative Scholarship program. **Contact:** 800-545-2433 or spectrum@ala.org

4446 ■ MLA Research, Development, and Demonstration Project Grants *(Graduate/Grant)*

Purpose: To fund a research or project that promotes excellence in the field of health sciences librarianship. **Focus:** Library and archival sciences; Health sciences. **Qualif.:** Applicants must have a graduate degree in library science; should be a practicing health sciences librarian with at least two years of professional experience; an individual member of the Medical Library Association; a U.S. or Canadian citizen or has permanent residence status. **Criteria:** Recipients of the awards will be evaluated based on the applicant and on the proposal criteria set by the Awards committee.

Funds Avail.: $100 to $1,000. **To Apply:** Application forms are available from the website. Proposals must contain title, goals, objectives, methodology, significance and budget. Nine copies of the completed application form and all related documents should be submitted to: Medical Library Association, Professional Development Department, 65 E. Wacker Place, Ste. 1900, Chicago, IL 60601-7246, email: mlapd2@mlahq.org. **Deadline:** December 1. **Contact:** mlapd2@mlahq.org.

4447 ■ MLA Scholarships for Minority Students *(Graduate/Scholarship)*

Purpose: To promote the education on health information management. **Focus:** Library and archival sciences; Health sciences. **Qualif.:** Applicant must be a U.S. or Canadian citizen or have permanent residence status; a member of a minority group (African-American, Hispanic, Asian, Native American, or Pacific Islander); entering an ALA-accredited graduate library school; must have completed no more than half of the graduate program. **Criteria:** Preference is given to those who have not been a recipient of the award.

Funds Avail.: $5,000. **To Apply:** Applicant must submit seven copies of the completed application form available at the website; 2-3 letters of reference from persons not related to the applicant; and an official transcript (sent directly by the respective institution to the MLA office). Nine copies of the completed application form and essay, and single copy of all related documents, must be returned to: Medical Library Association, Professional Development Department, 65 E. Wacker Place, Ste. 1900, Chicago, IL 60601-7246, email: mlapd2@mlahq.org. **Deadline:** December 1. **Contact:** mlapd2@mlahq.org.

4448 ■ Thomson Scientific/MLA Doctoral Fellowships *(Doctorate/Fellowship)*

Purpose: To fund a doctoral work in health sciences librarianship or information science. **Focus:** Health sciences;

Awards are arranged alphabetically below their administering organizations

Information science and technology; Library and archival sciences. **Qualif.:** Applicant must be a graduate of an ALA-accredited school of library science; a candidate in a Ph.D. program emphasizing on biomedical and health-related information science; and a U.S. or Canadian citizen of permanent residence status. **Criteria:** Preference is given to applicants who have completed at least 75 percent of their course work and dissertation prospectus either approved or in the approval process.

Funds Avail.: $2,000. **To Apply:** Application form is available at the website. Applicant must prepare two letters of reference (submitted directly to MLA); transcript or proof of enrollment in the graduate program and list of completed courses (mailed directly to MLA); and the name, title, address, phone, and email of doctoral advisor. Applicants must submit nine copies of completed application and other supporting materials to: Medical Library Association, Professional Development Department, 65 E. Wacker Place, Ste. 1900, Chicago, IL 60601-7246, email: mlapd2@mlahq.org. **Deadline:** December 1. **Contact:** mlapd2@mlahq.org.

4449 ■ MediCorp Health System

2300 Fall Hill Ave., Ste. 401
Fredericksburg, VA 22401
Ph: (540)899-5411
Fax: (540)741-2571
Free: (866)860-0946
URL: http://www.medicorpcareers.org

4450 ■ MHS Health Career Scholarships *(Undergraduate/Scholarship)*

Purpose: To provide financial assistance to cover tuition, fees, housing, and textbooks for deserving students in their final year of education. **Focus:** Medical. **Qualif.:** Applicants must be rising seniors who have at least a minimum GPA of 2.75 in profession courses and in good standing attending an accredited BSN, CRNA, PT, OT, SLP, radiology tech, or pharmacist program. **Criteria:** Applicants are selected based on financial need.

Funds Avail.: No specific amount. **To Apply:** Applicants must submit resume; a copy of current CPR; two clinical letters of reference; top clinical areas of interest; statement of goals; current transcript; and the complete application packet.

4451 ■ Meeting Professionals International-Connecticut River Valley Chapter

49 Cedar Ln.
Colchester, CT 06415
Ph: (860)961-1905
Fax: (860)499-5006
E-mail: mpicrv@gmail.com
URL: http://www.crvmpi.org

4452 ■ MPI CRV Continuing Education Scholarships *(Professional Development/Scholarship)*

Purpose: To promote members' professional development and encourage their active participation in the chapter. **Focus:** General studies. **Qualif.:** Applicant must be a current MPI CRV member in good standing. **Criteria:** Applications will be reviewed by the Scholarship Committee based on chapter involvement, experience, financial need, and professional contribution.

Funds Avail.: $1000. **To Apply:** Applicants must submit a completed application form with the required materials to MassMutual Center, Melissa Voutour, 1277 Main St., Springfield, MA 01103, or fax to: 413787-6645, or email at: mvoutour@massconvention.com. **Deadline:** May 2.

4453 ■ Meeting Professionals International-Greater New York Chapter

7 Fox Run Rd.
Briarcliff Manor, NY 10510
Ph: (914)762-1456
Fax: (914)944-9227
E-mail: info@mpigny.org
URL: http://www.mpigny.org

4454 ■ Jay Magazine Memorial Fund (JMMF) College Scholarships *(Undergraduate/Scholarship)*

Purpose: To support the education of a student working towards degrees to enter into the hospitality industry. **Focus:** Hotel, institutional, and restaurant management. **Qualif.:** Applicant must be carrying a minimum class load of 6 credits in current semester or be working F/T with 3 credits in current semester. **Criteria:** Selection is based on the merits of the application.

Funds Avail.: Membership to the chapter - $40; $1000 reimbursement of school expenses; and $100 in "MPI Dollars" to attend MPI Educational Events. **To Apply:** Applicants must submit a completed application form along with the required documents to Donny Wancho at awards@mpigny.org, or via fax at 718361-09670. **Deadline:** Jan 31.

4455 ■ The Melissa Institute

6250 Sunset Dr., Ste. 204
Miami, FL 33143
Ph: (786)662-5210
Fax: (786)662-5211
URL: http://www.melissainstitute.org

4456 ■ Belfer-Aptman Dissertation Research Awards *(Doctorate/Grant)*

Purpose: To provide financial assistance to support expenses that are directly related to violence prevention research. **Focus:** Violence. **Qualif.:** Applicants must be students in an accredited doctoral dissertation program. Candidates may be from any academic discipline; must have their dissertation proposal approved by their dissertation committee prior to their application to the Melissa Institute. **Criteria:** Applicants will be evaluated by the Award Selection Committee.

Funds Avail.: $2,000. **To Apply:** Applicants must submit proposed thesis; a brief 300-word abstract of proposed study; letter of recommendation from dissertation advisor; and curriculum vitae, including any scientific publications and presentations with a brief description of career plans. **Deadline:** April 1.

4457 ■ Memorial Foundation for Jewish Culture

50 Broadway, 34th Fl.
New York, NY 10004
Ph: (212)425-6606
Fax: (212)425-6602
E-mail: office@mfic.org
URL: http://www.mfjc.org

Awards are arranged alphabetically below their administering organizations

4458 ■ International Doctoral Scholarships for Studies Specializing in Jewish Fields *(Doctorate/Scholarship)*

Purpose: To help train qualified individuals for careers in Jewish scholarship and research, and to help Jewish educational, religious, and communal workers obtain advanced training for leadership positions. **Focus:** Jewish studies. **Qualif.:** Applicant must be a graduate student specializing in a Jewish field and must be officially enrolled or registered in a doctoral program at a recognized university. **Criteria:** Application and references are evaluated by outside experts and then considered by appropriate committees of the foundation.

Funds Avail.: $10,000. **To Apply:** Applicant must submit a documentation of the university. **Deadline:** October 31.

4459 ■ International Fellowships in Jewish Studies *(Professional Development/Fellowship)*

Purpose: To assist well-qualified individuals in carrying out an independent scholarly, literary or art project in a field of Jewish specialization. **Focus:** Jewish studies. **Qualif.:** Applicant must be a qualified scholar, researcher, or artist who possesses the knowledge and experience to formulate and implement a project in a field of Jewish specialization. **Criteria:** Proposed projects are evaluated by outside experts. Applications are then considered by appropriate committees of the foundation.

Funds Avail.: $10,000. **To Apply:** Application materials can be obtained through individual written requests with a brief description of the project from the Memorial Foundation for Jewish Culture, 50 Broadway-34th Fl., New York, NY 10004. **Deadline:** October 31.

4460 ■ International Scholarship Program for Community Service *(Other/Scholarship)*

Purpose: To assist well-qualified individuals to train for careers in the rabbinate, Jewish education, social work, and as religious functionaries. **Focus:** Jewish studies; Social work; Religious education. **Qualif.:** Applicants must be undergoing (or planning to undergo) training in a recognized yeshiva, teacher training seminary, school of social work, university or other educational institution. Applicants must commit to serve in a community of need for a minimum of two to three years and must be knowledgeable in the language and culture. **Criteria:** Selection of recipients will be done by outside experts and appropriate committees of the foundation.

Funds Avail.: Amount of the grant varies, depending on the country in which the student will be trained. **To Apply:** Applications may be obtained through individual written requests with a brief description of the project from the Memorial Foundation for Jewish Culture, 50 Broadway-34th Fl., New York, NY 10004. **Deadline:** October 30.

4461 ■ Mental Health Association of Tarrant County

3136 W St.
Fort Worth, TX 76107
Ph: (817)335-5405
Fax: (817)334-0025
E-mail: mhatc@mhatc.org
URL: http://www.mhatc.org

4462 ■ Patricia Powder Conolly Memorial Scholarships *(Undergraduate/Scholarship)*

Purpose: To provide financial support to those students pursuing a degree in the mental health field. **Focus:** Psychiatry; Psychology; Sociology; Social work; Counseling; Rehabilitation counseling. **Qualif.:** Applicants must be college students pursuing a degree in the mental health field. **Criteria:** Preference will be given to those students who meet the criteria.

Funds Avail.: No specific amount. **To Apply:** Applicants must check the available website to download the application form. **Contact:** Mental Health Association of Tarrant County at the above address (see entry 4461).

4463 ■ Lillian Cooper Droke Memorial Scholarships *(Undergraduate/Scholarship)*

Purpose: To provide financial support to those students who have mental illnesses. **Focus:** General Studies. **Qualif.:** Applicants must be enrolled in college or technical training; must have a mental illness. If no eligible mental health consumer applies, other students pursuing a career in the mental health field may also be considered. **Criteria:** Preference will be given to those who meet the criteria.

Funds Avail.: No specific amount. **To Apply:** Applicants must check the available website online to download the application form. **Contact:** Mental Health Association of Tarrant County at the above address (see entry 4461).

4464 ■ Linda Lyons Memorial Scholarship Fund *(Undergraduate/Scholarship)*

Purpose: To provide financial support to those students pursuing a degree in the mental health field. **Focus:** Psychiatry; Psychology; Sociology; Social work; Counseling; Rehabilitation counseling. **Qualif.:** Applicants must be college students pursuing a degree in the mental health field. **Criteria:** Preference will be given to those students who meet the criteria.

Funds Avail.: No specific amount. **To Apply:** Applicants must check the available website to download the application form. **Contact:** Mental Health Association of Tarrant County at the above address (see entry 4461).

4465 ■ Mexican American Cultural Center

PO Box 28185
San Antonio, TX 78228-5104
Ph: (210)732-2156
Fax: (210)732-9072
URL: http://www.maccsa.org

4466 ■ MACC Scholarships *(Professional Development/Scholarship)*

Purpose: To support an individual's spiritual and educational journey. **Focus:** Religious education, Languages. **Qualif.:** Applicant must be a member of any religious community. **Criteria:** Priority will be given to applicants ministering in the United States with possible exceptions based on individual requests and based on applicant's need.

Funds Avail.: No specific amount. **To Apply:** Applicant must have the registration form and fee; must have two letters of recommendation from the applicant's superior, bishop, chancellor, pastor, or supervisor; must have one letter from the organization's executive director; must have 2-3 typed pages of autobiography (pastoral program only); must have a questionnaire and placement (language program only). Complete application must be mailed to: MACC Scholarship Committee, 3115 W Ashby Place, San Antonio, TX 78228.

4467 ■ Mexican American Grocers Association

405 N. San Fernando Rd.
Los Angeles, CA 90031

Awards are arranged alphabetically below their administering organizations

Ph: (323)227-1565
Fax: (323)227-6935
E-mail: maga727@sbcglobal.net
URL: http://www.maga.org

4468 ■ Mexican American Grocers Association Scholarships *(Undergraduate/Scholarship)*

Purpose: To provide financial assistance for financially needy students. **Focus:** General studies. **Qualif.:** Applicants must demonstrate financial need. **Criteria:** Priority will be given to applicants with financial need.

Funds Avail.: No specific amount. **To Apply:** Applicants must check the application process online. **Contact:** Mexican American Grocers Association at the above address (see entry 4467).

4469 ■ Mexican American Legal Defense and Educational Fund

634 S Spring St.
Los Angeles, CA 90014
Ph: (213)629-2512
URL: http://www.maldef.org

4470 ■ MALDEF Law School Scholarships *(Undergraduate/Scholarship)*

Purpose: To increase the number of Latinos in the legal profession. **Focus:** Law. **Qualif.:** Students must be enrolled full time in law school. **Criteria:** Scholarship will be awarded to candidates who have outstanding academic record, including participation and leadership in extracurricular activities.

Funds Avail.: $7,000. **To Apply:** Applicants must complete and send the following materials: a completed and signed MALDEF Scholarship form; current resume; a typed personal statement of 750 words or less, double-spaced, detailing professional objectives, plans after school, and describing your past involvement in activities which applicant believes have served or benefited the Latino community and how these activities relate to your decision to pursue a career in the legal profession; an official undergraduate transcript or photocopy of an official transcript; For law schoolstudents who have already completed one year or more of law school, please, also provide: an official law school transcript or photocopy of an official transcript; a letter of recommendation describing your involvement in the Latino community from a person familiar with that involvement; a letter of recommendation from a college, or law school professor; and a completed financial need statement (enclose) from the school applicant is attending that indicates the financial assistance provided to you by the school's financial aid office. **Deadline:** October 3. **Contact:** MALDEF Law School Scholarship Program at the above address (see entry 4469).

4471 ■ Michigan Association for Deaf and Hard Hearing

2929 Covington Court, Ste. 200
Lansing, MI 48912-4939
Ph: (517)487-0066
Fax: (517)487-2586
Free: 800-968-7327
E-mail: info@madhh.org
URL: http://www.madhh.org

4472 ■ Brian McCartney Scholarships *(Undergraduate/Scholarship)*

Purpose: To improve the quality of life for deaf and hard of hearing individuals in Michigan through advocacy, education, leadership, and service. **Focus:** Hearing and deafness. **Qualif.:** Applicants must be deaf or hard of hearing high school seniors who intend to further their education at a college, university, state-certified trade school or a state-certified technical school, or a high school senior who is presently speech and/or language impaired. Applicants must be citizens of the United States; must be of good character and self-motivated. **Criteria:** Recipients are selected based on academic performance.

Funds Avail.: $500. **To Apply:** Applicant must submit a copy of the applicant's IEPC or a letter from an appropriate school representative stating that the applicant meets the requirements; transcript of grades from senior year; three letters of recommendation from school representative, member of clergy, representative of community service organization, employer, or parent/guardian; must write an essay describing the volunteer activities and/or experiences that demonstrate their leadership skills, their career goals and plans to use the scholarship. Applicant must submit a letter of acceptance after the selection process. **Deadline:** March 31.

4473 ■ Michigan Association of Realtors

PO Box 40725
Lansing, MI 48901-7925
Ph: (517)372-8890
Fax: (517)334-5568
Free: 800-454-7842
E-mail: abates@mirealtors.com
URL: http://www.mirealtors.com

4474 ■ Michigan Association of Realtors Scholarship Trust *(Undergraduate/Scholarship)*

Purpose: To encourage and support outstanding, highly-motivated students to specialize in the study of real estate. **Focus:** Real estate. **Qualif.:** Applicants must have an average grade point of 2.0 on a 4.0 scale or equivalent of a "C" average and show evidence of academic achievement; must exemplify character, including demonstrated evidence of good citizenship; must agree to take courses which are related to the real estate field; must be full-time students, entering junior or senior year or post-graduate work at a major university or college. **Criteria:** Applicants are selected based on the committee's review of the application materials.

Funds Avail.: No specific amount. **To Apply:** Applicants must complete and submit the application before the deadline. Application form can be downloaded at the Michigan Association of Realtors web site. Applicants must also provide a copy of ACT or SAT test scores and a copy of their college transcript. **Deadline:** July 1. **Contact:** Andrea Bates at the above address (see entry 4473).

4475 ■ Michigan Council of Women in Technology

PO Box 214585
Auburn Hills, MI 48321
Ph: (248)654-3697
Fax: (248)281-5391
E-mail: info@mcwt.org

Awards are arranged alphabetically below their administering organizations

URL: http://www.mcwt.org

4476 ■ Michigan Council of Women in Technology College Scholarship Program *(Graduate, Undergraduate/Scholarship)*

Purpose: To provide financial assistance for deserving Michigan-based women. **Focus:** General studies. **Qualif.:** Applicants must be Michigan-based women who are currently or will be enrolled in college or university-level courses. **Criteria:** Preference will be given to applicants who meet the criteria.

Funds Avail.: $5,000. **To Apply:** Applicants must check the council's website for the required materials. **Deadline:** February 28. **Contact:** Michigan Council of Women in Technology at the above address (see entry 4475).

4477 ■ Michigan Council of Women in Technology High School Scholarships Program *(Undergraduate/Scholarship)*

Purpose: To provide educational assistance for high school girls who are currently or will be enrolled in college level courses. **Focus:** General studies. **Qualif.:** Applicants must be young women entering college. **Criteria:** Preference will be given to students who meet the criteria.

Funds Avail.: A total disbursement of up to $20,000. **To Apply:** Applicants must check the available website for the required materials. **Deadline:** February 28. **Contact:** Michigan Council of Women in Technology at the above address (see entry 4475).

4478 ■ Michigan Education Association

PO Box 2573
East Lansing, MI 48826-2573
Ph: (517)332-6551
Fax: (517)337-5587
Free: 800-292-1934
E-mail: mea-it@mea.org
URL: http://www.mea.org

4479 ■ Michigan Education Association Scholarships *(Undergraduate/Scholarship)*

Purpose: To provide education, advancement of quality education and security of the rights of education employees. **Focus:** General studies. **Qualif.:** Applicants must be graduates of public schools; must be attending a Michigan public community/junior college, four-year degree granting institution, or a certification or license granting institution; or attend one of the approved private institutions. **Criteria:** Recipients are selected based on academic achievement, extra-curricular activities, school and community service.

Funds Avail.: No specific amount. **To Apply:** Applicants must submit completed application form.

4480 ■ Michigan League for Nursing

2410 Woodlake Dr.
Okemos, MI 48864
Ph: (517)347-8091
Fax: (517)347-4096
E-mail: cstacy@mhc.org
URL: http://www.michleaguenursing.org

4481 ■ Michigan League for Nursing Scholarships *(Undergraduate/Scholarship)*

Purpose: To promote professional growth and continuous quality improvement of educators for the nursing workforce; to enhance collaboration between nursing education and healthcare delivery systems; and to support recruitment for the nursing workforce. **Focus:** Nursing. **Qualif.:** Applicants must be enrolled in a program leading to a Licensed Practical Nurse certification, an Associate Degree in Nursing, or a Bachelor of Science in Nursing. Applicants must have successfully completed at least one nursing course with a clinical component and must have received a "C" grade or better. **Criteria:** Recipients are selected based on quality of essay, academic performance and financial need.

Funds Avail.: $500. **Number Awarded:** 4. **To Apply:** Applicants must submit an unfolded, completed application form in an 8 1/2 x 11 envelope. Must also submit an unfolded letter of endorsement and essay. **Deadline:** March 15.

4482 ■ Michigan Nursery and Landscape Association

2149 Commons Pkwy.
Okemos, MI 48864
Ph: (517)381-0437
Fax: (517)381-0638
Free: 800-879-6652
E-mail: stonebridge@aol.com
URL: http://www.mnla.org

4483 ■ Michigan Nursery and Landscape Association Scholarships *(Undergraduate/Scholarship)*

Purpose: To further education of individuals pursuing careers in the Green Industry. **Focus:** Landscape architecture and design. **Qualif.:** Applicants must be students pursuing a degree in the area of landscaping. **Criteria:** Recipients are selected based on academic performance and financial need.

Funds Avail.: No specific amount. **To Apply:** Applicants must submit a completed application form, a cover letter, resume, two letters of recommendation and photos/information on industry work completed. **Deadline:** November 1.

4484 ■ Michigan Nurses Foundation

2310 Jolly Oak Rd.
Okemos, MI 48864
Ph: (517)349-5640
URL: http://www.michigannursesfoundation.org

4485 ■ Michigan Nurses Foundation Scholarships *(Undergraduate/Scholarship)*

Purpose: To assist deserving nursing students who want to pursue their studies. **Focus:** Nursing. **Qualif.:** Applicant must be a student currently enrolled in a Michigan college/school of nursing that grants a certificate or degree for practicing nursing; must be in good academic standing with demonstrated progress toward degree completion. **Criteria:** Preference will be given to applicants that meet the requirements.

Funds Avail.: $500. **To Apply:** Applicant must complete the application form and application requirements before the deadline; send to: Scholarship Committee, Michigan Nurses Foundation, 2310 Jolly Oak Rd., Okemos, MI 48864. **Deadline:** July 15.

4486 ■ Michigan Society of Professional Engineers

PO Box 5276
Lansing, MI 48901

Awards are arranged alphabetically below their administering organizations

Ph: (517)487-9388
Fax: (517)487-0635
E-mail: mspe@voyager.net
URL: http://www.michiganspe.org

4487 ■ Michigan Society of Professional Engineers Scholarships *(Undergraduate/Scholarship)*

Purpose: To encourage high school seniors with the talent and commitment to pursue an engineering degree. **Focus:** Engineering. **Qualif.:** Applicants must be accepted at a Michigan ABET accredited college or university and enroll in an engineering program; must be high school seniors, residents of Michigan and U.S. citizens at the time of application; must have at least 3.0 GPA based on 4.0 scale for the 10th and 11th grades; and must attain a minimum composite test score of 26 on the American College Testing (ACT Exam). **Criteria:** Recipients are selected based on candidate's high school records, participation in extracurricular activities, evidence of leadership, character and self-reliance and comments from teachers and administrators.

Funds Avail.: No specific amount. **To Apply:** Applicants must submit a completed application form which can be obtained from a guidance counselor, local chapters or the MSPE Headquarters; a list of senior classes being taken; and a documented high school transcript and ACT test scores. **Contact:** mspe@voyager.net.

4488 ■ Michigan State Horticultural Society

63806 90th Ave.
Hartford, MI 49057
Ph: (269)424-3990
Fax: (269)424-3096
E-mail: mihortsociety@aol.com
URL: http://www.mihortsociety.org

4489 ■ Fruits and Vegetable Industries Scholarships *(Undergraduate/Scholarship)*

Purpose: To encourage among the people a greater love for choice fruit products; to awaken a larger interest in Michigan's horticultural possibilities; to offer practical suggestions along modern cultural and marketing methods; and to encourage the improved methods in the production, harvest, handling, storage, marketing and utilization of fruit and vegetable crops as well as a full farm marketers program. **Focus:** Horticulture. **Qualif.:** Applicants must be students who intend to pursue a career in the Midwest fruit industry or vegetable industry. **Criteria:** Recipients are selected based on financial need and academic performance.

Funds Avail.: $1,000. **To Apply:** Applicants must complete the application form. **Deadline:** September 30. **Contact:** mihortsociety@aol.com.

4490 ■ Jordan B. Tatter Scholarships *(Undergraduate/Scholarship)*

Purpose: To encourage among the people a greater love for choice fruit products; to awaken a larger interest in Michigan's horticultural possibilities; to offer practical suggestions along modern cultural and marketing methods; and to encourage the improved methods in the production, harvest, handling, storage, marketing and utilization of fruit and vegetable crops as well as a full farm marketers program. **Focus:** Horticulture. **Qualif.:** Applicants must be graduates or junior undergraduate students who show interest in working in the fruit and/or vegetable industry. **Criteria:** Recipients are selected based on financial need.

Funds Avail.: No specific amount. **To Apply:** Applicants must complete the application form. **Deadline:** October 1. **Contact:** 517-355-5191.

4491 ■ Michigan Stormwater-Floodplain Association

PO Box 14265
Lansing, MI 48901-4265
Ph: (810)341-7500
E-mail: bhaneline@roweincorp.com
URL: http://mi.floods.org

4492 ■ Michigan Stormwater-Floodplain Association Scholarships *(Undergraduate/Scholarship)*

Purpose: To promote the common interest in floodplain and stormwater management; enhance cooperation among various local, state, and federal governmental agencies; encourage effective and innovative approaches to managing the state's floodplain and stormwater management systems; to mitigate the losses, costs, and human suffering caused by flooding and to promote wise use of the natural and beneficial functions of floodplains. **Focus:** Water supply industry. **Qualif.:** Applicants must be full-time juniors, seniors, or graduate students in biosystems, civil, or environmental engineering with a specialization related to the mission and goals of the MSFA. **Criteria:** Recipients are selected based on academic performance and financial need.

Funds Avail.: $1,500. **To Apply:** Applicants must submit a completed application form; a copy of their program of study showing courses remaining and photocopy of their transcript; a current resume that includes a statement of their career objectives and graduation date; a one page, typed essay highlighting their academic achievements, extracurricular activities, past and present work experiences, future occupation and commitment to the mission and goals of the MSFA; must submit a letter of recommendation from a faculty member of their department.

4493 ■ Michigan Sugar Company

2600 S Euclid Ave.
Bay City, MI 48706
Ph: (989)686-0161
Fax: (989)671-3695
E-mail: info@michigansugar.com
URL: http://www.michigansugar.com

4494 ■ Phil Brimhall Memorial Scholarships *(Undergraduate/Scholarship)*

Purpose: To provide academic support to high school seniors who have completed a documented Youth Sugarbeet Project. **Focus:** General studies. **Qualif.:** Applicants must be residents of a county where sugarbeets are grown; must be high school graduating seniors; must have participated in the Michigan Sugar Youth Sugarbeet Program at one time and have completed a Sugarbeet Project. **Criteria:** Applicants are selected based on the committee's review of the application materials.

Funds Avail.: $1,000. **To Apply:** Applicants must submit a completed application form available at Michigan Sugar

Awards are arranged alphabetically below their administering organizations

Company web site. **Deadline:** April 25.

4495 ■ Albert Flegenheimer Memorial Scholarships *(Undergraduate/Scholarship)*

Purpose: To provide academic support to high school seniors who have completed a documented Youth Sugarbeet Project. **Focus:** General studies. **Qualif.:** Applicants must be residents of a county where sugarbeets are grown; must be high school graduating seniors; must have participated in the Michigan Sugar Youth Sugarbeet Program at one time and have completed a Sugarbeet Project. **Criteria:** Applicants are selected based on the committee's review of the application materials.

Funds Avail.: $2,500. **To Apply:** Applicants must submit a completed application form available at the Michigan Sugar Company web site. **Deadline:** April 25.

4496 ■ Michigan Sugar Company Hotel Restaurant/Resort Management Scholarships *(Undergraduate/Scholarship)*

Purpose: To provide financial support to deserving students enrolled in the Hotel Restaurant/Resort Management program of study. **Focus:** Hotel, institutional, and restaurant management. **Qualif.:** Applicants must be enrolled full-time in the Hotel Restaurant/Resort Management program in any college or university. **Criteria:** Applicants are selected based on the committee's review of the application materials.

Funds Avail.: $1,000. **To Apply:** For an application please contact the Financial Aid Office at Northwood University. **Contact:** Northwood University, 989-837-4230.

4497 ■ Michigan Sugar Queen Scholarships *(Undergraduate/Scholarship)*

Purpose: To provide academic support to Sugar Queen participants. **Focus:** General studies. **Qualif.:** Applicants must be female, at least 18 years old and not older than 23; must never have been married and have no minor dependents; must be serving as Michigan Sugar Queen or Court attendant for a full year from crowning; must be friendly, courteous, and not use tobacco, alcoholic beverages, or drugs when appearing at official functions as Michigan Queen or Court attendant; must be residents of a county where sugarbeets are grown (Arenac, Bay, Clare, Clinton, Genesee, Gladwin, Gratiot, Huron, Ionia, Iosco, Isabella, Lapeer, Macomb, Midland, Montcalm, Ogemaw, Saginaw, Sanilac, Shiawassee, St. Clair and Tuscola). A parent/guardian will be required to attend any overnight events as a chaperone. **Criteria:** Applicants are selected based on the committee's review of the application materials.

Funds Avail.: $2,000. **To Apply:** Interested contestants need to complete an application and send it with a picture. Application form can be downloaded at MSC website. **Contact:** Barb Wallace, 989-686-0161.

4498 ■ Michigan Turfgrass Foundation

3225 W. St.Joseph
Lansing, MI 48917
Ph: (517)327-9207
Fax: (517)321-0495
E-mail: litchfi9@msu.edu
URL: http://www.michiganturfgrass.org

4499 ■ Robert Hancock Memorial Scholarship Award *(Undergraduate/Scholarship)*

Purpose: To support the ongoing research, education and extension in the area of professional turfgrass management that will benefit all individuals who manage turfgrasses or derive pleasure from the results of such management. **Focus:** Management. **Qualif.:** Applicant must be a senior undergraduate in the four-year Turfgrass Management Program; and must have a 3.0 GPA or higher. **Criteria:** Recipients are selected based on GPA.

Funds Avail.: $2,000. **Number Awarded:** 1. **To Apply:** Applicants must complete the application form and submit along with a cover letter, resume, questionnaire answers, and letter of recommendation. **Deadline:** November 21. **Contact:** litchfi9@msu.edu.

4500 ■ Norman Kramer Scholarship Award *(Undergraduate/Scholarship)*

Purpose: To support the ongoing research, education and extension in the area of professional turfgrass management that will benefit all individuals who manage turfgrasses or derive pleasure from the results of such management. **Focus:** General studies. **Qualif.:** Applicants must be students with a minimum of 42 credits completed and who have a 3.0 GPA or higher. **Criteria:** Recipients are selected based on GPA.

Funds Avail.: $2,500. **Number Awarded:** 1. **To Apply:** Applicants must complete the application form and submit along with a cover letter, resume, questionnaire answers, and letter of recommendation. **Deadline:** November 21. **Contact:** litchfi9@msu.edu

4501 ■ Kenyon T. Payne Outstanding Student Awards *(Undergraduate/Award/Prize)*

Purpose: To support the ongoing research, education and extension in the area of professional turfgrass management that will benefit all individuals who manage turfgrasses or derive pleasure from the results of such management. **Focus:** Management. **Qualif.:** Applicants must be second year students in the Turfgrass Management Program who have a 3.0 GPA or higher. **Criteria:** Recipients are selected based on GPA, demonstrated leadership, character and estimated potential for future.

Funds Avail.: $2,000. **To Apply:** Applicants must complete the application form and submit along with a cover letter, resume, questionnaire answers, and letter of recommendation. **Deadline:** November 21. **Contact:** litchfi9@msu.edu.

4502 ■ Michigan Water Environment Association

PO Box 397
Bath, MI 48808
Ph: (517)641-7377
Fax: (517)641-7388
E-mail: mwea@mi-wea.org
URL: http://www.mi-wea.org

4503 ■ Antenore C. "Buth" Davanzo Scholarships *(Undergraduate/Scholarship)*

Purpose: To educate and inform policy makers and the general public; to promote scientifically-sound environmental practices and regulation; to promote and advance the water quality profession; to promote public and ecological health by preserving and enhancing Michigan's water environment. **Focus:** Environmental Conservation. **Qualif.:** Applicants must be attending a Michigan college or university; must be part-time students and pursuing a course of study leading to a career in Wastewater Treatment or some aspect of the water environment field; must

Awards are arranged alphabetically below their administering organizations

be entering the second year of a two or four-year program in the year following receipt of the award or be in a graduate level course of study; must have at least a 2.5 GPA on a 4.0 scale; must be organization members at the time of the presentation of the award. **Criteria:** Recipients are selected based on academic performance and adherence to the requirements.

Funds Avail.: $500. **To Apply:** Applicants must submit a paper of between 500 and 600 words reflecting on their career interests and objectives and how they envision using their education to enhance water quality; must submit a current copy of their college or university transcript; resume with all full and part-time employment, education history and extracurricular activities; a letter of recommendation from their academic advisor or other appropriate official attesting to their course of study and other aspects of their application. **Deadline:** March 15. **Contact:** 810-231-1200.

4504 ■ John P. Hennessy Scholarships
(Undergraduate/Scholarship)

Purpose: To educate and inform policy makers and the general public; to promote scientifically-sound environmental practices and regulation; to promote and advance the water quality profession; to promote public and ecological health by preserving and enhancing Michigan's water environment. **Focus:** Environmental Conservation. **Qualif.:** Applicants must be attending a Michigan college or university; must be full-time students and pursuing a course of study leading to a career in Wastewater Treatment or some aspect of the water environment field; must be entering the second year of a two- or four-year program the year following receipt of the award, or be in a graduate level course of study; must have an at least 2.5 GPA on a 4.0 scale; must be organization members at the time of the presentation of the award. **Criteria:** Recipients are selected based on academic performance and adherence to the requirements.

Funds Avail.: $1,000. **To Apply:** Applicants must submit a paper of between 500 and 600 words reflecting on their career interests and objectives and how they envision using their education to enhance water quality; must submit a current copy of their college or university transcript; resume with all full and part-time employment, education history and extracurricular activities; a letter of recommendation from their academic advisor or other appropriate official attesting to their course of study and other aspects of their application. **Deadline:** March 15. **Contact:** 810-231-1200.

4505 ■ Jack H. Wagner Scholarships
(Undergraduate/Scholarship)

Purpose: To educate and inform policy makers and the general public; to promote scientifically-sound environmental practices and regulation; to promote and advance the water quality profession; to promote public and ecological health by preserving and enhancing Michigan's water environment. **Focus:** Environmental Conservation. **Qualif.:** Applicants must be enrolled full-time and pursuing a course of study leading to a career in Wastewater Treatment or some other aspect of the water environment and/or environmental engineering field; must be entering the third or fourth year of their undergraduate program or be in a graduate level course of study. Applicant must have an at least 2.5 GPA on a 4.0 scale; must be organization member at the time of the presentation of the award. **Criteria:** Recipients are selected based on academic performance and adherence to the requirements.

Funds Avail.: $1,000. **To Apply:** Applicants must submit: a paper of between 500 and 600 words reflecting on their career interests and objectives and how they envision using their education to enhance water quality; a current copy of their college or university transcript; a resume with all full and part-time employment, education history and extracurricular activities; letter of recommendation from their academic advisor or other appropriate official attesting to their course of study and other aspects of their application. **Deadline:** March 15. **Contact:** 810-231-1200.

4506 ■ Mid-Atlantic States Association of Avian Veterinarians

Memorial Bldg.
610 N Main St., Ste. 291
Blacksburg, VA 24060-3311
Ph: (540)951-2559
Fax: (540)953-0230
E-mail: office@masaav.org
URL: http://www.masaav.org

4507 ■ E.L. Stubbs Research Grants *(Graduate/Grant)*

Purpose: To promote the study of avian medicine and surgery. **Focus:** Veterinary science and medicine. **Qualif.:** Applicant must be conducting a clinical study in the field of avian medicine and surgery. **Criteria:** Recipients are selected based on the committee's review of all proposals.

Funds Avail.: Maximum of $2,000. **To Apply:** Applicant must send a completed application form; a four-page research proposal; and a budget. **Deadline:** Any time of the year.

Remarks: Established in honor of Evan L. Stubbs.

4508 ■ Midwest Archives Conference

4300 S U.S. Hywy 1, 203-293
Jupiter, FL 33477
E-mail: dmkellam@indiana.edu
URL: http://www.midwestarchives.org

4509 ■ MAC Emeritus Scholarships for First-Time Meeting Attendees *(All, Professional Development/Scholarship)*

Purpose: To provide travel and conference assistance for first-time MAC meeting attendees. **Focus:** General studies. **Qualif.:** Applicant must be attending his/her first MAC meeting. **Criteria:** Recipients are selected based on their statements.

Funds Avail.: One Scholarship of $500 or two scholarships of $250. **Number Awarded:** Varies. **To Apply:** Applicants must submit a completed application form available at the website; an essay (maximum of 500 words) on the importance of the MAC meeting to the applicant and a summary of financial requirements; and a letter of support (optional). Requirements must be sent to: Ann Bowers 13697 Cuckle Creek Rd. Bowling Green, OH 43402, (419)352-1921, abowers@bgsu.edu. **Deadline:** February 15.

4510 ■ MAC Louisa Bowen Memorial Scholarships for Graduate Students in Archival Administration *(Graduate/Scholarship)*

Purpose: To enhance education and career in archival administration. **Focus:** Library and archival sciences. **Qua-**

Awards are arranged alphabetically below their administering organizations

lif.: Applicants must be a resident or full-time student residing in: Illinois, Indiana, Iowa, Kansas, Kentucky, Michigan, Minnesota, Missouri, Nebraska, North Dakota, Ohio, South Dakota, and Wisconsin; enrolled or accepted in a graduate, multi-course program in archival administration; have a GPA of 3.0 on 4.0 scale. **Criteria:** Recipient is selected based on his or her merits.

Funds Avail.: $750 and a one-year membership. **Number Awarded:** 1. **To Apply:** Applicants must submit a completed application form available at the website; transcript of recent academic program; essay (maximum of 500 words) on the applicant's interests and future goals in archival administration; and two letters of recommendation. Requirements must be sent to: Kimberly Butler (2007-2009) Archivist/ Associate Director of Archives North Central College Archives 320 E School Ave. Naperville, IL 60540-4694. Phone: (630)637-5714, Fax: (630)637-5716, kjbutler@noctrl.edu. **Deadline:** April 1.

4511 ■ Archie Motley Memorial Scholarships for Minority Students *(Graduate/Scholarship)*

Purpose: To promote education and career in archival administration. **Focus:** Library and archival sciences. **Qualif.:** The applicant must be an African, American Indian, Asian or Pacific Islander, or Latino student; currently enrolled in a graduate, multi-course program in archival administration or accepted into such a program for the next academic year; have a GPA of at least 3.0 on a 4.0 scale. **Criteria:** Recipients are selected based on their merits.

Funds Avail.: $750 and 1-year membership to MAC. **Number Awarded:** 2. **To Apply:** Applicants must submit a completed application form available at the website; transcript of recent academic program; essay (maximum of 500 words) on the applicant's interests and future goals in archival administration; and two letters of recommendation. Requirements must be sent to: Requirements must be sent to: Kimberly Neuenschwander, Marianist Archives 310 Roesch Library University of Dayton 300 College Park Dayton, OH 45469-1360, Phone: 937229-5538, Fax: 937229-5142, Email: neuenskm@notes.udayton.edu. **Deadline:** April 1.

4512 ■ Midwest Dairy Association

2015 Rice St.
St. Paul, MN 55113
Free: 800-642-3895
URL: http://www.midwestdairy.com

4513 ■ Chicago Division Scholarships *(Undergraduate/Scholarship)*

Purpose: To provide financial assistance to college students within the Chicago Division. **Focus:** General Studies. **Qualif.:** Applicants must be enrolled in an accredited college; must be immediate family members of dairy farmers. **Criteria:** Preference will be given to those students who meet the criteria.

Funds Avail.: $1,000. **Number Awarded:** 2. **To Apply:** Applicants must check the available website for the required materials. **Deadline:** March 1. **Contact:** For more information, contact: Marla Behrends, Industry Relations Manager at 309-376-2196

4514 ■ Iowa Division Scholarships *(All/ Scholarship)*

Purpose: To provide financial assistance to Iowa students. **Focus:** General Studies. **Qualif.:** Applicants must be enrolled in an accredited college. Applicants must be immediate family members of dairy farmers. **Criteria:** Recipients will be chosen by the committee.

Funds Avail.: $1,000; $500. **Number Awarded:** 11. **To Apply:** Applicants must check the available website for the required materials. **Deadline:** March 1. **Contact:** For more information, contact: Kent Lehs, Industry Relations Manager at 800-642-3895 or direct at 515-965-4623

4515 ■ Kansas City Division Scholarships *(All/ Scholarship)*

Purpose: To provide financial assistance to those students who are in need. **Focus:** General Studies. **Qualif.:** Applicants must be enrolled in an accredited college; must be immediate family members of dairy farmers. **Criteria:** Recipients will be chosen by the committee.

Funds Avail.: $500. **Number Awarded:** 10. **To Apply:** Applicants must check the available website for the required materials. **Deadline:** March 1. **Contact:** For more information, contact: Kent Lehs, Industry Relations Manager at 800-642-3895 or direct 515-965-4623

4516 ■ Minnesota Division Scholarships *(Undergraduate/Scholarship)*

Purpose: To provide financial assistance to those students who are in need. **Focus:** General Studies. **Qualif.:** Applicants must be enrolled students at the University of Minnesota CFANS in St. Paul or in Crookston. **Criteria:** Recipients will be chosen by the University as part of their normal scholarship selection process.

Funds Avail.: $1,000-$3,000. **To Apply:** Applicants must check the available website for the required materials. **Contact:** Midwest Dairy Association at the above address (see entry 4512).

4517 ■ North Dakota Division Scholarships *(Undergraduate/Scholarship)*

Purpose: To provide financial assistance to those deserving students. **Focus:** Food Nutrition; Education. **Qualif.:** Applicants must be juniors or non-graduating seniors majoring in food nutrition, family and consumer science education or education. **Criteria:** Recipients will be chosen by the University.

Funds Avail.: $1,000. **Number Awarded:** 2. **To Apply:** Applicants must check the available website for the required materials. **Contact:** For more information, contact: Char Heer, Industry Relations Manager at 701-782-4154

4518 ■ Ozarks Division Scholarships *(Undergraduate/Scholarship)*

Purpose: To provide financial support to those students who are in need. **Focus:** General Studies. **Qualif.:** Applicants must be enrolled in an accredited college. Applicants must be immediate family members of dairy farmers. **Criteria:** Recipients will be chosen by the committee.

Funds Avail.: $500. **Number Awarded:** 4. **To Apply:** Applicants must check the available website for the required materials. **Deadline:** March 1. **Contact:** For more information, contact: Stacy Dohle, Industry Relations Manager at 417-267-5039

4519 ■ St. Louis Division Scholarships *(Undergraduate/Scholarship)*

Purpose: To provide financial support to those students who are in need. **Focus:** General Studies. **Qualif.:** Applicants must be enrolled in an accredited college. Applicants must be immediate family members of dairy farmers. **Criteria:** Recipients will be chosen by the committee.

Funds Avail.: $1,000. **Number Awarded:** 2. **To Apply:** Applicants must check the available website for the required materials. **Deadline:** March 1. **Contact:** For more information, contact: Marla Behrends, Industry Relations Manager at 309-376-2196

4520 ■ South Dakota Division Scholarships
(Undergraduate/Scholarship)

Purpose: To provide financial support to those students who are in need. **Focus:** Dairy Science. **Qualif.:** Applicants must be incoming freshmen majoring in Dairy Science who are admitted at Dakota State University in Brookings. **Criteria:** Recipients will be chosen by the SDSU selection committee.

Funds Avail.: $750. **Number Awarded:** 2. **To Apply:** Applicants must check the available website for the required materials. **Contact:** For more information, contact: Char Hovland, Industry Relations Manager at 605-692-4812

4521 ■ Midwest Food Processors Association

4600 American Pkwy., Ste. 110
Madison, WI 53718-8334
Ph: (608)255-9946
Fax: (608)255-9838
Free: 800-369-6220
E-mail: info@mwfpa.org
URL: http://www.mwfpa.org

4522 ■ Carleton A. Friday Memorial Scholarships *(Undergraduate/Scholarship)*

Purpose: To enhance and promote the business interests of the Midwest food processing industry. **Focus:** Agricultural sciences. **Qualif.:** Applicants must be undergraduate students who are majoring in agriculture or food science within the University of Wisconsin system. **Criteria:** Recipients are selected based on financial need.

Funds Avail.: Up to $1,500. **Number Awarded:** 3. **To Apply:** Applicants must submit completed application form indicating GPA; a letter of recommendation from advisor or other faculty member; a letter of interest; letter of recommendation from past employer; document/s indicating financial need; and contact information. **Deadline:** June 13.

4523 ■ Kenneth G. Weckel Scholarships
(Undergraduate/Scholarship)

Purpose: To enhance and promote the business interests of the Midwest food processing industry. **Focus:** Agricultural sciences. **Qualif.:** Applicants must be undergraduate students who are majoring in agriculture or food science within the University of Wisconsin system. **Criteria:** Recipients are selected based on financial need.

Funds Avail.: $1,500. **Number Awarded:** 3. **To Apply:** Applicants must submit completed application form indicating GPA; a letter of recommendation from advisor or other faculty member; a letter of interest from students; letter of recommendation from past employer; documents indicating financial need; and contact information. **Deadline:** June 13.

4524 ■ Milbank, Tweed, Hadley & McCloy LLP

1 Chase Manhattan Plz.
New York, NY 10005
Ph: (212)530-5000
Fax: (212)530-5219
URL: http://www.milbank.com/en

4525 ■ Milbank Diversity Scholarships
(Undergraduate/Scholarship)

Purpose: To inspire career pursuits and excellence in the field of law by providing educational support for qualified law students. **Focus:** Law. **Qualif.:** Applicants must be members of groups traditionally underrepresented in large law firms; must be in good standing at an ABA accredited law school; must have successfully completed their first year of a full-time JD program; may not be the recipient of a similar scholarship award from another law firm; and must have completed two years of a JD program. **Criteria:** Recipients will be selected based on academic achievement, demonstrated leadership ability, excellent writing and interpersonal skills.

Funds Avail.: $50,000. **Number Awarded:** 2. **To Apply:** Applicants must complete the application form available online and submit along with an essay, official law school transcript and resume. Application form and other supporting documents must be sent to Elizabeth A. Crispino, Manager of Campus Recruiting. **Deadline:** September 1.

4526 ■ Military Intelligence Corps Association

6339 S Ranch Rd.
Hereford, AZ 85615
Ph: (520)456-6232
E-mail: info@micorps.org
URL: http://www.micorps.org

4527 ■ Military Intelligence Corps Association Scholarships *(Undergraduate/Scholarship)*

Purpose: To provide educational assistance for family members of Active Duty, Reserve, National Guard and retired Military Intelligence Soldiers. **Focus:** General studies. **Qualif.:** Applicants or their sponsors must be current MICA members in good standing. They must be pursuing post-secondary education through a college, university, vocational school or technical institution and must be accepted or enrolled in a qualified education program and who agree to complete at least one course or class. **Criteria:** The Scholarship Chairman determines evaluation criteria to be used during the board process. The Scholarship Board will judge the applications solely on documentation provided in the application. Areas of evaluation that the Scholarship Board considers are: educational goals (essay); past performance (transcripts); and potential for future success (letters of recommendation).

Funds Avail.: $500 - $1,000. **To Apply:** Applications must contain the following documentation: scholarship application checklist; scholarship application signed by the applicant; copy of MICA Membership Card (if copy of membership card is not available, please provide some proof of current membership); three letters of Recommendation (all letters of recommendation must be signed and include full point of contact information); essay (include a one-page essay detailing the applicant's educational goals and program of study); transcripts; and proof of acceptance by an educational institution. **Deadline:** May 15. **Contact:** MICA Scholarship Chairman; 110 Rhea Street, Fort Huachuca, Arizona 85613-7080.

4528 ■ Military Officers Association of America

201 N Washington St.
Alexandria, VA 22314

Awards are arranged alphabetically below their administering organizations

Ph: (703)549-2311
Free: 800-234-6622
E-mail: msc@moaa.org
URL: http://www.moaa.org

4529 ■ MOAA American Patriot Scholarships *(Undergraduate/Scholarship)*

Purpose: To help children of Uniformed Services members who died or was severley disabled while in active service as a member of the Regular, Guard or Reserve Forces. **Focus:** General studies. **Qualif.:** Applicant must be a child of a member of the Uniformed Services who died while in active service; must be under the age of 24 at the time of application (the maximum age for students who are serving or have served in the Armed Forces before completing college will be increased by the number of years served, for up to five years of service or 29 years of age); must be planning to attend an accredited college/university as a full-time student seeking their first undergraduate degree; and must have a cumulative GPA of 3.0 or higher on a 4.0 scale. **Criteria:** Awards are given based on scholastic ability, activities, and financial need.

Funds Avail.: At least $2,500. **To Apply:** Applicants must apply for the scholarship online. **Deadline:** March 3.

4530 ■ MOAA Base/Post Scholarships *(Undergraduate/Scholarship)*

Purpose: To help children of active Uniformed Services members. **Focus:** General studies. **Qualif.:** Applicant must be the dependent son/daughter (under age 24) of an active duty officer and enlisted military personnel. **Criteria:** Recipients are randomly selected.

Funds Avail.: $1,000. **Number Awarded:** 25. **To Apply:** Applicants must apply for the scholarship online. **Deadline:** March 3.

4531 ■ General John Paul Ratay Educational Grants *(Undergraduate/Grant)*

Purpose: To help children of Uniformed Services members. **Focus:** General studies. **Qualif.:** Applicant must be the child of the surviving spouse of a retired officer. **Criteria:** Applicants must apply for a loan in order to be considered.

Funds Avail.: $4,000. **To Apply:** Applicants must apply online. **Deadline:** March 3.

4532 ■ Mill Creek Business Association

13300 Bothell-Everett Hwy.
Mill Creek, WA 98012
Ph: (425)673-6200
E-mail: info@millcreekbiz.com
URL: http://www.millcreekbiz.com

4533 ■ Mill Creek Business Association Scholarships *(Undergraduate/Scholarship)*

Purpose: To encourage and assist local high school students in their pursuit of higher learning in Business or Fine Arts. **Focus:** Business; Fine Arts. **Qualif.:** Applicants must live in Mill Creek and/or attend school at Jacksonville High school or Archbishop Murphy High School; must be senior students in good standing at the time of application; must be accepted to attend a full-time accredited college, university or Fine Arts school; must be planning an academic course of study in the field of business/fine arts and/or plan to pursue a career in business or fine arts. **Criteria:** Recipients are selected based on academic performance.

Funds Avail.: No specific amount. **To Apply:** Applicants must complete the application form; must submit two letters of reference and recommendation from teachers, advisors, and/or local business people; a copy of the letter of acceptance from their institution; must provide a 200 word, typed essay stating their academic and career plans. **Deadline:** May 1. **Contact:** 13300 Bothell-Everett Hwy., Mill Creek, WA 98012.

4534 ■ Glenn Miller Birthplace Society

PO Box 61
Clarinda, IA 51632
Ph: (712)542-2461
E-mail: gmbs@heartland.net
URL: http://www.glennmiller.org

4535 ■ Glenn Miller Scholarships *(Undergraduate/Scholarship)*

Purpose: To seek out and assist promising young talents in any field of applied music who may be musical leaders of tomorrow. **Focus:** Music. **Qualif.:** Applicants must be graduating high school seniors or first year college students intending to make music a central part of their future life and high school seniors, unless they have been previous first place winners. **Criteria:** Recipient will be select based on some designed criteria by the Scholarship Committee.

Funds Avail.: $1,000 to $4,000. **To Apply:** Applicants must submit an audition CD or tape and completed application. **Deadline:** March 15.

4536 ■ Miller Thomson LLP

PO Box 1011
Toronto, ON, Canada M5H 3S1
Ph: (416)595-8500
Fax: (416)595-8695
Free: 888-762-5559
E-mail: toronto@millerthomson.com
URL: http://www.millerthomson.com

4537 ■ Miller Thomson Foundation Scholarships *(Undergraduate/Scholarship)*

Purpose: To encourage and promote the attainment of higher education goals by top students in Canada. **Focus:** General studies. **Qualif.:** Applicant must be a graduating student attending Canadian secondary schools and must be one of the top students in Canada who have demonstrated a high level of academic achievement and have made positive contribution to their school or community. **Criteria:** Recipient will be selected based on academic achievement and involvement in extracurricular activities.

Funds Avail.: $1,000. **Number Awarded:** 200. **To Apply:** Applicants are advised to visit the foundation website at www.millerthomson.com for scholarship information and instructions or contact Mrs. Lesley A. Lawson, Executive Director, The Miller Thomson Foundation at llawson@millerthomson.com. **Deadline:** March 15.

Remarks: Scholarship was created by Miller Thomson LLP in 1995 and funded annually by its partners.

4538 ■ Mineralogical Association of Canada

490, rue de la Couronne
Quebec, QC, Canada G1K 9A9

Ph: (418)653-0333
Fax: (418)653-0777
E-mail: office@mineralogicalassociation.ca
URL: http://www.mineralogicalassociation.ca

4539 ■ Mineralogical Association of Canada Scholarships *(Postgraduate/Scholarship)*

Purpose: To support the graduate students engaged in research in any field currently supported by MAC. **Focus:** Mineralogy. **Qualif.:** Applicants must be students entering their second year of an M.Sc. program or the second or third year of a Ph.D. program at any Canadian university or students who are Canadian citizens attending a university located outside of Canada. **Criteria:** Applications will be assessed by a committee consisting of three members of MAC council chaired by the Chairman of MACF.

Funds Avail.: CDN$10,000. **To Apply:** Applications must be accompanied by an official academic transcript (undergraduate and graduate). Applicants must provide an outline of their thesis project using two pages of single text. Applications and other documents must be sent to: MAC Scholarships, Mineralogical Association of Canada, 409 rue de la Couronne, Quebec, QC, G1K 9A9. **Deadline:** May 1. **Contact:** Pierrete Tremblay at the above address (see entry 4538).

4540 ■ Minneapolis Jewish Federation

13100 Wayzata Blvd., Ste. 200
Minnetonka, MN 55305
Ph: (952)593-2600
Fax: (952)593-2544
E-mail: webmaster@ujfc.org
URL: http://twincities.ujcfedweb.org

4541 ■ Minneapolis Camp Scholarships *(Undergraduate/Scholarship)*

Purpose: To provide financial assistance to those children with high financial need. **Focus:** General studies. **Qualif.:** Applicants must be Jewish; must be residents of the greater Minneapolis area. **Criteria:** Scholarships will be awarded to children registered to attend a recognized residential Jewish camp. The camp must be located in the region unless a camper's special needs (such as accommodations for children with disabilities or same-gender camping) can only be accommodated in another locale.

Funds Avail.: No specific amount. **To Apply:** Applicants must submit a completed application form to the Minneapolis Jewish Federation office. **Deadline:** March 28. **Contact:** Applications must be submitted to: Norma Kaplan, Camp Scholarships, 13100 Wayzata Blvd., Ste. 200, Minnetonka, MN 55305, or email nkaplan@mplsfed.org or call at 952-417-2335. Forms may also be downloaded from the Twin Cities website at www.jewishminnesota.org.

4542 ■ UJFC and Council of St. Paul Annual Scholarships *(All/Scholarship)*

Purpose: To provide financial assistance to deserving students. **Focus:** General Studies. **Qualif.:** Applicants must be Minnesota residents; must demonstrate financial need; must be Jewish; and in good academic standing. **Criteria:** Priority will be given to those students who have demonstrated high financial need.

Funds Avail.: No specific amount. **To Apply:** Applicants must check the website for the application process and required materials. **Deadline:** April 15. **Contact:** Minneapolis Jewish Federation at the above address (see entry 4540).

4543 ■ Minnesota Association County Probation Officers

Sherburne County Court Services
13880 Hwy. 10
Elk River, MN 55330
Ph: (763)241-2819
E-mail: christopher.maas@co.sherburne.mn.us
URL: http://www.macpo.org

4544 ■ Minnesota Association County Probation Officers Scholarships *(Undergraduate/Scholarship)*

Purpose: To promote and attract quality students to consider Corrections as a career. **Focus:** Criminal justice. **Qualif.:** Applicants must be junior or senior students majoring in Corrections, Sociology, Criminal justice, Psychology, Social Work, or other related fields who will be/are currently involved in an internship; must have a 2.5 GPA; and must be enrolled at an accredited two-year of four-year college or university. **Criteria:** Recipients are selected based on academic attainment, demonstrated leadership, commitment to a career in Corrections, and community involvement.

Funds Avail.: $500. **To Apply:** Applicants must submit a completed application form; a school transcript; resume of related volunteer/community experience; one letter of reference; and a 500-word essay describing the impact as you prepare for a career in Corrections.

4545 ■ Minnesota Association of Public Accountants

1711 W County Rd. B, Ste. 300N
Roseville, MN 55113
Ph: (651)635-0706
Fax: (651)635-0307
Free: 800-501-4521
E-mail: admin@mapamn.com
URL: http://www.mapa-mn.com

4546 ■ Minnesota Association of Public Accountant Scholarships *(Undergraduate/Scholarship)*

Purpose: To further the knowledge of the practitioner and offer a source of current information and interplay of ideas among professionals. **Focus:** Accounting. **Qualif.:** Applicants must be undergraduate students entering their junior year; must be enrolled in a degree program at an accredited four-year college or university majoring in accounting with the intention to practice in the field of public accounting; must have at least a 2.5 or better grade point average; must be U.S. citizens attending a U.S. accredited school; and must be Minnesota residents. **Criteria:** Recipients are selected based on academic performance.

Funds Avail.: No specific amount. **To Apply:** Applicants must submit a completed application form; official transcript; and letters of recommendation from advisors or professors. **Deadline:** April 1.

4547 ■ Minnesota Association of Township

PO Box 267
St. Michael, MN 55376

Awards are arranged alphabetically below their administering organizations

Ph: (763)497-2330
Fax: (763)497-3361
Free: 800-228-0296
E-mail: info@mntownships.org
URL: http://www.mntownships.org

4548 ■ Minnesota Association of Township Scholarships *(Undergraduate/Scholarship)*

Purpose: To foster efficient, effective and economical town governmental services and to further awareness and education about the township government. **Focus:** Government. **Qualif.:** Applicants must be currently enrolled in the 11th grade and attending a Minnesota public, private, or parochial high school or a home study program and plan to further their education at a college, university, or vocational school. **Criteria:** Recipients are selected based on the written essay, originality, knowledge of the subject matter in relationship to the title, supporting statements, correct spelling and punctuation.

Funds Avail.: $1,000. **Number Awarded:** 4. **To Apply:** Applicants must complete an application form; a 450-500-word, typed, double-spaced written essay; a current high school transcript; and a letter of recommendation from a high school teacher or counselor. **Deadline:** May 1.

4549 ■ Minnesota Chapter American Planning Association

9288 Beverly Dr.
Breezy Point, MN 56472
Ph: (763)576-2722
Free: 888-882-5369
E-mail: mnapa_admin@tds.net
URL: http://www.mnapa.com

4550 ■ Gunnar Isberg Student Scholarships *(Undergraduate/Scholarship)*

Purpose: To foster the development of students in the planning field by providing student scholarship each year. **Focus:** General studies. **Qualif.:** Applicants must be pursuing education in planning or planning related fields in a degree program; must be residents of the State of Minnesota or attending a university or college within the State of Minnesota in a planning related program. **Criteria:** Recipients are selected based on academic record, planning goals and planning related activities or job skills.

Funds Avail.: $1,000. **To Apply:** Applicants must submit a proof of enrollment; a recent transcript; letter of recommendation from a professor or job supervisor; a current resume including education, work experience, organizations, school activities, and professional skills; and a cover letter stating anticipated graduation date and professional goals. **Deadline:** July 11. **Contact:** michele.mcpherson@co.mill-lacs.mn.us.

4551 ■ Minnesota Health Information Management Association

PO Box 356
Stillwater, MN 55082
Ph: (651)342-0019
E-mail: mhima@comcast.net
URL: http://www.mnhima.org

4552 ■ Minnesota Health Information Management Association Scholarships *(Undergraduate/Scholarship)*

Purpose: To promote high quality health information and benefit the public, health care providers, and other clinical data users. **Focus:** Health education. **Qualif.:** Applicants must be Minnesota residents enrolled in an in-state or out-of-state program or out-of-state students attending a Minnesota school; must have completed accredited Health Information Technology or Health Information Management program; must be in a graduate program related to HIM College or University and accredited by a nationally recognized accrediting agency that has a coding certificate program or AHIMA Coding Basics Interactive Campus program. Applicant must have a cumulative GPA of 3.0 out of 4.0. **Criteria:** Recipients are selected based on academic achievement.

Funds Avail.: No specific amount. **To Apply:** Applicants must submit an application form; one letter of recommendation from faculty advisor, faculty member or mentor; a verification program; an essay with 500 words; and an official transcript of grades indicating cumulative grades.

4553 ■ Minnesota Minority Junior Golf Association

230 TriTech Ctr.
331 2nd Ave. S
Minneapolis, MN 55401-2240
Ph: (612)333-7309
E-mail: info@mmjga.org
URL: http://www.mmjga.org

4554 ■ Evans Scholarships *(Undergraduate/Scholarship)*

Purpose: To support minority junior golf. **Focus:** Sports. **Qualif.:** Applicants must have completed two full years in the MMJGA Caddie Program; must document at least 40 loops of caddying in the two-year period (with at least 25 loops at a private country club in the two-year period); must be assisting in training new caddies; must achieve "A" level or above caddie status at a country club; must be accepted at a post-secondary educational program or enrolled at a post-secondary educational program; and must maintain 2.0 or better grade point average. **Criteria:** Recipients are selected based on merit.

Funds Avail.: No specific amount. **Number Awarded:** 3. **To Apply:** Applicants must complete an application form and provide an essay.

4555 ■ Minnesota State Archery Association

4021 W Tischer Rd.
Duluth, MN 55803
Ph: (218)393-4181
E-mail: president.msaa@mnachery.org
URL: http://www.mnarchery.org

4556 ■ Minnesota State Archery Association Scholarship Program *(Undergraduate/Scholarship)*

Purpose: To encourage outstanding students to prepare for worthwhile careers at the college of their choice and to promote the sport of archery. **Focus:** General studies. **Qualif.:** Applicants must be graduating high school students who are academically successful and who can also demonstrate a sincere interest in the sport of archery. **Criteria:** Recipients are selected based on financial need and participation in activities.

Funds Avail.: $250. **To Apply:** Applicants must submit a completed application form and a resume. **Deadline:** June 15.

Awards are arranged alphabetically below their administering organizations

4557 ■ Minority Corporate Counsel Association

1111 Pennsylvania Ave. NW
Washington, DC 20004
Ph: (202)739-5901
Fax: (202)739-5999
URL: http://www.mcca.com

4558 ■ MCCA Lloyd M. Johnson, Jr. Scholarships *(Undergraduate/Scholarship)*

Purpose: To provide scholarship opportunities for minority students seeking to study law. **Focus:** Law. **Qualif.:** Program is open to college seniors and graduate students that are interested in obtaining a law degree; must have a grade point average of at least 2.5 on a 4.0 scale; must be in financial need; and must be considered a minority. **Criteria:** Applicants will be scored by the MCCA and UNCF and provide a list of the top forty candidates to the LMJ Scholarship Committee to choose the winners.

Funds Avail.: $10,000. **Number Awarded:** 10. **To Apply:** Applicants must accomplish online application. **Deadline:** January 1.

4559 ■ MiraCosta College

1 Barnard Dr.
Oceanside, CA 92056
Ph: (760)757-2121
Free: 888-201-8480
URL: http://www.miracosta.cc.ca.us

4560 ■ MiraCosta College Two-Year Colleges Scholarships *(Undergraduate/Scholarship)*

Purpose: To provide educational support for qualified individuals intending to pursue a two-year degree. **Focus:** General studies. **Qualif.:** Applicants must be U.S. citizens or permanent residents; must have a minimum of a 2.5 at time of nomination; must be planning to enroll in at least two course during the fall term at a two-year degree granting institution; and must be actively engaged in volunteer service or employed at least part-time. **Criteria:** Selection of applicants will be based on their application materials and academic performance.

Funds Avail.: $1,000. **Number Awarded:** 350. **To Apply:** Applicants must contact the scholarship at www.ptk.org for application and deadline information. **Deadline:** May 31.

4561 ■ TYLENOL Scholarships *(Undergraduate/Scholarship)*

Purpose: To encourage educational pursuits among individuals inclined in the field of health. **Focus:** Health education. **Qualif.:** Applicants must be students intending to pursue their careers in health-related studies. **Criteria:** Applicants will be judged based on leadership qualities and academic performance.

Funds Avail.: $1,000-$5,000. **Number Awarded:** 170. **To Apply:** Application forms are available online. **Deadline:** May 15.

4562 ■ Moline Foundation

817 11th Ave.
Moline, IL 61265
Ph: (309)736-3800
Fax: (309)736-3721
E-mail: molinefoundation@gconline.com
URL: http://www.molinefoundation.org

4563 ■ Engineers for Tomorrow Scholarships Program *(Undergraduate/Scholarship)*

Purpose: To provide grants to health, human services, education, community development, the arts, and other charitable organizations which benefit the citizens of Moline Foundations. To encourage engineering as a career and provide an incentive for young college graduates to return to live and work in Quad cities. **Focus:** Engineering. **Qualif.:** Applicants must be graduating high school seniors, or community college students preparing to transfer to four-year colleges. Applicants must intend to pursue a bachelor's degree on a full-time basis. Applicants must demonstrate financial need. Applicants must have achieved high school scholastic performance in the upper one-third of their class, or community college grade performance of 2.5 on a 4.0 scale, or equivalent. **Criteria:** Recipients are selected based on financial need.

Funds Avail.: $16,000. **To Apply:** Applicants must complete the application form. **Contact:** 309-736-3800.

4564 ■ Cleam T. Hanson Scholarship Fund *(Undergraduate/Scholarship)*

Purpose: To provide grants to health, human services, education, community development, the arts, and other charitable organizations which benefit the citizens of Moline Foundations. **Focus:** General studies. **Qualif.:** Applicants must be graduating high school seniors, or community college students preparing to transfer to four-year colleges. Applicants must intend to pursue a bachelor's degree on a full-time basis in any career field. Applicants must demonstrate financial need. Applicants must have achieved high school scholastic performance in the upper one-third of their class, or community college grade performance of 2.5 on a 4.0 scale, or equivalent. **Criteria:** Recipients are selected based on financial need.

Funds Avail.: No specific amount. **To Apply:** Applicants must complete the application form. **Contact:** 309-736-3800.

4565 ■ Lee Womack Scholarships Fund *(Undergraduate/Scholarship)*

Purpose: To provide grants to health, human services, education, community development, the arts, and other charitable organizations which benefit the citizens of Moline Foundations. To provide funds to deserving students from Moline High School who plan to obtain a college degree in education. **Focus:** Education. **Qualif.:** Applicants must be graduating high school seniors, or community college students preparing to transfer to four-year colleges. Applicants must intend to pursue a bachelor's degree on a full-time basis. Applicants must demonstrate financial need. Applicants must have achieved high school scholastic performance in the upper one-third of thelr class, or community college grade performance of 2.5 on a 4.0 scale, or equivalent. **Criteria:** Recipients are selected based on financial need.

Funds Avail.: No specific amount. **To Apply:** Applicants must complete the application form. **Contact:** 309-736-3800.

4566 ■ Monsanto Company

800 N Lindbergh Blvd.
St. Louis, MO 63167
Ph: (314)694-1000

Awards are arranged alphabetically below their administering organizations

URL: http://www.monsanto.com

4567 ■ Monsanto Company Agriculture Scholarships *(Undergraduate/Scholarship)*

Purpose: To support the education of students who have long-term career interest in agriculture. **Focus:** Agricultural sciences. **Qualif.:** Applicant must be a high school senior from a farm family; must have an above-average academic record; and must plan to enroll as a full-time student in an agriculture-related academic major at an accredited school. **Criteria:** Awards are given based on high school records, standardized test results, extracurricular activities and personal application essays.

Funds Avail.: $1,500. **Number Awarded:** 100. **To Apply:** Applicants may contact the Program Administrator for the application.

Remarks: In association with the National Association of Farm Broadcasters (NAFB). **Contact:** Program Administrator, Commitment to Agriculture Scholarship Program, c/o National FFA Organization, Scholarship Office, PO Box 68960 Indianapolis, IN 46268-0960, Phone: 317-802-6060, or E-mail: scholarships@ffa.org.

4568 ■ Montana Broadcasters Association

HC 70, Box 90
Bonner, MT 59823
Ph: (406)244-4622
Fax: (406)244-5518
E-mail: mba@mtbroadcasters.org
URL: http://www.mtbroadcasters.org

4569 ■ Joe Durso Memorial Scholarships *(Undergraduate/Scholarship)*

Purpose: To promote the values of local, free over-the-air broadcasting to the business community, governmental bodies and the general public in Montana; and to support the Montana broadcasting industry by providing services, information, continuing education, recruitment and a strong unified voice. **Focus:** Broadcasting. **Qualif.:** Applicants must be students entering their senior year, majoring in Radio-TV or Broadcast Journalism. **Criteria:** Recipients are selected based on academic performance.

Funds Avail.: No specific amount. **To Apply:** Applicants must submit a completed application form.

4570 ■ Great Falls Broadcasters Association Scholarships *(Undergraduate/Scholarship)*

Purpose: To promote the values of local, free over-the-air broadcasting to the business community, governmental bodies and the general public in Montana; and to support the Montana broadcasting industry by providing services, information, continuing education, recruitment and a strong unified voice. **Focus:** Broadcasting. **Qualif.:** Applicants must be students who have graduated from North-Central Montana High School and are enrolled as at least second-year students in Radio-TV at any public or private Montana college or university. **Criteria:** Recipients are selected based on academic performance.

Funds Avail.: No specific amount. **To Apply:** Applicants must submit completed application form.

4571 ■ Montana Broadcasters Association Directors' Scholarships *(Undergraduate/Scholarship)*

Purpose: To promote the values of local, free over-the-air broadcasting to the business community, governmental bodies and the general public in Montana; and to support the Montana broadcasting industry by providing services, information, continuing education, recruitment and a strong unified voice. **Focus:** Broadcasting; Theater Arts. **Qualif.:** Applicants must be students majoring in media and theater arts. **Criteria:** Recipients are selected based on academic performance.

Funds Avail.: No specific amount. **To Apply:** Applicants must submit a completed application form.

4572 ■ Montana Broadcasters Association Engineers' Scholarships *(Undergraduate/Scholarship)*

Purpose: To promote the values of local, free over-the-air broadcasting to the business community, governmental bodies and the general public in Montana; and to support the Montana broadcasting industry by providing services, information, continuing education, recruitment and a strong unified voice. **Focus:** Broadcasting; Engineering. **Qualif.:** Applicants must be second year students, majoring in Engineering at the UM College of Technology, and interested in pursuing a career in Broadcast Engineering. **Criteria:** Recipients are selected based on academic performance.

Funds Avail.: No specific amount. **To Apply:** Applicants must submit completed application form.

4573 ■ Morris County Psychological Association

50 Maple Ave.
Morristown, NJ 07960
Ph: (973)644-0033
E-mail: info@mcpanj.com
URL: http://www.mcpanj.com

4574 ■ Morris County Psychological Association Scholarships *(Undergraduate/Scholarship)*

Purpose: To stimulate and encourage the study of the behavioral sciences in high school students. **Focus:** General Studies. **Qualif.:** Applicants must be high school students who are taking classes related to the behavioral sciences including psychology, human and animal behavior, child development, sociology. **Criteria:** Preference will be given to those who meet the criteria.

Funds Avail.: No specific amount. **To Apply:** Applicants must check the available website for the required materials. **Contact:** Morris County Psychological Association at the above address (see entry 4573).

4575 ■ James B. Morris Scholarship Fund

525 SW 5th St., Ste. A
Des Moines, IA 50309-4501
Ph: (515)282-8192
Fax: (515)282-9117
E-mail: morris@assoc-mgmt.com
URL: http://www.morrisscholarship.org

4576 ■ James B. Morris Scholarships *(Undergraduate/Scholarship)*

Purpose: To provide assistance, motivation, and internship opportunities for minority students pursuing post-secondary and graduate degrees. **Focus:** General studies. **Qualif.:** Program is open to individuals of minority ethnic status as defined by the Equal Employment Opportunity Commission who have a minimum 2.5 GPA. Eligible applicants may be: Iowa high school graduates and residents of Iowa who are attending any U.S. college or university; or non-Iowa residents who are attending Iowa colleges or universities. **Criteria:** Applicants will be selected based on financial need and selection criteria.

Funds Avail.: No specific amount. **To Apply:** Applicants must submit a copy of official high school transcripts (for graduating high school seniors only), official college transcript (most recent semester only); must provide one or more letters of references (at least one must be from an instructor); must provide a writing sample (an essay about the applicant and why they are applying for the scholarship); must complete the application form available online and must have a recent photograph (head and shoulder shot only). Application form and other supporting documents must be sent to Scholarship Committee Chairperson, James B. Morris Scholarship Fund, Inc., 525 SW 5th St., Ste. A, Des Moines, IA 50309-4501. **Deadline:** April 1.

4577 ▪ Mortar Board National College Senior Honor Society

1200 Chambers Rd., Ste. 201
Columbus, OH 43212
Fax: (614)488-4095
Free: 800-989-6266
E-mail: mortarboard@mortarboard.org
URL: http://www.mortarboard.org

4578 ▪ Mortar Board National Foundation Fellowships *(Postdoctorate/Fellowship)*

Purpose: To provide financial support for members who want to pursue a post-graduate education. **Focus:** General studies. **Qualif.:** Applicant must be a current or former member of Mortar board working toward a degree beyond his or her bachelor's. **Criteria:** Candidates will be judged based on their academic record, recommendations, goals and objectives, need and contribution/commitment to Mortar Board.

Funds Avail.: $60,000. **To Apply:** Applicants must complete online application, must submit one official transcript of all work completed on the college level and two recommendations, completed online. **Deadline:** January 31.

4579 ▪ John R. Mott Scholarship Foundation

2550 M St. NW
Washington, DC 20037
E-mail: info@mottscholarship.org
URL: http://www.mottscholarship.org

4580 ▪ John R. Mott Scholarships *(Undergraduate/Scholarship)*

Purpose: To provide scholarship for higher education to students who are natives of Calabria. **Focus:** General studies. **Qualif.:** Applicants must be natives to the region of Calabria, Italy who are enrolled to attend any accredited post-secondary school; must be seeking an education leading to a degree or professional certificate. **Criteria:** Recipients will be selected based on academic achievement and financial need. Preferences will be given to students from the town of Serra D'Aielo, and the city and province of Cosenza.

Funds Avail.: $10,000. **To Apply:** Applicants must complete the application form available online. Applicants must submit an official transcript from the university attesting to academic performance. Application form and requirements must be sent to NIAF Mott Scholarships, 1860 19th St. NW. Washington, DC 20009. **Deadline:** March 15.

4581 ▪ Mountain Plains Adult Education Association

Adult Learning Center
815 Front St.
Helena, MT 59602
Ph: (406)324-2118
E-mail: djohl@helena.k12.mt.us
URL: http://www.mpaea.org

4582 ▪ MPAEA Memorial Scholarships *(Graduate/Scholarship)*

Purpose: To provide financial assistance for students' tuition, books and school-related expenses. **Focus:** Adult education. **Qualif.:** Applicant must be a student enrolled in a graduate degree program in an MPAEA member state; must be pursuing a graduate degree in adult education or closely related field; or a graduate student who has not previously received the scholarship. **Criteria:** Applicants will be evaluated based on financial need.

Funds Avail.: $1,000. **To Apply:** Applicants must review the criteria for eligibility before applying for the scholarship. They are advised to contact state MPAEA Board member for a copy of the application or download it from the MPAEA website: www.mpaea.org. **Deadline:** February 15. **Contact:** Dianne Marquez; New Mexico Junior College, 5317 Lovington Highway, Hobbs, NM 88240; phone: 505-392-5411; fax: 505-392-5499; email: dmarquez@nmjc.edu.

4583 ▪ MPAEA Professional Development Scholarships *(All/Scholarship)*

Purpose: To provide financial assistance for an individual from each member state of the Mountain Plains Adult Education Association to be used in attending conferences or other staff development activities during the MPAEA year. **Focus:** Adult education. **Qualif.:** Applicant must be a current member of MPAEA. **Criteria:** Applicants will be evaluated by the MPAEA Professional Development Committee based on financial need.

Funds Avail.: $500. **To Apply:** Applicants must submit all required application information. **Deadline:** February 15. **Contact:** Dianne Marquez; 5317 Lovington HWY, Hobbs, New Mexico 88240; email: dmarquez@nmjc.edu.

4584 ▪ MPAEA State Association Professional Development Grants *(Other/Grant)*

Purpose: To encourage and support professional development activities designed to benefit the members of the state association. **Focus:** Adult education. **Qualif.:** Applicant must be a state and its association which must have current membership in MPAEA. **Criteria:** Recipient will be selected by the Grant Selection Committee.

Funds Avail.: $500. **To Apply:** Applicants must contact the state MPAEA Board members for a copy of the application or download it from the web. They must complete the application with all applicable and required information and documentation and also complete a two-page report on the activity. Mail materials to the MPAEA Scholarship Committee Chair within two weeks following the event. **Contact:** Dianne Marquez; 5317 Lovington HWY, Hobbs, New

Mexico 88240; email: dmarquez@nmjc.edu.

4585 ■ MPAEA Student Scholarships *(Other/ Scholarship)*

Purpose: To provide financial assistance for students who are going to attend conferences or to engage in other student leadership activities during the year which runs from the beginning of the MPAEA Annual Conference, through the MPAEA Annual Conference of the following year. **Focus:** Adult education. **Qualif.:** Applicant must be from a state organization that has paid its affiliate dues for the current year. **Criteria:** Applicant will be evaluated by the MPAEA Student Scholarship Selection Committee.

Funds Avail.: $500. **To Apply:** Applicant must submit all required application information.

4586 ■ Ryan Mullaly Second Chance Fund

26 Meadow Ln.
Pennington, NJ 08534
E-mail: the2dchancefund@aol.com
URL: http://ryan2dchancefund.org

4587 ■ Ryan Mullaly Second Chance Fund Scholarships *(Undergraduate/Scholarship)*

Purpose: To provide financial assistance to young people who are fighting cancer to attend college. **Focus:** Cancer. **Qualif.:** Applicants must be citizens or permanent residents of the United States; must be diagnosed with cancer or encounter a recurrence of cancer between age 13 and graduation from high school; must be under active treatment for cancer while in high school, resulting in a substantial impact on their ability to attend class; must have a treatment history which includes chemotherapy and/or radiation; must be age 22 or younger; must have not previously been awarded a scholarship from the fund; must be currently pursuing an associate's or bachelor's degree at an accredited 2-year or 4-year college or currently enrolled in an accredited post-secondary vocational or trade program which will culminate in certification. **Criteria:** Applicants are evaluated based on financial need.

Funds Avail.: $1,000. **To Apply:** Applicants who are students still undergoing treatment, those with permanent effects from treatment and those at the beginning of their post-high school education are given priority.

4588 ■ Anthony Munoz Foundation

Longworth Hall
700 West Pete Rose Way, Unit 54
Cincinnati, OH 45203
Ph: (513)772-4900
Fax: (513)772-4911
E-mail: info@munozfoundation.org
URL: http://munozfoundation.com

4589 ■ Anthony Munoz Scholarships *(Undergraduate/Scholarship)*

Purpose: To support Tri-State youth in achieving their dreams of attending a local college or university. **Focus:** General studies. **Qualif.:** Applicant must be: a resident of any of the Tri-State region (Kentucky, Indiana, and Ohio); attending a local, Tri-State region, non-proprietary college, university or technical college; a graduating high school senior with at least a 2.0 GPA (or a G.E.D. recipient under the age of 23); of any race but of socio-economic need; must maintain a post-secondary GPA of at least a 2.0. **Criteria:** Recipient is chosen by the Munoz Family based on the submitted application.

Funds Avail.: No specific amount. **To Apply:** Applicants must submit a completed scholarship application form along with a copy of recent transcript; Expected Family Contribution (EFC) from Student Aid Report (SAR), which comes as a result of filing the FAFSA; and a copy of Financial Aid Award Letter from their chosen college. **Deadline:** April 30.

Remarks: Faxed applications will not be considered. In partnership with The Cincinnati Scholarship Foundation.

4590 ■ Daniel Murphy Scholarship Fund

228 S Wabash, Ste. 600
Chicago, IL 60604
Ph: (312)455-7800
Fax: (312)455-7801
E-mail: andrew@dmsf.org
URL: http://www.dmsf.org

4591 ■ Daniel Murphy Scholarships *(High School/Scholarship)*

Purpose: To financially support disadvantaged Chicago students who demonstrate academic potential. **Focus:** General studies. **Qualif.:** Applicant must be a Chicago eighth grade student who has demonstrated academic potential, strong character and financial need; must reside within the city of Chicago. **Criteria:** Awards are given based on merit.

Funds Avail.: No specific amount. **Number Awarded:** 100-120. **To Apply:** Applicants must submit a completed scholarship application form. **Deadline:** November 2.

4592 ■ Muscular Dystrophy Association

3300 E Sunrise Dr.
Tucson, AZ 85718
Ph: (520)529-2000
Fax: (520)529-5454
E-mail: grants@mdausa.org
URL: http://www.mda.org

4593 ■ MDA Development Grants *(Doctorate/ Grant)*

Purpose: To support research intended to develop treatments for muscular dystrophies and related diseases of the neuromuscular system. **Focus:** Muscular dystrophy. **Qualif.:** Applicant must hold an MD, PhD, DSc or equivalent degree; must be a member of a research team at an appropriate institution; must be qualified to conduct a program of original research under the supervision of a principal investigator; must have an acceptable research plan for a specific disease in MDA's program; must have access to institutional resources necessary to conduct the proposed research project; must have 18 months of post-doctoral research laboratory training at the time of application. **Criteria:** Recipients are given based on the committee's review of the submitted proposals.

Funds Avail.: $45,000. **Number Awarded:** 2. **To Apply:** Applicants must send a completed pre-proposal form to formally request for an application form. **Deadline:** January 15 and July 15.

4594 ■ MDA Research Grants *(Doctorate/Grant)*

Purpose: To support research intended to develop treatments for muscular dystrophies and related diseases of the

Awards are arranged alphabetically below their administering organizations

neuromuscular system. **Focus:** Muscular dystrophy. **Qualif.:** Applicant must hold an MD, PhD, DSc or equivalent degree; must be a member of a research team at an appropriate institution; must be qualified to conduct a program of original research under the supervision of a principal investigator; must have an acceptable research plan for a specific disease in MDA's program; must have access to institutional resources necessary to conduct the proposed research project; must have 18 months of post-doctoral research laboratory training at the time of application. **Criteria:** Recipients are given based on the committee's review of the submitted proposals.

Funds Avail.: No specific amount. **Number Awarded:** 2. **To Apply:** Applicants must send a completed pre-proposal form to formally request for an application form. **Deadline:** For pre-application form, December 15. For completed application, July 15.

4595 ■ Music Library Association

8551 Research Way, Ste. 180
Middleton, WI 53562
Ph: (608)836-5825
Fax: (608)831-8200
E-mail: mla@areditions.com
URL: http://www.musiclibraryassoc.org

4596 ■ Carol June Bradley Awards *(All/Grant)*

Purpose: To promote education involving the history of music libraries or special collections. **Focus:** Music; Library and archival sciences. **Qualif.:** Award is open to all interested applicants regardless of age, nationality, profession, or institutional affiliation. **Criteria:** Proposals will be reviewed on the basis of merit.

Funds Avail.: $1,000. **To Apply:** Applicants must submit a project summary, a preliminary budget, a current vita, and three names of references that must be sent to: Roberta Ford, Music Library, Columbus State University, 4225 University Ave., Columbus, GA 31907. **Deadline:** June 15. **Contact:** Roberta Ford, ford_roberta@colstate.edu.

4597 ■ Dena Epstein Award for Archival and Library Research in American Music *(All/Grant)*

Purpose: To support research in archives or libraries internationally on any aspect of American music. **Focus:** Music; Library and archival sciences. **Qualif.:** Award is open to all applicants regardless of age, nationality, profession, or institutional affiliation. **Criteria:** Proposals will be reviewed based on merit.

Funds Avail.: $2100. **To Apply:** Applicants must submit a brief research proposal (maximum of 10 pages) which includes description, detailed budget indicating the amount, justification, and additional sources of funding; curriculum vitae; and 3 letters of support from librarians and/or scholars. Submissions made electronically must be in Microsoft Word or PDF format and sent as e-mail attachments. If submitting by mail, include four copies of all documents. All documentation must be sent to: Prof. Suzanne L. Moulton-Gertig, Lamont School of Music, Newman Center for the Performing Arts, 2344 E. Iliff Ave., Denver, CO 80208 or smoulton@du.edu. **Deadline:** July 1.

4598 ■ Kevin Freeman Travel Grants *(Graduate, Professional Development/Grant)*

Purpose: To support travel and accommodation expenses for attendees of the MLA annual meeting. **Focus:** Music; Library and archival sciences. **Qualif.:** Applicants must be members of MAL; a graduate student in library school pursuing to become a music librarian; or a recent graduate of a graduate program in librarianship. **Criteria:** Applicants are selected based on merits.

Funds Avail.: $750. **To Apply:** Applicant must submit an application form; a current vita; and two letters of support mailed directly by the recommenders. Send application and other supporting materials in .pdf to: Judy Tsou, jstsou@u.washington.edu. **Deadline:** July 15. **Contact:** Judy Tsou, jstsou@u.washington.edu.

4599 ■ Walter Gerboth Awards *(All/Grant)*

Purpose: To assist research-in-progress in music or music librarianship. **Focus:** Music; Library and archival sciences. **Qualif.:** Applicants must be members of MLA who are in the first five years of their professional library careers. **Criteria:** Applicants will be reviewed based on merits.

Funds Avail.: $1000. **To Apply:** Applicants must submit the project description and statement of significance; a detailed total budget; two recommendation letters (one for the applicant and one for the project); and a curriculum vitae. All required materials must be sent to: Joseph Boonin, 1173 Singingwood Ct No. 2, Walnut Creek, CA 94595-3200, or joe@boonin.net **Deadline:** June 15. **Contact:** Joseph Boonin, joe@boonin.net

4600 ■ Myasthenia Gravis Foundation of America

1821 University Ave. W, Ste. S256
St. Paul, MN 55104
Ph: (651)917-6256
Fax: (651)917-1835
Free: 800-541-5454
E-mail: mgfa@myasthenia.org
URL: http://www.myasthenia.org

4601 ■ MGFA Student Fellowships *(Undergraduate/Fellowship)*

Purpose: To provide financial support to current medical students or graduate students interested in the scientific basis of myasthenia gravis or related neuromuscular conditions, serving both to further scientific inquiries into the nature of these disorders and to encourage more research. **Focus:** Myasthenia Gravis. **Qualif.:** Applicants must be medical or graduate students. **Criteria:** Applicants will be evaluated based on criteria designed by the Fellowship Committee.

Funds Avail.: $5,000. **To Apply:** Applicants must submit one hardcopy or one PDF file of the letter of interest, summary of the research and its significance to myasthenia gravis or related neuromuscular conditions, proposed budget, curriculum vitae of applicant and sponsoring preceptor and letter of recommendation from preceptor that indicates acceptance of the candidate and outlines the proposed work plan for the research study. **Deadline:** March 15.

4602 ■ Myasthenia Gravis Foundation of America Nursing Fellowships *(Undergraduate/Fellowship)*

Purpose: To provide financial assistance to nurses or nursing students interested in studying problems encountered by patients with myasthenia gravis or related neuromuscular conditions. **Focus:** Myasthenia gravis. **Qualif.:** Ap-

Awards are arranged alphabetically below their administering organizations

plicants must be professional nurses or nursing students. **Criteria:** Applicants will be evaluated based on criteria designed by the Fellowship Committee.

Funds Avail.: $5,000. **To Apply:** Applicant must submit four copies of a cover letter and the completed application form to the Chief Executive of the MGFA national office. **Deadline:** October 15.

4603 ■ Myasthenia Gravis Foundation of America Post-Doctoral Fellowships
(Postdoctorate/Fellowship)

Purpose: To attract physicians, PhD scientists and allied health professionals into conducting research into myasthenia gravis or related conditions. **Focus:** Myasthenia Gravis. **Qualif.:** Applicant must be a permanent resident of the United States or Canada who has been accepted to work in the laboratory of an established investigator at an institution in the United States, Canada or abroad deemed appropriate by the Medical/Scientific Advisory Board of the Myasthenia Gravis Foundation of America, Inc.; or a foreign national who has been accepted to work in the laboratory of an established investigator at an institution in the United States or Canada deemed appropriate by the Medical/Scientific Advisory Board of the Myasthenia Gravis Foundation of America, Inc. **Criteria:** Applicants will be evaluated by The Fellowship Committee based on some criteria.

Funds Avail.: $50,000. **To Apply:** Applicants must submit nine copies of the proposal and additional information to Post-Doctoral Committee. **Deadline:** October 1.

4604 ■ NAACP Legal Defense and Educational Fund

99 Hudson St., Ste. 1600
New York, NY 10013
Ph: (212)965-2200
URL: http://www.naacpldf.org

4605 ■ Earl Warren Civil Rights Training Scholarships *(Graduate/Scholarship)*

Purpose: To promote study in law. **Focus:** Law. **Qualif.:** Applicant must be a U.S. citizen; must be entering first year of full-time study; and must be a college graduate with good academic records, outstanding community service, and strong recommendations. **Criteria:** Preference is given to applicants who have a well-defined interest in civil rights and community service.

Funds Avail.: $3,000. **Number Awarded:** 15-20. **To Apply:** Applications for LDF's law scholarships may be requested between November 1 and February 28 by writing to The Earl Warren Legal Training Program, Inc. Requests for applications should be from the applicant and should include information about the applicant's undergraduate background, expected graduation date, law school plans and career goals. **Deadline:** March 31.

Remarks: Created in 1972.

4606 ■ Earl Warren Shearman and Sterling Scholarships *(Graduate/Scholarship)*

Purpose: To promote study in law. **Focus:** Law. **Qualif.:** Applicant must be an African-American student entering law school; must have an outstanding undergraduate academic record and above average LSAT scores; and must have mature and definitive career objectives and present evidence of exceptional university and community service. **Criteria:** Awards are given based on merit.

Funds Avail.: $15,000. **Number Awarded:** 15-20. **To Apply:** Applications for college scholarships may be requested between November 1, and March 31 by writing to The Herbert Lehman Education Fund. All requests for applications should be from the applicant and should include information about the applicant's college plans and career goals. Applications will be sent only to students who meet basic program criteria. **Deadline:** March 31.

Remarks: Sponsored by Sherman and Sterling.

4607 ■ NAMM, the International Music Products Association

5790 Armada Dr.
Carlsbad, CA 92008
Ph: (760)438-8001
Fax: (760)438-7327
Free: 800-767-6266
E-mail: info@namm.com
URL: http://www.namm.org

4608 ■ William R. Gard Memorial Scholarships
(Undergraduate/Scholarship)

Purpose: To enhance education and careers in the music product industry. **Focus:** Music; Music education. **Qualif.:** Applicants must be a member of NAMM Member firm; have completed 400 hours of employment at the NAMM Member firm; and enrolled full-time college student. **Criteria:** Applicants will be evaluated based on the submitted application and supporting documents.

Funds Avail.: $2,000 per academic year. **To Apply:** Application form is available at the website. Applicants must prepare reference letters; grade transcripts; awards and community involvement; and photograph. Forward completed application form and other required materials to: NAMM, International Music Products Association, William R. Gard Memorial Scholarship, 5790 Armanda Drive, Carlsbad, CA 92008. **Deadline:** March 31. **Contact:** NAMM Professional Development Department, 800-767-6266/760-438-8007 or gard@namm.org.

4609 ■ Nashville Catholic Business Women's League

PO Box 50994
Nashville, TN 37205-0994
E-mail: info@ncbwl.org
URL: http://www.ncbwl.org

4610 ■ Aurella Varallo Mariani Scholarship Program *(Undergraduate/Scholarship)*

Purpose: To provide financial support to those students who are in need. **Focus:** General studies. **Qualif.:** Applicants must be deserving young Catholic women in the middle Tennessee area. **Criteria:** Preference will be given to those students who meet the criteria.

Funds Avail.: No specific amount. **To Apply:** Applicants must check the available website for details.

Remarks: The scholarships are named in memory of Aurelia Varallo Mariani, a faithful and loving NCBWL member who graduated from St. Cecilia Academy in 1951. Her love for her alma mater and for this league continued until her untimely death in 1997. **Contact:** Nashville Catholic Business Women's League at the above address (see entry 4609).

Awards are arranged alphabetically below their administering organizations

4611 ■ NCBWL Scholarships *(High School/ Scholarship)*

Purpose: To provide scholarship assistance to deserving female students. **Focus:** General studies. **Qualif.:** Applicants must be female students; must be enrolled at St. Cecilia Academy, Father Ryan High School or Pope John Paul II High School for their full four years of matriculation. **Criteria:** Preference will be given to those students who meet the criteria.

Funds Avail.: No specific amount. **To Apply:** Applicants must submit a completed application form. **Contact:** Nashville Catholic Business Women's League at the above address (see entry 4609).

4612 ■ National 4th Infantry (IVY) Division Association

c/o Gregory A. Rollinger, 8891 Aviary Path
Inver Grove Heights, MN 55077
Ph: (651)994-0556
Fax: (651)994-0576
E-mail: 4idaexecdirector@comcast.net
URL: http://www.4thinfantry.org

4613 ■ 4th Infantry Division Association Scholarships *(Four Year College, Postgraduate, Two Year College/Scholarship)*

Purpose: To provide educational assistance to association members and their blood relatives. **Focus:** General studies. **Qualif.:** Applicant must be a blood relative, stepchild or adopted child of a current association member in good standing; must be a U.S. citizen. **Criteria:** Recipients are chosen by lottery at the National Reunion.

Funds Avail.: $500-$1,000. **Number Awarded:** 1-3. **To Apply:** Applicant must submit complete application package. **Deadline:** June 15. **Contact:** Alexander Cooker, Scholarship Fund Treasurer, alexcooker@aol.com.

4614 ■ National Academic Advising Association

Kansas State University
2323 Anderson Avenue, Ste. 225
Manhattan, KS 66502-2912
Ph: (785)532-5717
Fax: (785)532-7732
E-mail: nacada@ksu.edu
URL: http://www.nacada.ksu.edu

4615 ■ Wesley R. Habley NACADA Summer Institute Scholarships *(Professional Development/ Scholarship)*

Purpose: To help NACADA members afford a professional development experience. **Focus:** General studies. **Qualif.:** Applicant must be a current NACADA member at the time of scholarship application; must demonstrate involvement in NACADA activities through commission, region, task force, and/or committee participation; must demonstrate involvement in NACADA regional and/or national conferences as a participant and/or presenter. Currently elected or appointed officer and officials of NACADA, as well as previous Summer Institute Scholarship recipients and participants are not eligible to apply. **Criteria:** The selection committee encourages applications from groups which are under-represented in the association.

Funds Avail.: No specific amount. **To Apply:** Applicants must submit application materials in Word format via e-mail attachment to nacada@ksu.edu with subject line: Summer Institute Scholarship Application. Application forms and information on other requirements are available in the website. **Deadline:** March 3.

4616 ■ NACADA Scholarships *(Doctorate, Graduate/Scholarship)*

Purpose: To help association members offset expenses for graduate education. **Focus:** General studies. **Qualif.:** Applicant must be a member of NACADA for more than two years; must be currently enrolled in either a master's or doctoral program; must have worked as an academic advisor for two years. **Criteria:** Selection is based on merit.

Funds Avail.: $1,000; $500. **Number Awarded:** 1 ($1,000); 4 ($500). **To Apply:** Applicants must complete and submit for sets of the completed application package which includes: a NACADA Scholarship Application Form covering Career Goals Statement and financial assessment; official transcripts; resume; Evaluation/Recommendation by Faculty Form (sent directly to NACADA by faculty); and Evaluation by Employer Form. **Deadline:** March 3.

4617 ■ The National Academies

500 5th St. NW
Washington, DC 20001
Ph: (202)334-2872
E-mail: infofell@nas.edu
URL: http://www.nationalacademies.org

4618 ■ Ford Foundation Diversity Fellowships *(Doctorate/Fellowship)*

Purpose: To increase the diversity of the nation's college and university faculties by increasing their ethnic and racial diversity; to maximize educational benefits of diversity; and to increase the number of professors who can and will use diversity as a resource for enriching the education of all students. **Focus:** General studies. **Qualif.:** Applicants must be nationals of the United States regardless of race, national origin, gender, age, disability, or sexual orientation; must be individuals which have evidence of superior academic achievement; must be committed to a career in teaching and research at the college or university level; must be enrolled in or planning to enroll in an eligible research-based program leading to a Ph.D. or Sc.D degree at a U.S. educational institution; and must have not earned a doctoral degree at any time in any field. **Criteria:** Recipients are selected based on the evidence of superior academic achievement; degree of promise of continuing achievement as scholars and teachers; capacity to respond in pedagogically productive ways to the learning needs of students from diverse backgrounds; sustained personal engagement with communities that are underrepresented in the academy and an ability to bring this asset to learning, teaching, and scholarship at the college or university level; and likelihood of using the diversity of human experience as an educational resource in teaching and scholarship. Recipients are also selected based on the academic records, essays, letters of recommendation, the application itself, and other appropriate materials that meet the eligibility requirements and the selection criteria.

Funds Avail.: varies. **To Apply:** Applicants must complete the online application form including personal and contact information; a two-page, double-spaced statement of previous research; an essay describing proposed plan of graduate study or research and the applicant's long-range career

Awards are arranged alphabetically below their administering organizations

goals; transcript showing baccalaureate degree or undergraduate work; Graduate School Transcript; letters of reference; Verification of Predoctoral Status form; and GRE General Test Scores. **Contact:** National Research Council at the above address (see entry 4617).

4619 ■ The National Academies Dissertation Fellowships *(Doctorate/Fellowship)*

Purpose: To increase the diversity of the nation's college and university faculties by increasing their ethnic and racial diversity; to maximize educational benefits of diversity; to increase the number of professors who can and will use diversity as a resource for enriching the education of all students. **Focus:** General studies. **Qualif.:** Applicants must be nationals of the United States regardless of race, national origin, gender, age, disability, or sexual orientation; must be individuals which have evidence of superior academic achievement; must be committed to a career in teaching and research at the college or university level; must be Ph.D. or Sc.D degree at a U.S. educational institution; and must have not earned a doctoral degree at any time in any field. **Criteria:** Recipients are selected based on evidence of superior academic achievement; degree of promise of continuing achievement as scholars and teachers; capacity to respond in pedagogically productive ways to the learning needs of students from diverse backgrounds; sustained personal engagement with communities that are underrepresented in the academy and an ability to bring this asset to learning, teaching, and scholarship at the college or university level; likelihood of using the diversity of human experience as an educational resource in teaching and scholarship. Recipients are also selected based on academic records, essays, letters of recommendation, the application itself, and other appropriate materials that meet the eligibility requirements and the selection criteria.

Funds Avail.: $21,000. **Number Awarded:** 60. **To Apply:** Applicants must complete the online application form including personal and contact information; a two-page, double-spaced statement of previous research; essay describing proposed plan of graduate study or research and the applicant's long-range career goals; transcript showing baccalaureate degree or undergraduate work; graduate school transcript; letters of reference; verification of Predoctoral Status form; and GRE General Test Scores. **Deadline:** November 29; January 18. **Contact:** National Research Council at the above address (see entry 4617).

4620 ■ National Academies Postdoctoral Fellowships *(Postdoctorate/Fellowship)*

Purpose: To increase the diversity of the nation's college and university faculties by increasing their ethnic and racial diversity; to maximize the educational benefits of diversity; to increase the number of professors who can and will use the diversity as a resource for enriching the education of all students. **Focus:** American Studies. **Qualif.:** Applicants must be citizens or nationals of the United States; must be individuals with the evidence of superior academic achievement; must be committed to a career in teaching and research at the college or university level; and must be awarded a Ph.D. or Sc.D degree. **Criteria:** Recipients are selected based on the evidence of superior academic achievement; degree of promise of continuing achievement as scholars and teachers; capacity to respond in pedagogically productive ways to the learning needs of students from diverse backgrounds; sustained personal engagement with the communities that are underrepresented in the academy and an ability to bring this asset to learning, teaching, and scholarship at the college and university level; likelihood of using the diversity of human experience as an educational resource in teaching and scholarship. Recipients are also selected based on academic records, essays, letters of recommendation, indications of competence as a teacher, the application itself and other materials that meet the eligibility requirements.

Funds Avail.: $40,000. **Number Awarded:** 20. **To Apply:** Applicants must complete the application form including personal and contact information; statement of previous research; Annotated biography; one-page limit abstract of dissertation; abstract of proposed plan of study or research and long-range goal. **Deadline:** November 29; January 18. **Contact:** National Research Council at the above address (see entry 4617).

4621 ■ The National Academies Predoctoral Fellowships *(Doctorate/Fellowship)*

Purpose: To increase the diversity of the nation's college and university faculties by increasing their ethnic and racial diversity; to maximize educational benefits of diversity; to increase the number of professors who can and will use diversity as a resource for enriching the education of all students. **Focus:** General studies. **Qualif.:** Applicants must be nationals of the United States regardless of race, national origin, gender, age, disability, or sexual orientation; must be individuals who have evidence of superior academic achievement; must be committed to a career in teaching and research at the college or university level; must be enrolled or planning to enroll in an eligible research-based leading to a Ph.D. or Sc.D degree at a U.S. educational institution; and must have not earned a doctoral degree at any time in any field. **Criteria:** Recipients are selected based on the evidence of superior academic achievement; degree of promise of continuing achievement as scholars and teachers; capacity to respond in pedagogically productive ways to the learning needs of students from diverse backgrounds; sustained personal engagement with communities that are underrepresented in the academy and an ability to bring this asset to learning, teaching, and scholarship at the college or university level; likelihood of using the diversity of human experience as an educational resource in teaching and scholarship. Recipients are also selected based on academic records, essays, letters of recommendation, the application itself, and other appropriate materials that meet the eligibility requirements and the selection criteria.

Funds Avail.: $20,000. **Number Awarded:** 60. **To Apply:** Applicants must complete the online application form including personal and contact information; a two-page, double-spaced statement of previous research; essay describing proposed plan of graduate study or research and the applicant's long-range career goals; transcript showing baccalaureate degree or undergraduate work; graduate School Transcript; letters of reference; verification of Predoctoral Status form; and GRE General Test Scores. **Deadline:** November 15; January 18. **Contact:** National Research Council at the above address (see entry 4617).

4622 ■ National Academy of Education

500 Fifth St. NW 333
Washington, DC 20001
Ph: (202)334-2341
Fax: (202)334-2350
E-mail: info@naeducation.org
URL: http://www.naeducation.org

Awards are arranged alphabetically below their administering organizations

4623 ■ Adolescent Literacy Predoctoral Fellowships *(Doctorate/Fellowship)*

Purpose: To strengthen and stimulate the field of adolescent literacy. **Focus:** Adult Education. **Qualif.:** Applicants must be studying for a doctoral degree at a graduate school within the United States; must have demonstrated interest in, and acquired knowledge of, adolescent literacy; must have demonstrated knowledge of, and sensitivity to, the characteristics of the populations. **Criteria:** Applicants will be selected based on eligibility requirements.

Funds Avail.: $25,000. **Number Awarded:** 20. **To Apply:** Applicants must complete the application materials including two letters of recommendation. **Deadline:** December.

4624 ■ National Academy of Education Scholarships *(Doctorate/Fellowship)*

Purpose: To support early career scholars working in critical areas of education research. **Focus:** Education. **Qualif.:** Applicants must have received their PhD, EdD or equivalent research degree; should have a demonstrated record of research experience in education; non-US citizens are welcome to apply. **Criteria:** Applicant will be selected based on the past research record; career; trajectory and the quality of the project described in the application.

Funds Avail.: $55,000. **Number Awarded:** 20. **To Apply:** Applicants must submit complete application materials including application form; two letters of recommendation; project description; abstract of proposed research project; career history; curriculum vitae/resume and example of past research relevant to education.

4625 ■ National Academy of Television Arts and Sciences

111 W 57th St., Ste. 600
New York, NY 10019
Ph: (212)586-8424
Fax: (212)246-8129
E-mail: axa24@psu.edu
URL: http://www.emmyonline.org

4626 ■ John Cannon Memorial Scholarships *(Undergraduate/Scholarship)*

Purpose: To provide educational assistance to an outstanding high school senior who intends to pursue a baccalaureate degree in communications with emphasis on any aspect of the television industry. **Focus:** Television. **Qualif.:** Applicant must be a college-bound student within the United States who has demonstrated exceptional talent as a creator of video programming. **Criteria:** Recipient is chosen based on outstanding achievement and potential for success in a highly competitive field.

Funds Avail.: $40,000. **Number Awarded:** 9. **To Apply:** Application forms can be downloaded from the Foundation's scholarship web site or applicants may write to: Scholarship Committee, National Academy of Television Arts and Sciences, 111 W 57th St., Ste. 600, New York, NY 10019. **Deadline:** November 5.

4627 ■ National Active and Retired Federal Employees Association

606 N Washington St.
Alexandria, VA 22314
Ph: (703)838-7760
Fax: (703)838-7785
URL: http://www.narfe.org

4628 ■ NARFE-FEEA Scholarship Awards Program *(Undergraduate/Scholarship)*

Purpose: To provide financial assistance for education of children and grandchildren of federal employees. **Focus:** General studies. **Qualif.:** Applicant must be a child, grandchild, stepchild or great-grandchild of any NARFE member in good standing currently in high school and has at least a 3.0 grade point average on a 4.0 scale. **Criteria:** Applicants are judged according to the residence of the NARFE member.

Funds Avail.: 1,000. **To Apply:** Applicant must submit copies of their American College Testing (ACT) or Scholastic Aptitude Testing (SAT) scores, or other entrance examination scores as applicable; a written letter of recommendation/character reference from a teacher, or counselor; a list and brief description of awards and/or community service activities on a separate page; a typed, double-spaced, essay on a specific topic determined in the "Official Scholarship Application"; and two stamped, self-addressed No. 10 business-size envelopes. **Deadline:** April 30.

4629 ■ National Air Filtration Association

PO Box 68639
Virginia Beach, VA 23471
Ph: (757)313-7400
Fax: (757)497-1895
E-mail: nafa@nafahq.org
URL: http://www.nafahq.org

4630 ■ National Air Filtration Association Scholarship Fund *(Undergraduate/Scholarship)*

Purpose: To honor students who demonstrate outstanding personal and academic characteristics. **Focus:** General studies. **Qualif.:** Applicants must be immediate family members of NAFA members in good standing, or family members of employees of NAFA member firms. Grandchildren of NAFA members are also qualified. Incoming Freshmen must have a minimum ACT score of 22 or SAT score of 900 and rank in the top 35% of the graduating class. Transfer students must have a cumulative GPA of 2.75 on a 4.0 scale. **Criteria:** Applicants are selected based on the NAFA Past Presidents' review of the application materials.

Funds Avail.: $1,000. Cash scholarships are used for college expenses. **Number Awarded:** 2. **To Apply:** Applicants must submit a recent photo for press release purposes; a written essay of 1-2 typewritten pages that gives a brief biographical sketch of the individual along with reasons why they feel they should receive the scholarship; and two letters of recommendation, one of which must be from a recent teacher. Neither recommendation should be from a family member. **Deadline:** August 1.

4631 ■ National Alliance of Preservation Commission

PO Box 1605
Athens, GA 30603
Ph: (706)542-4731
Fax: (706)583-0320
E-mail: napc@uga.edu
URL: http://www.sed.uga.edu

Awards are arranged alphabetically below their administering organizations

4632 ■ National Alliance of Preservation Commission Student Scholarships *(Undergraduate/Scholarship)*

Purpose: To provide financial assistance for graduating students in historic preservation. **Focus:** Historic Preservation. **Qualif.:** Applicants must be a graduate student in historic preservation or related fields to participate in the National Commission Forum. **Criteria:** Recipients are selected based on their academic standing.

Funds Avail.: No specific amount. **To Apply:** Applicants must submit a cover letter with name and contact information; a 500-word statement explaining interest and expectations in attending the Forum; an estimate of the Forum expenses and the anticipated financial contribution. Applicants must also submit a proof of current student status; current resume including two academic and/or professional references. **Deadline:** May 5. **Contact:** NAPC Forum Scholarship, PO Box 1605, Athens, GA 30603; napc@uga.edu.

4633 ■ National Alpha Lambda Delta

PO Box 4403
Macon, GA 31208-4403
Free: 800-9-ALPHA-1
E-mail: ald@nationalald.org
URL: http://www.nationalad.org

4634 ■ ALD Graduate Fellowships *(Undergraduate/Fellowship)*

Purpose: To provide financial support for ALD members pursuing a graduate or professional degree. **Focus:** General studies. **Qualif.:** Applicant must be a member of Alpha Lambda Delta who has maintained a GPA of 3.5 on a 4.0 scale or equivalent until graduation. **Criteria:** Candidates will be selected based on academic records, recommendations submitted, the applicant's stated purpose and campus and community activities.

Funds Avail.: $3,000 up to $7,500. **Number Awarded:** 23. **To Apply:** Applicants must submit typed application, official transcript of all academic work, and list of not more than three persons from whom have requested letters of recommendation. **Deadline:** January 31.

4635 ■ Jo Anne J. Trow Scholarships *(Undergraduate/Scholarship)*

Purpose: To provide financial assistance to qualified members for their education. **Focus:** General studies. **Qualif.:** Applicants must be members of Alpha Lambda Delta who have maintained the cumulative grade point average of 3.5 on a 4.0 scale or equivalent. **Criteria:** Candidates will be evaluated by the chapter's scholarship selection committee.

Funds Avail.: $1,000 up to $3,000. **To Apply:** Applicants must complete application form, prepare the supplemental materials, and submit original application and two complete photocopies of all application materials to ALD chapter's scholarship selection committee's advisor. **Deadline:** April 1.

4636 ■ National American Arab Nurses Association

PO Box 43
Dearborn Heights, MI 48127
Ph: (313)680-5049
E-mail: info@n-aana.org
URL: http://www.n-aana.org

4637 ■ National American Arab Nurses Association Scholarships *(Undergraduate/Scholarship)*

Purpose: To provide financial assistance to applicants who are engaged in studying nursing at the associate degree, bachelor's degree, and master's degree or RN-BSN levels. **Focus:** Nursing. **Qualif.:** Applicants must be U.S. residents enrolled in an accredited nursing program at the time of the application, should be pursuing a nursing program during the year for which the award is made. **Criteria:** Recipients are evaluated on the basis of demonstrated academic excellence; leadership; academic; professional.

Funds Avail.: No specific amount. **To Apply:** Applicants must submit a copy of the most recent college or university transcript; two letters of recommendation from nursing faculty members that addresses the overall academic performance of the student and leadership activities; a one-page essay by the applicant describing eligibility why he/she is deserving for the award; a typewritten scholarship information sheet. **Deadline:** June 20.

4638 ■ National Arab American Medical Association

801 S Adams Rd., Ste. 208
Birmingham, MI 48009
Ph: (248)646-3661
Fax: (248)646-0617
E-mail: naama@naama.com
URL: http://www.naama.com

4639 ■ NAAMA Scholarships *(Undergraduate/Scholarship)*

Purpose: To provide financial assistance to Arabic students who are studying in a medical, osteopathic, or dental school. **Focus:** Medicine, Osteopathic; Dentistry. **Qualif.:** Applicants must be Arabic students enrolled in a U.S. or Canadian medical, osteopathic, or dental school. **Criteria:** Awards are given based on academic excellence and financial need.

Funds Avail.: $1,000. **Number Awarded:** 2. **To Apply:** Applicants must send completed application form together with a brief description on the applicant's education; transcripts; description of financial need; description of involvement in the Arab American community after completing studies; and recent 1040 tax return (with spouse and parents). **Deadline:** July.

4640 ■ National Asian American Society of Accountants

PO Box 8689
New York, NY 10116
Ph: (212)248-4888
Fax: (212)344-5636
E-mail: info@naasa.org
URL: http://www.naasa.org

4641 ■ AICPA Scholarships for Graduate Accounting Students *(Postgraduate/Scholarship)*

Purpose: To enhance the presence and influence of minorities in the accounting and finance profession; to encourage the development of finance professionals and students

Awards are arranged alphabetically below their administering organizations

while serving as a collective voice for the minority communities in the field of accounting and finance; and to encourage their selection of accounting as a major and their ultimate entry into the profession. **Focus:** Accounting; Finance. **Qualif.:** Applicants must have been accepted to a masters-level accounting, finance, taxation or other related program; must at least obtain 3.3 GPA major and cumulative; must be Black or African American, Hispanic or Latino, Asian, American Indian or Alaska native, Native Hawaiian Islander, or two or more races; must be U.S. citizens or permanent residents; and must be AICPA student affiliate members. **Criteria:** Recipients are selected based on academic standing and financial need.

Funds Avail.: Maximum amount of $5,000. **To Apply:** Applicants must submit completed application form; one-page, typed essay; and one letter of recommendation. **Deadline:** June 2.

4642 ■ AICPA Scholarships for Minority Accounting Students *(Undergraduate/Scholarship)*

Purpose: To enhance the presence and influence of minorities in the accounting and finance profession; to encourage the development of finance professionals and students while serving as a collective voice for the minority communities in the field of accounting and finance; and to encourage their selection of accounting as a major and their ultimate entry into the profession. **Focus:** Accounting; Finance. **Qualif.:** Applicant must be a declared accounting major with the intention of pursuing the CPA credential; must be full-time undergraduate student with 12 semester hours or equivalent at a four year or upper division institution, unless completing his/her semester of study; must have successfully completed at least 30 semester hours or equivalent of college coursework including at least six semester hours in accounting; must at least obtain 3.3 GPA major and cumulative; must be Black or African American, Hispanic or Latino, Asian, American Indian or Alaska native, Native Hawaiian Islander, or two or more races; must be U.S. citizen or permanent resident; and must be an AICPA student affiliate member. **Criteria:** Recipients are selected based on academic standing and financial need.

Funds Avail.: Maximum amount of $5,000. **To Apply:** Applicants must complete the application form and submit along with a one-page, typed essay and a letter of recommendation. **Deadline:** June 2.

4643 ■ ASCEND/ING Scholarships *(Undergraduate/Scholarship)*

Purpose: To recognize and inspire outstanding students. **Focus:** Accounting; Finance. **Qualif.:** Applicants must be current and active Ascend student members who are undergraduate or graduate students. Must either be juniors or seniors majoring in accountancy, finance, taxation, management information systems or business-related program in the academic year. They must have a strong academic standing and a 3.2 GPA or higher and community volunteer experience. **Criteria:** Recipients are selected based on financial need and academic standing.

Funds Avail.: No specific amount. **To Apply:** Applicants must submit a resume including current GPA; minimum of 500-word personal essay describing career goals; and unofficial college or university transcript. **Deadline:** June 15. **Contact:** vanessa.manzano@naasa.org

4644 ■ Ernst and Young/Ascend Leadership Scholarship Program *(Undergraduate/Scholarship)*

Purpose: To enhance the presence and influence of Asian Americans in the accounting and finance profession and to encourage the development of finance professionals and students while serving as a collective voice for the Asian and Pacific Islander communities in the field of accounting and finance. **Focus:** Accounting; Finance. **Qualif.:** Applicants must be students who demonstrate a desire to pursue a career in accounting and professional services. **Criteria:** Recipients are selected based on academic achievement and financial need.

Funds Avail.: $5,000. **Number Awarded:** 5. **To Apply:** Applicants must complete the application form. **Deadline:** June 15. **Contact:** venessa.manzano@naasa.org.

4645 ■ National Asian Pacific American Bar Association

1612 K Street NW, Ste. 1400
Washington, DC 20006
Ph: (202)775-9555
Fax: (202)775-9333
E-mail: ed@napaba.org
URL: http://www.napaba.org

4646 ■ Anheuser-Busch NAPABA Law Foundation Presidential Scholarships *(Undergraduate/Scholarship)*

Purpose: To award law students who demonstrate an outstanding leadership potential to serve the Asian Pacific American community. **Focus:** Law. **Qualif.:** Applicants must be a student enrolled as a law degree candidate in an accredited law school in the United States at least half time as determined by the school is eligible. **Criteria:** Applicants are selected by the foundation in consultation with the president of NAPABA.

Funds Avail.: $7,500. **To Apply:** Applicants must submit complete application form; official copy of most recent law school transcript; resume; two letters of recommendation; a copy of application to law school for financial assistance. **Contact:** Parkin Lee, Esq; New York Life Investment Management, LLC; 51 Madison Avenue Room 1104; New York, New York 10010.

4647 ■ Lim, Ruger and Kim Scholarships *(Undergraduate/Scholarship)*

Purpose: To award to law students who demonstrate a commitment to serve or contribute to the Asian Pacific American community as future leaders. **Focus:** Law. **Qualif.:** Applicants must be a student enrolled as a law degree candidate in an accredited law school in the US at least half time as determined by the school. **Criteria:** Applicants must have demonstrated financial need.

Funds Avail.: $2,500. **To Apply:** Applicants must submit a completed and signed application form from foundation; official copy of the applicant's most recent law school transcript; resume; letter of recommendation from persons not related to the applicant.

Remarks: In 2004 the Foundation established its Lim, Ruger and Kim Scholarship through the generosity of the law firm of Lim, Ruger and Kim in Los Angeles.

4648 ■ NAPABA Law Foundation Scholarships *(Undergraduate/Scholarship)*

Purpose: To award law students who demonstrate a commitment to serve or contribute to the Asian Pacific American community as future leaders. **Focus:** Law. **Qualif.:** Applicants must be a student enrolled as a law degree

Awards are arranged alphabetically below their administering organizations

candidate in an accredited law school in the US at least half time as determined by the school. **Criteria:** Applicants must have demonstrated financial need.

Funds Avail.: $2,500. **To Apply:** Applicants must submit a completed and signed application form from foundation; official copy of the applicant's most recent law school transcript; resume; letter of recommendation from persons not related to the applicant.

Remarks: In 2003 the Foundation named one of these scholarships in memory of Chris Nakamura; a leader of the Asian Pacific legal community of Arizona.

4649 ■ Diane Yu Loan Repayment Assistance Program *(Undergraduate/Loan)*

Purpose: To assist recent law graduates who are working in Asia Pacific American legal service organizations to repay a portion of their student loans. **Focus:** Law. **Qualif.:** Applicants must be a student enrolled as a law degree candidate in an accredited law school in the US at least half time as determined by the school. **Criteria:** Applicants must have demonstrated financial need.

Funds Avail.: $5,500 for each of two years to be applied to their educational debt. **To Apply:** Applicants must submit a completed and signed application form from foundation; official copy of the applicant's most recent law school transcript; resume; letter of recommendation from persons not related to the applicant.

Remarks: Diane Yu is a long-time supporter of NAPABA and the NAPABA Law Foundation and generously funded a program in 2004.

4650 ■ National Association for the Advancement of Colored People

PO Box 1740
Alexandria, VA 22312
Ph: (703)684-6190
Fax: (703)619-0450
E-mail: naacp@naacpalexandria.org
URL: http://www.naacpalexandria.org

4651 ■ Annie B. Rose Educational Scholarships *(Undergraduate/Scholarship)*

Purpose: To provide financial aid for those who have successfully completed high school and are planning to continue their education in an institution of higher learning. **Focus:** General studies. **Qualif.:** Applicant must be a resident of the City of Alexandria; must have a minimum "C" grade point average (2.5 or better); be a graduating senior or current college enrolled; must have applied to and received official notice of acceptance by an accredited school; must be willing to receive the scholarship award through the business office of his/her respective institution; and willing to uphold the goals and objectives of the NAACP. **Criteria:** Applicants will be evaluated based on academic achievement.

Funds Avail.: $1,000. **Number Awarded:** 3. **To Apply:** Applicants must submit an official NAACP Scholarship Application; two letters of recommendation; official school transcript; and a 200-300 words personal essay. **Deadline:** May 1.

4652 ■ National Association of Agricultural Educators

300 Garrigus Bldg.
University of Kentucky
Lexington, KY 40546-0215
Ph: (859)257-2224
Free: 800-509-0204
URL: http://www.naae.org

4653 ■ Delmar Cengage Learning-NAAE Upper Division Scholarships *(Undergraduate/Scholarship)*

Purpose: To provide educational opportunities to students majoring in agricultural education. **Focus:** Education; Agricultural sciences. **Qualif.:** Applicants must be agricultural education majors who want to be agricultural teachers; must be members of NAAE. **Criteria:** Awards are given based on academics, character and perseverance to the field of teaching in agricultural education.

Funds Avail.: $750. **Number Awarded:** 15. **To Apply:** Applicants must submit original copy and eight copies of application form; description of applicant's leadership and service activities; an essay entitled "Why I Want to Teach Agriculture"; a letter of recommendation from an agricultural education teacher in the applicant's college or university or from an agricultural education teacher at the local, state or national level; official transcript; and a photograph in a CD. **Deadline:** May 15.

4654 ■ National Association of Black Accountants

7249-A Hanover Pkwy.
Greenbelt, MD 20770
Ph: (301)474-6222
Fax: (301)474-3114
Free: 888-571-2939
E-mail: customerservice@nabainc.org
URL: http://www.nabainc.org

4655 ■ Donald J. Bristow Memorial Scholarship Program *(Graduate, Undergraduate/Scholarship)*

Purpose: To support deserving students planning to enter a business related field. **Focus:** Business; Accounting; Finance. **Qualif.:** Applicant must be a member of an ethic minority; an active NABA student member; enrolled full-time at a four-year United States college or university; must be a freshman, sophomore, junior or first-year senior undergraduate pursuing a major in accounting, finance, or business; or a graduate student in a master's-level business program; must meet the minimum requirement of 3.5 major GPA and 3.3 overall GPA or equivalent. **Criteria:** Recipients are selected based on the application and other supporting materials.

Funds Avail.: $3,500. **To Apply:** Applicant must submit a completed National Scholarship Application (NSA) available at the website; a current official transcript; a copy of Student/Permanent Resident Visa (for non-U.S. citizen applicants); a resume; two letters of recommendation; a personal biography (maximum of 500 words) discussing career objectives, leadership skills, community activities, and involvement in NABA. **Deadline:** January 31.

4656 ■ Mark Miller Award *(Graduate, Undergraduate/Scholarship)*

Purpose: To support deserving students planning to enter a business related field. **Focus:** Business; Accounting; Finance. **Qualif.:** Applicant must be a member of an ethic minority; an active NABA student member; enrolled full-time at a four-year United States college or university; a freshman, sophomore, junior or first-year senior undergraduate pursuing a major in accounting, finance, or busi-

Awards are arranged alphabetically below their administering organizations

ness; or a graduate student in a master's-level business program; must meet the minimum requirement of 2.0 major GPA and 2.5 overall GPA or equivalent. **Criteria:** Recipient is selected based on the application and other supporting materials.

Funds Avail.: $2,500. **To Apply:** Applicant must submit a completed National Scholarship Application (NSA) available at the website; a current official transcript; a copy of Student/Permanent Resident Visa (for non-U.S. citizen applicants); a resume; two letters of recommendation; a personal biography (maximum of 500 words) discussing career objectives, leadership skills, community activities, and involvement in NABA. **Deadline:** January 31.

4657 ■ NABA Corporate Scholarship Program *(Graduate, Undergraduate/Scholarship)*

Purpose: To support deserving students planning to enter a business related field. **Focus:** Business; Accounting; Finance. **Qualif.:** Applicant must be a member of an ethic minority, an active NABA student member, enrolled full-time at a four-year United States college or university; must be a freshman, sophomore, junior or first-year senior undergraduate pursuing a major in accounting, finance, or business; or a graduate student in a master's-level business program; must meet the minimum requirement of 3.5 major GPA and 3.3 overall GPA or equivalent. **Criteria:** Recipient is selected based on the application and other supporting materials.

Funds Avail.: $2,000-$10,000. **To Apply:** Applicant must submit a completed National Scholarship Application (NSA) available at the website; a current official transcript; a copy of Student/Permanent Resident Visa (for non-U.S. citizen applicants); a resume; two letters of recommendation; a personal biography (maximum of 500 words) discussing career objectives, leadership skills, community activities, and involvement in NABA. **Deadline:** January 31.

4658 ■ NABA National Scholarship Program *(Graduate, Undergraduate/Scholarship)*

Purpose: To support deserving students planning to enter a business related field. **Focus:** Business; Accounting; Finance. **Qualif.:** Applicant must be a member of an ethic minority; an active NABA student member; enrolled full-time at a four-year United States college or university; must be a freshman, sophomore, junior or first-year senior undergraduate pursuing a major in accounting, finance, or business; or a graduate student in a master's-level business program; must meet the minimum requirement of 3.5 major GPA and 3.3 overall GPA or equivalent. **Criteria:** Recipients are selected based on the application and other supporting materials.

Funds Avail.: $3,000-$6,000. **To Apply:** Applicants must submit a completed National Scholarship Application (NSA) available at the website; a current official transcript; a copy of the Student/Permanent Resident Visa (for non-U.S. citizen applicants); a resume; two letters of recommendation; a personal biography (maximum of 500 words) discussing career objectives, leadership skills, community activities, and involvement in NABA. **Deadline:** January 31.

4659 ■ TDC Scholarship Program *(Graduate, Undergraduate/Scholarship)*

Purpose: To support deserving students planning to enter a business related field. **Focus:** Business; Accounting; Finance. **Qualif.:** Applicant must be a member of an ethic minority; an active NABA student member; enrolled full-time at a four-year United States college or university; must be a freshman, sophomore, junior or first-year senior undergraduate pursuing a major in accounting, finance, or business; or a graduate student in a master's-level business program; must meet the minimum requirement of 3.5 major GPA and 3.3 overall GPA or equivalent. **Criteria:** Recipient is selected based on the application and other supporting materials.

Funds Avail.: $1,000. **To Apply:** Applicant must submit a completed National Scholarship Application (NSA) available at the website; a current official transcript; a copy of Student/Permanent Resident Visa (for non-U.S. citizen applicants); a resume; two letters of recommendation; a personal biography (maximum of 500 words) discussing career objectives, leadership skills, community activities, and involvement in NABA. **Deadline:** January 31.

4660 ■ Ralph and Valerie Thomas Scholarship Program *(Graduate, Undergraduate/Scholarship)*

Purpose: To support deserving students planning to enter a business related field. **Focus:** Business; Accounting; Finance. **Qualif.:** Applicant must be a member of an ethic minority; an active NABA student member; enrolled full-time at a four-year United States college or university; must be a freshman, sophomore, junior or first-year senior undergraduate pursuing a major in accounting, finance, or business; or a graduate student in a master's-level business program; must meet the minimum requirement of 3.5 major GPA and 3.3 overall GPA or equivalent. **Criteria:** Recipient is selected based on the application and other supporting materials.

Funds Avail.: $1,000. **To Apply:** Applicant must submit a completed National Scholarship Application (NSA) available at the website; a current official transcript; a copy of Student/Permanent Resident Visa (for non-U.S. citizen applicants); a resume; two letters of recommendation; a personal biography (maximum of 500 words) discussing career objectives, leadership skills, community activities, and involvement in NABA. **Deadline:** January 31.

4661 ■ Travis C. Tomlin Memorial Scholarship Program *(Graduate, Undergraduate/Scholarship)*

Purpose: To support deserving students planning to enter a business related field. **Focus:** Business; Accounting; Finance. **Qualif.:** Applicant must be a member of an ethic minority; an active NABA student member; enrolled full-time at a four-year United States college or university; must be a freshman, sophomore, junior or first-year senior undergraduate pursuing a major in accounting, finance, or business; or a graduate student in a master's-level business program; must meet the minimum requirement of 3.5 major GPA and 3.3 overall GPA or equivalent. **Criteria:** Recipient is selected based on the application and other supporting materials.

Funds Avail.: $2,000. **To Apply:** Applicant must submit a completed National Scholarship Application (NSA) available at the website; a current official transcript; a copy of Student/Permanent Resident Visa (for non-U.S. citizen applicants); a resume; two letters of recommendation; a personal biography (maximum of 500 words) discussing career objectives, leadership skills, community activities, and involvement in NABA. **Deadline:** January 31.

4662 ■ Thomas S. Watson, Jr. Memorial Scholarships *(Graduate, Undergraduate/Scholarship)*

Purpose: To support deserving students planning to enter a business related field. **Focus:** Business; Accounting;

Finance. **Qualif.:** Applicant must be a member of an ethic minority; an active NABA student member; enrolled full-time at a four-year United States college or university; must be a freshman, sophomore, junior or first-year senior undergraduate pursuing a major in accounting, finance, or business; or a graduate student in a master's-level business program; must meet the minimum requirement of 3.5 major GPA and 3.3 overall GPA or equivalent. **Criteria:** Recipient is selected based on the application and other supporting materials.

Funds Avail.: $1,000. **To Apply:** Applicant must submit a completed National Scholarship Application (NSA) available at the website; a current official transcript; a copy of Student/Permanent Resident Visa (for non-U.S. citizen applicants); a resume; two letters of recommendation; a personal biography (maximum of 500 words) discussing career objectives, leadership skills, community activities, and involvement in NABA. **Deadline:** January 31.

4663 ■ National Association of Black Social Workers

2305 Martin Luther King Ave. SE
Washington, DC 20020
Ph: (202)678-4570
Fax: (202)678-4572
E-mail: nabsw.harambee@verizon.net
URL: http://www.nabsw.org

4664 ■ Emma and Meloid Algood Tuition Scholarships *(Undergraduate/Scholarship)*

Purpose: To provide financial assistance for African-American students who are active in community service and planning to work in the field of social work. **Focus:** Social work. **Qualif.:** Applicants must be African-American students who have a 2.5 grade point average on a 4.0 scale; must express research interest in the black community; and must be enrolled for full-time study at an accredited US Bachelors of Social Work program in the semester that the award will be granted. **Criteria:** Applicants are evaluated based on academic achievement; community service; and financial need.

Funds Avail.: $1,000. **Number Awarded:** 1. **To Apply:** Applicants must submit a purpose letter (two to three pages, double-spaced, typewritten) which must include the following: professional interests, future social work aspirations, previous social work experiences, honors and achievements, research interests within the black community; two letters of recommendation, preferably by a professor, field instructor, or a prestigious community-based leader; financial need statement with a breakdown of students' assets and liabilities; and an official academic transcript from the school.

4665 ■ Dr. Joyce Beckett Scholarships *(Undergraduate/Scholarship)*

Purpose: To provide financial assistance for individuals completing graduate work and to develop professional skills and talent to work in the African-American community. **Focus:** Social work. **Qualif.:** Applicants must be African-American students who have a 2.5 GPA on 4.0 scale; must express research interest in the black community; and must be enrolled for full-time study at an accredited US graduate social work program in the semester that the award will be granted. **Criteria:** Applicants are evaluated based on academic achievement; community service; and financial need.

Funds Avail.: $1,000. **Number Awarded:** 1. **To Apply:** Applicants must submit a purpose letter (two to three pages, double-spaced, typewritten) which must include the following: professional interests, future social work aspirations, previous social work experiences, honors and achievements, research interests within the black community; must submit two letters of recommendation, preferably by a professor, field instructor, or a prestigious community-based leader; financial need statement with a breakdown of students' assets and liabilities; and an official academic transcript from the school.

4666 ■ Selena Danette Brown Book Scholarships *(Undergraduate/Scholarship)*

Purpose: To provide financial assistance for African-American students who are active in community service. **Focus:** Social work. **Qualif.:** Applicants must be active, paid members of NABSW; must be African-American students who have a 2.5 Grade Point Average on a 4.0 scale; must express research interest in the black community; and must be enrolled for full-time study at an accredited US social work program in the semester that the award will be granted. **Criteria:** Applicants are evaluated based on academic achievement; community service; and financial need.

Funds Avail.: $250. **Number Awarded:** 4. **To Apply:** Applicants must submit a purpose letter (two to three pages, double-spaced, and typewritten) which must include the following: professional interests, future social work aspirations, previous social work experiences, honors and achievements, research interests within the black community; must submit two letters of recommendation, preferably by a professor, field instructor, or a prestigious community-based leader; financial need statement with a breakdown of students' assets and liabilities; and an official academic transcript from the school.

4667 ■ Guynn Family Foundation Book Scholarships *(Undergraduate/Scholarship)*

Purpose: To provide financial assistance for African-American students who are active in community service and planning to work in the field of social work. **Focus:** Social work. **Qualif.:** Applicants must be African-American students who have a 3.0 grade point average on a 4.0 scale; must perform 40 hours of community service in an underserved African-American community; must express research interest in the black community; and must be enrolled for full-time study at an accredited US social work program in the semester that the award will be granted. **Criteria:** Applicants are evaluated based on academic achievement; community service; and financial need.

Funds Avail.: $750. **Number Awarded:** 1. **To Apply:** Applicants must submit a purpose letter (two to three pages, double-spaced, typewritten) which must include the following: professional interests, future social work aspirations, previous social work experiences, honors and achievements, research interests within the black community; must submit two letters of recommendation, preferably by a professor, field instructor, or a prestigious community-based leader; financial need statement with a breakdown of students' assets and liabilities; and an official academic transcript from the school.

4668 ■ Cenie Jomo Williams Tuition Scholarships *(Undergraduate/Scholarship)*

Purpose: To provide financial assistance for African-American students who are active in community service.

Awards are arranged alphabetically below their administering organizations

Focus: Social work. **Qualif.:** Applicants must be active, paid members of NABSW; must be students who have a 2.5 grade point average on a 4.0 scale; must be African-American students with demonstrated community service; must be students who will conduct research of interest to the black community; and must be enrolled for full-time study at an accredited US social work program in the semester that the award will be granted. **Criteria:** Applicants are evaluated based on academic achievement; community service; and financial need.

Funds Avail.: $2,000. **Number Awarded:** 2. **To Apply:** Applicants must submit a purpose letter (two to three pages, double-spaced, and typewritten) which must include the following: professional interests, future social work aspirations, previous social work experiences, honors and achievements, research interests within the black community; must submit two letters of recommendation, preferably by a professor, field instructor, or a prestigious community-based leader; financial need statement with a breakdown of students' assets and liabilities; and an official academic transcript from the school.

4669 ■ National Association of Black Telecommunications Professionals

2020 Pennsylvania Ave. NW
Washington, DC 20006
Ph: 877-349-8869
Fax: 877-349-8869
E-mail: office@nabtp.org
URL: http://www.nabtp.org

4670 ■ NABTP Collegian *(Undergraduate/Scholarship)*

Purpose: To provide financial assistance for students who wish to study telecommunications or a related field. **Focus:** Telecommunications. **Qualif.:** Applicants have notable achievements in academics, extra-curricular and/or community activities. Applicants must also illustrate an interest in telecommunications or a related field. **Criteria:** Recipients will be selected based the content of the essays, GPA, notable achievements, and financial need.

Funds Avail.: $2,000. **To Apply:** Applicant may download and fill out an application form online. Applicants are also required to submit the following documents: Evidence of household income; NABTP Collegian Applicants official college-university transcripts in a sealed envelope from your educational institution(s); Two signed Letters of Recommendation in a sealed envelope with author's signature signed across the back flap of the envelope; and a maximum 2-page essay which can downloaded online. **Deadline:** July 23.

4671 ■ National Association of Campus Activities

13 Harbison Way
Columbia, SC 29212
Ph: (803)732-6222
Fax: (803)749-1047
E-mail: info@naca.org
URL: http://www.naca.org

4672 ■ Tese Caldarelli Memorial Scholarships *(Undergraduate/Scholarship)*

Purpose: To support undergraduate or graduate students. **Focus:** General studies. **Qualif.:** Applicants must be undergraduate students with a minimum cumulative GPA of 3.0 or better at the time of the application. **Criteria:** Recipients are selected based on the demonstrated leadership skills and abilities and significant contributions to their campus communities.

Funds Avail.: No specific amount. **To Apply:** Applicants must submit a current resume and complete the application form; at least two letters of recommendation; official verification of the applicant's current enrollment status. **Deadline:** November 1.

4673 ■ Markey Scholarships *(Undergraduate/Scholarship)*

Purpose: To support undergraduate or graduate students. **Focus:** General studies. **Qualif.:** Applicants must have a minimum of a 2.5 cumulative GPA; be junior, senior, or graduate students at a four-year school in the former NACA South Central Region. **Criteria:** Recipients are selected based on the involvement and contribution to NACA Central; demonstrated potential in the field of student activities; contribution to the field of student activities and/or student activities employment; involvement in and contribution to other organizations.

Funds Avail.: No specific amount. **To Apply:** Applicants must submit a current resume and any supporting materials that may enhance the applicant's candidacy. **Deadline:** September 1.

4674 ■ NACA East Coast Graduate Student Scholarships *(Postdoctorate/Scholarship)*

Purpose: To assist students pursuing a career in student activities or a related student services field. **Focus:** General studies. **Qualif.:** Applicants must be matriculated in a master's doctorate degree program in student personnel services or a related area. Applicants must have demonstrated experience and involvement in campus activities and be committed to pursue a career as a campus activities professional. **Criteria:** Recipients are selected based on the demonstrated leadership, academic record, and financial need.

Funds Avail.: No specific amount. **To Apply:** Applicants must submit at least two to four letters of reference from professors, advisors or employers who are familiar with the applicant's experience related to campus activities; one copy of the applicant's undergraduate and graduate academic; a summary of the applicant's volunteer and employment activities related to campus activities or resume; a summary of professional goals the applicant hopes to accomplish in one year, five years and ten years. **Deadline:** May 30.

4675 ■ NACA East Coast Higher Education Research Scholarships *(Postgraduate/Scholarship)*

Purpose: To assist students pursuing a career in student activities or a related student services field; to provide funds for research projects designed to add to the college student personnel knowledge base, particularly those projects which focus on campus activities, address issues challenging the student affairs practitioners and/or issues challenging higher education as they relate to campus activities. **Focus:** General studies. **Qualif.:** Applicants must show that their research will add to the college student personnel knowledge base, particularly campus activities, or address issues challenging student affairs practitioners or higher education as they relate to campus activities. Applicants must be pursuing a master's degree. **Criteria:** Recipients are selected based on the demonstrated leadership,

Awards are arranged alphabetically below their administering organizations

academic record, and financial need.

Funds Avail.: $500. **To Apply:** Applicants must submit a completed application form; a written statement from the applicant detailing a statement of the problem, papoose of the project, plan and timeline to address the question, anticipated results, including types of evidence to indicate objectives were achieved, a statement of the project's anticipated contribution to the profession, proposed budget that identifies anticipated income from all sources, qualifications of those conducting research, and plans to evaluate the project. Applicants should submit a letter of support from the applicant's supervisor, major professor, department head or other appropriate individual. **Deadline:** June 15.

4676 ■ NACA East Coast Undergraduate Scholarships for Student Leaders *(Undergraduate/Scholarship)*

Purpose: To assist students pursuing graduate or undergraduate studies leading to a career in student activities or a related student services field. **Focus:** General studies. **Qualif.:** Applicants must be matriculated undergraduates in good standing at the time of their application and during the semester in which the award is received; have a GPA of 2.5 on a 4.0 scale; have demonstrated significant leadership skills and ability; have made significant contributions via volunteer involvement, either on or off campus; be enrolled in a college or university within the former NACA East Coast region. **Criteria:** Recipients are selected based on demonstrated leadership, academic record, and financial need.

Funds Avail.: No specific amount. **To Apply:** Applicants must submit at least two letters of recommendation; resume or description of the applicant's leadership activities, skills, and ability, training, and accomplishment; official transcript of the applicant's current enrollment status from the college or university. **Deadline:** March 31.

4677 ■ NACA Foundation Graduate Student Scholarships *(Postdoctorate/Scholarship)*

Purpose: To assist students pursuing a career in student activities or a related student services field. **Focus:** General studies. **Qualif.:** Applicants must be matriculated in a master's doctorate degree program in student personnel services or a related area. Applicants must have demonstrated experience and involvement in campus activities and be committed to pursue a career as a campus activities professional. Applicants must have graduated from a four- year college or university with a minimum GPA of 2.5. **Criteria:** Recipients are selected based on the demonstrated leadership, academic record, and financial need.

Funds Avail.: No specific amount. **To Apply:** Applicants must submit at least two to four letters of reference from professors, advisors or employers who are familiar with the applicant's experience related to campus activities; one copy of the applicant's undergraduate and graduate academic; a summary of the applicant's volunteer and employment activities related to campus activities or resume; a summary of professional goals the applicant hopes to accomplish in one year, five years and ten years. **Deadline:** May 30.

4678 ■ NACA Regional Council Student Leadership Scholarships *(Undergraduate/Scholarship)*

Purpose: To assist students pursuing graduate or undergraduate studies leading to a career in student activities or a related student services field. **Focus:** General studies. **Qualif.:** Applicants must be matriculated undergraduate in good standing at the time of their application and during the semester in which the award is received; hold a significant leadership position on campus or in the community; have made significant contributions via volunteer involvement, either on or off the campus. **Criteria:** Recipients are selected based on the demonstrated leadership, academic record, and financial need.

Funds Avail.: No specific amount. **To Apply:** Applicants must submit at least two letters of recommendation; resume or description of the applicant's leadership activities, skills, and ability, training, and accomplishment; and official transcript of the applicant's current enrollment status from the college or university. **Deadline:** May 1.

4679 ■ NACA Southeast Student Leadership Scholarships *(Undergraduate/Scholarship)*

Purpose: To assist students pursuing graduate or undergraduate studies leading to a career in student activities or a related student services field; to recognize the achievements of undergraduate student leaders enrolled at colleges and universities in the former NACA Southeast Region. **Focus:** General Studies. **Qualif.:** Applicants must be matriculated undergraduates in good standing at the time of their application and during the semester in which the award is received; have a GPA of 2.5 on a 4.0 scale; have demonstrated significant leadership skills and ability; hold a significant leadership position on campus or in the community; have made significant contributions via volunteer involvement, either on or off the campus. **Criteria:** Recipients are selected based on the demonstrated leadership, academic record, and financial need.

Funds Avail.: No specific amount. **Number Awarded:** 4. **To Apply:** Applicants must submit at least two letters of recommendation; resume or description of the applicant's leadership activities, skills, and ability, training, and accomplishment; and official transcript of the applicant's current enrollment status from the college or university. **Deadline:** March 31.

4680 ■ National Association of Campus Activities Multicultural Scholarship Programs *(Undergraduate/Scholarship)*

Purpose: To assist students pursuing graduate or undergraduate studies leading to a career in student activities or a related student services field; to provide economic assistance to qualified underrepresented programmers; to increase the participation of ethnic minority individuals in the field of campus activities. **Focus:** General studies. **Qualif.:** Applicants must be matriculated undergraduates in good standing at the time of their application and during the semester in which the award is received; must be a member of the African-American, Latina/Latino, Native American, Asian American, or Pacific Islander ethnic minorities; hold a significant leadership position on campus or in the community; have made significant contributions via volunteer involvement, either on or off the campus. **Criteria:** Recipients are selected based on the demonstrated leadership, academic record, and financial need.

Funds Avail.: No specific amount. **To Apply:** Applicants must submit at least two letters of recommendation; resume or description of the applicant's leadership activities, skills, and ability, training, and accomplishment; official transcript of the applicant's current enrollment status from the college or university. Applicants must submit a 350-600-word statement describing their leadership program and how their participation met their professional development objectives. **Deadline:** May 1.

4681 ■ National Association of Campus Activities Scholarships for Student Leaders *(Undergraduate/Scholarship)*

Purpose: To support undergraduate or graduate students. **Focus:** General studies. **Qualif.:** Applicants must be undergraduate students in good standing at the time of the application and during the semester in which the award is received. **Criteria:** Recipients are selected based on the demonstrated leadership skills and abilities and significant contributions to their campus communities.

Funds Avail.: No specific amount. **To Apply:** Applicants must submit a current resume and a letter of recommendation from the candidate's current supervisor. **Deadline:** November 1.

4682 ■ Lori Rhett Memorial Scholarships *(Undergraduate/Scholarship)*

Purpose: To recognize the achievements of undergraduate or graduate student leaders enrolled in colleges and universities located in the former NACA Pacific Northwest Region. **Focus:** General studies. **Qualif.:** Applicants must be matriculated undergraduate or graduate students with a cumulative GPA of 2.5 or better at the time of application and during the semester in which the award is received. Applicants must demonstrate significant leadership skills and abilities; hold a significant leadership position on campus. Applicants must have made significant contributions via volunteer involvement, either on or off campus. Applicants must be enrolled in a college or university within the former NACA Pacific Northwest Region. **Criteria:** Recipients are selected based on financial need and academic record.

Funds Avail.: No specific amount. **To Apply:** Applicants must complete the application form; at least two letters of recommendation; a resume; official verification of the applicant's current enrollment status and a copy of academic transcripts from the college or university. **Deadline:** June 30.

4683 ■ Ross-Fahey Scholarships *(Postgraduate/Scholarship)*

Purpose: To support undergraduate or graduate students and new professionals employed at colleges and universities in the former NACA New England Region. **Focus:** General studies. **Qualif.:** Applicants must be graduate students and new professionals in the former NACA New England Region. **Criteria:** Recipients are selected based on enrollment or employment at a member school; demonstrated significant leadership skills and abilities; and significant contributions thrugh volunteer involvement, either on or off campus.

Funds Avail.: No specific amount. **Number Awarded:** 2. **To Apply:** Applicants must submit a current resume and a letter of recommendation from the candidate's current supervisor. **Deadline:** October 1.

4684 ■ Wisconsin Region Student Leadership Scholarships *(Undergraduate/Scholarship)*

Purpose: To assist students pursuing graduate or undergraduate studies leading to a related student services field. **Focus:** General studies. **Qualif.:** Applicants must be undergraduate or graduate students in good standing and enrolled in the equivalent of at least six semesters at the time of the application and during the semester in which the award is received; be either currently enrolled in or have received a degree from a college or university within Wisconsin or Upper Peninsula of Michigan; have demonstrated leadership skills and significant service to his/her campus and/or the community. **Criteria:** Recipients are selected based on the record of academic achievement; involvement in and contribution to NACA Northern Plains by a student from Wisconsin or Upper Peninsula of Michigan; potential success in the field of campus activities.

Funds Avail.: No specific amount. **To Apply:** Applicants must complete the application form; obtain a 100-word biographical sketch; submit a resume or description of relevant educational experiences; and submit an official transcript of record and three letters of reference. **Deadline:** January 15.

4685 ■ Zagunis Student Leader Scholarships *(Undergraduate/Scholarship)*

Purpose: To provide financial assistance to undergraduate or graduate student leaders enrolled in the former NACA Great Lakes Region. **Focus:** General studies. **Qualif.:** Applicants must be undergraduate students with a minimum cumulative GPA of 3.0 or better at the time of the application. **Criteria:** Recipients are selected based on the demonstrated leadership skills and abilities and significant contributions to their campus communities.

Funds Avail.: No specific amount. **To Apply:** Applicants must submit a current resume and complete the application form. **Deadline:** November 1.

4686 ■ National Association of Chain Drug Stores Foundation

413 N Lee St.
Alexandria, VA 22314
Ph: (703)837-4276
Fax: (703)683-3587
E-mail: foundation@nacds.org
URL: http://www.nacdsfoundation.org

4687 ■ Pharmacy Student Scholarship Program *(Postdoctorate/Scholarship)*

Purpose: To support the development of future leaders in chain community pharmacy. **Focus:** Pharmacy. **Qualif.:** Applicants must be enrolled as full-time pharmacy students in accredited U.S. colleges or schools of pharmacy, studying to obtain a doctor of pharmacy degree. Applicants must have completed at least one professional year of pharmacy school to apply; must have experience in chain community pharmacy as well as the desire to pursue a career in chain community pharmacy; must have a minimum "C" GPA. **Criteria:** Recipients are selected based on the student's letter on career goals and interest in chain community pharmacy practice; recommendation from their chain pharmacy employer; student's credentials including leadership activities, professional, and community involvement and chain community pharmacy experience.

Funds Avail.: $2,000. **Number Awarded:** 45. **To Apply:** Applicants must submit a completed application form; a current resume or curriculum vitae; a cover letter explaining their interest and career goals in chain community pharmacy practice (not more than two pages,typewritten); and a letter of recommendation from the current or recent community pharmacy employer that explains why the applicant is deserving of the scholarship. **Deadline:** October 19.

4688 ■ National Association for Chicana and Chicano Studies
PO Box 720052
San Jose, CA 95172-0052
Ph: (408)924-5310
Fax: (408)924-5700
E-mail: naccs@naccs.org
URL: http://www.naccs.org

4689 ■ Leonor R. Guerrero Memorial Scholarships *(Undergraduate/Scholarship)*

Purpose: To support students in their educational journey. **Qualif.:** Applicants must be a Chicana/Latino Decent. A part-time or full-time student. **Criteria:** Priority is given to students with financial needs.

Funds Avail.: $1,000. **To Apply:** Applicants must send personal information. Applicants must also answer the 500 word essay questions online, and send to LRG Memorial Scholarship. **Deadline:** May 4. **Contact:** LRG Memorial Scholarship, attn: Lourdes R. Guerrero, MSW 10423 Montgomery Ave., Granada Hills, CA 91344

4690 ■ National Association of Collegiate Directors of Athletics
24651 Detroit Rd.
Westlake, OH 44145
Ph: (440)892-4000
Fax: (440)892-4007
URL: http://nacda.cstv.com

4691 ■ John McLendon Memorial Minority Postgraduate Scholarships *(Postdoctorate/Scholarship)*

Purpose: To support minority students pursuing graduate degrees in athletics administration. **Focus:** Sports studies. **Qualif.:** Applicant must be full-time senior or an undergraduate degree with two years work experience, preferably in athletics administration; have a minimum GPA of 3.0 (on a 4.0 scale); official classification as a minority as defined by federal guidelines; intention to attend graduate school to earn a degree in athletics administration; and involvement on the college/university or community level. **Criteria:** Nominations will be sent to a Review Committee of collegiate athletics administrators and top candidates will be sent to a Blue Ribbon Committee that will choose the final five winners.

Funds Avail.: $10,000. **Number Awarded:** 5. **To Apply:** A completed nomination form must be submitted in order to be considered. Forms must be signed and approved by the student's academic advisor. **Deadline:** June 16.

4692 ■ National Association of Conservation District Employees
1607 W Jackson St.
Macomb, IL 61455
Ph: (309)833-1711
Fax: (309)837-1512
E-mail: cindy.moon@il.nacdnet.net
URL: http://www.ncdea.org

4693 ■ National Association of Conservation District Employees Scholarships *(Undergraduate/Scholarship)*

Purpose: To provide financial support to a district employee or member of their immediate family who is participating in a resource conservation curriculum while enrolled in an accredited college or university. **Focus:** Agriculture. **Qualif.:** Applicant must be currently employed for a period of one year by a conservation district of the United States. Applicant must demonstrate integrity, ability, and competence in their work and possess skills gained through training or experience; or applicant must be an immediate family member of a conservation district employee. He/she must demonstrate an interest in soil and water conservation and have the intent to pursue a course in natural resource conservation. **Criteria:** Recipients are selected based on the academic record and performance of the applicant when it comes in soil and water conservation.

Funds Avail.: $1,000. **To Apply:** Applicant must fill out the application form and provide proof that he/she is currently enrolled. **Deadline:** May 1. **Contact:** Rich Duesterhaus at 509 Capitol Court, NE Washington, DC 20002; 202-547-6223.

4694 ■ National Association of Container Distributors
1601 Bond St., Ste. 101
Naperville, IL 60563
Ph: (630)544-5052
Fax: (630)544-5055
E-mail: info@nacd.net
URL: http://www.nacd.net

4695 ■ Henry Hoffman Memorial Scholarship Fund *(Undergraduate/Scholarship)*

Purpose: To provide assistance to students with financial need. **Focus:** General studies. **Qualif.:** Applicants must be students who have completed their junior year in high school and are children of employees of member companies of NACD. Students must have a 3.0 grade point average and maintain a 2.5 GPA in college. As a pre-requisite for eligibility, a NACD member company must employ one of the applicant's parents at the time the application is made. **Criteria:** Scholarship recipients will be selected based on past academic performance, performance on tests designated to measure ability and aptitude for higher education, and the applicant's rank in school. Recommendations by instructors or other persons unrelated to the candidate, extra-curricular activities and leadership contributions will also be considered.

Funds Avail.: No specific amount. **To Apply:** Applicants must submit a completed application form. **Deadline:** February 1.

4696 ■ National Association for County Community and Economic Development
2025 M St. NW, Ste. 800
Washington, DC 20036-3309
Ph: (202)367-1149
Fax: (202)367-2149
E-mail: snusser@smithbucklin.com
URL: http://www.nacced.org

4697 ■ NACCED Annual John C. Murphy Scholarships *(Graduate, Undergraduate/Scholarship)*

Purpose: To provide financial assistance to undergraduate and graduate students. **Focus:** Housing. **Qualif.:** Applicants must be currently attending an American college or

Awards are arranged alphabetically below their administering organizations

university with a chosen field of study including course work in the areas of affordable housing and/or community and economic development. Applicants must also exhibit financial need. **Criteria:** Recipients will be selected based on the quality of their personal statement, financial need, grade point average and content of the letter of recommendation.

Funds Avail.: $2,000. **Number Awarded:** 1. **To Apply:** All applicants must be nominated by a NACCED member in good standing. Candidates must submit a completed scholarship application; official school transcript with official grade point average; certification of financial need - with an attached Financial Aide Award letter from the university; collegiate letter of acceptance stating the date of enrollment; personal statement of approximately 500 words introducing the applicant; letter of recommendation from a teacher, faculty or civic leader; support letter from a NACCED member in good standing. **Deadline:** August 1.

4698 ■ National Association for Equal Opportunity in Higher Education

209 3rd St. SE
Washington, DC 20003
Ph: (202)552-3300
Fax: (202)552-3330
URL: http://www.nafeo.org

4699 ■ NAFEO Internship Program *(Undergraduate/Internship)*

Purpose: To provide financial assistance for students and give them opportunities to gain valuable work experience to supplement coursework. **Focus:** General studies. **Qualif.:** Applicants must be sophomore U.S. citizen students with a 3.0 cumulative grade point average; good credit rating; free of drug use, misdemeanors, or felonies in the last three years. **Criteria:** Applicants are evaluated based on academic achievements.

Funds Avail.: No specific amount. **To Apply:** Applicants must submit completed application and resume to the NAFEO Internship Office. They should have their institutions forward an official transcript of their academic work and two letters of recommendation or recommendation forms completed by faculty members. **Deadline:** March 1.

4700 ■ National Association of Farm Service Agency County Office Employees

3300 N "A" Bldg. 4, Ste. 220
Midland, TX 79705
Ph: (432)684-6781
E-mail: webmaster@nascoe.org
URL: http://www.nascoe.org

4701 ■ NASCOE Scholarships *(Other/Scholarship)*

Purpose: To provide financial assistance to members who wish to enroll in adult education courses aimed at enhancing their careers with FSA. **Focus:** Adult education. **Qualif.:** Applicants must members who are permanent County Office employees. **Criteria:** Candidates will be evaluated based on the score sheet as established by the NASCOE Scholarship Committee.

Funds Avail.: $200. **Number Awarded:** 1. **To Apply:** Applicants must submit applications in hard copies with appropriate signatures. **Deadline:** March 1.

4702 ■ National Association of Fellowships Advisors

University of Louisville
Louisville, KY 40292
E-mail: info@nafadvisors.org
URL: http://www.nafadvisors.org

4703 ■ Ford Foundation Predoctoral Fellowships for Minorities *(Doctorate/Fellowship)*

Purpose: To increase the presence of underrepresented minorities in the nation's college and university faculties; to enhance diversity on campuses; and to address the persisting effects of past discrimination. **Focus:** Teaching. **Qualif.:** Applicants must be members of at least one of the six minority groups whose underrepresentation in the professoriate has been severe and long-standing. **Criteria:** Fellowships will be given to those who meet the qualifications.

Funds Avail.: No specific amount. **To Apply:** Applicants must check the available website for the required materials. **Contact:** National Association of Fellowships Advisors at the above address (see entry 4702).

4704 ■ Gates Cambridge Scholarships *(Doctorate, Postgraduate/Scholarship)*

Purpose: To award scholarships on the basis of a person's intellectual ability, leadership capacity and desire to use their knowledge to contribute to society throughout the world by providing service to their communities and applying their talents and knowledge to improve the lives of others. **Focus:** General studies. **Qualif.:** Applicants must apply to pursue one of the following full-time residential courses of study: Research leading to the PhD degree; One-year post-graduate courses (e.g. MPhil, LLM, Diploma, MBA etc.); 2-year MSc degree; Second Bachelor degree as an Affiliated Student; MBBChir Clinical Studies; must be admitted to Cambridge through the University's normal academic procedures; must have a first class or high second class honors degree, or its equivalent, from a recognized university; must be well-prepared for the Cambridge course for which they are applying and must meet the academic criteria for admission specified by the university. **Criteria:** Awards will be given to those who meet the scholarship's criteria.

Funds Avail.: No specific amount. **To Apply:** Applicants must check the available website for the required materials. **Contact:** National Association of Fellowships Advisors at the above address (see entry 4702).

4705 ■ Hertz Foundation's Graduate Fellowships *(Doctorate/Fellowship)*

Purpose: To build America's capacity for innovation by nurturing remarkable applied scientists and engineers who show the most promise to change the world. **Focus:** Science; Engineering. **Qualif.:** Applicants must be admitted in a graduate school and demonstrate satisfactory progress toward receipt of the Ph.D degree. **Criteria:** Awards will be given to those who meet the criteria.

Funds Avail.: $31,000-$36,000 plus personal stipend. **To Apply:** Applicants must check the available website for the electronic application. **Contact:** National Association of Fellowships Advisors at the above address (see entry 4702).

4706 ■ Howard Hughes Medical Institute Predoctoral Fellowships *(Graduate/Fellowship)*

Purpose: To provide financial support for students who will pursue an MS, a Ph.D or an SC.D degree in the biological

Awards are arranged alphabetically below their administering organizations

sciences. **Focus:** Biological Sciences. **Qualif.:** Applicants must have completed less than one year of graduate study toward an M.S., a Ph.D., or an Sc.D. degree in the biological sciences. Students who hold or are pursuing medical or dental degrees (M.D., D.O., D.V.M., D.D.S.) may also be eligible to apply for fellowship support for study toward a Ph.D. or an Sc.D. **Criteria:** Awards will be given to those who meet the fellowship criteria.

Funds Avail.: No specific amount. **To Apply:** Applicants must check the available website for more information. **Contact:** National Association of Fellowships Advisors at the above address (see entry 4702).

4707 ■ Jacob K. Javits Fellowships *(Doctorate, Master's/Fellowship)*

Purpose: To provide financial assistance for students with superior ability as demonstrated by their achievements and exceptional promise. **Focus:** Arts; Humanities; Social Sciences. **Qualif.:** Applicants must demonstrate financial need. **Criteria:** Awards will be based on criteria.

Funds Avail.: No specific amount. **To Apply:** Applicants must demonstrate financial need by filing the Free Application for Federal Student Aid. **Contact:** National Association of Fellowships Advisors at the above address (see entry 4702).

4708 ■ George J. Mitchell Postgraduate Scholarships *(Postgraduate/Scholarship)*

Purpose: To introduce and connect generations of future American leaders to the island of Ireland while recognizing and fostering intellectual achievement, leadership, and a commitment to public service and community. **Focus:** General studies. **Qualif.:** Applicants must be between ages 18-30. **Criteria:** Selection of scholars will be determined by the Selection Committee.

Funds Avail.: No specific amount. **To Apply:** Applicants must check the available website for more information. **Contact:** Questions about the Mitchell Scholarships can be addressed to the Director, Mary Lou Hartman, at 703-841-5843 or by email at hartman@us-irelandalliance.org.

4709 ■ NAFA International Dissertation Research Fellowships *(Graduate/Fellowship)*

Purpose: To support distinguished graduate students in the humanities and social sciences conducting dissertation research outside the United States. **Focus:** Humanities; Social Sciences. **Qualif.:** Applicants must have completed all Ph.D. requirements except on-site dissertation research by the time the fellowship begins. **Criteria:** Awards will be given to those who meet the qualifications.

Funds Avail.: No specific amount. **To Apply:** Applicants must visit the IDRF website at www.ssrc.org/programs/idrf or contact program staff at idrf@ssrc.org. **Contact:** National Association of Fellowships Advisors at the above address (see entry 4702).

4710 ■ National Association of Fellowships Advisors Graduate Scholar Awards *(Postgraduate, Professional Development/Fellowship)*

Purpose: To provide financial support for students who are in need. **Focus:** General studies. **Qualif.:** Applicants must be planning to enroll in a post baccalaureate or professional study at accredited institutions of higher learning. **Criteria:** Awards will be given based on academic merit.

Funds Avail.: $10,000. **Number Awarded:** 12. **To Apply:** Applicants must check the available website for the required materials.

Remarks: Members can apply up to five years after graduation; Applicants may continue to re-apply as long as they are eligible. **Contact:** National Association of Fellowships Advisors at the above address (see entry 4702).

4711 ■ National Association of Financial Aid and Administrators

1101 Connecticut Ave. NW, Ste. 1100
Washington, DC 20036-4303
Ph: (202)785-0453
Fax: (202)785-1487
E-mail: web@nasfaa.org
URL: http://www.nasfaa.org

4712 ■ National Association of Financial Aid and Administrators Nursing Scholarships *(Undergraduate/Scholarship)*

Purpose: To provide certain costs of education in exchange for service at a health care facility with a critical shortage of nurses. **Focus:** Nursing. **Qualif.:** Applicants must be U.S. citizens or nationals. Applicants must be enrolled or accepted for enrollment as full- or part-time students in an accredited school of nursing in a professional registered nurse program. **Criteria:** Recipients are selected based on financial need.

Funds Avail.: $1,233. **To Apply:** Applicants must submit an application form; a verification of acceptance; an authorization to release information; a student aid report. **Deadline:** June 6.

4713 ■ National Association of Financial Aid and Administrators Scholarships for Disadvantaged Students *(Undergraduate/Scholarship)*

Purpose: To provide financial aid to disadvantaged students. **Focus:** Nursing. **Qualif.:** Applicants must be full-time students from disadvantaged backgrounds, enrolled in health professions and nursing programs. Applicants must be citizens or permanent residents of the United States. **Criteria:** Recipients are selected based on financial need, and participation in school activities.

Funds Avail.: No specific amount. **To Apply:** Applicants must complete the application form.

4714 ■ National Association of Health Services Executives

1140 Connecticut Ave., NW
Suite 505
Washington, DC 20036
Ph: (202)429-6060
Fax: (202)429-6767
E-mail: nahsehq@nahse.org
URL: http://www.nahse.org

4715 ■ Ellis J. Bonner Scholarships *(Doctorate, Graduate, Undergraduate/Scholarship)*

Purpose: To financially assist minority students in health care management or related field. **Focus:** Health care services; Health services administration. **Qualif.:** Applicant must be a NAHSE member; enrolled in college/university in Bachelor of Science, Master of Science or Doctorate

Degree major in health care administration or related field; have minimum of 2.5 GPA for undergraduates and 3.0 for graduates; must have demonstrated financial need. **Criteria:** Awards are given based on academic merit and financial need.

Funds Avail.: No specific amount. **Number Awarded:** 1. **To Apply:** Applicant must submit a scholarship application; resume; transcripts (if applicable); three letters of reference; composition; tax returns; two pictures 3x5; membership application and dues. **Deadline:** July 1.

4716 ■ Florence S. Gaynor Scholarships

(Doctorate, Graduate, Undergraduate/Scholarship)

Purpose: To financially assist minority students in health care management or related field. **Focus:** Health care services; Health services administration. **Qualif.:** Applicant must be a NAHSE member; enrolled in college/university in Bachelor of Science, Master of Science or Doctorate Degree major in health care administration or related field; have minimum of 2.5 GPA for undergraduates and 3.0 for graduates; must have demonstrated financial need. **Criteria:** Awards are given based on academic merit and financial need.

Funds Avail.: No specific amount. **Number Awarded:** 1. **To Apply:** Applicant must submit a scholarship application; resume; transcripts (if applicable); three letters of reference; composition; tax returns; two pictures 3x5; membership application and dues. **Deadline:** July 1.

Remarks: The scholarship is established in memory of Mrs. Florence Small Gaynor.

4717 ■ Haynes Rice Scholarships *(Doctorate, Graduate, Undergraduate/Scholarship)*

Purpose: To financially assist minority students in health care management or related field. **Focus:** Health care services; Health services administration. **Qualif.:** Applicant must be a NAHSE member; enrolled in college/university in a Bachelor of Science, Master of Science or Doctorate Degree major in health care administration or related field; have minimum of 2.5 GPA for undergraduates and 3.0 for graduates; must have demonstrated financial need. **Criteria:** Awards are given based on academic merit and financial need.

Funds Avail.: No specific amount. **Number Awarded:** 1. **To Apply:** Applicant must submit a scholarship application; resume; transcripts (if applicable); three letters of reference; composition; tax returns; two pictures 3x5; membership application and dues. **Deadline:** July 1.

Remarks: The scholarship is established in memory of Mr. Haynes Rice.

4718 ■ National Association of Heating Service Managers

PO Box 67
East Petersburg, PA 17520-0067
Fax: (717)625-3077
Free: 888-552-0900
E-mail: info@naohsm.org
URL: http://www.naohsm.org

4719 ■ Dave Nelsen Scholarships

(Undergraduate/Scholarship)

Purpose: To educate and advance oil heat service professionals. **Focus:** Heating, air conditioning, and refrigeration. **Qualif.:** Applicants must be currently attending or planning to attend a technical college or trade school and must be involved in the Oil Heating industry. **Criteria:** Recipients are selected based on the submitted application form.

Funds Avail.: $2,000. **Number Awarded:** 9. **To Apply:** Applicants must submit completed application form and a 500-word essay stating their goals towards the heating industry. **Deadline:** May 20.

4720 ■ National Association of Negro Business and Professional Women's Clubs

1806 New Hampshire Ave. NW
Washington, DC 20009
Ph: (202)483-4206
E-mail: info@nanbpwc.org
URL: http://www.nanbpwc.org

4721 ■ Dorothy G. Allsop Scholarships

(Undergraduate/Scholarship)

Purpose: To provide financial assistance for African-American students pursuing their college education. **Focus:** General studies. **Qualif.:** Applicants must be graduating African-American high school seniors residing in Connecticut who have a cumulative grade point average of 2.5 or above on a 4.0 scale. **Criteria:** Applicants are evaluated based on academic achievement and financial need.

Funds Avail.: No specific amount. **To Apply:** Applicants must complete the scholarship application form online and must submit a typed essay of no less than 250 words on the topic "Why Cosmetology/Beauty Culture is important to me" **Deadline:** March 1.

4722 ■ Dr. Julianne Malveaux Scholarships

(Undergraduate/Scholarship)

Purpose: To provide financial assistance for African-American students pursuing their college education. **Focus:** General studies. **Qualif.:** Applicants must be United States citizens; must be African-American females; must be enrolled as college sophomores or juniors in an accredited college or university; must be majoring in journalism, economics or related field (public policy, creative writing, etc.); and must have a cumulative grade point average (GPA) of 3.0 or above on a 4.0 scale. **Criteria:** Applicants are evaluated based on academic achievement and financial need.

Funds Avail.: No specific amount. **To Apply:** Applicants must complete the scholarship application online and submit a 1000-word essay on their career plans and their relevance to the Dr. Julianne Malveaux Program Theme: "Black Women's Hands Can Rock the World." **Deadline:** March 1.

4723 ■ NANBPWC National Scholarships

(Undergraduate/Scholarship)

Purpose: To provide financial assistance for African-American students pursuing their college education. **Focus:** General studies. **Qualif.:** Applicants must be graduating African-American high school seniors who have a cumulative grade point average of 3.0 or above on a 4.0 scale by February 1st in the year of graduation. **Criteria:** Applicants are evaluated based on financial need.

Funds Avail.: No specific amount. **To Apply:** Applicants must complete the scholarship application form online and must submit a typed essay of no less than 300 words on the topic: "Why Education is Important to Me" **Deadline:** March 1.

4724 ■ NANBPWC Woman of Substance Scholarships *(Undergraduate/Scholarship)*

Purpose: To provide financial assistance for African American students pursuing their college education. **Focus:** General studies. **Qualif.:** Applicants must be African American females who are residents of Michigan; must be undergraduate students enrolled in an accredited college or university; and must have a cumulative grade point average (GPA) 3.0 or above on a 4.0 scale. **Criteria:** Applicants are evaluated based on academic achievement and financial need.

Funds Avail.: No specific amount. **To Apply:** Applicants must complete the scholarship application online and submit a 500-word essay on the topic: "Challenges to the Mature Student and How They'd Overcome Them." **Deadline:** March 1.

4725 ■ National Association of Pastoral Musicians

962 Wayne Ave., Ste. 210
Silver Spring, MD 20910-4461
Ph: (240)247-3000
Fax: (240)247-3001
URL: http://www.npm.org

4726 ■ National Association of Pastoral Musicians Academic Scholarships *(Graduate, Undergraduate/Scholarship)*

Purpose: To assist with the cost of education formation for pastoral musicians. **Focus:** Music. **Qualif.:** Applicants must be NPM members; part-time or full-time in an undergraduate or graduate degree program of studies related to the field of pastoral music during the 2008-2009 school year; and must intend to work at least two years in the field of pastoral music following graduation/program completion. **Criteria:** Candidates must demonstrate financial need.

Funds Avail.: $34,000. **To Apply:** Applicants must submit letter or short essay containing the following information: name and contact information including address, home and work phone, and email; definition of the term "pastoral musician"; description of talents; previous experience as pastoral musician; educational background, educational program enrolled; recording (cassette or CD format) demonstrating solo performance skills or those of an ensemble under applicants' direction; two letters of recommendation, including one written by pastor; and completed financial need statement. **Deadline:** March 7.

4727 ■ NPM Program Scholarships *(Undergraduate/Scholarship)*

Purpose: To assist pastoral musicians with limited financial resources in taking advantage of opportunities for continuing formation at NPM conventions and institutes. **Focus:** Music. **Qualif.:** Applicants must be NPM members and should be from economically disadvantaged parishes. **Criteria:** Recipient will be selected based on financial need.

Funds Avail.: No amount mentioned. **To Apply:** Applicants must submit completed NPM Program Scholarship Application and the NPM Program Scholarship Applicant's letter; and parish recommendation completed by your pastor or pastoral administrator.

4728 ■ National Association of Pediatric Nurse Practitioners

20 Brace Rd., Ste. 200
Cherry Hill, NJ 08034-2634
Ph: (856)857-9700
Fax: (856)857-1600
E-mail: info@napnap.org
URL: http://www.napnap.org

4729 ■ Reckitt Benckiser Student Scholarships *(Graduate/Scholarship)*

Purpose: To provide financial assistance to Pediatric Nurse Practitioner Student to allow for attendance at the NAPNAP Annual Meeting. **Focus:** Nursing. **Qualif.:** Applicant must be NAPNAP member, registered nurse and a graduate student who has completed at least 1 semester of graduate studies in a Pediatric Nurse Practitioner Program; enrolled in a recognized program of study (associated with an academic institution authorized to award a master's degree or DNP in nursing), leading to completion of qualifications for education and practice as a PNP (a program defined as one which primarily prepares an individual to deliver child health care services, either in primary care, specialty care or acute care settings). **Criteria:** Recipient will be selected by the NAPNAP Foundation Scholarship Committee.

Funds Avail.: $1,500. **To Apply:** Applicants must submit original plus four copies (total 5) of the completed application with all the support documents. **Deadline:** March 15.

4730 ■ Elaine Gelman Scholarship Award *(Undergraduate/Scholarship)*

Purpose: To support the education of a nurse practitioner student who demonstrating the ability to articulate and follow through an innovative solution through clinical competence, academic achievement and involvement in political activism relating to a pediatric health care issue. **Focus:** Nursing. **Qualif.:** Applicant must be a full or part time NP student enrolled in an accredited NP program with an expected graduation date of two years or less. **Criteria:** Applicants will be judged based on clinical competence, academic achievement and involvement in political activism relating to health care issues.

Funds Avail.: $1,000. **To Apply:** Applicants must submit completed Elaine Gelman Scholaship Award Application Form; personal statement (200 words or less) describing why the individual is competing for this award and specifically what goals would be accomplished if he/she receives the award; two letters of reference from a faculty member and professional colleague. **Deadline:** June 30.

4731 ■ NAPNAP McNeil Annual Scholarships *(Undergraduate/Scholarship)*

Purpose: To provide financial assistance to students enrolled in pediatric nurse practitioner programs. **Focus:** Nursing. **Qualif.:** Applicant must be a registered nursing student who has completed at least 2 semesters or quarters as defined by the university; enrolled at a recognized PNP program; and have no previous formal pediatric nurse practitioner education. **Criteria:** Applicants will be judged based on academic performance and financial need status.

Funds Avail.: $2,000. **To Apply:** Applicants must submit five copies of the application and accompanying needed materials to the NAPNAP Foundation. **Deadline:** April 30.

4732 ■ NAPNAP McNeil Rural and Underserved Scholarships *(Undergraduate/Scholarship)*

Purpose: To provide financial support to PNP students who plan on practicing in a rural or underserved geographi-

Awards are arranged alphabetically below their administering organizations

cal region for the first two years after he/she completes their PNP education. **Focus:** General studies. **Qualif.:** Applicants must be planning on practicing in a rural or undeserved geographical region for the first two years after PNP education completed; registered nurse who has completed at least 2 semesters or quarters as defined by the university; enrolled at recognized Master's degree program; has no previous formal pediatric nurse practitioner education; and demonstrated financial need. **Criteria:** Recipient will be selected based on academic performance and financial status.

Funds Avail.: $37,000. **To Apply:** Applicants must submit five copies of the application and needed materials to NAP-NAP Foundation. **Deadline:** June 15.

4733 ■ National Association for Pupil Transportation

1840 Western Ave.
Albany, NY 12203
Ph: (518)452-3611
Fax: (518)218-0867
Free: 800-989-NAPT
E-mail: info@napt.org
URL: http://www.napt.org

4734 ■ Continuing Education Awards *(All/Scholarship)*

Purpose: To provide financial support to NAPT members enrolling for further education in public transportation. **Focus:** Transportation. **Qualif.:** Applicant must be a NAPT member for 3 or more consecutive years; and who has not become a recipient of the award for the 4 preceding years. **Criteria:** Recipients are selected based on merit.

Funds Avail.: $1,000 for pre-approved tuition, travel, lodging, and meal expenses. **Number Awarded:** 2. **To Apply:** Applicant must mail completed application form (available at the NAPT website) to: NAPT Headquarters, 1840 Western Ave. Albany, NY 12203. **Deadline:** July 1.

4735 ■ National Association of Recreation Resource Planners

PO Box 221
Marienville, PA 16239
Ph: (814)927-8212
Fax: (814)927-6659
E-mail: info@narrp.org
URL: http://www.narrp.org

4736 ■ NARRP Student Conference Scholarships *(Graduate, Undergraduate/Scholarship)*

Purpose: To provide financial support for the advancement of recreation planning knowledge, skills and professional leadership of students in higher education. **Focus:** General studies. **Qualif.:** Applicants must be undergraduate or graduate students enrolled full-time in an NRPA accredited recreation management, planning or closely related degree program. **Criteria:** Applicant will be evaluated based on his or her clear and compelling statement of career goals related to the recreation planning profession; degree that the scholarship will help the person achieve their career goals; quality of past work performance and future potential as judged by university advisor; extent of other contributing financial support or in-kind contributions from other sources (e.g., university, personal, third party organizations); degree that the requested financial support is appropriate and reasonable.

Funds Avail.: $500. **To Apply:** Applicant must complete the application form along with the current resume and transcript; 500-word narrative statement of academic and career goals, and how attending the NARRP Conference will be helpful towards achieving these goals; and letter of recommendation from Major Professor/Academic Advisor. **Deadline:** March 14.

4737 ■ National Association of School Safety and Law Enforcement Officers

PO Box 210079
Milwaukee, WI 53221
Ph: (315)529-4858
Fax: 877-282-4860
E-mail: nassleo@nassleo.org
URL: http://www.nassleo.org

4738 ■ NASSLEO Scholarships *(Undergraduate/Scholarship)*

Purpose: To provide financial assistance to students who have chosen to further their education and are considering a career in school security and/or law enforcement. **Focus:** Law Enforcement. **Qualif.:** Applicant must be a senior graduating student from a public high school; will be attending an accredited college or university; has not received a full scholarship; has been outstanding in the area of citizenship and community service. **Criteria:** The committee will select one individual student from each region for the award.

Funds Avail.: $500. **To Apply:** The faculty member must submit the complete nomination form, which can be downloaded at the NASSLEO website. Faculty member must list the individual's accomplishments in the area of citizenship and community service, what he/she has done to improve safety in the school, the contributions the student has made to his/her school, and any recognition received from his/her peers and/or faculty of the school for personal or academic achievement during this past school year. The narrative report must be limited to a single page. **Deadline:** April 1. **Contact:** Peter Pochowski, Executive Director at the above address (see entry 4737).

4739 ■ National Association for the Self-Employed

PO Box 612067
DFW Airport, TX 75261-2067
Fax: 800-551-4446
Free: 800-232-6273
E-mail: koberlander@nase.org
URL: http://www.nase.org

4740 ■ NASE Future Entrepreneur Scholarships *(Undergraduate/Scholarship)*

Purpose: To promote entrepreneurial philosophy. **Focus:** Business. **Qualif.:** Applicants must be dependents of NASE members. **Criteria:** Applicants who demonstrate the characteristics of a future micro-business owner will be given preference.

Funds Avail.: $12,000 scholarship for the first year and $4,000 for the next three years. **Number Awarded:** 1. **To Apply:** Applicants must submit a completed application form and original copies of transcripts and test scores. **Deadline:** April 25.

4741 ■ National Association for the Self-Employed Scholarships *(Undergraduate/Scholarship)*

Purpose: To assist members in sending their children to college. **Focus:** General studies. **Qualif.:** Applicant must be a legal dependent of a NASE member, aged 16-24; must be a high school student or college undergraduate. **Criteria:** Applicants will be selected based on leadership ability, academic performance, teacher recommendations, career and educational background, and school and community participation.

Funds Avail.: $4,000. **Number Awarded:** 20. **To Apply:** Applicants must submit a completed application form and original copies of transcripts and test scores. **Deadline:** May 15.

4742 ■ National Association of Sewer Service Companies

11521 Cronridge Dr., Ste. J
Owings Mills, MD 21117
Ph: (410)486-3500
Fax: (410)486-6838
E-mail: marc@logiball.com
URL: http://www.nassco.org

4743 ■ The NASSCO Jeffrey D. Ralston Memorial Scholarships *(Undergraduate/Scholarship)*

Purpose: To improve the success rate of everyone involved in the pipeline rehabilitation industry through education, technical resources, and industry advocacy. **Focus:** General studies. **Qualif.:** Applicants must be a dependent of an active NASSCO member or an active participant in the sewer service industry. Applicants must have at least a 3.0 GPA. **Criteria:** Recipients are selected based on ethics, high integrity, work experience, community service, and leadership.

Funds Avail.: $2,000. **Number Awarded:** 1. **To Apply:** Applicants must submit a completed application form. **Deadline:** January 21. **Contact:** www.nassco.org

4744 ■ National Association of State Land Reclamationists

Coal Research Center
Southern Illinois University
Carbondale, IL 62901-4623
Ph: (618)536-5521
Fax: (618)453-7346
E-mail: aharrington@crc.siu.edu
URL: http://www.crc.siu.edu/naslr/home.htm

4745 ■ Mined Land Reclamation Educational Grant Program *(Undergraduate/Grant)*

Purpose: To provide deserving individuals with a financial grant that will cover costs associated with education and research regarding mined land reclamation. **Focus:** Land management. **Qualif.:** Applicants must be enrolled as full-time juniors, seniors or graduate students in an accredited college or university in the United States with course works like special studies, and/or research in the area of mined land reclamation or closely related fields. **Criteria:** Candidates will be evaluated based on college grades, quality and relevance of course work or research, proposed special project or research budget, information obtained from references and other related considerations.

Funds Avail.: $1,000. **To Apply:** Applicants must submit completed application form and all required materials. **Deadline:** August 15.

4746 ■ National Association of Teacher Educators for Family and Consumer Sciences

Department of Child and Development Family Relations
College of Human Ecology
East Carolina University
Greenville, NC 27835-4353
Ph: (252)328-5714
E-mail: pickardm@ecu.edu
URL: http://www.natefacs.org

4747 ■ FACS Graduate Fellowships *(Graduate/Fellowship)*

Purpose: To promote further education and professional development within family and consumer sciences education. **Focus:** Home Economics. **Qualif.:** Applicant must be a U.S. citizen; and a family and consumer sciences education graduate student. **Criteria:** Applications will be rated in consideration of the likelihood of completing the degree and the contribution to family and consumer science education; academic work; professional association involvement; professional experience and scholarly work; and references.

Funds Avail.: $2000 - $4000. **To Apply:** Applicants must submit a completed application form together with all required attachments. Send to Dr. Lela G. Goar, 225 CR 207A Burnet, TX 78611, lkgoar@earthlink.net, 512715-8249. **Deadline:** November 8.

4748 ■ National Association of Women in Construction

327 S Adams St.
Fort Worth, TX 76104
Ph: (817)877-5551
Fax: (817)877-0324
Free: 800-552-3506
E-mail: nawic@nawic.org
URL: http://www.nawic.org

4749 ■ Construction Trades Scholarships *(Undergraduate/Scholarship)*

Purpose: To promote education and contribute to the betterment of the construction industry. **Focus:** Construction. **Qualif.:** Applicant must be currently enrolled in a construction related degree program at a school in the United States or Canada. **Criteria:** Application will be reviewed and selected by the NAWIC Founders' Scholarship Foundation Awards Committee.

Funds Avail.: $1,000-$2,000. **To Apply:** Applicants must have the following: Complete and signed application form; must have the transcript of grades for three most recent semester; must have extracurricular activities and Employment history. Application and other supporting materials must be sent to: NAWIC Founders' Scholarship Foundation, 10130 Vivera Dr., La Mesa, CA 91941. **Deadline:** March 15. **Contact:** Linda Young at the above address (see entry 4748).

Awards are arranged alphabetically below their administering organizations

4750 ■ NAWIC Founders Undergraduate Scholarships *(Undergraduate/Scholarship)*

Purpose: To promote education and contribute to the betterment of the construction industry. To encourage women to pursue and establish careers in the construction industry. **Focus:** Construction. **Qualif.:** Applicant must be currently enrolled in a construction-related degree program at a school in the United States or Canada, and must have at least one term remaining in an course of study leading to a degree or an associate degree in a construction-related field. Applicant must desire a career in a construction related field; must be enrolled full-time; must have a current cumulative GPA of 3.0 or higher to be considered for awards. **Criteria:** Application will be reviewed and selected by the NAWIC Founders' Scholarship Foundation Awards Committee. Preference will be given to the applicant's interest in construction, grades, extracurricular activities, employment experience, and financial need.

Funds Avail.: $1,000-$2,000. **To Apply:** Applicants must have the following: Complete the signed application form; must have the transcript of grades for three most recent semester; must have extracurricular activities and employment history. Application and other supporting materials must be sent to: NAWIC Founders' Scholarship Foundation, 327 S Adams, Forth Worth, TX 76104. **Deadline:** March 15.

4751 ■ National Association of Women Judges

1341 Connecticut Ave. NW, Ste. 42
Washington, DC 20036-1834
Ph: (202)393-0222
Fax: (202)393-0125
E-mail: nawj@nawj.org
URL: http://www.nawj.org

4752 ■ Equal Access to Justice Scholarships *(Undergraduate/Scholarship)*

Purpose: To provide financial assistance for law students who have demonstrated a sustained commitment to diversity and equality in the system of justice. **Focus:** Law. **Qualif.:** Applicants must be enrolled second- or third-year law student in good academic standing who demonstrate a sustained and passionate commitment to the achievement of equality of opportunity and access in the system of justice. **Criteria:** Recipient is selected by the Scholarship Selection Committee.

Funds Avail.: No amount mentioned. **To Apply:** Applicant must submit the completed application form and a 500-word personal statement and a resume.

4753 ■ National Ataxia Foundation

2600 Fernbrook Ln., Ste. 119
Minneapolis, MN 55447-4752
Ph: (763)553-0020
Fax: (763)553-0167
E-mail: naf@ataxia.org
URL: http://www.ataxia.org

4754 ■ National Ataxia Foundation Research Fellowships *(Postdoctorate/Fellowship)*

Purpose: To support a research on hereditary ataxia. **Focus:** Medicine. **Qualif.:** Applicants must have at least completed one year of post-doctoral training but not more than two at the time of application. **Criteria:** Awards are given to studies that demonstrate better understanding of the ataxia process.

Funds Avail.: $35,000-$45,000. **To Apply:** Applicants must send pre-submission applications to naf@ataxia.com. Submit the original and four copies of the pre-submission application together with the completed application form to the Foundation's Office. Applicants must also send the application form in Application deadline: September 15.

4755 ■ National Ataxia Foundation Research Grants *(Postdoctorate/Fellowship)*

Purpose: To support a research on the hereditary and sporadic ataxia. **Focus:** Medicine. **Qualif.:** Applicants must have at least completed one year of post-doctoral training but not more than two at the time of application. **Criteria:** Awards are given to studies that demonstrate better understanding of the ataxia process.

Funds Avail.: $125,000. **To Apply:** Applicants must send pre-submission applications to naf@ataxia.com. Submit the original and four copies of the pre-submission application together with the completed application form to the Foundation's Office. Applicants must also send the application form in .pdf via email. **Deadline:** Pre-submission application deadline: July 15. Application, August.

4756 ■ National Beta Club

151 Beta Club Way
Spartanburg, SC 29306-3012
Fax: (864)542-9300
Free: 800-845-8281
URL: http://www.betaclub.org

4757 ■ National Beta Club Scholarships *(Undergraduate/Scholarship)*

Purpose: To provide financial assistance to Beta Club members in their senior year. **Focus:** General studies. **Qualif.:** Applicants must be senior high school students who are active National Beta Club members and are registered with the national headquarters as of June 3; must be nominated by their Beta Club chapters to participate. **Criteria:** Applicants are evaluated based on a number of factors with special emphasis placed upon academic excellence, demonstrated leadership, character and school/community service.

Funds Avail.: $1,000-$15,000. **Number Awarded:** 210. **To Apply:** Applicants must submit all the required application information. **Deadline:** December 10.

4758 ■ National Black Coalition of Federal Aviation Employees

77 Southgate Rd.
Valley Stream, NY 11581
URL: http://www.nbcfae.org

4759 ■ National Black Coalition of Federal Aviation Employees Scholarship *(Other/Scholarship)*

Purpose: To financially support students who want to pursue higher education for prospective college, university, vocational or technical school. **Focus:** Aviation. **Qualif.:** Applicants must be dependents of NBCFAE members; must be high school or returning to college students. **Criteria:** Recipients will be selected based on academic merits.

Funds Avail.: No amount mentioned. **To Apply:** Applicants

Awards are arranged alphabetically below their administering organizations

must submit completed application with signature, transcript, letter of recommendation, and college acceptance letter (if high school student). **Deadline:** June 13. **Contact:** NBCFAE Scholarship Committee, National Education, Recruitment, and Training Chairperson, 432 Delafield Pl. NW, Washington DC 20011.

4760 ■ National Black MBA Association

180 N Michigan Ave., Ste. 1400
Chicago, IL 60601
Ph: (312)236-2622
Fax: (312)236-0390
E-mail: mail@nbmbaa.org
URL: http://www.nbmbaa.org

4761 ■ NBMBAA Graduate Scholarship Programs *(Graduate/Scholarship)*

Purpose: To financially assist qualified business students who has the potential to make great contributions in the field of business. **Focus:** Business. **Qualif.:** Applicants must demonstrate academic excellence, exceptional leadership potential and be actively involved in their local communities through service to others; be enrolled in a full-time graduate business program in a college or university in the United States accredited by the AACSB (AACSB International); agree to become an active member of NBMBAA. **Criteria:** Scholarship recipients will be selected based on the Selection Committee's review of the application materials.

Funds Avail.: $15,000. **Number Awarded:** 25. **To Apply:** Applicants must submit a two-page, typed essay (double spaced, 12-point font), resume and official transcripts (must be stamped and sealed). **Deadline:** April 21.

Remarks: Essay and resume must be submitted through online process only (please visit the website). **Contact:** Lori Johnson.

4762 ■ NBMBAA PhD Fellowship Programs *(Doctorate/Fellowship)*

Purpose: To financially assist minority students enrolled in a full-time business, management, or related discipline doctoral program. **Focus:** Business; Management. **Qualif.:** Applicants must be minority students enrolled in a full-time doctoral business or management program or related discipline in the U.S. **Criteria:** Fellowship recipients will be selected based on the Selection Committee's review of the application materials.

Funds Avail.: Fellowship amount not specified. **Number Awarded:** 2. **To Apply:** Applicants must submit an original research paper (maximum of five pages excluding title pages, abstract, exhibits and reference list). Papers should be typed in 12-point font and double-spaced throughout, with a 1-inch margin on all sides. The abstract must not exceed for more than 50 words, and pages should be numbered. Applicants must also submit an official transcript. **Contact:** Lori Johnson.

4763 ■ National Black Nurses Association

8630 Fenton St., Ste. 330
Silver Spring, MD 20910-3803
Ph: (301)589-3200
Fax: (301)589-3223
Free: 800-575-6298
E-mail: NBNA@erols.com
URL: http://www.nbna.org

4764 ■ National Black Nurses Association Scholarships *(Undergraduate/Scholarship)*

Purpose: To provide funding for continuing education. **Focus:** Nursing. **Qualif.:** Applicants must be member of NBNA and a local chapter currently enrolled in a nursing program (B.S.N., A.D., Diploma or L.P.N./L.V.N.) and in good scholastic standing at the time of application and must have at least one full year of school remaining. **Criteria:** Applicants will be evaluated by the NBNA Scholarship Committee.

Funds Avail.: $500 to $2,000. **To Apply:** Applicants must submit official transcript from an accredited school of nursing; two (2) page written essay; two letters of recommendation (one from applicant's school of nursing and one from the local chapter, or a nurse in the area if a local chapter does not exist); letters of recommendation and essay must be attached to the application; additional items to accompany the application in support of the candidates eligibility and desirability may include documented evidence of: a. participation in student nurse activities and b. involvement in the African American Community, i.e., letters, news clippings, awards, certificates, etc.

4765 ■ National Black Police Association

30 Kennedy St. NW, Ste. 101
Washington, DC 20011
Ph: (202)986-2070
Fax: (202)986-0410
E-mail: nbpanatofc@worldnet.att.net
URL: http://www.blackpolice.org

4766 ■ Alphonso Deal Scholarship Awards *(Undergraduate/Scholarship)*

Purpose: To support students pursuing education in law enforcement, or other related field. **Focus:** Law enforcement. **Qualif.:** Applicant must be a high school senior and a U.S. citizen with good character. **Criteria:** Recipients will be selected based on adherence to contest/application rules.

Funds Avail.: Amount not specified. **To Apply:** Applicants must fill up the application form available at the website. Applicant must prepare a recommendation letter (from principal, counselor or teacher); a current high school transcript with picture; and an acceptance letter from a college/university. **Deadline:** June 1.

4767 ■ National Board of Boiler and Pressure Vessel Inspectors

7437 Pingue Dr.
Worthington, OH 43085
Ph: (614)888-8320
Fax: (614)848-3474
E-mail: getinfo@nationalboard.org
URL: http://www.nationalboard.org

4768 ■ The National Board Technical Scholarships *(Other/Scholarship)*

Purpose: To provide financial assistance to children, stepchildren, grandchildren, or great-grandchildren of past and present staff and members of the National Board and the past or present Commissioned Inspectors employed by a

Awards are arranged alphabetically below their administering organizations

member jurisdiction. **Focus:** Engineering. **Qualif.:** Applicant must be currently enrolled full-time in an accredited four-year college or university in the United States or Canada; or be enrolled as a full-time student for the 2008-2009 academic year with sufficient college credits to be classified as a sophomore, junior, or senior; major in mechanical, manufacturing, electrical, industrial, welding, or chemical engineering, or other closely related engineering major; possess a cumulative college GPA of 3.0 or higher on a 4.0 scale; a citizen of the United States or Canada; a child, step-child, grandchild, or great-grandchild of a past or present National Board member (living or deceased), of a past or present Commissioned Inspector (living or deceased), employed by a member jurisdiction, or of a past or present National Board employee (living or deceased). In order for the child, step-child, grandchild, or great-grandchild to be eligible, the National Board member must have been a member for at least one year, the Commissioned Inspector must have been employed by the member jurisdiction for at least one year, or the National Board employee must have been a full-time employee for at least one year. **Criteria:** Applicants will be evaluated on the strength of their academic performance, proficiencies and demonstrated skills in the areas of interest to the National Board and its members.

Funds Avail.: $6,000. **To Apply:** Applicant must read the application carefully and complete all sections; include a personal statement of 500-750 words expressing: a) how college experiences-academics, extracurricular activities, outside activities, and work/internship experiences-are shaping his/her educational and career goals; b) why he/she should be considered for this scholarship award; and c) other information that may be of importance to the selection committee in its review of the application; include, or request to have sent, two letters of recommendation from appropriate college instructors or other college representatives on official school letterhead; include, or request to have sent, a letter of recommendation from a current National Board member, that is the Chief Boiler inspector in a jurisdiction; a listing of current National Board members, including contact information, is shown on National Board's website: www.nationalboard.org (Members Listing); include-or request to have sent-an official transcript from your college; include the names and contact information for two persons (not family members) you have known for at least one year, to be used as personal references; sign the last page of the application; mail the completed application to the National Board at the address on the application form. **Deadline:** February 29.

4769 ■ National Business Aviation Association

1200 18th St. NW, Ste. 400
Washington, DC 20036-9000
Ph: (202)783-9000
Fax: (202)331-8364
E-mail: info@nbaa.org
URL: http://www.nbaa.org

4770 ■ Donald A. Baldwin Sr. Business Aviation Management Scholarships *(Undergraduate/Scholarship)*

Purpose: To promote professional development and business aviation careers and to benefit individuals seeking to become NBAA Certified Aviation Managers(CAMs). **Focus:** Aviation. **Qualif.:** Applicants must be eligible to take the CAM Exam within two years of the date of the scholarship award; must meet the minimum qualifications to take the CAM Exam; must be U.S. citizens; and must have a grade point average of 3.0 or above on a 4.0 scale. **Criteria:** Recipients are selected based on academic performance and financial need.

Funds Avail.: No specific amount. **To Apply:** Applicants must submit a completed application form; an official transcript of record; a 250-word, typed, double-spaced essay describing the applicant's interest in and goals for a career in the business aviation industry; two letters of recommendation from those who can comment on the career aspirations and qualifications of the applicant; and current resume. **Deadline:** November 1. **Contact:** Jay Evans at the above address (see entry 4769).

4771 ■ Janice K. Barden Aviation Scholarships *(Undergraduate/Scholarship)*

Purpose: To promote professional development and business aviation careers. **Focus:** Aviation. **Qualif.:** Applicants must be undergraduate sophomores, juniors, or seniors enrolled in an aviation-related two-year, four-year, or postgraduate degree program; must have a GPA of at least 3.0 on a 4.0 scale; and must be U.S. citizens. **Criteria:** Recipients are selected based on academic performance and financial need.

Funds Avail.: $5,000. **Number Awarded:** 5. **To Apply:** Applicants must submit completed application form; a typed, double-spaced essay of 250 words, describing the applicant's interest in and goals for a career in the business aviation industry; a letter of recommendation from a member of the aviation department faculty at the institution in which the applicant is currently enrolled; two professional letters of recommendation; and a current resume. **Deadline:** November 1. **Contact:** Jay Evans at the above address (see entry 4769).

4772 ■ Alan H. Conklin Business Aviation Management Scholarships *(Undergraduate/Scholarship)*

Purpose: To promote professional development and business aviation careers. **Focus:** Aviation. **Qualif.:** Applicants must be full-time undergraduate sophomore, junior, or senior students; officially enrolled or accepted for enrollment in an aviation management program; U.S. citizens; and must have a grade point average of 3.0 or above on a 4.0 scale. **Criteria:** Recipients are selected based on academic performance and financial need.

Funds Avail.: No specific amount. **To Apply:** Applicants must submit completed application form; an official transcript of record; a 500-word, typed, double-spaced essay describing the applicant's interest in and goals for a career in business aviation; two letters of recommendation from those qualified to comment on the career aspirations and qualifications of the applicant especially as they relate to business aviation; and current resume. **Deadline:** August 1. **Contact:** Jay Evans at the above address (see entry 4769).

4773 ■ Corporate Aviation Management Scholarships *(Professional Development/Scholarship)*

Purpose: To promote professional development and business aviation careers and to benefit individuals seeking to become NBAA Certified Aviation Managers (CAMs). **Focus:** Aviation. **Qualif.:** Applicants must be currently working in the business aviation industry or attending a university-level aviation program. **Criteria:** Recipients are selected based on academic performance, financial need, career planning and progress of the individual toward a career in business aviation.

Awards are arranged alphabetically below their administering organizations

Funds Avail.: $850. **To Apply:** Applicants must submit a completed application form; an official transcript of record; a 250-word, typed, double-spaced essay describing the applicant's interest in and goals for a career in the business aviation industry; two letters of recommendation from either an employee of an NBAA Member Company flight department or a professor at the university where the applicant currently is enrolled; and a current resume. **Deadline:** November 1. **Contact:** Jay Evans at the above address (see entry 4769).

4774 ■ David E. Ewald Journalism Scholarships *(Undergraduate/Scholarship)*

Purpose: To benefit a student intending to pursue a career in journalism, preferably with an aviation focus. **Focus:** Aviation; Journalism. **Qualif.:** Applicants must be either enrolled or accepted for enrollment in an accredited college or university program in journalism or a related area and must be U.S. citizens. **Criteria:** Recipients are selected based on academic performance and financial need.

Funds Avail.: $1,000. **To Apply:** Applicants must submit a completed application form; an official transcript of record; a proof of enrollment or acceptance, prior to the distribution of award; a 500-1,000-word, typed, double-spaced essay describing the applicant's interest in and goals for a career in journalism; two letters of recommendation from either a faculty member or other individual who is familiar with the applicant's capabilities; and a current resume. **Deadline:** August 15. **Contact:** Jay Evans at the above address (see entry 4769).

4775 ■ Exxon Mobil Aviation and the Avitats International Operators Scholarships *(All/Scholarship)*

Purpose: To promote education and training as a means for individuals to increase the safety and professionalism of their positions. **Focus:** Aviation. **Qualif.:** Applicants must be aviation professionals engaged in international operations. **Criteria:** Recipients are selected based on academic performance and financial need.

Funds Avail.: $1,000. **To Apply:** Applicants must submit completed application form; an official transcript of record; a proof of enrollment or acceptance, prior to the distribution of award; a 500-word or less, typed, double-spaced essay that clearly explains how the scholarship will help the applicant achieve their international aviation career goals and necessary funds to achieve these goals; and at least one professional letter of recommendation, preferably from an NBAA MembCompany Representative. **Deadline:** January 30. **Contact:** Jay Evans at the above address (see entry 4769).

4776 ■ William M. Fanning Maintenance Scholarships *(Undergraduate/Scholarship)*

Purpose: To promote professional development and business aviation careers. **Focus:** Aviation. **Qualif.:** Applicants must be students who are currently enrolled in an accredited airframe and powerplant program at an approved FAR Part 147 school or an individual who is not currently enrolled but has been accepted for enrollment in an A&P program; must be U.S. citizens; and must have a grade point average of 3.0 or above on a 4.0 scale. **Criteria:** Recipients are selected based on academic performance and financial need.

Funds Avail.: $2,500. **Number Awarded:** 2. **To Apply:** Applicants must submit a complete application form; an official transcript of record; a 250-word, typed, double-spaced essay describing the applicant's interest in and goals for a career in the aviation maintenance field; two letters of recommendation from a member or other individual who is familiar with the applicant's capabilities; and current resume. **Deadline:** August 1. **Contact:** Jay Evans at the above address (see entry 4769).

4777 ■ Flight Attendants/Flight Technician Scholarships *(Undergraduate/Scholarship)*

Purpose: To promote education and training as a means for business aviation flight attendants and flight technicians to enhance their professional careers. **Focus:** Aviation. **Qualif.:** Applicants must be flight attendants or flight technicians. **Criteria:** Recipients are selected based on academic performance and financial need.

Funds Avail.: No specific amount. **To Apply:** Applicants must submit a completed application form; one signed aviation or leadership-related letter of recommendation, dated within the last two years; a typed, 100-word essay answering the required question; and a current, one-page resume. **Deadline:** March 31. **Contact:** Jay Evans at the above address (see entry 4769).

4778 ■ Lawrence Ginocchio Aviation Scholarships *(Undergraduate/Scholarship)*

Purpose: To recognize individuals who have demonstrated honesty, integrity, and selflessness in their dealings with others. **Focus:** Aviation. **Qualif.:** Applicants must be full-time undergraduate sophomore, junior, or senior students officially enrolled or accepted for enrollment in an aviation related two-year, four-year or postgraduate degree program; must be U.S. citizens; and must have a grade point average of 3.0 or above on a 4.0 scale. **Criteria:** Recipients are selected based on academic performance and financial need.

Funds Avail.: $25,000. **Number Awarded:** 5. **To Apply:** Applicants must submit a complete application form; must submit an official transcript of record; a 500-to 1,000-word, typed, double-spaced essay describing the applicant's interest in and goals for a career in the business aviation industry and demonstrating the applicant's strength of character; two letters of recommendation from those qualified to comment on the career aspirations and qualifications of the applicant especially as they relate to business aviation; and current resume. **Deadline:** August 1. **Contact:** Jay Evans at the above address (see entry 4769).

4779 ■ NORDAM Dee Howard/Etienne Fage Scholarships *(Undergraduate/Scholarship)*

Purpose: To promote professional development and business aviation careers. **Focus:** Aviation; Aeronautics. **Qualif.:** Applicants must be full-time undergraduate sophomore, junior, or senior students enrolled in the aerospace engineering or aeronautical systems maintenance engineering major at Embry-Riddle Aeronautical University; must be U.S. citizens; and must have a grade point average of 3.0 or above on a 4.0 scale. **Criteria:** Recipients are selected based on academic performance and financial need.

Funds Avail.: $25,000. **Number Awarded:** 5. **To Apply:** Applicants must submit a completed application form; an official transcript of record; a 250-word, typed, double-spaced essay describing the applicant's interest in and goals for a career in the business aviation industry; two letters of recommendation from an Embry-Riddle faculty member who is familiar with the applicant's capabilities; and current resume. **Deadline:** August 1. **Contact:** Jay Evans at the above address (see entry 4769).

4780 ■ Maintenance Technical Reward and Career Scholarships *(Undergraduate/Scholarship)*

Purpose: To promote technical education and professional development as a means for business aviation maintenance technicians to enhance their careers. **Focus:** Aviation. **Qualif.:** Applicants must be current holder of an airframe and powerplant certificate; currently employed in general aviation; must either be currently enrolled in either an accredited A&P program or an approved FAR Part 147 school. **Criteria:** Recipients are selected based on academic performance and financial need.

Funds Avail.: No specific amount. **To Apply:** Applicants must submit completed application form; a 250-word, typed, double-spaced essay describing the applicant's interest in and goals for a career in the business aviation maintenance field; current resume; and a letter of recommendation from either a supervisor, faculty member or other individual who is familiar with the applicant's capabilities. **Deadline:** February 15. **Contact:** Jay Evans at the above address (see entry 4769).

4781 ■ Scheduler and Dispatchers Scholarships *(Professional Development/Scholarship)*

Purpose: To promote education and training as a means for individuals to increase the professionalism of their positions. **Focus:** Aviation. **Qualif.:** Applicants must have completed all professional/educational training. **Criteria:** Recipients are selected based on academic performance and financial need.

Funds Avail.: $10,000. **To Apply:** Applicants must submit completed application form; a typed essay of 500-words or less; two professional letters of recommendation; and a current resume. **Deadline:** October 5. **Contact:** Jay Evans at the above address (see entry 4769).

4782 ■ U.S. Aircraft Insurance Group Professional Development Program Scholarships *(Undergraduate/Scholarship)*

Purpose: To promote professional development and business aviation careers. **Focus:** Aviation. **Qualif.:** Applicants must be full-time undergraduate sophomore, junior, or senior students in academic year enrolled in an aviation-related two-year, four-year, or postgraduate degree program that incorporates the NBAA PDP; must be U.S. citizens; and must have a grade point average of 3.0 or above on a 4.0 scale. **Criteria:** Recipients are selected based on academic performance and financial need.

Funds Avail.: $1,000. **To Apply:** Applicants must submit a completed application form; an official transcript of record; a 250-word, typed, double-spaced essay describing the applicant's interest in and goals for a career in business aviation flight department; two letters of recommendation from a member of aviation department faculty at the institution where the applicant is currently enrolled; and current resume. **Deadline:** August 1. **Contact:** Jay Evans at the above address (see entry 4769).

4783 ■ National Business Travel Association

110 N Royal St., 4th Fl.
Alexandria, VA 22314
Ph: (703)684-0836
Fax: (703)684-0263
E-mail: info@nbta.org
URL: http://www.nbta.org

4784 ■ GLP Program Scholarships *(Other/Scholarship)*

Purpose: To provide a high-level education experience to individuals in the process of growth and development within their companies. **Focus:** Travel and Tourism. **Qualif.:** Applicant must be an active member of NBTA and must retain NBTA membership throughout the scholarship period. **Criteria:** The recipient will be selected based on educational background, stature and responsibilities of the individual within his/her company; industry involvement; awards and honors; leadership and participation in NBTA activities; statement of career objectives; and outside appraisals.

Funds Avail.: No specific amount. **Number Awarded:** 1. **Deadline:** May 30. **Contact:** NBTA Foundation, 110 N Royal St., 4th Fl., Alexandria, VA 22314.

4785 ■ Independent Studies Program Scholarships *(Other/Scholarship)*

Purpose: To provide educational opportunities for business travel professionals. **Focus:** Travel and tourism. **Qualif.:** Applicant must: be an NBTA member and retain NBTA membership throughout the grant period; be endorsed by his or her company that will allow him or her necessary time and funding to attend the courses or programs; comply with all schedules and requirements pertaining to the scholarship application process. **Criteria:** The recipient will be selected by the NBTA Foundation Scholarship Committee based on standard recipient selection procedures.

Funds Avail.: $5,000. **Number Awarded:** 3. **Deadline:** May 30.

4786 ■ Mike Kabo Global Scholarships *(Other/Scholarship)*

Purpose: To provide individuals with the opportunity to attend the two day Global Leadership Program (GLP) session and NBTA's International Convention and Exposition. **Focus:** Travel and tourism. **Qualif.:** Applicant must be: a corporate travel professional from the buyer community; a resident outside of the United States of America; a member of NBTA or one of its Paragon Partner Members. **Criteria:** Recipients will be selected by the NBTA Foundation and the National Business Travel Association based on standard recipient review and selection procedures.

Funds Avail.: No specific amount. **Number Awarded:** 1. **Deadline:** May 30.

4787 ■ National Cattlemen's Foundation

9110 E Nichols Ave., Ste. 300
Centennial, CO 80112
Ph: (303)694-0305
E-mail: ncf@beef.org
URL: http://www.nationalcattlemensfoundation.org

4788 ■ Beef Industry Scholarships *(Undergraduate/Scholarship)*

Purpose: To identify and encourage talented and thoughtful students who will emerge as industry leaders. **Focus:** Agricultural sciences. **Qualif.:** Applicant must be a graduating high school senior or full-time undergraduate student enrolled at a two or four-year institution and have demonstrated commitment to a career in the beef industry through classes, internships or life experiences. **Criteria:** Awards are given based on the essay, which is judged based on originality, grammar, clarity of expression, accuracy, relevance of topic and the solutions offered.

Awards are arranged alphabetically below their administering organizations

Funds Avail.: $1,500. **Number Awarded:** 10. **To Apply:** Applicants must submit proof of enrollment (as a full-time student); a one page letter of career goals; the essay (maximum of 750 words); and two letters of reference. **Deadline:** October 1.

4789 ■ W.D. Farr Scholarships *(Graduate/Scholarship)*

Purpose: To promote education in the animal industry. **Focus:** Animal science and behavior. **Qualif.:** Applicant must be a graduate student. **Criteria:** Awards are given based on the application.

Funds Avail.: $12,000. **Number Awarded:** 2. **To Apply:** Applicants must contact the NCF for more information about the program.

Remarks: Honors the life's work of the late W.D. Farr of Greeley, Colorado.

4790 ■ Fred Johnson Memorial Scholarships *(Graduate/Scholarship)*

Purpose: To promote education in the animal industry. **Focus:** Animal science and behavior; Genetics. **Qualif.:** Applicant must be a Master's or Ph.D. student studying meat animal science or genetics. **Criteria:** Awards are given based on the application.

Funds Avail.: No specific amount. **To Apply:** Applicants must contact the NCF for more information about the program.

Remarks: In memory of Frederick Hursh Johnson, Jr.

4791 ■ NCF Fort Dodge Animal Health Legacy Scholarships for Undergraduate Students *(Undergraduate/Scholarship)*

Purpose: To promote study in animal science with an emphasis in bovine practice. **Focus:** Animal science and behavior. **Qualif.:** Applicant must be a U.S. citizen; an undergraduate junior or senior enrolled at a two-or four-year institution of higher learning; have demonstrated commitment to a career in the beef industry through classes, internships or life experience. **Criteria:** Applicants will be judged on effective communication skills, clarity of expression, originality and interest/passion for the cattle industry.

Funds Avail.: $5,000 each. **Number Awarded:** 2. **To Apply:** Applicants must submit a completed scholarship application form together with the essay and two letters of recommendation. **Deadline:** April 30.

Remarks: In partnership with Fort Dodge Animal Health.

4792 ■ NCF Fort Dodge Animal Health Legacy Scholarships for Veterinary Students *(Undergraduate/Scholarship)*

Purpose: To promote veterinary study and encourage bovine practice. **Focus:** Veterinary science and medicine. **Qualif.:** Applicant must be a U.S. citizen, and a veterinary student with an emphasis in bovine practice. **Criteria:** Applicants will be judged on effective communication skills, clarity of expression, originality and interest/passion for the cattle industry.

Funds Avail.: $5,000 each. **Number Awarded:** 3. **To Apply:** Applicants must submit a completed scholarship application form together with the essay and two letters of recommendation. **Deadline:** April 30.

Remarks: In partnership with Fort Dodge Animal Health.

4793 ■ National Center for Farmworker Health

1770 FM 967
Buda, TX 78610
Ph: (512)312-2700
Free: 800-531-5120
E-mail: info@ncfh.org
URL: http://www.ncfh.org

4794 ■ Migrant Health Scholarships *(Professional Development/Scholarship)*

Purpose: To assist the recipients in pursuing their educational and professional goals. **Focus:** Health education. **Qualif.:** Applicants must be interested in pursuing or continuing a career in the migrant health field, and must be employees at a community/migrant health center. **Criteria:** Awards are given based on achievement and character. Applicants are selected by the committee and are recognized at the Annual National Farmworkers Health Conference.

Funds Avail.: $1,000. **To Apply:** Application forms are available from the website. Applicants must send an application form; resume; one-page personal statement; letter of reference. **Deadline:** April 7.

4795 ■ National Center for Learning Disabilities

381 Park Ave. S, Ste. 1401
New York, NY 10016
Ph: (212)545-7510
Fax: (212)545-9665
Free: 888-575-7373
URL: http://www.ncld.org

4796 ■ Anne Ford Scholarships *(Undergraduate/Scholarship)*

Purpose: To assist students who are facing the challenges of living with a learning disability. **Focus:** General studies. **Qualif.:** Applicant must have a GPA of 3.0 or higher; demonstrated financial assistance; a U.S. citizen; enrolled as a high school senior and pursuing a four year undergraduate degree. **Criteria:** The Anne Ford Scholarship Committee will select the recipient.

Funds Avail.: $10,000. **To Apply:** Applicants must submit a completed application form; a personal statement; a high school transcript; three letters of recommendations; a financial statement; copies of SAT/ACT scores; and a current documentation of a learning disability that includes evaluation reports. **Deadline:** December 31.

4797 ■ National Chapter of Canada IODE

40 Orchard View Blvd., Ste. 254
Toronto, ON, Canada M4R 1B9
Ph: (416)487-4416
Fax: (416)487-4417
E-mail: iodecanada@bellnet.ca
URL: http://www.iode.ca

4798 ■ War Memorial Doctoral Scholarships *(Postgraduate/Scholarship)*

Purpose: To provide bursaries for university studies in Canada to children of men killed or permanently disabled in the Great War. **Focus:** General studies. **Qualif.:** Applicants must be Canadian citizens and at least in the second year of their doctoral program; must be a graduate of a Canadian university, and must have done or be doing post-graduate work. **Criteria:** Application will be evaluated by the National Selection Committee. Selection of ap-

Awards are arranged alphabetically below their administering organizations

plicants is based on their school records, health and character, the war service of their father and the family's financial circumstances. Selection committee will give preference to a "returned man" or to an immediate relative of a man who served in World War I.

Funds Avail.: $15,000. **To Apply:** Applications must be submitted to the National Selection Committee chair. **Deadline:** July.

4799 ■ National Coal Transportation Association

4 W Meadow Lark Ln., Ste. 100
Littleton, CO 80127-5718
Ph: (303)979-2798
Fax: (303)973-1848
E-mail: tom@nationalcoaltransportation.org
URL: http://www.nationalcoaltransportation.org

4800 ■ National Coal Transportation Association At Large Scholarships *(Undergraduate/ Scholarship)*

Purpose: To provide financial assistance to the dependents of employees of NCTA member companies. **Focus:** General studies. **Qualif.:** Applicants must be dependents of full time employees of NCTA member companies; enrolled in college as a sophomore or junior. **Criteria:** Recipients are selected based on academic merit, test scores, extracurricular activities, and personal statement of career interest.

Funds Avail.: $1,500. **To Apply:** Applicants must send an application form with school transcripts. **Deadline:** June 30.

4801 ■ National Collegiate Athletic Association

PO Box 6222
Indianapolis, IN 46206-6222
Ph: (317)917-6222
Fax: (317)917-6888
E-mail: pmr@ncaa.org
URL: http://www2.ncaa.org

4802 ■ Walter Byers Postgraduate Scholarships *(Postgraduate/Scholarship)*

Purpose: To promote and encourage postgraduate education for student-athletes. **Focus:** Sports studies. **Qualif.:** Student-athlete must have an overall undergraduate cumulative GPA of 3.50 or better (based on a maximum 4.0), or the equivalent; have competed in intercollegiate athletics as a member of a varsity team at an NCAA member institution; a graduating senior or enrolled in graduate study at an NCAA member institution; have intentions of applying for admission into a graduate degree program at a properly accredited, nonprofit educational institution or into a post baccalaureate professional degree program at a professionally accredited law school, medical school, or the equivalent, without restriction as to the national site of the institution; committed to work on a full-time basis toward a graduate degree or toward a post baccalaureate professional degree; have evidenced superior character and leadership; have demonstrated that participation in athletics has been a positive influence in personal and intellectual development; and enrolled in a graduate degree program within five years of being named a Byer's Scholar. **Criteria:** The committee will review the nominations, contact the finalists for an interview and select the final recipients.

Funds Avail.: $21,500. **Number Awarded:** One male and one female. **To Apply:** Student-athletes must be nominated by the institution's Faculty Athletics Representative (FAR) or a FAR designee (an individual in academics). **Deadline:** January.

4803 ■ Ethnic Minority and Women's Enhancement Postgraduate Scholarships *(Graduate/ Scholarship)*

Purpose: To increase the pool of opportunities for qualified minority and female candidates in intercollegiate athletics. **Focus:** Sports studies. **Qualif.:** Applicant must be seeking admission or have been accepted into a sports administration or sports-related program that will assist in obtaining a career in intercollegiate athletics (athletics administrator, coach, athletic trainer or other career that provides a direct service to intercollegiate athletics); have not yet begin any initial postgraduate studies; U.S. citizen; and have performed with distinction as a student body member at their respective undergraduate institution. **Criteria:** A subcommittee from the NCAA Committee on Women's Athletics will select 13 award recipients, and a subcommittee from the NCAA Minorities Opportunities and Interests Committee will select 13 award recipients.

Funds Avail.: $6000. **Number Awarded:** 26. **To Apply:** Applicants must submit application materials. **Deadline:** December 6.

4804 ■ Freedom Forum-NCAA Sports-Journalism Scholarships *(Undergraduate/ Scholarship)*

Purpose: To foster freedom of speech and press while promoting quality sports journalism education at the collegiate level. **Focus:** Sports writing; Journalism. **Qualif.:** Applicant must be a junior college student with career goals in sports journalism, majors in journalism, or experience in campus sports journalism. **Criteria:** Applications will be reviewed by a selection committee.

Funds Avail.: $3000. **Number Awarded:** 8. **To Apply:** Applicants must submit a completed application form along with official grade transcripts; three published journalism samples relative to sports; at least one letter of recommendation; and the essay. **Deadline:** December 14.

Remarks: In cooperation with The Freedom Forum. **Contact:** Suzy Hays, at 317-917-6477.

4805 ■ National Collegiate Athletic Association Postgraduate Scholarships *(Postgraduate/ Scholarship)*

Purpose: To promote and encourage postgraduate education for student-athletes. **Focus:** General studies. **Qualif.:** Applicant must be a student-athletes at an active NCAA member institution and in the final season of NCAA athletics eligibility or will not be using any remaining athletics eligibility; have an overall undergraduate minimum cumulative GPA of 3.200 (based on a 4.000 scale) or its equivalent; have performed with distinction as a member of the varsity team in the sport in which the student-athlete is being nominated; intend to continue academic work beyond the baccalaureate degree and enroll in a graduate degree program on a part or full time basis at an accredited graduate or degree-granting professional school; and an outstanding citizen and excellent role model for the institution and intercollegiate athletics as a whole. **Criteria:** Nominations are initially reviewed by seven regional selection committees.

Awards are arranged alphabetically below their administering organizations

Funds Avail.: $7500. **Number Awarded:** 87 men; 87 women. **To Apply:** Student-athletes must be nominated by the institution's Faculty Athletics Representative (FAR) or a FAR designee (an individual in academics). **Deadline:** January 17; March 20; and May 15.

4806 ■ National Collegiate Cancer Foundation

PO Box 14190
Silver Spring, MD 20911
Ph: (717)215-0943
URL: http://www.collegiatecancer.org

4807 ■ National Collegiate Cancer Foundation Scholarships *(Undergraduate/Scholarship)*

Purpose: To provide financial support for college students who have a personal diagnosis with cancer and are seeking to continue their higher education. **Focus:** General studies. **Qualif.:** Applicants must be college students who have been diagnosed with cancer and are seeking to continue their higher education. **Criteria:** Awards will be based on four criteria: financial need, quality of essay and recommendations, displaying a "Will Win" attitude, and overall story of cancer survivorship.

Funds Avail.: $1,000. **To Apply:** Applicants must check the available website for the required materials. **Deadline:** September. **Contact:** National Collegiate Cancer Foundation at the above address (see entry 4806).

4808 ■ National Commission for Cooperative Education

360 Huntington Ave., 384 CP
Boston, MA 02115-5096
Ph: (617)373-3770
Fax: (617)373-3463
E-mail: ncce@neu.edu
URL: http://www.co-op.edu

4809 ■ National Co-op Scholarship Program *(Undergraduate/Scholarship)*

Purpose: To assist students pursuing education in science, mathematics, engineering and technology. **Focus:** Mathematics and mathematical sciences; Science; Engineering. **Qualif.:** Applicants must be have a high school GPA of 3.5 (B+) or better. **Criteria:** Selection is based on the application.

Funds Avail.: No specific amount. **To Apply:** Applicants must complete the National Co-op Scholarship program application including a typed one-page essay. Application materials and must be sent directly to the applicant's college or university. **Deadline:** February 15.

4810 ■ National Community Pharmacists Association

100 Daingerfield Rd.
Alexandria, VA 22314
Ph: (703)683-8200
Fax: (703)683-3619
Free: 800-544-7477
E-mail: info@ncpanet.org
URL: http://www.ncpanet.org

4811 ■ J.C. and Rheba Cobb Memorial Scholarships *(Undergraduate/Scholarship)*

Purpose: To promote the continuing growth and prosperity of independent community pharmacy in the United States. **Focus:** Pharmacy. **Qualif.:** Applicants must be full-time pharmacy students in an accredited United States college of pharmacy. **Criteria:** Recipients are selected based on leadership qualities and academic achievement.

Funds Avail.: $2,500. **Number Awarded:** 1. **To Apply:** Applicants must submit a copy of the most recent official transcript of record. Applicants must submit a letter from school official familiar with the students activities; a letter from a pharmacy owner or manager, preferably an NCPA member; a letter from the applicants to the NCPA Foundation Scholarships Award Committee outlining his or her school and civic accomplishments and objectives for the future; a resume or curriculum vitae describing the students work and professional experience. **Deadline:** March 15.

4812 ■ National Community Pharmacists Association Internship Programs *(Undergraduate/Internship)*

Purpose: To provide undergraduate pharmacy students with an opportunity to become more aware of the vast opportunities that exist in independent pharmacy practice. To provide an experience that demonstrates the importance of a national pharmacy association to the profession. **Focus:** Pharmacy. **Qualif.:** Applicants must be enrolled in a full-time pharmacy program in pursuit of their first professional pharmacy degree; applicants must have a minimum of 2.50 cumulative GPA at an accredited U.S. college of pharmacy; a demonstrated interest in independent pharmacy practice through school activities and work experience; exhibit an interest in organizational involvement through participation in student organizations in college and/or community organizations. **Criteria:** Recipients are selected based on academic standing.

Funds Avail.: No specific amount. **To Apply:** Applicants must submit a letter of recommendation explaining their interest in the internship, career goals, and how the internship will help to meet the goals; a resume or curriculum vitae; a school transcript to verify a cumulative GPA of at least 2.5; two letters of recommendation, one from pharmacy school dean and one from the state pharmacy association executive, current recent employer, or NCPA Faculty Liaison. **Deadline:** January 15.

4813 ■ National Community Pharmacists Association Presidential Scholarships *(Undergraduate/Scholarship)*

Purpose: To promote the continuing growth and prosperity of independent community pharmacy in the United States. **Focus:** Pharmacy. **Qualif.:** Applicants must be full-time pharmacy students at an accredited college of pharmacy. **Criteria:** Recipients are selected based on leadership qualities and academic achievement.

Funds Avail.: $2,000. **Number Awarded:** 15. **To Apply:** Applicants must submit a copy of the most recent official transcript of record. Applicants must submit a letter from a school official familiar with the students activities; a letter from a pharmacy owner or manager, preferably an NCPA member; a letter from the applicant to the NCPA Foundation Scholarships Award Committee outlining his or her school and civic accomplishments and objectives for the future; a resume or curriculum vitae describing the students work and professional experience. **Deadline:** March 15.

4814 ■ Neil Pruitt, Sr. Memorial Scholarships *(Undergraduate/Scholarship)*

Purpose: To promote the continuing growth and prosperity of independent community pharmacy in the United States.

Awards are arranged alphabetically below their administering organizations

Focus: Pharmacy. **Qualif.:** Applicants must be full-time pharmacy students at an accredited United States college of pharmacy. **Criteria:** Recipients are selected based on leadership qualities, academic achievement, and demonstrated interest in entrepreneurism.

Funds Avail.: $2,500. **Number Awarded:** 1. **To Apply:** Applicants must submit a copy of the most recent official transcript of record; a letter from a school official familiar with the students activities; a letter from a pharmacy owner or manager, preferably an NCPA member; a letter from the applicant to the NCPA Foundation Scholarships Award Committee outlining his or her school and civic accomplishments and objectives for the future; a resume or curriculum vitae describing the students work and professional experience. **Deadline:** March 15.

4815 ■ Williard B. Simmons Sr. Memorial Scholarships *(Undergraduate/Scholarship)*

Purpose: To promote the continuing growth and prosperity of independent community pharmacy in the United States. **Focus:** Pharmacy. **Qualif.:** Applicants must be full-time pharmacy students at an accredited United States college of pharmacy. **Criteria:** Recipients are selected based on leadership qualities, academic achievement, and demonstrated interest in independent pharmacy management.

Funds Avail.: $2,500. **Number Awarded:** 1. **To Apply:** Applicants must submit a copy of the most recent official transcript of record. Applicants must submit a letter from school official familiar with the students activities; a letter from a pharmacy owner or manager, preferably an NCPA member; a letter from the applicants to the NCPA Foundation Scholarships Award Committee outlining his or her school and civic accomplishments and objectives for the future; a resume or curriculum vitae describing the students work and professional experience. **Deadline:** March 15.

4816 ■ National Conference of Bar Examiners

302 S Bedford St.
Madison, WI 53703-3622
Ph: (608)280-8550
Fax: (608)280-8552
E-mail: contact@ncbex.org
URL: http://www.ncbex.org

4817 ■ The Joe E. Covington Award for Research on Bar Admissions Testing *(Doctorate/Award/Prize)*

Purpose: To provide support for graduate students in any discipline doing research germane to bar admissions. **Focus:** General studies. **Qualif.:** Applicant must be a student conducting a research who is enrolled in a doctoral program and has completed a minimum of one year of study towards a Ph.D. degree or just completing a Ph.D degree. **Criteria:** Recipient will be selected by the Award Committee.

Funds Avail.: $6,000. **To Apply:** Applicant must submit application which includes a) a curriculum vitae; b) a letter of intent from the student's project advisor; c) a brief research proposal of up to four pages; d) a cover letter to Dr. Michael Kane. **Deadline:** March 7.

4818 ■ National Conference of Editorial Writers

3899 N Front St.
Harrisburg, PA 17110
Ph: (717)703-3015
Fax: (717)703-3014
E-mail: cnew@pa-news.org
URL: http://www.ncew.org

4819 ■ Barry Bingham Sr. Fellowships *(Professional Development/Fellowship)*

Purpose: To recognize the educator's outstanding effort to encourage minority students in the field of journalism. **Focus:** Journalism. **Qualif.:** Applicant must be faculty member who has shown great initiative in mentoring minority college students; must be at the college or university level. **Criteria:** Selection of applicant will be based on their application form and fellowship criteria.

Funds Avail.: $1,000. **To Apply:** For further information about the fellowship, applicants are advice to contact Sherid Virnig, Director of Admission, 717703-3015.

4820 ■ Rosalynn Carter Fellowships *(Professional Development/Fellowship)*

Purpose: To enhance understanding of mental health or mental illness. **Focus:** Mental health. **Qualif.:** Applicant must have at least three years experience in print or electronic journalism; must be a U.S. journalist. **Criteria:** Selection of candidates will be based on the criteria of the committee.

Funds Avail.: $10,000. **Number Awarded:** 6. **To Apply:** Application guidelines can be found online and must be submitted at: One Copenhill, 453 Freedom Parkway, Atlanta, GA 30307. **Deadline:** April 28.

4821 ■ National Cosmetology Association

401 N Michigan Ave.
Chicago, IL 60611
Ph: (312)527-6765
Fax: (312)464-6118
Free: (866)871-0656
E-mail: nca1@ncacares.org
URL: http://www.ncacares.org

4822 ■ Sally Beauty Scholarships for High School Graduates *(Undergraduate/Scholarship)*

Purpose: To help students find satisfaction, build a career and reach out to others; to keep the cosmetology profession strong. **Focus:** Cosmetology. **Qualif.:** Applicants must be high school graduates under the age of 26 who want to enter the cosmetology profession. **Criteria:** Recipients are selected based on academic performance and interest in a cosmetology program.

Funds Avail.: $1,000. **Number Awarded:** 10. **To Apply:** Applicants must submit a completed application form. **Deadline:** January 15.

4823 ■ National Costumers Association

121 N Bosart Ave.
Indianapolis, IN 46201
Ph: (317)351-1940
Fax: (317)351-1941
Free: 800-NCA-1321
E-mail: office@costumers.org
URL: http://www.costumers.org

4824 ■ National Costumers Association Scholarships *(Undergraduate/Scholarship)*

Purpose: To promote the costume industry through education. **Focus:** General studies. **Qualif.:** Applicants must be

Awards are arranged alphabetically below their administering organizations

17 years old and above, with a GPA of 2.75 or higher and enrolled in an accredited university or school. **Criteria:** Awards are given based on academic merit.

Funds Avail.: Dollar amounts of awards will be determined by the amount of funds available and the number of applicants meeting qualifications at the time of submission of application. **Number Awarded:** Varies. **To Apply:** Applicants must submit a completed and signed application form; proof of GPA; copy of online transcript; and one photo - preferably a headshot. Candidates must also submit a 100-word (max) biography and a 500-word (min) essay of the candidate's field of study and how it applies to the costume industry. **Deadline:** April 1. **Contact:** Gary Broadrick at the above address (see entry 4823).

4825 ■ National Council of Teachers of English

1111 W Kenyon Rd.
Urbana, IL 61801-1096
Ph: (217)328-3870
Fax: (217)328-0977
Free: 877-369-6283
E-mail: public_info@ncte.org
URL: http://www.ncte.org

4826 ■ NCTE Research Foundation Grants *(Professional Development/Grant)*

Purpose: To support research projects about the teaching and learning of language and literacies. **Focus:** English language and literature. **Qualif.:** Applicants must be a member of NCTE in good standing conducting a research related to the teaching and learning of language and literacies. **Criteria:** Preference is given to the applicant who will best meet the requirements.

Funds Avail.: $12,500. **To Apply:** Applicants may download the Research Foundation Grant Application Cover Sheet and guidelines from the website www.ncte.org/groups/cee. Applicants must also submit a 150-word abstract (one page, double-spaced) that discusses the research project; an itemized budget; appendices. **Deadline:** June 15. **Contact:** NCTE Research Foundation at 800-369-6283 ext. 3675, e-mail at researchfoundation@ncte.org.

4827 ■ Edwyna Wheadon Postgraduate Training Scholarship Fund *(Professional Development/Scholarship)*

Purpose: To support postgraduate training to enhance teaching skills. **Focus:** English language and literature; Teaching. **Qualif.:** Applicants must be teachers of English/Language Arts in a publicly funded institution. **Criteria:** Recipients are selected based on the submitted requirements.

Funds Avail.: $500. **To Apply:** Applicants must complete the application form. Applicants must also indicate the professional development experience for which he/she seeks support (separate piece of paper, less than 500 words). **Deadline:** January 31.

Remarks: In memory of Edwyna Wheadon. **Contact:** giving@ncte.org.

4828 ■ National Council of Teachers of Mathematics

1906 Association Dr.
Reston, VA 20190-1502
Ph: (703)620-9840
Fax: (703)476-2970
E-mail: inquiries@nctm.org
URL: http://www.nctm.org

4829 ■ Emerging Teacher-Leaders in Elementary School Mathematics Grants for Grades K-5 Teachers *(Professional Development/Grant)*

Purpose: To increase the breadth and depth of mathematics content knowledge of elementary school teachers who have demonstrated commitment to mathematics teaching and learning. **Focus:** Applied mathematics. **Qualif.:** Applicant must have the support of the school principal in becoming a mathematics teacher-leader within her or his school or district; must be a current full individual or E-Member of NCTM; must be a full-time elementary school teacher with at least three years of experience; have mathematics as a regular teaching responsibility. **Criteria:** Recipients will be selected based on merit.

Funds Avail.: $6,000. **Number Awarded:** 1. **To Apply:** Applicants must submit a proposal which includes: statement of the applicant's commitment to the improvement of his or her content knowledge and to the overall strengthening of the mathematics program; brief description of the need for content-based staff development; specific plans for improving the mathematics content knowledge of the grant recipient and implementation of subsequent in-service programs led by the grant recipient; an itemized budget; explanation of the anticipated improvements in mathematics teaching and explanation of how the applicant plans to assess improvement in students' learning. Awardees are required to submit a brief report (not to exceed two double-spaced pages) and an itemized report of expenses. **Deadline:** November 2.

4830 ■ Prospective Secondary Teacher Course Work Scholarships *(Postgraduate/Scholarship)*

Purpose: To provide financial support to college students preparing for teaching secondary school mathematics. **Focus:** Applied mathematics. **Qualif.:** Applicants must be currently completing their sophomore year of college, scheduling for full-time study at a four- or five-year college or university in the next academic year, and pursuing a career goal of becoming a certified teacher of secondary school mathematics. **Criteria:** Preference will be given to applicants with definitive career objectives and present evidence of exceptional university and community service.

Funds Avail.: $10,000. **To Apply:** Applicants must submit a written proposal that includes evidence of the applicant's past academic achievement in a college or university and the applicant's commitment to pursue a teaching career in secondary school mathematics; a written proposal that identifies the remaining two or three years of collegiate coursework in mathematics or mathematics education required to earn certification; a detailed outline of the full-time study required to meet these requirements within three years of study, and the course titles and credits for mathematics and mathematics education courses already completed (must be typewritten, double-spaced and single-sided, with margins of at least one inch on 8.5" x 11" paper and font size must be no smaller than 10-point, Times New Roman, and width between characters should be normal; one original and four copies of the proposal should be included in a single packet addressed to the Mathematics Education Trust); a budget; a signed recommendation letter; official transcript; a two-page, double-spaced essay on

Awards are arranged alphabetically below their administering organizations

why the applicant has chosen to pursue a career as a secondary school mathematics teacher. **Deadline:** May 9.

4831 ■ School In-Service Training Grants for Grades 6-8 Teachers *(Graduate/Grant)*

Purpose: To provide financial assistance to middle schools for in-service education in mathematics. **Focus:** Applied mathematics. **Qualif.:** Schools with a current NCTM K-8 school membership are eligible. **Criteria:** Preference will be given to schools with the most financial need.

Funds Avail.: $4,000. **To Apply:** Applicants must submit a proposal with the following: a brief, specific description of the need for the proposed staff development; must have a specific plan for meeting the identified needs; must have an itemized budget (presented in a table format) listing both funds requested from the Mathematics Education Trust and other sources of funds; must explain how the school's staff plans to assess the project's impact; must have the principal's letter of support signed on school stationery. **Deadline:** May 9.

4832 ■ School In-Service Training Grants for Grades 9-12 Teachers *(Graduate/Grant)*

Purpose: To provide financial assistance to secondary schools for in-service education in Mathematics. **Focus:** Applied mathematics. **Qualif.:** Schools with a current NCTM K-8 school membership are eligible. **Criteria:** Preference will be given to schools with the most financial need.

Funds Avail.: $4,000. **To Apply:** Applicants must submit a proposal with the following: a brief, specific description of the need for the proposed staff development; must have a specific plan for meeting the identified needs; must have an itemized budget (presented in a table format) listing both funds requested from the Mathematics Education Trust and other sources of funds; must explain how the school's staff plans to assess the project's impact; must have the principal's letter of support signed on school stationery. **Deadline:** May 9.

4833 ■ School In-Service Training Grants for Grades K-5 Teachers *(Graduate/Grant)*

Purpose: To provide financial assistance to elementary schools for in-service education in mathematics. **Focus:** Applied mathematics. **Qualif.:** Schools with a current NCTM K-8 school membership are eligible. **Criteria:** Preference will be given to schools with the most financial need.

Funds Avail.: $4,000. **To Apply:** Applicants must submit a proposal with the following: a brief, specific description of the need for the proposed staff development; must have a specific plan for meeting the identified needs; must have an itemized budget (presented in a table format) listing both funds requested from the Mathematics Education Trust and other sources of funds; must explain how the school's staff plans to assess the project's impact; must have the principal's letter of support signed on school stationery. **Deadline:** May 9.

4834 ■ National Court Reporters Association

8224 Old Courthouse Rd.
Vienna, VA 22182-3808
Ph: (703)556-6272
Fax: (703)556-6291
E-mail: misc@ncrahq.org
URL: http://www.ncraonline.org

Awards are arranged alphabetically below their administering organizations

4835 ■ National Court Reporters Association Student Intern Scholarships *(Undergraduate/Scholarship)*

Purpose: To provide scholarships to NCRA students. **Focus:** General studies. **Qualif.:** The nominee must be a current NCRA student member and must be an intern in any of the three career paths: judicial, CART, and captioning. The nominee must also be enrolled in an NCRA-certified Court Reporter Training Program. The nominee in a judicial court reporting program must have passed at least one of the program's Q and A tests at a minimum of 190 words per minute. The nominee in a CART or captioning program must have passed at least one of the program's literary tests at a minimum of 160 words per minute. Nominee must have a GPA of at least 3.5 overall, based on a 4.0 standard or equivalent. **Criteria:** Selection will be based on the committee's criteria.

Funds Avail.: No specific amount. **To Apply:** Nominator may download a nomination form via NCRA web site. **Deadline:** October 31.

4836 ■ New Professional Reporter Grants *(Professional Development/Grant)*

Purpose: To support new employees in their first year out of school. **Focus:** General studies. **Qualif.:** The nominee must be a current NCRA student member and must be enrolled in an NCRA-certified court reporting program. The nominee must have passed at least one of the court reporting program's Q and A tests at a minimum of 200 words per minute; must have a GPA of at least 3.5 overall, based on a 4.0 standard; must have a demonstrated a need for financial assistance. The nominee must also possess all the qualities exemplified by a professional court reporter, including professional attitude, demeanor, dress and motivation. All criteria must be confirmed and verified by the submitting court reporting program. **Criteria:** The winner will be selected by random drawing of all qualified nominees and will be publicized in the JCR, Newsflash, Caselines, and online, and will be formally announced at the NCRA's annual convention.

Funds Avail.: $2,000. **To Apply:** Applicant must submit his/her name to NCRA's New Professionals Community of Interest within one month of receiving the grant. **Contact:** NCRF at the above address (see entry 4834).

4837 ■ Frank Sarli Memorial Scholarships *(Undergraduate/Scholarship)*

Purpose: To provide scholarships to NCRA students. **Focus:** General studies. **Qualif.:** The nominee must be a current NCRA student member and must be enrolled in an NCRA-certified court reporting program. The nominee must have also passed at least one of the court reporting program's Q and A tests at a minimum of 200 words per minute; must have a grade point average of at least a 3.5 overall, based on a 4.0 standard; must have a demonstrated need for financial assistance; must possess all the qualities exemplified by a professional court reporter, including professional attitude, demeanor, dress and motivation. All criteria must be confirmed and verified by the submitting court reporting program. **Criteria:** Scholarship is given based on the committee's criteria.

Funds Avail.: No specific amount. **To Apply:** Nominator may nominate a student who meets the criteria for the scholarship. **Contact:** B.J. Shorak, Deputy Executive Director, bjshorak@ncrahq.org.

4838 ■ National Dairy Herd Improvement Association

PO Box 930399
Verona, WI 53593-0399
Ph: (608)848-6455
Fax: (608)848-7675
E-mail: jmattison@requestltd.com
URL: http://www.dhia.org

4839 ■ National Dairy Herd Improvement Association Scholarship Program *(Undergraduate/Scholarship)*

Purpose: To provide financial assistance for the education of incoming and continuing students at technical and two-year and four-year institutions. **Focus:** General studies. **Qualif.:** Applicants must be family members or employees of a herd on DHIA testing, or family members of an employee, or employees of a DHIA affiliate. **Criteria:** Recipients will be selected based on scholastic achievements and leadership in school and community activities.

Funds Avail.: $500. **To Apply:** Applicants must submit all the required application information. **Deadline:** September 30.

4840 ■ National Dairy Shrine

1224 Alton Darby Creek Rd.
Columbus, OH 43228-9792
Ph: (614)878-5333
Fax: (614)870-2622
E-mail: shrine@cobaselect.com
URL: http://www.dairyshrine.org

4841 ■ Progressive Dairy Producers Award *(All/Grant)*

Purpose: To provide funds for educational travel. **Focus:** Agribusiness; Agricultural sciences; Business; Dairy science. **Qualif.:** Candidates must be an individual, couple, family or multiple partner operation dairy producer between 21-45 years of age at the time of the application due date. **Criteria:** Priority will be given to nominees who own or manage operations.

Funds Avail.: $2,000. **Number Awarded:** Varies. **To Apply:** Applicants must submit the following: two letters of support; 6 copies of nomination and supporting information. **Deadline:** March 15.

4842 ■ National Defense Transportation Association

50 S Picket St., Ste. 220
Alexandria, VA 22304-7206
Ph: (703)751-5011
Fax: (703)823-8761
E-mail: info@ndtahq.com
URL: http://www.ndtahq.com

4843 ■ Academic Scholarship Program A *(Undergraduate/Scholarship)*

Purpose: To encourage college students to study transportation and logistics. **Focus:** Transportation; Logistics. **Qualif.:** Applicants must be members of NDTA or dependents of an NDTA member in good standing. **Criteria:** The Forum, Education and Professional Development Committee will select scholarship recipients based upon the merit of each applicant as attested to by academic performance and extracurricular involvement in school and community life. Scholarships are limited to those seeking an undergraduate degree.

Funds Avail.: No specific amount. **To Apply:** Applicants must note that at the time of filing his/her application, the student must have satisfactorily completed 45 semester hours of work at regionally accredited colleges or universities. The regionally accredited college/university, which the applicant plans to attend must offer a minimum of 15 semester hours in transportation, supply chain management, or logistics or some combination of the above. The applicant must indicate on his/her application the transportation/physical distribution, logistics or information technology courses he/she plans to incorporate into his/her degree program. These courses must comprise at least 15 semester hours of the student's required hours for a degree. A brief statement from a responsible administrator stating that the proposed courses will constitute acceptable work toward a degree must be attached to the application. Blank application forms may be obtained by the NDTA member from: The forum, Education and Professional Development Committee; NDTA Headquarters; or his/her local Chapter. completed applications must be submitted to the Forum, Education and Professional Development Committee. **Deadline:** April 16.

4844 ■ Academic Scholarship Program B *(Undergraduate/Scholarship)*

Purpose: To assist freshmen college students and high school graduates to achieve academic goals. **Focus:** Transportation; Logistics. **Qualif.:** Applicants must be NDTA members or financial dependents under the IRS code of an NDTA member. **Criteria:** Selection will be based upon the merit of each applicant as attested to by academic performance and extracurricular involvement in school and community life.

Funds Avail.: No specific amount. **To Apply:** Blank application forms may be obtained by the NDTA member from: The forum, Education and Professional Development Committee; NDTA Headquarters; or his/her local Chapter. Completed applications must be submitted to the Forum, Education and Professional Development Committee. **Deadline:** April 16.

4845 ■ National Dental Hygienists' Association

PO Box 22463
Tampa, FL 33622
Free: 800-234-1096
E-mail: forndha@aol.com
URL: http://ndhaonline.org

4846 ■ National Dental Hygienists' Association Scholarships *(Undergraduate/Scholarship)*

Purpose: To increase interest in dental hygiene particularly among African American students by providing financial assistance. **Focus:** Dental hygiene. **Qualif.:** Applicant must be a current member of the NDHA; must be a U.S. citizen particularly African American; must have minimum of 2.5 GPA or greater. **Criteria:** Awards are given based on merit.

Funds Avail.: No specific amount. **To Apply:** Applicant must send completed application form (downloadable from the website); NDHA student membership of $35; a copy of official sealed transcript; a print verification of enrollment form signed by Registrar/Office of Dean of Students; a

Awards are arranged alphabetically below their administering organizations

passport type photo; two recommendation letters (one from a dental hygiene director and the other one from dental hygiene teacher or employer); proof of financial need; statement of leadership skills; and stated ideas on how to promote the profession of dental hygiene and the NDHA Organization. **Deadline:** March 15.

4847 ■ National Drug Enforcement Officers Association

PO Box 1475
Quantico, VA 22134-1475
Ph: (704)770-2050
Fax: (704)770-2051
E-mail: steven.r.peterson@usdoj.gov
URL: http://www.ndeoa.org

4848 ■ NDEOA Scholarships *(Undergraduate/Scholarship)*

Purpose: To financially support the education of a child of a NDEOA member. **Focus:** General Studies. **Qualif.:** Applicant must be graduating from high school; or a college student pursuing an undergraduate degree; have a GPA of 2.75 in a 4.0 scale; must be a dependent of an NDEOA member in good standing. **Criteria:** Selection is based on the application materials submitted.

Funds Avail.: $1,000. **To Apply:** Applicant must submit a completed application form; three letters of recommendation; transcript; and a written essay about the applicant's plans and goals, and why the applicant deserves the scholarship. **Deadline:** July 1.

4849 ■ National Eagle Scout Association

PO Box 152079
Irving, TX 75015-2079
Ph: (972)580-2114
E-mail: eagletter@netbsa.org
URL: http://www.nesa.org

4850 ■ American Legion Eagle Scout of the Year Scholarships *(High School/Scholarship)*

Purpose: To support the education of a student active in Boy Scouting, Varsity Scouting, or Venturing. **Focus:** General studies. **Qualif.:** Applicant must have received the Eagle Scout Award and the religious emblem awarded by his religious institution; have demonstrated practical citizenship in church, school, Scouting, and the community; son or grandson of an American Legion or American Legion Auxiliary member; or must be a member of a Scouting unit chartered to a Legion post, an Auxiliary unit, or a Sons of the American Legion squadron. **Criteria:** Selection is based on the committee's review on the applications.

Funds Avail.: $10,000 and $2500. **Number Awarded:** One recipient and three second placers. **To Apply:** Applicants must complete and file the nomination form. **Deadline:** March 1.

Remarks: Awarded by The American Legion. **Contact:** Contact the American Legion department in their state.

4851 ■ Rick Arkans Eagle Scout Scholarships *(High School/Scholarship)*

Purpose: To support the education of a student active in Boy Scouting, Varsity Scouting, or Venturing. **Focus:** General studies. **Qualif.:** Applicant must be currently registered and active in Boy Scouting, Varsity Scouting, or Venturing; have earned the Eagle Scout Award; have earned the Ner Tamid or Etz Chaim religious emblem; active in a synagogue; have demonstrated practical citizenship in the synagogue, school, Scouting unit, and community; have demonstrate financial need; and be enrolled in an accredited high school and in his final year. **Criteria:** Selection is based on the committee's review on the applications.

Funds Avail.: $1000. **Number Awarded:** 1. **To Apply:** Applicants must submit a complete application. **Deadline:** February 28.

Remarks: Sponsored by the National Jewish Committee on Scouting.

4852 ■ Birmingham-Southern College Eagle Scout Scholarships *(Undergraduate/Scholarship)*

Purpose: To assist the education of an Eagle scout student. **Focus:** General studies. **Qualif.:** Applicant must be an incoming freshmen at the Birmingham Southern College; and an Eagle Scout. **Criteria:** Selection.

Funds Avail.: $2500 per year. **To Apply:** Applicant must forward a letter of interest and student resume at the BSC Admissions Office. **Deadline:** January 15.

Remarks: Award is given by BirminghamSouthern College, Birmingham, Ala. **Contact:** Admission Office, Birmingham-Southern College Box 549008 Birmingham, AL 35254, at 800-523-5793.

4853 ■ Emmett J. Doerr Memorial Distinguished Scout Scholarships *(High School/Scholarship)*

Purpose: To support the education of high school seniors who are currently registered and active in Boy Scouting, Varsity Scouting, or Venturing. **Focus:** General studies. **Qualif.:** Applicants must be outstanding Catholic high-school seniors currently registered and active in Boy Scouting, Varsity Scouting, or Venturing; have earned the Eagle Scout Award or the Silver Award; have earned the Ad Altare Dei or Pope Pius XII religious emblem; have held a Scouting leadership position; and have served in parish. **Criteria:** Selection is based on the committee's review on the applications.

Funds Avail.: $1000-$2500. **Number Awarded:** 3. **To Apply:** Applicants must submit a complete application. **Deadline:** April 1.

Remarks: Sponsored by the National Catholic Committee on Scouting. **Contact:** Barb Nestel, National Catholic Committee on Scouting, nccs@netbsa.org.

4854 ■ Dofflemyer Scholarships *(Undergraduate/Scholarship)*

Purpose: To assist the education of an Eagle Scout student. **Focus:** General studies. **Qualif.:** Applicant must be an Eagle Scout entering Stanford University. **Criteria:** Selection is based on a family's demonstrated need.

Funds Avail.: Varies. **To Apply:** Applicants must follow the university's standard application process. **Deadline:** February 1.

Remarks: Awarded by Stanford University, Stanford, Calif. **Contact:** Financial Aid Office, Stanford University, Montag Hall 355 Galvez St. Stanford, CA 94305-6106, at 888-326-3773, or financialaid@stanford.edu.

4855 ■ Eastern Orthodox Scouting Scholarships *(High School/Scholarship)*

Purpose: To support the education of a student active in Scouting, Varsity Scouting, or Venturing. **Focus:** General studies. **Qualif.:** Applicant must be registered and active in Boy Scouting or Girl Scouting; must have earned the Eagle Scout Award (Boy Scouts) or the Gold Award (Girl Scouts); active in an Eastern Orthodox church; have earned the Alpha Omega religious emblem; and enrolled in an accredited high school, in the final year. **Criteria:** Selection is based on merit.

Funds Avail.: $1000. **Number Awarded:** 3. **To Apply:** Applicants must submit four letters of recommendation with the application. **Deadline:** May 1.

Remarks: Awarded by the Eastern Orthodox Committee on Scouting. **Contact:** George N. Boulukos, 862 Guy Lombardo Ave. Freeport, New York 11520, at 516-868-4050.

4856 ■ Epsilon Tau Pi's Soaring Eagle Scholarships *(Undergraduate/Scholarship)*

Purpose: To assist the education of an Eagle Scout student. **Focus:** General studies. **Qualif.:** Applicant must be an Eagle Scout entering as freshman at the University of Dayton; have demonstrated leadership ability in Scouting, and has a strong record of community participation beyond Scouting; have a SAT score of at least 1600 or an ACT score of at least 25. **Criteria:** Selection is based on the committee's review on the applications.

Funds Avail.: $500. **To Apply:** Applicants must visit the Epsilon Tau Pi Alpha Chapter website for the details of application. **Deadline:** August 3.

Remarks: Awarded by Epsilon Tau Pi Alpha Chapter, University of Dayton, Dayton, Ohio. **Contact:** Soaring Eagle Scholarship, Epsilon Tau Pi, 1915 Trinity Ave. Dayton, OH 45409

4857 ■ Gaebe Eagle Scout Awards *(Undergraduate/Scholarship)*

Purpose: To assist the education of an Eagle Scout student. **Focus:** General studies. **Qualif.:** Applicant must be entering as freshman at Johnson and Wales University and must be an Eagle Scout. **Criteria:** Selection is based on the application, proof of Eagle Scout status, and high school transcript.

Funds Avail.: $1000. **To Apply:** Applications are available at JWU's NSO Office; submit application and a transcript of grades to the NSO Office. **Deadline:** February 1.

Remarks: The scholarship may be used at JWU's campuses in Providence, R.I.; North Miami, Fla.; Denver, Colo.; and Charlotte, N.C. Awarded by Johnson and Wales University, Providence, R.I. **Contact:** National Student Organizations, Johnson and Wales University, 8 Abbott Park Place Providence, RI 02903, at 800-342-5598, x-2345.

4858 ■ Gold Award/Eagle Scout Scholarships *(Undergraduate/Scholarship)*

Purpose: To assist the education of a boy and girl scout student. **Focus:** General studies. **Qualif.:** Applicant must have a high-school core GPA of at least 2.5 as calculated by Mississippi State University, or at least 48 hours of transferable community college course credit with a minimum cumulative GPA of 2.5; a Mississippi resident or have received the Eagle Scout Award or Gold Award in a Mississippi-based Scouting council. **Criteria:** Selection is based on the committee's review on the applications.

Funds Avail.: $1000 ($500 per semester). **To Apply:** Applicants must follow the university's standard application process. **Deadline:** August 1.

Remarks: Awarded by the Mississippi State University, Mississippi State, Miss. **Contact:** Office of Admissions and Scholarships, Mississippi State University P.O. Box 6334 Mississippi State, MS 39762-6334, at 662-325-2224, or admit@msstate.edu.

4859 ■ Zenon C.R. Hansen Leadership Scholarships *(Undergraduate/Scholarship)*

Purpose: To assist the education of an Eagle Scout student. **Focus:** General studies. **Qualif.:** Applicant must be a full-time Doane College student who is an Eagle Scout; active in the Boy Scouts of America, and planning to remain active in Scouting and leadership activities. **Criteria:** Selection is based on the committee's review on the applications.

Funds Avail.: Amount dependent on cost of tuition. **To Apply:** Applicants must visit the Doane College website for the details of application. **Deadline:** March 10.

Remarks: Award given by Doane College, Crete, Neb. **Contact:** Financial Aid Office, Doane College 1014 Boswell Avenue Crete, NE 68333, at 800-333-6263. .

4860 ■ Arthur M. and Berdena King Eagle Scout Scholarships *(High School/Scholarship)*

Purpose: To support the education of Eagle Scouts. **Focus:** General studies. **Qualif.:** Applicant must be Eagle Scouts currently registered in Scouting and have not reached their 19th birthday. **Criteria:** Selection is based on the application.

Funds Avail.: $8000, $4000, and $2000. **Number Awarded:** 3. **To Apply:** applicants must submit a completed application form together with the Four Generation ancestor chart, and the 500-word essay. **Deadline:** Varies by state and chapter.

Remarks: Awarded by the National Society of the Sons of the American Revolution. **Contact:** Contact the SAR department in their state.

4861 ■ Lamar University College of Engineering Scholarships *(Undergraduate/Scholarship)*

Purpose: To assist the education of an Eagle Scout student. **Focus:** Engineering. **Qualif.:** Applicant must be a Lamar University undergraduate student, including entering freshmen, majoring in chemical, civil, electrical, industrial, or mechanical engineering. **Criteria:** Preference is given to an Eagle Scout student.

Funds Avail.: $5000 per year. **To Apply:** Applicants must submit a completed Scholarship application form. **Deadline:** February 1.

Remarks: Award is given by Lamar University College of Engineering, Beaumont, Texas. **Contact:** Ron Peevy, Director of Recruiting and Cooperative Education, Lamar University College of Engineering P.O. Box 10057 Beaumont, TX 77710, at 409-880-7870, or ronald.peevy@lamar.edu START HERE...

4862 ■ Lindenwood University Scouting Scholarships *(Undergraduate/Scholarship)*

Purpose: To assist the education of an Eagle Scout student. **Focus:** General studies. **Qualif.:** Applicants must be undergraduate residential students who have been Boy Scouts. **Criteria:** Selection is based on the committee's review of the applications.

Funds Avail.: $6000-$12,000 per year. **Number Awarded:** 3. **To Apply:** Applicants must visit the Lindenwood University website for the details of application.

Remarks: Awards given by Lindenwood University, St. Charles, Mo. **Contact:** Office of Undergraduate Admissions, Lindenwood University 209 South Kings Highway St. Charles, MO 63301-1695, at 636-949-4949, or admissions@lindenwood.edu.

4863 ■ McDaniel College Eagle Scout Scholarships *(Undergraduate/Scholarship)*

Purpose: To assist the education of an Eagle Scout student. **Focus:** General studies. **Qualif.:** Applicant must be enrolled full-time and have a minimum 2.50 cumulative GPA and a minimum SAT-I combined score of 1000. **Criteria:** Selection is based on the committee's review on the applications.

Funds Avail.: $2000. **To Apply:** Applicants must visit the McDaniel College website for the details of application. **Deadline:** February 1.

Remarks: Awarded by McDaniel College (formerly Western Maryland College), Westminster, Md. **Contact:** McDaniel College, 2 College Hill Westminster, MD 21157, at 410-848-7000.

4864 ■ Newman University Scouting Scholarships *(Undergraduate/Scholarship)*

Purpose: To assist the education of a boy and girl scout student. **Focus:** General studies. **Qualif.:** Applicant must be an Eagle Scout or a Girl Scout (Gold Award winners) with a high school GPA of 2.5 or higher on a 4.0 scale; a first-time freshmen at Newman University; full-time student and maintains a cumulative GPA of at least 2.25; and active in one or more campus organization each year. **Criteria:** Selection is based on the committee's review on the applications.

Funds Avail.: $1500 per year. **To Apply:** Applicants must visit the Newman University website for the details of application.

Remarks: Awarded by Newman University, Wichita, Kan. **Contact:** Newman University, 3100 McCormick Ave. Wichita, KS 67213, at 877-639-6268.

4865 ■ Saint Vincent College Eagle Scout Scholarships *(Undergraduate/Scholarship)*

Purpose: To assist the education of an Eagle Scout student. **Focus:** General studies. **Qualif.:** Applicant must be an Eagle Scout student admitted at Saint Vincent College. **Criteria:** All Eagle Scout student will be qualified.

Funds Avail.: $500. **To Apply:** Applicants must submit a documentation to the admission counselor as part of the admission process.

Remarks: Awards given by Saint Vincent College, Latrobe, Penn. **Contact:** Saint Vincent College, 300 Fraser Purchase Road Latrobe, PA 15650, at 800-782-5549.

4866 ■ University of Louisville Eagle Scout Scholarships *(Undergraduate/Scholarship)*

Purpose: To assist the education of an Eagle Scout student. **Focus:** General studies. **Qualif.:** Applicant must be an incoming freshmen; a resident of Kentucky or Indiana; achieved the rank of Eagle Scout in the Lincoln Heritage Council, Blue Grass Council, Shawnee Trails Council, Dan Beard Council, or Tri-State Area Council; have a minimum high-school GPA of 3.35 on a 4.0 scale and a minimum score of 24 on the ACT or 1090 on the SAT-I. **Criteria:** Selection is based on the committee's review on the applications.

Funds Avail.: $2000 to full in-state tuition. **To Apply:** Applicants must visit the University of Louisville website for the details of application. **Deadline:** January 15.

Remarks: Awarded by University of Louisville, Louisville, Ky. **Contact:** Student Financial Aid Office, University of Louisville, Louisville, KY 40292, at 502-852-5511, or finaid@louisville.edu.

4867 ■ Chester M. Vernon Memorial Eagle Scout Scholarships *(High School/Scholarship)*

Purpose: To support the education of a student active in Boy Scouting, Varsity Scouting, or Venturing. **Focus:** General studies. **Qualif.:** Applicant must be currently registered and active in Boy Scouting, Varsity Scouting, or Venturing; have earned the Eagle Scout Award; have earned the Ner Tamid or Etz Chaim religious emblem; active in a synagogue; have demonstrated practical citizenship in the synagogue, school, Scouting unit, and community; have demonstrated financial need; and be enrolled in an accredited high school and in his final year. **Criteria:** Selection is based on the committee's review on the applications.

Funds Avail.: $1000 per year. **Number Awarded:** 1. **To Apply:** Applicants must submit a complete application. **Deadline:** February 28.

Remarks: Sponsored by the National Jewish Committee on Scouting.

4868 ■ Veterans of Foreign Wars Scout of the Year *(High School/Scholarship)*

Purpose: To support the education of a student active in Boy Scouting, Varsity Scouting, or Venturing. **Focus:** General studies. **Qualif.:** Applicant must have received the Eagle Scout Award, the Venturing Silver Award, or the Sea Scout Quartermaster Award; have demonstrated practical citizenship in school, Scouting, and the community. **Criteria:** Selection is based on the committee's review on the applications.

Funds Avail.: $5000. **To Apply:** Application must be submitted through a single, local VFW post. **Deadline:** March 1.

Remarks: Awarded by The Veterans of Foreign Wars of the United States. **Contact:** Veterans of Foreign Wars, 406 W. 34th St. Kansas City, Missouri 64111 816-756-3390, info@vfw.org.

4869 ■ Frank L. Weil Memorial Eagle Scout Scholarships *(Undergraduate/Scholarship)*

Purpose: To support the education of a student active in Boy Scouting, Varsity Scouting, or Venturing. **Focus:** General studies. **Qualif.:** Applicant must be currently registered and active in Boy Scouting, Varsity Scouting, or Venturing; have earned the Eagle Scout Award; have earned the Ner Tamid or Etz Chaim religious emblem; active in a synagogue; have demonstrated practical citizenship in the synagogue, school, Scouting unit, and community; and be enrolled in an accredited high school and in his final year. **Criteria:** Selection is based on the committee's review on the applications.

Funds Avail.: $1000 and $500. **Number Awarded:** 1 recipient and 2 runners-up. **To Apply:** Applicants must submit a complete application. **Deadline:** February 28.

Remarks: Sponsored by the National Jewish Committee on Scouting.

4870 ■ National Electrical Manufacturers Representatives Association
600 White Plains Rd., Ste. 600
Tarrytown, NY 10591-1504
Ph: (914)524-8650
Fax: (914)524-8655
Free: 800-446-3672
E-mail: nemra@nemra.org
URL: http://www.nemra.org

4871 ■ NEMRA Educational Scholarship Foundation *(Undergraduate/Scholarship)*

Purpose: To reward the academic excellence of the sons and daughters of NEMRA members and their employees. **Focus:** General studies. **Qualif.:** Applicants must be children of members of NEMRA (or their employees) who are in good standing as of December 31, and attend, or plan to attend (full-time) an accredited college, university or vocational-technical school. **Criteria:** Scholarships are awarded based on academic record, as well as participation in school and community activities, work experience, and unusual personal or family circumstances with preference given to applicants demonstrating interest in club membership or majoring in Business administration, marketing and sales or electrical engineering-related fields.

Funds Avail.: No specific amount. **Number Awarded:** 18. **To Apply:** Applicants must submit a completed and signed application form; a current official transcript; a recommendation from an individual who can give an honest assessment of the applicant's academic and personal abilities such as a teacher, pastor or college advisor. Application materials must be placed in a stamped No. 10 business size envelope. Two first class stamps are required. **Deadline:** January 7.

Remarks: Founded in 1985 through a bequest of the late Donald Egan of the Daniel Woodhead Company.

4872 ■ National Environmental Health Association
720 S Colorado Blvd., Ste. 1000-N
Denver, CO 80246
Ph: (303)756-9090
Fax: (303)691-9490
E-mail: staff@neha.org
URL: http://www.neha.org

4873 ■ National Environmental Health Association Scholarship Fund *(Graduate, Undergraduate/Scholarship)*

Purpose: To encourage and support early commitment by students to a career in environmental health. **Focus:** Environmental science. **Qualif.:** Applicants must be enrolled in an undergraduate or graduate program of studies in environmental health sciences and/or public health. **Criteria:** Applicants are selected based on the committee's review of the application materials.

Funds Avail.: No specific amount. **To Apply:** Applicants must complete the official application form (no faxes, copies or email submissions will be accepted); must provide an official copy of academic transcript; submit two faculty letters of recommendation from the school in which they are currently enrolled; and submit a letter of recommendation from an active NEHA member (three letters of recommendation must be received for an application to be considered). **Deadline:** February 1. **Contact:** Nelson E. Fabian at the above address (see entry 4872).

4874 ■ National Federation of the Blind
1800 Johnson St.
Baltimore, MD 21230
Ph: (410)659-9314
Fax: (410)685-5653
URL: http://www.nfb.org

4875 ■ Hermoine Grant Calhoun Scholarships *(Undergraduate/Scholarship)*

Purpose: To recognize achievement of blind scholars and to create opportunity for all blind people. **Focus:** General studies. **Qualif.:** All applicants must be legally blind; he/she must be pursuing or planning to pursue a full-time, post-secondary course of study in a degree program at a United States institution; he/she must be participant in NFB national convention and in all scheduled scholarship program activities. **Criteria:** Committee of Scholarship Program will evaluate the application based on academic excellence, community service, and financial need.

Funds Avail.: $3,000. **Number Awarded:** 22. **To Apply:** Applicant must fill out the application form; he/she must submit two letters of recommendation from individuals that can describe the academic ability, leadership skills, and/or community involvement; copies of transcript of record and a photocopy of score reports for all standardized tests taken for college admission(ACT, SAT or other); applicant must provide a letter of proof of legal blindness from a qualified professional; and an affiliate President's letter. **Deadline:** March 31.

4876 ■ Jennica Ferguson Memorial Scholarships *(Undergraduate/Scholarship)*

Purpose: To recognize achievement by blind scholars and create opportunity for all blind people; to keep alive the memory of a young woman who dealt with blindness and terminal illness with grace and strength, she frequently assured others she drew from the Federation and from her faith in God. **Focus:** Education, Elementary; Education, Secondary. **Qualif.:** Applicant must be legally blind; he/she must be pursuing or planning a career in elementary, secondary, or postsecondary teaching; he/she must be participant in NFB national convention and in all scheduled scholarship program activities. **Criteria:** committee of Scholarship Program will evaluate the application based on academic excellence, community service, and financial need.

Funds Avail.: $5,000. **Number Awarded:** 14. **To Apply:** Applicant must fill out the application form; he/she must submit two letters of recommendation from individuals that can describe the academic ability, leadership skills, and/or community involvement; copies of transcript of record and a photocopy of score reports for all standardized tests taken for college admission(ACT, SAT or other); applicant must provide a letter of proof of legal blindness from a qualified professional; and an affiliate President's letter. **Deadline:** March 31.

4877 ■ Guide Dogs for the Blind Dorothea and Roland Bohde Leadership Scholarships *(Postgraduate/Scholarship)*

Purpose: To recognize achievement of blind scholars and to create opportunity for all blind people. **Focus:** Education. **Qualif.:** All applicants must be legally blind; he/she must be pursuing or planning to pursue a full-time, postgraduate education in any field; he/she must be participant in NFB national convention and in all scheduled scholarship program activities. **Criteria:** Committee of Scholarship Program will evaluate the application based on the academic excellence, community service, and financial need.

Funds Avail.: No specific amount. **To Apply:** Applicant must fill out the application form; he/she must submit two letters of recommendation from individuals that can describe the academic ability, leadership skills, and/or community involvement; copies of transcript of record and a photocopy of score reports for all standardized tests taken for college admission (ACT, SAT or other); an applicant must provide a letter of proof of legal blindness from a qualified professional; and an affiliate President's letter. **Deadline:** March 31.

4878 ■ Kenneth Jernigan Scholarships *(Undergraduate/Scholarship)*

Purpose: To recognize achievement by blind scholars and create opportunity for all blind people. **Focus:** General studies. **Qualif.:** All applicants must be legally blind; he/she must be pursuing or planning to pursue a full-time, postsecondary course of study in a Degree Program at a United States institution; he/she must be participant in NFB national convention and in all scheduled scholarship program activities. **Criteria:** Committee of Scholarship Program will evaluate the application based on the academic excellence, community service, and financial need.

Funds Avail.: $12,000. **Number Awarded:** 1. **To Apply:** Applicant must fill out the application form; he/she must submit two letters of recommendation from individuals that can describe the academic ability, leadership skills, and/or community involvement; copies of transcript of record and a photocopy of score reports for all standardized tests taken for college admission (ACT, SAT or other); applicant must provide a letter of proof of legal blindness from a qualified professional; and an affiliate President's letter. **Deadline:** March 31.

4879 ■ Kuchler-Killian Memorial Scholarships *(Undergraduate/Scholarship)*

Purpose: To recognize achievement of blind scholars and to create opportunity for all blind people. **Focus:** General studies. **Qualif.:** All applicants must be legally blind; he/she must be pursuing or planning to pursue a full-time, postsecondary course of study in a degree program at a United States institution; he/she must be participant in NFB national convention and in all scheduled scholarship program activities. **Criteria:** Committee of Scholarship Program will evaluate the application based on the academic excellence, community service, and financial need.

Funds Avail.: $3,000. **Number Awarded:** 22. **To Apply:** Applicant must fill out the application form; he/she must submit two letters of recommendation from individuals that can describe the academic ability, leadership skills, and/or community involvement; copies of transcript of record and a photocopy of score reports for all standardized tests taken for college admission(ACT, SAT or other); applicant must provide a letter of proof of legal blindness from a qualified professional; and an affiliate President's letter. **Deadline:** March 31.

4880 ■ Michael Marucci Memorial Scholarships *(Undergraduate/Scholarship)*

Purpose: To recognize achievement of blind scholars and to create opportunity for all blind people. **Focus:** History; Geography; Political science. **Qualif.:** Applicants must be legally blind; he/she must be pursuing or planning a career in history, geography, or political science with a concentration in international studies or study requiring study abroad; he/she must be participant in NFB national convention and in all scheduled scholarship program activities. **Criteria:** Committee of Scholarship Program will evaluate the application based on academic excellence, community service, and financial need.

Funds Avail.: $5,000. **To Apply:** Applicant must fill out the application form; he/she must submit two letters of recommendation from individuals that can describe the academic ability, leadership skills, and/or community involvement; copies of transcript of record and a photocopy of score reports for all standardized tests taken for college admission(ACT, SAT or other); applicant must provide a letter of proof of legal blindness from a qualified professional; and an affiliate President's letter. **Deadline:** March 31.

4881 ■ National Federation of the Blind Educator of Tomorrow Award *(Undergraduate/Scholarship)*

Purpose: To recognize achievement of blind scholars and to create opportunity for all blind people. **Focus:** Education, Elementary; Education, Secondary. **Qualif.:** All applicants must be legally blind; he/she must be pursuing or planning a career in elementary, secondary, or postsecondary teaching; he/she must be participant in NFB national convention and in all scheduled scholarship program activities. **Criteria:** Committee of Scholarship Program will evaluate the application based on academic excellence, community service, and financial need.

Funds Avail.: $3,000. **To Apply:** Applicant must fill out the application form; he/she must submit two letters of recommendation from individuals that can describe the academic ability, leadership skills, and/or community involvement; copies of transcript of record and a photocopy of score reports for all standardized tests taken for college admission (ACT, SAT or other); applicant must provide a letter of proof of legal blindness from a qualified professional; and an affiliate President's letter. **Deadline:** March 31.

4882 ■ Charles and Melva T. Owen Memorial Scholarships *(Undergraduate/Scholarship)*

Purpose: To recognize achievement of blind scholars and to create opportunity for all blind people. **Focus:** General studies. **Qualif.:** All applicants must be legally blind; he/she must be pursuing or planning to pursue a full-time, postsecondary course of study in a degree program at a United States institution; he/she must be participant in NFB national convention and in all scheduled scholarship program activities. **Criteria:** Committee of Scholarship Program will evaluate the application based on academic excellence, community service, and financial need.

Funds Avail.: $10,000. **Number Awarded:** 1. **To Apply:** Applicant must fill out the application form; he/she must submit two letters of recommendation from individuals that can describe the academic ability, leadership skills, and/or community involvement; copies of transcript of record and a photocopy of score reports for all standardized tests taken for college admission(ACT, SAT or other); applicant must provide a letter of proof of legal blindness from a qualified professional; and an affiliate President's letter. **Deadline:** March 31.

4883 ■ E.U. Parker Scholarships *(Undergraduate/Scholarship)*

Purpose: To recognize achievement of blind scholars and to create opportunity for all blind people. **Focus:** General studies. **Qualif.:** All applicants must be legally blind; he/she must be pursuing or planning to pursue a full-time, post-secondary course of study in a degree program at a United States institution; he must be participant in NFB national convention and in all scheduled scholarship program activities. **Criteria:** Committee of Scholarship Program will evaluate the application based on the academic excellence, community service, and financial need.

Funds Avail.: $3,000. **To Apply:** Applicant must fill out the application form; he/she must submit two letters of recommendation from individuals that can describe the academic ability, leadership skills, and/or community involvement; copies of transcript of record and a photocopy of score reports for all standardized tests taken for college admission (ACT, SAT or other); applicant must provide a letter of proof of legal blindness from a qualified professional; and an affiliate President's letter. **Deadline:** March 31.

4884 ■ Howard B. Rickard Scholarships *(Undergraduate/Scholarship)*

Purpose: To recognize achievement of blind scholars and to create opportunity for all blind people. **Focus:** Law; Medicine; Engineering; Architecture; Natural Science. **Qualif.:** All applicants must be legally blind; he/she must be pursuing or planning to study in the field of law, medicine, engineering, architecture or the natural science; he/she must be participant in NFB national convention and in all scheduled scholarship program activities. **Criteria:** Committee of Scholarship Program will evaluate the application based on academic excellence, community service, and financial need.

Funds Avail.: $3,000. **To Apply:** Applicant must fill out the application form; he/she must submit two letters of recommendation from individuals that can describe the academic ability, leadership skills, and/or community involvement; copies of transcript of record and a photocopy of score reports for all standardized tests taken for college admission (ACT, SAT or other); an applicant must provide a letter of proof of legal blindness from a qualified professional; and an affiliate President's letter. **Deadline:** March 31.

4885 ■ National Federation of Paralegal Associations

PO Box 2016
Edmonds, WA 98020
Ph: (425)967-0045
Fax: (425)771-9588
E-mail: info@paralegals.org
URL: http://www.paralegals.org

4886 ■ NFPA/PACE Scholarships *(Professional Development/Scholarship)*

Purpose: To promote a global presence for the paralegal profession and leadership in the community. **Focus:** Paralegal studies. **Qualif.:** Applicants must be NFPA members; must be eligible to take the PACE exam. **Criteria:** Recipients are selected based on the quality of the essay and financial needs.

Funds Avail.: No specific amount. **To Apply:** Applicants must complete the application form; must sign the affidavit; write an essay of no more than four-pages responding to the question "Why is it important to become a PACE Registered Paralegal?" **Deadline:** July 11. **Contact:** National Federation of Paralegal Associations at the above address (see entry 4885).

4887 ■ NFPA and Thomson West Scholarships *(Undergraduate/Scholarship)*

Purpose: To promote a global presence for the paralegal profession and leadership in the legal community. **Focus:** Paralegal studies. **Qualif.:** Applicant must be a part-time or full-time, currently-enrolled student or accepted student in an accredited paralegal education program or college level program with emphasis in paralegal studies. Applicants must demonstrate or maintain at least a "B" average. **Criteria:** Recipients are selected based on scholastic excellence, participation in campus and paralegal program leadership activities, community service, review of the writing samples, and financial need.

Funds Avail.: $5,000. **To Apply:** Applicants must submit original and three copies of application form; letter of recommendation from the director of paralegal education program or an employer; a double-spaced essay of required topics (not more than four pages); recent official transcript showing at least a "B" average. High school transcripts are acceptable only if an applicant has not completed a college semester. **Deadline:** In 2004, deadline was August 4. **Contact:** National Federation of Paralegal Associations at the above address (see entry 4885).

4888 ■ National Federation of Republican Women

124 N Alfred St.
Alexandria, VA 22314
Ph: (703)548-9688
Fax: (703)548-9836
E-mail: mail@nfrw.org
URL: http://www.nfrw.org

4889 ■ National Pathfinder Scholarships *(Graduate, Undergraduate/Scholarship)*

Purpose: To support students with their education. **Focus:** General studies. **Qualif.:** Applicant must be undergraduate sophomore, junior or senior, or student enrolled in a master's degree program. **Criteria:** Applications must be received by applicant's State Federation President and will choose an application and submit to NFRW.

Funds Avail.: $2500. **Number Awarded:** 3. **To Apply:** Applicants must submit a completed application form together with three letters of recommendation (include contact numbers of the authors); an official copy of recent college transcript; a 1-page typed essay stating why applicant deserves the scholarship; another 1-page typed essay on career goals; a photograph (optional); and State Federation President Certification. **Deadline:** June 15.

Remarks: Established in 1985 in honor of First Lady Nancy Reagan.

4890 ■ Betty Rendel Scholarships *(Undergraduate/Scholarship)*

Purpose: To support students with their education. **Focus:** Political science; Government; Economics. **Qualif.:** Applicant must be an undergraduate student majoring in political science, government or economics; and have completed at least two years of college coursework. **Criteria:** Applications must be received by applicant's State Federation

President and will choose an application and submit to NFRW.

Funds Avail.: $1000. **Number Awarded:** 3. **To Apply:** Applicants must submit a completed application form together with three letters of recommendation (include contact numbers of the authors); an official copy of recent college transcript; a 1-page typed essay stating why deserve the scholarship; another 1-page typed essay on career goals; a photograph (optional); and State Federation President Certification. **Deadline:** June 1.

Remarks: Established in 1995 in honor of NFRW Past President Betty Rendel's extraordinary leadership skills and dedication to the Republican Party in her home state of Indiana.

4891 ■ National Forum for Black Public Administrators

777 N Capitol St. NE, Ste. 807
Washington, DC 20002
Ph: (202)408-9300
Fax: (202)408-8558
E-mail: webmaster@nfbpa.org
URL: http://www.nfbpa.org

4892 ■ CIGNA Healthcare Graduate Scholarships *(Graduate/Scholarship)*

Purpose: To support the education and development of African-American students and prepare them for careers in public administration. **Focus:** Public administration. **Qualif.:** Applicants must be full-time students, working towards a graduate degree in public administration, political science, urban affairs, public policy, or a related field preferably at an HBCU with excellent interpersonal and analytical abilities, strong oral and written communication skills and a 3.0 or better GPA for at least 1 remaining full time semester. **Criteria:** Applicants will be evaluated based on some criteria designed by the Scholarship Selection Committee.

Funds Avail.: $5,000. **Number Awarded:** 2. **To Apply:** Applicants must submit cover letter describing status as a student and other relevant information that might be used in evaluating application (extra-curricula activities, volunteer activities, etc.); official copies of all graduate (if applicable) and undergraduate transcripts; two reference letters, at least one of which should be from a faculty member; three-page essay, detailing autobiography and career goals and objectives; and a current resume. **Deadline:** February 27.

4893 ■ CIGNA Healthcare Undergraduate Scholarships *(Undergraduate/Scholarship)*

Purpose: To support the education and development of African-American students and prepare them for careers in public administration. **Focus:** Public administration; Political science; Urban affairs/design/planning. **Qualif.:** Applicants must be full-time students, working towards an undergraduate degree in public administration, political science, urban affairs, public policy, or a related field preferably at an HBCU with excellent interpersonal and analytical abilities, strong oral and written communication skills and a 3.5 or better grade point average for completed 1 full-time college semester and at least 1 full-time academic year. **Criteria:** Recipient will be selected based on financial need.

Funds Avail.: $1,000. **Number Awarded:** 1. **To Apply:** Applicants must submit a cover letter describing your current student status and other relevant information that might be used in evaluating the application (extra-curricular activities, volunteer activities, etc); official copies of all undergraduate transcripts; scores from the American College Testing (ACT) program or the Scholastic Aptitude Test (SAT) administered by the College Entrance Examination Board; a copy of their Application for Federal Student Aid (FASFA); two (2) reference letters (at least one of which should be from a faculty member); three-page essay detailing his/her autobiography and career goals and objectives; three-page essay answering the question: In your opinion, what are the five most critical skills public administrators ought to possess, and why?; and a current resume. **Deadline:** February 27.

4894 ■ Johnnie L. Cochran, Jr./MWH Scholarships *(Undergraduate/Scholarship)*

Purpose: To help NFBPA further achieve its mission of attracting the best and brightest African Americans to careers in public service. **Focus:** Public service. **Qualif.:** Applicants must be full-time students working towards an undergraduate or graduate degree in public administration, political science, urban affairs, public policy, or a related field who have excellent interpersonal and analytical abilities, strong oral and written communication skills and have 3.0 or better GPA for at least 1 full time semester remaining. **Criteria:** Applicants will be evaluated based on the criteria designed by the Scholarship Committee.

Funds Avail.: $5,000. **To Apply:** Applicants must submit cover letter describing current student status and other relevant information that might be used in evaluating application; official copies of all graduate and undergraduate transcripts; two reference letters (at least one of which should be from a faculty member); three-page essay detailing autobiography and career goals and objectives; and current resume.

4895 ■ The Future Colleagues Scholarships *(Undergraduate/Scholarship)*

Purpose: To provide financial assistance for the education of undergraduate students pursuing a career in public service. **Focus:** Public service. **Qualif.:** Applicants must be full-time undergraduate students with average academic credentials (2.5 to 3.0) and strong written, oral and analytical abilities, and have at least 1 full-time semester remaining. **Criteria:** Applicants will be evaluated based on the criteria designed by the Scholarship Selection Committee.

Funds Avail.: $1,000. **To Apply:** Applicants must submit a cover letter describing the current student status and other relevant information that might be used in evaluating the application (extra-curricular activities, volunteer activities, etc); a 500-word essay which provides an example of prior public or community service involvement and how it has influenced your future aspirations in public administration; official copies of all undergraduate transcripts; two (2) reference letters (at least one of which should be from a faculty member); and a current resume. **Deadline:** February 27.

4896 ■ Land-Use Planning Scholarships *(Graduate/Scholarship)*

Purpose: To support the education and development of post-secondary African American students. **Focus:** Public service. **Qualif.:** Applicants must be full-time students working towards a graduate degree (master's or doctoral) in urban planning or a related field (such as transportation engineering, landscape architecture, environmental planning, etc.); must be enrolled in an accredited college or university and either have a home domicile in the state of Maryland or attend a college or university located in

Awards are arranged alphabetically below their administering organizations

Maryland; should have excellent interpersonal and analytical abilities, strong oral and written communication skills; should have a 3.0 or better grade point average and at least 1 full time semester remaining (after May 2008). **Criteria:** Applicants will be evaluated by the Scholarship Selection Committee.

Funds Avail.: $3,000. **To Apply:** Applicants must submit a cover letter describing current student status and other relevant information that might be used in evaluating applications; official copies of all graduate and undergraduate transcripts; two reference letters, at least one of which should be from a faculty member; three-page essay, detailing his/her autobiography and career goals and objectives and current resume.

4897 ■ Willie T. Loud - CH2M Hill Scholarships *(Undergraduate/Scholarship)*

Purpose: To assist NFBPA to further achieve its mission of grooming the next generation of African Americans for careers in public service. **Focus:** Public service. **Qualif.:** Applicants must be full-time students with 3.0 or better GPA who are at least 1 full-time semester remaining or working towards a Bachelor's or Master's degree in Public Administration or a related field and should have strong interpersonal skills, excellent writing, analytical, and oral communication abilities. **Criteria:** Applicants will be evaluated based on criteria designed by the Scholarship Committee.

Funds Avail.: No specific amount. **To Apply:** Applicant must submit a cover letter describing current student status and other relevant information that might be used in evaluating application; official copies of all graduate and undergraduate transcripts; two reference letters (at least one of which should be from a faculty member); three-page essay detailing his/her autobiography and career goals and objectives; and current resume.

4898 ■ McKinley Financial Scholarships *(Graduate, Undergraduate/Scholarship)*

Purpose: To support the education and development of African-American students and prepare them for careers in public administration. **Focus:** Public administration. **Qualif.:** Applicants must be full-time students, working towards an undergraduate or graduate degree in public administration, political science, urban affairs, public policy or a related field with excellent interpersonal and analytical abilities, strong oral and written communication skills and 3.0 or better grade point average for at least 1 full time remaining semester. **Criteria:** Applicants will be selected based on some criteria by the Scholarship Selection Committee.

Funds Avail.: $1,000. **To Apply:** Applicants must submit a cover letter describing current student status and other relevant information that might be used in evaluating the application (extra-curricular activities, volunteer activities, etc.); official copies of all graduate (if applicable) and undergraduate transcripts; two reference letters (at least one of which should be from a faculty member); three-page essay detailing his/her autobiography and career goals and objectives; and a current resume. **Deadline:** February 27.

4899 ■ NFBPA/CDM Scholarships *(Undergraduate/Scholarship)*

Purpose: To help NFBPA further achieve its mission of attracting the best and brightest African Americans to careers in public service. **Focus:** Public service. **Qualif.:** Applicants must be full-time students working towards an undergraduate or graduate degree in public administration, political science, urban affairs, public policy, or a related field with excellent interpersonal and analytical abilities, strong oral and written communication skills, have 3.0 GPA and/or have at least 1 full time semester remaining. **Criteria:** Applicants will be evaluated based on criteria designed by the Scholarship Committee.

Funds Avail.: $5,000. **To Apply:** Applicants must submit a cover letter describing current student status and other relevant information that might be used in evaluating application; official copies of all graduate and undergraduate transcripts; two reference letters (at least one of which should be from a faculty member); three-page essay, detailing his/her autobiography and career goals and objectives; and current resume.

4900 ■ RA Consulting Service Maria Riley Scholarships *(Graduate, Undergraduate/Scholarship)*

Purpose: To provide financial assistance for the education and development of public administrators serving in the engineering and information technology field. **Focus:** Engineering. **Qualif.:** Applicants must be full-time students, working towards an undergraduate or graduate degree in engineering or information technology with excellent interpersonal and analytical abilities, strong oral and written communication skills and a 3.0 or better grade point average for at least 1 remaining full time semester. **Criteria:** Applicants will be evaluated by the Scholarship Selection Committee.

Funds Avail.: $1,500. **To Apply:** Applicants must submit cover letter describing current student status, and other relevant information that might be used in evaluating your application (extra-curricula activities, volunteer activities, etc); official copies of all graduate (if applicable) and undergraduate transcripts (transcripts must be included in application package, not sent separately); two reference letters (at least one of which should be from a faculty member); three-page essay detailing his/her autobiography and career goals and objectives; and a current resume. **Deadline:** February 27.

4901 ■ National Foster Parent Association

7512 Stanich Ln., Ste. 6
Gig Harbor, WA 98335
Ph: (253)853-4000
Fax: (253)853-4001
E-mail: info@nfpaonline.org
URL: http://www.nfpainc.org

4902 ■ NFPA Youth Scholarships *(Undergraduate/Scholarship)*

Purpose: To support foster parents in achieving safety, permanence and well-being for the children and youth in their care. **Focus:** General Studies. **Qualif.:** Foster parents must be a member of NFPA. **Criteria:** Scholarships are awarded based on the academic performance of the students.

Funds Avail.: No specific amount. **To Apply:** Applicants must submit a completed application form; A minimum of two (2) letters of recommendation from: foster parents, social workers, residential center, principal/teacher/guidance counselor, employer, etc., will be required with each application. A typewritten statement in 300-500 words on "Why I want to further my education and why I should be considered for a National Foster Parent Association

Scholarship" will also required. **Deadline:** March 31. **Contact:** NFPA Scholarship Committee, NFPA at the above address (see entry 4901).

4903 ■ National Foundation for Infectious Diseases

4733 Bethesda Ave., Ste. 750
Bethesda, MD 20814
Ph: (301)656-0003
Fax: (301)907-0878
E-mail: info@nfid.org
URL: http://www.nfid.org

4904 ■ NFID Advanced Vaccinology Course Travel Grants *(Postdoctorate/Grant)*

Purpose: To support researches dedicated to the study of infectious diseases. **Focus:** Medical Research. **Qualif.:** Applicant must be a recent postdoctoral graduate with a demonstrated interest in a career in vaccinology; must be a citizen and resident of the United States at the time of the course; must be conducting research or working in a recognized and accredited US institution of higher learning or in a governmental agency. **Criteria:** Priority is given to applicants with demonstrated financial need.

Funds Avail.: 4,000. **Number Awarded:** 2. **To Apply:** Application package must include a letter from the applicant (not exceeding two pages) stating the applicant's long term interest in vaccinology, proposed research or work in vaccinology for the next 2-3 years, location of the proposed research or work and department or division chairman, and financial need; a letter of support from the department or division chairman (not exceeding one page) reiterating the applicant's research or work in vaccinology; applicant's curriculum vitae; and a copy of the applicant's application to the advanced vaccinology course. **Contact:** Katia Mielczarek, Fondation Merieux, 17 rue Bourgelat, 69002, Lyon France; email: katia.mielczarek@fondation-merieux.org; phone: 33 (0) 472407979; fax: 33 (0) 472407950.

4905 ■ National Funeral Directors and Morticians Association

13625 Bishop's Dr.
Brookfield, WI 53005
Ph: (262)789-1880
Fax: (262)789-6977
Free: 800-228-6332
E-mail: nfda@nfda.org
URL: http://www.nfda.org

4906 ■ Arkansas State University Mountain Home Scholarships *(Undergraduate/Scholarship)*

Purpose: To provide financial support to the students enrolled in ASUMH. **Focus:** General studies. **Qualif.:** Applicant must be enrolled at Arkansas State University Mountain Home; must be a resident of Arkansas; must have a GPA average of 2.5-3.0. **Criteria:** Selection of candidates will be based on the application materials and academic criteria.

Funds Avail.: $425. **Number Awarded:** 2. **To Apply:** Applicant must have three recommendation letters, and for more information regarding the scholarship, applicants are advised to contact the Arkansas State University Mountain Home, 1600 College St., Mountain Home, AR 72653.

4907 ■ Bishop State Community College Scholarships *(Undergraduate/Scholarship)*

Purpose: To provide financial support to the students in mortuary science or funeral service education. **Focus:** Funeral services, Mortuary science. **Qualif.:** Applicant must be a student enrolled in mortuary science or funeral service education. **Criteria:** Selection of candidates will be based on their application form.

Funds Avail.: $1,800. **To Apply:** For more information regarding the scholarship, applicants are advised to contact Bishop State Community College 351 Broad St., Mobile, AL, 36603.

4908 ■ Carl Sandburg College Scholarships *(Undergraduate/Scholarship)*

Purpose: To provide financial assistant to the deserving students in Illinois. **Focus:** General studies. **Qualif.:** Applicant must be Illinois resident. **Criteria:** Selection of applicant will be based on the scholarship criteria.

Funds Avail.: $500. **To Apply:** For further information about the scholarship, applicants are advised to contact the school at: Carl Sandburg College, 2232 Lake Storey Rd., Galesburg, IL 61401-9576. **Contact:** Tim Krause.

4909 ■ Vincennes University Scholarships *(Undergraduate/Scholarship)*

Purpose: To provide financial support to the students in funeral service education. **Focus:** Funeral services. **Qualif.:** Applicant must have completed one semester in funeral service education program at Vincennes University. **Criteria:** Selection of applicant will be based on scholarship criteria.

Funds Avail.: $500. **Number Awarded:** 5. **To Apply:** For further information about the scholarship, applicants are advised to contact the school at: Vincennes University, 1002 N 1st St., Vincennes, IN 47591. **Contact:** John Alsobrooks.

4910 ■ National Gay Pilots Association

PO Box 7271
Dallas, TX 75209-0271
Ph: (214)336-0873
Fax: (214)350-0447
URL: http://www.ngpa.org

4911 ■ NGPA Education Fund Scholarships *(Undergraduate/Scholarship)*

Purpose: To provide educational assistance to students pursuing aviation careers as professional pilots. **Focus:** Aviation. **Qualif.:** Applicants must be pursuing a career in the field of aviation; must be accepted or enrolled in an accredited college or university with an aviation related curriculum (aerospace; aerodynamics; engineering and airport management) in pursuit of a degree leading to a career as a professional pilot or undergoing a course of study in recognized professional pilot aviation training program in an institution of higher learning, aviation technical school or government approved flight school; must have demonstrated community involvement, including support of the gay, lesbian, bi-sexual and transgender (GLBT) community. **Criteria:** Recipients are chosen based on academic record, work experience, financial need, extra curricular activities and community involvement.

Funds Avail.: $2,000. **Number Awarded:** Varies. **To Ap-**

Awards are arranged alphabetically below their administering organizations

ply: Applicants must submit a formal application; academic records; list of work experience, extra curricular activities and or/community activities/honors/awards; proof of financial need; letter of recommendation; and essay on personal goals. Further instructions can be found in the NGPA website. **Deadline:** March 1.

4912 ■ National Government Publishing Association

207 Third Ave.
Hattiesburg, MS 39401
Ph: (601)582-3330
Fax: (601)582-3354
E-mail: info@govpublishing.org
URL: http://www.govpublishing.org

4913 ■ Don Bailey Scholarships *(Undergraduate/Scholarship)*

Purpose: To promote education in the printing and graphic communications industry. **Focus:** Printing trades and industries; Graphic art and design. **Qualif.:** Applicants must be pursuing a career in graphic communications, printing technology, printing management or publishing; must be a high school senior or high school graduate; must be enrolled in a two or four year accredited graphic or printing program at a technical school, college/university in the United States; a full-time student maintaining a cumulative GPA of 3.0 or higher. **Criteria:** Selection is based on the submitted materials.

Funds Avail.: $1,000-$50,000 per academic year. **To Apply:** Applicant must submit a completed application form; a copy of SAT scores; an official transcript; a photocopy of the intended course of study. **Deadline:** March 1 for high school and Apri1 1 for college students.

Remarks: In honor of Donald L. Bailey Sr.

4914 ■ National Ground Water Association

601 Dempsey Rd.
Westerville, OH 43081
Ph: (614)898-7791
Fax: (614)898-7786
Free: 800-551-7379
E-mail: ngwa@ngwa.org
URL: http://www.ngwa.org

4915 ■ Len Assante Scholarship Fund *(Undergraduate/Scholarship)*

Purpose: To advance the expertise of all ground water professionals and to further ground water awareness and protection through education and outreach. **Focus:** Water supply industry. **Qualif.:** Applicants must be full-time undergraduate students entering in the field of study that serves, supports, or promotes the ground water industry; must maintain a 2.5 GPA. **Criteria:** Recipients are selected based on academic performance and financial need.

Funds Avail.: No specific amount. **To Apply:** Applicants must complete the application form. **Deadline:** April 1. **Contact:** bhowell@ngwa.org.

4916 ■ National Hemophilia Foundation

116 W 32nd St., 11th Fl.
New York, NY 10001
Ph: (212)328-3700
Fax: (212)328-3777
Free: 800-424-2631
E-mail: handi@hemophilia.org
URL: http://www.hemophilia.org

4917 ■ Kevin Child Scholarships *(Undergraduate/Scholarship)*

Purpose: To encourage aspirations of higher education among individuals with bleeding disorders through providing financial assistance. **Focus:** General studies. **Qualif.:** Applicants must be individuals diagnosed with hemophilia or von Willebrand disease; must be high school seniors with aspirations of attending an institute of higher education or college students already pursuing post secondary education. **Criteria:** Recipients will be selected based on academic performance, participation in school or community activities and an essay detailing educational and career goals.

Funds Avail.: $1,000. **Number Awarded:** 1. **To Apply:** Applicants must send a complete copy of the application (available from the website) along with a current official transcript of grades and 1 recommendation from an individual not related to the applicant to Renee LaBrew, Department of Finance, Administration & MIS, National Hemophilia Foundation, 116 West 32nd St., 11th Fl., New York, NY 10001-3212. **Deadline:** June 27.

4918 ■ Soozie Courter Sharing a Brighter Tomorrow Hemophilia Scholarship Program *(Graduate, Undergraduate/Scholarship)*

Purpose: To provide educational assistance to people with hemophilia and their families. **Focus:** General studies. **Qualif.:** Applicants must have hemophilia A or B; must be a high school senior; must have a graduate equivalency diploma (GED); or be currently enrolled in an accredited junior college, undergraduate, graduate or vocational school. **Criteria:** Recipients are selected based on the required essay, recommendations, and academic standing.

Funds Avail.: $7,500 (graduate scholarships); $5,000 (college scholarships); $2,500 (vocational scholarships). **Number Awarded:** 2 graduate scholarships; 16 college scholarships; 2 vocational scholarships. **To Apply:** Applicants must visit the website for necessary forms and further instructions. **Deadline:** April 4. **Contact:** Wyeth/Genetics Institute, Inc. phone: 888-999-2349; website: www.hemophiliavillage.com.

4919 ■ Eric Delson Memorial Scholarships *(Graduate, High School, Undergraduate/Scholarship)*

Purpose: To encourage educational pursuits among students with bleeding disorders by providing financial support. **Focus:** General studies. **Qualif.:** Students who are clinically diagnosed with hemophilia or von Willebrand disease are eligible to apply. Applicants must be entering Grades 7 through 12 at private secondary schools or must be high school seniors, high school graduates or equivalent (GED), or post-secondary school students currently enrolled or planning to enroll in a full-time undergraduate or graduate course at an accredited two or four-year college, university or vocational-technical school in the United States. Students must be accepted by the institution during the year for which the scholarship is given and must be enrolled with the designated institution no later than September of the coming year. **Criteria:** Scholarship recipients are chosen on the basis of academic record,

Awards are arranged alphabetically below their administering organizations

potential to succeed, leadership, participation in school and community activities, honors, work experience, statement of educational and career goals, unusual personal and family circumstances, and recommendations.

Funds Avail.: $1,500 for private high school; $2,500 for college or trade school. **Number Awarded:** 1 for private high school; 3 for college or trade school. **To Apply:** Applicants must call Caremark request for an application and send it together with a current transcript of grades to: The Eric Delson Memorial Scholarship Program, Citizens' Scholarship Foundation of America, PO Box 297, St. Peter, Minnesota 56802. **Deadline:** July 1. **Contact:** Caremark: 866-792-2731.

4920 ■ Eric Dostie Memorial College Scholarships *(Four Year College, Two Year College, Undergraduate/Scholarship)*

Purpose: To provide financial assistance to students with hemophilia or a related bleeding disorder. **Focus:** General studies. **Qualif.:** Scholarship is open to students with hemophilia or a related bleeding disorder, or their family members. Applicants must be citizens of the United States and enrolled full-time in an accredited two or four-year college program. **Criteria:** Recipients are selected on the basis of scholastic achievement, community service and financial need.

Funds Avail.: $1,000. **Number Awarded:** 10. **To Apply:** Applicants must submit an essay describing how his or her education will be used to serve humankind and to encourage self-improvement and enrichment. Applicants must request for an application. **Deadline:** March 1. **Contact:** NuFACTOR, phone: 800-323-6832.

4921 ■ Education is Power Scholarships *(Undergraduate/Scholarship)*

Purpose: To inspire attainment of higher education among individuals with hemophilia and von Willbrand Disease by providing educational funds. **Focus:** General studies. **Qualif.:** Applicants must be individuals living with hemophilia and von Willebrand Disease; must be entering or attending a community college, junior college, four-year college, university, or vocational school; and must be a United States resident. **Criteria:** Scholarships will be awarded to the applicant who best meets the scholarship criteria.

Funds Avail.: $500-2,500. **Number Awarded:** 20-25. **To Apply:** Applicant must submit the completed application form available from the website; documentation from a physician/nurse of the applicant's bleeding disorder; copy of diploma or graduate equivalency diploma (GED); most recent transcript; proof of admission to the school; proof of school tuition; a separate document outlining the applicant's community involvement and/or volunteer work; an essay (no less than 250 words); and one letter of recommendation or character reference. **Deadline:** May 1.

Remarks: Prior applicants and winners are encouraged to reapply each year.

4922 ■ Joshua Gomes Memorial Scholarship Fund *(Graduate, Undergraduate/Scholarship)*

Purpose: To provide academic scholarships for young adults with HIV/AIDS. **Focus:** General studies. **Qualif.:** Applicants must be individuals living with HIV/AIDS; must be accepted or enrolled in a US college or university as a full-time undergraduate or graduate student. **Criteria:** Scholarship is awarded based on combined merit and need.

Funds Avail.: 1,000. **Number Awarded:** Varies. **To Apply:** Applicants must submit the completed application form available from the website; letter from a doctor certifying that the applicant is HIV positive or has AIDS; official transcripts from high school showing the applicant's cumulative GPA; letter of acceptance from a U.S. college or university; three letters of recommendation; and an attached 500-word essay. Mail all requirements to: The Joshua Gomes Memorial Scholarship Fund, 2700 South Emerson St., Englewood, CO 80113-1737. **Deadline:** July 15.

4923 ■ Millie Gonzalez Memorial Scholarships *(Undergraduate/Scholarship)*

Purpose: To encourage educational pursuits among women with bleeding disorders through providing financial assistance. **Focus:** General studies. **Qualif.:** Scholarship is open to women diagnosed with hemophilia or Von Willebrand Disease, and who are entering or attending a college or vocational school. **Criteria:** Recipients are chosen based on combined merit and need.

Funds Avail.: $1,000. **Number Awarded:** 2. **To Apply:** Applicants are encouraged to submit their applications online to: scholarships@factorsupport.com; all the necessary instructions and application forms can be downloaded from the website. **Deadline:** April 30. **Contact:** Factor Support Network Pharmacy, phone: 877-376-4968, email: scholarships@factorsupport.com.

4924 ■ Professor Ulla Hedner Scholarships *(Undergraduate/Scholarship)*

Purpose: To provide educational assistance to members of the bleeding disorders community. **Focus:** General studies. **Qualif.:** Program is open to high school seniors and college or vocational students under the age of 23. **Criteria:** Scholarship is awarded on a competitive basis.

Funds Avail.: $2,000-$7,000. **Number Awarded:** Varies. **To Apply:** Applicants may call 877NOVO-777 to request for an application. **Deadline:** April 30.

4925 ■ Hemophilia Health Services Memorial Scholarship Program *(Graduate, Undergraduate/Scholarship)*

Purpose: To encourage higher learning among individuals with bleeding disorders by providing financial assistance. **Focus:** General studies. **Qualif.:** Applicant must be a US citizen with hemophilia, VWD or other bleeding disorder. **Criteria:** Recipients are selected based on merits.

Funds Avail.: $1,500. **Number Awarded:** Varies. **To Apply:** Applicants must visit the website to apply online. **Deadline:** May 1. **Contact:** Sally Johnson, Special Programs Coordinator, phone: 615-850-5175.

4926 ■ Mike Hylton and Ron Niederman Memorial Scholarships *(Undergraduate/Scholarship)*

Purpose: To encourage educational pursuits among men with bleeding disorders through providing financial assistance. **Focus:** General studies. **Qualif.:** Scholarship is offered to males with hemophilia or Von Willebrand Disease and their immediate family members intending to pursue further learning. **Criteria:** Recipients are chosen based on combined merit and need.

Funds Avail.: $1,000. **Number Awarded:** 5. **To Apply:** Application requirements and instructions are available from the website. **Deadline:** April 30. **Contact:** Factor Support Network Pharmacy, phone: 877-376-4968, email: scholarships@factorsupport.com.

4927 ■ K-12 Edu-Grants *(High School/Grant)*

Purpose: To help children with hemophilia afford learning assistance. **Focus:** General studies. **Qualif.:** Grant is open to children in Kindergarten through 12th grade. **Criteria:** Recipient is chosen based on a review of all application documents.

Funds Avail.: Up to $500. **To Apply:** Applicants must submit the completed application form available from the website along with a notarized letter from the tutor outlining the tutoring work done and the fees charged. Copies of receipts indicating payment made to a commercial tutoring center may also be submitted. Forward application forms and supporting documents to: SevenSECURE, PO Box 18648, Louisville, KY 40261. **Contact:** SevenSECURE, 877-668-6777.

4928 ■ Dave Madeiros Scholarship Program - Continued Education *(Four Year College, Two Year College/Scholarship)*

Purpose: To inspire higher learning among individuals with a bleeding disorder and their immediate family by providing financial assistance. **Focus:** General studies. **Qualif.:** Program is open to individuals with bleeding disorders and their immediate family pursuing secondary education at a two or four-year institution or accredited technical or arts school. **Criteria:** Recipients are selected based on an essay (500 words or less) describing the applicant's goals and future plans for use of their education or training.

Funds Avail.: $2,000. **Number Awarded:** Varies. **To Apply:** Applicants must submit complete application package which includes an application form available from the website; essay on the applicant's goals and aspirations and how the bleeding disorder community has played a part in the applicant's life (500 words or less); two letters of reference (one personal and one from a local chapter, Hemophilia Treatment Center or physician); proof of academic standing (high school transcript); list of all additional loans, scholarships, and funding requested and received; copy of most recent tax return and proof of enrollment. Mail all documents to: Factor Foundation of America, Attn: Scholarship Committee, Peninsula Corporate Center, 950 Peninsula Corporate Circle, Ste. 3017, Boca Raton, FL 33487. **Deadline:** April 15. **Contact:** Factor Foundation of America, Phone: 866-843-3362.

4929 ■ Dave Madeiros Scholarship Program - Creative Arts *(Other/Grant)*

Purpose: To encourage exposure to arts and sports among young individuals with bleeding disorders by providing financial assistance. **Focus:** General studies. **Qualif.:** Program is open to children with bleeding disorders and their siblings ages 5 to 17 who would like to be exposed in trainings in arts and/or sports. **Criteria:** Recipients are selected based on financial need.

Funds Avail.: 1,000. **Number Awarded:** Varies. **To Apply:** Applicants must submit the completed application (available from the website); an essay (500 words or less) on the desire to take part in a creative art, and how this experience will benefit the child; two letters of reference (one personal and one from a local chapter, Hemophilia Treatment Center or physician); proof of academic standing (high school transcript); list of all additional loans, scholarships, and funding requested and received; copy of most recent tax return and proof of enrollment. Mail all documents to: Factor Foundation of America, Attn: Scholarship Committee, Peninsula Corporate Center, 950 Peninsula Corporate Circle, Ste. 3017, Boca Raton, FL 33487. **Deadline:** April 15. **Contact:** Factor Foundation of America, Phone: 866-843-3362.

4930 ■ Lawrence Madeiros Scholarships *(Undergraduate/Scholarship)*

Purpose: To inspire educational pursuits among individuals with bleeding disorders by providing financial aid. **Focus:** General studies. **Qualif.:** Applicants must be students with an inherited bleeding disorder or other chronic disorder attending an accredited college or university. **Criteria:** Recipients are chosen based on combined merit and need.

Funds Avail.: $1,000. **Number Awarded:** Varies. **To Apply:** Applicants must submit the completed application form available from the website along with a copy of current transcript and a statement of recommendation. Forward documents to: The Lawrence Madeiros Scholarship, c/o PO Box 11, Mayfield, NY 12117. **Deadline:** June 1.

4931 ■ Christopher Pitkin Memorial Scholarships *(Undergraduate/Scholarship)*

Purpose: To expand opportunities for members of the hemophilia community by providing funds for their educational pursuits. **Focus:** General studies. **Qualif.:** All members of the hemophilia and bleeding disorders community, including spouses, siblings and children, are eligible to apply. **Criteria:** Recipients will be selected based on goal orientation, drive and motivation.

Funds Avail.: $500-1,000. **To Apply:** Applicant must complete application package which includes an application form available from the website; two letters of recommendation from someone who can assess the applicant's academic potentials and knows the applicant in general terms (doctor, nurse, social worker, friend, relative, or community leader). Finalists will be asked to submit transcripts and evidence of enrollment in an educational or vocational institution. **Deadline:** July 25.

4932 ■ Project Red Flag Academic Scholarships for Women with Bleeding Disorders *(Undergraduate/Scholarship)*

Purpose: To assist women with bleeding disorders in their pursuit of post high school studies. **Focus:** General studies. **Qualif.:** Applicants must be female residents of the U.S. with a bleeding disorder (includes von Willebrand disease, hemophilia carrier or other clotting factor deficiencies). **Criteria:** Recipients are chosen based on combined merit and need.

Funds Avail.: $2,500. **Number Awarded:** 2. **To Apply:** Applicant may contact Anna DeSimone at adesimone@hemophilia.org for application information and instructions. **Deadline:** May 16.

4933 ■ Salvatore E. Quinci Foundation Scholarships *(Undergraduate/Scholarship)*

Purpose: To provide educational assistance to individuals with bleeding disorders. **Focus:** General studies. **Qualif.:** Applicants must be diagnosed with hemophilia or other bleeding disorder, and must be accepted into an accredited university, college or vocational/technical school. **Criteria:** Scholarships will be awarded based on quality of application, how well the applicant meets the criteria, and how well-rounded the applicant is.

Funds Avail.: $2,000. **Number Awarded:** 2. **To Apply:** Applicants must submit a completed application form, transcripts and letters of recommendation to: Salvatore E. Quinci Foundation, 178 Florence St., Melrose, MA 02176-3710. **Deadline:** April 4.

Awards are arranged alphabetically below their administering organizations

4934 ■ Michael Bendix Sutton Foundation
(Undergraduate/Scholarship)

Purpose: To encourage careers in the field of law among individuals with bleeding disorders. **Focus:** Law. **Qualif.:** Students with hemophilia pursuing pre-law studies are eligible to apply. **Criteria:** Recipients are chosen based on combined merit and need.

Funds Avail.: $2,000. **Number Awarded:** 2. **To Apply:** Applicants must write for applications addressed to: Michael Bendix Sutton Foundation, c/o Marion B. Sutton, 300 Maritime Ave., White Plains, NY 10601. **Deadline:** March 30.

4935 ■ Rachel Warner Memorial Scholarships
(Graduate, Undergraduate/Scholarship)

Purpose: To provide educational assistance to members of the bleeding disorders community. **Focus:** General studies. **Qualif.:** Program is open to individuals with any bleeding disorder with educational pursuits from high school through graduate school. **Criteria:** Recipients are chosen based on combined merit and need.

Funds Avail.: Varies. **Number Awarded:** Varies. **To Apply:** Applicants may visit the website for application information and instructions. **Deadline:** May 1. **Contact:** The Committee of Ten Thousand, Phone: 800-488-2688, email: cottdc@earthlink.net

4936 ■ National Hispanic Coalition of Federal Aviation Employees

PO Box 23276
Washington, DC 20026-3276
E-mail: nhcfae@nhcfae.org
URL: http://www.nhcfae.org

4937 ■ Rene Matos Memorial Scholarships
(Undergraduate/Scholarship)

Purpose: To assist dependents of NHCFAE members, students of minority, and women complete their higher education efforts by recognizing and rewarding academically superior performance and achievements, leadership, and community involvement. **Focus:** General Studies. **Qualif.:** Applicants must be accepted to or attending an accredited college, university, or vocational/ trade school at the time the scholarship is awarded. **Criteria:** Selection of scholars will be based on the following criteria: financial need, academic achievement, student activities, honors/ awards received, community involvement, leadership, personal qualities and strengths.

Funds Avail.: No specific amount. **To Apply:** Applicants must submit the following: completed application form; financial need statement; official transcript; letter of recommendation; and a recent photograph. **Contact:** NHCFAE Scholarship Selection Committee PO Box 23276 Washington, D.C. 20026-3276.

4938 ■ National Honor Society

1904 Association Dr.
Reston, VA 20191-1537
Ph: (703)860-0200
Fax: (703)476-5432
URL: http://www.nhs.us

4939 ■ NHS National Scholarships
(Undergraduate/Scholarship)

Purpose: To provide educational assistance to NHS members. **Focus:** General studies. **Qualif.:** Candidate must be a senior student member nominated by an active NHS chapter. **Criteria:** Selection is based on the outstanding scholarship, leadership, service, and character.

Funds Avail.: Total of $200,000. **Number Awarded:** 9. **To Apply:** Nomination forms will be mailed to all active chapter advisers in early November. **Deadline:** February 1.

Remarks: From among the nine Regional Winners, one National Winner will be identified to receive an additional $10,000 in college scholarship funding. **Contact:** Membership Department, 800-253-7746 x-214, or email at membership@nhs.us.

4940 ■ National Housing Endowment

1201 15th St. NW
Washington, DC 20005
Ph: 800-368-5242
URL: http://www.nationalhousingendowment.org

4941 ■ Lee S. Evans/National Housing Endowment Scholarship *(Graduate, Undergraduate/Scholarship)*

Purpose: To address the need for educating and training construction managers in the residential building industry. **Focus:** Construction. **Qualif.:** Applicant must be registered as a full-time undergraduate or graduate student for the Fall term; must have at least one full academic year of course work remaining after the scholarship is awarded; must demonstrate interest in obtaining employment in the residential construction industry upon graduation. **Criteria:** Selection criteria include financial need, career goals, academic achievement, employment history, extra curricular activities and recommendations; preference is given to students who are current members (or will be members in the upcoming semester) of a student chapter of the National Association of Home Builders; preference is also given to students enrolled in a four-year program emphasizing construction.

Funds Avail.: Up to $5,000. **To Apply:** Applicants must submit a completed application form available at the website; transcript(s) and course requirements; and recommendations. Mail to: The National Housing Endowment, Attn: Lee S. Evans Scholarship, 1201 15th St. NW, Washington, DC 20005-2800. **Deadline:** December 7.

4942 ■ Herman J. Smith Scholarships
(Undergraduate/Scholarship)

Purpose: To address the need for educating and training construction managers in the residential building industry. **Focus:** Construction. **Qualif.:** Applicant must be registered as a full-time undergraduate or graduate student; must have at least one full academic year of course work remaining after the scholarship is awarded; must be majoring in construction management, mortgage finance, or a construction related field in an accredited 4-year institution; must demonstrate an interest in obtaining employment in the construction industry, mortgage finance, or a construction related field upon graduation. **Criteria:** Selection criteria include financial need, career goals, academic achievement, employment history, extra curricular activities and recommendations; preference will be given to applicants who are legal residents of Texas, or juniors or seniors who attend an institution in Texas.

Funds Avail.: Up to $2,000. **To Apply:** Application package includes application form, transcript and recommendations. Mail to: The National Housing Endowment, Attn: Lee

Awards are arranged alphabetically below their administering organizations

S. Evans Scholarship, 1201 15th St. NW, Washington, DC 20005-2800. **Deadline:** May 5.

4943 ■ National Huguenot Society
9033 Lyndale Ave., Ste. 108
Bloomington, MN 55420-3535
Ph: (952)885-9776
E-mail: awards@huguenot.netnation.com
URL: http://www.huguenot.netnation.com

4944 ■ National Huguenot Society Scholarships *(Undergraduate/Scholarship)*

Purpose: To coordinate activities of member societies; to promote the principles and virtues of the Huguenots, commemorate Huguenot history, collect and preserve historical data and relics illustrative of Huguenot life, manners, and customs; to provide financial aid for higher education of students who are members of the National Huguenot Society. **Focus:** General studies. **Qualif.:** Applicants must be regular memberS of the National Huguenot Society; must be students at an accredited college or graduate school with at least two semesters of history which include at least in part a history of religion; applicants must have completed at least two years of college with a 3.0 GPA on a 4.0 scale. **Criteria:** Recipients are selected based on academic standing and financial need.

Funds Avail.: $5,000. **To Apply:** Applicants must complete the application form; attach proof of enrollment at an accredited college or graduate school; attach a transcript of college grades for last two years showing a 3.0 or better GPA; attach proof of membership in the National Huguenot Society. **Contact:** Richard Dana Smith, Chairman of Huguenot Scholarship Awards, 647 Brinston Bridge Rd., West Chester, PA 19382.

4945 ■ National Industrial Belting Association
N 19 W 24400 Riverwood Dr.
Waukesha, WI 53188
Ph: (262)523-9090
Fax: (262)523-9091
URL: http://www.niba.org

4946 ■ Employee Education Scholarships *(Other/Scholarship)*

Purpose: To support continuing and higher education through the NIBA Education Fund. **Focus:** Education. **Qualif.:** Applicant must be a current employee of a NIBA Distributor/Fabricator member company; must have business or industry related courses that the employer views as an asset to the industry or the company or those courses required for a degree. Applicant must not be a NIBA director, officer or NIBA committee chairperson or a member company's owner with five percent or greater holdings. **Criteria:** Applications will be entered into a drawing to be held at the NIBA Annual Convention.

Funds Avail.: $1,000. **Number Awarded:** 3. **To Apply:** Applicant must submit completed application form listing the name, address, employer, length of employment, duties, work experience, education background, community activities, and documentation of course(s) including cost.

4947 ■ Ray Snow Memorial Scholarships *(Undergraduate/Scholarship)*

Purpose: To provide financial assistance to an individual pursuing a minimum 2-year course at an accredited college, university or technical school. **Focus:** General studies. **Qualif.:** Applicants must be children of NIBA Distributor/Fabricator Member Company employees and must attend a two-year or more accredited college, university or technical school. **Criteria:** Candidates will be evaluated based on academic achievement, community service/activities, demonstration of leadership, and written thesis.

Funds Avail.: $4,000. **Number Awarded:** 2. **Deadline:** May 1.

4948 ■ National Institute of Health
2 Center Dr. Rm. 2E24, MSC 0230
Bethesda, MD 20892-0230
Ph: 888-352-3001
Fax: (301)480-3123
Free: 888-352-3001
E-mail: ugsp@nih.gov
URL: http://www.ugsp.nih.gov

4949 ■ National Institute of Health Undergraduate Scholarship Program *(Undergraduate/Scholarship)*

Purpose: To provide competitive scholarships for students from disadvantaged backgrounds. **Focus:** Biomedical research; Behavioral sciences; Social sciences. **Qualif.:** Applicants must be US citizens, nationals, or qualified noncitizens; must be enrolled or accepted for enrollment as full-time students for the current academic year at an accredited, 4-year undergraduate institution; must be from a disadvantaged background (disadvantage background means that the financial aid office has certified student as having "exceptional financial need"); and must have a 3.5 GPA or higher (on a 4.0 scale) or be within the top 5 percent of their class. **Criteria:** Selection will be based on the committee's criteria.

Funds Avail.: No specific amount. **To Apply:** Applicants are encouraged to apply online at www.ugsp.nih.gov or may visit the website for the application forms. **Deadline:** March 31. **Contact:** NIH Undergraduate Scholarship Program at the above address (see entry 4948).

4950 ■ National Investment Company Service Association
2 Mt. Royal Ave.
Marlborough, MA 01752
Ph: (508)485-1500
Fax: (508)485-1560
E-mail: info@nicsa.org
URL: http://www.nicsa.org

4951 ■ William T. Blackwell Scholarship Fund *(Undergraduate/Scholarship)*

Purpose: To financially support dependents of NICSA member company employees in their education. **Focus:** General studies. **Qualif.:** Applicants must be dependents of full-time employees of NICSA member companies. Applicants must be enrolled, or planning to enroll in a full-time degree seeking course at an accredited four-year college or university. **Criteria:** Recipients are selected based on academic record, leadership and participation in school and community activities, honors, work experience, statement of goals and aspirations, unusual personal or family circumstances, and an outside appraisal.

Funds Avail.: $2,000-$5,000. **To Apply:** Application form is available from the website. Applicants must prepare a current transcript of grades and an appraisal provided by the school (sent in a sealed envelope). **Deadline:** January 15.

Remarks: The program is administered by Scholarship America. **Contact:** Scholarship America, One Scholarship Way, PO Box 297, Saint Peter, MN 56082. Telephone: 507-931-1682.

4952 ■ National Iranian American Council

1411 K St. NW, Ste. 600
Washington, DC 20005
Ph: (202)386-6325
Fax: (202)386-6409
URL: http://www.niacouncil.org

4953 ■ The Iranian-American Scholarship Fund *(Undergraduate/Scholarship)*

Purpose: To provide scholarships to students of Iranian descent. **Focus:** Ethnic. **Qualif.:** Applicants must be of Iranian heritage; Undergraduate (sophomore or above); Graduate (Masters Program or equivalent); GPA 3.5 or above. **Criteria:** Selection will be based on merit.

Funds Avail.: $1,000-$3,000. **To Apply:** Applicants may download an application form at Iranian-American Scholarship Fund website. Applicant must submit the completed application and all supporting documents. **Deadline:** April 1. **Contact:** Iranian-American Scholarship Fund; PO Box 500835, San Diego, CA 92150.

4954 ■ Iranian Artist Scholarships *(Undergraduate/Scholarship)*

Purpose: To promote and facilitate the appreciation of Iranian-American artists. **Focus:** Fine arts. **Qualif.:** Applicants must be Iranian or Iranian-American artists living and studying fine arts in the United States. Applicant must be between the ages of 18 and 30. **Criteria:** Selection is based on eligibility and merit.

Funds Avail.: $1,000. **To Apply:** Interested applicants must submit the following: a current resume; ten (10) slides labeled with title, size and medium (CD-ROM and video accepted); articles/reviews about applicant's work or exhibitions; an artist statement about his/her work (500-1000 words); a self-addressed stamped envelope. **Deadline:** June 1. **Contact:** EP-Scholarship, 11118 Lakespray Way, Reston, VA 20191; 202-607-0754.

4955 ■ Iranian Association of Boston's IAB Scholarships *(Undergraduate/Scholarship)*

Purpose: To provide scholarships to students who are of Iranian descent. **Focus:** Ethnic. **Qualif.:** The applicant must not be a relative or close relation of any members of the Scholarship Committee; must have legal immigration status; must be of Iranian descent or have active interest in Iranian culture and heritage; The applicant must be a full-time student of an accredited New England graduate or undergraduate institution in any of the following states: ME, VT, NH, MA, CT, or RI. **Criteria:** Scholarship is given based on merit; however, student's financial needs will also be an important consideration for the award.

Funds Avail.: $3,000. **To Apply:** Applicant may download an application form at the NIAC website. Applicant must complete and submit the application and other requirements. **Deadline:** February 1. **Contact:** NIAC at the above address (see entry 4952).

4956 ■ Iranian Federated Women's Club Scholarships *(Undergraduate/Scholarship)*

Purpose: To provide scholarships to students of Iranian descent. **Focus:** Ethnic. **Qualif.:** Open to all students of Iranian descent attending an undergraduate and graduate course. **Criteria:** Selection will be based on submitted materials and other criteria.

Funds Avail.: $10,000. **To Apply:** Applicant may download an application form at the Iranian Federated Women's Club website. Applicant must submit the complete application form and a personal essay describing himself/herself, his/her goals, and his/her qualifications for this scholarship. Applicant must also submit the following: two letters of reference; parent's tax return (for each tax return you must include IRS Form 4506); official transcript. **Deadline:** July 21. **Contact:** ifwc@aol.com.

4957 ■ Momeni Foundation Scholarships *(Undergraduate/Scholarship)*

Purpose: To provide scholarships to students of Iranian descent. **Focus:** Ethnic. **Qualif.:** Applicants must be college students and graduating high school seniors of Iranian descent of any citizenry, anywhere in the world. **Criteria:** Selection will be based on merit.

Funds Avail.: $500-$1,000. **To Apply:** Applicants must submit a resume or list of extra curricular activities, community leadership or voluntarism, membership in clubs or organizations and any other evidence of outstanding achievement; must submit a short narrative describing goals and plans and motivation towards such. **Deadline:** June 30. **Contact:** Momeni Foundation 12720 SW Allen Blvd., Beaverton, OR 97005 USA; 503-349-4939.

4958 ■ National Iranian American Council Fellowships *(Graduate, Undergraduate/Fellowship)*

Purpose: To provide outstanding Iranian-American college students with internships in political and media organizations. **Focus:** Political science; Economics; International affairs and relations; Journalism. **Qualif.:** Applicant must be a college junior, senior, and graduate student who is a U.S. citizen or a legal permanent resident of Iranian descent. **Criteria:** Selection process is highly competitive. Applicants are judged on the basis of their academic credentials, demonstrated interest in community and public service, and the ability to fulfill the needs and expectations of the congressional office they will be placed in.

Funds Avail.: Travel expenses covered to and from DC; $500 monthly stipend; $700 monthly towards rent. **To Apply:** Applicant must submit the following requirements: a completed application form; three letters of recommendation (two academic and one from an employment supervisor); resume; current college transcript; a 500-word essay answering the question: "How has being Iranian-American influenced your decision to pursue a career in public service or journalism?" **Deadline:** February 15. **Contact:** NIAC at the above address (see entry 4952).

4959 ■ National Italian American Bar Association

c/o Philip R. Boncore - Pres.
1140 Saratoga St.
East Boston, MA 02128
Ph: (617)561-0999
Fax: (617)561-8385
E-mail: prblawoff@aol.com
URL: http://www.niaba.org

Awards are arranged alphabetically below their administering organizations

4960 ■ National Italian American Bar Association Scholarships *(Postgraduate/Scholarship)*

Purpose: To assist deserving and qualified students who wish to further their legal education at a law school. **Focus:** Law. **Qualif.:** Applicants must be enrolled at a Law School member of the National Italian Bar Association. **Criteria:** Recipients will be selected based on scholastic ability, character, activities, and any other information provided on or with the application. Financial need may also be considered.

Funds Avail.: $1,000. **Number Awarded:** 3. **To Apply:** Applicants must submit an official law school grade transcript for the most recent academic year; a personal letter in support of the application; and two letters of reference. Application form and other supporting materials may sent to: Pacia & Pacia, LTD. 50 Power Rd., Pawtucket, RI 02860-3451. **Deadline:** April 15.

4961 ■ National Italian American Foundation

1860 19th St. NW
Washington, DC 20009
Ph: (202)387-0600
Fax: (202)387-0800
E-mail: information@niaf.org
URL: http://www.niaf.org

4962 ■ NIAF Scholarships - General Category I *(Undergraduate/Scholarship)*

Purpose: To financially support the education of Italian American students. **Focus:** General studies. **Qualif.:** Applicant must be enrolled in a U.S. accredited institution of higher education for the fall; must have a GPA of at least 3.5 out of 4.0 (or the equivalent); must be a U.S. citizen or a permanent resident alien; and must be an Italian American student who demonstrates outstanding potential and high academic achievements. **Criteria:** Awards are given based on academic performance, field of study, career objectives, and the potential, commitment, and abilities applicants have demonstrated that would enable them to make significant contributions to their chosen field of study.

Funds Avail.: $2,500-$10,000. **To Apply:** Applicants must submit completed student application and Teacher Evaluation Form online, official school transcript and FAFSA Financial Aid Form (optional), submitted by mail. **Deadline:** March 7.

4963 ■ NIAF Scholarships - General Category II *(Undergraduate/Scholarship)*

Purpose: To promote the study of Italian American studies or a related field. **Focus:** Italian studies. **Qualif.:** Applicant must be enrolled in an U.S. accredited institution of higher education for the fall; must have a GPA of at least 3.5 out of 4.0 (or the equivalent); must be a U.S. citizen or a permanent resident alien; and must be from any ethnic background majoring or minoring in Italian language, Italian studies, Italian American studies or a related field who demonstrate outstanding potential and high academic achievements. **Criteria:** Awards are given based on academic performance, field of study, career objectives, and the potential, commitment, and abilities applicants have demonstrated that would enable them to make significant contributions to their chosen field of study.

Funds Avail.: $2,500-$10,000. **To Apply:** Applicants must submit completed student application and Teacher Evaluation Form online; and submit official school transcript and FAFSA Financial Aid Form (optional) by mail. **Deadline:** March 7.

4964 ■ National Judges Association

PO Box 627
Boley, OK 74829
Ph: (918)667-3711
E-mail: hhicks@wwtech.org
URL: http://www.nationaljudgesassociation.org

4965 ■ National Judges Association Scholarships *(Professional Development/Scholarship)*

Purpose: To provide support for, and the continuation of, the non-attorney judge in the United States judicial system. **Focus:** Law. **Qualif.:** Applicants must be an attorney or any individual who is related to law. **Criteria:** Recipients are selected based on financial need.

Funds Avail.: No specific amount. **To Apply:** Applicants must complete the application form and provide evidence that he or she is a member of the American judiciary. **Contact:** National Judges Association at the above address (see entry 4964).

4966 ■ National Junior Angus Association

3201 Frederick Ave.
St. Joseph, MO 64506
Ph: (816)383-5100
Fax: (816)233-9703
E-mail: mjenkins@angusfoundation.org
URL: http://www.angusfoundation.org

4967 ■ Angus Foundation Scholarships *(Undergraduate/Scholarship)*

Purpose: To support education, youth and research by giving scholarship to young men and women who are active in the angus breed pursuing higher education. **Focus:** General studies. **Qualif.:** Applicants must be a National Junior Angus Association members and currently a junior, regular or life member of American Angus Association graduating high school senior or must be enrolled in junior college, four-year college/university or other accredited institution of higher education for the fall term, and must have a minimum 2.0 GPA. **Criteria:** Candidates will be evaluated by the Angus Foundation's Scholarship Selection Committee.

Funds Avail.: $100,000. **To Apply:** Applicants must seek application forms available at www.angusfoundation.org. **Deadline:** May 1.

4968 ■ National Junior Horticultural Association

15 Railroad Ave.
Homer City, PA 15748-1378
Ph: (724)479-3254
E-mail: carole@njha.org
URL: http://www.njha.org

4969 ■ National Junior Horticultural Association Alumni Scholarships *(Undergraduate/Scholarship)*

Purpose: To help young people develop their skills and obtain an understanding of horticulture. **Focus:** Horticulture. **Qualif.:** Program is open to any youth intending to return to the NJHA convention to expand their knowledge within NJHA. **Criteria:** Recipients are selected based on demonstrated interest in the field of horticulture and financial need.

Funds Avail.: No specific amount. **To Apply:** Applicants must submit a resume which must include a one paragraph statement about self, one paragraph about NJHA involvement, one paragraph about non-NJHA involvement, one paragraph about financial need, and a letter of recommendation from an NJHA leader. Applicants are advised to contact Mike Ensor who may be reached at 2336 Mt. Carmel Rd., Parkton, MD 21120-9608; phone: 410-357-0315, email: mensor@umd.ecu. **Deadline:** September 1. **Contact:** mensor@umd.ecu.

4970 ■ National Junior Swine Association

PO Box 2517
West Lafayette, IN 47996
Ph: (765)463-3594
Fax: (765)497-2959
E-mail: nsr@nationalsine.com
URL: http://www.nationalswine.com

4971 ■ Gregory D. Johnson Memorial Scholarships *(Graduate, Undergraduate/Scholarship)*

Purpose: To provide a network uniting purebred swine enthusiast through a youth organization. **Focus:** Agricultural economics. **Qualif.:** Applicant must be a spring college graduate with a bachelor's degree in an agricultural field or a current graduate student pursuing a master's or doctorate degree in swine genetics, swine reproduction or swine nutrition. **Criteria:** Applications will be scored by a committee and shall independently review and score each application received and select the recipient(s) based on the their criteria.

Funds Avail.: $1,000. **To Apply:** Applicant must enclose one letter of recommendation from a college advisor who can verify participant's graduate school acceptance or enrollment, in addition to their college activities and involvement; Applicants must submit graduate school acceptance letter or proof of graduate school enrollment. **Deadline:** May 15. **Contact:** NSR at the above address (see entry 4970).

4972 ■ The Maschhoffs Inc. Pork Production Scholarships *(Undergraduate/Scholarship)*

Purpose: To provide a network uniting purebred swine enthusiast through a youth organization. **Focus:** Agricultural economics. **Qualif.:** Applicants must be a member of the National Junior Swine Association (NJSA). Applicants must be 18-21 years old and enrolled in an agricultural program at a recognized college/ university. **Criteria:** Application will be scored by a committee selected by the NSR Chief Executive Officer and the NSR Director of Junior Activities. The judging committee will determine the winners of the essay contest. Essays will be judged on overall thought process and merit.

Funds Avail.: $1,500 for the first-place and $1,000 For the second-place. **To Apply:** Applicants may download an application form online. **Deadline:** May 23. **Contact:** NSR at the above address (see entry 4970).

4973 ■ National Junior Swine Association Outstanding Member Scholarships *(Graduate/ Scholarship)*

Purpose: To provide a network uniting purebred swine enthusiast through a youth organization. **Focus:** Agricultural economics. **Qualif.:** Applicants must be a member of the National Junior Swine Association. **Criteria:** Applications will be scored by a committee selected by the NSR Chief Executive Officer and the NSR Director of Junior Activities. One NJSA scholarship will be awarded to a student in each of the following age divisions: Intermediate (13-16), Junior (9-12), and Novice (8 and under). Two NJSA scholarships will be awarded to a student in the Senior division (17-21).

Funds Avail.: $200 for novice, $300 junior, $500 intermediate, $1,000 senior. **To Apply:** Applicants may submit their application to the office together with the other requirements. **Deadline:** December 1. **Contact:** NJSA at the above address (see entry 4970).

4974 ■ NJSA Visionary Leader Scholarships *(Graduate/Scholarship)*

Purpose: To provide a network uniting purebred swine enthusiast through a youth organization. **Focus:** Agricultural economics. **Qualif.:** Applicants must be a member of the NJSA Board of Directors. **Criteria:** Application will be scored by a committee and independently review and score each application received.

Funds Avail.: $500. **To Apply:** Applications should be typed. Extra pages may be used as necessary. Applications must be signed by a parent or guardian who has knowledge of the applicant's involvement in the NJSA. **Deadline:** May 15. **Contact:** NSR at the above address (see entry 4970).

4975 ■ Claude Robinson Scholarships *(Undergraduate/Scholarship)*

Purpose: To provide a network uniting purebred swine enthusiast through a youth organization. **Focus:** Agricultural economics. **Qualif.:** Scholarship applicants must be a sophomore, junior or senior enrolled in a collegiate. **Criteria:** Each selection committee member shall independently review and score each application received and select the recipient(s) based on the criteria.

Funds Avail.: $1,000. **To Apply:** Applicant must send in two letters of reference. One letter should be written by their college coach, and the second letter should be written by a non-family member who has knowledge of the applicant's involvement in the livestock industry. **Deadline:** March 1. **Contact:** National Swine Registry at the above address (see entry 4970).

4976 ■ Jason Shipley Memorial Scholarships *(Undergraduate/Scholarship)*

Purpose: To provide a network uniting purebred swine enthusiast through a youth organization. **Focus:** Agricultural economics. **Qualif.:** Applicants must be incoming freshman, sophomore or junior enrolled in an agriculturally related field. **Criteria:** The selection committee member shall independently review and score each application received and select the recipient(s) based on the criteria.

Funds Avail.: No specific amount. **To Apply:** Applicant must send in two letters of reference. One letter should be written by an athletic coach, and the second letter should be written by a non-family member who has knowledge of the applicant's involvement in the swine industry. **Deadline:** May 15. **Contact:**

4977 ■ National Kindergarten Alliance

c/o Anna Rainville
Waldorf School of the Peninsula
11311 Mora Dr.
Los Altos, CA 94024

URL: http://www.nkateach.org

4978 ■ National Kindergarten Alliance Graduate Scholarships *(Graduate/Scholarship)*

Purpose: To provide educational assistance to classroom teachers pursuing an advanced degree in Early Childhood Education or a closely related field. **Focus:** Early childhood education. **Qualif.:** Applicants must be NKA members in good standing for at least one year. **Criteria:** Recipients will be selected based on the quality of application materials submitted.

Funds Avail.: $250. **To Apply:** Applicants must submit a completed application form; a narrative (2-3 pages) of professional work experience, extra curricular activities responsibilities, leadership, citizenship activities, awards and honors; reasons for choosing Early Childhood Education as a career; post graduation plans; a copy of transcripts; and two professional letters of recommendation. **Deadline:** March 1.

4979 ■ National Legal Aid and Defender Association

1140 Connecticut Ave. NW, Ste. 900
Washington, DC 20036
Ph: (202)452-0620
Fax: (202)872-1031
E-mail: info@nlada.org
URL: http://www.nlada.org

4980 ■ The C. Lyons Fellowship Program *(All/Fellowship)*

Purpose: To support emerging leaders in the equal justice community. **Focus:** Law. **Qualif.:** Applicant must be a member of the NLADA. **Criteria:** Applicants will be evaluated based on a demonstrated commitment to the delivery of legal services to the poor; a clearly-defined project or interest that is national in scope and that would be mutually beneficial to NLADA and the program from which the fellow represents; and the desire to learn about and explore national advocacy and public policy issues.

Funds Avail.: No amount specified. **To Apply:** Applicant must check the website of the National Legal Aid and Defender Association for more detailed information about the fellowship.

4981 ■ National Little Britches Rodeo Association

5050 Edison Ave., Ste. 105
Colorado Springs, CO 80915
Ph: (719)389-0333
Fax: (719)578-1367
Free: 800-763-3694
URL: http://www.nlbra.com

4982 ■ NLBRA/Wrangler Academic Scholarships *(Undergraduate/Scholarship)*

Purpose: To support student members in their education. **Focus:** General studies. **Qualif.:** Applicants must be high school seniors; a competing NLBRA member for the previous three years; and will complete their last year of high school prior to the 2008 National Little Britches Finals Rodeo. **Criteria:** Selection is based on academics.

Funds Avail.: $1,000-$2,000. **Number Awarded:** 6. **To Apply:** Applicants must submit a completed application form along with a certified copy of high school transcripts. **Deadline:** June 30.

4983 ■ Rainwater Family Scholarships *(Undergraduate/Scholarship)*

Purpose: To support student members in their education. **Focus:** General studies. **Qualif.:** Applicant must be a NLBRA member for three years minimum; have a GPA of 3.0 or better; and a NLBRA member in the senior division. **Criteria:** Selection is based on merit.

Funds Avail.: $500. **Number Awarded:** 4 (2 boys and 2 girls). **To Apply:** Applicants must fill out the entry form and submit it together with an official transcript. **Deadline:** April 20.

Remarks: Established by Warren and Toni Rainwater, in memory of their son, Winn Hal Rainwater, and daughter, Carla Suzanne Rainwater.

4984 ■ National Medical Fellowships

5 Hanover Sq., 15th Fl.
New York, NY 10004
Ph: (212)483-8880
Fax: (212)483-8897
E-mail: info@nmfonline.org
URL: http://www.nmfonline.org

4985 ■ California Community Service Scholarships *(Undergraduate/Scholarship)*

Purpose: To encourage future physicians to establish community-based primary care practices in California. **Focus:** Medicine. **Qualif.:** Applicant must be a third or fourth year student; enrolled at MD degree granting schools in California; an African-American, mainland Puerto Rican, Mexican-American, Native Hawaiian, Alaska Native, or American Indian; a U.S. citizen; and must demonstrate commitment to practice in California. **Criteria:** Selection is based on demonstrated commitment to practice in California, interest in community-based primary care, satisfactory academic performance, leadership, and financial need.

Funds Avail.: $7500. **To Apply:** Applicants must submit a completed application form together with the required materials. **Deadline:** January. **Contact:** CSSP Interim Program Coordinator, Mary Wade at 415-397-2526 or marywade@nmfonline.org.

4986 ■ California Community Service Scholarships - Bay Area *(Undergraduate/Scholarship)*

Purpose: To encourage future physicians to establish community-based primary care practices in California. **Focus:** Medicine. **Qualif.:** Applicant must be a third or fourth year student; enrolled at MD degree granting schools in California; an African-American, mainland Puerto Rican, Mexican-American, Native Hawaiian, Alaska Native, or American Indian; a U.S. citizen; and must demonstrate commitment to practice in the San Francisco Bay Area. **Criteria:** Selection is based on demonstrated commitment to practice in California, interest in community-based primary care, satisfactory academic performance, leadership, and financial need.

Funds Avail.: $7500-$15,000. **To Apply:** Applicants must submit a completed application form together with the required materials. **Deadline:** January. **Contact:** CSSP Interim Program Coordinator, Mary Wade at 415-397-2526 or marywade@nmfonline.org.

4987 ■ Gerber Fellowships in Pediatric Nutrition *(Undergraduate/Fellowship)*

Purpose: To provide support for a minority medical student or resident doing ongoing research in the area of pediatric nutrition. **Focus:** Medicine, Pediatric. **Qualif.:** Applicant must be a second or third year student; an African-American, mainland Puerto Rican, Mexican-American, Native Hawaiian, Alaska Native, or American Indian; a U.S. citizen attending a M.D. degree-granting institutions accredited by the Liaison Committee on Medical Education of the Association of American Medical Colleges, or in D.O. degree-granting colleges of osteopathic medicine accredited by the Bureau of Professional Education of the American Osteopathic Association; and pursuing careers in pediatric nutrition research. **Criteria:** The Program Advisory Committee will review each application.

Funds Avail.: $3000. **Number Awarded:** 1. **To Apply:** Applicants must submit a competed application form together with a letter of recommendation from medical school dean or director; a letter of commitment; an official academic transcript; a curriculum vitae; a personal statement on career goals; and a description of the research project. **Deadline:** October.

Remarks: Created in 1997 with support from the Gerber Companies Foundation.

4988 ■ W.K. Kellogg Foundation Doctoral Fellowships in Health Policy *(Professional Development/Fellowship)*

Purpose: To provide opportunity to complete advanced training in research methodology, including quantitative and qualitative methods. **Focus:** Public health. **Qualif.:** Applicant must be enrolled in, or accepted for enrollment at the RAND Graduate School, The University of Michigan School of Public Health, Brandeis University, The Heller Graduate School, UCLA School of Public Health, The Mailman School of Public Health at Columbia University, The Harvard School of Public Health, The Johns Hopkins School of Hygiene and Public Health or The University of Pennsylvania; an African-American, Asian, Hispanic, or Native American; a U.S. citizen or permanent resident; demonstrates commitment to work with underserved populations upon completion of the doctorate; and exhibit willingness to complete relevant dissertation research. **Criteria:** The National Advisory Committee will select based on academic accomplishments, research potentials, demonstrated interest and ability in health policy research, and commitment to working with underserved populations.

Funds Avail.: Covers tuition, fees and a partial living stipend. **Number Awarded:** 1. **To Apply:** Applicants must submit a competed application form together with the required materials. **Deadline:** June.

4989 ■ National Medical Fellowships Need-Based Scholarships *(Undergraduate/Scholarship)*

Purpose: To support medical students in educational pursuits. **Focus:** Medicine. **Qualif.:** Applicants must be first or second year medical student; an African-American, Mexican-American, Native American, Alaska Native, Native Hawaiian, or mainland Puerto Ricans who permanently reside within the 50 U.S. states; and accepted to AAMC or AOA-accredited U.S. medical schools for study leading to M.D. or D.O. degrees. Applicants born outside of the U.S. must submit a proof of citizenship. **Criteria:** Selection is based on financial need.

Funds Avail.: $500-$10,000. **To Apply:** Applicants must submit a completed application together with the required documents. **Deadline:** June 30.

4990 ■ National Military Intelligence Association

PO Box 479
Hamilton, VA 20159
Ph: (540)338-1143
E-mail: admin@nmia.org
URL: http://www.nmia.org

4991 ■ NMIA Scholarship Program *(Undergraduate/Scholarship)*

Purpose: To support the growth of professional studies in the field of military intelligence and to recognize and reward excellence in the development and transfer of knowledge about military and associated intelligence disciplines. **Focus:** Military science and education. **Qualif.:** Applicants must be dependents of NMIA active members, mobilized reserve and national guard personnel, and other reserve or National Guard members, eligible for college entrance in the class of 2011. **Criteria:** Recipient will be selected based on academic achievement, SAT or ACT scores, extra-curricular activities, and career objectives.

Funds Avail.: $1,000. **Number Awarded:** 3. **To Apply:** Applicants must submit application form, supporting transcripts and SAT or ACT scores. **Deadline:** August 1.

4992 ■ National Organization of Black Law Enforcement Executives

Hubert T. Bell Jr. Office Complex,
4609-F Pinecrest Office Park Dr.
Alexandria, VA 22312-1442
Ph: (703)658-1529
Fax: (703)658-9479
E-mail: jakers@noblenatl.org
URL: http://www.noblenational.org

4993 ■ NOBLE Fellowship Program *(All/Fellowship)*

Purpose: To ensure that minorities will have equal opportunities in participating in different levels of law enforcement. **Focus:** Law enforcement. **Qualif.:** Applicant must be a NOBLE member and a full-time active law enforcement official holding a college degree. **Criteria:** Applications are screened by a review committee and the Executive Director of NOBLE.

Funds Avail.: No specific amount. **To Apply:** Applicants must submit a statement of proposed project/activity for the Fellowship period.

Remarks: The employer of the applicant must agree to pay the fellow's salary and fringe benefits during the fellowship.

4994 ■ NOBLE Southern California Chapter Scholarship Program *(Undergraduate/Scholarship)*

Purpose: To assist Southern California students in their education. **Focus:** General studies. **Qualif.:** Applicant must be a Southern California resident or student attending a college, university, or academy accredited by the Scholarship Committee. **Criteria:** Recipients are selected based on merits.

Funds Avail.: $1,000. **Number Awarded:** 2. **To Apply:** Application forms are available at the website. Applicants

Awards are arranged alphabetically below their administering organizations

must submit a completed application form, a recent photograph, and two letters of recommendation to SCC NOBLE Scholarship Committee. **Deadline:** January 12.

4995 ■ National Organization for Human Services

90 Madison St., Ste. 206
Denver, CO 80206
Ph: (303)320-5430
Fax: (303)322-1455
URL: http://www.nationalhumanservices.org

4996 ■ David C. Maloney Scholarship Program *(Undergraduate/Scholarship)*

Purpose: To support the education of a student in a human service program. **Focus:** Humanities; Human relation. **Qualif.:** Applicant must be an Associate, Baccalaureate, or Master's student member of NOHS; have a GPA of 3.0 and above on a 4.0 scale; enrolled in a Human Services studies program. **Criteria:** Consideration will be given to applicants with special established needs or minority status.

Funds Avail.: No specific amount. **To Apply:** Applicants must submit an official transcript (sent by the university in a sealed envelope); a resume; an essay (500-words) about the applicant's commitment to the field of helping and quality of Human Service Education; copy of current NOHS membership card; and two reference letters. Send applications as email attachments to Linda Wark, PhD, LMFT, Chair, Professional Development Committee at warkl@ipfw.edu. **Deadline:** May 1.

4997 ■ National Organization of Industrial Trade Unions

148-06 Hillside Ave.
Jamaica, NY 11435
Ph: (718)291-3434
Fax: (718)526-2920
URL: http://www.noitu.org

4998 ■ Daniel Lasky Scholarship Fund *(Undergraduate/Scholarship)*

Purpose: To provide financial assistance to sons and daughters of the Union. **Focus:** Industrial. **Qualif.:** Applicants must be sons or daughters of a NOITU member who will graduate from high school this year and planning to attend an accredited college in the coming fall term. **Criteria:** Candidates will be judged by the Scholarship Committee.

Funds Avail.: No amount mentioned. **To Apply:** Applicants must submit the following requirements: a) Scholastic Aptitude Test (SAT I) scores; b) verification of acceptance by a college or university approved by the Federation of Regional Accrediting commission of Higher Education; c) letters of recommendation from (2) faculty members in the high school you are attending; high school transcript (showing final grades of the graduating year); and the name and address of the college applicants will be attending. **Deadline:** July 1.

4999 ■ National Organization of Italian-American Women

25 W 43rd St., Rm. 1005
New York, NY 10036
Ph: (212)642-2003
Fax: (212)642-2006
URL: http://www.noiaw.org

5000 ■ National Organization of Italian-American Women Scholarships *(All/Scholarship)*

Purpose: To provide financial support for Italian-American women in need of additional support for the education of their choice. **Focus:** General studies. **Qualif.:** Applicant must be a female student, matriculating full-time and have at least one parent of Italian American descent. **Criteria:** Candidates will be evaluated based on minimum cumulative 3.5 GPA and financial need.

Funds Avail.: $10,000. **Number Awarded:** 5. **To Apply:** Applicants must submit completed application form and a one page typewritten bio. **Deadline:** February 28.

5001 ■ National Orientation Directors Association

1313 5th St. SE, Ste. 323A
Minneapolis, MN 55414
Ph: (612)627-0150
Fax: (612)627-0153
Free: (866)521-NODA
E-mail: noda@umn.edu
URL: http://www.nodaweb.org

5002 ■ Norman K. Russell Scholarships *(Graduate/Scholarship)*

Purpose: To assist students committed to orientation-related fields. **Focus:** General studies. **Qualif.:** Applicant must be enrolled in a graduate program. **Criteria:** Selection is based on the application and other supporting documents.

Funds Avail.: $1,000. **Number Awarded:** 3. **To Apply:** Applicants must submit a Norman K. Russell Scholarship application form; a statement (double-spaced, three pages); a resume; an official transcript (must state enrollment in a graduate program, or graduation from a graduate program); official verification of present enrollment; and two letters of recommendations **Deadline:** September 5. **Contact:** Orientation Services, Director, Andy Cinoman.

5003 ■ National Osteoporosis Foundation

1232 22nd St. NW
Washington, DC 20037-1202
Ph: (202)223-2226
Fax: (202)223-1726
Free: 800-231-4222
URL: http://www.nof.org

5004 ■ National Osteoporosis Foundation Research Grants *(Doctorate, Graduate/Grant)*

Purpose: To support research investigation on osteoporosis. **Focus:** Medical research. **Qualif.:** Applicants must have an MD, PhD or equivalent average and must be within 4 years post-completion of the postdoctoral training period; must have U.S. citizenship or permanent status and affiliated with a U.S.based, not-for-profit academic or research institution. **Criteria:** Preference will be given to investigators who have not yet received the award.

Funds Avail.: $57,000. **Number Awarded:** 3. **To Apply:**

Applicants must submit a letter of intent (1 page) describing the proposed research project and objectives and submit it to: Robert Recker, MD, Chairman, Research Subcommittee, National Osteoporosis Foundation 1232 22nd St. NW, Washington, DC 20037, or fax to: 202223-1726 Attn: Betty Hawkins, or email to: researchgrants@nof.org. **Deadline:** December 1 for letter of intent and February 20 for the complete proposals. **Contact:** Betty Hawkins, Research Coordinator, Phone: 202-223-2226, researchgrants@nof.org.

5005 ■ National Parking Association

1112 16th St. NW, Ste. 840
Washington, DC 20036
Ph: (202)296-4336
Fax: (202)296-3102
Free: 800-647-PARK
E-mail: info@npapark.org
URL: http://www.npapark.org

5006 ■ BioRx/Hemophilia of North Carolina Educational Scholarships *(Undergraduate/Scholarship)*

Purpose: To provide financial assistance to people with bleeding disorders in their pursuit to obtain higher education degree. **Focus:** General Studies. **Qualif.:** Applicant must be caregivers of children affected with bleeding disorders, a person who has been diagnosed with hemophilia, or a sibling of a person diagnosed with hemophilia. **Criteria:** Priority is given to a hemophilia community member, parent and family members seeking healthcare related education from an accredited college or university or certified training program.

Funds Avail.: $2,000. **Number Awarded:** 3. **To Apply:** Applicants may call or write for application; program instructions are available at the website. **Deadline:** May 1. **Contact:** BioRx, Phone: 866-442-4679, email cbarnex@biorx.net.

5007 ■ Beth Carew Memorial Scholarships *(Undergraduate/Scholarship)*

Purpose: To provide assistance and support to individual and families affected by chronic illness and help these students obtain higher education degree. **Focus:** General Studies. **Qualif.:** Any student with hemophilia, von Willebrand disease, or a related inherited bleeding disorder is eligible to apply for this Scholarship; high school seniors who have been accepted to an accredited college or university may apply; College freshmen, sophomores, and juniors may also apply. **Criteria:** Recipient is chosen based on merit.

Funds Avail.: $2,000. **Number Awarded:** 10. **To Apply:** Applicants must call, write, or e-mail for application or download application from the website. **Deadline:** April 4. **Contact:** Colburn-Keenan Foundation, Inc, phone: 800-966-2431

5008 ■ Bill McAdam Scholarships *(Undergraduate/Scholarship)*

Purpose: To provide financial assistance to people with bleeding disorders in their pursuit to obtain higher education degree. **Focus:** General Studies. **Qualif.:** Scholarship is open to a person with hemophilia, VWD or other hereditary bleeding disorder or the person's spouse, partner, child or sibling planning to attend an accredited college or university or certified training program. **Criteria:** Recipient is chosen based on financial need.

Funds Avail.: $2,000. **Number Awarded:** 1. **To Apply:** Applicants may call or write for application. **Deadline:** May 15. **Contact:** Cathy McAdam Scholarship Fund, 22226 Doxtator, Dearborn, MI 48128 Phone: 313-563-1412, mcmcadam@comcast.net

5009 ■ Parking Industry Institute Scholarship Program *(Undergraduate/Scholarship)*

Purpose: To provide financial aid to support the association's commitment to advance educational opportunities. **Focus:** General studies. **Qualif.:** Applicants must be undergraduate students enrolled at an accredited two or four year college/university; a child or spouse of a full-time employee of a firm which is a member of the National Parking Association; a full-time or part-time employee of a firm which is a member of the National Parking Association. **Criteria:** Applicants will be selected on the basis of merits as well as scholastic and extracurricular achievement.

Funds Avail.: $1,000-$3,000. **To Apply:** Applicants must submit a completed application form, and related materials such as transcripts and recommendations to the Trustees of The Parking Industry Institute. **Deadline:** March 1.

5010 ■ National Parkinson Foundation

1501 NW 9th Ave./Bob Hope Rd.
Miami, FL 33136-1494
Ph: (305)243-6666
Fax: (305)243-5595
Free: 800-327-4545
E-mail: contact@parkinson.org
URL: http://www.parkinson.org

5011 ■ Individual-Investigator Grants Program *(Postdoctorate/Grant)*

Purpose: To support projects that are directly relevant to the study of causes and cures for Parkinson's disease. **Focus:** Medical research. **Qualif.:** Candidates must be postdoctoral fellows or residents in recognized training programs, or tenure-track and researchtrack faculty at colleges, universities or research institutes. Candidates must be planning to conduct research on the causes and cures for Parkinson's disease. Both basic and clinical researches are eligible for the grant. **Criteria:** Preference is given to scientists who are at the early stage of their professional careers.

Funds Avail.: Up to $50,000. **To Apply:** Applicants may visit the website for application forms, instructions and research proposal format. **Deadline:** March 17. **Contact:** National Parkinson's Foundation, tel: 305-243-6666.

5012 ■ National Poultry and Food Distributors Association

958 McEver Rd. Ext., Unit B-8
Gainesville, GA 30504
Ph: (770)535-9901
Fax: (770)535-7385
Free: 877-845-1545
E-mail: info@npfda.org
URL: http://www.npfda.org

5013 ■ National Poultry and Food Distributors Association Scholarships *(Undergraduate/Scholarship)*

Purpose: To help build "people resources" for the poultry and food industries. **Focus:** Poultry Science; Food science

Awards are arranged alphabetically below their administering organizations

and technology; Dietetics; Agribusiness; Agricultural economics; Agriculture, Economic aspects; Agricultural sciences. **Qualif.:** Applicant must be a full time junior or senior at a U.S. institution for the upcoming award year, and must be pursuing a poultry or related agricultural degree. **Criteria:** Recipients are selected based on the committee's review of their application.

Funds Avail.: $2,000. **Number Awarded:** 5. Cash prizes will go to the top four; the fifth student chosen will be the alternate student should one of the award recipients not use all of his/her funds (early graduation). **To Apply:** Applicant must submit an application form; official transcript; letter of recommendation from his/her Dean; and a one-page letter describing his/her goals and aspirations. **Deadline:** May 31.

Remarks: This scholarship foundation was established in 1979.

5014 ■ National Preservation Institute

PO Box 1702
Alexandria, VA 22313
Ph: (703)765-0100
E-mail: info@npi.org
URL: http://www.npi.org

5015 ■ National Preservation Institute Scholarships *(Other/Scholarship)*

Purpose: To provide financial assistance to individuals who wish to attend the NPI seminars. **Focus:** General studies. **Qualif.:** Applicants must work at least 20 hours a week (paid or volunteer) at the organization that they will represent; must be full-time students. **Criteria:** Recipient will be selected based on merits.

Funds Avail.: No amount specified.

5016 ■ National Press Photographers Association

3200 Croasdaile Dr., Ste. 306
Durham, NC 27705
Ph: (919)383-7246
Fax: (919)383-7261
E-mail: info@nppa.org
URL: http://www.nppa.org

5017 ■ Bob Baxter Scholarships *(Undergraduate/Scholarship)*

Purpose: To improve and facilitate the administration of press photography. To promote the study of press photography and research therein, and to continue the education of press photographers. **Focus:** Photography. **Qualif.:** Applicants must be full-time students at a school in the United States and intend to pursue a career in photojournalism. **Criteria:** Recipients are selected based on academic standing and financial need.

Funds Avail.: $1,000. **To Apply:** Applicants must submit a portfolio; six or more photos; picture editors must send three tearsheets. Video journalists must submit a tape of three short but complete stories. **Deadline:** March 1. **Contact:** richards@northjersey.com

5018 ■ Reid Blackburn Scholarships *(Undergraduate/Scholarship)*

Purpose: To improve and facilitate the administration of press photography. To promote the study of press photography and research therein, and to continue the education of press photographers. **Focus:** Photography. **Qualif.:** Applicants must have completed one year at a recognized four-year college or university with courses in photojournalism and must be continuing in a program leading to bachelor's degree. Applicants must have at least one half year of undergraduate schooling remaining at time of award. **Criteria:** Recipients are selected based on academic standing and financial need.

Funds Avail.: No specific amount. **To Apply:** Applicants must submit a portfolio; six or more photos; picture editors must send three tearsheets. Video journalists must submit a tape of three short but complete stories. Applicants must submit an essay stating the philosophy and goals of their work. **Deadline:** March 1. **Contact:** fay.blackburn@columbian.com

5019 ■ Bob East Scholarships *(Undergraduate/Scholarship)*

Purpose: To improve and facilitate the administration of press photography. To promote the study of press photography and research therein, and to continue the education of press photographers. **Focus:** Photography. **Qualif.:** Applicants must either be undergraduates in the first three-and-a-half years of college, or planning to pursue post-graduate work and able to offer some indication of acceptance in such program. **Criteria:** Recipients are selected based on academic standing, financial need, and quality of the portfolio.

Funds Avail.: $2,000. **To Apply:** Applicants must submit a five-single-image portfolio; six or more photos. Picture editors must send three tearsheets. Video journalists must submit a tape of three short but complete stories. **Deadline:** March 1. **Contact:** 305-376-2015

5020 ■ Kit C. King Graduate Scholarships *(Postgraduate/Scholarship)*

Purpose: To improve and facilitate the administration of press photography. To promote the study of press photography and research therein, and to continue the education of press photographers. **Focus:** Photography. **Qualif.:** Applicants must be pursuing an advanced degree in journalism with an emphasis in photojournalism. **Criteria:** Recipients are selected based on the academic standing, financial need, and quality of the portfolio.

Funds Avail.: $1,000. **To Apply:** Applicants must submit a portfolio with six or more photos, and state their goals and philosophy relating to documentary photojournalism. Picture editors must send three tearsheets. Video journalists must submit a tape of three short but complete stories. **Deadline:** March 1. **Contact:** sines@commercialappeal.com

5021 ■ Still Photographer Scholarships *(Undergraduate/Scholarship)*

Purpose: To improve and facilitate the administration of press photography. To promote the study of press photography and research therein, and to continue the education of press photographers. **Focus:** Photography. **Qualif.:** Applicants must have completed one year at a recognized four-year college or university with courses in photojournalism and must be continuing in a program leading to a bachelor's degree. Applicants must have at least one half of undergraduate schooling remaining at the time of award. **Criteria:** Recipients are selected based on academic standing, financial need, and quality of the portfolio.

Funds Avail.: $2,000. **To Apply:** Applicants must submit a

Awards are arranged alphabetically below their administering organizations

portfolio with six or more photos and state their goals and philosophy relating to documentary photojournalism. Picture editors must send three tearsheets. Video journalists must submit a tape of three short but complete stories. **Deadline:** March 1. **Contact:** wsanders@citizen-times.com

5022 ■ Television News Scholarships *(Undergraduate/Scholarship)*

Purpose: To improve and facilitate the administration of press photography. To promote the study of press photography and research therein, and to continue the education of press photographers. **Focus:** Photography. **Qualif.:** Applicants must be enrolled in a recognized four-year college or university with courses in TV news photojournalism. Applicants must be continuing in a program leading to a bachelor's degree. Applicants must be in their junior or senior year at the time award is given. **Criteria:** Recipients are selected based on academic standing, financial need, and quality of the portfolio.

Funds Avail.: $1,000. **To Apply:** Applicants must submit a portfolio with six or more photos. Picture editors must send three tearsheets. Video journalists must submit a tape of three short but complete stories. Applicants must complete the entry form and submit it along with a videotape containing examples of his or her work. Applicants must include a one-page biographical sketch including a personal statement addressing their professional goals. **Deadline:** March 1. **Contact:** dooks@verizon.net

5023 ■ National Private Truck Council

950 N Glebe Road, Ste. 530
Arlington, VA 22203-4183
Ph: (703)683-1300
Fax: (703)683-1217
URL: http://www.nptc.org

5024 ■ CTP Scholarship Program *(Professional Development/Scholarship)*

Purpose: To promote continuous learning and professional development by providing financial aid for individuals lacking the necessary corporate funding to pursue the CTP designation. **Focus:** Transportation; Management. **Qualif.:** Applicants must be members in good standing of the National Private Truck Council; must be currently employed in a fleet management position; must have at least five years of fleet management experience; must be able to fully participate in all offerings included in the CTP Scholarship. **Criteria:** Award is given based on merit.

Funds Avail.: $195 (waiver of the CTP Examination fee); $2,050 (complimentary registration for the five-day Fleet Management Institute); $330 (complimentary registration for the one-day CTP examination workshop in January). **To Apply:** Applicants must submit a resume which indicates the candidate's history of accomplishments, active participation in transportation/logistics organizations, a continuing pursuit of knowledge and learning and participation in community service or volunteer organizations; two letters of recommendation from a member of the NPTC or from a management personnel within the candidate's company who is familiar with the candidate's job performance; an original essay of not less than 300 words on "Why I Want a Certified Transportation Professional (CTP) Scholarship." Mail to: Institute for Truck Transportation Management, 2200 Mill Rd. Ste. 350, Alexandria, VA 22314. **Deadline:** September 1. **Contact:** National Private Truck Council, tel: 703-683-1300.

5025 ■ National Public Employer Labor Relations Association

1012 S Coast Hwy., Ste. M
Oceanside, CA 92054
Ph: (760)433-1686
Fax: (760)433-1687
Free: 877-673-5721
URL: http://npelra.org

5026 ■ The Anthony C. Russo Scholarships *(Graduate/Scholarship)*

Purpose: To provide financial assistance to deserving graduate students studying labor and employee relations or a closely related field. **Focus:** Labor relations. **Qualif.:** Applicants must be a U.S. citizen who is a graduate student currently enrolled and seeking a graduate degree in human resources, labor and industrial relations, public administration or political science, with a strong and documented interest in the public sector. **Criteria:** Recipients will be selected based on financial need.

Funds Avail.: $3,000. **Number Awarded:** 5. **To Apply:** Applicants must submit application forms with neatly typed information; resume; recommendations from at least two faculty members; and final undergraduate transcript and most recent graduate school transcript. **Deadline:** September 28.

5027 ■ National Recreation and Park Association

22377 Belmont Ridge Rd.
Ashburn, VA 20148
Ph: (703)858-0784
Fax: (703)858-0794
E-mail: info@nrpa.org
URL: http://www.nrpa.org

5028 ■ National Recreation and Park Association Diversity Scholarships *(Undergraduate/Scholarship)*

Purpose: To encourage NRPA Congress and Exposition attendance by members of ethnic minorities; to emphasize the value of involvement in the organization; to develop minority communities to promote the benefits of NRPA. **Focus:** Parks and Recreation. **Qualif.:** Applicant must be a person of an ethnic minority; be a professional, citizen or student member of NRPA at the time of application; be currently employed as a professional in parks and recreation agency or a student currently enrolled in a park and recreation degree program. **Criteria:** Recipients are selected based on their compliance with basic eligibility requirements set by the National Recreation and Park Association.

Funds Avail.: No stated amount. **To Apply:** Applicants must submit an application form; two references; and letters of recommendation directly to the National Recreation and Park Association. **Deadline:** April 25. **Contact:** NRPA Awards Coordinator at the above address (see entry 5027).

5029 ■ National Recycling Coalition

805 15th St. NW, Ste. 425
Washington, DC 20005
Ph: (202)789-1430
Fax: (202)789-1431

Awards are arranged alphabetically below their administering organizations

E-mail: info@nrc-recycle.org
URL: http://www.nrc-recycle.org

5030 ■ National Recycling Coalition Congress Scholarships *(Undergraduate/Scholarship)*

Purpose: To sponsor scholarships for college students. **Focus:** General studies. **Qualif.:** Applicants must be interested in a professional career and gaining exposure to the recycling field. **Criteria:** Priority will be given to students with financial need.

Funds Avail.: No specific amount. **Number Awarded:** 5. **To Apply:** Applicants should submit the completed application form; must have a letter of recommendation from their school's staff or faculty to the NRC. **Deadline:** July 25.

Remarks: The scholarships are intended as a way for college students interested in a professional career to gain exposure to the recycling field. They will have the opportunity to attend over 35 conference sessions, workshops and tours, as well as to meet and network with community, state and national recycling leaders. **Contact:** For more information about the scholarship, contact Alec Cooley at alecc@nrc-recycle.org.

5031 ■ National Restaurant Association Educational Foundation

175 W Jackson Blvd., Ste. 1500
Chicago, IL 60604-2702
Ph: (312)715-1010
Free: 800-765-2122
E-mail: info@nraef.org
URL: http://www.nraef.org

5032 ■ Al Schuman Ecolab Undergraduate Entrepreneurial Scholarships *(Undergraduate/Scholarship)*

Purpose: To support post-secondary students with strong entrepreneurial commitment who are dedicated to furthering their education and enhancing their careers in the restaurant and food service industry. **Focus:** Food service careers. **Qualif.:** Applicant must be a citizen or a permanent resident of the United States of America or be a resident of American Samoa, Guam, Puerto Rico or the U.S. Virgin Islands; must be pursuing a degree in the restaurant and food service industry; must be accepted or enrolled in the following schools: California State Polytechnic University - Pomona, Cornell University, Culinary Institute of America, Johnson and Wales University, Kendall College, Lynn University, Michigan State University, New York University, Pennsylvania State University, Purdue University, University of Denver, University of Houston, University of Nevada (Las Vegas) or University of Massachusetts-Amherst. Applicant must have a minimum grade point average of 3.0 on a 4.0 scale, or a GED average standard score of 470 or higher. Applicant must also be enrolled for two consecutive semesters and not entering his/her last term before graduating. **Criteria:** Recipients are selected based on the judges' review of application focusing on presentation, entrepreneurial project, academic merit and letters of recommendation.

Funds Avail.: Bronze - $3,500; Silver $5,500; Gold - $7,500. **Number Awarded:** 3. **To Apply:** Applicants must submit an application packet which includes completed online application, an entrepreneurial project as described in the application, a copy of college curriculum with the number of credit hours detailed, transcript from current school or a copy of the GED certificate and three letters of recommendation from current or previous employer(s) in the restaurant and/or food service industries, current teachers/professors or personal references. **Deadline:** March 7.

5033 ■ National Roofing Contractors Association

10255 W Higgins Rd., Ste. 600
Rosemont, IL 60018-5607
Ph: (847)299-9070
Fax: (847)299-1183
URL: http://www.nrca.net

5034 ■ Melvin Kruger Endowed Scholarship Program *(Undergraduate/Scholarship)*

Purpose: To provide financial support for students continuing their education and training beyond high school. **Focus:** General studies. **Qualif.:** Applicant must be a student who needs financial assistant to continue his/her education. **Criteria:** Scholarship recipients are selected base on the academic record and financial need.

Funds Avail.: $5,000. **To Apply:** Applicant must visit the NRCA for further instruction and information regarding with the scholarship.

5035 ■ Roofing Industry Scholarships *(Graduate, Undergraduate/Scholarship)*

Purpose: To assist employees, immediate family of employees or immediate family of NRCA contractor members, who plan to pursue post-secondary education in college and vocational programs. **Focus:** General studies. **Qualif.:** Applicants must be full-time employees, dependent children or spouse of NRCA contractor members who have a minimum of one year of employment with the company as of the application deadline date. Member companies must have been a contractor member of NRCA for a minimum of one year as of the application deadline date. Applicants must be seniors or graduates who plan to enroll or students who are already enrolled in a full-time undergraduate course of study at an accredited two or four year college, university or vocational technical school. **Criteria:** Scholarship recipients are selected based on academic record, potential to succeed, leadership and participation in school and community activities, honors, work experience, a statement of educational and career goals, and an outside appraisal. Financial need is not considered. Final selection of recipients is made by the Alliance board of trustees.

Funds Avail.: $1,000. **To Apply:** Applicant must complete the application form on the website and mail it along with a current complete official transcript of grades to Scholarship America, One Scholarship Way, PO Box 297, Saint Peter, MN, 56082. **Deadline:** January 31.

5036 ■ National Sculpture Society

237 Park Ave., Ground Fl.
New York, NY 10017
E-mail: info@nationalsculpture.org
URL: http://www.nationalsculpture.org

5037 ■ Alex J. Ettl Grants *(Professional Development/Grant)*

Purpose: To honor sculptors who demonstrate commitment and exceptional ability in their work. **Focus:** Sculpture.

Awards are arranged alphabetically below their administering organizations

Qualif.: Applicants must be U.S. citizens; and non-professional members of National Sculpture Society. **Criteria:** Awards are given based on the quality of the materials submitted.

Funds Avail.: $4,000. **To Apply:** Applicants must submit at least 10 images of their work (of at least eight different works) and a brief biographical sketch or resume. The images should be submitted in a CD in .tif format, 300 dpi resolution, and approximately 800 pixels long (longest side of the image); or in 8"x10" photographs indicated at the back the name of the sculptor, title, size, medium, and date of execution. Applicants must also provide a self-addressed stamped envelope for the return of the photographs. **Deadline:** January 10.

5038 ■ National Sculpture Society Scholarships *(Undergraduate/Scholarship)*

Purpose: To provide financial assistance to those studying figurative or representational sculpture. **Focus:** Sculpture. **Qualif.:** Applicant must be enrolled in a sculpture school. **Criteria:** Awards are given based on the quality of the materials submitted.

Funds Avail.: $2,000. **To Apply:** Applicants must submit a letter of application including a brief biography and the background in sculpture; two letters of recommendation; 8-10 images of work on CD with at least three works shown; and a proof of financial need. Submit all materials to: Scholarship National Sculpture Society, 237 Park Ave., Ground Fl. New York, NY 10017. **Deadline:** May 31.

Remarks: Applicants must also provide a self-addressed stamped envelope for the return of the materials.

5039 ■ National Sheriffs' Association

1450 Duke St.
Alexandria, VA 22314
Ph: (703)836-7827
Fax: (703)683-6541
Free: 800-424-7827
URL: http://www.sheriffs.org

5040 ■ NSA Scholarship Program *(Undergraduate/Scholarship)*

Purpose: To provide educational assistance to employees of a sheriff's office or their dependents. **Focus:** Criminal justice; Law. **Qualif.:** Applicant must be applying or enrolled in an undergraduate or graduate college program majoring in a criminal justice-related subject area; must be employed by a sheriff's office or a dependent of an individual employed by a sheriff's office; and must not be a previous recipient of the NSA scholarship. **Criteria:** Scholarship is granted to applicants with complete requirements as reviewed by the NSA Awards and Scholarship Committee.

Funds Avail.: $1,000. **To Apply:** Applicants must provide a completed Official NSA scholarship application form available at the website; a transcript from high school or college (if already attending college); two letters of recommendation (one must be from a principal, teacher, guidance counselor, or advisor); endorsement letter from the sheriff of applicant's county; statement of financial need; and an essay (minimum of 150 words) about the applicant's intents in pursuing a career in law enforcement. Required materials must be photocopied and forwarded to the NSA Awards and Scholarship Committee while the application form must be mailed to: Hilary Burgess, National Sheriff's Association 1450 Duke St. Alexandria, VA 22314, Attn: NSA Scholarship Program. **Deadline:** April 1.

5041 ■ National Sleep Foundation

1522 K St. NW, Ste. 500
Washington, DC 20005
Ph: (202)347-3471
Fax: (202)347-3472
E-mail: nsf@sleepfoundation.org
URL: http://www.sleepfoundation.org

5042 ■ NSF Pickwick Postdoctoral Research Fellowships *(Postdoctorate/Fellowship)*

Purpose: To promote research and studies in sleep or sleep disorders. **Focus:** Sleep and sleep disorders. **Qualif.:** Applicant must have a sponsor and plan to conduct research in recognized U.S. or Canadian programs of study; have received either an MD, DVM, PhD or DO degree completed within the past five years by the time the fellowship. Individuals who have a National Institute of Health or National Science Foundation Research Grant, or hold a faculty position are not qualified. **Criteria:** Selection is based on demonstrated evidence of aptitude for and proficiency in research and interest in pursuing a career in sleep research.

Funds Avail.: $36,996-$45,048 plus $7000 allowance. **To Apply:** Applicants must complete NSF Pickwick Postdoctoral Fellowship application along with the required materials. **Deadline:** November 1.

Remarks: Started in 1995. **Contact:** Jessica Steinitz at jsteinitz@sleepfoundation.org.

5043 ■ National Slovak Society of the USA

351 Valley Brook Rd.
McMurray, PA 15317-3337
Ph: (724)731-0094
Fax: (724)731-0145
Free: 800-488-1890
E-mail: dblazek@nsslife.org
URL: http://www.nsslife.org

5044 ■ National Slovak Society of the USA Scholarships *(Undergraduate/Scholarship)*

Purpose: To financially assist members in attending college or trade school. **Focus:** Nursing; Education, Vocational-technical **Qualif.:** Applicant must be a member of the National Slovak Society for a minimum of two years; completed high school; have a minimum of $10,000 of permanent life insurance in force, or $5000 annuity; accepted by a college or university; a junior college, nursing, trade, technical or business school (2 years); or other institutions approved by the NSS Board of Directors. **Criteria:** Applications is reviewed by the Fraternal Growth Committee of the NSS Board of Directors.

Funds Avail.: $400 per year. **Number Awarded:** Varies. **To Apply:** Applicants must submit completed applications along with latest transcript; proof of acceptance as a full-time student; a resume/biographical sketch with recent photograph; and proof of fraternal activities. **Deadline:** May 1.

5045 ■ National Slovak Society of the USA Senior Scholarships *(Undergraduate/Scholarship)*

Purpose: To encourage older members to continue their education and to make fuller use of their leisure time.

Awards are arranged alphabetically below their administering organizations

Focus: Education, Vocational-technical. **Qualif.:** Applicant must be a member of the National Slovak Society; 55 years and above; enrolled and successfully completed a continuing education or adult education course. Continuing education classes for the attainment or maintenance of a degree or certification are not qualified. **Criteria:** Applications are reviewed by the National Officer.

Funds Avail.: One-half reimbursement of the tuition, limited up to $100. **To Apply:** Applicants must enroll and pay for the course of their choice, after the applicant have finished the class, they must submit an application, along with the verification that the class was successfully completed.

5046 ■ National Society of Accountants

1010 N Fairfax St.
Alexandria, VA 22314
Ph: (703)549-6400
Fax: (703)549-2984
Free: 800-966-6679
E-mail: members@nsacct.org
URL: http://www.nsacct.org

5047 ■ National Society of Accountants Scholarship Program *(Undergraduate/Scholarship)*

Purpose: To assist college students pursuing an accounting major. **Focus:** Accounting. **Qualif.:** Applicant must be a full-time or part-time student majoring in accounting at any U.S. accredited institution; have a "B" (3.0 on a 4.0 scale) or better GPA; be a U.S. or Canadian citizen. **Criteria:** Recipients are selected on the basis of academic record, demonstrated leadership and participation in school and community activities, honors, work experience, statement of goals and aspirations, unusual personal or family circumstances and an outside appraisal. Financial need is also considered.

Funds Avail.: $500, $1,000 or $2,000. **Number Awarded:** 32. **To Apply:** Applicants must complete the application form (visit the website) and mail it with a transcript of records. **Deadline:** March 10.

Remarks: Administered by Scholarship Management Services, a department of Scholarship America. **Contact:** Scholarship America, One Scholarship Way, PO Box 297 Saint Peter, MN 56082; Phone: (507)931-1682.

5048 ■ The Stanley H. Stearman Awards *(Undergraduate/Scholarship)*

Purpose: To provide financial assistance to students majoring in accounting. **Focus:** Accounting. **Qualif.:** Applicants must be a dependent or spouse, niece, nephew, son- or daughter-in-law of an active/retired, living or deceased NSA member. **Criteria:** Recipients are selected based on the submitted application.

Funds Avail.: $2,000. **To Apply:** Applicants must complete the application form (visit the website) and mail it with a transcript of records. **Deadline:** March 10.

Remarks: The award is to honor retired NSA Executive Vice President Stanley H. Stearman. **Contact:** Scholarship America, One Scholarship Way, PO Box 297 Saint Peter, MN 56082; Phone: (507)931-1682.

5049 ■ National Society of Black Physicists

1100 N. Glebe Rd., Ste. 1010
Arlington, VA 22201
Ph: (703)536-4207
Fax: (703)536-4203
E-mail: headquarters@nsbp.org
URL: http://www.nsbp.org

5050 ■ Michael P. Anderson Scholarships in Space Science *(Undergraduate/Scholarship)*

Purpose: To support interest in physics by providing educational assistance to skilled physics majors. **Focus:** Physics. **Qualif.:** Applicants must be physics majors in their junior or senior year. **Criteria:** Recipient is selected based on merit and evaluation of the applicant's scientific abilities and potential which includes versatility, ability to make sound judgments, major academic strengths and weaknesses (if any) and performance in an independent study (if any) as manifested through documents submitted.

Funds Avail.: $1,000. **Number Awarded:** 1. **To Apply:** Applicant must send the complete application package along with official transcripts and a stamped envelope to: Scholarship Committee Chair, National Society of Black Physicists, 6704G Lee Highway, Arlington, VA 22205. **Deadline:** January 12.

Remarks: Established to commemorate Dr. Michael P. Anderson, an accomplished physicist and a NASA astronaut who perished in a space shuttle accident.

5051 ■ APS Scholarships for Minority Undergraduate Physics Majors *(Undergraduate/Scholarship)*

Purpose: To inspire pursuits in physics education specifically among minority undergraduates. **Focus:** Physics. **Qualif.:** Any African-American, Hispanic American, or Native American U.S. citizen or permanent resident who is majoring or planning to major in physics; a high school senior, college freshman, or sophomore is eligible to apply for the scholarship. **Criteria:** Recipient is selected based on the committee's review of their academic eligibility.

Funds Avail.: $2,000 (for new minority scholars); $3,000 (for renewal students) to be used for tuition, room & board and educational materials. **To Apply:** Applicants may download application materials in the website. **Deadline:** February 6.

Remarks: Established in 1980.

5052 ■ Harvey Washington Banks Scholarships in Astronomy *(Undergraduate/Scholarship)*

Purpose: To support interest in physics by providing educational assistance to skilled physics majors. **Focus:** Physics. **Qualif.:** Applicants must be physics majors in their junior or senior year. **Criteria:** Recipient is selected based on merit and evaluation of the applicant's scientific abilities and potential which includes versatility, ability to make sound judgments, major academic strengths and weaknesses (if any) and performance in an independent study (if any) as manifested through documents submitted.

Funds Avail.: $1,000. **Number Awarded:** 1. **To Apply:** Applicant must send the complete application package along with official transcripts and a stamped envelope to: Scholarship Committee Chair, National Society of Black Physicists, 6704G Lee Highway, Arlington, VA 22205. **Deadline:** January 12.

Remarks: Established to commemorate Dr. Harvey Washington Banks, the first African-American to receive a Ph.D. degree in astronomy.

5053 ■ Charles S. Brown Scholarships in Physics *(Graduate, Undergraduate/Scholarship)*

Purpose: To inspire the next generation of physicians by providing financial assistance to individuals pursuing further studies in the field of physics. **Focus:** Physics. **Qualif.:** Graduate students and undergraduate students with a declared major in physics are eligible for this scholarship. **Criteria:** Recipient is selected based on merit and evaluation of the applicant's scientific abilities and potential which includes versatility, ability to make sound judgments, major academic strengths and weaknesses (if any) and performance in an independent study (if any) as manifested through documents submitted.

Funds Avail.: $1,000. **Number Awarded:** 1. **To Apply:** Applicant must send complete application package available in the website with official transcript and supply a stamped envelope addressed to: Scholarship Committee Chair, National Society of Black Physicists, 6704G Lee Highway, Arlington, VA 22205. **Deadline:** January 12.

Remarks: Established to commemorate Dr. Charles S. Brown, who had extensive contributions in the development of science and technology in Africa.

5054 ■ Robert A. Ellis Scholarships in Physics *(Undergraduate/Scholarship)*

Purpose: To support interest in physics by providing educational assistance to skilled physics majors. **Focus:** Physics. **Qualif.:** Applicants must be physics majors in their junior or senior year. **Criteria:** Recipient is selected based on merit and evaluation of the applicant's scientific abilities and potential which includes versatility, ability to make sound judgments, major academic strengths and weaknesses (if any) and performance in an independent study (if any) as manifested through documents submitted.

Funds Avail.: $1,000. **Number Awarded:** 1. **To Apply:** Applicant must send the complete application package along with official transcripts and a stamped envelope to: Scholarship Committee Chair, National Society of Black Physicists, 6704G Lee Highway, Arlington, VA 22205. **Deadline:** January 12.

Remarks: Established to commemorate Dr. Robert A. Ellis, an internationally-recognized pioneer in modern experimental plasma physics.

5055 ■ Elmer S. Imes Scholarships in Physics *(Undergraduate/Scholarship)*

Purpose: To support interest in physics by providing educational assistance to skilled physics majors. **Focus:** Physics. **Qualif.:** Applicants must be physics majors in their junior or senior year. **Criteria:** Recipient is selected based on merit and evaluation of the applicant's scientific abilities and potential which includes versatility, ability to make sound judgments, major academic strengths and weaknesses (if any) and performance in an independent study (if any) as manifested through documents submitted.

Funds Avail.: $1,000. **Number Awarded:** 1. **To Apply:** Applicant must send the complete application package along with official transcripts and a stamped envelope to: Scholarship Committee Chair, National Society of Black Physicists, 6704G Lee Highway, Arlington, VA 22205. **Deadline:** January 12.

Remarks: Established to honor Elmer S. Imes, one of the first African-Americans to receive a Ph.D. degree in physics.

5056 ■ Walter Samuel McAfee Scholarships in Space Physics *(Undergraduate/Scholarship)*

Purpose: To support interest in physics by providing educational assistance to skilled physics majors. **Focus:** Physics. **Qualif.:** Applicants must be physics majors in their junior or senior year. **Criteria:** Recipient is selected based on merit and evaluation of the applicant's scientific abilities and potential which includes versatility, ability to make sound judgments, major academic strengths and weaknesses (if any) and performance in an independent study (if any) as manifested through documents submitted.

Funds Avail.: $1,000. **Number Awarded:** 1. **To Apply:** Applicant must send the complete application package along with official transcripts and a stamped envelope to: Scholarship Committee Chair, National Society of Black Physicists, 6704G Lee Highway, Arlington, VA 22205. **Deadline:** January 12.

Remarks: Established to commemorate Dr. Walter Samuel McAfee and his significant contributions in space communications, radar, and general understanding of electromagnetic propagation.

5057 ■ Ronald E. McNair Scholarships in Space and Optical Physics *(Undergraduate/Scholarship)*

Purpose: To support interest in physics by providing educational assistance to skilled physics majors. **Focus:** Physics. **Qualif.:** Applicants must be physics majors in their junior or senior year. **Criteria:** Recipient is selected based on merit and evaluation of the applicant's scientific abilities and potential which includes versatility, ability to make sound judgments, major academic strengths and weaknesses (if any) and performance in an independent study (if any) as manifested through documents submitted.

Funds Avail.: $1,000. **Number Awarded:** 1. **To Apply:** Applicant must send the complete application package along with official transcripts and a stamped envelope to: Scholarship Committee Chair, National Society of Black Physicists, 6704G Lee Highway, Arlington, VA 22205. **Deadline:** January 12.

Remarks: Established to commemorate Dr. Ronald E. McNair, an accomplished physicist and a NASA astronaut who perished in a space shuttle accident.

5058 ■ Willie Hobbs Moore Scholarships *(Undergraduate/Scholarship)*

Purpose: To support interest in physics by providing educational assistance to skilled physics majors. **Focus:** Physics. **Qualif.:** Applicants must be physics majors in their junior or senior year. **Criteria:** Recipient is selected based on merit and evaluation of the applicant's scientific abilities and potential which includes versatility, ability to make sound judgments, major academic strengths and weaknesses (if any) and performance in an independent study (if any) as manifested through documents submitted.

Funds Avail.: $1,000. **Number Awarded:** 1. **To Apply:** Applicant must send the complete application package along with official transcripts and a stamped envelope to: Scholarship Committee Chair, National Society of Black Physicists, 6704G Lee Highway, Arlington, VA 22205. **Deadline:** January 12.

Remarks: Established to commemorate Dr. Willie Hobbs Moore, the first African-American female to earn a Ph.D. degree in physics.

5059 ■ Harry L. Morrison Scholarships *(Undergraduate/Scholarship)*

Purpose: To support interest in physics by providing educational assistance to skilled physics majors. **Focus:** Physics. **Qualif.:** Applicants must be physics majors in their junior or senior year. **Criteria:** Recipient is selected based on merit and evaluation of the applicant's scientific abilities and potential which includes versatility, ability to make sound judgments, major academic strengths and weaknesses (if any) and performance in an independent study (if any) as manifested through documents submitted.

Funds Avail.: $1,000. **Number Awarded:** 1. **To Apply:** Applicant must send the complete application package along with official transcripts and a stamped envelope to: Scholarship Committee Chair, National Society of Black Physicists, 6704G Lee Highway, Arlington, VA 22205. **Deadline:** January 12.

Remarks: Established to commemorate Dr. Harry L. Morrison, a legendary figure in mathematical statistical physics.

5060 ■ Arthur BC Walker Scholarships *(Undergraduate/Scholarship)*

Purpose: To support interest in physics by providing educational assistance to skilled physics majors. **Focus:** Physics. **Qualif.:** Applicants must be physics majors in their junior or senior year. **Criteria:** Recipient is selected based on merit and evaluation of the applicant's scientific abilities and potential which includes versatility, ability to make sound judgments, major academic strengths and weaknesses (if any) and performance in an independent study (if any) as manifested through documents submitted.

Funds Avail.: $1,000. **Number Awarded:** 1. **To Apply:** Applicant must send the complete application package along with official transcripts and a stamped envelope to: Scholarship Committee Chair, National Society of Black Physicists, 6704G Lee Highway, Arlington, VA 22205. **Deadline:** January 12.

Remarks: Established to commemorate Dr. Arthur BC Walker, one of the most brilliant x-ray spectroscopists who ever lived.

5061 ■ National Society, Daughters of the American Revolution

1776 D St. NW
Washington, DC 20006-5303
Ph: (202)628-1776
URL: http://www.dar.org

5062 ■ American History Scholarships *(Undergraduate/Scholarship)*

Purpose: To promote the study of American history among students. **Focus:** American history. **Qualif.:** Applicants must be graduating students who want to pursue an undergraduate degree with a concentrated study of a minimum of 24 credit hours in American History and American Government. **Criteria:** Recipients will be selected by the scholarship committee based on the quality of the application materials submitted.

Funds Avail.: $2,000. **To Apply:** Applicants must obtain a letter of sponsorship from their local DAR chapter. Application forms and other supporting documents must be completed correctly and submitted in one package. **Deadline:** February 15.

5063 ■ J.E. Caldwell Centennial Scholarships *(Undergraduate/Scholarship)*

Purpose: To provide financial assistance to individuals who wish to pursue their degrees. **Focus:** Historic preservation. **Qualif.:** Applicants must be students who plan to pursue their course of graduate study in the field of historic preservation. **Criteria:** Recipients will be selected by the scholarship committee based on the quality of the application materials submitted.

Funds Avail.: $2,000. **To Apply:** Applicants must obtain a letter of sponsorship from their local DAR chapter. Application forms and other supporting documents must be completed correctly and submitted in one package. **Deadline:** February 15.

5064 ■ Enid Hall Griswold Memorial Scholarships *(Undergraduate/Scholarship)*

Purpose: To encourage students to pursue an undergraduate degree. **Focus:** Political science; History; Government; Economics. **Qualif.:** Applicants must be juniors or seniors enrolled in an accredited college or university in the United States; pursuing a major in political science, history, government, or economics. **Criteria:** Recipients will be selected by the scholarship committee based on the quality of the application materials submitted.

Funds Avail.: $1,000. **To Apply:** Applicants must obtain a letter of sponsorship from their local DAR chapter. Application forms and other supporting documents must be completed correctly and submitted in one package. **Deadline:** February 15.

5065 ■ National Society of High School Scholars

1936 N Druid Hills Rd.
Atlanta, GA 30319
Free: (866)343-1800
URL: http://www.nshss.org

5066 ■ Abercrombie and Fitch Global Diversity Scholar Awards *(High School/Scholarship)*

Purpose: To support members to attain higher education. **Focus:** General studies. **Qualif.:** Applicant must be a NSHSS member. **Criteria:** Selection is based on the submitted essay, and will be judged on ingenuity and quality.

Funds Avail.: $1000. **Number Awarded:** 10. **To Apply:** Applicants must submit a completed application form and required materials. **Deadline:** April 30.

5067 ■ Class Nobel Academic Scholarships for Members *(High School/Scholarship)*

Purpose: To support the education of student members. **Focus:** General studies. **Qualif.:** Applicants must be high school student members. **Criteria:** Selection is based on academic performance; demonstrated leadership; school and extracurricular activities; and community service.

Funds Avail.: $5000. **To Apply:** Apply online by going to the member log in page. **Deadline:** November 30.

5068 ■ Griffith College Scholarships for NSHSS Members *(High School/Scholarship)*

Purpose: To support members to attain higher education. **Focus:** General studies. **Qualif.:** Applicant must be a NSHSS member. **Criteria:** Selection is based on the application.

Funds Avail.: $1000. **Number Awarded:** 5. **To Apply:** Applicants must submit a completed application form and required materials. **Deadline:** April 30.

Remarks: Sponsored by Griffith College, Dublin.

5069 ■ Kaplan Test Prep and Admission Scholarships for NSHSS Members *(High School/Scholarship)*

Purpose: To support members to attain higher education. **Focus:** General studies. **Qualif.:** Applicant must be a

Awards are arranged alphabetically below their administering organizations

NSHSS member. **Criteria:** Selection is based on the application.

Funds Avail.: $1000. **Number Awarded:** 2. **To Apply:** Applicants must submit a completed application form together with the required materials and a stamped, self-addressed postcard. **Deadline:** April 30.

Remarks: Sponsored by Kaplan Test Prep and Admissions.

5070 ■ NSHSS Academic Paper Awards *(High School/Scholarship)*

Purpose: To support the education of student members. **Focus:** General studies. **Qualif.:** Applicant must be a NSHSS member. **Criteria:** Selection is based on the submitted materials.

Funds Avail.: $250. **Number Awarded:** Depends on the quantity and quality of entries. **To Apply:** Applicants must submit their written high school academic paper (research paper, original essay, or analytical paper) accompanied by the Academic Paper Awards entry form. **Deadline:** May 1.

Remarks: Applicants may submit one paper per year.

5071 ■ NSHSS National Scholar Awards *(High School/Scholarship)*

Purpose: To support the education of student members. **Focus:** General studies. **Qualif.:** Applicant must be a high school student member. **Criteria:** Selection is based on academic performance; demonstrated leadership; school and extracurricular activities; and community service.

Funds Avail.: $1000. **To Apply:** Apply online by going to the member log in page. **Deadline:** November 30.

Remarks: Award will be given to selected finalist for the Class Nobel Academic Scholarships.

5072 ■ Robert P. Sheppard Leadership Awards *(High School/Scholarship)*

Purpose: To support the education of student members. **Focus:** General studies. **Qualif.:** Applicant must be a high school student member. **Criteria:** Awards are given to the applicant who demonstrated outstanding commitment to community service and initiative in volunteer activities.

Funds Avail.: $1000. **To Apply:** Applicants must submit a completed application form together with the required materials. **Deadline:** February 1.

5073 ■ National Society for Histotechnology

10320 Little Patuxent Pkwy., Ste. 804
Columbia, MD 21044
Ph: (443)535-4060
Fax: (443)535-4055
E-mail: histo@nsh.org
URL: http://www.nsh.org

5074 ■ Robert A. Clark Memorial Educational Scholarships *(Other/Scholarship)*

Purpose: To provide educational scholarships and student scholarships to recipients on a reimbursement basis. **Focus:** Histology. **Qualif.:** Applicants must be pursuing advanced education and knowledge within the profession of histotechnology. **Criteria:** Recipients will be selected based on their sincere efforts and not necessarily upon academic merit.

Funds Avail.: $1,000. **Number Awarded:** 5. **To Apply:** Applicants must complete online application together with supporting documentation. **Deadline:** May 1. **Contact:** The Award Committee Chair, Jean Mitchell at the above address (see entry 5073).

5075 ■ Fisher Healthcare Educational Scholarships *(Other/Scholarship)*

Purpose: To provide educational scholarships and student scholarships to recipients on a reimbursement basis. **Focus:** Histology. **Qualif.:** Applicants must be pursuing advanced education and knowledge within the profession of histotechnology. **Criteria:** Recipients will be selected based on their sincere efforts and not necessarily upon academic merit.

Funds Avail.: $1,000. **Number Awarded:** 5. **To Apply:** Applicants must complete online application together with supporting documentation. **Deadline:** May 1. **Contact:** The Award Committee Chair, Jean Mitchell at the above address (see entry 5073).

5076 ■ Irwin S. Lerner Student Scholarships *(Undergraduate/Scholarship)*

Purpose: To provide educational scholarships and student scholarships to recipients on a reimbursement basis. **Focus:** General studies. **Qualif.:** Applicants must be students from approved histotechnology schools. **Criteria:** Applicants will be selected according to their academic ability and financial need.

Funds Avail.: $500. **Number Awarded:** 4. **To Apply:** Applicants must complete online application and submit with supporting documentation. **Deadline:** May 1. **Contact:** Award Committee Chair, Jean Mitchell at the above address (see entry 5073).

5077 ■ Newcomer Supply Student Scholarships *(Undergraduate/Scholarship)*

Purpose: To provide educational scholarships and student scholarships to recipients on a reimbursement basis. **Focus:** General studies. **Qualif.:** Applicants must be students from approved histotechnology schools. **Criteria:** Applicants will be selected according to their academic ability and financial need.

Funds Avail.: $500. **Number Awarded:** 4. **To Apply:** Applicants must complete online application and submit with supporting documentation. **Deadline:** May 1. **Contact:** Award Committee Chair, Jean Mitchell at the above address (see entry 5073).

5078 ■ Leonard Noble Educational Scholarships *(Other/Scholarship)*

Purpose: To provide educational scholarships and student scholarships to recipients on a reimbursement basis. **Focus:** Histology. **Qualif.:** Applicants must be pursuing advanced education and knowledge within the profession of histotechnology. **Criteria:** Recipients will be selected based on their sincere efforts and not necessarily upon academic merit.

Funds Avail.: $1,000. **Number Awarded:** 5. **To Apply:** Applicants must complete online application together with supporting documentation. **Deadline:** May 1. **Contact:** The Award Committee Chair, Jean Mitchell at the above address (see entry 5073).

5079 ■ Sakura Finetek Student Scholarships *(Undergraduate/Scholarship)*

Purpose: To provide educational scholarships and student scholarships to recipients on a reimbursement basis. **Fo-**

cus: General studies. **Qualif.:** Applicants must be students from approved histotechnology schools. **Criteria:** Applicants will be selected according to their academic ability and financial need.

Funds Avail.: $500. **Number Awarded:** 4. **To Apply:** Applicants must complete online application and submit with supporting documentation. **Deadline:** May 1. **Contact:** Award Committee Chair, Jean Mitchell at the above address (see entry 5073).

5080 ■ Dezna C. Sheehan Memorial Educational Scholarships *(Other/Scholarship)*

Purpose: To provide educational scholarships and student scholarships to recipients on a reimbursement basis. **Focus:** Histology. **Qualif.:** Applicants must be pursuing advanced education and knowledge within the profession of histotechnology. **Criteria:** Recipients will be selected based on their sincere efforts and not necessarily upon academic merit.

Funds Avail.: $1,000. **Number Awarded:** 5. **To Apply:** Applicants must complete online application together with supporting documentation. **Deadline:** May 1. **Contact:** The Award Committee Chair, Jean Mitchell at the above address (see entry 5073).

5081 ■ Sigma Diagnostics Student Scholarships *(Undergraduate/Scholarship)*

Purpose: To provide educational scholarships and student scholarships to recipients on a reimbursement basis. **Focus:** General studies. **Qualif.:** The applicants must be students from approved histotechnology schools. **Criteria:** Applicants will be selected according to their academic ability and financial need.

Funds Avail.: $500. **Number Awarded:** 4. **To Apply:** Applicants must complete online application together with supporting documentation. **Deadline:** May 1. **Contact:** The Award Committee Chair, Jean Mitchell at the above address (see entry 5073).

5082 ■ Thermo Scientific Educational Scholarships *(Other/Scholarship)*

Purpose: To provide educational scholarships and student scholarships to recipients on a reimbursement basis. **Focus:** Histology. **Qualif.:** Applicants must be pursuing advanced education and knowledge within the profession of histotechnology. **Criteria:** Recipients will be selected based on their sincere efforts and not necessarily upon academic merit.

Funds Avail.: $1,000. **Number Awarded:** 5. **To Apply:** Applicants must complete online application together with supporting documentation. **Deadline:** May 1. **Contact:** The Award Committee Chair, Jean Mitchell at the above address (see entry 5073).

5083 ■ Ventana Medical Systems In Situ Hybridization Awards *(Other/Award/Prize)*

Purpose: To provide educational scholarships and student scholarships to recipients on a reimbursement basis. **Focus:** Histology. **Qualif.:** The applicant must be pursuing an advanced education within the profession of histotechnology. **Criteria:** Recipient will be selected based on working achievement and/or academic merit.

Funds Avail.: $1,000. **Number Awarded:** 1. **To Apply:** Applicants must complete online application together with supporting documentation. **Deadline:** May 1. **Contact:** The Award Committee Chair, Jean Mitchell at the above address (see entry 5073).

5084 ■ National Space Club

2025 M St. NW, Ste. 800
Washington, DC 20006
Ph: (202)973-8661
E-mail: info@spaceclub.org
URL: http://www.spaceclub.org

5085 ■ Dr. Robert H. Goddard Memorial Scholarships *(Graduate, Undergraduate/Scholarship)*

Purpose: To stimulate the interest of students in the opportunity to advance scientific knowledge through space research and exploration. **Focus:** Engineering; Science. **Qualif.:** Applicant must be a U.S. citizen, in at least the junior year of an accredited university, and have the intention of pursuing undergraduate or graduate studies in science or engineering during the interval of the scholarship. **Criteria:** Recipients will be selected based on the NSC Committee on Scholarships' review of the application materials.

Funds Avail.: $10,000. **Number Awarded:** 1. **To Apply:** Applicants must submit an official transcript of college record; letters of recommendation from faculty; accomplishments demonstrating personal qualities of creativity and leadership; scholastic plans that would lead to future participation in some phase of the aerospace sciences and technology; and past research and participation in space-related science and engineering. **Deadline:** January 6.

5086 ■ National Speleological Society

2813 Cave Ave.
Huntsville, AL 35810-4431
Ph: (256)852-1300
Fax: (256)851-9241
E-mail: nss@caves.org
URL: http://www.caves.org

5087 ■ NSS Sara Corrie Memorial Grants *(All/Grant)*

Purpose: TO support cave exploration in the U.S territories. **Focus:** Cave studies. **Qualif.:** Applicants must be NSS members. **Criteria:** Selection is based on the application materials submitted.

Funds Avail.: $250. **To Apply:** Applicants must send a letter to the Chairman of the U.S Exploration Committee explaining the importance and usage of the grant as well as the amount needed. **Contact:** Thomas Shifflett, Committee Chairman, 540-554-2314.

5088 ■ NSS Conservation Grants *(All/Grant)*

Purpose: To support a cave conservation-linked research. **Focus:** Cave studies. **Qualif.:** Open to all individuals conducting a cave conservation-linked research, including student projects. **Criteria:** Selection is based on merit, impact of research and the qualifications of the applicant.

Funds Avail.: $5,000. **To Apply:** Application form is available from the website. Submit completed applications to: John E. Pearson, Administrator, NSS Conservation Grants 329 Brownstown Rd., Renick WV 24966-9649, fax to: 304497-3939, email to: jpearson@rcc.com.

Remarks: Submission through email is preferred. **Contact:**

Awards are arranged alphabetically below their administering organizations

Jim C. Werker, 505-895-5050, werks@zianet.com

5089 ■ NSS Education Grants *(All/Grant)*

Purpose: To promote cave and karst education. **Focus:** Cave studies. **Qualif.:** Applicant must be a private individual or organization. **Criteria:** Awards are given based on merit.

Funds Avail.: No specific amount. **To Apply:** Application form is available at the website. Applicants must submit the completed application form and send it electronically in MS Word or PDF file to amybern@juno.com. **Deadline:** March and September. **Contact:** Education Division Chief, Amy Bern, amybern@juno.com.

5090 ■ Ralph W. Stone Graduate Fellowships *(Graduate/Grant)*

Purpose: To support cave-related thesis research. **Focus:** Cave studies. **Qualif.:** Applicants must be NSS members currently pursuing graduate studies. **Criteria:** Recipients are selected based on the committee's review of submitted proposals.

Funds Avail.: $1,700. **To Apply:** Applicants must send a proposal which includes a project description; a resume with NSS number; a transcript; two letters of recommendation (one from the thesis advisor); a budget and its justification. Send proposals electronically in Word or Adobe Acrobat files to dmcfarla@jsd.claremont.edu. **Deadline:** March 25. **Contact:** Chair, NSS Research Advisory Committee, dmcfarla@jsd.claremont.edu.

5091 ■ Young Investigator Grants *(Undergraduate/Grant)*

Purpose: To support research done by younger members of the society. **Focus:** Cave studies. **Qualif.:** Applicant must be a NSS member under 22 years old. **Criteria:** Recipients are selected based on the committee's review of submitted proposals proposal.

Funds Avail.: $500. **To Apply:** Applicants must send an application including a narrative (four pages, double-spaced) about the motivation of the study, objectives and methodology, and a brief discussion of related literature. The application must also include a detailed budget; transcript; a brief statement of experience and interest (maximum of 250 words); and two letters of recommendation. Submit applications electronically (Word or .pdf files) to the Chair of the NSS Research Advisory Committee, dmcfarla@jsd.claremont.edu. **Deadline:** February 1.

5092 ■ National Sporting Clays Association

5931 Roft Rd.
San Antonio, TX 78253
Ph: (210)688-3371
Fax: (210)688-3014
Free: 800-877-5338
E-mail: nssa@nssa-nsca.com
URL: http://www.mynsca.com

5093 ■ NSSA/NSCA Collegiate Scholarships *(Undergraduate/Scholarship)*

Purpose: To support the education of a student active in sporting clays. **Focus:** General studies. **Qualif.:** Applicant must be a graduating high school senior; an NSCA member; pursuing a 4-year degree program; and active NSCA registered sporting clays participant. **Criteria:** Selection is based on scholarship, citizenship and participation in NSCA activities.

Funds Avail.: $5000. **Number Awarded:** 1. **To Apply:** Applicants must submit a completed Scholarship Application; an essay (maximum of 250 words) describing goals and reasons why deserve the scholarship; a letter of personal recommendation; copy of class rank/high school grades from the school registrar; and a copy of past shooting history and accomplishments. **Deadline:** May 31. **Contact:** Glynne Moseley.

5094 ■ National Stone Sand and Gravel Association

1605 King St.
Alexandria, VA 22314
Ph: (703)525-8788
URL: http://www.nssga.org

5095 ■ The Jennifer Curtis Byler Scholarships *(Undergraduate/Scholarship)*

Purpose: To provide scholarships to students who plan to pursue a career in the aggregates industry. **Focus:** Public affairs. **Qualif.:** Applicants must be graduating high school seniors or students enrolled in a public affairs major. Applicants must also be dependents of an aggregates company employee. **Criteria:** Recipients will be selected based on commitment to a career in public affairs.

Funds Avail.: No specific amount. **To Apply:** Applicants must submit a completed form; a letter of recommendation from a faculty advisor; a 300 to 500-word statement about the plans for a career in public affairs; a letter or recommendation from employer (if the applicant worked in public affairs as a summer employee). **Deadline:** May 31.

5096 ■ Samuel C. Kraus, Jr. Memorial Scholarships *(Undergraduate/Scholarship)*

Purpose: To provide scholarships to students pursuing a career in the crushed stone industry. **Focus:** Engineering, Mining and Mineral; Geology. **Qualif.:** Applicant must be a mining engineering or geology student at the University of Missouri Rolla. **Criteria:** Recipients are selected based on the committee's review of all portfolios.

Funds Avail.: No specific amount. **To Apply:** Contact the School of Mines and Metallurgy, University of Missouri Rolla for the application procedures. **Contact:** 64501-0249.

5097 ■ National Stroke Association

9707 E Easter Ln.
Centennial, CO 80112
Ph: (303)754-0902
Fax: (303)649-1328
Free: 800-787-6537
E-mail: info@stroke.org
URL: http://www.stroke.org

5098 ■ National Stroke Association Research Fellowships in Cerebrovascular Disease *(Doctorate/Fellowship)*

Purpose: To provide opportunities for promising investigators to develop and focus their research interests and efforts on the causes, mechanisms and treatment of cerebrovascular disease. **Focus:** Medicine, Cerebrovascular. **Qualif.:** Applicants must be medicine students with a specialization in cerebrovascular disease. **Criteria:** Preference will be given to applicants who meet the qualifications.

Awards are arranged alphabetically below their administering organizations

Funds Avail.: No specific amount. **To Apply:** Applicants must check the available website for the required materials. **Contact:** National Stroke Association at the above address (see entry 5097).

5099 ■ National Student Nurses' Association

45 Main St., Ste. 606
Brooklyn, NY 11201
Ph: (718)210-0705
Fax: (718)210-0710
E-mail: nsna@nsna.org
URL: http://www.nsna.org

5100 ■ The Foundation of the National Student Nurses' Association Scholarships *(Graduate, Undergraduate/Scholarship)*

Purpose: To promote education in nursing. **Focus:** Nursing. **Qualif.:** Applicant must be U.S. citizen enrolled in a State-approved school of nursing or pre-nursing in associate degree, baccalaureate, diploma, generic doctorate, and generic master's programs. **Criteria:** Selection is based on academic achievement; financial need; and involvement in nursing student organizations and community activities related to health care.

Funds Avail.: $1000-$2500. **To Apply:** Applicants must submit a copy of recent nursing school and college transcripts; proof of membership (for NSNA members); and a copy of RN license (if applicable). **Deadline:** January 9.

Remarks: In Memory of Frances Tompkins. **Contact:** FNSNA at (718) 210-0705.

5101 ■ National Swimming Pool Foundation

4775 Granby Circle
Colorado Springs, CO 80919-3131
Ph: (719)540-9119
Fax: (719)540-2787
URL: http://www.nspf.org

5102 ■ NSPF Ray B. Essick Scholarship Awards *(Other/Scholarship)*

Purpose: To encourage healthier living through aquatic education and research. **Focus:** Health education. **Qualif.:** Applicant must be a Certified Pool/Spa Operator; a Certified Pool/Spa Operator Instructor; or have an immediate family member possessing CPO certification. **Criteria:** Selection is based on the applications and supporting materials.

Funds Avail.: $2,000. **Number Awarded:** 1 per fall semester. **To Apply:** Application forms are available at the website. Applicants must prepare a biographical sketch (maximum of 300 words); a resume; a 2" x 3" photograph; an essay of no more than five double-spaced, 12 font size, type-written pages; official academic transcripts; a copy of recent SAT or ACT scores; two letters of recommendation from teachers or college professors. **Deadline:** June 1.

5103 ■ NSPF Board of Directors' Scholarship Awards *(Other/Scholarship)*

Purpose: To encourage healthier living through aquatic education and research. **Focus:** Health education. **Qualif.:** Applicant must be a Certified Pool/Spa Operator; a Certified Pool/Spa Operator Instructor; or have an immediate family member possessing CPO certification. **Criteria:** Selection is based on the applications and supporting materials.

Funds Avail.: $1,000. **Number Awarded:** 8 per fall semester. Application forms are available at the website. Applicants must prepare a biographical sketch (maximum of 300 words); a resume; a 2" x 3" photograph; an essay of no more than five double-spaced, 12 font size, type-written pages; official academic transcripts; a copy of recent SAT or ACT scores; two letters of recommendation from teachers or college professors. **Deadline:** June 1.

5104 ■ NSPF Scholarship Awards *(Other/Scholarship)*

Purpose: To encourage healthier living through aquatic education and research. **Focus:** Health education. **Qualif.:** Applicant must be a Certified Pool/Spa Operator; a Certified Pool/Spa Operator Instructor; or have an immediate family member possessing CPO certification. **Criteria:** Selection is based on the applications and supporting materials.

Funds Avail.: $1,000. **Number Awarded:** 8 per fall semester. Application forms are available at the website. Applicants must prepare a biographical sketch (maximum of 300 words); a resume; a 2" x 3" photograph; an essay of no more than five double-spaced, 12 font size, type-written pages; official academic transcripts; a copy of recent SAT or ACT scores; two letters of recommendation from teachers or college professors. **Deadline:** June 1.

5105 ■ National Taxidermists Association

108 Branch Dr.
Slidell, LA 70461
Ph: (866)662-9054
Fax: (985)641-9463
E-mail: ntahq@aol.com
URL: http://www.nationaltaxidermists.com

5106 ■ Charlie Fleming Education Fund Scholarships *(Undergraduate/Scholarship)*

Purpose: To provide cash scholarships for qualified NTA members, or their dependents, to further their education in Taxidermy, or to attain higher education. **Focus:** Taxonomy. **Qualif.:** Applicants must be NTA members and/or their children; member must be in the third year of continuous NTA membership. **Criteria:** Recipients are selected based on the scholarship committee's review of all applications.

Funds Avail.: $500 **To Apply:** Applicants must complete application form and file a statement outlining the reasons for furthering their education, as well as an explanation of how this education will benefit their future in the field of taxidermy. **Deadline:** April 30.

5107 ■ National Technical Honor Society

PO Box 1336
Flat Rock, NC 28731
Ph: (828)698-8011
Fax: (828)698-8564
URL: http://www.nths.org

5108 ■ HOSA Scholarships *(Undergraduate/Scholarship)*

Purpose: To promote career opportunities in health care; to enhance the delivery of quality health care to all people. **Focus:** Health care services. **Qualif.:** Applicant must be either a senior secondary or postsecondary student who plans to continue his/her education in the health care field; **Criteria:** Scholarship committee will evaluate the application based on the enrolled education; documents such as proof of acceptance into a program of health occupation/ health science education for the following academic year, leadership activities and recognition, community involvement, references, and personal statement.

Funds Avail.: $2,000. **To Apply:** Applicants must submit and mail in one envelope the typed, word-processed or legible handwriting application; he/she must submit letters of reference, and official transcript of record; all applications must be submitted directly to the National HOSA Headquarters; there is no limit to the number of applications per school or per state association. **Deadline:** April 20.

5109 ■ Leaders at Work Scholarship in Textiles and Apparel *(Undergraduate/Scholarship)*

Purpose: To help students set goals, makes plans, become leaders at work, and prepare for career success. **Focus:** General studies. **Qualif.:** Applicants must be high school seniors; must have been active members of Family, Career, and Community Leaders of America for a minimum of one year; must have paid national and state dues no later than March 1, 2008. **Criteria:** Recipients will be selected based on the grades, demonstrated leadership ability, ability to communicate well, and active participation and membership in an FCCLA Chapter.

Funds Avail.: $500. **Number Awarded:** 4. **To Apply:** Applicant must fill out the on-line application form; must complete the requirements for Outstanding Leader Recognition found on the Career Connection and Leaders at Work CD; must attach recent official high school transcript; a letter of recommendation from the food production and services, or Hospitality, Tourism, and Recreation instructor; and must submit a two-minute videotape (VHS or DVD format) which address the question "How will the leadership skills you have developed through FCCLA help you reach the Family and Consumer Sciences career goal?" and a copy of the chapter affiliation form verifying national dues payment by March 1.

5110 ■ Beth Middleton Memorial Scholarships *(Undergraduate/Scholarship)*

Purpose: To expand leadership potential and develop skills for lifeplanning, goal setting, problem solving, decision making and interpersonal communications. **Focus:** General studies. **Qualif.:** Applicant must be a member for a minimum of two years (not necessarily consecutive); a current or former FCCLA state or national officer; he/she must be senior and have a 3.5 GPA activities and have made a significant contribution to a state or national project exemplary of the goals and ideals of FCCLA. **Criteria:** Recipients will be selected based on academic records and contributions made as an officer.

Funds Avail.: $400 for tuition, room and/or board. **Number Awarded:** 1. **To Apply:** Applicant must fill out the on-line application form using a 10pt. Times New Roman font; must attach the most recent official high school transcript of record including the first semester of the senior year including standardized college entrance exam scores(ACT and/or SAT); must provide a copy of the chapter affiliation verifying national dues paid by December 1, 2007; applicants must include recommendations from their local adviser, state adviser, and one other person knowledgeable of student's non-FCCLA activities; **Deadline:** December 1.

5111 ■ National Technical Honor Society Scholarships *(Undergraduate/Scholarship)*

Purpose: To promote educational excellence; to enhance career opportunities for the NTHS membership. **Focus:** General studies. **Qualif.:** Applicant must be a member who has held the office of the President of the State FCCLA Association; must be a senior and must have taken the ACT or SAT examination; must have applied to a degree granting institution leading to an associate's or bachelor's degree in any field of study. **Criteria:** Recipients will be selected based on outstanding leadership, academic excellence, and significant volunteer experience; also, judges will base the evaluation to the style and expression as well as content.

Funds Avail.: $1,000. **To Apply:** Applicant must fill out the online application form using the 10pt. Times new Roman font; most recent official high school transcript including the first semester grades of the senior year and standardized college entrance exam scores(ACT and/or SAT); a copy of the chapter affiliation verifying national dues paid by January 1, 2008; applicants must include a letter of recommendation from their local adviser, state adviser, and one other person knowledgeable of student's non-FCCLA activities; all signatures must be included. **Deadline:** March 1.

5112 ■ Wiley Publishing Inc. Scholarships *(Undergraduate/Scholarship)*

Purpose: To help students set goals, makes plans, become leaders at work, and prepare for career success. **Focus:** General studies. **Qualif.:** Applicants must be students who have outstanding leadership qualities gain through FCCLA membership and other experiences in family, school, and community; applicants must be seniors who have affiliated with national FCCLA by March 1; must have taken the ACT or SAT examination; must have applied to a degree-granting institution leading to an associate's or bachelor's degree in any field of study. **Criteria:** Scholarship Committee will evaluate the application based on the style and expression as well as content.

Funds Avail.: $1,000. **Number Awarded:** 4. **To Apply:** Applicant must fill out the online application form; he/she must completed the requirements for Outstanding Leader Recognition found on the Career Connection and Leaders at Work CD; an applicant must submit the completed Outstanding Leader application form; he/she must attach recent official high school transcript; a letter of recommendation from the food production and services, or hospitality, tourism, and recreation instructor; and must submit a two-minute videotape(VHS or DVD format) which addresses the question "How will the leadership skills you have developed through FCCLA help you reach the family and consumer sciences career goal?"; and a copy of the chapter affiliation form verifying national dues payment by May 1.

5113 ■ National Throw Coaches Association

PO Box 14114
Palm Desert, CA 92255-4114
Ph: 888-527-6772
Fax: 800-859-4335
E-mail: rlasorsa@dc.rr.com
URL: http://www.nationalthrowcoachesassociation.org

5114 ■ John O'Connor Memorial Scholarship Fund *(Undergraduate/Scholarship)*

Purpose: To support and encourage children of NTCA members who wish to pursue higher learning. **Focus:**

General studies. **Qualif.:** Applicants must be children of NTCA members who are presently attending college or will be entering college next fall. **Criteria:** Selection of recipient is based on merit.

Funds Avail.: No specific amount. **To Apply:** Application can be obtained by calling the NTCA at (888) 527-6772.

5115 ■ National Union of Public and General Employees

15 Auriga Dr.
Nepean, ON, Canada K2E 1B7
Ph: (613)228-9800
Fax: (613)228-9801
E-mail: national@nupge.ca
URL: http://www.nupge.ca

5116 ■ Tommy Douglas Scholarships
(Undergraduate/Scholarship)

Purpose: To provide financial assistance for the post-secondary education of children of NUPGE members. **Focus:** General studies. **Qualif.:** Applicants must be children (including foster children) of National Union of Public and General Employees members who plan to enter the first year of a Canadian public post-secondary education institution. **Criteria:** Recipient will be selected based on an essay (750-1000 words) on "How Tommy Douglas contributed to making Canada a more just and equitable society.".

Funds Avail.: $1,500. **To Apply:** Application forms are available at the website. Applicants must submit an essay and completed application form to: Tommy Douglas Scholarship, National Union of Public and General Employees, 15 Auriga Dr., Nepean, ON K2E 1B7. **Deadline:** June 30.

5117 ■ Terry Fox Memorial Scholarships
(Undergraduate/Scholarship)

Purpose: To inspire the educational endeavors of students with disabilities. **Focus:** General studies. **Qualif.:** Applicants must be disabled children (including foster children) of NAPGE members entering as freshmen in a Canadian public post-secondary educational institution. **Criteria:** Recipient will be selected based on an essay (750-1000 words) on "The importance of quality public services in enhancing the quality of life of people with disabilities.".

Funds Avail.: $1,500. **To Apply:** Application forms are available at the website. Applicants must submit an essay completed application form to: Terry Fox Memorial Scholarship, National Union of Public and General Employees, 15 Auriga Dr., Nepean, ON K2E 1B7. **Deadline:** June 30.

5118 ■ Scholarships for Aboriginal Canadians
(Undergraduate/Scholarship)

Purpose: To assist Aboriginal Canadian students in their educational endeavors. **Focus:** General studies. **Qualif.:** Applicant must be aboriginal Canadian children (including foster children) of National Union of Public and General Employees members entering as freshmen in a Canadian public post-secondary educational institution. **Criteria:** Recipients will be selected based on an essay (750-1000 words) on "The importance of quality public services in enhancing the quality of life of Aboriginal Canadians.".

Funds Avail.: $1,500. **To Apply:** Application forms are available at the website. Applicants must submit an essay along with completed application form to: Scholarships for Aboriginal Canadians, National Union of Public and General Employees, 15 Auriga Dr., Nepean, ON K2E 1B7. **Deadline:** June 30.

5119 ■ Scholarships for Visible Minorities
(Undergraduate/Scholarship)

Purpose: To assist all visible minority students in their education. **Focus:** General studies. **Qualif.:** Applicants must be visible minority children (including foster children) of National Union of Public and General Employees members entering as freshmen in a Canadian public post-secondary educational institution. **Criteria:** Recipients will be selected based on an essay (750-1000 words) on "The importance of quality public services in enhancing the quality of life of visible minorities.".

Funds Avail.: $1,500. **To Apply:** Application forms are available at the website. Applicants must submit an essay along with completed application form to Scholarships for Visible Minorities, National Union of Public and General Employees, 15 Auriga Dr., Nepean, ON K2E 1B7. **Deadline:** June 30.

5120 ■ National Volunteer Fire Council

7852 Walker Dr., Ste. 450
Greenbelt, MD 20770
Ph: (202)887-5700
Fax: (202)887-5291
E-mail: nvfcoffice@nvfc.org
URL: http://www.nvfc.org

5121 ■ Junior Firefighter Scholarships
(Undergraduate/Scholarship)

Purpose: To provide resources on how to establish a program, a network for connecting with other program, and to increase recruitment and retention to junior firefighters. **Focus:** Fires and fire prevention. **Qualif.:** Applicant must be a high school senior, or a high school graduate within the past three years who is enrolled or will be enrolled in the following school year at an accredited two- or four-year institution of higher learning, a trade school or a certification program; be a pat or current junior firefighter in a department that is registered with the NVFC National Junior Firefighter Program. Applicants must also have proven to be an active and vital member of a junior firefighter program for at least one year and currently be active either as a junior firefighter or in some other capacity. Applicants must also have demonstrated intent to pursue emergency services. **Criteria:** Recipients are selected based on the objective judgment of the scholarship committee as to which candidates demonstrate the greatest potential for future involvement in emergency services as exhibited by their past emergency service record.

Funds Avail.: $5,000. **Number Awarded:** 10. **To Apply:** Applicants must complete the scholarship application form; must submit an official transcript from the institution most recently attended; complete a 250-word essay outlining how being a junior firefighter has impacted the applicant's life, how the scholarship will further field of study, and plans for the future involvement in emergency services; must submit two letters of recommendation; recent photo to be used for NVFC newsletter, website if selected; fire department must submit a 250-word essay outlining its current junior firefighter program and how a $5,000 grant would benefit the department. **Deadline:** May 15. **Contact:** nvfcoffice@nvfc.org.

5122 ■ National Women's Studies Association

7100 Baltimore Ave., Ste. 502
College Park, MD 20740
Ph: (301)403-0407
E-mail: nsaoffice@nwsa.org
URL: http://www.nwsa.org

5123 ■ Jewish Caucus Scholarships
(Undergraduate/Scholarship)

Purpose: To encourage the participation in NWSA of individuals whose presence enrich the diversity of and increase participation by underrepresented constituencies in the NWSA. **Focus:** Jewish studies. **Qualif.:** Applicants must be graduate students who are enrolled for the current academic year and who have a special interest in the lives, work and culture of Jewish women. **Criteria:** Recipients are selected based on the brief statement of financial need; feminist or community activities; and relevance of the research to NWSA goals. Preference will be given to those whose research show evidence of the application of feminist methodology to the study of Jewish women's experience or expression.

Funds Avail.: $1,000. **To Apply:** Applicants must complete the application form including name and contact information; dissertation/thesis title; two-to-three page abstract of the work; and two letters of recommendation. The Scholarship Review Committee would like applicants to attach a statement of no more than five pages addressing the following: demonstrate your preparation for conducting research in Jewish Women's Studies (please include a one-page abstract of your thesis or dissertation proposal); how have your activities demonstrated your interest in Jewish life and feminist life on campus or in your community; and what additional information about you, such as your background and other influences, might shed light on how you understand the relationship of feminism and Judaism. **Deadline:** March 1.

5124 ■ National Women's Studies Association Lesbian Scholarships *(Doctorate, Graduate/Scholarship)*

Purpose: To provide a $500 research award in recognition of a Master's Thesis or Doctoral Dissertation research project that resonates with the mission of NWSA and the goals of the Lesbian Caucus. **Focus:** General studies. **Qualif.:** Applicants must be graduate students embarking on the doctoral dissertation phase of their academic career. The field of degree is open, but the work should focus on lesbian (defined broadly) lives, identities, or realities and make a contribution to the fields of lesbian and sexuality studies. **Criteria:** Recipients are selected based on the clarity of project description; relevance to mission of NWS, goals of Lesbian Caucus, and field of Women's and Gender Studies; engagement of feminist analytical frameworks and methodologies; and potential impact on the fields of lesbian/sexuality studies.

Funds Avail.: $500. **To Apply:** Applicants must complete the application form including name and contact information; dissertation/thesis title; two-to-three page abstract of the work; and two (2) letters of recommendation. **Contact:** lcchair@lists.nwsa.org

5125 ■ NWSA Distinguished Fellowships *(All/Fellowship)*

Purpose: To promote research that contributes to the scholarship or public knowledge about feminism, women of color, Women's Studies, NWSA, or Women's Centers by providing NWSA members with opportunities to complete extended projects. **Focus:** General studies. **Qualif.:** Applicants must be members of NWSA and retain their membership through their fellowship if selected; must be faculty or staff members at colleges or universities or independent scholars or writers; must be at least five years into their professional work and must plan to complete the fellowship five or more years before retirement. **Criteria:** Recipients are selected based on the qualifications of candidates and impact of the proposal statement.

Funds Avail.: No specific amount. **To Apply:** Applicants must submit electronically a completed cover form; a vita not more than eight pages; a proposal statement (maximum of three pages); and three (3) letters of recommendation. **Deadline:** October 1.

5126 ■ NWSA Graduate Scholarships *(Graduate/Scholarship)*

Purpose: To encourage the participation in NWSA of individuals whose presence enrich the diversity of and increase participation by underrepresented constituencies in the NWSA. **Focus:** General studies. **Qualif.:** Program is open to members of NWSA who, in the fall of the year of the award, will be engaged in the research or writing stages of a Master's Thesis or Ph.D. Dissertation in the interdisciplinary field of women's studies. The research project must be on women and must enhance the NWSA mission. **Criteria:** Recipients are selected based on the brief statement of financial need; feminist or community activities; and relevance of the research to NWSA goals.

Funds Avail.: $1,000. **To Apply:** Applicants must complete the application form including name and contact information; dissertation/thesis title; two-to-three page of abstract of the work; and two letters of recommendation.

5127 ■ Native Women's Association of Canada

PO Box 331
1721 Chiefswood Rd.
Ohsweken, ON, Canada N0A 1M0
Ph: (519)445-0990
Fax: (519)445-0924
Free: (866)796-6053
URL: http://www.nwac-hq.org/en

5128 ■ Helen Bassett Commemorative Scholarships *(Undergraduate/Scholarship)*

Purpose: To provide financial support for students intending to pursue their law careers. **Focus:** Law. **Qualif.:** Applicants must be post-secondary students, specifically Aboriginal females, pursuing a law career; must be under 31 years old; must demonstrate financial need; and must demonstrate commitment to improving the situation of Aboriginal women and youth in Canada politically, culturally, economically or otherwise. **Criteria:** Applicants will be selected based on financial need and academic standing.

Funds Avail.: $1,000. **Number Awarded:** 4. **To Apply:** Applicants must submit application form, proof of age, and proof of Aboriginal descent; must have a proof of attending post-secondary studies: acceptance letter from a post-secondary institution; must have the most recent official transcript, proof of community involvement/interest and dedication in working on Aboriginal women's issues; one reference letter of support from a local community organization, or school, or any relevant organization/person; must

Awards are arranged alphabetically below their administering organizations

provide a short essay of 1-2 pages, and statement of financial need in a letter, plus monthly or yearly budget and a list of other funding sources and scholarships. Application form and all other required documents must be sent to CDC-Youth Native Women's Association of Canada, 1292 Wellington St., W, Ottawa, ON K1Y 3A9. **Deadline:** July 11.

5129 ■ Natural Hazards Research and Applications Information Center

482 UCB
Boulder, CO 80309-0482
Ph: (303)492-6818
Fax: (303)492-2151
E-mail: hazctr@colorado.edu
URL: http://www.colorado.edu/hazards

5130 ■ Mary Fran Myers Scholarships *(All/Grant)*

Purpose: To support individual commitment to disaster research. **Focus:** Emergency and disaster services. **Qualif.:** Applicants must be researchers, students, practitioners in disaster management. **Criteria:** Priority is given to applicants with financial need.

Funds Avail.: No specific amount. **To Apply:** Applicant must send four copies of the application form. **Deadline:** April. **Contact:** Lori Peek, lori.peek@colostate.edu.

5131 ■ Naval Intelligence Professionals

PO Box 11579
Burke, VA 22009-1579
E-mail: navintpro@aol.com
URL: http://www.navintpro.org

5132 ■ Vice Admiral Donald D. Engen Scholarships *(Undergraduate/Scholarship)*

Purpose: To provide financial assistance for higher education of NIP members. **Focus:** General studies. **Qualif.:** Applicants must be eligible for college entrance or be enrolled as full-time students in an undergraduate college program or must be active duty enlisted personnel enrolled as full-time students in either an accredited associate or bachelor degree program. **Criteria:** Recipient will be selected based on academic achievement (GPA); SAT or ACT scores; extra-curricular activities; and career objectives.

Funds Avail.: $1,000. **To Apply:** Applicants must submit completed application form along with supporting transcripts and SAT or ACT scores. **Deadline:** April 15.

5133 ■ Captain Anthony D. Sesow Scholarships *(Undergraduate/Scholarship)*

Purpose: To provide financial assistance for the education of NIP members. **Focus:** General studies. **Qualif.:** Applicants must be eligible for college entrance or be enrolled as full-time students in an undergraduate college program or must be active duty enlisted personnel enrolled as either full-time students in an accredited associate or bachelor degree program. **Criteria:** Recipients will be selected based on academic achievement (GPA); SAT or ACT scores; extra curricular activities; and career objectives.

Funds Avail.: $1,000. **To Apply:** Applicants must submit completed application form along with supporting transcripts and SAT or ACT scores. **Deadline:** April 15.

5134 ■ Commander Dan F. Shanower Scholarships *(Undergraduate/Scholarship)*

Purpose: To provide financial assistance for higher education of NIP members. **Focus:** General studies. **Qualif.:** Applicants must be eligible for college entrance or be enrolled as full-time students in an undergraduate college program or must be active duty enlisted personnel enrolled as either full-time students in an accredited associate or bachelor degree program. **Criteria:** Recipients will be selected based on academic achievement (GPA); SAT or ACT scores; extra-curricular activities; and career objectives.

Funds Avail.: $1,000. **To Apply:** Applicants must submit completed application form along with supporting transcripts and SAT or ACT scores. **Deadline:** April 15.

5135 ■ Naval Reserve Association

1619 King St.
Alexandria, VA 22314-2793
Ph: (703)548-5800
Fax: (866)683-3647
Free: (866)672-4968
E-mail: admin@navy-reserve.org
URL: http://www.navy-reserve.org

5136 ■ Naval Reserve Association Scholarships *(Undergraduate/Scholarship)*

Purpose: To provide educational assistance for the sons and daughters of members of the Naval Reserve Association. **Focus:** General studies. **Qualif.:** Applicants must be children of a NRA member in good standing; must be US citizens; must be under 24 years of age; and must be enrolled in or accepted for full-time enrollment at an accredited college, university or a fully-accredited technical school. **Criteria:** Selection will be based on the committee's criteria.

Funds Avail.: No specific amount. **To Apply:** Applicants may download an application form available at the NRA web site. **Deadline:** May 1.

5137 ■ Navy League of the United States

2300 Wilson Blvd., Ste. 200
Arlington, VA 22201-5424
Ph: (703)528-1775
Fax: (703)528-2333
Free: 800-356-5760
E-mail: execdirector@navyleague.org
URL: http://www.navyleague.org

5138 ■ John G. Brokaw Scholarships *(Undergraduate/Scholarship)*

Purpose: To assist in the college/university expenses of the dependents of sea service personnel. **Focus:** General studies. **Qualif.:** Applicant must be a U.S. citizen; a dependent or direct descendant of an active, reserve, retired or honorably discharged member of the US Navy, Coast Guard, US-Flag Merchant Marine, Marine Corps or US Naval Sea Cadet Corps; completing the final year of high school; and will be entering an accredited college/university. **Criteria:** Recipients will be selected based on the application materials submitted and other supporting documents.

Funds Avail.: $2,500. **To Apply:** Applicants must prepare a copy of all applicable transcripts (grade 9-present); two letters of recommendation; copy of SAT/ACT scores; FAFSA information; proof of qualifying sea service duty; a personal statement (one page) on the reasons to be considered for the program; and a list of extracurricular/

scholastic activities (maximum of two pages). **Deadline:** March 3.

5139 ■ Wesley C. Cameron Scholarships *(Undergraduate/Scholarship)*

Purpose: To assist in the college/university expenses of the dependents of sea service personnel. **Focus:** General studies. **Qualif.:** Applicant must be a U.S. citizen; a dependent or direct descendant of an active, reserve, retired or honorably discharged member of the US Navy, Coast Guard, US-Flag Merchant Marine, Marine Corps or US Naval Sea Cadet Corps; completing the final year of high school; and will be entering an accredited college/ university. **Criteria:** Recipients will be selected based on the application materials submitted and other supporting documents.

Funds Avail.: $2,500. **To Apply:** Applicants must prepare a copy of all applicable transcripts (grade 9-present); two letters of recommendation; copy of SAT/ACT scores; FAFSA information; proof of qualifying sea service duty; a personal statement (one page) on the reasons to be considered for the program; and a list of extracurricular/ scholastic activities (maximum of two pages). **Deadline:** March 3.

5140 ■ Ann E. Clark Foundation Scholarships *(Undergraduate/Scholarship)*

Purpose: To financially assist the dependents of sea service personnel for college/university expenses. **Focus:** General studies. **Qualif.:** Applicant must be a U.S. citizen; currently residing in the state of California; a dependent or direct descendant of an active, reserve, retired or honorably discharged member of the US Navy, Coast Guard, US-Flag Merchant Marine, Marine Corps or US Naval Sea Cadet Corps; completing his/her final year of high school and will be entering an accredited college/university. **Criteria:** Preference is given to applicants residing in California.

Funds Avail.: $2,500. **To Apply:** Applicants must prepare a copy of all applicable transcripts (grade 9-present); two letters of recommendation; copy of SAT/ACT scores; FAFSA information; proof of qualifying sea service duty; a personal statement (one page) on the reasons to be considered for the program; and a list of extracurricular/ scholastic activities (maximum of two pages). **Deadline:** March 3.

5141 ■ Capt. Winifred Quick Collins Scholarships *(Undergraduate/Scholarship)*

Purpose: To assist in the college/university expenses of the dependents of sea service personnel. **Focus:** General studies. **Qualif.:** Applicant must be a U.S. citizen; a dependent or direct descendant of an active, reserve, retired or honorably discharged member of the US Navy, Coast Guard, US-Flag Merchant Marine, Marine Corps or US Naval Sea Cadet Corps; completing the final year of high school; and will be entering an accredited college/ university. **Criteria:** Recipients will be selected based on the application materials submitted and other supporting documents.

Funds Avail.: $2,500. **To Apply:** Applicants must prepare a copy of all applicable transcripts (grade 9-present); two letters of recommendation; copy of SAT/ACT scores; FAFSA information; proof of qualifying sea service duty; a personal statement (one page) on the reasons to be considered for the program; and a list of extracurricular/ scholastic activities (maximum of two pages). **Deadline:** March 3.

5142 ■ Gladys Ann Smith Greater Los Angeles Women's Council Scholarships *(Undergraduate/ Scholarship)*

Purpose: To financially assist the dependents of sea service personnel for college/university expenses. **Focus:** General studies. **Qualif.:** Applicant must be a U.S. citizen; currently residing in the state of California; a dependent or direct descendant of an active, reserve, retired or honorably discharged member of the US Navy, Coast Guard, US-Flag Merchant Marine, Marine Corps or US Naval Sea Cadet Corps; completing his/her final year of high school and will be entering an accredited college/university. **Criteria:** Preference is given to applicants residing in California.

Funds Avail.: $2,500. **To Apply:** Applicants must prepare a copy of all applicable transcripts (grade 9-present); two letters of recommendation; copy of SAT/ACT scores; FAFSA information; proof of qualifying sea service duty; a personal statement (one page) on the reasons to be considered for the program; and a list of extracurricular/ scholastic activities (maximum of two pages). **Deadline:** March 3.

5143 ■ Subic Bay-Cubi Point 1 Scholarships *(Undergraduate/Scholarship)*

Purpose: To assist in the college/university expenses of the dependents of sea service personnel. **Focus:** General studies. **Qualif.:** Applicant must be a U.S. citizen; a dependent or direct descendant of an active, reserve, retired or honorably discharged member of the US Navy, Coast Guard, US-Flag Merchant Marine, Marine Corps or US Naval Sea Cadet Corps; completing the final year of high school; and will be entering an accredited college/ university. **Criteria:** Recipients will be selected based on the application materials submitted and other supporting documents.

Funds Avail.: $2,500. **To Apply:** Applicants must prepare a copy of all applicable transcripts (grade 9-present); two letters of recommendation; copy of SAT/ACT scores; FAFSA information; proof of qualifying sea service duty; a personal statement (one page) on the reasons to be considered for the program; and a list of extracurricular/ scholastic activities (maximum of two pages). **Deadline:** March 3.

5144 ■ William A. Sullivan Scholarships *(Undergraduate/Scholarship)*

Purpose: To assist in the college/university expenses of the dependents of sea service personnel. **Focus:** General studies. **Qualif.:** Applicant must be a U.S. citizen; a dependent or direct descendant of an active, reserve, retired or honorably discharged member of the US Navy, Coast Guard, US-Flag Merchant Marine, Marine Corps or US Naval Sea Cadet Corps; completing the final year of high school; and will be entering an accredited college/ university. **Criteria:** Preference will be given to residents of San Diego, California.

Funds Avail.: $2,500. **To Apply:** Applicants must prepare a copy of all applicable transcripts (grade 9-present); two letters of recommendation; copy of SAT/ACT scores; FAFSA information; proof of qualifying sea service duty; a personal statement (one page) on the reasons to be considered for the program; and a list of extracurricular/ scholastic activities (maximum of two pages). **Deadline:** March 3.

5145 ■ Navy-Marine Corps Relief Society

875 N Randolph St., Ste. 225
Arlington, VA 22203-1757

Ph: (703)696-4904
Fax: (703)696-0744
URL: http://www.nmcrs.org

5146 ■ Admiral Mike Boorda Scholarship Program *(Undergraduate/Scholarship)*

Purpose: To help eligible Navy and Marine Corps families pursue their academic goals by providing education grants and interest-free loans. **Focus:** General studies. **Qualif.:** Student must be enrolled in either: Marine Enlisted Commissioning Education Program (MECEP), Medical Enlisted Commissioning Program (MECP), or Meritorious Commissioning Program (MCP); must be a high school graduate (or equivalent) and enrolled or accepted as a full-time undergraduate student in a traditional classroom setting at a post-secondary, technical, or vocational institution participating in the U.S. Department of Education's Federal grant and loan program; must have a minimum cumulative GPA of 2.0 on a 4.0 scale; and must possess a current Navy or Marine Corps Military Identification Card. **Criteria:** Recipients are selected based on financial need.

Funds Avail.: $500-$2,500. **To Apply:** Application instructions and forms are available from the website. **Deadline:** May 1. **Contact:** NMCRS Education Division, phone: 703-696-4960 or DSN 426-4960, email: education@hq.nmcrs.org.

5147 ■ Dependents of Deceased Service Members Scholarship Program *(Undergraduate/Scholarship)*

Purpose: To provide educational assistance to spouses and children of members of the Society. **Focus:** General studies. **Qualif.:** Applicants must possess a current military dependent's Uniformed Services Identification and Privilege Card; must have a minimum cumulative GPA of 2.0 on a 4.0 scale; must be the immediate relative of an active duty Sailor or Marine who died as a result of the May 17, 1987 attack on the USS Stark, or the spouse of a service member disabled due to the terrorist attack on the USS STARK; the September 11, 2001 attack on the Pentagon; or the death of a Sailor or Marine due to hostile fire in a theater of combat operation during the Global War on Terrorism (GWOT). **Criteria:** Recipients will be selected based on merits.

Funds Avail.: No specific amount. **To Apply:** Application instructions and forms are available at the website. **Deadline:** March 1. **Contact:** NMCRS Education Division, phone: 703-696-4960 or DSN 426-4960, email: education@hq.nmcrs.org.

5148 ■ Spouse Tuition Aids Program *(Graduate, Undergraduate/Scholarship)*

Purpose: To help eligible Navy and Marine Corps families pursue their academic goals by providing education grants and interest-free loans. **Focus:** General studies. **Qualif.:** Program is open only to spouses residing with active duty service members stationed at overseas locations. **Criteria:** Recipients are selected based on financial need.

Funds Avail.: Up to 50% of tuition for on-base education programs; up to a maximum of $300 per undergraduate term or $350 per graduate term. Not to exceed $1,500/$1,750 per academic year. **To Apply:** Application forms and instructions are available from the website. **Contact:** Nearest overseas NMCRS location.

5149 ■ USS Tennessee Scholarship Fund *(Undergraduate/Scholarship)*

Purpose: To help eligible Navy and Marine Corps families pursue their academic goals by providing education grants and interest-free loans. **Focus:** General studies. **Qualif.:** Program is open to unmarried dependent children of sailors currently serving, or have served, aboard the USS Tennessee. Applicants must possess a current military dependent's Uniformed Services Identification and Privilege Card; must be a high school graduate (or equivalent) and enrolled or accepted as a full-time undergraduate student in a traditional classroom setting at a post-secondary, technical, or vocational institution participating in the U.S. Department of Education's Federal grant and loan program; must have a minimum cumulative GPA of 2.0 (on a 4.0 scale). **Criteria:** Recipients are selected based on financial need.

Funds Avail.: up to $2,000. **To Apply:** Application instructions and information are available at the society's website. **Deadline:** March 1. **Contact:** NMCRS Education Division, phone: 703-696-4960 or DSN 426-4960, email: education@hq.nmcrs.org.

5150 ■ Nazareth Association

PO Box 224
Nazareth, MI 49074
Ph: (269)342-1191
Fax: (269)381-0343
E-mail: office@nazarethassociation.org
URL: http://www.nazarethassociation.org

5151 ■ The Nazareth Scholarships *(Undergraduate/Scholarship)*

Purpose: To provide financial support for eligible undergraduate students of junior or senior status wishing to complete their degree at approved Catholic colleges in Michigan. **Focus:** General studies. **Qualif.:** Applicants must be currently enrolled at an approved Catholic college/university; must be undergraduate junior or senior students; and must have cumulative GPA of 3.0 or better on a 4.0 scale at the conclusion of the present year and be in good standing with their academic institution. **Criteria:** Recipients are selected based on demonstration of academic performance, extracurricular volunteer activities and/or community services.

Funds Avail.: $1,000. **To Apply:** Applicants must complete the application form and submit along with transcript of records, a 500-word essay and three letters of recommendation.

5152 ■ Nebraska Association of Legal Assistants

PO Box 24943
Omaha, NE 68124
E-mail: info@neala.org
URL: http://www.neala.org

5153 ■ Nebraska Association of Legal Assistants Student Scholarships *(Undergraduate/Scholarship)*

Purpose: To encourage and assist men and women in pursuit of training for careers as legal assistants. **Focus:** Law. **Qualif.:** Applicants must be Nebraska residents admitted and committed to enroll as half-time or full-time students in a university, college, community college or business college located in Nebraska that offers an accredited legal assistant program; must be in good standing with at least 3.0 GPA at the time of application. **Criteria:** Recipients are selected based on academic performance.

Awards are arranged alphabetically below their administering organizations

Funds Avail.: No specific amount. **To Apply:** Applicants must submit a completed application form, resume, two letters of recommendation from instructors, employers or community leaders, a copy of a letter of acceptance to a Nebraska legal assistant program, a statement of good academic standing for the most recent college term; recipients must pass the interview. **Deadline:** May 18.

5154 ■ Nebraska Farm Bureau

PO Box 80299
Lincoln, NE 68501
Fax: (402)421-4432
URL: http://www.nefb.org

5155 ■ Nebraska Farm Bureau Young Farmers and Ranchers Greater Horizon Scholarships

(Undergraduate/Scholarship)

Purpose: To encourage and assist young people between the ages of 18 and 35 to meet their personal goals of higher education. **Focus:** General studies. **Qualif.:** Applicants must be members or family of members of the county of Farm Bureau in Nebraska; must be residents of Nebraska; must have intention of enrolling full-time in a college or university's agricultural field of studies; must demonstrate leadership potential through extracurricular activities and work experiences; and must be 18 to 35 years of age. **Criteria:** Applicants are evaluated based on the criteria designed by the Selection Committee, comprised of three YF&R committee members, associate director/member services and assistant treasurer.

Funds Avail.: $1,000. **To Apply:** Applicants must submit the completed application form; three letters of reference; and copy of most recent transcript. **Deadline:** March 31.

5156 ■ Nebraska Grain Sorghum Producers Association

PO Box 94982
Lincoln, NE 68509
Ph: (402)471-3552
Fax: (402)470-3040
E-mail: sorghum@nrcdec.nrc.state.ne.us
URL: http://nesorghum.nol.org

5157 ■ Nebraska Grain Sorghum Producers Association Scholarships *(Undergraduate/Scholarship)*

Purpose: To aid and promote higher education in agriculture; to promote the study of sorghum and its impact on agriculture. **Focus:** Agricultural economics. **Qualif.:** Applicants must be graduating high school seniors or students who are currently enrolled in post-secondary education; must plan to pursue a course of study which will prepare him or her a career in agriculture or an ag-related field. **Criteria:** Recipients are selected based on interest in the field of agriculture.

Funds Avail.: $400. **To Apply:** Applicants must submit a completed application form; must submit a copy of transcript of records; letter of recommendation from a counselor or advisor with necessary signatures. Applicant must have membership status. **Deadline:** February 1. **Contact:** 402-471-3552.

5158 ■ Nebraska High School Rodeo Association

PO Box 10
Arnold, NE 69120
Ph: (308)848-2664
Fax: (308)848-2544
E-mail: becky.dailey@hotmail.com
URL: http://www.hsrodeo-nebraska.com

5159 ■ Tom Boots Memorial Scholarships

(Undergraduate/Scholarship)

Purpose: To assist graduating seniors of Nebraska High School Rodeo Association. **Focus:** General studies. **Qualif.:** Applicants must be graduating seniors of Nebraska High School. **Criteria:** Recipients are selected based on academic performance.

Funds Avail.: $500. **To Apply:** Applicants must submit a completed application form. **Contact:** 404 S Cleveland Ave. PO Box 101, Mullen, NE 69152.

5160 ■ Sharon Kreikemeier Memorial Scholarships *(Undergraduate/Scholarship)*

Purpose: To assist a senior boy or girl in the Nebraska High School Rodeo Association. **Focus:** General studies. **Qualif.:** Applicants must be enrolled in Nebraska High School. **Criteria:** Recipients are selected based on academic performance.

Funds Avail.: $500. **To Apply:** Applicants must complete the application form. **Contact:** 1327 D. Rd. West Point, NE 68788.

5161 ■ Brittany Mueller Memorial Scholarships

(High School/Scholarship)

Purpose: To assist a graduating senior girl who participates in the Break-A-Way Roping event in the Nebraska State High School. **Focus:** General studies. **Qualif.:** Applicants must be graduating senior girls in Nebraska High School with a 95% GPA. **Criteria:** Recipients are selected based on academic performance.

Funds Avail.: $500. **To Apply:** Applicants must submit a cover sheet including name, address and GPA; must submit an at least one page essay stating their career goals, one letter of recommendation and a copy of their grade transcripts. **Deadline:** June 1. **Contact:** 1600 N Prairie Trace Rd., Sutherland NE 69165.

5162 ■ Swede Swanson Memorial Scholarships

(Undergraduate/Scholarship)

Purpose: To assist a graduating student who participates in Steer Wrestling at Nebraska High School. **Focus:** Sports. **Qualif.:** Applicants must be graduating senior boys who participate in the Steer Wrestling event in the Nebraska High School Rodeo Association. **Criteria:** Recipients are selected based on academic performance.

Funds Avail.: $500. **To Apply:** Applicants must submit a cover sheet including name, address and GPA; must submit at least one page essay stating their career goals, one letter of recommendation and a copy of their grade transcripts. **Deadline:** June 1. **Contact:** 8696 S. Hershey Dickens Road Hershey, NE 69143.

5163 ■ Nebraska Hospital Association

3255 Salt Creek Circle, Ste. 100
Lincoln, NE 68504-4761
Ph: (402)742-8140
Fax: (402)742-8191
E-mail: info@nhanet.org
URL: http://www.nhanet.org

Awards are arranged alphabetically below their administering organizations

5164 ■ Nebraska Hospital Association Tuition Aid and Scholarships *(Undergraduate/Scholarship)*

Purpose: To advance the improvement of the health of the people of Nebraska through the provision of better health care; to foster and sponsor educational programs for training of health career personnel; to provide financial aid for Nebraska hospital employees needing assistance in the pursuit of an education in the health care field; to promote and sponsor research in health care issues. **Focus:** Medical education. **Qualif.:** Applicants must be enrolled in an accredited program leading to registration, licensure or a clinical laboratory science degree; must be employed by a member hospital of the Nebraska Hospital Association. **Criteria:** Recipients are selected based on academic performance and interest in a health career.

Funds Avail.: No specific amount. **To Apply:** Applicants must complete the application form.

5165 ■ Nebraska State Bar Association

PO Box 81809
Lincoln, NE 68501
Ph: (402)475-7091
Fax: (402)475-7098
Free: 800-927-0117
URL: http://www.nebar.com

5166 ■ Fraser Stryker Diversity Scholarship Program *(Undergraduate/Scholarship)*

Purpose: To provide college tuition assistance and paid internships at the firm for students of African-American, Asian, Latino and Native American origins from low-income families in the Omaha metro area. **Focus:** Law. **Qualif.:** Applicants must be pursuing law studies; must be African-American, Asian, Latino or Native American students; must be from low-income families in the Omaha metro area. **Criteria:** Preference will be given to those students who meet the criteria.

Funds Avail.: $2,500 per academic year. **To Apply:** Applicants must check the available website for the application process online. **Deadline:** March 9. **Contact:** For more information or application for the Fraser Stryker Diversity Scholarship Program, please visit www.fraserstryker.com.

5167 ■ New England Club Managers Association

300 Arnold Palmer Blvd., Ste. 227
Norton, MA 02766-1365
Ph: (774)430-9050
Fax: (774)430-9051
E-mail: necma@necma.org
URL: http://www.necma.org

5168 ■ Hospitality Food Service Scholarships *(Undergraduate/Scholarship)*

Purpose: To support students of hospitality studies and those interested in the club management profession. **Focus:** Service food careers. **Qualif.:** Applicants must be full-time students in a degree program with a minimum 3.0 GPA; must be currently working in the club industry and demonstrate an interest in continuing to work in the field. **Criteria:** Recipients are selected based on achievement.

Funds Avail.: No specific amount. **To Apply:** Applicants must submit a completed and neat application form; a transcript; references; and an essay. **Deadline:** September 14.

5169 ■ David Meador Student Scholarships *(Undergraduate/Scholarship)*

Purpose: To support students of hospitality studies and those interested in the club management profession. **Focus:** General studies. **Qualif.:** Applicants must be full-time students currently working within the club industry, while studying. **Criteria:** Recipients are selected based on achievement.

Funds Avail.: No specific amount. **To Apply:** Applicants must submit a completed and neat application form; a transcript; references; and an essay. **Deadline:** September 14.

5170 ■ New Hampshire Automotive Dealers Association

PO Box 2337, 507 S St.
Concord, NH 03302-2337
Ph: (603)224-2369
Fax: (603)225-4895
Free: 800-852-3372
E-mail: pmcnamara@nhada.com
URL: http://www.nhada.com

5171 ■ The Medallion Fund Scholarships *(Undergraduate/Scholarship)*

Purpose: To assist individuals who are interested in attending accredited vocational or technical programs; to improve the workforce skills, especially in areas of need, in the state of New Hampshire. **Focus:** Automotive technology. **Qualif.:** Applicants must be legal residents of New Hampshire; must have a keen desire to work in a vocational/technical career. **Criteria:** Recipients are selected based on demonstrated clear vision for how their education will help them achieve or improve their employment goals and on commitment to their educational program, both financially and otherwise.

Funds Avail.: No specific amount. **To Apply:** Applicants must submit a completed application form, high school or college transcript, a signed letter of recommendation from an Automotive Technology or other technical instructor and a signed letter of recommendation from a high school math, science or English teacher, verifying applicants' ability to do satisfactory academic work at the postsecondary level. **Contact:** 37 Pleasant St., concord, NH 03301-4005.

5172 ■ New Hampshire Snowmobile Association

614 Laconia Rd., Unit 4
Tilton, NH 03276
Ph: (603)273-0220
Fax: (603)273-0218
E-mail: nhsaoffice@nhsa.com
URL: http://www.nhsa.com

5173 ■ New Hampshire Snowmobile Association Scholarships *(Undergraduate/Scholarship)*

Purpose: To assist the education of a dependent of a NHSA member. **Focus:** General studies. **Qualif.:** Applicant must be a graduating high school senior, accepted at a college, junior college, or vocational school; or a college student already enrolled. **Criteria:** The scholarship commit-

Awards are arranged alphabetically below their administering organizations

tee will review applications and will select based on academic achievement, extracurricular involvement, community service and the quality of the original essay.

Funds Avail.: $1000. **Number Awarded:** 1. **To Apply:** Applicants must submit a completed application form along with the required documents. Send materials to Jim Strickland, Chairman, NHSA Scholarship, PO Box 417, Marlow, NH 03456. **Deadline:** March 1.

5174 ■ New Jersey Association of Osteopathic Physicians and Surgeons

1 Distribution Way, Ste. 201
Monmouth Junction, NJ 08852
Ph: (732)940-9000
Fax: (732)940-8899
E-mail: njaops@njosteo.com
URL: http://www.njosteo.com

5175 ■ New Jersey Association of Osteopathic Physicians and Surgeons Scholarships
(Undergraduate/Scholarship)

Purpose: To promote public health, unite professionals for the maintenance of high standards of practice and osteopathic education; to promote scientific research. **Focus:** Osteopathic medicine. **Qualif.:** Applicants must be students entering their first year in an osteopathic college; must be residents of New Jersey and have completed four years of pre-medical education. **Criteria:** Recipients are selected based on undergraduate academic achievement, financial need, motivation and professional promise.

Funds Avail.: No specific amount. **To Apply:** Applicants must submit a completed application form, four completed reference evaluation forms, MCAT scores, pre-med college transcript and an essay stating their reasons for becoming an osteopathic physician. **Deadline:** April 30. **Contact:** njaops@njosteo.com.

5176 ■ New Jersey Performing Arts Center

36 Park Place
Newark, NJ 07102
Ph: (973)642-8989
Free: 888-466-5722
E-mail: ticketservices@njpac.org
URL: http://www.njpac.org

5177 ■ Jeffrey Carollo Music Scholarships
(Undergraduate/Scholarship)

Purpose: To motivate talented young artists seeking an outlet for musical expression. **Focus:** Music. **Qualif.:** Applicants must be enrolled in the music program at the Newark Community School of the Arts. **Criteria:** Recipients are selected based on demonstrated interest in the field of music.

Funds Avail.: No specific amount. **To Apply:** Applicants must submit a completed application form. **Contact:** 973-353-8009.

5178 ■ Star-Ledger Scholarships for the Performing Arts *(Undergraduate/Scholarship)*

Purpose: To provide higher education opportunities for the young people of Newark; to provide an opportunity to gain practical experience at the New Jersey Performing Arts Center through internships. **Focus:** Performing Arts. **Qualif.:** Applicants must be high school seniors who wish to realize their potential by attending college but who may not be able to attend because of financial limitations. **Criteria:** Recipients are selected based on merit and demonstrated potential to become leading arts professionals.

Funds Avail.: No specific amount. **To Apply:** Applicants must submit a completed application form.

5179 ■ New Jersey Press Foundation

840 Bear Tavern Rd., Ste. 305
West Trenton, NJ 08628-1019
Ph: (609)406-0600
Fax: (609)406-0300
E-mail: jjobrien@njpa.org
URL: http://www.njpa.org

5180 ■ Richard Drukker Memorial Scholarships
(Undergraduate/Scholarship)

Purpose: To promote journalism careers and newspaper readership among New Jersey residents. **Focus:** Journalism. **Qualif.:** Applicants must be journalism minors and staff members of the Montclarion. **Criteria:** Recipients are selected based on academic standing and financial need.

Funds Avail.: $2,000. **To Apply:** Applicants must complete the application form and submit an academic transcript for all college work completed; three samples of journalistic writing that has appeared in any newspaper or was done for class assignments; a statement of interest in a newspaper career, written as an autobiographical sketch describing their journalistic skills and achievements (not more than 500 words); and a statement of financial or family circumstances. **Deadline:** February 28.

5181 ■ Bernard Kilgore Memorial Scholarships
(Undergraduate/Scholarship)

Purpose: To promote journalism career and newspaper readership among New Jersey residents. **Focus:** Journalism. **Qualif.:** Applicants must be graduating high school seniors. Applicants must be planning to study journalism in college and to pursue a journalism career; must have at least a 3.0 GPA on a 4.0 scale and have participated in high school journalism for at least two years. **Criteria:** Recipients are selected based on academic record and financial need.

Funds Avail.: $5,000. **To Apply:** Applicants must submit an official entry form; a self-analytical evaluation of the journalistic life using a creative form; and one action photo of themselves in a journalistic role; and an official copy of their transcript. Applicants should secure three to four letters of recommendation from advisers, teachers familiar with their leadership and journalistic abilities, or practitioners with whom they have worked. **Deadline:** February 15.

5182 ■ Isaac Roth Newspaper Carrier Scholarships Program *(Undergraduate/Scholarship)*

Purpose: To promote journalism careers and newspaper readership among New Jersey residents. **Focus:** Journalism. **Qualif.:** Applicants must be adult carriers who are currently enrolled as full-time college students and plan to continue as full-time students. **Criteria:** Recipients are selected based on financial need and academic standing.

Funds Avail.: $2,000. **To Apply:** Applicants must complete the application form. Applicants must submit an essay of 150 words; a copy of thier transcript; and up to five letters

Awards are arranged alphabetically below their administering organizations

of recommendation from the carrier's route customers. **Deadline:** April 30.

5183 ■ New Jersey Psychological Association

414 Eagle Rock Ave., Ste.211
West Orange, NJ 07052
Ph: (973)243-9800
Free: 800-281-6572
E-mail: njpa@psychologynj.org
URL: http://www.psychologynj.org

5184 ■ New Jersey Psychological Association Scholarships for Minority Graduate Students *(Postgraduate/Scholarship)*

Purpose: To support the needs of underserved communities through research or service. **Focus:** Psychology. **Qualif.:** Applicants must be graduate students enrolled at at a New Jersey university or college at the master's or doctoral level of study, or an intern at a New Jersey facility; must be minority group members as defined by federal guidelines; must be students in good standing at their college or university. **Criteria:** Recipients are selected based on social significance of the study, scientific rigor of the study, originality of the study, feasibility and clarity of written expression.

Funds Avail.: $2,000. **To Apply:** Applicants must submit four copies of a 1,000-1,500 word project proposal to the NJPA Foundation; must submit a completed application form; must substantiate his/her claim to minority status according to federal guidelines. **Deadline:** July 14.

5185 ■ Dorothy D. Palmer Scholarship for the Study of Optimal Aging in Women *(Postdoctorate/Scholarship)*

Purpose: To support the training of psychologists. **Focus:** Psychology. **Qualif.:** Applicants must be doctoral students enrolled in a New Jersey university. **Criteria:** Recipients are selected based on demonstrated interest in gerontology and women's studies, and attitude in working with aging women at a comprehensive retirement facility.

Funds Avail.: $5,000. **To Apply:** Applicants must submit a brief statement of professional goals as well as specific training goals consistent with the nature of the scholarship; must submit a completed application form. **Deadline:** July 14.

5186 ■ New Mexico Association for Bilingual Education

PO Box 5190
Clovis, NM 88102-5190
Ph: (505)309-3599
Fax: (505)769-0742
E-mail: nmabe@suddenlink.net
URL: http://www.nmabe.net

5187 ■ New Mexico Association for Bilingual Education Scholarships *(Undergraduate/Scholarship)*

Purpose: To provide financial support for deserving students intending to pursue studies in the area of bilingual education. **Focus:** Bilingual Education. **Qualif.:** Applicants must be juniors or seniors in a New Mexico university bilingual education teacher preparation program. Applicants must have a GPA of 3.0 or better for initial consideration and for renewals. They must reapply by the appropriate deadline for consideration each semester. **Criteria:** Preference will be given to those students who meet the criteria.

Funds Avail.: No specific amount. **To Apply:** Applicants must submit the completed application form; two letters of recommendation; a written essay in Spanish or a Native American language outlining their reasons for entering the field of Bilingual Education; and current university transcripts. **Contact:** New Mexico Association for Bilingual Education at the above address (see entry 5186).

5188 ■ New York Financial Writers Association

PO Box 338
Ridgewood, NJ 07451-0338
Ph: (201)612-0100
Fax: (201)612-9915
E-mail: info@nyfwa.org
URL: http://www.nyfwa.org

5189 ■ New York Financial Writers' Associations Scholarships *(Graduate, Undergraduate/Scholarship)*

Purpose: To provide financial assistance to those studying business, finance, and journalism. **Focus:** Business; Finance; Journalism. **Qualif.:** Undergraduate or graduate journalism students in the Metropolitan New York area who are seriously interested in pursuing a career in business and financial journalism. **Criteria:** Recipients are chosen based on the application materials submitted.

Funds Avail.: No specific amount. **To Apply:** Applicants must send an application form together with an essay explaining why the applicant is pursuing a career in business and financial journalism, current resume, list of other scholarships received and samples of financial writings and clippings created. If an application form is unavailable, applicants may submit a cover letter with the requirements listed. **Deadline:** April 15. **Contact:** NYFWS Scholarship Committee at the above address (see entry 5188).

5190 ■ New York School Nutrition Association

125 Wolf Rd.
Albany, NY 12205
Ph: (518)446-9061
Fax: (518)446-0113
E-mail: suzanne@nyssfsa.org
URL: http://www.nyssfsa.org

5191 ■ Jeff Siegel Scholarships *(Undergraduate/Scholarship)*

Purpose: To help defray the cost of food service education for students; to provide means of recognition for the school food service department. **Focus:** Service food careers. **Qualif.:** Applicants must be recommended by a NYSNA member who has been an active member for at least one year; must be high school graduating students in the year the scholarship is awarded, from the school where the Director is employed; must have been accepted at a college with a program in food service and intend to pursue a career in the food service industry. **Criteria:** Recipients are selected based on the required documents and academic performance.

Funds Avail.: No specific amount. **To Apply:** Applicants

Awards are arranged alphabetically below their administering organizations

must attach a letter of recommendation from the NYSNA member who submitted their name for the award; must attach a 200 word essay on how/why they chose food service as their future career; must attach a letter of recommendation from a school official, guidance counselor, principal etc.; must attach a copy of letter of acceptance from college; must submit a copy of high school transcript, including first semester of the senior year; must attach any additional comments or information that will be helpful. **Deadline:** May 1. **Contact:** 125 Wolf Rd., Ste. 315, Albany, NY 12205.

5192 ■ New York State Association of Agricultural Fairs

714 Nellis St.
Watertown, NY 13601
Ph: (315)771-3003
E-mail: carousels4@aol.com
URL: http://www.nyfairs.org

5193 ■ New York State Association of Agricultural Fairs Scholarships *(Undergraduate/Scholarship)*

Purpose: To provide financial assistance to those high school and college students who have been active in their local fairs and who intend to pursue higher education in an agricultural or fair management related field. **Focus:** Agricultural economics. **Qualif.:** Applicants must be in their senior year of high school in New York State or New York residents planning to pursue or already attending college in an agricultural or fair management-related field at an accredited institution of higher education. **Criteria:** Recipients are selected based on quality of the essay, citizenship and leadership, fair participation, field of study, presentation of application and academic achievements.

Funds Avail.: $1,000. **To Apply:** Applicants must complete the application form.

5194 ■ The New York Times Company Foundation

230 W 41st St., Ste. 1300
New York, NY 10036-7207
Ph: (212)556-1091
URL: http://www.nytco.com/company/foundation

5195 ■ The New York Times College Scholarships *(Undergraduate/Scholarship)*

Purpose: To support students who have overcome exceptional hardship to achieve excellence in New York City high schools. **Focus:** General studies. **Qualif.:** Applicants must be seniors who are attending public, parochial or private high schools in New York City; must have demonstrated academic achievement, commitment to learning-especially in the face of financial and other obstacles, and community service. **Criteria:** Awards are given based on merit and need.

Funds Avail.: $7,500. **Number Awarded:** 8. **To Apply:** Applicants may contact The New York Times Company Foundation for the application. **Contact:** at the above address (see entry 5194).

5196 ■ New York Water Environment Association

525 Plum St., Ste. 102
Syracuse, NY 13204
Ph: (315)422-7811
Fax: (315)422-3851
E-mail: mail@nywea.org
URL: http://www.nywea.org

5197 ■ N.G. Kaul Memorial Scholarships *(Postdoctorate/Scholarship)*

Purpose: To help lead the way toward existing state and national clean water programs. **Focus:** Environmental science. **Qualif.:** Applicants must be students pursuing graduate or doctoral degrees in environmental/civil engineering or environmental science, concentrating on water quality; must show commitment to government service. **Criteria:** Recipients are selected based on demonstrated interest in or commitment to pursue government service, relevance of career objective to the environmental field related to water quality, academic potential, character and other activities.

Funds Avail.: $2,500. **To Apply:** Applicants must complete the application form; must provide letter verifying enrollment or acceptance in a college environmental program on college stationary; must attach transcripts, and two requested essays. **Deadline:** February 28.

5198 ■ New York Water Environment Association Scholarships *(Undergraduate/Scholarship)*

Purpose: To help lead the way toward existing state and national clean water programs. **Focus:** Environmental science. **Qualif.:** Applicants must be students enrolled at a college or university where there is a NYWEA student chapter or high school students who will be enrolled in an environmentally related program in a four year college or university. **Criteria:** Recipients are selected based on academic performance.

Funds Avail.: $1,500. **To Apply:** Applicants must complete the application form; must submit a requested essay; official school transcript; and a minimum of two letters of recommendation, from which one must come from a teacher and the other from someone not related to the applicant. **Deadline:** January 22.

5199 ■ New York Women in Communications Foundation

355 Lexington Ave., 15th Fl.
New York, NY 10017-6603
Ph: (212)297-2133
Fax: (212)370-9047
URL: http://www.nywici.org

5200 ■ New York Women in Communications, Inc. Foundation Scholarships *(Graduate, Undergraduate/Scholarship)*

Purpose: To provide financial assistance for the education of the residents of NY, NJ, CT, or PA. **Focus:** Advertising; Broadcasting; Communications; Media arts; Journalism; Marketing and distribution; Media arts; Public relations. **Qualif.:** Applicants must be high school seniors, or college undergraduate or graduate students who are permanent residents of NY, NJ, CT or PA majoring or declaring a major in a communications-related field, including but not limited to advertising, broadcasting, communications, English, film, journalism, marketing, new media, or public relations. Applicants must have an overall GPA of 3.2 or better (or the high school equivalent). **Criteria:** Recipients are selected based on academic achievement, need, demonstrated leadership, participation in school and community-service

Awards are arranged alphabetically below their administering organizations

activities, honors and other awards or recognitions, work experience, statement of goals and aspirations, and unusual personal and/or family circumstances.

Funds Avail.: No specific amount. **To Apply:** Applicants must submit completed application form and all other required application information and materials. **Deadline:** January 30.

5201 ■ The Newspaper Guild

501 3rd St. NW, 6th Fl.
Washington, DC 20001-2797
Ph: (202)434-7177
Fax: (202)434-1472
URL: http://www.newsguild.org

5202 ■ The Irving Leuchter Memorial Scholarships *(All/Scholarship)*

Purpose: To provide training related to the executive and administrative responsibilities of union officers as well as their community role as trade unionists. **Focus:** General studies. **Qualif.:** Applicants must be full-time union staff of locals or TNG in good standing. **Criteria:** Recipients must be adjudged capable of meeting the instructional standards of the program and of benefiting from such a course of study.

Funds Avail.: $10,500. **To Apply:** Applicants must submit complete application. **Deadline:** November 1.

5203 ■ Newswomen's Club of New York

15 Gramercy Park S
New York, NY 10003
Ph: (212)777-1610
URL: http://www.newswomensclubnewyork.com

5204 ■ Anne O'Hare McCormick Scholarship Fund *(Undergraduate/Scholarship)*

Purpose: To provide financial assistance to aspiring journalists to pursue their careers. **Focus:** Journalism. **Qualif.:** Applicants must be journalists attending Columbia University's Graduate School of Journalism; must be citizens of the United States and have financial need. **Criteria:** Selections are based on the trustee's estimate of each candidate's ability, determination to succeed, and potential for a career in journalism.

Funds Avail.: $5,000. **Number Awarded:** 2. **To Apply:** Application form must be print or type clearly. Applicant must submit the list of job-related experience, with dates of employment; must have a brief statement of financial resources, including needs for tuition and living expenses during the academic year; must have two letters of recommendation that focus on the applicants qualifications for the field of journalism; must prepare an autobiographical essay mentioning family, educational background, journalistic experience and goals; must have one or two examples of the applicant's writing. Application and other documents must be sent to: Anne O'Hare McCormick Journalism Scholarship Fund, Newswomen's Club of New York, 15 Gramercy Park S, 2nd Flr., New York, NY 10003. **Deadline:** June 1.

5205 ■ Ninety-Nines, International Organization of Women Pilots

4300 Amelia Earhart Rd.
Oklahoma City, OK 73159
Ph: (405)685-7969
Fax: (405)685-7985
Free: 800-994-1929
E-mail: 99s@ninety-nines.org
URL: http://www.ninety-nines.org

5206 ■ AE Flight Training Scholarships *(Professional Development/Scholarship)*

Purpose: To assist licensed pilot members who wish to complete an additional pilot certificate and pilot training course. **Focus:** Aviation. **Qualif.:** Applicant must be a member of The Ninety-Nines Inc.; a current pilot with appropriate medical certificate; must have sufficient flight time experience to meet or exceed the fight time requirement for the certificate; must demonstrate financial need; must be qualified as a pilot. **Criteria:** Awards are given based on credentials and financial need.

Funds Avail.: Covers entire cost of the pilot training course or additional pilot certificate or pilot rating. **To Apply:** Applicant must complete the application form (please visit website) on an 8 1/2x11 paper (clipped or stapled) and submit it to the Section AE Scholarship Chairman or to Section Governor. **Contact:** Joy Parker-Blackwood, AEMSF Chairman aechair@ninety-nines.org, 905-841-7930.

5207 ■ AE Jet Type Rating Scholarships *(Professional Development/Scholarship)*

Purpose: To assist licensed pilot members who wish to complete type rating certification in any jet aircraft. **Focus:** Aviation. **Qualif.:** Applicant must be a member of The Ninety-Nines Inc.; a current Airline Transport Pilot with first-class medical certificate; must have a minimum of 100 hours multi-engine flight time or combined multi-engine and turbine time. **Criteria:** Awards are given based on credentials and financial need.

Funds Avail.: Covers one complete training course for a jet type rating. **To Apply:** Applicant must complete the application form (please visit website) on an 8 1/2x11 paper (clipped or stapled) and submit it to the Section AE Scholarship Chairman or to Section Governor. **Contact:** Joy Parker-Blackwood, AEMSF Chairman aechair@ninety-nines.org, 905-841-7930.

5208 ■ AE Technical Training Scholarships *(Professional Development/Scholarship)*

Purpose: To assist licensed pilot members to complete an aerospace technical training or certification course. **Focus:** Aviation. **Qualif.:** Applicant must be a member of The Ninety-Nines Inc.; a current Airline Transport Pilot with first-class medical certificate; have a minimum of 100-hours multi-engine flight time or combined multi-engine and turbine time. **Criteria:** Awards are given based on credentials and financial need.

Funds Avail.: No specific amount. **To Apply:** Applicant must complete the application form (please visit website) on an 8 1/2x11 paper (clipped or stapled) and submit it to the Section AE Scholarship Chairman or to Section Governor. **Contact:** Joy Parker-Blackwood, AEMSF Chairman aechair@ninety-nines.org, 905-841-7930.

5209 ■ Amelia Earhart Memorial Academic Scholarships *(Undergraduate/Scholarship)*

Purpose: To provide financial assistance for students pursuing education in the field of aviation and aerospace **Focus:** Aviation. **Qualif.:** Applicant must be currently enrolled in a degree seeking institution in the field of

Awards are arranged alphabetically below their administering organizations

aerospace and aviation; must be a member of The Ninety-Nines Inc. Associates and bachelor degree students must have a cumulative GPA of 3.0 or better on a 4.0 scale, or equivalent; and must demonstrate financial need. **Criteria:** Awards are given based on credentials and financial need.

Funds Avail.: $5,000. **To Apply:** Applicant must complete the application form (please visit website) on an 8 1/2x11 paper (clipped or stapled) and submit it to Section AE Scholarship Chairman or to Section Governor. **Contact:** Joy Parker-Blackwood, AEMSF Chairman aechair@ninety-nines.org, 905-841-7930.

5210 ■ Non Commissioned Officers Association

PO Box 33790
San Antonio, TX 78265-3790
Ph: (210)653-6161
Free: 800-662-2620
E-mail: execdir@ncoausa.org
URL: http://www.ncoausa.org

5211 ■ NCOA Scholarships *(Undergraduate/Scholarship)*

Purpose: To assist the children and spouses of NCOA members who wish to pursue their education. **Focus:** General studies. **Qualif.:** Applicant must be a spouse or child of a NCOA member and must be 25 years old and below (for children of members). **Criteria:** Recipients will be selected by the committee of educators.

Funds Avail.: $900 (nine children and four spouses), two special awards of $1,000, and one $1,000 from all applications. **Number Awarded:** 16. **To Apply:** Children of NCOA members must submit a completed application form; two letters of recommendation; a handwritten autobiography; personal letter of recommendation; transcripts; copy of ACT/SAT scores; and a composition (maximum of 200 words) about Americanism. Spouses of NCOA members must submit a completed application form; a copy of high school diploma or GED; transcript of completed college courses (if any); a certificate of completion for other training courses; a brief biography; and a letter of intent on: degree course of study, plans for completion of a degree program, and a paragraph about "What a College Degree Means to Me." Mail all documents in one complete package to: NCOA Scholarship Fund, Inc., PO Box 33610, San Antonio, TX 78265. **Deadline:** March 31.

Remarks: Students must maintain a B average to be considered for renewal.

5212 ■ Bettsy Ross Educational Fund *(All, Professional Development/Scholarship)*

Purpose: To assist division members who wish to improve their skills by taking a course at a local business or technical school. **Focus:** Data processing. **Qualif.:** Applicant must be a NCOA Auxiliary Division member. **Criteria:** Applicant selection is based on the submitted applications.

Funds Avail.: $250. **Number Awarded:** 6. **To Apply:** Applicant must submit an application form and forward it to: NCOA Scholarships 10635 IH 35 N San Antonio, TX 78233.

Remarks: The scholarship is named after NCOA International Auxiliary President, Bettsy Ross. **Contact:** tkish@ncoausa.org.

5213 ■ Nor' Easters Snowmobile Club

PO Box 517
Hollis, NH 03049
E-mail: hollisnoreasters@yahoo.com
URL: http://www.noreasters.org

5214 ■ Nor' Easters Scholarships - Four-year Program *(Undergraduate/Scholarship)*

Purpose: To support the education of a student member. **Focus:** General studies. **Qualif.:** Applicant must be a high school senior of exemplary character; a club member; must demonstrate an active interest primarily in the sport of snowmobiling, or secondarily in trail management and maintenance; and must exemplify a commitment to community service. **Criteria:** Selection is based on the application.

Funds Avail.: $1000. **Number Awarded:** 1-2. **To Apply:** Applicants must submit a completed application form along with the required documents. **Deadline:** May 2.

5215 ■ Nor' Easters Scholarships - Two-year Program *(Undergraduate/Scholarship)*

Purpose: To support the education of a student member. **Focus:** General studies. **Qualif.:** Applicant must be a high school senior of exemplary character; a club member; must demonstrate an active interest primarily in the sport of snowmobiling, or secondarily in trail management and maintenance; and must exemplify a commitment to community service. **Criteria:** Selection is based on the application.

Funds Avail.: $500. **Number Awarded:** 1-2. **To Apply:** Applicants must submit a completed application form along with the required documents. **Deadline:** May 2.

5216 ■ North American Conference on British Studies

1600 Woodland Rd.
Abington, PA 19001
Ph: (215)881-7584
Fax: (215)881-7333
E-mail: axa24@psu.edu
URL: http://www.nacbs.org

5217 ■ NACBS Dissertation Year Fellowships *(Postdoctorate/Fellowship)*

Purpose: To support dissertation research in the British Isles on any topic of British history or British studies. **Focus:** History. **Qualif.:** Applicant must be a citizen or permanent resident of the United States or Canada; enrolled in a PhD program in a U.S. or Canadian institution; has completed all degree requirements for dissertation; must be nominated by a dissertation advisor; must need to travel to the British Isles for the purpose of dissertation research and must conduct full-time research in the British Isles for a period of at least six months. **Criteria:** Selection is based on merit and importance of research.

Funds Avail.: $6,000. **Number Awarded:** 1. **To Apply:** Nomination must be supported by a letter of recommendation; application consists of the two letters of nomination and recommendation, one-page curriculum vitae, a 1000-word research proposal which should explain the importance of the topic to the field of British history. Send materials to: Professor Nadja Durbach, University of Utah, 318 Carlson Hall, 380 S 1400 E, Rm. 00211, Salt Lake City, UT, 84112. **Deadline:** March 15. **Contact:** Professor Nadja Durbach, n.durbach@utah.edu.

5218 ■ NACBS-Huntington Library Fellowships *(Postdoctorate/Fellowship)*

Purpose: To aid in dissertation research in British studies using the collections of the library. **Focus:** History. **Qualif.:**

Awards are arranged alphabetically below their administering organizations

Applicants must be U.S. or Canadian citizens or permanent residents; must be enrolled in a PhD program in a U.S. or Canadian institution; the time of fellowship tenure must be spent in residence at the Huntington Library. **Criteria:** Selection is based on merit and importance of research.

Funds Avail.: $2,000. **To Apply:** Applications should consist of a curriculum vitae, two supporting letters (one from applicant's dissertation advisor) and a description of the research project. A copy of the application package must be sent to each member of the Huntington Library Fellowship Committee. **Deadline:** November 30.

5219 ■ North American Interfraternal Foundation

1750 Royalton Dr.
Carmel, IN 46032-9620
Ph: (317)595-9613
URL: http://www.nif-inc.net

5220 ■ Jack Anson Fellowships *(Graduate/Fellowship)*

Purpose: To support a current or former staff member of a national social fraternity or sorority who is currently enrolled or has applied for a graduate study at an accredited college or university. **Focus:** General studies. **Qualif.:** Applicants must be pursuing degrees in student personnel, college administrative work or contemplating work for their sorority or fraternity professional staff. **Criteria:** Applicants will be selected based on the screening and award process.

Funds Avail.: $1,000. **Number Awarded:** 2. **To Apply:** Applicants must submit a completed application form; letters of recommendation; official transcript; graduate or professional school acceptance letter.

Remarks: To honor Jack Anson of Phi Kappa Tau Fraternity for his years of dedicated service to his fraternity and to the interfraternal movement.

5221 ■ Lloyd G. Balfour Fellowships *(Graduate/Fellowship)*

Purpose: To provide financial assistance to full-time students who are enrolled in accredited graduate or professional schools. **Focus:** General studies. **Qualif.:** Applicants must be graduate students who are members of NIC; NPC; NPHC and PFA fraternities. **Criteria:** Applicants will be selected based on scholastic achievement, campus and community involvement and leadership within one's fraternity/sorority.

Funds Avail.: $1,000-$5,000. **Number Awarded:** 10. **To Apply:** Applicants must submit complete application; official transcript from college or university; copy of graduate or professional school acceptance letter. **Deadline:** April.

Remarks: Initiated in 1985 in honor of Lloyd G. Balfour of Sigma Chi Fraternity.

5222 ■ James H. McLaughlin Scholarships *(Undergraduate/Scholarship)*

Purpose: To provide funding for individuals with outstanding fraternal leadership who are enrolled in Canadian universities. **Focus:** General studies. **Qualif.:** Applicants must be undergraduate students who are attending or are agreeable to transfer to a Canadian university; must be a founding member or new member of a Canadian colony or interest group; or must be an IFC or Panhellenic officer at a Canadian University. **Criteria:** Award is given based on results of screening and award processing.

Funds Avail.: $500. **Number Awarded:** 1. **To Apply:** Applicants must submit a completed application and official transcript from college or university. **Deadline:** April.

5223 ■ Mary Louise Roller Panhellenic Scholarships *(Undergraduate/Scholarship)*

Purpose: To provide educational funding to undergraduate female students intending to pursue graduate studies. **Focus:** General studies. **Qualif.:** Applicants must be undergraduate women with desire to attend graduate school. **Criteria:** Award is given based on demonstrated outstanding service to applicant's local college panhellenic during her undergraduate year.

Funds Avail.: $1,500. **Number Awarded:** 1. **To Apply:** Applicants must submit a completed application; official transcript from college or university; letter of endorsement from Panhellenic Council; letter of endorsement from Panhellenic Advisor; and copy of acceptance letter from graduate school.

Remarks: Scholarship is funded by a grant from Alpha Omicron Pi Fraternity in honor of Mary Louise Roller's 33 year tenure on AOPi's Panhellenic Delegation.

5224 ■ North American Serials Interest Group

PMB 305
1902 Ridge Rd.
West Seneca, NY 14224
E-mail: info@nasig.org
URL: http://www.nasig.org

5225 ■ NASIG Conference Student Grants *(Postdoctorate/Grant)*

Purpose: To encourage participation in the serials information chain. **Focus:** Computer and information sciences. **Qualif.:** Applicants must be full or part-time students who are currently enrolled at the graduate level at an ALA-accredited library school. **Criteria:** Applicants must not have attended a previous NASIG conference, but may have participated in a NASIG conference as a local volunteer.

Funds Avail.: No amount mentioned. **To Apply:** Applicants must submit a completed application form and a reference questionnaire. **Deadline:** February 15.

5226 ■ Fritz Schwartz Serials Education Scholarships *(Other/Scholarship)*

Purpose: To advance the serials profession by providing educational opportunities for students with prior serials experience. **Focus:** Internet design and development. **Qualif.:** Applicants must be students in any NASIG member country (defined for this purpose as the United States, Canada, Mexico, and Greenland). **Criteria:** Priority is given to applicants with serials-related work experience and a desire to pursue a professional serials career after earning the graduate library degree.

Funds Avail.: $3,000. **Deadline:** February 15.

5227 ■ North American Society for the Sociology of Sport

PO Box 291
Bowling Green, OH 43402
Ph: (419)352-1928
Fax: (419)354-2957
E-mail: treasurer@nasss.org
URL: http://www.nasss.org

Awards are arranged alphabetically below their administering organizations

5228 ■ NASSS Graduate Minority Scholarships *(Graduate/Scholarship)*

Purpose: To support ethnic minority graduate students who are doing research in the area of sport sociology. **Focus:** Sociology. **Qualif.:** Applicants must be NASSS members. **Criteria:** Recipient selection will be performed by the NASSS Diversity and Climate Committee.

Funds Avail.: $500. **To Apply:** Applicants must submit a one-page essay stating how they would contribute to the field of sociology, along with a faculty recommendation from someone who is familiar with the applicant's work and aspirations. **Deadline:** August 8.

5229 ■ North Carolina American Water Works Association

3701 National Dr., Ste. 205
Raleigh, NC 27612
Ph: (919)784-9030
Fax: (919)784-9032
E-mail: sshoaf@ci.burlington.nc.us
URL: http://www.ncsafewater.org

5230 ■ Carol Bond College Scholarships *(Undergraduate/Scholarship)*

Purpose: To encourage interest in environmental education. **Focus:** Environmental science. **Qualif.:** Applicants must be future or current community college students; must be either high school seniors accepted for enrollment or current community college students enrolled at a North Carolina community college; must be pursuing a degree in Environmental Sciences or Water Resources Management concentrations; must be U.S. citizens. **Criteria:** Recipients are selected based on potential to provide leadership in the environmental sciences and environmental engineering fields and potential to positively impact the fields.

Funds Avail.: $1,000. **To Apply:** Applicants must submit: an official application form; one copy of an official, sealed transcript of all university education; two letters of recommendation from professors, employers, or academic advisors; a 500-750 word typed or legibly written essay that discusses why theyu should be a scholarship recipient; proof of U.S. citizenship. **Deadline:** June 1.

5231 ■ Carol Bond Environmental Educator Scholarships *(Professional Development/ Scholarship)*

Purpose: To encourage interest in environmental education. **Focus:** Environmental science. **Qualif.:** Applicants must be environmental educators; must be North Carolina accredited teachers; must be U.S. citizens. **Criteria:** Recipients are selected based on potential to provide leadership and to promote knowledge of the environmental science and/or engineering fields.

Funds Avail.: $500. **To Apply:** Applicants must submit: an official application form; one reference letter from non-family member, limited to one page, submitted in a sealed envelope with referee's signature on the flap; a 500-750 word typed or legibly written essay that discusses why they should be a scholarship recipient and what motivates them to educate others about the environment; proof of U.S. citizenship. **Deadline:** September 1.

5232 ■ Carol Bond University Scholarships *(Undergraduate/Scholarship)*

Purpose: To encourage interest in environmental education. **Focus:** Environmental science. **Qualif.:** Program is open to four-year university students pursuing a bachelor's degree in either Environmental Sciences or Environmental Engineering. Applicants must have a minimum overall 2.75 GPA and must be U.S. citizens. **Criteria:** Recipients are selected based on academic record and potential to provide leadership in the environmental sciences and environmental engineering fields.

Funds Avail.: $1,000. **To Apply:** Applicants must submit: an official application form; a copy of an official, sealed transcript of all university education; two letters of recommendation from professors, employers, or academic advisors; a 500-750 word typed or legibly written essay that discusses why they should be a scholarship recipient; proof of U.S. citizenship. **Deadline:** April 1.

5233 ■ North Carolina Association of Health Care Recruiters

High Point Regional Hospital PO Box HP-5
High Point, NC 27261
Ph: (336)878-6029
Fax: (336)878-6709
E-mail: cglover@hprhs.com
URL: http://www.ncahcr.org

5234 ■ North Carolina Association of Health Care Recruiters Scholarships *(Undergraduate/ Scholarship)*

Purpose: To assist, encourage and enable deserving students currently enrolled in an accredited program for health professions. **Focus:** Health care services. **Qualif.:** Applicants must be full-time students in North Carolina who have been accepted into an accredited ADN, BSN or allied health program. **Criteria:** Recipients are selected based on academic performance.

Funds Avail.: $500. **To Apply:** Applicants must complete the application form.

5235 ■ North Carolina Commercial Flower Growers Association

PO Box 58220
Raleigh, NC 27658
Ph: (919)334-0093
Fax: (919)877-0940
E-mail: smgbryan@aol.com
URL: http://www.nccfga.org

5236 ■ North Carolina Commercial Flower Growers Association Floriculture Scholarships *(Undergraduate/Scholarship)*

Purpose: To support research on biological control of sweet potato and other integrated pest management approaches for greenhouse insect control. **Focus:** Horticulture. **Qualif.:** Applicants must be full-time horticulture, entomology, or plant pathology students with an emphasis in greenhouse floriculture production; must be in their final year at a two-year, four-year or graduate institution. **Criteria:** Recipients are selected based on academic performance.

Funds Avail.: $500. **To Apply:** Applicants must submit a completed application form.

5237 ■ North Carolina Economic Developers Association

1201 Edward Mill Rd., Ste. 102
Raleigh, NC 27607

Awards are arranged alphabetically below their administering organizations

Ph: (919)882-1961
Fax: (919)882-1902
Free: 888-246-2332
E-mail: nceda@capstrat.com
URL: http://www.nceda.org

5238 ■ Jack Ervin EDI Scholarships *(Professional Development/Scholarship)*

Purpose: To recognize and support the advancement of outstanding practitioners; to offer an advanced level of training on a broad range of subjects and skills required to carry out an effective economic development program; to prepare participants for professional certification eligibility; and to provide graduates the necessary level of education. **Focus:** Economics. **Qualif.:** Applicants must be residing and working in North Carolina; must be members of NCEDA for duration of the program; and must have completed two years of economic development work. Additionally, applicants must show completion of or plans to complete the Basic Course, a prerequisite to the Economic Development Institute. **Criteria:** Recipients are selected based on financial need and professional development.

Funds Avail.: $1,950 (total value). **To Apply:** Application package must include documents demonstrating need for financial assistance as well as documents demonstrating planned career path in the profession (past, present and future) and how the program fits into those plans; letters of recommendation are suggested. Four (4) original copies of all documents must be submitted to: Amy Jackson at the above address. **Deadline:** February 20. **Contact:** Amy Jackson at the above address (see entry 5237).

5239 ■ Governor James E. Holshouser Professional Development Scholarships *(Professional Development/Scholarship)*

Purpose: To recognize and support the advancement of outstanding practitioners. **Focus:** Economics. **Qualif.:** Applicants must be residing and working in North Carolina; must be members of NCEDA for duration of the program; and must have demonstrated financial need. Additionally, applicants must show completion of or plans to complete the Basic Course, a prerequisite to the Economic Development Institute. **Criteria:** Recipients are selected based on financial need.

Funds Avail.: $1,000. **To Apply:** Application package must include documents demonstrating need for financial assistance as well as documents demonstrating planned career path in the profession (past, present and future) and how the program fits into those plans; letters of recommendation are suggested. Four (4) original copies of all documents must be submitted to: Amy Jackson at the above address. **Deadline:** February 20. **Contact:** Amy Jackson at the above address (see entry 5237).

5240 ■ The Dan Stewart Scholarships *(Professional Development/Scholarship)*

Purpose: To recognize and support the advancement of outstanding practitioners by paying tuition to the one-week basic economic development course at UNC-Chapel Hill. **Focus:** Economics. **Qualif.:** Applicants must be: residing and working in North Carolina; members of NCEDA for the duration of the program; and willing to complete all coursework. **Criteria:** Recipients are selected based primarily on financial need, followed by demonstrated professional development and presentation of the application itself.

Funds Avail.: $575. **To Apply:** Application package must include documents demonstrating need for financial assistance as well as documents demonstrating chosen career path in the profession (past, present and future) and how the program fits into those plans; letters of recommendation are suggested. Four (4) original copies of all documents must be submitted to: Amy Jackson at the above address. **Deadline:** February 20. **Contact:** Amy Jackson at the above address (see entry 5237).

5241 ■ North Carolina Nursery and Landscape Association

968 Trinity Rd.
Raleigh, NC 27607
Ph: (919)816-9119
Fax: (919)816-9118
E-mail: rgelvin@ncan.com
URL: http://www.ncnla.com

5242 ■ Certified Landscape Technician Scholarships *(Undergraduate/Scholarship)*

Purpose: To identify and reward horticulture students who exemplify scholastic aptitude, positive attitude and industry potential. **Focus:** Landscape technology. **Qualif.:** Applicants must be full-time students enrolled in a horticulture curriculum and interested in becoming CLT-certified. **Criteria:** Recipients are selected based on academic performance and demonstrated interest in landscaping.

Funds Avail.: $250. **To Apply:** Applicants must complete the application form. **Deadline:** April 24. **Contact:** 919-816-9119.

5243 ■ North Carolina Nursery and Landscape Association Horticulture Scholarships *(Undergraduate/Scholarship)*

Purpose: To identify and reward horticulture students who exemplify scholastic aptitude, positive attitude and industry potential. **Focus:** Horticulture. **Qualif.:** Applicants must be full-time students who are enrolled in a two-to-four year horticulture program in North Carolina. **Criteria:** Recipients are selected based on academic performance, attitude and leadership potential.

Funds Avail.: No specific amount. **To Apply:** Applicants must complete the application form; must submit a resume, transcripts and a wallet size black and white photograph. **Deadline:** May 14.

5244 ■ North Carolina Simmental Association

1341 Hwy. 21
Hamptonville, NC 27020
Ph: (336)468-1679
Fax: (336)468-1686
E-mail: ncsa@yadtel.net
URL: http://www.ncsimmental.com

5245 ■ Jim Graham Scholarships *(Undergraduate/Scholarship)*

Purpose: To develop and promote the Simmental breed of cattle in the state of North Carolina; to help members of the North Carolina Simmental Association promote, improve and market their cattle. **Focus:** Agricultural sciences. **Qualif.:** Applicants must be high school or college students planning to pursue or pursuing a career in an agricultural-related field of study; must maintain a 2.0 GPA. **Criteria:**

Awards are arranged alphabetically below their administering organizations

must submit a completed application form with a one-page resume in English; a 200-word statement in English; and a recommendation letter in a signed and sealed envelope, from the department chair, principal or dean. Send all materials to Cemanahuac Summer Study Scholarships, Northeast Conference c/o Dickinson College PO Box 1773 Carlisle, PA 17013-2896. **Deadline:** December 1. **Contact:** nectfl@dickinson.edu.

5264 ■ French Embassy Scholarships *(Other/Scholarship)*

Purpose: To support the teaching of French in the United States. **Focus:** Education, Bilingual and cross-cultural; Foreign languages. **Qualif.:** Applicants must be full-time teachers in a public or private school, at any level; must teach in the Northeast Conference region (CT, DE, ME, MD, MA, NH, NJ, NY, PA, RI, VT, VA, WV, DC); must carry a teaching load of at least 50% Spanish classes; and have attended at least one Northeast Conference. **Criteria:** Selection is based on merits and the need for an experience in Mexico.

Funds Avail.: No specific amount. **To Apply:** Applicants must submit a completed application form with a one-page resume in English; a 200-word statement in English; and a recommendation letter in a signed and sealed envelope, from the department chair, principal or dean. Send all materials to Cemanahuac Summer Study Scholarships, Northeast Conference c/o Dickinson College PO Box 1773 Carlisle, PA 17013-2896. **Deadline:** December 1. **Contact:** nectfl@dickinson.edu.

5265 ■ Goethe-Institut AATG Scholarships *(Other/Scholarship)*

Purpose: To support the teaching of German in the United States. **Focus:** Education, Bilingual and cross-cultural; Foreign languages. **Qualif.:** Applicants must be full-time teachers in a public or private school, at any level; must teach in the Northeast Conference region (CT, DE, ME, MD, MA, NH, NJ, NY, PA, RI, VT, VA, WV, DC); must carry a teaching load of at least 50% Spanish classes; and have attended at least one Northeast Conference. **Criteria:** Selection is based on merits and the need for an experience in Mexico.

Funds Avail.: No specific amount. **To Apply:** Applicants must submit a completed application form with a one-page resume in English; a 200-word statement in English; and a recommendation letter in a signed and sealed envelope, from the department chair, principal or dean. Send all materials to Cemanahuac Summer Study Scholarships, Northeast Conference c/o Dickinson College PO Box 1773 Carlisle, PA 17013-2896. **Deadline:** December 1. **Contact:** nectfl@dickinson.edu.

5266 ■ Mead Leadership Fellows Program *(Professional Development/Fellowship)*

Purpose: To identify potential leaders in education and to support the development of their potential. **Focus:** Education, Bilingual and cross-cultural; Foreign languages. **Qualif.:** Candidates must be foreign language teachers who demonstrate leadership potential at their schools, colleges or universities. **Criteria:** Selection is based on work experience and merits.

Funds Avail.: No amount specified. **To Apply:** Candidates must submit a completed application from; a resume or curriculum vitae (maximum of two pages); a letter of nomination (maximum of two pages) from the nominating body declaring the leadership potential of the candidate; and a written commitment containing a draft of specific plan of action. **Deadline:** December 1.

5267 ■ Spanish Embassy Scholarships *(Graduate, Other/Scholarship)*

Purpose: To support the teaching of Spanish in the United States. **Focus:** Education, Bilingual and cross-cultural; Foreign languages. **Qualif.:** Applicants must be full-time teachers in a public or private school, at any level; must teach in the Northeast Conference region (CT, DE, ME, MD, MA, NH, NJ, NY, PA, RI, VT, VA, WV, DC); must carry a teaching load of at least 50% Spanish classes; and have attended at least one Northeast Conference. **Criteria:** Selection is based on merits and the need for an experience in Mexico.

Funds Avail.: No specific amount. **To Apply:** Applicants must submit a completed application form with a one-page resume in English; a 200-word statement in English; and a recommendation letter in a signed and sealed envelope, from the department chair, principal or dean. Send all materials to Cemanahuac Summer Study Scholarships, Northeast Conference c/o Dickinson College PO Box 1773 Carlisle, PA 17013-2896. **Deadline:** December 1. **Contact:** nectfl@dickinson.edu.

5268 ■ Northern Arizona Native-American Foundation

411 W Cherry Ave.
Flagstaff, AZ 86001
Ph: (928)527-9860
URL: http://www.tnanaf.org

5269 ■ Northern Arizona Native-American Foundation Scholarships *(Undergraduate/Scholarship)*

Purpose: To encourage educational pursuits by providing financial assistance for high school seniors. **Focus:** General studies. **Qualif.:** Applicants must be freshmen, sophomores, or juniors in high school who are interested in attending a four-year college, community college, art school, or vocational school. **Criteria:** Applicants are evaluated based on merit and financial need.

Funds Avail.: $250 up to $2,000. **To Apply:** Applicants must submit all the required application information.

5270 ■ Northern Indiana Community Foundation

PO Box 807
Rochester, IN 46975
Ph: (574)223-2227
Fax: (574)224-3709
Free: 877-432-6423
URL: http://www.nicf.org

5271 ■ Frederick Rakestraw Law Scholarships *(Undergraduate/Scholarship)*

Purpose: To provide scholarships for qualified college graduates pursuing a degree in law. **Focus:** Law. **Qualif.:** Applicants must be residents of Fulton County Indiana for at least three years during their high school career. **Criteria:** Selection of recipients is based on merit.

Funds Avail.: $1,000. **To Apply:** Applicants must submit a completed scholarship form; an acceptance letter or other proof of enrollment in any school of law in the US; a cur-

Awards are arranged alphabetically below their administering organizations

rent transcript; and three letters of recommendation. **Deadline:** June 19.

5272 ■ Northwest Michigan Home Builders Association

PO Box 171
Cadillac, MI 49601
Ph: (231)775-5256
Fax: (231)775-2134
E-mail: info@nwmhba.com
URL: http://www.nwmhba.com

5273 ■ R.D. Neuman Memorial Scholarships *(Undergraduate/Scholarship)*

Purpose: To help build one's business. **Focus:** Construction. **Qualif.:** Applicant must be a resident of Wexford, Missaukee or Oseloa County; must be pursuing a degree in construction, architecture, or engineering or an associate's degree in drafting or building; applicants must have a minimum of 2.5 GPA and be attending school in Michigan. **Criteria:** Recipients are selected based on academic performance and financial need.

Funds Avail.: $500-$1,000. **To Apply:** Applicants must submit a written paragraph on goals and aspirations; must submit a list of extracurricular activities/work history. **Deadline:** May 1.

5274 ■ Northwest-Shoals Community College

PO Box 2545
Muscle Shoals, AL 35662
Ph: (256)331-5200
Fax: (256)331-5222
Free: 800-645-8967
URL: http://www.nwscc.edu

5275 ■ Alabama Power Scholarships *(Undergraduate/Scholarship)*

Purpose: To support NW-SCC students in their educational pursuit. **Focus:** General studies. **Qualif.:** Applicant must be a high school student entering Northwest-Shoals Community College. **Criteria:** Students must be selected by high school counselors or by the NW-SCC Foundation Scholarship Committee.

Funds Avail.: No specific amount. **To Apply:** Applicants must submit a completed application form together with the required materials and information. **Deadline:** March 2. **Contact:** Northwest Shoals Foundation at 256-331-5240.

5276 ■ Billy Bowling Memorial Scholarships *(Undergraduate/Scholarship)*

Purpose: To support NW-SCC students in their educational pursuit. **Focus:** General studies. **Qualif.:** Applicant must be a high school student entering Northwest-Shoals Community College. **Criteria:** Students must be selected by high school counselors or by the NW-SCC Foundation Scholarship Committee.

Funds Avail.: No specific amount. **To Apply:** Applicants must submit a completed application form together with the required materials and information. **Deadline:** March 2. **Contact:** Northwest Shoals Foundation at 256-331-5240.

5277 ■ Cecil Earl Clapp, Sr. Memorial Scholarships *(Undergraduate/Scholarship)*

Purpose: To support NW-SCC students in their educational pursuit. **Focus:** General studies. **Qualif.:** Applicant must be a high school student entering Northwest-Shoals Community College. **Criteria:** Students must be selected by high school counselors or by the NW-SCC Foundation Scholarship Committee.

Funds Avail.: No specific amount. **To Apply:** Applicants must submit a completed application form together with the required materials and information. **Deadline:** March 2. **Contact:** Northwest Shoals Foundation at 256-331-5240.

5278 ■ Marvin E. Daly Memorial Scholarships *(Undergraduate/Scholarship)*

Purpose: To support NW-SCC students in their educational pursuit. **Focus:** General studies. **Qualif.:** Applicant must be a Lauderdale County senior student entering Northwest-Shoals Community College. **Criteria:** Students must be selected by high school counselors or by the NW-SCC Foundation Scholarship Committee.

Funds Avail.: No specific amount. **To Apply:** Applicants must submit a completed application form together with the required materials and information. **Deadline:** March 2. **Contact:** Northwest Shoals Foundation at 256-331-5240.

5279 ■ Michael Denton Scholarships *(Undergraduate/Scholarship)*

Purpose: To support NW-SCC students in their educational pursuit. **Focus:** General studies. **Qualif.:** Applicant must be a Colbert Heights High School senior student entering Northwest-Shoals Community College. **Criteria:** Students must be selected by high school counselors or by the NW-SCC Foundation Scholarship Committee.

Funds Avail.: No specific amount. **To Apply:** Applicants must submit a completed application form together with the required materials and information. **Deadline:** March 2. **Contact:** Northwest Shoals Foundation at 256-331-5240.

5280 ■ Homajean Grisham Memorial Scholarships *(Undergraduate/Scholarship)*

Purpose: To support NW-SCC students with their educational pursuit. **Focus:** General studies. **Qualif.:** Applicants must be Cherokee High School Senior students entering Northwest-Shoals Community College. **Criteria:** Students must be selected by high school counselors or by the NW-SCC Foundation Scholarship Committee.

Funds Avail.: No specific amount. **To Apply:** Applicants must submit a completed application form together with the required materials and information. **Deadline:** March 2. **Contact:** Northwest Shoals Foundation at 256-331-5240.

5281 ■ Howell Heflin Memorial Scholarships *(Undergraduate/Scholarship)*

Purpose: To support NW-SCC students in their educational pursuit. **Focus:** General studies. **Qualif.:** Applicant must be a high school student entering Northwest-Shoals Community College. **Criteria:** Students must be selected by high school counselors or by the NW-SCC Foundation Scholarship Committee.

Funds Avail.: No specific amount. **To Apply:** Applicants must submit a completed application form together with the required materials and information. **Deadline:** March 2. **Contact:** Northwest Shoals Foundation at 256-331-5240.

5282 ■ June Hester Memorial Scholarships *(Undergraduate/Scholarship)*

Purpose: To support NW-SCC students in their educational pursuit. **Focus:** General studies. **Qualif.:** Applicant must be

American citizen with no criminal records; a high school graduate or GED equivalent; and a child or grandchild of parent or grandparent who is a member, or a deceased member of the Florence/Lauderdale Post 11 of the American Legion. **Criteria:** Selection is based on financial need.

Funds Avail.: No specific amount. **To Apply:** Applicants must submit a completed American Legion Scholarship Application along with the required materials and information. **Deadline:** March 30. **Contact:** American Legion, at 256-764-5122.

5301 ■ D. Mitchell Self Memorial Scholarships *(Undergraduate/Scholarship)*

Purpose: To support NW-SCC students in their educational pursuit. **Focus:** General studies. **Qualif.:** Applicant must be a high school student entering Northwest-Shoals Community College. **Criteria:** Students must be selected by high school counselors or by the NW-SCC Foundation Scholarship Committee.

Funds Avail.: No specific amount. **To Apply:** Applicants must submit a completed application form together with the required materials and information. **Deadline:** March 2. **Contact:** Northwest Shoals Foundation at 256-331-5240.

5302 ■ Shoals Home Builders Association Scholarships *(Undergraduate/Scholarship)*

Purpose: To support NW-SCC students with their educational pursuit. **Focus:** General studies. **Qualif.:** Applicant must be high school Senior student entering Northwest-Shoals Community College majoring in Building trade. **Criteria:** Students are selected by high school counselors or by the NW-SCC Foundation Scholarship Committee.

Funds Avail.: No specific amount. **To Apply:** Applicants must submit a completed application form together with the required materials and information. **Deadline:** March 2. **Contact:** Northwest Shoals Foundation at 256-331-5240.

5303 ■ Aaron B. Singleton Memorial Scholarships *(Undergraduate/Scholarship)*

Purpose: To support NW-SCC students in their educational pursuit. **Focus:** General studies. **Qualif.:** Applicant must be a Muscle Shoals High School senior student entering Northwest-Shoals Community College. **Criteria:** Students must be selected by high school counselors or by the NW-SCC Foundation Scholarship Committee.

Funds Avail.: No specific amount. **To Apply:** Applicants must submit a completed application form together with the required materials and information. **Deadline:** March 2. **Contact:** Northwest Shoals Foundation at 256-331-5240.

5304 ■ Tuscumbia Kiwanis Scholarships *(Undergraduate/Scholarship)*

Purpose: To support NW-SCC students with their educational pursuit. **Focus:** General studies. **Qualif.:** Applicants must be Deshler High School Senior students entering Northwest-Shoals Community College. **Criteria:** Students must be selected by high school counselors or by the NW-SCC Foundation Scholarship Committee.

Funds Avail.: No specific amount. **To Apply:** Applicants must submit a completed application form together with the required materials and information. **Deadline:** March 2. **Contact:** Northwest Shoals Foundation at 256-331-5240.

5305 ■ Wayne County Bank Scholarships *(Undergraduate/Scholarship)*

Purpose: To support NW-SCC students with their educational pursuit. **Focus:** General studies. **Qualif.:** Applicants must be Wayne County High School Senior students entering Northwest-Shoals Community College. **Criteria:** Students must be selected by high school counselors or by the NW-SCC Foundation Scholarship Committee.

Funds Avail.: No specific amount. **To Apply:** Applicants must submit a completed application form together with the required materials and information. **Deadline:** March 2. **Contact:** Northwest Shoals Foundation at 256-331-5240.

5306 ■ Nova Scotia Salmon Association

PO Box 396
Chester, NS, Canada B0J 1J0
E-mail: nssalmo@yahoo.ca
URL: http://www.novascotiasalmon.ns.ca

5307 ■ Nova Scotia Salmon Association Scholarships *(All/Scholarship)*

Purpose: To financially support students in their academic and in-river pursuits. **Focus:** Aquaculture. **Qualif.:** Applicants must have undertaken, or be in the process of undertaking, a scholarly pursuit related to the enhancement or conservation of the Atlantic salmon and/or trout; must propose to publish, or have published, an article or scientific paper in any field which features the enhancement of the Atlantic salmon and/or trout; must promote the cause of the Atlantic salmon and trout by outstanding leadership or participation; be engaged in endeavors of an association which results to the conservation of the Atlantic salmon and trout. **Criteria:** Applicants will be evaluated based on the criteria designed by the NSSA Scholarship Committee.

Funds Avail.: $500. **Number Awarded:** 2. **To Apply:** Applicants must complete all the needed information in the application form. **Deadline:** October 30.

5308 ■ NPELRA Foundation

1012 S Coast Hwy., Ste. M
Oceanside, CA 92054
Ph: (760)433-1686
Fax: (760)433-1687
Free: 877-673-5721
URL: http://npelra.org

5309 ■ NPELRA Foundation Scholarships *(Graduate/Scholarship)*

Purpose: To provide educational assistance to U.S. citizen graduate students. **Focus:** Personnel administration/human resources; Industrial and labor relations; Public administration; Political science. **Qualif.:** Applicants must be students currently enrolled in graduate studies in human resources, labor and industrial relations, public administration or political science with strong documented interest in the public sector. **Criteria:** Applicants who are students currently working for state, local, or special district governments will be given preference.

Funds Avail.: $3,000. **Number Awarded:** 5. **To Apply:** Applicants must submit a completed application form and other required information and materials for the award. **Deadline:** September 26.

5310 ■ Nurses Educational Fund

304 Park Ave. S, 11th Fl.
New York, NY 10010
Ph: (212)590-2443

Awards are arranged alphabetically below their administering organizations

Fax: (212)590-2446
E-mail: info@n-e-f.org
URL: http://www.n-e-f.org

5311 ■ NEF Scholarships for Leadership *(Doctorate/Scholarship)*

Purpose: To increase the supply of nurses qualified for administrative, supervisory, teaching or research positions and clinical specialization in nursing. **Focus:** Nursing. **Qualif.:** Applicants must be registered nurses; members of a professional nursing association; enrolled full-time in a professionally NLNAC- or CCNE-accredited nursing masters degree program or as full- or part-time students in a doctoral program in nursing or a nursing-related field. Applicants must be U.S. citizens or have declared official intention of becoming one. **Criteria:** Recipients are selected on the basis of excellence in academics, which is given first priority; and potential for contributing to the profession.

Funds Avail.: No specific amount. **To Apply:** Applicants must submit the application; Professional Nursing Membership Verification; National Student Nurses' Association Form; and four Reference Forms. **Deadline:** March 1.

5312 ■ Occupational Physicians Scholarship Fund

25 NW Point Blvd., Ste. 700
Elk Grove Village, IL 60007-1030
Ph: (847)818-1800
Fax: (847)818-9289
E-mail: opsf@opsf.org
URL: http://www.opsf.org

5313 ■ Occupational Physicians Scholarship Fund *(Undergraduate/Scholarship)*

Purpose: To help alleviate the shortage of properly trained and skilled occupational physicians. **Focus:** Occupational Therapy. **Qualif.:** Applicants must be capable of making a significant contribution in their field and wish to pursue a well-rounded residency education in occupational medicine. **Criteria:** Preference will be given to those students who meet the criteria.

Funds Avail.: No specific amount. **To Apply:** Applicants are required to submit the following: a completed OPSF application downloaded from the website; all undergraduate college transcripts; records of previous medical and post-medical school performance; copies of any publications that the applicant has authored; three letters of recommendation, including letters from the directors of any previous training programs; a letter of support from the applicant's current program director, if accepted in an occupational medicine program. **Deadline:** November 2. **Contact:** Occupational Physicians Scholarship Fund at the above address (see entry 5312).

5314 ■ Office Products Wholesaler Association

5024-R Campbell Blvd.
Baltimore, MD 21236-5974
Ph: (410)931-8100
Fax: (410)931-8111
URL: http://www.opwa.org

5315 ■ OPWA Educational Scholarships *(Undergraduate/Scholarship)*

Purpose: To provide educational assistance to individuals affiliated with the office products industry. **Focus:** General studies. **Qualif.:** Applicant must be an employee, or relative of an employee of an OPWA member company; or a member group or relative of the member group affiliated with the office product industry. **Criteria:** Selection is based on academic success, interest, abilities, and financial need.

Funds Avail.: $5,000, $2,500 and $1,000. **To Apply:** Application form is available at the website. Applicant must prepare a transcript of grades and credits; a letter of recommendation from a person employed by a firm in the office products industry (must hold an executive or managerial position) and another from a teacher, professor or other educational professional. **Deadline:** March 10.

5316 ■ Ohio Association of Broadcasters

88 E Broad St., Ste.1180
Columbus, OH 43215
Ph: (614)228-4052
Fax: (614)228-8133
Free: (866)228-5794
E-mail: oab@oab.org
URL: http://www.oab.org

5317 ■ Ohio Association of Broadcaster's Kids Scholarships *(Undergraduate/Scholarship)*

Purpose: To encourage high standards of professionalism in the industry; to foster a stronger relationship between higher education and the profession; to promote a greater understanding of the ethics and societal responsibility of broadcasters; to support potential and commitment in promising future broadcasters; to advance a continuing commitment to diversity in the industry. **Focus:** Broadcasting. **Qualif.:** Applicants must be high school seniors who are children of a full-time employee of an OAB member station; must plan to enroll in a postsecondary institution. **Criteria:** Recipients are selected based on academic performance.

Funds Avail.: $1,500. **To Apply:** Applicants must submit a completed application form; a two page essay; a copy of high school transcript and one letter of recommendation. **Deadline:** March 28. **Contact:** oab@oab.org.

5318 ■ Ohio Association of Broadcasters Scholarships *(Undergraduate/Scholarship)*

Purpose: To encourage high standards of professionalism in the industry; to foster a stronger relationship between higher education and the profession; to promote a greater understanding of the ethics and societal responsibility of broadcasters; to support potential and commitment in promising future broadcasters; to advance a continuing commitment to diversity in the industry. **Focus:** Broadcasting. **Qualif.:** Applicants must be college students interested in pursuing a career in broadcasting; must be residents of Ohio; must be working toward a major or minor in their school's radio or television broadcasting or communications program; must have a minimum of 2.75 on a 4.0 scale, or the equivalent. **Criteria:** Recipients are selected based on academic performance.

Funds Avail.: No specific amount. **Number Awarded:** 3. **To Apply:** Applicants must complete the application form, transcripts and letters of recommendation. **Deadline:** March 28. **Contact:** oab@oab.org.

5319 ■ Ohio Farm Bureau Federation

280 Plaza
PO Box 182383
Columbus, OH 43218-2383

Awards are arranged alphabetically below their administering organizations

Ph: (614)249-2400
URL: http://ofbf.org

5320 ■ Women's Leadership in Agriculture Scholarship Program *(Undergraduate/Scholarship)*

Purpose: To provide financial support to deserving women. **Focus:** Agricultural Sciences. **Qualif.:** Applicants must be enrolled in an accredited college or university. **Criteria:** Selection will be based on community involvement.

Funds Avail.: No specific amount. **To Apply:** Applicants must submit a completed application form. **Contact:** Ohio Farm Bureau Federation at the above address (see entry 5319).

5321 ■ Ohio Newspaper Association

1335 Dublin Rd., Ste. 216-B
Columbus, OH 43215
Ph: (614)486-6677
Fax: (614)486-4940
URL: http://www.ohionews.org

5322 ■ Harold K. Douhhit Regional Scholarships *(Undergraduate/Scholarship)*

Purpose: To provide educational assistance for students from Northern Ohio. **Focus:** Journalism. **Qualif.:** Applicants must have graduated from a high school in Cuyahog, Lorain, Huron, Erie, Wood, Geauga, Sandusky, Ottawa or Lucas county; must be enrolled as sophomores, juniors or seniors at an Ohio college or university; must have a minimum grade point average of 3.0 (B); and must clearly demonstrate ability to write. **Criteria:** Selection will be based on the committee's criteria.

Funds Avail.: $1,500. **To Apply:** Applicants must submit completed application form typed or printed legibly by the applicant; official university or college transcript; an autobiography of 750 to 1,000 words describing academic and career interests, awards, extracurricular activities and any journalism-related activities; and two letters of recommendation from college or university faculty members familiar with the student's work and career interests, with special emphasis on the student's financial need. Students are encouraged to provide writing samples or articles that have been published. **Deadline:** March 31. **Contact:** Ohio Newspaper Foundation at the above address (see entry 5321).

5323 ■ Ohio Newspaper Association Minority Scholarships *(Undergraduate/Scholarship)*

Purpose: To provide educational assistance for minority high school seniors in Ohio intending to pursue a newspaper journalism career. **Focus:** Journalism. **Qualif.:** Applicants must be graduating seniors at an Ohio high school; must be enrolled as college freshmen at an Ohio college or university; must have a minimum high school grade point average of 2.5 (C+); must clearly demonstrate ability to write; and must be African American, Hispanic, Asian American or American Indian. **Criteria:** Selection will be based on the committee's criteria.

Funds Avail.: $1,500. **To Apply:** Applicants must submit completed application form typed or printed legibly by the applicant; an autobiography of 750 to 1,000 words describing academic and career interest, awards, extracurricular activities and any journalism-related activities; and two letters of recommendation from high school faculty members familiar with the student's work and career interests. Students may provide additional information such as samples or articles that have been published. **Deadline:** March 31. **Contact:** Ohio Newspaper Foundation at the above address (see entry 5321).

5324 ■ Ohio Newspaper Association University Journalism Scholarships *(Undergraduate/Scholarship)*

Purpose: To provide educational assistance for students demonstrating a career commitment to newspaper journalism. **Focus:** Journalism. **Qualif.:** Applicants must be enrolled as sophomores, juniors or seniors at an Ohio college or university; must have a minimum grade point average of 2.5 (C+); and must clearly demonstrate ability to write. **Criteria:** Preference will be given to students demonstrating a career commitment to newspaper journalism.

Funds Avail.: $1,500. **To Apply:** Applicants must submit completed application form typed or printed legibly by the applicant; official college or university transcript; an autobiography of 750 to 1,000 words describing academic and career interests, awards, extracurricular activities and any journalism-related activities (emphasis should be given to newspaper or print journalism); two letters of recommendation from college or university faculty members familiar with the student's work and career interests; and writing samples or articles that have been published. **Deadline:** March 31. **Contact:** Ohio News Foundation at the above address (see entry 5321).

5325 ■ Ohio Newspaper Association Women's Scholarships *(Undergraduate/Scholarship)*

Purpose: To provide educational assistance for students in an Ohio college or university. **Focus:** Journalism. **Qualif.:** Applicants must be enrolled as juniors or seniors at an Ohio college or university. **Criteria:** Selection will be based on the committee's criteria.

Funds Avail.: $1,500. **To Apply:** Applicants must submit completed application form together with official college or university transcript; two letters of recommendation; three to four news clippings; and statements answering the three application questions. **Deadline:** March 31. **Contact:** Ohio Newspaper Foundation at the above address (see entry 5321).

5326 ■ Oklahoma Association for the Improvement of Developmental Education

10300 E 81st St. S
Tulsa, OK 74133
Ph: (918)595-8615
E-mail: kdaily@tulsacc.edu
URL: http://www.osu-okmulgee.edu

5327 ■ OKAIDE Scholarships *(Undergraduate/Scholarship)*

Purpose: To provide financial assistance to those deserving students. **Focus:** General Studies. **Qualif.:** Applicants must be Oklahoma residents of a year or more; must be currently enrolled full-time in an Oklahoma institution of higher education (2 yr. or 4 yr.); during the twelve months prior to application, students must have taken at least one developmental course (0 level), successfully completed all developmental courses taken, and have an overall GPA of 3.3 or higher. **Criteria:** Priority will be given to those students who meet the criteria.

Awards are arranged alphabetically below their administering organizations

Funds Avail.: $250. **Number Awarded:** 2. **To Apply:** Applicants must submit a completed application form and write a one-page statement explaining why they should be considered for this scholarship; a faculty letter of recommendation and two other faculty references with telephone numbers or e-mail address. **Deadline:** October 15.

Remarks: Only complete applications will be considered. **Contact:** Applications should be submitted to: Kathy Daily Tulsa.

5328 ■ Oklahoma City University School of Law

251 N Blackwelder Ave.
Oklahoma City, OK 73106
Ph: (405)208-5337
URL: http://www.okcu.edu/law/

5329 ■ Kerr Foundation Scholarships *(Undergraduate/Scholarship)*

Purpose: To provide financial assistance for qualified law students intending to pursue their studies. **Focus:** Law. **Qualif.:** Applicants must be upper class students who have high GPA (generally 3.5 or above) and high LSAT (generally at the 80th percentile or above). **Criteria:** Selection of applicants is based on academic performance, service to the school, financial need and character.

Funds Avail.: No specific amount. **Number Awarded:** 20. **To Apply:** Applicants must complete the application form available online and submit along with their undergraduate transcript and letters of recommendation.

5330 ■ Oklahoma City University Merit Scholarships *(Undergraduate/Scholarship)*

Purpose: To provide financial assistance for qualified law students intending to pursue their studies. **Focus:** Law. **Qualif.:** Applicants must have a high GPA (generally 3.5 or above) and high LSAT (generally at the 80th percentile or above). **Criteria:** Selection is based on LSAT and GPA average.

Funds Avail.: Covers 2/3 of tuition. **To Apply:** Applicants must complete the application form available online and must also submit the undergraduate transcript and letters of recommendation. **Deadline:** April 1.

5331 ■ Hatton W. Sumners Scholarships *(Undergraduate/Scholarship)*

Purpose: To provide financial assistance for qualified law students intending to pursue their studies. **Focus:** Law. **Qualif.:** Applicants must be U.S. citizens; must rank in the top quarter of their class; and must be residents of or students/graduates of colleges or universities in Oklahoma, Arkansas, Kansas, Missouri, Texas, Louisiana, Nebraska, or New Mexico. **Criteria:** Selection is based on academic proficiency, extra-curricular achievement and demonstrated capacity for public service.

Funds Avail.: Covers all tuition and other fees, $400 book allowance and $2,500 living stipend. **To Apply:** Applicants must complete the application form available online must also submit their undergraduate transcript and letters of recommendation. **Deadline:** February 15.

5332 ■ Olympia Tumwater Foundation

PO Box 4098
Tumwater, WA 98501
Ph: (360)943-2550
Fax: (360)943-6755
E-mail: otf@olytumfoundation.org
URL: http://www.olytumfoundation.org

5333 ■ Olympia Tumwater Foundation Traditional Scholarships *(Undergraduate/Scholarship)*

Purpose: To provide support for qualified students. **Focus:** General studies. **Qualif.:** Applicant must be graduating from a Thurston County high school; must be a Thurston County resident; must be planning to attend a public or private school in Washington State; must have a GPA of 3.0 or better; must show a need for financial aid and academic promise; and must have a strong work ethic and be involved in the community. **Criteria:** Recipient will be selected based on the criteria designed by the Scholarship Selection Committee.

Funds Avail.: $90,000. **To Apply:** Applicants are advised to contact Olympia Tumwater Foundation, PO Box 4098, Tumwater, WA 98501 for scholarship information and instructions. **Deadline:** March 1.

5334 ■ Olympia Tumwater Foundation Transitional (non-traditional) Scholarships *(Undergraduate/Scholarship)*

Purpose: To provide educational assistance for non-traditional students at South Puget Sound Community College, The Evergreen State College and Saint Martin's University. **Focus:** General studies. **Qualif.:** Applicant must be a resident of Thurston County; must have completed at least 50% of his/her degree or certificate program and have an established plan for completion of the program; and must be in good academic standing. **Criteria:** Recipients will be selected based on the criteria set by the Scholarship Selection Committee.

Funds Avail.: $90,000. **To Apply:** Applicants are advised to contact Olympia Tumwater Foundation, PO Box 4098, Tumwater, WA 98501 for scholarship information and instructions. **Deadline:** March 1.

5335 ■ Omaha Education Association

4202 S 57th St.
Omaha, NE 68137
Ph: (402)346-0400
Fax: (402)346-8410
URL: http://www.omahoea.org

5336 ■ Horace Mann Insurance Scholarships *(High School/Scholarship)*

Purpose: To provide financial assistance to those students who are in need. **Focus:** General Studies. **Qualif.:** Applicants must be high school seniors who are children or legal dependents of U.S. public education employees. **Criteria:** Preference will be given to those who meet the criteria.

Funds Avail.: $30,000. **To Apply:** Applicants must check the available website for the required materials. **Deadline:** February. **Contact:** Omaha Education Association at the above address (see entry 5335).

5337 ■ Omohundro Institute of Early American History and Culture

PO Box 8781
Williamsburg, VA 23187-8781

Awards are arranged alphabetically below their administering organizations

Ph: (757)221-1110
Fax: (757)221-1047
E-mail: ieahc1@wm.edu
URL: http://oieahc.wm.edu

5338 ■ Institute-NEH Postdoctoral Fellowships
(Doctorate, Professional Development/Fellowship)

Purpose: To promote study in any area of early American studies. **Focus:** American studies. **Qualif.:** Applicant must have completed the Ph.D. by the date the fellowship begins; must be a U.S. citizen or have lived in the U.S. for the 3 years preceding the fellowship award (required for NEH funding); have not previously published a scholarly book or have entered into a contract for the publication of a scholarly monograph; proposed fellowship project must not be under contract with another publisher. **Criteria:** A principal criterion for selection is that the candidate's dissertation or other manuscript have significant potential as a distinguished, book-length contribution to scholarship.

Funds Avail.: $40,000. **To Apply:** Applicants must submit a completed application form; curriculum vitae; abstract of the project; Statement of Proposed Work; Manuscript (written a substantial portion of the dissertation or proposed book project, at least 100 pages); table of contents (list of the chapters in the manuscript); and three references sent directly to the Director, Omohundro Institute of Early American History and Culture. **Deadline:** November 1. **Contact:** ieahc1@wm.edu.

5339 ■ Institute Andrew W. Mellon Postdoctoral Research Fellowships *(Professional Development/ Fellowship)*

Purpose: To promote study in any area of early American studies. **Focus:** American studies. **Qualif.:** Applicant must have received their Ph.D. at least 12 months prior to the fellowship; have not previously published a book or have entered into a contract for the publication of a scholarly monograph; proposed fellowship project must not be under contract with another publisher. **Criteria:** The principal criterion for selection is that the manuscript have significant potential for publication as a distinguished, book-length contribution to scholarship.

Funds Avail.: $45,000. **To Apply:** Applicants must submit a one copy of a completed dissertation or book manuscript; completed application form (four copies); curriculum vitae (four copies); samples of work; statement of proposed work; abstract (four copies); and three references sent directly to Beverly Smith, Manager, Institute Administration, Mellon Fellowship. **Deadline:** November 1. **Contact:** ieahc1@wm.edu.

5340 ■ Ontario Trucking Association

555 Dixon Rd.
Toronto, ON, Canada M9W 1H8
Ph: (416)249-7401
Fax: (416)245-6152
E-mail: info@ontruck.org
URL: http://www.ontruck.org

5341 ■ Bison Transport Scholarships
(Undergraduate/Scholarship)

Purpose: To assist the deserving students who demonstrate exemplary commitment to their academic studies and community. **Focus:** Transportation; Logistics; Human resources; Business. **Qualif.:** Applicant must be a postsecondary student who demonstrates an exemplary commitment to his/her academic studies and community; must be enrolled in full-time studies in Transportation, Logistics, Human resources, or a Business program at a recognized university or college in Canada. **Criteria:** Applicant will be selected based on their academic success.

Funds Avail.: $1,000. **To Apply:** Applicants must complete the Bison Transport Commitment to People Scholarship Statement of Volunteer Work/Community Services form; must attach a letter that explains how they help people in ways other than through volunteer/charitable work or community service; must submit an official transcript of their most recent marks; must include an essay of 500 words or less that explains what motivated them to embark on studies in their chosen field and their career aspirations. **Deadline:** August 15.

5342 ■ Erb Group Companies Service to Community Scholarships *(Undergraduate/Scholarship)*

Purpose: To educate an individual who demonstrates a commitment to his/her community. **Focus:** General studies. **Qualif.:** Applicant must be a first-year postsecondary student enrolled in a recognized college or university, who demonstrates a commitment to his/her community through his/her involvement in community and/or charitable volunteer work. **Criteria:** Recipient will be selected based on the scholarship criteria.

Funds Avail.: No specific amount. **To Apply:** Applicant must submit: an official transcript of record; a curriculum vitae of past volunteer and charity work; a minimum of two reference letters related to applicant's volunteer and charity work; a letter of no more than 500 words that describes why he/she has a strong commitment to community service and details future aspirations relevant to ongoing community service and/or charitable work. Application form and other supporting documents must be sent to OTA Education Foundation, Inc., 555 Dixon Rd., Toronto, ON M9W 1H8. **Deadline:** July 15.

5343 ■ J.O. Goodman Scholarship Awards
(Undergraduate/Scholarship)

Purpose: To provide scholarship assistance to Ontario students who have demonstrated commitment to academic success and community service, and who have planned to have an affiliation with the trucking industry. **Focus:** General studies. **Qualif.:** Applicants must be: outstanding first-year students entering college directly from high school; enrolled in approved programs at approved post-secondary institutions; twenty-five years of age or under. **Criteria:** Applicants will be selected based on their academic success.

Funds Avail.: $1,500. **To Apply:** Applicants must submit a written letter of 400 words or less stating why they feel they should be considered for the award; must state their academic and personal accomplishments, contributions to community, extracurricular activities, personal, academic and career goals and other relevant information; must complete the application form available online; must submit the official transcript of marks for the current academic year; must submit the complete Scholarship Sponsorship form; must provide a written essay of 500 words or less that answers, "For the movement of freight, why is trucking considered the most efficient and effective means of transport in North America?". Application form and other supporting documents must be sent to OTA Education Foundation, Inc., 555 Dixon Rd., Toronto, ON M9W 1H8. **Deadline:** July 15.

Awards are arranged alphabetically below their administering organizations

Remarks: Award is named for Mr. Joe Goodman, who for forty-four years was Senior Staff Executive of the Ontario Trucking Association (OTA).

5344 ■ C.V. Hoar Scholarship Awards
(Undergraduate/Scholarship)

Purpose: To provide scholarship assistance to Ontario students who have demonstrated commitment to academic success and community service, and who have planned to have an affiliation with the trucking industry. **Focus:** General studies. **Qualif.:** Applicants must be: outstanding first-year students entering a university directly from high school; enrolled in approved programs at approved post-secondary institutions; twenty-five years of age or under. **Criteria:** Applicants will be selected based on their academic success.

Funds Avail.: $1,000. **To Apply:** Applicants must submit a written letter of 400 words or less stating why they feel they should be considered for the award; must state their academic and personal accomplishments, contributions to community, extracurricular activities, personal, academic and career goals and other relevant information; must complete the application form available online. Applicants must submit: the official transcript of marks for the current academic year; complete Scholarship Sponsorship form; an essay of 500 words or less that answers, "For the movement of freight, why is trucking considered the most efficient and effective means of transport in North America?". Application form and other supporting documents must be sent to OTA Education Foundation, Inc., 555 Dixon Rd., Toronto, ON M9W 1H8. **Deadline:** July 15.

Remarks: Award is named for Mr. C.V. (Charles) Hoar, who is one of the founding members of the OTA Education Foundation and who led the Foundation into its current form when he helped establish the J.O. Goodman Awards in 1979 following the retirement of Mr. Goodman as Senior Staff Executive of the Ontario Trucking Association.

5345 ■ OTA Education Foundation Scholarships
(Undergraduate/Scholarship)

Purpose: To provide scholarship assistance to Ontario students who have demonstrated commitment to academic success and community service, and who have planned to have an affiliation with the trucking industry. **Focus:** General studies. **Qualif.:** Applicants must be Ontario students enrolled in approved programs at approved post-secondary institutions; must be twentyfive years of age or under. **Criteria:** Applicant will be selected based on their academic success.

Funds Avail.: 1,000-1,500. **To Apply:** Applicant must submit: the application form available online; the official transcript of marks for the current academic year; the complete Scholarship Sponsorship form; an essay of 500 words or less that answers, "For the movement of freight, why is trucking considered the most efficient and effective means of transport in North America?". Application form and other supporting documents must be sent to OTA Education Foundation, Inc., 555 Dixon Rd., Toronto, ON M9W 1H8. **Deadline:** July 15.

5346 ■ Open Society Institute
400 W 59th St.
New York, NY 10019
Ph: (212)548-0600
URL: http://www.soros.org

5347 ■ Open Society Fellowships *(Professional Development/Fellowship)*

Purpose: To support outstanding individuals from around the world. **Focus:** General Studies. **Qualif.:** Applicants must be innovative professionals working on projects that inspire meaningful public debate, shape public policy, and generate intellectual ferment within the Open Society Institute. **Criteria:** Criteria for selection include, but are not limited to, the applicant's experience, the project's relevance to the goals of the fellowship, and the applicant's potential to accomplish such goals.

Funds Avail.: No specific amount. **To Apply:** Applicants must check the available website to download the application form and learn the application process. **Contact:** Open Society Institute at the above address (see entry 5346).

5348 ■ Opera Foundation
712 Fifth Ave., 32nd Flr.
New York, NY 10019
Ph: (212)664-8843
Fax: (212)664-8415
E-mail: gala@operafoundation.org
URL: http://www.operafoundation.org

5349 ■ Opera Foundation Scholarships *(Professional Development/Scholarship)*

Purpose: To provide opportunity to American singers to work and study at Deutsche Oper Berlin and Teatro Regio Torino. **Focus:** Music, Opera. **Qualif.:** Scholarship competition is open to American citizens and permanent residents between the ages of 18 and 30 who are beginning their professional careers. Selected candidates will be invited to participate in auditions at a location to be announced by the Foundation. Transportation to and from New York is at the candidate's own expense. **Criteria:** Selection will be based on the committee's criteria.

Funds Avail.: No specific amount. **To Apply:** Applicants may download or request an application online. Applicants can also request an application directly by contacting the Foundation. Applications must be accompanied by all of the following requirements: a photocopy of birth certificate, Green Card or Passport; two letters of recommendation from a music professional (manager, teacher, coach) dated no later than the deadline; a recent photograph; an application processing fee of $40.00 (non-refundable) paid by certified bank check or money order, payable to The Opera Foundation, Inc. **Deadline:** February 12. **Contact:** Manheim LLC, at the above address (see entry 5348).

5350 ■ Operation Homefront
8930 Fourwinds Dr., Ste. 340
San Antonio, TX 78239
Ph: (210)659-7756
Fax: (210)566-7544
Free: 800-722-6098
E-mail: info@operationhomefront.net
URL: http://www.operationhomefront.net

5351 ■ Operation Homefront Scholarships
(Undergraduate/Scholarship)

Purpose: To provide financial assistance to the spouses and children of active-duty personnel. **Focus:** Vocational-technical education. **Qualif.:** Applicants must be spouses

Awards are arranged alphabetically below their administering organizations

and children of active-duty military personnel who plan to pursue post-secondary education, including college, vocational and technical training. **Criteria:** Recipients are selected based on financial need.

Funds Avail.: $1,000 up to $5,000. **To Apply:** Applicants must submit all the required application information. **Deadline:** May 30.

5352 ▪ Orange County Association of Educational Office Professionals

550 Blumont St.
Laguna Beach, CA 92651
Ph: (949)497-7700
Fax: (949)497-7710
E-mail: acutler@lagunabeachschools.org
URL: http://www.caeop.org/ocaeop.htm

5353 ▪ OCAEOP Community Service Scholarship Program *(Undergraduate/Scholarship)*

Purpose: To assist business education students who intend to continue with higher education and pursue a career in business administration or education. **Focus:** Business administration. **Qualif.:** Applicant must have applied for admission to a post-high school accredited institution and plan to enter following the granting of the scholarship, or already be enrolled in an accredited college or university; must be a resident of the State of California; and must intend to continue his/her education in the field of business administration or education. **Criteria:** Applicants will be evaluated based on need for financial assistance; scholastic achievement; initiative; extracurricular activities; and quality and completeness of application materials.

Funds Avail.: $1,000. **To Apply:** Applicants must submit completed application and biographical information forms; official copy of high school transcript (or university/college transcript for higher education applicants); one-page essay on "Why the applicant is choosing a career in Business or Education"; three letters of recommendation from a language arts or math teacher, principal, counselor or other school administrator describing the candidate's activities, leadership record, character, personality, initiative and home background. **Deadline:** March 31.

5354 ▪ Orange County Community Foundation

30 Corporate Park, Ste. 410
Irvine, CA 92606
Ph: (949)553-4202
Fax: (949)553-4211
E-mail: cmontesano@oc-cf.org
URL: http://www.oc-cf.org

5355 ▪ Larry Acterman Public Education Awards *(Undergraduate/Scholarship)*

Purpose: To support outstanding students in pursuing a career as a public school teacher. **Focus:** Education. **Qualif.:** Applicants must: be a high school senior graduating from the Long Beach Unified School District; plan to enroll in a full-time course of study at an accredited four-year public college or university in the state of California to attain a degree and a teaching credential; demonstrate outstanding scholastic ability and a determination to graduate from college and become a public school teacher, Financial need will be considered as well. **Criteria:** Selection will be based on the committee's criteria.

Funds Avail.: $2,000. **To Apply:** Interested applicant may download an application from the Foundation's website. in a maximum one-page essay, write about any one of the following topics: Your interest in becoming a public school teacher; The importance of a strong public education system for society and democracy; How you would improve public schools and/or public education in California. **Deadline:** March 28. **Contact:** Claudia Montesano, 949-553-4202 ext. 46; cmontesano@oc-cf.org.

5356 ▪ Frank and Ruth Bila Scholarships *(Undergraduate/Scholarship)*

Purpose: to provide scholarship to the students currently pursuing a career in the restaurant/hotel management field. **Focus:** Hotel, institutional, and restaurant management. **Qualif.:** Applicant must: be a full-time student and have maintained a GPA greater than or equal to 3.0 for the preceding two years of high school or college; be a United States citizen; an outstanding student between the ages of 17 and 30 years old. **Criteria:** Selection will be based on financial need.

Funds Avail.: $5,000. **To Apply:** Interested applicant may download an application from the Foundation Web site. In a maximum of 250 words, write abut our academic interests, educational plan, and the way in which your educational plan is appropriate to your situation, abilities and long-term goals. **Deadline:** May 4. **Contact:** Claudia Montesano, 949-553-4202 ext. 46; cmontesano@oc-cf.org.

5357 ▪ Lee Brennan Memorial Scholarships *(Undergraduate/Scholarship)*

Purpose: To provide scholarship opportunities to the eligible undergraduate students. **Focus:** General studies. **Qualif.:** Applicant must: be a graduating senior from Aliso Miguel High School, who is active in athletics or an active participant of a US Diving Southern Pacific Association Diving Team (please make sure to include this information in the application form); be a student who plans to enroll full-time at an accredited college or university and students who enroll in trade schools, for careers such as law enforcement, fire fighting, auto or computer repair, etc.; have at least a C average GPA. **Criteria:** Selection will be based on the committee's criteria.

Funds Avail.: $2,000. **Number Awarded:** 1-2. **To Apply:** Interested applicant may download an application from the Foundation's website. Applicant must also submit a 350-word essay describing the following: How athletics have influenced your life; Your academic plan and ways in which your plan is appropriate to your situation, abilities and long-term goals; Any special circumstances which have impacted or may impact your academic performance, community service or leadership activities. **Deadline:** March 15. **Contact:** Claudia Montesano, 949-553-4202 ext. 46; cmontesano@oc-cf.org.

5358 ▪ Case-Swayne Company Scholarships *(Undergraduate/Scholarship)*

Purpose: To help local students, with financial difficulties, continue their education. **Focus:** General studies. **Qualif.:** Applicants must: be high school seniors who are graduating from Santa Ana or Corona-Norco School Districts; must be students wishing to enroll full-time at an accredited two- or four-year college, university, or vocational/trade school; must demonstrate outstanding scholastic ability and/or leadership, financial need and determination to graduate from college. **Criteria:** Selection will be based on the committee's criteria.

Awards are arranged alphabetically below their administering organizations

Funds Avail.: $800. **Number Awarded:** 1-2. **To Apply:** Applicants may download an application from the Foundation's website. Applicants must submit an essay with maximum of 250-words. **Deadline:** March 15. **Contact:** Claudia Montesano, 949-553-4202 ext. 46; cmontesano@oc-cf.org.

5359 ■ Brad Evans Memorial Scholarships *(Undergraduate/Scholarship)*

Purpose: To assist talented and versatile students with first year expenses at the University of California, Berkeley. **Focus:** General studies. **Qualif.:** Applicants must: be Orange County high school graduating seniors who are attending school in the Newport Mesa Unified School District; have been accepted to an accredited program at the University of California, Berkeley; have demonstrated record of community service and leadership; have a minimum of 3.0 GPA. **Criteria:** Selections will be based on the committee's criteria.

Funds Avail.: $3,000. **Number Awarded:** 1. **To Apply:** Applicants must submit 250 words containing academic interests and educational plan (must be appropriate to situation, abilities and long-term goals). Applicants must completely fill out and sign the attached application. Applicants must submit official transcript of records; 2 letters of recommendation sealed and signed by the writer across the seal. Submit the following to the Foundation in one large envelope: Original plus two copies of your application and essay; Two letters of recommendation, each still sealed; Official Transcript of Grades. **Deadline:** April 30. **Contact:** Claudia Montesano, 949-553-4202 ext. 46; cmontesano@oc-cf.org.

5360 ■ MacPherson Scholarships *(Undergraduate/Scholarship)*

Purpose: To help local youth pursue vocational, technical or advanced education. **Focus:** General studies. **Qualif.:** Applicant must: be a high school senior graduating from an Orange County high school or attending an accredited Orange County community college; have a minimum 2.5 GPA; demonstrate financial need; be planning to attend an accredited job training or community college. **Criteria:** Selection will be based on the committee's criteria.

Funds Avail.: $500-$5,000. **To Apply:** Interested applicant may download an application from the Foundation's website. Applicant must write at least one page, typed and double-space, answering the following questions: What are your career goals and how do you plan to reach those goals; Describe any classes that you have taken or accomplishments you have achieved that will help you realize your goals; Describe any special circumstances that you have experienced and how they have helped or deterred you from realizing your goals; Where do you picture yourself in five years; Please explain why it is important for you to receive this award. **Deadline:** $500-$5,000. **Contact:** Claudia Montesano, 949-553-4202 ext. 46; cmontesano@oc-cf.org.

5361 ■ New Opportunities Through Retraining Scholarship Fund *(Undergraduate/Scholarship)*

Purpose: To assist people who have decided to make a change for the better, through education. **Focus:** General studies. **Qualif.:** Applicant must be: male or female, over the age of 25 years old; interested in improving job and/or educational skills; already applied to, or will apply to, a local junior college, vocational/trade school, or four-year college or university. **Criteria:** Selection will be based on the committee's criteria.

Funds Avail.: $1,500. **Number Awarded:** 3. **To Apply:** Applicant must submit an essay answering to the following question with a brief paragraph: Please describe your current financial status; What impact will this scholarship have on your situation; What type of retraining or education do you seek and why; How will retraining and furthering your education assist you in accomplishing your long-term goals. Answers must be typed and double-spaced, with the applicant's full name appearing in the upper right hand corner on all pages that are attached. **Deadline:** March 28.

Remarks: Established in 2001. **Contact:** Claudia Montesano, 949-553-4202 ext. 46; cmontesano@oc-cf.org.

5362 ■ Orange County Centennial Academic Scholarships *(Undergraduate/Scholarship)*

Purpose: To award scholarship to the students who are residents of Orange County. **Focus:** Genera studies. **Qualif.:** Applicants must: be local high school graduating seniors who are residents of Orange County, California, and who are completing their last three years of high school in the county; be students who are planning to enroll full-time at an accredited college or university; be outstanding students, with a combined math, writing, and critical reading SAT score of at least 2100 and who have also demonstrated a record of community service and leadership in the area. **Criteria:** Selection will be based on the committee's criteria.

Funds Avail.: $2,500. **Number Awarded:** 6. **To Apply:** Interested applicants must include in their application a 250 words or less essay. Write about your academic interests and plans and the way in which your plan is appropriate to your situation, abilities and long-term goals. **Deadline:** March 15. **Contact:** Claudia Montesano, 949-553-4202 ext. 46; cmontesano@oc-cf.org.

5363 ■ Orange County Centennial Arts Scholarships *(Undergraduate/Scholarship)*

Purpose: To award scholarship to the students who are residents of Orange County. **Focus:** Performing arts; Visual Arts; Theater arts; Music. **Qualif.:** Applicants must: be local high school graduating seniors who are residents of Orange County, California, and who are completing their last three years of high school in the county; be students who are planning to enroll full-time at an accredited college or university and majoring in the arts. Example of acceptable majors include: dance, voice, opera, theater arts, musical theater, visual arts and music; demonstrated record of community service and leadership. particular attention will be given to training, honors and achievements in the arts. **Criteria:** Selection will be based on the committee's criteria.

Funds Avail.: $2,000. **Number Awarded:** 3. **To Apply:** Applicants must include a 250-word essay in their application. Applicants must write about their interests and plans and the way in which their plan is appropriate to their situation, abilities and long-term goals. **Deadline:** March 15. **Contact:** Claudia Montesano, 949-553-4202 ext. 46; cmontesano@oc-cf.org.

5364 ■ Orange County Centennial Certification Scholarships *(Undergraduate/Scholarship)*

Purpose: To award scholarship to the students who are residents of Orange County. **Focus:** General studies. **Qualif.:** Applicants must: be local high school graduating seniors who are residents of Orange County, California and who are completing their last three years of high school in the county; be students who are planning to enter the work force after completing a two-year vocational program; have

Awards are arranged alphabetically below their administering organizations

a demonstrated record of community service and leadership in the area. **Criteria:** Selection will be based on the committee's criteria.

Funds Avail.: No specific amount. **To Apply:** Interested applicants may download an application from the Foundation's website. Applicants must include a 250 words essay in their application. Applicants must write about their academic interest and plans and the way in which their plan is appropriate to their situation, abilities and long-term goals. **Deadline:** March 15. **Contact:** Claudia Montesano, 949-553-4202 ext. 46; cmontesano@oc-cf.org.

5365 ■ Orange County Tourism Council Scholarships *(Undergraduate/Scholarship)*

Purpose: To assist people who have decided to make a change for the better, through education. **Focus:** Travel and tourism. **Qualif.:** Applicant must: be male or female age 18 or over; be enrolled or accepted transfer student to California State University, Fullerton; be an Orange County resident; have demonstrated employment in the entertainment/tourism industry, either full-time, part-time or seasonally; Intent to pursue a career in the entertainment/tourism industry; have a minimum of 2.5 GPA. **Criteria:** Selection will be based on the committee's criteria.

Funds Avail.: $2,500. **Number Awarded:** 2. **To Apply:** Interested applicants may download an application from the Foundation's website and include a minimum of 200 words essay answering the following questions: Please describe your current financial status; What impact will this scholarship have on your situation; Please explain why you have chosen to have a career in the entertainment/tourism industry; How will retraining and furthering your education assist you in accomplishing your long-term goals. **Deadline:** March 31. **Contact:** Claudia Montesano, 949-553-4202 ext. 46; cmontesano@oc-cf.org.

5366 ■ Margaret E. Oser Scholarships for Women *(Undergraduate/Scholarship)*

Purpose: To provide scholarship to the women with high academic ability and significant financial need. **Focus:** General studies. **Qualif.:** Applicant must: be enrolled at an accredited Orange County community college at the time of application; have completed at least 12 units of academic work, that are transferable to the California College or university system, within the previous two semesters; have maintained at least a 3.0 GPA in the transferable coursework; have identified a possible educational focus and have obtained a written recommendation from an instructor in that field. If selected for this program, demonstrate ability and intent to earn a bachelor's or advanced degree as a full-time student. **Criteria:** Selection will be based on the committee's criteria.

Funds Avail.: $6,000. **Number Awarded:** 3-4. **To Apply:** Interested applicant may download an application from the Foundation's website. Applicant must also write a maximum of 350 words essay in each of the following: Your academic plans, if you were to receive this stipend through your college graduation; Ways in which your strategy is appropriate to your situation, abilities and long-term goals; a difficult obstacle you have had to overcome in life and how you responded to the challenge. **Deadline:** April 15. **Contact:** Claudia Montesano, 949-553-4202 ext. 46; cmontesano@oc-cf.org.

5367 ■ D.R. Segal Memorial Scholarships for Journalistic Excellence *(Undergraduate/Scholarship)*

Purpose: To provide scholarship to the students interested in pursuing a career in journalism. **Focus:** Journalism. **Qualif.:** Applicants must be Orange County high school graduating seniors or current college students wishing to pursue a career in journalism. **Criteria:** Selection will be based on the committee's criteria.

Funds Avail.: $2,000. **Number Awarded:** 4. **To Apply:** Interested applicant may download an application from the Foundation's website. As an attachment to your application, write about your father and how he has influenced your life. The essay should be a maximum of one page, typed and double-spaced. **Deadline:** March 28. **Contact:** Claudia Montesano, 949-553-4202 ext. 46; cmontesano@oc-cf.org.

5368 ■ Mark P. Tiner Education Scholarships *(Undergraduate/Scholarship)*

Purpose: to provide graduating seniors with substantial financial assistance to pursue their undergraduate degree. **Focus:** General studies. **Qualif.:** Applicant must; be Orange County seniors from public and private high schools; have a minimum GPA of at least a 3.75; plan to enroll in a 4-year accredited college or university and fulfill one of the requirements during their senior year of high school; demonstrate financial need. **Criteria:** Selection will be based on the committee's criteria.

Funds Avail.: $500. **To Apply:** Interested applicant may download an application from the Foundation's website. Applicant must also write a 250-500 word essay, describing your academic goals and plans, describe how your plan is appropriate to your situation, abilities and overall goal. **Deadline:** March 15. **Contact:** Claudia Montesano, 949-553-4202 ext. 46; cmontesano@oc-cf.org.

5369 ■ James L. Warner Scholarships *(Undergraduate/Scholarship)*

Purpose: To provide financial assistance to students that graduated from the Whittier Union High School district. **Focus:** General studies. **Qualif.:** Students must have attended on the following high schools in the Whittier Union High School: California High School, Santa Fe High School, Whittier High School, Frontier High School or Pioneer High School. Students must plan to attend on w of the following colleges: Pomona College, Whittier College, University of Southern California; Stanford University or any campus of the University of California system. Students must demonstrate financial need. **Criteria:** Selection will be based on the committee's criteria.

Funds Avail.: $1,000-$2,000. **To Apply:** Interested applicant may download an application from the Foundation's website. A minimum of a one-page, typed, double-spaced essay should address the following: what are your goals in college; Describe your service to your school and community; Explain why you should be awarded this scholarship; How you have benefited from attending high school; Describe any special family or personal circumstance that has affected your achievement in school, work or your participation in school or community service. **Deadline:** April 30. **Contact:** Claudia Montesano, 949-553-4202 ext. 46; cmontesano@oc-cf.org.

5370 ■ Charles H. and Ethel E. Wolfe Scholarships *(Undergraduate/Scholarship)*

Purpose: To award scholarship to the undergraduate student who is an Orange County resident. **Focus:** Genera studies. **Qualif.:** Student must: be recommended by the principal of the high school from which the student is graduating; demonstrate high scholastic achievement, financial need, and community involvement; proceed to

Awards are arranged alphabetically below their administering organizations

enroll and study at a non-profit institution of higher learning within the continental United States. **Criteria:** Selection will be based on the committee's criteria.

Funds Avail.: $2,000. **Number Awarded:** 1. **To Apply:** Interested applicant may download an application from the Foundation's website. In a maximum of 250 words, write about your academic interests, educational plan, and the way in which your educational plan is appropriate to your situation, abilities and long-term goals. **Deadline:** March 15. **Contact:** Claudia Montesano, 949-553-4202 ext. 46; cmontesano@oc-cf.org.

5371 ■ Order Sons of Italy in America

219 E St. NE
Washington, DC 20002
Ph: (202)547-2900
Fax: (202)546-8168
URL: http://www.osia.org

5372 ■ Italian Language Scholarships *(Undergraduate/Scholarship)*

Purpose: To provide financial support for education of the US citizens of Italian descent. **Focus:** General studies. **Qualif.:** Applicants must be US citizens of Italian descent (at least one Italian or Italian American grandparent) their junior or senior year of undergraduate study for the Fall of 2008 term, majoring or minoring in Italian language studies at an accredited academic institution. **Criteria:** SIF scholarship recipients are not eligible.

Funds Avail.: $5,000 to $25,000. **To Apply:** Applicants must submit cover sheet; official transcript; test scores; resume outlining extracurricular activities, work, experience, volunteer service and honors, especially as they relate to Italian language, culture and heritage; letters of recommendation; type-written original essay of 500-700 words in Italian on why learning Italian is important in today's world and plan of how to use the language degree; and the processing fee. **Deadline:** February 28.

5373 ■ Order Sons of Italy Foundation General Scholarships *(Graduate, Undergraduate/Scholarship)*

Purpose: To provide financial support for the education of eligible individuals for the scholarship. **Focus:** General studies. **Qualif.:** Applicants must be U.S. citizens of Italian descent enrolled in an undergraduate or graduate program at a four-year, accredited academic institution for the Fall 2008 term. **Criteria:** Recipient of the NELA scholarship must be in a matriculated program of study either on the undergraduate or graduate level.

Funds Avail.: $5,000 to $25,000. **To Apply:** Applicants must submit cover sheet, official transcript, test scores, resume, letters of recommendation, essay, and the processing fee. **Deadline:** February 28.

5374 ■ Henry Salvatori Scholarships *(Undergraduate/Scholarship)*

Purpose: To provide financial support to college bound high school senior demonstrating exceptional leadership, deep understanding and respect for the principles of the nation - liberty, freedom and equality. **Focus:** General studies. **Qualif.:** Applicants must be U.S. citizens of Italian descent in their senior year of high school and planning to attend a four-year, accredited institution for the Fall 2008 term. **Criteria:** Previous SIF scholarship recipients are not eligible.

Funds Avail.: $5,000 to $25,000. **To Apply:** Applicants must submit cover sheet, official transcript, test scores, resume, two letters of recommendation from public figures whose careers have demonstrated a commitment to the principles the scholarship embodies, type-written original essay of 750-1,000 words concerning the declaration of independence, the constitution and the bill of rights - discussion of the relevance of these documents to the principles of liberty, freedom and equality in the United States and the processing fee. **Deadline:** February 28.

5375 ■ Oregon Association of Broadcasters

7150 SW Hampton St., Ste. 240
Portland, OR 97223-8366
Ph: (503)443-2299
Fax: (503)443-2488
E-mail: theoab@theoab.org
URL: http://www.theoab.org

5376 ■ Oregon Association of Broadcasters Scholarships *(Undergraduate/Scholarship)*

Purpose: To promote, enhance, strengthen and defend the broadcast industry. To encourage and promote sound broadcast customs and practices. **Focus:** Broadcasting. **Qualif.:** Applicants must be graduating high school students, or students enrolled in two- or four-year college broadcast programs. Applicants must be Oregon residents, enrolled or intending to enroll at an Oregon college or university. **Criteria:** Recipients are selected based on academic record and financial need.

Funds Avail.: Varies. **To Apply:** Applicants must complete the application form. Applicants must include an essay explaining the student's reasons for choosing a career in broadcasting or a related field. **Contact:** theoab@theoab.org

5377 ■ Oregon Association of Nurseries

29751 SW Town Center Loop W
Wilsonville, OR 97070
Ph: (503)682-5089
Fax: (503)682-5099
Free: 800-342-6401
E-mail: info@oan.org
URL: http://www.oan.org

5378 ■ Christmas Tree Chapter Scholarship Awards *(Undergraduate/Scholarship)*

Purpose: To provide opportunities for education, research and business development to members, including landscapers and allied businesses, that supply goods and services to those who grow, handle and retail ornamental horticultural products in Oregon. **Focus:** Horticulture. **Qualif.:** Applicants must be students pursuing a degree in the field of horticulture. **Criteria:** Recipients are selected based on academic performance and financial need.

Funds Avail.: $500. **To Apply:** Applicants must submit one copy of official transcript of records and three current letters of reference supporting the applicant's horticulture abilities. **Deadline:** April 1. **Contact:** 29751 SW Town Center Loop W, Wilsonville, OR 97070.

5379 ■ Clackamas Chapter Scholarship Awards *(Undergraduate/Scholarship)*

Purpose: To provide opportunities for education, research and business development to members, including landscap-

Awards are arranged alphabetically below their administering organizations

ers and allied businesses, that supply goods and services to those who grow, handle and retail ornamental horticultural products in Oregon. **Focus:** Horticulture. **Qualif.:** Applicants must be freshmen students in an ornamental horticulture field. **Criteria:** Recipients are selected based on academic performance and financial need.

Funds Avail.: $1,000. **To Apply:** Applicants must submit one copy of official transcript of records and three current letters of reference supporting the applicant's horticulture abilities. **Deadline:** April 1. **Contact:** 29751 SW Town Center Loop W, Wilsonville, OR 97070.

5380 ■ Bill Egan Scholarship Program *(Undergraduate/Scholarship)*

Purpose: To provide opportunities for education, research and business development to members, including landscapers and allied businesses, that supply goods and services to those who grow, handle and retail ornamental horticultural products in Oregon. **Focus:** Horticulture. **Qualif.:** Applicants must be college students majoring in horticulture with an emphasis on the greenhouse/floriculture areas. **Criteria:** Recipients are selected based on academic performance and financial need.

Funds Avail.: $500. **To Apply:** Applicants must submit one copy of official transcript of records and three current letters of reference supporting the applicant's horticulture abilities. **Deadline:** April 1. **Contact:** 29751 SW Town Center Loop W, Wilsonville, OR 97070.

5381 ■ Emerald Empire Chapter Scholarship Awards *(Undergraduate/Scholarship)*

Purpose: To provide opportunities for education, research and business development to members, including landscapers and allied businesses, that supply goods and services to those who grow, handle and retail ornamental horticultural products in Oregon. **Focus:** Horticulture. **Qualif.:** Applicants must be junior or senior college students majoring in horticulture, landscape architecture or landscape construction who have graduated from an Oregon high school. **Criteria:** Recipients are selected based on academic performance and financial need.

Funds Avail.: $500. **To Apply:** Applicants must submit one copy of official transcript of records and three current letters of reference supporting the applicant's horticulture abilities. **Deadline:** April 1. **Contact:** 29751 SW Town Center Loop W, Wilsonville, OR 97070.

5382 ■ Martin Holmason Memorial Scholarship Awards *(Undergraduate/Scholarship)*

Purpose: To provide opportunities for education, research and business development to members, including landscapers and allied businesses, that supply goods and services to those who grow, handle and retail ornamental horticultural products in Oregon. **Focus:** Horticulture. **Qualif.:** Applicants must be college junior or senior students majoring in ornamental horticulture. **Criteria:** Recipients are selected based on academic performance and financial need.

Funds Avail.: $500. **To Apply:** Applicants must submit one copy of official transcript of records and three current letters of reference supporting the applicant's horticulture abilities. **Deadline:** April 1. **Contact:** 29751 SW Town Center Loop W, Wilsonville, OR 97070.

5383 ■ Joseph H. Klupenger Scholarship Awards *(Undergraduate/Scholarship)*

Purpose: To provide opportunities for education, research and business development to members, including landscapers and allied businesses that supply goods and services to those who grow, handle and retail ornamental horticultural products in Oregon. **Focus:** Horticulture. **Qualif.:** Applicants must be students majoring in ornamental horticulture; must intend to work in the ornamental industry. **Criteria:** Recipients are selected based on academic performance and financial need.

Funds Avail.: $550. **To Apply:** Applicants must submit one copy of official transcript of records and three current letters of reference supporting the applicant's horticulture abilities. **Deadline:** April 1. **Contact:** 29751 SW Town Center Loop W, Wilsonville, OR 97070.

5384 ■ Mt. Hood Chapter Scholarship Awards *(Undergraduate/Scholarship)*

Purpose: To provide opportunities for education, research and business development to members, including landscapers and allied businesses, that supply goods and services to those who grow, handle and retail ornamental horticultural products in Oregon. **Focus:** Horticulture. **Qualif.:** Applicants must be college students majoring in ornamental horticulture. **Criteria:** Recipients are selected based on academic performance and financial need.

Funds Avail.: $1,000. **To Apply:** Applicants must submit one copy of official transcript of records and three current letters of reference supporting the applicant's horticulture abilities. **Deadline:** April 1. **Contact:** 29751 SW Town Center Loop W, Wilsonville, OR 97070.

5385 ■ Nurseries Foundation Scholarship Awards *(Undergraduate/Scholarship)*

Purpose: To provide opportunities for education, research and business development to members, including landscapers and allied businesses, that supply goods and services to those who grow, handle and retail ornamental horticultural products in Oregon. **Focus:** Horticulture. **Qualif.:** Applicants must be college students majoring in the field of horticulture. **Criteria:** Recipients are selected based on academic performance and financial need.

Funds Avail.: $1,000. **To Apply:** Applicants must submit one copy of official transcript of records and three current letters of reference supporting the applicant's horticulture abilities. **Deadline:** April 1. **Contact:** 29751 SW Town Center Loop W, Wilsonville, OR 97070.

5386 ■ Nurseries Memorial Scholarship Awards *(Graduate/Scholarship)*

Purpose: To provide opportunities for education, research and business development to members, including landscapers and allied businesses, that supply goods and services to those who grow, handle and retail ornamental horticultural products in Oregon. **Focus:** Horticulture. **Qualif.:** Applicants must be graduate students pursuing researchs project pertaining to ornamental horticulture. **Criteria:** Recipients are selected based on academic performance and financial need.

Funds Avail.: $1,000. **To Apply:** Applicants must submit one copy of official transcript of records and three current letters of reference supporting the applicant's horticulture abilities. **Deadline:** April 1. **Contact:** 29751 SW Town Center Loop W, Wilsonville, OR 97070.

5387 ■ Oregon Association of Nurseries Scholarship Program *(Undergraduate/Scholarship)*

Purpose: To provide opportunities for education, research and business development to members, including landscap-

Awards are arranged alphabetically below their administering organizations

ers and allied businesses, that supply goods and services to those who grow, handle and retail ornamental horticultural products in Oregon. **Focus:** Horticulture. **Qualif.:** Applicants must be students preparing for a career in ornamental horticulture and related fields. **Criteria:** Recipients are selected based on academic performance and financial need.

Funds Avail.: No specific amount. **To Apply:** Applicants must submit one copy of official transcript of records and three current letters of reference supporting the applicants' horticulture abilities. **Deadline:** April 1. **Contact:** 29751 SW Town Center Loop W, Wilsonville, OR 97070.

5388 ■ Retail Chapter Scholarship Awards *(Undergraduate/Scholarship)*

Purpose: To provide opportunities for education, research and business development to members, including landscapers and allied businesses, that supply goods and services to those who grow, handle and retail ornamental horticultural products in Oregon. **Focus:** Horticulture. **Qualif.:** Applicants must be students majoring in ornamental horticulture and related fields. **Criteria:** Recipients are selected based on academic performance and financial need.

Funds Avail.: $1,000. **To Apply:** Applicants must submit one copy of official transcript of records and three current letters of reference supporting applicant's horticulture abilities. **Deadline:** April 1. **Contact:** 29751 SW Town Center Loop W, Wilsonville, OR 97070.

5389 ■ Willamette Chapter Scholarship Awards *(Undergraduate/Scholarship)*

Purpose: To provide opportunities for education, research and business development to members, including landscapers and allied businesses, that supply goods and services to those who grow, handle and retail ornamental horticultural products in Oregon. **Focus:** Horticulture. **Qualif.:** Applicants must be students majoring in ornamental horticulture and related fields. **Criteria:** Recipients are selected based on academic performance and financial need.

Funds Avail.: $1,000. **To Apply:** Applicants must submit one copy of official transcript of records and three current letters of reference supporting the applicant's horticulture abilities. **Deadline:** April 1. **Contact:** 29751 SW Town Center Loop W, Wilsonville, OR 97070.

5390 ■ Ed Wood Memorial Scholarship Awards *(Undergraduate/Scholarship)*

Purpose: To provide opportunities for education, research and business development to members, including landscapers and allied businesses, that supply goods and services to those who grow, handle and retail ornamental horticultural products in Oregon. **Focus:** Horticulture. **Qualif.:** Applicants must be currently enrolled in a college horticulture program in Oregon. **Criteria:** Recipients are selected based on the promise and commitment they show toward making significant future contributions to the nursery industry.

Funds Avail.: $1,500. **To Apply:** Applicants must submit one copy of official transcript of records and three current letters of reference supporting the applicant's horticulture abilities. **Deadline:** April 1. **Contact:** 29751 SW Town Center Loop W, Wilsonville, OR 97070.

5391 ■ Oregon Farm Bureau

3415 Commercial St. SE
Salem, OR 97302
Ph: (503)399-1701
Fax: (503)399-8082
Free: 800-334-6323
E-mail: annemarie@oregonfb.org
URL: http://www.oregonfb.org

5392 ■ Clackamas County Farm Bureau Scholarships *(Undergraduate/Scholarship)*

Purpose: To promote involvement in agriculture; to help those interested in an agricultural future; to further the education of those involved in the field, thus promoting a stronger future for the industry. **Focus:** Agricultural economics. **Qualif.:** Applicants must be residents of Clackamas County at the time of the application; must be interested in pursuing a career in agriculture or a related field; must have a GPA of at least 2.8. **Criteria:** Recipients are selected based on academic performance.

Funds Avail.: $1,000. **Number Awarded:** 3. **To Apply:** Applicants must submit: two letters of recommendation, from which one must come from an Ag Advisor or teacher and the other from another non-relative; transcript of records from most recent school attended; written statement detailing reasons for interest in an agricultural profession, leadership, community service experience and experience in agriculture. **Deadline:** April 1. **Contact:** 33814 S Meridian Rd., Woodburn, OR 97071.

5393 ■ Oregon Farm Bureau Memorial Scholarships *(Undergraduate/Scholarship)*

Purpose: To promote educational improvement, economic opportunity and social achievement for its members and the farming, ranching and natural resources industry as a whole. **Focus:** Agricultural economics. **Qualif.:** Applicants must be full-time students pursuing an agriculture-related major. **Criteria:** Recipients are selected based on academic performance and financial need.

Funds Avail.: $1,000. **To Apply:** Applicants must complete an application form; must submit a transcript of records and three letters of recommendation. **Deadline:** April 1. **Contact:** Dana Eckfield at the above address (see entry 5391).

5394 ■ Washington County Farm Bureau Scholarships *(Undergraduate/Scholarship)*

Purpose: To promote educational improvement, economic opportunity and social achievement for its members and the farming, ranching and natural resources industry as a whole. **Focus:** Agricultural economics. **Qualif.:** Applicants must be graduating high school seniors or college students enrolled in an agriculture degree program. **Criteria:** Recipients are selected based on academic performance, financial need, and community involvement.

Funds Avail.: $1,000. **Number Awarded:** 5. **To Apply:** Applicants must submit a completed application form. **Deadline:** May 5. **Contact:** 503-648-9442.

5395 ■ Willamette Valley AG Association Scholarships *(Undergraduate/Scholarship)*

Purpose: To support Oregon High School graduates that plan to attend an Oregon university to study an area that would have a positive impact on production agriculture or other agricultural related fields. **Focus:** Agricultural economics. **Qualif.:** Applicants must be full-time students who are college level juniors or seniors pursuing an agriculture-related major at an Oregon college or university, and students seeking a graduate level teaching degree. **Criteria:** Recipients are selected based on academic performance and financial need.

Funds Avail.: $1,000. **To Apply:** Applicants must submit a completed application form; a transcript of records and three letters of recommendation. **Deadline:** April 1. **Contact:** Dana Eckfield at the above address (see entry 5391).

5396 ■ Yamhill County Farm Bureau Scholarships *(Undergraduate/Scholarship)*

Purpose: To assist Yamhill County high school graduates in furthering their education. **Focus:** Agricultural economics. **Qualif.:** Applicants must be full-time students who have successfully completed at least one year of higher education at an accredited college or university; must have plans to continue their education at an accredited college; must have a major in agriculture or related field; must have a minimum of 2.5 GPA for the last college term; must have a minimum of 12 credits per term; must be graduates of Yamhill County. **Criteria:** Recipients are selected based on academic performance.

Funds Avail.: $1,500. **Number Awarded:** 2. **To Apply:** Applicants must submit a completed and signed application form, two letters of recommendation from non-related persons and official transcripts from all colleges attended. **Deadline:** August 1. **Contact:** 1215 N Adams St., Ste. C, McMinnville, OR 97128.

5397 ■ Oregon Medical Association

11740 SW, 68th Pkwy., Ste.100
Portland, OR 97223
Ph: (503)619-8000
Fax: (503)619-0609
E-mail: oma@theoma.org
URL: http://www.theoma.org

5398 ■ Linn Benton Scholarships *(Undergraduate/Scholarship)*

Purpose: To advance medical science through education. **Focus:** Medicine. **Qualif.:** Applicants must be high school seniors or graduates seeking a career in medicine or nursing. **Criteria:** Recipients are selected based on academic performance.

Funds Avail.: $1,000. **Number Awarded:** 3. **To Apply:** Applicants must complete the application form. **Deadline:** April 1.

5399 ■ Organization of American States

1889 F St. NW
Washington, DC 20006
Ph: (202)458-6166
E-mail: scholarships@aos.org
URL: http://www.educoas.org

5400 ■ Organization of American States Academic Scholarships *(Undergraduate/Scholarship)*

Purpose: To assist the member states with their domestic efforts in pursuit of integral development goals by supporting human resource development in the priority areas; to promote and support human capacity development and the strengthening of bonds among peoples in the hemisphere by maximizing the number of scholarships awarded in reputable educational institutions in its member states with the resources available. **Focus:** General studies. **Qualif.:** Applicants must be involved in undergraduate or graduate studies that lead to a degree and/or graduate research at a university or higher learning institution in a member state. **Criteria:** Recipients are selected based on financial need.

Funds Avail.: No specific amount. **To Apply:** Applicants must accomplish application form. **Contact:** scholarships@aos.org

5401 ■ Organization of American States AOS-Placed Scholarships *(Undergraduate/Scholarship)*

Purpose: To assist the member states with their domestic efforts in pursuit of integral development goals by supporting human resource development in the priority areas; to promote and support human capacity development and the strengthening of bonds among people in the hemisphere by maximizing the number of scholarships awarded in reputable educational institutions in its member states with the resources available. **Focus:** General studies. **Qualif.:** Applicants must be enrolled in a university, college, or institution. **Criteria:** Recipients are selected based on financial need.

Funds Avail.: No specific amount. **To Apply:** Applicants must complete the application form. **Contact:** scholarships@aos.org

5402 ■ Organization of American States Graduate Scholarships *(Undergraduate/Scholarship)*

Purpose: To assist the member states with their domestic efforts in pursuit of integral development goals by supporting human resource development in the priority areas; to promote and support human capacity development and the strengthening of bonds among people in the hemisphere by maximizing the number of scholarships awarded in reputable educational institutions in its member states with the resources available. **Focus:** General studies. **Qualif.:** Applicants must be enrolled in a master's or doctorate degree program. **Criteria:** Recipients are selected based on financial need.

Funds Avail.: $30,000. **To Apply:** Applicants must complete the application form. **Contact:** scholarships@aos.org

5403 ■ Organization of American States Self-Placed Scholarships *(Undergraduate/Scholarship)*

Purpose: To assist the member states with their domestic efforts in pursuit of integral development goals by supporting human resource development in the priority areas; to promote and support human capacity development and the strengthening of bonds among peoples in the hemisphere by maximizing the number of scholarships awarded in reputable educational institutions in its member states with the resources available. **Focus:** General studies. **Qualif.:** Applicants must be enrolled in a university, college, or institution. **Criteria:** Recipients are selected based on financial need.

Funds Avail.: No specific amount. **To Apply:** Applicants must complete the application form. **Contact:** scholarships@aos.org

5404 ■ Leo S. Rowe Pan American Fund *(Undergraduate/Loan)*

Purpose: To help finance higher educational pursuits in the United States. **Focus:** Latin American Studies; Arts; Science. **Qualif.:** Applicants must be undergraduate or graduate students from Latin American or Caribbean AOS member countries who are studying or have been admitted for studies in the United States to a program leading to a

Awards are arranged alphabetically below their administering organizations

university degree in an institution of higher learning accredited by the corresponding regional or national council; or must be students and professionals who are either currently pursuing or wish to pursue advanced studies, research, or technical activities in the arts or sciences in institution in the United States; must able to demonstrate, to the Committee's satisfaction their need for assistance, the usefulness of their studies, and ability to successfully complete them; must be nationals of Latin American or Carribbean member State of the AOS; must have a grade point average of at least 3.0 or "B" from their current or most recent academic institution; and must agree to return to their origin after completion of their studies. **Criteria:** Recipients are selected based on academic records and financial need.

Funds Avail.: $15,000 (in total). **To Apply:** Applicants must submit original, duly sealed, stamped, or notarized transcript of grades; diplomas; and foreign student advisor form.

5405 ■ Organization of Black Airline Pilots

8630 Fenton St., Ste. 126
Silver Spring, MD 20910
Free: 800-JET-OBAP
E-mail: nationaloffice@obap.org
URL: http://www.obap.org

5406 ■ Edward L. Horne, Jr. Scholarships *(All/ Scholarship)*

Purpose: To promote education in the aviation industry. **Focus:** Aviation. **Qualif.:** Applicant must be an OBAP member pursuing a career in the aviation industry. **Criteria:** Selection is based on the application materials.

Funds Avail.: No specific amount. **To Apply:** Applicants must provide an evidence of participation in at least one OBAP event; a copy of Private Pilot's license; a resume with photo; two letters of recommendations (one must be from an OBAP member); a copy of medical permit; and an essay (maximum of 1000 words) about the applicant's greatest challenge in life. **Deadline:** June 15.

Remarks: Sponsored by Captain Edward L. Horne, Jr. **Contact:** Clarence Grisham.

5407 ■ OBAP Fellowships - Airline Transport (ATP) *(Professional Development/Fellowship)*

Purpose: To promote education and training in the aviation industry. **Focus:** Aviation. **Qualif.:** Applicant must be an OBAP member in good standing; can read, write and speak English fluently; must be a U.S. citizen, or has established authorization to work in the U.S; must have participated in any of the ACE Camp or Pilots-in Schools events; must have participated in any event that supports the ideals and initiatives of OBAP. **Criteria:** Fellowship is awarded on a first come, first served basis.

Funds Avail.: Up to $1,500. **To Apply:** Applicant must submit a completed application form together with two letters of recommendation (one must be from an OBAP member) and a 2-page essay. Applicants may also apply online.

5408 ■ OBAP Fellowships - Commercial *(Professional Development/Fellowship)*

Purpose: To promote education and training in the aviation industry. **Focus:** Aviation. **Qualif.:** Applicant must be an OBAP member in good standing; can read, write and speak English fluently; must be a U.S. citizen, or has established authorization to work in the U.S; must have participated in any of the ACE Camp or Pilots-in Schools events; must have participated in any event that supports the ideals and initiatives of OBAP. **Criteria:** Fellowship is awarded on a first come, first served basis.

Funds Avail.: Up to $1,500. **To Apply:** Applicant must submit a completed application form together with two letters of recommendation (one must be from an OBAP member) and a 2-page essay. Applicants may also apply online.

5409 ■ OBAP Fellowships - Instructor rating (CFI/CFII/MEI) *(Professional Development/ Fellowship)*

Purpose: To promote education and training in the aviation industry. **Focus:** Aviation. **Qualif.:** Applicant must be an OBAP member in good standing; can read, write and speak English fluently; must be a U.S. citizen, or has established authorization to work in the U.S; must have participated in any of the ACE Camp or Pilots-in Schools events; must have participated in any event that supports the ideals and initiatives of OBAP. **Criteria:** Fellowship is awarded on a first come, first served basis.

Funds Avail.: Up to $1,500. **To Apply:** Applicant must submit a completed application form together with two letters of recommendation (one must be from an OBAP member) and a 2-page essay. Applicants may also apply online.

5410 ■ OBAP Fellowships - Multi-Engine *(Professional Development/Fellowship)*

Purpose: To promote education and training in the aviation industry. **Focus:** Aviation. **Qualif.:** Applicant must be an OBAP member in good standing; can read, write and speak English fluently; must be a U.S. citizen, or has established authorization to work in the U.S; must have participated in any of the ACE Camp or Pilots-in Schools events; must have participated in any event that supports the ideals and initiatives of OBAP. **Criteria:** Fellowship is awarded on a first come, first served basis.

Funds Avail.: Up to $1,500. **To Apply:** Applicant must submit a completed application form together with two letters of recommendation (one must be from an OBAP member) and a 2-page essay. Applicants may also apply online.

5411 ■ OBAP General Scholarships *(All/ Scholarship)*

Purpose: To promote education in the aviation industry. **Focus:** Aviation. **Qualif.:** Applicant must be an OBAP member pursuing a career in the aviation industry. **Criteria:** Selection is based on the application materials.

Funds Avail.: $4,000. **Number Awarded:** 5. **To Apply:** Applicants must provide an evidence of participation in at least one OBAP event; a copy of Private Pilot's license; a resume; two letters of recommendations (one must be from an OBAP member); a copy of medical permit; a 2-page autobiography with recent photo; and an essay on, "What is/has been your greatest life challenge, and how has it enriched you or someone else's life?" **Deadline:** June 15. **Contact:** Clarence Grisham.

5412 ■ Organization of Chinese Americans

1322 18th St. NW
Washington, DC 20036-1803
Ph: (202)223-5500

Fax: (202)296-0540
E-mail: oca@ocanational.org
URL: http://www.ocanatl.org

5413 ■ OCA Scholarships *(Undergraduate/Scholarship)*

Purpose: To provide financial assistance to APA high school seniors entering their first year of college in the upcoming Fall Quarter or Semester. **Focus:** General studies. **Qualif.:** Applicants must be a current APA high school senior entering their first year of college in the upcoming 2008 Fall Semester/Quarter, demonstrate financial need, a permanent resident or U.S. citizen, and have a cumulative Grade Point Average (GPA) of 3.0 or above (on a 4.0 scale). **Criteria:** Candidates will be evaluated by the Scholarship Committee.

Funds Avail.: No amount mentioned. **To Apply:** Applicants must submit resume, one page essay, high school transcript, letter of acceptance from college or university, printout of student aid report (SAR), and financial Aid Award notification (FAN) from college or university. **Deadline:** April 18.

5414 ■ Orphan Foundation of America

21351 Gentry Dr., Ste. 130
Sterling, VA 20166
Ph: (571)203-0270
Fax: (571)203-0273
E-mail: help@orphan.org
URL: http://www.orphan.org

5415 ■ Casey Family Scholars Scholarships *(Undergraduate/Scholarship)*

Purpose: To provide opportunities and resources for America's foster youth to pursue their education and succeed in life. **Focus:** Health care services. **Qualif.:** Applicants must be accepted or enrolled in an accredited post-secondary program at the undergraduate level in a college, university, vocational or technical institute. Applicants must be children under the age of 25, who have spent at least 12 months in foster care and who were not subsequently adopted. **Criteria:** Recipients are selected based on financial needs and scholastic standing.

Funds Avail.: $10,000. **To Apply:** Applicants must complete the application form. **Contact:** scholarships@orphan.org

5416 ■ Orthopaedic Trauma Association

6300 N River Road, Ste. 727
Rosemont, IL 60018-4226
Ph: (847)698-1631
Fax: (847)823-0536
E-mail: ota@aaos.org
URL: http://www.ota.org

5417 ■ OTA Research Grants *(Graduate/Grant)*

Purpose: To promote excellence in care for the injured patient, through provision of scientific forums. **Focus:** Orthopaedic. **Qualif.:** Applicant must have pre-proposals. **Criteria:** Grants are available to any research issue related to musculoskeletal trauma, excluding product development.

Funds Avail.: Clinical Research Grants ($40,000/year, 2 year grant cycle); Basic Research Grants ($25,000, 1 year grant cycle); Resident Research Grants ($10,000, 1 year grant cycle). **To Apply:** Research grants pre-proposal applications are available online. **Deadline:** April 1; **Contact:** OTA at the above address (see entry 5416).

5418 ■ Ottawa Centre for Research and Innovation

2625 Queensview Dr., Ste. 200
Ottawa, ON, Canada K2B 8K2
Ph: (613)828-6274
Fax: (613)726-3440
E-mail: worldclass@ocri.ca
URL: http://www.ocri.ca

5419 ■ Black Canadian Scholarships *(Undergraduate/Scholarship)*

Purpose: To provide support for Black Canadian students intending to pursue their education. **Focus:** General studies. **Qualif.:** Applicant must be a Black Canadian student graduating from a high school in the city of Ottawa; must be admissible to a recognized Canadian university; must demonstrate a need of financial assistance; must be a Canadian citizen; and must demonstrate leadership in community involvement. **Criteria:** Selection of applicants will be based on the scholarship selection criteria.

Funds Avail.: $5,000. **To Apply:** Applicants must submit a two-page essay explaining why the scholarship is important to the applicant and how the applicant will satisfy the eligibility criteria; must provide a photocopy of the applicant's latest official transcript of 6 Grade 12 courses with a 75%+average; must have a letter of recommendation from a teacher/guidance counselor in current academic year; must have proof of community service; must have proof of Canadian citizenship; and must have a detailed statement indicating the amount of money expected from various sources. Application form and requirements must be sent to Black Canadian Scholarship Fund, PO Box 8002, Ottawa, ON K1G 5H6. **Deadline:** May 31.

5420 ■ George Joseph Cooper Awards *(Undergraduate/Scholarship)*

Purpose: To provide financial assistance for qualified individuals intending to pursue their studies. **Focus:** General studies. **Qualif.:** Applicant must be a graduating student from a high school in the region of Ottawa; must have applied to a recognized college or university; must be entering a full-time program; and must demonstrate financial need and academic achievements. **Criteria:** Selection of applicants will be based on the scholarship selection criteria.

Funds Avail.: $1,000. **To Apply:** Applicants must complete the application form, available online; must provide a letter of reference from a teacher/ guidance counselor; and must submit a copy of the latest transcript of record. **Deadline:** April 14.

5421 ■ Lord Dundonald Chapter (IODE) Scholarships *(Undergraduate/Scholarship)*

Purpose: To provide financial assistance for qualified Ottawa students. **Focus:** General studies. **Qualif.:** Applicant must be a student from a high school in the region of Ottawa; must have applied to a recognized college or university; must be entering a full-time program; and must demonstrate financial need and academic achievements. **Criteria:** Applicants will be selected based on academic and financial standing.

Awards are arranged alphabetically below their administering organizations

Funds Avail.: $500. **To Apply:** Applicants must complete the application form, available online; must provide a letter of reference from a teacher/guidance counselor; and must submit a copy of the latest transcript of record. **Deadline:** April 14.

5422 ■ Elizabeth Heath Post-Secondary Awards *(Undergraduate/Scholarship)*

Purpose: To provide financial support for deserving Ottawa students. **Focus:** General studies. **Qualif.:** Applicant must be a graduating student from a high school in the region of Ottawa; must have applied to a recognized college or university; must be entering a full-time program; and must demonstrate financial need and academic achievements. **Criteria:** Selection of recipients will be based on financial need and academic standing.

Funds Avail.: $2,500. **Number Awarded:** 2. **To Apply:** Applicants must complete the application form, available online; must provide a letter of reference from a teacher/ guidance counselor; and must submit a copy of the latest transcript of record. **Deadline:** April 14.

5423 ■ Elizabeth Heath Technical, Trades Training and Development Awards *(Undergraduate/ Scholarship)*

Purpose: To provide financial assistance for graduating high school students in the Ottawa region. **Focus:** General studies. **Qualif.:** Applicant must be a student graduating from the apprenticeship Cooperative Education Studies program at a high school in the region of Ottawa; must be pursuing further education or training in an apprenticeship or skilled employment program; must demonstrate a need for financial assistance; and must have demonstrated diligence and determination both "on the job" and at school. **Criteria:** Selection of applicants will be based on financial need and academic standing.

Funds Avail.: $1,500. **Number Awarded:** 3. **To Apply:** Applicants must complete the application form available online; must provide a letter of reference from a teacher/ guidance counselor; and must submit a copy of the latest transcript of record. **Deadline:** April 14.

5424 ■ Barbara Ingram, Janet W. McCarthy and W.J.P. Jack Robertson Memorial Scholarships *(Undergraduate/Scholarship)*

Purpose: To provide financial assistance to qualified individuals intending to pursue their education. **Focus:** General studies. **Qualif.:** Applicant must be a graduating student from a high school in the region of Ottawa; must have applied to a recognized college or university; must be entering a full-time program; and must be a person with a physical disability. **Criteria:** Consideration will be given to students demonstrating financial need.

Funds Avail.: $1,500. **Number Awarded:** 2. **To Apply:** Applicants must complete the application form, available online; must provide a letter of reference from a teacher/ guidance counselor; and must submit a copy of the latest transcript of record. **Deadline:** April 14.

5425 ■ Kildonan Education Awards *(Undergraduate/Scholarship)*

Purpose: To provide financial assistance for qualified Ottawa students. **Focus:** General studies. **Qualif.:** Applicant must be a graduating student from a high school in the region of Ottawa; must have applied to a recognized college or university; must be entering a full-time program; and must demonstrate both financial need and academic achievements. **Criteria:** Selection of applicants will be based on financial need and academic standing.

Funds Avail.: $4,000. **Number Awarded:** 3. **To Apply:** Applicants must complete the application form, available online; must provide a letter of reference from a teacher/ guidance counselor; and must submit a copy of the latest transcript of record. **Deadline:** April 14.

5426 ■ Jack Meadows Memorial Awards *(Undergraduate/Scholarship)*

Purpose: To provide financial assistance for qualified Ottawa students. **Focus:** General studies. **Qualif.:** Applicant must be a graduating student from a high school in the region of Ottawa; must have applied to a recognized college or university; must be entering a full-time program; and must demonstrate financial need and academic achievements. **Criteria:** Selection of applicants will be based on financial and academic standing.

Funds Avail.: $2,500 (if attending college), $3,000 (if attending university). **Number Awarded:** 6. **To Apply:** Applicants must complete the application form, available online; must provide a letter of reference from a teacher/ guidance counselor; and must submit a copy of the latest transcript of record. **Deadline:** April 14.

5427 ■ Outdoor Power Equipment Aftermarket Association

1726 M St. NW, Ste. 1101
Washington, DC 20036
Ph: (202)775-8605
Fax: (202)833-1577
E-mail: opeaa@opeaa.org
URL: http://www.opeaa.org

5428 ■ Bill Nelson Scholarship Endowment *(Undergraduate/Scholarship)*

Purpose: To provide financial assistance for the educational pursuits of employees of OPEEA members and their dependents. **Focus:** General studies. **Qualif.:** Applicants must be children, stepchildren, grandchildren and adopted children of employees of OPEEA members; and must be at least senior students in high school. **Criteria:** Awards are given based on academic merit and tests results.

Funds Avail.: $1,000. **To Apply:** Applicants must fill out application form available in OPEEA website and submit along with sponsor information, essay (in 250 words) describing academic aspirations and two letters of reference.

5429 ■ Outdoor Writers Association of America

121 Hickory St., Ste. 1
Missoula, MT 59801
Ph: (406)728-7434
Fax: (406)728-7445
E-mail: krhoades@owaa.org
URL: http://www.owaa.org

5430 ■ Bodie McDowell Scholarships *(Graduate, Undergraduate/Scholarship)*

Purpose: To provide educational services to members. **Focus:** Writing. **Qualif.:** Applicant must be an undergraduate or graduate students from any discipline and all schools;

Awards are arranged alphabetically below their administering organizations

must have a career goal in outdoor communications. **Criteria:** Selection of applicant will be based on talent, promise and firsthand outdoor knowledge and will be rated on clarity, organization and originality. GPA average is also considered.

Funds Avail.: $1,000 to $4,000. **To Apply:** Applicant must submit a completed application, letter of recommendation from school, transcript, example of outdoor communication work, a one to two page statement of career goals, and optional letters of recommendation from others familiar with applicant's work. **Deadline:** March 1. **Contact:** Kevin Rhoades at krhoades@owaa.org.

5431 ■ Outward Bound

100 Mystery Point Rd.
Garrison, NY 10524
Ph: (845)424-4000
Fax: (845)424-4121
E-mail: info@outwardbound.org
URL: http://www.outwardbound.org

5432 ■ Marmot Leadership Scholarships *(Postgraduate, Professional Development, Undergraduate/Scholarship)*

Purpose: To recognize outstanding students who have leadership potential and are in need of financial assistance. **Focus:** Community leadership. **Qualif.:** Applicant must be a graduating high school senior (age 17+) or a college/university student (age 23 maximum) who demonstrates leadership potential and financial need. **Criteria:** Preference will be given to applicants who best meet the requirements.

Funds Avail.: Funds must be used for tuition only. **To Apply:** Applicants must submit a complete Marmot Leadership Scholarship Application, Essay Questions, and Financial Application; a $100 application fee; a letter of recommendation that can attest to the applicant's leadership qualities, experience and/or potential; a copy of the applicant's (or parents) most recent 1040 Federal Tax Form, including all schedules. For students under 21 or not self-supporting, both parents' income information is required. Send application to: Email scholarships@outwardbound.org, Subject: OBLS Application: Name; Fax (866)851-7738, Attention: Scholarship Awards Coordinator, Marmot Application; Mail - Scholarship Awards Coordinator, Marmot Application, Outward Bound Wilderness, 910 Jackson St., Golden, CO 80401. **Deadline:** April 16. **Contact:** Scholarship Awards Coordinator toll free number: 888-837-5204, email scholarships@outwardbound.org.

5433 ■ Outward Bound Leadership Scholarships for Educators *(Professional Development/Scholarship)*

Purpose: For teachers who will incorporate experiential learning techniques into their schools. **Focus:** Community leadership. **Qualif.:** Teachers must be at least 23 years-old and should teach at the same school from which they applied; former Outward Bound scholars are not qualified. **Criteria:** Preference will be given to applicants who best meet the requirements.

Funds Avail.: Funds must be used for tuition only. **To Apply:** Applicants must submit a complete Outward Bound Leadership Scholarship Application and Essay Questions, available at the website www.outwardboundwilderness.org; a $100 application fee; a letter of recommendation that can attest to the applicant's leadership qualities, experience and/or potential. Send application to: Email scholarships@outwardbound.org, Subject: OBLS Application: Name; Fax (866)851-7738, Attention: Scholarship Awards Coordinator, Marmot Application; Mail - Scholarship Awards Coordinator, Marmot Application, Outward Bound Wilderness, 910 Jackson St., Golden, CO 80401. **Deadline:** March 15. **Contact:** Scholarship Awards Coordinator toll free number: 888-837-5204, email: scholarships@outwardbound.org.

5434 ■ Outward Bound Wilderness Leadership Awards *(High School, Professional Development/Award/Prize)*

Purpose: For students who have demonstrated interest in community service and display potential leadership. **Focus:** Community leadership. **Qualif.:** Candidates must be junior high school students; must be identified as candidates by a teacher or a staff. **Criteria:** Applicants are selected based on student presentations/interviews and jury's review of application materials. Applicants are also nominated by a former Outward Bound Alumni, school staff, or teachers.

Funds Avail.: No specific amount. **To Apply:** Applicants must submit completed application with answers to essay questions posted in the website. **Contact:** Lisa Mattis, lmattis@outwardbound.org.

5435 ■ Owner-Operator Independent Drivers Association

1 NW OOIDA Dr.
Grain Valley, MO 64029
Ph: (816)229-5791
Fax: (816)427-4468
E-mail: ooida@ooida.com
URL: http://www.ooida.com

5436 ■ Owner-Operator Independent Drivers Association Scholarships *(Undergraduate/Scholarship)*

Purpose: To assist the children, grandchildren and legal dependents of OOIDA members in their effort to gain higher education. **Focus:** General studies. **Qualif.:** Applicants must be immediate family members of OOIDA. Scholarships are available for children, grandchildren, and legal dependents of OOIDA members. **Criteria:** Awards are given based on academic merit. Applicants are selected in a blind evaluation conducted by the Scholarship Advisory Committee.

Funds Avail.: $1,000. **To Apply:** Applicants must submit a 500-word essay; official certified high school transcript; proof of enrollment from institution of higher education. Application form and guidelines can be obtained from the OOIDA office or can be downloaded from the OOIDA website. **Deadline:** February 1.

5437 ■ Pacific-10 Conference

1350 Treat Blvd., Ste. 500
Walnut Creek, CA 94597-8853
Ph: (925)932-4411
Fax: (925)932-4601
URL: http://www.pac-10.org

5438 ■ The Pac-10 Postgraduate Scholarships *(Graduate/Scholarship)*

Purpose: To honor outstanding student-athletes from member institutions who also are outstanding scholars.

Awards are arranged alphabetically below their administering organizations

Focus: General studies. **Qualif.:** Applicants must have an overall undergraduate minimum cumulative GPA of 3.00 (based on a 4.00 scale) or its equivalent; in the final season of intercollegiate athletics eligibility and competition under Pac-10 legislation; have performed with distinction as a member of the varsity team in the sport in which the student-athlete has been nominated; intend to continue academic work beyond the baccalaureate degree as a full-time graduate student; have behaved, both on and off the field, in a manner that has brought credit to the student-athlete, the institution and intercollegiate athletics. **Criteria:** Selection is based on participation in campus or community service activities.

Funds Avail.: $3000. **Number Awarded:** 40. **To Apply:** Applicants must contact the Faculty Athletics Representative or the Life Skills Coordinator at their institution.

Remarks: One male and one female from the pool of 40 Pac-10 Postgraduate Scholarship winners will receive the Oroweat "Healthy Minds" Scholarships of $10,000. **Contact:** Chris Dawson.

5439 ■ Pacific Legal Foundation

3900 Lennane Dr., Ste. 200
Sacramento, CA 95834
Ph: (916)419-7111
Fax: (916)419-7747
Free: 800-847-7719
E-mail: plf@pacificlegal.org
URL: http://www.community.pacificlegal.org

5440 ■ Legal Scholarship for Law Students
(Undergraduate/Scholarship)

Purpose: To encourage legal scholarships related to Pacific Legal Foundation's Litigation. **Focus:** Law. **Qualif.:** Applicants must be enrolled in law schools in the United States. **Criteria:** Recipients are selected based on the quality of the essay.

Funds Avail.: $5,000. **To Apply:** Applicants must submit original essays related to one or more of the legal objectives. **Deadline:** July 1. **Contact:** Pacific Legal Foundation at the above address (see entry 5439).

5441 ■ Legal Scholarship for Non-Tenured Law Professors *(All/Scholarship)*

Purpose: To encourage legal scholarship related to Pacific Legal Foundation's Litigation. **Focus:** Law. **Qualif.:** Applicants must be junior faculty members at American Law schools to add the body of legal-academic scholarship in support of freedom and free enterprise. **Criteria:** Recipients are selected based on the quality of the proposal.

Funds Avail.: $5,000. **To Apply:** Applicants must submit proposals for research leading to the publication of a law review article or comparable legal scholarship. **Deadline:** July 1. **Contact:** Pacific Legal Foundation at the above address (see entry 5439).

5442 ■ Legal Scholarship for Tenured Law Professors *(All/Scholarship)*

Purpose: To encourage legal scholarship related to Pacific Legal Foundation's Litigation. **Focus:** Law. **Qualif.:** Applicants must be tenured professors at law schools in the United States. **Criteria:** Recipients are selected based on the quality of the proposal.

Funds Avail.: $5,000. **To Apply:** Applicants must submit proposals for research leading to the publication of a law review article or comparable legal scholarship. **Deadline:** July 1. **Contact:** Pacific Legal Foundation at the above address (see entry 5439).

5443 ■ Pacific Legal Foundation Faculty Grants
(All/Grant)

Purpose: To encourage legal scholarship related to Pacific Legal Foundation's Litigation. **Focus:** Law. **Qualif.:** Applicants must be engaged in original research reasonably expected to lead to publication on important legal issues relating to PLF's litigation program. **Criteria:** Recipients are selected based on the quality of the research.

Funds Avail.: $10,000. **Number Awarded:** 4. **To Apply:** Applicants must complete the application form. **Deadline:** Not stated. **Contact:** Pacific Legal Foundation at the above address (see entry 5439).

5444 ■ Painting and Decorating Contractors of America

1801 Park 270 Dr., Ste. 220
St. Louis, MO 63146
Ph: (314)514-7322
Fax: (314)514-9417
Free: 800-332-7322
E-mail: ihoren@pdca.org
URL: http://www.pdca.org

5445 ■ A.E. Robert Friedman Scholarships
(Postgraduate, Undergraduate/Scholarship)

Purpose: To assist students who wish to further their education. **Focus:** Adult education; Education, Vocational-technical. **Qualif.:** Applicants must be at least seniors in high school, no more than 26 years old; nominated by an active PDCA member, unrelated to a PDCA member or employee and otherwise unconnected with the PDCA. **Criteria:** Applicants are selected based on financial need and eligibility.

Funds Avail.: $1,500. **Number Awarded:** Varies. **To Apply:** Applicants must submit a completed application form; essays; letters of recommendation and transcript. **Deadline:** October 1.

Remarks: Scholarships are in honor of A.E. Robert Friedman, a legal counsel of PDCA and supporter of education.

5446 ■ Palos Fine Arts Association

8901 W 123rd St.
Palos Park, IL 60464
Ph: (708)671-3755
E-mail: info@palosfinearts.com
URL: http://www.palosfinearts.com

5447 ■ Felicia De Bow Memorial Scholarships
(All/Scholarship)

Purpose: To further interest in and study of arts. **Focus:** Fine arts. **Qualif.:** Applicants must be females of at least 21 years of age; must reside or work within the boundaries of High School District 230 or 218; must attend a regular meeting of the Palos Fine Arts Council to share their experiences from the use of the scholarship. **Criteria:** Recipients are selected based on academic performance and financial need.

Funds Avail.: $500. **To Apply:** Applicants must submit: a

Awards are arranged alphabetically below their administering organizations

completed application form; release form; art materials in the form of CD, tape, slides, audio or manuscript; a 1,000 word essay including a brief self-history, goals, when and where the class or workshops will be held and reasons for interest in attending the class.

5448 ■ Palos Fine Arts Association Scholarships *(Undergraduate/Scholarship)*

Purpose: To further interest in and study of arts. **Focus:** Fine Arts. **Qualif.:** Applicants must be junior or senior high school students residing within the boundaries of high school districts 230 or 218; must attend Stagg, Sandburg, Andrew, Shepard, Chicago Christian, Marist, McCauly, Sacred Heart or be home-schooled. **Criteria:** Recipients are selected based on academic performance and financial need.

Funds Avail.: $500. **Number Awarded:** 2. **To Apply:** Applicants must submit: a completed application form; release form; art materials in the form of CD, tape, slides, audio or manuscript; a 1,000 word essay including a brief self-history, goals, when and where the class or workshops will be held and reasons for interest in attending the class.

5449 ■ Paper Stock Industries

3300 PGA Blvd., Ste. 635
Palm Beach Gardens, FL 33410-2811
Ph: (561)627-9191
E-mail: nktraders@tradersintl.net
URL: http://www.paperstockindustries.org

5450 ■ Paper Stock Industries/RRF Scholarships *(Undergraduate/Scholarship)*

Purpose: To provide financial assistance to students who wish to continue their education. **Focus:** General studies. **Qualif.:** Applicant must be a employee, son, daughter or spouse of an individual who has been employed for at least one year in a member firm of a PSI Chapter; must have at least a C+ average in high school and meet all the qualifications for admission to a regionally accredited two-year or four-year post secondary institution. **Criteria:** Recipients will be evaluated based on merit.

Funds Avail.: $1,000. **To Apply:** Applicants must submit a completed scholarship application; official transcripts of all high school and/or college grades, SAT, and/or ACT scores; two letters of recommendation; resume of the applicant's personal history; and a one-page short essay entitled "Why College is important to Me." **Deadline:** March 15. **Contact:** Nini Krever at the above address (see entry 5449).

5451 ■ Paper Stock Industries Chapter of ISRI

3300 PGA Blvd, Ste. 635
Palm Beach Gardens, FL 33410-2811
Ph: (561)627-9191
E-mail: nktraders@tradersintl.net
URL: http://www.paperstockindustries.org

5452 ■ Paper Stock Industries Chapter of ISRI Scholarship Program *(Undergraduate/Scholarship)*

Purpose: To provide financial aid for employees of the Paper Stock Industries Chapter and their immediate families intending to pursue education. **Focus:** General studies. **Qualif.:** Applicant must be an employee, or an immediate relative (child or spouse) of an individual who has been employed for at least one year by a member firm of the PSI Chapter; and must have at least a C+ average in high school. **Criteria:** Scholarship beneficiaries will be selected by the PSI Chapter Scholarship Committee based on merit.

Funds Avail.: $1,000. **Number Awarded:** 4. **To Apply:** Applicants must submit completed the scholarship application (downloadable from PSI website); official transcript of records (high school and college); standardized test scores: SAT and/or ACT; two letters of recommendation; a personal resume; and a one-page minimum essay on "Why College is Important to Me." Applicants must send an original and two copies of all necessary documents to: Nini Krever c/o Traders International Corp. 3300 PGA Blvd. Ste. 635, Palm Beach Gardens Florida 33410. **Deadline:** March 15. **Contact:** Nini Krever.

5453 ■ Parapsychological Association

1390 N McDowell Blvd., Ste. G-208
Petaluma, CA 94954
E-mail: business@parapsych.org
URL: http://www.parapsych.org

5454 ■ Parapsycological Association Research Endowment *(All/Grant)*

Purpose: To encourage parapsychological research by students and other researchers. **Focus:** Parapsychology. **Qualif.:** Any individual interested in the field of parapsychology. **Criteria:** The awards will be administered by the Board of the Parapsychology Association, via committee established to evaluate scholarship and grant requests.

Funds Avail.: $2,000-$5,000. **To Apply:** Applicant must submit a brief but formal proposal (less than 3000 words), in either plain text or a word document. **Deadline:** June 30. **Contact:** Roger Nelson, rdnelson@princeton.edu.

5455 ■ Parapsychology Foundation

PO Box 1562
New York, NY 10021
Ph: (212)628-1550
Fax: (212)628-1559
E-mail: info@parapsychology.org
URL: http://www.parapsychology.org

5456 ■ Frances P. Bolton Fellowships *(Doctorate/Fellowship)*

Purpose: To support a dissertation/thesis dealing with some aspect of parapsychological phenomena. **Focus:** Psychology. **Qualif.:** Program is open to doctorate students in good standing; must be currently enrolled full-time in an accredited school/university; must demonstrate interest in parapsychology; must be working on a dissertation or thesis related with some aspect of psychological phenomena; and must be members of the foundation. **Criteria:** Selection is done on the basis of academic achievement, community involvement, work experience and recommendations.

Funds Avail.: $3,000. **Number Awarded:** 1. **To Apply:** Applicants must submit a completed application form together with letters of recommendation and a copy of the doctoral dissertation/thesis. **Deadline:** February 15.

5457 ■ Eileen J. Garrett Scholarships *(Undergraduate/Scholarship)*

Purpose: To promote education in the field of psychology while stimulating interest in the field of Parapsychology.

Focus: Psychology. **Qualif.:** Applicants must be currently enrolled full-time in an accredited school or university; must be pursuing academic study in parapsychology; and must be members of the foundation. **Criteria:** Awards are given based on academic record, personal promise, character and financial need. Selection of recipients is made by the colleges in accordance with their established procedures.

Funds Avail.: $3,000. **Number Awarded:** 1. **To Apply:** Applicants must submit an application form together with letters of reference from individuals familiar with the applicant's work or studies in parapsychology. **Deadline:** July 15.

5458 ■ Charles T. and Judith A. Tart Student Incentive Awards *(Graduate, Postdoctorate, Undergraduate/Grant)*

Purpose: To support a research that deals directly with some aspect of parapsychology. **Focus:** Psychology. **Qualif.:** Applicants must be undergraduate, graduate or postgraduate students seeking either psychology course or any related field; must be enrolled full-time in an accredited school or university; and must have a great interest in parapsychology. **Criteria:** Priority is given to students with financial need.

Funds Avail.: $500. **Number Awarded:** 1. **To Apply:** Applicants must submit an application form together with letters of recommendation from individuals familiar with the applicant's work and studies; a project description (maximum of 2 pages); and a one-page statement of budget needed for the research. **Deadline:** October 15.

5459 ■ Park Law Enforcement Association

520 N Stevenson
Olathe, KS 66061
Ph: (239)332-6975
E-mail: info@parkranger.com
URL: http://www.parkranger.com

5460 ■ Newell S. Rand Jr. Memorial Scholarships *(Undergraduate/Scholarship)*

Purpose: To promote park law enforcement. **Focus:** Law Enforcement. **Qualif.:** Applicants must be enrolled in a field of study related to park law enforcement. **Criteria:** Recipients are chosen by the PLEA Board or Committee appointed by the PLEA board.

Funds Avail.: $500. **To Apply:** Applicants must submit current resume including education, work experience, and civic activity; a letter showing their interest in the Park Law Enforcement field and explaining why they are worthy of the PLEA Scholarship; a letter of recommendation from an instructor or advisor in their field of study; and proof of enrollment. Applications must be submitted to the PLEA President. **Deadline:** October 1.

5461 ■ Parkersburg Area Community Foundation

501 Avery St.
Parkersburg, WV 26101
Ph: (304)428-4438
Fax: (304)428-1200
Free: (866)428-4438
E-mail: info@pacfwv.com
URL: http://www.pacfwv.com

5462 ■ Bob Adkins Memorial Scholarships *(Undergraduate/Scholarship)*

Purpose: To provide financial assistance for qualified senior high school students from Point Pleasant High School. **Focus:** General studies. **Qualif.:** Applicant must be a graduating senior from Point Pleasant High School; must have a minimum 2.0 GPA; must have financial need for assistance and must have participated in high school athletics (including team participation and/or support services to team, such as manager). **Criteria:** Selection of applicants will be based on the length of time and variety of sports participated in, participation in the school community, and financial need.

Funds Avail.: $250-$500. **To Apply:** Applicants must submit a cover sheet (3 pages) and application form (4 pages); must have a personal essay; must have high school and/or post-secondary transcripts; must provide a letter of recommendation and a signed copy of the page of their or their parent's most recent tax return that indicates adjusted gross income; and must have a Student Aid Report showing estimated family contribution from FAFSA. Application form and other supporting documents must be sent to Our Community's Foundation, P.O Box 1762, Parkersburg, WV 26102. **Deadline:** March 20.

5463 ■ Martin K. Alsup Scholarships *(Undergraduate/Scholarship)*

Purpose: To provide financial assistance for qualified high school seniors from Parkersburg High School. **Focus:** Music. **Qualif.:** Applicant must be a graduating senior from Parkersburg High School; must have a strong commitment to the field of instrumental music and music-related activities as demonstrated by participation in orchestra or the Big Red Band. **Criteria:** Preference is given to students interested in majoring in music.

Funds Avail.: $1,200. **To Apply:** Applicants must submit a cover sheet (3 pages) and application form (4 pages); must have a personal essay; must have high school and/or post-secondary transcripts; must provide a letter of recommendation; copy of the page of their or their parent's most recent tax return that indicates adjusted gross income; and must have a Student Aid Report, showing estimated family contribution, from FAFSA. Application form and other supporting documents must be sent to Our Community's Foundation, P.O Box 1762, Parkersburg, WV 26102. **Deadline:** March 20.

5464 ■ Ambrose-Ramsey Trust Scholarships *(Undergraduate/Scholarship)*

Purpose: To provide financial assistance for qualified students from Parkersburg, Parkersburg South, Parkersburg Catholic, or Williamstown High School. **Focus:** Ministry. **Qualif.:** Applicant must be a graduate from Parkersburg, Parkersburg South, Parkersburg Catholic, or Williamstown High School with the desire to further their education in the study of the Methodist Ministry. **Criteria:** Selection of applicants will be based on the application requirements and scholarship selection criteria.

Funds Avail.: $1,000-$3,000. **To Apply:** Applicants must submit a cover sheet (3 pages) and application form (4 pages); a personal essay; a high school and/or post-secondary transcript; a letter of recommendation; signed copy of the page of their or their parent's most recent tax return that indicates adjusted gross income; and a Student Aid Report showing estimated family contribution from FAFSA. Application form and other supporting documents must be sent to Our Community's Foundation, P.O Box

Awards are arranged alphabetically below their administering organizations

1762, Parkersburg, WV 26102. **Deadline:** March 20.

5465 ■ Joe Barbarow Memorial Scholarships
(Undergraduate/Scholarship)

Purpose: To provide financial support for deserving graduate seniors at Parkersburg High School. **Focus:** General studies. **Qualif.:** Applicant must be a high school graduating senior and must have attended Hamilton Junior High in Wood County. **Criteria:** Selection of applicants will be based on academic achievement, school citizenship, moral character, and financial need.

Funds Avail.: $760. **To Apply:** Applicants must submit a cover sheet (3 pages) and application form (4 pages); a personal essay; a high school and/or post-secondary transcript; a letter of recommendation; a signed copy of the page of their or their parent's most recent tax return that indicates adjusted gross income; and a Student Aid Report showing estimated family contribution from FAFSA. Application form and other supporting documents must be sent to Our Community's Foundation, P.O Box 1762, Parkersburg, WV 26102. **Deadline:** March 20.

5466 ■ Lewis and Gurry Batten Scholarships
(Undergraduate/Scholarship)

Purpose: To provide financial assistance for qualified senior high school at Parkersburg High School. **Focus:** General studies. **Qualif.:** Applicant must be a Parkersburg High School graduating senior; must have a minimum of 2.5 GPA; and must be attending a four-year course in college or university. **Criteria:** Selection of recipients will be based on merit and financial need.

Funds Avail.: $600. **To Apply:** Applicants must submit a cover sheet (3 pages) and application form (4 pages); a personal essay; a high school and/or post-secondary transcript; a letter of recommendation; a signed copy of the page of their or their parent's most recent tax return that indicates adjusted gross income; and a Student Aid Report showing estimated family contribution from FAFSA. Application form and other supporting documents must be sent to Our Community's Foundation, P.O Box 1762, Parkersburg, WV 26102. **Deadline:** March 20.

5467 ■ William (Billbo) Boston Scholarships
(Undergraduate/Scholarship)

Purpose: To provide financial assistance for qualified individuals intending to pursue their undergraduate degree. **Focus:** Computer and information sciences. **Qualif.:** Applicants must be graduating seniors or current undergraduates who previously graduated from a Wood County high school and are pursuing undergraduate degree in computer science at an accredited post-secondary school in West Virginia or Ohio with a minimum of 3.0 GPA. **Criteria:** Selection of recipients will be based on financial need, class rank, school activities, and achievement.

Funds Avail.: $450. **To Apply:** Applicants must submit a cover sheet (3 pages) and application form (4 pages); a personal essay; a high school and/or post-secondary transcript; a letter of recommendation; a signed copy of the page of their or their parent's most recent tax return that indicates adjusted gross income; and a Student Aid Report, showing estimated family contribution, from FAFSA. Application form and other supporting documents must be sent to Our Community's Foundation, P.O Box 1762, Parkersburg, WV 26102. **Deadline:** March 20.

5468 ■ Chester H. Bruce Memorial Scholarships
(Undergraduate/Scholarship)

Purpose: To provide financial support for qualified students of Wirt County High School. **Focus:** Christian education. **Qualif.:** Applicant must be a graduating senior of Wirt County High School; must be pursuing vocational or trade studies or Christian ministry or service; must be enrolled as a full-time student in an undergraduate two-or-four-year program or a vocational program or graduate school; must have a minimum of 2.5 GPA; and must have a strong work ethic. **Criteria:** Selection of recipients will be based on the scholarship selection criteria.

Funds Avail.: $750. **To Apply:** Applicants must submit a cover sheet (3 pages) and application form (4 pages); must have a personal essay; must have a high school and/or post-secondary transcript; must provide a letter of recommendation and a signed copy of the page of their or their parent's most recent tax return that indicates adjusted gross income; and must have a Student Aid Report showing estimated family contribution from FAFSA. Application form and other supporting documents must be sent to Our Community's Foundation, P.O Box 1762, Parkersburg, WV 26102. **Deadline:** March 20.

5469 ■ Bryce-Lietzke Martin Scholarships
(Undergraduate/Scholarship)

Purpose: To provide financial assistance for qualified individuals in Wood County. **Focus:** General studies. **Qualif.:** Applicant must be a Wood County resident; must have an interest in golf; must have a minimum of 2.5 GPA; and must be accepted or attending a post-secondary education. **Criteria:** Selection of recipients will be based on good moral character, involvement in extracurricular activities, and financial need.

Funds Avail.: $500-$750. **To Apply:** Applicants must submit a cover sheet (3 pages) and application form (4 pages); must have a personal essay; must have a high school and/or postsecondary transcript; must provide a letter of recommendation and a signed copy of the page of their or their parent's most recent tax return that indicates adjusted gross income; and must have a Student Aid Report showing estimated family contribution, from FAFSA. Application form and other supporting documents must be sent to Our Community's Foundation, P.O Box 1762, Parkersburg, WV 26102. **Deadline:** March 20.

5470 ■ Freda Burge Scholarships
(Undergraduate/Scholarship)

Purpose: To encourage graduating students of Williamstown High School to pursue their education. **Focus:** General studies. **Qualif.:** Applicant must be a Williamstown High School graduating senior; must be planning to attend West Virginia University-Parkersburg full-time; and must have a minimum of 2.5 GPA. **Criteria:** Selection of recipients will be based on financial need and application materials.

Funds Avail.: $600. **To Apply:** Applicants must submit a cover sheet (3 pages) and application form (4 pages); must have a personal essay; must have a high school and/or post-secondary transcript; must provide a letter of recommendation and a signed copy of the page of their or their parent's most recent tax return that indicates adjusted gross income; and must have a Student Aid Report showing estimated family contribution, from FAFSA. Application form and other supporting documents must be sent to Our Community's Foundation P.O Box 1762, Parkersburg, WV 26102. **Deadline:** March 20.

5471 ■ George H. Clinton Scholarship Fund
(Undergraduate/Scholarship)

Purpose: To provide support for graduating or graduate students from a Wood County, WV high school. **Focus:**

Awards are arranged alphabetically below their administering organizations

Communications. **Qualif.:** Applicants must be graduating or have graduated from a Wood County, WV, high school; must be attending college full-time and majoring in the media communications field; must have a minimum of 3.0 GPA. **Criteria:** Selection of applicants will be based on the scholarship selection criteria.

Funds Avail.: $1,000. **To Apply:** Applicants must submit a cover sheet (3 pages) and application form (4 pages); must have a personal essay; must have a high school and/or post-secondary transcript; must provide a letter of recommendation and a signed copy of the page of their or their parent's most recent tax return that indicates adjusted gross income; and must have a Student Aid Report showing estimated family contribution from FAFSA. Application form and other supporting documents must be sent to Our Community's Foundation, P.O. Box 1762, Parkersburg, WV 26102. **Deadline:** March 20.

5472 ■ Dwight O. Conner and Ellen Conner Lepp Scholarships *(Undergraduate/Scholarship)*

Purpose: To provide financial assistance for qualified graduating high school students at Parkersburg High School. **Focus:** General studies. **Qualif.:** Applicant must be a Parkersburg High School graduating senior. **Criteria:** Selection of applicants will be based on financial need.

Funds Avail.: $240. **To Apply:** Applicants must submit a cover sheet (3 pages) and application form (4 pages); must have a personal essay; must have a high school and/or post-secondary transcript; must provide a letter of recommendation in a signed, copy of the page of their or their parent's most recent tax return that indicates adjusted gross income; and must have a Student Aid Report showing estimated family contribution from FAFSA. Application form and other supporting documents must be sent to Our Community's Foundation, P.O Box 1762, Parkersburg, WV 26102. **Deadline:** March 20.

5473 ■ Dave Couch Memorial Scholarships *(Undergraduate/Scholarship)*

Purpose: To provide financial assistance for qualified individuals intending to pursue studies involving massage therapy or physical or occupational therapy. **Focus:** Physical therapy; Occupational therapy. **Qualif.:** Applicant must be a resident of Wood, Wirt, Jackson, Pleasants, Ritchie, Roane, Mason, Calhoun, Gilmer, or Doddridge in WV or Washington County, OH; must be actively pursuing a course of study involving massage therapy or physical or occupational therapy. **Criteria:** Selection of applicants will be based on personal commitment to service for individuals whose lives are affected by ALS or other neuromuscular or disabling disease, as evidenced by related volunteer or community service to individuals whose lives are affected by these diseases or for organizations serving individuals whose lives are affected.

Funds Avail.: $500. **To Apply:** Applicants must submit a cover sheet (3 pages) and application form (4 pages); must have a personal essay; must have high school and/or post-secondary transcripts; must provide a letter of recommendation in a signed and sealed envelope; a copy of the page of their or their parent's most recent tax return that indicates adjusted gross income; must have a Student Aid Report, showing estimated family contribution, from FAFSA. Application form and other supporting documents must be sent to Our Community's Foundation, P.O Box 1762, Parkersburg, WV 26102. **Deadline:** March 20.

5474 ■ Jennifer Coulter Memorial Scholarships *(Undergraduate/Scholarship)*

Purpose: To encourage the graduating seniors of Parkersburg High School to pursue their career in teaching. **Focus:** Teaching. **Qualif.:** Applicant must be a graduating senior from Parkersburg High School interested in pursuing a career in teaching and must be involved in extracurricular and/or community service activities. **Criteria:** Selection of recipients will be based on academic achievement or potential to achieve academically with evidence of at least a 2.5 GPA, and financial need. Preference will be given to students who have displayed interest in foreign language study during their high school career.

Funds Avail.: $1,000. **To Apply:** Applicants must submit a cover sheet (3 pages) and application form (4 pages); must have a personal essay; must have a high school and/or post-secondary transcript; must provide a letter of recommendation and a signed copy of the page of their or their parent's most recent tax return that indicates adjusted gross income; and must have a Student Aid Report showing estimated family contribution from FAFSA. Application form and other supporting documents must be sent to Our Community's Foundation, P.O Box 1762, Parkersburg, WV 26102. **Deadline:** March 20.

5475 ■ Cindy Curry Memorial Scholarships *(Undergraduate/Scholarship)*

Purpose: To encourage the graduating students to pursue their education. **Focus:** General studies. **Qualif.:** Applicants must be graduating high school seniors from any Wood County high school; must be planning to attend an accredited West Virginia college or university full-time; must have a minimum of 3.0 GPA; and must have a strong motivation to attend school. **Criteria:** Recipients will be selected based on the scholarship selection criteria.

Funds Avail.: $1,000. **To Apply:** Applicants must submit a cover sheet (3 pages) and application form (4 pages); must have a personal essay; must have a high school and/or post- secondary transcript; must provide a letter of recommendation and a signed copy of the page of their or their parent's most recent tax return that indicates adjusted gross income; and must have a Student Aid Report, showing estimated family contribution, from FAFSA. Application form and other supporting documents must be sent to Our Community's Foundation, P.O Box 1762, Parkersburg, WV 26102. **Deadline:** March 20.

5476 ■ Kenneth D. and Katherine D. Davis Scholarships *(Undergraduate/Scholarship)*

Purpose: To encourage graduating seniors of Wirt County High School to pursue their education. **Focus:** Business. **Qualif.:** Applicant must be a Wirt County High School graduating senior pursuing a career or major in business. **Criteria:** Recipients will be selected based on financial need, academic achievement, potential and character.

Funds Avail.: $225. **To Apply:** Applicants must submit a cover sheet (3 pages) and application form (4 pages); must have a personal essay; must have a high school and/or post- secondary transcript; must provide a letter of recommendation and a signed, copy of the page of their or their parent's most recent tax return that indicates adjusted gross income; and must have a Student Aid Report showing estimated family contribution from FAFSA. Application form and other supporting documents must be sent to Our Community's Foundation, P.O Box 1762, Parkersburg, WV 26102. **Deadline:** March 20.

5477 ■ Lawrence E. Davis Scholarships
(Undergraduate/Scholarship)

Purpose: To encourage the graduating seniors of Parkersburg High School to pursue their education in either the state of West Virginia or Ohio. **Focus:** General studies. **Qualif.:** Applicants must be graduating seniors from Parkersburg High School who have been admitted to attend an accredited four-year institution of higher education in either the state of West Virginia or Ohio as full-time students, with a minimum 2.5 GPA. **Criteria:** Selection of recipients will be based on financial need.

Funds Avail.: $900. **To Apply:** Applicants must submit a cover sheet (3 pages) and application form (4 pages); must have a personal essay; must have a high school and/or post-secondary transcript; must provide a letter of recommendation in a signed, copy of the page of their or their parent's most recent tax return that indicates adjusted gross income; and must have a Student Aid Report showing estimated family contribution from FAFSA. Application form and other supporting documents must be sent to Our Community's Foundation, P.O Box 1762, Parkersburg, WV 26102. **Deadline:** March 20.

5478 ■ Doddridge County Promise Scholarships
(Undergraduate/Scholarship)

Purpose: To encourage the graduating students of Doddridge County High School to pursue their education. **Focus:** General studies. **Qualif.:** Applicants must be graduating high school seniors or graduates of Doddridge County High School who have been admitted to the college of their choice; must have a GPA of 3.2 or above, be in the top 20% of the class, ACT of 21 or above or SAT of 1100 or above; must have followed a college-bound curriculum; and must have financial need. **Criteria:** Recipients will be selected based on the evaluation of the scholarship selection committee.

Funds Avail.: $500-$1,000. **To Apply:** Applicants must submit a cover sheet (3 pages) and application form (4 pages); must have a personal essay; must have a high school and/or post-secondary transcript; must provide a letter of recommendation and a signed copy of the page of their or their parent's most recent tax return that indicates adjusted gross income; and must have a Student Aid Report showing estimated family contribution from FAFSA. Application form and other supporting documents must be sent to Our Community's Foundation, P.O Box 1762, Parkersburg, WV 26102. **Deadline:** March 20.

5479 ■ Deborah Gandee Dudding Memorial Scholarships *(Undergraduate/Scholarship)*

Purpose: To provide financial assistance for qualified graduating seniors at Ravenswood High School. **Focus:** General studies. **Qualif.:** Applicant must be a Ravenswood High School graduating senior; must have a minimum of 2.5 GPA. **Criteria:** Preference will be given to students with financial need who have exhibited a record of community service, a balance of academic and extracurricular interest, and a commitment to the growth, development, and/ or the well-being of children.

Funds Avail.: $250-$500. **To Apply:** Applicants must submit a cover sheet (3 pages) and application form (4 pages); must have a personal essay; must have high school and/or post-secondary transcripts; must provide a letter of recommendation and a signed copy of the page of their or their parent's most recent tax return that indicates adjusted gross income; and must have a Student Aid Report showing estimated family contribution, from FAFSA. Application form and other supporting documents must be sent to Our Community's Foundation, P.O Box 1762, Parkersburg, WV 26102. **Deadline:** March 20.

5480 ■ David Edward Farson Scholarships
(Undergraduate/Scholarship)

Purpose: To encourage graduating seniors at Parkersburg High School to pursue their education. **Focus:** General studies. **Qualif.:** Applicant must be a Parkersburg High School graduating senior; must be planning to attend Marshall University. **Criteria:** Selection of applicants will be based on financial need and academic achievements.

Funds Avail.: $1,500. **To Apply:** Applicants must submit a cover sheet (3 pages) and application form (4 pages); must have a personal essay; must have high school and/or post-secondary transcripts; must provide a letter of recommendation and a signed copy of the page of their or their parent's most recent tax return that indicates adjusted gross income; and must have a Student Aid Report showing estimated family contribution, from FAFSA. Application form and other supporting documents must be sent to Our Community's Foundation, P.O Box 1762, Parkersburg, WV 26102. **Deadline:** March 20.

5481 ■ Fostering Hope Scholarship Fund
(Undergraduate/Scholarship)

Purpose: To provide financial assistance for qualified individuals intending to pursue their education. **Focus:** General studies. **Qualif.:** Applicants must be students who are actively enrolled, or have been enrolled, in the foster care system; must be WV residents; must be admitted to a course of study at a post-high school educational institution for the upcoming year. **Criteria:** Selection of applicants will be based on academic promise, good character, good citizenship and financial need.

Funds Avail.: $250-$500. **To Apply:** Applicants must submit a cover sheet (3 pages) and application form (4 pages); must have a personal essay; must have high school and/or post-secondary transcripts; must provide a letter of recommendation and a signed copy of the page of their or their parent's most recent tax return that indicates adjusted gross income; and must have a Student Aid Report showing estimated family contribution, from FAFSA. Application form and other supporting documents must be sent to Our Community's Foundation, P.O Box 1762, Parkersburg, WV 26102. **Deadline:** March 20.

5482 ■ William E. "Bill" Gallagher Scholarships
(Undergraduate/Scholarship)

Purpose: To provide financial assistance for qualified graduating seniors at Parkersburg South High School. **Focus:** General studies. **Qualif.:** Applicants must be graduating seniors at Parkersburg South High School who have been admitted to attend Glenville State College in Glenville, WV, or Alderson Broaddus College in Philippi, WV. **Criteria:** Selection of applicants will be based on the knowledge and a love of people as attested to by the guidance counselors and as evidenced by candidate's participation in extracurricular activities and community service.

Funds Avail.: $500. **To Apply:** Applicants must submit a cover sheet (3 pages) and application form (4 pages); must have a personal essay; must have high school and/or post-secondary transcripts; must provide a letter of recommendation and a signed copy of the page of their or their parent's most recent tax return that indicates adjusted gross income; and must have a Student Aid Report, showing estimated family contribution from FAFSA. Application form and other supporting documents must be sent to Our Community's Foundation, P.O Box 1762, Parkersburg, WV 26102. **Deadline:** March 20.

5483 ■ Laverne L. Gibson Memorial Scholarships *(Undergraduate/Scholarship)*

Purpose: To provide financial assistance for qualified graduating seniors intending to pursue their career in education. **Focus:** Education; Special education. **Qualif.:** Applicant must be a graduating senior from Wood County West Virginia or Washington County Ohio; must be majoring in education, and special education. **Criteria:** Selection of applicants will be based on academic achievement or potential to achieve, honesty and good moral character, involvement in extracurricular and/or community service activities, and financial need.

Funds Avail.: $390. **To Apply:** Applicants must submit a cover sheet (3 pages) and application form (4 pages); must have a personal essay; must have high school and/or post-secondary transcripts; must provide a letter of recommendation and a signed copy of the page of their or their parent's most recent tax return that indicates adjusted gross income; must have a Student Aid Report, showing estimated family contribution, from FAFSA. Application form and other supporting documents must be sent to Our Community's Foundation, P.O Box 1762, Parkersburg, WV 26102. **Deadline:** March 20.

5484 ■ Shane Gilbert Memorial Scholarships *(Undergraduate/Scholarship)*

Purpose: To encourage graduating students to pursue their post-secondary education. **Focus:** General studies. **Qualif.:** Applicant must be a Wood County Technical/Caperton Canter graduating senior intending to pursue post-secondary education. **Criteria:** Selection of applicants will be based on achievements, ability, financial need, citizenship, and recommendation.

Funds Avail.: $1,000. **To Apply:** Applicants must submit a cover sheet (3 pages) and application form (4 pages); must have a personal essay; must have a high school and/or post-secondary transcript; must provide a letter of recommendation and a signed copy of the page of their or their parent's most recent tax return that indicates adjusted gross income; and must have a Student Aid Report showing estimated family contribution from FAFSA. Application form and other supporting documents must be sent to Our Community's Foundation, P.O Box 1762, Parkersburg, WV 26102. **Deadline:** March 20.

5485 ■ S. William & Martha R. Golf Educational Scholarships *(Undergraduate/Scholarship)*

Purpose: To encourage individuals to pursue their career in medical school. **Focus:** Medical education. **Qualif.:** Applicants must have attended high school in Wood County and must be entering or currently in medical school. **Criteria:** Selection of applicants will be based on merit and need.

Funds Avail.: $2,000. **To Apply:** Applicants must submit a cover sheet (3 pages) and application form (4 pages); must have a personal essay; must have a high school and/or postsecondary transcript; must provide a letter of recommendation and a signed copy of the page of their or their parent's most recent tax return that indicates adjusted gross income; and must have a Student Aid Report showing estimated family contribution from FAFSA. Application form and other supporting documents must be sent to Our Community's Foundation, P.O Box 1762, Parkersburg, WV 26102. **Deadline:** March 20.

5486 ■ Russ Grant Memorial Scholarship for Tennis *(Undergraduate/Scholarship)*

Purpose: To encourage graduating seniors to pursue higher level education. **Focus:** General studies. **Qualif.:** Applicants must be graduating seniors from Parkersburg High School, Parkersburg South High School or Parkersburg Catholic High School; must have shown evidence of an interest in tennis; must be pursuing higher level education; and must have a minimum of 2.5 GPA. **Criteria:** Selection of recipients will be based on commitment to tennis, academic achievement, and financial need.

Funds Avail.: $800. **To Apply:** Applicants must submit a cover sheet (3 pages) and application form (4 pages); must have a personal essay; must have a high school and/or post-secondary transcript; must provide a letter of recommendation and a signed copy of the page of their or their parent's most recent tax return that indicates adjusted gross income; and must have a Student Aid Report showing estimated family contribution from FAFSA. Application form and other supporting documents must be sent to Our Community's Foundation, P.O Box 1762, Parkersburg, WV 26102. **Deadline:** March 20.

5487 ■ Sarah Gwisdalla Memorial Scholarships *(Undergraduate/Scholarship)*

Purpose: To encourage the graduating students of Ripley High School to pursue their education. **Focus:** General studies. **Qualif.:** Applicant must be a Ripley High School graduating senior with a minimum of 3.0 GPA. **Criteria:** Preference will be given to students with financial need and a strong record of community service.

Funds Avail.: $250-$500. **To Apply:** Applicants must submit a cover sheet (3 pages) and application form (4 pages); must have a personal essay; must have a high school and/or post-secondary transcript; must provide a letter of recommendation in a signed, copy of the page of their or their parent's most recent tax return that indicates adjusted gross income; must have a Student Aid Report, showing estimated family contribution from FAFSA. Application form and other supporting documents must be sent to Our Community's Foundation, P.O Box 1762, Parkersburg, WV 26102. **Deadline:** March 20.

5488 ■ Nathaniel Hafer Memorial Scholarships *(Undergraduate/Scholarship)*

Purpose: To encourage the graduate students of Ravenswood High School to pursue their studies. **Focus:** General studies. **Qualif.:** Applicant must be a Ravenswood High School graduating senior; must have a minimum 2.0 GPA. **Criteria:** Preference will be given to students with financial need and a strong record of community service.

Funds Avail.: $250-$500. **To Apply:** Applicants must submit a cover sheet (3 pages) and application form (4 pages); must have a personal essay; must have a high school and/or post-secondary transcript; must provide a letter of recommendation and a signed copy of the page of their or their parent's most recent tax return that indicates adjusted gross income; and must have a Student Aid Report showing estimated family contribution from FAFSA. Application form and other supporting documents must be sent to Our Community's Foundation, P.O. Box 1762, Parkersburg, WV 26102. **Deadline:** March 20.

5489 ■ Clayburn and Garnet R. Hanna Scholarships *(Undergraduate/Scholarship)*

Purpose: To provide financial assistance for the residents or graduates of Wirt County. **Focus:** General studies. **Qua-**

Awards are arranged alphabetically below their administering organizations

lif.: Applicant must be a resident of Wirt County or graduate of Wirt County High School; must be planning to attend a post-secondary educational institution full-time. **Criteria:** Selection of applicants will be based on financial need, likelihood of completion of degree, and leadership. Preference will be given to students who are not likely to receive other significant scholarship awards.

Funds Avail.: $540. **To Apply:** Applicants must submit a cover sheet (3 pages) and application form (4 pages); must have a personal essay; must have a high school and/or post-secondary transcript; must provide a letter of recommendation and a signed copy of the page of their or their parent's most recent tax return that indicates adjusted gross income; and must have a Student Aid Report showing estimated family contribution from FAFSA. Application form and other supporting documents must be sent to Our Community's Foundation, P.O Box 1762, Parkersburg, WV 26102. **Deadline:** Maorch 20.

5490 ■ H.G. Hardbarger Science and Mathematics Awards *(Undergraduate/Scholarship)*

Purpose: To provide financial assistance for graduating seniors from Ritchie County High School. **Focus:** General studies. **Qualif.:** Applicant must be a graduating senior from Ritchie County High School who has demonstrated achievement in the fields of Math/Science. **Criteria:** Applicants will be selected based on the scholarship criteria.

Funds Avail.: $670. **To Apply:** Applicants must submit a cover sheet (3 pages) and application form (4 pages); must have a personal essay; must have high school and/or post-secondary transcripts; must provide a letter of recommendation and a signed copy of the page of their or their parent's most recent tax return that indicates adjusted gross income; and must have a Student Aid Report showing estimated family contribution, from FAFSA. Application form and other supporting documents must be sent to Our Community's Foundation, P.O Box 1762, Parkersburg, WV 26102. **Deadline:** March 20.

5491 ■ Ruth Harris Memorial Scholarships *(Undergraduate/Scholarship)*

Purpose: To provide financial support for qualified graduating female high school students of Wood County, WV. **Focus:** General studies. **Qualif.:** Applicant must be a graduating female high school student who is a resident of Wood County, WV, not to be over 20 years of age at first selection and must be planning to attend West Virginia University. **Criteria:** Selection of applicants will be based on the application requirements and scholarship selection criteria.

Funds Avail.: $1,000. **To Apply:** Applicants must submit a cover sheet (3 pages) and application form (4 pages); must have a personal essay; must have high school and/or post-secondary transcripts; must provide a letter of recommendation and a signed copy of the page of their or their parent's most recent tax return that indicates adjusted gross income; must have a Student Aid Report, showing estimated family contribution, from FAFSA. Application form and other supporting documents must be sent to Our Community's Foundation, P.O Box 1762, Parkersburg, WV 26102. **Deadline:** March 20.

5492 ■ Harrisville Lions Club Scholarships *(Undergraduate/Scholarship)*

Purpose: To provide financial support for qualified individuals in Ritchie County intending to pursue their studies. **Focus:** Education, Vocationaltechnical. **Qualif.:** Applicant must be a resident of Ritchie County; must be pursuing vocational, technical, or trade related education through an accredited institution or program; and must have a minimum 2.0 GPA (if a graduating senior or presently enrolled in school). **Criteria:** Preference will be given to students with financial need.

Funds Avail.: $500. **To Apply:** Applicants must submit a cover sheet (3 pages) and application form (4 pages); must have a personal essay; must have high school and/or post-secondary transcripts; must provide a letter of recommendation; copy of the page of their or their parent's most recent tax return that indicates adjusted gross income; and must have a Student Aid Report showing estimated family contribution, from FAFSA. Application form and other supporting documents must be sent to Our Community's Foundation, P.O Box 1762, Parkersburg, WV 26102. **Deadline:** March 20.

5493 ■ Harry C. Hartleben III. Scholarships *(Undergraduate/Scholarship)*

Purpose: To provide financial assistance for qualified graduating seniors from Parkersburg High School intending to pursue higher education. **Focus:** General studies. **Qualif.:** Applicant must be a graduating senior from Parkersburg High School who plans to pursue higher education; and must have a minimum 3.0 GPA. **Criteria:** Recipients of the scholarships will be selected based on academic achievement, motivation, character, and involvement in school and community activities. Financial need is not a primary consideration.

Funds Avail.: $300. **To Apply:** Applicants must submit a cover sheet (3 pages) and application form (4 pages); must have a personal essay; must have high school and/or post-secondary transcripts; must provide a letter of recommendation; copy of the page of their or their parent's most recent tax return that indicates adjusted gross income; and must have a Student Aid Report showing estimated family contribution, from FAFSA. Application form and other supporting documents must be sent to Our Community's Foundation, P.O Box 1762, Parkersburg, WV 26102. **Deadline:** March 20.

5494 ■ Gail Hartshorn Scholarships *(Undergraduate/Scholarship)*

Purpose: To provide financial assistance for qualified Wood County residents intending to pursue their studies. **Focus:** Emergency and disaster services; Paramedics. **Qualif.:** Applicants must be Wood County residents who are pursuing emergency medical technician or paramedic training. **Criteria:** Selection of applicants will be based on financial need and commitment to career in emergency services.

Funds Avail.: $240. **To Apply:** Applicants must submit a cover sheet (3 pages) and application form (4 pages); must have a personal essay; must have a high school and/or post-secondary transcript; must provide a letter of recommendation; copy of the page of their or their parent's most recent tax return that indicates adjusted gross income; and a Student Aid Report, showing estimated family contribution, from FAFSA. Application form and other supporting documents must be sent to Our Community's Foundation, P.O Box 1762, Parkersburg, WV 26102. **Deadline:** March 20.

5495 ■ Gregory Lynn Haught Citizenship Awards *(Undergraduate/Award/Prize)*

Purpose: To encourage the graduating students of Ritchie County High School to pursue their education. **Focus:**

Awards are arranged alphabetically below their administering organizations

General studies. **Qualif.:** Applicant must be a Ritchie County High School graduating senior. **Criteria:** Selection of applicants will be based on academic achievement, good moral character, service to others, and service in religious activities and endeavors.

Funds Avail.: $1,000. **To Apply:** Applicants must submit a cover sheet (3 pages) and application form (4 pages); must have a personal essay; must have a high school and/or postsecondary transcript; must provide a letter of recommendation and a signed copy of the page of their or their parent's most recent tax return that indicates adjusted gross income; and must have a Student Aid Report showing estimated family contribution from FAFSA. Application form and other supporting documents must be sent to Our Community's Foundation, P.O Box 1762, Parkersburg, WV 26102. **Deadline:** March 20.

5496 ■ Dorcas Edmonson Haught Scholarships *(Undergraduate/Scholarship)*

Purpose: To provide financial support for qualified students intending to attend Marietta College. **Focus:** General studies. **Qualif.:** Applicant must be a graduating Parkersburg High School senior who plans to attend Marietta College. **Criteria:** Selection of applicants will be based on financial need, achievements, and character.

Funds Avail.: $250. **To Apply:** Applicants must submit a cover sheet (3 pages) and application form (4 pages); must have a personal essay; must have a high school and/or post-secondary transcript; must provide a letter of recommendation; copy of the page of their or their parent's most recent tax return that indicates adjusted gross income; and a Student Aid Report showing estimated family contribution, from FAFSA. Application form and other supporting documents must be sent to Our Community's Foundation, P.O Box 1762, Parkersburg, WV 26102. **Deadline:** March 20.

5497 ■ Ella Beren Hersch Scholarships *(Undergraduate/Scholarship)*

Purpose: To encourage graduating students to pursue their education. **Focus:** General studies. **Qualif.:** Applicants must be a Parkersburg High School graduating senior. **Criteria:** Applicants will be selected based on financial need.

Funds Avail.: $1,400. **To Apply:** Applicants must submit a cover sheet (3 pages) and application form (4 pages); must have a personal essay; must have a high school and/or post-secondary transcript; must provide a letter of recommendation and a signed copy of the page of their or their parent's most recent tax return that indicates adjusted gross income; and must have a Student Aid Report showing estimated family contribution from FAFSA. Application form and other supporting documents must be sent to Our Community's Foundation, P.O Box 1762, Parkersburg, WV 26102. **Deadline:** March 20.

5498 ■ Holly Jackson-Wuller Memorial Scholarships *(Undergraduate/Scholarship)*

Purpose: To encourage the graduating seniors of Parkersburg South High School to pursue their college degree. **Focus:** General studies. **Qualif.:** Applicant must be a graduating senior from Parkersburg South High School planning to attend Marshall University, with minimum 2.5 GPA. **Criteria:** Selection of applicants will be based on financial need and participation in school, church and community activities.

Funds Avail.: $500. **To Apply:** Applicants must submit a cover sheet (3 pages) and application form (4 pages); must have a personal essay; must have a high school and/or post-secondary transcript; must provide a letter of recommendation and a signed copy of the page of their or their parent's most recent tax return that indicates adjusted gross income; and must have a Student Aid Report showing estimated family contribution, from FAFSA. Application form and other supporting documents must be sent to Our Community's Foundation, P.O Box 1762, Parkersburg, WV 26102. **Deadline:** March 20.

5499 ■ K.A.S.A Memorial Scholarships *(Undergraduate/Scholarship)*

Purpose: To provide financial support for graduating high school seniors or graduates of Doddridge County High School. **Focus:** General studies. **Qualif.:** Applicant must be a graduating high school senior or graduate of Doddridge County High School; must have a minimum GPA of 2.5. **Criteria:** Preference will be given to a student who has been admitted to attend a public college in West Virginia, and to a well-rounded, hard working individual with financial need who is not receiving substantial scholarship aid from other sources.

Funds Avail.: $1,100. **To Apply:** Applicants must submit a cover sheet (3 pages) and application form (4 pages); must have a personal essay; must have a high school and/or post-secondary transcript; must provide a letter of recommendation; copy of the page of their or their parent's most recent tax return that indicates adjusted gross income; and a Student Aid Report showing estimated family contribution from FAFSA. Application form and other supporting documents must be sent to Our Community's Foundation, P.O Box 1762, Parkersburg, WV 26102. **Deadline:** March 20.

5500 ■ Dr. Charles Kelly Memorial Scholarships *(Undergraduate/Scholarship)*

Purpose: To provide financial assistance for qualified graduating seniors of Ravenswood High School. **Focus:** General studies. **Qualif.:** Applicant must be a Ravenswood High School graduating senior planning to attend Marshall University. **Criteria:** Selection of applicants will be based on financial need.

Funds Avail.: $250-$500. **To Apply:** Applicants must submit a cover sheet (3 pages) and application form (4 pages); must have a personal essay; must have a high school and/or post-secondary transcript; must provide a letter of recommendation; copy of the page of their or their parent's most recent tax return that indicates adjusted gross income; and a Student Aid Report showing estimated family contribution from FAFSA. Application form and other supporting documents must be sent to Our Community's Foundation, P.O Box 1762, Parkersburg, WV 26102. **Deadline:** March 20.

5501 ■ Judge Oliver Kessel Memorial Scholarship-Ripley Rotary *(Undergraduate/Scholarship)*

Purpose: To assist Ripley High School graduating seniors. **Focus:** General studies. **Qualif.:** Applicant must be a Ripley High School graduating senior with a minimum GPA of 2.0. **Criteria:** Selection of recipients will be based on financial need and strong record of community service.

Funds Avail.: $500. **To Apply:** Applicants must submit a cover sheet (3 pages) and application form (4 pages); must have a personal essay; must have a high school and/or postsecondary transcript; must provide a letter of recommendation; copy of the page of their or their parent's most

Awards are arranged alphabetically below their administering organizations

recent tax return that indicates adjusted gross income; and a Student Aid Report showing estimated family contribution from FAFSA. Application form and other supporting documents must be sent to Our Community's Foundation, P.O Box 1762, Parkersburg, WV 26102. **Deadline:** March 20.

5502 ■ Rhonda Knopp Memorial Scholarships
(Undergraduate/Scholarship)

Purpose: To provide financial assistance for qualified graduating seniors intending to pursue their degree in health care field. **Focus:** Health care services. **Qualif.:** Applicant must be a Roane County High School graduating senior pursuing a degree in the health care field with a minimum of 2.0 GPA. **Criteria:** Applicants will be selected based on their financial need. Preference will be given to students with record of community service.

Funds Avail.: $250-$500. **To Apply:** Applicants must submit a cover sheet (3 pages) and application form (4 pages); must have a personal essay; must have a high school and/or post-secondary transcript; must provide a letter of recommendation; copy of the page of their or their parent's most recent tax return that indicates adjusted gross income; and a Student Aid Report showing estimated family contribution from FAFSA. Application form and other supporting documents must be sent to Our Community's Foundation, P.O Box 1762, Parkersburg, WV 26102. **Deadline:** March 20.

5503 ■ Harold Knopp Scholarships
(Undergraduate/Scholarship)

Purpose: To provide financial assistance for qualified graduating students from Wood County. **Focus:** Journalism. **Qualif.:** Applicant must be a graduating senior from Wood County; must have excelled in journalism in high school; and must be planning to pursue a career in journalism. **Criteria:** Applicants will be selected based on their application materials.

Funds Avail.: $450. **To Apply:** Applicants must submit a cover sheet (3 pages) and application form (4 pages); must have a personal essay; must have a high school and/or post-secondary transcript; must provide a letter of recommendation; copy of the page of their or their parent's most recent tax return that indicates adjusted gross income; and a Student Aid Report showing estimated family contribution from FAFSA. Application form and other supporting documents must be sent to Our Community's Foundation, P.O Box 1762, Parkersburg, WV 26102. **Deadline:** March 20.

5504 ■ Langfitt-Ambrose Trust Fund
(Undergraduate/Scholarship)

Purpose: To provide financial assistance for deserving students intending to pursue their education. **Focus:** General studies. **Qualif.:** Applicant must be a graduate from Parkersburg, Parkersburg South, Parkersburg Catholic, or Williamstown High School; must have excelled in the combined fields of Mathematics and English desiring to further their education in those fields. **Criteria:** Recipients will be selected based on their application materials.

Funds Avail.: $500-$1,000. **To Apply:** Applicants must submit a cover sheet (3 pages) and application form (4 pages); a personal essay; a high school and/or post-secondary transcript; a letter of recommendation; copy of the page of their or their parent's most recent tax return that indicates adjusted gross income; and a Student Aid Report showing estimated family contribution from FAFSA. Application form and other supporting documents must be sent to Our Community's Foundation, P.O Box 1762, Parkersburg, WV 26102. **Deadline:** March 20.

5505 ■ Megan Nicole Longwell Scholarships
(Undergraduate/Scholarship)

Purpose: To encourage the graduating seniors of Parkersburg South High School to pursue their college degree. **Focus:** General studies. **Qualif.:** Applicants must be Parkersburg South High School graduating seniors who have been admitted to an accredited institution of higher learning as full-time students with a minimum 2.5 GPA. **Criteria:** Selection of applicants will be based on financial need and participation in school athletics. Special consideration will be given to applicants whose families have experienced extraordinary special need.

Funds Avail.: $1,385. **To Apply:** Applicants must submit a cover sheet (3 pages) and application form (4 pages); must have a personal essay; must have a high school and/or post-secondary transcript; must provide a letter of recommendation and a signed copy of the page of their or their parent's most recent tax return that indicates adjusted gross income; and must have a Student Aid Report showing estimated family contribution from FAFSA. Application form and other supporting documents must be sent to Our Community's Foundation, P.O. Box 1762, Parkersburg, WV 26102. **Deadline:** March 20.

5506 ■ Dudley Mullins/Cabot Corporation Scholarships *(Undergraduate/Scholarship)*

Purpose: To assist graduating seniors of Williamstown High School in their educational pursuits. **Focus:** General studies. **Qualif.:** Applicant must be a Williamstown graduating senior; must have attended Waverly Elementary School for a minimum of one year and graduated from Waverly Elementary; must have a minimum of 2.0 GPA. **Criteria:** Selection of applicants will be based on involvement in school and civic activities, academic achievement, and potential.

Funds Avail.: $1,000. **To Apply:** Applicants must submit a cover sheet (3 pages) and application form (4 pages); a personal essay; a high school and/or post-secondary transcript; a letter of recommendation; a signed copy of the page of their or their parent's most recent tax return that indicates adjusted gross income; and a Student Aid Report showing estimated family contribution from FAFSA. Application form and other supporting documents must be sent to Our Community's Foundation, P.O Box 1762, Parkersburg, WV 26102. **Deadline:** March 20.

5507 ■ Pennsboro Alumni Scholarship Fund
(Undergraduate/Scholarship)

Purpose: To provide financial assistance for graduating seniors of Ritchie County High School intending to pursue their education. **Focus:** General studies. **Qualif.:** Applicant must be a Ritchie County High School graduating senior who demonstrates financial need. **Criteria:** Preference will be given to students who demonstrated academic promise, good character, good citizenship and financial need.

Funds Avail.: $500. **To Apply:** Applicants must submit a cover sheet (3 pages) and application form (4 pages); a personal essay; a high school and/or post-secondary transcript; a letter of recommendation; a signed copy of the page of their or their parent's most recent tax return that indicates adjusted gross income; and a Student Aid Report showing estimated family contribution from FAFSA. Application form and other supporting documents must be sent to Our Community's Foundation, P.O Box 1762, Parkersburg, WV 26102. **Deadline:** March 20.

5508 ■ Pepsi Wood County Technical/Caperton Center Scholarship Fund *(Undergraduate/Scholarship)*

Purpose: To assist graduating seniors in their educational pursuits. **Focus:** General studies. **Qualif.:** Applicants must be graduating seniors attending Wood County Technical/Caperton Canter who are admitted to a post-secondary education institution. **Criteria:** Selection of applicants will be based on GPA, financial need, and recommendations.

Funds Avail.: $900. **To Apply:** Applicants must submit a cover sheet (3 pages) and application form (4 pages); a personal essay; a high school and/or post-secondary transcript; a letter of recommendation; a signed copy of the page of their or their parent's most recent tax return that indicates adjusted gross income; and a Student Aid Report showing estimated family contribution from FAFSA. Application form and other supporting documents must be sent to Our Community's Foundation, P.O Box 1762, Parkersburg, WV 26102. **Deadline:** March 20.

5509 ■ William R. Pfalzgraf Scholarships *(Undergraduate/Scholarship)*

Purpose: To assist graduating students in their educational pursuits. **Focus:** Law; Education, English as a second language; Music. **Qualif.:** Applicant must be a Parkersburg High School graduating senior with a minimum of 3.0 GPA. **Criteria:** Selection of applicants will be based on merit, motivation toward higher education, character, and financial need. Preference will be given to students with interest in or achievement in the areas of law, debating, English or music.

Funds Avail.: $760. **To Apply:** Applicants must submit a cover sheet (3 pages) and application form (4 pages); a personal essay; a high school and/or post-secondary transcript; a letter of recommendation; a signed copy of the page of their or their parent's most recent tax return that indicates adjusted gross income; and a Student Aid Report showing estimated family contribution from FAFSA. Application form and other supporting documents must be sent to Our Community's Foundation, P.O Box 1762, Parkersburg, WV 26102. **Deadline:** March 20.

5510 ■ Herschel Pifer Memorial Scholarships *(Undergraduate/Scholarship)*

Purpose: To encourage graduating students to pursue their education. **Focus:** General studies. **Qualif.:** Applicants must be Ritchie County High School graduating seniors. **Criteria:** Selection of applicants will be based on financial need, academic achievement, and activities.

Funds Avail.: $500. **To Apply:** Applicants must submit a cover sheet (3 pages) and application form (4 pages); must have a personal essay; must have a high school and/or post-secondary transcript; must provide a letter of recommendation and a signed copy of the page of their or their parent's most recent tax return that indicates adjusted gross income; and must have a Student Aid Report showing estimated family contribution, from FAFSA. Application form and other supporting documents must be sent to Our Community's Foundation, P.O. Box 1762, Parkersburg, WV 26102. **Deadline:** March 20.

5511 ■ William Reaser Scholarships *(Undergraduate/Scholarship)*

Purpose: To encourage graduating students to pursue their college postsecondary education. **Focus:** Vocational-technical. **Qualif.:** Applicant must be a Ritchie County High School graduating senior planning to pursue post-secondary education in a technical or vocational field. **Criteria:** Selection of recipients will be based on academic achievement or potential in the area of vocational/technical studies, honesty and good moral character, community service, and financial need.

Funds Avail.: $500. **To Apply:** Applicants must submit a cover sheet (3 pages) and application form (4 pages); must have a personal essay; must have a high school and/or postsecondary transcript; must provide a letter of recommendation and a signed copy of the page of their or their parent's most recent tax return that indicates adjusted gross income; and must have a Student Aid Report showing estimated family contribution from FAFSA. Application form and other supporting documents must be sent to Our Community's Foundation, P.O. Box 1762, Parkersburg, WV 26102. **Deadline:** March 20.

5512 ■ James H. Roberts Athletic Scholarships *(Undergraduate/Scholarship)*

Purpose: To encourage graduating students to continue their education. **Focus:** General studies. **Qualif.:** Applicant must be a graduating senior from Wirt County High School; must be planning to attend a four-year program of study at a higher education institution in West Virginia; must be a student athlete; and must have a minimum of 2.0 GPA. **Criteria:** Selection of recipients will be based on commitment to athletics, GPA and test scores.

Funds Avail.: $1,000. **To Apply:** Applicants must submit a cover sheet (3 pages) and application form (4 pages); a personal essay; a high school and/or post-secondary transcript; a letter of recommendation; a signed copy of the page of their or their parent's most recent tax return that indicates adjusted gross income; and a Student Aid Report showing estimated family contribution from FAFSA. Application form and other supporting documents must be sent to Our Community's Foundation, P.O Box 1762, Parkersburg, WV 26102. **Deadline:** March 20.

5513 ■ Thomas Warren Roberts Scholarships *(Undergraduate/Scholarship)*

Purpose: To encourage graduating students to continue their education. **Focus:** General studies. **Qualif.:** Applicant must be a Belpre High School graduating senior. **Criteria:** Selection of recipient will be based on financial need, academic achievement, involvement in school activities, and character.

Funds Avail.: $650. **To Apply:** Applicants must submit a cover sheet (3 pages) and application form (4 pages); a personal essay; a high school and/or post-secondary transcript; a letter of recommendation; a signed copy of the page of their or their parent's most recent tax return that indicates adjusted gross income; and a Student Aid Report showing estimated family contribution from FAFSA. Application form and other supporting documents must be sent to Our Community's Foundation, P.O Box 1762, Parkersburg, WV 26102. **Deadline:** March 20.

5514 ■ James Robinson Memorial Scholarships *(Undergraduate/Scholarship)*

Purpose: To provide support for graduating students intending to pursue their education. **Focus:** General studies. **Qualif.:** Applicant must be a Ripley High School, Jackson County, graduating senior pursuing full-time enrollment or person of any age currently enrolled full-time at WVU Parkersburg Jackson County Center with a minimum of 2.0 GPA. **Criteria:** Selection of recipients will be based

Awards are arranged alphabetically below their administering organizations

on financial need and records of community service.

Funds Avail.: $500. **To Apply:** Applicants must submit a cover sheet (3 pages) and application form (4 pages); a personal essay; a high school and/or post-secondary transcript; a letter of recommendation; a signed copy of the page of their or their parent's most recent tax return that indicates adjusted gross income; and a Student Aid Report showing estimated family contribution from FAFSA. Application form and other supporting documents must be sent to Our Community's Foundation, P.O Box 1762, Parkersburg, WV 26102. **Deadline:** March 20.

5515 ■ Carl M. Rose Memorial Scholarship Fund *(Undergraduate/Scholarship)*

Purpose: To encourage graduating students to pursue their education. **Focus:** Education, Secondary. **Qualif.:** Applicant must be a Parkersburg South High School graduating senior; must have a 3.0 GPA; and must be planning to pursue a major in secondary education. **Criteria:** Selection will be based on financial need, personal statement, and academic achievement. Consideration will be given to applicants majoring in math and science secondary education.

Funds Avail.: $390. **To Apply:** Applicants must submit a cover sheet (3 pages) and application form (4 pages); a personal essay; a high school and/or post-secondary transcript; a letter of recommendation; a signed copy of the page of their or their parent's most recent tax return that indicates adjusted gross income; and a Student Aid Report showing estimated family contribution from FAFSA. Application form and other supporting documents must be sent at Our Community's Foundation, P.O Box 1762, Parkersburg, WV 26102. **Deadline:** March 20.

5516 ■ S. Byrl Ross Memorial Scholarship Fund *(Undergraduate/Scholarship)*

Purpose: To encourage graduating students to pursue their education. **Focus:** Music. **Qualif.:** Applicant must be a graduating senior of Wood or Ritchie Counties pursuing a major in music or a music-related field at a post-secondary educational institution. **Criteria:** Scholarship recipients are chosen on the basis of financial need, academic achievement, potential, and character.

Funds Avail.: $1,150. **To Apply:** Applicants must submit a cover sheet (3 pages) and application form (4 pages); a personal essay; a high school and/or post-secondary transcript; a letter of recommendation; a signed copy of the page of their or their parent's most recent tax return that indicates adjusted gross income; and a Student Aid Report showing estimated family contribution from FAFSA. Application form and other supporting documents must be sent to Our Community's Foundation, P.O Box 1762, Parkersburg, WV 26102. **Deadline:** March 20.

5517 ■ Mike Ruben Scholarships *(Undergraduate/Scholarship)*

Purpose: To encourage graduating students to pursue their education. **Focus:** General studies. **Qualif.:** Applicant must be a high school graduating senior. **Criteria:** Preference will be given to deserving students who have demonstrated excellence in academics and athletics.

Funds Avail.: $250-$500. **To Apply:** Applicants must submit a cover sheet (3 pages) and application form (4 pages); a personal essay; a high school and/or post-secondary transcript; a letter of recommendation; a signed copy of the page of their or their parent's most recent tax return that indicates adjusted gross income; and a Student Aid Report showing estimated family contribution from FAFSA. Application form and other supporting documents must be sent to Our Community's Foundation, P.O Box 1762, Parkersburg, WV 26102. **Deadline:** March 20.

5518 ■ St. Joseph's Hospital School of Nursing Alumnae Scholarships *(Undergraduate/Scholarship)*

Purpose: To encourage graduating students to pursue their education. **Focus:** Nursing. **Qualif.:** Applicant must be a resident of Wood, Ritchie, Wirt, Calhoun, Jackson, Gilmer, Roane, Pleasants, or Doddridge in WV or Washington County, OH; must be planning to attend an accredited college/nursing school to become a RN; must have a financial need and a minimum of 2.0 GPA; must be willing to make a written pledge attesting to their intention to return to the area covered by the service region of the Foundation to practice for at least two years. **Criteria:** Recipients will be selected based on financial need and other scholarship selection criteria.

Funds Avail.: $500. **To Apply:** Applicants must submit a cover sheet (3 pages) and application form (4 pages); a personal essay; a high school and/or post-secondary transcript; a letter of recommendation; a signed copy of the page of their or their parent's most recent tax return that indicates adjusted gross income; and a Student Aid Report showing estimated family contribution from FAFSA. Application form and other supporting documents must be sent to Our Community's Foundation, P.O Box 1762, Parkersburg, WV 26102. **Deadline:** March 20.

5519 ■ Everett Oscar Shimp Memorial Scholarships *(Undergraduate/Scholarship)*

Purpose: To encourage graduating students to pursue their education. **Focus:** Agriculture, Economic aspects; History. **Qualif.:** Applicant must be a graduate of Jackson or Roane County high schools who is currently enrolled full-time and has completed college credits equivalent to junior or senior status; must have a minimum of 3.0 college GPA; and must be majoring in agriculture or history or pursuing an education degree majoring in agriculture or history. **Criteria:** Applicants will be selected based on the scholarship criteria.

Funds Avail.: $500-$1,000. **To Apply:** Applicants must submit a cover sheet (3 pages) and application form (4 pages); a personal essay; a high school and/or post-secondary transcript; a letter of recommendation; a signed copy of the page of their or their parent's most recent tax return that indicates adjusted gross income; and a Student Aid Report showing estimated family contribution from FAFSA. Application form and other supporting documents must be sent to Our Community's Foundation, P.O Box 1762, Parkersburg, WV 26102. **Deadline:** March 20.

5520 ■ Pat Shimp Memorial Scholarships *(Undergraduate/Scholarship)*

Purpose: To encourage graduating students to pursue their degree in the business or agriculture field. **Focus:** Business; Agriculture, Economic aspects. **Qualif.:** Applicant must be a Roane County High School graduating senior pursuing a degree in the business or agriculture field with a minimum of 2.0 GPA. **Criteria:** Preference will be given to students with record of community service.

Funds Avail.: $500. **To Apply:** Applicants must submit a cover sheet (3 pages) and application form (4 pages); a personal essay; a high school and/or post-secondary transcript; a letter of recommendation; a signed copy of the page of their or their parent's most recent tax return that indicates adjusted gross income; and a Student Aid Report showing estimated family contribution from FAFSA. Application form and other supporting documents must be sent to Our Community's Foundation, P.O Box 1762, Parkersburg, WV 26102. **Deadline:** March 20.

5521 ■ Simonton Windows Scholarship Fund
(Undergraduate/Scholarship)

Purpose: To provide educational assistance to high school graduates or the equivalent who demonstrate academic potential. **Focus:** General studies. **Qualif.:** Applicants must be currently enrolled in undergraduate studies; must have graduated from high school or the equivalent and shall desire to attend a post-secondary educational institution, such as a college, university, technical or trade school, vocational school, business school; and must have a good academic standing with a minimum 2.5 GPA on a 4.0 scale. **Criteria:** Selection of applicants will be based on financial need, academic achievement, and leadership abilities and activities.

Funds Avail.: Amount of the scholarship may vary depending on the type of institution the student is attending and relative cost. **To Apply:** Applicants must complete the application form, available online; must submit a personal essay, high school and/or post-secondary transcript; must have a copy of the page of their or their parent's most recent tax return that indicates adjusted gross income, a copy of the page from their Student Aid Report from FAFSA that shows their Estimated Family Contribution; must have financial aid award letter from their top-choice post-secondary educational institution. Application form and other supporting documents must be sent to Our Community's Foundation, P.O Box 1762, Parkersburg, WV 26102. **Deadline:** April 1.

5522 ■ Bill Six Memorial Scholarship Fund
(Undergraduate/Scholarship)

Purpose: To encourage graduating seniors to pursue their education. **Focus:** General studies. **Qualif.:** Applicants must be graduating seniors or previous high school graduates who are permanent residents of Vienna, WV, who have at least a 2.0 GPA. **Criteria:** Selection of recipients is based on financial need and potential for successful achievement beyond high school. Preference will be given to the student who appears to be a hard worker and is likely to succeed, yet does not necessarily maintain a superior GPA.

Funds Avail.: $500. **To Apply:** Applicants must submit a cover sheet (3 pages) and application form (4 pages); a personal essay; a high school and/or post-secondary transcript; a letter of recommendation; a signed copy of the page of their or their parent's most recent tax return that indicates adjusted gross income; and a Student Aid Report showing estimated family contribution from FAFSA. Application form and other supporting documents must be sent to Our Community's Foundation, P.O Box 1762, Parkersburg, WV 26102. **Deadline:** March 20.

5523 ■ Mary K. Smith Rector Scholarships
(Undergraduate/Scholarship)

Purpose: To encourage graduating seniors to pursue their education. **Focus:** Vocational-technical education. **Qualif.:** Applicants must be graduating seniors from Gilmer County High School; must be planning to attend an accredited college or university in West Virginia; must have a minimum of 2.5 GPA. **Criteria:** Selection of recipients will be based on academic achievement and financial need.

Funds Avail.: $500-$1,500. **To Apply:** Applicants must submit a cover sheet (3 pages) and application form (4 pages); must have a personal essay; must have high school and/or post-secondary transcripts; must provide a letter of recommendation; copy of the page of their or their parent's most recent tax return that indicates adjusted gross income; and a Student Aid Report showing estimated family contribution from FAFSA. Application form and other supporting documents must be sent at Our Community's Foundation, P.O Box 1762, Parkersburg, WV 26102. **Deadline:** March 20.

5524 ■ C.R. Thomas Scholarships
(Undergraduate/Scholarship)

Purpose: To encourage graduating students to pursue their education. **Focus:** General studies. **Qualif.:** Applicant must be a graduating senior of Parkersburg High School and must be willing to help the community and others. **Criteria:** Recipients will be selected based on financial need and application materials.

Funds Avail.: $650. **To Apply:** Applicants must submit a cover sheet (3 pages) and application form (4 pages); a personal essay; a high school and/or post-secondary transcript; a letter of recommendation; a signed copy of the page of their or their parent's most recent tax return that indicates adjusted gross income; and a Student Aid Report showing estimated family contribution from FAFSA. Application form and other supporting documents must be sent to Our Community's Foundation, P.O Box 1762, Parkersburg, WV 26102. **Deadline:** March 20.

5525 ■ Charles A. Townsend Scholarships
(Undergraduate/Scholarship)

Purpose: To encourage graduating students to pursue their career as education professionals. **Focus:** Education. **Qualif.:** Applicant must be a graduating senior of Wood County schools planning to attend an accredited post-secondary school; must be interested in pursuing a career as an education professional; and must be pursuing a degree at St. John's College in Annapolis, MD, or Santa Fe, NM. **Criteria:** Selection of recipients will be based on financial need, achievement, and character.

Funds Avail.: $985. **To Apply:** Applicants must submit a cover sheet (3 pages) and application form (4 pages); a personal essay; a high school and/or post-secondary transcript; a letter of recommendation; a signed copy of the page of their or their parent's most recent tax return that indicates adjusted gross income; and a Student Aid Report, showing estimated family contribution, from FAFSA. Application form and other supporting documents must be sent to Our Community's Foundation, P.O Box 1762, Parkersburg, WV 26102. **Deadline:** March 20.

5526 ■ Wayne-Meador-Elliott Scholarships
(Undergraduate/Scholarship)

Purpose: To encourage graduating seniors of Ritchie County High School to pursue their education. **Focus:** General studies. **Qualif.:** Applicant must be a Ritchie County High School graduating senior; must be enrolled as a fulltime student to attend an accredited four-year college or university; and must have a minimum of 3.0 GPA. **Criteria:** Preference will be given to students planning to major in the field of education administration, music, geology/ petroleum engineering or education. Selection of recipients will be based on ability to overcome obstacles, strong work ethic, interest in community service and leadership, and financial need.

Awards are arranged alphabetically below their administering organizations

Funds Avail.: $500. **To Apply:** Applicants must submit a cover sheet (3 pages) and application form (4 pages); a personal essay; a high school and/or post-secondary transcript; a letter of recommendation; a signed copy of the page of their or their parent's most recent tax return that indicates adjusted gross income; and a Student Aid Report showing estimated family contribution from FAFSA. Application form and other supporting documents must be sent to Our Community's Foundation, P.O Box 1762, Parkersburg, WV 26102. **Deadline:** March 20.

5527 ■ West Virginia Nurses Association District No. 3 Scholarships *(Undergraduate/Scholarship)*

Purpose: To provide support for qualified individuals intending to pursue their nursing degree. **Focus:** Nursing. **Qualif.:** Applicants must reside in Wood, Wirt, Calhoun, Jackson, or Roane Counties and must be pursuing an associate nursing degree as full-time students. **Criteria:** Selection of recipients will be based on merit.

Funds Avail.: $800. **To Apply:** Applicants must submit a cover sheet (3 pages) and application form (4 pages); a personal essay; a high school and/or post-secondary transcript; a letter of recommendation; a signed copy of the page of their or their parent's most recent tax return that indicates adjusted gross income; and a Student Aid Report showing estimated family contribution from FAFSA. Application form and other supporting documents must be sent to Our Community's Foundation, P.O Box 1762, Parkersburg, WV 26102. **Deadline:** March 20.

5528 ■ Whitaker-Minard Memorial Scholarships *(Undergraduate/Scholarship)*

Purpose: To encourage graduating seniors to pursue their degrees in any field specializing in services for individuals with disabilities. **Focus:** Disabilities. **Qualif.:** Applicant must be a graduating high school senior admitted to attend college, or a currently enrolled college student; must be pursuing associate or bachelor level degrees in any field specializing in services for individuals with disabilities; must have a minimum of 2.5 GPA; must be a resident of Wood, Pleasants, Ritchie, Wirt, Gilmer, Calhoun, Jackson, Roane or Tyler Counties, West Virginia or Washington County, Ohio. **Criteria:** Preference will be given to applicants who show willingness to volunteer/participate or has previously volunteer/participated in one of Wood County Society's programs, the year the scholarship is received or the following year.

Funds Avail.: $1,000. **To Apply:** Applicants must submit a cover sheet (3 pages) and application form (4 pages); must have a personal essay; must have a high school and/or post-secondary transcript; must provide a letter of recommendation and a signed copy of the page of their or their parent's most recent tax return that indicates adjusted gross income; and must have a Student Aid Report showing estimated family contribution from FAFSA. Application form and other supporting documents must be sent to Our Community's Foundation, P.O Box 1762, Parkersburg, WV 26102. **Deadline:** March 20.

5529 ■ Glenn Wilson Broadcast Journalism Scholarships *(Undergraduate/Scholarship)*

Purpose: To provide financial support for qualified individuals intending to pursue their education. **Focus:** Journalism; Communications; Marketing and distribution. **Qualif.:** Applicants must be current or previous Wood or Pleasant County, WV, or Washington County, OH, high school students; must be studying broadcast journalism, journalism, communications or marketing; and must have a minimum 2.5 GPA. **Criteria:** Preference will be given to students whose main interest is broadcast journalism as demonstrated by candidate's school activities or through study of this field.

Funds Avail.: $560. **To Apply:** Applicants must submit a cover sheet (3 pages) and application form (4 pages); a personal essay; a high school and/or post- secondary transcript; a letter of recommendation; a signed copy of the page of their or their parent's most recent tax return that indicates adjusted gross income; and a Student Aid Report showing estimated family contribution from FAFSA. Application form and other supporting documents must be sent to Our Community's Foundation, P.O Box 1762, Parkersburg, WV 26102. **Deadline:** March 20.

5530 ■ Wood County Bar Association Memorial Scholarships *(Undergraduate/Scholarship)*

Purpose: To provide financial assistance for qualified individuals intending to pursue their law degree. **Focus:** Law. **Qualif.:** Applicant must be a student attending an accredited law school in the United States and must have certain minimal contacts with Wood, Jackson, Ritchie, Wirt, or Pleasant Counties in West Virginia. **Criteria:** Selection of recipients will be based on the scholarship selection criteria.

Funds Avail.: $250-$500. **To Apply:** Applicants must submit a cover sheet (3 pages) and application form (4 pages); a personal essay; a high school and/or post-secondary transcript; a letter of recommendation; a signed copy of the page of their or their parent's most recent tax return that indicates adjusted gross income; and a Student Aid Report showing estimated family contribution from FAFSA. Application form and other supporting documents must be sent to Our Community's Foundation, P.O Box 1762, Parkersburg, WV 26102. **Deadline:** March 20.

5531 ■ Parkinson's Disease Foundation

1359 Broadway, Ste. 1509
New York, NY 10018
Ph: (212)923-4700
Fax: (212)923-4778
Free: 800-457-6676
E-mail: info@pdf.org
URL: http://www.pdf.org

5532 ■ Clinician Scientist Development Awards *(Postgraduate/Fellowship)*

Purpose: To provide financial assistance to support three years of research training in an environment where talented young clinicians address problems in Parkinson's Disease with the most current scientific tools. **Focus:** Parkinson's disease. **Qualif.:** Applicants must hold an MD, DO, or equivalent clinical degree from an accredited institution and must have completed residency training but be less than seven years from completion of residency when funding begins. **Criteria:** Applicants will be evaluated by the Scientific Advisory Committee of the PDF and the Clinical Research Subcommittee of the Science Committee of the AAN based on the following criteria: ability and promise as a clinician scientist based on previous training and career plan, letters of reference and curriculum vitae; quality and nature of the training to be provide and the institutional, departmental and mentor-specific training environment; quality and originality of the research plan.

Funds Avail.: May 1. **To Apply:** Applicants must submit a letter of nomination; letter of intent to pursue a three-year program indicating the specific clinical focus, the proposed institution and preceptor and future goals; three-page research plan, including brief statements of aims, background, and the contemplated approaches to methodology and data; copy of current curriculum vitae; letters of reference supporting his/her potential for a clinical, academic research career, and qualifications for the fellowship; listing of the applicant's and mentor's current and pending support, other than this award, using NIH format; letter from the proposed mentor detailing his/her support of and commitment to the applicant and the proposed research and training plan, specifically indicate the mentor's role in the development and preparation of the applicant's research plan. The letter should describe: how the proposed research fits into the mentor's research program: expertise and experience in the area of research proposed and the nature of the mentor's proposed time commitment to the supervision and training of the applicant: and the mentor's prior experience in the supervision, training, and successful mentoring of clinician scientists; copy of mentor's NIH biosketch; document describing arrangements for formal course work to include: quantitative clinical epidemiology, biostatistics, study design, data analysis, and ethics. The documentation must outline: hours and content of the proposed formal instruction; availability of tutorial assistance for the research project; and computer approaches to statistical analysis at the host institution; document describing the level of interaction between the applicant and subjects in your research project. **Deadline:** January 15. **Contact:** Erin Jackson, 1080 Montreal Ave., St. Paul, MN 55116; Phone: 651-695-2704; Fax: 651-361-4804; Email: ejackson@aan.com.

5533 ■ PDF International Research Grants Program *(Postdoctorate/Grant)*

Purpose: To provide financial assistance for projects of the highest scientific caliber from around the world. **Focus:** Parkinson's disease. **Qualif.:** Applicants must have completed a PhD or MD and qualified to serve as a principal investigator for the project which is basic, translational and clinical research. **Criteria:** Applicant's proposal will be peer-reviewed and competitively evaluated based on the quality of the research proposal and its pertinence to Parkinson's disease.

Funds Avail.: $700,000. **To Apply:** Applicants must submit the application package which includes: the completed PDF application form, including the signature of the applicant and the relevant institutional authority; letter of recommendation consisting the background of proposed study, specific aims, details of proposed experiment including methods, statement describing relevance of proposed studies, budget and justification, curriculum vitae and references. **Deadline:** February 1.

5534 ■ Patient Advocate Foundation

700 Thimble Shoals Blvd., Ste. 200
Newport News, VA 23606
Fax: (757)873-8999
Free: 800-532-5274
E-mail: help@patientadvocate.org
URL: http://www.patientadvocate.org

5535 ■ Patient Advocate Foundations Scholarships *(Undergraduate/Scholarship)*

Purpose: To provide financial support to individuals under the age of 25 who have been diagnosed with cancer or another life-threatening disease. **Focus:** General studies. **Qualif.:** Applicants must be survivors or current patients diagnosed with cancer or another life-threatening disease; must write an essay on how their diagnosis has impacted their lives and their future goals, (1000 word maximum); must submit a copy of an acceptance letter from their chosen college, university, or vocational-technical school; must submit written documentation from physician of medical history; must provide two letters of recommendation from non-related persons (examples: teachers, coaches, community leaders). Please ask that each reference include their name, address and phone number within the letter; must provide an official high school and/or current college transcript (with school seal); financial form that demonstrates financial need with a copy of the first two pages of tax returns. **Criteria:** Preference will be given to those who meet the criteria.

Funds Avail.: $3,000. **To Apply:** Applicants must maintain an overall 3.0 G.P.A.; must be full-time students; must sign an agreement to complete 20 hours of community service for the year the scholarship will be dispensed and provide PAF with a written confirmation from a supervisor when that service has been completed. **Contact:** Patient Advocate Foundation at the above address (see entry 5534).

5536 ■ PBR Forces Veterans Association

6097 Davon St.
Jacksonville, FL 32244-3178
Ph: (419)281-4711
URL: http://www.pbr-fva.org

5537 ■ James Elliott Williams Scholarship Fund *(Undergraduate/Scholarship)*

Purpose: To assist the direct descendants of members. **Focus:** Army. **Qualif.:** Candidates must be a direct descent of an active Vietnam Veteran member of PBR Forces Veterans Association; must be enrolled in a two or four-year accredited college/technical school.

Funds Avail.: Varies depending on available funds. **To Apply:** Applicants must fill out the application form; form must be printed using blue or black ink; and application must be countersigned by the Sponsor.

5538 ■ Pediatric AIDS Fund

1140 Connecticut Ave. NW, Ste. 200
Washington, DC 20036
Ph: (202)296-9165
Fax: (202)296-9185
E-mail: dc@pedaids.org
URL: http://www.pedaids.org

5539 ■ Elizabeth Glaser Scientist Award *(Other/Award/Prize)*

Purpose: To allow scientists to focus on their long-term efforts on issues specific to pediatric HIV/AIDS by providing funding support for research. **Focus:** Acquired immune deficiency syndrome. **Qualif.:** Applicants must be scientists who represent the best and brightest investigators from the international medical science community. **Criteria:** Recipient will be selected based on their knowledge, innovation, and dedication.

Funds Avail.: $682,500. **To Apply:** Applicants must submit completed form designed for the award.

5540 ■ International Scholar Awards *(Postdoctorate/Award/Prize)*

Purpose: To render financial support for deserving clinicians and scientists in developing countries. **Focus:**

Awards are arranged alphabetically below their administering organizations

Acquired immune deficiency syndrome. **Qualif.:** Applicants must be health care professionals who have specific training or experience with HIV/AIDS; must hold an MD or PhD; and must demonstrate commitment to continuing to work in developing country on HIV/ AIDS. **Criteria:** Preference is given to candidates from developing countries.

Funds Avail.: $57,225. **To Apply:** Applicants must work with a qualified experienced sponsor (faculty member with advanced degree) to oversee, provide guidance and evidence of the institution's commitment to his career development.

5541 ■ Pediatric Endocrinology Nursing Society

7794 Grow Dr.
Pensacola, FL 32514
Ph: (850)484-5223
Fax: (850)484-8762
Free: 877-936-7367
E-mail: pens@puetzamc.com
URL: http://www.pens.org

5542 ■ Pediatric Endocrinology Nursing Society Academic Education Scholarships
(Undergraduate/Scholarship)

Purpose: To promote the study and development of pediatric endocrine nursing. **Focus:** Nursing, Pediatric. **Qualif.:** Applicant must be an active PENS member for at least three years; currently employed in pediatric endocrine nursing; and pursuing a nursing degree. **Criteria:** Applicants who are pursuing their BS(N) and applying for the scholarship for the first-time will be given preference.

Funds Avail.: $1,000. **To Apply:** Applicants must submit a completed application form; copy of RN License; curriculum vitae or resume; receipt of registration from college or university; transcript of records or acceptance letter. **Deadline:** April and September.

5543 ■ Pediatric Endocrinology Nursing Society Continuing Education Scholarships
(Undergraduate/Scholarship)

Purpose: To promote the study and development of pediatric endocrine nursing. **Focus:** Nursing, Pediatric. **Qualif.:** Applicant must be an active PENS member for at least three years. **Criteria:** Recipients are selected based on the committee's review of the application materials.

Funds Avail.: $1,000. **To Apply:** Applicants must send a completed application form and a 2-4 page clinical exemplar. Send documents via email. **Deadline:** January 15. **Contact:** Patricia Barlow, pmbarlow@puetzamc.com.

5544 ■ Pedorthic Footwear Association

2025 M St. NW, Ste. 800
Washington, DC 20036
Ph: (202)367-1145
Fax: (202)367-2145
Free: 800-673-8447
E-mail: info@pedorthics.org
URL: http://www.pedorthics.org

5545 ■ The Eneslow Pedorthic Institute Scholarships *(Undergraduate/Scholarship)*

Purpose: For students committed to attending the New York College of Podiatric Medicine/EPI course. **Focus:** Orthotics prosthetics technology; Pathology. **Qualif.:** Applicants must be at least 18 years old and have at least a high school diploma or equivalent; have an experience related to footwear for foot care; must describe their educational plans, including the school(s), the approximate timetable, the approximate date on which they plan to take the pedorthic certification exam (Applicants need not be enrolled in a course at the time of application); must sit for the certification exam within two years of completing course work supported by the Foundation scholarship; must agree in advance that, if selected to receive a scholarship, they will serve as advisors to the Foundation Scholarship Committee for two years immediately after receipt of a scholarship (such service shall not exceed 16 hours of consultation, generally by telephone or e-mail, over the course of those years); must describe their preferred area of concentration in pedorthics. **Criteria:** Applicants are selected based on, but not limited to, evidence of commitment to a career in pedorthics; financial need; applicant's preferred pedorthic interest area.

Funds Avail.: $500-$2,500. **To Apply:** Applicants must submit a completed application form to the Scholarship Review Committee. Applicants must also submit three recommendations from individuals not related to them. **Deadline:** January 15.

5546 ■ The Dawn Janisse Scholarships
(Undergraduate/Scholarship)

Purpose: To provide financial assistance to students who are interested in a career in pedorthics. **Focus:** Orthotics prosthetics technology; Pathology. **Qualif.:** Applicants must be at least 18 years old and have at least a high school diploma or equivalent; have an experience related to footwear for foot care; must describe their educational plans, including the school(s), the approximate timetable, the approximate date on which they plan to take the pedorthic certification exam (Applicants need not be enrolled in a course at the time of application); must sit for the certification exam within two years of completing course work supported by the Foundation scholarship; must agree in advance that, if selected to receive a scholarship, they will serve as advisors to the Foundation Scholarship Committee for two years immediately after receipt of a scholarship (such service shall not exceed 16 hours of consultation, generally by telephone or e-mail, over the course of those years); must describe their preferred area of concentration in pedorthics. **Criteria:** Applicants are selected based on, but not limited to, evidence of commitment to a career in pedorthics; financial need; applicant's preferred pedorthic interest area.

Funds Avail.: $500-$2,500. **To Apply:** Applicants must submit a completed application form to the Scholarship Review Committee. Applicants must also submit three recommendations from individuals not related to them. **Deadline:** January 15.

5547 ■ The Aristotle Mirones Scholarships
(Undergraduate/Scholarship)

Purpose: To financially assist students interested in a career in pedorthics. **Focus:** Orthotics prosthetics technology; Pathology. **Qualif.:** Applicants must be at least 18 years old and have at least a high school diploma or equivalent; have an experience related to footwear for foot care; must describe their educational plans, including the school(s), the approximate timetable, the approximate date on which they plan to take the pedorthic certification exam (Applicants need not be enrolled in a course at the time of application); must sit for the certification exam within two

Awards are arranged alphabetically below their administering organizations

years of completing course work supported by the Foundation scholarship; must agree in advance that, if selected to receive a scholarship, they will serve as advisors to the Foundation Scholarship Committee for two years immediately after receipt of a scholarship (such service shall not exceed 16 hours of consultation, generally by telephone or e-mail, over the course of those years); must describe their preferred area of concentration in pedorthics. **Criteria:** Applicants are selected based on, but not limited to, evidence of commitment to a career in pedorthics; financial need; applicant's preferred pedorthic interest area.

Funds Avail.: $500-$2,500. **To Apply:** Applicants must submit a completed application form to the Scholarship Review Committee. Applicants must also submit three recommendations from individuals not related to them.

Remarks: In memory of Aristotle Mirones, founder of ARIMED Orthotics, Prosthetics and Pedorthics.

5548 ■ The Oklahoma State University at Okmulgee Scholarships *(Undergraduate/Scholarship)*

Purpose: To students pursuing Fundamentals Course at Oklahoma State University. **Focus:** Orthotics prosthetics technology; Pathology. **Qualif.:** Applicants must be at least 18 years old and have at least a high school diploma or equivalent; have an experience related to footwear for foot care; must describe their educational plans, including the school(s), the approximate timetable, the approximate date on which they plan to take the pedorthic certification exam (Applicants need not be enrolled in a course at the time of application); must sit for the certification exam within two years of completing course work supported by the Foundation scholarship; must agree in advance that, if selected to receive a scholarship, they will serve as advisors to the Foundation Scholarship Committee for two years immediately after receipt of a scholarship (such service shall not exceed 16 hours of consultation, generally by telephone or e-mail, over the course of those years); must describe their preferred area of concentration in pedorthics. **Criteria:** Applicants are selected based on, but not limited to, evidence of commitment to a career in pedorthics; financial need; applicant's preferred pedorthic interest area.

Funds Avail.: $500-$2,500. **To Apply:** Applicants must submit a completed application form to the Scholarship Review Committee. Applicants must also submit three recommendations from individuals not related to them. **Deadline:** January 15.

5549 ■ The Sidney M. Pols Scholarships *(Undergraduate/Scholarship)*

Purpose: To provide financial assistance to students who are interested in a career in pedorthics. **Focus:** Orthotics prosthetics technology; Pathology. **Qualif.:** Applicants must be at least 18 years old and have at least a high school diploma or equivalent; have an experience related to footwear for foot care; must describe their educational plans, including the school(s), the approximate timetable, the approximate date on which they plan to take the pedorthic certification exam (Applicants need not be enrolled in a course at the time of application); must sit for the certification exam within two years of completing course work supported by the Foundation scholarship; must agree in advance that, if selected to receive a scholarship, they will serve as advisors to the Foundation Scholarship Committee for two years immediately after receipt of a scholarship (such service shall not exceed 16 hours of consultation, generally by telephone or e-mail, over the course of those years); must describe their preferred area of concentration in pedorthics. **Criteria:** Applicants are selected based on, but not limited to, evidence of commitment to a career in pedorthics; financial need; applicant's preferred pedorthic interest area.

Funds Avail.: $500-$2,500. **To Apply:** Applicants must submit a completed application form to the Scholarship Review Committee. Applicants must also submit three recommendations from individuals not related to them. **Deadline:** January 15.

Remarks: Scholarship is created by P.W. Minor and Son, Inc.

5550 ■ The Dr. William M. Scholl College of Podiatric Medicine Scholarships *(Undergraduate/Scholarship)*

Purpose: To students pursuing Basic Course at Finch University. **Focus:** Orthotics prosthetics technology; Pathology. **Qualif.:** Applicants must be at least 18 years old and have at least a high school diploma or equivalent; have an experience related to footwear for foot care; must describe their educational plans, including the school(s), the approximate timetable, the approximate date on which they plan to take the pedorthic certification exam (Applicants need not be enrolled in a course at the time of application); must sit for the certification exam within two years of completing course work supported by the Foundation scholarship; must agree in advance that, if selected to receive a scholarship, they will serve as advisors to the Foundation Scholarship Committee for two years immediately after receipt of a scholarship (such service shall not exceed 16 hours of consultation, generally by telephone or e-mail, over the course of those years); must describe their preferred area of concentration in pedorthics. **Criteria:** Applicants are selected based on, but not limited to, evidence of commitment to a career in pedorthics; financial need; applicant's preferred pedorthic interest area.

Funds Avail.: $500-$2,500. **To Apply:** Applicants must submit a completed application form to the Scholarship Review Committee. Applicants must also submit three recommendations from individuals not related to them. **Deadline:** January 15.

5551 ■ The Xtra Depth University Scholarships *(Undergraduate/Scholarship)*

Purpose: To provide financial assistance to students who are interested in a career in pedorthics. **Focus:** Orthotics prosthetics technology; Pathology. **Qualif.:** Applicants must be at least 18 years old and have at least a high school diploma or equivalent; have an experience related to footwear for foot care; must describe their educational plans, including the school(s), the approximate timetable, the approximate date on which they plan to take the pedorthic certification exam (Applicants need not be enrolled in a course at the time of application); must sit for the certification exam within two years of completing course work supported by the Foundation scholarship; must agree in advance that, if selected to receive a scholarship, they will serve as advisors to the Foundation Scholarship Committee for two years immediately after receipt of a scholarship (such service shall not exceed 16 hours of consultation, generally by telephone or e-mail, over the course of those years); must describe their preferred area of concentration in pedorthics. **Criteria:** Applicants are selected based on, but not limited to, evidence of commitment to a career in pedorthics; financial need; applicant's preferred pedorthic interest area.

Funds Avail.: $500-$2,500. **To Apply:** Applicants must submit a completed application form to the Scholarship Review Committee. Applicants must also submit three recommendations from individuals not related to them. **Deadline:** January 15.

Remarks: Scholarship is created by P.W. Minor and Son, Inc.

5552 ■ Penndelphia Scholarship Foundation

PO Box 42791
Philadelphia, PA 19101
Ph: (215)576-1216
URL: http://www.penndelsf.org

5553 ■ Penndelphia Scholarships Foundation *(Undergraduate/Scholarship)*

Purpose: To provide financial assistance to deserving students who want to pursue their studies. **Focus:** General studies. **Qualif.:** Applicant must be a high school senior, high school graduate or registered as an undergraduate student at an accredited college or post-secondary vocational/technical institution. **Criteria:** Recipient will be selected based on financial need and academic excellence.

Funds Avail.: $1,000. **To Apply:** Applicant must submit: a financial statement and photograph; scholastic record or complete transcript of record; recommendation letter. Application form is available online and must be sent to Penndelphia Scholarship Foundation, PO Box 42791, Philadelphia, PA 19101. **Deadline:** April 15.

5554 ■ Pennsylvania Association of Arson Investigators

RR2 Box 195
Martinsburg, PA 16662
Ph: (717)278-4854
E-mail: cjpi77@aol.com
URL: http://www.paai.org

5555 ■ Pennsylvania Association of Arson Investigators Scholarships *(Undergraduate/Scholarship)*

Purpose: To support members of the association with their educational pursuits. **Focus:** Fires and fire prevention. **Qualif.:** Applicants must be paid-up members in good standing or an immediate family of paid-up member in good standing or children of deceased members; must be enrolled, or planning to enroll, in the next scheduled semester of a two- or four-year accredited college/university that offers courses in police or fire sciences including, fire investigation and related subjects. **Criteria:** Applications will be reviewed by the Scholarship Committee.

Funds Avail.: No specific amount. **To Apply:** Applicants must submit a completed application form with the required materials to the Chairman of the Scholarship Committee, Thomas W. Dolan, Jr., 2 Luke Lane, Carlisle PA 17013. **Deadline:** May 15. **Contact:** Thomas W. Dolan.

5556 ■ Pennsylvania Land Surveyors Foundation

2040 Linglestown Rd., Ste. 200
Harrisburg, PA 17110
Ph: (717)540-6811
Fax: (717)540-6815
E-mail: hmorijah@psls.org
URL: http://www.psls.org

5557 ■ Pennsylvania Land Surveyors Foundation Scholarships *(Undergraduate/Scholarship)*

Purpose: To promote, improve and encourage the profession and practice of land surveying in the Commonwealth of Pennsylvania by providing financial assistance to those persons intending to pursue or who are currently pursuing an education in surveying with an ultimate goal of becoming practicing Professional Land Surveyors. **Focus:** Surveying. **Qualif.:** Applicants must: be citizens of the United States and be residents of the Commonwealth of Pennsylvania; be enrolled in or accepted in a two-year Surveying Technology Program or a four-year Bachelor of Science Program in Land Surveying; submit copies of SAT scores and high school or college transcripts with completed Transcript Release Form from Guidance Office or Registrar's Office. **Criteria:** Selection will be based on performance factors, applicant's activities, application preparation, Guidance Counselor/Advisor evaluation, applicant's potential as a Professional Land Surveyor.

Funds Avail.: $20,000. **To Apply:** Application form can be downloaded online. Each portion of the application has a specific point value. Judges will score each section separately. Incomplete applications will not be considered. Forms must be typed or neatly printed. Use of separate paper will be accepted. Points may be lost for poor grammar, incorrect spelling, illegibility, or lack of neatness. Proofread carefully. Applicants must submit a recommendation form to their Guidance Counselor/Advisor. **Deadline:** February 1. **Contact:** Pennsylvania Land Surveyors' Foundation at the above address (see entry 5556).

5558 ■ Pennsylvania Library Association

220 Cumberland Pkwy., Ste. 10
Mechanicsburg, PA 17055
Ph: (717)766-7663
Fax: (717)766-5440
Free: 800-622-3308
E-mail: glenn@palibraries.org
URL: http://www.palibraries.org

5559 ■ Pennsylvania Library Association Scholarships for MLS Students *(Undergraduate/Scholarship)*

Purpose: To provide opportunities for professional growth, leadership development and continuing education for librarians. **Focus:** Library science. **Qualif.:** Applicants must be Pennsylvania residents who are seeking a master's degree in the Library Science field that will earn them professional status; must have completed 12 credit hours toward the degree during the scholarship year. **Criteria:** Recipients are selected based on academic performance.

Funds Avail.: $1,500. **Number Awarded:** 3. **To Apply:** Applicants must submit a completed application form and a verification of enrollment in an ALA accredited graduate program. **Deadline:** May 15.

5560 ■ Pennsylvania Society of Professional Engineers

908 N 2nd St.
Harrisburg, PA 17102
Ph: (717)441-6051
Fax: (717)236-2046

Awards are arranged alphabetically below their administering organizations

E-mail: pspeinfo@pspe.org
URL: http://www.pspe.org

5561 ■ Pennsylvania Society of Professional Engineers Scholarships *(Undergraduate/ Scholarship)*

Purpose: To provide financial assistance for freshmen students to pursue their academic goals in the engineering field of study. **Focus:** Engineering. **Qualif.:** Applicants must be freshmen attending their first semester of college at an ABET-accredited engineering School in the Commonwealth of Pennsylvania. **Criteria:** Applicants are evaluated based on financial need.

Funds Avail.: $4,000. **Number Awarded:** 6. **To Apply:** Applicants must submit all the required application information.

5562 ■ Pennsylvania State System of Higher Education Foundation

2986 N 2nd St.
Harrisburg, PA 17110
Ph: (717)720-4086
Fax: (717)720-7082
URL: http://www.thepafoundation.org

5563 ■ Wayne G. Failor Scholarships *(High School/Scholarship)*

Purpose: To provide educational assistance to high school seniors graduating from a West Shore School District high school and planning to major in business or a related field at one of the State System universities. **Focus:** Business. **Qualif.:** Applicants must be students who are graduating seniors of a West Shore School District high school; full-time undergraduate students who plan to enroll at a State System university; must plan to major in business or a related field; must have a "B" average or better by the end of their junior year in high school. **Criteria:** Recipients are selected on the basis of financial need.

Funds Avail.: No specific amount. **To Apply:** Applicants must submit all the required application information. **Deadline:** May 1.

5564 ■ James Hughes Memorial Scholarship Fund *(Undergraduate/Scholarship)*

Purpose: To provide recognition and financial assistance to low-income, disadvantaged students residing in the city of Philadelphia who attended any of the public high schools or charter schools in the school district of Philadelphia and who wish to enroll in universities of the Pennsylvania State System of Higher Education. **Focus:** General studies. **Qualif.:** Applicants must have graduated from any public high school or charter school in the school district of Philadelphia; must be full-time undergraduate students accepted at a PASSHE university, with priority given to incoming freshmen. **Criteria:** Recipients are selected based on financial need.

Funds Avail.: $1,500. **To Apply:** Applicants must submit the James Hughes Memorial Scholarship (JHMS) application form; two written references using the letter of reference form (one academic/professional and one personal); current high school transcript; 250-word essay on why they feel they are deserving of the Hughes scholarship, their desire to achieve academically and how they have overcome adversities in their lives. **Deadline:** March 31.

5565 ■ Robert Noyce Scholarship Program *(Undergraduate/Scholarship)*

Purpose: To provide financial assistance to increase the number of basic education teachers with strong content knowledge in science, technology, engineering, and mathematics (STEM). **Focus:** Science; Technology; Engineering; Mathematics and mathematical sciences. **Qualif.:** Applicants must have a qualifying cumulative GPA of 3.00, with preference for those with a GPA of 3.5 or higher; must be transfer students or post-baccalaureates who completed a semester or more of coursework at a State System university to establish the qualifying GPA of 3.00; must be full-time students during each semester for which the award is received. **Criteria:** Applicants are evaluated based on academic achievement.

Funds Avail.: $10,000. **To Apply:** Applicants must submit completed application form; official transcripts from all institutions attended; a two page essay describing personal and professional goals, commitment to teaching and personal philosophy of teaching; three letters of recommendation that must address, but are not limited to: a) the scholarship of the applicant, b) the character of the applicant, c) the interpersonal skills of the applicant relative to teaching, and d) the general interpersonal skills of the applicant; and a resume. **Deadline:** April 20.

5566 ■ Minnie Patton Stayman Scholarships *(Undergraduate/Scholarship)*

Purpose: To provide educational assistance to all the students who are enrolled at PASSHE universities. **Focus:** General studies. **Qualif.:** Applicants must: be residents of Altoona; be full-time undergraduate students who plan to enroll at a Pennsylvania State System of Higher Education university. **Criteria:** Recipients are selected based on financial need.

Funds Avail.: $1,000. **To Apply:** Applicants must submit all the required application information.

5567 ■ Pension Real Estate Association

100 Pearl St., 13th Fl.
Hartford, CT 06103
Ph: (860)692-6341
Fax: (860)692-6351
E-mail: membership@prea.org
URL: http://www.prea.org

5568 ■ Pension Real Estate Association Scholarships *(Undergraduate/Scholarship)*

Purpose: To promote understanding of institutional investment in real estate. **Focus:** Real estate. **Qualif.:** Applicants must be students studying real estate at the undergraduate and graduate levels. **Criteria:** Recipients are selected based on financial need.

Funds Avail.: Total amount of $60,000. **To Apply:** Applicants must submit a completed application form.

5569 ■ People To People International

911 Main St., Ste. 2110
Kansas City, MO 64105
Ph: (816)531-4701
Fax: (816)561-7502
E-mail: ptpi@ptpi.org
URL: http://www.ptpi.org

5570 ■ Joyce C. Hall College Scholarships *(Undergraduate/Scholarship)*

Purpose: To encourage youth participation in international activities. **Focus:** General Studies. **Qualif.:** Applicants must be current members of People to People International with experience in at least one of the many programs offered during the past four years. Applicants must also be full-time college students or high school seniors maintaining a 3.0 grade point average on a 4.0 scale. **Criteria:** Recipients will be selected based on the evaluation of all application materials.

Funds Avail.: $2,000. Funds must be used to pay tuition first, before books and supplies. **Number Awarded:** 5. **To Apply:** Applicants must send an application form accompanied by: a statement of the applicant's participation in a People to People International activity, and what that experience meant to increasing his/her understanding of intercultural relations among the peoples of the world; an original essay not more than 1,000 words regarding "Why I believe international friendships are important and how my experiences have improved my understanding of people from other countries/cultures;" Statement of Financial Need Form; three letters of recommendation; transcript. High school seniors must provide proof that they are actively applying to a college or university. **Deadline:** October 15.

5571 ■ Pepperdine University School of Law

24255 Pacific Coast Highway
Malibu, CA 90263
Ph: (310)506-4611
E-mail: soladmis@pepperdine.edu
URL: http://law.pepperdine.edu

5572 ■ Associated Women for Pepperdine (AWP) Scholarships *(Undergraduate/Scholarship)*

Purpose: To assist students at Pepperdine University School. **Focus:** Education; Psychology; Law. **Qualif.:** Applicants must be admitted at Pepperdine University; and be members of the Church of Christ. **Criteria:** Recipient selection is based financial need, merit, character, and church membership.

Funds Avail.: No specific amount. **To Apply:** Applicants must submit a completed scholarship application form together with a resume, letter of qualifications, and a letter confirming active membership in a local Church of Christ congregation. **Deadline:** October 31.

5573 ■ Beck-Pfann Memorial Scholarships *(Undergraduate/Scholarship)*

Purpose: To assist students at Pepperdine University School of Law. **Focus:** Law. **Qualif.:** Applicants must be second-year students. **Criteria:** Recipient selection is based on community service, academic achievement, financial need, and extracurricular activities.

Funds Avail.: No specific amount. **To Apply:** Applicants must submit a completed scholarship application form together with a resume and a letter of qualifications. **Deadline:** October 31.

Remarks: Established in honor of R. Michael Beck and C. Lori Pfann.

5574 ■ David and Camille Boatwright Endowed Scholarships *(Undergraduate/Scholarship)*

Purpose: To assist students at Pepperdine University School of Law. **Focus:** Law. **Qualif.:** Applicants must be a Pepperdine University School of Law students. **Criteria:** Recipient of the award is determined by the Scholarship Committee.

Funds Avail.: No specific amount. **To Apply:** Applicants must submit a completed scholarship application form together with a resume, and letter of qualifications. **Deadline:** October 31.

5575 ■ Ann Marie Bredefeld Scholarships *(Undergraduate/Scholarship)*

Purpose: To assist students at Pepperdine University School of Law. **Focus:** Law. **Qualif.:** Applicants must be students who share the Christian values of Pepperdine. **Criteria:** Award is given based on merit.

Funds Avail.: No specific amount. **To Apply:** Applicants must submit a completed scholarship application form together with a resume and a letter of qualifications. **Deadline:** October 31.

5576 ■ Margaret Martin Brock Scholarships in Law *(Undergraduate/Scholarship)*

Purpose: To assist students at Pepperdine University School of Law. **Focus:** Law. **Qualif.:** Applicants must be Pepperdine University School of Law students. **Criteria:** Recipient of the award is determined by the Scholarship Committee.

Funds Avail.: No specific amount. **To Apply:** Applicants must submit a completed scholarship application form together with a resume and a letter of qualifications. **Deadline:** October 31.

Remarks: Scholarship fund was established by the late Mrs. Margaret Martin Brock.

5577 ■ Kae and Kay Brockermeyer Endowed Scholarships *(Undergraduate/Scholarship)*

Purpose: To assist students at Pepperdine University School of Law. **Focus:** Law. **Qualif.:** Applicants must be law students interested in trial advocacy. Applicant must also be a resident of the state of Texas. **Criteria:** Award is given based on merit.

Funds Avail.: No specific amount. **To Apply:** Applicants must submit a completed scholarship application form together with a resume and a letter of qualifications. **Deadline:** October 31.

5578 ■ Shirley J. Brooke Endowed Scholarships *(Undergraduate/Scholarship)*

Purpose: To assist students at Pepperdine University School of Law. **Focus:** Law. **Qualif.:** Applicants must be female law students who demonstrate above average academic achievement. **Criteria:** Award is given based on merit.

Funds Avail.: No specific amount. **To Apply:** Applicants must submit a completed scholarship application form together with a resume and a letter of qualifications. **Deadline:** October 31.

5579 ■ Athalie Clarke Endowed Scholarships *(Undergraduate/Scholarship)*

Purpose: To assist students at Pepperdine University School of Law. **Focus:** Law. **Qualif.:** Applicants must be Pepperdine University School of Law students. **Criteria:** Recipient of the award is determined by the Scholarship Committee.

Funds Avail.: No specific amount. **To Apply:** Applicants

Awards are arranged alphabetically below their administering organizations

must submit a completed scholarship application form together with a resume and a letter of qualifications. **Deadline:** October 31.

Remarks: Funded by the late Athalie Irvine Clarke.

5580 ■ Brian Dane Cleary Memorial Scholarships *(Undergraduate/Scholarship)*

Purpose: To assist students at Pepperdine University School of Law. **Focus:** Law. **Qualif.:** Applicants must be Pepperdine University School of Law students. **Criteria:** Recipients will be selected based on financial need.

Funds Avail.: No specific amount. **To Apply:** Applicants must submit a completed scholarship application form together with a resume and a letter of qualifications. **Deadline:** October 31.

Remarks: Established by the family members and friends of Brian Dane Cleary, member of the Class of 1991, died in a car accident 18 days before graduation.

5581 ■ Hugh and Hazel Darling Dean Scholarships *(Undergraduate/Scholarship)*

Purpose: To encourage students to remain enrolled at the School of Law. **Focus:** Law. **Qualif.:** Applicants must be Pepperdine University School of Law students. **Criteria:** Recipients are selected based on academic excellence as well as school and community involvement.

Funds Avail.: No specific amount. **To Apply:** Applicants must submit a completed scholarship application form together with a resume and a letter of qualifications. **Deadline:** October 31.

5582 ■ Darling Foundation Endowed School of Law Scholarships *(Undergraduate/Scholarship)*

Purpose: To assist students at Pepperdine University School of Law. **Focus:** Law. **Qualif.:** Applicants must be Pepperdine University School of Law students. **Criteria:** Recipients will be selected based on financial need.

Funds Avail.: No specific amount. **To Apply:** Applicants must submit a completed scholarship application form together with a resume and a letter of qualifications. **Deadline:** October 31.

5583 ■ Martha Delman and Milton Arthur Krug Endowed Scholarships *(Undergraduate/Scholarship)*

Purpose: To assist students at Pepperdine University School of Law. **Focus:** Law. **Qualif.:** Applicants must be Pepperdine University School of Law students. **Criteria:** Recipient of the award is determined by the Scholarship Committee.

Funds Avail.: No specific amount. **To Apply:** Applicants must submit a completed scholarship application form together with a resume and a letter of qualifications. **Deadline:** October 31.

Remarks: Funded by the late Martha Delman Krug.

5584 ■ Edward D. Di Loreto-Odell S. McConnell Scholarships *(Undergraduate/Scholarship)*

Purpose: To assist students at Pepperdine University School of Law. **Focus:** Law. **Qualif.:** Applicants must be Pepperdine University School of Law students with high scholastic standing. **Criteria:** Recipients will be selected based on financial need.

Funds Avail.: No specific amount. **To Apply:** Applicants must submit a completed scholarship application form together with a resume and a letter of qualifications. **Deadline:** October 31.

5585 ■ R. Wayne Estes Endowed Scholarships *(Undergraduate/Scholarship)*

Purpose: To assist students at Pepperdine University School of Law. **Focus:** Law. **Qualif.:** Applicants must be Pepperdine University School of Law students. **Criteria:** Recipient of the award is determined by the Scholarship Committee.

Funds Avail.: No specific amount. **To Apply:** Applicants must submit a completed scholarship application form together with a resume and a letter of qualifications. **Deadline:** October 31.

Remarks: Established by former students, colleagues and friends of Professor Emeritus R. Wayne Estes.

5586 ■ Judge McIntyre Faries Scholarships *(Undergraduate/Scholarship)*

Purpose: To assist students at Pepperdine University School of Law. **Focus:** Law. **Qualif.:** Applicants must be Pepperdine University School of Law students. **Criteria:** Recipient of the award is determined by the Scholarship Committee.

Funds Avail.: No specific amount. **To Apply:** Applicants must submit a completed scholarship application form together with a resume and a letter of qualifications. **Deadline:** October 31.

Remarks: Established by John Herlotz to honor California jurist, Judge McIntyre Faries.

5587 ■ Froberg-Suess JD/MBA Scholarships *(Undergraduate/Scholarship)*

Purpose: To assist students at Pepperdine University School of Law. **Focus:** Law. **Qualif.:** Applicants must have successfully completed at least one semester of law school and one semester of business school. **Criteria:** Recipients are selected based on merit.

Funds Avail.: No specific amount. **To Apply:** Applicants must submit a completed scholarship application form together with a resume and a letter of qualifications. **Deadline:** October 31.

Remarks: Applicants are required to make a moral pledge to give back to the scholarship fund within five years of the date of graduation from Pepperdine's School of Law.

5588 ■ Gerald Garner Memorial Scholarships *(Undergraduate/Scholarship)*

Purpose: To assist students at Pepperdine University School of Law. **Focus:** Law. **Qualif.:** Applicants must be Pepperdine University School of Law students. **Criteria:** Recipient of the award is determined by the Scholarship Committee.

Funds Avail.: No specific amount. **To Apply:** Applicants must submit a completed scholarship application form together with a resume and a letter of qualifications. **Deadline:** October 31.

Remarks: Established in memory of Gerald Garner.

5589 ■ Terry M. Giles Honor Scholarships *(Undergraduate/Scholarship)*

Purpose: To assist students at Pepperdine University School of Law. **Focus:** Law. **Qualif.:** Applicants must be

Awards are arranged alphabetically below their administering organizations

third-year students. **Criteria:** Recipients are selected based on scholastic achievement, co-curricular and extracurricular activities, personality and character.

Funds Avail.: No specific amount. **To Apply:** Applicants must submit a completed scholarship application form together with a resume and a letter of qualifications. **Deadline:** October 31.

Remarks: Sponsored by Terry M. Giles (class of 1974).

5590 ■ Guy P. Greenwald Jr. Endowed Scholarships *(Undergraduate/Scholarship)*

Purpose: To assist students at Pepperdine University School of Law. **Focus:** Law. **Qualif.:** Applicants must be Pepperdine University School of Law students. **Criteria:** Recipients will be selected based on financial need.

Funds Avail.: No specific amount. **To Apply:** Applicants must submit a completed scholarship application form together with a resume and a letter of qualifications. **Deadline:** October 31.

Remarks: Established by the late Guy P. Greenwald, attorney and Pepperdine friend.

5591 ■ Warren and Rosalie Gummow Endowed Scholarships *(Undergraduate/Scholarship)*

Purpose: To assist students at Pepperdine University School of Law. **Focus:** Law. **Qualif.:** Applicants must be Pepperdine University School of Law students. **Criteria:** Recipients will be selected based on financial need.

Funds Avail.: No specific amount. **To Apply:** Applicants must submit a completed scholarship application form together with a resume and a letter of qualifications. **Deadline:** October 31.

Remarks: Funded by Rosalie and the late Warren Gummow.

5592 ■ Mark and Michelle Hiepler Endowed Scholarships *(Undergraduate/Scholarship)*

Purpose: To assist students at Pepperdine University School of Law. **Focus:** Law. **Qualif.:** Applicants must be the writers of the Best Respondent's Brief and Best Petitioner's Brief in the yearly Vincent S. Dalsimer Moot Court Competition. **Criteria:** Scholarships will be awarded based on financial need, academic study, community involvement, and health care law interest or health care background.

Funds Avail.: Total of $1,000. **To Apply:** Applicants must submit a completed scholarship application form together with a resume and a letter of qualifications. **Deadline:** October 31.

Remarks: Established by Mark (class of 1988) and Michelle (class of 1989) Hiepler, in memory of Nelene Hiepler Fox.

5593 ■ JD/MBA Scholarships *(Undergraduate/Scholarship)*

Purpose: To assist students at Pepperdine University School of Law. **Focus:** Law; Business. **Qualif.:** Applicant must be a student enrolled in the joint JD and MBA program at the School of Law and Graziadio School of Business and Management. Applicant must be in good standing in all areas of the University. **Criteria:** Award is given based on merit.

Funds Avail.: No specific amount. **To Apply:** Applicants must submit a completed scholarship application form together with a resume and a letter of qualifications. **Deadline:** October 31.

5594 ■ JSR Foundation Endowed School of Law Scholarships *(Undergraduate/Scholarship)*

Purpose: To assist students at Pepperdine University School of Law. **Focus:** Law. **Qualif.:** Applicants must be Pepperdine University School of Law students. **Criteria:** Recipients will be selected based on financial need.

Funds Avail.: No specific amount. **To Apply:** Applicants must submit a completed scholarship application form together with a resume and a letter of qualifications. **Deadline:** October 31.

Remarks: Funded by JSR (Joan Stuart Richard) Foundation.

5595 ■ Woodrow Judkins Endowed Scholarships *(Undergraduate/Scholarship)*

Purpose: To assist students at Pepperdine University School of Law. **Focus:** Law. **Qualif.:** Applicants must be Pepperdine University School of Law students with good academic standing. **Criteria:** Recipient of the award is determined by the Scholarship Committee.

Funds Avail.: No specific amount. **To Apply:** Applicants must submit a completed scholarship application form together with a resume and a letter of qualifications. **Deadline:** October 31.

5596 ■ Kerrigan Scholarships *(Undergraduate/Scholarship)*

Purpose: To assist students at Pepperdine University School of Law. **Focus:** Law. **Qualif.:** Applicant must be a single-parent mother at the School of Law. **Criteria:** Award is given based on merit and need.

Funds Avail.: No specific amount. **To Apply:** Applicants must submit a completed scholarship application form together with a resume and a letter of qualifications. **Deadline:** October 31.

Remarks: Established by Sharon Kerrigan, 1992 School of Law alumna.

5597 ■ Krist-Reavley Minority Scholarships *(Undergraduate/Scholarship)*

Purpose: To assist students at Pepperdine University School of Law. **Focus:** Law. **Qualif.:** Applicant must be an ethnically diverse student. **Criteria:** Award is given based on merit and need.

Funds Avail.: No specific amount. **To Apply:** Applicants must submit a completed scholarship application form together with a resume and a letter of qualifications. **Deadline:** October 31.

Remarks: Established by noted trial attorney Ronald D. Krist and his wife, Carole.

5598 ■ Julia Kwan Endowed Scholarships *(Graduate/Scholarship)*

Purpose: To assist students at Pepperdine University School of Law. **Focus:** Law. **Qualif.:** Applicants must be Pepperdine University School of Law students pursuing a graduate degree. **Criteria:** Recipients will be selected based on financial need.

Funds Avail.: No specific amount. **To Apply:** Applicants must submit a completed scholarship application form together with a resume and a letter of qualifications. **Deadline:** October 31.

Remarks: Funded by Julia Kwan.

5599 ■ Albert J. and Mae Lee Memorial Scholarships *(Undergraduate/Scholarship)*

Purpose: To assist students at Pepperdine University School of Law. **Focus:** Law. **Qualif.:** Applicants must be Pepperdine University School of Law students with above average scholastic ability, and who are in need of financial assistance. **Criteria:** Award is given based on merit and financial need.

Funds Avail.: No specific amount. **To Apply:** Applicants must submit a completed scholarship application form together with a resume and a letter of qualifications. **Deadline:** October 31.

5600 ■ Greg Matthews Memorial Scholarships *(Undergraduate/Scholarship)*

Purpose: To assist students at Pepperdine University School of Law. **Focus:** Law. **Qualif.:** Applicants must be Pepperdine University School of Law students. **Criteria:** Recipients will be selected based on financial need.

Funds Avail.: No specific amount. **To Apply:** Applicants must submit a completed scholarship application form together with a resume and a letter of qualifications. **Deadline:** October 31.

5601 ■ J. McDonald and Judy Williams School of Law Scholarships *(Undergraduate/Scholarship)*

Purpose: To assist students at Pepperdine University School of Law. **Focus:** Law. **Qualif.:** Applicants must be admitted at Pepperdine University; and must be members of the Church of Christ. **Criteria:** Award is given based on merit and financial need.

Funds Avail.: No specific amount. **To Apply:** Applicants must submit a completed scholarship application form together with a resume, letter of qualifications, and a letter confirming active membership in a local Church of Christ congregation. **Deadline:** October 31.

5602 ■ John Merrick Law Scholarships *(Undergraduate/Scholarship)*

Purpose: To assist students at Pepperdine University School of Law. **Focus:** Law. **Qualif.:** Applicants must be Pepperdine University School of Law students. **Criteria:** Preference is given to those with an interest in public service.

Funds Avail.: No specific amount. **To Apply:** Applicants must submit a completed scholarship application form together with a resume and a letter of qualifications. **Deadline:** October 31.

Remarks: Established in honor of long-time Malibu judge John Merrick.

5603 ■ Charles I. Nelson Endowed Scholarships *(Undergraduate/Scholarship)*

Purpose: To assist students at Pepperdine University School of Law. **Focus:** Law. **Qualif.:** Applicants must be Pepperdine University School of Law students. **Criteria:** Recipient of the award is determined by the Scholarship Committee.

Funds Avail.: No specific amount. **To Apply:** Applicants must submit a completed scholarship application form together with a resume and a letter of qualifications. **Deadline:** October 31.

Remarks: Established by Kae Brockemeyer in honor of Professor Emeritus Charles I. Nelson.

5604 ■ Gunnar Nicholson Endowed Scholarships *(Undergraduate/Scholarship)*

Purpose: To assist students at Pepperdine University School of Law. **Focus:** Law. **Qualif.:** Applicants must be Pepperdine University School of Law students. **Criteria:** Recipient of the award is determined by the Scholarship Committee.

Funds Avail.: No specific amount. **To Apply:** Applicants must submit a completed scholarship application form together with a resume and a letter of qualifications. **Deadline:** October 31.

5605 ■ Pepperdine University Armenian Student Scholarships *(Undergraduate/Scholarship)*

Purpose: To assist students at Pepperdine University School of Law. **Focus:** Law. **Qualif.:** Applicants must be law students of Armenian heritage; and must be admitted at Pepperdine University School of Law. **Criteria:** Award is given based on merit.

Funds Avail.: No specific amount. **To Apply:** Applicants must submit a completed application form together with a resume and a letter of qualifications. **Deadline:** October 31.

Remarks: Established by Khajak Kassabian, a 1997 School of Law alum.

5606 ■ Pepperdine University Dean's Scholarships *(Doctorate, Graduate/Scholarship)*

Purpose: To assist students in the Juris Doctor program at Pepperdine University School of Law. **Focus:** Law. **Qualif.:** Applicants must be admitted as full-time students at the Juris Doctor program at Pepperdine University School of Law in fall or spring semesters only; must have an undergraduate GPA of 3.5 or higher; and an LSAT score in the 88th percentile. **Criteria:** Award is given based on merit.

Funds Avail.: Varies. **To Apply:** Applicants admitted full-time will be automatically considered.

5607 ■ Pepperdine University Diversity Scholarships *(Doctorate, Graduate/Scholarship)*

Purpose: To assist students at Pepperdine University School of Law. **Focus:** Law. **Qualif.:** Applicants must be admitted as full-time students of the Juris Doctor program at Pepperdine University School of Law in the fall or spring semesters only. Applicants must have the ability to bring significant diversity to the student body. **Criteria:** Award is given based on merit.

Funds Avail.: Varies. **To Apply:** Applicants must submit a completed Diversity Scholarship application to the Admissions Office. **Deadline:** February 1.

5608 ■ Pepperdine University Faculty Scholarships *(Doctorate, Graduate/Scholarship)*

Purpose: To assist students in the Juris Doctor program at Pepperdine University School of Law. **Focus:** Law. **Qualif.:** Applicants must be admitted as full-time students at the Juris Doctor program at Pepperdine University School of Law in the fall or spring semesters only; have a minimum undergraduate GPA of 3.5; and an LSAT score in the 93rd percentile. **Criteria:** Recipients are selected based on academic excellence and personal achievement, without regard to financial need.

Funds Avail.: Full tuition plus a $5,000 stipend. **To Apply:** Applicants must submit a complete admission file; faculty scholar application; and a letter to the Office of Admissions. **Deadline:** January 10.

5609 ■ Jamie Phillips Endowed Scholarships *(Undergraduate/Scholarship)*

Purpose: To assist students at Pepperdine University School of Law. **Focus:** Law. **Qualif.:** Applicants must be Pepperdine University School of Law students. **Criteria:** Recipient of the award is determined by the Scholarship Committee.

Funds Avail.: No specific amount. **To Apply:** Applicants must submit a completed scholarship application form together with a resume and a letter of qualifications. **Deadline:** October 31.

Remarks: Established in memory of Jamie Phillips, wife of School of Law Dean Emeritus Ronald F. Phillips.

5610 ■ John Purfield Endowed Scholarships *(Undergraduate/Scholarship)*

Purpose: To assist students at Pepperdine University School of Law. **Focus:** Law. **Qualif.:** Applicants must be Pepperdine University School of Law students. **Criteria:** Award is given based on academic excellence.

Funds Avail.: No specific amount. **To Apply:** Applicants must submit a completed scholarship application form together with a resume and a letter of qualifications. **Deadline:** October 31.

Remarks: Established by John Purfield. .

5611 ■ Barbara A. Shacochis Scholarships *(Undergraduate/Scholarship)*

Purpose: To assist students at Pepperdine University School of Law. **Focus:** Law. **Qualif.:** Applicants must be Pepperdine University School of Law students and members of the Law Review. **Criteria:** Preference will be given to third year Law Review students or editors of the Law Review.

Funds Avail.: No specific amount. **To Apply:** Applicants must submit a completed scholarship application form together with a resume and a letter of qualifications. **Deadline:** October 31.

5612 ■ Benjamin G. Shatz Scholarships *(Undergraduate/Scholarship)*

Purpose: To assist students at Pepperdine University School of Law. **Focus:** Law. **Qualif.:** Applicants must be second or third-year students and an active members of the Jewish Law Student Association. **Criteria:** Award is given based on merit and financial need.

Funds Avail.: No specific amount. **To Apply:** Applicants must submit a completed scholarship application form together with a resume and a letter of qualifications. **Deadline:** October 31.

Remarks: Sponsored by Benjamin G. Shatz (class of 1992).

5613 ■ Stuart Silverman Scholarships *(Undergraduate/Scholarship)*

Purpose: To assist students at Pepperdine University School of Law. **Focus:** Law. **Qualif.:** Applicants must be Pepperdine University School of Law students pursuing a Juris Doctorate degree at the School of Law; and must have overcome a major tragedy or hardship. **Criteria:** Award is given based on need.

Funds Avail.: No specific amount. **To Apply:** Applicants must submit a completed scholarship application form together with a resume and a letter of qualifications. **Deadline:** October 31.

5614 ■ Special Law School Scholarships *(Undergraduate/Scholarship)*

Purpose: To assist students at Pepperdine University School of Law. **Focus:** Law. **Qualif.:** Applicants must be Pepperdine University School of Law students with a special financial need. **Criteria:** Award is given based on financial need.

Funds Avail.: No specific amount. **To Apply:** Applicants must submit a completed scholarship application form together with a resume and a letter of qualifications. **Deadline:** October 31.

5615 ■ Honorable Raymond Thompson Endowed Scholarships *(Undergraduate/Scholarship)*

Purpose: To assist students at Pepperdine University School of Law. **Focus:** Law. **Qualif.:** Applicants must be Pepperdine University School of Law students. **Criteria:** Award is given based on public service, extracurricular activities, financial need and merit.

Funds Avail.: No specific amount. **To Apply:** Applicants must submit a completed scholarship application form together with a resume and a letter of qualifications. **Deadline:** October 31.

Remarks: Established in memory of Raymond H. Thompson, Superior Court Judge and Professor Emeritus at the School of Law.

5616 ■ Thomas and Glenna Trimble Endowed Scholarships *(Undergraduate/Scholarship)*

Purpose: To assist students at Pepperdine University School. **Focus:** Law. **Qualif.:** Applicants must be admitted at Pepperdine University; and must be members of the Church of Christ. **Criteria:** Award is given based on financial need, merit, character, and church membership.

Funds Avail.: No specific amount. **To Apply:** Applicants must submit a completed scholarship application form together with a resume, letter of qualifications, and a letter confirming active membership in a local Church of Christ congregation. **Deadline:** October 31.

Remarks: Established by Tom and Glenna Trimble.

5617 ■ Brian J. White Endowed Law Scholarships *(Undergraduate/Scholarship)*

Purpose: To assist students at Pepperdine University School. **Focus:** Law. **Qualif.:** Applicants must be practicing Christians committed to pursuing a career in criminal defense; must actively worship with a local congregation and be committed to Christ. **Criteria:** Award is given based on a review of all application materials.

Funds Avail.: No specific amount. **To Apply:** Applicants must submit a completed scholarship application form together with a resume, letter of qualifications, and a letter of confirmation from a minister or priest. **Deadline:** October 31.

Remarks: Established by Brian White.

5618 ■ Howard A. White Endowed Scholarships *(Undergraduate/Scholarship)*

Purpose: To assist students at Pepperdine University School of Law. **Focus:** Law. **Qualif.:** Applicants must be

Awards are arranged alphabetically below their administering organizations

Pepperdine University School of Law students. **Criteria:** Award is given based on merit.

Funds Avail.: No specific amount. **To Apply:** Applicants must submit a completed scholarship application form together with a resume and a letter of qualifications. **Deadline:** October 31.

Remarks: Established in honor of Howard A. White, President Emeritus of Pepperdine University.

5619 ■ Petroleum Packaging Council

1219 Ganado
San Clemente, CA 92673
Ph: (949)369-7102
Fax: (949)498-6496
E-mail: ppc@atdmanagement.com
URL: http://www.ppcouncil.org

5620 ■ Petroleum Packaging Council Scholarships *(Undergraduate/Scholarship)*

Purpose: To provide technical leadership and education for the petroleum packaging industry. **Focus:** Packaging. **Qualif.:** Must be a member of PPC with good standing. **Criteria:** Scholarships are given based on the academic performance of the student.

Funds Avail.: $2,500. **To Apply:** Applications are available online. Applicant must be a member to access the links. **Deadline:** April 1. **Contact:** Brenda Baker 949-369-7102.

5621 ■ Phi Beta Kappa

1606 New Hampshire Ave. NW
Washington, DC 20009
Ph: (202)265-3808
Fax: (202)986-1601
E-mail: info@pbk.org
URL: http://staging.pbk.org

5622 ■ Walter J. Jensen Fellowships *(Professional Development/Fellowship)*

Purpose: To help educators and researchers improve education in standard French language, literature and culture as well as in the study of standard French in the United States. **Focus:** French studies. **Qualif.:** Candidates must be U.S. citizens under the age of 40 who can demonstrate their career does or will involve active use of the French language; must have earned a bachelor's degree from an accredited four-year institution with 3.0 minimum GPA in French language and literature as a major; and must demonstrate superior competence in French according to the standards established by the American Association of Teachers of French. **Criteria:** Preference may be given to members of Phi Beta Kappa and educators at the secondary school level or higher.

Funds Avail.: $10,000. **To Apply:** Further information may be obtained from the Awards Coordinators.

5623 ■ Mary Isabel Sibley Fellowships *(Doctorate/Fellowship)*

Purpose: To increase interest in the study of Greek language, history, literature or archaeology, or the study of French language or literature. **Focus:** French studies, Greek studies. **Qualif.:** Candidates must be unmarried women 25 to 35 years of age who have demonstrated their ability to carry on with an original research; must hold a doctoral degree or have fulfilled all the requirements for a doctorate except for the dissertation; must be planning to full-time work to research during the fellowship year; and must be Phi Beta Kappa members or U.S citizens. **Criteria:** Selection of the applicants will be based on the criteria of the Fellowship Committee.

Funds Avail.: $20,000. **To Apply:** Further information may be obtained from the Awards Coordinators. **Deadline:** January 15.

5624 ■ Phi Chi Theta

1508 E Beltline Rd., Ste. 104
Carrollton, TX 75006
Ph: (972)245-7202
E-mail: executivedirector@phichitheta.org
URL: http://www.phichitheta.org

5625 ■ Anna E. Hall Memorial Scholarships *(Undergraduate/Scholarship)*

Purpose: To support students who have made a substantial contribution and impact to the organization or local community intending to pursue a degree in the fields of business and/or economics. **Focus:** Business; Economics. **Qualif.:** Applicants must be national members of Phi Chi Theta in good standing; must be students who have completed at least one semester or two quarters of college in the United States and will be enrolled in and attending classes during the forthcoming academic year at an approved college or university in the United States (in pursuit of a degree in the fields of Business and/or Economics). **Criteria:** Candidates will be selected based on: achievements and contributions to the Phi Chi Theta; scholastic achievement as demonstrated in transcript; courses enrolled in during the Spring Semester of 2008; school and community achievement and activities; letters of recommendation from a Phi Chi Theta Fraternity officer; an essay explaining of how do they see themselves, using their Phi Chi Theta experience and scholastic achievement, realizing their career goals in the next 3-5 years; and resume.

Funds Avail.: $500. **To Apply:** Applicants may visit the Phi Chi Theta Educational Foundation's website for application information and instructions. **Deadline:** May 1.

5626 ■ Helen D. Snow Memorial Scholarships *(Undergraduate/Scholarship)*

Purpose: To support students who have made a substantial contribution and impact to the organization or local community pursuing a degree in the fields of business and/or economics. **Focus:** Business; Economics. **Qualif.:** Applicants must be national members of Phi Chi Theta in good standing; must be students who have completed at least one semester or two quarters of college in the United States and will be enrolled in and attending classes during the forthcoming academic year at an approved college or university in the United States in pursuit of a degree in the fields of business and/or economics. **Criteria:** Candidates will be selected based on: achievements and contributions to the Phi Chi Theta; scholastic achievement as demonstrated in transcript; courses enrolled in during the Spring Semester of 2008; school and community achievement and activities; letters of recommendation from a Phi Chi Theta Fraternity officer; an essay explaining of how do they see themselves, using their Phi Chi Theta experience and scholastic achievement, realizing their career goals in the next 3-5 years; and resume.

Funds Avail.: $500. **To Apply:** Applicants may visit the Phi

Chi Theta Educational Foundation's website for application information and instructions. **Deadline:** May 1.

5627 ■ Phi Kappa Phi

7576 Goodwood Blvd.
Baton rouge, LA 70806
Ph: (225)388-4917
Fax: (225)388-4900
Free: 800-804-9880
E-mail: info@phikappaphi
URL: http://www.phikappaphi.org

5628 ■ Phi Kappa Phi Emerging Scholar Awards *(Undergraduate/Award/Prize)*

Purpose: To recognize and encourage academic achievement in all disciplines. **Focus:** General studies. **Qualif.:** Applicant must have a cumulative GPA of 3.75 on 4.0 scale and at least earned 30 semester hours as a full-time student during 2007 and spring 2008 academic year at an institution that has an active Phi Kappa Phi chapter. **Criteria:** Applicants will be evaluated based on academic recognition, awards, community activity and leadership.

Funds Avail.: $250. **Number Awarded:** 60. **To Apply:** Applicant must answer and submit type-written applications downloadable on the organization's website. **Deadline:** July 14.

5629 ■ Phi Kappa Phi Fellowships *(Other/Fellowship)*

Purpose: To provide financial support for members entering the first year of graduate or professional study. **Focus:** General studies. **Qualif.:** Applicants must be active members of Phi Kappa Phi and have applied to enroll as a full-time student in a post-baccalaureate program of study for the 2008-2009 academic year, at an accredited American Institution of higher learning. **Criteria:** Candidates will be evaluated based on academic achievement, including transcripts, honors and awards, relevant research experience, standardized test scores, and samples of creative work, service and leadership experience, on and off campus letters of recommendation, personal statement and career goals, and acceptance at an approved graduate or professional program.

Funds Avail.: $5,000. **Number Awarded:** 60. **To Apply:** Applicants must complete application online, print, and submit it with the other required materials to respective chapters. **Deadline:** February 1.

5630 ■ Phi Kappa Sigma

2 Timber Drive
Chester Springs, PA 19425
Ph: (610)469-3282
Fax: (610)469-3286
URL: http://www.pks.org

5631 ■ Phi Kappa Sigma Need-Based Scholarships *(Undergraduate/Scholarship)*

Purpose: To support student members with their educational pursuits. **Focus:** General studies. **Qualif.:** Applicant must be an officially registered member of Phi Kappa Sigma Fraternity; with initiation fee having been remitted by the chapter to the Fraternity Headquarters; and must be in undergraduate level. **Criteria:** Selection is based on financial need and scholastic achievement.

Funds Avail.: No specific amount. **To Apply:** Applicants must submit completed application forms along with the required materials. Official transcript of grades must be forwarded directly by the college registrar. All materials must be submitted to Reynold R. Hagel 6701 Sixth Avenue South Seattle, WA 98108, 206499-2393 or scholarship@pks.org. **Deadline:** May 31.

5632 ■ Phi Kappa Sigma Participation-Based Scholarships *(Undergraduate/Scholarship)*

Purpose: To support student members with their educational pursuits. **Focus:** General studies. **Qualif.:** Applicant must be an officially registered member of Phi Kappa Sigma Fraternity; with initiation fee having been remitted by the chapter to the Fraternity Headquarters; and must be in undergraduate level. **Criteria:** Selection is based on campus and community involvement and scholastic achievement.

Funds Avail.: No specific amount. **To Apply:** Applicants must submit completed application forms along with the required materials. Official transcript of grades must be forwarded directly by the college registrar. All materials must be submitted to Reynold R. Hagel 6701 Sixth Avenue South Seattle, WA 98108, 206499-2393 or scholarship@pks.org. **Deadline:** May 31.

5633 ■ Phi Sigma Epsilon

3747 S Howell Ave.
Milwaukee, WI 53207
Ph: (414)328-1952
Fax: (414)328-1953
Free: 800-761-9350
E-mail: pse@pse.org
URL: http://www.pse.org

5634 ■ Anchor Plastics Scholarships *(Graduate, Undergraduate/Scholarship)*

Purpose: To advance education of Pi Sigma Epsilon student member in sales and marketing. **Focus:** Marketing and distribution. **Qualif.:** Applicant must be enrolled in an undergraduate program and working toward an undergraduate degree with at least one semester, two quarters or summer session left before graduation; or enrolled or planning to enroll in a Graduate Program and working toward a post graduate degree (such as an MBA) with at least one semester, two quarters or summer session left before graduation; or a graduating senior with outstanding loans to his/her university. **Criteria:** Selection is based on Pi Sigma Epsilon activities; career objectives/ educational goals; educational financing; overall and major GPA; and non-PSE activities/work experience.

Funds Avail.: $1000. **Number Awarded:** 1. **To Apply:** Applicants must submit a completed application form together with a one page description of qualifications (Pi Sigma Epsilon activities; Mu Kappa Tau activities; Career objectives; Educational goals; Campus/Community activities; Special achievements/awards; Employment history; Percent of education financed by self, parents, scholarships, other); and two letters of recommendation. send materials electronically to scholarships@pse.org. **Deadline:** January 18.

Remarks: Sponsored by Anchor Plastics.

5635 ■ Anheuser-Busch International Scholarships *(Graduate, Undergraduate/Scholarship)*

Purpose: To advance education of Pi Sigma Epsilon student member in sales and marketing. **Focus:** Marketing and distribution. **Qualif.:** Applicant must be enrolled in an undergraduate program and working toward an undergraduate degree with at least one semester, two quarters or summer session left before graduation; or enrolled or planning to enroll in a Graduate Program and working toward a post graduate degree (such as an MBA) with at least one semester, two quarters or summer session left before graduation; or a graduating senior with outstanding loans to his/her university. **Criteria:** Selection is based on Pi Sigma Epsilon activities; career objectives/ educational goals; educational financing; overall and major GPA; and non-PSE activities/work experience.

Funds Avail.: $1500. **Number Awarded:** 1. **To Apply:** Applicants must submit a completed application form together with a one page description of qualifications (Pi Sigma Epsilon activities; Mu Kappa Tau activities; Career objectives; Educational goals; Campus/Community activities; Special achievements/awards; Employment history; Percent of education financed by self, parents, scholarships, other); and two letters of recommendation. send materials electronically to scholarships@pse.org. **Deadline:** January 18.

Remarks: Sponsored by Anheuser-Busch.

5636 ■ Enterprise Rent-A-Car Scholarships
(Graduate, Undergraduate/Scholarship)

Purpose: To advance education of Pi Sigma Epsilon student member in sales and marketing. **Focus:** Marketing and distribution. **Qualif.:** Applicant must be enrolled in an undergraduate program and working toward an undergraduate degree with at least one semester, two quarters or summer session left before graduation; or enrolled or planning to enroll in a Graduate Program and working toward a post graduate degree (such as an MBA) with at least one semester, two quarters or summer session left before graduation; or a graduating senior with outstanding loans to his/her university. **Criteria:** Selection is based on Pi Sigma Epsilon activities; career objectives/ educational goals; educational financing; overall and major GPA; and non-PSE activities/work experience.

Funds Avail.: $1500. **Number Awarded:** 1. **To Apply:** Applicants must submit a completed application form together with a one page description of qualifications (Pi Sigma Epsilon activities; Mu Kappa Tau activities; Career objectives; Educational goals; Campus/Community activities; Special achievements/awards; Employment history; Percent of education financed by self, parents, scholarships, other); and two letters of recommendation. send materials electronically to scholarships@pse.org. **Deadline:** January 18.

Remarks: Sponsored by Enterprise Rent-A-Car.

5637 ■ Federated Insurance Scholarships
(Graduate, Undergraduate/Scholarship)

Purpose: To advance education of Pi Sigma Epsilon student member in sales and marketing. **Focus:** Marketing and distribution. **Qualif.:** Applicant must be enrolled in an undergraduate program and working toward an undergraduate degree with at least one semester, two quarters or summer session left before graduation; or enrolled or planning to enroll in a Graduate Program and working toward a post graduate degree (such as an MBA) with at least one semester, two quarters or summer session left before graduation; or a graduating senior with outstanding loans to his/her university. **Criteria:** Selection is based on Pi Sigma Epsilon activities; career objectives/ educational goals; educational financing; overall and major GPA; and non-PSE activities/work experience.

Funds Avail.: $1000. **Number Awarded:** 1. **To Apply:** Applicants must submit a completed application form together with a one page description of qualifications (Pi Sigma Epsilon activities; Mu Kappa Tau activities; Career objectives; Educational goals; Campus/Community activities; Special achievements/awards; Employment history; Percent of education financed by self, parents, scholarships, other); and two letters of recommendation. send materials electronically to scholarships@pse.org. **Deadline:** January 18.

Remarks: Sponsored by Federated Insurance.

5638 ■ William H. Harris Memorial Scholarships
(Graduate, Undergraduate/Scholarship)

Purpose: To advance education of Pi Sigma Epsilon student member in sales and marketing. **Focus:** Marketing and distribution. **Qualif.:** Applicant must be enrolled in an undergraduate program and working toward an undergraduate degree with at least one semester, two quarters or summer session left before graduation; or enrolled or planning to enroll in a Graduate Program and working toward a post graduate degree (such as an MBA) with at least one semester, two quarters or summer session left before graduation; or a graduating senior with outstanding loans to his/her university. **Criteria:** Selection is based on Pi Sigma Epsilon activities; career objectives/ educational goals; educational financing; overall and major GPA; and non-PSE activities/work experience.

Funds Avail.: $1500. **Number Awarded:** 1. **To Apply:** Applicants must submit a completed application form together with a one page description of qualifications (Pi Sigma Epsilon activities; Mu Kappa Tau activities; Career objectives; Educational goals; Campus/Community activities; Special achievements/awards; Employment history; Percent of education financed by self, parents, scholarships, other); and two letters of recommendation. send materials electronically to scholarships@pse.org. **Deadline:** January 18.

Remarks: In memory of PSE co-founder, William H. Harris.

5639 ■ Debbie Khalil Memorial Scholarships
(Graduate, Undergraduate/Scholarship)

Purpose: To advance education of Pi Sigma Epsilon student member in sales and marketing. **Focus:** Marketing and distribution. **Qualif.:** Applicant must be enrolled in an undergraduate program and working toward an undergraduate degree with at least one semester, two quarters or summer session left before graduation; or enrolled or planning to enroll in a Graduate Program and working toward a post graduate degree (such as an MBA) with at least one semester, two quarters or summer session left before graduation; or a graduating senior with outstanding loans to his/her university. **Criteria:** Selection is based on Pi Sigma Epsilon activities; career objectives/ educational goals; educational financing; overall and major GPA; and non-PSE activities/work experience.

Funds Avail.: $1500. **Number Awarded:** 1. **To Apply:** Applicants must submit a completed application form together with a one page description of qualifications (Pi Sigma Epsilon activities; Mu Kappa Tau activities; Career objectives; Educational goals; Campus/Community activities; Special achievements/awards; Employment history; Percent of education financed by self, parents, scholarships, other); and two letters of recommendation. send materials electronically to scholarships@pse.org. **Deadline:** January 18.

Remarks: In memory of Debbie Khalil.

5640 ■ Mach 1 Air Services Scholarships
(Graduate, Undergraduate/Scholarship)

Purpose: To advance education of Pi Sigma Epsilon student member in sales and marketing. **Focus:** Marketing and distribution. **Qualif.:** Applicant must be enrolled in an undergraduate program and working toward an undergraduate degree with at least one semester, two quarters or summer session left before graduation; or enrolled or planning to enroll in a Graduate Program and working toward a post graduate degree (such as an MBA) with at least one semester, two quarters or summer session left before graduation; or a graduating senior with outstanding loans to his/her university. **Criteria:** Selection is based on Pi Sigma Epsilon activities; career objectives/ educational goals; educational financing; overall and major GPA; and non-PSE activities/work experience.

Funds Avail.: $2000. **Number Awarded:** 1. **To Apply:** Applicants must submit a completed application form together with a one page description of qualifications (Pi Sigma Epsilon activities; Mu Kappa Tau activities; Career objectives; Educational goals; Campus/Community activities; Special achievements/awards; Employment history; Percent of education financed by self, parents, scholarships, other); and two letters of recommendation. send materials electronically to scholarships@pse.org. **Deadline:** January 18.

Remarks: Sponsored by Mach 1 Air Services.

5641 ■ MPower Scholarships *(Graduate, Undergraduate/Scholarship)*

Purpose: To advance education of Pi Sigma Epsilon student member in sales and marketing. **Focus:** Marketing and distribution. **Qualif.:** Applicant must be enrolled in an undergraduate program and working toward an undergraduate degree with at least one semester, two quarters or summer session left before graduation; or enrolled or planning to enroll in a Graduate Program and working toward a post graduate degree (such as an MBA) with at least one semester, two quarters or summer session left before graduation; or a graduating senior with outstanding loans to his/her university. **Criteria:** Selection is based on Pi Sigma Epsilon activities; career objectives/ educational goals; educational financing; overall and major GPA; and non-PSE activities/work experience.

Funds Avail.: $1000. **Number Awarded:** 1. **To Apply:** Applicants must submit a completed application form together with a one page description of qualifications (Pi Sigma Epsilon activities; Mu Kappa Tau activities; Career objectives; Educational goals; Campus/Community activities; Special achievements/awards; Employment history; Percent of education financed by self, parents, scholarships, other); and two letters of recommendation. send materials electronically to scholarships@pse.org. **Deadline:** January 18.

Remarks: Sponsored by MPower.

5642 ■ Northwestern Mutual Financial Network Scholarships *(Graduate, Undergraduate/Scholarship)*

Purpose: To advance education of Pi Sigma Epsilon student member in sales and marketing. **Focus:** Marketing and distribution. **Qualif.:** Applicant must be enrolled in an undergraduate program and working toward an undergraduate degree with at least one semester, two quarters or summer session left before graduation; or enrolled or planning to enroll in a Graduate Program and working toward a post graduate degree (such as an MBA) with at least one semester, two quarters or summer session left before graduation; or a graduating senior with outstanding loans to his/her university. **Criteria:** Selection is based on Pi Sigma Epsilon activities; career objectives/ educational goals; educational financing; overall and major GPA; and non-PSE activities/work experience.

Funds Avail.: $1500. **Number Awarded:** 1. **To Apply:** Applicants must submit a completed application form together with a one page description of qualifications (Pi Sigma Epsilon activities; Mu Kappa Tau activities; Career objectives; Educational goals; Campus/Community activities; Special achievements/awards; Employment history; Percent of education financed by self, parents, scholarships, other); and two letters of recommendation. send materials electronically to scholarships@pse.org. **Deadline:** January 18.

Remarks: Sponsored by Northwestern Mutual Life Insurance Company.

5643 ■ Phi Sigma Epsilon Innovation Scholarships *(Graduate, Undergraduate/Scholarship)*

Purpose: To advance education of Pi Sigma Epsilon student member in sales and marketing. **Focus:** Marketing and distribution. **Qualif.:** Applicant must be enrolled in an undergraduate program and working toward an undergraduate degree with at least one semester, two quarters or summer session left before graduation; or enrolled or planning to enroll in a Graduate Program and working toward a post graduate degree (such as an MBA) with at least one semester, two quarters or summer session left before graduation; or a graduating senior with outstanding loans to his/her university. **Criteria:** Selection is based on Pi Sigma Epsilon activities; career objectives/ educational goals; educational financing; overall and major GPA; and non-PSE activities/work experience.

Funds Avail.: $1500. **Number Awarded:** 1. **To Apply:** Applicants must submit a completed application form together with a one page description of qualifications (Pi Sigma Epsilon activities; Mu Kappa Tau activities; Career objectives; Educational goals; Campus/Community activities; Special achievements/awards; Employment history; Percent of education financed by self, parents, scholarships, other); and two letters of recommendation. send materials electronically to scholarships@pse.org. **Deadline:** January 18.

Remarks: Presented by 3M Corporation.

5644 ■ Phi Sigma Epsilon Past National President Scholarships *(Graduate, Undergraduate/Scholarship)*

Purpose: To advance education of Pi Sigma Epsilon student member in sales and marketing. **Focus:** Marketing and distribution. **Qualif.:** Applicant must be enrolled in an undergraduate program and working toward an undergraduate degree with at least one semester, two quarters or summer session left before graduation; or enrolled or planning to enroll in a Graduate Program and working toward a post graduate degree (such as an MBA) with at least one semester, two quarters or summer session left before graduation; or a graduating senior with outstanding loans to his/her university. **Criteria:** Selection is based on Pi Sigma Epsilon activities; career objectives/ educational goals; educational financing; overall and major GPA; and non-PSE activities/work experience.

Funds Avail.: $1500. **Number Awarded:** 1. **To Apply:** Applicants must submit a completed application form together with a one page description of qualifications (Pi Sigma Epsilon activities; Mu Kappa Tau activities; Career objectives; Educational goals; Campus/Community activities; Special achievements/awards; Employment history; Percent of education financed by self, parents, scholarships, other); and two letters of recommendation. send materials electronically to scholarships@pse.org. **Deadline:** January 18.

Remarks: Contributions came from past PSE National Presidents.

5645 ■ Sales and Marketing Executives International Scholarships *(Graduate, Undergraduate/Scholarship)*

Purpose: To assist in the development of future sales and marketing professionals. **Focus:** Marketing and distribution. **Qualif.:** Applicant must be enrolled in an undergraduate program and working toward an undergraduate degree with at least one semester, two quarters or summer session left before graduation; or enrolled or planning to enroll in a Graduate Program and working toward a post graduate degree (such as an MBA) with at least one semester, two quarters or summer session left before graduation; or a graduating senior with outstanding loans to his/her university. **Criteria:** Selection is based on Pi Sigma Epsilon activities; career objectives/ educational goals; educational financing; overall and major GPA; and non-PSE activities/ work experience.

Funds Avail.: $1500. **Number Awarded:** 1. **To Apply:** Applicants must submit a completed application form together with a one page description of qualifications (Pi Sigma Epsilon activities; Mu Kappa Tau activities; Career objectives; Educational goals; Campus/Community activities; Special achievements/awards; Employment history; Percent of education financed by self, parents, scholarships, other); and two letters of recommendation. send materials electronically to scholarships@pse.org. **Deadline:** January 18.

Remarks: Sponsored by Sales and Marketing Executives International.

5646 ■ The Standard Scholarships *(Graduate, Undergraduate/Scholarship)*

Purpose: To advance education of Pi Sigma Epsilon student member in sales and marketing. **Focus:** Marketing and distribution. **Qualif.:** Applicant must be enrolled in an undergraduate program and working toward an undergraduate degree with at least one semester, two quarters or summer session left before graduation; or enrolled or planning to enroll in a Graduate Program and working toward a post graduate degree (such as an MBA) with at least one semester, two quarters or summer session left before graduation; or a graduating senior with outstanding loans to his/her university. **Criteria:** Selection is based on Pi Sigma Epsilon activities; career objectives/ educational goals; educational financing; overall and major GPA; and non-PSE activities/work experience.

Funds Avail.: $1000. **Number Awarded:** 1. **To Apply:** Applicants must submit a completed application form together with a one page description of qualifications (Pi Sigma Epsilon activities; Mu Kappa Tau activities; Career objectives; Educational goals; Campus/Community activities; Special achievements/awards; Employment history; Percent of education financed by self, parents, scholarships, other); and two letters of recommendation. send materials electronically to scholarships@pse.org. **Deadline:** January 18.

Remarks: Sponsored by The Standard.

5647 ■ Student Media Group Scholarships *(Graduate, Undergraduate/Scholarship)*

Purpose: To advance education of Pi Sigma Epsilon student member in sales and marketing. **Focus:** Marketing and distribution. **Qualif.:** Applicant must be enrolled in an undergraduate program and working toward an undergraduate degree with at least one semester, two quarters or summer session left before graduation; or enrolled or planning to enroll in a Graduate Program and working toward a post graduate degree (such as an MBA) with at least one semester, two quarters or summer session left before graduation; or a graduating senior with outstanding loans to his/her university. **Criteria:** Selection is based on Pi Sigma Epsilon activities; career objectives/ educational goals; educational financing; overall and major GPA; and non-PSE activities/work experience.

Funds Avail.: $1000. **Number Awarded:** 1. **To Apply:** Applicants must submit a completed application form together with a one page description of qualifications (Pi Sigma Epsilon activities; Mu Kappa Tau activities; Career objectives; Educational goals; Campus/Community activities; Special achievements/awards; Employment history; Percent of education financed by self, parents, scholarships, other); and two letters of recommendation. send materials electronically to scholarships@pse.org. **Deadline:** January 18.

Remarks: Sponsored by Student Media Group.

5648 ■ Swivel Media Scholarships *(Graduate, Undergraduate/Scholarship)*

Purpose: To advance education of Pi Sigma Epsilon student member in sales and marketing. **Focus:** Marketing and distribution. **Qualif.:** Applicant must be enrolled in an undergraduate program and working toward an undergraduate degree with at least one semester, two quarters or summer session left before graduation; or enrolled or planning to enroll in a Graduate Program and working toward a post graduate degree (such as an MBA) with at least one semester, two quarters or summer session left before graduation; or a graduating senior with outstanding loans to his/her university. **Criteria:** Selection is based on Pi Sigma Epsilon activities; career objectives/ educational goals; educational financing; overall and major GPA; and non-PSE activities/work experience.

Funds Avail.: $2000. **Number Awarded:** 1. **To Apply:** Applicants must submit a completed application form together with a one page description qualifications (Pi Sigma Epsilon activities; Mu Kappa Tau activities; Career objectives; Educational goals; Campus/Community activities; Special achievements/awards; Employment history; Percent of education financed by self, parents, scholarships, other); and two letters of recommendation. send materials electronically to scholarships@pse.org. **Deadline:** January 18.

Remarks: Sponsored by Swivel Media.

5649 ■ Thrivent Financial Scholarships *(Graduate, Undergraduate/Scholarship)*

Purpose: To advance education of Pi Sigma Epsilon student member in sales and marketing. **Focus:** Marketing and distribution. **Qualif.:** Applicant must be enrolled in an undergraduate program and working toward an undergraduate degree with at least one semester, two quarters or summer session left before graduation; or enrolled or planning to enroll in a Graduate Program and working toward a post graduate degree (such as an MBA) with at least one semester, two quarters or summer session left before graduation; or a graduating senior with outstanding loans to his/her university. **Criteria:** Selection is based on Pi Sigma Epsilon activities; career objectives/ educational goals; educational financing; overall and major GPA; and non-PSE activities/work experience.

Funds Avail.: $1000. **Number Awarded:** 1. **To Apply:** Applicants must submit a completed application form together with a one page description of qualifications (Pi Sigma Epsilon activities; Mu Kappa Tau activities; Career objectives; Educational goals; Campus/Community activities; Special achievements/awards; Employment history; Percent

Awards are arranged alphabetically below their administering organizations

of education financed by self, parents, scholarships, other); and two letters of recommendation. send materials electronically to scholarships@pse.org. **Deadline:** January 18.

Remarks: Sponsored by Thrivent Financial.

5650 ■ Valpak Scholarships *(Graduate, Undergraduate/Scholarship)*

Purpose: To advance education of Pi Sigma Epsilon student member in sales and marketing. **Focus:** Marketing and distribution. **Qualif.:** Applicant must be enrolled in an undergraduate program and working toward an undergraduate degree with at least one semester, two quarters or summer session left before graduation; or enrolled or planning to enroll in a Graduate Program and working toward a post graduate degree (such as an MBA) with at least one semester, two quarters or summer session left before graduation; or a graduating senior with outstanding loans to his/her university. **Criteria:** Selection is based on Pi Sigma Epsilon activities; career objectives/ educational goals; educational financing; overall and major GPA; and non-PSE activities/work experience.

Funds Avail.: $1500. **Number Awarded:** 1. **To Apply:** Applicants must submit a completed application form together with a one page description of qualifications (Pi Sigma Epsilon activities; Mu Kappa Tau activities; Career objectives; Educational goals; Campus/Community activities; Special achievements/awards; Employment history; Percent of education financed by self, parents, scholarships, other); and two letters of recommendation. send materials electronically to scholarships@pse.org. **Deadline:** January 18.

Remarks: Sponsored by Valpak.

5651 ■ Vector Marketing Scholarships *(Graduate, Undergraduate/Scholarship)*

Purpose: To advance education of Pi Sigma Epsilon student member in sales and marketing. **Focus:** Marketing and distribution. **Qualif.:** Applicant must be enrolled in an undergraduate program and working toward an undergraduate degree with at least one semester, two quarters or summer session left before graduation; or enrolled or planning to enroll in a Graduate Program and working toward a post graduate degree (such as an MBA) with at least one semester, two quarters or summer session left before graduation; or a graduating senior with outstanding loans to his/her university. **Criteria:** Selection is based on Pi Sigma Epsilon activities; career objectives/ educational goals; educational financing; overall and major GPA; and non-PSE activities/work experience.

Funds Avail.: $1000. **Number Awarded:** 1. **To Apply:** Applicants must submit a completed application form together with a one page description of qualifications (Pi Sigma Epsilon activities; Mu Kappa Tau activities; Career objectives; Educational goals; Campus/Community activities; Special achievements/awards; Employment history; Percent of education financed by self, parents, scholarships, other); and two letters of recommendation. send materials electronically to scholarships@pse.org. **Deadline:** January 18.

Remarks: Sponsored by Vector Marketing.

5652 ■ Whan Memorial Scholarships *(Graduate, Undergraduate/Scholarship)*

Purpose: To advance education of Pi Sigma Epsilon student member in sales and marketing. **Focus:** Marketing and distribution. **Qualif.:** Applicant must be enrolled in an undergraduate program and working toward an undergraduate degree with at least one semester, two quarters or summer session left before graduation; or enrolled or planning to enroll in a Graduate Program and working toward a post graduate degree (such as a MBA) with at least one semester, two quarters or summer session left before graduation; or a graduating senior with outstanding loans to his/her university. **Criteria:** Selection is based on Pi Sigma Epsilon activities; career objectives/ educational goals; educational financing; overall and major GPA; and non-PSE activities/work experience.

Funds Avail.: $1500. **Number Awarded:** 2. **To Apply:** Applicants must submit a completed application form together with a one page description of qualifications (Pi Sigma Epsilon activities; Mu Kappa Tau activities; Career objectives; Educational goals; Campus/Community activities; Special achievements/awards; Employment history; Percent of education financed by self, parents, scholarships, other); and two letters of recommendation. send materials electronically to scholarships@pse.org. **Deadline:** January 18.

Remarks: In memory of Tony Whan, Past President of Sales & Marketing Executives International.

5653 ■ Xilinx Scholarships *(Graduate, Undergraduate/Scholarship)*

Purpose: To advance education of Pi Sigma Epsilon student member in sales and marketing. **Focus:** Marketing and distribution. **Qualif.:** Applicant must be enrolled in an undergraduate program and working toward an undergraduate degree with at least one semester, two quarters or summer session left before graduation; or enrolled or planning to enroll in a Graduate Program and working toward a post graduate degree (such as an MBA) with at least one semester, two quarters or summer session left before graduation; or a graduating senior with outstanding loans to his/her university. **Criteria:** Selection is based on Pi Sigma Epsilon activities; career objectives/ educational goals; educational financing; overall and major GPA; and non-PSE activities/work experience.

Funds Avail.: $1000. **Number Awarded:** 1. **To Apply:** Applicants must submit a completed application form together with a one page description of qualifications (Pi Sigma Epsilon activities; Mu Kappa Tau activities; Career objectives; Educational goals; Campus/Community activities; Special achievements/awards; Employment history; Percent of education financed by self, parents, scholarships, other); and two letters of recommendation. send materials electronically to scholarships@pse.org. **Deadline:** January 18.

Remarks: Sponsored by Xilinx.

5654 ■ Phi Sigma Pi National Honor Fraternity

2119 Ambassador Circle
Lancaster, PA 17603
Ph: (717)299-4710
Fax: (717)390-3054
E-mail: pspoffice@phisigmapi.org
URL: http://www.phisigmapi.org

5655 ■ Richard Cecil Todd and Clauda Pennock Todd Tripod Scholarships *(Graduate, Undergraduate/Scholarship)*

Purpose: To promote the future academic opportunity of Phi Sigma Pi Brothers. **Focus:** General studies. **Qualif.:** Applicant must be undergraduate student pursuing a Bachelor's Degree; or graduating senior entering a graduate school (must provide a proof of enrollment to a graduate program); an active Phi Sigma Pi member; and have a

Awards are arranged alphabetically below their administering organizations

GPA of 3.00. **Criteria:** Selection is based on application.

Funds Avail.: No specific amount. **To Apply:** Applicants must submit a completed application form; letters of recommendation; official transcript; and notification from the Financial Aid Office (if applicable). **Deadline:** April 15.

Remarks: All required materials must be typewritten.

5656 ■ Rolla F. Wood Graduate Scholarships *(Graduate/Scholarship)*

Purpose: To encourage the educational advancement of an alumni member. **Focus:** General studies. **Qualif.:** Applicants must be Phi Sigma Pi alumnus graduated in good standing and pursuing a postgraduate degree or certification (Proof of enrollment in a graduate/professional school program must be submitted); a member of the National Alumni Association; and have a GPA of 3.0. **Criteria:** Selection is based on the application.

Funds Avail.: No specific amount. **To Apply:** Applicants must submit a completed application form; letters of recommendation; official transcript; an essay; and notification from the Financial Aid Office (if applicable). **Deadline:** April 15.

Remarks: Established in 2004.

5657 ■ Phi Upsilon Omicron

PO Box 329
Fairmont, WV 26555
Ph: (304)368-0612
E-mail: info@phiu.org
URL: http://www.phiu.org

5658 ■ S. Penny Chappell Scholarships *(Undergraduate/Scholarship)*

Purpose: To promote education in advance family and consumer sciences and related areas. **Focus:** Fashion design; Textile science. **Qualif.:** Applicant must be a Phi U member; pursuing a baccalaureate degree in fashion design and construction, textile design and development and/or textile preservation. **Criteria:** Selection is based on the applicant's scholastic record; participation in Phi U and other collegiate activities; a statement of professional aims and goals; professional services; and recommendations.

Funds Avail.: No specific amount. **To Apply:** Applicants must submit an application; transcripts; recommendations. Application documents must be assembled in order, clipped together with a paper clip and placed in a 10" x 13" envelope. Enclose a self-addressed stamped postcard. **Deadline:** February 1.

Remarks: Applicants may apply for more than one fellowship.

5659 ■ Geraldine Clewell Fellowships - Doctoral Student *(Graduate/Fellowship)*

Purpose: To promote education in advance family and consumer sciences and related areas. **Focus:** Family planning; Consumer affairs. **Qualif.:** Applicant must be a Phi U member; a doctoral student in family and consumer sciences or a related area. **Criteria:** Selection is based on applicant's scholastic record; honors and recognitions; participation in honor society, professional, community, and other organizations; scholarly work; statement of professional goals; and recommendations. Preference is given to a student who desires to teach at the college/university level.

Funds Avail.: No specific amount. **To Apply:** Applicants must submit an application; transcripts; recommendations (at least one must be from major advisor). Application documents must be assembled in order, clipped together with a paper clip and placed in a 10" x 13" envelope. Enclose a self-addressed stamped postcard. **Deadline:** February 1.

Remarks: Applicants may apply for more than one fellowship.

5660 ■ Geraldine Clewell Fellowships - Masteral *(Graduate/Fellowship)*

Purpose: To promote education in advance family and consumer sciences and related areas. **Focus:** Family planning; Consumer affairs. **Qualif.:** Applicant must be a Phi U member; pursuing a master's degree in family and consumer sciences or related area. **Criteria:** Selection is based on applicant's scholastic record; honors and recognitions; participation in honor society, professional, community, and other organizations; scholarly work; statement of professional goals; and recommendations. Preference is given to a student majoring in family and consumer sciences education and who desires to teach at the elementary/secondary level.

Funds Avail.: No specific amount. **To Apply:** Applicants must submit an application; transcripts; recommendations (at least one must be from major advisor). Application documents must be assembled in order, clipped together with a paper clip and placed in a 10" x 13" envelope. Enclose a self-addressed stamped postcard. **Deadline:** February 1.

Remarks: Applicants may apply for more than one fellowship.

5661 ■ Geraldine Clewell Scholarships - Undergraduate *(Undergraduate/Scholarship)*

Purpose: To promote education in advance family and consumer sciences and related areas. **Focus:** Family planning; Consumer affairs. **Qualif.:** Applicant must be a Phi U member; enrolled full-time in a baccalaureate degree program in family and consumer sciences or a related area. **Criteria:** Selection is based on the applicant's scholastic record; participation in Phi U and other collegiate activities; a statement of professional aims and goals; professional services; and recommendations.

Funds Avail.: No specific amount. **To Apply:** Applicants must submit an application; transcripts; recommendations. Application documents must be assembled in order, clipped together with a paper clip and placed in a 10" x 13" envelope. Enclose a self-addressed stamped postcard. **Deadline:** February 1.

Remarks: Applicants may apply for more than one fellowship.

5662 ■ Closs/Parnitzke/Clarke Scholarships *(Undergraduate/Scholarship)*

Purpose: To promote education in advance family and consumer sciences and related areas. **Focus:** Family planning; Consumer affairs. **Qualif.:** Applicant must be a Phi U member; enrolled full-time in a baccalaureate degree program in family and consumer sciences or a related area. **Criteria:** Selection is based on the applicant's scholastic record; participation in Phi U and other collegiate activities; a statement of professional aims and goals; professional services; and recommendations.

Funds Avail.: No specific amount. **To Apply:** Applicants must submit an application; transcripts; recommendations. Application documents must be assembled in order, clipped together with a paper clip and placed in a 10" x 13" envelope. Enclose a self-addressed stamped postcard. **Deadline:** February 1.

Remarks: Applicants may apply for more than one fellowship.

5663 ■ Jean Dearth Dickerscheid Fellowships
(Graduate/Fellowship)

Purpose: To promote education in advance family and consumer sciences and related areas. **Focus:** Family planning; Consumer affairs. **Qualif.:** Applicant must be a Phi U member; pursuing a Ph.D. in family and consumer sciences or related area and has earned at least one other degree in family and consumer sciences; and interested for a career in academia. **Criteria:** Selection is based on applicant's scholastic record; honors and recognitions; participation in honor society, professional, community, and other organizations; scholarly work; statement of professional goals; and recommendations.

Funds Avail.: No specific amount. **To Apply:** Applicants must submit an application; transcripts; recommendations. Application documents must be assembled in order, clipped together with a paper clip and placed in a 10" x 13" envelope. Enclose a self-addressed stamped postcard. **Deadline:** February 1.

Remarks: Applicants may apply for more than one fellowship.

5664 ■ Margaret Drew Alpha Fellowships
(Graduate/Fellowship)

Purpose: To promote education in advance family and consumer sciences and related areas. **Focus:** Family planning; Consumer affairs; Nutrition. **Qualif.:** Applicant must be a Phi U member; in a graduate study in the field of family and consumer sciences. **Criteria:** Selection is based on applicant's scholastic record; honors and recognitions; participation in honor society, professional, community, and other organizations; scholarly work; statement of professional goals; and recommendations. Preference is given to a dietetics or food and nutrition major.

Funds Avail.: No specific amount. **To Apply:** Applicants must submit an application; transcripts; recommendations. Application documents must be assembled in order, clipped together with a paper clip and placed in a 10" x 13" envelope. Enclose a self-addressed stamped postcard. **Deadline:** February 1.

Remarks: Applicants may apply for more than one fellowship.

5665 ■ Genevieve Forthun Scholarships
(Undergraduate/Scholarship)

Purpose: To promote education in advance family and consumer sciences and related areas. **Focus:** Family planning; Consumer affairs. **Qualif.:** Applicant must be a Phi U member; enrolled full-time in a baccalaureate degree program in family and consumer sciences or a related area. **Criteria:** Selection is based on the applicant's scholastic record; participation in Phi U and other collegiate activities; a statement of professional aims and goals; professional services; and recommendations.

Funds Avail.: No specific amount. **To Apply:** Applicants must submit an application; transcripts; recommendations. Application documents must be assembled in order, clipped together with a paper clip and placed in a 10" x 13" envelope. Enclose a self-addressed stamped postcard. **Deadline:** February 1.

Remarks: Applicants may apply for more than one fellowship.

5666 ■ Mary Weiking Franken Scholarships
(Undergraduate/Scholarship)

Purpose: To promote education in advance family and consumer sciences and related areas. **Focus:** Family planning; Consumer affairs. **Qualif.:** Applicant must be a Phi U member; enrolled full-time in a baccalaureate degree program in family and consumer sciences or a related area. **Criteria:** Preference is given to students majoring in child/family or family and consumer sciences education.

Funds Avail.: No specific amount. **To Apply:** Applicants must submit an application; transcripts; recommendations. Application documents must be assembled in order, clipped together with a paper clip and placed in a 10" x 13" envelope. Enclose a self-addressed stamped postcard. **Deadline:** February 1.

Remarks: Applicants may apply for more than one fellowship.

5667 ■ Tommie J. Hamner Scholarships
(Undergraduate/Scholarship)

Purpose: To promote education in advance family and consumer sciences and related areas. **Focus:** Family planning; Consumer affairs. **Qualif.:** Applicant must be a Phi U member; enrolled full-time in a baccalaureate degree program in family and consumer sciences or a related area; and have shown exemplary commitment to Phi Upsilon Omicron. **Criteria:** Selection is based on the applicant's scholastic record; participation in Phi U and other collegiate activities; a statement of professional aims and goals; professional services; and recommendations.

Funds Avail.: No specific amount. **To Apply:** Applicants must submit an application; transcripts; recommendations. Application documents must be assembled in order, clipped together with a paper clip and placed in a 10" x 13" envelope. Enclose a self-addressed stamped postcard. **Deadline:** February 1.

Remarks: Applicants may apply for more than one fellowship.

5668 ■ Jackman Scholarships *(Undergraduate/Scholarship)*

Purpose: To promote education in advance family and consumer sciences and related areas. **Focus:** Family planning; Consumer affairs. **Qualif.:** Applicant must be a Phi U member; enrolled full-time in a baccalaureate degree program in family and consumer sciences or a related area; and have shown exemplary commitment to Phi Upsilon Omicron. **Criteria:** Selection is based on the applicant's scholastic record; participation in Phi U and other collegiate activities; a statement of professional aims and goals; professional services; and recommendations.

Funds Avail.: No specific amount. **To Apply:** Applicants must submit an application; transcripts; recommendations. Application documents must be assembled in order, clipped together with a paper clip and placed in a 10" x 13" envelope. Enclose a self-addressed stamped postcard. **Deadline:** February 1.

Remarks: Applicants may apply for more than one fellowship.

5669 ■ Martha Combs Jenkins Scholarships
(Undergraduate/Scholarship)

Purpose: To promote education in advance family and consumer sciences and related areas. **Focus:** Family planning; Consumer affairs. **Qualif.:** Applicant must be a Phi U member; pursuing a baccalaureate degree in family and consumer sciences or one of its related areas; and has shown exemplary commitment to Phi Upsilon Omicron. **Criteria:** Selection is based on the applicant's scholastic record; participation in Phi U and other collegiate activities; a statement of professional aims and goals; professional services; and recommendations.

Funds Avail.: No specific amount. **To Apply:** Applicants must submit an application; transcripts; recommendations. Application documents must be assembled in order, clipped together with a paper clip and placed in a 10" x 13" envelope. Enclose a self-addressed stamped postcard. **Deadline:** February 1.

Remarks: Applicants may apply for more than one fellowship.

5670 ■ Treva C. Kintner Scholarships *(Undergraduate/Scholarship)*

Purpose: To promote education in advance family and consumer sciences and related areas. **Focus:** Family planning; Consumer affairs. **Qualif.:** Applicant must be a Phi U member; a non-traditional student; completed at least half of the academic work toward a baccalaureate degree in family and consumer sciences or a related area. **Criteria:** Selection is based on the applicant's scholastic record; participation in Phi U and other collegiate activities; a statement of professional aims and goals; professional services; and recommendations.

Funds Avail.: No specific amount. **To Apply:** Applicants must submit an application; transcripts; recommendations. Application documents must be assembled in order, clipped together with a paper clip and placed in a 10" x 13" envelope. Enclose a self-addressed stamped postcard. **Deadline:** February 1.

Remarks: Applicants may apply for more than one fellowship.

5671 ■ Phi Upsilon Omicron Candle Fellowships *(Graduate/Fellowship)*

Purpose: To promote education in advance family and consumer sciences and related areas. **Focus:** Family planning; Consumer affairs. **Qualif.:** Applicant must be a Phi U member; enrolled or planning to enroll in a graduate school; and study leading to a master's degree in family and consumer sciences. **Criteria:** Selection is based on applicant's scholastic record; honors and recognitions; participation in honor society, professional, community, and other organizations; scholarly work; statement of professional goals; and recommendations.

Funds Avail.: No specific amount. **To Apply:** Applicants must submit an application; transcripts; recommendations. Application documents must be assembled in order, clipped together with a paper clip and placed in a 10" x 13" envelope. Enclose a self-addressed stamped postcard. **Deadline:** February 1.

Remarks: Applicants may apply for more than one fellowship.

5672 ■ Phi Upsilon Omicron Challenge Scholarships *(Undergraduate/Scholarship)*

Purpose: To promote education in advance family and consumer sciences and related areas. **Focus:** Family planning; Consumer affairs. **Qualif.:** Applicant must be a Phi U member; enrolled full-time in a baccalaureate degree program in family and consumer sciences or a related area. **Criteria:** Selection is based on the applicant's scholastic record; participation in Phi U and other collegiate activities; a statement of professional aims and goals; professional services; and recommendations.

Funds Avail.: No specific amount. **To Apply:** Applicants must submit an application; transcripts; recommendations. Application documents must be assembled in order, clipped together with a paper clip and placed in a 10" x 13" envelope. Enclose a self-addressed stamped postcard. **Deadline:** February 1.

Remarks: Applicants may apply for more than one fellowship.

5673 ■ Phi Upsilon Omicron Diamond Anniversary Fellowships *(Graduate/Fellowship)*

Purpose: To promote education in advance family and consumer sciences and related areas. **Focus:** Family planning; Consumer affairs. **Qualif.:** Applicant must be a Phi U member; accepted into or currently enrolled in a graduate program; studying at the master's or doctoral level in family and consumer sciences or a related area. **Criteria:** Selection is based on applicant's scholastic record; honors and recognitions; participation in honor society, professional, community, and other organizations; scholarly work; statement of professional goals; and recommendations.

Funds Avail.: No specific amount. **To Apply:** Applicants must submit an application; transcripts; recommendations. Application documents must be assembled in order, clipped together with a paper clip and placed in a 10" x 13" envelope. Enclose a self-addressed stamped postcard. **Deadline:** February 1.

Remarks: Applicants may apply for more than one fellowship.

5674 ■ Phi Upsilon Omicron Founders Fellowships *(Graduate/Fellowship)*

Purpose: To promote education in advance family and consumer sciences and related areas. **Focus:** Family planning; Consumer affairs. **Qualif.:** Applicant must be a Phi U member; have completed at least half the credit-hour requirements toward the doctorate in some area of family and consumer sciences and have had several years of successful employment in the profession. **Criteria:** Selection is based on applicant's scholastic record; honors and recognitions; participation in honor society, professional, community, and other organizations; scholarly work; statement of professional goals; and recommendations.

Funds Avail.: No specific amount. **To Apply:** Applicants must submit an application; transcripts; recommendations. Application documents must be assembled in order, clipped together with a paper clip and placed in a 10" x 13" envelope. Enclose a self-addressed stamped postcard. **Deadline:** February 1.

Remarks: Applicants may apply for more than one fellowship.

5675 ■ Phi Upsilon Omicron Golden Anniversary Scholarships *(Undergraduate/Scholarship)*

Purpose: To promote education in advance family and consumer sciences and related areas. **Focus:** Family planning; Consumer affairs. **Qualif.:** Applicant must be a Phi U member; enrolled full-time in a baccalaureate degree program in family and consumer sciences or a related area. **Criteria:** Selection is based on the applicant's scholastic record; participation in Phi U and other collegiate activities;

a statement of professional aims and goals; professional services; and recommendations.

Funds Avail.: No specific amount. **To Apply:** Applicants must submit an application; transcripts; recommendations. Application documents must be assembled in order, clipped together with a paper clip and placed in a 10" x 13" envelope. Enclose a self-addressed stamped postcard. **Deadline:** February 1.

Remarks: Applicants may apply for more than one fellowship.

5676 ■ Phi Upsilon Omicron Past Presidents Scholarships *(Undergraduate/Scholarship)*

Purpose: To promote education in advance family and consumer sciences and related areas. **Focus:** Family planning; Consumer affairs. **Qualif.:** Applicant must be a Phi U member; enrolled full-time in a baccalaureate degree program in family and consumer sciences or a related area. **Criteria:** Selection is based on the applicant's scholastic record; participation in Phi U and other collegiate activities; a statement of professional aims and goals; professional services; and recommendations.

Funds Avail.: No specific amount. **To Apply:** Applicants must submit an application; transcripts; recommendations. Application documents must be assembled in order, clipped together with a paper clip and placed in a 10" x 13" envelope. Enclose a self-addressed stamped postcard. **Deadline:** February 1.

Remarks: Applicants may apply for more than one fellowship.

5677 ■ Phi Upsilon Omicron Presidents Research Fellowships *(Graduate/Fellowship)*

Purpose: To promote education in advance family and consumer sciences and related areas. **Focus:** Family planning; Consumer affairs. **Qualif.:** Applicant must be a Phi U member; on a graduate research at the master's, doctoral or post-doctoral level in family and consumer sciences or a related area. **Criteria:** Selection is based on applicant's scholastic record; honors and recognitions; participation in honor society, professional, community, and other organizations; scholarly work; statement of professional goals; and recommendations.

Funds Avail.: No specific amount. **To Apply:** Applicants must submit an application; transcripts; recommendations; and include a research prospectus exhibiting organization and need for the research. Application documents must be assembled in order, clipped together with a paper clip and placed in a 10" x 13" envelope. Enclose a self-addressed stamped postcard. **Deadline:** February 1.

Remarks: Applicants may apply for more than one fellowship.

5678 ■ Nell Bryant Robinson Scholarships *(Undergraduate/Scholarship)*

Purpose: To promote education in advance family and consumer sciences and related areas. **Focus:** Family planning; Consumer affairs; Nutrition. **Qualif.:** Applicant must be a Phi U member; pursuing a baccalaureate degree in family and consumer sciences or one of its related areas. **Criteria:** Preference is given to student majoring in dietetics or food and nutrition.

Funds Avail.: No specific amount. **To Apply:** Applicants must submit an application; transcripts; recommendations. Application documents must be assembled in order, clipped together with a paper clip and placed in a 10" x 13" envelope. Enclose a self-addressed stamped postcard. **Deadline:** February 1.

Remarks: Applicants may apply for more than one fellowship.

5679 ■ Lucile Rust Scholarships *(Undergraduate/Scholarship)*

Purpose: To promote education in advance family and consumer sciences and related areas. **Focus:** Family planning; Consumer affairs. **Qualif.:** Applicant must be a Phi U member; enrolled full-time in a baccalaureate degree program in family and consumer sciences or a related area. **Criteria:** Selection is based on the applicant's scholastic record; participation in Phi U and other collegiate activities; a statement of professional aims and goals; professional services; and recommendations.

Funds Avail.: No specific amount. **To Apply:** Applicants must submit an application; transcripts; recommendations. Application documents must be assembled in order, clipped together with a paper clip and placed in a 10" x 13" envelope. Enclose a self-addressed stamped postcard. **Deadline:** February 1.

Remarks: Applicants may apply for more than one fellowship.

5680 ■ Margaret Jerome Sampson Scholarships *(Undergraduate/Scholarship)*

Purpose: To promote education in advance family and consumer sciences and related areas. **Focus:** Family planning; Consumer affairs; Nutrition. **Qualif.:** Applicant must be a Phi U member; enrolled full-time in a baccalaureate degree program in family and consumer sciences or a related area. **Criteria:** Selection is based on the applicant's scholastic record; participation in Phi U; professional aims and goals. Preference is given to student majoring in dietetics or food and nutrition.

Funds Avail.: $3000. **Number Awarded:** 4. **To Apply:** Applicants must submit an application; transcripts; recommendations (one must be from the Phi U chapter advisor). Application documents must be assembled in order, clipped together with a paper clip and placed in a 10" x 13" envelope. Enclose a self-addressed stamped postcard, a financial statement and one double-spaced typewritten page about the reasons for needing an additional financial assistance. **Deadline:** February 1.

Remarks: Applicants may apply for more than one fellowship.

5681 ■ Lillian P. Schoephoerster Scholarships *(Undergraduate/Scholarship)*

Purpose: To promote education in advance family and consumer sciences and related areas. **Focus:** Family planning; Consumer affairs. **Qualif.:** Applicant must be a Phi U member; a non-traditional student enrolled full-time in a baccalaureate degree program in family and consumer sciences or a related area. **Criteria:** Selection is based on the applicant's scholastic record; participation in Phi U and other collegiate activities; a statement of professional aims and goals; professional services; and recommendations.

Funds Avail.: $1000. **Number Awarded:** 2. **To Apply:** Applicants must submit an application; transcripts; recommendations. Application documents must be assembled in order, clipped together with a paper clip and placed in a 10" x 13" envelope. Enclose a self-addressed stamped postcard. **Deadline:** February 1.

Remarks: Applicants may apply for more than one fellowship.

5682 ■ Sutherland/Purdy Scholarships
(Undergraduate/Scholarship)

Purpose: To promote education in advance family and consumer sciences and related areas. **Focus:** Fashion design; Textile science. **Qualif.:** Applicant must be a Phi U member; pursuing a baccalaureate degree in clothing and textiles or a related area such as apparel design or fashion merchandising; have held a leadership position in her/his Phi U chapter; and have earned at least a 3.0 out of 4.0 overall point average. **Criteria:** Selection is based on the applicant's scholastic record; participation in Phi U and other collegiate activities; a statement of professional aims and goals; professional services; and recommendations.

Funds Avail.: No specific amount. **To Apply:** Applicants must submit an application; transcripts; recommendations. Application documents must be assembled in order, clipped together with a paper clip and placed in a 10" x 13" envelope. Enclose a self-addressed stamped postcard. **Deadline:** February 1.

Remarks: Applicants may apply for more than one fellowship.

5683 ■ Philanthropic Educational Organization

3700 Grand Ave.
Des Moines, IA 50312
Ph: (515)255-3153
Fax: (515)255-3820
E-mail: glane@peodsm.org
URL: http://www.peointernational.org

5684 ■ International Peace Scholarships
(Undergraduate/Scholarship)

Purpose: To provide scholarships for selected women from other countries for study in the United States and Canada. **Focus:** General studies. **Qualif.:** Applicants must be qualified for admission to full-time graduate study, working toward a graduate degree in the college or university. **Criteria:** Recipients are selected based on a non-discriminatory basis without consideration of race, national origin, religious affiliation, or disability.

Funds Avail.: $10,000 (total). **To Apply:** Applicants must submit completed application form; a copy of confirmation of admission; and a witnessed statement certifying that upon completion of their degree programs they will return to their own country within 60 days. **Deadline:** April 1.

5685 ■ PEO Educational Loan Funds *(Graduate, Undergraduate/Loan)*

Purpose: To promote educational opportunities for women who desire higher education and are in need of financial assistance. **Focus:** General studies. **Qualif.:** Applicants must be recommended by a local chapter of the P.E.O. sisterhood and must be within two years of completing their course of study. Program is also open for applicants who are graduate students in medical or law schools, seniors seeking a bachelor's degree or students enrolled in a hospital professional nurse training program, a non-collegiate, technical program, or vocational program in a college or university. **Criteria:** Recipients are selected based on financial need.

Funds Avail.: $9,000 (in total). **To Apply:** Applicants must submit a cover letter; application form with a packet checklist and instructions; school information form or proof of enrollment; transcript of records; request for permission to obtain credit report; acknowledgement of loan terms; and memo of indebtedness.

5686 ■ The Phillips Foundation

1 Massachusetts Ave. NW, Ste. 620
Washington, DC 20001
Ph: (202)250-3887
E-mail: jhollingsworth@thephillipsfoundation.org
URL: http://www.thephillipsfoundation.org

5687 ■ Ronald Reagan College Leaders Scholarship Program *(Undergraduate/Scholarship)*

Purpose: To assist students in alleviating financial burdens associated with higher education. **Focus:** General studies. **Qualif.:** Applicants must be U.S. citizens enrolled full-time in good standing at any accredited, four-year degree-granting institution in the United States or its territories. Those attending two-year schools may apply as juniors for a one-time scholarship for the senior year, upon transfer to a four-year institution. **Criteria:** Applicants are evaluated based on merit.

Funds Avail.: No specific amount. **To Apply:** Applicants must submit an essay of 500 to 750 words describing their backgrounds, career objectives and scope of participation in leadership activities promoting freedom, American values and constitutional principles.

5688 ■ PHS Commissioned Officers Foundation

8201 Corporate Dr., Ste. 200
Landover, MD 20785
Ph: (301)731-9080
Fax: (301)731-9084
E-mail: info@phscof.org
URL: http://www.phscof.org

5689 ■ Scholarship for Junior PHS Commissioned Officers *(Undergraduate/Scholarship)*

Purpose: To provide financial assistance to dependent children or dependent spouses of active duty, retired, or deceased officers of the USPHS Commissioned Corps. **Focus:** General studies. **Qualif.:** Applicants must be dependent children or spouses of active duty, retired or deceased officers of the USPHS Commissioned Corps; must be current or entering college/vocational students who have a minimum cumulative grade point average of 3.0 (on a 4.0 scale). **Criteria:** Applicants are evaluated based on criteria designed by the Scholarship Selection Committee.

Funds Avail.: No specific amount. **To Apply:** Applicants must submit all the required application information. **Deadline:** June 1.

5690 ■ Pi Gamma Mu

1001 Millington, Ste. B
Winfield, KS 67156
Ph: (620)221-3128
Fax: (620)221-7124
E-mail: pgm@sckans.edu
URL: http://www.pigammamu.org

5691 ■ Pi Gamma Mu Scholarships *(Graduate/Scholarship)*

Purpose: To provide financial support to qualified individuals to pursue education. **Focus:** Sociology, Anthropology,

Political science, History, Economics, International affairs and relations, Public administration, Criminal justice, Law, Social work, Psychology, Geography. **Qualif.:** Applicant must be a first or second year graduate student in the areas of sociology, anthropology, political science, history, economics, international relations, public administration, criminal justice, law, social work, psychology, and human/ cultural geography. **Criteria:** Application will be evaluated based upon the degree to which the social sciences are an integral component of the overall course of study.

Funds Avail.: $2,000 or $1,000 award to attend graduate school. **Number Awarded:** No more than 3. **To Apply:** Applicant must submit a program description outlining requirements and coursework; must have transcripts, a statement explaining why the scholarship is desired, a resume, and three letters of recommendation from professors or work supervisors in the field in which the applicant intends to work. **Deadline:** January 30.

5692 ■ Pierce College District 11

9401 Farwest Dr. SW
Lakewood, WA 98498
Ph: (253)964-6500
URL: http://www.pierce.ctc.edu

5693 ■ Pierce College Foundation Coca-Cola Scholarships *(Undergraduate/Scholarship)*

Purpose: To support Pierce College students with their education. **Focus:** General studies. **Qualif.:** Applicants must be U.S. citizens; must have a 2.5 minimum GPA; must be engaged in community service within the previous 12 months or employed full or part-time; must be enrolled in at least two courses. Applicants may not be the children or grandchildren of a Coca-Cola employee. **Criteria:** Nominees will be selected by the Pierce College Scholarship Committee (one from Fort Steilacoom and one from Puyallup).

Funds Avail.: $1,000. **To Apply:** Applicants must submit a completed application form with the required materials to Pierce College Puyallup Attn: Ruth Ann Hatchett 1601 39th Ave SE, Gaspard Building Room No. 108 Puyallup, WA 98374-2222, or to Pierce College Fort Steilacoom Attn: Paula Henson-Williams 9401 Farwest Drive S.W Cascade Building Room No. 325-J Lakewood, WA 98498-1999. **Deadline:** May 9.

5694 ■ Pierce County Retired Teachers Scholarships *(Undergraduate/Scholarship)*

Purpose: To support Pierce College students with their education. **Focus:** Teaching. **Qualif.:** Applicants must be community college students in the second year of program and who will graduate with an AA degree; must be planning to transfer to a four-year university/college as full-time students; must be intending to pursue a career in teaching or education; and must have a minimum 2.5 GPA. **Criteria:** Selection is based on the application.

Funds Avail.: $1,000. **Number Awarded:** 1. **To Apply:** Applicants must complete the application form and submit together with the required materials to Ruth Ann Hatchett Pierce College District Rm. 108 Gaspard Building 1601 39th Ave. SE, Puyallup, WA 98374. **Deadline:** May 2.

Remarks: Funded by the Retired Teacher Association - WSRTA Affiliate No. 27.

5695 ■ Post 4137 Veterans Foundation Scholarships *(Undergraduate/Scholarship)*

Purpose: To render financial assistance for the veterans, children, grandchildren and great-grandchildren of U.S. veterans. **Focus:** General studies. **Qualif.:** Applicants must be honorably discharged veterans or, children, grandchildren, or great-grandchildren of an honorably discharged veteran; must be enrolled at or admitted to a private secondary educational institution, or a university, including community colleges. **Criteria:** Selection of recipient is based on merit.

Funds Avail.: $5,000. **Number Awarded:** 1. **To Apply:** Applicants must complete and submit the application form with the required documents and supporting materials to Post 4137 Veterans Foundation C/O Invicta Law Group, PLLC, 1000 Second Avenue, Suite 3310 Seattle, WA 98115. **Deadline:** May 30. **Contact:** scholarship@invictalaw.com.

5696 ■ Pinnacle West Capital Corporation

PO Box 53999
Phoenix, AZ 85072-3999
Ph: (602)250-1000
Free: 800-457-2983
URL: http://www.pinnaclewest.com

5697 ■ APS/ASU Scholarships *(Undergraduate/Scholarship)*

Purpose: To provide financial assistance to qualified individuals who want to pursue their career. **Focus:** Chemical engineering; Electrical engineering; Mechanical engineering; Civil engineering; Construction; Telecommunications systems; Accounting; Finance; Economics; Information science and technology; Education, Elementary; Education, Secondary; Special education; Nursing. **Qualif.:** Applicant must be an Arizona resident; must have a cumulative GPA of at least 3.0; must demonstrate financial need. **Criteria:** Recipient will be selected based on the scholarship application requirements.

Funds Avail.: $2,000. **Number Awarded:** 10. **To Apply:** Applicant must complete the application form available online and send it to ASU Scholarship Office, Arizona State University, PO Box 470412, Tempe, AZ 85287-0412. **Deadline:** March 1. **Contact:** Louise Moskowitz at louise.moskowitz@aps.com.

5698 ■ APS/Maricopa County Community Colleges Scholarships *(Undergraduate/Scholarship)*

Purpose: To provide financial assistance to qualified individuals who want to pursue their career. **Focus:** Mechanical engineering; Electrical engineering; Civil engineering; Chemical engineering; Trades training; Information science and technology; Marketing and distribution; Accounting; Finance; Economics; Management; Education; Health care services. **Qualif.:** Applicant must be an Arizona resident; must have a cumulative GPA of at least 3.0; must demonstrate financial need; must be a high school senior or current Maricopa Community College student; must be enrolled in a minimum of nine credit hours per semester. **Criteria:** Recipient will be selected based on the scholarship application requirements.

Funds Avail.: $1,000. **Number Awarded:** 25. **To Apply:** Applicant must complete the application form available online and must be sent to ASU Scholarship Office, Arizona State University, PO Box 470412, Tempe, AZ 85287-0412. **Contact:** Louise Moskowitz at louise.moskowitz@aps.com.

5699 ■ Plumbing-Heating-Cooling Contractors Association

PO Box 6808
Falls Church, VA 22046

Awards are arranged alphabetically below their administering organizations

Ph: (703)237-8100
Fax: (703)237-7442
Free: 800-533-7694
E-mail: naphcc@naphcc.org
URL: http://www.phccweb.org

5700 ■ American Standard Scholarships *(Undergraduate/Scholarship)*

Purpose: To establish a framework for the industry's first apprenticeship system and to spearhead education programs to keep pace with technological change. **Focus:** Business. **Qualif.:** Applicants must be citizens of the United States or Canada and must be in a full-time undergraduate degree program at an accredited four-year college or university with a major directly relating to plumbing-heating-cooling profession. **Criteria:** Recipients are selected based on academic performance.

Funds Avail.: $2,500. **Number Awarded:** 4. **To Apply:** Applicants must complete the application form and submit an official transcript of the high school grades; letter of recommendation from high school principal or counselor, college/university dean, academic advisor, or apprentice program instructor; SAT and ACT scores and cumulative GPA; and a letter of recommendation from an active member of the plumbing-heating-cooling contractors. **Deadline:** May 1.

5701 ■ Delta Faucet Scholarships *(Undergraduate/Scholarship)*

Purpose: To establish a framework for the industry's first apprenticeship system and to spearhead education programs to keep pace with technological change. **Focus:** Business. **Qualif.:** Applicants must be citizens of the United States or Canada and currently enrolled in or planning to enroll in plumbing, heating, cooling contractors; or must be enrolled full-time in an undergraduate degree program at an accredited four-year college or university with a major directly relating to the plumbing-heating-cooling profession. **Criteria:** Recipients are selected based on academic performance.

Funds Avail.: $2,500. **Number Awarded:** 6. **To Apply:** Applicants must complete the application form; must submit an official transcript of the high school grades; letter of recommendation from high school principal or counselor, college/university dean, academic advisor, or apprentice program instructor; SAT and ACT scores and cumulative GPA. **Deadline:** May 1.

5702 ■ Plumbing-Heating-Cooling Contractors Association Educational Foundation Massachusetts Auxiliary Scholarships *(Undergraduate/Scholarship)*

Purpose: To establish a framework for the industry's first apprenticeship system and to spearhead educational programs to keep pace with technological change. **Focus:** Business. **Qualif.:** Applicants must be high school seniors who are citizens of the United States and residents of the Commonwealth of Massachusetts, planning to enroll in a full-time undergraduate degree program at an accredited four-year college or university. **Criteria:** Recipients are selected based on academic performance and financial need.

Funds Avail.: $1,500. **Number Awarded:** 1. **To Apply:** Applicants must complete the application form and submit an official transcript of high school grades; letter of recommendation from high school principal or counselor; SAT and ACT scores and cumulative GPA; and a letter of recommendation from an active member of the Plumbing-Heating-Cooling Contractors Association National Auxiliary. **Deadline:** May 1.

5703 ■ Plumbing-Heating-Cooling Contractors Association Educational Foundation Need-Based Scholarships *(Undergraduate/Scholarship)*

Purpose: To establish a framework for the industry's first apprenticeship system and to spearhead educational programs to keep pace with technological change. **Focus:** Business. **Qualif.:** Applicants must be citizens of the United States or Canada planning to enroll in a full-time undergraduate degree program at an accredited four-year college or university. **Criteria:** Recipients are selected based on academic performance and financial need.

Funds Avail.: $2,500. **Number Awarded:** 1. **To Apply:** Applicants must complete the application form and submit an official transcript of high school grades; letter of recommendation from high school principal or counselor; SAT and ACT scores and cumulative GPA; and a letter of recommendation from an active member of the Plumbing-Heating-Cooling Contractors Association National Association. **Deadline:** May 1.

5704 ■ Plumbing-Heating-Cooling Contractors Association Educational Foundation Scholarships *(Undergraduate/Scholarship)*

Purpose: To establish a framework for the industry's first apprenticeship system and to spearhead educational programs to keep pace with technological change. **Focus:** Business. **Qualif.:** Applicants must be citizens of the United States or Canada and are planning to enroll in a full-time undergraduate degree program at an accredited four-year college or university. **Criteria:** Recipients are selected based on academic performance and financial need.

Funds Avail.: $3,000; $12,000. **Number Awarded:** 5. **To Apply:** Applicants must complete the application form and submit an official transcript of the high school grades; letter of recommendation from high school principal or counselor; SAT and ACT scores and cumulative GPA; and a letter of recommendation from an active member of the Plumbing-Heating-Cooling Contractors Association National Association. **Deadline:** May 1.

5705 ■ A.O. Smith Scholarships *(Undergraduate/Scholarship)*

Purpose: To establish a framework for the industry's first apprenticeship system and to spearhead education programs to keep pace with technological change. **Focus:** Business. **Qualif.:** Applicants must be citizens of the United States or Canada and must be enrolled full-time in an undergraduate degree program at an accredited four-year college or university with a major directly relating to plumbing-heating-cooling profession. **Criteria:** Recipients are selected based on academic performance.

Funds Avail.: $2,500. **Number Awarded:** 2. **To Apply:** Applicants must complete the application form and must submit an official transcript of the high school grades; letter of recommendation from high school principal or counselor, college/university dean, academic advisor, or apprentice program instructor; SAT and ACT scores as well as cumulative GPA; and a letter of recommendation from an active member of the plumbing-heating-cooling contractors. **Deadline:** May 1.

5706 ■ Bradford White Scholarships
(Undergraduate/Scholarship)

Purpose: To establish a framework for the industry's first apprenticeship system and to spearhead education programs to keep pace with technological change. **Focus:** Business. **Qualif.:** Applicants must be citizens of the United States or Canada and must be enrolled full-time in an undergraduate degree program at an accredited two-year community college, technical college or trade school with a major directly related to the plumbing-heating-cooling profession. **Criteria:** Recipients are selected based on academic performance.

Funds Avail.: $2,500. **Number Awarded:** 3. **To Apply:** Applicants must complete the application form and submit an official transcript of the high school grades; letter of recommendation from high school principal or counselor, college/university dean, academic advisor, or apprentice program instructor; SAT and ACT scores and cumulative GPA; and a letter of recommendation from an active member of the plumbing-heating-cooling contractors. **Deadline:** May 1.

5707 ■ Plus Foundation

5353 Wayzata Blvd., Ste. 600
Minneapolis, MN 55416
Ph: (952)746-2590
Fax: (952)746-2599
URL: http://www.plusfoundation.org

5708 ■ Leo Gilmartin Scholarships *(High School/ Scholarship)*

Purpose: To assist deserving PLUS member students with their college education. **Focus:** General studies. **Qualif.:** Applicants must be high school seniors who are children of current PLUS members or children of employees of current PLUS corporate sponsors. **Criteria:** Applicants are evaluated based on scholastic merit and extracurricular activity.

Funds Avail.: $10,000. **To Apply:** Applicants must submit college entrance exam scores; GPA and class rank; essay and letters of recommendation; list of extracurricular and community service activities. **Deadline:** March 15.

5709 ■ PLUS Foundation Financial Aid Grants
(Undergraduate/Scholarship)

Purpose: To assist deserving PLUS member students with their college education. **Focus:** General studies. **Qualif.:** Applicants must be high school seniors who are children of current PLUS members or children of employees of current PLUS corporate sponsors. **Criteria:** Recipients are selected based on family financial need and proof of average to above average high school performance.

Funds Avail.: $10,000. **To Apply:** Applicants must submit the household adjusted gross income; total number in household and number of dependent children attending college; estimated cost of tuition; GPA, class rank, college entrance exams scores. **Deadline:** March 15.

5710 ■ PMCA: An International Association of Confectioners

2980 Linden St., Ste. E3
Bethlehem, PA 18017
Ph: (610)625-4655
Fax: (610)625-4567
E-mail: info@pmca.com
URL: http://www.pmca.com

5711 ■ AACT Undergraduate Scholarships
(Undergraduate/Scholarship)

Purpose: To foster education students involved in confectionery technology. **Focus:** Food science and technology; Chemistry; Biology. **Qualif.:** Applicants must be sophomores, juniors or seniors majoring in food science, chemical science, biological science, or related field at an accredited four-year college or university in North America; must have a GPA of 3.0; and must be interested in confectionery technology. **Criteria:** Applicants are selected based on the committee's review of the application materials.

Funds Avail.: $5,000 (two $2,500 installments). **To Apply:** Applicants must submit a completed application form together with a letter of recommendation; copy of college transcript; and a list of academic activities, experience, other activities, honors and awards, and a short statement of personal and professional goals. Send materials to Kevin Silva, Warrell Corp. 2150 Slate Hill Road Camp Hill, PA 17011. **Deadline:** April 18. **Contact:** Kevin Silva, kevins@warrellcorp.com

5712 ■ PMCA Graduate Fellowships at Pennsylvania State University *(Graduate/ Fellowship)*

Purpose: To foster education and training of students involved in confectionery technology. **Focus:** Food science and technology. **Qualif.:** Applicants must be graduate students pursuing a career in the confectionery industry or students with an undergraduate degree and confectionery experience and are interested in furthering education. **Criteria:** Selection is based on merit.

Funds Avail.: No specific amount. **To Apply:** Applicants should contact Dr. Greg Ziegler of The Pennsylvania State University, grz1@psu.edu, 814863-2960.

5713 ■ Point Foundation

PO Box 60108
Los Angeles, CA 90060-0108
Ph: (323)933-1234
Fax: (866)33-POINT
E-mail: info@pointfoundation.org
URL: http://thepointfoundation.org

5714 ■ Merle Aronson Point Scholarships
(Graduate, Undergraduate/Scholarship)

Purpose: To support the LGBT community. **Focus:** General studies. **Qualif.:** Applicant must be LGBT or have a history of leadership in the LGBT community and plan to be a LGBT leader in the future. **Criteria:** Award is given based on the application.

Funds Avail.: No specific amount. **Number Awarded:** 1. **To Apply:** Applicants must complete the online scholarship application by March 1. If chosen as semi-finalists, students are requested to submit supplemental materials, in one envelope: two to three letters of recommendation; official transcripts; test score verification; and resume. **Deadline:** March 1.

Remarks: Point Foundation will not return submitted supplemental materials. **Contact:** ginger@pointfoundation.org, or 775-782-5659, fax: 775-782-5690.

5715 ■ Norman Blachford Point Scholarships
(Graduate, Undergraduate/Scholarship)

Purpose: To support the LGBT community. **Focus:** General studies. **Qualif.:** Applicant must be from the area of San

Diego, California; LGBT; or have a history of leadership in the LGBT community and plan to be a LGBT leader in the future. **Criteria:** Award is given based on the application.

Funds Avail.: No specific amount. **To Apply:** Applicants must complete the online scholarship application by March 1. If chosen as semi-finalist, students are requested to submit supplemental materials, in one envelope: two to three letters of recommendation; official transcripts; test score verification; and resume. **Deadline:** March 1.

Remarks: Point Foundation will not return submitted supplemental materials. **Contact:** ginger@pointfoundation.org, or 775-782-5659, fax: 775-782-5690.

5716 ■ Carlos Enrique Cisneros Point Scholarships *(Graduate, Undergraduate/Scholarship)*

Purpose: To support the LGBT community. **Focus:** General studies. **Qualif.:** Applicant must be a LGBT student of distinction attending American University, Washington, DC or have a history of leadership in the LGBT community and plan to be a LGBT leader in the future. **Criteria:** Award is given based on academic achievement and leadership development.

Funds Avail.: No specific amount. **To Apply:** Applicants must complete the online scholarship application by March 1. If chosen as semi-finalists, students are requested to submit supplemental materials, in one envelope: two to three letters of recommendation; official transcripts; test score verification; and resume. **Deadline:** March 1.

Remarks: Point Foundation will not return submitted supplemental materials. **Contact:** ginger@pointfoundation.org, or 775-782-5659, fax: 775-782-5690.

5717 ■ Elsie De Wolfe Point Scholarships *(Graduate, Undergraduate/Scholarship)*

Purpose: To support the LGBT community. **Focus:** General studies. **Qualif.:** Applicant must be LGBT; or have a history of leadership in the LGBT community and plan to be a LGBT leader in the future. **Criteria:** Award is given based on the application.

Funds Avail.: No specific amount. **To Apply:** Applicants must complete the online scholarship application by March 1. If chosen as semi-finalists, students are requested to submit supplemental materials, in one envelope: two to three letters of recommendation; official transcripts; test score verification; and resume. **Deadline:** March 1.

Remarks: Point Foundation will not return submitted supplemental materials. **Contact:** ginger@pointfoundation.org, or 775-782-5659, fax: 775-782-5690.

5718 ■ Walter M. Decker Point Scholarships *(Graduate, Undergraduate/Scholarship)*

Purpose: To support the LGBT community. **Focus:** General studies. **Qualif.:** Applicant must be LGBT; or have a history of leadership in the LGBT community and plan to be a LGBT leader in the future. **Criteria:** Award is given based on the application.

Funds Avail.: No specific amount. **Number Awarded:** one or more. **To Apply:** Applicants must complete the online scholarship application by March 1. If chosen as semi-finalists, students are requested to submit supplemental materials, in one envelope: two to three letters of recommendation; official transcripts; test score verification; and resume. **Deadline:** March 1.

Remarks: Point Foundation will not return submitted supplemental materials. **Contact:** ginger@pointfoundation.org, or 775-782-5659, fax: 775-782-5690.

5719 ■ Dr. Joan W. Fernandez Point Scholarships *(Graduate, Undergraduate/Scholarship)*

Purpose: To support the LGBT community. **Focus:** General studies. **Qualif.:** Applicant must be lesbian, aspiring to be a theater director and graduate with the MFA degree. **Criteria:** Award is given based on the application.

Funds Avail.: No specific amount. **To Apply:** Applicants must complete the online scholarship application by March 1. If chosen as semi-finalists, students are requested to submit supplemental materials, in one envelope: two to three letters of recommendation; official transcripts; test score verification; and resume. **Deadline:** March 1.

Remarks: Point Foundation will not return submitted supplemental materials. **Contact:** ginger@pointfoundation.org, or 775-782-5659, fax: 775-782-5690.

5720 ■ David B. Goodstein Point Scholarships *(Graduate, Undergraduate/Scholarship)*

Purpose: To support the LGBT community. **Focus:** General studies. **Qualif.:** Applicant must be LGBT; or have a history of leadership in the LGBT community and plan to be a LGBT leader in the future. **Criteria:** Award is given based on the application.

Funds Avail.: No specific amount. **To Apply:** Applicants must complete the online scholarship application by March 1. If chosen as semi-finalists, students are requested to submit supplemental materials, in one envelope: two to three letters of recommendation; official transcripts; test score verification; and resume. **Deadline:** March 1.

Remarks: Point Foundation will not return submitted supplemental materials. **Contact:** ginger@pointfoundation.org, or 775-782-5659, fax: 775-782-5690.

5721 ■ Evelyn W. Harrison Point Scholarships *(Graduate, Undergraduate/Scholarship)*

Purpose: To support the LGBT community. **Focus:** General studies. **Qualif.:** Applicant must be LGBT or have a history of leadership in the LGBT community and plan to be a LGBT leader in the future. **Criteria:** Award is given based on the application. Preference is given to applications from Southeastern part of U.S.

Funds Avail.: No specific amount. **To Apply:** Applicants must complete the online scholarship application by March 1. If chosen as semi-finalists, students are requested to submit supplemental materials, in one envelope: two to three letters of recommendation; official transcripts; test score verification; and resume. **Deadline:** March 1.

Remarks: Point Foundation will not return submitted supplemental materials. **Contact:** ginger@pointfoundation.org, or 775-782-5659, fax: 775-782-5690.

5722 ■ HBO Point Scholarships *(Graduate, Undergraduate/Scholarship)*

Purpose: To support the LGBT community. **Focus:** General studies. **Qualif.:** Applicant must be LGBT or have a history of leadership in the LGBT community and plan to be a LGBT leader in the future and be pursuing a career in the media. **Criteria:** Award is given based on the application.

Funds Avail.: No specific amount. **To Apply:** Applicants must complete the online scholarship application by March 1. If chosen as semi-finalists, students are requested to submit supplemental materials, in one envelope: two to three letters of recommendation; official transcripts; test score verification; and resume. **Deadline:** March 1.

Remarks: Point Foundation will not return submitted supplemental materials. **Contact:** ginger@pointfoundation.org, or 775-782-5659, fax: 775-782-5690.

5723 ■ Kevin Hummer Point Scholarships *(Graduate, Undergraduate/Scholarship)*

Purpose: To support the LGBT community. **Focus:** General studies. **Qualif.:** Applicant must be LGBT; or have a history of leadership in the LGBT community and plan to be a LGBT leader in the future. **Criteria:** Award is given based on the application.

Funds Avail.: No specific amount. **To Apply:** Applicants must complete the online scholarship application by March 1. If chosen as semi-finalists, students are requested to submit supplemental materials, in one envelope: two to three letters of recommendation; official transcripts; test score verification; and resume. **Deadline:** March 1.

Remarks: Point Foundation will not return submitted supplemental materials. **Contact:** ginger@pointfoundation.org, or 775-782-5659, fax: 775-782-5690.

5724 ■ Bryan L. Knapp Point Scholarships *(Graduate, Undergraduate/Scholarship)*

Purpose: To support the LGBT community. **Focus:** General studies. **Qualif.:** Applicant must be an undergraduate LGBT student of distinction from the New York City area attending Cornell University, Ithaca, New York.

Funds Avail.: No specific amount. **To Apply:** Applicants must complete the online scholarship application by March 1. If chosen as semi-finalists, students are requested to submit supplemental materials, in one envelope: two to three letters of recommendation; official transcripts; test score verification; and resume. **Deadline:** March 1.

Remarks: Point Foundation will not return submitted supplemental materials. **Contact:** ginger@pointfoundation.org, or 775-782-5659, fax: 775-782-5690.

5725 ■ Jonathan D. Lewis Point Scholarships *(Graduate, Undergraduate/Scholarship)*

Purpose: To support the LGBT community. **Focus:** General studies. **Qualif.:** Applicant must be LGBT or have a history of leadership in the LGBT community and plan to be a LGBT leader in the future. **Criteria:** Award is given based on the application.

Funds Avail.: No specific amount. **To Apply:** Applicants must complete the online scholarship application by March 1. If chosen as semi-finalists, students are requested to submit supplemental materials, in one envelope: two to three letters of recommendation; official transcripts; test score verification; and resume. **Deadline:** March 1.

Remarks: Point Foundation will not return submitted supplemental materials. **Contact:** ginger@pointfoundation.org, or 775-782-5659, fax: 775-782-5690.

5726 ■ Casey Sakir Point Scholarships *(Graduate, Undergraduate/Scholarship)*

Purpose: To support the LGBT community. **Focus:** Fashion design; Arts. **Qualif.:** Applicant must be LGBT; or have a history of leadership in the LGBT community and plan to be a LGBT leader in the future, and planning a future in the fields of design, fashion or the arts. **Criteria:** Award is given based on the application.

Funds Avail.: No specific amount. **To Apply:** Applicants must complete the online scholarship application by March 1. If chosen as semi-finalists, students are requested to submit supplemental materials, in one envelope: two to three letters of recommendation; official transcripts; test score verification; and resume. **Deadline:** March 1.

Remarks: Point Foundation will not return submitted supplemental materials. **Contact:** ginger@pointfoundation.org, or 775-782-5659, fax: 775-782-5690.

5727 ■ Time Warner Point Scholarships *(Graduate, Undergraduate/Scholarship)*

Purpose: To support the LGBT community. **Focus:** General studies. **Qualif.:** Applicant must be LGBT or have a history of leadership in the LGBT community and plan to be a LGBT leader in the future. **Criteria:** Award is given based on the application.

Funds Avail.: No specific amount. **To Apply:** Applicants must complete the online scholarship application by March 1. If chosen as semi-finalists, students are requested to submit supplemental materials, in one envelope: two to three letters of recommendation; official transcripts; test score verification; and resume. **Deadline:** March 1.

Remarks: Point Foundation will not return submitted supplemental materials. **Contact:** ginger@pointfoundation.org, or 775-782-5659, fax: 775-782-5690.

5728 ■ Polish American Engineers Association

5835 W Irving Park Rd.
Chicago, IL 60634
E-mail: contact@polishengineers.org
URL: http://www.polishengineers.org

5729 ■ Ralph Modjeski Scholarships *(Graduate, Undergraduate/Scholarship)*

Purpose: To provide financial assistance for qualified engineering students. **Focus:** Engineering. **Qualif.:** Applicant must be an engineering student at 4-year college or university or can also be a graduate engineering who demonstrates excellent academic achievements and proven commitment to engineering. **Criteria:** Scholarship committee gives particular consideration to applicants of Polish heritage.

Funds Avail.: No specific amount. **To Apply:** Applicants must complete the application form, available online; must submit an official transcript, 200-word letter describing the student's short and long term goals with any other information deemed pertinent; and must have three references with addresses and telephone numbers. Application form and requirements must be sent to Polish American Engineers Association, 5835 W Irving Park Rd., Chicago, IL 60634. **Deadline:** June 30.

5730 ■ Polish Falcons of America

615 Iron City Dr.
Pittsburgh, PA 15205-4397
Ph: (412)922-2244
Fax: (412)922-5029
Free: 800-535-2071
URL: http://www.polishfalcons.org

5731 ■ Falcon Achievement Scholarships *(Undergraduate/Scholarship)*

Purpose: To provide financial support for deserving Falcon members aspiring to attend institutions of higher learning.

Awards are arranged alphabetically below their administering organizations

Focus: Polish studies. **Qualif.:** Candidates must be graduating high school seniors or presently enrolled undergraduates intending to pursue further education as a full time student in an accredited two or four year college, university or trade school; must have a minimum cumulative GPA of 2.0 out of 4.0. **Criteria:** Selection of applicant will be based on the academic achievements and leadership qualities.

Funds Avail.: $1,000. **To Apply:** Applicant must complete and sign the application form available online; must provide a community service information, essay, and photo; must submit the official transcript, counselor recommendation, and net information form and letter. **Deadline:** February 1.

5732 ■ General Falcon Scholarships
(Undergraduate/Scholarship)

Purpose: To provide financial support for deserving Falcon members who are aspiring to attend institutions of higher learning. **Focus:** General studies. **Qualif.:** Candidates must be graduating high school seniors or presently enrolled undergraduates intending to pursue further education as a full time student in an accredited two or four year college, university or trade school; must have a minimum cumulative GPA of 2.0 out of 4.0; must have taken an active participants in the Polish Falcon programs. **Criteria:** Selection of applicant will be based on the criteria of the selection committee.

Funds Avail.: $500. **To Apply:** Applicant must complete and sign the application form available online; must provide a community service information, essay, and photo; must submit the official transcript, counselor recommendation, and net information form and letter. **Deadline:** February 1.

5733 ■ Richard C. Gorecki Scholarships
(Undergraduate/Scholarship)

Purpose: To provide financial assistance for deserving individuals intending to pursue their education. **Focus:** General studies. **Qualif.:** Applicant must be a PFA member for six years; must have a minimum GPA of 3.0 out of 4.0; Applicant must be enrolled full-time in a four-year college or university, or full-time post-graduate studies. **Criteria:** Selection of applicant will be based on the academic achievements and leadership qualities. Decisions of the selection board are subject to the approval of the National Board of Directors.

Funds Avail.: $15,000. **To Apply:** Applicant must complete the scholarship application; must have a two part essay (minimum 500 words for each part); must provide at least three letters of recommendation. **Deadline:** May 27.

5734 ■ Portable Sanitation Association International

7800 Metro Pkwy., Ste. 104
Bloomington, MN 55425-1514
Ph: (952)854-8300
Fax: (952)854-7560
Free: 800-822-3020
E-mail: info@psai.org
URL: http://www.psai.org

5735 ■ PSAI Scholarship Funds *(Undergraduate/Scholarship)*

Purpose: To assist individuals intending to pursue higher education. **Focus:** Technology. **Qualif.:** Applicants must be graduating high school students or current undergraduate college students; must be employees of PSAI company or their dependents; must be college undergraduates; must have at least a GPA of 3.0 or above; must demonstrate the importance and value of portable sanitation; must have at least minimum of two (2) years employed by PSAI member company; and must maintain a minimum SAT Score 1000 or ACT 21. **Criteria:** Selections are done on the basis of academic achievement, community involvement, work experience and recommendations.

Funds Avail.: $2,500 to cover college expenses. **To Apply:** Applicants must submit a copy of transcript; a 500 to 1000 word essay; a completed hard copy of application form; and profile sheet with the PSAI office. **Deadline:** March 15.

5736 ■ Portuguese American Leadership Council of the United States

1316 Pennsylvania Ave. SE, Capitol Hill
Washington, DC 20003
Ph: (202)466-4664
Fax: (202)466-4661
E-mail: palcus@palcus.org
URL: http://www.palcus.org

5737 ■ Cabrillo Clubs of California Scholarships
(Undergraduate/Scholarship)

Purpose: To provide financial support to high school seniors of Portuguese heritage. **Focus:** General studies. **Qualif.:** Applicant must be of Portuguese descent; must have maintained a 3.50 or better GPA and be a graduating senior and citizen of the U.S. **Criteria:** Scholarship will be awarded based on the criteria of the Scholarship Committee.

Funds Avail.: $400. **To Apply:** Applicant must mail all completed application packets to: Cabrillo Civic Clubs of California, 1455 Willow St., San Diego, CA 92106-2122.

5738 ■ Portuguese-American Scholarship Foundation *(Undergraduate/Scholarship)*

Purpose: To provide financial assistance to qualified New Jersey students of Portuguese ancestry, who wants to further their post-secondary school education and gain greater access to a better way of life. **Focus:** General studies. **Qualif.:** Applicants must be New Jersey High School seniors that are Portuguese-born or that have a parent or grandparent that is Portuguese-born; must be a U.S. citizen or U.S. permanent residents; must demonstrate financial need; must be a New Jersey high school senior applying to, or accepted in, a four-year college or university curriculum leading to a baccalaureate degree; must meet the minimum PASF academic standards, including a grade point average of B or better. **Criteria:** Scholarship will be evaluated based on the academic achievement and financial need.

Funds Avail.: $7,000. **To Apply:** Application must be completed and sent to: Portuguese-American Scholarship Foundation of NJ, Chairperson, Scholarship Review Board, PO Box 7169, Colonia, NJ 07067. **Deadline:** February 15.

5739 ■ Portuguese American Police Association

PO Box 51523
New Bedford, MA 02745-0045
Ph: (508)994-5390
E-mail: info@papamass.org

Awards are arranged alphabetically below their administering organizations

URL: http://www.papamass.org

5740 ■ Portuguese American Police Association Scholarships *(Undergraduate/Scholarship)*

Purpose: To provide support for deserving students intending to pursue a career in either Health Care, Social Service, Law Enforcement, or other related fields. **Focus:** Health care services, Social work, Law enforcement. **Qualif.:** Applicant must be a Portuguese descent; must be a resident of Massachusetts; must be enrolled full-time in an accredited college or university or a graduating senior applying to full-time status in an accredited or another college or university; must be majoring in either health care, social services, law enforcement or another related field; must maintain a GPA of 2.0 or higher. **Criteria:** Candidates will be selected based on their academic standing.

Funds Avail.: $500. **Number Awarded:** 6. **To Apply:** Application forms are available online. Applicant must submit an essay of no more than three paragraphs stating the reason stating their career goals; must have a high school transcript that includes the class rank; must have the current college/university transcript; must have a letter of reference from each of the following: (1) Guidance counselor or advisor and (2) Personal reference, preferably from someone with whom the applicants have work. Application materials must be sent to: Scholarship Committee, Portuguese American Police Association, Inc., PO Box 51523, New Bedford, MA 02745-0045. **Deadline:** June 1.

5741 ■ Practising Law Institute

810 Seventh Ave., 21st Fl.
New York, NY 10019
Ph: (212)824-5700
Fax: (212)824-5733
URL: http://www.pli.edu

5742 ■ Practising Law Institute Law Student Scholarships *(Undergraduate/Scholarship)*

Purpose: To provide financial assistance to qualified students who want to pursue their career. **Focus:** Law. **Qualif.:** Applicants must be legal aid and government attorneys, judges, judicial clerks, and employees of nonprofit organizations. **Criteria:** Recipients will be selected based on all application requirements.

Funds Avail.: Scholarship award will cover the full or partial tuition cost. **To Apply:** Applicants must complete the application forms available online; must have a legible copy of a student ID for the current term; and must complete the Statement of Need on the respective letter head. Application forms other supporting documents must be sent to PLI, 810 7th Ave., New York, NY 10019 or faxed to 888560-4852.

5743 ■ Presbyterian Association of Musicians

100 Witherspoon St.
Louisville, KY 40202-1396
Ph: (502)569-8465
URL: http://www.presbymusic.org

5744 ■ Presbyterian Association of Musicians Scholarships *(Other/Scholarship)*

Purpose: To provide financial assistance for students for summer worship and music conferences. **Focus:** Music. **Qualif.:** Applicants must be adult, children, youth members of the association. **Criteria:** Recipient will be selected based on financial need.

Funds Avail.: No amount mentioned. **To Apply:** Adult applicants must write and submit a short essay of qualifications as an applicant and why applicant would like to attend a PAM conference and a letter of recommendation from pastor or music director; for children and youth applicants, music directors must write an evaluation statement of the applicants including the applicant's musical experience and involvement in the church, how the applicant would benefit from the conference and perception of the applicant's financial need. **Deadline:** February 15.

5745 ■ Prescott Fine Arts Association

208 N Marina St.
Prescott, AZ 86301
Ph: (928)541-0209
E-mail: pfaadirector@qwestoffice.net
URL: http://www.pfaa.net

5746 ■ Prescott Fine Arts Association Scholarship Program *(Undergraduate/Scholarship)*

Purpose: To recognize and support the talented young people of Yavapai County. **Focus:** Fine Arts. **Qualif.:** Applicants must be high school students who reside in Yavapai County. **Criteria:** Recipients are selected based on financial need.

Funds Avail.: $500. **Number Awarded:** 7. **To Apply:** Applicants must complete the application form.

5747 ■ President's Commission on White House Fellowships

1900 E St. NW, Rm.B431
Washington, DC 20415
Ph: (202)606-1818
URL: http://www.whitehouse.gov

5748 ■ White House Fellows *(Professional Development/Fellowship)*

Purpose: To provide gifted and highly motivated young Americans with some first hand experience in the process of governing the Nation and a sense of personal involvement in the leadership of society. To enhance the leadership and other learning experiences in the work assignment. **Focus:** General studies. **Qualif.:** Applicant must be a U.S. citizen; must be a employees of the federal government are not eligible unless they are career military personnel; must have completed their undergraduate education and be working in their chosen professions. **Criteria:** Selection of applicant will be based on the following criteria: (1) A record of remarkable professional achievement early in one's career; (2) Evidence of leadership skills and the potential for further growth; (3) A demonstrated commitment to public service; (4) The knowledge and skills necessary to contribute successfully at the highest levels of the federal government.

Funds Avail.: No specific amount. **To Apply:** Application forms are available online and must be sent together with the other supporting documents at The President's Commission on White House Fellows, c/o O.P.M. - Shiela Coates, 1900 E St., NW, Rm. B431, Washington, DC 20415. **Deadline:** February 1.

5749 ■ Pride Foundation

PO Box 2194, 1122 E Pike St. PMB 1001
Seattle, WA 98112

Awards are arranged alphabetically below their administering organizations

Ph: (206)323-3318
Fax: (206)323-1017
Free: 800-735-7287
E-mail: prideweb@pridefoundation.org
URL: http://www.pridefoundation.org

5750 ■ Paul Arnold Memorial Scholarships *(Undergraduate/Scholarship)*

Purpose: To provide scholarship to the students who have been stigmatized, isolated or closeted because of sexual identity issues. **Focus:** Interior design; Fashion design; Graphic art and design. **Qualif.:** Applicants must be young men and women studying interior, fashion, graphic design. **Criteria:** Selection will be based on the committee's criteria.

Funds Avail.: No specific amount. **To Apply:** Qualified students are asked to submit an application to determine eligibility for scholarships. Applicants may download an application form from the Foundation's website. **Contact:** Pride Foundation at the above address (see entry 5749).

5751 ■ Asian and Pacific Islander Queers Sisters Scholarships *(Undergraduate/Scholarship)*

Purpose: To provide scholarship to students who have been stigmatized, isolated or closeted because of sexual identity issues. **Focus:** General studies. **Qualif.:** Applicants must be Asian/Pacific Islander lesbians, bisexual females, or transgender (both MTF and FTM spectrum). **Criteria:** Selection will be based on the committee's criteria.

Funds Avail.: No specific amount. **To Apply:** Qualified students are asked to submit an application to determine eligibility for scholarships. Applicants may download an application form from the Foundation's website. **Contact:** Pride Foundation at the above address (see entry 5749).

5752 ■ Associates in Behavioral Health Scholarships *(Graduate/Scholarship)*

Purpose: To provide scholarship to the students who have been stigmatized, isolated or closeted because of sexual identity issues. **Focus:** Psychology; Psychiatry; Social work; Nursing, Psychiatric. **Qualif.:** Applicants must be LGBT students pursuing graduate education in psychology, psychiatry, social work, or psychiatric nursing. Preference given to individuals with demonstrated financial needs and to those entering or already enrolled in an accredited graduate program. **Criteria:** Selection will be based on the committee's criteria.

Funds Avail.: No specific amount. **To Apply:** Qualified students are asked to submit an application to determine eligibility for scholarships. Applicants may download an application form from the Foundation's website. **Contact:** Pride Foundation at the above address (see entry 5749).

5753 ■ Athletic Excellence Scholarships *(Undergraduate/Scholarship)*

Purpose: To provide scholarship to the students who have been stigmatized, isolated or closeted because of sexual identity issues. **Focus:** Sports studies. **Qualif.:** Applicant must be an LGBT individual who plans to pursue or study athletics through college, or for athletes pursuing national/international excellence in sports through an accredited institution or program. **Criteria:** Selection will be based on the committee's criteria.

Funds Avail.: No specific amount. **To Apply:** Qualified students are asked to submit an application to determine eligibility for scholarships. Applicants may download an application form from the Foundation's website. **Contact:** Pride Foundation at the above address (see entry 5749).

5754 ■ Barbara Bailey Scholarships *(Undergraduate/Scholarship)*

Purpose: To provide scholarship to the students who have been stigmatized, isolated or closeted because of sexual identity issues. **Focus:** General studies. **Qualif.:** Applicant must be a lesbian from the state of Washington. **Criteria:** Selection will be based on the committee's criteria.

Funds Avail.: No specific amount. **To Apply:** Qualified students are asked to submit an application to determine eligibility for scholarships. Applicants may download an application form from the Foundation's website. **Contact:** Pride Foundation at the above address (see entry 5749).

5755 ■ Charly Baker and Heath Merriwether Memorial Scholarships *(Undergraduate/Scholarship)*

Purpose: To provide scholarship to the students who have been stigmatized, isolated or closeted because of sexual identity issues. **Focus:** Theater arts. **Qualif.:** Applicant must be a student under the age of 25 who graduated from any West Seattle high school or are studying theater art. **Criteria:** Selection will be based on the committee's criteria.

Funds Avail.: No specific amount. **To Apply:** Qualified students are asked to submit an application to determine eligibility for scholarships. Applicants may download an application form from the Foundation's website. **Contact:** Pride Foundation at the above address (see entry 5749).

5756 ■ Bellevue PFLAG Scholarships *(Undergraduate/Scholarship)*

Purpose: To provide scholarship to the students who have been stigmatized, isolated or closeted because of sexual identity issues. **Focus:** General Studies. **Qualif.:** Applicant must be a graduating high school seniors currently attending a greater East King County high school. **Criteria:** Selection will be based on the committee's criteria.

Funds Avail.: No specific amount. **To Apply:** Qualified students are asked to submit an application to determine eligibility for scholarships. Applicants may download an application form from the Foundation's website. **Contact:** Pride Foundation at the above address (see entry 5749).

5757 ■ Bill Bendiner and Doug Morgenson Scholarships *(Undergraduate/Scholarship)*

Purpose: To provide scholarship to the students who have been stigmatized, isolated or closeted because of sexual identity issues. **Focus:** Human relations; Health sciences; Visual arts. **Qualif.:** Applicant must be pursing a career in human services, health sciences or visual arts. **Criteria:** Selection will be based on the committee's criteria.

Funds Avail.: No specific amount. **To Apply:** Qualified students are asked to submit an application to determine eligibility for scholarships. Applicants may download an application form from the Foundation's website. **Contact:** Pride Foundation at the above address (see entry 5749).

5758 ■ Robert Browning Scholarships *(Undergraduate/Scholarship).*

Purpose: To provide scholarship to the students who have been stigmatized, isolated or closeted because of sexual identity issues. **Focus:** Health sciences. **Qualif.:** Applicant must be majoring in health sciences program. **Criteria:** Selection will be based on the committee's criteria.

Funds Avail.: No specific amount. **To Apply:** Qualified students are asked to submit an application to determine eligibility for scholarships. Applicants may download an application form from the Foundation's website. **Contact:** Pride Foundation at the above address (see entry 5749).

5759 ▪ Deloris Carter Hampton Scholarships *(Undergraduate/Scholarship)*

Purpose: To provide scholarship to the students who have been stigmatized, isolated or closeted because of sexual identity issues. **Focus:** Education; Dance. **Qualif.:** Applicants must be women of color who have a demonstrated history of activism and/or leadership in the LGBT community and are pursuing a degree in education, women's health, or dance. **Criteria:** Selection will be based on the committee's criteria.

Funds Avail.: No specific amount. **To Apply:** Qualified students are asked to submit an application to determine eligibility for scholarships. Applicants may download an application form from the Foundation's website. **Contact:** Pride Foundation at the above address (see entry 5749).

5760 ▪ Donald O. Coffman Scholarships *(Undergraduate/Scholarship)*

Purpose: To provide scholarship to the students who have been stigmatized, isolated or closeted because of sexual identity issues. **Focus:** General studies. **Qualif.:** Applicant must be a current and future LGBT and straight-ally leaders and role models. **Criteria:** Selection will be based on the committee's criteria.

Funds Avail.: No specific amount. **To Apply:** Qualified students are asked to submit an application to determine eligibility for scholarships. Applicants may download an application form from the Foundation's website. **Contact:** Pride Foundation at the above address (see entry 5749).

5761 ▪ Cole Family Scholarships *(Undergraduate/Scholarship)*

Purpose: To provide scholarship to the students who have been stigmatized, isolated or closeted because of sexual identity issues. **Focus:** General studies. **Qualif.:** Applicant must be a Washington resident under the age of 25 and raised by one or more lesbian or gay parent. **Criteria:** Selection will be based on the committee's criteria.

Funds Avail.: No specific amount. **To Apply:** Qualified students are asked to submit an application to determine eligibility for scholarships. Applicants may download an application form from the Foundation's website. **Contact:** Pride Foundation at the above address (see entry 5749).

5762 ▪ Dennis Coleman Choral Conducting Scholarships *(Undergraduate/Scholarship)*

Purpose: To provide scholarship to the students who have been stigmatized, isolated or closeted because of sexual identity issues. **Focus:** Music. **Qualif.:** Applicant must be a LGBT student studying choral conducting or music with preference given to those committed to creating social change through music. **Criteria:** Selection will be based on the committee's criteria.

Funds Avail.: No specific amount. **To Apply:** Qualified students are asked to submit an application to determine eligibility for scholarships. Applicants may download an application form from the Foundation's website. **Contact:** Pride Foundation at the above address (see entry 5749).

5763 ▪ Compassionate Care Scholarships *(Undergraduate/Scholarship)*

Purpose: To provide scholarship to students who have been stigmatized, isolated or closeted because of sexual identity issues. **Focus:** General studies. **Qualif.:** Applicant must be a student committed to offering compassionate support services to those dealing with illness, death, grief or trauma, especially where violent acts such as suicide must be addressed. **Criteria:** Selection will be based on the committee's criteria.

Funds Avail.: No specific amount. **To Apply:** Qualified students are asked to submit an application to determine eligibility for scholarships. Applicants may download an application form from the Foundation's website. **Contact:** Pride Foundation at the above address (see entry 5749).

5764 ▪ Brian M. Day Scholarships *(Undergraduate/Scholarship)*

Purpose: To provide scholarship to the students who have been stigmatized, isolated or closeted because of sexual identity issues. **Focus:** General studies. **Qualif.:** Applicants must be Puget Sound area gay men of color who have significant financial need and demonstrate activism in the gay/lesbian community and their communities of color. **Criteria:** Selection will be based on the committee's criteria.

Funds Avail.: No specific amount. **To Apply:** Qualified students are asked to submit an application to determine eligibility for scholarships. Applicants may download an application form from the Foundation's website. **Contact:** Pride Foundation at the above address (see entry 5749).

5765 ▪ Derivative Duo Scholarships *(Undergraduate/Scholarship)*

Purpose: To provide scholarship to the students who have been stigmatized, isolated or closeted because of sexual identity issues. **Focus:** Mental health; Human relations. **Qualif.:** Applicant must be a resident of Washington studying mental health or human services. **Criteria:** Selection will be based on the committee's criteria.

Funds Avail.: No specific amount. **To Apply:** Qualified students are asked to submit an application to determine eligibility for scholarships. Applicants may download an application form from the Foundation's website. **Contact:** Pride Foundation at the above address (see entry 5749).

5766 ▪ Imperial Sovereign Court of Tacoma Scholarships *(Professional Development/ Scholarship)*

Purpose: To provide scholarship to the students who have been stigmatized, isolated or closeted because of sexual identity issues. **Focus:** General Studies. **Qualif.:** Applicant must be a resident of Pierce County working to enhance the leadership of the LGBT and straight-ally community. **Criteria:** Selection will be based on the committee's criteria.

Funds Avail.: No specific amount. **To Apply:** Qualified students are asked to submit an application to determine eligibility for scholarships. Applicants may download an application form from the Foundation's website. **Contact:** Pride Foundation at the above address (see entry 5749).

5767 ▪ Inland Northwest Business Alliance (INBA) Scholarships *(Undergraduate/Scholarship)*

Purpose: To provide scholarship to the students who have been stigmatized, isolated or closeted because of sexual identity issues. **Focus:** General studies. **Qualif.:** Applicant must be an undergraduate student who is also a resident of Eastern Washington, Idaho, or Montana. **Criteria:** Selection will be based on the committee's criteria.

Funds Avail.: No specific amount. **To Apply:** Qualified students are asked to submit an application to determine eligibility for scholarships. Applicants may download an application form from the Foundation's website. **Contact:** Pride Foundation at the above address (see entry 5749).

5768 ■ Patricia Van Kirk Scholarships *(Undergraduate/Scholarship)*

Purpose: To provide scholarship to the students who have been stigmatized, isolated or closeted because of sexual identity issues. **Focus:** Theater arts; Visual arts. **Qualif.:** Applicant must be a lesbian studying theater or visual arts. Preference is given to students who are self-identified lesbian, gay, bisexual or transgender (LGBT). **Criteria:** Selection will be based on the committee's criteria.

Funds Avail.: No specific amount. **To Apply:** Qualified students are asked to submit an application to determine eligibility for scholarships. Applicants may download an application form from the Foundation's website. **Contact:** Pride Foundation at the above address (see entry 5749).

5769 ■ McFarffels Scholarships *(Undergraduate/Scholarship)*

Purpose: To provide scholarship to the students who have been stigmatized, isolated or closeted because of sexual identity issues. **Focus:** General studies. **Qualif.:** Applicant must be a lesbian with financial need entering a field that promotes social change and/or social justice. Preference is given to students who are self-identified lesbian, gay, bisexual or transgender (LGBT). **Criteria:** Selection will be based on the committee's criteria.

Funds Avail.: No specific amount. **To Apply:** Qualified students are asked to submit an application to determine eligibility for scholarships. Applicants may download an application form from the Foundation's website. **Contact:** Pride Foundation at the above address (see entry 5749).

5770 ■ Jacinta McKoy Memorial Scholarships *(Undergraduate/Scholarship)*

Purpose: To provide scholarship to the students who have been stigmatized, isolated or closeted because of sexual identity issues. **Focus:** Education. **Qualif.:** Applicant must be a student from the Black Hills community pursuing education in the healing arts. Preference is given to students who are self-identified lesbian, gay, bisexual or transgender (LGBT). **Criteria:** Selection will be based on the committee's criteria.

Funds Avail.: No specific amount. **To Apply:** Qualified students are asked to submit an application to determine eligibility for scholarships. Applicants may download an application form from the Foundation's website. **Contact:** Pride Foundation at the above address (see entry 5749).

5771 ■ Jack D. Motteler Scholarships *(Undergraduate/Scholarship)*

Purpose: To provide scholarship to the students who have been stigmatized, isolated or closeted because of sexual identity issues. **Focus:** Visual arts. **Qualif.:** Applicant must be an undergraduate student in the visual arts. **Criteria:** Selection will be based on the committee's criteria.

Funds Avail.: No specific amount. **To Apply:** Qualified students are asked to submit an application to determine eligibility for scholarships. Applicants may download an application form from the Foundation's website. **Contact:** Pride Foundation at the above address (see entry 5749).

5772 ■ Obrzut Ling Scholarships *(Undergraduate/Scholarship)*

Purpose: To provide scholarship to the students who have been stigmatized, isolated or closeted because of sexual identity issues. **Focus:** General studies. **Qualif.:** Applicant must be a student enrolled or entering a vocational or technical program at an accredited learning institution. Preference is given to students who are self-identified lesbian, gay, bisexual or transgender (LGBT). **Criteria:** Selection will be based on the committee's criteria.

Funds Avail.: No specific amount. **To Apply:** Qualified students are asked to submit an application to determine eligibility for scholarships. Applicants may download an application form from the Foundation's website. **Contact:** Pride Foundation at the above address (see entry 5749).

5773 ■ Political Leadership Scholarships *(Undergraduate/Scholarship)*

Purpose: To provide scholarship to the students who have been stigmatized, isolated or closeted because of sexual identity issues. **Focus:** Law; Political science; Public Administration. **Qualif.:** Applicant must be studying law, political science, public policy or public administration with the goal of improving rights for LGBT people. Preference is given to students who are self-identified lesbian, gay, bisexual or transgender (LGBT). **Criteria:** Selection will be based on the committee's criteria.

Funds Avail.: No specific amount. **To Apply:** Qualified students are asked to submit an application to determine eligibility for scholarships. Applicants may download an application form from the Foundation's website. **Contact:** Pride Foundation at the above address (see entry 5749).

5774 ■ Pride Foundation Regional Scholarships *(Undergraduate/Scholarship)*

Purpose: To provide scholarship to the students who have been stigmatized, isolated or closeted because of sexual identity issues. **Focus:** General studies. **Qualif.:** Applicant must be a resident of areas outside of King County where Pride Foundation is working to enhance the leadership of the LGBT and straight-ally community: Whatcom/Skagit, Kitsap County, Pierce County, Clark County, Black Hills, Inland Northwest, Southern Idaho and Columbia Basin. **Criteria:** Selection will be based on the committee's criteria.

Funds Avail.: No specific amount. **To Apply:** Qualified students are asked to submit an application to determine eligibility for scholarships. Applicants may download an application form from the Foundation's website. **Contact:** Pride Foundation at the above address (see entry 5749).

5775 ■ Don Renschler Scholarships *(Graduate/Scholarship)*

Purpose: To provide scholarship to the students who have been stigmatized, isolated or closeted because of sexual identity issues. **Focus:** Mental Health. **Qualif.:** Applicant must be a resident of Washington who is a graduate student in the study of mental health. **Criteria:** Selection will be based on the committee's criteria.

Funds Avail.: No specific amount. **To Apply:** Qualified students are asked to submit an application to determine eligibility for scholarships. Applicants may download an application form from the Foundation's website. **Contact:** Pride Foundation at the above address (see entry 5749).

5776 ■ Richard C. Rolfs Scholarships *(Undergraduate/Scholarship)*

Purpose: To provide scholarship to the students who have been stigmatized, isolated or closeted because of sexual identity issues. **Focus:** General studies. **Qualif.:** Applicants must be Eastern Washington residents, or undergraduate students attending college in Eastern Washington. **Criteria:** Selection will be based on the committee's criteria.

Funds Avail.: No specific amount. **To Apply:** Qualified students are asked to submit an application to determine eligibility for scholarships. Applicants may download an application form from the Foundation's website. **Contact:** Pride Foundation at the above address (see entry 5749).

5777 ■ Rosenberg-Ibarra Scholarships *(Undergraduate/Scholarship)*

Purpose: To provide scholarship to the students who have been stigmatized, isolated or closeted because of sexual identity issues. **Focus:** General studies. **Qualif.:** Applicant must be a LGBT student who either graduated from a high school in Idaho or will be attending a college or university within the state of Idaho. **Criteria:** Selection will be based on the committee's criteria.

Funds Avail.: No specific amount. **To Apply:** Qualified students are asked to submit an application to determine eligibility for scholarships. Applicants may download an application form from the Foundation's website. **Contact:** Pride Foundation at the above address (see entry 5749).

5778 ■ Social Work Scholarships *(Graduate, Undergraduate/Scholarship)*

Purpose: To provide scholarship to the students who have been stigmatized, isolated or closeted because of sexual identity issues. **Focus:** Social work. **Qualif.:** Applicants must be gay, lesbian or transgender students enrolled or admitted to a C.S.W.E. accredited bachelors or masters social work degree program or to a doctoral program in social work. Preference given to students of color. **Criteria:** Selection will be based on the committee's criteria.

Funds Avail.: No specific amount. **To Apply:** Qualified students are asked to submit an application to determine eligibility for scholarships. Applicants may download an application form from the Foundation's website. **Contact:** Pride Foundation at the above address (see entry 5749).

5779 ■ Kathy Spadoni Memorial Scholarships *(Undergraduate/Scholarship)*

Purpose: To provide scholarship to the students who have been stigmatized, isolated or closeted because of sexual identity issues. **Focus:** General studies. **Qualif.:** Applicant must be a graduating high school senior entering a bachelor's degree program who has demonstrated leadership skills and have a passion for making positive social change. Preference is given to students who are self-identified lesbian, gay, bisexual or transgender (LGBT). **Criteria:** Selection will be based on the committee's criteria.

Funds Avail.: No specific amount. **To Apply:** Qualified students are asked to submit an application to determine eligibility for scholarships. Applicants may download an application form from the Foundation's website. **Contact:** Pride Foundation at the above address (see entry 5749).

5780 ■ Phil Sullivan Scholarships *(Undergraduate/Scholarship)*

Purpose: To provide scholarship to the students who have been stigmatized, isolated or closeted because of sexual identity issues. **Focus:** General studies. **Qualif.:** Applicant must be a student under the age of 21 who demonstrates significant financial need, with preference to those that have been homeless. **Criteria:** Selection will be based on the committee's criteria.

Funds Avail.: No specific amount. **To Apply:** Qualified students are asked to submit an application to determine eligibility for scholarships. Applicants may download an application form from the Foundation's website. **Contact:** Pride Foundation at the above address (see entry 5749).

5781 ■ True North Land Surveying Scholarships *(Undergraduate/Scholarship)*

Purpose: To provide scholarship to the students who have been stigmatized, isolated or closeted because of sexual identity issues. **Focus:** Mathematics and mathematical sciences. **Qualif.:** Applicant must be a student pursuing a career in Land Surveying (Geomatics) or majoring in mathematics. **Criteria:** Selection will be based on the committee's criteria.

Funds Avail.: No specific amount. **To Apply:** Qualified students are asked to submit an application to determine eligibility for scholarships. Applicants may download an application form from the Foundation's website. **Contact:** Pride Foundation at the above address (see entry 5749).

5782 ■ Ric Ulrich and Chuck Pischke Scholarships *(Undergraduate/Scholarship)*

Purpose: To provide scholarship to the students who have been stigmatized, isolated or closeted because of sexual identity issues. **Focus:** Visual arts. **Qualif.:** Candidate must intend to study in visual arts and design. Preference is given to students who are self-identified lesbian, gay, bisexual or transgender (LGBT). **Criteria:** Selection will be based on the committee's criteria.

Funds Avail.: No specific amount. **To Apply:** Qualified students are asked to submit an application to determine eligibility for scholarships. Applicants may download an application form from the Foundation's website. **Contact:** Pride Foundation at the above address (see entry 5749).

5783 ■ Wells Fargo Scholarships *(Undergraduate/Scholarship)*

Purpose: To provide scholarship to the students who have been stigmatized, isolated or closeted because of sexual identity issues. **Focus:** General studies. **Qualif.:** Applicant must be a current or future LGBT and straight-ally leaders and role models. **Criteria:** Selection will be based on the committee's criteria.

Funds Avail.: No specific amount. **To Apply:** Qualified students are asked to submit an application to determine eligibility for scholarships. Applicants may download an application form from the Foundation's website. **Contact:** Pride Foundation at the above address (see entry 5749).

5784 ■ Whidbey Island Giving Circle Scholarships *(Undergraduate/Scholarship)*

Purpose: To provide scholarship to the students who have been stigmatized, isolated or closeted because of sexual identity issues. **Focus:** General studies. **Qualif.:** Applicant must be a current and future LGBT and straight-ally leaders and role models, with preference given to residents of Whidbey Island. **Criteria:** Selection will be based on the committee's criteria.

Funds Avail.: No specific amount. **To Apply:** Qualified students are asked to submit an application to determine eligibility for scholarships. Applicants may download an application form from the Foundation's website. **Contact:** Pride Foundation at the above address (see entry 5749).

5785 ■ James and Colin Lee Wozumi Scholarships *(Undergraduate/Scholarship)*

Purpose: To provide scholarship to the students who have been stigmatized, isolated or closeted because of sexual

Awards are arranged alphabetically below their administering organizations

identity issues. **Focus:** General studies. **Qualif.:** Applicant must be an undergraduate student who is goal-oriented, HIV positive, and/or focusing on the treatment and/or eradication of HIV. Preference is given to students who are self-identified lesbian, gay, bisexual or transgender (LGBT). **Criteria:** Selection will be based on the committee's criteria.

Funds Avail.: No specific amount. **To Apply:** Qualified students are asked to submit an application to determine eligibility for scholarships. Applicants may download an application form from the Foundation's website. **Contact:** Pride Foundation at the above address (see entry 5749).

5786 ■ You Go Girl! Scholarships
(Undergraduate/Scholarship)

Purpose: To provide scholarship to the students who have been stigmatized, isolated or closeted because of sexual identity issues. **Focus:** General studies. **Qualif.:** Applicants must be lesbians who have completed their sophomore year of college. **Criteria:** Selection will be based on the committee's criteria.

Funds Avail.: No specific amount. **To Apply:** Qualified students are asked to submit an application to determine eligibility for scholarships. Applicants may download an application form from the Foundation's website. **Contact:** Pride Foundation at the above address (see entry 5749).

5787 ■ Urashi Zen Scholarships *(Undergraduate/Scholarship)*

Purpose: To provide scholarship to the students who have been stigmatized, isolated or closeted because of sexual identity issues. **Focus:** Business administration; Computer and information sciences; Political science. **Qualif.:** Applicant must be a student studying business administration, computer science, or political science. **Criteria:** Selection will be based on the committee's criteria.

Funds Avail.: No specific amount. **To Apply:** Qualified students are asked to submit an application to determine eligibility for scholarships. Applicants may download an application form from the Foundation's website. **Contact:** Pride Foundation at the above address (see entry 5749).

5788 ■ Professional Aviation Maintenance Association

400 Commonwealth Dr.
Warrendale, PA 15096
Ph: (724)772-4092
Fax: (724)772-4064
Free: (866)865-7262
E-mail: hq@pama.org
URL: http://www.pama.org

5789 ■ PAMA Foundation Scholarship Program
(Graduate, Undergraduate/Scholarship)

Purpose: To provide educational assistance as a reward and recognition to qualified students pursuing careers in aviation maintenance. **Focus:** Aviation; Aeronautics. **Qualif.:** Applicants who are applying individually must be enrolled in a FAR Part 147 certificated educational institution in pursuit of an Airframe and Powerplant (A&P) license or a degree in aerospace maintenance and management; must have completed 25 percent of the required curriculum; must have a B average or equivalent; and must have a need for financial assistance. Applicants pursuing a Chapter application must be active; and not a relative of any PAMA board member. The chapter must also be recognized by PAMA. **Criteria:** Recipients are selected based on educational performance, work experience, participation in school and community activities, career commitment and future potential, financial need, and recommendation by a counselor, advisor, aviation maintenance instructor, or current employer.

Funds Avail.: $1,000. **To Apply:** Individual applicants must submit a certificate of current enrollment or avionics certification; completed Form SS-APP-880(typewritten and signed) and letter(s) of reference(s); Chapter applicants must submit completed Form CH-APP-880 (typewritten and signed) and are encouraged to present CH-APP-880 Forms of students awarded the previous year (if applicable). All requirements must be forwarded to PAMA Foundation Scholarships, 400 Commonwealth Dr. Warrendale, PA 15096. **Deadline:** October 31.

5790 ■ Professional Construction Estimators Association of America

PO Box 680336
Charlotte, NC 28216
Ph: (704)489-1494
Fax: (704)489-1495
Free: 877-521-7232
E-mail: pcea@pcea.org
URL: http://www.pcea.org

5791 ■ Ted C. Wilson Memorial Scholarships
(Undergraduate/Scholarship)

Purpose: To provide financial assistance to those who plan to further their education in the construction industry. **Focus:** Engineering; Construction. **Qualif.:** Applicant must be a high school senior, college freshman, sophomore or junior student planning to further his/her education in the construction industry. Applicant must be a resident of, or plan to attend a school or university in North Carolina, South Carolina, Virginia, Georgia and Florida where PCEA has an established chapter. **Criteria:** Applicants are selected based on the academic ability, need and desire to enter the construction industry.

Funds Avail.: $1,500. **To Apply:** Applicants must submit a completed application form; one evaluation form completed by the high school Guidance Counselor or College Faculty Advisor, whichever is applicable at time of application; one evaluation form completed by an adult not related to the applicant; official transcript of high school/college grades and latest S.A.T. scores if available. Finalists may be interviewed by the Scholarship Committee. **Deadline:** March 15.

Remarks: Established in May 21, 1988 in memory of Ted Wilson (1932-1987), the first National Executive Director of the PCEA.

5792 ■ Professional Institute of the Public Service of Canada

250 Tremblay Rd.
Ottawa, ON, Canada K1G 3J8
Ph: (613)228-6310
Fax: (613)228-9048
URL: http://www.portal.pipsc.ca

5793 ■ Professional Institute of the Public Service of Canada Expanded Scholarships
(Undergraduate/Scholarship)

Purpose: To provide educational assistance for students through three series: The President's Series; The Leader's

Awards are arranged alphabetically below their administering organizations

Series; and The Founders' Series. **Focus:** General studies. **Qualif.:** Applicants must be children or grandchildren of regular or retired members in good standing or members who were in good standing at the time of their death. Applicants must be entering their first year of post-secondary education, in a full-time program at an educational institution which is a member of the Association of Universities and Colleges in Canada. **Criteria:** Awards will be granted by an impartial selection panel using the following factors: academic achievement (transcript required); typed statement by the candidates indicating why they deserve a scholarship and outlining their goals for future education and career; documented leadership ability and community service involvement; essay of 750-1000 words on "professionalism". A suggested topic is "What does it mean to be professional in your career" but other specific topics on professionalism are welcomed.

Funds Avail.: $5,000 (President's Series); $3,500 (Leaders' Series); $1,500 (Founders' Series). **To Apply:** Application must include the following: official PIPSC Scholarship Application Form; a copy of the official transcript of marks from the learning institution most recently attended; a statement about why you should receive the scholarship and your future education and career goals; a typed statement about your leadership abilities and community service involvement with supporting evidence; and a 750-1000 word essay on "professionalism". Applicants must submit the application by mail or fax with other supporting documents. **Deadline:** July 11.

5794 ■ Public Agency Risk Managers Association

PO Box 6810
San Jose, CA 95150
Fax: 888-412-5913
Free: 888-90-PARMA
E-mail: brenda.reisinger@parma.com
URL: http://www.parma.com

5795 ■ PARMA Scholarships *(Undergraduate/Scholarship)*

Purpose: To promote, develop, and facilitate education and leadership in public agency risk management. **Focus:** Management. **Qualif.:** Applicant should be an employee of a member public agency pursuing an associate in Risk Management, Risk Management for Public Entities, Associate in Risk Pool Management. **Criteria:** The member of the Committee appointed by the president of PARMA will select the candidates based on the statement of his or her ultimate life goals in risk management and other related information.

Funds Avail.: $500 **Number Awarded:** 4. **To Apply:** An applicant must fill out the application form; attach a written sponsorship statement by a PARMA member agency; must submit of his/her ultimate own goals in the field of risk management; a description of the participation in PARMA including the local Chapter level; and attach any other related experience or information you may wish to submit in support of your scholarship request. **Contact:** PARMA Secretary Treasurer PO Box 711894 Santee, CA 92072-1894.

5796 ■ Public Education Foundation

3360 W Sahara Ave., Ste. 160
Las Vegas, NV 89102
Ph: (702)799-1042
Fax: (702)799-5247
E-mail: steelej@ccpef.org
URL: http://ccpef.org

5797 ■ Evelyn Abrams Memorial Scholarships *(Undergraduate/Scholarship)*

Purpose: To support individuals aiming to acquire a degree in education or business. **Focus:** Education; Business. **Qualif.:** Applicants must be CCSD female seniors interested in pursuing a degree in education or business at an accredited college/university; must have a minimum 3.0 unweighted cumulative GPA; and must demonstrate financial need. **Criteria:** Selection is based on merit.

Funds Avail.: $750. **Number Awarded:** 1. **To Apply:** Applicants must submit a completed application form together with the required materials. **Deadline:** March 7. **Contact:** Shana Venenga at 702-799-1042.

5798 ■ Adelson Family Scholarships *(Undergraduate/Scholarship)*

Purpose: To assist the education of the dependents of Venetian Resort Hotel Casino Employees. **Focus:** General studies. **Qualif.:** Applicants must be CCSD seniors; must be dependents of a Venetian Resort Hotel Casino employee; must be planning to attend an accredited college/university; must have a minimum 3.5 cumulative GPA; and must demonstrate financial need. **Criteria:** Awards are given based on need.

Funds Avail.: $2,500. **Number Awarded:** 3. **To Apply:** Applicants must submit a completed application form together with an essay, two letters of recommendation, transcript and a resume of awards. **Deadline:** April 4. **Contact:** Shana Venenga at 702-799-1042.

5799 ■ Adelson Scholarships *(Undergraduate/Scholarship)*

Purpose: To support individuals pursuing a career in the field of health services. **Focus:** Health care services. **Qualif.:** Applicants must be CCSD seniors interested in pursuing a career in the field of health services at an accredited college/university; must have a minimum 3.5 cumulative GPA; and must demonstrate financial need. **Criteria:** Selection is based on merit.

Funds Avail.: $2,000. **Number Awarded:** 3. **To Apply:** Applicants must submit a completed application form together with an essay, two letters of recommendation, transcript and a resume of awards. **Deadline:** March 4. **Contact:** Shana Venenga at 702-799-1042.

5800 ■ Alliance of Black Culinarians Scholarships *(Undergraduate/Scholarship)*

Purpose: To promote education in culinary arts. **Focus:** Culinary arts. **Qualif.:** Applicants must be CCSD seniors; must have a minimum 2.5 GPA; and must demonstrate financial need. **Criteria:** Preference is given to minority students and those interested in a career in culinary arts.

Funds Avail.: $1,000. **Number Awarded:** 3. **To Apply:** Applicants must submit a completed application form together with an essay, two letters of recommendation, transcript and a resume. **Deadline:** March 31. **Contact:** Shana Venenga at 702-799-1042.

5801 ■ American Nuclear Society Nevada Section Scholarships *(Undergraduate/Scholarship)*

Purpose: To promote education in the field of nuclear science. **Focus:** Engineering, Nuclear; Nuclear science. **Qua-**

Awards are arranged alphabetically below their administering organizations

lif.: Applicants must be CCSD seniors planning to major in nuclear engineering or a nuclear science related field at UNLV with a minimum 3.8 cumulative GPA. **Criteria:** Awards are given based on merit.

Funds Avail.: $1,000. **Number Awarded:** 2. **To Apply:** Applicants must submit a completed application form together with an essay, two letters of recommendation, transcript and a resume of awards. **Deadline:** March 7. **Contact:** Shana Venenga at 702-799-1042.

5802 ■ Susan Ayers Memorial Scholarships *(Undergraduate/Scholarship)*

Purpose: To provide educational opportunities for individuals intending to pursue higher studies. **Focus:** General studies. **Qualif.:** Applicants must be CCSD seniors who have attended the Estes McDoniel Elementary School; must be planning to attend an accredited post-secondary college/university; and must have a minimum 3.0 unweighted cumulative GPA. **Criteria:** Award is given based on the application materials.

Funds Avail.: $500. **Number Awarded:** 1. **To Apply:** Applicants must submit a completed application form together with an essay, two letters of recommendation, and transcript. **Deadline:** March 7. **Contact:** Shana Venenga at 702-799-1042.

5803 ■ Jeannette Bautista Memorial Scholarships *(Undergraduate/Scholarship)*

Purpose: To provide educational opportunities for individuals intending to pursue higher studies. **Focus:** Education. **Qualif.:** Applicants must be CCSD seniors planning to attend an accredited post-secondary institution in the field of education; must have a minimum 3.5 cumulative GPA; and must demonstrate financial need. **Criteria:** Special preference is given to secondary education mathematics majors.

Funds Avail.: $250. **Number Awarded:** 1. **To Apply:** Applicants must submit a completed application form together with an essay, two letters of recommendation, transcript and a resume of awards. **Deadline:** March 7. **Contact:** Shana Venenga at 702-799-1042.

5804 ■ Blues Ambassador Scholarships *(Undergraduate/Scholarship)*

Purpose: To provide educational opportunities for individuals intending to pursue higher studies. **Focus:** General studies. **Qualif.:** Applicants must be CCSD seniors who have demonstrated an interest and achievement in the arts or shown leadership in encouraging understanding among people of diverse backgrounds; must have a minimum 2.5 cumulative GPA; must be planning to attend an accredited institution of higher learning; and must demonstrate financial need. **Criteria:** Award is given based on the application materials.

Funds Avail.: $10,000 for a four-year program or $5,000 for a two-year program. **Number Awarded:** 1. **To Apply:** Applicants must submit a completed application form together with an essay, two letters of recommendation, transcript and a resume of awards. **Deadline:** March 7. **Contact:** Shana Venenga at 702-799-1042.

5805 ■ Donald Franklin Bradley Memorial Scholarships *(Undergraduate/Scholarship)*

Purpose: To promote education related in photography. **Focus:** Photography. **Qualif.:** Applicants must be CCSD seniors planning to attend the University of Nevada, Las Vegas as full-time students for a major related to photography; must have a minimum 3.0 cumulative GPA (weighted or unweighted). **Criteria:** Preference will be given to students that demonstrate financial need.

Funds Avail.: $1,000. **Number Awarded:** 1. **To Apply:** Applicants must submit a completed application form together with an essay, transcript, a letter of recommendation, and copies of best photographs taken. **Deadline:** March 31. **Contact:** Shana Venenga at 702-799-1042.

5806 ■ Susan Brager Occupational Education Scholarships *(Undergraduate/Scholarship)*

Purpose: To provide educational opportunities for individuals intending to pursue higher studies. **Focus:** Education. **Qualif.:** Applicants must be CCSD seniors; must have completed a minimum of two years of an established occupational education program; must have a minimum 2.5 cumulative GPA; and must be planning to attend a school in the Nevada Higher Education System within Clark County. **Criteria:** Award is given based on the application materials.

Funds Avail.: $1,000. **Number Awarded:** 1. **To Apply:** Applicants must submit a completed application form together with an essay, a letter of recommendation, transcript and a resume of awards. **Deadline:** March 7. **Contact:** Shana Venenga at 702-799-1042.

5807 ■ Agustin Cano Memorial Scholarships *(Undergraduate/Scholarship)*

Purpose: To provide educational opportunities for individuals intending to pursue higher studies. **Focus:** General studies. **Qualif.:** Applicants must be Valley High School seniors planning to attend an accredited college/university as full-time students. **Criteria:** Award is given based on the application materials.

Funds Avail.: $500. **Number Awarded:** 1. **To Apply:** Applicants must submit a completed application form together with an essay, two letters of recommendation, and a resume of awards. **Deadline:** March 7. **Contact:** Shana Venenga at 702-799-1042.

5808 ■ John Caoile Memorial Scholarships *(Undergraduate/Scholarship)*

Purpose: To provide educational opportunities for individuals intending to pursue higher studies. **Focus:** General studies. **Qualif.:** Applicants must be Durango High School AFJROTC program seniors planning to attend an accredited post-secondary institution and have excelled in the areas of leadership, community service and extra-curricular activities and must have a minimum 3.0 GPA. **Criteria:** Award is given based on the application materials.

Funds Avail.: $1,000. **Number Awarded:** 1. **To Apply:** Applicants must submit a completed application form together with a letter of recommendation, transcript and a resume of awards. **Deadline:** March 7. **Contact:** Shana Venenga at 702-799-1042.

5809 ■ CCSD School Counselors' Scholarships *(Undergraduate/Scholarship)*

Purpose: To provide educational opportunities for individuals intending to pursue higher studies. **Focus:** General studies. **Qualif.:** Applicants must be CCSD seniors who have met and overcome a serious personal challenge or adversity; must have a minimum 2.5 unweighted GPA; and must be planning to attend an accredited post-secondary institution. **Criteria:** Award is given based on the application materials.

Awards are arranged alphabetically below their administering organizations

Funds Avail.: $1,000. **Number Awarded:** 1. **To Apply:** Applicants must submit a completed application form together with an essay, two letters of recommendation, transcript and a resume of awards. **Deadline:** March 7. **Contact:** Shana Venenga at 702-799-1042.

5810 ▪ Cheyenne High School Faculty Memorial Scholarships *(Undergraduate/Scholarship)*

Purpose: To provide educational opportunities for individuals intending to pursue higher studies. **Focus:** General studies. **Qualif.:** Applicants must be Cheyenne High School seniors planning to attend an accredited post-secondary institution and have a minimum 3.1 unweighted GPA. **Criteria:** Awards are given based on the application materials.

Funds Avail.: $1000. **Number Awarded:** 2. **To Apply:** Applicants must submit a completed application form together with an essay, a resume of awards, and two letters of recommendation. **Deadline:** March 7. **Contact:** Shana Venenga at 702-799-1042.

5811 ▪ Nate Mack/Cindi Turner Scholarships *(Undergraduate/Scholarship)*

Purpose: To provide educational opportunities for individuals intending to pursue higher studies. **Focus:** General studies. **Qualif.:** Applicants must be CCSD seniors who attended Nate Mack Elementary School for at least three years; must be planning to attend an accredited college/university; must have a minimum 2.8 cumulative GPA; and must demonstrate financial need. **Criteria:** Award is given based on the application materials.

Funds Avail.: $500. **Number Awarded:** 1. **To Apply:** Applicants must submit a completed application form along with an essay, two letters of recommendation, transcript, and resume of awards. **Deadline:** March 7. **Contact:** Shana Venenga at 702-799-1042.

5812 ▪ Clark High School Academy of Finance Scholarships *(Undergraduate/Scholarship)*

Purpose: To promote education in business, economics or finance. **Focus:** Business; Economics; Finance. **Qualif.:** Applicants must be Clark High School Academy of Finance (AOF) seniors interested in pursuing a degree in business, economics or finance at an accredited college/university and who have a minimum 3.0 GPA. **Criteria:** Award is given based on merit.

Funds Avail.: $2,000. **Number Awarded:** 1. **To Apply:** Applicants must submit a completed application form together with an essay, three letters of recommendation, transcript, resume of awards, and a copy of AOF Internship Evaluation. **Deadline:** March 7. **Contact:** Shana Venenga at 702-799-1042.

5813 ▪ Clark High School Alumni Leadership Circle Scholarships *(Undergraduate/Scholarship)*

Purpose: To promote education in business, economics or finance. **Focus:** Business; Economics; Finance. **Qualif.:** Applicants must be Clark High School Academy of Finance (AOF) seniors interested in pursuing a degree in business, economics or finance at an accredited college/university and who have a minimum 3.0 GPA. **Criteria:** Award is given based on the application materials.

Funds Avail.: $500. **Number Awarded:** 1. **To Apply:** Applicants must submit a completed application form together with an essay, two letters of recommendation, transcript, resume of awards, and a copy of AOF Internship Evaluation. **Deadline:** March 7. **Contact:** Shana Venenga at 702-799-1042.

5814 ▪ Clark High School Teacher Education Academy Scholarships *(Undergraduate/Scholarship)*

Purpose: To provide educational opportunities for individuals intending to pursue higher studies. **Focus:** Education. **Qualif.:** Applicants must be Teacher Education Academy at Clark High School (TEACH) seniors interested in pursuing a degree in education at an accredited college/university; must have a minimum 2.8 cumulative GPA; and must be currently enrolled in the TEACH Educational Internship and Seminar course. **Criteria:** Award is given based on the application materials.

Funds Avail.: $500. **Number Awarded:** 1. **To Apply:** Applicants must submit a completed application form together with an essay, transcript, and resume of awards. **Deadline:** March 7.

Remarks: In memory of Eleine Flemming-Smith. **Contact:** Shana Venenga at 702-799-1042.

5815 ▪ Corbett-Porter Building Bridges Scholarships *(Undergraduate/Scholarship)*

Purpose: To provide educational opportunities for individuals intending to pursue higher studies. **Focus:** General studies. **Qualif.:** Applicants must be CCSD seniors who have worked to create a school environment free of discrimination, harassment and intolerance by building bridges between the gay/lesbian and straight communities; must have a 2.5 minimum GPA; and must be planning to attend an accredited post-secondary institution. **Criteria:** Consideration is given to students with financial need.

Funds Avail.: $1,000. **Number Awarded:** 1. **To Apply:** Applicants must submit a completed application form together with an essay, two letters of recommendation, transcript, and resume of awards. **Deadline:** March 7. **Contact:** Shana Venenga at 702-799-1042.

5816 ▪ Robin M. Daniels Memorial Scholarships *(Undergraduate/Scholarship)*

Purpose: To provide educational opportunities for individuals intending to pursue higher studies. **Focus:** General studies. **Qualif.:** Applicants must be CCSD seniors who have met and overcome a serious personal challenge or adversity and plan to attend an accredited post-secondary institution in Nevada. **Criteria:** Award is given based on merit.

Funds Avail.: $1,000. **Number Awarded:** 1. **To Apply:** Applicants must submit a completed application form together with an essay, and two letters of recommendation. **Deadline:** March 7. **Contact:** Shana Venenga at 702-799-1042.

5817 ▪ Harvey N. Dondero Communication and Journalism Excellence Scholarships *(Undergraduate/Scholarship)*

Purpose: To promote education in communication. **Focus:** Journalism; Communications. **Qualif.:** Applicants must be CCSD seniors planning to attend an accredited post-secondary institution pursuing a degree in journalism or communications. **Criteria:** Award is given based on merit.

Funds Avail.: $1,200. **Number Awarded:** 1. **To Apply:** Applicants must submit a completed application form together with an essay, transcript, and a recommendation written by a journalism or English teacher. **Deadline:** March 31. **Contact:** Shana Venenga at 702-799-1042.

Awards are arranged alphabetically below their administering organizations

5818 ■ Mickey Donnelly Memorial Scholarships *(Undergraduate/Scholarship)*

Purpose: To provide educational opportunities for individuals intending to pursue higher studies. **Focus:** General studies. **Qualif.:** Applicants must be CCSD seniors who have attended Walter Johnson Junior High School for a minimum of one year and are planning to attend an accredited post-secondary institution in Nevada; must have a minimum 2.5 unweighted cumulative GPA. **Criteria:** Award is given based on merit.

Funds Avail.: $500. **Number Awarded:** 1. **To Apply:** Applicants must submit a completed application form together with an essay, two letters of recommendation, transcript, and resume of awards. **Deadline:** March 7. **Contact:** Shana Venenga at 702-799-1042.

5819 ■ Travis Dunning Memorial Scholarships *(Undergraduate/Scholarship)*

Purpose: To provide educational opportunities for individuals intending to pursue higher studies. **Focus:** General studies. **Qualif.:** Applicants must be high school seniors from Green Valley, Coronado, Foothill, Silverado or Liberty planning to attend an accredited four-year college/university and who have a 3.0 weighted or unweighted GPA. **Criteria:** Award is given based on need.

Funds Avail.: $1,500. **Number Awarded:** 1. **To Apply:** Applicants must submit a completed application form together with an essay, two letters of recommendation, transcript, and resume of awards. **Deadline:** March 31. **Contact:** Shana Venenga at 702-799-1042.

5820 ■ Palo Verde High School - Barbara Edwards Memorial Scholarships *(Undergraduate/Scholarship)*

Purpose: To provide educational opportunities for individuals intending to pursue higher studies. **Focus:** Foreign languages. **Qualif.:** Applicants must be Palo Verde High School seniors who have completed seven semesters of the same foreign language and demonstrated academic excellence; must be planning to attend an accredited college or university; and must have a minimum 3.5 cumulative GPA. **Criteria:** Award is given based on the application materials.

Funds Avail.: $1,000. **Number Awarded:** 1. **To Apply:** Applicants must submit a completed application form along with an essay, transcript, resume of awards, and Foreign Language Teacher Evaluation Sheet. **Deadline:** March 7. **Contact:** Shana Venenga at 702-799-1042.

5821 ■ Don English Memorial Scholarships *(Undergraduate/Scholarship)*

Purpose: To promote education in photography and journalism. **Focus:** Photography; Journalism. **Qualif.:** Applicants must be CCSD seniors planning to attend an accredited college, university, or institute as full-time students in the field of photography, media arts, or journalism; must have a minimum 3.0 cumulative GPA. **Criteria:** Preference is given to students who demonstrate financial need.

Funds Avail.: $4,100. **Number Awarded:** 1. **To Apply:** Applicants must submit a completed application form together with an essay, two letters of recommendation, transcript, and resume of awards. **Deadline:** March 7. **Contact:** Shana Venenga at 702-799-1042.

5822 ■ Epicurean Charitable Foundation Scholarships *(Undergraduate/Scholarship)*

Purpose: To promote education in Hotel Management and Food and Beverage. **Focus:** Hotel, institutional, and restaurant management. **Qualif.:** Applicants must be high school seniors in Clark County planning to attend an accredited post-secondary institution; must be planning to obtain a bachelor's degree and major in Hotel Management or Food & Beverage programs; must have demonstrated financial need; and must have a cumulative GPA of 2.75. **Criteria:** Award is given based on merit.

Funds Avail.: $5,000-$10,000. **Number Awarded:** Up to 8. **To Apply:** Applicants must submit a completed application form together with an essay, career goal statement, two letters of recommendation, transcript, and resume of awards. **Deadline:** March 7. **Contact:** Shana Venenga at 702-799-1042.

5823 ■ Evening Mesquite Club Scholarships *(Undergraduate/Scholarship)*

Purpose: To provide educational opportunities for individuals intending to pursue higher studies. **Focus:** General studies. **Qualif.:** Applicants must be CCSD female seniors planning to attend an accredited post-secondary institution in Nevada as a full-time student; must have a minimum 3.0 GPA; and must have demonstrated financial need. **Criteria:** Award is given based on need.

Funds Avail.: $1,200. **Number Awarded:** 1. **To Apply:** Applicants must submit a completed application form together with an essay, two letters of recommendation, transcript, and resume of awards. **Deadline:** March 7. **Contact:** Shana Venenga at 702-799-1042.

5824 ■ Gordy Fink Memorial Scholarships *(Undergraduate/Scholarship)*

Purpose: To provide educational opportunities for individuals intending to pursue higher studies. **Focus:** General studies. **Qualif.:** Applicants must be Valley High School seniors planning to attend the University of Nevada, Las Vegas as full-time students. **Criteria:** Consideration is given to students with financial need.

Funds Avail.: $1,000. **Number Awarded:** 2. **To Apply:** Applicants must submit a completed application form together with an essay, two letters of recommendation, transcript, resume of awards, and letter of admission from UNLV. **Deadline:** March 7. **Contact:** Shana Venenga at 702-799-1042.

5825 ■ Flora English Creative Writing Scholarships *(Undergraduate/Scholarship)*

Purpose: To provide educational opportunities for individuals intending to pursue higher studies. **Focus:** Education, English as a second language. **Qualif.:** Applicants must be CCSD seniors interested in pursuing a degree in English at an accredited college or university; must have a minimum 3.0 cumulative GPA; and must demonstrate financial need. **Criteria:** Award is given based on need.

Funds Avail.: $1,000. **Number Awarded:** 1. **To Apply:** Applicants must submit a completed application form together with an essay, two letters of recommendation, transcript, and resume of awards. **Deadline:** March 7. **Contact:** Shana Venenga at 702-799-1042.

5826 ■ Fraser Family Scholarships *(Undergraduate/Scholarship)*

Purpose: To provide educational opportunities for individuals intending to pursue higher studies. **Focus:** Education. **Qualif.:** Applicants must be high school seniors from Durango with a 3.5 cumulative GPA planning to attend an accredited college/university and pursuing a degree in education or related field. **Criteria:** Award is given based on the application materials.

Funds Avail.: $1,000. **Number Awarded:** 1. **To Apply:** Applicants must submit a completed application form together with an essay, two letters of recommendation, transcript, and resume of awards. **Deadline:** March 7. **Contact:** Shana Venenga at 702-799-1042.

5827 ■ Veronica Gantt Memorial Scholarships
(Undergraduate/Scholarship)

Purpose: To provide educational opportunities for individuals intending to pursue higher studies. **Focus:** General studies. **Qualif.:** Applicants must be Del Sol High School seniors active in sports and community; must be planning to attend an accredited college or university; and must have a minimum 3.0 cumulative GPA. **Criteria:** Awards are given based on the application materials.

Funds Avail.: $500. **Number Awarded:** 2. **To Apply:** Applicants must submit a completed application form together with an essay and a recommendation letter. **Deadline:** March 7. **Contact:** Shana Venenga at 702-799-1042.

5828 ■ Dr. Virginia Gilbert Memorial Scholarships *(Undergraduate/Scholarship)*

Purpose: To promote education in the field of mathematics. **Focus:** Mathematics and mathematical sciences. **Qualif.:** Applicants must be CCSD seniors who have demonstrated an interest in mathematics and planning to attend a Southern Nevada accredited college/university. **Criteria:** Awards are given based on the application materials.

Funds Avail.: $10,000. **Number Awarded:** 2. **To Apply:** Applicants must submit a completed application form together with an essay, a recommendation letter, and a transcript. **Deadline:** March 7. **Contact:** Shana Venenga at 702-799-1042.

5829 ■ Nick Giorgione Hope for Hearts Scholarships *(Undergraduate/Scholarship)*

Purpose: To provide educational opportunities for individuals intending to pursue higher studies. **Focus:** General studies. **Qualif.:** Applicants must be CCSD seniors with a minimum 2.8 cumulative GAP, affected by a heart disease. **Criteria:** Consideration is given to students with financial need.

Funds Avail.: $1,500. **Number Awarded:** 1. **To Apply:** Applicants must submit a completed application form together with an essay, a letter of recommendation, transcript, and a documentation from a school health office or doctor verifying heart condition. **Deadline:** March 7. **Contact:** Shana Venenga at 702-799-1042.

5830 ■ Glazing Industry Scholarships
(Undergraduate/Scholarship)

Purpose: To support the education of students having a parent or grandparent participating in the glazing industry. **Focus:** General studies. **Qualif.:** Applicants must be High school seniors or post-secondary students in Nevada who are children or grandchildren of individuals actively participating in the glazing industry; must have a desire to achieve excellence through education, planning to attend a post-secondary program; and must have a minimum 2.8 unweighted cumulative GPA. **Criteria:** Awards are given based on application materials.

Funds Avail.: $500. **Number Awarded:** 6. **To Apply:** Applicants must submit a completed application form together with an essay, a letter of recommendation, and transcript. **Deadline:** March 7. **Contact:** Shana Venenga at 702-799-1042.

5831 ■ Gretchen Hauff Memorial Scholarships
(Undergraduate/Scholarship)

Purpose: To promote education in physical education. **Focus:** Physical education. **Qualif.:** Applicants must be CCSD female seniors interested in pursuing a degree in physical education at an accredited college/university; must have a minimum 2.5 unweighted cumulative GPA; and must have demonstrated financial need. **Criteria:** Award is given based on need.

Funds Avail.: $1,000. **Number Awarded:** 1. **To Apply:** Applicants must submit a completed application form together with an essay, three letters of recommendation, transcript, and resume of awards. **Deadline:** March 7. **Contact:** Shana Venenga at 702-799-1042.

5832 ■ Michael J. Hoggard Memorial Scholarships *(Undergraduate/Scholarship)*

Purpose: To provide educational opportunities for individuals intending to pursue higher studies. **Focus:** General studies. **Qualif.:** Applicants must be Green Valley High School seniors who have been on the school's soccer team for at least two years (including senior year); must be planning to attend an accredited post-secondary college/university; and must have a minimum 3.0 cumulative GPA. **Criteria:** Award is given based on need.

Funds Avail.: $1,000. **Number Awarded:** 1. **To Apply:** Applicants must submit a completed application form with the essay, two letters of recommendation, transcript, and resume of awards. **Deadline:** March 7. **Contact:** Shana Venenga at 702-799-1042.

5833 ■ JMA Architecture Studios Scholarships
(Undergraduate/Scholarship)

Purpose: To promote education in architecture. **Focus:** Architecture. **Qualif.:** Applicants must be CCSD seniors interested in pursuing a career in architecture; must be planning to attend a university with an accredited School of Architecture; must demonstrate financial need; and must have a minimum 3.0 unweighted cumulative GPA. **Criteria:** Preferential consideration will be given to students who have participated in the Clark County School District's drafting program.

Funds Avail.: $3,500. **Number Awarded:** 1. **To Apply:** Applicants must submit a completed application form along with a work sample, two letters of recommendation, transcript, resume of awards, and a college/university admission acceptance letter. **Deadline:** March 7. **Contact:** Shana Venenga at 702-799-1042.

5834 ■ Knights of Pythias Scholarships
(Undergraduate/Scholarship)

Purpose: To provide educational opportunities for individuals intending to pursue higher studies. **Focus:** General studies. **Qualif.:** Applicants must be CCSD seniors who have demonstrated exemplary participation in community service and planning to attend an accredited post-secondary institution. **Criteria:** Award is given based on merit.

Funds Avail.: $1,000. **Number Awarded:** 1. **To Apply:** Applicants must submit a completed application form with the essay, two letters of recommendation, and resume of awards. **Deadline:** March 7. **Contact:** Shana Venenga at 702-799-1042.

Awards are arranged alphabetically below their administering organizations

5835 ■ Las Vegas Chinatown Scholarships *(Undergraduate/Scholarship)*

Purpose: To provide educational opportunities for individuals intending to pursue higher studies. **Focus:** Business. **Qualif.:** Applicants must be CCSD seniors of Asian descent planning to attend an accredited college/university in Nevada and must have a minimum 3.0 cumulative GPA. **Criteria:** Preference will be given to students planning to major in Business.

Funds Avail.: $1,000. **Number Awarded:** 2. **To Apply:** Applicants must submit a completed application form with an essay, two letters of recommendation, transcript, and resume of awards. **Deadline:** March 7. **Contact:** Shana Venenga at 702-799-1042.

5836 ■ Las Vegas Elks Scholarships *(Undergraduate/Scholarship)*

Purpose: To provide educational opportunities for individuals intending to pursue higher studies. **Focus:** General studies. **Qualif.:** Applicants must be CCSD seniors planning to attend an accredited college, university or vocational school; must have a GPA which is adequate for entry to the school; must be citizens of the U.S.; and must live at an address in Las Vegas, Nevada. **Criteria:** Awards are given based on scholastic records with consideration of grade point, as well as SAT or ACT scores.

Funds Avail.: $1,500. **Number Awarded:** 5. **To Apply:** Applicants must submit a completed application form along with the essay, transcript and resume of awards. The essay, resume and reference must not be more than six pages. **Deadline:** March 7. **Contact:** Shana Venenga at 702-799-1042.

5837 ■ Las Vegas Elks Scholarships for the Physically Challenged *(Undergraduate/Scholarship)*

Purpose: To provide educational assistance for physically challenged students. **Focus:** General studies. **Qualif.:** Applicants must be CCSD seniors who are physically challenged; must be planning to attend an accredited college, university or vocational school; must have a GPA adequate for entry to the school; must be citizens of the U.S.; and must live at an address in Las Vegas, Nevada. **Criteria:** Awards are given based on need.

Funds Avail.: $5,000. **Number Awarded:** 4. **To Apply:** Applicants must submit a completed application form along with an essay, transcript and resume of awards. The essay, resume and reference must not be more than six pages. **Deadline:** March 7. **Contact:** Shana Venenga at 702-799-1042.

5838 ■ Melissa A. Lyles Memorial Scholarships *(Undergraduate/Scholarship)*

Purpose: To provide educational opportunities for individuals intending to pursue higher studies. **Focus:** General studies. **Qualif.:** Applicants must be CCSD seniors who have demonstrated an academic achievement in a minimum of eleven Honors or Advanced Placement courses; must be planning to attend an accredited college/university; and must have a minimum 4.0 weighted cumulative GPA. **Criteria:** Award is given based on merit.

Funds Avail.: $5,000. **Number Awarded:** 1. **To Apply:** Applicants must submit a completed application form along with an essay, transcript and resume of awards. **Deadline:** March 7. **Contact:** Shana Venenga at 702-799-1042.

5839 ■ Corporal Joseph Martinez U.S. Army Memorial Scholarships *(Undergraduate/Scholarship)*

Purpose: To provide educational opportunities for individuals intending to pursue higher studies. **Focus:** Maritime studies. **Qualif.:** Applicants must be Durango High School AFJROTC program seniors planning to attend an accredited post-secondary institution either during or immediately following enlistment in any branch of the U.S. military may apply. **Criteria:** Award is given based on the application materials.

Funds Avail.: $500-$1,000. **Number Awarded:** 1 or 2. **To Apply:** Applicants must submit a completed application form along with the letter from military recruiter, one letter of recommendation, transcript, and resume. **Deadline:** March 7. **Contact:** Shana Venenga at 702-799-1042.

5840 ■ Aaron Matusek Memorial Scholarships *(Undergraduate/Scholarship)*

Purpose: To provide educational opportunities for individuals intending to pursue higher studies. **Focus:** General studies. **Qualif.:** Applicants must be CCSD seniors with a minimum 2.75 cumulative GPA and planning to attend an accredited college/university in Nevada. **Criteria:** Award is given based on need.

Funds Avail.: $800. **Number Awarded:** 1. **To Apply:** Applicants must submit a completed application form along with an essay, two letters of recommendation, transcript, and resume of awards. **Deadline:** March 7. **Contact:** Shana Venenga at 702-799-1042.

5841 ■ Ronald McDonald House Charities of Las Vegas Scholarships *(Undergraduate/Scholarship)*

Purpose: To provide educational opportunities for individuals intending to pursue higher studies. **Focus:** General studies. **Qualif.:** Applicants must be high school seniors in Clark or Nye County in Nevada; must be eligible to attend an accredited post-secondary educational institute (includes colleges, universities, junior colleges, vocational institutes and trade schools); and must have a minimum 2.5 cumulative GPA-unweighted. **Criteria:** Awards are given based on the application materials.

Funds Avail.: Varies. **Number Awarded:** Varies. **To Apply:** Applicants must submit a complete application form together with certified high school transcript; personal statement; letter of recommendation; and a copy of parent's/guardian's IRS Form W2. **Deadline:** march 7.

Remarks: Sponsored by RMHC Charities.

5842 ■ MSPT Sports Medicine Scholarships *(Undergraduate/Scholarship)*

Purpose: To provide educational opportunities for individuals intending to pursue higher studies. **Focus:** Health care services; Sports medicine. **Qualif.:** Applicants must be CCSD seniors intending to pursue a career in healthcare/sports medicine; must be planning to attend at an accredited post-secondary institution; and must have a minimum 3.2 unweighted cumulative GPA. **Criteria:** Awards are given based on the application materials.

Funds Avail.: $2,500. **Number Awarded:** 2. **To Apply:** Applicants must submit a completed application form along with an essay, transcript, and resume of awards. **Deadline:** March 7. **Contact:** Shana Venenga at 702-799-1042.

5843 ■ National Security Technologies Engineering and Science Scholarships *(Undergraduate/Scholarship)*

Purpose: To promote education in the field of engineering or science. **Focus:** Engineering; Science. **Qualif.:** Applicants must be CCSD seniors planning to major in engineering or science at a four-year institution with a minimum 3.5 cumulative GPA. **Criteria:** Awards are given based on the application materials.

Funds Avail.: $5,000. **Number Awarded:** Up to 10. **To Apply:** Applicants must submit a completed application form along with an essay, transcript, and three letters of recommendation. **Deadline:** March 7. **Contact:** Shana Venenga at 702-799-1042.

5844 ■ Nevada Black Police Association Scholarships *(Undergraduate/Scholarship)*

Purpose: To assist the education of African American students. **Focus:** General studies. **Qualif.:** Applicants must be CCSD African American seniors planning to attend a college/university; must have a 2.5 GPA; and must demonstrate financial need. **Criteria:** Awards are given based on need.

Funds Avail.: $1,000. **Number Awarded:** 4. **To Apply:** Applicants must submit a completed application form along with an essay, two letters of recommendation, transcript, resume of awards, and a college letter of admission. **Deadline:** March 7. **Contact:** Shana Venenga at 702-799-1042.

5845 ■ Nevada Parent Teacher Association Scholarships *(Undergraduate/Scholarship)*

Purpose: To provide educational opportunities for individuals intending to pursue higher studies. **Focus:** Education. **Qualif.:** Applicants must be CCSD seniors who have attended a PTSA high school or Teacher Education Academy at Clark High School (TEACH); must be pursuing a degree in education; must be planning to attend a post-secondary college or university; and must have a minimum 2.8 cumulative GPA. **Criteria:** Award is given based on the application materials.

Funds Avail.: $500. **Number Awarded:** 1. **To Apply:** Applicants must submit a completed application form along with an essay, transcript, and resume of awards. **Deadline:** March 7. **Contact:** Shana Venenga at 702-799-1042.

5846 ■ North Las Vegas Firefighters - William J. Harnedy Memorial Scholarships *(Undergraduate/Scholarship)*

Purpose: To provide educational opportunities for individuals intending to pursue higher studies. **Focus:** General studies. **Qualif.:** Applicants must be CCSD seniors who have attended a North Las Vegas High School; must be enrolled in the Credit Retrieval Program; must have a minimum cumulative 2.5 GPA; must have demonstrated financial need; and must be planning to attend an accredited post-secondary institution. **Criteria:** Award is given based on the application materials.

Funds Avail.: $1,000. **Number Awarded:** 1. **To Apply:** Applicants must submit a completed application form together with an essay and transcript. **Deadline:** March 7. **Contact:** Shana Venenga at 702-799-1042.

5847 ■ Palo Verde High School Faculty Follies Scholarships *(Undergraduate/Scholarship)*

Purpose: To provide educational opportunities for individuals intending to pursue higher studies. **Focus:** Theater arts. **Qualif.:** Applicants must be Palo Verde High School seniors who have completed six semesters of theater classes; must be planning to attend an accredited college/university; and must have a minimum 2.5 cumulative GPA. **Criteria:** Award is given based on the application materials.

Funds Avail.: $500. **Number Awarded:** 1. **To Apply:** Applicants must submit a completed application form along with an essay, transcript, resume of awards, and Leadership, Activities and Achievement Information. **Deadline:** March 7. **Contact:** Shana Venenga at 702-799-1042.

5848 ■ Panther Cafe Scholarships *(Undergraduate/Scholarship)*

Purpose: To provide educational opportunities for individuals intending to pursue higher studies. **Focus:** General studies. **Qualif.:** Applicants must be Palo Verde High School seniors who have participated in a class that is directly associated with the operation of the Panther Cafe and must be planning to attend an accredited post-secondary college or institution. **Criteria:** Awards are given based on the application materials.

Funds Avail.: $500. **Number Awarded:** 2. **To Apply:** Applicants must submit a completed application form along with an essay, two letters of recommendation, transcript, and resume of awards. **Deadline:** March 7. **Contact:** Shana Venenga at 702-799-1042.

5849 ■ Pardee Community Building Scholarships *(Undergraduate/Scholarship)*

Purpose: To provide educational opportunities for individuals intending to pursue higher studies. **Focus:** Business; Civil engineering; Architecture; Construction. **Qualif.:** Applicants must be CCSD seniors who have demonstrated an interest in home building and community development; must be planning to attend a Nevada accredited college or university; must be pursuing studies in areas of business, civil engineering, architecture or landscape architecture and construction management; and must have a minimum 2.8 cumulative GPA. **Criteria:** Awards are given based on merit.

Funds Avail.: $1,500. **Number Awarded:** 10. **To Apply:** Applicants must submit a completed application form along with an essay, two letters of recommendation, transcript, and resume of awards. **Deadline:** March 7. **Contact:** Shana Venenga at 702-799-1042.

5850 ■ Penn-Bird Family Memorial Scholarships *(Undergraduate/Scholarship)*

Purpose: To provide educational opportunities for individuals intending to pursue higher studies. **Focus:** Education. **Qualif.:** Applicants must be CCSD seniors pursuing a degree in education and with a minimum 3.0 cumulative GPA. **Criteria:** Awards are given based on the application materials.

Funds Avail.: $1,000. **Number Awarded:** 2. **To Apply:** Applicants must submit a completed application form along with the essay, transcript, and college letter of admission. **Deadline:** March 7. **Contact:** Shana Venenga at 702-799-1042.

5851 ■ Josef Princ Memorial Scholarships *(Undergraduate/Scholarship)*

Purpose: To provide educational opportunities for individuals intending to pursue higher studies. **Focus:** Engineering; Mathematics and mathematical sciences. **Qualif.:** Applicants must be CCSD male seniors of European descent;

must be maintaining a minimum 3.5 cumulative GPA; must be demonstrating financial need; and must be planning to attend an accredited post-secondary college/university majoring in engineering, mathematics or science. **Criteria:** Awards are given based on need.

Funds Avail.: $2,000. **Number Awarded:** 3. **To Apply:** Applicants must submit a completed application form along with an essay, two letters of recommendation, transcript, and resume of awards. **Deadline:** March 7. **Contact:** Shana Venenga at 702-799-1042.

5852 ■ R.M. Princ Scholarships *(Undergraduate/Scholarship)*

Purpose: To provide educational opportunities for individuals intending to pursue higher studies. **Focus:** Education, Elementary; Education, Secondary. **Qualif.:** Applicants must be CCSD female seniors who have maintained a minimum 3.5 cumulative GPA; must demonstrate financial need; and must be planning to attend an accredited post-secondary college or university majoring in the field of education (elementary or secondary). **Criteria:** Awards are given based on need.

Funds Avail.: $2,000. **Number Awarded:** 3. **To Apply:** Applicants must submit a completed application form along with an essay, two letters of recommendation, transcript, and resume of awards. **Deadline:** March 7. **Contact:** Shana Venenga at 702-799-1042.

5853 ■ Procida Tile Importers Scholarships *(Undergraduate/Scholarship)*

Purpose: To provide educational opportunities for individuals intending to pursue higher studies. **Focus:** General studies. **Qualif.:** Applicants must be CCSD seniors with a minimum 3.5 cumulative GPA and adverse family situations; must be planning to attend the University of Nevada, Las Vegas; and must demonstrate financial need. **Criteria:** Awards are given based on need.

Funds Avail.: $1,000. **Number Awarded:** Up to 10. **To Apply:** Applicants must submit a completed application form along with an essay, transcript, resume of awards, and Adult Nominating Form. **Deadline:** March 31. **Contact:** Shana Venenga at 702-799-1042.

5854 ■ Public Education Foundation Opportunity Scholarships *(Undergraduate/Scholarship)*

Purpose: To provide educational opportunities for individuals intending to pursue higher studies. **Focus:** General studies. **Qualif.:** Applicants must be CCSD seniors planning to attend an accredited post-secondary institution in Nevada and must maintain a minimum GPA of 3.0. **Criteria:** Awards are given based on need.

Funds Avail.: Full-ride scholarship. **Number Awarded:** 2. **To Apply:** Applicants must submit a completed application form along with an essay, two letters of recommendation, transcript, and resume of awards. **Deadline:** March 31. **Contact:** Shana Venenga at 702-799-1042.

5855 ■ Republic Services Environmental Studies Scholarships *(Undergraduate/Scholarship)*

Purpose: To promote education in the area of environmental studies/sciences. **Focus:** Environmental science. **Qualif.:** Applicants must be CCSD seniors planning to major in Environmental Studies/Sciences at a four-year institution with a minimum 3.5 cumulative GPA. **Criteria:** Award is given based on the application materials.

Funds Avail.: $1,500. **Number Awarded:** 1. **To Apply:** Applicants must submit a completed application form along with the essay, a letter of recommendation, and resume. **Deadline:** March 31. **Contact:** Shana Venenga at 702-799-1042.

5856 ■ Elizabeth Shafer Memorial Scholarships *(Undergraduate/Scholarship)*

Purpose: To provide educational opportunities for individuals intending to pursue higher studies. **Focus:** Culinary arts. **Qualif.:** Applicants must be CCSD seniors pursuing a degree in the culinary field; must have a minimum 2.0 cumulative GPA; and must be U.S. citizens either by birth or naturalization. **Criteria:** Award is given based on the application materials.

Funds Avail.: $1,000. **Number Awarded:** 1. **To Apply:** Applicants must submit a completed application form along with an essay, transcript, resume of awards, and a visible sample of artwork or culinary talents. **Deadline:** March 7. **Contact:** Shana Venenga at 702-799-1042.

5857 ■ Silver Nugget Family Scholarships *(Undergraduate/Scholarship)*

Purpose: To provide educational opportunities for individuals intending to pursue higher studies. **Focus:** General studies. **Qualif.:** Applicants must be CCSD seniors; must be dependents of a Silver Nugget Gaming Team member; and must be planning to attend an accredited college/university. **Criteria:** Award is given based on the application materials.

Funds Avail.: $3,000. **Number Awarded:** 1. **To Apply:** Applicants must submit a completed application together with an essay (400-500 words). **Deadline:** March 31. **Contact:** Shana Venenga at 702-799-1042.

5858 ■ Silver Nugget Gaming Ambassadors Scholarships *(Undergraduate/Scholarship)*

Purpose: To promote education in arts and business. **Focus:** Arts; Business. **Qualif.:** Applicants must be CCSD seniors who attended Rancho High School, Desert Pines High School, Community College East or Area Technical Trade Center; must have demonstrated an interest in the arts and business; and must have shown leadership skills. **Criteria:** Award is given based on the application materials.

Funds Avail.: $3,000. **Number Awarded:** 1. **To Apply:** Applicants must submit a completed application form together with an essay (400-500 words). **Deadline:** March 31. **Contact:** Shana Venenga at 702-799-1042.

5859 ■ Smith's Personal Best Scholarships *(Undergraduate/Scholarship)*

Purpose: To provide educational opportunities for individuals intending to pursue higher studies. **Focus:** General studies. **Qualif.:** Applicants must be CCSD seniors who have met and overcome a serious personal challenge or adversity; must plan to attend an accredited post-secondary institution. **Criteria:** Awards are given based on the application materials.

Funds Avail.: $1,000. **Number Awarded:** 10. **To Apply:** Applicants must submit complete application package which include the Applicant's General Information, the Certifications and Authorizations form, the Short Answer Questionnaire and the nomination form completed by an adult who knows the student well - a teacher, counselor, club advisor, employer, etc. **Deadline:** March 7. **Contact:** Shana Venenga at 702-799-1042.

5860 ■ Southern Nevada Sports Hall of Fame Athletic Scholarships *(Undergraduate/Scholarship)*

Purpose: To provide educational opportunities for individuals intending to pursue higher studies. **Focus:** General studies. **Qualif.:** Applicants must be CCSD seniors who have participated in athletics for the past four years with a minimum 3.2 unweighted cumulative GPA. **Criteria:** Awards are given based on the submitted materials.

Funds Avail.: $2,000. **Number Awarded:** 2. **To Apply:** Applicants must submit a completed application form along with an essay, two letters of recommendation, transcript, and resume. **Deadline:** March 7. **Contact:** Shana Venenga at 702-799-1042.

5861 ■ Spartan Staff Scholarships *(Undergraduate/Scholarship)*

Purpose: To provide educational opportunities for individuals intending to pursue higher studies. **Focus:** General studies. **Qualif.:** Applicants must be Cimarron-Memorial High School seniors interested in pursuing a degree at an accredited college or university; must have a minimum 3.0 unweighted cumulative GPA; and must demonstrate financial need. **Criteria:** Awards are given based on need.

Funds Avail.: $500. **Number Awarded:** 8. **To Apply:** Applicants must submit a completed application form along with an essay, two letters of recommendation, transcript, and resume of awards. **Deadline:** April. **Contact:** Shana Venenga at 702-799-1042.

5862 ■ Striving for Success Scholarships *(Undergraduate/Scholarship)*

Purpose: To provide educational opportunities for individuals intending to pursue higher studies. **Focus:** General studies. **Qualif.:** Applicants must be Northeast Region High School special education seniors planning to attend an accredited post-secondary institution. **Criteria:** Award is given based on the application materials.

Funds Avail.: $500. **Number Awarded:** 1. **To Apply:** Applicants must submit a completed application form along with an essay, two letters of recommendation, transcript, and resume of awards. **Deadline:** March 7. **Contact:** Shana Venenga at 702-799-1042.

5863 ■ Tall Awareness Scholarships *(Undergraduate/Scholarship)*

Purpose: To provide educational opportunities for individuals intending to pursue higher studies. **Focus:** General studies. **Qualif.:** Applicants must be CCSD seniors attending an accredited post-secondary school; must have met the minimum height requirement of 5'10" for female students and 6'2" for male students. **Criteria:** Selection is based on height requirement, financial need, academic achievement, volunteer work, school activities and service to the community.

Funds Avail.: $1,000. **Number Awarded:** 1. **To Apply:** Applicants must submit a completed application form along with an essay, a letter of recommendation, and transcript. **Deadline:** March 7. **Contact:** Shana Venenga at 702-799-1042.

5864 ■ Sheila Tarr-Smith Memorial Scholarships *(Undergraduate/Scholarship)*

Purpose: To provide educational opportunities for individuals intending to pursue higher studies. **Focus:** Public service. **Qualif.:** Applicants must be CCSD seniors planning to attend the University of Nevada, Las Vegas, as full-time students; must have a major related to public service; must have a minimum 3.4 unweighted cumulative GPA; and must demonstrate community service and financial need. **Criteria:** Awards are given based on the application materials.

Funds Avail.: $2,500. **Number Awarded:** 2. **To Apply:** Applicants must submit a completed application form along with an essay, two letters of recommendation, transcript, and resume of awards. **Deadline:** March 7. **Contact:** Shana Venenga at 702-799-1042.

5865 ■ TEACH Scholarships *(Undergraduate/Scholarship)*

Purpose: To provide educational opportunities for individuals intending to pursue higher studies. **Focus:** Education. **Qualif.:** Applicants must be Teacher Education Academy at Clark High School (TEACH) seniors interested in pursuing a degree in education at an accredited college/university; must have a minimum 2.8 cumulative GPA; and must be currently enrolled in the TEACH Educational Internship and Seminar course. **Criteria:** Awards are given based on the application materials.

Funds Avail.: $500. **Number Awarded:** 3. **To Apply:** Applicants must submit a completed application form along with an essay, transcript, resume of awards, and a copy of recent TEACH Internship Evaluation. **Deadline:** March 7. **Contact:** Shana Venenga at 702-799-1042.

5866 ■ Tsutako Curo Scholarships *(Undergraduate/Scholarship)*

Purpose: To support single mothers desiring to advance their education. **Focus:** General studies. **Qualif.:** Applicants must be CCSD seniors who are single mothers desiring to advance their education at an accredited post-secondary institution; must have a minimum 2.5 cumulative GPA; and must demonstrate financial need. **Criteria:** Award is given based on need.

Funds Avail.: $1,500. **Number Awarded:** 1. **To Apply:** Applicants must submit a completed application form together with an essay, two letters of recommendation, and transcript. **Deadline:** March 7. **Contact:** Shana Venenga at 702-799-1042.

5867 ■ Judith Warner Memorial Scholarships *(Undergraduate/Scholarship)*

Purpose: To provide educational opportunities for individuals intending to pursue higher studies. **Focus:** General studies. **Qualif.:** Applicants must be Rancho High School seniors planning to attend the University of Nevada, Las Vegas as full-time students; must have a minimum 2.5 cumulative GPA; and must demonstrate financial need. **Criteria:** Award is given based on merit.

Funds Avail.: $600. **Number Awarded:** 1. **To Apply:** Applicants must submit a completed application form along with an essay, two letters of recommendation, transcript, resume of awards, and letter of admission from UNLV. **Deadline:** March 7. **Contact:** Shana Venenga at 702-799-1042.

5868 ■ Edwin F. Wiegand Science and Technology Scholarships *(Undergraduate/Scholarship)*

Purpose: To provide educational opportunities for individuals intending to pursue higher studies. **Focus:** Computer and information sciences. **Qualif.:** Applicants must be CCSD seniors pursuing a degree in science, technology, computer science or related field at the University of

Awards are arranged alphabetically below their administering organizations

Nevada, Las Vegas, or the University of Nevada, or Reno, with a minimum of 3.0 cumulative GPA. **Criteria:** Priority will be given to students who have been involved with CyberCorps or CCSD's InterAct Online Learning Community.

Funds Avail.: $1,250. **Number Awarded:** 2. **To Apply:** Applicants must submit a completed application form along with an essay, two letters of recommendation, transcript, and a resume of awards. **Deadline:** March 7. **Contact:** Shana Venenga at 702-799-1042.

5869 ■ Williams Foundation Scholarships
(Undergraduate/Scholarship)

Purpose: To provide educational opportunities for individuals intending to pursue higher studies. **Focus:** General studies. **Qualif.:** Applicants must be CCSD seniors planning to attend an accredited post-secondary institution for which they meet entry level requirements. **Criteria:** Awards are given based on the application materials.

Funds Avail.: $1,000. **Number Awarded:** 5. **To Apply:** Applicants must submit a completed application form along with an essay, two letters of recommendation, transcript, and resume of awards. **Deadline:** March 7. **Contact:** Shana Venenga at 702-799-1042.

5870 ■ Public Library Association

American Library Association
50 E Huron St.
Chicago, IL 60611
Fax: (312)280-5029
Free: 800-545-2433
E-mail: pla@ala.org
URL: http://www.pla.org

5871 ■ DEMCO New Leaders Travel Grants *(All/Grant)*

Purpose: To improve the expertise and professional development of public librarians. **Focus:** Library and archival sciences. **Qualif.:** Applicants must be members of the Public Library Association; must be practicing librarians for five years or less; must not be officers or members of the PLA Board of Directors; and must not be members or supervisors of the New Leaders Travel Grant Jury. **Criteria:** Selection is based on the quality of the submitted proposals.

Funds Avail.: $2,500. **To Apply:** Applicants are advised to visit the website for the PLA's awards online application. **Deadline:** December 3.

5872 ■ Grow your Own @ Your Library Institutional Scholarships *(Graduate, Professional Development/Scholarship)*

Purpose: To support the education needs of public library staff intending to obtain master's degree in library and information science. **Focus:** Library and archival sciences. **Qualif.:** Institutions which are applying must be public libraries in the U.S. and must be recognized under state law. **Criteria:** Applications will be reviewed by a committee appointed by the PLA president.

Funds Avail.: $8,000. **To Apply:** Application materials are available at the website and must be completed by a member of the institution staff, typically the library director or designated staff. **Deadline:** December 3.

Remarks: Institutions that receive funds under this program are responsible for administering the tuition reimbursement of employees.

5873 ■ Public Relations Society of America

33 Maiden Ln., 11th Fl.
New York, NY 10038-5150
Ph: (212)460-1474
Fax: (212)995-0757
E-mail: prssa@prsa.org
URL: http://www.prssa.org

5874 ■ Betsy Plank/PRSSA Scholarships
(Undergraduate/Scholarship)

Purpose: To provide educational support for deserving students intending to pursue a career in public relations. **Focus:** Public relations. **Qualif.:** Program is open to PRSSA members who are enrolled in programs of public relations studies and are in their junior or senior year of undergraduate studies. **Criteria:** Applicants will be selected based on their academic achievement in public relations and overall studies, demonstrated leadership, practical experience and commitment to public relations, particularly as expressed in the candidate's statement.

Funds Avail.: $4,250. **To Apply:** Application form and other supporting documents must be sent to PRSSA, Betsy Plank/PRSSA Scholarship, 33 Maiden Ln., 11th Fl., New York, NY 10038. **Deadline:** June 2.

5875 ■ Stephen D. Pisinski Memorial Scholarships *(Undergraduate/Scholarship)*

Purpose: To provide educational assistance for qualified students intending to pursue a career in the field of public relations. **Focus:** Public relations; Journalism; Communications. **Qualif.:** Applicants must be majoring in journalism, communications, or public relations; must be junior or senior level only; must have at least a 3.3 overall GPA on a 4.0 system; must be members of the Public Relations Student Society of America, and leadership positions are a plus. **Criteria:** Applicants will be selected by criteria of the selection committee.

Funds Avail.: $1,500. **To Apply:** Applicants must submit a resume including any academic honors, special projects, activities and/or work experience or training; an official transcript of all college studies, including grades of the preceding semester; an essay of 1,000 words or less stating your career goals; two strong writing samples; and two letters of academic and/or professional recommendations. Application form and other required items must be sent to PRSSA Headquarters by Stephen D. Pininski Memorial Scholarship, Public Relations Student Society of America, 33 Maiden Ln., 11th Fl., New York, NY 10038. **Deadline:** June 2.

5876 ■ Gary Yoshimura Scholarships
(Undergraduate/Scholarship)

Purpose: To provide support to qualified PRSSA members who demonstrate a financial need for the pursuit of higher education in the public relations field. **Focus:** Public relations. **Qualif.:** Applicants must have a minimum GPA of 3.0; must be a PRSSA member. **Criteria:** Applicants will be selected based on their academic performance and application materials.

Funds Avail.: $2,400. **To Apply:** Application forms are available at the website. Applicants must submit an official transcript, a letter of recommendation from an internship supervisor/employer or faculty advisor; must prepare a 1,000-word essay describing a challenge they have faced, either personally or professionally, and how they overcame it; must complete the statement of intent and financial need section. **Deadline:** January 31.

5877 ■ Public Service Alliance of Canada

233 Gilmour St.
Ottawa, ON, Canada K2P 0P1
Ph: (613)560-4200
Free: 888-604-7722
E-mail: terranc@psac-afpc.com
URL: http://www.psac.com

5878 ■ J.R. (Joe) Power National Scholarships
(Postgraduate/Scholarship)

Purpose: To provide financial assistance to children and dependents of PSAC members. **Focus:** General studies. **Qualif.:** Applicants must be PSAC members or their children who are returning to university, college or a recognized institute of higher learning; must have a good standing in PSAC as of May 31 of the current year. **Criteria:** Scholarships are awarded based on the impact of the 800-word essay, scholastic achievement, and community and union involvement as reviewed by the PSAC scholarship committee.

Funds Avail.: $2,000. **Number Awarded:** 1. **To Apply:** Applicant must submit an 800-word essay on the topic chosen by the PSAC scholarship committee and a transcript of the most current academic standing. Applicant must also prepare proof of registration with the name of the university, college or institute of higher learning. Application forms are available from the website and must be completed and emailed, mailed or faxed to: Public Service Alliance of Canada, 233 Gilmour St., Ste. 904, Ottawa, ON K2P OP1. **Deadline:** July 16.

5879 ■ PSAC - Coughlin National Scholarships
(Postgraduate/Scholarship)

Purpose: To provide financial assistance to children and dependents of PSAC members. **Focus:** General studies. **Qualif.:** Applicants must be PSAC members or their children who are returning to university, college or a recognized institute of higher learning; must have a good standing in PSAC as of May 31 of the current year. **Criteria:** Scholarships are awarded based on the impact of the 800-word essay, scholastic achievement, and community and union involvement as reviewed by the PSAC scholarship committee.

Funds Avail.: $3,000-$4,000. **To Apply:** Applicant must submit an 800-word essay on the topic chosen by the PSAC scholarship committee and a transcript of the most current academic standing. Applicant must also prepare proof of registration with the name of the university, college or institute of higher learning. Application forms are available from the website and must be completed and emailed, mailed or faxed to: Public Service Alliance of Canada, 233 Gilmour St., Ste. 904, Ottawa, ON K2P OP1. **Deadline:** July 16.

5880 ■ PSAC - Groulx National Scholarships
(Postgraduate/Scholarship)

Purpose: To provide financial assistance to children and dependents of PSAC members. **Focus:** General studies. **Qualif.:** Applicants must be PSAC members or their children who are returning to university, college or a recognized institute of higher learning; must have a good standing in PSAC as of May 31 of the current year. **Criteria:** Scholarships are awarded based on the impact of the 800-word essay, scholastic achievement, and community and union involvement as reviewed by the PSAC scholarship committee.

Funds Avail.: $3,000-$4,000. **To Apply:** Applicant must submit an 800-word essay on the topic chosen by the PSAC scholarship committee and a transcript of the most current academic standing. Applicant must also prepare proof of registration with the name of the university, college or institute of higher learning. Application forms are available from the website and must be completed and emailed, mailed or faxed to: Public Service Alliance of Canada, 233 Gilmour St., Ste. 904, Ottawa, ON K2P OP1. **Deadline:** July 16.

5881 ■ PSAC National Scholarships
(Postgraduate/Scholarship)

Purpose: To provide financial assistance to children and dependents of PSAC members. **Focus:** General studies. **Qualif.:** Applicants must be PSAC members or their children who are returning to university, college or a recognized institute of higher learning; must have a good standing in PSAC as of May 31 of the current year. **Criteria:** Scholarships are awarded based on the impact of the 800-word essay, scholastic achievement, and community and union involvement as reviewed by the PSAC scholarship committee.

Funds Avail.: $1,000. **Number Awarded:** 1. **To Apply:** Applicant must submit an 800-word essay on the topic chosen by the PSAC scholarship committee and a transcript of the most current academic standing. Applicant must also prepare proof of registration with the name of the university, college or institute of higher learning. Application forms are available from the website and must be completed and emailed, mailed or faxed to: Public Service Alliance of Canada, 233 Gilmour St., Ste. 904, Ottawa, ON K2P OP1. **Deadline:** July 16.

5882 ■ PSAC Regional Scholarships
(Postgraduate/Scholarship)

Purpose: To provide financial assistance to children and dependents of PSAC members. **Focus:** General studies. **Qualif.:** Applicants must be PSAC members or their children who are returning to university, college or a recognized institute of higher learning; must have a good standing in PSAC as of May 31 of the current year. **Criteria:** Scholarships are awarded based on the impact of the 800-word essay, scholastic achievement, and community and union involvement as reviewed by the PSAC scholarship committee.

Funds Avail.: $1,000. **Number Awarded:** 7. **To Apply:** Applicant must submit an 800-word essay on the topic chosen by the PSAC scholarship committee and a transcript of the most current academic standing. Applicant must also prepare proof of registration with the name of the university, college or institute of higher learning. Application forms are available from the website and must be completed and emailed, mailed or faxed to: Public Service Alliance of Canada, 233 Gilmour St., Ste. 904, Ottawa, ON K2P OP1. **Deadline:** July 16.

5883 ■ Puerto Rican Legal Defense and Education Fund

99 Hudson St., 14th Fl.
New York, NY 10013
Ph: (212)219-3360
Fax: (212)431-4276

Free: 800-328-2322
E-mail: info@prldef.org
URL: http://www.prldef.org

5884 ■ Puerto Rican Bar Association Scholarships *(Undergraduate/Scholarship)*

Purpose: To protect opportunities for all Latinos to succeed in school and work, fulfill their dreams, and sustain their families and communities. **Focus:** Law. **Qualif.:** Applicants must be first or second year students in a JD degree program at an American Bar Association (ABA) approved law school. **Criteria:** Recipients will be selected based on financial need, community involvement and academic promise.

Funds Avail.: $1500-$2000. **To Apply:** Applicants must complete the applications. **Deadline:** March 1.

5885 ■ Quality Function Deployment (QFD) Institute

1140 Morehead Ct.
Ann Arbor, MI 48103
Ph: (734)995-0847
Fax: (206)203-0733
E-mail: registration@qfdi.org
URL: http://www.qfdi.org

5886 ■ Akao Scholarships for QFD *(Undergraduate/Scholarship)*

Purpose: To stimulate QFD research and education at higher education institutions worldwide by rewarding the university student who has written and submitted the best "Student QFD Paper" of the year. **Focus:** Education. **Qualif.:** Applicants must be full-time working students; currently enrolled in an accredited university/college degree program. **Criteria:** Selection is determined by the Akao Scholarship Committee.

Funds Avail.: No specific amount. **To Apply:** Applicants must submit a paper reporting their own QFD application case study and/or research findings (must include QFD work objects and data, method(s) used, applicants' own analysis, conclusion and references, information about the applicant as well as any student co-authors). Working students must include their employers' name, employment location and short description of their job; recommendation letter from a professor of their school; proof of enrollment status issued by their school's registrar office. **Deadline:** May 1.

5887 ■ Quarter Century Wireless Association

PO Box 3247
Framingham, MA 01705
Ph: (508)405-1930
Fax: (508)405-1965
URL: http://www.qcwa.org

5888 ■ QCWA Memorial Scholarships *(Undergraduate/Scholarship)*

Purpose: To provide financial support for students intending to pursue higher education. **Focus:** Radio and television. **Qualif.:** Applicants must be radio amateurs enrolled or planning to enroll in a full-time course which leads to a degree at an accredited college/university. **Criteria:** Applications will be reviewed by the Foundation for Amateur Radio.

Funds Avail.: $500-$3,000. **To Apply:** Applications are requested from the Foundation for Amateur Radio Scholarship Committee; applicant must be recommended by a QCWA member. **Deadline:** April 30.

Remarks: Established in 1977. **Contact:** Lalend Buddy Smith, QCWA Memorial Scholarship Fund, 504-721-4684, w4ye@aol.com.

5889 ■ Quill and Scroll Society

100 Adler Journalism Bldg.
Iowa City, IA 52242
Ph: (319)335-3457
Fax: (319)335-3989
E-mail: quill-scroll@uiowa.edu
URL: http://www.uiowa.edu

5890 ■ Lester G. Benz Memorial Scholarships for College Journalism Study *(Other/Scholarship)*

Purpose: To identify and reward experienced journalism teachers and publication advisers who seek the opportunity to upgrade journalism skills, teaching methodologies and advising techniques. **Focus:** Journalism. **Qualif.:** Applicants must be high-school journalism teachers and newspaper and yearbook advisers who have had at least six semester hours of journalism courses; a minimum of four years of teaching experience and advising school publications; currently teaching a journalistic writing class; and a definite commitment to return to the high school classroom and publication. **Criteria:** Candidates will be selected by Scholarship Committee.

Funds Avail.: $500 for actual tuition, room, board and transportation costs. **To Apply:** Applicants must submit the completed application form, two letters of recommendation that will attest to their journalism teaching skills, publication advising, quality of the journalistic writing courses the applicants teach and the quality of the publications the applicant advises. **Deadline:** April 15.

5891 ■ Edward J. Nell Memorial Scholarships in Journalism *(Undergraduate/Scholarship)*

Purpose: To provide financial assistance to well-qualified individuals to attend any college or university that offers a major in journalism. **Focus:** Journalism. **Qualif.:** Applicant must be a student in freshman year. **Criteria:** Recipient will be selected based on some criteria designed by the Scholarship Committee.

Funds Avail.: $500 to $1,500. **To Apply:** Applicant must submit three separate forms (Form I - Principal or Counselor, Form II - Student and Form III - Journalism Adviser) together with the supporting material (official transcript, applicant's letter regarding journalistic experience, and five selections of student's published work and letters of endorsement from principal, counselor and/or adviser). **Deadline:** May 10.

5892 ■ Radio Advisory Board of Canada

811-116 Albert St.
Ottawa, ON, Canada K1P 5G3
Ph: (613)230-3261
Free: 888-902-5768
E-mail: rabc.gm@on.aibn.com
URL: http://www.rabc-cccr.ca

5893 ■ Future Leader in Radiocommunications Scholarships *(Postgraduate/Scholarship)*

Purpose: To encourage careers in telecommunications especially among engineering students. **Focus:** Telecom-

Awards are arranged alphabetically below their administering organizations

munications systems. **Qualif.:** Applicants must be enrolled in an accredited Canadian university and must have completed at least the second year in an engineering programme. **Criteria:** Selection of applicants will be based on their academic excellence and community involvement.

Funds Avail.: $3,500. **To Apply:** Scholarship applications may be obtained by contacting RABC; completed applications must be submitted to RABC. **Deadline:** July 31.

5894 ■ Railway Tie Association

115 Commerce Dr., Ste. C
Fayetteville, GA 30214
Ph: (770)460-5553
Fax: (770)460-5573
E-mail: ties@rta.org
URL: http://www.rta.org

5895 ■ John Mabry Forestry Scholarships
(Undergraduate/Award/Prize)

Purpose: To provide financial support for students attending technical schools, colleges and universities. **Focus:** General studies. **Qualif.:** Applicants must be students in accredited second year technical schools or juniors and seniors attending four-year colleges and universities. **Criteria:** Recipients are selected based on leadership qualities, career objectives, scholastic achievement, and financial need.

Funds Avail.: $1,500. **Number Awarded:** 2. **To Apply:** Applicants must submit completed application along with personal narrative, one black and white photo, and a copy of transcript. **Deadline:** June 30.

5896 ■ Jeannette Rankin Foundation

PO Box 6653
Athens, GA 30604-6653
Ph: (706)208-1211
Fax: (706)548-0202
E-mail: info@rankinfoundation.org
URL: http://www.rankinfoundation.org

5897 ■ Jeannette Rankin Scholarships
(Undergraduate/Scholarship)

Purpose: To financially support the education of a low-income female student who wishes to pursue her educational goals. **Focus:** General studies. **Qualif.:** Applicant must be female, age 35 or older; a U.S. citizen; enrolled in, or accepted to an accredited school; pursuing a technical or vocational education, an associate's degree, or a first bachelor's degree; and have low-income according to the U.S. Department of Labor's Lower Living Standard. **Criteria:** Awards are given based on goals; plans in reaching those goals; challenges the applicant may have faced; and financial situation.

Funds Avail.: No specific amount. **To Apply:** Applicants must submit a completed scholarship application along with a personal statement; two letters of recommendation; and proof of enrollment or acceptance. Applicants are requested to submit two complete sets of the application materials. **Contact:** at the above address (see entry 5896).

5898 ■ Raytheon Company

870 Winter Street
Waltham, MA 02451
Ph: (781)522-3000
URL: http://www.raytheon.com

5899 ■ Raytheon Scholarship Program
(Undergraduate/Scholarship)

Purpose: To assist employee's children who plan to continue their education in college. **Focus:** General studies. **Qualif.:** Applicants must be under the age of 24; dependent children of active employees who work 20 hours or more per week and have at least one year of service with the company by the application deadline; college freshmen, sophomores and juniors who plan to enroll in a full-time undergraduate course of study at an accredited two-year or four-year college or university. **Criteria:** Recipients are selected on the basis of academic record, demonstrated leadership, participation in school and community activities, honors, work experience, statement of goals and aspirations, and unusual personal or family circumstances.

Funds Avail.: $1,000. **To Apply:** Applicants must submit the application and current complete official transcript of grades to Scholarship America. **Deadline:** April 30.

5900 ■ Reach Out for Youth with Ileitis and Colitis

84 Northgate Circle
Melville, NY 11747
Ph: (631)293-3102
E-mail: info@reachourforyouth.org
URL: http://www.reachoutforyouth.org

5901 ■ ROFY Scholarships *(Undergraduate/Scholarship)*

Purpose: To encourage students to set high educational standards. **Focus:** Ileitis and Colitis. **Qualif.:** Applicant must be graduating from high school; must be from a family with a paid membership. **Criteria:** Awards are given based on the academic performance of an applicant.

Funds Avail.: No specific amount. **To Apply:** Students applying for the scholarship must submit an essay of approximately 1000 words to the organization about living with IBD or how Reach Out for Youth helped them deal with their illness. **Deadline:** June 1. **Contact:** ROfY at the above address (see entry 5900).

5902 ■ Redlands Community Scholarship Foundation

c/o Kathleen Venegas-Boge, Admin. Asst.
PO Box 1683
Redlands, CA 92373
Ph: (909)307-9892
Fax: (909)307-9892
URL: http://www.redlandsscholarships.org

5903 ■ Ruth Adams Memorial Scholarships
(Undergraduate/Scholarship)

Purpose: To encourage educational pursuits among Redlands Unified School District graduates by providing educational assistance. **Focus:** General studies. **Qualif.:** Applicant must be a female graduating senior who has been accepted at and will be attending the University of Redlands as a full-time student. **Criteria:** Award is given based on merit.

Funds Avail.: $500. **Number Awarded:** 1. **To Apply:** Ap-

Awards are arranged alphabetically below their administering organizations

plicants must submit: completed application form with the scantron sheet; cover sheet; student activity and community activity sheets; personal essay; and a copy of unofficial transcript (signed by the counselor). **Deadline:** February 20.

Remarks: No electronic submissions of application will be accepted. Submit two printed copies of the application and use a No. 2 pencil on the scantron sheet.

5904 ■ Patty Ahearn Victoria Elementary Scholarships *(Undergraduate/Scholarship)*

Purpose: To encourage educational pursuits among Redlands Unified School District graduates by providing educational assistance. **Focus:** General studies. **Qualif.:** Applicant must be a graduating senior; must have a 2.5 GPA or higher; must have attended Victoria Elementary School for at least three years; and must have continued to follow the "Victoria Peace Builder's Pledge." **Criteria:** Award is given based on merit.

Funds Avail.: $500. **Number Awarded:** 1. **To Apply:** Applicants must submit a completed application form together with the scantron sheet; cover sheet; student activity and community activity sheets; personal essay; and a copy of unofficial transcript (signed by the counselor). **Deadline:** February 20.

Remarks: No electronic submissions of application will be accepted. Submit two printed copies of the application and use a No. 2 pencil on the scantron sheet.

5905 ■ Robinson G. Allen Athletic Memorial Scholarships *(Undergraduate/Scholarship)*

Purpose: To encourage educational pursuits among Redlands Unified School District graduates by providing educational assistance. **Focus:** General studies. **Qualif.:** Applicant must be a senior whose athletic prowess has been limited, for the most part, to junior varsity teams and who plans to attend an institution of higher learning on a full-time basis. **Criteria:** Award is given based on sportsmanship, citizenship, scholarship and financial need.

Funds Avail.: $500. **Number Awarded:** 1. **To Apply:** Applicants must submit a completed application form together with the scantron sheet; cover sheet; student activity and community activity sheets; personal essay; and a copy of unofficial transcript (signed by the counselor). **Deadline:** February 20.

Remarks: No electronic submissions of application will be accepted. Submit two printed copies of the application and use a No. 2 pencil on the scantron sheet.

5906 ■ William A. Allen Memorial Metal Shop/ Auto Body Scholarships *(Undergraduate/ Scholarship)*

Purpose: To encourage educational pursuits among Redlands Unified School District graduates by providing educational assistance. **Focus:** General studies. **Qualif.:** Applicant must be an outstanding metal shop or auto body student who displays dedication, skill and desire to become a true craftsman. Student must demonstrate creativity, show problem solving abilities, and exhibit good social skills. **Criteria:** Award is given based on merit.

Funds Avail.: $300. **Number Awarded:** 1. **To Apply:** Applicants must submit a completed application form together with the scantron sheet; cover sheet; student activity and community activity sheets; personal essay; and a copy of unofficial transcript (signed by the counselor). **Deadline:** February 20.

Remarks: No electronic submissions of application will be accepted. Submit two printed copies of the application and use a No. 2 pencil on the scantron sheet.

5907 ■ Cindy Andrews Educational Scholarships *(Undergraduate/Scholarship)*

Purpose: To encourage educational pursuits among Redlands Unified School District graduates by providing educational assistance. **Focus:** General studies. **Qualif.:** Applicant must be a graduating senior who has been a CSF member for at least 4 semesters and is planning to be a teacher and eventually an administrator in the public school system. **Criteria:** Award is given based on merit.

Funds Avail.: $300. **Number Awarded:** 1. **To Apply:** Applicants must submit a completed application form together with the scantron sheet; cover sheet; student activity and community activity sheets; personal essay; and a copy of unofficial transcript (signed by the counselor). **Deadline:** February 20.

Remarks: No electronic submissions of application will be accepted. Submit two printed copies of the application and use a No. 2 pencil on the scantron sheet.

5908 ■ Aquatics Booster Club Scholarships *(Undergraduate/Scholarship)*

Purpose: To encourage educational pursuits among Redlands Unified School District graduates by providing educational assistance. **Focus:** Aquaculture. **Qualif.:** Applicant must be a graduating senior who has participated for at least three consecutive years in the water polo and/or swimming program. Student must have maintained at least a 3.0 GPA and be planning to continue in an aquatic program in college. **Criteria:** Award is given based on merit.

Funds Avail.: No specific amount. **To Apply:** Applicants must submit a completed application form together with the scantron sheet; cover sheet; student activity and community activity sheets; personal essay; and a copy of unofficial transcript (signed by the counselor). **Deadline:** February 20.

Remarks: No electronic submissions of application will be accepted. Submit two printed copies of the application and use a No. 2 pencil on the scantron sheet.

5909 ■ Frank G. Araujo Memorial Scholarships *(Undergraduate/Scholarship)*

Purpose: To encourage educational pursuits among Redlands Unified School District graduates by providing educational assistance. **Focus:** General studies. **Qualif.:** Applicant must be a student of Mexican-American descent; must have a 3.0 or higher GPA; must demonstrate good citizenship; and must participate in school or community activities. **Criteria:** Award is given based on merit.

Funds Avail.: $600. **Number Awarded:** 1. **To Apply:** Applicants must submit a completed application form together with the scantron sheet; cover sheet; student activity and community activity sheets; personal essay; and a copy of unofficial transcript (signed by the counselor). **Deadline:** February 20.

Remarks: No electronic submissions of application will be accepted. Submit two printed copies of the application and use a No. 2 pencil on the scantron sheet.

5910 ■ Connie "Chelo" Armendariz Memorial Scholarships *(Undergraduate/Scholarship)*

Purpose: To encourage educational pursuits among Redlands Unified School District graduates by providing

educational assistance. **Focus:** General studies. **Qualif.:** Applicant must be a graduating senior planning to continue education at a vocational school, junior college, or university. **Criteria:** Preference is given to a student who attended the former Saint Mary's Catholic Church in Redlands.

Funds Avail.: $500. **Number Awarded:** 1. **To Apply:** Applicants must submit a completed application form together with the scantron sheet; cover sheet; student activity and community activity sheets; personal essay; and a copy of unofficial transcript (signed by the counselor). **Deadline:** February 20.

Remarks: No electronic submissions of application will be accepted. Submit two printed copies of the application and use a No. 2 pencil on the scantron sheet.

5911 ■ Baha'i Faith Scholarships for Racial Harmony *(Undergraduate/Scholarship)*

Purpose: To encourage educational pursuits among Redlands Unified School District graduates by providing educational assistance. **Focus:** General studies. **Qualif.:** Applicant must be a graduating senior who has promoted racial and intercultural harmony on campus. **Criteria:** Award is given based on merit.

Funds Avail.: $200. **Number Awarded:** 1. **To Apply:** Applicants must submit a completed application form together with the scantron sheet; cover sheet; student activity and community activity sheets; personal essay; and a copy of unofficial transcript (signed by the counselor). **Deadline:** February 20.

Remarks: No electronic submissions of application will be accepted. Submit two printed copies of the application and use a No. 2 pencil on the scantron sheet.

5912 ■ Timothy Baylink Good Fellowship Awards *(Undergraduate/Scholarship)*

Purpose: To encourage educational pursuits among Redlands Unified School District graduates by providing educational assistance. **Focus:** General studies. **Qualif.:** Applicant must be a graduating senior who possesses some of the attributes of Dr. Timothy Baylink, which include athleticism, sense of adventure, friendliness, free spirit, interest in computers, and commitment to learning. **Criteria:** Award is given based on merit.

Funds Avail.: $1,000. **Number Awarded:** 1. **To Apply:** Applicants must submit: a completed application form together with the scantron sheet; cover sheet; student activity and community activity sheets; personal essay; and a copy of unofficial transcript (signed by the counselor). **Deadline:** February 20.

Remarks: No electronic submissions of application will be accepted. Submit two printed copies of the application and use a No. 2 pencil on the scantron sheet.

5913 ■ Beau Gunn Redlands Baseball For Youth Scholarships *(Undergraduate/Scholarship)*

Purpose: To encourage educational pursuits among Redlands Unified School District graduates by providing educational assistance. **Focus:** General studies. **Qualif.:** Applicant must be a senior who has participated in the Redlands Baseball for Youth Program (including score keeping and umpiring) for a minimum of three years and has exemplified good sportsmanship and academic achievement. **Criteria:** Award is given based on merit.

Funds Avail.: $500. **Number Awarded:** 1. **To Apply:** Applicants must submit a completed application form together with the scantron sheet; cover sheet; student activity and community activity sheets; personal essay; and a copy of unofficial transcript (signed by the counselor). **Deadline:** February 20.

Remarks: No electronic submissions of application will be accepted. Submit two printed copies of the application and use a No. 2 pencil on the scantron sheet.

5914 ■ Beaver Medical Clinic-Glen Adams Scholarship Awards *(Undergraduate/Scholarship)*

Purpose: To encourage educational pursuits among Redlands Unified School District graduates by providing educational assistance. **Focus:** General studies. **Qualif.:** Applicant must be a graduating senior seeking a career in the field of medicine and must be outstanding academically, in leadership skills, and in sports participation. **Criteria:** Award is given based on merit.

Funds Avail.: $750. **Number Awarded:** 1. **To Apply:** Applicants must submit a completed application form together with the scantron sheet; cover sheet; student activity and community activity sheets; personal essay; and a copy of unofficial transcript (signed by the counselor). **Deadline:** February 20.

Remarks: No electronic submissions of application will be accepted. Submit two printed copies of the application and use a No. 2 pencil on the scantron sheet.

5915 ■ Beaver Medical Clinic-H.E.A.R.T. Scholarship Awards *(Undergraduate/Scholarship)*

Purpose: To encourage educational pursuits among Redlands Unified School District graduates by providing educational assistance. **Focus:** General studies. **Qualif.:** Applicant must be a graduating senior seeking a career in the field of medicine who participated in the HEART Academy program for three years. **Criteria:** Award is given based on merit.

Funds Avail.: $750. **Number Awarded:** 1. **To Apply:** Applicants must submit a completed application form together with the scantron sheet; cover sheet; student activity and community activity sheets; personal essay; and a copy of unofficial transcript (signed by the counselor). **Deadline:** February 20.

Remarks: No electronic submissions of application will be accepted. Submit two printed copies of the application and use a No. 2 pencil on the scantron sheet.

5916 ■ Beaver Medical Clinic-Premed Scholarship Awards *(Undergraduate/Scholarship)*

Purpose: To encourage educational pursuits among Redlands Unified School District graduates by providing educational assistance. **Focus:** General studies. **Qualif.:** Applicant must be a graduating senior seeking a career in the field of medicine. Student must be outstanding both academically and in leadership skills. **Criteria:** Award is given based on merit.

Funds Avail.: $4,000. **Number Awarded:** 1. **To Apply:** Applicants must submit a completed application form together with the scantron sheet; cover sheet; student activity and community activity sheets; personal essay; and a copy of unofficial transcript (signed by the counselor). **Deadline:** February 20.

Remarks: No electronic submissions of application will be accepted. Submit two printed copies of the application and use a No. 2 pencil on the scantron sheet.

5917 ■ Garvin L. Beck Scholarships *(Undergraduate/Scholarship)*

Purpose: To encourage educational pursuits among Redlands Unified School District graduates by providing

Awards are arranged alphabetically below their administering organizations

educational assistance. **Focus:** General studies. **Qualif.:** Applicant must be enrolled at a four-year college, junior college or trade school. **Criteria:** Award is given based on merit.

Funds Avail.: $1000. **Number Awarded:** 1. **To Apply:** Applicants must submit a completed application form together with the scantron sheet; cover sheet; student activity and community activity sheets; written documentation of registration at the college or a valid registration to a junior college or trade school; proof of a letter of junior varsity sport during the last two years of high school; a one-page essay; and a copy of unofficial transcript (signed by the counselor). **Deadline:** February 20.

Remarks: No electronic submissions of application will be accepted. Submit two printed copies of the application and use a No. 2 pencil on the scantron sheet.

5918 ■ Raymond and Donald Beeler Memorial Scholarships *(Undergraduate/Scholarship)*

Purpose: To encourage educational pursuits among Redlands Unified School District graduates by providing educational assistance. **Focus:** General studies. **Qualif.:** Applicant must be a student with at least a 3.0 GPA intending to attend a community or four-year college on a full-time basis. **Criteria:** Awards are given based on merit. Financial need is also a consideration.

Funds Avail.: $500; $1000. **Number Awarded:** 2; 2. **To Apply:** Applicants must submit a completed application form together with the scantron sheet; cover sheet; student activity and community activity sheets; personal essay; and a copy of unofficial transcript (signed by the counselor). **Deadline:** February 20.

Remarks: No electronic submissions of application will be accepted. Submit two printed copies of the application and use a No. 2 pencil on the scantron sheet.

5919 ■ David Beltran Memorial Scholarships *(Undergraduate/Scholarship)*

Purpose: To encourage educational pursuits among Redlands Unified School District graduates by providing educational assistance. **Focus:** Theater arts. **Qualif.:** Applicant must be a college-bound graduating senior planning to major in drama, theater arts or thespian studies. **Criteria:** Awards are given based on merit.

Funds Avail.: $500. **Number Awarded:** 2. **To Apply:** Applicants must submit a completed application form together with the scantron sheet; cover sheet; student activity and community activity sheets; personal essay; and a copy of unofficial transcript (signed by the counselor). **Deadline:** February 20.

Remarks: No electronic submissions of application will be accepted. Submit two printed copies of the application and use a No. 2 pencil on the scantron sheet.

5920 ■ Benchwarmers of Redlands-Jess Mercado Football Scholarships *(Undergraduate/Scholarship)*

Purpose: To encourage educational pursuits among Redlands Unified School District graduates by providing educational assistance. **Focus:** General studies. **Qualif.:** Applicant must be a three-year member of the Terrier football team who has been a starter for at least one year, exhibits good citizenship and dedication, and has an eligible GPA. **Criteria:** Award is given based on merit.

Funds Avail.: $500. **Number Awarded:** 1. **To Apply:** Applicants must submit a completed application form together with the scantron sheet; cover sheet; student activity and community activity sheets; personal essay; and a copy of unofficial transcript (signed by the counselor). **Deadline:** February 20.

Remarks: No electronic submissions of application will be accepted. Submit two printed copies of the application and use a No. 2 pencil on the scantron sheet.

5921 ■ Barbara Bonnema Memorial Scholarships *(Undergraduate/Scholarship)*

Purpose: To encourage educational pursuits among Redlands Unified School District graduates by providing educational assistance. **Focus:** General studies. **Qualif.:** Applicant must be a college-bound graduating senior who will be attending school on a full-time basis. **Criteria:** Awards are given based academic excellence and financial need.

Funds Avail.: $500; $1000. **Number Awarded:** 2; 1. **To Apply:** Applicants must submit a completed application form together with the scantron sheet; cover sheet; student activity and community activity sheets; personal essay; and a copy of unofficial transcript (signed by the counselor). **Deadline:** February 20.

Remarks: No electronic submissions of application will be accepted. Submit two printed copies of the application and use a No. 2 pencil on the scantron sheet.

5922 ■ Boy Scouts of America Troop 3 Scholarships - Art Till/Nathan E. Smith Memorial Scholarships *(Undergraduate/Scholarship)*

Purpose: To encourage educational pursuits among Redlands Unified School District graduates by providing educational assistance. **Focus:** General studies. **Qualif.:** Applicant must be a graduating senior with at least a 3.0 GPA; must be planning to attend an accredited college, university, or vocational program; and must have continuous involvement in scouting and community service. **Criteria:** Preference is given to individuals who have attained the rank of Eagle Scout.

Funds Avail.: $300. **To Apply:** Applicants must submit a completed application form together with the scantron sheet; cover sheet; student activity and community activity sheets; personal essay; and a copy of unofficial transcript (signed by the counselor). **Deadline:** February 20.

Remarks: No electronic submissions of application will be accepted. Submit two printed copies of the application and use a No. 2 pencil on the scantron sheet.

5923 ■ Quincy Brown Memorial Scholarships *(Undergraduate/Scholarship)*

Purpose: To encourage educational pursuits among Redlands Unified School District graduates by providing educational assistance. **Focus:** Business; Teaching. **Qualif.:** Applicant must be a graduating senior enrolled as a full-time student in a four-year college or university; must be pursuing a business or teaching career; must have a 3.0 or higher GPA; and must have attended Redlands High School for at least three consecutive years. **Criteria:** Awards are given based on merit.

Funds Avail.: $600; $1000. **Number Awarded:** 7. **To Apply:** Applicants must submit a completed application form together with the scantron sheet; cover sheet; student activity and community activity sheets; personal essay; and a copy of unofficial transcript (signed by the counselor). **Deadline:** February 20.

Remarks: No electronic submissions of application will be accepted. Submit two printed copies of the application and use a No. 2 pencil on the scantron sheet.

5924 ■ Kathy Bush Memorial Scholarships
(Undergraduate/Scholarship)

Purpose: To encourage educational pursuits among Redlands Unified School District graduates by providing educational assistance. **Focus:** General studies. **Qualif.:** Applicant must be a graduating senior who has been outstanding in the field of instrumental music. **Criteria:** Award is given based on merit.

Funds Avail.: $300. **Number Awarded:** 1. **To Apply:** Applicants must submit a completed application form together with the scantron sheet; cover sheet; student activity and community activity sheets; personal essay; and a copy of unofficial transcript (signed by the counselor). **Deadline:** February 20.

Remarks: No electronic submissions of application will be accepted. Submit two printed copies of the application and use a No. 2 pencil on the scantron sheet.

5925 ■ Robert G. Campbell Scholarships
(Undergraduate/Scholarship)

Purpose: To encourage educational pursuits among Redlands Unified School District graduates by providing educational assistance. **Focus:** General studies. **Qualif.:** Applicant must be an above-average student who is highly motivated to pursue his/her career. **Criteria:** Award is given based on merit.

Funds Avail.: $1,250 each year. **Number Awarded:** 1. **To Apply:** Applicants must submit a completed application form together with the scantron sheet; cover sheet; student activity and community activity sheets; personal essay; and a copy of unofficial transcript (signed by the counselor). **Deadline:** February 20.

Remarks: No electronic submissions of application will be accepted. Submit two printed copies of the application and use a No. 2 pencil on the scantron sheet.

5926 ■ Cesar E. Chavez Scholarships
(Undergraduate/Scholarship)

Purpose: To encourage educational pursuits among Redlands Unified School District graduates by providing educational assistance. **Focus:** General studies. **Qualif.:** Applicant must be a graduating senior who is in need of financial assistance in order to attend an institution of higher learning. **Criteria:** Award is given based on merit.

Funds Avail.: $1,000. **Number Awarded:** 1. **To Apply:** Applicants must submit a completed application form together with the scantron sheet; cover sheet; student activity and community activity sheets; personal essay; and a copy of unofficial transcript (signed by the counselor). **Deadline:** February 20.

Remarks: No electronic submissions of application will be accepted. Submit two printed copies of the application and use a No. 2 pencil on the scantron sheet.

5927 ■ Contemporary Club Scholarships
(Undergraduate/Scholarship)

Purpose: To encourage educational pursuits among Redlands Unified School District graduates by providing educational assistance. **Focus:** Music. **Qualif.:** Applicant must be a graduating senior intending to continue his/her studies in music. **Criteria:** Award is given based on merit.

Funds Avail.: $500. **Number Awarded:** 1. **To Apply:** Applicants must submit a completed application form together with the scantron sheet; cover sheet; student activity and community activity sheets; personal essay; and a copy of unofficial transcript (signed by the counselor). **Deadline:** February 20.

Remarks: No electronic submissions of application will be accepted. Submit two printed copies of the application and use a No. 2 pencil on the scantron sheet.

5928 ■ Cope Middle School PTSA Scholarships
(Undergraduate/Scholarship)

Purpose: To encourage educational pursuits among Redlands Unified School District graduates by providing educational assistance. **Focus:** General studies. **Qualif.:** Applicant must be a graduating senior who attended Cope Middle School for three years. **Criteria:** Priority will be given to a student whose parents were PTA volunteers.

Funds Avail.: $300. **Number Awarded:** 1. **To Apply:** Applicants must submit a completed application form together with the scantron sheet; cover sheet; student activity and community activity sheets; personal essay; and a copy of unofficial transcript (signed by the counselor). **Deadline:** February 20.

Remarks: No electronic submissions of application will be accepted. Submit two printed copies of the application and use a No. 2 pencil on the scantron sheet.

5929 ■ Crafton Elementary School PTA Scholarships *(Undergraduate/Scholarship)*

Purpose: To encourage educational pursuits among Redlands Unified School District graduates by providing educational assistance. **Focus:** General studies. **Qualif.:** Applicant must be a graduating senior who attended Crafton Elementary School for at least a year. **Criteria:** Preference is given to a student living in the school area.

Funds Avail.: $300. **Number Awarded:** 1. **To Apply:** Applicants must submit a completed application form together with the scantron sheet; cover sheet; student activity and community activity sheets; personal essay; and a copy of unofficial transcript (signed by the counselor). **Deadline:** February 20.

Remarks: No electronic submissions of application will be accepted. Submit two printed copies of the application and use a No. 2 pencil on the scantron sheet.

5930 ■ Crafton Hills College Foundation Scholarships *(Undergraduate/Scholarship)*

Purpose: To encourage educational pursuits among Redlands Unified School District graduates by providing educational assistance. **Focus:** General studies. **Qualif.:** Applicant must be a graduating senior enrolled at Crafton Hills College; must have a minimum 3.0 GPA; and must be attending college on a full-time basis. **Criteria:** Scholarship will be given to those who best meet the qualifications.

Funds Avail.: $500. **Number Awarded:** Varies. **To Apply:** Applicants must submit a completed application form together with the scantron sheet; cover sheet; student activity and community activity sheets; personal essay; and a copy of unofficial transcript (signed by the counselor). **Deadline:** February 20.

Remarks: No electronic submissions of application will be accepted. Submit two printed copies of the application and use a No. 2 pencil on the scantron sheet.

5931 ■ Arthur H. Daniels Scholarships
(Undergraduate/Scholarship)

Purpose: To encourage educational pursuits among Redlands Unified School District graduates by providing

educational assistance. **Focus:** General studies. **Qualif.:** Applicant must be a graduating senior demonstrating good citizenship, academic accomplishment, contribution to school and community and the intention to attend a college/ university on a full-time basis. **Criteria:** Awards are given based on merit.

Funds Avail.: $300, $500 and $1000. **Number Awarded:** 15. **To Apply:** Applicants must submit a completed application form together with the scantron sheet; cover sheet; student activity and community activity sheets; personal essay; and a copy of unofficial transcript (signed by the counselor). **Deadline:** February 20.

Remarks: No electronic submissions of application will be accepted. Submit two printed copies of the application and use a No. 2 pencil on the scantron sheet.

5932 ■ ROP - Dr. Linda Denver Scholarships *(Undergraduate/Scholarship)*

Purpose: To encourage educational pursuits among Redlands Unified School District graduates by providing educational assistance. **Focus:** General studies. **Qualif.:** Applicant must be a senior who has taken at least one ROP class; must have received a recommendation from a teacher; and must be able to demonstrate in a short essay how his/her ROP class has helped carry out his/her future career plans. **Criteria:** Award is given based on merit.

Funds Avail.: $100. **Number Awarded:** 1. **To Apply:** Applicants must submit a completed application form together with the scantron sheet; cover sheet; student activity and community activity sheets; personal essay; and a copy of unofficial transcript (signed by the counselor). **Deadline:** February 20.

Remarks: No electronic submissions of application will be accepted. Submit two printed copies of the application and use a No. 2 pencil on the scantron sheet.

5933 ■ Pat Dermargosian Memorial Scholarships *(Undergraduate/Scholarship)*

Purpose: To encourage educational pursuits among Redlands Unified School District graduates by providing educational assistance. **Focus:** General studies. **Qualif.:** Applicant must be a graduating senior whose parent has been actively involved in the PTA throughout his/her school years. **Criteria:** Award is given based on merit.

Funds Avail.: No specific amount. **Number Awarded:** 1. **To Apply:** Applicants must submit a completed application form together with the scantron sheet; cover sheet; student activity and community activity sheets; personal essay; and a copy of unofficial transcript (signed by the counselor). **Deadline:** February 20.

Remarks: No electronic submissions of application will be accepted. Submit two printed copies of the application and use a No. 2 pencil on the scantron sheet.

5934 ■ James Mackenzie Fallows Scholarships Honoring Gertrude Baccus *(Undergraduate/Scholarship)*

Purpose: To encourage educational pursuits among Redlands Unified School District graduates by providing educational assistance. **Focus:** General studies. **Qualif.:** Applicant must write an essay, article, speech, or some other work of non-fiction designed to explore an idea or explain a situation with the clarity and logic that Mrs. Baccus insisted on from her students. **Criteria:** Award is given to student who produces the best piece of expository writing.

Funds Avail.: $1,000. **Number Awarded:** 1. **To Apply:** Applicants must submit a completed application form together with the scantron sheet; cover sheet; student activity and community activity sheets; personal essay; and a copy of unofficial transcript (signed by the counselor). **Deadline:** February 20.

Remarks: No electronic submissions of application will be accepted. Submit two printed copies of the application and use a No. 2 pencil on the scantron sheet.

5935 ■ Arthur and Juna Fisher Memorial Track Scholarships *(Undergraduate/Scholarship)*

Purpose: To encourage educational pursuits among Redlands Unified School District graduates by providing educational assistance. **Focus:** General studies. **Qualif.:** Applicant must be a graduating senior who has been active in track activities for at least two years and has maintained a 3.0 or better GPA. **Criteria:** Award is given based on merit.

Funds Avail.: $500. **Number Awarded:** 1. **To Apply:** Applicants must submit a completed form together with the scantron sheet; cover sheet; student activity and community activity sheets; personal essay; and a copy of unofficial transcript (signed by the counselor). **Deadline:** February 20.

Remarks: No electronic submissions of application will be accepted. Submit two printed copies of the application and use a No. 2 pencil on the scantron sheet.

5936 ■ Franklin Elementary School PTA Scholarships *(Undergraduate/Scholarship)*

Purpose: To encourage educational pursuits among Redlands Unified School District graduates by providing educational assistance. **Focus:** General studies. **Qualif.:** Applicants must be students who attended Franklin Elementary School and have extensive volunteer service in both school and community. **Criteria:** Award is given based on merit.

Funds Avail.: $250. **Number Awarded:** 1. **To Apply:** Applicants must submit a completed application form together with the scantron sheet; cover sheet; student activity and community activity sheets; personal essay; and a copy of unofficial transcript (signed by the counselor). **Deadline:** February 20.

Remarks: No electronic submissions of application will be accepted. Submit two printed copies of the application and use a No. 2 pencil on the scantron sheet.

5937 ■ Friends and Family of Jennifer Balber Scholarships *(Undergraduate/Scholarship)*

Purpose: To encourage educational pursuits among Redlands Unified School District graduates by providing educational assistance. **Focus:** Marine biology; Oceanography. **Qualif.:** Applicant must be a graduating senior who has a cumulative GPA of 2.5 or higher; must demonstrate financial need; must be involved in school and community activities; must demonstrate strong character and citizenship; and must be pursuing a career in marine biology, oceanography, or a closely-related field. **Criteria:** Award is given based on the application.

Funds Avail.: $500. **Number Awarded:** 1. **To Apply:** Applicants must submit a completed application form together with the scantron sheet; cover sheet; student activity and community activity sheets; personal essay; and a copy of unofficial transcript (signed by the counselor). **Deadline:** February 20.

Remarks: No electronic submissions of application will be accepted. Submit two printed copies of the application and use a No. 2 pencil on the scantron sheet.

5938 ■ Gail Garner R.I.S.E. Memorial Scholarships *(Undergraduate/Scholarship)*

Purpose: To encourage educational pursuits among Redlands Unified School District graduates by providing educational assistance. **Focus:** General studies. **Qualif.:** Applicant must be a student graduating through the Redlands Independent Study Education (R.I.S.E.) program. **Criteria:** Award is given based on merit.

Funds Avail.: $500. **Number Awarded:** 1. **To Apply:** Applicants must submit a completed application form together with the scantron sheet; cover sheet; student activity and community activity sheets; personal essay; and a copy of unofficial transcript (signed by the counselor). **Deadline:** February 20.

Remarks: No electronic submissions of application will be accepted. Submit two printed copies of the application and use a No. 2 pencil on the scantron sheet.

5939 ■ Ann and Brad Glassco Scholarships *(Undergraduate/Scholarship)*

Purpose: To encourage educational pursuits among Redlands Unified School District graduates by providing educational assistance. **Focus:** General studies. **Qualif.:** Applicant must be a student who has performed in at least two acts in the YMCA's Great "Y" Circus in junior or senior year of high school. Student must have a 2.5 GPA or better. **Criteria:** Award is given based on merit.

Funds Avail.: $500. **Number Awarded:** 1. **To Apply:** Applicants must submit a completed application form together with the scantron sheet; cover sheet; student activity and community activity sheets; personal essay; and a copy of unofficial transcript (signed by the counselor). **Deadline:** February 20.

Remarks: No electronic submissions of application will be accepted. Submit two printed copies of the application and use a No. 2 pencil on the scantron sheet.

5940 ■ Rachel Graham Memorial Scholarships *(Undergraduate/Scholarship)*

Purpose: To encourage educational pursuits among Redlands Unified School District graduates by providing educational assistance. **Focus:** General studies. **Qualif.:** Applicant must be a graduating senior attending a four-year college/university on a full-time basis; must have maintained at least a 3.0 GPA; must show good citizenship; and must participate in school and community activities. **Criteria:** Awards are given based on merit.

Funds Avail.: $600. **Number Awarded:** 8. **To Apply:** Applicants must submit a completed application form together with the scantron sheet; cover sheet; student activity and community activity sheets; personal essay; and a copy of unofficial transcript (signed by the counselor). **Deadline:** February 20.

Remarks: No electronic submissions of application will be accepted. Submit two printed copies of the application and use a No. 2 pencil on the scantron sheet.

5941 ■ Community Bank - Lee Guggisberg Foundation Memorial Scholarships *(Undergraduate/Scholarship)*

Purpose: To encourage educational pursuits among Redlands Unified School District graduates by providing educational assistance. **Focus:** Business; Accounting. **Qualif.:** Applicant must complete the graduation requirements of the Redlands Unified School District; must be enrolled as a full-time student at an accredited college/university prior to Community Bank releasing the scholarship money; and must plan to further education in the field of business management or accounting. **Criteria:** Awards are given based on merit.

Funds Avail.: $300. **Number Awarded:** 3. **To Apply:** Applicants must submit a completed application form together with the scantron sheet; cover sheet; student activity and community activity sheets; personal essay; and a copy of unofficial transcript (signed by the counselor). **Deadline:** February 20.

Remarks: No electronic submissions of application will be accepted. Submit two printed copies of the application and use a No. 2 pencil on the scantron sheet.

5942 ■ Guzkowski Family Scholarships *(Undergraduate/Scholarship)*

Purpose: To encourage educational pursuits among Redlands Unified School District graduates by providing educational assistance. **Focus:** General studies. **Qualif.:** Applicant must be a graduating senior student. **Criteria:** Award is given based on merit.

Funds Avail.: $300. **Number Awarded:** 1. **To Apply:** Applicants must submit a completed application form together with the scantron sheet; cover sheet; student activity and community activity sheets; personal essay; and a copy of unofficial transcript (signed by the counselor). **Deadline:** February 20.

Remarks: No electronic submissions of application will be accepted. Submit two printed copies of the application and use a No. 2 pencil on the scantron sheet.

5943 ■ William T. Hartzell Memorial Scholarships *(Undergraduate/Scholarship)*

Purpose: To encourage educational pursuits among Redlands Unified School District graduates by providing educational assistance. **Focus:** General studies. **Qualif.:** Applicant must be a graduating senior who maintains at least a 3.5 GPA; must have shown leadership in school activities; must plan to attend a college/university on a full-time basis; and must have attended Redlands area schools for six years or more. **Criteria:** Award is given based on merit.

Funds Avail.: $500. **Number Awarded:** 1. **To Apply:** Applicants must submit a completed application form together with the scantron sheet; cover sheet; student activity and community activity sheets; personal essay; and a copy of unofficial transcript (signed by the counselor). **Deadline:** February 20.

Remarks: No electronic submissions of application will be accepted. Submit two printed copies of the application and use a No. 2 pencil on the scantron sheet.

5944 ■ R. Garn Haycock Memorial Scholarships *(Undergraduate/Scholarship)*

Purpose: To encourage educational pursuits among Redlands Unified School District graduates by providing educational assistance. **Focus:** General studies. **Qualif.:** Applicant must be a deserving senior who displays good citizenship, character, and academic potential, has a need for financial assistance and is intending to attend an institution of higher learning on a full-time basis. **Criteria:** Award is given based on merit.

Awards are arranged alphabetically below their administering organizations

Funds Avail.: $1,000. **Number Awarded:** 1. **To Apply:** Applicants must submit a completed application form together with the scantron sheet; cover sheet; student activity and community activity sheets; personal essay; and a copy of unofficial transcript (signed by the counselor). **Deadline:** February 20.

Remarks: No electronic submissions of application will be accepted. Submit two printed copies of the application and use a No. 2 pencil on the scantron sheet.

5945 ■ Holy Name Of Jesus Parish Scholarships *(Undergraduate/Scholarship)*

Purpose: To encourage educational pursuits among Redlands Unified School District graduates by providing educational assistance. **Focus:** General studies. **Qualif.:** Applicant must be a graduating senior who is active in parish youth activities; must be above-average in academic standing; must be a registered member of the parish; and must be attending a college/university in the fall. **Criteria:** Award is given based on merit.

Funds Avail.: $500. **Number Awarded:** 1. **To Apply:** Applicants must submit a completed application form together with the scantron sheet; cover sheet; student activity and community activity sheets; personal essay; and a copy of unofficial transcript (signed by the counselor). **Deadline:** February 20.

Remarks: No electronic submissions of application will be accepted. Submit two printed copies of the application and use a No. 2 pencil on the scantron sheet.

5946 ■ Eric L. Jacobson Memorial Scholarships *(Undergraduate/Scholarship)*

Purpose: To encourage educational pursuits among Redlands Unified School District graduates by providing educational assistance. **Focus:** General studies. **Qualif.:** Applicant must be a graduating senior who has maintained a 3.0 or higher GPA; must have participated on the speech or debate team for at least two years (one of which must be the senior year); and must be planning to attend a four-year college/university on a full-time basis. **Criteria:** Consideration is given to a student who demonstrates a variety of interests and performs service to school and community.

Funds Avail.: $1,000. **Number Awarded:** 1. **To Apply:** Applicants must submit a completed application form together with the scantron sheet; cover sheet; student activity and community activity sheets; personal essay; and a copy of unofficial transcript (signed by the counselor). **Deadline:** February 20.

Remarks: No electronic submissions of application will be accepted. Submit two printed copies of the application and use a No. 2 pencil on the scantron sheet.

5947 ■ Mike Jensen R.I.S.E. Memorial Scholarships *(Undergraduate/Scholarship)*

Purpose: To encourage educational pursuits among Redlands Unified School District graduates by providing educational assistance. **Focus:** General studies. **Qualif.:** Applicant must be a graduating senior student. **Criteria:** Awards are given based on positive attitude, cooperation and responsibility while in attendance at the R.I.S.E. program.

Funds Avail.: $500. **Number Awarded:** 2. **To Apply:** Applicants must submit a completed application form together with the scantron sheet; cover sheet; student activity and community activity sheets; personal essay; and a copy of unofficial transcript (signed by the counselor). **Deadline:** February 20.

Remarks: No electronic submissions of application will be accepted. Submit two printed copies of the application and use a No. 2 pencil on the scantron sheet.

5948 ■ Brian Jimenez Memorial Scholarships *(Undergraduate/Scholarship)*

Purpose: To encourage educational pursuits among Redlands Unified School District graduates by providing educational assistance. **Focus:** Criminal justice. **Qualif.:** Applicant must be a male senior who has participated in baseball or soccer, has a GPA of 2.5 or higher, and is intending to attend an institution of higher learning on a full-time basis. **Criteria:** Preference is given to a student who plans to major in criminal justice or criminal law.

Funds Avail.: $500. **Number Awarded:** 1. **To Apply:** Applicants must submit a completed application form together with the scantron sheet; cover sheet; student activity and community activity sheets; personal essay; and a copy of unofficial transcript (signed by the counselor). **Deadline:** February 20.

Remarks: No electronic submissions of application will be accepted. Submit two printed copies of the application and use a No. 2 pencil on the scantron sheet.

5949 ■ Junior Women of the Contemporary Club Scholarships *(Undergraduate/Scholarship)*

Purpose: To encourage educational pursuits among Redlands Unified School District graduates by providing educational assistance. **Focus:** General studies. **Qualif.:** Applicant must be a graduating senior who shows financial need, has a respectable GPA, and has a definite goal in mind. **Criteria:** Award is given based on merit.

Funds Avail.: $300. **Number Awarded:** 1. **To Apply:** Applicants must submit a completed application form together with the scantron sheet; cover sheet; student activity and community activity sheets; personal essay; and a copy of unofficial transcript (signed by the counselor). **Deadline:** February 20.

Remarks: No electronic submissions of application will be accepted. Submit two printed copies of the application and use a No. 2 pencil on the scantron sheet.

5950 ■ Annette and Ernest Keith Scholarships *(Undergraduate/Scholarship)*

Purpose: To encourage educational pursuits among Redlands Unified School District graduates by providing educational assistance. **Focus:** General studies. **Qualif.:** Applicant must be a graduating senior belonging to the top ten percent of their class who will be attending a four-year California college/university on a full-time basis. **Criteria:** Awards are given based on merit.

Funds Avail.: $600. **Number Awarded:** 5. **To Apply:** Applicants must submit a completed application form together with the scantron sheet; cover sheet; student activity and community activity sheets; personal essay; and a copy of unofficial transcript (signed by the counselor). **Deadline:** February 20.

Remarks: No electronic submissions of application will be accepted. Submit two printed copies of the application and use a No. 2 pencil on the scantron sheet.

5951 ■ Kimberly Elementary School PTA Scholarships *(Undergraduate/Scholarship)*

Purpose: To encourage educational pursuits among Redlands Unified School District graduates by providing

educational assistance. **Focus:** General studies. **Qualif.:** Applicant must be a graduating senior who attended Kimberly Elementary School for a minimum of three years; must be an average or above-average achiever; and must demonstrate good citizenship. **Criteria:** Award is given based on merit.

Funds Avail.: $300. **Number Awarded:** 1. **To Apply:** Applicants must submit a completed application form together with the scantron sheet; cover sheet; student activity and community activity sheets; personal essay; and a copy of unofficial transcript (signed by the counselor). **Deadline:** February 20.

Remarks: No electronic submissions of application will be accepted. Submit two printed copies of the application and use a No. 2 pencil on the scantron sheet.

5952 ■ Kingsbury Elementary School PTA Scholarships *(Undergraduate/Scholarship)*

Purpose: To encourage educational pursuits among Redlands Unified School District graduates by providing educational assistance. **Focus:** General studies. **Qualif.:** Applicant must be a student who attended Kingsbury Elementary School for at least three years; must have a minimum of a "C" average; must have demonstrated good citizenship and leadership; must show financial need; and must demonstrate involvement in extracurricular and community activities. **Criteria:** Award is given based on merit.

Funds Avail.: No specific amount. **Number Awarded:** 1. **To Apply:** Applicants must submit a completed application form together with the scantron sheet; cover sheet; student activity and community activity sheets; personal essay; and a copy of unofficial transcript (signed by the counselor). **Deadline:** February 20.

Remarks: No electronic submissions of application will be accepted. Submit two printed copies of the application and use a No. 2 pencil on the scantron sheet.

5953 ■ Christopher J. Kohlmeier Scholarships *(Undergraduate/Scholarship)*

Purpose: To encourage educational pursuits among Redlands Unified School District graduates by providing educational assistance. **Focus:** Law enforcement. **Qualif.:** Applicant must be a graduating senior planning to attend a two-year or four-year college or university; must have strong test scores, but whose "C" average in high school could easily have been higher. **Criteria:** Preference is given to a student interested in a career in law enforcement or firefighting.

Funds Avail.: $300. **Number Awarded:** 1. **To Apply:** Applicants must submit a completed application form together with the scantron sheet; cover sheet; student activity and community activity sheets; personal essay; and a copy of unofficial transcript (signed by the counselor). **Deadline:** February 20.

Remarks: No electronic submissions of application will be accepted. Submit two printed copies of the application and use a No. 2 pencil on the scantron sheet.

5954 ■ Harold Leeming Memorial Scholarships *(Undergraduate/Scholarship)*

Purpose: To encourage educational pursuits among Redlands Unified School District graduates by providing educational assistance. **Focus:** Engineering; Physical sciences. **Qualif.:** Applicant must be a graduating senior who has an interest in engineering or physical science; must have played an active part in school and community activities; and must be enrolled in engineering or physical science courses. **Criteria:** Preference is given to students who have an interest in aerospace engineering or science.

Funds Avail.: $1,000. **Number Awarded:** 2. **To Apply:** Applicants must submit a completed application form together with the scantron sheet; cover sheet; student activity and community activity sheets; personal essay; and a copy of unofficial transcript (signed by the counselor). **Deadline:** February 20.

Remarks: No electronic submissions of application will be accepted. Submit two printed copies of the application and use a No. 2 pencil on the scantron sheet.

5955 ■ Doreen Legg Memorial Scholarships *(Undergraduate/Scholarship)*

Purpose: To encourage educational pursuits among Redlands Unified School District graduates by providing educational assistance. **Focus:** Business; Teaching. **Qualif.:** Applicant must be a graduating senior enrolling full-time at a four-year college or university; must be pursuing a business or teaching career; must have a minimum 3.0 GPA; and must have attended Redlands High School for at least three consecutive years. **Criteria:** Awards are given based on merit.

Funds Avail.: $600 and $1000. **Number Awarded:** 9. **To Apply:** Applicants must submit a completed application form together with the scantron sheet; cover sheet; student activity and community activity sheets; personal essay; and a copy of unofficial transcript (signed by the counselor). **Deadline:** February 20.

Remarks: No electronic submissions of application will be accepted. Submit two printed copies of the application and use a No. 2 pencil on the scantron sheet.

5956 ■ Jack A. and Louise S. Levine Memorial Scholarships *(Undergraduate/Scholarship)*

Purpose: To encourage educational pursuits among Redlands Unified School District graduates by providing educational assistance. **Focus:** General studies. **Qualif.:** Applicant must be a graduating senior planning to continue education; must have a 3.0 or higher GPA; must demonstrate good citizenship; and must have participated in school and/or community activities. **Criteria:** Award is given based on merit.

Funds Avail.: $500. **Number Awarded:** 1. **To Apply:** Applicants must submit a completed application form together with the scantron sheet; cover sheet; student activity and community activity sheets; personal essay; and a copy of unofficial transcript (signed by the counselor). **Deadline:** February 20.

Remarks: No electronic submissions of application will be accepted. Submit two printed copies of the application and use a No. 2 pencil on the scantron sheet.

5957 ■ Lugonia Alumni/Harrison Lightfoot Scholarships *(Undergraduate/Scholarship)*

Purpose: To encourage educational pursuits among Redlands Unified School District graduates by providing educational assistance. **Focus:** General studies. **Qualif.:** Applicant must be a graduating senior who attended Lugonia Elementary School. Student must have extensive community service and/or be involved in school activities; must demonstrate good citizenship; and must have a GPA of 2.5 or higher. **Criteria:** Award is given based on merit.

Funds Avail.: No specific amount. **Number Awarded:** 1.

Awards are arranged alphabetically below their administering organizations

To Apply: Applicants must submit a completed application form together with the scantron sheet; cover sheet; student activity and community activity sheets; personal essay; and a copy of unofficial transcript (signed by the counselor). **Deadline:** February 20.

Remarks: No electronic submissions of application will be accepted. Submit two printed copies of the application and use a No. 2 pencil on the scantron sheet.

5958 ■ James Mackenzie Fallows Scholarship Honoring William Cunningham *(Undergraduate/ Scholarship)*

Purpose: To encourage educational pursuits among Redlands Unified School District graduates by providing educational assistance. **Focus:** General studies. **Qualif.:** Applicant must be a student who shows great promise for public service in his/her career. **Criteria:** Award is given based on merit.

Funds Avail.: $1,000. **Number Awarded:** 1. **To Apply:** Applicants must submit a completed application form together with the scantron sheet; cover sheet; student activity and community activity sheets; personal essay; and a copy of unofficial transcript (signed by the counselor). **Deadline:** February 20.

Remarks: No electronic submissions of application will be accepted. Submit two printed copies of the application and use a No. 2 pencil on the scantron sheet.

5959 ■ Mariposa Elementary School PTA Scholarships *(Undergraduate/Scholarship)*

Purpose: To encourage educational pursuits among Redlands Unified School District graduates by providing educational assistance. **Focus:** General studies. **Qualif.:** Applicant must be a graduating senior who attended Mariposa Elementary School for at least two years and must have demonstrated serious scholarship, good citizenship, and a desire for further education either in academics or a vocational trade. **Criteria:** Award is given based on merit.

Funds Avail.: $300. **Number Awarded:** 1. **To Apply:** Applicants must submit a completed application form together with the scantron sheet; cover sheet; student activity and community activity sheets; personal essay; and a copy of unofficial transcript (signed by the counselor). **Deadline:** February 20.

Remarks: No electronic submissions of application will be accepted. Submit two printed copies of the application and use a No. 2 pencil on the scantron sheet.

5960 ■ McKinley Elementary School PTA Scholarships *(Undergraduate/Scholarship)*

Purpose: To encourage educational pursuits among Redlands Unified School District graduates by providing educational assistance. **Focus:** General studies. **Qualif.:** Applicant must be a graduating senior who attended McKinley Elementary School for at least three years and plan to attend a college, university, or vocational school. **Criteria:** Awards are given based on merit.

Funds Avail.: $300. **Number Awarded:** 2. **To Apply:** Applicants must submit a completed application form together with the scantron sheet; cover sheet; student activity and community activity sheets; personal essay; and a copy of unofficial transcript (signed by the counselor). **Deadline:** February 20.

Remarks: No electronic submissions of application will be accepted. Submit two printed copies of the application and use a No. 2 pencil on the scantron sheet.

5961 ■ Augustine and Sandra Medina Memorial Scholarships *(Undergraduate/Scholarship)*

Purpose: To encourage educational pursuits among Redlands Unified School District graduates by providing educational assistance. **Focus:** General studies. **Qualif.:** Applicant must be a graduating senior; must have a minimum 2.5 GPA; must be involved in community and/or school activities; must have financial need; and must intend to pursue a two or four-year college degree. **Criteria:** Award is given based on merit.

Funds Avail.: $350. **Number Awarded:** 1. **To Apply:** Applicants must submit a completed application form together with the scantron sheet; cover sheet; student activity and community activity sheets; personal essay; a copy of unofficial transcript (signed by the counselor); and a short statement regarding a hardship that they experienced and how it impacted their life. **Deadline:** February 20.

Remarks: No electronic submissions of application will be accepted. Submit two printed copies of the application and use a No. 2 pencil on the scantron sheet.

5962 ■ Dorothy Mitchell Scholarships *(Undergraduate/Scholarship)*

Purpose: To encourage educational pursuits among Redlands Unified School District graduates by providing educational assistance. **Focus:** General studies. **Qualif.:** Applicant must be a graduating senior planning to enter the teaching profession. **Criteria:** Award is given based on merit.

Funds Avail.: $300. **Number Awarded:** 1. **To Apply:** Applicants must submit a completed application form together with the scantron sheet; cover sheet; student activity and community activity sheets; personal essay; and a copy of unofficial transcript (signed by the counselor). **Deadline:** February 20.

Remarks: No electronic submissions of application will be accepted. Submit two printed copies of the application and use a No. 2 pencil on the scantron sheet.

5963 ■ Moore Middle School PTA Scholarships *(Undergraduate/Scholarship)*

Purpose: To encourage educational pursuits among Redlands Unified School District graduates by providing educational assistance. **Focus:** General studies. **Qualif.:** Applicant must be a graduating senior who has attended Moore Middle School for three years and plans to attend college or a trade school. **Criteria:** Award is given based on merit.

Funds Avail.: $300. **Number Awarded:** 1. **To Apply:** Applicants must submit a completed application form together with the scantron sheet; cover sheet; student activity and community activity sheets; personal essay; and a copy of unofficial transcript (signed by the counselor). **Deadline:** February 20.

Remarks: No electronic submissions of application will be accepted. Submit two printed copies of the application and use a No. 2 pencil on the scantron sheet.

5964 ■ Harry Munoz Memorial Scholarships *(Undergraduate/Scholarship)*

Purpose: To encourage educational pursuits among Redlands Unified School District graduates by providing educational assistance. **Focus:** General studies. **Qualif.:**

Applicant must be a graduate who has demonstrated academic achievement, outstanding citizenship, and a desire to continue his/her education. **Criteria:** Award is given based on merit.

Funds Avail.: $1,000. **Number Awarded:** 1. **To Apply:** Applicants must submit a completed application form together with the scantron sheet; cover sheet; student activity and community activity sheets; personal essay; and a copy of unofficial transcript (signed by the counselor). **Deadline:** February 20.

Remarks: No electronic submissions of application will be accepted. Submit two printed copies of the application and use a No. 2 pencil on the scantron sheet.

5965 ■ Rick Munoz Memorial Scholarships *(Undergraduate/Scholarship)*

Purpose: To support Redlands Unified School District graduates with their educational pursuit. **Focus:** General studies. **Qualif.:** Applicant must be a graduating senior who demonstrates high academic achievement, outstanding citizenship, and a desire to continue his/her education. **Criteria:** Award is given based on merit.

Funds Avail.: $500. **Number Awarded:** 1. **To Apply:** Applicants must submit a completed application form together with the scantron sheet; cover sheet; student activity and community activity sheets; personal essay; a copy of unofficial transcript (signed by the counselor); proof of letter in at least one sport in senior year. **Deadline:** February 20.

Remarks: No electronic submissions of application will be accepted. Submit two printed copies of the application and use a No. 2 pencil on the scantron sheet.

5966 ■ Jack Nagasaka Memorial Scholarships *(Undergraduate/Scholarship)*

Purpose: To encourage educational pursuits among Redlands Unified School District graduates by providing educational assistance. **Focus:** General studies. **Qualif.:** Applicant must be a graduating senior who has outstanding performance in the field of math or science. **Criteria:** Awards are given based on grades and achievement test scores in chemistry, physics and/or math.

Funds Avail.: $300. **Number Awarded:** 2. **To Apply:** Applicants must submit a completed application form together with the scantron sheet; cover sheet; student activity and community activity sheets; personal essay; and a copy of unofficial transcript (signed by the counselor). **Deadline:** February 20.

Remarks: No electronic submissions of application will be accepted. Submit two printed copies of the application and use a No. 2 pencil on the scantron sheet.

5967 ■ Robyn Nance Memorial Scholarships *(Undergraduate/Scholarship)*

Purpose: To encourage educational pursuits among Redlands Unified School District graduates by providing educational assistance. **Focus:** General studies. **Qualif.:** Applicant must be a graduating senior active in dramatic arts; must have utilized talents to the utmost; must display a love and enthusiasm for the theatre; and must participate whenever and wherever needed. **Criteria:** Award is given based on merit.

Funds Avail.: $500. **Number Awarded:** 1. **To Apply:** Applicants must submit a completed application form together with the scantron sheet; cover sheet; student activity and community activity sheets; personal essay; and a copy of unofficial transcript (signed by the counselor). **Deadline:** February 20.

Remarks: No electronic submissions of application will be accepted. Submit two printed copies of the application and use a No. 2 pencil on the scantron sheet.

5968 ■ Mike Niemeyer Memorial Football Scholarships *(Undergraduate/Scholarship)*

Purpose: To encourage educational pursuits among Redlands Unified School District graduates by providing educational assistance. **Focus:** General studies. **Qualif.:** Applicant must be a graduating senior who is a member of the Redlands High School Terrier football team and must demonstrate academic achievement and good citizenship. **Criteria:** Preference is given to a high academic achiever or to an offensive or defensive lineman.

Funds Avail.: $500. **Number Awarded:** 1. **To Apply:** Applicants must submit a completed application form together with the scantron sheet; cover sheet; student activity and community activity sheets; personal essay; and a copy of unofficial transcript (signed by the counselor). **Deadline:** February 20.

Remarks: No electronic submissions of application will be accepted. Submit two printed copies of the application and use a No. 2 pencil on the scantron sheet.

5969 ■ Optimist Club Of Redlands - Ralph Maloof Scholarships *(Undergraduate/Scholarship)*

Purpose: To encourage educational pursuits among Redlands Unified School District graduates by providing educational assistance. **Focus:** General studies. **Qualif.:** Applicant must be a graduating male senior who has a minimum 3.0 GPA, a positive attitude, and involvement in service to the community. **Criteria:** Award is given based on merit.

Funds Avail.: $1,500. **Number Awarded:** 1. **To Apply:** Applicants must submit a completed application form together with the scantron sheet; cover sheet; student activity and community activity sheets; personal essay; and a copy of unofficial transcript (signed by the counselor). **Deadline:** February 20.

Remarks: No electronic submissions of application will be accepted. Submit two printed copies of the application and use a No. 2 pencil on the scantron sheet.

5970 ■ Optimist Club of Redlands - Virginia Elliott Scholarships *(Undergraduate/Scholarship)*

Purpose: To encourage educational pursuits among Redlands Unified School District graduates by providing educational assistance. **Focus:** General studies. **Qualif.:** Applicant must be a female graduating senior who has a minimum 3.0 GPA, a positive attitude, and involvement in service to the community. **Criteria:** Award is given based on merit.

Funds Avail.: $1,500. **Number Awarded:** 1. **To Apply:** Applicants must submit a completed application form together with the scantron sheet; cover sheet; student activity and community activity sheets; personal essay; and a copy of unofficial transcript (signed by the counselor). **Deadline:** February 20.

Remarks: No electronic submissions of application will be accepted. Submit two printed copies of the application and use a No. 2 pencil on the scantron sheet.

5971 ■ PCH Architects/Steven J. Lehnhof Memorial Architectural Scholarships *(Undergraduate/Scholarship)*

Purpose: To encourage educational pursuits among Redlands Unified School District graduates by providing educational assistance. **Focus:** Architecture; Architectural engineering. **Qualif.:** Applicant must be a graduating senior who will be majoring in architecture or architectural engineering at an accredited college/university. **Criteria:** Award is given based on merit.

Funds Avail.: $1000. **Number Awarded:** 1. **To Apply:** Applicants must submit a completed application form together with the scantron sheet; cover sheet; student activity and community activity sheets; personal essay; and a copy of unofficial transcript (signed by the counselor). **Deadline:** February 20.

Remarks: No electronic submissions of application will be accepted. Submit two printed copies of the application and use a No. 2 pencil on the scantron sheet.

5972 ■ Marshall Phelps Athletic Memorial Scholarships *(Undergraduate/Scholarship)*

Purpose: To encourage educational pursuits among Redlands Unified School District graduates by providing educational assistance. **Focus:** General studies. **Qualif.:** Applicant must be a graduating male or female with proven athletic ability and interest in a career involving some phase of athletics (sports medicine, coaching, or physical therapy) and is enrolling in a two-year or four-year college program with a minimum 2.0 GPA. **Criteria:** Award is given based on merit.

Funds Avail.: $1,000. **Number Awarded:** 1. **To Apply:** Applicants must submit a completed application form together with the scantron sheet; cover sheet; student activity and community activity sheets; personal essay; and a copy of unofficial transcript (signed by the counselor). **Deadline:** February 20.

Remarks: No electronic submissions of application will be accepted. Submit two printed copies of the application and use a No. 2 pencil on the scantron sheet.

5973 ■ Howard and Mildred Phoenix Scholarships *(Undergraduate/Scholarship)*

Purpose: To encourage educational pursuits among Redlands Unified School District graduates by providing educational assistance. **Focus:** General studies. **Qualif.:** Applicant must be a graduating senior who has demonstrated good citizenship, academic accomplishment, contribution to school and community; must be planning to further career in a business field; and must have attended Redlands High School for at least three semesters. **Criteria:** Award is given based on merit.

Funds Avail.: $400. **Number Awarded:** 1. **To Apply:** Applicants must submit a completed application form together with the scantron sheet; cover sheet; student activity and community activity sheets; personal essay; and a copy of unofficial transcript (signed by the counselor). **Deadline:** February 20.

Remarks: No electronic submissions of application will be accepted. Submit two printed copies of the application and use a No. 2 pencil on the scantron sheet.

5974 ■ Gail Porterfield Memorial Scholarships *(Undergraduate/Scholarship)*

Purpose: To encourage educational pursuits among Redlands Unified School District graduates by providing educational assistance. **Focus:** General studies. **Qualif.:** Applicant must be a graduating young woman who has a minimum 3.5 GPA; must be planning to enter a medical or scientific field; and must have financial need. **Criteria:** Award is given based on merit.

Funds Avail.: $500. **Number Awarded:** 1. **To Apply:** Applicants must submit a completed application form together with the scantron sheet; cover sheet; student activity and community activity sheets; personal essay; and a copy of unofficial transcript (signed by the counselor). **Deadline:** February 20.

Remarks: No electronic submissions of application will be accepted. Submit two printed copies of the application and use a No. 2 pencil on the scantron sheet.

5975 ■ The Power to Continue Learning Scholarships *(Undergraduate/Scholarship)*

Purpose: To encourage educational pursuits among Redlands Unified School District graduates by providing educational assistance. **Focus:** General studies. **Qualif.:** Applicant must be a graduating young woman; must have a minimum 2.5 GPA; must have participated in at least one school activity; must have demonstrated some type of community service; and must be planning to attend a two-year or four-year college or a vocational program. **Criteria:** Preference is given to a student who will be the first in her family to obtain a college degree or professional-level training.

Funds Avail.: $500. **Number Awarded:** 1. **To Apply:** Applicants must submit a completed application form together with the scantron sheet; cover sheet; student activity and community activity sheets; personal essay; and a copy of unofficial transcript (signed by the counselor). **Deadline:** February 20.

Remarks: No electronic submissions of application will be accepted. Submit two printed copies of the application and use a No. 2 pencil on the scantron sheet.

5976 ■ Raul Ramirez Memorial Scholarships *(Undergraduate/Scholarship)*

Purpose: To encourage educational pursuits among Redlands Unified School District graduates by providing educational assistance. **Focus:** General studies. **Qualif.:** Applicant must be a graduating varsity letterman in wrestling, shot put, or track; must show dedication to sports, enthusiasm, an effort to improve, and respect for other athletes and teammates; must have satisfactory grades. **Criteria:** Award is given based on merit.

Funds Avail.: $700. **Number Awarded:** 1. **To Apply:** Applicants must submit a completed application form together with the scantron sheet; cover sheet; student activity and community activity sheets; personal essay; and a copy of unofficial transcript (signed by the counselor). **Deadline:** February 20.

Remarks: No electronic submissions of application will be accepted. Submit two printed copies of the application and use a No. 2 pencil on the scantron sheet.

5977 ■ Redlands Area Interfaith Council Scholarships *(Undergraduate/Scholarship)*

Purpose: To encourage educational pursuits among Redlands Unified School District graduates by providing educational assistance. **Focus:** General studies. **Qualif.:** Applicant must be a graduating student. **Criteria:** Award is given based on merit.

Funds Avail.: $500. **Number Awarded:** 1. **To Apply:** Applicants must submit a completed application form together with the scantron sheet; cover sheet; student activity and community activity sheets; a 1-page essay explaining "How I can be an agent of peace"; and a copy of unofficial transcript (signed by the counselor). **Deadline:** February 20.

Remarks: No electronic submissions of application will be accepted. Submit two printed copies of the application and use a No. 2 pencil on the scantron sheet.

5978 ■ Redlands Community Scholarship Foundation Scholarships *(Undergraduate/Scholarship)*

Purpose: To encourage educational pursuits among Redlands Unified School District graduates by providing educational assistance. **Focus:** General studies. **Qualif.:** Applicant must be a graduating senior student. **Criteria:** Awards are given based on merit.

Funds Avail.: $500. **Number Awarded:** 15. **To Apply:** Applicants must submit a completed application form together with the scantron sheet; cover sheet; student activity and community activity sheets; personal essay; and a copy of unofficial transcript (signed by the counselor). **Deadline:** February 20.

Remarks: No electronic submissions of application will be accepted. Submit two printed copies of the application and use a No. 2 pencil on the scantron sheet.

5979 ■ Redlands Council PTA - Dorothy Jolley Memorial Scholarships *(Undergraduate/Scholarship)*

Purpose: To encourage educational pursuits among Redlands Unified School District graduates by providing educational assistance. **Focus:** General studies. **Qualif.:** Applicant must be a graduating senior; must have a minimum 3.0 GPA; and must be active in a non-school service group such as church, scouts, or a community service club. **Criteria:** Award is given based on merit.

Funds Avail.: $300. **Number Awarded:** 1. **To Apply:** Applicants must submit a completed application form together with the scantron sheet; cover sheet; student activity and community activity sheets; personal essay; and a copy of unofficial transcript (signed by the counselor). **Deadline:** February 20.

Remarks: No electronic submissions of application will be accepted. Submit two printed copies of the application and use a No. 2 pencil on the scantron sheet.

5980 ■ Redlands Footlighters, Inc. - Merle and Peggy Williams Scholarships *(Undergraduate/Scholarship)*

Purpose: To encourage educational pursuits among Redlands Unified School District graduates by providing educational assistance. **Focus:** General studies. **Qualif.:** Applicant must be a graduating senior who has made major contributions in theatre, either as an actor or as a theatre technician, and intends to continue involvement in theatre activities in the future. **Criteria:** Award is given based on merit.

Funds Avail.: $750. **Number Awarded:** 1. **To Apply:** Applicants must submit a completed application form together with the scantron sheet; cover sheet; student activity and community activity sheets; personal essay; and a copy of unofficial transcript (signed by the counselor). **Deadline:** February 20.

Remarks: No electronic submissions of application will be accepted. Submit two printed copies of the application and use a No. 2 pencil on the scantron sheet.

5981 ■ Redlands High School Academic Decathalon Scholarships *(Undergraduate/Scholarship)*

Purpose: To encourage educational pursuits among Redlands Unified School District graduates by providing educational assistance. **Focus:** General studies. **Qualif.:** Applicant must be an outstanding senior who participated in the Academic Decathlon program. **Criteria:** Awards are given based on the application.

Funds Avail.: $300. **Number Awarded:** 3. **To Apply:** Applicants must submit a completed application form together with the scantron sheet; cover sheet; student activity and community activity sheets; personal essay; and a copy of unofficial transcript (signed by the counselor). **Deadline:** February 20.

Remarks: No electronic submissions of application will be accepted. Submit two printed copies of the application and use a No. 2 pencil on the scantron sheet.

5982 ■ Redlands High School Boy's Varsity Volleyball Scholarships *(Undergraduate/Scholarship)*

Purpose: To encourage educational pursuits among Redlands Unified School District graduates by providing educational assistance. **Focus:** General studies. **Qualif.:** Applicant must be a graduating senior who is a member of the Boy's Varsity Volleyball team. **Criteria:** Award is given based on merit.

Funds Avail.: $300. **Number Awarded:** 1. **To Apply:** Applicants must submit a completed application form together with the scantron sheet; cover sheet; student activity and community activity sheets; personal essay; and a copy of unofficial transcript (signed by the counselor). **Deadline:** February 20.

Remarks: No electronic submissions of application will be accepted. Submit two printed copies of the application and use a No. 2 pencil on the scantron sheet.

5983 ■ Redlands High School Class of 1957 *(Undergraduate/Scholarship)*

Purpose: To encourage educational pursuits among Redlands Unified School District graduates by providing educational assistance. **Focus:** General studies. **Qualif.:** Applicant must be a graduating senior; must have a 3.0 or better GPA; must be planning to continue education on a full-time basis at a vocational school, community college, or university; must have good character and citizenship; and must have demonstrated involvement in service to the community. **Criteria:** Preference is given to students who are descendants of members of the RHS Class of 1957.

Funds Avail.: $500. **Number Awarded:** 1. **To Apply:** Applicants must submit a completed application form together with the scantron sheet; cover sheet; student activity and community activity sheets; personal essay; and a copy of unofficial transcript (signed by the counselor). **Deadline:** February 20.

Remarks: No electronic submissions of application will be accepted. Submit two printed copies of the application and use a No. 2 pencil on the scantron sheet.

5984 ■ Redlands High School Drama Boosters Award *(Undergraduate/Scholarship)*

Purpose: To encourage educational pursuits among Redlands Unified School District graduates by providing

Awards are arranged alphabetically below their administering organizations

educational assistance. **Focus:** Performing arts. **Qualif.:** Applicant must be a graduating senior pursuing a performing arts degree in college. **Criteria:** Award is given based on merit.

Funds Avail.: $200. **Number Awarded:** 1. **To Apply:** Applicants must submit: a completed application form together with the scantron sheet; cover sheet; student activity and community activity sheets; personal essay; and a copy of unofficial transcript (signed by the counselor). **Deadline:** February 20.

Remarks: No electronic submissions of application will be accepted. Submit two printed copies of the application and use a No. 2 pencil on the scantron sheet.

5985 ■ Redlands High School Girls' Volleyball Boosters Scholarship Awards *(Undergraduate/Scholarship)*

Purpose: To encourage educational pursuits among Redlands Unified School District graduates by providing educational assistance. **Focus:** General studies. **Qualif.:** Applicant must be a graduating senior volleyball player with good academic standing and citizenship; must be a dedicated team player; and must have positive leadership skills and a positive attitude. **Criteria:** Award is given based on the application.

Funds Avail.: $750. **To Apply:** Applicants must submit a completed application form together with the scantron sheet; cover sheet; student activity and community activity sheets; personal essay; and a copy of unofficial transcript (signed by the counselor). **Deadline:** February 20.

Remarks: No electronic submissions of application will be accepted. Submit two printed copies of the application and use a No. 2 pencil on the scantron sheet.

5986 ■ Redlands High School Mock Trial Scholarships *(Undergraduate/Scholarship)*

Purpose: To encourage educational pursuits among Redlands Unified School District graduates by providing educational assistance. **Focus:** General studies. **Qualif.:** Applicant must be a graduating senior and a member of the RHS Mock Trial team (either Varsity or Junior Varsity) whose performances have contributed to a successful program. **Criteria:** Awards are given based on merit.

Funds Avail.: $300 and $500. **Number Awarded:** 2. **To Apply:** Applicants must submit a completed application form together with the scantron sheet; cover sheet; student activity and community activity sheets; personal essay; and a copy of unofficial transcript (signed by the counselor). **Deadline:** February 20.

Remarks: No electronic submissions of application will be accepted. Submit two printed copies of the application and use a No. 2 pencil on the scantron sheet.

5987 ■ Redlands High School-PTSA Scholarships *(Undergraduate/Scholarship)*

Purpose: To encourage educational pursuits among Redlands Unified School District graduates by providing educational assistance. **Focus:** General studies. **Qualif.:** Applicant must be a graduating senior pursuing a career in a vocational field with a 2.0 or higher GPA; or a graduating senior pursuing a career in a four-year college with a 3.0 or higher GPA. Student must demonstrate good citizenship, a high work capacity, and service to school and/or community. **Criteria:** Awards are given based on merit.

Funds Avail.: $400. **To Apply:** Applicants must submit a completed application form together with the scantron sheet; cover sheet; student activity and community activity sheets; personal essay; and a copy of unofficial transcript (signed by the counselor). **Deadline:** February 20.

Remarks: No electronic submissions of application will be accepted. Submit two printed copies of the application and use a No. 2 pencil on the scantron sheet.

5988 ■ Redlands High School Soccer Boosters Scholarship Awards *(Undergraduate/Scholarship)*

Purpose: To encourage educational pursuits among Redlands Unified School District graduates by providing educational assistance. **Focus:** General studies. **Qualif.:** Applicants must be graduating seniors who have participated in a minimum of two seasons in the Redlands High School soccer program, lettered in their senior year; must have demonstrated good citizenship; and must have a minimum 3.3 GPA. **Criteria:** Awards are given based on the application.

Funds Avail.: $350. **Number Awarded:** 4. **To Apply:** Applicants must submit a completed application form together with the scantron sheet; cover sheet; student activity and community activity sheets; personal essay; and a copy of unofficial transcript (signed by the counselor). **Deadline:** February 20.

Remarks: No electronic submissions of application will be accepted. Submit two printed copies of the application and use a No. 2 pencil on the scantron sheet.

5989 ■ Redlands High School Softball Booster Scholarship Awards *(Undergraduate/Scholarship)*

Purpose: To encourage educational pursuits among Redlands Unified School District graduates by providing educational assistance. **Focus:** General studies. **Qualif.:** Applicants must be graduating seniors who have earned a varsity letter in senior year and who have a minimum 3.25 weighted GPA. **Criteria:** Award is given based on the application.

Funds Avail.: $250. **Number Awarded:** 2. **To Apply:** Applicants must submit a completed application form together with the scantron sheet; cover sheet; student activity and community activity sheets; personal essay; and a copy of unofficial transcript (signed by the counselor). **Deadline:** February 20.

Remarks: No electronic submissions of application will be accepted. Submit two printed copies of the application and use a No. 2 pencil on the scantron sheet.

5990 ■ Redlands High School Speech Boosters Scholarship Awards *(Undergraduate/Scholarship)*

Purpose: To encourage educational pursuits among Redlands Unified School District graduates by providing educational assistance. **Focus:** General studies. **Qualif.:** Applicant must be an outstanding speech team member. **Criteria:** Award is given based on the votes of the team members and coaches.

Funds Avail.: $1,000. **Number Awarded:** 6. **To Apply:** Applicants must submit a completed application form together with the scantron sheet; cover sheet; student activity and community activity sheets; personal essay; and a copy of unofficial transcript (signed by the counselor). **Deadline:** February 20.

Remarks: No electronic submissions of application will be accepted. Submit two printed copies of the application and use a No. 2 pencil on the scantron sheet.

5991 ■ Redlands High School Spiritleaders Scholarships *(Undergraduate/Scholarship)*

Purpose: To encourage educational pursuits among Redlands Unified School District graduates by providing educational assistance. **Focus:** General studies. **Qualif.:** Applicant must be a graduating senior who has been in Spiritleaders for a minimum of two years. **Criteria:** Awards are given based on GPA.

Funds Avail.: $300. **To Apply:** Applicants must submit a completed application form together with the scantron sheet; cover sheet; student activity and community activity sheets; personal essay; and a copy of unofficial transcript (signed by the counselor). **Deadline:** February 20.

Remarks: No electronic submissions of application will be accepted. Submit two printed copies of the application and use a No. 2 pencil on the scantron sheet.

5992 ■ Redlands High School Terrier Band Boosters Club Scholarships *(Undergraduate/Scholarship)*

Purpose: To encourage educational pursuits among Redlands Unified School District graduates by providing educational assistance. **Focus:** General studies. **Qualif.:** Applicant must be a graduating senior who participated in the Redlands High School instrumental music program and plans to continue with instrumental music in some capacity (not necessarily majoring in music). **Criteria:** Award is given based on the application.

Funds Avail.: $250. **To Apply:** Applicants must submit a completed application form together with the scantron sheet; cover sheet; student activity and community activity sheets; personal essay; and a copy of unofficial transcript (signed by the counselor). **Deadline:** February 20.

Remarks: No electronic submissions of application will be accepted. Submit two printed copies of the application and use a No. 2 pencil on the scantron sheet.

5993 ■ Redlands High School Vocal Music Boosters Scholarship Awards *(Undergraduate/Scholarship)*

Purpose: To encourage educational pursuits among Redlands Unified School District graduates by providing educational assistance. **Focus:** General studies. **Qualif.:** Applicant must be a graduating senior who has participated in the Redlands High School choral program and plans to continue with music in some capacity. **Criteria:** Awards are given based on the application.

Funds Avail.: $500 and $400. **Number Awarded:** 2. **To Apply:** Applicants must submit a completed application form together with the scantron sheet; cover sheet; student activity and community activity sheets; personal essay; and a copy of unofficial transcript (signed by the counselor). **Deadline:** February 20.

Remarks: No electronic submissions of application will be accepted. Submit two printed copies of the application and use a No. 2 pencil on the scantron sheet.

5994 ■ Redlands Morning Kiwanis Club Foundation Scholarships *(Undergraduate/Scholarship)*

Purpose: To encourage educational pursuits among Redlands Unified School District graduates by providing educational assistance. **Focus:** General studies. **Qualif.:** Applicant must be a graduating senior; must have at least a 3.0 GPA; and must be planning to attend an accredited college, university, or vocational program. **Criteria:** Preference is given to individuals who have demonstrated their past involvement in community service projects and willingness to serve as community volunteers.

Funds Avail.: $2,000. **Number Awarded:** 1. **To Apply:** Applicants must submit a completed application form together with the scantron sheet; cover sheet; student activity and community activity sheets; a 1-page essay on "What I feel is the importance of volunteerism, and how community service will/may affect my future."; and a copy of unofficial transcript (signed by the counselor). **Deadline:** February 20.

Remarks: No electronic submissions of application will be accepted. Submit two printed copies of the application and use a No. 2 pencil on the scantron sheet.

5995 ■ Redlands Noon Kiwanis Club Foundation Scholarships *(Undergraduate/Scholarship)*

Purpose: To encourage educational pursuits among Redlands Unified School District graduates by providing educational assistance. **Focus:** General studies. **Qualif.:** Applicant must be a graduating senior with good citizenship, extracurricular activity involvement, and demonstrated leadership abilities. **Criteria:** Recipients will be selected through an interview process conducted by the Redlands Noon Kiwanis Club scholarship committee.

Funds Avail.: $5,000. **Number Awarded:** 3. **To Apply:** Applicants must submit a completed application form together with the scantron sheet; cover sheet; student activity and community activity sheets; personal essay; and a copy of unofficial transcript (signed by the counselor). **Deadline:** February 20.

Remarks: No electronic submissions of application will be accepted. Submit two printed copies of the application and use a No. 2 pencil on the scantron sheet.

5996 ■ Redlands Noon Kiwanis Club - Martin and Dorothy Munz Scholarships *(Undergraduate/Scholarship)*

Purpose: To encourage educational pursuits among Redlands Unified School District graduates by providing educational assistance. **Focus:** General studies. **Qualif.:** Applicant must be a graduating senior; must be a COMPACT student for at least his/her senior year; must have a 3.0 GPA in all subjects; must have an interest or aptitude for education or a business career; must be involved in community service such as scouting, church, etc.; must be involved in extracurricular school activities; must be highly motivated to obtain a four-year college degree; and must demonstrate a financial need. **Criteria:** Award is given based on the application.

Funds Avail.: $1,250. **Number Awarded:** 1. **To Apply:** Applicants must submit a completed application form together with the scantron sheet; cover sheet; student activity and community activity sheets; personal essay; and a copy of unofficial transcript (signed by the counselor). **Deadline:** February 20.

Remarks: No electronic submissions of application will be accepted. Submit two printed copies of the application and use a No. 2 pencil on the scantron sheet.

5997 ■ Redlands Rotary Club - Donald C. Anderson Scholarships *(Undergraduate/Scholarship)*

Purpose: To encourage educational pursuits among Redlands Unified School District graduates by providing educational assistance. **Focus:** General studies. **Qualif.:**

Awards are arranged alphabetically below their administering organizations

Applicant must be a graduating senior demonstrating high academic achievement, outstanding citizenship, and service to school and community. **Criteria:** Recipient will be selected through an interview process conducted by the Redlands Rotary Club scholarship committee.

Funds Avail.: $2000. **Number Awarded:** 1. **To Apply:** Applicants must submit a completed application form together with the scantron sheet; cover sheet; student activity and community activity sheets; personal essay; and a copy of unofficial transcript (signed by the counselor). **Deadline:** February 20.

Remarks: No electronic submissions of application will be accepted. Submit two printed copies of the application and use a No. 2 pencil on the scantron sheet.

5998 ■ Redlands Rotary Club - Ernest L. Cronemeyer Memorial Scholarships *(Undergraduate/Scholarship)*

Purpose: To encourage educational pursuits among Redlands Unified School District graduates by providing educational assistance. **Focus:** General studies. **Qualif.:** Applicant must be a graduating senior with high academic achievement, outstanding citizenship, and service to school and community. **Criteria:** Recipient will be selected through an interview process conducted by the Redlands Rotary Club scholarship committee.

Funds Avail.: $4,000. **Number Awarded:** 1. **To Apply:** Applicants must submit a completed application form together with the scantron sheet; cover sheet; student activity and community activity sheets; personal essay; and a copy of unofficial transcript (signed by the counselor). **Deadline:** February 20.

Remarks: No electronic submissions of application will be accepted. Submit two printed copies of the application and use a No. 2 pencil on the scantron sheet.

5999 ■ Redlands Rotary Club Foundation Discretionary Scholarships *(Undergraduate/Scholarship)*

Purpose: To encourage educational pursuits among Redlands Unified School District graduates by providing educational assistance. **Focus:** General studies. **Qualif.:** Applicant must be a graduating senior who has demonstrated high academic achievement, outstanding citizenship, and service to school and community. **Criteria:** Recipients will be selected through an interview process conducted by the Redlands Rotary Club scholarship committee.

Funds Avail.: $1,000. **Number Awarded:** 2. **To Apply:** Applicants must submit a completed application form together with the scantron sheet; cover sheet; student activity and community activity sheets; personal essay; and a copy of unofficial transcript (signed by the counselor). **Deadline:** February 20.

Remarks: No electronic submissions of application will be accepted. Submit two printed copies of the application and use a No. 2 pencil on the scantron sheet.

6000 ■ Redlands Teachers Association Scholarships *(Undergraduate/Scholarship)*

Purpose: To encourage educational pursuits among Redlands Unified School District graduates by providing educational assistance. **Focus:** General studies. **Qualif.:** Applicant must be a graduating senior; must have a minimum 3.0 GPA or better; must be active in school and community; must have demonstrated outstanding citizenship; must be enrolled in college; and must make a presentation to the Sunrise Rotary Club. **Criteria:** Awards are given based on merit.

Funds Avail.: $500. **To Apply:** Applicants must submit a completed application form together with the scantron sheet; cover sheet; student activity and community activity sheets; personal essay; and a copy of unofficial transcript (signed by the counselor). **Deadline:** February 20.

Remarks: No electronic submissions of application will be accepted. Submit two printed copies of the application and use a No. 2 pencil on the scantron sheet.

6001 ■ Liz Roberts Memorial Scholarships *(Undergraduate/Scholarship)*

Purpose: To encourage educational pursuits among Redlands Unified School District graduates by providing educational assistance. **Focus:** Nursing. **Qualif.:** Applicant must be a graduating senior who will attend a training school, college, or university; must be pursuing a degree in nursing; must demonstrate financial need; must have maintained a 3.0 GPA; must have good citizenship; must have demonstrated community service; and must have a desire to help others. **Criteria:** Award is given based on merit.

Funds Avail.: $500. **Number Awarded:** 1. **To Apply:** Applicants must submit a completed application form together with the scantron sheet; cover sheet; student activity and community activity sheets; personal essay; and a copy of unofficial transcript (signed by the counselor). **Deadline:** February 20.

Remarks: No electronic submissions of application will be accepted. Submit two printed copies of the application and use a No. 2 pencil on the scantron sheet.

6002 ■ Charles and Ruth Ronin Memorial Scholarships *(Undergraduate/Scholarship)*

Purpose: To encourage educational pursuits among Redlands Unified School District graduates by providing educational assistance. **Focus:** Political science; History; Education. **Qualif.:** Applicant must be a graduating senior with a 3.5 or higher GPA who will attend a four-year college/university on a full-time basis in pursuit of a bachelor's degree in political science, history, or education. **Criteria:** Award is given based on merit.

Funds Avail.: $1,000. **Number Awarded:** 1. **To Apply:** Applicants must submit a completed application form together with the scantron sheet; cover sheet; student activity and community activity sheets; personal essay; and a copy of unofficial transcript (signed by the counselor). **Deadline:** February 20.

Remarks: No electronic submissions of application will be accepted. Submit two printed copies of the application and use a No. 2 pencil on the scantron sheet.

6003 ■ ROP - Ambassadors Scholarships *(Undergraduate/Scholarship)*

Purpose: To encourage educational pursuits among Redlands Unified School District graduates by providing educational assistance. **Focus:** General studies. **Qualif.:** Applicant must be a senior who participates in the ROP Ambassador program and submits and presents before a panel of judges a marketing concept that helps to promote ROP and its programs. **Criteria:** Award is given based on the application.

Funds Avail.: $250. **To Apply:** Applicants must submit a completed application form together with the scantron sheet; cover sheet; student activity and community activity sheets; personal essay; and a copy of unofficial transcript (signed by the counselor). **Deadline:** February 20.

Remarks: No electronic submissions of application will be accepted. Submit two printed copies of the application and use a No. 2 pencil on the scantron sheet.

6004 ■ ROP - Rob Bruce Memorial Scholarships *(Undergraduate/Scholarship)*

Purpose: To encourage educational pursuits among Redlands Unified School District graduates by providing educational assistance. **Focus:** General studies. **Qualif.:** Applicant must be a graduating senior who has done outstanding work in an ROP class. **Criteria:** Awards are given based on the application.

Funds Avail.: $200. **To Apply:** Applicants must submit a completed application form together with the scantron sheet; cover sheet; student activity and community activity sheets; personal essay; and a copy of unofficial transcript (signed by the counselor). **Deadline:** February 20.

Remarks: No electronic submissions of application will be accepted. Submit two printed copies of the application and use a No. 2 pencil on the scantron sheet.

6005 ■ Michael A. Russo Memorial Scholarships *(Undergraduate/Scholarship)*

Purpose: To encourage educational pursuits among Redlands Unified School District graduates by providing educational assistance. **Focus:** General studies. **Qualif.:** Applicant must be a graduating senior pursuing a career in a medical or medically-allied profession or career. **Criteria:** Award is given based on merit.

Funds Avail.: $1,000. **Number Awarded:** 1. **To Apply:** Applicants must submit a completed application form together with the scantron sheet; cover sheet; student activity and community activity sheets; personal essay; and a copy of unofficial transcript (signed by the counselor). **Deadline:** February 20.

Remarks: No electronic submissions of application will be accepted. Submit two printed copies of the application and use a No. 2 pencil on the scantron sheet.

6006 ■ Schoolsfirst Federal Credit Union Scholarships *(Undergraduate/Scholarship)*

Purpose: To encourage educational pursuits among Redlands Unified School District graduates by providing educational assistance. **Focus:** General studies. **Qualif.:** Applicants must be high school seniors. **Criteria:** Award is given based on scholarship, participation in school and community activities, and school personnel recommendation.

Funds Avail.: No specific amount. **To Apply:** Applicants must submit a completed application form together with the scantron sheet; cover sheet; student activity and community activity sheets; personal essay; and a copy of unofficial transcript (signed by the counselor). **Deadline:** February 20.

Remarks: No electronic submissions of application will be accepted. Submit two printed copies of the application and use a No. 2 pencil on the scantron sheet.

6007 ■ Felix R. Sepulveda Memorial Scholarships - Northside Booster Club *(Undergraduate/Scholarship)*

Purpose: To encourage educational pursuits among Redlands Unified School District graduates by providing educational assistance. **Focus:** General studies. **Qualif.:** Applicant must be a graduating male or female who has maintained at least a 2.5 GPA and participated in at least one sport. **Criteria:** Award is given based on merit.

Funds Avail.: $500. **Number Awarded:** 1. **To Apply:** Applicants must submit a completed application form together with the scantron sheet; cover sheet; student activity and community activity sheets; personal essay; and a copy of unofficial transcript (signed by the counselor). **Deadline:** February 20.

Remarks: No electronic submissions of application will be accepted. Submit two printed copies of the application and use a No. 2 pencil on the scantron sheet.

6008 ■ Shervin Tehranchi Wrestling Scholarships *(Undergraduate/Scholarship)*

Purpose: To encourage educational pursuits among Redlands Unified School District graduates by providing educational assistance. **Focus:** General studies. **Qualif.:** Applicant must be a graduating senior; must have been a member of the wrestling team for at least two years; must have a minimum 2.7 GPA; and must demonstrate good citizenship. **Criteria:** Award is given based on merit.

Funds Avail.: $300. **Number Awarded:** 1. **To Apply:** Applicants must submit completed application form together with the scantron sheet; cover sheet; student activity and community activity sheets; personal essay; and a copy of unofficial transcript (signed by the counselor). **Deadline:** February 20.

Remarks: No electronic submissions of application will be accepted. Submit two printed copies of the application and use a No. 2 pencil on the scantron sheet.

6009 ■ Rajadi Sjarif Memorial Scholarships *(Undergraduate/Scholarship)*

Purpose: To encourage educational pursuits among Redlands Unified School District graduates by providing educational assistance. **Focus:** General studies. **Qualif.:** Applicant must be an ELL student with a GPA of 3.0 or higher. **Criteria:** Award is given based on merit.

Funds Avail.: $300. **Number Awarded:** 1. **To Apply:** Applicants must submit a completed application form together with the scantron sheet; cover sheet; student activity and community activity sheets; personal essay; and a copy of unofficial transcript (signed by the counselor). **Deadline:** February 20.

Remarks: No electronic submissions of application will be accepted. Submit two printed copies of the application and use a No. 2 pencil on the scantron sheet.

6010 ■ Smiley Elementary School PTA - Beverly Roberts Memorial Scholarships *(Undergraduate/Scholarship)*

Purpose: To encourage educational pursuits among Redlands Unified School District graduates by providing educational assistance. **Focus:** General studies. **Qualif.:** Applicant must be a graduating senior in the upper half of the senior class who attended Smiley Elementary School and is a well-rounded student. **Criteria:** Award is given based on merit.

Funds Avail.: $500. **Number Awarded:** 1. **To Apply:** Applicants must submit a completed application form together with the scantron sheet; cover sheet; student activity and community activity sheets; personal essay; and a copy of unofficial transcript (signed by the counselor). **Deadline:** February 20.

Remarks: No electronic submissions of application will be accepted. Submit two printed copies of the application and use a No. 2 pencil on the scantron sheet.

6011 ■ Soroptimist International of Redlands Scholarships *(Undergraduate/Scholarship)*

Purpose: To encourage educational pursuits among Redlands Unified School District graduates by providing educational assistance. **Focus:** Health care services; Law; Engineering; Computer and information sciences; Education; Business. **Qualif.:** Applicant must be a graduating senior who has participated in community service and who will be attending an accredited college on a full-time basis and is planning to major in one of the following fields: health care, law, engineering, computer science, education and/or business administration. **Criteria:** Award is given based on merit.

Funds Avail.: $750. **Number Awarded:** 1. **To Apply:** Applicants must submit a completed application form together with the scantron sheet; cover sheet; student activity and community activity sheets; personal essay; and a copy of unofficial transcript (signed by the counselor). **Deadline:** February 20.

Remarks: No electronic submissions of application will be accepted. Submit two printed copies of the application and use a No. 2 pencil on the scantron sheet.

6012 ■ Redlands Evening Lions Club - Barbara Westen Scholarships *(Undergraduate/Scholarship)*

Purpose: To encourage educational pursuits among Redlands Unified School District graduates by providing educational assistance. **Focus:** General studies. **Qualif.:** Applicant must be a graduating senior student who has demonstrated scholastic ability and financial need. **Criteria:** Award is given based on merit.

Funds Avail.: $350. **Number Awarded:** 1. **To Apply:** Applicants must submit a completed application form together with the scantron sheet; cover sheet; student activity and community activity sheets; personal essay; and a copy of unofficial transcript (signed by the counselor). **Deadline:** February 20.

Remarks: No electronic submissions of application will be accepted. Submit two printed copies of the application and use a No. 2 pencil on the scantron sheet.

6013 ■ Reflex Sympathetic Dystrophy Syndrome Association of America

PO Box 502
Milford, CT 06460
Ph: (203)877-3790
Fax: (203)882-8362
Free: 877-662-7737
E-mail: info@rsds.org
URL: http://www.rsds.org

6014 ■ RSDSA Research Grants *(Postdoctorate, Professional Development/Grant)*

Purpose: To seek relevant research that will improve understanding and treatment of RSD/CRPS-1. **Focus:** Medicine. **Qualif.:** Applicants must be health science professionals with interest in study and treatment of painful conditions; must be residents, fellows and Ph.D. holders who are under the direct sponsorship and supervision of a senior scientist or faculty member. **Criteria:** Recipients are selected based on a committee's review of the proposal.

Funds Avail.: $50,000. **To Apply:** Applicants must send research grant application; letter of support from head of host institution; copies of approved documents from the host institution; copy of proposed informed consent form; letter from the department chair indicating the career development of the applicant; and RSDSA Research Grant Application Declaration signed by all investigators. Mail three copies or send electronically as MSWord document on a CD-ROM or as an attachment in MSWord to: info@rsds.org, subject: Research Grant Application. **Deadline:** November 1.

6015 ■ REFORMA: National Association to Promote Library and Information Services

PO Box 4386
Fresno, CA 93744
Ph: (480)734-4460
Fax: (480)471-7442
E-mail: reformaoffice@riosbalderrama.com
URL: http://www.reforma.org

6016 ■ REFORMA Scholarship Program *(Graduate/Scholarship)*

Purpose: To encourage Spanish-speaking individuals to pursue or advance a career in library and information science. **Focus:** Library and archival sciences. **Qualif.:** Applicants must be U.S. citizens; must be Spanish-speaking; must be current or entering graduate library school students; and must show evidence of commitment to a career in librarianship. **Criteria:** Recipients are selected based on educational background, intellectual abilities and personal character.

Funds Avail.: $1,500. **Number Awarded:** Varies. **To Apply:** Application materials are available at the website. Applicants must submit a completed application form together with official copies of college transcripts, resume and two letters of reference from professors, employers, librarians or other professionals to: REFORMA Scholarship Committee, Ramona Grijalva, Chair, PO Box 7543 Tucson, AZ 85725, ramonagrijalva@yahoo.com. **Deadline:** March 15.

6017 ■ Registry of Interpreters for the Deaf

333 Commerce St.
Alexandria, VA 22314
Ph: (703)838-0030
Fax: (703)838-0454
URL: http://www.rid.org

6018 ■ Elizabeth Benson Scholarship Awards *(Undergraduate/Scholarship)*

Purpose: To provide financial assistance to members enrolled to ITP or IPP. **Focus:** Hearing and deafness. **Qualif.:** Applicants must have dual membership; enrolled full-time or 9-hours in an interpreter or transliterator program; must have completed at least one semester of ITP or IPP; have 3.0 GPA in ITP or IPP. **Criteria:** Awards are given based on credentials.

Funds Avail.: $500. **To Apply:** Applicants must submit eight copies of a letter of interest specifying financial need; an application form (can be downloaded from the website); transcripts; three letters of recommendation (must be from an ITP or IPP chair, instructor and personal reference); copies of current RID and affiliate chapter membership card. **Deadline:** April.

Awards are arranged alphabetically below their administering organizations.

6019 ■ Daniel H. Pokorny Memorial Scholarship Awards *(Undergraduate/Scholarship)*

Purpose: To provide financial support to members applying for a certification. **Focus:** Hearing and deafness. **Qualif.:** Applicant must be a member for least one year. **Criteria:** Awards are given based on the committee's votes.

Funds Avail.: No specific amount. **To Apply:** Applicant must send eight copies of the application form (can be downloaded from the website). **Deadline:** April 1.

Remarks: If not chosen as a recipient, the applicant may re-apply for the next cycle.

6020 ■ Religion Newswriters Association

PO Box 2037
Westerville, OH 43086-2037
Ph: (614)891-9001
Fax: (614)891-9774
E-mail: masondl@rna.org
URL: http://www.rna.org

6021 ■ Lily Scholarships in Religion for Journalists *(Professional Development/Scholarship)*

Purpose: To help journalists achieve excellence in writing and reporting in faith, values, ethics and spirituality in the news media. **Focus:** Journalism. **Qualif.:** Applicants must be full-time print and broadcast journalists working at general circulation or non-religious media. Freelance journalists are also eligible to apply. **Criteria:** Recipients are selected based on demonstrated interest in the field of journalism.

Funds Avail.: $5,000. **To Apply:** Applicants must submit a completed application form and must show an evidence of employment as full-time journalists in a secular news media. **Deadline:** January 1; April 1; July 1 and October 1. **Contact:** Amy Schiska at the above address (see entry 6020).

6022 ■ Reserve Officers Association of the United States

1 Constitution Ave. NE
Washington, DC 20002-5618
Ph: (202)479-2200
Fax: (202)547-1641
Free: 800-809-9448
E-mail: info@roa.org
URL: http://www.roa.org

6023 ■ Henry J. Reilly Memorial Scholarships - For Freshmen in College *(Undergraduate/Scholarship)*

Purpose: To assist in the educational pursuits of members of ROA, ROAL, and their dependents. **Focus:** General studies. **Qualif.:** Applicants must be dependents of an active or associate ROA or ROAL member; must be 21 years old or below; must be accepted for full-time undergraduate study at a regional accredited four-year U.S. college/university; must be in the top 1/4th of the graduating class; and must have a GPA of 3.3 or higher (on a 4.0 scale). **Criteria:** Award is given based on the merit.

Funds Avail.: $500. **To Apply:** Application materials are available at the website. Applicants must complete the application form and submit together with an official high school transcript; recent official college transcript; test score verification; and a 500-word essay on their career goals. All materials must be submitted in one envelope at one time only. **Deadline:** April 10. **Contact:** Ms. Betsy Allen, 800-809-9448 x-756, or scholarship@roa.org.

6024 ■ Henry J. Reilly Memorial Scholarships - For Graduating High School Seniors *(Undergraduate/Scholarship)*

Purpose: To assist in the educational pursuits of members of ROA, ROAL, and their dependents. **Focus:** General studies. **Qualif.:** Applicants must be dependents of an active or associate ROA or ROAL member; must be 21 years old or below; must be accepted for full-time undergraduate study at a regional accredited four-year U.S. college/university; must be in the top 1/4th of the graduating class; and must have a GPA of 3.3 and above on a 4.0 scale. **Criteria:** Award is given based on the merit.

Funds Avail.: $500. **To Apply:** Application materials are available at the website. Applicants must submit completed application along with an official high school transcript; copy of acceptance letter; test scores; Verification and Assessment Report and Academic and Personal Assessment Report; an essay on the applicant's career goals (500 words). All materials must be submitted in one envelope at one time only. **Deadline:** April 10. **Contact:** Ms. Betsy Allen, 800-809-9448 x-756, or scholarship@roa.org.

6025 ■ Henry J. Reilly Memorial Scholarships - For Sophomores and Juniors in College *(Undergraduate/Scholarship)*

Purpose: To assist in the educational pursuits of members of ROA, ROAL, and their dependents. **Focus:** General studies. **Qualif.:** Applicants must be dependents of an active or associate ROA or ROAL member; must be 26 years old or below; must be accepted for full-time undergraduate study at a regional accredited four-year U.S. college/university; must have a GPA of 3.3 or higher on a 4.0 scale; and must have evidence of acceptance (for community college students transferring to a four-year college/university). **Criteria:** Award is given based on the merit.

Funds Avail.: $500. **To Apply:** Application materials are available at the website. Applicants must complete the application form and submit together with an official high school transcript; recent official college transcript; test score verification; and a 500-word essay on their career goals. All materials must be submitted in one envelope at one time only. **Deadline:** April 10. **Contact:** Ms. Betsy Allen, 800-809-9448 x-756, or scholarship@roa.org.

6026 ■ Henry J. Reilly Memorial Scholarships - Graduate Program *(Graduate, Professional Development/Scholarship)*

Purpose: To assist in the educational pursuits of members of ROA, ROAL, and their dependents. **Focus:** General studies. **Qualif.:** Applicants must be active or associate ROA or ROAL members; must be accepted for graduate study at a regional accredited four-year U.S. college/university; must have an undergraduate GPA of 3.2 and above on a 4.0 scale; and must be enrolled in 2 graduate courses. **Criteria:** Award is given based on the merit.

Funds Avail.: $500. **To Apply:** Application form is available at the website. Applicants must complete the application form and submit along with three recommendation letters; curriculum vitae; and an evidence of a 3.3 GPA in the graduate work. All materials must be submitted in one

Awards are arranged alphabetically below their administering organizations

envelope at one time only. **Deadline:** April 10. **Contact:** Ms. Betsy Allen, 800-809-9448 x-756, or scholarship@roa.org.

6027 ■ Retail Packaging Association

PO Box 17656
Covington, KY 41017
Ph: (859)341-9623
Fax: (859)341-6211
E-mail: info@retailpackaging.org
URL: http://www.retailpackaging.org

6028 ■ RPA Scholarships *(Undergraduate/Scholarship)*

Purpose: To provide educational assistance to dependents of members of the association. **Focus:** General studies. **Qualif.:** Applicants must be high school seniors or college freshmen, sophomores and juniors who are dependents of a fulltime RPA member. **Criteria:** Grantees will be selected according to academic records, test scores, extracurricular involvement and financial need.

Funds Avail.: $1,000. **Number Awarded:** 2. **To Apply:** Applicants are advised to visit the website for the online application process. **Deadline:** May 15.

6029 ■ Retail Print Music Dealers Association

14070 Proton Rd., Ste. 100
Dallas, TX 75244
Ph: (972)233-9107
Fax: (972)490-4219
E-mail: office@printmusic.org
URL: http://www.printmusic.org

6030 ■ Ed Adams Memorial Scholarships *(Professional Development/Scholarship)*

Purpose: To encourage individuals to advance further studies in the print music industry. **Focus:** Music. **Qualif.:** Applicants must be currently working for an RPMDA member or associate member establishment; must have worked for a minimum of 400 hours in the print music industry; and must exhibit a strong desire to continue to work in the print music industry. **Criteria:** Scholarship recipients will be selected by RPMDA based on college or high school records; financial need; honors; awards; community service; recommendations; personal qualifications; quality of essay from the applicant; and sponsoring company.

Funds Avail.: $1,000. **To Apply:** Applicants must submit a completed RPMDA/Ed Adams Scholarship Award application; three letters of reference; a completed Employment Verification Form a Sponsoring RPDMA members or assistance member; SAT or ACT scores (optional); sponsor statement of endorsement (200 words); a 300-word essay; and a photo (optional).

Remarks: In memory of Ed Adams, a man whose dedicated service to the print music industry touched lives across the United States.

6031 ■ Retired League Postmasters of the National League of Postmasters

One Beltway Center
5904 Richmond Highway, Ste. 500
Alexandria, VA 22303-1864
Ph: (703)329-4550
Fax: (703)329-0466
E-mail: information@postmasters.org
URL: http://www.postmasters.org

6032 ■ Retired League Postmasters Scholarship Program *(Undergraduate/Scholarship)*

Purpose: To provide financial assistance for the education of children or grandchildren of an active Postmasters or retired postmasters, who are members of the National League of Postmasters. **Focus:** General studies. **Qualif.:** Applicants must be high school graduates accepted as first year students, for fall admission to an accredited college, university or trade school; must have a 3.0 GPA over all or a 3.0 average for the last full year of high school. **Criteria:** Applicants will be evaluated based on academic performance.

Funds Avail.: No specific amount. **To Apply:** Applicants must submit transcript of grades covering the most recent year of school and list of awards or community service during previous school terms. **Deadline:** June 30.

6033 ■ Rhode Island Foundation

One Union Sta.
Providence, RI 02903
Ph: (401)274-4564
Fax: (401)331-8085
URL: http://www.rifoundation.org/matriarch/default.asp

6034 ■ Bach Organ and Keyboard Music Scholarships *(Undergraduate/Scholarship)*

Purpose: To provide financial assistance for promising music students to pursue their career. **Focus:** Education, Music. **Qualif.:** Applicant must be a Rhode Island resident enrolled in college as a music major; must be a church organist and an American Guild of Organists member; and must demonstrate financial need. **Criteria:** Selection of applicants will be based on financial need.

Funds Avail.: $1,000. **To Apply:** Applicants must complete the application form, available online; must submit one essay, recent high school or college transcript (music majors); must have a copy of their final Student Aid Report, financial aid award letter, and one recommendation from their organ/keyboard teacher or church official. Application forms and other supporting documents must be sent to Libby Monahan, GFWC Women's Club of South County Scholarship, Rhode Island Foundation, One Union Station, Providence, RI 02903. **Deadline:** June 9.

6035 ■ Antonio Cirino Memorial Art Education Fellowships *(Undergraduate/Fellowship)*

Purpose: To provide financial assistance for qualified individuals pursuing graduate education toward a master's or doctorate in order to pursue a teaching career in the arts. **Focus:** Arts. **Qualif.:** Applicant must be a Rhode Island resident; must be an artist pursuing graduate education toward a master's or doctorate in order to pursue a teaching career in the arts; must demonstrate financial need; and must have lived in Rhode Island for at least five years prior to applying for the award. **Criteria:** Preference will be given to visual art artists.

Funds Avail.: $74,500. **Number Awarded:** 16. **To Apply:** Application forms are available online and must be submit to www.callforentry.org. **Deadline:** May 23.

Awards are arranged alphabetically below their administering organizations

6036 ■ Constant Memorial Scholarship for Aquidneck Island Resident *(Undergraduate/Scholarship)*

Purpose: To provide support for deserving visual art or music major students intending to pursue their education. **Focus:** Visual arts; Education, Music. **Qualif.:** Applicants must be Aquidneck Island residents for at least three years; must demonstrate a serious interest in visual arts and/or music; must have a proof of enrollment in an arts or music major at an accredited institution of higher education; and must be able to demonstrate financial need. **Criteria:** Selection of applicants will be based on the scholarship selection criteria.

Funds Avail.: $2,000-$5,000. **Number Awarded:** 2. **To Apply:** Applicants must complete the application form, available online; must have a copy of their financial aid award letter; must submit a recent official college transcript; three proofs of Rhode Island residency; one essay; copy of their final Student Aid Report; one letter of recommendation; and a sample of work done within the last 12 months. Application forms and other supporting documents must be sent to Libby Monahan, GFWC Women's Club of South County Scholarship, Rhode Island Foundation, One Union Station, Providence, RI 02903. **Deadline:** June 9.

6037 ■ Edward Leon Duhamel Freemasons Scholarships *(Undergraduate/Scholarship)*

Purpose: To provide financial assistance to descendants of members of the Franklin Lodge of Freemasons in Wesley, RI. **Focus:** General studies. **Qualif.:** Applicants must be descendants of a member of Franklin Lodge in Wesley, Rhode Island, or descendants of other Freemansons who are RI residents; must be able to demonstrate scholastic achievement and good citizenship; and must be enrolled in an accredited post-secondary institution. **Criteria:** Applicants will be selected based on the scholarship selection criteria. Preference will be given to prior year's recipients.

Funds Avail.: $500-$1,000. **To Apply:** Applicants must complete the application form, available online; must submit a financial aid award letter, recent official transcript, essay, and a copy of their final student aid report. Application form and other supporting documents must be sent to Libby Monahan, Duhamel Scholarship, Rhode Island Foundation, One Union Station, Providence, RI 02903. **Deadline:** May 19.

6038 ■ GFWC Women's Club of South County Scholarships *(Undergraduate/Scholarship)*

Purpose: To provide support for females living in Washington County who need financial assistance in order to pursue education or job training. **Focus:** General studies. **Qualif.:** Applicants must be able to demonstrate financial need; must be a resident of Washington County; must be a female, age 25 or older; and must be enrolled or registered in an educational or job skills training program and working toward their first degree or certificate. **Criteria:** Preference will be given to highly motivated, low-income single women with children who need further education or training to become self-supporting.

Funds Avail.: $1,000. **Number Awarded:** 2. **To Apply:** Applicants must complete the application form available online; must submit a financial aid award letter, a copy of final Student Aid Report, one essay, recent official transcript, and letter of recommendation. Application forms and other supporting documents must be sent to Libby Monahan, GFWC Women's Club of South County Scholarship, Rhode Island Foundation, One Union Station, Providence, RI 02903. **Deadline:** June 2.

6039 ■ MJSA Educational Foundation Jewelry Scholarships *(Undergraduate/Scholarship)*

Purpose: To provide financial assistance for qualified students enrolled at colleges, universities, or nonprofit technical schools on the post-secondary level in the US. **Focus:** Metallurgy. **Qualif.:** Applicant must be a student enrolled in tool-making, design, metals fabrication, or other jewelry-related courses. **Criteria:** Selection of recipients will be based on their academic standing and application requirements.

Funds Avail.: No specific amount. **To Apply:** Applicants must complete and submit the application form and materials to www.callforentry.org. **Deadline:** May 14.

6040 ■ Rhode Island Association of Former Legislators Scholarships *(Undergraduate/Scholarship)*

Purpose: To provide financial assistance for promising students with a distinguished record of public services. **Focus:** General studies. **Qualif.:** Applicant must be a graduating high school senior and resident of Rhode Island; must have a history of substantial voluntary involvement in community service; must have been accepted into an accredited post-secondary institution; must be able to demonstrate financial need. **Criteria:** Selection of applicants will be based on Scholarship selection criteria.

Funds Avail.: $1,500. **To Apply:** Applicants must complete the application form, available online; must submit a copy of financial aid award letter, most recent official high school transcript, one letter of recommendation, one essay, and a copy of their final Student Aid Report. Application forms and other supporting documents must be sent to Libby Monahan, GFWC Women's Club of South County Scholarship, Rhode Island Foundation, One Union Station, Providence, RI 02903. **Deadline:** June 4.

6041 ■ Rhode Island Commission on Women/ Freda H. Goldman Education Awards *(Undergraduate/Award/Prize)*

Purpose: To provide support for individuals intending to pursue their education or job training. **Focus:** General studies. **Qualif.:** Applicants must be enrolled or registered in an educational or job skills training program; must be Rhode Island residents; and must be able to demonstrate financial need. **Criteria:** Preference will be given to highly motivated, self-supporting low-income women who are completing their first undergraduate degree or certificate program.

Funds Avail.: No specific amount. **To Apply:** Applicants must complete the application form, available online; must have their financial aid award letter, a copy of their final Student Aid Report, one essay, most recent official academic transcript, letter of recommendation, and resume. Application forms and other supporting documents must be sent to Libby Monahan, GFWC Women's Club of South County Scholarship, Rhode Island Foundation, One Union Station, Providence, RI 02903. **Deadline:** June 12.

6042 ■ Lily and Catello Sorrentino Memorial Scholarships *(Undergraduate/Scholarship)*

Purpose: To encourage older students to return to undergraduate school for further education. **Focus:** General studies. **Qualif.:** Applicant must be a Rhode Island resident who is at least 45 years of age; must be attending any degree-conferring, non-parochial educational college or university within Rhode Island towards an undergraduate degree; must be able to demonstrate financial need; must

Awards are arranged alphabetically below their administering organizations

not have any relationship with the Sorrentino family or the Rhode Island Foundation that can be construed in any way as influencing the fund's recommendation. **Criteria:** Selection of applicants will be based on the selection criteria.

Funds Avail.: $350-$1,000. **To Apply:** Applicants must complete the application form, available online; must have a copy of their financial aid award letter, official transcript, one essay, copy of their final student aid report, and two letters of recommendation. Application form and other supporting documents must be sent to Libby Monahan Sorrentino Scholarships, Rhode Island Foundation, 1 Union Station, Providence, RI 02903. **Deadline:** May 15.

6043 ■ Bruce and Marjorie Sundlun Scholarships *(Undergraduate/Scholarship)*

Purpose: To assist single parents in the pursuit of education beyond high school. **Focus:** General studies. **Qualif.:** Applicants must be single parents, either male or female, who are currently enrolled in a Rhode Island institution of higher learning or continuing education; must be Rhode Island residents and able to demonstrate financial need. **Criteria:** Preference will be given to applicants who are completing their first degree or certificate program.

Funds Avail.: $1,000. **Number Awarded:** 3-5. **To Apply:** Applicants must complete the application form, available online; must submit a copy of their financial aid award letter, and a recent official transcript; must prepare one essay; must have a copy of their final Student Aid Report and letter of recommendation. Application forms and other supporting documents must be sent to Libby Monahan, GFWC Women's Club of South County Scholarship, Rhode Island Foundation, One Union Station, Providence, RI 02903. **Deadline:** June 13.

6044 ■ Marilyn Graboys Wool Scholarships *(Undergraduate/Scholarship)*

Purpose: To provide tuition support to women with financial need planning to attend graduate school to attain a law degree at an accredited institution. **Focus:** Law. **Qualif.:** Applicants must be females planning to attend or registered in an accredited law school; must be Rhode Island residents; must be accepted into an accredited law school; and must be able to demonstrate financial need. **Criteria:** Selection of applicants will be based on the scholarship selection criteria.

Funds Avail.: $2,000. **To Apply:** Applicants must complete the application form, available online; must have a copy of their financial aid award letter and a recent official transcript; and must provide one essay, a copy of their Student Aid Report, and letter of recommendation. Application forms and other supporting documents must be sent to Libby Monahan, GFWC Women's Club of South County Scholarship, Rhode Island Foundation, One Union Station, Providence, RI 02903. **Deadline:** June 20.

6045 ■ Roanoke Bar Association

PO Box 18183
Roanoke, VA 24014
Ph: (540)342-4905
Fax: (540)342-1252
E-mail: roanokebar@earthlink.net
URL: http://www.roanokebar.com

6046 ■ Jane S. Glenn Memorial Endowed Scholarships *(Undergraduate/Scholarship)*

Purpose: To provide financial assistance to those deserving law students. **Focus:** Law. **Qualif.:** Applicants must be law students who are enrolled at an accredited law school in the Commonwealth of Virginia; must maintain a minimum 2.5 GPA. **Criteria:** Preference is given to those who graduated from William and Mary, and who have demonstrated financial need.

Funds Avail.: No specific amount. **To Apply:** Applicants must submit a completed application form. **Contact:** Roanoke Bar Association at the above address (see entry 6045).

6047 ■ James N. Kincanon Scholarships *(Undergraduate/Scholarship)*

Purpose: To provide financial assistance to those students who demonstrate diligence and commitment to their studies, academic excellence and an interest in the pursuit of law. **Focus:** Law. **Qualif.:** Applicants must be residents of the City of Roanoke, the City of Salem, or the County of Roanoke, or graduates of a high school located in those jurisdictions. Applicants must have a grade point average of at least 3.0 during high school (and college or law school, if applicable) and must be accepted, or expect to be accepted prior to the fall semester, into post-secondary training, pursuing education in the law. **Criteria:** Applicants are selected based on the committee's review of the application materials.

Funds Avail.: No specific amount. **To Apply:** Applicants must submit a completed application form online. **Deadline:** February 1. **Contact:** Roanoke Bar Association at the above address (see entry 6045).

6048 ■ Jackie Robinson Foundation

1 Hudson Sq.
75 Varick St., 2nd Fl.
New York, NY 10013-1917
Ph: (212)290-8600
Fax: (212)290-8081
E-mail: general@jackierobinson.org
URL: http://www.jackierobinson.org

6049 ■ Jackie Robinson Scholarships *(Undergraduate/Scholarship)*

Purpose: To financially support minority students in attaining higher educational pursuits. **Focus:** General studies. **Qualif.:** Applicant must be a minority high school student showing leadership potential and demonstrating financial need to attend an accredited 4-year college or university. **Criteria:** Awards are given based on merit and need.

Funds Avail.: $7,500. **To Apply:** Applicants must submit a letter of recommendation, official transcript (with raised seal), and SAT or ACT scores. **Deadline:** March 31.

6050 ■ Rocky Mountain Coal Mining Institute

8057 S Yukon Way
Littleton, CO 80128-5510
Ph: (303)948-3300
Fax: (303)948-1132
E-mail: mail@rmcmi.org
URL: http://www.rmcmi.org

6051 ■ Rocky Mountain Coal Mining Institute Engineering/Geology Scholarships *(Undergraduate/Scholarship)*

Purpose: To provide financial aid to junior and senior year students who are career-pathed in mining related industries.

Awards are arranged alphabetically below their administering organizations

Focus: Engineering, Geological; Engineering. **Qualif.:** Applicant must be a full-time college sophomore or junior at the time of selection; both a U.S. citizen and a legal resident of one of the Rocky Mountain Coal Mining Institute member states Arizona, Colorado, Montana, New Mexico, North Dakota, Texas, Utah, or Wyoming; pursuing a degree in a mining-related field or in the engineering disciplines; interested in coal as a career path. **Criteria:** Recipients are selected based on the scholarship committee's review of the application materials.

Funds Avail.: $2,000. **Number Awarded:** 1 candidate from each state. **To Apply:** Applicants must submit a completed application form that can be downloaded from www.rmcmi-.org. **Deadline:** February 1.

Remarks: Established in 1984. **Contact:** Karen Inzano, RMCMI Executive Director, or Beth Coen.

6052 ■ Rocky Mountain Coal Mining Institute Technical Scholarships *(Undergraduate/ Scholarship)*

Purpose: To students in technical programs who would like to pursue their education in the coal industry. **Focus:** Education, Vocational-technical; Trades training **Qualif.:** Applicant must be a first-year student at a two-year Technical/Trade School in a good standing at the time of selection; both a U.S. citizen and a legal resident of one of the Rocky Mountain Coal Mining Institute member states - Arizona, Colorado, Montana, New Mexico, North Dakota, Texas, Utah, or Wyoming; studying an applicable trade; interested in coal as a career path. **Criteria:** Recipients are selected based on the scholarship committee's review of the application materials.

Funds Avail.: $1,000. **Number Awarded:** 1 candidate from each state. **To Apply:** Applicants must submit a completed application form that can be downloaded from www.rmcmi-.org. **Deadline:** February 1.

Remarks: The fund is directly sent to the college, university, or technical school as tuition credit. **Contact:** Karen Inzano, RMCMI Executive Director, or Beth Coen.

6053 ■ Rocky Mountain Mineral Law Foundation

9191 Sheridan Blvd., Ste. 203
Westminster, CO 80031
Ph: (303)321-8100
Fax: (303)321-7657
E-mail: info@rmmlf.org
URL: http://www.rmmlf.org

6054 ■ Joe Rudd Scholarships *(Undergraduate/ Scholarship)*

Purpose: To encourage the study of natural resources law by well-qualified law students who have the potential to make significant contributions to scholarship in natural resources law. **Focus:** Law. **Qualif.:** Applicants must be a law student enrolled at one of the foundation's governing law schools and can demonstrate a commitment to study natural resources law. **Criteria:** Recipients are selected based on potential to make a significant contribution to the field of natural resources law, academic ability, leadership ability, year in law school and financial need.

Funds Avail.: A total amount of $100,000 per year. **To Apply:** Applicants must submit the requirements. **Deadline:** April 1.

6055 ■ Rocky Mountain Nature Association

48 Alpine Cir.
Estes Park, CO 80517
Ph: (970)586-0108
E-mail: membership.rmna@rmna.org
URL: http://www.rmna.org

6056 ■ Rocky Mountain Research Fellowships *(Graduate/Fellowship)*

Purpose: To convey the importance of communicating park research to the public. **Focus:** General studies. **Qualif.:** Applicants must be currently enrolled in, or in the process of graduating from, a graduate level program at an accredited college or university; must show proven excellence in scholarship and research, or training in the fields of natural and/or cultural resources; must have goals that include an interest in a career with national or state parks in interpretation, natural or cultural resources, resource management, or environmental education; should exhibit the ability to communicate effectively to both general and public audiences; should exhibit a willingness to contribute to the purposes of the Rocky Mountain Fellowship Program and assist the National Park Service by sharing knowledge, skill and enthusiasm. **Criteria:** Preference will be given to those who meet the scholarship criteria.

Funds Avail.: No specific amount. **Number Awarded:** 1. **To Apply:** Applicants must submit a preliminary research proposal and the chosen fellow will be expected to convey research findings to the general public as well as to professional audiences.

Remarks: It is an endowed program funded by the Justine and Leslie Fidel Bailey Trust. **Contact:** Rocky Mountain Nature Association at the above address (see entry 6055).

6057 ■ Roofing Industry Alliance for Progress

10255 W Higgins Rd., Ste. 600
Rosemont, IL 60018-5607
Ph: (847)299-9070
Fax: (847)299-1183
E-mail: bjudson@roofingindustryalliance.net
URL: http://www.nrca.net/rp/related/nrf

6058 ■ Roofing Industry Alliance for Progress Scholarships *(Graduate, Undergraduate/ Scholarship)*

Purpose: To provide financial support to immediate families of NRCA members to be able to attend college or vocational programs. **Focus:** General studies. **Qualif.:** Applicant must be dependents of full-time employees or spouses of NRCA contractor members or companies that have been NRCA members for at least one year; high school seniors or graduates or undergraduates enrolled full-time in a course of study in an accredited two- or four-year college/university or vocational school; relatives of Alliance trustees or officers are not eligible. **Criteria:** Awards are given based on academic record, potential to succeed, leadership and participation in school and community, honors, work experience, statement of educational and career goals and outside appraisal.

Funds Avail.: $1000. **To Apply:** Applicant must send a completed application form together with a transcript. **Deadline:** January 31. **Contact:** The Roofing Industry Alliance for Progress Scholarship Program, Scholarship America, One Scholarship Way, P.O. Box 297, Saint Peter, MN 56082, Telephone: (507)931-1682, ext. 629

6059 ■ Roothbert Fund

475 Riverside Dr., Rm. 252
New York, NY 10115

Ph: (212)870-3116
E-mail: mail@roothbertfund.org
URL: http://www.roothbertfund.org

6060 ■ Roothbert Fund Scholarships
(Undergraduate/Scholarship)

Purpose: To provide financial assistance to people motivated by spiritual values. **Focus:** General studies. **Qualif.:** Scholarship is open to all people in the United States regardless of sex, age, color, nationality or religious background. **Criteria:** Preference will be given to those who can satisfy high scholastic requirements and are considering careers in education.

Funds Avail.: $2,000-$3,000. **To Apply:** Applicants must submit all the application information.

6061 ■ The Rotary Foundation

1560 Sherman Ave.
Evanston, IL 60201
Ph: (847)866-3000
Fax: (847)328-8554
E-mail: jennifer.deters@rotary.org
URL: http://www.rotary.org

6062 ■ The Rotary Foundation Ambassadorial Scholarships *(Undergraduate/Scholarship)*

Purpose: To further international understanding and friendly relations among people of different countries and geographical areas. **Focus:** General studies. **Qualif.:** Applicants must be currently enrolled in a university, college, or institution. **Criteria:** Recipients are selected based on their academic records.

Funds Avail.: No specific amount. **To Apply:** Applicants must complete the application form; applicants must provide an essay including a brief autobiography, work experience, and volunteer activities; a detailed statement of intent (not more than three pages); a list of principal interests and activities (not more than one page); applicants must submit a transcript of records. **Deadline:** March 1; August 15.

6063 ■ Rowan Business Alliance

PO Box 1907
Salisbury, NC 28145-1907
Ph: (704)636-3629
Fax: (704)633-4970
URL: http://www.rowanalliance.com

6064 ■ Julian C. Johnston Memorial Scholarships *(Undergraduate/Scholarship)*

Purpose: To help young people further their education. **Focus:** General Studies. **Qualif.:** Applicants must have demonstrated leadership in school and volunteer community activities or work experience, awards or honors; must have a minimum of 3.0 GPA; must have a minimum SAT score of 910 or ACT composite score of 19; must be of good character. **Criteria:** Preference will be given to those students who meet the criteria.

Funds Avail.: No specific amount. **To Apply:** Applicant must submit the following: signed and dated official scholarship award application form; activity sheet; an original letter (no photocopies) from the student, addressed to the RBA Selection Committee, stating why and where he or she intends to further their education and what he or she plans to do upon graduation. Applicant must also submit school transcripts, including SAT and/or ACT scores, class rank, grade point average (and weighted average if available); a written summary to the selection committee of how student plans to pay for his or her total college education; and a photograph. **Deadline:** March 16.

Remarks: JCJ Scholarships are not solely chosen on academic scores or need. Personal interviews are required.

6065 ■ Royal Bank of Canada

260 Adelaide St. E
Toronto, ON, Canada M5A 1N1
Free: (866)363-1722
E-mail: 4edu@sympatico.ca
URL: http://www.rbcroyalbank.com

6066 ■ RBC Royal Bank Scholarships for First Year Medical & Dental Students *(Undergraduate/Scholarship)*

Purpose: To provide scholarship assistance to qualified individuals who want to pursue their studies. **Focus:** Medical education; Dentistry. **Qualif.:** Applicants must be Canadian citizens or permanent residents of Canada; must be accepted into the first year of a recognized medical or dental program at a university in Canada for the academic year; must be full-time students studying to become an accredited medical doctors or dentists. **Criteria:** Recipients will be selected based on the scholarship application criteria.

Funds Avail.: $5,000. **Number Awarded:** 27. **To Apply:** Applicants must complete the application form available online; must provide basic contact details, including their email, address, phone number, mailing address, and must provide information on their current undergraduate or graduate school, as well as details on the medical or dental school they will be attending. **Deadline:** September 30.

6067 ■ RBC Royal Bank Scholarships for New Canadians *(Undergraduate/Scholarship)*

Purpose: To provide scholarship assistance to qualified individuals who wants to pursue their studies. **Focus:** General studies. **Qualif.:** Applicants must be Canadian citizens or permanent residents of Canada; must be in graduating year in Canadian high school or CEGEP; intends to enroll or enter in an accredited Canadian college or university as full-time students; must have achieved at least a 70% average in their previous year of study. **Criteria:** Recipients will be selected based on the scholarship application criteria.

Funds Avail.: $2,000. **Number Awarded:** 12. **To Apply:** Applicants must complete the application form available online; must provide basic contact details, including their email address, phone number, mailing address, and must provide information about their citizenship status, place of birth and year of arrival in Canada; must provide information about their current school, grade average, extracurricular activities and future educational plans. **Deadline:** June 8.

6068 ■ RBC Royal Bank Scholarships for Undergraduates *(Undergraduate/Scholarship)*

Purpose: To provide scholarship assistance to qualified individuals who want to pursue their studies. **Focus:** Business; Science; Visual arts. **Qualif.:** Applicants must be

Awards are arranged alphabetically below their administering organizations

Canadian citizens or permanent residents; must be enrolled as full-time students in an accredited Canadian college or university; must be entering their second through final program year; must have minimum cumulative GPA equivalent to 70% average. **Criteria:** Recipients will be evaluated on a combination of creativity, practical application, relevance to their field and inventiveness.

Funds Avail.: Gold: $5,000; Silver: $3,000; Bronze: $2,000. **Number Awarded:** 9. **To Apply:** Applicants must provide basic contact details, including their email address, phone numbers, mailing address, and must provide information about their college or university, program of study, and cumulative GPA. **Deadline:** June 9.

6069 ■ Royal Canadian Golf Association

1333 Dorval Dr., Ste. 1
Oakville, ON, Canada L6M 4X7
Ph: (905)849-9700
Fax: (905)845-7040
E-mail: ssimmons@rcga.org
URL: http://www.rcga.org

6070 ■ Suzanne Beauregard Scholarships
(Undergraduate/Scholarship)

Purpose: To support young golfers who wish to pursue their studies. **Focus:** General studies. **Qualif.:** Applicants must have completed at least one full year in a post-secondary degree program and show a minimum average of 70%; must be a full-time student at a university, college or CEGEP; must demonstrate a record of athletic and academic excellence; must be a member in good standing of Golf Quebec; must demonstrate regular participation in community and or extracurricular activities. **Criteria:** Candidates will be judged based on the information contained within their applications and support materials.

Funds Avail.: $1,000. **To Apply:** Application forms are available online and must be sent to RCGA, 1333 Dorval Dr., Ste. 1, Oakville, ON L6M 4X7. **Deadline:** June 30.

6071 ■ Canadian Seniors Golf Association Scholarships *(Undergraduate/Scholarship)*

Purpose: To provide financial assistance to young Canadian men and women. **Focus:** General studies. **Qualif.:** Applicants must be Canadian men and women who elect to obtain an education and participate in the golf program at a RCGA Foundation-recognized university in Canada; must have successfully completed at least one full year in a post-secondary degree program and show a minimum average of 70% in each year of the program; must have experience in competitive golf at a regional, provincial or national level; must have been accepted at and plan to attend an RCGA Foundation recognized college or university, and must have been named or be becoming named to the institution's golf team. **Criteria:** Candidates will be judged based on the information contained in their applications and support materials.

Funds Avail.: $3,000. **Number Awarded:** 4. **To Apply:** Application forms are available online and must be sent to RCGA, 1333 Dorval Dr., Ste. 1, Oakville, ON L6M 4X7. **Deadline:** June 30.

6072 ■ Connor/Spafford Scholarships
(Undergraduate/Scholarship)

Purpose: To assist promising Nova Scotia Atlantic Canada men and women to obtain a degree and participate in the golf program at a university. **Focus:** General studies. **Qualif.:** Applicants must be a Canadian citizen or a resident in Atlantic Canada; must have successfully completed at least one full year in a postsecondary degree program and have maintained a minimum average of 70%; must have been accepted at a university or college and have been named or will be named to the institution's golf team; must have experience in competitive golf at a regional, provincial or natural level. **Criteria:** Preference will be given to applicants who were born in or are residents in Nova Scotia.

Funds Avail.: $5,000. **Number Awarded:** 2. **To Apply:** Application forms are available online and must be sent to RCGA, 1333 Dorval Dr., Ste. 1, Oakville, ON L6M 4X7. **Deadline:** June 30.

6073 ■ Mary Ellen Driscoll Scholarships
(Undergraduate/Scholarship)

Purpose: To provide financial assistance to Canadian women. **Focus:** General studies. **Qualif.:** Applicant must be a female Canadian citizen or a resident in New Brunswick; must have successfully completed at least one full year in a post-secondary degree program at a recognized educational institution; must have been accepted at a university or college and have been named or will be named to the institution's golf team; must have experience in competitive golf at the regional, provincial or national level. **Criteria:** Preference will be given to applicants who have been accepted to a college or university in Canada with a recognized golf program.

Funds Avail.: $1,000. **To Apply:** Application forms are available online and must be sent to RCGA, 1333 Dorval Dr., Ste. 1, Oakville, ON L6M 4X7. **Deadline:** June 30.

6074 ■ Georgia Hilton Academic Scholarships
(Undergraduate/Scholarship)

Purpose: To assist a promising university student. **Focus:** Sports studies; Business administration. **Qualif.:** Applicants must be university students studying towards a degree in sport/business administration; must show a minimum average of 80% in the last two years of high school, or CEGEP, and have attained a graduation diploma (minimum Grade 12). Must also have completed at least one full year of education in a post-secondary degree program at a recognized institution; must intend to continue in an undergraduate or graduate program in sport/business administration; must have experience in competitive golf at a regional, provincial, or national level; must have participated in community and/or extracurricular activities; must be a Canadian citizen or landed immigrant. **Criteria:** Candidates will be judged based on the information contained in their applications and support materials.

Funds Avail.: $5,000. **To Apply:** Application forms are available online and must be sent to RCGA, 1333 Dorval Dr., Ste. 1, Oakville, ON L6M 4X7. **Deadline:** June 30.

6075 ■ Nu-Gro Corporation Turfgrass Scholarships (Graduate) *(Graduate, Postgraduate/ Scholarship)*

Purpose: To assist promising students toward a postgraduate degree in turfgrass management. **Focus:** Turfgrass management. **Qualif.:** Applicant must be a student of turfgrass agronomy or turfgrass management; must have completed a relevant undergraduate program at a recognized university or college; must have been accepted as a full-time student in a graduate or postgraduate degree in agronomy/turfgrass management; must have experience in the game of golf and a desire to pursue a career in the golf industry; must have participated in community and/or extracurricular activities. **Criteria:** Candidates will be judged based on the information contained in their applications and support materials.

Funds Avail.: $5,000. **To Apply:** Application forms are available online and must be sent to RCGA, 1333 Dorval Dr., Ste. 1, Oakville, ON L6M 4X7. **Deadline:** June 30.

6076 ■ Nu-Gro Corporation Turfgrass Scholarships (Undergraduate) *(Undergraduate/Scholarship)*

Purpose: To assist promising students towards an undergraduate degree in turfgrass management. **Focus:** Turfgrass management. **Qualif.:** Applicant must be a student of turfgrass agronomy or turfgrass management; must have completed at least one full year in a postsecondary degree/diploma program at a recognized institution and show a minimum average of 75%; must have experience in the game of golf and a desire to pursue a career in the golf industry; must have participated in community and/or extracurricular activities. **Criteria:** Candidates will be judged based on the information contained in their applications and support materials.

Funds Avail.: $5,000. **To Apply:** Application forms are available online and must be sent to RCGA, 1333 Dorval Dr., Ste. 1, Oakville, ON L6M 4X7. **Deadline:** June 30.

6077 ■ Marlene Streit Golf Scholarships *(Undergraduate/Scholarship)*

Purpose: To support the Canadian female golfers attending Canadian universities and colleges recognized by the RCGA Foundation. **Focus:** General studies. **Qualif.:** Applicants must be Canadian female golfers; must have a minimum of 70% in the last two years of high school/CEGEP and have graduated (minimum grade 12). Applicant musts also complete at least one full year in a post-secondary degree program and show a minimum average of 70%; must have experience in competitive golf at a regional, provincial or national level; must have been accepted at an RCGA Foundation recognized college or university, and have been named or will be named to the institution's golf team; must be Canadian citizens or landed immigrants. **Criteria:** Candidates will be judged based on the information contained in their applications and support materials.

Funds Avail.: $3,500. **Number Awarded:** 2. **To Apply:** Application forms are available online and must be sent to RCGA, 1333 Dorval Dr., Ste. 1, Oakville, ON L6M 4X7. **Deadline:** June 30.

6078 ■ Rubber Division American Chemical Society

PO Box 499
Akron, OH 44309-0499
Ph: (330)972-7814
Fax: (330)972-5269
URL: http://www.rubber.org

6079 ■ Rubber Division American Chemical Society Scholarships *(Undergraduate/Scholarship)*

Purpose: To provide financial assistance to students pursuing a college degree related to rubber technology, polymer science or the chemical profession. **Focus:** Chemistry; Physics; Chemical engineering; Mechanical engineering. **Qualif.:** Applicants must be enrolled in an accredited university or college where rubber division has a partner organization; must be students majoring in chemistry, physics, chemical engineering, mechanical engineering, polymer science or any other field related to the rubber industry. **Criteria:** Awards are given based on academic merit.

Funds Avail.: $5,000. **To Apply:** Applicants must send application form; two nomination letters; and transcript mailed by school registrar via regular mail. **Deadline:** March. **Contact:** Christie Robinson, Education & Publications Manager, 330-972-7815.

6080 ■ Damon Runyon Cancer Research Foundation

One Exchange Plaza
55 Broadway, Ste. 302
New York, NY 10006
Ph: (212)455-0520
Free: 877-877-7CANCER
E-mail: award@drcrf.org
URL: http://www.cancerresearchfund.org

6081 ■ Damon Runyon Cancer Research Foundation Fellowships *(Postdoctorate/Fellowship)*

Purpose: To support the training of the brightest postdoctoral scientists as they embark upon their research careers. **Focus:** Medical Research. **Qualif.:** Applicants must have completed one or more degrees or its equivalent: MD, PhD, MD/Phd, DDS, DVM (applicants must include a copy of their diploma to confirm date of conferral); application must be under the guidance of a Sponsor - a scientist (tenured, tenure-track or equivalent position); applicants who have already accepted a postdoctoral research fellowship award are not eligible. **Criteria:** Selection is based on the quality of the research proposal; qualifications, experience and productivity of both the candidate and the Sponsor; and the quality of the research training environment in which the proposed research is to be conducted.

Funds Avail.: $43,000 1st year; $45,000 2nd year; $46,000 3rd year. **Number Awarded:** varies. **To Apply:** Applicants may visit the website for detailed instructions and information. **Deadline:** March 17; August 15.

6082 ■ Damon Runyon Clinical Investigator Awards *(Postdoctorate/Fellowship)*

Purpose: To increase the number of physicians capable of moving seamlessly between the laboratory and the patient's bedside in search of breakthrough treatments. **Focus:** Medical research. **Qualif.:** Applicants must be U.S. citizens or permanent legal residents; must be nominated by their institution; must have received an MD or MD/PhD degree(s) from an accredited institution and are board-eligible; must be committed to spending 80% of their time conducting research; must apply in conjunction with a mentor who is established in the field of clinical translational cancer research. **Criteria:** Recipients are chosen based on excellence of the applicant and the mentor; innovation, creativity, quality and originality of research proposal; commitment of the mentor and institution to the development and training of the applicant as an independent clinical research investigator; evidence of the applicant's commitment to clinical translational and/or cancer prevention research and their ability to apply these advances; importance of the proposed research; and adherence of the proposal to the definition of clinical research.

Funds Avail.: $100,000 stipend and $50,000 research allowance each year. **To Apply:** Applicants may visit website for detailed instructions and fellowship information. **Deadline:** March 3.

6083 ■ Damon Runyon-Rachleff Innovation Awards *(Postdoctorate/Fellowship)*

Purpose: To provide funding for extraordinary early career researchers who have an innovative new idea but lack sufficient preliminary data to obtain traditional funding. **Focus:** Medical research. **Qualif.:** Applicants, including non-U.S. citizens, must be conducting independent research at a U.S. research institution; institutional nominations are not required; basic and translational/clinical projects will be considered; applicants with a background in multiple disciplines are encouraged to apply; joint submission from collaborators working in different disciplines will be considered; applicants must belong to either: tenure-track Assistant Professors within the first three years of obtaining the position, Clinical Instructors and Senior Clinical Fellows (with an MD) pursuing a period of independent research before taking a faculty position, or Postdoctoral Fellows and highly motivated recent PhD and MD graduates pursuing a period of independent research before taking a faculty position; must commit 80% of their time to conducting research; and must demonstrate access to the resources and infrastructures necessary to conduct the research. **Criteria:** Recipients are chosen based on the applicant's capacity to conduct bold, exceptionally creative research; the novelty and potential for breakthrough innovation of the proposed research; the likelihood of impact to cancer understanding if research is successful; and the applicant's lack of resources to pursue the proposed research.

Funds Avail.: $150,000 per year. **To Apply:** Applicants may visit website for detailed instructions and information. **Deadline:** June 2.

6084 ■ Rural Telephone Company

892 W Madison Ave.
Glenns Ferry, ID 83623
Ph: (208)366-2614
Fax: (208)366-2615
Free: 888-366-7821
URL: http://www.rtci.net

6085 ■ Rural Telephone Company Scholarships *(Undergraduate/Scholarship)*

Purpose: To provide fund for the education of high school senior whose parents or legal guardian is a subscriber to any of the following Rural Telephone Company services. **Focus:** General studies. **Qualif.:** Applicants must be high school seniors whose parents or legal guardians are subscribers to any of the following Rural Telephone Company services: Cable, Telephone, Cellular PCS, Wireless Internet or Satellite Internet. **Criteria:** Awards are given based on the submitted application.

Funds Avail.: $250, $500 and $1,000. **Number Awarded:** 7. **To Apply:** Applicants must submit completed scholarship application. **Deadline:** May 8. **Contact:** susan.case@ruraltelphone.com.

6086 ■ Russian Brotherhood Organization of the USA

1733 Spring Garden St.
Philadelphia, PA 19130
Ph: (215)563-2537
Free: 800-726-8721
E-mail: info@rbo.org
URL: http://www.rbo.org

6087 ■ Mihaly Russin Scholarship Awards *(Graduate/Scholarship)*

Purpose: To offer aid to students seeking higher education. **Focus:** General studies. **Qualif.:** Applicants must have life insurance policy of $10,000 or more with the RBO; remained active within the society; must be a Christian. **Criteria:** Selection is based on the application.

Funds Avail.: $1000. **To Apply:** Applicants must submit a completed application form together with two letters of recommendation, a picture, a copy of transcripts and acceptance letter. **Deadline:** September 30.

6088 ■ Saints Cyril and Methodius Scholarships *(Undergraduate/Scholarship)*

Purpose: To support the education of a student member. **Focus:** General studies. **Qualif.:** Applicant must be a high school graduate or prep school; hold a Russian Brotherhood Organization life insurance certificate of not less than $3000; and a member of the society in good standing. **Criteria:** Recipients are selected by an independent scholarship committee.

Funds Avail.: Depends on the financial need of the student's family. **To Apply:** Applicants must submit a completed application form and send it to SS. Cyril and Methodius Scholarships.

6089 ■ SACHS Foundation

90 S Cascade Ave., Ste. 1410
Colorado Springs, CO 80903
Ph: (719)633-2353
URL: http://www.sachsfoundation.org

6090 ■ SACHS Foundation Graduate Scholarships *(Graduate/Scholarship)*

Purpose: To provide educational assistance to deserving Colorado Black students. **Focus:** General studies. **Qualif.:** Applicants must be students who are receiving an undergraduate degree. **Criteria:** Applicants are evaluated based on academic merit and financial need.

Funds Avail.: $5,000. **To Apply:** Applicants must submit Graduate Application form; SACHS FOUNDATION financial statement; copy of parents' or (if over 21 and not a dependent) their own most current completed federal tax return including W-2(s) (IRS form 1040); certified copy of final undergraduate grade transcript. **Deadline:** March 1.

6091 ■ SACHS Foundation Undergraduate Scholarships for Colorado Black Students *(High School/Scholarship)*

Purpose: To provide educational assistance to deserving Colorado black students. **Focus:** General studies. **Qualif.:** Applicants must be African-American students who are residents of Colorado for a minimum of 5 years; current high school seniors, or those who have graduated not more than 3 years prior to the application and did not or are not currently attending college. **Criteria:** Applicants are evaluated based on academic achievement.

Funds Avail.: $4,000. **To Apply:** Applicants must submit the completed application form; SACHS Foundation financial statement; copy of parents' most recent completed

Awards are arranged alphabetically below their administering organizations

federal tax return including W-2(s), (IRS Form 1040); certified copy of high school grade transcript; three current letters of recommendation from persons not related to them; recent small photograph; and the copy of Colorado enrollment form, which indicates racial category. **Deadline:** March 1.

6092 ■ Safe Schools Coalition

1002 E Seneca St.
Seattle, WA 98122-4203
Ph: (206)957-1621
Fax: (206)325-2689
URL: http://www.safeschoolscoalition.org

6093 ■ AIDS Awareness Scholarships *(Undergraduate/Scholarship)*

Purpose: To provide financial assistance for students who have a commitment or involvement in AIDS awareness. **Focus:** General studies. **Qualif.:** Applicants must be enrolled at Golden Gate University. **Criteria:** Preference will be given to those who meet the criteria.

Funds Avail.: No specific amount. **To Apply:** Applicants must check the available website for the required materials. **Deadline:** April. **Contact:** Golden Gate University Financial Aid Office at 536 Mission Street San Francisco, CA 94105 Phone: 1-415-442-7270 Fax: 1-415-442-7807.

6094 ■ Albuquerque Lesbian and Gay Chamber of Commerce Scholarships *(Undergraduate/Scholarship)*

Purpose: To provide financial assistance for LGBT undergraduate students. **Focus:** General studies. **Qualif.:** Applicants must be gay or lesbian undergraduate students at the University of New Mexico or the Technical Vocation Institute of Albuquerque and residents of New Mexico for at least one year. **Criteria:** Preference will be given to those who demonstrate financial need, academic achievement and community involvement.

Funds Avail.: $1,000. **Number Awarded:** 6. **To Apply:** Applicants must check the available website for more information. **Deadline:** May 15. **Contact:** Albuquerque Lesbian & Gay Chamber of Commerce Scholarships PO Box 27207 Albuquerque, NM 87125 Phone: 505-243-6767.

6095 ■ Allen (Dan) Memorial Scholarships *(Undergraduate/Scholarship)*

Purpose: To provide financial assistance for students demonstrating service to or achievement in the gay-lesbian community. **Focus:** General studies. **Qualif.:** Applicants must be enrolled at City College of San Francisco (CA) and have a GPA of 2.5 or better. **Criteria:** Preference will be given to those students who meet the criteria.

Funds Avail.: $600. **To Apply: Deadline:** October 31 for Fall semester and April 1 for Spring semester. **Contact:** Safe Schools Coalition at the above address (see entry 6092).

6096 ■ Apple Scholars *(Undergraduate/Scholarship)*

Purpose: To support transgendered students by helping them financially by awarding scholarships to transgendered students for the innovative use of technology in their schoolwork. **Focus:** General studies. **Qualif.:** Applicants must be high school seniors. **Criteria:** Selection of scholars will be based on criteria.

Funds Avail.: $2,000. **Number Awarded:** 10. **To Apply:** Applicants must check the available website for the required materials. **Deadline:** May 30.

Remarks: Recipients will also receive a MacBook Pro and iPod nano. **Contact:** Safe Schools Coalition at the above address (see entry 6092).

6097 ■ Asian/Pacific Gays and Friends Scholarships *(Undergraduate/Scholarship)*

Purpose: To provide financial support for gay students. **Focus:** General studies. **Qualif.:** Applicants must be male Asian/Pacific Islanders involved in gay community leadership/activities in Southern California (counties of Los Angeles, Orange, Riverside, San Bernardino, Ventura). **Criteria:** Awards will be given to those who meet the scholarship criteria.

Funds Avail.: $1,000. **To Apply:** Applicants must check the available website for the required materials. **Deadline:** September 15. **Contact:** The Fund for Lesbian and Gay Scholarships PO Box 48320 Los Angeles, CA 90048. Phone: 1-213-650-5752.

6098 ■ BIGALA (Bisexual Gay and Lesbian Alliance) Scholarships *(Undergraduate/Scholarship)*

Purpose: To provide financial assistance to students demonstrating service to or achievement in the gay, lesbian, bisexual or transgender community. **Focus:** General studies. **Qualif.:** Applicants must be enrolled at City College of San Francisco and have a GPA of 3.0 or better. **Criteria:** Preference will be given to those who meet the criteria.

Funds Avail.: $200 per year. **To Apply:** Applicants must check the available website for the required materials. **Contact:** Safe Schools Coalition at the above address (see entry 6092).

6099 ■ Carolina's Gay & Lesbian Scholarships *(Undergraduate/Scholarship)*

Purpose: To encourage and reward involvement and activism by members of the LGBT community at Duke University. **Focus:** General studies. **Qualif.:** Applicants must be gay, lesbian, bisexual and transgender students from North or South Carolina who are attending Duke University. **Criteria:** Awards will be based on financial need and student involvement in the LGBT community.

Funds Avail.: No specific amount. **To Apply:** Applicants must check the available website for the required materials.

6100 ■ George Choy Memorial/Gay Asian Pacific Alliance (GAPA) Scholarships *(Undergraduate/Scholarship)*

Purpose: To provide financial assistance for lesbian, gay, bisexual and transgender (LGBT) Asian and Pacific Islanders (API) who are in the process of applying to or are currently attending a post-secondary institution. **Focus:** General studies. **Qualif.:** Applicants must be an Asian/Pacific Islander graduating from a Bay Area high school (counties of Alameda, Contra Costa, Marin, San Francisco, San Mateo, Santa Clara, Napa, Sonoma and Solano) with a GPA of 3.0 or better. **Criteria:** Selection of scholars will be based on criteria.

Funds Avail.: No specific amount. **To Apply:** Applicants must check the contact information for inquiries. **Deadline:** June 15. **Contact:** The Horizons Foundation 870 Market Street, Suite 1155 San Francisco, CA 94102 Phone: 1-415-398-2333.

Awards are arranged alphabetically below their administering organizations

6101 ■ College of Marin Gay and Lesbian Student Scholarships *(Undergraduate/Scholarship)*

Purpose: To provide financial support for those who are in need. **Focus:** General studies. **Qualif.:** Applicant must be a gay or lesbian student enrolled at the College of Marin. **Criteria:** Preference will be given to those who meet the criteria.

Funds Avail.: $250 per year. **To Apply:** Applicants must check the contact information for inquiries. **Deadline:** March. **Contact:** College of Marin Foundation Development Office at PO Box 446 Kentfield, CA 94914 Phone: 1-415-485-9382.

6102 ■ Deaf Queer Youth Scholarships *(Undergraduate/Scholarship)*

Purpose: To sponsor scholarships for deaf lesbian, gay, bisexual, transgender, intersex or queer students who are out about their sexual orientation/ identity. **Focus:** General studies. **Qualif.:** Applicants must be currently enrolled in high school or college; must be under the age of 25; and must have a minimum 2.5 GPA. US Citizenship is required. **Criteria:** Selection is based on a written or video essay.

Funds Avail.: $500. **To Apply:** Applicants must check the available website for the required materials. **Deadline:** July 15. **Contact:** Safe Schools Coalition at the above address (see entry 6092).

6103 ■ Lee Dubin Scholarship Fund *(Undergraduate/Scholarship)*

Purpose: To provide financial support for gay, lesbian, bisexual and transgendered students who are in need. **Focus:** General studies. **Qualif.:** Applicants must be children of lesbian, gay, bisexual and transgendered parents and guardians who have worked to affect change in the LGBT community and the community at large. **Criteria:** Selection of scholars will be based on criteria.

Funds Avail.: $1,000. **Number Awarded:** 3-5. **To Apply:** Applicants must check the available website for more information. **Deadline:** April 15.

6104 ■ eQuality Scholarships *(Undergraduate/Scholarship)*

Purpose: To provide financial assistance for graduating high school seniors from Northern and Central California who have promoted understanding of and equality for the lesbian, gay, bisexual, transgender community. **Focus:** General studies. **Qualif.:** Applicants must be LGBT students. **Criteria:** Selection of scholars will be based on criteria.

Funds Avail.: $1,500. **To Apply:** Applicants must check the available website for the required materials.

6105 ■ First Friday Breakfast Club Scholarships *(Undergraduate/Scholarship)*

Purpose: To provide financial assistance for high school seniors who have worked to reduce homophobia and increase awareness and tolerance of gay and lesbian issues. **Focus:** General studies. **Qualif.:** Applicants must be high school seniors. **Criteria:** Preference will be given to those who meet the criteria.

Funds Avail.: Maximum of $3,000. **Number Awarded:** 1. **To Apply:** Applicants must check the available website for the required materials. **Deadline:** March 31. **Contact:** Safe Schools Coalition at the above address (see entry 6092).

6106 ■ Gay and Lesbian Business Association of Santa Barbara Scholarships *(Undergraduate/Scholarship)*

Purpose: To provide financial assistance for LGBT students. **Focus:** General studies. **Qualif.:** Applicants must show financial need, academic achievement, community involvement and extracurricular activities. **Criteria:** Priority will be given to those who are in need.

Funds Avail.: Varies. **To Apply:** Applicants must check the available website for the required materials. **Deadline:** July 1. **Contact:** Gay and Lesbian Business Association of Santa Barbara PO Box 90907 Santa Barbara, CA 93190.

6107 ■ Gill Foundation Scholarships (Colorado) *(Undergraduate/Scholarship)*

Purpose: To provide financial assistance for LGBT students. **Focus:** General studies. **Qualif.:** Applicants must be gay, lesbian, bisexual or transgendered students attending Colorado colleges. **Criteria:** Awards will be based on past involvement in LGBT issues and other criteria.

Funds Avail.: $2,000. **To Apply:** Applicants must check the available website for the required materials. **Contact:** For more inquiries just contact your college's financial aid office or Dean of students office.

6108 ■ GLSEN Connecticut Chapter Scholarships *(Undergraduate/Scholarship)*

Purpose: To provide financial support for gay, lesbian, bisexual or transgendered students. **Focus:** General studies. **Qualif.:** Applicant must be a Connecticut resident between 16 and 21 years old. **Criteria:** Preference will be given to those who meet the scholarship criteria.

Funds Avail.: $500. **To Apply:** Applicants must check the available website for the required materials. **Deadline:** April 15. **Contact:** Ronnie Kim G. H. Robertson School 227 Cross Street Coventry, CT 06238.

6109 ■ Bobby Griffith Memorial Scholarships *(Undergraduate/Scholarship)*

Purpose: To provide financial assistance for gay, lesbian, bisexual and transgender youth who contribute to the community by improving the environment for GLBT youth. **Focus:** General studies. **Qualif.:** Applicants must be residents of Contra Costa County and must be graduating seniors. **Criteria:** Awards will be based on criteria.

Funds Avail.: No specific amount. **To Apply:** Applicants must check the available website for the required materials. **Contact:** Gay, Lesbian and Straight Education Network San Francisco Bay Area Chapter (formerly BANGLE) PO Box 30482 Walnut Creek, CA 94598.

6110 ■ Jaye Haddad Memorial Fund *(Undergraduate/Scholarship)*

Purpose: To provide financial assistance for students who have been diagnosed with cancer or AIDS or students with physical disabilities. **Focus:** General Studies. **Qualif.:** Must be enrolled at UCSD as an undergraduate student. **Criteria:** Preference will be given to those who meet the criteria.

Funds Avail.: No specific amount. **To Apply:** Applicants must check the available website for the required materials. **Deadline:** November 30. **Contact:** Safe Schools Coalition at the above address (see entry 6092).

6111 ■ James J. Harvey Dissertation Fellowships *(Doctorate/Fellowship)*

Purpose: To provide financial assistance for graduate students studying male or female homosexuality, including but not limited to sociological, medical, political, historical and legal ramifications or to the study of the life and work of James J. Harvey. **Focus:** Sexuality. **Qualif.:** Applicant must be a Ph.D. candidate at UCI. **Criteria:** Awards will be given to those who meet the criteria.

Funds Avail.: No specific amount. **Number Awarded:** 2-3. **To Apply:** Applicants must check the available website for the required materials. **Contact:** Steve Johnson, Director of Graduate Financial Support; Research and Graduate Studies University of California, Irvine 120 Administration Irvine, CA 92697 Phone: 1-714-824-4223.

6112 ■ Peter Kaufman Memorial Scholarships *(Undergraduate/Scholarship)*

Purpose: To provide financial assistance for gay, lesbian, bisexual and transgendered students. **Focus:** General studies. **Qualif.:** Program is open to gay, lesbian, bisexual or transgender high school seniors who have worked with the GLBT community. **Criteria:** Preference will be given to those who meet the criteria.

Funds Avail.: $1,000. **To Apply:** Applicants must check the available website for the required materials. **Contact:** Kathy J. Gill, Director Gay & Lesbian Education Commission Los Angeles Unified School District, Room 242 450 N. Grand Avenue Los Angeles, CA 90012 Phone: 1-213-625-6392.

6113 ■ Bill Kidder Fund Awards *(Undergraduate/Scholarship)*

Purpose: To provide financial support for students who are in need. **Focus:** General studies. **Qualif.:** Applicants must be enrolled as an undergraduate or graduate student at UNH and demonstrate service to the lesbian, gay, bisexual and transgendered community. **Criteria:** Preference will be given to those who meet the criteria.

Funds Avail.: $1,500. **To Apply:** Applicants must check the available website for the required materials. **Deadline:** April.

6114 ■ Lambda Alumni (UCLA Lesbian & Gay Alumni Association) Scholarships Program *(Undergraduate/Scholarship)*

Purpose: To provide financial assistance for students showing academic excellence and service to the lesbian, gay and bisexual community, regardless of sexual orientation. **Focus:** General studies. **Qualif.:** Applicants must demonstrate financial need and be enrolled at UCLA. **Criteria:** Preference will be given to those who meet the criteria.

Funds Avail.: $1,000 per year. **To Apply:** Applicants must check the available website for the required materials. **Deadline:** March. **Contact:** UCLA Lambda Alumni Association at PO Box 24075 Los Angeles, CA 90024.

6115 ■ Jonathan Lax Scholarship Fund for Gay Men *(Undergraduate/Scholarship)*

Purpose: To encourage gay men to obtain additional education, aspire to positions in which they contribute to society, be open about their sexual preference and act as role models for other gay men with similar potential. **Focus:** General studies. **Qualif.:** Applicants must be gay students. **Criteria:** Selection of scholars will be based on criteria.

Funds Avail.: $20,000 for 1 scholar and $5,000 for multiple scholars. **To Apply:** Applicants must check the available website for the required materials.

6116 ■ LEAGUE Foundation Scholarships *(Undergraduate/Scholarship)*

Purpose: To provide financial assistance for lesbian, gay, bisexual and transgender high school seniors. **Focus:** General studies. **Qualif.:** Applicants must be lesbian, gay, bisexual and transgender high school seniors; must have a minimum of 3.0 GPA; and must be actively and substantially involved in community service. **Criteria:** Selection of scholars will be based on criteria.

Funds Avail.: No specific amount. **To Apply:** Applicants must check the available website for the required materials. **Deadline:** April.

Remarks: Scholarships include the Matthew Shepard Memorial Scholarship (name used with permission of the Shepard family), named for the Wyoming college student murdered in 1998 for his sexual orientation, and the Laurel Hester Memorial Scholarship.

6117 ■ Lesbians for Change Scholarships *(Undergraduate/Scholarship)*

Purpose: To provide financial assistance for lesbians in New Mexico pursuing higher education. **Focus:** General studies. **Qualif.:** Applicants must be residents of New Mexico involved politically in the lesbian community. **Criteria:** Preference will be given to those who meet the criteria.

Funds Avail.: $500. **Number Awarded:** 2. **To Apply:** Applicants must check the available website for the required materials. **Deadline:** June. **Contact:** Lesbians for Change PO Box 27664 Albuquerque, NM 87125 Phone: 1-505-292-2219 (Sonia Bettez).

6118 ■ Live Out Loud Annual Scholarships *(Undergraduate/Scholarship)*

Purpose: To provide scholarships for gay, bisexual and transgender students and allies who have made significant contributions to society by "living out loud" and supporting the LGBT community. **Focus:** General studies. **Qualif.:** Applicants must be graduating high school seniors and students who deferred attending an educational institution for one year following graduation. **Criteria:** Selection of scholars will be based on academic credentials, an essay, leadership and community service involvement, an interview, two letters of recommendation, financial need and future goals.

Funds Avail.: $2,500. **Number Awarded:** 3. **To Apply:** Applicants must check the available contact information for inquiries. **Deadline:** March 31.

6119 ■ Audre Lord Scholarships *(Graduate, Undergraduate/Scholarship)*

Purpose: To recognize out lesbians, gay, bisexual and transgender students of color who are making significant contributions to their communities by supporting them financially. **Focus:** General studies. **Qualif.:** Applicants must be gay and lesbian undergraduate and graduate students of African descent. **Criteria:** Preference will be given to those who meet the criteria.

Funds Avail.: $1,000. **To Apply:** Applicants must check the contact information for inquiries. **Deadline:** May 15.

Remarks: Zami is Atlanta's premiere organization for lesbians of African descent, and the award's emphasis is on service to the lesbian community.

6120 ■ Markowski-Leach Scholarships Fund *(Graduate, Undergraduate/Scholarship)*

Purpose: To provide financial assistance for gay and lesbian undergraduate and graduate students who help enhance the greater society's perception of gay and lesbian people. **Focus:** General studies. **Qualif.:** Applicant must be

Awards are arranged alphabetically below their administering organizations

enrolled as an undergraduate or graduate student at San Francisco State University, the University of California at Berkeley or Stanford University, with a GPA of 2.5 or better. **Criteria:** Selection of scholars will be based on criteria.

Funds Avail.: $1,250. **To Apply:** Applicants must check the available website for the required materials. **Deadline:** April.

6121 ■ Barry H. Marshal Scholarships
(Undergraduate/Scholarship)

Purpose: To provide recognition and financial assistance for outstanding undergraduate students enrolled or planning to enroll at Penn State University who have demonstrated need for funds to meet their necessary college expenses and who advocate for or contribute to the lesbian, gay, bisexual, transgender (LGBT) community. **Focus:** General studies. **Qualif.:** Applicants must be undergraduate students at Penn State University. **Criteria:** Preference will be given to those students from New York.

Funds Avail.: No specific amount. **To Apply:** Applicants must check the available website for the required materials.

6122 ■ Michael L. Marx and Donald K. Marshall Scholarships *(Undergraduate/Scholarship)*

Purpose: To recognize students who have made a contribution to the gay and lesbian community. **Focus:** General studies. **Qualif.:** Applicants must be enrolled at UCSD at the sophomore, junior, or senior level. **Criteria:** Preference will be given to those who meet the criteria.

Funds Avail.: $1,000. **To Apply:** Applicants must check the available website for the required materials. **Deadline:** February. **Contact:** University of California, San Diego Scholarship Office 0013 La Jolla, CA 92093-0013 Phone: 1-619-534-3263.

6123 ■ Messenger-Anderson Journalism Scholarships and Internships Program
(Undergraduate/Scholarship)

Purpose: To sponsor scholarships for gay, lesbian, bisexual and transgendered students pursuing a degree in journalism and communications at an accredited four-year college or university. **Focus:** Journalism; Communications. **Qualif.:** Applicants must be high school seniors or current undergraduate students with a cumulative 2.8 GPA or better. **Criteria:** Selection will be based on criteria.

Funds Avail.: $5,000 for the first year and $2,500 for the second and third years. **To Apply:** Applicants may check the available contact information for inquiries. **Deadline:** February.

Remarks: The award is sponsored by the National Gay and Lesbian Task Force (NGLTF). Winners are required to participate in the Messenger-Anderson Scholarship Intern Program at NGLTF offices in Washington, DC, or New York City during the summer.

6124 ■ Harvey Milk/Tom Homann Gay and Lesbian Student Scholarships *(Undergraduate/Scholarship)*

Purpose: To help San Diego area students achieve their goals of vocational, technical or professional careers. **Focus:** General studies. **Qualif.:** Program is open to lesbian, gay, bisexual or transgender residents of San Diego County. **Criteria:** Preference will be given to those who meet the criteria.

Funds Avail.: $250-$1,000. **To Apply:** Applicants must check the available website for the required materials. **Deadline:** June. **Contact:** The Harvey Milk/Tom Homann Gay and Lesbian Student Scholarship c/o The Imperial Court de San Diego, Inc. PO Box 33915 San Diego, CA 92163 Phone: 1-619-692-1967 Fax: 1-619-295-7829.

6125 ■ Minnesota GLBT Educational Fund
(Undergraduate/Scholarship)

Purpose: To recognize outstanding gay, lesbian, bisexual and transgender youth and friends and to support their continuing education. **Focus:** General studies. **Qualif.:** Applicants must be residents of Minnesota or residents from elsewhere who are attending (or planning to attend) a Minnesota educational institution. **Criteria:** Awards will be given to those who meet the criteria.

Funds Avail.: $1,000-$2,000. **To Apply:** Applicants must check the available website for the required materials. **Contact:** Awards Committee Minnesota GLBT Educational Fund 1409 Willow St, Suite 305 Minneapolis, MN 55403-3251 Phone: 1-612-870-1806 Fax: 1-612-871-6587.

6126 ■ National Lesbian and Gay Journalists Association (NLGJA) Scholarships
(Undergraduate/Scholarship)

Purpose: To provide scholarships and awards for LGBT students interested in journalism. **Focus:** Journalism. **Qualif.:** Applicants must be LGBT journalism students. **Criteria:** Selection of recipients is based on merit.

Funds Avail.: $5,000 for Leroy F. Aarons Scholarships; $1,000 for Bob Ross Scholarships. **To Apply:** Applicants must check the available website for more scholarship information. **Deadline:** February; July. **Contact:** Safe Schools Coalition at the above address (see entry 6092).

6127 ■ NWSA Graduate Scholarships in Lesbian Studies *(Doctorate, Graduate/Fellowship)*

Purpose: To provide financial assistance for graduate students doing master's thesis or Ph.D. dissertation research in lesbian studies. **Focus:** General studies. **Qualif.:** Applicants must be members of the National Women's Studies Association. **Criteria:** Preference is given to applicants who are NWSA members.

Funds Avail.: $500. **To Apply:** Applicants must check the available website for the required materials. **Deadline:** February 15. **Contact:** Loretta Younger National Women's Studies Association 7100 Baltimore Avenue, Suite 301 College Park, MD 20742 Phone: 1-301-403-0525 Fax: 1-301-403-4137.

6128 ■ NYNEX Diversity Scholarship Awards
(Undergraduate/Scholarship)

Purpose: To provide financial assistance for students pursuing higher education from diverse cultural, ethnic, educational and special needs backgrounds. **Focus:** General studies. **Qualif.:** Applicants must reside in the NYNEX service territory. **Criteria:** Preference will be given to those who meet the criteria.

Funds Avail.: $2,500. **To Apply:** Applicants must check the available website for the required materials. **Contact:** For more information, call 1-800-537-4180.

6129 ■ Sheldon Oppenheim Memorial Scholarships *(Undergraduate/Scholarship)*

Purpose: To provide financial assistance for a gay, lesbian, bisexual or transgender individual intending to pursue their college education. **Focus:** General studies. **Qualif.:** Ap-

Awards are arranged alphabetically below their administering organizations

plicants must be identified as GLBT; must register as a matriculated student; and must register for at least 6 credits in a degree or certificate program at RCC. **Criteria:** Preference will be given to those who meet the criteria.

Funds Avail.: $250-$500. **To Apply:** Applicants must submit the following: an essay describing any obstacles they may have overcome, their educational goals; any community service, or special circumstances; two letters of recommendation are optional. **Deadline:** June.

6130 ■ OSU Gay, Lesbian, Bisexual and Transgender Alumni Society (PFLAG Scholarships) *(Undergraduate/Scholarship)*

Purpose: To provide financial support for students who have dedicated time and energy to the GLBT community and toward GLBT and HIV/AIDS issues. **Focus:** General studies. **Qualif.:** Applicants should have a minimum GPA of 2.0. **Criteria:** Preference will be given to those students with financial need.

Funds Avail.: No specific amount. **To Apply:** Applicants must complete and submit the application form, accompanied by a letter of recommendation. **Deadline:** February. **Contact:** Safe Schools Coalition at the above address (see entry 6092).

6131 ■ Dr. Connell Persico Scholarships *(Undergraduate/Scholarship)*

Purpose: To provide financial assistance for a student who is making or has made significant contributions to the LGBT community. **Focus:** General studies. **Qualif.:** Applicants must be students who made significant contributions to the lesbian, gay, bisexual and transgender community. **Criteria:** Preference will be given to those students who meet the criteria.

Funds Avail.: $2,500. **To Apply:** Applicants must check the available website for the required materials. **Contact:** Safe Schools Coalition at the above address (see entry 6092).

6132 ■ PFLAG/HATCH Youth Scholarship Foundation *(Undergraduate/Scholarship)*

Purpose: To provide financial assistance for LGBT students who are in need. **Focus:** General studies. **Qualif.:** Applicants must be Houston area students or students from outside the Houston area who will attend Houston colleges. **Criteria:** Preference will be given to those who meet the scholarship criteria.

Funds Avail.: $2,000 for over 2 years and $10,000 for over 4 years. **To Apply:** Applicants must check the available website for the required materials. **Deadline:** May 1. **Contact:** PFLAG/HATCH Youth Scholarship Foundation P.O. Box 667010 Houston, TX 77266-7010 Phone: 1-713-467-3524.

6133 ■ Point Foundation Scholarships *(Graduate, Postgraduate, Undergraduate/Scholarship)*

Purpose: To provide financial support and hope for meritorious undergraduate, graduate and postgraduate students who are marginalized because of their sexual orientation or gender identity. **Focus:** General studies. **Qualif.:** Applicants must be LGBT students with a 3.5 GPA. **Criteria:** Awards will be based on need and criteria.

Funds Avail.: $5,000-$28,000. **To Apply:** Applicants must check the available contact information for more inquiries. **Deadline:** March 1. **Contact:** The Point Foundation PO Box 11210 Chicago, IL 60611 Phone: 1-866-33-POINT (1-866-337-6468) Fax: 1-866-39-POINT (1-866-397-6468).

6134 ■ Pride Foundation Scholarships *(Undergraduate/Scholarship)*

Purpose: To provide financial assistance for gay, lesbian, bisexual and transgender students pursuing higher education. **Focus:** Business Administration; Computer Science; Political Science; Visual arts. **Qualif.:** Applicants must be gay, lesbian, bisexual and transgendered students in these fields of studies. **Criteria:** Preference will be given to those who meet the scholarship criteria.

Funds Avail.: Range from $500 to $10,000. **To Apply:** Applicants must check the available website for the required materials. **Deadline:** January.

6135 ■ Puget Sound LGBT Leadership Scholarships Fund *(Undergraduate/Scholarship)*

Purpose: To complement successful academic experiences by providing financial support for student leadership and involvement in the LGBT community at Puget Sound. **Focus:** General studies. **Qualif.:** Applicants who identify themselves as lesbian, gay, bisexual, transgender or allies are welcome and eligible for this award. **Criteria:** Preference will be given to those who meet the criteria.

Funds Avail.: $2,000. **To Apply:** Applicants must check the available website for the required materials. **Deadline:** April.

6136 ■ Davis Putter Scholarships Fund *(Undergraduate/Scholarship)*

Purpose: To provide scholarships for individuals who are able to do academic work at the university level and who are part of the progressive movement on the campus and in the community. **Focus:** General studies. **Qualif.:** Applicants must be students actively working for peace and justice; must be enrolled in an accredited school and receiving college credit for the time period covered by their grants; and must be living in the United States and planning to enroll in school in the U.S. in order to apply. **Criteria:** Selection will be based on academic merit and financial need.

Funds Avail.: Maximum of $8,000 and may be considerably smaller depending on the applicant's circumstances and the amount of funding available. **To Apply:** Applicants must submit a completed application form with a short personal statement, transcripts, letters of support from two people able to evaluate the applicant's current political work, an official financial statement (i.e., FAFSA or SAR), and a passport-like photograph suitable for reproduction. **Deadline:** April. **Contact:** Safe Schools Coalition at the above address (see entry 6092).

6137 ■ Roy Scrivner Research Grants *(Graduate, Postdoctorate/Grant)*

Purpose: To provide grants for graduate and postdoctoral research concerning the study of lesbian, gay and bisexual family psychology and family therapy. **Focus:** Family Therapy. **Qualif.:** Applicants must be graduate and postdoctoral students. **Criteria:** Selection will be based on merit.

Funds Avail.: $1,000 for graduate student grants and up to $10,000 for postdoctoral grant. **Number Awarded:** 2 (Graduate grants); 1 (Postdoctoral grant). **To Apply:** Applicants must check the available contact information for more inquiries. **Deadline:** November 1.

6138 ■ Matthew Shepard Scholarships *(Undergraduate/Scholarship)*

Purpose: To provide financial assistance for gay and lesbian high school seniors from Iowa planning to attend

Awards are arranged alphabetically below their administering organizations

an Iowa Board of Regions university (Iowa State, University of Iowa or the University of Northern Iowa). **Focus:** General studies. **Qualif.:** Applicants must be gay and lesbian high school seniors planning to be admitted in an Iowa Board of Regions University. **Criteria:** Awards will be based on academic achievement, community involvement or service and financial need.

Funds Avail.: No specific amount. **To Apply:** Applicants must check the available website for the required materials. **Deadline:** March 31. **Contact:** Safe Schools Coalition at the above address (see entry 6092).

6139 ■ Wiggsy Sivertsen Scholarships *(Undergraduate/Scholarship)*

Purpose: To provide financial assistance for gay and lesbian students or students who have provided service to or worked on behalf of gay and lesbian issues. **Focus:** General studies. **Qualif.:** Applicants must be enrolled at San Jose State University and demonstrate financial need. **Criteria:** Priority will be given to those students who demonstrate financial need.

Funds Avail.: $750. **To Apply:** Applicants must check the available website for the required materials. **Contact:** Dr. Jill Steinberg SJSU Counseling Center Phone: 408-924-5910.

6140 ■ Team DC Student-Athlete Scholarships *(Undergraduate/Scholarship)*

Purpose: To provide financial assistance for self-identified lesbian, gay, bisexual or transgender (LGBT) student-athletes who have enhanced the perception of the LGBT community through contributions and involvement in one or more sports. **Focus:** General studies. **Qualif.:** Applicants must be high school seniors in the Washington DC metropolitan area who will be attending an accredited two-year or four-year college or university in the United States with demonstrated academic and athletic excellence as well as potential to serve as a positive LGBT role model. **Criteria:** Preference will be based on qualifications.

Funds Avail.: $1,500. **To Apply:** Applicants must check the available contact information for inquiries about the requirements. **Deadline:** April 1.

6141 ■ Joseph Towner Fund for Gay and Lesbian Families *(Undergraduate/Scholarship)*

Purpose: To provide financial assistance for children of gay and lesbian families. **Focus:** General studies. **Qualif.:** Applicant must be a postsecondary student with at least one gay or lesbian parent residing in the Bay Area (counties of Alameda, Contra Costa, Marin, San Francisco, San Mateo, Santa Clara, Napa, Sonoma and Solano); must be 25 years old or younger and have a GPA of 2.5 or better. **Criteria:** Preference will be given to those who meet the criteria.

Funds Avail.: There is a maximum award of $500 per term; $1,000 per academic year; With a lifetime maximum of $4,000. **To Apply:** Applicants must check the available contact information for inquiries. **Deadline:** June 15. **Contact:** The Horizons Foundation 870 Market Street, Suite 1155 San Francisco, CA 94102 Phone: 1-415-398-2333.

6142 ■ Transgender Scholarships and Education Legacy Fund *(Undergraduate/Scholarship)*

Purpose: To provide financial assistance for transgender-identified students. **Focus:** Social Services; Health Care Services; Religious Education; Teaching; Law. **Qualif.:** Applicants must be students of one of these fields of studies. **Criteria:** Preference will be given to those who meet the qualifications.

Funds Avail.: No specific amount. **To Apply:** Applicants must check the contact information for more inquiries. **Deadline:** February 1.

Remarks: The awards are sponsored by the International Foundation for Gender Education. **Contact:** International Foundation for Gender Education (IFGE) TSELF Awards Committee PO Box 540229 Waltham, MA 02454-0229 Phone: 781-899-2212; Fax: 781-899-2212 URL: www.tself.org.

6143 ■ United Teachers Los Angeles Stonewall Scholarship Fund *(Undergraduate/Scholarship)*

Purpose: To provide financial assistance for deserving high school students to further their educational goals. **Focus:** General studies. **Qualif.:** Applicants must be students of the Los Angeles Unified School District (LAUSD) or enrolled in a high school completion program. **Criteria:** Preference will be given to those who meet the criteria.

Funds Avail.: The scholarship amount varies, but is generally $250 to $500. **To Apply:** Applicants must check the contact information for inquiries. **Deadline:** April. **Contact:** Judith Bruner at 3303 Wilshire Blvd., 10th floor Los Angeles, CA 90010 Phone: 1-800-556-8852 or 1-213-487-5560.

6144 ■ University of California LGBT Alumni (UCGALA) scholarships *(Undergraduate/Scholarship)*

Purpose: To provide financial assistance for students with good academic achievement. **Focus:** General studies. **Qualif.:** Applicants must be LGBT alumni at the University of California. **Criteria:** Preference will be given to those who meet the criteria.

Funds Avail.: No specific amount. **To Apply:** Applicants must check the available website for the required materials. **Contact:** University of California, Berkeley, Alumni House Berkeley, CA 94720-7450 Phone: 1-510-643-2315.

6145 ■ Bruce Wade Memorial Scholarships for Lesbian, Gay and Bisexual *(Undergraduate/Scholarship)*

Purpose: To provide financial assistance for UCI lesbian, gay and bisexual students who contribute in improving the campus environment for other lesbian, gay and bisexual students. **Focus:** General studies. **Qualif.:** Applicants must be enrolled as undergraduate or graduate students at UCI and demonstrate service to the lesbian, gay and bisexual campus community. **Criteria:** Preference will be given to those who meet the criteria.

Funds Avail.: $1,200. **Number Awarded:** 2. **To Apply:** Applicants must check the available website for the required materials. **Deadline:** April. **Contact:** Pat Walsh; UCI Lesbian, Gay, Bisexual Resource Center at University of California, Irvine 106 Gateway Commons Irvine, CA 92697 Phone: 1-714-824-3277.

6146 ■ White Rose Scholarships *(Undergraduate/Scholarship)*

Purpose: To provide financial assistance for LGBT students who are in need. **Focus:** General studies. **Qualif.:** Applicants must demonstrate financial need and must have earned a cumulative of 3.0 GPA. **Criteria:** Priority will be given to students with financial need.

Funds Avail.: No specific amount. **To Apply:** Applicants must check the contact information for inquiries. **Deadline:** January 15. **Contact:** For more information, visit the web site of the Imperial Court of the Rocky Mountain Empire, or write to White Rose Scholarship Foundation, Attn: Scholarship Selection Committee, PO Box 100811, Denver, CO 80250-0811.

6147 ■ Tim Wolfred Scholarships
(Undergraduate/Scholarship)

Purpose: To provide financial assistance for those who are in need. **Focus:** General studies. **Qualif.:** Applicants must be students who are taking at least one class in the Gay, Lesbian and Bisexual Studies Department at City College of San Francisco. **Criteria:** Preference will be given to those who meet the criteria.

Funds Avail.: $50 based on need. **To Apply:** Applicants must check the available website for the required materials. **Contact:** Elaine Mannon, Coordinator, Scholarship Office at City College of San Francisco Batmale Hall, Room 366 50 Phelan Avenue, Box L230 San Francisco, CA 94112 Phone: 1-415-239-3339.

6148 ■ Michael A. Zamperini/W. Clay Burchell Scholarships *(Undergraduate/Scholarship)*

Purpose: To provide financial assistance for a lesbian/gay student beginning his or her final fall semester of law school. **Focus:** Law. **Qualif.:** Applicants must be enrolled at Golden Gate University School of Law. **Criteria:** Preference will be given to those who meet the criteria.

Funds Avail.: The scholarship amount varies, but is typically $1,000 to $2,000. **To Apply:** Applicants must check the available website for the required materials. **Contact:** Golden Gate University School of Law; Financial Aid Office at 536 Mission Street San Francisco, CA 94105 Phone: 1-415-442-6635 Fax: 1-415-442-6609.

6149 ■ Saint Andrew's Society of the State of New York

150 E 55 St., Ste. 3
New York, NY 10022
Ph: (212)223-4248
Fax: (212)223-0748
E-mail: office@standrewsny.org
URL: http://www.standrewsny.org

6150 ■ Saint Andrews Scholarships
(Undergraduate/Scholarship)

Purpose: To promote cultural interchange and goodwill between Scotland and the United States. **Focus:** General studies. **Qualif.:** Applicants must be senior undergraduate students who will obtain a Bachelor's degree from an accredited college or university and who can demonstrate the significance of studying in Scotland; must reside or attend school within 250 miles of New York State. **Criteria:** Recipients are selected based on academic achievement, extracurricular activities, financial need, statement of personal objectives, Scottish descent and proof of citizenship.

Funds Avail.: $20,000. **To Apply:** Applicants must submit application and letters of reference from appropriate professors.

6151 ■ Saint Paul University Canada

223 Main St.
Ottawa, ON, Canada K1S 1C4
Ph: (613)236-1393
Free: 800-637-6859
E-mail: info@ustpaul.ca
URL: http://www.ustpaul.ca

6152 ■ Saint Paul University Excellence Scholarships *(Undergraduate/Scholarship)*

Purpose: To provide educational assistance for the students of Saint Paul University. **Focus:** General studies. **Qualif.:** Program is open to all students in Saint Paul University. **Criteria:** Scholarships are awarded by a committee upon reception of recommended candidacies from the various academic units.

Funds Avail.: $1,000. **Number Awarded:** 8. **To Apply:** Applicants must submit a request for scholarships to a national council. **Deadline:** May 1 and September 30. **Contact:** Saint Paul University at the above address (see entry 6151).

6153 ■ Saint Paul University Financial Aid Bursaries *(Undergraduate/Scholarship)*

Purpose: To provide educational assistance for all students in Saint Paul University. **Focus:** General studies. **Qualif.:** Applicants must be full-time students enrolled in a program of 1st, 2nd and 3rd cycles of Saint Paul University. Bursaries are offered to Canadian citizens, permanent residents and foreign students alike. **Criteria:** Requests are evaluated by a committee according to financial necessity or very special conditions.

Funds Avail.: No specific amount. **To Apply:** Applicants may get an application form six weeks before the deadline at the Scholarships Office or at the Saint Paul University website. **Deadline:** May 1. **Contact:** Saint Paul University Scholarships Office, room 150-A, Guigues Hall.

6154 ■ Sallie Mae Fund

12061 Bluemont Way
Reston, VA 20190
Ph: (703)533-4834
URL: http://www.salliemaefund.org

6155 ■ American Dream Scholarship Program
(Undergraduate/Scholarship)

Purpose: To assist African-American students with financial need. **Focus:** General studies. **Qualif.:** Applicant must be a U.S. citizen; with a GPA of 2.5 on a 4.0 scale; meet the criteria of Pell Grant eligibility; must be enrolled full-time at an accredited, undergraduate institution. **Criteria:** Applicants who will meet the Federal Pell Grant eligibility and demonstrate financial need will be given preference.

Funds Avail.: $500-$5,000. **To Apply:** Applicants must apply online at www.salliemaefund.org. **Deadline:** April 15.

Remarks: In partnership with the United Negro College Fund.

6156 ■ First in My Family Scholarship Program
(Undergraduate/Scholarship)

Purpose: To help finance first in the family Hispanic American students pursue their college education. **Focus:** General studies. **Qualif.:** Applicants must be U.S. citizen Hispanic Americans; have a GPA of 3.0 on a 4.0 scale; must be enrolled as full-time undergraduates at accredited institutions. **Criteria:** Applicants will be selected based on financial need.

Awards are arranged alphabetically below their administering organizations

Funds Avail.: $500-$5,000. **To Apply:** Applicants must mail an official transcript; proof of family income and citizenship status. Submit online: a letter of recommendation; resume; an essay. A Financial Aid Verification is needed for applicants chosen as finalists. **Deadline:** April 15.

Remarks: In partnership with the Hispanic College Fund. **Contact:** Hispanic College Fund 1301 K St. NW, Ste. 450-A West Washington, DC 20005, Telephone: 800-644-4223.

6157 ■ The Sallie Mae 911 Education Fund *(Undergraduate/Scholarship)*

Purpose: To assist in the financial needs of children of the victims of the September 11, 2001 terrorist attack. **Focus:** General studies. **Qualif.:** Applicant must be a dependent of a September 11, 2001 victim; must be enrolled full-time and having a satisfactory academic process at: a Public two years, or a Private/Proprietary two years, or a Public or Public four years. **Criteria:** Applicants are selected based on proof of eligibility and relative financial need.

Funds Avail.: $2,500. **To Apply:** Applicants must complete an application form available at the website (www.salliemaefund.org) and submit to the Financial Aid Director of the applicant's school. Mail completed applications to: The Sallie Mae 911 Educational Fund Scholarship Program c/o The Community foundation for the National Capital Region 1201 15th St. NW, Ste. 420 Washington, DC 20005. **Deadline:** May 15.

6158 ■ Unmet Need Scholarships *(Undergraduate/Scholarship)*

Purpose: To support students with more than $1,000 short of financial need. **Focus:** General studies. **Qualif.:** Applicant must be a U.S. citizen; must have a $30,000 or less family adjusted gross income; have a GPA of 2.5 on a 4.0 scale or minimum 42 GED average test score; a high school senior or graduate or a student enrolled as a full-time undergraduate in an accredited post secondary institution; must demonstrate unmet financial need of at least $1,000 after the financial aid award package has been determined. **Criteria:** Recipients will be selected based on financial need.

Funds Avail.: $1,000-$3,800. **To Apply:** Applicants must complete an application form available at the website www.salliemaefund.org and mail it together with: current, complete transcript of grades (Official transcript of grades; or unofficial transcript that includes that student and school's name; or Student-generated online transcript that includes that student name, school name, grade and credit hours earned for each course, and term in which each course was taken; or GED test score results); Student Aid Report (SAR) or Institutional Student Information Report (ISIR) (Complete SAR Print Summary from the FAFSA website; or student copy of the complete SAR; or school's complete ISIR). The application and all documents must be mailed in one envelope to: Scholarship America The Sallie Mae Fund Unmet Need Scholarship Program One Scholarship Way, PO Box 297 Saint Peter, MN 56082. **Deadline:** May 31. **Contact:** 507-931-1682.

6159 ■ Writers of Passage Scholarship Program *(Undergraduate/Prize)*

Purpose: To focus on the importance of developing good writing skills. **Focus:** General studies. **Qualif.:** Applicant must be an enrolled full-time undergraduate at a Historically Black College or University (HBCU) or Predominantly Black College (PBI); must demonstrate financial need as defined by the applicant's college or university; have a minimum GPA of 2.5 on a 4.0 scale; must have filed the Free Application for Federal Student Aid (FAFSA) at www-.fafsa.ed.gov. **Criteria:** Winners are selected based on the applicants' essays.

Funds Avail.: $5,000 for the recipient and $20,000 grant to the winner's university. **To Apply:** Applicants must complete and submit the application form available at the website www.nafeo.org/home.php; Certification and Authorization Form; "Writers of Passage" essay; transcripts (college transcripts for students who have completed one or more semesters of post-secondary education); copy of complete academic year Student Aid report (SAR). All documents must be in an envelope and mailed to: The "Writers of Passage" Essay Competition National Association for Equal Opportunity in Higher Education (NAFEO) 209 Third Street, SE Washington, DC 20003. **Deadline:** February 1.

Remarks: In partnership with the National Association for Equal Opportunity in Higher Education (NAFEO). **Contact:** Rachel Cooke (202)552-3300 email: rcooke@nafeo.org.

6160 ■ The San Diego Foundation

2508 Historic Decatur Rd., Ste. 200
San Diego, CA 92106
Ph: (619)235-2300
Fax: (619)239-1710
E-mail: info@sdfoundation.org
URL: http://www.sdfoundation.org

6161 ■ 92109 Community Fund-Mark and Karla Stuart Family Scholarships *(Undergraduate/Scholarship)*

Purpose: To support the education of students from California. **Focus:** General studies. **Qualif.:** Applicant must be a resident of San Diego County (military personnel and dependents are exempt); must be a citizen or legal resident of the United States; must attend an accredited two-year college, four-year university or licensed trade and vocational school in the U.S.; must be a full-time student (unless otherwise noted); must have a measure of academic and civic achievement; must be of good moral and personal character; must be a graduate from Mission Bay High School, San Diego, CA; have a minimum 3.0 GPA on a 4.0 scale; and committed in serving the community through involvement in community service, church or extra-curricular activities. **Criteria:** Awards are given based on the application materials.

Funds Avail.: No specific amount. **Number Awarded:** To be determined. **To Apply:** Applicants must submit a completed Common Scholarship Application together with personal statement; two letters of recommendation on official letterhead (written within the last six months); official transcript in an official and sealed envelope; and a copy of 2006 or most recent tax form (Form 1040-pages 1 & 2; Form 1040A-pages 1 & 2; Form 1040EZ-page 1). **Deadline:** January 28. **Contact:** Arzo Mansury, Dir. Scholarships at 619-814-1343, or scholarships@sdfoundation.org.

6162 ■ AeA Scholarships *(Undergraduate/Scholarship)*

Purpose: To support the education of students from California. **Focus:** Mathematics and mathematical sciences; Science; Engineering; Computer and information sciences. **Qualif.:** Applicant must be a resident of San Diego County (military personnel and dependents are exempt); a citizen or legal resident of the United States; at-

Awards are arranged alphabetically below their administering organizations

tend an accredited two-year college, four-year university or licensed trade and vocational school in the U.S.; a full-time student (unless otherwise noted); have a measure of academic and civic achievement; be of good moral and personal character; graduate from a San Diego County public high school; have a minimum 3.75 GPA on a 4.0 scale; and be majoring in math, science, engineering, or computers. **Criteria:** Awards are given based on the application materials.

Funds Avail.: $1000. **Number Awarded:** 2. **To Apply:** Applicants must submit a completed Common Scholarship Application together with personal statement; two letters of recommendation on official letterhead (written within the last six months); official transcript in an official and sealed envelope; copy of 2006 or most recent tax form (Form 1040-pages 1 & 2; Form 1040A-pages 1 & 2; Form 1040EZ-page 1); and an unofficial copy of SAT score results. **Deadline:** January 28. **Contact:** Arzo Mansury, Dir. Scholarships at 619-814-1343, or scholarships@sdfoundation.org.

6163 ■ After-the-Fires Scholarships *(Undergraduate/Scholarship)*

Purpose: To support the education of students from California. **Focus:** General studies. **Qualif.:** Applicant must be a resident of San Diego County (military personnel and dependents are exempt); a citizen or legal resident of the United States; attend an accredited two-year college, four-year university or licensed trade and vocational school in the U.S.; a full-time student (unless otherwise noted); have a measure of academic and civic achievement; be of good moral and personal character; have a minimum 2.50 GPA on a 4.0 scale; demonstrated financial need; and lost homes and/or source of income in the 2007 wildfires. **Criteria:** Awards are given based on the application materials.

Funds Avail.: $500-$2500. **Number Awarded:** To be determined. **To Apply:** Applicants must submit a completed Common Scholarship Application together with personal statement; two letters of recommendation on official letterhead (written within the last six months); official transcript in an official and sealed envelope; copy of most recent tax form (Form 1040-pages 1 & 2; Form 1040A-pages 1 & 2; Form 1040EZ-page 1); and a formal documentation or a letter on official letterhead from FEMA (insurance company), or high school/college guidance counselor/principal indicating the loss of home in the 2007 wildfires and/or a letter from employer indicating loss of income. **Deadline:** January 28. **Contact:** Arzo Mansury, Dir. Scholarships at 619-814-1343, or scholarships@sdfoundation.org

6164 ■ Julie Allen World Classroom Scholarships *(Undergraduate/Scholarship)*

Purpose: To support the education of students from California. **Focus:** International affairs and relations; Business; Economics; Civil rights; Foreign languages. **Qualif.:** Applicant must be an undergraduate student enrolled at the University of San Diego, UC San Diego, or San Diego State University; have a minimum 2.50 GPA on a 4.0 scale; demonstrated financial need; planning to study abroad for a minimum of one semester in a Second or Third World Country whose culture, language and customs are different than their own. **Criteria:** Preference is given to students who are interested in studying in fields such as, but not limited to, international relations, business, economics, social development, humanitarian and civil rights, foreign languages, or other similar fields.

Funds Avail.: $1,000. **Number Awarded:** 1. **To Apply:** Applicants must submit a completed Common Scholarship Application together with personal statement; two letters of recommendation on official letterhead (written within the last six months); official transcript in an official and sealed envelope; copy of most recent tax form (Form 1040-pages 1 & 2; Form 1040A-pages 1 & 2; Form 1040EZ-page 1); and an essay (maximum one page, typed, double-spaced) addressing applicant's reason(s) for studying abroad, or coming to San Diego to pursue an education from the student's native country. **Deadline:** January 28. **Contact:** Arzo Mansury, Dir. Scholarships at 619-814-1343, or scholarships@sdfoundation.org.

6165 ■ Marvin Arnold and Irene Jaquetta Heye Scholarships *(Undergraduate/Scholarship)*

Purpose: To support the education of students from California. **Focus:** Engineering. **Qualif.:** Applicant must be a graduating high school senior planning to attend California Polytechnic State University or current student attending California Polytechnic State University. Student must be majoring in engineering; have a minimum 3.33 grade point average on a 4.0 scale; have a demonstrated financial need; and be actively involved in extra-curricular activities, community service, or work experience. **Criteria:** Preference will be given to the dependents of active military personnel.

Funds Avail.: $17,500. **Number Awarded:** 1. **To Apply:** Applicants may obtain a copy of the Marvin Arnold and Irene Jaquetta Heye Scholarship Application by sending through e-mail the applicant's name and address to scholarships@sdfoundation.org. **Contact:** 619-814-1343 or scholarships@sdfoundation.org.

6166 ■ ARREOLA/CBSPM Scholarships *(Undergraduate/Scholarship)*

Purpose: To support the education of students from California. **Focus:** General studies. **Qualif.:** Applicant must be a graduating senior from Montgomery and Southwest high schools in the Sweetwater Union High School District; have a minimum 3.25 GPA on a 4.0 scale; planning to attend an accredited two-year college, four-year university, or licensed trade/vocational school in the U.S.; have demonstrated financial need and strong commitment to contribute to the community as demonstrated by the involvement in extra-curricular/church activities, or work/volunteer experience. **Criteria:** Preference will be given to students who are ambitious, have shown success and potential in the courses related to their chosen career, and persevere in spite of their obstacles.

Funds Avail.: $1,000. **Number Awarded:** 2. **To Apply:** Applicants must submit a completed Common Scholarship Application together with personal statement; two letters of recommendation on official letterhead (written within the last six months); official transcript in an official and sealed envelope; and a copy of most recent tax form (Form 1040-pages 1 & 2; Form 1040Apages 1 & 2; Form 1040EZ-page 1). **Deadline:** January 28. **Contact:** Arzo Mansury, Dir. Scholarships at 619-814-1343, or scholarships@sdfoundation.org.

6167 ■ William and Lucille Ash Scholarships *(Undergraduate/Scholarship)*

Purpose: To support the education of students from California. **Focus:** General studies. **Qualif.:** Applicant must be an adult re-entry student; have a minimum 3.0 GPA on a 4.0 scale; demonstrated financial need; planning to attend an accredited two-year college, four-year university, or licensed trade/vocational school in the state of California; and employed (minimum part-time) and involved in serving the community as demonstrated by involvement in extra-curricular activities, community/church service, or work experience. **Criteria:** Special consideration will be given to individuals who have been in foster care.

Funds Avail.: $1,000-$5,000. **Number Awarded:** 3. **To Apply:** Applicants must submit a completed Common Scholarship Application together with personal statement; two letters of recommendation on official letterhead (written within the last six months); official transcript in an official and sealed envelope; a copy of most recent tax form (Form 1040-pages 1 & 2; Form 1040A-pages 1 & 2; Form 1040EZ-page 1); a letter from the applicant's workplace supervisor, on official letterhead, verifying employment, either part-time or full-time (letter must title, job responsibilities, and the length of time have been employed). If the applicant have been in the foster care system, include a letter of recommendation from social worker indicating that the applicant have been in foster care. **Deadline:** January 28. **Contact:** Arzo Mansury, Dir. Scholarships at 619-814-1343, or scholarships@sdfoundation.org.

6168 ■ Frank H. Ault Scholarships
(Undergraduate/Scholarship)

Purpose: To support the education of students from California. **Focus:** Accounting. **Qualif.:** Applicant must be a graduating high school student or junior college student; planning to major in accounting or finance at an accredited four-year university; or a current college student (sophomore, junior, or senior year) have declared a major in finance or accounting. Students must minimum 3.0 GPA on a 4.0 scale; and have participated in extra-curricular or community service activities. **Criteria:** Preference will be given to students who are active members of or have taken leadership in their school's accounting society.

Funds Avail.: $1,500 each. **Number Awarded:** 6. **To Apply:** Applicants must submit a completed Common Scholarship Application together with personal statement; two letters of recommendation on official letterhead (written within the last six months); official transcript in an official and sealed envelope; and copy of most recent tax form (Form 1040-pages 1 & 2; Form 1040A-pages 1 & 2; Form 1040EZ-page 1). **Deadline:** January 28. **Contact:** Arzo Mansury, Dir. Scholarships at 619-814-1343, or scholarships@sdfoundation.org.

6169 ■ Ballard Family Foundation Scholarships
(Undergraduate/Scholarship)

Purpose: To support the education of students from California. **Focus:** General studies. **Qualif.:** Applicant must be a student between the ages of 17-25; have been in foster care; have demonstrated financial need; have a minimum high school GPA of 2.50 on a 4.0 scale or a 2.75 college GPA on a 4.0 scale; and be attending an accredited four-year university, two-year college or licensed trade/vocational school in the U.S. **Criteria:** Special consideration will be given to African-American students.

Funds Avail.: $1000. **Number Awarded:** 4. **To Apply:** Applicants must submit a completed Common Scholarship Application together with personal statement; two letters of recommendation on official letterhead (written within the last six months); official transcript in an official and sealed envelope; and a letter of recommendation from the applicant's social worker indicating the applicant is or has been in foster care. **Deadline:** January 28. **Contact:** Arzo Mansury, Dir. Scholarships at 619-814-1343, or scholarships@sdfoundation.org.

6170 ■ Barta-Lehman Musical Scholarships
(Undergraduate/Scholarship)

Purpose: To support the education of students from California. **Focus:** Music. **Qualif.:** Applicant must be a graduating high school senior, or current undergraduate or graduate college student; must be a serious and talented musician; planning to pursue a career in music and/or play professionally (string instruments preferred); have a minimum 3.0 GPA on a 4.0 scale; and planning to attend an accredited four-year university or music academy in the U.S. **Criteria:** Awards are given based on the application materials.

Funds Avail.: $2,000. **Number Awarded:** 4. **To Apply:** Applicants must submit a completed Common Scholarship Application together with personal statement; two letters of recommendation on official letterhead (written within the last six months); official transcript in an official and sealed envelope; copy of most recent tax form (Form 1040-pages 1 & 2; Form 1040A-pages 1 & 2; Form 1040EZ -page 1); a letter of recommendation on letterhead must come from a music teacher indicating level of talent and seriousness about pursuing music as a career; and a CD or video of the applicant's music. **Deadline:** January 28. **Contact:** Arzo Mansury, Dir. Scholarships at 619-814-1343, or scholarships@sdfoundation.org.

6171 ■ Ray and Mary Bell Memorial Scholarships *(Undergraduate/Scholarship)*

Purpose: To support the education of students from California. **Focus:** General studies. **Qualif.:** Applicant must be a graduating high school senior from Fallbrook High School in Fallbrook, CA; will attend an accredited two-year college or four-year university in the U.S; have a minimum 3.0 GPA on a 4.0 scale; and have a commitment to serving the community through involvement in community service, church or extra-curricular activities. **Criteria:** Awards are given based on the application materials.

Funds Avail.: $1,000. **Number Awarded:** 1. **To Apply:** Applicants must submit a completed Common Scholarship Application together with personal statement; two letters of recommendation on official letterhead (written within the last six months); official transcript in an official and sealed envelope; and a copy of most recent tax form (Form 1040-pages 1 & 2; Form 1040A-pages 1 & 2; Form 1040EZ-page 1); and an essay (maximum one page, typed, double-spaced) describing the world the applicant came from. **Deadline:** January 28. **Contact:** Arzo Mansury, Dir. Scholarships at 619-814-1343, or scholarships@sdfoundation.org.

6172 ■ James R. and Geraldine F. Bertelsen Scholarships *(Undergraduate/Scholarship)*

Purpose: To support the education of students from California. **Focus:** General studies. **Qualif.:** Applicant must be a practicing Roman Catholic who is: a graduating high school senior who has applied to, been accepted by, and will attend a four-year Roman Catholic college/university in the U.S.; or a student currently enrolled at a Catholic college/university in the U.S. Student must be resident of Carlsbad, CA for a minimum of one full year and be enrolling in or currently be enrolled in a course of instruction that will enable to obtain an undergraduate degree within four years. Student in senior year of college, who will graduate early and not complete a full academic year, are not eligible. **Criteria:** Award is given based on achievement with need being a secondary consideration.

Funds Avail.: Minimum of $5,000. **Number Awarded:** 3. **To Apply:** Applicants must submit a completed Common Scholarship Application together with personal statement; two letters of recommendation on official letterhead (written within the last six months); official transcript in an official and sealed envelope; copy of 2006 or most recent taxes (Form 1040-pages 1 & 2; Form 1040A-pages 1 & 2; Form 1040EZ -page 1); a letter of recommendation on official letterhead from the applicant's parish priest, deacon or other church official who can verify the applicant is a practicing Catholic; and a form verifying Carlsbad residency for each period of 2006 and 2007, or 2007 and 2008 (utility bills, insurance forms, etc.). **Deadline:** January 28. **Contact:** Arzo Mansury, Dir. Scholarships at 619-814-1343, or scholarships@sdfoundation.org.

6173 ■ Biocom Scholarships *(Undergraduate/Scholarship)*

Purpose: To support the education of students from California. **Focus:** Biology; Chemistry; Biomedical engineering. **Qualif.:** Applicant must be a graduating high school senior with a minimum 3.50 GPA on a 4.0 scale; planning to attend an accredited two-year college or four-year university in the U.S.; must demonstrate a likelihood of achieving academic success with primary emphasis in biology, chemistry, physical and computational biosciences or biomedical engineering; committed in serving San Diego life sciences community; maintain a minimum 3.20 cumulative GPA on a 4.0 scale while in college; and exhibit the traits modeled by BIOCOM co-founder, James McGraw (leadership, passion for life sciences, integrity, and community service). **Criteria:** Awards are given based on the application materials.

Funds Avail.: $1,500. **Number Awarded:** 5. **To Apply:** Applicants must submit a completed Common Scholarship Application together with personal statement; two letters of recommendation on official letterhead (written within the last six months); official transcript in an official and sealed envelope; and copy of most recent tax form (Form 1040-pages 1 & 2; Form 1040A-pages 1 & 2; Form 1040EZ-page 1). **Deadline:** January 28.

Remarks: In memory of James McGraw. **Contact:** Arzo Mansury, Dir. Scholarships at 619-814-1343, or scholarships@sdfoundation.org.

6174 ■ Dorothy M. Bolyard Memorial Scholarships *(Undergraduate/Scholarship)*

Purpose: To support the education of students from California. **Focus:** General studies. **Qualif.:** Applicant must be a San Diego resident (age 25 years and older); pursuing a degree at an accredited two-year college or four-year university in San Diego County; have a minimum 3.0 GPA on a 4.0 scale; and demonstrated financial need. **Criteria:** Preference is given to applicants who have a record of involvement in their community as demonstrated by their extra-curricular activities, community or church service, or work experience.

Funds Avail.: $1,000. **Number Awarded:** 5. **To Apply:** Applicants must submit a completed Common Scholarship Application together with personal statement; two letters of recommendation on official letterhead (written within the last six months); official transcript in an official and sealed envelope; and copy of most recent tax form (Form 1040-pages 1 & 2; Form 1040A-pages 1 & 2; Form 1040EZ-page 1). **Deadline:** January 28. **Contact:** Arzo Mansury, Dir. Scholarships at 619-814-1343, or scholarships@sdfoundation.org.

6175 ■ Breslauer Family Scholarships *(Undergraduate/Scholarship)*

Purpose: To support the education of students from California. **Focus:** General studies. **Qualif.:** Applicant must be a graduating senior from San Diego High School in downtown San Diego; have a minimum 3.0 GPA on a 4.0 scale; demonstrated financial needs; planning to attend an accredited four-year university in the U.S. **Criteria:** Awards are given based on the application materials.

Funds Avail.: $500-$750. **Number Awarded:** 4. **To Apply:** Applicants must submit a completed Common Scholarship Application together with personal statement; two letters of recommendation on official letterhead (written within the last six months); official transcript in an official and sealed envelope; and copy of 2006 or most recent tax form (Form 1040-pages 1 & 2; Form 1040A-pages 1 & 2; Form 1040EZ-page 1). **Deadline:** January 28. **Contact:** Arzo Mansury, Dir. Scholarships at 619-814-1343, or scholarships@sdfoundation.org.

6176 ■ Louise A. Broderick San Diego County Scholarships *(Undergraduate/Scholarship)*

Purpose: To support the education of students from California. **Focus:** General studies. **Qualif.:** Applicant must be a single parent with dependent children who are re-entering college or are already in college. Applicants must have a minimum 2.0 GPA on a 4.0 scale; demonstrated financial need; and plan to attend a two-year community college, four-year university, or trade and vocational school. **Criteria:** Award is given based on the application materials.

Funds Avail.: $2,000. **Number Awarded:** 2. **To Apply:** Applicants must submit a completed Common Scholarship Application together with personal statement; two letters of recommendation on official letterhead (written within the last six months); official transcript in an official and sealed envelope; and a copy of most recent tax form (Form 1040-pages 1 & 2; Form 1040A-pages 1 & 2; Form 1040EZ-page 1). **Deadline:** January 28. **Contact:** Arzo Mansury, Dir. Scholarships at 619-814-1343, or scholarships@sdfoundation.org.

6177 ■ California Association of Family and Consumer Sciences (CAFCS)-San Diego Chapter Scholarships *(Graduate, Undergraduate/Scholarship)*

Purpose: To support the education of students from California. **Focus:** Food science and technology; Diabetes; Nutrition; Food service careers; Home Economics; Fashion design; Textile science; Housing; Management. **Qualif.:** Applicant must be a graduating high school senior, current college student, or graduate student majoring in Food Sciences; Dietetics; Nutrition; Food Services; Hospitality; Human, Child and Family Development; Apparel, Fashion and Textile Services; Housing and Interiors; Consumer Economics; Management and Resources; or Family and Consumer Science Education. Student must have a minimum 2.50 GPA on a 4.0 scale; planning to attend an accredited two-year college, four-year university, or licensed trade-vocational school in the U.S. Undergraduate student must be enrolled in school full-time (12 units per semester or 9 per quarter). Graduate student may be enrolled full-time or part-time with awards allocated appropriately based upon enrollment units. **Criteria:** Awards are given based on the application materials.

Funds Avail.: To be determined. **Number Awarded:** To be determined. **To Apply:** Applicants must submit a completed

Common Scholarship Application together with personal statement; two letters of recommendation on official letterhead (written within the last six months); official transcript in an official and sealed envelope; copy of 2006 or most recent tax form (Form 1040-pages 1 & 2; Form 1040A-pages 1 & 2; Form 1040EZ -page 1); and a letter of recommendation on official letterhead from an instructor or professional indicating the applicant's interest in pursing one of the above listed fields. **Deadline:** January 28. **Contact:** Arzo Mansury, Dir. Scholarships at 619-814-1343, or scholarships@sdfoundation.org.

6178 ■ Cheerful Giver Scholarships
(Undergraduate/Scholarship)

Purpose: To support the education of students from California. **Focus:** General studies. **Qualif.:** Applicant must be a graduating high school senior, a child of a single parent; or a child of parents who serve the community (pastor, church staff, teacher/educator, police officer, firefighter, military, etc.). Students must have a minimum 2.0 GPA and plan to attend an accredited four-year university in the U.S. **Criteria:** Award is given based on the application materials.

Funds Avail.: No specific amount. **To Apply:** Applicants must submit a completed Scholarship Application together with a typed personal statement (maximum of two pages); a copy of transcripts; and a copy of most recent tax form (Form 1040-pages 1 & 2; Form 1040A-pages 1 & 2; Form 1040EZpage 1). **Deadline:** March 10. **Contact:** scholarships@sdfoundation.org.

6179 ■ The Club at Morningside Scholarships
(Undergraduate/Scholarship)

Purpose: To support the education of students from California. **Focus:** General studies. **Qualif.:** Applicant must be a graduating high school senior, student already in college, or planning to attend an accredited two-year college, four-year university, graduate school, or licensed trade/vocational school in the U.S. High school senior and student currently enrolled in school must have a cumulative GPA of 2.50 or higher on a 4.0 scale. **Criteria:** Award is given based on the application materials.

Funds Avail.: No specific amount. **To Apply:** Applicants must submit a completed Scholarship Application together with a typed personal statement (maximum of two pages); two letters or recommendation on official letterhead; official transcripts in a sealed envelope; a copy of most recent tax form (Form 1040-pages 1 & 2; Form 1040A-pages 1 & 2; Form 1040EZ-page 1); and a letter verifying the applicants or applicant's parent(s) are employed by The Club at Morningside. **Deadline:** January 28. **Contact:** Arzo Mansury, Dir. Scholarships at 619-814-1343, or scholarships@sdfoundation.org.

6180 ■ Madison and Edith Cooper Scholarships
(Undergraduate/Scholarship)

Purpose: To support the education of students from California. **Focus:** General studies. **Qualif.:** Applicant must be young adult in San Diego County (to age 24); have been in the foster care system; planning to attend an accredited two-year college, four-year university, or licensed trade/vocational school in the U.S.; have a minimum 2.50 GPA on a 4.0 scale; demonstrated financial need; and involved in serving the community through extra-curricular activities, community service, or work experience. **Criteria:** Awards are given based on the application materials.

Funds Avail.: $1,000. **Number Awarded:** 10. **To Apply:** Applicants must submit a completed Common Scholarship Application together with personal statement; two letters of recommendation on official letterhead (written within the last six months); official transcript in an official and sealed envelope; a copy of most recent tax form (Form 1040-pages 1 & 2; Form 1040A-pages 1 & 2; Form 1040EZ-page 1); and a letter of recommendation on official letterhead from a social worker indicating that the applicant have been in foster care. **Deadline:** January 28. **Contact:** Arzo Mansury, Dir. Scholarships at 619-814-1343, or scholarships@sdfoundation.org.

6181 ■ Crawford Scholarships *(Undergraduate/Scholarship)*

Purpose: To support the education of students from California. **Focus:** General studies. **Qualif.:** Applicant must be a graduating senior from the Crawford Educational Complex; have a minimum 2.50 GPA on a 4.0 scale; planning to attend an accredited two-year college or four-year university in the U.S.; have demonstrated financial need; and engaged in the community through involvement in extra-curricular/church/volunteer activities or work experience. **Criteria:** Awards are given based on the application materials.

Funds Avail.: $4,000 each. **Number Awarded:** 12. **To Apply:** Applicants must submit a completed Common Scholarship Application together with personal statement; two letters of recommendation on official letterhead (written within the last six months); official transcript in an official and sealed envelope; and copy of 2006 or most recent tax form (Form 1040-pages 1 & 2; Form 1040A-pages 1 & 2; Form 1040EZ-page 1). **Deadline:** January 28. **Contact:** Arzo Mansury, Dir. Scholarships at 619-814-1343, or scholarships@sdfoundation.org.

6182 ■ Daddy Longlegs Scholarships
(Undergraduate/Scholarship)

Purpose: To support the education of students from California. **Focus:** General studies. **Qualif.:** Applicant must be a young adult in San Diego County (to age 25) who have been in foster care; planning to attend an accredited two-year college, four-year university, or licensed trade/vocational school in the U.S.; have a minimum 2.0 GPA on a 4.0 scale; and demonstrated financial need. **Criteria:** Awards are given based on the application materials.

Funds Avail.: $500-$2,000. **Number Awarded:** 4. **To Apply:** Applicants must submit a completed Common Scholarship Application together with personal statement; two letters of recommendation on official letterhead (written within the last six months); official transcript in an official and sealed envelope; copy of most recent tax form (Form 1040-pages 1 & 2; Form 1040A-pages 1 & 2; Form 1040EZ-page 1); and a letter of recommendation on official letterhead from the applicant's social worker indicating he/she is currently or has been in the foster care system. **Deadline:** January 28. **Contact:** Arzo Mansury, Dir. Scholarships at 619-814-1343, or scholarships@sdfoundation.org.

6183 ■ Davis Family Scholarships
(Undergraduate/Scholarship)

Purpose: To support the education of students from California. **Focus:** General studies. **Qualif.:** Applicant must be a graduating Latino high school senior from a San Diego County public school; planning to attend an accredited four-year public university in the state of California; have demonstrated financial need; and have an unweighted GPA between 3.00 to 3.50 GPA on a 4.0 scale. **Criteria:** Special consideration will be given to applicants who are committed to their communities through their involvement in community service, extra-curricular activities and/or work experience.

Funds Avail.: $1,000. **Number Awarded:** 3. **To Apply:** Applicants must submit a completed Common Scholarship Application together with personal statement; two letters of recommendation on official letterhead (written within the last six months); official transcript in an official and sealed envelope; and copy of 2006 or most recent tax (Form 1040-pages 1 & 2; Form 1040A-pages 1 & 2; Form 1040EZ-page 1). **Deadline:** January 28. **Contact:** Arzo Mansury, Dir. Scholarships at 619-814-1343, or scholarships@sdfoundation.org.

6184 ■ Ruth DeMoss Scholarships
(Undergraduate/Scholarship)

Purpose: To support the education of students from California. **Focus:** General studies. **Qualif.:** Applicant must be an African-American, Native American, or Latino student currently attending an accredited two-year college in San Diego County and will transfer to a four-year university in San Diego County. Student must have a minimum 2.50 GPA on a 4.0 scale; have demonstrated financial need, and a commitment to the community as shown by leadership and volunteer activities. **Criteria:** Award is given based on the application materials.

Funds Avail.: $1,000. **Number Awarded:** 1. **To Apply:** Applicants must submit a completed Common Scholarship Application together with personal statement; two letters of recommendation on official letterhead (written within the last six months); official transcript in an official and sealed envelope; a copy of most recent tax form (Form 1040-pages 1 & 2; Form 1040A-pages 1 & 2; Form 1040EZ-page 1); and a letter of acceptance on official letterhead from the four-year university in San Diego County to which he/she will be transferring upon receipt of this scholarship. **Deadline:** January 28. **Contact:** Arzo Mansury, Dir. Scholarships at 619-814-1343, or scholarships@sdfoundation.org.

6185 ■ Herman H. Derksen Scholarships
(Undergraduate/Scholarship)

Purpose: To support the education of students from California. **Focus:** General studies. **Qualif.:** Applicant must be a San Diego resident pursuing a trade or vocation; will attend an accredited two-year college or licensed trade/vocational school in San Diego County; have a minimum 2.0 GPA on a 4.0 scale; and demonstrated financial need. **Criteria:** Special consideration is given to applicants who have a record of involvement in their community as demonstrated by their extra-curricular activities, community or church service, or work experience.

Funds Avail.: $2,000. **Number Awarded:** 4. **To Apply:** Applicants must submit a completed Common Scholarship Application together with personal statement; two letters of recommendation on official letterhead (written within the last six months); official transcript in an official and sealed envelope; copy of most recent tax form (Form 1040-pages 1 & 2; Form 1040A-pages 1 & 2; Form 1040EZ-page 1); and an essay (maximum one page, typed, double spaced) detailing applicant's reasons for, and interest in, pursuing a vocational education. **Deadline:** January 28. **Contact:** Arzo Mansury, Dir. Scholarships at 619-814-1343, or scholarships@sdfoundation.org.

6186 ■ Hans H. and Margaret B. Doe Scholarships *(Graduate, Undergraduate/Scholarship)*

Purpose: To support the education of students from California. **Focus:** General studies. **Qualif.:** Applicant must be a biological, adopted or stepchild of an employee at the Vista Irrigation District. Student may attend a trade/vocational school, two-year college, four-year university or graduate school, including medical and law. **Criteria:** Award is given based on academic achievement, financial need, extra-curricular activities/work experience, demonstrated leadership, good citizenship, and potential for future development.

Funds Avail.: Covers the entire cost of college. **To Apply:** Applicants must contact The San Diego Foundation for obtaining the application form and guidelines. **Deadline:** March 10. **Contact:** 619-814-1343 or scholarships@sdfoundation.org.

6187 ■ Dokmo Family Scholarships
(Undergraduate/Scholarship)

Purpose: To support the education of students from California. **Focus:** General studies. **Qualif.:** Applicant must be a graduating senior attending a high school in the Poway Unified School District; planning to attend an accredited two-year college or four-year university in San Diego County; have an unweighted GPA of 2.50 on a 4.0 scale; have demonstrated financial need; and actively involved in serving the community through involvement in extra-curricular activities, community and church service, or work experience. **Criteria:** Awards are given based on the application materials.

Funds Avail.: $1,000 each. **Number Awarded:** 5. **To Apply:** Applicants must submit a completed Common Scholarship Application together with personal statement; two letters of recommendation on official letterhead (written within the last six months); official transcript in an official and sealed envelope; copy of most recent tax form (Form 1040-pages 1 & 2; Form 1040A-pages 1 & 2; Form 1040EZ -page 1); and a form verifying residency in Rancho Bernardo or Poway from for each period of 2004, 2005, 2006 and 2007, or 2005, 2006, 2007 and 2008 (phone/utility bills or property tax information). **Deadline:** January 28. **Contact:** Arzo Mansury, Dir. Scholarships at 619-814-1343, or scholarships@sdfoundation.org.

6188 ■ Drinkwater Family Scholarships
(Undergraduate/Scholarship)

Purpose: To support the education of students from California. **Focus:** General studies. **Qualif.:** Applicant must be a graduating high school senior; the first in the family to attend an accredited four-year university in the U.S.; have a minimum unweighted GPA of 3.25 on a 4.0 scale; demonstrated financial need; and actively involved in serving the community as shown by participation in extra-curricular, church activities, or community service. **Criteria:** Awards are given based on the application materials.

Funds Avail.: $1,000. **Number Awarded:** 4. **To Apply:** Applicants must submit a completed Common Scholarship Application together with personal statement; two letters of recommendation on official letterhead (written within the last six months); official transcript in an official and sealed envelope; copy of 2006 or most recent tax form (Form 1040-pages 1 & 2; Form 1040A-pages 1 & 2; Form 1040EZ -page 1); and a letter of recommendation from the applicant's high school counselor indicating he/she is the first person in his/her family to attend college. **Deadline:** January 28. **Contact:** Arzo Mansury, Dir. Scholarships at 619-814-1343, or scholarships@sdfoundation.org.

6189 ■ Reuben H. Fleet Memorial Scholarships
(Undergraduate/Scholarship)

Purpose: To support the education of students from California. **Focus:** Science; Engineering; Mathematics and mathematical sciences. **Qualif.:** Applicant must be a college student pursuing an undergraduate degree in science, engineering or math. Students must have completed 54 semester units or 72 quarter units; maintained a minimum 3.0 GPA on a 4.0 scale; enrolled at a four-year university in San Diego County; or be a San Diego County resident attending a four-year university in the U.S. **Criteria:** Awards are given based on the application materials.

Funds Avail.: $5,000. **Number Awarded:** 3. **To Apply:** Applicants must submit a completed Common Scholarship Application together with personal statement; two letters of recommendation on official letterhead (written within the last six months); official transcript in an official and sealed envelope; and a copy of most recent tax form (Form 1040-pages 1 & 2; Form 1040A-pages 1 & 2; Form 1040EZ-page 1). If attending a two-year college, applicants must submit a letter of acceptance on official letterhead from the four-year university which the applicant will be transferring. **Deadline:** January 28. **Contact:** Arzo Mansury, Dir. Scholarships at 619-814-1343, or scholarships@sdfoundation.org.

6190 ■ Jonathan Hastings Foster Scholarships
(Undergraduate/Scholarship)

Purpose: To support the education of students from California. **Focus:** Teaching. **Qualif.:** Applicant must be a graduating senior from Point Loma High School; or current San Diego State University student pursuing a career in teaching; must have a minimum 3.50 GPA on a 4.0 scale; and attending an accredited four-year university in the United States. **Criteria:** Consideration will be given to applicants who are actively involved in their community, as demonstrated by their involvement in extra-curricular activities, community service, and/or work experience.

Funds Avail.: $1,500. **Number Awarded:** 1. **To Apply:** Applicants must submit a completed Common Scholarship Application together with personal statement; two letters of recommendation on official letterhead (written within the last six months); official transcript in an official and sealed envelope; and a copy of most recent tax form (Form 1040-pages 1 & 2; Form 1040A-pages 1 & 2; Form 1040EZ-page 1). **Deadline:** January 28. **Contact:** Arzo Mansury, Dir. Scholarships at 619-814-1343, or scholarships@sdfoundation.org.

6191 ■ Leslie Jane Hahn Memorial Scholarships
(Undergraduate/Scholarship)

Purpose: To support the education of students from California. **Focus:** General studies. **Qualif.:** Applicant must be a graduating high school senior girl from a public school; attending an accredited four-year college/university in the U.S.; have at least a 3.75 GPA on a 4.0 scale; demonstrated financial need; and have a history of active involvement in athletics, other extracurricular activities, community service or work experience. **Criteria:** Preference will be given to applicants who most closely embody Jane's qualities and reflect her background described above.

Funds Avail.: $3,000. **Number Awarded:** 1. **To Apply:** Applicants must submit a completed Common Scholarship Application together with personal statement; two letters of recommendation on official letterhead (written within the last six months); official transcript in an official and sealed envelope; and a copy of most recent tax form (Form 1040-pages 1 & 2; Form 1040A-pages 1 & 2; Form 1040EZ-page 1). **Deadline:** January 28. **Contact:** Arzo Mansury, Dir. Scholarships at 619-814-1343, or scholarships@sdfoundation.org.

6192 ■ Helm Family Scholarships
(Undergraduate/Scholarship)

Purpose: To support the education of students from California. **Focus:** Biology; Computer and information sciences; Chemistry; Technology; Engineering; Physics. **Qualif.:** Applicant must be an entering junior or senior student at San Diego State University or the University of California, San Diego; have declared a major in mathematics or a scientific field such as, but not limited to, biology, computer science, chemistry, technology, engineering, physics, etc.; have a minimum 3.0 GPA on a 4.0 scale; and have demonstrated financial need. **Criteria:** Consideration will be given to students who are employed or have participated in extra-curricular activities or community service.

Funds Avail.: $5,00. **Number Awarded:** 2. **To Apply:** Applicants must submit a completed Common Scholarship Application together with personal statement; two letters of recommendation on official letterhead (written within the last six months); official transcript in an official and sealed envelope; and a copy of most recent tax form (Form 1040-pages 1 & 2; Form 1040Apages 1 & 2; Form 1040EZ-page 1). **Deadline:** January 28. **Contact:** Arzo Mansury, Dir. Scholarships at 619-814-1343, or scholarships@sdfoundation.org.

6193 ■ Doris Hendren Memorial Scholarships
(Undergraduate/Scholarship)

Purpose: To support the education of students from California. **Focus:** Liberal arts. **Qualif.:** Applicant must be a student attending an accredited two-year college or four-year university in San Diego County; pursuing a degree in a field of liberal arts; have a minimum 3.0 GPA on a 4.0 scale; demonstrated financial need; have commitment to the San Diego community through work experience, community, church, or school activities. **Criteria:** Awards are given based on the application materials.

Funds Avail.: $1,000. **Number Awarded:** 5. **To Apply:** Applicants must submit a completed Common Scholarship Application together with personal statement; two letters of recommendation on official letterhead (written within the last six months); official transcript in an official and sealed envelope; and copy of most recent tax form (Form 1040-pages 1 & 2; Form 1040A-pages 1 & 2; Form 1040EZ-page 1). **Deadline:** January 28. **Contact:** Arzo Mansury, Dir. Scholarships at 619-814-1343, or scholarships@sdfoundation.org.

6194 ■ Albert W. and Mildred Hubbard Scholarships *(Undergraduate/Scholarship)*

Purpose: To support the education of students from California. **Focus:** General studies. **Qualif.:** Applicant must be a graduating senior attending high school in Escondido or Valley Center; a resident of Escondido or Valley Center already in college; or a student currently attending the San Pasqual Academy in Escondido, CA. Applicant must have a minimum 2.50 GPA on a 4.0 scale; a resident of Escondido, CA or Valley Center, CA for the past four years (excluding students attending San Pasqual Academy); have demonstrated financial need; and plan to attend an accredited two-year college or four-year university in the U.S. **Criteria:** Awards are given based on the application materials.

Funds Avail.: May be the actual amount of tuition charged by the respective college/university, but no more than the actual amount of tuition charged by the University of California system. **Number Awarded:** 8. **To Apply:** Applicants must submit a completed Common Scholarship

Application together with personal statement; two letters of recommendation on official letterhead (written within the last six months); official transcript in an official and sealed envelope; copy of most recent tax form (Form 1040-pages 1 & 2; Form 1040A-pages 1 & 2; Form 1040EZ-page 1); and any form verifying residency in Escondido or Valley Center for each period of 2004, 2005, 2006, and 2007, or 2005, 2006, 2007 and 2008 (i.e. bank statements, utility bills, insurance forms, etc.). **Deadline:** January 28. **Contact:** Arzo Mansury, Dir. Scholarships at 619-814-1343, or scholarships@sdfoundation.org.

6195 ■ Frederick George James Memorial Scholarships *(Undergraduate/Scholarship)*

Purpose: To support the education of students from California. **Focus:** Law enforcement. **Qualif.:** Applicant must be a graduating senior from Sweetwater Union High School, located in National City, CA; a exemplary member of the National City Police Department Explorer Post No. 2859; have a minimum 2.85 GPA on a 4.0 scale; and have demonstrated a strong desire to achieve a degree in Police Science at an accredited two-year college or four-year university in the U.S. **Criteria:** Award is given based on the application materials.

Funds Avail.: $500. **Number Awarded:** 1. **To Apply:** Applicants must submit a completed Common Scholarship Application together with personal statement; two letters of recommendation on official letterhead (written within the last six months); official transcript in an official and sealed envelope; copy of most recent tax form (Form 1040-pages 1 & 2; Form 1040A-pages 1 & 2; Form 1040EZ-page 1); a letter of recommendation from a Sweetwater High School administrator or academic teacher; and another letter of recommendation from an officer affiliated with the National City Police Department Explorers Program. **Deadline:** January 28.

Remarks: Letters must be on official letterhead written within the last six months. **Contact:** Arzo Mansury, Dir. Scholarships at 619-814-1343, or scholarships@sdfoundation.org.

6196 ■ Ruth E. Jenkins Scholarships *(Undergraduate/Scholarship)*

Purpose: To support the education of students from California. **Focus:** General studies. **Qualif.:** Applicant must be a graduating African-American high school senior from San Diego County attending an accredited four-year university in the U.S. Student must have a 3.0 GPA on a 4.0 scale; have demonstrated financial need; and be involved in serving the communities through extra-curricular activities, work, church, or community service. **Criteria:** Preference is given to applicants who will attend a historically African-American college or university.

Funds Avail.: $1,000. **Number Awarded:** 1. **To Apply:** Applicants must submit a completed Common Scholarship Application together with personal statement; two letters of recommendation on official letterhead (written within the last six months); official transcript in an official and sealed envelope; and a copy of most recent tax form (Form 1040-pages 1 & 2; Form 1040A-pages 1 & 2; Form 1040EZ-page 1). **Deadline:** January 28. **Contact:** Arzo Mansury, Dir. Scholarships at 619-814-1343, or scholarships@sdfoundation.org.

6197 ■ Napoleon A. Jones, III Memorial Scholarships *(Undergraduate/Scholarship)*

Purpose: To support the education of students from California. **Focus:** General studies. **Qualif.:** Applicant must be a graduating high school senior residing within the zip codes of 92113, 92114, and 92115; or a graduating senior attending one of the following public high schools: Crawford, Hoover, Lincoln, Morse, San Diego High (located in downtown San Diego), and School for the Creative and Performing Arts. Student must have a minimum 3.0 GPA on a 4.0 scale; planning to attend an accredited four-year university in the U.S.; have financial need; and engaged in serving the community as demonstrated by involvement in extra-curricular, work, church, or volunteer activities. **Criteria:** Award is given based on the application materials.

Funds Avail.: $2,000-$3,000. **Number Awarded:** 1. **To Apply:** Applicants must submit a completed Common Scholarship Application together with personal statement; two letters of recommendation on official letterhead (written within the last six months); official transcript in an official and sealed envelope; and a copy of most recent tax form (Form 1040-pages 1 & 2; Form 1040A-pages 1 & 2; Form 1040EZ-page 1). **Deadline:** January 28. **Contact:** Arzo Mansury, Dir. Scholarships at 619-814-1343, or scholarships@sdfoundation.org.

6198 ■ Kawano Family Scholarships *(Undergraduate/Scholarship)*

Purpose: To support the education of students from California. **Focus:** General studies. **Qualif.:** Applicant must be a student from San Diego County who have arthritis or have an immediate family member affected by arthritis, which impacts the applicant on a daily basis. Student must have a minimum 3.0 GPA on a 4.0 scale; demonstrated financial need; and planning to attend, or attending an accredited four-year university in the U.S. **Criteria:** Awards are given based on the application materials.

Funds Avail.: $1,000-$2,000. **Number Awarded:** 1-2. **To Apply:** Applicants must submit a completed Common Scholarship Application together with personal statement; two letters of recommendation on official letterhead (written within the last six months); official transcript in an official and sealed envelope; and a copy of most recent tax form (Form 1040-pages 1 & 2; Form 1040A-pages 1 & 2; Form 1040EZ-page 1); and an essay (maximum of two pagess, typed, double-spaced) clearly addressing who has arthritis and how life has been affected by it. **Deadline:** January 28. **Contact:** Arzo Mansury, Dir. Scholarships at 619-814-1343, or scholarships@sdfoundation.org.

6199 ■ Kiwanis Club of Escondido Scholarships I *(Undergraduate/Scholarship)*

Purpose: To support the education of students from California. **Focus:** General studies. **Qualif.:** Applicant must be a graduating high school senior in the Escondido High School District; planning to attend an accredited four-year university in the U.S.; have a minimum 3.0 GPA on a 4.0 scale; an active member of a Key Club (sponsored by an Escondido Kiwanis Club); have demonstrated financial need; and be actively involved in serving the community through involvement in extra-curricular activities, community service, sports, or work experience. **Criteria:** Awards are given based on the application materials.

Funds Avail.: $1,000. **Number Awarded:** 2. **To Apply:** Applicants must submit a completed Common Scholarship Application together with personal statement; two letters of recommendation on official letterhead (written within the last six months); official transcript in an official and sealed envelope; a copy of most recent tax form (Form 1040-pages 1 & 2; Form 1040A-pages 1 & 2; Form 1040EZ-page 1); and a letter of recommendation from the applicant's Key

Club Advisor indicating the student's degree of involvement. **Deadline:** January 28. **Contact:** Arzo Mansury, Dir. Scholarships at 619-814-1343, or scholarships@ sdfoundation.org.

6200 ■ Kiwanis Club of Escondido Scholarships II *(Undergraduate/Scholarship)*

Purpose: To support the education of students from California. **Focus:** General studies. **Qualif.:** Applicant must be a graduating high school senior in the Escondido High School District; planning to attend a two-year college or licensed trade/vocational school in the U.S.; have a minimum 2.0 GPA on a 4.0 scale; active member of a Key Club (sponsored by an Escondido Kiwanis Club); have demonstrated financial need; and actively involved in serving the community through involvement in extra-curricular activities, community service, sports, or work experience. **Criteria:** Awards are given based on the application materials.

Funds Avail.: $1,000. **Number Awarded:** 2. **To Apply:** Applicants must submit a completed Common Scholarship Application together with personal statement; two letters of recommendation on official letterhead (written within the last six months); official transcript in an official and sealed envelope; a copy ofmost recent tax form (Form 1040-pages 1 & 2; Form 1040A-pages 1 & 2; Form 1040EZ-page 1); and a letter of recommendation from the applicant's Key Club Advisor indicating the student's degree of involvement. **Deadline:** January 28. **Contact:** Arzo Mansury, Dir. Scholarships at 619-814-1343, or scholarships@ sdfoundation.org.

6201 ■ Judith Keller Marx Krumholz Scholarships *(Undergraduate/Scholarship)*

Purpose: To support the education of students from California. **Focus:** General studies. **Qualif.:** Applicant must be a student attending San Diego City College who have completed one full academic semester; have a minimum 2.50 GPA on a 4.0 scale; demonstrated financial need; and attending San Diego City College. **Criteria:** Preference will be given to applicants who have taken either Fundamentals of Mathematics 032 or Personal Growth 127.

Funds Avail.: $500. **Number Awarded:** 5. **To Apply:** Applicants must submit a completed Common Scholarship Application together with personal statement; two letters of recommendation on official letterhead (written within the last six months); official transcript in an official and sealed envelope; and a copy of most recent tax form (Form 1040-pages 1 & 2; Form 1040A-pages 1 & 2; Form 1040EZ-page 1). **Deadline:** January 28. **Contact:** Arzo Mansury, Dir. Scholarships at 619-814-1343, or scholarships@ sdfoundation.org.

6202 ■ Joseph C. Larson Entrepreneurial Scholarships *(Undergraduate/Scholarship)*

Purpose: To support the education of students from California. **Focus:** General studies. **Qualif.:** Applicant must be a graduating high school senior who will attend an accredited four-year university; or a student who have successfully completed at least one full academic year towards undergraduate degree at an accredited four-year university in the U.S. Student must have a minimum 3.0 GPA on a 4.0 scale. **Criteria:** Special consideration is given to students who can demonstrate their interest in entrepreneurial endeavors through the creation of their own business or consulting venue, mirroring that of Mr. Larson.

Funds Avail.: $2,500. **Number Awarded:** 3. **To Apply:** Applicants must submit a completed Common Scholarship Application together with personal statement; two letters of recommendation on official letterhead (written within the last six months); official transcript in an official and sealed envelope; copy of most recent tax form (Form 1040-pages 1 & 2; Form 1040A-pages 1 & 2; Form 1040EZ-page 1); and an essay (maximum two pages, typed, double-spaced) explaining the applicant's plan in using education in furthering entrepreneurial goals. **Deadline:** January 28. **Contact:** Arzo Mansury, Dir. Scholarships at 619-814-1343, or scholarships@sdfoundation.org.

6203 ■ Patrick Ledden Honorary Scholarships *(Undergraduate/Scholarship)*

Purpose: To support the education of students from California. **Focus:** General studies. **Qualif.:** Applicant must be a graduating senior at The Preuss School, UCSD; have a minimum 3.50 GPA on a 4.0 scale; and planning to attend a public or private four-year university in the state of California. **Criteria:** Special consideration is given to students who have participated in extra-curricular activities and community service or have work experience.

Funds Avail.: $3,000. **Number Awarded:** 4. **To Apply:** Applicants must submit a completed Common Scholarship Application together with personal statement; two letters of recommendation on official letterhead (written within the last six months); official transcript in an official and sealed envelope; a copy of most recent tax form (Form 1040-pages 1 & 2; Form 1040A-pages 1 & 2; Form 1040EZ -page 1); and an essay (maximum one page, typed, double-spaced) answering "What have you learned from your experience at The Preuss School, UCSD that you feel will best benefit you in college?". **Deadline:** January 28. **Contact:** Arzo Mansury, Dir. Scholarships at 619-814-1343, or scholarships@sdfoundation.org.

6204 ■ Ken Lee Memorial Scholarships *(Undergraduate/Scholarship)*

Purpose: To support the education of students from California. **Focus:** General studies. **Qualif.:** Applicant must be a graduating senior; a resident of Chula Vista, CA; attending a public or private Chula Vista high school; have a minimum 3.50 GPA on a 4.0 scale; planning to attend an accredited four-year university in the U.S.; have demonstrated commitment to the Chula Vista community through involvement in extra-curricular activities, community service, sports, or work experience. **Criteria:** Awards are given based on the application materials.

Funds Avail.: $1,000. **Number Awarded:** One scholarship to each high school in Chula Vista that submits at least three applications. **To Apply:** Applicants must submit a completed Common Scholarship Application together with personal statement; two letters of recommendation on official letterhead (written within the last six months); official transcript in an official and sealed envelope; and a copy of most recent tax form (Form 1040-pages 1 & 2; Form 1040A-pages 1 & 2; Form 1040EZ-page 1); and a form verifying residency in Chula Vista for each period of 2004, 2005, 2006 and 2007 or 2005, 2006, 2007 and 2008 must be submitted (phone/utility bills or property tax information). **Deadline:** January 28. **Contact:** Arzo Mansury, Dir. Scholarships at 619-814-1343, or scholarships@ sdfoundation.org.

6205 ■ Lehman Family Scholarships *(Undergraduate/Scholarship)*

Purpose: To support the education of students from California. **Focus:** General studies. **Qualif.:** Applicant must

Awards are arranged alphabetically below their administering organizations

be a graduating senior from Lincoln, Morse, or San Diego (downtown San Diego) high Schools; have a minimum 3.00 GPA on a 4.0 scale; planning to attend an accredited four-year university in the U.S; have financial need; and have demonstrated commitment to the through involvement in extra-curricular activities, work or volunteer experience, or church activities. **Criteria:** Awards are given based on the application materials.

Funds Avail.: $1,500. **Number Awarded:** 4. **To Apply:** Applicants must submit a completed Common Scholarship Application together with personal statement; two letters of recommendation on official letterhead (written within the last six months); official transcript in an official and sealed envelope; and a copy of most recent tax form (Form 1040-pages 1 & 2; Form 1040A-pages 1 & 2; Form 1040EZ-page 1). **Deadline:** January 28. **Contact:** Arzo Mansury, Dir. Scholarships at 619-814-1343, or scholarships@sdfoundation.org.

6206 ■ The Lemon Grove Education Foundation Scholarships *(Undergraduate/Scholarship)*

Purpose: To support the education of students from California. **Focus:** General studies. **Qualif.:** Applicant must be a graduating high school senior or adult (ages 18 or over); reside within the boundaries of the Lemon Grove School District; have a minimum 2.0 GPA on a 4.0 scale; attending a four-year public university, two-year community college, licensed trade/vocational school, or regional occupational program in San Diego County. **Criteria:** Awards are given based on the application materials.

Funds Avail.: $1,000. **Number Awarded:** 3. **To Apply:** Applicants must submit a completed Common Scholarship Application together with personal statement; two letters of recommendation on official letterhead (written within the last six months); official transcript in an official and sealed envelope; copy of most recent tax form (Form 1040-pages 1 & 2; Form 1040A-pages 1 & 2; Form 1040EZ-page 1); and a form verifying residency within the boundaries of the Lemon Grove School District for each period of 2005 and 2006, or 2006 and 2007 (phone/utility bills, property tax forms, etc.) **Deadline:** January 28. **Contact:** Arzo Mansury, Dir. Scholarships at 619-814-1343, or scholarships@sdfoundation.org.

6207 ■ Anneka McMillan Creative Arts Scholarships *(Undergraduate/Scholarship)*

Purpose: To support the education of students from California. **Focus:** Creative arts. **Qualif.:** Applicant must be a student from San Diego County who is continuing training or pursuing a career or degree in a creative arts (creative writing, photography, art, drama, music, or dance); have a minimum 2.50 GPA on a 4.0 scale; demonstrated financial need; and planning to attend an accredited educational institution or arts academy in the U.S. **Criteria:** Awards are given based on the application materials.

Funds Avail.: $1,000. **Number Awarded:** 1-2. **To Apply:** Applicants must submit a completed Common Scholarship Application together with personal statement; two letters of recommendation on official letterhead (written within the last six months); official transcript in an official and sealed envelope; copy of most recent tax form (Form 1040-pages 1 & 2; Form 1040A-pages 1 & 2; Form 1040EZ -page 1); and copies of creative arts materials (portfolio with illustrations, a video, an audio recording, etc.) which demonstrates achievements. Materials will not be returned. **Deadline:** January 28. **Contact:** Arzo Mansury, Dir. Scholarships at 619-814-1343, or scholarships@sdfoundation.org

6208 ■ Mission Bay Hospital Auxiliary Scholarships *(Undergraduate/Scholarship)*

Purpose: To support the education of students from California. **Focus:** Medicine. **Qualif.:** Applicant must be a graduating college senior pursuing a career in medicine; a resident of San Diego County; planning to attend an accredited medical school in the U.S.; have a minimum 3.50 GPA on a 4.0 scale; and demonstrated financial need. **Criteria:** Award is given based on the application materials.

Funds Avail.: $5,000. **Number Awarded:** 1. **To Apply:** Applicants must submit a completed Common Scholarship Application together with personal statement; two letters of recommendation on official letterhead (written within the last six months); official transcript in an official and sealed envelope; and a copy of most recent tax form (Form 1040-pages 1 & 2; Form 1040A-pages 1 & 2; Form 1040EZ-page 1). **Deadline:** January 28. **Contact:** Arzo Mansury, Dir. Scholarships at 619-814-1343, or scholarships@sdfoundation.org.

6209 ■ MKC Scholarships *(Undergraduate/Scholarship)*

Purpose: To support the education of students from California. **Focus:** General studies. **Qualif.:** Applicant must be a graduating senior or a student who have already graduated from The Preuss School, UCSD. Student must have financial need; planning to attend an accredited two-year college or four-year university in the U.S.; have a minimum 3.0 GPA on a 4.0 scale; and involved in the community through participation in extra-curricular or religious activities or volunteer or work experience. **Criteria:** Award is given based on the application materials.

Funds Avail.: $1,000-$3,000. **Number Awarded:** Varies. **To Apply:** Applicants must submit a completed Common Scholarship Application together with personal statement; two letters of recommendation on official letterhead (written within the last six months); official transcript in an official and sealed envelope; a copy of most recent tax form (Form 1040-pages 1 & 2; Form 1040A-pages 1 & 2; Form 1040EZ-page 1); an essay (one page, typed, double-spaced) answering "What would you say to a student thinking of entering The Preuss School, UCSD, and what has been the most important aspect of your experience while attending?"; (for students who have already graduated and are currently attending a college or university) a copy of high school transcript from The Preuss School, UCSD. **Deadline:** January 28. **Contact:** Arzo Mansury, Dir. Scholarships at 619-814-1343, or scholarships@sdfoundation.org.

6210 ■ Native American Charter High Schools After-the-Fires Scholarships *(Undergraduate/Scholarship)*

Purpose: To support the education of students from California. **Focus:** General studies. **Qualif.:** Applicant must be a graduating high school senior enrolled in a Tribal Charter High School in San Diego County whose family was financially impacted by the 2007 wildfires. Student must have a minimum 2.0 GPA on a 4.0 scale and planning to attend an accredited two-year college, four-year university, or licensed trade/vocational school in the U.S. **Criteria:** Awards are given based on the application materials.

Funds Avail.: To be determined. **Number Awarded:** To be determined. **To Apply:** Applicants must submit a completed Common Scholarship Application together with personal statement; two letters of recommendation on official letterhead (written within the last six months); official transcript in an official and sealed envelope; a copy of most recent tax form (Form 1040-pages 1 & 2; Form 1040A-pages 1 & 2; Form 1040EZ-page 1); and a formal documentation or a letter on official letterhead from FEMA (insurance company), or high school guidance counselor/principal indicating the loss of home in the 2007 wildfires and/or letter from parents' or parent's employer(s) indicating loss of income. **Deadline:** January 28. **Contact:** Arzo Mansury, Dir. Scholarships at 619-814-1343, or scholarships@sdfoundation.org.

6211 ■ Stuart L. Noderer Memorial Scholarships
(Undergraduate/Scholarship)

Purpose: To support the education of students from California. **Focus:** Science; Engineering; Architecture. **Qualif.:** Applicant must be graduating senior from Mission Bay High School; planning to attend an accredited four-year university in the U.S.; have a minimum 3.50 GPA on a 4.0 scale; and will major in science, engineering or architecture. **Criteria:** Awards are given based on the application materials.

Funds Avail.: $1,000. **Number Awarded:** 2. **To Apply:** Applicants must submit a completed Common Scholarship Application together with personal statement; two letters of recommendation on official letterhead (written within the last six months); official transcript in an official and sealed envelope; and a copy of 2006 or most recent tax form (Form 1040-pages 1 & 2; Form 1040Apages 1 & 2; Form 1040EZ-page 1). **Deadline:** January 28. **Contact:** Arzo Mansury, Dir. Scholarships at 619-814-1343, or scholarships@sdfoundation.org.

6212 ■ Pearman Family Scholarships
(Undergraduate/Scholarship)

Purpose: To support the education of students from California. **Focus:** General studies. **Qualif.:** Applicant must be a graduating African-American high school senior from San Diego County; have a minimum 3.0 GPA on a 4.0 scale; planning to attend an accredited four-year university in the U.S.; and have demonstrated financial need. **Criteria:** Award is given based on the application materials.

Funds Avail.: $750. **Number Awarded:** 1. **To Apply:** Applicants must submit a completed Common Scholarship Application together with personal statement; two letters of recommendation on official letterhead (written within the last six months); official transcript in an official and sealed envelope; and a copy of most recent tax form (Form 1040-pages 1 & 2; Form 1040A-pages 1 & 2; Form 1040EZ-page 1). **Deadline:** January 28. **Contact:** Arzo Mansury, Dir. Scholarships at 619-814-1343, or scholarships@sdfoundation.org.

6213 ■ Steve Petix Journalism Scholarship
(Undergraduate/Scholarship)

Purpose: To support the education of students from California. **Focus:** Journalism. **Qualif.:** Applicant must be graduating senior attending schools in the Grossmont Union High School District interested in pursuing a career in journalism or related writing career; have a minimum 2.50 GPA on a 4.0 scale; and planning to attend an accredited two-year college or four-year university in the U.S. **Criteria:** Preference will be given to students who have been involved in their school newspaper or serve as yearbook staff.

Funds Avail.: $1,000. **Number Awarded:** 2. **To Apply:** Applicants must submit a completed Common Scholarship Application together with personal statement; two letters of recommendation on official letterhead (written within the last six months); official transcript in an official and sealed envelope; and a copy of most recent tax form (Form 1040-pages 1 & 2; Form 1040A-pages 1 & 2; Form 1040EZ-page 1). **Deadline:** January 28. **Contact:** Arzo Mansury, Dir. Scholarships at 619-814-1343, or scholarships@sdfoundation.org.

6214 ■ Pollard-Bailey Scholarships
(Undergraduate/Scholarship)

Purpose: To support the education of students from California. **Focus:** General studies. **Qualif.:** Applicant must be a graduating high school senior who will attend Grossmont or Cuyamaca Community College; must have a minimum 2.50 GPA on a 4.0 scale; demonstrated financial need; and engaged in serving the community through involvement in extra-curricular activities/church/volunteer activities or work experience. **Criteria:** Awards are given based on the application materials.

Funds Avail.: $1,000. **Number Awarded:** 5. **To Apply:** Applicants must submit a completed Common Scholarship Application together with personal statement; two letters of recommendation on official letterhead (written within the last six months); official transcript in an official and sealed envelope; and a copy of most recent tax form (Form 1040-pages 1 & 2; Form 1040A-pages 1 & 2; Form 1040EZ-page 1). **Deadline:** January 28. **Contact:** Arzo Mansury, Dir. Scholarships at 619-814-1343, or scholarships@sdfoundation.org.

6215 ■ Port with No Borders Scholarships
(Undergraduate/Scholarship)

Purpose: To support the education of students from California. **Focus:** General studies. **Qualif.:** Applicants must be San Diego Port tenants, sub-tenants, or Port of San Diego employees or their children who are residents of San Diego County. Applicants must be graduating high school seniors, or currently enrolled college students; having a minimum 2.50 GPA on a 4.0 scale; working towards their undergraduate degree; have a demonstrated financial need; and plan to attend an accredited two-year college or four-year university in the U.S. **Criteria:** Awards are given based on the application materials.

Funds Avail.: $2,000. **Number Awarded:** 6. **To Apply:** Applicants must submit a completed Common Scholarship Application together with personal statement; two letters of recommendation on official letterhead (written within the last six months); official transcript in an official and sealed envelope; a copy of 2006 or most recent tax form (Form 1040-pages 1 & 2; Form 1040A-pages 1 & 2; Form 1040EZ-page 1); a letter from the employer on official letterhead verifying the applicant is an employee of a tenant or sub-tenant of the Port of San Diego or his/her parent is employed by a tenant or sub-tenant of the Port of San Diego; and an essay (maximum one page, typed, double-spaced) addressing how the applicant's studies could lead to a career related to the business and operations of a port. **Deadline:** January 28. **Contact:** Arzo Mansury, Dir. Scholarships at 619-814-1343, or scholarships@sdfoundation.org.

6216 ■ Qualcomm San Diego Science, Technology, Engineering and Mathematics Scholarships
(Undergraduate/Scholarship)

Purpose: To support the education of students from California. **Focus:** General studies. **Qualif.:** Applicant must be a graduating high school senior; or a student currently attending a local community college and transferring to

Awards are arranged alphabetically below their administering organizations

either the University of California, San Diego, San Diego State University or California State University, San Marcos. Student must have a minimum of 3.50 GPA on a 4.0 scale and demonstrated financial need. **Criteria:** Awards are given based on the application materials.

Funds Avail.: $2,500. **Number Awarded:** 5. **To Apply:** Applicants must submit a completed Common Scholarship Application together with personal statement; two letters of recommendation on official letterhead (written within the last six months); official transcript in an official and sealed envelope; and a copy of most recent tax form (Form 1040-pages 1 & 2; Form 1040A-pages 1 & 2; Form 1040EZ-page 1). **Deadline:** January 28. **Contact:** Arzo Mansury, Dir. Scholarships at 619-814-1343, or scholarships@sdfoundation.org.

6217 ■ Rancho Bernardo/Smith Scholarships
(Undergraduate/Scholarship)

Purpose: To support the education of students from California. **Focus:** General studies. **Qualif.:** Applicant must be a graduating high school senior from Rancho Bernardo; will attend an accredited, public four-year university in the state of California; must have a minimum 3.50 GPA on a 4.0 scale; and demonstrated commitment to the Rancho Bernardo community through involvement in extra-curricular activities, community service, sports, or work experience. **Criteria:** Special consideration will be given to applicants who have lost one or both parents while in high school.

Funds Avail.: $1,000. **Number Awarded:** 2. **To Apply:** Applicants must submit a completed Common Scholarship Application together with personal statement; two letters of recommendation on official letterhead (written within the last six months); official transcript in an official and sealed envelope; a copy of most recent tax form (Form 1040-pages 1 & 2; Form 1040A-pages 1 & 2; Form 1040EZ-page 1); and a form verifying residency in Rancho Bernardo for at least one year for each period of 2006-2007 or 2007-2008 (bank statements, utility bills, insurance forms, etc.). **Deadline:** January 28. **Contact:** Arzo Mansury, Dir. Scholarships at 619-814-1343, or scholarships@sdfoundation.org.

6218 ■ The Remington Club Scholarships
(Undergraduate/Scholarship)

Purpose: To support the education of students from California. **Focus:** General studies. **Qualif.:** Applicants must be employees, and the children of employees at The Remington Club. Applicants must have a minimum 2.50 GPA on a 4.0 scale; planning to attend an accredited two-year college, four-year university, or licensed trade/vocational school in the U.S.; have a commitment to the community as demonstrated through involvement in extra-curricular activities, community service, sports, or work experience; may be graduating high school seniors, students already in school, or adults re-entering school. Employees must be employed at The Remington Club for a minimum of six consecutive months. **Criteria:** Awards are given based on the application materials.

Funds Avail.: $1,000-$4,000. **Number Awarded:** To be determined. **To Apply:** Applicants must submit a completed Common Scholarship Application together with personal statement; two letters of recommendation on official letterhead (written within the last six months); official transcript in an official and sealed envelope; a copy of most recent tax form (Form 1040-pages 1 & 2; Form 1040A-pages 1 & 2; Form 1040EZ -page 1); and a letter from The Remington Club (on official letterhead and signed by personnel in Human Resources or an immediate supervisor) indicating how long the employee has been employed at The Remington Club, the position he/she holds and, if applicable, the name of the son/daughter who is applying for the scholarship. **Deadline:** January 28. **Contact:** Arzo Mansury, Dir. Scholarships at 619-814-1343, or scholarships@sdfoundation.org.

6219 ■ The Rotary Club of Rancho Bernardo Sunrise Abraxas Student Scholarships
(Undergraduate/Scholarship)

Purpose: To support the education of students from California. **Focus:** General studies. **Qualif.:** Applicant must be graduating high school senior of Abraxas High School in Poway, CA; have a minimum 2.50 GPA on a 4.0 scale; and planning to attend an accredited two-year college, four-year university or licensed trade/vocational school in the U.S. **Criteria:** Awards are given based on the application materials.

Funds Avail.: To be determined. **Number Awarded:** To be determined. **To Apply:** Applicants must submit a completed Common Scholarship Application together with personal statement; two letters of recommendation on official letterhead (written within the last six months); official transcript in an official and sealed envelope; a copy of most recent tax form (Form 1040-pages 1 & 2; Form 1040A-pages 1 & 2; Form 1040EZ -page 1); and a letter of recommendation from an administrator or teacher from Abraxas High School. **Deadline:** January 28. **Contact:** Arzo Mansury, Dir. Scholarships at 619-814-1343, or scholarships@sdfoundation.org.

6220 ■ Rubinstein Family Scholarships
(Undergraduate/Scholarship)

Purpose: To support the education of students from California. **Focus:** General studies. **Qualif.:** Applicant must be a graduating high school senior; or a student enrolled at an institution of higher education who have been diagnosed with a chronic illness (e.g. Crohn's & Colitis, Diabetes, Asthma, etc.). Student must have a minimum 3.0 GPA on a 4.0 scale; and planning to attend an accredited two-year college or four-year university in the U.S. **Criteria:** Preference will be given to applicants planning to attend school outside San Diego County.

Funds Avail.: $1,000. **Number Awarded:** 1. **To Apply:** Applicants must submit a completed Common Scholarship Application together with personal statement; two letters of recommendation on official letterhead (written within the last six months); official transcript in an official and sealed envelope; a copy of most recent tax form (Form 1040-pages 1 & 2; Form 1040A-pages 1 & 2; Form 1040EZ-page 1); and a one page essay on how the applicant has coped with their chronic illness. **Deadline:** January 28. **Contact:** Arzo Mansury, Dir. Scholarships at 619-814-1343, or scholarships@sdfoundation.org.

6221 ■ San Diego City College Study Abroad Scholarships *(Undergraduate/Scholarship)*

Purpose: To support the education of students from California. **Focus:** General studies. **Qualif.:** Applicant must be a student enrolled in at least 6 units (online courses are not applicable) at San Diego City College, have completed a minimum of 12 college level units; have a cumulative GPA of 2.50 or higher on a 4.0 scale; must have no previous study abroad experience; a citizen or permanent resident of the U.S.; and have a demonstrated financial need. **Criteria:** Preference may be given to students who have never traveled outside of North America.

Funds Avail.: $500-$1,000. **Number Awarded:** 2 for Italy and 2 for Spain. **To Apply:** Applicants must submit a completed scholarship application form, along with a typed personal statement (maximum of two pages); a copy of transcripts; and a copy of most recent tax form(s) used to complete financial information (Form 1040-pages 1 & 2; Form 1040A-pages 1 & 2: Form 1040EZ-page 1). **Deadline:** September 15. **Contact:** 619-814-1343 or scholarships@sdfoundation.org.

6222 ■ The San Diego Foundation Community Scholarship II *(Undergraduate/Scholarship)*

Purpose: To support the education of students from California. **Focus:** General studies. **Qualif.:** Applicant must be graduating high school senior; have a minimum 2.50 GPA on a 4.0 scale; and will attend an accredited two-year college in San Diego County. **Criteria:** Priority will be given to students who have demonstrated financial need and have contributed to their community as demonstrated by their involvement in extra-curricular activities, work, religious, or volunteer activities.

Funds Avail.: $500-$1,000. **Number Awarded:** 10-20. **To Apply:** Applicants must submit a completed Common Scholarship Application together with personal statement; two letters of recommendation on official letterhead (written within the last six months); official transcript in an official and sealed envelope; and a copy of most recent tax form (Form 1040-pages 1 & 2; Form 1040A-pages 1 & 2; Form 1040EZ-page 1). **Deadline:** January 28. **Contact:** Arzo Mansury, Dir. Scholarships at 619-814-1343, or scholarships@sdfoundation.org.

6223 ■ The San Diego Foundation Community Scholarships I *(Undergraduate/Scholarship)*

Purpose: To support the education of students from California. **Focus:** General studies. **Qualif.:** Applicant must be a senior graduating from a San Diego County continuation high school; must have a minimum 2.0 GPA on a 4.0 scale; and will attend an accredited two-year college, four-year university, or licensed trade/vocational school in the U.S. **Criteria:** Priority will be given to students who have a demonstrated financial need and have contributed to their community as demonstrated by their involvement in extra-curricular activities, work, religious, or volunteer activities.

Funds Avail.: $1,000. **Number Awarded:** 5. **To Apply:** Applicants must submit a completed Common Scholarship Application together with personal statement; two letters of recommendation on official letterhead (written within the last six months); official transcript in an official and sealed envelope; and a copy of most recent tax form (Form 1040-pages 1 & 2; Form 1040A-pages 1 & 2; Form 1040EZ-page 1). **Deadline:** January 28. **Contact:** Arzo Mansury, Dir. Scholarships at 619-814-1343, or scholarships@sdfoundation.org.

6224 ■ San Diego National Bank Scholarships *(Undergraduate/Scholarship)*

Purpose: To support the education of students from California. **Focus:** General studies. **Qualif.:** Applicant must be adult with low and moderate income levels less than or equal to 80% of the prevailing San Diego County Metropolitan Statistical Area HUD median income level (currently $34,700); 21 years of age or over with a high school diploma or GED; have financial need; working towards undergraduate degree; planning to attend an accredited two-year college, four-year university, or licensed trade/vocational school in San Diego County; and committed to the community as demonstrated by participation in community, church or school activities. **Criteria:** Awards are given based on the application materials.

Funds Avail.: $500-$2,500. **Number Awarded:** 5. **To Apply:** Applicants must submit a completed Common Scholarship Application together with personal statement; two letters of recommendation on official letterhead (written within the last six months); official transcript in an official and sealed envelope; and a copy of most recent tax form (Form 1040-pages 1 & 2; Form 1040A-pages 1 & 2; Form 1040EZ-page 1). **Deadline:** January 28. **Contact:** Arzo Mansury, Dir. Scholarships at 619-814-1343, or scholarships@sdfoundation.org.

6225 ■ San Diego Pathways to College Scholarships *(Undergraduate/Scholarship)*

Purpose: To support the education of students from California. **Focus:** General studies. **Qualif.:** Applicant must be graduating high school senior attending a four-year university in the state of California; have a minimum 3.0 GPA on a 4.0 scale; demonstrated financial need; and actively involved in extra-curricular activities, community service, religious activities, work experience, or athletics. **Criteria:** Awards are given based on the application materials.

Funds Avail.: To be determined. **Number Awarded:** To be determined. **To Apply:** Applicants must submit a completed Common Scholarship Application together with personal statement; two letters of recommendation on official letterhead (written within the last six months); official transcript in an official and sealed envelope; and a copy of 2006 or most recent tax form (Form 1040-pages 1 & 2; Form 1040A-pages 1 & 2; Form 1040EZ-page 1). **Deadline:** January 28. **Contact:** Arzo Mansury, Dir. Scholarships at 619-814-1343, or scholarships@sdfoundation.org.

6226 ■ San Diego Regional Aviation Association Scholarships *(Undergraduate/Scholarship)*

Purpose: To support the education of students from California. **Focus:** Aviation. **Qualif.:** Applicant must be a Southern California resident enrolled at an accredited two-year college or four-year university in Southern California, studying aviation-related curricula. Student must have a minimum 2.50 GPA on a 4.0 scale. **Criteria:** Preference may be given to applicants with a demonstrated record of community service. Special consideration will be given to those students with current or previous military service.

Funds Avail.: No specific amount. **To Apply:** Applicants must submit a completed scholarship application form, along with a typed personal statement (maximum of two pages); two letters of recommendation on official letterhead (one letter must come from a member of the aviation community or aviation department faculty at the institution in which the applicant is currently enrolled); a official transcripts in a sealed envelope; and a copy of most recent tax form(s) used to complete financial information (Form 1040-pages 1 & 2; Form 1040A-pages 1 & 2: Form 1040EZ-page 1). **Deadline:** March 21. **Contact:** 619-814-1343 or scholarships@sdfoundation.org.

6227 ■ San Pasqual Academy Scholarships *(Undergraduate/Scholarship)*

Purpose: To support the education of students from California. **Focus:** General studies. **Qualif.:** Applicant must be graduating high school senior at San Pasqual Academy; must have a minimum 2.50 GPA on a 4.0 scale; and planning to attend an accredited two-year college, four-year university, or licensed trade/vocational school in the U.S. **Criteria:** Awards are given based on the application materials.

Funds Avail.: $1,000. **Number Awarded:** 5. **To Apply:** Applicants must submit a completed Common Scholarship Application together with personal statement; two letters of recommendation on official letterhead (written within the last six months); official transcript in an official and sealed envelope; a copy of most recent tax form (Form 1040-pages 1 & 2; Form 1040A-pages 1 & 2; Form 1040EZ-page 1); and a letter of recommendation on official letterhead from the staff or faculty at San Pasqual Academy indicating the student is enrolled at the school. **Deadline:** January 28. **Contact:** Arzo Mansury, Dir. Scholarships at 619-814-1343, or scholarships@sdfoundation.org.

6228 ■ Malini E. Sathyadev Memorial Scholarships *(Undergraduate/Scholarship)*

Purpose: To support the education of students from California. **Focus:** General studies. **Qualif.:** Applicant must be a graduating high school senior from Horizon High School and Cathedral Catholic High School; have a minimum 3.50 GPA on a 4.0 scale; attending an accredited four-year university in the U.S.; and involved in serving the community as demonstrated by involvement in community service and extra-curricular activities such as sports and music. **Criteria:** Awards are given based on the application materials.

Funds Avail.: $1,500. **Number Awarded:** 3. **To Apply:** Applicants must submit a completed Common Scholarship Application together with personal statement; two letters of recommendation on official letterhead (written within the last six months); official transcript in an official and sealed envelope; a copy of most recent tax form (Form 1040-pages 1 & 2; Form 1040A-pages 1 & 2; Form 1040EZ-page 1); and an essay (one page, typed, double-spaced) on the role that Jesus Christ plays in the applicant's life. **Deadline:** January 28. **Contact:** Arzo Mansury, Dir. Scholarships at 619-814-1343, or scholarships@sdfoundation.org.

6229 ■ SDF Community College Transfer Scholarships for Math and Science *(Undergraduate/Scholarship)*

Purpose: To support the education of students from California. **Focus:** Science; Engineering; Mathematics and mathematical sciences. **Qualif.:** Applicant must be a San Diego Community College student transferring to an accredited four-year university in the U.S.; majoring in science, engineering, or mathematics; and have a minimum 3.0 GPA on a 4.0 scale in community college work. **Criteria:** Awards are given based on the application materials. Financial need will be strongly considered.

Funds Avail.: $2,500. **Number Awarded:** 5. **To Apply:** Applicants must submit a completed Common Scholarship Application together with personal statement; two letters of recommendation on official letterhead (written within the last six months); official transcript in an official and sealed envelope; copy of 2006 or most recent tax form (Form 1040-pages 1 & 2; Form 1040A-pages 1 & 2; Form 1040EZ-page 1); and s letter of acceptance on official letterhead from the accredited four-year university. **Deadline:** January 28. **Contact:** Arzo Mansury, Dir. Scholarships at 619-814-1343, or scholarships@sdfoundation.org

6230 ■ Harvey L. Simmons Memorial Scholarships *(Undergraduate/Scholarship)*

Purpose: To support the education of students from California. **Focus:** General studies. **Qualif.:** Applicant must be a graduating high school senior; will attend an accredited two-year college or four-year university in the U.S.; have a minimum 3.0 GPA on a 4.0 scale; have demonstrated financial need; and committed in serving the community through involvement in community service, church or extra-curricular activities. **Criteria:** Preference will be given to applicants who have participated in high school sports for at least three years, two at the varsity level, and are intending to play at the college level.

Funds Avail.: $500. **Number Awarded:** 2. **To Apply:** Applicants must submit a completed Common Scholarship Application together with personal statement; two letters of recommendation on official letterhead (written within the last six months); official transcript in an official and sealed envelope; copy of 2006 or most recent tax form (Form 1040-pages 1 & 2; Form 1040A-pages 1 & 2; Form 1040EZ-page 1); and a letter of recommendation on letterhead from the applicant's coach detailing the sport(s) played, level and years of participation, and achievements. **Deadline:** January 28. **Contact:** Arzo Mansury, Dir. Scholarships at 619-814-1343, or scholarships@sdfoundation.org.

6231 ■ Gwen Stefani After-the-Fires Scholarships *(Undergraduate/Scholarship)*

Purpose: To support the education of students from California. **Focus:** General studies. **Qualif.:** Applicant must be a graduating high school senior or a current college student who lost homes and/or source of income in the 2007 wildfires. Student must have a minimum 2.50 GPA on a 4.0 scale; have demonstrated financial need; and plan to attend or currently attending an accredited two-year college or four-year university in the U.S. **Criteria:** Award is given based on the application materials.

Funds Avail.: To be determined. **Number Awarded:** To be determined. **To Apply:** Applicants must submit a completed Common Scholarship Application together with personal statement; two letters of recommendation on official letterhead (written within the last six months); official transcript in an official and sealed envelope; copy of most recent tax form (Form 1040-pages 1 & 2; Form 1040A-pages 1 & 2; Form 1040EZ-page 1); and a formal documentation or a letter on official letterhead from FEMA (insurance company), or high school/college guidance counselor/principal indicating the loss of home in the 2007 wildfires and/or a letter from the applicant's employer indicating loss of income. **Deadline:** January 28. **Contact:** Arzo Mansury, Dir. Scholarships at 619-814-1343, or scholarships@sdfoundation.org.

6232 ■ Step Up Scholarships *(Undergraduate/Scholarship)*

Purpose: To support the education of students from California. **Focus:** General studies. **Qualif.:** Applicant must be a resident of San Diego County pursuing a teaching credential at a four-year university in San Diego County; must have a minimum 3.20 GPA on a 4.0 scale; a U.S. citizen and resident of California. **Criteria:** Award is given based on the application materials.

Funds Avail.: $2,000. **Number Awarded:** 1. **To Apply:** Applicants must submit a completed Common Scholarship Application together with personal statement; two letters of recommendation on official letterhead (written within the last six months); official transcript in an official and sealed envelope; and a copy of most recent tax form (Form 1040-pages 1 & 2; Form 1040A-pages 1 & 2; Form 1040EZ-page 1). **Deadline:** January 28. **Contact:** Arzo Mansury,

Dir. Scholarships at 619-814-1343, or scholarships@sdfoundation.org.

6233 ■ Raymond A. Tice Scholarships I
(Undergraduate/Scholarship)

Purpose: To support the education of students from California. **Focus:** General studies. **Qualif.:** Applicant must be a graduating high school senior; attending an accredited two-year college or four-year university in San Diego County; have a minimum 2.25 to 3.50 GPA on a 4.0 scale and demonstrated financial need; actively involved in serving the community as demonstrated by involvement in extra-curricular activities, community/church service, or work experience. **Criteria:** Awards are given based on the application materials.

Funds Avail.: $1,000-$2,500. **Number Awarded:** 15. **To Apply:** Applicants must submit a completed Common Scholarship Application together with personal statement; two letters of recommendation on official letterhead (written within the last six months); official transcript in an official and sealed envelope; and a copy of most recent tax form (Form 1040-pages 1 & 2; Form 1040A-pages 1 & 2; Form 1040EZ-page 1). **Deadline:** January 28. **Contact:** Arzo Mansury, Dir. Scholarships at 619-814-1343, or scholarships@sdfoundation.org.

6234 ■ Raymond A. Tice Scholarships II
(Undergraduate/Scholarship)

Purpose: To support the education of students from California. **Focus:** General studies. **Qualif.:** Applicant must be a student attending an accredited two-year college or four-year university in San Diego County who will continue college education in San Diego. Student must have a minimum 2.75 to 3.75 GPA on a 4.0 scale; demonstrated financial need; involved in serving the community as demonstrated by involvement in extra-curricular activities, community/church service, or work experience. **Criteria:** Awards are given based on the application materials.

Funds Avail.: $1,000-$2,500. **Number Awarded:** 15. **To Apply:** Applicants must submit a completed Common Scholarship Application together with personal statement; two letters of recommendation on official letterhead (written within the last six months); official transcript in an official and sealed envelope; and a copy of most recent tax form (Form 1040-pages 1 & 2; Form 1040A-pages 1 & 2; Form 1040EZ-page 1). **Deadline:** January 28. **Contact:** Arzo Mansury, Dir. Scholarships at 619-814-1343, or scholarships@sdfoundation.org.

6235 ■ Vincent Trotter Health Care Scholarships
(Undergraduate/Scholarship)

Purpose: To support the education of students from California. **Focus:** Health care services. **Qualif.:** Applicant must be a graduating high school senior or adult re-entry student pursuing a career in the health care field (nurse, doctor, health care aid, or medical researcher) who will attend an accredited four-year university, two-year college or licensed trade/vocational school in the U.S. Student must have a minimum 2.50 GPA or better on a 4.0 scale. **Criteria:** Awards are given based on the application materials.

Funds Avail.: $1,000-$2,000. **Number Awarded:** 1-2. **To Apply:** Applicants must submit a completed Common Scholarship Application together with personal statement; two letters of recommendation on official letterhead (written within the last six months); official transcript in an official and sealed envelope; a copy of most recent tax form (Form 1040-pages 1 & 2; Form 1040A-pages 1 & 2; Form 1040EZ-page 1); and an essay (maximum one page, typed, double-spaced) describing how the applicant has made a real difference in somebody's life or getting something significant accomplished. **Deadline:** January 28. **Contact:** Arzo Mansury, Dir. Scholarships at 619-814-1343, or scholarships@sdfoundation.org.

6236 ■ The UCSD Black Alumni Scholarship for Arts and Humanities *(Undergraduate/Scholarship)*

Purpose: To support the education of students from California. **Focus:** Humanities; Arts. **Qualif.:** Applicant must be an African-American student currently attending the University of California, San Diego (UCSD); or prospective African-American student enrolling at UCSD. Student must be majoring in the arts or humanities. High school student must have a 3.0 GPA on a 4.0 scale while current UCSD students must maintain at least a 2.75 GPA on a 4.0 scale. **Criteria:** Awards are given based on the application materials.

Funds Avail.: $1,000-$2,500. **Number Awarded:** 5. **To Apply:** Applicants must submit a completed Common Scholarship Application together with personal statement; two letters of recommendation on official letterhead (written within the last six months); official transcript in an official and sealed envelope; and a copy of most recent tax form (Form 1040-pages 1 & 2; Form 1040A-pages 1 & 2; Form 1040EZ-page 1). **Deadline:** January 28. **Contact:** Arzo Mansury, Dir. Scholarships at 619-814-1343, or scholarships@sdfoundation.org.

6237 ■ The UCSD Black Alumni Scholarships for Engineering, Mathematics and Science
(Undergraduate/Scholarship)

Purpose: To support the education of students from California. **Focus:** Humanities; Arts. **Qualif.:** Applicant must be an African-American student currently attending the University of California, San Diego (UCSD); or prospective African-American student who will be enrolling at UCSD. Students must be majoring in the arts or humanities. High school students must have a 3.0 GPA on a 4.0 scale while current UCSD students must have maintained at least a 2.75 GPA on a 4.0 scale. **Criteria:** Awards are given based on the application materials.

Funds Avail.: $1,000-$2,500. **Number Awarded:** 5. **To Apply:** Applicants must submit a completed Common Scholarship Application together with personal statement; two letters of recommendation on official letterhead (written within the last six months); official transcript in an official and sealed envelope; and a copy of most recent tax form (Form 1040-pages 1 & 2; Form 1040A-pages 1 & 2; Form 1040EZ-page 1). **Deadline:** January 28. **Contact:** Arzo Mansury, Dir. Scholarships at 619-814-1343, or scholarships@sdfoundation.org.

6238 ■ USA Freestyle Martial Arts Scholarships
(Undergraduate/Scholarship)

Purpose: To support the education of students from California. **Focus:** General studies. **Qualif.:** Applicant must be a student currently attending or have attended USA Freestyle Martial Arts for at least two years; must have a minimum 2.50 GPA on a 4.0 scale; and either be graduating high school senior or current college student planning to attend an accredited two-year college, four-year university, or licensed trade/vocational school in the U.S. **Criteria:** Preference will be given to students with a demonstrated financial need and/or have persevered in spite of any obstacles.

Funds Avail.: $1,000-3,000. **Number Awarded:** 2. **To Apply:** Applicants must submit a completed Common Scholarship Application together with personal statement; two letters of recommendation on official letterhead (written within the last six months); official transcript in an official and sealed envelope; a copy of most recent tax form (Form 1040-pages 1 & 2; Form 1040A-pages 1 & 2; Form 1040EZ-page 1); essay (maximum one page, typed, double-spaced) addressing "How you anticipate utilizing the skills you have learned from the study of Martial Arts to inspire a caring world"; and a letter on official letterhead from USA Freestyle Martial Arts verifying the applicant is/was a student at the school. **Deadline:** January 28. **Contact:** Arzo Mansury, Dir. Scholarships at 619-814-1343, or scholarships@sdfoundation.org.

6239 ■ Weissbuch Family Scholarships
(Undergraduate/Scholarship)

Purpose: To support the education of students from California. **Focus:** General studies. **Qualif.:** Applicant must be a student enrolled at the University of California, San Diego (UCSD); be in freshman, sophomore or junior year; and have a minimum 2.50 GPA on a 4.0 scale. Student must be employed part-time and have a demonstrated financial need. Applicants must be a resident of San Diego County for a minimum of four years. **Criteria:** Awards are given based on the application materials.

Funds Avail.: $1,500. **Number Awarded:** 2. **To Apply:** Applicants must submit a completed Common Scholarship Application together with personal statement; two letters of recommendation on official letterhead (written within the last six months); official transcript in an official and sealed envelope; a copy of most recent tax form (Form 1040-pages 1 & 2; Form 1040A-pages 1 & 2; Form 1040EZ-page 1); a form verifying residency in San Diego County for at least four years for each period of 2004, 2005, 2006 and 2007, or 2005, 2006, 2007 and 2008 (bank statements, utility bills, insurance forms, high school transcripts, etc.); and a letter from current employer on official letterhead verifying employment. **Deadline:** January 28. **Contact:** Arzo Mansury, Dir. Scholarships at 619-814-1343, or scholarships@sdfoundation.org.

6240 ■ Leon Williams Scholarships
(Undergraduate/Scholarship)

Purpose: To support the education of students from California. **Focus:** Health care services. **Qualif.:** Applicant must be a graduating African-American high school senior from San Diego County; have a minimum 2.50 GPA on a 4.0 scale; attending an accredited four-year university in the U.S.; involved in communities as demonstrated by extra-curricular, work, church, or volunteer activities; have demonstrated financial need; and pursuing a career in health or the healthcare field. **Criteria:** Award is given based on the application materials.

Funds Avail.: $1,000. **Number Awarded:** 1. **To Apply:** Applicants must submit a completed Common Scholarship Application together with personal statement; two letters of recommendation on official letterhead (written within the last six months); official transcript in an official and sealed envelope; and a copy of most recent tax form (Form 1040-pages 1 & 2; Form 1040A-pages 1 & 2; Form 1040EZ-page 1); and an essay (maximum of two pagess, typed, double-spaced) on "Improving the Health of our Underserved Community." **Deadline:** January 28. **Contact:** Arzo Mansury, Dir. Scholarships at 619-814-1343, or scholarships@sdfoundation.org.

6241 ■ Randy Williams Scholarships
(Undergraduate/Scholarship)

Purpose: To support the education of students from California. **Focus:** General studies. **Qualif.:** Applicant must be a graduating high school senior; have participated in high school and/or club competitive swimming programs; planning to attend an accredited two-year college, four-year university or licensed trade/vocational school in the U.S.; and have a minimum 2.50 GPA on a 4.0 scale. **Criteria:** Award is given based on the application materials.

Funds Avail.: $1,000. **Number Awarded:** 1. **To Apply:** Applicants must submit a completed Common Scholarship Application together with personal statement; two letters of recommendation on official letterhead (written within the last six months); official transcript in an official and sealed envelope; a copy of most recent tax form (Form 1040-pages 1 & 2; Form 1040A-pages 1 & 2; Form 1040EZ -page 1); a letter of recommendation on official letterhead from the applicant's swim coach; and an essay (maximum one page, typed, double-spaced) describing the benefits enjoyed from being involved in competitive swimming and emphasizing how to utilize the skills learned in swimming in reaching the applicant's goals. **Deadline:** January 28. **Contact:** Arzo Mansury, Dir. Scholarships at 619-814-1343, or scholarships@sdfoundation.org.

6242 ■ Jean Wright-Elson Scholarships *(Graduate, Undergraduate/Scholarship)*

Purpose: To support the education of students from California. **Focus:** Nursing. **Qualif.:** Applicant must be a college student who completed two full academic years (60 semester units or 72 quarter units); pursuing a career in nursing; have a minimum 3.0 GPA on a 4.0 scale; demonstrated financial need; a resident of San Diego County; attending an accredited two-year college or four-year university in the U.S. Scholarship is also open to a student pursuing Masters degree or Ph.D. in nursing. **Criteria:** Awards are given based on the application materials.

Funds Avail.: $1,000. **Number Awarded:** 2. **To Apply:** Applicants must submit a completed Common Scholarship Application together with personal statement; two letters of recommendation on official letterhead (written within the last six months); official transcript in an official and sealed envelope; copy of most recent tax form (Form 1040-pages 1 & 2; Form 1040A-pages 1 & 2; Form 1040EZ-page 1); a letter of recommendation on official letterhead from a health-related employer or volunteer supervisor; and an essay (maximum one page, typed, double-spaced) emphasizing applicant's career goals in nursing. **Deadline:** January 28. **Contact:** Arzo Mansury, Dir. Scholarships at 619-814-1343, or scholarships@sdfoundation.org.

6243 ■ Santa Barbara Dance Alliance

PO Box 22256
Santa Barbara, CA 93121
Ph: (805)966-6950
Fax: (805)966-6950
E-mail: dance@sbdancealliance.org
URL: http://www.sbdancealliance.org

6244 ■ Dance Education Scholarship Program
(High School/Scholarship)

Purpose: To provide financial support to talented students. **Focus:** Dance. **Qualif.:** Applicants must be students ages 8-16 years old; must have talent, dedication and financial

Awards are arranged alphabetically below their administering organizations

need. Applicants may dance in any form; must have studied for at least 2 years, and be recommended by their instructors or studios. **Criteria:** Preference will be given to those students who meet the criteria.

Funds Avail.: No specific amount. **To Apply:** Applicants must submit a completed application form. **Deadline:** May 9. **Contact:** Santa Barbara Dance Alliance at the above address (see entry 6243).

6245 ■ Bert Saperstein Communications Scholarship Fund

PO Box 42-Wykagyl Sta.
New Rochelle, NY 10804
Ph: (914)636-1281
E-mail: info@bsc-scholarshipfund.org
URL: http://www.bsc-scholarshipfund.org

6246 ■ Bert Saperstein Communication Scholarships *(Undergraduate/Scholarship)*

Purpose: To promote and increase interest in the field of Communication Arts which include film and television, creative writing, advertising, public relations, and communication design. **Focus:** Communication arts. **Qualif.:** Applicants must be enrolled full-time in any college/university. **Criteria:** Selection will be based on the criteria set by the Board of Trustees.

Funds Avail.: $500-$2,000. **To Apply:** Applicants may submit their application letters and other requirements to the office. **Contact:** Bert Saperstein Communication at the above address (see entry 6245).

6247 ■ Saratoga County Bar Association

PO Box 994
Saratoga Springs, NY 12866
Ph: (518)587-5829
E-mail: pclute@saratogacountybar.org
URL: http://www.saratogacountybar.org

6248 ■ Saratoga County Bar Association Law Student Scholarships *(All/Scholarship)*

Purpose: To support the efforts of students studying or entering the legal profession. **Focus:** Law. **Qualif.:** Applicants must be residents of Saratoga County who are in their second or third year of law school. **Criteria:** Recipients are selected based on class rank, demonstrated leadership, community involvement and financial need.

Funds Avail.: $1,000. **Number Awarded:** 2. **To Apply:** Applicants must submit a completed application form. **Deadline:** November 1. **Contact:** pclute@saratogacountybar.org.

6249 ■ Saskatchewan Trucking Association

1335 Wallace St.
Regina, SK, Canada S4N 3Z5
Ph: (306)569-9696
Fax: (306)569-1008
Free: 800-563-7623
URL: http://www.sasktrucking.com

6250 ■ Saskatchewan Trucking Association Scholarships *(Undergraduate/Scholarship)*

Purpose: To provide support to the employees and children of employees of association members. **Focus:** General studies. **Qualif.:** Applicant must be a grade 12 graduate who is an employee or a child of an employee, a carrier or associate trade member of the association; must be a student returning to post-secondary education after an absence of more than five years. **Criteria:** Applicants will be selected based on financial need and scholastic ability. Scholarship will be awarded without regards to sex, race, colour, national origin or religion.

Funds Avail.: $5,000. **Number Awarded:** 7. **To Apply:** Applicants must submit a transcript of record and the application form and must send it to Scholarship Applications, c/o Saskatchewan Trucking Association, 1335 Wallace St., Regina, Saskatchewan S4N 3Z5. **Deadline:** June 30.

6251 ■ Scholarship Foundation of Santa Barbara

PO Box 3620
Santa Barbara, CA 93130
Ph: (805)687-6065
Fax: (805)687-6031
E-mail: info@sbscholarship.org
URL: http://www.sbscholarship.org

6252 ■ Scholarship Foundation of Santa Barbara Art Scholarship Program *(High School/Scholarship)*

Purpose: To provide financial assistance to students who are planning to major in Art or an art-related major at college. **Focus:** Arts. **Qualif.:** Applicants must be graduating high school seniors who have attended at least four of the six secondary grade school years in Southern Santa Barbara County, comprised of Goleta, Santa Barbara, and Carpinteria; must be planning to major in Art or an art-related field in college. **Criteria:** Applicants are assessed based on academic merit.

Funds Avail.: No specific amount. **To Apply:** Applicants must submit all the required application information. **Deadline:** November 15.

6253 ■ South Coast Area High School Senior Honors Scholarship Program *(High School/Scholarship)*

Purpose: To provide assistance to deserving students for continuing their education. **Focus:** General studies. **Qualif.:** Applicants must be graduating high school seniors who have attended at least four of the six secondary grade school years in Southern Santa Barbara County (Goleta, Santa Barbara, Carpinteria). **Criteria:** Applicants are evaluated based on academic achievement.

Funds Avail.: No specific amount. **To Apply:** Applicants must submit completed application form; personal statement/essay; academic transcript; academic recommendation letter; and employer/supervisor recommendation letter in order to qualify for an interview. **Deadline:** November 15.

6254 ■ Undergraduate and Medical/Graduate General Scholarship and Loan Program *(Graduate/Scholarship)*

Purpose: To assist applicants studying in standard academic programs on a traditional academic calendar. **Focus:** General studies. **Qualif.:** Applicants must be U.S. citizens or documented legal permanent U.S. residents; must have attended at least four of the six secondary grade school years at a Santa Barbara County school and have graduated or will graduate from a Santa Barbara County high school; must be planning to attend full-time (12 units minimum per term) at an approved vocational school, 2-year college or 4-year college and must maintain a minimum 2.0 GPA. **Criteria:** Applicants are evaluated based on financial need, potential and motivation.

Funds Avail.: No specific amount. **To Apply:** Applicants must submit all the required application information. **Deadline:** January 31.

6255 ■ School Nutrition Association

700 South Washington St., Ste. 300
Alexandria, VA 22314
Ph: (703)739-3900
Fax: (703)739-3915
Free: 800-877-8822
E-mail: servicecenter@schoolnutrition.org
URL: http://www.schoolnutrition.org/Index.aspx?id=1075

6256 ■ Nancy Curry Scholarships *(Postgraduate/Scholarship)*

Purpose: To provide School Nutrition Association members with the opportunity to explore higher education options with the help of financial assistance. **Focus:** Food service careers. **Qualif.:** Applicant must be a member or dependent of a member of SNA for at least one year; pursuing a school foodservicerelated field; accepted at technical/vocational institution or university/ college; have a satisfactory academic record; and must express the desire to make school foodservice a career. **Criteria:** Selection is based on the application.

Funds Avail.: No specific amount. **Number Awarded:** 1. **To Apply:** Applicants must submit a completed application along with the required materials and informations. **Deadline:** April 15.

Remarks: Funded by Handgards, Inc. and friends of Nancy Curry.

6257 ■ GED Jump Start Scholarships *(Other/Scholarship)*

Purpose: To empower SNA members to stay in school foodservice and advance their careers, and make members eligible for college-level scholarships. **Focus:** Food service careers. **Qualif.:** Applicant must be a member of SNA; have not yet receive a high school diploma or a GED; planning on getting GED within one year of receiving the scholarship; and must not have received a GED Jump Start Scholarship in the past. **Criteria:** The Financial Aid Committee will review applications.

Funds Avail.: $200. **Number Awarded:** 20. **To Apply:** Applicants must submit a completed application form along with the required materials and information. **Deadline:** Applications are accepted throughout the year. **Contact:** Sasha Bleifield, at 800-877-8822 x-104, or sbleifield@schoolnutrition.org.

6258 ■ Schwan's Food Service Scholarships *(Undergraduate/Scholarship)*

Purpose: To provide School Nutrition Association members with the opportunity to explore higher education options with the help of financial assistance. **Focus:** Food service careers. **Qualif.:** Applicant must be a member or dependent of a member of SNA for at least one year; pursuing a school foodservicerelated field; accepted at technical/vocational institution or university/ college; have a satisfactory academic record; and must express the desire to make school foodservice a career. **Criteria:** Selection is based on the application.

Funds Avail.: No specific amount. **To Apply:** Applicants must submit a completed application along with the required materials and information. **Deadline:** April 15.

Remarks: Funded by Schwan's Food Service.

6259 ■ SNF Professional Growth Scholarships *(Graduate, Undergraduate/Scholarship)*

Purpose: To provide School Nutrition Association members with the opportunity to explore higher education options with the help of financial assistance. **Focus:** Food service careers. **Qualif.:** Applicant must be a member or dependent of a member of SNA for at least one year; pursuing undergraduate or graduate studies; have a satisfactory academic record; and must express the desire to make school foodservice a career. **Criteria:** Selection is based on the application.

Funds Avail.: No specific amount. **To Apply:** Applicants must submit a completed application along with the required materials and information. **Deadline:** April 15.

6260 ■ Winston Scholarships *(Graduate, Undergraduate/Scholarship)*

Purpose: To provide School Nutrition Association members with the opportunity to explore higher education options with the help of financial assistance. **Focus:** Food service careers. **Qualif.:** Applicant must be employed as a School Food Service Professional; or a the dependent of an employee, employed as a School Food Service Professional; a registered, or have plans to attend an accredited college, university or vocational/technical institution. **Criteria:** Selection is based on the application.

Funds Avail.: $2500. **To Apply:** Applicants must submit a completed Winston Scholarship application form along with the required materials and information. **Deadline:** April 15.

6261 ■ Schulich School of Business

4700 Keele St.
Toronto, ON, Canada M3J 1P3
Ph: (416)736-2100 x.77979
E-mail: cschewell@schulich.yorku.ca
URL: http://www.schulich.yorku.ca

6262 ■ Lawrence Bloomberg Entrance Awards *(Postgraduate/Award/Prize)*

Purpose: To recognize an incoming MBA student who has demonstrated the highest academic standing. **Focus:** General studies. **Qualif.:** Applicants must be female MBA students who are currently enrolled in the second year of study; must be active in their community; must have demonstrated leadership either in the workplace or through extracurricular activities; must have at least two years of working experience. **Criteria:** Applicants are selected based on academic excellence and financial need.

Funds Avail.: $10,000. **To Apply:** Applicants are advised to visit the organization for the application procedure. **Deadline:** February 1.

6263 ■ Louis J. Brody Q.C. Entrance Scholarships *(Postgraduate/Scholarship)*

Purpose: To recognize an incoming MBA student who has demonstrated the highest academic standing. **Focus:**

General studies. **Qualif.:** Applicants must be female MBA students who are currently enrolled in the second year of study and have demonstrated academic excellence in previous studies. **Criteria:** Applicants are evaluated based on academic excellence and financial need.

Funds Avail.: $5,000. **To Apply:** Applicants are advised to visit the organization for the application procedure. **Deadline:** February 1.

Remarks: Established in 1996 in memory of Louis Brody.

6264 ■ Peter F. Bronfman Entrance Awards
(Postgraduate/Award/Prize)

Purpose: To recognize an incoming MBA student who has demonstrated the highest academic standing. **Focus:** General studies. **Qualif.:** Applicants must be female MBA students who are currently enrolled in the second year of study; must be active in their community; must have demonstrated leadership either in the workplace or through extracurricular activities; must have at least two years of working experience. **Criteria:** Applicants are selected based on academic excellence and financial need.

Funds Avail.: $5,000. **To Apply:** Applicants are advised to visit the organization for the application procedure. **Deadline:** February 1.

6265 ■ Peter F. Bronfman Scholarships of Merit
(Postgraduate/Scholarship)

Purpose: To recognize an incoming MBA student who has demonstrated the highest academic standing. **Focus:** General studies. **Qualif.:** Applicants must be female MBA students who are currently enrolled in the second year of study; must be active in their community; must have demonstrated leadership either in the workplace or through extracurricular activities; must have at least two years of working experience. **Criteria:** Applicants are selected based on academic excellence and financial need.

Funds Avail.: $10,000. **To Apply:** Applicants are advised to visit the organization for the application procedure. **Deadline:** February 1.

6266 ■ CAWEE International Student Fellowships *(Postgraduate/Fellowship)*

Purpose: To recognize an incoming MBA student who has demonstrated the highest academic standing. **Focus:** General studies. **Qualif.:** Applicants must be female MBA students who are currently enrolled in the second year of study; must demonstrate academic excellence, leadership, or entrepreneurship. **Criteria:** Applicants are evaluated based on academic excellence and financial need.

Funds Avail.: $5,000. **To Apply:** Applicants are advised to visit the organization for the application procedure. **Deadline:** February 1.

6267 ■ Marshall A. Cohen Entrance Awards
(Postgraduate/Award/Prize)

Purpose: To recognize an incoming MBA student who has demonstrated the highest academic standing. **Focus:** General studies. **Qualif.:** Applicants must be female MBA students who are currently enrolled in the second year of study; must be active in their community; must have demonstrated academic excellence in previous studies; and must have at least two years of working experience. **Criteria:** Applicants are selected based on community involvement and extracurricular activities which have contributed to the well-being of others, academic excellence, and financial need.

Funds Avail.: $10,000. **To Apply:** Applicants are advised to visit the organization for the application procedure. **Deadline:** February 1.

6268 ■ Bernie Kom Memorial Awards
(Postgraduate/Award/Prize)

Purpose: To recognize an incoming MBA student who has demonstrated the highest academic standing. **Focus:** General studies. **Qualif.:** Applicants must be female MBA students who are currently enrolled in the second year of study and have demonstrated academic excellence in previous studies. **Criteria:** Applicants are evaluated based on academic excellence and financial need.

Funds Avail.: $5,000. **To Apply:** Applicants are advised to visit the organization for the application procedure. **Deadline:** February 1.

6269 ■ Allen T. Lambert Scholarships
(Postgraduate/Scholarship)

Purpose: To recognize an incoming MBA student who has demonstrated the highest academic standing. **Focus:** General studies. **Qualif.:** Applicants must be female MBA students who are currently enrolled in the second year of study and have demonstrated academic excellence in previous studies. **Criteria:** Applicants are evaluated based on academic excellence and financial need.

Funds Avail.: $5,000. **To Apply:** Applicants are advised to visit the organization for the application procedure. **Deadline:** February 1.

6270 ■ Kenneth Laundy Entrance Scholarships
(Postgraduate/Scholarship)

Purpose: To recognize an incoming MBA student who has demonstrated the highest academic standing. **Focus:** General studies. **Qualif.:** Applicants must be female MBA students who are currently enrolled in the second year of study and have achieved outstanding academic performance in preparation for the joint program. **Criteria:** Applicants are selected based on academic excellence and financial need.

Funds Avail.: $2,500. **To Apply:** Applicants are advised to visit the organization for the application procedure. **Deadline:** February 1.

6271 ■ Carol Anne Letheren Entrance Awards
(Postgraduate/Award/Prize)

Purpose: To recognize an incoming MBA student who has demonstrated the highest academic standing. **Focus:** General studies. **Qualif.:** Applicants must be female MBA students who are currently enrolled in the second year of study; must be active in their community and must demonstrate leadership either in the workplace or through extracurricular activities; must have at least two years of working experience. **Criteria:** Applicants are selected based on academic excellence and financial need.

Funds Avail.: $5,000. **To Apply:** Applicants are advised to visit the organization for the application procedure. **Deadline:** February 1.

6272 ■ Ian Lithgow Memorial Awards
(Postgraduate/Award/Prize)

Purpose: To recognize an incoming MBA student who has demonstrated the highest academic standing. **Focus:** General studies. **Qualif.:** Applicants must be female MBA students who are currently enrolled in the second year of study and have demonstrated academic excellence in previous studies. **Criteria:** Applicants are selected based on academic excellence and financial need.

Funds Avail.: $5,000. **To Apply:** Applicants are advised to visit the organization for the application procedure. **Deadline:** February 1.

6273 ■ Irwin Allen Nadal Entrance Awards *(Postgraduate/Award/Prize)*

Purpose: To recognize an incoming MBA student who has demonstrated the highest academic standing. **Focus:** General studies. **Qualif.:** Applicants must be female MBA students who are currently enrolled in the second year of study; must have a minimum cumulative grade of 6.0 (B+). **Criteria:** Applicants are evaluated based on academic achievements and financial need.

Funds Avail.: $2,500. **To Apply:** Applicants are advised to visit the organization for the application procedure. **Deadline:** February 1.

6274 ■ Miles Spencer Nadal Entrance Awards *(Postgraduate/Award/Prize)*

Purpose: To recognize an incoming MBA student who has demonstrated the highest academic standing. **Focus:** General studies. **Qualif.:** Applicants must be female MBA students who are currently enrolled in the second year of study; must have a minimum cumulative grade of 6.0 (B+). **Criteria:** Applicants are evaluated based on academic achievements and financial need.

Funds Avail.: $2,500. **To Apply:** Applicants are advised to visit the organization for the application procedure. **Deadline:** February 1.

6275 ■ Tanna H. Schulich MBA Entrance Scholarships *(Postgraduate/Scholarship)*

Purpose: To recognize an incoming MBA student who has demonstrated the highest academic standing. **Focus:** General studies. **Qualif.:** Applicants must be female MBA students who are currently enrolled in the second year of study; must be active in their community; and have demonstrated leadership either in the workplace or through extracurricular activities; must have at least two years of working experience. **Criteria:** Applicants are selected based on academic excellence and financial need.

Funds Avail.: $20,000. **To Apply:** Applicants are advised to visit the organization for the application procedure. **Deadline:** February 1.

6276 ■ Harry Steele Entrance Awards *(Postgraduate/Award/Prize)*

Purpose: To recognize an incoming MBA student who has demonstrated the highest academic standing. **Focus:** General studies. **Qualif.:** Applicants must be female MBA students who are currently enrolled in the second year of study; must be active in their community; must have demonstrated leadership either in the workplace or through extracurricular activities; must have at least two years of working experience. **Criteria:** Applicants are selected based on academic excellence and financial need.

Funds Avail.: $10,000. **To Apply:** Applicants are advised to visit the organization for the application procedure. **Deadline:** February 1.

6277 ■ York Graduate Scholarships *(Graduate/Scholarship)*

Purpose: To recognize an incoming MBA student who has demonstrated the highest academic standing. **Focus:** General studies. **Qualif.:** Applicants must be students at the masteral or doctoral level; must have an unequivocal "A" standing in their previous two years of study. **Criteria:** Applicants are evaluated based on demonstrated academic excellence and financial need.

Funds Avail.: $4,000. **To Apply:** Applicants are advised to visit the organization for the application procedure. **Deadline:** February 1.

6278 ■ Scleroderma Foundation

300 Rosewood Dr., Ste. 105
Danvers, MA 01923
Ph: (978)463-5843
Fax: (978)463-5809
Free: 800-722-4673
E-mail: sfinfo@scleroderma.org
URL: http://www.scleroderma.org

6279 ■ Scleroderma Foundation Established Investigator Grants *(Doctorate/Grant)*

Purpose: To provide assistance for established investigators in areas of research related to SSc who are pursuing highly innovative and meritorious pilot projects. **Focus:** Medicine, Osteopathic. **Qualif.:** Applicants must have a doctoral degree in Medicine, Osteopathy, Veterinary Medicine or one of the sciences and must have completed a postdoctoral fellowship. **Criteria:** Recipients are selected based on a committee's review of the proposal.

Funds Avail.: $150,000. **To Apply:** Applicants must submit one original copy in PDF format via CD and five hard copies of completed application along with five sets of appendices. **Deadline:** September 15.

6280 ■ Scleroderma Foundation New Investigator Grants *(Doctorate/Grant)*

Purpose: To provide financial assistance to promising new investigators in areas of research related to SSc. **Focus:** Medicine, Osteopathic. **Qualif.:** Applicants must have a doctoral degree in Medicine, Osteopathy, Veterinary Medicine or one of the sciences and must have completed a postdoctoral fellowship. **Criteria:** Recipients are selected based on a committee's review of the proposal.

Funds Avail.: $150,000. **To Apply:** Applicants must submit one original copy in PDF format via CD and five hard copies of completed application and five sets of appendices. **Deadline:** September 15.

6281 ■ Scleroderma Research Foundation

220 Montgomery St., Ste. 1411
San Francisco, CA 94104
Ph: (415)834-9444
Fax: (415)834-9177
Free: 800-441-CURE
URL: http://www.srfcure.org

6282 ■ SRF Post-doctoral Fellowships *(Postdoctorate/Fellowship)*

Purpose: To raise interest in exploring new approaches and hypotheses on the pathogenesis of scleroderma among young scientists by providing funding support. **Focus:** Biomedical research. **Qualif.:** Applicants must be U.S. citizens or permanent residents and must be Ph.D. or M.D. degree holders. Applicants must also identify a sponsoring

Awards are arranged alphabetically below their administering organizations

private or public non-profit institution and an individual who will serve as a sponsor and will directly supervise and document everything that are involved in the training and research experience of the candidate. **Criteria:** Award is given based on merit.

Funds Avail.: $35,000-$55,000. **Number Awarded:** 2. **To Apply:** Applicants must submit completed and signed application along with letter from sponsoring principle investigator; relevant supplemental material appended to application; research proposal; and three letters of recommendation. **Deadline:** November 30.

6283 ■ Scottish Rite Foundation of Colorado

1370 Grant St.
Denver, CO 80203-2347
Ph: (303)861-2410
Fax: (303)861-2411
Free: (866)289-6797
E-mail: ritecare@scottishfoundation.org
URL: http://www.scottishritefoundation.org

6284 ■ Dwight A. Hamilton Scottish Rite Foundation of Colorado Graduate Scholarships

(Graduate/Scholarship)

Purpose: To provide financial assistance to graduate students in speech-language pathology to further their studies in the field. **Focus:** Speech and language pathology/audiology. **Qualif.:** Applicants must have successfully completed the first year of graduate study in speech-language pathology with a grade point average of 3.5 (B+) or higher; must be enrolled as second-year graduate students in speech-language pathology at either the University of Colorado-Boulder or the University of Northern Colorado; must be recognized as Colorado residents by the university; must be committed to a career in treating children with childhood language disorders; must be planning to remain in Colorado after graduation to serve children in the state. **Criteria:** Applicants who are interested in serving children in rural or underserved areas of Colorado are given preference.

Funds Avail.: $5,000. **Number Awarded:** 2. **To Apply:** Applicants must submit official transcript or academic progress report (first year graduate study); proof of Colorado residency as defined by the university's criteria; one-page, double-spaced statement on career goals and aspirations including a description of students' interest in serving children with language disorders and intention to remain in Colorado; one letter of recommendation from university faculty; one letter of recommendation from clinical supervisor; one-page professional resume; application checklist showing application completeness. **Deadline:** June 15.

6285 ■ Scouts Canada

1345 Baseline Rd.
Ottawa, ON, Canada K2C 0A7
Ph: (613)224-5131
Fax: (613)224-3571
URL: http://www.scouts.ca

6286 ■ Reginald K. Groome Memorial Scholarships

(Postgraduate/Scholarship)

Purpose: To enhance the mission of Scouts Canada through recognition of scholastic and other achievement by youth members of Scouts Canada; to encourage continuous self-development on the part of active youth members of Scouts Canada through institutions of post secondary education. **Focus:** General studies. **Qualif.:** Program is open to individuals who have not reached their 25th birthday; must have the leadership contribution to scouting; and must have scholastic achievements up to the time of application. **Criteria:** Candidates will be selected based on merit.

Funds Avail.: No specific amount. **To Apply:** Application form is available at the website. Applicants must submit an official transcript of record and must attach a typed statement (200 words) discussing the value of scouting in their life. **Deadline:** April 1.

6287 ■ Screen Actors Guild

5757 Wilshire Blvd.
Los Angeles, CA 90036
Ph: (323)549-6708
E-mail: saginfo@sag.org
URL: http://www.sagfoundation.org

6288 ■ The John L. Dales Scholarship Fund

(Undergraduate/Scholarship)

Purpose: To assist students in their chosen field. **Focus:** Performing Arts. **Qualif.:** The scholarship applies only to accredited and licensed universities, colleges, junior colleges, adult specialty schools or trade/vocational schools. **Criteria:** Applicant for scholarship awards of the John L. Dales Scholarship Fund will be selected in accordance of the criteria.

Funds Avail.: No specific amount. **To Apply:** Applicant shall submit a transcript of all high school, college and university course and evaluations, SAT scores, and any other relevant information; Applicant shall submit the Confidential Financial Aid Form for applicant and a copy of their most recent Federal Income Tax Returns for applicant and parent; If either applicant or parents are incorporated, the Corporate Tax Return must be submitted. All submitted tax returns must be complete; Applicant shall submit an essay of 350 to 750 words on one of the topics provided with the application; and a two personal letters of recommendation. **Deadline:** March 15. **Contact:** Davidson Lloyd, Administrative Director, 323-549-6649, dlloyd@sag.org.

6289 ■ Scrollsaw Association of the World

116 E Lynn St.
Botkins, OH 45306
Ph: (937)693-3309
URL: http://www.saw-online.com

6290 ■ Patrick Spielman Memorial Scholarship Program

(Undergraduate/Scholarship)

Purpose: To promote activities within Local Chapter that will enhance the groups scrolling knowledge. **Focus:** Arts. **Qualif.:** Applicant must be undergraduate or a senior high school student; he/she is at least 24 age and under enrolled in a full time undergraduate course study at an accredited two or four year college, university, or vocational-technical school.

Funds Avail.: $1,000 **Number Awarded:** 2. **To Apply:** Applicant must request an application form to be sent by writing the SAW Office. **Deadline:** March 15.

6291 ■ Seaspace Incorporation

PO Box 3753
Houston, TX 77253-3753

Awards are arranged alphabetically below their administering organizations

Ph: (713)467-6675
E-mail: seaspace@seaspace.org
URL: http://www.seaspace.org

6292 ■ Seaspace Scholarships *(Postgraduate, Undergraduate/Scholarship)*

Purpose: To support marine-related courses of study. **Focus:** General studies. **Qualif.:** Applicants must be undergraduate students entering their junior or senior year and graduate students with an overall GPA of at least 3.3 on a 4.0 scale; must be enrolled or accepted full-time in an accredited U.S. college or university. **Criteria:** Recipients are selected based on financial need.

Funds Avail.: No specific amount. **To Apply:** Applicants must submit a completed application form. **Contact:** Jesse Cancelmo at jesse@cancelmophoto.com.

6293 ■ Section for Women in Public Administration

1301 Pennsylvania Ave. NW, Ste. 840
Washington, DC 20004
Ph: (202)393-7878
E-mail: pyearwood@aspanet.org
URL: http://www.swpanet.org

6294 ■ Rita Mae Kelly Awards *(All/Award/Prize)*

Purpose: To promote research about gender-related issues. **Focus:** Public administration; Women's studies. **Qualif.:** Candidates must be conducting a research on an issue significant to the role of women in public administration. **Criteria:** Award recipients will be selected based on the National Awards Chair's review of the application materials.

Funds Avail.: No specific amount. **To Apply:** Nominators must submit a cover letter that addresses the question of why the candidate deserves the award; and a curriculum vitae of the nominee with current contact information. Nominations must be sent to Patricia Alt, Awards Chair at palt@towson.edu. **Deadline:** December 15.

6295 ■ Serbian Bar Association of America

1000 N Lake Shore Dr., Unit 2204
Chicago, IL 60611
E-mail: dbalac@aol.com
URL: http://www.serbbar.org

6296 ■ Serbian Bar Association of America Scholarships *(Undergraduate/Scholarship)*

Purpose: To promote the best interests of the Serbian American community. **Focus:** Law. **Qualif.:** Applicants must be of Serbian birth or ancestry and/or their spouses who are enrolled in an accredited law school in the US. **Criteria:** Selection is based on merit.

Funds Avail.: $500-$2000. **To Apply:** Applicants must submit a typed essay of no more than 250 words detailing how they plan to use their legal education within the Serbian American community and submit a certified copy of their law school transcript. **Deadline:** October.

6297 ■ Seton Hall University School of Law

1 Newark Ctr.
Newark, NJ 07102
Ph: (973)642-8850
Fax: (973)642-8876
Free: 888-415-7271
E-mail: law_financial@shu.edu
URL: http://law.shu.edu

6298 ■ Seton Hall Law School's Merit Scholarship Program *(Undergraduate/Scholarship)*

Purpose: To reward the hard work and academic success of students. **Focus:** Law. **Qualif.:** Prospective recipient must be an incoming law student of the university. **Criteria:** Recipients are selected based on the Law School Admission Test (LSAT) scores, undergraduate academic performance, and academic promise.

Funds Avail.: $4,500 to full tuition. **To Apply:** All applicants for school admission are considered an applicant for the program. **Deadline:** End of enrollment in fall.

Remarks: No separate application is required. Scholarship is renewable by maintaining a required GPA standard.

6299 ■ Sheet Metal And Air Conditioning Contractors' National Association

4201 Lafayette Center Dr.
Chantilly, VA 20151-1209
Ph: (703)803-2980
Fax: (703)803-3732
E-mail: info@smacna.org
URL: http://www.smacna.org

6300 ■ SMACNA College of Fellows Scholarships *(Undergraduate/Scholarship)*

Purpose: To provide financial assistance for the discovery, interpretation, and dissemination of new knowledge that promotes leadership development and personal growth. **Focus:** Metallurgy. **Qualif.:** Applicants must be students seeking to further their education in an undergraduate course of study in an accredited institution of higher education; must be planning to pursue any course of study, however, studies in a field related to the sheet metal industry are preferred. Entering freshmen and undergraduate students seeking a degree from an accredited four-year program, college, or university are eligible. **Criteria:** Recipients are selected based on demonstrated academic excellence; academic goals; involvement in extracurricular activities; community involvement; leadership ability; good character; and financial need.

Funds Avail.: $2,000. **Number Awarded:** 3. **To Apply:** Applicants must submit all the required application information. **Deadline:** April 30.

6301 ■ Shell Oil Company

PO Box 2463
Houston, TX 77252
Ph: (713)241-6161
Free: 888-467-4355
E-mail: shellcustomercare@shell.com
URL: http://www.shell.com

6302 ■ Shell Incentive Scholarships Fund *(Undergraduate/Scholarship)*

Purpose: To offer scholarships to selected students pursuing two and four-year college degrees in certain engineering or geosciences disciplines at certain colleges. **Focus:** Engineering; Geosciences. **Qualif.:** Applicants must be un-

Awards are arranged alphabetically below their administering organizations

derrepresented students pursuing a four-year degree in a specific technical field of study at certain colleges. **Criteria:** Recipients are selected based on financial need.

Funds Avail.: $5,000. **To Apply:** Applicants must submit a completed application form.

6303 ■ Shell Process Technology Scholarships *(Undergraduate/Scholarship)*

Purpose: To help students who seek an education to obtain employment in the industries that use and control mechanical, physical or chemical processes to produce a final product. **Focus:** Engineering; Geosciences. **Qualif.:** Applicants must be currently enrolled or planning to enroll in the Process Technology two-year degree program. **Criteria:** Recipients are selected based on financial need.

Funds Avail.: $2,000. **To Apply:** Applicants must submit a completed application form.

6304 ■ Shell Technical Scholarships *(Undergraduate/Scholarship)*

Purpose: To offer scholarships to selected students pursuing two and four-year college degrees in certain engineering or geosciences disciplines at certain colleges. **Focus:** Engineering; Geosciences. **Qualif.:** Applicants must be students pursuing a four-year college degree in certain engineering or geosciences disciplines at certain colleges. **Criteria:** Recipients are selected based on academic performance and financial need.

Funds Avail.: $5,000. **To Apply:** Applicants must submit a completed application form.

6305 ■ Shoreline Community College Foundation

16101 Greenwood Ave. N, Ste. 1005
Shoreline, WA 98133-5696
Ph: (206)546-4755
Fax: (206)546-5826
E-mail: rmanchester@shoreline.edu
URL: http://www.shoreline.edu

6306 ■ Beta Sigma Phi-VCT Scholarships *(Undergraduate/Scholarship)*

Purpose: To increase access and success of Shoreline Community College students; to attract, encourage and assist talented students enrolled in Fine Arts programs at SCC. **Focus:** Fine Arts. **Qualif.:** Applicants must be full-time or part-time students at the Shoreline/Lake Forest Park area who are enrolling at SCC; applicants must have demonstrated strong academic improvement in the last three semesters. **Criteria:** Recipients are selected based on the academic performance and financial needs.

Funds Avail.: No specific amount. **To Apply:** Applicants must complete the application form.

6307 ■ Boeing Company Scholarships *(Undergraduate/Scholarship)*

Purpose: To increase access and success of Shoreline Community College students. **Focus:** Manufacturing; Engineering; Information Science and Technology. **Qualif.:** Applicants must be full-time or part-time students at the Shoreline/Lake Forest Park area who are enrolling at SCC. **Criteria:** Recipients are selected based on academic performance and financial needs.

Funds Avail.: $500. **Number Awarded:** 2. **To Apply:** Applicants must complete the application form.

6308 ■ Ivan Braga Scholarships *(Undergraduate/Scholarship)*

Purpose: To increase access and success of Shoreline Community College students. **Focus:** Surgery. **Qualif.:** Applicants must be part-time or full-time students who are currently enrolled at Shoreline Community College. **Criteria:** Recipients are selected based on the academic performance and financial needs.

Funds Avail.: No specific amount. **To Apply:** Applicants must complete the application form.

6309 ■ Co Dental Hygiene Scholarships *(Undergraduate/Scholarship)*

Purpose: To increase access and success of Shoreline Community College students. **Focus:** Dental hygiene. **Qualif.:** Applicants must be full-time or part-time students at the Shoreline/Lake Forest Park area who are enrolling at SCC. **Criteria:** Recipients are selected based on academic performance and financial needs.

Funds Avail.: $500. **To Apply:** Applicants must complete the application form.

6310 ■ Dr. Princeton L. Co Emergency Fund for Dental Hygiene Scholarships *(Undergraduate/Scholarship)*

Purpose: To increase access and success of Shoreline Community College students; to provide emergency assistance for Shoreline Community College dental hygiene students who are in need of financial assistance. **Focus:** Dental hygiene. **Qualif.:** Applicants must be currently enrolled as full-time dental hygiene students at Shoreline Community College; must be survivors of domestic abuse; must be Washington State residents for a minimum of one year; must not have previous two or four year college degree; must earn and maintain minimum cumulative GPA of 2.50 (minimum GPA of 3.0 in dental hygiene coursework); and must not be currently included on the Scholarship Selection Committee or related (first degree) to a person on the Selection Committee. **Criteria:** Recipients are selected based on academic standing and financial needs.

Funds Avail.: $300. **To Apply:** Applicants must complete the application form; must submit statement or documentation of income and need; unofficial SCC transcript; and current class schedule. **Contact:** mbaker@shoreline.edu

6311 ■ Carli Edwards Memorial Scholarships *(Undergraduate/Scholarship)*

Purpose: To increase access and success of Shoreline Community College students. **Focus:** Criminal Justice. **Qualif.:** Applicants must be returning or part-time students at Shoreline Community College; must be survivors of domestic abuse; must be Washington State residents for a minimum of one year; must not have previous two or four year college degree; must be criminal justice majors; must earn and maintain a minimum cumulative GPA of 3.0 (GPA of 3.5 in criminal justice coursework); and must not be currently included on the Scholarship Selection Committee or related (first degree) to a person on the Selection Committee. **Criteria:** Recipients are selected based on academic standing and financial needs.

Funds Avail.: $200. **To Apply:** Applicants must complete application form; must submit letter of recommendation from teacher, professor or employer (excluding criminal

Awards are arranged alphabetically below their administering organizations

justice faculty); statement or documentation of income and need; and unofficial SCC transcript.

6312 ■ Friends of Mary Automotive Scholarships *(Undergraduate/Scholarship)*

Purpose: To increase access and success of Shoreline Community College students; to provide financial assistance to women in the automotive program. **Focus:** Automotive technology. **Qualif.:** Applicants must be full-time or part-time students at the Shoreline/Lake Forest Park area who are enrolling at SCC. **Criteria:** Recipients are selected based on academic performance and financial needs.

Funds Avail.: No specific amount. **To Apply:** Applicants must complete the application form.

6313 ■ Dr. Bill Johnson Scholarships *(Undergraduate/Scholarship)*

Purpose: To increase access and success of Shoreline Community College students. **Focus:** Mathematics and mathematical science. **Qualif.:** Applicants must be full-time or part-time students at the Shoreline/Lake Forest Park area who are enrolling at SCC. **Criteria:** Recipients are selected based on academic performance and financial needs.

Funds Avail.: No specific amount. **To Apply:** Applicants must complete the application form.

6314 ■ Ina Knutsen Scholarships *(Undergraduate/Scholarship)*

Purpose: To increase access and success of Shoreline Community College students. **Focus:** General studies. **Qualif.:** Applicants must be full-time or part-time students at the Shoreline/Lake Forest Park area who are enrolling at SCC. **Criteria:** Recipients are selected based on academic performance and financial needs.

Funds Avail.: No specific amount. **To Apply:** Applicants must complete the application form.

6315 ■ Ken LaFountaine First Nations Scholarships *(Undergraduate/Scholarship)*

Purpose: To increase access and success of Shoreline Community College students; to provide First Nation students (indigenous to the Americas and associated territories) with financial assistance in times of need. **Focus:** General studies. **Qualif.:** Applicants must be returning or part-time students at Shoreline Community College; must have demonstrated active involvement in the First Nation community in the Puget Sound area, either on campus or in the broader community; and must not be currently included on the Scholarship Selection Committee or related (first degree) to a person on the Selection Committee. **Criteria:** Recipients are selected based on academic standing and financial needs.

Funds Avail.: $300. **To Apply:** Applicants must submit evidence of likelihood of academic success with a minimum of 2.0 GPA or 2.0 during most recent quarter attended; evidence of the other venues of financial support; letter of recommendation from a teacher, professor, or employer. **Contact:** bpeace-g@shoreline.edu

6316 ■ Ron LaFreniere Business Scholarships *(Undergraduate/Scholarship)*

Purpose: To increase access and success of Shoreline Community College students. **Focus:** Business Administration. **Qualif.:** Applicants must be part-time or full-time students who are currently enrolled at Shoreline Community College. **Criteria:** Recipients are selected based on academic performance and financial needs.

Funds Avail.: No specific amount. **To Apply:** Applicants must complete the application form.

6317 ■ Mallet Nursing Scholarships *(Undergraduate/Scholarship)*

Purpose: To increase access and success of Shoreline Community College students; to assist promising students to continue their studies at an accredited four year college or university. **Focus:** Nursing. **Qualif.:** Applicants must be part-time or full-time students who are currently enrolled at Shoreline Community College. **Criteria:** Recipients are selected based on academic performance, financial needs, merit and community involvement.

Funds Avail.: No specific amount. **To Apply:** Applicants must complete the application form.

6318 ■ Eric Niemitalo Scholarships in Earth and Environmental Science *(Undergraduate/Scholarship)*

Purpose: To increase access and success of Shoreline Community College students. **Focus:** Environmental Science. **Qualif.:** Applicants must be full-time or part-time students at the Shoreline/Lake Forest Park area who are enrolling at SCC. **Criteria:** Recipients are selected based on academic performance and financial needs.

Funds Avail.: No specific amount. **To Apply:** Applicants must complete the application form.

6319 ■ Joseph Wood Rogers Memorial Scholarships *(Undergraduate/Scholarship)*

Purpose: To increase access and success of Shoreline Community College students; to assist promising students to continue their studies in Mathematics at an accredited four year college or university. **Focus:** Mathematics and mathematical science. **Qualif.:** Applicants must be part-time or full-time students who are currently enrolled at Shoreline Community College. **Criteria:** Recipients are selected based on academic performance and financial needs.

Funds Avail.: No specific amount. **To Apply:** Applicants must complete the application form.

6320 ■ Shoreline Community College Academic Excellence Scholarships for Graduating High School Seniors *(Undergraduate/Scholarship)*

Purpose: To increase access and success of Shoreline Community College students. **Focus:** General studies. **Qualif.:** Applicants must be graduating high school seniors in the Shoreline/Lake Forest Park area who are enrolling at SCC; must have demonstrated strong academic performance. **Criteria:** Recipients are selected based on academic performance, leadership qualities and involvement in school and community activities.

Funds Avail.: No specific amount. **To Apply:** Applicants must complete the application form.

6321 ■ Shoreline Community College Academic Improvement Scholarships for Graduating High School Seniors *(Undergraduate/Scholarship)*

Purpose: To increase access and success of Shoreline Community College students. **Focus:** General studies. **Qualif.:** Applicants must be graduating high school seniors

Awards are arranged alphabetically below their administering organizations

in the Shoreline/Lake Forest Park area who are enrolling at SCC; must have demonstrated strong academic improvement in the last three semesters. **Criteria:** Recipients are selected based on academic performance and financial needs.

Funds Avail.: No specific amount. **To Apply:** Applicants must complete the application form.

6322 ■ Shoreline Community College Continuing Students Scholarships *(Undergraduate/Scholarship)*

Purpose: To increase access and success of Shoreline Community College students. **Focus:** General studies. **Qualif.:** Applicants must be part-time or full-time students who are currently enrolled at Shoreline Community College. **Criteria:** Recipients are selected based on academic performance, financial needs, involvement in school and community activities.

Funds Avail.: No specific amount. **To Apply:** Applicants must complete the application form.

6323 ■ Shoreline Community College Part-Time Students Scholarships *(Undergraduate/Scholarship)*

Purpose: To increase access and success of Shoreline Community College students. **Focus:** General studies. **Qualif.:** Applicants must be part-time students who are currently enrolled at Shoreline Community College. **Criteria:** Recipients are selected based on the academic performance, financial needs, involvement in school and community activities.

Funds Avail.: No specific amount. **To Apply:** Applicants must complete the application form.

6324 ■ Margaret Svec Scholarships *(Undergraduate/Scholarship)*

Purpose: To increase access and success of Shoreline Community College students; to assist promising students to continue their studies in mathematics at an accredited four year college or university. **Focus:** Mathematics and mathematical science. **Qualif.:** Applicants must be part-time or full-time students who are currently enrolled at Shoreline Community College. **Criteria:** Recipients are selected based on academic performance and financial needs.

Funds Avail.: No specific amount. **To Apply:** Applicants must complete the application form.

6325 ■ Elizabeth Thomas Scholarships *(Undergraduate/Scholarship)*

Purpose: To increase access and success of Shoreline Community College students. **Focus:** General studies. **Qualif.:** Applicants must be full-time or part-time students at the Shoreline/Lake Forest Park area who are enrolling at SCC. **Criteria:** Recipients are selected based on academic performance and financial needs.

Funds Avail.: No specific amount. **To Apply:** Applicants must complete the application form.

6326 ■ Sickle Cell Disease Association of America

31 East Baltimore St., Ste. 800
Baltimore, MD 21202
Ph: (410)528-1555
Fax: (410)528-1495
Free: 800-421-8453
E-mail: scdaa@sicklecelldisease.org
URL: http://www.sicklecelldisease.org

6327 ■ Kermit B. Nash Academic Scholarships *(Undergraduate/Scholarship)*

Purpose: To promote educational pursuits of individuals with sickle cell disease. **Focus:** General studies. **Qualif.:** Applicants must be individuals with sickle cell disease (individuals with sickle cell trait are not eligible); and must be graduating high school seniors. **Criteria:** Award is given based on the applicant's GPA, academic achievement, SAT scores, community service, quality of essay, and academic obstacles caused by the disease.

Funds Avail.: $5,000 per academic year. **Number Awarded:** 1. **To Apply:** Applicants must submit an application form; transcripts; physician's certification of sickle cell status; and an essay. **Deadline:** May. **Contact:** Mr. Manning, 800-421-8453 or lmanning@sicklecelldisease.org.

6328 ■ SCDAA Post-Doctoral Research Fellowships *(Doctorate/Fellowship)*

Purpose: To provide financial support for young investigators conducting research in sickle cell disease. **Focus:** Specific disease. **Qualif.:** Applicants must have completed a doctoral degree (MD, PhD or equivalent); must have completed clinical training; must not have more than a total of five years of post-doctoral research experience by the award date; and must be affiliated with a non-profit institution of higher learning or non-profit research facility in the United States. **Criteria:** Awards will be given based on evidence of the applicant's commitment to a research career in sickle cell disease, quality and originality of the proposed research, and importance of the research to the field.

Funds Avail.: $25,000 ($20,000 salary and $5,000 supplies) per year. **To Apply:** Applicants must submit three copies of application and research mentor's supporting documents including a letter of commitment and the biographical sketch of the mentor. **Deadline:** May 1. **Contact:** Sonya I. Ross, Vice President, Programs and Services, 410-528-1555.

6329 ■ Siemens Foundation

170 Wood Ave., S.
Iselin, NJ 08830
Fax: (732)603-5890
Free: 877-822-5233
E-mail: foundation.us@siemens.com
URL: http://www.siemens-foundation.org

6330 ■ Siemens Teacher Scholarships *(Graduate, Undergraduate/Scholarship)*

Purpose: To encourage minority students to consider careers teaching math and science; to provide financial assistance to those students who are in need. **Focus:** Education. **Qualif.:** Applicants must be undergraduate or graduate students pursuing education; must be enrolled at one of the historically black colleges or universities. **Criteria:** Preference will be given to those who meet the criteria.

Funds Avail.: No specific amount. **To Apply:** Applicants must check the application process online.

6331 ■ Sierra Student Coalition

600 14th St. NW, Ste. 750
Washington, DC 20005

Awards are arranged alphabetically below their administering organizations

Fax: (202)637-0410
Free: 888-564-6772
E-mail: sierra.student@sierraclub.org
URL: http://www.ssc.org

6332 ■ Drum Major Institute Scholars *(Undergraduate/Scholarship)*

Purpose: To provide financial support and to advocate for fairness, equity and strong communities. **Focus:** General studies. **Qualif.:** Applicants must be sophomore and junior college students and must be 18 years old. **Criteria:** Preference will be given to those who meet the criteria.

Funds Avail.: No specific amount. **To Apply:** Applicants must check the available website for the required materials.

Remarks: DMI Scholars is a "Public Policy 101" for young people who want to shape the direction of our country. **Contact:** Sierra Student Coalition at the above address (see entry 6331).

6333 ■ NWF's Women for Sustainable Development (WSD) Scholarships *(Undergraduate/Scholarship)*

Purpose: To provide financial assistance for deserving students and to offer career building skills and educational opportunities for participants as well as the opportunity to use these skills to build awareness about international sustainable development issues on their campuses and in their communities. **Focus:** General studies. **Qualif.:** Applicants must be females enrolled in undergraduate schools in the U.S. and Mexico. **Criteria:** Preference will be given to those who meet the criteria.

Funds Avail.: No specific amount. **To Apply:** Applicants must check the available website for the required materials.

6334 ■ SSC-Building Environmental Campus Community (BECC) Fellowships *(Undergraduate/Scholarship)*

Purpose: To support talented student organizers to implement the "Building Environmental Campus Community" (BECC) project during the upcoming fall semester on selected campuses nationwide and to conduct a hard-hitting campaign for clean energy on campus. **Focus:** General studies. **Qualif.:** Applicants must meet the following criteria: currently enrolled full-time in a college or university; president or leader of an environmental group; demonstrated leadership and recruitment skills; willing and able to use the Sierra Student Coalition name for environmental group, or indicate affiliation with the SSC in campaign materials, media outreach, meetings, and events; and commitment to the BECC model of face-to-face outreach and contact to get students on campus involved in energy issues. **Criteria:** Preference will be given to those who meet the criteria.

Funds Avail.: $1,500. **To Apply:** Applicants must check the available website for the required materials. **Contact:** Sierra Student Coalition at the above address (see entry 6331).

6335 ■ Young People For (YP4) Scholarships *(Undergraduate/Fellowship)*

Purpose: To provide financial support, technical support and media assistance while a student implements a self-designed blueprint for social justice. **Focus:** General studies. **Qualif.:** Applicants must be undergraduate students at twoand four-year institutions. **Criteria:** Preference will be given to those who meet the criteria.

Funds Avail.: No specific amount. **Number Awarded:** 200. **To Apply:** Applicants must check the available website for the required materials. **Contact:** Sierra Student Coalition at the above address (see entry 6331).

6336 ■ Sigma Delta Chi Foundation

3909 N Meridian St.
Indianapolis, IN 46208
Ph: (317)927-8000
Fax: (317)920-4789
URL: http://www.spj.org

6337 ■ Eugene C. Pulliam Fellowships for Editorial Writing *(All/Fellowship)*

Purpose: To provide financial assistance to outstanding editorial writers to help broaden their journalistic horizons and knowledge of the world. **Focus:** Editors and editing. **Qualif.:** Applicants must be a full-time editorial writer at a news publication located in the United States; with at least three years experience as an editorial writer; demonstrate outstanding writing and analytical abilities and ability and intent to publish work within 18 months of selection. **Criteria:** Applicants entry will be reviewed and evaluated by a panel of judges.

Funds Avail.: $75,000. **To Apply:** Applicants must submit a cover letter (containing complete contact information) stating the purpose and nature of the proposed study, a time line for accomplishing the work and a plan for how the stipend will be used; editor's endorsement; a one-page professional biography and summary of professional experience; and five samples of editorials. **Deadline:** July 1.

6338 ■ Sigma Delta Epsilon, Graduate Women in Science

PO Box 291
Avon, MA 02322
Ph: (919)668-1439
E-mail: marie_drottar@msn.com
URL: http://www.gwis.org

6339 ■ Eloise Gerry Fellowships *(Graduate, Postdoctorate/Fellowship)*

Purpose: To encourage research careers in the sciences for women. **Focus:** Science. **Qualif.:** Applicant must be enrolled as a graduate student, or engaged in post-doctoral or early-stage junior faculty academic research, and demonstrate financial need. **Criteria:** Selection is based on scientific merit, fields of study and requested funding amounts.

Funds Avail.: Total of $14,494. **Number Awarded:** 4. **To Apply:** Applicants must submit a completed application from together with the abstract of the proposed project (maximum of 200 words, 12 point font, 0.75 in margins); a project proposal description; a proposed budget; two letters of recommendation (sent directly by the authors to fellowships applications@gwis.org, with the name of the applicant as the subject line); copies of animal/human subjects approval or collecting permits; an application process fee of $20. Send entire application (except the recommendation letters and fee) electronically as a single, complete PDF document with "SDE/GWIS Application" and applicant's name in the subject line to fellowships applications@gwis.org. **Deadline:** January 15.

6340 ■ Nell I. Mondy Fellowships *(Graduate, Postdoctorate/Fellowship)*

Purpose: To encourage research careers in the sciences for women. **Focus:** Science. **Qualif.:** Applicant must be enrolled as a graduate student, or engaged in post-doctoral or early-stage junior faculty academic research, and demonstrate financial need. **Criteria:** Selection is based on scientific merit, fields of study and requested funding amounts.

Funds Avail.: Total of $3000. **Number Awarded:** 1. **To Apply:** Applicants must submit a completed application from together with the abstract of the proposed project (maximum of 200 words, 12 point font, 0.75 in margins); a project proposal description; a proposed budget; two letters of recommendation (sent directly by the authors to fellowships applications@gwis.org, with the name of the applicant as the subject line); copies of animal/human subjects approval or collecting permits; an application process fee of $20. Send entire application (except the recommendation letters and fee) electronically as a single, complete PDF document with "SDE/GWIS Application" and applicant's name in the subject line to fellowships applications@gwis.org. **Deadline:** January 15.

6341 ■ Vessa Notchev Fellowships *(Graduate, Postdoctorate/Fellowship)*

Purpose: To encourage research careers in the sciences for women. **Focus:** Science. **Qualif.:** Applicant must be enrolled as a graduate student, or engaged in post-doctoral or early-stage junior faculty academic research, and demonstrate financial need. **Criteria:** Selection is based on scientific merit, fields of study and requested funding amounts.

Funds Avail.: Total of $14,494. **Number Awarded:** 4. **To Apply:** Applicants must submit a completed application from together with the abstract of the proposed project (maximum of 200 words, 12 point font, 0.75 in margins); a project proposal description; a proposed budget; two letters of recommendation (sent directly by the authors to fellowships applications@gwis.org, with the name of the applicant as the subject line); copies of animal/human subjects approval or collecting permits; an application process fee of $20. Send entire application (except the recommendation letters and fee) electronically as a single, complete PDF document with "SDE/GWIS Application" and applicant's name in the subject line to fellowships applications@gwis.org. **Deadline:** January 15.

6342 ■ Sigma Delta Epsilon Fellowships *(Graduate, Postdoctorate/Fellowship)*

Purpose: To encourage research careers in the sciences for women. **Focus:** Science. **Qualif.:** Applicant must be enrolled as a graduate student, or engaged in post-doctoral or early-stage junior faculty academic research, and demonstrate financial need. **Criteria:** Selection is based on scientific merit, fields of study and requested funding amounts.

Funds Avail.: Total of $10,489. **Number Awarded:** 3. **To Apply:** Applicants must submit a completed application from together with the abstract of the proposed project (maximum of 200 words, 12 point font, 0.75 in margins); a project proposal description; a proposed budget; two letters of recommendation (sent directly by the authors to fellowships applications@gwis.org, with the name of the applicant as the subject line); copies of animal/human subjects approval or collecting permits; an application process fee of $20. Send entire application (except the recommendation letters and fee) electronically as a single, complete PDF document with "SDE/GWIS Application" and applicant's name in the subject line to fellowships applications@gwis.org. **Deadline:** January 15.

6343 ■ Sigma Kappa Foundation

8733 Founder Rd.
Indianapolis, IN 46268
Ph: (317)872-3275
E-mail: alewis@sigmakappa.org
URL: http://www.sigmakappafoundation.org

6344 ■ Margaret J. Andrew Memorial Scholarships *(Undergraduate/Scholarship)*

Purpose: To encourage and support the scholastic development of the collegiate and alumnae sisters of the foundation. **Focus:** Food science and technology. **Qualif.:** Applicants must be in good standing as a junior, senior, or graduate student; must be studying food science/food technology or a related major (nutrition, dietetics); must have a minimum cumulative GPA: 3.0. **Criteria:** Selection of candidates will be based on GPA and other basic demographic criteria.

Funds Avail.: $750. **Number Awarded:** 2. **To Apply:** Application forms are available online. Applicant must submit the transcript and recommendation letter through online. **Deadline:** March 1.

6345 ■ Frances Warren Baker Memorial Scholarships *(Undergraduate/Scholarship)*

Purpose: To encourage and support the scholastic development of the collegiate and alumnae sisters of the foundation. **Focus:** Journalism, Communications. **Qualif.:** Applicant must be a member in good standing enrolled in an undergraduate program in the fields of journalism or communication (print media); must have a minimum cumulative GPA: 3.0. **Criteria:** Preference will be given to sophomores and juniors with at least one year's study remaining.

Funds Avail.: $500. **Number Awarded:** 1. **To Apply:** Application forms are available online. Applicant must submit the transcript and recommendation letter through online. **Deadline:** March 1.

6346 ■ Beta Nu/Caryl Cordis D'hondt Scholarships *(Undergraduate/Scholarship)*

Purpose: To encourage and support the scholastic development of the collegiate and alumnae sisters of the foundation. **Focus:** General studies. **Qualif.:** Applicants must be a initiated members in good standing (scholastic, financial, membership) of Beta Nu Chapter (Bradley University); must be in need of financial assistance; must be involved in Sigma Kappa and the Bradley University campus. **Criteria:** Applicants will be judge based on their active participation in a variety of the foundation and academic activities.

Funds Avail.: $500. **Number Awarded:** 1. **To Apply:** Application forms are available online. Applicant must submit the transcript and recommendation letter through online. **Deadline:** March 1.

6347 ■ Beta Omega Scholarships *(Undergraduate/Scholarship)*

Purpose: To encourage and support the scholastic development of the collegiate and alumnae sisters of the foundation. **Focus:** General studies. **Qualif.:** Applicants must be initiated, active members in good standing of Beta Omega

Chapter (University of Nebraska, Omaha); must be a junior or senior class status (mid-year graduating seniors are eligible); must have a minimum cumulative GPA: 3.0; must be in need of financial assistance. **Criteria:** Applicants will be judge based on their active participation in a variety of the foundation and academic activities.

Funds Avail.: $1,000. **Number Awarded:** 1. **To Apply:** Application forms are available online. Applicant must submit the transcript and recommendation letter through online. **Deadline:** March 1.

6348 ■ Beta Sigma Scholarships *(Undergraduate/Scholarship)*

Purpose: To encourage and support the scholastic development of the collegiate and alumnae sisters of the foundation. **Focus:** General studies. **Qualif.:** Applicants must be an active, initiated members in good standing of Beta Sigma Chapter (Purdue University); must be a sophomore, junior, or senior class status (mid-year graduating seniors are eligible); must have a minimum cumulative GPA: 2.5; must be in need of financial assistance; must be Residing in the chapter house; must demonstrate leadership in their chapter and on campus. **Criteria:** Applicants will be judge based on their active participation in a variety of the foundation and academic activities.

Funds Avail.: $500. **Number Awarded:** 1. **To Apply:** Application forms are available online. Applicant must submit the transcript and recommendation letter through online. **Deadline:** March 1.

6349 ■ Walta Wilkinson Carmichael Scholarships *(Undergraduate/Scholarship)*

Purpose: To encourage and support the scholastic development of the collegiate and alumnae sisters of the foundation. **Focus:** General studies. **Qualif.:** Applicant must be a alumnae members in good standing, enrolled in a graduate program, who have demonstrated participation in collegiate chapter activities from their beginning year and continuing through the senior year of membership; must have a minimum undergraduate GPA: 3.0. **Criteria:** Candidates will be selected based on their academic standing.

Funds Avail.: $500. **Number Awarded:** 1. **To Apply:** Application forms are available online. Applicant must submit the transcript and recommendation letter through online. **Deadline:** March 1.

6350 ■ Christine Kerr Cawthorne Scholarships *(Undergraduate/Scholarship)*

Purpose: To encourage and support the scholastic development of the collegiate and alumnae sisters of the foundation. **Focus:** General studies. **Qualif.:** Applicants must be initiated collegiate members in good standing of Alpha Chi Chapter (Georgetown College); must be a matriculated rising sophomore at the time the application is completed, and therefore a matriculated junior in the academic year for which the scholarship is issued; must have a minimum cumulative GPA: 3.0. **Criteria:** Applicants will be judged on leadership and service provided to the chapter and campus community.

Funds Avail.: $1,000. **Number Awarded:** 1. **To Apply:** Application forms are available online. Applicant must submit the transcript and recommendation letter through online. **Deadline:** March 1.

6351 ■ Maridell Braham Condon Scholarships *(Undergraduate/Scholarship)*

Purpose: To encourage and support the scholastic development of the collegiate and alumnae sisters of the foundation. **Focus:** Education. **Qualif.:** Applicants must be initiated, active members in good standing; must be majoring in education; must have a minimum cumulative GPA: 3.0. **Criteria:** Applicants will be judged based on the demonstrated financial need and active participation in a variety of Sigma Kappa and academic activities. Preference will be given to juniors and seniors with at least one year study remaining.

Funds Avail.: $500. **Number Awarded:** 1. **To Apply:** Application forms are available online. Applicant must submit the transcript and recommendation letter through online. **Deadline:** March 1.

6352 ■ Delta Chi Alumnae Memorial Scholarships *(Undergraduate/Scholarship)*

Purpose: To encourage and support the scholastic development of the collegiate and alumnae sisters of the foundation. **Focus:** General studies. **Qualif.:** Applicants must be a initiated members of Delta Chi Chapter (University of Central Oklahoma); must be a junior or senior class status; must have a minimum cumulative GPA: 3.25; must be currently enrolled in 12 hours or more. **Criteria:** Consideration will be given for leadership and service provided to the chapter and to the campus community.

Funds Avail.: $400. **Number Awarded:** 1. **To Apply:** Application forms are available online. Applicant must submit the transcript and recommendation letter through online. **Deadline:** March 1.

6353 ■ Wilma Sackett Dressel Scholarships *(Undergraduate/Scholarship)*

Purpose: To encourage and support the scholastic development of the collegiate and alumnae sisters of the foundation. **Focus:** General studies. **Qualif.:** Applicant must be a initiated member in good standing of Alpha Tau Chapter (Michigan State University); must demonstrate financial need. **Criteria:** Selection of applicant will be based on their financial need.

Funds Avail.: $500. **Number Awarded:** 1. **To Apply:** Application forms are available online. Applicant must submit the transcript and recommendation letter through online. **Deadline:** March 1.

6354 ■ Epsilon Epsilon Scholarships *(Undergraduate/Scholarship)*

Purpose: To encourage and support the scholastic development of the collegiate and alumnae sisters of the foundation. **Focus:** General studies. **Qualif.:** Applicant must be a initiated member in good standing of Epsilon Epsilon Chapter (University of Georgia); must be a junior or senior class status; must have a minimum cumulative GPA 3.00. **Criteria:** Candidates will be selected based on their leadership qualities as an officer or former officer of the chapter and financial need.

Funds Avail.: $500. **Number Awarded:** 1. **To Apply:** Application forms are available online. Applicant must submit the transcript and recommendation letter through online. **Deadline:** March 1.

6355 ■ Epsilon Tau Scholarships *(Undergraduate/Scholarship)*

Purpose: To encourage and support the scholastic development of the collegiate and alumnae sisters of the foundation. **Focus:** General studies. **Qualif.:** Applicant must be a initiated member in good standing (scholastic, financial, membership) of Epsilon Tau Chapter (California State

University at Fullerton); must demonstrate financial need and involvement in Sigma Kappa, campus, and the community. **Criteria:** Candidates will be selected based on their financial need and involvement to the foundation.

Funds Avail.: $500. **Number Awarded:** 1. **To Apply:** Application forms are available online. Applicant must submit the transcript and recommendation letter through online. **Deadline:** March 1.

6356 ■ Marian Johnson Frutiger Scholarships *(Undergraduate/Scholarship)*

Purpose: To encourage and support the scholastic development of the collegiate and alumnae sisters of the foundation. **Focus:** General studies. **Qualif.:** Candidates must be a initiated member in good financial standing of the foundation; must have a minimum cumulative GPA: 3.0; must exemplifies the ideals and standards of Sigma Kappa; must exhibits outstanding sisterhood and must demonstrate leadership in the Greek system. **Criteria:** Candidates will be judged based on leadership, academic excellence and financial standing.

Funds Avail.: $1,000. **Number Awarded:** 3. **To Apply:** Application forms are available online. Applicant must submit the transcript and recommendation letter through online. **Deadline:** March 1.

6357 ■ Gamma Iota Scholarships - Gamma Tau *(Undergraduate/Scholarship)*

Purpose: To encourage and support the scholastic development of the collegiate and alumnae sisters of the foundation. **Focus:** General studies. **Qualif.:** Applicants must be a initiated members attending Kappa Eta (Texas Christian University), Zeta Nu (University of Texas at San Antonio), Gamma Tau (Midwestern State), or Zeta Kappa (Angelo State); must have a minimum cumulative GPA: 3.0; must held or currently hold a Sorority position; must demonstrate involvement in campus and community activities; must be in need of financial assistance. **Criteria:** Candidates will be selected based on their financial need and involvement to the foundation.

Funds Avail.: $500. **Number Awarded:** 1. **To Apply:** Application forms are available online. Applicant must submit the transcript and recommendation letter through online. **Deadline:** March 1.

6358 ■ Gamma Iota Scholarships - Kappa Eta *(Undergraduate/Scholarship)*

Purpose: To encourage and support the scholastic development of the collegiate and alumnae sisters of the foundation. **Focus:** General studies. **Qualif.:** Applicants must be a initiated members attending Kappa Eta (Texas Christian University), Zeta Nu (University of Texas at San Antonio), Gamma Tau (Midwestern State), or Zeta Kappa (Angelo State); must have a minimum cumulative GPA: 3.0; must have held or currently hold a Sorority position; must demonstrate involvement in campus and community activities; must be in need of financial assistance. **Criteria:** Candidates will be selected based on their financial need and involvement to the foundation.

Funds Avail.: $500. **Number Awarded:** 1. **To Apply:** Application forms are available online. Applicant must submit the transcript and recommendation letter through online. **Deadline:** March 1.

6359 ■ Gamma Iota Scholarships - Zeta Kappa *(Undergraduate/Scholarship)*

Purpose: To encourage and support the scholastic development of the collegiate and alumnae sisters of the foundation. **Focus:** General studies. **Qualif.:** Applicants must be a initiated members attending Kappa Eta (Texas Christian University), Zeta Nu (University of Texas at San Antonio), Gamma Tau (Midwestern State), or Zeta Kappa (Angelo State); must have a minimum cumulative GPA: 3.0; must have held or currently hold a Sorority position; must demonstrate involvement in campus and community activities; must be in need of financial assistance. **Criteria:** Candidates will be selected based on their financial need and involvement to the foundation.

Funds Avail.: $500. **Number Awarded:** 1. **To Apply:** Application forms are available online. Applicant must submit the transcript and recommendation letter through online. **Deadline:** March 1.

6360 ■ Gamma Iota Scholarships - Zeta Nu *(Undergraduate/Scholarship)*

Purpose: To encourage and support the scholastic development of the collegiate and alumnae sisters of the foundation. **Focus:** General studies. **Qualif.:** Applicant must be a initiated members attending Kappa Eta (Texas Christian University), Zeta Nu (University of Texas at San Antonio), Gamma Tau (Midwestern State), or Zeta Kappa (Angelo State); must have a minimum cumulative GPA: 3.0; must have held or currently hold a Sorority position; must have demonstrate involvement in campus and community activities; must be in need of financial assistance. **Criteria:** Candidates will be selected based on their financial need and involvement to the foundation.

Funds Avail.: $500. **Number Awarded:** 1. **To Apply:** Application forms are available online. Applicant must submit the transcript and recommendation letter through online. **Deadline:** March 1.

6361 ■ Lucile Cheever Graubart/Lambda Scholarships *(Undergraduate/Scholarship)*

Purpose: To encourage and support the scholastic development of the collegiate and alumnae sisters of the foundation. **Focus:** General studies. **Qualif.:** Applicants must be a initiated members of Lambda Chapter (University of California, Berkeley) in good standing; must be in need of financial assistance. **Criteria:** Candidates will be selected based on their financial need.

Funds Avail.: $750. **Number Awarded:** 2. **To Apply:** Application forms are available online. Applicant must submit the transcript and recommendation letter through online. **Deadline:** March 1.

6362 ■ Elise Reed Jenkins Memorial Scholarships - Gamma Lambda *(Undergraduate/Scholarship)*

Purpose: To encourage and support the scholastic development of the collegiate and alumnae sisters of the foundation. **Focus:** General studies. **Qualif.:** Applicants must be an undergraduate member of either Alpha Delta Chapter (University of Tennessee, Knoxville), Gamma Lambda Chapter (East Tennessee State University), or Gamma Psi Chapter (Tennessee Wesleyan); must be a loyal members of Sigma Kappa for at least two, and preferably three years; must have a minimum cumulative GPA of: 3.0. **Criteria:** Applicants will be selected based on their performance and service provided to the chapter and to the campus community.

Funds Avail.: $500. **Number Awarded:** 1. **To Apply:** Application forms are available online. Applicant must submit the transcript and recommendation letter through online. **Deadline:** March 1.

Awards are arranged alphabetically below their administering organizations

6363 ■ Elise Reed Jenkins Memorial Scholarships - Gamma Psi *(Undergraduate/Scholarship)*

Purpose: To encourage and support the scholastic development of the collegiate and alumnae sisters of the foundation. **Focus:** General studies. **Qualif.:** Applicants must be an undergraduate member of either Alpha Delta Chapter (University of Tennessee, Knoxville), Gamma Lambda Chapter (East Tennessee State University), or Gamma Psi Chapter (Tennessee Wesleyan); must be loyal members of Sigma Kappa for at least two, and preferably three years; must have a minimum cumulative GPA of: 3.0. **Criteria:** Consideration will be given for leadership and service provided to the chapter and to the campus community.

Funds Avail.: $500. **Number Awarded:** 1. **To Apply:** Application forms are available online. Applicant must submit the transcript and recommendation letter through online. **Deadline:** March 1.

6364 ■ Kappa Zeta Scholarships *(Undergraduate/Scholarship)*

Purpose: To encourage and support the scholastic development of the collegiate and alumnae sisters of the foundation. **Focus:** General studies. **Qualif.:** Applicants must be a initiated members of Kappa Zeta Chapter (Elon University) in good standing; must demonstrate outstanding leadership and service to the chapter, Panhellenic, and the University; must have a minimum cumulative GPA: 3.4. **Criteria:** Candidates will be selected based on their academic achievements and involvement to the foundation.

Funds Avail.: $750. **Number Awarded:** 1. **To Apply:** Application forms are available online. Applicant must submit the transcript and recommendation letter through online. **Deadline:** March 1.

6365 ■ Joan Reagin McNeill Scholarships - Alpha Theta *(Undergraduate/Scholarship)*

Purpose: To encourage and support the scholastic development of the collegiate and alumnae sisters of the foundation. **Focus:** General studies. **Qualif.:** Applicants must be an active sophomore, junior, or senior members of Alpha Theta Chapter (University of Louisville) or Theta Phi Chapter (University of Tennessee, Chattanooga) in good standing with at least one year remaining for completion of an undergraduate degree; must have a minimum cumulative GPA: 3.25. **Criteria:** Financial need will be considered.

Funds Avail.: $500. **Number Awarded:** 1. **To Apply:** Application forms are available online. Applicant must submit the transcript and recommendation letter through online. **Deadline:** March 1.

6366 ■ Joan Reagin McNeill Scholarships - Theta Phi *(Undergraduate/Scholarship)*

Purpose: To encourage and support the scholastic development of the collegiate and alumnae sisters of the foundation. **Focus:** General studies. **Qualif.:** Applicants must be a active sophomore, junior, or senior members of Alpha Theta Chapter (University of Louisville) or Theta Phi Chapter (University of Tennessee, Chattanooga) in good standing with at least one year remaining for completion of an undergraduate degree; must have a minimum cumulative GPA: 3.25. **Criteria:** Financial need will be considered.

Funds Avail.: $500. **Number Awarded:** 1. **To Apply:** Application forms are available online. Applicant must submit the transcript and recommendation letter through online. **Deadline:** March 1.

6367 ■ Evelyn S. Nish Scholarships *(Undergraduate/Scholarship)*

Purpose: To encourage and support the scholastic development of the collegiate and alumnae sisters of the foundation. **Focus:** General studies. **Qualif.:** Applicants must be initiated, active members in good standing of the Theta Chapter (University of Illinois); must be a junior or senior student enrolled during the academic year that the scholarship is granted; must have a minimum cumulative GPA: 3.0. **Criteria:** Consideration will be given for leadership and service provided to the chapter and to the campus community.

Funds Avail.: $1,000. **Number Awarded:** 1. **To Apply:** Application forms are available online. Applicant must submit the transcript and recommendation letter through online. **Deadline:** March 1.

6368 ■ Mary Turnbull Schacht Memorial Scholarships *(Undergraduate/Scholarship)*

Purpose: To encourage and support the scholastic development of the collegiate and alumnae sisters of the foundation. **Focus:** General studies. **Qualif.:** Applicants must be initiated, active members in good standing of the Lambda Chapter (University of California, Berkeley); must demonstrate outstanding leadership and service provided to the chapter, panhellenic and the University of California, Berkeley; must have a minimum cumulative GPA: 3.0. **Criteria:** Candidates will be selected based on their involvement to the foundation.

Funds Avail.: $500. **Number Awarded:** 1. **To Apply:** Application forms are available online. Applicant must submit the transcript and recommendation letter through online. **Deadline:** March 1.

6369 ■ Sigma Kappa Foundation Alumnae Continuing Education Scholarships *(Undergraduate/Scholarship)*

Purpose: To encourage and support the scholastic development of the collegiate and alumnae sisters of the foundation. **Focus:** General studies. **Qualif.:** Applicant must be a alumnae currently possessing an undergraduate degree from a four-year institution and having been accepted/enrolled in an advanced degree program; must have a minimum cumulative GPA: 3.0. **Criteria:** Selection of candidates will be based on academic standing.

Funds Avail.: $1,000. **Number Awarded:** 5. **To Apply:** Application forms are available online. Applicant must submit the transcript and recommendation letter through online. **Deadline:** March 1.

6370 ■ Sigma Kappa Foundation Alzheimer's/Gerontology Scholarships *(Undergraduate/Scholarship)*

Purpose: To encourage and support the scholastic development of the collegiate and alumnae sisters of the foundation. **Focus:** Alzheimer's disease, Gerontology. **Qualif.:** Applicant must be a graduate students or alumnae studying Alzheimer, Gerontology (the study of aging), or a related field. **Criteria:** Selection of candidates will be based on the scholarship criteria.

Funds Avail.: $1,000. **Number Awarded:** 3. **To Apply:** Application forms are available online. Applicant must submit the transcript and recommendation letter through online. **Deadline:** March 1.

6371 ■ Sigma Kappa Foundation Founders' Scholarships *(Undergraduate/Scholarship)*

Purpose: To encourage and support the scholastic development of the collegiate and alumnae sisters of the foundation. **Focus:** General studies. **Qualif.:** Applicants should be active, initiated, continuing members in good standing; must have a minimum cumulative GPA: 3.0; must demonstrate a leadership role on campus (student government, chapter officer, Panhellenic officer). **Criteria:** Preference will be given to sophomores and juniors with at least one year study remaining.

Funds Avail.: $1,000. **Number Awarded:** 5. **To Apply:** Application forms are available online. Applicant must submit the transcript and recommendation letter through online. **Deadline:** March 1.

6372 ■ Sigma Kappa Foundation Gerontology Scholarships *(Undergraduate/Scholarship)*

Purpose: To encourage and support the scholastic development of the collegiate and alumnae sisters of the foundation. **Focus:** Gerontology. **Qualif.:** Applicant must be a junior, senior, or graduate student with at least one year study remaining; must be a member in good standing, majoring in Gerontology (the study of aging) or a related field; must have a minimum cumulative GPA: 3.0. **Criteria:** Selection of candidates will be based on GPA and other basic demographic criteria.

Funds Avail.: $1,000. **Number Awarded:** 1. **To Apply:** Application forms are available online. Applicant must submit the transcript and recommendation letter through online. **Deadline:** March 1.

6373 ■ Sigma Kappa Foundation Michigan Scholarships *(Undergraduate/Scholarship)*

Purpose: To encourage and support the scholastic development of the collegiate and alumnae sisters of the foundation. **Focus:** General studies. **Qualif.:** Applicant must be a Michigan resident as defined by the university of attendance; must be initiated in Sigma Kappa, currently active, and in good standing with the chapter at a College or University in Michigan; must have at least two semesters of undergraduate study remaining at the time of the award; must have a minimum GPA: 2.5 and in good standing with the university of enrollment. Applicant may not have received the scholarship previously. **Criteria:** Candidates will be selected based on their academic achievements and involvement to the foundation.

Funds Avail.: $250. **Number Awarded:** 1. **To Apply:** Application forms are available online. Applicant must submit the transcript and recommendation letter through online. **Deadline:** March 1.

6374 ■ Elin J. Stene/Xi Scholarships *(Undergraduate/Scholarship)*

Purpose: To encourage and support the scholastic development of the collegiate and alumnae sisters of the foundation. **Focus:** General studies. **Qualif.:** Applicants must be initiated, active members in good standing of Xi Chapter (University of Kansas); must be a junior or senior class status (mid-year graduating seniors are eligible); must have a minimum cumulative GPA: 3.0; must be in need of financial assistance. **Criteria:** Consideration will be given for leadership and service provided to the chapter and to the campus community.

Funds Avail.: $1,000. **Number Awarded:** 2. **To Apply:** Application forms are available online. Applicant must submit the transcript and recommendation letter through online. **Deadline:** March 1.

6375 ■ Lorraine E. Swain Scholarships *(Undergraduate/Scholarship)*

Purpose: To encourage and support the scholastic development of the collegiate and alumnae sisters of the foundation. **Focus:** General studies. **Qualif.:** Applicant must initiated in Sigma Kappa, currently active, and in good standing with the chapter at a College or University in Colorado. **Criteria:** Consideration will be given for leadership and service provided to the chapter and to the campus community.

Funds Avail.: $500. **Number Awarded:** 1. **To Apply:** Application forms are available online. Applicant must submit the transcript and recommendation letter through online. **Deadline:** March 1.

6376 ■ Theta/Caryl Cordis D'hondt Scholarships *(Undergraduate/Scholarship)*

Purpose: To encourage and support the scholastic development of the collegiate and alumnae sisters of the foundation. **Focus:** General studies. **Qualif.:** Applicants must be initiated, active members in good standing with Theta Tau Chapter (Kansas State University); must be a junior or senior class status (mid-year graduating seniors are also eligible); must have a minimum cumulative GPA: 3.0; must be in need of financial assistance. **Criteria:** Financial need will be considered.

Funds Avail.: $500. **Number Awarded:** 1. **To Apply:** Application forms are available online. Applicant must submit the transcript and recommendation letter through online. **Deadline:** March 1.

6377 ■ Theta Tau Scholarships *(Undergraduate/Scholarship)*

Purpose: To encourage and support the scholastic development of the collegiate and alumnae sisters of the foundation. **Focus:** General studies. **Qualif.:** Applicant must be initiated, active members in good standing with Theta Tau Chapter (Kansas State University); must be a junior or senior class status (mid-year graduating seniors are also eligible); must have a minimum cumulative GPA: 3.0; must be in need of financial assistance. **Criteria:** Candidates will be selected based on their merit and financial need.

Funds Avail.: $1,000. **Number Awarded:** 1. **To Apply:** Application forms are available online. Applicant must submit the transcript and recommendation letter through online. **Deadline:** March 1.

6378 ■ Barber Owen Thomas Scholarships *(Undergraduate/Scholarship)*

Purpose: To encourage and support the scholastic development of the collegiate and alumnae sisters of the foundation. **Focus:** General studies. **Qualif.:** Applicant must be an active members in good standing of the Beta Sigma Chapter (Purdue University); must be a junior or senior in class status (mid-year graduating seniors are also eligible); must have a minimum cumulative GPA: 2.5; must be in need of financial assistance; must be residing in the chapter house. **Criteria:** Applicants will be judge based on their active participation in a variety of the foundation and academic activities.

Funds Avail.: $500. **Number Awarded:** 1. **To Apply:** Application forms are available online. Applicant must submit the transcript and recommendation letter through online. **Deadline:** March 1.

6379 ■ Irma E. Voigt Memorial Scholarships *(Undergraduate/Scholarship)*

Purpose: To encourage and support the scholastic development of the collegiate and alumnae sisters of the foundation. **Focus:** General studies. **Qualif.:** Applicants must be a initiated members of Beta Upsilon Chapter (Ohio University) in good standing; must be a junior class status, currently enrolled in 12 or more hours; must have a minimum cumulative GPA: 3.0; must be actively involved in her chapter, on campus, and in the community. **Criteria:** Candidates will be selected based on their academic achievements and involvement to the foundation.

Funds Avail.: $500. **Number Awarded:** 1. **To Apply:** Application forms are available online. Applicant must submit the transcript and recommendation letter through online. **Deadline:** March 1.

6380 ■ Alice Hersey Wick Scholarships
(Undergraduate/Scholarship)

Purpose: To encourage and support the scholastic development of the collegiate and alumnae sisters of the foundation. **Focus:** General studies. **Qualif.:** Applicant must be initiated collegiate members in good standing; must have a minimum cumulative GPA of 3.0. **Criteria:** Applications will be judged based on leadership and service provided to the chapter, campus, and community.

Funds Avail.: $500. **Number Awarded:** 1. **To Apply:** Application forms are available online. Applicant must submit the transcript and recommendation letter through online. **Deadline:** March 1.

6381 ■ Andrea Will Memorial Scholarships
(Undergraduate/Scholarship)

Purpose: To encourage and support the scholastic development of the collegiate and alumnae sisters of the foundation. **Focus:** General studies. **Qualif.:** Applicants must be a new initiates in good standing of Gamma Mu Chapter, matriculating at Eastern Illinois University; must have a minimum cumulative GPA: 3.0; must demonstrate involvement in co-curricular activities, and evidence of leadership qualities and experience. **Criteria:** Applicants will be judge based on their active participation in a variety of the foundation and academic activities.

Funds Avail.: $500. **Number Awarded:** 1. **To Apply:** Application forms are available online. Applicant must submit the transcript and recommendation letter through online. **Deadline:** March 1.

6382 ■ Sigma Theta Tau International Honor Society of Nursing

550 W North St.
Indianapolis, IN 46202
Free: 888-634-7575
URL: http://www.nursingsociety.org

6383 ■ Patricia Smith Christensen Scholarships
(Postdoctorate/Scholarship)

Purpose: To assist graduate nursing students who are pursuing nursing education in the area of maternal-child or pediatric nursing. **Focus:** Nursing. **Qualif.:** Applicants must be Canadian residents; Sigma Theta Tau International members; registered nurses with current licenses; and enrolled in a master's or doctoral program in nursing. **Criteria:** Applicants are evaluated based on academic achievement and financial need.

Funds Avail.: $1,000. **To Apply:** Applicants must submit a letter outlining the reasons for pursuing advanced nursing education in the area of maternal-child or pediatric nursing and providing details about their current program and future career plans; curriculum vitae; two letters of reference: one clinical and one academic; official transcripts. **Deadline:** March 1.

6384 ■ Silicon Valley Community Foundation

2240 W El Camino Real Ste. 300
Mountain View, CA 94040-1498
Ph: (650)450-5400
Fax: (650)450-5401
URL: http://www.siliconvalleycf.org

6385 ■ Hazel Reed Baumeister Scholarship Program *(Undergraduate/Scholarship)*

Purpose: To support high school graduates of high academic achievement who would be unable to pursue higher education without financial assistance. **Focus:** General Studies. **Qualif.:** Applicants must be current graduating seniors or graduates of a public or private high school in San Mateo County or Santa Clara County; must be United States citizens; must have demonstrated financial hardship; must have earned a minimum cumulative grade point average of 3.3. **Criteria:** Preference will be given to those students who meet the criteria.

Funds Avail.: maximum award amount: $5,000. **Number Awarded:** 15. **To Apply:** Applicants must check the available website for the required materials. **Deadline:** March 5. **Contact:** Silicon Valley Community Foundation at the above address (see entry 6384).

6386 ■ Crain Educational Grants Program
(Undergraduate/Scholarship)

Purpose: To enable high school graduates to pursue courses of study they would otherwise be unable to follow due to limited financial means. **Focus:** General Studies. **Qualif.:** Applicants must be current graduating seniors or graduates of a public or private high school in San Mateo County or Santa Clara County; must be United States citizens; must have demonstrated financial hardship; must have a minimum cumulative grade point average of 3.3. **Criteria:** Priority will be given to those students with financial need.

Funds Avail.: Maximum award amount: $5,000. **Number Awarded:** 10. **To Apply:** Applicants must check the available website to download the application form online. **Deadline:** March 5. **Contact:** Silicon Valley Community Foundation at the above address (see entry 6384).

6387 ■ Curry Award for Girls and Young Women
(Undergraduate/Scholarship)

Purpose: To provide financial support to those students who are in need. **Focus:** General Studies. **Qualif.:** Applicants must be current residents of San Mateo County; must be United States citizens or legal residents; must be young women 16 to 26 years old. **Criteria:** Preference will be given to those students who meet the criteria.

Funds Avail.: $ 1,000 per award. **Number Awarded:** 10. **To Apply:** Applicants must check the available website for the required materials. **Deadline:** March 5. **Contact:** Silicon Valley Community Foundation at the above address (see entry 6384).

6388 ■ Eustace-Kwan Family Foundation Scholarships *(Undergraduate/Scholarship)*

Purpose: To help promising high school and junior college students pursue higher education at an accredited two- or four-year college or vocational school. **Focus:** General

Awards are arranged alphabetically below their administering organizations

Studies. **Qualif.:** Applicants must be current residents of San Mateo County or Northern Santa Clara County; must be current graduating high school seniors planning to attend an accredited two- or four-year college or vocational school or current community college students planning to transfer to a four-year college; must be United States citizens or legal residents; must have a cumulative grade point average of 3.5 on a 4.0 scale; must have demonstrated community involvement. **Criteria:** Preference will be given to those students who meet the criteria.

Funds Avail.: Maximum award amount: $2,500. **Number Awarded:** 12. **To Apply:** Applicants must check the available website for more information. **Deadline:** March 5. **Contact:** Silicon Valley Community Foundation at the above address (see entry 6384).

6389 ■ Dr. Mary Finegold Scholarships *(Undergraduate/Scholarship)*

Purpose: To provide financial assistance to those students who are in need. **Focus:** Science. **Qualif.:** Applicants must be senior females graduating from a public or private high school in San Mateo or Northern Santa Clara County; must be United States citizens; must intend to complete a four-year degree in the sciences; must have a minimum cumulative grade point average of 3.0 on a 4.0 scale; must have demonstrated financial hardship; must be active in athletics. **Criteria:** Preference will be given to those students who meet the criteria.

Funds Avail.: $3,000. **Number Awarded:** 1. **To Apply:** Applicants must check the available website for the required materials. **Deadline:** March 5. **Contact:** Silicon Valley Community Foundation at the above address (see entry 6384).

6390 ■ Bobette Bibo Gugliotta Memorial Scholarships for Creative Writing *(Undergraduate/Scholarship)*

Purpose: To provide financial assistance to those students who are in need. **Focus:** General Studies. **Qualif.:** Applicants must be current graduating seniors or graduates of a public or private high school in San Mateo County or Northern Santa Clara County; must be accepted to or awaiting acceptance to a two- or four- year college or university; must be United States citizens. **Criteria:** Preference will be given to those students who meet the criteria.

Funds Avail.: $2,000 for undergraduate; $1,000 for graduating high school seniors. **To Apply:** Applicants must check the available website for the required materials. **Deadline:** March 5. **Contact:** Silicon Valley Community Foundation at the above address (see entry 6384).

6391 ■ Dr. James L. Hutchinson and Evelyn Ribbs Hutchinson Medical School Scholarship Fund *(Undergraduate/Scholarship)*

Purpose: To recognize students who demonstrate excellence in both character and academic achievement by giving them scholarships. **Focus:** Medicine. **Qualif.:** Applicants must be United States citizens; must be college seniors and accepted to medical school, or currently enrolled full-time in an accredited medical school program; must demonstrate personal motivation for excellence in both character and academic achievement. Personal integrity, as exemplified by leadership, community involvement, and concern for others, will be considered. **Criteria:** Preference will be given to those students who meet the criteria.

Funds Avail.: $2,000. **Number Awarded:** 1. **To Apply:** Applicants must check the available website for the required materials. **Deadline:** May 16. **Contact:** Silicon Valley Community Foundation at the above address (see entry 6384).

6392 ■ Kumin Scholars Program *(Undergraduate/Scholarship)*

Purpose: To support current community college students who wish to transfer to a four-year institution. **Focus:** General Studies. **Qualif.:** Applicants must be United States citizens or legal residents; must be enrolled part-time or full-time in a community college; must have completed at least 20 graded semester or quarter units; must have earned a minimum GPA of 2.5. **Criteria:** Preference will be given to those students who meet the criteria.

Funds Avail.: Maximum award amount: $18,000. **Number Awarded:** 15. **To Apply:** Applicants must check the available website for the required materials. **Deadline:** June 25. **Contact:** Silicon Valley Community Foundation at the above address (see entry 6384).

6393 ■ Rambus Scholarship Fund *(Undergraduate/Scholarship)*

Purpose: To broaden the educational opportunities of students who, by virtue of their academic and extracurricular achievement, demonstrate a passion for science and technology that extends beyond the classroom. **Focus:** General Studies. **Qualif.:** Applicants must be graduating students from high schools located in either Mountain View or Los Altos, California, and planning to attend a four year college/university. Applicants must have a minimum of 3.0 GPA (on a 4.0 scale) for grades 10-12. **Criteria:** Preference will be given to those students who meet the criteria.

Funds Avail.: Maximum award amount: $10,000. **Number Awarded:** 8. **To Apply:** Applicants must check the available website for the required materials. **Contact:** For more information and application visit: http://www.rambus.com/scholarship

6394 ■ Fauneil J. Rinn Scholarships *(Undergraduate/Scholarship)*

Purpose: To provide financial assistance to those students who are in need. **Focus:** Political Science; Public Administration. **Qualif.:** Applicants must be women who are current students in good standing in the Political Science or Master of Public Administration programs at San Jose State University. **Criteria:** Selection will be based on their achievements and abilities as reflected in a brief application form, a resume and a 500-word essay on a subject relevant to the political or governmental role of women.

Funds Avail.: Up to $1,250. **Number Awarded:** 1. **To Apply:** Applicants must check the available website for the required materials. **Contact:** Contact Terry Christensen, Professor, Department of Political Science, San Jose State University, at 408-924-5565 or at Terry.Christensen@sjsu.edu for more information or an application.

6395 ■ Ruppert Educational Grant Program *(Undergraduate/Scholarship)*

Purpose: To provide financial assistance to those students who are in need. **Focus:** General Studies. **Qualif.:** Applicants must be United States citizens; must be current graduating seniors attending high schools in San Mateo County or Northern Santa Clara County (Daly City through Mountain View). Applicants must demonstrate: financial hardship; evidence of partial self-support (e.g., savings from summer jobs, part-time work, etc.); community involvement; academic promise and GPA improvement during high school years. **Criteria:** Preference will be given to those who meet the criteria.

Funds Avail.: $2,000. **Number Awarded:** 30. **To Apply:** Applicants must check the available website for the required materials. **Deadline:** March 5. **Contact:** Silicon Valley Community Foundation at the above address (see entry 6384).

6396 ■ Leo and Trinidad Sanchez Scholarships *(Undergraduate/Scholarship)*

Purpose: To provide financial support to those students who are in need. **Focus:** Architecture. **Qualif.:** Applicants must be Hispanic/American (with at least one parent of Hispanic or Hispanic/American heritage); must be residents of Santa Clara or Santa Cruz County; must be seniors in high school or students at West Valley College enrolled in a program leading to a degree in architecture, or students in any architectural school. **Criteria:** Preference will be given to those who meet the criteria.

Funds Avail.: Maximum award amount: $4,500. **Number Awarded:** 1. **To Apply:** Applicants must check the available website for more information regarding this award. **Contact:** Silicon Valley Community Foundation at the above address (see entry 6384).

6397 ■ Sand Hill Scholars Program *(Undergraduate/Scholarship)*

Purpose: To provide financial assistance to those students who are in need. **Focus:** General Studies. **Qualif.:** Applicants must be eighth-grade graduates of the Ravenswood City School District; must be current graduating seniors attending a high school in San Mateo County or Northern Santa Clara County. **Criteria:** Preference is given to students who have shown motivation and leadership, have overcome hardships to remain in school, or have been involved in educational, job-related, or community activities outside the school environment.

Funds Avail.: $4,000. **Number Awarded:** 5. **To Apply:** Applicants must check the available website for the required materials. **Deadline:** March 5. **Contact:** Silicon Valley Community Foundation at the above address (see entry 6384).

6398 ■ Simon Youth Foundation

225 W Washington St.
Indianapolis, IN 46204
Ph: (317)636-1600
Fax: (317)263-2371
Free: 800-509-3676
E-mail: syf@simon.com
URL: http://www.syf.org

6399 ■ Education Resource Center (ERC) Scholarships *(Undergraduate/Scholarship)*

Purpose: To provide scholarships to the promising at-risk students enrolled in Education Resource Centers across the country. **Focus:** General studies. **Qualif.:** Applicants for the SYF Education Resource Center Scholarship Program must be graduating ERC students who plan to enroll in a full-time undergraduate course of study at an accredited two- or four-year college, university, or vocational/technical school. **Criteria:** Selection will be based on committee's criteria.

Funds Avail.: $1,500-$2,500. **To Apply:** Applicants must submit their application together with other required documents to the Foundation. **Contact:** SYF at the above address (see entry 6398).

6400 ■ Simon Youth Foundation Community Scholarships *(Undergraduate/Scholarship)*

Purpose: To provide scholarships to the promising students in communities that host Simon properties. **Focus:** General studies. **Qualif.:** Scholarship is available to students who plan to enroll in a full-time undergraduate course of study at an accredited two- or four-year college, university, or vocational/technical school. **Criteria:** Selection will be based on the committee's criteria. In addition, four-year renewable Awards of Excellence are awarded in eight communities: Atlanta, Boston, Dallas, Indianapolis, Miami, New York, Orange County and Orlando.

Funds Avail.: $1,500. **To Apply:** Applicants may submit an application and other required documents to the Foundation. **Contact:** SYF at the above address (see entry 6398).

6401 ■ DW Simpson Global Actuarial Recruitment

1800 W Larchmont Ave.
Chicago, IL 60613
Ph: (312)867-2300
Fax: (312)951-8386
Free: 800-837-8338
E-mail: actuaries@dwsimpson.com
URL: http://www.actuaryjobs.com

6402 ■ DW Simpson Actuarial Science Scholarship Program *(Undergraduate/Scholarship)*

Purpose: To provide financial support for deserving students who are pursuing study in actuarial science. **Focus:** Actuarial science. **Qualif.:** Applicants must be entering their senior year of undergraduate study in actuarial science, have maintained a GPA of 3.2 or higher in their major and an overall GPA of 3.0 or better and have passed at least 1 actuarial examination, and be eligible to work in the United States. **Criteria:** Applicants will be evaluated on the basis of academic performance.

Funds Avail.: $1,000. **To Apply:** Applicants must complete the application form available online at the DW Simpsons Global Actuarial Recruitment. **Deadline:** April 30 for the Fall scholarship; October 31 for the Spring scholarship.

6403 ■ SINFONIA Educational Foundation

10600 Old State Rd.
Evansville, IN 47711-1399
Ph: 800-473-2649
Fax: (812)867-0633
E-mail: foundationinfo@sinfonia.org
URL: http://www.sinfonia.org

6404 ■ Delta Iota Alumni Scholarships *(Undergraduate/Scholarship)*

Purpose: To provide educational assistance for American college students. **Focus:** General studies. **Qualif.:** Applicants must have been college students for at least two semesters; must be in good standing; must maintain good standing status during the academic year of scholarship. **Criteria:** Applicants are evaluated based on merit.

Funds Avail.: $500. **Number Awarded:** 1. **To Apply:** Applicants must submit typed or computer-generated applica-

Awards are arranged alphabetically below their administering organizations

tion with 2-4 page essay on the topic: How Sinfonians take active roles in building of better men in society; two letters of support, one from a Sinfonian and one from a non-Sinfonian, that address evidence of the applicant's integrity, ethics, initiative and overall devotion to the Object of Phi Mu Alpha Sinfonia Fraternity; composite style coat and tie photo for promotional purposes only; name and address of hometown newspaper for promotional purposes. **Deadline:** February 1.

6405 ■ W. Eldridge and Emily Lowe Scholarships *(Undergraduate/Scholarship)*

Purpose: To provide educational assistance for American college students. **Focus:** General studies. **Qualif.:** Applicants must have been college students for at least two semesters; must be in good standing; must maintain good standing status during the academic year of scholarship. **Criteria:** Applicants are evaluated based on merit.

Funds Avail.: $1,000. **Number Awarded:** 1. **To Apply:** Applicants must submit typed or computer-generated application with 2-4 page essay on the topic: How Sinfonians take active roles in building of better men in society; two letters of support, one from a Sinfonian and one from a non-Sinfonian, that address evidence of the applicant's integrity, ethics, initiative and overall devotion to the Object of Phi Mu Alpha Sinfonia Fraternity; composite style coat and tie photo for promotional purposes only; name and address of hometown newspaper for promotional purposes. **Deadline:** February 1.

6406 ■ James H. Patrenos Memorial Scholarships *(Undergraduate/Scholarship)*

Purpose: To provide educational assistance for American college students. **Focus:** General studies. **Qualif.:** Applicants must have attended college for at least two semesters; must be in good standing; must maintain good standing status during the academic year of scholarship. **Criteria:** Applicants are evaluated based on merit.

Funds Avail.: $1,000. **Number Awarded:** 1. **To Apply:** Applicants must submit typed or computer-generated application with 2-4 page essay on the topic: How Sinfonians take active roles in building of better men in society; two letters of support, one from a Sinfonian and one from a non-Sinfonian, that address evidence of the applicant's integrity, ethics, initiative and overall devotion to the Object of Phi Mu Alpha Sinfonia Fraternity; composite style coat and tie photo for promotional purposes only; name and address of hometown newspaper for promotional purposes. **Deadline:** February 1.

6407 ■ Sino-American Pharmaceutical Professionals Association

PO Box 282
Nanuet, NY 10954
E-mail: information@sapaweb.org
URL: http://www.sapaweb.org

6408 ■ SAPA Scholarships *(Undergraduate/Scholarship)*

Purpose: To recognize and support excellence on the part of outstanding high school students, and to encourage the finest high school graduates to develop career in life science. **Focus:** Life sciences. **Qualif.:** Applicant must be a full-time high school graduate who plans full-time undergraduate study at an accredited four-year college in the upcoming academic year; must have GPA above 3.3, a minimum SAT 1400 and be in the top tenth of the class; must be a United States citizen, or a legal resident alien; must demonstrated a potential for and commitment to a career in life sciences. **Criteria:** Applicant will be evaluated based on their merit and outstanding potential and intend to pursue careers in life sciences. SAPA Scholars are selected by the Board of SAPA Scholarship and Excellence in Education for Life Science Foundation.

Funds Avail.: $1,000. **To Apply:** Applicant must submit an essay of approximately 600 words, two letters of recommendation from teachers who can discuss the nominee's potential for a career in life sciences including a teacher in the applicant's field of study and another who can attest the nominee's potential; must have a list of awards received; must have a list of Advanced Placement of Honors courses with grades. **Deadline:** April 30.

6409 ■ Sjogrens Syndrome Foundation

6707 Democracy Blvd. Ste. 325
Bethesda, MD 20817
Ph: (301)530-4420
Fax: (301)530-4415
Free: 800-475-6473
E-mail: tms@sjogrens.org
URL: http://www.sjogrens.org

6410 ■ SSF Research Grants *(Doctorate/Grant)*

Purpose: To encourage therapeutic development in Sjogren's syndrome by funding potential researches on further treatment and understanding of the disease. **Focus:** Medical research. **Qualif.:** Applicant must be a basic scientist and clinical investigator; or a junior or senior investigator conducting research at an institution in the United States. **Criteria:** Applicants are selected based on the application package.

Funds Avail.: $50,000. **To Apply:** Applicants must submit a complete application package which includes: an Application Face page; abstract for the research proposal; publications; budget; letters of recommendation; statement of guarantee of adequate facilities and budget for the research proposal; and a principal investigators signed statement of responsibility. Applicants must send the documents electronically to research@sjogrens.org with a subject line: Applicant NameResearch Grant Application, or send on a CD to: Sjogren's Syndrome Foundation Attn: Research Grant 6707 Democracy Blvd., Ste. 325 Bethesda, MD 20817. **Deadline:** February 1.

6411 ■ SSF Student Fellowships *(Graduate, Undergraduate/Fellowship)*

Purpose: To provide financial support for students working on a semester or summer research project in Sjogren's Syndrome. **Focus:** Medical research. **Qualif.:** Applicants must be medical, dental, or PhD graduate and undergraduate students; must be conducting research at an institution in the United States. **Criteria:** Applicants are selected based on the application package.

Funds Avail.: $2,000. **To Apply:** Applicants must submit a complete application package which includes: an Application Face page; abstract for the research proposal; publications; budget; letters of recommendation; statement of guarantee of adequate facilities and budget for the research proposal; and a principal investigators signed statement of responsibility. Applicants must send the documents electronically to research@sjogrens.org with a subject line:

Applicant NameResearch Grant Application, or send on a CD to: Sjogren's Syndrome Foundation Attn: Research Grant 6707 Democracy Blvd., Ste. 325 Bethesda, MD 20817. **Deadline:** February 1.

6412 ■ Snowmobile Association of Massachusetts

PO Box 386
Conway, MA 01341
Ph: (413)369-8092
Fax: (413)369-0203
E-mail: webmaster@sledmass.com
URL: http://www.sledmass.com

6413 ■ Snowmobile Association of Massachusetts Scholarships *(Undergraduate/Scholarship)*

Purpose: To develop and maintain an expanding interconnected snowmobile trail system, allowing snowmobile enthusiasts to travel from Worcester County. **Focus:** Transportation. **Qualif.:** Applicants must be high school seniors or college students. **Criteria:** Recipients are selected based on academic performance and financial need.

Funds Avail.: $2,500. **Number Awarded:** 2. **To Apply:** Applicants must submit a completed application form; an official high school or college transcript; recommendations in writing by at lest two teachers; recommendations in writing by one or two friends, employers, or clergy; proof of acceptance at the listed college, university or vocational school; a written essay about snowmobiling in the state. All required documents must be provided in five copies. **Deadline:** March 25.

6414 ■ Social Science Research Council

810 Seventh Ave.
New York, NY 10019
Ph: (212)377-2700
Fax: (212)377-2727
E-mail: info@ssrc.org
URL: http://www.ssrc.org

6415 ■ Dissertation Proposal Development Fellowships *(Doctorate/Fellowship)*

Purpose: To supports early-stage graduate students in formulating successful doctoral dissertation proposals. **Focus:** Social sciences, Humanities. **Qualif.:** Applicant must be a student in the humanities and social sciences undertaking doctoral dissertation research; must be a second or third year PhD student enrolled in U.S institutions, who have not yet submitted and will not submit their dissertation proposal until after the fall workshop; must be a student who have completed their comprehensive, general, and qualifying exams. Faculty must apply as teams; must be tenured at the time of application; must be trained in different disciplines; must experiences supervisors of dissertation research. **Criteria:** Student applications will be evaluated based on the following criteria: (1) Originality and appropriateness of the topic; (2) Preparation of the student; (3) Summer Predissertation Research Plan ; (4) Summer Funding. Research directors and their proposed research fields are evaluated based on the following criteria: (1) Originality; (2) Appropriateness; (3) Research Directors; (4) Impact.

Funds Avail.: $10,000. **To Apply:** Applicant must submit a proposed research about the dissertation topic. Applications have to be submitted by two tenured faculty from different US universities and, as relevant, different disciplines. **Deadline:** October 3.

6416 ■ Korean Studies Dissertation Workshop Funds *(Graduate/Grant)*

Purpose: To foster a sustained network of advanced graduate students and faculty engaged in research on Korea. **Focus:** Social sciences, Humanities. **Qualif.:** Applicant must be a full-time advanced graduate student enrolled at a U.S. or Canadian institution; must have an approved dissertation prospectus at the time of application, but cannot have completed writing for final submission. **Criteria:** Special consideration will be given to students from universities that are not major Korea Studies institutions. Selection of applicant will be based on the narrative project descriptions as part of the application.

Funds Avail.: Funds for the program are provided by the Korea Foundation. **To Apply:** Applicant must complete and sign two-page application form; must have a summary of the dissertation proposal; must submit a curriculum vitae. Application form and other supporting documents must be sent to: Social Science Research Council, Korean Studies Dissertation Workshop, 810 Seventh Ave., 31st Fl., New York, NY 10019. **Deadline:** May 1.

6417 ■ Social Sciences and Humanities Research Council of Canada

350 Albert St.
PO Box 1610
Ottawa, ON, Canada K1P 6G4
Ph: (613)995-4273
E-mail: webgrant@sshrc.ca
URL: http://www.crsh.ca

6418 ■ Canada Graduate Scholarships Program *(Graduate/Scholarship)*

Purpose: To develop research skills and assist in the training of highly-qualified personnel by supporting students in the social sciences and humanities who demonstrate a high standard of achievement in undergraduate and early graduate studies. **Focus:** Humanities; Social sciences. **Qualif.:** Applicant must: be a citizen or permanent resident of Canada; be applying for support to pursue his/her first graduate degree and have not completed more than 12 months of full-time graduate study at the proposed start date of the award; have achieved a first-class average, as determined by his or her university, in each of the last two years of full-time study; have not already received an award for master's-level study from SSHRC, Natural Sciences and Engineering Research Council or Canadian Institute of Health Research; must not be applying for graduate funding from NSERC or CIHR; not be pursuing a degree program that combines undergraduate and graduate studies. At the time of taking up the award applicants must: be registered full-time at a recognized Canadian university; be in the first year of a master's program in the social sciences or humanities that includes advanced research training. **Criteria:** Selection will be based on the academic excellence, research potential and communication skills.

Funds Avail.: $17,500. **To Apply:** Applicants must complete the application form and the required attachments. Applicants will find the application instructions inside their application when they begin to create it online. Applicants must determine their current applicant status and submit their complete application to the appropriate institution. **Contact:** Canada Graduate Scholarships, SSHRC, 613-943-7777, cgs@sshrc.ca.

6419 ■ Major Collaborative Research Initiatives Grants *(Graduate/Grant)*

Purpose: To support leading edge research with true potential breakthrough that addresses broad and critical issues of intellectual, social, economic, and cultural significance through the effective coordination and integration of diverse research activities and research results. **Focus:** Humanities; Social sciences. **Qualif.:** Applicants must be Project Directors, Research Teams or Foreign Researchers. Applications must be submitted by the director on behalf of the research team. The project director must satisfy all the regular eligibility requirements for an applicant as set out in the definitions section. The research team must represent a minimum of two Canadian postsecondary institutions (including the Canadian host institution) and must include sufficient members to cover the diverse perspective and expertise required by the breadth of the research questions outlined in the proposal. The team may include co-applicants (co-investigators) and collaborators in accordance with SSHRC definitions. In accordance with SSHRC's policy of encouraging international collaboration, provided that their benefit to the project is demonstrated, researchers affiliated with foreign institutions may be invited to join MCRI teams as co-applicants and have access to research funds for work carried out as part of Canadian-led teams. **Criteria:** Selection will be based on the following criteria: quality, significance, breadth and scope of the proposed research; strength and skills of the Project Director; strength and expertise of the team; student training; dissemination strategies; and budget justification.

Funds Avail.: No specific amount. **To Apply:** For the letter of intent stage, the applicants must complete a web-page application. This includes an outline of the proposal that clearly identifies the critical issue or issues to be addressed and that takes into account all the program's evaluation criteria. Only those successful applicants at the letter of intent stage are invited to submit a formal application. **Deadline:** January 31 - Letter of Intent. **Contact:** Brenda Werrell, MCRI Program Coordinator, 613-947-9659, brenda.werrell@sshrc.ca.

6420 ■ Social Sciences and Humanities Research Council of Canada Standard Research Grants *(Doctorate, Graduate/Grant)*

Purpose: To support research and develop excellence in the social sciences and humanities. **Focus:** Humanities; Social Sciences. **Qualif.:** For standard research grants, there are two categories of eligible applicants: applicant/principal investigator; co-applicant/co-investigator. There are three other categories of eligible participants: research collaborator, student assistant, and other assistants and support staff. Postdoctoral applicants must establish an affiliation with an eligible postsecondary institution. Students enrolled in a program of study are not eligible to apply. A PhD candidate, however, whether holding a faculty position or not, is eligible to receive a Standard Research Grant if he or she: has met all requirements for the PhD by the year in which the grant is awarded; has established a formal affiliation with a Canadian postsecondary institution and maintains such an affiliation for the duration of the grant period. **Criteria:** Selection will be based on a competitive process.

Funds Avail.: Maximum of $100,000. **To Apply:** Successful applicants may submit only one application as a principal investigator within any three-year period. Researchers applying for programs of research of less than three years must explain why a shorter period is appropriate. Under normal circumstances, if an applicant submits a request for one- or two-year funding and is granted an award, he/she is not eligible to apply again as a principal investigator until the next three-year cycle. If, however, the applicant believes there are exceptional and substantive scholarly reasons for re-applying within the three-year cycle, he or she may submit an application accompanied by a one-page letter justifying the exceptional circumstances. If an applicant submits a request for three-year funding, but on the scholarly recommendation of the adjudication committee is granted an award for one or two years only, the applicant is automatically eligible to re-apply within the three-year period. **Deadline:** October 15. **Contact:** SSHRC at the above address (see entry 6417).

6421 ■ SSHRC Doctoral Fellowships Program *(Doctorate/Fellowship, Scholarship)*

Purpose: To develop research skills and assist in the training of highly-qualified academic personnel by supporting students who demonstrate a high standard of scholarly achievement in undergraduate and graduate studies in the social sciences and humanities. **Focus:** Humanities; Social sciences. **Qualif.:** Applicant must: be a citizen or permanent resident of Canada; be applying for support to pursue their first PhD; be pursuing doctoral studies (or a combined MA/PhD) in the social sciences and humanities; not have already received a scholarship or fellowship from SSHRC, NSERC or CIHR to undertake or complete a doctoral degree or combined MA/PhD; not be applying in the current academic year to NSERC or CIHR; and not be pursuing a degree program that combines undergraduate and graduate degrees. CGS Doctoral Scholarships are tenable only at recognized universities in Canada; SSHRC Doctoral Fellowships are tenable at any recognized university in Canada or abroad, provided that the award holder has completed at least one previous degree at a Canadian university. On the proposed start date of the award, applicants must: be registered as a full-time student undertaking or continuing a doctoral program in the social sciences or humanities; and not have exceeded the allowable number of months already spent in doctoral study, as set out in the section above. **Criteria:** Selection will be based on academic merit.

Funds Avail.: $35,000/annum - Doctoral Scholarships; $20,000 - SSHRC Doctoral Fellowships. **To Apply:** Applicants must ensure that they meet the requirements; complete and submit only one application form with the required attachments. Applicants will find the application instructions inside their application when they begin to create it online. Applicants must determine their current registration status and submit their complete application to the appropriate institution. Candidates eligible for both the CGS Doctoral Scholarship and the SSHRC Doctoral Fellowship will be considered for both awards. All candidates will be assigned a rank order on the basis of the selection committee's recommendations. **Contact:** Fellowships and Institutional Grants Division, SSHRC, 613-943-7777, fellowships@sshrc.ca

6422 ■ Society of Allied Weight Engineers

PO Box 60024, Terminal Annex
Los Angeles, CA 90060
Ph: (562)596-2873

Fax: (562)596-2874
URL: http://www.sawe.org

6423 ■ Frank Fong Scholarships *(Undergraduate/Scholarship)*

Purpose: To provide financial assistance for the education of the dependents of SAWE members. **Focus:** Engineering; Physics; Mathematics and mathematical sciences; Computer and information sciences. **Qualif.:** Applicants must be children or grandchildren of SAWE members; must be aged 25 or below; full-time undergraduate students; pursuing a technical course of study (engineering, physics, mathematics, computer sciences, etc.). **Criteria:** Awards are given based on academic merit; work experience; extra curricular activities; and goal for the application.

Funds Avail.: $1000. **Number Awarded:** 5. **To Apply:** Application forms are available at the website. Applicants must submit completed application form and send together with a complete transcript of grades. **Deadline:** April. **Contact:** Ginny Miller, Scholarship Management Services, Telephone: (507)931-1682, Toll-free: (800)537-4180.

6424 ■ SAWE Scholarships *(Undergraduate/Scholarship)*

Purpose: To provide financial assistance for the education of the dependents of SAWE members. **Focus:** General studies. **Qualif.:** Applicants must be children or grandchildren of SAWE members; must be aged 25 or below; and must full-time undergraduate students. **Criteria:** Awards are given based on academic merit; work experience; extra curricular activities; and goal for the application.

Funds Avail.: $1000. **Number Awarded:** 5. **To Apply:** Application forms are available at the website. Applicants must submit completed application form and send together with a complete transcript of grades. **Deadline:** April. **Contact:** Ginny Miller, Scholarship Management Services, Telephone: (507)931-1682, Tollfree: (800)537-4180.

6425 ■ Society of Architectural Historians

1365 North Astor St.
Chicago, IL 60610-2144
Ph: (312)573-1365
Fax: (312)573-1141
E-mail: info@sah.org
URL: http://www.sah.org

6426 ■ Beverly Willis Architecture Foundation Dissertation Fellowships *(Doctorate/Fellowship)*

Purpose: To provide assistance for the professional development of graduate students in architectural history. **Focus:** Architecture. **Qualif.:** Applicants must be enrolled in a PhD program conducting a dissertation research about the contribution of women to the production of architecture in the United States in the mid-twentieth century (should be submitted in English). **Criteria:** Recipient is selected based on the submitted applications.

Funds Avail.: $10,000. **Number Awarded:** 1. **To Apply:** Applicants are advised to visit the website for the online Fellowship Application. Applicants must also submit via email to ksturm@sah.org a Word document which contains a summary or abstract; a budget detailing the use of the funds (one to two pages); a curriculum vitae; and two letters of recommendation. **Deadline:** February 15.

Remarks: A joint program of the Society of Architectural Historians and Beverly Willis Architecture Foundation Dissertation Fellowship.

6427 ■ Edilia and Francois Auguste de Montequin Fellowships *(Doctorate/Scholarship)*

Purpose: To support research on Spanish, Portuguese, or Ibero-American architecture. **Focus:** Architectural engineering. **Qualif.:** Applicant must be a member of the Society of Architectural Historians; a full-time junior graduate student engaged in a doctoral dissertation research; or a senior graduate student with a completed PhD or equivalent with a research focusing on Spanish, Portuguese, or Ibero-American architecture. **Criteria:** Awards are given based on the submitted applications.

Funds Avail.: $2,000 for junior scholars and $6,000 for senior scholars. **Number Awarded:** 1. **To Apply:** Application form is available at the SAH office and at the website. **Deadline:** October 20.

6428 ■ Samuel H. Kress Foundation Dissertation Fellowships *(Doctorate/Fellowship)*

Purpose: To provide assistance for the professional development of graduate students in architectural history. **Focus:** Architecture. **Qualif.:** Applicant must be a U.S. Citizen; enrolled at an American university; a doctoral candidate with a dissertation that focuses on European architecture before 1850. **Criteria:** Applicants must be nominated by their university department.

Funds Avail.: $15,000. **Number Awarded:** 1. **To Apply:** Applicants are advised to visit the website for the online Fellowship Application. **Deadline:** January 15.

Remarks: A joint program of the Society of Architectural Historians and Samuel H. Kress Foundation.

6429 ■ SAH Study Tour Fellowships *(Doctorate/Fellowship)*

Purpose: To provide travel opportunities that focus on the history of architecture and landscapes. **Focus:** Architecture. **Qualif.:** Applicant must be a member of the Society of Architectural Historians and a PhD student. **Criteria:** Recipients are selected by a committee by the SAH President.

Funds Avail.: Amount not specified. **To Apply:** Applicants are advised to visit the website for the online Study Tour Fellowship application.

6430 ■ Society for Canadian Women in Science and Technology

No. 471-411 Dunsmuir St.
Vancouver, BC, Canada V6B 1X4
Ph: (604)893-8657
Fax: (604)893-8692
URL: http://www.scwist.ca

6431 ■ M. Hildred Blewett Scholarships *(Postdoctorate/Scholarship)*

Purpose: To enable early-career women to return to physics research career after having had to interrupt their careers for family reasons. **Focus:** Physics. **Qualif.:** Applicants must be currently legal residents or resident aliens of the United States or Canada; must be currently in Canada or the United States; must have an affiliation with a research-active educational institution or national laboratory; and must have completed work toward a PhD. **Crite-**

Awards are arranged alphabetically below their administering organizations

ria: Applicants are selected based on a committee's review of the application materials.

Funds Avail.: $45,000. **To Apply:** Application form is available at the website. Completed application form and other supporting documents must be sent electronically to: blewett@aps.org. **Deadline:** June 2. **Contact:** Sue Otwell.

6432 ■ CEMF Claudette MacKay-Lassonde Scholarships *(Postdoctorate/Scholarship)*

Purpose: To encourage Canadian women to pursue careers in the field of engineering. **Focus:** Engineering. **Qualif.:** Applicants must be Canadian women who are pursuing studies in engineering at the PhD level. **Criteria:** Applicants are selected based on the committee's review of the application materials.

Funds Avail.: $15,000. **To Apply:** Applicants are advised to visit the website for the online application system. **Deadline:** January.

6433 ■ CN Scholarships for Women *(Postgraduate/Scholarship)*

Purpose: To encourage women to pursue non-traditional careers in areas such as trade, technology and operations and to promote employment equity in Canada. **Focus:** Technology. **Qualif.:** Applicants must be Canadian students in the field of trade, technology and operation; and must demonstrate their desire for a career in trades, technology or operation by providing a brief description of their career interest. **Criteria:** Applicants will be evaluated on the basis of their demonstrated interests in a non-traditional career. Scholarships are awarded regardless of whatever other financial assistance applicants may have obtained and may be used by the recipients to ease financial constraints while studying.

Funds Avail.: $600. **To Apply:** Applicants must submit letter of recommendation and other supporting documents to the educational institution that will in turn remit the money to the recipient. **Deadline:** October 12.

6434 ■ NSERC Canada Graduate Scholarships *(Graduate, Postdoctorate/Scholarship)*

Purpose: To provide financial support for the most outstanding eligible scholars pursuing master's or doctoral studies in a Canadian university; to assist recent recipients of doctoral degrees in adding to their research experience; and to stimulate the interest of undergraduate students in research. **Focus:** Natural sciences, Engineering. **Qualif.:** Applicants must be Canadian citizens or permanent residents of Canada; must hold (or expect to hold) a degree in science or engineering from a university whose standing is acceptable to NSERC; and must have obtained a first-class average in each of the last two years of study. **Criteria:** Applicants are evaluated and selected according to the criteria in the categories: academic excellence, research ability or potential, communication, interpersonal and leadership abilities.

Funds Avail.: $17,500-$35,000. **To Apply:** Application form and instructions are available at the website. **Deadline:** October 15.

6435 ■ NSERC Postgraduate Scholarships *(Graduate, Postdoctorate/Scholarship)*

Purpose: To provide financial support to high-calibre scholars who are engaged in master's or doctoral programs in the natural sciences or engineering; to assist recent recipients of doctoral degrees in adding to their research experience; and to stimulate the interest of undergraduate students in research. **Focus:** Natural sciences, Engineering. **Qualif.:** Applicants must be Canadian citizens or permanent residents of Canada; must hold (or expect to hold) a degree in science or engineering from a university whose standing is acceptable to NSERC; and must have obtained a first-class average in each of the last two years of study. **Criteria:** Applicants are evaluated and selected according to the criteria in the categories: academic excellence, research ability or potential, communication, interpersonal and leadership abilities.

Funds Avail.: $17,300. **To Apply:** Application form is available at the website. **Deadline:** October 15.

6436 ■ Society of Dance History Scholars

3416 Primm Ln.
Birmingham, AL 35216
Ph: (205)978-1404
Fax: (205)823-2760
E-mail: ashanti@sdhs.org
URL: http://www.sdhs.org

6437 ■ Graduate Student Travel Grants *(Graduate, Professional Development/Grant)*

Purpose: To help graduate students to defray costs of attending the annual conference. **Focus:** Dance. **Qualif.:** Applicants must be student members of SDHS; must be enrolled in a graduate degree program; and must be engaged in dance research. **Criteria:** Recipients are selected based on the committee's review of application materials.

Funds Avail.: $300. **Number Awarded:** 3. **To Apply:** Applicants must submit application form; estimated budget; proposal of maximum 250 words; and a curriculum vitae. **Deadline:** March 31. **Contact:** Jim Ranieri, Accounts Manager; sdhs@primemanagement.net.

6438 ■ Society for Economic Botany

PO Box 299
St. Louis, MO 63166-0299
E-mail: sebmembership@econbot.org
URL: http://www.econbot.org

6439 ■ Richard E. Schultes Research Awards *(Graduate/Grant)*

Purpose: To provide funding support for a research related to economic botany. **Focus:** Botany. **Qualif.:** Applicants must be graduate students who have received their degree within a year and must be members of the society. **Criteria:** Recipients are selected based on the submitted proposal.

Funds Avail.: $2,500. **To Apply:** Applicants' major advisor must confirm current MS, PhD or Post-doctoral status of the applicant through email message at schultesaward@econbot.org and must also provide a recommendation letter. Applicants must prepare in MS Word the description of the proposed research (2 pages); a tabular budget (1 page); and a one-page resume. Files must be named using first initial_lastname and must be sent electronically at schultesaward@econbot.org. **Deadline:** February 28.

Remarks: Established in honor of Dr. Richard Evans Schultes, society's economic botanist. **Contact:** schultesaward@econbot.org.

6440 ■ Society of Exploration Geophysicists

PO Box 702740
Tulsa, OK 74170-2740

Ph: (918)497-5500
Fax: (918)497-5557
E-mail: membership@seg.org
URL: http://www.seg.org

6441 ■ Society of Exploration Geophysicists Foundation Scholarships *(Graduate, Undergraduate/Scholarship)*

Purpose: To reduce the financial burden of tuition of geoscience students and promote study in geoscience. **Focus:** Geosciences. **Qualif.:** Applicant must be a student pursuing a college curriculum directed toward a career in applied geophysics, or a closely related field such as geosciences, physics, geology, or earth and environmental sciences; must be attending high school and planning to enter college next fall or be an undergraduate or graduate college student whose grades are above average. **Criteria:** Awards are given based on the application materials.

Funds Avail.: $500-$14,000. **To Apply:** Applicants must submit a completed scholarship application form and materials. **Deadline:** February 1. **Contact:** scholarships@seg.org

6442 ■ Society For Human Resource Management

1800 Duke St.
Alexandria, VA 22314
Ph: (703)548-3440
Fax: (703)535-6490
Free: 800-283-SHRM
URL: http://www.shrm.org

6443 ■ Barbara Sanchez Scholarships *(Undergraduate/Scholarship)*

Purpose: To provide educational fund for pursuing college degree in human resources or a related field. **Focus:** Personnel administration/human resources; Media arts. **Qualif.:** Applicants must be SHRM members; must be working full-time in human resources media field. **Criteria:** Recipients are selected based on merit.

Funds Avail.: $1500. **Number Awarded:** 5. **To Apply:** Applicants must return the signed application form with a letter of acceptance from the college and two letters of reference. **Deadline:** July 15.

Remarks: The scholarship was created to honor the late Barbara Sanchez, an HR Director at Newsday and dedicated member of the Media Human Resources Association board of directors.

6444 ■ SHRM Certification Scholarships - Individual *(Graduate/Scholarship)*

Purpose: To provide education scholarships to individuals pursuing study in Human Resource Management. **Focus:** Personnel administration/human resources. **Qualif.:** Applicants must be working full-time in human resources; must be working towards certification as professional in human resources (a global professional in Human Resources or a senior professional in Human Resources). **Criteria:** Recipients are selected based on work experiences and commitment to human resources.

Funds Avail.: $750. **Number Awarded:** 12. **To Apply:** Applicants must return the signed application form with a copy of resume; list of past SHRM volunteer leadership roles; and an essay. **Deadline:** July 15.

6445 ■ SHRM Foundation Regional Academic Scholarships *(Graduate, Undergraduate/Scholarship)*

Purpose: To encourage interest and education in the field of human resources. **Focus:** Personnel administration/human resources. **Qualif.:** Applicants must be working full-time in the field of human resources or pursuing graduate college degree in a Human Resource related field in an accredited institution of higher learning (full-time, part-time, online and distance learning programs are acceptable). Previous applicants and past scholarship recipients are eligible to re-apply. **Criteria:** Scholarship recipients will be selected based primarily on merit and will be evaluated according to the criteria set by the reviewing committee.

Funds Avail.: $1,375. **Number Awarded:** 8. **To Apply:** Applicants must return the signed application form with a letter of acceptance from the college and two letters of reference. **Deadline:** July 15.

6446 ■ Society of Georgia Archivists

PO Box 133085
Atlanta, GA 30333
Ph: (404)651-2477
Fax: (404)651-4314
E-mail: vicepresident@soga.org
URL: http://www.soga.org

6447 ■ Brenda S. Bank Educational Workshop Scholarships *(Undergraduate/Scholarship)*

Purpose: To enhance archival education. **Focus:** General studies. **Qualif.:** Eligible applicants are those who are engaged in compensated or volunteer archival work at any level in an institution in the state of Georgia, SGA members employed outside the state of Georgia, graduate students preparing for a career in archives at a college or university in Georgia or SGA students studying outside of Georgia. **Criteria:** Recipients are selected based on the academic performance and financial need.

Funds Avail.: No specific amount. **To Apply:** Applicants must submit: completed application form; a cover letter; letter of recommendation; resume; 500-word or less essay discussing how scholarship will enhance their overall professional development and/or what they hope to bring back to their current and/or anticipated work from the experience. **Deadline:** May 19. **Contact:** PO Box 1027 Savannah, GA 31402.

6448 ■ Anthony R. Dees Educational Workshop Scholarships *(Undergraduate/Scholarship)*

Purpose: To enhance archival education. **Focus:** General studies. **Qualif.:** Eligible applicants are those who are engaged in compensated or volunteer archival work at any level in an institution in the state of Georgia, SGA members employed outside the state of Georgia, graduate students preparing for a career in archives at a college or university in Georgia or SGA students studying outside of Georgia. **Criteria:** Recipients are selected based on the academic performance and financial need.

Funds Avail.: No specific amount. **To Apply:** Applicants must submit: completed application form; a cover letter; letter of recommendation; resume; a 500-word or less essay discussing how scholarship will enhance their overall professional development and/or what they hope to bring back to their current and/or anticipated work from the experience. **Contact:** PO Box 1027 Savannah, GA 31402.

6449 ■ Larry Gulley Scholarships
(Undergraduate/Scholarship)

Purpose: To enhance archival education, membership and participation in the profession. **Focus:** General studies. **Qualif.:** Eligible applicants are those who are engaged in compensated or volunteer archival work at any level in an institution in the state of Georgia, SGA members employed outside the state of Georgia, graduate students preparing for a career in archives at a college or university in Georgia or SGA students studying outside of Georgia. **Criteria:** Recipients are selected based on the academic performance and financial need.

Funds Avail.: No specific amount. **To Apply:** Applicants must submit: completed application form; a cover letter; letter of recommendation; resume; a 500-word or less essay discussing how scholarship will enhance their overall professional development and/or what they hope to bring back to their current and/or anticipated work from the experience. **Deadline:** February 15. **Contact:** PO Box 1027 Savannah, GA 31402.

6450 ■ Carroll Hart Scholarships *(Graduate/Scholarship)*

Purpose: To enhance archival education and membership. **Focus:** General studies. **Qualif.:** Eligible applicants are those engaged in compensated or volunteer archival work at any level in an institution in the state of Georgia, SGA members employed outside the state of Georgia, graduate students preparing for a career in archives at a college or university in Georgia or SGA students studying outside of Georgia. **Criteria:** Recipients are selected based on the academic performance and financial need.

Funds Avail.: $500. **To Apply:** Applicants must submit: completed application form; a cover letter; letter of recommendation; resume; 500 or less word essay discussing how scholarship will enhance their overall professional development and/or what they hope to bring back to their current and/or anticipated work from the experience. **Deadline:** March 1. **Contact:** PO Box 1027 Savannah, GA 31402.

6451 ■ Society for Historians of American Foreign Relations

106 Dulles Hall
230 W 17th Ave.
Department of History
Ohio State University
Columbus, OH 43210
Ph: (614)292-1951
Fax: (614)292-2282
E-mail: shafr@osu.edu
URL: http://www.shafr.org

6452 ■ Samuel Flagg Bemis Research Grants
(Doctorate, Graduate/Grant)

Purpose: To help defray the costs of domestic or international travel in conducting a research on a significant scholarly project. **Focus:** International affairs and relations. **Qualif.:** Applicants must be working on a dissertation dealing with some aspect of U.S. foreign relations history and must have completed all requirements for the doctoral degree except the dissertation. **Criteria:** Selection is based on a review of the submitted materials.

Funds Avail.: $2,000. **To Apply:** Graduate students must apply for the Holt Fellowships to be considered for the Samuel F. Bemis Research Grants. Untenured faculty members and recent Ph.D.s working as professional historians must submit a dissertation prospectus including a paragraph or two on how funds would be expended (8-12 pages), a concise curriculum (1-2 pages), a budget (1 page); and a recommendation letter to be submitted separately (all documents must be submitted through email). **Deadline:** February 1.

6453 ■ Stuart L. Bernath Dissertation Grants
(Doctorate/Grant)

Purpose: To help defray expenses in writing dissertations. **Focus:** International affairs and relations. **Qualif.:** Applicants must be working on dissertations dealing with some aspect of U.S. foreign relations history and have completed all requirements for the doctoral degree except the dissertation. **Criteria:** Selection is based on merit. Applicants will also be considered for the Gelfand-Rappaport Fellowship.

Funds Avail.: $4,000. **Number Awarded:** 1. **To Apply:** Applicants must submit a dissertation prospectus with a paragraph or two on how funds would be expended (8-12 pages); a concise c.v. (1-2 pages); and a budget (1 page). Dissertation adviser must write a letter of recommendation which must be submitted separately. All documents must be submitted through email. **Deadline:** November 15.

Remarks: Established through Dr. Gerald J. and Myrna F. Bernath, in memory of their late son, Stuart L. Bernath, Ph.D. **Contact:** Andrew L. Johns, Department of History, Brigham Young University, andrew_johns@byu.edu.

6454 ■ Myrna F. Bernath Fellowships *(Doctorate, Graduate/Fellowship)*

Purpose: To defray the costs of scholarly research by women. **Focus:** International affairs and relations. **Qualif.:** Applicants must be women from U.S. universities or women abroad pursuing a research in the United States. **Criteria:** Preference will be given to graduate students who will be finishing their Ph.Ds within five years.

Funds Avail.: $ 5,000. **To Apply:** Applicants must submit a dissertation prospectus including a paragraph or two on how funds would be expended (8-12 pages), a curriculum vitae (1-2 pages), a budget (1 page), and a letter of recommendation (to be submitted separately). All documents must be submitted through email. **Deadline:** December 1. **Contact:** Darlene Rivas, Pepperdine University, darlene.rivas@pepperdine.edu.

6455 ■ Robert A. and Barbara Divine Graduate Student Travel Grants *(Graduate/Grant)*

Purpose: To support the travel of graduate students. **Focus:** International affairs and relations. **Qualif.:** Applicants must be graduate students who will present papers at the annual meetings of SHAFR. **Criteria:** Program committee shall evaluate applications and allocate the available funds. Selection is based on merit and not on financial need.

Funds Avail.: Funds vary each year. **To Apply:** Application details are publicized in each annual Call For Papers for the annual meeting.

Remarks: Established in 2006 to honor Professor and Mrs. Robert A. Divine, a long-time professor at the University of Texas.

6456 ■ Lawrence Gelfand - Armin Rappaport Fellowships *(Doctorate, Graduate/Grant)*

Purpose: To defray the costs of travel in conducting a research on a significant dissertation project. **Focus:**

Awards are arranged alphabetically below their administering organizations

International affairs and relations. **Qualif.:** Applicants must be working on a dissertation dealing with some aspect of United States foreign relations history and have completed all requirements for the doctoral degree except the dissertation. **Criteria:** Selection is based on a review of the submitted materials.

Funds Avail.: $4,000. **To Apply:** Applicants must submit a dissertation prospectus including a paragraph or two on how funds would be expended (8-12 pages), a concise curriculum vitae (1-2 pages), and a budget (1 page). Dissertation advisers must write a letter of recommendation and submit it separately via e-mail. **Deadline:** November 15.

Remarks: Applicants are also considered for the Bernath Dissertation Grants. Established in honor of Lawrence Gelfand, founding member and former SHAFR president and Armin Rappaport, founding editor of Diplomatic History. **Contact:** Andrew L. Johns, Department of History, Brigham Young University, andrew_johns@byu.edu.

6457 ■ Michael J. Hogan Fellowships *(Graduate/Fellowship)*

Purpose: To encourage researches on foreign languages. **Focus:** Foreign languages. **Qualif.:** Applicants must be graduate students conducting research on some aspect of U.S. foreign relations history. **Criteria:** Membership in SHAFR is not required but could be considered.

Funds Avail.: $4,000. **To Apply:** Applicants must submit a detailed plan in using the fellowship to achieve the purposes of the program (5-7 pages); a curriculum vitae (1-2 pages); and a one-page budget. Graduate adviser must write a recommendation letter and submit it separately (all documents must be submitted through email to the committee chair). **Deadline:** February 1.

Remarks: Established in honor of Michael J. Hogan, a long-time editor of Diplomatic History. **Contact:** Kristin Ahlberg, Hogan Committee Chair, ahlbergkl@state.gov.

6458 ■ W. Stull Holt Dissertation Fellowships *(Doctorate, Graduate/Grant)*

Purpose: To defray the costs of travel in conducting a research on a significant dissertation project. **Focus:** International affairs and relations. **Qualif.:** Applicants must be working on a dissertation dealing with some aspect of U.S. foreign relations history and must have completed all requirements for the doctoral degree except the dissertation. **Criteria:** Selection is based on the submitted dissertation prospectus.

Funds Avail.: $4,000. **To Apply:** Applicants must submit a dissertation prospectus including a paragraph or two on how funds would be expended (8-12 pages), a concise curriculum (1-2 pages), and a budget (1 page). Dissertation adviser must write a recommendation letter and submit it separately (all documents must be submitted through email). **Deadline:** February 1. **Contact:** Kristin Ahlberg, Holt Committee Chair, ahlbergkl@state.gov.

6459 ■ SHAFR Dissertation Completion Fellowships *(Doctorate/Fellowship)*

Purpose: To support the writing and completion of doctoral dissertation. **Focus:** International affairs and relations. **Qualif.:** Applicants must be candidates for the PhD in a humanities or social science program; must be at the writing stage of the dissertation with a topic in the field of U.S. foreign relations history or international history; and must be members of SHAFR. **Criteria:** Selection is based on the submitted applications and other supporting materials.

Funds Avail.: $20,000. **Number Awarded:** 2. **To Apply:** Applicants must submit an application letter stating the project's significance, applicant's status, and other received support; a statement of research (3 pages, 750 words); a curriculum vitae; and a recommendation letter from the doctoral advisor. Send applications electronically to Emily S. Rosenberg at erosenbe@uci.edu (Subject: Last Name: SHAFR Dissertation Completion Fellowship). **Deadline:** April 1. **Contact:** Dissertation Completion Fellowship Chair, Emily S. Rosenberg, erosenbe@uci.edu.

6460 ■ Society for the History of Technology

618 Ross Hall Iowa State University
Ames, IA 50011
Ph: (515)294-8469
Fax: (515)294-6390
E-mail: shot@istate.edu
URL: http://www.historyoftechnology.org

6461 ■ Brooke Hindle Postdoctoral Fellowships *(Postdoctorate/Fellowship)*

Purpose: To promote the history of technology as a field of scholarly endeavor. **Focus:** History. **Qualif.:** Applicants must hold a doctorate in the history of technology or a related field. **Criteria:** Recipient of this award are based on the committee's criteria.

Funds Avail.: $10,000. **To Apply:** Applicant must submit their 2,500 word summary of the dissertation an a sample chapter; A plan of work (1000-1500 words) for the period of the fellowship; Two letters of recommendation. For applicants in full-time employment, one letter must include confirmation that an appropriate period of release will be granted. **Deadline:** April 15. **Contact:** Amy Bix, SHOT Secretary, 515-294-8469.

6462 ■ Melvin Kranzberg Dissertation Fellowships *(Doctorate/Fellowship)*

Purpose: To promote the history of technology as a field of scholarly endeavor. **Focus:** History. **Qualif.:** Applicants must be working on projects in the history of technology; Applicants must have completed all requirements for their doctorate except for the dissertation by September 1 of the year of the award is made. **Criteria:** The recipient of this award is based on the committee's criteria.

Funds Avail.: $4,000. **To Apply:** Applicants must submit their curriculum vitae; a 3-5 page (750-1250 words) summary of abstract of the proposed dissertation which applicants should describe how their research contributes to the history of technology; A 1-2 page (250-500 words) description of how the applicant intends to use the funds; A letter of recommendation from the student's dissertation director. **Deadline:** April 15. **Contact:** Amy Brix, SHOT Secretary, 515-294-8469.

6463 ■ SHOT-NASA Fellowships *(Doctorate, Postdoctorate/Fellowship)*

Purpose: To promote the history of technology as a field of scholarly endeavor. **Focus:** History. **Qualif.:** Applicant must possess a doctorate in history of technology or in a closely related field, or be enrolled as a student in a doctoral degree program and have completed all requirements for the Ph.D., except the dissertation, in history of technology or a related field. **Criteria:** Recipients of this award are on the basis of the committee's criteria.

Funds Avail.: $17,000. **To Apply:** Applicant must submit

Awards are arranged alphabetically below their administering organizations

an application form, curriculum vitae, two letters of recommendation, and a research proposal of not more than six pages, double-spaced. **Deadline:** April 1. **Contact:** Amy Brix, shot@iastate.edu.

6464 ■ Society for Judgment and Decision Making

PO Box 3061110
Tallahassee, FL 32306-1110
E-mail: bfennema@cob.fsu.edu
URL: http://www.sjdm.org

6465 ■ Jane Beattie Memorial Scholarships *(All/Scholarship)*

Purpose: To provide funding to subsidize travel to the U.S. for purposes of scholarly activity by foreign scholars in the area of judgment and decision research. **Focus:** General studies. **Qualif.:** Applicants must be scholars living and working in a country other than the United States. **Criteria:** Candidates will be evaluated based on the committee's estimate of the prospective value of the proposed activity, its relevance to the field of judgment and decision research, the scholarly credentials of the applicant, and the extent to which the award would contribute to the success of the applicant including considerations of financial and academic need.

Funds Avail.: $400 to $700. **To Apply:** Applicants must submit one-page application form, a one-page (single-spaced) description of the planned scholarly activity and a copy of their curriculum vitae. The activity may consist of attendance at a relevant conference in the U.S., or a visit to a U.S. institution. The description of activities should indicate the nature of the planned scholarly activity, with whom the applicant plans to work (if applicable), what the applicant hopes to accomplish with the visit, and why travel to the U.S. is important to its accomplishment.

6466 ■ Einhorn New Investigator Awards *(Undergraduate/Award/Prize)*

Purpose: To encourage outstanding work by new researchers. **Focus:** General studies. **Qualif.:** Applicants must be individuals who have not yet completed their PhD. **Criteria:** Candidates will be evaluated based on the criteria designed by the committee appointed by the President of the Committee.

Funds Avail.: No specific amount. **To Apply:** Applicants must submit four copies of a journal-style manuscript on any topic related to judgment and decision making accompanied by: (1) four copies of a summary or extended abstract of the paper, not to exceed four pages in length and (2) a cover letter that includes the name of the investigator's graduate advisor and the date that the Ph.D. was awarded (if applicable). In the case of co-authored papers, if the authors are all new investigators they can be considered jointly; otherwise, the new investigator(s) must be the primary author(s) and should be the primary source of ideas. **Deadline:** July 1. **Contact:** Craig R. M. McKenzie, 9500 Gilman Dr. MC 0109, University of California, San Diego La Jolla, CA, 92093-0109, USA.

6467 ■ Society of Louisiana Certified Public Accountants

2400 Veterans Blvd., Ste. 500
Kenner, LA 70062
Ph: (504)464-1040
Free: 800-288-5272
E-mail: ghazel@lcpa.org
URL: http://www.lcpa.org

6468 ■ Society of Louisiana Certified Public Accountants Scholarships *(Undergraduate/Scholarship)*

Purpose: To further develop the accounting education and the accounting profession. **Focus:** Accounting. **Qualif.:** Applicants must have 2.5 academic grade point average; must be Louisiana domiciled; must be enrolled in an accounting program in a Louisiana four year college or university; and must be an at least fifth semester student. **Criteria:** Recipients are selected based on academic achievement and financial need.

Funds Avail.: No specific amount. **To Apply:** Applicants must complete the application form and submit an official college transcript and essay. **Deadline:** June 7.

6469 ■ Society of Manufacturing Engineers Education Foundation

PO Box 930
Dearborn, MI 48121-0930
Ph: (313)425-3300
Fax: (313)425-3411
Free: 800-733-4763
E-mail: foundation@sme.org
URL: http://www.sme.org/cgi-bin/smeefhtml.pl?/foundation/foundation_hp.htm&&&SEF&

6470 ■ Walt Bartram Memorial Education Awards (Region 12 and Chapter 119) *(Undergraduate/Scholarship)*

Purpose: To promote higher education to students from New Mexico, Arizona or Southern California. **Focus:** Manufacturing. **Qualif.:** Applicant must be a graduating high school senior enrolling as a full-time college or university student; must be a current SME Chapter member (except high school students); must pursue a degree in manufacturing engineering or related field in New Mexico, Arizona or Southern California; have a GPA of 3.5 on a 4.0 scale. **Criteria:** Preference is given to the applicants who will best meet the requirements.

Funds Avail.: $1,000. Scholarship funds may be used for credit toward books, fees or tuition only. **To Apply:** Visit the website for the online scholarship application process.

6471 ■ Caterpillar Scholars Award *(Undergraduate/Scholarship)*

Purpose: To assist high school seniors and undergraduate students in their college education. **Focus:** Manufacturing. **Qualif.:** Applicant must be enrolled as a full-time undergraduate student in a degree program in manufacturing engineering in the U.S. or Canada; must have completed a minimum of 30 college credit hours (minority applicants may apply as incoming freshmen); have GPA of 3.0 on a 4.0 scale. **Criteria:** Preference is given to applicants who participated in a STEPS camp.

Funds Avail.: $1,000. Scholarship funds may be used for credit toward books, fees or tuition only. **To Apply:** Applicants must contact the Foundation for applications.

6472 ■ Arthur and Gladys Cervenka Scholarships *(Undergraduate/Scholarship)*

Purpose: To promote higher education to students. **Focus:** Manufacturing; Technology. **Qualif.:** Applicant must be an

Awards are arranged alphabetically below their administering organizations

undergraduate student enrolled fulltime in a degree program in manufacturing engineering or technology; have completed a minimum of 30 college credit hours; have a GPA of 3.0 on a 4.0 scale. **Criteria:** Preference is given, but not limited to, the students in the state of Florida.

Funds Avail.: $1,000. Scholarship funds may be used for credit toward books, fees or tuition only. **To Apply:** Visit the website for the online scholarship application process.

Remarks: In memory of Arthur and Gladys Cervenka.

6473 ■ Chapter 4 - Lawrence A. Wacker Memorial Awards *(Undergraduate/Scholarship)*

Purpose: To assist high school seniors and undergraduate students to continue their education. **Focus:** Manufacturing; Mechanical engineering; Engineering, Industrial. **Qualif.:** Applicant must pursue a bachelor's degree in manufacturing, mechanical or industrial engineering; have a GPA of 3.0 on a 4.0 scale; must reside and attend an accredited institution in the U.S. or Canada. **Criteria:** Scholarship committee will give special considerations for: First preference: applicants who are Chapter 4 members (spouses, children or grandparents); Second preference: applicants who reside within Wisconsin counties (Milwaukee, Ozaukee, Washington and Waukesha); Third preference: applicants who reside within the state of Wisconsin.

Funds Avail.: $1,000. Scholarship funds may be used for credit toward books, fees or housing only. **Number Awarded:** 2. One to a graduating senior, and another to a current undergraduate student. **To Apply:** Visit the website for the Scholarship Application Process.

6474 ■ Chapter 6 Fairfield County Scholarships *(Undergraduate/Scholarship)*

Purpose: To financially support students in their education. **Focus:** Manufacturing; Technology. **Qualif.:** Applicants must be undergraduate students enrolled full-time in a degree program in manufacturing, technology, or a closely related field in the U.S. or Canada; have a GPA of 3.0 on a 4.0 scale. **Criteria:** Preference is given, but not limited to, applicants residing in the eastern part of the U.S.

Funds Avail.: $1,000. Scholarship funds may be used for credit toward books, fees or tuition only. **To Apply:** Visit the website for the online scholarship application process.

6475 ■ Chapter 17 - St. Louis Scholarships *(Undergraduate/Scholarship)*

Purpose: To financially support students who wish to pursue their education. **Focus:** Manufacturing; Engineering, Industrial. **Qualif.:** Applicants must be enrolled full-time or part-time undergraduate in a manufacturing engineering, industrial technology or other manufacturing related degree program; have a GPA of 2.5 on a 4.0 scale. **Criteria:** Recipient selection is based on: First preference: residing within the boundaries of St. Lewis Chapter 17; Second preference: residing within the state of Missouri.

Funds Avail.: $1,000. Scholarship funds may be used for credit toward books, fees or tuition only. **To Apply:** Visit the website for the online scholarship application process.

6476 ■ Chapter 23 - Quad Cities Iowa/Illinois Scholarships *(Undergraduate/Scholarship)*

Purpose: To assist high school seniors and undergraduate students in their education. **Focus:** Manufacturing. **Qualif.:** Applicant must be an undergraduate student or entering freshman pursuing a bachelor's degree in manufacturing engineering or related field on an accredited college or university in Iowa or Illinois; have a GPA of 2.5 on a 4.0 scale. **Criteria:** Recipient is selected based on: First preference: a child/grandchild/step child of a registered SME member or student member; Second preference: residing and attending college or university at Iowa or Illinois; Third preference: attending a college located in Iowa or Illinois.

Funds Avail.: $1,000. Scholarship funds may be used for credit toward books, fees or tuition only. **To Apply:** Visit the website for the online scholarship application process.

6477 ■ Chapter 31 - Peoria Endowed Scholarships *(Undergraduate/Scholarship)*

Purpose: To financially support students in their education. **Focus:** Manufacturing; Engineering, Industrial. **Qualif.:** Applicants must be pursuing a bachelor's degree in manufacturing engineering, industrial engineering, manufacturing technology or a manufacturing related degree program at Bradley University (Peoria, Illinois) or Illinois University (Normal, Illinois); have a GPA of 3.0 on a 4.0 scale. **Criteria:** Recipient is selected based on: First preference: a North Central Peoria-Chapter 31 member (spouse/child/grandchild); Second preference: an Illinois Central College transfer student; Third preference: SME student chapter members.

Funds Avail.: $1,000. Scholarship funds may be used for credit toward books, fees or tuition only. **To Apply:** Visit the website for the online scholarship application process.

6478 ■ Chapter 52 - Wichita Scholarships *(Graduate, Undergraduate/Scholarship)*

Purpose: To financially support students in their education. **Focus:** Manufacturing; Engineering, Industrial. **Qualif.:** Applicants must pursue an associate's degree, bachelor's degree or graduate degree in manufacturing, mechanical or industrial engineering, engineering technology or industrial technology at an accredited public or private college or university in Kansas, Oklahoma or Missouri; have a GPA of 2.5 on a 4.0 scale. **Criteria:** Recipient is selected based on: First preference: a child/grandchild/relative of a current SME Wichita Chapter No. 52 member; Second preference: resident of Kansas, Oklahoma or Missouri; Third preference: applicants planning to attend college or university at the state of Kansas.

Funds Avail.: $1,000. Scholarship funds may be used for credit toward books, fees or tuition only. **To Apply:** Visit the website for the online scholarship application process.

6479 ■ Chapter 56 - Fort Wayne Scholarships *(Graduate, Undergraduate/Scholarship)*

Purpose: To financially support students in their education. **Focus:** Manufacturing; Engineering, Industrial. **Qualif.:** Applicant must pursue an associate's degree, bachelor's degree or graduate degree in manufacturing, mechanical or industrial engineering, engineering technology or industrial technology at an accredited public or private college or university in Indiana; have a GPA of 2.5 on a 4.0 scale. **Criteria:** Recipient is selected based on: First preference: a child/grandchild of a current SME Fort Wayne Chapter No. 56 member; Second preference: a SME student member of student chapters that SME Fort Wayne Chapter No. 56 sponsor; Third preference: residents of Indiana; Fourth preference: planning to attend a college or university in the state of Indiana.

Funds Avail.: $1,000. Scholarship funds may be used for credit toward books, fees or tuition only. **To Apply:** Visit the website for the online scholarship application process.

6480 ■ Chapter 63 - Portland James E. Morrow Scholarships *(Graduate, Undergraduate/Scholarship)*

Purpose: To financially support students in their education. **Focus:** Manufacturing. **Qualif.:** Applicant must be a student pursuing a career in manufacturing or any related field; have a GPA of 2.5 on a 4.0 scale. **Criteria:** Recipient is selected based on: First preference: a child/grandchild/step child of a current Chapter 63 member; Second preference: a SME student chapter member in Oregon or southwest Washington; Third preference: applicants planning to attend school in Oregon or southwest Washington; Fourth preference: applicants residing within Oregon and Washington.

Funds Avail.: $1,000. Scholarship funds may be used for credit toward books, fees or tuition only. **To Apply:** Visit the website for the online scholarship application process.

6481 ■ Chapter 63 - Portland Uncle Bud Smith Scholarships *(Graduate, Undergraduate/Scholarship)*

Purpose: To financially support students in their education. **Focus:** Manufacturing. **Qualif.:** Applicant must be a student pursuing a career in manufacturing or any related field; have a GPA of 2.5 on a 4.0 scale. **Criteria:** selection is based on: First preference: a child/grandchild/step child of a current Chapter 63 member; Second preference: a SME student chapter member in Oregon or southwest Washington; Third preference: planning to attend school in Oregon or southwest Washington; Fourth preference: applicants residing within Oregon and Washington.

Funds Avail.: $1,000. Scholarship funds may be used for credit toward books, fees or tuition only. **To Apply:** Visit the website for the online scholarship application process.

6482 ■ Chapter 67 - Phoenix Scholarships *(Undergraduate/Scholarship)*

Purpose: To assist high school seniors and undergraduate students to continue college. **Focus:** Manufacturing; Engineering, Industrial. **Qualif.:** Applicant must be a high school senior planning to enroll in a manufacturing program technology course; or an undergraduate student currently enrolled in a manufacturing engineering technology; manufacturing technology, industrial technology or related program at an accredited college or university in Arizona; have a GPA of 2.5 on a 4.0 scale. **Criteria:** Preference is given to applicants who best meet the requirements.

Funds Avail.: $1,000. Scholarship funds may be used for credit toward books, fees or housing only. **To Apply:** Visit the website for the Scholarship Application Process.

6483 ■ Chapter 93 - Albuquerque Scholarships *(Undergraduate/Scholarship)*

Purpose: To assist high school seniors and undergraduate students in New Mexico to attend college. **Focus:** Manufacturing. **Qualif.:** Applicant must be a freshman or undergraduate student pursuing a bachelor's degree in manufacturing engineering or related field at an accredited college or university in New Mexico; have a GPA of 2.5 on a 4.0 scale. **Criteria:** Scholarship committee will give consideration to: First preference: a child/grandchild/step child of a current Chapter 93 member; Second preference: an SME student member attending New Mexico university; Third preference: resident of the state of New Mexico; Fourth preference: student planning to attend an engineering college or university in the state of New Mexico; Fifth preference: student planning to pursue an associate's degree.

Funds Avail.: $1,000. Scholarship funds may be used for credit toward books, fees or tuition only. **To Apply:** Visit the website for the online Scholarship Application Process.

6484 ■ Chapter 198 - Downriver Detroit Scholarships *(Graduate, Undergraduate/Scholarship)*

Purpose: To financially support students in their education. **Focus:** Manufacturing; Mechanical engineering; Industrial engineering. **Qualif.:** Applicant must be enrolled full-time seeking an associate's degree, bachelor's degree or graduate degree in manufacturing, mechanical or industrial engineering, engineering technology, or industrial technology at an accredited public or private college/university in the state of Michigan; have a GPA of 2.5 on a 4.0 scale. **Criteria:** Recipients are selected based on: First preference: a child/grandchild of a current SME Downriver Chapter No. 198 member; Second preference: a SME student member of student chapter that SME Downriver Chapter No. 198 sponsors; Third preference: applicants who are residents of Michigan; Fourth preference: applicants who plan to attend a college/university in the state of Michigan.

Funds Avail.: $1,000. Scholarship funds may be used for credit toward books, fees or tuition only. **To Apply:** Visit the website for the online scholarship application process.

6485 ■ Chapter 311 - Tri City Scholarships *(Undergraduate/Scholarship)*

Purpose: To assist high school seniors and undergraduate students in Michigan to attend college. **Focus:** Manufacturing; Engineering, Industrial. **Qualif.:** Applicants must pursue a bachelor's degree in manufacturing engineering, industrial engineering, manufacturing technology engineering or related field; have a GPA of 3.0 on a 4.0 scale. **Criteria:** Scholarship committee will give consideration to: First preference: residents of Michigan; Second preference: students enrolled in a college or university in Michigan.

Funds Avail.: $1,000. Scholarship funds may be used for credit toward books, fees and tuition only. **To Apply:** Visit the website for the online Scholarship Application Process.

6486 ■ Chapter One - Detroit Founding Chapter Scholarships *(Graduate, Undergraduate/Scholarship)*

Purpose: To financially support students in their education. **Focus:** Manufacturing. **Qualif.:** Applicants must be graduate or undergraduate students enrolled full-time or part-time in a manufacturing, manufacturing engineering technology or any related degree or certificate program in the following institutions: Wayne State University, Student Chapter S004; Lawrence Technological University, Student Chapter S011; University of Detroit-Mercy, Student Chapter S081; Focus: Hope, Center for Advanced Technologies, Student Chapter S279; Henry Ford Community College, Student Chapter S331; Macomb Community College, Student Chapter S071; University of Michigan - Dearborn, Student Chapter S326. Applicants must have a minimum GPA of 3.0 on a 4.0 scale; and must demonstrate good character and leadership. **Criteria:** Preference is given to applicants who are active in SME Student Chapter activities at their respective institutions or SME-Detroit Chapter One - The Founding Chapter.

Funds Avail.: $1,000. Scholarship funds may be used for credit toward books, fees or tuition only. **Number Awarded:** 3. One award for three academic levels (Associates, Bac-

Awards are arranged alphabetically below their administering organizations

calaureate, Graduate). **To Apply:** Visit the website for the online scholarship application process.

6487 ■ Chapter 116 - Kalamazoo - Roscoe Douglas Scholarships *(Undergraduate/Scholarship)*

Purpose: To financially support students in their education. **Focus:** Manufacturing. **Qualif.:** Applicant must be a full-time undergraduate student at the Western Michigan University; must have completed at least 30 college credit hours; be pursuing a career in manufacturing engineering or manufacturing engineering technology; have a GPA of 3.0 on a 4.0 scale. **Criteria:** Preference is given to applicants who will best meet the requirements.

Funds Avail.: $1,000. Scholarship funds may be used for credit toward books, fees or tuition only. **To Apply:** Visit the website for the online scholarship application process.

Remarks: The scholarship is named after the professor of emeritus of mechanical engineering Roscoe H. Douglas at Western Michigan University.

6488 ■ Future Leaders of Manufacturing Scholarships *(Graduate, Undergraduate/Scholarship)*

Purpose: To financially support students in their education. **Focus:** Manufacturing; Engineering; Engineering, Industrial. **Qualif.:** Candidates must be SME Student Chapter members; must be nominated by their faculty advisors; must be enrolled full-time undergraduate or graduate students; must be in manufacturing engineering, engineering technology, industrial technology, technical or related majors. **Criteria:** Preference is given to candidates who best meet the requirements.

Funds Avail.: $1,000. Scholarship funds may be used for credit toward books, fees or tuition only. **To Apply:** Candidates must submit a completed Nomination/Application form; a recommendation letter from the faculty advisor; a resume; transcripts. **Deadline:** February 1. **Contact:** SME Foundation at 313-425-3300.

6489 ■ Connie and Robert T. Gunter Scholarships *(Undergraduate/Scholarship)*

Purpose: To financially support students in their education. **Focus:** Manufacturing. **Qualif.:** Applicant must be enrolled as a full-time undergraduate student in a degree program in manufacturing engineering or technology; must have completed a minimum of 30 college credit hours; must have a GPA of 3.5 on a 4.0 scale. **Criteria:** Preference is given to applicants who will best meet the requirements.

Funds Avail.: $1,000. Scholarship funds may be used for credit toward books, fees or tuition only. **To Apply:** Visit the website for the online scholarship application process.

Remarks: Started in 1997.

6490 ■ Gene Haas Foundation Manufacturing Technology Scholarships *(Undergraduate/Scholarship)*

Purpose: To encourage students to attend the "Careers in Technology" event. **Focus:** Manufacturing. **Qualif.:** Applicant must be a graduating high school senior or undergraduate student seeking an associate or baccalaureate degree in manufacturing engineering, manufacturing engineering technology or a related field; must have a GPA of 2.5 on a 4.0 scale; must attend the SME Great lakes Advanced Productivity Careers in Technology. **Criteria:** Preference is given to applicants who pursue degrees in the state of Michigan and from a school in the state of Michigan.

Funds Avail.: $1,000. Scholarship funds may be used for credit toward books, fees or tuition only. **To Apply:** Applicants must use the on-line SME-EF scholarship application process to apply.

6491 ■ Clinton J. Helton Manufacturing Scholarships *(Undergraduate/Scholarship)*

Purpose: To financially support students in their education. **Focus:** Manufacturing. **Qualif.:** Applicant must be enrolled as a full-time undergraduate student in a degree seeking program in manufacturing engineering, technology or related field at an approved Colorado college (Colorado State University or University of Colorado); must have completed a minimum of 30 college credit hours; must have a GPA of 3.0 on a 4.0 scale. **Criteria:** Preference is given to applicants who will best meet the requirements.

Funds Avail.: No specific amount. **To Apply:** Visit the website for the online scholarship application process.

Remarks: Scholarship funds may be used for credit toward books, fees or tuition only. Established in 1979.

6492 ■ Henry Ford Academy Scholarships *(Undergraduate/Scholarship)*

Purpose: To assist high school seniors and undergraduate students to attend college. **Focus:** Engineering; Technology. **Qualif.:** Applicants must be graduating high school seniors from Henry Ford Academy pursuing a bachelor/associate degree in engineering or technology at an accredited college or university in the U.S.; have a GPA of 3.0 on a 4.0 scale. **Criteria:** Applicants who attend University of Michigan-Dearborn will be given preference.

Funds Avail.: $1,000. Scholarship funds may be used for credit toward books, fees or tuition only. **To Apply:** Applicants must submit two reference letters, one from a Henry Ford Academy instructor.

Remarks: Renewal of scholarship requires a GPA of 3.0.

6493 ■ Lucile B. Kaufman Women's Scholarships *(Undergraduate/Scholarship)*

Purpose: To financially support students in their education. **Focus:** Manufacturing; Technology. **Qualif.:** Applicants must be enrolled full-time undergraduate students in a degree program in manufacturing engineering, technology, or related field in the U.S. or Canada; must be female; have a GPA of 3.0 on a 4.0 scale; have completed at least 30 college credits; pursuing a career in manufacturing engineering or manufacturing technology. **Criteria:** Preference is given to applicants who best meet the requirements.

Funds Avail.: $1,000. Scholarship funds may be used for credit toward books, fees or tuition only. **To Apply:** Visit the website for the online scholarship application process.

Remarks: The scholarship was established by Professor Emeritus of Engineering Lucile B. Kaufman at Arizona State University.

6494 ■ E. Wayne Kay Co-op Scholarships *(Undergraduate/Scholarship)*

Purpose: To financially support students in their education. **Focus:** Manufacturing. **Qualif.:** Applicant must be enrolled as a full-time undergraduate student in a manufacturing engineering or technology degree program in the U.S. or Canada; must be working through a co-op program in a manufacturing related environment; must have completed a minimum of 30 college credit hours; have a GPA of 3.0 on a 4.0 scale; must provide evidence of demonstrated excellence related to manufacturing engineering or technology that may include a project completed for the applicant's employer. **Criteria:** Preference is given to applicants who best meet the requirements.

Funds Avail.: $1,000. Scholarship funds may be used for credit toward books, fees or tuition only. **To Apply:** Visit the website for the online scholarship application process. Applicants must present a letter of recommendation from their employer and a letter of support from a faculty at their college or university.

6495 ■ E. Wayne Kay Community College Scholarships *(Undergraduate/Scholarship)*

Purpose: To assist high school seniors and undergraduate students to attend college. **Focus:** Manufacturing. **Qualif.:** Applicant must be a graduating high school senior or a full-time undergraduate student enrolled in a degree program in manufacturing or related field at a two year Community College or trade school in the U.S. or Canada; freshman or sophomore with less than 60 college credit hours completed and pursuing a career in manufacturing engineering or technology; have a GPA of 3.0 on a 4.0 scale. **Criteria:** Preference is given to applicants who best meet the requirements.

Funds Avail.: $1,000. Scholarship funds may be used for credit toward books, fees or tuition only. **To Apply:** Visit the website for the online Scholarship Application Process.

6496 ■ E. Wayne Kay High School Scholarships *(Undergraduate/Scholarship)*

Purpose: To assist high school seniors to attend college. **Focus:** Manufacturing. **Qualif.:** Applicant must be a graduating high school senior who commits to enroll as a full-time freshman in a manufacturing engineering or technology program at an accredited college or university; have an overall GPA of 3.0 on a 4.0 scale for high school senior year. **Criteria:** Preference is given to applicants who best meet the requirements.

Funds Avail.: $1,000. Scholarship funds may be used for credit toward books, fees or tuition only. **To Apply:** Visit the website for the online Scholarship Application Process.

6497 ■ Giuliano Mazzetti Scholarships *(Undergraduate/Scholarship)*

Purpose: To financially support students in their education. **Focus:** Manufacturing; Technology. **Qualif.:** Applicants must be enrolled full-time undergraduate students in a degree program in manufacturing engineering, technology, or related field in the U.S. or Canada; must have completed at least 30 college credit hours; must be pursuing a career in manufacturing engineering or technology; must have a GPA of 3.0 on a 4.0 scale. **Criteria:** Preference is given to applicants who best meet the requirements.

Funds Avail.: $1,000. Scholarship funds may be used for credit toward books, fees or tuition only. **To Apply:** Visit the website for the online scholarship application process.

6498 ■ Clarence and Josephine Myers Scholarships *(Graduate, Undergraduate/Scholarship)*

Purpose: To financially support students in their education. **Focus:** Manufacturing; Mechanical engineering; Industrial engineering. **Qualif.:** Applicant must be a graduate or undergraduate student pursuing an associate, bachelor or graduate degree in manufacturing, machinable or industrial engineering in the state of Indiana; have a GPA of 3.0 on a 4.0 scale. **Criteria:** Applicants who plan to attend or are currently attending a college/university in Indiana; who attended Arsenal Technological High School in Indianapolis; SME student members of SME Chapter 37 sponsored chapters; a children/grandchildren of a current SME Chapter 37 member, will be given special consideration by the Scholarships Committee.

Funds Avail.: $1,000; Scholarship funds may be used for credit toward books, fees or tuition only. **To Apply:** Visit the website for the online scholarship application process.

Remarks: In memory of Josephine and Clarence J. Myers.

6499 ■ North Central (Region 9) Scholarships *(Undergraduate/Scholarship)*

Purpose: To financially support students in their education. **Focus:** Manufacturing; Mechanical engineering; Engineering, Industrial. **Qualif.:** Applicant must be an enrolled full-time undergraduate student pursuing a bachelor's degree or associate's degree in manufacturing, mechanical, industrial engineering or industrial engineering or industrial technology at a two- or four-year college/university within the North Central Region (Iowa, Minnesota, Nebraska, North Dakota, South Dakota, Wisconsin and upper peninsula of Michigan); have a GPA of 3.0 on a 4.0 scale. **Criteria:** Preference is based on: First preference: applicants who are SME members, their spouses or children/grandchildren from the North Central Region; Second Preference: applicants who reside in North Central Region (Iowa, Minnesota, Nebraska, North Dakota, South Dakota, Wisconsin and upper peninsula of Michigan).

Funds Avail.: $1,000. Scholarship funds may be used for credit toward books, fees or tuition only. **To Apply:** Visit the website for the online scholarship application process.

6500 ■ Edward S. Roth Manufacturing Engineering Scholarships *(Graduate, Undergraduate/Scholarship)*

Purpose: To assist high school seniors and undergraduate students to attend college. **Focus:** Manufacturing. **Qualif.:** Applicant must be a U.S. citizen; must be a graduating high school senior or a current full-time graduate or undergraduate student pursuing a bachelor's or master's degree in manufacturing engineering from an ABET-accredited school (California Polytechnic State University, CA; California State Polytechnic University, CA; University of Miami, FL; Bradley University, IL; Central State University, OH; Miami University, OH; Boston University, MA; Worcester Polytechnic Institute, MA; University of Massachusetts, MA; St. Cloud State University, MN; The University of Texas - Pan American, TX; Brigham Young University, UT; Utah State University, UT); must have a GPA of 3.0 on a 4.0 scale. **Criteria:** Preference is given to applicants with demonstrated financial need, minority students, and students participating in a Co-Op program.

Funds Avail.: $1,000. Scholarship funds may be used for credit toward books, fees or tuition only.

6501 ■ Prof. George Schneider, Jr. Manufacturing Technology Education Scholarships *(Undergraduate/Scholarship)*

Purpose: To financially support students in their education. **Focus:** Manufacturing. **Qualif.:** Applicants must be enrolled at least 6 credit hours per semester; pursuing a bachelor's degree in manufacturing engineering, manufacturing engineering technology or related field at the Lawrence

Awards are arranged alphabetically below their administering organizations

Technological University; have a GPA of 2.5 on a 4.0 scale; have completed at least 60 college credit hours. **Criteria:** Preference is given to applicants who will best the requirements.

Funds Avail.: $1,000. Scholarship funds may be used for credit toward books, fees or tuition only. **To Apply:** The College of Engineering Dean at Lawrence Technological University will recommend two to three candidates for the scholarship annually. A letter of recommendation for the nominated student is provided by the Chair of the School of Technology at Lawrence Technological University.

6502 ■ SME Directors Scholarships
(Undergraduate/Scholarship)

Purpose: To financially support students in their education. **Focus:** Manufacturing. **Qualif.:** Applicants must be enrolled full-time undergraduate students in a manufacturing degree program at a U.S. or Canadian college; have completed at least 30 college credit hours; pursuing a career in manufacturing; have a GPA of 3.5 on a 4.0 scale. **Criteria:** Preference is given to applicants who demonstrate leadership skills in a community, academic, or professional environment.

Funds Avail.: $1,000. Scholarship funds may be used for credit toward books, fees or tuition only. **To Apply:** Visit the website for the online scholarship application process.

6503 ■ SME Education Foundation Family Scholarships *(Undergraduate/Scholarship)*

Purpose: To support the children or grandchildren of SME members. **Focus:** Manufacturing. **Qualif.:** Applicant must pursue a degree in manufacturing engineering, manufacturing engineering technology, or a related manufacturing field of study; must be a resident and attending in an accredited institution in the U.S. or Canada; must have at least one parent or grandparent that became an SME member for 2 years in good standing; must be graduating high school senior or undergraduate with up to 30 credit hours completed; enrolling full-time at a college or university; have a GPA of 3.0 on a 4.0 scale; have a minimum 1000 SAT score and/or 21 ACT score. **Criteria:** Recipient selection is based on academic excellence; communication and interpersonal skills; interest in manufacturing engineering, manufacturing engineering technology, or related field; and on extracurricular activities.

Funds Avail.: $1,000. **To Apply:** Applicants must complete the Scholarship Application Process; and submit a 300-word student statement letter explaining: career objectives in manufacturing engineering, manufacturing engineering technology, or related fields; educational objectives; how the scholarship will help with the objectives; reason for entering this field. Applicants must also include a 2-page resume; official transcripts; two letters of recommendation from current or former employers or teachers; a copy of SAT or ACT test results; an essay about the applicant's favorite manufacturing engineer. **Deadline:** February 1.

6504 ■ SME Ford PAS Scholarships
(Undergraduate/Scholarship)

Purpose: To assist high school seniors and undergraduate students in their college education. **Focus:** Engineering; Technology. **Qualif.:** Applicant must be a current or former student of a Ford PAS program at their high school or in a Ford PAS after-school/weekend/summer/college program; must be pursuing a bachelor/associate degree in engineering or technology at an accredited college or university in the U.S.; have a GPA of 3.0 on a 4.0 scale. **Criteria:** Preference is given to applicants who attend a Ford Advanced Education Program partner school or university.

Funds Avail.: $1,000. Scholarship funds may be used for credit toward books, fees or tuition only. **To Apply:** Applicants must submit two reference letters, one from a Ford PAS instructor.

Remarks: Renewal of scholarship requires a GPA of 3.0.

6505 ■ Myrtle and Earl Walker Scholarships
(Undergraduate/Scholarship)

Purpose: To financially support students in their education. **Focus:** Manufacturing; Technology. **Qualif.:** Applicant must be an enrolled full-time undergraduate student in a degree program in manufacturing engineering or technology in the U.S. or Canada; must have completed at least 15 college credit hours or one semester; must be pursuing a career in manufacturing engineering or technology; must have a GPA of 3.0 on a 4.0 scale. **Criteria:** Preference is given to applicants who best meet the requirements.

Funds Avail.: $1,000. Scholarship funds may be used for credit toward books, fees or tuition only. **To Apply:** Visit the website for the online scholarship application process.

6506 ■ Allen and Loureena Weber Scholarships
(Undergraduate/Scholarship)

Purpose: To assist high school seniors and undergraduate students in their college education. **Focus:** Manufacturing; Mechanical engineering; Engineering; Industrial Engineering. **Qualif.:** Applicant must be a student of the University of Northern Kentucky or pursuing an associate's degree or bachelor's degree in manufacturing, mechanical, industrial engineering, engineering technology or industrial technology with a satisfactory GPA; should reflect the interest of the donor in "individuals who possess technical aptitude and desire for education and practical learning". **Criteria:** Recipients are selected based on: First preference: graduates of Dayton High School (Dayton, KY); Second preference: other high schools in the Dayton, KY area including Newport High School (Newport, KY).

Funds Avail.: $1,000. Scholarship funds may be used for credit toward books, fees or tuition only. **To Apply:** Visit the website for the scholarship application process.

6507 ■ William E. Weisel Scholarships
(Undergraduate/Scholarship)

Purpose: To financially support students in their education. **Focus:** Engineering; Technology. **Qualif.:** Applicants must be U.S. citizens; enrolled full-time undergraduate students in an engineering or technology program in the U.S or Canada; have completed at least 30 college credit hours; have a GPA of 3.0 on a 4.0 scale. **Criteria:** Preference is given to applicants who intend to apply their knowledge in the sub-specialty of medical robotics.

Funds Avail.: $1,000. Scholarship funds may be used for credit toward books, fees or tuition only. **To Apply:** Visit the website for the online scholarship application process.

Remarks: The scholarship is a living tribute to the memory of William E. Weisel's career in manufacturing.

6508 ■ Albert E. Wischmeyer Memorial Scholarships *(Undergraduate/Scholarship)*

Purpose: To assist high school seniors and undergraduate students in their education. **Focus:** Manufacturing; Mechanical engineering. **Qualif.:** Applicants must be graduating high school seniors or undergraduates pursuing a degree in manufacturing engineering, manufacturing engineering technology, or mechanical technology; attending an accredited institution in New York State; must be residents of Western New York; have a GPA of 2.5 on a 4.0 scale. **Criteria:** Recipients will be selected based on the application materials submitted.

Funds Avail.: $1,000. Scholarship funds may be used for credit toward books, fees or tuition only. **To Apply:** Students must write for applications.

Remarks: In memory of Albert E. Wischmeyer.

6509 ■ Society of Marine Port Engineers

111 Broad St.
PO Box 369
Eatontown, NJ 07724
Ph: (732)389-2009
Fax: (732)389-2264
E-mail: dmoore@smpe.org
URL: http://www.smpe.org

6510 ■ Society of Marine Port Engineers Scholarship Loans *(Undergraduate/Scholarship/Forgivable Loan)*

Purpose: To assist members of SMPE and their families in pursuing higher studies. **Focus:** General Studies. **Qualif.:** Program is open to children of SMPE members with a minimum of three years membership; and must be attending or accepted as full-time students in the next regular term of indicated institutions of higher education. **Criteria:** Recipients are selected based on merit.

Funds Avail.: No specific amount. **To Apply:** Application forms and instructions are available at the SMPE website. **Deadline:** July 15.

6511 ■ Society for the Maternal-Fetal Medicine

409 12th St. SW
Washington, DC 20024
Ph: (202)863-2476
Fax: (202)554-1132
E-mail: smfm@smfm.org
URL: http://www.smfm.org

6512 ■ SMFM/AAOGF Scholarship Award *(Graduate/Scholarship)*

Purpose: To support a single scholarship in maternal-fetal medicine. **Focus:** Gynecological and Obstetrical. **Qualif.:** Applicants must be a member of SMFM. **Criteria:** Scholarship is awarded based on the committee's criteria.

Funds Avail.: $100,000 per year of which at least $5,000 but not more than $15,000 must be used for employee benefits where the scholarship is awarded.

Remarks: With the enthusiastic support of the Board of Directors of the SMFM and the Council of the American Association of Obstetrical society and the Endowment Fund Committee of the American Association of Obstetricians and Gynecologists Foundation (AAOGF), the SMFM and AAOGF has entered into a partnership to support a single scholarship in maternal-fetal medicine. **Contact:** SMFM at the above address (see entry 6511).

6513 ■ Society for Military History

Journal of Military History
George C. Marshall Library
Virginia Military Institute
Lexington, VA 24450
Ph: (540)464-7468
Fax: (540)464-7330
E-mail: jmhsmh@vmi.edu
URL: http://www.smh-hq.org

6514 ■ ABC-Clio Research Grants *(Graduate/Grant)*

Purpose: To promote research on military history. **Focus:** Military history. **Qualif.:** Applicant must be a member of the Society for Military History; a graduate student enrolled in a doctoral program; or employed full-time as a professional historian without a doctoral degree. **Criteria:** Grant recipients will be selected based on the jury's review of the application materials.

Funds Avail.: $500. **Number Awarded:** 2. **To Apply:** Applicants must submit a curriculum vitae (maximum of 5 pages) which includes a statement of 500 words about the project description, uses of funds, and other sources of financial support already received. Applicants must also submit a (one page) bibliography of the recent relevant secondary work on the topic. **Deadline:** November 1.

6515 ■ Society for Mining, Metallurgy and Exploration

8307 Shaffer Pkwy.
Littleton, CO 80127-4102
Ph: (303)973-9550
Fax: (303)973-3845
Free: 800-763-3132
E-mail: estrada@smenet.org
URL: http://www.smenet.org

6516 ■ SME Coal and Energy Division Scholarships *(Undergraduate/Scholarship)*

Purpose: To provide support to students seeking advanced education in the minerals industry profession and field. **Focus:** Metallurgy; Mineralogy; Mining; Engineering, Mining and Mineral. **Qualif.:** Applicants must be junior or senior students majoring in mining or mineral engineering programs that are accredited by the Accreditation Board for Engineering and Technology (ABET). Applicants must be a student member of SME and must have a minimum cumulative 2.50 GPA. Applicants who have received a previous Coal and Energy Division Scholarship may, upon submitting a new application, be granted a scholarship, subject to the recommendations of the college or university the recipient is attending and review by the Scholarship Committee. **Criteria:** Scholarship recipients are selected based on the academic record, character and financial need.

Funds Avail.: $1,500. **Number Awarded:** 15. **To Apply:** Applicants must submit a completed application form, transcript and two letters of recommendation, one of which must be from the Program Chair or Department Head. Application form should include a brief outline of the applicant's participation in mining industry-related activities (such as the student chapter or local section of SME), coal industry employment or employment commitment, scholastic achievements and an explanation why the applicant is interested in a career in coal and is deserving of Coal and Energy Division support. **Deadline:** October 30. **Contact:** Ann Marie Estrada at the above address (see entry 6515).

Awards are arranged alphabetically below their administering organizations

6517 ■ SME Environmental Division Scholarships *(Undergraduate/Scholarship)*

Purpose: To provide support to students seeking advanced education in the minerals industry profession and field. **Focus:** Metallurgy; Mineralogy; Mining; Engineering, Mining and Mineral. **Qualif.:** Candidates must be promising college students who desire to develop their skills related to mining and the environment. Candidates must be of good character and must have demonstrated scholastic aptitude; must be a member of SME, attending a college or university of his or her choice that provides a curriculum leading to an undergraduate degree related to mining and the environment and a faculty advisor with special interests in an environmentally oriented program. **Criteria:** Scholarship recipients are selected based on scholastic ability, potential, professional interest, character and financial need.

Funds Avail.: $2,000. **To Apply:** Applicants must submit a completed application form, transcript and two references from faculty members, people from industry, or others who can write about his/her academic potential and professional interests. **Deadline:** October 30. **Contact:** Ann Marie Estrada at the above address (see entry 6515).

6518 ■ Society of Naval Architects and Marine Engineers

601 Pavonia Ave.
Jersey City, NJ 07306
Ph: (201)798-4800
Fax: (201)798-4975
Free: 800-798-2188
E-mail: ldavis@sname.org
URL: http://www.sname.org

6519 ■ Mandell and Lester Rosenblatt and Robert N. Herbert Undergraduate Scholarships *(Undergraduate/Scholarship)*

Purpose: To encourage study in naval architecture, marine engineering, ocean engineering or marine industry-related fields. **Focus:** Architecture, Naval; Marine engineering; Ocean engineering. **Qualif.:** Applicants must be U.S. or Canadian citizens who are actively involved with SNAME and other professional organizations. **Criteria:** Recipients are selected based on the scholarship committee's recommendations and the executive committee's approval.

Funds Avail.: $6,000. **To Apply:** Applicants must complete the application form; Applicants must provide an evidence of sound academic achievement; a 500-600 word application essay; three letters of professional recommendations in which the two must be NA/ME/OE faculty who have had the student in class and at least two of whom are SNAME members. **Deadline:** June 1. **Contact:** efaustino@sname.org.

6520 ■ Society of Naval Architects and Marine Engineers Undergraduate Scholarships *(Undergraduate/Scholarship)*

Purpose: To encourage study in naval architecture, marine engineering, ocean engineering or marine industry-related fields. **Focus:** Architecture, Naval; Marine engineering; Ocean engineering. **Qualif.:** Applicants must be planning to study in the U.S. or Canada; applicants must study toward a degree in naval architecture, marine engineering, ocean engineering or marine industry related fields at an accredited school; applicants must be entering junior or senior year. **Criteria:** Recipients are selected based on/or in accordance with the colleges' established procedures.

Funds Avail.: $2,000. **To Apply:** Applicants must complete the online application form; applicants must submit a transcript of records or any proof that he/she is currently enrolled or have been accepted by the school, colleges, or universities. **Contact:** efaustino@sname.org.

6521 ■ Society of Nuclear Medicine

1850 Samuel Morse Dr.
Reston, VA 20190
Ph: (703)708-9000
Fax: (703)708-9015
URL: http://www.snm.org

6522 ■ Paul Cole Scholarships *(Undergraduate/Scholarship)*

Purpose: To provide financial support to students for educational careers in line with nuclear medicine technology. **Focus:** Nuclear medicine. **Qualif.:** Applicants must demonstrate financial need; be enrolled or accepted in an institution accredited through the Joint Review Committee on Educational Programs in Nuclear Medicine Technology (JRCNMT); have a minimum cumulative GPA of 2.5 or better (on a 4.0 scale) or B average in a nuclear medicine technology core curriculum. **Criteria:** Applicants will be evaluated based on financial need, statement of goals, academic performance, and program director recommendations.

Funds Avail.: $1,000. **To Apply:** Applicants must submit complete application, which includes statement and program director's signature; official transcripts of all format education; letter of recommendation from the program director verifying the applicant's acceptance into or enrollment in the nuclear medicine technology program. **Deadline:** October 17.

6523 ■ SNMTS Bachelor's Degree Completion Scholarships *(Undergraduate/Scholarship)*

Purpose: To support students pursuing a Bachelor's degree completion program related to their nuclear medicine career. **Focus:** General studies. **Qualif.:** Applicants must demonstrate financial need; hold a certificate or associate's degree in nuclear medicine technology; currently enrolled in a bachelor's level program to advance their career in nuclear medicine; have a minimum cumulative GPA of 2.5 or better (on 4.0 scale) or B average in the program's core curriculum, and member of the SNMTS. **Criteria:** Candidates will be judged based on the criteria designed by the Scholarship Committee.

Funds Avail.: $5,000. **To Apply:** Applicants must submit a completed application, which includes applicant's statement and recommenders' signature; official transcripts of all formal education (high school transcripts are not necessary if transcripts of college level work are submitted); a letter of recommendation from an educational or professional reference; an official transcript or letter from the institution's registrar's office verifying the applicant's enrollment or acceptance in the Bachelor's degree program. **Deadline:** May 30.

6524 ■ SNMTS Clinical Advancement Scholarships *(Other/Scholarship)*

Purpose: To support technologists who are pursuing clinical advancement through didactic educational programs. **Focus:** Clinical sciences. **Qualif.:** Applicants must demon-

Awards are arranged alphabetically below their administering organizations

strate financial need; be currently enrolled in didactic educational programs (ex. CT, DEXA, physics, statistics); complete the said class or program; and member of the SNMTS. **Criteria:** Candidates will be judged based on the criteria designed by the Scholarship Committee.

Funds Avail.: $500. **To Apply:** Applicants must submit a completed application, which includes applicant's statement and recommenders' signature; official transcripts of all formal education (high school transcripts are not necessary if transcripts of college level work are submitted); letter of recommendation from an educational or professional reference; an official transcript or letter from the institution's registrar's office verifying the applicant's enrollment or acceptance in the educational programs. **Deadline:** May 30.

6525 ■ Society Of Broadcast Engineers

9102 North Meridian St., Ste. 150
Indianapolis, IN 46260
Ph: (317)846-9000
Fax: (317)846-9120
E-mail: mclappe@sbe.org
URL: http://www.sbe.org

6526 ■ Harold E. Ennes Scholarships *(Professional Development/Scholarship)*

Purpose: To provide educational fund to deserving candidates who aspire to a career in the technical aspects of broadcasting. **Focus:** Broadcasting; Engineering. **Qualif.:** Applicants must be SBE members; have a career interest in the technical aspect of broadcasting; have work experience in broadcasting engineering. **Criteria:** Preferences are given to those who are employed in broadcast engineering.

Funds Avail.: $1000 - $3000. **Number Awarded:** 3. **To Apply:** Application forms are available at the website. Complete only the A and C sections of the application form and send together with a brief autobiography; a summary of technical changes; and a copy of recent college transcripts (if applicable). **Deadline:** July 1.

Remarks: Established in memory of Harold E. Enned.

6527 ■ Robert D. Greenberg Scholarships *(Professional Development/Scholarship)*

Purpose: To provide educational fund to deserving candidates who aspire to a career in the technical aspects of broadcasting. **Focus:** Broadcasting; Engineering. **Qualif.:** Applicants must be SBE members; have a career interest in the technical aspect of broadcasting; have work experience in broadcasting engineering. **Criteria:** Preferences are given to those who are employed in broadcast engineering.

Funds Avail.: $1000 - $3000. **Number Awarded:** 3. **To Apply:** Application forms are available at the website. Complete only the A and C sections of the application form and send together with a brief autobiography; a summary of technical changes; and a copy of recent college transcripts (if applicable). **Deadline:** July 1.

6528 ■ Youth Scholarships *(Undergraduate/Scholarship)*

Purpose: To provide educational fund to deserving candidates who aspire to a career in the technical aspects of broadcasting. **Focus:** Broadcasting; Engineering. **Qualif.:** Applicants must be high school seniors; planning to enroll at a technical school; pursuing studies leading to a career in broadcasting engineering or related field. **Criteria:** Recipients are selected based on the committee's review of application materials.

Funds Avail.: $1000 $3000. **Number Awarded:** 3. **To Apply:** Application forms are available at the website. Complete only the B and C sections of the application form and send together with a brief autobiography; a summary of technical changes; and a copy of recent college transcripts (if applicable). **Deadline:** July 1.

6529 ■ Society of Pediatric Nurses

1194 Grow Dr.
Pensacola, FL 32514
Ph: (850)494-9467
Fax: (850)484-8762
Free: 800-723-2902
E-mail: spn@puetzamc.com
URL: http://www.pednurses.org

6530 ■ Society of Pediatric Nurses Educational Scholarship *(Graduate, Professional Development/Scholarship)*

Purpose: To help SPN members further their professional education. **Focus:** Nursing. **Qualif.:** Applicant must be a member engaged in a BSN completion program or a graduate program that will advance the health of children. **Criteria:** Applicants will be evaluated by the Scholarship Selection Committee.

Funds Avail.: $500. **To Apply:** Applicant must submit a complete application which includes the following: documentation of current enrollment/acceptance in BSN completion or graduate program; a curriculum vitae; a letter of recommendation from an SPN member. The letter must address the following: the nominator's relationship to the nominee, the nominee's position and responsibility, the nominee's interest in and/or commitment to the care of children and their families, a letter of recommendation from a faculty member who can evaluate the nominee's potential to meet professional goals **Deadline:** November 14.

6531 ■ Society of Pediatric Psychology

PO Box 170231
Atlanta, GA 30317
E-mail: pedpsychol@aol.com
URL: http://www.apa.org/divisions/div54

6532 ■ Lizette Peterson Homer Injury Prevention Grant Awards *(Professional Development, Undergraduate/Grant)*

Purpose: To provide assistance to research related to prevention of injuries to children and adolescents. **Focus:** Pediatric medicine. **Qualif.:** Applicants must be students and faculty members. **Criteria:** Recipients are selected based on committee's review of proposal.

Funds Avail.: $1500. **To Apply:** Applicants must submit a seven pages summary of proposed research which includes abstract (maximum of 100 words), project descriptions with introduction, budget, reference; curriculum vitae; letter of recommendation by faculty supervisor; and proof of IRB approval send by email at palermot@ohsu.edu on one single Word format. **Deadline:** October 1. **Contact:** Tonya Palermo, PhD, Phone: 503-494-0848, Fax: 503-494-5945, palermo@ohsu.edu.

Awards are arranged alphabetically below their administering organizations

6533 ■ Routh Student Research Grants *(Undergraduate/Grant)*

Purpose: To provide assistance to research related to field of pediatric psychology. **Focus:** Pediatric medicine. **Qualif.:** Applicants must be student members of APA. **Criteria:** Recipients are selected based on committee's review of proposal.

Funds Avail.: $1000. **To Apply:** Applicants must submit summary of proposed research (maximum of 100 words); project objectives (maximum of 7 pages); a detailed budget; a statement about the qualifications, training, membership of the applicant; and a letter of recommendation by faculty supervisor, send materials by email in MS Word format to: palermot@ohsu.edu. **Deadline:** October 1. **Contact:** Tonya Palermo, PhD, Phone: 503-494-0848, Fax: 503-494-5945, palermo@ohsu.edu.

6534 ■ Society for Pediatric Radiology

1891 Preston White Dr.
Reston, VA 20191
Ph: (703)648-0680
E-mail: spr@acr.org
URL: http://www.pedrad.org

6535 ■ Society for Pediatric Radiology Research Fellows *(Graduate, Professional Development/ Fellowship)*

Purpose: To provide young investigators an opportunity to gain further insight into scientific investigation and to develop competence in research techniques and methods. **Focus:** Radiology. **Qualif.:** Applicant must be a member of the Society for the Pediatric Radiology (SPR); holds a full-time faculty position in an educational institution; and in a department of diagnostic radiology, radiation oncology or nuclear medicine and have completed all advanced training. **Criteria:** Selection is based on scientific merit and appropriateness.

Funds Avail.: $30,000. **To Apply:** Applicants must submit one printed copy (with signatures) and one electronic version of the completed application submitted to jboylan@acr.org. **Deadline:** March 15.

6536 ■ Society for Pediatric Radiology Seed Grants *(Graduate, Professional Development/Grant)*

Purpose: To foster research and education in pediatric radiology. **Focus:** Radiology. **Qualif.:** One of the member of the investigator team must be a member of the Society for the Pediatric Radiology (SPR); holds a full-time faculty position in an educational institution; and in a department of diagnostic radiology, radiation oncology or nuclear medicine and have completed all advanced training. **Criteria:** Selection is based on scientific merit and appropriateness.

Funds Avail.: Maximum of $10,000. **To Apply:** Applicants must submit one printed copy (with signatures) and one electronic version of the completed application submitted to jboylan@acr.org. **Deadline:** March 15 and October 15.

6537 ■ Society for Pediatric Urology

900 Cummings Center, Ste. 221-U
Beverly, MA 01915
Ph: (978)927-8330
Fax: (978)524-8890
URL: http://www.spuonline.org

6538 ■ John W. Duckett Jr., AFUD Pediatric Research Scholarships *(Undergraduate/ Scholarship)*

Purpose: to promote pediatric urology, appropriate practice, education as well as exchanges between practitioners involve din the treatment of genito urinary disorders of children. **Focus:** Pediatric medicine. **Qualif.:** Applicant must be taking up pediatric medicine. **Criteria:** Application will be evaluated by the Scholarship Committee.

Funds Avail.: $10,000. **To Apply:** Applicant must fill out the application form and submit to the American Foundation of Urologic Disease.

6539 ■ Society for Pediatric Urology Research Grant Program *(Undergraduate/Grant)*

Purpose: To promote pediatric urology, an appropriate practice, education as well as exchanges between practitioners involved in the treatment of genito urinary disorders in children. **Focus:** Pediatric medicine. **Qualif.:** Applicant must have a knowledge in pediatric urology and must be officially enrolled in an accredited institution. **Criteria:** Recipients will be selected based on the synopsis of the research plan.

Funds Avail.: $30,000. **To Apply:** Applicants must attach a copy of Principal Investigator's Curriculum Vitae; a letter of commitment from the chair of the Principal Investigator's Department; must attach an abstract of the research plan which summarizes the long-term objectives, scientific aims, and methodology; a grant budget; and must provide a justification which describes any large or unusual expenses in any category or any cost of the need which may not be obvious. **Deadline:** February 20.

6540 ■ Society of Physics Students

One Physics Ellipse
College Park, MD 20740
Ph: (301)209-3007
Fax: (301)209-0839
E-mail: sps@aip.org
URL: http://www.spsnational.org

6541 ■ Peggy Dixon Two-Year Scholarships *(Undergraduate/Scholarship)*

Purpose: To support students from a two-year college transitioning into a physics bachelor's degree program. **Focus:** Physics. **Qualif.:** Applicants must have completed at least one semester or quarter of the introductory physics sequence; and currently registered in the appropriate subsequent physics courses. **Criteria:** Applicants are selected based on high scholarship performance both in physics and overall studies; exhibition of the potential and intention for continued scholastic development in physics; active participation in SPS programs.

Funds Avail.: $2000. **To Apply:** Application forms are available online. Applicants must submit completed application form; certified and official transcript (submitted directly by the applicant's college/university); letters from at least two full-time members of the faculty. **Deadline:** February 15.

Remarks: The scholarship is established in memory of Dr. Peggy A. Dixon, SPS and Sigma Pi Sigma Historian from 19922003.

6542 ■ Herbert Levy Memorial Endowment Fund Scholarships *(Undergraduate/Scholarship)*

Purpose: To provide financial assistance to promising physics students. **Focus:** Physics. **Qualif.:** Applicants must

Awards are arranged alphabetically below their administering organizations

be full-time undergraduate students applying in their junior year (except for two-year college applicants who should apply after completing one semester of physics); and must be SPS members. **Criteria:** Applicants are selected based on high scholarship performance both in physics and overall studies; exhibition of the potential and intention for continued scholastic development in physics; and active participation in SPS programs.

Funds Avail.: $2,000. **To Apply:** Application forms are available online. Applicants must submit completed application form; certified and official transcript (submitted directly by the applicant's college/university); letters from at least two full-time members of the faculty. **Deadline:** February 15.

Remarks: Scholarships establish by Margaret Sussman Levy in memory of her husband Dr. Herbert Levy.

6543 ■ Sigma Pi Sigma Undergraduate Research Awards *(Undergraduate/Grant)*

Purpose: To support local chapter activities that would contribute to the strengthening of the SPS program. **Focus:** Physics. **Qualif.:** Applicants must be active chapter members of SPS. **Criteria:** Proposals will be judged by a panel of physicists.

Funds Avail.: $2000. **To Apply:** Applicants must submit a proposal containing a budget and must be signed by the advisor and officers of the chapter. **Deadline:** November 15.

6544 ■ SPS Future Teacher Scholarships *(Undergraduate/Scholarship)*

Purpose: To award SPS members participating in a teacher education program and pursuing a career in physics education. **Focus:** Physics. **Qualif.:** Applicants must be undergraduate students applying in their junior year majoring in physics; and must be SPS members. **Criteria:** Applicants are selected based on high scholarship performance both in physics and overall studies; exhibition of the potential and intention for continued scholastic development in physics; and active participation in SPS programs.

Funds Avail.: $2000. **To Apply:** Application forms are available online. Applicants must submit completed application form; certified and official transcript (submitted directly by the applicant's college/university); letters from at least two full-time members of the faculty; and a statement from an SPS advisor that certifies the applicant's participation in a teacher education program. **Deadline:** February 15.

6545 ■ SPS Leadership Scholarships *(Undergraduate/Scholarship)*

Purpose: To encourage the students to pursue their career in study of physics. **Focus:** Physics. **Qualif.:** Applicants must be full-time undergraduate students applying in their junior year (except for two-year college applicants who should apply after completing one semester of physics); and must be SPS members. **Criteria:** Applicants are selected based on high scholarship performance both in physics and overall studies; exhibition of the potential and intention for continued scholastic development in physics; and active participation in SPS programs.

Funds Avail.: $5000 and $2000. **To Apply:** Application forms are available online. Applicants must submit completed application form; certified and official transcript (submitted directly by the applicant's college/university); letters from at least two full-time members of the faculty. **Deadline:** February 15.

6546 ■ Society of Plastics Engineers

14 Fairfield Dr.
Brookfield, CT 06804-0403
Ph: (203)775-0471
Fax: (203)775-8490
E-mail: info@4spe.org
URL: http://www.4spe.org

6547 ■ Blow Molding Division Memorial Scholarships *(Graduate, Undergraduate/Scholarship)*

Purpose: To promote scientific and engineering knowledge relating to plastics. **Focus:** Science; Engineering. **Qualif.:** Applicants must be undergraduate and graduate students in institutions, colleges, or universities; applicants must have demonstrated or expressed interest in the plastic industry; applicants must be in good academic standing. **Criteria:** Recipients are selected based on financial need and academic standing.

Funds Avail.: $8,000. **Number Awarded:** 2. **To Apply:** Applicants must complete the application form; applicants must submit three letters of recommendation, two of which are from a teacher or school official and one from an employer or non-relative; a high school and/or college transcript for the past two years; a list of current and past school activities, community activities, and honors; a listing of employment history; a one-to-two-page typewritten statement telling why they are applying for the scholarship, qualifications, educational and career goals in the plastic industry. **Deadline:** January 15. **Contact:** foundation@4spe.org

6548 ■ Robert E. Cramer Scholarships *(Graduate, Undergraduate/Scholarship)*

Purpose: To promote scientific and engineering knowledge relating to plastics. **Focus:** Science; Engineering. **Qualif.:** Applicants must be undergraduate and graduate students in institutions, colleges, or universities; applicants must have demonstrated or expressed interest in the plastic industry; applicants must be in good academic standing. **Criteria:** Recipients are selected based on financial need and academic standing.

Funds Avail.: $1,000. **Number Awarded:** 1. **To Apply:** Applicants must complete the application form; applicants must submit three letters of recommendation, two of which are from a teacher or school official and one from an employer or non-relative; a high school and/or college transcript for the past two years; a list of current and past school activities, community activities, and honors; A listing of employment history; a one-to-two-page typewritten statement telling why they are applying for the scholarship, qualifications, educational and career goals in the plastic industry. **Deadline:** January 15. **Contact:** foundation@4spe.org

6549 ■ Robert G. Dailey Scholarships *(Graduate, Undergraduate/Scholarship)*

Purpose: To promote scientific and engineering knowledge relating to plastics. **Focus:** Science; Engineering. **Qualif.:** Applicants must be undergraduate and graduate students in institutions, colleges, or universities; Applicants must have demonstrated or expressed interest in the plastic industry; applicants must be in good academic standing. **Criteria:** Recipients are selected based on financial need and academic standing.

Funds Avail.: $4,000. **Number Awarded:** 1. **To Apply:**

Applicants must complete the application form; applicants must submit three letters of recommendation, two of which are from a teacher or school official and one from an employer or non-relative; a high school and/or college transcript for the past two years; a list of current and past school activities, community activities, and honors; a listing of employment history; a one-to-two-page typewritten statement telling why they are applying for the scholarship, qualifications, educational and career goals in the plastic industry. **Deadline:** January 15. **Contact:** foundation@4spe.org

6550 ■ Fleming/Blaszcak Scholarships *(Graduate, Undergraduate/Scholarship)*

Purpose: To promote scientific and engineering knowledge relating to plastics. **Focus:** Science; Engineering. **Qualif.:** Applicants must be undergraduate and graduate students in institutions, colleges, or universities; applicants must have demonstrated or expressed interest in the plastic industry; applicants must be in good academic standing; applicants must be of Mexican descent and citizens or legal residents of the United States. **Criteria:** Recipients are selected based on financial need and academic standing.

Funds Avail.: $2,000. **Number Awarded:** 1. **To Apply:** Applicants must complete the application form; applicants must submit three letters of recommendation, two of which are from a teacher or school official and one from an employer or non-relative; a high school and/or college transcript for the past two years; a list of current and past school activities, community activities, and honors; a listing of employment history; a one-to-two-page typewritten statement telling why they are applying for the scholarship, qualifications, educational and career goals in the plastic industry; applicants must provide a documentation of their Mexican heritage and their citizenship status such as a birth certificate or a U.S. passport. **Deadline:** January 15. **Contact:** foundation@4spe.org

6551 ■ Harold Giles Scholarships *(Graduate, Undergraduate/Scholarship)*

Purpose: To promote scientific and engineering knowledge relating to plastics. **Focus:** Science; Engineering. **Qualif.:** Applicants must be undergraduate and graduate students in institutions, colleges, or universities; applicants must have demonstrated or expressed interest in the plastic industry; applicants must be in good academic standing; applicants must have experience in the composites industry such as courses taken, research conducted, or jobs held. **Criteria:** Recipients are selected based on financial need and academic standing.

Funds Avail.: $1,000. **Number Awarded:** 1. **To Apply:** Applicants must complete the application form; applicants must submit three letters of recommendation, two of which are from a teacher or school official and one from an employer or non-relative; a high school and/or college transcript for the past two years; a list of current and past school activities, community activities, and honors; a listing of employment history; a one-to-two-page typewritten statement telling why they are applying for the scholarship, qualifications, educational and career goals in the plastic industry. **Deadline:** January 15. **Contact:** foundation@4spe.org

6552 ■ Gulf Coast Hurricane Scholarships *(Graduate, Undergraduate/Scholarship)*

Purpose: To promote scientific and engineering knowledge relating to plastics. **Focus:** Science; Engineering. **Qualif.:** Applicants must be undergraduate and graduate students in institutions, colleges, or universities; Applicants must have demonstrated or expressed interest in the plastic industry; applicants must be in good academic standing; applicants must maintain a 2.0 GPA and enroll in at least six credit hours per semester. **Criteria:** Recipients are selected based on financial need and academic standing.

Funds Avail.: $6,000 for four-year university; $2,000 for two-year junior college. **Number Awarded:** 1. **To Apply:** Applicants must complete the application form; applicants must submit three letters of recommendation, two of which are from a teacher or school official and one from an employer or non-relative; a high school and/or college transcript for the past two years; a list of current and past school activities, community activities, and honors; a listing of employment history; a one-to-two-page typewritten statement telling why they are applying for the scholarship, qualifications, educational and career goals in the plastic industry; applicants must provide proof of residence in a Gulf Coast County declared a national disaster area by the President. **Deadline:** January 15. **Contact:** foundation@4spe.org

6553 ■ Injection Molding Division Scholarships *(Graduate, Undergraduate/Scholarship)*

Purpose: To promote scientific and engineering knowledge relating to plastics. **Focus:** Science; Engineering. **Qualif.:** Applicants must be undergraduate and graduate students in institutions, colleges, or universities; applicants must have demonstrated or expressed interest in the plastic industry; applicants must be in good academic standing; applicants must have experience in the molding industry such as courses taken, research conducted or jobs held. **Criteria:** Recipients are selected based on financial need and academic standing.

Funds Avail.: $3,000. **To Apply:** Applicants must complete the application form; Applicants must submit three letters of recommendation, two of which are from a teacher or school official and one from an employer or non-relative; a high school and/or college transcript for the past two years; a list of current and past school activities, community activities, and honors; a listing of employment history; a one-to-two-page typewritten statement telling why they are applying for the scholarship, qualifications, educational and career goals in the plastic industry. **Deadline:** January 15. **Contact:** foundation@4spe.org

6554 ■ Erwin Lew Memorial Scholarships *(Graduate, Undergraduate/Scholarship)*

Purpose: To promote scientific and engineering knowledge relating to plastics. **Focus:** Science; Engineering. **Qualif.:** Applicants must be undergraduate and graduate students in institutions, colleges, or universities; applicants must have demonstrated or expressed interest in the plastic industry; applicants must be in good academic standing in their respective schools; applicants must be working on a senior or MS project which the scholarship will support. **Criteria:** Recipients are selected based on financial need and academic standing.

Funds Avail.: $2,500. **Number Awarded:** 1. **To Apply:** Applicants must complete the application form; three letters of recommendation, two of which are from a teacher or school official and one from an employer or non-relative; a high school and/or college transcript for the past two years; a list of current and past school activities, community activities, and honors; a listing of employment history; a one-to-two-page typewritten statement telling why they are applying for the scholarship, qualifications, educational and career goals in the plastic industry. **Deadline:** January 15. **Contact:** foundation@4spe.org

6555 ■ James I. MacKenzie Memorial Scholarships *(Graduate, Undergraduate/Scholarship)*

Purpose: To promote scientific and engineering knowledge relating to plastics. **Focus:** Science; Engineering. **Qualif.:** Applicants must be undergraduate and graduate students in institutions, colleges, or universities. Applicants must have demonstrated or expressed interest in the plastic industry; applicants must be in good academic standing; applicants must have experience in the thermoplastic elastomers industry, such as courses taken, research conducted, or jobs held. **Criteria:** Recipients are selected based on financial need and academic standing.

Funds Avail.: $2,500. **Number Awarded:** 1. **To Apply:** Applicants must complete the application form; applicants must submit three letters of recommendation, two of which are from a teacher or school official and one from an employer or non-relative; a high school and/or college transcript for the past two years; a list of current and past school activities, community activities, and honors; a listing of employment history; a one-to-two-page typewritten statement telling why they are applying for the scholarship, qualifications, educational and career goals in the plastic industry; applicants must include a statement detailing their exposure to the thermoses industry. **Deadline:** January 15. **Contact:** foundation@4spe.org

6556 ■ Ted and Ruth Neward Scholarships *(Graduate, Undergraduate/Scholarship)*

Purpose: To promote scientific and engineering knowledge relating to plastics. **Focus:** Science; Engineering. **Qualif.:** Applicants must be undergraduate and graduate students in institutions, colleges, or universities; applicants must have demonstrated or expressed interest in the plastic industry; applicants must be in good academic standing. **Criteria:** Recipients are selected based on financial need and academic standing.

Funds Avail.: $3,000. **Number Awarded:** 3. **To Apply:** Applicants must complete the application form; applicants must submit three letters of recommendation, two of which are from a teacher or school official and one from an employer or non-relative; a high school and/or college transcript for the past two years; a list of current and past school activities, community activities, and honors; a listing of employment history; a one-to-two-page typewritten statement telling why they are applying for the scholarship, qualifications, educational and career goals in the plastic industry. **Deadline:** January 15. **Contact:** foundation@4spe.org

6557 ■ Plastics Pioneers Association Scholarships *(Graduate, Undergraduate/Scholarship)*

Purpose: To promote scientific and engineering knowledge relating to plastics. **Focus:** Science; Engineering. **Qualif.:** Applicants must be undergraduate and graduate students in institutions, colleges, or universities including those enrolled in associate degree or technical degree programs who are committed to becoming hands-on workers in the plastics industry and who are dedicated to careers as plastics technicians or engineers. Applicants must have demonstrated or expressed interest in the plastic industry; applicants must be in good academic standing. **Criteria:** Recipients are selected based on financial need and academic standing.

Funds Avail.: $3,000. **To Apply:** Applicants must complete the application form; applicants must submit three letters of recommendation, two of which are from a teacher or school official and one from an employer or non-relative; a high school and/or college transcript for the past two years; a list of current and past school activities, community activities, and honors; a listing of employment history; A one-to-two-page typewritten statement telling why they are applying for the scholarship, qualifications, educational and career goals in the plastic industry. **Deadline:** January 15. **Contact:** foundation@4spe.org

6558 ■ Polymer Modifiers and Additives Division Scholarships *(Graduate, Undergraduate/Scholarship)*

Purpose: To promote scientific and engineering knowledge relating to plastics. **Focus:** Science; Engineering. **Qualif.:** Applicants must be undergraduate and graduate students in institutions, colleges, or universities; applicants must have demonstrated or expressed interest in the plastic industry; applicants must be in good academic standing. **Criteria:** Recipients are selected based on financial need and academic standing.

Funds Avail.: $4,000. **Number Awarded:** 3. **To Apply:** Applicants must complete the application form; applicants must submit three letters of recommendation, two of which are from a teacher or school official and one from an employer or non-relative; a high school and/or college transcript for the past two years; a list of current and past school activities, community activities, and honors; a listing of employment history; a one-to-two-page typewritten statement telling why they are applying for the scholarship, qualifications, educational and career goals in the plastic industry. **Deadline:** January 15. **Contact:** foundation@4spe.org

6559 ■ Society of Plastics Engineers General Scholarships *(Graduate, Undergraduate/Scholarship)*

Purpose: To promote scientific and engineering knowledge relating to plastics. **Focus:** Science; Engineering. **Qualif.:** Applicants must be undergraduate and graduate students in institutions, colleges, or universities; applicants must have demonstrated or expressed interest in the plastic industry; applicants must be in good academic standing. **Criteria:** Recipients are selected based on financial need and academic standing.

Funds Avail.: $4,000. **To Apply:** Applicants must complete the application form; applicants must submit three letters of recommendation, two of which are from a teacher or school official and one from an employer or non-relative; a high school and/or college transcript for the past two years; a list of current and past school activities, community activities, and honors; a listing of employment history; a one-to-two-page typewritten statement telling why they are applying for the scholarship, qualifications, educational and career goals in the plastic industry. **Deadline:** January 15. **Contact:** foundation@4spe.org

6560 ■ Society of Plastics Engineers Pittsburgh Scholarships *(Graduate, Undergraduate/Scholarship)*

Purpose: To promote scientific and engineering knowledge relating to plastics. **Focus:** Science; Engineering. **Qualif.:** Applicants must be undergraduate and graduate students in institutions, colleges, or universities; applicants must have demonstrated or expressed interest in the plastic industry; applicants must be in good academic standing; **Criteria:** Recipients are selected based on financial need and academic standing.

Funds Avail.: $2,000. **Number Awarded:** 2. **To Apply:** Applicants must complete the application form; applicants must submit three letters of recommendation, two of which are from a teacher or school official and one from an employer or non-relative; a high school and/or college transcript for the past two years; a list of current and past school activities, community activities, and honors; a listing of employment history; A one-to-two-page typewritten statement telling why they are applying for the scholarship, qualifications, educational and career goals in the plastic industry; applicants must provide proof of graduation from high school. **Deadline:** January 15. **Contact:** foundation@4spe.org

6561 ■ Thermoforming Scholarships *(Graduate, Undergraduate/Scholarship)*

Purpose: To promote scientific and engineering knowledge relating to plastics. **Focus:** Science; Engineering. **Qualif.:** Applicants must be undergraduate and graduate students in institutions, colleges, or universities including those enrolled in associate degree or technical degree programs who are committed to becoming hands-on workers in the plastics industry and who are dedicated to careers as plastics technicians or engineers. Applicants must have demonstrated or expressed interest in the plastic industry; applicants must be in good academic standing; applicants must have experience in the thermoplastic elastomers industry, such as courses taken, research conducted, or jobs held. **Criteria:** Recipients are selected based on financial need and academic standing.

Funds Avail.: $7,500. **To Apply:** Applicants must complete the application form; applicants must submit three letters of recommendation, two of which are from a teacher or school official and one from an employer or non-relative; a high school and/or college transcript for the past two years; a list of current and past school activities, community activities, and honors; a listing of employment history; a one-to-two-page typewritten statement telling why they are applying for the scholarship, qualifications, educational and career goals in the plastic industry. **Deadline:** January 15. **Contact:** foundation@4spe.org

6562 ■ Thermoplastic Materials and Foams Division Scholarships *(Graduate, Undergraduate/Scholarship)*

Purpose: To promote scientific and engineering knowledge relating to plastics. **Focus:** Science; Engineering. **Qualif.:** Applicants must be undergraduate and graduate students in institutions, colleges, or universities; applicants must have demonstrated or expressed interest in the plastic industry; applicants must be in good academic standing. **Criteria:** Recipients are selected based on financial need and academic standing.

Funds Avail.: $1,000. **Number Awarded:** 1. **To Apply:** Applicants must complete the application form; applicants must submit three letters of recommendation, two of which are from a teacher or school official and one from an employer or non-relative; a high school and/or college transcript for the past two years; a list of current and past school activities, community activities, and honors; a listing of employment history; a one-to-two-page typewritten statement telling why they are applying for the scholarship, qualifications, educational and career goals in the plastic industry. **Deadline:** January 15. **Contact:** foundation@4spe.org

6563 ■ Thermoplastics Elastomers Special Interest Group Scholarships *(Graduate, Undergraduate/Scholarship)*

Purpose: To promote scientific and engineering knowledge relating to plastics. **Focus:** Science; Engineering. **Qualif.:** Applicants must be undergraduate and graduate students in institutions, colleges, or universities. Applicants must have demonstrated or expressed interest in the plastic industry; applicants must be in good academic standing; applicants must have experience in the thermoplastic elastomers industry, such as courses taken, research conducted, or jobs held. **Criteria:** Recipients are selected based on financial need and academic standing.

Funds Avail.: $1,000. **Number Awarded:** 1. **To Apply:** Applicants must complete the application form; applicants must submit three letters of recommendation, two of which are from a teacher or school official and one from an employer or non-relative; a high school and/or college transcript for the past two years; a list of current and past school activities, community activities, and honors; a listing of employment history; a one-to-two-page typewritten statement telling why they are applying for the scholarship, qualifications, educational and career goals in the plastic industry. **Deadline:** January 15. **Contact:** foundation@4spe.org

6564 ■ Vinyl Plastics Division Scholarships *(Graduate, Undergraduate/Scholarship)*

Purpose: To promote scientific and engineering knowledge relating to plastics. **Focus:** Science; Engineering. **Qualif.:** Applicants must be undergraduate and graduate students in institutions, colleges, or universities; applicants must have demonstrated or expressed interest in the plastic industry; applicants must be in good academic standing. **Criteria:** Recipients are selected based on financial need and academic standing.

Funds Avail.: $3,000. **Number Awarded:** 1. **To Apply:** Applicants must complete the application form; applicants must submit three letters of recommendation, two of which are from a teacher or school official and one from an employer or non-relative; a high school and/or college transcript for the past two years; a list of current and past school activities, community activities, and honors; a listing of employment history; a one-to-two-page typewritten statement telling why they are applying for the scholarship, qualifications, educational and career goals in the plastic industry. **Deadline:** January 15. **Contact:** foundation@4spe.org

6565 ■ Society for the Preservation of Old Mills

PO Box 22
East Meredith, NY 13757
URL: http://www.spoom.org

6566 ■ SPOOM Research Grants *(Graduate/Grant)*

Purpose: To provide financial assistance to researches on mills or milling-related subjects. **Focus:** Preservation. **Qualif.:** Program is open to individuals seeking support for their research on mills or milling-related subject. Applicants must be active members of SPOOM; must be full-time students and in good standing. **Criteria:** Awards are granted based on the significance of the contribution that the proposed project will make to the preservation or understanding of mills or milling; conception, definition, organization and description of the requested project; likelihood that the applicants will complete the entire project; and support of a mill related group with the eligibility criteria.

Funds Avail.: No specific amount. **Number Awarded:** 1. **To Apply:** Applicants must prepare a one-page outline of the project; official graduate transcript; resume detailing applicable work experiences; and must complete application form available in the SPOOM office or website. **Deadline:** September 1.

6567 ■ Society of Professional Journalists

Eugene S. Pulliam National Journalism Center
3909 N Meridian St.
Indianapolis, IN 46208
Ph: (317)927-8000
Fax: (317)920-4789
E-mail: tharper@spj.org
URL: http://www.spj.org

6568 ■ Fred Archibald Communications Internships *(Undergraduate/Internship)*

Purpose: To encourage the free practice of journalism and stimulate high standards of ethical behavior. **Focus:** Journalism. **Qualif.:** Applicants must be juniors or seniors pursuing a degree in journalism, marketing, communications or public relations at a college or university, or a recent college graduate; must be willing to relocate to Indianapolis for ten weeks if not a resident; must have writing and/or reporting experience; Should be able to manage multiple tasks, remain organized and meet deadlines; must have decision making, problem solving, and research skills; must possess ability to express ideas and opinions with willingness to take initiative and work cooperatively with others; must have proficient computer skills; must have strong work ethics and a positive attitude. **Criteria:** Recipients are selected based on academic performance.

Funds Avail.: $400 per week. **To Apply:** Applicants must submit a completed application form and attach a cover letter, current resume, three to five writing samples and a one-page essay detailing their future goals and objectives. **Contact:** bking@apj.org

6569 ■ Pulliam/Kilgore Freedom of Information Internships *(Undergraduate/Internship)*

Purpose: To encourage the free practice of journalism and stimulate high standards of ethical behavior. **Focus:** Journalism. **Qualif.:** Applicants must be journalism students who are entering or just completing their senior year, graduate journalism students, or law students with a journalism background. **Criteria:** Recipients are selected based on strong background in writing and reporting and academic performance.

Funds Avail.: $400 per week. **To Apply:** Applicant must submit a completed application form along with resume and one-page essay that illustrates their understanding of Freedom of Information issues and what they expect to gain from the internship (not more than five writings). **Deadline:** January 5. **Contact:** quill@spj.org.

6570 ■ The Working Press Internships *(Undergraduate/Internship)*

Purpose: To encourage the free practice of journalism and stimulate high standards of ethical behavior. **Focus:** Journalism. **Qualif.:** Applicants must be student writers, photographers, and designers. **Criteria:** Recipients are selected based on academic performance.

Funds Avail.: $400 per week. **Number Awarded:** 12. **To Apply:** Applicant must submit two copies of the following: completed application form; a resume; three clips, lay-outs or published photos. **Deadline:** April 19. **Contact:** jskeel@spj.org

6571 ■ Society for the Psychological Study of Lesbian, Gay and Bisexual Issues

American Psychological Association, 750 First St. NE
Washington, DC 20002-4242
Ph: (202)216-7602
Fax: (202)218-3599
E-mail: div44@apa.org
URL: http://www.apadivision44.org

6572 ■ Bisexual Foundation Scholarships *(Graduate/Scholarship)*

Purpose: To promote research on the psychology of bisexuality. **Focus:** Psychology. **Qualif.:** Applicant must be a full-time graduate student in a Department of Psychology. **Criteria:** Recipients are selected based on the application materials submitted.

Funds Avail.: Maximum of $1,000. **To Apply:** Applicants must submit an application consisting of: one cover sheet; curriculum vitae; one copy of IRB approval notice (if applicable); six copies of the application; and two self-addressed stamped envelopes. Send application materials to: Cisco Sanchez, PhD; Department of Human Genetics UCLA School of Medicine; 695 Charles Young Dr. S, No. 5524 Los Angeles, CA 900957088. Phone:310267-2456, Fax: 310794-5446, Email: fjsanchez@mednet.ucla.edu. **Deadline:** February.

6573 ■ Malyon-Smith Scholarships *(Graduate/Scholarship)*

Purpose: To promote education in psychology. **Focus:** Psychology. **Qualif.:** Applicant must be a full-time graduate student in a Department of Psychology. **Criteria:** Recipients are selected based on the proposals.

Funds Avail.: Maximum of $1,000. **To Apply:** Applicants must submit an application consisting of: one cover sheet; curriculum vitae; one copy of IRB approval notice (if applicable); six copies of the application; and two self-addressed stamped envelopes. Send application materials to: Cisco Sanchez, PhD; Department of Human Genetics UCLA School of Medicine; 695 Charles Young Dr. S, No. 5524 Los Angeles, CA 900957088. Phone:310267-2456, Fax: 310794-5446, Email: fjsanchez@mednet.ucla.edu. **Deadline:** February.

6574 ■ Society for the Psychological Study for Social Issues

208 I St. NE
Washington, DC 20002-4340
Ph: (202)675-6956
Fax: (202)675-6902
E-mail: spssi@spssi.org
URL: http://www.spssi.org

6575 ■ Clara Mayo Grants *(Graduate/Grant)*

Purpose: To support masters' theses or pre-dissertation research on aspects of sexism, racism, or prejudice. **Focus:** Psychology; Social sciences. **Qualif.:** Applicant must be an

SPSSI member; matriculated in graduate programs in psychology, applied social science, and related disciplines. **Criteria:** Preference is given to student enrolled in a terminal master's program.

Funds Avail.: $1000. **Number Awarded:** 4. **To Apply:** Applicants are advised to visit the website for the online scholarship application. **Deadline:** May 1.

Remarks: Sponsored by SPSSI's Clara Mayo Memorial Fund.

6576 ■ SPPSI Grants-In-Aid Program *(Graduate, Postdoctorate/Grant)*

Purpose: To support scientific research in social problem areas related to the basic interests and goals of SPSSI. **Focus:** Psychology. **Qualif.:** Applicant must be an SPSSI member. **Criteria:** Preference is given to students at the dissertation stage of the graduate career.

Funds Avail.: $1000-$2000. **To Apply:** Applicants are advised to visit the website for the online scholarship application. **Deadline:** May 1 and October 15.

Remarks: Sponsored by The Sophie and Shirley Cohen Memorial Fund and SPSSI membership contributions.

6577 ■ Society for Range Management

10030 W 27th Ave.
Wheat Ridge, CO 80215-6601
Ph: (303)986-3309
Fax: (303)986-3892
E-mail: info@rangelands.org
URL: http://www.rangelands.org

6578 ■ Masonic-Range Science Scholarships *(Undergraduate/Scholarship)*

Purpose: To financially assist students with their education. **Focus:** Science. **Qualif.:** Applicant must be a high school senior, or college freshman or sophomore planning to major in/currently majoring in range science or a closely related field; and must be sponsored by a member of the Society for Range Management (SRM), the National Association of Conservation Districts (NACD), or the Soil and Water Conservation Society (SWCS). **Criteria:** Selection is based on the application.

Funds Avail.: Varies each year. **To Apply:** Applicants must submit a completed application form together with a copy of high school and college transcripts; official copy of SAT and ACT scores; two letters of references. Send materials to Paul Loeffler Texas General Land Office 500 West Ave H, Suite 101, Box 2 Alpine, TX 79830-6008. **Deadline:** January 15. **Contact:** vtrujillo@rangelands.org.

6579 ■ Society of Satellite Professionals International

55 Broad St., 14th Fl.
New York, NY 10004
Ph: (212)809-5199
Fax: (212)825-0075
E-mail: tbond@sspi.org
URL: http://www.hessberger.com/sspi/index.html

6580 ■ The Access Intelligence Scholarships *(Graduate, Undergraduate/Scholarship)*

Purpose: To recognize innovative work in the satellite field. **Focus:** Telecommunications systems; Broadcasting. **Qualif.:** Applicant must be an SSPI member; pursue education in the satellite industry or a field making direct use of satellite technology; have academic and leadership achievement; show potential for significant contribution to the satellite communications industry; enrolled in an accredited college or university program at the time of the scholarship issuance. **Criteria:** Applicant who will best meet the requirements will be given preference.

Funds Avail.: No specific amount. **To Apply:** Applicants may mail or fax their applications together with a current transcript. **Deadline:** December 31. **Contact:** Membership Director Tamara Bond at the above address (see entry 6579).

6581 ■ The A.W. Perigard Fund *(Graduate, Undergraduate/Scholarship)*

Purpose: To assist students with financial need. **Focus:** Telecommunications systems. **Qualif.:** Applicant must be an SSPI member; must pursue education in the satellite industry or a field making direct use of satellite technology; have academic and leadership achievement; have potential for significant contribution to the satellite communications industry; enrolled in an accredited college or university program at the time of the scholarship issuance. **Criteria:** Applicant who will best meet the requirements will be given preference.

Funds Avail.: No specific amount. **To Apply:** Applicants my mail or fax their applications together with a current transcript. **Deadline:** December 31. **Contact:** Membership Director Tamara Bond at the above address (see entry 6579).

6582 ■ The PSSC Legacy Fund *(Graduate, Undergraduate/Scholarship)*

Purpose: To provide financial assistance to those who wish to study international satellite applications and distance education. **Focus:** Telecommunications systems. **Qualif.:** Applicant must be an SSPI member; pursue education in the satellite industry or a field making direct use of satellite technology; have academic and leadership achievement; show potential for significant contribution to the satellite communications industry; enrolled in an accredited college or university program at the time of the scholarship issuance. **Criteria:** Applicant who will best meet the requirements will be given preference.

Funds Avail.: No specific amount. **To Apply:** Applicants may mail or fax their applications together with a current transcript. **Deadline:** December 31. **Contact:** Membership Director Tamara Bond at the above address (see entry 6579).

6583 ■ The SSPI Mid-Atlantic Chapter Scholarships *(Graduate, Undergraduate/Scholarship)*

Purpose: To provide financial assistance to those studying telecommunications systems. **Focus:** Telecommunications systems. **Qualif.:** Applicant must be an SSPI member; pursue education in the satellite industry or a field making direct use of satellite technology; have academic and leadership achievement; show potential for significant contribution to the satellite communications industry; enrolled in an accredited college or university program at the time of the scholarship issuance. **Criteria:** Applicant who will best meet the requirements will be given preference.

Funds Avail.: No specific amount. **To Apply:** Applicants may mail or fax their applications together with a current

Awards are arranged alphabetically below their administering organizations

transcript. **Deadline:** December 31. **Contact:** Membership Director Tamara Bond at the above address (see entry 6579).

6584 ■ The SSPI Northeast Chapter Scholarships *(Graduate, Undergraduate/Scholarship)*

Purpose: To provide financial assistance to those studying telecommunications systems. **Focus:** Telecommunications systems. **Qualif.:** Applicant must be an SSPI member; pursue education in the satellite industry or a field making direct use of satellite technology; have academic and leadership achievement; potential for significant contribution to the satellite communications industry; enrolled in an accredited college or university program at the time of the scholarship issuance. **Criteria:** Applicant who will best meet the requirements will be given preference.

Funds Avail.: No specific amount. **To Apply:** Applicants may mail or fax their applications together with a current transcript. **Deadline:** December 31. **Contact:** Membership Director Tamara Bond at the above address (see entry 6579).

6585 ■ The SSPI Southern California Scholarships *(Graduate, Undergraduate/Scholarship)*

Purpose: To assist students with financial need. **Focus:** Telecommunications systems. **Qualif.:** Applicant must be a female SSPI member; current graduate or undergraduate of Southern California University System with a GPA of 3.2 or higher, pursue education in the satellite industry or a field making direct use of satellite technology; have academic and leadership achievement; show potential for significant contribution to the satellite communications industry; enrolled in an accredited college or university program at the time of the scholarship issuance. **Criteria:** Applicant who will best meet the requirements will be given preference.

Funds Avail.: No specific amount. **To Apply:** Applicants may mail or fax their applications together with a current transcript to: Cynthia M. Dinkins, Vice President of Business and Program Development, T. Howard Foundation 601 13th St. NW, Ste. 710N Washington, DC 20005. **Deadline:** December 31. **Contact:** Vice President of Business and Program Development Cynthia M. Dinkins e-mail at cdinkins@t-howard.org.

6586 ■ Society for the Scientific Study of Sexuality

PO Box 416
Allentown, PA 18105-0416
Ph: (610)530-2483
Fax: (610)530-2485
E-mail: thesociety@sexscience.org
URL: http://www.sexscience.org

6587 ■ Society for the Scientific Study of Sexuality Student Research Grants *(Undergraduate/Grant)*

Purpose: To advance knowledge of sexuality; to advance the quality and quantity of the knowledge base in sexual science; to foster the recognition of sexual science within the scientific community, public policy makers, and the general public; to communicate the implications of sexual science. **Focus:** Sexuality. **Qualif.:** Applicants must be students who are doing human sexuality research. **Criteria:** Recipients are selected based on submitted requirements.

Funds Avail.: $1,000. **Number Awarded:** 2. **To Apply:** Applicants must obtain IRB approval for the project; applicants must prepare a 150-word abstract of the proposed research; prepare a short biographical sketch suitable for the use of the society's newsletter; applicants must prepare a ten-page, double-spaced abstract of the proposed research and bibliography in MS Word; applicants must prepare a proposed budget for the project. **Contact:** mlpeters@sexscience.org.

6588 ■ Society of University of Surgeons

341 N Maitland Ave., Ste. 130
Maitland, FL 32751
Ph: (407)647-7714
Fax: (407)629-2502
E-mail: info@susweb.com
URL: http://www.susweb.org

6589 ■ SUS Foundation Junior Faculty Grants *(Graduate/Grant)*

Purpose: To support the research of surgeons whose work involves the basic science that underlies a surgical disease. **Focus:** Surgery. **Qualif.:** Applicants must be tenure-track faculty member in a Department of Surgery; Within three years of his/her first facility appointment. **Criteria:** Grant is awarded based on the eligibility of the applicant.

Funds Avail.: $30,000. **Deadline:** August 31. **Contact:** SUS at the above address (see entry 6588).

6590 ■ SUS - Wyeth Clinical Scholar Award *(Graduate/Award/Prize)*

Purpose: To support the research of surgeon whose work involves the basic science that underlies a surgical disease. **Focus:** Surgery. **Qualif.:** Applicant must be a faculty member in a Department of surgery; and within three years of his/her first faculty appointment. **Criteria:** Selections based on the scientific merit of the proposal and the potential of the applicant.

Funds Avail.: $30,000. **To Apply:** Applicant must submit his/her application online using submission system. Applicant must download and print a hard-copy of the Award Authorizations Form which will verify various institutional requirements and approvals. A completed Award Authorization form must be submitted via mail to the Society offices prior to the application deadline. **Deadline:** August 31. **Contact:** SUS at the above address (see entry 6588).

6591 ■ Society of Women Engineers

230 East Ohio St., Ste. 400
Chicago, IL 60611
Ph: (312)596-5223
E-mail: hq@swe.org
URL: http://www.swe.org

6592 ■ Society of Women Engineers Scholarships *(Undergraduate/Scholarship)*

Purpose: To help individuals achieve full potential in careers as engineers and leaders; to expand the image of the engineering profession as a positive force improving the quality of life; to demonstrate the value of diversity. **Focus:** Engineering. **Qualif.:** Applicants must be incoming freshmen women who are accepted for enrollment in a baccalaureate ABET/CSAB accredited engineering or computer science degree program; must have a minimum

Awards are arranged alphabetically below their administering organizations

GPA of 3.5/4.0 scale for freshmen applicants; must not be the current recipients of a renewable SWE Scholarship; must be full-time students; must be U.S. citizens or permanent residents of the US for some scholarships; and must not be receiving full funding for education from another organization. **Criteria:** Recipients are selected based on academic standing.

Funds Avail.: $400,000. **To Apply:** Applicants must fill out the online application form; send a current school stamp and signature official transcript from high school or where you have taken courses; a copy of letter of acceptance from ABET accredited college or university indicating acceptance into an engineering or computer science curriculum for the coming academic year; and two letters of recommendation of which one must be from a high school teacher and the other must be from a person who has known the applicant for two or more years and who is not a relative or member of the applicant's family. **Deadline:** May 15. **Contact:** Society of Women Engineers at the above address (see entry 6591).

6593 ■ Sokol USA

PO Box 189
East Orange, NJ 07019-0189
Ph: (973)676-0280
Fax: (973)676-3348
Free: 888-253-0362
E-mail: sokolusahqs@aol.com
URL: http://www.Sokolusa.org

6594 ■ Milan Getting Scholarships *(Undergraduate/Scholarship)*

Purpose: To support Sokol USA student members in furthering their education. **Focus:** General studies. **Qualif.:** Applicant must be a Sokol USA member; furthering education in a four-year college or university. **Criteria:** Selection is based on the application.

Funds Avail.: $500. **To Apply:** Applicants must request scholarship application at the Sokol USA Headquarters. **Deadline:** March 1.

6595 ■ Solid Waste Association of North America

1100 Wayne Ave., Ste. 700
Silver Spring, MD 20910
Ph: 800-467-9262
Fax: (301)589-7068
URL: http://www.swana.org

6596 ■ Grant H. Flint International Scholarships - Category I *(Undergraduate/Scholarship)*

Purpose: To promote education and professional development by providing financial aid. **Focus:** General Studies. **Qualif.:** Applicants must be sons, daughters, grandsons or granddaughters of members (sponsors) and in good standing at the time of recommendation, selection and award; graduating high school seniors or graduate equivalent certified candidates who have been accepted for enrollment in a junior college, a four-year college, or a university (any program). **Criteria:** Awards are given based on academic achievement, participation in community activities, extracurricular activities and quality of written discussion.

Funds Avail.: $2,000. **Number Awarded:** 3. **To Apply:** Applicants may visit SWANA website for scholarship forms and instructions. **Deadline:** May 1. **Contact:** Kathy Callaghan, Staff Administrator, at the above address (see entry 6595)tel 240-494-2248, email: kcallaghan@swana.org.

6597 ■ Grant H. Flint International Scholarships - Category II *(Undergraduate/Scholarship)*

Purpose: To promote education and professional development by providing financial aid. **Focus:** Environmental Science; Engineering. **Qualif.:** Applicants can be SWANA student members who are currently enrolled full-time students and/or entering their junior or senior undergraduate year; must be pursuing a degree in environmental science, engineering, or other suitable major related to solid waste management. **Criteria:** Awards are given to the applicants with the highest ranking on combined academic achievement (30%), volunteer activities (20%) and relation of studies to solid waste management (50%).

Funds Avail.: $2,000. **Number Awarded:** 1. **To Apply:** Application forms and instructions are available at SWANA website. **Deadline:** May 1. **Contact:** Kathy Callaghan, Staff Administrator, at the above address (see entry 6595)tel 240-494-2248, email: kcallaghan@swana.org.

6598 ■ Robert P. Stearns/SCS Engineers Awards *(Graduate/Scholarship)*

Purpose: To promote education and professional development in areas of solid waste management by providing financial aid. **Focus:** Environmental Science; Engineering. **Qualif.:** Applicants can be SWANA student members who are currently enrolled full-time and/or graduate school students pursuing a degree in environmental science, engineering or other suitable major related to solid waste management. (SWANA employees and members of their families are not eligible to apply). **Criteria:** Recipients are selected based on merit.

Funds Avail.: $5,000. **Number Awarded:** 1. **To Apply:** Application forms and instructions are available at SWANA website. **Deadline:** May 1. **Contact:** Kathy Callaghan, Staff Administrator, at the above address (see entry 6595)tel: 240-494-2248, email: kcallaghan@swana.org.

6599 ■ Veolia ES Waste-to-Energy/Terrence L. Guest Memorial Awards *(Graduate/Scholarship)*

Purpose: To promote education and professional development in areas of solid waste management by providing financial aid. **Focus:** Environmental Science; Engineering. **Qualif.:** Applicants can be SWANA student members who are full-time students entering and/or graduate school students pursuing a degree in environmental science, engineering or other suitable major related to solid waste management. (SWANA employees and members of their families are not eligible to apply). **Criteria:** Recipients are selected based on merit.

Funds Avail.: $3,000. **Number Awarded:** 1. **To Apply:** Application forms and instructions are available in the SWANA website. **Deadline:** May 1. **Contact:** Kathy Callaghan, Staff Administrator, at the above address (see entry 6595)tel: 240-494-2248, email: kcallaghan@swana.org.

6600 ■ Sons of Confederate Veterans

PO Box 59
Columbia, TN 38402
Ph: 800-380-1896
Fax: (931)831-6712
URL: http://www.scv.org

Awards are arranged alphabetically below their administering organizations

6601 ■ Stand Watie Scholarships
(Undergraduate/Scholarship)

Purpose: To encourage educational pursuits by providing educational assistance. **Focus:** General studies. **Qualif.:** Applicants must be members of: Sons of Confederate Veterans, Children of the Confederacy, or United Daughters of the Confederacy; must be students in an accredited junior college or 4-year college or university. **Criteria:** Decision by the selection committee is based on information provided in the application letter and associated documents.

Funds Avail.: $1,000. **To Apply:** Application package includes a personal letter of application, proof of membership in one of the organizations named, a complete personal data, three letters of recommendation. Send complete application package to: Stand Watie Scholarship Fund, Chairman Michael Hann Hayes, 4335 Hwy. 63, Malcolm, IA 50157. **Contact:** phone: 641-528-4409; iowa_rebel@yahoo.com.

6602 ■ Sons of Norway Foundation

1455 W Lake St.
Minneapolis, MN 55408-2666
Ph: (612)827-3611
Fax: (612)827-0658
E-mail: foundation@sofn.com
URL: http://www.sofn.com

6603 ■ Nancy Lorraine Jensen Memorial Scholarships *(Undergraduate/Scholarship)*

Purpose: To promote the heritage and the culture of Norway. To encourage young women to enter the field of science and engineering. **Focus:** Science; Engineering. **Qualif.:** Applicant must be an American citizen not younger than 17 and not older than 35 on the date the scholarship application is submitted. Applicant must be a current female member or the daughter or granddaughter of a current member of the Sons of Norway, and have held such membership for at least three years duration, on the date the application is submitted. Applicants must be full-time undergraduates who have completed at least one term (quarter, semester) of her studies. **Criteria:** Recipients are selected based on their long-term career goals and clarity of their study plan; academic potential and evidence of ability to succeed; and letters of recommendation giving specific evidence of good character, eagerness, earnestness and ambition in the field of science and engineering.

Funds Avail.: No specific amount. **Number Awarded:** 3. **To Apply:** Applicants must submit an application form. Applicants must send SAT or ACT scores; a 500-word essay giving proof of their accomplishments and describing how they intend to pursue their career; sealed, official copy of their latest grade transcript; and three sealed letters of recommendation. **Deadline:** April 1.

6604 ■ Sons of Norway Foundation Scholarships to Oslo International School
(Undergraduate/Scholarship)

Purpose: To support students who attend Oslo International Summer School. **Focus:** Engineering; Science. **Qualif.:** Applicants must be admitted to Oslo International Summer School. Applicants must be current members of the Sons of Norway, or the children or grandchildren of current members. **Criteria:** Recipients are selected based on financial need, their essay, GPA and letters of recommendation.

Funds Avail.: $1,500. **Number Awarded:** 2. **To Apply:** Applicants must submit an application form; essay; letters of recommendation. **Deadline:** March 1.

6605 ■ Sons of Union Veterans of the Civil War

PO Box 1865
Harrisburg, PA 17105
Ph: (717)232-7000
URL: http://www.suvcw.org

6606 ■ SUVCW Scholarships *(Undergraduate/Scholarship)*

Purpose: To inspire higher learning by providing educational opportunities. **Focus:** General studies. **Qualif.:** Male applicants must be current members or Associate of Sons of Union Veterans of the Civil War; female applicants must be the daughters or granddaughters of a current member or Associate of Sons of Union Veterans of the Civil War and must be current members of at least one of the following organizations: Woman's Relief Corps, Ladies of the Grand Army of the Republic, Daughters of Union Veterans of the Civil War 1861-1865, or Auxiliary to the Sons of Union Veterans of the Civil War; must rank in the upper one-fourth of high school graduating class, preferably in the upper one-tenth; must have a record of performance in activities both in school and in the community; must have a sound interest and positive attitude toward college work. **Criteria:** Recipients are chosen based on merit.

Funds Avail.: $1,000. **Number Awarded:** 2. **To Apply:** Applicants can download forms from the website. **Deadline:** March 31.

6607 ■ South Asian Journalists Association

c/o Sreenath Sreenivasan
Columbia Graduate School of Journalism
2950 Broadway
New York, NY 10027
Ph: (212)854-0191
E-mail: saja@columbia.edu
URL: http://www.saja.org

6608 ■ SAJA Journalism Scholarships
(Undergraduate/Scholarship)

Purpose: To provide educational fund to students pursuing journalism as a career. **Focus:** Journalism. **Qualif.:** Applicants must be South Asian descents; a high school seniors; must be enrolled or current students in an accredited college or university (two-year or four year) in the United States or Canada and/or entering a graduate-level program in the United States or Canada. **Criteria:** Recipients are selected based on: applicant's interest in journalism; writing skills; reasons for entering journalism; and financial need.

Funds Avail.: $1000 for high school senior about to enter college; $1500 for undergraduate college student (four-year or community college); $2000 for graduate-level students; $2000 for undergraduate or graduate student in broadcast or journalism. **Number Awarded:** 5. **To Apply:** Applicants must fill out online application form available at the website. **Deadline:** February 15.

6609 ■ South Carolina Association for Financial Professionals

301 University Ridge, Ste. 600
Greenville, SC 29601

Awards are arranged alphabetically below their administering organizations

Ph: (864)467-7210
E-mail: jkintigh@greenvillecounty.org
URL: http://www.scafponline.org

6610 ▪ South Carolina Association for Financial Professionals Certified Treasury Professional Scholarships *(Professional Development/Scholarship)*

Purpose: To establish an additional scholarship award for students to obtain Treasury Professional certification. **Focus:** Finance. **Qualif.:** Applicants must be employed in South Carolina; must be prepared to lead the treasury and finance profession in pursuit of excellence. **Criteria:** Recipients are selected based on their performance and demonstrated interest in the field of treasury and finance.

Funds Avail.: No specific amount. **To Apply:** Applicants must complete the application form; must submit a one page summary of specific treasury qualifications; must provide resume of work history; must provide a three-to-five page, double-spaced discussion document based on the latest developments in the Treasury Management field and why they should be awarded the scholarship.

6611 ▪ South Carolina Association for Financial Professionals College Education Scholarships *(Undergraduate/Scholarship)*

Purpose: To provide a forum for the exchange of ideas and discussion of legislative, regulatory, and banking issues and developments and the opportunity to network with other Treasury Management professionals; to award an academic scholarship to an outstanding undergraduate student pursuing a degree in business in the areas including, but not limited to, accounting, economics, finance, business administration and management. **Focus:** Finance. **Qualif.:** Applicants must be South Carolina residents; must be U.S. citizens or legal permanent residents; must earn a cumulative 3.0 GPA on a 4.0 scale and a GPA in their major area of 3.5 on a 4.0 scale; must be enrolled as degree-seeking students at eligible South Carolina public or independent (private) institutions; must not be current recipients of a full-tuition scholarship. **Criteria:** Recipients are selected based on their academic performance.

Funds Avail.: $1,000. **Number Awarded:** 2-5. **To Apply:** Applicants must complete the application form; must submit a one page summary of academic achievement including the applicant's GPA (overall and major area) and a list of all relevant courses in the Treasury Management field; must submit a letter of recommendation from their major field faculty member; must provide a three-to-five page, double-spaced discussion of the Treasury Management field.

6612 ▪ South Carolina Public Health Association

1215 Anthony Ave.
Columbia, SC 29201
Ph: (803)540-7531
Fax: (803)254-3773
E-mail: scpha@queencommunicationsllc.com
URL: http://www.scpha.com

6613 ▪ Malcolm U. Dantzler Scholarships *(Professional Development/Scholarship)*

Purpose: To protect and promote personal, community and environmental health; to exercise leadership in health policy development and action; to foster scientific and professional development among its members. **Focus:** Public Health. **Qualif.:** Applicants must be current members in good standing of the South Carolina Public Health Association for at least the year in which the scholarship application is submitted; must be enrolled in a course of study leading to a degree in a health-related field; must have documentation of at least six hours of study remaining before graduation; must demonstrate great academic and professional promise; must achieve and maintain a GPA of 3.5 or better based on the 4.0 scale; must exhibit significant commitment to the public health profession through volunteer and/or professional activity such as involvement in community and scholarly activities and participation in related professional and/or student organizations. **Criteria:** Recipients are selected based on academic performance and demonstrated involvement in community activities.

Funds Avail.: $500. **To Apply:** Applicants must complete the application form; must write a personal statement of 250 words or less about their career goals and professional aspirations; must include current official transcript of records; must include proof of hours remaining before graduation. **Deadline:** March 31. **Contact:** 803-545-4464.

6614 ▪ South Carolina Public Health Association Scholarships *(Undergraduate/Scholarship)*

Purpose: To protect and promote personal, community and environmental health; to exercise leadership in health policy development and action; to foster scientific and professional development among its members. **Focus:** Public Health. **Qualif.:** Applicants must be students enrolled in an accredited School of Public Health; must be current members in good standing of the South Carolina Public Health Association for at least the year in which the scholarship application is submitted; must have documentation of at least six hours of study remaining before graduation; must demonstrate great academic and professional promise; must achieve and maintain a GPA of 3.5 or better based on the 4.0 scale; must exhibit significant commitment to the public health profession through volunteer and/or professional activity such as involvement in community and scholarly activities and participation in related professional and/or student organizations. **Criteria:** Recipients are selected based on academic performance and demonstrated involvement in community activities.

Funds Avail.: $750. **To Apply:** Applicants must complete the application form; must write a personal statement of 250 words or less about their career goals and professional aspirations; must include current official transcript of records; must include proof of hours remaining before graduation. **Deadline:** March 31. **Contact:** 803-545-4464.

6615 ▪ South Carolina Scholastic Press Association

University of South Carolina
College of Mass Communications and Information Studies
Columbia, SC 29208
Ph: (803)777-6284
Fax: (803)777-4103
E-mail: flowersk@mailbox.sc.edu
URL: http://www.sc.edu

6616 ▪ McClatchy Scholarships *(Undergraduate/Scholarship)*

Purpose: To provide financial assistance to those students who are in need. **Focus:** Journalism. **Qualif.:** Applicants must be minority students pursuing print journalism careers

Awards are arranged alphabetically below their administering organizations

in the School of Journalism and Mass Communications. **Criteria:** Scholarships will be awarded based on need and merit as determined by the School of Journalism.

Funds Avail.: No specific amount. **To Apply:** Applicants must check the available website for more information. **Contact:** South Carolina Scholastic Press Association at the above address (see entry 6615).

6617 ■ SCSPA Scholarships *(Undergraduate/Scholarship)*

Purpose: To provide financial support to deserving students. **Focus:** Journalism. **Qualif.:** Applicants must be graduating seniors who have been admitted and plan to attend the USC School of Journalism and Mass Communications. **Criteria:** Awards will be based on scholastic journalism involvement as well as applicants' academic achievements while in high school.

Funds Avail.: No specific amount. **To Apply:** Applicants must check the available website for the required materials. **Contact:** South Carolina Scholastic Press Association at the above address (see entry 6615).

6618 ■ SCSPA Yearbook Scholarships *(Undergraduate/Scholarship)*

Purpose: To provide financial assistance to deserving students. **Focus:** Journalism. **Qualif.:** Applicants must be graduating high school seniors who have shown academic excellence and plan to attend the University of South Carolina main campus in Columbia. **Criteria:** Preference will be given to those students who meet the criteria.

Funds Avail.: No specific amount. **To Apply:** Applicants must check the available website for more information. **Contact:** South Carolina Scholastic Press Association at the above address (see entry 6615).

6619 ■ South Central Power Company

PO Box 250
Lancaster, OH 43130
Ph: (740)653-4422
Fax: (740)681-4488
Free: 800-282-5064
E-mail: feedback@scp.utilities.com
URL: http://www.southcentralpower.com

6620 ■ South Central Power Scholarships *(Undergraduate/Scholarship)*

Purpose: To help high school seniors pursuing their education at a college, vocational or technical school. **Focus:** General studies. **Qualif.:** Applicants must be graduating seniors who have basic credits for entering college or a proper vocational or technical school; have current career GPA of at least 3.6 on a 4.0 scale and a combined ACT score of at least 22; must be accepted or will be accepted at an accredited college or proper vocational or technical school; and must live at the South Central Power account location. Parents/guardians of the students must be members/consumers of South Central Power Company. Applicants who have received a full tuition scholarship to the school of their choice are not qualified. **Criteria:** Awards are given based on scholastic record; personal achievement, school and community activities; poise, personality and appearance; and knowledge of cooperatives based on an OREC fact book provided by South Central Power Company.

Funds Avail.: $400-$2,500. **Number Awarded:** 6. **To Apply:** Each high school in South Central Power Company's service area will nominate one boy and one girl to represent the school in the contest. Nominated students must submit a completed official scholarship application form (must be typed), together with the complete high school grade transcript. **Deadline:** March 7. **Contact:** Rita Tate, Office Services Support Specialist, at 740-653-4422 x-6167, or 800-282-5064 x-6167.

6621 ■ Touchstone Special Achievement Scholarships *(Undergraduate/Scholarship)*

Purpose: To help high school seniors pursuing their education at a college, vocational or technical school. **Focus:** General studies. **Qualif.:** Applicants must be graduating high school senior students whose parents or guardians are electric members of an Ohio rural electric cooperative. **Criteria:** Students are judged on how well their activities reflect the Touchstone Energy core values of accountability, integrity, innovation and commitment to community, as well as their drive and dedication to achieving a college education despite personal obstacles or challenges.

Funds Avail.: $750 and $1,500. **Number Awarded:** 2 first place, and 2 second place. **To Apply:** Applicants must submit a completed scholarship application to Ohio Rural Electric Cooperative (OREC). **Contact:** Rita Tate, Office Services Support Specialist, at 740-653-4422 x-6167, or 800-282-5064 x-6167.

6622 ■ South Jersey Golf Association

10 Bennington Dr.
Medford, NJ 08055
Ph: (609)953-6873
E-mail: golfoffice@sjgolf.org
URL: http://www.sjgolf.org

6623 ■ South Jersey Golf Association Scholarships *(Undergraduate/Scholarship)*

Purpose: To provide support for deserving high school seniors intending to pursue their education. **Focus:** General studies. **Qualif.:** Applicant must be a graduating high school senior of Atlantic, Burlington, Camden, Cape May, Cumberland, Gloucester, Ocean or Salem County high schools; must have plans to enroll as a full-time undergraduate student at an accredited college or university within the United States. **Criteria:** Selection of applicants will be based on academic standing.

Funds Avail.: $500-$750. **To Apply:** Applicants must have a copy of their college/university letter of acceptance or waitlist deferral; must provide a copy of their transcript which must include midyear grades through the fall semester of senior year; must provide a copy of their SATI or ACT Score Reports; must have a typed essay, three letters of recommendation, completed resume, and a senior yearbook photograph. Application form and requirements must be sent to 3 Southern Dr., Tinton Falls, NJ 07724. **Deadline:** April 30.

6624 ■ South Kentucky Rural Electric Cooperative Corporation

PO Box 910
Somerset, KY 42502
Ph: (606)678-4121
Fax: (606)679-8279
Free: 800-264-5112
URL: http://www.skrecc.com

Awards are arranged alphabetically below their administering organizations

6625 ■ Sam J. Hord Memorial Scholarships *(Undergraduate/Scholarship)*

Purpose: To provide financial assistance for students to continue college education. **Focus:** General studies. **Qualif.:** Applicants must be students who are members of South Kentucky Rural Electric Cooperative, or whose parents are members. **Criteria:** Applicants are evaluated based on the criteria designed by the Scholarship Selection Committee.

Funds Avail.: No specific amount. **To Apply:** Applicants must submit a completed scholarship application; copy of grade transcript; copy of most recent family federal tax return; and, ACT, SAT or COMPASS results. **Deadline:** March 1.

6626 ■ South Kentucky RECC High School Senior Scholarships *(Undergraduate/Scholarship)*

Purpose: To provide financial assistance for high school seniors to continue college education. **Focus:** General studies. **Qualif.:** Applicants must be full-time high school seniors whose principal residence has an active account with South Kentucky RECC. **Criteria:** Applicants are evaluated based on criteria of the Scholarship Committee without regard to race, religion, sex, age or physical capability.

Funds Avail.: $1,000. **To Apply:** Applicants must submit a completed application form along with an essay about how Rural Electrification has affected their lives, their home communities and their local economy.

Remarks: Scholarship is paid directly to the accredited educational institution of the student's choice upon enrollment.

6627 ■ Woman In Rural Electrification Scholarships *(Undergraduate/Scholarship)*

Purpose: To provide financial assistance for Kentucky students to continue college education. **Focus:** General studies. **Qualif.:** Applicants must be students whose immediate family is served by a Kentucky rural electric cooperative, such as South Kentucky RECC; must be full-time juniors or seniors with at least 60 hours of credits at a Kentucky college or university by the start of the fall term. **Criteria:** Applicants will be evaluated based on criteria designed by the committee of the Kentucky W.I.R.E. and chosen applicants will be notified.

Funds Avail.: $1,000. **To Apply:** Applicants must contact their local South Kentucky RECC office or call the toll-free number found in the cooperative's website, for further information.

6628 ■ Southeastern Library Association

PO Box 950
Rex, GA 30273
Ph: (770)961-3520
Fax: (770)961-3712
URL: http://selaonline.org

6629 ■ The Ginny Frankenthaler Memorial Scholarship *(Undergraduate/Scholarship)*

Purpose: To recruit beginning professional librarians who have potential for leadership and have made a commitment to service in the libraries of the Southeastern United States; to provide financial assistance towards the completion of their graduate degree in library science from an institution accredited by the American Library Association. **Focus:** Science. **Qualif.:** Applicants must be completing their senior year at an accredited college or university or be graduates of such an institution; must be accepted as students in a degree program accredited by the American Library Association; must be ready to begin the program of study no later than the fall term of the year in which the scholarship is awarded; must indicate their intention to complete the degree requirements within three years; must maintain a "B" GPA throughout the program and must agree to work within one year following the graduation from library school. **Criteria:** Recipients are selected based on academic performance, financial need and interest in work and study related to library science.

Funds Avail.: $1,000. **To Apply:** Applicants must submit an official application form, three letters of acceptance from a library school accredited by the American Library Association, three letters of reference sent directly by the references, and an official transcript of all academic works. **Deadline:** May 1.

6630 ■ Southeastern Theatre Conference

PO Box 9868
Greensboro, NC 27429
Ph: (336)272-3645
Fax: (336)272-8810
E-mail: setc@setc.org
URL: http://www.setc.org

6631 ■ Leighton M. Ballew Directing Scholarships *(Undergraduate/Scholarship)*

Purpose: To provide services and educational programs for those individuals and organizations engaged in theatre in the southeast. **Focus:** Theatre arts. **Qualif.:** Applicants must have completed their undergraduate work at an accredited institution within the SETC region; and be entering graduate school in any region for the time or be currently enrolled in a graduate directing program in a college or university in any region. **Criteria:** Selections will be based on the replies and recommendations as candidates for the award.

Funds Avail.: $3,300. **To Apply:** the following information should be provided by all applicants: Personal letter outlining plans and objectives for graduate work or internship; A complete resume, including work in stage management or play direction; Names, addresses, and telephone numbers of three references who have had agreed, at the request of the award committee, to write letters recommending the applicant; Complete undergraduate and graduate transcripts; Letter of acceptance by an accredited graduate program in directing. **Deadline:** January 15. **Contact:** Marc Powers, University of South Florida, University of Theatre and Dance, 4202 E. Fowler Ave., TAR 230 Tampa, FL 33620; mpowers@arts.usf.edu.

6632 ■ Polly Holliday Scholarships *(Undergraduate/Scholarship)*

Purpose: To provide services and educational programs for those individuals and organized engaged in theatre in the southeast. **Focus:** Theatre arts. **Qualif.:** Any high school senior in the southeastern Theatre Conference Region who is planning to attend a college or university with the intent of majoring in theatre arts. **Criteria:** Selection is based on the financial need, talent, and the potential for academic success in college.

Funds Avail.: $1,000. **To Apply:** Applicants must provide the following: An official transcript, along with verification of class rank and available SAT or ACT scores from the high school guidance counselor or principal; Three completed recommendation forms, with one being from the nominee's high school principal; The students completed nominee resume form. **Deadline:** January 15. **Contact:** Roy Hudson 3541 Oakdale Drive, Birmingham, AL 35223; rhudson@jefcoed.com.

6633 ▪ Robert Porterfield Graduate Scholarships *(Graduate/Scholarship)*

Purpose: To provide services and educational programs for those individuals and organizations engaged in theatre in the southeast. **Focus:** Theatre arts. **Qualif.:** Applicant must have completed undergraduate work at an institution within the SETC region; and be attending or entering an accredited graduate school the fall term following the convention at which the award is announced. **Criteria:** Applicants may be selected as finalist on the basis of their materials.

Funds Avail.: $3,400. **To Apply:** Applicant must provide the following materials: Completed Application form; Personal letter outlining plans and objectives; a complete resume; Three reference letters speaking specifically to the applicant's potential as a graduate student; Complete, official transcripts from all colleges/universities attended. **Deadline:** January 15. **Contact:** Brenda May Ito, Columbus State University, Department of Theatre, 4225 University Avenue, Columbus, GA 31907; 706-507-8410; may_brenda@colstate.edu.

6634 ▪ Marian A. Smith Scholarships *(Graduate/Scholarship)*

Purpose: To provide services and educational programs for those individuals and organizations engaged in theatre in the southeast. **Focus:** Theatre arts. **Qualif.:** Applicants must have completed undergraduate work at an institution within the SETC region; and be entering graduate school for the first time. **Criteria:** Selection will be based on their replies and recommendations as the candidates for the award.

Funds Avail.: $2,300. **To Apply:** the following materials and information should be provided by all applicants via email or standard mail: Completed application form; Personal letter outlining plans and objectives; A complete resume; Ten slides or photographs of completed work or renderings; Names, addresses and phone numbers of three to five references; Complete college transcripts. **Deadline:** February 8. **Contact:** Carey Hanson, University of Mississippi, Department of Theatre, Isom Hall, Room 110 A, University, MS 38677; 662-915-6990; costumes@olemiss.edu.

6635 ▪ Southeastern Theatre Conference Secondary School Scholarships *(Undergraduate/Scholarship)*

Purpose: To provide services and educational programs for those individuals and organizations engaged in theatre in the southeast. **Focus:** Theatre arts. **Qualif.:** Any high school senior in the southeastern theatre conference region who is planning to attend a college or university in the SETC region with the intent of majoring in Theatre Arts. **Criteria:** Selection is based on the aptitude in theatrical practices and the potential for academic success in college.

Funds Avail.: $2,100. **To Apply:** Applicant must provide the following: An official transcript, along with verification of class rank and available SAT or ACT scores from the high-school guidance counselor or principal; Three completed recommendation forms, with one being from the nominee's high-school principal; The student's completed nominee resume form. **Deadline:** January 15. **Contact:** SETC at the above address (see entry 6630).

6636 ▪ William E. Wilson Scholarships *(Graduate/Scholarship)*

Purpose: To provide services and educational programs for those individuals and organizations engaged in theatre in the southeast. **Focus:** Theatre arts. **Qualif.:** Applicants must be legal residents of a state in the SETC region, and must have at least one year of experience as a full-time teacher and director of theatre in regionally accredited secondary school in the SETC region. The award recipient must enroll in a regionally accredited graduate program within one year of being selected for the scholarship. **Criteria:** Selection will be based on their replies and recommendations as the candidates for the award.

Funds Avail.: $6,500. **To Apply:** Applicants must provide the following: Complete application form; official transcript; resume. **Deadline:** January 15. **Contact:** Sandra Cockrell, 9063 Narcissus Ave, Seminole, FL 33777; Scockrel@tampabay.rr.com.

6637 ▪ Southern Scholarship Foundation

322 Stadium Dr.
Tallahassee, FL 32304
Ph: (850)222-3833
Fax: (850)222-6750
Free: 800-253-2769
URL: http://www.southernscholarship.org

6638 ▪ Southern Scholarship Foundation Scholarships *(Undergraduate/Scholarship)*

Purpose: To support students attending the four major universities in Florida. **Focus:** General studies. **Qualif.:** Applicant must be attending one of the four major universities in Florida (Florida A&M University, Florida Gulf Coast University, Florida State University, and the University of Florida); demonstrate financial need (submit the FAFSA); and have at least a 3.00 GPA. **Criteria:** Recipients will be selected based on the application materials.

Funds Avail.: No specific amount. **To Apply:** Applicants must submit a completed scholarship application form, recent photograph, an acceptance letter, a list of honors and activities, transcript, three letters of recommendation, the essay, financial information, and resume. **Deadline:** March and November.

6639 ▪ Southwest Florida Community Foundation

8260 College Pkwy., Ste. 101
Fort Myers, FL 33919
Ph: (239)274-5900
Fax: (239)274-5930
URL: http://www.floridacommunity.com

6640 ▪ Judge Isaac Anderson, Jr. Scholarships *(Undergraduate/Scholarship)*

Purpose: To provide to a two-year regionally accredited college or university to a Lee County high school senior who can demonstrate financial need. **Focus:** General studies. **Qualif.:** Applicant must be a graduate from public or

Awards are arranged alphabetically below their administering organizations

private high school in Lee County; must have financial need; must maintain a GPA of 3.0 or higher; must demonstrate strong ties to the community through extracurricular activities, religious endeavors or community service; and must plan to attend a two-or-four year regionally accredited college or university. **Criteria:** Selection of recipients will be based on academic performance and financial need.

Funds Avail.: $1,000. **To Apply:** Applicants must complete the application forms available online and must have a letter of interest, transcript and letter of recommendation. **Deadline:** March 26. **Contact:** Kathryn Clinton at kcintron@floridacommunity.com.

6641 ■ Lewis B. Barber Memorial Scholarships
(Undergraduate/Scholarship)

Purpose: To fund books and tuition for students pursuing either of the following educational paths: (1) certification to teach the deaf and blind; (2) seminary or pre-seminary school to study church, Christian music or Christian education. **Focus:** Christian education; Church occupations. **Qualif.:** Applicants must graduate from public or private high school in Charlotte, Collier, Glades, Hendry or Lee County; must maintain satisfactory grades; must acknowledge and express Jesus Christ as Lord and Savior; and must demonstrate financial need. **Criteria:** Scholarship recipients are selected based upon the specific criteria made by each fund's donor. Scholarship application is reviewed by the Scholarship Committee. Selection of applicants will be based on academic standing and financial need.

Funds Avail.: $1,200. **To Apply:** Application forms are available online. Applicants must submit a letter of interest, transcript, and letter of recommendation. **Deadline:** February 15.

6642 ■ James Bilder Scholarships
(Undergraduate/Scholarship)

Purpose: To fund tuition for high school students intending to pursue vocational or technical studies. **Focus:** General studies. **Qualif.:** Applicants must have graduated from public high school in Lee County; must pursue 2-year degree at community college or technical certification at certified technical school; and must demonstrate financial need. **Criteria:** Scholarship recipients are selected based upon the specific criteria made by each fund's donor. Scholarship application is reviewed by the Scholarship Committee. Selection of applicants will be based on academic standing and financial need.

Funds Avail.: $1,000. **To Apply:** Applicants must submit a letter of interest, transcript, and letter of recommendation. **Deadline:** February 15.

6643 ■ Jordan ABDO/Michael Bluett Memorial Scholarships *(Undergraduate/Scholarship)*

Purpose: To fund scholarships for a North Fort Myers High School male or female student athlete. **Focus:** General studies. **Qualif.:** Applicants must have graduated from North Fort Myers High School; must be student athletes with a GPA of at least 3.5. **Criteria:** Scholarship recipients are selected based upon the specific criteria made by each fund's donor. Scholarship application is reviewed by the Scholarship Committee. Selection of applicants will be based on academic standing and financial need.

Funds Avail.: $1,000. **To Apply:** Applicants must complete the application form available online and submit a letter of interest, transcript, and letter of recommendation. **Deadline:** February 15.

6644 ■ Carl E. Brooks Scholarships
(Undergraduate/Scholarship)

Purpose: To fund tuition for college-bound students of one or more immigrant parents. **Focus:** General studies. **Qualif.:** Applicants must have graduated from public or private high school in Charlotte, Collier, Glades, Hendry or Lee County. **Criteria:** Scholarship recipients are selected based upon the specific criteria made by each fund's donor. Scholarship application is reviewed by the Scholarship Committee. Selection of applicants will be based on academic standing and financial need.

Funds Avail.: $2,000. **Number Awarded:** 2. **To Apply:** Applicants must provide proof of parent's immigrant status and must submit a letter of interest, transcript, and letter of recommendation. **Deadline:** February 15.

6645 ■ John and Ruth Childe Scholarships
(Undergraduate/Scholarship)

Purpose: To fund education of students with physical disability intending to pursue higher education in a college, university or technical school. **Focus:** General studies. **Qualif.:** Applicants must be graduates from a public or private high school in Lee county; must have a disability; and must have good academic standing. **Criteria:** Consideration is made for middle-income families.

Funds Avail.: No specific amount. **To Apply:** Applicants must complete application form, available online and must have a letter of interest, transcript and letter of recommendation. Application form and other supporting documents must be sent to Southwest Florida, Community Foundation, 8260 College Pkwy., Ste. 101, Fort Myers, FL 33919. **Deadline:** February 15.

6646 ■ City of Sanibel Employee Dependent Scholarships *(Undergraduate/Scholarship)*

Purpose: To provide financial assistance for qualified dependents of Sanibel City employees to attend a college or university. **Focus:** General studies. **Qualif.:** Applicant must be a dependent of a Sanibel City Employee (includes City Clerk's office, finance, legal, legislative, planning, police, building, natural resources, public works, management information systems, utility, recreation, and administrative services); must demonstrate financial need and academic achievement. **Criteria:** Scholarship recipients are selected based upon the specific criteria made by each fund's donor. Scholarship application is reviewed by the Scholarship Committee.

Funds Avail.: $1,000. **To Apply:** Applicants must complete the application form, available online; must have a student letter of interest, financial need documentation, transcript, and two letters of recommendation. Application form and other supporting documents must be sent to Community Foundation of Sanibel-Captiva, 8260 College Pkwy., Ste. 101, Fort Myers, FL 33919. **Deadline:** February 15. **Contact:** Kathryn Cintron at the above address (see entry 6639).

6647 ■ COUSE-Gram Scholarships
(Undergraduate/Scholarship)

Purpose: To provide educational assistance for Moore Haven High School students pursuing post-secondary education. **Focus:** General studies. **Qualif.:** Applicant must be a Moore Haven High School senior; must pursue post-secondary education. **Criteria:** Application materials are reviewed by a member of the Community Foundation's Scholarship Reading Committee. Selection of applicants will be based on academic standing and financial need.

Funds Avail.: No specific amount. **To Apply:** Applicants must submit a letter of interest, transcript, and letter of recommendation. Application forms are available online. **Deadline:** February 15.

6648 ■ D&A Florida Scholarships
(Undergraduate/Scholarship)

Purpose: To fund a student who will attend: FGCU, university of Florida/ Gainesville, Florida State University/ Tallahassee, Flagler College, Stetson University/Deland, University of Miami, University of Tampa, or Embry Riddle Aeronautical University/Daytona Beach. **Focus:** Architecture; Business; Engineering; International affairs and relations; Journalism; Computer and information sciences; Law; Literature; Medicine; Physics; Chemistry; Political science. **Qualif.:** Applicants must have graduated from a public or private high school in Charlotte, Glades, Hendry or Lee County; must pursue a degree in Architecture, Business, Engineering, International affairs and relations, Journalism, Computer and information sciences, Law, Literature, Medicine, Physics, Chemistry, or Political science. **Criteria:** Scholarship recipients are selected based upon the specific criteria made by each fund's donor. Scholarship application is reviewed by the Scholarship Committee. Selection of applicants will be based on academic standing and financial need.

Funds Avail.: $10,000. **To Apply:** Application forms are available online. Applicants must submit a letter of interest and letter of recommendation, a transcript and financial need documentation. **Deadline:** February 15.

6649 ■ Doctors IRA & UDAYA Nursing Scholarships *(Undergraduate/Scholarship)*

Purpose: To fund a student studying nursing at Edison College or Florida Gulf Coast University. **Focus:** Nursing. **Qualif.:** Applicants must plan to attend or be attending Edison College or Florida Gulf Coast University; must be enrolled in a nursing program; and must demonstrate financial need. **Criteria:** Scholarship recipients are selected based upon the specific criteria made by each fund's donor. Scholarship application is reviewed by the Scholarship Committee. Selection of applicants will be based on academic standing and financial need.

Funds Avail.: No specific amount. **To Apply:** Applicants must submit a student letter of interest, documentation of financial need, transcript, and letter of recommendation. **Deadline:** February 15.

6650 ■ Dunbar Heritage Scholarships
(Undergraduate/Scholarship)

Purpose: To fund a Dunbar High School graduating student of African-American descent in pursuing a bachelor's degree at an accredited college. **Focus:** General studies. **Qualif.:** Applicant must be a graduating member of Dunbar High School; must be of African-American descent; must have financial need; must have a GPA of 2.5 or higher; and must enter college within the year following high school graduation. **Criteria:** Scholarship recipients are selected based upon the specific criteria made by each fund's donor. Scholarship application is reviewed by the Scholarship Committee. Selection of applicants will be based on academic standing and financial need.

Funds Avail.: Amount of scholarship is determined each year by the Selection Committee. **To Apply:** Applicants must submit a letter of interest, transcript, and letter of recommendation. Application forms are available online. **Deadline:** February 15.

6651 ■ Anne M. Fassett Scholarships
(Undergraduate/Scholarship)

Purpose: To fund post-high school educational opportunities at the college, community college, or technical school level for males and females with a physical disability and who use a wheelchair. **Focus:** General studies. **Qualif.:** Applicants must have graduated from a public or private high school in Charlotte, Collier, Glades, Hendry or Lee County; must be currently enrolled or planning to attend a Florida state college, community college or technical school; must have a physical disability and use a wheelchair; and must demonstrate financial need. **Criteria:** Scholarship recipients are selected based upon the specific criteria made by each fund's donor. Scholarship application is reviewed by the Scholarship Committee. Selection of applicants will be based on academic standing and financial need.

Funds Avail.: Scholarship award amount is determined by committee. **To Apply:** Application forms are available online. Applicants must submit a letter of recommendation, letter of interest, financial need documentation, and transcript. **Deadline:** March 20.

6652 ■ Paul B. & Aline Flynn Scholarships
(Undergraduate/Scholarship)

Purpose: To fund high school or undergraduate/graduate students planning to study at a 4-year accredited college in the area of Communications or Journalism. **Focus:** Communications; Journalism. **Qualif.:** Applicants must have graduated from a public or private high school in Charlotte, Collier, Glades, Hendry or Lee County; must pursue a degree in Communications, English or Journalism; and must maintain satisfactory grades. **Criteria:** Scholarship recipients are selected based upon the specific criteria made by each fund's donor. Scholarship application is reviewed by the Scholarship Committee. Selection of recipients will be based on academic standing and financial need.

Funds Avail.: No specific amount. **To Apply:** Application forms are available online. Applicants must submit a student letter of interest, high school/college transcript, and letter of recommendation. **Deadline:** February 15.

6653 ■ Charles and Margaret Foster Scholarships *(Undergraduate/Scholarship)*

Purpose: To provide financial assistance for qualified students in Florida. **Focus:** Environmental technology; Music. **Qualif.:** Applicant must be a resident of Lee County and must be studying environmental studies or environmental education at the University of Florida or studying music at Florida State University. **Criteria:** Scholarship recipients are selected based upon the specific criteria made by each fund's donor. Scholarship application is reviewed by the Scholarship Committee.

Funds Avail.: $300. **Number Awarded:** 2. **To Apply:** Applicants must have the application form, available online, and must submit a transcript, letter of interest and letter of recommendation. **Deadline:** February 15.

6654 ■ Dorris W. Frey Memorial Scholarships
(Undergraduate/Scholarship)

Purpose: To fund students studying Christian ministry/ youth ministry, Christian counseling, nursing and medicine.

Awards are arranged alphabetically below their administering organizations

Focus: Ministry; Christian education; Nursing; Medicine. **Qualif.:** Applicants must have graduated from a public or private high school in Charlotte, Collier, Glades, Hendry or Lee County; must pursue one of the above named degrees of study; must maintain satisfactory grades; must be committed to Jesus Christ and show commitment through action in ministering to others; and must have recognized ability and academic performance with standard measures of grades and appropriate test scores. **Criteria:** Scholarship recipients are selected based on the specific criteria made by each fund's donor. Scholarship application is reviewed by the Scholarship Committee. Selection of applicants will be based on academic standing and financial need.

Funds Avail.: Scholarship amount is determined by selection committee. **To Apply:** Applicants must submit an essay of future commitment, transcript, and references. **Deadline:** February 15.

6655 ■ American Association of University Women-Mary Sue Gottcent Memorial Scholarships *(Undergraduate/Scholarship)*

Purpose: To fund Lee County females who are enrolled in accredited programs of study at either 2-year or 4-year accredited institutions. **Focus:** General studies. **Qualif.:** Applicants must be residents of Lee County who demonstrate financial need. **Criteria:** Preference will be given to females over 25 years of age.

Funds Avail.: $1,000. **To Apply:** Application forms are available online. Applicants must submit a personal statement essay, proof of financial need, high school/college transcript, and three letters of recommendation. **Deadline:** March 20. **Contact:** Kathryn Cintron at the above address (see entry 6639).

6656 ■ William L. Graddy Law School Scholarships *(Undergraduate/Scholarship)*

Purpose: To fund scholarships for students who have completed their first year of course load at an accredited law school. **Focus:** Law. **Qualif.:** Applicants must have completed first year of law school; must have a GPA of 2.8 or above and be in the top 25% of class; must have been a resident of Charlotte, Collier, Glades, Hendry or Lee for at least 3 years; and must demonstrate financial need. **Criteria:** Scholarship recipients are selected based upon the specific criteria made by each fund's donor. Scholarship application is reviewed by the Scholarship Committee. Selection of applicants will be based on academic standing and financial need.

Funds Avail.: $1,000. **To Apply:** Application forms are available online. Applicants must submit a letter of interest, letter of recommendation from college instructor, transcript and financial need documentation. **Deadline:** March 20.

6657 ■ Francis Harris Gresham Scholarships *(Undergraduate/Scholarship)*

Purpose: To fund tuition for college-bound seniors from Lee County high schools. **Focus:** General studies. **Qualif.:** Applicants must have graduated from a public or private high school in Lee County. **Criteria:** Scholarship recipients are selected based upon the specific criteria made by each fund's donor. Scholarship application is reviewed by the Scholarship Committee. Selection of applicants will be based on academic standing and financial need.

Funds Avail.: $1,000. **To Apply:** Applicants must submit a letter of interest, transcript, and letter of recommendation. Application forms are available online. **Deadline:** February 15.

6658 ■ Matt Harmon Memorial Scholarships *(Undergraduate/Scholarship)*

Purpose: To fund books and tuition for college-bound male baseball players. **Focus:** General studies. **Qualif.:** Applicants must be graduates of a public school in Lee County; must be male; must demonstrate financial need; and must have played baseball in high school. **Criteria:** Scholarship recipients are selected based upon the specific criteria made by each fund's donor. Scholarship application is reviewed by the Scholarship Committee.

Funds Avail.: $500. **To Apply:** Applicants must submit a letter of interest, transcript, and letter of recommendation. Application forms are available online. **Deadline:** February 15.

6659 ■ Chip Johnson Scholarships *(Undergraduate/Scholarship)*

Purpose: To fund scholarships for students who have completed 60 hours of college and plan to attend one of named colleges. **Focus:** General studies. **Qualif.:** Applicants must have completed 60 semester hours of college and plan to continue study toward a 4-year degree at Barry University, FGCU, Nova, Edison College or International College, or a regionally-accredited college in the 5-county area; must have a GPA of 3.5 or above and an outstanding record of academic achievement; must have lived in the 5-county area served by the Community Foundation (Charlotte, Collier, Glades, Hendry and Lee); and must have demonstrated leadership, community service and service to school. **Criteria:** Scholarship recipients are selected based upon the specific criteria made by each fund's donor. Scholarship application is reviewed by the scholarship committee. Selection of applicants will be based on academic standing and financial need.

Funds Avail.: $1,200. **Number Awarded:** 7. **To Apply:** Applicants must complete the application forms available online; must submit a letter of recommendation from college instructor and letter of interest; must have a transcript of record. **Deadline:** March 20.

6660 ■ George E. Judd Scholarships *(Undergraduate/Scholarship)*

Purpose: To fund tuition for graduating seniors pursuing higher education in the fine or performing arts. **Focus:** Fine arts; Performing arts. **Qualif.:** Applicants must graduate from public or private high school in Lee County and must pursue a degree in the fine or performing arts. **Criteria:** Scholarship recipients are selected based upon the specific criteria made by each fund's donor. Scholarship application is reviewed by the scholarship Committee.

Funds Avail.: $1,000. **To Apply:** Applicants must submit a letter of interest, transcript, and letter of recommendation. Application forms are available online. **Deadline:** February 15.

6661 ■ Doc Keen Memorial Scholarships *(Undergraduate/Scholarship)*

Purpose: To fund a scholarship for college or vocational school for a student who was an active member of 4-H or a FFA Organization for two consecutive years and has attended a Moore Haven, Clewiston, or LaBelle high school. **Focus:** General studies. **Qualif.:** Applicant must be a graduate from a Moore Haven, Clewinston or LaBelle high school; must pursue higher education; must maintain satisfactory grades; and must have been an active member of 4-H or a FFA Organization for two consecutive years. **Criteria:** Application materials are reviewed by a member of the Community Foundation's Scholarship Reading Committee. Selection of applicants will be based on academic standing and financial need.

Funds Avail.: $1,000. **To Apply:** Application forms are available online. Applicants must submit a letter of interest, transcript, list of 4-H or FFA activities, and letter of recommendation. **Deadline:** February 15.

6662 ■ Isabel Mayer Kirkpatrick Scholarships
(Undergraduate/Scholarship)

Purpose: To fund tuition for high school graduates with a "B" average of 3.03.7. **Focus:** General studies. **Qualif.:** Applicants must graduate from public or private high school in Lee County; must be well-rounded in terms of education, community service, sports and leadership activities; and must have a GPA of 3.0-3.7 (anything higher will disqualify the student). **Criteria:** Application materials must be reviewed by a member of the Community Foundation's Scholarship Reading Committee. Selection of applicants will be based on academic standing and financial need.

Funds Avail.: $1,000. **To Apply:** Applicants must submit a letter of interest, transcript, and letter of recommendation. Application forms are available online. **Deadline:** February 15.

6663 ■ Robert A. Kleckner Scholarships
(Undergraduate/Scholarship)

Purpose: To fund high school and undergraduate/graduate students who are pursuing a career in finance or accounting. **Focus:** Finance; Accounting. **Qualif.:** Applicants must be residents of Charlotte, Glades, Hendry or Lee County pursuing a degree in finance or accounting. **Criteria:** Scholarship recipients are selected based upon the specific criteria made by each fund's donor. Scholarship application is reviewed by the Scholarship Committee. Selection of applicants will be based on academic standing and financial need.

Funds Avail.: $1,200. **To Apply:** Application forms are available online. Applicants must submit a letter of interest, high school/college transcript, and letter of recommendation. **Deadline:** February 15.

6664 ■ Love of Bonita Empowerment Scholarships *(Undergraduate/Scholarship)*

Purpose: To fund books, tuition and/or course fees for Bonita Spring residents to attend a college or technical school. **Focus:** General studies. **Qualif.:** Applicant must be a resident of Bonita Spring and must demonstrate financial need. **Criteria:** Scholarship recipients are selected based upon the specific criteria made by each fund's donor. Scholarship application is reviewed by the Scholarship Committee. Selection of applicants will be based on academic standing and financial need.

Funds Avail.: $1,000. **To Apply:** Applicants must submit a letter of interest, financial need documentation, transcript, and letter of recommendation. Applicants must submit the application forms and other supporting documents to Kathryn Cintron, Donor Services, Bonita Spring Community Foundation, 8260 College Pkwy., Ste. 101, Fort Myers, FL 33919. **Deadline:** February 15.

6665 ■ Ruth Messmer Memorial Scholarships
(Undergraduate/Scholarship)

Purpose: To fund tuition for females pursuing a business career in college. **Focus:** Business. **Qualif.:** Applicants must have graduated from a public or private high school in Lee County with a documented "B" average; must be females pursuing a business career in college. **Criteria:** Scholarship recipients are selected based upon the specific criteria made by each fund's donor. Scholarship application is reviewed by the scholarship committee. Selection of recipients will be based on academic standing and financial need.

Funds Avail.: $1,000. **To Apply:** Applicants must submit a letter of interest, transcript, and letter of recommendation. Application forms are available online. **Deadline:** February 15.

6666 ■ Judge William J. Nelson Scholarships
(Undergraduate/Scholarship)

Purpose: To provide financial assistance for qualified high school seniors who will be attending the University of Florida. **Focus:** General studies. **Qualif.:** Applicant must be a resident of Charlotte, Collier, Glades, Hendry or Lee County; must have overcome adversity in some way; and must attend the University of Florida. **Criteria:** Scholarship recipients are selected based upon the specific criteria made by each fund's donor. Scholarship application is reviewed by the Scholarship Committee. Selection of applicants will be based on academic standing and financial need.

Funds Avail.: $1,000. **To Apply:** Applicants must submit a letter of interest, transcript, and letter of recommendation. Application forms are available online. **Deadline:** February 15.

6667 ■ Robert B. and Dorothy Pence Scholarships *(Undergraduate/Scholarship)*

Purpose: To fund tuition for economically-disadvantaged students to attend college or technical school. **Focus:** General studies. **Qualif.:** Applicants must have graduated from a public or private high school in Lee County and must be an industrious student with good moral character and document financial need. **Criteria:** Scholarship recipients are selected based upon the specific criteria made by each fund's donor. Scholarship application is reviewed by the Scholarship Committee. Selection of applicants will be based on academic standing and financial need.

Funds Avail.: $1,000. **To Apply:** Applicants must submit a letter of interest, transcript, and letter of recommendation. Application forms are available online. **Deadline:** February 15.

6668 ■ Chet and Jannett Perry Scholarships
(Undergraduate/Scholarship)

Purpose: To provide funding support for students pursuing a career in accounting. **Focus:** Accounting. **Qualif.:** Applicant must be graduating from a public or private high school in Charlotte, Hendry, Glades or Lee County; must pursue a degree in accounting; and must enter college within a year following high school graduation. **Criteria:** Scholarship recipients are selected based upon the specific criteria made by each fund's donor. Scholarship application is reviewed by the Scholarship Committee. Selection of applicants will be based on academic standing and financial need.

Funds Avail.: $1,000. **To Apply:** Applicants must submit a letter of interest, transcript, and letter of recommendation. Application forms are available online. **Deadline:** February 15.

6669 ■ Faye Lynn Roberts Educational Scholarships *(Undergraduate/Scholarship)*

Purpose: To fund scholarships for female students pursuing a career in technical studies, court reporting, computer training or nursing. **Focus:** Technical training; Computer and information sciences; Nursing. **Qualif.:** Applicants must be 21 years of age or older; must be residents of Lee County; and must demonstrate financial need. **Criteria:** Scholarship recipients are selected based upon the specific criteria made by each fund's donor. Scholarship application is reviewed by the Scholarship Committee. Selection of applicants will be based on academic standing and financial need.

Funds Avail.: $5,000. **To Apply:** Application forms are available online. Applicants must submit a personal essay, financial need documentation, high school/college transcript and letter of recommendation. **Deadline:** March 20.

6670 ■ David G. Robinson Arts Scholarships *(Undergraduate/Scholarship)*

Purpose: To fund tuition for high school seniors who plan to study the arts in an accredited school. **Focus:** Arts. **Qualif.:** Applicants must graduate from a public school in Lee County; must be an industrious student with good moral character; must document financial need; and must show leadership and community service. **Criteria:** Scholarship recipients are selected based upon the specific criteria made by each fund's donor. Scholarship application is reviewed by the Scholarship Committee. Selection of applicants will be based on academic standing and financial need.

Funds Avail.: $1,000. **To Apply:** Applicants must submit a letter of interest, transcript, and letter of recommendation. Application forms are available online. **Deadline:** February 15.

6671 ■ Rockin' Christmas Fund Scholarships *(Undergraduate/Scholarship)*

Purpose: To fund a student who has displayed high levels of excellence in academic and/or athletics and who has lost a parent due to an illness or sudden death and to help qualified students to pay for education in a college, university or technical school. **Focus:** General studies. **Qualif.:** Applicants must have graduated from a public or private high school in Lee or Collier to receive the award which will be based upon satisfactory evidence of matriculation to a college, university or technical school; must provide evidence of a academic athletic achievement from any coach at school or from any league participated in, if not at school; and must demonstrate financial need. Applicants do not have to have played high school sports but rather must demonstrate that athletics are a part of their life. **Criteria:** Scholarship recipients are selected based upon the specific criteria made by each fund's donor. Scholarship application is reviewed by the Scholarship Committee. Selection of applicants will be based on academic standing and financial need.

Funds Avail.: No specific amount. **To Apply:** Applicants must provide a letter from guidance counselors of the high school signed by the counselor on how the student qualifies under the loss of parent criteria; must submit a letter of interest, transcript, and letter of recommendation. Application forms are available online. **Deadline:** February 15.

6672 ■ Robert C. and Margaret A. Schikora Scholarships *(Undergraduate/Scholarship)*

Purpose: To provide tuition for high school graduates' post-secondary educational opportunities, including trade/technical school, undergraduate work, post-graduate work, and professional education. **Focus:** General studies. **Qualif.:** Applicants must graduate from public or private high school in Lee County with documented "B" average; must be well-rounded in terms of education, community service, sports and leadership activities; and must demonstrate financial need. **Criteria:** Scholarship recipients are selected based upon the specific criteria made by each fund's donor. Scholarship application is reviewed by the scholarship committee. Selection of applicants will be based on academic standing and financial need.

Funds Avail.: $1,000. **To Apply:** Applicants must submit a letter of interest, transcript, and letter of recommendation. Application forms are available online. **Deadline:** February 15.

6673 ■ John M. and Mary A. Shanley Memorial Scholarships *(Undergraduate/Scholarship)*

Purpose: To fund students pursuing degrees or advanced degrees in medicine, law, dentistry, teaching (math and science), ministry, engineering, accounting, architecture and computer science. **Focus:** Medicine; Law; Dentistry; Teaching; Ministry; Engineering; Accounting; Agriculture; Economic aspects; Architecture; Computer and information sciences. **Qualif.:** Applicant must be a resident of Charlotte, Hendry or Lee County. **Criteria:** Financial need is not required.

Funds Avail.: $5,000. **To Apply:** Application forms are available online. Applicants must submit a letter of interest, letter of recommendation and transcript. **Deadline:** February 15.

6674 ■ Southwest Florida Community Foundation College Assistance Scholarships *(Undergraduate/Scholarship)*

Purpose: To fund books, laboratory fees, or any expenses related to student's academic costs. **Focus:** General studies. **Qualif.:** Applicants must reside in Charlotte, Lee, Glades, Hendry or Collier County and must demonstrate financial need. **Criteria:** Application materials are reviewed by a member of the Community Foundation's Scholarship Reading Committee. Selection of applicants will be based on academic standing and financial need.

Funds Avail.: $500. **To Apply:** Applicants must submit a letter of interest, transcript, and financial need documentation. **Deadline:** February 15.

6675 ■ Anne Sturrock Nursing Scholarships *(Undergraduate/Scholarship)*

Purpose: To endow nursing scholarships for members or children of members of St. Andrew Catholic Church in Cape Coral. **Focus:** Nursing. **Qualif.:** Applicant must be a member or a child of a member of St. Andrew Catholic Church; must pursue a career in nursing; and must demonstrate financial need. **Criteria:** Scholarship recipients are selected based upon the specific criteria made by each fund's donor. Scholarship application is reviewed by the Scholarship Committee. Selection of applicants will be based on academic standing and financial need.

Funds Avail.: Scholarship award amount is determined by committee. **To Apply:** Application forms are available online. Applicants must submit a letter of interest, letter of recommendation from pastor of St. Andrew, transcript and financial need documentation. **Deadline:** February 15.

6676 ■ SWFL Deputy Sheriffs Association Fund Scholarships *(Undergraduate/Scholarship)*

Purpose: To provide financial funds for qualified high school students who are dependents of law enforcement

Awards are arranged alphabetically below their administering organizations

officers. **Focus:** General studies. **Qualif.:** Applicant must be a graduate from high school in Charlotte, Collier, Lee, Hendry or Glades Counties; must be a dependent of a law enforcement officer in the above counties; and must list name of law enforcement officer. **Criteria:** Scholarship recipients are selected based upon the specific criteria made by each fund's donor. Scholarship application is reviewed by the scholarship committee.

Funds Avail.: No specific amount. **To Apply:** Applicants must complete the application form, available online, and submit a letter of interest, transcript, and letter of recommendation. **Deadline:** February 15.

6677 ■ SWFL Professional Golfers Association Scholarships *(Undergraduate/Scholarship)*

Purpose: To provide tuition for high school graduates who played competitive golf in their senior year and at least one other year during high school. **Focus:** General studies. **Qualif.:** Applicants must have graduated from a public or private high school in Charlotte, Lee or Collier County; must have played competitive golf in their senior year and at least one other year during high school; and must have academic achievement and show evidence of community service and outside activities. **Criteria:** Scholarship recipients are selected based upon the specific criteria made by each fund's donor. Scholarship application is reviewed by the Scholarship Committee. Selection of applicants will be based on academic standing and financial need.

Funds Avail.: $1,000. **To Apply:** Applicants must submit a letter of interest, transcript, and letter of recommendation. Application forms are available online. **Deadline:** February 15.

6678 ■ John I. and Madeleine R. Taeni Scholarships *(Undergraduate/Scholarship)*

Purpose: To fund students pursuing degrees in teaching, nursing, paramedic training or emergency medical technician training. **Focus:** Teaching; Nursing; Paramedics; Emergency and disaster services. **Qualif.:** Applicant must be a resident of Charlotte, Collier, Glades, Hendry or Lee County; must be highly motivated; must pursue teaching, nursing paramedic training, or emergency medical technician training; and must have graduated high school at least two years ago. **Criteria:** Scholarship recipients are selected based upon the specific criteria made by each fund's donor. Scholarship application is reviewed by the Scholarship Committee. Selection of applicants will be based on academic standing and financial need.

Funds Avail.: $1,000. **To Apply:** Application forms are available online. Applicants must submit a letter of interest, letter of recommendation, and transcript. **Deadline:** March 20.

6679 ■ Special Libraries Association

331 S Patrick St.
Alexandria, VA 22314-3501
Ph: (703)647-4900
Fax: (703)647-4901
E-mail: sla@sla.org
URL: http://www.sla.org

6680 ■ Affirmative Action Scholarships *(Graduate/Scholarship)*

Purpose: To promote education in the Special Librarian field. **Focus:** Library and archival sciences; Information science and technology. **Qualif.:** Applicant must be a U.S. citizen; a member of a minority group defined as Black (African American), Hispanic, Asian or Pacific Islander, American Indian, Aleutian (Alaskan) native or native Hawaiian; and must be pursuing a graduate study in librarianship leading to a master's degree at a recognized school of library or information science. **Criteria:** Preference is given to applicants who display great interest in special library work.

Funds Avail.: $6,000. **Number Awarded:** 1. **To Apply:** Applicants must prepare an official transcript or letter of acceptance; three reference letters; statement of financial need; and an essay (500-1000 words). **Deadline:** September 30.

Remarks: Matriculated school applicants must submit an official transcript of library school record to date. **Contact:** scholarship@sla.org.

6681 ■ Mary Adeline Conner Professional Development Scholarships *(Graduate/Scholarship)*

Purpose: To promote education in the Special Librarian field. **Focus:** Library and archival sciences; Information science and technology. **Qualif.:** Applicant must be a member of the SLA with an M.L.S. degree and must have worked in a special library; accepted into a certificate or degree program at an accredited college/university or by a professional association/society. **Criteria:** Preference is given to applicants who display great interest in special library work.

Funds Avail.: $1,000. **Number Awarded:** 1. **To Apply:** Applicants must prepare an official transcript or letter of acceptance; three reference letters; statement of financial need; and an essay (500-1000 words). **Deadline:** September 30. **Contact:** scholarship@sla.org.

6682 ■ Institute for Scientific Information (ISI) Scholarships *(Doctorate, Graduate/Scholarship)*

Purpose: To promote education in the Special Librarian field. **Focus:** Library and archival sciences; Information science and technology. **Qualif.:** Applicant must be a member of SLA with working experience in a special library; and pursuing a graduate study leading to a PhD from a recognized program in library science, information science or related fields of study. **Criteria:** Preference is given to applicants who display great interest in special library work.

Funds Avail.: $1,000. **Number Awarded:** 1. **To Apply:** Applicants must prepare an official transcript or letter of acceptance; three reference letters; statement of financial need; and an essay (500-1000 words). **Deadline:** September 30. **Contact:** scholarship@sla.org.

6683 ■ Plenum Scholarships *(Doctorate/Scholarship)*

Purpose: To promote education in the Special Librarian field. **Focus:** Library and archival sciences; Information science and technology. **Qualif.:** Applicant must be a member of the SLA with working experience in a special library; and a doctoral candidate with an approved dissertation topic enrolled in a course of study. **Criteria:** Preference is given to applicants who display great interest in special library work.

Funds Avail.: $1,000. **Number Awarded:** 1. **To Apply:** Applicants must prepare an evidence of dissertation topic approval; an official transcript or letter of acceptance; three reference letters; statement of financial need; and an essay (500-1000 words). **Deadline:** September 30. **Contact:** scholarship@sla.org.

6684 ■ SLA Scholarships *(Graduate/Scholarship)*

Purpose: To promote education in the Special Librarian field. **Focus:** Library and archival sciences. **Qualif.:** Applicant must be a college graduate or college senior with an interest in special librarianship. **Criteria:** Preference is given to applicants who display great interest in special library work.

Funds Avail.: $6,000. **Number Awarded:** 3. **To Apply:** Applicants must prepare an official transcript or letter of acceptance; three reference letters; statement of financial need; and an essay (500-1000 words). **Deadline:** September 30. **Contact:** scholarship@sla.org.

6685 ■ Specialized Carriers and Rigging Association

2750 Prosperity Ave., Ste. 620
Fairfax, VA 22031-4312
Ph: (703)698-0291
Fax: (703)698-0297
E-mail: info@scranet.org
URL: http://www.scranet.org

6686 ■ SC and R Foundation Grant Program *(Undergraduate/Grant)*

Purpose: To support a research by technical/vocational college students. **Focus:** Transportation. **Qualif.:** Applicants must have at least one term of undergraduate study remaining or have applied to technical/vocational college; must have study leading to an associate degree in the field of specialized carriers and rigging industry; an employees or a relative of an employees of SC and RA Member Company. **Criteria:** Scholarship committee performed blind evaluations of all the applications.

Funds Avail.: $1500. **To Apply:** Applicants must complete the application form together with two letters of recommendation (one letter from an academic advisor or employer); official transcripts; recent photograph; and contact information. **Contact:** Scholarship Subcommittee, rpage@scranet.org.

6687 ■ SC and R Foundation Scholarships *(Undergraduate/Scholarship)*

Purpose: To provides career opportunities and scholarship to its members. **Focus:** Transportation. **Qualif.:** Applicants must have at least one term of undergraduate study remaining or have applied to a college/university; must have study leading to bachelor degree in fields related to specialized carriers and rigging industry; must be employees or relatives of employees of SC and RA Member Company. **Criteria:** Scholarship committee performed blind evaluations of all the applications.

Funds Avail.: $3000. **Number Awarded:** 1. **To Apply:** Applicants must complete the application form together with two letters of recommendation (one letter from an academic advisor or employer); official transcripts; recent photograph; and contact information. **Contact:** Scholarship Subcommittee, rpage@scranet.org.

6688 ■ Specialty Equipment Market Association

PO Box 4910
Diamond Bar, CA 91765-0910
Ph: (909)396-0289
Fax: (909)860-1709
E-mail: sema@sema.org
URL: http://www.sema.org

6689 ■ Loan Forgiveness Scholarships *(Undergraduate/Scholarship)*

Purpose: To foster industry leadership by supporting the education of students pursuing careers in the automotive aftermarket. **Focus:** Automotive technology. **Qualif.:** Applicants must be post-graduate students with one year minimum employment by a SEMA member company. **Criteria:** Recipients are selected based on the review of the completed application.

Funds Avail.: $1,000. **To Apply:** Applicants must submit a completed application form; resume; official, sealed transcripts for all college or post-secondary course work completed through the first quarter or semester of the current year; must provide documentation of outstanding student loans; personal essay; two letters of recommendation from professors, career counselors, or employers; must submit a current photo for publication and promotional use. **Contact:** education@sema.org.

6690 ■ Specialty Equipment Market Association Scholarships *(Undergraduate/Scholarship)*

Purpose: To foster industry leadership by supporting the education of students pursuing careers in the automotive aftermarket; to foster leadership in the specialty equipment marketplace and to support educational goals for students pursuing careers in the automotive aftermarket. **Focus:** Automotive technology. **Qualif.:** Applicants must be graduates, or undergraduate sophomores, juniors or seniors, in a vocational or technical degree program in a two-to-four year accredited university or college in the United States or Canada. Applicants must have a minimum 2.5 grade point average; must be pursuing studies leading to a career in the automotive aftermarket or a related field. **Criteria:** Recipients are selected based on academic performance.

Funds Avail.: Varies. **Number Awarded:** 4. **To Apply:** Applicants must submit a completed application form; must submit a personal essay outlining reasons the applicant wants to pursue a career in the automotive aftermarket or related fields; must submit an official sealed transcript from all college or post-secondary course work completed; two letters of recommendation from a non-family member on company letterhead. **Deadline:** April 20.

6691 ■ Spencer Foundation

625 North Michigan Ave., Ste. 1600
Chicago, IL 60611
Ph: (312)337-7000
Fax: (312)337-0282
E-mail: abrinkman@spencer.org
URL: http://www.spencer.org

6692 ■ Spencer Foundation Dissertation Fellowship Program *(Postdoctorate/Fellowship)*

Purpose: To encourage a new generation of scholars from a wide range of disciplines and professional fields to undertake research relevant to the improvement of education. **Focus:** General studies. **Qualif.:** Applicants need not be U.S. citizens; must be candidates for the doctoral degree at a graduate school within the United States. **Criteria:** Recipients are selected based on academic standing and submitted requirements.

Funds Avail.: $25,000. **To Apply:** Applicants must complete the application form and submit along with a list of

Awards are arranged alphabetically below their administering organizations

publications/presentations; a dissertation abstract; a personal statement; a narrative discussion of the dissertation; a work plan; two letters of recommendation; and graduate transcript of records. **Deadline:** June 1. **Contact:** 312-274-6526.

6693 ■ Spencer Foundation Research Grants
(All/Grant)

Purpose: To provide funding for research projects that study education in the United States and abroad. **Focus:** General studies. **Qualif.:** Applicants must be principal investigators who are affiliated with a school district, a college or university, a research facility, or a cultural institution. **Criteria:** Recipients are selected based on the provided proposal.

Funds Avail.: $40,000. **To Apply:** Applicants must submit a proposal cover sheet; proposal narrative including the description of the project, a brief summary of the relevant literature, a concise summary of the conceptual framework, research methods, an explanation how the proposed work fits within one or more of the Spencer focus areas or unique contribution of the work, and a clear identification of the principal investigators and role of any supporting researchers; proposed budget; and curriculum vitae. **Contact:** Spencer Foundation at the above address (see entry 6691).

6694 ■ SPIE (The International Society for Optical Engineering)

PO Box 10
Bellingham, WA 98227-0010
Ph: (360)676-3290
Fax: (360)647-1445
Free: 888-504-8171
E-mail: customerservice@spie.org
URL: http://www.spie.org

6695 ■ BACUS Scholarships *(Graduate, Undergraduate/Scholarship)*

Purpose: To provide education assistance to students in field of microlithography. **Focus:** Optical engineering; Optics. **Qualif.:** Applicants must be student members of SPIE; must be enrolled full-time, undergraduate or graduate students in the field of microlithography emphasizing on optical tooling or semiconductor manufacturing technologies. **Criteria:** Applicants are selected based on merit, experiences and education level.

Funds Avail.: $4000. **Number Awarded:** 2. **To Apply:** Applicants must submit a completed scholarship application form (available at the website); a 450-word essay; and two letters of recommender sent separately by the recommender. Application materials must not exceed more than ten pages. **Deadline:** January 11.

Remarks: Scholarships are sponsored by BACUS, the International Technical Group of SPIE dedicated to the advancement of photomask technology. **Contact:** scholarships@spie.org.

6696 ■ Michael Kidger Memorial Scholarships in Optical Design *(Graduate/Scholarship)*

Purpose: To provide education assistance to a student in optical design. **Focus:** Optics; Optical engineering. **Qualif.:** Applicants must be graduate students; must be SPIE members; must be enrolled full-time in an optics, photonics, imaging or optoelectronics program or related discipline at the University of Central Florida. **Criteria:** Applicants are selected based on merit, experiences and education level.

Funds Avail.: $5000. **To Apply:** Applicants must submit a completed scholarship application form (available at the website); a 450-word essay; and two letters of recommendation sent separately by the recommender. Application materials must not exceed more than ten pages. **Deadline:** January 11.

Remarks: Established in honor of Michael John Kidger, a well-respected educator and member of the optical science and engineering community. **Contact:** scholarships@spie.org.

6697 ■ Laser Technology, Engineering and Applications Scholarships *(Graduate, Undergraduate/Scholarship)*

Purpose: To promote education in laser technology, engineering, or applications. **Focus:** Engineering; Technology. **Qualif.:** Applicants must be student members of SPIE; must be enrolled full-time in an optics photonics imaging or optoelectronics program or related discipline at an accredited school; must be in high school or secondary school, undergraduate or post-secondary school, or graduate school. **Criteria:** Applicants are selected based on merit, experiences and education level.

Funds Avail.: $4000. **To Apply:** Applicants must submit a completed scholarship application form (available at the website); a 450-word essay; and two letters of recommendation sent separately by the recommender. Application materials must not exceed more than ten pages. **Deadline:** January 11.

Remarks: Sponsored in part by a gift from the former Forum for Military Applications of Directed Energy. **Contact:** scholarships@spie.org.

6698 ■ D.J. Lovell Scholarships *(Graduate, Undergraduate/Scholarship)*

Purpose: To provide education assistance to a student in optical design. **Focus:** Optics; Optical engineering. **Qualif.:** Applicants must be student members of SPIE; must be enrolled full-time in an optics photonics imaging or optoelectronics program or related discipline at an accredited school; must be in high school or secondary school, undergraduate or post-secondary school, or graduate school. **Criteria:** Applicants are selected based on merit, experiences and education level.

Funds Avail.: $11,000. **To Apply:** Applicants must submit a completed scholarship application form (available at the website); a 450-word essay; and two letters of recommendation sent separately by the recommender. Application materials must not exceed more than ten pages. **Deadline:** January 11.

Remarks: The scholarship is sponsored in part by SPIE with contributions from Labsphere Inc. **Contact:** scholarships@spie.org.

6699 ■ William H. Price Scholarships *(Graduate, Undergraduate/Scholarship)*

Purpose: To provide education assistance to a student in optical design. **Focus:** Optical engineering; Optics. **Qualif.:** Applicants must be student members of SPIE; must be enrolled full-time, undergraduate or graduate in an optical design and engineering. **Criteria:** Applicants are selected based on merit, experiences and education level.

Funds Avail.: $3000. **To Apply:** Applicants must submit a completed scholarship application form (available at the

Awards are arranged alphabetically below their administering organizations

website); a 450-word essay; and two letters of recommendation sent separately by the recommender. Application materials must not exceed more than ten pages. **Deadline:** January 11.

Remarks: Established in 1985 in honor of Bill Price, a well-respected member of the SPIE technical community. **Contact:** scholarships@spie.org.

6700 ■ Student Travel Grants *(Graduate, Undergraduate/Grant)*

Purpose: To supplement travel support for students presenting a paper at any of SPIE's meetings. **Focus:** Optical engineering; Optics. **Qualif.:** Applicants must be fulltime student members of SPIE; must be authors of an accepted paper presented at the conference; and must have not received any SPIE funding in the past 12 months. **Criteria:** The conference chair will indicate if the applicant's paper presentation is necessary to the success of the conference.

Funds Avail.: Covers travel expenses. **To Apply:** Applicant must submit a student travel grant application form (available at the website); a letter of recommendation from faculty advisor or head department; and a written support from the chair of the conference which the paper will be presented.

6701 ■ Spina Bifida Association of America

4590 MacArthur Blvd. NW
Washington, DC 20007
Ph: (202)944-3285
Fax: (202)944-3295
Free: 800-621-3141
E-mail: sbaa@sbaa.org
URL: http://www.sbaa.org

6702 ■ SBA Four-Year Scholarships Program *(Undergraduate/Scholarship)*

Purpose: To assist persons born with Spina Bifida to achieve their full potential through higher education. **Focus:** General studies. **Qualif.:** Applicants must have Spina Bifida (present a physician's statement of disability); must be high school seniors; enrolled in, or accepted by a college or university; must demonstrate financial need. **Criteria:** Recipients are selected based on the committee's review of application materials.

Funds Avail.: $5000. **Number Awarded:** 1. **To Apply:** Scholarship application forms are available at the website. Applicants must file a completed application together with the physician's statement of disability (includes the physician's address and phone number); official school transcript; test scores (SAT, ACT, GRE); acceptance letter by school or college; three recommendation letters, two from faculty members; personal statement about educational goals (3 pages) and send to: SBA, Attn: Scholarship Committee 4590 MacArthur Boulevard, NW Ste. 250, Washington, DC 20007-4226. **Deadline:** March 7.

Remarks: Immediate family members of SBA Board, Scholarship Committee and Staff are not eligible for the awards. **Contact:** Tanya Coogan, tcoogan@sbaa.org.

6703 ■ SBA One-Year Scholarships Program *(Undergraduate/Scholarship)*

Purpose: To assist persons born with Spina Bifida to achieve their full potential through higher education. **Focus:** General studies. **Qualif.:** Applicants must have Spina Bifida (present a physician's statement of disability); must be high school graduates or possess a General Education Development (GED) test; must be enrolled in a four year university, junior college, approved trade, vocational, or business school. **Criteria:** Recipients are selected based on the committee's review of application materials.

Funds Avail.: $2000. **Number Awarded:** 5. **To Apply:** Scholarship application forms are available at the website. Applicants must file a completed application together with the physician's statement of disability (includes the physician's address and phone number); official school transcript; test scores (SAT, ACT, GRE); acceptance letter by school or college; three recommendation letters, two from faculty members; personal statement about educational goals (3 pages) and send to: SBA, Attn: Scholarship Committee 4590 MacArthur Boulevard, NW, Ste. 250, Washington, DC 20007-4226. **Deadline:** March 7.

Remarks: Immediate family members of SBA Board, Scholarship Committee and Staff are not eligible for the awards. **Contact:** Tanya Coogan, tcoogan@sbaa.org.

6704 ■ Stanford University Knight Fellowships

450 Serra Mall, Bldg. 120, Rm. 424
Stanford University
Stanford, CA 94305-2050
Ph: (650)723-4937
Fax: (650)725-6154
E-mail: knight-info@lists.stanford.edu
URL: http://knight.stanford.edu

6705 ■ John S. Knight Fellowships *(Professional Development/Fellowship)*

Purpose: To provide financial assistance for U.S. journalists who have already done first-rate work and who have the potential of reaching the top ranks in their specialties. **Focus:** Journalism. **Qualif.:** Applicants must have at least seven years of full-time professional experience; There are no educational prerequisites; No college degree is required; must be currently working full-time as journalists: employees of newspapers, wire services, television or radio news departments, Web sites, magazines covering news, commentary, or public affairs, and full-time freelancers. Eligible journalists include those who write or edit news, commentary, or editorials; critics and reviewers, photojournalists, editorial cartoonists and supervising editors, anchors, and producers; journalism business and management executives whose decisions affect editorial quality - for example, publishers, general managers, news directors and station managers - or who are likely to be in such positions are also eligible. Such applicants must be committed to improving editorial quality in their news organizations, and not merely in improving a particular business skill or specialty. **Criteria:** Applicants will be evaluated by three reviewers - the Program Director, the Deputy Director, and a third experienced journalist.

Funds Avail.: $55,000. **Number Awarded:** 12. **To Apply:** Applicants must submit written essays: an intellectual autobiography, and a statement of how they propose to spend the fellowship year, indicating specific areas of study; must submit a letter from their employer endorsing their application and granting a leave of absence if chosen for a fellowship. Three letters of recommendation, including one from the applicant's immediate supervisor, are required as well as work samples. **Deadline:** February 1.

6706 ■ Stark Community Foundation

400 Market Ave. N, Ste. 200
Canton, OH 44702-2107

Awards are arranged alphabetically below their administering organizations

Ph: (330)454-3426
Fax: (330)454-5855
URL: http://www.starkcommunityfoundation.org

6707 ■ Wayne D. Ackerman Family Scholarship Fund *(Undergraduate/Scholarship)*

Purpose: To provide scholarship assistance to qualified individuals who want to pursue their studies. **Focus:** General studies. **Qualif.:** Applicants must be senior students attending high school in Stark County, OH; must be enrolled as full-time students; must have GPA of at least 3.0 on 4.0 scale; must demonstrate outstanding involvement both in academics and extracurricular activities; must have been accepted into a four-year college or university. **Criteria:** Selection of applicants will be based on the Scholarship selection criteria.

Funds Avail.: No specific amount. **To Apply:** Application forms are available online and must be sent to Stark Community Foundation, 400 Market Ave. N, Ste. 200, Canton, OH 44702. **Deadline:** May 1.

6708 ■ American Guild of Organists, Canton Chapter Charitable Fund *(Undergraduate/Scholarship)*

Purpose: To provide scholarship assistance to qualified individuals who want to pursue their studies. **Focus:** Music. **Qualif.:** Applicants must be students residing in Stark County, without regard to gender, race, color, creed or nationality who are pursuing a four-year bachelor degree program at an accredited college or university in music with a major in instrument; must show an evidence of competent technique and musicianship. **Criteria:** Selection of applicants will be based on the scholarship selection criteria.

Funds Avail.: No specific amount. **To Apply:** Application forms are available online. Applicants must submit a letters of reference and a submitted tape and/or audition including one Bach work or movement, one French work or movement, and a third work of applicant's choice. Application form and requirements must be sent to Mr. Greg L. Hollinger, Treas. at 9264 Shipton Circle NW, North Canton, OH 44720. **Deadline:** April 15.

6709 ■ Joan Blend Scholarship Fund *(Undergraduate/Scholarship)*

Purpose: To provide scholarship assistance to qualified individuals who want to pursue their studies. **Focus:** Nursing. **Qualif.:** Applicants must be attending or planning to attend university or nursing school offering a Registered Nursing Degree; must have GPA of 2.5 or higher; must demonstrate financial need. **Criteria:** Recipients are selected based on academic standing and financial need.

Funds Avail.: No specific amount. **To Apply:** Applicants must complete and submit the application form and other supporting documents to Mr. Dan Blend, 1684 Markley St. NW N. Canton, OH 44720. **Deadline:** April 15.

6710 ■ Sheriff W. Bruce Umpleby Law Enforcement Scholarship Fund *(Undergraduate/Scholarship)*

Purpose: To provide scholarship assistance to qualified individuals who want to pursue their studies. **Focus:** Law enforcement. **Qualif.:** Applicants must be students who are seniors attending high school either inside or outside Stark County, who will graduate with their class, or are graduates of a high school either inside or outside Stark County; must be enrolled as full-time students; must have achieved cumulative GPA of at least 3.0 on a 4.0 scale; must have demonstrated outstanding involvement both in academics and extra curricular activities; must have been accepted, into a post secondary institution with plans to major in law enforcement. **Criteria:** Recipient will be selected based on academic standing and extracurricular activities.

Funds Avail.: No specific amount. **To Apply:** Applicants must submit a written statement (at least 2 paragraphs) and three letters of recommendations from their teacher and/or teacher. Application form and other supporting documents must be sent to Stark Community Foundation, 400 Market Ave. N, Ste. 200, Canton, OH 44702. **Deadline:** March 15.

6711 ■ Harry D. Callahan Educational Trust *(Undergraduate/Scholarship)*

Purpose: To provide scholarship assistance to qualified individuals who want to pursue their studies. **Focus:** General studies. **Qualif.:** Applicants must be students residing in Stark County who are pursuing a two-year or four-year college degree at an accredited school within approximately 150 miles of Canton; must have participation in athletics, government and other extracurricular and community activities; and must demonstrate leadership qualities. **Criteria:** Recipients will be selected based on financial need and scholastic ability.

Funds Avail.: No specific amount. **To Apply:** Applicants must submit completed application form and other supporting documents to Catholic Youth Council, 1330 Park Ave., NW, Canton, OH 44708. **Deadline:** April 30. **Contact:** Kris Baum.

6712 ■ George H. and Anna Casper Fund *(Undergraduate/Scholarship)*

Purpose: To provide scholarship assistance to qualified individuals who want to pursue their studies. **Focus:** General studies. **Qualif.:** Applicants must be students residing in Stark County; must be attending college full or part-time; must demonstrate financial need and academic excellence. **Criteria:** Recipients will be selected based on financial need and academic standing.

Funds Avail.: No specific amount. **To Apply:** Applicants must complete and submit the application form and requirements to Robert Martelet, Sec., 836 Market Ave. N, Canton, OH 44702. **Deadline:** May 20.

6713 ■ Ruth M. Cogan Scholarship Fund *(Undergraduate/Scholarship)*

Purpose: To provide scholarship assistance to qualified applicants from Stark County, Ohio. **Focus:** Music. **Qualif.:** Applicants must be high school students and present college students with an interest in studying music, have an inner feeling for music and whose lives have reflected the spiritual qualities, depth, understanding and love. **Criteria:** Recipients will be selected based on financial need and scholastic ability.

Funds Avail.: Amount of award will be determined by the Selection committee. **To Apply:** Applicants must complete the application form available online and must be sent to Stark Community Foundation, 400 Market Ave. N, Ste. 200, Canton, OH 44702. **Deadline:** April 15.

6714 ■ Julio C. Diaz Memorial Scholarship Fund *(Undergraduate/Scholarship)*

Purpose: To provide scholarship assistance to qualified individuals who want to pursue their studies. **Focus:**

Awards are arranged alphabetically below their administering organizations

General studies. **Qualif.:** Applicants must be attending or who have been accepted at St. Thomas Aquinas High School; must have GPA of at least 3.0 on a 4.0 scale. **Criteria:** Recipients are selected based on the following criteria: (1) Completion of scholarship application; (2) Demonstration of financial need; (3) Achievement of minimum cumulative GPA of at least 3.0 on a 4.0 scale; (4) Demonstration of involvement in extracurricular activities or community service project; (5) Demonstration of commitment to anti-tobacco use. Consideration will be given to qualified candidates of Hispanic descent.

Funds Avail.: No specific amount. **To Apply:** Applicants must have and completed the application form and two letters of recommendation from the following: teacher, school administrators, or guidance counselors. Application form and requirements must be sent to St. Thomas Aquinas High School, Victoria Frustaci/Business Office, 2121 Reno Dr., Louisville, OH 44641. **Deadline:** May 1.

6715 ■ Rob Digiacomo Scholarship Fund
(Undergraduate/Scholarship)

Purpose: To provide scholarship assistance to qualified individuals who want to pursue their studies. **Focus:** General studies. **Qualif.:** Applicants must be graduating seniors residing at the Lake Local School District; must demonstrate commitment to excellence in academic and athletic accomplishments; must have exceptional moral and personal characteristics; must have leadership skills; and must demonstrate devotion to family. **Criteria:** Recipients will be selected based on financial need and scholastic ability.

Funds Avail.: $600. **Number Awarded:** 1. **To Apply:** Applicants must complete the application form available online and must be sent to Edmond J. DiGiacomo and Sandra E. DiGiacomo, 755 Oneida Trail, Hartville, OH 44632. **Deadline:** April 15.

6716 ■ Emergency Medicine Physician Scholarships for Health Information Management Program *(Undergraduate/Scholarship)*

Purpose: To provide scholarship assistance to qualified individuals who want to pursue their studies. **Focus:** Health education. **Qualif.:** Applicants must be students beginning the second year of study at Stark State College and enrolled full time in the Health Information Management Technology program; must have minimum GPA of 3.0 on a 4.0 scale; must complete his/her education at the conclusion of spring semester; must have interview with the EMP Manager of Coding and Senior Executives. **Criteria:** Recipients will be selected based on the scholarship selection criteria.

Funds Avail.: No specific amount. **To Apply:** Applicants must submit an employment history, attitude and work ethic together with the application form to EMP Scholarship Program, Emergency Medicine Physicians, 4535 Dressler Rd. NW, Canton, OH 44718. **Deadline:** July 27.

6717 ■ Emergency Medicine Physicians Scholarship Fund for Non-Physician Employee Dependents *(Undergraduate/Scholarship)*

Purpose: To provide scholarship assistance to qualified individuals who want to pursue their studies. **Focus:** General studies. **Qualif.:** Applicants must be dependent children of non-physician employees of Emergency Medicine Physicians, Inc. who are pursuing or applying for college level studies. **Criteria:** Selection of applicant must be based on academic performance, extracurricular activities, and leadership and community activities or services.

Funds Avail.: $2,500-$5,000. **Number Awarded:** 2. **To Apply:** Applicants must submit two letters of recommendation and an educational or professional essay; must complete the application form together with the application requirements to EMP Scholarship Program, Emergency Medicine Physicians 4535 Dressler Rd. NW, Canton, OH 44718. **Deadline:** August 10.

6718 ■ Jack B. Fisher Scholarship Fund
(Undergraduate/Scholarship)

Purpose: To provide scholarship assistance to qualified individuals who want to pursue their studies. **Focus:** Fisheries sciences/management. **Qualif.:** Applicants must be graduate of a Stark County High school and current employees of Fisher Foods in good standing (If employed during high school, a minimum of one year of employment is required. If employed after graduation from high school, a minimum of 2 years of employment is required); must have above average accomplishment in high school; must demonstrate good moral and personal characteristics. **Criteria:** Recipients will be selected based on the scholarship selection criteria.

Funds Avail.: $250. **Number Awarded:** 4. **To Apply:** Applicants must submit a recommendation letter from a store manager, and application form to Fisher Foods Marketing, Inc. 4855 Frank Rd. NW N, Canton, OH 44720. **Deadline:** July 23.

6719 ■ Alice J. Foit Scholarships
(Undergraduate/Scholarship)

Purpose: To provide scholarship assistance to qualified individuals who want to pursue their studies. **Focus:** General Studies. **Qualif.:** Applicants must be high school graduates or seniors residing in Carroll County, German Township, Harrison County, OH; must be enrolled as full time students; must have achieved high school cumulative GPA of at least 2.5 on a 4.0 scale, and if attending college a cumulative GPA of at least 2.0 on a 4.0 scale; must have demonstrated involvement, both in extracurricular activities or community and religious activities; must have been accepted into a two or four year college on university program leading to a degree; must intend to live in or work in either Carroll or Harrison County, OH for a minimum of two year after completion of their education. **Criteria:** Selection of applicants will be based on financial need and potential.

Funds Avail.: No specific amount. **To Apply:** Applicants must complete and submit the application form and requirements to Richard Lee Rumbaugh, 63 E Main St., Carrollton, OH 44615. **Deadline:** November.

6720 ■ Thomas W. Gallagher Scholarship Fund
(Undergraduate/Scholarship)

Purpose: To provide scholarship assistance to qualified individuals who want to pursue their studies. **Focus:** Pharmacy. **Qualif.:** Applicants must be seniors attending Minerva High School, Minerva, OH or will be graduated with his/her class; must be full-time students who have been accepted into a four-year college or university to pursue a degree in pharmacy; must be full-time students who have been accepted into a four-year college or university to study in the field of science (if no students pursuing a degree in pharmacy have applied). **Criteria:** Consideration will be given to students pursuing a degree in pharmacy.

Funds Avail.: No specific amount. **To Apply:** Applicants

must complete and submit the application form available online at Guidance High School, 501 Almeda Ave., Minerva, OH 44657. **Deadline:** April 10.

6721 ■ David A. and Pamela A. Gault Charitable Fund *(Undergraduate/Scholarship)*

Purpose: To provide scholarship assistance to qualified individuals who want to pursue their studies. **Focus:** General studies. **Qualif.:** Applicants must be graduates of Stark County High School with residency in Stark County for a minimum of 5 years; must be enrolled at Otterbein College or Walsh University, pursuing a graduate or undergraduate degree in business; must have a minimum of 2.5 GPA on a 4.0 scale. **Criteria:** Recipients will be selected based on the scholarship selection criteria.

Funds Avail.: No specific amount. **Number Awarded:** 2. **To Apply:** Applicants must have a recommendation letter by Otterbein College or Walsh University. Application forms are available online and must be sent to Stark Community Foundation, 400 market Ave. N, Canton, OH 44702. **Deadline:** April 1.

6722 ■ Margaret S. Gilbert Scholarship Fund *(Undergraduate/Scholarship)*

Purpose: To provide scholarship assistance to qualified individuals who want to pursue their studies. **Focus:** Natural sciences; Mathematics and mathematical sciences; History. **Qualif.:** Applicants must be Stark County public high school female graduates who attend or will attend Oberlin College; must have a major in one of the natural sciences, mathematics, or history; must have extracurricular activities, especially those demonstrating interest in science; must demonstrate diligent effort, responsibility and financial need. **Criteria:** Recipients will be selected based on the scholarship selection criteria.

Funds Avail.: $37,000. **Number Awarded:** 2. **To Apply:** Applicants must have academic record; must submit the application form and requirements at 400 Market Ave. N, Ste. 200, Canton, OH 44702. **Deadline:** May 1.

6723 ■ James H. and Shirley L. Green Scholarship Fund *(Undergraduate/Scholarship)*

Purpose: To provide scholarship assistance to qualified individuals who want to pursue their studies. **Focus:** General studies. **Qualif.:** Applicants must be seniors attending Canton South High School, Canton, OH; must have been accepted into a two-year or four-year college or university; must demonstrate financial need. **Criteria:** Selection of applicants will be based on the scholarship selection criteria.

Funds Avail.: No specific amount. **To Apply:** Application forms are available online and must be sent to Barbara Tscholl, Canton South High School, 600 Faircrest St. SE, Canton OH 44707. **Deadline:** April 1.

6724 ■ Velma Shotwell Griffin Memorial Scholarship Fund *(Undergraduate/Scholarship)*

Purpose: To provide scholarship assistance to qualified individuals who want to pursue their studies. **Focus:** History; Writing; Music. **Qualif.:** Applicants must be graduates of Conotton Valley High School or Carrollton High School; must be planning to enroll, or currently enrolled, at an accredited college or university to pursue further education in the following fields: (1) History; (2) Writing, not limited to, English Journalism, Language Arts, Communications and programs in Mass Media; (3) Music, not limited to vocal music, instrumental music, music history, music education, and music performance; (4) Any other program or field of study approved by the selection committee. **Criteria:** Recipients will be selected based on the following criteria: (1) Academic merit; (2) Participation in extracurricular school and civic activities related to History, Writing or Music, good moral and personal characteristics; (3) Good moral and personal characteristics, including integrity and an interest in their communities; (4) Demonstrated interest in History, Writing or Music and commitment to the further study of these subject; (5) Demonstrate financial need.

Funds Avail.: $1,000. **Number Awarded:** 1. **To Apply:** Applicants must submit completed application form and are advised to contact Carrollton High School Guidance Office, Connotton Valley High School Guidance Office. **Deadline:** April 28.

6725 ■ Dr. James H. Heckaman Memorial Scholarship Fund *(Undergraduate/Scholarship)*

Purpose: To provide scholarship assistance to qualified individuals who want to pursue their studies. **Focus:** General studies. **Qualif.:** Applicants must be Hoover High School graduating seniors; must have above average accomplishment in high school; must have demonstrated financial need; must be planning to a four-year degree program in any field of study; must demonstrate good moral and personal characteristics. **Criteria:** Selection of applicants will be based on the scholarship selection criteria.

Funds Avail.: No specific amount. **To Apply:** Application forms are available online and must be sent to Barbara Tarantino, Dir. of Guidance, Hoover Canton, OH 44720.

6726 ■ Dale O. Heimberger CRNA Memorial Scholarship Fund *(Graduate/Scholarship)*

Purpose: To provide scholarship assistance to qualified individuals who want to pursue their studies. **Focus:** Anesthesiology. **Qualif.:** Applicants must be accepted into the University of Akron, College of Nursing-Graduate Anesthesia Program; must have scholastic aptitude; must demonstrate financial need. **Criteria:** Selection of applicants will be based on financial need and academic excellence.

Funds Avail.: Amount of awards will be determined by the Selection Committee. **To Apply:** Applicants must complete and submit the application form and requirements to University of Akron, Nurse-Anesthesia Program, 209 Carroll St., Akron, OH 44325-3701. **Deadline:** November 15.

6727 ■ Raymond T. Hoge Scholarship Fund *(Undergraduate/Scholarship)*

Purpose: To provide scholarship assistance to qualified individuals who want to pursue their studies. **Focus:** Business; Education. **Qualif.:** Applicants must be graduating senior members of Perry High School or alumni who plan to attend an institution of higher learning; must be in good academic standing; must be planning to pursue a degree in the field of business or education; must demonstrate financial need. **Criteria:** Recipients will be selected based on the scholarship selection criteria; community service; and work experience.

Funds Avail.: No specific amount. **To Apply:** Applicants must complete and submit the application form at Perry High School Guidance Office, 3737 13th St. SW, Massillon, OH 44646. **Deadline:** April 15.

6728 ■ Minnie Hopkins Memorial Scholarship Fund of Lathrop/Compton School *(Undergraduate/Scholarship)*

Purpose: To provide scholarship assistance to qualified individuals who want to pursue their studies. **Focus:** General studies. **Qualif.:** Applicants must have graduated from Lathrop/Compton School and attended Lathrop/Compton for at least three years; must have graduated from Stark County public high school and been accepted into a college, university, or technical school; must have leadership skills; must have academic ability and achievement; must have initiative and motivation; must demonstrate financial need. **Criteria:** Recipients will be selected based on scholarship selection criteria.

Funds Avail.: No specific amount. **To Apply:** Applicants must provide statement about his/ her family background. Application form and requirements must be sent to Stark Community Foundation, 400 Market Ave. N, Ste. 200, Canton, OH 44702. **Deadline:** April 15.

6729 ■ Judge and Mrs. Robert D. Horowitz Legal Scholarship Fund *(Graduate/Scholarship)*

Purpose: To provide scholarship assistance to qualified individuals who want to pursue their studies. **Focus:** Paralegal studies. **Qualif.:** Applicants must be graduate of high school in Stark, Columbiana, Carroll, Tuscarawas, Wayne or Holmes County, OH; must be enrolled or accepted as full-time or parttime students in a doctorate program; must demonstrate public service through volunteer activities or work experience; must demonstrate financial need. **Criteria:** Selection of applicants will be based on the scholarship application criteria.

Funds Avail.: No specific amount. **To Apply:** Applicants must have at least two letter of reference documenting their public service and/or volunteer activities and have completed a short essay on their personal public service and/or volunteer experience; must complete and submit the application form and requirements to Jennifer L. Santuk, 19 Andrea Circle Needham, MA 02494. **Deadline:** March 24.

6730 ■ Virginia C. Jack and Ralph L. Jack Scholarships *(Undergraduate/Scholarship)*

Purpose: To provide scholarship assistance to qualified individuals who want to pursue their studies. **Focus:** Vocational-technical education; Nursing. **Qualif.:** Applicants must be Stark County residents; must be admitted to technical school, college or university, or school of nursing; must be full or part time students; must be traditional or non-traditional students; must have 2.50 or higher GPA on a 4.0 scale. **Criteria:** Selection of applicants will be based on financial need and academic excellence.

Funds Avail.: $2,000. **To Apply:** Applicants must submit two letters of recommendation and essay. Application form and other supporting documents must be sent to Stark Community Foundation, 400 Market Ave. N, Ste. 200, Canton, OH 44702. **Deadline:** April 1.

6731 ■ Jackson High School Alumni Scholarship Fund *(Undergraduate/Scholarship)*

Purpose: To provide scholarship assistance to qualified individuals who want to pursue their studies. **Focus:** General studies. **Qualif.:** Applicants must be graduating seniors at Jackson High School or Jackson High School graduates who are currently enrolled as full-time college students; must have minimum GPA of 2.5 or above. **Criteria:** Selection of applicants will be based on their demonstration of community service, involvement in extracurricular activities, academic standing, and personal interview with Selection Committee.

Funds Avail.: No specific amount. **To Apply:** Application forms are available online and must be sent to Mr. Dan Headland, 5585 Stoney Ridge Rd., Canton, OH 44718. **Deadline:** April.

6732 ■ Junior Achievement of East Central Ohio, Inc. Scholarship Fund *(Undergraduate/Scholarship)*

Purpose: To provide scholarship assistance to qualified individuals who want to pursue their studies. **Focus:** General studies. **Qualif.:** Applicants must be high school seniors who have participated in Junior Achievement of Stark County. **Criteria:** Recipients will be selected based on the following criteria: (1) Participation in J.A.; (2) Demonstrated support of free enterprise system; (3) Academic achievement; (4) Extracurricular activities; (5) Service to school and community; (6) Service to school and community; (7) Anticipated ability to succeed in college.

Funds Avail.: No specific amount. **To Apply:** Applicants must complete and submit the application form and other supporting documents to Jody L. Levitt, JA of East Central Ohio, Inc., 4353 Executive Circle NW, Canton, OH 44718. **Deadline:** March 1.

6733 ■ David A. Kaiser Memorial Scholarship Fund *(Undergraduate/Scholarship)*

Purpose: To provide scholarship assistance to qualified individuals who want to pursue their studies. **Focus:** General studies. **Qualif.:** Applicants must be fulltime students in high school in the Canton City School District; must be accepted into an accredited college or university; must be planning to pursue a four-year degree. **Criteria:** Selection of applicants will be based on the following criteria: (1) Minimum GPA of 3.8; (2) Personal integrity; (3) Evidence of leadership skills; (4) participation in extracurricular activities.

Funds Avail.: $3,000. **To Apply:** Application forms are available online at www.starkcommunityfoundation.org or for more information applicants are advice to contact the foundation at Stark Community Foundation, 400 Market Ave. N, Ste. 200, Canton, OH 44702. **Deadline:** March 15.

6734 ■ Louise Nader Khourey/Kappa Delta Pi Scholarships *(Undergraduate/Scholarship)*

Purpose: To provide scholarship assistance to qualified individuals who want to pursue their studies. **Focus:** Education; Foreign languages. **Qualif.:** Applicants must be graduating seniors from Stark County high schools who plan to attend an institution of higher learning; must be planning to pursue a degree in the field of education. **Criteria:** Priority will be given to applicants who aspire toward a degree in Foreign Language Education. Recipients will be selected based on their personal traits, leadership qualities and academic goals consistent with the standard of Kappa Delta Pi.

Funds Avail.: No specific amount. **To Apply:** Applicants must submit completed application forms and are advised to visit the High School Guidance Counselor. **Deadline:** January.

6735 ■ Samuel Krugliak Legal Scholarship Fund *(Graduate/Scholarship)*

Purpose: To provide scholarship assistance to qualified individuals who want to pursue their studies. **Focus:**

Awards are arranged alphabetically below their administering organizations

Paralegal studies. **Qualif.:** Applicants must be currently enrolled and attending law school accredited by the American Bar Association or have enrolled and will be attending in the fall; must have shown an active commitment to their community; must display strong academic achievement; must reside or have formerly resided in the Stark, Wayne, Carroll, Holmes, Summit, Tuscarawas, Columbiana, or Mahoning Counties when not attending law school; must desire to pursue the practice of law in the Stark County Region. **Criteria:** Selection of applicants will be based on the scholarship application criteria.

Funds Avail.: No specific amount. **To Apply:** Applicants must attach transcript of records and resume. Application form and other supporting documents must be submitted to Krugliak, Wilkins, Griffiths & Dougherty Co., L.P.A. 4475 Munson St. NW, Canton, OH 44735-6963. **Deadline:** April 15.

6736 ■ Lake Dollars for Scholars Endowment Fund *(Undergraduate/Scholarship)*

Purpose: To provide scholarship assistance to qualified individuals who want to pursue their studies. **Focus:** Education, Vocational-technical; Nursing. **Qualif.:** Applicants must be graduating seniors residing within the boundaries of the Lake Local District, Lake Township, and Stark County, OH; must have been accepted into a two-year or four-year college or university, nursing school, or other post high school vocational education program; must meet the requirements of the application form provided by Lake Dollars For Scholars. **Criteria:** Selection of applicants will be based on the scholarship application criteria.

Funds Avail.: No specific amount. **To Apply:** Applicants must submit completed application form and are advised to contact the Lake High School Guidance Office at 330877-4285. **Deadline:** March 20.

6737 ■ Jay C. and B. Nadine Leggett Charitable Scholarship Fund *(Undergraduate/Scholarship)*

Purpose: To assist qualified individuals who want to pursue their studies. **Focus:** General studies. **Qualif.:** Applicants must be graduates of Conotton Valley High School or high school seniors who applied to and have been accepted by college, university, or recognized educational institution of higher learning, or presently enrolled in college. **Criteria:** Recipients are selected based on academic excellence and financial need.

Funds Avail.: No specific amount. **To Apply:** Applicants must be complete and submit the application form and requirements to Judson Lada, Guidance Counselor, Conotton Valley High School, 7205 Cumberland Rd. SW, Bowerston, OH 44695. **Deadline:** April 1.

6738 ■ Lillian Grace Mahan Scholarship Fund *(Undergraduate/Scholarship)*

Purpose: To provide scholarship assistance to qualified individuals who want to pursue their studies. **Focus:** Library and archival sciences. **Qualif.:** Applicants must be graduate or undergraduate students of library science who are residents of Stark County; must have an outstanding academic performance and aptitude and/or are in need of financial assistance to pursue a degree in library science; must have demonstrated academic performance record and other activities. **Criteria:** Selection of applicants will be based on the following criteria.

Funds Avail.: $4,895. **Number Awarded:** 8. **To Apply:** Application forms are available online and must be sent to Canton Student Loan Foundation, 4974 Higbee Ave. NW, Canton, OH 44718. **Deadline:** April 1.

6739 ■ Manzer-Keener-Wefler Scholarships *(Undergraduate/Scholarship)*

Purpose: To provide scholarship assistance to qualified individuals who want to pursue their studies. **Focus:** Photography; Visual arts. **Qualif.:** Applicants must have been accepted by, or are currently attending, a two-year or four-year college or university or art institute within the United States; that their chosen field of study is in the field of or related to photography or visual arts; either seniors attending a high school in Stark County, OH, or counties contiguous to Stark, who will graduate the year the scholarship is awarded or college undergraduate students originally from Stark County, OH, or counties contiguous to Stark, who are currently attending a two-year or four-year college or university or art institute full time or non-traditional college students originally from Stark County, OH, or counties contiguous to Stark, who are currently attending a two-year or four-year college or university or art institute part-time; and first time applicants must have a minimum GPA of at least 2.5 on a 4.0. **Criteria:** Recipients are selected based on financial need; and demonstrated involvement both in academics and extracurricular activities related to their chosen field of study.

Funds Avail.: No specific amount. **To Apply:** Applicants must submit a two letters of recommendation letter. Application from and other supporting documents must be sent to Stark Community Foundation, 400 Market Ave. N, Ste. 200, Canton, OH 44702. **Deadline:** May 1.

6740 ■ Markley Family Scholarship Fund *(Undergraduate/Scholarship)*

Purpose: To provide scholarship assistance to qualified individuals who want to pursue their studies. **Focus:** General studies. **Qualif.:** Applicants must be full time undergraduate students of Walsh University, North Canton, OH. **Criteria:** Applicants will be selected based on academic performance and financial need.

Funds Avail.: No specific amount. **To Apply:** Applicants must complete and submit the application form to Assistant Director of Financial Aid, Walsh University, 2020 Easton NW, North Canton, OH 44720. **Deadline:** April 1.

6741 ■ Bill McCarthy Scout Scholarship Fund *(Undergraduate/Scholarship)*

Purpose: To provide scholarship assistance to qualified individuals who want to pursue their studies. **Focus:** General studies. **Qualif.:** Applicants must be male students who are or have been Boy Scouts; having belonged to a troop in the Tuslaw District; and who have attained at least the rank of a First Class Scout; and who ranks at least among the highest ten boys in his graduating class in high school. **Criteria:** Recipients will be selected based on the scholarship selection criteria.

Funds Avail.: No specific amount. **To Apply:** Applicants must complete and submit the application requirements to Mr. Andy McGeee, Tuslaw High School Guidance Counselor, 1847 Manchester NW, Massillon, OH 44647. **Deadline:** April 1.

6742 ■ Sanders J. Mestel Legal Scholarship Fund *(Undergraduate/Scholarship)*

Purpose: To provide scholarship assistance to qualified individuals who want to pursue their studies. **Focus:** Law.

Qualif.: Applicants must be law students whose residence is in Stark County. **Criteria:** Selection of applicants will be based on financial need, academic standing and written statement.

Funds Avail.: No specific amount. **To Apply:** Applicants must submit written statement of 250-300 words by the applicant indicating his/her special interest, extracurricular activities and future career aspirations in law. Application form and other supporting documents must be sent to Stark Community Foundation, 400 Market Ave. N, Canton, OH 44702. **Deadline:** May 1.

6743 ■ Harry Mestel Memorial Accounting Scholarship Fund *(Undergraduate/Scholarship)*

Purpose: To provide scholarship assistance to qualified individuals who want to pursue their studies. **Focus:** Accounting. **Qualif.:** Applicants must be accounting students enrolled in an Ohio college or university in their final year, in pursuit of a Bachelor of Science in Accounting Degree, whose permanent address is in Stark County; must demonstrate financial need; must demonstrate involvement in community activities; must have achieved a cumulative GPA of at least 3.0 on a 4.0 scale. **Criteria:** Selection of applicant will be based on financial need and academic standing.

Funds Avail.: No specific amount. **To Apply:** Applicants must complete and submit the application form and requirements to Stark Community Foundation, 400 Market Ave. N, Canton, OH 44702. **Deadline:** May 1.

6744 ■ John G. and Betty J. Mick Scholarship Fund *(Undergraduate/Scholarship)*

Purpose: To provide scholarship assistance to qualified individuals who want to pursue their studies. **Focus:** Engineering. **Qualif.:** Applicants must be seniors attending a high school in Stark County, OH; must have been accepted as a full-time students in Stark State College of Technology engineering Program for a two year degree program which will also transfer to a four year degree program at another university at the discretion of the students; must have been accepted as full-time students into the Engineering program at any university or college in the State of Ohio; nontraditional students furthering their education after entering the workforce will be considered secondarily; must have cumulative GPA of at least 2.0 on a 4.0 scale. **Criteria:** Recipients will be selected based on academic achievement, personal interview, and recommendation by at least one of their teachers, counselors, or principals.

Funds Avail.: No specific amount. **To Apply:** Applicants must complete and submit the application form and requirements to Stark Community Foundation, 400 Market Ave. N, Ste. 200, Canton, OH 44702. **Deadline:** April 15.

6745 ■ Fizz and Dutch Miller Scholarship Fund *(Undergraduate/Scholarship)*

Purpose: To provide scholarship assistance to qualified individuals who want to pursue their studies. **Focus:** Vocational-technical education; Nursing. **Qualif.:** Applicants must be graduates of Strasburg High School or current residents of Strasburg; must have been admitted to and enrolled in a college, university, technical school, vocational school or nursing school; must demonstrate participation in school and community activities; must demonstrate good citizenship; must demonstrate financial assistance to pursue the best level of education. **Criteria:** Selection of applicants will be based on the criteria of the Scholarship Selection Committee.

Funds Avail.: No specific amount. **To Apply:** Applicants must submit two letters of reference. Application form and other supporting documents must be sent to The Strasburg High School Guidance Office. **Deadline:** May 10.

6746 ■ Lt. Colonel Robert G. Moreland Vocational/Technical Fund *(Undergraduate/Scholarship)*

Purpose: To provide scholarship assistance to qualified individuals who want to pursue their studies. **Focus:** Education, Vocational-technical. **Qualif.:** Applicants must be residents of Stark County, OH; must be graduating high school seniors; must be older students desiring vocational/technical training or retraining GED certificate; must intend to pursue vocational or technical education or training in a school or college within the State of Ohio; must demonstrate financial assistance. **Criteria:** Recipients will be selected based on the Scholarship Selection Committee.

Funds Avail.: No specific amount. **To Apply:** Applicants must complete and submit the application form and requirements to Lt. Colonel Robert G. Moreland Scholarship, Stark Community Foundation, 400 Market Ave. N, Ste. 200, Canton, OH 44702-2107. **Deadline:** April 10.

6747 ■ Notre Dame Club of Canton Scholarships *(Undergraduate/Scholarship)*

Purpose: To provide scholarship assistance to qualified individuals who want to pursue their studies. **Focus:** General studies. **Qualif.:** Applicants must be students who have attended Stork County or Tuscarawas County, Ohio High School, Dalton High School, or Orville High School in Wayne County, Ohio, or Central Kidron Christian School in Kidron, OH; must have GPA of at least 3.0 on a 4.0 scale while in high school; must demonstrate outstanding involvement both in academics and extracurricular activities; must have been accepted to attend the University of Notre Dame, Notre Dame, Indiana. **Criteria:** Recipients will be selected based on academic standing and extracurricular activities.

Funds Avail.: No specific amount. **To Apply:** Applicants must complete and submit the application form to Stark Community Foundation, 400 Market Ave. N, Ste. 200, Canton, OH 44702. **Deadline:** June 15.

6748 ■ O'Jays Scholarship Fund *(Undergraduate/Scholarship)*

Purpose: To provide scholarship assistance to qualified individuals who want to pursue their studies. **Focus:** General studies. **Qualif.:** Applicants must be seniors attending high school in Stark County who will graduate the year the scholarship is awarded, or residents of Stark County who have previously attained high school diploma or Graduate Equivalency Diploma; must be accepted by or presently attending a two-year college or university, nursing school, or other post high school vocational educational program; must have cumulative GPA of 2.5 on a 4.0 scale; must demonstrate extracurricular activities or community activities; must demonstrate financial need. **Criteria:** Selection of applicants will be based on the scholarship application criteria.

Funds Avail.: No specific amount. **To Apply:** Applicants must complete and submit the application form to Stark Community Foundation, 400 Market Ave. N, Ste. 200, Canton, OH 44702. **Deadline:** April 30.

6749 ■ Perry Township School Memorial Scholarship Fund *(Undergraduate/Scholarship)*

Purpose: To provide scholarship assistance to qualified individuals who want to pursue their studies. **Focus:**

General studies. **Qualif.:** Applicants must be high school graduates or high school seniors who have permanent residency in Perry Township, Carroll County, OH or who have permanent residency on the date they began their post high school education; must have been accepted at and planning to enroll, or are currently enrolled, at an accredited college, university, or technical school with at least a two year course of study to pursue further education; must have good moral and personal characteristics; must demonstrate involvement in community and religious activities; must demonstrate financial need. **Criteria:** Recipients will be selected by the criteria of the Scholarship Selection Committee.

Funds Avail.: No specific amount. **To Apply:** Applicants must submit completed application form and are advice to contact Carrollton High School Guidance Office. **Deadline:** March 14.

6750 ■ August M. Rocco Scholarship Fund
(Undergraduate/Scholarship)

Purpose: To provide scholarship assistance to qualified individuals who want to pursue their studies. **Focus:** General studies. **Qualif.:** Applicants must be male or female graduates of Canton Central Catholic High School or St. Thomas Aquinas High School and of the Catholic faith; must be accepted to attend college at University of Notre Dame, South Bend, IN; must have good scholastic record and character traits. **Criteria:** Selection of applicants will be based on scholastic ability and character traits.

Funds Avail.: No specific amount. **To Apply:** Applicants must complete and submit the application form and other supporting documents to Stark Community Foundation, 400 Market Ave. N, Canton, OH 44702. **Deadline:** June 5.

6751 ■ Aaron Seesan Memorial Scholarship Fund *(Graduate/Scholarship)*

Purpose: To provide scholarship assistance to qualified individuals who want to pursue their studies. **Focus:** General studies. **Qualif.:** Applicants must be graduating seniors from Massillon Washington High School and any other Stark County High Schools; must demonstrate financial need; must have minimum 3.0 cumulative GPA on a 4.0 scale; must demonstrate an involvement in extracurricular activities or community service. **Criteria:** Selection of applicants will be based on the scholarship selection criteria.

Funds Avail.: No specific amount. **To Apply:** Applicants must submit an essay and letter of recommendation from the following: one from school personnel and one from outside source such as employer, community service organization, church official. Application form and requirements must be sent to Massillon Washington High School, One Paul E. Brown Dr. SE, Massillon, OH 44646. **Deadline:** April 15.

6752 ■ Don and Madalyn Sickafoose Educational Trust *(Undergraduate/Scholarship)*

Purpose: To provide scholarship assistance to qualified individuals who want to pursue their studies. **Focus:** General studies. **Qualif.:** Applicants must be students living in Southeastern Stark County, Northwestern Carroll County and Northern Tuscarawas County which would include the following district: Brown Local, Canton Local, Osnaburg Local, Fairless Local, Sandy Valley, Tusky Valley and Carrollton Exempted Village. **Criteria:** Recipients will be selected based on financial need, demonstrated aptitude for college work, and academic standing.

Funds Avail.: No specific amount. **To Apply:** Applicants must complete and submit the application form and requirements to Stark Community Foundation, 400 Market Ave. N, Ste. 200, Canton, OH 44702. **Deadline:** May 15.

6753 ■ R. Skeeles Memorial Scholarship Fund
(Undergraduate/Scholarship)

Purpose: To provide scholarship assistance to qualified individuals who want to pursue their studies. **Focus:** General studies. **Qualif.:** Applicants must have attended Worley School for at least four years; must have good academic accomplishment in high school; must have good moral and personal characteristic. **Criteria:** Recipients are selected based on Scholarship Selection Committee's review of application.

Funds Avail.: No specific amount. **To Apply:** Applicants must complete and submit the application form and requirements to Worley School PTA President, 424 21st St. NW, Canton, OH 44709. **Deadline:** April 1.

6754 ■ Stark County Bar Association Fund
(Undergraduate/Scholarship)

Purpose: To provide scholarship assistance to qualified individuals who want to pursue their studies. **Focus:** Law. **Qualif.:** Applicants must be law students enrolled at accredited law schools; must be from the Stark County area. **Criteria:** Selection of applicants will be based on the criteria of the selection committee.

Funds Avail.: No specific amount. **To Apply:** Applicants must complete and submit the application form and requirements to Stark County Bar Association, 116 Cleveland Ave. NW, Ste. 400, Canton, OH 44702. **Deadline:** April 1.

6755 ■ Stark County Dairy Promoters Scholarships *(Undergraduate/Scholarship)*

Purpose: To provide scholarship assistance to qualified individuals who want to pursue their studies. **Focus:** Dairy science; Animal science and behavior; Medicine, Veterinary; Nutrition; Food science and technology. **Qualif.:** Applicants must be residents of Stark County, OH; must be pursuing college-level study in the field of dairy science, animal science, veterinary medicine, human nutrition, or food science; must have 2.5 high school GPA; must have demonstrated financial need. **Criteria:** Recipients are selected based on Scholarship Selection Committee's review of application.

Funds Avail.: No specific amount. **To Apply:** Applicants must complete and submit the application form and requirements to Stark County Diary Promoters Scholarship Committee, Stark Community Foundation, 400 Market Ave. N, Ste. 200, Canton, OH 44702. **Deadline:** April 15.

6756 ■ Jeffery Tyler Sweitzer Wrestling Memorial Scholarship Fund *(Undergraduate/Scholarship)*

Purpose: To provide scholarship assistance to qualified individuals who want to pursue their studies. **Focus:** General studies. **Qualif.:** Applicants must be male residents of Stark County, OH; must have achieved passing GPA on a 4.0 scale; must be graduating students from Hoover High School, North Canton, OH, have participated in the wrestling program; must be students attending West Liberty College, Wheeling, WV; must be students graduating from any Stark County area high school who have participated in a wrestling program. **Criteria:** Recipients will be selected based on the Scholarship Selection Criteria.

Funds Avail.: No specific amount. **To Apply:** Applicants

must submit completed application form and requirements to Canton Hoover High School Wrestling Booster Club.

6757 ■ Timothy S. Sweterlitsch Memorial Scholarship Fund *(Undergraduate/Scholarship)*

Purpose: To provide scholarship assistance to qualified individuals who want to pursue their studies. **Focus:** General studies. **Qualif.:** Applicants must be graduates of Washington High School, Massillon, OH; must have an academic accomplishment; must have good moral and personal characteristics. **Criteria:** Recipient will be selected based on academic standing and character.

Funds Avail.: $6,000. **Number Awarded:** 2. **To Apply:** Applicants must complete and submit the application form and other supporting documents to Mr. Frank Sweterlitsch, 802 Deerfield Lane NE, Massillon, OH 44646. **Deadline:** April 15.

6758 ■ Tim Triner Letter Carriers Scholarship Fund *(Undergraduate/Scholarship)*

Purpose: To provide scholarship assistance to qualified individuals who want to pursue their studies. **Focus:** General studies. **Qualif.:** Applicants must be seniors enrolled as full-time students; must have scholastic achievements; must be children or legal wards of Donor's active, retired or deceased members of Branch No. 238, National Association of Letter; must have a proof of acceptance into a post-secondary college, university or technical training program. **Criteria:** Recipients are selected based on the Scholarship Selection Committee's review of application.

Funds Avail.: No specific amount. **To Apply:** Applicants must complete and submit the application form and requirements to Scholarship Chairman, Branch No. 238 NALC, P.O Box 20248, Canton, OH 44701-0248. **Deadline:** May 31.

6759 ■ Norman J. Tschantz/Walter C. Deuble Scholarships *(Undergraduate/Scholarship)*

Purpose: To provide scholarship assistance to qualified individuals who want to pursue their studies. **Focus:** General studies. **Qualif.:** Applicants must have served at least one year as a caddy at Congress Lake Country Club; must have academic achievement in high school, college, or trade school; must have extracurricular activities. **Criteria:** Selection of applicants will be based on academic standing, extracurricular activities, and overall character and demonstration of responsibility and diligent effort.

Funds Avail.: No specific amount. **To Apply:** Applicants must submit completed application form and are advised to contact Congress Lake Pro Shop at 330877-0576.

6760 ■ Ira G. Turpin Scholar Fund *(Undergraduate/Scholarship)*

Purpose: To provide scholarship assistance to qualified individuals who want to pursue their studies. **Focus:** General studies. **Qualif.:** Applicants must be students attending Stark Country schools. **Criteria:** Selection of applicants will be based on their perseverance, high standards, and hard work toward achieving their career goals.

Funds Avail.: No specific amount. **To Apply:** Application forms are available online and must be sent to: Judge David E. Stucki, Stark County Family Court, 110 Central Plaza S, Ste. 601, Canton, OH 447021414.

6761 ■ John R. and Joan F. Warren Scholarship Fund *(Undergraduate/Scholarship)*

Purpose: To provide scholarship assistance to qualified individuals who want to pursue their studies. **Focus:** General studies. **Qualif.:** Applicants must be students planning to enroll or are presently enrolled at Grove City College. **Criteria:** Preferences are given to freshmen and current students who are Stark County residents. Recipients will be selected based on the scholarship standards established by Grove City College.

Funds Avail.: $500-$1,000. **To Apply:** Applicants must complete and submit the application form and requirements to Financial Aid Office, 100Campus Dr., Grove City, PA 16127. **Deadline:** April 15.

6762 ■ Lester and Eleanor Webster Charitable Trust Fund *(Undergraduate/Scholarship)*

Purpose: To provide scholarship assistance to qualified individuals who want to pursue their studies. **Focus:** General studies. **Qualif.:** Applicants must be students residing in Stark County who are pursuing a two-year or four-year college degree at an accredited school within the State of Ohio and who have attained sophomore status in college at time of award. **Criteria:** Recipients will be selected based on financial need, high school and/or college activities, scholastic aptitude and competence.

Funds Avail.: No specific amount. **To Apply:** Applicants must complete and submit the application form and requirements to Stark Community Foundation, 400 Market Ave. N, Ste. 200, Canton, OH 44702. **Deadline:** June 1.

6763 ■ Mary Kean White Memorial Scholarship Fund *(Undergraduate/Scholarship)*

Purpose: To provide scholarship assistance to qualified individuals who want to pursue their studies. **Focus:** Education, Elementary. **Qualif.:** Applicants must be graduates of Malvern High School or Carrollton High School; must be currently enrolled as full time students at an accredited college or university; must have cumulative GPA of at least 3.0 on a 4.0 scale; must be pursuing a career in elementary education or related field; must demonstrate financial need. **Criteria:** Recipients will be selected based on academic standing and financial need.

Funds Avail.: No specific amount. **To Apply:** Applicants must complete and submit the application form and requirements to Carrollton High School Guidance Office, Malvern High School Guidance Office. **Deadline:** April 1.

6764 ■ Workshop, Inc. and Stark MRDD Fostering Diversity Through Special Needs Scholarship Fund *(Undergraduate/Scholarship)*

Purpose: To provide scholarship assistance to qualified individuals who want to pursue their studies. **Focus:** Special education. **Qualif.:** Applicants must be residents of Stark County; must have at least a 3.0 cumulative GPA; must be majoring in Special Education or related field; must be juniors or seniors at a college or university. **Criteria:** Recipients will be selected based on academic achievement, volunteer/paid work experience and/or involvement in campus/community activities or organizations, essay review, and personal interview.

Funds Avail.: No specific amount. **To Apply:** Applicants must submit a 500-word essay, which describes, "Why you chose to major in special education or related field", and an essay review. Application form and other supporting documents must be sent to The Workshops, Inc. 2950 Whipple Ave. NW, Canton, OH 44708. **Deadline:** June 15. **Contact:** Leslie Thomas at the above address (see entry 6706).

6765 ■ Steuben County Community Foundation

1701 N Wayne St.
Angola, IN 46703

Ph: (260)665-6656
Fax: (260)665-8420
URL: http://www.steubenfoundation.org

6766 ■ Clifford V. Abbott Memorial Scholarships
(Undergraduate/Scholarship)

Purpose: To provide financial support to outstanding students. **Focus:** General Studies. **Qualif.:** Applicants must be residents of Steuben County; must be graduating seniors from Fremont High School. **Criteria:** Applicants are selected based on the committee's review of the application materials.

Funds Avail.: No specific amount. **To Apply:** Applicants must check the website for the application process online. **Deadline:** March 15. **Contact:** Steuben County Community Foundation at the above address (see entry 6765).

6767 ■ Mandel & Lauretta Abrahamer Scholarships *(Undergraduate/Scholarship)*

Purpose: To provide financial support to those students in health-related fields. **Focus:** Nursing. **Qualif.:** Applicants must be residents of Steuben County; must be entering in a Nursing School; must have a cumulative 3.0 GPA; must demonstrate financial need. **Criteria:** Scholarship recipients are selected based on the committee's review of the application materials.

Funds Avail.: No specific amount. **To Apply:** Applicants must submit the following: copy of school transcripts; any supporting statement from former teachers or supervisors of any paid or volunteer work in your chosen field will be considered; an essay answering the question, "What characteristics are necessary to be a successful nurse?". **Deadline:** March 15. **Contact:** Steuben County Community Foundation at the above address (see entry 6765).

6768 ■ Tara Lynne Arnold Scholarships
(Undergraduate/Scholarship)

Purpose: To provide financial support to those students who will be entering a four-year college or university with intent of pursuing a Bachelor's Degree. **Focus:** Psychology; Women's Studies. **Qualif.:** Applicants must attend or have attended Angola High School; must be in good academic standing. **Criteria:** Preference will be given to those students who will take up psychology or women's studies.

Funds Avail.: No specific amount. **To Apply:** Applicants must check the website for the application process online and required materials. **Deadline:** March 15.

6769 ■ Richard L. Baker Memorial Scholarships
(Undergraduate/Scholarship)

Purpose: To provide financial support to those graduating students of Fremont High School. **Focus:** General Studies. **Qualif.:** Applicants must be graduating seniors from Fremont High School; must be residing within the Fremont Community School District; must be admitted to a college or university as full-time students; must receive Academic Honors from Fremont High School. **Criteria:** Applicants are selected based on the committee's review of the application materials.

Funds Avail.: No specific amount. **To Apply:** Applicants must submit a completed application form; a 250-word essay; and high school transcripts. **Deadline:** March 15. **Contact:** Steuben County Community Foundation at the above address (see entry 6765).

6770 ■ Verna Curry Boyer Scholarships
(Undergraduate/Scholarship)

Purpose: To provide financial assistance to those students who are in need. **Focus:** General Studies. **Qualif.:** Applicants must be graduates of any Steuben County High School, including Prairie Heights, Fremont, Hamilton or MSD of Steuben County. **Criteria:** Applicants are selected based on the committee's review of the application materials.

Funds Avail.: No specific amount. **To Apply:** Applicants must check the website for the application process online. **Deadline:** March 15. **Contact:** Steuben County Community Foundation at the above address (see entry 6765).

6771 ■ Builders Association of Northeast Indiana (BANI) Scholarships *(Undergraduate/Scholarship)*

Purpose: To provide financial support to those students who are in need. **Focus:** General Studies. **Qualif.:** Applicants must be graduating seniors attending a high school and residing in Steuben County. **Criteria:** Applicants are selected based on the committee's review of the application materials.

Funds Avail.: No specific amount. **To Apply:** Applicants must check the website for the application process online. **Deadline:** March 15. **Contact:** Steuben County Community Foundation at the above address (see entry 6765).

6772 ■ Ellen Eberhardt Memorial Scholarships
(Undergraduate/Scholarship)

Purpose: To provide financial assistance to those deserving students. **Focus:** General Studies. **Qualif.:** Applicants must be residents of Steuben County; must be graduating seniors from a Steuben County High School; must be entering a four-year college or university with the intent to pursue a career in environmental education, biology, earth science or elementary education; must demonstrate financial need. **Criteria:** Applicants are selected based on the committee's review of the application materials.

Funds Avail.: No specific amount. **To Apply:** Applicants must check the website for the application process and required materials. **Deadline:** March 15. **Contact:** Steuben County Community Foundation at the above address (see entry 6765).

6773 ■ Farmers State Bank Scholarships
(Undergraduate/Scholarship)

Purpose: To provide financial assistance to deserving students. **Focus:** General Studies. **Qualif.:** Applicants must be residents of Steuben County; must be seniors at Angola High School, Fremont High School or Hamilton High School planning to enroll in a full-time undergraduate course at an accredited two or four-year college, university, or vocational-technical school in the fall following graduation; must have a documented GPA at the time of application between 2.5 and 3.5 on a scale of 4.0. **Criteria:** Applicants are selected based on the Scholarship Committee's review of the application materials.

Funds Avail.: No specific amount. **To Apply:** Applicants must check the website for the application process online. **Deadline:** March 15. **Contact:** Steuben County Community Foundation at the above address (see entry 6765).

6774 ■ Don and Eileen Fulton Nursing Scholarships *(Undergraduate/Scholarship)*

Purpose: To provide financial assistance to those students who will be continuing their education through an accredited

Awards are arranged alphabetically below their administering organizations

nursing program at any Indiana institution of higher education. **Focus:** Nursing. **Qualif.:** Applicants must be graduating seniors or have graduated from a Steuben County High School; must provide two references, preferably demonstrating nursing experience. **Criteria:** Applicants are selected based on the committee's review of the application materials.

Funds Avail.: No specific amount. **To Apply:** Applicants must check the website for the application process and required materials. **Deadline:** March 15. **Contact:** Steuben County Community Foundation at the above address (see entry 6765).

6775 ■ Helen R. Greenamyer Memorial Scholarships *(Undergraduate/Scholarship)*

Purpose: To provide financial support to those students who are pursuing a career in Nursing. **Focus:** Nursing. **Qualif.:** Applicants must be graduates of any Steuben County High School, including Prairie Heights, Fremont, Hamilton or MSD of Steuben County; must be pursuing a career in Nursing. **Criteria:** Applicants are selected based on the committee's review of the application materials.

Funds Avail.: No specific amount. **To Apply:** Applicants must check the website for the application process and required materials. **Deadline:** March 15. **Contact:** Steuben County Community Foundation at the above address (see entry 6765).

6776 ■ Ed Haas Memorial Scholarships
(Undergraduate/Scholarship)

Purpose: To provide financial assistance to those students who are in need. **Focus:** Education; Humanities; Arts. **Qualif.:** Applicants must be residents of Steuben County; must be graduating seniors from Angola High School; must be pursuing degree in the field of Education, Humanities or Arts. **Criteria:** Applicants are selected based on the committee's review of the application materials.

Funds Avail.: No specific amount. **To Apply:** Applicants must submit any supporting statements from former teachers or supervisors of any paid or volunteer work in your chosen field will be considered; copy of school transcripts; an essay answering the questions "why do you want to pursue a career in Education, Humanities or the Arts?" and "what influenced your decision?" Applicants must check the website for the application process and required materials. **Deadline:** March 15. **Contact:** Steuben County Community Foundation at the above address (see entry 6765).

6777 ■ H. Pauline Hand Memorial Scholarships
(Undergraduate/Scholarship)

Purpose: To provide financial support to those graduating students from Angola High School, Fremont, Hamilton or Prairie Heights High School. **Focus:** General Studies. **Qualif.:** Applicants must be residents of Steuben County; must be full-time students at any accredited college or university. **Criteria:** Recipients will be selected based on academic achievement, leadership abilities and character.

Funds Avail.: No specific amount. **To Apply:** Applicants must check the website for the application process and required materials. **Deadline:** March 15. **Contact:** Steuben County Community Foundation at the above address (see entry 6765).

6778 ■ Dr. M.G. "Doc" Headley Scholarships
(Undergraduate/Scholarship)

Purpose: To provide financial assistance to those students who are in need. **Focus:** Agriculture; Veterinary Science. **Qualif.:** Applicants must be pursuing a certified or degreed agricultural or veterinarian program at an institution of higher education. Applicants must be graduating students from Angola, Fremont, Hamilton or Prairie Heights High School. **Criteria:** Priority will be given to those students in the field of veterinary medicine.

Funds Avail.: No specific amount. **Number Awarded:** Minimum of 3 persons. **To Apply:** Applicants must check the website for the application process and required materials. **Deadline:** March 15. **Contact:** Steuben County Community Foundation at the above address (see entry 6765).

6779 ■ Dale Hughes, Jr. Memorial Scholarships
(Undergraduate/Scholarship)

Purpose: To provide financial assistance to those students who are in need. **Focus:** General Studies. **Qualif.:** Applicants must be residents of Steuben County; must be graduating from Prairie Heights High School; must be continuing their education through an accredited program at any institution of higher education. **Criteria:** Applicants are selected based on the committee's review of the application materials. Preference will be given to students pursuing agricultural education opportunities.

Funds Avail.: No specific amount. **To Apply:** Applicants must check the website for the application process and required materials. **Deadline:** March 15. **Contact:** Steuben County Community Foundation at the above address (see entry 6765).

6780 ■ Sylvia E. Jackson Scholarships
(Undergraduate/Scholarship)

Purpose: To provide financial support to those students who are in need. **Focus:** General Studies. **Qualif.:** Applicants must be residents of Steuben County and must be enrolled as seniors in Angola High School on or before October 1 of their senior year; must attend an accredited school within the boundaries of the United States. **Criteria:** Recipients will be selected based on academic potential, academic achievement and general citizenship.

Funds Avail.: No specific amount. **To Apply:** Applicants must check the website for the application process and required materials. **Deadline:** March 15. **Contact:** Steuben County Community Foundation at the above address (see entry 6765).

6781 ■ John W. Kelley Memorial Scholarships
(Undergraduate/Scholarship)

Purpose: To provide financial support to those students who are interested in earning a degree in Law Enforcement Education. **Focus:** Law Enforcement. **Qualif.:** Applicants must be residents of Steuben County; must be graduating seniors from any Steuben County High School; must be pursuing a degree in Law Enforcement Education. **Criteria:** Applicants are selected based on the committee's review of the application materials.

Funds Avail.: No specific amount. **To Apply:** Applicants must check the website for the application process and required materials. **Deadline:** March 15. **Contact:** Steuben County Community Foundation at the above address (see entry 6765).

6782 ■ Las Limas Community Scholarships
(Undergraduate/Scholarship)

Purpose: To provide financial assistance to students having difficulty financing their education. **Focus:** General Studies. **Qualif.:** Applicants must be residents of Steuben,

Awards are arranged alphabetically below their administering organizations

6803 ■ StraightForward Media's Minority Scholarships *(Undergraduate/Scholarship)*

Purpose: To financially assist students in their educational pursuits. **Focus:** General studies. **Qualif.:** Applicant must be a minority student. **Criteria:** Awards are given based on merit.

Funds Avail.: $500. **Number Awarded:** 4. **To Apply:** Applicants must complete scholarship application online. **Deadline:** March, June, September, December.

Remarks: Awards are given four times a year.

6804 ■ StraightForward Media's Nursing School Scholarships *(Undergraduate/Scholarship)*

Purpose: To financially assist students in their educational pursuits. **Focus:** Nursing. **Qualif.:** Applicant must be a nursing student. **Criteria:** Awards are given based on merit.

Funds Avail.: $500. **To Apply:** Applicants must complete the scholarship application online. **Deadline:** January, April, July, October.

Remarks: Awards are given four times a year.

6805 ■ StraightForward Media's Science Scholarships *(Undergraduate/Scholarship)*

Purpose: To financially assist students in their educational pursuits. **Focus:** Science. **Qualif.:** Applicant must be a student pursuing a degree in a science-related field. **Criteria:** Awards are given based on merit.

Funds Avail.: $500. **Number Awarded:** 4. **To Apply:** Applicants must complete scholarship application online.

Remarks: Awards are given four times a year.

6806 ■ StraightForward Media's Teacher Scholarships *(Undergraduate/Scholarship)*

Purpose: To financially assist students in their educational pursuits. **Focus:** Teaching. **Qualif.:** Applicant must be a student planning to be a teacher. **Criteria:** Awards are given based on merit.

Funds Avail.: $500. **To Apply:** Applicants must complete the Online Scholarship Application. **Deadline:** January, April, July, October.

Remarks: Awards are given four times a year.

6807 ■ StraightForward Media's Vocational-Technical School Scholarships *(Undergraduate/Scholarship)*

Purpose: To financially assist students in their educational pursuits. **Focus:** Education, Vocational-technical. **Qualif.:** Applicants must be a students pursuing degrees, licenses or certificates at vocational schools. **Criteria:** Awards are given based on merit.

Funds Avail.: $500. **To Apply:** Applicants must complete the Online Scholarship Application. **Deadline:** November, February, May, August.

Remarks: Awards are given four times a year.

6808 ■ Fraser Stryker

500 Energy Plaza, 409 S 17th St.
Omaha, NE 68102-2663
Ph: (402)341-6000
Fax: (402)341-8290
E-mail: sbruckner@fraserstryker.com
URL: http://www.fraserstryker.com

6809 ■ Fraser Stryker Diversity Scholarships *(Undergraduate/Scholarship)*

Purpose: To provide financial assistance in the form of college tuition and provide paid internships to students. **Focus:** General studies. **Qualif.:** Applicants must be of African-American, Asian, Latino or Native-American origins who are graduating seniors at any of the public or private high schools in the greater Omaha area; must have been accepted to an accredited college or university located in the united States; must be college students who have received Fraser Diversity Scholarships in prior years. **Criteria:** Recipients are selected based on interest in pursuing a career in law, financial need, top 20% in class rank, SAT scores and academic performance.

Funds Avail.: $2,500. **To Apply:** Applicants must submit a completed application form and evidence of enrollment. **Contact:** 402-341-6000.

6810 ■ Student Osteopathic Medical Association

142 E Ontario St.
Chicago, IL 60611
Ph: (312)202-8193
Fax: (312)202-8200
Free: 800-621-1773
E-mail: somanat@studentdo.com
URL: http://www.studentdo.com

6811 ■ Humanism in Medicine Scholarships *(Undergraduate/Scholarship)*

Purpose: To help medical students pursue their studies. **Focus:** Osteopathic Medicine. **Qualif.:** Applicant must be a third- or fourth-year osteopathic medical student attending any accredited osteopathic medical colleges. **Criteria:** Recipients are selected based on demonstrated character; leadership and dedication; compassion and empathy; spirit and enthusiasm.

Funds Avail.: No specific amount. **To Apply:** Applicants must complete the application form. Applicants must submit a 500-word essay. Applicants must submit a curriculum vitae. **Deadline:** September 22. **Contact:** sabeena.rahman@nv.touro.edu

6812 ■ Student Osteopathic Medical Student Fellowships and Research *(Undergraduate/Fellowship)*

Purpose: To provide funds for medical students who are currently or will be conducting a research project in the field of osteopathy. **Focus:** Osteopathic medicine. **Qualif.:** Applicants must be osteopathic medical students. **Criteria:** Recipients are selected based on the significance of the research project.

Funds Avail.: $2,000. **To Apply:** Applicants must present an abstract. **Deadline:** January 4. **Contact:** allisaco@pcom.edu

6813 ■ Marvin H. and Kathleen G. Teget Leadership Scholarships *(Undergraduate/Scholarship)*

Purpose: To benefit students pursuing a career in specialty medicine. **Focus:** Specialty Medicine. **Qualif.:** Applicants must be currently enrolled in a specialty medicine program at an institution, college, or university. **Criteria:** Recipients are selected based on their personal statement.

Funds Avail.: $500. **Number Awarded:** 2. **To Apply:** Applicants must submit a personal statement and complete the application form. **Deadline:** March 15.

6814 ■ Suicide Prevention Action Network USA

1025 Vermont Ave., NW, Ste. 1066
Washington, DC 20005

Awards are arranged alphabetically below their administering organizations

Ph: (202)449-3600
Fax: (202)449-3601
E-mail: info@spanusa.org
URL: http://www.spanusa.org

6815 ■ Eleanor Benett Scholarships *(All/ Scholarship)*

Purpose: To assist suicide survivors and attempt to help survivors in their efforts to advance suicide prevention by helping underwrite activities relevant to suicide prevention. **Focus:** Suicide. **Qualif.:** Applicants must be current members of SPAN USA "Partner for Action" who seek financial assistance to participate in an activity relevant to suicide prevention within the United States. **Criteria:** Applicants are evaluated based on criteria designed by the Scholarship Selection Committee.

Funds Avail.: $500. **To Apply:** Applicants must complete the form and attach a 250-word essay describing how the activity for which they are seeking scholarship support will further their own education and/or contribute to the advancement of suicide prevention, be it at the community, state or nation level. This essay should include something about the individual's experience as a suicide survivor and/or attempt survivor and membership in SPAN USA.

6816 ■ Sun Country Amateur Golf Association

1440 Rio Rancho Blvd.
Rio Rancho, NM 87124
Ph: (505)897-0864
Fax: (505)897-3494
Free: 800-346-5319
E-mail: mwilliams@newmexicogolf.org
URL: http://www.newmexicogolf.org

6817 ■ Sun Country Amateur Golf Association Scholarships *(Undergraduate/Scholarship)*

Purpose: To provide financial support to those deserving students. **Focus:** General Studies. **Qualif.:** Applicants must have completed their junior year in high school or at least one year in college; have achieved 3.0 or higher cumulative grade point average; and must have connection to golf. **Criteria:** Recipients are selected based on personal character as evidenced by student's participation in extracurricular activities or involvement in the local community; and financial need.

Funds Avail.: No specific amount. **To Apply:** Applicants must check the available website for the required materials. **Contact:** For more information please contact: Barbara Saia at (505) 897-0864.

6818 ■ Sunshine Lady Foundation

4900 Randall Pkwy., Ste. H
Wilmington, NC 28403
Ph: (910)397-0023
Fax: (910)397-0023
Free: (866)255-7742
E-mail: nancy@sunshinelady.org
URL: http://www.sunshinelady.org

6819 ■ Change Your World Scholarships *(Undergraduate/Scholarship)*

Purpose: To help support the battered woman to overcome barriers to their education, which is necessary for their becoming employable and financially stable. **Focus:** General studies. **Qualif.:** Applicants must be direct survivors of domestic violence or partner abuse. Applicants must be citizens or legal residents of the United States. Applicants must be officially accepted to an accredited university or institution in the United States. Applicants must be 17 to 25 years old. Applicants must maintain a 3.0 GPA and a full-time enrollment status. **Criteria:** Recipients are selected based on academic ability and financial need.

Funds Avail.: No specific amount. **To Apply:** Applicants must complete the application form and provide evidence of enrollment. **Deadline:** July 1.

6820 ■ Women's Independence Scholarship Programs *(Undergraduate/Scholarship)*

Purpose: To help survivors of domestic violence obtain an education that will in turn offer them the chance to secure employment, personal independence and self-sufficiency. To help battered women overcome barriers to the education necessary for their becoming employable and financially stable. To help single mothers with young children who have the greatest financial challenges to gain work so they can support their families. **Focus:** General studies. **Qualif.:** Applicants must be direct survivors of domestic violence or partner abuse. Applicants must be citizens or legal residents of the United States. Applicants must be officially accepted into an accredited course of study at a United States institution. **Criteria:** Recipients are selected based on the demonstrated critical need for financial assistance and determination to complete a training and/or academic program. They should demonstrate a definite plan to use the desired training to upgrade skills for career advancement, to train for new career field, or to enter or reenter the job market.

Funds Avail.: No specific amount. **To Apply:** Applicants must complete the application form and provide the necessary documents such as transcripts. **Contact:** nancy@sunshinelady.org

6821 ■ Supreme Council, Ancient Accepted Scottish Rite of Free-Masonry

PO Box 519
Lexington, MA 02420-0519
Ph: (781)862-4410
Fax: (781)863-1833
E-mail: info@supremecouncil.org
URL: http://www.supremecouncil.org

6822 ■ Abbott Scholarships *(Undergraduate/ Scholarship)*

Purpose: To support the continuing education of young men and women from Scottish Rite families and Masonic-related youth groups. **Focus:** General studies. **Qualif.:** Applicant must be currently enrolled at an accredited college or university; have a GPA of 2.75; a child or grandchild of a Scottish Rite Mason in the Northern Masonic Jurisdiction; or a member of a youth organization sponsored by the Masonic fraternity in the Northern Masonic Jurisdiction; or a graduate of one of the 32nd degree Masonic Learning Centers for Children in the Northern Masonic Jurisdiction. **Criteria:** Selection is based on the application.

Funds Avail.: No specific amount. **To Apply:** Applicants must submit a completed application form together with a copy of current college transcript; a letter of recommendation; and current FAFSA form. Mail applications to the Val-

Awards are arranged alphabetically below their administering organizations

ley providing for their eligibility.

Remarks: Named after Leon M. Abbott, Sovereign Grand Commander from 1921-1932.

6823 ■ Surety and Fidelity Association of America

1101 Connecticut Ave. NW, Ste. 800
Washington, DC 20036
Ph: (202)463-0600
Fax: (202)463-0606
URL: http://www.surety.org

6824 ■ Surety Industry Scholarship Program for Minority Students *(Undergraduate/Scholarship)*

Purpose: To provide financial assistance to outstanding minority students to support their studies in the areas of insurance/risk management, accounting, or business/finance and to encourage their consideration of the surety industry and surety underwriting as a career choice. **Focus:** Insurance and insurance-related fields; Management; Accounting; Business; Finance. **Qualif.:** Applicants must be majoring in insurance/risk management, accounting, or business/finance; must have an overall and major grade point average (GPA) of at least 3.0 on 4.0 scale; must be minority students who have satisfactorily completed at least 30 semester hours and at least 6 semester hours in their declared major; must be enrolled as full-time undergraduate students (minimum of 12 semester hours or equivalent) at an accredited four-year institution. **Criteria:** Applicants are evaluated based on academic achievement and financial need.

Funds Avail.: $2,500. **To Apply:** Applicants must submit all the required application information. **Deadline:** April 30.

6825 ■ Surface Officer Spouses

PO Box 9902
Norfolk, VA 23505-9902
URL: http://www.surfaceofficerspousesnorfolk.com

6826 ■ Anchor Scholarship Foundation *(Undergraduate/Scholarship)*

Purpose: To provide financial assistance for academically qualified dependents of current and former members of the Naval Surface Forces, Atlantic. **Focus:** General studies. **Qualif.:** Applicants must attend an accredited, four-year college or university in the United States and intend to work toward their first bachelor's degree on a full time basis; must be high school seniors or college students in an accredited school or equivalent educational institution; must be dependent children or spouses whose service member meets the following requirements: a) sponsor is active duty or retired US Navy; b) sponsor has served a minimum of six years in a unit under the administrative control of Commander, Naval Surface Force, US Atlantic Fleet or US Pacific Fleet. **Criteria:** Recipients are selected based on academic proficiency, extracurricular activities, character and all-around ability and financial need.

Funds Avail.: $500. **To Apply:** Applicants must submit all the needed materials for the scholarship.

6827 ■ Swiss Benevolent Society of New York

500 Fifth Ave., Rm. 1800
New York, NY 10110
Ph: (212)246-0655
Fax: (212)246-1366
E-mail: info@sbsny.com
URL: http://www.sbsny.org

6828 ■ Sonia S. Maguire Outstanding Scholastic Achievement Awards *(Graduate, Undergraduate/Scholarship)*

Purpose: To provide financial support to college seniors or graduate students who have demonstrated sustained academic excellence in a demanding study program. **Focus:** General studies. **Qualif.:** Applicants or one of their parents must be Swiss nationals; must be domiciled in New York, New Jersey, Connecticut, Pennsylvania or Delaware; must demonstrate the need for financial support; must be in good academic standing and show aptitude in their chosen fields of study. **Criteria:** Applicants are selected based on the committee's review of the application materials.

Funds Avail.: No specific amount. **To Apply:** Application forms can be downloaded at the SBSNY web site. Applicants must submit the following required documents: general and scholastic pages of application packet; official transcripts of all high school, college and graduate grades when applying for the first time, official updates thereafter; SAT or GRE results when applying for the first time; proof of Swiss citizenship of applicant or one parent when applying for the first time; proof of U.S. citizenship or visa status when applying for the first time; two letters of recommendation from professors in the applicant's major area of study, on official letterhead. **Deadline:** January 31. **Contact:** SBSNY at the above address (see entry 6827).

6829 ■ Medicus Student Exchange *(Graduate, Undergraduate/Scholarship)*

Purpose: To provide partial financial support for U.S. residents at the junior, senior or graduate college level who have been accepted to study at a Swiss University or Federal Institute of Technology. **Focus:** General studies. **Qualif.:** Applicants must be residents of the United States and must be in good academic standing and show aptitude in their chosen fields of study. **Criteria:** Applicants are selected based on the committee's review of the application materials.

Funds Avail.: No specific amount. **To Apply:** Application forms can be downloaded at the SBSNY web site. Applicants must submit the following required documents: general and scholastic pages of application packet; official transcripts of all high school, college and graduate grades when applying for the first time, official updates thereafter; SAT or GRE results when applying for the first time; proof of Swiss citizenship of applicant or one parent when applying for the first time; proof of U.S. citizenship or visa status when applying for the first time; letter of acceptance from Swiss University or Federal Institute of Technology or Technical College; two letters of recommendation from professors in the applicant's major area of study, on official letterhead; proof of proficiency in the language of instruction; statement of sufficient total funding. For studies in the U.S.: official transcript of records of at least one year of study in the U.S.; transcripts of education in Switzerland; letter of recommendation from a professor in the applicant's major area of study, on official letterhead. **Deadline:** January 31. **Contact:** SBSNY at the above address (see entry 6827).

6830 ■ Pellegrini Scholarships *(Graduate, Undergraduate/Scholarship)*

Purpose: To provide financial support to post-secondary school level students for vocational, undergraduate or graduate academic studies at an accredited school. **Focus:** General studies. **Qualif.:** Applicants or one of their parents must be Swiss nationals; must be domiciled in New York, New Jersey, Connecticut, Pennsylvania or Delaware; must demonstrate the need for financial support; must be in good academic standing and show aptitude in their chosen fields of study. **Criteria:** Applicants are selected based on need and academic merit.

Funds Avail.: No specific amount. **To Apply:** Application forms can be downloaded at the SBSNY web site. Applicants must submit the following required documents: general and scholastic pages of application packet; official transcripts of all high school, college and graduate grades when applying for the first time, official updates thereafter; SAT or GRE results when applying for the first time; proof of Swiss citizenship of applicant or one parent when applying of the first time; proof of U.S. citizenship or visa status when applying for the first time; financial pages of application packet, including all requested information, unless applying for merit portion only; signed copy of all pages and schedules of Federal Income Tax returns, and of W-2 forms of applicant and supporting party and/or spouse, where applicable; proof of cost for tuition and room and board, copy of bursar's bill (high school applicants provide figures of anticipated cost); letter of reference from a high school principal or a guidance counselor, or from a professor in the applicant's major area of study, on official letterhead. **Deadline:** January 31. **Contact:** SBSNY at the above address (see entry 6827).

6831 ■ Zimmermann Scholarships *(Graduate/ Scholarship)*

Purpose: To provide financial assistance to graduate students with the highest cumulative grade point average. **Focus:** General studies. **Qualif.:** Applicants or one of their parents must be Swiss nationals. Applicants must be domiciled in New York, New Jersey, Connecticut, Pennsylvania or Delaware. Applicants must be in good academic standing and show aptitude in their chosen fields of study. **Criteria:** Applicants are selected based on the committee's review of the application materials.

Funds Avail.: No specific amount. **To Apply:** Application forms can be downloaded at the SBSNY web site. Applicants must submit the following required documents: general and scholastic pages of application packet; official transcripts of all high school, college and graduate grades when applying for the first time, official updates thereafter; SAT or GRE results when applying for the first time; proof of Swiss citizenship of applicant or one parent when applying for the first time; proof of U.S. citizenship or visa status when applying for the first time; two letters of recommendation from professors. **Deadline:** January 31. **Contact:** SBSNY at the above address (see entry 6827).

6832 ■ Tag and Label Manufacturers Institute

40 Shuman Blvd., Ste. 295
Naperville, IL 60563
Ph: (630)357-9222
Fax: (630)357-0192
Free: 800-533-8564
E-mail: office@tlmi.com
URL: http://www.tlmi.com

6833 ■ TLMI Scholarships - Four-Year Colleges *(Undergraduate/Scholarship)*

Purpose: To promote education in the flexographic industry. **Focus:** Management; Marketing and distribution; Graphic art and design. **Qualif.:** Applicant must be a second or third year full-time college student pursuing a career in the tag and table manufacturing industry; majoring in management, sales/ marketing, graphic arts, graphic design, or production; and must maintain a 3.00 or higher GPA. **Criteria:** Applicants are selected based on the application materials.

Funds Avail.: $5,000. **Number Awarded:** 6. **To Apply:** Applicants must fill out the application online; must prepare a personal statement (one page) on personal information, work experiences, family financial report, career and educational goals and reasons why they deserve the award; a school transcript; three references; and samples of work (not mandatory). **Deadline:** January 1-March 31. **Contact:** Karen Planzat.

6834 ■ TLMI Scholarships - Two-Year Colleges *(Undergraduate/Scholarship)*

Purpose: To promote education in the flexographic industry. **Focus:** Industrial design. **Qualif.:** Applicants must be enrolled full-time in a flexographic printing program at a two-year college or technical program that grants degrees; and must maintain a 3.00 or higher GPA. **Criteria:** Applicants will be selected based on the application materials.

Funds Avail.: $1,000. **Number Awarded:** 4. **To Apply:** Application forms are available at the website. Committee will not accept applications direct from a student, applicants must present the application form together with an official college transcript and a personal statement to his/her educator for submission to the TLMI. Educators must forward complete application package to TLMI **Deadline:** January 1-March 31. **Contact:** Karen Planzat, 800-533-8564.

6835 ■ Tailhook Association

9696 Businesspark Ave.
San Diego, CA 92131
Ph: (858)689-9223
Free: 800-322-4665
E-mail: thookassn@aol.com
URL: http://www.tailhook.org

6836 ■ Tailhook Educational Foundation Scholarships Program *(Undergraduate/ Scholarship)*

Purpose: To educate the public with the history and present day activities of US navy carrier aviation. **Focus:** Aviation. **Qualif.:** Applicants must be high school graduates and dependents of current or former (US Navy/US Marines Corps/US Coast Guards) Naval Aviators, Naval Flight Officers, or Naval Aircrewmen; must be dependents of individuals who are serving or have served on board as US Navy Aircraft carriers. **Criteria:** Recipients are selected based on their application materials.

Funds Avail.: $2000-$10000. **To Apply:** Application forms are available at the website. Applicants must complete the application form together with a certified copy of high school transcript; documentation of SAT or ACT score; an essay on career goals (1 page); endorsement letter; letter of acceptance at a college/university; and an aircrew designation letter (if applicable). Mail application and other support-

Awards are arranged alphabetically below their administering organizations

ing materials to: The Tailhook Educational Foundation, Scholarship Applications 9696 Businesspark Ave. San Diego, CA 92131-1643. **Deadline:** March 17.

6837 ■ Taiwanese American Citizens League

3001 Walnut Grove Ave., No. 7
Rosemead, CA 91770
Ph: (626)202-0170
E-mail: tacl@tacl.org
URL: http://www.tacl.org

6838 ■ Taiwanese American Community Scholarships *(Undergraduate/Scholarship)*

Purpose: To recognize high school seniors with leadership qualities as well as a public service and to encourage them to pursue higher education. **Focus:** General studies. **Qualif.:** Applicants should be college bound senior graduating class from one of the ten high schools: Irvine High School, Northwood High School, Canyon High School, University High School, Woodbridge High School, Villa Park High School, Laguna High School, Aliso Niguel High School, Troy High School and Fountain Valley High School. **Criteria:** Awards are given based on the committee's criteria.

Funds Avail.: $500. **To Apply:** Applicant may download an application form from the website. Applicant must submit a one-page biography that includes activities and volunteer work during your high school years; A typed essay of no more than 1000 words, on the topic: "Indicate a person who has as a significant influence on you and describe that influence"; One recommendation letter form on of your school teachers or counselors; A copy of your official high school transcript. **Deadline:** April 18. **Contact:** TACL at the above address (see entry 6837).

6839 ■ Tall Clubs International

PO Box 441
Portland, OR 97207
Ph: 888-468-2552
E-mail: admin@tall.org
URL: http://www.tall.org

6840 ■ Tall Clubs International Student Scholarships *(Undergraduate/Scholarship)*

Purpose: To promote tall awareness among tall men and women, and in the community. **Focus:** General studies. **Qualif.:** Applicant must be under 21 years of age and attending their first year of college in the following fall. The recipient must also meet the TCI height requirement minimums of 5'10 for women and 6'2 for men. **Criteria:** Selections are based on the academic performance of an applicant.

Funds Avail.: $1,000. **To Apply:** To a club meeting simply select a known student as a candidate for a TCI scholarship award. TCI has forms that are downloadable by any Club member in the Member Services Console pertaining to student scholarship.

6841 ■ Tanana Valley Campus

604 Barnette St.
Fairbanks, AK 99701
Ph: (907)455-2800
Free: 877-882-8827
URL: http://www.tvc.uaf.edu

6842 ■ Mary Ghezzi Nursing Scholarships *(Undergraduate/Scholarship)*

Purpose: To provide financial support for qualified students intending to pursue their nursing education. **Focus:** Nursing. **Qualif.:** Applicants must be enrolled in Tahana Valley Campus; must be students who want to pursue their career in Nursing. **Criteria:** Applicants will be selected based on their application requirements.

Funds Avail.: $2,000. **To Apply:** Applicants are advised to contact Allied Health at 455-2822 for further information about the scholarship application.

6843 ■ Stacy Kaiser Memorial Funds *(Undergraduate/Scholarship)*

Purpose: To provide support for deserving students intending to pursue their careers in radiologic technology. **Focus:** Radiology. **Qualif.:** Applicants must be residents of Alaska; must be in the second year of program in radiologic technology. **Criteria:** Applicants will be selected based on their application requirements.

Funds Avail.: $1,000. **To Apply:** Scholarship applications are available online and must be completed and sent to: uaonline.alaska.edu (to access the scholarship application, applicant must choose to "Login to secured area "if they have a UA ID or apply for admission for the new students).

6844 ■ William C. Leary Memorial Emergency Services Scholarships *(Undergraduate/Scholarship)*

Purpose: To encourage students to pursue their career in emergency service program. **Focus:** Emergency and disaster services. **Qualif.:** Applicants must be students enrolled in emergency service program. **Criteria:** Selection of applicants will be based on the decision of the scholarship committee.

Funds Avail.: $500. **To Apply:** Scholarship applications are available at uaonline.alaska.edu (to access the scholarship application, you must choose "Login to secure area" if they have a UA ID or apply for admission for the new students).

6845 ■ Ruth Lister Scholarships *(Undergraduate/Scholarship)*

Purpose: To provide financial support for deserving individuals intending to pursue their educational goals. **Focus:** General studies. **Qualif.:** Applicants must be residents of Alaska; must be enrolled in a vocational program. **Criteria:** Preference will be given to Alaska residents and students enrolled in vocational programs.

Funds Avail.: $2,000. **To Apply:** Scholarship applications are available online at uaonline.alaska.edu (to access the scholarship application, applicant must choose "Login to secured area" if they have a UA ID or apply for admission for the new students).

6846 ■ Rachael Patterson Memorial Scholarships *(Undergraduate/Scholarship)*

Purpose: To provide educational support for qualified students intending to pursue their education. **Focus:** Technology, Criminal justice, Fires and fire prevention. **Qualif.:** Applicants must be sophomores or above; must be enrolled in justice, fire science or office management and technology; must be residents of Alaska (at least two years) and are intending to remain in Alaska. **Criteria:** Preference will be given to residents of Alaska.

Awards are arranged alphabetically below their administering organizations

Funds Avail.: No specific amount. **To Apply:** Scholarship applications are available online at uaonline.alaska.edu (to access the scholarship application, applicant must choose "Login to secured area" if they have a UA ID or apply for admission for the new students).

6847 ■ Schaible Health Care Services Scholarships *(Undergraduate/Scholarship)*

Purpose: To assist students in the health care services field at Tahana Valley Campus and/or Kuskokwim Campus within the college of Rural and Community Development at UAF. **Focus:** Health care services. **Qualif.:** Applicants must be attending at Kuskokwom Campus or Tahana Valley Campus; must be enrolled in health care service. **Criteria:** Selection of applicants will be based on their application requirements.

Funds Avail.: $500. **To Apply:** Scholarship applications are available online at uaonline.alaska.edu (to access the scholarship application, applicant must choose "Login to secured area" if they have a UA ID or apply for admission for the new students).

6848 ■ Anna Doris Southall Nursing Scholarships *(Undergraduate/Scholarship)*

Purpose: To provide support for deserving students intending to pursue their degree in pre-medicine or nursing. **Focus:** Nursing. **Qualif.:** Applicants must be second year students enrolled in a pre-medicine or nursing program. **Criteria:** Selection of recipients will be based on the application and eligibility requirements.

Funds Avail.: $1,000. **To Apply:** The applicants are advised to contact Allied Health at 455-2822 for further scholarship information and instructions.

6849 ■ Tanana Valley Campus Culinary Arts Scholarships *(Undergraduate/Scholarship)*

Purpose: To provide support for deserving students intending to pursue their study in culinary arts. **Focus:** Culinary arts. **Qualif.:** Applicants must be students intending to pursue a career in culinary arts in Alaska. **Criteria:** Applicants will be selected based on their application requirements.

Funds Avail.: Varies. **To Apply:** Applicants are advised to contact the Culinary Arts at 455-2902 for further information about the application requirements and procedure.

6850 ■ Technical Women's Organization

6905 S 1300 E No. 124
Midvale, UT 84047
Ph: (405)954-3247
E-mail: Emily.M.Godinet@faa.gov
URL: http://www.technicalwomen.org

6851 ■ TWO Scholarship Program *(Undergraduate/Scholarship)*

Purpose: To encourage students to take every opportunity to participate in training and education that will enhance or advance careers. **Focus:** Technical Training. **Qualif.:** Applicants must be in a training program that will advance or enhance the individual's career in a technical area. **Criteria:** Preference will be given to those students who meet the criteria.

Funds Avail.: $500. **To Apply:** Applicants must check the available website for more information. **Deadline:** May 15. **Contact:** Application Mailing Address: Brenda Smith-Keene P.O. Box 20802 Kansas City, MO 64195

6852 ■ Technology Student Association

1914 Association Dr.
Reston, VA 20191-1540
Ph: (703)860-9000
Fax: (703)758-4852
URL: http://www.tsaweb.org

6853 ■ William P. Elrod Memorial Scholarships *(Undergraduate/Scholarship)*

Purpose: To provide financial support for the outstanding service in the field of technology to a TSA student who is college or vocational/tech school bound and who is in good academic standing. **Focus:** Technology. **Qualif.:** Applicants must be: TSA graduating high school seniors or alumni still enrolled in an undergraduate program or vo/tech school with a GPA of 3.0 or better; must have performed services on the local, state and national level and active member of an affiliated TSA chapter; able to express financial need for the scholarship; accepted or enrolled in a four-year college, university, or vo/tech school to receive the funds; and able to describe their future educational goals. **Criteria:** Candidates will be evaluated by the Awards Committee.

Funds Avail.: $500. **To Apply:** Applicants must submit a completed application to the TSA Awards Committee. **Deadline:** May 1.

6854 ■ TSA Teach Technology Scholarships *(Undergraduate/Scholarship)*

Purpose: To support the technology education profession by encouraging TSA students to pursue careers as K-12 technology teachers. **Focus:** Technology. **Qualif.:** Applicants must have participated in an active TSA chapter for a minimum of two (2) consecutive years; served as a TSA officer at the local, state and/or national level for a minimum of one (1) academic year; attended and participated in at least one (1) TSA conference at the state or national level-.Participated in an active TSA chapter for a minimum of two (2) consecutive years; served as a TSA officer at the local, state and/or national level for a minimum of one (1) academic year; attended and participated in at least one (1) TSA conference at the state or national level. **Criteria:** Recipient will be selected by TSA Award Selection Committee.

Funds Avail.: $500. **Number Awarded:** 1. **To Apply:** Applicants must submit: a signed cover letter that includes the following: a detailed description of the applicant's involvement in TSA, based on the above criteria; SAT score and/or ACT score: high school class rank (indicate how many in the class); no more than three (3) letters of reference, one of which must come from a technology teacher; a single-sided, one-page typed essay on his/her career plans for becoming a teacher in the technology education profession. **Deadline:** December 31.

6855 ■ Telecommunications Association of Michigan

600 W Shiawassee St.
Lansing, MI 48933
Ph: (517)482-4166
Fax: (517)482-3548
URL: http://telecommich.org

Awards are arranged alphabetically below their administering organizations

6856 ■ Telecommunications Association of Michigan Scholarship Fund *(Undergraduate/Scholarship)*

Purpose: To elevate the technical and business competence of young people by providing them with assistance to acquire meaningful and marketable skills; to provide educational incentive to deserving students who will ultimately provide leadership for the professions in business, education and public service. **Focus:** General Studies. **Qualif.:** Applicants must be member of a non-Michigan high school or enrolled in an accredited, degree-granting, non-Michigan college or university. **Criteria:** Selection is based on academic excellence, financial need and ability.

Funds Avail.: No specific amount. **To Apply:** Applicants must check the available website for the required materials. **Contact:** Telecommunications Association of Michigan Foundation, Inc. at the above address (see entry 6855).

6857 ■ Telluride Association

217 West Ave.
Ithaca, NY 14850
Ph: (607)273-5011
Fax: (607)272-2667
E-mail: ithaca_info@tellurideassociation.org
URL: http://www.tellurideassociation.org

6858 ■ Telluride Association Summer Program Scholarships *(High School/Scholarship)*

Purpose: To provide a unique educational opportunity to students from all social and financial backgrounds. **Focus:** General studies. **Qualif.:** Applicant must be a junior high school; must be nominated by a teacher, counselor, and other educators. **Criteria:** Applicants who will meet the requirements will be prioritized.

Funds Avail.: Covers all cost for the Telluride Association Summer Program (except travel cost). May also offer $500 as stipend to replace summer work earnings for students who would otherwise be unable to attend the program. **To Apply:** Teachers, educators, or counselors can nominate up to five candidates. TASP Nomination Form is available at the website. **Deadline:** December 3. **Contact:** Ellen Baer, Administrative Director: ellen.baer@tellurideassociation.org

6859 ■ Texas Association of Developing Colleges

1140 Empire Central, Ste. 550
Dallas, TX 75247
Ph: (214)630-2511
Fax: (214)631-2030
E-mail: info@txadc.org
URL: http://www.txadc.org

6860 ■ The Urban Scholarships Fund *(Undergraduate/Scholarship)*

Purpose: To strategically plan, organize and direct cooperative opportunities and programs for its members and serve as administrator of educational and community programs. **Focus:** General studies. **Qualif.:** Applicants must be U.S. citizens; must be full-time undergraduate students in good standing or graduating high school students. **Criteria:** Recipients are selected based on financial need.

Funds Avail.: $700 for community college; $2,000 for private four-year college students. **To Apply:** Applicants must submit a completed application form and a copy of high school or college transcript.

6861 ■ Texas Music Educators Association

7900 Centre Park
Austin, TX 78754
Ph: (512)452-0710
Fax: (512)451-9213
E-mail: rfloyd@tmea.org
URL: http://www.tmea.org

6862 ■ Bill Cormack Scholarships *(Undergraduate/Scholarship)*

Purpose: To provide professional growth opportunities; to encourage interaction among music education professionals; to foster public support for music in school; to offer quality musical experiences for students; to cultivate universal appreciation and lifetime involvement in music; to develop and maintain productive working relationships with other professional organizations. **Focus:** Music. **Qualif.:** Applicants must be entering freshmen in a Texas college or university; must major in a music degree program leading to Texas teacher-certification with music as the primary teaching field. **Criteria:** Recipients are selected based on academic performance.

Funds Avail.: $2,500. **To Apply:** Applicant must submit: completed application form; a high school transcript; a one-to-two page essay that describes his/her reasons for becoming a teacher, commitment to music education and future career goals; three-to-five evaluations from individuals who can assess the applicant's potential for success in an undergraduate music education program and as a music educator, music skills and abilities, work ethic and other personal qualities; must submit a verification from student's advisor that the applicant will teach within the semester indicated on the application. **Deadline:** November 15. **Contact:** Kay Vanlandingham at the above address (see entry 6861).

6863 ■ Texas Music Educators Association Past-Presidents Memorial Scholarships *(Undergraduate/Scholarship)*

Purpose: To provide professional growth opportunities; to encourage interaction among music education professionals; to foster public support for music in school; to offer quality musical experiences for students; to cultivate universal appreciation and lifetime involvement in music; to develop and maintain productive working relationships with other professional organizations. **Focus:** Music. **Qualif.:** Applicants must be entering freshmen at a Texas college or university; must major in a music degree program leading to Texas teacher-certification with music as the primary teaching field. **Criteria:** Recipients are selected based on academic performance.

Funds Avail.: $2,000. **To Apply:** Applicants must submit: completed application form; high school transcript; a one-to-two-page essay that describes his or her reasons for becoming a teacher, commitment to music education and future career goals; three-to-five evaluations from individuals who can assess the applicant's potential for success in an undergraduate music education program and as a music educator, music skills and abilities, work ethic and other personal qualities; must submit a verification by student's advisor that the applicant will teach within the semester indicated on the application. **Deadline:** November 15. **Contact:** Kay Vanlandingham at the above address (see entry 6861).

6864 ■ Texas Mutual Insurance Company
6210 E Hwy. 290
Austin, TX 78723-1098
Ph: (512)224-3800
Free: 800-583-5995
E-mail: information@texasmutual.com
URL: http://www.texasmutual.com

6865 ■ Texas Mutual Scholarship Program *(Undergraduate/Scholarship)*

Purpose: To provide financial support for the surviving family members of employees who died from an on-the-job accident, and/or whose injuries qualify for lifetime income benefits, to have the chance to pursue education and training to help them build better futures. **Focus:** Vocational-technical education. **Qualif.:** Applicants must be unmarried surviving children of an individual who died as a result of a work-related injury or whose severe injuries qualify them for a lifetime income benefits (LIBs) under the Texas Worker's Compensation Act. **Criteria:** Applicants will be evaluated based on age (must be unmarried and be between the ages of 16 and 25) and academic performance.

Funds Avail.: $4,000. **To Apply:** Applicants must complete the application form available at the website of Texas Mutual Insurance Company and submit along with the other materials needed to qualify for the scholarship.

6866 ■ Texas Scottish Rite Hospital for Children
2222 Welborn St.
Dallas, TX 75219
Ph: (214)559-5000
Fax: (214)559-7428
Free: 800-421-1121
E-mail: tsrhpress@tsrh.org
URL: http://www.tsrhc.org

6867 ■ Legacy Scholarship Program *(Undergraduate/Scholarship)*

Purpose: To provide educational assistance for former patients of Texas Scottish Rite Hospital for Children. **Focus:** General studies. **Qualif.:** Applicants must be present or former patients of TSRHC; must have applied and been accepted to an undergraduate program in a university, junior college or approved technical training program. **Criteria:** Recipients are selected based on financial need; academic record; and challenges met.

Funds Avail.: No specific amount. **To Apply:** Applicants must submit all the required application information. **Deadline:** March 10.

6868 ■ Texas Society of Professional Engineers
PO Box 2145
Austin, TX 78768
Ph: (512)472-9286
Fax: (512)472-2934
Free: 800-580-8973
E-mail: trishb@tspe.org
URL: http://www.tspe.org

6869 ■ Texas Society of Professional Engineers Scholarships *(Undergraduate/Scholarship)*

Purpose: To provide financial assistance to students studying to become engineers in an engineering program at an ABET-accredited college or university. **Focus:** Engineering. **Qualif.:** Applicants must be United States citizens; high school seniors with a 3.0 or higher GPA entering college in the coming school year; have scored at least 600 in math, 550 in critical reading and 500 in writing on the SAT, or a 29 in math and 25 in English on the ACT; and enrolled in an ABET program. **Criteria:** Applicants are evaluated based on academic performance.

Funds Avail.: No specific amount. **To Apply:** Applicants must submit the completed application form; essay; two recommendations from non-relatives (high school teachers preferred); and an official transcript. **Deadline:** January 21.

6870 ■ Texas State University - San Marcos Development Foundation
601 University Dr., JCK 960
San Marcos, TX 78666
Ph: (512)245-3860
Fax: (512)245-4929
URL: http://www.developmentfoundation.com

6871 ■ Max Godwin Endowed Scholarships *(Undergraduate/Scholarship)*

Purpose: To provide financial assistance to students who want to pursue accounting in college. **Focus:** Accounting. **Qualif.:** Applicants must be enrolled full-time (12 hours or more) in the undergraduate accounting program, in good standing with the San Marcos Accounting Club; must have at least one semester remaining before graduation and a 2.50 overall GPA; must have completed Principles of Financial Accounting and Principles of Managerial Accounting with at least a "B". **Criteria:** Applicants are evaluated based on academic achievement.

Funds Avail.: $500. **To Apply:** Applicants must submit all the required application information.

6872 ■ Texas Telephone Association
1001 Congress Ave., Ste. 450
Austin, TX 78701
Ph: (512)472-1183
Fax: (512)472-1293
E-mail: braddenton@tta.org
URL: http://www.tta.org

6873 ■ Texas Telephone Association Foundation Scholarships *(Undergraduate/Scholarship)*

Purpose: To provide financial assistance to those students with financial hardship. **Focus:** General Studies. **Qualif.:** Applicants must be U.S citizens; must have earned a cumulative GPA of 3.0 or higher; must plan to attend a Texas college or university. **Criteria:** Preference will be based on criteria.

Funds Avail.: $1,500. **To Apply:** Applicants must submit completed application, postmarked before March 14. Application must include a current transcript; a letter of acceptance from a Texas college or university; a copy of student's SAR (Student Aid Report).

Awards are arranged alphabetically below their administering organizations

Remarks: Special consideration will be given to students who will be pursuing a college degree in fields of study relevant to telecommunications (math, business, engineering, and computer science). **Contact:** Texas Telephone Association Foundation at the above address (see entry 6872).

6874 ■ Textile Care Allied Trades Association

271 Rte. 46 W No. D203
Fairfield, NJ 07004
Ph: (973)244-1790
Fax: (973)244-4455
E-mail: info@tcata.org
URL: http://www.tcata.org

6875 ■ TCATA College Scholarship Program *(Undergraduate/Scholarship)*

Purpose: To provide financial support for students interested in pursuing a degree at any accredited U.S. college or university on a full-time basis. **Focus:** General studies. **Qualif.:** Applicant must be a full-time employee, or a son or daughter of a full-time employee, of a member company in good standing of the Textile Care Allied Trades Association for three years. **Criteria:** Recipient will be selected based on academic achievement, leadership qualities, and courses of study.

Funds Avail.: $1,000. **To Apply:** Applicants must complete an application form and provide a copy of Scholarship Aptitude Text (SAT) or American College Test (ACT) scores; transcripts of all high school grades and any college grades if applicable; a letter from their high school principal - or other highest official equivalent - describing their leadership qualities, extra-curricular activities and other relevant information; and a letter describing past personal accomplishments, immediate goals and future academic and career objectives. **Deadline:** April 1.

6876 ■ ThanksUSA

1390 Chain Bridge Rd., No. 260
McLean, VA 22101
Free: 888-849-8720
URL: http://www.thanksusa.org

6877 ■ ThanksUSA Scholarships *(Undergraduate/Scholarship)*

Purpose: To support the dependents and spouses of active duty U.S. military service personnel with their educational pursuits. **Focus:** General studies. **Qualif.:** Applicants must be dependent children, age 24 and under, or spouses of active-duty U.S. military service personnel; planning to enroll full-time in an accredited two-year or four-year college, university, vocational school or technical school; have at least a 2.5 cumulative GPA on a 4.0 scale, or its equivalent, on relevant academic record (high-school record for incoming freshmen or post-secondary school record for those already enrolled in a college, university or vocational/technical school). **Criteria:** Recipients are selected based on financial need, academic record and demonstrated leadership and participation in school and community activities. Preference is given to children or spouses of service personnel killed or injured during active duty.

Funds Avail.: $3,000. **Number Awarded:** 500. **To Apply:** Applicants must submit a completed application along with transcripts and evidence of active military duty to verify eligibility. Copies of military I.D. are not acceptable. Mail application to ThanksUSA Scholarship Program, Scholarship America, c/o Shellee Hintz, One Scholarship Way, PO Box 297, St. Peter, MN 56082. **Deadline:** May 15. **Contact:** Scholarship Management Services at 507-931-0408, or shintz@scholarshipamerica.org.

6878 ■ Theatre for Young Audiences/USA

1602 Belle View Blvd., No. 810
Alexandria, VA 22307
Ph: (703)671-0640
E-mail: info@tya/usa.org
URL: http://www.assitej-usa.org

6879 ■ Anne Shaw Fellowships *(Graduate/Fellowship)*

Purpose: To support career development opportunities for theater artists and administrators committed to Theatre for Young Audiences. **Focus:** Theater arts. **Qualif.:** All active ASSITEJ/USA members are eligible to apply. **Criteria:** Priority is given to those applicants (at any stage of their TYA and theatre career) who state clear objectives for career developments and thoughtfully describe a process for active participation with another person, institution or organization.

Funds Avail.: $2,000. **To Apply:** Individuals may submit their proposal specifying a particular host or partner, or may request assistance matching their project proposal with a member of organization. Once an application has been given, the applicant should submit a one-page narrative, a budget, letters of support, and a professional resume. Applicants should articulate the purpose of the project and how it relates to their personal mission or the mission of the theater. **Deadline:** December 15. **Contact:** Leonora Inez Brown, Co-Chair Ann Shaw Fellowship; LBrown23@depaul.edu.

6880 ■ Third Wave Foundation

25 E 21st St., 4th Fl.
New York, NY 10010
Ph: (212)228-8311
Fax: (212)780-9181
E-mail: info@thirdwavefoundation.org
URL: http://thirdwavefoundation.org

6881 ■ The Lela Breitbart Memorial Scholarship Fund *(All/Scholarship)*

Purpose: To support organizations working on issues of reproductive justice around the country. **Focus:** Environmental law. **Qualif.:** Applicants must be women and transgender people between the ages of 15 and 30. **Criteria:** Recipients are selected based on financial need.

Funds Avail.: $3,000. **To Apply:** Applicants must submit a resume. Applicants must fill out the application form.

6882 ■ Thunder Bay Community Foundation

PO Box 20120
Thunder Bay, ON, Canada P7E 6P2
Ph: (807)475-7279
E-mail: tbcf@tbaytel.net
URL: http://www.tbcf.org

6883 ■ Helen L. Dewar Scholarships *(Undergraduate/Scholarship)*

Purpose: To provide scholarship assistance to qualified graduating students from Hammarskjold, Hillcrest and St.

Awards are arranged alphabetically below their administering organizations

Ignatius High Schools. **Focus:** General studies. **Qualif.:** Applicant must be from Hammerskfold High School, Hillcrest High School, or St. Ignatius High School; must have a minimum overall average of 80% in grade 12 credits; must be seeking full-time admission to a Canadian university that is accredited by the Association of Universities and Colleges of Canada. **Criteria:** Nominees will be evaluated based on marks, community involvement, each of the three reference letters, and the response to the essay question.

Funds Avail.: No specific amount. **Number Awarded:** 3. **To Apply:** Applicant must submit: completed application form (available online); three reference letters (one from a school source, one from extracurricular source, and one from the nominating committee/individual sponsoring their application for the scholarship); must submit all required documents to the Thunder Bay Community Foundation. **Deadline:** April 15.

6884 ■ Joshua Dyke Family Scholarships
(Undergraduate/Scholarship)

Purpose: To provide scholarship assistance to qualified graduating students from Dennis Franklin Cromarty, Geraldton Composite, La Verendrye, Lake Superior, Manitouwadge, Marathon, and Nipigon-Red Rock District High Schools. **Focus:** General studies. **Qualif.:** Applicants must be from Sir Winston Churchill C&VI, St. Patrick High School or Westgate C&VI; must be in their graduating year of secondary school; must have a minimum overall average of 80% in grade 12 credits; must be seeking full-time admission to a Canadian university that is accredited by the Association of Universities and Colleges of Canada. **Criteria:** Applicants will be evaluated based on marks, community involvement, each of the three reference letters, and the response to the essay question.

Funds Avail.: No specific amount. **Number Awarded:** 3. **To Apply:** Applicants must submit: completed application form (available online); three reference letters (one from a school source, one from extracurricular source, and one from the nominating committee/individual sponsoring their application for the scholarship); must submit all required documents to the Thunder Bay Community Foundation. **Deadline:** April 15.

6885 ■ Marathon Pulp Inc. Education Achievement Scholarships *(Undergraduate/Scholarship)*

Purpose: To provide scholarship assistance to graduating students who meet the requirements set out by Marathon Pulp Inc. **Focus:** General studies. **Qualif.:** Applicant must have completed the last year of secondary school less than 12 months prior; must have obtained an average of 75% in the last two years of schooling; must be seeking admission on a full-time basis to a university that is a member or affiliated to a member of the Association of University and Colleges of Canada. **Criteria:** Application will be evaluated by the scholarship committee based on complete high school academic record as well as a confidential report from the student's school, letter of reference, and details of the applicant's involvement in nonsport activities, community activities, athletics and other special interests.

Funds Avail.: $6,000. **To Apply:** Information and application forms are available at Marathon High School Student Services or may be obtained by written request to the Thunder Bay Community Foundation. Application and other supporting documents must be sent to the Thunder Bay Community Foundation. **Deadline:** April 30.

6886 ■ John Alexander McLean Scholarships
(Undergraduate/Scholarship)

Purpose: To provide scholarship assistance to qualified graduating students from the Bachelor of Education program at Lakehead University. **Focus:** Education. **Qualif.:** Applicant must be in their final year before graduation from the Bachelor of Education program at Lakehead University; must be pursuing a career in education; must have a minimum overall average of 80% in all university credits. **Criteria:** Applicant will be evaluated based on marks, community involvement, each of the three reference letters, and the response to the essay question.

Funds Avail.: No specific amount. **To Apply:** Applicant must submit: completed application form (available online); three reference letters (one from a school source, one from extracurricular source, and one from the nominating committee/individual sponsoring their application for the scholarship); must submit all required documents to the Thunder Bay Community Foundation. **Deadline:** April 15.

6887 ■ Geraldine Ruth Rogers Scholarships
(Undergraduate/Scholarship)

Purpose: To provide scholarship assistance to qualified graduating students from Dennis Franklin Cromarty, Geraldton Composite, La Verendrye, Lake Superior, Manitouwadge, Marathon, and Nipigon-Red Rock District High School. **Focus:** General studies. **Qualif.:** Applicants must be from Dennis Franklin Cromarty High School, Geraldton Composite High School, Ecole secondaire catholique de la Verendrye, Lake Superior High School, Manitouwadge High School, Marathon High School or Nipigon-Red Rock District High School; must be in their graduating year of secondary school; must have a minimum overall average of 80% in Grade 12 credits; must be seeking full-time admission to a Canadian university that accredited by the Association of Universities and Colleges of Canada. **Criteria:** Applicant will be evaluated based on marks, community involvement, each of the three reference letters, and the response to the essay question.

Funds Avail.: No specific amount. **Number Awarded:** 5. **To Apply:** Applicants must submit: completed application form (available online); three reference letters (one from a school source, one from extracurricular source, and one from the nominating committee/individual sponsoring their application for the scholarship); must submit all required documents to the Thunder Bay Community Foundation. **Deadline:** April 15.

6888 ■ Ross A. Wilson Science Scholarships
(Undergraduate/Scholarship)

Purpose: To provide scholarship assistance to qualified graduating students at Hammarskjold High School who excel in science. **Focus:** Science. **Qualif.:** Applicant must be: from Hammarskjold High School; pursuing a university degree and career in the sciences; in their graduating year of secondary school. Applicant must have a minimum overall average of 80% in Grade 12 credits; must be seeking full-time admission to a Canadian university that is accredited by the Association of Universities and Colleges of Canada. **Criteria:** Applicant will be evaluated based on marks, community involvement, each of the three reference letters, and the response to the essay question.

Funds Avail.: No specific amount. **Number Awarded:** 3. **To Apply:** Applicant must submit: completed application form (available online); three reference letters (one from a school source, one from extracurricular source, and one from the nominating committee/individual sponsoring their application for the scholarship); must submit all required documents to the Thunder Bay Community Foundation. **Deadline:** April 15.

6889 ■ Tidewater Builders Association

2117 Smith Ave.
Chesapeake, VA 23320-2515
Ph: (757)420-2434
Fax: (757)424-5954
E-mail: cpfieffer@tbaonline.org
URL: http://www.tbaonline.org

6890 ■ Tidewater Builders Association Scholarships *(Undergraduate/Scholarship)*

Purpose: To improve climate for quality housing for all incomes; to promote the growth and development of the shelter industry; to promote excellence and professionalism among members through educational and networking opportunities; to support and enhance the community through charitable projects. **Focus:** General studies. **Qualif.:** Applicants must be local high school seniors residing in the TBA service area; must be U.S. citizens; must attend an accredited four-year undergraduate degree program as a full-time student during the four-year period of continual and uninterrupted studies. **Criteria:** Recipients are selected based on financial need and academic standing.

Funds Avail.: No specific amount. **To Apply:** Applicants must complete the application form. **Deadline:** March 21. **Contact:** mhearring@tbaonline.org.

6891 ■ Touro Synagogue Foundation

85 Touro St.
Newport, RI 02840
Ph: (401)847-4794
Fax: (401)845-8790
E-mail: info@tourosynagogue.org
URL: http://www.tourosynagogue.org

6892 ■ The Aaron and Rita Slom Scholarships *(Undergraduate/Scholarship)*

Purpose: To educate future generations. **Focus:** Historical preservation. **Qualif.:** Applicants must be a high school graduating students. **Criteria:** The scholarships are for high school seniors who plan to enroll in an institute of higher learning for a minimum of six credits. The institution can be public or private, and has no geographic limitations.

Funds Avail.: $500. **To Apply:** Students must submit an interpretative work (i.e. written submission, audio visual, documentary, film, Powerpoint...) focusing on the George Washington letter in context with the present time. Written submissions such as essays, stories, poems (no less than 500 words and no more than 1000 words), or audio-visual submissions such as documentaries, films or computer presentations (no more than 10 minutes) will be considered. **Deadline:** April 4. **Contact:** Touro Synagogue Foundation at the above address (see entry 6891).

6893 ■ Toyota Motor Sales

19001 S Western Ave. Dept. WC11
Torrance, CA 90501
Fax: (310)468-7814
Free: 800-331-4331
URL: http://www.toyota.com

6894 ■ Toyota Community Scholars *(Undergraduate/Scholarship)*

Purpose: To provide financial support to those students who are in need. **Focus:** General studies. **Qualif.:** Applicants must be high school seniors; must be in good academic standing; must have leadership skills and commitment to community service. **Criteria:** Selection will be based on criteria.

Funds Avail.: $10,000; $20,000. **Number Awarded:** 100. **To Apply:** Applicants must see their high school guidance counselors or administration office for an application. **Contact:** High School Guidance Counselor: For more information, please contact: Educational Testing Service P. O. Box 6730 Princeton, NJ 08541 at 609-771-7878; 609-771-7750; (f) or email: srp-csr@ets.org.

6895 ■ Transport Workers Union of America

1700 Broadway
New York, NY 10019
Ph: (212)259-4900
Fax: (212)265-4537
URL: http://www.twu.org

6896 ■ Michael J. Quill Scholarships *(Undergraduate/Scholarship)*

Purpose: To provide professional legal, education, research and public relations services to the local and divisions. **Focus:** General studies. **Qualif.:** Applicants must be senior high school students of son, daughter, dependent brothers and sisters of present, retired, or deceased TWU members who will enter an accredited college of their own choice. **Criteria:** Recipients are selected based on applicant's capability to do the college work under the High School Principal certification.

Funds Avail.: $1,200. **Number Awarded:** 15. **To Apply:** Applicants must fill out the coupon on the back page of the January, February, or March TWU Express. **Deadline:** May 1. **Contact:** Transport Worker's Union of America at the above address (see entry 6895).

6897 ■ Transportation Association of Canada

2323 St., Laurent Blvd.
Ottawa, ON, Canada K1G 4J8
Ph: (613)736-1350
Fax: (613)736-1395
E-mail: secretariat@tac-act.ca
URL: http://www.tac-atc.ca

6898 ■ TAC Foundation-3M Canada Company *(Postgraduate, Undergraduate/Scholarship)*

Purpose: To recognize the importance of education in the transportation field. **Focus:** Transportation. **Qualif.:** Applicants must be Canadian citizens or landed immigrants. **Criteria:** Preference will be given to candidates with relevant work experience.

Funds Avail.: $5,000. **To Apply:** Applicant must complete the application form available online; must provide academic references and relevant employment information; must have an electronic version of their transcript of record. Application form and requirements must be sent to the TAC Foundation. **Deadline:** March 3.

6899 ■ TAC Foundation-Albert M. Stevens Scholarships *(Postgraduate/Scholarship)*

Purpose: To support the students in Canada pursuing postgraduate studies in transportation. **Focus:** Transporta-

Awards are arranged alphabetically below their administering organizations

tion. **Qualif.:** Applicants must be admissible to a postgraduate studies program or already registered as full-time graduate students; must be studying in the field of transportation and meet the conditions which apply to the scholarships; must be in the top quarter of their class in addition to having a minimum GPA of B. **Criteria:** Selection of applicants will be based on academic standing and application requirements.

Funds Avail.: $5,000. **To Apply:** Applicant must complete the application form available online; must provide academic references and relevant employment information; must have an electronic version of their transcript of record. Application form and requirements must be sent to the TAC Foundation. **Deadline:** March 3.

6900 ■ TAC Foundation-Armtec Scholarships *(Undergraduate/Scholarship)*

Purpose: To encourage engineering students to focus on the vital aspects of Canada's landscape. **Focus:** Civil engineering; Transportation. **Qualif.:** Applicant must be entering third or fourth year studies; must intend to pursue a career in some aspect of the transportation field and meet the conditions of the scholarships; must have achieved an overall B level or equivalent average mark in their previous academic year. **Criteria:** Preference will be given to candidates with relevant work experience.

Funds Avail.: $5,000. **To Apply:** Applicant must complete the application form (available online); must provide academic references and relevant employment information; must have an electronic version of their transcript of record. Application form and requirements must be sent to the TAC Foundation. **Deadline:** March 3.

6901 ■ TAC Foundation-BA Group Scholarships *(Postgraduate, Undergraduate/Scholarship)*

Purpose: To encourage students to acquire the full range of technical skills required for contributing to the development of superior transportation solutions. **Focus:** Transportation. **Qualif.:** Applicants must be Canadian citizens or landed immigrants. **Criteria:** Preference will be given to candidates with relevant work experience.

Funds Avail.: $5,000. **To Apply:** Applicant must complete the application form available online; must provide academic references and relevant employment information; must have an electronic version of their transcript of record. Application form and requirements must be sent to the TAC Foundation. **Deadline:** March 3.

6902 ■ TAC Foundation-Cement Association of Canada Scholarships *(Postgraduate, Undergraduate/Scholarship)*

Purpose: To recognize the importance of education in the transportation field. **Focus:** Transportation. **Qualif.:** Applicants must be Canadian citizens or landed immigrants. **Criteria:** Preference will be given to candidates with relevant work experience.

Funds Avail.: $5,000. **To Apply:** Applicant must complete the application form available online; must provide academic references and relevant employment information; must have an electronic version of their transcript of record. Application form and requirements must be sent to the TAC Foundation. **Deadline:** March 3.

6903 ■ TAC Foundation-Delcan Corporation Scholarships *(Postgraduate, Undergraduate/Scholarship)*

Purpose: To recognize the importance of education in the transportation field. **Focus:** Transportation. **Qualif.:** Applicants must be Canadian citizens or landed immigrants. **Criteria:** Preference will be given to candidates with relevant work experience.

Funds Avail.: $5,000. **To Apply:** Applicant must complete the application form available online; must provide academic references and relevant employment information; must have an electronic version of their transcript of record. Application form and requirements must be sent to the TAC Foundation. **Deadline:** March 3.

6904 ■ TAC Foundation-Dillon Consulting Scholarships *(Undergraduate/Scholarship)*

Purpose: To provide support and encouragement to those interested in pursuing a career in transportation planning or transportation engineering. **Focus:** Transportation. **Qualif.:** Applicant must be entering third or fourth year studies; must intend to pursue a career in some aspect of the transportation field and meet the conditions of the scholarships; must have achieved an overall B level or equivalent average mark in their previous academic year. **Criteria:** Preference will be given to candidates with relevant work experience.

Funds Avail.: $5,000. **To Apply:** Applicant must complete the application form (available online); must provide academic references and relevant employment information; must have an electronic version of their transcript of record. Application form and requirements must be sent to the TAC Foundation. **Deadline:** March 3.

6905 ■ TAC Foundation-EBA Engineering Consultants Ltd. Scholarships *(Postgraduate, Undergraduate/Scholarship)*

Purpose: To provide scholarship to graduate and postgraduate students who are doing research in transportation infrastructure and systems. **Focus:** Transportation. **Qualif.:** Applicants must be Canadian citizens or landed immigrants. **Criteria:** Preference is given for research in the areas of design, construction, maintenance and operation of roadway transportation systems in rural and urban environments.

Funds Avail.: $5,000. **To Apply:** Applicant must complete the application form available online; must provide academic references and relevant employment information; must have an electronic version of their transcript of record. Application form and requirements must be sent to the TAC Foundation. **Deadline:** March 3.

6906 ■ TAC Foundation-IBI Group Scholarships *(Postgraduate, Undergraduate/Scholarship)*

Purpose: To provide scholarship to graduate and postgraduate students who are pursuing a degree in transportation. **Focus:** Transportation. **Qualif.:** Applicants must be Canadian citizens or landed immigrants. **Criteria:** Preference will be given to candidates with relevant work experience.

Funds Avail.: $5,000. **To Apply:** Applicant must complete the application form (available online); must provide academic references and relevant employment information; must have an electronic version of their transcript of record. Application form and requirements must be sent to the TAC Foundation. **Deadline:** March 3.

6907 ■ TAC Foundation-iTRANS Consulting Scholarships *(Postgraduate/Scholarship)*

Purpose: To provide financial support to students pursuing postgraduate studies in transportation planning and transportation engineering. **Focus:** Transportation. **Qualif.:** Applicants must be admissible to a postgraduate studies program or already registered as full-time students; must be studying in the field of transportation and meet the conditions which apply to the scholarship; must be in the top quarter of their class in addition to having a minimum GPA of B. **Criteria:** Selection of applicants will be based on academic standing and application requirements.

Funds Avail.: $10,000. **To Apply:** Applicant must complete the application form (available online); must provide academic references and relevant employment information; must have an electronic version of their transcript of record. Application form and requirements must be sent to the TAC Foundation. **Deadline:** March 3.

6908 ■ TAC Foundation-McCormick Rankin Corporation Scholarships *(Undergraduate/Scholarship)*

Purpose: To recognize the importance of education in the transportation field. **Focus:** Transportation. **Qualif.:** Applicant must be entering third or fourth year studies; must intend to pursue a career in some aspect of the transportation field and meet the conditions of the scholarships; must have achieved an overall B level or equivalent average mark in their previous academic year. **Criteria:** Preference will be given to candidates with relevant work experience.

Funds Avail.: $5,000. **To Apply:** Applicant must complete the application form available online; must provide academic references and relevant employment information; must have an electronic version of their transcript of record. Application form and requirements must be sent to the TAC Foundation. **Deadline:** March 3.

6909 ■ TAC Foundation-MMM Group Limited Scholarships *(Postgraduate, Undergraduate/Scholarship)*

Purpose: To recognize the importance of education in the transportation field. **Focus:** Transportation. **Qualif.:** Applicants must be Canadian citizens or landed immigrants. **Criteria:** Preference will be given to a student who intends to pursue a career in the private sector.

Funds Avail.: $5,000. **To Apply:** Applicant must complete the application form (available online); must provide academic references and relevant employment information; must have an electronic version of their transcript of record. Application form and requirements must be sent to the TAC Foundation. **Deadline:** March 3.

6910 ■ TAC Foundation-Municipalities Scholarships *(Postgraduate, Undergraduate/Scholarship)*

Purpose: To recognize the importance of education in the transportation field. **Focus:** Transportation. **Qualif.:** Applicants must be Canadian citizens or landed immigrants. **Criteria:** Preference will be given to candidates with relevant work experience.

Funds Avail.: $3,000. **To Apply:** Applicant must complete the application form (available online); must provide academic references and relevant employment information; must have an electronic version of their transcript of record. Application form and requirements must be sent to the TAC Foundation. **Deadline:** March 3.

6911 ■ TAC Foundation-Provinces and Territories Scholarships *(Postgraduate, Undergraduate/Scholarship)*

Purpose: To recognize the importance of education in the transportation field. **Focus:** Transportation. **Qualif.:** Applicants must be Canadian citizens or landed immigrants. **Criteria:** Preference will be given to candidates with relevant work experience.

Funds Avail.: $5,000. **To Apply:** Applicant must complete the application form (available online); must provide academic references and relevant employment information; must have an electronic version of their transcript of record. Application form and requirements must be sent to the TAC Foundation. **Deadline:** March 3.

6912 ■ TAC Foundation Scholarships *(Postgraduate, Undergraduate/Scholarship)*

Purpose: To recognize the importance of education in the transportation field. **Focus:** Transportation. **Qualif.:** Applicants must be Canadian citizens or landed immigrants. **Criteria:** Preference will be given to candidates with relevant work experience.

Funds Avail.: $5,000. **To Apply:** Applicant must complete the application form available online; must provide academic references and relevant employment information; must have an electronic version of their transcript of record. Application form and requirements must be sent to the TAC Foundation. **Deadline:** March 3.

6913 ■ TAC Foundation-Stantec Consulting Scholarships *(Postgraduate/Scholarship)*

Purpose: To encourage students to continue their postgraduate studies in the field of transportation engineering and to contribute to the cost-effective mobility upon which our society is based. **Focus:** Transportation. **Qualif.:** Applicants must be admissible to a postgraduate studies program or already registered as full-time graduate students; must be studying in the field of transportation and meet the conditions which apply to the scholarships; must be in the top quarter of their class in addition to having a minimum GPA of B. **Criteria:** Selection of applicants will be based on academic standing and application requirements.

Funds Avail.: $5,000. **To Apply:** Applicant must complete the application form available online; must provide academic references and relevant employment information; must have an electronic version of their transcript of record. Application form and requirements must be sent to the TAC Foundation. **Deadline:** March 3.

6914 ■ TAC Foundation-UMA Engineering Ltd. Scholarships *(Undergraduate/Scholarship)*

Purpose: To provide scholarship to the individuals working towards a career in the transportation industry as engineers, planners, program mangers or other technical specialties. **Focus:** Transportation. **Qualif.:** Applicant must be entering third or fourth year studies; must intend to pursue a career in some aspect of the transportation field and meet the conditions of the scholarships; must have achieved an overall B level or equivalent average mark in their previous academic year. **Criteria:** Preference will be given to candidates with relevant work experience.

Funds Avail.: $5,000. **To Apply:** Applicant must complete the application form available online; must provide academic references and relevant employment information; must have an electronic version of their transcript of record. Application form and requirements must be sent to the TAC Foundation. **Deadline:** March 3.

6915 ■ TAC Foundation-Waterloo Alumni Scholarships *(Postgraduate/Scholarship)*

Purpose: To provide financial support to students pursuing postgraduate studies in transportation. **Focus:** Transportation. **Qualif.:** Applicants must be admissible to a postgraduate studies program or already be registered as full-time graduate students; must be studying in the field of transportation and meet the conditions which apply to the scholarships; must be in the top quarter of their class in addition to having a minimum GPA of B. **Criteria:** Preference will be given to qualified candidates pursuing their work in the pavement field.

Funds Avail.: $7,500. **To Apply:** Applicant must complete the application form available online; must provide academic references and relevant employment information; must have an electronic version of their transcript of record. Application form and requirements must be sent to the TAC Foundation. **Deadline:** March 3.

6916 ■ Transportation Clubs International

PO Box 2223
Ocean Shores, WA 98569
Ph: 877-858-8627
Free: (187)78588628
E-mail: info@transporationclubsinternational.com
URL: http://www.transportationclubsinternational.com

6917 ■ Ginger and Fred Deines Canada Scholarships *(Undergraduate/Scholarship)*

Purpose: To create, stimulate, and perpetuate discussion of topics relating to local and national transportation issues; to promote member clubs, companies, and individuals the importance of transportation and transportation logistics; to promote the general welfare of member clubs and their membership; to provide an international forum for local transportation and logistics organizations; to stimulate and perpetuate dialogue among its members on subjects of national and international transportation importance; and to promote education in the transportation industry. **Focus:** Transportation; Logistics; Traffic Management. **Qualif.:** Applicants must be enrolled in an educational program in an accredited institution of higher learning in a vocational or degree program in the fields of Transportation, Logistics or Traffic Management or related fields intending to prepare for a career in these areas. They must be of Canadian nationality and enrolled in a school in Canada or the U.S. **Criteria:** Recipients are selected based on scholastic ability, potential, professional interest, character, and financial need.

Funds Avail.: $2,000. **To Apply:** Applicants must submit a certified copy of the college/university transcript; three letters of recommendation; a small, current photograph to be used for publication; an essay of not more than 200-words, explaining why you have chosen transportation or an allied field as a career path; and outline of the objectives. **Deadline:** May 31. **Contact:** Transportation Clubs International Scholarships Attn: Bill Blair, Zimmer Worldwide Logistics at 15710 JFK Blvd., Houston, Texas 77032; bblair@zimmerworlwide.com

6918 ■ Ginger and Fred Deines Mexico Scholarships *(Undergraduate/Scholarship)*

Purpose: To create, stimulate, and perpetuate discussion of topics relating to local and national transportation issues; to promote member clubs, companies, and individuals the importance of transportation and transportation logistics; to promote the general welfare of member clubs and their membership; to provide an international forum for local transportation and logistics organizations; to stimulate and perpetuate dialogue among its members on subjects of national and international transportation importance; and to promote education in the transportation industry. **Focus:** Transportation; Logistics; Traffic Management. **Qualif.:** Applicants must be enrolled in an educational program in an accredited institution of higher learning in a vocational or degree program in the fields of Transportation, Logistics or Traffic Management or related fields intending to prepare for a career in these areas. They must be of Mexican nationality and enrolled in a school in Mexico or the U.S. **Criteria:** Recipients are selected based on scholastic ability, potential, professional interest, character, and financial need.

Funds Avail.: $2,000. **To Apply:** Applicants must submit a certified copy of the college/university transcript; three letters of recommendation; a small, current photograph to be used for publication; an essay of not more than 200 words explaining why you have chosen transportation or an allied field as a career path; and outline of the objectives. **Deadline:** May 31. **Contact:** Transportation Clubs International Scholarships Attn: Bill Blair, Zimmer Worldwide Logistics at 15710 JFK Blvd., Houston, Texas 77032; bblair@zimmerworlwide.com

6919 ■ Hooper Memorial Scholarships *(Undergraduate/Scholarship)*

Purpose: To create, stimulate, and perpetuate discussion of topics relating to local and national transportation issues; to promote member clubs, companies, and individuals the importance of transportation and transportation logistics; to promote the general welfare of member clubs and their membership; to provide an international forum for local transportation and logistics organizations; to stimulate and perpetuate dialogue among its members on subjects of national and international transportation importance; and to promote education in the transportation industry. **Focus:** Transportation; Logistics; Traffic Management. **Qualif.:** Applicants must be enrolled in an educational program in an accredited institution of higher learning in a vocational or degree program in the fields of Transportation, Logistics or Traffic Management or related fields intending to prepare for a career in these areas. **Criteria:** Recipients are selected based on scholastic ability, potential, professional interest, character, and financial need.

Funds Avail.: $2,000. **To Apply:** Applicants must submit a certified copy of the college/university transcript; three letters of recommendation; a small, current photograph to be use for publication; an essay of not more than 200-words, explaining why you have chosen transportation or an allied field as a career path; and outline of the objectives. **Deadline:** May 31. **Contact:** Transportation Clubs International Scholarships Attn: Bill Blair, Zimmer Worldwide Logistics at 15710 JFK Blvd., Houston, Texas 77032; bblair@zimmerworlwide.com

6920 ■ Denny Lydic Scholarships *(Undergraduate/Scholarship)*

Purpose: To create, stimulate, and perpetuate discussion of topics relating to local and national transportation issues; to promote member clubs, companies, and individuals the importance of transportation and transportation logistics; to promote the general welfare of member clubs and their membership; to provide an international forum for local transportation and logistics organizations; to stimulate and perpetuate dialogue among its members on subjects of national and international transportation importance; and to promote education in the transportation industry. **Focus:** Transportation; Logistics; Traffic Management. **Qualif.:** Applicants must be enrolled in an educational program in an accredited institution of higher learning in a vocational or degree program in the fields of Transportation, Logistics or Traffic Management or related fields intending to prepare for a career in these areas. **Criteria:** Recipients are selected based on scholastic ability, potential, professional interest, character, and financial need.

Funds Avail.: $1,000. **To Apply:** Applicants must submit a certified copy of the college/university transcript; three letters of recommendation; a small, current photograph to be used for publication; an essay not more than 200-words explaining why you have chosen transportation or an allied field as a career path; and outline of the objectives. **Deadline:** May 31. **Contact:** Transportation Clubs International Scholarships Attn: Bill Blair, Zimmer Worldwide Logistics at 15710 JFK Blvd., Houston, Texas 77032; bblair@zimmerworlwide.com

6921 ■ Texas Transportation Scholarships
(Undergraduate/Scholarship)

Purpose: To create, stimulate, and perpetuate discussion of topics relating to local and national transportation issues; to promote member clubs, companies, and individuals the importance of transportation and transportation logistics; to promote the general welfare of member clubs and their membership; to provide an international forum for local transportation and logistics organizations; To stimulate and perpetuate dialogue among members on subjects of national and international transportation importance; and to promote education in the transportation industry. **Focus:** Transportation; Logistics; Traffic Management. **Qualif.:** Applicants must be enrolled in an educational program in an accredited institution of higher learning in a vocational or degree program in the fields of Transportation, Logistics or Traffic Management or related fields intending to prepare for a career in these areas. **Criteria:** Recipients are selected based on scholastic ability, potential, professional interest, character, and financial need.

Funds Avail.: $1,500. **To Apply:** Applicants must submit a certified copy of the college/university transcript; three letters of recommendation; a small, current photograph to be used for publication; an essay not more than 200-words explaining why you have chosen transportation or an allied field as a career path; and outline of the objectives. **Deadline:** May 31. **Contact:** Transportation Clubs International Scholarships Attn: Bill Blair, Zimmer Worldwide Logistics at 15710 JFK Blvd., Houston, Texas 77032; bblair@zimmerworlwide.com

6922 ■ Alice Glaisyer Warfield Scholarships
(Undergraduate/Scholarship)

Purpose: To create, stimulate, and perpetuate discussion of topics relating to local and national transportation issues; to promote member clubs, companies, and individuals the importance of transportation and transportation logistics; to promote the general welfare of member clubs and their membership; to provide an international forum for local transportation and logistics organizations; To stimulate and perpetuate dialogue among its members on subjects of national and international transportation importance; and to promote education in the transportation industry. **Focus:** Transportation; Logistics; Traffic Management. **Qualif.:** Applicants must be enrolled in an educational program in an accredited institution of higher learning in a vocational or degree program in the fields of Transportation, Logistics or Traffic Management or related fields intending to prepare for a career in these areas. **Criteria:** Recipients are selected based on scholastic ability, potential, professional interest, character, and financial need.

Funds Avail.: $1,500. **To Apply:** Applicants must submit a certified copy of the college/university transcript; three letters of recommendation; a small, current photograph to be used for publication; an essay of not more than 200 words explaining why you have chosen transportation or an allied field as a career path; and outline of the objectives. **Deadline:** May 31. **Contact:** Transportation Clubs International Scholarships Attn: Bill Blair, Zimmer Worldwide Logistics at 15710 JFK Blvd., Houston, Texas 77032; bblair@zimmerworlwide.com

6923 ■ Truck Renting and Leasing Association

675 N Washington St., Ste. 410
Alexandria, VA 22314
Ph: (703)299-9120
Fax: (703)299-9115
E-mail: pvroom@trala.com
URL: http://www.trala.org

6924 ■ TRALA Scholarships Program
(Undergraduate/Scholarship)

Purpose: To provide financial assistance for the education of the dependents of TRALA members. **Focus:** General studies. **Qualif.:** Applicant must be a high school senior; a dependent of a full-time employee of TRALA member companies; and have a GPA of 3.0 or higher in a 4.0 scale. **Criteria:** Selection of recipients will be administered by Scholarship America.

Funds Avail.: $5000. **Number Awarded:** 2. **To Apply:** Application form is available at the website. Applicants must submit a completed application form together with a current transcript of grades to: TRALA Scholarship Fund, Scholarship America, One Scholarship Way PO Box 297 St. Peter, MN 56082. **Deadline:** = January 15. **Contact:** Scholarship America, Telephone: (507)931-1682; Fax: (507)931-9168.

6925 ■ Truckload Carriers Association

555 E Braddock Rd.
Alexandria, VA 22314
Ph: (703)838-1950
Fax: (703)838-6610
E-mail: tca@truckload.org
URL: http://www.truckload.org

6926 ■ Truckload Carriers Association Scholarships *(Undergraduate/Scholarship)*

Purpose: To provide financial assistance for the education of TCA members. **Focus:** General studies. **Qualif.:** Applicants must be a college junior or senior in good standing, who is a child, grandchild or spouse of an employee of a trucking company, or the child, grandchild or spouse of an independent contractor or an independent contractor affiliated with a trucking company and attending an accredited four-year college or university. **Criteria:** The recipient will be selected based on financial need, excellence in scholastic achievement in freshman and sophomore years (minimum of 3.3 cumulative GPA), full-time student status with high character and integrity. Students pursuing transportation and business degrees will be given special consideration.

Funds Avail.: $2,000 up to $5,000. **To Apply:** Applicants must send their complete application, official complete transcript of all college courses and grades, course schedule including tuition and fees for upcoming term. **Deadline:** May 16.

Awards are arranged alphabetically below their administering organizations

6927 ■ Pierre Elliott Trudeau Foundation

1514 Doctor Penfield Ave., 2nd Flr.
Montreal, QC, Canada H3G 1B9
Ph: (514)938-0001
Fax: (514)938-0046
E-mail: tfinfo@trudeaufoundation.ca
URL: http://www.trudeaufoundation.ca

6928 ■ Trudeau Foundation Doctoral Scholarships *(Doctorate/Scholarship)*

Purpose: To support qualified individuals who want to pursue their research on a present-day concern. **Focus:** Humanities; Social sciences. **Qualif.:** Applicants must be Canadian citizens and landed immigrants pursuing fulltime doctoral studies in Canada; must be applying for the first year of a doctoral program, or be registered in the first or second year of such a program. **Criteria:** Selection of candidates will be based on the following criteria: (1) Academic achievement; (2) Outstanding ability to engage in lively exchange with other researchers and scholars; and (3) Intention to work in an area related to one or more of the four themes of the foundation and a desire to contribute to public dialogue about those themes.

Funds Avail.: $240,000. **To Apply:** Applicant must complete the application form available online; must submit the official transcript and reference letters. **Deadline:** January 9. **Contact:** Josee St-Martin, stmartin@trudeaufoundation.ca.

6929 ■ The Harry S. Truman Scholarship Foundation

712 Jackson Pl. NW
Washington, DC 20006
Ph: (202)395-4831
Fax: (202)395-6995
E-mail: office@truman.gov
URL: http://www.truman.gov

6930 ■ Harry S. Truman Scholarships *(Postgraduate/Scholarship)*

Purpose: To provide financial assistance to college students who are planning to pursue careers in government or elsewhere in public service. **Focus:** Public service. **Qualif.:** Candidates must be nominated by their current institution of higher education or by their two-year institution if they are transfer students from community colleges or junior colleges; must be a full-time junior-level student at a four-year institution pursuing a bachelor's degree; must be a student in his/her second or third year of collegiate study who expects to graduate, or a senior-level student who is a resident of Puerto Rico or the Islands; committed to a career in public service; in the upper quarter of his or her class; a U.S. citizen or a United States national from American Samoa or the Commonwealth of the Northern Mariana Islands. **Criteria:** Applicants are selected based on the jury's review of the application materials.

Funds Avail.: $30,000 merit-based. **Number Awarded:** 60-65. **To Apply:** Applicants must submit a completed application form which can be downloaded at www.truman.gov. **Deadline:** February 5.

6931 ■ Truss Plate Institute

218 N Lee St., Ste. 312
Alexandria, VA 22314
Ph: (703)683-1010
E-mail: mcassidy@tpinst.org
URL: http://www.tpinst.org

6932 ■ Truss Plate Institute Scholarships *(Doctorate/Scholarship)*

Purpose: To support a graduate-level research involving metal plate connected (MPC) wood trusses. **Focus:** Engineering. **Qualif.:** Applicant must be a graduate student (MS or PhD) maintaining a 3.0 GPA. **Criteria:** The RS Selection Committee will review all applications and awards the RS.

Funds Avail.: $25,000. **To Apply:** Applicants must submit an application form (downloadable from the website); transcript of college/university records; a biographical sketch (maximum of 200 words); an essay (maximum of 1500 words) about the purposed research. **Deadline:** January.

Remarks: Established in 1999. **Contact:** Executive Director, Michael A. Cassidy at the above address (see entry 6931).

6933 ■ Turf and Ornamental Communicators Association

120 W Main St.
New Prague, MN 56071
Ph: (952)758-6340
Fax: (952)758-5813
E-mail: tocaassociation@aol.com
URL: http://www.toca.org

6934 ■ Turf and Ornamental Communicators Association Scholarship Program *(Undergraduate/Scholarship)*

Purpose: To provide financial support for undergraduate college students pursuing a career in green industry communications. **Focus:** Communications. **Qualif.:** Applicants must major or minor in technical communications or a green industry related field such as horticulture, plant sciences, botany, agronomy, plant pathology, etc; must demonstrate an interest in using this course of study in the field of communications; must have overall GPA of 2.5 or above and a 3.0 in the major area of study (based on 4.0 scale). **Criteria:** Applicants will be evaluated by the Scholarship Committee.

Funds Avail.: $2,500. **To Apply:** Applicants must submit complete application form together with references, writing/editing sample, essay, resume, and transcript. **Deadline:** March 1.

6935 ■ Turkish Coalition of America

1025 Connecticut Ave. NW, Ste. 1000
Washington, DC 20036
Ph: (202)370-1399
Fax: (202)370-1398
E-mail: info@turkishcoalitionofamerica.org
URL: http://www.turkishcoalition.org

6936 ■ American Turkish Society Arif Mardin Music Fellowships *(Professional Development/Fellowship)*

Purpose: To provide financial assistance for promising musicians from Turkey and to give them the chance to study in the United States. **Focus:** Music. **Qualif.:** Ap-

Awards are arranged alphabetically below their administering organizations

plicants must be promising musicians from Turkey. **Criteria:** Consideration for the fellowship will be based on merit and potential to benefit from the program in current or future music career.

Funds Avail.: No specific amount. **Number Awarded:** 1. **To Apply:** Applicants must check the available website for more information.

Remarks: In honor of Arif Mardin (1932-2006), world-renowned producer/arranger and vice chairman of the American Turkish Society for many years. **Contact:** For more information on this program, please visit the American Turkish Society website at: www.americanturkishsociety-.org.

6937 ■ Ahmet Ertegun Memorial Scholarships *(Graduate, Undergraduate/Scholarship)*

Purpose: To provide financial support for deserving students of Turkish descent pursuing undergraduate or graduate studies in music. **Focus:** Music. **Qualif.:** Applicants must be music students at Juilliard School in New York City. **Criteria:** Preference will be given to those who meet the criteria.

Funds Avail.: No specific amount. **To Apply:** Applicants must check the available website for the required materials.

Remarks: One of the seminal figures in the history of popular music, Ahmet Ertegun was also a prominent philanthropist dedicated to enhancing relations and cultural understanding between the United States and his native country, Turkey.

6938 ■ TCA-BAACBH Scholarships *(Undergraduate/Scholarship)*

Purpose: To foster friendship, understanding and cooperation between the United States and Turkey and to explore the historical and cultural links between Turkey and Bosnia Herzegovina. **Focus:** General studies. **Qualif.:** Applicants must be Bosnian-American students. **Criteria:** Selection is based on merit.

Funds Avail.: No specific amount. **To Apply:** Applicants must check the available website for more information. **Contact:** Turkish Coalition of America at the above address (see entry 6935).

6939 ■ TCA Turkish American Scholarships *(Undergraduate/Scholarship)*

Purpose: To engage and cultivate a new generation of young Turkish American leaders. **Focus:** Public Affairs; Political Science; International Affairs and Relations; Communications; Printing Trades; Public Relations. **Qualif.:** Applicants must meet the following criteria: be a U.S. citizen or permanent resident (green card holder); have, and maintain through the course of the scholarship period, a cumulative minimum 3.3 GPA on a 4.0 scale; evidence of leadership commitment through participation in community service, particularly within the Turkish American community; and be a high school senior applying to an accredited college or university, or college student who plans to continue undergraduate study; or a college senior or graduate enrolled or about to enroll in graduate school. Graduate students who apply for the TCA must plan to pursue studies and a career in public affairs. **Criteria:** Candidates will be selected on the basis of academic achievement, interest in Turkish American issues as demonstrated by involvement in Turkish American community affairs, and individual leadership qualities conducive to pursuing a career in public affairs, media and public relations. Priority will be given to students who are admitted to top national universities or liberal arts schools.

Funds Avail.: No specific amount. **To Apply:** Applicants must submit three (3) collated, non-stapled, paperclipped copies of each of the following items: (1) Completed Application Form (2) Resume: Each copy should be submitted on one single-sided 8.5" x 11" sheet of paper. (3) Short essay: The essay should not exceed 500 words, must be typed and double-spaced. **Deadline:** June 6. **Contact:** Turkish Coalition of America at the above address (see entry 6935).

6940 ■ TCA-UMD Scholarships *(Undergraduate/Scholarship)*

Purpose: To foster friendship, understanding and cooperation between the United States and Turkey and to explore the historical and cultural links between Turkey and Macedonia. **Focus:** General studies. **Qualif.:** Applicants must be full time Macedonian-American undergraduates. **Criteria:** Preference will be given to those who meet the criteria.

Funds Avail.: $2,000. **Number Awarded:** 10. **To Apply:** Applicants must check the available website for the required materials. **Contact:** Turkish Coalition of America at the above address (see entry 6935).

6941 ■ J.L. Turner Legal Association

PO Box 134002
Dallas, TX 75313-4002
Ph: (214)761-1707
URL: http://www.jltla.org

6942 ■ JLTLA Scholarships *(Undergraduate/Scholarship)*

Purpose: To inspire educational pursuits in the field of law among law students. **Focus:** Law. **Qualif.:** Program is open to second or third year law students that are from or attending law school in the Dallas-Fort Worth Metroplex. **Criteria:** Selection will be based on financial need and merit.

Funds Avail.: No specific amount. **To Apply:** Applicants must submit the following requirements: application; a short biographical sketch (5-7 sentences, written in third person for inclusion in gala booklet if selected); photograph (3x5 or larger of head and shoulders, photograph should be suitable for inclusion in gala booklet if selected); a certified copy of law school transcript; letters of reference; and a brief essay. Applicants may download an application form at J.L Turner website. **Deadline:** September 28. **Contact:** Star A. Carter; 214-746-7899; Star.Carter@weil.com.

6943 ■ JLTLA Texas Bar Review Scholarships *(Undergraduate/Scholarship)*

Purpose: To inspire educational pursuits in the field of law among minority law students. **Focus:** Law. **Qualif.:** Applicants must be in their 3L year and must be taking the Texas Bar Examination. **Criteria:** Scholarship is given based on both merit and financial need.

Funds Avail.: No specific amount. **To Apply:** Applicants must submit the following requirements: application; financial statement; resume; essay; and letter of reference; certified copy of law school transcript; short biographical sketch (5-7 sentences length, and written in third person); photograph (size 3x5 or larger of head and shoulders only. Photograph should be suitable for inclusion in a professional publication). **Deadline:** March 31. **Contact:** Star A.

Awards are arranged alphabetically below their administering organizations

Carter; 214-746-7899; Star.Carter@weil.com.

6944 ■ Morris K. Udall Foundation

130 S Scott Ave.
Tucson, AZ 85701-1922
Ph: (520)901-8500
Fax: (520)670-5530
E-mail: info@udall.gov
URL: http://www.udall.gov

6945 ■ Morris K. Udall Scholarships *(Undergraduate/Scholarship)*

Purpose: To provide scholarship assistance for qualified individuals. **Focus:** Environmental technology; Native American studies. **Qualif.:** Applicant must be a student who has demonstrated commitment to a career related to the environment; or must be a Native American or Alaska Native student who has demonstrated commitment to a career related to tribal public policy or Native health care; must be a sophomore or junior level college student; must have a college GPA of at least 3.0 or the equivalent; and must be a U.S citizen, U.S national, or U.S permanent resident. **Criteria:** Recipients will be selected based on the following criteria: (1) demonstrated commitment to environmental or natural resources, tribal public policy, or Native American health care; (2) course of study and proposed career; (3) leadership, character, desire to make a difference, and general wellroundedness.

Funds Avail.: No specific amount. **To Apply:** Applicants must complete and sign Udall Scholarship Application and submit along with an 800-word essay (signed and dated), a current official college transcript and transcripts for other colleges attended, and three letters of recommendation. **Deadline:** March 4.

6946 ■ Unitarian Universalist Association of Congregations

25 Beacon St.
Boston, MA 02108
Ph: (617)742-2100
E-mail: info@uua.org
URL: http://www.uua.org

6947 ■ Martha and Robert Atherton Ministerial Scholarships *(Graduate, Master's/Scholarship)*

Purpose: To provide financial assistance to promising ministerial students in their second or third year of seminary. **Focus:** Ministry. **Qualif.:** Applicant must be student in the second or third year of seminary; and a citizen of the United States or Canada. **Criteria:** Priority is given to students that have demonstrated outstanding ministerial ability secondarily to students with the greatest financial need, especially persons of color.

Funds Avail.: No specific amount. **To Apply:** Applicants must apply for financial aid to be automatically considered for scholarships with no additional material is required, except where noted. **Deadline:** April 15.

Remarks: Established in 1997, through the generous contributions of Martha and Robert Atherton.

6948 ■ Olympia Brown and Max Kapp Awards *(Graduate/Scholarship)*

Purpose: To support the education of a student in a Masters of Divinity degree program leading to fellowship as a Unitarian Universalist (UU) minister. **Focus:** Ministry. **Qualif.:** Applicant must be student enrolled full-time or at least half time in a Masters of Divinity degree program leading to fellowship as a Unitarian Universalist (UU) minister; and a citizen of the United States or Canada. **Criteria:** Priority is given to students that have demonstrated outstanding ministerial ability secondarily to students with the greatest financial need, especially persons of color.

Funds Avail.: $2500. **Number Awarded:** one woman and one man. Applicants must apply for financial aid to be automatically considered for scholarships. In addition, applicants must submit a winning paper, sermon, or other special project on some aspect of Universalism. **Deadline:** April 15.

6949 ■ Children of Unitarian Universalist Ministers College Scholarships *(Undergraduate/Scholarship)*

Purpose: To defray undergraduate college expenses of the children of Unitarian Universalist Ministers. **Focus:** General studies. **Qualif.:** Applicant must be college undergraduate and a dependent of a Unitarian Universalist Minister. **Criteria:** Priority is given to applicants with family income not exceeding $50,000.

Funds Avail.: No specific amount. **To Apply:** Applicants must complete the online Application process and submit a proof of college enrollment to the UUA Office of Church Staff Finances. **Deadline:** September 30.

6950 ■ Pauly D'Orlando Memorial Art Scholarships *(Graduate, Undergraduate/Scholarship)*

Purpose: To support Unitarian Universalist students with their educational pursuit. **Focus:** Fine arts. **Qualif.:** Applicant must be a Unitarian Universalist graduate or undergraduate student pursuing a career in fine arts. Performing arts majors are not eligible. **Criteria:** Selection is based on active relationship with Unitarian Universalism, financial need, and enrollment in an accredited institution.

Funds Avail.: Varies. **Number Awarded:** Varies. **To Apply:** Applicants must submit a completed application form along with the supporting documentation. **Deadline:** February 15.

Remarks: Funded by a trust set up by the First Unitarian Church of New Orleans.

6951 ■ David Eaton Scholarships *(Graduate, Master's/Scholarship)*

Purpose: To support the education of a student in a Masters of Divinity degree program leading to fellowship as a Unitarian Universalist (UU) minister. **Focus:** Ministry. **Qualif.:** Applicant must be student enrolled full-time or at least half time in a Masters of Divinity degree program leading to fellowship as a Unitarian Universalist (UU) minister; a citizen of the United States or Canada; and a woman from a historically marginalized group who share the same vision as David Eaton. **Criteria:** Priority is given to students that have demonstrated outstanding ministerial ability secondarily to students with the greatest financial need, especially persons of color.

Funds Avail.: No specific amount. **To Apply:** Applicants must apply for financial aid to be automatically considered for scholarships with no additional materials required, except where noted. **Deadline:** April 15.

Remarks: Established in memory of Rev. David Hilliard Eaton.

Awards are arranged alphabetically below their administering organizations

6952 ■ David Pohl Scholarships *(Graduate, Master's/Scholarship)*

Purpose: To support the education of a student in a Masters of Divinity degree program leading to fellowship as a Unitarian Universalist (UU) minister. **Focus:** Ministry. **Qualif.:** Applicant must be student enrolled full-time or at least half time in a Masters of Divinity degree program leading to fellowship as a Unitarian Universalist (UU) minister; and a citizen of the United States or Canada. **Criteria:** Priority is given to students that have demonstrated outstanding ministerial ability secondarily to students with the greatest financial need, especially persons of color.

Funds Avail.: No specific amount. **To Apply:** Applicants must apply for financial aid to be automatically considered for scholarships with no additional material is required, except where noted. **Deadline:** April 15.

Remarks: Established in memory of Rev. David Pohl.

6953 ■ Roy H. Pollack Scholarships *(Graduate, Master's/Scholarship)*

Purpose: To support the education of a student in a Masters of Divinity degree program leading to fellowship as a Unitarian Universalist (UU) minister. **Focus:** Ministry. **Qualif.:** Applicant must be a second or third-year student having strong academic records and a promising candidate for the Unitarian Universalist ministry; must be a citizen of the United States or Canada. **Criteria:** Priority is given to students that have demonstrated outstanding ministerial ability secondarily to students with the greatest financial need, especially persons of color.

Funds Avail.: No specific amount. **To Apply:** Applicants must apply for financial aid to be automatically considered for scholarships with no additional material is required, except where noted. **Deadline:** April 15.

Remarks: Created in 1998.

6954 ■ Alice Schulman Simmons Scholarships for UU Women *(Undergraduate/Scholarship)*

Purpose: To support the education of a UU woman with education. **Focus:** General studies. **Qualif.:** Applicant must be a Unitarian Universalist Women attending Simmons College in Boston. **Criteria:** UUA will validate all candidates.

Funds Avail.: $25,000. **Number Awarded:** 2. **To Apply:** Applicants must apply and submit the Information Profile for Endowed Scholarships through the Office of Student Financial Services at Simmons College. **Contact:** Stewardship and Development Office, at 617-948-4655.

6955 ■ Joseph Sumner Smith Scholarships *(All/Scholarship)*

Purpose: To support the education of a Unitarian Universalist (UU) student. **Focus:** General studies. **Qualif.:** Applicant must be a Unitarian Universalist student attending Anitoch or Harvard. **Criteria:** Priority is given to students who will pursue the ministry after graduation.

Funds Avail.: $500-$1000. **To Apply:** Applicants must contact the Scholarship Administrator of the UU Funding Program for the application process. **Deadline:** April 30.

6956 ■ Marion Barr Stanfield Art Scholarships *(Graduate, Undergraduate/Scholarship)*

Purpose: To support Unitarian Universalist students with their educational pursuit. **Focus:** Fine arts. **Qualif.:** Applicant must be a Unitarian Universalist graduate or undergraduate student pursuing a career in fine arts. Performing arts majors are not eligible. **Criteria:** Selection is based on active relationship with Unitarian Universalism, financial need, and enrollment in an accredited institution.

Funds Avail.: Varies. **Number Awarded:** Varies. **To Apply:** Applicants must submit a completed application form along with the supporting documentation. **Deadline:** February 15.

6957 ■ Otto M. Stanfield Law Scholarships *(Graduate/Scholarship)*

Purpose: To support Unitarian Universalist students with their educational pursuits. **Focus:** Law. **Qualif.:** Applicant must be a Unitarian Universalist student entering or in law school. Pre-law students or political science majors are not eligible. **Criteria:** Selection is based on active relationship with Unitarian Universalism, financial need, and enrollment in an accredited institution.

Funds Avail.: Varies. **Number Awarded:** Varies. **To Apply:** Applicants must submit a completed application form along with the supporting documentation. **Deadline:** February 15.

Remarks: Established by Marion Barr Stanfield in memory of her husband.

6958 ■ Rev. Chuck and Nancy Thomas Scholarships *(Graduate, Master's/Scholarship)*

Purpose: To support the education of a student in a Masters of Divinity degree program leading to fellowship as a Unitarian Universalist (UU) minister. **Focus:** Ministry. **Qualif.:** Applicant must be a first-year student showing an outstanding commitment to Unitarian Universalism as a lay leader before preparing for ordained ministry; and must be a citizen of the United States or Canada. **Criteria:** Priority is given to students that have demonstrated outstanding ministerial ability secondarily to students with the greatest financial need, especially persons of color.

Funds Avail.: $11,000. **Number Awarded:** 1. **To Apply:** Applicants must apply for financial aid to be automatically considered for scholarships. In addition, applicants must submit a completed application form with the required materials. Those who wish to submit a nomination should write a letter of recommendation showing a connection between the applicant's ministry and their life goals along with examples of their strong leadership skills. **Deadline:** April 2.

Remarks: Established in 1998 by Lorella and Todd Hess in honor of Lorella's father, Rev. Charles Thomas.

6959 ■ Von Ogden Vogt Scholarships *(Graduate, Master's/Scholarship)*

Purpose: To support the intellectual, spiritual, and professional development of future Unitarian Universalist ministers attending Meadville Lombard Theological School. **Focus:** Ministry. **Qualif.:** Applicant must be student enrolled full-time or at least half time in a Masters of Divinity degree program leading to fellowship as a Unitarian Universalist (UU) minister; attending Meadville Lombard Theological School; and a citizen of the United States or Canada. **Criteria:** Priority is given to students that have demonstrated outstanding ministerial ability secondarily to students with the greatest financial need, especially persons of color.

Funds Avail.: No specific amount. **To Apply:** Applicants must apply for financial aid to be automatically considered for scholarships with no additional material is required, except where noted. **Deadline:** April 15.

Remarks: Established in 2001 by Ogden and Carolyn Vogt to honor Carolyn's father, Rev. Dr. Von Ogden Vogt.

6960 ■ United Engineering Foundation

PO Box 70
Mount Vernon, VA 22121-0070
Ph: (973)244-2328
Fax: (973)882-5155
E-mail: engfnd@aol.com
URL: http://www.uefoundation.org

6961 ■ United Engineering Foundation Grants *(All/Grant)*

Purpose: To support engineering and education for the advancement of engineering arts and sciences. **Focus:** Engineering. **Qualif.:** Any non-profit organization, individual, and group is eligible for the grant. **Criteria:** The UEF Grants Committee will prioritize the proposals and forward prioritized proposals to the UEF Board of Trustees.

Funds Avail.: No specific amount. **To Apply:** Applicants must submit a detailed proposal and a two-page concept paper (submitted in PDF format to engfnd@aol.com, and a copy to davidlbelden@cs.com). **Deadline:** June 1.

6962 ■ United Foods and Commercial Workers International Union

1775 K St., NW
Washington, DC 20006
Ph: (202)223-3111
Free: 800-551-4010
URL: http://www.ufcw.org

6963 ■ UFCW Scholarships *(Undergraduate/Scholarship)*

Purpose: To financially support UFCW members and their unmarried dependents with their educational pursuit. **Focus:** General studies. **Qualif.:** Applicants must be UFCW members or their unmarried dependents under age of 20. **Criteria:** Selection is based on scholastic achievements, community involvement, and on the essay.

Funds Avail.: $2,000. **To Apply:** Applicants must complete the UFCW Scholarship Application online or request by writing to the UFCW International Union, Attn: Scholarship Program. **Deadline:** March 15. **Contact:** scholarship@ufcw.org.

6964 ■ United Methodist Communications

PO Box 320
Nashville, TN 37202-0320
Ph: (615)742-5400
E-mail: umcom@umcom.org
URL: http://www.umcom.org

6965 ■ Leonard M. Perryman Communications Scholarships for Ethnic Minority Students *(Undergraduate/Scholarship)*

Purpose: To provide financial assistance to students who intend to pursue a career in religion journalism for communications. **Focus:** Religion; Journalism; Communications. **Qualif.:** Applicants must be undergraduate United Methodist students, who intend to pursue a career in religion journalism for study at an accredited U.S. college or university. **Criteria:** Applicants are evaluated based on financial need.

Funds Avail.: $2,500. **To Apply:** Applicants must submit all the required application information. **Deadline:** March 15.

6966 ■ United Methodist Youth Organization

PO Box 340003
Nashville, TN 37203
Ph: (615)340-7079
Free: 877-899-2780
E-mail: youngpeople@gbod.org
URL: http://www.gbod.org/youngpeople

6967 ■ David W. Self Scholarships *(Undergraduate/Scholarship)*

Purpose: To aid United Methodist students who are continuing their self-development through higher education. **Focus:** Church occupations. **Qualif.:** Applicant must be U.S. citizen or permanent resident; a racial/ethnic minority youth active in local United Methodist Church for at least one year; graduating high school senior entering first year of undergraduate study; admitted to a full-time degree program in an accredited college or university; maintaining at least "C" average in high school; pursuing a church-related career; and established financial need. **Criteria:** selection is based on the application.

Funds Avail.: Up to $1000. **To Apply:** Applicants must submit a completed application form. **Deadline:** June 1.

6968 ■ Richard S. Smith Scholarships *(Undergraduate/Scholarship)*

Purpose: To aid United Methodist students continuing their self-development through higher education. **Focus:** Church occupations. **Qualif.:** Applicant must be U.S. citizen or permanent resident; a racial/ethnic minority youth active in local United Methodist Church for at least one year; graduating high school senior entering first year of undergraduate study; admitted to a full-time degree program in an accredited college or university; maintaining at least "C" average in high school; pursuing a church-related career; and established financial need. **Criteria:** selection is based on the application.

Funds Avail.: Up to $1000. **To Apply:** Applicants must submit a completed application form. **Deadline:** June 1.

6969 ■ United South and Eastern Tribes

711 Stewarts Ferry Pike, Ste. 100
Nashville, TN 37214
Ph: (615)872-7900
Fax: (615)872-7417
E-mail: mcook@usetinc.org
URL: http://www.usetinc.org

6970 ■ United South and Eastern Tribes Scholarship Fund *(Undergraduate/Scholarship)*

Purpose: To provide financial assistance to Indian students in the USET service area. **Focus:** General studies. **Qualif.:** Applicants must be Indian students who are enrolled members of one of twenty-four USET member tribes. **Criteria:** Applicants will be judged based on demonstrated need for financial assistance, satisfactory scholastic standing

Awards are arranged alphabetically below their administering organizations

and current enrollment or acceptance in a post-secondary educational institution.

Funds Avail.: $500. **To Apply:** Applicants must complete the application found on the website of USET. **Deadline:** April 30.

6971 ■ U.S. Air Force ROTC

551 E Maxwell Blvd.
Maxwell AFB, AL 36112-5917
Ph: (334)953-6167
Fax: (866)423-7682
URL: http://www.afrotc.com

6972 ■ Air Force ROTC Enhanced HBCU Scholarships *(Undergraduate/Scholarship)*

Purpose: To meet officer production requirements and enhance enrollment at HBCUs. **Focus:** General studies. **Qualif.:** Applicants must be enrolled at the following colleges/universities: Jackson State University; Tuskegee University; Alabama State University; Howard University; North Carolina A&T State University; Fayetteville State University; Tennessee State University. **Criteria:** Recipients will be selected based on merit.

Funds Avail.: Tuition capped at $15,000; Books at $900. per year. **To Apply:** Applicants may start the application process for the scholarship program by contacting the Air Force ROTC detachment at the school that they wish to enroll in.

6973 ■ Hispanic Serving Institution Scholarships *(Undergraduate/Scholarship)*

Purpose: To meet officer production requirements and enhance enrollment at HSIs. **Focus:** General studies. **Qualif.:** Applicants must be students enrolled as HSIs (Hispanic Serving Institution), including those schools which host an Air force ROTC detachment and those which are crosstowns of another school that hosts a detachment. **Criteria:** Applicants do not have to meet a selection board for this scholarship.

Funds Avail.: Tuition capped at $15,000; Books at $900 per year. **To Apply:** Applicants may start the application process for the scholarship program by contacting the Air Force ROTC detachment at the school that they wish to attend.

6974 ■ Historically Black College or University Scholarships *(Undergraduate/Scholarship)*

Purpose: To meet officer production requirements and enhance enrollment at HBCUs. **Focus:** General studies. **Qualif.:** Applicants must be enrolled at an HBCU (Historically Black College or University), including those schools which host an Air Force ROTC detachment and those which are crosstowns of another school that hosts a detachment. **Criteria:** Applicants do not have to meet a selection board.

Funds Avail.: Tuition capped at $15,000; Books at $900. **To Apply:** Applications for the HBCU Scholarship are processed and approved at the detachment level. Applicant must contact the detachment serving the school, and the school will work to nominate the applicant for the appropriate scholarship program. Applications are accepted at any time each year.

6975 ■ U.S. Air Force ROTC Enhanced HSI Scholarship *(Undergraduate/Scholarship)*

Purpose: To meet officer production requirements and enhance enrollment at HSIs. **Focus:** General studies. **Qualif.:** Applicants must be enrolled at the following colleges/universities: California State University; New Mexico State University; University of New Mexico; University of Puerto Rico- Rio Piedras; University of Puerto Rico-Mayaguez; University of Texas - San Antonio. **Criteria:** Recipients will be selected based on merit.

Funds Avail.: Tuition capped at $15,000; Books at $900. per year. **To Apply:** Applicants may start the application process for the scholarship program by contacting the Air Force ROTC detachment at the school that they wish to enroll in. at the above address.

6976 ■ U.S. Air Force ROTC Express Scholarships *(Undergraduate/Scholarship)*

Purpose: To provide financial assistance for college students enrolled in specific fields. **Focus:** Engineering; Aerospace sciences; Aeronautics; Atmospheric sciences. **Qualif.:** Applicants must be United States citizens by the end of the projected term of activation; must pass the Air Force Officer Qualifying Test; must pass the Air Force ROTC Physical Fitness Test; must have at least a 2.5 cumulative college grade point average; must a physical examination and be certified; must not be a contracted scholarship recipient; and must meet the age, moral and other scholarship eligibility requirements for Air force ROTC. **Criteria:** The Express Scholarship program is operated on a fully qualified basis - those who meet the qualifications are awarded the scholarship and do not meet a scholarship selection board.

Funds Avail.: $15,000. **To Apply:** Applications for the Express Scholarship are processed and approved at the detachment level. Applicant must contact the detachment serving the school that he/she wishes to attend and the school will work to nominate the student for the appropriate scholarship program.

6977 ■ U.S. Air Force ROTC High School Scholarships *(Undergraduate/Scholarship)*

Purpose: To provide financial assistance to high school seniors. **Focus:** General studies. **Qualif.:** Applicants must be United States citizens or able to obtain citizenship by the last day of the first term of the freshman year for 4-year offers, or the first term of the sophomore year for 3-year offers; must be a high school graduate or have an equivalent certificate; must be 17-31 years old prior to scholarship activation; and must not be enrolled full-time at a college or a university except for joint high school college programs. **Criteria:** Recipient selection will be based on leadership and work experience; extracurricular activities; results from the personal interview; questionnaire results; and academic scores.

Funds Avail.: Type 1-$900; Type 2-$15,000: Type 7-$9,000. **To Apply:** Applicants must submit their application online and include the following forms: Counselor Certification, Personal Statement, Physical Fitness Assessment, and resume. Applicants must have their high school transcripts with raised seal or signature as well as their SAT or ACT scores. **Deadline:** December 1.

6978 ■ U.S. Air Force ROTC In-College Scholarships *(Undergraduate/Scholarship)*

Purpose: To provide scholarships to college freshmen and sophomores in any major. **Focus:** General studies. **Qualif.:** Applicants must be United States citizens by the end of the projected term of activation; must pass the Air Force Officer Qualifying Test; must meet the Air Force ROTC weight and body fat standards; must pass the Air Force ROTC Physi-

Awards are arranged alphabetically below their administering organizations

cal Fitness Test; have at least a 2.5 cumulative college grade point average; pass a physical examination; must not be a contracted scholarship recipient; and must meet the age, moral and other scholarship eligibility requirements for Air force ROTC. **Criteria:** Selection will be based on academic performance.

Funds Avail.: Type 2-$15,000; Type 3-$9,000; Type 6-$3,000. **To Apply:** Applicants must fill out the application request form online.

6979 ■ United States Army Warrant Officers Association

462 Herndon Pkwy., Ste. 207
Herndon, VA 20170-5235
Ph: (703)742-7727
Fax: (703)742-7728
Free: 800-587-2962
URL: http://www.penfed.org/usawoa

6980 ■ USAWOASF/Grantham University On-Line Scholarships *(Graduate, Undergraduate/Scholarship)*

Purpose: To give financial awards to deserving candidates. **Focus:** General studies. **Qualif.:** Applicant must be a member, or a spouse of a member of the association, or their dependents under 23 years of age (high school seniors and above); planning to attend full-time or continue education at an accredited American college or university or a vocational technical institution; and has a GPA of 3.0 or higher on a 4.0 scale. **Criteria:** Applicants will be selected based on the application materials.

Funds Avail.: No specific amount. **To Apply:** Application form is available at the website. Applicant must submit a complete application packet consisting of: the application form; an essay (800-100 words, include word count) on educational goals; circumstances which may effect the applicant's school attendance; list of extracurricular activities; recommendation letter (from instructor, faculty advisor, etc.); National Test Scores, SAT, ACT, etc.; transcript of grades; and a 4x6 photograph (view head and shoulders). **Deadline:** May 1.

6981 ■ USAWOASF Regular Scholarships *(Undergraduate/Scholarship)*

Purpose: To give financial awards to deserving candidates. **Focus:** General studies. **Qualif.:** Applicant must be a spouse or dependent of a USAWOA member, 23 years old and below; must be planning to attend full-time or continue education at an accredited American college or university, or a vocational technical institution; and has a GPA of 3.0 or higher on a 4.0 scale. **Criteria:** Selection committee's decision is based on the whole-person concept.

Funds Avail.: $1000. **To Apply:** Application form is available at the website. Applicant must submit a complete application packet consisting of: the application form (typewritten format); an essay (800-100 words, include word count) on educational goals; circumstances which may effect the applicant's school attendance; list of extracurricular activities; a recommendation letter (from instructor, faculty advisor, etc.); National Test Scores, SAT, ACT, etc.; and a 4x6 photograph (view head and shoulders). **Deadline:** May 1.

6982 ■ United States Capitol Historical Society

200 Maryland Ave. NE
Washington, DC 20002
Fax: (202)544-8244
Free: 800-887-9318
E-mail: uschs@uschs.org
URL: http://www.uschs.org

6983 ■ United States Capitol Historical Society Fellowships *(Graduate/Fellowship)*

Purpose: To provide financial support to scholars researching important topics in the art and architectural history of the United States Capitol Complex. **Focus:** History, United States; Art history; American studies; Museum science. **Qualif.:** Applicant must be a graduate student enrolled in a degree program in art or architectural history, American history, American studies, museum studies, or decorative arts, and scholars with a proven record of research and publication. **Criteria:** Applications are judged based on the qualifications of the applicant, the significance of the topic, the degree of need for the proposed research, the feasibility of the research plan, and the likelihood that the research will lead to publication.

Funds Avail.: $2,000 per month, up to $24,000 for a full year. **To Apply:** Applicants must submit a curriculum vitae; transcripts of graduate work; two supporting letters; dates for which the fellowship is requested, with estimated time period for each phase of the proposed research; list of expected sources of income during the proposed period; and research proposal (maximum 5 pages). Submit materials by regular mail to Dr. Donald Kennon, or by fax or email to Dr. Barbara Wolanin, 202228-4602, bwolanin@aoc.gov. **Deadline:** March 15.

6984 ■ U.S. Department of Homeland Security

12th & C St. SW
Washington, DC 20024
Ph: (202)245-2499
E-mail: dhsed@orau.org
URL: http://www.orau.gov/dhsed

6985 ■ The Homeland Security Graduate Fellowships *(Graduate/Fellowship)*

Purpose: To pursue basic science and technology innovations that can be applied to the DHS mission. **Focus:** Science technologies; Engineering; Mathematics and mathematical sciences. **Qualif.:** Applicants must be a U.S. citizen as of the application deadline; applicants must have a cumulative undergraduate GPA from the institution granting the bachelor's degree of 3.30 or higher on a 4.00 scale; applicants must have a cumulative graduate GPA of 3.30 or higher on a 4.00 scale if currently enrolled in graduate school; applicants must be pursuing a doctoral or masters degree with a thesis requirement in a homeland security science, technology, engineering or mathematics field with interest in a homeland security research area; applicants must also be a college senior as of the application deadline; applicants must also be bachelor's degree but not currently enrolled and completed not more than two graduate courses since completion of the bachelor's degree; or if applicant is enrolled full-time in the first year of a master's program and completed not more than two graduate courses since completion of a bachelor's degree or if enrolled part-time in graduate courses and wish to enroll full-time in a Ph.D. master's program, completed not more than two graduate courses since completion of a bachelor's degree; and if an applicant is a veterinary medical student who is enrolled at an accredited school or college of veterinary medicine and who is currently in the fourth year

Awards are arranged alphabetically below their administering organizations

of professional curriculum leading to a DVM or VMD degree and begin a postgraduate course of study are also eligible to apply. **Criteria:** Recipients are selected based on the candidate's academic record; reference report; GRE test scores; research experience essay; current research interest essay; and contribution to public service.

Funds Avail.: $2,300. **To Apply:** Applicants must complete the online application form; two online reference report forms; applicants must submit an official academic transcript from all postsecondary institutions attended. **Deadline:** January 7 for online application form; January 14 for reference report and required documents.

6986 ■ The Homeland Security Undergraduate Scholarships *(Undergraduate/Scholarship)*

Purpose: To pursue basic science and technology innovations that can be applied to the DHS mission. **Focus:** Science technologies; Engineering; Mathematics and mathematical sciences. **Qualif.:** Applicants must be a U.S. citizen as of the application deadline; applicants must have a cumulative undergraduate GPA of 3.30 or higher on a 4.00 scale; applicants must be majoring in a homeland security science, technology, engineering or mathematics field with interest in a homeland security research area; applicants must be in second year of college if been attending college full-time; applicants must have completed a total of at least 45 but not more than 60 semester hours if been attending on a part-time, or combination or part-time and full-time basis. **Criteria:** Recipients are selected based on the candidate's academic record; reference report; SAT or ACT test scores; Research experience essay; current research interests essay; and contribution to public service essay.

Funds Avail.: $1,000; **To Apply:** Applicants must complete the online application form; applicants must submit two online reference report forms; applicants must submit official academic transcript from all postsecondary institutions attended. **Deadline:** January 7 for online application form; January 14 for documents.

6987 ■ United States Geospatial Intelligence Foundation

2325 Dulles Corner Blvd., Ste. 450
Herndon, VA 20171
Ph: (703)793-0109
Fax: (703)793-9069
Free: 800-698-7443
E-mail: stu.shea@usgif.org
URL: http://www.usgif.org

6988 ■ United States Geospatial Intelligence Foundation Graduate Scholarships *(Postgraduate/Scholarship)*

Purpose: To help further the geospatial tradecraft. To assist promising students interested in the geospatial sciences. **Focus:** Geosciences. **Qualif.:** Applicants must be graduate students interested in geospatial sciences. **Criteria:** Recipients are selected based on academic standing, financial need, and quality of the applicant's essay.

Funds Avail.: No specific amount. **To Apply:** Applicants must complete the application form. Applicants must submit an essay describing their understanding of the geospatial intelligence tradecraft, future goals and how they relate to geospatial tradecraft, their understanding of the variety of careers and opportunities available within the geospatial intelligence tradecraft, and their motivation for pursuing this field. Applicants must submit two letters of recommendation. **Deadline:** May 30. **Contact:** scholar ships@usgif.org

6989 ■ United States Geospatial Intelligence Foundation High School Scholarships *(Undergraduate/Scholarship)*

Purpose: To help further the geospatial tradecraft. To assist promising students interested in the geospatial sciences. **Focus:** Geosciences. **Qualif.:** Applicants must be senior high school students interested in geospatial sciences. **Criteria:** Recipients are selected based on academic standing, financial need, and quality of the applicant's essay.

Funds Avail.: No specific amount. **To Apply:** Applicants must complete the application form. Applicants must submit an essay describing their understanding of the geospatial intelligence tradecraft, future goals and how they relate to geospatial tradecraft, their understanding of the variety of careers and opportunities available within the geospatial intelligence tradecraft, and their motivation for pursuing this field. Applicants must submit two letters of recommendation. **Deadline:** May 30.

6990 ■ United States Geospatial Intelligence Foundation Undergraduate Scholarships *(Undergraduate/Scholarship)*

Purpose: To help further the geospatial tradecraft. To assist promising students interested in the geospatial sciences. **Focus:** Geosciences. **Qualif.:** Applicants must be undergraduate students interested in geospatial sciences. **Criteria:** Recipients are selected based on academic standing, financial need, and quality of the applicant's essay.

Funds Avail.: No specific amount. **To Apply:** Applicants must complete the application form. Applicants must submit an essay describing their understanding of the geospatial intelligence tradecraft, future goals and how they relate to geospatial tradecraft, their understanding of the variety of careers and opportunities available within the geospatial intelligence tradecraft, and their motivation for pursuing this field. Applicants must submit two letters of recommendation. **Deadline:** May 30. **Contact:** scholarships@usgif.org

6991 ■ United States Golf Association

PO Box 708
Far Hills, NJ 07931
Ph: (908)234-2300
Fax: (908)234-9687
E-mail: koconnor@usga.org
URL: http://www.usga.org

6992 ■ United States Golf Association Fellowship Program *(All/Fellowship)*

Purpose: To develop recent college graduates' professional skills such as leadership and organizational efficiency; to educate them in the role of philanthropy and the non-profit sector and offer experience in the golf world. **Focus:** Athletics. **Qualif.:** Applicants must have: strong leadership potential, interest in public service, desire for personal and professional growth; strong analytical, written and verbal skills; appreciation for the impact of the game; personal initiative and commitment to teamwork; willingness and ability to travel; and eligibility to work in the United States. **Criteria:** Recipients are selected based on demonstrated interest in golf.

Funds Avail.: No specific amount. **To Apply:** Applicants

must submit: a one-to-two page cover letter describing their interest in the program; resume or C.V.; an official transcript of records; two letters of recommendation with an index card including the proponents' name and contact information. **Deadline:** December 15. **Contact:** fellowship@usga.org.

6993 ■ United States Golf Association Scholarship Program *(Undergraduate/Scholarship)*

Purpose: To provide opportunity for participants to think critically about leadership skills and become more engaged and invested citizens in their respective communities. **Focus:** Athletics. **Qualif.:** Applicants must be 15 to 19 years old; must be "Honor Roll" students or maintain a strong GPA; must play or be qualified to play at a varsity level; must demonstrate leadership, must have an active involvement in community activities/service and have proven ability in an event of size and magnitude. **Criteria:** Recipients are selected based on academic performance and involvement in extracurricular activities.

Funds Avail.: No specific amount. **To Apply:** Applicants must submit a completed application form. **Deadline:** May 5. **Contact:** mkeys@usgagrants.org.

6994 ■ United States Hunter Jumper Association

4047 Iron Works Pky.
Lexington, KY 40511
Ph: (859)225-2055
Fax: (859)258-9033
E-mail: sdotson@ushja.org
URL: http://www.ushja.org

6995 ■ USHJA Athletic Scholarships *(Undergraduate/Scholarship)*

Purpose: To recognize athlete students by supporting them financially. **Focus:** General Studies. **Qualif.:** Applicants must be full-time undergraduate students attending Midway College who will participate in one of the following sports: Equestrian, Tennis, Basketball, Softball or Soccer. **Criteria:** Preference will be given to those who meet the criteria.

Funds Avail.: No specific amount. **To Apply:** Applicants must check the available website for details. **Contact:** United States Hunter Jumper Association at the above address (see entry 6994).

6996 ■ USHJA General Scholarships *(Undergraduate/Scholarship)*

Purpose: To provide financial support to those students who are in need. **Focus:** General Studies. **Qualif.:** Applicants must be graduating high school seniors or current undergraduate students who are pursuing postsecondary studies. **Criteria:** Selection will be based on academic achievement, financial need, extracurricular activities, community service, involvement with American Saddlebred horses and recommendations.

Funds Avail.: $5,000. **Number Awarded:** 4. **To Apply:** Applicants must check the available website for the required materials. **Deadline:** April 30. **Contact:** For more information, please visit: http://www.asha.net

6997 ■ USHJA Postgraduate Scholarships *(Postgraduate/Scholarship)*

Purpose: To recognize intercollegiate student-athletes by supporting them in their educational expenses. **Focus:** General Studies. **Qualif.:** Applicants must be male or female intercollegiate full-time student-athletes who are in the final year of NCAA eligibility and plan to enroll in graduate school upon completion of their four-year degree. Students must have a minimum 3.2 GPA, be nominated by a faculty athletic representative or director of athletics of a NCAA member institution in the final season of competition, and have performed with distinction as a member of a varsity team in the sport for which they are nominated. Awards are seasonal according to sport, as follows: FALL -badminton (W), cross country, equestrian (W), football, soccer, water polo (M), volleyball (W), and field hockey (W); WINTER archery (W), basketball, bowling (W), fencing, gymnastics, ice hockey, rifle, skiing, squash (W), swimming & diving, team handball (W), indoor track & field, and wrestling (M); and SPRING - baseball, golf, lacrosse, rowing (W), softball, synchronized swimming (W), tennis, volleyball (M), outdoor track & field, and water polo. **Criteria:** Recipients will be selected based on the committee's decision.

Funds Avail.: Maximum award amount: $7,500. **Number Awarded:** 174. **To Apply:** Applicants must check the available website for more information. **Contact:** For inquiries please visit: http://www.ncaa.org

6998 ■ U.S.-Ireland Alliance

2800 Clarendon Blvd., No. 502 West
Arlington, VA 22201
E-mail: vargo@us-irelandalliance.org
URL: http://us-irelandalliance.org

6999 ■ George J. Mitchell Scholarships *(Undergraduate/Scholarship)*

Purpose: To introduce and connect generations of future American leaders to the island of Ireland, while recognizing and fostering intellectual achievement, leadership, and a commitment to public service and community. **Focus:** Business. **Qualif.:** Applicant must be a U.S. citizen between 18-30 years old. **Criteria:** Applicants will be judged based on academic excellence and intellectual distinction, outstanding record of leadership, sustained commitment to service and community and must hold a bachelor's degree from an accredited college or university.

Funds Avail.: No specific amount. **To Apply:** Applicants must apply online. **Deadline:** October 6.

7000 ■ United States Marine Corps Drill Instructors Association

PO Box 5401
Parris Island, SC 29905
Ph: (912)632-4557
Fax: (912)632-4557
URL: http://www.usmcdiassn.com

7001 ■ L.D. "Crow" Crawford Scholarships *(Undergraduate/Scholarship)*

Purpose: To support the members' children to pursue their careers. **Focus:** General studies. **Qualif.:** Applicant must be a members' dependent child under 21 years of age; must be pursuing undergraduate work; must maintain a "B" grade point average. **Criteria:** Selection of applicant will be based on the application materials.

Funds Avail.: $500. **Number Awarded:** 2. **To Apply:** Applicant must have the letter from college or university stating that the applicant are accepted to attend their institutions; must have a transcript from the last school attended; must have a 500 word or less essay about the applicant's educational goals (new applicant only). Scholarship applications are available through National Headquarters. **Deadline:** July 31.

7002 ■ U.S. Pan Asian American Chamber of Commerce

1329 18th St., NW
Washington, DC 20036
Ph: (202)296-5221
Fax: (202)296-5225
Free: 800-696-7818
E-mail: info@uspaacc.com
URL: http://www.uspaacc.com

7003 ■ Paul Shearman Allen and Associate Scholarships *(Undergraduate/Scholarship)*

Purpose: To provide financial assistance to Asian American high school seniors who have demonstrated scholastic achievement and financial need and will pursue post-secondary education at an accredited educational institution in the United States. **Focus:** General studies. **Qualif.:** Applicants must be: at least 16 years of age at the time of application; of Asian Pacific Island heritage; citizens or permanent residents of the United States; beginning full-time study at an accredited post-secondary educational institution in the United States; must have a 3.3 grade point average. **Criteria:** Recipients are selected based on academic achievement; leadership in extracurricular activities; involvement in community service; and financial need.

Funds Avail.: $5,000. **To Apply:** Applicants must submit: completed online application with photo attached on the top right hand corner; short biography; essay; transcript; household tax return (signed by taxpayers); recommendations; additional attachments; post-secondary institution information. **Deadline:** February 22.

7004 ■ Asian American Scholarships *(Undergraduate/Scholarship)*

Purpose: To provide financial assistance to Asian American high school seniors who have demonstrated scholastic achievement and financial need and will pursue post-secondary education at an accredited educational institution in the United States. **Focus:** General studies. **Qualif.:** Applicants must be: at least 16 years of age at the time of application; of Asian Pacific Island heritage; citizens or permanent residents of the United States; beginning full-time study at an accredited post-secondary educational institution in the United States; must have a 3.3 grade point average or higher. **Criteria:** Applicants are evaluated on the basis of academic achievement; leadership in extracurricular activities; involvement in community service; and financial need.

Funds Avail.: $5,000. **To Apply:** Applicants must submit: completed online application with photo attached on the top right hand corner; short biography; essay; transcript; household tax return; recommendations; additional attachments; and post-secondary institution information. **Deadline:** February 22.

7005 ■ Darden Restaurants Scholarships *(Undergraduate/Scholarship)*

Purpose: To provide financial assistance to Asian American high school seniors who have demonstrated scholastic achievement and financial need and will pursue post-secondary education at an accredited educational institution in the United States. **Focus:** General studies. **Qualif.:** Applicants must be: at least 16 years of age at the time of application; of Asian Pacific Island heritage; citizens or permanent residents of the United States; beginning full-time study at an accredited post-secondary educational institution in the United States; must have a GPA of 3.3 or higher. **Criteria:** Applicants are evaluated based on academic achievement; leadership in extracurricular activities; involvement in community service; and, financial need.

Funds Avail.: $5,000. **To Apply:** Applicants must submit: completed online application with photo attached on the top right hand corner; short biography; essay; transcript; household tax return (signed by taxpayers); recommendations; additional attachments; post-secondary institution information. **Deadline:** February 22.

7006 ■ Home Depot Scholarships *(Undergraduate/Scholarship)*

Purpose: To provide financial assistance to Asian American high school seniors who have demonstrated scholastic achievement and financial need and will pursue post-secondary education at an accredited educational institution in the United States. **Focus:** General studies. **Qualif.:** Applicants must be: at least 16 years of age at the time of application; of Asian Pacific Island heritage; citizens or permanent residents of the United States; beginning full-time study at an accredited post-secondary educational institution in the United States; must have a GPA of 3.3 or higher. **Criteria:** Applicants are evaluated based on academic achievement; leadership in extracurricular activities; involvement in community service; and financial need.

Funds Avail.: $5,000. **To Apply:** Applicants must submit: completed online application with photo attached on the top right hand corner; short biography; essay; transcript; household tax return (signed by taxpayers); recommendations; additional attachments; post-secondary institution information. **Deadline:** February 22.

7007 ■ Bruce Lee Scholarships *(Undergraduate/Scholarship)*

Purpose: To provide financial assistance to a student with strong character, who has persevered and prevailed over adversity, and who will pursue post-secondary education at an accredited educational institution in the United States. **Focus:** General studies. **Qualif.:** Applicants must be: at least 16 years of age at the time of application; of Asian Pacific Island heritage; citizens or permanent residents of the United States; beginning full-time study at an accredited post-secondary educational institution in the United States; must have a GPA of 3.0 or higher. **Criteria:** Applicants are evaluated based on strong character; the ability to persevere and prevail over adversity; academic excellence; community service involvement; and financial need.

Funds Avail.: $5,000. **To Apply:** Applicants must submit: completed online application with photo attached on the top right hand corner; short biography; essay; transcript; household tax return (signed by taxpayers); recommendations; additional attachments; post-secondary institution information. **Deadline:** February 22.

7008 ■ LeePapa and Associates Scholarship for Travel *(Graduate, Undergraduate/Scholarship)*

Purpose: To encourage the students to travel back to the land of their birth or heritage during summer break and share the experience with the greater USPAAC community.

Focus: General studies. **Qualif.:** Applicants must be of Asian Pacific Island heritage; must be citizens of United States; must be undergraduate or graduate students, with minimum of 3.3 grade point average at an accredited post-secondary educational institution in the United States. **Criteria:** Applicants are evaluated based on academic achievement; leadership in extracurricular activities; involvement in community service; and financial need.

Funds Avail.: $5,000. **To Apply:** Applicants must submit: downloaded application for the award; photo; additional attachment describing extracurricular activities, academic honors, and community service activities; 100-word biography; essay of 500 words on I Need This Scholarship (typed, double-spaced and signed by the applicants and their academic guidance counselors); transcripts from undergrad or post-grad school; copy of most recent household tax return signed by taxpayers; two letters of recommendation from those listed as references in the application. **Deadline:** March 17.

7009 ■ Ruth Mu-Lan and James S.C. Chao Scholarship *(Undergraduate/Scholarship)*

Purpose: To provide financial assistance to female Asian American high school seniors who will be pursuing post-secondary education at an accredited educational institution in the United States. **Focus:** General studies. **Qualif.:** Applicants must be: females and at least 16 years of age at the of application; of Asian Pacific Island heritage; citizens or permanent residents of the United States; beginning full-time study at an accredited post-secondary educational institution in the United States; must have a GPA of 3.5 or higher. **Criteria:** Applicants are evaluated based on academic excellence; leadership in extracurricular activities; involvement in community service; and financial need.

Funds Avail.: $3,000. **To Apply:** Applicants must submit: completed online application with photo attached on the top right hand corner; short biography; essay; transcript; household tax return (signed by taxpayers); recommendations; additional attachments; post-secondary institution information. **Deadline:** February 22.

7010 ■ Pepsico Scholarships *(Undergraduate/Scholarship)*

Purpose: To provide financial assistance to Asian American high school seniors who have demonstrated scholastic achievement and financial need and will pursue post-secondary education at an accredited educational institution in the United States. **Focus:** General studies. **Qualif.:** Applicants must be: at least 16 years of age at the time of application; of Asian Pacific Island heritage; citizens or permanent residents of the United States; beginning full-time study at an accredited post-secondary educational institution in the United States; must have a GPA of 3.3 or higher. **Criteria:** Applicants are evaluated based on academic achievement; leadership in extracurricular activities; involvement in community service; and, financial need.

Funds Avail.: $5,000. **To Apply:** Applicants must submit: completed online application with photo attached on the top right hand corner; short biography; essay; transcript; household tax return (signed by taxpayers); recommendations; additional attachments; post-secondary institution information. **Deadline:** February 22.

7011 ■ Philip Morris USA Scholarships *(Undergraduate/Scholarship)*

Purpose: To provide financial assistance to Asian American high school seniors who have demonstrated scholastic achievement and financial need and will pursue post-secondary education at an accredited educational institution in the United States. **Focus:** General studies. **Qualif.:** Applicants must be: at least 16 years of age at the time of application; of Asian Pacific Island heritage; citizens or permanent residents of the United States; beginning full-time study at an accredited post-secondary educational institution in the United States; must have a GPA of 3.3 or higher. **Criteria:** Applicants are evaluated based on academic achievement; leadership in extracurricular activities; involvement in community service; and financial need.

Funds Avail.: $5,000. **To Apply:** Applicants must submit: completed online application with photo attached on the top right hand corner; short biography; essay; transcript; household tax return (signed by taxpayers); recommendations; additional attachments; post-secondary institution information. **Deadline:** February 22.

7012 ■ Ken and Pam Pong Scholarships *(Undergraduate/Scholarship)*

Purpose: To provide financial assistance to Asian American high school seniors who have demonstrated scholastic achievement and financial need and will pursue post-secondary education at an accredited educational institution in the United States. **Focus:** General studies. **Qualif.:** Applicants must be: at least 16 years of age at the time of application; of Asian Pacific Island heritage; citizens or permanent residents of the United States; beginning full-time study at an accredited post-secondary educational institution in the United States; must have a 3.3 GPA or higher. **Criteria:** Applicants are evaluated based on academic achievement; leadership in extracurricular activities; involvement in community service; and financial need.

Funds Avail.: $2,000. **To Apply:** Applicants must submit: completed online application with photo attached on the top right hand corner; short biography; essay; transcript; household tax return (signed by taxpayers); recommendations; additional attachments; post-secondary institution information. **Deadline:** February 22.

7013 ■ Drs. Poh Shien and Judy Young Scholarships *(Undergraduate/Scholarship)*

Purpose: To provide financial assistance to Asian American high school seniors who have demonstrated scholastic achievement and financial need and will pursue post-secondary education at an accredited educational institution in the United States. **Focus:** General studies. **Qualif.:** Applicants must be: at least 16 years of age at the time of application; of Asian Pacific Island heritage; citizens or permanent residents of the United States; beginning full-time study at an accredited post-secondary educational institution in the United States; must have a GPA of 3.3 or higher. **Criteria:** Applicants are evaluated based on academic achievement; leadership in extracurricular activities; involvement in community service; and financial need.

Funds Avail.: $4,000. **To Apply:** Applicants must submit: completed online application with photo attached on the top right hand corner; short biography; essay; transcript; household tax return (signed by taxpayers); recommendations; additional attachments; post-secondary institution information. **Deadline:** February 22.

7014 ■ Telamon Scholarships *(Undergraduate/Scholarship)*

Purpose: To provide financial assistance to Asian American high school seniors who have demonstrated scholastic achievement and financial need and will pursue post-

Awards are arranged alphabetically below their administering organizations

secondary education at an accredited educational institution in the United States. **Focus:** General studies. **Qualif.:** Applicants must be: at least 16 years of age at the time of application; of Asian Pacific Island heritage; citizens or permanent residents of the United States; beginning full-time study at an accredited post-secondary educational institution in the United States; must have a GPA of 3.3 or higher. **Criteria:** Applicants are evaluated based on academic achievement; leadership in extracurricular activities; involvement in community service; and, financial need.

Funds Avail.: $2,000. **To Apply:** Applicants must submit: completed online application with photo attached on the top right hand corner; short biography; essay; transcript; household tax return (signed by taxpayers); recommendations; additional attachments; post-secondary institution information. **Deadline:** February 22.

7015 ■ U.S. Pan Asian American Chamber of Commerce CBS Scholarships *(Undergraduate/Scholarship)*

Purpose: To provide financial assistance to Asian American high school seniors who have demonstrated scholastic achievement and financial need and will pursue post-secondary education at an accredited educational institution in the United States. **Focus:** General studies. **Qualif.:** Applicants must be: at least 16 years of age at the time of application; of Asian Pacific Island heritage; citizens or permanent residents of the United States; beginning full-time study at an accredited post-secondary educational institution in the United States; must have a GPA of 3.3 or higher. **Criteria:** Applicants are evaluated based on academic achievement; leadership in extracurricular activities; involvement in community service; and financial need.

Funds Avail.: $5,000. **To Apply:** Applicants must submit: completed online application with photo attached on the top right hand corner; short biography; essay; transcript; household tax return (signed by taxpayers); recommendations; additional attachments; post-secondary institution information. **Deadline:** February 22.

7016 ■ U.S. Pan Asian American Chamber of Commerce McDonald's Scholarships *(Undergraduate/Scholarship)*

Purpose: To provide financial assistance to Asian American high school seniors who have demonstrated scholastic achievement and financial need and will pursue post-secondary education at an accredited educational institution in the United States. **Focus:** General studies. **Qualif.:** Applicants must be: at least 16 years of age at the time of application; of Asian Pacific Island heritage; citizens or permanent residents of the United States; beginning full-time study at an accredited post-secondary educational institution in the United States; must have a GPA 3.3 GPA or higher. **Criteria:** Applicants are evaluated based on academic achievement; leadership in extracurricular activities; involvement in community service; and financial need.

Funds Avail.: $3,000. **To Apply:** Applicants must submit completed online application with photo attached on the top right hand corner; short biography; essay; transcript; household tax return (signed by taxpayers); recommendations; additional attachments; post-secondary institution information. **Deadline:** February 22.

7017 ■ U.S. Pan Asian American Chamber of Commerce UPS Scholarships *(Undergraduate/Scholarship)*

Purpose: To provide financial assistance to Asian American high school seniors who have demonstrated scholastic achievement and financial need and will pursue post-secondary education at an accredited educational institution in the United States. **Focus:** General studies. **Qualif.:** Applicants must be: at least 16 years of age at the time of application; of Asian Pacific Island heritage; citizens or permanent residents of the United States; beginning full-time study at an accredited post-secondary educational institution in the United States; must have a GPA of 3.3 or higher. **Criteria:** Applicants are evaluated based on academic achievement; leadership in extracurricular activities; involvement in community service; and financial need.

Funds Avail.: $5,000. **To Apply:** Applicants must submit: completed online application with photo attached on the top right hand corner; short biography; essay; transcript; household tax return (signed by taxpayers); recommendations; additional attachments; post-secondary institution information. **Deadline:** February 22.

7018 ■ United States Tour Operators Association

275 Madisn Ave., Ste. 2014
New York, NY 10016
Ph: (212)599-6599
Fax: (212)599-6744
E-mail: information@ustoa.com
URL: http://www.ustoa.com

7019 ■ United States Tour Operators Association Scholarships *(Undergraduate/Scholarship)*

Purpose: To educate the travel industry; to foster professionalism within the tour operator industry; to facilitate and develop travel on a worldwide basis. **Focus:** Travel and Tourism. **Qualif.:** Applicants must be students enrolled at an accredited four-year college or university in the United States or Canada; must have a degree emphasis in travel or be in a tourism-related program with a 3.0 GPA. **Criteria:** Recipients are selected based on academic performance.

Funds Avail.: $2,500. **To Apply:** Applicants must submit a completed application form; a typed resume; an official copy of transcript sent from the school detailing courses completed, academic standing and GPA; and one letter of recommendation from a tourism professor. **Deadline:** April 1.

7020 ■ U.S.-Ukraine Foundation

1701 K St. NW Ste. 903
Washington, DC 20006
Ph: (202)223-2228
Fax: (202)223-1224
E-mail: info@usukraine.org
URL: http://www.usukraine.org

7021 ■ Mychajlo Dmytrenko Fine Arts Foundation Scholarships *(Undergraduate/Scholarship)*

Purpose: To support the education of Art students from the Academy of Fine Arts in Kyiv. **Focus:** Fine Arts. **Qualif.:** Applicants must be art students at the academy of Fine Arts in Kyiv. **Criteria:** Selection is based on criteria.

Funds Avail.: No specific amount. **To Apply:** Applicants must submit a completed application form. **Contact:** 1425 La Perla Long Beach CA 90815 USA and look for Mark Dmytrenko, President or call at Tel: 877-813-4591; Fax: 562-986-5770 Email: foundation@dmytrenko.org

Awards are arranged alphabetically below their administering organizations

7022 ■ European College of Liberal Arts (ECLA) Scholarships *(Undergraduate/Scholarship)*

Purpose: To offer full scholarships on a need-blind basis. **Focus:** General Studies. **Qualif.:** Applicants must study German while attending ECLA; must have earned 30 credit hours in a full year program and 8 credits in the summer program; should be between ages 18-24 with the right background and interests, proficient academic performance and good values. **Criteria:** Preference will be given to those students who meet the criteria.

Funds Avail.: No specific amount. **To Apply:** Applicants must check the available website for more information. **Contact:** For more information about ECLA and the scholarship program, see www.ecla.de. For other questions, please email Dick Shriver at rhsusa@yahoo.com.

7023 ■ University of Maryland International Student Scholarships *(Undergraduate/Scholarship)*

Purpose: To provide scholarships to those deserving undergraduate international students. **Focus:** General Studies. **Qualif.:** Applicants must be undergraduate international students; must have demonstrated a strong record of academic achievement and proficient English skills. **Criteria:** Preference will be given to students who meet the criteria.

Funds Avail.: No specific amount. **To Apply:** Applicants must check the available website for more information. **Deadline:** June 1. **Contact:** For more information just contact the Office of International Admissions at 410-704-6069 or visit their website for complete details: www.towson.edu/intladm

7024 ■ USA/USA-Ukramerazha Scholarships *(Undergraduate/Scholarship)*

Purpose: To provide financial support to talented high school students in Ukraine. **Focus:** General Studies. **Qualif.:** Applicants must be talented high school students in Ukraine heading to preparatory schools and colleges in the U.S., Canada or the United Kingdom. **Criteria:** Preference will be given to those students who meet the criteria.

Funds Avail.: No specific amount. **To Apply:** Applicants must check the available website for more information. **Remarks:** USA/USA Program services help selected students understand the requirements and procedures of Western educational institutions by offering advisory workshops and scholarships for entrance exams. **Contact:** U.S.Ukraine Foundation at the above address (see entry 7020).

7025 ■ Unites States Institute of Peace

1200 17th St. NW
Washington, DC 20036
Ph: (202)457-1700
Fax: (202)429-6063
URL: http://www.usip.org

7026 ■ The Jennings Randolph Peace Scholar Dissertation Program *(All/Scholarship)*

Purpose: To recognize practitioners, scholars, policymakers, journalists and other professionals so that they can conduct research on conflict and peace while in residence at the Institute. **Focus:** General studies. **Qualif.:** Applicants must be citizens of any country. **Criteria:** Recipients are selected based on project significance; project design; implementation; potential as a peace scholar.

Funds Avail.: $20,000. **To Apply:** Applicants must complete the application form; applicants must submit a proposed project. **Deadline:** January 5.

7027 ■ Unites States Institute of Peace JR Senior Fellowships Program *(All/Fellowship)*

Purpose: To recognize practitioners, scholars, policymakers, journalists and other professionals so that they can conduct research on conflict and peace while in residence at the Institute. **Focus:** General studies. **Qualif.:** Applicants must be citizens of any country. **Criteria:** Recipients are selected based on overall project significance; project design; implementation; track record and reputation; potential as fellows.

Funds Avail.: $80,000. **To Apply:** Applicants must complete the application form; applicants must submit a proposed project. **Deadline:** September 8.

7028 ■ University of Alaska Anchorage

3211 Providence Dr.
Anchorage, AK 99508
Ph: (907)786-1800
URL: http://www.uaa.alaska.edu

7029 ■ Alaska Community Foundation Sven E. & Lorraine Eriksson Scholarships *(Undergraduate/Scholarship)*

Purpose: To provide financial assistance for tuition and other related educational expenses to full-time students of the University of Alaska Anchorage who are formally admitted to an undergraduate engineering or music degree-seeking program. **Focus:** Engineering; Music. **Qualif.:** Applicant must demonstrate motivation, academic and leadership potential; must be an Alaskan resident who has graduated from an Alaskan high school; must be a United States citizen; must be an incoming college freshman must have a minimum high school GPA of 2.5; must have a minimum cumulative grade point average of 3.0 from college and have had a 2.5 GPA from high school; must be formally admitted to an undergraduate engineering or music degree-seeking program at the University of Alaska Anchorage; must demonstrate financial need; must be an incoming or continuing student at the University of Alaska Anchorage. **Criteria:** Preference will be given to University of Alaska Anchorage applicants and to applicant who plan to pursue a career in Alaska as demonstrated by a personal essay.

Funds Avail.: No specific amount. **To Apply:** Applicants must complete the application form available online. **Deadline:** February 15.

7030 ■ Chugach Gem & Mineral Society Scholarships *(Undergraduate/Scholarship)*

Purpose: To provide financial assistance for tuition and other related educational expenses to University of Alaska Anchorage or University of Alaska Fairbanks students who are admitted in a Geology degree-seeking program. **Focus:** Geology. **Qualif.:** Applicant must be in good academic standing with a minimum cumulative GPA of 2.0; must demonstrate motivation, academic and leadership potential; must be formally admitted to an undergraduate Geology major or minor degree-seeking program at the University of Alaska Anchorage or Fairbanks by the start of the fall semester; must plan on enrolling at least half-time (six

Awards are arranged alphabetically below their administering organizations

credits) at the University of Alaska Anchorage or the University of Alaska Fairbanks; must be junior or senior standing; must be an Alaska resident; must be enrolled in the semester for which the award is made. **Criteria:** Selection of applicants will be based on the application requirement.

Funds Avail.: $2,000. **Number Awarded:** 2. **To Apply:** Applicant must complete the UAA Scholarship Application Form available online; must attach a list of activities/ community service in which the applicant have participated; must submit a resume and personal essay; must have two letters of recommendation and transcript; must provide a proof of Alaska residency. Application must be received by the UAA Office of Student Financial Aid, Attn: CGMS Rasmusson Memorial Earth Science Scholarship, PO Box 141608, Anchorage, AK 99514. **Deadline:** October 6.

7031 ■ Benjamin A. Gilman International Scholarship *(Undergraduate/Scholarship)*

Purpose: To encourage students to choose non-traditional study destinations abroad, especially those outside of Western Europe and Australia; to support students who have been traditionally under-represented in study abroad, including but not limited to, students with high financial need, community college students, students in under-represented fields such as the sciences and engineering, students with diverse ethnic backgrounds, and students with disabilities. **Focus:** Engineering; Science; General studies. **Qualif.:** Applicants must be U.S. citizen undergraduate students who are receiving Federal Pell Grant funding at a 2-year or 4-year college or university to participate in study abroad programs worldwide; must be receiving a Federal Pell Grant or provide proof that he/she will be receiving a Pell Grant at the time of application or during the term of their study abroad; must be applying to or has been accepted into a study abroad program eligible for credit by the student's accredited institution of higher education in the U.S; must be studying abroad for at least 4 weeks in one country; must be studying abroad in any country except Cuba or a country on the State Department's current travel warning list; must be studying in the fall, spring, or academic year terms including winter intersessions. **Criteria:** Selection criteria are based on the Gilman Scholarship Program goals that may differ from other scholarship programs. Award recipients are selected using the following criteria: (1) Diversity of Applicant; (2) Statement of Purpose Essay; (3) Follow-on Project Proposal Essay; (4) Academic Progress and Performance;(5) Fields of Study; (6) Country of Destination; (7) U.S. Institution and State Distribution; (8) Length of Study; (9) Lack Previous Undergraduate Study Abroad Experience.

Funds Avail.: Award amounts will vary depending on length of study and student need, with the average award being $4,000. **To Apply:** Applicants must submit a completed application form with other requirements or supporting documents. **Deadline:** April and September.

7032 ■ Lenore & George Hedla Accounting Scholarships *(Undergraduate/Scholarship)*

Purpose: To provide financial assistance for tuition and other related educational expenses to a UAA student who is enrolled full-time or parttime with a declared major in accounting. **Focus:** Accounting. **Qualif.:** Applicants must demonstrate motivation, academic and leadership potential; must be in good academic standing with a minimum cumulative GPA of 2.0; must be formally admitted to an undergraduate accounting degreeseeking program at the UAA; must plan on enrolling at least full-time or part-time at the UAA; may be a U.S. citizen, non-U.S. citizen, Alaska resident, or out-of-state resident; must be enrolled in the semester for which the award is made. **Criteria:** Applicants will be selected base on their academic standing and application materials.

Funds Avail.: No specific amount. **To Apply:** Applicants must complete the electronic scholarship application available online at www.uaa.alaska.edu/scholarships/hedla.cfm. **Deadline:** February 15.

7033 ■ Killam Fellowships Program *(Undergraduate/Fellowship)*

Purpose: To encourage undergraduate students in the United States and Canada by providing a unique opportunity for academic exchange. **Focus:** General studies. **Qualif.:** Applicant must be a citizen of Canada or the United States; must be a full-time undergraduate student in good standing at a degree-granting institution in Canada or the United States; must meet the eligibility requirements of their home university; must be fluent in English; must have a superior academic record; must complete all the steps of the application process prior to the published deadlines, and, in the case of the direct exchange applicants; must be nominated by his/her university to receive a Killam Fellowship. **Criteria:** Selection is open and competitive, based on a combination of academic standing, personal statement, and letters of reference. Applications are reviewed by an independent adjudication committee comprised of faculty members from Canadian and American universities.

Funds Avail.: $10,000. **To Apply:** Applications and instructions can be obtained online at www.killamfellowships.com. **Deadline:** January 31.

7034 ■ Arlene Kuhner Memorial Scholarships *(Undergraduate/Scholarship)*

Purpose: To provide financial assistance for tuition and other related educational expenses to a University of Alaska Anchorage student who has a declared major in English. **Focus:** Education, English as a second language. **Qualif.:** Applicant must demonstrate academic excellence; must be in good academic standing with at least a cumulative GPA of 3.0; must be a student attending the University of Alaska Anchorage with a declared major in English; must take a minimum of six credits per semester. **Criteria:** Preference will be given to students who have been in residence at UAA for at least a year.

Funds Avail.: No specific amount. **To Apply:** For further information about the scholarship, applicants are advised to visit the website at www.uaa.alaska.edu/scholarships/ arlene.cfm. **Deadline:** February 15.

7035 ■ Providence Alaska Medical Center Auxiliary Scholarships *(Undergraduate/ Scholarship)*

Purpose: To provide financial support to students who want to pursue their degree in the field of medicine. **Focus:** Medicine. **Qualif.:** Applicant must be admitted to a degree-seeking clinical major; must be currently enrolled as a first year student or beyond at one of the institutions of higher education in Alaska; must have a minimum GPA of 2.7. **Criteria:** Selection of applicants will be based on their application and academic standing.

Funds Avail.: $1,000. **To Apply:** Applicants must complete the scholarship application form; must have the current official transcript of grades; must have two letters of recommendation from university or college faculty members; must have a two- or three-page statement that includes: (1) Name, permanent address, phone number, social security number and student ID number; (2) A short history of the applicant and family; (3) A statement of goals; (4) A summary of interest and community involvement; (5) A summary of work experience and financial need. Application must be sent to: Providence Alaska Medical Center Auxiliary, Scholarship Committee, 3200 Providence Dr., PO Box 196604, Anchorage, AK 99519-6604. **Deadline:** June 30.

7036 ■ Lillian Smith Scholarship for Teaching Students *(Graduate, Undergraduate/Scholarship)*

Purpose: To provide financial assistance to students at UAA who are studying to become teachers. **Focus:** Education. **Qualif.:** Applicants must demonstrate motivation, academic and leadership potential; must be in good academic standing with a minimum cumulative GPA of 2.0 for undergraduate and 3.0 for graduate; must be a full-time student attending the UAA (12 credits for undergraduates, 9 credits for graduates); must be fully admitted to the Education degree program at the UAA; may be an incoming or continuing student at the University of Alaska Anchorage; may be a U.S. citizen, non-U.S. citizen, Alaskan resident, or out-of-state resident. **Criteria:** Preference will be given to students who demonstrate financial need.

Funds Avail.: $500. **Number Awarded:** 2. **To Apply:** Applicants must complete the electronic scholarship application available online. **Deadline:** February 15.

7037 ■ Sheri Stears Education Scholarships *(Undergraduate/Scholarship)*

Purpose: To provide financial assistance for tuition and other educational expenses to students admitted to pre-service teacher education programs at UAA. **Focus:** Education. **Qualif.:** Applicants must be in good academic standing with a minimum cumulative GPA of 3.0; must be involved in extracurricular activities; must be formally admitted to the College of Education pursuing an undergraduate education degree or the Master of Arts in Teaching at the UAA; must plan on enrolling at least half-time (6 credits) at the UAA; may be an incoming or continuing student at the UAA; may be a U.S. citizen, non-U.S. citizen, Alaska resident, or out-of-state resident. **Criteria:** Preference will be given to: (1) Applicants who are Alaska residents; (2) Applicants who demonstrate financial need; (3) Applicants who address best how they see themselves advancing education in Alaska; (4) Undergraduate applicants.

Funds Avail.: $500-$2,500. **To Apply:** Applicants must submit an essay responding to these questions: (1) How do you see yourself further advancing education in Alaska?; (2) How do your extracurricular activities enhance your educational experience?; Applicants must complete the electronic scholarship application available online at www.uaa.alaska.edu/scholarships/sheri.cfm. **Deadline:** February 15.

7038 ■ Sturgulewski Family Scholarships *(Graduate, Undergraduate/Scholarship)*

Purpose: To provide financial assistance for tuition and other educational expenses to full-time students who are formally admitted to a journalism, engineering, or education degree-seeking program at the University of Alaska Anchorage. **Focus:** Journalism; Engineering; Education. **Qualif.:** Applicants must demonstrate motivation, academic and leadership potential; must be in good academic standing with a minimum cumulative GPA of 2.0 for undergraduates and 3.0 for graduates; must be formally admitted to a journalism, engineering, or education undergraduate, graduate, certificate, and/or vocational degree-seeking program at the University of Alaska Anchorage; must have plan on enrolling full-time (12 credits for undergraduates and 9 for graduates) at the University of Alaska Anchorage; may be an incoming or continuing student at the University of Alaska Anchorage; may be a U.S citizen, non-US citizen, Alaska resident, or out-of-state resident; must be enrolled in the semester for which the award is made. **Criteria:** Selection of applicants will be based on their application materials and academic standing.

Funds Avail.: $500. **To Apply:** Applicants must complete the electronic scholarship application available online at www.uaa.alaska.edu/scholarships/sturgulewski_family.cfm. **Deadline:** February 15.

7039 ■ UAA Accounting Club Scholarships *(Undergraduate/Scholarship)*

Purpose: To provide financial assistance for tuition and other related educational expenses to a University of Alaska Anchorage student who is enrolled in at least nine credits with a declared major in accounting, and to encourage non-traditional students to pursue academic endeavors. **Focus:** Accounting. **Qualif.:** Applicants must demonstrate motivation, academic and leadership potential; must be in good academic standing with a minimum cumulative GPA of 3.0; must be formally admitted to an undergraduate Accounting degree-seeking program at the UAA; must plan on enrolling at least nine credits at the UAA; must demonstrate an involvement in extracurricular activities, with specific involvement in the UAA Accounting Club; must be junior or senior standing and have completed a 300-level accounting course or be enrolled in a 300-level accounting course during the semester of the award; may be a U.S. citizen, non-U.S. citizen, Alaska resident, or out-of-state resident; must be enrolled in the semester for which the award is made. **Criteria:** Preference will be given to applicants demonstrating financial need and to non-traditional students.

Funds Avail.: $500. **To Apply:** Applicants must complete the electronic scholarship application available online. **Deadline:** February 15.

7040 ■ UAA Alaska Kidney Foundation Scholarships *(Graduate, Undergraduate/Scholarship)*

Purpose: To provide scholarships in the name of the Alaska Kidney Foundation to prepare new nurses to provide safe and effective care to individuals experiencing chronic kidney disease in Alaska. **Focus:** Nursing. **Qualif.:** Applicants must have been a resident of Alaska for three years prior to the start of the semester the award is given; must be formally admitted to a nursing degree program that leads to RN licensure; must plan on being enrolled at least part-time (six credits); must have completed one clinical nursing course by the start of the semester the award is given, unless a new student. Applicants who have successfully completed a clinical nursing course must have a minimum cumulative GPA of 2.5 and nursing course minimum cumulative GPA of 2.0. Applicants who are new students beginning clinical studies and have not completed a clinical nursing course must have a minimum cumulative GPA of 2.8. **Criteria:** Preference will be given to applicants who write an essay that: (1) Reflects a career plan that includes working with a clientele that could result in working with individuals with chronic or acute kidney disease or with clients at risk for the development of chronic renal disease; (2) Reflects a plan to remain to practice in Alaska.

Funds Avail.: $1,000-$2,400. **Number Awarded:** 19. **To Apply:** Applicants must submit a brief essay (250 words max) describing the following: (1) A career plan that includes working with a clientele that could result in working with individuals with chronic or acute kidney disease or with clients at risk for the development of chronic renal disease; (2) A plan to remain in practice in Alaska. Applicants must complete the electronic scholarship application available online at www.uaa.alaska.edu/scholarships/kidney.cfm. **Deadline:** February 15.

7041 ■ UAA Alumni Association Scholarships *(Undergraduate/Scholarship)*

Purpose: To provide financial assistance to students who want to pursue their education at UAA. **Focus:** General studies. **Qualif.:** Applicants must demonstrate motivation, academic, and leadership potential; must be in good academic standing with a minimum cumulative GPA of 2.5 for undergraduates and 3.0 for graduates; must be formally admitted to a degree- or certificate-seeking program within one of the following UAA schools/ colleges: College of Business, College of Business and Public Policy, College of Arts and Sciences, College of Health and Social Welfare, Community & Technical College, School of Engineering, and the College of Education; must plan on enrolling full-time (12 credits for undergraduates, 9 credits for graduates) at UAA; must be an incoming or continuing student at UAA; may be a U.S citizen, non-U.S citizen, Alaska resident, or out-ofstate resident. **Criteria:** Recipient will be chosen based on their monetary need, scholastic success, community volunteer involvement, and leadership. Preference will be given to students who are Alaska high school graduates, continuing UAA students, and/or students whose parent(s) graduated with a degree from the University of Alaska and to those who demonstrate financial need.

Funds Avail.: $1,000. **Number Awarded:** 6. **To Apply:** Application forms are available online. **Deadline:** February 15.

7042 ■ UAA Anchorage Daily News Minority Journalism Scholarships *(Undergraduate/Scholarship)*

Purpose: To provide financial assistance for tuition and other educational expenses to minority students who are formally admitted to the journalism degree-seeking program at the University of Alaska Anchorage. **Focus:** Journalism. **Qualif.:** Applicants must demonstrate motivation, academic and leadership potential; must be in good academic standing with a minimum cumulative GPA of 2.0; must be formally admitted to a journalism degreeseeking program at the University of Alaska Anchorage; must plan on enrolling full-time (12 credits for undergraduates) at the University of Alaska Anchorage; may be an incoming or continuing student at the University of Alaska Anchorage; must be enrolled in the semester for which the award is made. **Criteria:** Preference will be given to Alaska Native students.

Funds Avail.: $500-$1,000. **To Apply:** Applicants must complete the electronic scholarship application available online at www.uaa.alaska.edu/scholarships/adn.cfm. **Deadline:** February 15.

7043 ■ UAA April Relyea Scholarships *(Graduate, Undergraduate/Scholarship)*

Purpose: To provide financial assistance for tuition and other educational expenses to students who are formally admitted to a degree-seeking program at the University of Alaska Anchorage who have an intent to explore human-nature relationships through writing or other creative expression. **Focus:** Human relations. **Qualif.:** Applicants must demonstrate environmental interest with intent to explore the topic of human-nature relationships through writing or other creative expressions; must be in good academic standing with a minimum cumulative GPA of 2.0 for undergraduates and 3.0 for graduates; must be formally admitted to an undergraduate, graduate, certificate, and/or vocational degree-seeking program at the University of Alaska Anchorage; may be a U.S citizen, non-U.S citizen, Alaska resident, or out-of-state resident; must complete a project to receive a second semester scholarship. **Criteria:** Preference will be given to students with an intent to produce work for the Student Showcase and students with a demonstrated interest in writing nature books for children.

Funds Avail.: $500. **To Apply:** Applicants must submit an essay about their interest in human-nature relationships and how they intend to pursue that interest at UAA; must submit two letters of reference from source having knowledge of their environmental interest. Application forms and other supporting documents must be sent to the UAA Office of Student Financial Assistance, April Relyea Scholarship, PO Box 141608, Anchorage, AK 99503. **Deadline:** February 15.

7044 ■ UAA Ardell French Memorial Scholarships *(Undergraduate/Scholarship)*

Purpose: To provide financial assistance for tuition and other educational expenses to full-time students who are formally admitted to a chemistry degree-seeking program at the University of Alaska Anchorage. **Focus:** Chemistry. **Qualif.:** Applicants must demonstrate motivation, academic and leadership potential; must be in good academic standing with a minimum cumulative GPA of 2.0; must be formally admitted to a undergraduate chemistry degree-seeking program at the University of Alaska Anchorage; must plan on enrolling full-time (12 credits) at the University of Alaska Anchorage; may be a U.S citizen, non-U.S citizen, Alaska resident, or out-of-state resident; must be enrolled in the semester for which the award is made. **Criteria:** Preference will be given to applicants who demonstrate financial need and to applicants from Alaska.

Funds Avail.: $1,000-$2,000. **To Apply:** Applicants must complete the electronic scholarship application available online at www.uaa.alaska.edu/scholarships/ardell.cfm. **Deadline:** February 15.

7045 ■ UAA Brown Schoenheit Memorial Scholarships *(Undergraduate/Scholarship)*

Purpose: To provide financial assistance for tuition and other educational expenses to students who are formally admitted to a music degree-seeking program at the University of Alaska Anchorage. **Focus:** Music. **Qualif.:** Applicants must demonstrate motivation, academic and leadership potential, and musical ability; must be in good academic standing with a minimum cumulative GPA of 2.0; must be formally admitted to a music degree-seeking program at the University of Alaska Anchorage by the start of the semester for which the award is to be made; must be a Music major with emphasis in an orchestral instrument; must plan on enrolling at least half-time (6 credits) at the University of Alaska Anchorage for the semester in which the award is made; may be an incoming or continuing student at the University of Alaska Anchorage; may be a U.S. citizen, non-U.S. citizen, Alaska resident, or out-of-state resident. **Criteria:** Preference will be given to a flute student and to applicants who intend to pursue a career in Alaska upon graduating.

Funds Avail.: No specific amount. **To Apply:** Applicants must complete the electronic scholarship application available online at www.uaa.alaska.edu/scholarships/brown.cfm. **Deadline:** February 15.

7046 ■ UAA Chris L. Kleinke Scholarships
(Graduate, Undergraduate/Scholarship)

Purpose: To provide a monetary award to an outstanding student in the UAA Master of Science in Clinical Psychology program. **Focus:** Psychology. **Qualif.:** Applicants must demonstrate motivation, academic and leadership potential; must be in good academic standing with a minimum cumulative GPA of 3.0; must be formally admitted to the Master of Science in Clinical Psychology program at the UAA; must plan on enrolling full-time (nine credits of graduate course work) at the University of Alaska Anchorage; applicant may be an incoming or continuing student at the UAA; may be a U.S citizen, non-U.S. citizen, Alaska resident, or out-of-state resident; must be enrolled in the semester for which the award is made. **Criteria:** Preference will be given to students who have completed at least one year in the Master of Science in Clinical Psychology program. Applicants will be judged by the UAA Clinical Training Committee by the following criteria: (1) Academic performance in the MS in Clinical Psychology program as measured by current UAA graduate GPA, and undergraduate GPA in Psychology courses (not necessarily from UAA); (2) Potential for success in the field of clinical psychology as measured by clinical community, and/or research experience and letters of recommendation from a professional in the field; (3) The strength of personal statement detailing the applicant's plans for a future career in psychology.

Funds Avail.: $1,500. **To Apply:** Applicants must provide two letters of recommendation from professors and/or professionals in the clinical psychology field; must complete the electronic scholarship application available online at www.uaa.alaska.edu/scholarships/chris.cfm. **Deadline:** February 15.

7047 ■ UAA College of Business & Public Policy Scholarships *(Graduate, Undergraduate/Scholarship)*

Purpose: To provide financial assistance for tuition and other educational expenses to full-time students who are formally admitted to a degreeseeking program within the College of Business & Public Policy at the UAA. **Focus:** Business; Public service. **Qualif.:** Applicants must demonstrate motivation, academic and leadership potential; must be in good academic standing with a minimum cumulative GPA of 2.0 for undergraduates and 3.0 for graduates; must be formally admitted to an undergraduate, graduate, certificate, and/or vocational degree-seeking program within the College of Business & Public Policy at the UAA; must plan on enrolling full-time (12 credits for undergraduate and nine credits for graduate) at the UAA; may be an incoming or continuing student at the UAA; may be a U.S. citizen, non-U.S. citizen, Alaska resident, or out-of-state resident. **Criteria:** Applicants will be selected based on their academic standing and application materials.

Funds Avail.: $500. **Number Awarded:** 3. **To Apply:** Applicants must complete the electronic scholarship application. **Deadline:** February 15.

7048 ■ UAA Diane Olsen Memorial Scholarships
(Undergraduate/Scholarship)

Purpose: To provide financial assistance to junior and senior students at UAA to help them pay for tuition and other related expenses. **Focus:** Economics. **Qualif.:** Applicants must demonstrate motivation, academic and leadership potential; must be in good academic standing with a minimum cumulative GPA of 2.75; must have a junior or senior standing; must be a declared economics major or have an interest in economics as demonstrated by the completion of at least 12 credits in economic courses; must plan on enrolling full-time (twelve credits for undergraduate) at the UAA; must be active in student clubs, student organizations or student governance; may be an incoming or continuing student at the UAA; may be a U.S. citizen, non-U.S. citizen, Alaska resident, or out-of-state resident. **Criteria:** Preference will be given to non-traditional students.

Funds Avail.: $500. **To Apply:** Applicants must complete the electronic scholarship application available online at www.uaa.alaska.edu/scholarships/diane.cfm. **Deadline:** February 15.

7049 ■ UAA Dr. Jon Baker Memorial Scholarships *(Graduate, Undergraduate/Scholarship)*

Purpose: To offer financial assistance for tuition and other educational expenses to full-time University of Alaska Anchorage students who are admitted to the Psychology program. **Focus:** Psychology. **Qualif.:** Applicants must demonstrate motivation, academic and leadership potential; must be in good academic standing with a minimum cumulative GPA of 2.0 for undergraduate and 3.0 for graduate; must be formally admitted to an undergraduate, graduate, certificate, and/or vocational degree-seeking program at the University of Alaska Anchorage; may be a U.S. citizen, nonU.S. citizen, Alaska resident, or out-of-state resident. **Criteria:** Preference will be given to students who are formally admitted to the Psychology program.

Funds Avail.: $500. **Number Awarded:** 2. **To Apply:** Applicants must complete the electronic scholarship application available online at www.uaa.alaska.edu/scholarships/jon.cfm. **Deadline:** February 15.

7050 ■ UAA Edward Rollin Clinton Memorial for Music *(Undergraduate/Scholarship)*

Purpose: To provide financial assistance for tuition and other educational expenses to full-time students who are formally admitted to a music degree-seeking program at the University of Alaska Anchorage. **Focus:** Music. **Qualif.:** Applicant must be in good academic standing with a minimum cumulative GPA of 3.0; must be formally admitted to a music degree-seeking program at the University of Alaska Anchorage; must plan on enrolling at least full-time (12 credits) at the University of Alaska Anchorage; may be an incoming or continuing student at the University of Alaska Anchorage; may be a U.S citizen, non-U.S citizen, Alaska resident, or out-of-state resident. **Criteria:** Class standing preferences will be as follows: (1) Preference will be given to an entering freshman planning to study piano; (2) Preference will be given to upper division students studying piano; (3) Preference will be given to freshman planning to study any instrument; (4) Preference will be given to upper division students studying any instrument; (5) Preference will be given to students who demonstrate financial need.

Funds Avail.: $1,000. **To Apply:** Applicants must submit a compact disc recording which must include a minimum of two (2) selections from the standard classical repertoire. Application form and other supporting documents must be sent to UAA Office of Student Financial Assistance, Edward Rollin Clinton Scholarship, PO Box 141608, Anchorage, AK

99514. **Deadline:** February 15.

7051 ■ UAA Elaine Atwood Scholarships
(Undergraduate/Scholarship)

Purpose: To provide financial assistance to University of Alaska Anchorage students who are formally admitted to the journalism & public communication degree-seeking program. **Focus:** Journalism; Public affairs. **Qualif.:** Applicants must demonstrate motivation, academic and leadership potential; must be in good academic standing with a minimum cumulative GPA of 3.0; must be formally admitted to the Journalism and Public Communication degree program at UAA; must plan on enrolling full-time (12 credits) at the University of Alaska Anchorage; may be an incoming or continuing student at the University of Alaska Anchorage; must be an Alaska resident who will pursue a career in Alaska. **Criteria:** Applicants will be selected based on their academic standing and application documents.

Funds Avail.: $2,500-5,000. **To Apply:** Applicants must complete the electronics scholarship application available online at www.uaa.alaska.edu/scholarships/elaine.cfm. **Deadline:** February 15.

7052 ■ UAA Emi Chance Memorial Scholarships
(Undergraduate/Scholarship)

Purpose: To provide financial assistance for tuition and other related educational expenses to a full-time student attending the University of Alaska Anchorage who are junior-standing art majors. **Focus:** Art. **Qualif.:** Applicants must demonstrate motivation, talent, academic, and leadership potential; must have demonstrated a commitment to his/her community; must be in good academic standing with a minimum cumulative GPA of 3.0; must be a full-time student (12 credits) at the University of Alaska Anchorage; must be formally admitted to an art degree-seeking program at the University of Alaska Anchorage; must be a drawing and/or painting major with a junior class standing; must submit one drawing and/or painting with application; may be a U.S. citizen, non-U.S. citizen, Alaska resident, or out-of-state resident; must be enrolled in the semester for which the award is made. **Criteria:** Selection of applicants will be based on their academic standing and application materials.

Funds Avail.: No specific amount. **To Apply:** Applicants must submit one drawing and/or painting to the UAA Office of Student Financial Assistance. Application forms are available online and must be sent to UAA Office of Student Financial Assistance, EMI Chance Memorial Scholarships, PO Box 141608, AK 99514-1608. **Deadline:** February 15.

7053 ■ UAA Eveline Schuster Memorial Award/ Scholarships *(Graduate, Undergraduate/ Scholarship)*

Purpose: To provide financial assistance to cover a student-designated sociology project to be conducted while the student is enrolled at UAA and to encourage the students to pursue sociology as a career. **Focus:** Sociology. **Qualif.:** Applicants must demonstrate motivation, academic, and leadership potential; must be in good academic standing with a 3.0 GPA and a sociology GPA of 3.3 or better; must be formally admitted to a sociology degree-seeking program or interdisciplinary master's degree-seeking program with sociology as one of the disciplines, at the UAA; must plan on enrolling full-time (12 credits for undergraduates, 9 credits for graduates) at the UAA; must have at least a junior class standing; must have been enrolled in at least six (6) credits prior to the semester the award is granted; may be a U.S citizen, non-U.S. citizen, Alaska resident, or out-of-state resident. **Criteria:** Selection of applicants will be based on their academic standing and application documents.

Funds Avail.: No specific amount. **To Apply:** Applicants must submit a cover letter indicating if they are applying for the scholarship or for project funding; must submit two (2) letters of recommendation; must submit a project budget and statement indicating the project intent; must complete the electronic scholarship application available online at www.uaa.alaska.edu/scholarships/eveline.cfm. **Deadline:** February 15.

7054 ■ UAA Friends of the Performing Arts Scholarships *(Undergraduate/Scholarship)*

Purpose: To provide financial assistance for tuition and other education related expenses to a full-time University of Alaska Anchorage student who has shown a proven interest in the performing arts. **Focus:** Performing arts. **Qualif.:** Applicants must demonstrate motivation, academic and leadership potential; must be in good academic standing in an undergraduate performing arts degree-seeking program at the University of Alaska Anchorage; must plan on enrolling full-time (12 credits) at the University of Alaska Anchorage; must show proven interest in the performing arts; may be an incoming or continuing student at the University of Alaska Anchorage; may be a U.S. citizen, non-U.S. citizen, Alaska resident, or out-of-state resident; must be enrolled in the semester for which the award is made. **Criteria:** Applicants will be selected based on their application materials and academic standing.

Funds Avail.: $750. **To Apply:** Applicants must complete the scholarship application available online at www.uaa.alaska.edu/scholarships/friends_arts.cfm. **Deadline:** February 15.

7055 ■ UAA GCI, Inc. Scholarships
(Undergraduate/Scholarship)

Purpose: To provide financial assistance for tuition and other educational expenses to full-time students who are formally admitted to a journalism & public communications degree-seeking program at the University of Alaska Anchorage and who are in financial need. **Focus:** Journalism; Public affairs. **Qualif.:** Applicants must demonstrate motivation, academic and leadership potential; must be in good academic standing with a minimum cumulative GPA of 3.0; must be formally admitted to a journalism & public communications degree-seeking program at the University of Alaska Anchorage; must plan on enrolling full-time (12 credits) at the University of Alaska Anchorage; must be able to demonstrate financial need; must be enrolled in the semester for which the award is made; may be an incoming or continuing student at the University of Alaska Anchorage; may be a U.S citizen, non-U.S citizen, Alaska resident, or out-of-state resident. **Criteria:** Applicants will be selected based on their application materials and academic standing.

Funds Avail.: No specific amount. **To Apply:** Applicants must complete the electronic scholarship application available online at www.uaa.alaska.edu/scholarships/sturgulewski_family.cfm. **Deadline:** February 15.

7056 ■ UAA Governor William A. Egan Scholarships *(Undergraduate/Scholarship)*

Purpose: To provide financial assistance for tuition and other educational expenses to students who are formally

Awards are arranged alphabetically below their administering organizations

admitted to a political science or history degree-seeking program or who are members of the Forty-Ninth State Fellows Program at the University of Alaska Anchorage. **Focus:** Political science; History. **Qualif.:** Applicant must demonstrate motivation, academic and leadership potential; must demonstrate a commitment to their community; must be in good academic standing with a minimum cumulative GPA of 2.0; must be formally admitted to a political science or history degreeseeking program at the University of Alaska Anchorage; must plan on enrolling full-time (12 credits) at the University of Alaska Anchorage; may be an incoming or continuing student at the University of Alaska Anchorage; may be a U.S citizen, non-U.S citizen, Alaska resident, out-of-state resident; must be enrolled in the semester for which the award is made. **Criteria:** Preference will be given to applicants who are Alaska residents and have shown a potential for public service.

Funds Avail.: $560. **To Apply:** Applicants must complete the electronic scholarship application available online at www.uaa.alaska.edu/scholarships/egan.cfm. **Deadline:** February 15.

7057 ■ UAA Jack & Martha Roderick Scholarships *(Graduate, Undergraduate/Scholarship)*

Purpose: To provide financial assistance for tuition and other educational expenses to students who are formally admitted to a degree-seeking program within the College of Arts & Sciences at the University of Alaska Anchorage. **Focus:** Art; Science. **Qualif.:** Applicants must be in good academic standing with a minimum cumulative GPA of 2.0 for undergraduates and 3.0 for graduates; must be formally admitted to an undergraduate, graduate, and/or certificate degree-seeking program within the College of Arts & Science at the University of Alaska Anchorage; must plan on enrolling at least part-time (six credits for undergraduate or five for graduate) at the University of the Alaska Anchorage; may be a U.S citizen, non-U.S citizen, Alaska resident, or out-of-state resident; must be able to demonstrate financial need; must be enrolled in the semester for which the award is made. **Criteria:** Selection of applicants will be based on their financial need and academic standing.

Funds Avail.: $500-$1,000. **Number Awarded:** 2. **To Apply:** Application forms are available at www.uaa.alaska.edu/scholarships/jack.cfm. **Deadline:** February 15.

7058 ■ UAA Jan & Glenn Fredericks Scholarships *(Graduate, Undergraduate/Scholarship)*

Purpose: To provide financial assistance for tuition and other educational expenses to full-time students who are formally admitted to a business degree-seeking program at the UAA. **Focus:** Business. **Qualif.:** Applicants must demonstrate motivation, academic and leadership potential; must be in good academic standing with a minimum cumulative GPA of 2.0 for undergraduates and 3.0 for graduates; must be formally admitted to a business degreeseeking program at the UAA by the start of the semester; must plan on enrolling full-time (12 credits for undergraduate and nine credits for graduate) at the UAA by the start of the semester of the award; must have at least a junior, senior, or graduate class-standing by the start of the semester of the award; may be a U.S. citizen, non-U.S. citizen, Alaska resident, or out-of-state resident. **Criteria:** Preference will be given to students who are of Alaskan ethnicity.

Funds Avail.: No specific amount. **To Apply:** Applicants must complete the electronic scholarship application available online at www.uaa.alaska.edu/scholarships/jan.cfm. **Deadline:** February 15.

7059 ■ UAA Ken Gray Endowment Scholarships *(Undergraduate/Scholarship)*

Purpose: To provide financial assistance for tuition and other educational expenses to full-time junior or senior students who are formally admitted into a Bachelor of Arts or Bachelor of Fine Arts program in the area of sculpture and/or performance art at the University of Alaska Anchorage. **Focus:** Performing arts, Sculpture. **Qualif.:** Applicants must exhibit an innovative, experimental, and conceptual direction in his/her artwork that stretches the limits of traditional sculpture; must demonstrate motivation, academic and leadership potential; must be in good academic standing with a minimum cumulative GPA of 3.25 and a cumulative GPA of 3.5 in the area of concentration; must formally be admitted to a Bachelor of Arts or Bachelor of Fine Arts at the University of Alaska Anchorage; must plan on enrolling full-time at the University of Alaska Anchorage; must submit a portfolio of work consisting of twenty slides, three letters of reference from practitioners in the sculpture area and/or faculty, and a two-page artist's statement reflecting the criteria for selection; must be enrolled in the semester for which the award is made; may be a U.S. citizen, non-U.S. citizen, Alaska resident, or out-of-state resident. **Criteria:** Applicants will be selected based on their application materials and academic standing.

Funds Avail.: $500-$800. **To Apply:** Applicants must submit a portfolio of work consisting of 20 slides; must have three letters of reference from practitioners in the sculpture area and/or UAA faculty; must have a two-page artist's statement reflecting the criteria for selection. Application materials must be sent to UAA Office of Student Financial Assistance, Ken Gray Scholarships, PO Box 141608, Anchorage, AK 99514-1608. **Deadline:** February 15.

7060 ■ UAA Kimura Scholarship Fund (Photography Scholarships) *(Undergraduate/Scholarship)*

Purpose: To provide financial assistance for tuition and other related educational expenses to full-time students at the University of Alaska Anchorage with a declared major in art or journalism & public communications. **Focus:** Art; Journalism; Photography. **Qualif.:** Applicant must be a full-time student attending the University of Alaska Anchorage with a declared major in art or with a declared major in journalism & public communication with an emphasis in photography; must be in their junior year and has completed at least nine credits in studio photography classes at the 200 level or above; must be in good academic standing with at least a 3.0 GPA. **Criteria:** Applicants will be selected based on their application and academic standing.

Funds Avail.: No specific amount. **Number Awarded:** 2. **To Apply:** Applicants must submit a proof of their photography work. Application documents and other supporting documents must submit to UAA Office of Student Financial Assistance, Kimura Scholarships, PO Box 141608, Anchorage, AK 99514. **Deadline:** February 15.

7061 ■ UAA Kimura Scholarship Funds (Illustration Scholarships) *(Undergraduate/Scholarship)*

Purpose: To provide financial assistance for tuition and other related educational expenses to full-time students at the University of Alaska Anchorage with a declared major in art or journalism & public communications. **Focus:** Art; Journalism; Illustrators and illustrations. **Qualif.:** Applicants must be a full-time student (12 credits per semester) attending the University of Alaska Anchorage with a declared

Awards are arranged alphabetically below their administering organizations

major in art with an emphasis in illustration; must be in their junior year and have completed at least nine credits in illustration classes at the 200 level or above; must be in good academic standing with at least a 3.0 GPA. **Criteria:** Applicants will be selected based on their application materials and academic standing.

Funds Avail.: No specific amount. **Number Awarded:** 2. **To Apply:** Applicants must submit a proof of their photography work. Application documents and other supporting documents must submit to UAA Office of Student Financial Assistance, Kimura Scholarships, PO Box 141608, Anchorage, AK 99514. **Deadline:** February 15.

7062 ■ UAA Kris Knudson Memorial Scholarships *(Graduate, Undergraduate/Scholarship)*

Purpose: To provide financial assistance for tuition and other educational expenses to full-time students who are formally admitted to a degreeseeking program in the area of biochemistry, immunology, or microbiology at the University of Alaska Anchorage. **Focus:** Biochemistry; Immunology; Microbiology. **Qualif.:** Applicant must demonstrate motivation, academic and leadership potential; must be in good academic standing with a minimum cumulative GPA of 3.0; must be formally admitted to an undergraduate or graduate degree-seeking program in the area of biochemistry, immunology, or microbiology at the University of Alaska Anchorage; must plan on enrolling full-time (12 credits) for undergraduate and (9 credits) for graduate at the University of Alaska Anchorage; must have completed at least fifteen credits in chemistry, biological sciences, and/or natural sciences; must be involved in a research project within the area of biochemistry, immunology, or microbiology; may be a U.S citizen, non-U.S. citizen, Alaska resident, or out-of-state resident; must be enrolled in the semester for which the award is made. **Criteria:** Selection of applicants will be based on the criteria of the scholarship committee and by their academic standing.

Funds Avail.: $500-$885. **To Apply:** Applicants must submit a brief essay (250 words max) describing their involvement in a research project related to biochemistry, immunology, or microbiology. Application forms are available at www.uaa.alaska.edu/scholarships/kris.cfm. **Deadline:** February 15.

7063 ■ UAA Mark A. Beltz Scholarships *(Graduate, Undergraduate/Scholarship)*

Purpose: To provide financial assistance for tuition and other educational expenses to students who are in financial need. **Focus:** Political science; Economics; Business administration; Science technologies. **Qualif.:** Applicants must demonstrate motivation, academic and leadership potential; must be in good academic standing with a minimum cumulative GPA of 2.0 for undergraduates and 3.0 for graduates; must be formally admitted to a political science, economics, business administration, business and corporate law, or science and technology undergraduate, graduate, certificate, and/or vocational degree-seeking program at the University of Alaska Anchorage; must plan on enrolling at least half-time (6 credits) at the University of Alaska Anchorage; may be an incoming or continuing student at the University of Alaska Anchorage; may be a U.S. citizen, nonU.S. citizen, Alaska resident, or out-of-state resident. **Criteria:**.

Funds Avail.: $500$1,000. **To Apply:** Applicants must complete the electronics scholarship application available online. **Deadline:** February 15.

7064 ■ UAA Melissa J. Wolf Scholarships *(Undergraduate/Scholarship)*

Purpose: To provide financial assistance for tuition and other educational expenses to full-time students who are formally admitted to the Accounting degree program at the UAA. **Focus:** Accounting. **Qualif.:** Applicants must demonstrate motivation, academic and leadership potential; must be in good academic standing with a minimum cumulative grade point average of 2.0; must be formally admitted to an Accounting degree at the UAA; must plan on enrolling full-time (twelve credits) at the UAA; may be a U.S. citizen, non-U.S. citizen, Alaska resident, or out-of-state resident; must be enrolled in the semester for which the award is made. **Criteria:** Preference will be given to students who demonstrate a financial need.

Funds Avail.: No specific amount. **To Apply:** Applicants must complete the electronic scholarship application online. **Deadline:** February 15.

7065 ■ UAA Michael Baring-Gould Memorial Scholarships *(Graduate, Undergraduate/Scholarship)*

Purpose: To provide financial assistance for tuition and other educational expenses to full-time students who are formally admitted to an undergraduate social sciences program or enrolled in an interdisciplinary masters program which includes sociology as one of the disciplines. **Focus:** Social sciences; Sociology. **Qualif.:** Applicants must be in good academic standing with a minimum cumulative GPA of 2.5 for undergraduates and 3.0 for graduates; must be formally admitted to an undergraduate social sciences major or an Interdisciplinary Master's degree program that includes sociology as one of the disciplines at the University of Alaska Anchorage; must have completed at least thirty credits (undergraduate applicants); must have completed at least six credits prior to the semester of the award at the University of Alaska Anchorage; must plan on enrolling full-time (12 credits for undergraduates and nine credits for graduates) at the University of Alaska Anchorage the semester the award is granted; must demonstrate involvement in a project or area of study which reflects a commitment to social justice, peace, equality, and/or empowerment of minorities; may be a U.S. citizen, non-U.S. citizen, Alaska resident, or out-of-state resident. **Criteria:** Applicants will be selected based on their application materials, financial need and academic standing.

Funds Avail.: No specific amount. **To Apply:** Applicants must submit two letters of recommendation and an essay (250 words) describing the student's involvement in a project or area of study which reflects a commitment to social justice, peace, equality, and/or empowerment of minorities. Application material must be mailed to the UAA Office of Student Financial Assistance, PO Box 141608, Anchorage, AK 99514-1608. **Deadline:** February 15.

7066 ■ UAA Michael D. Ford Memorial Scholarships *(Graduate, Undergraduate/Scholarship)*

Purpose: To encourage an Alaskan student to enter the field of business and to provide financial assistance for tuition and other educational expenses to full-time students who are formally admitted to a business degree-seeking program at the University of Alaska Anchorage. **Focus:** Business. **Qualif.:** Applicants must have been born in Alaska and be a current Alaska resident; must be in good academic standing with a minimum cumulative GPA of 3.0; must be formally admitted to a business degree-seeking program at the University of UAA; must plan on enrolling full-time (12 credits for undergraduate and nine credits for graduate) at the UAA. **Criteria:** Preference will be given to minority students who needs financial assistant.

Funds Avail.: No specific amount. **To Apply:** Applicants must complete the electronic scholarship application available online at www.uaa.alaska.edu/scholarships/michael.cfm. **Deadline:** February 15.

7067 ■ UAA Muriel Hannah Scholarships in Art
(Undergraduate/Scholarship)

Purpose: To provide financial assistance for tuition and other educational expenses to full-time students who are formally admitted to a degreeseeking program at the University of Alaska Anchorage and who have a demonstrated talent in art. **Focus:** Art. **Qualif.:** Applicants must demonstrate motivation, academic and leadership potential; must be in good academic standing with a minimum cumulative GPA of 2.0 for undergraduate and 3.0 for graduate; must be formally admitted to an undergraduate, graduate, certificate, and/or vocational degree-seeking program at the University of Alaska Anchorage; must plan on enrolling full-time (12 credits) for undergraduate and (nine credits) for graduate at the University of Alaska Anchorage; must be able to demonstrate a talent in art; must be enrolled in the semester for which the award is made; must be an incoming or continuing student at the University of Alaska Anchorage; must be a U.S. citizen, non-U.S. citizen, Alaska resident, or out-of-state resident. **Criteria:** Preference will be given to students of one-quarter or more Alaska Native ethnicity.

Funds Avail.: $500-$1,000. **To Apply:** Applicants must provide ten (10) slides of artwork to demonstrate their talent in art. Application forms are available at the website and must be sent to UAA Office of Student Financial Assistance, PO Box 141608, Anchorage, AK 99514-1608. **Deadline:** February 15.

7068 ■ UAA Pat Brakke Political Science Scholarships *(Undergraduate/Scholarship)*

Purpose: To provide financial assistance for tuition and other educational expenses to a full-time student majoring in political science. **Focus:** Political science. **Qualif.:** Applicants must be in good academic standing with a minimum cumulative GPA of 3.0; must be formally admitted to the Political Science program at the University of Alaska Anchorage; must plan on enrolling at least full-time (12 credits) at the University of Alaska Anchorage; may be a U.S. citizen, non-U.S. citizen, Alaska resident, or out-of-state resident; must demonstrate motivation, academic and leadership potential. **Criteria:** Applicants will be selected based on their academic standing and application materials.

Funds Avail.: $650. **To Apply:** Applicants must complete the electronic scholarship application available online at www.uaa.alaska.edu/scholarships/pat.cfm. **Deadline:** February 15.

7069 ■ UAA Paul G. Landis Scholarships
(Undergraduate/Scholarship)

Purpose: To provide an annual scholarship to art majors at the University of Alaska Anchorage. **Focus:** Art. **Qualif.:** Applicants must demonstrate motivation, talent, academic, and leadership potential; must be in good academic standing with a minimum cumulative GPA of 2.0; must be attending at least part-time (6 credits); must be formally admitted to an art degree-seeking program at the University of Alaska Anchorage; must submit one drawing and/ or painting; may be a U.S citizen, non-U.S citizen, Alaska resident, or out-of-state resident; must be enrolled in the semester for which the award is made. **Criteria:** Recipient will be selected based on merit. Preference will be given to students whose work is focused in painting or drawing.

Funds Avail.: $1,000. **To Apply:** Applicant must submit ten (10) visual examples of their art work in slides or digital imagery using CD ROM/DVD formats; must submit a brief statement (125 words max) indicating the conceptual and formal direction pertinent to the student's current body of work. **Deadline:** February 15.

7070 ■ UAA Pignalberi Public Policy Scholarships *(Graduate/Scholarship)*

Purpose: To provide financial assistance for tuition and other educational expenses to students enrolled in a graduate degree program in the UAA College of Business and Public Policy. **Focus:** Business; Public service. **Qualif.:** Applicants must demonstrate motivation, academic and leadership potential; must be in good academic standing with a minimum cumulative GPA of 3.0; must be a full-time graduate student (9 credits per semester) formally admitted to the College of Business and Public Policy; must be an Alaskan resident with the intent to stay and be involved in local business and/or politics; may be an incoming or continuing student at the UAA. **Criteria:** Preference will be given to students who demonstrate financial need.

Funds Avail.: No specific amount. **To Apply:** Applicants must submit a brief essay (250 words) answering the following question: "In your opinion, what is the most important political issue in Alaska today?"; must complete the electronic scholarship application available online at www.uaa.alaska.edu/scholarships/pignalberi_pp.cfm. **Deadline:** February 15.

7071 ■ UAA Quanterra Scholarships
(Undergraduate/Scholarship)

Purpose: To provide financial assistance for tuition and other educational expenses to full-time or part-time students who are formally admitted to an engineering or science degree-seeking program at the University of Alaska Anchorage and who are of Alaska Native ethnicity. **Focus:** Engineering; Science. **Qualif.:** Applicants must demonstrate motivation, academic and leadership potential; must be in good academic standing with a minimum cumulative GPA of 2.5 for undergraduate and 3.0 for graduate; must be formally admitted to a engineering or science degree-seeking program at the University of Alaska Anchorage by the start of the semester of the award; may also be in the Masters of Civil Engineering Program, Master of Science Program; Associate of Applied Science Program for Petroleum Engineering Aide or Petroleum Technology, or working toward a Petroleum Technology Certificate; must plan on enrolling at least half-time (6 credits) at the University of Alaska Anchorage; must be able to demonstrate financial need; must be enrolled in the semester for which the award is made; must be Alaska Native ethnicity; must provide proof of Native Corporation Affiliation and Lineage Verification; may be an incoming or continuing student at the University of Alaska Anchorage. **Criteria:** Preference will be given to students in the Petroleum Technology Program or the Chemistry Program.

Funds Avail.: No specific amount. **To Apply:** Applicant must provide a proof of Native Corporation Affiliation and Lineage Verification. **Deadline:** February 15.

7072 ■ UAA RRANN Program Scholarships
(Undergraduate/Scholarship)

Purpose: To provide financial assistance for tuition and other educational expenses to students currently enrolled in a nursing degree program through the Recruitment and Retention of Alaska Natives into Nursing at the UAA. **Focus:** Nursing. **Qualif.:** Applicants must be in good academic standing with a minimum cumulative GPA of 2.0; must be formally admitted to a degree program within the School of Nursing through the RRANN program; may be an incoming or continuing student at the UAA; must be an Alaskan resident; must be enrolled in the semester for which the award is to be in effect. **Criteria:** Preference will be given to Alaska Natives or American Indian students.

Funds Avail.: $639-$1,500. **Number Awarded:** 18. **To Apply:** Applicants must complete the electronic scholarship application available online at www.uaa.alaska.edu/scholarships/rrann.cfm. **Deadline:** February 15.

7073 ■ UAA Wells Fargo Career Scholarships
(Graduate/Scholarship)

Purpose: To provide financial assistance for tuition and other educational expenses to students who are seriously interested in a career with Wells Fargo. **Focus:** Food service careers. **Qualif.:** Applicants must demonstrate motivation, academic and leadership potential; must be in good academic standing with a minimum cumulative GPA of 3.0; must be seriously interested in a career with Wells Fargo; must meet all internship requirements through the UAA Career Services Center; must be a junior or senior student attending the University of Alaska Anchorage; must be enrolled full-time (12 credits) during the semester of the award; must be admitted to an undergraduate degree program within the College of Business and Public Policy. **Criteria:** Preference will be given to candidates in Business Management, Finance, Economics, or Accounting majors or minors.

Funds Avail.: $4,950-$9,900. **Number Awarded:** 2. **To Apply:** Applicants must submit a brief essay (250 words) describing their interest in a career with Wells Fargo; must complete the electronic scholarship application available online at www.uaa.alaska.edu/scholarships/wells.cfm. **Deadline:** February 15.

7074 ■ University of Alaska Fairbanks Alumni Association

PO Box 750126
Fairbanks, AK 99775
Ph: (907)474-7081
Free: 800-770-ALUM
E-mail: fvalum@uaf.edu
URL: http://www.uaf.edu/alumni

7075 ■ Jim Doogan Memorial Scholarships
(Undergraduate/Scholarship)

Purpose: To support students with their educational pursuit. **Focus:** General studies. **Qualif.:** Applicant must be a sophomore student or above. **Criteria:** Scholarship recipients are selected based on the volunteer alumni scholarship committee's review of the application materials.

Funds Avail.: No specific amount. **To Apply:** Applicants may apply using the Supplement for Scholarship Application. **Deadline:** February 15.

Remarks: Established in memory of Jim Doogan, a supporter of UAF and an active member of the UAF Alumni Association. **Contact:** Scholarship Coordinator, 907-474-5372.

7076 ■ Fairbanks Chapter Legacy Scholarships
(Undergraduate/Scholarship)

Purpose: To support students in their educational pursuits. **Focus:** General studies. **Qualif.:** Applicant must be a sophomore student or above. **Criteria:** Recipients are selected by the volunteer alumni scholarship committee.

Funds Avail.: No specific amount. **To Apply:** Applicants may apply using the Supplement for Scholarship Application. **Deadline:** February 15. **Contact:** Scholarship Coordinator, 907-474-5372.

7077 ■ Jay Hammond Memorial Scholarships
(Undergraduate/Scholarship)

Purpose: To support students with their educational pursuit. **Focus:** General studies. **Qualif.:** Applicant must exhibit leadership and desire to make a difference in Alaska. **Criteria:** Scholarship recipients are selected based on the volunteer alumni scholarship committee's review of the application materials.

Funds Avail.: No specific amount. **To Apply:** Applicants may apply using the Supplement for Scholarship Application. **Deadline:** February 15.

Remarks: The scholarship is named after Jay Hammond, former governor. **Contact:** Scholarship Coordinator, 907-474-5372.

7078 ■ Audrey Loftus Memorial Scholarships
(Undergraduate/Scholarship)

Purpose: To support students with their educational pursuit. **Focus:** General studies. **Qualif.:** Applicants must be freshmen or transfer students, demonstrated experience in and future commitment to extracurricular/ community activities; and have a GPA of 3.0 and above. **Criteria:** Selection is based on leadership skills and potentiality.

Funds Avail.: No specific amount. **To Apply:** Applicants may apply using the Supplement for Scholarship Application. **Deadline:** February 15.

Remarks: Established in memory of Adrey Loftus, founding director of the UAFAA. **Contact:** Scholarship Coordinator, 907-474-5372.

7079 ■ UAF Alumni Association Scholarships
(Undergraduate/Scholarship)

Purpose: To support the education of a dependent of an alumni. **Focus:** General studies. **Qualif.:** Applicants must be undergraduate sophomores, juniors and seniors; dependents of active alumni association members; and have a GPA of 2.5-3.5 range. **Criteria:** Recipients are selected by the volunteer alumni scholarship committee.

Funds Avail.: No specific amount. **To Apply:** Applicants may apply using the Supplement for Scholarship Application. **Deadline:** February 15.

Remarks: Recipients are expected to be involved in the alumni development after graduation. Previous awardees may re-apply. **Contact:** Scholarship Coordinator, 907-474-5372.

7080 ■ University Aviation Association

3410 Skyway Dr.
Auburn, AL 36830-6444
Ph: (334)844-2434

Awards are arranged alphabetically below their administering organizations

URL: http://www.uaa.aero

7081 ■ Joseph Frasca Excellence in Aviation Scholarships *(Undergraduate/Scholarship)*

Purpose: To encourage a high level of achievement in aviation studies through education assistance. **Focus:** Aviation. **Qualif.:** Applicants must have a minimum of 3.0 GPA; must have Federal Aviation Administration certification in either aviation maintenance or flight; a member of at least one Aviation organization; and juniors or seniors currently enrolled in a UAA member institution. **Criteria:** Preference is given to applicants with demonstrated interest or experience in aviation simulation; aircraft restoration; aerobatics; with work experience in aviation; with work experience while in school; and exhibits financial need.

Funds Avail.: 1,500. **Number Awarded:** 2. **To Apply:** Applicants must submit five copies of completed application form; a brief essay; transcript; FAA certificates; one letter of reference; documents about financial status and other supporting documents. **Deadline:** April 4.

7082 ■ Eugene S. Kropf Scholarships *(Undergraduate/Scholarship)*

Purpose: To encourage careers in aviation and other related fields through educational assistance. **Focus:** Aviation. **Qualif.:** Applicants must be U.S. citizens; enrolled in or planning to pursue two- or four-year degrees in the field of aviation; must be officially enrolled in a UAA member institution; and have a 3.0 GPA. **Criteria:** Awards are given based on academic merit and character.

Funds Avail.: $500. **To Apply:** Applicants must submit application form; proof of enrollment; transcript; an essay (250 words typewritten, double-spaced) on "How Can I Improve Aviation Education". **Deadline:** May 31. **Contact:** Kevin R. Kuhlmann, Professor of Aviation and Aerospace Science, Metropolitan State College of Denver, Campus Box 30, PO Box 173362, Denver, CO 802173362.

7083 ■ Paul A. Whelan Aviation Scholarships *(Undergraduate/Scholarship)*

Purpose: To promote educational pursuits in the field of aviation or space-related fields through financial assistance. **Focus:** Aviation. **Qualif.:** Applicants must be U.S. citizens; sophomore, junior, senior or graduate students; enrolled in a UAA member institution; and must have 2.5 overall GPA and 3.0 in Aviation. **Criteria:** Priority is given to applicants who have an FAA certification as a pilot or mechanic; formerly or currently in military service via active duty, ROTC, the Air National Guard or Reserves while in school; and member of an aviation-related association or professional group such as the UAA.

Funds Avail.: $2,000. **Number Awarded:** 1. **To Apply:** Applicants must submit original copies and five copies of application form; official transcript; and recommendation letter from the institution. **Deadline:** May 15.

Remarks: Established in memory of Paul A. Whelan, an aviation educator. **Contact:** Dr. David A. NewMyer, Chair, University Aviation Association Scholarship Committee, Southern Illinois University Carbondale, 1365 Douglas Drive, ASA Carbondale, IL 62901-6623.

7084 ■ University of California, Berkeley

301B Campbell Hall No. 2922
Berkeley, CA 94720-2922
Ph: (510)643-6929
E-mail: scholarships@learning.berkeley.edu
URL: http://www.berkeley.edu

7085 ■ Beinecke Brothers Memorial Scholarships *(Undergraduate/Scholarship)*

Purpose: To encourage a junior student to continue studies in the arts, humanities, or social sciences. **Focus:** Arts, Humanities, Social sciences. **Qualif.:** Applciant must be a junior student; must be a U.S citizen or U.S national from American Samoa or the Commonwealth of Northern Mariana Islands; must have a superior intellectual ability (typically a minimum 3.5 GPA); must have a financial need. **Criteria:** Applicants will be evaluated based on their academic standing and by their plans to pursue their career in college teaching and/or research. Preference is given to candidates for whom the scholarship would enable her/him to attend graduate school.

Funds Avail.: $34,000. **To Apply:** Applicant must complete a application form (available online); must have a current resume; must provide a 1000-word personal statement describing background, interests, career goals, and plan for graduate study; must have a official copies of all college transcripts; must have three letters of recommendation from faculty members. **Deadline:** February 15.

7086 ■ Jack Kent Coke Graduate Scholarships *(Graduate/Scholarship)*

Purpose: To provide financial support for qualified students intending to continue their education in graduate school. **Focus:** General studies. **Qualif.:** Applicant must be a senior or recent graduate from an accredited college or university in the U.S; must have a cumulated GPA of 3.5 or better; must have a plan to attend graduate school. **Criteria:** Applicants will be evaluated based on their ability and achievements, unmet financial need, a will to succeed, leadership and public service, critical thinking ability, and an appreciation for or participation in the arts and humanities.

Funds Avail.: $50,000. **To Apply:** Applicant must complete the application form online; must have the parent financial information forms, signed applicant and both his or her parents, with two copies of all requested attachments; must provide a two recommendation letter; must have the official copies of transcripts from all colleges attended; must have the resume/curriculum vita; must have a portfolio (for applicants in the Arts). **Deadline:** February 14.

7087 ■ John Gardner Fellowships *(Undergraduate/Fellowship)*

Purpose: To encourage the graduating seniors to pursue the public service career of their choice. **Focus:** Public service. **Qualif.:** Applicant must be a senior graduating from the University of California, Berkeley; must be a United States citizen. **Criteria:** Applicants are evaluated based on the following criteria: (1) Demonstrated commitment to public service; (2) Record of academic accomplishment; (3) Maturity, personal integrity, and sense of responsibility; (4) Creativity, energy, and initiative; (5) Leadership potential: the ability to inspire others to action.

Funds Avail.: $27,500. **Number Awarded:** 3. **To Apply:** Applicant must submit one copy of the complete application form (available online); must have a formal resume; must have an official academic transcript; must have three letters of recommendation, at least one of which must be from a faculty member who is familiar with the applicant's university level work. Application materials must be sent to: Institute of Governmental Program, 111 Moses Hall, No. 2370, Berkeley, CA 94720-2370. **Deadline:** February 27.

7088 ■ Donald A. Strauss Scholarships *(Undergraduate/Scholarship)*

Purpose: To encourage junior students to pursue a public service career of their choice. **Focus:** Public service. **Qualif.:** Applicant must be a full-time junior; must be in the upper third class (typically a minimum 3.3 GPA); must have plan to devote significant part of life to public service. **Criteria:** Applicants will be evaluated based on their public service project proposal, outstanding leadership potential, effective communication skills and who "wish to make a difference" in local, regional, or national communities.

Funds Avail.: $10,000. **To Apply:** Applicant must complete the application form (available online); must have one-page resume that includes work history and community service experience; must have one-page autobiographical statement; must have four-page proposal for a community service project; must have completed the acceptance form; must have two or three letters of recommendation from individuals who are well-acquainted worth the student's academic and/or service work; must have an official copies of all college transcripts. **Deadline:** February 15.

7089 ■ Udall Scholarships *(Undergraduate/Scholarship)*

Purpose: To provide financial support for outstanding sophomore and junior students. **Focus:** Environmental science, Health care services. **Qualif.:** Applicant must be a student who studies the environmental and related fields; must be a Native American or Alaska Native in fields related to health care or tribal public policy; Applicant must be a full-time sophomore or junior students; must be a U.S. citizen or resident alien; must have a minimum of 3.0 GPA. **Criteria:** Applicants will be selected based on how they demonstrate the area of study and public or community service activities, commitment to and potential for making significant contributions to their fields.

Funds Avail.: $5,000 for educational expenses. UC Berkeley selection committee will select the university's nominee based on the application materials and criteria. **To Apply:** Applicant must complete the application form; must have a 800-word essay discussing a significant public speech, legislative act, or public policy statement by Congressman Udall and its relationship to the applicant's interest or coursework; must have a three letters of recommendation from: (1) a faculty member who can discuss the applicant's potential; (2) a faculty member in the applicant's of study; (3) another individual who can attest to the applicant's capabilities; must have the official college transcripts. **Deadline:** February 20.

7090 ■ University Film and Video Association

PO Box 1777
Edwardsville, IL 62026
Free: (866)647-8382
E-mail: ufvahome@aol.com
URL: http://www.ufva.org

7091 ■ UFVA Carole Fielding Student Grants *(Graduate, Undergraduate/Grant)*

Purpose: To support a student research project. **Focus:** Video; Media arts. **Qualif.:** Applicants must be an undergraduate or graduate student (a faculty member who is also a member of the association must sponsor the applicant). **Criteria:** Applicants are selected based on eligibility and merit.

Funds Avail.: No specific amount. **To Apply:** Applicants must submit six stapled copies of the application form as cover sheet (available at the website); a one-page description of the project; a one-page resume; a statement by the sponsoring UFVA member; and a one-page budget statement to: Professor Robert Johnson Jr., UFVA Carole Fielding Students Grants Chairman, Framingham State College, 100 State St., Framingham, MA 01701-9101. **Deadline:** December 15. **Contact:** Professor Robert Johnson, Jr.

7092 ■ University of Hawaii at Manoa

2500 Campus Rd., Hawaii Hall 202
Honolulu, HI 96822
Ph: (808)956-8111
URL: http://www.uhm.hawaii.edu

7093 ■ National Security Education Program Fellowships *(Undergraduate/Fellowship)*

Purpose: To provide support for outstanding U.S. graduate students intending to pursue a career in language study. **Focus:** Foreign languages. **Qualif.:** Applicant must be a U.S graduate student who wants to pursue their area of specialization in language study; must be a U.S. citizen. **Criteria:** Selection of applicants will be based on their application requirements.

Funds Avail.: $2,000. **To Apply:** For applications and information, applicants are advice to contact Dr. Chizuko Allen, Undergraduate and Fellowships Advisor, School of Pacific & Asian Studies, University of Hawaii, Honolulu, HI 96822, 808.956.2210. **Deadline:** Early November.

7094 ■ Starr Foundation Graduate Fellowship in Asian Studies *(Graduate/Grant)*

Purpose: To support continuing graduate students for such activities as field study, summer language study, or research/conference travel. **Focus:** Foreign languages, General studies. **Qualif.:** Applicant must be a graduate student who does not hold FLAS awards. **Criteria:** Selection will be based on the application requirements.

Funds Avail.: $2,000. **To Apply:** For further information and application materials, applicants are advised to contact the SPAS Office of student Academic Services, 315 Moore Hall. **Deadline:** November 15.

7095 ■ University of Hawaii at Manoa East-West Center Graduate Fellowships *(Graduate, Postdoctorate/Fellowship)*

Purpose: To provide support for qualified individuals intending to participate in the educational and research programs at the EWC. **Focus:** General studies. **Qualif.:** Applicant must be a citizen and legal resident of an Asian or Pacific country, or the United States; must be interested in participating in the educational and research programs at EWC while pursuing a master's or doctoral degree at the University of Hawaii. **Criteria:** Preference is given to those in a master's degree program.

Funds Avail.: No specific amount. **To Apply:** Application must be made to the Center's in-country program representative. For further information, applicants may write to the EastWest Center, Office of Award Service, Rm. 2066, 1601 East-West Rd., Honolulu, HI 96848. **Deadline:** November 1.

7096 ■ University of Hawaii at Manoa Graduate Assistantship Awards *(Graduate/Award/Prize)*

Purpose: To assist graduate students with their education. **Focus:** Teaching. **Qualif.:** Applicant must have a strong

Awards are arranged alphabetically below their administering organizations

background in Asian Studies; must have a high scholastic record; must be admitted as a graduate student; must have a high level of English proficiency; must carry at least 6 units of credit each semester and maintain a minimum of 3.0 GPA. **Criteria:** Selection will be based on the academic standing of the applicant.

Funds Avail.: No specific amount. **To Apply:** Applicant must submit a letter of application, resume, and names, addresses and telephone numbers of three references to: Chair of Asian Studies, Moore Hall 412, University of Hawaii at Manoa, 1890 East-West Rd., Honolulu, HI 96822. **Deadline:** March 3.

7097 ■ University of Hawaii at Manoa Graduate Student Organization Travel Funds *(Graduate/ Grant)*

Purpose: To provide assistance to UH graduate students making scholarly or artistic presentations at conferences and professional meetings on the mainland and elsewhere. **Focus:** General studies. **Qualif.:** Applicant must be classified graduate student. **Criteria:** Selection of applicant will be based on their application requirements.

Funds Avail.: No specific amount. **Number Awarded:** 3. **To Apply:** For application forms and more detailed information on the amount of stipends contact the GSO at 808956-8776/8018/4832, Hemenway Hall 212. **Deadline:** January 1, June 1, September 1.

7098 ■ University of Hawaii at Manoa Japan Travel Bureau Scholarships *(Graduate, Undergraduate/Scholarship)*

Purpose: To promote understanding between peoples and nations of the world through higher education. **Focus:** International affairs and relations, Crosscultural studies. **Qualif.:** Candidate must be a full-time classified UHM graduate student or upper class undergraduate interested in international relations or cross-cultural studies and have demonstrated high scholastic achievement. **Criteria:** Candidates will be selected based on their academic standing.

Funds Avail.: $1,000. **To Apply:** Information and application materials may be obtained from the SPAS Office of Student Academic Services, 315 Moore Hall. **Deadline:** March 1.

7099 ■ University of Louisville Alumni Association

Malcolm B. Chancey Center
Alumni Office
Louisville, KY 40292
Ph: (502)852-6186
Fax: (502)852-6920
Free: 800-813-8635
E-mail: jimmy.ford@louisville.edu
URL: http://www.alumni.louisville.edu

7100 ■ Beth K. Fields Scholarships *(Undergraduate/Scholarship)*

Purpose: To financially support students in their educational pursuit. **Focus:** General studies. **Qualif.:** Applicant must be 25 years old and below; have a minimum of 12 semester hours college credit; have a 3.0 GPA; be a full-time student; and must be supporting at least one dependent. **Criteria:** Applications will be reviewed by the Scholarship Committee of the Board of Directors.

Funds Avail.: No specific amount. **To Apply:** Applicants must submit a completed application form together with a copy of official transcripts; a 300-word essay; and two letters of recommendations. **Deadline:** March 15. **Contact:** Amanda Thompson, 502-852-4956 or ajthom01@gwise.louisville.edu.

7101 ■ Raymond A. Kent-Navy V-12/ROTC *(Undergraduate/Scholarship)*

Purpose: To support direct descendants of an individuals who served in the Navy V-12 program or the Naval ROTC program at UofL. **Focus:** General studies. **Qualif.:** Applicant must be a direct descendant an individual who served the Navy V-12 program or the Naval ROTC program. **Criteria:** Applications will be reviewed by the Scholarship Committee of the Board of Directors.

Funds Avail.: No specific amount. **To Apply:** Applicants must submit a completed application form together with a copy of official transcripts; a 300-word essay; and two letters of recommendations. **Deadline:** March 15. **Contact:** Amanda Thompson, 502-852-4956 or ajthom01@gwise.louisville.edu.

7102 ■ Kentucky Alumni Club Scholarships - Capital Region Alumni Club *(Undergraduate/ Scholarship)*

Purpose: To support students in their educational pursuits. **Focus:** General studies. **Qualif.:** Applicant must reside in the state of Kentucky specifically in Anderson, Franklin, Henry, Owen, Mercer, Shelby, and Spencer counties; and must maintain a GPA of 3.0. **Criteria:** Selection is based on the submitted applications.

Funds Avail.: $500 for the first year. **Number Awarded:** 1. **To Apply:** Applicant must complete the application with an essay; official copies of transcripts; test scores; and two letters of recommendation (one from a teacher) submitted to the Scholarship Committee. **Deadline:** March 15. **Contact:** 502-852-6186.

7103 ■ Kentucky Alumni Club Scholarships - Central Kentucky Alumni Club *(Undergraduate/ Scholarship)*

Purpose: To support students in their educational pursuits. **Focus:** General studies. **Qualif.:** Applicant must reside in the state of Kentucky specifically in Fayette, Jessamine, Woodford, Clark, Bourbon, Scott, Harrison and Madison counties. **Criteria:** Selection is based on the submitted applications.

Funds Avail.: Full tuition. **To Apply:** Applicant must complete the application with an essay; official copies of transcripts; test scores; and two letters of recommendation (one from a teacher) submitted to Paul W. Graf, 3367 Ridgecane Rd. Lexington, KY 40513. **Deadline:** April 15.

7104 ■ Kentucky Alumni Club Scholarships - Lake Cumberland Alumni Club *(Undergraduate/ Scholarship)*

Purpose: To support students in their educational pursuits. **Focus:** General studies. **Qualif.:** Applicant must reside in the state of Kentucky specifically in Adair, Casey, Clinton, Cumberland, Laurel, McCreary, Pulaski, Rockcastle, Russell and Wayne counties; must be admitted to University of Louisville; have a GPA of 3.5 or above and an ACT/SAT equivalent of 24 or higher. **Criteria:** Selection is based on the submitted applications.

Funds Avail.: $500. **Number Awarded:** 1. **To Apply:** Ap-

plicant must complete the application with an essay; official copies of transcripts; test scores; and two letters of recommendation (one from a teacher) submitted to Dr. Sonya Jones, PO Box 289 Somerset, KY 42502. **Deadline:** April 1. **Contact:** Susan Hughes, 606-348-4086 or shugdes@wayne.k12.ky.us.

7105 ■ Kentucky Alumni Club Scholarships - Northern Kentucky Alumni Club *(Undergraduate/Scholarship)*

Purpose: To support students in their educational pursuits. **Focus:** General studies. **Qualif.:** Applicant must reside in the state of Kentucky specifically in Boone, Kenton, Campbelle, Grant, Carroll, Pendleton, and Gallatin counties or in Hamilton County in Ohio; must maintain a GPA of 3.0; and an ACT/SAT equivalent of 20 or above. **Criteria:** Selection is based on the submitted applications.

Funds Avail.: $500. **Number Awarded:** 1. **To Apply:** Applicant must complete the application with an essay; official copies of transcripts; test scores; and two letters of recommendation (one from a teacher) submitted to Kathleen Annear Carnes, 332 Forest Hill Dr., Lexington, KY 40509-1970.

7106 ■ Outstanding Undergraduate Scholarships (SOAR) *(Undergraduate/Scholarship)*

Purpose: To support students in their educational pursuits. **Focus:** General studies. **Qualif.:** Applicant must be registered full-time for the semester. **Criteria:** Selection is based on the submitted applications.

Funds Avail.: $1,000. **Number Awarded:** 1. **To Apply:** Applicants must submit a completed application form together with a copy of official transcripts; a 300-word essay; and two letters of recommendations. **Deadline:** March 15. **Contact:** Amanda Thompson, 502-852-4956 or ajthom01@gwise.louisville.edu.

7107 ■ Rodney Williams Legacy Scholarships *(Undergraduate/Grant)*

Purpose: To support the children and grandchildren of UofL alumni. **Focus:** General studies. **Qualif.:** Applicant must be related to a UofL graduate; incoming freshman or transfer student; have a 3.0 GPA; and must be a full-time student for the semester. **Criteria:** Selection is based on the submitted applications.

Funds Avail.: No specific amount. **To Apply:** Applicants must submit a completed application form together with a copy of official transcripts; a 300-word essay; and two letters of recommendations. **Deadline:** March 15. **Contact:** Amanda Thompson, 502-852-4956 or ajthom01@gwise.louisville.edu.

7108 ■ University of Memphis

Cecil C. Humphreys School of Law
3715 Central Ave.
Memphis, TN 38152
Ph: (901)678-2421
Fax: (901)678-5210
E-mail: lawadmissions@memphis.edu
URL: http://www.law.memphis.edu

7109 ■ Tillie B. Alperin Scholarships *(Undergraduate/Scholarship)*

Purpose: To support the education of female law students at the University of Memphis. **Focus:** Law. **Qualif.:** Applicant must be a female law student who has successfully completed her first year with a B average; has demonstrated a commitment to the legal profession; and demonstrates financial need. **Criteria:** Selection is based academic performance, leadership, character, personal achievements, and financial need. Preference will be given to applicants who have overcome significant obstacles in pursuit of their education.

Funds Avail.: No specific amount. **To Apply:** Applicants must complete the online scholarship application form along with a personal statement; resume; scholarship statement; and recommendation letters. Applicants must also complete the FAFSA Form. **Deadline:** March 15.

Remarks: Named in honor of the late Tillie Blen Alperin, a 1935 graduate of the old University of Memphis Law School and one of the first women to practice law in Tennessee. **Contact:** Dr. Sue Ann McClellan, Assistant Dean of Admissions, at 901-678-5403, or smcclell@memphis.edu; Ms. DebraAnn Brown, Assistant Director for Student Financial Aid, at 901-678-3737, or dbrown@memphis.edu.

7110 ■ Claude T. Coffman Memorial Scholarships *(Undergraduate/Scholarship)*

Purpose: To support the education of law students at the University of Memphis. **Focus:** Law. **Qualif.:** Applicant must be admitted at the University of Memphis Cecil C. Humphreys School of Law. **Criteria:** Selection is based on academic merit and financial need.

Funds Avail.: No specific amount. **To Apply:** Applicants must complete the online scholarship application form along with a personal statement; resume; scholarship statement; and recommendation letters. Applicants must also complete the FAFSA Form. **Deadline:** March 15.

Remarks: The scholarship is named in honor of the late professor and former interim dean of the Cecil C. Humphreys School of Law. **Contact:** Dr. Sue Ann McClellan, Assistant Dean of Admissions, at 901-678-5403, or smcclell@memphis.edu; Ms. DebraAnn Brown, Assistant Director for Student Financial Aid, at 901-678-3737, or dbrown@memphis.edu.

7111 ■ Cleveland Drennon, Jr. Memorial Scholarships *(Undergraduate/Scholarship)*

Purpose: To support the education of law students at the University of Memphis. **Focus:** Law. **Qualif.:** Applicant must be admitted as full-time student at the University of Memphis Cecil C. Humphreys School of Law. **Criteria:** Selection is based on academic merit and financial need. Special consideration will be given to student-athlete graduates of The University of Memphis or Vanderbilt University.

Funds Avail.: No specific amount. **To Apply:** Applicants must complete the online scholarship application form along with a personal statement; resume; scholarship statement; and recommendation letters. Applicants must also complete the FAFSA Form. **Deadline:** March 15.

Remarks: Funded by Humphrey E. Folk, Jr. and the Drennon family and friends. **Contact:** Dr. Sue Ann McClellan, Assistant Dean of Admissions, at 901-678-5403, or smcclell@memphis.edu; Ms. DebraAnn Brown, Assistant Director for Student Financial Aid, at 901-678-3737, or dbrown@memphis.edu.

7112 ■ East Tennessee Foundation Scholarships *(Undergraduate/Scholarship)*

Purpose: To support the education of law students at the University of Memphis. **Focus:** Law. **Qualif.:** Applicant must

Awards are arranged alphabetically below their administering organizations

be a second- or third-year student who demonstrates community involvement or commitment to public service. **Criteria:** Selection is based academic performance, leadership, character, personal achievements, and financial need.

Funds Avail.: No specific amount. **Number Awarded:** 1. **To Apply:** Applicants must complete the online scholarship application form along with a personal statement; resume; scholarship statement; and recommendation letters. Applicants must also complete the FAFSA Form. **Deadline:** March 15.

Remarks: Scholarship is made possible by a grant from the Tennessee Judicial Conference Foundation. The scholarship is awarded every four years, rotating among the other law schools in the state. **Contact:** Dr. Sue Ann McClellan, Assistant Dean of Admissions, at 901-678-5403, or smcclell@memphis.edu; Ms. DebraAnn Brown, Assistant Director for Student Financial Aid, at 901-678-3737, or dbrown@memphis.edu.

7113 ■ Evans and Petree Law Firm Scholarships *(Undergraduate/Scholarship)*

Purpose: To support the education of law students at the University of Memphis. **Focus:** Law. **Qualif.:** Applicant must be an African American law student. **Criteria:** Selection is based academic performance, leadership, character, personal achievements, and financial need. Preference will be given to a returning African American student with financial need.

Funds Avail.: No specific amount. **Number Awarded:** 1. **To Apply:** Applicants must complete the online scholarship application form along with the personal statement; resume; scholarship statement; and recommendation letters. Applicants must also complete the FAFSA Form. **Deadline:** March 15.

Remarks: Established in Honor of Percy Harvey, Esq. by the Evans and Petree Law Firm. **Contact:** Dr. Sue Ann McClellan, Assistant Dean of Admissions, at 901-678-5403, or smcclell@memphis.edu; Ms. DebraAnn Brown, Assistant Director for Student Financial Aid, at 901-678-3737, or dbrown@memphis.edu.

7114 ■ Federal Court Bench and Bar Scholarships *(Undergraduate/Scholarship)*

Purpose: To broaden the Middle District of Tennessee bar through expanded opportunities for law students from all backgrounds. **Focus:** Law. **Qualif.:** Applicants must be economically disadvantaged law students from the Middle District of Tennessee; in good academic standing at the law school or the most recent school attended; have demonstrated financial need; and must have graduated from a high school in, or resided for the previous three years as a non-full time student in one of the following Tennessee Counties: Cannon, Cheatham, Clay, Cumberland, Davidson, DeKalb, Dickson, Fentress, Giles, Hickman, Houston, Humphreys, Jackson, Lawrence, Lewis, Macon, Marshall, Maury, Montgomery, Overton, Pickett, Putnam, Robertson, Rutherford, Smith, Stewart, Sumner, Trousdale, Wayne, White, Williamson, or Wilson. **Criteria:** Recipients will be selected based on financial need.

Funds Avail.: No specific amount. **To Apply:** Applicants must complete the online scholarship application form along with a personal statement; resume; scholarship statement; and recommendation letters. Applicants must also complete the FAFSA Form. **Deadline:** March 15. **Contact:** Dr. Sue Ann McClellan, Assistant Dean of Admissions, at 901-678-5403, or smcclell@memphis.edu; Ms. DebraAnn Brown, Assistant Director for Student Financial Aid, at 901-678-3737, or dbrown@memphis.edu.

7115 ■ Wilford Hayes Gowen Scholarships *(Undergraduate/Scholarship)*

Purpose: To support the education of law students at the University of Memphis. **Focus:** Law. **Qualif.:** Applicant must be a second- or third-year law student. **Criteria:** Selection is based academic performance, financial need, and personal determination.

Funds Avail.: No specific amount. **To Apply:** Applicants must complete the online scholarship application form along with a personal statement; resume; scholarship statement; and recommendation letters. Applicants must also complete the FAFSA Form. **Deadline:** March 15.

Remarks: Established in memory of Wilford Hayes Gowen, through the Community Foundation of Western North Carolina. **Contact:** Dr. Sue Ann McClellan, Assistant Dean of Admissions, at 901-678-5403, or smcclell@memphis.edu; Ms. DebraAnn Brown, Assistant Director for Student Financial Aid, at 901-678-3737, or dbrown@memphis.edu.

7116 ■ Herbert Herff Presidential Law Scholarships *(Undergraduate/Scholarship)*

Purpose: To support the education of law students at the University of Memphis. **Focus:** Law. **Qualif.:** Applicants must be admitted at the University of Memphis Cecil C. Humphreys School of Law; have demonstrated high academic or professional achievement; and show potential for an outstanding law career. **Criteria:** Selection is based on academic merit and financial need.

Funds Avail.: No specific amount. **To Apply:** Applicants must complete the online scholarship application form along with a personal statement; resume; scholarship statement; and recommendation letters. Applicants must also complete the FAFSA Form. **Deadline:** March 15.

Remarks: Funded by the Herbert Herff Trust. **Contact:** Dr. Sue Ann McClellan, Assistant Dean of Admissions, at 901-678-5403, or smcclell@memphis.edu; Ms. DebraAnn Brown, Assistant Director for Student Financial Aid, at 901-678-3737, or dbrown@memphis.edu.

7117 ■ Robert and Elaine Hoffman Memorial Scholarships *(Undergraduate/Scholarship)*

Purpose: To support the education of law students at the University of Memphis. **Focus:** Law. **Qualif.:** Applicants must be admitted at the University of Memphis Cecil C. Humphreys School of Law. **Criteria:** Selection is based on academic merit and financial need.

Funds Avail.: No specific amount. **To Apply:** Applicants must complete the online scholarship application form along with a personal statement; resume; scholarship statement; and recommendation letters. Applicants must also complete the FAFSA Form. **Deadline:** March 15.

Remarks: The scholarship is named in honor of the late Chancellor Robert Hoffman and his sister Elaine. **Contact:** Dr. Sue Ann McClellan, Assistant Dean of Admissions, at 901-678-5403, or smcclell@memphis.edu; Ms. DebraAnn Brown, Assistant Director for Student Financial Aid, at 901-678-3737, or dbrown@memphis.edu.

7118 ■ Kathryn Hookanson Law Fellowships *(Undergraduate/Scholarship)*

Purpose: To support the education of law students at the University of Memphis. **Focus:** Law. **Qualif.:** Applicant must be a student at the University of Memphis. **Criteria:** Preference may be given to female students and those in financial need.

Funds Avail.: No specific amount. **To Apply:** Applicants must complete the online scholarship application form along with a personal statement; resume; scholarship statement; and recommendation letters. Applicants must also complete the FAFSA Form. **Deadline:** March 15.

Remarks: Established by Ms. Hookanson, her family, friends and colleagues. **Contact:** Dr. Sue Ann McClellan, Assistant Dean of Admissions, at 901-678-5403, or smcclell@memphis.edu; Ms. DebraAnn Brown, Assistant Director for Student Financial Aid, at 901-678-3737, or dbrown@memphis.edu.

7119 ■ John C. "Jack" Hough Memorial Law Scholarships *(Undergraduate/Scholarship)*

Purpose: To support the education of law students at the University of Memphis. **Focus:** Law. **Qualif.:** Applicant must be a second- or third-year law student who demonstrates financial need and is working as a volunteer or in a law school externship in the office of the Shelby County Public Defender. **Criteria:** Selection is based academic performance, leadership, character, personal achievements, and financial need. Preference will be given to applicants who express an interest in a career in government service as a public defender or prosecutor, or in the field of criminal law.

Funds Avail.: No specific amount. **To Apply:** Applicants must complete the online scholarship application form along with a personal statement; resume; scholarship statement; and recommendation letters. Applicants must also complete the FAFSA Form. **Deadline:** March 15.

Remarks: Scholarship is named in honor of the late John C. "Jack" Hough, a former member of the Shelby County Public Defender's Office. **Contact:** Dr. Sue Ann McClellan, Assistant Dean of Admissions, at 901-678-5403, or smcclell@memphis.edu; Ms. DebraAnn Brown, Assistant Director for Student Financial Aid, at 901-678-3737, or dbrown@memphis.edu.

7120 ■ Cecil C. Humphreys Law Fellowships *(Undergraduate/Scholarship)*

Purpose: To support the education of law students at the University of Memphis. **Focus:** Law. **Qualif.:** Applicant must be a second- or third-year student. **Criteria:** Selection is based on demonstrated outstanding academic performance, leadership, good citizenship, and scholarly achievements.

Funds Avail.: Free waiver for half the cost of in-state tuition. **To Apply:** Applicants must complete the online scholarship application form along with a personal statement; resume; scholarship statement; and recommendation letters. Applicants must also complete the FAFSA Form. **Deadline:** March 15.

Remarks: Fellowship is funded through a grant from the Plough Foundation. Humphreys Fellows are required to work 15 hours per week as a research assistant to faculty members. **Contact:** Dr. Sue Ann McClellan, Assistant Dean of Admissions, at 901-678-5403, or smcclell@memphis.edu; Ms. DebraAnn Brown, Assistant Director for Student Financial Aid, at 901-678-3737, or dbrown@memphis.edu.

7121 ■ Judge William B. Leffler Scholarships *(Undergraduate/Scholarship)*

Purpose: To support the education of law students at the University of Memphis. **Focus:** Law. **Qualif.:** Applicants must be admitted at the University of Memphis Cecil C. Humphreys School of Law. **Criteria:** Selection is based on academic merit and financial need.

Funds Avail.: No specific amount. **To Apply:** Applicants must complete the online scholarship application form along with the personal statement; resume; scholarship statement; and recommendation letters. Applicants must also complete the FAFSA Form. **Deadline:** March 15.

Remarks: The award is funded through the Leffler family, the donations of friends, and proceeds from the annual bankruptcy law seminar in Judge Leffler's memory. **Contact:** Dr. Sue Ann McClellan, Assistant Dean of Admissions, at 901-678-5403, or smcclell@memphis.edu; Ms. DebraAnn Brown, Assistant Director for Student Financial Aid, at 901-678-3737, or dbrown@memphis.edu.

7122 ■ H.H. McKnight Memorial Scholarships *(Undergraduate/Scholarship)*

Purpose: To support the education of law students at the University of Memphis. **Focus:** Law. **Qualif.:** Applicants must be veterans of the United States Armed Forces interested in pursuing a career in criminal law. **Criteria:** Selection is based on academic merit and financial need.

Funds Avail.: No specific amount. **Number Awarded:** 2. **To Apply:** Applicants must complete the online scholarship application form along with a personal statement; resume; scholarship statement; and recommendation letters. Applicants must also complete the FAFSA Form. **Deadline:** March 15. **Contact:** Dr. Sue Ann McClellan, Assistant Dean of Admissions, at 901-678-5403, or smcclell@memphis.edu; Ms. DebraAnn Brown, Assistant Director for Student Financial Aid, at 901-678-3737, or dbrown@memphis.edu.

7123 ■ Sam A. Myar, Jr. Law Scholarships *(Undergraduate/Scholarship)*

Purpose: To support the education of law students at the University of Memphis. **Focus:** Law. **Qualif.:** Applicant must be the Editor-in-Chief and the Managing Editor of the University of Memphis Law Review. **Criteria:** Selection is based academic performance, leadership, character, personal achievements, and financial need.

Funds Avail.: No specific amount. **To Apply:** Applicants must complete the online scholarship application form along with a personal statement; resume; scholarship statement; and recommendation letters. Applicants must also complete the FAFSA Form. **Deadline:** March 15.

Remarks: Established in 1960. **Contact:** Dr. Sue Ann McClellan, Assistant Dean of Admissions, at 901-678-5403, or smcclell@memphis.edu; Ms. DebraAnn Brown, Assistant Director for Student Financial Aid, at 901-678-3737, or dbrown@memphis.edu.

7124 ■ Donald and Susie Polden Dean's Scholarships *(Undergraduate/Scholarship)*

Purpose: To support the education of law students at the University of Memphis. **Focus:** Law. **Qualif.:** Applicants must be law students; must be committed to community or public service; and must express a desire to serve the community during or following law school. **Criteria:** Recipients will be selected based on academic merit and financial need.

Funds Avail.: No specific amount. **To Apply:** Applicants must complete the online scholarship application form along with a personal statement; resume; scholarship statement; and recommendation letters. Applicants must also complete the FAFSA Form. **Deadline:** March 15. **Contact:** Dr. Sue Ann McClellan, Assistant Dean of Admissions, at 901-678-5403, or smcclell@memphis.edu; Ms. DebraAnn Brown, Assistant Director for Student Financial Aid, at 901-678-3737, or dbrown@memphis.edu.

7125 ■ Ratner and Sugarmon Scholarships *(Undergraduate/Scholarship)*

Purpose: To support the education of law students at the University of Memphis. **Focus:** Law. **Qualif.:** Applicants must be second or third year law students. **Criteria:** Award is given to the student who best exemplifies a commitment to the needs of the underrepresented in society.

Funds Avail.: No specific amount. **To Apply:** Applicants must complete the online scholarship application form along with a personal statement; resume; scholarship statement; and recommendation letters. Applicants must also complete the FAFSA Form. **Deadline:** March 15. **Contact:** Dr. Sue Ann McClellan, Assistant Dean of Admissions, at 901-678-5403, or smcclell@memphis.edu; Ms. DebraAnn Brown, Assistant Director for Student Financial Aid, at 901-678-3737, or dbrown@memphis.edu.

7126 ■ Joseph Henry Shepherd Scholarships *(Undergraduate/Scholarship)*

Purpose: To support the education of law students at the University of Memphis. **Focus:** Law. **Qualif.:** Applicant must be admitted at the University of Memphis Cecil C. Humphreys School of Law. **Criteria:** Selection is based on academic merit and financial need.

Funds Avail.: No specific amount. **Number Awarded:** 3. **To Apply:** Applicants must complete the online scholarship application form along with a personal statement; resume; scholarship statement; and recommendation letters. Applicants must also complete the FAFSA Form. **Deadline:** March 15.

Remarks: Sponsored by Dorothy S. Shepherd. **Contact:** Dr. Sue Ann McClellan, Assistant Dean of Admissions, at 901-678-5403, or smcclell@memphis.edu; Ms. DebraAnn Brown, Assistant Director for Student Financial Aid, at 901-678-3737, or dbrown@memphis.edu.

7127 ■ Amy E. Spain Memorial Scholarships *(Undergraduate/Scholarship)*

Purpose: To support the education of law students at the University of Memphis. **Focus:** Law. **Qualif.:** Applicants must be law students with demonstrated academic merit. **Criteria:** Recipients will be selected based on academic merit.

Funds Avail.: No specific amount. **Number Awarded:** 2. **To Apply:** Applicants must complete the online scholarship application form along with a personal statement; resume; scholarship statement; and recommendation letters. Applicants must also complete the FAFSA Form. **Deadline:** March 15.

Remarks: Established by the family and friends of Amy Elizabeth Spain, who died at age 30 by a car accident in 1997. **Contact:** Dr. Sue Ann McClellan, Assistant Dean of Admissions, at 901-678-5403, or smcclell@memphis.edu; Ms. DebraAnn Brown, Assistant Director for Student Financial Aid, at 901-678-3737, or dbrown@memphis.edu.

7128 ■ James F. and Donna Springfield Scholarships *(Undergraduate/Scholarship)*

Purpose: To support the education of law students at the University of Memphis. **Focus:** Law. **Qualif.:** Applicant must be a graduate of Rhodes College. **Criteria:** Selection is based on academic merit.

Funds Avail.: No specific amount. **Number Awarded:** 1. **To Apply:** Applicants must complete the online scholarship application form along with the personal statement; resume; scholarship statement; and recommendation letters. Applicants must also complete the FAFSA Form. **Deadline:** March 15.

Remarks: Scholarship is made possible by an endowment fund established by Mr. and Mrs. Springfield. **Contact:** Dr. Sue Ann McClellan, Assistant Dean of Admissions, at 901-678-5403, or smcclell@memphis.edu; Ms. DebraAnn Brown, Assistant Director for Student Financial Aid, at 901-678-3737, or dbrown@memphis.edu.

7129 ■ Tennessee Bar Foundation IOLTA Law School Scholarships *(Undergraduate/Scholarship)*

Purpose: To support the education of law students at the University of Memphis. **Focus:** Law. **Qualif.:** Applicants must be Tennessee residents and rising third year students in good standing. **Criteria:** Selection is based on demonstrated concern for public interest law, financial need, and diversity representation.

Funds Avail.: No specific amount. **To Apply:** Applicants must complete the online scholarship application form along with a personal statement; resume; scholarship statement; and recommendation letters. Applicants must also complete the FAFSA Form. **Deadline:** March 15.

Remarks: Scholarship is funded by the Tennessee Bar Foundation. **Contact:** Dr. Sue Ann McClellan, Assistant Dean of Admissions, at 901-678-5403, or smcclell@memphis.edu; Ms. DebraAnn Brown, Assistant Director for Student Financial Aid, at 901-678-3737, or dbrown@memphis.edu.

7130 ■ Tennessee Board of Regents Law Scholarships *(Undergraduate/Scholarship)*

Purpose: To support the education of law students at the University of Memphis. **Focus:** Law. **Qualif.:** Applicant must be a Tennessee resident. **Criteria:** Selection is based on academic merit and financial need.

Funds Avail.: No specific amount. **To Apply:** Applicants must complete the online scholarship application form along with a personal statement; resume; scholarship statement; and recommendation letters. Applicants must also complete the FAFSA Form. In addition, attach a separate statement explaining in detail the circumstances that qualify the student to be considered for the scholarship. **Deadline:** March 15. **Contact:** Dr. Sue Ann McClellan, Assistant Dean of Admissions, at 901-678-5403, or smcclell@memphis.edu; Ms. DebraAnn Brown, Assistant Director for Student Financial Aid, at 901-678-3737, or dbrown@memphis.edu.

7131 ■ Wyatt, Tarrant and Combs, LLP Scholarships *(Undergraduate/Scholarship)*

Purpose: To support the education of law students at the University of Memphis. **Focus:** Law. **Qualif.:** Applicant must be admitted as full-time student at the University of Memphis Cecil C. Humphreys School of Law. **Criteria:** Selection is based on academic merit and financial need. Preference is given to a Tennessee or Kentucky resident.

Funds Avail.: No specific amount. **To Apply:** Applicants must complete the online scholarship application form along with a personal statement; resume; scholarship statement; and recommendation letters. Applicants must also complete the FAFSA Form. **Deadline:** March 15.

Remarks: Scholarship is made possible by Wyatt, Tarrant & Combs, LLP. The scholarship will be offered every three years. **Contact:** Dr. Sue Ann McClellan, Assistant Dean of Admissions, at 901-678-5403, or smcclell@memphis.edu; Ms. DebraAnn Brown, Assistant Director for Student Financial Aid, at 901-678-3737, or dbrown@memphis.edu.

7132 ■ University of Minnesota

240 Williamson Hall
231 Pillsbury Dr. SE
Minneapolis, MN 55455-0213
Ph: (612)625-2008
Fax: (612)626-1693
Free: 800-752-1000
URL: http://www1.umn.edu/twincities

7133 ■ Carol E. Macpherson Memorial Scholarship and Alumnae Society Scholarships *(Graduate, Undergraduate/Scholarship)*

Purpose: To provide support for qualified individuals intending to pursue an educational career. **Focus:** General studies. **Qualif.:** Applicant must be a female student who has had a five-year or longer break in their postsecondary education; must demonstrate financial need; must have a admission or pending admission to an undergraduate or graduate/professional degree or credit certificate program at any University of Minnesota campus; must meet half-time enrollment status minimum; must provide academic transcripts of all college/post-secondary enrollment; must have a good academic standing at the University of Minnesota; must submit a support letters from two references who have known the applicants and their educational goals. **Criteria:** Applicant selection is weighted by the following characteristics: (1) First generation in family to attend college; (2) First undergraduate degree; (3) Student parent status.

Funds Avail.: $1,000-$4,000. **To Apply:** Applicant must submit the complete application, including their personal statement and a copy of their Student Aid Report; must have a transcript of all college/post-secondary enrollment; must have two Applicant Appraisal Forms (to be sent directly from references or attached to application in a sealed envelope signed by the writer across the seal). **Deadline:** April 30.

7134 ■ University of Minnesota Women Student Travel Grants *(Graduate, Undergraduate/Grant)*

Purpose: To help the students in University of Minnesota to pursue their education. **Focus:** General studies. **Qualif.:** Applicant must be a University of Minnesota, Twin Cities undergraduate or graduate student in good standing with his/her college; must have a cumulative GPA of 3.00. **Criteria:** Priority will be given to students attending national conferences, their first conference and/or presenting at a conference (conference presentation is a preferred requirement of graduate student applicants).

Funds Avail.: $100-$300. **To Apply:** Application forms are available in the website. Applicant must attach conference program information and proof of registration; must provide the student-issued University transcript, and information about other sources of funding. Application form and other application materials must be sent to: Office for University Women, 185 Klaeber Court, 320 16th Ave., SE, Minneapolis, MN 55455. **Deadline:** August 1 and December 1.

7135 ■ Upper Midwest Human Rights Fellowship Program *(Professional Development/Fellowship)*

Purpose: To encourages residents of the Upper Midwest to undertake practical experiences/internships in human rights organizations. To promote social justice by providing practical training in the varied aspects of human rights work worldwide. **Focus:** Human rights. **Qualif.:** Applicants must be residents of the Upper Midwest with a particular focus on Minnesota, Montana, North Dakota, South Dakota, and Wisconsin; must have adequate proficiency in the relevant languages. **Criteria:** Primary criterion for selection is a demonstrated interest in, and commitment to, the promotion of international human rights. Subcommittee of the Human Rights Center's Advisory Board will select the grant recipients. Awards will be determined by considering an individual's qualifications and interests together with the needs of the supervising organization.

Funds Avail.: $1,000-$4,500 money will help pay transportation, lodging, and food expenses incurred during the fellowship period. **To Apply:** Applicant submit a complete application form, available online; must provide the confirmation letter from host; transcript (from last ten years only); resume; essay (2-3 pages), should detail the following: (1) Fellowship placement; (2) Proposed host organization; (3) Significance of the experience for your academic or professional training; (4) Relationship of the fellowship to your future goals; (5) How the host organization will benefit from a fellowship; (6) Description of the key aspects of a current human rights issue in the country/location of your proposed fellowship and how the sponsoring organization addresses it; (7) Description of how you will use your new human rights experiences in your community upon your return home. **Deadline:** February 25.

7136 ■ University of New Hampshire

Office of Admission
4 Garrison Ave.
Durham, NH 03824
Ph: (603)862-1360
Fax: (603)862-0077
E-mail: admission@unh.edu
URL: http://www.unh.edu

7137 ■ CEPS-Tyco Scholarships *(Undergraduate/Scholarship)*

Purpose: To provide financial assistance to students who want to continue their education at UNH. **Focus:** Engineering; Physical sciences. **Qualif.:** Applicants must be high school seniors admitted to the University's College of Engineering and Physical Sciences. **Criteria:** Selection criteria include: (1) Rigorous programs of study including a minimum of five years of mathematics and four years of science, with preference given to Advanced Placement and International Baccalaureate Courses; (2) Grades that indicate excellence; (3) Class rank in the top 10 percent (for students attending schools that provide class rank) or equivalent; (4) SAT Reasoning Test scores of 1310+ (Critical Reading and Math only) or a 30+ composite on the ACT with writing test.

Funds Avail.: $10,000. **Number Awarded:** 2. **To Apply:** Applicants must have an application for admission to a major within the College of Engineering and Physical Sciences at the University of New Hampshire; must have official high school transcripts, including the first marking period of senior year; must have the official test scores for

Awards are arranged alphabetically below their administering organizations

either the SAT Reasoning Test or ACT with writing test; must submit an additional scholarship essay through the online form; must submit a Free Application for Federal Student Aid (FAFSA) form. Application form and other supporting documents must be sent to University of New Hampshire, Office of Admission/CEPS-Tyco Scholarship, Grant House, 4 Garrison Ave., Durham, NH 03824. **Deadline:** November 15.

7138 ■ UNH Alumni Association Legacy Scholarships *(Undergraduate/Scholarship)*

Purpose: To provide financial assistance to students who want to continue their education at UNH. **Focus:** General studies. **Qualif.:** Applicants must be enrolled or accepted as full-time students in a four-year degree program at UNH, Durham campus; must possess leadership potential as demonstrated through involvement in academic, co-curricular and/or work activities; must have a relative who is an alumnus/a of the University of Hampshire who must have been a dues-paying member at the time of his or her death; and must have a cumulative GPA of 3.2. **Criteria:** The scholarship Committee will judge the applicants based on the following evaluation criteria: (1) Academic record; (2) Leadership potential; (3) Breadth of academic, co-curricular and employment activities; (4) Quality and content of the application, essay, strength of recommendation and interview, if applicable; (5) Length of membership and/or level of service to UNH or the Alumni Association by the related dues-paying member.

Funds Avail.: $3,000. **To Apply:** Applicants must complete the application form available online; and must have a letter of recommendation from a high school teacher, guidance counselor or UNH faculty member. **Deadline:** March 31.

7139 ■ UNH Parent's Association Endowment Scholarship Fund *(Undergraduate/Scholarship)*

Purpose: To provide financial assistance to students who want to continue their education at UNH. **Focus:** General studies. **Qualif.:** Applicants must demonstrate academic achievement; must be of good character; must have a minimum cumulative GPA of 2.8; must be involved in community service projects or in the university community; and must be making financial contributions to their education through employment. **Criteria:** Selection of recipients will be based on financial need.

Funds Avail.: $5,000-$9,000. **To Apply:** Applicants must submit a University Community and/or Community Service verification letter; an employment verification Letter; a background information statement (maximum of 1 page double spaced); and must have a faculty recommendation. Application forms are available online and must be sent to University of New Hampshire Parent's Association.

7140 ■ University of North Carolina School of Journalism and Mass Communication

University of North Carolina, Carol Hall CB 3365
Chapel Hill, NC 27599-3365
Ph: (919)962-1204
Fax: (919)962-0620
E-mail: jomc@unc.edu
URL: http://www.jomc.unc.edu

7141 ■ Floyd S. Alford Jr. Scholarships *(Undergraduate/Scholarship)*

Purpose: To educate journalists; to recognize students who demonstrate outstanding journalistic talent and a strong commitment to improving the community through honest and accurate work. **Focus:** Journalism. **Qualif.:** Applicants must be undergraduate students majoring in journalism. **Criteria:** Recipients are selected based on the academic performance, and financial need.

Funds Avail.: $500. **To Apply:** Applicants must complete the application form.

7142 ■ Peggy Allen Community Newspaper Internships *(Undergraduate/Internship)*

Purpose: To educate journalists. **Focus:** Journalism; Communication. **Qualif.:** Applicants must be enrolled or plan to enroll in university and have an at least 2.9 GPA. **Criteria:** Recipients are selected based on the academic performance, financial need, and potential for journalism-mass communication careers.

Funds Avail.: $5,000. **To Apply:** Applicants must complete the application form. **Deadline:** February 1. **Contact:** PO Box 1080, Chapel Hill, NC 27514-1080.

7143 ■ Phillip Alston Scholarships *(Undergraduate/Scholarship)*

Purpose: To educate journalists. **Focus:** Journalism; Communications. **Qualif.:** Applicants must be undergraduate students in university. **Criteria:** Recipients are selected based on the academic performance, and financial need.

Funds Avail.: $500. **To Apply:** Applicants must complete the application form.

7144 ■ Jim Batten Community Newspaper Internships *(Undergraduate/Internship)*

Purpose: To provide financial assistance to news-editorial journalism and community journalism students. **Focus:** Journalism; Communication. **Qualif.:** Applicants must be enrolled or plan to enroll in university and have at least 2.9 GPA. **Criteria:** Recipients are selected based on the academic performance, financial need and potential for journalism-mass communication careers.

Funds Avail.: $5,000. **To Apply:** Applicants must submit a completed application form. Applicants must contact the school's director of graduate studies for other application requirements. **Deadline:** February 1. **Contact:** PO Box 1080, Chapel Hill, NC 27514-1080.

7145 ■ BellSouth Business Internship Awards *(Postgraduate/Internship)*

Purpose: To provide financial assistance to undergraduate or graduate students interested in business journalism. **Focus:** Journalism. **Qualif.:** Applicants must have arranged a business journalism internship and must be in the BellSouth service area. **Criteria:** Recipients are selected based on the academic performance, and financial need.

Funds Avail.: $1,000. **To Apply:** Applicants must submit a completed application form.

7146 ■ Margaret Blanchard Dissertation Support Fund *(Postgraduate/Grant)*

Purpose: To educate journalists. **Focus:** Communications. **Qualif.:** Applicants must be graduate student who are U.S. citizens. **Criteria:** Recipients are selected based on the academic performance, and financial need.

Funds Avail.: varies. **To Apply:** Applicants must complete the application form; applicants must contact the school's director of graduate studies. **Deadline:** January 1.

7147 ■ Tom Bost Scholarships *(Undergraduate/Scholarship)*

Purpose: To educate journalists. **Focus:** Journalism; Communications. **Qualif.:** Applicants must be undergraduate students in university. **Criteria:** Recipients are selected based on the academic performance, and financial need.

Funds Avail.: $500. **To Apply:** Applicants must complete the application form.

7148 ■ Rick Brewer Scholarships *(Undergraduate/Scholarship)*

Purpose: To educate journalists. **Focus:** Broadcasting; Journalism; Public relations. **Qualif.:** Applicants must be undergraduate students with a keen interest in pursuing a career in sports journalism, broadcasting, or public relations. **Criteria:** Recipients are selected based on the academic performance, and financial need.

Funds Avail.: $1,000. **To Apply:** Applicants must complete the application form.

7149 ■ Elton Casey Scholarships *(Undergraduate/Scholarship)*

Purpose: To educate journalists. **Focus:** Journalism. **Qualif.:** Applicants must be students who are interested in pursuing a career in sports journalism with a preference given to students from Orange or Durham counties. **Criteria:** Recipients are selected based on the academic performance, and financial need.

Funds Avail.: $750. **To Apply:** Applicants must complete the application form.

7150 ■ Ardis Cohoon Scholarships *(Undergraduate/Scholarship)*

Purpose: To provide educational assistance for journalists intending to achieve better communication skills. **Focus:** Communications; Journalism. **Qualif.:** Applicants must be currently enrolled or plan to enroll in university with at least a 2.9 GPA. **Criteria:** Recipients are selected based on academic performance and financial need.

Funds Avail.: $500. **To Apply:** Applicants must complete the application package.

7151 ■ Louis M. Connor Jr. Scholarships *(Undergraduate/Scholarship)*

Purpose: To educate journalists. **Focus:** Public relations. **Qualif.:** Applicants must be enrolled or plan to enroll in university and have an at least 2.9 GPA. **Criteria:** Recipients are selected based on the academic performance, and financial need.

Funds Avail.: $3,000. **To Apply:** Applicants must complete the application form. **Deadline:** February 1. **Contact:** PO Box 1080, Chapel Hill, NC 27514-1080.

7152 ■ Kathryn M. Cronin Scholarships *(Undergraduate/Scholarship)*

Purpose: To educate journalists. **Focus:** Journalism; Communications. **Qualif.:** Applicants must be enrolled or plan to enroll in university and have an at least 2.9 GPA. **Criteria:** Recipients are selected based on the academic performance, financial need, and potential for journalism-mass communication careers.

Funds Avail.: $3,000. **To Apply:** Applicants must complete the application form; see Professor Tom Linden. **Deadline:** March 1. **Contact:** PO Box 1080, Chapel Hill, NC 27514-1080.

7153 ■ Don and Barbara Curtis Excellence Fund for Extracurricular Student Activities *(Undergraduate/Grant)*

Purpose: To educate journalists; to support undergraduates who participate in meaningful out-of class activities that will help them in their mass communications careers. **Focus:** Journalism; Communication. **Qualif.:** Applicants must be students who are currently enrolled at the University of North Carolina and/or as a member of a student organization. **Criteria:** Recipients are selected based on the academic performance, financial need, and potential for journalism-mass communication careers.

Funds Avail.: $25,000. **To Apply:** Applicants must complete the application form. **Deadline:** October and February. **Contact:** PO Box 1080, Chapel Hill, NC 27514-1080.

7154 ■ James Davis Scholarships *(Undergraduate/Internship)*

Purpose: To educate journalists. **Focus:** Journalism; Communication. **Qualif.:** Applicants must be enrolled or plan to enroll in university and have an at least 2.9 GPA; Applicants must be studying North Carolina history, and North Carolina natives. **Criteria:** Recipients are selected based on the academic performance, financial need, and potential for journalism-mass communication careers.

Funds Avail.: $4,000. **To Apply:** Applicants must complete the application form. **Deadline:** February 1. **Contact:** PO Box 1080, Chapel Hill, NC 27514-1080.

7155 ■ Robert Winchester Dodson Scholarships *(Undergraduate/Scholarship)*

Purpose: To educate journalists. **Focus:** Communication. **Qualif.:** Applicants must be students who are currently enrolled or plan to enroll in university. **Criteria:** Recipients are selected based on the academic performance, and financial need.

Funds Avail.: $1,500. **To Apply:** Applicants must complete the application form.

7156 ■ Vivian Edmonds Scholarships *(Undergraduate/Scholarship)*

Purpose: To provide financial assistance to journalism students. **Focus:** Journalism; Communication. **Qualif.:** Applicants must be sophomore students and must have a minimum of 2.9 GPA. **Criteria:** Recipients are selected based on the academic performance, financial need and potential for journalism-mass communication careers.

Funds Avail.: $1,000. **To Apply:** Applicants must submit a completed application form. **Deadline:** February 1. **Contact:** PO Box 1080, Chapel Hill, NC 27514-1080.

7157 ■ Reese Felts Scholarships *(Undergraduate/Scholarship)*

Purpose: To educate journalists. **Focus:** Communication; Journalism. **Qualif.:** Applicants must be currently enrolled or plan to enroll in university. **Criteria:** Recipients are selected based on the academic performance, and financial need.

Funds Avail.: $2,500. **To Apply:** Applicants must complete the application form.

7158 ■ Ameel J. Fisher Scholarships *(Undergraduate/Scholarship)*

Purpose: To educate journalists. **Focus:** Journalism; Communication. **Qualif.:** Applicants must be enrolled or plan to enroll in university and have an at least 2.9 GPA. **Criteria:** Recipients are selected based on the academic performance, financial need, and potential for journalism-mass communication careers.

Funds Avail.: $4,000. **To Apply:** Applicants must complete the application form. **Deadline:** February 1. **Contact:** PO Box 1080, Chapel Hill, NC 27514-1080.

7159 ■ Victoria M. Gardner Scholarships *(Undergraduate/Scholarship)*

Purpose: To educate journalists so that they can communicate about science and medicine effectively. **Focus:** Medical. **Qualif.:** Applicants must be students interested in families, children, and medical issues. **Criteria:** Recipients are selected based on the academic performance, and financial need.

Funds Avail.: $5,500. **To Apply:** Applicants must complete the application form. **Deadline:** October 1.

7160 ■ Kays Gary Scholarships *(Undergraduate/Scholarship)*

Purpose: To educate journalists. **Focus:** Communications; Journalism. **Qualif.:** Applicants must be currently enrolled or plan to enroll in university and have an at least 2.9 GPA. **Criteria:** Recipients are selected based on the academic performance, and financial need.

Funds Avail.: $500. **To Apply:** Applicants must complete the application form.

7161 ■ Stephen Gates Scholarships *(Undergraduate/Scholarship)*

Purpose: To educate journalists. **Focus:** Communication; Broadcasting. **Qualif.:** Applicants must be student currently enrolled or planing to enroll in university. **Criteria:** Recipients are selected based on the academic performance, and financial need.

Funds Avail.: $2,000. **To Apply:** Applicants must complete the application form.

7162 ■ Joy Gibson Scholarships *(Undergraduate/Scholarship)*

Purpose: To educate journalists. **Focus:** Journalism; Communications. **Qualif.:** Applicants must be undergraduate students in university. **Criteria:** Recipients are selected based on the academic performance, and financial need.

Funds Avail.: $500. **To Apply:** Applicants must complete the application form.

7163 ■ L.C. Gifford Distinguished Journalism Scholarships *(Undergraduate/Scholarship)*

Purpose: To educate journalists. **Focus:** Communication; Journalism. **Qualif.:** Applicants must be journalism students from the University of North Carolina Chapel Hill. **Criteria:** Recipients are selected based on the academic performance, and financial need.

Funds Avail.: $2,000. **To Apply:** Applicants must complete the application form.

7164 ■ Charles Hauser Scholarships *(Undergraduate/Scholarship)*

Purpose: To educate journalists. **Focus:** Communications; Journalism. **Qualif.:** Applicants must be currently enrolled or plan to enroll in university and have an at least 2.9 GPA. **Criteria:** Recipients are selected based on the academic performance, and financial need.

Funds Avail.: $500. **To Apply:** Applicants must complete the application form.

7165 ■ Paul Green Houston Scholarships *(Undergraduate/Scholarship)*

Purpose: To educate journalists. **Focus:** Communication; Journalism. **Qualif.:** Applicants must be students majoring in news editorial journalism. **Criteria:** Recipients are selected based on the academic performance, and financial need.

Funds Avail.: $1,500. **To Apply:** Applicants must complete the application form.

7166 ■ James F. Hurley III Bicentennial Merit Scholarships *(Undergraduate/Scholarship)*

Purpose: To provide financial assistance to journalism students. **Focus:** Journalism; Communication. **Qualif.:** Applicants must be enrolled or plan to enroll in university and have an at least 2.9 GPA. **Criteria:** Preference is given to students with a newspaper career interest.

Funds Avail.: $7,250. **To Apply:** Applicants must submit a completed application form. Applicants must contact the school's director of graduate studies for other application requirements. **Deadline:** February 1. **Contact:** PO Box 1080, Chapel Hill, NC 27514-1080.

7167 ■ Fred Hutchison Travel Scholarships *(Undergraduate/Scholarship)*

Purpose: To educate journalists; to help defray expenses associated with travel to foreign countries for courses. **Focus:** Journalism; Communication. **Qualif.:** Applicants must be students who are currently enrolled or plan to enroll in university. **Criteria:** Recipients are selected based on the academic performance, financial need, and potential for journalism-mass communication careers.

Funds Avail.: No specific amount. **To Apply:** Applicants must complete the application form; see Professor Tom Linden. **Deadline:** March 1. **Contact:** jyopp@email.unc.edu.

7168 ■ Edward Jackson International Scholarships *(Undergraduate/Scholarship)*

Purpose: To educate journalists; to support undergraduate students in traveling to a European country to learn about it's politics, culture, and mass media by working there. **Focus:** Communication; Journalism. **Qualif.:** Applicants must be news editorial undergraduate students, preferably from North Carolina. **Criteria:** Recipients are selected based on the academic performance, and financial need.

Funds Avail.: $2,500. **To Apply:** Applicants must complete the application form. **Deadline:** February 1.

7169 ■ Gene Jackson Scholarships *(Undergraduate/Scholarship)*

Purpose: To educate journalists. **Focus:** Communication; Journalism. **Qualif.:** Applicants must be graduate students of the school whve had a distinguished career in newspaper and worked in the University of North Carolina Chapel Hill Development Office. **Criteria:** Recipients are selected based on the academic performance, and financial need.

Funds Avail.: $1,250. **To Apply:** Applicants must complete the application form.

7170 ■ Peter Lars Jacobson Scholarships *(Undergraduate/Scholarship)*

Purpose: To provide educational assistance for journalists to help them achieve effective communication in the fields of science and medicine. **Focus:** Journalism; Communications. **Qualif.:** Applicants must be journalism and mass communication students who are able to write the best medical story. **Criteria:** Recipients are selected based on academic performance and financial need.

Funds Avail.: $500. **To Apply:** Applicants must submit completed application form; applicants must submit a story or stories with name, address, telephone number and class year to Professor Tom Linden. **Deadline:** February 1.

7171 ■ Glenn Keever Scholarships *(Undergraduate/Scholarship)*

Purpose: To educate journalists. **Focus:** Communication; Journalism. **Qualif.:** Applicants must be undergraduate students, preferably in North Carolina. **Criteria:** Recipients are selected based on the academic performance, and financial need.

Funds Avail.: $2,500. **To Apply:** Applicants must complete the application form.

7172 ■ Charles Kuralt Fellowships in International Broadcasting *(Postgraduate/Scholarship)*

Purpose: To educate journalists. **Focus:** Broadcasting. **Qualif.:** Applicant must be a recent school graduate, with a bachelor's or master's degree who excelled in electronic communication. **Criteria:** Recipients are selected based on the academic performance, financial need, and potential for journalism-mass communication careers.

Funds Avail.: No specific amount. **To Apply:** Applicants must complete the application form; see Professor Tom Linden. **Deadline:** October 1.

7173 ■ Norval Neil Luxon Prize for Scholarship to a Junior Scholarships *(Undergraduate/Scholarship)*

Purpose: To educate journalists. **Focus:** Communications. **Qualif.:** Applicant must be junior with the highest grade point of average; applicants must have at least 36 credit hours of graded course work at the University of North Carolina and have completed approximately 90 credit hours by the end of the spring semester. **Criteria:** Recipients are selected based on the academic performance, and financial need.

Funds Avail.: $500. **To Apply:** Applicants must complete the application form.

7174 ■ Mackey-Byars Scholarships for Communication Excellence *(Undergraduate/Scholarship)*

Purpose: To educate journalists. **Focus:** Communications. **Qualif.:** Applicants must be minority or disadvantaged students majoring in mass communications. **Criteria:** Recipients are selected based on academic performance and financial need.

Funds Avail.: $500. **To Apply:** Applicants must complete the application form.

7175 ■ Raleigh Mann Scholarships *(Undergraduate/Scholarship)*

Purpose: To educate journalists. **Focus:** Journalism; Communications. **Qualif.:** Applicants must be undergraduate students in university. **Criteria:** Recipients are selected based on academic performance and financial need.

Funds Avail.: $500. **To Apply:** Applicants must complete the application package.

7176 ■ Donald Mauer Scholarships *(Undergraduate/Scholarship)*

Purpose: To educate journalists. **Focus:** Advertising. **Qualif.:** Applicants must be rising junior in the advertising sequence. **Criteria:** Recipients are selected based on the academic performance, and financial need.

Funds Avail.: $500. **To Apply:** Applicants must complete the application form.

7177 ■ Maxwell Graduate Scholarships in Medical Journalism *(Postgraduate/Scholarship)*

Purpose: To educate journalists so that they can communicate about science and medicine effectively. **Focus:** Journalism. **Qualif.:** Applicants must be master's students in the medical journalism program. **Criteria:** Recipients are selected based on the academic performance, and financial need.

Funds Avail.: $1,000. **To Apply:** Applicants must complete the application form.

7178 ■ Molly McKay Scholarships *(Undergraduate/Scholarship)*

Purpose: To educate journalists. **Focus:** Religion. **Qualif.:** Applicants must be students interested in religion. **Criteria:** Recipients are selected based on the academic performance, and financial need.

Funds Avail.: $1,000. **To Apply:** Applicants must complete the application form.

7179 ■ C.A. "Pete" McKnight Scholarships *(Undergraduate/Scholarship)*

Purpose: To educate journalists. **Focus:** Journalism. **Qualif.:** Applicants must be currently enrolled or plan to enroll in university. **Criteria:** Recipients are selected based on the academic performance, and financial need.

Funds Avail.: $2,500. **To Apply:** Applicants must complete the application form.

7180 ■ Edward Heywood Megson Scholarships *(Undergraduate/Scholarship)*

Purpose: To educate journalists. **Focus:** Journalism; Communications. **Qualif.:** Applicants must be graduates of University of North Carolina- Chapel Hill. **Criteria:** Recipients are selected based on the academic performance, and financial need.

Funds Avail.: $750. **To Apply:** Applicants must complete the application form.

7181 ■ Quincy Sharpe Mills Scholarships *(Undergraduate/Scholarship)*

Purpose: To provide financial assistance to minority and disadvantaged students. **Focus:** Journalism; Communication. **Qualif.:** Applicants must be currently enrolled in or planning to attend university and must have a minimum of 2.9 GPA. **Criteria:** Recipients are selected based on the academic performance, financial need and potential for journalism-mass communication careers. Preference is also given to minority and disadvantaged students.

Funds Avail.: $3,000. **To Apply:** Applicants must submit a completed application form. **Deadline:** February 1. **Contact:** PO Box 1080, Chapel Hill, NC 27514-1080.

7182 ■ Minority Presence Grant Program for Doctoral Study *(Undergraduate/Grant)*

Purpose: To educate journalists. **Focus:** General studies. **Qualif.:** Applicants must be black residents of North

Carolina; applicants must be full-time students pursuing doctoral degrees, law degree, or degrees in veterinary medicine at East Carolina University, Carolina State University, University of North Carolina at Chapel Hill, at Greensboro, or at Charlotte Campus. **Criteria:** Recipients are selected based on the academic performance, financial need, and potential for journalism-mass communication careers.

Funds Avail.: $4,000. **To Apply:** Applicants must complete the application form. **Deadline:** March 1. **Contact:** PO Box 1080, Chapel Hill, NC 27514-1080.

7183 ■ Alexander Morisey Scholarships
(Undergraduate/Scholarship)

Purpose: To provide financial assistance to journalism students. **Focus:** Journalism; Communication. **Qualif.:** Applicants must be first year students and must have a minimum of 2.9 GPA. **Criteria:** Recipients are selected based on the academic performance, financial need and potential for journalism-mass communication careers.

Funds Avail.: $1,000. **To Apply:** Applicants must submit a completed application form. **Deadline:** February 1. **Contact:** PO Box 1080, Chapel Hill, NC 27514-1080.

7184 ■ N.C. Psychoanalytic Foundation Journalism Scholarships *(Postgraduate/Scholarship)*

Purpose: To educate journalists so that they can communicate about science and medicine effectively. **Focus:** Journalism. **Qualif.:** Applicants must be master's students in the medical journalism program. **Criteria:** Recipients are selected based on the academic performance, and financial need.

Funds Avail.: $1,000. **To Apply:** Applicants must complete the application form; applicants must submit a 200-word proposal for a project in any medium on mental health. **Deadline:** March 1.

7185 ■ Pfizer Minority Medical Journalism Scholarships *(Postgraduate/Scholarship)*

Purpose: To provide financial assistance to medical journalism students. **Focus:** Journalism; Communication. **Qualif.:** Applicants must be incoming master's students in the medical journalism program. **Criteria:** Recipients are selected based on the academic performance, financial need, and potential for journalism-mass communication careers. Preference is given to minority and disadvantaged students.

Funds Avail.: $6,000. **To Apply:** Applicants must submit a completed application form. **Deadline:** February 1. **Contact:** PO Box 1080, Chapel Hill, NC 27514-1080.

7186 ■ Robert Pittman Scholarships
(Undergraduate/Scholarship)

Purpose: To provide financial assistance to journalism students. **Focus:** Journalism; Communication. **Qualif.:** Applicants must be enrolled or plan to enroll in university and have at least 2.9 GPA; applicants must have an internship at St. Petersburg Times. **Criteria:** Recipients are selected based on the academic performance, financial need, and potential for journalism-mass communication careers. Preference is given to a student with an interest in newspapers.

Funds Avail.: $7,000. **To Apply:** Applicants must submit a completed application form. Applicants must contact the School's Director of graduate studies for other application requirements. **Deadline:** February 1. **Contact:** PO Box 1080, Chapel Hill, NC 27514-1080.

7187 ■ Erwin Potts Scholarships
(Undergraduate/Scholarship)

Purpose: To provide financial assistance to Latino students studying newspaper journalism. **Focus:** Journalism; Communication. **Qualif.:** Applicants must be currently enrolled or plan to attend in university and must have a minimum of 2.9 GPA. **Criteria:** Recipients are selected based on the academic performance, financial need and potential for journalism-mass communication careers.

Funds Avail.: $2,000. **To Apply:** Applicants must submit a completed application form. **Deadline:** February 1. **Contact:** PO Box 1080, Chapel Hill, NC 27514-1080.

7188 ■ Peter DeWitt Pruden and Phyliss Harrill Pruden Scholarships *(Undergraduate/Scholarship)*

Purpose: To provide financial assistance to journalism students. **Focus:** Journalism; Communication. **Qualif.:** Applicants must be enrolled or plan to enroll in a university in North Carolina, Tennessee, or Virginia and have an at least 2.9 GPA. **Criteria:** Preference goes to students from Virginia, Tennessee or North Carolina with strong character, excellent academic performance and financial need.

Funds Avail.: $10,000. **To Apply:** Applicants must submit a completed application form. Applicants must contact the school's director of graduate studies for other application requirements. **Deadline:** February 1. **Contact:** PO Box 1080, Chapel Hill, NC 27514-1080.

7189 ■ Bob Quincy Scholarships
(Undergraduate/Scholarship)

Purpose: To educate journalists. **Focus:** Communication; Journalism. **Qualif.:** Applicants must be currently enrolled or plan to enroll in university. **Criteria:** Recipients are selected based on the academic performance, and financial need.

Funds Avail.: $2,500. **To Apply:** Applicants must complete the application form.

7190 ■ Marjorie Usher Regan Scholarships
(Undergraduate/Scholarship)

Purpose: To educate journalists. **Focus:** Communication; Journalism. **Qualif.:** Applicants must be women with a career interest in print journalism. **Criteria:** Recipients are selected based on the academic performance, and financial need.

Funds Avail.: $2,000. **To Apply:** Applicants must complete the application form.

7191 ■ Eugene L. Roberts Jr. Prize
(Undergraduate/Prize)

Purpose: To educate journalists so that they can communicate effectively. **Focus:** Journalism. **Qualif.:** Applicants must be undergraduate students interested in print journalism who propose the best idea for a Gene Roberts-type story; applicants must be returning to the School for at least one semester, when he or she will research and write the story in JOMC 296. The course is "Independent Study" supervised by a faculty member for three credits. **Criteria:** Recipients are selected based on the academic performance, and financial need.

Funds Avail.: $5,500. **To Apply:** Applicants must complete the application form. **Deadline:** February 1.

7192 ■ A.C. Snow Scholarships *(Undergraduate/Scholarship)*

Purpose: To educate journalists. **Focus:** Journalism. **Qualif.:** Applicants must be news editorial students with an interest in grammar. **Criteria:** Recipients are selected based on the academic performance, and financial need.

Funds Avail.: $750. **To Apply:** Applicants must complete the application form.

7193 ■ Hal Tanner Jr. Scholarships *(Undergraduate/Scholarship)*

Purpose: To educate journalists. **Focus:** Communication; Advertising. **Qualif.:** Applicants must be rising senior students majoring in advertising. **Criteria:** Recipients are selected based on the academic performance, and financial need.

Funds Avail.: $1,500. **To Apply:** Applicants must complete the application form.

7194 ■ Jim and Pat Thacker Sports Communication Internships *(Undergraduate/Internship)*

Purpose: To educate journalists; to pay expenses for a student who has secured a summer internship in sports communication. **Focus:** Communication. **Qualif.:** Applicants must be currently enrolled or plan to enroll in university. **Criteria:** Recipients are selected based on the academic performance, and financial need.

Funds Avail.: $2,500. **To Apply:** Applicants must complete the application form; applicants must contact Professor John Sweeney for details.

7195 ■ Tucker Family Scholarships *(Undergraduate/Scholarship)*

Purpose: To provide financial assistance to journalism students. **Focus:** Journalism; Communication. **Qualif.:** Applicants must be enrolled or plan to enroll in university and have at least 2.9 GPA. **Criteria:** Recipients are selected based on the academic performance, financial need and potential for journalism-mass communication careers. Preference is given to students in print or broadcast.

Funds Avail.: $5,000. **To Apply:** Applicants must submit a completed application form. **Deadline:** February 1. **Contact:** PO Box 1080, Chapel Hill, NC 27514-1080.

7196 ■ David Julian Wichard Scholarships *(Undergraduate/Scholarship)*

Purpose: To educate journalists. **Focus:** Communication; Journalism. **Qualif.:** Applicants must be currently enrolled or planning to enroll in university; applicants must be residents of North Carolina. **Criteria:** Recipients are selected based on the academic performance, and financial need.

Funds Avail.: $2,000. **To Apply:** Applicants must complete the application form.

7197 ■ Tom Wicker Scholarships *(Undergraduate/Scholarship)*

Purpose: To provide financial assistance to news-editorial graduate students. **Focus:** Journalism; Communication. **Qualif.:** Applicants must be enrolled or plan to enroll in university and have an at least 2.9 GPA. **Criteria:** Recipients are selected based on the academic performance, financial need and potential for journalism-mass communication careers.

Funds Avail.: $1,000. **To Apply:** Applicants must submit a completed application form. Applicants must contact the school's director of graduate studies for other application requirements. **Deadline:** February 1. **Contact:** PO Box 1080, Chapel Hill, NC 27514-1080.

7198 ■ WKIX Alumni Association Scholarships *(Undergraduate/Scholarship)*

Purpose: To educate journalists. **Focus:** Communications. **Qualif.:** Applicants must be student in the electronic communication sequence. **Criteria:** Recipients are selected based on the academic performance, and financial need.

Funds Avail.: $1,000. **To Apply:** Applicants must complete the application form.

7199 ■ WTVD Endowment Scholarships *(Undergraduate/Scholarship)*

Purpose: To provide financial assistance to journalism students. **Focus:** Journalism; Communication. **Qualif.:** Applicants must be enrolled or plan to enroll in university and have at least 2.9 GPA. **Criteria:** Recipients are selected based on the academic performance, financial need and potential for journalism-mass communication careers.

Funds Avail.: $1,000. **To Apply:** Applicants must submit a completed application form. **Deadline:** February 1. **Contact:** PO Box 1080, Chapel Hill, NC 27514-1080.

7200 ■ University of Oregon

1217 University of Oregon
Eugene, OR 97403
Ph: (541)346-1000
Fax: (541)346-5815
Free: 800-232-3825
E-mail: stl@uoregon.edu
URL: http://www.uoregon.edu

7201 ■ Oregon Community Credit Union Scholarships *(Undergraduate/Scholarship)*

Purpose: To provide financial support for undergraduate students with financial need. **Focus:** General studies. **Qualif.:** Applicants must be students from Oregon who demonstrate academic excellence and contribute to the community in which they live. Applicants must have graduated from high school in one of the following Oregon counties: Benton, Columbia, Lane, Linn, Marion, Multnumah, Polk, Washington or Yamhill; and must have a high school GPA of 3.50 or higher. **Criteria:** Selection of recipients will be based on academic achievements, community involvement, and financial need.

Funds Avail.: $4,800. **To Apply:** Applicants must submit an extra-curricular activities listing, one short statement, and one essay as part of the University of Oregon Scholarship Application. **Deadline:** January 15.

7202 ■ Robert W. and Bernice Ingalls Staton Scholarships *(Undergraduate/Scholarship)*

Purpose: To provide financial support to students who desire to further their education without financial burden. **Focus:** Humanities; Fine arts; Education; Music. **Qualif.:** Applicants must be Oregon residents and must have an extraordinary financial need. **Criteria:** Recipients are selected based on financial need. Preference is given to students who declare a major in the Humanities, Department of Fine Arts, the College of Education, or the School of Music.

Funds Avail.: $5,000. **To Apply:** Applicants must submit the Admission application available online to the Office of Admission. **Deadline:** January 15.

7203 ■ University of Oregon Dean's Scholarships *(Undergraduate/Scholarship)*

Purpose: To encourage qualified individuals to pursue their studies in the University of Oregon. **Focus:** General studies. **Qualif.:** Applicants must be entering freshmen; must have a minimum cumulative high school GPA of 3.6; must meet all current UO freshman admission requirements; must have not attended another college after graduation from high school. **Criteria:** Recipients will be selected based on high school GPA and coursework.

Funds Avail.: $500-$6,000. **To Apply:** Applicants must submit the UO Undergraduate Admission Application available online to the Office of Admission. **Deadline:** January 15.

7204 ■ University of Oregon Diversity-Building Scholarships *(Graduate, Undergraduate/ Scholarship)*

Purpose: To encourage the undergraduate and graduate students to enhance their educational experience by sharing diverse cultural experiences. **Focus:** General studies. **Qualif.:** Applicants must be U.S citizens or permanent residents; must be currently enrolled as UO students in good academic standing; must meet the DBS minimum GPA requirements; must have a minimum cumulative GPA of 3.0 for freshmen, and 2.50 for other applicants. **Criteria:** UO Diversity - Building Scholarship Committee gives priority to students who demonstrate the following: (1) Strong academic background as documented by official high school and/or college transcript; (2) Financial need as defined by federal guidelines; (3) Family educational history; (4) Residency status; (5) Commitment to diversity through documented history of community service, leadership, or other activities.

Funds Avail.: No specific amount. **To Apply:** Application forms are available online. Applicants must submit a personal statement, letter of recommendation and official transcripts. Application form and other supporting materials must be submitted to the Office of Student Financial Aid & Scholarships. **Deadline:** January 15.

7205 ■ University of Oregon General University Scholarships *(Undergraduate/Scholarship)*

Purpose: To support qualified individuals who wish to pursue their education. **Focus:** General studies. **Qualif.:** Applicants must have a minimum GPA of 3.50. **Criteria:** Selection of applicants will be based on academic performance, SAT or ACT scores (Freshmen), extracurricular involvement, faculty recommendation (junior, senior, and graduate students), as well as writing ability and creativity as demonstrated in the career aspirations and scholarship essay.

Funds Avail.: $1,000-$2,700. **To Apply:** Applicants must complete the Scholarship Application Form and submit high school transcripts as well as SAT or ACT scores. **Deadline:** January 15.

7206 ■ University of Oregon Presidential Scholarships *(Undergraduate/Scholarship)*

Purpose: To provide financial support to the state's brightest students. **Focus:** General studies. **Qualif.:** Applicants must be Oregon residents; must be entering freshmen; must have a minimum GPA of 3.5. **Criteria:** Applications will be judged by the Scholarship Committee based on academic performance, SAT or ACT scores, extracurricular involvement, as well as writing ability and creativity as demonstrated in the career aspirations and scholarship essay.

Funds Avail.: $6,500. **To Apply:** Applicants must complete the Scholarship Application forms available online; and must submit official high school transcripts and SAT or ACT scores to the Office of Admissions. **Deadline:** January 15.

7207 ■ University of Toronto

315 Bloor St. W
Toronto, ON, Canada M5S 1A3
Ph: (416)978-2011
E-mail: information.commonsats@utoronto.ca
URL: http://www.utoronto.ca

7208 ■ Dr. Anderson Abbott Awards *(Undergraduate/Scholarship)*

Purpose: To support students with their educational pursuit. **Focus:** Medicine; Health sciences. **Qualif.:** Applicant must be a black student of UofT. **Criteria:** The selection committee may give preference to student in the medical program or in a related health science program.

Funds Avail.: $4000. **Number Awarded:** 1. **To Apply:** Applicants must submit a completed Abbot application form along with the required materials and information. **Deadline:** March 28.

7209 ■ Al Mercury Scholarships *(Undergraduate/ Scholarship)*

Purpose: To support students with their educational pursuits. **Focus:** General studies. **Qualif.:** Applicant must be a UofT student demonstrated community involvement, academic excellence, integrity and an appreciation and interest in music. **Criteria:** Selection is based on general proficiency or outstanding achievements.

Funds Avail.: Approximately $700. **To Apply:** Applicants must submit a completed application form along with the required materials and information. **Deadline:** March 28.

7210 ■ Stephanie Ali Memorial Scholarships *(Undergraduate/Scholarship)*

Purpose: To support students with their educational pursuits. **Focus:** General studies. **Qualif.:** Applicant must be a student of U of T; in financial need; and have demonstrated commitment to community work or participation in charitable activities. **Criteria:** Preference is given to student who are past or present members of the University of Toronto Gospel Choir.

Funds Avail.: Approximately $200. **To Apply:** Applicants must submit a completed Stephanie Ali Memorial Scholarships application form along with the required materials and information. **Deadline:** March 28.

7211 ■ J.P. Bickell Mining Scholarships *(Undergraduate/Scholarship)*

Purpose: To support students with their educational pursuits. **Focus:** Geology; Geophysics; Earth sciences; Mining; Environmental science. **Qualif.:** Applicant must be a student of U of T; an undergraduate student in second or higher years studying mining (including the geological and geophysical fields as well as environmental sciences, geological sciences, earth science programs and mining engineering); have a minimum GPA of B or better and have demonstrated interest in the mining industry or field. **Criteria:** Selection is based on general proficiency or outstanding achievements.

Funds Avail.: Approximately $2000. **To Apply:** Applicants must submit a letter of application together with a letter outlining the interest in the mining industry. **Deadline:** October 31.

Awards are arranged alphabetically below their administering organizations

7212 ■ Leon C. Bynoe Memorial Scholarships *(Undergraduate/Scholarship)*

Purpose: To support students with their educational pursuits. **Focus:** General studies. **Qualif.:** Applicant must be a student of U of T; an undergraduate student enrolled in an undergraduate degree program; and must demonstrate outstanding service to the Afro-Canadian community. **Criteria:** Selection is based on financial need and outstanding academic achievement. Preference is given to students from the Afro-Canadian community and MTHA residents.

Funds Avail.: Approximately $1300. **To Apply:** Applicants must submit a completed Leon C. Bynoe Memorial Scholarships application form along with the required materials and information. **Deadline:** November 30.

7213 ■ Canadian Federation of University Women Etobicoke Bursary *(Graduate, Undergraduate/Scholarship)*

Purpose: To support students with their educational pursuits. **Focus:** General studies. **Qualif.:** Applicant must be a female undergraduate or graduate student of U of T; a resident of Etobicoke; and in need of financial assistance for education. **Criteria:** Selection is based on general proficiency or outstanding achievements.

Funds Avail.: $1000 and $650. **Number Awarded:** 1 first year undergraduate student; 1 second or higher year undergraduate student; and 1 graduate student. **To Apply:** Applicants must submit a completed Canadian Federation of University Women Etobicoke Bursary application form along with the required materials and information. **Deadline:** October 31.

7214 ■ Canadian Macedonian Federation Scholarships *(Undergraduate/Scholarship)*

Purpose: To support students with their educational pursuits. **Focus:** General studies. **Qualif.:** Applicants must be a student of U of T in second, third or fourth year of any degree program with a minimum GPA of 3.5; a member of the Canadian Macedonian Federation, or have made a major commitment to any of its member service organizations through community service, contribution of a minimum of one year. **Criteria:** Selection is based on general proficiency or outstanding achievements.

Funds Avail.: Approximately $250. **To Apply:** Applicants must submit a letter outlining the qualifications; attach a transcript of results, with a list of involvement or contribution to the Canadian Macedonian Federation or its member service organizations; and a proof of membership in the Federation (if applicable). **Deadline:** March 28.

7215 ■ Chinese-Canadian History and Culture Fellowships *(Graduate/Fellowship)*

Purpose: To support a master's or doctoral research on Chinese-Canadian community. **Focus:** Area and ethnic studies. **Qualif.:** Applicant must be master's or doctoral students planning to engage in research at the University of Toronto in the history, cultural or social make-up of a Chinese-Canadian community; and must be fluent in a Chinese dialect. **Criteria:** Preference is given to students who have not previously held the award.

Funds Avail.: $6000 (Masters student) or $7000 (Doctoral student). **Number Awarded:** 1. **To Apply:** Applicants must submit a completed application form along with official transcripts of academic results of all university studies; three letters of recommendation; and a comprehensive description of the research which will be performed during the period of the fellowship. **Deadline:** April 25.

7216 ■ City of Toronto Graduate Scholarships for Women in Mathematics *(Graduate/Scholarship)*

Purpose: To support students with their educational pursuits. **Focus:** Mathematics and mathematical sciences. **Qualif.:** Applicants must be a female student of UofT enrolled in a master's or doctoral program in mathematics. **Criteria:** Selection is based on financial need, academic merit and demonstrated interest in issues related to women in mathematics.

Funds Avail.: Annual income (no less than $9000). **To Apply:** Applicants must submit a completed application form along with the required materials and information. **Deadline:** November 1. **Contact:** osap.staff@utoronto.ca.

7217 ■ City of Toronto Queen Elizabeth II Sesquicentennial Scholarships in Community Health Nursing (Graduate) *(Graduate/Scholarship)*

Purpose: To support students with their educational pursuit. **Focus:** Nursing. **Qualif.:** Applicant must be a graduate student enrolled in the Graduate Department of Nursing Science; have completed courses in community health and demonstrate a commitment to this aspect of nursing. **Criteria:** Selection is based on general proficiency or outstanding achievements.

Funds Avail.: $3000. **Number Awarded:** 1. **To Apply:** Applicants must submit a completed application form along with the required materials and information. **Deadline:** September 29.

7218 ■ City of Toronto Queen Elizabeth II Sesquicentennial Scholarships in Community Health Nursing (Undergraduate) *(Undergraduate/Scholarship)*

Purpose: To support students with their educational pursuits. **Focus:** Nursing. **Qualif.:** Applicant must be undergraduate student completing the first year of the second-entry two year BScN program. **Criteria:** Preference may be given to students proficient in a language besides English and whose interest is to work with multicultural families.

Funds Avail.: $5000. **Number Awarded:** 1. **To Apply:** Applicants must submit a completed application form along with the required materials and information. **Deadline:** June 30. **Contact:** osap.staff@utoronto.ca.

7219 ■ City of Toronto Scholarships for Aboriginal Students *(Graduate, Undergraduate/Scholarship)*

Purpose: To support students with their educational pursuit. **Focus:** Health services administration. **Qualif.:** Applicants must be an undergraduate or graduate aboriginal student studying in any of the health professional programs. **Criteria:** Selection is based on financial need, academic merit and demonstrated community leadership skills.

Funds Avail.: Approximately $4500. **To Apply:** Applicants must submit a completed application form along with the required materials and informations. **Deadline:** October 31.

7220 ■ City of Toronto Women's Studies Scholarships *(Graduate, Undergraduate/Scholarship)*

Purpose: To support students with their educational pursuits. **Focus:** Women's studies. **Qualif.:** Applicants must

Awards are arranged alphabetically below their administering organizations

be undergraduate or graduate students in Women's Studies. **Criteria:** Selection is based on financial need and academic merit.

Funds Avail.: Undergraduate - $5000; Graduate scholarship valued at the balance of the annual income. **Number Awarded:** 1 undergraduate; and 1 graduate student. **To Apply:** Applicants must submit a completed application form along with the required materials and information. **Deadline:** Undergraduate: June 30; Graduate: November 1.

7221 ■ Mary Jane Hendrie Memorial Scholarships *(Graduate, Undergraduate/Scholarship)*

Purpose: To support students with their educational pursuits. **Focus:** Japanese studies. **Qualif.:** Applicant must be a senior undergraduate or graduate student of U of T; interested in relations between Japan and Canada with studies in business, law, economics, international relations, or political science. **Criteria:** Selection is based on general proficiency or outstanding achievements.

Funds Avail.: Approximately $3500. **To Apply:** Applicants must submit a completed application form along with the required materials and information. **Deadline:** March 28.

Remarks: Faculty members can nominate a student by writing a letter to the Scholarship Selection Committee describing the student's qualifications for the award.

7222 ■ Irving J. Hoffman Memorial Scholarships *(Undergraduate/Scholarship)*

Purpose: To support students with their educational pursuits. **Focus:** General studies. **Qualif.:** Applicant must be a physically handicapped student, enrolled on either a full-time or part-time basis, demonstrates superior academic achievement; have completed at least five university level courses, or the equivalent. Students registered in OISE are not qualified. **Criteria:** Selection is based on academic achievement and financial need.

Funds Avail.: Approximately $500. **To Apply:** Applicants must submit a completed application form along with the required materials and information. **Deadline:** March 28.

7223 ■ Hosinec Family Scholarships *(Graduate, Undergraduate/Scholarship)*

Purpose: To support students with their educational pursuits. **Focus:** General studies. **Qualif.:** Applicant must be undergraduate or graduate student of the U of T. **Criteria:** Selection is based on need and academic merit.

Funds Avail.: $3000. **Number Awarded:** 5. **To Apply:** Applicants must submit a completed application form and required materials and information. **Deadline:** November 30.

Remarks: Funded by the Hosinec Family Endowment Fund.

7224 ■ In-course Scholarships - Chinese Dance Workshop Scholarships *(Undergraduate/Scholarship)*

Purpose: To support students with their educational pursuits. **Focus:** Dance. **Qualif.:** Applicant must be a student of U of T and have attended a recognized dance institute for at least three years. **Criteria:** Selection is based on academic excellence and demonstrated dance experience.

Funds Avail.: Approximately $2400. **To Apply:** Applicants must submit a letter of application verifying at least three years of attendance at a recognized dance institute along with a transcript of marks. **Deadline:** October 31.

7225 ■ Khaki University and Y.M.C.A. Memorial Scholarships *(Undergraduate/Scholarship)*

Purpose: To support students with their educational pursuits. **Focus:** General studies. **Qualif.:** Applicant must be enrolled in the second or higher year of an undergraduate course proceeding to a degree; have at least first class honours standing. **Criteria:** Preference is given to students who are descendent from one who has served in the armed forces.

Funds Avail.: Variable. **To Apply:** Applicants must submit a completed application form along with the required materials and information. **Deadline:** November 30.

7226 ■ Lo Family Scholarships *(Undergraduate/Scholarship)*

Purpose: To support students with their educational pursuits. **Focus:** General studies. **Qualif.:** Applicant must be a Canadian citizen, permanent resident or protected person (recognized convention refugee) and will be enrolled full-time; an active leader, respected and considered to be well-rounded citizen in school and community, and have demonstrated financial need. **Criteria:** Selection is based on financial need and academic merit.

Funds Avail.: No specific amount. **To Apply:** Applicants must submit an online UTAPS application and a letter outlining community activity and demonstrated leadership skills; and a letter of support from school. **Deadline:** January.

7227 ■ Gertrude and Edith Lowidt and Mary Catherine Preiss Memorial Bursaries in Nutritional Sciences *(Undergraduate/Scholarship)*

Purpose: To support students with their educational pursuit. **Focus:** Nutrition. **Qualif.:** Applicant must be a UofT student registered in the Faculty of Arts and Science, St. George Campus entering or in a third or fourth year course offered by the Department of Nutritional Sciences. **Criteria:** Selection is based on financial need. Preference is given to students intending to complete the Specialist Program in Nutritional Sciences.

Funds Avail.: $500. **Number Awarded:** 2. **To Apply:** Applicants must submit a completed application form along with the required materials and informations. **Deadline:** November 30.

7228 ■ John Macara, Barrister of Goderich, Scholarships *(Undergraduate/Scholarship)*

Purpose: To support students with their educational pursuits. **Focus:** General studies. **Qualif.:** Applicant must be a Canadian citizen, permanent resident or protected person (recognized convention refugee) and will be enrolled full-time. **Criteria:** Preference is given to applicants who can establish that they are the blood kin of the late Mrs. Jean Glasgow.

Funds Avail.: No specific amount. **To Apply:** Applicants must submit an online UTAPS application and a letter explaining how they are related to the late Mrs. Glasgow. **Deadline:** January.

7229 ■ Joseph McCulley Educational Scholarships *(Graduate, Undergraduate/Scholarship)*

Purpose: To support students with their educational pursuits. **Focus:** Social work. **Qualif.:** Applicant must be a

U of T graduate or undergraduate student whose programs of study and career interests lie in the area of public life or social work, emphasizing on penology. **Criteria:** Selection is based on financial need.

Funds Avail.: Variable in value, to the total of the annual income. **To Apply:** Applicants must submit a completed application form together with the required materials and information. **Deadline:** November 30.

7230 ■ John H. Moss Scholarships
(Undergraduate/Scholarship)

Purpose: To support students with their educational pursuits. **Focus:** Arts; Science. **Qualif.:** Applicant must be a U of T student having a minimum GPA of 3.3 (B+); demonstrates outstanding academic and extra-curricular leadership; in the graduating year in Arts and Science at the University of Toronto (St. George, Mississauga and Scarborough campuses) and intending to pursue a second degree or studies at the graduate level. **Criteria:** Selection is based on general proficiency or outstanding achievements.

Funds Avail.: Up to $16,650. **To Apply:** Applicants must submit a completed application form together with the required materials and information. **Deadline:** November 26.

7231 ■ Nortel Institute Undergraduate Scholarships *(Undergraduate/Scholarship)*

Purpose: To support students with their educational pursuits. **Focus:** Applied art; Engineering. **Qualif.:** Applicant must be a U of T student and a Canadian citizen or landed immigrant and a resident of Ontario; must be in the second or third year in the Faculty of Applied Science and Engineering, the Faculty of Arts and Science, University of Toronto Mississauga and University of Toronto Scarborough. **Criteria:** Selection is based on financial need, academic merit and on the essay.

Funds Avail.: Approximately $5000. **To Apply:** Applicants must submit a completed application form together with the required materials and information. **Deadline:** November 1.

7232 ■ Ontario Hockey Association War Memorial Scholarships *(Undergraduate/Scholarship)*

Purpose: To support students with their educational pursuits. **Focus:** General studies. **Qualif.:** Applicant must be a Canadian citizen, permanent resident or protected person (recognized convention refugee) and will be enrolled full-time; and a descendent of one who has served with the Canadian forces. **Criteria:** Selection is based on financial need and academic merit.

Funds Avail.: No specific award. **To Apply:** Applicants must submit an online UTAPS application and the proof of service. **Deadline:** January.

7233 ■ Taylor Statten Memorial Fellowships
(Graduate/Scholarship)

Purpose: To support students with their educational pursuits. **Focus:** Education, Physical; Social work. **Qualif.:** Applicant must be a U of T student in post-baccalaureate study in professional field or career related to youth services (such as physical and health education, psychology, teaching, the ministry and social work). **Criteria:** Consideration is given to academically qualified students with career goals and past interests and experience indicate a serious commitment to working with young people.

Funds Avail.: Approximately $2000. **To Apply:** Applicants must submit a completed application form together with the required documents and information. **Deadline:** March 28.

7234 ■ Evald Torokvei Foundation Scholarships
(Graduate/Scholarship)

Purpose: To support students with their educational pursuits. **Focus:** Chemical engineering. **Qualif.:** Applicant must be a graduate student engaged in research in chemicals and plastics. **Criteria:** Selection is based on academic standing, community and university involvement and financial need.

Funds Avail.: $1000. **Number Awarded:** 2. **To Apply:** Applicants must submit a letter of application that includes the applicant's name, address, phone number, student number; area of research, name of Research Director; details of the applicant's involvement in the University community; a statement of financial need (if applicable); transcript of marks; and letters of reference. **Deadline:** November 30.

7235 ■ University of Toronto Accenture Scholarships *(Undergraduate/Scholarship)*

Purpose: To support students with their educational pursuits. **Focus:** Engineering; Computer and information sciences. **Qualif.:** Applicant must be a student of U of T; enrolled in an Engineering, Computer Science or Bachelor of Commerce Degree; a third year student entering the final year of study; have maintained a strong academic background - minimum GPA of 3.0; and actively involved in two or more extracurricular activities. **Criteria:** Selection is based on general proficiency or outstanding achievements.

Funds Avail.: $1500. **To Apply:** Applicants must submit a completed Accenture Scholarship application form along with the required materials and information. **Deadline:** April 25.

7236 ■ University of Toronto SAC Undergraduate Grants *(Undergraduate/Grant)*

Purpose: To support students with their educational pursuits. **Focus:** General studies. **Qualif.:** Applicant must be a UofT full-time undergraduate student maintaining a minimum academic standing of "C". **Criteria:** Selection is based on financial need, and extracurricular involvement in the University Community.

Funds Avail.: $1300. **To Apply:** Applicants must submit a completed application form together with the required materials and information. **Deadline:** November 30.

7237 ■ Frank M. Waddell Scholarships *(Graduate, Undergraduate/Scholarship)*

Purpose: To support students with their educational pursuits. **Focus:** General studies. **Qualif.:** Applicant must be a U of T student coming from Brant County, Ontario; and have a minimum average of B-. **Criteria:** Preference is given to students who have not previously been awarded a Frank M. Waddell Scholarship.

Funds Avail.: $5000. **Number Awarded:** 1. **To Apply:** Applicant must submit a letter outlining how the applicant meet the "Brant County" criteria. **Deadline:** April 25.

7238 ■ University of Virginia

PO Box 400160
Charlottesville, VA 22904-4160
Ph: (434)924-0311
URL: http://www.virginia.edu

7239 ■ Bayly-Tiffany Scholarships
(Undergraduate/Scholarship)

Purpose: To support students at the University of Virginia with their educational pursuits. **Focus:** General studies.

Awards are arranged alphabetically below their administering organizations

Qualif.: Applicants must be students of the University of Virginia and residents of Accomack or Northampton counties in Virginia. **Criteria:** Selection is based on need.

Funds Avail.: No specific amount. **To Apply:** Students do not need to complete a separate application form but are considered automatically when admitted. **Contact:** Student Financial Services, 434-982-6000/866-391-0063, or at faid@virginia.edu.

7240 ■ V. Thomas Forehand, Jr. Scholarships *(Undergraduate/Scholarship)*

Purpose: To support students at the University of Virginia with their educational pursuits. **Focus:** General studies. **Qualif.:** Applicants must be University of Virginia undergraduate students from the city of Chesapeake, and attended Oscar F. Smith High School, Norfolk Academy, or Nansemond-Suffolk Academy. **Criteria:** Selection is based on need.

Funds Avail.: No specific amount. **To Apply:** Students do not need to complete a separate application form but are considered automatically when admitted. **Contact:** Student Financial Services, 434-982-6000, 866-391-0063, or at faid@virginia.edu.

7241 ■ Kaprielian Memorial Scholarships *(Undergraduate/Scholarship)*

Purpose: To support students at the University of Virginia with their educational pursuits. **Focus:** General studies. **Qualif.:** Applicants must be University of Virginia students; U.S. citizens or registered permanent residents of Armenian descent. **Criteria:** Selection is based on financial need.

Funds Avail.: No specific amount. **To Apply:** Students do not need to complete a separate application form but are considered automatically when admitted. **Contact:** Student Financial Services, 434-982-6000, 866-391-0063, or at faid@virginia.edu.

7242 ■ John Allen Love Scholarships *(Graduate, Undergraduate/Scholarship)*

Purpose: To support students at the University of Virginia with their educational pursuits. **Focus:** General studies. **Qualif.:** Applicants must be University of Virginia undergraduate or graduate students residing in Missouri. **Criteria:** Preference is given to applicants residing in St. Louis or St. Louis County, and also to those enrolled in courses in the Department of Government and Foreign Affairs.

Funds Avail.: No specific amount. **To Apply:** Students do not need to complete a separate application form but are considered automatically when admitted. **Contact:** Student Financial Services, 434-982-6000/866-391-0063, or at faid@virginia.edu.

7243 ■ Margaret E. Phillips Scholarships *(Undergraduate/Scholarship)*

Purpose: To support students at the University of Virginia with their educational pursuits. **Focus:** General studies. **Qualif.:** Applicants must be University of Virginia students preparing for and proposing to becoming a minister of the Protestant Episcopal Church in America. **Criteria:** Selection is based on need.

Funds Avail.: No specific amount. **To Apply:** Students do not need to complete a separate application form but are considered automatically when admitted. **Contact:** Student Financial Services, 434-982-6000/866-391-0063, or at faid@virginia.edu.

7244 ■ Charles Fred Wonson Scholarships *(Undergraduate/Scholarship)*

Purpose: To support students at the University of Virginia with their educational pursuits. **Focus:** General studies. **Qualif.:** Applicants must be graduates of Robert E. Lee High School in Staunton, Virginia. **Criteria:** Selection is based on need.

Funds Avail.: No specific amount. **To Apply:** Students do not need to complete a separate application form but are considered automatically when admitted. **Contact:** Student Financial Services, 434-982-6000/866-391-0063, or at faid@virginia.edu.

7245 ■ University of Wisconsin-Madison

432 N Murray St.
Madison, WI 53706-1496
Ph: (608)262-3060
Fax: (608)262-9068
E-mail: askbucky@uwmad.wisc.edu
URL: http://www.wisc.edu

7246 ■ Victor Albright Scholarships-Dane County *(Undergraduate/Scholarship)*

Purpose: To support Wisconsin students in their education. **Focus:** General studies. **Qualif.:** Applicants must be graduates of a Dane County public high school. **Criteria:** Selection is based on merit.

Funds Avail.: $100. **Number Awarded:** Varies. **To Apply:** Students must be nominated by their high school principals or guidance counselors.

7247 ■ Victor Albright Scholarships *(Undergraduate/Scholarship)*

Purpose: To support Wisconsin students in their education. **Focus:** General studies. **Qualif.:** Applicants must be graduates of public high schools within Wisconsin counties (excluding Dane). **Criteria:** Selection is based on merit.

Funds Avail.: $500-$1,000. **Number Awarded:** 2. **To Apply:** Students must be nominated by their high school principals or guidance counselors.

7248 ■ Bascom Hill Society Scholarships *(Undergraduate/Scholarship)*

Purpose: To support students in their education. **Focus:** General studies. **Qualif.:** Applicants must be full-time juniors or seniors with outstanding volunteer contributions to the university and/or their community while maintaining a solid academic record; must have a cumulative GPA of at least a 3.2. Wisconsin and Minnesota residents must have an unmet need of at least $1,000 and out-of-state students must have an unmet need of at least $5,000. **Criteria:** Selection is based on merit and financial need.

Funds Avail.: No amount specified. **Number Awarded:** 1. **To Apply:** Applicants must contact the Office of Undergraduate Academic Awards for more information. **Deadline:** End of March. **Contact:** Office of Undergraduate Academic Awards, Julie Stubbs, at 608-890-0370, or stubbs@wisc.edu.

7249 ■ Mary Ann Brichta Scholarships *(Undergraduate/Scholarship)*

Purpose: To support UW-Madison students in their education. **Focus:** Education, Secondary. **Qualif.:** Applicants must be UW-Madison sophomore, junior, or senior under-

Awards are arranged alphabetically below their administering organizations

represented students of color majoring in elementary or secondary education. **Criteria:** Selection is based on academic excellence.

Funds Avail.: No specific amount. **Number Awarded:** Varies. **To Apply:** Scholarship applications are available from the Office of the Dean. **Deadline:** February.

7250 ■ Patricia Buchanan Memorial Scholarships *(Undergraduate/Scholarship)*

Purpose: To support UW-Madison students in their education. **Focus:** Education, Secondary. **Qualif.:** Applicants must be UW-Madison sophomore, junior, or senior underrepresented students of color majoring in elementary or secondary education. **Criteria:** Selection is based on academic excellence.

Funds Avail.: No specific amount. **Number Awarded:** Varies. **To Apply:** Scholarship applications are available from the Office of the Dean. **Deadline:** February.

7251 ■ Engineering Departmental Scholarships *(Undergraduate/Scholarship)*

Purpose: To support UW-Madison students in their education. **Focus:** Engineering. **Qualif.:** Applicants must be UW-Madison students admitted into a degree-granting department. **Criteria:** Selection is based on academic achievement.

Funds Avail.: Varies. **Number Awarded:** Varies. **To Apply:** Students must contact the specific department office about the application process. **Deadline:** March 15. **Contact:** College of Engineering, Engineering Student Services Office, at 608-262-2473, or hansen@engr.wisc.edu.

7252 ■ Engineering Diversity Affairs Scholarships *(All/Scholarship)*

Purpose: To support UW-Madison students in their education. **Focus:** Engineering. **Qualif.:** Applicants must be UW-Madison women and students of color; must be U.S. citizens or permanent residents enrolled in the College of Engineering. **Criteria:** Selection is based on academic achievement.

Funds Avail.: Varies. **Number Awarded:** Varies. **To Apply:** Students must contact the specific department office or the Engineering Student Services office about the application process. **Deadline:** March 15. **Contact:** College of Engineering, Engineering Student Services Office, at 608-262-2473, or hansen@engr.wisc.edu.

7253 ■ Evjue Foundation, Inc./Capital Times Scholarships *(Undergraduate/Scholarship)*

Purpose: To provide financial assistance to students who wish to pursue their education. **Focus:** General studies. **Qualif.:** Applicant must be a dependent of a regular full-time employee of The Capital Times. **Criteria:** Recipient selection will be based on academic performance.

Funds Avail.: No amount specified. **Number Awarded:** Varies. **To Apply:** Applicants must contact the Evjue Foundation for more information about the scholarship. **Deadline:** February. **Contact:** The Evjue Foundation, Inc., at 608-252-6401.

7254 ■ Edward R. and Hazel N. Felber Scholarships *(Undergraduate/Scholarship)*

Purpose: To financial assistance to students who wish to pursue their education. **Focus:** General studies. **Qualif.:** Applicant must be a dependent of a Madison Gas and Electric (MG&E) employee. **Criteria:** Recipients will be selected based on academic record, leadership, participation in extracurricular activities, and work experience. Financial need is not considered.

Funds Avail.: $2,000. **Number Awarded:** Varies. **To Apply:** Applicants must contact MG&E at 608252-7392 to request for an application. **Deadline:** May 1.

7255 ■ Gay, Lesbian, Bisexual, Transgender Alumni Council Scholarships *(Undergraduate/Scholarship)*

Purpose: To support UW-Madison students in their education. **Focus:** General studies. **Qualif.:** Applicants must be committed to the gay, lesbian, bisexual, and transgender community, and maintaining an outstanding academic achievement. **Criteria:** Priority will be given to the student with the most financial need.

Funds Avail.: Up to $2,000. **Number Awarded:** Varies. **To Apply:** Applicants must contact the Wisconsin Alumni Association for information about the program. **Deadline:** spring. **Contact:** Wisconsin Alumni Association, at 608-262-2551, or glbtac@uwalumni.com, visit the website www.uwalumni.com/glbtac.

7256 ■ Barry M. Goldwater Scholarships *(Undergraduate/Scholarship)*

Purpose: To provide financial assistance to mathematics, science, and engineering students who wish to pursue their education. **Focus:** Mathematics and mathematical sciences; Science; Engineering. **Qualif.:** Applicants must be full-time juniors or seniors with outstanding potential for a career in mathematics, science, or engineering; have at least a B average; rank in the upper quarter of the high schools class; be U.S. citizens or U.S. nationals; and nominated by UW-Madison. **Criteria:** Selection is based on merit.

Funds Avail.: $7500. **Number Awarded:** 300. **To Apply:** Applicants must contact the Office of Undergraduate Academic Awards for information about the scholarship. **Deadline:** November. **Contact:** Office of Undergraduate Academic Awards, Julie Stubbs, at 608-890-0370, or stubbs@wisc.edu.

7257 ■ Human Ecology Continuing Undergraduate Student Scholarships *(Undergraduate/Scholarship)*

Purpose: To support UW-Madison students in their education. **Focus:** Ecology. **Qualif.:** Applicants must be UW-Madison sophomores, juniors, or seniors enrolled in the School of Human Ecology. **Criteria:** Selection is based on scholastic and extracurricular achievement.

Funds Avail.: $2,000. **Number Awarded:** Up to 35. **To Apply:** Applicants must submit the School of Human Ecology Continuing Undergraduate Student Scholarship Application, along with three letters of recommendation, official transcripts, and a resume. **Deadline:** February 15. **Contact:** School of Human Ecology, Office of Student Academic Affairs, at 608-262-2608.

7258 ■ James Jesinski Scholarships *(Undergraduate/Scholarship)*

Purpose: To support students in their education. **Focus:** General studies. **Qualif.:** Applicant must be a dependent of a member of Wisconsin Teamsters Union Locals 43, 56, 75, 200, 344, 354, 446, 563, 579, 662, 695, or 1081. Applicants must also be affiliated with Teamsters Joint Council

39. **Criteria:** Recipient selection will be based on financial need.

Funds Avail.: $2,000. **Number Awarded:** 2. **To Apply:** Applicants must apply for UW-Madison financial aid by March 1. **Deadline:** March 31. **Contact:** Office of Student Financial Services, Scholarship Section, at 608-262-9996, or finaid@finaid.wisc.edu.

7259 ■ Kemper K. Knapp Scholarships *(Undergraduate/Scholarship)*

Purpose: To support UW-Madison students in their education. **Focus:** General studies. **Qualif.:** Student must be Wisconsin residents entering UW-Madison as freshmen. **Criteria:** Recipient selection will be based on academic excellence.

Funds Avail.: Up to $5,000. **Number Awarded:** Varies. **To Apply:** Students do not need to complete a separate application form but are considered automatically when admitted. **Deadline:** Varies. **Contact:** Office of Student Financial Services, Scholarship Section, at 608-262-9996, or finaid@finaid.wisc.edu.

7260 ■ George Koeppel and Roland W. Zinns Scholarships *(Undergraduate/Scholarship)*

Purpose: To support UW-Madison students in their education. **Focus:** Education, Secondary. **Qualif.:** Applicant must be UW-Madison freshmen students; must be Wisconsin residents with permanent home address in Milwaukee County. **Criteria:** Selection is based on academic excellence.

Funds Avail.: No specific amount. **Number Awarded:** Varies. **To Apply:** Scholarship applications are available from the Office of the Dean. **Deadline:** February.

7261 ■ Lawton Minority Retention Grants *(Undergraduate/Scholarship)*

Purpose: To support UW-Madison students in their education. **Focus:** General studies. **Qualif.:** Applicants must be underrepresented students of color; must be Wisconsin or Minnesota residents; and must be sophomore, junior, or senior students. **Criteria:** Recipients will be selected based on financial need.

Funds Avail.: Up to $2,500. **Number Awarded:** Varies. **To Apply:** Applicants must file an application at FAFSA in order to be considered. In addition, applicants must contact the Minority and Disadvantaged Coordinator in the UW-Madison school or college where they are enrolled. **Deadline:** July 15.

7262 ■ McBurney Disability Scholarships *(Undergraduate/Scholarship)*

Purpose: To support UW-Madison students in their education. **Focus:** General studies. **Qualif.:** Applicants must have a documented disability (physical, psychological, sensory, or learning) as verified by the McBurney Disability Resource Center. **Criteria:** Recipients will be selected based on the application materials submitted.

Funds Avail.: $500-$2,500. **Number Awarded:** Up to 20. **To Apply:** Applicants must submit a completed McBurney Scholarship Application along with two letters of recommendation and a current transcript. **Deadline:** April 15.

7263 ■ John P. and Tashia F. Morgridge Scholarships *(Undergraduate/Scholarship)*

Purpose: To support UW-Madison students in their education. **Focus:** Education, Secondary. **Qualif.:** Applicants must be UW-Madison sophomores, juniors, or seniors who are underrepresented students of color. Applicants must be preparing for a teaching career, preferably at the elementary level. **Criteria:** Selection is based on academic achievement and financial need; with preference given to graduates of Wisconsin high schools.

Funds Avail.: Varies. **Number Awarded:** 6. **To Apply:** Scholarship applications are available from the Office of the Dean. **Deadline:** February. **Contact:** School of Education, Office of the Dean, at 608-262-6137, or soeinfo@education.wisc.edu.

7264 ■ Charles S. Pearce Scholarships *(Undergraduate/Prize, Scholarship)*

Purpose: To support students in their education. **Focus:** General studies. **Qualif.:** Applicants must be admitted and enrolled at the university, and must be winners of the JSEHS research competition. **Criteria:** Selection is made by the symposium committee.

Funds Avail.: Wisconsin resident tuition. **Number Awarded:** 1. **To Apply:** Students must contact the Engineering Learning Center. **Deadline:** December. **Contact:** Engineering Learning Center, Sandy Courter, at 608-265-9767, or courter@engr.wisc.edu.

7265 ■ Pi Lambda Theta Scholarships *(Undergraduate/Scholarship)*

Purpose: To support UW-Madison students in their education. **Focus:** Education. **Qualif.:** Applicants must be UW-Madison junior students having the highest GPA in the School of Education; and must have completed at least one full semester (12 credits). **Criteria:** Recipient selection is based on academic excellence.

Funds Avail.: Varies. **Number Awarded:** 2. **To Apply:** Scholarship applications are available from the Office of the Dean. **Deadline:** February. **Contact:** School of Education, Office of the Dean, at 608-262-6137, soeinfo@education.wisc.edu.

7266 ■ Powers-Knapp Scholarships *(Undergraduate/Scholarship)*

Purpose: To support UW-Madison students in their education. **Focus:** General studies. **Qualif.:** Applicants must be incoming freshmen, underrepresented, students of color with an outstanding academic achievement. **Criteria:** Recipients will be selected based on academic achievements.

Funds Avail.: Wisconsin resident tuition for Wisconsin and Minnesota residents. Non-residents receive the difference between resident and non-resident tuition. **Number Awarded:** Up to 60. **To Apply:** Contact the Chancellor's Scholarships Program for more information. **Deadline:** February 1. **Contact:** 608-262-9315.

7267 ■ Reserve Officers Training Corps (ROTC) Scholarships *(Undergraduate/Scholarship)*

Purpose: To support UW-Madison students in their education. **Focus:** Military science and education. **Qualif.:** Applicants must be U.S. citizens enrolled in ROTC programs. **Criteria:** Selection is based on merit.

Funds Avail.: Full tuition and fees, book allowance, and a monthly tax-free stipend. **Number Awarded:** Varies. **To Apply:** Applicants may contact Air Force Aerospace Studies, Air Force ROTC; Military Science, Army ROTC; Naval Sciences, Navy ROTC for more information about the program. **Deadline:** December 1. **Contact:** Air Force

Aerospace Studies, Air Force ROTC at 608-262-3440; Military Science, Army ROTC, at 608-262-3411; Naval Sciences, Navy ROTC, at 608-262-3794 or 800-443-2672.

7268 ■ School of Education Scholarships for Students from Underrepresented Groups *(Undergraduate/Scholarship)*

Purpose: To support UW-Madison students in their education. **Focus:** Education. **Qualif.:** Applicants must be UW-Madison underrepresented students of color with demonstrated financial need majoring in Education. **Criteria:** Selection is based on academic achievement and financial need.

Funds Avail.: Varies. **Number Awarded:** Varies. **To Apply:** Scholarship applications are available from the Office of the Dean. **Contact:** School of Education, Office of the Dean, at 608-262-6137, soeinfo@education.wisc.edu.

7269 ■ School of Pharmacy Continuing Student Scholarships *(Undergraduate/Scholarship)*

Purpose: To support UW-Madison students in their education. **Focus:** Pharmacology; Toxicology; Pharmacy. **Qualif.:** Applicants must be students who are continuing their education in the School of Pharmacy. **Criteria:** Selection is based on academic achievement, extracurricular activities, and financial need.

Funds Avail.: Varies. **Number Awarded:** More than 60. **To Apply:** Applicants must contact the Student Services Office for the details and application materials. **Deadline:** Third week of April. **Contact:** School of Pharmacy at 608-262-6234, or pharminfo@pharmacy.wisc.edu.

7270 ■ University of Wisconsin-Madison Academic Excellence Scholarships *(Undergraduate/Scholarship)*

Purpose: To support Wisconsin students in their education. **Focus:** General studies. **Qualif.:** Applicants must be incoming freshmen; must be Wisconsin residents with the highest GPA in high school class; enrolled as first-year students at a post-secondary institution in Wisconsin. **Criteria:** Selection is based on merit.

Funds Avail.: $2,250. **Number Awarded:** 1-6 per high school. **To Apply:** Applicants must contact their high school guidance counselor for information about the scholarship. **Deadline:** February 15.

7271 ■ University of Wisconsin-Madison African American Alumni Scholarships *(Undergraduate/Scholarship)*

Purpose: To support UW-Madison students in their education. **Focus:** General studies. **Qualif.:** Applicants must be African American full-time students. **Criteria:** Recipients will be selected based on financial need.

Funds Avail.: Varies. **Number Awarded:** 1-2. **To Apply:** Applicants must contact Wisconsin Alumni Association for the application materials and procedures. **Deadline:** June 1. **Contact:** Wisconsin Alumni Association at 608-262-2551, or waa@uwalumni.com.

7272 ■ University of Wisconsin-Madison American Indian Alumni Scholarships *(Undergraduate/Scholarship)*

Purpose: To support UW-Madison students in their education. **Focus:** General studies. **Qualif.:** Applicants must be American Indian full-time students. **Criteria:** Recipients will be selected based on financial need.

Funds Avail.: No specific amount. **Number Awarded:** Varies. **To Apply:** Applicants must file the FAFSA. **Deadline:** July 1. **Contact:** Wisconsin Alumni Association at 608-262-2551, or waa@uwalumni.com.

7273 ■ University of Wisconsin-Madison/CALS Continuing Student Scholarships *(Undergraduate/Scholarship)*

Purpose: To support UW-Madison students in their education. **Focus:** Agricultural sciences; Life sciences. **Qualif.:** Applicant must be a UW-Madison sophomore, junior, or senior student enrolled in the College of Agricultural and Life Sciences (CALS). **Criteria:** Selection is based on academic excellence.

Funds Avail.: $500-$3,000. **Number Awarded:** Up to 200. **To Apply:** Applicants must submit a completed application form together with a letter of recommendation. **Deadline:** February 1.

7274 ■ University of Wisconsin-Madison/CALS Minority Scholarships *(Undergraduate/Scholarship)*

Purpose: To support UW-Madison students in their education. **Focus:** Agricultural sciences; Life sciences. **Qualif.:** Applicants must be UW-Madison students of color enrolled in the College of Agricultural and Life Sciences (CALS). **Criteria:** Selection is based on academic excellence.

Funds Avail.: $500-$2,000. **Number Awarded:** Varies. **To Apply:** Students must submit a completed CALS Scholarship Application along with the letter of recommendation. **Deadline:** January 15.

7275 ■ University of Wisconsin-Madison Chancellor's Scholarships *(Undergraduate/Scholarship)*

Purpose: To support UW-Madison students in their education. **Focus:** General studies. **Qualif.:** Applicants must be incoming freshmen, underrepresented, students of color with outstanding academic achievements. **Criteria:** Recipients will be selected based on academic achievements.

Funds Avail.: Full tuition and an annual book stipend of $800. **Number Awarded:** Up to 40. **To Apply:** Contact the Chancellor's Scholarships Program for more information. **Deadline:** February 1. **Contact:** 608-262-9315.

7276 ■ University of Wisconsin-Madison Hispanic/Latino Alumni Scholarships *(Undergraduate/Scholarship)*

Purpose: To support UW-Madison students in their education. **Focus:** General studies. **Qualif.:** Applicants must be Hispanic or Latino full-time students. **Criteria:** Priority will be given to the student with the most financial need.

Funds Avail.: Varies. **Number Awarded:** 1-2. **To Apply:** Applicants must contact the Wisconsin Alumni Association for information about the program. **Deadline:** June 1. **Contact:** Wisconsin Alumni Association, at 608-262-2551, or glbtac@uwalumni.com, visit the website www.uwalumni.com/glbtac.

7277 ■ University of Wisconsin-Madison Minority Teacher Loans *(Professional Development, Undergraduate/Loan, Scholarship)*

Purpose: To support UW-Madison students in their education. **Focus:** Education, Secondary. **Qualif.:** Applicants must be UW-Madison juniors or seniors from underrepre-

Awards are arranged alphabetically below their administering organizations

sented groups enrolled full-time in a teacher preparation program; must be Wisconsin residents planning to teach in selected school districts in Wisconsin; or degree-holders enrolled in a teacher certification program. **Criteria:** Recipients are selected based on academic excellence.

Funds Avail.: $250-$3000. **Number Awarded:** Varies. **To Apply:** Scholarship applications are available from the Office of the Dean. **Deadline:** Varies.

Remarks: 25 percent of the loan is forgiven for each year the recipient teaches in the selected school district. Teaching for 4 years eliminates 100 percent of the debt. Recipients who do not teach in selected districts must repay the loan at an interest rate of 5 percent.

7278 ■ University of Wisconsin-Madison Music Scholarships *(Undergraduate/Scholarship)*

Purpose: To support UW-Madison students in their education. **Focus:** Music. **Qualif.:** Applicants must be Wisconsin outstanding musicians as demonstrated by a musical background and an audition with the School of Music. **Criteria:** Consideration is based on musical ability, scholarly accomplishments, or a combination of both.

Funds Avail.: $1,000-$5,000. **Number Awarded:** Varies. **To Apply:** Applicants must fill out the School of Music application and attend the audition. **Deadline:** February. **Contact:** School of Music, at 608-263-5986, or baabrams@wisc.edu.

7279 ■ University of Wisconsin-Madison National Merit Scholarships *(Undergraduate/Scholarship)*

Purpose: To support UW-Madison students in their education. **Focus:** General studies. **Qualif.:** Applicants must be entering UW-Madison as freshman; and must have taken the Preliminary SAT/National Merit Scholarship Qualifying Test (PSAT/NMSQT) during the spring semester of the sophomore year or the fall semester of the junior year. **Criteria:** Recipients will be selected based on a review of all applications.

Funds Avail.: $750-$2,000. **Number Awarded:** 5. **To Apply:** Students must file a FAFSA to be considered. **Contact:** Office of Student Financial Services, Scholarship Section, at 608-262-9996, or finaid@finaid.wisc.edu.

7280 ■ University of Wisconsin-Madison Pharmacy New Student Scholarships *(Undergraduate/Scholarship)*

Purpose: To support UW-Madison students in their education. **Focus:** Pharmacology; Toxicology; Pharmacy. **Qualif.:** Applicants must be Wisconsin students entering as first year students in the School of Pharmacy. **Criteria:** Recipients will be selected based on academic achievement, extracurricular activities, and financial need.

Funds Avail.: Varies. **To Apply:** Applicants must contact the Student Services Office for the details and application materials. **Deadline:** First week of May. **Contact:** School of Pharmacy, at 608-262-6234, or pharminfo@pharmacy.wisc.edu.

7281 ■ University of Wisconsin-Madison Single Parent and Adult Scholarships *(Undergraduate/Scholarship)*

Purpose: To support students in their education. **Focus:** General studies. **Qualif.:** Applicants must be single parents or adults enrolled in at least 9 credit units; must be in good academic standing; must be U.S. citizens or permanent residents; must show proof of financial need; and must demonstrate probability for academic success. **Criteria:** Selection is based on merit and need.

Funds Avail.: $1,000-$2,000. **Number Awarded:** Varies. **To Apply:** Applicants must contact the Adult and Student Services Center for more information. **Deadline:** March 1.

7282 ■ Vilas Equity Scholarships *(Undergraduate/Scholarship)*

Purpose: To support UW-Madison students in their education. **Focus:** General studies. **Qualif.:** Applicants must be entering UW-Madison as freshmen. **Criteria:** Recipient selection is based on academic excellence.

Funds Avail.: $400. **Number Awarded:** Varies. **To Apply:** Students are considered automatically when admitted. **Contact:** Office of Student Financial Services, Scholarship Section, at 608-262-9996, or finaid@finaid.wisc.edu.

7283 ■ William F. Vilas Scholarships *(Undergraduate/Scholarship)*

Purpose: To support UW-Madison students in their education. **Focus:** General studies. **Qualif.:** Students must be entering UW-Madison as freshmen; and must have a strong academic performance based on class rank and GPA. **Criteria:** Selection is based on academic excellence.

Funds Avail.: $400. **Number Awarded:** Varies. **To Apply:** Students do not need to complete a separate application form but are considered automatically when admitted. **Contact:** Office of Student Financial Services, Scholarship Section, at 608-262-9996, or finaid@finaid.wisc.edu.

7284 ■ Wisconsin High School Scholarships *(Undergraduate/Scholarship)*

Purpose: To support Wisconsin students in their education. **Focus:** General studies. **Qualif.:** Applicants must be graduates of participating Wisconsin high schools. **Criteria:** Selection is based on merit.

Funds Avail.: No specific amount. **Number Awarded:** Varies. **To Apply:** Applicants must contact their high school guidance councilors for more information.

7285 ■ Wisconsin-Madison Journalism Scholarships *(Undergraduate/Scholarship)*

Purpose: To support UW-Madison students in their education. **Focus:** Journalism. **Qualif.:** Applicants must be UW-Madison junior or senior journalism students who demonstrated academic merit and have gained professional experience. **Criteria:** Consideration is given to underrepresented students of color and students with demonstrated financial need.

Funds Avail.: $500-$1,500. **Number Awarded:** Varies. **To Apply:** Applicants must complete the electronic application available online. **Deadline:** Varies. **Contact:** School of Journalism, Placement Office, at 608-263-4858, or salkin@facstaff.wisc.edu.

7286 ■ Wisconsin-Madison Music Clinic Scholarships *(Undergraduate/Scholarship)*

Purpose: To support UW-Madison students in their education. **Focus:** Music. **Qualif.:** Applicants must be Wisconsin high school graduates with outstanding musical talent who attended the UW-Madison Summer Music Clinic both summers before enrolling at UW-Madison. **Criteria:** Recipients will be selected based on musical ability, scholarly accomplishments, or a combination of both.

Funds Avail.: Wisconsin resident tuition for four years of study. **Number Awarded:** 10. **To Apply:** Applicants must contact the Music Clinic Coordinator for information. **Deadline:** May 15 of junior year in high school. **Contact:** School of Music, Music Clinic Coordinator, at 608-263-2242, or maaley@facstaff.wisc.edu.

7287 ■ Upsilon Pi Epsilon Association

158 Wetlands Edge Rd.
American Canyon, CA 94503
Ph: (530)518-8488
Fax: (707)647-3560
URL: http://upe.acm.org

7288 ■ UPE/ACM Scholarship Awards *(Graduate, Undergraduate/Award/Prize)*

Purpose: To encourage academic excellence for students in the computing discipline. To raise the importance of academic achievement and professional commitment in our future computer professionals. **Focus:** Computer and information sciences. **Qualif.:** Applicant must be a graduate or undergraduate students, who are ACM members and members of the ACM student chapter at their academic institution. **Criteria:** Applicants will be selected based on their application form and other supporting documents.

Funds Avail.: $1,000. **To Apply:** Applicant must submit a three letter of recommendation (one letter indicating class rank from Department Chair or Advisor); must have a certificate copy of the three years (minimum) official academic transcripts; must have a statement of your participation in the ACM student chapter at their academic institution. Application forms are available in the website address and must be sent together with the other application materials to: ACM Local Activities, 1515 Broadway, New York, NY 10036.

7289 ■ UPE Scholarship Awards *(Graduate, Undergraduate/Award/Prize)*

Purpose: To promote computing sciences and to encourage its contribution to the enhancement of knowledge. **Focus:** Computer and information sciences. **Qualif.:** Applicant must be in graduate or undergraduate student levels. **Criteria:** Application form and other documents will be evaluated by the Executive Council of UPE.

Funds Avail.: No specific amount. **To Apply:** Application forms are available in the website address and must be sent to: Upsilon Pi Epsilon, California State University, Chico, 158 Wetlands Edge Rd., American Canyon, CA, 94503. **Deadline:** June 15.

7290 ■ Urban Affairs Association

298 Graham Hall, University of delaware
Newark, DE 19716
Ph: (302)831-1681
Fax: (302)831-4225
E-mail: uaa@udel.edu
URL: http://www.udel.edu

7291 ■ Alma H. Young Emerging Scholar Award *(Doctorate/Scholarship)*

Purpose: To support the development of university education, research, and service programs in urban affairs. **Focus:** General studies. **Qualif.:** Applicants must be pursuing doctoral research in urban affairs, regardless of academic discipline; must have finished the required course work; passed the comprehensive examinations; and have an approved dissertation proposal. **Criteria:** Recipients are selected based on scholarship and commitment to urban issues.

Funds Avail.: $1,000. **To Apply:** Applicant must submit a nomination letter from a current UAA member; a provide two-to-three page, double-spaced personal statement by the applicant describing urban interests, engagement, and career plans; a curriculum vitae; a prospectus for the dissertation of 1,500-2,000 words that indicate the research questions, argument or hypotheses, literature and data resources, methodology, and nature of expected findings. **Deadline:** February 18.

7292 ■ Urban Financial Services Coalition

1200 G St., Ste. 800
Washington, DC 20005
Ph: (202)289-8335
Fax: (202)682-3058
Free: 800-996-8335
E-mail: ufsc@ufscnet.org
URL: http://www.ufscnet.org

7293 ■ Herbert W. Whiteman, Jr. Scholarships *(Graduate, Undergraduate/Scholarship)*

Purpose: To provide assistance to minority students in their education. **Focus:** Banking; Finance. **Qualif.:** Applicants must have a 3.0 GPA on a 4.0 scale; pursuing an undergraduate or advanced degree in finance or business at an accredited college/university. **Criteria:** Applicants will be selected based on leadership, career goals and on the essay.

Funds Avail.: No specific amount. **To Apply:** Application form is available at the website. Applicants must submit a completed application form together with a reference letter; acceptance letter from the college/university; and a 400- to 500-word essay to: UFSC Foundation, Attn: Herbert W. Whiteman, Jr. Scholarship Fund, 2121 K. St. NW, Suite 800, Washington, DC 20037.

7294 ■ Urban and Land Institute

1025 Thomas Jefferson St. NW, Ste. 500
Washington, DC 20007
Ph: (202)624-7000
Fax: (202)624-7140
Free: 800-321-5011
E-mail: customerservice@uli.org
URL: http://www.uli.org

7295 ■ Kenneth M. Good Graduate Students Fellowship Program *(Undergraduate/Fellowship)*

Purpose: To promote interdisciplinary education and to encourage excellence in real estate-related studies. **Focus:** Real Estate. **Qualif.:** Applicants must be graduating students who are studying real estate, real estate development, or related subjects at a major North American university. **Criteria:** Recipients are selected based on financial need of the applicant and result of the nomination.

Funds Avail.: $5,000. **Number Awarded:** 8. **To Apply:** Applicants must submit evidence that they are currently at-

Awards are arranged alphabetically below their administering organizations

tending a real estate degree program.

7296 ■ Urban League of Metropolitan Denver

5900 E 39th Ave.
Denver, CO 80207
Ph: (303)388-5861
E-mail: adminassistant@denverurbanleague.org
URL: http://www.denverurbanleague.org

7297 ■ University of Phoenix First Chance Scholarship Fund *(Undergraduate/Scholarship)*

Purpose: To promote the life changing benefits of education and honor individuals who have shown desire to improve their lives and the lives of those around them through education. **Focus:** General studies. **Qualif.:** Applicants must meet one of the following criteria: must be legal residents of the United States; have a valid visa that does not prohibit educational studies; have been granted temporary protection status along with approved Notice of Action issued by Citizen Immigration Services and verified through CIS Form g-845; or have been granted asylum along with the approved Notice of Action issued by the Citizen Immigration Services; are not receiving 100% tuition reimbursement; are not employees or family members of Apollo Group, Inc. University of Phoenix, Western International University, Institute for Professional Development or any other subsidiary of Apollo Group Inc. **Criteria:** Preference will be given to those students who have met one of the criteria.

Funds Avail.: No specific amount. **To Apply:** Applicants must submit the following: a complete, signed application, together with all supporting documentation, if any, by the deadline date listed below. The completion of the application form does not create an obligation to award a scholarship to applicant. Submit a complete questionnaire. High importance will be placed on the applicant's desire to advance in their education, with an emphasis on furthering their careers, and their impact in the community for which they reside. To be considered the essay must meet the following requirements: Each of the four questions should be answered in complete sentences and paragraph format with approximately 4-7 sentences, Double spaced, 12 point font 8 x 11 paper, and pages must be paper-clipped together (no staples). **Deadline:** June 29. **Contact:** Urban League of Metropolitan Denver Inc. at the above address (see entry 7296).

7298 ■ USDA Animal and Plant Health Inspection Service

USDA, APHIS, Human Resources/Employment
4700 River Rd., Unit 106
Riverdale, MD 20737
Ph: (301)734-5596
URL: http://www.aphis.usda.gov

7299 ■ PPQ William F. Helms Student Scholarships *(Undergraduate/Scholarship)*

Purpose: To provide financial assistance to academically qualified students who are enrolled in college-level programs related to agriculture or the biological sciences. **Focus:** General studies. **Qualif.:** Applicants must be: United States citizens; enrolled in an accredited college or university within the U.S.; sophomores or juniors in good academic standing (must maintain an at least 2.5 grade point average); enrolled in programs related to agriculture or the biological sciences; must agree to work for the agency during school breaks (both summer and holiday periods) a minimum of 640 hours prior to completion of studies. **Criteria:** Applicants are evaluated based on academic achievement.

Funds Avail.: No specific amount. **To Apply:** Applicants must submit completed application which contains an Optional Application for Federal Employment (OF-612) or resume; a personal letter that describes their interests, goals and chosen career plans, explains how they envision their ability will contribute to the PPQ mission, outlines why they should be selected for this program over other candidates, and lists the permanent addresses at which they can be contacted all year. Applicants must also submit transcripts of their college work to date; three letters of recommendation from people not related to them; documentation of service, if they have served in the U.S. Armed Forces. **Deadline:** March 1.

7300 ■ Saul T. Wilson, Jr. Scholarships *(Graduate, Undergraduate/Scholarship)*

Purpose: To provide financial assistance to graduates and undergraduates of veterinary medicine and biomedical sciences. **Focus:** Veterinary; Medicine, Veterinary; Biomedical sciences. **Qualif.:** Applicants must be U.S. citizens enrolled in an accredited college or university within the United States as full-time students in good academic standing; must be undergraduate students who have completed at least 2 years (60 semester or 90 quarter hours) of a 4-year preveterinary medicine or other biomedical science curriculum or graduate students who have completed not more than 1 year (18 semester or 27 quarter hours) of study in veterinary medicine; must be willing to work for the agency during school breaks (both summer and holiday periods). **Criteria:** Applicants are evaluated based on academic achievement.

Funds Avail.: $5,000 up to $10,000. **To Apply:** Applicants must submit resume, including current and summer addresses and telephone numbers; transcripts of all college courses completed; letter of acceptance, if entering graduate school; three letters of recommendation from college officials; original essay, not exceeding 500 words on the topic: "Why I should receive a Saul T. Wilson, Jr., Scholarship and what contributions I would make to APHIS, Veterinary Services"; documentation of service, if they have served in the U.S. Armed Forces. **Deadline:** March 1.

7301 ■ USTA Tennis and Education Foundation

70 W Road Oak Ln.
White Plains, NY 10604
Ph: (914)696-7223
E-mail: eliezer@usta.com
URL: http://www.usta.com

7302 ■ Marian Wood Baird Scholarships *(Undergraduate/Scholarship)*

Purpose: To provide scholarships to deserving youngsters who have participated in the United States Tennis Association. **Focus:** General studies. **Qualif.:** Applicants must have a strong involvement in extracurricular activities, course work and community service; must exhibit Financial Need; must be involved in an organized community tennis program such as USTA School Tennis, NJTL, USTA Team Tennis, etc.; must be entering first year of undergraduate work as a full-time student in a four-year college/university program; must have a minimum of 3.0 GPA on a 4.0 scale.

Criteria: Scholarship is given based on academic performance.

Funds Avail.: $15,000. **To Apply:** Applicants must submit in one envelope the following required forms and supporting documents: A typed or clearly printed application signed by the applicant and parent or guardian; A typed or clearly printed endorsement from a faculty member from the applicant's high school and from a coach/program director; A typed endorsement from an individual of the applicant's choice; An official high school transcript; ACT/SAT examination scores; The applicant's official financial aid form; and a current photograph of the applicant. **Deadline:** February 8.

7303 ■ Dwight F. Davis Memorial Scholarships *(Undergraduate/Scholarship)*

Purpose: To provide scholarships to qualified high school seniors. **Focus:** General studies. **Qualif.:** Applicants must be high school seniors with strong involvement in extracurricular activities, course work and community service; must exhibit financial need; must be actively involved in an organized community tennis program such as USTA School Tennis, NJTL, USTA Team Tennis, etc.; must be entering the first year of undergraduate work as a full-time student in a four-year college/university program. **Criteria:** Scholarship is given based on academic performance.

Funds Avail.: $7,500. **Number Awarded:** 2. **To Apply:** Applicants must submit in one envelope the following required forms and supporting documents: A typed or clearly printed application signed by the applicant and parent or guardian; a typed or clearly printed endorsement from a faculty member from the applicant's high school and from a coach/program director; a typed endorsement from an individual of the applicant's choice; an official high school transcript; ACT/SAT examination scores; applicant's official financial aid form; and a current photograph. **Deadline:** February 8.

7304 ■ Eve Kraft Education and College Scholarships *(Undergraduate/Scholarship)*

Purpose: To provide scholarships to qualified high school seniors. **Focus:** General studies. **Qualif.:** Applicants must be high school seniors with strong involvement in extracurricular activities, course work and community service; must exhibit financial need; must be actively involved in an organized community tennis program such as USTA School Tennis, NJTL, USTA Team Tennis, etc.; must be entering the first year of undergraduate work as a full-time student in a four-year college/university program. **Criteria:** Scholarship is given based on academic performance.

Funds Avail.: $2,500. **To Apply:** Applicants must submit in one envelope the following required forms and supporting documents: A typed or clearly printed application signed by the applicant and parent or guardian; a typed or clearly printed endorsement from a faculty member from the applicant's high school and from a coach/program director; a typed endorsement from an individual of the applicant's choice; an official high school transcript; ACT/SAT examination scores; applicant's official financial aid form; and a current photograph. **Deadline:** February 8.

Remarks: The scholarship is partially supported by Robert Kraft and family.

7305 ■ Dwight Mosley Scholarships *(Undergraduate/Scholarship)*

Purpose: To provide scholarship to high school seniors of ethnically diverse heritage. **Focus:** General studies. **Qualif.:** Applicants must be high school seniors with strong involvement in extracurricular activities, course work and community service; must exhibit financial need; must be actively involved in an organized community tennis program such as USTA School Tennis, NJTL, USTA Team Tennis, etc.; must be entering the first year of undergraduate work as a full-time student in a four-year college/university program. **Criteria:** Scholarship is given based on academic performance.

Funds Avail.: $10,000. **Number Awarded:** 2. **To Apply:** Applicants must submit in one envelope the following required forms and supporting documents: A typed or clearly printed application signed by the applicant and parent or guardian; a typed or clearly printed endorsement from a faculty member from the applicant's high school and from a coach/program director; a typed endorsement from an individual of the applicant's choice; an official high school transcript; ACT/SAT examination scores; applicant's official financial aid form; and a current photograph. **Deadline:** February 8.

7306 ■ USTA Tennis and Education Foundation College Education Scholarships *(Undergraduate/Scholarship)*

Purpose: To provide scholarships to qualified high schools. **Focus:** General Studies. **Qualif.:** Applicants must be high school seniors with strong involvement in extracurricular activities, course work and community service; must exhibit financial need; must be actively involved in an organized community tennis program such as USTA School Tennis, NJTL, USTA Team Tennis, etc.; must be entering the first year of undergraduate work as a full-time student in a four-year college/university program. **Criteria:** Scholarship is given based on academic performance.

Funds Avail.: $6,000. **To Apply:** Applicants must submit in one envelope the following required forms and supporting documents: A typed or clearly printed application signed by the applicant and parent or guardian; a typed or clearly printed endorsement from a faculty member from the applicant's high school and from a coach/program director; a typed endorsement from an individual of the applicant's choice; an official high school transcript; ACT/SAT examination scores; applicant's official financial aid form; and a current photograph. **Deadline:** February 8.

7307 ■ USTA Tennis and Education Foundation College Textbook Scholarships *(Undergraduate/Scholarship)*

Purpose: To provide a one-time award to assist students in purchasing textbooks or supplies. **Focus:** General studies. **Qualif.:** Applicants must be high school seniors with strong involvement in extracurricular activities, course work and community service; must exhibit financial need; must be actively involved in an organized community tennis program such as USTA School Tennis, NJTL, USTA Team Tennis, etc.; must be entering the first year of undergraduate work as a full-time student in a four-year college/university program. **Criteria:** Scholarship is given based on academic performance.

Funds Avail.: $1,000. **To Apply:** Applicants must submit in one envelope the following required forms and supporting documents: A typed or clearly printed application signed by the applicant and parent or guardian; a typed or clearly printed endorsement from a faculty member from the applicant's high school and from a coach/program director; a typed endorsement from an individual of the applicant's choice; an official high school transcript; ACT/SAT examination scores; applicant's official financial aid form; and a current photograph. **Deadline:** February 8.

7308 ■ Utility Workers Union of America

815 16th St. NW
Washington, DC 20006
Ph: (202)974-8200
Fax: (202)974-8201
E-mail: webmaster@uwua.net
URL: http://www.uwua.net

7309 ■ Utility Workers Union of America Scholarship Program *(Undergraduate/Scholarship)*

Purpose: To identify and honor exceptionally able high school students; to provide a system of services for corporations, foundations, and other organizations that wish to sponsor college undergraduate scholarships for outstanding students who interest them. **Focus:** General studies. **Qualif.:** Applicants must be high school students who are sons and daughters of active members of UWUA; must be a U.S. citizen and have a permanent residence in the United States. **Criteria:** Recipients will be selected based on academic record throughout high school, significant activities and contributions to the school community, test scores, recommendations, and the student's essay about personal characteristics, activities, plan, and goals.

Funds Avail.: $500-$2,000. **To Apply:** Applicants must fill out the application form; must take the PSAT/NMSQT; must obtain a copy of the Official Student Guide to the PSAT/NMSQT from the high school counselor and make arrangements with the school to take the PSAT/NMSQT. **Deadline:** December 31.

7310 ■ Vector Marketing Corporation

5301 Limestone Rd., Ste. 105
Wilmington, DE 19808
Ph: (302)372-8020
E-mail: campus@cutco.com
URL: http://www.vectorscholarships.com

7311 ■ All-American Vector Marketing Scholarship Program *(Undergraduate/Scholarship)*

Purpose: To recognize students who have excelled in their roles as sales representatives. **Focus:** Marketing and distribution. **Qualif.:** Applicants must be full-time students at an accredited college or university; active in the business at the conclusion of the Scholarship Race. **Criteria:** Selection will be based on sales performance. Scholastic achievement and financial need are not taken into consideration.

Funds Avail.: $250-$1,000. **To Apply:** Applicants must provide current official transcript as well as a copy of current semester registration. Applicants may contact Vector Marketing Corporation for other requirements. **Contact:** Vector Marketing Corporation at the above address (see entry 7310).

7312 ■ Vector Marketing Canadian Scholarship Awards *(Undergraduate/Scholarship)*

Purpose: To provide financial assistance to student sales representatives and the institutions of higher education they attend. **Focus:** Marketing and distribution. **Qualif.:** Applicants must be full-time university or college students working with Vector. **Criteria:** Scholarship recipients are selected based on the committee's review of the application materials.

Funds Avail.: No specific amount. **To Apply:** Applicants must provide current official transcript as well as a copy of current semester registration. Applicants may contact Vector Marketing Corporation for other requirements. **Contact:** Vector Marketing Corporation at the above address (see entry 7310).

7313 ■ Ventura County Medical Association Alliance

601 E Daily Dr.
Camarillo, CA 93010
Ph: (805)484-6822
E-mail: info@vcma-alliance.com
URL: http://www.vcma-alliance.com

7314 ■ Ventura County Medical Association Alliance Scholarships *(Undergraduate/Scholarship)*

Purpose: To educate and protect the health and well-being of the people of Ventura County. **Focus:** Medicine. **Qualif.:** Applicants must be accepted or currently enrolled in a health career program; must be students of Ventura County. **Criteria:** Recipients are selected based on academic performance and financial need.

Funds Avail.: No specific amount. **To Apply:** Applicants must submit a copy of health career acceptance notification, most recent transcript or progress report (for students attending technical/vocational school), brief biography, recent photo, completed application form and letter of recommendation from a person who can speak to the character and motivation of applicant. **Deadline:** June 20.

7315 ■ Vesalius Trust

20751 W Chartwell Dr.
Kildeer, IL 60047
Ph: (847)540-8671
Fax: (847)540-8681
E-mail: vesaliustrust@aol.com
URL: http://www.vesaliustrust.org

7316 ■ Inez Demonet Scholarships *(Graduate/Scholarship)*

Purpose: To support students with promising contributions to the profession of medical illustration. **Focus:** Visual arts. **Qualif.:** Applicant must be a second year student in a graduate program in medical illustration accredited by the Association of Medical Illustrators. **Criteria:** Applicants are evaluated based on academic performance, quality of artwork and references, and evidence of accomplishments.

Funds Avail.: $2,000. **To Apply:** Application forms are available at the website. Applicants must prepare a resume (1 page); transcripts; references; portfolio of five portfolio pieces; and an essay. **Deadline:** February 8. **Contact:** Wendy Hiller Gee, VT Student Grants and Scholarships, 650-244-4320 or wendy.hillergee@krames.com.

7317 ■ Vesalius Trust Student Scholarships *(Undergraduate/Scholarship)*

Purpose: To support students enrolled in medical illustration programs. **Focus:** Visual arts. **Qualif.:** Applicants must be enrolled in a medical illustration program and must have

Awards are arranged alphabetically below their administering organizations.

completed one year of the curriculum. **Criteria:** Applicants are judged based on background, education and project concept, design and production plan.

Funds Avail.: No specific amount. **To Apply:** Applicants must submit an application form; a resume; graduate project description; budget and timeline; transcripts; preceptor form and faculty advisor form. **Deadline:** November 9. **Contact:** Wendy Hiller Gee, VT Student Grants and Scholarships, 650-244-4320 or wendy.hillergee@krames.com.

7318 ■ Vietnam Veterans of America

8605 Cameron St., Ste. 400
Silver Spring, MD 20910
Ph: (301)585-4000
Fax: (301)585-0519
Free: (180)0882-1316
E-mail: jrowan@vva.org
URL: http://www.vva.org

7319 ■ Mike Nash Memorial Scholarships *(Undergraduate/Scholarship)*

Purpose: To provide support and assistance to veterans in securing earned benefits from the Department of Veterans Affairs. **Focus:** General studies. **Qualif.:** Applicants must be dependent children, grandchildren, orphans, and widows of deceased Vietnam Veterans. **Criteria:** Recipients are selected based on the completeness of the application, demonstrated need, and grade point average.

Funds Avail.: No amount specified. **Number Awarded:** 1. **To Apply:** Applicants must submit a completed application form; a high school or college transcript; photocopy of SAT, ACT, or other acknowledged testing source results; a letter of acceptance from a college, university or post-secondary training institution; a copy of form DD-214 and death certificate from the related Vietnam era veteran, if the veteran is deceased. Applicants must provide a statement describing financial need; include a copy of the applicant's parent and the applicant's most current personal income tax form; two letters of reference from current or former teachers, academic advisors, employers, or ministers attesting the applicant's character; and a letter in the applicant's own words, expressing current educational goals and objectives, individual accomplishments and any other personal information that may assist in the selection process. **Deadline:** May 31.

7320 ■ Vietnamese American Scholarship Foundation

PO Box 429
Stafford, TX 77497
E-mail: scholarships@vietscholarships.org
URL: http://www.vietscholarships.org

7321 ■ Danny T. Le Memorial Scholarships *(High School, Undergraduate/Scholarship)*

Purpose: To provide financial assistance to students of Vietnamese descent from the Greater Houston area for pursuing further education. **Focus:** General studies. **Qualif.:** Applicants must be of Vietnamese descent; must be graduated or graduating from a high school in the Greater Houston Area and pursuing degree at an accredited 4-year college or university. **Criteria:** Applicants are evaluated based on academic excellence; compassion and desire to help others; strong will and determination to achieve their goals.

Funds Avail.: $1,250. **To Apply:** Applicants must download and complete the application form and submit it with their resume, an essay and a letter of recommendation. **Deadline:** May 5.

7322 ■ Le Hoang Nguyen (LHN) College Scholarships *(High School/Scholarship)*

Purpose: To provide financial assistance to outstanding graduating high school seniors attending college in the upcoming fall semester. **Focus:** General studies. **Qualif.:** Applicants must be Vietnamese descendants and residents of the state of Texas; must be graduating high school seniors with a GPA of 3.0 or higher; must be ranked in the top 10% of graduating high school class; must attend the first semester at an accredited college or university immediately following notification of the scholarship award. **Criteria:** Applicants are evaluated based on academic achievement and financial need.

Funds Avail.: $500. **Number Awarded:** 1. **To Apply:** Applicants must complete the online application; upload resume and essays with online application and submit recommendation online. **Deadline:** May 5.

7323 ■ The Thuy Nguyen Scholarships *(High School/Scholarship)*

Purpose: To provide financial assistance to high school senior students for furthering their education. **Focus:** General studies. **Qualif.:** Applicants must be graduating high school seniors from Houston or the surrounding area; must have a cumulative GPA of 3.5 or higher; must be descendants of at least one Vietnamese parent; and must have a family annual income of less than $50,000. **Criteria:** Applicants are evaluated based on financial need.

Funds Avail.: No specific amount. **To Apply:** Applicants must complete online application form; upload resume and essay with online application and submit recommendation online. **Deadline:** May 5.

7324 ■ Vera Tran Memorial Scholarships *(Undergraduate/Scholarship)*

Purpose: To provide financial assistance to graduating high school seniors of Vietnamese descent wishing to pursue further education. **Focus:** General studies. **Qualif.:** Applicants must be of Vietnamese descent, graduating high school seniors from Houston or the surrounding area who are planning to pursue an education at an accredited 4-year college or university. **Criteria:** Applicants are evaluated based on demonstrated dedication to academic excellence; passion for learning; compassion and desire to help others; pursuit of their dreams; and proven leadership.

Funds Avail.: $2,000. **To Apply:** Applicants must complete the online application and submit it with their resume; must also send one transcript and recommendation. **Deadline:** May 5.

7325 ■ Violin Society of America

48 Academy St.
Poughkeepsie, NY 12601
Ph: (845)452-7557
URL: http://www.vsa.to

7326 ■ Violin Society of America Scholarships *(Undergraduate/Scholarship)*

Purpose: To provide financial assistance for needy and deserving students of the art of violin and bow making and

Awards are arranged alphabetically below their administering organizations

restoration. **Focus:** Music. **Qualif.:** Applicant must be a student U.S. citizen, have satisfactorily completed at least one full year of study in the program, have shown serious effort, talent and future promise and have financial need. **Criteria:** Applicants will be evaluated by the administrator of the program and will be recommended to the VSA.

Funds Avail.: No amount mentioned. **To Apply:** Teachers and faculty of leading American violin making schools annually submit the names of those students most worthy of scholarship aid.

7327 ■ Virginia Foundation for Independent Colleges

8010 Ridge Rd., Ste. B
Richmond, VA 23229-7288
Ph: (804)288-6609
Fax: (804)282-4635
Free: 800-230-6757
E-mail: info@vfic.org
URL: http://www.vfic.org

7328 ■ Hilb, Rogal and Hobbs Scholarships *(Undergraduate/Scholarship)*

Purpose: To provide financial assistance to students who will be juniors at a VFIC member college. **Focus:** Marketing and distribution; Business; Economics; Finance; Mathematics and Mathematical sciences. **Qualif.:** Applicants must be full-time students at one of the fifteen private colleges/universities associated with the Virginia Foundation for Independent Colleges; must be first-semester juniors at the time of application with a cumulative grade point average of at least 3.0 on a 4.0 scale, who have declared, or intend to declare a major in one of the following disciplines: marketing, business, economics, finance, mathematics or related fields; must be U.S. citizens. **Criteria:** Applicants will be evaluated based on demonstrated financial need and academic achievement.

Funds Avail.: $2,500. **To Apply:** Applicants must submit all the required application information. **Deadline:** November 1.

7329 ■ Norfolk Southern Scholarships *(Undergraduate/Scholarship)*

Purpose: To provide financial assistance to students who will be juniors at a VFIC member college to defray educational expenses. **Focus:** Economics; Business; Finance; Accounting. **Qualif.:** Applicants must be full-time students at one of the fifteen private colleges/universities associated with the VFIC; first semester juniors at the time of application with a cumulative GPA of at least 3.0 on a 4.0 scale and declared major in economics, business, finance, accounting or related fields, and interested in a career in a Fortune 500 corporate setting; must be United States citizens. **Criteria:** Applicants will be evaluated based on academic achievement and financial need.

Funds Avail.: $5,000. **To Apply:** Applicants must submit resume, college transcript, two letters of recommendation and the completed application form. **Deadline:** November 1.

7330 ■ Phillip Morris USA Scholarships *(Undergraduate/Scholarship)*

Purpose: To provide financial assistance for the students in their junior year at a VFIC college or university. **Focus:** Accounting; Biology; Business; Chemistry; Computer and information sciences; Economics; Engineering; Finance; Physics. **Qualif.:** Applicants must be U.S. citizens and current full-time sophomores attending a VFIC college or university (students from underrepresented populations are encouraged to apply); have minimum of 3.5 cumulative GPA; committed to applying for an internship with Phillip Morris USA for the summer after junior year; have declared, or intend to declare, a major in one of the following disciplines: accounting, biology, business, chemistry, computer science, economics, engineering, finance, or physics. **Criteria:** Applicants are evaluated based on academic achievement and financial need.

Funds Avail.: $5,000. **To Apply:** Applicants must submit completed application form along with two letters of recommendation and other required application information. **Deadline:** November 1.

7331 ■ Witt Mares Scholarships *(Undergraduate/Scholarship)*

Purpose: To provide financial assistance for students who are current juniors of VFIC institutions. **Focus:** Accounting. **Qualif.:** Applicants must be full-time students at one of the five pre-selected private colleges/universities associated with the Virginia Foundation for Independent Colleges: Lynchburg College, Shenandoah University, Marymount University, Virginia Wesleyan College, Randolph-Macon College; must have a cumulative grade point average of at least a 3.0 on a 4.0 scale; be a junior at the time of application; be an accounting major, or have a related major or minor with coursework which includes completion of the Introductory Accounting sequence (sophomore year) and planning to complete the Intermediate Accounting sequence in their junior year; must be citizens of the United States of America. **Criteria:** Recipients will be selected by the staff of the Virginia Foundation for Independent Colleges with consultation from the Witt Mares Human Resources Manager.

Funds Avail.: $2,500. **To Apply:** Applicants must submit all the required application information. **Deadline:** November 1.

7332 ■ Virginia Tech Multicultural Programs and Services

150 Squires Student Center
Blacksburg, VA 24061
Ph: (540)231-8584
Fax: (540)231-0945
E-mail: mps@vt.edu
URL: http://www.mps.vt.edu

7333 ■ Emma L. Bowen Foundation Scholarships for Minority Interests in Media work/study Program *(Undergraduate/Scholarship)*

Purpose: To create a career opportunities in media industry for minority youth that focuses on scholastic achievement, direct work experience and professional development. **Focus:** General studies. **Qualif.:** Applicant must be African American, Hispanic, Asian or Native American rising high school senior, graduating high school senior or college freshman; must have a cumulative GPA of at least 3.0 and interest in pursuing a career in media industry; must be planning to attend a four-year accredited college or university; must be a U.S. citizen or a legal resident of United States and can speak and write English fluently. **Criteria:** Recipients are selected based on academic

Awards are arranged alphabetically below their administering organizations

performance and financial need.

Funds Avail.: No specific amount. **To Apply:** Applicants must submit an official transcript, at least two educational references from teachers and advisors and a 500 to 1,000 word essay; must submit an original and two copies of application in an envelope. **Deadline:** May 9.

7334 ■ Brown and Caldwell Minority Scholarships *(Undergraduate/Scholarship)*

Purpose: To assist Virginia Tech in creating a welcoming environment that affirms and celebrates the diversity of its community particularly those from underrepresented and historically marginalized populations. **Focus:** General studies. **Qualif.:** Applicants must be full-time minority students in their junior year of study; must have a minimum 3.0 GPA and must be majoring in engineering and science-related studies; must be U.S. citizens or permanent residents; must be able to commit to an eight-week summer internship. **Criteria:** Recipients are selected based on academic performance and financial need.

Funds Avail.: $3,000. **To Apply:** Applicants must submit a 250 word essay stating the reasons of choosing environmental disciplines as major. **Deadline:** May 1.

7335 ■ The Voice Foundation

1721 Pine St.
Philadelphia, PA 19103
Ph: (215)735-7999
Fax: (215)735-9293
E-mail: office@voicefoundation.org
URL: http://www.voicefoundation.org

7336 ■ Institutional Grants: Educational and Research Projects *(All/Grant)*

Purpose: TO support voice research and care. **Focus:** Music, Vocal. **Qualif.:** Applicants must be conducting research or projects about human voice. **Criteria:** Proposals are reviewed by a panel selected by the Chairman of the Scientific Advisory Board.

Funds Avail.: $10,000-15,000. **To Apply:** Applicants must complete the online application process.

7337 ■ Voluntary Protection Programs Participants' Association

7600-E Leesburg Pike, Ste. 440
Falls Church, VA 22043-2004
Ph: (703)761-1146
Fax: (703)761-1148
E-mail: administrator@vpppa.org
URL: http://www.vpppa.org

7338 ■ Delta/VPPPA Safety, Health and Environmental Scholarships *(Undergraduate/Scholarship)*

Purpose: To encourage students' active participation in occupational safety, health and/or environmental outreach programs in their schools, community and/or workplace. **Focus:** Environmental conservation; Occupational safety and health. **Qualif.:** Applicants must be students who are enrolled or enrolling in a college or university (graduate or undergraduate level) or a vocational school pursuing a degree in the environmental, occupational safety and/or health field; they must be either employed at a VPPPA Full, Corporate or Associate member company or the child or grandchild of an employee; and must have had or have at least a 2.5 GPA on a scale of 4.0. **Criteria:** Recipients are chosen on the basis of demonstrated occupational safety, health and/or environmental outreach efforts in their schools, communities and/or workplace, leadership skills, extracurricular activities, involvement in professional organizations, communication skills and other awards and honors earned at educational institutions or at their place of employment; Preference is given to applicants from airline and associated aviation industries.

Funds Avail.: No specific amount. **To Apply:** Applicants must submit a completed application form and supporting documents to: VPPPA, Inc., Attn: Awards Committee, 7600-E Leesburg Pike, Ste. 440, Falls Church, VA 22043-2004; or fax to: (703) 761-1148, Attn: Awards Committee. **Deadline:** May 1.

Remarks: The scholarship supports Delta's "Force for Global Good" initiative that focuses on Breast Cancer Awareness, The Red Cross, Habitat for Humanity and environmental responsibility.

7339 ■ VPPPA William Sullivan Scholarships *(Graduate, Undergraduate/Scholarship)*

Purpose: To recognize an employee at a VPPPA full member site who has made significant contributions to the VPP program at his or her site. **Focus:** Environmental conservation; Occupational safety and health. **Qualif.:** Applicants must be a current employee at a VPP site (the site must be a VPPPA full member in good standing); must demonstrate their contributions to the VPP site; must be pursuing a degree (undergraduate or graduate) either part-time or full-time; and must have at least a 2.5 GPA on a scale of 4.0. **Criteria:** Recipient is chosen based on merit.

Funds Avail.: No specific amount. **To Apply:** Applicants must submit a completed application form, an official transcript and a reference letter relating to your VPP involvement at your site from a site VPP coordinator, operations manager, site EHS staff, OSHA, Regional VPPPA Chapter Chairperson, and others. Forward to: VPPPA, Inc., Attn: Awards Committee, 7600-E Leesburg Pike, Ste. 440, Falls Church, VA 22043-2004; or fax to: (703) 761-1148, Attn: Awards Committee. **Deadline:** May 1.

7340 ■ VPPPA June Brothers Scholarships *(Graduate, Undergraduate/Scholarship)*

Purpose: To encourage careers in the areas of safety, health and environment by providing educational support. **Focus:** Environmental conservation; Occupational safety and health. **Qualif.:** Applicants must be students who either work at a current VPP site or the children/grandchildren of an employee of a VPP site (the site must be a VPPPA full member in good standing); must be pursuing a degree (undergraduate or graduate) in the environmental, safety and health areas (either part-time or full-time); must have at least a 2.5 GPA on a scale of 4.0. **Criteria:** Recipients are chosen on the basis of demonstrated occupational safety, health and/or environmental outreach efforts in their schools, communities and/or workplace, leadership skills, extracurricular activities, involvement in professional organizations, communication skills and other awards and honors earned at educational institutions or at their place of employment.

Funds Avail.: No specific amount. **Number Awarded:** Varies. **To Apply:** Applicants must submit completed application form available in the website; a typewritten biography of at least 300 words describing interests and accomplishments or current resume; copy of current transcript; reference letters from the VPPPA site employee and from high school teacher, university's department head, professor or supervisor at current job. Forward all requirements to: VPPPA, Inc., Attn: Awards Committee, 7600-E Leesburg Pike, Ste. 440, Falls Church, VA 22043-2004; or fax to: (703) 761-1148, Attn: Awards Committee. **Deadline:** May 1.

7341 ■ VPPPA Stephen Brown Scholarships
(Graduate, Undergraduate/Scholarship)

Purpose: To encourage careers in the areas of safety, health and environment by providing educational support. **Focus:** Environmental conservation; Occupational safety and health. **Qualif.:** Applicants must be students who either work at a current VPP site or the children/grandchildren of an employee of a VPP site (the site must be a VPPPA full member in good standing); must be pursuing a degree (undergraduate or graduate) in the environmental, safety and health areas (either part-time or full-time); must have at least a 2.5 GPA on a scale of 4.0. **Criteria:** Recipients are chosen on the basis of demonstrated occupational safety, health and/or environmental outreach efforts in their schools, communities and/or workplace, leadership skills, extracurricular activities, involvement in professional organizations, communication skills and other awards and honors earned at educational institutions or at their place of employment.

Funds Avail.: No specific amount. **Number Awarded:** 1. **To Apply:** Applicants must submit completed application form available in the website; a typewritten biography of at least 300 words describing interests and accomplishments; copy of current transcript; reference letters from the VPPPA site employee and from high school teacher, university's department head, professor or supervisor at current job. Forward all requirements to: VPPPA, Inc., Attn: Awards Committee, 7600-E Leesburg Pike, Ste. 440, Falls Church, VA 22043-2004; or fax to: (703) 761-1148, Attn: Awards Committee. **Deadline:** May 1.

7342 ■ Warner Norcross & Judd LLP

900 Fifth Third Ctr.
111 Lyon St. NW
Grand Rapids, MI 49503-2487
Ph: (616)752-2000
Fax: (616)752-2500
URL: http://www.wnj.com

7343 ■ Warner Norcross & Judd LLP Law School Studies Scholarships *(Undergraduate/Scholarship)*

Purpose: To provide encouragement and financial assistance to students of racial and ethnic minority heritage pursuing a career in Law. **Focus:** Law. **Qualif.:** Applicants must be currently attending an accredited law school within the United States area; must be former or current residents of Michigan or attend a Michigan Law school; must have a cumulative GPA of 2.5 or above at their college or law school; must demonstrate financial need. **Criteria:** Applicants will be selected based on academic standing and financial need.

Funds Avail.: $5,000. **To Apply:** Applicants must provide a statement of goals and aspirations related to their studies in the legal profession; must prepare a statement of goals indicating the reason why they choose the legal profession/field as their area of study; must demonstrate financial need; must have two letters of reference. Applicants must complete the application forms available online and send it to 161 Ottawa Ave. NW, Ste. 209-C, Grand Rapids, MI 49503. **Deadline:** April 15. **Contact:** Ruth Bishop, Scholarship Coordinator at the above address (see entry 7342).

7344 ■ Earl Warren Legal Training Program

99 Hudson St., Ste. 1600
New York, NY 10013
Ph: (212)965-2200
URL: http://www.naacpldf.org

7345 ■ Herbert Lehman Education Scholarships
(Undergraduate/Scholarship)

Purpose: To provide students financial assistance in entering college. **Focus:** General studies. **Qualif.:** Applicants must be students entering four-year college as a full-time student for the first time; a U.S. citizens; be of excellent character with recommendations from teachers, community representatives or employers; have exceptional leadership potential with an ability to work well in diverse settings. **Criteria:** Award is given to a candidate with an outstanding potential as evidenced by high school academic records, test scores, and personal essays.

Funds Avail.: $ 2000. **To Apply:** Applications must be requested by writing to The Herbert Lehman Education Fund; application materials must be typed or neatly printed in ink and they must conform to program guidelines. **Deadline:** April 30.

Remarks: Named after the former Governor and United States Senator from New York State;

7346 ■ Washburn University School of Law

1700 SW College Ave.
Topeka, KS 66621
Ph: (785)670-1060
Fax: (785)670-3249
URL: http://washburnlaw.edu

7347 ■ Business and Transactional Law Center Scholarships *(Undergraduate/Scholarship)*

Purpose: To financially assist Washburn University students with their education. **Focus:** Law. **Qualif.:** Applicants must be admitted to Washburn Law; and must have an interest in business law or transactional law. **Criteria:** Recipients are selected based on the quality of all application materials submitted.

Funds Avail.: Maximum of $15,000 per year. **To Apply:** Applicants must attach a 1-2 paragraph description of interest, background or qualifications related to the scholarship specific area.

7348 ■ Child and Family Advocacy Fellowships
(Undergraduate/Scholarship)

Purpose: To financially assist Washburn University students with their education. **Focus:** Law. **Qualif.:** Applicants must be admitted to Washburn Law and must pursue careers in child and family advocacy. **Criteria:** Award is given based on the application materials.

Funds Avail.: Maximum of $14,000 per year. **To Apply:** Applicants must attach a 1-2 paragraph description of interest, background or qualifications related to the scholarship specific area.

7349 ■ Judge Delmas C. Hill Scholarships
(Undergraduate/Scholarship)

Purpose: To financially assist Washburn University students with their education. **Focus:** Law. **Qualif.:** Ap-

Awards are arranged alphabetically below their administering organizations

plicants must be admitted as full-time students in Washburn Law; must be in the top ten percent of the class; and must have a 2.5 GPA. **Criteria:** Award is given based on the application materials.

Funds Avail.: Full-tuition and a stipend of $2,000 per year. **Number Awarded:** 1. **To Apply:** Applicants must submit a statement showing: the reason for interest in the law as a profession; public and community service activities; leadership activities; and potential for leadership.

7350 ■ Koch Scholarships *(Undergraduate/Scholarship)*

Purpose: To financially assist Washburn University students with their education. **Focus:** Law. **Qualif.:** Applicants must be admitted as full-time students in Washburn Law; must be in the top ten percent of the class; and must have a 3.0 GPA. **Criteria:** Award is given based on the application materials.

Funds Avail.: Full-tuition for three years of law school; student fees; and a stipend of $6,000 for the first year of law school and $3,000 per year in the second and third years. **Number Awarded:** 1. **To Apply:** Applicants must submit a statement showing: the reason for interest in the law as a profession; public and community service activities; leadership activities; and potential for leadership.

7351 ■ Pittsburg State University Distinguished Graduate Scholarships *(Undergraduate/Scholarship)*

Purpose: To help defray some of the costs of a legal education for a Pittsburg State University student elected to attend Washburn Law. **Focus:** Law. **Qualif.:** Applicants must be PSU students admitted to Washburn Law. **Criteria:** Award is given based on merit.

Funds Avail.: No specific amount. **To Apply:** PSU applicants admitted to Washburn Law will be automatically considered.

Remarks: Established by David Pierce, Washburn Law Professor and Pittsburg State University graduate.

7352 ■ Polsinelli Diversity Scholarships *(Undergraduate/Scholarship)*

Purpose: To financially assist Washburn University minority students with their education. **Focus:** Law. **Qualif.:** Applicants must be incoming first-year minority law students. **Criteria:** Award is given based on merit.

Funds Avail.: $7,500. **Number Awarded:** 1. **To Apply:** Applicants admitted to Washburn Law will be automatically considered.

Remarks: Created through the contributions of the Polsinelli Shalton Flanigan Suelthause PC law firm.

7353 ■ Shamberg Scholarships *(Undergraduate/Scholarship)*

Purpose: To financially assist Washburn University students with their education. **Focus:** Law. **Qualif.:** Applicants must be admitted to Washburn Law. **Criteria:** Selection is based on academic achievements and leadership potential.

Funds Avail.: Full-tuition and a $1,000 stipend. **Number Awarded:** 3.

Remarks: Students admitted to Washburn Law will be automatically considered.

7354 ■ J.L. Weigand, Jr. Legal Education Trust Scholarships *(Undergraduate/Scholarship)*

Purpose: To promote excellence in legal education and to encourage the most scholastically qualified students who are long term Kansas residents to remain in or return to Kansas to practice law. **Focus:** Law. **Qualif.:** Applicants must be admitted full-time to Washburn Law; must be in the top ten percent of the class; and have been a legal resident of Kansas for at least ten years prior to their admission to law school. **Criteria:** Selection is based on merit.

Funds Avail.: No specific amount. **To Apply:** Applicants admitted to Washburn Law will be automatically considered.

Remarks: Established by John L. Weigand, Jr.

7355 ■ The Washington Group

720 Park Blvd.
PO Box 73
Boise, ID 83729
Ph: (208)386-5000
E-mail: membership@washingtongroup.org
URL: http://www.wgint.com

7356 ■ Alberta Ukrainian Centennial Commemorative Scholarships *(Undergraduate/Scholarship)*

Purpose: To encourage active participation in Ukrainian community. **Focus:** General studies. **Qualif.:** Applicants must be graduate students intending to study in Alberta or Canadian graduate students from Alberta intending to study in Ukraine. **Criteria:** Recipients are selected based on academic records.

Funds Avail.: No specific amount. **To Apply:** Applicants must fill out the application and supporting materials. **Deadline:** February 1. **Contact:** Alberta Heritage Scholarship Fund at 9940 106th Street, Edmonton, Alberta, T5K 2V1, Canada; 1403-427-5538; 1403-422-4516.

7357 ■ Canada-Ukraine Parliamentary Program (CUPP) Internship Scholarships *(Undergraduate/Scholarship)*

Purpose: To encourage active participation in Ukrainian community. **Focus:** General studies. **Qualif.:** Program is open for individuals seeking scholarships for a three-month internship for Ukrainian undergraduates with a Member of Parliament of the House of Commons in Ottawa, Canada. This internship is open only to citizens of Ukraine. Proficiency in English or French as well as in Ukrainian is a requirement. **Criteria:** Recipients are selected based on academic records.

Funds Avail.: No specific amount. **To Apply:** Application is available online. **Deadline:** February 1. **Contact:** Ukrainian Studies Foundation, 620 Spadina Avenue, Toronto, Ontario, Canada M5S 2H4; 416-234-9114; cupp@infoukes.com.

7358 ■ Chopivsky Fellowships *(Undergraduate/Scholarship)*

Purpose: To encourage active participation in Ukrainian community. **Focus:** Forestry; Environmental Studies; Economics. **Qualif.:** Applicants must be Ukrainian citizens and must be first admitted to the appropriate faculties at Yale; must be in graduate degree program leading to master's degree at the Yale School of Management at the Yale School of Forestry and Environmental Studies, and in the Departments of International Relations, International Economics, and Developmental Studies. **Criteria:** Recipients are selected based on academic records.

Funds Avail.: No specific amount. **Number Awarded:** 2.

To Apply: Applicants must fill out the application form and supporting materials. **Deadline:** January 1. **Contact:** PO Box 208206, New Haven, CT 06520-8606; 1203-432-3423; 12034325963.

7359 ■ Eugene & Elinor Kotur Scholarship Trust Fund *(Undergraduate/Scholarship)*

Purpose: To encourage active participation in Ukrainian community. **Focus:** General studies. **Qualif.:** Applicants must be enrolled in the sophomore or higher year or graduate school of about thirty leading colleges and universities in the USA listed on the application form. Applicants may have to be members of the Ukrainian Fraternal Association for two years. **Criteria:** Recipients are selected based on academic records.

Funds Avail.: $1,000. **To Apply:** Applicants must write for application. **Contact:** Ukrainian Fraternal Association Scholarship Program, PO Box 350, Scranton, PA 18501-0350; 1717-342-0937.

7360 ■ The Ivan Shandor Memorial Ukrainian American Bar Association Scholarships *(Undergraduate/Scholarship)*

Purpose: To encourage active participation in Ukrainian community. **Focus:** Law. **Qualif.:** Applicants must be enrolled in the masters of law degree program at Georgetown University Law center; must be resident or resided in Ukraine; must be fluent in Ukrainian language; and must demonstrate a desire to promote democracy and uphold the rule of law in Ukraine. **Criteria:** Recipients are selected based on academic records.

Funds Avail.: No specific amount. **To Apply:** Applicants must fill out the application form. **Contact:** Scholarships for International Students, Georgetown university Law Center, Office of development, 600 New Jersey Avenue, N.W., Washington, DC 20001; 202-662-9000.

7361 ■ Marusia Yaworska Entrance Scholarships *(Undergraduate/Scholarship)*

Purpose: To encourage active participation in Ukrainian community. **Focus:** Music. **Qualif.:** Applicants must be high school seniors already attending an accredited college or university; must be members of the Ukrainian Fraternal Association for two years. **Criteria:** Recipients are selected based on academic records.

Funds Avail.: $5,000. **Number Awarded:** 2. **To Apply:** Applicants must fill out the application and supporting materials. **Deadline:** March 31. **Contact:** Department of Music, faculty of Arts, University of Ottawa, 50 University Private, Ottawa, Ontario, K1N 5N5, Canada.

7362 ■ Washington Higher Education Coordinating Board

PO Box 43430
Olympia, WA 98504-3430
Ph: (360)753-7800
E-mail: info@hecb.wa.gov
URL: http://www.hecb.wa.gov

7363 ■ American Indian Endowed Scholarships *(Graduate, Undergraduate/Scholarship)*

Purpose: To help financially needy students with close social and cultural ties to a Native American community to pursue undergraduate and graduate studies. **Focus:** General studies. **Qualif.:** Applicant must have demonstrated financial need based on a completed FAFSA; a Washington state resident; enrolled full-time as an undergraduate or graduate student in an eligible program; and not pursuing a degree in theology. **Criteria:** Selection is based on academic merit and commitment to serve the American Indian community.

Funds Avail.: $500-$2000. **Number Awarded:** 15. **To Apply:** Applicants must submit an American Indian Endowed Scholarship application form together with the required materials and information. **Deadline:** February 1.

Remarks: Students can use the scholarships at public colleges and universities and accredited independent colleges, universities, and career schools in Washington.

7364 ■ Future Teachers Conditional Scholarships and Loan Repayment *(Professional Development, Undergraduate/Loan)*

Purpose: To encourage outstanding students and paraprofessionals to become teachers, and to encourage current teachers to obtain additional endorsements in teacher shortage subjects. **Focus:** Teaching. **Qualif.:** Applicant must be a resident student of Washington state; planning to complete an approved program leading to a residency teacher certificate or an additional shortage subject endorsement; planning to be employed as a certificated classroom teacher in Washington K-12 public schools; planning to attend an eligible college at least half-time; and not pursuing or planning to pursue a degree in theology. **Criteria:** Selection is based on academic ability; bilingual ability; contributions to school systems; potential to serve as a positive role model for students; length of time until completion of the educational program; and commitment to serve as a Washington public classroom teacher.

Funds Avail.: Varies. **To Apply:** Applicants must contact the Future Teachers Conditional Scholarship and Loan Repayment Program in order to apply.

Remarks: In return for conditional scholarships or loan repayments, participants agree to teach in Washington K-12 public schools.

7365 ■ GET Ready for Math and Science Conditional Scholarships *(Four Year College, Two Year College, Undergraduate/Scholarship)*

Purpose: To support low-income and middle-income high school students with top math and science test scores to apply college for free. **Focus:** Mathematics and mathematical sciences; Science. **Qualif.:** Applicants must score a 4 on the math or science section of the high school WASL or score above the 95th percentile on the math section of the SAT or ACT; have a family income at or below 125 percent of the state median family income at the time of application; a Washington state resident; agrees to earn a bachelor's degree in a qualified math or science program at an eligible Washington college/university; and agree to work full-time in a math or science occupation in Washington for at least three years following college graduation. **Criteria:** Applicants must meet all the qualifications and requirements.

Funds Avail.: Full-tuition. **To Apply:** Applications will be available April 2009. **Deadline:** June.

Remarks: In partnership with the Office of the Superintendent of Public Instruction and the College Success Foundation.

7366 ■ Washington College Bound Scholarships *(Undergraduate/Scholarship)*

Purpose: To provide hope and incentive for students and families who otherwise might not consider college as an option because of its cost. **Focus:** General studies. **Qualif.:** Applicants must be seventh-grade students from families eligible for free or reduced-priced lunches who sign the pledge. Their family income must remain at 65 percent or less of the state's median income by the time of high school graduation. **Criteria:** Student must have signed a pledge in 7th grade promising to graduate from high school and demonstrate good citizenship.

Funds Avail.: Covers the cost of college tuition, fees and books. **To Apply:** The online application and brochure are being finalized. Materials will be sent to all middle schools, including a link to the online application.

7367 ■ Washington Higher Education Coordinating Board Educational Opportunity Grants
(Undergraduate/Grant)

Purpose: To encourage financially needy students to complete a bachelor's degree. **Focus:** General studies. **Qualif.:** Applicants must have place bound circumstances (having personal barriers which unable the student to continue education); a Washington resident; have at least junior standing before the first term of enrollment at an eligible four-year college; have financial need; and a junior or senior transfer student (student cannot receive EOG to continue at the current college). **Criteria:** Selection is based on the student's place bound circumstances and financial need.

Funds Avail.: $5000. **To Apply:** Applicants must submit a completed application form along with the required materials and information. **Deadline:** October 1; February 1; April 1; and June 1.

7368 ■ Washington Higher Education Coordinating Board Health Professional Scholarships
(Undergraduate/Scholarship)

Purpose: To attract and retain health professionals to serve in critical shortage areas in Washington state. **Focus:** Physics; Nursing; Midwifery; Pharmacy; Dentistry. **Qualif.:** Applicant must be a student training to become a primary care health professional in an eligible profession; a U.S. citizen; have completed all prerequisite course work; not be in default on any educational loans; and must sign a Promissory Note agreeing to serve for a minimum of three years in a designated shortage area in Washington state or pay back funds with double penalty plus interest. **Criteria:** Priority is given to those applicants enrolled in Undergraduate Nursing, Nursing Faculty, Dental, Dental Hygienist, and Pharmacist programs who demonstrate a commitment to rural communities and underserved populations as outlined in the narrative portion of the application.

Funds Avail.: Varies by educational program. **To Apply:** Applicants must submit a completed application form along with the required materials and information. **Deadline:** April 30.

Remarks: Participants must agree, in return for the assistance, to provide primary care health care in rural or underserved urban areas with designated shortages for a minimum of three years.

7369 ■ Washington Higher Education Coordinating Board State Need Grants *(Undergraduate/Grant)*

Purpose: To help state's lowest-income undergraduate students pursue degrees, hone skills, or retrain for new careers. **Focus:** General studies. **Qualif.:** Applicant must have a family income of equal to or less than 70 percent of the state median; a Washington State resident; enrolled as an undergraduate student in an eligible program, at a minimum of 3 credits; pursuing a certificate, bachelor's degree, or first associate degree; and not pursuing a degree in theology. **Criteria:** Selection is based on the applicant's family income.

Funds Avail.: Amounts vary by the type of school the applicant's attending. **To Apply:** Applicants must file a FAFSA (Free Application for Federal Student Aid) to be considered.

7370 ■ Washington Hospital Health Care System

2000 Mowry Ave.
Fremont, CA 94538
Ph: (510)797-1111
E-mail: foundation@whhs.com
URL: http://www.whhs.com

7371 ■ Medical Staff Scholarships
(Undergraduate/Scholarship)

Purpose: To meet the healthcare needs of the district residents through medical services, education and research. **Focus:** Health sciences. **Qualif.:** Applicants must be students residing within the Washington Township Health Care District who are pursuing careers in the health sciences field. **Criteria:** Recipients are selected based on academic performance and demonstrated interest in a health-related field.

Funds Avail.: $1,500. **Number Awarded:** 2. **To Apply:** Applicants must submit a completed application form. **Contact:** 510-791-3446.

7372 ■ Service League Volunteer Scholarships
(Undergraduate/Scholarship)

Purpose: To meet the healthcare needs of district residents through medical services, education and research. **Focus:** Health care services. **Qualif.:** Applicants must be graduating high school seniors or college students who are pursuing studies in a health-related field; must have 2.50 GPA or higher; must be U.S. citizens and residents of Washington Hospital District; must have been accepted by an accredited school, college or university offering a bachelor or higher degree program in a health-related field; must be full-time students and must have comleted 100 hours of volunteer service or employment in a health-related field. **Criteria:** Recipients are selected based on academic performance.

Funds Avail.: $1,000. **Number Awarded:** 2. **To Apply:** Applicants must submit: completed application form; current letters of recommendation from a Director of Volunteer Services, employer, counselor, advisor or teacher; high school or college transcript and proof of citizenship. **Deadline:** April 1. **Contact:** 510-791-3465.

7373 ■ Washington Metropolitan Scholars

110 Maryland Ave. NE, Ste. 502
Washington, DC 20002
Ph: (202)544-8301
Fax: (202)318-0761
E-mail: geoff@wmscholars.org
URL: http://www.wmscholars.org

7374 ■ Washington Metropolitan Scholarships
(Undergraduate/Scholarship)

Purpose: To assist students with their college admission, scholarship seminars, college counseling, academic support and retention services, internships and career development workshops. **Focus:** General studies. **Qualif.:** Applicants must be African American; must have at least a cumulative GPA of 3.5 on a 4.0 scale, or is in the top twenty-five percent of his or her senior class; must be a citizen or a legal permanent resident of the United States, and resides in the Washington metropolitan area; must be a prospective graduating senior from an accredited public, private, or parochial school in the metropolitan area; must also be entering an accredited college or university as a full-time, degree-seeking freshmen in the upcoming year; must demonstrate leadership abilities through participation in community service, extracurricular or other activities; must exhibit financial need. **Criteria:** Recipients are selected based on scholastic attainment; success in an extracurricular activities; character, commitment, seriousness of purpose and determination to excel in his or her chosen field; selection will also be judged based on the content and quality of their nomination materials.

Funds Avail.: Maximum amount of $5,000. **To Apply:** Applicants must fill out the online application form; submit an official recommendation from a teacher or counselor who has personal knowledge of the student's abilities and must be signed by the principal; submit an official transcript of records. **Deadline:** November 3. **Contact:** geoff@wmscholars.org.

7375 ■ Washington Scholarship Fund

1100 17th St. NW, Ste. 330
Washington, DC 20036
Ph: (202)222-0535
Fax: (202)222-0543
E-mail: scholarships@washingtonscholarshipfund.org
URL: http://www.washingtonscholarshipfund.org

7376 ■ D.C. Opportunity Scholarship Program *(Undergraduate/Scholarship)*

Purpose: To increase educational opportunities for low-income students and families in Washington, D.C. **Focus:** General studies. **Qualif.:** Applicants must be living in Washington, D.C.; must currently be attending a public school; must be five years old or entering kindergarten; must have a household income at or below 185 percent of poverty. **Criteria:** Recipients are selected based on financial need.

Funds Avail.: $7,500. **To Apply:** Applicants must submit a report card or other school document from the school year showing the child's name, current grade, and school name; applicants must submit a birth certificate for any child who will be entering kindergarten. **Contact:** scholarships@washingtonscholarshipfund.org.

7377 ■ Washington Scholarship Fund Signature Scholarships Program *(Undergraduate/Scholarship)*

Purpose: To increase educational opportunities for low-income students and families in Washington, D.C. **Focus:** General studies. **Qualif.:** Applicants must be living in Washington, D.C.; must currently be attending a public school; must be five years old or entering kindergarten; must have a household income at or below 270 percent of poverty. **Criteria:** Recipients are selected based on financial need.

Funds Avail.: $3,000. **To Apply:** Applicants must submit a report card or other school document from the school year showing the child's name, current grade, and school name; applicants must submit a birth certificate for any child who will be entering kindergarten. **Contact:** scholarships@washingtonscholarshipfund.org.

7378 ■ Washington State Business Education Association

c/o Lori Finn
800 Abbott Rd.
Walla Walla, WA 99362
Ph: (509)526-8606
Fax: (509)526-8690
E-mail: lfinn@wwps.org
URL: http://www.wsbea.org

7379 ■ Dr. F. Ross Byrd Scholarships *(Graduate/Scholarship)*

Purpose: To provide financial support to those students who are in need. **Focus:** Business. **Qualif.:** Applicants must be graduate students with a minimum of one quarter or one semester of graduate classes to complete. Applicants must be pursuing an advanced degree in business education or a related education field (Vocational Administration, Business & Marketing, Curriculum, etc.). **Criteria:** Preference will be given to those who meet the criteria.

Funds Avail.: No specific amount. **To Apply:** Applicants must submit a completed application form and 3 letters of recommendation, one of which must be from a member of the student's graduate advisory committee, another one from a local vocational director/vocational administrator/administrator, and one from a member of WSBEA. **Deadline:** May 1. **Contact:** Jackie Floetke, WSBEA Scholarship Committee at PO Box 138 Wilson Creek, WA 98860

7380 ■ Doris Y. and John J. Gerber Scholarships *(Undergraduate/Scholarship)*

Purpose: To provide financial assistance to those students who are in need. **Focus:** Business. **Qualif.:** Applicants must be junior or senior students majoring in Business Education. Applicants must be nominated by their advisor who is a current dues-paying member of WSBEA. **Criteria:** Preference will be given to those who meet the criteria.

Funds Avail.: No specific amount. **To Apply:** Applicants must inquire online for the application process. **Deadline:** December 1. **Contact:** Jackie Floetke, WSBEA Scholarship Committee at PO Box 138 Wilson Creek, WA 98860

7381 ■ Washington State Lake Protection Association

PO Box 4245
Seattle, WA 98194
Ph: (206)263-6242
E-mail: info@walpa.org
URL: http://www.walpa.org

7382 ■ WALPA Lake Scholarships *(Graduate, Undergraduate/Scholarship)*

Purpose: To support undergraduate and graduate students in their pursuit of degrees specializing in the fields of Environmental Science. **Focus:** Environmental Science. **Qualif.:** Applicants must be enrolled as part or full time undergraduate or graduate students in an accredited college or university in Washington or Idaho and be completing course work or research related to biology, hydrology, ecology and management or restoration of lakes and watersheds in Washington and Idaho. **Criteria:** Preference will be given to those students who meet the criteria.

Funds Avail.: $750-$1,000. **Number Awarded:** 2. **To Apply:** Applicants must check the available website for the required materials. **Contact:** Washington State Lake Protection Association at the above address (see entry 7381).

7383 ■ Washington University Law School

Campus Box 1120
One Brookings Dr.
St. Louis, MO 63130-4899
Ph: (314)935-6400
E-mail: eckrich@wulaw.wustl.edu
URL: http://www.law.wustl.edu

7384 ■ Buder Scholarship for American Indian Law Students *(Undergraduate/Scholarship)*

Purpose: To provide financial assistance to law students. **Focus:** Law. **Qualif.:** Applicants must be American Indian Law students. **Criteria:** Recipient selection will be based on demonstrated potential for success in law school as evidenced by undergraduate academic performance.

Funds Avail.: No specific amount. **To Apply:** Applicants must submit an application letter and other requirements to the office.

7385 ■ Walter Moran Farmer Scholarships *(Undergraduate/Scholarship)*

Purpose: To provide financial assistance to public service students who wish to continue their education. **Focus:** Public service. **Qualif.:** Applicants must be the first generation of their families to attend college or graduate school. **Criteria:** Recipient selection will be based on intellectual, leadership and community service achievement; demonstrated commitment to bringing diverse people together; and demonstrated achievement in the face of personal challenges.

Funds Avail.: No specific amount. **To Apply:** Applicant must submit an application letter and other requirements.

7386 ■ Washington University Law School Chancellor's Graduate Fellowships *(Graduate/Fellowship)*

Purpose: To provide encouragement as well as financial support to students interested in careers as college or university professors. **Focus:** Arts and Sciences; Business; Social Work; Engineering; Law. **Qualif.:** Students must have earned or be in the process of earning an undergraduate degree from a U.S. institution. **Criteria:** Recipients will be selected based on potential contributions to the diversity of graduate education at Washington University.

Funds Avail.: No specific amount. **To Apply:** Applicants may download an application form from the website. **Deadline:** January 15. **Contact:** Joyce Edwards.

7387 ■ Washington University Law School Olin Fellowships for Women *(Graduate/Fellowship)*

Purpose: To provide financial assistance to women who wish to have careers in higher education. **Focus:** General studies. **Qualif.:** Applicants must be women. **Criteria:** Recipients will be selected based on the committee's review of all applications.

Funds Avail.: No specific amount. **To Apply:** Applicants must submit a completed application form; a one-page information form; a curriculum vitae; an essay; three letters of recommendation; a transcript; and test scores. **Deadline:** February 1. **Contact:** Joyce Edwards Campus Box 1187, One Brookings Dr., St. Louis, MO 63130-4899; 314-935-6821.

7388 ■ Webster Society Scholarships *(Undergraduate/Scholarship)*

Purpose: To provide financial assistance to public service students who wish to continue their education. **Focus:** Public service. **Qualif.:** Applicants must be entering first-year JD students with exemplary academic credentials and an established commitment to public service. **Criteria:** Selection will be based on academic merit.

Funds Avail.: Full tuition scholarship. **To Apply:** Interested applicants should write a short statement summarizing their involvement in public service activities. **Deadline:** February 1.

7389 ■ Water and Sewer Distributors of America

100 North 20th St., 4th floor
Philadelphia, PA 19103-1443
Ph: (215)564-3484
Fax: (215)963-9785
E-mail: wasda@fernley.com
URL: http://www.wasda.com

7390 ■ Matt Stager Memorial Scholarship Fund *(Undergraduate/Scholarship)*

Purpose: To promote the waterworks/wastewater products distribution industry; to improve the image of WASDA and the industry. **Focus:** General studies. **Qualif.:** Applicant must have been employed by a company which was or is a regular Member of WASDA; must have an office in Canada, United States, or Puerto Rico; must have knowledge in distribution selling in waterworks, and sewer or storm drainage pipes. **Criteria:** Recipients will be selected based on the review of all application materials submitted.

Funds Avail.: No specific amount. **To Apply:** Applicants must prepare a one-page detailed narrative description of the academic plans for the future and the career goals; must attach two letters of recommendation from teachers who are not related or members of the Matt Stager Scholarship Section Committee who have knowledge in academic achievements and who are able to comment on the academic motivation and character; must have a WASDA member contact verify parent's employment; have the Counselor fill out the counselor's report; submit the required scores and forward all requirements to the WASDA Headquarters. **Deadline:** April 1.

7391 ■ Watson-Brown Foundation

310 Tom Watson Way
Thomson, GA 30824
Ph: (706)595-8886
Fax: (706)595-3948
URL: http://www.watson-brown.org

7392 ■ Watson-Brown Scholarships *(Undergraduate/Scholarship)*

Purpose: To assist Georgia and South Carolina students with their educational pursuits. **Focus:** General studies.

Awards are arranged alphabetically below their administering organizations

Qualif.: Applicants must be students from Georgia or South Carolina; must be high school seniors or current undergraduate students. **Criteria:** Scholarship recipients are selected based on merit and need.

Funds Avail.: $3,000 and $5,000. **Number Awarded:** Approximately 200. **To Apply:** Applicants must complete the online scholarship application and submit supporting documents (essay, financial need statement, letters of recommendation, high school/college transcript, IRS Form 1040 or 1040 EZ) which must be mailed separately. **Deadline:** February 15. **Contact:** Sarah Katherine McNeil, Director of Scholarships and Alumni Relations, at skmcneil@watson-brown.org.

7393 ■ West Virginia Coal Association

PO Box 3923
Charleston, WV 25309
Ph: (304)342-4153
Fax: (304)342-7651
E-mail: braney@wvcoal.com
URL: http://www.wvcoal.com

7394 ■ Friends of Coal Scholarships
(Undergraduate/Scholarship)

Purpose: To provide a strong and dependable infrastructure for the continued mining of West Virginia coal. **Focus:** General studies. **Qualif.:** Applicants must be high school honor graduates; must have high GPA's in high school; must be living in West Virginia. **Criteria:** Recipients are selected based on academic performance and financial need.

Funds Avail.: $2,500. **To Apply:** Applicants must submit a filled-out application form.

7395 ■ West Virginia Congress of Parents and Teachers

PO Box 3557
Parkersburg, WV 26103
Ph: (304)420-9576
Fax: (304)420-9577
E-mail: wv_office@pta.org
URL: http://www.wvpta.net

7396 ■ West Virginia PTA Scholarships
(Undergraduate/Scholarship)

Purpose: To support the education of WV students. **Focus:** General studies. **Qualif.:** Applicants must be high school seniors in a WV school; and have at least a 2.0 grade point average. **Criteria:** Selection is based on the overall presence of the essay and application; volunteer service; honors received; extracurricular activities; GPA, ACT and SAT scores.

Funds Avail.: $500. **To Apply:** Applicant's must submit the completed application form with supporting documents. One original, and four copies must be submitted to the Scholarship Committee. **Deadline:** February 15.

7397 ■ West Virginia Hospitality and Travel Association

PO Box 2391
Charleston, WV 25328
Ph: (304)342-6511
E-mail: sharonhrowe@charter.net
URL: http://www.wvhta.com

7398 ■ Peter Meyer Memorial Scholarships
(Undergraduate/Scholarship)

Purpose: To complete the educational pathway already underway in West Virginia. **Focus:** Travel and tourism. **Qualif.:** Applicants must be high school seniors who plan to enroll in a hospitality degree program. **Criteria:** Recipients are selected based on academic performance, industry related work experience, strength of letters of recommendation, content, style, and required essay question and presentation of application.

Funds Avail.: $500. **To Apply:** Applicants must submit a typed or neatly printed application; an official transcript from high school attended; proof of hospitality and travel-related work experience with a minimum of 250 hours verified by copies of paycheck stubs or letters from employer stipulating number of hours worked; one letter of recommendation on letterhead from a current/previous employer; and acceptance letter from the post-secondary institution. **Deadline:** May 31. **Contact:** edfdn@wvhta.com

7399 ■ West Virginia Educational Foundation Hospitality Business Alliance Scholarships
(Undergraduate/Scholarship)

Purpose: To complete the educational pathway already underway in West Virginia. **Focus:** Travel and tourism. **Qualif.:** Applicants must be prostart and lodging management program high school senior students who plan to enroll in a hospitality degree program. Applicants must be West Virginia residents and may be planning to attend out-of-state schools. **Criteria:** Recipients are selected based on academic performance and financial need.

Funds Avail.: $1,000. **To Apply:** Applicants must submit a completed application form.

7400 ■ West Virginia Hospitality and Travel Association General Scholarships *(Undergraduate/Scholarship)*

Purpose: To complete the educational pathway already underway in West Virginia. **Focus:** Travel and tourism. **Qualif.:** Applicants must be graduating seniors in a West Virginia High School; must have a minimum grade point of average of 2.75 on a 4.0 scale; must have performed a minimum of 250 hours of hospitality and travel industry related work experience; must have applied to a hospitality, travel, or recreation management program in a post-secondary institution, either full-time or substantial part-time with the intent to enroll in a minimum of 2 terms. **Criteria:** Recipients are selected based on academic performance, industry-related work experience, strength of letters of recommendation, content, style, and required essay question and presentation of application.

Funds Avail.: $1,000. **To Apply:** Applicants must submit a typed or neatly printed application; an official transcript from high school attended; proof of hospitality and travel-related work experience with a minimum of 250 hours verified by copies of paycheck stubs or letters from employer stipulating number of hours worked; one letter of recommendation on letterhead from a current/previous employer; and acceptance letter from the post-secondary institution. **Deadline:** May 31. **Contact:** edfdn@wvhta.com.

7401 ■ West Virginia Rural Health Education Partnerships

PO Box 9003
Morgantown, WV 26506-9003

Awards are arranged alphabetically below their administering organizations

Ph: (304)293-6753
E-mail: klrobinson@hsc.wvu.edu
URL: http://www.wvrhep.org

7402 ■ Health Sciences Scholarship Program *(Undergraduate/Scholarship)*

Purpose: To increase the number of primary care providers in rural West Virginia. **Focus:** Health sciences. **Qualif.:** Applicants must be fourth year medical students at a West Virginia school of medicine or osteopathy who are entering primary care internship or residency programs in West Virginia; applicants must either be students who are in the final year of a primary care educational program in West Virginia for nurse practitioners or physician assistants, or a master's degree nursing education; or students who are in the final year of a graduate program in physical therapy. **Criteria:** Recipients are selected based on recommendations of an advisory panel.

Funds Avail.: $20,000. **To Apply:** Applicants must submit a complete application form. **Contact:** tyler@hepc.wvnet.edu.

7403 ■ Medical Students Loan Program *(Undergraduate/Loan)*

Purpose: To provide loans to students at schools of medicine or osteopathy in West Virginia. **Focus:** Health sciences. **Qualif.:** Applicants must be accepted for enrollment or be enrolled full-time in a West Virginia school of medicine or osteopathy. **Criteria:** Recipients are selected based on academic performance.

Funds Avail.: $10,000. **To Apply:** Applicants must submit completed application form.

7404 ■ Western Golf Association

1 Briar Rd.
Golf, IL 60029
Ph: (847)724-4600
Fax: (847)724-7133
E-mail: evansscholars@wgaesf.com
URL: http://www.westerngolfassociation.com

7405 ■ Chuck Evans Scholarships *(Undergraduate/Scholarship)*

Purpose: To help caddies to pursue education. **Focus:** General studies. **Qualif.:** Applicant must be caddies nominated by their club and have caddied, successfully and regularly, for a minimum of two years and also expected to caddie or work at their sponsoring club during the summer prior to the application; have completed junior year of high school with above B average in college preparatory courses and are required to take the ACT; have clearly establish their need for financial assistance; and have an outstanding character. **Criteria:** Scholarship Committee will select finalist and will conduct an interview.

Funds Avail.: Full-tuition. **To Apply:** Caddies must be nominated by their respective clubs.

7406 ■ Western Michigan Society of Health-System Pharmacists

8835 Summerset Woods Ct., SE
Alto, MI 49302
Ph: (616)752-6676
E-mail: danastaat@ferris.edu
URL: http://www.wmshp.net

7407 ■ Western Michigan Society of Health-System Pharmacists Scholarships *(All/Scholarship)*

Purpose: To develop community and health-system pharmacists, technicians and students. **Focus:** Pharmacy. **Qualif.:** Applicants must be in good standing with the College of Pharmacy; must be a native or current resident of the Western Michigan area. **Criteria:** Recipients are selected based on demonstrated interest in health-system pharmacy and involvement in or leadership positions with professional organizations.

Funds Avail.: $1,000. **To Apply:** Applicants must complete the application form. **Deadline:** March 31. **Contact:** Brad Miller at the above address (see entry 7406).

7408 ■ White House Correspondents' Association

600 New Hampshire Ave.
Washington, DC 20037
Ph: (202)266-7453
Fax: (202)266-7454
URL: http://www.whca.net

7409 ■ The Frank Cormier Scholarships *(Undergraduate/Scholarship)*

Purpose: To provide financial assistance to promising journalism students. **Focus:** Journalism. **Qualif.:** Applicants must be undergraduate journalism students at Phillip Merrill College of Journalism at the University of Maryland. **Criteria:** Awards are given based on academic merit.

Funds Avail.: $24,000.

Remarks: Established in 1991, in 1994 it was named in honor of Frank Cormier, legendary White House correspondent for The Associated Press.

7410 ■ The Deborah Orin-Eilbeck Scholarships *(Graduate/Scholarship)*

Purpose: To provide financial assistance to those studying journalism. **Focus:** Journalism. **Qualif.:** Applicants must be graduate journalism students at Northwestern University Medill School of Journalism. **Criteria:** Awards are given based on academic merit.

Funds Avail.: $5,000 each. **Number Awarded:** 2.

Remarks: Awards established in honor of Deborah Orin-Eilbeck, the tenacious White House correspondent for The New York Post and Medill graduate who died of cancer in 2006.

7411 ■ Wilkinson & Company LLP

PO Box 757
Belleville, ON, Canada K8N 5B5
Ph: (613)966-5105
Fax: (613)962-7072
Free: 888-728-3890
URL: http://www.wilkinson.net

7412 ■ Wilkinson & Company LLP Secondary School Scholarships *(Undergraduate/Scholarship)*

Purpose: To provide financial support for students. **Focus:** Business-related course. **Qualif.:** Applicants must have highest mark in business-related course. **Criteria:** Priority will be based on scholastic records.

Awards are arranged alphabetically below their administering organizations

Funds Avail.: $300. **To Apply:** Applicants must submit a completed application form. **Contact:** Wilkinson & Company LLP at the above address (see entry 7411).

7413 ■ Willamette University

900 State St.
Salem, OR 97301
Ph: (503)370-6300
URL: http://www.willamette.edu

7414 ■ Melvin Henderson-Rubio Scholarships

(Undergraduate/Scholarship)

Purpose: To provide financial support to individuals who wish to pursue their studies. **Focus:** General studies. **Qualif.:** Applicants must be student enrolling from a home address in the greater Los Angeles area. **Criteria:** Applicants will be selected based on academic credentials and financial need.

Funds Avail.: $5,000. **To Apply:** For more information about the scholarship, applicants must contact the Office of Financial Aid. **Deadline:** January 1.

7415 ■ Mary Stuart Rogers Scholarships

(Undergraduate/Scholarship)

Purpose: To provide financial support to individuals who wish to pursue their studies. **Focus:** General studies. **Qualif.:** Applicants must have a 3.0 GPA to be considered. **Criteria:** Applicants will be selected based on academic credentials, leadership and financial need.

Funds Avail.: $4,000. **Number Awarded:** 14. **To Apply:** For more information about the scholarship, applicants must contact the Office of Financial Aid. **Deadline:** January 1.

7416 ■ John G. Williams Foundation

PO Box 1229
Camp Hill, PA 17001-1229
Ph: (717)763-1333
Fax: (717)763-1336
E-mail: amgrpmld@aol.com
URL: http://www.jgwfoundation.org

7417 ■ John G. Williams Scholarships Fund

(Undergraduate/Scholarship)

Purpose: To provide financial assistance to Pennsylvania residents for their pursuit of college, post-graduate, and/or professional education opportunities, in courses and at educational institutions that they select and that are acceptable to the Board of Trustees. **Focus:** General studies. **Qualif.:** Applicants must be a resident of Pennsylvania. Applicants must be high school graduates and enrolled full-time. Applicants must have and maintain at all times a minimum GPA of 3.0 or its equivalent. **Criteria:** Recipients are selected based on demonstrated financial need, personal initiative, and civic responsibility.

Funds Avail.: No specific amount. **To Apply:** Applicants must complete the standard financial need and financial aid form. Applicants must submit a transcript of grades for the most recent academic year. Applicants must provide evidence of acceptance and attendance by college or graduate school and two character recommendations. **Deadline:** June 15.

7418 ■ Winston-Salem Foundation

860 W Fifth St.
Winston-Salem, NC 27101-2506
Ph: (336)725-2382
Fax: (336)727-0581
E-mail: info@wsfoundation.org
URL: http://www.wsfoundation.org

7419 ■ William H. Andrews/HAWS Scholarships

(Undergraduate/Scholarship)

Purpose: To assist graduating high school seniors and adults in their studies. **Focus:** General studies. **Qualif.:** Applicants must be graduating high school seniors or adults wishing to continue in post-secondary education; must be residents living in a property owned or managed by HAWS. **Criteria:** Recipients are selected based on the committee's review of applications.

Funds Avail.: No specific amount. **To Apply:** Applicants may download an application form at WSF website or send request to Scholarship coordinator. **Deadline:** March 15. **Contact:** Michelle Greene, 336-399-3579.

7420 ■ Chester Arzell and Helen Miller Montgomery Scholarships *(Undergraduate/Scholarship)*

Purpose: To graduating high school seniors from Stokes County public high schools. **Focus:** General studies. **Qualif.:** Applicants must have a minimum, cumulative, unweighted GPA of 2.0; participate in community service; demonstrate good character; participate in extracurricular activities; demonstrate financial need. **Criteria:** Selection will be based on the committee's criteria.

Funds Avail.: $1,000. **To Apply:** Scholarship applications are available online or in the guidance offices of the three Stokes county high schools. **Deadline:** April 1. **Contact:** WSF Student Aid Department, 336-714-3445.

7421 ■ F.A. and Charlotte Blount Scholarships

(Undergraduate/Scholarship)

Purpose: To assist graduating high school students of Forsyth County. **Focus:** General studies. **Qualif.:** Applicants must be graduating Forsyth County high school students who will pursue a baccalaureate degree at an accredited college or university. **Criteria:** Preference will be given to minority students.

Funds Avail.: $750. **To Apply:** Applicants must submit a completed application form; grade transcript through first semester of the 12th grade; and one recommendation. **Deadline:** March 31. **Contact:** Winston-Salem Foundation at the above address (see entry 7418).

7422 ■ Sam L. Booke, Sr. Scholarships

(Undergraduate/Scholarship)

Purpose: To encourage students to pursue careers in the Mathematics field. **Focus:** Mathematics and mathematical sciences. **Qualif.:** Applicants must be graduating seniors from public high schools in the Winston-Salem/Forsyth County School; must demonstrate interest in Mathematics. **Criteria:** Recipients are selected based on: evidence of excellence in Mathematics through both course selection and grades; intent to pursue a career in Mathematics; potential to achieve career goal; and academic excellence.

Funds Avail.: No specific amount. **To Apply:** Applicants must complete online application form. Applicants must also submit one teacher recommendation from math teacher; and official high school grade transcript (through at least first semester of the 12th grade and including SAT scores and class rank). **Deadline:** March 31. **Contact:**

Winston-Salem Foundation at the above address (see entry 7418).

7423 ■ Tien Bui Memorial Scholarships
(Undergraduate/Scholarship)

Purpose: To assist graduating high school seniors who have attended the Winston-Salem/Forsyth County Schools' Career Center. **Focus:** General studies. **Qualif.:** Applicants must: demonstrate a minimum cumulative GPA of 3.5; must have strong SAT scores and challenging academic course selection as a graduating high school senior; must demonstrate financial need (award not restricted to lowest family income); have attended the Winston-Salem/Forsyth County Schools' Career Center during their high school and successfully completed either advanced placement in Math or Science. **Criteria:** Recipients are selected based on the committee's review of application materials.

Funds Avail.: No specific amount. **To Apply:** Scholarship applications are available online. Applicants must complete the Tien Bui Memorial Scholarship application; must submit grade transcript through 1st semester of 12th grade; and submit letter of acceptance from NCSU that specifies enrollment in the College of Engineering. **Deadline:** March 31. **Contact:** Foundation's Student Aid Department, 336-714-3445.

7424 ■ Wes Burton Memorial Scholarships
(Undergraduate/Scholarship)

Purpose: To assist graduating high school seniors of Mt. Tabor High School. **Focus:** Mathematics and mathematical science; Computer and information sciences; Business administration; Engineering. **Qualif.:** Applicants must have a minimum GPA of 3.5; must demonstrate community and school service; must have an intent to pursue a career in Mathematics, Computer Science, Business Administration, or Engineering; demonstrate financial need (award is not restricted to lowest family incomes). **Criteria:** Award is given based on the committee's criteria.

Funds Avail.: No specific amount. **To Apply:** Student must complete the application in its entirety and include supplemental items and information requested in the various sections of the application. The supplemental items include: an interview with the Foundation; a grade transcript; a resume or list of student activities; one letter of recommendation from a math teacher, business teacher, or computer science teacher. **Deadline:** March 31. **Contact:** WSF Student Aid Department, 336-714-3445.

7425 ■ Andrew Blake Clark Memorial Scholarships *(Undergraduate/Scholarship)*

Purpose: To provide college scholarships to worthy graduating high school seniors at Mt. Tabor High School. **Focus:** General studies. **Qualif.:** Applicants must be gradauting seniors at Mt. Tabor High School. **Criteria:** Selection will be based on the academic promise, financial need, and school and/or community leadership.

Funds Avail.: $1,000. **To Apply:** Students interested in being considered for the scholarship award should submit the following to Stan Huck in the Mt. Tabor Guidance Office: transcript of high school courses through 1st semester 12th grade; high school resume; personal statement describing accomplishments and future plans. **Deadline:** April 4. **Contact:** WSF Student Aid Department, 336-714-3445.

7426 ■ Elmer and Rosa Lee Collins Scholarships *(Undergraduate/Scholarship)*

Purpose: To provide a college scholarship to a worthy graduating high school senior from a Forsyth County high school. **Focus:** General studies. **Qualif.:** Applicants must demonstrate character and purpose as evidenced in school, community, church, and work activities; academic success by achieving a minimum, unweighted, cumulative GPA of 3.5 with strong course selection; financial need (however, the scholarship is not restricted to lower family incomes); and must be US citizens. **Criteria:** Selection will be based on the committee's criteria.

Funds Avail.: $2,500. **To Apply:** Eligible high school seniors may complete an application online. Applicants are responsible for submitting the completed application and all supplemental items to the Foundation. Supplemental items include: grade transcript through the 1st semester of the 12th grade; one recommendation from a teacher, guidance couselor, coach, principal, employer, clergy, or other community leader who has supervised, counseled or coached applicant in some capacity. **Deadline:** March 31. **Contact:** WSF Student Aid Department, 336-714-3445.

7427 ■ Lloyd E. and Rachel S. Collins Scholarships *(Undergraduate/Scholarship)*

Purpose: To award scholarships to worthy graduating high school seniors form North, South, and West Stokes High Schools who will attend an accredited two or four-year college or university. **Focus:** General studies. **Qualif.:** Applicants must demonstrate academic achievement, participate in community service, demonstrate good character, participate in extracurricular activities, demonstrate financial need. **Criteria:** Selection will be based on the committee's criteria.

Funds Avail.: $1,000. **To Apply:** Applications for the scholarship are available in the guidance offices of the three Stokes County high schools. **Deadline:** April 1.

Remarks: Established in 1991. **Contact:** WSF Student Aid Department, 336-714-3445.

7428 ■ D.C. Cornelius Memorial Scholarships
(Undergraduate/Scholarship)

Purpose: To award scholarship to a graduating high school senior from Forbush High School. **Focus:** General studies. **Qualif.:** Applicants must demonstrate, character, leadership, compassion for all people and dedication to service of community and school. Applicants must have a minimum GPA of 2.8. Demonstration of financial need is preferred. Applicants must be a US citizen. **Criteria:** Award is given based on the committee's criteria.

Funds Avail.: $1,000. **To Apply:** Scholarship applications will be available in the guidance office at Forbush High School and also online. Students must complete the application in its entirety; include grade transcripts with the application at time of submittal; and include recommendations with the application. **Deadline:** April 15. **Contact:** WSF Student Aid Department, 336-714-3445.

7429 ■ Serena D. Dalton Scholarships
(Undergraduate/Scholarship)

Purpose: To provide financial aid for needy students. **Focus:** General studies. **Qualif.:** Applicants must have adjusted gross income within the table guidelines (table is based on up to 330% above the federal poverty level); be a resident of Forsyth County; must have achieved a current cumulative GPA of at least 2.0; must be enrolled a minimum of six credit hours/semester during the academic year in a program leading to a first time two or four year degree, certificate, or diploma from an accredited institution which participates in the federal student aid program; must be a

Awards are arranged alphabetically below their administering organizations

US citizen. **Criteria:** Selection will be based on the committee's criteria.

Funds Avail.: No specific amount. **To Apply:** The following items are required to complete the application process: Submittal of completed application and signed signature page; Signed copy of parents'/guardians'/family's previous year's 1040, 1040A, or 1040EZ income tax return (for dependent students); Signed copy of applicant's previous year's tax return; Official high school grade transcript through at least 1st semester of the 12th grade or year-end college grade transcript, whichever is the most recent (request from the school's Registrar and forward to the Foundation); Copy of the Student Aid Report if applicant has applied for federal aid; Copy of the financial aid award letter. Please submit the application on-line and follow with additional items as soon as you receive them. **Deadline:** March 31. **Contact:** WSF Student Aid Department, 336-714-3445.

7430 ■ Dean Prim Scholarships *(Undergraduate/Scholarship)*

Purpose: To provide travel and college scholarships to high school juniors and seniors. **Focus:** General studies. **Qualif.:** Qualified candidates must be: at least 16 years of age; a high school junior or high school senior; must demonstrate excellence in schoolwork as evidenced by course selection and grades (minimum unweighted GPA of 3.0); must participate in extracurricular school activities, community and/or church activities, and school or community athletics; must demonstrate good character and show interest in and concern for being an active member of society; must be committed to traveling and studying in China and have the full support of parent(s) to participate. The scholarship is available to students regardless of race, sex, national, origin, or religion. **Criteria:** Selection will be based on the committee's criteria.

Funds Avail.: $500. **To Apply:** The Prim scholarship application is on The Winston-Salem Foundation's web site. It is the student's responsibility to make sure that, along with submittal for the electronic application completed in its entirety, all supplemental materials are in the office of The Winston-Salem Foundation by the deadline. Supplemental materials include: a grade transcript, through 10th grade for juniors and 11th grade for seniors; two recommendations as described in the application; a recent photograph (include student's name on back of photo); **Deadline:** October 31. **Contact:** WSF Student Aid Department, 336-714-3445.

7431 ■ Wade and Marcelene Duncan Scholarships *(Undergraduate/Scholarship)*

Purpose: to provide scholarships to worthy high school seniors graduating from either North Stokes or South Stokes High schools. **Focus:** General studies. **Qualif.:** Applicant must be a graduating senior from either North Stokes or South Stokes High School who will attend an accredited four-year educational institution. Applicants must demonstrate leadership, participate in community service, participate in athletics and be generally well-rounded. **Criteria:** The applications will be reviewed by the Wade and Marcelene Duncan Scholarship Fund Committee at each high school. Upon determination of the scholarship recipient each year, the selection committee will notify The Winston-Salem Foundation of that individual's name, address, college of choice, social security number, and telephone number.

Funds Avail.: $250. **To Apply:** Applications and all required materials must be delivered to your high school guidance office. Students should contact the guidance office at North Stokes High School or South Stokes High School to request applications. Applications are also available online. **Deadline:** March 31. **Contact:** North Stokes High School, 336-593-8134; South Stokes High School, 336-994-2995.

7432 ■ Virginia Elizabeth and Alma Vane Taylor Student Nurse Scholarships *(Undergraduate/Scholarship)*

Purpose: Provides scholarships for N.C. residents pursuing two and four-year Nursing degrees at accredited N.C. colleges. **Focus:** Nursing. **Qualif.:** Applicants must: be accepted into an accredited North Carolina school of nursing program, as verified by an acceptance letter; have a family adjusted gross income that does not exceed $80,000; have a high school/college cumulative GPA of at least 2.5. Preference will be given to those seeking first time associate or baccalaureate degrees; those with masters degrees in any area will be ineligible to apply. **Criteria:** Selection will be based on the committee's criteria.

Funds Avail.: $1,200. **To Apply:** The Winston-Salem Foundation's General Financial Aid Application will be used to apply for this scholarship. The General Financial Aid Application is available online or you may request an application to the Foundation's Student Aid Committee. **Deadline:** March 31. **Contact:** WSF Student Aid Department, 336-714-3445.

7433 ■ Forsyth County Nursing Scholarships *(Undergraduate/Scholarship)*

Purpose: To provide educational need-based scholarships for Forsyth County residents seeking nursing degrees at accredited two year and four year colleges and who will, upon completing a degree, practice nursing in Forsyth County, N.C. Preference will be given to those seeking first-time associate or baccalaureate nursing degree. **Focus:** Nursing. **Qualif.:** Applicants must have a family adjusted gross income within the table guidelines (table is based on up to 330% above the federal poverty level); have achieved a current cumulative grade point average of at least 2.0; be a US citizen; be a child of a living or deceased Vietnam veteran; be a Forsyth County N.C. resident; and provide a letter of acceptance into a nursing program. **Criteria:** Selection will be based on the committee's criteria.

Funds Avail.: No specific amount. **To Apply:** The following items are required to complete the application process: Submittal of completed application and signed signature page; Signed copy of parents'/guardians'/family's previous year's 1040, 1040A, or 1040EZ income tax return (for dependent students); Signed copy of applicant's previous year's tax return; Official high school grade transcript through at least 1st semester of the 12th grade or college grade transcript, whichever is the most recent (request from the school's Registrar and forward to the Foundation); Copy of the Student Aid Report if applicant has applied for federal aid; Copy of the financial aid award letter. Please submit the application on-line and follow with additional items as soon as you receive them. **Deadline:** March 31. **Contact:** WSF Student Aid Department, 336-714-3445.

7434 ■ Denise Franklin Journalism Scholarships *(Undergraduate/Scholarship)*

Purpose: To provide a merit scholarship to high school senior planning to pursue a career in journalism. **Focus:** Journalism. **Qualif.:** Students must have a minimum, unweighted, grade point average of 3.0. Applicants should have a minimum of two years involvement in a journalism project or involvement in two different types of journalistic media. Students of color with a strong academic record and desire to pursue a career in journalism are encouraged to apply. Applicant must be a US citizen. **Criteria:** Selection will be based on the committee's criteria.

Funds Avail.: $500. **To Apply:** Applicants must complete and submit an application online at the Foundation's Web site. In addition to submittal of the application, applicants must also provide the following to be considered: Provide a letter of recommendation from a current journalism instructor; Submit up to three samples of journalism work such as published newspaper articles, audio or videotapes, a website or a photo essay (samples will not be returned); High school grade transcript through first semester, 12th grade. **Deadline:** March 31.

Remarks: Established in 2004. **Contact:** Edna Barker, 336-714-3445; Kay Dillon, 336-714-3446.

7435 ■ Gaddy Student Scholarships
(Undergraduate/Scholarship)

Purpose: To give priority consideration to those students who will attend Davidson College or Wake Forest University. **Focus:** General studies. **Qualif.:** This renewable scholarship seeks to identify those students: who are graduating high school seniors from R.J. Reynolds High School; who demonstrate academic promise; who are US citizens; who have participated as athletes or in support positions in high school athletics (broad consideration); who have financial need (broad consideration given - not restricted to lower family incomes). **Criteria:** Selection will be based on the committee's criteria.

Funds Avail.: $1,000. **To Apply:** Students must provide the following: A completed application; grade transcript through 1st semester, 12th grade; one recommendation as described in the application guidelines. Schedule an interview, if so advised. **Deadline:** March 31.

Remarks: Established in 1997. **Contact:** WSF Student Aid Department, 336-714-3445.

7436 ■ Garden Club Council of Winston-Salem and Forsyth County Council *(Undergraduate/Scholarship)*

Purpose: To provide financial support for educational opportunities to legal residents of North Carolina who will attend a two and/or four year college and have been accepted into the Horticulture Technology or Landscape Architecture curriculums at Forsyth Technical Community College or other accredited post-secondary schools in North Carolina. **Focus:** Horticulture; Landscape architecture and design. **Qualif.:** Applicants must demonstrate academic potential; financial need; full-time attendance (minimum of 12 credit hours/semester); pursuit of undergraduate associate or baccalaureate degree (first-time degrees preferred); must be US citizens. The scholarship is renewable for a second consecutive year if student maintains a cumulative college GPA of 2.0, continues full-time enrollment and continues in horticulture or landscape architecture; otherwise, scholarship is forfeited. Available to traditional and non-traditional age students. **Criteria:** Decisions are made by The Winston-Salem Foundation's Student Aid Committee. Individual will be selected on a first come, first served basis but must meet all qualifications. Number and size of scholarship(s) will depend on available income.

Funds Avail.: No specific amount. **To Apply:** Application must be completed and submitted with all required materials to the Student Aid Department at The Winston-Salem Foundation. Supplemental materials listed on the last page of the application include previous year's federal tax return for student and parent, if student is a dependent; academic year-end grade transcript; Federal Student Aid Report; federal award notice and interview with student aid staff. **Deadline:** March 31. **Contact:** Edna Barker, 336-714-3445; Kay Dillon, 336-714-3446.

7437 ■ John L. Gilmer Educational Grants
(Undergraduate/Scholarship)

Purpose: To provide scholarships to the graduating high school seniors from accredited public, private, or parochial schools, who will attend accredited higher education institutions seeking undergraduate degrees. **Focus:** General studies. **Qualif.:** Applicants must be Forsyth County residents; be graduating high school seniors; have achieved a minimum, unweighted cumulative GPA of 3.0; have a family adjusted gross income not exceeding $80,000. **Criteria:** Selection will be based on the committee's criteria.

Funds Avail.: $1,000. **To Apply:** Eligible high school seniors may complete an application online. Applicants are responsible for submitting the completed application and all supplemental items, except the family federal tax return, to the Foundation by March 31. The family federal tax return must be submitted by April 15. Supplemental items include: Grade transcript through the 1st semester of the 12th grade; Family federal tax return from last year; An interview if so advised. Those recipients completing an undergraduate degree in three years will forfeit the fourth year's scholarship. **Deadline:** March 31. **Contact:** WSF Student Aid Department, 336-714-3445.

7438 ■ John L. Gilmer Merit Based Scholarships
(Undergraduate/Scholarship)

Purpose: To provide scholarships to the graduating high school seniors from accredited public, private, or parochial schools, who will attend accredited higher education institutions seeking undergraduate degrees. **Focus:** General studies. **Qualif.:** Applicants must be Forsyth County residents; graduating high school seniors; must have achieved a minimum, unweighted cumulative GPA of 3.5. **Criteria:** Selection will be based on the committee's criteria. Awards are renewable for three consecutive years as long as recipients maintain full-time enrollment and a cumulative minimum college GPA of 2.75, as ascertained by academic year-end grade transcript. An official grade transcript is required each summer. Any student failing to maintain a minimum cumulative GPA of 2.75 at current academic year end may be considered again for renewal at the end of the next academic year, with overall consideration for renewal not exceeding the time frame of the scholarship.

Funds Avail.: No specific amount. **To Apply:** Eligible high school seniors may complete an application online. Applicants are responsible for submitting the completed application and all supplemental items to the Foundation. Supplemental items include: Grade transcript through the 1st semester of the 12th grade; One recommendation from a teacher, guidance counselor, coach, principal, employer, clergy, or other community leader who has supervised, counseled or coached applicant in some capacity; An interview if so advised. Those recipients completing an undergraduate degree in three years will forfeit the fourth year's scholarship. **Deadline:** March 31. **Contact:** WSF Student Aid Department, 336-714-3445.

7439 ■ L. Gordon, Jr. and June D. Pfefferkorn Scholarships *(Undergraduate/Scholarship)*

Purpose: To award worthy graduating high school seniors in Forsyth County. **Focus:** General studies. **Qualif.:** Applicants must: attend an accredited four-year college or university in North Carolina; be a resident of Forsyth County; have achieved a current cumulative, unweighted GPA of at least 3.5; demonstrate significant promise in leadership, community service, and school service; be US citizens; demonstrate financial need, (award not restricted to lowest family incomes); be graduating high school seniors. **Criteria:** Selection will be based on the committee's criteria.

Funds Avail.: No specific amount. **To Apply:** The following items are required to complete the application process: submittal of completed application and signed signature page; signed copy of parents'/guardians'/ family's previous year's 1040, 1040A, 1040EZ income tax return; signed copy of applicant's previous year's tax return; official high school grade transcript through at least 1st semester of the 12th grade; one recommendation from a teacher, guidance, coach, principal, employer, clergy, or other community leader who has supervised, counseled or coached applicant in some capacity. **Deadline:** March 31. **Contact:** WSF Student Aid Department, 336-714-3445.

7440 ■ Claude B. Hart Memorial Scholarships *(Undergraduate/Scholarship)*

Purpose: To award scholarship to worthy graduating high school seniors from Elkin High School who are US citizens. **Focus:** Mathematics and mathematical sciences; Engineering. **Qualif.:** Applicants must demonstrate significant promise in academics, leadership, community service and school service and intend to major in mathematics (accounting, computer science, business administration) and/or engineering (mechanical, civil, chemical, etc.) in college. Demonstration of financial need is preferred, but award is not restricted to lowest family incomes. Renewal of the award after the first year will require that the student be a full-time undergraduate student at an accredited four-year institution, maintain a minimum cumulative grade point average of 2.5, and continue to major in mathematics or engineering. **Criteria:** Selection will be based on the committee's criteria.

Funds Avail.: No specific amount. **To Apply:** Scholarship applications will be provided in the guidance office at Elkin High School. Student must complete the application, requested transcripts, and financial information before being considered by the Elkin High School Scholarship Committee. The Scholarship Committee will submit up to 5 candidates to The Winston-Salem Foundation for review by the Elkin Advisory Committee or its appointed subcommittee. **Contact:** WSF Student Aid Department, 336-714-3445.

7441 ■ Oliver Joel and Ellen Pell Denny Healthcare Scholarship Fund *(Undergraduate/Scholarship)*

Purpose: To provide grants to the North Carolina residents pursuing education in the allied health fields. **Focus:** Health care services. **Qualif.:** Applicants must be seeking a two or four year degree or be enrolled in a program leading to a certificate or diploma; be attending an accredited North Carolina school pursuing healthcare education such as, but not limited, registered nursing, licensed practical nursing, nuclear medicine, radiography, and respiratory therapy; provide an acceptance letter for all programs; have a family adjusted gross income that does not exceed $80,000; have a high school/college cumulative GPA of at least 2.5 for all healthcare programs, including nursing. Students must be North Carolina residents and US citizens. Preference will be given to those living in Forsyth, Davidson, Davie, Stokes, Surry, and Yadkin counties. **Criteria:** Selection will be based on the committee's criteria.

Funds Avail.: $1,200. **To Apply:** The Winston-Salem Foundation's General Financial Aid Application will be used to apply for this scholarship. The General Financial Aid Applications are available in high school guidance office and on the website. **Deadline:** March 31. **Contact:** WSF Student Aid Department, 336-714-3445.

7442 ■ Jimmy Johnson Memorial Scholarships *(Undergraduate/Scholarship)*

Purpose: To provide financial support for a graduating high school senior from Forsyth County who will attend Forsyth Technical Community College. **Focus:** Construction. **Qualif.:** This fund seeks to identify those high school seniors who: demonstrate significant promise in academics and involvement in community service; have a minimum, unweighted high school GPA of 3.0; demonstrate financial need (preferred, but not restricted to lowest family incomes); are enrolled full-time at Forsyth Technical Community College in a construction or a house-build related program. Applicants must be US citizens; Forsyth County residents; graduating high school seniors. **Criteria:** Selection will be based on the committee's criteria.

Funds Avail.: No specific amount. **To Apply:** Applications are available online. First time applicants must complete the application in its entirety and provide the following supplemental items as they are obtained by the applicant: parent/guardian's tax return from previous year; applicant's tax return from previous year; official high school grade transcript through the first semester of the 12th grade; resume; one recommendation; copy of Student Aid Report if applicant applied for federal aid; copy of Financial Aid Award Notice. **Deadline:** March 31. **Contact:** WSF Student Aid Department, 336-714-3445.

7443 ■ Stella B. Johnson Scholarships *(Undergraduate/Scholarship)*

Purpose: To provide educational aid for college to qualified traditional and non-traditional age applicants from charitable funds established by generous supporters of the community. **Focus:** General studies. **Qualif.:** Applicants must: have a family adjusted gross income within the table guidelines (table is based on up to 330% above the federal poverty level); be residents of Forsyth County; have achieved a current cumulative grade point average of at least 2.0; must be enrolled a minimum of six credit hours/ semester during the academic year in a program leading to a first time two or four year degree, certificate, or diploma from an accredited institution which participates in the federal student aid program; must be US citizens. **Criteria:** Selection will be based on the committee's criteria.

Funds Avail.: No specific amount. **To Apply:** The following items are required to complete the application process: submittal of completed application and signed signature page; signed copy of parents'/guardians'/family's previous year's 1040, 1040A, or 1040EZ income tax return (for dependent students); signed copy of applicant's previous year's tax return; official high school grade transcript through at least 1st semester of the 12th grade or year-end college grade transcript, whichever is the most recent (request from the school's Registrar and forward to the

Foundation); copy of the Student Aid Report if applicant has applied for federal aid; copy of the financial aid award letter; interview if so advised. Please submit the application on-line **Deadline:** March 31. **Contact:** WSF Student Aid Department, 336-714-3445.

7444 ■ Douglas Gray Kinel Scholarships
(Undergraduate/Scholarship)

Purpose: To award freshman who will pursue a degree in music from one of the following institutions: North Carolina School of the Arts, Salem College, Wake Forest University, or Winston-Salem State University. **Focus:** Music. **Qualif.:** This scholarship seeks to identify those students who: will pursue a degree in music; demonstrate a minimum, cumulative, unweighted GPA of 3.5; have financial need (scholarship is not restricted to lowest family incomes); are residents of Forsyth County; are Moravian, preferably; are studying to enter a church-related vocation, preferably. **Criteria:** Selection will be based on the committee's criteria.

Funds Avail.: $500. **To Apply:** Scholarship applications will be available online. Students must: complete the scholarship application; provide grade transcript through the 1st semester of 12th grade; submit one recommendation as outlined on the application; attend an interview if so advised. **Deadline:** March 31. **Contact:** WSF Student Aid Department, 336-714-3445.

7445 ■ Johny Lineberry Memorial Scholarships
(Undergraduate/Scholarship)

Purpose: To award a worthy Forbush High School senior who will go directly to an accredited vocational/technical school, community college, or college/university in pursuit of a certificate, diploma or baccalaureate degree. **Focus:** General science. **Qualif.:** Applicants must be graduating high school seniors from Forsbush High School in East Bend, N.C.; demonstrate a minimum, cumulative, unweighted GPA of at least 2.5; demonstrate strong character and community involvement; intend to study the field of electronics, preferably. **Criteria:** Selection will be based on the committee's criteria.

Funds Avail.: $500. **To Apply:** Applications for the scholarship are available in the guidance office at Forbush High School and from The Winston-Salem Foundation's web site. Completed applications should be submitted to the guidance office. **Deadline:** March 31. **Contact:** WSF Student Aid Department, 336-714-3445.

7446 ■ L.D. and Elsie Long Memorial Scholarships *(Undergraduate/Scholarship)*

Purpose: To provide educational scholarships for residents of Forsyth County to attend Wake Forest University. **Focus:** General studies. **Qualif.:** Applicant must have a family adjusted gross income within the table guidelines (table is based on up to 330% above the federal poverty level); be a resident of Forsyth County; have achieved a current cumulative GPA of at least 2.0; must be enrolled a minimum of six credits hours/semester during the academic year in a program leading to a graduate degree from Wake Forest University. **Criteria:** Selection will be based on the committee's criteria.

Funds Avail.: No specific amount. **To Apply:** The following items are required to complete the application process: submittal of completed application and signed signature page; signed copy of applicant's previous year's tax return; official high school grade transcript through at least 1st semester of the 12th grade or year-end college grade transcript, whichever is the most recent (request from the school's Registrar and forward to the Foundation); copy of the Student Aid Report (SAR) if applicant has applied for federal aid; copy of the financial award letter; interview if so advised. **Deadline:** March 31. **Contact:** WSF Student Aid Department, 336-714-3445.

7447 ■ Millennium Charter Academy College Scholarships *(Undergraduate/Scholarship)*

Purpose: To award worthy graduating high school senior who attended Millennium Charter Academy in Mount Airy, North Carolina in grades six through eight. **Focus:** General studies. **Qualif.:** Applicants must be graduating seniors pursuing a bachelor's degree at a college or university; have attended Millennium Charter Academy for at least three years; exemplify noteworthy academic success, strong moral character and a keen sense of community. **Criteria:** Selection will be based on the committee's criteria.

Funds Avail.: No specific amount. **To Apply:** The following items must be submitted to the Millennium Charter Academic Scholarship Committee: a grade transcript with class rank, as well as weighted and unweighted GPA; one educational reference and two non-family character references; records of leadership and extra-curricular school and community activities; a 100-300 word typed essay that describes applicant's personal and professional goals. **Deadline:** February 28. **Contact:** Kirby R. McCrary, Headmaster Millennium Charter Academy 500 Old Springs Road Mt. Airy, N.C. 27030.

7448 ■ N.W. Mitchell-Piedmont Federal Savings and Loans Endowed Scholarships
(Undergraduate/Scholarship)

Purpose: To provide merit-based scholarships for worthy students attending Forsyth Technical Community College. **Focus:** General studies. **Qualif.:** The renewable scholarship seeks to identify those students who: demonstrate academic success; are residents of Forsyth, Davie, Davidson, Stokes, Surry, Watauge, or Yadkin counties; are first semester students enrolled in a minimum of 12 course hours per semester; are US citizens or eligible noncitizens (as verified by the Student Aid Report); show interest and concern for being an active member of society. **Criteria:** Selection will be based on the committee's criteria.

Funds Avail.: $1,000. **Number Awarded:** 2. **To Apply:** Students should complete the application in its entirety and submit it by the deadline. In addition, the following supplemental items must also be submitted by the deadline: official year-end grade transcript; one recommendation; and student aid report. **Deadline:** July 31. **Contact:** WSF Student Aid Department, 336-714-3445.

7449 ■ Orthopaedic Specialists Nursing Scholarships *(Undergraduate/Scholarship)*

Purpose: To provide educational need-based scholarships for Forsyth County residents seeking nursing degrees at Forsyth Technical Community College or Winston-Salem State University. **Focus:** Nursing. **Qualif.:** Applicants must be pursuing a first-time associate degree or a bachelors degree in nursing. Must provide a copy of letter of admission to the nursing program at FTCC or WSSU (students ineligible until accepted into nursing program); demonstration of academic promise. Must have achieved 3.0 cumulative, unweighted GPA for graduating high school senior or 2.6 cumulative GPA as a college student; demonstrate financial need based on 300% of federal poverty guidelines. Scholarship recipients are expected to make themselves available for scholarship presentation events. **Criteria:**

Selection will be based on the committee's criteria.

Funds Avail.: No specific amount. **To Apply:** Scholarship application may be obtained online and submitted after January 1 each year for the next academic year. In addition to the application, the following items are required for first-time applicants: signed copy of parent/guardian federal income tax return (for dependent students); signed copy of applicant's federal income tax return; current official transcript of academic record (obtain from school Registrar); copy of Student Aid Report if student applied for federal aid; copy of financial aid notice from college if student applied for federal aid. **Deadline:** March 31. **Contact:** Edna Barker, 336-714-3445.

7450 ■ Alice Conger Patterson Scholarships *(Undergraduate/Scholarship)*

Purpose: To help deserving adult women achieve their educational goals. **Focus:** General studies. **Qualif.:** Scholarship seeks to identify those: who demonstrate financial need; who are female students, twenty-three years of age or older; who have earned a high school diploma or equivalent certificate (GED, home school completion, adult high school diploma); who are applying to or are currently enrolled in a four-year college or university in the Piedmont Triad of North Carolina in pursuit of an undergraduate degree. Preference will be given to students at Salem College who demonstrate a strong purpose in pursuing a liberal arts degree. **Criteria:** Selection will be based on the committee's criteria.

Funds Avail.: No specific amount. **To Apply:** Scholarship applications will be available online. Students must submit: completed application and signed signature page; copy of federal tax return for previous year; copy of the financial aid award letter for upcoming year; grade transcripts with class ranking in high school and transcripts for all college or university work to date; one recommendation. **Deadline:** March 31. **Contact:** WSF Student Aid Department, 336-714-3445.

7451 ■ William H. and Lena M. Petree Scholarships *(Undergraduate/Scholarship)*

Purpose: To provide college scholarships for worthy Forsyth County residents. **Focus:** General studies. **Qualif.:** Applicants must be graduating high-school seniors; demonstrate academic promise during high-school; have a minimum, cumulative, unweighted GPA of 3.5 through 1st semester, 12th grade; demonstrate a willingness for self-help during high school; demonstrate leadership, school service, and community service during high school; demonstrate financial need for upcoming college expenses (award not restricted to lowest family incomes); be US citizens. **Criteria:** Selection will be based on the committee's criteria.

Funds Avail.: No specific amount. **To Apply:** Application may be downloaded from the Foundation's web site. In addition to completing the application, students must: submit one recommendation; submit a grade transcript through first semester, 12th grade; be present for an interview. **Deadline:** March 31. **Contact:** WSF Student Aid Department, 336-714-3445.

7452 ■ Pfafftown Jaycees/Lynn Canada Memorial Scholarships *(Undergraduate/Scholarship)*

Purpose: To provide scholarships for Forsyth County residents seeking nursing degrees at Forsyth Technical Community College. **Focus:** General studies. **Qualif.:** Applicants must be enrolled on a full-time basis in the pursuit of a first associate or a first baccalaureate degree; provide a copy of letter of admission into the nursing program at FTCC (ineligible until accepted into nursing program); maintain an unweighted high school or college cumulative GPA of 2.5; not exceed annual adjusted gross family income of $80,000; be US citizens. **Criteria:** Selection will be based on the committee's criteria.

Funds Avail.: No specific amount. **To Apply:** Eligible applicants may obtain a scholarship application from The Winston-Salem Foundation's website. In addition to the completed/signed application, the applicants is responsible for providing the following required supplemental items: signed copy of parent/guardian's federal income tax return; signed copy of student's federal income tax return, if applicable; applicant's official high school (as of 1st semester, 12th grade) or official college grade transcript (as of academic year-end); copy of Student Aid Report and financial aid notice if student applied for federal aid. **Deadline:** March 31. **Contact:** Edna Barker, 336-714-3445.

7453 ■ John S. and Jacqueline P. Rider Scholarships *(Undergraduate/Scholarship)*

Purpose: To provide an award to a graduating high school senior in Forsyth County N.C. **Focus:** General studies. **Qualif.:** Applicants must: demonstrate financial need (not restricted to lower family incomes); be a resident of Forsyth County; have achieved a current cumulative grade point average of at least 3.5; must be enrolled full-time in a program leading to a two or four year degree, certificate, or diploma from an accredited institution which participates in the federal student aid program; be a graduating high school senior. **Criteria:** Selection will be based on merit and financial need though need is not restricted to lower incomes.

Funds Avail.: $500. **To Apply:** The following items are required to complete the application process: submittal of completed application and signed signature page; signed copy of parent's/guardians'/family's previous year's 1040, 1040A, or 1040EZ income tax return; signed copy of applicant's previous year's tax return; official high school grade transcript through at least 1st semester of the 12th grade (request from the school's registrar and forward to the Foundation); one recommendation from a teacher, guidance counselor, coach, principal, employer, clergy, or other community leader who has supervised, counseled or coached applicant in some capacity. **Deadline:** March 31. **Contact:** WSF Student Aid Department, 336-714-3445.

7454 ■ Ray and Pearly Sams Scholarships *(Undergraduate/Scholarship)*

Purpose: To provide financial assistance for college tuition, fees and room and board for worthy graduating high school seniors in Forsyth County. **Focus:** General studies. **Qualif.:** This fund seeks to identify the well-rounded graduating high-school senior who: has achieved excellence in school work as evidence by course selection and grades (minimum cumulative unweighted GPA of 3.5 on a 4.0 scale, or equivalent) through 1st semester of the 12th grade; has participated in school service clubs and/or other school activities; has participated in non-school community service activities; demonstrates good moral character; demonstrates evidence of financial need, although award is not restricted to lower incomes; is a United States citizen. **Criteria:** Selection will be based on the committee's criteria.

Funds Avail.: $2,500. **To Apply:** High school seniors may complete and submit the application online. The application and the following items must be received in the foundation's

Awards are arranged alphabetically below their administering organizations

office by the deadline: official grade transcript through the 1st semester of the 12 grade; one recommendation from a teacher, guidance counselor, coach, principal, employer, clergy, or other community leader who has supervised, counseled or coached applicant in some capacity; an interview with the Foundation's Director of Student Aid, if so advised **Deadline:** May 1. **Contact:** WSF Student Aid Department, 336-714-3445.

7455 ■ Bruce Shelton Scholarships *(Undergraduate/Scholarship)*

Purpose: To provide an award to a graduating high school student from a Forsyth County school who displays the traits of athletic excellence, academic achievement, leadership, and social responsibility. **Focus:** General studies. **Qualif.:** The renewable scholarship seeks to identify students who exhibit the following qualities in equal measure: athletic excellence the student must have excelled in at least one varsity sport; social responsibility - the student must have participated in at least one extracurricular or community activity; academic success - the student must have a minimum, unweighted high school cumulative grade point average of at least 3.0, as of the 1st semester of the 12th grade and be ranked in the top 25% of the senior class; leadership - the student must possess qualities that exhibit a willingness to "go the extra mile". Recipients receiving renewal awards must maintain a minimum cumulative GPA of 2.5 and full time enrollment of at least 12 hours each semester at accredited four-year institutions. Official grade transcripts must be submitted each summer by July 1 for verification of acceptable academic pace and GPA. Recipients should request grade transcripts from the Registrar for themselves and forward to the Foundation. **Criteria:** Selection will be based on the committee's criteria.

Funds Avail.: $1,000. **To Apply:** Students should complete the application in its entirety and submit it by the deadline. In addition, the following supplemental items must be submitted: a grade transcript through the first semester of the 12th grade; one recommendation as described in the application. **Deadline:** March 31. **Contact:** WSF Student Aid Department, 336-714-3445.

7456 ■ Tom Shown Scholarships *(Undergraduate/Scholarship)*

Purpose: To award worthy students from the counties of Forsyth, Wikes, Surry, Yahkin, and Davie who plan to attend an accredited two or four year college or university, preferably in North Carolina. **Focus:** General studies. **Qualif.:** Applicants must: demonstrate financial need (award not restricted to lower incomes); have a cumulative, minimum high school or college GPA of 2.7; must be employed a minimum of 20 hours, monthly (including college work study); be US citizens. **Criteria:** Selection will be based on the committee's criteria.

Funds Avail.: $1,000-$2,000. **To Apply:** The General Financial Aid Application should be completed for this scholarship and is available online. Applicants are responsible for submitting the completed application and all supplemental items. Supplemental items include: Parent/guardian's tax return (for dependent students); applicant's tax return; official high school grade transcript through at least the first semester of the 12th grade or year-end college grade transcript; a copy of your Student Aid Report and financial aid notice if student applied for federal aid; an interview at The Winston-Salem Foundation. **Deadline:** July 31. **Contact:** WSF Student Aid Department, 336-714-3445.

7457 ■ Stultz Scholarships *(Undergraduate/Scholarship)*

Purpose: To provide educational aid to qualified traditional and non-traditional age applicants from charitable funds established by generous supporters of the community. **Focus:** General studies. **Qualif.:** Applicant must: have a family adjusted gross income within the table guidelines (table is based on up to 330% above the federal poverty level); be a resident of Forsyth County; have achieved a current cumulative grade point of at least 2.0; be enrolled a minimum of six credit hours/semester during the academic year, in a program leading to a first time two or four year degree, certificate, or diploma from an accredited institution which participates in the federal student aid program; be a US citizen. **Criteria:** Selection will be based on the committee's criteria.

Funds Avail.: No specific amount. **To Apply:** The following items are required to complete the application process: submittal of completed application and signed signature page; signed copy of parent's/guardians'/family's previous year's 1040, 1040A, or 1040EZ income tax return; signed copy of applicant's previous year's tax return; official high school grade transcript through at least 1st semester of the 12th grade or year-end college grade transcript, whichever is the most recent, (request from the school's Registrar and forward to the Foundation); copy of the Student Aid Report (SAR) and financial aid award letter if applicant has applied for federal aid; interview if so advised. **Deadline:** July 31. **Contact:** WSF Student Aid Department, 336-714-3445.

7458 ■ Jeff Turner-Forsyth Audubon Society Scholarships *(Undergraduate/Scholarship)*

Purpose: To support worthy graduating high school seniors from a Forsyth County High School and admitted to a four year accredited college or university. **Focus:** General studies. **Qualif.:** Applicants must demonstrate character, leadership, and solid academic skills (minimum unweighted GPA of 3.0). Demonstration of financial need will be considered but is not required. US citizenship is required. **Criteria:** Selection will be based on committee's criteria.

Funds Avail.: $500. **To Apply:** Scholarship Applications will be available online. Student must: complete the Winston-Salem Foundation application in its entirety, including an attached listing of student activities as well as personal statement; provide grade transcript through 1st semester of 12th grade with the application, at time of submittal; include at least one letter of reference (3 maximum) which addresses the applicant's character as well as environmental interest/experiences. **Deadline:** April 30.

Remarks: Established in May of 2005. **Contact:** WSF Student Aid Department, 336-714-3445.

7459 ■ Nell and Spencer Waggoner Scholarships *(Undergraduate/Scholarship)*

Purpose: To award merit-based scholarships to worthy graduating high school seniors in Forsyth County who intend to pursue baccalaureate degrees at accredited universities and colleges. **Focus:** General studies. **Qualif.:** Preference is given to students who: demonstrate evidence of excellence through course selection and academic achievement with a minimum cumulative GPA of 3.0 (D's are undesirable in any coursework in grades 9-12); outstanding community and school leadership; demonstrate community service and/or school service and concern for being a contributing member of society (work experience recognized for those who have less community involvement due to work obligations). The scholarships are for four consecutive years, provided requirements for renewal are met. Renewing recipients must provide an official academic year-end grade transcript to the Foundation each year. Students must request grade transcripts for themselves from the college registrar and then forward the transcript to the Foundation. **Criteria:** Selection will be based on the committee's criteria.

Funds Avail.: No specific amount. **To Apply:** In addition to a completed application, the following items are required: a high school grade transcript through at least the first semester of the 12th grade; an interview if so advised; one recommendation. **Deadline:** March 31. **Contact:** WSF Student Aid Department, 336-714-3445.

7460 ■ Art and Dannie Weber Scholarships *(Undergraduate/Scholarship)*

Purpose: To provide a consecutive four-year renewable award to a graduating high school senior form a Forsyth County high school who will pursue post-secondary education. **Focus:** General studies. **Qualif.:** Applicants must: have demonstrated character and purpose as evidenced in school, community, church, and work activities; have financial need (however, the scholarship is not restricted to lower family incomes); demonstrate academic success by having achieved minimum, unweighted high school cumulative grade point average (GPA) between 2.5-3.5. **Criteria:** Selection will be based on the committee's criteria.

Funds Avail.: $750. **To Apply:** Students who are interested in applying for this scholarship should complete the application in its entirety and submit it by the deadline. In addition, the following supplemental items must be submitted: a grade transcript through the first semester of the 12th grade; family federal tax return for last year (deadline April 15); one recommendation from a teacher, guidance counselor, coach, principal, employer, clergy, or other community leader who has supervised, counseled or coached applicant in some capacity. **Deadline:** March 31. **Contact:** WSF Student Aid Department, 336-714-3445.

7461 ■ Edward Kent Welch Memorial Scholarships *(Undergraduate/Scholarship)*

Purpose: To provide college scholarships to graduating high school seniors at Mt. Tabor High School who will attend the University of North Carolina at Chapel Hill. **Focus:** General studies. **Qualif.:** Students must: have academic promise; evidence of strong moral character; have a genuine concern for others; have school and/or community leadership. The scholarship is available to students regardless of race, sex, national origin, religion, or handicap. **Criteria:** Selection will be based on the committee's criteria.

Funds Avail.: $1,500. **To Apply:** The Mt. Tabor Guidance Office will select the recipient of this award from its pool of students admitted by and planning to attend UNC-Chapel Hill. **Contact:** WSF Student Aid Department, 336-714-3445.

7462 ■ Elizabeth T. Williams Scholarships *(Undergraduate/Scholarship)*

Purpose: To award worthy graduating high school seniors who plan to attend the University of North Carolina at Chapel Hill. **Focus:** General studies. **Qualif.:** This fund seeks to identify the well-rounded individual who: has achieved academic success (minimum, cumulative, unweighted GPA of 3.0 on a 4.0 scale, or equivalent through first semester, 12th grade with appropriate course selection); has participated in student service clubs and/or other school activities; has participated in non-school community service activities; has participated directly in athletics or in support positions for athletics; may or may not have part-time work experience; demonstrates good moral character; shows evidence of financial need (not restricted to lowest incomes); and is a United States citizen. **Criteria:** Selection will be based on the committee's criteria.

Funds Avail.: No specific amount. **To Apply:** Applications may be submitted by accessing the Foundation's web site. Applicants are responsible for submitting the application and getting the supplemental items to The Winston-Salem Foundation on or before the deadline. The application packet will contain the following components: the completed application; grade transcript; two recommendations; list of student activities. **Deadline:** March 31. **Contact:** WSF Student Aid Department, 336-714-3445.

7463 ■ Edwin H. and Louise N. Williamson Endowed Scholarships *(Undergraduate/Scholarship)*

Purpose: To provide scholarships to a graduating high school senior who will pursue a bachelor's degree at the University of North Carolina-Greensboro. **Focus:** General studies. **Qualif.:** This scholarship seeks to identify those students who: demonstrate a minimum, cumulative, unweighted GPA of 3.0; have a financial need, however, the scholarship is not restricted to lowest family incomes; will attend the University of North Carolina-Greensboro; are graduating from a Forsyth County high school. **Criteria:** Selection will be based on the committee's criteria.

Funds Avail.: $1,500. **To Apply:** Scholarship applications are available online. Students must: complete application in its entirety; provide grade transcript through the 1st semester of 12th grade; provide one recommendation, as described in the application; attend an interview, if so advised. **Deadline:** February 15. **Contact:** WSF Student Aid Department, 336-714-3445.

7464 ■ Winston-Salem Foundation Scholarships *(Undergraduate/Scholarship)*

Purpose: To provide scholarships to Forsyth County graduating seniors who will pursue post-secondary education at accredited institutions. **Focus:** General studies. **Qualif.:** Applicants must have a minimum, cumulative, unweighted GPA of 2.5 to 3.0; a challenging course selection; must demonstrate leadership, school service, and community involvement; must demonstrate financial need (award is not restricted to lower family incomes). **Criteria:** Selection will be based on the committee's criteria.

Funds Avail.: No specific amount. **To Apply:** Scholarship application will be available online. Students must: complete the scholarship application in its entirely; provide grade transcript through the 1st semester of the 12th grade. **Deadline:** March 31. **Contact:** WSF Student Aid Department, 336-714-3445.

7465 ■ Blanche Raper Zimmerman Scholarships *(Professional Development/Scholarship)*

Purpose: To assist public or private teachers specializing in social science studies or history. **Focus:** History. **Qualif.:** Applicants must be history or social studies teachers of any grade, kindergarten through twelfth; must have a minimum of three years full-time teaching experience in Forsyth County. **Criteria:** Recipients are selected based on committee's review of application materials.

Funds Avail.: No specific amount. **To Apply:** Applicants should write a letter of application (no more than two pages single-spaced, typewritten) to Kay Dillon, describing the proposed participation in a conference, workshop or foreign travel, as specified in the purpose and requirements; should prepare an itemized statement of all costs associated with a conference, workshop, or travel, including costs of registration, transportation, housing, and meals; and should provide letter of recommendation from his or her principal which includes a verification of the number of years of teaching experience. **Deadline:** April 4. **Contact:** Kay Dillon, 336-714-3446; Edna Barker, 336-714-3445.

7466 ■ Winterthur Museum and Country Estate

Rte. 52
Winterthur, DE 19735
Ph: (302)888-4600
Free: 800-448-3883
E-mail: tourinfo@winterthur.org
URL: http://www.winterthur.org

7467 ■ McNeil Dissertation Fellowships *(All/Fellowship)*

Purpose: To provide financial assistance to humanities students who wish to pursue advanced research. **Focus:** Humanities. **Qualif.:** Applicants must be U.S. citizens or residents for three years prior to the application. **Criteria:** Recipients are selected based on the significance of the research.

Funds Avail.: $7,000. **To Apply:** Applicants must submit the application cover sheet; prepare an application essay of no more than 1500 words that opens with a concise overview of the project; a copy of the curriculum vitae; and two letters of reference addressing the previous scholarly record and current project. Applicants must mail six copies of the completed application package.

7468 ■ Winterthur Research Fellowships *(All/Fellowship)*

Purpose: To provide financial assistance to humanities students who wish to pursue advanced research. **Focus:** Humanities. **Qualif.:** Applicants must be U.S. citizens or residents for three years prior to the application. **Criteria:** Recipients are selected based on the significance of the research.

Funds Avail.: $1,500. **To Apply:** Applicants must submit the application cover sheet; prepare an application essay of no more than 1500 words that opens with a concise overview of the project; a copy of the curriculum vitae; and two letters of reference addressing the previous scholarly record and current project. Applicants must mail six copies of the completed application package.

7469 ■ Wisconsin Association for Food Protection

PO Box 329
Sun Prairie, WI 53590
Ph: (608)833-6181
E-mail: info@wafp-wi.org
URL: http://www.wafp-wi.org

7470 ■ E.H. Marth Food and Environmental Scholarships *(Undergraduate/Scholarship)*

Purpose: To promote and sustain interest in fields of study that may lead to a career in dairy, food, or environmental sanitation. **Focus:** Food science and technology. **Qualif.:** Applicants must be accepted or enrolled in an accredited post high school undergraduate degree or diploma program (university, college, or technical college) in Wisconsin or an out-of-state school with a reciprocal enrollment agreement with Wisconsin. They must be full-time students enrolled in a dairy science, food science, environmental sanitation or closely related major who are residents of Wisconsin. **Criteria:** Recipients are selected based on academic performance, professional potential, activities, and financial need.

Funds Avail.: No specific amount. **To Apply:** Applicants must submit a complete application form; a copy of official transcript; recommendation of advisor or instructor which should address scholastic ability, professional potential, applicable work experience, extra-curricular activities, financial need and other relevant information. **Contact:** nelsong@uwstout.edu.

7471 ■ Wisconsin Broadcasters Association

44 E Mifflin St., Ste. 900
Madison, WI 53703
Ph: (608)255-2600
Fax: (608)256-3986
Free: 800-236-1922
E-mail: mendicott@wi-broadcasters.org
URL: http://www.wi-broadcasters.org

7472 ■ Wisconsin Broadcasters Association Scholarships *(Undergraduate/Scholarship)*

Purpose: To assist students enrolled in broadcasting-related educational programs at four-year public or private colleges and universities. **Focus:** Broadcasting. **Qualif.:** Applicants must have completed 60 credits and must be majoring in broadcasting, communications, or related field at a four-year public or private college or university; must have Wisconsin connection in that they must have either graduated from a Wisconsin high school or be attending a Wisconsin college or university; and must be planning a career in radio or television broadcasting. **Criteria:** Recipients are selected based on academic performance and quality of the essay.

Funds Avail.: $2,000. **Number Awarded:** 4. **To Apply:** Applicants must submit a completed application form; a current official transcript of college/university grades; two brief letters of recommendation supporting the application; maximum of three pages, original, typed, double-spaced essay written by the applicant forecasting what the broadcasting industry will be like in five years and how the applicant believes he or she will contribute to radio or television during that time. **Deadline:** October 19. **Contact:** John Laabs at the above address (see entry 7471).

7473 ■ Wolf Trap Foundation for the Performing Arts

1645 Trap Rd.
Vienna, VA 22182
Ph: (703)255-1900
E-mail: wolftrap@wolftrap.org
URL: http://www.wolf-trap.org

7474 ■ Wolf Trap Foundation Scholarship Program for Performing Arts Teachers *(Professional Development/Scholarship)*

Purpose: To enhance the strategies of teachers in teaching arts education. **Focus:** Performing arts. **Qualif.:** Ap-

Awards are arranged alphabetically below their administering organizations

plicants must be performing arts public high school teachers. **Criteria:** Selection is based on proposals.

Funds Avail.: $2500. **To Apply:** Proposals by invitation only. **Contact:** Wolf Trap's Education Department at 703-255-1933.

7475 ■ The Wolf Trap Internship Program
(Graduate, Professional Development, Undergraduate/Internship)

Purpose: To provide training program for the performing arts. **Focus:** Performing arts. **Qualif.:** Applicants must be undergraduate students (completed one year of study or equivalent), graduate students, or recent graduates (up to two years out of school); career-changers enrolled in a degree program; and international students (J-1 or F-1 Visa required). **Criteria:** Committee will review submitted materials.

Funds Avail.: No specific amount. **To Apply:** Applicants must submit a cover letter with a brief personal statement and an outline of career goals; a resume; two academic or professional recommendations; two contrasting writing samples, (maximum of 3 pages each). Applicants must send the requirements to Internship Program Wolf Trap Foundation for the Performing Arts, 1645 Trap Road, Vienna, VA 22182, 703255-1924 (fax), internships@wolftrap.org (e-mail). **Deadline:** March 1, July 1, and November 1. **Contact:** (703)255-1933, (800)404-8461, or e-mail internships@wolftrap.org.

7476 ■ Women in Federal Law Enforcement

2200 Wilson Blvd.
Arlington, VA 22201
Ph: (703)548-9211
Fax: (410)451-7373
Free: (866)399-4353
E-mail: wifle@comcast.net
URL: http://www.wifle.org

7477 ■ The WIFLE Scholarship Fund *(Graduate, Postdoctorate, Undergraduate/Scholarship)*

Purpose: To provide financial assistance to women interested in law enforcement careers. **Focus:** Law enforcement. **Qualif.:** Applicants must be U.S. citizens; must be full-time students at an accredited four-year college or university, or a fully accredited community college with the intention of transferring to a four-year degree; must have completed at least one full academic year of college work; must major in Criminal Justice or a related discipline such as social sciences, public administration, computer science, finance, linguistic arts, chemistry, or physics leading to a four-year degree; have a minimum 3.0 overall grade point average (GPA). **Criteria:** Recipients will be selected based on academic potential, achievement and commitment to serving communities in the field of law enforcement.

Funds Avail.: $2,500. **To Apply:** Applicants must complete the application with a 500-word essay describing the applicant's involvement in a community project and the results or impact of that involvement to the community. If the applicant is currently serving or has served an internship with a law enforcement agency, preferably a federal law enforcement agency, the applicant must provide details including the name of the agency, the dates served and the value of the experience and the accomplishment through the internship in a 500-word essay. Applicants must have at least one community leader or member of a community or police official sponsor their applications with a written statement of support. **Deadline:** May 1.

7478 ■ Women In Defense

2111 Wilson Blvd., Ste. 400
Arlington, VA 22201-3061
Ph: (703)247-2552
Fax: (703)522-1885
E-mail: wid@ndia.org
URL: http://wid.ndia.org

7479 ■ Women In Defense HORIZONS Scholarships *(Graduate, Undergraduate/Scholarship)*

Purpose: To provide financial assistance to further educational objectives of women either employed or planning careers in defense or national security areas. **Focus:** National security; Military history; Government; Engineering; Computer and information sciences; Physics; Mathematics and mathematical sciences; Business; Law; International affairs and relations; Political science; Economics. **Qualif.:** Applicant must be currently enrolled at an accredited university/college, either full-time or part-time; must have junior, senior or graduate status; demonstrate interest in pursuing a career related to national security or defense; demonstrate financial need; have a minimum GPA of 3.25. Applicant must be a female citizen of the United States. **Criteria:** Awards are given based on academic achievement, participation in defense and national security activities, field of study, work experience, statements of objectives, recommendations, and financial need.

Funds Avail.: No specific amount. **To Apply:** Applicants must submit a completed scholarship application form with the essays, recommendations, and transcripts. **Deadline:** July 1.

Remarks: Established in 1988.

7480 ■ Women Marines Association

PO Box 8405
Falls Church, VA 22041-8405
Free: 888-525-1943
E-mail: wma@womenmarines.org
URL: http://www.womenmarines.org

7481 ■ LaRue A. Ditmore Music Scholarships
(Undergraduate/Scholarship)

Purpose: To financially assist students with their educational pursuits. **Focus:** Maritime studies. **Qualif.:** Applicant must have served, or be serving in the U.S. Marine Corps or Reserve; or a direct descendant by blood, or legal adoption or stepchild of a Marine on active duty, or who has served in the U.S. Marine Corps, Regular or Reserve; or a sibling or a descendant of a sibling by blood, or legal adoption or stepchild of a Marine on active duty, or who has served in the U.S. Marine Corps, Regular or Reserve; or have completed two years in a Marine Corps JROTC program. High school applicant must have maintained a B+ average for the sophomore or junior years; have a SAT score of 1100 (combined Math/Verbal); have an ACT score of 25 (combined Math/Verbal). College students must have a GPA of 3.5. Applicant must have a WMA member sponsor. **Criteria:** A selection board of five members will review qualified applications.

Funds Avail.: $1500. **To Apply:** Applicants must submit a completed application form together with a copy of Sponsor's National Membership Card; a wallet size photo (name written on lower back); three letters of reference from a school personnel (on official letterhead signed and sealed envelope); proof of relationship to a U.S. Marine; and a permanent and alternate Email addresses. High school students must also send official transcripts (mailed directly from the school) and a letter of acceptance for the following year. College freshmen students must send an additional official final high school transcript (including SAT/ACT scores) and current college transcript. Send all materials to Luann Weeks, 251 SW 1300th Road, Chilhowee, MO 64733-8133, ldweeks@pocketmail.com. **Deadline:** March 31.

Remarks: Male applicants must submit a proof of draft registration when applying on or after their eighteenth birthday.

7482 ■ Lily H. Gridley Memorial Scholarships
(Undergraduate/Scholarship)

Purpose: To financially assist students with their educational pursuits. **Focus:** Maritime studies. **Qualif.:** Applicant must have served, or be serving in the U.S. Marine Corps or Reserve; or a direct descendant by blood, or legal adoption or stepchild of a Marine on active duty, or has served in the U.S. Marine Corps, Regular or Reserve; or a sibling or a descendant of a sibling by blood, or legal adoption or stepchild of a Marine on active duty, or who has served in the U.S. Marine Corps, Regular or Reserve; or have completed two years in a Marine Corps JROTC program. High school applicant must have maintained a B+ average for the sophomore or junior years; have a SAT score of 1100 (combined Math/Verbal); have an ACT score of 25 (combined Math/Verbal). College students must have a GPA of 3.5. Applicant must have a WMA member sponsor. **Criteria:** A selection board of five members will review qualified applications.

Funds Avail.: $1500. **To Apply:** Applicants must submit a completed application form together with a copy of Sponsor's National Membership Card; a wallet size photo (name written on lower back); three letters of reference from a school personnel (on official letterhead signed and sealed envelope); proof of relationship to a U.S. Marine; and a permanent and alternate Email addresses. High schools students must also send official transcripts (mailed directly from the school) and a letter of acceptance for the following year. College freshmen students must send an additional official final high school transcript (including SAT/ACT scores) and current college transcript. Send all materials to Luann Weeks, 251 SW 1300th Road, Chilhowee, MO 64733-8133, ldweeks@pocketmail.com. **Deadline:** March 31.

Remarks: Male applicants must submit a proof of draft registration when applying on or after their eighteenth birthday.

7483 ■ Ethyl and Armin Wiebke Memorial Scholarships *(Undergraduate/Scholarship)*

Purpose: To financially assist students with their educational pursuits. **Focus:** Maritime studies. **Qualif.:** Applicant must have served, or be serving in the U.S. Marine Corps or Reserve; or a direct descendant by blood, or legal adoption or stepchild of a Marine on active duty, or who has served in the U.S. Marine Corps, Regular or Reserve; or a sibling or a descendant of a sibling by blood, or legal adoption or stepchild of a Marine on active duty, or who has served in the U.S. Marine Corps, Regular or Reserve; or have completed two years in a Marine Corps JROTC program. High school applicant must have maintained a B+ average for the sophomore or junior years; have a SAT score of 1100 (combined Math/Verbal); have an ACT score of 25 (combined Math/Verbal). College students must have a GPA of 3.5. Applicant must have a WMA member sponsor. **Criteria:** A selection board of five members will review qualified applications.

Funds Avail.: $1500. **Number Awarded:** 1. **To Apply:** Applicants must submit a completed application form together with a copy of Sponsor's National Membership Card; a wallet size photo (name written on lower back); three letters of reference from a school personnel (on official letterhead signed and sealed envelope); proof of relationship to a U.S. Marine; and a permanent and alternate Email addresses. High schools students must also send official transcripts (mailed directly from the school) and a letter of acceptance for the following year. College freshmen students must send an additional official final high school transcript (including SAT/ACT scores) and current college transcript. Send all materials to Luann Weeks, 251 SW 1300th Road, Chilhowee, MO 64733-8133, ldweeks@pocketmail.com. **Deadline:** March 31.

Remarks: Male applicants must submit a proof of draft registration when applying on or after their eighteenth birthday.

7484 ■ WMA Memorial Scholarships
(Undergraduate/Scholarship)

Purpose: To financially assist students with their educational pursuits. **Focus:** Maritime studies. **Qualif.:** Applicant must have served, or be serving in the U.S. Marine Corps or Reserve; or a direct descendant by blood, or legal adoption or stepchild of a Marine on active duty, or who has served in the U.S. Marine Corps, Regular or Reserve; or a sibling or a descendant of a sibling by blood, or legal adoption or stepchild of a Marine on active duty, or who has served in the U.S. Marine Corps, Regular or Reserve; or have completed two years in a Marine Corps JROTC program. High school applicant must have maintained a B+ average for the sophomore or junior years; have a SAT score of 1100 (combined Math/Verbal); have an ACT score of 25 (combined Math/Verbal). College students must have a GPA of 3.5. Applicant must have a WMA member sponsor. **Criteria:** A selection board of five members will review qualified applications.

Funds Avail.: $1500. **To Apply:** Applicants must submit a completed application form together with a copy of Sponsor's National Membership Card; a wallet size photo (name written on lower back); three letters of reference from a school personnel (on official letterhead signed and sealed envelope); proof of relationship to a U.S. Marine; and a permanent and alternate Email addresses. High schools students must also send official transcripts (mailed directly from the school) and a letter of acceptance for the following year. College freshmen students must send an additional official final high school transcript (including SAT/ACT scores) and current college transcript. Send all materials to Luann Weeks, 251 SW 1300th Road, Chilhowee, MO 64733-8133, ldweeks@pocketmail.com. **Deadline:** March 31.

Remarks: Male applicants must submit a proof of draft registration when applying on or after their eighteenth birthday.

7485 ■ Women's Army Corps Veterans Association

PO Box 5577
Fort McClellan, AL 36205-5577
Ph: (256)820-6824
E-mail: info@armywomen.org
URL: http://www.armywomen.org

7486 ■ Women's Army Corps Veterans Association Scholarships *(Undergraduate/Scholarship)*

Purpose: To provide educational assistance to relatives of Army Service Women. **Focus:** General studies. **Qualif.:** Program is open to relatives of Army Service Women. **Criteria:** Selection is based on academic achievement, leadership as expressed through co-curricular activities and community involvement, biographical sketch and recommendations.

Funds Avail.: $1,500. **To Apply:** Applicants must submit the completed application form available from the website, an official 7-semester high school transcript, three letters of recommendation (one of which must be written by a teacher, counselor or principal); biographical sketch; and documentation of sponsor's military service. Forward materials to: Women's Army Corps Veteran's Association, Women's Army Corps Veterans Scholarship, PO Box 5577, Fort McClellan, Alabama 36205-5577.

7487 ■ Women's Association of the Mining Industry of Canada Foundation

PO Box 207, Postal Station "A"
Toronto, ON, Canada M5W 1B2
E-mail: scholarships@cogeco.ca
URL: http://www.pdac.ca/wamic/about.html

7488 ■ National Geophysics Scholarships *(Postgraduate/Scholarship)*

Purpose: To support undergraduate students enrolled in mining related or earth science programs in Canadian universities. **Focus:** Earth sciences, Mining. **Qualif.:** Applicants must be currently registered in third year geophysics; must be undergraduate students who have attained the highest academic average on completion of their year in an accredited geophysics program at a qualified Canadian university. **Criteria:** Applicants are selected based on academic standing and financial need.

Funds Avail.: $1,000. **To Apply:** Application must include: student's name; official transcript of the student's marks (including his/her third year marks); student's sessional and permanent home addresses; student's social insurance number; professor's recommendations; and other scholarships, bursaries or awards that the student has applied for and received. Application forms and other documents must be submitted to the chairperson of the Awards Committee, Women's Association of the Mining Industry of Canada Foundation, PO Box 207, Postal Station A, Toronto, ON M5W 1B2. **Deadline:** June 4.

7489 ■ National Scholarships *(Postgraduate/Scholarship)*

Purpose: To support undergraduate students enrolled in mining related or earth science programs in Canadian universities. **Focus:** Earth sciences, Mining. **Qualif.:** Applicants must be currently registered in third year geophysics; must be undergraduate students who have attained the highest academic average on completion of their year in an accredited geophysics program at a qualified Canadian university. **Criteria:** Applicants are selected based on academic standing and financial need.

Funds Avail.: $1,000. **To Apply:** Application must include: student's name and curriculum vitae; official transcript of the student's marks (including his/her third year marks); student's sessional and permanent home addresses; student's social insurance number; professor's recommendations; and other scholarships, bursaries or awards that the student has applied for and received. Application forms and other documents must be submitted to the chairperson of the Awards Committee, Women's Association of the Mining Industry of Canada Foundation, PO Box 207, Postal Station A, Toronto, ON M5W 1B2. **Deadline:** June 4.

7490 ■ Wood Bursary Awards *(Postgraduate/Award/Prize)*

Purpose: To support undergraduate students enrolled in mining related or earth science programs in Canadian universities. **Focus:** Earth sciences; Mining. **Qualif.:** Applicants must be third or fourth year undergraduate students who are enrolled in an accredited mining related program in a Canadian university. **Criteria:** Applicants will be evaluated based on academic standing and financial need.

Funds Avail.: $6,000. **To Apply:** Application forms and other documents must be submitted to the chairperson of the Awards Committee, Women's Association of the Mining Industry of Canada Foundation, PO Box 207, Postal Station A, Toronto, ON M5W 1B2. **Deadline:** June 4.

7491 ■ Women's Business Enterprise National Council

1120 Connecticut Ave. NW, Ste. 1000
Washington, DC 20036
Ph: (202)872-5515
Fax: (202)872-5505
E-mail: ldenny@wbenc.org
URL: http://www.wbenc.org

7492 ■ Dorothy B. Brothers Executive Scholarship Program *(High School/Scholarship)*

Purpose: To provide financial assistance and opportunities for women to attend an executive level course. **Focus:** General Studies. **Qualif.:** Applicants must be currently certified as a woman business enterprise by WBENC; must have at least three-to-five years experience running a business; must employ at least three full-time employees; must maintain a minimum annual sales volume of $500,000 (the range is $500,000-$50,000); must not have previously attended a comparable executive management program (TUK-WBENC Executive Program). **Criteria:** Recipients are selected based on the quality of the essay.

Funds Avail.: $4,500. **To Apply:** Applicants must fill out the application form and submit an essay stating the applicant's career goals related to business. **Deadline:** April 30.

7493 ■ Women's International Network of Utility Professionals

PO Box 817
Fergus Falls, MN 56538-0817
Ph: (218)731-1659

Awards are arranged alphabetically below their administering organizations

E-mail: drexler@runestone.net
URL: http://www.winup.org

7494 ■ Julia Kiene Fellowship in Electrical Energy *(Graduate/Fellowship)*

Purpose: To support students engaging in graduate work toward an advanced degree in any phase of electrical energy. **Focus:** Electrical engineering. **Qualif.:** Applicant must be a graduate student in an advanced degree in electrical energy. **Criteria:** Selection is based on the application.

Funds Avail.: $2000. **To Apply:** Applicants must submit a completed application form along with the required materials. **Deadline:** March 1.

Remarks: Established in memory of Julia Kiene, past president of the organization.

7495 ■ Lyle Mamer Fellowships *(Graduate/Fellowship)*

Purpose: To support students engaging in graduate work toward an advanced degree in any phase of electrical energy. **Focus:** Electrical engineering. **Qualif.:** Applicant must be a graduate student earning an advanced degree in electrical energy. **Criteria:** Selection is based on the application.

Funds Avail.: $1000. **To Apply:** Applicants must submit a completed application form along with the required materials. **Deadline:** March 1.

Remarks: Established in memory of Lyle Mamer who served as an Associate Professor at the University of Tennessee College of Home Economics for 35 years.

7496 ■ WINUP Member Scholarships *(Professional Development/Scholarship)*

Purpose: To assist members in furthering their education. **Focus:** Electrical engineering. **Qualif.:** Applicants must be a WINUP member. **Criteria:** Selection is based on the application.

Funds Avail.: $500. **To Apply:** Applicants must submit a completed application form with the required materials and information. **Deadline:** March 1.

7497 ■ Women's Jewelry Association

7000 W Southwest Hwy.
Chicago Ridge, IL 60415
Ph: (708)361-6000
Fax: (708)361-6166
E-mail: info@womensjewelry.org
URL: http://www.womensjewelry.org

7498 ■ Women's Jewelry Association Member Grants *(All/Grant)*

Purpose: To provide educational financial assistance for students in the international jewelry, watch and related industries. **Focus:** Fashion design; Design. **Qualif.:** Applicants must be a WJA member. **Criteria:** Applicants are selected through a random drawing of the WJA Member Grant Committee.

Funds Avail.: $500. **To Apply:** Applicants must provide in a printed text limited to one 8 1/2 x 11 page: a short statement about applicant's personal information, work, the course and how the grant will benefit the applicant (mandatory); applicant's signature to accept all terms and conditions of the WJA Grants (mandatory); a brief description of the applicant's contributions to the jewelry and/or related industries (optional). Applicants must submit a completed application form and all supporting documents to WJA Member Grant Committee. **Deadline:** January 31. **Contact:** Sue Seider, Member Grant Committee Chair.

7499 ■ Women's Jewelry Association Scholarships *(Undergraduate/Scholarship)*

Purpose: To provide educational financial assistance for students in the international jewelry, watch and related industries. **Focus:** Fashion design; Design. **Qualif.:** Applicants must be students enrolled in fine jewelry and watch design courses in the United States. **Criteria:** Recipients are selected based on the jury's review of the application materials.

Funds Avail.: A total amount of $25,000 is available. **To Apply:** Applicants must submit a completed application form to the WJA Scholarship Committee. **Contact:** Lisa Slovis, Student Scholarship Committee Chair.

7500 ■ Women's Missionary Council of the Christian Methodist Episcopal Church

11321 South Aberdeen
Chicago, IL 60643
Ph: (773)264-2273
Fax: (773)264-2274
E-mail: hamb@sbcglobal.ne
URL: http://www.cme-church.org/Missionary_Council

7501 ■ The Helena B. Cobb Annual Scholarships *(Undergraduate/Scholarship)*

Purpose: To emphasizes the importance of educational training beyond the high school level. **Focus:** General studies. **Qualif.:** Applicant must be a member of the Christian Methodist Episcopal Church; a high school graduate; and enrolled in a college, university, or vocational-technical school. **Criteria:** Selection is based on the application.

Funds Avail.: $100. **To Apply:** Applicants must submit a completed application form. **Deadline:** December 31.

Remarks: The program was named for the first Vice President of the Council, Helena B. Cobb.

7502 ■ The Helena B. Cobb Four-Year Higher Education Grants *(Undergraduate/Scholarship)*

Purpose: To emphasizes the importance of educational training beyond the high school level. **Focus:** General studies. **Qualif.:** Applicant must be a member of the Christian Methodist Episcopal Church; a high school graduate; and enrolled in a college, university, or vocational-technical school. **Criteria:** Applicants are chosen through a four-year progressive competitive system from the local to Episcopal levels.

Funds Avail.: $1000-$4000. **Number Awarded:** 10. **To Apply:** Applicants must submit a completed application form. **Deadline:** December 31.

Remarks: The program was named for the first Vice President of the Council, Helena B. Cobb.

7503 ■ Women's National Book Association

PO Box 237, FDR Sta.
New York, NY 10150-0231
Ph: (212)208-4629
Fax: (212)208-4629

Awards are arranged alphabetically below their administering organizations

E-mail: publicity@bookbuzz.com
URL: http://www.wnba-books.org

7504 ■ WNBA Eastman Grants *(Professional Development/Grant)*

Purpose: To provide funds for librarians who are interested in learning about the publishing process. **Focus:** Publishing. **Qualif.:** Applicants must be an MLS or its equivalent, and have at least two years of post-master's work experience in a library. **Criteria:** Recipients are selected based on the likelihood of career benefit to the person taking the course.

Funds Avail.: $750. **Number Awarded:** 1. **To Apply:** Applicants must provide a current resume; a personal statement of not more than 300 words concerning an ongoing interest in the publishing process and how a better understanding of this process would enhance the applicant's library career; a list of publishing courses to which the applicant would apply; and a signed acknowledgement of intent to submit to ALA and WNBA a simple report and verification of attendance at the chosen publishing course. **Deadline:** November 1.

Remarks: Established in 1997 and honors Ann Heidbreder Eastman, a prominent member of both the publishing and library communities and a member of both WNBA and ALA until her death in 1993. **Contact:** Mary Jo Bolduc at the above address (see entry 7503).

7505 ■ Women's Overseas and Service League

PO Box 7124
Washington, DC 20044-7124
E-mail: carolhabgood@sbcglobal.net
URL: http://www.wosl.org

7506 ■ Women's Overseas and Service League Scholarships for Women *(Undergraduate/Scholarship)*

Purpose: To assist women who have served overseas in or with the Armed Forces. **Focus:** General studies. **Qualif.:** Applicants must be women who are committed to the advancement in military or other public service careers; must have demonstrated such commitment through life experiences; have successfully completed a minimum of 12 semester(18 quarter) hours of study in any institution of higher Education with a minimum of 2.5 grade point average; must be admitted for study in an institution of higher learning program leading to an academic degree (Associate Degree or higher). The program must be professional or technical in nature; must agree to enroll for a minimum of six semester(nine quarter) hours of study each academic period; and she must agree to maintain academic standards. **Criteria:** Scholarship Committee of the Women's Overseas Service League Board of Directors will evaluate the student's application based on academic records.

Funds Avail.: $500-$1,000.00. **To Apply:** Applicants must fill out the application form; must include all needed documents such as resume, transcripts, essays and references. **Deadline:** March 1.

7507 ■ Women's Transportation Seminar

1701 K St. NW, Ste. 800
Washington, DC 20006
Ph: (202)955-5085
Fax: (202)955-5088
E-mail: membership@wtsinternational.org
URL: http://www.wtsinternational.org

7508 ■ Sharon D. Banks Undergraduate Memorial Scholarships *(Undergraduate/Scholarship)*

Purpose: To introduce cultural and organizational changes aimed at motivating the public transit work force. **Focus:** Transportation; Finance; Logistics. **Qualif.:** Applicants must be women pursuing undergraduate studies in transportation engineering, planning, finance or logistics, or related fields. Applicants must have at least a GPA of 3.0 or higher. **Criteria:** Recipients are selected based on specific transportation goals, academic record, transportation-related activities, or job skills.

Funds Avail.: $3,000. **To Apply:** Applicants must fill out the scholarship application form **Deadline:** May 15.

7509 ■ Anne Koby Legacy Scholarships *(Undergraduate/Scholarship)*

Purpose: To provide financial assistance to women who wish to further their careers as leaders in the transportation industry. **Focus:** Transportation; Finance; Logistics. **Qualif.:** Applicants must be women pursuing undergraduate studies in transportation engineering, planning, finance or logistics, or related fields; and must have a GPA of at least 3.0 or higher. **Criteria:** Recipients are selected based on specific transportation goals, academic record, transportation-related activities or job skills.

Funds Avail.: $3,000. **To Apply:** Applicants must fill out the scholarship application form and submit them to local WTS Chapters. **Deadline:** May 15.

7510 ■ Helen M. Overly Memorial Scholarships *(Undergraduate/Scholarship)*

Purpose: To introduce cultural and organizational changes aimed at motivating the public transit work force. **Focus:** Transportation; Finance; Logistics. **Qualif.:** Applicants must be women pursuing undergraduate studies in transportation engineering, planning, finance or logistics, or related fields. Applicants must have at least a GPA of 3.0 or higher. **Criteria:** Recipients are selected based on specific transportation goals, academic record, transportation-related activities, or job skills.

Funds Avail.: $6,000. **To Apply:** Applicants must fill out the scholarship application form **Deadline:** May 15.

7511 ■ Worcester District Medical Society

Mechanics Hall, 321 Main St.
Worcester, MA 01608
Ph: (508)753-1579
Fax: (508)754-6246
E-mail: info@wdms.org
URL: http://www.wdms.org

7512 ■ Worcester District Medical Society Scholarship Fund *(Undergraduate/Scholarship)*

Purpose: To provide educational assistance to medical students. **Focus:** Medicine. **Qualif.:** Applicants must be second, third, or fourth year students enrolled, (with tuition obligation), in an accredited medical or osteophathic school and legal residents of Central Massachusetts at the time of applying to medical school. **Criteria:** Recipients are selected based on academic achievement; community service; and financial need.

Awards are arranged alphabetically below their administering organizations

Funds Avail.: No specific amount. **To Apply:** Applicants must submit completed application form; current transcript; two letters of recommendation; and an essay stating the reasons for selecting a career in medicine and why they feel deserving of the award. **Deadline:** August 31.

7513 ■ Working Against Cancer

PO Box 70233
Pasadena, CA 91107
Ph: (626)914-2914
E-mail: contactus@workingagainstcancer.org
URL: http://www.workingagainstcancer.org

7514 ■ Survival Scholarship Program
(Undergraduate/Scholarship)

Purpose: To assist young adult cancer survivors (ages 30 yrs and under) by providing awards toward academic and vocational education. **Focus:** General Studies. **Qualif.:** Applicants must be cancer survivors or recently diagnosed with cancer. **Criteria:** Priority will be given to those who meet the criteria.

Funds Avail.: $500 (2) and $1,000 (1). **Number Awarded:** 3. **To Apply:** Applicants must check the available website for other requirements. **Contact:** Working Against Cancer at the above address (see entry 7513).

7515 ■ Working for Farmers' Success

PO Box 68
Truman, MN 56088
Ph: (507)524-4130
Fax: (507)776-2871
Free: 800-776-2871
E-mail: wfsinfo@wfsag.com
URL: http://www.wfsag.com

7516 ■ Working for Farmers' Success Scholarships *(Undergraduate/Scholarship)*

Purpose: To encourage young people to pursue an agricultural career. **Focus:** Agricultural economics. **Qualif.:** Applicants must be senior students who are graduating from the WFS trade territory. **Criteria:** Recipients will be selected based on academic performance, qualities of leadership, integrity and good community citizenship.

Funds Avail.: $500. **Number Awarded:** 20. **To Apply:** Applicants must submit a completed application form. **Deadline:** March 30. **Contact:** Jo Ann Gumto at the above address (see entry 7515).

7517 ■ World Council of Credit Unions

601 Pennsylvania Ave. NW
South Bldg., Ste. 600
Washington, DC 20004-2601
Ph: (202)638-0205
Fax: (202)638-3410
E-mail: mail@woccu.org
URL: http://www.woccu.org

7518 ■ WYCUP Scholarships *(Professional Development/Scholarship)*

Purpose: To engage and promote the next generation of credit union professionals and volunteers in the international credit union movement. **Focus:** General studies. **Qualif.:** Applicant must be 35 years of age or younger; must be actively involved either as an employee or volunteer with a credit union or credit organization affiliated with the international credit union movement; must demonstrate personal commitment and the ability to significantly influence credit unions in his/her country; must exhibit the potential to advance the international credit union system; must not have been a previous WYCUP Scholarship recipient. **Criteria:** Individual selected for the scholarship are those the committee believes have the greatest potential to contribute to the international credit union system.

Funds Avail.: Scholarship covers all costs associated with the event, including conference registration fee, travel costs, hotel accommodation and metals. **To Apply:** Applicant must have a two Nomination Form (attached) completed by the nominee and the sponsor; must provide the proof of age (photocopy of passport, driver's license, birth certificate or other official document); must prepare a brief 500-words essay describing contribution made to the development of the candidate's credit union or credit union organization. **Deadline:** June 2.

7519 ■ Worldwide Assurance for Employees of Public Agencies

7651 Leesburg Pike
Falls Church, VA 22043
Ph: (703)790-8010
Free: 800-368-3484
E-mail: info@waepa.org
URL: http://www.waepa.org

7520 ■ WAEPA Scholarship Program
(Undergraduate/Scholarship)

Purpose: To assist policy holders' children who plan to continue education in college or vocational school programs. **Focus:** General studies. **Qualif.:** Applicants must be children, under the age of 23, of WAEPA life insurance policy holders; must be high school seniors or graduates who plan to enroll or are already enrolled full-time in an accredited two-year or four-year college, university or vocational-technical school; must have a minimum grade point average of 3.0 on a 4.0 scale or its equivalent. **Criteria:** Recipients are selected based on academic record, demonstrated leadership and participation in school, community and volunteer activities, honors, work experience, statement of goals and aspirations, unusual personal or family circumstances and an outside appraisal.

Funds Avail.: $1,000 to $4,000. **Number Awarded:** 50. **To Apply:** Applicants must complete the application and mail it along with a current and complete transcript of grades to Scholarship America. **Deadline:** February 1. **Contact:** WAEPA Scholarship Program; Scholarship America; One Scholarship Way, PO Box 297, Saint Peter, MN 56082; Telephone: 507-931-1682.

7521 ■ Wound, Ostomy and Continence Nurses Society

15000 Commerce Pkwy., Ste. C
Mount Laurel, NJ 08054
Free: 888-224-9626
URL: http://www.wocn.org

7522 ■ WOCN Accredited Nursing Education Scholarships *(Graduate, Undergraduate/Scholarship)*

Purpose: To support individuals seeking education in wound, ostomy and continence nursing specialties. **Focus:**

Awards are arranged alphabetically below their administering organizations

Nursing. **Qualif.:** Applicants must be pursuing an education in wound, ostomy and continence nursing care; accepted in a WOCN-accredited WOC Educational Program. **Criteria:** WOCN Scholarship Committee will review completed applications.

Funds Avail.: No specific amount. **To Apply:** Application form is available at the website. **Deadline:** November and May 1.

7523 ■ WOCN Advanced Education Scholarships *(Doctorate, Graduate, Undergraduate/Scholarship)*

Purpose: To support individual seeking education in wound, ostomy and continence nursing specialties. **Focus:** Nursing. **Qualif.:** Applicant must be seeking a baccalaureate, master's or doctoral degree or NP certificate; a member of WOCN; employed (for at least three years) as a wound, ostomy or continence nurse; accepted in an NLN-accredited nursing program or other accredited college/university program for non-nursing degree. **Criteria:** WOCN Scholarship Committee will review completed applications.

Funds Avail.: No specific amount. **To Apply:** Application form is available at the website. **Deadline:** November and May 1.

7524 ■ Xavier University

3800 Victory Pky.
Cincinnati, OH 45207
Ph: (513)745-3000
Free: 800-344-GOXU
URL: http://www.xavier.edu

7525 ■ Catholic Healthcare Partners Scholarships *(Undergraduate/Scholarship)*

Purpose: To financially support students with their education. **Focus:** Nursing. **Qualif.:** Applicant must be an incoming student majoring in nursing. **Criteria:** Selection is based on academic merit and financial need.

Funds Avail.: $10,000. **To Apply:** Applicants must apply for financial aid by completing the FAFSA and submit a completed application form. **Deadline:** FAFSA: February 15; Application: March 1.

Remarks: In partnership with The Catholic Healthcare Partners.

7526 ■ Edgecliff Alumni Awards *(Undergraduate/Scholarship)*

Purpose: To financially support students with their education. **Focus:** General studies. **Qualif.:** Applicants must be the children, grandchildren, nieces or nephews of a Edgecliff College alumni. **Criteria:** Selection is based on academic merit and financial need.

Funds Avail.: Begins at $500. **To Apply:** Applicants admitted at the Xavier University are automatically considered. **Deadline:** February 1.

7527 ■ Edgecliff McAuley Art Scholarships *(Undergraduate/Scholarship)*

Purpose: To financially support students with their education. **Focus:** Arts. **Qualif.:** Applicant must be an incoming first year student with good academic achievement and outstanding artistic talent, and have declared a major in the Arts. **Criteria:** Selection is based on the submitted portfolio.

Funds Avail.: 1 Full-tuition, and 2 half-tuition. **Number Awarded:** 3. **To Apply:** Students admitted at the Xavier University are automatically considered. Applicants must submit a Portfolio (minimum of eight or maximum of twelve examples of applicant's best work). Portfolios must be clearly labeled with the applicant's name, home phone number, school, and must include an inventory list and a one page personal resume. All pieces must be matted (white mats are mandatory) unless in slide/digital format. All work must be original. **Deadline:** December 1. **Contact:** 513-745-3811.

7528 ■ Edgecliff McAuley Music Scholarships *(Undergraduate/Scholarship)*

Purpose: To financially support students with their education. **Focus:** Music. **Qualif.:** Applicant must be an incoming student. **Criteria:** Selection is based on musical talent and achievement.

Funds Avail.: Full-tuition. **Number Awarded:** 1. **To Apply:** Students admitted at the Xavier University are automatically considered. Applicants must pass the audition held on January 26, February 2, and February 23.

7529 ■ James E. Hoff, S.J. Scholars *(Undergraduate/Scholarship)*

Purpose: To financially support students with their education. **Focus:** General studies. **Qualif.:** Applicants must be the children, grandchildren, nieces or nephews of a Edgecliff College alumni; must demonstrate exceptional leadership, vision, courage, service and compassion in academic and personal life. **Criteria:** Selection is based on academic merit and financial need.

Funds Avail.: Varies. **To Apply:** Applicants admitted at the Xavier University are automatically considered. **Deadline:** February 1.

Remarks: Award may be given to an Edgecliff alumni award recipient.

7530 ■ Indiana Alumni Scholarships *(Undergraduate/Scholarship)*

Purpose: To financially support students with their education. **Focus:** General studies. **Qualif.:** Applicant must be an incoming freshmen from Indiana. **Criteria:** Selection is based on need.

Funds Avail.: $2000. **Number Awarded:** 2. **To Apply:** Applicants must apply for financial aid by completing the FAFSA. **Deadline:** FAFSA deadline: February 15; Application deadline: March 1.

7531 ■ Ohio War Orphan Scholarships *(Undergraduate/Scholarship)*

Purpose: To financially support students with their education. **Focus:** General studies. **Qualif.:** Applicant must be student with a parent who served at least 90 days of active duty during wartime and is disabled or deceased as a result of service. **Criteria:** Qualified students are automatically considered.

Funds Avail.: $660. **To Apply:** Applications available from high school guidance counselors or veterans offices.

7532 ■ Miguel Pro Scholarships *(Undergraduate/Scholarship)*

Purpose: To financially support students with their education. **Focus:** General studies. **Qualif.:** Applicant must be a Hispanic/Latino first-year student with excellent academic achievement. **Criteria:** Selection is based on merit.

Funds Avail.: Up to full-tuition. **To Apply:** Applicants admitted at the Xavier University are automatically considered. **Deadline:** December 1.

Remarks: Selected students will be interviewed on the campus. The scholarship is named in honor of Miguel Pro, S.J., a Mexican priest who was martyred by the Mexican government in 1927 for his practice and teaching of the Catholic faith.

7533 ■ Trustee, Schawe, Presidential and Honor Scholarships *(Undergraduate/Scholarship)*

Purpose: To financially support students with their education. **Focus:** General studies. **Qualif.:** Applicant must be an incoming first-year student with excellent academic achievement (rank at least in the top 25 percent of high school class, have appropriately high grades, and have a minimum SAT of 1130, 25 ACT). **Criteria:** Selection is based on merit.

Funds Avail.: $8000-$12,000. **To Apply:** Applicants admitted at the Xavier University are automatically considered.

7534 ■ Francis X. Weninger Scholarships *(Undergraduate/Scholarship)*

Purpose: To financially support students with their education. **Focus:** General studies. **Qualif.:** Applicant must be an African American first-year student with excellent academic achievement. **Criteria:** Selection is base don merit.

Funds Avail.: Up to full-tuition. **To Apply:** Applicants admitted at the Xavier University are automatically considered. **Deadline:** December 1.

Remarks: Selected students will be interviewed on the campus. The Scholarship is named in honor of Francis Xavier Weninger, S.J., founder of St. Ann Parish in 1865.

7535 ■ St. Francis Xavier Scholarships *(Undergraduate/Scholarship)*

Purpose: To financially support students with their education. **Focus:** General studies. **Qualif.:** Applicant must be an incoming first-year student with exceptional academic achievement and outstanding leadership involvement in the community or school. **Criteria:** Selection is based on merit.

Funds Avail.: Full-tuition. **Number Awarded:** 10. **To Apply:** Applicants admitted at the Xavier University are automatically considered. **Deadline:** December 1.

Remarks: Selected students will be interviewed in the campus.

7536 ■ Xavier Service Fellowships *(Undergraduate/Fellowship)*

Purpose: To financially support students with their education. **Focus:** General studies. **Qualif.:** Applicant must be incoming first-year student who have demonstrated high academic achievement, outstanding service to community, school, or church, and leadership in encouraging others to serve. **Criteria:** Preference is given to students demonstrating exemplary involvement in volunteer service; have shown potential for leading other students in service; have attained a minimum score of 29 on the ACT composite or 1280 on the SAT; and in the top ten percent of the high school senior class.

Funds Avail.: Full tuition, room and board. **Number Awarded:** 5. **To Apply:** Applicants admitted at the Xavier University are automatically considered. **Deadline:** December 1.

Remarks: Selected students will be interviewed on the campus.

7537 ■ Xavier University Chancellor Scholarships *(Undergraduate/Scholarship)*

Purpose: To financially support students with their education. **Focus:** General studies. **Qualif.:** Applicant must be an incoming first-year student with excellent academic achievement. **Criteria:** Selection is based on merit.

Funds Avail.: $15,000. **Number Awarded:** 15. **To Apply:** Applicants admitted at the Xavier University are automatically considered. **Deadline:** December 1.

Remarks: Selected students will be interviewed in the campus. Named in honor of Xavier's late Chancellor James E. Hoff, S.J.

7538 ■ Xavier University Departmental Scholarships *(Undergraduate/Scholarship)*

Purpose: To financially support students with their education. **Focus:** Chemistry; Classical studies; History; Mathematics and mathematical sciences; Modern languages; Physics. **Qualif.:** Applicant must top the score in either of the six departmental exams (chemistry, classics (Latin), history, mathematics, modern languages (French, German or Spanish) and physics). Student must major in the area for which the scholarship is awarded. **Criteria:** Scholarship is given to the highest scorer on the exams.

Funds Avail.: $2500. **To Apply:** Participants will take an exam in the appropriate subject area and have an opportunity to speak with faculty and learn more about the department.

7539 ■ Xavier University Honors Bachelor of Arts Scholarships *(Undergraduate/Scholarship)*

Purpose: To financially support students with their education. **Focus:** Arts. **Qualif.:** Applicant must be a student enrolled in the honor bachelor of arts program. **Criteria:** Selection is based on merit.

Funds Avail.: One-quarter tuition. **To Apply:** Applicants admitted at the Xavier University are automatically considered.

7540 ■ Xavier University Legacy Scholarships *(Undergraduate/Scholarship)*

Purpose: To financially support students with their education. **Focus:** General studies. **Qualif.:** Applicants must be full-time undergraduate student who are children or grandchildren of Xavier alumni. **Criteria:** Selection is based on academic merit, leadership and service activities.

Funds Avail.: $3000. **Number Awarded:** 2. **To Apply:** Applicants must submit a completed Legacy Scholarship Application along with the requires supporting materials. **Deadline:** March 21.

7541 ■ Xavier University ROTC Scholarships - Air Force ROTC *(Undergraduate/Scholarship)*

Purpose: To financially support students with their education. **Focus:** Aerospace sciences. **Qualif.:** Applicants must be high school students pursuing an Air Force ROTC or college freshmen and sophomores pursuing an in-college Air Force ROTC. **Criteria:** Selection is based on merit.

Funds Avail.: Covers the cost of remaining tuition, room and board. **To Apply:** Applicants must contact the Detachment 665 Unit Admission Officer for the application process. **Contact:** 513-556-2237.

7542 ■ Xavier University ROTC Scholarships - Army ROTC *(Undergraduate/Scholarship)*

Purpose: To financially support students with their education. **Focus:** Military science and education. **Qualif.:** Applicant may be a freshman, sophomore, junior, or senior student pursuing military science at Xavier University. Nursing students can also compete for an Army ROTC nursing scholarship and upon graduation become an Army Nurse. **Criteria:** Selection is based on a student's merit and grades, not financial need.

Funds Avail.: Full-tuition, $900 yearly book allowance and a monthly stipend starting at $350/month during the academic school year. **To Apply:** High School students may apply online for an Army ROTC Scholarship at www.goarmy.com/rotc. **Deadline:** March 1. **Contact:** Major Tim Diley, at 513-745-1062.

7543 ■ Xavier University Williams Scholarships *(Undergraduate/Scholarship)*

Purpose: To financially support students with their education. **Focus:** Business. **Qualif.:** Applicant must be a first year student declared a major in the Williams College of Business. **Criteria:** Selection is based on merit.

Funds Avail.: $3000. **Number Awarded:** 4. **To Apply:** Applicants admitted at the Xavier University are automatically considered. **Deadline:** February 15.

7544 ■ Young Menswear Association

36 W 20th St., 3rd Fl.
New York, NY 10011
Ph: (212)594-6422
E-mail: hharrison@ymafashionscholarshipfund.org
URL: http://the-yma.com

7545 ■ YMA Fashion Scholarships *(Undergraduate/Scholarship)*

Purpose: To promote education in the fashion industry. **Focus:** Fashion design; Business. **Qualif.:** Applicant must be a full-time junior or senior student with a GPA of 3.0 or above in a 4.0 GPA system. **Criteria:** Applicants will be reviewed by the YMA Scholarship Committee.

Funds Avail.: No specific amount. **To Apply:** Educators can nominate up to eight applicants per school. Nominated applicants must submit all the student records and transcript; and an essay. For Design students, submit a portfolio (at least 2 designs/projects) not to exceed 8 1/2"x 11" folder size. For Business students, submit a project about merchandising, marketing or finance not to exceed 8 1/2"x 11" folder size. Application form is to be sent electronically to hharrison@ymafashionscholarshipfund.org; a box per school containing all other materials of the applicants must be sent to: The YMA Fashion Scholarship Fund, 36 West 20th St., 3rd Fl., New York, NY 10011. **Deadline:** January 15.

7546 ■ Youth Maritime Training Association

PO Box 70425
Seattle, WA 98127-0425
Ph: (206)782-1080
E-mail: info@ymta.net
URL: http://www.ymta.net

7547 ■ Norm Manly - YMTA Maritime Educational Scholarships *(Undergraduate/Scholarship)*

Purpose: To support students pursuing maritime training and education. **Focus:** Maritime studies. **Qualif.:** Applicants must have attended at least one semester or quarter in an YMTA-supported program or be a current active member of a Sea Scout ship for the past 6 months; must be under 21 at time of application; must be enrolled as a senior in a high school in the State of Washington; and have GPA of at least 2.5. Relatives of YMTA Executive, Honorary and Advisory Board members are not eligible for YMTA Scholarships. **Criteria:** Recipients will be selected based on a review of all the application materials submitted.

Funds Avail.: $1,000, $3,000, and $5,000. **Number Awarded:** 4. **To Apply:** Applicants are required to complete the application form and submit along with the required documents to Youth Maritime Training Association PO Box 70425 Seattle, WA 98127. **Deadline:** February and April. **Contact:** Carleen See, arleeninballard@yahoo.com.

7548 ■ Youth for Understanding

6400 Goldsboro Rd., Ste. 100
Bethesda, MD 20817
Ph: (240)235-2100
Fax: (240)235-2104
Free: (866)4YFU-USA
E-mail: admission@yfu.org
URL: http://www.yfu-usa.org

7549 ■ Youth for Understanding Scholarships *(Undergraduate/Scholarship)*

Purpose: To provide deserving individuals with the best international exchange experience. **Focus:** Travel and tourism. **Qualif.:** Applicants must be between the ages of 15 and 18 and have maintained a minimum 3.0 GPA for a year or semester program or 2.0 GPA for a summer program, and be in good health. **Criteria:** Recipient will be selected based on a comprehensive evaluation process done by the Selection Committee at the YFU USA national office.

Funds Avail.: No specific amount. **To Apply:** Applicant must file an application online at the website of YFU.

7550 ■ Yukon Law Foundation

Box 31789
Whitehorse, YT, Canada T1A 6L3
Ph: (867)667-7500
Fax: (867)393-3904
E-mail: lsy@yknet.yk.ca
URL: http://www.yukonlawfoundation.com

7551 ■ Yukon Law Foundation Scholarships *(Undergraduate/Scholarship)*

Purpose: To provide financial assistance to qualified students who want to pursue their studies. **Focus:** Law. **Qualif.:** Applicants must be students attending law or law related studies. **Criteria:** Recipients will be selected based on academic achievement, residency, community involvement, and financial need.

Funds Avail.: $5,000. **To Apply:** Applicants must complete the application form available online; submit a transcript of record and two letters of recommendation. Application form and other supporting documents must be sent to Yukon Law Foundation, 202-302 Steele St., Whitehorse, YT CA Y1A 2C5.

7552 ■ Zeta Phi Beta Sorority

1734 New Hampshire Ave. NW
Washington, DC 20009

Awards are arranged alphabetically below their administering organizations

Ph: (202)387-3103
Fax: (202)232-4593
E-mail: ihq@zphib1920.org
URL: http://www.zphib1920.org

7553 ■ Mildred Cater Bradham Social Work Fellowships *(Graduate/Fellowship)*

Purpose: To support students in pursuit of higher education. **Focus:** Social work. **Qualif.:** Applicant must be a Zeta Phi Beta Sorority, Inc. member; pursuing a full-time graduate or professional degree in social work in an accredited college or university program. **Criteria:** Selection is based on the application and supporting documents.

Funds Avail.: $500-$1000. **Number Awarded:** 1. **To Apply:** Applicants must submit completed application forms along with the required materials. **Deadline:** February 1.

7554 ■ Lullelia W. Harrison Scholarships in Counseling *(Graduate, Undergraduate/Scholarship)*

Purpose: To support students in pursuit of higher education. **Focus:** Counseling/Guidance. **Qualif.:** Applicant must be a full-time graduate or undergraduate level student enrolled in a degree program in counseling. **Criteria:** Selection is based on the application and supporting documents.

Funds Avail.: $500-$1000. **Number Awarded:** 1. **To Apply:** Applicants must submit completed application forms along with the required materials. **Deadline:** February 1.

7555 ■ Isabel M. Herson Scholarships in Education *(Graduate, Undergraduate/Scholarship)*

Purpose: To support students in pursuit of higher education. **Focus:** Education, Elementary; Education—Curricula. **Qualif.:** Applicant must be in graduate or undergraduate level student enrolled full-time in a degree program in either elementary or secondary education. **Criteria:** Selection is based on the application and supporting documents.

Funds Avail.: $500-$1000. **Number Awarded:** 1. **To Apply:** Applicants must submit completed application forms along with the required materials. **Deadline:** February 1.

7556 ■ Zora Neale Hurston Scholarships *(Graduate/Scholarship)*

Purpose: To support students in pursuit of higher education. **Focus:** Anthropology. **Qualif.:** Applicant must be a graduate student enrolled full-time pursuing a degree in anthropology. **Criteria:** Selection is based on the application and supporting documents.

Funds Avail.: $500-$1000. **Number Awarded:** 1. **To Apply:** Applicants must submit completed application forms along with the required materials. **Deadline:** February 1.

7557 ■ S. Evelyn Lewis Memorial Scholarships in Medical Health Sciences *(Graduate, Undergraduate/Scholarship)*

Purpose: To support students in pursuit of higher education. **Focus:** Medicine; Health sciences. **Qualif.:** Applicant must be a full-time graduate or undergraduate woman enrolled in a program leading to a degree in medicine or health sciences. **Criteria:** Selection is based on the application and supporting documents.

Funds Avail.: $500-$1000. **Number Awarded:** 1. **To Apply:** Applicants must submit completed application forms along with the required materials. **Deadline:** February 1.

7558 ■ Nancy B. Woolridge McGee Graduate Fellowships *(Graduate/Fellowship)*

Purpose: To support students in pursuit of higher education. **Focus:** General studies. **Qualif.:** Applicant must be a Zeta Phi Beta Sorority, Inc. member; pursuing a full-time graduate or professional degree in an accredited college or university program. **Criteria:** Selection is based on the application and supporting documents.

Funds Avail.: $500-$1000. **Number Awarded:** 1. **To Apply:** Applicants must submit completed application forms along with the required materials. **Deadline:** February 1.

7559 ■ Deborah Partridge Wolfe International Fellowships *(Graduate, Undergraduate/Fellowship)*

Purpose: To support students in pursuit of higher education. **Focus:** General studies. **Qualif.:** Applicant must be a full-time graduate or undergraduate U.S. student studying abroad; or full-time graduate or undergraduate foreign student studying in the U.S. **Criteria:** Selection is based on the application and supporting documents.

Funds Avail.: $500-$1000. **To Apply:** Applicants must submit a completed application forms along with the required materials. **Deadline:** February 1.

7560 ■ Zeta Phi Beta Sorority General Graduate Scholarships *(Graduate, Postdoctorate/Scholarship)*

Purpose: To support students for the pursuit of higher education. **Focus:** General studies. **Qualif.:** Applicant must be a full-time graduate woman on a professional degree, masters, doctoral or enrolled in post-doctoral study. **Criteria:** Selection is based on the application.

Funds Avail.: $2500 per year. **Number Awarded:** 1. **To Apply:** Applicants must submit a completed application forms along with the required materials. **Deadline:** February 1.

7561 ■ Zeta Phi Beta Sorority General Undergraduate Scholarships *(Undergraduate/Scholarship)*

Purpose: To support students for the pursuit of higher education. **Focus:** General studies. **Qualif.:** Applicant must be a full-time undergraduate freshman, sophomore, junior, senior or graduating high school planning to enter college. **Criteria:** Selection is based on the application and supporting documents.

Funds Avail.: $500-$1000. **Number Awarded:** 1. **To Apply:** Applicants must submit completed application form along with the required materials. **Deadline:** February 1.

7562 ■ Zonta Club of Hilo

PO Box 1915
Hilo, HI 96721-1915
Ph: (808)959-2711
E-mail: info@hilozonta.org
URL: http://zontahilo.org

7563 ■ Amelia Earhart Fellowship Program *(Postdoctorate/Fellowship)*

Purpose: To provide financial support for qualified females intending to pursue their graduate Ph.D./doctoral degrees in aerospace-related science and aerospace-related engineering. **Focus:** Engineering, Aerospace; Aerospace sciences. **Qualif.:** Applicants must be registered in an accredited Ph.D/doctoral program in a qualifying area of science or engineering closely related to advanced studies in aerospace-related engineering; must demonstrate a superior academic record at a recognized university or college with accredited courses in aerospace-related studies as verified by transcripts and recommendation; must provide evidence of a well-defined research program in aerospace-related science or aerospace-related engineering as described in the application essay, research and publication; must clearly demonstrate the relationship of the research to aerospace and furnish verification of the research program through at least one of the reference letters required with the application; and must be registered in a Ph.D/ doctorate program by the time the fellowship is awarded. **Criteria:** Selection of applicants will be based on the application requirements.

Funds Avail.: $10,000. **To Apply:** Applicants must submit transcripts of grades and school verification form; must have the list of schools attended and degrees received, employment history, plans for intended study, essay on academic and professional goals, and three recommendations from teachers or supervisors. **Deadline:** November 15.

Awards are arranged alphabetically below their administering organizations

Field of Study Index

This index classifies awards by one or more of some 400 specific subject categories. Citations are arranged alphabetically under all appropriate subject categories. Each citation is followed by the study level and award type, which appear in parentheses. The number following the parenthetical information indicates the book entry number for a particular award, not a page number.

Accounting

ACUA Scholarships *(Graduate, Undergraduate/Scholarship)* [1381]
African American Network - Carolinas Scholarship Fund *(Undergraduate/Scholarship)* [3037]
AICPA Scholarships for Graduate Accounting Students *(Postgraduate/Scholarship)* [4641]
AICPA Scholarships for Minority Accounting Students *(Undergraduate/Scholarship)* [4642]
ALPFA Scholarship Programs *(Postgraduate, Undergraduate/Scholarship)* [1492]
American Society of Military Comptrollers National Scholarship Program *(Undergraduate/Scholarship)* [1011]
APS/ASU Scholarships *(Undergraduate/Scholarship)* [5697]
APS/Maricopa County Community Colleges Scholarships *(Undergraduate/Scholarship)* [5698]
ASCEND/ING Scholarships *(Undergraduate/Scholarship)* [4643]
ASWA 2-Year College Scholarships *(Undergraduate/Scholarship)* [1091]
ASWA Undergraduate Scholarships *(Undergraduate/Scholarship)* [1092]
Frank H. Ault Scholarships *(Undergraduate/Scholarship)* [6168]
Avista Corporation Minds in Motion Scholarships *(Undergraduate/Scholarship)* [4163]
Bill & Nell Biggs Scholarships *(Undergraduate/Scholarship)* [4348]
T. Frank Booth Memorial Scholarship Fund *(Undergraduate/Scholarship)* [3043]
Donald J. Bristow Memorial Scholarship Program *(Graduate, Undergraduate/Scholarship)* [4655]
Stuart Cameron and Margaret McLeod Memorial Scholarships (SCMS) *(Graduate, Undergraduate/Scholarship/Forgivable Loan)* [3744]
Mable B. Crawford Memorial Scholarships *(Undergraduate/Scholarship)* [4354]
Ernst and Young/Ascend Leadership Scholarship Program *(Undergraduate/Scholarship)* [4644]
Max Godwin Endowed Scholarships *(Undergraduate/Scholarship)* [6871]
Goodman and Company, LLP Annual Scholarships *(Undergraduate/Scholarship)* [3262]
Community Bank - Lee Guggisberg Foundation Memorial Scholarships *(Undergraduate/Scholarship)* [5941]
Lenore & George Hedla Accounting Scholarships *(Undergraduate/Scholarship)* [7032]
HSBC-North America Scholarship Program *(Undergraduate/Scholarship)* [3592]
HSF/General Motors Scholarship Program *(Undergraduate/Scholarship)* [3595]
HSF/Wal-Mart Stores Inc. Scholarship Program *(Graduate, Undergraduate/Scholarship)* [3599]
Idaho Society of CPA's Scholarships *(Undergraduate/Scholarship)* [3647]
IMA FAR Doctoral Student Grant Program *(Doctorate/Grant)* [3745]
IMA Memorial Education Fund Scholarships (MEF) *(Graduate, Undergraduate/Scholarship/Forgivable Loan)* [3746]
Journyx Scholarships *(Graduate, Undergraduate/Scholarship)* [4035]
Robert A. Kleckner Scholarships *(Undergraduate/Scholarship)* [6663]
KPMG Foundation Minority Accounting Doctoral Scholarships *(Postdoctorate/Scholarship)* [4097]
Michael B. Kruse Scholarships *(Undergraduate/Scholarship)* [2428]
Paul J. Laninga Memorial Scholarship Fund *(Undergraduate/Scholarship)* [3290]
Lewis-Clark State College/Idaho Society of CPAs Scholarships Fund *(Undergraduate/Scholarship)* [4196]
Marathon Oil Corporation College Scholarship Program *(Graduate, Undergraduate/Scholarship)* [3600]
Michele L. McDonald Scholarships *(Undergraduate/Scholarship)* [2832]
Harry Mestel Memorial Accounting Scholarship Fund *(Undergraduate/Scholarship)* [6743]
Mark Miller Award *(Graduate, Undergraduate/Scholarship)* [4656]
Minnesota Association of Public Accountant Scholarships *(Undergraduate/Scholarship)* [4546]
NABA Corporate Scholarship Program *(Graduate, Undergraduate/Scholarship)* [4657]
NABA National Scholarship Program *(Graduate, Undergraduate/Scholarship)* [4658]
National Society of Accountants Scholarship Program *(Undergraduate/Scholarship)* [5047]
Hubert A. Nelson Scholarships *(Undergraduate/Scholarship)* [2787]
Norfolk Southern Scholarships *(Undergraduate/Scholarship)* [7329]
Chet and Jannett Perry Scholarships *(Undergraduate/Scholarship)* [6668]
Phillip Morris USA Scholarships *(Undergraduate/Scholarship)* [7330]
Rowling, Dold and Associates LLP Scholarships *(Undergraduate/Scholarship)* [2833]
Seattle Chapter ASWA Scholarships *(All/Scholarship)* [2834]
John M. and Mary A. Shanley Memorial Scholarships *(Undergraduate/Scholarship)* [6673]
Snodgrass Scholarships *(Undergraduate/Scholarship)* [4384]
Society of Louisiana Certified Public Accountants Scholarships *(Undergraduate/Scholarship)* [6468]
The Stanley H. Stearman Awards *(Undergraduate/Scholarship)* [5048]
Surety Industry Scholarship Program for Minority Students *(Undergraduate/Scholarship)* [6824]
Talbert Family Memorial Accounting Scholarships *(Undergraduate/Scholarship)* [2291]
TDC Scholarship Program *(Graduate, Undergraduate/Scholarship)* [4659]
Ralph and Valerie Thomas Scholarship Program *(Graduate, Undergraduate/Scholarship)* [4660]
Travis C. Tomlin Memorial Scholarship Program *(Graduate, Undergraduate/Scholarship)* [4661]
Toyota High School Scholarship Program *(Undergraduate/Scholarship)* [3603]
UAA Accounting Club Scholarships *(Undergraduate/Scholarship)* [7039]
UAA Melissa J. Wolf Scholarships *(Undergraduate/Scholarship)* [7064]
Verizon Scholarship Program *(Undergraduate/Scholarship)* [3607]
Wachovia Scholarship Awards *(Undergraduate/Scholarship)* [3571]
Wall-Mart Stores, Inc. Fellowships - Graduate *(Undergraduate/Scholarship)* [643]
Thomas S. Watson, Jr. Memorial Scholarships *(Graduate, Undergraduate/Scholarship)* [4662]
Wells Fargo American Indian Scholarship for Graduates *(Graduate/Scholarship)* [644]
Witt Mares Scholarships *(Undergraduate/Scholarship)* [7331]
Women In Need Scholarships *(Undergraduate/Scholarship)* [2835]
Women In Transition Scholarships *(Undergraduate/Scholarship)* [2836]
Harry and Angel Zerigian Scholarships *(Undergraduate/Scholarship)* [1295]

Acquired immune deficiency syndrome

Elizabeth Glaser Scientist Award *(Other/Award/Prize)* [5539]
International Scholar Awards *(Postdoctorate/Award/Prize)* [5540]

Actuarial science

Actuarial Scholarships for Minority Students *(Undergraduate/Scholarship)* [383]
HSBC-North America Scholarship Program *(Undergraduate/Scholarship)* [3592]
International Association of Black Actuaries Scholarships *(Undergraduate/Scholarship)* [3786]
DW Simpson Actuarial Science Scholarship Program *(Undergraduate/Scholarship)* [6402]
Toyota High School Scholarship Program *(Undergraduate/Scholarship)* [3603]

Adult education

Adolescent Literacy Predoctoral Fellowships *(Doctorate/Fellowship)* [4623]
A.E. Robert Friedman Scholarships *(Postgraduate, Undergraduate/Scholarship)* [5445]
International Graduate Student Awards *(Graduate/Scholarship)* [26]
MPAEA Memorial Scholarships *(Graduate/Scholarship)* [4582]
MPAEA Professional Development Scholarships *(All/Scholarship)* [4583]
MPAEA State Association Professional Development Grants *(Other/Grant)* [4584]
MPAEA Student Scholarships *(Other/Scholarship)* [4585]
NASCOE Scholarships *(Other/Scholarship)* [4701]

Advertising (See also: Public relations)

American Advertising Federation-Cleveland College Scholarships *(Undergraduate/Scholarship)* [291]

American Advertising Federation-Cleveland High School Scholarships *(Undergraduate/Scholarship)* [292]
HSBC-North America Scholarship Program *(Undergraduate/Scholarship)* [3592]
The Lagrant Foundation - Graduate Students Scholarships *(Graduate/Scholarship)* [4104]
The Lagrant Foundation - Undergraduate Students Scholarship *(Undergraduate/Scholarship)* [4105]
Donald Mauer Scholarships *(Undergraduate/Scholarship)* [7176]
New York Women in Communications, Inc. Foundation Scholarships *(Graduate, Undergraduate/Scholarship)* [5200]
Jim Springer Memorial Scholarships *(Undergraduate/Scholarship)* [2289]
Hal Tanner Jr. Scholarships *(Undergraduate/Scholarship)* [7193]
Toyota High School Scholarship Program *(Undergraduate/Scholarship)* [3603]

Aeronautics (See also: Aviation)

AIAA Foundation Scholarship Program *(Undergraduate/Scholarship)* [646]
AMA/Charles H. Grant Scholarships *(Undergraduate/Scholarship)* [18]
Amelia Earhart Memorial Academic Scholarships *(Undergraduate/Scholarship)* [5209]
NORDAM Dee Howard/Etienne Fage Scholarships *(Undergraduate/Scholarship)* [4779]
PAMA Foundation Scholarship Program *(Graduate, Undergraduate/Scholarship)* [5789]
Sig Memorial Scholarships *(Undergraduate/Scholarship)* [19]
Telford Scholarships *(Undergraduate/Scholarship)* [20]
U.S. Air Force ROTC Express Scholarships *(Undergraduate/Scholarship)* [6976]

Aerospace sciences

AFROTC Scholarships *(Undergraduate/Scholarship)* [46]
Air Force Association Excellence Scholarships *(Undergraduate/Scholarship)* [47]
Air Force Association/Grantham Scholarships *(Undergraduate/Scholarship)* [48]
Air Force Association Spouse Scholarships *(Undergraduate/Scholarship)* [49]
Jodi Callahan Memorial Scholarships *(Undergraduate/Scholarship)* [50]
Descendant Scholarships *(Undergraduate/Scholarship)* [2606]
Amelia Earhart Fellowship Program *(Postdoctorate/Fellowship)* [7563]
John and Alice Egan Multi-Year Mentioning Scholarships *(Undergraduate/Scholarship)* [2607]
Matching Scholarships Program *(Undergraduate/Scholarship)* [2608]
Navy, Army or Air Force ROTC Scholarship Program *(Undergraduate/Scholarship)* [2609]
Pitsenbarger Awards *(Undergraduate/Scholarship)* [52]
U.S. Air Force ROTC Express Scholarships *(Undergraduate/Scholarship)* [6976]
Xavier University ROTC Scholarships - Air Force ROTC *(Undergraduate/Scholarship)* [7541]

African-American studies (See also: Area and ethnic studies)

Muddy Waters Scholarships *(Undergraduate/Scholarship)* [1768]

Aggression and violence (See also: Sociology)

Belfer-Aptman Dissertation Research Awards *(Doctorate/Grant)* [4456]
Gail Burns-Smith "Dare to Dream" Fund *(Undergraduate/Scholarship)* [3452]

Agribusiness (See also: Agricultural sciences)

Alberta Agricultural Economics Association Scholarships *(Graduate/Scholarship)* [137]
Alberta Agricultural Economics Association Undergraduate Scholarships *(Undergraduate/Scholarship)* [138]
Douglas McRorie Memorial Scholarships *(Doctorate, Graduate/Scholarship)* [37]
National Poultry and Food Distributors Association Scholarships *(Undergraduate/Scholarship)* [5013]
Progressive Dairy Producers Award *(All/Grant)* [4841]

Agricultural sciences (See also: specific areas of study, e.g. Horticulture)

Myron Asplin Foundation Scholarships *(Undergraduate/Scholarship)* [3687]
Beef Industry Scholarships *(Undergraduate/Scholarship)* [4788]
Eugene Boyko Scholarships *(Undergraduate/Scholarship)* [140]
Delmar Cengage Learning-NAAE Upper Division Scholarships *(Undergraduate/Scholarship)* [4653]
College of Agriculture and Natural Resources Scholarships *(Undergraduate/Scholarship)* [3432]
Charles Dobbins FTA Scholarships *(Undergraduate/Scholarship)* [3154]
Edon Farmers Cooperative Scholarships *(Undergraduate/Scholarship)* [2826]
Florida Fertilizer and Agrichemical Association Scholarships *(Undergraduate/Scholarship)* [3010]
Carleton A. Friday Memorial Scholarships *(Undergraduate/Scholarship)* [4522]
Jim Graham Scholarships *(Undergraduate/Scholarship)* [5245]
Cecil Lane Family Scholarships *(Undergraduate/Scholarship)* [114]
Monsanto Company Agriculture Scholarships *(Undergraduate/Scholarship)* [4567]
National Poultry and Food Distributors Association Scholarships *(Undergraduate/Scholarship)* [5013]
North Dakota Farmers Union Agricultural Studies Scholarships *(Undergraduate/Scholarship)* [5252]
Ina E. Powell Memorial Scholarships *(Undergraduate/Scholarship)* [115]
Progressive Dairy Producers Award *(All/Grant)* [4841]
University of Wisconsin-Madison/CALS Continuing Student Scholarships *(Undergraduate/Scholarship)* [7273]
University of Wisconsin-Madison/CALS Minority Scholarships *(Undergraduate/Scholarship)* [7274]
The Wax Company Scholarships *(Undergraduate/Scholarship)* [121]
Kenneth G. Weckel Scholarships *(Undergraduate/Scholarship)* [4523]
Women's Leadership in Agriculture Scholarship Program *(Undergraduate/Scholarship)* [5320]

Agriculture, Economic aspects

Kyutaro & Yasuo Abiko Memorial Scholarships *(Undergraduate/Scholarship)* [4015]
Agriculture Future of America Community Scholarships *(Undergraduate/Scholarship)* [39]
Agriculture Future of America Scholarship Program *(Undergraduate/Scholarship)* [40]
Alberta Agricultural Economics Association Scholarships *(Graduate/Scholarship)* [137]
Clackamas County Farm Bureau Scholarships *(Undergraduate/Scholarship)* [5392]
Keith Gilmore Foundation - Diploma Scholarships *(Professional Development/Scholarship)* [3240]
Keith Gilmore Foundation - Postgraduate Scholarships *(Postgraduate/Scholarship)* [3241]
Keith Gilmore Foundation - Undergraduate Scholarships *(Undergraduate/Scholarship)* [3242]
Dr. M.G. "Doc" Headley Scholarships *(Undergraduate/Scholarship)* [6778]
IPSA Student Recognition Awards *(Undergraduate/Scholarship)* [3688]
Gregory D. Johnson Memorial Scholarships *(Graduate, Undergraduate/Scholarship)* [4971]
Sam S. Kuwahara Memorial Scholarships *(Undergraduate/Scholarship)* [4019]
The Maschhoffs Inc. Pork Production Scholarships *(Undergraduate/Scholarship)* [4972]
National Association of Conservation District Employees Scholarships *(Undergraduate/Scholarship)* [4693]
National Junior Swine Association Outstanding Member Scholarships *(Graduate/Scholarship)* [4973]
National Poultry and Food Distributors Association Scholarships *(Undergraduate/Scholarship)* [5013]
Nebraska Grain Sorghum Producers Association Scholarships *(Undergraduate/Scholarship)* [5157]
New York State Association of Agricultural Fairs Scholarships *(Undergraduate/Scholarship)* [5193]
NJSA Visionary Leader Scholarships *(Graduate/Scholarship)* [4974]
Oregon Farm Bureau Memorial Scholarships *(Undergraduate/Scholarship)* [5393]
Claude Robinson Scholarships *(Undergraduate/Scholarship)* [4975]
John M. and Mary A. Shanley Memorial Scholarships *(Undergraduate/Scholarship)* [6673]
Dr. Robert and Anna Shaw Scholarships *(Undergraduate/Scholarship)* [184]
Everett Oscar Shimp Memorial Scholarships *(Undergraduate/Scholarship)* [5519]
Pat Shimp Memorial Scholarships *(Undergraduate/Scholarship)* [5520]
Jason Shipley Memorial Scholarships *(Undergraduate/Scholarship)* [4976]
Stanley W. Strew Educational Fund Scholarship *(Undergraduate/Scholarship)* [1812]
Samuel Upchurch Memorial Scholarships *(Undergraduate/Scholarship)* [119]
Washington County Farm Bureau Scholarships *(Undergraduate/Scholarship)* [5394]
Willamette Valley AG Association Scholarships *(Undergraduate/Scholarship)* [5395]
Working for Farmers' Success Scholarships *(Undergraduate/Scholarship)* [7516]
Yamhill County Farm Bureau Scholarships *(Undergraduate/Scholarship)* [5396]

Alzheimer's disease

Sigma Kappa Foundation Alzheimer's/Gerontology Scholarships *(Undergraduate/Scholarship)* [6370]

Anesthesiology

Baxter Corporation Canadian Research Awards in Anesthesia *(Professional Development/Award/Prize)* [1912]
Canadian Anesthesiologists' Society Research Awards *(Professional Development/Award/Prize)* [1913]
CAS/Vitaid-LMA Residents' Research Grant Competition *(Professional Development/Award/Prize)* [1915]
Dale O. Heimberger CRNA Memorial Scholarship Fund *(Graduate/Scholarship)* [6726]
David S. Sheridan Canadian Research Awards *(Professional Development/Award/Prize)* [1918]
Smiths Medical Canada Ltd. Research Awards *(Professional Development/Award/Prize)* [1919]

Animal rights

ABA Scholarships *(Undergraduate/Scholarship)* [437]
Richard E. Andrews Memorial Scholarships *(Undergraduate/Scholarship)* [438]

WildBird/Clements Memorial Scholarships (Undergraduate/Scholarship) [439]

Animal science and behavior (See also: Zoology)

ABA Scholarships (Undergraduate/Scholarship) [437]
Richard E. Andrews Memorial Scholarships (Undergraduate/Scholarship) [438]
Auburn Animal Science Department Graduate Student Scholarships (Graduate/Scholarship) [112]
W.D. Farr Scholarships (Graduate/Scholarship) [4789]
Fred Johnson Memorial Scholarships (Graduate/Scholarship) [4790]
NCF Fort Dodge Animal Health Legacy Scholarships for Undergraduate Students (Undergraduate/Scholarship) [4791]
Ratcliffe Hicks School of Agriculture Heritage Scholarships (Undergraduate/Scholarship) [3492]
Stark County Dairy Promoters Scholarships (Undergraduate/Scholarship) [6755]
Samuel Upchurch Memorial Scholarships (Undergraduate/Scholarship) [119]
Ed Wadsworth Memorial Scholarships (Undergraduate/Scholarship) [120]
WildBird/Clements Memorial Scholarships (Undergraduate/Scholarship) [439]

Anthropology

Zora Neale Hurston Scholarships (Graduate/Scholarship) [7556]
Pi Gamma Mu Scholarships (Graduate/Scholarship) [5691]

Aquaculture

Aquatics Booster Club Scholarships (Undergraduate/Scholarship) [5908]
Lloyd Bridges Scholarships (Graduate/Scholarship) [2077]
Nova Scotia Salmon Association Scholarships (All/Scholarship) [5307]

Archeology

Kenan Erim Fellowships for Research at Ancient Aphrodisiacs (Postdoctorate/Fellowship) [893]
Kress Pre-Doctoral Fellowships in the History of Art and Archeology in Turkey (Postdoctorate/Fellowship) [898]
National Endowment for the Humanities Advanced Fellowship for Research in Turkey (Postdoctorate/Fellowship) [900]
Jane C. Waldbaum Archaeological Field School Scholarships (Undergraduate/Scholarship) [1195]

Architecture (See also: Landscape architecture and design)

AAUW Legal Advocacy Fund Selected Professions Fellowships (Doctorate, Graduate/Fellowship) [7]
AIAS/AIA Trust Scholarships for Emerging Professionals (Postgraduate/Scholarship) [648]
Architects Association of PEI Scholarships (Undergraduate/Scholarship) [2496]
Association for Women in Architecture Scholarships (Undergraduate/Scholarship) [1506]
Beverly Willis Architecture Foundation Dissertation Fellowships (Doctorate/Fellowship) [6426]
Connecticut Building Congress Scholarships (Undergraduate/Scholarship) [3436]
Tom Cory Memorial Scholarships (Undergraduate/Scholarship) [1197]
D&A Florida Scholarships (Undergraduate/Scholarship) [6648]
Charles Dubose Scholarships (Undergraduate/Scholarship) [3446]
Kenan Erim Fellowships for Research at Ancient Aphrodisiacs (Postdoctorate/Fellowship) [893]
Gen III Scholarships (Undergraduate/Scholarship) [2822]
IALD Scholarship Programs (Graduate, Undergraduate/Scholarship) [3809]
JMA Architecture Studios Scholarships (Undergraduate/Scholarship) [5833]
Samuel H. Kress Foundation Dissertation Fellowships (Doctorate/Fellowship) [6428]
Kress Pre-Doctoral Fellowships in the History of Art and Archeology in Turkey (Postdoctorate/Fellowship) [898]
Stuart L. Noderer Memorial Scholarships (Undergraduate/Scholarship) [6211]
Pardee Community Building Scholarships (Undergraduate/Scholarship) [5849]
PCH Architects/Steven J. Lehnhof Memorial Architectural Scholarships (Undergraduate/Scholarship) [5971]
Howard B. Rickard Scholarships (Undergraduate/Scholarship) [4884]
The RTKL Traveling Fellowships (Undergraduate/Fellowship) [310]
SAH Study Tour Fellowships (Doctorate/Fellowship) [6429]
Leo and Trinidad Sanchez Scholarships (Undergraduate/Scholarship) [6396]
John M. and Mary A. Shanley Memorial Scholarships (Undergraduate/Scholarship) [6673]
Study Scholarships for Artists or Musicians (Graduate/Scholarship) [3230]
Toyota High School Scholarship Program (Undergraduate/Scholarship) [3603]
Dimitri J. Ververelli Memorial Scholarships (Undergraduate/Scholarship) [3536]

Architecture, Naval

Mandell and Lester Rosenblatt and Robert N. Herbert Undergraduate Scholarships (Undergraduate/Scholarship) [6519]
Society of Naval Architects and Marine Engineers Undergraduate Scholarships (Undergraduate/Scholarship) [6520]

Area and ethnic studies (See also: specific areas of study, e.g. Latin American studies)

Chinese-Canadian History and Culture Fellowships (Graduate/Fellowship) [7215]
Houtan Scholarships (Graduate/Scholarship) [3623]
The Iranian-American Scholarship Fund (Undergraduate/Scholarship) [4953]
Iranian Association of Boston's IAB Scholarships (Undergraduate/Scholarship) [4955]
Iranian Federated Women's Club Scholarships (Undergraduate/Scholarship) [4956]
Momeni Foundation Scholarships (Undergraduate/Scholarship) [4957]

Armenian studies (See also: Area and ethnic studies)

AGBU Scholarships (Graduate/Loan) [1255]
Karekin DerAvedision Memorial Endowment Fund (Undergraduate/Scholarship) [1276]
Garikian Scholarship Fund (Undergraduate/Scholarship) [1279]
Knights of Vartan, Fresno Lodge No. 9 Scholarships (Undergraduate/Scholarship) [1287]

Art (See also: Performing arts; Visual arts; specific areas of study, e.g. Painting)

Academic Promise Scholarships (Undergraduate/Scholarship) [3697]
American Watercolor Society Scholarship Program for Art Teachers (Professional Development/Scholarship) [1147]
Art Institute of Colorado Scholarships (Undergraduate/Scholarship) [1310]
Art Institute's Best Teen Chef in America Culinary Scholarships (Undergraduate/Scholarship) [1311]
Joan Auld Scholarships (Undergraduate/Scholarship) [2497]
James Beard Foundation/Art Institute of Colorado Scholarships (Undergraduate/Scholarship) [1312]
Beta Sigma Phi-VCT Scholarships (Undergraduate/Scholarship) [6306]
Anne-Marie Bonner Scholarships (Undergraduate/Scholarship) [3994]
Chautauqua Scholarship Program (All/Scholarship) [3882]
Paul Collins Scholarships (Undergraduate/Scholarship) [3325]
Colorado PROSTART/Art Institute of Colorado Art Scholarships for High School Seniors (Undergraduate/Scholarship) [1313]
Colorado Springs Pikes Peak Region School District Young Peoples Art Show Scholarships (Undergraduate/Scholarship) [1314]
Convergence Assistantship Grants (Undergraduate/Grant) [3394]
Dewey Lee Curtis Scholarship Fund (Doctorate, Graduate/Scholarship) [2631]
Felicia De Bow Memorial Scholarships (All/Scholarship) [5447]
Denver Public School Art Award/Scholarships for High School Seniors (Undergraduate/Scholarship) [1315]
Walt Disney Company Foundation Scholarships (Undergraduate/Scholarship) [4037]
Mychajlo Dmytrenko Fine Arts Foundation Scholarships (Undergraduate/Scholarship) [7021]
Pauly D'Orlando Memorial Art Scholarships (Graduate, Undergraduate/Scholarship) [6950]
Douglas County Art Awards Scholarship for High School Seniors (Undergraduate/Scholarship) [1316]
The "Drawn to Art" Fellowships (Doctorate/Fellowship) [301]
Adrienne Zoe Fedok Art and Music Scholarships (Undergraduate/Scholarship) [3099]
Fine Arts Association Minority Scholarships (Undergraduate/Scholarship) [2932]
Fine Arts Association United Way Scholarships (Undergraduate/Scholarship) [2933]
Fine Arts and Music Scholarships (Undergraduate/Scholarship) [2420]
Mearl K. Gable II Memorial Grants (Professional Development/Grant) [3395]
Mathilda & Carolyn Gallmeyer Scholarships (Undergraduate/Scholarship) [3330]
Guntley-Lorimer Science and Arts Scholarships (Undergraduate/Scholarship) [1733]
Ed Haas Memorial Scholarships (Undergraduate/Scholarship) [6776]
HGA and Dendel Scholarships (Undergraduate/Scholarship) [3396]
Regina Higdon Scholarships (Undergraduate/Scholarship) [2423]
Lucy Hilty Research Grants (All/Grant) [813]
Indiana State Alumni Association Creative and Performing Arts Award (Undergraduate/Scholarship) [3701]
Iranian Artist Scholarships (Undergraduate/Scholarship) [4954]
Donald Wills Jacobs Scholarships (Undergraduate/Scholarship) [4362]
Gregori Jakovina Endowment Scholarships (Undergraduate/Scholarship) [2884]
Jefferson County Art Awards Scholarship for High school Seniors (Undergraduate/Scholarship) [1317]
George E. Judd Scholarships (Undergraduate/Scholarship) [6660]
Jay and Deborah Last Fellowships (Doctorate/Fellowship) [304]
Larry McDonald Scholarships (Undergraduate/Scholarship) [2888]
McNamara Family Creative Arts Project Grants (Graduate, Undergraduate/Grant) [3601]
Mill Creek Business Association Scholarships (Undergraduate/Scholarship) [4533]
National Endowment for the Humanities Advanced Fellowship for Research in Turkey (Postdoctorate/Fellowship) [900]
Palos Fine Arts Association Scholarships (Undergraduate/Scholarship) [5448]
Marvin R. and Pearl E. Patterson Family Scholarships Fund (Undergraduate/Scholarship) [3296]
Silvio and Eugenio Petrini Grants (Professional Development/Grant) [3397]

Phi Theta Kappa Scholarships *(Undergraduate/Scholarship)* [3712]
David G. Robinson Arts Scholarships *(Undergraduate/Scholarship)* [6670]
Dr. Robert and Anna Shaw Scholarships *(Undergraduate/Scholarship)* [184]
Marion Barr Stanfield Art Scholarships *(Graduate, Undergraduate/Scholarship)* [6956]
Robert W. and Bernice Ingalls Staton Scholarships *(Undergraduate/Scholarship)* [7202]
Study Scholarships for Artists or Musicians *(Graduate/Scholarship)* [3230]
UAA Emi Chance Memorial Scholarships *(Undergraduate/Scholarship)* [7052]
UAA Jack & Martha Roderick Scholarships *(Graduate, Undergraduate/Scholarship)* [7057]
UAA Kimura Scholarship Fund (Photography Scholarships) *(Undergraduate/Scholarship)* [7060]
UAA Muriel Hannah Scholarships in Art *(Undergraduate/Scholarship)* [7067]
UAA Paul G. Landis Scholarships *(Undergraduate/Scholarship)* [7069]
Philip F. Vineberg Travelling Fellowship in the Humanities *(Graduate/Scholarship)* [4432]
Washington University Law School Chancellor's Graduate Fellowships *(Graduate/Fellowship)* [7386]
Wyoming Art Symposium Scholarships *(Undergraduate/Scholarship)* [1318]
Gwen Yarnell Theatre Scholarships *(Undergraduate/Scholarship)* [2934]

Art conservation
Kress Conservation Fellowships *(Graduate/Fellowship)* [4099]

Art, Greek
Hellenic University Club of Philadelphia Founders Scholarships *(Undergraduate/Scholarship)* [3530]

Art history
Kenan Erim Fellowships for Research at Ancient Aphrodisiacs *(Postdoctorate/Fellowship)* [893]
Hench Post-Dissertation Fellowships *(Postdoctorate/Fellowship)* [303]
Kress Pre-Doctoral Fellowships in the History of Art and Archeology in Turkey *(Postdoctorate/Fellowship)* [898]
United States Capitol Historical Society Fellowships *(Graduate/Fellowship)* [6983]

Art industries and trade
Michael Beaudry Scholarships *(Graduate/Scholarship)* [3173]
Paul Collins Scholarships *(Undergraduate/Scholarship)* [3325]
Nortel Institute Undergraduate Scholarships *(Undergraduate/Scholarship)* [7231]
Matthew A. Runci, MJSA Scholarships *(Undergraduate/Scholarship)* [3197]
Dr. Robert and Anna Shaw Scholarships *(Undergraduate/Scholarship)* [184]
S.H. Silver Scholarships *(Graduate/Scholarship)* [3198]
Kurt Wayne Scholarships *(Graduate/Scholarship)* [3201]

Art, Roman
Estelle Shohet Brettman Fellowship *(Postdoctorate/Fellowship)* [3821]

Art therapy
AATA Anniversary Scholarships *(Graduate/Scholarship)* [312]
The Dave Family "Humor Studies" Scholarships *(Undergraduate/Scholarship)* [1364]
Ed Dunkelblau Scholarships *(All/Scholarship)* [1365]
Hartford Foundation for Public Giving Occupational Therapy Scholarships *(Undergraduate/Scholarship)* [3459]
Margie Klein "Paper Plate" Scholarships *(All/Scholarship)* [1366]
Myra Levick Scholarships *(Graduate/Scholarship)* [313]
William Philpott Scholarships *(All/Scholarship)* [1712]
Lenny Ravich "Shalom" Scholarships *(All/Scholarship)* [1367]
Rawley Silver Award for Excellence *(Graduate/Scholarship)* [314]
Patty Wooten Scholarships *(Undergraduate/Scholarship)* [1368]

Arts
Art Graduate Scholarships *(Graduate/Scholarship)* [148]
Arts for Career Development Scholarships *(Professional Development/Internship)* [149]
William E. Barto Scholarships *(Undergraduate/Scholarship)* [2772]
Beinecke Brothers Memorial Scholarships *(Undergraduate/Scholarship)* [7085]
Antonio Cirino Memorial Art Education Fellowships *(Undergraduate/Fellowship)* [6035]
Edgecliff McAuley Art Scholarships *(Undergraduate/Scholarship)* [7527]
Helen R. Finley-Loescher Scholarships *(Undergraduate/Scholarship)* [2464]
Jacob K. Javits Fellowships *(Doctorate, Master's/Fellowship)* [4707]
Jewish Federation Academic Scholarships *(Graduate, Undergraduate/Scholarship)* [4029]
Anneka McMillan Creative Arts Scholarships *(Undergraduate/Scholarship)* [6207]
John H. Moss Scholarships *(Undergraduate/Scholarship)* [7230]
Virginia Nicklas Scholarships *(Undergraduate/Scholarship)* [2658]
Northwest-Shoals Community College Fine Arts Scholarships - Art *(Undergraduate/Scholarship)* [5293]
Prescott Fine Arts Association Scholarship Program *(Undergraduate/Scholarship)* [5746]
Leo S. Rowe Pan American Fund *(Undergraduate/Loan)* [5404]
Casey Sakir Point Scholarships *(Graduate, Undergraduate/Scholarship)* [5726]
Scholarship Foundation of Santa Barbara Art Scholarship Program *(High School/Scholarship)* [6252]
Silver Nugget Gaming Ambassadors Scholarships *(Undergraduate/Scholarship)* [5858]
Patrick Spielman Memorial Scholarship Program *(Undergraduate/Scholarship)* [6290]
StraightForward Media's Art School Scholarships *(Undergraduate/Scholarship)* [6795]
The UCSD Black Alumni Scholarship for Arts and Humanities *(Undergraduate/Scholarship)* [6236]
The UCSD Black Alumni Scholarships for Engineering, Mathematics and Science *(Undergraduate/Scholarship)* [6237]
Xavier University Honors Bachelor of Arts Scholarships *(Undergraduate/Scholarship)* [7539]

Astronautics
AIAA Foundation Scholarship Program *(Undergraduate/Scholarship)* [646]

Astronomy and astronomical sciences
American Astronomical Society Small Research Grants *(Doctorate/Grant)* [428]
AWIS College Scholarships *(Undergraduate/Scholarship)* [1519]
Chretien International Research Grants *(Doctorate, Professional Development/Grant)* [429]

Athletics
Earl and Countess of Wessex - World Championships in Athletics Scholarships *(Undergraduate/Scholarship)* [155]
The Gene and John Athletic Scholarships *(Undergraduate/Scholarship)* [6789]
The Tacoma Athletic Commission Scholarships *(Undergraduate/Scholarship)* [3379]
United States Golf Association Fellowship Program *(All/Fellowship)* [6992]
United States Golf Association Scholarship Program *(Undergraduate/Scholarship)* [6993]

Atmospheric science
U.S. Air Force ROTC Express Scholarships *(Undergraduate/Scholarship)* [6976]

Automotive technology
AIA and the Global Automotive Aftermarket Symposium Scholarships *(Undergraduate/Scholarship)* [1569]
APSAIL's Ralph Silverman Memorial Scholarships *(Undergraduate/Scholarship)* [1542]
ISA Aerospace Industries Division - William H. Atkinson Scholarships *(Graduate, Undergraduate/Scholarship)* [3940]
Automotive Technician Scholarship Program *(Undergraduate/Scholarship)* [4334]
Automotive Women's Alliance Foundation Scholarships *(Undergraduate/Scholarship)* [1577]
Larry H. Averill Memorial Scholarships *(Undergraduate/Scholarship)* [1549]
AVI Scholarships *(Undergraduate/Scholarship)* [1543]
Tom Babcox Memorial Scholarships *(All/Scholarship)* [1544]
Rob Copeland Memorial Scholarships *(Undergraduate/Scholarship)* [4172]
Richard Cossette/Gale Memorial Scholarships *(All/Scholarship)* [1545]
Harold Dieckmann Draper, Sr. Scholarships *(Undergraduate/Scholarship)* [1550]
John E. Echlin Memorial Scholarships *(Undergraduate/Scholarship)* [1551]
Florida Automotive Industry Scholarships *(Undergraduate/Scholarship)* [1546]
Carlyle Fraser/Wilton Looney Scholarships *(Undergraduate/Scholarship)* [1552]
Friends of Mary Automotive Scholarships *(Undergraduate/Scholarship)* [6312]
John Goerlich Memorial Scholarships *(Undergraduate/Scholarship)* [1553]
Charles V. Hagler Scholarships *(Undergraduate/Scholarship)* [1554]
Zenon C.R. Hansen Memorial Scholarships *(Undergraduate/Scholarship)* [1555]
Bob and Dawn Hardy Automotive Scholarship *(Undergraduate/Scholarship)* [3982]
Norman E. Huston Scholarships *(Graduate, Undergraduate/Scholarship)* [3941]
ISA Educational Foundation Scholarships *(Graduate, Undergraduate/Scholarship)* [3942]
ISA Executive Board Scholarships *(Graduate, Undergraduate/Scholarship)* [3943]
ISA Section and District Scholarships - Birmingham *(Graduate, Undergraduate/Scholarship)* [3944]
ISA Section and District Scholarships - Houston *(Graduate, Undergraduate/Scholarship)* [3945]
ISA Section and District Scholarships - Lehigh Valley *(Graduate, Undergraduate/Scholarship)* [3946]
ISA Section and District Scholarships - New Jersey *(Graduate, Undergraduate/Scholarship)* [3947]
ISA Section and District Scholarships - Niagara Frontier *(Graduate, Undergraduate/Scholarship)* [3948]
ISA Section and District Scholarships - Northern California *(Graduate, Undergraduate/Scholarship)* [3949]
ISA Section and District Scholarships - Richmond (Hopewell) *(Graduate, Undergraduate/Scholarship)* [3950]
ISA Section and District Scholarships - Savannah River *(Graduate, Undergraduate/Scholarship)* [3951]
ISA Section and District Scholarships - Southwestern Wyoming *(Graduate, Undergraduate/Scholarship)* [3952]
ISA Section and District Scholarships - Texas, Louisiana and Mississippi *(Graduate, Undergraduate/Scholarship)* [3953]

ISA Section and District Scholarships - Wilmington (Graduate, Undergraduate/Scholarship) [3954]
ISA Technical Division Scholarships - Analysis Division (Graduate, Undergraduate/Scholarship) [3955]
ISA Technical Division Scholarships - Chemical and Petroleum Industries Division (Graduate, Undergraduate/Scholarship) [3956]
ISA Technical Division Scholarships - Computer Technology Division (Graduate, Undergraduate/Scholarship) [3957]
ISA Technical Division Scholarships - Food and Pharmaceutical Industries Division (Graduate, Undergraduate/Scholarship) [3958]
ISA Technical Division Scholarships - Power Industry Division (Graduate, Undergraduate/Scholarship) [3959]
ISA Technical Division Scholarships - Process Measurement and Control Division (Graduate, Undergraduate/Scholarship) [3960]
ISA Technical Division Scholarships - Pulp and Paper Industry Division (Graduate, Undergraduate/Scholarship) [3961]
ISA Technical Division Scholarships - Test Measurement Division (Graduate, Undergraduate/Scholarship) [3962]
ISA Technical Division Scholarships - Water and Wastewater Industries Division (Graduate, Undergraduate/Scholarship) [3963]
Bob and Mary Ives Scholarships (Graduate, Undergraduate/Scholarship) [3964]
Ken and Romaine Kauffman Scholarship Fund (Undergraduate/Scholarship) [3108]
John W. Koons, Sr. Memorial Scholarships (Undergraduate/Scholarship) [1556]
Ken Krum/Bud Kouts Memorial Scholarships (Undergraduate/Scholarship) [1557]
Lewis-Clark State College Presidential Technical Out-of-State Scholarships (Undergraduate/Scholarship) [4199]
Loan Forgiveness Scholarships (Undergraduate/Scholarship) [6689]
Leon I. Lock and Barbara R. Lock Scholarship Fund (Undergraduate/Scholarship) [3109]
Hans McCorriston Motive Power Machinist Grant Programs (Postgraduate/Scholarship) [1570]
Brouwer D. McIntyre Memorial Scholarships (Undergraduate/Scholarship) [1558]
The Medallion Fund Scholarships (Undergraduate/Scholarship) [5171]
Jim Moran Scholarships (Undergraduate/Scholarship) [1559]
Arthur Paulin Automotive Aftermarket Scholarship Awards (Postgraduate/Scholarship) [1571]
Kenneth Rogers Memorial Scholarships (Undergraduate/Scholarship) [4213]
Dorothy M. Ross Memorial Scholarships (Undergraduate/Scholarship) [1560]
SEMA Memorial Scholarships (Graduate/Scholarship) [1573]
Sloan Northwood Heavy-Duty Scholarships (Undergraduate/Scholarship) [1547]
Stuart H. Snyder Memorial Scholarships (Undergraduate/Scholarship) [1561]
Society of Automotive Analyst Scholarships (Undergraduate/Scholarship) [1562]
Specialty Equipment Market Association Scholarships (Undergraduate/Scholarship) [6690]
Walter W. Stillman Scholarships (Undergraduate/Scholarship) [1563]
Toyota High School Scholarship Program (Undergraduate/Scholarship) [3603]
TRW Foundation Scholarships (Undergraduate/Scholarship) [1564]
Universal Underwriters Scholarships (Undergraduate/Scholarship) [1565]
J. Irving Whalley Memorial Scholarships (Undergraduate/Scholarship) [1566]
M.H. Yager Memorial Scholarships (Undergraduate/Scholarship) [1567]

Aviation (See also: Aeronautics)

AE Flight Training Scholarships (Professional Development/Scholarship) [5206]
AE Jet Type Rating Scholarships (Professional Development/Scholarship) [5207]
AE Technical Training Scholarships (Professional Development/Scholarship) [5208]
Aircraft Owners and Pilots Association Scholarships (Undergraduate/Scholarship) [66]
AMACESP Student Scholarships (Undergraduate/Scholarship) [92]
David Arver Memorial Scholarships (Undergraduate/Scholarship) [67]
Dutch and Ginger Arver Scholarships (Undergraduate/Scholarship) [68]
Association of Flight Attendants Scholarship Fund (Undergraduate/Scholarship) [1419]
Aviation Distributors and Manufacturers Association Scholarship Fund (All/Scholarship) [1579]
Donald A. Baldwin Sr. Business Aviation Management Scholarships (Undergraduate/Scholarship) [4770]
Janice K. Barden Aviation Scholarships (Undergraduate/Scholarship) [4771]
Alan H. Conklin Business Aviation Management Scholarships (Undergraduate/Scholarship) [4772]
Corporate Aviation Management Scholarships (Professional Development/Scholarship) [4773]
John P. Culhane Memorial Scholarships (Undergraduate/Scholarship) [125]
Johnny Davis Memorial Scholarships (Undergraduate/Scholarship) [69]
Arlene Davis Scholarships (Undergraduate/Scholarship) [2685]
Distinguished Flying Cross Society Scholarship (Undergraduate/Scholarship) [2724]
F. Atlee Dodge Maintenance Scholarships (Undergraduate/Scholarship) [126]
Duncan Aviation Scholarships (Undergraduate/Scholarship) [70]
Amelia Earhart Memorial Academic Scholarships (Undergraduate/Scholarship) [5209]
David E. Ewald Journalism Scholarships (Undergraduate/Scholarship) [4774]
Exxon Mobil Aviation and the Avitats International Operators Scholarships (All/Scholarship) [4775]
William M. Fanning Maintenance Scholarships (Undergraduate/Scholarship) [4776]
Field Aviation Co., Inc. Scholarships (Undergraduate/Scholarship) [71]
Flight Attendants/Flight Technician Scholarships (Undergraduate/Scholarship) [4777]
Joseph Frasca Excellence in Aviation Scholarships (Undergraduate/Scholarship) [7081]
Garmin Scholarships (Undergraduate/Scholarship) [72]
Lowell Gaylor Memorial Scholarships (Undergraduate/Scholarship) [73]
Lawrence Ginocchio Aviation Scholarships (Undergraduate/Scholarship) [4778]
Bud Glover Memorial Scholarships (Undergraduate/Scholarship) [74]
Gogos Scholarships (Undergraduate/Scholarship) [2302]
Leon Harris/Les Nichols Memorial Scholarships to Spartan College of Aeronautics & Technology (Undergraduate/Scholarship) [75]
Don C. Hawkins Memorial Scholarships (Undergraduate/Scholarship) [76]
Helicopter Foundation International Commercial Helicopter Rating Scholarships (All/Scholarship) [3520]
Helicopter Foundation International Maintenance Technician Certificate Scholarships (Professional Development/Scholarship) [3521]
Honeywell Avionics Scholarships (Undergraduate/Scholarship) [77]
Edward L. Horne, Jr. Scholarships (All/Scholarship) [5406]
NORDAM Dee Howard/Etienne Fage Scholarships (Undergraduate/Scholarship) [4779]
The ISASI Rudolf Kapustin Memorial Scholarships (Undergraduate/Scholarship) [3902]
Eugene S. Kropf Scholarships (Undergraduate/Scholarship) [7082]
L-3 Avionics Systems Scholarships (Undergraduate/Scholarship) [78]
Maintenance Technical Reward and Career Scholarships (Undergraduate/Scholarship) [4780]
Mid-Continent Instrument Scholarships (Undergraduate/Scholarship) [79]
Joshua Esch Mitchell Aviation Scholarships (Undergraduate/Scholarship) [3342]
Monte R. Mitchell Global Scholarships (Undergraduate/Scholarship) [80]
National Black Coalition of Federal Aviation Employees Scholarship (Other/Scholarship) [4759]
NGPA Education Fund Scholarships (Undergraduate/Scholarship) [4911]
Michelle North Scholarships for Safety (Professional Development/Scholarship) [3522]
OBAP Fellowships - Airline Transport (ATP) (Professional Development/Fellowship) [5407]
OBAP Fellowships - Commercial (Professional Development/Fellowship) [5408]
OBAP Fellowships - Instructor rating (CFI/CFII/MEI) (Professional Development/Fellowship) [5409]
OBAP Fellowships - Multi-Engine (Professional Development/Fellowship) [5410]
OBAP General Scholarships (All/Scholarship) [5411]
PAMA Foundation Scholarship Program (Graduate, Undergraduate/Scholarship) [5789]
Chuck Peacock Memorial Scholarships (Undergraduate/Scholarship) [81]
Plane and Pilot Magazine/Garmin Scholarships (Undergraduate/Scholarship) [82]
Bob Reeve Professional Aviation Management Scholarships (Undergraduate/Scholarship) [127]
Rockwell Collins Scholarships (Undergraduate/Scholarship) [83]
Marty Rosness Student Scholarships (Undergraduate/Scholarship) [1204]
San Diego Regional Aviation Association Scholarships (Undergraduate/Scholarship) [6226]
Bill Sanderson Aviation Maintenance Technician Scholarship (Professional Development/Scholarship) [3523]
Scheduler and Dispatchers Scholarships (Professional Development/Scholarship) [4781]
Scholarship Challenge Flight (Undergraduate/Scholarship) [3409]
Thomas J. Slocum Memorial Scholarships to Westwood College of Aviation Technology (Undergraduate/Scholarship) [84]
Southeast Aerospace Inc. Scholarships (Undergraduate/Scholarship) [85]
Sporty's Pilot Shop/Cincinnati Avionics Scholarships (Undergraduate/Scholarship) [86]
Tailhook Educational Foundation Scholarships Program (Undergraduate/Scholarship) [6836]
Kei Takemoto Memorial Scholarships (Undergraduate/Scholarship) [87]
Lee Tarbox Memorial Scholarships (Undergraduate/Scholarship) [88]
Tom Taylor Memorial Scholarships to Spartan College of Aeronautics and Technology (Undergraduate/Scholarship) [89]
Texas State Technical College Scholarships (Undergraduate/Scholarship) [90]
U.S. Aircraft Insurance Group Professional Development Program Scholarships (Undergraduate/Scholarship) [4782]
Paul A. Whelan Aviation Scholarships (Undergraduate/Scholarship) [7083]
Dr. Harold S. Wood Award for Excellence (Undergraduate/Award/Prize) [3207]

Banking (See also: Accounting; Finance)

Conference of State Bank Supervisors Graduate School Scholarships (Graduate/Award/Prize) [2527]
Tribal Business Management Program (TBM) Scholarships (Undergraduate/Scholarship) [2069]
Wall-Mart Stores, Inc. Fellowships - Graduate (Undergraduate/Scholarship) [643]
Wells Fargo American Indian Scholarship for Graduates (Graduate/Scholarship) [644]
Wells Fargo Scholarship Program (Graduate, Undergraduate/Scholarship) [3608]

Herbert W. Whiteman, Jr. Scholarships *(Graduate, Undergraduate/Scholarship)* [7293]

Behavioral sciences

Owen F. Aldis Scholarship Fund *(Graduate/Scholarship)* [3904]
Behavioral Sciences Post-Doctoral Fellowships *(Postdoctorate/Fellowship)* [2867]
Behavioral Sciences Student Fellowships *(Graduate, Undergraduate/Fellowship)* [2868]
Epilepsy Foundation Research Grants *(All/Grant)* [2871]
National Institute of Health Undergraduate Scholarship Program *(Undergraduate/Scholarship)* [4949]
Targeted Research Initiative for Health Outcomes *(Doctorate/Grant)* [2875]
Targeted Research Initiative for Mood Disorders *(Doctorate/Grant)* [2876]
Targeted Research Initiative for Seniors *(Doctorate/Grant)* [2877]

Bible studies (See also: Religion; Theology)

Catholic Biblical Association of America Scholarships *(Undergraduate/Scholarship)* [2071]

Biochemistry (See also: Chemistry)

Epilepsy Foundation Pre-doctoral Research Training Fellowships *(Graduate/Grant)* [2870]
UAA Kris Knudson Memorial Scholarships *(Graduate, Undergraduate/Scholarship)* [7062]

Biological and clinical sciences (See also: Biology)

Daland Fellowships in Clinical Investigation *(Doctorate/Fellowship)* [767]
Endowment Fund for Education Grants *(Undergraduate/Grant)* [1707]
Endowment Fund for Education (Loan) *(Undergraduate/Loan)* [1708]
Endowment Fund for Education (Loan/Grants for Equipment) *(Undergraduate/Grant)* [1709]
Endowment Fund for Education (Loans/Grants for Educational Materials) *(Undergraduate/Grant)* [1710]
Howard Hughes Medical Institute Predoctoral Fellowships *(Graduate/Fellowship)* [4706]
Lewis and Clark Fund for Exploration and Field Research *(Doctorate/Grant)* [770]
National Candy Technologist Scholarship Program *(Undergraduate/Scholarship)* [332]
SNMTS Clinical Advancement Scholarships *(Other/Scholarship)* [6524]

Biology (See also: Biological and clinical sciences)

AACT Undergraduate Scholarships *(Undergraduate/Scholarship)* [5711]
Alaska Support Industry Alliance Scholarships *(Undergraduate/Scholarship)* [4341]
Avista Corporation Minds in Motion Scholarships *(Undergraduate/Scholarship)* [4163]
AWIS College Scholarships *(Undergraduate/Scholarship)* [1519]
Catherine H. Beattie Fellowships *(Graduate/Fellowship)* [2089]
Stan Beck Fellowships *(Undergraduate/Fellowship)* [2861]
Biocom Scholarships *(Undergraduate/Scholarship)* [6173]
BioQuip Scholarships *(Undergraduate/Scholarship)* [2862]
John and Elisabeth Buck Endowed Scholarships *(Undergraduate/Scholarship)* [4283]
C. Lalor Burdick Scholarships *(Undergraduate/Scholarship)* [4284]
Max M. Burger Endowed Scholarships in Embryology *(Undergraduate/Scholarship)* [4285]
Julian E. Carnes Scholarship Fund *(Undergraduate/Scholarship)* [3046]
Charles Dobbins FTA Scholarships *(Undergraduate/Scholarship)* [3154]
Robertson Lola Ellis Scholarships *(Undergraduate/Scholarship)* [4286]
Thomas B. Grave and Elizabeth F. Grave Scholarships *(Undergraduate/Scholarship)* [4287]
Caswell Grave Scholarships *(Undergraduate/Scholarship)* [4288]
William Randolph Hearst Educational Endowments *(Undergraduate/Scholarship)* [4289]
Helm Family Scholarships *(Undergraduate/Scholarship)* [6192]
Benjamin Kaminer Endowed Scholarships in Physiology *(Undergraduate/Scholarship)* [4290]
Arthur Klorfein Scholarships and Fellowship Funds *(Undergraduate/Scholarship)* [4291]
Lakselaget Foundation Scholarships *(Graduate, Undergraduate/Scholarship)* [4107]
Lewis-Clark State College Presidential Technical Out-of-State Scholarships *(Undergraduate/Scholarship)* [4199]
Frank R. Lillie Fellowships and Scholarships *(Undergraduate/Scholarship)* [4292]
Marine Biological Laboratory Pioneers Fund *(Undergraduate/Scholarship)* [4293]
S.O. Mast Founder's Scholarships *(Undergraduate/Scholarship)* [4294]
Merck Undergraduate Science Research Scholarships *(Undergraduate/Scholarship)* [318]
Frank Morrell Endowed Memorial Scholarships *(Undergraduate/Scholarship)* [4295]
Pfizer Inc. Endowed Scholarships *(Undergraduate/Scholarship)* [4297]
Phillip Morris USA Scholarships *(Undergraduate/Scholarship)* [7330]
Pioneer Hi-Bred International Graduate Student Fellowships *(Graduate/Fellowship)* [2863]
Herbert W. Rand Fellowships and Scholarships *(Undergraduate/Scholarship)* [4298]
Florence C. Rose and S. Meryl Rose Scholarships *(Undergraduate/Scholarship)* [4299]
Ruth Sager Scholarships *(Undergraduate/Scholarship)* [4300]
Milton L. Shifman Endowed Scholarships *(Undergraduate/Scholarship)* [4301]
Julia Viola Simms Science Scholarships *(Postgraduate/Scholarship)* [1742]
Horace W. Stunkard Scholarships *(Undergraduate/Scholarship)* [4302]
J.P. Madeline Trinkaus Endowed Scholarships in Embryology *(Undergraduate/Scholarship)* [4303]

Biology, Marine

Atlantic Salmon Federation Olin Fellowships *(All/Fellowship)* [1536]
Friends and Family of Jennifer Balber Scholarships *(Undergraduate/Scholarship)* [5937]
IWFA Scholarships *(Graduate/Scholarship)* [3925]
Marine Technology Society ROV Scholarships *(Undergraduate/Scholarship)* [4310]
Marine Technology Society Scholarships for Graduate and Undergraduate Students *(Undergraduate/Scholarship)* [4311]
Marine Technology Society Student Scholarships for Graduating High School Seniors *(Undergraduate/Scholarship)* [4312]
Marine Technology Society Student Scholarships for Two-year Technical, Engineering and Community College Students *(Undergraduate/Scholarship)* [4313]
The Paros-Digiquartz Scholarships *(Undergraduate/Scholarship)* [4314]
Ronald L. Schmied Scholarships *(Professional Development, Undergraduate/Grant)* [3388]

Biology, Molecular

Robert W. Allington Fellowships *(Doctorate, Postdoctorate/Fellowship)* [2106]

Biomedical research (See also: Medical research)

Clinical Pharmacy Post-Pharm.D. Fellowships in the Biomedical Research Sciences *(Postdoctorate/Fellowship)* [580]
Donald A. B. Lindberg Research Fellowships *(Doctorate, Graduate/Fellowship)* [4444]
Long-Term Postdoctoral Fellowships for Biomedical and Behavioral Research in Japan *(Professional Development/Fellowship)* [1715]
National Institute of Health Undergraduate Scholarship Program *(Undergraduate/Scholarship)* [4949]
SRF Post-doctoral Fellowships *(Postdoctorate/Fellowship)* [6282]

Biomedical sciences

Saul T. Wilson, Jr. Scholarships *(Graduate, Undergraduate/Scholarship)* [7300]

Botany

GCA Awards in Tropical Botany *(Doctorate/Award/Prize)* [3158]
Mary Pelmutter Scholarships *(Postgraduate/Award/Prize)* [2022]
Dennis Raveling Scholarships *(Undergraduate/Scholarship)* [1862]
Richard E. Schultes Research Awards *(Graduate/Grant)* [6439]

British studies (See also: Scottish studies)

Carl H. Pforzheimer, Jr., Research Grants *(Graduate/Grant)* [4057]

Broadcasting (See also: Media arts)

AAJA/CNN Scholar Program *(Graduate, Undergraduate/Scholarship)* [1328]
AAJA/COX Foundation Scholarships *(Graduate, Undergraduate/Scholarship)* [1329]
The Access Intelligence Scholarships *(Graduate, Undergraduate/Scholarship)* [6580]
John Bayliss Broadcast Foundation Internship Programs *(Undergraduate/Internship)* [1603]
BBM Canada Scholarships *(Undergraduate/Scholarship)* [1922]
Rick Brewer Scholarships *(Undergraduate/Scholarship)* [7148]
Mary L. Brown Scholarships *(Undergraduate/Scholarship)* [3929]
Joe Durso Memorial Scholarships *(Undergraduate/Scholarship)* [4569]
Harold E. Ennes Scholarships *(Professional Development/Scholarship)* [6526]
Harold E. Fellows Scholarships *(All/Scholarship)* [1784]
Stephen Gates Scholarships *(Undergraduate/Scholarship)* [7161]
Great Falls Broadcasters Association Scholarships *(Undergraduate/Scholarship)* [4570]
Robert D. Greenberg Scholarships *(Professional Development/Scholarship)* [6527]
Ruth Hancock Scholarships *(Undergraduate/Scholarship)* [1923]
Indiana Broadcasters Association for College Scholarship Program *(Undergraduate/Scholarship)* [3690]
Indiana Broadcasters Association High School Scholarship Program *(Undergraduate/Scholarship)* [3691]
John Bayliss Broadcast Foundation Scholarships *(Undergraduate/Scholarship)* [1604]
Charles Kuralt Fellowships in International Broadcasting *(Postgraduate/Scholarship)* [7172]
LIN Television Corporation Minority Scholarships and Training Program *(Undergraduate/Scholarship)* [4247]
McNamara Family Creative Arts Project Grants *(Graduate, Undergraduate/Grant)* [3601]
Montana Broadcasters Association Directors' Scholarships *(Undergraduate/Scholarship)* [4571]
Montana Broadcasters Association Engineers' Scholarships *(Undergraduate/Scholarship)* [4572]
New York Women in Communications, Inc. Foundation Scholarships *(Graduate, Undergraduate/Scholarship)* [5200]

Ohio Association of Broadcaster's Kids Scholarships *(Undergraduate/Scholarship)* [5317]
Ohio Association of Broadcasters Scholarships *(Undergraduate/Scholarship)* [5318]
Oregon Association of Broadcasters Scholarships *(Undergraduate/Scholarship)* [5376]
Walter S. Patterson Scholarships *(All/Scholarship)* [1785]
Producers Academy Scholarships *(All/Scholarship)* [2543]
Helen J. Sioussat/Fay Wells Scholarships *(All/Scholarship)* [1786]
Small Station Training Scholarships *(Professional Development/Scholarship)* [2544]
Leo Suarez Journalism Scholarships *(Undergraduate/Scholarship)* [2601]
Alexander M. Tanger Scholarships *(All/Scholarship)* [1787]
Two Year/Community Broadcast Education Association Scholarships Award *(All/Scholarship)* [1788]
Abe Voron Scholarships *(All/Scholarship)* [1789]
Vincent T. Wasilewski Scholarships *(All/Scholarship)* [1790]
Wisconsin Broadcasters Association Scholarships *(Undergraduate/Scholarship)* [7472]
Youth Scholarships *(Undergraduate/Scholarship)* [6528]

Business

Evelyn Abrams Memorial Scholarships *(Undergraduate/Scholarship)* [5797]
Accenture American Indian Scholarship Program *(Graduate, Undergraduate/Scholarship)* [640]
Alaska Aerospace Development Corporation Scholarships *(Undergraduate/Scholarship)* [4338]
Julie Allen World Classroom Scholarships *(Undergraduate/Scholarship)* [6164]
ALPFA Scholarship Programs *(Postgraduate, Undergraduate/Scholarship)* [1492]
American Business Women's Association Sarasota Chapter Scholarships *(Undergraduate/Scholarship)* [2503]
American Standard Scholarships *(Undergraduate/Scholarship)* [5700]
ARA Scholarship Awards *(Undergraduate/Scholarship)* [1575]
ASBPE Young Leaders Scholarships *(All, Professional Development/Scholarship)* [925]
Avista Corporation Minds in Motion Scholarships *(Undergraduate/Scholarship)* [4163]
Bank of America Junior Achievement Scholarship Fund *(Undergraduate/Scholarship)* [3040]
Banner Bank Business Scholarships *(Undergraduate/Scholarship)* [4164]
Bison Transport Scholarships *(Undergraduate/Scholarship)* [5341]
Boeing Business Scholarships *(Undergraduate/Scholarship)* [3250]
Donald J. Bristow Memorial Scholarship Program *(Graduate, Undergraduate/Scholarship)* [4655]
Dr. F. Ross Byrd Scholarships *(Graduate/Scholarship)* [7379]
C200 Scholar Awards *(All/Scholarship)* [2337]
Catching the Dream Scholarship *(Graduate, Undergraduate/Scholarship)* [632]
C.C.H.R.M.A. Scholarships *(High School, Undergraduate/Scholarship)* [2268]
Clark High School Academy of Finance Scholarships *(Undergraduate/Scholarship)* [5812]
Clark High School Alumni Leadership Circle Scholarships *(Undergraduate/Scholarship)* [5813]
Congressional Scholarships Award *(Undergraduate/Scholarship)* [3147]
Connecticut Mortgage Bankers Scholarships-Social Affairs Committee *(Undergraduate/Scholarship)* [3439]
Mable B. Crawford Memorial Scholarships *(Undergraduate/Scholarship)* [4354]
Critical Language Scholarships for Intensive Summer Institutes *(Graduate, Undergraduate/Scholarship)* [892]
D&A Florida Scholarships *(Undergraduate/Scholarship)* [6648]
Kenneth D. and Katherine D. Davis Scholarships *(Undergraduate/Scholarship)* [5476]
Delta Faucet Scholarships *(Undergraduate/Scholarship)* [5701]
Cindy P. Dennis Scholarship Fund *(Undergraduate/Scholarship)* [2534]
Wayne G. Failor Scholarships *(High School/Scholarship)* [5563]
First Security Foundation Business Scholarships *(Undergraduate/Scholarship)* [4178]
Floto-Peel Family Scholarships Fund *(Undergraduate/Scholarship)* [3278]
Gen III Scholarships *(Undergraduate/Scholarship)* [2822]
Doris Y. and John J. Gerber Scholarships *(Undergraduate/Scholarship)* [7380]
GIA Endowment Scholarships - School of Business *(Undergraduate/Scholarship)* [3179]
William R. Goldfarb Memorial Scholarships *(Undergraduate/Scholarship)* [834]
Community Bank - Lee Guggisberg Foundation Memorial Scholarships *(Undergraduate/Scholarship)* [5941]
Anna E. Hall Memorial Scholarships *(Undergraduate/Scholarship)* [5625]
Hilb, Rogal and Hobbs Scholarships *(Undergraduate/Scholarship)* [7328]
Hispanic College Fund Scholarship Programs *(Undergraduate/Scholarship)* [3583]
Raymond T. Hoge Scholarship Fund *(Undergraduate/Scholarship)* [6727]
HSBC-North America Scholarship Program *(Undergraduate/Scholarship)* [3592]
HSF/Nissan Community College Transfer Scholarship Program *(Undergraduate/Scholarship)* [3598]
HSF/Wal-Mart Stores Inc. Scholarship Program *(Graduate, Undergraduate/Scholarship)* [3599]
IAAP Wings Chapter Scholarships *(Undergraduate/Scholarship)* [3782]
Insurance Women of Portland Scholarships *(Graduate/Scholarship)* [3767]
International Dairy-Deli-Bakery Association Undergraduate Scholarships *(Graduate, Undergraduate/Scholarship)* [3835]
International Management Council (IMC) Scholarships *(Undergraduate/Scholarship)* [2472]
Jamaica National Building Society Scholarships *(Undergraduate/Scholarship)* [4001]
JD/MBA Scholarships *(Undergraduate/Scholarship)* [5593]
The Jhaveri Scholarships *(Graduate/Scholarship)* [3184]
Margaret G. Johnson and Marge J. Stout Scholarships *(Undergraduate/Scholarship)* [4188]
Johnson and Wales University Scholarships *(Undergraduate/Scholarship)* [4039]
Paul J. Laninga Memorial Scholarship Fund *(Undergraduate/Scholarship)* [3290]
Las Vegas Chinatown Scholarships *(Undergraduate/Scholarship)* [5835]
Rick and Beverly Lattin Education Scholarships Fund *(Undergraduate/Scholarship)* [3291]
Doreen Legg Memorial Scholarships *(Undergraduate/Scholarship)* [5955]
Luso-American Education Foundation C-1 General Scholarships *(Undergraduate/Scholarship)* [4261]
Kaia Lynn Markwalter Endowed Scholarships *(Undergraduate/Scholarship)* [4204]
MESBEC Scholarships *(Undergraduate/Scholarship)* [2067]
Ruth Messmer Memorial Scholarships *(Undergraduate/Scholarship)* [6665]
Michael Jewelers Foundation Scholarships for Athletes *(Undergraduate/Scholarship)* [3483]
Mill Creek Business Association Scholarships *(Undergraduate/Scholarship)* [4533]
Mark Miller Award *(Graduate, Undergraduate/Scholarship)* [4656]
George J. Mitchell Scholarships *(Undergraduate/Scholarship)* [6999]
Robert E. and Judy More Scholarship Fund *(Undergraduate/Scholarship)* [2967]
NABA Corporate Scholarship Program *(Graduate, Undergraduate/Scholarship)* [4657]
NABA National Scholarship Program *(Graduate, Undergraduate/Scholarship)* [4658]
NAPMW Mat-Su Valley Alaska Scholarships *(Undergraduate/Scholarship)* [4372]
NASE Future Entrepreneur Scholarships *(Undergraduate/Scholarship)* [4740]
National Honor Roll Scholarships *(Undergraduate/Scholarship)* [1808]
NBMBAA Graduate Scholarship Programs *(Graduate/Scholarship)* [4761]
NBMBAA PhD Fellowship Programs *(Doctorate/Fellowship)* [4762]
Paul and Ruth Neidhold Business Scholarship *(Undergraduate/Scholarship)* [2477]
Hubert A. Nelson Scholarships *(Undergraduate/Scholarship)* [2787]
Dr. Ezra Nesbeth Scholarships *(Undergraduate/Scholarship)* [4002]
New York Financial Writers' Associations Scholarships *(Graduate, Undergraduate/Scholarship)* [5189]
Norfolk Southern Scholarships *(Undergraduate/Scholarship)* [7329]
North Carolina Vending Association Academic Scholarships *(Undergraduate/Scholarship)* [5247]
Peggy (Kommer) Novosad Scholarships *(Graduate, Postgraduate/Scholarship)* [3344]
Office Depot Scholarships *(Undergraduate/Scholarship)* [3569]
Pardee Community Building Scholarships *(Undergraduate/Scholarship)* [5849]
Phillip Morris USA Scholarships *(Undergraduate/Scholarship)* [7330]
Plumbing-Heating-Cooling Contractors Association Educational Foundation Massachusetts Auxiliary Scholarships *(Undergraduate/Scholarship)* [5702]
Plumbing-Heating-Cooling Contractors Association Educational Foundation Need-Based Scholarships *(Undergraduate/Scholarship)* [5703]
Plumbing-Heating-Cooling Contractors Association Educational Foundation Scholarships *(Undergraduate/Scholarship)* [5704]
Progressive Dairy Producers Award *(All/Grant)* [4841]
RBC Royal Bank Scholarships for Undergraduates *(Undergraduate/Scholarship)* [6068]
Dr. Felix H. Reyler Memorial Scholarships *(Undergraduate/Scholarship)* [2599]
Dorothy Worden Ronken Scholarships *(Graduate/Scholarship)* [2698]
Wendell Scott Awards *(Graduate, Undergraduate/Scholarship)* [3570]
David and Sharon Seaver Family Scholarship Fund *(Undergraduate/Scholarship)* [3305]
Pat Shimp Memorial Scholarships *(Undergraduate/Scholarship)* [5520]
Silver Nugget Gaming Ambassadors Scholarships *(Undergraduate/Scholarship)* [5858]
A.O. Smith Scholarships *(Undergraduate/Scholarship)* [5705]
Helen D. Snow Memorial Scholarships *(Undergraduate/Scholarship)* [5626]
Soroptimist International of Redlands Scholarships *(Undergraduate/Scholarship)* [6011]
Morgan Stanley Tribal Scholars Program *(Undergraduate/Scholarship)* [626]
StraightForward Media's Business School Scholarships *(Undergraduate/Scholarship)* [6796]
Edward P. Suchecki Family Scholarship Fund *(Undergraduate/Scholarship)* [3310]
Surety Industry Scholarship Program for Minority Students *(Undergraduate/Scholarship)* [6824]
TDC Scholarship Program *(Graduate, Undergraduate/Scholarship)* [4659]
The Rodney Thaxton Justice Fund *(Undergraduate/Scholarship)* [2602]
Ralph and Valerie Thomas Scholarship Program *(Graduate, Undergraduate/Scholarship)* [4660]
Travis C. Tomlin Memorial Scholarship Program *(Graduate, Undergraduate/Scholarship)* [4661]
Toyota High School Scholarship Program *(Undergraduate/Scholarship)* [3603]
Tribal Business Management Program (TBM) Scholarships *(Undergraduate/Scholarship)* [2069]
Jacki Tuckfield Memorial Graduate Business Scholarship Fund *(Undergraduate/Scholarship)* [2603]
UAA College of Business & Public Policy Scholarships *(Graduate, Undergraduate/Scholarship)* [7047]
UAA Jan & Glenn Fredericks Scholarships *(Gradu-*

ate, Undergraduate/Scholarship) [7058]
UAA Michael D. Ford Memorial Scholarships (Graduate, Undergraduate/Scholarship) [7066]
UAA Pignalberi Public Policy Scholarships (Graduate/Scholarship) [7070]
Urban Financial Services Coalition Scholarships (Undergraduate/Scholarship) [1744]
Verizon Scholarship Program (Undergraduate/Scholarship) [3607]
Thomas S. Watson, Jr. Memorial Scholarships (Graduate, Undergraduate/Scholarship) [4662]
Seitlin Franklin E. Wheeler Scholarship Fund (Undergraduate/Scholarship) [2604]
Bradford White Scholarships (Undergraduate/Scholarship) [5706]
Wilkinson & Company LLP Secondary School Scholarships (Undergraduate/Scholarship) [7412]
Women In Defense HORIZONS Scholarships (Graduate, Undergraduate/Scholarship) [7479]
Xavier University Williams Scholarships (Undergraduate/Scholarship) [7543]
YMA Fashion Scholarships (Undergraduate/Scholarship) [7545]

Business administration

AAUW Legal Advocacy Fund Selected Professions Fellowships (Doctorate, Graduate/Fellowship) [7]
African American Network - Carolinas Scholarship Fund (Undergraduate/Scholarship) [3037]
American Society of Military Comptrollers National Scholarship Program (Undergraduate/Scholarship) [1011]
ARS Undergraduate Scholarships (Four Year College, Two Year College, Undergraduate/Scholarship) [1259]
Lawrence Bayer Business Administration Scholarships (Undergraduate/Scholarship) [4346]
Mary Elizabeth Lockwood Beneventi MBA Scholarships (Graduate/Scholarship) [3422]
Bill & Nell Biggs Scholarships (Undergraduate/Scholarship) [4348]
Wes Burton Memorial Scholarships (Undergraduate/Scholarship) [7424]
The Rick Crane Group Real Estate Scholarships Fund (Undergraduate/Scholarship) [4173]
Walt Disney Company Foundation Scholarships (Undergraduate/Scholarship) [4037]
Richard Gregory Freeland, II Educational Scholarships (High School/Scholarship) [1762]
Fuchs-Harden Educational Scholarships Fund (Undergraduate/Scholarship) [3375]
HACU/Wal-Mart Achievers Scholarships (Undergraduate/Scholarship) [3567]
Georgia Hilton Academic Scholarships (Undergraduate/Scholarship) [6074]
HSF/Citi Fellows Program (Undergraduate/Scholarship) [3594]
HSF/General Motors Scholarship Program (Undergraduate/Scholarship) [3595]
Ron LaFreniere Business Scholarships (Undergraduate/Scholarship) [6316]
George A. Nielsen Public Investor Scholarships (Graduate, Undergraduate/Scholarship) [3267]
OCAEOP Community Service Scholarship Program (Undergraduate/Scholarship) [5353]
Pride Foundation Scholarships (Undergraduate/Scholarship) [6134]
RBC Financial Group Scholarships (Graduate/Scholarship) [1740]
Scotiabank Scholarships (Graduate/Scholarship) [1741]
Snodgrass Scholarships (Undergraduate/Scholarship) [4384]
Society of Automotive Analyst Scholarships (Undergraduate/Scholarship) [1562]
UAA Mark A. Beltz Scholarships (Graduate, Undergraduate/Scholarship) [7063]
Wachovia Scholarship Awards (Undergraduate/Scholarship) [3571]
Urashi Zen Scholarships (Undergraduate/Scholarship) [5787]

Canadian studies (See also: Area and ethnic studies)

Graduate Student Scholarships (Postgraduate/Scholarship) [3833]

Cartography/Surveying

AAGS Graduate Fellowship Award (Undergraduate/Fellowship) [481]
AAGS Joseph F. Dracup Scholarship Award (Undergraduate/Scholarship) [482]
ACSM Fellowship Scholarships (Undergraduate/Scholarship) [483]
The Bernsten International Scholarships in Surveying Technology (Undergraduate/Scholarship) [484]
Connecticut Association of Land Surveyors Memorial Scholarships (Undergraduate/Scholarship) [2529]
Nettie Dracup Memorial Scholarships (Undergraduate/Scholarship) [485]
Kris M. Kunze Memorial Scholarships (Undergraduate/Scholarship) [486]
The Lowell H. and Dorothy Loving Undergraduate Scholarships (Undergraduate/Scholarship) [487]
MALSE Scholarships (Undergraduate/Scholarship) [4326]
The Cady McDonnell Memorial Scholarships (Undergraduate/Scholarship) [488]
Norman Nicholson Scholarships (Undergraduate/Scholarship) [1937]
NSPS Board of Governors Scholarships (Undergraduate/Scholarship) [489]
The NSPS Scholarships (Undergraduate/Scholarship) [490]
Pennsylvania Land Surveyors Foundation Scholarships (Undergraduate/Scholarship) [5557]
The Schonstedt Scholarships in Surveying (Undergraduate/Scholarship) [491]

Cave studies

NSS Sara Corrie Memorial Grants (All/Grant) [5087]
NSS Conservation Grants (All/Grant) [5088]
NSS Education Grants (All/Grant) [5089]
Ralph W. Stone Graduate Fellowships (Graduate/Grant) [5090]
Young Investigator Grants (Undergraduate/Grant) [5091]

Chemistry (See also: Biochemistry)

AACT Undergraduate Scholarships (Undergraduate/Scholarship) [5711]
Robert W. Allington Fellowships (Doctorate, Postdoctorate/Fellowship) [2106]
ASBC Foundation Graduate Scholarships (Doctorate, Graduate/Scholarship) [922]
AWIS College Scholarships (Undergraduate/Scholarship) [1519]
Biocom Scholarships (Undergraduate/Scholarship) [6173]
Gordon Cain Fellowships in Technology, Policy, and Entrepreneurship (Doctorate, Postdoctorate/Fellowship) [2107]
Julian E. Carnes Scholarship Fund (Undergraduate/Scholarship) [3046]
CHF Travel Grants (All/Grant) [2108]
D&A Florida Scholarships (Undergraduate/Scholarship) [6648]
DEPS Graduate Scholarship Program (Graduate/Scholarship) [2715]
Robert E. Dougherty Scholarships (Undergraduate/Scholarship) [2525]
Sidney M. Edelstein Fellowships (Doctorate, Postdoctorate/Fellowship) [2109]
Robert W. Gore Fellowships in Materials Innovation (Doctorate, Postdoctorate/Fellowship) [2110]
John C. Haas Fellowships in the History of Chemical Industries (Doctorate, Postdoctorate/Fellowship) [2111]
Helm Family Scholarships (Undergraduate/Scholarship) [6192]
Larson Aquatic Research Support (Graduate/Scholarship) [1144]
Lewis-Clark State College/American Chemical Society Scholars Program (Undergraduate/Scholarship) [4192]
Lewis-Clark State College Presidential Technical Out-of-State Scholarships (Undergraduate/Scholarship) [4199]
Merck Undergraduate Science Research Scholarships (Undergraduate/Scholarship) [318]
Roy G. Neville Fellowships (Doctorate, Postdoctorate/Fellowship) [2112]
Phillip Morris USA Scholarships (Undergraduate/Scholarship) [7330]
Charles C. Price Fellowships in Polymer History (Doctorate, Postdoctorate/Fellowship) [2113]
Rubber Division American Chemical Society Scholarships (Undergraduate/Scholarship) [6079]
Julia Viola Simms Science Scholarships (Postgraduate/Scholarship) [1742]
UAA Ardell French Memorial Scholarships (Undergraduate/Scholarship) [7044]
Xavier University Departmental Scholarships (Undergraduate/Scholarship) [7538]

Child care

Early Childhood Educators Scholarship Program (Undergraduate/Scholarship) [4332]

Child development

Huenefeld/Denton Scholarships (Undergraduate/Scholarship) [2692]

Chinese studies (See also: Area and ethnic studies)

Louise Wallace Hackney Fellowship for the Study of Chinese Art (Doctorate/Fellowship) [744]

Christian education

Lewis B. Barber Memorial Scholarships (Undergraduate/Scholarship) [6641]
Chester H. Bruce Memorial Scholarships (Undergraduate/Scholarship) [5468]
Dorris W. Frey Memorial Scholarships (Undergraduate/Scholarship) [6654]

Cinema

Gerald Pratley Awards (Doctorate, Graduate/Award/Prize) [2930]

Civil rights

Julie Allen World Classroom Scholarships (Undergraduate/Scholarship) [6164]
Kalmen Kaplansky Scholarships in Economic and Social Rights (Graduate/Scholarship) [2730]
Minoru Yasui Memorial Scholarship (Graduate/Scholarship) [4022]

Classical studies (See also: Area and ethnic studies)

Glenn Knudsvig Memorial Scholarships (Graduate, Undergraduate/Scholarship) [460]
Arthur Patch McKinlay Scholarships (Graduate, Undergraduate/Scholarship) [461]
Ed Phinney Commemorative Scholarships (Graduate, Undergraduate/Scholarship) [462]
Clair Shirey Scholarships (Undergraduate/Scholarship) [4382]
Xavier University Departmental Scholarships (Undergraduate/Scholarship) [7538]

Clinical laboratory sciences

Alpha Mu Tau Undergraduate Scholarships (Undergraduate/Scholarship) [931]
The AMTF Graduate Scholarships (Graduate/Scholarship) [932]
Ruth M. French Graduate Scholarships (Doctorate,

Graduate/Scholarship) [933]
Dorothy Morrison Undergraduate Scholarships (Undergraduate/Scholarship) [934]
Ida and May Reilly Graduate Scholarships (Doctorate, Graduate/Scholarship) [935]

Communications

Advertising Production Club Scholarship Awards (Graduate, Undergraduate/Scholarship) [28]
AFCEA Distance Learning/Online Scholarships (Undergraduate/Scholarship) [1236]
AFCEA General John A. Wickham Scholarships (Undergraduate/Scholarship) [1238]
AFCEA Scholarship for Working Professionals (Graduate/Scholarship) [1240]
AGBU Scholarships (Graduate/Loan) [1255]
Peggy Allen Community Newspaper Internships (Undergraduate/Internship) [7142]
Phillip Alston Scholarships (Undergraduate/Scholarship) [7143]
APC High School Scholarships (Undergraduate/Scholarship) [29]
ARRLF Mississippi Scholarships (Undergraduate/Scholarship) [819]
Avista Corporation Minds in Motion Scholarships (Undergraduate/Scholarship) [4163]
Frances Warren Baker Memorial Scholarships (Undergraduate/Scholarship) [6345]
Jim Batten Community Newspaper Internships (Undergraduate/Internship) [7144]
Margaret Blanchard Dissertation Support Fund (Postgraduate/Grant) [7146]
Tom Bost Scholarships (Undergraduate/Scholarship) [7147]
William E. "Buck" Bragunier Scholarships (Undergraduate/Scholarship) [1241]
LT.G. Douglas D. Buchholz Memorial Scholarships (Undergraduate/Scholarship) [1242]
Elton Casey Scholarships (Undergraduate/Scholarship) [7149]
George H. Clinton Scholarship Fund (Undergraduate/Scholarship) [5471]
Ardis Cohoon Scholarships (Undergraduate/Scholarship) [7150]
Irvine W. Cook WA0CGS Scholarships (Undergraduate/Scholarship) [829]
Milton E. Cooper/Young AFCEAN Graduate Scholarships (Graduate/Scholarship) [1243]
Charles Clarke Cordle Memorial Scholarships (Undergraduate/Scholarship) [830]
Kathryn M. Cronin Scholarships (Undergraduate/Scholarship) [7152]
Don and Barbara Curtis Excellence Fund for Extracurricular Student Activities (Undergraduate/Grant) [7153]
James Davis Scholarships (Undergraduate/Internship) [7154]
Disabled War Veterans Scholarships (Undergraduate/Scholarship) [1244]
Robert Winchester Dodson Scholarships (Undergraduate/Scholarship) [7155]
Harvey N. Dondero Communication and Journalism Excellence Scholarships (Undergraduate/Scholarship) [5817]
Vivian Edmonds Scholarships (Undergraduate/Scholarship) [7156]
Reese Felts Scholarships (Undergraduate/Scholarship) [7157]
Charles N. Fisher Memorial Scholarships (Undergraduate/Scholarship) [833]
Ameel J. Fisher Scholarships (Undergraduate/Scholarship) [7158]
Florida Outdoor Writers Association Scholarships (Undergraduate/Scholarship) [3016]
Paul B. & Aline Flynn Scholarships (Undergraduate/Scholarship) [6652]
Kays Gary Scholarships (Undergraduate/Scholarship) [7160]
Stephen Gates Scholarships (Undergraduate/Scholarship) [7161]
Joy Gibson Scholarships (Undergraduate/Scholarship) [7162]
L.C. Gifford Distinguished Journalism Scholarships (Undergraduate/Scholarship) [7163]
Keith Gilmore Foundation - Diploma Scholarships (Professional Development/Scholarship) [3240]
Keith Gilmore Foundation - Postgraduate Scholarships (Postgraduate/Scholarship) [3241]
Keith Gilmore Foundation - Undergraduate Scholarships (Undergraduate/Scholarship) [3242]
Paul and Helen L. Grauer Scholarships (Undergraduate/Scholarship) [835]
Charles Hauser Scholarships (Undergraduate/Scholarship) [7164]
Paul Green Houston Scholarships (Undergraduate/Scholarship) [7165]
HSF/Nissan Community College Transfer Scholarship Program (Undergraduate/Scholarship) [3598]
James F. Hurley III Bicentennial Merit Scholarships (Undergraduate/Scholarship) [7166]
Fred Hutchison Travel Scholarships (Undergraduate/Scholarship) [7167]
International Foodservice Editorial Council Scholarships (Graduate, Undergraduate/Scholarship) [3852]
Iowa Journalism Institute Scholarships (Undergraduate/Scholarship) [3935]
Harriet Irsay Scholarships (Graduate, Undergraduate/Scholarship) [674]
Edward Jackson International Scholarships (Undergraduate/Scholarship) [7168]
Gene Jackson Scholarships (Undergraduate/Scholarship) [7169]
Peter Lars Jacobson Scholarships (Undergraduate/Scholarship) [7170]
Glenn Keever Scholarships (Undergraduate/Scholarship) [7171]
Dr. James L. Lawson Memorial Scholarships (Undergraduate/Scholarship) [841]
Lockheed Martin IT Scholarships (Undergraduate/Scholarship) [1245]
Norval Neil Luxon Prize for Scholarship to a Junior Scholarships (Undergraduate/Scholarship) [7173]
Mackey-Byars Scholarships for Communication Excellence (Undergraduate/Scholarship) [7174]
Raleigh Mann Scholarships (Undergraduate/Scholarship) [7175]
Lockheed Martin Graduate Scholarships (Graduate/Scholarship) [1246]
Fred R. McDaniel Memorial Scholarships (Undergraduate/Scholarship) [842]
McNamara Family Creative Arts Project Grants (Graduate, Undergraduate/Grant) [3601]
Edward Heywood Megson Scholarships (Undergraduate/Scholarship) [7180]
Messenger-Anderson Journalism Scholarships and Internships Program (Undergraduate/Scholarship) [6123]
Quincy Sharpe Mills Scholarships (Undergraduate/Scholarship) [7181]
Alexander Morisey Scholarships (Undergraduate/Scholarship) [7183]
New York Women in Communications, Inc. Foundation Scholarships (Graduate, Undergraduate/Scholarship) [5200]
AFCEA General Emmett Paige Scholarships (Undergraduate/Scholarship) [1247]
Leonard M. Perryman Communications Scholarships for Ethnic Minority Students (Undergraduate/Scholarship) [6965]
Chuck Pezzano Scholarships (Undergraduate/Scholarship) [1770]
Pfizer Minority Medical Journalism Scholarships (Postgraduate/Scholarship) [7185]
PGSF-GATF Scholarships (Graduate, Undergraduate/Scholarship) [31]
Stephen D. Pisinski Memorial Scholarships (Undergraduate/Scholarship) [5875]
Robert Pittman Scholarships (Undergraduate/Scholarship) [7186]
Erwin Potts Scholarships (Undergraduate/Scholarship) [7187]
Peter DeWitt Pruden and Phyliss Harrill Pruden Scholarships (Undergraduate/Scholarship) [7188]
Bob Quincy Scholarships (Undergraduate/Scholarship) [7189]
Marjorie Usher Regan Scholarships (Undergraduate/Scholarship) [7190]
Bert Saperstein Communication Scholarships (Undergraduate/Scholarship) [6246]
Deedee Segel - Hartford Courant Internships (Undergraduate/Internship) [3495]
StraightForward Media's Media and Communications Scholarships (Undergraduate/Scholarship) [6801]
Leo Suarez Journalism Scholarships (Undergraduate/Scholarship) [2601]
Hal Tanner Jr. Scholarships (Undergraduate/Scholarship) [7193]
TCA Turkish American Scholarships (Undergraduate/Scholarship) [6939]
Jim and Pat Thacker Sports Communication Internships (Undergraduate/Internship) [7194]
Tucker Family Scholarships (Undergraduate/Scholarship) [7195]
Turf and Ornamental Communicators Association Scholarship Program (Undergraduate/Scholarship) [6934]
Veterans of Enduring Freedom (Afghanistan) and Iraqi Freedom Scholarships (Undergraduate/Scholarship) [1250]
David Julian Wichard Scholarships (Undergraduate/Scholarship) [7196]
L. Phil Wicker Scholarships (Undergraduate/Scholarship) [861]
Tom Wicker Scholarships (Undergraduate/Scholarship) [7197]
Glenn Wilson Broadcast Journalism Scholarships (Undergraduate/Scholarship) [5529]
Marine Corps Sgt. Jeannette L. Winters Memorial Scholarships (Undergraduate/Scholarship) [1251]
WKIX Alumni Association Scholarships (Undergraduate/Scholarship) [7198]
WTVD Endowment Scholarships (Undergraduate/Scholarship) [7199]

Communications technologies

Electronic Document Systems Foundation Scholarships (Undergraduate/Scholarship) [2846]
Carol A. Ratza Memorial Scholarships (Undergraduate/Scholarship) [3365]

Computer and information sciences

AAUW Legal Advocacy Fund Selected Professions Fellowships (Doctorate, Graduate/Fellowship) [7]
AeA Scholarships (Undergraduate/Scholarship) [6162]
African American Network - Carolinas Scholarship Fund (Undergraduate/Scholarship) [3037]
Air Products and Chemicals, Inc. Scholarships (Undergraduate/Scholarship) [1429]
Stephanie Ali Memorial Scholarships (Undergraduate/Scholarship) [7210]
Delores A. Auzenne Fellowship (Postgraduate/Fellowship) [2995]
Avista Corporation Minds in Motion Scholarships (Undergraduate/Scholarship) [4163]
AWIS College Scholarships (Undergraduate/Scholarship) [1519]
William (Billbo) Boston Scholarships (Undergraduate/Scholarship) [5467]
Wes Burton Memorial Scholarships (Undergraduate/Scholarship) [7424]
Julian E. Carnes Scholarship Fund (Undergraduate/Scholarship) [3046]
Chambersburg/Fannett-Metal School District Scholarship Fund (Undergraduate/Scholarship) [3092]
D&A Florida Scholarships (Undergraduate/Scholarship) [6648]
Electronic Document Systems Foundation Scholarships (Undergraduate/Scholarship) [2846]
ESA Foundation Computer and Video Game Scholarship Program (Undergraduate/Scholarship) [2859]
Frank Fong Scholarships (Undergraduate/Scholarship) [6423]
Richard Gregory Freeland, II Educational Scholarships (High School/Scholarship) [1762]
William R. Goldfarb Memorial Scholarships (Undergraduate/Scholarship) [834]
Jimmy Guild Memorial Scholarships (Undergraduate/Scholarship) [4182]
Dr. Stan Heaps Memorial Scholarships (Undergraduate/Scholarship) [3719]

Helm Family Scholarships (Undergraduate/Scholarship) [6192]
HSBC-North America Scholarship Program (Undergraduate/Scholarship) [3592]
HSF/Hewlett Packard (HP) Diversity in Education Scholarship Program (Undergraduate/Scholarship) [3596]
HSF/Wal-Mart Stores Inc. Scholarship Program (Graduate, Undergraduate/Scholarship) [3599]
Informatics Circle of Research Excellence Scholarships (Doctorate, Graduate/Scholarship) [159]
Lewis-Clark State College Presidential Technical Out-of-State Scholarships (Undergraduate/Scholarship) [4199]
MESBEC Scholarships (Undergraduate/Scholarship) [2067]
NASIG Conference Student Grants (Postdoctorate/Grant) [5225]
Dr. Ezra Nesbeth Scholarships (Undergraduate/Scholarship) [4002]
Edsel Newman Scholarship (Undergraduate/Scholarship) [4228]
Ray, NORP and Katie, WOKTE Pautz Scholarships (Undergraduate/Scholarship) [847]
PHD ARA Scholarships (Undergraduate/Scholarship) [849]
Phillip Morris USA Scholarships (Undergraduate/Scholarship) [7330]
Pride Foundation Scholarships (Undergraduate/Scholarship) [6134]
Faye Lynn Roberts Educational Scholarships (Undergraduate/Scholarship) [6669]
John M. and Mary A. Shanley Memorial Scholarships (Undergraduate/Scholarship) [6673]
Snodgrass Scholarships (Undergraduate/Scholarship) [4384]
Soroptimist International of Redlands Scholarships (Undergraduate/Scholarship) [6011]
Henry D. and Ruth G. Swartz Family Scholarship Fund (Undergraduate/Scholarship) [3311]
Toyota High School Scholarship Program (Undergraduate/Scholarship) [3603]
Vice Adm. Jerry O. Tuttle, USN (Ret.) and Mrs. Barbara A. Tuttle Science and Technology Scholarships (Undergraduate/Scholarship) [1249]
University of Toronto Accenture Scholarships (Undergraduate/Scholarship) [7235]
UPE/ACM Scholarship Awards (Graduate, Undergraduate/Award/Prize) [7288]
UPE Scholarship Awards (Graduate, Undergraduate/Award/Prize) [7289]
Verizon Scholarship Program (Undergraduate/Scholarship) [3607]
Edwin F. Wiegand Science and Technology Scholarships (Undergraduate/Scholarship) [5868]
Women In Defense HORIZONS Scholarships (Graduate, Undergraduate/Scholarship) [7479]
Ralph Yetka Memorial Scholarships (Undergraduate/Scholarship) [4391]
Urashi Zen Scholarships (Undergraduate/Scholarship) [5787]

Construction

Herb Adrian Memorial Scholarship Fund (Undergraduate/Scholarship) [3036]
AGC Foundation Outstanding Educator Awards (Professional Development/Award/Prize) [1344]
APS/ASU Scholarships (Undergraduate/Scholarship) [5697]
ASSE Construction Safety Scholarships (Undergraduate/Scholarship) [1047]
Associated General Contractors of Connecticut Scholarships (Undergraduate/Scholarship) [2531]
Bechtel Group Foundation Scholarship for Safety & Health (Undergraduate/Scholarship) [1049]
O.J. Beck, Jr. Memorial Scholarships (Undergraduate/Scholarship) [2263]
Construction Trades Scholarships (Undergraduate/Scholarship) [4749]
John Costello Memorial Scholarships (Undergraduate/Scholarship) [2532]
Cindy P. Dennis Scholarship Fund (Undergraduate/Scholarship) [2534]
Lee S. Evans/National Housing Endowment Scholarship (Graduate, Undergraduate/Scholarship) [4941]
HSF/Wal-Mart Stores Inc. Scholarship Program (Graduate, Undergraduate/Scholarship) [3599]
Jimmy Johnson Memorial Scholarships (Undergraduate/Scholarship) [7442]
Charles McMahon Memorial Construction Management/Engineering Scholarship Awards (Undergraduate/Scholarship) [1320]
NAWIC Founders Undergraduate Scholarships (Undergraduate/Scholarship) [4750]
R.D. Neuman Memorial Scholarships (Undergraduate/Scholarship) [5273]
Pardee Community Building Scholarships (Undergraduate/Scholarship) [5849]
Herman J. Smith Scholarships (Undergraduate/Scholarship) [4942]
Toyota High School Scholarship Program (Undergraduate/Scholarship) [3603]
Washington Group International Safety Scholarships (Undergraduate/Scholarship) [1074]
Ted C. Wilson Memorial Scholarships (Undergraduate/Scholarship) [5791]

Consumer affairs

Geraldine Clewell Fellowships - Doctoral Student (Graduate/Fellowship) [5659]
Geraldine Clewell Fellowships - Masteral (Graduate/Fellowship) [5660]
Geraldine Clewell Scholarships - Undergraduate (Undergraduate/Scholarship) [5661]
Closs/Parnitzke/Clarke Scholarships (Undergraduate/Scholarship) [5662]
Jean Dearth Dickerscheid Fellowships (Graduate/Fellowship) [5663]
Margaret Drew Alpha Fellowships (Graduate/Fellowship) [5664]
Lydia Fohn-Hansen/Lola Hill Memorial Scholarships (Undergraduate/Scholarship) [4357]
Genevieve Forthun Scholarships (Undergraduate/Scholarship) [5665]
Mary Weiking Franken Scholarships (Undergraduate/Scholarship) [5666]
Tommie J. Hamner Scholarships (Undergraduate/Scholarship) [5667]
Jackman Scholarships (Undergraduate/Scholarship) [5668]
Martha Combs Jenkins Scholarships (Undergraduate/Scholarship) [5669]
Treva C. Kintner Scholarships (Undergraduate/Scholarship) [5670]
Phi Upsilon Omicron Candle Fellowships (Graduate/Fellowship) [5671]
Phi Upsilon Omicron Challenge Scholarships (Undergraduate/Scholarship) [5672]
Phi Upsilon Omicron Diamond Anniversary Fellowships (Graduate/Fellowship) [5673]
Phi Upsilon Omicron Founders Fellowships (Graduate/Fellowship) [5674]
Phi Upsilon Omicron Golden Anniversary Scholarships (Undergraduate/Scholarship) [5675]
Phi Upsilon Omicron Past Presidents Scholarships (Undergraduate/Scholarship) [5676]
Phi Upsilon Omicron Presidents Research Fellowships (Graduate/Fellowship) [5677]
Nell Bryant Robinson Scholarships (Undergraduate/Scholarship) [5678]
Lucile Rust Scholarships (Undergraduate/Scholarship) [5679]
Margaret Jerome Sampson Scholarships (Undergraduate/Scholarship) [5680]
Lillian P. Schoephoerster Scholarships (Undergraduate/Scholarship) [5681]

Cooley's anemia

Cooley's Anemia Foundation Research Fellowships (Doctorate/Fellowship) [2539]

Cosmetology

Sally Beauty Scholarships for High School Graduates (Undergraduate/Scholarship) [4822]
California Association of Private Postsecondary Schools Scholarships (Undergraduate/Scholarship) [1814]
Melissa Eleonor Ernest Scholarship (Undergraduate/Scholarship) [3978]
Joe Francis Haircare Scholarships (Undergraduate/Scholarship) [3141]
Helen F. "Jerri" Rand Memorial Scholarships (Undergraduate/Scholarship) [2509]
H. Wayne Van Agtmael Cosmetology Scholarship Fund (Undergraduate/Scholarship) [3312]

Counseling/Guidance

ASHA Scholarships (Graduate, Undergraduate/Scholarship) [915]
ASHA Student Research Grants (Graduate, Undergraduate/Scholarship) [916]
Patricia Pownder Conolly Memorial Scholarships (Undergraduate/Scholarship) [4462]
Lullelia W. Harrison Scholarships in Counseling (Graduate, Undergraduate/Scholarship) [7554]
Linda Lyons Memorial Scholarship Fund (Undergraduate/Scholarship) [4464]
Native American Leadership Education (NALE) Scholarships (Postdoctorate, Undergraduate/Scholarship) [2068]
Ross Trust Graduate Student Scholarships (Graduate/Scholarship) [517]
Toyota High School Scholarship Program (Undergraduate/Scholarship) [3603]

Crafts

Joan Auld Scholarships (Undergraduate/Scholarship) [2497]

Creative writing

Armistead Maupin Creative Writing Scholarship Fund (Undergraduate/Scholarship) [2887]
Eleanor M. Wolfson Memorial Scholarship Fund (Undergraduate/Scholarship) [2981]

Criminal justice

American Criminal Justice Association Scholarships (Undergraduate/Scholarship) [519]
Officer Brian A. Aselton Memorial Scholarships (Undergraduate/Scholarship) [3419]
Robert C. Carson Memorial Bursary (Undergraduate/Scholarship) [153]
Connecticut Association of Women Police Scholarships (Undergraduate/Scholarship) [3435]
Jorge Espejal Contreras Memorial Scholarships (Graduate, Undergraduate/Scholarship) [3804]
Correctional Education Association Scholarships (Graduate, Undergraduate/Scholarship) [2546]
Colonel Richard M. Dawson Scholarships (Undergraduate/Scholarship) [2417]
Carli Edwards Memorial Scholarships (Undergraduate/Scholarship) [6311]
Brian Jimenez Memorial Scholarships (Undergraduate/Scholarship) [5948]
Minnesota Association County Probation Officers Scholarships (Undergraduate/Scholarship) [4544]
NSA Scholarship Program (Undergraduate/Scholarship) [5040]
Ottawa Police 150th Anniversary Scholarships (Undergraduate/Scholarship) [1772]
Rachael Patterson Memorial Scholarships (Undergraduate/Scholarship) [6846]
Pi Gamma Mu Scholarships (Graduate/Scholarship) [5691]
Emmett H. Turner Scholarships (Undergraduate/Scholarship) [2450]

Criminology

Robert C. Carson Memorial Bursary (Undergraduate/Scholarship) [153]

Criticism (Art, Drama, Literary)

Northwest-Shoals Community College Fine Arts Scholarships - Drama (Undergraduate/Scholarship) [5294]

Wendy Y. Wolfson Memorial Scholarship Fund (Undergraduate/Scholarship) [2982]

Cross-cultural studies

University of Hawaii at Manoa Japan Travel Bureau Scholarships (Graduate, Undergraduate/Scholarship) [7098]

Culinary arts

L'Academie de Cuisine Culinary Arts Scholarships (All, Professional Development/Scholarship) [2568]
Alliance of Black Culinarians Scholarships (Undergraduate/Scholarship) [5800]
American Culinary Federation Chair's Scholarship Grants (All/Scholarship) [521]
American Culinary Federation Educational Scholarship Grants (All/Scholarship) [522]
Balestreri/Cutino Scholarships (Undergraduate/Scholarship) [523]
Harry A. Bell Travel Grants (All/Grant) [2569]
Canadian Hospitality Foundation College Entrance Scholarships (Undergraduate/Scholarship) [1976]
Chaine des Rotisseurs Scholarships (Undergraduate/Scholarship) [524]
Julia Child Memorial Scholarships (Undergraduate/Scholarship) [525]
Geri Coccodrilli Culinary Scholarship Fund (Undergraduate/Scholarship) [3272]
Cuisinart Culinary Study Scholarships (All, Professional Development/Scholarship) [2570]
Culinary (1-Year Program) Scholarships (Undergraduate/Scholarship) [1978]
Culinary and Hospitality Foundation of San Benito County Scholarships (Undergraduate/Scholarship) [2566]
The Culinary Trust's Memorial Journalism Scholarships (Professional Development/Grant) [2571]
Linda Cullen Memorial Scholarships (High School/Scholarship) [526]
The eGullet Society for Culinary Arts and Letters Brian and Thelma Moore Memorial Culinary Journalist Independent Study Scholarships (Professional Development/Grant) [2572]
The eGullet Society for Culinary Arts and Letters Culinary Journalist Independent Study Scholarships (Professional Development/Grant) [2573]
The eGullet Society for Culinary Arts and Letters Matthew X. Hassett Memorial Culinary Arts Scholarships (All, Professional Development/Scholarship) [2574]
The eGullet Society for Culinary Arts and Letters Professional Chef Independent Study Scholarships (Other, Professional Development/Grant) [2575]
Senior Chef Frank Farello Scholarships (Professional Development/Scholarship) [527]
The French Culinary Institute Classic Pastry Arts Scholarships (All, Professional Development/Scholarship) [2576]
The French Culinary Institute Culinary Arts Scholarships (All, Professional Development/Scholarship) [2577]
The French Culinary Institute's Food and Technology Scholarships - Magic Potions Transglutaminase (Professional Development/Scholarship) [2578]
International Dairy-Deli-Bakery Association Undergraduate Scholarships (Graduate, Undergraduate/Scholarship) [3835]
International Foodservice Editorial Council Scholarships (Graduate, Undergraduate/Scholarship) [3852]
Stanley "Doc" Jensen Scholarships (High School/Scholarship) [528]
Johnson and Wales University Scholarships (Undergraduate/Scholarship) [4039]
Kendall College Bachelor of Arts in Culinary Arts Scholarships (Undergraduate/Scholarship) [2579]
Le Cordon Bleu Ottawa Culinary Arts Institute Basic Cuisine Certificate Scholarships (All, Professional Development/Scholarship) [2580]
Andrew Macrina Scholarships (High School/Scholarship) [529]
Ray and Gertrude Marshall Scholarships (Undergraduate/Scholarship) [530]
Karl Mehlmann Scholarships (Undergraduate/Scholarship) [2306]
New England Culinary Institute Scholarships (All/Scholarship) [2581]
Prostart National Certificate of Achievement Scholarships (Undergraduate/Scholarship) [3617]
Hermann G. Rusch Scholarships (Professional Development/Scholarship) [531]
Elizabeth Shafer Memorial Scholarships (Undergraduate/Scholarship) [5856]
South Carolina Undergraduate Scholarships (Undergraduate/Scholarship) [3619]
Spice Box Grants (Professional Development/Grant) [532]
Tanana Valley Campus Culinary Arts Scholarships (Undergraduate/Scholarship) [6849]
Tomato Fest Scholarship Grants (Undergraduate/Scholarship) [533]
Charlie Trotters's Culinary Education Foundation Culinary Study Scholarships (All, Professional Development/Scholarship) [2582]
Zwilling, J.A. Henckels Culinary Arts Scholarships (All, Professional Development/Scholarship) [2583]

Culture

AAS Fellowships for Creative and Performing Artists and Writers (All/Fellowship) [296]
Leo Baeck Fellowships Program (Doctorate, Postdoctorate/Fellowship) [2079]
Stephen Botein Fellowships (Doctorate/Fellowship) [300]
The "Drawn to Art" Fellowships (Doctorate/Fellowship) [301]
Jay and Deborah Last Fellowships (Doctorate/Fellowship) [304]
The Legacy Fellowships (Doctorate/Fellowship) [305]
Kate B. and Hall J. Peterson Fellowships (Doctorate/Fellowship) [306]
The Joyce Tracy Fellowships (Doctorate/Fellowship) [308]

Dairy science

Progressive Dairy Producers Award (All/Grant) [4841]
South Dakota Division Scholarships (Undergraduate/Scholarship) [4520]
Stark County Dairy Promoters Scholarships (Undergraduate/Scholarship) [6755]

Dance (See also: Performing arts)

Ruth Abernathy Presidential Scholarships (Graduate, Undergraduate/Scholarship) [351]
Artistic Scholarship Awards (Undergraduate/Scholarship) [1598]
Deloris Carter Hampton Scholarships (Undergraduate/Scholarship) [5759]
Dance Education Scholarship Program (High School/Scholarship) [6244]
Rebecca Davis Scholarships (Professional Development/Scholarship) [2619]
Graduate Student Travel Grants (Graduate, Professional Development/Grant) [6437]
In-course Scholarships - Chinese Dance Workshop Scholarships (Undergraduate/Scholarship) [7224]
Indiana State Alumni Association Creative and Performing Arts Award (Undergraduate/Scholarship) [3701]
Study Scholarships for Artists or Musicians (Graduate/Scholarship) [3230]

Data processing (See also: Computer and information sciences)

Bettsy Ross Educational Fund (All, Professional Development/Scholarship) [5212]

Dental hygiene

Co Dental Hygiene Scholarships (Undergraduate/Scholarship) [6309]
Dr. Princeton L. Co Emergency Fund for Dental Hygiene Scholarships (Undergraduate/Scholarship) [6310]
IADR David B. Scott Fellowships (Undergraduate/Fellowship) [3790]
Ken LaFountaine First Nations Scholarships (Undergraduate/Scholarship) [6315]
National Dental Hygienists' Association Scholarships (Undergraduate/Scholarship) [4846]
Dr. Sidney Rafal Memorial Scholarships (Undergraduate/Scholarship) [3491]

Dental laboratory technology

Chinese American Medical Society Summer Research Outreach Programs (Undergraduate/Grant) [2135]
Esther Lim Memorial Scholarships (Undergraduate/Scholarship) [2136]
Ruth Liu Memorial Scholarships (Undergraduate/Scholarship) [2137]

Dentistry

American Academy of Periodontology Educator Scholarships (Postdoctorate/Scholarship) [283]
American Academy of Periodontology Foundation Education Fellowships (Postdoctorate/Fellowship) [284]
American Academy of Periodontology Teaching Fellowships (Postdoctorate/Fellowship) [285]
American Dental Association Dental Assisting Scholarship Program (Undergraduate/Scholarship) [535]
American Dental Association Dental Hygiene Scholarship Program (Undergraduate/Scholarship) [536]
American Dental Association Dental Laboratory Technology Scholarship Program (Undergraduate/Scholarship) [537]
American Dental Association Dental Student Scholarship (Undergraduate/Scholarship) [538]
American Dental Association Minority Dental Student Scholarships (Undergraduate/Scholarship) [539]
ASHA Scholarships (Graduate, Undergraduate/Scholarship) [915]
ASHA Student Research Grants (Graduate, Undergraduate/Scholarship) [916]
Abram and Sylvia Chasens Teaching and Research Fellowships (Postdoctorate/Fellowship) [286]
DAAD Study Scholarship Awards (Graduate/Scholarship) [3223]
Nicholas S. Hetos, DDS, Memorial Graduate Scholarships (Graduate/Scholarship) [3531]
Howard B. Higgins South Carolina Dental Scholarships (Undergraduate/Scholarship) [3061]
IADR John Clarkson Fellowships (Postdoctorate/Fellowship) [3791]
IADR John Gray Fellowships (Professional Development/Fellowship) [3792]
IADR Norton Ross Fellowships (Professional Development/Fellowship) [3793]
Jason Lang Scholarship (Undergraduate/Scholarship) [163]
Richard J. Lazzara Fellowships in Advanced Implant Surgery (Postdoctorate/Fellowship) [287]
Dr. Mac Scholarships (Undergraduate/Scholarship) [2431]
NAAMA Scholarships (Undergraduate/Scholarship) [4639]
IADR Toshio Nakao Fellowships (Professional Development/Fellowship) [3794]
Nicholas J. Piergrossi Scholarships (Undergraduate/Scholarship) [3489]
Dr. Sidney Rafal Memorial Scholarships (Undergraduate/Scholarship) [3491]
RBC Royal Bank Scholarships for First Year Medical & Dental Students (Undergraduate/Scholarship) [6066]
Scholarships for Emigres in the Health Sciences (Undergraduate/Scholarship) [4025]
Jeptha Wade Schureman Scholarship Program (Undergraduate/Scholarship) [2521]
John M. and Mary A. Shanley Memorial Scholar-

ships *(Undergraduate/Scholarship)* [6673]
Dr. Kiyoshi Sonoda Memorial Scholarships *(Graduate/Scholarship)* [4021]
Bud and Linda Tarrson Fellowships *(Postdoctorate/Fellowship)* [288]
Washington Higher Education Coordinating Board Health Professional Scholarships *(Undergraduate/Scholarship)* [7368]

Design

Joan Auld Scholarships *(Undergraduate/Scholarship)* [2497]
MJSA Education Foundation Scholarship Fund *(Undergraduate/Scholarship)* [4278]
Women's Jewelry Association Member Grants *(All/Grant)* [7498]
Women's Jewelry Association Scholarships *(Undergraduate/Scholarship)* [7499]

Diabetes

The Youth Scholarship Program *(Undergraduate/Scholarship)* [2095]

Disabilities

American Speech Language Hearing Foundation Clinical Research Grants *(Doctorate/Grant)* [1098]
American Speech Language Hearing Foundation Endowed Scholarships *(Postdoctorate/Scholarship)* [1099]
American Speech Language Hearing Foundation General Scholarships *(Postgraduate/Scholarship)* [1100]
American Speech Language Hearing Foundation Scholarships for International Students *(Graduate/Scholarship)* [1101]
American Speech Language Hearing Foundation Scholarships for Students with Disability *(All/Scholarship)* [1102]
ASHFA Scholarships for Minority Students *(Postgraduate/Scholarship)* [1103]
The Eric Marder Scholarships *(Undergraduate/Scholarship)* [3678]
New Century Scholars Doctoral Scholarships *(Postdoctorate/Scholarship)* [1104]
New Century Scholars Research Grants *(Doctorate/Grant)* [1105]
Whitaker-Minard Memorial Scholarships *(Undergraduate/Scholarship)* [5528]

Drafting

Toyota High School Scholarship Program *(Undergraduate/Scholarship)* [3603]

Earth sciences

American Association of Stratigraphic Palynologists Student Scholarships *(Graduate/Scholarship)* [404]
J.P. Bickell Mining Scholarships *(Undergraduate/Scholarship)* [7211]
Canadian Society of Petroleum Geologists Regional Undergraduate Scholarships *(Undergraduate/Scholarship)* [2044]
Earthquake Engineering Research Institute/Fema Graduate Fellowships *(Graduate/Scholarship)* [2804]
Lewis-Clark State College Presidential Technical Out-of-State Scholarships *(Undergraduate/Scholarship)* [4199]
National Geophysics Scholarships *(Postgraduate/Scholarship)* [7488]
National Scholarships *(Postgraduate/Scholarship)* [7489]
Paleontological Society Student Research Grants *(Graduate, Undergraduate/Grant)* [405]
Wood Bursary Awards *(Postgraduate/Award/Prize)* [7490]

Ecology (See also: Environmental science)

Human Ecology Continuing Undergraduate Student Scholarships *(Undergraduate/Scholarship)* [7257]
Maude Keisling/Cumberland County Extension Homemakers Scholarships *(Undergraduate/Scholarship)* [2425]
Dennis Raveling Scholarships *(Undergraduate/Scholarship)* [1862]
Mary and Elliot Wood Foundation Graduate Scholarship Fund *(Graduate/Scholarship)* [3085]

Economics

Alberta Agricultural Economics Association Undergraduate Scholarships *(Undergraduate/Scholarship)* [138]
Julie Allen World Classroom Scholarships *(Undergraduate/Scholarship)* [6164]
American Society of Comparative Law TransCoop Programs *(All/Fellowship)* [937]
American Society of Military Comptrollers National Scholarship Program *(Undergraduate/Scholarship)* [1011]
APS/ASU Scholarships *(Undergraduate/Scholarship)* [5697]
APS/Maricopa County Community Colleges Scholarships *(Undergraduate/Scholarship)* [5698]
ARS Undergraduate Scholarships *(Four Year College, Two Year College, Undergraduate/Scholarship)* [1259]
Avista Corporation Minds in Motion Scholarships *(Undergraduate/Scholarship)* [4163]
Chopivsky Fellowships *(Undergraduate/Scholarship)* [7358]
Clark High School Academy of Finance Scholarships *(Undergraduate/Scholarship)* [5812]
Clark High School Alumni Leadership Circle Scholarships *(Undergraduate/Scholarship)* [5813]
Mable B. Crawford Memorial Scholarships *(Undergraduate/Scholarship)* [4354]
Jack Ervin EDI Scholarships *(Professional Development/Scholarship)* [5238]
Randy Green Memorial Scholarship Fund *(High School/Scholarship)* [2598]
Enid Hall Griswold Memorial Scholarships *(Undergraduate/Scholarship)* [5064]
Anna E. Hall Memorial Scholarships *(Undergraduate/Scholarship)* [5625]
Hilb, Rogal and Hobbs Scholarships *(Undergraduate/Scholarship)* [7328]
Governor James E. Holshouser Professional Development Scholarships *(Professional Development/Scholarship)* [5239]
HSBC-North America Scholarship Program *(Undergraduate/Scholarship)* [3592]
HSF/Citi Fellows Program *(Undergraduate/Scholarship)* [3594]
HSF/General Motors Scholarship Program *(Undergraduate/Scholarship)* [3595]
Kalmen Kaplansky Scholarships in Economic and Social Rights *(Graduate/Scholarship)* [2730]
Douglas McRorie Memorial Scholarships *(Doctorate, Graduate/Scholarship)* [37]
National Iranian American Council Fellowships *(Graduate, Undergraduate/Fellowship)* [4958]
Norfolk Southern Scholarships *(Undergraduate/Scholarship)* [7329]
Phillip Morris USA Scholarships *(Undergraduate/Scholarship)* [7330]
Pi Gamma Mu Scholarships *(Graduate/Scholarship)* [5691]
Betty Rendel Scholarships *(Undergraduate/Scholarship)* [4890]
Helen D. Snow Memorial Scholarships *(Undergraduate/Scholarship)* [5626]
Society of Automotive Analyst Scholarships *(Undergraduate/Scholarship)* [1562]
The Dan Stewart Scholarships *(Professional Development/Scholarship)* [5240]
Toyota High School Scholarship Program *(Undergraduate/Scholarship)* [3603]
Tribal Business Management Program (TBM) Scholarships *(Undergraduate/Scholarship)* [2069]
UAA Diane Olsen Memorial Scholarships *(Undergraduate/Scholarship)* [7048]
UAA Mark A. Beltz Scholarships *(Graduate, Undergraduate/Scholarship)* [7063]
Urban Financial Services Coalition Scholarships *(Undergraduate/Scholarship)* [1744]
Verizon Scholarship Program *(Undergraduate/Scholarship)* [3607]
Women In Defense HORIZONS Scholarships *(Graduate, Undergraduate/Scholarship)* [7479]
Mary and Elliot Wood Foundation Graduate Scholarship Fund *(Graduate/Scholarship)* [3085]

Editors and editing

ASBPE Young Leaders Scholarships *(All, Professional Development/Scholarship)* [925]
Aubespin Scholarships *(Undergraduate/Scholarship)* [495]
Eugene C. Pulliam Fellowships for Editorial Writing *(All/Fellowship)* [6337]

Education (See also: specific areas of study, e.g. Education, Bilingual and cross-cultural)

Larry Acterman Public Education Awards *(Undergraduate/Scholarship)* [5355]
AERA-AIR Fellows Program *(Postdoctorate/Fellowship)* [543]
AERA Minority Fellowship Program in Education Research *(Postdoctorate/Fellowship)* [545]
Akao Scholarships for QFD *(Undergraduate/Scholarship)* [5886]
William Tasse Alexander Scholarship Fund *(Undergraduate/Scholarship)* [3038]
Margaret M. Alkek Scholarship *(Undergraduate/Scholarship)* [2637]
American Quarter Horse Foundation Scholarships *(Undergraduate/Scholarship)* [811]
AMS Teacher Education Scholarships *(Undergraduate/Scholarship)* [718]
Charles Lee Anderson Memorial Scholarship *(Undergraduate/Scholarship)* [2455]
APS/Maricopa County Community Colleges Scholarships *(Undergraduate/Scholarship)* [5698]
Mike Ardaw Scholarships *(Undergraduate/Scholarship)* [4345]
ARTC Glenn Moon Scholarships *(Undergraduate/Scholarship)* [3418]
Associated Women for Pepperdine (AWP) Scholarships *(Undergraduate/Scholarship)* [5572]
Avery Bayle Barth Scholarships *(Undergraduate/Scholarship)* [2642]
Diane Basilone-Engle Memorial Scholarships *(Undergraduate/Scholarship)* [1889]
Jeannette Bautista Memorial Scholarships *(Undergraduate/Scholarship)* [5803]
Susan Brager Occupational Education Scholarships *(Undergraduate/Scholarship)* [5806]
Brown Foundation Academic Scholarships *(Undergraduate/Scholarship)* [1796]
Brown Foundation College Scholarship *(Undergraduate/Scholarship)* [631]
Cecil E. Burney Scholarships *(High School, Undergraduate/Scholarship)* [2267]
Career Colleges Scholarships *(Undergraduate/Scholarship)* [3672]
Deloris Carter Hampton Scholarships *(Undergraduate/Scholarship)* [5759]
Catching the Dream Scholarship *(Graduate, Undergraduate/Scholarship)* [632]
Delmar Cengage Learning-NAAE Upper Division Scholarships *(Undergraduate/Scholarship)* [4653]
Clark High School Teacher Education Academy Scholarships *(Undergraduate/Scholarship)* [5814]
Lula Faye Clegg Memorial Scholarship Fund *(Undergraduate/Scholarship)* [3052]
Maridell Braham Condon Scholarships *(Undergraduate/Scholarship)* [6351]
Judy Crocker Memorial Scholarship Fund *(Undergraduate/Scholarship)* [3055]
CSA Fraternal Life Scholarships *(Undergraduate/Scholarship)* [2564]
June Danby and Pat Pearse Education Scholarship *(Undergraduate/Scholarship)* [3975]
Antonia Dellas Memorial Scholarship *(Undergraduate/Scholarship)* [3976]
Employee Education Scholarships *(Other/Scholarship)* [4946]
E.V. Erickson Field of Interest Education Scholarships Fund *(Undergraduate/Scholarship)* [3274]

Bertha M. Fase Memorial Scholarship Fund *(Undergraduate/Scholarship)* [3276]
Fordham Fellowships *(Undergraduate/Fellowship)* [3027]
Fordham Scholarships *(Doctorate/Scholarship)* [3028]
Fraser Family Scholarships *(Undergraduate/Scholarship)* [5826]
Garikian Scholarship Fund *(Undergraduate/Scholarship)* [1279]
The Gates Millennium Scholars *(Undergraduate/Scholarship)* [3590]
Laverne L. Gibson Memorial Scholarships *(Undergraduate/Scholarship)* [5483]
Guide Dogs for the Blind Dorothea and Roland Bohde Leadership Scholarships *(Postgraduate/Scholarship)* [4877]
Martha and Oliver Hansen Memorial Scholarship *(Undergraduate/Scholarship)* [3981]
Karen Harter Recruitment Scholarship Grant *(Undergraduate/Scholarship)* [2469]
Karen Harter Recruitment Scholarship Grant *(Undergraduate/Scholarship)* [2470]
Dick and Pat Hazel Minority Scholarships *(Professional Development/Scholarship)* [2377]
High School Councilors Scholarships *(Undergraduate/Scholarship)* [3673]
Raymond T. Hoge Scholarship Fund *(Undergraduate/Scholarship)* [6727]
Huenefeld/Denton Scholarships *(Undergraduate/Scholarship)* [2692]
Imagine America Scholarships *(Undergraduate/Scholarship)* [3675]
Insurance Women of Portland Scholarships *(Graduate/Scholarship)* [3767]
Harriet Irsay Scholarships *(Graduate, Undergraduate/Scholarship)* [674]
Jewish Federation Academic Scholarships *(Graduate, Undergraduate/Scholarship)* [4029]
Maude Keisling/Cumberland County Extension Homemakers Scholarships *(Undergraduate/Scholarship)* [2425]
Louise Nader Khourey/Kappa Delta Pi Scholarships *(Undergraduate/Scholarship)* [6734]
Leila Klinger Kurtzman Mamorial Scholarship Fund *(Undergraduate/Scholarship)* [3558]
Edna Martin Scholarships *(Undergraduate/Scholarship)* [2432]
Jacinta McKoy Memorial Scholarships *(Undergraduate/Scholarship)* [5770]
John Alexander McLean Scholarships *(Undergraduate/Scholarship)* [6886]
MESBEC Scholarships *(Undergraduate/Scholarship)* [2067]
Microbiology Undergraduate Teaching Fellowships *(Undergraduate/Fellowship)* [1008]
National Academy of Education Scholarships *(Doctorate/Fellowship)* [4624]
Native American Leadership Education (NALE) Scholarships *(Postdoctorate, Undergraduate/Scholarship)* [2068]
Nevada Parent Teacher Association Scholarships *(Undergraduate/Scholarship)* [5845]
North Dakota Division Scholarships *(Undergraduate/Scholarship)* [4517]
North Mecklenburg Teachers' Memorial Scholarships *(Undergraduate/Scholarship)* [3071]
Parents Scholarships *(Undergraduate/Scholarship)* [3676]
Penn-Bird Family Memorial Scholarships *(Undergraduate/Scholarship)* [5850]
Pi Lambda Theta Scholarships *(Undergraduate/Scholarship)* [7265]
Rechsteiner Family Scholarship Fund *(Undergraduate/Scholarship)* [2971]
Charles and Ruth Ronin Memorial Scholarships *(Undergraduate/Scholarship)* [6002]
Dorothy Worden Ronken Scholarships *(Graduate/Scholarship)* [2698]
School of Education Scholarships for Students from Underrepresented Groups *(Undergraduate/Scholarship)* [7268]
Marion A. And Ruth Sherwood Family Fund Education Scholarships *(Undergraduate/Scholarship)* [3307]
Siemens Teacher Scholarships *(Graduate, Undergraduate/Scholarship)* [6330]
Lillian Smith Scholarship for Teaching Students *(Graduate, Undergraduate/Scholarship)* [7036]
Soroptimist International of Redlands Scholarships *(Undergraduate/Scholarship)* [6011]
Robert W. and Bernice Ingalls Staton Scholarships *(Undergraduate/Scholarship)* [7202]
Sheri Stears Education Scholarships *(Undergraduate/Scholarship)* [7037]
Peter T. Steinwedell Scholarships *(Undergraduate/Scholarship)* [3498]
Sturgulewski Family Scholarships *(Graduate, Undergraduate/Scholarship)* [7038]
John A. Sullivan Scholarships *(Undergraduate/Scholarship)* [2795]
TEACH Scholarships *(Undergraduate/Scholarship)* [5865]
Charles A. Townsend Scholarships *(Undergraduate/Scholarship)* [5525]
Toyota High School Scholarship Program *(Undergraduate/Scholarship)* [3603]
Philip F. Vineberg Travelling Fellowship in the Humanities *(Graduate/Scholarship)* [4432]
Richard M. Weaver Fellowships *(Graduate/Fellowship)* [3774]
Faye and Rendell Webb Scholarships *(High School, Undergraduate/Scholarship)* [2292]
Art and Dannie Weber Scholarships *(Undergraduate/Scholarship)* [7460]
Louise Wachter Wichman Scholarship Fund *(Undergraduate/Scholarship)* [3314]
Dr. Dana Williams Scholarships *(High School, Undergraduate/Scholarship)* [2294]
Winston-Salem Foundation Scholarships *(Undergraduate/Scholarship)* [7464]
Paul R. Wolf Memorial Scholarships *(Graduate/Scholarship)* [1033]
Lee Womack Scholarships Fund *(Undergraduate/Scholarship)* [4565]
Mary and Elliot Wood Foundation Graduate Scholarship Fund *(Graduate/Scholarship)* [3085]
Geofrey H. Wood Scholarships *(Undergraduate/Scholarship)* [2032]
Minoru Yasui Memorial Scholarship *(Graduate/Scholarship)* [4022]

Education, Bilingual and cross-cultural

Cemanahuac Educational Community Scholarships *(Other/Scholarship)* [5263]
French Embassy Scholarships *(Other/Scholarship)* [5264]
Goethe-Institut AATG Scholarships *(Other/Scholarship)* [5265]
Mead Leadership Fellows Program *(Professional Development/Fellowship)* [5266]
New Mexico Association for Bilingual Education Scholarships *(Undergraduate/Scholarship)* [5187]
Spanish Embassy Scholarships *(Graduate, Other/Scholarship)* [5267]
Toyota High School Scholarship Program *(Undergraduate/Scholarship)* [3603]

Education—Curricula

Evelyn Abrams Memorial Scholarships *(Undergraduate/Scholarship)* [5797]
Copper and Brass Service Center Inc. Scholarship Program *(Undergraduate/Scholarship)* [2541]
Ed Haas Memorial Scholarships *(Undergraduate/Scholarship)* [6776]
Isabel M. Herson Scholarships in Education *(Graduate, Undergraduate/Scholarship)* [7555]
Edith Cantor Morrison Memorial Scholarships *(Graduate, Undergraduate/Scholarship)* [1671]
Ina E. Powell Memorial Scholarships *(Undergraduate/Scholarship)* [115]
Audrey L. Wright Scholarships *(Undergraduate/Scholarship)* [3358]

Education, Early childhood

Early Childhood Development Scholarships *(Undergraduate/Scholarship)* [1701]
Patty Hamilton Early Childhood Development Scholarships *(Undergraduate/Scholarship)* [4360]
John Hoffbauer Memorial Scholarships *(Undergraduate/Scholarship)* [2780]
Carol Hoy Scholarship fund *(Undergraduate/Scholarship)* [3106]
Irene Brand Lieberman Scholarship *(Postgraduate/Scholarship)* [3560]
Molly Ann Mishler Memorial Scholarships *(Undergraduate/Scholarship)* [4371]
National Kindergarten Alliance Graduate Scholarships *(Graduate/Scholarship)* [4978]
Toyota High School Scholarship Program *(Undergraduate/Scholarship)* [3603]

Education, Elementary

APS/ASU Scholarships *(Undergraduate/Scholarship)* [5697]
Gina L. Barnhart Memorial Scholarship Fund *(Undergraduate/Scholarship)* [2942]
Marian Jones Donaldson Scholarship Fund *(Undergraduate/Scholarship)* [2952]
Lindsay M. Entz Memorial Scholarships *(Undergraduate/Scholarship)* [2953]
Jennica Ferguson Memorial Scholarships *(Undergraduate/Scholarship)* [4876]
Norma Gotwalt Scholarship Fund *(Undergraduate/Scholarship)* [3102]
Isabel M. Herson Scholarships in Education *(Graduate, Undergraduate/Scholarship)* [7555]
Carol Hoy Scholarship fund *(Undergraduate/Scholarship)* [3106]
Carie and George Lyter Scholarship Fund *(Undergraduate/Scholarship)* [3110]
National Federation of the Blind Educator of Tomorrow Award *(Undergraduate/Scholarship)* [4881]
Ruth Cook Pfautz Memorial Scholarship Fund *(Undergraduate/Scholarship)* [3115]
R.M. Princ Scholarships *(Undergraduate/Scholarship)* [5852]
Mary Kean White Memorial Scholarship Fund *(Undergraduate/Scholarship)* [6763]
Ralph Yetka Memorial Scholarships *(Undergraduate/Scholarship)* [4391]

Education, English as a second language

Douglas-Coldwell Foundation Scholarships in Social Affairs *(Graduate/Scholarship)* [2729]
Flora English Creative Writing Scholarships *(Undergraduate/Scholarship)* [5825]
Sarah Jane Houston Scholarships *(Undergraduate/Scholarship)* [2691]
Arlene Kuhner Memorial Scholarships *(Undergraduate/Scholarship)* [7034]
William R. Pfalzgraf Scholarships *(Undergraduate/Scholarship)* [5509]

Education, Industrial

American Rental Association Foundation Scholarships *(Undergraduate/Scholarship)* [888]
Gary L. Buffington Memorial Scholarships *(Undergraduate/Scholarship)* [3717]
Bus and Mary Ellen Durant Timberline High School Endowed Scholarships *(Undergraduate/Scholarship)* [4177]
Flexible Packaging Academic Scholarships & Summer Internship Program *(Undergraduate/Internship)* [2988]
Daniel Lasky Scholarship Fund *(Undergraduate/Scholarship)* [4998]
Lewis-Clark State College Presidential Technical Out-of-State Scholarships *(Undergraduate/Scholarship)* [4199]
Ron Marshall Scholarships *(Undergraduate/Scholarship)* [889]
Material Handling Institute of America Scholarships *(Graduate, Undergraduate/Scholarship)* [4395]

Dorothy Wellnitz Canadian Scholarships *(Undergraduate/Scholarship)* [890]

Education, Medical

AMA Foundation Minority Scholars Award *(Undergraduate/Scholarship)* [712]
AMA Foundation Physicians of Tomorrow Scholarships *(Undergraduate/Scholarship)* [713]
Davis Educational Scholarship Fund *(Undergraduate/Scholarship)* [2506]
Victoria M. Gardner Scholarships *(Undergraduate/Scholarship)* [7159]
S. William & Martha R. Golf Educational Scholarships *(Undergraduate/Scholarship)* [5485]
Alice Newell Joslyn Medical Fund *(Undergraduate/Scholarship)* [1612]
John and Lois Lamont Graduate Scholarships *(Postgraduate/Award/Prize)* [1957]
Lapeer County Medical Scholarships Fund *(Undergraduate/Scholarship)* [4142]
Karen E. Latt Memorial Scholarship *(Undergraduate/Scholarship)* [3559]
Albert and Eloise Midyette Memorial Scholarship Fund *(Undergraduate/Scholarship)* [3068]
Nebraska Hospital Association Tuition Aid and Scholarships *(Undergraduate/Scholarship)* [5164]
Herbert W. Nickens Medical Student Scholarships *(Undergraduate/Scholarship)* [1362]
Novo Nordisk NP Doctoral Education Scholarships *(Doctorate/Scholarship)* [271]
Pharmavite LLC NP Doctoral Education Scholarships *(Doctorate/Scholarship)* [273]
RBC Royal Bank Scholarships for First Year Medical & Dental Students *(Undergraduate/Scholarship)* [6066]
Ventura County Medical Association Alliance Scholarships *(Undergraduate/Scholarship)* [7314]
Jerome P. Webster Fellowships *(Professional Development/Fellowship)* [3927]
The Arthur N. Wilson, MD, Scholarships *(Undergraduate/Scholarship)* [714]

Education, Music

AOSA Research Grants *(All/Grant)* [739]
Bach Organ and Keyboard Music Scholarships *(Undergraduate/Scholarship)* [6034]
Constant Memorial Scholarship for Aquidneck Island Resident *(Undergraduate/Scholarship)* [6036]
William R. Gard Memorial Scholarships *(Undergraduate/Scholarship)* [4608]
Donald and Idabelle Mohr Scholarships *(Undergraduate/Scholarship)* [2241]
Muddy Waters Scholarships *(Undergraduate/Scholarship)* [1768]

Education, Physical

Ruth Abernathy Presidential Scholarships *(Graduate, Undergraduate/Scholarship)* [351]
American Sokol Merit Awards *(Undergraduate/Scholarship)* [1096]
Gretchen Hauff Memorial Scholarships *(Undergraduate/Scholarship)* [5831]
Indiana State Alumni Association Creative and Performing Arts Award *(Undergraduate/Scholarship)* [3701]
Bonnie Sorenson Scudder Scholarship *(Undergraduate/Scholarship)* [2486]
Taylor Statten Memorial Fellowships *(Graduate/Scholarship)* [7233]

Education, Religious

Mary E. Bivins Foundation Religious Scholarship Program *(Graduate, Undergraduate/Scholarship)* [1719]
Emmanuel Bible College Scholarships *(Undergraduate/Scholarship)* [1278]
International Scholarship Program for Community Service *(Other/Scholarship)* [4460]
MACC Scholarships *(Professional Development/Scholarship)* [4466]
Transgender Scholarships and Education Legacy Fund *(Undergraduate/Scholarship)* [6142]
Philip F. Vineberg Travelling Fellowship in the Humanities *(Graduate/Scholarship)* [4432]

Education, Secondary

APS/ASU Scholarships *(Undergraduate/Scholarship)* [5697]
The Bailey Family Foundation High School Scholarship Program *(Undergraduate/Scholarship)* [1587]
Mary Ann Brichta Scholarships *(Undergraduate/Scholarship)* [7249]
Patricia Buchanan Memorial Scholarships *(Undergraduate/Scholarship)* [7250]
COUSE-Gram Scholarships *(Undergraduate/Scholarship)* [6647]
Marian Jones Donaldson Scholarship Fund *(Undergraduate/Scholarship)* [2952]
Jennica Ferguson Memorial Scholarships *(Undergraduate/Scholarship)* [4876]
Mollie Harter Memorial Fund *(Undergraduate/Scholarship)* [2958]
George Koeppel and Roland W. Zinns Scholarships *(Undergraduate/Scholarship)* [7260]
La Voz Latina Scholarships *(Undergraduate/Scholarship)* [2474]
John P. and Tashia F. Morgridge Scholarships *(Undergraduate/Scholarship)* [7263]
National Federation of the Blind Educator of Tomorrow Award *(Undergraduate/Scholarship)* [4881]
Noyce Scholarships for Secondary Math and Science Education *(Undergraduate/Scholarship)* [3711]
R.M. Princ Scholarships *(Undergraduate/Scholarship)* [5852]
Carl M. Rose Memorial Scholarship Fund *(Undergraduate/Scholarship)* [5515]
University of Wisconsin-Madison Minority Teacher Loans *(Professional Development, Undergraduate/Loan, Scholarship)* [7277]
Ralph Yetka Memorial Scholarships *(Undergraduate/Scholarship)* [4391]

Education, Special

ACRES Scholarships *(Postgraduate, Professional Development/Scholarship)* [513]
APS/ASU Scholarships *(Undergraduate/Scholarship)* [5697]
Laverne L. Gibson Memorial Scholarships *(Undergraduate/Scholarship)* [5483]
Illinois Special Education Teacher Tuition Waiver Scholarships *(Undergraduate/Scholarship)* [3664]
Military Order of the Perpetual Heart Foundation Scholarships *(Undergraduate/Scholarship)* [4206]
Toyota High School Scholarship Program *(Undergraduate/Scholarship)* [3603]
Workshop, Inc. and Stark MRDD Fostering Diversity Through Special Needs Scholarship Fund *(Undergraduate/Scholarship)* [6764]

Education, Vocational-technical

ALOA Scholarship Foundation *(Undergraduate/Scholarship)* [1346]
APS/Maricopa County Community Colleges Scholarships *(Undergraduate/Scholarship)* [5698]
ARA Scholarship Awards *(Undergraduate/Scholarship)* [1575]
Bus and Mary Ellen Durant Timberline High School Endowed Scholarships *(Undergraduate/Scholarship)* [4177]
Laura M. Fleming Scholarship Fund *(Undergraduate/Scholarship)* [3058]
A.E. Robert Friedman Scholarships *(Postgraduate, Undergraduate/Scholarship)* [5445]
Harrisville Lions Club Scholarships *(Undergraduate/Scholarship)* [5492]
Wilbert L. and Zora F. Holmes Scholarship Endowment Fund *(Undergraduate/Scholarship)* [3062]
IOIA Andrew Rutherford Scholarships *(Professional Development/Scholarship)* [3684]
IOIA Organic Community Initiative Scholarship *(Other/Scholarship)* [3685]
Virginia C. Jack and Ralph L. Jack Scholarships *(Undergraduate/Scholarship)* [6730]
Margaret G. Johnson and Marge J. Stout Scholarships *(Undergraduate/Scholarship)* [4188]
Lake Dollars for Scholars Endowment Fund *(Undergraduate/Scholarship)* [6736]
The Leaders of Tomorrow Scholarships *(Undergraduate/Scholarship)* [2813]
Fizz and Dutch Miller Scholarship Fund *(Undergraduate/Scholarship)* [6745]
Lt. Colonel Robert G. Moreland Vocational/Technical Fund *(Undergraduate/Scholarship)* [6746]
National Dairy Herd Improvement Association Scholarship Program *(Undergraduate/Scholarship)* [4839]
National Slovak Society of the USA Scholarships *(Undergraduate/Scholarship)* [5044]
National Slovak Society of the USA Senior Scholarships *(Undergraduate/Scholarship)* [5045]
Northwest-Shoals Community College Applied Technology Scholarships *(Undergraduate/Scholarship)* [5290]
Operation Homefront Scholarships *(Undergraduate/Scholarship)* [5351]
William Reaser Scholarships *(Undergraduate/Scholarship)* [5511]
Faye Lynn Roberts Educational Scholarships *(Undergraduate/Scholarship)* [6669]
Rocky Mountain Coal Mining Institute Technical Scholarships *(Undergraduate/Scholarship)* [6052]
Bill Sawyer Memorial Scholarships *(Undergraduate/Scholarship)* [4214]
Ethel Shinn Alumni-Vocational Scholarships *(Undergraduate/Scholarship)* [4216]
Mary K. Smith Rector Scholarships *(Undergraduate/Scholarship)* [5523]
Beatrice Drinnan Spence Scholarships *(Undergraduate/Scholarship)* [2814]
StraightForward Media's Vocational-Technical School Scholarships *(Undergraduate/Scholarship)* [6807]
Texas Mutual Scholarship Program *(Undergraduate/Scholarship)* [6865]
Turner Family Scholarship Fund *(Undergraduate/Scholarship)* [3080]
TWO Scholarship Program *(Undergraduate/Scholarship)* [6851]
The Wilmore Scholarship Fund *(Undergraduate/Scholarship)* [3084]

Educational administration

ACUA Scholarships *(Graduate, Undergraduate/Scholarship)* [1381]
AGBU Scholarships *(Graduate/Loan)* [1255]
Native American Leadership Education (NALE) Scholarships *(Postdoctorate, Undergraduate/Scholarship)* [2068]

Electronics

AFCEA Distance Learning/Online Scholarships *(Undergraduate/Scholarship)* [1236]
AFCEA General John A. Wickham Scholarships *(Undergraduate/Scholarship)* [1238]
ARRLF Mississippi Scholarships *(Undergraduate/Scholarship)* [819]
William E. "Buck" Bragunier Scholarships *(Undergraduate/Scholarship)* [1241]
Irvine W. Cook WA0CGS Scholarships *(Undergraduate/Scholarship)* [829]
Milton E. Cooper/Young AFCEAN Graduate Scholarships *(Graduate/Scholarship)* [1243]
Charles Clarke Cordle Memorial Scholarships *(Undergraduate/Scholarship)* [830]
Charles N. Fisher Memorial Scholarships *(Undergraduate/Scholarship)* [833]
Paul and Helen L. Grauer Scholarships *(Undergraduate/Scholarship)* [835]
IRARC Memorial Joseph P. Rubino WA4MMD Scholarships *(Undergraduate/Scholarship)* [840]
Dr. James L. Lawson Memorial Scholarships *(Undergraduate/Scholarship)* [841]
Johny Lineberry Memorial Scholarships *(Undergraduate/Scholarship)* [7445]
Fred R. McDaniel Memorial Scholarships *(Undergraduate/Scholarship)* [842]
Ray, NORP and Katie, WOKTE Pautz Scholarships *(Undergraduate/Scholarship)* [847]
PHD ARA Scholarships

(Undergraduate/Scholarship) [849]
Carol A. Ratza Memorial Scholarships (Undergraduate/Scholarship) [3365]
Toyota High School Scholarship Program (Undergraduate/Scholarship) [3603]
L. Phil Wicker Scholarships (Undergraduate/Scholarship) [861]

Emergency and disaster services

Gail Hartshorn Scholarships (Undergraduate/Scholarship) [5494]
International Association of Emergency Managers Scholarships (Undergraduate/Scholarship) [3796]
William C. Leary Memorial Emergency Services Scholarships (Undergraduate/Scholarship) [6844]
Mary Fran Myers Scholarships (All/Grant) [5130]
John I. and Madeleine R. Taeni Scholarships (Undergraduate/Scholarship) [6678]

Energy-related areas

American Association of Blacks in Energy Scholarships (Undergraduate/Scholarship) [324]
Association of Desk and Derrick Clubs Education Trust Scholarships (Undergraduate/Scholarship) [1388]
Association of Energy Engineers Foundation Scholarship Program (Graduate, Undergraduate/Scholarship) [1407]
DEED Student Research Grant/Internships (Graduate, Undergraduate/Grant) [804]
EMLF Law Student Scholarships (Undergraduate/Scholarship) [2855]
Environment, Natural Resource and Energy (ENRE) Division Fellowships (Graduate/Scholarship) [779]

Engineering (See also: specific areas of study, e.g. Engineering, Chemical)

AAAS Mass Media Science and Engineering Fellowships (Graduate, Postgraduate, Undergraduate/Fellowship) [316]
AAAS Science and Technology Policy Fellowships (Postdoctorate/Fellowship) [317]
AACE International Competitive Scholarships (Undergraduate/Scholarship) [1350]
AAUW Legal Advocacy Fund Selected Professions Fellowships (Doctorate, Graduate/Fellowship) [7]
Accenture American Indian Scholarship Program (Graduate, Undergraduate/Scholarship) [640]
Henry Adams Scholarships (Undergraduate/Scholarship) [962]
AeA Scholarships (Undergraduate/Scholarship) [6162]
AFCEA Distance Learning/Online Scholarships (Undergraduate/Scholarship) [1236]
AFCEA Fellowships (Doctorate, Graduate/Fellowship) [1237]
AFCEA General John A. Wickham Scholarships (Undergraduate/Scholarship) [1238]
AFCEA Scholarship for Working Professionals (Graduate/Scholarship) [1240]
African American Network - Carolinas Scholarship Fund (Undergraduate/Scholarship) [3037]
AIST Baltimore Chapter Scholarships (Undergraduate/Scholarship) [1438]
AIST Detroit Chapter Scholarships (Undergraduate/Scholarship) [1439]
AIST Northwest Chapter Scholarships (Undergraduate/Scholarship) [1440]
AIST Ronald E. Lincoln Memorial Scholarships (Undergraduate/Scholarship) [1441]
AIST William E. Schwabe Memorial Scholarships (Undergraduate/Scholarship) [1443]
AIST Willy Korf Memorial Fund (Undergraduate/Scholarship) [1444]
Alaska Aerospace Development Corporation Scholarships (Undergraduate/Scholarship) [4338]
Alaska Community Foundation Sven E. & Lorraine Eriksson Scholarships (Undergraduate/Scholarship) [7029]
Stephanie Ali Memorial Scholarships (Undergraduate/Scholarship) [7210]
AMEC Aboriginal Undergraduate Scholarships (Undergraduate/Scholarship) [1947]
AMEC Masters Scholarships (Graduate/Scholarship) [1948]
American Council of Engineering Companies of Illinois Scholarships (Doctorate, Graduate, Undergraduate/Scholarship) [497]
American Lebanese Engineering Society Scholarship Program (Other/Scholarship) [692]
American Society of Heating, Refrigerating, and Air-Conditioning Memorial Scholarships (Undergraduate/Scholarship) [963]
American Society of Heating, Refrigerating, and Air-Conditioning Undergraduate Scholarships (Undergraduate/Scholarship) [964]
ISPE/M.E. Amstutz Memorial Award (Undergraduate/Scholarship) [3658]
Mike Ardaw Scholarships (Undergraduate/Scholarship) [4345]
AREMA Committee Scholarships 18 - Light Density & Short Line Railways (Undergraduate/Scholarship) [865]
AREMA Committee Scholarships 24 - Education and Training (Undergraduate/Scholarship) [866]
AREMA Committee Scholarships 33 - Electric Energy Utilization (Undergraduate/Scholarship) [867]
AREMA Presidential Spouse Scholarships (Undergraduate/Scholarship) [868]
AREMA Scholarships (Undergraduate/Scholarship) [869]
AREMA Staff Scholarships (Undergraduate/Scholarship) [870]
Marvin Arnold and Irene Jaquetta Heye Scholarships (Undergraduate/Scholarship) [6165]
ASNT Fellow Awards (Postdoctorate/Fellowship) [1021]
Astronaut Scholarship Foundation Scholarships (Undergraduate/Scholarship) [1527]
Audio Engineering Society Educational Foundation Scholarships (Undergraduate/Grant) [1538]
Delores A. Auzenne Fellowship (Postgraduate/Fellowship) [2995]
Avista Corporation Minds in Motion Scholarships (Undergraduate/Scholarship) [4163]
AWIS College Scholarships (Undergraduate/Scholarship) [1519]
B&W Y-12 Scholarship Fund (Undergraduate/Scholarship) [2806]
Beginning Freshmen Awards (Undergraduate/Scholarship) [4056]
Charles E. Behlke Engineering Memorial Scholarships (Undergraduate/Scholarship) [4347]
Bill & Nell Biggs Scholarships (Undergraduate/Scholarship) [4348]
Blow Molding Division Memorial Scholarships (Graduate, Undergraduate/Scholarship) [6547]
Boeing Company Scholarships (Undergraduate/Scholarship) [6307]
Boeing Engineering Scholarships (Undergraduate/Scholarship) [3251]
William E. "Buck" Bragunier Scholarships (Undergraduate/Scholarship) [1241]
Henry Broughton, K2AE Memorial Scholarships (Undergraduate/Scholarship) [822]
LT.G. Douglas D. Buchholz Memorial Scholarships (Undergraduate/Scholarship) [1242]
Dorothy and Dick Burgess Scholarship (Undergraduate/Scholarship) [3974]
Wes Burton Memorial Scholarships (Undergraduate/Scholarship) [7424]
Cesar A. Calas/FES Miami Chapter Scholarships (Undergraduate/Scholarship) [3000]
Julian E. Carnes Scholarship Fund (Undergraduate/Scholarship) [3046]
Willis H. Carrier Scholarships (Undergraduate/Scholarship) [965]
Catching the Dream Scholarship (Graduate, Undergraduate/Scholarship) [632]
CEMF Claudette MacKay-Lassonde Scholarships (Postdoctorate/Scholarship) [6432]
CEMF Undergraduate Engineering Scholarships (Undergraduate/Scholarship) [1949]
CEPS-Tyco Scholarships (Undergraduate/Scholarship) [7137]
Channabasappa Memorial Scholarships (Graduate, Professional Development/Scholarship) [3837]
The Churchill Scholarships (Postgraduate/Scholarship) [2147]
Frank M. Coda Scholarships (Undergraduate/Scholarship) [966]
Paul I. and Elena H. Cohen Scholarships (Graduate, Undergraduate/Scholarship) [871]
College and Trade/Technical School Scholarships (Undergraduate/Scholarship) [2898]
Committee 12 - Rail Transit Scholarships (Undergraduate/Scholarship) [872]
Committee 27 - Maintenance-of-Way Work Equipment Scholarships (Undergraduate/Scholarship) [873]
Connecticut Building Congress Scholarships (Undergraduate/Scholarship) [3436]
Holly A. Cornell Scholarships (Graduate/Scholarship) [1143]
Richard P. Covert, Ph.D./FHIMSS Scholarships for Management Systems (Other/Scholarship) [3516]
Robert E. Cramer Scholarships (Graduate, Undergraduate/Scholarship) [6548]
Critical Language Scholarships for Intensive Summer Institutes (Graduate, Undergraduate/Scholarship) [892]
CSX Scholarships (Undergraduate/Scholarship) [874]
John J. Cunningham Memorial Scholarships (Undergraduate/Scholarship) [875]
Robert G. Dailey Scholarships (Graduate, Undergraduate/Scholarship) [6549]
D&A Florida Scholarships (Undergraduate/Scholarship) [6648]
Disabled War Veterans Scholarships (Undergraduate/Scholarship) [1244]
Robert E. Dougherty Scholarships (Undergraduate/Scholarship) [2525]
John R. Eidson Jr., Scholarships (Undergraduate/Scholarship) [2274]
Electronic Document Systems Foundation Scholarships (Undergraduate/Scholarship) [2846]
Engineering Departmental Scholarships (Undergraduate/Scholarship) [7251]
Engineering Diversity Affairs Scholarships (All/Scholarship) [7252]
Engineers for Tomorrow Scholarships Program (Undergraduate/Scholarship) [4563]
Harold E. Ennes Scholarships (Professional Development/Scholarship) [6526]
Larry L. Etherton Scholarships (Graduate, Undergraduate/Scholarship) [876]
AIST Benjamin F. Fairless Scholarships (AIME) (Undergraduate/Scholarship) [1445]
Fecon Scholarships (Undergraduate/Scholarship) [3001]
Lt. Col. Romeo and Josephine Bass Ferretti Scholarships (Undergraduate/Scholarship) [51]
FICE Scholarships (Undergraduate/Scholarship) [3002]
Herb Fincher Memorial Scholarship (Undergraduate/Scholarship) [2373]
Reuben H. Fleet Memorial Scholarships (Undergraduate/Scholarship) [6189]
Fleming/Blaszcak Scholarships (Graduate, Undergraduate/Scholarship) [6550]
Grant H. Flint International Scholarships - Category II (Undergraduate/Scholarship) [6597]
Florida Engineering Society Junior College Scholarships (Undergraduate/Scholarship) [3003]
Florida Engineering Society University Scholarships (Undergraduate/Scholarship) [3004]
FMA Foundation Scholarships (Undergraduate/Scholarship) [3022]
Frank Fong Scholarships (Undergraduate/Scholarship) [6423]
Michael W. and Jean D. Franke Family Foundation Scholarships (Graduate, Undergraduate/Scholarship) [877]
Richard Gregory Freeland, II Educational Scholarships (High School/Scholarship) [1762]
Fuchs-Harden Educational Scholarships Fund (Undergraduate/Scholarship) [3375]
Future Leaders of Manufacturing Scholarships (Graduate, Undergraduate/Scholarship) [6488]
Michael and Gina Garcia Rail Engineering Scholarships (Undergraduate/Scholarship) [879]

The Gates Millennium Scholars *(Undergraduate/Scholarship)* [3590]
Gautier Family Scholarships Fund *(Undergraduate/Scholarship)* [3281]
Gen III Scholarships *(Undergraduate/Scholarship)* [2822]
Georgia Engineering Foundation Scholarships *(Undergraduate/Scholarship)* [3212]
Harold Giles Scholarships *(Graduate, Undergraduate/Scholarship)* [6551]
Midwest Chapter Scholarships - Jack Gill *(Undergraduate/Scholarship)* [1446]
Benjamin A. Gilman International Scholarship *(Undergraduate/Scholarship)* [7031]
Dr. Robert H. Goddard Memorial Scholarships *(Graduate, Undergraduate/Scholarship)* [5085]
William R. Goldfarb Memorial Scholarships *(Undergraduate/Scholarship)* [834]
Barry M. Goldwater Scholarships *(Undergraduate/Scholarship)* [7256]
GREAT MINDS Collegiate Scholarship Program *(Undergraduate/Scholarship)* [236]
Robert D. Greenberg Scholarships *(Professional Development/Scholarship)* [6527]
Gulf Coast Hurricane Scholarships *(Graduate, Undergraduate/Scholarship)* [6552]
Hamilton Industrial Environmental Association Bursaries-Mohawk College *(Undergraduate/Scholarship)* [3390]
Duane Hanson Scholarships *(Undergraduate/Scholarship)* [967]
Chris Harding Scholarships *(Undergraduate/Scholarship)* [880]
Claude B. Hart Memorial Scholarships *(Undergraduate/Scholarship)* [7440]
Helm Family Scholarships *(Undergraduate/Scholarship)* [6192]
Henry Ford Academy Scholarships *(Undergraduate/Scholarship)* [6492]
Hertz Foundation's Graduate Fellowships *(Doctorate/Fellowship)* [4705]
Hewlett-Packard Undergraduate Scholarships *(Undergraduate/Scholarship)* [1950]
Hispanic College Fund Scholarship Programs *(Undergraduate/Scholarship)* [3583]
The Homeland Security Graduate Fellowships *(Graduate/Fellowship)* [6985]
The Homeland Security Undergraduate Scholarships *(Undergraduate/Scholarship)* [6986]
Jane Hood Memorial Fund *(Undergraduate/Scholarship)* [2959]
HSF/Nissan Community College Transfer Scholarship Program *(Undergraduate/Scholarship)* [3598]
IDA Fellowship Award *(Professional Development/Fellowship)* [3838]
Informatics Circle of Research Excellence Scholarships *(Doctorate, Graduate/Scholarship)* [159]
Injection Molding Division Scholarships *(Graduate, Undergraduate/Scholarship)* [6553]
International Association of Foundation Drilling Scholarships for Civil Engineering Students *(Postgraduate/Scholarship)* [3798]
ISPE Advantage Award/Foundation Scholarships *(Undergraduate/Scholarship)* [3659]
Nancy Lorraine Jensen Memorial Scholarships *(Undergraduate/Scholarship)* [6603]
Joseph C. Johnson Memorial Grants *(Undergraduate/Scholarship)* [927]
Carl A. Kountz Engineering Scholarships *(Undergraduate/Scholarship)* [4109]
Lam Research Corporation - San Jose State University Scholarships *(Undergraduate/Scholarship)* [4112]
Lamar University College of Engineering Scholarships *(Undergraduate/Scholarship)* [4861]
Laser Technology, Engineering and Applications Scholarships *(Graduate, Undergraduate/Scholarship)* [6697]
Harold Leeming Memorial Scholarships *(Undergraduate/Scholarship)* [5954]
Gerald J. Levandoski Memorial Scholarship Fund *(Undergraduate/Scholarship)* [2962]
Erwin Lew Memorial Scholarships *(Graduate, Undergraduate/Scholarship)* [6554]
Lewis-Clark State College Presidential Technical Out-of-State Scholarships *(Undergraduate/Scholarship)* [4199]
Lockheed Martin IT Scholarships *(Undergraduate/Scholarship)* [1245]
David F. Ludovici Scholarships *(Undergraduate/Scholarship)* [3005]
James I. MacKenzie Memorial Scholarships *(Graduate, Undergraduate/Scholarship)* [6555]
Marine Corps Engineer Association Assistance Fund *(Graduate, High School, Undergraduate/Scholarship)* [4306]
Lockheed Martin Graduate Scholarships *(Graduate/Scholarship)* [1246]
Charles McMahon Memorial Construction Management/Engineering Scholarship Awards *(Undergraduate/Scholarship)* [1320]
MESBEC Scholarships *(Undergraduate/Scholarship)* [2067]
Bernard Michel Scholarships *(Undergraduate/Scholarship)* [1908]
Michigan Society of Professional Engineers Scholarships *(Undergraduate/Scholarship)* [4487]
Michigan Tech Alumni Scholarships *(Undergraduate/Scholarship)* [881]
John G. and Betty J. Mick Scholarship Fund *(Undergraduate/Scholarship)* [6744]
Midwest Chapter Scholarships - Betty McKern *(Undergraduate/Scholarship)* [1448]
Midwest Chapter Scholarships - Don Nelson *(Undergraduate/Scholarship)* [1449]
Midwest Chapter Scholarships - Engineering *(Undergraduate/Scholarship)* [1450]
Midwest Chapter Scholarships - Mel Nickel *(Undergraduate/Scholarship)* [1451]
Raymond W. Miller, PE and Alice E. Miller Scholarships *(Undergraduate/Scholarship)* [3006]
Raymond W. Miller, PE Scholarships *(Undergraduate/Scholarship)* [3007]
Ralph Modjeski Scholarships *(Graduate, Undergraduate/Scholarship)* [5729]
Montana Broadcasters Association Engineers' Scholarships *(Undergraduate/Scholarship)* [4572]
Robert E. and Judy More Scholarship Fund *(Undergraduate/Scholarship)* [2967]
Gary B. Multanen/CM Magazine Scholarships *(All/Scholarship)* [479]
The National Board Technical Scholarships *(Other/Scholarship)* [4768]
National Co-op Scholarship Program *(Undergraduate/Scholarship)* [4809]
National Security Technologies Engineering and Science Scholarships *(Undergraduate/Scholarship)* [5843]
Ted and Ruth Neward Scholarships *(Graduate, Undergraduate/Scholarship)* [6556]
Edsel Newman Scholarship *(Undergraduate/Scholarship)* [4228]
Alwin B. Newton Scholarships *(Undergraduate/Scholarship)* [968]
Donald E. Nichols Scholarships *(Undergraduate/Scholarship)* [969]
Stuart L. Noderer Memorial Scholarships *(Undergraduate/Scholarship)* [6211]
Norfolk Southern Foundation Scholarships *(Undergraduate/Scholarship)* [882]
Nortel Institute Undergraduate Scholarships *(Undergraduate/Scholarship)* [7231]
Northeastern Ohio Chapter Scholarships - Alfred B. Glossbrenner and John Klusch Scholarships *(Undergraduate/Scholarship)* [1454]
Robert Noyce Scholarship Program *(Undergraduate/Scholarship)* [5565]
NSERC Canada Graduate Scholarships *(Graduate, Postdoctorate/Scholarship)* [6434]
NSERC Postgraduate Scholarships *(Graduate, Postdoctorate/Scholarship)* [6435]
Ohio Valley Chapter Scholarships *(Undergraduate/Scholarship)* [1455]
Patricia & Armen Oumedian Scholarships *(Undergraduate/Scholarship)* [3345]
AFCEA General Emmett Paige Scholarships *(Undergraduate/Scholarship)* [1247]
Joseph M. Parish Memorial Grants *(Undergraduate/Scholarship)* [928]
PB Rail Engineering Scholarships *(Undergraduate/Scholarship)* [883]
Pennsylvania Society of Professional Engineers Scholarships *(Undergraduate/Scholarship)* [5561]
Phillip Morris USA Scholarships *(Undergraduate/Scholarship)* [7330]
William Pigott Memorial Scholarship *(Undergraduate/Scholarship)* [2480]
Plastics Pioneers Association Scholarships *(Graduate, Undergraduate/Scholarship)* [6557]
Polymer Modifiers and Additives Division Scholarships *(Graduate, Undergraduate/Scholarship)* [6558]
Eric Primavera Memorial Scholarships *(Undergraduate/Scholarship)* [3008]
Josef Princ Memorial Scholarships *(Undergraduate/Scholarship)* [5851]
RA Consulting Service Maria Riley Scholarships *(Graduate, Undergraduate/Scholarship)* [4900]
REMSA Scholarships *(Undergraduate/Scholarship)* [884]
Howard B. Rickard Scholarships *(Undergraduate/Scholarship)* [4884]
Rocky Mountain Coal Mining Institute Engineering/Geology Scholarships *(Undergraduate/Scholarship)* [6051]
Barnes W. Rose, Jr. and Eva Rose Nichol Scholarship Fund *(Undergraduate/Scholarship)* [194]
AIST David H. Samson Scholarships *(Undergraduate/Scholarship)* [1456]
Scholarships for Technology Students *(Postgraduate/Scholarship)* [1945]
Wendell Scott Awards *(Graduate, Undergraduate/Scholarship)* [3570]
SDF Community College Transfer Scholarships for Math and Science *(Undergraduate/Scholarship)* [6229]
The John and Marion Selby Engineering Scholarship *(Undergraduate/Scholarship)* [3987]
John M. and Mary A. Shanley Memorial Scholarships *(Undergraduate/Scholarship)* [6673]
Dr. Robert and Anna Shaw Scholarships *(Undergraduate/Scholarship)* [184]
Shell Incentive Scholarships Fund *(Undergraduate/Scholarship)* [6302]
Shell Process Technology Scholarships *(Undergraduate/Scholarship)* [6303]
Shell Technical Scholarships *(Undergraduate/Scholarship)* [6304]
Marion A. and Ruth K. Sherwood Family Fund Engineering Scholarships *(Undergraduate/Scholarship)* [3308]
Small Cash Grants *(Undergraduate/Scholarship)* [929]
SME Ford PAS Scholarships *(Undergraduate/Scholarship)* [6504]
Society of Plastics Engineers General Scholarships *(Graduate, Undergraduate/Scholarship)* [6559]
Society of Plastics Engineers Pittsburgh Scholarships *(Graduate, Undergraduate/Scholarship)* [6560]
Society of Women Engineers Scholarships *(Undergraduate/Scholarship)* [6592]
Sons of Norway Foundation Scholarships to Oslo International School *(Undergraduate/Scholarship)* [6604]
Soroptimist International of Redlands Scholarships *(Undergraduate/Scholarship)* [6011]
Southeast Member Chapter Scholarships *(Undergraduate/Scholarship)* [1457]
Robert P. Stearns/SCS Engineers Awards *(Graduate/Scholarship)* [6598]
StraightForward Media's Engineering Scholarships *(Undergraduate/Scholarship)* [6797]
Sturgulewski Family Scholarships *(Graduate, Undergraduate/Scholarship)* [7038]
Texas Society of Professional Engineers Scholarships *(Undergraduate/Scholarship)* [6869]
Anil and Neema Thakrar Family Fund *(Undergraduate/Scholarship)* [3122]
Thermoforming Scholarships *(Graduate, Undergraduate/Scholarship)* [6561]
Thermoplastic Materials and Foams Division Scholarships *(Graduate, Undergraduate/Scholarship)* [6562]
Thermoplastics Elastomers Special Interest Group Scholarships *(Graduate, Undergraduate/Scholarship)* [6563]
Thompson Scholarship for Women in Safety

(Graduate/Scholarship) [1072]
Reuben Trane Scholarships (Undergraduate/Scholarship) [970]
Transfer Engineering Student Awards (Undergraduate/Scholarship) [4058]
Truss Plate Institute Scholarships (Doctorate/Scholarship) [6932]
Vice Adm. Jerry O. Tuttle, USN (Ret.) and Mrs. Barbara A. Tuttle Science and Technology Scholarships (Undergraduate/Scholarship) [1249]
UAA Quanterra Scholarships (Undergraduate/Scholarship) [7071]
United Engineering Foundation Grants (All/Grant) [6961]
U.S. Air Force ROTC Express Scholarships (Undergraduate/Scholarship) [6976]
University of Toronto Accenture Scholarships (Undergraduate/Scholarship) [7235]
Vale Inco Limited Masters Scholarships (Graduate/Scholarship) [1952]
Veolia ES Waste-to-Energy/Terrence L. Guest Memorial Awards (Graduate/Scholarship) [6599]
Dimitri J. Ververelli Memorial Scholarships (Undergraduate/Scholarship) [3536]
Lari Ann Vest Memorial Scholarships (Undergraduate/Scholarship) [809]
Veterans of Enduring Freedom (Afghanistan) and Iraqi Freedom Scholarships (Undergraduate/Scholarship) [1250]
Vinyl Plastics Division Scholarships (Graduate, Undergraduate/Scholarship) [6564]
Gary Wagner, K3OMI Scholarships (Undergraduate/Scholarship) [859]
Washington University Law School Chancellor's Graduate Fellowships (Graduate/Fellowship) [7386]
Allen and Loureena Weber Scholarships (Undergraduate/Scholarship) [6506]
William E. Weisel Scholarships (Undergraduate/Scholarship) [6507]
Ted C. Wilson Memorial Scholarships (Undergraduate/Scholarship) [5791]
Marine Corps Sgt. Jeannette L. Winters Memorial Scholarships (Undergraduate/Scholarship) [1251]
Women In Defense HORIZONS Scholarships (Graduate, Undergraduate/Scholarship) [7479]
Yasme Foundation Scholarships (Undergraduate/Scholarship) [863]
Ralph Yetka Memorial Scholarships (Undergraduate/Scholarship) [4391]

Engineering, Aerospace/Aeronautical/ Astronautical

DEPS Graduate Scholarship Program (Graduate/Scholarship) [2715]
Amelia Earhart Fellowship Program (Postdoctorate/Fellowship) [7563]

Engineering, Agricultural

International Code Council Foundation General Scholarship Fund (Undergraduate/Scholarship) [3828]
J.W. "Bill" Neese Scholarships (Undergraduate/Scholarship) [3829]
William J. Tangye Scholarships (Undergraduate/Scholarship) [3831]

Engineering, Architectural

AISC/Carolina Steel Scholarships (Undergraduate/Scholarship) [676]
AISC/Fred R. Havens Fellowships (Graduate, Undergraduate/Fellowship) [677]
AISC/Great Lakes Fabricators and Erectors Association Fellowships (Graduate/Fellowship) [678]
AISC/Rocky Mountain Steel Construction Association Fellowships (Graduate/Fellowship) [679]
AISC/Southern Association of Steel Fabricators Fellowships (Graduate/Fellowship) [680]
AISC/Southern Association of Steel Fabricators Scholarships (Undergraduate/Scholarship) [681]
AISC/Structural Steel Education Council Fellowships (Graduate/Fellowship) [682]
AISC/US Steel Fellowships (Graduate/Fellowship) [683]
Michael Baker Corporation Scholarship Program (Undergraduate/Scholarship) [1430]
Edilia and Francois Auguste de Montequin Fellowships (Doctorate/Scholarship) [6427]
HDR Engineering, Inc. Scholarship for Diversity in Engineering (Undergraduate/Scholarship) [1432]
PCH Architects/Steven J. Lehnhof Memorial Architectural Scholarships (Undergraduate/Scholarship) [5971]
Snodgrass Scholarships (Undergraduate/Scholarship) [4384]

Engineering, Automotive

Larry H. Averill Memorial Scholarships (Undergraduate/Scholarship) [1549]
Harold Dieckmann Draper, Sr. Scholarships (Undergraduate/Scholarship) [1550]
John E. Echlin Memorial Scholarships (Undergraduate/Scholarship) [1551]
Carlyle Fraser/Wilton Looney Scholarships (Undergraduate/Scholarship) [1552]
John Goerlich Memorial Scholarships (Undergraduate/Scholarship) [1553]
Charles V. Hagler Scholarships (Undergraduate/Scholarship) [1554]
Zenon C.R. Hansen Memorial Scholarships (Undergraduate/Scholarship) [1555]
John W. Koons, Sr. Memorial Scholarships (Undergraduate/Scholarship) [1556]
Ken Krum/Bud Kouts Memorial Scholarships (Undergraduate/Scholarship) [1557]
Brouwer D. McIntyre Memorial Scholarships (Undergraduate/Scholarship) [1558]
Jim Moran Scholarships (Undergraduate/Scholarship) [1559]
Dorothy M. Ross Memorial Scholarships (Undergraduate/Scholarship) [1560]
Stuart H. Snyder Memorial Scholarships (Undergraduate/Scholarship) [1561]
Society of Automotive Analyst Scholarships (Undergraduate/Scholarship) [1562]
Walter W. Stillman Scholarships (Undergraduate/Scholarship) [1563]
TRW Foundation Scholarships (Undergraduate/Scholarship) [1564]
Universal Underwriters Scholarships (Undergraduate/Scholarship) [1565]
J. Irving Whalley Memorial Scholarships (Undergraduate/Scholarship) [1566]
M.H. Yager Memorial Scholarships (Undergraduate/Scholarship) [1567]

Engineering, Biomedical

Biocom Scholarships (Undergraduate/Scholarship) [6173]
Toyota High School Scholarship Program (Undergraduate/Scholarship) [3603]

Engineering, Chemical

AIChE/Donald F. and Mildred Topp Othmer National Scholarship Awards (Undergraduate/Scholarship) [655]
Air Products and Chemicals, Inc. Scholarships (Undergraduate/Scholarship) [1429]
APS/ASU Scholarships (Undergraduate/Scholarship) [5697]
APS/Maricopa County Community Colleges Scholarships (Undergraduate/Scholarship) [5698]
DEPS Graduate Scholarship Program (Graduate/Scholarship) [2715]
Marathon Oil Corporation College Scholarship Program (Graduate, Undergraduate/Scholarship) [3600]
John J. McKetta Undergraduate Scholarships (Undergraduate/Scholarship) [656]
Minority Scholarship Awards for College Students (Undergraduate/Scholarship) [657]
Minority Scholarship Awards for Incoming College Freshmen (Undergraduate/Scholarship) [658]
Rubber Division American Chemical Society Scholarships (Undergraduate/Scholarship) [6079]
Evald Torokvei Foundation Scholarships (Graduate/Scholarship) [7234]
Toyota High School Scholarship Program (Undergraduate/Scholarship) [3603]

Engineering, Civil

AGC New York State Chapter Scholarship Program (Undergraduate/Scholarship) [1427]
AISC/Carolina Steel Scholarships (Undergraduate/Scholarship) [676]
AISC/Fred R. Havens Fellowships (Graduate, Undergraduate/Fellowship) [677]
AISC/Great Lakes Fabricators and Erectors Association Fellowships (Graduate/Fellowship) [678]
AISC/Rocky Mountain Steel Construction Association Fellowships (Graduate/Fellowship) [679]
AISC/Southern Association of Steel Fabricators Fellowships (Graduate/Fellowship) [680]
AISC/Southern Association of Steel Fabricators Scholarships (Undergraduate/Scholarship) [681]
AISC/Structural Steel Education Council Fellowships (Graduate/Fellowship) [682]
AISC/US Steel Fellowships (Graduate/Fellowship) [683]
Amos Joe Alter ASCE Section Alaska Section Scholarships (Undergraduate/Scholarship) [4344]
Arsham Amirikian Engineering Scholarships (Undergraduate/Scholarship) [1155]
APS/Maricopa County Community Colleges Scholarships (Undergraduate/Scholarship) [5698]
APWA Engineering Scholarships (Undergraduate/Scholarship) [806]
ASDSO Undergraduate Scholarships (Undergraduate/Scholarship) [1497]
Michael Baker Corporation Scholarship Program (Undergraduate/Scholarship) [1430]
Warren E. "Whitey" Cole American Society of Highway Engineers Scholarships (Undergraduate/Scholarship) [2947]
HDR Engineering, Inc. Scholarship for Diversity in Engineering (Undergraduate/Scholarship) [1432]
HSF/Wal-Mart Stores Inc. Scholarship Program (Graduate, Undergraduate/Scholarship) [3599]
International Association of Foundation Drilling Scholarships for Part-time Civil Engineering Graduate School Students (Postgraduate/Scholarship) [3799]
MALSE Scholarships (Undergraduate/Scholarship) [4326]
Marathon Oil Corporation College Scholarship Program (Graduate, Undergraduate/Scholarship) [3600]
Pardee Community Building Scholarships (Undergraduate/Scholarship) [5849]
Charles Smith Memorial Scholarship Awards (Undergraduate/Scholarship) [1321]
TAC Foundation-Armtec Scholarships (Undergraduate/Scholarship) [6900]
Toyota High School Scholarship Program (Undergraduate/Scholarship) [3603]
Verizon Scholarship Program (Undergraduate/Scholarship) [3607]
Larry Wilson Scholarships for Undergraduate Civil Engineering Students (Undergraduate/Scholarship) [1228]

Engineering, Computer

Zachary Barriger Memorial Scholarships (High School/Scholarship) [2262]
Chambersburg/Fannett-Metal School District Scholarship Fund (Undergraduate/Scholarship) [3092]
HSBC-North America Scholarship Program (Undergraduate/Scholarship) [3592]
HSF/Hewlett Packard (HP) Diversity in Education Scholarship Program (Undergraduate/Scholarship) [3596]
IBM Canada Undergraduate Scholarships (Undergraduate/Scholarship) [1951]
Toyota High School Scholarship Program (Undergraduate/Scholarship) [3603]

Verizon Scholarship Program (Undergraduate/Scholarship) [3607]

Engineering, Electrical

APS/ASU Scholarships (Undergraduate/Scholarship) [5697]
APS/Maricopa County Community Colleges Scholarships (Undergraduate/Scholarship) [5698]
Zachary Barriger Memorial Scholarships (High School/Scholarship) [2262]
DEPS Graduate Scholarship Program (Graduate/Scholarship) [2715]
Belknap Freeman Carnegie Mellon Scholarships (Undergraduate/Scholarship) [878]
Perry F. Hadlock Memorial Scholarships (Undergraduate/Scholarship) [837]
HSF/General Motors Scholarship Program (Undergraduate/Scholarship) [3595]
HSF/Hewlett Packard (HP) Diversity in Education Scholarship Program (Undergraduate/Scholarship) [3596]
HSF/Wal-Mart Stores Inc. Scholarship Program (Graduate, Undergraduate/Scholarship) [3599]
IBM Canada Undergraduate Scholarships (Undergraduate/Scholarship) [1951]
Julia Kiene Fellowship in Electrical Energy (Graduate/Fellowship) [7494]
Lyle Mamer Fellowships (Graduate/Fellowship) [7495]
Marathon Oil Corporation College Scholarship Program (Graduate, Undergraduate/Scholarship) [3600]
Edmond A. Metzger Scholarships (Undergraduate/Scholarship) [843]
NASA Aeronautics Scholarship Undergraduate Program (Undergraduate/Scholarship) [956]
Verizon Scholarship Program (Undergraduate/Scholarship) [3607]
WINUP Member Scholarships (Professional Development/Scholarship) [7496]

Engineering, Geological

HDR Engineering, Inc. Scholarship for Diversity in Engineering (Undergraduate/Scholarship) [1432]
Marliave Scholarship Fund (Undergraduate/Scholarship) [1409]
Rocky Mountain Coal Mining Institute Engineering/Geology Scholarships (Undergraduate/Scholarship) [6051]
Martin L. Stout Scholarships (Undergraduate/Scholarship) [1410]

Engineering, Hydraulic

Channabasappa Memorial Scholarships (Graduate, Professional Development/Scholarship) [3837]
IDA Fellowship Award (Professional Development/Fellowship) [3838]

Engineering, Industrial

Chapter 4 - Lawrence A. Wacker Memorial Awards (Undergraduate/Scholarship) [6473]
Chapter 17 - St. Louis Scholarships (Undergraduate/Scholarship) [6475]
Chapter 31 - Peoria Endowed Scholarships (Undergraduate/Scholarship) [6477]
Chapter 52 - Wichita Scholarships (Graduate, Undergraduate/Scholarship) [6478]
Chapter 56 - Fort Wayne Scholarships (Graduate, Undergraduate/Scholarship) [6479]
Chapter 67 - Phoenix Scholarships (Undergraduate/Scholarship) [6482]
Chapter 198 - Downriver Detroit Scholarships (Graduate, Undergraduate/Scholarship) [6484]
Chapter 311 - Tri City Scholarships (Undergraduate/Scholarship) [6485]
John S.W. Fargher Scholarships (Graduate/Scholarship) [3730]
Future Leaders of Manufacturing Scholarships (Graduate, Undergraduate/Scholarship) [6488]
Dwight D. Gardner Scholarships (Undergraduate/Scholarship) [3731]
Gilbreth Memorial Fellowships (Graduate/Scholarship) [3732]
HSF/General Motors Scholarship Program (Undergraduate/Scholarship) [3595]
HSF/Wal-Mart Stores Inc. Scholarship Program (Graduate, Undergraduate/Scholarship) [3599]
IIE Council of Fellows Undergraduate Scholarships (Undergraduate/Scholarship) [3733]
John L. Imhoff Scholarships (Graduate, Undergraduate/Scholarship) [3734]
Harold and Inge Marcus Scholarships (Undergraduate/Scholarship) [3735]
Marvin Mundel Memorial Scholarships (Undergraduate/Scholarship) [3736]
Clarence and Josephine Myers Scholarships (Graduate, Undergraduate/Scholarship) [6498]
Presidents Scholarships (Undergraduate/Scholarship) [3737]
A.O. Putnam Memorial Scholarships (Undergraduate/Scholarship) [3738]
Tom D. Ralls Memorial Scholarships (Professional Development/Scholarship) [3020]
United Parcel Service Scholarship for Female Students (Undergraduate/Scholarship) [3740]
United Parcel Service Scholarship for Minority Students (Undergraduate/Scholarship) [3741]
Verizon Scholarship Program (Undergraduate/Scholarship) [3607]
Allen and Loureena Weber Scholarships (Undergraduate/Scholarship) [6506]
Lisa Zaken Award For Excellence (Graduate, Undergraduate/Award/Prize) [3742]

Engineering, Marine

Marine Technology Society Student Scholarships for Two-year Technical, Engineering and Community College Students (Undergraduate/Scholarship) [4313]
Mandell and Lester Rosenblatt and Robert N. Herbert Undergraduate Scholarships (Undergraduate/Scholarship) [6519]
Society of Naval Architects and Marine Engineers Undergraduate Scholarships (Undergraduate/Scholarship) [6520]

Engineering, Materials

Electronics Division Lewis C. Hoffman Scholarships (Undergraduate/Scholarship) [453]

Engineering, Mechanical

Air Products and Chemicals, Inc. Scholarships (Undergraduate/Scholarship) [1429]
APS/Maricopa County Community Colleges Scholarships (Undergraduate/Scholarship) [5698]
Association of Desk and Derrick Clubs Education Trust Scholarships (Undergraduate/Scholarship) [1388]
Auxiliary Undergraduate Scholarships (Undergraduate/Scholarship) [995]
Chapter 4 - Lawrence A. Wacker Memorial Awards (Undergraduate/Scholarship) [6473]
Chapter 198 - Downriver Detroit Scholarships (Graduate, Undergraduate/Scholarship) [6484]
Lucy and Charles W.E. Clarke Scholarships (Undergraduate/Scholarship) [996]
HSF/General Motors Scholarship Program (Undergraduate/Scholarship) [3595]
Marathon Oil Corporation College Scholarship Program (Graduate, Undergraduate/Scholarship) [3600]
Clarence and Josephine Myers Scholarships (Graduate, Undergraduate/Scholarship) [6498]
NASA Aeronautics Scholarship Undergraduate Program (Undergraduate/Scholarship) [956]
Elizabeth M. and Winchell M. Parson Scholarships (Doctorate/Scholarship) [997]
Rice-Cullimore Scholarships (Graduate/Scholarship) [998]
Marjorie Roy Rothermel Scholarship (Graduate/Scholarship) [999]
Rubber Division American Chemical Society Scholarships (Undergraduate/Scholarship) [6079]
Verizon Scholarship Program (Undergraduate/Scholarship) [3607]
Allen and Loureena Weber Scholarships (Undergraduate/Scholarship) [6506]
Albert E. Wischmeyer Memorial Scholarships (Undergraduate/Scholarship) [6508]

Engineering, Mining and Mineral

Samuel C. Kraus, Jr. Memorial Scholarships (Undergraduate/Scholarship) [5096]
SME Coal and Energy Division Scholarships (Undergraduate/Scholarship) [6516]
SME Environmental Division Scholarships (Undergraduate/Scholarship) [6517]

Engineering, Naval

ASNE Scholarships (Graduate, Undergraduate/Scholarship) [1015]

Engineering, Nuclear

American Nuclear Society Incoming Freshman Scholarships (High School/Scholarship) [723]
American Nuclear Society Nevada Section Scholarships (Undergraduate/Scholarship) [5801]
American Nuclear Society Undergraduates Scholarships (Undergraduate/Scholarship) [724]
Association of Desk and Derrick Clubs Education Trust Scholarships (Undergraduate/Scholarship) [1388]

Engineering, Ocean

Mandell and Lester Rosenblatt and Robert N. Herbert Undergraduate Scholarships (Undergraduate/Scholarship) [6519]
Society of Naval Architects and Marine Engineers Undergraduate Scholarships (Undergraduate/Scholarship) [6520]

Engineering, Optical

BACUS Scholarships (Graduate, Undergraduate/Scholarship) [6695]
DEPS Graduate Scholarship Program (Graduate/Scholarship) [2715]
Michael Kidger Memorial Scholarships in Optical Design (Graduate/Scholarship) [6696]
D.J. Lovell Scholarships (Graduate, Undergraduate/Scholarship) [6698]
William H. Price Scholarships (Graduate, Undergraduate/Scholarship) [6699]
Student Travel Grants (Graduate, Undergraduate/Grant) [6700]

Engineering, Petroleum

Alaska Support Industry Alliance Scholarships (Undergraduate/Scholarship) [4341]
Association of Desk and Derrick Clubs Education Trust Scholarships (Undergraduate/Scholarship) [1388]
Marathon Oil Corporation College Scholarship Program (Graduate, Undergraduate/Scholarship) [3600]

English language and literature (See also: Literature; Linguistics)

Dick Depaolis Memorial Scholarships (Undergraduate/Scholarship) [2512]
Indiana State Alumni Association Creative and Performing Arts Award (Undergraduate/Scholarship) [3701]
NCTE Research Foundation Grants (Professional Development/Grant) [4826]
Susan P. Schroeder Memorial Scholarships (Undergraduate/Scholarship) [4215]
Edwyna Wheadon Postgraduate Training Scholarship Fund (Professional Development/Scholarship) [4827]

Entomology

AAPA Research Scholarships

(Undergraduate/Award/Prize) [393]

Environmental conservation

Bat Conservation International Student Research Scholarships *(Undergraduate/Scholarship)* [1601]
Antenore C. "Buth" Davanzo Scholarships *(Undergraduate/Scholarship)* [4503]
Delta/VPPPA Safety, Health and Environmental Scholarships *(Undergraduate/Scholarship)* [7338]
John P. Hennessy Scholarships *(Undergraduate/Scholarship)* [4504]
VPPPA William Sullivan Scholarships *(Graduate, Undergraduate/Scholarship)* [7339]
VPPPA June Brothers Scholarships *(Graduate, Undergraduate/Scholarship)* [7340]
VPPPA Stephen Brown Scholarships *(Graduate, Undergraduate/Scholarship)* [7341]
Jack H. Wagner Scholarships *(Undergraduate/Scholarship)* [4505]
Frederick K. Weyerhaeuser Forest History Fellowships *(Graduate/Fellowship)* [3031]

Environmental law

The Lela Breitbart Memorial Scholarship Fund *(All/Scholarship)* [6881]

Environmental science (See also: Ecology)

Avista Corporation Minds in Motion Scholarships *(Undergraduate/Scholarship)* [4163]
J.P. Bickell Mining Scholarships *(Undergraduate/Scholarship)* [7211]
Carol Bond College Scholarships *(Undergraduate/Scholarship)* [5230]
Carol Bond Environmental Educator Scholarships *(Professional Development/Scholarship)* [5231]
Carol Bond University Scholarships *(Undergraduate/Scholarship)* [5232]
The Robert A Catlin/David W. Long Memorial Scholarship *(Undergraduate/Scholarship)* [2996]
Chopivsky Fellowships *(Undergraduate/Scholarship)* [7358]
Frank L. Dautriel Memorial Scholarships (Graduate) *(Graduate/Scholarship)* [4257]
Frank L. Dautriel Memorial Scholarships (Undergraduate) *(Undergraduate/Scholarship)* [4258]
EMLF Law Student Scholarships *(Undergraduate/Scholarship)* [2855]
Grant H. Flint International Scholarships - Category II *(Undergraduate/Scholarship)* [6597]
Marjorie M. Hendricks Environmental Education Scholarships Fund *(Undergraduate/Scholarship)* [3285]
N.G. Kaul Memorial Scholarships *(Postdoctorate/Scholarship)* [5197]
Randall Matthis for Environmental Studies Scholarships *(Graduate, Undergraduate/Scholarship)* [1226]
Ben Meadows Natural Resource Scholarships - Academic Achievement Scholarships *(Undergraduate/Scholarship)* [1620]
Ben Meadows Natural Resource Scholarships - Leadership Scholarships *(Undergraduate/Scholarship)* [1621]
National Environmental Health Association Scholarship Fund *(Graduate, Undergraduate/Scholarship)* [4873]
New York Water Environment Association Scholarships *(Undergraduate/Scholarship)* [5198]
Eric Niemitalo Scholarships in Earth and Environmental Science *(Undergraduate/Scholarship)* [6318]
Republic Services Environmental Studies Scholarships *(Undergraduate/Scholarship)* [5855]
Royal Palm Audobon Society Environmental Fellowships *(Postgraduate/Fellowship)* [2998]
Miller G. Sherwood Family Scholarship Fund *(Undergraduate/Scholarship)* [3309]
Robert P. Stearns/SCS Engineers Awards *(Graduate/Scholarship)* [6598]
Judith A. Towle Environmental Studies Fund *(Undergraduate/Fellowship)* [3966]
Udall Scholarships *(Undergraduate/Scholarship)* [7089]
Veolia ES Waste-to-Energy/Terrence L. Guest Memorial Awards *(Graduate/Scholarship)* [6599]
WALPA Lake Scholarships *(Graduate, Undergraduate/Scholarship)* [7382]
Larry Wilson for Environmental Studies Scholarships *(Graduate, Undergraduate/Scholarship)* [1227]
Mary and Elliot Wood Foundation Graduate Scholarship Fund *(Graduate/Scholarship)* [3085]

Environmental technology

Arkansas Society of Professional Sanitarians Scholarships *(Undergraduate/Scholarship)* [1234]
Jim Bourque Scholarships *(Postgraduate/Scholarship)* [1200]
Frank L. Dautriel Memorial Scholarships (Graduate) *(Graduate/Scholarship)* [4257]
Frank L. Dautriel Memorial Scholarships (Undergraduate) *(Undergraduate/Scholarship)* [4258]
Charles and Margaret Foster Scholarships *(Undergraduate/Scholarship)* [6653]
Hamilton Industrial Environmental Association Bursaries-Mohawk College *(Undergraduate/Scholarship)* [3390]
Thompson Scholarship for Women in Safety *(Graduate/Scholarship)* [1072]
Morris K. Udall Scholarships *(Undergraduate/Scholarship)* [6945]

Epilepsy

Behavioral Sciences Post-Doctoral Fellowships *(Postdoctorate/Fellowship)* [2867]
Behavioral Sciences Student Fellowships *(Graduate, Undergraduate/Fellowship)* [2868]
Epilepsy Foundation Post-doctoral Research Fellowships *(Postdoctorate, Professional Development/Grant)* [2869]
Epilepsy Foundation Pre-doctoral Research Training Fellowships *(Graduate/Grant)* [2870]
Epilepsy Foundation Research Grants *(All/Grant)* [2871]
Epilepsy Foundation Research and Training Fellowships for Clinicians *(Doctorate, Professional Development/Grant)* [2872]
Health Sciences Student Fellowships *(Doctorate, Graduate/Fellowship)* [2873]
Partnership for Pediatric Epilepsy Research *(Doctorate/Grant)* [2874]
Targeted Research Initiative for Health Outcomes *(Doctorate/Grant)* [2875]
Targeted Research Initiative for Mood Disorders *(Doctorate/Grant)* [2876]
Targeted Research Initiative for Seniors *(Doctorate/Grant)* [2877]

Equine studies

Alabama Horse Council Scholarships *(Undergraduate/Scholarship)* [111]

Ethics and bioethics

ARRS/Leonard Berlin Scholarships in Medical Professionalism *(Professional Development/Scholarship)* [907]

European studies

Leo Baeck Fellowships Program *(Doctorate, Postdoctorate/Fellowship)* [2079]
ECA Alumni Small Grants Program *(Professional Development/Grant)* [3894]
Dr. Guido Goldman Fellowships *(Doctorate, Postdoctorate/Fellowship)* [503]
Individual Advanced Research Opportunities Program (IARO) For Master's Student *(Graduate/Grant)* [3895]
Individual Advanced Research Opportunities Program (IARO) For Pre-doctoral Students *(Postgraduate/Grant)* [3896]
Individual Advanced Research Opportunities Program (IARO) For Professionals *(Professional Development/Grant)* [3897]
Individual Advanced Research Opportunities Program (IARO) for Postdoctoral Scholars *(Postdoctorate/Grant)* [3898]
Kade-Heideking Fellowships *(Doctorate/Fellowship)* [3235]
Kress Curatorial Fellowships *(Doctorate/Fellowship)* [4100]
Kress Fellowships in Art History at Foreign Institutions *(Doctorate/Fellowship)* [4101]
Kress Travel Fellowships in the History of Art *(Doctorate/Fellowship)* [4102]
McGill University Scholarships for Research Trips to Europe *(Graduate/Scholarship)* [4431]
Thyssen-Heideking Fellowships *(Postdoctorate/Fellowship)* [3236]

Family/Marital therapy (See also: Rehabilitation, Physical/Psychological)

Roy Scrivner Research Grants *(Graduate, Postdoctorate/Grant)* [6137]

Family planning

Geraldine Clewell Fellowships - Doctoral Student *(Graduate/Fellowship)* [5659]
Geraldine Clewell Fellowships - Masteral *(Graduate/Fellowship)* [5660]
Geraldine Clewell Scholarships - Undergraduate *(Undergraduate/Scholarship)* [5661]
Closs/Parnitzke/Clarke Scholarships *(Undergraduate/Scholarship)* [5662]
Jean Dearth Dickerscheid Fellowships *(Graduate/Fellowship)* [5663]
Margaret Drew Alpha Fellowships *(Graduate/Fellowship)* [5664]
Lydia Fohn-Hansen/Lola Hill Memorial Scholarships *(Undergraduate/Scholarship)* [4357]
Genevieve Forthun Scholarships *(Undergraduate/Scholarship)* [5665]
Mary Weiking Franken Scholarships *(Undergraduate/Scholarship)* [5666]
Tommie J. Hamner Scholarships *(Undergraduate/Scholarship)* [5667]
Phyllis P. Harris Scholarships *(Postgraduate/Award/Prize)* [1956]
Jackman Scholarships *(Undergraduate/Scholarship)* [5668]
Martha Combs Jenkins Scholarships *(Undergraduate/Scholarship)* [5669]
Treva C. Kintner Scholarships *(Undergraduate/Scholarship)* [5670]
Dr. Henry Morgentaler Future Choice Scholarships *(Postgraduate/Award/Prize)* [1958]
Phi Upsilon Omicron Candle Fellowships *(Graduate/Fellowship)* [5671]
Phi Upsilon Omicron Challenge Scholarships *(Undergraduate/Scholarship)* [5672]
Phi Upsilon Omicron Diamond Anniversary Fellowships *(Graduate/Fellowship)* [5673]
Phi Upsilon Omicron Founders Fellowships *(Graduate/Fellowship)* [5674]
Phi Upsilon Omicron Golden Anniversary Scholarships *(Undergraduate/Scholarship)* [5675]
Phi Upsilon Omicron Past Presidents Scholarships *(Undergraduate/Scholarship)* [5676]
Phi Upsilon Omicron Presidents Research Fellowships *(Graduate/Fellowship)* [5677]
Nell Bryant Robinson Scholarships *(Undergraduate/Scholarship)* [5678]
Lucile Rust Scholarships *(Undergraduate/Scholarship)* [5679]
Margaret Jerome Sampson Scholarships *(Undergraduate/Scholarship)* [5680]
Lillian P. Schoephoerster Scholarships *(Undergraduate/Scholarship)* [5681]

Fashion design

Paul Arnold Memorial Scholarships *(Undergraduate/Scholarship)* [5750]
California Association of Family and Consumer Sciences (CAFCS)-San Diego Chapter Scholarships *(Graduate, Undergraduate/Scholarship)* [6177]
S. Penny Chappell Scholarships

(Undergraduate/Scholarship) [5658]
Hadar J. Chemtob Scholarship (Undergraduate/Scholarship) [3556]
GAP, Inc. Scholarships Award (Undergraduate/Scholarship) [3566]
Edith Head Scholarships (Undergraduate/Scholarship) [2688]
HSF/Wal-Mart Stores Inc. Scholarship Program (Graduate, Undergraduate/Scholarship) [3599]
Casey Sakir Point Scholarships (Graduate, Undergraduate/Scholarship) [5726]
Sutherland/Purdy Scholarships (Undergraduate/Scholarship) [5682]
Women's Jewelry Association Member Grants (All/Grant) [7498]
Women's Jewelry Association Scholarships (Undergraduate/Scholarship) [7499]
YMA Fashion Scholarships (Undergraduate/Scholarship) [7545]

Filmmaking (See also: Media arts)

AAS Fellowships for Creative and Performing Artists and Writers (All/Fellowship) [296]
David Rose Scholarships (Undergraduate/Scholarship) [942]
Steve Kaplan TV and Film Studies Scholarships (Professional Development/Scholarship) [946]
MANAA Media Scholarships (Graduate, Undergraduate/Scholarship) [4439]
McNamara Family Creative Arts Project Grants (Graduate, Undergraduate/Grant) [3601]

Finance (See also: Banking; Accounting)

ACUA Scholarships (Graduate, Undergraduate/Scholarship) [1381]
Herb Adrian Memorial Scholarship Fund (Undergraduate/Scholarship) [3036]
African American Network - Carolinas Scholarship Fund (Undergraduate/Scholarship) [3037]
AICPA Scholarships for Graduate Accounting Students (Postgraduate/Scholarship) [4641]
AICPA Scholarships for Minority Accounting Students (Undergraduate/Scholarship) [4642]
ALPFA Scholarship Programs (Postgraduate, Undergraduate/Scholarship) [1492]
American Society of Military Comptrollers National Scholarship Program (Undergraduate/Scholarship) [1011]
APS/ASU Scholarships (Undergraduate/Scholarship) [5697]
APS/Maricopa County Community Colleges Scholarships (Undergraduate/Scholarship) [5698]
ASCEND/ING Scholarships (Undergraduate/Scholarship) [4643]
ASWA 2-Year College Scholarships (Undergraduate/Scholarship) [1091]
ASWA Undergraduate Scholarships (Undergraduate/Scholarship) [1092]
Sharon D. Banks Undergraduate Memorial Scholarships (Undergraduate/Scholarship) [7508]
Donald J. Bristow Memorial Scholarship Program (Graduate, Undergraduate/Scholarship) [4655]
Stuart Cameron and Margaret McLeod Memorial Scholarships (SCMS) (Graduate, Undergraduate/Scholarship/Forgivable Loan) [3744]
Clark High School Academy of Finance Scholarships (Undergraduate/Scholarship) [5812]
Clark High School Alumni Leadership Circle Scholarships (Undergraduate/Scholarship) [5813]
Ernst and Young/Ascend Leadership Scholarship Program (Undergraduate/Scholarship) [4644]
Daniel B. Goldberg Scholarships (Other/Scholarship) [3264]
Frank L. Greathouse Government Accounting Scholarships (Other/Scholarship) [3265]
Hilb, Rogal and Hobbs Scholarships (Undergraduate/Scholarship) [7328]
Hispanic College Fund Scholarship Programs (Undergraduate/Scholarship) [3583]
HSBC-North America Scholarship Program (Undergraduate/Scholarship) [3592]
HSF/Citi Fellows Program (Undergraduate/Scholarship) [3594]
HSF/General Motors Scholarship Program (Undergraduate/Scholarship) [3595]
HSF/Wal-Mart Stores Inc. Scholarship Program (Graduate, Undergraduate/Scholarship) [3599]
IMA Memorial Education Fund Scholarships (MEF) (Graduate, Undergraduate/Scholarship/Forgivable Loan) [3746]
Robert A. Kleckner Scholarships (Undergraduate/Scholarship) [6663]
Anne Koby Legacy Scholarships (Undergraduate/Scholarship) [7509]
Douglas McRorie Memorial Scholarships (Doctorate, Graduate/Scholarship) [37]
Mark Miller Award (Graduate, Undergraduate/Scholarship) [4656]
Minorities in Government Finance Scholarships (Graduate, Undergraduate/Scholarship) [3266]
Robert E. and Judy More Scholarship Fund (Undergraduate/Scholarship) [2967]
NABA Corporate Scholarship Program (Graduate, Undergraduate/Scholarship) [4657]
NABA National Scholarship Program (Graduate, Undergraduate/Scholarship) [4658]
Networks Scholarships College of Business (Undergraduate/Scholarship) [3710]
New York Financial Writers' Associations Scholarships (Graduate, Undergraduate/Scholarship) [5189]
George A. Nielsen Public Investor Scholarships (Graduate, Undergraduate/Scholarship) [3267]
Norfolk Southern Scholarships (Undergraduate/Scholarship) [7329]
Helen M. Overly Memorial Scholarships (Undergraduate/Scholarship) [7510]
Phillip Morris USA Scholarships (Undergraduate/Scholarship) [7330]
Public Employee Retirement Research and Administration Scholarships (Graduate/Scholarship) [3268]
Dr. Felix H. Reyler Memorial Scholarships (Undergraduate/Scholarship) [2599]
Society of Automotive Analyst Scholarships (Undergraduate/Scholarship) [1562]
South Carolina Association for Financial Professionals Certified Treasury Professional Scholarships (Professional Development/Scholarship) [6610]
South Carolina Association for Financial Professionals College Education Scholarships (Undergraduate/Scholarship) [6611]
Surety Industry Scholarship Program for Minority Students (Undergraduate/Scholarship) [6824]
TDC Scholarship Program (Graduate, Undergraduate/Scholarship) [4659]
Ralph and Valerie Thomas Scholarship Program (Graduate, Undergraduate/Scholarship) [4660]
Travis C. Tomlin Memorial Scholarship Program (Graduate, Undergraduate/Scholarship) [4661]
Tribal Business Management Program (TBM) Scholarships (Undergraduate/Scholarship) [2069]
Urban Financial Services Coalition Scholarships (Undergraduate/Award/Prize) [1744]
Verizon Scholarship Program (Undergraduate/Scholarship) [3607]
Wachovia Scholarship Awards (Undergraduate/Scholarship) [3571]
Wall-Mart Stores, Inc. Fellowships - Graduate (Undergraduate/Scholarship) [643]
Thomas S. Watson, Jr. Memorial Scholarships (Graduate, Undergraduate/Scholarship) [4662]
Wells Fargo American Indian Scholarship for Graduates (Graduate/Scholarship) [644]
Wells Fargo Scholarship Program (Graduate, Undergraduate/Scholarship) [3608]
Herbert W. Whiteman, Jr. Scholarships (Graduate, Undergraduate/Scholarship) [7293]

Fires and fire prevention

Randall Brown and Associates Awards (Postgraduate/Award/Prize) [1962]
Fire Safety Awards (Postgraduate/Award/Prize) [1963]
Junior Firefighter Scholarships (Undergraduate/Scholarship) [5121]
Leber Rubes Inc. Awards (Postgraduate/Award/Prize) [1964]
Joseph C. Menezes Scholarships (Undergraduate/Scholarship) [4276]
Nadine International Inc. Awards (Postgraduate/Award/Prize) [1965]
Rachael Patterson Memorial Scholarships (Undergraduate/Scholarship) [6846]
Pennsylvania Association of Arson Investigators Scholarships (Undergraduate/Scholarship) [5555]
Snodgrass Scholarships (Undergraduate/Scholarship) [4384]
Peter Stainsby Awards (Postgraduate/Award/Prize) [1973]
Thompson Scholarship for Women in Safety (Graduate/Scholarship) [1072]
Underwriters' Laboratories of Canada Awards (Postgraduate/Award/Prize) [1966]
John Charles Wilson Scholarships (Undergraduate/Scholarship) [3784]

Fisheries sciences/management

Jack B. Fisher Scholarship Fund (Undergraduate/Scholarship) [6718]
Ben Meadows Natural Resource Scholarships - Academic Achievement Scholarships (Undergraduate/Scholarship) [1620]
Ben Meadows Natural Resource Scholarships - Leadership Scholarships (Undergraduate/Scholarship) [1621]
Ronald L. Schmied Scholarships (Professional Development, Undergraduate/Grant) [3388]

Folklore

Muddy Waters Scholarships (Undergraduate/Scholarship) [1768]

Food science and technology

AACT Undergraduate Scholarships (Undergraduate/Scholarship) [5711]
American Institute of Baking Scholarships (Undergraduate/Scholarship) [650]
Margaret J. Andrew Memorial Scholarships (Undergraduate/Scholarship) [6344]
California Association of Family and Consumer Sciences (CAFCS)-San Diego Chapter Scholarships (Graduate, Undergraduate/Scholarship) [6177]
Delta Daily Food (Canada) Inc. Scholarships (Undergraduate/Scholarship) [3847]
Food Engineering Scholarships (Postdoctorate, Postgraduate/Scholarship) [3024]
William A. Hipp Scholarships (All/Scholarship) [4336]
Institute of Food Technologists Graduate Scholarships (Graduate/Scholarship) [3724]
Institute of Food Technologists Junior/Senior Scholarships (Undergraduate/Scholarship) [3725]
Institute of Food Technologists Sophomore Scholarships (Undergraduate/Scholarship) [3726]
International Foodservice Editorial Council Scholarships (Graduate, Undergraduate/Scholarship) [3852]
E.H. Marth Food and Environmental Scholarships (Undergraduate/Scholarship) [7470]
National Candy Technologist Scholarship Program (Undergraduate/Scholarship) [332]
National Poultry and Food Distributors Association Scholarships (Undergraduate/Scholarship) [5013]
PMCA Graduate Fellowships at Pennsylvania State University (Graduate/Fellowship) [5712]
V. Duane Rath Graduate Research Fellowships (Doctorate, Graduate, Postdoctorate/Fellowship) [3025]
Stark County Dairy Promoters Scholarships (Undergraduate/Scholarship) [6755]
John D. Utterback Undergraduate Scholarships (Undergraduate/Scholarship) [230]

Food service careers

Harvey and Laura Alpert Scholarship Award (Undergraduate/Scholarship) [3845]
California Association of Family and Consumer Sci-

ences (CAFCS)-San Diego Chapter Scholarships *(Graduate, Undergraduate/Scholarship)* [6177]
Leticia B. Carter Scholarships *(All/Scholarship)* [4321]
Nancy Curry Scholarships *(Postgraduate/Scholarship)* [6256]
Food Engineering Scholarships *(Postdoctorate, Postgraduate/Scholarship)* [3024]
GED Jump Start Scholarships *(Other/Scholarship)* [6257]
Marcia S. Harris Legacy Fund Scholarships *(Undergraduate/Scholarship)* [4322]
The Erika A. Hayes Scholarships *(Undergraduate/Scholarship)* [4323]
Hospitality Food Service Scholarships *(Undergraduate/Scholarship)* [5168]
IFSEA Worthy Goal Scholarships *(Four Year College, Two Year College/Scholarship)* [3850]
International Dairy-Deli-Bakery Association Undergraduate Scholarships *(Graduate, Undergraduate/Scholarship)* [3835]
International Foodservice Editorial Council Scholarships *(Graduate, Undergraduate/Scholarship)* [3852]
Maryland Hospitality Education Foundation Co-Branded Scholarships *(Undergraduate/Scholarship)* [4324]
V. Duane Rath Graduate Research Fellowships *(Doctorate, Graduate, Postdoctorate/Fellowship)* [3025]
Al Schuman Ecolab Undergraduate Entrepreneurial Scholarships *(Undergraduate/Scholarship)* [5032]
Schwan's Food Service Scholarships *(Undergraduate/Scholarship)* [6258]
Jeff Siegel Scholarships *(Undergraduate/Scholarship)* [5191]
SNF Professional Growth Scholarships *(Graduate, Undergraduate/Scholarship)* [6259]
UAA Wells Fargo Career Scholarships *(Graduate/Scholarship)* [7073]
Winston Scholarships *(Graduate, Undergraduate/Scholarship)* [6260]

Foreign languages

Julie Allen World Classroom Scholarships *(Undergraduate/Scholarship)* [6164]
Pete and Ellen Bensley Memorial Scholarship Fund *(Undergraduate/Scholarship)* [3041]
Cemanahuac Educational Community Scholarships *(Other/Scholarship)* [5263]
Palo Verde High School - Barbara Edwards Memorial Scholarships *(Undergraduate/Scholarship)* [5820]
French Embassy Scholarships *(Other/Scholarship)* [5264]
German Society Scholarships *(Undergraduate/Scholarship)* [3238]
Goethe-Institut AATG Scholarships *(Other/Scholarship)* [5265]
Michael J. Hogan Fellowships *(Graduate/Fellowship)* [6457]
ISCALC International Scholarship Fund *(Undergraduate/Scholarship)* [2960]
Louise Nader Khourey/Kappa Delta Pi Scholarships *(Undergraduate/Scholarship)* [6734]
Language Teacher Bursary Program Awards *(Professional Development/Award/Prize)* [164]
Languages In Teacher Education Scholarships *(Professional Development/Scholarship)* [165]
MACC Scholarships *(Professional Development/Scholarship)* [4466]
Mead Leadership Fellows Program *(Professional Development/Fellowship)* [5266]
National Security Education Program Fellowships *(Undergraduate/Fellowship)* [7093]
Spanish Embassy Scholarships *(Graduate, Other/Scholarship)* [5267]
Starr Foundation Graduate Fellowship in Asian Studies *(Graduate/Grant)* [7094]
Audrey L. Wright Scholarships *(Undergraduate/Scholarship)* [3358]

Forestry

Chopivsky Fellowships *(Undergraduate/Scholarship)* [7358]
Robert E. Dougherty Scholarships *(Undergraduate/Scholarship)* [2525]
James L. and Genevieve H. Goodwin Scholarships *(Undergraduate/Scholarship)* [3454]
Ben Meadows Natural Resource Scholarships - Academic Achievement Scholarships *(Undergraduate/Scholarship)* [1620]
Ben Meadows Natural Resource Scholarships - Leadership Scholarships *(Undergraduate/Scholarship)* [1621]
Dr. Harry V. Pfautz Memorial Scholarship Fund *(Undergraduate/Scholarship)* [3114]
Ina E. Powell Memorial Scholarships *(Undergraduate/Scholarship)* [115]
Frederick K. Weyerhaeuser Forest History Fellowships *(Graduate/Fellowship)* [3031]

French studies (See also: Area and ethnic studies)

Alliance Francaise of Hartford Harpin/Rohinsky Scholarships *(Undergraduate/Scholarship)* [3413]
Fellowships for Full-time Studies in French *(Undergraduate/Fellowship)* [156]
Walter J. Jensen Fellowships *(Professional Development/Fellowship)* [5622]
Mary Isabel Sibley Fellowships *(Doctorate/Fellowship)* [5623]

Funeral services (See also: Mortuary science)

ABFSE National Scholarship Program *(Undergraduate/Scholarship)* [441]
Bishop State Community College Scholarships *(Undergraduate/Scholarship)* [4907]
NFDA Professional Women's Conference Scholarships *(Undergraduate/Scholarship)* [3152]
Vincennes University Scholarships *(Undergraduate/Scholarship)* [4909]

Gaming industry

Wall-Mart Stores, Inc. Fellowships - Graduate *(Undergraduate/Scholarship)* [643]
Wells Fargo American Indian Scholarship for Graduates *(Graduate/Scholarship)* [644]

Gemology

Jack Abelson Scholarships *(Graduate/Scholarship)* [3171]
William Argo Scholarships *(Undergraduate/Scholarship)* [3172]
Michael Beaudry Scholarships *(Graduate/Scholarship)* [3173]
ColorMasters Scholarships *(Undergraduate/Scholarship)* [3174]
Dennis Foltz Scholarships *(Graduate/Scholarship)* [3175]
Eye On Jewels Scholarships *(Undergraduate/Scholarship)* [3176]
GIA Endowment Scholarships - Distance Education *(Graduate/Scholarship)* [3177]
GIA Endowment Scholarships - On Campus *(Graduate/Scholarship)* [3178]
GIA Endowment Scholarships - School of Business *(Undergraduate/Scholarship)* [3179]
Ray Glynn Scholarships *(Undergraduate/Scholarship)* [3180]
Marion H. Halfacre Scholarships *(Graduate/Scholarship)* [3181]
Morris Hanauer Scholarships *(Undergraduate/Scholarship)* [3182]
The Jhaveri Scholarships *(Graduate/Scholarship)* [3184]
George W. Juno Memorial Scholarships *(Graduate/Scholarship)* [3185]
Robert Kammerling Scholarships *(Graduate/Scholarship)* [3186]
Kazanjian Scholarships *(Undergraduate/Scholarship)* [3187]
Richard Kern Scholarships *(Undergraduate/Scholarship)* [3188]
Richard T. Liddicoat Scholarships *(Graduate/Scholarship)* [3189]
James R. Lucey Scholarships *(Graduate/Scholarship)* [3191]
Irene Mack Scholarships *(Undergraduate/Scholarship)* [3192]
Vincent Manson Scholarships *(Graduate/Scholarship)* [3193]
Mikimoto Scholarships *(Graduate/Scholarship)* [3194]
Matthew A. Runci, MJSA Scholarships *(Undergraduate/Scholarship)* [3197]
S.H. Silver Scholarships *(Graduate/Scholarship)* [3198]
Daniel Swarovski and Company Scholarships *(Graduate/Scholarship)* [3199]
Trillion Diamond Company Scholarships *(Undergraduate/Scholarship)* [3200]
Kurt Wayne Scholarships *(Graduate/Scholarship)* [3201]
William Goldberg Diamond Corp. Scholarships *(Undergraduate/Scholarship)* [3203]

Genealogy

ASG Scholar Awards *(Professional Development/Scholarship)* [960]

General studies/Field of study not specified

4th Infantry Division Association Scholarships *(Four Year College, Postgraduate, Two Year College/Scholarship)* [4613]
The "21" Endowed Scholarships *(Undergraduate/Scholarship)* [4160]
92109 Community Fund-Mark and Karla Stuart Family Scholarships *(Undergraduate/Scholarship)* [6161]
AAAA Scholarship Program *(Undergraduate/Scholarship)* [1299]
AABA Read Carlock Memorial Scholarship Fund *(Professional Development/Scholarship)* [1206]
AAIB Scholarships *(Undergraduate/Scholarship)* [355]
AAS-American Society for Eighteenth Century Studies Fellowships *(Postdoctorate/Fellowship)* [295]
AAS CIAC Small Grants *(Graduate, Other/Grant)* [1370]
AAS Korean Studies Scholarship Program *(Doctorate, Graduate/Scholarship)* [1371]
AAUW Legal Advocacy Fund American Fellowships *(Doctorate/Fellowship)* [4]
AAUW Legal Advocacy Fund Career Development Grants *(Professional Development/Grant)* [5]
AAUW Legal Advocacy Fund International Fellowships *(Doctorate, Graduate/Fellowship)* [6]
ABA Members Scholarships (ABA Bus and Tour Operators Only) *(Undergraduate/Scholarship)* [447]
Anthony Abbene Scholarships *(Undergraduate/Scholarship)* [3635]
Clifford V. Abbott Memorial Scholarships *(Undergraduate/Scholarship)* [6766]
Abbott Scholarships *(Undergraduate/Scholarship)* [6822]
Alejandro "Alex" Abecia Reaching High Scholarships *(Undergraduate/Scholarship)* [2259]
Abercrombie and Fitch Global Diversity Scholar Awards *(High School/Scholarship)* [5066]
The Frederick B. Abramson Memorial Foundation Scholarships *(Undergraduate/Scholarship)* [11]
ACE K-12 Scholarships Program *(High School/Scholarship)* [234]
ACHE/American Legion Auxiliary Scholarships *(Undergraduate/Scholarship)* [98]
ACHE/American Legion Scholarships *(Undergraduate/Scholarship)* [99]
ACHE Junior and Community College Athletic Scholarships *(Undergraduate/Scholarship)* [100]
ACHE Police Officers and Firefighters Survivors' Educational Assistance Programs

(Undergraduate/Scholarship) [102]
ACHE Senior Adult Scholarships (Two Year College, Undergraduate/Scholarship) [103]
ACHE Two-Year College Academic Scholarships (Two Year College, Undergraduate/Scholarship) [104]
Ken and Pat Ackerman Family Scholarship Fund (Undergraduate/Scholarship) [2938]
Wayne D. Ackerman Family Scholarship Fund (Undergraduate/Scholarship) [6707]
Nancy Ashley Adams/Ashley Adams Koetje Scholarships (Undergraduate/Scholarship) [2635]
Adams Family Scholarships (Undergraduate/Scholarship) [2636]
Ruth D. Adams Fund (Undergraduate/Scholarship) [2939]
Mamie Adams Memorial Awards (Undergraduate/Scholarship) [4161]
The Clarke B. Adams Memorial Foundation Lapeer County Community Foundation Fund (Undergraduate/Scholarship) [4138]
Lt. Holly Adams Memorial Scholarship (Undergraduate/Scholarship) [2404]
Ruth Adams Memorial Scholarships (Undergraduate/Scholarship) [5903]
Henry S. and Carolyn Adams Scholarship Fund (Undergraduate/Scholarship) [3035]
Frederick G. Adams Scholarships (Undergraduate/Scholarship) [3411]
Carl Joseph Adelhardt Memorial Scholarships (Undergraduate/Scholarship) [3167]
Adelson Family Scholarships (Undergraduate/Scholarship) [5798]
ADGEF Scholarships (All/Scholarship) [246]
Bob Adkins Memorial Scholarships (Undergraduate/Scholarship) [5462]
Chris Nance Adler Scholarship Fund (High School/Scholarship) [2260]
Adoptive Families Today Commemorative Scholarships (Undergraduate/Scholarship) [24]
Adults Students in Scholastic Transition (ASIST) (All/Scholarship) [2894]
AFIA Scholarships (Undergraduate/Scholarship) [573]
AFSA Chapter 155 Division 1 Scholarships - Category 1 (Undergraduate/Scholarship) [56]
AFSA Chapter 155 Division 1 Scholarships - Category 2 (Undergraduate/Scholarship) [57]
AFSA Chapter 155 Division 1 Scholarships - Category 3 (Undergraduate/Scholarship) [58]
AFSA Scholarship Program (Undergraduate/Scholarship) [54]
After-the-Fires Scholarships (Undergraduate/Scholarship) [6163]
Patty Ahearn Victoria Elementary Scholarships (Undergraduate/Scholarship) [5904]
Ahepa Buckeye Scholarship Awards (Undergraduate/Scholarship) [42]
Ahepa District No. 1 Scholarship Program (Graduate, Undergraduate/Scholarship) [44]
AIBS Junior Fellowships (Doctorate/Fellowship) [652]
AIBS Senior Fellowships (Doctorate, Postdoctorate/Fellowship) [653]
AIDS Awareness Scholarships (Undergraduate/Scholarship) [6093]
AIGC Fellowship for Graduates (Graduate/Fellowship) [641]
AIMS Long-term Research Grants (Postdoctorate/Grant) [667]
AIMS Short-term Research Grants (Postdoctorate/Grant) [668]
Air Force ROTC Enhanced HBCU Scholarships (Undergraduate/Scholarship) [6972]
Airports Council International-North America Scholarship (Graduate, Undergraduate/Scholarship) [94]
AIST San Francisco Chapter Scholarships (Undergraduate/Scholarship) [1442]
Al Mercury Scholarships (Undergraduate/Scholarship) [7209]
Alabama Gi Dependents Educational Benefit Programs (Undergraduate/Scholarship) [105]
Alabama National Guard Educational Assistance Programs (Undergraduate/Scholarship) [106]
Alabama Power Scholarships (Undergraduate/Scholarship) [5275]
Alabama Scholarships for Dependents of Blind Parents (Undergraduate/Scholarship) [107]
Alabama Student Assistance Programs (Undergraduate/Scholarship) [108]
Alabama Student Grant Programs (Undergraduate/Grant) [109]
Alaska Kidney Foundation-ASN Research Grants (Doctorate/Grant) [1017]
Alaska Native Medical Center Auxiliary Scholarships (Undergraduate/Scholarship) [4339]
Alaska Yukon Pioneer Memorial Scholarships (Undergraduate/Scholarship) [4343]
Alberta Centennial Premier's Scholarships - Alberta (Undergraduate/Scholarship) [146]
Alberta Press Council Scholarships (Undergraduate/Scholarship) [187]
Alberta Ukrainian Centennial Commemorative Scholarships (Undergraduate/Scholarship) [7356]
Victor Albright Scholarships-Dane County (Undergraduate/Scholarship) [7246]
Victor Albright Scholarships (Undergraduate/Scholarship) [7247]
Albuquerque Lesbian and Gay Chamber of Commerce Scholarships (Undergraduate/Scholarship) [6094]
ALD Graduate Fellowships (Undergraduate/Fellowship) [4634]
Anne L. Alexander and Blaise Robert Alexander Memorial Scholarships (Undergraduate/Scholarship) [2940]
Hon. Lincoln Alexander Scholarships (Undergraduate/Scholarship) [1724]
Horatio Alger Ak-Sar-Ben Scholarships (Undergraduate/Scholarship) [198]
Horatio Alger Alabama Scholarships (Undergraduate/Scholarship) [199]
Horatio Alger California and California Orange County Scholarships (Undergraduate/Scholarship) [200]
Horatio Alger Delaware Scholarships (Undergraduate/Scholarship) [201]
Horatio Alger District of Columbia, Maryland, and Virginia Scholarships (Undergraduate/Scholarship) [202]
Horatio Alger Florida Scholarships (Undergraduate/Scholarship) [203]
Horatio Alger Franklin Scholarships (Undergraduate/Scholarship) [204]
Horatio Alger Georgia Scholarships (Undergraduate/Scholarship) [205]
Horatio Alger Idaho University Scholarships (Undergraduate/Scholarship) [206]
Horatio Alger Illinois Scholarships (Undergraduate/Scholarship) [207]
Horatio Alger Indiana Scholarships (Undergraduate/Scholarship) [208]
Horatio Alger Iowa Scholarships (Undergraduate/Scholarship) [209]
Horatio Alger Kentucky Scholarships (Undergraduate/Scholarship) [210]
Horatio Alger Lola and Duane Hagadone Idaho Scholarships (Undergraduate/Scholarship) [211]
Horatio Alger Louisiana Scholarships (Undergraduate/Scholarship) [212]
Horatio Alger Minnesota Scholarships (Undergraduate/Scholarship) [213]
Horatio Alger Mississippi Scholarships (Undergraduate/Scholarship) [214]
Horatio Alger Missouri Scholarships (Undergraduate/Scholarship) [215]
Horatio Alger Montana Scholarships (Undergraduate/Scholarship) [216]
Horatio Alger National Scholarships (Undergraduate/Scholarship) [217]
Horatio Alger New Jersey Scholarships (Undergraduate/Scholarship) [218]
Horatio Alger New York Scholarships (Undergraduate/Scholarship) [219]
Horatio Alger North Dakota Scholarships (Undergraduate/Scholarship) [220]
Horatio Alger Oregon Scholarships (Undergraduate/Scholarship) [221]
Horatio Alger Pennsylvania Scholarships (Undergraduate/Scholarship) [222]
Horatio Alger South Dakota Scholarships (Undergraduate/Scholarship) [223]
Horatio Alger Texas - Fort Worth Scholarships (Undergraduate/Scholarship) [224]
Horatio Alger Texas Scholarships (Undergraduate/Scholarship) [225]
Horatio Alger Utah Scholarships (Undergraduate/Scholarship) [226]
Horatio Alger Washington Scholarships (Undergraduate/Scholarship) [227]
Horatio Alger Wyoming Scholarships (Undergraduate/Scholarship) [228]
Paul Shearman Allen and Associate Scholarships (Undergraduate/Scholarship) [7003]
Robinson G. Allen Athletic Memorial Scholarships (Undergraduate/Scholarship) [5905]
Allen (Dan) Memorial Scholarships (Undergraduate/Scholarship) [6095]
William A. Allen Memorial Metal Shop/Auto Body Scholarships (Undergraduate/Scholarship) [5906]
Allen - Marty Allen Scholarships (High School, Undergraduate/Scholarship) [2261]
Alliance for Academic Achievement Program Scholarships (Undergraduate/Scholarship) [3412]
Dorothy G. Allsop Scholarships (Undergraduate/Scholarship) [4721]
Alpha Chi Sigma Scholarship Award (Graduate, Undergraduate/Award/Prize) [244]
Alpha Eta Scholarships (Undergraduate/Scholarship) [2638]
Alpha Kappa Alpha - Educational Advancement Foundation Financial Need-Based Scholarships (Graduate, Undergraduate/Scholarship) [248]
Alpha Kappa Alpha - Educational Advancement Foundation Merit Scholarships (Graduate, Undergraduate/Scholarship) [249]
Alpha Rho Leadership Scholarships (Undergraduate/Scholarship) [2639]
Justin Scot Alston Memorial Scholarships (Undergraduate/Scholarship) [3636]
Altrusa International of Grand Rapids Scholarships (Undergraduate/Scholarship) [3319]
Lou Amen Legacy Scholarship (Undergraduate/Scholarship) [1819]
American Association of University Women International Fellowships (All/Fellowship) [425]
American Composites Manufacturers Association Scholarships (Undergraduate/Scholarship) [477]
American Composites Manufacturers Association Western Chapter Scholarships (Undergraduate/Scholarship) [478]
American Council of Learned Societies Fellowships (Postdoctorate/Fellowship) [508]
American Dream Scholarship Program (Undergraduate/Scholarship) [6155]
American Fire Sprinkler Association Scholarships (Undergraduate/Scholarship) [3414]
American Foreign Service Association Scholarship Fund (Undergraduate/Scholarship) [575]
American GI Forum of San Jose Scholarships (Undergraduate/Scholarship) [595]
American Indian Endowed Scholarships (Graduate, Undergraduate/Scholarship) [7363]
American Kidney Fund's Patient Scholarship Program (Other/Scholarship) [690]
American Legion Boys/Girls State Scholarships (Undergraduate/Scholarship) [4162]
American Legion Eagle Scout of the Year Scholarships (High School/Scholarship) [4850]
The American Legion Legacy Scholarships (Undergraduate/Scholarship) [694]
The American Legion National High School Oratorical Scholarships Contest (Undergraduate/Scholarship) [695]
American Paint Horse Foundation Scholarships (Undergraduate/Scholarship) [755]
American Savings Foundation Scholarships (Undergraduate/Scholarship) [3416]
American Society for Microbiology Undergraduate Research Fellowships (Undergraduate/Fellowship) [1004]
American Water Ski Educational Foundation Scholarships (Undergraduate/Scholarship) [1140]
Americans for Informed Democracy Global Scholar Tuition (Undergraduate/Scholarship) [1176]
Amherst College Connecticut Alumni Scholarships (Undergraduate/Scholarship) [3417]

Bernard Amtmann Fellowships *(Postgraduate/Grant)* [1698]
AMVETS National Scholarships - Entering College Freshmen *(Undergraduate/Scholarship)* [1133]
AMVETS National Scholarships - For Veterans *(Undergraduate/Scholarship)* [1134]
AMVETS National Scholarships - JROTC *(Undergraduate/Scholarship)* [1135]
Anaheim Police Survivors and Scholarship Fund *(Undergraduate/Scholarship)* [1178]
Anchor Scholarship Foundation *(Undergraduate/Scholarship)* [6826]
Andersen Nontraditional Scholarship for Women's Education and Retraining *(Undergraduate/Scholarship)* [3039]
Judge Isaac Anderson, Jr. Scholarships *(Undergraduate/Scholarship)* [6640]
Wilbur H. Anderson Memorial Scholarships *(Undergraduate/Scholarship)* [1182]
Jane E. Anderson Scholarships *(Undergraduate/Scholarship)* [2640]
Kathy D. and Stephen J. Anderson Scholarships *(Undergraduate/Scholarship)* [2405]
Warren M. Anderson Scholarships *(Undergraduate/Scholarship)* [3698]
Cindy Andrews Educational Scholarships *(Undergraduate/Scholarship)* [5907]
William H. Andrews/HAWS Scholarships *(Undergraduate/Scholarship)* [7419]
Angus Foundation Scholarships *(Undergraduate/Scholarship)* [4967]
Jack Anson Fellowships *(Graduate/Fellowship)* [5220]
APA Minority Fellowships Program *(Postdoctorate/Fellowship)* [1334]
APC Scholarships *(Undergraduate/Scholarship)* [131]
APC Tuition-Assist Scholarship Awards *(Graduate, Undergraduate/Scholarship)* [30]
APDA Research Grants *(Professional Development/Grant)* [758]
APIASF Scholarships *(Undergraduate/Scholarship)* [1340]
Apple Scholars *(Undergraduate/Scholarship)* [6096]
APPMA's Jules Schwimmer Scholarship Program *(Undergraduate/Scholarship)* [765]
APT US&C Scholarships *(All/Scholarship)* [1483]
Frank G. Araujo Memorial Scholarships *(Undergraduate/Scholarship)* [5909]
A.R.F.O.R.A. Undergraduate Scholarships for Women *(Undergraduate/Scholarship)* [909]
Arizona Christian School Tuition Organization Scholarships *(Undergraduate/Scholarship)* [1214]
Rick Arkans Eagle Scout Scholarships *(High School/Scholarship)* [4851]
Arkansas State University Mountain Home Scholarships *(Undergraduate/Scholarship)* [4906]
Connie "Chelo" Armendariz Memorial Scholarships *(Undergraduate/Scholarship)* [5910]
Armenian American Citizen's League Scholarships *(Undergraduate/Scholarship)* [1266]
Armenian General Athletic Union Scholarships *(Undergraduate/Scholarship)* [1269]
Armenian Professional Society Scholarship Fund *(Graduate/Scholarship)* [1257]
Armenian Relief Society Scholarships *(Graduate, Undergraduate/Scholarship)* [1270]
Armenian Scholarship Foundation Scholarships *(Graduate, Undergraduate/Scholarship)* [1262]
Aaron Edward Arnoldsen Memorial Scholarships *(Undergraduate/Scholarship)* [1308]
Judge Sidney M. Aronovitz Memorial Scholarships *(High School/Scholarship)* [2594]
Merle Aronson Point Scholarships *(Graduate, Undergraduate/Scholarship)* [5714]
A.R.O.Y. Stanitz Scholarships *(Undergraduate/Scholarship)* [910]
ARREOLA/CBSPM Scholarships *(Undergraduate/Scholarship)* [6166]
Chester Arzell and Helen Miller Montgomery Scholarships *(Undergraduate/Scholarship)* [7420]
ASBA College Scholarship Program *(Undergraduate/Scholarship)* [918]
ASBC Foundation Undergraduate Scholarships *(Undergraduate/Scholarship)* [923]
William and Lucille Ash Scholarships *(Undergraduate/Scholarship)* [6167]
Asian American Scholarships *(Undergraduate/Scholarship)* [7004]
Asian/Pacific Gays and Friends Scholarships *(Undergraduate/Scholarship)* [6097]
Asian and Pacific Islander Queers Sisters Scholarships *(Undergraduate/Scholarship)* [5751]
ASIS Foundation Chapter Matching Scholarships *(Undergraduate/Scholarship)* [1342]
Michael M. Assarian Scholarships *(Undergraduate/Scholarship)* [1271]
Darrell and Palchie Asselin Scholarships *(Undergraduate/Scholarship)* [2771]
Association for the Advancement of Baltic Studies Dissertation Grants for Graduate Students *(Doctorate/Grant)* [1348]
Association on American Indian Affairs Emergency Aid Scholarship *(Undergraduate/Scholarship)* [630]
Association for Compensatory Educators of Texas Paraprofessionals Scholarships *(Undergraduate/Scholarship)* [1385]
Association for Compensatory Educators of Texas Scholarships *(Undergraduate/Scholarship)* [1386]
Association of Universities and Colleges of Canada Public Scholarships *(Undergraduate/Scholarship)* [1504]
Athletic Equipment Managers Association College Scholarships *(Undergraduate/Scholarship)* [1531]
Atlanta Alumnae Achievement Scholarships *(Undergraduate/Scholarship)* [2641]
Atlantic Provinces Library Association Memorial Awards *(Professional Development/Scholarship)* [1533]
John L. Avila Memorial Scholarships *(Professional Development/Scholarship)* [4260]
Susan Ayers Memorial Scholarships *(Undergraduate/Scholarship)* [5802]
John M. Azarian Memorial Armenian Youth Scholarships Fund *(Undergraduate/Scholarship)* [1272]
B-Brave McMahon/Stratton Scholarship Fund *(Undergraduate/Scholarship)* [2941]
BAEO Children's Scholarship Fund *(High School/Scholarship)* [1721]
BAFTX Early Starters Awards *(Undergraduate/Scholarship)* [1779]
BAFTX Graduate Awards *(Undergraduate/Scholarship)* [1780]
BAFTX Junior Achievers Awards *(Undergraduate/Scholarship)* [1781]
BAFTX Undergraduate Awards *(Undergraduate/Scholarship)* [1782]
Baha'i Faith Scholarships for Racial Harmony *(Undergraduate/Scholarship)* [5911]
Lincoln C. Bailey Memorial Scholarship Fund *(Undergraduate/Scholarship)* [3900]
Bambey Bailey Scholarships *(Undergraduate/Scholarship)* [2391]
Barbara Bailey Scholarships *(Undergraduate/Scholarship)* [5754]
Sandra Sebrell Bailey Scholarships *(Undergraduate/Scholarship)* [2683]
Marian Wood Baird Scholarships *(Undergraduate/Scholarship)* [7302]
Richard L. Baker Memorial Scholarships *(Undergraduate/Scholarship)* [6769]
Robby Baker Memorial Scholarships *(Undergraduate/Scholarship)* [189]
Lloyd G. Balfour Fellowships *(Graduate/Fellowship)* [5221]
Ballard Family Foundation Scholarships *(Undergraduate/Scholarship)* [6169]
G. Thomas Balsbaugh Memorial Scholarship Fund *(Undergraduate/Scholarship)* [3090]
Brenda S. Bank Educational Workshop Scholarships *(Undergraduate/Scholarship)* [6447]
Barakat Trust and Barakat Foundation Scholarships *(Graduate/Scholarship)* [1192]
Joe Barbarow Memorial Scholarships *(Undergraduate/Scholarship)* [5465]
Robbie Baron Memorial Scholarships *(Undergraduate/Scholarship)* [3091]
Laura Beckley Barsotti Memorial Scholarships *(Undergraduate/Scholarship)* [3637]
Leon and Talin Barsoumian Scholarships *(Graduate, Undergraduate/Scholarship)* [1263]
Elsa Barton Educational Scholarships Fund *(Undergraduate/Scholarship)* [791]
Bascom Hill Society Scholarships *(Undergraduate/Scholarship)* [7248]
Charles A. Bassett Endowed Memorial Scholarship Fund *(Undergraduate/Scholarship)* [3270]
William H. Bates Oxford Cup Scholarships *(Graduate, Undergraduate/Scholarship)* [1641]
Lewis and Gurry Batten Scholarships *(Undergraduate/Scholarship)* [5466]
Hazel Reed Baumeister Scholarship Program *(Undergraduate/Scholarship)* [6385]
Timothy Baylink Good Fellowship Awards *(Undergraduate/Scholarship)* [5912]
Bayly-Tiffany Scholarships *(Undergraduate/Scholarship)* [7239]
BCCC Foundation Scholarships *(Undergraduate/Scholarship)* [1591]
BCCC Foundation Workforce Scholarships *(Undergraduate/Scholarship)* [1592]
Beacon of Hope Scholarships *(Undergraduate/Scholarship)* [1608]
Jane Beattie Memorial Scholarships *(All/Scholarship)* [6465]
Beau Gunn Redlands Baseball For Youth Scholarships *(Undergraduate/Scholarship)* [5913]
Suzanne Beauregard Scholarships *(Undergraduate/Scholarship)* [6070]
Beaver Medical Clinic-Glen Adams Scholarship Awards *(Undergraduate/Scholarship)* [5914]
Beaver Medical Clinic-H.E.A.R.T. Scholarship Awards *(Undergraduate/Scholarship)* [5915]
Beaver Medical Clinic-Premed Scholarship Awards *(Undergraduate/Scholarship)* [5916]
Don C. Beaver Memorial Scholarship *(Undergraduate/Scholarship)* [1820]
BECA Foundation-CUSM Scholarships *(Undergraduate/Scholarship)* [1610]
BECA Foundation General Scholarships Fund *(Undergraduate/Scholarship)* [1611]
Stephen D. Bechtel Oxford Cup Scholarships *(Graduate, Undergraduate/Scholarship)* [1642]
Dennis J. Beck Memorial Scholarship *(Undergraduate/Scholarship)* [3973]
Garvin L. Beck Scholarships *(Undergraduate/Scholarship)* [5917]
Beecroft Family Scholarships *(High School/Scholarship)* [2264]
Raymond and Donald Beeler Memorial Scholarships *(Undergraduate/Scholarship)* [5918]
Notah Begay III Scholarship Program *(Undergraduate/Scholarship)* [190]
John Bell and Lawrence Thornton Scholarship Fund *(Undergraduate/Scholarship)* [3421]
Ray and Mary Bell Memorial Scholarships *(Undergraduate/Scholarship)* [6171]
Alfred D. Bell Travel Grants *(All/Grant)* [3030]
Bellevue PFLAG Scholarships *(Undergraduate/Scholarship)* [5756]
Benchwarmers of Redlands-Jess Mercado Football Scholarships *(Undergraduate/Scholarship)* [5920]
Benedict Fellowships *(Graduate/Fellowship)* [238]
Dr. Francis Anthony Beneventi Medical Scholarships *(Undergraduate/Scholarship)* [3423]
Louise Bennett-Coverley Scholarships *(Undergraduate/Scholarship)* [1725]
Bertram W. Bennett Memorial Scholarships *(Graduate, Undergraduate/Scholarship)* [1643]
Reverend E.F. Bennett Scholarships *(High School/Scholarship)* [2265]
Bergman Scholarships *(Undergraduate/Scholarship)* [5249]
Richard L. Bernardi Memorial Scholarship *(Undergraduate/Scholarship)* [2456]
Donald H. Bernstein/John B. Talbert, Jr. Scholarship Fund *(Undergraduate/Scholarship)* [3042]
James R. and Geraldine F. Bertelsen Scholarships *(Undergraduate/Scholarship)* [6172]
Beta Gamma Memorial Scholarship Fund *(Undergraduate/Scholarship)* [2643]
Beta Nu/Caryl Cordis D'hondt Scholarships *(Undergraduate/Scholarship)* [6346]
Beta Omega Scholarships *(Undergraduate/Scholarship)* [6347]
Beta Sigma Scholarships *(Undergraduate/Scholarship)* [6348]

Bethune-Cookman University Excelsior Scholarships *(Undergraduate/Scholarship)* [1690]
Bethune-Cookman University Presidential Scholarships *(Undergraduate/Scholarship)* [1691]
BIA Higher Education Grants *(Undergraduate/Grant)* [1208]
BIE-Loan for Service for Graduates *(Graduate/Loan)* [642]
BIGALA (Bisexual Gay and Lesbian Alliance) Scholarships *(Undergraduate/Scholarship)* [6098]
James Bilder Scholarships *(Undergraduate/Scholarship)* [6642]
BioRx/Hemophilia of North Carolina Educational Scholarships *(Undergraduate/Scholarship)* [5006]
Birmingham-Southern College Eagle Scout Scholarships *(Undergraduate/Scholarship)* [4852]
Birmingham Student Scholarship Fund Association *(Undergraduate/Scholarship)* [1717]
BISA's Scholarship Assistance Program *(Undergraduate/Scholarship)* [1759]
BISA's Scholarships Assistance Program *(High School/Scholarship)* [1761]
Lebbeus F. Bissell Scholarships *(Undergraduate/Scholarship)* [3424]
Norman Blachford Point Scholarships *(Graduate, Undergraduate/Scholarship)* [5715]
Black Canadian Scholarships *(Undergraduate/Scholarship)* [5419]
Black Student Fund *(High School/Scholarship)* [1722]
William T. Blackwell Scholarship Fund *(Undergraduate/Scholarship)* [4951]
Bloch-Selinger Education Fund *(Undergraduate/Scholarship)* [2943]
Lawrence Bloomberg Entrance Awards *(Postgraduate/Award/Prize)* [6262]
F.A. and Charlotte Blount Scholarships *(Undergraduate/Scholarship)* [7421]
Blues Ambassador Scholarships *(Undergraduate/Scholarship)* [5804]
Jordan ABDO/Michael Bluett Memorial Scholarships *(Undergraduate/Scholarship)* [6643]
Harry and Edith Blunt Scholarships *(Undergraduate/Scholarship)* [457]
BMO Financial Group Scholarships *(Undergraduate/Scholarship)* [1726]
Sandra Bobbitt Continuing Education Scholarships *(Undergraduate/Scholarship)* [1474]
Edith and Arnold N. Bodtker Grant *(All/Grant)* [2613]
Hagop Bogigian Scholarship Fund *(Undergraduate/Scholarship)* [1273]
Therese and David Bohbot Scholarship *(Undergraduate/Scholarship)* [3553]
Bolick Foreign Student Scholarships *(Undergraduate/Scholarship)* [4349]
Dorothy M. Bolyard Memorial Scholarships *(Undergraduate/Scholarship)* [6174]
BOMA/NY Scholarships *(Undergraduate/Scholarship)* [1802]
Steve Bonk Scholarships *(Postgraduate/Scholarship)* [2050]
Lorne and Ruby Bonnell Scholarships *(Undergraduate/Scholarship)* [2498]
Barbara Bonnema Memorial Scholarships *(Undergraduate/Scholarship)* [5921]
Scott Bonners Memorial Scholarships *(Undergraduate/Scholarship)* [1890]
Admiral Mike Boorda Scholarship Program *(Undergraduate/Scholarship)* [5146]
Diane Booth Memorial Scholarships *(Undergraduate/Scholarship)* [2944]
Tom Boots Memorial Scholarships *(Undergraduate/Scholarship)* [5159]
David L. Boren Undergraduate Scholarships *(Graduate, Undergraduate/Scholarship)* [1424]
Geraldine Geistert Boss Scholarships *(Undergraduate/Scholarship)* [3321]
Dr. George T. Bottomley Scholarships *(Undergraduate/Scholarship)* [4414]
Miranda Bouldin General Scholarships *(Undergraduate/Scholarship)* [4255]
Emma L. Bowen Foundation Scholarships for Minority Interests in Media work/study Program *(Undergraduate/Scholarship)* [7333]
William R. Bowen Scholarship *(Undergraduate/Scholarship)* [2368]
Billy Bowling Memorial Scholarships *(Undergraduate/Scholarship)* [5276]
Boy Scouts of America General Scholarships *(Undergraduate/Scholarship)* [3426]
Boy Scouts of America Troop 3 Scholarships - Art Till/Nathan E. Smith Memorial Scholarships *(Undergraduate/Scholarship)* [5922]
Dr. Betty J. Boyd-Beu & Edwin G. Beu, Jr. Scholarships *(Undergraduate/Scholarship)* [4350]
W. Scott Boyd Group Grants *(All/Grant)* [3813]
Dody Boyd Scholarships *(Undergraduate/Scholarship)* [2408]
Verna Curry Boyer Scholarships *(Undergraduate/Scholarship)* [6770]
Charles Bradley Memorial Scholarships *(Undergraduate/Scholarship)* [3403]
W. Philip Braender and Nancy Coleman Braender Scholarships *(Undergraduate/Scholarship)* [3427]
The Helen and Edward Brancati Teacher Development Scholarships *(Professional Development/Scholarship)* [2054]
Marlene Brand Memorial Scholarship *(Undergraduate/Scholarship)* [3554]
Kenneth H. Breeden Scholarships *(Undergraduate/Scholarship)* [4132]
Marion Luna Brem/Pat McNeil Teen Parent Scholarships *(Undergraduate/Scholarship)* [2266]
Lee Brennan Memorial Scholarships *(Undergraduate/Scholarship)* [5357]
Breslauer Family Scholarships *(Undergraduate/Scholarship)* [6175]
Hilda E. Bretzlaff Foundation Scholarships *(Undergraduate/Grant)* [1777]
Phil Brimhall Memorial Scholarships *(Undergraduate/Scholarship)* [4494]
Louise A. Broderick San Diego County Scholarships *(Undergraduate/Scholarship)* [6176]
Louis J. Brody Q.C. Entrance Scholarships *(Postgraduate/Scholarship)* [6263]
Ross P. Broesamle Educational Scholarships Fund *(Undergraduate/Scholarship)* [4139]
John G. Brokaw Scholarships *(Undergraduate/Scholarship)* [5138]
Peter F. Bronfman Entrance Awards *(Postgraduate/Award/Prize)* [6264]
Peter F. Bronfman Scholarships of Merit *(Postgraduate/Scholarship)* [6265]
Seth R. and Corrine H. Brooks Memorial Scholarships *(Graduate, Undergraduate/Scholarship)* [1644]
Carl E. Brooks Scholarships *(Undergraduate/Scholarship)* [6644]
Dorothy B. Brothers Executive Scholarship Program *(High School/Scholarship)* [7492]
Brown and Caldwell Minority Scholarships *(Undergraduate/Scholarship)* [7334]
Brown Dental Scholarships *(Undergraduate/Scholarship)* [3995]
Diana Brown Endowed Scholarships *(Undergraduate/Scholarship)* [4165]
Marjorie M. Brown Fellowships Program *(Postdoctorate/Fellowship)* [4052]
The John Carter Brown Library Long-Term Fellowships *(All/Fellowship)* [2061]
The John Carter Brown Library Short-Term Fellowships *(Doctorate, Postdoctorate/Fellowship)* [2062]
Quincy Brown Memorial Scholarships *(Undergraduate/Scholarship)* [5923]
Jesse Brown Memorial Youth Scholarship Program *(Undergraduate/Scholarship)* [2722]
JoAhn Brown-Nash Memorial Scholarships *(Undergraduate/Scholarship)* [2409]
Edward M. Brown Oxford Cup Memorial Scholarships *(Graduate, Undergraduate/Scholarship)* [1645]
Ron Brown Scholars Program *(High School/Scholarship)* [1798]
Bernic and Gordon Brown Scholarship *(All/Scholarship)* [3555]
James W. Jr.and Jane T. Brown Scholarship Fund *(Undergraduate/Scholarship)* [3271]
Jack H. Brown Scholarship *(Undergraduate/Scholarship)* [1821]
The Robert W. Brunsman Memorial Scholarships *(Graduate, Undergraduate/Scholarship)* [3875]
Bernard and Mary Brusin Scholarships *(Undergraduate/Scholarship)* [2773]
William and Clara Bryan Scholarships *(Undergraduate/Scholarship)* [2410]
Bryce-Lietzke Martin Scholarships *(Undergraduate/Scholarship)* [5469]
Susan Thompson Buffett Foundation Scholarships *(Undergraduate/Scholarship)* [1800]
Tien Bui Memorial Scholarships *(Undergraduate/Scholarship)* [7423]
Builders Association of Northeast Indiana (BANI) Scholarships *(Undergraduate/Scholarship)* [6771]
Armen H. Bululian Scholarships *(Undergraduate/Scholarship)* [1274]
Charles E. Bunnell Scholarships *(Undergraduate/Scholarship)* [4351]
William T. Burbage Family Memorial Scholarship *(Undergraduate/Scholarship)* [2369]
George M. Burditt Scholarships *(Undergraduate/Scholarship)* [1421]
Adam S. Burford Memorial Scholarships *(Graduate, Undergraduate/Scholarship)* [1646]
Freda Burge Scholarships *(Undergraduate/Scholarship)* [5470]
Loyal D. Burkett Memorial Scholarships *(Undergraduate/Scholarship)* [4352]
Kathy Bush Memorial Scholarships *(Undergraduate/Scholarship)* [5924]
Lindsay Buster Memorial Scholarship *(Undergraduate/Scholarship)* [2457]
Leon C. Bynoe Memorial Scholarships *(Undergraduate/Scholarship)* [7212]
Joe Bynum/Raymond James Investment Services Technical Excellence Scholarships Fund *(Undergraduate/Scholarship)* [2346]
Robert C. Byrd Honors Scholarships *(Undergraduate/Scholarship)* [3662]
Thad Byrne Memorial Scholarships *(Graduate, Undergraduate/Scholarship)* [1647]
George J. Bysiewicz Scholarship Fund *(Undergraduate/Scholarship)* [2392]
Cabrillo Clubs of California Scholarships *(Undergraduate/Scholarship)* [5737]
Dr. Aurelio M. Caccomo Family Foundation Memorial Scholarships *(Undergraduate/Scholarship)* [1136]
Cal State San Macros Alumna Scholarships *(Undergraduate/Scholarship)* [1859]
Tese Caldarelli Memorial Scholarships *(Undergraduate/Scholarship)* [4672]
Calhoun County Auduburn University Scholarships *(Undergraduate/Scholarship)* [2347]
Calhoun Scholarships *(Undergraduate/Scholarship)* [1810]
Hermoine Grant Calhoun Scholarships *(Undergraduate/Scholarship)* [4875]
California Groundwater Association Scholarships *(Undergraduate/Scholarship)* [1837]
California Scottish Rite Foundation Scholarships *(Undergraduate/Scholarship)* [1852]
California Shopping Cart Retrieval Corporation Inc. Scholarships *(Undergraduate/Scholarship)* [1822]
Calista Scholarships *(Undergraduate/Scholarship)* [1864]
Harry D. Callahan Educational Trust *(Undergraduate/Scholarship)* [6711]
Calvin Alumni Association Arizona Central Chapter Scholarships *(Undergraduate/Scholarship)* [1866]
Calvin Alumni Association-Black Alumni Chapter Scholarships *(Undergraduate/Scholarship)* [1867]
Calvin Alumni Association British Columbia Scholarships *(Undergraduate/Scholarship)* [1868]
Calvin Alumni Association California- Bay Area Scholarships *(Undergraduate/Scholarship)* [1869]
Calvin Alumni Association Colorado Chapter Scholarships *(Undergraduate/Scholarship)* [1870]
Calvin Alumni Association Florida-Gulf Coast Scholarships *(Undergraduate/Scholarship)* [1871]
Calvin Alumni Association-Illinois Scholarships *(Undergraduate/Scholarship)* [1872]
Calvin Alumni Association-Iowa/Pella Scholarships *(Undergraduate/Scholarship)* [1873]
Calvin Alumni Association-Maryland/Baltimore Scholarships *(Undergraduate/Scholarship)* [1874]
Calvin Alumni Association-Michigan Lakeshore Scholarships *(Undergraduate/Scholarship)* [1875]
Calvin Alumni Association-Michigan, Lansing Schol-

arships (Undergraduate/Scholarship) [1876]
Calvin Alumni Association-New Jersey Scholarships (Undergraduate/Scholarship) [1877]
Calvin Alumni Association-New York, Rochester Scholarships (Undergraduate/Scholarship) [1878]
Calvin Alumni Association-South Florida Scholarships (Undergraduate/Scholarship) [1879]
Calvin Alumni Association-South Florida Sophomore Scholarships (Undergraduate/Scholarship) [1880]
Calvin Alumni Association-Southeast Michigan Scholarships (Undergraduate/Scholarship) [1881]
Calvin Alumni Association-Southeastern Wisconsin Scholarships (Undergraduate/Scholarship) [1882]
Calvin Alumni Association Southern California Chapter Scholarships (Undergraduate/Scholarship) [1883]
Calvin Alumni Association-Southwest Michigan, Kalamazoo Scholarships (Undergraduate/Scholarship) [1884]
Calvin Alumni Association-Washington, D.C. Scholarships (Undergraduate/Scholarship) [1885]
Calvin Alumni Association-Washington, Lynden Scholarships (Undergraduate/Scholarship) [1886]
Calvin Alumni Association-Washington-Seattle/Tacoma Scholarships (Undergraduate/Scholarship) [1887]
Camden County College Employee Memorial Scholarships (Undergraduate/Scholarship) [1891]
Camden County College Foundation Scholarships (Undergraduate/Scholarship) [1892]
Camden County Retired Educators Association Scholarships (Undergraduate/Scholarship) [1893]
Cameco Northern Scholarships - Technical Institute (Undergraduate/Scholarship) [1906]
Cameco Northern Scholarships - University (Undergraduate/Scholarship) [1907]
Wesley C. Cameron Scholarships (Undergraduate/Scholarship) [5139]
Lois Campbell Scholarship Award (Undergraduate/Scholarship) [3846]
Theodore R. Campbell Scholarship (Undergraduate/Scholarship) [150]
Robert G. Campbell Scholarships (Undergraduate/Scholarship) [5925]
Canada Millennium Bursary (Undergraduate/Scholarship) [151]
Canada Millennium Scholarship Foundation Millennium Bursary Award (Undergraduate/Award/Prize) [1910]
Canada Study Grant for the Accommodation of Students with Permanent Disabilities (Undergraduate/Grant) [4156]
Canada-Ukraine Parliamentary Program (CUPP) Internship Scholarships (Undergraduate/Scholarship) [7357]
Canadian Federation of University Women Etobicoke Bursary (Graduate, Undergraduate/Scholarship) [7213]
Canadian Hard of Hearing Association Scholarships (Undergraduate/Scholarship) [1968]
Canadian Macedonian Federation Scholarships (Undergraduate/Scholarship) [7214]
Canadian Parking Association Scholarships (Undergraduate/Scholarship) [2027]
Canadian Sanitation Supply Association Scholarships (Undergraduate/Scholarship) [2029]
Canadian Seniors Golf Association Scholarships (Undergraduate/Scholarship) [6071]
Cancer Survivors' Fund Scholarships (Undergraduate/Scholarship) [2052]
Agustin Cano Memorial Scholarships (Undergraduate/Scholarship) [5807]
John Caoile Memorial Scholarships (Undergraduate/Scholarship) [5808]
Cape Fear Community College Merit Scholarships (Undergraduate/Scholarship) [2057]
Kasie Ford Capling Memorial Scholarship Endowment Fund (Undergraduate/Scholarship) [3045]
Career Advancement Scholarships (Undergraduate/Scholarship) [1806]
Beth Carew Memorial Scholarships (Undergraduate/Scholarship) [5007]
Glen and Babs Carlson Endowed Scholarships (Undergraduate/Scholarship) [4166]
Carmangay Home and School Association Scholarships (Undergraduate/Scholarship) [152]
Walta Wilkinson Carmichael Scholarships (Undergraduate/Scholarship) [6349]
Herb Carnegie Scholarships (Undergraduate/Scholarship) [1727]
Joe Carnes Scholarship (Undergraduate/Scholarship) [2458]
Carolina Panthers Scholarship Fund (Graduate/Scholarship) [3047]
Carolina's Gay & Lesbian Scholarships (Undergraduate/Scholarship) [6099]
Carolinas-Virginias Retail Hardware Scholarship Fund (Undergraduate/Scholarship) [3048]
Walter & Elsie Carr Endowed Scholarships (Undergraduate/Scholarship) [4167]
Commander James Carr Forensic Science Scholarships (Undergraduate/Scholarship) [252]
Cartwright Scholarships Program (Undergraduate/Scholarship) [618]
Casabella Family Memorial Scholarships (Undergraduate/Scholarship) [3430]
Case-Swayne Company Scholarships (Undergraduate/Scholarship) [5358]
Local 827 Peter J. Casey Scholarships (Undergraduate/Scholarship) [3819]
Fraser Milner Casgrain LLP Scholarships (Undergraduate/Scholarship) [1728]
George H. and Anna Casper Fund (Undergraduate/Scholarship) [6712]
Orrie & Dorothy Cassada Scholarships (Undergraduate/Scholarship) [3322]
Thomas D. and Karen Cassady Scholarships (Graduate, Undergraduate/Scholarship) [1648]
May Cassioppi Scholarship (Undergraduate/Scholarship) [2459]
Marshall Cavendish Scholarships (Graduate/Scholarship) [699]
CAWEE International Student Fellowships (Postgraduate/Fellowship) [6266]
Christine Kerr Cawthorne Scholarships (Undergraduate/Scholarship) [6350]
CCSD School Counselors' Scholarships (Undergraduate/Scholarship) [5809]
CCU Alumni Endowed Scholarships (Undergraduate/Scholarship) [2304]
Cedarcrest Farms Scholarships (Undergraduate/Scholarship) [687]
Certified Municipal Clerk Scholarships (CMC) (Professional Development/Scholarship) [3872]
CEW Scholarships (All/Scholarship) [2081]
CFERP Masters Fellowships (Graduate/Fellowship) [2343]
CFIG National Scholarships (Undergraduate/Scholarship) [1954]
Emily Chaison Gold Award Scholarships (Undergraduate/Scholarship) [3431]
Logan S. Chambers Individual Scholarships (Professional Development/Scholarship) [3814]
Mary Anne Chambers Scholarships (Undergraduate/Scholarship) [3996]
Change Your World Scholarships (Undergraduate/Scholarship) [6819]
Harry H. and Floy B. Chapin Scholarship (Undergraduate/Scholarship) [2460]
Oscar Chapman Memorial Scholarships (Graduate, Undergraduate/Scholarship) [1649]
Charlotte Housing Authority Scholarship Fund (CHASF) (Undergraduate/Scholarship) [3049]
Charlotte-Mecklenburg Schools Scholarship Incentive Program (Undergraduate/Scholarship) [3050]
Cesar E. Chavez Scholarships (Undergraduate/Scholarship) [5926]
Cheatham County Scholarships (Undergraduate/Scholarship) [2412]
Cheerful Giver Scholarships (Undergraduate/Scholarship) [6178]
Sgt. Michael F. Cherven Memorial Scholarships (Undergraduate/Scholarship) [4330]
Cheyenne High School Faculty Memorial Scholarships (Undergraduate/Scholarship) [5810]
Chi Chapter Undergraduate Scholarships (Undergraduate/Scholarship) [2644]
Chi Phi Educational Trust (Undergraduate/Scholarship) [2117]
Chicago Division Scholarships (Undergraduate/Scholarship) [4513]
Chicana Latina Scholarship Fund (Graduate, Undergraduate/Scholarship) [2121]
Child of Alumni Book Voucher Awards (Undergraduate/Scholarship) [3699]
Kevin Child Scholarships (Undergraduate/Scholarship) [4917]
John and Ruth Childe Scholarships (Undergraduate/Scholarship) [6645]
Children of Unitarian Universalist Ministers College Scholarships (Undergraduate/Scholarship) [6949]
Children's Scholarship Fund of Charlotte (High School/Scholarship) [3051]
Choose Your Future Scholarships (Undergraduate/Scholarship) [2413]
George Choy Memorial/Gay Asian Pacific Alliance (GAPA) Scholarships (Undergraduate/Scholarship) [6100]
Andrew G. Chressanthis Memorial Scholarships (Undergraduate/Scholarship) [3527]
Chrysler Technical Scholarships Fund (Undergraduate/Scholarship) [2633]
CHS - Bursary Program Scholarships (Undergraduate/Scholarship) [1970]
CHS - Mature Student Bursary Program Scholarships (Professional Development/Scholarship) [1971]
CHS Scholarships (Undergraduate/Scholarship) [1972]
Church Family Scholarships (Undergraduate/Scholarship) [4169]
CIA Undergraduate Scholarships (Undergraduate/Scholarship) [1425]
CIBC Scholarships (Undergraduate/Scholarship) [1729]
Cincinnati High School Scholarships (High School/Scholarship) [2149]
Cincinnati Scholarship Foundation CFT/ACPSOP Scholarships (Undergraduate/Scholarship) [2150]
Nate Mack/Cindi Turner Scholarships (Undergraduate/Scholarship) [5811]
CIP Fellow's Travel Scholarships (Postgraduate/Scholarship) [1980]
Carlos Enrique Cisneros Point Scholarships (Graduate, Undergraduate/Scholarship) [5716]
Citi Foundation Scholarships Program (Undergraduate/Scholarship) [619]
City of Sanibel Employee Dependent Scholarships (Undergraduate/Scholarship) [6646]
Civitan Shropshire Scholarships (Undergraduate/Scholarship) [2243]
Cecil Earl Clapp, Sr. Memorial Scholarships (Undergraduate/Scholarship) [5277]
Ann E. Clark Foundation Scholarships (Undergraduate/Scholarship) [5140]
Fisher Clark Memorial Endowed Scholarships (Undergraduate/Scholarship) [4170]
Andrew Blake Clark Memorial Scholarships (Undergraduate/Scholarship) [7425]
Class Nobel Academic Scholarships for Members (High School/Scholarship) [5067]
Classic Wines of California Scholarships (Undergraduate/Scholarship) [1823]
Cleveland Alumni Association Scholarships (Graduate, Undergraduate/Scholarship) [1650]
David H. Clift Scholarships (Graduate/Scholarship) [700]
Bryan Cline Memorial Soccer Scholarship Program (Undergraduate/Scholarship) [191]
Irene Culver Cllins and Louis Franklin Collins Scholarship (Undergraduate/Scholarship) [2370]
L. Robert Clough Memorial Scholarships (Graduate, Undergraduate/Scholarship) [1651]
The Club at Morningside Scholarships (Undergraduate/Scholarship) [6179]
CMAA Student Conference Travel Grants (All/Grant) [2251]
The Helena B. Cobb Annual Scholarships (Undergraduate/Scholarship) [7501]
The Helena B. Cobb Four-Year Higher Education Grants (Undergraduate/Scholarship) [7502]
Coca-Cola First Generation Scholarships (Undergraduate/Scholarship) [620]
Coca-Cola Scholars Foundation Four-Year Award for Seniors (Undergraduate/Scholarship) [2296]
CODY Foundation Fund (Undergraduate/Scholarship) [3093]
Coeur d'Alene Alumni Scholarships

(Undergraduate/Scholarship) [4171]
Steven L. Coffey Memorial Scholarships (Undergraduate/Scholarship) [2809]
Thomas D. Coffield Scholarships (Undergraduate/Scholarship) [3324]
Donald O. Coffman Scholarships (Undergraduate/Scholarship) [5760]
COHEAO Scholarships (Undergraduate/Scholarship) [2257]
Marshall A. Cohen Entrance Awards (Postgraduate/Award/Prize) [6267]
Jack Kent Coke Graduate Scholarships (Graduate/Scholarship) [7086]
Cole Family Scholarships (Undergraduate/Scholarship) [5761]
Cole Foundation Undergraduate Scholarship Program (Undergraduate/Scholarship) [3053]
The College Club of Hartford Scholarships (Undergraduate/Scholarship) [3433]
College Education Loan Scholarships For U.S. Resident Students (Undergraduate/Loan) [3779]
College of Marin Gay and Lesbian Student Scholarships (Undergraduate/Scholarship) [6101]
Capt. Winifred Quick Collins Scholarships (Undergraduate/Scholarship) [5141]
Elmer and Rosa Lee Collins Scholarships (Undergraduate/Scholarship) [7426]
Erma Collins Scholarships (Undergraduate/Scholarship) [1730]
Lloyd E. and Rachel S. Collins Scholarships (Undergraduate/Scholarship) [7427]
Columbus Citizens Foundation College Scholarships (Undergraduate/Scholarship) [2334]
Columbus Citizens Foundation High School Scholarships (High School/Scholarship) [2335]
Commonwealth "Good Citizen" Scholarships (Undergraduate/Scholarship) [1431]
Communal Studies Association Research Fellowships (Graduate/Grant) [2339]
Communications Workers of America Scholarships (Undergraduate/Scholarship) [2341]
Community-based Natural Resource Management Assistantships (All/Internship) [2344]
The Community Foundation DBI Scholarships (Undergraduate/Scholarship) [2415]
Community Foundation of the Fox River Valley Scholarships (Undergraduate/Scholarship) [2389]
Community Foundation of Sarasota County Adult Learner Scholarships (Undergraduate/Scholarship) [2505]
Community Foundation Scholarships (Undergraduate/Scholarship) [2461]
The Community Foundation Student Education Loans (Undergraduate/Loan) [2416]
Community Foundation of Western Massachusetts Community Scholarship Program (Undergraduate/Scholarship) [2523]
Compassionate Care Scholarships (Undergraduate/Scholarship) [5763]
Connecticut Association of Latinos in Higher Education Scholarships (Undergraduate/Scholarship) [3434]
Connecticut Capitol Scholarship Program (Undergraduate/Scholarship) [3437]
Connecticut Nurserymen's Foundation Scholarships (Undergraduate/Scholarship) [3440]
Dwight O. Conner and Ellen Conner Lepp Scholarships (Undergraduate/Scholarship) [5472]
Connor/Spafford Scholarships (Undergraduate/Scholarship) [6072]
Constantinople Armenian Relief Society (C.A.R.S.) Scholarships (Undergraduate/Scholarship) [1275]
The Continental Group Scholarship Fund (High School/Scholarship) [2596]
James & Maryetta Cook Scholarships (Undergraduate/Scholarship) [1894]
George Joseph Cooper Awards (Undergraduate/Scholarship) [5420]
Madison and Edith Cooper Scholarships (Undergraduate/Scholarship) [6180]
Cope Middle School PTSA Scholarships (Undergraduate/Scholarship) [5928]
Copnick/Hilliard Scholarships (Professional Development/Scholarship) [2024]
Corbett-Porter Building Bridges Scholarships (Undergraduate/Scholarship) [5815]
Cornaro Scholarships for Graduate Studies (Graduate/Scholarship) [4042]
D.C. Cornelius Memorial Scholarships (Undergraduate/Scholarship) [7428]
Cost-of-Books Relief Scholarships (Undergraduate/Scholarship) [1860]
Cotner Family Scholarships (Undergraduate/Scholarship) [2948]
Council on Social Work Education Minority Fellowship Programs (Postdoctorate/Fellowship) [2553]
Council on Social Work Education Scholars Program (Postdoctorate/Scholarship) [2554]
Soozie Courter Sharing a Brighter Tomorrow Hemophilia Scholarship Program (Graduate, Undergraduate/Scholarship) [4918]
Reuben R. Cowles Youth Awards (Undergraduate/Award/Prize) [688]
Justin Forrest Cox "Beat the Odds" Memorial Scholarships (Undergraduate/Scholarship) [2269]
Crafton Elementary School PTA Scholarships (Undergraduate/Scholarship) [5929]
Crafton Hills College Foundation Scholarships (Undergraduate/Scholarship) [5930]
Margaret T. Craig Community Service Scholarship (Undergraduate/Scholarship) [2462]
Crain Educational Grants Program (Undergraduate/Scholarship) [6386]
Crawford Scholarships (Undergraduate/Scholarship) [6181]
L.D. "Crow" Crawford Scholarships (Undergraduate/Scholarship) [7001]
Creative Glass Center of America Fellowships (All/Fellowship) [2557]
R.G Crossno Memorial Scholarships (Undergraduate/Scholarship) [2810]
Crowder Scholarship Fund (Undergraduate/Scholarship) [3056]
CRS Scholarships (Undergraduate/Scholarship) [2145]
Lydia Cruz and Sandra Maria Ramos Scholarships (Undergraduate/Scholarship) [2681]
The Crystal Green Blood Assurance Scholarships (Undergraduate/Scholarship) [1766]
CSF Ach Family Scholarships (Undergraduate/Scholarship) [2151]
CSF Barr Foundation Scholarships (Undergraduate/Scholarship) [2152]
CSF Barrett Family Scholarships (Undergraduate/Scholarship) [2153]
CSF Bigg's/Curtis Breeden Scholarships (Undergraduate/Scholarship) [2154]
CSF Bob and Linda Kohlhepp Scholarships (Undergraduate/Scholarship) [2155]
CSF Borden Inc. Scholarships (Undergraduate/Scholarship) [2156]
CSF Carl H. Linder Family Scholarships (Undergraduate/Scholarship) [2157]
CSF Castellini Foundation Scholarships (Undergraduate/Scholarship) [2158]
CSF Charles and Claire Phillips Scholarships (Undergraduate/Scholarship) [2159]
CSF Charlotte R. Schmidlapp Scholarships (Undergraduate/Scholarship) [2160]
CSF Christopher Todd Grant Memorial Scholarships (Undergraduate/Scholarship) [2161]
CSF Cincinnati Bell Scholarships (Undergraduate/Scholarship) [2162]
CSF Cincinnati Financial Corporation Scholarships (Undergraduate/Scholarship) [2163]
CSF Cincinnati Milacron Scholarships (Undergraduate/Scholarship) [2164]
CSF Corwin Nixon Scholarships (Undergraduate/Scholarship) [2165]
CSF Crosset Family Scholarships (Undergraduate/Scholarship) [2166]
CSF Dater Foundation Scholarships (Undergraduate/Scholarship) [2167]
CSF David J. Joseph Company Scholarships (Undergraduate/Scholarship) [2168]
CSF Dee Wacksman Memorial Scholarships (Undergraduate/Scholarship) [2169]
CSF Duke Energy Scholarships (Undergraduate/Scholarship) [2170]
CSF Dwight Hibbard Scholarships (Undergraduate/Scholarship) [2171]
CSF Ella Wilson Johnson Scholarships (Undergraduate/Scholarship) [2172]
CSF Estelle Davis Memorial Scholarships (Undergraduate/Scholarship) [2173]
CSF Eugene Carroll Scholarships (Undergraduate/Scholarship) [2174]
CSF E.W. Scripps Scholarships (Undergraduate/Scholarship) [2175]
CSF Farmer Family Foundation Scholarships (Undergraduate/Scholarship) [2176]
CSF Fifth Third Bank Combined Scholarships (Undergraduate/Scholarship) [2177]
CSF Fletemeyer Family Scholarships (Undergraduate/Scholarship) [2178]
CSF Florette B. Hoffheimer Scholarships (Undergraduate/Scholarship) [2179]
CSF Frank Foster Skillman Scholarships (Undergraduate/Scholarship) [2180]
CSF Gardner Foundation Scholarships (Undergraduate/Scholarship) [2181]
CSF G.E. Aircraft Engines Scholarships (Undergraduate/Scholarship) [2182]
CSF George and Amy Polley Scholarships (Undergraduate/Scholarship) [2183]
CSF Goldman, Sachs and Company Scholarships (Undergraduate/Scholarship) [2184]
CSF Greater Cincinnati Scholarships Association (Undergraduate/Scholarship) [2185]
CSF H.C. Schott Foundation Scholarships (Undergraduate/Scholarship) [2186]
CSF HCRTA/Glen O. and Wyllabeth Wise Scholarships (Undergraduate/Scholarship) [2187]
CSF Heidelberg Distributing Co. Scholarships (Undergraduate/Scholarship) [2188]
CSF Heinz Pet Products Scholarships (Undergraduate/Scholarship) [2189]
CSF Helen Steiner Rice Scholarships (Undergraduate/Scholarship) [2190]
CSF Johnny Bench Scholarships (Undergraduate/Scholarship) [2191]
CSF Joseph S. Stern, Jr. Scholarships (Undergraduate/Scholarship) [2192]
CSF Judge Benjamin Schwartz Scholarships (Undergraduate/Scholarship) [2193]
CSF Juilfs Foundation Scholarships (Undergraduate/Scholarship) [2194]
CSF Kroger Cincinnati/Dayton Scholarships (Undergraduate/Scholarship) [2195]
CSF L and T Woolfolk Memorial Scholarships (Undergraduate/Scholarship) [2196]
CSF Lazarus/Federated Scholarships (Undergraduate/Scholarship) [2197]
CSF L.B. Zapoleon Scholarships (Undergraduate/Scholarship) [2198]
CSF Lowe Simpson Scholarships (Undergraduate/Scholarship) [2199]
CSF Lyle and Arlene Everingham Scholarships (Undergraduate/Scholarship) [2200]
CSF Lyle Everingham Scholarships (Undergraduate/Scholarship) [2201]
CSF M and E Brown Scholarships (Undergraduate/Scholarship) [2202]
CSF M. Kantor and Brothers Scholarships (Undergraduate/Scholarship) [2203]
CSF Martha W. Tanner Memorial Scholarships (Undergraduate/Scholarship) [2204]
CSF Marvin Rammelsberg Memorial Scholarships (Undergraduate/Scholarship) [2205]
CSF Mary Roberts Scholarships (Undergraduate/Scholarship) [2206]
CSF McCall Educational Scholarships (Undergraduate/Scholarship) [2207]
CSF Michael Bany Memorial Scholarships (Undergraduate/Scholarship) [2208]
CSF Midland Company Scholarships (Undergraduate/Scholarship) [2209]
CSF Nelson Schwab Jr. Family Scholarships (Undergraduate/Scholarship) [2210]
CSF Nethercott Family Scholarships (Undergraduate/Scholarship) [2211]
CSF Ohio National Foundation Scholarships (Undergraduate/Scholarship) [2212]
CSF Pepper Family Scholarships (Undergraduate/Scholarship) [2213]
CSF Pichler Family Scholarships (Undergraduate/Scholarship) [2214]
CSF PNC Bank Scholarships

(*Undergraduate/Scholarship*) [2215]
CSF Priscilla Gamble Scholarships (*Undergraduate/Scholarship*) [2216]
CSF Procter and Gamble Scholarships (*Undergraduate/Scholarship*) [2217]
CSF Raymond and Augusta Klink Scholarships (*Undergraduate/Scholarship*) [2218]
CSF Richard Heekin Scholarships (*Undergraduate/Scholarship*) [2219]
CSF Robert H. Reakirt Foundation Scholarships (*Undergraduate/Scholarship*) [2220]
CSF Roger and Joyce Howe Family Scholarships (*Undergraduate/Scholarship*) [2221]
CSF S. David Shor Scholarships (*Undergraduate/Scholarship*) [2222]
CSF SC Johnson, A Family Company Scholarships (*Undergraduate/Scholarship*) [2223]
CSF Scripps Headliners Scholarships (*Undergraduate/Scholarship*) [2224]
CSF Semple Foundation Scholarships (*Undergraduate/Scholarship*) [2225]
CSF Thomas J. Emery Memorial Scholarships (*Undergraduate/Scholarship*) [2226]
CSF T.L. Conlan Memorial Scholarships (*Undergraduate/Scholarship*) [2227]
CSF Union Central 135th Anniversary Scholarships (*Undergraduate/Scholarship*) [2228]
CSF U.S. Bank N.A. Scholarships (*Undergraduate/Scholarship*) [2229]
CSF Walter and Marilyn Bartlett Scholarships (*Undergraduate/Scholarship*) [2230]
CSF Western-Southern Foundation Scholarships (*Undergraduate/Scholarship*) [2231]
CSF William A. Friedlander Scholarships (*Undergraduate/Scholarship*) [2232]
CSF Wm. J. Rielly/MCURC Scholarships (*Undergraduate/Scholarship*) [2233]
CSF Woodward Trustees Scholarships (*Undergraduate/Scholarship*) [2234]
CSF Wynne Family Memorial Scholarships (*Undergraduate/Scholarship*) [2235]
Murtha Cullina Scholarships (*Undergraduate/Scholarship*) [2393]
Brian Cummins Memorial Scholarships (*Undergraduate/Scholarship*) [3441]
Laura Moore Cunningham Foundation General Scholarships (*Undergraduate/Scholarship*) [4174]
Curry Award for Girls and Young Women (*Undergraduate/Scholarship*) [6387]
Cindy Curry Memorial Scholarships (*Undergraduate/Scholarship*) [5475]
Michael D. Curtin Renaissance Student Memorial Scholarships (*Undergraduate/Scholarship*) [2811]
Cystic Fibrosis Foundation Scholarships (*Undergraduate/Scholarship*) [2585]
DAAD Undergraduate Scholarship Program (*Undergraduate/Scholarship*) [3224]
Daddy Longlegs Scholarships (*Undergraduate/Scholarship*) [6182]
Daggy Youth/Student Scholarships (*Professional Development/Scholarship*) [3915]
Daimler Chrysler Scholarships Award (*Undergraduate/Scholarship*) [3565]
Serena D. Dalton Scholarships (*Undergraduate/Scholarship*) [7429]
Marvin E. Daly Memorial Scholarships (*Undergraduate/Scholarship*) [5278]
Robin M. Daniels Memorial Scholarships (*Undergraduate/Scholarship*) [5816]
Arthur H. Daniels Scholarships (*Undergraduate/Scholarship*) [5931]
Danville Education Association Scholarship Fund (*Undergraduate/Scholarship*) [2949]
Danville High School Class of 1963 Scholarship Fund (*Undergraduate/Scholarship*) [2950]
Danville Rotary Scholarships (*Undergraduate/Scholarship*) [2951]
Darden Restaurants Scholarships (*Undergraduate/Scholarship*) [7005]
Datatel Angelfire Scholarships (*Graduate, Undergraduate/Scholarship*) [2615]
Datatel Scholarships (*Graduate, Undergraduate/Scholarship*) [2616]
Daughters of the American Revolution American Indian Scholarships (*Undergraduate/Scholarship*) [633]
Kenneth and Kathleen Davis Endowed Scholarships (*Undergraduate/Scholarship*) [4175]
Davis Family Scholarships (*Undergraduate/Scholarship*) [6183]
The William H. Davis, Jr. Scholarship Fund (*Undergraduate/Scholarship*) [2399]
Davis Memorial Foundation Scholarship Award Program (*Graduate, Undergraduate/Scholarship*) [2621]
Dwight F. Davis Memorial Scholarships (*Undergraduate/Scholarship*) [7303]
Lawrence E. Davis Scholarships (*Undergraduate/Scholarship*) [5477]
Larry Dean Davis Scholarships Program (*Undergraduate/Scholarship*) [1775]
William W. Dawson Memorial Scholarships (*Graduate, Undergraduate/Scholarship*) [1652]
Brian M. Day Scholarships (*Undergraduate/Scholarship*) [5764]
D.C. Opportunity Scholarship Program (*Undergraduate/Scholarship*) [7376]
D.C. and Virginia Brown Scholarships (*High School, Undergraduate/Scholarship*) [2270]
Elsie De Wolfe Point Scholarships (*Graduate, Undergraduate/Scholarship*) [5717]
Deaf Queer Youth Scholarships (*Undergraduate/Scholarship*) [6102]
Dean Prim Scholarships (*Undergraduate/Scholarship*) [7430]
B.J. Dean Scholarships (*Undergraduate/Scholarship*) [2418]
Derek Lee Dean Soccer Scholarships (*High School/Scholarship*) [2271]
Don Debolt Franchising Scholarship Program (*Undergraduate/Scholarship*) [3856]
Walter M. Decker Point Scholarships (*Graduate, Undergraduate/Scholarship*) [5718]
Laurence Decore Awards for Student Leadership (*Undergraduate/Scholarship*) [154]
Anthony R. Dees Educational Workshop Scholarships (*Undergraduate/Scholarship*) [6448]
Jan DiMartino Delany Memorial Scholarship Fund (*Undergraduate/Scholarship*) [3094]
Vine Deloria Jr. Memorial Scholarships (*Graduate/Scholarship*) [621]
Eric Delson Memorial Scholarships (*Graduate, High School, Undergraduate/Scholarship*) [4919]
Delta Chi Alumnae Memorial Scholarships (*Undergraduate/Scholarship*) [6352]
Delta Iota Alumni Scholarships (*Undergraduate/Scholarship*) [6404]
Delta Phi Epsilon Educational Foundation Scholarships (*Undergraduate/Scholarship*) [2679]
Delta Sigma Theta Hartford Alumnae Scholarships (*Undergraduate/Scholarship*) [3442]
Delta Tau Chapter Scholarships (*Graduate, Undergraduate/Scholarship*) [1653]
Delta Zeta Undergraduate Scholarships (*Undergraduate/Scholarship*) [2686]
C. Rodney Demarest Memorial Scholarships (*Undergraduate/Scholarship*) [3443]
Christopher Demetris Scholarships (*Undergraduate/Scholarship*) [3528]
Ruth DeMoss Scholarships (*Undergraduate/Scholarship*) [6184]
Michael Denton Scholarships (*Undergraduate/Scholarship*) [5279]
Denver Scholarship Foundation Scholarships (*Undergraduate/Scholarship*) [2705]
ROP - Dr. Linda Denver Scholarships (*Undergraduate/Scholarship*) [5932]
Tommy Depaola Scholarship Award (*Undergraduate/Scholarship*) [3848]
Dependents of Deceased Service Members Scholarship Program (*Undergraduate/Scholarship*) [5147]
Depression and ADHD Fellowships (*Professional Development/Fellowship*) [4078]
Herman H. Derksen Scholarships (*Undergraduate/Scholarship*) [6185]
Pat Dermargosian Memorial Scholarships (*Undergraduate/Scholarship*) [5933]
Achille & Irene Despres, William & Andre Scholarships (*Undergraduate/Scholarship*) [3326]
Detroit Economic Club Scholarships (*Undergraduate/Scholarship*) [2513]
Detroit Tigers Willie Horton Scholarships (*Undergraduate/Scholarship*) [2514]
Helen L. Dewar Scholarships (*Undergraduate/Scholarship*) [6883]
Albert and Jane Dewey Scholarships (*Undergraduate/Scholarship*) [3444]
Julio C. Diaz Memorial Scholarship Fund (*Undergraduate/Scholarship*) [6714]
Bill Dickey Scholarship Association Scholarships (*Undergraduate/Scholarship*) [2711]
Rob Digiacomo Scholarship Fund (*Undergraduate/Scholarship*) [6715]
The E.R. and Lilian B. Dimmette Scholarship Fund (*Undergraduate/Scholarship*) [3057]
Dr. Allan A. Dixon Memorial Scholarships (*Postgraduate/Scholarship*) [2034]
Doddridge County Promise Scholarships (*Undergraduate/Scholarship*) [5478]
Hans H. and Margaret B. Doe Scholarships (*Graduate, Undergraduate/Scholarship*) [6186]
Emmett J. Doerr Memorial Distinguished Scout Scholarships (*High School/Scholarship*) [4853]
Dofflemyer Scholarships (*Undergraduate/Scholarship*) [4854]
Dokmo Family Scholarships (*Undergraduate/Scholarship*) [6187]
Dolphin Scholarships (*Undergraduate/Scholarship*) [2726]
Harry A. Donn Scholarships (*Undergraduate/Scholarship*) [3445]
Mickey Donnelly Memorial Scholarships (*Undergraduate/Scholarship*) [5818]
Jim Doogan Memorial Scholarships (*Undergraduate/Scholarship*) [7075]
Doraine Pursuit of Educational Excellence Scholarships (*High School/Scholarship*) [2272]
Dorizas Memorial Scholarships (*Undergraduate/Scholarship*) [3529]
Eric Dostie Memorial College Scholarships (*Four Year College, Two Year College, Undergraduate/Scholarship*) [4920]
Father Connie Dougherty Scholarships (*Undergraduate/Scholarship*) [2507]
Tommy Douglas Scholarships (*Undergraduate/Scholarship*) [5116]
Jay Downes Memorial Scholarships (*High School/Scholarship*) [2273]
Wilma Sackett Dressel Scholarships (*Undergraduate/Scholarship*) [6353]
Drinkwater Family Scholarships (*Undergraduate/Scholarship*) [6188]
Mary Ellen Driscoll Scholarships (*Undergraduate/Scholarship*) [6073]
Lillian Cooper Droke Memorial Scholarships (*Undergraduate/Scholarship*) [4463]
Drum Major Institute Scholars (*Undergraduate/Scholarship*) [6332]
Sergeant Major Douglas R. Drum Memorial Scholarship Fund (*Undergraduate/Scholarship*) [716]
Lee Dubin Scholarship Fund (*Undergraduate/Scholarship*) [6103]
Deborah Gandee Dudding Memorial Scholarships (*Undergraduate/Scholarship*) [5479]
Edward Leon Duhamel Freemasons Scholarships (*Undergraduate/Scholarship*) [6037]
Duluth Building and Construction Trades Council Scholarships (*Undergraduate/Scholarship*) [2774]
Duluth Central HS Alumni Scholarships (*Undergraduate/Scholarship*) [2775]
Dunbar Heritage Scholarships (*Undergraduate/Scholarship*) [6650]
John Holt Duncan Memorial Scholarships (*Graduate, Undergraduate/Scholarship*) [1654]
Wade and Marcelene Duncan Scholarships (*Undergraduate/Scholarship*) [7431]
Lord Dundonald Chapter (IODE) Scholarships (*Undergraduate/Scholarship*) [5421]
Travis Dunning Memorial Scholarships (*Undergraduate/Scholarship*) [5819]
Durning Sisters Scholarships (*Graduate/Scholarship*) [2645]
Joshua Dyke Family Scholarships (*Undergraduate/Scholarship*) [6884]
Eastern Orthodox Scouting Scholarships (*High School/Scholarship*) [4855]
Eastern Shore Builder's Association Scholarships

(Undergraduate/Scholarship) [2371]
Ellen Eberhardt Memorial Scholarships (Undergraduate/Scholarship) [6772]
Edgecliff Alumni Awards (Undergraduate/Scholarship) [7526]
Melanie and Todd Edmonson Memorial Scholarship (Undergraduate/Scholarship) [2348]
Edmonton Epilepsy Continuing Education Scholarships (Undergraduate/Scholarship) [2824]
Education is Power Scholarships (Undergraduate/Scholarship) [4921]
Education Resource Center (ERC) Scholarships (Undergraduate/Scholarship) [6399]
Educational Administration Scholarships Award (Postgraduate/Scholarship) [397]
Educational Enrichment Awards (Undergraduate/Scholarship) [1209]
Educational Leadership Foundation Grants (Undergraduate/Grant) [2300]
Educational Opportunity Fund (Undergraduate/Scholarship) [3097]
Educational Portal of the Americas Graduate Scholarships (Postgraduate/Scholarship) [2838]
Educational Portal of the Americas Undergraduate Scholarships (Undergraduate/Scholarship) [2839]
Educational and Professional Achievement Scholarships (Undergraduate/Scholarship) [451]
Jimmy Edwards Scholarships (Undergraduate/Scholarship) [2419]
Christine H. Eide Memorial Scholarships (Graduate, Undergraduate/Scholarship) [4242]
Einhorn New Investigator Awards (Undergraduate/Award/Prize) [6466]
ELA Foundation Scholarships (Graduate/Scholarship) [1297]
George & Isabelle Elanjian Scholarships (Undergraduate/Scholarship) [1277]
W. Eldridge and Emily Lowe Scholarships (Undergraduate/Scholarship) [6405]
Todd Elias Memorial Scholarships (Graduate, Undergraduate/Scholarship) [1655]
Elks National Foundation Scholarships (Undergraduate/Scholarship) [2848]
Dr. Robert Elliott Memorial Scholarships (Undergraduate/Scholarship) [4415]
Pauline Elliott Scholarships (Undergraduate/Scholarship) [4416]
Emergency Medicine Physicians Scholarship Fund for Non-Physician Employee Dependents (Undergraduate/Scholarship) [6717]
Emerging Leaders Scholarships (Undergraduate/Scholarship) [1841]
Priscilla Maxwell Endicott Scholarships (Undergraduate/Scholarship) [3447]
Vice Admiral Donald D. Engen Scholarships (Undergraduate/Scholarship) [5132]
Epsilon Epsilon Scholarships (Undergraduate/Scholarship) [6354]
Epsilon Tau Pi's Soaring Eagle Scholarships (Undergraduate/Scholarship) [4856]
Epsilon Tau Scholarships (Undergraduate/Scholarship) [6355]
Alan R. Epstein "Reach for the Stars" Scholarships (Undergraduate/Scholarship) [2597]
eQuality Scholarships (Undergraduate/Scholarship) [6104]
Erb Group Companies Service to Community Scholarships (Undergraduate/Scholarship) [5342]
Robert C. Erb Sr. Scholarships (Undergraduate/Scholarship) [4417]
Harriet Erich Graduate Fellowships (Graduate/Scholarship) [2646]
Ernest Hemingway Research Grants (Professional Development/Grant) [3538]
The Eleonor A. Ernest Scholarship (Undergraduate/Scholarship) [3977]
Robert P. Ernest Scholarship (Undergraduate/Scholarship) [3979]
Boomer Esiason Foundation Scholarship Program (All/Scholarship) [2587]
European College of Liberal Arts (ECLA) Scholarships (Undergraduate/Scholarship) [7022]
Eustace-Kwan Family Foundation Scholarships (Undergraduate/Scholarship) [6388]
Brad Evans Memorial Scholarships (Undergraduate/Scholarship) [5359]
Chuck Evans Scholarships (Undergraduate/Scholarship) [7405]
Evening Mesquite Club Scholarships (Undergraduate/Scholarship) [5823]
Evjue Foundation, Inc./Capital Times Scholarships (Undergraduate/Scholarship) [7253]
Excel Staffing Companies Scholarships for Excellence in Continuing Education (Undergraduate/Scholarship) [192]
Executive Women International Fellows Program (Graduate/Fellowship) [2895]
Executive Women International Scholarship Program (EWISP) (High School/Scholarship) [2896]
Exercise For Life Athletic Scholarships Program (Undergraduate/Scholarship) [2588]
FACT Graduating Senior Scholarship Program (Undergraduate/Scholarship) [2920]
Faculty Research Visit Grant (Doctorate/Grant) [3225]
Fairbanks Chapter Legacy Scholarships (Undergraduate/Scholarship) [7076]
James Mackenzie Fallows Scholarships Honoring Gertrude Baccus (Undergraduate/Scholarship) [5934]
Families of Freedom Scholarship Fund - America Scholarships (Undergraduate/Scholarship) [2902]
Farmers State Bank Scholarships (Undergraduate/Scholarship) [6773]
Farmers Union Marketing and Processing Foundation Stanley Moore Scholarships (Undergraduate/Scholarship) [5250]
Farmington UNICO Scholarships (Undergraduate/Scholarship) [3448]
David Edward Farson Scholarships (Undergraduate/Scholarship) [5480]
Anne M. Fassett Scholarships (Undergraduate/Scholarship) [6651]
FCBA Foundation Scholarships (Undergraduate/Scholarship) [2909]
Federal Employee Education and Assistance Fund Scholarships (Other/Scholarship) [2913]
Federalsburg Rotary Club Scholarships (Undergraduate/Scholarship) [2372]
FEEA Scholarship Program (Other/Scholarship) [2914]
Nolan W. Feeser Scholarship Fund (Undergraduate/Scholarship) [2954]
Virginia Valk Fehsenfeld Scholarships (Undergraduate/Scholarship) [3327]
Symee Ruth Feinburg Memorial Scholarships (Undergraduate/Scholarship) [3449]
Edward R. and Hazel N. Felber Scholarships (Undergraduate/Scholarship) [7254]
Fellowships for Intensive Advanced Turkish Language Study in Turkey (Undergraduate/Fellowship) [895]
Dr. Joan W. Fernandez Point Scholarships (Graduate, Undergraduate/Scholarship) [5719]
Beth K. Fields Scholarships (Undergraduate/Scholarship) [7100]
Film Arts Foundation Development Grants (All/Grant) [2928]
Gordy Fink Memorial Scholarships (Undergraduate/Scholarship) [5824]
First Church of Christ in Wethersfield - Metcalf Scholarships (Undergraduate/Scholarship) [3450]
First Friday Breakfast Club Scholarships (Undergraduate/Scholarship) [6105]
First in My Family Scholarship Program (Undergraduate/Scholarship) [6156]
Arthur and Juna Fisher Memorial Track Scholarships (Undergraduate/Scholarship) [5935]
Fitzgerald Fellowships (Undergraduate/Fellowship) [2672]
Carol C. Fitzgerald Scholarship Program (Professional Development/Scholarship) [2911]
Fitzgerald Scholarships (Undergraduate/Scholarship) [2673]
Gloria Flaherty Scholarships (Graduate/Scholarship) [3248]
Albert Flegenheimer Memorial Scholarships (Undergraduate/Scholarship) [4495]
FLEOA Foundation Scholarship Program (Undergraduate/Scholarship) [2916]
Grant H. Flint International Scholarships - Category I (Undergraduate/Scholarship) [6596]
Florida Atlantic Planning Society Graduate Fellowships for Academic Excellence (Postgraduate/Fellowship) [2997]
John Flynn Memorial Scholarship (Undergraduate/Scholarship) [2465]
Barney Flynn Memorial Scholarships (High School/Scholarship) [2275]
FMA-FEEA Scholarship Program (Undergraduate/Scholarship) [2918]
Alice J. Foit Scholarships (Undergraduate/Scholarship) [6719]
Food for Thought Scholarships (High School/Scholarship) [2276]
Ford Foundation Diversity Fellowships (Doctorate/Fellowship) [4618]
Ford Motor Company Scholarship Program (Undergraduate/Scholarship) [3589]
Anne Ford Scholarships (Undergraduate/Scholarship) [4796]
V. Thomas Forehand, Jr. Scholarships (Undergraduate/Scholarship) [7240]
Foresters Scholarships (Undergraduate/Scholarship) [3682]
Forsyth County United Way Scholarships (Undergraduate/Scholarship) [4133]
Forward Face Scholarships (Professional Development/Scholarship) [3033]
Fostering Hope Scholarship Fund (Undergraduate/Scholarship) [5481]
Foundation for the Advancement of Aboriginal Youth Bursary Program (Undergraduate/Scholarship) [1939]
Foundation for the Advancement of Aboriginal Youth Scholarships (Undergraduate/Scholarship) [1940]
Foundation for the Carolinas Rotary Scholarship Fund (Undergraduate/Scholarship) [3059]
Foundation of the Federal Bar Association Public Service Scholarships (Undergraduate/Scholarship) [3125]
Foundation Scholarships (Undergraduate/Scholarship) [4064]
Terry Fox Memorial Scholarships (Undergraduate/Scholarship) [5117]
Jacob and Lewis Fox Scholarships (Undergraduate/Scholarship) [3451]
Joey and Florence Franco Legacy Scholarship (Undergraduate/Scholarship) [1824]
Joe Francomano Scholarships (Undergraduate/Scholarship) [4038]
Johnny and Sarah Frank Scholarships (Undergraduate/Scholarship) [4358]
John Hope Franklin Dissertation Fellowships (Doctorate/Fellowship) [768]
James Franklin and Dorothy J. Warnell Scholarship Fund (Undergraduate/Scholarship) [2508]
Franklin Elementary School PTA Scholarships (Undergraduate/Scholarship) [5936]
Franklin Research Grants (Doctorate/Grant) [769]
John and Victory E. Frantz Scholarship Fund (Undergraduate/Scholarship) [3279]
Freedom Alliance Scholarships (Undergraduate/Scholarship) [3143]
Dale E. Fridell Memorial Scholarships (Undergraduate/Scholarship) [6793]
Phil Friel Scholarships (Undergraduate/Scholarship) [4418]
Joel R. Friend Scholarship (Undergraduate/Scholarship) [1626]
Friends of Coal Scholarships (Undergraduate/Scholarship) [7394]
Friends of Megan Bolton Memorial Fund (Undergraduate/Scholarship) [3100]
Friendship Scholarship Fund (Undergraduate/Scholarship) [3101]
Dean A. Froehlich Endowed Scholarships (Undergraduate/Scholarship) [4179]
Melbourne & Alice E. Frontjes Scholarships (Undergraduate/Scholarship) [3328]
Marian Johnson Frutiger Scholarships (Undergraduate/Scholarship) [6356]
Gerard Swartz Fudge Memorial Scholarships (Undergraduate/Scholarship) [3638]
Fulbright New Century Scholars Program (Professional Development/Scholarship) [1714]
Daniel G. and Helen I. Fultz Scholarship Fund (Undergraduate/Scholarship) [2955]

Gaddy Student Scholarships (Undergraduate/Scholarship) [7435]
Gaebe Eagle Scout Awards (Undergraduate/Scholarship) [4857]
Harry Gairey Scholarships (Undergraduate/Scholarship) [1731]
Farley Moody Galbraith Scholarship Fund (Undergraduate/Scholarship) [2350]
Louise Bales Gallagher Scholarships (Undergraduate/Scholarship) [2647]
William E. "Bill" Gallagher Scholarships (Undergraduate/Scholarship) [5482]
Whitney Laine Gallahar Memorial Scholarship Fund (Undergraduate/Scholarship) [2351]
Carolyn Gallmeyer Scholarships (Undergraduate/Scholarship) [3329]
Gallo Blue Chip Scholarships (Undergraduate/Scholarship) [3404]
Gamma Iota Scholarships - Gamma Tau (Undergraduate/Scholarship) [6357]
Gamma Iota Scholarships - Kappa Eta (Undergraduate/Scholarship) [6358]
Gamma Iota Scholarships - Zeta Kappa (Undergraduate/Scholarship) [6359]
Gamma Iota Scholarships - Zeta Nu (Undergraduate/Scholarship) [6360]
GANA Scholarship Program (Undergraduate/Scholarship) [3258]
Veronica Gantt Memorial Scholarships (Undergraduate/Scholarship) [5827]
Garden State Rotary Club of Cherry Hill Scholarships (Undergraduate/Scholarship) [1895]
Peter M. Gargano Scholarship Fund (Undergraduate/Scholarship) [2776]
Gail Garner R.I.S.E. Memorial Scholarships (Undergraduate/Scholarship) [5938]
Marcus Garvey Scholarships (Undergraduate/Scholarship) [3453]
Marcus Mosiah Garvey Scholarships (Undergraduate/Scholarship) [3997]
Gaston Scholarships (Undergraduate/Scholarship) [239]
Gates Cambridge Scholarships (Doctorate, Postgraduate/Scholarship) [4704]
Raffin Gathercole Scholarships (Undergraduate/Scholarship) [3168]
David A. and Pamela A. Gault Charitable Fund (Undergraduate/Scholarship) [6721]
James L. Gavin Memorial Scholarships (Graduate, Undergraduate/Scholarship) [1656]
A.R.F.O.R.A. Martha Gavrila Scholarships for Women (Graduate/Scholarship) [912]
Gay, Lesbian, Bisexual, Transgender Alumni Council Scholarships (Undergraduate/Scholarship) [7255]
Gay and Lesbian Business Association of Santa Barbara Scholarships (Undergraduate/Scholarship) [6106]
Irma Gelhausen Scholarship Fund (Undergraduate/Scholarship) [4140]
General Falcon Scholarships (Undergraduate/Scholarship) [5732]
General Mills Foundation Scholarships (Undergraduate/Scholarship) [622]
Gerber Foundation Merit Scholarships (Undergraduate/Scholarship) [3219]
Daniel Gerber, Sr. Medallion Scholarships (Undergraduate/Scholarship) [3220]
Getty Research Exchange Fellowship Program for Cultural Heritage Preservation (Doctorate/Fellowship) [896]
GFWC Women's Club of South County Scholarships (Undergraduate/Scholarship) [6038]
GHI Fellowships at the Horner Library (Doctorate/Fellowship) [3234]
Tim Gifford Scholarship Fund (Undergraduate/Scholarship) [3282]
Shane Gilbert Memorial Scholarships (Undergraduate/Scholarship) [5484]
William Harrison Gill Education Fund (Undergraduate/Scholarship) [1627]
Gill Foundation Scholarships (Colorado) (Undergraduate/Scholarship) [6107]
Benjamin A. Gilman International Scholarship (Undergraduate/Scholarship) [7031]
Leo Gilmartin Scholarships (High School/Scholarship) [5708]
John L. Gilmer Educational Grants (Undergraduate/Scholarship) [7437]
John L. Gilmer Merit Based Scholarships (Undergraduate/Scholarship) [7438]
Susan Kay Munson Gilmore Memorial Scholarship (Undergraduate/Scholarship) [2467]
Nick Giorgione Hope for Hearts Scholarships (Undergraduate/Scholarship) [5829]
Alex Gissler Memorial Scholarships (Undergraduate/Scholarship) [4419]
Ann and Brad Glassco Scholarships (Undergraduate/Scholarship) [5939]
Glazing Industry Scholarships (Undergraduate/Scholarship) [5830]
Gleaner Life Insurance Scholarship Foundation (Undergraduate/Scholarship) [3244]
GLSEN Connecticut Chapter Scholarships (Undergraduate/Scholarship) [6108]
Irene Carlson Gnaedinger Memorial Scholarships (Undergraduate/Scholarship) [4180]
Godparents for Tanzania Scholarships (Undergraduate/Scholarship) [3246]
Gold Award/Eagle Scout Scholarships (Undergraduate/Scholarship) [4858]
Gold Key Scholarships (Undergraduate/Scholarship) [4065]
Golden Key International Honour Society New Graduate Member Scholarships (Undergraduate/Scholarship) [3252]
Golden Key International Honour Society Study Abroad Scholarships (Undergraduate/Scholarship) [3253]
Golden Key International Honour Society Undergraduate Research Grants (Undergraduate/Grant) [3254]
Goldmann Scholarships Fund (Undergraduate/Scholarship) [3645]
Joshua Gomes Memorial Scholarship Fund (Graduate, Undergraduate/Scholarship) [4922]
Millie Gonzalez Memorial Scholarships (Undergraduate/Scholarship) [4923]
J.O. Goodman Scholarship Awards (Undergraduate/Scholarship) [5343]
David B. Goodstein Point Scholarships (Graduate, Undergraduate/Scholarship) [5720]
Richard Goolsby Scholarship Fund (Undergraduate/Scholarship) [3060]
Lucille May Gopie Scholarships (Undergraduate/Scholarship) [1732]
L. Gordon, Jr. and June D. Pfefferkorn Scholarships (Undergraduate/Scholarship) [7439]
Thomas Boston Gordon Memorial Scholarships (Graduate, Undergraduate/Scholarship) [1658]
Pauline LaFon Gore Scholarships (Undergraduate/Scholarship) [2421]
Richard C. Gorecki Scholarships (Undergraduate/Scholarship) [5733]
Nettie and Jesse Gorov Scholarship (Undergraduate/Scholarship) [2468]
American Association of University Women-Mary Sue Gottcent Memorial Scholarships (Undergraduate/Scholarship) [6655]
Carl W. Gottschalk Research Scholar Grants (Doctorate/Grant) [1018]
Charles F. Gould Endowment Scholarships (Undergraduate/Scholarship) [4359]
Graduate Education Loan Scholarships (Graduate/Loan) [3780]
Graduate Student Scholarship (Graduate/Scholarship) [157]
Rachel Graham Memorial Scholarships (Undergraduate/Scholarship) [5940]
Grand Rapids Scholarship Association (Undergraduate/Scholarship) [3331]
Grande Prairie 4-H District Scholarships (Undergraduate/Scholarship) [133]
Granger Business Association College Scholarships (Undergraduate/Scholarship) [3362]
Russ Grant Memorial Scholarship for Tennis (Undergraduate/Scholarship) [5486]
Lucile Cheever Graubart/Lambda Scholarships (Undergraduate/Scholarship) [6361]
Greater Seattle Business Association Scholarships (Undergraduate/Scholarship) [3367]
Green Hill Yacht and Country Club Scholarships (Undergraduate/Scholarship) [2374]
Green Knight Economic Development Corporation (GKEDC) Scholarships (Undergraduate/Scholarship) [3381]
James H. and Shirley L. Green Scholarship Fund (Undergraduate/Scholarship) [6723]
Curt Greene Memorial Scholarships (Undergraduate/Scholarship) [3405]
Francis Harris Gresham Scholarships (Undergraduate/Scholarship) [6657]
Griffin Foundation Scholarships (Undergraduate/Scholarship) [3383]
Griffith College Scholarships for NSHSS Members (High School/Scholarship) [5068]
Bobby Griffith Memorial Scholarships (Undergraduate/Scholarship) [6109]
Russ Griffith Memorial Scholarships (Graduate, Undergraduate/Scholarship) [2617]
Homajean Grisham Memorial Scholarships (Undergraduate/Scholarship) [5280]
Reginald K. Groome Memorial Scholarships (Postgraduate/Scholarship) [6286]
Jack & Mary Lou Gruber Scholarships (Undergraduate/Scholarship) [4181]
Gruwell Scholarships (Undergraduate/Scholarship) [2375]
Melissa Guerra Scholarships (Undergraduate/Scholarship) [2277]
Bobette Bibo Gugliotta Memorial Scholarships for Creative Writing (Undergraduate/Scholarship) [6390]
GuildScholar Awards (Undergraduate/Scholarship) [4027]
Hai Guin Scholarships Association (Undergraduate/Scholarship) [1280]
Guin-Stanford Scholarships (Professional Development/Scholarship) [2352]
Calouste Gulbenkian Foundation Scholarships (Graduate, Undergraduate/Scholarship) [1281]
Larry Gulley Scholarships (Undergraduate/Scholarship) [6449]
Patricia S. Gustafson '56 Memorial Scholarships (Undergraduate/Scholarship) [2777]
Guzkowski Family Scholarships (Undergraduate/Scholarship) [5942]
Sarah Gwisdalla Memorial Scholarships (Undergraduate/Scholarship) [5487]
Wesley R. Habley NACADA Summer Institute Scholarships (Professional Development/Scholarship) [4615]
Jaye Haddad Memorial Fund (Undergraduate/Scholarship) [6110]
Nathaniel Hafer Memorial Scholarships (Undergraduate/Scholarship) [5488]
Sophia Hagopian Memorial Fund (Undergraduate/Scholarship) [1282]
Leslie Jane Hahn Memorial Scholarships (Undergraduate/Scholarship) [6191]
Hall of Achievement Scholarships (Undergraduate/Scholarship) [1825]
Joyce C. Hall College Scholarships (Undergraduate/Scholarship) [5570]
Chappie Hall Scholarship Program (Graduate, Postgraduate, Undergraduate/Scholarship) [2]
Guy D. & Mary Edith Halladay Graduate Scholarships (Undergraduate/Scholarship) [3332]
Al Hamilton Scholarships (Undergraduate/Scholarship) [1734]
George and Mary Josephine Hamman Foundation Scholarships (High School/Scholarship) [3392]
Jay Hammond Memorial Scholarships (Undergraduate/Scholarship) [7077]
Adam Hampton Memorial Scholarship Fund (Undergraduate/Scholarship) [2956]
Hancock Family Snow Hill High School Scholarships (Undergraduate/Scholarship) [2376]
H. Pauline Hand Memorial Scholarships (Undergraduate/Scholarship) [6777]
Ilse and George Hanfmann Fellowships (Doctorate/Fellowship) [897]
Byron Hanke Fellowships (Undergraduate/Fellowship) [3088]
Clayburn and Garnet R. Hanna Scholarships (Undergraduate/Scholarship) [5489]
Hanover-Horton High School Youth of Promise Scholarships (Undergraduate/Scholarship) [3980]
Zenon C.R. Hansen Leadership Scholarships

(Undergraduate/Scholarship) [4859]
Cleam T. Hanson Scholarship Fund (Undergraduate/Scholarship) [4564]
H.G. Hardbarger Science and Mathematics Awards (Undergraduate/Scholarship) [5490]
Charles Henry Hardin Memorial Scholarships (Graduate, Undergraduate/Scholarship) [1659]
Matt Harmon Memorial Scholarships (Undergraduate/Scholarship) [6658]
Harness Tracks of America Scholarship Fund (Undergraduate/Scholarship) [3407]
Walter and Lucille Harper Scholarship (Undergraduate/Scholarship) [4066]
Ruth Harris Memorial Scholarships (Undergraduate/Scholarship) [5491]
Frank and Charlene Harris Scholarships (Undergraduate/Scholarship) [2422]
Peg Hart Harrison Memorial Scholarships (Undergraduate/Scholarship) [2648]
Evelyn W. Harrison Point Scholarships (Graduate, Undergraduate/Scholarship) [5721]
Morton Harrison Scholarship Fund (Undergraduate/Scholarship) [2957]
Harry and Lucille Brown Scholarships (Undergraduate/Scholarship) [3334]
Carroll Hart Scholarships (Graduate/Scholarship) [6450]
Hartford Foundation College Scholarship Program (Undergraduate/Scholarship) [3458]
Hartford Grammar School Scholarships (Undergraduate/Scholarship) [3460]
Hartford Whalers Booster Club Scholarships (Undergraduate/Scholarship) [3462]
Harry C. Hartleben III. Scholarships (Undergraduate/Scholarship) [5493]
William T. Hartzell Memorial Scholarships (Undergraduate/Scholarship) [5943]
Gregory Lynn Haught Citizenship Awards (Undergraduate/Award/Prize) [5495]
Dorcas Edmonson Haught Scholarships (Undergraduate/Scholarship) [5496]
R. Garn Haycock Memorial Scholarships (Undergraduate/Scholarship) [5944]
HBO Point Scholarships (Graduate, Undergraduate/Scholarship) [5722]
Erin Kumelos Heard Memorial Scholarships (Undergraduate/Scholarship) [2649]
Elizabeth Heath Post-Secondary Awards (Undergraduate/Scholarship) [5422]
Elizabeth Heath Technical, Trades Training and Development Awards (Undergraduate/Scholarship) [5423]
Dr. James H. Heckaman Memorial Scholarship Fund (Undergraduate/Scholarship) [6725]
Professor Ulla Hedner Scholarships (Undergraduate/Scholarship) [4924]
Howell Heflin Memorial Scholarships (Undergraduate/Scholarship) [5281]
Lavonne Heghinian Scholarships (Undergraduate/Scholarship) [2689]
Ronald, Randall and Roger Helman Scholarships (Graduate, Undergraduate/Scholarship) [1660]
PPQ William F. Helms Student Scholarships (Undergraduate/Scholarship) [7299]
Jeanne H. Hemmingway Scholarships (Undergraduate/Scholarship) [2778]
Hemophilia Health Services Memorial Scholarship Program (Graduate, Undergraduate/Scholarship) [4925]
Henderson Memorial Endowed Scholarships (Undergraduate/Scholarship) [4183]
Melvin Henderson-Rubio Scholarships (Undergraduate/Scholarship) [7414]
John B. Henderson Scholarships (Undergraduate/Scholarship) [4361]
Michael Herman Memorial Scholarship Fund (Undergraduate/Scholarship) [3286]
Manuel Hernandez, Jr. Foundation Scholarships (High School/Scholarship) [2278]
Ella Beren Hersch Scholarships (Undergraduate/Scholarship) [5497]
Peter Hess Scholarships (Undergraduate/Scholarship) [3183]
June Hester Memorial Scholarships (Undergraduate/Scholarship) [5282]
Jim Hierlihy Memorial Scholarships (Undergraduate/Scholarship) [2879]
Highway Worker Memorial Scholarship Program (Undergraduate/Scholarship) [904]
Doris E. Higley Memorial Scholarships (Undergraduate/Scholarship) [3464]
Douglas W. Hill, Jr. Memorial Scholarships (Graduate, Undergraduate/Scholarship) [1661]
John A. Hill Memorial Scholarships (Graduate, Undergraduate/Scholarship) [1662]
Gus and Henrietta Hill Scholarships (Graduate/Scholarship) [2779]
Cecilia Hillman Scholarships (Undergraduate/Scholarship) [3465]
Hilton Tribal College Diversity Scholarships (Undergraduate/Scholarship) [623]
D. Glenn Hilts Scholarships Program (Graduate, Undergraduate/Scholarship) [1493]
Jim & Nancy Hinkle Travel Grants (Postdoctorate/Grant) [3539]
Ernest and Charlotte Hirst Family Scholarships (Undergraduate/Scholarship) [3466]
Hispanic Association of Colleges and Universities Scholarships (Undergraduate/Scholarship) [3568]
Hispanic Association on Corporate Responsibility Scholarship Program (Undergraduate/Scholarship) [3573]
Hispanic Scholarship Fund (HSF) College Scholarship Program (Graduate, Undergraduate/Scholarship) [3591]
Hispanic Serving Institution Scholarships (Undergraduate/Scholarship) [6973]
Historically Black College or University Scholarships (Undergraduate/Scholarship) [6974]
Lucy Hsu Ho Scholarship (Undergraduate/Scholarship) [1628]
C.V. Hoar Scholarship Awards (Undergraduate/Scholarship) [5344]
James E. Hoff, S.J. Scholars (Undergraduate/Scholarship) [7529]
Hoffman Family Scholarships Fund (Undergraduate/Scholarship) [3288]
Henry Hoffman Memorial Scholarship Fund (Undergraduate/Scholarship) [4695]
Irving J. Hoffman Memorial Scholarships (Undergraduate/Scholarship) [7222]
The Thelma S. Hoge Memorial Scholarship Fund (Undergraduate/Scholarship) [2400]
Michael J. Hoggard Memorial Scholarships (Undergraduate/Scholarship) [5832]
Cleve Holloway Memorial Scholarship Fund (Undergraduate/Scholarship) [2353]
Robert Holmes Scholarships (Undergraduate/Scholarship) [2515]
Holy Name Of Jesus Parish Scholarships (Undergraduate/Scholarship) [5945]
Home Depot Scholarships (Undergraduate/Scholarship) [7006]
Herbert Hoover Uncommon Student Awards (Undergraduate/Scholarship) [3613]
Hopi Education Awards (All/Award/Prize) [1210]
Frank and Gladys Hopkins Endowed Scholarships (Undergraduate/Scholarship) [4185]
Minnie Hopkins Memorial Scholarship Fund of Lathrop/Compton School (Undergraduate/Scholarship) [6728]
Sam J. Hord Memorial Scholarships (Undergraduate/Scholarship) [6625]
Hormel Foods Charitable Trust Scholarships (Undergraduate/Scholarship) [3615]
Hosinec Family Scholarships (Graduate, Undergraduate/Scholarship) [7223]
Max and Julia Houghton Duluth Central Scholarships (Undergraduate/Scholarship) [2781]
Houston Alumnae Chapter Graduate Fellowships (Graduate/Fellowship) [2650]
Houston Alumnae Undergraduate Tri Delta Scholarships (Undergraduate/Scholarship) [2651]
Kaspar Hovannisian Memorial Scholarships (Graduate/Scholarship) [1283]
Hirair and Anna Hovnanian Foundation Presidential Scholarships (Undergraduate/Scholarship) [1284]
Hirair and Anna Hovnanian Foundation Scholarships (Undergraduate/Scholarship) [1285]
C.D. Howard Scholarships (Undergraduate/Scholarship) [3827]
Christopher Hoy/ERT Scholarships (Graduate/Scholarship) [701]
HSF/Atrisco Heritage Foundation Scholarship Program (Graduate, Undergraduate/Scholarship) [3593]
HSF/IDT Hope High School Scholarship Program (Undergraduate/Scholarship) [3597]
Albert W. and Mildred Hubbard Scholarships (Undergraduate/Scholarship) [6194]
William Peyton Hubbard Scholarships (Undergraduate/Scholarship) [1735]
Amber Huber Memorial Scholarship (Undergraduate/Scholarship) [2471]
Dale Hughes, Jr. Memorial Scholarships (Undergraduate/Scholarship) [6779]
Roger K. Hughes Legacy Scholarship (Undergraduate/Scholarship) [1826]
James Hughes Memorial Scholarship Fund (Undergraduate/Scholarship) [5564]
Paul A. Hughes Memorial Scholarship (Undergraduate/Scholarship) [1827]
Humane Studies Fellowships (Graduate/Fellowship) [3728]
Humber College Institute of Technology and Advanced Learning Scholarships (Undergraduate/Scholarship) [3998]
Kevin Hummer Point Scholarships (Graduate, Undergraduate/Scholarship) [5723]
Donald & Florence Hunting Scholarships (Undergraduate/Scholarship) [3335]
Clay Huntington Sports Communications Scholarships (Undergraduate/Scholarship) [3376]
Doc Hurley Scholarships (Undergraduate/Scholarship) [3468]
Mike Hylton and Ron Niederman Memorial Scholarships (Undergraduate/Scholarship) [4926]
I Have a Dream Scholarships (Undergraduate/Scholarship) [3999]
IAESTE United States Scholarships (Undergraduate/Scholarship) [1435]
IAHCSMM - Purdue University Scholarship Awards (Professional Development/Scholarship) [3801]
Ice Skating Institute of America Education Foundation (Undergraduate/Scholarship) [3642]
Idaho Attorney General Scholarships (Undergraduate/Scholarship) [4186]
Idaho Promise Category B Scholarships (Undergraduate/Scholarship) [4187]
IEHA Education Foundation Scholarship Awards (Undergraduate/Scholarship) [3842]
Illinois Association of Chamber of Commerce Executives Scholarships (Postdoctorate/Scholarship) [3654]
Illinois Student Assistance Commission Merit Recognition Scholarships (Undergraduate/Scholarship) [3666]
Illuminator Educational Foundation Scholarships (Undergraduate/Scholarship) [1828]
Imagine America Online Scholarships (Undergraduate/Scholarship) [3674]
Imperial Sovereign Court of Tacoma Scholarships (Professional Development/Scholarship) [5766]
Independent Lubricant Manufacturers Association Scholarships (Undergraduate/Scholarship) [3680]
Indiana Alumni Scholarships (Undergraduate/Scholarship) [7530]
Indiana State Alumni Association Dean's Scholarships (Undergraduate/Scholarship) [3702]
Indiana State Alumni Association Incentive Scholarships (Undergraduate/Scholarship) [3703]
Indiana State Alumni Association President's Academic Excellence Scholarships (Undergraduate/Scholarship) [3704]
Indiana State Alumni Association President's Scholarships (Undergraduate/Scholarship) [3705]
Indiana State Alumni Association Transfer Student Scholarships (Undergraduate/Scholarship) [3707]
Indiana Top Scholar Award (Undergraduate/Scholarship) [3708]
Barbara Ingram, Janet W. McCarthy and W.J.P. Jack Robertson Memorial Scholarships (Undergraduate/Scholarship) [5424]
Jennifer Ingrum Scholarships (Undergraduate/Scholarship) [2424]
INIA Scholarship Program (All/Scholarship) [3880]
Inland Northwest Business Alliance (INBA) Scholarships (Undergraduate/Scholarship) [5767]

Institute of Turkish Studies Undergraduate Study Grants *(Undergraduate/Grant)* [3755]
International Door Association Scholarship Awards *(Undergraduate/Scholarship)* [3840]
International Education Awards - Ukraine *(Undergraduate/Scholarship)* [160]
International Grenfell Association Bursary *(Undergraduate/Scholarship)* [3863]
International Grenfell Association Secondary/High School Scholarships *(Undergraduate/Scholarship)* [3864]
International Grenfell Association University/College Scholarships *(Undergraduate/Scholarship)* [3865]
International Harvester Collectors Scholarships *(Undergraduate/Scholarship)* [3867]
International Order of the King's Daughters and Sons North American Indian Scholarship Program *(Undergraduate/Scholarship)* [635]
International Peace Scholarships *(Undergraduate/Scholarship)* [5684]
International Sanitary Supply Association Foundation Scholarships *(High School/Scholarship)* [2030]
Interracial Scholarship Fund of Greater Hartford *(Undergraduate/Scholarship)* [3469]
Iowa Division Scholarships *(All/Scholarship)* [4514]
Greg Irons Student Scholarships *(Undergraduate/Scholarship)* [2782]
IRTS Foundation Summer Fellowship Program *(Graduate, Undergraduate/Fellowship)* [3886]
Martha Isabell Memorial Scholarships *(Undergraduate/Scholarship)* [5283]
Hazel D. Isbell Fellowships *(Graduate/Fellowship)* [2652]
Gunnar Isberg Student Scholarships *(Undergraduate/Scholarship)* [4550]
Broughton Isom Memorial Scholarships *(Undergraduate/Scholarship)* [5284]
Italian Language Scholarships *(Undergraduate/Scholarship)* [5372]
J and K Foundation Scholarships *(Undergraduate/Scholarship)* [3470]
Jack Family Scholarships *(Undergraduate/Scholarship)* [3336]
The Jackson Club Scholarships *(Undergraduate/Scholarship)* [2783]
Jackson High School Alumni Scholarship Fund *(Undergraduate/Scholarship)* [6731]
Sylvia E. Jackson Scholarships *(Undergraduate/Scholarship)* [6780]
Holly Jackson-Wuller Memorial Scholarships *(Undergraduate/Scholarship)* [5498]
Freddy L. Jacobs Scholarships *(Undergraduate/Scholarship)* [3815]
Eric L. Jacobson Memorial Scholarships *(Undergraduate/Scholarship)* [5946]
Dwight P. Jacobus Scholarships *(Undergraduate/Scholarship)* [1488]
Cory Jam Awards *(Undergraduate/Scholarship)* [2784]
Jamaica Day Basil Duncan Memorial Scholarships *(Undergraduate/Scholarship)* [4000]
Jamail/Long Challenge Grant Scholarships *(Graduate, Undergraduate/Scholarship)* [3576]
Carl and Lucille Jarrett Scholarship Fund *(Graduate, Undergraduate/Scholarship)* [2961]
Right Hon. Michaelle Jean Scholarships *(Undergraduate/Scholarship)* [1736]
Erin L. Jenkins Memorial Scholarship Fund *(Undergraduate/Scholarship)* [3107]
Elise Reed Jenkins Memorial Scholarships - Gamma Lambda *(Undergraduate/Scholarship)* [6362]
Elise Reed Jenkins Memorial Scholarships - Gamma Psi *(Undergraduate/Scholarship)* [6363]
Ruth E. Jenkins Scholarships *(Undergraduate/Scholarship)* [6196]
Mike Jensen R.I.S.E. Memorial Scholarships *(Undergraduate/Scholarship)* [5947]
Kenneth Jernigan Scholarships *(Undergraduate/Scholarship)* [4878]
Harry Jerome Scholarships *(Undergraduate/Scholarship)* [1737]
James Jesinski Scholarships *(Undergraduate/Scholarship)* [7258]
JFEW/UJA-Federation Rose Biller Scholarships *(Undergraduate/Scholarship)* [4024]
James V. Johnson Scholarship Fund *(Undergraduate/Scholarship)* [3063]
Camilla C. Johnson Scholarships *(Undergraduate/Scholarship)* [3337]
Chip Johnson Scholarships *(Undergraduate/Scholarship)* [6659]
Stella B. Johnson Scholarships *(Undergraduate/Scholarship)* [7443]
Julian C. Johnston Memorial Scholarships *(Undergraduate/Scholarship)* [6064]
Napoleon A. Jones, III Memorial Scholarships *(Undergraduate/Scholarship)* [6197]
Annabel Lambeth Jones Scholarship Fund *(Undergraduate/Scholarship)* [3064]
Junior Achievement of East Central Ohio, Inc. Scholarship Fund *(Undergraduate/Scholarship)* [6732]
Junior Women of the Contemporary Club Scholarships *(Undergraduate/Scholarship)* [5949]
Just Out Scholarship Fund *(Undergraduate/Scholarship)* [2885]
Juvenile Arthritis Scholarships *(Undergraduate/Scholarship)* [3471]
K-12 Edu-Grants *(High School/Grant)* [4927]
David A. Kaiser Memorial Scholarship Fund *(Undergraduate/Scholarship)* [6733]
Martin S. Kane Memorial Community Service Award Scholarships *(Undergraduate/Scholarship)* [2378]
Kansas City Division Scholarships *(All/Scholarship)* [4515]
Walter Kapala Scholarships *(Undergraduate/Scholarship)* [3472]
Don Kaplan Legacy Scholarship *(Undergraduate/Scholarship)* [1829]
Kaplan Test Prep and Admission Scholarships for NSHSS Members *(High School/Scholarship)* [5069]
Kappa Chapter Centennial Scholarships *(Undergraduate/Scholarship)* [2653]
Kappa Kappa Gamma Graduate Scholarships *(Graduate/Scholarship)* [4044]
Kappa Kappa Gamma Undergraduate Scholarships *(Undergraduate/Scholarship)* [4045]
Kappa Omicron Nu Honor Society Scholars Program Grants *(Undergraduate/Grant)* [4053]
Kappa Zeta Scholarships *(Undergraduate/Scholarship)* [6364]
Kaprielian Memorial Scholarships *(Undergraduate/Scholarship)* [7241]
K.A.S.A Memorial Scholarships *(Undergraduate/Scholarship)* [5499]
KASF Chair Scholarships *(Graduate, Undergraduate/Scholarship)* [4085]
KASF Designated Scholarships *(Graduate, Undergraduate/Scholarship)* [4086]
KASF General Scholarships *(Graduate, Undergraduate/Scholarship)* [4087]
Peter Kaufman Memorial Scholarships *(Undergraduate/Scholarship)* [6112]
William and Beatrice Kavanaugh Scholarship *(Undergraduate/Scholarship)* [3983]
Kawano Family Scholarships *(Undergraduate/Scholarship)* [6198]
Norair M. Kebabjian Memorial Scholarships *(Undergraduate/Scholarship)* [1264]
Doc Keen Memorial Scholarships *(Undergraduate/Scholarship)* [6661]
Annette and Ernest Keith Scholarships *(Undergraduate/Scholarship)* [5950]
Kellogg Company Career Scholarships *(Undergraduate/Scholarship)* [4067]
Dr. Charles Kelly Memorial Scholarships *(Undergraduate/Scholarship)* [5500]
Raymond A. Kent-Navy V-12/ROTC *(Undergraduate/Scholarship)* [7101]
Kentucky Alumni Club Scholarships - Capital Region Alumni Club *(Undergraduate/Scholarship)* [7102]
Kentucky Alumni Club Scholarships - Central Kentucky Alumni Club *(Undergraduate/Scholarship)* [7103]
Kentucky Alumni Club Scholarships - Lake Cumberland Alumni Club *(Undergraduate/Scholarship)* [7104]
Kentucky Alumni Club Scholarships - Northern Kentucky Alumni Club *(Undergraduate/Scholarship)* [7105]
Kentucky Educational Excellence Scholarships *(Graduate, Undergraduate/Scholarship)* [1702]
Kentucky Tuition Grants *(Undergraduate/Grant)* [1703]
Judge Oliver Kessel Memorial Scholarship-Ripley Rotary *(Undergraduate/Scholarship)* [5501]
Dr. Leizon and Barbara Kessel Scholarships *(Undergraduate/Scholarship)* [3473]
Ashley E. Ketcher Memorial Scholarships *(Undergraduate/Scholarship)* [2473]
Luella Akins Key Scholarships *(Undergraduate/Scholarship)* [2654]
KFC Colonel's Scholars Program *(Undergraduate/Scholarship)* [4070]
Khaki University and Y.M.C.A. Memorial Scholarships *(Undergraduate/Scholarship)* [7225]
Bill Kidder Fund Awards *(Undergraduate/Scholarship)* [6113]
Mary and Millard Kiker Scholarship Fund *(Undergraduate/Scholarship)* [3065]
Kilbuck Family Native American Scholarship *(Undergraduate/Scholarship)* [1629]
Kildonan Education Awards *(Undergraduate/Scholarship)* [5425]
Helen and George Kilik Scholarship *(Undergraduate/Scholarship)* [161]
Killam Fellowships Program *(Undergraduate/Fellowship)* [7033]
Kimberly Elementary School PTA Scholarships *(Undergraduate/Scholarship)* [5951]
Dr. Martin Luther King & Coretta Scott King Student Leadership Scholarships *(Undergraduate/Scholarship)* [1896]
Arthur M. and Berdena King Eagle Scout Scholarships *(High School/Scholarship)* [4860]
Mackenzie King Open Scholarships *(Graduate/Scholarship)* [4428]
Kingsbury Elementary School PTA Scholarships *(Undergraduate/Scholarship)* [5952]
James P. Kirkgasser Memorial Scholarships *(Graduate, Undergraduate/Scholarship)* [1663]
Isabel Mayer Kirkpatrick Scholarships *(Undergraduate/Scholarship)* [6662]
Dr. Elemer and Eva Kiss Scholarships Fund *(Undergraduate/Scholarship)* [3629]
Kiwanis Club of Escondido Scholarships I *(Undergraduate/Scholarship)* [6199]
Kiwanis Club of Escondido Scholarships II *(Undergraduate/Scholarship)* [6200]
Lewiston Clarkston Kiwanis Club Scholarships *(Undergraduate/Scholarship)* [4189]
Gerda and Kurt Klein Scholarships *(High School/Scholarship)* [3621]
Bryan L. Knapp Point Scholarships *(Graduate, Undergraduate/Scholarship)* [5724]
J. Merrill Knapp Research Fellowships *(Undergraduate/Fellowship)* [597]
Kemper K. Knapp Scholarships *(Undergraduate/Scholarship)* [7259]
Iver & Cora Knapstad Scholarships *(Undergraduate/Scholarship)* [4363]
Knights of Pythias Scholarships *(Undergraduate/Scholarship)* [5834]
Knox-Hume Scholarships *(Undergraduate/Scholarship)* [2426]
John Reily Knox Memorial Scholarships *(Graduate, Undergraduate/Scholarship)* [1664]
Ina Knutsen Scholarships *(Undergraduate/Scholarship)* [6314]
Seth Koehler Central High School Scholarship Fund *(Undergraduate/Scholarship)* [3289]
Anna and John Kolesay Memorial Scholarship *(Undergraduate/Scholarship)* [162]
Bernie Kom Memorial Awards *(Postgraduate/Award/Prize)* [6268]
Susan G. Komen Breast Cancer Foundation College Scholarship Awards *(Undergraduate/Award/Prize)* [4080]
Herman P. Kopplemann Scholarships *(Undergraduate/Scholarship)* [3474]
Robert Wade Korn Endowed Scholarships *(Undergraduate/Scholarship)* [4364]
Eugene & Elinor Kotur Scholarship Trust Fund *(Undergraduate/Scholarship)* [7359]

Eve Kraft Education and College Scholarships *(Undergraduate/Scholarship)* [7304]
Norman Kramer Scholarship Award *(Undergraduate/Scholarship)* [4500]
Sharon Kreikemeier Memorial Scholarships *(Undergraduate/Scholarship)* [5160]
Robert Krembil Scholarships of Merit *(Postgraduate/Scholarship)* [2082]
Carl A. Kroch Oxford Cup Memorial Scholarships *(Graduate, Undergraduate/Scholarship)* [1665]
Melvin Kruger Endowed Scholarship Program *(Undergraduate/Scholarship)* [5034]
Judith Keller Marx Krumholz Scholarships *(Undergraduate/Scholarship)* [6201]
Kuchler-Killian Memorial Scholarships *(Undergraduate/Scholarship)* [4879]
Heloise Werthan Kuhn Scholarships *(Undergraduate/Scholarship)* [2429]
Kumin Scholars Program *(Undergraduate/Scholarship)* [6392]
Chris Kurzweil Scholarships *(Undergraduate/Scholarship)* [2516]
La Unidad Latina Foundation Scholarships *(Graduate, Undergraduate/Scholarship)* [3586]
Gretchen Laatsch Scholarships *(Undergraduate/Scholarship)* [1379]
Lavina Laible Scholarships *(Undergraduate/Scholarship)* [3338]
Casey Laine Armed Forces Scholarships *(High School/Scholarship)* [2279]
Lam Research Corporation Core Value and Performance Scholarships for Interns *(Undergraduate/Scholarship)* [4110]
Lam Research Corporation Core Values Scholarships *(Undergraduate/Scholarship)* [4111]
Lambda Alumni (UCLA Lesbian & Gay Alumni Association) Scholarships Program *(Undergraduate/Scholarship)* [6114]
Allen T. Lambert Scholarships *(Postgraduate/Scholarship)* [6269]
Frank S. Land Scholarships *(Undergraduate/Scholarship)* [2702]
Otho E. Lane Memorial Scholarships *(Graduate, Undergraduate/Scholarship)* [1666]
Langfitt-Ambrose Trust Fund *(Undergraduate/Scholarship)* [5504]
Lanier Merit Scholarships *(Undergraduate/Scholarship)* [4134]
Lanier Need-Based Scholarships *(Undergraduate/Scholarship)* [4135]
Stephen Lankester Scholarships *(Undergraduate/Scholarship)* [3339]
The Otis and Florence Lapham Memorial Scholarship *(Undergraduate/Scholarship)* [3984]
Peter and Jody Larkin Legacy Scholarship *(Undergraduate/Scholarship)* [1830]
Joseph C. Larson Entrepreneurial Scholarships *(Undergraduate/Scholarship)* [6202]
Las Limas Community Scholarships *(Undergraduate/Scholarship)* [6782]
Las Vegas Elks Scholarships *(Undergraduate/Scholarship)* [5836]
Las Vegas Elks Scholarships for the Physically Challenged *(Undergraduate/Scholarship)* [5837]
Austin E. Lathrop Scholarships *(Undergraduate/Scholarship)* [4365]
Kenneth Laundy Entrance Scholarships *(Postgraduate/Scholarship)* [6270]
Lawton Minority Retention Grants *(Undergraduate/Scholarship)* [7261]
Jonathan Lax Scholarship Fund for Gay Men *(Undergraduate/Scholarship)* [6115]
Sue Kay Lay Memorial Scholarships *(High School/Scholarship)* [2280]
Lazarian Graduate Scholarships *(Graduate/Scholarship)* [1260]
Lazarus Foundation Scholarships *(Undergraduate/Scholarship)* [3475]
Danny T. Le Memorial Scholarships *(High School, Undergraduate/Scholarship)* [7321]
Franklin M. Leach Scholarships *(Undergraduate/Scholarship)* [4366]
Leaders at Work Scholarship in Textiles and Apparel *(Undergraduate/Scholarship)* [5109]
LEAGUE Foundation Scholarships *(Undergraduate/Scholarship)* [6116]
Jack W. Leatherman Family Scholarship Fund *(Undergraduate/Scholarship)* [3292]
Patrick Ledden Honorary Scholarships *(Undergraduate/Scholarship)* [6203]
Ken Lee Memorial Scholarships *(Undergraduate/Scholarship)* [6204]
Bruce Lee Scholarships *(Undergraduate/Scholarship)* [7007]
LeePapa and Associates Scholarship for Travel *(Graduate, Undergraduate/Scholarship)* [7008]
Legacy Scholarship Program *(Undergraduate/Scholarship)* [6867]
Jay C. and B. Nadine Leggett Charitable Scholarship Fund *(Undergraduate/Scholarship)* [6737]
Legislative Incentive for Future Excellence (LIFE) Scholarships *(Undergraduate/Scholarship)* [232]
Herbert Lehman Education Scholarships *(Undergraduate/Scholarship)* [7345]
Lehman Family Scholarships *(Undergraduate/Scholarship)* [6205]
Imelda and Ralph LeMar Scholarship Program *(Undergraduate/Scholarship)* [2517]
The Lemon Grove Education Foundation Scholarships *(Undergraduate/Scholarship)* [6206]
Stan Lencki Scholarships *(Undergraduate/Scholarship)* [4420]
Franklin A. Lentesty Scholarships *(Undergraduate/Scholarship)* [5285]
V.A. Leonard Scholarships *(Graduate, Undergraduate/Scholarship)* [253]
Leopold Education Project Scholarships *(Undergraduate/Scholarship)* [2475]
Shepard L. & Mabel C. Lepard Scholarships *(Undergraduate/Scholarship)* [3340]
Irwin S. Lerner Student Scholarships *(Undergraduate/Scholarship)* [5076]
Lesbians for Change Scholarships *(Undergraduate/Scholarship)* [6117]
Carol Anne Letheren Entrance Awards *(Postgraduate/Award/Prize)* [6271]
The Irving Leuchter Memorial Scholarships *(All/Scholarship)* [5202]
Jack A. and Louise S. Levine Memorial Scholarships *(Undergraduate/Scholarship)* [5956]
Lewis-Clark Coin Club Endowed Scholarships *(Undergraduate/Scholarship)* [4191]
Lewis-Clark State College Foundation Scholars Scholarships *(Undergraduate/Scholarship)* [4193]
Lewis-Clark State College Freshman Scholarships *(Undergraduate/Scholarship)* [4194]
Lewis-Clark State College Non-Traditional Student Scholarships *(Undergraduate/Scholarship)* [4197]
Lewis-Clark State College Presidential Out-of-State Scholarships *(Undergraduate/Scholarship)* [4198]
Lewis-Clark State College Provost Scholarships *(Undergraduate/Scholarship)* [4200]
Lewis-Clark State College Transfer Scholarships *(Undergraduate/Scholarship)* [4201]
Lewis-Clark State College Valley Scholarships *(Undergraduate/Scholarship)* [4202]
George T. Lewis, Jr. Academic Scholarship Fund *(Undergraduate/Scholarship)* [3067]
Jonathan D. Lewis Point Scholarships *(Graduate, Undergraduate/Scholarship)* [5725]
Marvin Lewis Scholarships *(Undergraduate/Scholarship)* [4222]
Lewiston Service League Memorial Scholarships *(Undergraduate/Scholarship)* [4203]
Lexington Alumni Scholarships *(Undergraduate/Scholarship)* [4224]
Lexington Community Foundation Annual Scholarships *(Undergraduate/Scholarship)* [4225]
Lexington Community Foundation/CCC Scholarships *(Undergraduate/Scholarship)* [4226]
Lexington Teacher Appreciation Scholarships *(Professional Development/Scholarship)* [4227]
George C. Liacouras Memorial Scholarships *(Undergraduate/Scholarship)* [3532]
LIFE Lessons Scholarships Program *(Undergraduate/Scholarship)* [4240]
Lighthouse International Scholarships - College-bound Awards *(High School/Scholarship)* [4243]
Lighthouse International Scholarships - Graduate Awards *(Graduate/Scholarship)* [4244]
Lighthouse International Scholarships - Undergraduate Awards *(Undergraduate/Scholarship)* [4245]
Lilly Fellow Scholarships *(Undergraduate/Fellowship)* [3709]
Lindenwood University Scouting Scholarships *(Undergraduate/Scholarship)* [4862]
David Linton Memorial Scholarships *(Graduate, Undergraduate/Scholarship)* [1667]
Ruth Lister Scholarships *(Undergraduate/Scholarship)* [6845]
Listerhill Credit Union Scholarships *(Undergraduate/Scholarship)* [5286]
LIT Scholarships *(Graduate, Undergraduate/Scholarship)* [4116]
Ian Lithgow Memorial Awards *(Postgraduate/Award/Prize)* [6272]
Live Out Loud Annual Scholarships *(Undergraduate/Scholarship)* [6118]
E.C. Lloyd and J.C.U. Johnson Scholarships Fund *(Undergraduate/Scholarship)* [2355]
Lo Family Scholarships *(Undergraduate/Scholarship)* [7226]
Virgil K. Lobring Scholarships *(Undergraduate/Scholarship)* [2518]
Audrey Loftus Memorial Scholarships *(Undergraduate/Scholarship)* [7078]
Stephen Logan Memorial Scholarships *(Undergraduate/Scholarship)* [3169]
Lone Star GIA Associate and Alumni Scholarships *(Undergraduate/Scholarship)* [3190]
L.D. and Elsie Long Memorial Scholarships *(Undergraduate/Scholarship)* [7446]
Megan Nicole Longwell Scholarships *(Undergraduate/Scholarship)* [5505]
Audre Lord Scholarships *(Graduate, Undergraduate/Scholarship)* [6119]
Sir James Lougheed Awards of Distinction *(Doctorate, Graduate/Award/Prize)* [166]
Love of Bonita Empowerment Scholarships *(Undergraduate/Scholarship)* [6664]
First Lieutenant Scott McClean Love Memorial Scholarship - Children of Soldiers *(Undergraduate/Scholarship)* [1303]
First Lieutenant Scott McClean Love Memorial Scholarship - Spouses of Soldiers *(Undergraduate/Scholarship)* [1304]
John Allen Love Scholarships *(Graduate, Undergraduate/Scholarship)* [7242]
Diane G. Lowe and John Gomez, IV Scholarships *(Undergraduate/Scholarship)* [2430]
H.B. Paul Lowenberg Lions Scholarships *(Undergraduate/Scholarship)* [3476]
Horace G. Lozier Memorial Scholarships *(Graduate, Undergraduate/Scholarship)* [1668]
Elsa Ludeke Graduate Scholarships *(Graduate/Scholarship)* [2694]
Lugonia Alumni/Harrison Lightfoot Scholarships *(Undergraduate/Scholarship)* [5957]
Luso-American Fraternal Federation B-2 Scholarships *(Postgraduate/Scholarship)* [4265]
Luso-American Fraternal Federation B-3 Scholarships *(All/Scholarship)* [4266]
Luso-American Fraternal Federation B-4 Scholarships *(All/Scholarship)* [4267]
Melissa A. Lyles Memorial Scholarships *(Undergraduate/Scholarship)* [5838]
John Mabry Forestry Scholarships *(Undergraduate/Award/Prize)* [5895]
MAC Emeritus Scholarships for First-Time Meeting Attendees *(All, Professional Development/Scholarship)* [4509]
Bill MacAloney Legacy Scholarship *(Undergraduate/Scholarship)* [1831]
John Macara, Barrister of Goderich, Scholarships *(Undergraduate/Scholarship)* [7228]
James Mackenzie Fallows Scholarship Honoring William Cunningham *(Undergraduate/Scholarship)* [5958]
Carol E. Macpherson Memorial Scholarship and Alumnae Society Scholarships *(Graduate, Undergraduate/Scholarship)* [7133]
MacPherson Scholarships *(Undergraduate/Scholarship)* [5360]
Dave Madeiros Scholarship Program - Continued Education *(Four Year College, Two Year College/Scholarship)* [4928]
Dave Madeiros Scholarship Program - Creative Arts *(Other/Grant)* [4929]

Lawrence Madeiros Scholarships *(Undergraduate/Scholarship)* [4930]
John T. & Frances Maghielse Scholarships *(Undergraduate/Scholarship)* [3341]
Sonia S. Maguire Outstanding Scholastic Achievement Awards *(Graduate, Undergraduate/Scholarship)* [6828]
Rick Mahoney Scholarships *(Undergraduate/Scholarship)* [4421]
Mary Main Memorial Scholarships *(Undergraduate/Scholarship)* [3478]
Dr. Julianne Malveaux Scholarships *(Undergraduate/Scholarship)* [4722]
Manchester Scholarship Foundation Scholarships *(Undergraduate/Scholarship)* [3479]
Mangasar M. Mangasarian Scholarship Fund *(Graduate/Scholarship)* [1288]
Horace Mann Insurance Scholarships *(High School/Scholarship)* [5336]
Marathon Pulp Inc. Education Achievement Scholarships *(Undergraduate/Scholarship)* [6885]
Stephen T. Marchello Scholarships *(Undergraduate/Scholarship)* [4280]
Aurella Varallo Mariani Scholarship Program *(Undergraduate/Scholarship)* [4610]
Marine Corps League National Scholarships *(Undergraduate/Scholarship)* [4308]
Mariposa Elementary School PTA Scholarships *(Undergraduate/Scholarship)* [5959]
Markey Scholarships *(Undergraduate/Scholarship)* [4673]
Markley Family Scholarship Fund *(Undergraduate/Scholarship)* [6740]
Markowski-Leach Scholarships Fund *(Graduate, Undergraduate/Scholarship)* [6120]
Carl J. Marrara Memorial Scholarship Fund *(Undergraduate/Scholarship)* [2963]
Barry H. Marshal Scholarships *(Undergraduate/Scholarship)* [6121]
Samuel Taylor Marshall Memorial Scholarships *(Graduate, Undergraduate/Scholarship)* [1669]
Sarah Shinn Marshall Scholarships *(Undergraduate/Scholarship)* [2655]
Marshall Undergraduate Scholars Programs *(Undergraduate/Award/Prize)* [4319]
Martin Sisters Scholarships *(Undergraduate/Scholarship)* [2656]
John S. Martinez and Family Scholarships Fund *(Undergraduate/Scholarship)* [2394]
Michael L. Marx and Donald K. Marshall Scholarships *(Undergraduate/Scholarship)* [6122]
Beverly Mascoll Scholarships *(Undergraduate/Scholarship)* [1738]
Master Municipal Clerks Academy Scholarships *(Professional Development/Scholarship)* [3873]
Matanuska-Susitna College Regent's Scholarships *(Undergraduate/Scholarship)* [4368]
Rene Matos Memorial Scholarships *(Undergraduate/Scholarship)* [4937]
The Renardo A. Matteucci Scholarship Fund *(Undergraduate/Scholarship)* [2401]
Antonio Mattos Memorial Scholarships *(Undergraduate/Scholarship)* [4268]
Mature Student Scholarships *(Undergraduate/Scholarship)* [2880]
Aaron Matusek Memorial Scholarships *(Undergraduate/Scholarship)* [5840]
Edmund F. Maxwell Scholarships *(Undergraduate/Scholarship)* [4405]
Juliann and Joseph Maxwell Scholarships *(Undergraduate/Scholarship)* [2433]
Juliann King Maxwell Scholarships for Students in White County, Arkansas *(Undergraduate/Scholarship)* [2434]
John E. Mayfield ABLE Scholarships *(Undergraduate/Scholarship)* [2435]
John E. Mayfield Scholarships for Cheatham County Central High School *(Undergraduate/Scholarship)* [2436]
John E. Mayfield Scholarships for Harpeth High School *(Undergraduate/Scholarship)* [2437]
John E. Mayfield Scholarships Pleasant View Christian School *(Undergraduate/Scholarship)* [2438]
John E. Mayfield Scholarships for Sycamore High School *(Undergraduate/Scholarship)* [2439]
Bill McAdam Scholarships *(Undergraduate/Scholarship)* [5008]
McBurney Disability Scholarships *(Undergraduate/Scholarship)* [7262]
Bill McCarthy Scout Scholarship Fund *(Undergraduate/Scholarship)* [6741]
Walter A. and Nan C. McCloskey Memorial Scholarships *(Undergraduate/Scholarship)* [2964]
Dave McCloud Aviation Memorial Scholarships *(Undergraduate/Scholarship)* [4369]
Dr. Cladwell McCoy, Jr. Memorial Scholarships *(Undergraduate/Scholarship)* [3482]
McDaniel College Eagle Scout Scholarships *(Undergraduate/Scholarship)* [4863]
Ronald McDonald House Charities of Las Vegas Scholarships *(Undergraduate/Scholarship)* [5841]
McDonald's USA National Employee Scholarship Program *(Undergraduate/Scholarship)* [4412]
McFarffels Scholarships *(Undergraduate/Scholarship)* [5769]
Nancy B. Woolridge McGee Graduate Fellowships *(Graduate/Fellowship)* [7558]
Lucile E. McGee Scholarship *(Undergraduate/Scholarship)* [3985]
McGill University Alma Mater Student Travel Grants *(Graduate/Grant)* [4430]
McKelvey Foundation Entrepreneurial Scholarships *(Undergraduate/Scholarship)* [4434]
McKelvey Scholarships *(Undergraduate/Scholarship)* [4435]
McKinley Elementary School PTA Scholarships *(Undergraduate/Scholarship)* [5960]
John L. and Eleanore I. Mckinley Scholarships *(Undergraduate/Scholarship)* [2695]
Louise McKinney Post-secondary Scholarship *(Undergraduate/Scholarship)* [167]
McKinney Sisters Undergraduate Scholarships *(Undergraduate/Scholarship)* [2657]
Elizabeth McKissick Memorial Scholarships *(Undergraduate/Scholarship)* [4205]
James H. McLaughlin Scholarships *(Undergraduate/Scholarship)* [5222]
David McMeans Memorial Scholarships *(Undergraduate/Scholarship)* [5287]
Joan Reagin McNeill Scholarships - Alpha Theta *(Undergraduate/Scholarship)* [6365]
Joan Reagin McNeill Scholarships - Theta Phi *(Undergraduate/Scholarship)* [6366]
David Meador Student Scholarships *(Undergraduate/Scholarship)* [5169]
Jack Meadows Memorial Awards *(Undergraduate/Scholarship)* [5426]
Medicus Student Exchange *(Graduate, Undergraduate/Scholarship)* [6829]
Augustine and Sandra Medina Memorial Scholarships *(Undergraduate/Scholarship)* [5961]
Dr. Ernest and Minnie Mehl Scholarship *(Undergraduate/Scholarship)* [168]
Richard Mellon Endowment Scholarships *(Undergraduate/Scholarship)* [4370]
Mellon Post-Doctoral Fellowships in Turkey for East European Scholars *(Doctorate/Fellowship)* [899]
Steven Craig Merrill Memorial Scholarships *(Graduate, Undergraduate/Scholarship)* [1670]
Mesothelioma Memorial Scholarships *(Undergraduate/Scholarship)* [6794]
Mexican American Grocers Association Scholarships *(Undergraduate/Scholarship)* [4468]
MHS Health Career Scholarships *(Undergraduate/Scholarship)* [4450]
Michaels Jewelers Foundation General Scholarships *(Undergraduate/Scholarship)* [3484]
Michigan Council of Women in Technology College Scholarship Program *(Graduate, Undergraduate/Scholarship)* [4476]
Michigan Council of Women in Technology High School Scholarships Program *(Undergraduate/Scholarship)* [4477]
Michigan Education Association Scholarships *(Undergraduate/Scholarship)* [4479]
Michigan Sugar Queen Scholarships *(Undergraduate/Scholarship)* [4497]
Beth Middleton Memorial Scholarships *(Undergraduate/Scholarship)* [5110]
Midwest Chapter Scholarships - Non-Engineering *(Undergraduate/Scholarship)* [1452]
Midwest Chapter Scholarships - Western States Award *(Undergraduate/Scholarship)* [1453]
Keith Miffioli Scholarship *(Undergraduate/Scholarship)* [2476]
Mihaly Russin Scholarship Awards *(Graduate/Scholarship)* [6087]
Milan Getting Scholarships *(Undergraduate/Scholarship)* [6594]
Eunice Miles Scholarships *(Undergraduate/Scholarship)* [3195]
Military Intelligence Corps Association Scholarships *(Undergraduate/Scholarship)* [4527]
Harvey Milk/Tom Homann Gay and Lesbian Student Scholarships *(Undergraduate/Scholarship)* [6124]
Millennium Alberta Rural Incentive Bursary Award *(Undergraduate/Award/Prize)* [169]
Millennium Charter Academy College Scholarships *(Undergraduate/Scholarship)* [7447]
Robbie Miller Memorial Scholarships *(Undergraduate/Scholarship)* [4207]
Brian and Colleen Miller Scholarships *(High School/Scholarship)* [2281]
Carolina Panthers Players Sam Mills Memorial Scholarship Fund *(Undergraduate/Scholarship)* [3069]
Minerva Scholarships *(Undergraduate/Scholarship)* [1739]
Minneapolis Camp Scholarships *(Undergraduate/Scholarship)* [4541]
Minnesota Division Scholarships *(Undergraduate/Scholarship)* [4516]
Minnesota GLBT Educational Fund *(Undergraduate/Scholarship)* [6125]
Minnesota Power Community Involvement Scholarships *(Undergraduate/Scholarship)* [2785]
MiraCosta College Two-Year Colleges Scholarships *(Undergraduate/Scholarship)* [4560]
Missigman Scholarship Fund *(Undergraduate/Scholarship)* [2966]
N.W. Mitchell-Piedmont Federal Savings and Loans Endowed Scholarships *(Undergraduate/Scholarship)* [7448]
George J. Mitchell Postgraduate Scholarships *(Postgraduate/Scholarship)* [4708]
Dorothy Mitchell Scholarships *(Undergraduate/Scholarship)* [5962]
Robert L. & Hilda Treasure Mitchell Scholarships *(Undergraduate/Scholarship)* [3343]
Sam Mizrahi Memorial Scholarships *(Undergraduate/Scholarship)* [3111]
MKC Scholarships *(Undergraduate/Scholarship)* [6209]
MOAA American Patriot Scholarships *(Undergraduate/Scholarship)* [4529]
MOAA Base/Post Scholarships *(Undergraduate/Scholarship)* [4530]
Modern Woodmen of America Scholarships *(Undergraduate/Scholarship)* [2786]
Cary Moore Memorial Scholarship Fund *(Undergraduate/Scholarship)* [2519]
Moore Middle School PTA Scholarships *(Undergraduate/Scholarship)* [5963]
Stanley Moore Scholarships *(Undergraduate/Scholarship)* [5251]
Kyle Moreland Memorial Endowment Scholarships Fund *(Undergraduate/Scholarship)* [3294]
Herbie Morici Memorial Scholarships *(Undergraduate/Scholarship)* [1843]
Leo F. Moro Baseball Memorial Scholarships *(Undergraduate/Scholarship)* [3112]
Morris County Psychological Association Scholarships *(Undergraduate/Scholarship)* [4574]
James B. Morris Scholarships *(Undergraduate/Scholarship)* [4576]
Mortar Board National Foundation Fellowships *(Postdoctorate/Fellowship)* [4578]
Dwight Mosley Scholarships *(Undergraduate/Scholarship)* [7305]
John R. Mott Scholarships *(Undergraduate/Scholarship)* [4580]
MPI CRV Continuing Education Scholarships *(Professional Development/Scholarship)* [4452]
Ruth Mu-Lan and James S.C. Chao Scholarship *(Undergraduate/Scholarship)* [7009]
Brittany Mueller Memorial Scholarships *(High School/Scholarship)* [5161]
Dudley Mullins/Cabot Corporation Scholarships

(Undergraduate/Scholarship) [5506]
Muncy Rotary Club Scholarship Fund (Undergraduate/Scholarship) [2968]
Muncy Scholars Award Fund (Undergraduate/Award/Prize) [2969]
Harry Munoz Memorial Scholarships (Undergraduate/Scholarship) [5964]
Rick Munoz Memorial Scholarships (Undergraduate/Scholarship) [5965]
Anthony Munoz Scholarships (Undergraduate/Scholarship) [4589]
Daniel Murphy Scholarships (High School/Scholarship) [4591]
Carolyn Murray Memorial Scholarships (Undergraduate/Scholarship) [1897]
Muscle Shoals Kiwanis/Wal-Mart Scholarships (Undergraduate/Scholarship) [5288]
NACA East Coast Graduate Student Scholarships (Postdoctorate/Scholarship) [4674]
NACA East Coast Higher Education Research Scholarships (Postgraduate/Scholarship) [4675]
NACA East Coast Undergraduate Scholarships for Student Leaders (Undergraduate/Scholarship) [4676]
NACA Foundation Graduate Student Scholarships (Postdoctorate/Scholarship) [4677]
NACA Regional Council Student Leadership Scholarships (Undergraduate/Scholarship) [4678]
NACA Southeast Student Leadership Scholarships (Undergraduate/Scholarship) [4679]
NACADA Scholarships (Doctorate, Graduate/Scholarship) [4616]
Irwin Allen Nadal Entrance Awards (Postgraduate/Award/Prize) [6273]
Miles Spencer Nadal Entrance Awards (Postgraduate/Award/Prize) [6274]
NAFEO Internship Program (Undergraduate/Internship) [4699]
Jack Nagasaka Memorial Scholarships (Undergraduate/Scholarship) [5966]
NANBPWC National Scholarships (Undergraduate/Scholarship) [4723]
NANBPWC Woman of Substance Scholarships (Undergraduate/Scholarship) [4724]
Robyn Nance Memorial Scholarships (Undergraduate/Scholarship) [5967]
NAPNAP McNeil Rural and Underserved Scholarships (Undergraduate/Scholarship) [4732]
NARFE-FEEA Scholarship Awards Program (Undergraduate/Scholarship) [4628]
NARRP Student Conference Scholarships (Graduate, Undergraduate/Scholarship) [4736]
Kermit B. Nash Academic Scholarships (Undergraduate/Scholarship) [6327]
Archie Hartwell Nash Memorial Scholarships (Undergraduate/Scholarship) [2440]
Mike Nash Memorial Scholarships (Undergraduate/Scholarship) [7319]
The NASSCO Jeffrey D. Ralston Memorial Scholarships (Undergraduate/Scholarship) [4743]
National AAHAM Scholarships (Undergraduate/Scholarship) [353]
The National Academies Dissertation Fellowships (Doctorate/Fellowship) [4619]
The National Academies Predoctoral Fellowships (Doctorate/Fellowship) [4621]
National Air Filtration Association Scholarship Fund (Undergraduate/Scholarship) [4630]
National Association for Armenian Studies and Research Scholarships (Undergraduate/Scholarship) [1289]
National Association of Campus Activities Multicultural Scholarship Programs (Undergraduate/Scholarship) [4680]
National Association of Campus Activities Scholarships for Student Leaders (Undergraduate/Scholarship) [4681]
National Association of Fellowships Advisors Graduate Scholar Awards (Postgraduate, Professional Development/Fellowship) [4710]
National Association for the Self-Employed Scholarships (Undergraduate/Scholarship) [4741]
National Beta Club Scholarships (Undergraduate/Scholarship) [4757]
National Coal Transportation Association At Large Scholarships (Undergraduate/Scholarship) [4800]
National College Scholarship Award (Undergraduate/Scholarship) [3970]
National Collegiate Athletic Association Postgraduate Scholarships (Postgraduate/Scholarship) [4805]
National Collegiate Cancer Foundation Scholarships (Undergraduate/Scholarship) [4807]
National Costumers Association Scholarships (Undergraduate/Scholarship) [4824]
National Court Reporters Association Student Intern Scholarships (Undergraduate/Scholarship) [4835]
National Huguenot Society Scholarships (Undergraduate/Scholarship) [4944]
National Organization of Italian-American Women Scholarships (All/Scholarship) [5000]
National Pathfinder Scholarships (Graduate, Undergraduate/Scholarship) [4889]
National Preservation Institute Scholarships (Other/Scholarship) [5015]
National Recycling Coalition Congress Scholarships (Undergraduate/Scholarship) [5030]
National Technical Honor Society Scholarships (Undergraduate/Scholarship) [5111]
National Women's Studies Association Lesbian Scholarships (Doctorate, Graduate/Scholarship) [5124]
Native American Charter High Schools After-the-Fires Scholarships (Undergraduate/Scholarship) [6210]
Native American Education Grants (Graduate, Undergraduate/Grant) [636]
Naval Reserve Association Scholarships (Undergraduate/Scholarship) [5136]
The Nazareth Scholarships (Undergraduate/Scholarship) [5151]
NCBWL Scholarships (High School/Scholarship) [4611]
NCOA Scholarships (Undergraduate/Scholarship) [5211]
NDEOA Scholarships (Undergraduate/Scholarship) [4848]
H.N. Neal Memorial Scholarships (Undergraduate/Scholarship) [1898]
Nebraska Farm Bureau Young Farmers and Ranchers Greater Horizon Scholarships (Undergraduate/Scholarship) [5155]
Douglas J. Neeley Memorial Scholarships (Graduate, Undergraduate/Scholarship) [1672]
Bill Nelson Scholarship Endowment (Undergraduate/Scholarship) [5428]
Judge William J. Nelson Scholarships (Undergraduate/Scholarship) [6666]
NEMRA Educational Scholarship Foundation (Undergraduate/Scholarship) [4871]
Andrew Nerland Endowment Scholarships (Undergraduate/Scholarship) [4373]
Amelia and Emanuel Nessell Scholarships (Undergraduate/Scholarship) [2788]
Reverend John S. Nettled Scholarship (Undergraduate/Scholarship) [2358]
Nevada Black Police Association Scholarships (Undergraduate/Scholarship) [5844]
New Hampshire Snowmobile Association Scholarships (Undergraduate/Scholarship) [5173]
New Mexico Manufactured Housing Association Scholarship Program (Undergraduate/Scholarship) [193]
New Opportunities Through Retraining Scholarship Fund (Undergraduate/Scholarship) [5361]
New Professional Reporter Grants (Professional Development/Grant) [4836]
The New York Times College Scholarships (Undergraduate/Scholarship) [5195]
Newcomer Supply Student Scholarships (Undergraduate/Scholarship) [5077]
Frank Newman Leadership Awards (Undergraduate/Scholarship) [1916]
Newman University Scouting Scholarships (Undergraduate/Scholarship) [4864]
Jerry Newson Scholarships (Undergraduate/Scholarship) [2441]
NFPA Youth Scholarships (Undergraduate/Scholarship) [4902]
Le Hoang Nguyen (LHN) College Scholarships (High School/Scholarship) [7322]
The Thuy Nguyen Scholarships (High School/Scholarship) [7323]
NHPGA Apprentice Scholarships (Undergraduate/Scholarship) [4422]
NHS National Scholarships (Undergraduate/Scholarship) [4939]
NIAF Scholarships - General Category I (Undergraduate/Scholarship) [4962]
Mike Niemeyer Memorial Football Scholarships (Undergraduate/Scholarship) [5968]
Evelyn S. Nish Scholarships (Undergraduate/Scholarship) [6367]
Anderson Niskanen Scholarships (Undergraduate/Scholarship) [2789]
Nissan North America, Inc. Scholarships (Undergraduate/Scholarship) [624]
NLBRA/Wrangler Academic Scholarships (Undergraduate/Scholarship) [4982]
Charles S. Noble Scholarships for Study at Harvard (Undergraduate/Scholarship) [170]
NOBLE Southern California Chapter Scholarship Program (Undergraduate/Scholarship) [4994]
Edna A. Noblin Dawsonville Lions Club Scholarships (Undergraduate/Scholarship) [4136]
Nolle Scholarships (Undergraduate/Scholarship) [240]
Nor' Easters Scholarships - Four-year Program (Undergraduate/Scholarship) [5214]
Nor' Easters Scholarships - Two-year Program (Undergraduate/Scholarship) [5215]
Norall Scholarships Trust (Undergraduate/Scholarship) [4229]
Nordic Ski Association of Anchorage Scholarships (Undergraduate/Scholarship) [129]
North Dakota Farmers Union Co-op House Scholarships (Undergraduate/Scholarship) [5253]
North Dakota Farmers Union Scholarships (Undergraduate/Scholarship) [5254]
North Las Vegas Firefighters - William J. Harnedy Memorial Scholarships (Undergraduate/Scholarship) [5846]
North Texas GIA Alumni Association Scholarships (Undergraduate/Scholarship) [3196]
Northern Alberta Development Council Bursary Award (Undergraduate/Award/Prize) [171]
Northern Alberta Development Council Bursary Partnership Program (Undergraduate/Award/Prize) [173]
Northern Arizona Native-American Foundation Scholarships (Undergraduate/Scholarship) [5269]
Northern Student Supplement (Undergraduate/Award/Prize) [175]
Northern Virginia Alumnae Chapter Scholarships (Undergraduate/Scholarship) [2659]
Eugene Northrup Scholarships (Undergraduate/Scholarship) [4208]
Northwest Community Center Scholarships (Undergraduate/Scholarship) [2478]
Northwest-Shoals Community College Academic Scholarships (Undergraduate/Scholarship) [5289]
Northwest-Shoals Community College Athletic Scholarships (Undergraduate/Scholarship) [5291]
Northwest-Shoals Community College Bank Independent Scholarships (Undergraduate/Scholarship) [5292]
Northwest-Shoals Community College High School Academic Scholarships (Undergraduate/Scholarship) [5296]
Northwest-Shoals Community College Independent Computer Scholarships (Undergraduate/Scholarship) [5297]
Northwest-Shoals Community College Student Activities Scholarships (Undergraduate/Scholarship) [5298]
Notre Dame Club of Canton Scholarships (Undergraduate/Scholarship) [6747]
NSHSS Academic Paper Awards (High School/Scholarship) [5070]
NSHSS National Scholar Awards (High School/Scholarship) [5071]
NSSA/NSCA Collegiate Scholarships (Undergraduate/Scholarship) [5093]
NW-SCC/American Cancer Society College Scholarships (Undergraduate/Scholarship) [5299]
NW-SCC American Legion Scholarships - Florence/Lauderdale Post No. 11 (Undergraduate/Scholarship) [5300]

NWF's Women for Sustainable Development (WSD) Scholarships *(Undergraduate/Scholarship)* [6333]
NWSA Distinguished Fellowships *(All/Fellowship)* [5125]
NWSA Graduate Scholarships *(Graduate/Scholarship)* [5126]
NWSA Graduate Scholarships in Lesbian Studies *(Doctorate, Graduate/Fellowship)* [6127]
NYNEX Diversity Scholarship Awards *(Undergraduate/Scholarship)* [6128]
Obrzut Ling Scholarships *(Undergraduate/Scholarship)* [5772]
Katharine H. Obye Scholarship Award *(Undergraduate/Scholarship)* [2479]
OCA Scholarships *(Undergraduate/Scholarship)* [5413]
John O'Connor Memorial Scholarship Fund *(Undergraduate/Scholarship)* [5114]
Odd Fellows Lodge No. 8 Endowed Scholarships *(Undergraduate/Scholarship)* [4209]
Captain Jennifer Shafer Odom Memorial Scholarships - Children of Soldiers *(Undergraduate/Scholarship)* [1305]
Captain Jennifer Shafer Odom Memorial Scholarships - Spouses of Soldiers *(Undergraduate/Scholarship)* [1306]
Don & Jan O'Dowd/SWAA Scholarships *(Undergraduate/Scholarship)* [4375]
Ohio War Orphan Scholarships *(Undergraduate/Scholarship)* [7531]
O'Jays Scholarship Fund *(Undergraduate/Scholarship)* [6748]
OKAIDE Scholarships *(Undergraduate/Scholarship)* [5327]
Roy C. and Dorothy Jean Olson Memorial Scholarships *(Undergraduate/Scholarship)* [3876]
Olympia Tumwater Foundation Traditional Scholarships *(Undergraduate/Scholarship)* [5333]
Olympia Tumwater Foundation Transitional (non-traditional) Scholarships *(Undergraduate/Scholarship)* [5334]
O'Meara Foundation Scholarships *(Undergraduate/Scholarship)* [3485]
Charlie O'Meilia Scholarships *(Undergraduate/Scholarship)* [3830]
Ontario Hockey Association War Memorial Scholarships *(Undergraduate/Scholarship)* [7232]
Open Society Fellowships *(Professional Development/Fellowship)* [5347]
Sheldon Oppenheim Memorial Scholarships *(Undergraduate/Scholarship)* [6129]
Optimist Club Of Redlands - Ralph Maloof Scholarships *(Undergraduate/Scholarship)* [5969]
Optimist Club of Redlands - Virginia Elliott Scholarships *(Undergraduate/Scholarship)* [5970]
OPWA Educational Scholarships *(Undergraduate/Scholarship)* [5315]
Orange County Centennial Academic Scholarships *(Undergraduate/Scholarship)* [5362]
Orange County Centennial Certification Scholarships *(Undergraduate/Scholarship)* [5364]
Orchard-Hoyman Fund for GLBT Student Scholarships *(Undergraduate/Scholarship)* [2889]
Order Sons of Italy Foundation General Scholarships *(Graduate, Undergraduate/Scholarship)* [5373]
Oregon Community Credit Union Scholarships *(Undergraduate/Scholarship)* [7201]
Oregon Logging Conference Scholarships *(Undergraduate/Scholarship)* [4210]
Organization of American States Academic Scholarships *(Undergraduate/Scholarship)* [5400]
Organization of American States AOS-Placed Scholarships *(Undergraduate/Scholarship)* [5401]
Organization of American States Graduate Scholarships *(Undergraduate/Scholarship)* [5402]
Organization of American States Self-Placed Scholarships *(Undergraduate/Scholarship)* [5403]
Orin Carver Scholarships *(Undergraduate/Scholarship)* [2499]
Margaret E. Oser Scholarships for Women *(Undergraduate/Scholarship)* [5366]
OSU Gay, Lesbian, Bisexual and Transgender Alumni Society (PFLAG Scholarships) *(Undergraduate/Scholarship)* [6130]
OTA Education Foundation Scholarships *(Undergraduate/Scholarship)* [5345]
Alvin G. Ott Fish and Wildlife Scholarships *(Undergraduate/Scholarship)* [4376]
Ted H. Ousley Scholarship Fund *(Undergraduate/Scholarship)* [3072]
Outstanding Undergraduate Scholarships (SOAR) *(Undergraduate/Scholarship)* [7106]
Charles and Melva T. Owen Memorial Scholarships *(Undergraduate/Scholarship)* [4882]
Owner-Operator Independent Drivers Association Scholarships *(Undergraduate/Scholarship)* [5436]
Ozarks Division Scholarships *(Undergraduate/Scholarship)* [4518]
The Pac-10 Postgraduate Scholarships *(Graduate/Scholarship)* [5438]
Dr. Nicholas Padis Memorial Graduate Scholarships *(Graduate/Scholarship)* [3533]
E. William Palmer Memorial Scholarships *(Graduate, Undergraduate/Scholarship)* [1673]
The PanHellenic Scholarships *(Undergraduate/Scholarship)* [3525]
Panther Cafe Scholarships *(Undergraduate/Scholarship)* [5848]
Paper Stock Industries Chapter of ISRI Scholarship Program *(Undergraduate/Scholarship)* [5452]
Paper Stock Industries/RRF Scholarships *(Undergraduate/Scholarship)* [5450]
Cissy McDaniel Parker Scholarships *(Undergraduate/Scholarship)* [2660]
E.U. Parker Scholarships *(Undergraduate/Scholarship)* [4883]
Parking Industry Institute Scholarship Program *(Undergraduate/Scholarship)* [5009]
Fitzroy and Mildred Parkinson Memorial Scholarships *(Undergraduate/Scholarship)* [3486]
James H. Patrenos Memorial Scholarships *(Undergraduate/Scholarship)* [6406]
Gail Patrick Charitable Trust Scholarships *(Undergraduate/Scholarship)* [2697]
Alice Conger Patterson Scholarships *(Undergraduate/Scholarship)* [7450]
Paul and Inger Friend 4-H Scholarships *(Undergraduate/Scholarship)* [6783]
Charles S. Pearce Scholarships *(Undergraduate/Prize, Scholarship)* [7264]
Minnie Pearl Scholarship Program *(Undergraduate/Scholarship)* [2802]
Pearman Family Scholarships *(Undergraduate/Scholarship)* [6212]
Peierls Rising Star Scholarship Program *(Undergraduate/Scholarship)* [3602]
Pellegrini Scholarships *(Graduate, Undergraduate/Scholarship)* [6830]
Dorothy E. Hofmann Pembroke Scholarships *(Undergraduate/Scholarship)* [3488]
Robert B. and Dorothy Pence Scholarships *(Undergraduate/Scholarship)* [6667]
Penndelphia Scholarships Foundation *(Undergraduate/Scholarship)* [5553]
Pennsboro Alumni Scholarship Fund *(Undergraduate/Scholarship)* [5507]
P.E.O. Chapter Scholarship Fund *(Undergraduate/Scholarship)* [3297]
PEO Educational Loan Funds *(Graduate, Undergraduate/Loan)* [5685]
Pepsi Wood County Technical/Caperton Center Scholarship Fund *(Undergraduate/Scholarship)* [5508]
Pepsico Scholarships *(Undergraduate/Scholarship)* [7010]
Joaquin Pereira Memorial Scholarships *(Undergraduate/Scholarship)* [4269]
Zoe Gore Perrin Scholarships *(Undergraduate/Scholarship)* [2661]
Eleanor Perry Memorial Endowed Scholarships *(Undergraduate/Scholarship)* [4212]
Perry Township School Memorial Scholarship Fund *(Undergraduate/Scholarship)* [6749]
Dr. Connell Persico Scholarships *(Undergraduate/Scholarship)* [6131]
Persons Case Scholarships *(Undergraduate/Scholarship)* [176]
Charles E. Peterson Research Senior Fellowships *(Professional Development/Fellowship)* [1529]
William H. and Lena M. Petree Scholarships *(Undergraduate/Scholarship)* [7451]
Pfafftown Jaycees/Lynn Canada Memorial Scholarships *(Undergraduate/Scholarship)* [7452]
PFLAG/HATCH Youth Scholarship Foundation *(Undergraduate/Scholarship)* [6132]
Marshall Phelps Athletic Memorial Scholarships *(Undergraduate/Scholarship)* [5972]
Phi Kappa Phi Emerging Scholar Awards *(Undergraduate/Award/Prize)* [5628]
Phi Kappa Phi Fellowships *(Other/Fellowship)* [5629]
Phi Kappa Sigma Need-Based Scholarships *(Undergraduate/Scholarship)* [5631]
Phi Kappa Sigma Participation-Based Scholarships *(Undergraduate/Scholarship)* [5632]
Philip Morris USA Scholarships *(Undergraduate/Scholarship)* [7011]
Walter T. Philippy Scholarships *(Undergraduate/Scholarship)* [4423]
Phillips Scholarships *(Undergraduate/Scholarship)* [2500]
Margaret E. Phillips Scholarships *(Undergraduate/Scholarship)* [7243]
Howard and Mildred Phoenix Scholarships *(Undergraduate/Scholarship)* [5973]
Pierce College Foundation Coca-Cola Scholarships *(Undergraduate/Scholarship)* [5693]
Herschel Pifer Memorial Scholarships *(Undergraduate/Scholarship)* [5510]
Christopher Pitkin Memorial Scholarships *(Undergraduate/Scholarship)* [4931]
Day Pitney LLP Scholarships *(Undergraduate/Scholarship)* [3490]
Peter George Pitsakis Memorial Scholarships *(Undergraduate/Scholarship)* [3534]
Al Plamann Legacy Scholarship *(Undergraduate/Scholarship)* [1832]
TFC Edward A. Plank, Jr. Memorial Scholarship *(Undergraduate/Scholarship)* [2379]
PLUS Foundation Financial Aid Grants *(Undergraduate/Scholarship)* [5709]
Henry DeWitt Plyler Scholarship Fund *(Undergraduate/Scholarship)* [3073]
Point Foundation Scholarships *(Graduate, Postgraduate, Undergraduate/Scholarship)* [6133]
Point Lay Memorial Scholarships *(Undergraduate/Scholarship)* [4377]
Pollard-Bailey Scholarships *(Undergraduate/Scholarship)* [6214]
David J. Pollini Scholarships *(Undergraduate/Scholarship)* [4424]
Ken and Pam Pong Scholarships *(Undergraduate/Scholarship)* [7012]
Buster Pool Memorial Scholarships *(Undergraduate/Scholarship)* [2443]
Pope Scholarships Award *(Undergraduate/Scholarship)* [4425]
Port with No Borders Scholarships *(Undergraduate/Scholarship)* [6215]
Gail Porterfield Memorial Scholarships *(Undergraduate/Scholarship)* [5974]
Portland Area Business Association Scholarships *(Undergraduate/Scholarship)* [2890]
Portuguese-American Scholarship Foundation *(Undergraduate/Scholarship)* [5738]
Post 4137 Veterans Foundation Scholarships *(Undergraduate/Scholarship)* [5695]
Barbara Potter Scholarships *(All/Scholarship)* [741]
Gerald Powell Scholarship *(Undergraduate/Scholarship)* [2360]
The Power to Continue Learning Scholarships *(Undergraduate/Scholarship)* [5975]
J.R. (Joe) Power National Scholarships *(Postgraduate/Scholarship)* [5878]
Powers-Knapp Scholarships *(Undergraduate/Scholarship)* [7266]
Master Sergeant Neal E. Powers Memorial Scholarships *(Undergraduate/Scholarship)* [59]
Prairie Baseball Academy Scholarships *(Undergraduate/Scholarship)* [177]
Pride Foundation Regional Scholarships *(Undergraduate/Scholarship)* [5774]
Pride of the Rose Scholarships Fund *(Undergraduate/Scholarship)* [2891]
Private High School Awards *(Undergraduate/Award/Prize)* [1211]
Miguel Pro Scholarships

(Undergraduate/Scholarship) [7532]
Procida Tile Importers Scholarships (Undergraduate/Scholarship) [5853]
Professional Institute of the Public Service of Canada Expanded Scholarships (Undergraduate/Scholarship) [5793]
Progress Lane Scholarships (Undergraduate/Scholarship) [2380]
Project Red Flag Academic Scholarships for Women with Bleeding Disorders (Undergraduate/Scholarship) [4932]
Provincial and Regional 4-H Scholarships (Undergraduate/Scholarship) [134]
ProWorld Study Abroad Scholarships (Undergraduate/Scholarship) [3256]
Pryor Graduate Fellowships (Graduate/Fellowship) [241]
Cheryl White Pryor Memorial Scholarships (Undergraduate/Scholarship) [2662]
PSAC - Coughlin National Scholarships (Postgraduate/Scholarship) [5879]
PSAC - Groulx National Scholarships (Postgraduate/Scholarship) [5880]
PSAC National Scholarships (Postgraduate/Scholarship) [5881]
PSAC Regional Scholarships (Postgraduate/Scholarship) [5882]
Public Agency Training Council Criminal Justice Scholarships (Undergraduate/Scholarship) [254]
Public Education Foundation Opportunity Scholarships (Undergraduate/Scholarship) [5854]
Puedo Scholarships - Joseph Huerta (High School/Scholarship) [2282]
Duane V. Puerde Memorial Scholarship (Undergraduate/Scholarship) [2381]
Puget Sound LGBT Leadership Scholarships Fund (Undergraduate/Scholarship) [6135]
Elizabeth Pusey Scholarship (Undergraduate/Scholarship) [2382]
Davis Putter Scholarships Fund (Undergraduate/Scholarship) [6136]
Qualcomm San Diego Science, Technology, Engineering and Mathematics Scholarships (Undergraduate/Scholarship) [6216]
Quality Initiative Grant-in-Aid (Doctorate, Graduate/Grant) [951]
Queen Elizabeth II Graduate Scholarship Program (Doctorate, Graduate/Scholarship) [178]
Michael J. Quill Scholarships (Undergraduate/Scholarship) [6896]
Salvatore E. Quinci Foundation Scholarships (Undergraduate/Scholarship) [4933]
Dr. J. Glenn Radcliffe Memorial Scholarships (Undergraduate/Scholarship) [6784]
J.J. Rains Memorial Scholarships (High School/Scholarship) [2283]
Rainwater Family Scholarships (Undergraduate/Scholarship) [4983]
Rambus Scholarship Fund (Undergraduate/Scholarship) [6393]
Raul Ramirez Memorial Scholarships (Undergraduate/Scholarship) [5976]
Rancho Bernardo/Smith Scholarships (Undergraduate/Scholarship) [6217]
The Jennings Randolph Peace Scholar Dissertation Program (All/Scholarship) [7026]
Jeannette Rankin Scholarships (Undergraduate/Scholarship) [5897]
General John Paul Ratay Educational Grants (Undergraduate/Grant) [4531]
Dr. Mark Rathke Family Scholarships (Undergraduate/Scholarship) [2790]
Mary C. Rawlins Scholarships (Undergraduate/Scholarship) [3493]
W.B. Ray HS Class of '56 Averill Johnson Scholarships (High School/Scholarship) [2284]
Raytheon Scholarship Program (Undergraduate/Scholarship) [5899]
RBC Royal Bank Scholarships for New Canadians (Undergraduate/Scholarship) [6067]
Ronald Reagan College Leaders Scholarship Program (Undergraduate/Scholarship) [5687]
Redlands Area Interfaith Council Scholarships (Undergraduate/Scholarship) [5977]
Redlands Community Scholarship Foundation Scholarships (Undergraduate/Scholarship) [5978]
Redlands Council PTA - Dorathy Jolley Memorial Scholarships (Undergraduate/Scholarship) [5979]
Redlands Footlighters, Inc. - Merle and Peggy Williams Scholarships (Undergraduate/Scholarship) [5980]
Redlands High School Academic Decathalon Scholarships (Undergraduate/Scholarship) [5981]
Redlands High School Boy's Varsity Volleyball Scholarships (Undergraduate/Scholarship) [5982]
Redlands High School Class of 1957 (Undergraduate/Scholarship) [5983]
Redlands High School Girls' Volleyball Boosters Scholarship Awards (Undergraduate/Scholarship) [5985]
Redlands High School Mock Trial Scholarships (Undergraduate/Scholarship) [5986]
Redlands High School-PTSA Scholarships (Undergraduate/Scholarship) [5987]
Redlands High School Soccer Boosters Scholarship Awards (Undergraduate/Scholarship) [5988]
Redlands High School Softball Booster Scholarship Awards (Undergraduate/Scholarship) [5989]
Redlands High School Speech Boosters Scholarship Awards (Undergraduate/Scholarship) [5990]
Redlands High School Spiritleaders Scholarships (Undergraduate/Scholarship) [5991]
Redlands High School Terrier Band Boosters Club Scholarships (Undergraduate/Scholarship) [5992]
Redlands High School Vocal Music Boosters Scholarship Awards (Undergraduate/Scholarship) [5993]
Redlands Morning Kiwanis Club Foundation Scholarships (Undergraduate/Scholarship) [5994]
Redlands Noon Kiwanis Club Foundation Scholarships (Undergraduate/Scholarship) [5995]
Redlands Noon Kiwanis Club - Martin and Dorothy Munz Scholarships (Undergraduate/Scholarship) [5996]
Redlands Rotary Club - Donald C. Anderson Scholarships (Undergraduate/Scholarship) [5997]
Redlands Rotary Club - Ernest L. Cronemeyer Memorial Scholarships (Undergraduate/Scholarship) [5998]
Redlands Rotary Club Foundation Discretionary Scholarships (Undergraduate/Scholarship) [5999]
Redlands Teachers Association Scholarships (Undergraduate/Scholarship) [6000]
Vern W. Reeder Memorial Scholarships (Undergraduate/Scholarship) [3574]
Registered Apprenticeship Program (RAP) Scholarships (Undergraduate/Scholarship) [179]
Henry J. Reilly Memorial Scholarships - For Freshmen in College (Undergraduate/Scholarship) [6023]
Henry J. Reilly Memorial Scholarships - For Graduating High School Seniors (Undergraduate/Scholarship) [6024]
Henry J. Reilly Memorial Scholarships - For Sophomores and Juniors in College (Undergraduate/Scholarship) [6025]
Henry J. Reilly Memorial Scholarships - Graduate Program (Graduate, Professional Development/Scholarship) [6026]
Jacob L. Reinecke Memorial Scholarship Fund (Undergraduate/Scholarship) [3299]
Daniel L. Reiss Memorial Scholarship Fund (Undergraduate/Scholarship) [3300]
The Remington Club Scholarships (Undergraduate/Scholarship) [6218]
Retired League Postmasters Scholarship Program (Undergraduate/Scholarship) [6032]
Lori Rhett Memorial Scholarships (Undergraduate/Scholarship) [4682]
Rhode Island Association of Former Legislators Scholarships (Undergraduate/Scholarship) [6040]
Rhode Island Commission on Women/Freda H. Goldman Education Awards (Undergraduate/Award/Prize) [6041]
John J. and Elizabeth Rhodes Scholarships (Graduate, Undergraduate/Scholarship) [1674]
Ben C. Rich Memorial Scholarships (Graduate, Undergraduate/Scholarship) [1675]
Barbara Hagan Richards Scholarships (Undergraduate/Scholarship) [2444]
James Edward "Bill" Richards Scholarships (Undergraduate/Scholarship) [2445]
Philip Guy Richardson Memorial Scholarship (Undergraduate/Scholarship) [3986]
John S. and Jacqueline P. Rider Scholarships (Undergraduate/Scholarship) [7453]
Jasper Ridge Restoration Fellowships Jasper Ridge Biological Preserve (Graduate, Postdoctorate/Fellowship) [2816]
Jerrothia Allenfonzo Riggs & Anna & Dorothy Mae Barnes Scholarships (Undergraduate/Scholarship) [1899]
Susan E. Riley Scholarships (Undergraduate/Scholarship) [2663]
Lana K. Rinehart Scholarship (Undergraduate/Scholarship) [2383]
Harold and Eleonor Ringelberg Scholarship Fund (Undergraduate/Scholarship) [3301]
Josephine Ringold Scholarships (Undergraduate/Scholarship) [3346]
Jean Wiggin Roach Scholarships (Undergraduate/Scholarship) [2664]
James H. Roberts Athletic Scholarships (Undergraduate/Scholarship) [5512]
Marion Roberts Memorial Scholarships (Postgraduate/Scholarship) [1572]
Thomas Warren Roberts Scholarships (Undergraduate/Scholarship) [5513]
A.D. 'Al' Robertson Memorial Scholarships (Undergraduate/Scholarship) [4378]
Ben Robinette Scholarship Endowment Fund (Undergraduate/Scholarship) [3074]
Jackie Robinson Foundation Minority Scholarship (Undergraduate/Scholarship) [637]
James Robinson Memorial Scholarships (Undergraduate/Scholarship) [5514]
Jackie Robinson Scholarships (Undergraduate/Scholarship) [6049]
August M. Rocco Scholarship Fund (Undergraduate/Scholarship) [6750]
Rockford Area Habitat for Humanity College Scholarships (Undergraduate/Scholarship) [2482]
Rockford Chapter Daughters of the American Revolution Memorial Scholarships (Undergraduate/Scholarship) [2483]
Rockin' Christmas Fund Scholarships (Undergraduate/Scholarship) [6671]
Rocky Mountain Research Fellowships (Graduate/Fellowship) [6056]
R.O.E.A. Dumitru Golea Goldy-Gemu Scholarships (Undergraduate/Scholarship) [913]
Kimberly Marie Rogers Memorial Scholarship Fund (Undergraduate/Scholarship) [2972]
Pat and Cliff Rogers Nursing Scholarships (Undergraduate/Scholarship) [4379]
Geraldine Ruth Rogers Scholarships (Undergraduate/Scholarship) [6887]
Mary Stuart Rogers Scholarships (Undergraduate/Scholarship) [7415]
Richard C. Rolfs Scholarships (Undergraduate/Scholarship) [5776]
Mary Louise Roller Panhellenic Scholarships (Undergraduate/Scholarship) [5223]
Ronald McDonald House Charities African American Future Achievers Scholarships (Undergraduate/Scholarship) [4407]
Ronald McDonald House Charities of Hispanic Heritage (Undergraduate/Scholarship) [4408]
Ronald McDonald House Charities Scholarships (Undergraduate/Scholarship) [4409]
Ronald McDonald House Charities Scholarships in Asia (Undergraduate/Scholarship) [4410]
Roofing Industry Alliance for Progress Scholarships (Graduate, Undergraduate/Scholarship) [6058]
Roofing Industry Scholarships (Graduate, Undergraduate/Scholarship) [5035]
Roothbert Fund Scholarships (Undergraduate/Scholarship) [6060]
ROP - Ambassadors Scholarships (Undergraduate/Scholarship) [6003]
ROP - Rob Bruce Memorial Scholarships (Undergraduate/Scholarship) [6004]
Annie B. Rose Educational Scholarships (Undergraduate/Scholarship) [4651]
Dr. Wayne F. Rose Scholarship Fund (Undergraduate/Scholarship) [2973]
Ollie Rosenberg Educational Trust (Undergraduate/Scholarship) [3117]
Rosenberg-Ibarra Scholarships

(Undergraduate/Scholarship) [5777]
Jean and Tom Rosenthal Scholarship Program (Undergraduate/Scholarship) [2520]
Ross-Fahey Scholarships (Postgraduate/Scholarship) [4683]
The Rotary Club of Cape Coral Goldcoast Scholarships Fund (Undergraduate/Scholarship) [2055]
Rotary Club of Corpus Christi Scholarships (High School/Scholarship) [2285]
The Rotary Club of Rancho Bernardo Sunrise Abraxas Student Scholarships (Undergraduate/Scholarship) [6219]
The Rotary Foundation Ambassadorial Scholarships (Undergraduate/Scholarship) [6062]
Bernard Rotberg Memorial Scholarships (Undergraduate/Scholarship) [4031]
Robin Rousseau Memorial Mountain Achievement Scholarship (Undergraduate/Scholarship) [180]
RPA Scholarships (Undergraduate/Scholarship) [6028]
Mike Ruben Scholarships (Undergraduate/Scholarship) [5517]
Rubinstein Family Scholarships (Undergraduate/Scholarship) [6220]
Lawrence E. & Mabel Jackson Rudberg Scholarships (Undergraduate/Scholarship) [2791]
Anna M. Rundguist Memorial Scholarship (Undergraduate/Scholarship) [3378]
Ruppert Educational Grant Program (Undergraduate/Scholarship) [6395]
Rural Telephone Company Scholarships (Undergraduate/Scholarship) [6085]
Norman K. Russell Scholarships (Graduate/Scholarship) [5002]
Michael A. Russo Memorial Scholarships (Undergraduate/Scholarship) [6005]
Rutherford Scholars (Undergraduate/Scholarship) [181]
Alexander Rutherford Scholarships for High School Achievement (Undergraduate/Scholarship) [182]
Michael Clarkson Ryan Memorial Scholarships (Graduate, Undergraduate/Scholarship) [1676]
Charles and Eleonor Rycenga Education Scholarships Fund (Undergraduate/Scholarship) [3302]
Deborah Jean Rydberg Memorial Scholarship (Undergraduate/Scholarship) [2484]
Ryerson Scholarships (Undergraduate/Scholarship) [4003]
Jeanne Graves Ryland Scholarships (Undergraduate/Scholarship) [2665]
SACHS Foundation Graduate Scholarships (Graduate/Scholarship) [6090]
SACHS Foundation Undergraduate Scholarships for Colorado Black Students (High School/Scholarship) [6091]
Sacks For CF Scholarships (All/Scholarship) [2589]
Julie Anne Sadlier Memorial Scholarships (Undergraduate/Scholarship) [2666]
Virginia Hartford Saharov Memorial Scholarships (Undergraduate/Scholarship) [2667]
Saint Andrews Scholarships (Undergraduate/Scholarship) [6150]
St. James Armenian Church Memorial Scholarships (Undergraduate/Scholarship) [1290]
St. Louis Division Scholarships (Undergraduate/Scholarship) [4519]
Saint Paul University Excellence Scholarships (Undergraduate/Scholarship) [6152]
Saint Paul University Financial Aid Brasseries (Undergraduate/Scholarship) [6153]
St. Stephen A.M.E. Allison E. Fisher Book Awards (Undergraduate/Scholarship) [2985]
Saint Vincent College Eagle Scout Scholarships (Undergraduate/Scholarship) [4865]
Saints Cyril and Methodius Scholarships (Undergraduate/Scholarship) [6088]
Joseph and Amelia Saks Scholarship Fund (Undergraduate/Scholarship) [2361]
Sakura Finetek Student Scholarships (Undergraduate/Scholarship) [5079]
The Sallie Mae 911 Education Fund (Undergraduate/Scholarship) [6157]
Marie V. Saltwick Scholarships (Undergraduate/Scholarship) [2792]
Henry Salvatori Scholarships (Undergraduate/Scholarship) [5374]
Samalot - Sebastian Scholarship Fund (High School/Scholarship) [2600]
The Walter Samek III Memorial Scholarship Fund (Undergraduate/Scholarship) [2402]
Ray and Pearly Sams Scholarships (Undergraduate/Scholarship) [7454]
Samsung American Legion Scholarships (Undergraduate/Scholarship) [697]
San Diego City College Study Abroad Scholarships (Undergraduate/Scholarship) [6221]
The San Diego Foundation Community Scholarship II (Undergraduate/Scholarship) [6222]
The San Diego Foundation Community Scholarships I (Undergraduate/Scholarship) [6223]
San Diego National Bank Scholarships (Undergraduate/Scholarship) [6224]
San Diego Pathways to College Scholarships (Undergraduate/Scholarship) [6225]
San Pasqual Academy Scholarships (Undergraduate/Scholarship) [6227]
Sand Hill Scholars Program (Undergraduate/Scholarship) [6397]
Carl Sandburg College Scholarships (Undergraduate/Scholarship) [4908]
Frank Sarli Memorial Scholarships (Undergraduate/Scholarship) [4837]
Saskatchewan Trucking Association Scholarships (Undergraduate/Scholarship) [6250]
Roger C. Sathre Memorial Scholarship Fund (Undergraduate/Scholarship) [3649]
Malini E. Sathyadev Memorial Scholarships (Undergraduate/Scholarship) [6228]
Save Mart Legacy Scholarships (Undergraduate/Scholarship) [1833]
John A. Savoy Scholarship Fund (Undergraduate/Scholarship) [2975]
SAWE Scholarships (Undergraduate/Scholarship) [6424]
Mark Dauglas Sawyer Memorial Scholarship (High School/Scholarship) [2362]
SBA Four-Year Scholarships Program (Undergraduate/Scholarship) [6702]
SBA One-Year Scholarships Program (Undergraduate/Scholarship) [6703]
Leslie and Mary Ella Scales Memorial Scholarship (Undergraduate/Scholarship) [2363]
Edith Scandlyn/Sammie Lynn Scandlyn Puett Memorial Scholarships (Undergraduate/Scholarship) [2668]
Mary Turnbull Schacht Memorial Scholarships (Undergraduate/Scholarship) [6368]
David W. Schacht Native American Student Scholarship (Undergraduate/Scholarship) [1630]
Millicent M. Schaffner Endowed Memorial Scholarship (Undergraduate/Scholarship) [3303]
William C. Scheetz Family Scholarships (Graduate, Undergraduate/Scholarship) [1677]
Dr. Oskar and Sally Schickler Scholarship (Undergraduate/Scholarship) [3561]
Robert C. and Margaret A. Schikora Scholarships (Undergraduate/Scholarship) [6672]
Esther Schlundt Memorial Scholarships (Undergraduate/Scholarship) [3694]
Richard J. Schnell Memorial Scholarship (Postdoctorate/Scholarship) [2485]
Scholarship Award of The Aliant Pioneer Volunteers (Postgraduate/Scholarship) [1989]
Scholarship for Junior PHS Commissioned Officers (Undergraduate/Scholarship) [5689]
Scholarships for Aboriginal Canadians (Undergraduate/Scholarship) [5118]
Scholarships of the Arts (Graduate, Undergraduate/Scholarship) [2590]
Scholarships for Visible Minorities (Undergraduate/Scholarship) [5119]
Schoolsfirst Federal Credit Union Scholarships (Undergraduate/Scholarship) [6006]
Tanna H. Schulich MBA Entrance Scholarships (Postgraduate/Scholarship) [6275]
Alice Schulman Simmons Scholarships for UU Women (Undergraduate/Scholarship) [6954]
David and Ginny Schultz Family Scholarship Fund (Undergraduate/Scholarship) [3304]
Carl A. Scott Book Scholarships (Undergraduate/Scholarship) [2555]
Seaman Family Scholarships (High School/Scholarship) [2286]
Seaspace Scholarships (Postgraduate, Undergraduate/Scholarship) [6292]
Fred A. Seaton Memorial Scholarships (Graduate, Undergraduate/Scholarship) [1678]
Margery J. Seeger Scholarships (Undergraduate/Scholarship) [3347]
Elisabeth Seegmiller Recruitment Scholarship Grant (Undergraduate/Scholarship) [2487]
Aaron Seesan Memorial Scholarship Fund (Graduate/Scholarship) [6751]
Detective Cheryl Seiden Memorial Scholarships (Undergraduate/Scholarship) [255]
D. Mitchell Self Memorial Scholarships (Undergraduate/Scholarship) [5301]
Senior Memorial Scholarships (Undergraduate/Scholarship) [2488]
William "Buddy" Sentner Scholarship Awards (Undergraduate/Scholarship) [391]
Felix R. Sepulveda Memorial Scholarships - Northside Booster Club (Undergraduate/Scholarship) [6007]
Servus Credit Union 4-H Scholarships (Undergraduate/Scholarship) [135]
Captain Anthony D. Sesow Scholarships (Undergraduate/Scholarship) [5133]
Hubert K. Seymour Scholarships (Undergraduate/Scholarship) [5255]
Judge Terry Shamsie Scholarships (High School/Scholarship) [2287]
William H. Shannon Fellowships (Professional Development/Fellowship) [3916]
Commander Dan F. Shanower Scholarships (Undergraduate/Scholarship) [5134]
Ken and Sandy Sharkey Family Scholarship Fund (Undergraduate/Scholarship) [3306]
W.L. Shattuck Scholarship (Undergraduate/Scholarship) [3650]
Regina B. Shearn Scholarships (Graduate, Undergraduate/Scholarship) [256]
Jim Sheerin Scholarships (Undergraduate/Scholarship) [4426]
Nettie and Edward Shelah Scholarships (Undergraduate/Scholarship) [6785]
Bruce Shelton Scholarships (Undergraduate/Scholarship) [7455]
Matthew Shepard Scholarships (Undergraduate/Scholarship) [6138]
Robert P. Sheppard Leadership Awards (High School/Scholarship) [5072]
Shervin Tehranchi Wrestling Scholarships (Undergraduate/Scholarship) [6008]
Drs. Poh Shien and Judy Young Scholarships (Undergraduate/Scholarship) [7013]
Shoals Home Builders Association Scholarships (Undergraduate/Scholarship) [5302]
Misty and Sally Shoop Scholarships (Graduate, Undergraduate/Scholarship) [1679]
Shoreline Community College Academic Excellence Scholarships for Graduating High School Seniors (Undergraduate/Scholarship) [6320]
Shoreline Community College Academic Improvement Scholarships for Graduating High School Seniors (Undergraduate/Scholarship) [6321]
Shoreline Community College Continuing Students Scholarships (Undergraduate/Scholarship) [6322]
Shoreline Community College Part-Time Students Scholarships (Undergraduate/Scholarship) [6323]
Tom Shown Scholarships (Undergraduate/Scholarship) [7456]
Ralph W. Shrader Diversity Scholarships (Graduate/Scholarship) [1248]
Phil Shykes Memorial Scholarships (Undergraduate/Scholarship) [2793]
Don and Madalyn Sickafoose Educational Trust (Undergraduate/Scholarship) [6752]
Norman Siegel Research Scholar Grants (Doctorate/Grant) [1019]
Sigma Diagnostics Student Scholarships (Undergraduate/Scholarship) [5081]
Sigma Kappa Foundation Alumnae Continuing Education Scholarships (Undergraduate/Scholarship) [6369]
Sigma Kappa Foundation Founders' Scholarships (Undergraduate/Scholarship) [6371]
Sigma Kappa Foundation Michigan Scholarships

(Undergraduate/Scholarship) [6373]
Silver Nugget Family Scholarships (Undergraduate/Scholarship) [5857]
Meyer and Dorothy Silverman Scholarships (Undergraduate/Scholarship) [2446]
Harvey L. Simmons Memorial Scholarships (Undergraduate/Scholarship) [6230]
Simon Youth Foundation Community Scholarships (Undergraduate/Scholarship) [6400]
Simonton Windows Scholarship Fund (Undergraduate/Scholarship) [5521]
Bro. Dr. Frank T. Simpson (Undergraduate/Scholarship) [3497]
John R. Simpson Memorial Scholarships (Graduate, Undergraduate/Scholarship) [1680]
Aaron B. Singleton Memorial Scholarships (Undergraduate/Scholarship) [5303]
Wiggsy Sivertsen Scholarships (Undergraduate/Scholarship) [6139]
Bill Six Memorial Scholarship Fund (Undergraduate/Scholarship) [5522]
Rajadi Sjarif Memorial Scholarships (Undergraduate/Scholarship) [6009]
R. Skeeles Memorial Scholarship Fund (Undergraduate/Scholarship) [6753]
Francelene Skinner Memorial Scholarship (Undergraduate/Scholarship) [4230]
Sledge Fellowships (Graduate/Fellowship) [242]
J. Ward Sleichter and Frances F. Sleichter Memorial Scholarship Fund (Undergraduate/Scholarship) [3119]
Smiley Elementary School PTA - Beverly Roberts Memorial Scholarships (Undergraduate/Scholarship) [6010]
Eva Smith Bursary (Undergraduate/Scholarship) [4004]
Gladys Ann Smith Greater Los Angeles Women's Council Scholarships (Undergraduate/Scholarship) [5142]
Drew Smith Memorial Scholarship (Undergraduate/Scholarship) [2384]
Tacy Ana Smith Memorial Scholarship Fund (Undergraduate/Scholarship) [3076]
James George Smith Memorial Scholarships (Graduate, Undergraduate/Scholarship) [1681]
Smith-Reynolds Founder Fellowships (Graduate/Fellowship) [3540]
Brian Smith Scholarship (Undergraduate/Scholarship) [1773]
Esther M. Smith Scholarship (Undergraduate/Scholarship) [2385]
Ralph and Josephine Smith Scholarship Fund (Undergraduate/Scholarship) [2976]
Helen J. and Harold Gilman Smith Scholarship (Graduate, Undergraduate/Scholarship) [1631]
Joseph Sumner Smith Scholarships (All/Scholarship) [6955]
Smith's Personal Best Scholarships (Undergraduate/Scholarship) [5859]
Gladys Snauble Scholarships (Undergraduate/Scholarship) [3348]
SNMTS Bachelor's Degree Completion Scholarships (Undergraduate/Scholarship) [6523]
Ray Snow Memorial Scholarships (Undergraduate/Scholarship) [4947]
Society of Marine Port Engineers Scholarship Loans (Undergraduate/Scholarship/Forgivable Loan) [6510]
Dale and Betty George Sola Scholarships (Undergraduate/Scholarship) [2794]
Christine Soper Scholarships (Undergraduate/Scholarship) [3349]
Soroptimist International of Chambersburg Scholarship Fund (Undergraduate/Scholarship) [3120]
Lily and Catello Sorrentino Memorial Scholarships (Undergraduate/Scholarship) [6042]
Sourdough Reunion Memorial Scholarships (Undergraduate/Scholarship) [4385]
South Central Power Scholarships (Undergraduate/Scholarship) [6620]
South Coast Area High School Senior Honors Scholarship Program (High School/Scholarship) [6253]
South Jersey Golf Association Scholarships (Undergraduate/Scholarship) [6623]
South Kentucky RECC High School Senior Scholarships (Undergraduate/Scholarship) [6626]
South Texas Lighthouse for the Blind Scholarships (Undergraduate/Scholarship) [2288]
Southern Nevada Sports Hall of Fame Athletic Scholarships (Undergraduate/Scholarship) [5860]
Southern Scholarship Foundation Scholarships (Undergraduate/Scholarship) [6638]
Southwest Florida Community Foundation College Assistance Scholarships (Undergraduate/Scholarship) [6674]
Sovereign Nations Scholarship Fund (Undergraduate/Scholarship) [625]
Master Sergeant William Sowers Memorial Scholarships (Undergraduate/Scholarship) [60]
Kathy Spadoni Memorial Scholarships (Undergraduate/Scholarship) [5779]
Nathan Sparks Memorial Scholarship (Undergraduate/Scholarship) [2364]
Spartan Scholarship Awards (Undergraduate/Scholarship) [3843]
Spartan Staff Scholarships (Undergraduate/Scholarship) [5861]
Faith Speckhard Scholarships (Undergraduate/Scholarship) [3989]
Spencer Foundation Dissertation Fellowship Program (Postdoctorate/Fellowship) [6692]
Spencer Foundation Research Grants (All/Grant) [6693]
Lawrence Alan Spiegel Remembrance Scholarships (Undergraduate/Scholarship) [3611]
Spirit of Allison Graduation Award (High School/Award/Prize) [2986]
The Spirit Square Center for Arts and Education Scholarship Fund (Undergraduate/Scholarship) [3077]
Spouse Tuition Aids Program (Graduate, Undergraduate/Scholarship) [5148]
SSC-Building Environmental Campus Community (BECC) Fellowships (Undergraduate/Scholarship) [6334]
Ernest and Charlene Stachowiak Memorial Scholarship (Undergraduate/Scholarship) [2489]
Matt Stager Memorial Scholarship Fund (Undergraduate/Scholarship) [7390]
H.T. and Terrell Stanford Scholarship (Undergraduate/Scholarship) [2365]
Starr Foundation Graduate Fellowship in Asian Studies (Graduate/Grant) [7094]
State of Idaho Scholarships Category A (Undergraduate/Scholarship) [4217]
Minnie Patton Stayman Scholarships (Undergraduate/Scholarship) [5566]
Harry Steele Entrance Awards (Postgraduate/Award/Prize) [6276]
Gwen Stefani After-the-Fires Scholarships (Undergraduate/Scholarship) [6231]
Mireille and Murray Steinberg Scholarship (Postgraduate/Scholarship) [3562]
Ralph Steinhauer Awards of Distinction (Doctorate, Graduate/Award/Prize) [185]
Elin J. Stene/Xi Scholarships (Undergraduate/Scholarship) [6374]
Step Up Scholarships (Undergraduate/Scholarship) [6232]
H. Hiram Stephenson Oxford Cup Scholarships (Graduate, Undergraduate/Scholarship) [1682]
Hugh E. Stephenson Oxford Cup Scholarships (Graduate, Undergraduate/Scholarship) [1683]
Elizabeth Coulter Stephenson Scholarships (Undergraduate/Scholarship) [2699]
Richie Stevenson Scholarships (Undergraduate/Scholarship) [2448]
Stewart Title Firefighters Scholarships (High School, Undergraduate/Scholarship) [2290]
Mary Stewart and William T. Covington, Jr. Scholarship Fund (Undergraduate/Scholarship) [3078]
Dr. Gunnar B. Stickler Scholarships (Undergraduate/Scholarship) [6787]
James E. Stoner Memorial Scholarships (Undergraduate/Scholarship) [1417]
Stop Hunger Scholarships (Undergraduate/Scholarship) [398]
StraightForward Media's Minority Scholarships (Undergraduate/Scholarship) [6803]
Bonnie Strangio Education Scholarships (Graduate, Undergraduate/Scholarship) [2591]
Marlene Streit Golf Scholarships (Undergraduate/Scholarship) [6077]
Striving for Success Scholarships (Undergraduate/Scholarship) [5862]
Fraser Stryker Diversity Scholarships (Undergraduate/Scholarship) [6809]
Stultz Scholarships (Undergraduate/Scholarship) [7457]
Subic Bay-Cubi Point 1 Scholarships (Undergraduate/Scholarship) [5143]
Phil Sullivan Scholarships (Undergraduate/Scholarship) [5780]
William A. Sullivan Scholarships (Undergraduate/Scholarship) [5144]
Summerside-Natick Hockey Scholarships (Undergraduate/Scholarship) [2501]
Sun Country Amateur Golf Association Scholarships (Undergraduate/Scholarship) [6817]
Sun Life Financial Peer Support Scholarships (Professional Development/Scholarship) [2025]
Bruce and Marjorie Sundlun Scholarships (Undergraduate/Scholarship) [6043]
Survival Scholarship Program (Undergraduate/Scholarship) [7514]
Sussman-Miller Educational Assistance Award Program (Undergraduate/Scholarship) [195]
SUVCW Scholarships (Undergraduate/Scholarship) [6606]
Lorraine E. Swain Scholarships (Undergraduate/Scholarship) [6375]
Hugh B. Sweeny Scholarships (Undergraduate/Scholarship) [4040]
Jeffery Tyler Sweitzer Wrestling Memorial Scholarship Fund (Undergraduate/Scholarship) [6756]
Timothy S. Sweterlitsch Memorial Scholarship Fund (Undergraduate/Scholarship) [6757]
SWFL Deputy Sheriffs Association Fund Scholarships (Undergraduate/Scholarship) [6676]
SWFL Professional Golfers Association Scholarships (Undergraduate/Scholarship) [6677]
Sycamore Scholar Awards (Undergraduate/Scholarship) [3713]
Hazaros Tabakoglu Scholarship Fund (Undergraduate/Scholarship) [1291]
The Tabat Scholarship Fund (Graduate/Scholarship) [2922]
Tagged for Greatness Scholarships (Undergraduate/Scholarship) [116]
Taiwanese American Community Scholarships (Undergraduate/Scholarship) [6838]
Tall Awareness Scholarships (Undergraduate/Scholarship) [5863]
Tall Clubs International Student Scholarships (Undergraduate/Scholarship) [6840]
Jack Tate/ThinkCOLLEGE Scholarship Fund (Undergraduate/Scholarship) [3079]
Ryan "Munchie" Taylor Memorial Scholarships (Undergraduate/Scholarship) [4270]
TCA-BAACBH Scholarships (Undergraduate/Scholarship) [6938]
TCA-UMD Scholarships (Undergraduate/Scholarship) [6940]
TCATA College Scholarship Program (Undergraduate/Scholarship) [6875]
Team DC Student-Athlete Scholarships (Undergraduate/Scholarship) [6140]
Telamon Scholarships (Undergraduate/Scholarship) [7014]
Telecommunications Association of Michigan Scholarship Fund (Undergraduate/Scholarship) [6856]
Telluride Association Summer Program Scholarships (High School/Scholarship) [6858]
Tennessee Trucking Association Scholarships (Undergraduate/Scholarship) [2449]
Charles L. Terrell/New Haven Savings Bank Scholarship Fund (Undergraduate/Scholarship) [2396]
Texas Telephone Association Foundation Scholarships (Undergraduate/Scholarship) [6873]
ThanksUSA Scholarships (Undergraduate/Scholarship) [6877]
Theta/Caryl Cordis D'hondt Scholarships (Undergraduate/Scholarship) [6376]
Theta Tau Scholarships (Undergraduate/Scholarship) [6377]
Barbara Thomas Bursary (Undergraduate/Scholarship) [4005]

Barber Owen Thomas Scholarships *(Undergraduate/Scholarship)* [6378]
C.R. Thomas Scholarships *(Undergraduate/Scholarship)* [5524]
Dorothy B. & Charles E. Thomas Scholarships *(Undergraduate/Scholarship)* [3351]
Elizabeth Thomas Scholarships *(Undergraduate/Scholarship)* [6325]
Madlyn D. Thompson Memorial Scholarships *(Undergraduate/Scholarship)* [1900]
Barbara and Howard Thompson Scholarship *(Undergraduate/Scholarship)* [3991]
Miller Thomson Foundation Scholarships *(Undergraduate/Scholarship)* [4537]
Thornberg/Havens Scholarships *(Undergraduate/Scholarship)* [2700]
Dorothy J. Thurston Graduate Scholarships *(Undergraduate/Scholarship)* [3352]
Raymond A. Tice Scholarships I *(Undergraduate/Scholarship)* [6233]
Raymond A. Tice Scholarships II *(Undergraduate/Scholarship)* [6234]
Tidewater Builders Association Scholarships *(Undergraduate/Scholarship)* [6890]
Time Warner Point Scholarships *(Graduate, Undergraduate/Scholarship)* [5727]
Time Warner Tribal Scholars Program *(Undergraduate/Scholarship)* [627]
Mark P. Tiner Education Scholarships *(Undergraduate/Scholarship)* [5368]
TMCF Scholarships *(Undergraduate/Scholarship)* [4316]
Mario J. Tocco Hydrocephalus Foundation Scholarships *(Undergraduate/Scholarship)* [3639]
Richard Cecil Todd and Clauda Pennock Todd Tripod Scholarships *(Graduate, Undergraduate/Scholarship)* [5655]
Michael W. Toennis Scholarships *(Graduate, Undergraduate/Scholarship)* [1684]
Togiak Village Scholarships *(Undergraduate/Scholarship)* [4386]
Aram Torossian Memorial Scholarships *(Undergraduate/Scholarship)* [1292]
Touchstone Special Achievement Scholarships *(Undergraduate/Scholarship)* [6621]
Town and County Club Scholarships *(Undergraduate/Scholarship)* [3499]
Joseph Towner Fund for Gay and Lesbian Families *(Undergraduate/Scholarship)* [6141]
Toyota Community Scholars *(Undergraduate/Scholarship)* [6894]
Traditional Student Scholarships *(Undergraduate/Scholarship)* [2510]
TRALA Scholarships Program *(Undergraduate/Scholarship)* [6924]
Vera Tran Memorial Scholarships *(Undergraduate/Scholarship)* [7324]
Traub-Dicker Rainbow Scholarships *(Undergraduate/Scholarship)* [6790]
Trelut Family Legacy Scholarships *(Undergraduate/Scholarship)* [1834]
Marie Tremaine Fellowships *(Postgraduate/Grant)* [1699]
Tribal Priority Scholarships *(Undergraduate/Scholarship)* [1212]
Tim Triner Letter Carriers Scholarship Fund *(Undergraduate/Scholarship)* [6758]
Mildred E. Troske Music Scholarships *(Undergraduate/Scholarship)* [3353]
Jo Anne J. Trow Scholarships *(Undergraduate/Scholarship)* [4635]
Troy University Rodeo Team Scholarships *(Graduate/Scholarship)* [117]
Truckload Carriers Association Scholarships *(Undergraduate/Scholarship)* [6926]
Trustee, Schawe, Presidential and Honor Scholarships *(Undergraduate/Scholarship)* [7533]
Trustee Scholarships *(Undergraduate/Scholarship)* [4068]
Norman J. Tschantz/Walter C. Deuble Scholarships *(Undergraduate/Scholarship)* [6759]
Tschudy Family Scholarships *(Undergraduate/Scholarship)* [4219]
Tsutako Curo Scholarships *(Undergraduate/Scholarship)* [5866]
Richard R. Tufenkian Memorial Scholarships *(Undergraduate/Scholarship)* [1253]
Tunxis Community College Foundation Scholarships *(Undergraduate/Scholarship)* [3500]
Jeff Turner-Forsyth Audubon Society Scholarships *(Undergraduate/Scholarship)* [7458]
Mark and Vera Turner Memorial Scholarship *(Undergraduate/Scholarship)* [4231]
Ira G. Turpin Scholar Fund *(Undergraduate/Scholarship)* [6760]
Tuscumbia Kiwanis Scholarships *(Undergraduate/Scholarship)* [5304]
TU@UT HSF College Scholarship Program *(Undergraduate/Scholarship)* [3604]
UAA Alumni Association Scholarships *(Undergraduate/Scholarship)* [7041]
UAF Alumni Association Scholarships *(Undergraduate/Scholarship)* [7079]
UFCW Scholarships *(Undergraduate/Scholarship)* [6963]
UJFC and Council of St. Paul Annual Scholarships *(All/Scholarship)* [4542]
Umialik Scholarships *(Undergraduate/Scholarship)* [4387]
Undergraduate and Medical/Graduate General Scholarship and Loan Program *(Graduate/Scholarship)* [6254]
UNH Alumni Association Legacy Scholarships *(Undergraduate/Scholarship)* [7138]
UNH Parent's Association Endowment Scholarship Fund *(Undergraduate/Scholarship)* [7139]
Union of Marash Armenian Scholarships *(Graduate, Undergraduate/Scholarship)* [1293]
Union Plus Scholarship Program *(Undergraduate/Scholarship)* [3922]
United South and Eastern Tribes Scholarship Fund *(Undergraduate/Scholarship)* [6970]
U.S. Air Force ROTC Enhanced HSI Scholarship *(Undergraduate/Scholarship)* [6975]
U.S. Air Force ROTC High School Scholarships *(Undergraduate/Scholarship)* [6977]
U.S. Air Force ROTC In-College Scholarships *(Undergraduate/Scholarship)* [6978]
U.S. Bates Scholarship Program *(Undergraduate/Scholarship)* [3923]
U.S. BIA Indian Higher Education Grants *(Undergraduate/Grant)* [638]
U.S. Pan Asian American Chamber of Commerce CBS Scholarships *(Undergraduate/Scholarship)* [7015]
U.S. Pan Asian American Chamber of Commerce McDonald's Scholarships *(Undergraduate/Scholarship)* [7016]
U.S. Pan Asian American Chamber of Commerce UPS Scholarships *(Undergraduate/Scholarship)* [7017]
United Teachers Los Angeles Stonewall Scholarship Fund *(Undergraduate/Scholarship)* [6143]
Unites States Institute of Peace JR Senior Fellowships Program *(All/Fellowship)* [7027]
University of Alaska Scholars Program *(Undergraduate/Scholarship)* [4388]
University Alliance HSF/UGA College Scholarship Program *(Undergraduate/Scholarship)* [3605]
University of California LGBT Alumni (UCGALA) scholarships *(Undergraduate/Scholarship)* [6144]
University of Hawaii at Manoa East-West Center Graduate Fellowships *(Graduate, Postdoctorate/Fellowship)* [7095]
University of Hawaii at Manoa Graduate Student Organization Travel Funds *(Graduate/Grant)* [7097]
University of Louisville Eagle Scout Scholarships *(Undergraduate/Scholarship)* [4866]
University of Maryland International Student Scholarships *(Undergraduate/Scholarship)* [7023]
University of Minnesota Women Student Travel Grants *(Graduate, Undergraduate/Grant)* [7134]
University of Oregon Dean's Scholarships *(Undergraduate/Scholarship)* [7203]
University of Oregon Diversity-Building Scholarships *(Graduate, Undergraduate/Scholarship)* [7204]
University of Oregon General University Scholarships *(Undergraduate/Scholarship)* [7205]
University of Oregon Presidential Scholarships *(Undergraduate/Scholarship)* [7206]
University of Phoenix First Chance Scholarship Fund *(Undergraduate/Scholarship)* [7297]
University of Phoenix Touchdown Mondays Scholarship Program *(All/Scholarship)* [2592]
University of Toronto SAC Undergraduate Grants *(Undergraduate/Grant)* [7236]
University of West Alabama Rodeo Team Scholarships *(Graduate/Scholarship)* [118]
University of Wisconsin-Madison Academic Excellence Scholarships *(Undergraduate/Scholarship)* [7270]
University of Wisconsin-Madison African American Alumni Scholarships *(Undergraduate/Scholarship)* [7271]
University of Wisconsin-Madison American Indian Alumni Scholarships *(Undergraduate/Scholarship)* [7272]
University of Wisconsin-Madison Chancellor's Scholarships *(Undergraduate/Scholarship)* [7275]
University of Wisconsin-Madison Hispanic/Latino Alumni Scholarships *(Undergraduate/Scholarship)* [7276]
University of Wisconsin-Madison National Merit Scholarships *(Undergraduate/Scholarship)* [7279]
University of Wisconsin-Madison Single Parent and Adult Scholarships *(Undergraduate/Scholarship)* [7281]
Unmet Need Scholarships *(Undergraduate/Scholarship)* [6158]
The Urban Scholarships Fund *(Undergraduate/Scholarship)* [6860]
USA Freestyle Martial Arts Scholarships *(Undergraduate/Scholarship)* [6238]
USA/USA-Ukramerazha Scholarships *(Undergraduate/Scholarship)* [7024]
USAWOASF/Grantham University On-Line Scholarships *(Graduate, Undergraduate/Scholarship)* [6980]
USAWOASF Regular Scholarships *(Undergraduate/Scholarship)* [6981]
USHJA Athletic Scholarships *(Undergraduate/Scholarship)* [6995]
USHJA General Scholarships *(Undergraduate/Scholarship)* [6996]
USHJA Postgraduate Scholarships *(Postgraduate/Scholarship)* [6997]
USS Tennessee Scholarship Fund *(Undergraduate/Scholarship)* [5149]
USTA Tennis and Education Foundation College Education Scholarships *(Undergraduate/Scholarship)* [7306]
USTA Tennis and Education Foundation College Textbook Scholarships *(Undergraduate/Scholarship)* [7307]
Utility Workers Union of America Scholarship Program *(Undergraduate/Scholarship)* [7309]
Valley Alliance of Mentors for Opportunities and Scholarship (VAMOS) Program *(Undergraduate/Scholarship)* [3606]
Hurad Van Der Bedrosian Memorial Scholarships *(Graduate/Scholarship)* [1294]
Keith C. Vanderhyde Scholarships *(Undergraduate/Scholarship)* [3354]
Jacob R. & Mary M. VanLoo & Lenore K. VanLoo Scholarships *(Undergraduate/Scholarship)* [3355]
Chester M. Vernon Memorial Eagle Scout Scholarships *(High School/Scholarship)* [4867]
Veterans of Foreign Wars Scout of the Year *(High School/Scholarship)* [4868]
Vilas Equity Scholarships *(Undergraduate/Scholarship)* [7282]
William F. Vilas Scholarships *(Undergraduate/Scholarship)* [7283]
Gupton A. Vogt Oxford Cup Memorial Scholarships *(Graduate, Undergraduate/Scholarship)* [1685]
Irma E. Voigt Memorial Scholarships *(Undergraduate/Scholarship)* [6379]
Frank M. Waddell Scholarships *(Graduate, Undergraduate/Scholarship)* [7237]
Bruce Wade Memorial Scholarships for Lesbian, Gay and Bisexual *(Undergraduate/Scholarship)* [6145]
Robert R. Wade Scholarship *(Undergraduate/Scholarship)* [4232]
Mercedes Laurie Wade Scholarships *(Undergraduate/Scholarship)* [1901]
WAEPA Scholarship Program

(Undergraduate/Scholarship) [7520]
Nell and Spencer Waggoner Scholarships (Undergraduate/Scholarship) [7459]
Laramie Walden Memorial Fund (Undergraduate/Scholarship) [3082]
Margaret E. Waldron Scholarship Fund (Undergraduate/Scholarship) [2977]
War Memorial Doctoral Scholarships (Postgraduate/Scholarship) [4798]
Rachel Warner Memorial Scholarships (Graduate, Undergraduate/Scholarship) [4935]
James L. Warner Scholarships (Undergraduate/Scholarship) [5369]
John R. and Joan F. Warren Scholarship Fund (Undergraduate/Scholarship) [6761]
Washington College Bound Scholarships (Undergraduate/Scholarship) [7366]
Washington Higher Education Coordinating Board Educational Opportunity Grants (Undergraduate/Grant) [7367]
Washington Higher Education Coordinating Board State Need Grants (Undergraduate/Grant) [7369]
Washington Metropolitan Scholarships (Undergraduate/Scholarship) [7374]
Washington Reciprocity Out-of-State Scholarships (Undergraduate/Scholarship) [4220]
Washington Scholarship Fund Signature Scholarships Program (Undergraduate/Scholarship) [7377]
Washington University Law School Olin Fellowships for Women (Graduate/Fellowship) [7387]
Stand Watie Scholarships (Undergraduate/Scholarship) [6601]
Watson-Brown Scholarships (Undergraduate/Scholarship) [7392]
Watsontown Volunteer Fire Company Scholarships (Undergraduate/Scholarship) [1902]
Wayne County Bank Scholarships (Undergraduate/Scholarship) [5305]
Wayne-Meador-Elliott Scholarships (Undergraduate/Scholarship) [5526]
Lester and Eleanor Webster Charitable Trust Fund (Undergraduate/Scholarship) [6762]
Frank L. Weil Memorial Eagle Scout Scholarships (Undergraduate/Scholarship) [4869]
The Bee Winkler Weinstein Scholarship Fund (All/Scholarship) [6791]
Weissbuch Family Scholarships (Undergraduate/Scholarship) [6239]
Edward Kent Welch Memorial Scholarships (Undergraduate/Scholarship) [7461]
Wells Fargo Scholarships (Undergraduate/Scholarship) [5783]
Donald M. Wells Scholarships (Undergraduate/Scholarship) [3356]
Teri Wenglein-Callender Undergraduate Scholarships (Undergraduate/Scholarship) [2669]
Francis X. Weninger Scholarships (Undergraduate/Scholarship) [7534]
West Indian Migrant Farm Workers Memorial Scholarships (Undergraduate/Scholarship) [3501]
West Virginia PTA Scholarships (Undergraduate/Scholarship) [7396]
Redlands Evening Lions Club - Barbara Westen Scholarships (Undergraduate/Scholarship) [6012]
Western Governors University Scholarship Program (Undergraduate/Scholarship) [3609]
Robert B. Westover Scholarships (Undergraduate/Scholarship) [3202]
Wheelchair Success Foundation Scholarships (Undergraduate/Scholarship) [2293]
Whidbey Island Giving Circle Scholarships (Undergraduate/Scholarship) [5784]
White House Fellows (Professional Development/Fellowship) [5748]
White Rose Scholarships (Undergraduate/Scholarship) [6146]
Portia White Scholarships (Undergraduate/Scholarship) [1745]
Robert B. and Sophia Whiteside Scholarships (Undergraduate/Scholarship) [2796]
Ann Cook Whitman Scholarships for Perry High School (Undergraduate/Scholarship) [2843]
Ann Cook Whitman Washington, DC Scholarships (Undergraduate/Scholarship) [2844]
Donna Axum Whitworth Scholarships (Undergraduate/Scholarship) [2670]
Dwight Whylie Scholarships (Undergraduate/Scholarship) [1746]
Alice Hersey Wick Scholarships (Undergraduate/Scholarship) [6380]
Wicomico High School Class of '55 Scholarships (Undergraduate/Scholarship) [2386]
Barbara Wiedner and Dorothy Vandercook Memorial Peace Scholarships (Undergraduate/Scholarship) [3360]
Elmo Wierenga Alumni Scholarships (Undergraduate/Scholarship) [3357]
Fred C. Wikoff, Jr. Scholarship Fund (Undergraduate/Scholarship) [3083]
Teddy Wilburn Scholarships (Undergraduate/Scholarship) [2451]
Wiley Publishing Inc. Scholarships (Undergraduate/Scholarship) [5112]
Andrea Will Memorial Scholarships (Undergraduate/Scholarship) [6381]
M. William and Frances J. Tilghman Scholarship (Undergraduate/Scholarship) [2387]
Williams Foundation Scholarships (Undergraduate/Scholarship) [5869]
Rodney Williams Legacy Scholarships (Undergraduate/Grant) [7107]
CSM Virgil R. Williams Scholarships (Undergraduate/Scholarship) [2857]
Elizabeth T. Williams Scholarships (Undergraduate/Scholarship) [7462]
John G. Williams Scholarships Fund (Undergraduate/Scholarship) [7417]
Randy Williams Scholarships (Undergraduate/Scholarship) [6241]
Edwin H. and Louise N. Williamson Endowed Scholarships (Undergraduate/Scholarship) [7463]
Mary Katherine "Kathy" Williamson Scholarship Fund (Undergraduate/Scholarship) [2366]
Williamsport High School Class of 1970 Scholarship Fund (Undergraduate/Scholarship) [2979]
Williamsport-Lycoming Community Foundation - Benjamin Franklin Scholarships (Undergraduate/Scholarship) [2980]
Bob Wilson Legacy Scholarship (Undergraduate/Scholarship) [1835]
Wisconsin High School Scholarships (Undergraduate/Scholarship) [7284]
Wisconsin Region Student Leadership Scholarships (Undergraduate/Scholarship) [4684]
Woksape Oyate: "Wisdom of the People" Distinguished Scholars Award (Undergraduate/Scholarship) [628]
Milton Wolf Scholarships (Undergraduate/Scholarship) [3204]
Deborah Partridge Wolfe International Fellowships (Graduate, Undergraduate/Fellowship) [7559]
Charles H. and Ethel E. Wolfe Scholarships (Undergraduate/Scholarship) [5370]
Tim Wolfred Scholarships (Undergraduate/Scholarship) [6147]
Woman In Rural Electrification Scholarships (Undergraduate/Scholarship) [6627]
Woman's Club of Grand Haven Scholarships Fund (Undergraduate/Scholarship) [3315]
The Woman's Club of Nashville Scholarships (Undergraduate/Scholarship) [2452]
Women's Army Corps Veterans Association Scholarships (Undergraduate/Scholarship) [7486]
Women's Independence Scholarship Programs (Undergraduate/Scholarship) [6820]
Women's Overseas and Service League Scholarships for Women (Undergraduate/Scholarship) [7506]
Carolyn Wones Recruitment Scholarships Grant (Undergraduate/Scholarship) [2492]
Charles Fred Wonson Scholarships (Undergraduate/Scholarship) [7244]
Mary and Elliot Wood Foundation Undergraduate Scholarship Fund (Undergraduate/Scholarship) [3086]
Rolla F. Wood Graduate Scholarships (Graduate/Scholarship) [5656]
Hugh and Helen Wood Nepales Scholarship (Undergraduate/Scholarship) [1632]
Betsy B. Woodward Scholarships (Undergraduate/Scholarship) [1422]
James and Colin Lee Wozumi Scholarships (Undergraduate/Scholarship) [5785]
Writers of Passage Scholarship Program (Undergraduate/Prize) [6159]
WYCUP Scholarships (Professional Development/Scholarship) [7518]
Margaret Wyeth Scholarship (Undergraduate/Scholarship) [2493]
St. Francis Xavier Scholarships (Undergraduate/Scholarship) [7535]
Xavier Service Fellowships (Undergraduate/Fellowship) [7536]
Xavier University Chancellor Scholarships (Undergraduate/Scholarship) [7537]
Xavier University Legacy Scholarships (Undergraduate/Scholarship) [7540]
William J. Yankee Memorial Scholarships (Undergraduate/Scholarship) [789]
Vera Yip Memorial Scholarships (Undergraduate/Scholarship) [2133]
York Graduate Scholarships (Graduate/Scholarship) [6277]
York Regional Police Scholarships (Undergraduate/Scholarship) [4006]
York Rite Grand Chapter Royal Arch Masons Scholarships (Undergraduate/Scholarship) [2703]
Jack and Edna May Yost Scholarship Fund (Undergraduate/Scholarship) [3123]
You Go Girl! Scholarships (Undergraduate/Scholarship) [5786]
Alma H. Young Emerging Scholar Award (Doctorate/Scholarship) [7291]
Young People For (YP4) Scholarships (Undergraduate/Fellowship) [6335]
Donnell B. Young Scholarships (Undergraduate/Scholarship) [4074]
Mary Jo Young Scholarships (Undergraduate/Scholarship) [1705]
Elmer Cooke Young - Taylor Young Scholarships (Undergraduate/Scholarship) [3502]
Youth Affairs Committee Rising Star Scholarships (Undergraduate/Scholarship) [4007]
Youth Leadership Scholarships (Undergraduate/Scholarship) [1844]
Youth Partners Accessing Capital (P.A.C.) (Graduate, Undergraduate/Scholarship) [250]
Zagunis Student Leader Scholarships (Undergraduate/Scholarship) [4685]
Zale Corporation Scholarships (Undergraduate/Scholarship) [3205]
Zenko Family Scholarship Fund (Undergraduate/Scholarship) [3316]
Zeta Chapter Memorial Scholarships Award (Undergraduate/Scholarship) [2494]
Zeta Phi Beta Sorority General Graduate Scholarships (Graduate, Postdoctorate/Scholarship) [7560]
Zeta Phi Beta Sorority General Undergraduate Scholarships (Undergraduate/Scholarship) [7561]
Zimmermann Scholarships (Graduate/Scholarship) [6831]
A.R. Zipf Fellowships (Graduate/Fellowship) [2551]
Morris and Rebecca Ziskind Memorial Scholarships (Undergraduate/Scholarship) [3640]
Ruth and Sherman Zudekoff Scholarships (Undergraduate/Scholarship) [2397]

Genetics

Epilepsy Foundation Pre-doctoral Research Training Fellowships (Graduate/Grant) [2870]
Fred Johnson Memorial Scholarships (Graduate/Scholarship) [4790]

Geography (See also: Cartography/Surveying)

AAG IGIF Graduate Research Awards (Graduate, Undergraduate/Scholarship) [1352]
AAG IGIF Student Travel Grants (Graduate, Undergraduate/Grant) [1353]
Darrel Hess Community College Geography Scholarships (Undergraduate/Scholarship) [1354]
Excellence in Geographic Information Systems Scholarships (Undergraduate/Scholarship) [4356]
Michael Marucci Memorial Scholarships

(Undergraduate/Scholarship) [4880]
Pi Gamma Mu Scholarships (Graduate/Scholarship) [5691]

Geology

American Association of Stratigraphic Palynologists Student Scholarships (Graduate/Scholarship) [404]
Association of Desk and Derrick Clubs Education Trust Scholarships (Undergraduate/Scholarship) [1388]
J.P. Bickell Mining Scholarships (Undergraduate/Scholarship) [7211]
Cameco Corporation Scholarships in the Geological Sciences - Continuing Students (Undergraduate/Scholarship) [1904]
Cameco Corporation Scholarships in the Geological Sciences - Entering Students (Undergraduate/Scholarship) [1905]
Canadian Society of Petroleum Geologists Regional Graduate Scholarships (Doctorate, Graduate/Scholarship) [2043]
Chugach Gem & Mineral Society Scholarships (Undergraduate/Scholarship) [7030]
Farouk El-Baz Student Research Grants (Doctorate, Graduate, Undergraduate/Grant) [3209]
Geological Society of America Graduate Student Research Grants (Doctorate, Graduate/Grant) [3210]
HSF/Wal-Mart Stores Inc. Scholarship Program (Graduate, Undergraduate/Scholarship) [3599]
Samuel C. Kraus, Jr. Memorial Scholarships (Undergraduate/Scholarship) [5096]
Marathon Oil Corporation College Scholarship Program (Graduate, Undergraduate/Scholarship) [3600]
McColl Family Fellowships (Professional Development/Fellowship) [593]
Paleontological Society Student Research Grants (Graduate, Undergraduate/Grant) [405]

Geophysics (See also: Physics)

Association of Desk and Derrick Clubs Education Trust Scholarships (Undergraduate/Scholarship) [1388]
J.P. Bickell Mining Scholarships (Undergraduate/Scholarship) [7211]
CSEG Scholarship Trust Fund (Postgraduate/Scholarship) [2038]
Marathon Oil Corporation College Scholarship Program (Graduate, Undergraduate/Scholarship) [3600]

Geosciences

AWG Maria Luisa Crawford Field Camp Scholarships (Undergraduate/Scholarship) [1508]
AWG Minority Scholarships (Undergraduate/Scholarship) [1509]
AWIS College Scholarships (Undergraduate/Scholarship) [1519]
Canadian Aboriginal Science and Technology Society Scholarships (Undergraduate/Scholarship) [2042]
Chrysalis Scholarships (Graduate/Grant) [1510]
Penelope Hanshaw Scholarships (Graduate, Undergraduate/Scholarship) [1511]
Puget Sound Chapter Scholarships (Undergraduate/Scholarship) [1512]
Glen Ruby Memorial Scholarships (Undergraduate/Scholarship) [2045]
William Rucker Greenwood Scholarships (Graduate, Undergraduate/Scholarship) [1513]
Shell Incentive Scholarships Fund (Undergraduate/Scholarship) [6302]
Shell Process Technology Scholarships (Undergraduate/Scholarship) [6303]
Shell Technical Scholarships (Undergraduate/Scholarship) [6304]
Society of Exploration Geophysicists Foundation Scholarships (Graduate, Undergraduate/Scholarship) [6441]
United States Geospatial Intelligence Foundation Graduate Scholarships (Postgraduate/Scholarship) [6988]
United States Geospatial Intelligence Foundation High School Scholarships (Undergraduate/Scholarship) [6989]
United States Geospatial Intelligence Foundation Undergraduate Scholarships (Undergraduate/Scholarship) [6990]

German studies (See also: Area and ethnic studies)

Leo Baeck Institute - DAAD Fellowship (Doctorate/Fellowship) [3222]
Doctoral and Postdoctoral Fellowships (Doctorate, Postgraduate/Fellowship) [3233]
German Society Scholarships (Undergraduate/Scholarship) [3238]
German Studies Research Grant (Undergraduate/Grant) [3226]
Dr. Guido Goldman Fellowships (Doctorate, Postdoctorate/Fellowship) [503]
Dr. Richard M. Hunt Fellowships (Doctorate, Postdoctorate/Fellowship) [504]
Intensive Language Course Grants (Doctorate/Grant) [3227]
Kade-Heideking Fellowships (Doctorate/Fellowship) [3235]
Learn German in Germany (Doctorate/Grant) [3229]
Thyssen-Heideking Fellowships (Postdoctorate/Fellowship) [3236]
University Summer Course Grants (Undergraduate/Grant) [3231]

Gerontology

CAG Donald Menzies Bursary Awards (Postgraduate/Award/Prize) [1927]
CAG Margery Boyce Bursary Awards (Postgraduate/Award/Prize) [1928]
Extendicare Scholarships (Graduate/Scholarship) [1998]
Hoffman-Laroche Scholarships (Graduate/Scholarship) [2001]
Military Nurses Association Scholarships (Graduate/Scholarship) [2007]
Helen Mussallem Scholarships (Graduate/Scholarship) [2009]
New Brunswick Nurses Association Scholarships (Graduate/Scholarship) [2010]
Sigma Kappa Foundation Alzheimer's/Gerontology Scholarships (Undergraduate/Scholarship) [6370]
Sigma Kappa Foundation Gerontology Scholarships (Undergraduate/Scholarship) [6372]

Government (See also: Political science)

ARS Undergraduate Scholarships (Four Year College, Two Year College, Undergraduate/Scholarship) [1259]
George Oliver Benton Memorial Scholarships (Undergraduate/Scholarship) [2407]
Center for Women in Government and Civil Society Fellowships (Postgraduate/Fellowship) [2091]
Congressional Research Awards (Graduate/Award/Prize) [2719]
Enid Hall Griswold Memorial Scholarships (Undergraduate/Scholarship) [5064]
Bryce Harlow Fellowship Program (Undergraduate/Fellowship) [3401]
Ray and Kathy LaHood Scholarships for the Study of American Government (Undergraduate/Scholarship) [2720]
Minnesota Association of Township Scholarships (Undergraduate/Scholarship) [4548]
Police Explorer Scholarships Program (Undergraduate/Scholarship) [3018]
Betty Rendel Scholarships (Undergraduate/Scholarship) [4890]
Women In Defense HORIZONS Scholarships (Graduate, Undergraduate/Scholarship) [7479]
Mary and Elliot Wood Foundation Graduate Scholarship Fund (Graduate/Scholarship) [3085]

Graphic art and design (See also: Art)

Advertising Production Club Scholarship Awards (Graduate, Undergraduate/Scholarship) [28]
APC High School Scholarships (Undergraduate/Scholarship) [29]
Paul Arnold Memorial Scholarships (Undergraduate/Scholarship) [5750]
Don Bailey Scholarships (Undergraduate/Scholarship) [4913]
Cadmus Communications Corporation Graphics Scholarship Endowment Fund (Undergraduate/Scholarship) [3044]
ESA Foundation Computer and Video Game Scholarship Program (Undergraduate/Scholarship) [2859]
International Foodservice Editorial Council Scholarships (Graduate, Undergraduate/Scholarship) [3852]
Lewis-Clark State College Presidential Technical Out-of-State Scholarships (Undergraduate/Scholarship) [4199]
PGSF-GATF Scholarships (Graduate, Undergraduate/Scholarship) [31]
TLMI Scholarships - Four-Year Colleges (Undergraduate/Scholarship) [6833]

Greek studies (See also: Area and ethnic studies)

Mary Isabel Sibley Fellowships (Doctorate/Fellowship) [5623]

Health care services

ACMPE Scholarship Fund Program (Graduate, Undergraduate/Scholarship) [22]
Adelson Scholarships (Undergraduate/Scholarship) [5799]
APS/Maricopa County Community Colleges Scholarships (Undergraduate/Scholarship) [5698]
Leslie Baranowski Scholarships for Professional Excellence (All/Scholarship) [3721]
Ellis J. Bonner Scholarships (Doctorate, Graduate, Undergraduate/Scholarship) [4715]
Maria Borrero Scholarships (Undergraduate/Scholarship) [3425]
Joe Q. Bryant American Council on Exercise Educational Scholarships (Undergraduate/Scholarship) [499]
Rhea Sourifman Caplin Memorial Scholarships (Undergraduate/Scholarship) [3429]
Leigh Carter Scholarships (Undergraduate/Scholarship) [2411]
Casey Family Scholars Scholarships (Undergraduate/Scholarship) [5415]
CD-HCF Chair's Scholarships (Professional Development/Scholarship) [2536]
CentraState Associated Auxiliaries Scholarships (Undergraduate/Scholarship) [2099]
CentraState Healthcare Foundation Health Professional Scholarships (Undergraduate/Scholarship) [2101]
Albert W. Dent Graduate Student Scholarships (Undergraduate/Scholarship) [466]
Eagles Fly for Leukemia Scholarships (Undergraduate/Scholarship) [2127]
Gardner Foundation INS Education Scholarship (All/Scholarship) [3722]
Florence S. Gaynor Scholarships (Doctorate, Graduate, Undergraduate/Scholarship) [4716]
John Glaser Scholarships (Undergraduate/Scholarship) [2298]
Tim and Tom Gullikson Foundation Scholarships (Undergraduate/Scholarship) [2129]
Health and Aging Policy Fellows (Professional Development/Fellowship) [786]
HOSA Scholarships (Undergraduate/Scholarship) [5108]
Michael A. Hunter Memorial Scholarships (Undergraduate/Scholarship) [2130]
Gaynold Jensen Education Stipends (Postdoctorate,

Professional Development/Scholarship) [2537]
Oliver Joel and Ellen Pell Denny Healthcare Scholarship Fund *(Undergraduate/Scholarship)* [7441]
The Robert Wood Johnson Health Policy Fellowship Program *(All/Fellowship)* [787]
Kaiser Permanente Northwest Pride Scholarships *(Undergraduate/Scholarship)* [2886]
Rhonda Knopp Memorial Scholarships *(Undergraduate/Scholarship)* [5502]
David A. Kronick Travelling Fellowships *(Doctorate/Fellowship)* [4443]
Donald A. B. Lindberg Research Fellowships *(Doctorate, Graduate/Fellowship)* [4444]
Mat-Su Health Foundation Scholarships *(Undergraduate/Scholarship)* [4367]
Foster G. McGaw Graduate Student Scholarships *(Undergraduate/Scholarship)* [467]
William J. Merriman American Council on Exercise Educational Scholarships *(Undergraduate/Scholarship)* [500]
MSPT Sports Medicine Scholarships *(Undergraduate/Scholarship)* [5842]
North Carolina Association of Health Care Recruiters Scholarships *(Undergraduate/Scholarship)* [5234]
Northern California Chapter of HIMSS Scholarships *(Other/Scholarship)* [3518]
George Phillips Scholarships *(Undergraduate/Scholarship)* [4251]
Portuguese American Police Association Scholarships *(Undergraduate/Scholarship)* [5740]
Haynes Rice Scholarships *(Doctorate, Graduate, Undergraduate/Scholarship)* [4717]
Schaible Health Care Services Scholarships *(Undergraduate/Scholarship)* [6847]
Service League Volunteer Scholarships *(Undergraduate/Scholarship)* [7372]
William Shannon American Council on Exercise Certification Scholarships *(Professional Development, Undergraduate/Scholarship)* [501]
The Eileen J. Smith, R.N. Memorial Scholarship *(Undergraduate/Scholarship)* [3988]
Soroptimist International of Redlands Scholarships *(Undergraduate/Scholarship)* [6011]
Ken Stanley Memorial Scholarships *(Undergraduate/Scholarship)* [4253]
Matt Stauffer Memorial Scholarships *(Undergraduate/Scholarship)* [2131]
StraightForward Media's Medical Professions Scholarships *(Undergraduate/Scholarship)* [6802]
Paul Tejada Memorial Scholarship *(Undergraduate/Scholarship)* [3990]
Transgender Scholarships and Education Legacy Fund *(Undergraduate/Scholarship)* [6142]
Vincent Trotter Health Care Scholarships *(Undergraduate/Scholarship)* [6235]
Udall Scholarships *(Undergraduate/Scholarship)* [7089]
Leon Williams Scholarships *(Undergraduate/Scholarship)* [6240]
Marilyn Yetso Memorial Scholarships *(Undergraduate/Scholarship)* [2132]

Health education

Ruth Abernathy Presidential Scholarships *(Graduate, Undergraduate/Scholarship)* [351]
ACS/ASA Health Policy and Management Scholarships *(Professional Development/Scholarship)* [1117]
ASHA Scholarships *(Graduate, Undergraduate/Scholarship)* [915]
ASHA Student Research Grants *(Graduate, Undergraduate/Scholarship)* [916]
Association of American Indian Physicians Scholarships *(Graduate, Undergraduate/Scholarship)* [1360]
Emergency Medicine Physician Scholarships for Health Information Management Program *(Undergraduate/Scholarship)* [6716]
NSPF Ray B. Essick Scholarship Awards *(Other/Scholarship)* [5102]
Steven Huesing Scholarships *(Undergraduate/Scholarship)* [2255]
Randall Matthis for Environmental Studies Scholarships *(Graduate, Undergraduate/Scholarship)* [1226]
Migrant Health Scholarships *(Professional Development/Scholarship)* [4794]
Minnesota Health Information Management Association Scholarships *(Undergraduate/Scholarship)* [4552]
NSPF Board of Directors' Scholarship Awards *(Other/Scholarship)* [5103]
NSPF Scholarship Awards *(Other/Scholarship)* [5104]
Terry Linda Potter Scholarship Fund *(Undergraduate/Scholarship)* [3298]
TYLENOL Scholarships *(Undergraduate/Scholarship)* [4561]

Health sciences

Dr. Anderson Abbott Awards *(Undergraduate/Scholarship)* [7208]
Allied Health Care Professional Scholarships *(Undergraduate/Scholarship)* [3661]
ASET Student Education Grants *(All/Grant)* [954]
Bill Bendiner and Doug Morgenson Scholarships *(Undergraduate/Scholarship)* [5757]
Robert Browning Scholarships *(Undergraduate/Scholarship)* [5758]
Joseph R. Calder, Jr., MD Scholarship Fund *(Undergraduate/Scholarship)* [2946]
CentraState Band Aid Open Committee Scholarships *(Undergraduate/Scholarship)* [2100]
Gordon W. and Agnes P. Cobb Scholarships *(Undergraduate/Scholarship)* [2808]
College of Agriculture and Natural Resources Scholarships *(Undergraduate/Scholarship)* [3432]
DCH Freehold Toyota Scholarships *(Undergraduate/Scholarship)* [2102]
Health Sciences Scholarship Program *(Undergraduate/Scholarship)* [7402]
Health Sciences Student Fellowships *(Doctorate, Graduate/Fellowship)* [2873]
HLS/MLA Professional Development Grants *(Doctorate/Grant)* [4442]
Houston/Nancy Holliman Scholarships *(Undergraduate/Scholarship)* [2690]
Indian Health Service Scholarship Program *(Undergraduate/Scholarship)* [634]
The Robert Wood Johnson Health Policy Fellowship Program *(All/Fellowship)* [787]
S. Evelyn Lewis Memorial Scholarships in Medical Health Sciences *(Graduate, Undergraduate/Scholarship)* [7557]
Medical Staff Scholarships *(Undergraduate/Scholarship)* [7371]
Medical Students Loan Program *(Undergraduate/Loan)* [7403]
MLA/NLM Spectrum Scholarship Program *(Graduate/Scholarship)* [4445]
MLA Research, Development, and Demonstration Project Grants *(Graduate/Grant)* [4446]
MLA Scholarships for Minority Students *(Graduate/Scholarship)* [4447]
Dr. Ezra Nesbeth Scholarships *(Undergraduate/Scholarship)* [4002]
Helen Woodruff Nolop Scholarship in Audiology and Allied Fields *(Graduate/Scholarship)* [2696]
Norkus Charitable Foundation Scholarships *(Undergraduate/Scholarship)* [2103]
Scholarships for Disadvantaged Students *(Undergraduate/Scholarship)* [3513]
Dr. Robert Norman Shaw Scholarship *(Undergraduate/Scholarship)* [183]
Thomson Scientific/MLA Doctoral Fellowships *(Doctorate/Fellowship)* [4448]
Star and Barry Tobias Scholarships *(Undergraduate/Scholarship)* [2104]

Health services administration

Ellis J. Bonner Scholarships *(Doctorate, Graduate, Undergraduate/Scholarship)* [4715]
City of Toronto Scholarships for Aboriginal Students *(Graduate, Undergraduate/Scholarship)* [7219]
Florence S. Gaynor Scholarships *(Doctorate, Graduate, Undergraduate/Scholarship)* [4716]
GE Healthcare Management Scholarship Program *(Postgraduate/Scholarship)* [1039]
Haynes Rice Scholarships *(Doctorate, Graduate, Undergraduate/Scholarship)* [4717]

Hearing and deafness

Elizabeth Benson Scholarship Awards *(Undergraduate/Scholarship)* [6018]
College Scholarship Awards *(Undergraduate/Scholarship)* [1614]
Houston/Nancy Holliman Scholarships *(Undergraduate/Scholarship)* [2690]
Brian McCartney Scholarships *(Undergraduate/Scholarship)* [4472]
George H. Nofer Scholarships for Law and Public Policy *(Doctorate, Graduate/Scholarship)* [1615]
Daniel H. Pokorny Memorial Scholarship Awards *(Undergraduate/Scholarship)* [6019]
School Age Financial Aid Program *(Undergraduate/Scholarship)* [1616]

Heating, air conditioning, and refrigeration

Lewis-Clark State College Presidential Technical Out-of-State Scholarships *(Undergraduate/Scholarship)* [4199]
Dave Nelsen Scholarships *(Undergraduate/Scholarship)* [4719]
Snodgrass Scholarships *(Undergraduate/Scholarship)* [4384]

Hematology

Aplastic, Anemia and Myelosdysplasia Scholarships *(Graduate/Scholarship)* [1991]

Hemophilia

Hemophilia Federation of America Educational Scholarships *(Undergraduate/Scholarship)* [3542]

Hispanic American studies

Latin American Educational Foundation Scholarships *(Undergraduate/Scholarship)* [4145]
LULAC GE Scholarships *(Undergraduate/Scholarship)* [4151]
LULAC GM Scholarships *(Graduate, High School, Undergraduate/Award/Prize)* [4152]
LULAC National Scholarship Fund *(Graduate, High School, Undergraduate/Scholarship)* [4153]
Pepsi Escribe tu Futuro Scholarships *(Undergraduate/Scholarship)* [4154]

Histology

Robert A. Clark Memorial Educational Scholarships *(Other/Scholarship)* [5074]
Fisher Healthcare Educational Scholarships *(Other/Scholarship)* [5075]
Leonard Noble Educational Scholarships *(Other/Scholarship)* [5078]
Dezna C. Sheehan Memorial Educational Scholarships *(Other/Scholarship)* [5080]
Thermo Scientific Educational Scholarships *(Other/Scholarship)* [5082]
Ventana Medical Systems In Situ Hybridization Awards *(Other/Award/Prize)* [5083]

Historic preservation

Association for Preservation Technology International Student Scholarships *(All/Scholarship)* [1518]
J.E. Caldwell Centennial Scholarships *(Undergraduate/Scholarship)* [5063]
Death Valley '49ers Scholarships *(Undergraduate/Scholarship)* [2627]
National Alliance of Preservation Commission Student Scholarships *(Undergraduate/Scholarship)* [4632]

The Aaron and Rita Slom Scholarships (Undergraduate/Scholarship) [6892]

History

ARS Undergraduate Scholarships (Four Year College, Two Year College, Undergraduate/Scholarship) [1259]
Leo Baeck Fellowships Program (Doctorate, Postdoctorate/Fellowship) [2079]
Cecil E. Burney Scholarships (High School, Undergraduate/Scholarship) [2267]
Dick Depaolis Memorial Scholarships (Undergraduate/Scholarship) [2512]
Douglas-Coldwell Foundation Scholarships in Social Affairs (Graduate/Scholarship) [2729]
Fellowships in Aerospace History (Doctorate/Fellowship) [605]
Margaret S. Gilbert Scholarship Fund (Undergraduate/Scholarship) [6722]
Velma Shotwell Griffin Memorial Scholarship Fund (Undergraduate/Scholarship) [6724]
Enid Hall Griswold Memorial Scholarships (Undergraduate/Scholarship) [5064]
Hench Post-Dissertation Fellowships (Postdoctorate/Fellowship) [303]
Brooke Hindle Postdoctoral Fellowships (Postdoctorate/Fellowship) [6461]
Harriet Irsay Scholarships (Graduate, Undergraduate/Scholarship) [674]
The J. Franklin Jameson Fellowship in American History (Doctorate/Fellowship) [606]
Melvin Kranzberg Dissertation Fellowships (Doctorate/Fellowship) [6462]
Michael Marucci Memorial Scholarships (Undergraduate/Scholarship) [4880]
NACBS Dissertation Year Fellowships (Postdoctorate/Fellowship) [5217]
NACBS-Huntington Library Fellowships (Postdoctorate/Fellowship) [5218]
National Endowment for the Humanities Advanced Fellowship for Research in Turkey (Postdoctorate/Fellowship) [900]
Pi Gamma Mu Scholarships (Graduate/Scholarship) [5691]
Charles and Ruth Ronin Memorial Scholarships (Undergraduate/Scholarship) [6002]
Everett Oscar Shimp Memorial Scholarships (Undergraduate/Scholarship) [5519]
UAA Governor William A. Egan Scholarships (Undergraduate/Scholarship) [7056]
Frederick K. Weyerhaeuser Forest History Fellowships (Graduate/Fellowship) [3031]
Xavier University Departmental Scholarships (Undergraduate/Scholarship) [7538]
Blanche Raper Zimmerman Scholarships (Professional Development/Scholarship) [7465]

History, American

AAS Fellowships for Creative and Performing Artists and Writers (All/Fellowship) [296]
AAS-Northeast Modern Language Association Fellowships (All/Fellowship) [298]
American History Scholarships (Undergraduate/Scholarship) [5062]
Stephen Botein Fellowships (Doctorate/Fellowship) [300]
Cromwell Fellowships (Undergraduate/Fellowship) [991]
Doctoral and Postdoctoral Fellowships (Doctorate, Postgraduate/Fellowship) [3233]
Kade-Heideking Fellowships (Doctorate/Fellowship) [3235]
The Legacy Fellowships (Doctorate/Fellowship) [305]
Kate B. and Hall J. Peterson Fellowships (Doctorate/Fellowship) [306]
Tadeusz Sendzimir Scholarships (Undergraduate/Scholarship) [3496]
Thyssen-Heideking Fellowships (Postdoctorate/Fellowship) [3236]
The Joyce Tracy Fellowships (Doctorate/Fellowship) [308]
United States Capitol Historical Society Fellowships (Graduate/Fellowship) [6983]

History, Ancient

Fellowships in the Humanities and Social Sciences in Turkey (Postdoctorate/Fellowship) [894]

History, Economic

AFCEA Fellowships (Doctorate, Graduate/Fellowship) [1237]
Arthur H. Cole Grants in Aid (Doctorate/Grant) [2818]
Exploratory Travel and Data Grants (Doctorate/Grant) [2819]
Graduate Dissertation Fellowships (Doctorate/Fellowship) [2820]

History, Military

ABC-Clio Research Grants (Graduate/Grant) [6514]
American Division Veterans Association Scholarships (Undergraduate/Scholarship) [541]
Marshall-Baruch Fellowships (Doctorate/Fellowship) [4318]
Women In Defense HORIZONS Scholarships (Graduate, Undergraduate/Scholarship) [7479]

Home Economics

Hettie M. Anthony Fellowships (Postdoctorate/Fellowship) [4051]
California Association of Family and Consumer Sciences (CAFCS)-San Diego Chapter Scholarships (Graduate, Undergraduate/Scholarship) [6177]
FACS Graduate Fellowships (Graduate/Fellowship) [4747]
Kappa Omicron Nu National Alumni Fellowships (Graduate/Fellowship) [4047]
Eileen C. Maddex Fellowships (Graduate/Fellowship) [4049]
Omicron Nu Research Fellowships (Postdoctorate/Fellowship) [4054]

Homosexuality

CLAGS Fellowships (Graduate/Fellowship) [2085]
Martin Duberman Fellowships (Professional Development/Fellowship) [2086]
GAPA Scholarships (Undergraduate/Scholarship) [3165]
Joan Heller-Diane Bernard Fellowships (Graduate, Undergraduate/Fellowship) [2087]

Horticulture

American Conifer Society Scholarships (Undergraduate/Scholarship) [493]
American Floral Endowment Scholarships (Undergraduate/Scholarship) [549]
American Society for Horticultural Science Student Travel Grants (Graduate, Undergraduate/Grant) [972]
Arizona Nursery Association Scholarships (Undergraduate/Scholarship) [1219]
ASHS Industry Division Student Travel Grants (Graduate, Undergraduate/Grant) [973]
ASHS Scholars Awards (Undergraduate/Scholarship) [974]
Ball Horticultural Company Scholarships (Undergraduate/Scholarship) [550]
Vic and Margaret Ball Student Intern Scholarships (Undergraduate/Internship) [551]
Catherine H. Beattie Fellowships (Graduate/Fellowship) [2089]
Harold Bettinger Scholarships (Undergraduate/Scholarship) [552]
Leonard Bettinger Scholarships (Undergraduate/Scholarship) [553]
James Bridenbaugh Memorial Scholarship (Undergraduate/Scholarship) [554]
John Carew Memorial Scholarships (Undergraduate/Scholarship) [555]
Christmas Tree Chapter Scholarship Awards (Undergraduate/Scholarship) [5378]
Clackamas Chapter Scholarship Awards (Undergraduate/Scholarship) [5379]
Howard A. Clark Horticulture Scholarships (Undergraduate/Scholarship) [2414]
Class Fund Ornamental Horticulture Scholarship Program (Undergraduate/Scholarship) [980]
James H. Davis Scholarships (Undergraduate/Scholarship) [3012]
Earl Deadman Memorial Scholarships (Undergraduate/Scholarship) [556]
Dosatron International Inc. Scholarships (Undergraduate/Scholarship) [557]
Bill Egan Scholarship Program (Undergraduate/Scholarship) [5380]
Emerald Empire Chapter Scholarship Awards (Undergraduate/Scholarship) [5381]
Miklos Faust International Travel Awards (Postdoctorate/Fellowship) [975]
Paris Fracasso Production Floriculture Scholarships (Undergraduate/Scholarship) [558]
Fruits and Vegetable Industries Scholarships (Undergraduate/Scholarship) [4489]
Garden Club Council of Winston-Salem and Forsyth County Council (Undergraduate/Scholarship) [7436]
Katherine M. Grosscup Scholarships (Graduate, Undergraduate/Scholarship) [3159]
John Holden Vocational Scholarships (Undergraduate/Scholarship) [559]
Martin Holmason Memorial Scholarship Awards (Undergraduate/Scholarship) [5382]
Idaho Nursery and Landscape Association Scholarships (Undergraduate/Scholarship) [3652]
Illinois Landscape Contractors Association Scholarships (Undergraduate/Scholarship) [3656]
Joseph H. Klupenger Scholarship Awards (Undergraduate/Scholarship) [5383]
Ed Markham International Scholarships (Undergraduate/Scholarship) [560]
The Master Gardeners of Pierce County Scholarships (Undergraduate/Scholarship) [3377]
Mossmiller Student Intern Scholarships Program (Undergraduate/Internship) [561]
Mt. Hood Chapter Scholarship Awards (Undergraduate/Scholarship) [5384]
Nashville Unit Scholarships (Undergraduate/Scholarship) [3544]
National Greenhouse Manufacturers Association Scholarships (Undergraduate/Scholarship) [562]
National Junior Horticultural Association Alumni Scholarships (Undergraduate/Scholarship) [4969]
North Carolina Commercial Flower Growers Association Floriculture Scholarships (Undergraduate/Scholarship) [5236]
North Carolina Nursery and Landscape Association Horticulture Scholarships (Undergraduate/Scholarship) [5243]
Mike and Flo Novovesky Scholarships (Undergraduate/Scholarship) [563]
Nurseries Foundation Scholarship Awards (Undergraduate/Scholarship) [5385]
Nurseries Memorial Scholarship Awards (Graduate/Scholarship) [5386]
Lawrence "Bud" Ohlman Memorial Scholarships (Undergraduate/Scholarship) [564]
Oregon Association of Nurseries Scholarship Program (Undergraduate/Scholarship) [5387]
Pennsylvania Heartland Unit Scholarships (Undergraduate/Scholarship) [3545]
Jim Perry Vocational Scholarships (Undergraduate/Scholarship) [565]
Rain Bird Intelligent Use of Water Scholarships (Undergraduate/Scholarship) [4127]
Ratcliffe Hicks School of Agriculture Heritage Scholarships (Undergraduate/Scholarship) [3492]
James K. Rathmell Jr. Scholarships (Undergraduate/Scholarship) [566]
Bertha and Byron L. Reppert Scholarship Fund (Undergraduate/Scholarship) [3116]
Retail Chapter Scholarship Awards (Undergraduate/Scholarship) [5388]
Seed Companies Scholarships (Undergraduate/Scholarship) [567]
South Texas Unit Scholarships (Undergraduate/Scholarship) [3546]
Marco Polo Stufano Garden Conservancy Fellow-

ships *(Professional Development/Fellowship)* [3161]
Jordan B. Tatter Scholarships *(Undergraduate/Scholarship)* [4490]
John Tomasovic, Sr. Scholarships *(Undergraduate/Scholarship)* [568]
Edward Tuinier Memorial Scholarships *(Undergraduate/Scholarship)* [569]
Jacob VanNamen-Vans Marketing Scholarships *(Undergraduate/Scholarship)* [570]
West Michigan Nursery and Landscape Association Scholarships Fund *(Undergraduate/Scholarship)* [3313]
Western Michigan Greenhouse Association Scholarships *(Undergraduate/Scholarship)* [571]
Western Reserve Herb Society Scholarships *(Undergraduate/Scholarship)* [3547]
Willamette Chapter Scholarship Awards *(Undergraduate/Scholarship)* [5389]
Ed Wood Memorial Scholarship Awards *(Undergraduate/Scholarship)* [5390]
Francis Sylvia Zverina Scholarship *(Undergraduate/Scholarship)* [3548]

Hospitals—Administration

Jessica King Scholarships *(Undergraduate/Scholarship)* [1436]

Hotel, institutional, and restaurant management

The AAA (American Automobile Association) Five Diamond Hospitality Scholarships *(Undergraduate/Scholarship)* [608]
American Express Professional Development Scholarships *(Professional Development/Scholarship)* [609]
The American Express Scholarship Competition *(Undergraduate/Scholarship)* [610]
Applied Hospitality Degree Scholarships *(Undergraduate/Scholarship)* [1975]
Frank and Ruth Bila Scholarships *(Undergraduate/Scholarship)* [5356]
Canadian Hospitality Foundation College Entrance Scholarships *(Undergraduate/Scholarship)* [1976]
Canadian Hospitality Foundation University Entrance Scholarships *(Undergraduate/Scholarship)* [1977]
Caribbean Hotel Association Academic Scholarships *(Undergraduate/Scholarship)* [2059]
Epicurean Charitable Foundation Scholarships *(Undergraduate/Scholarship)* [5822]
FHSMAI Scholarship Program *(Graduate/Scholarship)* [3127]
R.W. "Bob" Holden Scholarships *(Undergraduate/Scholarship)* [3508]
The Hyatt Hotels Fund For Minority Lodging Management Students *(Undergraduate/Scholarship)* [611]
The Steve Hymans Extended Stay Scholarship Program *(Undergraduate/Scholarship)* [612]
International Foodservice Editorial Council Scholarships *(Graduate, Undergraduate/Scholarship)* [3852]
Clem Judd Jr. Memorial Scholarships *(Undergraduate/Scholarship)* [3509]
Lodging Management Program (LMP) Scholarships *(Undergraduate/Scholarship)* [613]
Jay Magazine Memorial Fund (JMMF) College Scholarships *(Undergraduate/Scholarship)* [4454]
Michigan Sugar Company Hotel Restaurant/Resort Management Scholarships *(Undergraduate/Scholarship)* [4496]
Native Hawaiian Scholarships *(Undergraduate/Scholarship)* [3510]
New England Culinary Institute Scholarships *(All/Scholarship)* [2581]
The Arthur J. Packard Memorial Scholarship Competition *(Undergraduate/Scholarship)* [614]
Pepsi Scholarships *(Undergraduate/Scholarship)* [615]
Rama Scholarships for the American Dream *(Graduate, Undergraduate/Scholarship)* [616]
Tribal Business Management Program (TBM) Scholarships *(Undergraduate/Scholarship)* [2069]

Housing

California Association of Family and Consumer Sciences (CAFCS)-San Diego Chapter Scholarships *(Graduate, Undergraduate/Scholarship)* [6177]
NACCED Annual John C. Murphy Scholarships *(Graduate, Undergraduate/Scholarship)* [4697]

Human relations

Bill Bendiner and Doug Morgenson Scholarships *(Undergraduate/Scholarship)* [5757]
Derivative Duo Scholarships *(Undergraduate/Scholarship)* [5765]
Phyllis P. Harris Scholarships *(Postgraduate/Award/Prize)* [1956]
David C. Maloney Scholarship Program *(Undergraduate/Scholarship)* [4996]
UAA April Relyea Scholarships *(Graduate, Undergraduate/Scholarship)* [7043]

Human rights

Alberta Award for the Study of Canadian Human Rights and Multiculturalism *(Doctorate, Graduate/Award/Prize)* [145]
Beverlee Bell Scholarships in Human Rights and Democracy *(Graduate/Scholarship)* [2728]
Henigson Human Rights Fellowships *(Undergraduate/Fellowship)* [3504]
HRP Global Human Rights Fellowships *(Graduate/Fellowship)* [3505]
Satter Human Rights Fellowships *(Graduate/Fellowship)* [3506]
Upper Midwest Human Rights Fellowship Program *(Professional Development/Fellowship)* [7135]
Minoru Yasui Memorial Scholarship *(Graduate/Scholarship)* [4022]

Humanities

AAS National Endowment for the Humanities Long-Term Fellowships *(Postdoctorate/Fellowship)* [297]
ACLS Frederick Burkhardt Fellowships *(Professional Development/Fellowship)* [299]
American Society of Comparative Law TransCoop Programs *(All/Fellowship)* [937]
Beinecke Brothers Memorial Scholarships *(Undergraduate/Scholarship)* [7085]
Canada Graduate Scholarships Program *(Graduate/Scholarship)* [6418]
Critical Language Scholarships for Intensive Summer Institutes *(Graduate, Undergraduate/Scholarship)* [892]
Dissertation Proposal Development Fellowships *(Doctorate/Fellowship)* [6415]
Fellowships in the Humanities and Social Sciences in Turkey *(Postdoctorate/Fellowship)* [894]
Harry Frank Guggenheim Fellowships *(Doctorate/Fellowship)* [3385]
Harry Frank Guggenheim Foundation Grants *(All/Grant)* [3386]
Ed Haas Memorial Scholarships *(Undergraduate/Scholarship)* [6776]
Lois Hole Humanities and Social Sciences Scholarship *(Undergraduate/Scholarship)* [158]
International Society for Humor Studies Graduate Student Awards (GSA) *(Graduate/Award/Prize)* [3906]
International Society for Humor Studies Scholarly Contribution Awards (SCA) *(Graduate/Award/Prize)* [3907]
Jacob K. Javits Fellowships *(Doctorate, Master's/Fellowship)* [4707]
Korean Studies Dissertation Workshop Funds *(Graduate/Grant)* [6416]
Henry Luce Foundation Dissertation Fellowships in American Art *(Doctorate/Fellowship)* [509]
Major Collaborative Research Initiatives Grants *(Graduate/Grant)* [6419]
David C. Maloney Scholarship Program *(Undergraduate/Scholarship)* [4996]
Larry McDonald Scholarships *(Undergraduate/Scholarship)* [2888]
McNeil Dissertation Fellowships *(All/Fellowship)* [7467]
Andrew W. Mellon Dissertation Completion Fellowships *(Doctorate/Fellowship)* [510]
Mellon Fellowships *(Doctorate, Graduate/Fellowship)* [2550]
NAFA International Dissertation Research Fellowships *(Graduate/Fellowship)* [4709]
National Endowment for the Humanities Advanced Fellowship for Research in Turkey *(Postdoctorate/Fellowship)* [900]
Persian Language Study in Tehran *(Doctorate, Graduate/Fellowship)* [663]
Post-Doctoral Summer Travel-Research Grants *(Doctorate/Grant)* [3756]
Charles A. Ryskamp Research Fellowships *(Doctorate/Fellowship)* [511]
Short-term senior fellowships in Iranian Studies *(Doctorate, Graduate/Fellowship)* [665]
Social Sciences and Humanities Research Council of Canada Standard Research Grants *(Doctorate, Graduate/Grant)* [6420]
SSHRC Doctoral Fellowships Program *(Doctorate/Fellowship, Scholarship)* [6421]
Robert W. and Bernice Ingalls Staton Scholarships *(Undergraduate/Scholarship)* [7202]
Summer Language Study Grants in Turkey *(Graduate/Grant)* [3758]
Summer Research Grants in Turkey *(Graduate/Grant)* [3759]
Trudeau Foundation Doctoral Scholarships *(Doctorate/Scholarship)* [6928]
The UCSD Black Alumni Scholarship for Arts and Humanities *(Undergraduate/Scholarship)* [6236]
The UCSD Black Alumni Scholarships for Engineering, Mathematics and Science *(Undergraduate/Scholarship)* [6237]
Winterthur Research Fellowships *(All/Fellowship)* [7468]
Mary and Elliot Wood Foundation Graduate Scholarship Fund *(Graduate/Scholarship)* [3085]

Huntington's disease

HDSA Research Fellowships *(Postdoctorate/Fellowship)* [3631]
HDSA Research Grants *(Other/Grant)* [3632]
Hereditary Disease Foundation Research Grants *(Postdoctorate/Grant)* [3550]
Don King Student Fellowships *(Undergraduate/Fellowship)* [3633]
John J. Wasmuth Postdoctoral Fellowships *(Postdoctorate/Fellowship)* [3551]

Ileitis and colitis

ROFY Scholarships *(Undergraduate/Scholarship)* [5901]

Illustrators and illustrations

UAA Kimura Scholarship Funds (Illustration Scholarships) *(Undergraduate/Scholarship)* [7061]

Immunology

UAA Kris Knudson Memorial Scholarships *(Graduate, Undergraduate/Scholarship)* [7062]

Indian studies (Asia)

SHOT-NASA Fellowships *(Doctorate, Postdoctorate/Fellowship)* [6463]

Industrial design

Flexible Packaging Academic Scholarships & Summer Internship Program *(Undergraduate/Internship)* [2988]
TLMI Scholarships - Two-Year Colleges *(Undergraduate/Scholarship)* [6834]

Industrial hygiene

Thompson Scholarship for Women in Safety *(Graduate/Scholarship)* [1072]

Industrial and labor relations

Mackenzie King Travelling Scholarships *(Graduate/Scholarship)* [4429]
NPELRA Foundation Scholarships *(Graduate/Scholarship)* [5309]
The Anthony C. Russo Scholarships *(Graduate/Scholarship)* [5026]

Information science and technology

AFFIRM University Scholarships *(Undergraduate/Scholarship)* [1414]
Affirmative Action Scholarships *(Graduate/Scholarship)* [6680]
APALA Scholarship Program *(Doctorate, Graduate/Scholarship)* [1336]
APS/ASU Scholarships *(Undergraduate/Scholarship)* [5697]
APS/Maricopa County Community Colleges Scholarships *(Undergraduate/Scholarship)* [5698]
Black Data Processing Associates Scholarships *(High School/Scholarship)* [1606]
Boeing Company Scholarships *(Undergraduate/Scholarship)* [6307]
Dvora Brodie Scholarships *(Other/Scholarship)* [3515]
Mary Adeline Conner Professional Development Scholarships *(Graduate/Scholarship)* [6681]
Healthcare Information Management Systems Scholarships *(Other/Scholarship)* [3517]
HSF/Wal-Mart Stores Inc. Scholarship Program *(Graduate, Undergraduate/Scholarship)* [3599]
Institute for Scientific Information (ISI) Scholarships *(Doctorate, Graduate/Scholarship)* [6682]
Iowa Library Association Foundation Scholarships *(Graduate/Scholarship)* [3931]
Christian Larew Memorial Scholarships *(Graduate/Scholarship)* [4236]
Lewis-Clark State College Presidential Technical Out-of-State Scholarships *(Undergraduate/Scholarship)* [4199]
Robert V. McKenna Scholarships *(Undergraduate/Scholarship)* [3369]
Arthur L. Norberg Travel Grants *(All/Grant)* [1583]
Office Depot Scholarships *(Undergraduate/Scholarship)* [3569]
Plenum Scholarships *(Doctorate/Scholarship)* [6683]
Thomson Scientific/MLA Doctoral Fellowships *(Doctorate/Fellowship)* [4448]
Jack E. Tillson Scholarships *(Graduate/Scholarship)* [3932]
The Adelle and Erwin Tomash Fellowships *(Doctorate/Fellowship)* [1584]
Urban Financial Services Coalition Scholarships *(Undergraduate/Scholarship)* [1744]
Verizon Scholarship Program *(Undergraduate/Scholarship)* [3607]
Wall-Mart Stores, Inc. Fellowships - Graduate *(Undergraduate/Scholarship)* [643]
Wells Fargo American Indian Scholarship for Graduates *(Graduate/Scholarship)* [644]
Lisa Winkler Memorial Scholarships *(Undergraduate/Scholarship)* [1415]

Insurance and insurance-related fields

CPCU Laman Educational Foundation Scholarships *(Professional Development/Scholarship)* [3761]
Founders Circle Professional Scholarships *(Professional Development/Scholarship)* [3762]
Gongaware Scholarships College of Business *(Undergraduate/Scholarship)* [3700]
Insurance Scholarship Foundation of America College Scholarships *(Undergraduate/Scholarship)* [3763]
Insurance Scholarship Foundation of America Professional Scholarships *(Professional Development/Scholarship)* [3764]
Insurance Women of Portland Scholarships *(Graduate/Scholarship)* [3767]
Intermediaries and Reinsurance Underwriters Association Scholarships *(Undergraduate/Internship)* [3777]
Marsh College Scholarships *(Undergraduate/Scholarship)* [3765]
Surety Industry Scholarship Program for Minority Students *(Undergraduate/Scholarship)* [6824]
The Rodney Thaxton Justice Fund *(Undergraduate/Scholarship)* [2602]
Seitlin Franklin E. Wheeler Scholarship Fund *(Undergraduate/Scholarship)* [2604]

Intelligence service

Jorge Espejal Contreras Memorial Scholarships *(Graduate, Undergraduate/Scholarship)* [3804]
The Henley Putnam University Scholarships *(Professional Development/Scholarship)* [3805]

Interdisciplinary studies

General Scholarship Awards *(Undergraduate/Scholarship)* [1599]

Interior design

Paul Arnold Memorial Scholarships *(Undergraduate/Scholarship)* [5750]
IFDA Part-time Student Scholarships *(Undergraduate/Scholarship)* [3860]
Charles D. Mayo Student Scholarships *(Undergraduate/Scholarship)* [3861]
Eloise Pitts O'More Scholarships *(Undergraduate/Scholarship)* [2442]

International affairs and relations

AGBU Scholarships *(Graduate/Loan)* [1255]
Julie Allen World Classroom Scholarships *(Undergraduate/Scholarship)* [6164]
Samuel Flagg Bemis Research Grants *(Doctorate, Graduate/Grant)* [6452]
Stuart L. Bernath Dissertation Grants *(Doctorate/Grant)* [6453]
Myrna F. Bernath Fellowships *(Doctorate, Graduate/Fellowship)* [6454]
D&A Florida Scholarships *(Undergraduate/Scholarship)* [6648]
Robert A. and Barbara Divine Graduate Student Travel Grants *(Graduate/Grant)* [6455]
Mayme and Herb Frank Scholarship Program *(Graduate, Undergraduate/Scholarship)* [1323]
Lawrence Gelfand - Armin Rappaport Fellowships *(Doctorate, Graduate/Grant)* [6456]
Burton L. Gerber Scholarships *(Graduate, Undergraduate/Scholarship)* [1657]
W. Stull Holt Dissertation Fellowships *(Doctorate, Graduate/Grant)* [6458]
Harriet Irsay Scholarships *(Graduate, Undergraduate/Scholarship)* [674]
ISCALC International Scholarship Fund *(Undergraduate/Scholarship)* [2960]
Mackenzie King Travelling Scholarships *(Graduate/Scholarship)* [4429]
National Iranian American Council Fellowships *(Graduate, Undergraduate/Fellowship)* [4958]
Pi Gamma Mu Scholarships *(Graduate/Scholarship)* [5691]
SHAFR Dissertation Completion Fellowships *(Doctorate/Fellowship)* [6459]
TCA Turkish American Scholarships *(Undergraduate/Scholarship)* [6939]
University of Hawaii at Manoa Japan Travel Bureau Scholarships *(Graduate, Undergraduate/Scholarship)* [7098]
Women In Defense HORIZONS Scholarships *(Graduate, Undergraduate/Scholarship)* [7479]

International trade

Malcolm Baldridge Scholarships *(Undergraduate/Scholarship)* [3420]
HSBC-North America Scholarship Program *(Undergraduate/Scholarship)* [3592]

Internet design and development

Fritz Schwartz Serials Education Scholarships *(Other/Scholarship)* [5226]

Interracial studies

Short-term senior fellowships in Iranian Studies *(Doctorate, Graduate/Fellowship)* [665]

Italian studies (See also: Area and ethnic studies)

NIAF Scholarships - General Category II *(Undergraduate/Scholarship)* [4963]

Japanese studies (See also: Area and ethnic studies)

Mary Jane Hendrie Memorial Scholarships *(Graduate, Undergraduate/Scholarship)* [7221]
Japan Foundation, New York Doctoral Fellowship Program *(Doctorate/Fellowship)* [4009]
Japan Foundation, New York Research Fellowship Program *(Undergraduate/Fellowship)* [4010]
Japan Foundation, New York Short-Term Fellowship Program *(Doctorate/Fellowship)* [4011]
JAUW Fellowship Awards *(Postgraduate/Fellowship)* [1960]
The Shincho Graduate Fellowships for Study in Japan *(Graduate/Fellowship)* [4060]

Jewish studies (See also: Area and ethnic studies)

Hebrew Ladies Sheltering Home Scholarships *(Undergraduate/Scholarship)* [3463]
International Doctoral Scholarships for Studies Specializing in Jewish Fields *(Doctorate/Scholarship)* [4458]
International Fellowships in Jewish Studies *(Professional Development/Fellowship)* [4459]
International Scholarship Program for Community Service *(Other/Scholarship)* [4460]
Jewish Caucus Scholarships *(Undergraduate/Scholarship)* [5123]

Journalism

AAJA/CNN Scholar Program *(Graduate, Undergraduate/Scholarship)* [1328]
AAJA/COX Foundation Scholarships *(Graduate, Undergraduate/Scholarship)* [1329]
AAJA/S.I. Newhouse Foundation Scholarships *(Graduate, Undergraduate/Scholarship)* [1330]
AAS Fellowships for Creative and Performing Artists and Writers *(All/Fellowship)* [296]
Kyutaro & Yasuo Abiko Memorial Scholarships *(Undergraduate/Scholarship)* [4015]
Al Muammar Scholarships for Journalism *(Undergraduate/Scholarship)* [1191]
Alaska Press Club Scholarships *(Undergraduate/Scholarship)* [4340]
Floyd S. Alford Jr. Scholarships *(Undergraduate/Scholarship)* [7141]
Jim Allard Broadcast Journalism Scholarships *(Undergraduate/Scholarship)* [1921]
Peggy Allen Community Newspaper Internships *(Undergraduate/Internship)* [7142]
Phillip Alston Scholarships *(Undergraduate/Scholarship)* [7143]
American Political Science Association Journalists Fellowships *(Professional Development/Fellowship)* [783]
American Political Science Association/MCI Scholarships *(Postdoctorate/Scholarship)* [784]
American Quarter Horse Foundation Scholarships *(Undergraduate/Scholarship)* [811]
Fred Archibald Communications Internships *(Undergraduate/Internship)* [6568]
ARS Undergraduate Scholarships *(Four Year Col-*

lege, Two Year College, Undergraduate/Scholarship) [1259]
Association of Electronic Journalists President's Scholarships *(Undergraduate/Scholarship)* [1392]
Frances Warren Baker Memorial Scholarships *(Undergraduate/Scholarship)* [6345]
Jim Batten Community Newspaper Internships *(Undergraduate/Internship)* [7144]
N.S. Beinstock Fellowships *(Undergraduate/Fellowship)* [1393]
BellSouth Business Internship Awards *(Postgraduate/Internship)* [7145]
Pete and Ellen Bensley Memorial Scholarship Fund *(Undergraduate/Scholarship)* [3041]
Lester G. Benz Memorial Scholarships for College Journalism Study *(Other/Scholarship)* [5890]
Barry Bingham Sr. Fellowships *(Professional Development/Fellowship)* [4819]
Tom Bost Scholarships *(Undergraduate/Scholarship)* [7147]
Ed Bradley Scholarships *(Undergraduate/Scholarship)* [1394]
Rick Brewer Scholarships *(Undergraduate/Scholarship)* [7148]
Broadcast News Management Fellowships *(Undergraduate/Scholarship)* [1395]
Michelle Clark Fellowships *(Undergraduate/Fellowship)* [1396]
Ardis Cohoon Scholarships *(Undergraduate/Scholarship)* [7150]
The Frank Cormier Scholarships *(Undergraduate/Scholarship)* [7409]
Kathryn M. Cronin Scholarships *(Undergraduate/Scholarship)* [7152]
D&A Florida Scholarships *(Undergraduate/Scholarship)* [6648]
James Davis Scholarships *(Undergraduate/Internship)* [7154]
Harvey N. Dondero Communication and Journalism Excellence Scholarships *(Undergraduate/Scholarship)* [5817]
Harold K. Douhhit Regional Scholarships *(Undergraduate/Scholarship)* [5322]
Richard Drukker Memorial Scholarships *(Undergraduate/Scholarship)* [5180]
Vivian Edmonds Scholarships *(Undergraduate/Scholarship)* [7156]
Don English Memorial Scholarships *(Undergraduate/Scholarship)* [5821]
David E. Ewald Journalism Scholarships *(Undergraduate/Scholarship)* [4774]
Reese Felts Scholarships *(Undergraduate/Scholarship)* [7157]
Allison E. Fisher Scholarships *(Undergraduate/Scholarship)* [2984]
Ameel J. Fisher Scholarships *(Undergraduate/Scholarship)* [7158]
Florida Outdoor Writers Association Scholarships *(Undergraduate/Scholarship)* [3016]
Paul B. & Aline Flynn Scholarships *(Undergraduate/Scholarship)* [6652]
George Foreman Tribute to Lyndon B. Johnson Scholarships *(Undergraduate/Scholarship)* [1397]
Denise Franklin Journalism Scholarships *(Undergraduate/Scholarship)* [7434]
Freedom Forum-NCAA Sports-Journalism Scholarships *(Undergraduate/Scholarship)* [4804]
Garikian Scholarship Fund *(Undergraduate/Scholarship)* [1279]
Kays Gary Scholarships *(Undergraduate/Scholarship)* [7160]
Joy Gibson Scholarships *(Undergraduate/Scholarship)* [7162]
L.C. Gifford Distinguished Journalism Scholarships *(Undergraduate/Scholarship)* [7163]
Keith Gilmore Foundation - Diploma Scholarships *(Professional Development/Scholarship)* [3240]
Keith Gilmore Foundation - Postgraduate Scholarships *(Postgraduate/Scholarship)* [3241]
Keith Gilmore Foundation - Undergraduate Scholarships *(Undergraduate/Scholarship)* [3242]
Charles Hauser Scholarships *(Undergraduate/Scholarship)* [7164]
Paul Green Houston Scholarships *(Undergraduate/Scholarship)* [7165]
James F. Hurley III Bicentennial Merit Scholarships *(Undergraduate/Scholarship)* [7166]
Fred Hutchison Travel Scholarships *(Undergraduate/Scholarship)* [7167]
INF Scholarships *(Undergraduate/Scholarship)* [3934]
Inter American Press Association Scholarships *(Undergraduate/Scholarship)* [3771]
International Foodservice Editorial Council Scholarships *(Graduate, Undergraduate/Scholarship)* [3852]
InternXchange *(Undergraduate/Internship)* [3228]
Iowa Journalism Institute Scholarships *(Undergraduate/Scholarship)* [3935]
Harriet Irsay Scholarships *(Graduate, Undergraduate/Scholarship)* [674]
Edward Jackson International Scholarships *(Undergraduate/Scholarship)* [7168]
Gene Jackson Scholarships *(Undergraduate/Scholarship)* [7169]
Peter Lars Jacobson Scholarships *(Undergraduate/Scholarship)* [7170]
Sister Rita Jeanne Scholarships *(Undergraduate/Scholarship)* [4033]
Ken Kashiwara Scholarships *(Undergraduate/Scholarship)* [1398]
Glenn Keever Scholarships *(Undergraduate/Scholarship)* [7171]
Bernard Kilgore Memorial Scholarships *(Undergraduate/Scholarship)* [5181]
John S. Knight Fellowships *(Professional Development/Fellowship)* [6705]
Harold Knopp Scholarships *(Undergraduate/Scholarship)* [5503]
Lily Scholarships in Religion for Journalists *(Professional Development/Scholarship)* [6021]
LIN Television Corporation Minority Scholarships and Training Program *(Undergraduate/Scholarship)* [4247]
Raleigh Mann Scholarships *(Undergraduate/Scholarship)* [7175]
Maxwell Graduate Scholarships in Medical Journalism *(Postgraduate/Scholarship)* [7177]
Durwood McAlister Scholarships *(Undergraduate/Scholarship)* [3214]
McClatchy Scholarships *(Undergraduate/Scholarship)* [6616]
Anne O'Hare McCormick Scholarship Fund *(Undergraduate/Scholarship)* [5204]
C.A. "Pete" McKnight Scholarships *(Undergraduate/Scholarship)* [7179]
Edward Heywood Megson Scholarships *(Undergraduate/Scholarship)* [7180]
Messenger-Anderson Journalism Scholarships and Internships Program *(Undergraduate/Scholarship)* [6123]
Quincy Sharpe Mills Scholarships *(Undergraduate/Scholarship)* [7181]
Jacque I. Minnotte Health Reporting Fellowships *(Undergraduate/Fellowship)* [1399]
Alexander Morisey Scholarships *(Undergraduate/Scholarship)* [7183]
Morris Newspaper Corp. Scholarships *(Undergraduate/Scholarship)* [3215]
Muddy Waters Scholarships *(Undergraduate/Scholarship)* [1768]
National Iranian American Council Fellowships *(Graduate, Undergraduate/Fellowship)* [4958]
National Lesbian and Gay Journalists Association (NLGJA) Scholarships *(Undergraduate/Scholarship)* [6126]
N.C. Psychoanalytic Foundation Journalism Scholarships *(Postgraduate/Scholarship)* [7184]
Edward J. Nell Memorial Scholarships in Journalism *(Undergraduate/Scholarship)* [5891]
New York Financial Writers' Associations Scholarships *(Graduate, Undergraduate/Scholarship)* [5189]
New York Women in Communications, Inc. Foundation Scholarships *(Graduate, Undergraduate/Scholarship)* [5200]
Ohio Newspaper Association Minority Scholarships *(Undergraduate/Scholarship)* [5323]
Ohio Newspaper Association University Journalism Scholarships *(Undergraduate/Scholarship)* [5324]
Ohio Newspaper Association Women's Scholarships *(Undergraduate/Scholarship)* [5325]
The Deborah Orin-Eilbeck Scholarships *(Graduate/Scholarship)* [7410]
Leonard M. Perryman Communications Scholarships for Ethnic Minority Students *(Undergraduate/Scholarship)* [6965]
Steve Petix Journalism Scholarship *(Undergraduate/Scholarship)* [6213]
Pfizer Minority Medical Journalism Scholarships *(Postgraduate/Scholarship)* [7185]
PHD ARA Scholarships *(Undergraduate/Scholarship)* [849]
Stephen D. Pisinski Memorial Scholarships *(Undergraduate/Scholarship)* [5875]
Robert Pittman Scholarships *(Undergraduate/Scholarship)* [7186]
Carter Pitts Scholarships *(Undergraduate/Scholarship)* [3936]
Erwin Potts Scholarships *(Undergraduate/Scholarship)* [7187]
Lou and Carole Prato Sports Reporting Scholarships *(Undergraduate/Scholarship)* [1400]
Peter DeWitt Pruden and Phyliss Harrill Pruden Scholarships *(Undergraduate/Scholarship)* [7188]
Pulliam/Kilgore Freedom of Information Internships *(Undergraduate/Internship)* [6569]
Bob Quincy Scholarships *(Undergraduate/Scholarship)* [7189]
Marjorie Usher Regan Scholarships *(Undergraduate/Scholarship)* [7190]
Nike Reynolds Journalism Scholarships *(Undergraduate/Scholarship)* [1401]
Eugene L. Roberts Jr. Prize *(Undergraduate/Prize)* [7191]
William C. Rogers Scholarships *(Undergraduate/Scholarship)* [3216]
Isaac Roth Newspaper Carrier Scholarships Program *(Undergraduate/Scholarship)* [5182]
SAJA Journalism Scholarships *(Undergraduate/Scholarship)* [6608]
Abe Schecter Graduate Scholarships *(Postgraduate/Scholarship)* [1402]
SCSPA Scholarships *(Undergraduate/Scholarship)* [6617]
SCSPA Yearbook Scholarships *(Undergraduate/Scholarship)* [6618]
D.R. Segal Memorial Scholarships for Journalistic Excellence *(Undergraduate/Scholarship)* [5367]
Deedee Segel - Hartford Courant Internships *(Undergraduate/Internship)* [3495]
Carole Simpson Scholarships *(Undergraduate/Scholarship)* [1403]
Ward Sims Memorial Scholarships *(Undergraduate/Scholarship)* [4383]
Drue Smith/Society of Professional Journalists Scholarships *(Undergraduate/Scholarship)* [2447]
A.C. Snow Scholarships *(Undergraduate/Scholarship)* [7192]
Sturgulewski Family Scholarships *(Graduate, Undergraduate/Scholarship)* [7038]
Leo Suarez Journalism Scholarships *(Undergraduate/Scholarship)* [2601]
Kirk Sutlive Scholarships *(Undergraduate/Scholarship)* [3217]
Taylor/Blakeslee University Fellowships *(Undergraduate/Fellowship)* [2548]
Tucker Family Scholarships *(Undergraduate/Scholarship)* [7195]
UAA Anchorage Daily News Minority Journalism Scholarships *(Undergraduate/Scholarship)* [7042]
UAA Elaine Atwood Scholarships *(Undergraduate/Scholarship)* [7051]
UAA GCI, Inc. Scholarships *(Undergraduate/Scholarship)* [7055]
UAA Kimura Scholarship Fund (Photography Scholarships) *(Undergraduate/Scholarship)* [7060]
David Julian Wichard Scholarships *(Undergraduate/Scholarship)* [7196]
Tom Wicker Scholarships *(Undergraduate/Scholarship)* [7197]
Glenn Wilson Broadcast Journalism Scholarships *(Undergraduate/Scholarship)* [5529]
Pete Wilson Graduate Scholarships *(Postgraduate/Scholarship)* [1404]
Pete Wilson Journalism Scholarships *(Undergraduate/Scholarship)* [1405]
Wisconsin-Madison Journalism Scholarships

(Undergraduate/Scholarship) [7285]
The Working Press Internships (Undergraduate/Internship) [6570]
WTVD Endowment Scholarships (Undergraduate/Scholarship) [7199]

Korean studies

Fall Fellowships in Korean Studies (Professional Development/Fellowship) [4082]
Korean Language Study Awards (Graduate/Scholarship) [4083]

Land management

Appraisal Institute Education Trust Scholarships (Graduate, Undergraduate/Scholarship) [1189]
Marathon Oil Corporation College Scholarship Program (Graduate, Undergraduate/Scholarship) [3600]
Mined Land Reclamation Educational Grant Program (Undergraduate/Grant) [4745]

Landscape architecture and design

American Society of Landscape Architects Council of Fellow Scholarships (Undergraduate/Scholarship) [979]
ASLA Council of Fellows Scholarships (Undergraduate/Scholarship) [4118]
California Landscape Contractors Association Scholarships (Undergraduate/Scholarship) [1839]
Certified Landscape Technician Scholarships (Undergraduate/Scholarship) [5242]
CLASS Fund Irrigation Scholarship Program (Graduate, Undergraduate/Scholarship) [4119]
CLASS Fund Landscape Architecture Scholarship Program (Graduate, Undergraduate/Scholarship) [4120]
Class Fund Ornamental Horticulture Scholarship Program (Undergraduate/Scholarship) [980]
CLASS Fund University Scholarship Program (Graduate, Undergraduate/Scholarship) [4121]
The Dangermond Fellowships (Postgraduate/Fellowship) [981]
Garden Club Council of Winston-Salem and Forsyth County Council (Undergraduate/Scholarship) [7436]
Hawaii Chapter/David T. Woolsey Scholarships (Graduate, Undergraduate/Scholarship) [4122]
Edith H. Henderson Scholarships (Undergraduate/Scholarship) [982]
IFDA Educational Foundation (Undergraduate/Scholarship) [3859]
Steven G. King Play Environments Scholarships (Undergraduate/Scholarship) [4123]
LAF/Class Fund AILA/YAMAGAMI/Hope Fellowships (Postgraduate/Fellowship) [983]
Landscape Forms Design for People Scholarships (Undergraduate/Scholarship) [4124]
William J. Locklin Scholarships (Undergraduate/Scholarship) [984]
Michigan Nursery and Landscape Association Scholarships (Undergraduate/Scholarship) [4483]
Raymond E. Page Scholarships (Undergraduate/Scholarship) [985]
Courtland Paul Scholarships (Undergraduate/Scholarship) [4125]
Peridian International, Inc./Rae L. Price, FASLA Scholarships (Undergraduate/Scholarship) [4126]
Rae L. Price Scholarships (Undergraduate/Scholarship) [986]
Rain Bird Intelligent Use of Water Scholarships (Undergraduate/Scholarship) [4127]
Rain Bird Scholarships (Undergraduate/Scholarship) [987]
Douglas Dockery Thomas Fellowships (Graduate/Fellowship) [4128]
Harriet Barnhart Wimmer Scholarships (Undergraduate/Scholarship) [988]
David T. Woolsey Scholarships (Undergraduate/Scholarship) [989]

Latin American studies (See also: Area and ethnic studies)

American Society for Microbiology International Fellowships for Latin America (Postdoctorate/Fellowship) [1003]
FAIC Latin American and Caribbean Scholars Program (Professional Development/Scholarship) [660]
Foundation of American Institute for Conservation Lecture Grants (Professional Development/Grant) [661]
Leonor R. Guerrero Memorial Scholarships (Undergraduate/Scholarship) [4689]
Leo S. Rowe Pan American Fund (Undergraduate/Loan) [5404]

Law

AAJ Trial Advocacy Scholarships (Undergraduate/Scholarship) [357]
AAUW Legal Advocacy Fund Selected Professions Fellowships (Doctorate, Graduate/Fellowship) [7]
ABA Legal Opportunity Scholarship Funds (Undergraduate/Scholarship) [3582]
ABA Legal Scholarships (Graduate/Scholarship) [382]
ABF Doctoral Fellowships (Doctorate, Graduate/Fellowship) [433]
The Frederick B. Abramson Public Interest Fellowships Award (All/Fellowship) [12]
Accenture American Indian Scholarship Program (Graduate, Undergraduate/Scholarship) [640]
Affirmative Action Mini Grant and Student Scholarships (All/Grant) [14]
AGBU Scholarships (Graduate/Loan) [1255]
Akron Bar Association Foundation Scholarships (Undergraduate/Scholarship) [96]
Tillie B. Alperin Scholarships (Undergraduate/Scholarship) [7109]
American Counsel Association Scholarships (Undergraduate/Scholarship) [515]
American Society of Comparative Law TransCoop Programs (All/Fellowship) [937]
Anheuser-Busch NAPABA Law Foundation Presidential Scholarships (Undergraduate/Scholarship) [4646]
Arent Fox Diversity Scholarships (Undergraduate/Scholarship) [1202]
ARS Undergraduate Scholarships (Four Year College, Two Year College, Undergraduate/Scholarship) [1259]
Asian American Lawyers Associations of Massachusetts Scholarships (Undergraduate/Scholarship) [1332]
Asian/Pacific Bar Association of Sacramento Law Foundation Scholarships (Undergraduate/Scholarship) [1338]
ASIL Helton Fellowship Program (All/Fellowship) [977]
Associated Women for Pepperdine (AWP) Scholarships (Undergraduate/Scholarship) [5572]
Attorney-CPA Foundation Scholarships (Undergraduate/Scholarship) [322]
William Stone Ayres Scholarships (Undergraduate/Scholarship) [2732]
The Bailey Family Foundation College Scholarship Program (Undergraduate/Scholarship) [1586]
Donald W. Banner Corporate Intern Scholarships (Undergraduate/Scholarship) [3769]
Donald W. Banner Diversity Scholarship for Law Students (Undergraduate/Scholarship) [1594]
Barbri Scholarships for Bar Preparation (Undergraduate/Scholarship) [3578]
Helen Bassett Commemorative Scholarships (Undergraduate/Scholarship) [5128]
Bay Area Minority Law Student Scholarships (Graduate, Undergraduate/Scholarship) [1596]
Beck-Pfann Memorial Scholarships (Undergraduate/Scholarship) [5573]
Peggy Bernheim Memorial Scholarships (Undergraduate/Scholarship) [1792]
Beverly Estate Scholarships (Undergraduate/Scholarship) [2733]
Black Women Lawyers Association of Los Angeles Scholarships (Undergraduate/Scholarship) [1757]
David and Camille Boatwright Endowed Scholarships (Undergraduate/Scholarship) [5574]
George and Mary Brammer Scholarships (Undergraduate/Scholarship) [2734]
Ann Marie Bredefeld Scholarships (Undergraduate/Scholarship) [5575]
Margaret Martin Brock Scholarships in Law (Undergraduate/Scholarship) [5576]
Kae and Kay Brockermeyer Endowed Scholarships (Undergraduate/Scholarship) [5577]
Shirley J. Brooke Endowed Scholarships (Undergraduate/Scholarship) [5578]
The Allen E. Broussard Scholarships (Undergraduate/Scholarship) [431]
Gregory Brunk Scholarships (Undergraduate/Scholarship) [2735]
Buder Scholarship for American Indian Law Students (Undergraduate/Scholarship) [7384]
Sam Bull Memorial Scholarships (Undergraduate/Scholarship) [142]
Business and Transactional Law Center Scholarships (Undergraduate/Scholarship) [7347]
Donald C. and Doris K. Byers Scholarships (Undergraduate/Scholarship) [2736]
Johnston Cabaniss Scholarships (Undergraduate/Scholarship) [123]
California Bar Foundation Diversity Scholarships (Undergraduate/Scholarship) [1325]
California Bar Law Foundation Scholarships (Undergraduate/Scholarship) [1326]
CALL/ACBD Education Reserve Fund Grants (Graduate/Grant) [1930]
Canadian Association of Law Libraries CALL Research Grants (Graduate/Grant) [1931]
Robert C. Carson Memorial Bursary (Undergraduate/Scholarship) [153]
Child and Family Advocacy Fellowships (Undergraduate/Scholarship) [7348]
Vincent Chin Memorial Fund Scholarships (Graduate/Scholarship) [455]
Athalie Clarke Endowed Scholarships (Undergraduate/Scholarship) [5579]
Brian Dane Cleary Memorial Scholarships (Undergraduate/Scholarship) [5580]
Claude T. Coffman Memorial Scholarships (Undergraduate/Scholarship) [7110]
Columbian Lawyers Association of Westchester County Scholarships (Undergraduate/Scholarship) [2331]
Mable B. Crawford Memorial Scholarships (Undergraduate/Scholarship) [4354]
Angela D. Dales Merit Scholarship Program (Undergraduate/Loan) [1187]
Dallas Hispanic Bar Association Scholarships (Undergraduate/Scholarship) [2611]
D&A Florida Scholarships (Undergraduate/Scholarship) [6648]
Hugh and Hazel Darling Dean Scholarships (Undergraduate/Scholarship) [5581]
Darling Foundation Endowed School of Law Scholarships (Undergraduate/Scholarship) [5582]
Davis Wright Tremaine 1L Diversity Scholarships (Undergraduate/Scholarship) [2623]
Alexander A. DelleCese Memorial Scholarships (Undergraduate/Scholarship) [1793]
Martha Delman and Milton Arthur Krug Endowed Scholarships (Undergraduate/Scholarship) [5583]
Edward D. Di Loreto-Odell S. McConnell Scholarships (Undergraduate/Scholarship) [5584]
Carol DiMaiti Scholarship Awards (Undergraduate/Scholarship) [4328]
Raymond DiPaglia Endowment Scholarships (Undergraduate/Scholarship) [2737]
Grace O. Doane Scholarships (Undergraduate/Scholarship) [2738]
Joseph M. Dorgan Scholarships (Undergraduate/Scholarship) [2739]
Drake University Law School Law Opportunity Scholarships - Disadvantage (Undergraduate/Scholarship) [2740]
Drake University Law School Law Opportunity Scholarships - Diversity (Undergraduate/Scholarship) [2741]

Drake University Law School Public Service Scholarships *(Undergraduate/Scholarship)* [2742]
Cleveland Drennon, Jr. Memorial Scholarships *(Undergraduate/Scholarship)* [7111]
DRI Law Student Diversity Scholarships *(Undergraduate/Scholarship)* [1755]
Robert E. Early Memorial Scholarships *(Undergraduate/Scholarship)* [2743]
East Tennessee Foundation Scholarships *(Undergraduate/Scholarship)* [7112]
Electric Cooperative Pioneer Trust Fund Scholarships *(Undergraduate/Scholarship)* [2744]
Herman E. Elgar Memorial Scholarships *(Undergraduate/Scholarship)* [2745]
Equal Access to Justice Scholarships *(Undergraduate/Scholarship)* [4752]
Equal Justice Works Fellowship Program *(Graduate, Undergraduate/Fellowship)* [2882]
R. Wayne Estes Endowed Scholarships *(Undergraduate/Scholarship)* [5585]
Evans and Petree Law Firm Scholarships *(Undergraduate/Scholarship)* [7113]
Faegre & Benson Diversity Scholarships *(Undergraduate/Scholarship)* [2900]
D.J. Fairgrave Education Trust *(Undergraduate/Scholarship)* [2746]
Farella Braun Martel LLP Diversity Scholarships *(Undergraduate/Scholarship)* [2904]
Judge McIntyre Faries Scholarships *(Undergraduate/Scholarship)* [5586]
Federal Court Bench and Bar Scholarships *(Undergraduate/Scholarship)* [7114]
Fellowships to Promote Research on the Legal Framework for Civil Society in Latin America, Africa and Asia *(All/Fellowship)* [3823]
Finnegan, Henderson, Farabow, Garrett & Dunner, LLP Diversity Scholarships *(Undergraduate/Scholarship)* [2936]
Scott A. Flahive Memorial Scholarship Fund *(Undergraduate/Scholarship)* [3277]
Leland Stanford Forrest Scholarships *(Undergraduate/Scholarship)* [2747]
Howard Fox Memorial Law Scholarship *(Undergraduate/Scholarship)* [1634]
Franchise Law Diversity Scholarship Awards *(Undergraduate/Scholarship)* [3857]
Froberg-Suess JD/MBA Scholarships *(Undergraduate/Scholarship)* [5587]
Gerald Garner Memorial Scholarships *(Undergraduate/Scholarship)* [5588]
William H. Gates Public Service Law Scholarships *(Undergraduate/Scholarship)* [3163]
Joseph H. Gellert/Dutchess County Bar Association Scholarships *(Undergraduate/Scholarship)* [2798]
Terry M. Giles Honor Scholarships *(Undergraduate/Scholarship)* [5589]
Senator James Gladstone Memorial Scholarships *(Undergraduate/Scholarship)* [143]
Jane S. Glenn Memorial Endowed Scholarships *(Undergraduate/Scholarship)* [6046]
Wilford Hayes Gowen Scholarships *(Undergraduate/Scholarship)* [7115]
William L. Graddy Law School Scholarships *(Undergraduate/Scholarship)* [6656]
Greater Philadelphia Law Library Association Scholarships *(Undergraduate/Scholarship)* [3371]
Philip F. Greco Memorial Scholarships *(Undergraduate/Scholarship)* [4272]
Guy P. Greenwald Jr. Endowed Scholarships *(Undergraduate/Scholarship)* [5590]
Warren and Rosalie Gummow Endowed Scholarships *(Undergraduate/Scholarship)* [5591]
The Richard D. Hailey AAJ Law Student Scholarships *(Undergraduate/Scholarship)* [358]
Lex and Scott Hawkins Endowed Scholarships *(Undergraduate/Scholarship)* [2748]
Thomas T. Hayashi Memorial Scholarships *(Graduate, Undergraduate/Scholarship)* [4017]
Edward and Cora Hayes Scholarships *(Undergraduate/Scholarship)* [2749]
Annamae Heaps Law Scholarships *(Undergraduate/Scholarship)* [2750]
John M. Helmick Law Scholarships *(Undergraduate/Scholarship)* [2751]
Herbert Herff Presidential Law Scholarships *(Undergraduate/Scholarship)* [7116]
Alia Herrera Memorial Scholarships *(Undergraduate/Scholarship)* [359]
Mark and Michelle Hiepler Endowed Scholarships *(Undergraduate/Scholarship)* [5592]
Hierholzer-Fojtik Scholarship Fund *(Undergraduate/Scholarship)* [3287]
Judge Delmas C. Hill Scholarships *(Undergraduate/Scholarship)* [7349]
Hispanic Lawyers Association of Illinois Public Interest Fellowships *(Undergraduate/Scholarship)* [3579]
HNBF Princeton Review Duard Bradshaw Memorial Scholarships *(Undergraduate/Scholarship)* [3584]
Robert and Elaine Hoffman Memorial Scholarships *(Undergraduate/Scholarship)* [7117]
Kathryn Hookanson Law Fellowships *(Undergraduate/Scholarship)* [7118]
John C. "Jack" Hough Memorial Law Scholarships *(Undergraduate/Scholarship)* [7119]
HSF/Wal-Mart Stores Inc. Scholarship Program *(Graduate, Undergraduate/Scholarship)* [3599]
John Peter Humphrey Student Fellowships *(Graduate/Fellowship)* [1942]
Cecil C. Humphreys Law Fellowships *(Undergraduate/Scholarship)* [7120]
IBA Law Student Scholarships Foundation *(Undergraduate/Scholarship)* [3715]
International Association of Law Libraries Scholarship Program *(Professional Development/Scholarship)* [3807]
International Municipal Lawyers Association Canadian Scholarships *(Professional Development/Scholarship)* [3878]
Internships in International Civil Society Law *(Undergraduate/Internship)* [3824]
Iranian American Bar Association Scholarships *(Undergraduate/Scholarship)* [3938]
James P. Irish Scholarships *(Undergraduate/Scholarship)* [2752]
Italian American Lawyers Association Annual Scholarships *(Undergraduate/Scholarship)* [3968]
Jamaica National Building Society Scholarships *(Undergraduate/Scholarship)* [4001]
Japanese American Bar Association Scholarships *(Undergraduate/Scholarship)* [4013]
JD/MBA Scholarships *(Undergraduate/Scholarship)* [5593]
Jewish Federation Academic Scholarships *(Graduate, Undergraduate/Scholarship)* [4029]
JLTLA Scholarships *(Undergraduate/Scholarship)* [6942]
JLTLA Texas Bar Review Scholarships *(Undergraduate/Scholarship)* [6943]
Edward H. Jones Scholarships *(Undergraduate/Scholarship)* [2753]
JSR Foundation Endowed School of Law Scholarships *(Undergraduate/Scholarship)* [5594]
Woodrow Judkins Endowed Scholarships *(Undergraduate/Scholarship)* [5595]
Justicia En Diversidad Scholarships *(Undergraduate/Scholarship)* [3585]
Kaplan Scholarships *(Undergraduate/Scholarship)* [3580]
Kegler Brown Minority Merit Scholarships *(Undergraduate/Scholarship)* [4062]
Kerr Foundation Scholarships *(Undergraduate/Scholarship)* [5329]
Kerrigan Scholarships *(Undergraduate/Scholarship)* [5596]
James N. Kincanon Scholarships *(Undergraduate/Scholarship)* [6047]
Martin Luther King Law Scholarships *(Undergraduate/Scholarship)* [2754]
Forest A. King Scholarships *(Undergraduate/Scholarship)* [2755]
Koch Scholarships *(Undergraduate/Scholarship)* [7350]
Senator Carl O. Koella, Jr. Memorial Scholarships *(Undergraduate/Scholarship)* [2427]
Krist-Reavley Minority Scholarships *(Undergraduate/Scholarship)* [5597]
Julia Kwan Endowed Scholarships *(Graduate/Scholarship)* [5598]
James D. Lang Memorial Scholarships *(Graduate/Scholarship)* [1932]
Jason Lang Scholarship *(Undergraduate/Scholarship)* [163]
Law Foundation of British Columbia Graduate Fellowships *(Undergraduate/Fellowship)* [4147]
Law and Social Science Dissertation Fellowship and Mentoring Program *(Doctorate, Graduate/Fellowship)* [434]
Verne Lawyer Scholarships *(Undergraduate/Scholarship)* [2756]
League of Attorneys' Wives Scholarships *(Undergraduate/Scholarship)* [2757]
Albert J. and Mae Lee Memorial Scholarships *(Undergraduate/Scholarship)* [5599]
The Leesfield/AAJ Law Student Scholarships *(Undergraduate/Scholarship)* [360]
Judge William B. Leffler Scholarships *(Undergraduate/Scholarship)* [7121]
Legal Research Service Scholarships *(Undergraduate/Scholarship)* [2758]
Legal Scholarship for Law Students *(Undergraduate/Scholarship)* [5440]
Legal Scholarship for Non-Tenured Law Professors *(All/Scholarship)* [5441]
Legal Scholarship for Tenured Law Professors *(All/Scholarship)* [5442]
Craig Lensch Memorial Scholarships *(Undergraduate/Scholarship)* [1794]
Frederick D. Lewis Jr. Scholarships *(Undergraduate/Scholarship)* [2759]
Lim, Ruger and Kim Scholarships *(Undergraduate/Scholarship)* [4647]
The C. Lyons Fellowship Program *(All/Fellowship)* [4980]
Gordon and Delores Madson Scholarships *(Undergraduate/Scholarship)* [2760]
MALDEF Law School Scholarships *(Undergraduate/Scholarship)* [3587]
MALDEF Law School Scholarships *(Undergraduate/Scholarship)* [4470]
Howard T. Markey Memorial Scholarships *(Undergraduate/Scholarship)* [2906]
Abraham Lincoln Marovitz Public Interest Law Scholarships *(Undergraduate/Scholarship)* [2119]
Greg Matthews Memorial Scholarships *(Undergraduate/Scholarship)* [5600]
MCCA Lloyd M. Johnson, Jr. Scholarships *(Undergraduate/Scholarship)* [4558]
J. McDonald and Judy Williams School of Law Scholarships *(Undergraduate/Scholarship)* [5601]
H.H. McKnight Memorial Scholarships *(Undergraduate/Scholarship)* [7122]
John Merrick Law Scholarships *(Undergraduate/Scholarship)* [5602]
Sanders J. Mestel Legal Scholarship Fund *(Undergraduate/Scholarship)* [6742]
Milbank Diversity Scholarships *(Undergraduate/Scholarship)* [4525]
Minority Presence Grant Program for Doctoral Study *(Undergraduate/Grant)* [7182]
Jake S. More Scholarships *(Undergraduate/Scholarship)* [2761]
Thomas More Scholarships *(Undergraduate/Scholarship)* [3260]
Sam A. Myar, Jr. Law Scholarships *(Undergraduate/Scholarship)* [7123]
NAPABA Law Foundation Scholarships *(Undergraduate/Scholarship)* [4648]
National Italian American Bar Association Scholarships *(Postgraduate/Scholarship)* [4960]
National Judges Association Scholarships *(Professional Development/Scholarship)* [4965]
Nebraska Association of Legal Assistants Student Scholarships *(Undergraduate/Scholarship)* [5153]
Charles I. Nelson Endowed Scholarships *(Undergraduate/Scholarship)* [5603]
Gunnar Nicholson Endowed Scholarships *(Undergraduate/Scholarship)* [5604]
Helen W. Nies Scholarships *(Undergraduate/Scholarship)* [2907]
Peggy (Kommer) Novosad Scholarships *(Graduate, Postgraduate/Scholarship)* [3344]
NSA Scholarship Program *(Undergraduate/Scholarship)* [5040]
Oklahoma City University Merit Scholarships *(Undergraduate/Scholarship)* [5330]
Dwight D. Opperman Scholarships *(Undergraduate/Scholarship)* [2762]

PACE/Columbian Lawyers Association of Westchester County Endowed Scholarships (Undergraduate/Scholarship) [2332]
Pacific Legal Foundation Faculty Grants (All/Grant) [5443]
Pathways to Success Scholarships (Undergraduate/Scholarship) [3113]
Pepperdine University Armenian Student Scholarships (Undergraduate/Scholarship) [5605]
Pepperdine University Dean's Scholarships (Doctorate, Graduate/Scholarship) [5606]
Pepperdine University Diversity Scholarships (Doctorate, Graduate/Scholarship) [5607]
Pepperdine University Faculty Scholarships (Doctorate, Graduate/Scholarship) [5608]
Jerome S. Petz, S.J., Scholarships (Undergraduate/Scholarship) [2763]
William R. Pfalzgraf Scholarships (Undergraduate/Scholarship) [5509]
Jamie Phillips Endowed Scholarships (Undergraduate/Scholarship) [5609]
Pi Gamma Mu Scholarships (Graduate/Scholarship) [5691]
Pittsburg State University Distinguished Graduate Scholarships (Undergraduate/Scholarship) [7351]
Donald and Susie Polden Dean's Scholarships (Undergraduate/Scholarship) [7124]
Political Leadership Scholarships (Undergraduate/Scholarship) [5773]
Polsinelli Diversity Scholarships (Undergraduate/Scholarship) [7352]
George V. Powell Diversity Scholarships (Undergraduate/Scholarship) [4130]
Practising Law Institute Law Student Scholarships (Undergraduate/Scholarship) [5742]
Diana M. Priestly Memorial Scholarships (Undergraduate/Scholarship) [1933]
Prince Edward Island Law Student Scholarships (Undergraduate/Scholarship) [4149]
Public Interest Scholarships (Undergraduate/Scholarship) [1816]
Puerto Rican Bar Association Scholarships (Undergraduate/Scholarship) [5884]
John Purfield Endowed Scholarships (Undergraduate/Scholarship) [5610]
Frederick Rakestraw Law Scholarships (Undergraduate/Scholarship) [5271]
Ratner and Sugarmon Scholarships (Undergraduate/Scholarship) [7125]
Janet Reynoldson Memorial Scholarships (Undergraduate/Scholarship) [2764]
Howard B. Rickard Scholarships (Undergraduate/Scholarship) [4884]
Isador M. Robinson Endowment Scholarships (Undergraduate/Scholarship) [2765]
Rosenthal Bar Exam Scholarships (Undergraduate/Scholarship) [1817]
Joe Rudd Scholarships (Undergraduate/Scholarship) [6054]
Saratoga County Bar Association Law Student Scholarships (All/Scholarship) [6248]
Jeptha Wade Schureman Scholarship Program (Undergraduate/Scholarship) [2521]
Walter and Rita Selvy Scholarships (Undergraduate/Scholarship) [2766]
Serbian Bar Association of America Scholarships (Undergraduate/Scholarship) [6296]
Seton Hall Law School's Merit Scholarship Program (Undergraduate/Scholarship) [6298]
Barbara A. Shacochis Scholarships (Undergraduate/Scholarship) [5611]
Shamberg Scholarships (Undergraduate/Scholarship) [7353]
The Ivan Shandor Memorial Ukrainian American Bar Association Scholarships (Undergraduate/Scholarship) [7360]
John M. and Mary A. Shanley Memorial Scholarships (Undergraduate/Scholarship) [6673]
Benjamin G. Shatz Scholarships (Undergraduate/Scholarship) [5612]
Bill and Ann Sheperd Legal Scholarships Fund (Undergraduate/Scholarship) [2892]
Joseph Henry Shepherd Scholarships (Undergraduate/Scholarship) [7126]
Stuart Silverman Scholarships (Undergraduate/Scholarship) [5613]
Soroptimist International of Redlands Scholarships (Undergraduate/Scholarship) [6011]
Amy E. Spain Memorial Scholarships (Undergraduate/Scholarship) [7127]
Special Law School Scholarships (Undergraduate/Scholarship) [5614]
Spring Internship in International NGO Law (Undergraduate/Internship) [3825]
James F. and Donna Springfield Scholarships (Undergraduate/Scholarship) [7128]
Otto M. Stanfield Law Scholarships (Graduate/Scholarship) [6957]
Stark County Bar Association Fund (Undergraduate/Scholarship) [6754]
StraightForward Media's Law School Scholarships (Undergraduate/Scholarship) [6799]
Fraser Stryker Diversity Scholarship Program (Undergraduate/Scholarship) [5166]
Summer Research Diversity Fellowships in Law and Social Science (Undergraduate/Fellowship) [435]
Hatton W. Sumners Scholarships (Undergraduate/Scholarship) [5331]
Michael Bendix Sutton Foundation (Undergraduate/Scholarship) [4934]
Charles "Buck" and Dora Taylor Endowed Law Scholarships (Undergraduate/Scholarship) [2767]
Tennessee Bar Foundation IOLTA Law School Scholarships (Undergraduate/Scholarship) [7129]
Tennessee Board of Regents Law Scholarships (Undergraduate/Scholarship) [7130]
Honorable Raymond Thompson Endowed Scholarships (Undergraduate/Scholarship) [5615]
Transgender Scholarships and Education Legacy Fund (Undergraduate/Scholarship) [6142]
Thomas and Glenna Trimble Endowed Scholarships (Undergraduate/Scholarship) [5616]
Trustees College Scholarships (Undergraduate/Scholarship) [4273]
Trustees Law School Scholarships (Undergraduate/Scholarship) [4274]
Philip F. Vineberg Travelling Fellowship in the Humanities (Graduate/Scholarship) [4432]
The Viscount Bennett Fellowships (Graduate/Fellowship) [1935]
Gary Walker Memorial Scholarships (Professional Development/Scholarship) [3788]
Warner Norcross & Judd LLP Law School Studies Scholarships (Undergraduate/Scholarship) [7343]
Earl Warren Civil Rights Training Scholarships (Graduate/Scholarship) [4605]
Earl Warren Shearman and Sterling Scholarships (Graduate/Scholarship) [4606]
Washington University Law School Chancellor's Graduate Fellowships (Graduate/Fellowship) [7386]
J.L. Weigand, Jr. Legal Education Trust Scholarships (Undergraduate/Scholarship) [7354]
Haemer Wheatcraft Scholarships (Undergraduate/Scholarship) [2768]
Brian J. White Endowed Law Scholarships (Undergraduate/Scholarship) [5617]
Howard A. White Endowed Scholarships (Undergraduate/Scholarship) [5618]
Sidney B. Williams, Jr. Scholarships (Undergraduate/Scholarship) [685]
Women In Defense HORIZONS Scholarships (Graduate, Undergraduate/Scholarship) [7479]
Wood County Bar Association Memorial Scholarships (Undergraduate/Scholarship) [5530]
Marilyn Graboys Wool Scholarships (Undergraduate/Scholarship) [6044]
Wyatt, Tarrant and Combs, LLP Scholarships (Undergraduate/Scholarship) [7131]
Minoru Yasui Memorial Scholarship (Graduate/Scholarship) [4022]
Diane Yu Loan Repayment Assistance Program (Undergraduate/Loan) [4649]
Yukon Law Foundation Scholarships (Undergraduate/Scholarship) [7551]
Michael A. Zamperini/W. Clay Burchell Scholarships (Undergraduate/Scholarship) [6148]
Zarley, McKee, Thomte, Voorhees, Sease Law Scholarships (Undergraduate/Scholarship) [2769]

Law enforcement

Jack Ackroyd Scholarships (Professional Development/Scholarship) [1925]
American Association of State Troopers Scholarship Foundation First Scholarships (Undergraduate/Scholarship) [400]
American Association of State Troopers Scholarship Foundation Second Scholarships (Undergraduate/Scholarship) [401]
American Federation of Police and Concerned Citizen Scholarships (Undergraduate/Scholarship) [547]
Sheriff W. Bruce Umpleby Law Enforcement Scholarship Fund (Undergraduate/Scholarship) [6710]
Alphonso Deal Scholarship Awards (Undergraduate/Scholarship) [4766]
Louise J. Franchini Rockford Police Department Scholarships (Undergraduate/Scholarship) [2466]
Wayne Hildebrant Police Scholarships Fund (Undergraduate/Scholarship) [4141]
IAWP International Recognition and Scholarship Award (Professional Development/Scholarship) [3811]
Frederick George James Memorial Scholarships (Undergraduate/Scholarship) [6195]
V.J. Johnson Memorial Scholarships (Undergraduate/Scholarship) [402]
John W. Kelley Memorial Scholarships (Undergraduate/Scholarship) [6781]
Christopher J. Kohlmeier Scholarships (Undergraduate/Scholarship) [5953]
Law Enforcement Memorial Scholarship Fund (Undergraduate/Scholarship) [3066]
NASSLEO Scholarships (Undergraduate/Scholarship) [4738]
NOBLE Fellowship Program (All/Fellowship) [4993]
Portuguese American Police Association Scholarships (Undergraduate/Scholarship) [5740]
Newell S. Rand Jr. Memorial Scholarships (Undergraduate/Scholarship) [5460]
StraightForward Media's Law Enforcement Scholarships (Professional Development, Undergraduate/Scholarship) [6798]
The WIFLE Scholarship Fund (Graduate, Postdoctorate, Undergraduate/Scholarship) [7477]

Leadership, Institutional and community

Diversity Executive Leadership Program Scholarships (Professional Development/Scholarship) [920]
Kappa Omicron Nu Undergraduate Scholarships (Undergraduate/Scholarship) [4048]
Marmot Leadership Scholarships (Postgraduate, Professional Development, Undergraduate/Scholarship) [5432]
Outward Bound Leadership Scholarships for Educators (Professional Development/Scholarship) [5433]
Outward Bound Wilderness Leadership Awards (High School, Professional Development/Award/Prize) [5434]
Scholarships for Leadership Training and Coaching (Professional Development/Scholarship) [2717]

Leukemia

E.D. Thomas Post Doctoral Fellowships (Postdoctorate/Fellowship) [3145]

Liberal arts

Cecil E. Burney Scholarships (High School, Undergraduate/Scholarship) [2267]
Elizabeth M. Gruber Scholarships (Graduate/Scholarship) [2687]
Doris Hendren Memorial Scholarships (Undergraduate/Scholarship) [6193]
Harriet Irsay Scholarships (Graduate, Undergraduate/Scholarship) [674]
Armistead Maupin Creative Writing Scholarship

Fund (Undergraduate/Scholarship) [2887]
Bernard Michel Scholarships (Undergraduate/Scholarship) [1908]
StraightForward Media's Liberal Arts Scholarships (Undergraduate/Scholarship) [6800]

Library and archival sciences

AALL Scholarships for Continuing Education Classes (Postgraduate/Scholarship) [362]
AALL Scholarships for Library School Graduates Seeking a Non-Law Degree (Postgraduate/Scholarship) [363]
AALL & Thomson West - George A. Strait Minority Scholarship Endowment (Postgraduate/Scholarship) [364]
Above and Beyond Scholarships (Graduate/Scholarship) [1846]
Affirmative Action Scholarships (Graduate/Scholarship) [6680]
AJL Convention Travel Grants (All/Grant) [1459]
AJL Scholarship Program (Undergraduate/Scholarship) [1460]
American Association of Law Libraries Library School Scholarships (Postgraduate/Scholarship) [365]
APALA Scholarship Program (Doctorate, Graduate/Scholarship) [1336]
John Blanchard Memorial Scholarships (Graduate/Scholarship) [1847]
Bound to Stay Bound Books (BTSB) Scholarships (Graduate/Scholarship) [1464]
Rev. Andrew L. Bouwhuis Memorial Scholarship Program (Graduate/Scholarship) [2073]
Carol June Bradley Awards (All/Grant) [4596]
CFI Sid Solow Scholarships (Graduate/Scholarship) [1467]
Rick Chace Foundation Scholarships (Graduate/Scholarship) [1468]
CLA/ACB Dafoe Scholarships (Graduate/Scholarship) [1985]
Mary Adeline Conner Professional Development Scholarships (Graduate/Scholarship) [6681]
James F. Connolly LexisNexis Academic & Library Solutions Scholarships (Postgraduate/Scholarship) [366]
Continuing Education Awards (Graduate/Grant) [4441]
DEMCO New Leaders Travel Grants (All/Grant) [5871]
Dena Epstein Award for Archival and Library Research in American Music (All/Grant) [4597]
Kevin Freeman Travel Grants (Graduate, Professional Development/Grant) [4598]
Jewels Gardiner Scholarships (Undergraduate/Scholarship) [1848]
Eugene Garfield Doctoral Dissertation Fellowships (Doctorate, Graduate/Fellowship) [1636]
The Gates Millennium Scholars (Undergraduate/Scholarship) [3590]
Walter Gerboth Awards (All/Grant) [4599]
Grow your Own @Your Library Institutional Scholarships (Graduate, Professional Development/Scholarship) [5872]
D. Glenn Hilts Scholarships Program (Graduate, Undergraduate/Scholarship) [1493]
HLS/MLA Professional Development Grants (Doctorate/Grant) [4442]
Huenefeld/Denton Scholarships (Undergraduate/Scholarship) [2692]
Indiana Library Federation AIME Scholarships (Undergraduate/Scholarship) [3693]
Institute for Scientific Information (ISI) Scholarships (Doctorate, Graduate/Scholarship) [6682]
Iowa Library Association Foundation Scholarships (Graduate/Scholarship) [3931]
Kodak Fellowships in Film Preservation (Graduate/Scholarship) [1469]
Christian Larew Memorial Scholarships (Graduate/Scholarship) [4236]
Library Media Teacher Scholarships (Graduate/Scholarship) [1849]
LITA and LSSI Minority Scholarships (Graduate/Scholarship) [4237]
LITA/OCLC Minority Scholarships (Graduate/Scholarship) [4238]
Lucius Littauer Foundation Travel Grants (All/Grant) [1461]
MAC Louisa Bowen Memorial Scholarships for Graduate Students in Archival Administration (Graduate/Scholarship) [4510]
Lillian Grace Mahan Scholarship Fund (Undergraduate/Scholarship) [6738]
Frederic G. Melcher Scholarships (Graduate/Scholarship) [1465]
MLA Research, Development, and Demonstration Project Grants (Graduate/Grant) [4446]
MLA Scholarships for Minority Students (Graduate/Scholarship) [4447]
Archie Motley Memorial Scholarships for Minority Students (Graduate/Scholarship) [4511]
Doris Orenstein Memorial Convention Travel Grants (All/Grant) [1462]
Katharine Pantzer Senior Fellowships in the British Book Trades (Professional Development/Fellowship) [1696]
Mary Pickford Scholarships (Graduate/Scholarship) [1470]
Plenum Scholarships (Doctorate/Scholarship) [6683]
Sarah Rebecca Reed Scholarships (Graduate/Scholarship) [1637]
REFORMA Scholarship Program (Graduate/Scholarship) [6016]
School Library Paraprofessional Scholarships (Graduate/Scholarship) [1850]
Frank B. Sessa Scholarships for Continuing Professional Education (Professional Development/Scholarship) [1638]
SLA Scholarships (Graduate/Scholarship) [6684]
Carin Alma E. Somers Scholarship Trust (Undergraduate/Scholarship) [1534]
Sony Pictures Scholarships (Graduate/Scholarship) [1471]
Thomson Scientific/MLA Doctoral Fellowships (Doctorate/Fellowship) [4448]
Jack E. Tillson Scholarships (Graduate/Scholarship) [3932]
Universal Studios Preservation Scholarships (Graduate/Scholarship) [1472]
Philip F. Vineberg Travelling Fellowship in the Humanities (Graduate/Scholarship) [4432]
Sue Marsh Weller Memorial Scholarships (Graduate, Postgraduate, Undergraduate/Scholarship) [3695]
H.W. Wilson Scholarships (Graduate/Scholarship) [1986]
Blance E. Woolls Scholarships (Graduate/Scholarship) [1639]
World Book Graduate Scholarships in Library and Information Science (Graduate/Scholarship) [1987]

Life sciences (See also: specific areas of study, e.g. Biology)

Merck Undergraduate Science Research Scholarships (Undergraduate/Scholarship) [318]
SAPA Scholarships (Undergraduate/Scholarship) [6408]
University of Wisconsin-Madison/CALS Continuing Student Scholarships (Undergraduate/Scholarship) [7273]
University of Wisconsin-Madison/CALS Minority Scholarships (Undergraduate/Scholarship) [7274]

Lighting science

IALD Scholarship Programs (Graduate, Undergraduate/Scholarship) [3809]

Linguistics

National Endowment for the Humanities Advanced Fellowship for Research in Turkey (Postdoctorate/Fellowship) [900]

Literature

D&A Florida Scholarships (Undergraduate/Scholarship) [6648]
Hench Post-Dissertation Fellowships (Postdoctorate/Fellowship) [303]
National Endowment for the Humanities Advanced Fellowship for Research in Turkey (Postdoctorate/Fellowship) [900]
Virginia Nicklas Scholarships (Undergraduate/Scholarship) [2658]
Ameen Rihani Scholarship Program (Undergraduate/Scholarship) [1193]

Local government

Congressional Scholarships Award (Undergraduate/Scholarship) [3147]

Logistics

Academic Scholarship Program A (Undergraduate/Scholarship) [4843]
Academic Scholarship Program B (Undergraduate/Scholarship) [4844]
Sharon D. Banks Undergraduate Memorial Scholarships (Undergraduate/Scholarship) [7508]
Bison Transport Scholarships (Undergraduate/Scholarship) [5341]
James Costello Memorial Scholarships (Undergraduate/Scholarship) [3920]
Ginger and Fred Deines Canada Scholarships (Undergraduate/Scholarship) [6917]
Ginger and Fred Deines Mexico Scholarships (Undergraduate/Scholarship) [6918]
Delta Nu Alpha Foundation Scholarships (Undergraduate/Scholarship) [2677]
Hooper Memorial Scholarships (Undergraduate/Scholarship) [6919]
Anne Koby Legacy Scholarships (Undergraduate/Scholarship) [7509]
Denny Lydic Scholarships (Undergraduate/Scholarship) [6920]
Marathon Oil Corporation College Scholarship Program (Graduate, Undergraduate/Scholarship) [3600]
Helen M. Overly Memorial Scholarships (Undergraduate/Scholarship) [7510]
Texas Transportation Scholarships (Undergraduate/Scholarship) [6921]
Alice Glaisyer Warfield Scholarships (Undergraduate/Scholarship) [6922]

Management

Herb Adrian Memorial Scholarship Fund (Undergraduate/Scholarship) [3036]
APS/Maricopa County Community Colleges Scholarships (Undergraduate/Scholarship) [5698]
George M. Brooker Collegiate Scholarships for Minorities (Graduate, Postgraduate, Undergraduate/Scholarship) [3748]
California Association of Family and Consumer Sciences (CAFCS)-San Diego Chapter Scholarships (Graduate, Undergraduate/Scholarship) [6177]
Stuart Cameron and Margaret McLeod Memorial Scholarships (SCMS) (Graduate, Undergraduate/Scholarship/Forgivable Loan) [3744]
Club Managers Association of America (CMAA) Research Grants (All/Grant) [2250]
CTP Scholarship Program (Professional Development/Scholarship) [5024]
Diversity Executive Leadership Program Scholarships (Professional Development/Scholarship) [920]
Donald M. Furbush Scholarships (Professional Development/Scholarship) [3749]
GAP, Inc. Scholarships Award (Undergraduate/Scholarship) [3566]
Griffith Foundation Scholarships (Undergraduate/Scholarship) [902]
HACU/Wal-Mart Achievers Scholarships (Undergraduate/Scholarship) [3567]
Robert Hancock Memorial Scholarship Award (Undergraduate/Scholarship) [4499]
HSBC-North America Scholarship Program (Undergraduate/Scholarship) [3592]
HSF/Wal-Mart Stores Inc. Scholarship Program (Graduate, Undergraduate/Scholarship) [3599]
IMA Memorial Education Fund Scholarships (MEF)

(Graduate, Undergraduate/Scholarship/Forgivable Loan) [3746]
IREM Foundation Minority Outreach Scholarships (Professional Development/Scholarship) [3750]
Willmoore H. Kendall Scholarships (Postgraduate/Scholarship) [2252]
David A. Kronick Travelling Fellowships (Doctorate/Fellowship) [4443]
Val Mason Scholarships (Postgraduate/Scholarship) [2036]
NBMBAA PhD Fellowship Programs (Doctorate/Fellowship) [4762]
PARMA Scholarships (Undergraduate/Scholarship) [5795]
Kenyon T. Payne Outstanding Student Awards (Undergraduate/Award/Prize) [4501]
Joe Perdue Scholarships (Undergraduate/Scholarship) [2253]
Paul H. Rittle Sr. Memorial Scholarships (Professional Development/Scholarship) [3751]
Wendell Scott Awards (Graduate, Undergraduate/Scholarship) [3570]
Surety Industry Scholarship Program for Minority Students (Undergraduate/Scholarship) [6824]
TLMI Scholarships - Four-Year Colleges (Undergraduate/Scholarship) [6833]
Tribal Business Management Program (TBM) Scholarships (Undergraduate/Scholarship) [2069]
Wall-Mart Stores, Inc. Fellowships - Graduate (Undergraduate/Scholarship) [643]
Wells Fargo American Indian Scholarship for Graduates (Graduate/Scholarship) [644]

Manufacturing

Malcolm Baldridge Scholarships (Undergraduate/Scholarship) [3420]
Walt Bartram Memorial Education Awards (Region 12 and Chapter 119) (Undergraduate/Scholarship) [6470]
Boeing Company Scholarships (Undergraduate/Scholarship) [6307]
Caterpillar Scholars Award (Undergraduate/Scholarship) [6471]
Arthur and Gladys Cervenka Scholarships (Undergraduate/Scholarship) [6472]
Chapter 4 - Lawrence A. Wacker Memorial Awards (Undergraduate/Scholarship) [6473]
Chapter - 6 Fairfield County Scholarships (Undergraduate/Scholarship) [6474]
Chapter 17 - St. Louis Scholarships (Undergraduate/Scholarship) [6475]
Chapter 23 - Quad Cities Iowa/Illinois Scholarships (Undergraduate/Scholarship) [6476]
Chapter 31 - Peoria Endowed Scholarships (Undergraduate/Scholarship) [6477]
Chapter 52 - Wichita Scholarships (Graduate, Undergraduate/Scholarship) [6478]
Chapter 56 - Fort Wayne Scholarships (Graduate, Undergraduate/Scholarship) [6479]
Chapter 63 - Portland James E. Morrow Scholarships (Graduate, Undergraduate/Scholarship) [6480]
Chapter 63 - Portland Uncle Bud Smith Scholarships (Graduate, Undergraduate/Scholarship) [6481]
Chapter 67 - Phoenix Scholarships (Undergraduate/Scholarship) [6482]
Chapter 93 - Albuquerque Scholarships (Undergraduate/Scholarship) [6483]
Chapter 198 - Downriver Detroit Scholarships (Graduate, Undergraduate/Scholarship) [6484]
Chapter 311 - Tri City Scholarships (Undergraduate/Scholarship) [6485]
Chapter One - Detroit Founding Chapter Scholarships (Graduate, Undergraduate/Scholarship) [6486]
College and Trade/Technical School Scholarships (Undergraduate/Scholarship) [2898]
Dake Community Manufacturing Scholarships (Undergraduate/Scholarship) [3273]
Chapter 116 - Kalamazoo - Roscoe Douglas Scholarships (Undergraduate/Scholarship) [6487]
FMA Foundation Scholarships (Undergraduate/Scholarship) [3022]
Future Leaders of Manufacturing Scholarships (Graduate, Undergraduate/Scholarship) [6488]
Connie and Robert T. Gunter Scholarships (Undergraduate/Scholarship) [6489]
Gene Haas Foundation Manufacturing Technology Scholarships (Undergraduate/Scholarship) [6490]
Clinton J. Helton Manufacturing Scholarships (Undergraduate/Scholarship) [6491]
HSF/General Motors Scholarship Program (Undergraduate/Scholarship) [3595]
Lucile B. Kaufman Women's Scholarships (Undergraduate/Scholarship) [6493]
E. Wayne Kay Co-op Scholarships (Undergraduate/Scholarship) [6494]
E. Wayne Kay Community College Scholarships (Undergraduate/Scholarship) [6495]
E. Wayne Kay High School Scholarships (Undergraduate/Scholarship) [6496]
Giuliano Mazzetti Scholarships (Undergraduate/Scholarship) [6497]
Clarence and Josephine Myers Scholarships (Graduate, Undergraduate/Scholarship) [6498]
North Central (Region 9) Scholarships (Undergraduate/Scholarship) [6499]
Edward S. Roth Manufacturing Engineering Scholarships (Graduate, Undergraduate/Scholarship) [6500]
Prof. George Schneider, Jr. Manufacturing Technology Education Scholarships (Undergraduate/Scholarship) [6501]
SME Directors Scholarships (Undergraduate/Scholarship) [6502]
SME Education Foundation Family Scholarships (Undergraduate/Scholarship) [6503]
Myrtle and Earl Walker Scholarships (Undergraduate/Scholarship) [6505]
Allen and Loureena Weber Scholarships (Undergraduate/Scholarship) [6506]
Albert E. Wischmeyer Memorial Scholarships (Undergraduate/Scholarship) [6508]
Women of Today's Manufacturing Scholarships (Undergraduate/Scholarship) [2491]

Maritime studies

LaRue A. Ditmore Music Scholarships (Undergraduate/Scholarship) [7481]
Lily H. Gridley Memorial Scholarships (Undergraduate/Scholarship) [7482]
Corporal Joseph Martinez U.S. Army Memorial Scholarships (Undergraduate/Scholarship) [5839]
Ed Monk Scholarships (Professional Development/Scholarship) [2093]
Norm Manly - YMTA Maritime Educational Scholarships (Undergraduate/Scholarship) [7547]
Ethyl and Armin Wiebke Memorial Scholarships (Undergraduate/Scholarship) [7483]
WMA Memorial Scholarships (Undergraduate/Scholarship) [7484]

Marketing and distribution

All-American Vector Marketing Scholarship Program (Undergraduate/Scholarship) [7311]
American Marketing Association-Connecticut Chapter, Anna C. Klune Memorial Scholarships (Graduate/Scholarship) [3415]
Anchor Plastics Scholarships (Graduate, Undergraduate/Scholarship) [5634]
Anheuser-Busch International Scholarships (Graduate, Undergraduate/Scholarship) [5635]
Enterprise Rent-A-Car Scholarships (Graduate, Undergraduate/Scholarship) [5636]
Federated Insurance Scholarships (Graduate, Undergraduate/Scholarship) [5637]
Richard A. Hammill Scholarships Fund (Undergraduate/Scholarship) [708]
William H. Harris Memorial Scholarships (Graduate, Undergraduate/Scholarship) [5638]
Hilb, Rogal and Hobbs Scholarships (Undergraduate/Scholarship) [7328]
HSBC-North America Scholarship Program (Undergraduate/Scholarship) [3592]
HSF/Wal-Mart Stores Inc. Scholarship Program (Graduate, Undergraduate/Scholarship) [3599]
Debbie Khalil Memorial Scholarships (Graduate, Undergraduate/Scholarship) [5639]
The Lagrant Foundation - Graduate Students Scholarships (Graduate/Scholarship) [4104]
The Lagrant Foundation - Undergraduate Students Scholarship (Undergraduate/Scholarship) [4105]
Robert J. Lavidge Nonprofit Marketing Research Scholarships (Professional Development/Scholarship) [709]
Mach 1 Air Services Scholarships (Graduate, Undergraduate/Scholarship) [5640]
Marathon Oil Corporation College Scholarship Program (Graduate, Undergraduate/Scholarship) [3600]
MPower Scholarships (Graduate, Undergraduate/Scholarship) [5641]
New York Women in Communications, Inc. Foundation Scholarships (Graduate, Undergraduate/Scholarship) [5200]
Northwestern Mutual Financial Network Scholarships (Graduate, Undergraduate/Scholarship) [5642]
Office Depot Scholarships (Undergraduate/Scholarship) [3569]
Sanky Perlowin Memorial Scholarships (Undergraduate/Scholarship) [2713]
Phi Sigma Epsilon Innovation Scholarships (Graduate, Undergraduate/Scholarship) [5643]
Phi Sigma Epsilon Past National President Scholarships (Graduate, Undergraduate/Scholarship) [5644]
Sales and Marketing Executives International Scholarships (Graduate, Undergraduate/Scholarship) [5645]
Society of Automotive Analyst Scholarships (Undergraduate/Scholarship) [1562]
Jim Springer Memorial Scholarships (Undergraduate/Scholarship) [2289]
The Standard Scholarships (Graduate, Undergraduate/Scholarship) [5646]
Student Media Group Scholarships (Graduate, Undergraduate/Scholarship) [5647]
Swivel Media Scholarships (Graduate, Undergraduate/Scholarship) [5648]
Thrivent Financial Scholarships (Graduate, Undergraduate/Scholarship) [5649]
TLMI Scholarships - Four-Year Colleges (Undergraduate/Scholarship) [6833]
Valpak Scholarships (Graduate, Undergraduate/Scholarship) [5650]
Valuing Diversity PhD Scholarships (Doctorate/Scholarship) [710]
Vector Marketing Canadian Scholarship Awards (Undergraduate/Scholarship) [7312]
Vector Marketing Scholarships (Graduate, Undergraduate/Scholarship) [5651]
Verizon Scholarship Program (Undergraduate/Scholarship) [3607]
Whan Memorial Scholarships (Graduate, Undergraduate/Scholarship) [5652]
Glenn Wilson Broadcast Journalism Scholarships (Undergraduate/Scholarship) [5529]
Xilinx Scholarships (Graduate, Undergraduate/Scholarship) [5653]

Materials research/science

ASNT Fellowship Awards (Graduate/Fellowship) [1022]
DEPS Graduate Scholarship Program (Graduate/Scholarship) [2715]
Electronics Division Lewis C. Hoffman Scholarships (Undergraduate/Scholarship) [453]
Robert B. Oliver ASNT Scholarships (Undergraduate/Scholarship) [1023]

Mathematics and mathematical sciences

AeA Scholarships (Undergraduate/Scholarship) [6162]
AFCEA Distance Learning/Online Scholarships (Undergraduate/Scholarship) [1236]
AFCEA Fellowships (Doctorate, Graduate/Fellowship) [1237]
AFCEA General John A. Wickham Scholarships (Undergraduate/Scholarship) [1238]
AFCEA Math and Science Teachers Scholarships

(Graduate/Scholarship) [1239]
AFCEA Scholarship for Working Professionals (Graduate/Scholarship) [1240]
African American Network - Carolinas Scholarship Fund (Undergraduate/Scholarship) [3037]
Alaska Aerospace Development Corporation Scholarships (Undergraduate/Scholarship) [4338]
Avista Corporation Minds in Motion Scholarships (Undergraduate/Scholarship) [4163]
AWIS College Scholarships (Undergraduate/Scholarship) [1519]
B&W Y-12 Scholarship Fund (Undergraduate/Scholarship) [2806]
Bill & Nell Biggs Scholarships (Undergraduate/Scholarship) [4348]
Sam L. Booke, Sr. Scholarships (Undergraduate/Scholarship) [7422]
William E. "Buck" Bragunier Scholarships (Undergraduate/Scholarship) [1241]
LT.G. Douglas D. Buchholz Memorial Scholarships (Undergraduate/Scholarship) [1242]
Wes Burton Memorial Scholarships (Undergraduate/Scholarship) [7424]
The Churchill Scholarships (Postgraduate/Scholarship) [2147]
City of Toronto Graduate Scholarships for Women in Mathematics (Graduate/Scholarship) [7216]
Mike Crapo Math and Science Scholarship Fund (Undergraduate/Scholarship) [3644]
Disabled War Veterans Scholarships (Undergraduate/Scholarship) [1244]
Emerging Teacher-Leaders in Elementary School Mathematics Grants for Grades K-5 Teachers (Professional Development/Grant) [4829]
Kevin Ernst Memorial Scholarship Fund (Undergraduate/Scholarship) [3275]
Reuben H. Fleet Memorial Scholarships (Undergraduate/Scholarship) [6189]
Frank Fong Scholarships (Undergraduate/Scholarship) [6423]
The Gates Millennium Scholars (Undergraduate/Scholarship) [3590]
GET Ready for Math and Science Conditional Scholarships (Four Year College, Two Year College, Undergraduate/Scholarship) [7365]
Dr. Virginia Gilbert Memorial Scholarships (Undergraduate/Scholarship) [5828]
Margaret S. Gilbert Scholarship Fund (Undergraduate/Scholarship) [6722]
Golden Key Math Scholarships (Undergraduate/Scholarship) [3255]
Barry M. Goldwater Scholarships (Undergraduate/Scholarship) [7256]
GREAT MINDS Collegiate Scholarship Program (Undergraduate/Scholarship) [236]
Jimmy Guild Memorial Scholarships (Undergraduate/Scholarship) [4182]
Claude B. Hart Memorial Scholarships (Undergraduate/Scholarship) [7440]
Hilb, Rogal and Hobbs Scholarships (Undergraduate/Scholarship) [7328]
The Homeland Security Graduate Fellowships (Graduate/Fellowship) [6985]
The Homeland Security Undergraduate Scholarships (Undergraduate/Scholarship) [6986]
Jane Hood Memorial Fund (Undergraduate/Scholarship) [2959]
Dr. Bill Johnson Scholarships (Undergraduate/Scholarship) [6313]
Lakselaget Foundation Scholarships (Graduate, Undergraduate/Scholarship) [4107]
Lewis-Clark State College Presidential Technical Out-of-State Scholarships (Undergraduate/Scholarship) [4199]
Lockheed Martin IT Scholarships (Undergraduate/Scholarship) [1245]
Carie and George Lyter Scholarship Fund (Undergraduate/Scholarship) [3110]
Lockheed Martin Graduate Scholarships (Graduate/Scholarship) [1246]
Mentoring Travel Grants for Women (Postdoctorate/Scholarship) [1515]
MESBEC Scholarships (Undergraduate/Scholarship) [2067]
National Co-op Scholarship Program (Undergraduate/Scholarship) [4809]
Robert Noyce Scholarship Program (Undergraduate/Scholarship) [5565]
Noyce Scholarships for Secondary Math and Science Education (Undergraduate/Scholarship) [3711]
AFCEA General Emmett Paige Scholarships (Undergraduate/Scholarship) [1247]
Josef Princ Memorial Scholarships (Undergraduate/Scholarship) [5851]
Prospective Secondary Teacher Course Work Scholarships (Postgraduate/Scholarship) [4830]
Joseph Wood Rogers Memorial Scholarships (Undergraduate/Scholarship) [6319]
School In-Service Training Grants for Grades 6-8 Teachers (Graduate/Grant) [4831]
School In-Service Training Grants for Grades 9-12 Teachers (Graduate/Grant) [4832]
School In-Service Training Grants for Grades K-5 Teachers (Graduate/Grant) [4833]
SDF Community College Transfer Scholarships for Math and Science (Undergraduate/Scholarship) [6229]
Julia Viola Simms Science Scholarships (Postgraduate/Scholarship) [1742]
Margaret Svec Scholarships (Undergraduate/Scholarship) [6324]
Anil and Neema Thakrar Family Fund (Undergraduate/Scholarship) [3122]
Travel Grants for Women Researchers (Postdoctorate/Scholarship) [1516]
True North Land Surveying Scholarships (Undergraduate/Scholarship) [5781]
Veterans of Enduring Freedom (Afghanistan) and Iraqi Freedom Scholarships (Undergraduate/Scholarship) [1250]
Marine Corps Sgt. Jeannette L. Winters Memorial Scholarships (Undergraduate/Scholarship) [1251]
Women In Defense HORIZONS Scholarships (Graduate, Undergraduate/Scholarship) [7479]
Woodcock Family Education Scholarship Program (Undergraduate/Scholarship) [196]
Xavier University Departmental Scholarships (Undergraduate/Scholarship) [7538]
Leo Zupin Memorial Scholarship Fund (Undergraduate/Scholarship) [3317]

Mechanics and repairs

Caterpillar Scholarships in Diesel Mechanics (Undergraduate/Scholarship) [4168]
ISOPE Offshore Mechanics Scholarships for Outstanding Students (Graduate/Scholarship) [3909]

Media arts

AAAS Mass Media Science and Engineering Fellowships (Graduate, Postgraduate, Undergraduate/Fellowship) [316]
Association for Women in Sports Media Internship Program (Graduate, Undergraduate/Internship) [1521]
UFVA Carole Fielding Student Grants (Graduate, Undergraduate/Grant) [7091]
HSF/Nissan Community College Transfer Scholarship Program (Undergraduate/Scholarship) [3598]
Harriet Irsay Scholarships (Graduate, Undergraduate/Scholarship) [674]
McNamara Family Creative Arts Project Grants (Graduate, Undergraduate/Grant) [3601]
New York Women in Communications, Inc. Foundation Scholarships (Graduate, Undergraduate/Scholarship) [5200]
Barbara Sanchez Scholarships (Undergraduate/Scholarship) [6443]
StraightForward Media's Media and Communications Scholarships (Undergraduate/Scholarship) [6801]
Sandy Ulm Scholarships (Undergraduate/Scholarship) [2993]

Medical assisting

Northampton County Medical Society Alliance Scholarships (Undergraduate/Scholarship) [5261]
Maxine Williams Scholarships (Postdoctorate/Scholarship) [368]

Medical laboratory technology

Dade Behring Student Scholarship Awards (Postgraduate/Scholarship) [2040]
The Joe E. Covington Award for Research on Bar Admissions Testing (Doctorate/Award/Prize) [4817]

Medical research (See also: Biomedical research)

AHNS-ACS Career Development Awards (Professional Development/Grant) [599]
AHNS Pilot Research Grants (Professional Development/Grant) [600]
AHNS Young Investigator Awards (Professional Development/Grant) [601]
American Liver Foundation Liver Scholar Awards (Doctorate/Award/Prize) [703]
American Liver Foundation Special Research Initiatives (Doctorate/Award/Prize) [704]
Ballantyne Resident Research Grants (Professional Development/Grant) [602]
CAS/GE Healthcare Canada Inc. Research Awards (Professional Development/Award/Prize) [1914]
Cystic Fibrosis Cholestatic Liver Disease Liver Scholarships (Doctorate/Award/Prize) [705]
Deafness Research Foundation Research Grants (Doctorate/Grant) [2625]
Individual-Investigator Grants Program (Postdoctorate/Grant) [5011]
ITNS Research Grants (Professional Development/Grant) [3918]
National Osteoporosis Foundation Research Grants (Doctorate, Graduate/Grant) [5004]
NFID Advanced Vaccinology Course Travel Grants (Postdoctorate/Grant) [4904]
Novo Nordisk Canada-CAS Research Awards (Professional Development/Award/Prize) [1917]
Postdoctoral Research Fellowships (Doctorate/Award/Prize) [706]
Damon Runyon Cancer Research Foundation Fellowships (Postdoctorate/Fellowship) [6081]
Damon Runyon Clinical Investigator Awards (Postdoctorate/Fellowship) [6082]
Damon Runyon-Rachleff Innovation Awards (Postdoctorate/Fellowship) [6083]
SSF Research Grants (Doctorate/Grant) [6410]
SSF Student Fellowships (Graduate, Undergraduate/Fellowship) [6411]
Surgeon Scientist Career Development Awards (Professional Development/Grant) [603]
Tarrson Regeneration Scholarships (Postdoctorate/Scholarship) [289]
E.D. Thomas Post Doctoral Fellowships (Postdoctorate/Fellowship) [3145]

Medical technology

Chinese American Medical Society Summer Research Outreach Programs (Undergraduate/Grant) [2135]
Margaret Dowell-Gravatt, M.D. Scholarship (Undergraduate/Scholarship) [1625]
Illinois Student Assistance Commission Medical Student Scholarships (Graduate/Scholarship) [3665]
Esther Lim Memorial Scholarships (Undergraduate/Scholarship) [2136]
Ruth Liu Memorial Scholarships (Undergraduate/Scholarship) [2137]
SPSmedical CS Scholarships (Other/Scholarship) [3802]

Medicine (See also: specific areas of study, e.g. Oncology; specific diseases, e.g. Diabetes)

AAUW Legal Advocacy Fund Selected Professions Fellowships (Doctorate, Graduate/Fellowship) [7]
Dr. Anderson Abbott Awards (Undergraduate/Scholarship) [7208]

Accenture American Indian Scholarship Program (Graduate, Undergraduate/Scholarship) [640]
Advanced Cardiovascular Surgery Fellowships (Graduate, Postdoctorate/Fellowship) [415]
AFPPA Student Scholarships (Undergraduate/Scholarship) [1412]
AGBU Scholarships (Graduate/Loan) [1255]
Allegheny County Medical Society (ACMS) Medical Student Scholarship (Undergraduate/Scholarship) [3134]
Alliance Medical Education Scholarship Fund (AMES) (Undergraduate/Scholarship) [3135]
American Association for Thoracic Surgery Clinical Fellowships (Graduate/Fellowship) [416]
APDA Summer Fellowships (Doctorate/Fellowship) [759]
Armenian American Medical Association Scholarships (Undergraduate/Scholarship) [1267]
ARS Undergraduate Scholarships (Four Year College, Two Year College, Undergraduate/Scholarship) [1259]
ASHA Scholarships (Graduate, Undergraduate/Scholarship) [915]
ASHA Student Research Grants (Graduate, Undergraduate/Scholarship) [916]
Dr. Noyes L. Avery, Jr. & Ann E. Avery Scholarships (Undergraduate/Scholarship) [3320]
Benign Essential Blepharospasm Research Foundation Research Grant (Postdoctorate/Grant) [1623]
Linn Benton Scholarships (Undergraduate/Scholarship) [5398]
Eleanor McWilliams Burke Fund (Undergraduate/Scholarship) [2945]
Joseph R. Calder, Jr., MD Scholarship Fund (Undergraduate/Scholarship) [2946]
California Community Service Scholarships (Undergraduate/Scholarship) [4985]
California Community Service Scholarships - Bay Area (Undergraduate/Scholarship) [4986]
Career Mobility Scholarship Awards (Doctorate, Undergraduate/Scholarship) [16]
CCFA Career Development Awards (Doctorate, Graduate/Grant) [2559]
CCFA Research Fellowship Awards (Doctorate, Graduate/Fellowship) [2560]
CCFA Student Research Fellowship Awards (Graduate, Undergraduate/Grant) [2561]
CDC Foundation Scholarships (Undergraduate/Scholarship) [2075]
Edward D. Churchill Research Scholarships (Professional Development/Scholarship) [417]
Clinical Laboratory Management Association High School Senior Scholarships (High School/Scholarship) [2247]
Clinical Laboratory Management Association Undergraduate Scholarships (Undergraduate/Scholarship) [2248]
Dr. Mark Cohen Scholarship (Undergraduate/Scholarship) [3557]
Crohn's and Colitis Foundation of America Senior Research Awards (Doctorate, Graduate/Grant) [2562]
DAAD Study Scholarship Awards (Graduate/Scholarship) [3223]
D&A Florida Scholarships (Undergraduate/Scholarship) [6648]
Margaret Dowell-Gravatt, M.D. Scholarship (Undergraduate/Scholarship) [1625]
Family and Children's Services of Lebanon County Fund (Undergraduate/Scholarship) [3098]
Dorris W. Frey Memorial Scholarships (Undergraduate/Scholarship) [6654]
William R. Goldfarb Memorial Scholarships (Undergraduate/Scholarship) [834]
Scott A. Gunder, MD, DCMS Presidential Scholarships (Undergraduate/Scholarship) [3136]
Ryan Hill Thoracoesophageal Fellowships (Graduate/Fellowship) [418]
Dr. James L. Hutchinson and Evelyn Ribbs Hutchinson Medical School Scholarship Fund (Undergraduate/Scholarship) [6391]
Jewish Federation Academic Scholarships (Graduate, Undergraduate/Scholarship) [4029]
Magoichi & Shizuko Kato Memorial Scholarships (Graduate/Scholarship) [4018]
Jason Lang Scholarship (Undergraduate/Scholarship) [163]
Rebecca Lee, M.D. Scholarships (Undergraduate/Scholarship) [1373]
S. Evelyn Lewis Memorial Scholarships in Medical Health Sciences (Graduate, Undergraduate/Scholarship) [7557]
Lycoming County Medical Society (LCMS) Scholarships (Undergraduate/Scholarship) [3137]
Irene and Daisy MacGregor Memorial Scholarships (Graduate/Scholarship) [3477]
Dr. Edward May Magruder Medical Scholarships (Other/Scholarship) [458]
Dr. Frank and Florence Marino Scholarships (Undergraduate/Scholarship) [3480]
Massachusetts General Hospital Summer Scholars Program (Undergraduate/Fellowship) [419]
Mission Bay Hospital Auxiliary Scholarships (Undergraduate/Scholarship) [6208]
Montgomery County Medical Society (MCMS) Scholarships (Undergraduate/Scholarship) [3138]
National Ataxia Foundation Research Fellowships (Postdoctorate/Fellowship) [4754]
National Ataxia Foundation Research Grants (Postdoctorate/Fellowship) [4755]
National Medical Fellowships Need-Based Scholarships (Undergraduate/Scholarship) [4989]
Northern Alberta Development Council Bursary for Medical Students (Undergraduate/Award/Prize) [172]
Sylvia Parkinson Scholarships (Undergraduate/Scholarship) [3487]
Providence Alaska Medical Center Auxiliary Scholarships (Undergraduate/Scholarship) [7035]
Howard B. Rickard Scholarships (Undergraduate/Scholarship) [4884]
Alice W. Rooke Scholarships (Undergraduate/Scholarship) [3494]
RSDSA Research Grants (Postdoctorate, Professional Development/Grant) [6014]
Scholarships for Emigres in the Health Sciences (Undergraduate/Scholarship) [4025]
Jeptha Wade Schureman Scholarship Program (Undergraduate/Scholarship) [2521]
G. Helner Sell Research and Training Grants (Professional Development/Grant) [1110]
John M. and Mary A. Shanley Memorial Scholarships (Undergraduate/Scholarship) [6673]
Myrtle Siegfried, MD and Michael Vigilante, MD Scholarships (Undergraduate/Scholarship) [3139]
Julia Viola Simms Science Scholarships (Postgraduate/Scholarship) [1742]
Dr. William E. & Norma Sprague Scholarships (Undergraduate/Scholarship) [3350]
Summer Intern Scholarships in Cardiothoracic Surgery (Undergraduate/Scholarship) [420]
Dr. Peter A. Theodos Memorial Graduate Scholarships (Graduate/Scholarship) [3535]
Thompson Scholarship for Women in Safety (Graduate/Scholarship) [1072]
Sam Tughan Scholarships (Undergraduate/Scholarship) [2031]
The Sibyl Jennings Vorheis Memorial Scholarship Program (Undergraduate/Scholarship) [3081]
Worcester District Medical Society Scholarship Fund (Undergraduate/Scholarship) [7512]

Medicine, Cardiology

APACVS Scholarships (Professional Development/Scholarship) [1479]
Cardiac Sonographer Education Development Grants (Professional Development, Undergraduate/Grant) [950]
DeBakey International Society Fellowship Awards (Professional Development/Award/Prize) [2629]

Medicine, Cerebrovascular

National Stroke Association Research Fellowships in Cerebrovascular Disease (Doctorate/Fellowship) [5098]

Medicine, Chiropractic

Beatrice K. Blair Scholarships (Undergraduate/Scholarship) [1764]
F. Maynard Lipe Scholarship Award (Postdoctorate/Award/Prize) [464]

Medicine, Geriatric

APDA Postdoctoral Fellowships (Professional Development/Fellowship) [757]
Deets-Laine Geriatric NP Student Scholarships (Doctorate, Graduate/Scholarship) [267]
Pharmacy Faculty Fellowships in Geriatric Pharmacy/Geriatric Pharmaceutical Science (Postdoctorate/Fellowship) [584]

Medicine, Gynecological and obstetrical

SMFM/AAOGF Scholarship Award (Graduate/Scholarship) [6512]

Medicine, Internal

Epilepsy Foundation Research and Training Fellowships for Clinicians (Doctorate, Professional Development/Grant) [2872]

Medicine, Nuclear

Paul Cole Scholarships (Undergraduate/Scholarship) [6522]

Medicine, Orthopedic

AOA Research Fellowships (Doctorate/Fellowship) [33]
AOA Research Grants (Graduate/Grant) [34]
AOFAS Research Grants Program (Graduate/Grant) [746]
Orthopedic Foot and Ankle Fellowships (Graduate/Fellowship) [747]
OTA Research Grants (Graduate/Grant) [5417]

Medicine, Osteopathic

AACOM Scholar in Residence Program (Graduate, Undergraduate/Scholarship) [339]
William G. Anderson, DO, Minority Scholarship (Undergraduate/Scholarship) [749]
Humanism in Medicine Scholarships (Undergraduate/Scholarship) [6811]
Illinois Student Assistance Commission Medical Student Scholarships (Graduate/Scholarship) [3665]
Russell C. McCaughan, DO, Education Scholarships (Undergraduate/Scholarship) [750]
NAAMA Scholarships (Undergraduate/Scholarship) [4639]
New Jersey Association of Osteopathic Physicians and Surgeons Scholarships (Undergraduate/Scholarship) [5175]
Procter and Gamble Complex PE Scholars Grant (Undergraduate/Award/Prize) [751]
Savvy Student Traveler Grant Program (Undergraduate/Grant) [752]
Scleroderma Foundation Established Investigator Grants (Doctorate/Grant) [6279]
Scleroderma Foundation New Investigator Grants (Doctorate/Grant) [6280]
Student Osteopathic Medical Student Fellowships and Research (Undergraduate/Fellowship) [6812]
Marvin H. and Kathleen G. Teget Leadership Scholarships (Undergraduate/Scholarship) [6813]
Welch Scholars Grants (Undergraduate/Grant) [753]

Medicine, Pediatric

APSNA Educational Scholarships (Professional Development/Scholarship) [763]
ASHA Scholarships (Graduate, Undergraduate/Scholarship) [915]
ASHA Student Research Grants (Graduate, Undergraduate/Scholarship) [916]
Daland Fellowships in Clinical Investigation (Doctorate/Fellowship) [767]
John W. Duckett Jr., AFUD Pediatric Research Scholarships (Undergraduate/Scholarship) [6538]
Gerber Fellowships in Pediatric Nutrition (Undergraduate/Fellowship) [4987]

Lizette Peterson Homer Injury Prevention Grant Awards *(Professional Development, Undergraduate/Grant)* [6532]
Routh Student Research Grants *(Undergraduate/Grant)* [6533]
Society for Pediatric Urology Research Grant Program *(Undergraduate/Grant)* [6539]

Medicine, Sports

Evans Scholarships *(Undergraduate/Scholarship)* [4554]
Minnesota State Archery Association Scholarship Program *(Undergraduate/Scholarship)* [4556]
MSPT Sports Medicine Scholarships *(Undergraduate/Scholarship)* [5842]
Swede Swanson Memorial Scholarships *(Undergraduate/Scholarship)* [5162]

Medieval studies

Fellowships in the Humanities and Social Sciences in Turkey *(Postdoctorate/Fellowship)* [894]

Mental health

Anxiety Disorders Association of America Career Development Travel Awards *(Professional Development/Award/Prize)* [1184]
Anxiety Disorders Association of America Junior Faculty Research Grants *(Professional Development/Grant)* [1185]
ASA Minority Fellowships Program *(Doctorate, Master's/Fellowship)* [1094]
Rosalynn Carter Fellowships *(Professional Development/Fellowship)* [4820]
CVS/All Kids Can Scholars Program *(Undergraduate/Scholarship)* [1540]
Derivative Duo Scholarships *(Undergraduate/Scholarship)* [5765]
Family and Children's Services of Lebanon County Fund *(Undergraduate/Scholarship)* [3098]
Don Renschler Scholarships *(Graduate/Scholarship)* [5775]
Scholarships for Lutheran College Students *(Undergraduate/Scholarship)* [1687]
Scholarships for Lutheran Nursing Students *(Undergraduate/Scholarship)* [1688]

Metallurgy

AIST Baltimore Chapter Scholarships *(Undergraduate/Scholarship)* [1438]
AIST Detroit Chapter Scholarships *(Undergraduate/Scholarship)* [1439]
AIST Ronald E. Lincoln Memorial Scholarships *(Undergraduate/Scholarship)* [1441]
AIST William E. Schwabe Memorial Scholarships *(Undergraduate/Scholarship)* [1443]
AIST Willy Korf Memorial Fund *(Undergraduate/Scholarship)* [1444]
Edward J. Dulis Scholarships *(Undergraduate/Scholarship)* [4397]
AIST Benjamin F. Fairless Scholarships (AIME) *(Undergraduate/Scholarship)* [1445]
Dayton E. Finnigan Scholarship *(Undergraduate/Scholarship)* [3374]
Globe-Trotters Chapter Scholarships *(Undergraduate/Scholarship)* [1447]
Nicholas J. Grant Scholarships *(Undergraduate/Scholarship)* [4398]
John M. Haniak Scholarships *(Undergraduate/Scholarship)* [4399]
Materials Information Society National Merit Scholarships *(Undergraduate/Scholarship)* [4400]
MJSA Educational Foundation Jewelry Scholarships *(Undergraduate/Scholarship)* [6039]
Northeastern Ohio Chapter Scholarships - Alfred B. Glossbrenner and John Klusch Scholarships *(Undergraduate/Scholarship)* [1454]
Ohio Valley Chapter Scholarships *(Undergraduate/Scholarship)* [1455]
William Park Woodside Founder's Scholarships *(Undergraduate/Scholarship)* [4401]
George A. Roberts Scholarships *(Undergraduate/Scholarship)* [4402]
SMACNA College of Fellows Scholarships *(Undergraduate/Scholarship)* [6300]
SME Coal and Energy Division Scholarships *(Undergraduate/Scholarship)* [6516]
SME Environmental Division Scholarships *(Undergraduate/Scholarship)* [6517]
Lucille and Charles A. Wert Scholarships *(Undergraduate/Scholarship)* [4403]

Microbiology (See also: Biology)

American Society for Microbiology International Fellowships for Africa *(Postdoctorate/Fellowship)* [1001]
American Society for Microbiology International Fellowships for Asia *(Postdoctorate/Fellowship)* [1002]
ASM/CCID Program in Infectious Disease and Public Health Microbiology *(Postdoctorate/Fellowship)* [1005]
Margaret Dowell-Gravatt, M.D. Scholarship *(Undergraduate/Scholarship)* [1625]
Microbiology Undergraduate Research Fellowships *(Undergraduate/Fellowship)* [1007]
UAA Kris Knudson Memorial Scholarships *(Graduate, Undergraduate/Scholarship)* [7062]
Selma A. Waksman Endowed Scholarships in Microbial Diversity *(Undergraduate/Scholarship)* [4304]
Robert D. Watkins Graduate Research Fellowships *(Postdoctorate/Fellowship)* [1009]

Midwifery

ACNM Foundation, Inc. Fellowship for Graduate Education *(Doctorate, Postdoctorate/Fellowship)* [469]
Basic Midwifery Student Scholarship Program *(Undergraduate/Scholarship)* [470]
Hazel Corbin/Childbirth Connection Grant for Evidence-based Midwifery Care *(Professional Development/Award/Prize)* [471]
Washington Higher Education Coordinating Board Health Professional Scholarships *(Undergraduate/Scholarship)* [7368]

Military science and education

Sergeant Douglas and Charlotte DeHorse Scholarships *(Undergraduate/Scholarship)* [2066]
Burton L. Gerber Scholarships *(Graduate, Undergraduate/Scholarship)* [1657]
NMIA Scholarship Program *(Undergraduate/Scholarship)* [4991]
Reserve Officers Training Corps (ROTC) Scholarships *(Undergraduate/Scholarship)* [7267]
Colonel Nate Smith Memorial Scholarships *(Graduate, Undergraduate/Scholarship)* [4437]
Xavier University ROTC Scholarships - Army ROTC *(Undergraduate/Scholarship)* [7542]

Mineralogy

EMLF Law Student Scholarships *(Undergraduate/Scholarship)* [2855]
Mineralogical Association of Canada Scholarships *(Postgraduate/Scholarship)* [4539]
SME Coal and Energy Division Scholarships *(Undergraduate/Scholarship)* [6516]
SME Environmental Division Scholarships *(Undergraduate/Scholarship)* [6517]

Mining (See also: Engineering, Mining and Mineral)

American Society of Mining and Reclamation Memorial Scholarships *(Undergraduate/Scholarship)* [1013]
J.P. Bickell Mining Scholarships *(Undergraduate/Scholarship)* [7211]
National Geophysics Scholarships *(Postgraduate/Scholarship)* [7488]
National Scholarships *(Postgraduate/Scholarship)* [7489]
SME Coal and Energy Division Scholarships *(Undergraduate/Scholarship)* [6516]
SME Environmental Division Scholarships *(Undergraduate/Scholarship)* [6517]
Wood Bursary Awards *(Postgraduate/Award/Prize)* [7490]

Modern languages

Fellowships in the Humanities and Social Sciences in Turkey *(Postdoctorate/Fellowship)* [894]
Xavier University Departmental Scholarships *(Undergraduate/Scholarship)* [7538]

Mortuary science (See also: Funeral services)

ABFSE National Scholarship Program *(Undergraduate/Scholarship)* [441]
Bishop State Community College Scholarships *(Undergraduate/Scholarship)* [4907]
Joseph E. Hagan Memorial Scholarships *(Undergraduate/Scholarship)* [3150]
Key Memories Scholarships *(Undergraduate/Scholarship)* [3151]
NFDA Professional Women's Conference Scholarships *(Undergraduate/Scholarship)* [3152]

Motherhood

Childbirth Educator Program Scholarships *(Other/Scholarship)* [4114]

Muscular dystrophy

Dystonia Medical Research Foundation Fellowships *(Postdoctorate/Fellowship)* [2800]
MDA Development Grants *(Doctorate/Grant)* [4593]
MDA Research Grants *(Doctorate/Grant)* [4594]

Museum science

CFI Sid Solow Scholarships *(Graduate/Scholarship)* [1467]
Rick Chace Foundation Scholarships *(Graduate/Scholarship)* [1468]
Kodak Fellowships in Film Preservation *(Graduate/Scholarship)* [1469]
Betsy B. and Garold A. Leach Scholarship for Museum Studies *(Undergraduate/Scholarship)* [2693]
Lee Kimche McGrath Worldwide Fellowships *(Professional Development/Fellowship)* [1490]
Mary Pickford Scholarships *(Graduate/Scholarship)* [1470]
Sony Pictures Scholarships *(Graduate/Scholarship)* [1471]
United States Capitol Historical Society Fellowships *(Graduate/Fellowship)* [6983]
Universal Studios Preservation Scholarships *(Graduate/Scholarship)* [1472]

Music

Ed Adams Memorial Scholarships *(Professional Development/Scholarship)* [6030]
Alaska Community Foundation Sven E. & Lorraine Eriksson Scholarships *(Undergraduate/Scholarship)* [7029]
Margaret M. Alkek Scholarship *(Undergraduate/Scholarship)* [2637]
Martin K. Alsup Scholarships *(Undergraduate/Scholarship)* [5463]
American Guild of Organists, Canton Chapter Charitable Fund *(Undergraduate/Scholarship)* [6708]
American Turkish Society Arif Mardin Music Fellowships *(Professional Development/Fellowship)* [6936]
The Anderson Group Summer Institute Scholarships *(Other/Scholarship)* [1180]
AOSA Research Grants *(All/Grant)* [739]
AOSA Research Partnership Grants *(All/Grant)* [740]
Louis Armstrong Scholarships *(High School/Scholarship)* [939]
Artistic Scholarship Awards *(Undergraduate/Scholarship)* [1598]
Bernt Balchen, Jr. Hardingfele Scholarships *(All, Professional Development/Scholarship)* [3399]

Barta-Lehman Musical Scholarships *(Undergraduate/Scholarship)* [6170]
Norbert J. Beihoff Scholarships *(Undergraduate/Scholarship)* [2238]
Belmont University Commercial Music Scholarships *(Undergraduate/Scholarship)* [2406]
Charlotte V. Bergen Scholarships *(Undergraduate/Scholarship)* [940]
Carol June Bradley Awards *(All/Grant)* [4596]
Cecil E. Burney Scholarships *(High School, Undergraduate/Scholarship)* [2267]
Jeffrey Carollo Music Scholarships *(Undergraduate/Scholarship)* [5177]
Llewellyn L. Cayvan String Instrument Scholarships *(Undergraduate/Scholarship)* [3323]
Cherry Lane Foundation/Music Alive! Scholarships *(Undergraduate/Scholarship)* [941]
Ruth M. Cogan Scholarship Fund *(Undergraduate/Scholarship)* [6713]
Dennis Coleman Choral Conducting Scholarships *(Undergraduate/Scholarship)* [5762]
Contemporary Club Scholarships *(Undergraduate/Scholarship)* [5927]
Bill Cormack Scholarships *(Undergraduate/Scholarship)* [6862]
David Rose Scholarships *(Undergraduate/Scholarship)* [942]
Fran Morgenstern Davis Scholarships *(Undergraduate/Scholarship)* [943]
John Denver Music Scholarships *(Undergraduate/Scholarship)* [944]
Louis Dreyfus Warner-Chappell City College Scholarships *(Undergraduate/Scholarship)* [945]
Edgecliff McAuley Music Scholarships *(Undergraduate/Scholarship)* [7528]
Dena Epstein Award for Archival and Library Research in American Music *(All/Grant)* [4597]
Ahmet Ertegun Memorial Scholarships *(Graduate, Undergraduate/Scholarship)* [6937]
Adrienne Zoe Fedok Art and Music Scholarships *(Undergraduate/Scholarship)* [3099]
Fine Arts and Music Scholarships *(Undergraduate/Scholarship)* [2420]
Charles and Margaret Foster Scholarships *(Undergraduate/Scholarship)* [6653]
Kevin Freeman Travel Grants *(Graduate, Professional Development/Grant)* [4598]
William R. Gard Memorial Scholarships *(Undergraduate/Scholarship)* [4608]
Garikian Scholarship Fund *(Undergraduate/Scholarship)* [1279]
Walter Gerboth Awards *(All/Grant)* [4599]
Velma Shotwell Griffin Memorial Scholarship Fund *(Undergraduate/Scholarship)* [6724]
Henry and Janet Guareillo Scholarship Fund *(Undergraduate/Scholarship)* [3103]
Guy D. & Mary Edith Halladay Music Scholarships *(Graduate, Undergraduate/Scholarship)* [3333]
Hench Post-Dissertation Fellowships *(Postdoctorate/Fellowship)* [303]
Indiana State Alumni Association Creative and Performing Arts Award *(Undergraduate/Scholarship)* [3701]
Ruth K. Jacobs Memorial Scholarship Fund *(Graduate, Undergraduate/Scholarship)* [2141]
Alvin H. Johnson AMS Dissertation Fellowships *(Undergraduate/Fellowship)* [720]
Steve Kaplan TV and Film Studies Scholarships *(Professional Development/Scholarship)* [946]
Douglas Gray Kinel Scholarships *(Undergraduate/Scholarship)* [7444]
Leiber and Stoller Music Scholarships *(Undergraduate/Scholarship)* [947]
Harold A. Levin Scholarships *(Undergraduate/Scholarship)* [2240]
Paul Mansur Scholarships *(Undergraduate/Scholarship)* [3869]
Howard Mayer Brown Fellowships *(Postdoctorate/Fellowship)* [721]
Christopher Mesi Music Scholarships *(Undergraduate/Scholarship)* [2064]
Glenn Miller Scholarships *(Undergraduate/Scholarship)* [4535]
Muddy Waters Scholarships *(Undergraduate/Scholarship)* [1768]
Albert and Alice Nacinovich Music Scholarships *(Undergraduate/Scholarship)* [2970]
National Association of Pastoral Musicians Academic Scholarships *(Graduate, Undergraduate/Scholarship)* [4726]
Northwest-Shoals Community College Fine Arts Scholarships - Music *(Undergraduate/Scholarship)* [5295]
NPM Program Scholarships *(Undergraduate/Scholarship)* [4727]
Orange County Centennial Arts Scholarships *(Undergraduate/Scholarship)* [5363]
Rudy Perez Songwriting Scholarships *(Undergraduate/Scholarship)* [948]
William R. Pfalzgraf Scholarships *(Undergraduate/Scholarship)* [5509]
Presbyterian Association of Musicians Scholarships *(Other/Scholarship)* [5744]
Mark A. Reid Memorial Scholarship Grant *(Undergraduate/Scholarship)* [2481]
S. Byrl Ross Memorial Scholarship Fund *(Undergraduate/Scholarship)* [5516]
Curtis M. Saulsbury Scholarship Fund *(Undergraduate/Scholarship)* [2395]
Shields-Gillespie Scholarships *(All/Scholarship)* [742]
Robert W. and Bernice Ingalls Staton Scholarships *(Undergraduate/Scholarship)* [7202]
Joseph L. and Vivian E. Steele Music Scholarship Fund *(Undergraduate/Scholarship)* [3121]
Study Scholarships for Artists or Musicians *(Graduate/Scholarship)* [3230]
Texas Music Educators Association Past-Presidents Memorial Scholarships *(Undergraduate/Scholarship)* [6863]
Barry Tuckwell Scholarships *(All/Scholarship)* [3870]
UAA Brown Schoenheit Memorial Scholarships *(Undergraduate/Scholarship)* [7045]
UAA Edward Rollin Clinton Memorial for Music *(Undergraduate/Scholarship)* [7050]
University of Wisconsin-Madison Music Scholarships *(Undergraduate/Scholarship)* [7278]
Philip F. Vineberg Travelling Fellowship in the Humanities *(Graduate/Scholarship)* [4432]
Violin Society of America Scholarships *(Undergraduate/Scholarship)* [7326]
Willa Beach-Porter Music Scholarships *(Undergraduate/Scholarship)* [2097]
Gary S. Wilmer RAMI Music Scholarship *(Undergraduate/Scholarship)* [2490]
Wisconsin-Madison Music Clinic Scholarships *(Undergraduate/Scholarship)* [7286]
Wendy Y. Wolfson Memorial Scholarship Fund *(Undergraduate/Scholarship)* [2982]
John W. Work III Memorial Foundation Scholarships *(Undergraduate/Scholarship)* [2453]
Marusia Yaworska Entrance Scholarships *(Undergraduate/Scholarship)* [7361]

Music, Classical

Lou Drane Fund *(Undergraduate/Scholarship)* [3095]

Music, Jazz

Hartford Jazz Society Scholarships *(Undergraduate/Scholarship)* [3461]

Music, Piano

Nellie Love Butcher Scholarships *(Undergraduate/Scholarship)* [3428]
Chopin Foundation of the United States Scholarships *(Undergraduate/Scholarship)* [2139]

Music therapy

Hartford Foundation for Public Giving Occupational Therapy Scholarships *(Undergraduate/Scholarship)* [3459]

Music, Vocal

John D. Anello Sr. and Albert A. Silverman Memorial Scholarships *(Undergraduate/Scholarship)* [2237]
Elizabeth W. Boyce Scholarships *(Undergraduate/Scholarship)* [2239]
Institutional Grants: Educational and Research Projects *(All/Grant)* [7336]

Myasthenia Gravis

MGFA Student Fellowships *(Undergraduate/Fellowship)* [4601]
Myasthenia Gravis Foundation of America Nursing Fellowships *(Undergraduate/Fellowship)* [4602]
Myasthenia Gravis Foundation of America Post-Doctoral Fellowships *(Postdoctorate/Fellowship)* [4603]

National security

Rieser Fellowships *(Undergraduate/Fellowship)* [1804]
Women In Defense HORIZONS Scholarships *(Graduate, Undergraduate/Scholarship)* [7479]

Native American studies

Phillips Fund Grant for Native American Research *(Graduate/Grant)* [771]
Allogan Slagle Memorial Scholarships *(Graduate/Scholarship)* [1357]
Morris K. Udall Scholarships *(Undergraduate/Scholarship)* [6945]
Adolph Van Pelt Special Fund for Indians Scholarships *(Undergraduate/Scholarship)* [1358]

Natural resources

Avista Corporation Minds in Motion Scholarships *(Undergraduate/Scholarship)* [4163]
EMLF Law Student Scholarships *(Undergraduate/Scholarship)* [2855]
Environment, Natural Resource and Energy (ENRE) Division Fellowships *(Graduate/Scholarship)* [779]
Grand Haven Offshore Challenge Scholarships Fund *(Undergraduate/Scholarship)* [3283]
Great Lakes Commission Sea Grant Fellowships *(Graduate/Scholarship)* [3364]
Randall Matthis for Environmental Studies Scholarships *(Graduate, Undergraduate/Scholarship)* [1226]
Ben Meadows Natural Resource Scholarships - Academic Achievement Scholarships *(Undergraduate/Scholarship)* [1620]
Ben Meadows Natural Resource Scholarships - Leadership Scholarships *(Undergraduate/Scholarship)* [1621]
Guy A. Woodings Scholarships *(Undergraduate/Scholarship)* [4390]

Natural sciences

Lorraine Allison Scholarships *(Postgraduate/Scholarship)* [1199]
Margaret S. Gilbert Scholarship Fund *(Undergraduate/Scholarship)* [6722]
NSERC Canada Graduate Scholarships *(Graduate, Postdoctorate/Scholarship)* [6434]
NSERC Postgraduate Scholarships *(Graduate, Postdoctorate/Scholarship)* [6435]
Laura Ann Peck Memorial Endowed Scholarships *(Undergraduate/Scholarship)* [4211]
Howard B. Rickard Scholarships *(Undergraduate/Scholarship)* [4884]
Susan P. Schroeder Memorial Scholarships *(Undergraduate/Scholarship)* [4215]

Near Eastern studies

Garikian Scholarship Fund *(Undergraduate/Scholarship)* [1279]

Neurology

AANS Medical Student Summer Research Fellowships (MSSRF) *(Undergraduate/Fellowship)* [370]
ACS/NREF-AANS Faculty Career Development Award *(Professional Development/Award/Prize)* [371]
Basic Research Fellowships *(Postdoctorate/Fellowship)* [443]

Clinical Research Training Fellowships (Other/Fellowship) [260]
George C. Cotzias, MD Memorial Fellowships (Professional Development/Fellowship) [760]
Daland Fellowships in Clinical Investigation (Doctorate/Fellowship) [767]
Roger C. Duvoisin, MD Research Grants (Professional Development/Grant) [761]
Epilepsy Foundation Research and Training Fellowships for Clinicians (Doctorate, Professional Development/Grant) [2872]
Medical Student Summer Research Scholarships (Undergraduate/Scholarship) [261]
William P. Van Wagenen Fellowships (Undergraduate/Fellowship) [372]

Neuroscience

ASET Educational Seminars, Courses and Program Scholarships (All, Professional Development/Scholarship) [953]
Certified Neuroscience Registered Nurse (CNRN) Recertification Grants Program (Professional Development/Grant) [374]
Epilepsy Foundation Post-doctoral Research Fellowships (Postdoctorate, Professional Development/Grant) [2869]
Epilepsy Foundation Pre-doctoral Research Training Fellowships (Graduate/Grant) [2870]
Integra Foundation NNF Research Grants Award (Professional Development/Grant) [375]
Klingenstein Fellowships in the Neurosciences (Doctorate, Professional Development/Fellowship) [4076]
NNF Scholarships Program (Graduate, Undergraduate/Scholarship) [376]

Nuclear science

American Nuclear Society Nevada Section Scholarships (Undergraduate/Scholarship) [5801]
American Nuclear Society Undergraduates Scholarships (Undergraduate/Scholarship) [724]

Nursing

AACN Scholarships (Undergraduate/Scholarship) [320]
AACN Excellence in Academics Nursing Scholarships (Undergraduate/Scholarship) [334]
AACN Minority Nurse Faculty Scholarships (Graduate/Scholarship) [335]
Mandel & Lauretta Abrahamer Scholarships (Undergraduate/Scholarship) [6767]
ACNP Nurse Practitioner Student Scholarship Awards (Undergraduate/Scholarship) [473]
AfterCollege/AACN Nursing Scholarships (Graduate, Undergraduate/Scholarship) [336]
American Association of Critical-Care Nurses BSN Scholarships (Undergraduate/Scholarship) [341]
American Association of Critical-Care Nurses Graduate Scholarships (Doctorate, Graduate/Scholarship) [342]
American Quarter Horse Foundation Scholarships (Undergraduate/Scholarship) [811]
ANCA Scholarships (Graduate, Undergraduate/Scholarship) [1301]
Roy Anderson Memorial Scholarships (Graduate, Undergraduate/Scholarship) [2308]
AORN Foundation Scholarship Program (Undergraduate/Scholarship) [1477]
APS/ASU Scholarships (Undergraduate/Scholarship) [5697]
APSNA Educational Scholarships (Professional Development/Scholarship) [763]
Arizona Nurses Foundation Scholarships (Graduate, Undergraduate/Scholarship) [1221]
Arkansas Nursing Foundation - Dorothea Funk Scholarships (Professional Development/Scholarship) [1230]
Arkansas Nursing Foundation - Mary Gray Scholarships (Professional Development/Scholarship) [1231]
ASHA Scholarships (Graduate, Undergraduate/Scholarship) [915]
ASHA Student Research Grants (Graduate, Undergraduate/Scholarship) [916]
Association of Rehabilitation Nurses Scholarship Program (Undergraduate/Scholarship) [1485]
Astra Zeneca RURAL Scholarships (Doctorate/Scholarship) [1992]
Howard Baker Foundation Scholarships (Undergraduate/Scholarship) [1589]
Dr. Johnella Banks Memorial Scholarships (Undergraduate/Scholarship) [1750]
Banner Health System - McKee Medical Center, Loveland: Nightingale Scholarships (Graduate, Undergraduate/Scholarship) [2309]
Banner Health System - North Colorado Medical Center, Greeley: Nightingale Scholarships (Graduate, Undergraduate/Scholarship) [2310]
Leslie Baranowski Scholarships for Professional Excellence (All/Scholarship) [3721]
Basic Midwifery Student Scholarship Program (Undergraduate/Scholarship) [470]
BCEN Undergraduate Scholarships (Undergraduate/Scholarship) [2850]
Ann Beckingham Scholarships (Doctorate/Scholarship) [1993]
Reckitt Benckiser Student Scholarships (Graduate/Scholarship) [4729]
Marcy and Bruce Benson: Nightingale Scholarships (Graduate, Undergraduate/Scholarship) [2311]
Dr. Noorali & Sabiya Bharwani Endowment (Undergraduate/Scholarship) [1693]
Hussein Jina Bharwani Memorial Endowment (Undergraduate/Scholarship) [1694]
Birks Family Foundation Scholarships (Undergraduate/Scholarship) [1994]
Joan Blend Scholarship Fund (Undergraduate/Scholarship) [6709]
Breakthrough to Nursing Scholarships (Undergraduate/Scholarship) [3129]
Ruby A. Brown Memorial Scholarships (Undergraduate/Scholarship) [2807]
Eleanor McWilliams Burke Fund (Undergraduate/Scholarship) [2945]
byourself Scholarship Fund (Undergraduate/Scholarship) [2504]
Joseph R. Calder, Jr., MD Scholarship Fund (Undergraduate/Scholarship) [2946]
The California Endowment and AACN Minority Nurse Faculty Scholarships (Graduate/Scholarship) [337]
Canadian Nurses Foundation - Baxter Corporation Scholarships (Graduate/Scholarship) [1995]
Canadian Nurses Foundation Northern Scholarships (Undergraduate/Scholarship) [1996]
Canadian Nurses Foundation Scholarships (Undergraduate/Scholarship) [1997]
Rhea Sourifman Caplin Memorial Scholarships (Undergraduate/Scholarship) [3429]
Career Mobility Scholarship Awards (Doctorate, Undergraduate/Scholarship) [16]
Career Mobility Scholarships (Graduate, Undergraduate/Scholarship) [3130]
Catholic Healthcare Partners Scholarships (Undergraduate/Scholarship) [7525]
Certified Neuroscience Registered Nurse (CNRN) Recertification Grants Program (Professional Development/Grant) [374]
CFIDS Association of America NP Student Scholarships (Graduate/Scholarship) [263]
Patricia Smith Christensen Scholarships (Postdoctorate/Scholarship) [6383]
City of Toronto Queen Elizabeth II Sesquicentennial Scholarships in Community Health Nursing (Graduate) (Graduate/Scholarship) [7217]
City of Toronto Queen Elizabeth II Sesquicentennial Scholarships in Community Health Nursing (Undergraduate) (Undergraduate/Scholarship) [7218]
Frank Cole Memorial Emergency NP Student Scholarships (Graduate/Scholarship) [264]
Jennet Colliflower Nursing Scholarships (Undergraduate/Scholarship) [2595]
Colorado Nurses Association: Nightingale Scholarships (Graduate, Undergraduate/Scholarship) [2312]
Colorado Nurses Association: Virginia Paulson Memorial Scholarships (Graduate, Undergraduate/Scholarship) [2313]
Colorado Nurses Foundation Nightingale Scholarships (Graduate, Undergraduate/Scholarship) [2314]
Colorado Organization of Nursing Leaders Scholarships (Graduate, Undergraduate/Scholarship) [2315]
Connecticut League of Nursing Scholarships (Undergraduate/Scholarship) [3438]
Hazel Corbin/Childbirth Connection Grant for Evidence-based Midwifery Care (Professional Development/Award/Prize) [471]
Cranberry Institute NP Student Scholarships (Graduate/Scholarship) [265]
Daiichi Sankyo Inc. NP Student Scholarships (Graduate/Scholarship) [266]
Arthur L. Davis Publishing Agency Scholarships (Graduate, Undergraduate/Scholarship) [2316]
Deets-Laine Geriatric NP Student Scholarships (Doctorate, Graduate/Scholarship) [267]
Jane Delano Society Scholarships (Undergraduate/Scholarship) [886]
Gretchen Dimico Memorial Scholarships (Undergraduate/Scholarship) [4176]
Doctors IRA & UDAYA Nursing Scholarships (Undergraduate/Scholarship) [6649]
Margaret Dowell-Gravatt, M.D. Scholarship (Undergraduate/Scholarship) [1625]
Bus and Mary Ellen Durant Timberline High School Endowed Scholarships (Undergraduate/Scholarship) [4177]
Virginia Elizabeth and Alma Vane Taylor Student Nurse Scholarships (Undergraduate/Scholarship) [7432]
Emergency Nurses Association Undergraduate Scholarships (Undergraduate/Scholarship) [2851]
ENA Foundation Advanced Practice Scholarships (Undergraduate/Scholarship) [2852]
Ruth Murphy Evans Scholarship (Undergraduate/Scholarship) [3373]
Faculty Doctoral Scholarships (Doctorate/Scholarship) [2853]
Family and Children's Services of Lebanon County Fund (Undergraduate/Scholarship) [3098]
Red and Lola Fehr: Nightingale Scholarships (Graduate, Undergraduate/Scholarship) [2317]
Fitzgerald Health Education Associates NP Student Scholarships (Graduate/Scholarship) [268]
Florida Association District of Nursing Administration Scholarships (Undergraduate/Scholarship) [2990]
Florida Nurses Association Scholarships (Professional Development/Scholarship) [3014]
Forsyth County Nursing Scholarships (Undergraduate/Scholarship) [7433]
Barbara Palo Foster Memorial Scholarships (Undergraduate/Scholarship) [2128]
The Foundation of the National Student Nurses' Association Scholarships (Graduate, Undergraduate/Scholarship) [5100]
Dorris W. Frey Memorial Scholarships (Undergraduate/Scholarship) [6654]
Don and Eileen Fulton Nursing Scholarships (Undergraduate/Scholarship) [6774]
Gadsden State/McClellan Campus Nursing Scholarships Award (Undergraduate/Scholarship) [2349]
Gardner Foundation INS Education Scholarship (All/Scholarship) [3722]
Elaine Gelman Scholarship Award (Undergraduate/Scholarship) [4730]
Mary Ghezzi Nursing Scholarships (Undergraduate/Scholarship) [6842]
Helen Glass Scholarships (Doctorate/Scholarship) [1999]
William R. Goldfarb Memorial Scholarships (Undergraduate/Scholarship) [834]
Goodfellow Nursing Scholarships (Undergraduate/Scholarship) [4249]
Goodfellow Professional Development Fund (Professional Development/Scholarship) [4250]
Baxter Corporation - Jean Goodwill Scholarships (Postgraduate/Scholarship) [9]
William G. and Mayme J. Green Scholarships (Undergraduate/Scholarship) [3455]
Helen R. Greenamyer Memorial Scholarships (Undergraduate/Scholarship) [6775]
Amy and Horace Hagedorn Trust: Nightingale Scholarships (Graduate, Undergraduate/Scholarship) [2318]

Gordon B. and Josephine Hewlet Memorial Fund *(Undergraduate/Scholarship)* [3104]
Judy Hill Scholarships *(Undergraduate/Scholarship)* [2000]
Caroline Holt Nursing Scholarships *(Undergraduate/Scholarship)* [3467]
Roberta L. Houpt Scholarship Fund *(Undergraduate/Scholarship)* [3105]
Idaho Nursing Scholarships *(Undergraduate/Scholarship)* [3646]
Illinois Student Assistance Commission Nurse Educator Scholarships *(Undergraduate/Scholarship)* [3667]
Illinois Student Assistance Commission Nursing Education Scholarships *(Undergraduate/Scholarship)* [3668]
Imogene Ward Nursing Scholarships *(Undergraduate/Scholarship)* [2991]
Integra Foundation NNF Research Grants Award *(Professional Development/Grant)* [375]
Virginia C. Jack and Ralph L. Jack Scholarships *(Undergraduate/Scholarship)* [6730]
Jamaica National Building Society Scholarships *(Undergraduate/Scholarship)* [4001]
Johnson and Johnson: Nightingale Scholarships *(Graduate, Undergraduate/Scholarship)* [2319]
Johnson & Johnson Scholarships *(Undergraduate/Scholarship)* [2002]
Kaiser Permanente: Nightingale Scholarships *(Graduate, Undergraduate/Scholarship)* [2320]
Dorothy Kergin Scholarships *(Doctorate/Scholarship)* [2003]
Edyie G. Kirby Nursing Scholarships Award *(Undergraduate/Scholarship)* [2354]
Lake Dollars for Scholars Endowment Fund *(Undergraduate/Scholarship)* [6736]
Tecla Lin & Nelia Laroza Memorial Scholarships *(Undergraduate/Scholarship)* [2004]
Gertie S. Lowe Nursing Scholarships Award *(Undergraduate/Scholarship)* [2356]
Mallet Nursing Scholarships *(Undergraduate/Scholarship)* [6317]
Eleanor Martin Scholarships *(Graduate/Scholarship)* [2005]
Katherine Portnoy Mattleson Scholarships *(Undergraduate/Scholarship)* [3481]
McKesson Scholarships *(Undergraduate/Scholarship)* [3131]
McLean Scholarships *(Undergraduate/Scholarship)* [1433]
Jerry Medforth Nursing Scholarships Award *(Undergraduate/Scholarship)* [2357]
Meloche-Monnex Scholarships *(Doctorate/Scholarship)* [2006]
Metropolitan State College of Denver, President's Office: Nightingale Scholarships *(Graduate, Undergraduate/Scholarship)* [2321]
Michigan League for Nursing Scholarships *(Undergraduate/Scholarship)* [4481]
Michigan Nurses Foundation Scholarships *(Undergraduate/Scholarship)* [4485]
Albert and Eloise Midyette Memorial Scholarship Fund *(Undergraduate/Scholarship)* [3068]
Mary Ann Mikulic Scholarships *(Undergraduate/Scholarship)* [1486]
Fizz and Dutch Miller Scholarship Fund *(Undergraduate/Scholarship)* [6745]
Joseph and Catherine Missigman Memorial Nursing Scholarships *(Undergraduate/Scholarship)* [2965]
H.M. Muffly Memorial Scholarships *(Graduate, Undergraduate/Scholarship)* [2322]
Margaret Munro Scholarships *(Undergraduate/Scholarship)* [2008]
NAPNAP McNeil Annual Scholarships *(Undergraduate/Scholarship)* [4731]
National American Arab Nurses Association Scholarships *(Undergraduate/Scholarship)* [4637]
National Association of Financial Aid and Administrators Nursing Scholarships *(Undergraduate/Scholarship)* [4712]
National Association of Financial Aid and Administrators Scholarships for Disadvantaged Students *(Undergraduate/Scholarship)* [4713]
National Black Nurses Association Scholarships *(Undergraduate/Scholarship)* [4764]
National Heartburn Alliance NP Student Scholarships *(Graduate/Scholarship)* [269]
National Slovak Society of the USA Scholarships *(Undergraduate/Scholarship)* [5044]
NEF Scholarships for Leadership *(Doctorate/Scholarship)* [5311]
Sharon Nield Memorial Scholarships *(Undergraduate/Scholarship)* [2011]
The Nightingale Scholarships Award *(Undergraduate/Scholarship)* [2359]
NNF Scholarships Program *(Graduate, Undergraduate/Scholarship)* [376]
North Carolina League for Nursing Academic Scholarship Fund *(Graduate/Scholarship)* [3070]
North Ottawa Hospital Auxiliary Scholarships Fund *(Undergraduate/Scholarship)* [3295]
Northampton County Medical Society Alliance Scholarships *(Undergraduate/Scholarship)* [5261]
Novartis Pharmaceutical Corporation NP Student Scholarships *(Graduate/Scholarship)* [270]
Novo Nordisk NP Doctoral Education Scholarships *(Doctorate/Scholarship)* [271]
Nursing Scholarship Program *(Undergraduate/Scholarship)* [3512]
Orthopaedic Specialists Nursing Scholarships *(Undergraduate/Scholarship)* [7449]
Senator Norman Paterson Fellowship Scholarships *(Doctorate/Scholarship)* [2012]
Margaret Pemberton Scholarships *(Undergraduate/Scholarship)* [1751]
Pfizer Inc. 2007 NP Student Scholarships *(Graduate/Scholarship)* [272]
Pharmavite LLC NP Doctoral Education Scholarships *(Doctorate/Scholarship)* [273]
Poudre Valley Health System, Fort Collins: Nightingale Scholarships *(Graduate, Undergraduate/Scholarship)* [2323]
Pat Redden Memorial Scholarships *(Undergraduate/Scholarship)* [4252]
Faye Lynn Roberts Educational Scholarships *(Undergraduate/Scholarship)* [6669]
Liz Roberts Memorial Scholarships *(Undergraduate/Scholarship)* [6001]
Rocky Mountain Region of Wound Ostomy Continence Nurses Society Scholarships *(Graduate, Undergraduate/Scholarship)* [2324]
Rose Medical Center, Denver: Nightingale Scholarships *(Graduate, Undergraduate/Scholarship)* [2325]
St. Anthony's Hospitals, Denver: Nightingale Scholarships *(Graduate, Undergraduate/Scholarship)* [2326]
St. Joseph's Hospital School of Nursing Alumnae Scholarships *(Undergraduate/Scholarship)* [5518]
St. Mary's Hospital and Medical Center, Grand Junction: Nightingale Scholarships *(Graduate, Undergraduate/Scholarship)* [2327]
Sanofi Pasteur Scholarships *(Graduate/Scholarship)* [2013]
Scholarships for Emigres in the Health Sciences *(Undergraduate/Scholarship)* [4025]
Scholarships for Lutheran Nursing Students *(Undergraduate/Scholarship)* [1688]
Jeptha Wade Schureman Scholarship Program *(Undergraduate/Scholarship)* [2521]
Seedworks Fund: Nightingale Scholarships *(Graduate, Undergraduate/Scholarship)* [2328]
Sigma Theta Tau International Scholarships *(Doctorate/Scholarship)* [2014]
Hazel Simms Nursing Scholarship *(Professional Development/Scholarship)* [4143]
Society of Pediatric Nurses Educational Scholarship *(Graduate, Professional Development/Scholarship)* [6530]
Anna Doris Southall Nursing Scholarships *(Undergraduate/Scholarship)* [6848]
Specialty Nursing Scholarships *(Undergraduate/Scholarship)* [3132]
The Mabel Keaton Staupers National Scholarship Award *(Doctorate, Graduate, Undergraduate/Scholarship)* [2115]
StraightForward Media's Nursing School Scholarships *(Undergraduate/Scholarship)* [6804]
Anne Sturrock Nursing Scholarships *(Undergraduate/Scholarship)* [6675]
John I. and Madeleine R. Taeni Scholarships *(Undergraduate/Scholarship)* [6678]
UAA Alaska Kidney Foundation Scholarships *(Graduate, Undergraduate/Scholarship)* [7040]
UAA RRANN Program Scholarships *(Undergraduate/Scholarship)* [7072]
UCB, Inc. NP Student Scholarships *(Graduate/Scholarship)* [274]
John Vanderlee Scholarships *(Undergraduate/Scholarship)* [2015]
The Sibyl Jennings Vorheis Memorial Scholarship Program *(Undergraduate/Scholarship)* [3081]
Sue Walicki Nursing Scholarship *(Undergraduate/Scholarship)* [3992]
Patty Walter Memorial Scholarships *(Graduate, Undergraduate/Scholarship)* [2329]
Washington Higher Education Coordinating Board Health Professional Scholarships *(Undergraduate/Scholarship)* [7368]
West Virginia Nurses Association District No. 3 Scholarships *(Undergraduate/Scholarship)* [5527]
WOCN Accredited Nursing Education Scholarships *(Graduate, Undergraduate/Scholarship)* [7522]
WOCN Advanced Education Scholarships *(Doctorate, Graduate, Undergraduate/Scholarship)* [7523]
Jean Wright-Elson Scholarships *(Graduate, Undergraduate/Scholarship)* [6242]
Joan C. Yoder Memorial Nursing Scholarships *(Undergraduate/Scholarship)* [4392]
Yukon Delta Fisheries Development Association Scholarships *(Undergraduate/Scholarship)* [4393]

Nursing, Cardiovascular and cerebrovascular

Epilepsy Foundation Pre-doctoral Research Training Fellowships *(Graduate/Grant)* [2870]

Nursing, Pediatric

Eight and Forty Lung and Respiratory Disease Nursing Scholarships *(Professional Development/Scholarship)* [696]
Pediatric Endocrinology Nursing Society Academic Education Scholarships *(Undergraduate/Scholarship)* [5542]
Pediatric Endocrinology Nursing Society Continuing Education Scholarships *(Undergraduate/Scholarship)* [5543]

Nursing, Psychiatric

Associates in Behavioral Health Scholarships *(Graduate/Scholarship)* [5752]
Irene and Daisy MacGregor Memorial Scholarships *(Graduate/Scholarship)* [3477]

Nutrition

ASHA Scholarships *(Graduate, Undergraduate/Scholarship)* [915]
ASHA Student Research Grants *(Graduate, Undergraduate/Scholarship)* [916]
Eleanor McWilliams Burke Fund *(Undergraduate/Scholarship)* [2945]
California Association of Family and Consumer Sciences (CAFCS)-San Diego Chapter Scholarships *(Graduate, Undergraduate/Scholarship)* [6177]
Margaret Drew Alpha Fellowships *(Graduate/Fellowship)* [5664]
International Foodservice Editorial Council Scholarships *(Graduate, Undergraduate/Scholarship)* [3852]
Gertrude and Edith Lowidt and Mary Catherine Preiss Memorial Bursaries in Nutritional Sciences *(Undergraduate/Scholarship)* [7227]
National Poultry and Food Distributors Association Scholarships *(Undergraduate/Scholarship)* [5013]
North Dakota Division Scholarships *(Undergraduate/Scholarship)* [4517]
Nell Bryant Robinson Scholarships *(Undergraduate/Scholarship)* [5678]
Margaret Jerome Sampson Scholarships *(Undergraduate/Scholarship)* [5680]
Stark County Dairy Promoters Scholarships *(Undergraduate/Scholarship)* [6755]

Mary and Elliot Wood Foundation Graduate Scholarship Fund *(Graduate/Scholarship)* [3085]

Occupational safety and health

AAOHN Academic Study Scholarships *(Graduate, Undergraduate/Scholarship)* [378]
AAOHN Continuing Education Scholarships *(Professional Development/Scholarship)* [379]
America Responds Memorial Scholarships *(Undergraduate/Scholarship)* [1046]
ASSE Construction Safety Scholarships *(Undergraduate/Scholarship)* [1047]
ASSE Diversity Committee Scholarships *(Graduate, Undergraduate/Scholarship)* [1048]
Bechtel Group Foundation Scholarship for Safety & Health *(Undergraduate/Scholarship)* [1049]
Warren K. Brown Scholarships *(Undergraduate/Scholarship)* [1050]
Central Indiana ASSE Scholarships *(Graduate, Undergraduate/Scholarship)* [1051]
CNA Foundation Scholarships *(Graduate, Undergraduate/Scholarship)* [1052]
Delta/VPPPA Safety, Health and Environmental Scholarships *(Undergraduate/Scholarship)* [7338]
Scott Dominguez - Craters of the Moon Chapter Scholarships *(Graduate, Undergraduate/Scholarship)* [1053]
Georgia Chapter of ASSE Annual Scholarships *(Undergraduate/Scholarship)* [1054]
Gold Country Section & Region II Scholarships *(Graduate, Undergraduate/Scholarship)* [1055]
Greater Baton Rouge Chapter - Don Jones Excellence in Safety Scholarships *(Undergraduate/Scholarship)* [1056]
Gulf Coast Past President's Scholarships *(Undergraduate/Scholarship)* [1057]
George Gustafson HSE Memorial Scholarships *(Graduate, Undergraduate/Scholarship)* [1058]
David Iden Memorial Safety Scholarships *(Undergraduate/Scholarship)* [1059]
Karl A. Jacobson Scholarships *(Undergraduate/Scholarship)* [1060]
James P. Kohn Memorial Scholarships *(Graduate/Scholarship)* [1061]
Leadership Development Scholarships *(Professional Development/Scholarship)* [380]
Liberty Mutual Scholarships *(Undergraduate/Scholarship)* [1062]
Dick Martin Scholarships *(Postgraduate/Scholarship)* [1943]
Medina Scholarships for Hispanics in Safety *(Graduate, Undergraduate/Scholarship)* [1063]
North Florida Chapter Safety Education Scholarships *(Graduate, Undergraduate/Scholarship)* [1064]
Northeastern Illinois Chapter Scholarships *(Graduate, Undergraduate/Scholarship)* [1065]
PDC Scholarships *(Undergraduate/Scholarship)* [1066]
Harold F. Polston Scholarships *(Undergraduate/Scholarship)* [1067]
William C. Ray, CIH, CSP Arizona Scholarships *(Graduate, Undergraduate/Scholarship)* [1068]
Marsh Risk Consulting Scholarships *(Undergraduate/Scholarship)* [1069]
Julie Schmid Research Scholarships *(All/Scholarship)* [1475]
Southwest Chapter Roy Kinslow Scholarships *(Undergraduate/Scholarship)* [1070]
VPPPA William Sullivan Scholarships *(Graduate, Undergraduate/Scholarship)* [7339]
Harry Taback 9/11 Memorial Scholarships *(Undergraduate/Scholarship)* [1071]
Thompson Scholarship for Women in Safety *(Graduate/Scholarship)* [1072]
UPS Diversity Scholarships *(Undergraduate/Scholarship)* [1073]
VPPPA June Brothers Scholarships *(Graduate, Undergraduate/Scholarship)* [7340]
VPPPA Stephen Brown Scholarships *(Graduate, Undergraduate/Scholarship)* [7341]
Washington Group International Safety Scholarships *(Undergraduate/Scholarship)* [1074]

Occupational therapy

Renee Achter Scholarship Program *(Postgraduate/Scholarship)* [726]
Naida Ackley Scholarship Program *(Postgraduate/Scholarship)* [727]
Diane Blicksilver Aja Memorial Scholarship Program *(Postgraduate/Scholarship)* [728]
AMBUCS Scholarships for Therapists Program *(Graduate, Undergraduate/Scholarship)* [258]
Ethel Beard Burstein Scholarship Program *(Postgraduate/Scholarship)* [729]
Canadian Occupational Therapy Foundation Graduate Scholarships *(Graduate/Scholarship)* [2017]
Canadian Occupational Therapy Foundation Invacare Master's Scholarships *(Graduate/Scholarship)* [2018]
Thelma Cardwell Scholarships *(Graduate/Scholarship)* [2019]
Dave Couch Memorial Scholarships *(Undergraduate/Scholarship)* [5473]
Margaret Dowell-Gravatt, M.D. Scholarship *(Undergraduate/Scholarship)* [1625]
Goldwin Howland Scholarships *(Graduate/Scholarship)* [2020]
Kappa Delta Phi Scholarship Program *(Postgraduate/Scholarship)* [730]
Susan Lang Scholarship Program *(Postgraduate/Scholarship)* [731]
Janice McGraw Memorial Scholarship Program *(Postgraduate/Scholarship)* [732]
Mary Minglen Scholarship Program *(Postgraduate/Scholarship)* [733]
NorthCoast Medical Scholarship Program *(Postgraduate/Scholarship)* [734]
Occupational Physicians Scholarship Fund *(Undergraduate/Scholarship)* [5313]
Frank Oppenheimer Scholarship Program *(Postgraduate/Scholarship)* [735]
Willard and Spackman Scholarship Program *(Postgraduate/Scholarship)* [736]
Edith Weingarten Scholarship Program *(Postgraduate/Scholarship)* [737]

Oceanography

Friends and Family of Jennifer Balber Scholarships *(Undergraduate/Scholarship)* [5937]

Oncology

American College of Radiation Oncology Resident Scholarships *(Graduate/Scholarship)* [475]
Aplastic, Anemia and Myelosdysplasia Scholarships *(Graduate/Scholarship)* [1991]
Childhood Cancer Foundation Candlelighters Canada Scholarships *(All/Scholarship)* [2125]
Childhood Cancer Foundation Scholarships *(Undergraduate/Scholarship)* [2123]
Ryan Mullaly Second Chance Fund Scholarships *(Undergraduate/Scholarship)* [4587]
Patient Advocate Foundations Scholarships *(Undergraduate/Scholarship)* [5535]
E.D. Thomas Post Doctoral Fellowships *(Postdoctorate/Fellowship)* [3145]

Opera

Opera Foundation Scholarships *(Professional Development/Scholarship)* [5349]

Operations research

Gary B. Multanen/CM Magazine Scholarships *(All/Scholarship)* [479]

Optics

BACUS Scholarships *(Graduate, Undergraduate/Scholarship)* [6695]
Michael Kidger Memorial Scholarships in Optical Design *(Graduate/Scholarship)* [6696]
D.J. Lovell Scholarships *(Graduate, Undergraduate/Scholarship)* [6698]
William H. Price Scholarships *(Graduate, Undergraduate/Scholarship)* [6699]
Student Travel Grants *(Graduate, Undergraduate/Grant)* [6700]

Optometry

The William C. Ezell Fellowships *(Postgraduate/Fellowship)* [276]
Terrance Ingraham Pediatric Optometry Residency Award *(Graduate/Award/Prize)* [277]
VISTAKON George Mertz and Sheldon Wechsler Residency Awards *(All/Award/Prize)* [278]
Antoinette M. Molinari Memorial Scholarships *(Doctorate/Scholarship)* [279]
VISTAKON Research Grants *(All/Grant)* [280]
VSP Research Grants *(All/Grant)* [281]

Orthotics prosthetics technology

The Eneslow Pedorthic Institute Scholarships *(Undergraduate/Scholarship)* [5545]
The Dawn Janisse Scholarships *(Undergraduate/Scholarship)* [5546]
The Aristotle Mirones Scholarships *(Undergraduate/Scholarship)* [5547]
The Oklahoma State University at Okmulgee Scholarships *(Undergraduate/Scholarship)* [5548]
The Sidney M. Pols Scholarships *(Undergraduate/Scholarship)* [5549]
The Dr. William M. Scholl College of Podiatric Medicine Scholarships *(Undergraduate/Scholarship)* [5550]
The Xtra Depth University Scholarships *(Undergraduate/Scholarship)* [5551]

Packaging

Richard F. Heaney Memorial Scholarship Fund *(Graduate, Undergraduate/Scholarship)* [3817]
Petroleum Packaging Council Scholarships *(Undergraduate/Scholarship)* [5620]

Painting (See also: Art)

American Watercolor Society Scholarship Program for Art Teachers *(Professional Development/Scholarship)* [1147]

Paralegal studies

American Institute for Paralegal Studies Alumni Achievement Scholarships *(Undergraduate/Scholarship)* [670]
American Institute for Paralegal Studies Alumni Competitive Scholarships *(Undergraduate/Scholarship)* [671]
American Institute for Paralegal Studies Merit Scholarships *(Undergraduate/Scholarship)* [672]
Therese A. Cannon Educational Scholarships *(Professional Development/Scholarship)* [3884]
Judge and Mrs. Robert D. Horowitz Legal Scholarship Fund *(Graduate/Scholarship)* [6729]
Kentucky Paralegal Association Student Scholarships *(Undergraduate/Scholarship)* [4072]
Samuel Krugliak Legal Scholarship Fund *(Graduate/Scholarship)* [6735]
NFPA/PACE Scholarships *(Professional Development/Scholarship)* [4886]
NFPA and Thomson West Scholarships *(Undergraduate/Scholarship)* [4887]
Pathways to Success Scholarships *(Undergraduate/Scholarship)* [3113]

Paramedics

Gail Hartshorn Scholarships *(Undergraduate/Scholarship)* [5494]
John I. and Madeleine R. Taeni Scholarships *(Undergraduate/Scholarship)* [6678]

Parapsychology

Parapsycological Association Research Endowment *(All/Grant)* [5454]

Parkinson's disease
APDA Postdoctoral Fellowships *(Professional Development/Fellowship)* [757]
Clinician Scientist Development Awards *(Postgraduate/Fellowship)* [5532]
PDF International Research Grants Program *(Postdoctorate/Grant)* [5533]

Parks and recreation
Arizona Parks and Recreation Educational Scholarship Program *(Graduate, Undergraduate/Scholarship)* [1223]
National Recreation and Park Association Diversity Scholarships *(Undergraduate/Scholarship)* [5028]
Michael A. Ramnes Professional Scholarships *(Professional Development/Scholarship)* [1224]

Pathology
The Eneslow Pedorthic Institute Scholarships *(Undergraduate/Scholarship)* [5545]
The Dawn Janisse Scholarships *(Undergraduate/Scholarship)* [5546]
The Aristotle Mirones Scholarships *(Undergraduate/Scholarship)* [5547]
The Oklahoma State University at Okmulgee Scholarships *(Undergraduate/Scholarship)* [5548]
The Sidney M. Pols Scholarships *(Undergraduate/Scholarship)* [5549]
The Dr. William M. Scholl College of Podiatric Medicine Scholarships *(Undergraduate/Scholarship)* [5550]
The Xtra Depth University Scholarships *(Undergraduate/Scholarship)* [5551]

Peace studies
Post-Doctoral or Sabbatical Fellowships *(Doctorate/Fellowship)* [4158]
Rieser Fellowships *(Undergraduate/Fellowship)* [1804]
Mary and Elliot Wood Foundation Graduate Scholarship Fund *(Graduate/Scholarship)* [3085]

Performing arts
AAS Fellowships for Creative and Performing Artists and Writers *(All/Fellowship)* [296]
ACHE Junior and Community College Performing Arts Scholarships *(Undergraduate/Scholarship)* [101]
ASTR Research Fellowships *(All/Grant)* [1077]
The John L. Dales Scholarship Fund *(Undergraduate/Scholarship)* [6288]
George E. Judd Scholarships *(Undergraduate/Scholarship)* [6660]
Liberace Scholarship Fund *(Undergraduate/Scholarship)* [4234]
McNamara Family Creative Arts Project Grants *(Graduate, Undergraduate/Grant)* [3601]
Muddy Waters Scholarships *(Undergraduate/Scholarship)* [1768]
Orange County Centennial Arts Scholarships *(Undergraduate/Scholarship)* [5363]
Redlands High School Drama Boosters Award *(Undergraduate/Scholarship)* [5984]
Star-Ledger Scholarships for the Performing Arts *(Undergraduate/Scholarship)* [5178]
UAA Friends of the Performing Arts Scholarships *(Undergraduate/Scholarship)* [7054]
UAA Ken Gray Endowment Scholarships *(Undergraduate/Scholarship)* [7059]
Wolf Trap Foundation Scholarship Program for Performing Arts Teachers *(Professional Development/Scholarship)* [7474]
The Wolf Trap Internship Program *(Graduate, Professional Development, Undergraduate/Internship)* [7475]

Persian studies
Research Fellowships in Iranian Studies (Resident Director-Tehran) *(Doctorate, Graduate/Fellowship)* [664]

Personnel administration/human resources
Bison Transport Scholarships *(Undergraduate/Scholarship)* [5341]
C.C.H.R.M.A. Scholarships *(High School, Undergraduate/Scholarship)* [2268]
HSF/General Motors Scholarship Program *(Undergraduate/Scholarship)* [3595]
NPELRA Foundation Scholarships *(Graduate/Scholarship)* [5309]
Barbara Sanchez Scholarships *(Undergraduate/Scholarship)* [6443]
SHRM Certification Scholarships - Individual *(Graduate/Scholarship)* [6444]
SHRM Foundation Regional Academic Scholarships *(Graduate, Undergraduate/Scholarship)* [6445]
Verizon Scholarship Program *(Undergraduate/Scholarship)* [3607]

Pharmaceutical sciences
American Foundation for Pharmaceutical Education Gateway Research Scholarships *(Professional Development/Scholarship)* [577]
American Foundation for Pharmaceutical Education Pre-Doctoral Fellowships in the Pharmaceutical Sciences *(Doctorate/Fellowship)* [578]
American Foundation for Pharmaceutical Education Pre-Doctoral Fellowships in the Pharmaceutical Sciences *(Doctorate/Fellowship)* [579]
Minority Pharmacy Faculty New Investigator Grants *(Professional Development/Grant)* [581]
Pharmacy Faculty Fellowships in Community Pharmacy Practice *(Postdoctorate/Fellowship)* [583]
Pharmacy Faculty Fellowships in Geriatric Pharmacy/Geriatric Pharmaceutical Science *(Postdoctorate/Fellowship)* [584]

Pharmacology
Epilepsy Foundation Pre-doctoral Research Training Fellowships *(Graduate/Grant)* [2870]
School of Pharmacy Continuing Student Scholarships *(Undergraduate/Scholarship)* [7269]
University of Wisconsin-Madison Pharmacy New Student Scholarships *(Undergraduate/Scholarship)* [7280]

Pharmacy
Armenian American Pharmacists' Association Scholarships *(Doctorate, Graduate/Scholarship)* [1268]
Eleanor McWilliams Burke Fund *(Undergraduate/Scholarship)* [2945]
Joseph R. Calder, Jr., MD Scholarship Fund *(Undergraduate/Scholarship)* [2946]
Christian Pharmacist Fellowship International Scholarships *(Professional Development/Fellowship)* [2143]
J.C. and Rheba Cobb Memorial Scholarships *(Undergraduate/Scholarship)* [4811]
DAAD Study Scholarship Awards *(Graduate/Scholarship)* [3223]
Epilepsy Foundation Pre-doctoral Research Training Fellowships *(Graduate/Grant)* [2870]
Thomas W. Gallagher Scholarship Fund *(Undergraduate/Scholarship)* [6720]
Jason Lang Scholarship *(Undergraduate/Scholarship)* [163]
Minority Pharmacy Faculty New Investigator Grants *(Professional Development/Grant)* [581]
Minority Student Gateway to Research Scholarships *(Professional Development/Scholarship)* [582]
National Community Pharmacists Association Internship Programs *(Undergraduate/Internship)* [4812]
National Community Pharmacists Association Presidential Scholarships *(Undergraduate/Scholarship)* [4813]
Northern Alberta Development Council Bursary for Pharmacy Students *(Undergraduate/Scholarship)* [174]
Pharmacy Faculty Fellowships in Community Pharmacy Practice *(Postdoctorate/Fellowship)* [583]
Pharmacy Faculty New Investigator Grants Program *(Doctorate/Grant)* [585]
Pharmacy Student Scholarship Program *(Postdoctorate/Scholarship)* [4687]
Neil Pruitt, Sr. Memorial Scholarships *(Undergraduate/Scholarship)* [4814]
Scholarships for Emigres in the Health Sciences *(Undergraduate/Scholarship)* [4025]
School of Pharmacy Continuing Student Scholarships *(Undergraduate/Scholarship)* [7269]
Williard B. Simmons Sr. Memorial Scholarships *(Undergraduate/Scholarship)* [4815]
University of Wisconsin-Madison Pharmacy New Student Scholarships *(Undergraduate/Scholarship)* [7280]
Washington Higher Education Coordinating Board Health Professional Scholarships *(Undergraduate/Scholarship)* [7368]
Western Michigan Society of Health-System Pharmacists Scholarships *(All/Scholarship)* [7407]

Philosophy
Ameen Rihani Scholarship Program *(Undergraduate/Scholarship)* [1193]

Photogrammetry
Robert E. Altenhofen Memorial Scholarships *(Graduate, Undergraduate/Scholarship)* [1025]
Intergraph Scholarships *(Graduate/Scholarship)* [1028]
Leica Geosystems Internships *(Graduate/Internship)* [1029]
Francis H. Moffitt Memorial Scholarships *(Graduate, Undergraduate/Scholarship)* [1031]
The Kenneth J. Osborn Memorial Scholarships *(Undergraduate/Scholarship)* [1032]
Paul R. Wolf Memorial Scholarships *(Graduate/Scholarship)* [1033]

Photography
Bob Baxter Scholarships *(Undergraduate/Scholarship)* [5017]
Reid Blackburn Scholarships *(Undergraduate/Scholarship)* [5018]
Donald Franklin Bradley Memorial Scholarships *(Undergraduate/Scholarship)* [5805]
Bob East Scholarships *(Undergraduate/Scholarship)* [5019]
Don English Memorial Scholarships *(Undergraduate/Scholarship)* [5821]
Allison E. Fisher Scholarships *(Undergraduate/Scholarship)* [2984]
International Foodservice Editorial Council Scholarships *(Graduate, Undergraduate/Scholarship)* [3852]
Kit C. King Graduate Scholarships *(Postgraduate/Scholarship)* [5020]
Manzer-Keener-Wefler Scholarships *(Undergraduate/Scholarship)* [6739]
Still Photographer Scholarships *(Undergraduate/Scholarship)* [5021]
Television News Scholarships *(Undergraduate/Scholarship)* [5022]
UAA Kimura Scholarship Fund (Photography Scholarships) *(Undergraduate/Scholarship)* [7060]

Photography, Journalistic
AAJA/COX Foundation Scholarships *(Graduate, Undergraduate/Scholarship)* [1329]

Physical sciences
American Council of Independent Laboratories Scholarships *(Undergraduate/Scholarship)* [506]
American Sokol Merit Awards *(Undergraduate/Scholarship)* [1096]
Casey Bennett Scholarships *(Undergraduate/Scholarship)* [2926]
CEPS-Tyco Scholarships *(Undergraduate/Scholarship)* [7137]
Harold Leeming Memorial Scholarships *(Undergraduate/Scholarship)* [5954]

Ohio Valley Chapter Scholarships *(Undergraduate/Scholarship)* [1455]

Physical therapy

AMBUCS Scholarships for Therapists Program *(Graduate, Undergraduate/Scholarship)* [258]
Eleanor McWilliams Burke Fund *(Undergraduate/Scholarship)* [2945]
Dave Couch Memorial Scholarships *(Undergraduate/Scholarship)* [5473]
Margaret Dowell-Gravatt, M.D. Scholarship *(Undergraduate/Scholarship)* [1625]
Hartford Foundation for Public Giving Occupational Therapy Scholarships *(Undergraduate/Scholarship)* [3459]
Scholarships for Emigres in the Health Sciences *(Undergraduate/Scholarship)* [4025]
The Sibyl Jennings Vorheis Memorial Scholarship Program *(Undergraduate/Scholarship)* [3081]
Monica M. Weaver Memorial Fund *(Undergraduate/Scholarship)* [2978]

Physics

AFCEA Distance Learning/Online Scholarships *(Undergraduate/Scholarship)* [1236]
AFCEA Fellowships *(Doctorate, Graduate/Fellowship)* [1237]
AFCEA General John A. Wickham Scholarships *(Undergraduate/Scholarship)* [1238]
AFCEA Scholarship for Working Professionals *(Graduate/Scholarship)* [1240]
Alaska Aerospace Development Corporation Scholarships *(Undergraduate/Scholarship)* [4338]
American Physical Society Undergraduate Scholarships *(Undergraduate/Scholarship)* [773]
Michael P. Anderson Scholarships in Space Science *(Undergraduate/Scholarship)* [5050]
APS Scholarships for Minority Undergraduate Physics Majors *(Undergraduate/Scholarship)* [5051]
AWIS College Scholarships *(Undergraduate/Scholarship)* [1519]
Harvey Washington Banks Scholarships in Astronomy *(Undergraduate/Scholarship)* [5052]
M. Hildred Blewett Scholarships *(Postdoctorate/Scholarship)* [6431]
William E. "Buck" Bragunier Scholarships *(Undergraduate/Scholarship)* [1241]
Charles S. Brown Scholarships in Physics *(Graduate, Undergraduate/Scholarship)* [5053]
LT.G. Douglas D. Buchholz Memorial Scholarships *(Undergraduate/Scholarship)* [1242]
Julian E. Carnes Scholarship Fund *(Undergraduate/Scholarship)* [3046]
D&A Florida Scholarships *(Undergraduate/Scholarship)* [6648]
DEPS Graduate Scholarship Program *(Graduate/Scholarship)* [2715]
Disabled War Veterans Scholarships *(Undergraduate/Scholarship)* [1244]
Peggy Dixon Two-Year Scholarships *(Undergraduate/Scholarship)* [6541]
Robert A. Ellis Scholarships in Physics *(Undergraduate/Scholarship)* [5054]
Frank Fong Scholarships *(Undergraduate/Scholarship)* [6423]
Helm Family Scholarships *(Undergraduate/Scholarship)* [6192]
Elmer S. Imes Scholarships in Physics *(Undergraduate/Scholarship)* [5055]
Herbert Levy Memorial Endowment Fund Scholarships *(Undergraduate/Scholarship)* [6542]
Lockheed Martin IT Scholarships *(Undergraduate/Scholarship)* [1245]
Barbara Lotze Scholarships for Future Teachers *(Undergraduate/Scholarship)* [385]
Lockheed Martin Graduate Scholarships *(Graduate/Scholarship)* [1246]
Walter Samuel McAfee Scholarships in Space Physics *(Undergraduate/Scholarship)* [5056]
Ronald E. McNair Scholarships in Space and Optical Physics *(Undergraduate/Scholarship)* [5057]
Willie Hobbs Moore Scholarships *(Undergraduate/Scholarship)* [5058]
Harry L. Morrison Scholarships *(Undergraduate/Scholarship)* [5059]
Northampton County Medical Society Alliance Scholarships *(Undergraduate/Scholarship)* [5261]
AFCEA General Emmett Paige Scholarships *(Undergraduate/Scholarship)* [1247]
Phillip Morris USA Scholarships *(Undergraduate/Scholarship)* [7330]
Rubber Division American Chemical Society Scholarships *(Undergraduate/Scholarship)* [6079]
Sigma Pi Sigma Undergraduate Research Awards *(Undergraduate/Grant)* [6543]
Julia Viola Simms Science Scholarships *(Postgraduate/Scholarship)* [1742]
SPS Future Teacher Scholarships *(Undergraduate/Scholarship)* [6544]
SPS Leadership Scholarships *(Undergraduate/Scholarship)* [6545]
Veterans of Enduring Freedom (Afghanistan) and Iraqi Freedom Scholarships *(Undergraduate/Scholarship)* [1250]
Arthur BC Walker Scholarships *(Undergraduate/Scholarship)* [5060]
Washington Higher Education Coordinating Board Health Professional Scholarships *(Undergraduate/Scholarship)* [7368]
Marine Corps Sgt. Jeannette L. Winters Memorial Scholarships *(Undergraduate/Scholarship)* [1251]
Women In Defense HORIZONS Scholarships *(Graduate, Undergraduate/Scholarship)* [7479]
Xavier University Departmental Scholarships *(Undergraduate/Scholarship)* [7538]

Physiology

Bruce and Betty Alberts Endowed Scholarships in Physiology *(Undergraduate/Scholarship)* [4282]
Epilepsy Foundation Pre-doctoral Research Training Fellowships *(Graduate/Grant)* [2870]
Indiana State Alumni Association Rural Health Scholarships *(Undergraduate/Scholarship)* [3706]
Mountain Memorial Scholarships *(Undergraduate/Scholarship)* [4296]
Scholarships for Emigres in the Health Sciences *(Undergraduate/Scholarship)* [4025]

Plastic surgery

American Association of Plastic Surgeons Academic Scholars Program *(Graduate/Grant)* [387]

Podiatry

Illinois Student Assistance Commission Podiatric Scholarship Program *(Undergraduate/Scholarship)* [3669]
Zelda Walling Vicha Memorial Scholarships *(Undergraduate/Scholarship)* [1035]

Polish studies (See also: Area and ethnic studies)

Falcon Achievement Scholarships *(Undergraduate/Scholarship)* [5731]
Harriet Irsay Scholarships *(Graduate, Undergraduate/Scholarship)* [674]
Kosciuszko Foundation Graduate Study and Research in Poland Scholarships *(Graduate/Scholarship)* [4089]
Kosciuszko Foundation Tuition Scholarships *(Undergraduate/Scholarship)* [4090]
Kosciuszko Foundation Year Abroad Scholarships *(Undergraduate/Scholarship)* [4091]
Massachusetts Federation of Polish Women's Clubs Scholarships *(Undergraduate/Scholarship)* [4092]
Polish American Club of North Jersey Scholarships *(Undergraduate/Scholarship)* [4093]
Polish National Alliance of Brooklyn, USA Scholarships *(Undergraduate/Scholarship)* [4094]
Tadeusz Sendzimir Scholarships *(Undergraduate/Scholarship)* [3496]
Dr. Marie E. Zakrzewski Medical Scholarships *(Undergraduate/Scholarship)* [4095]

Political science

American Political Science Association Federal Executives Fellowships *(Professional Development/Fellowship)* [782]
American Political Science Association/MCI Scholarships *(Postdoctorate/Scholarship)* [784]
American Political Science Association Political Scientists Fellowships *(All/Fellowship)* [785]
ARS Undergraduate Scholarships *(Four Year College, Two Year College, Undergraduate/Scholarship)* [1259]
Avista Corporation Minds in Motion Scholarships *(Undergraduate/Scholarship)* [4163]
Sam Bull Memorial Scholarships *(Undergraduate/Scholarship)* [142]
Cecil E. Burney Scholarships *(High School, Undergraduate/Scholarship)* [2267]
CIGNA Healthcare Graduate Scholarships *(Graduate/Scholarship)* [4892]
CIGNA Healthcare Undergraduate Scholarships *(Undergraduate/Scholarship)* [4893]
D&A Florida Scholarships *(Undergraduate/Scholarship)* [6648]
Douglas-Coldwell Foundation Scholarships in Social Affairs *(Graduate/Scholarship)* [2729]
Garikian Scholarship Fund *(Undergraduate/Scholarship)* [1279]
Senator James Gladstone Memorial Scholarships *(Undergraduate/Scholarship)* [143]
Randy Green Memorial Scholarship Fund *(High School/Scholarship)* [2598]
Enid Hall Griswold Memorial Scholarships *(Undergraduate/Scholarship)* [5064]
Hench Post-Dissertation Fellowships *(Postdoctorate/Fellowship)* [303]
John Peter Humphrey Student Fellowships *(Graduate/Fellowship)* [1942]
McKinley Financial Scholarships *(Graduate, Undergraduate/Scholarship)* [4898]
National Iranian American Council Fellowships *(Graduate, Undergraduate/Fellowship)* [4958]
NPELRA Foundation Scholarships *(Graduate/Scholarship)* [5309]
Pi Gamma Mu Scholarships *(Graduate/Scholarship)* [5691]
Political Leadership Scholarships *(Undergraduate/Scholarship)* [5773]
Pride Foundation Scholarships *(Undergraduate/Scholarship)* [6134]
Betty Rendel Scholarships *(Undergraduate/Scholarship)* [4890]
Bertha and Byron L. Reppert Scholarship Fund *(Undergraduate/Scholarship)* [3116]
Ameen Rihani Scholarship Program *(Undergraduate/Scholarship)* [1193]
Fauneil J. Rinn Scholarships *(Undergraduate/Scholarship)* [6394]
Charles and Ruth Ronin Memorial Scholarships *(Undergraduate/Scholarship)* [6002]
John Streiff Memorial Scholarships *(Undergraduate/Scholarship)* [4218]
TCA Turkish American Scholarships *(Undergraduate/Scholarship)* [6939]
UAA Governor William A. Egan Scholarships *(Undergraduate/Scholarship)* [7056]
UAA Mark A. Beltz Scholarships *(Graduate, Undergraduate/Scholarship)* [7063]
UAA Pat Brakke Political Science Scholarships *(Undergraduate/Scholarship)* [7068]
Women In Defense HORIZONS Scholarships *(Graduate, Undergraduate/Scholarship)* [7479]
Urashi Zen Scholarships *(Undergraduate/Scholarship)* [5787]

Population studies

Phyllis P. Harris Scholarships *(Postgraduate/Award/Prize)* [1956]

Portuguese studies (See also: Area and ethnic studies)

Luso-American Education Foundation G-1 Grants *(Professional Development/Grant)* [4262]
Luso-American Education Foundation G-2 Grants *(Professional Development/Grant)* [4263]
Luso-American Education Foundation G-3 Grants *(Postgraduate/Grant)* [4264]

Poultry science

National Poultry and Food Distributors Association Scholarships *(Undergraduate/Scholarship)* [5013]

Preservation

SPOOM Research Grants *(Graduate/Grant)* [6566]

Printing—History

Katharine Pantzer Senior Fellowships in the British Book Trades *(Professional Development/Fellowship)* [1696]

Printing trades and industries

Don Bailey Scholarships *(Undergraduate/Scholarship)* [4913]
TCA Turkish American Scholarships *(Undergraduate/Scholarship)* [6939]

Printmaking

Lewis-Clark State College Presidential Technical Out-of-State Scholarships *(Undergraduate/Scholarship)* [4199]

Psychiatry

Associates in Behavioral Health Scholarships *(Graduate/Scholarship)* [5752]
Patricia Pownder Conolly Memorial Scholarships *(Undergraduate/Scholarship)* [4462]
Daland Fellowships in Clinical Investigation *(Doctorate/Fellowship)* [767]
Epilepsy Foundation Research and Training Fellowships for Clinicians *(Doctorate, Professional Development/Grant)* [2872]
Linda Lyons Memorial Scholarship Fund *(Undergraduate/Scholarship)* [4464]

Psychology

APAGS-CLGBTC Grant Program *(Graduate/Grant)* [795]
APAGS' Committee on Ethic Minority Affairs (CEMA) Grant Program *(Graduate/Grant)* [796]
APS Student Grants *(Graduate, Undergraduate/Grant)* [1481]
Tara Lynne Arnold Scholarships *(Undergraduate/Scholarship)* [6768]
ASPPB Larry J. Bass Jr., PhD. Memorial Scholarship Awards *(Graduate, Undergraduate/Grant)* [797]
Associated Women for Pepperdine (AWP) Scholarships *(Undergraduate/Scholarship)* [5572]
Associates in Behavioral Health Scholarships *(Graduate/Scholarship)* [5752]
Delores A. Auzenne Fellowship *(Postgraduate/Fellowship)* [2995]
AWIS College Scholarships *(Undergraduate/Scholarship)* [1519]
Bisexual Foundation Scholarships *(Graduate/Scholarship)* [6572]
Ellin Bloch and Pierre Ritchie Honorary Scholarships *(Doctorate, Graduate/Grant)* [798]
Frances P. Bolton Fellowships *(Doctorate/Fellowship)* [5456]
Patricia Pownder Conolly Memorial Scholarships *(Undergraduate/Scholarship)* [4462]
Meredith P. Crawford Fellowship in I/O Psychology *(Undergraduate/Fellowship)* [3627]
Diversity Dissertation Scholarships *(Doctorate/Fellowship)* [799]
Epilepsy Foundation Pre-doctoral Research Training Fellowships *(Graduate/Grant)* [2870]
Nancy B. Forest and L. Michael Honaker Master's Scholarships for Research *(Doctorate, Graduate/Scholarship)* [800]
Garikian Scholarship Fund *(Undergraduate/Scholarship)* [1279]
Eileen J. Garrett Scholarships *(Undergraduate/Scholarship)* [5457]
Linda Lyons Memorial Scholarship Fund *(Undergraduate/Scholarship)* [4464]
Malyon-Smith Scholarships *(Graduate/Scholarship)* [6573]
Clara Mayo Grants *(Graduate/Grant)* [6575]
Scott Mesh Honorary Scholarships for Research in Psychology *(Graduate/Fellowship)* [801]
Minority Medical Student Fellowships in HIV Psychiatry *(Undergraduate/Fellowship)* [793]
New Jersey Psychological Association Scholarships for Minority Graduate Students *(Postgraduate/Scholarship)* [5184]
Dorothy D. Palmer Scholarship for the Study of Optimal Aging in Women *(Postdoctorate/Scholarship)* [5185]
Pi Gamma Mu Scholarships *(Graduate/Scholarship)* [5691]
David Pilon Scholarships for Training in Professional Psychology *(Doctorate, Graduate/Scholarship)* [802]
SPPSI Grants-In-Aid Program *(Graduate, Postdoctorate/Grant)* [6576]
Charles T. and Judith A. Tart Student Incentive Awards *(Graduate, Postdoctorate, Undergraduate/Grant)* [5458]
Taylor Statten Memorial Fellowships *(Graduate/Scholarship)* [7233]
UAA Chris L. Kleinke Scholarships *(Graduate, Undergraduate/Scholarship)* [7046]
UAA Dr. Jon Baker Memorial Scholarships *(Graduate, Undergraduate/Scholarship)* [7049]

Public administration

AGBU Scholarships *(Graduate/Loan)* [1255]
American Society of Military Comptrollers National Scholarship Program *(Undergraduate/Scholarship)* [1011]
Marvin A. Andrews Scholarships/Internships *(Graduate/Scholarship)* [1216]
Center for Congressional and Presidential Studies (CPPS) Endowment *(Graduate, Undergraduate/Scholarship)* [1123]
CIGNA Healthcare Graduate Scholarships *(Graduate/Scholarship)* [4892]
CIGNA Healthcare Undergraduate Scholarships *(Undergraduate/Scholarship)* [4893]
Charles A. Esser Memorial Scholarships *(Graduate/Scholarship)* [1217]
Rita Mae Kelly Awards *(All/Award/Prize)* [6294]
Michael Koizumi APWA Scholarships *(Undergraduate/Scholarship)* [808]
McKinley Financial Scholarships *(Graduate, Undergraduate/Scholarship)* [4898]
George A. Nielsen Public Investor Scholarships *(Graduate, Undergraduate/Scholarship)* [3267]
NPELRA Foundation Scholarships *(Graduate/Scholarship)* [5309]
Pi Gamma Mu Scholarships *(Graduate/Scholarship)* [5691]
Political Leadership Scholarships *(Undergraduate/Scholarship)* [5773]
Fauneil J. Rinn Scholarships *(Undergraduate/Scholarship)* [6394]

Public affairs

The Jennifer Curtis Byler Scholarships *(Undergraduate/Scholarship)* [5095]
Jane R. Glaser Scholarships *(Undergraduate/Scholarship)* [1124]
Bryce Harlow Fellowship Program *(Undergraduate/Fellowship)* [3401]
Clifford Roberts Graduate Fellowships *(Doctorate/Fellowship)* [2842]
TCA Turkish American Scholarships *(Undergraduate/Scholarship)* [6939]
UAA Elaine Atwood Scholarships *(Undergraduate/Scholarship)* [7051]
UAA GCI, Inc. Scholarships *(Undergraduate/Scholarship)* [7055]

Public health

Arkansas Public Health Association Scholarships *(Undergraduate/Scholarship)* [1233]
Elizabeth and Sherman Asche Memorial Scholarship Fund *(Graduate, Undergraduate/Scholarship)* [1356]
Malcolm U. Dantzler Scholarships *(Professional Development/Scholarship)* [6613]
Frank L. Dautriel Memorial Scholarships (Graduate) *(Graduate/Scholarship)* [4257]
Frank L. Dautriel Memorial Scholarships (Undergraduate) *(Undergraduate/Scholarship)* [4258]
The Gates Millennium Scholars *(Undergraduate/Scholarship)* [3590]
Great Lakes Commission Sea Grant Fellowships *(Graduate/Scholarship)* [3364]
Jewish Federation Academic Scholarships *(Graduate, Undergraduate/Scholarship)* [4029]
W.K. Kellogg Foundation Doctoral Fellowships in Health Policy *(Professional Development/Fellowship)* [4988]
Scholarships for Leadership Training and Coaching *(Professional Development/Scholarship)* [2717]
South Carolina Public Health Association Scholarships *(Undergraduate/Scholarship)* [6614]

Public relations (See also: Advertising)

Betsy Plank/PRSSA Scholarships *(Undergraduate/Scholarship)* [5874]
Rick Brewer Scholarships *(Undergraduate/Scholarship)* [7148]
Louis M. Connor Jr. Scholarships *(Undergraduate/Scholarship)* [7151]
HSBC-North America Scholarship Program *(Undergraduate/Scholarship)* [3592]
International Foodservice Editorial Council Scholarships *(Graduate, Undergraduate/Scholarship)* [3852]
Harriet Irsay Scholarships *(Graduate, Undergraduate/Scholarship)* [674]
The Lagrant Foundation - Graduate Students Scholarships *(Graduate/Scholarship)* [4104]
The Lagrant Foundation - Undergraduate Students Scholarship *(Undergraduate/Scholarship)* [4105]
New York Women in Communications, Inc. Foundation Scholarships *(Graduate, Undergraduate/Scholarship)* [5200]
Stephen D. Pisinski Memorial Scholarships *(Undergraduate/Scholarship)* [5875]
Wendell Scott Awards *(Graduate, Undergraduate/Scholarship)* [3570]
Jim Springer Memorial Scholarships *(Undergraduate/Scholarship)* [2289]
TCA Turkish American Scholarships *(Undergraduate/Scholarship)* [6939]
Gary Yoshimura Scholarships *(Undergraduate/Scholarship)* [5876]

Public service

ARS Undergraduate Scholarships *(Four Year College, Two Year College, Undergraduate/Scholarship)* [1259]
March and Ruti Bell Foundation Scholarships *(Undergraduate/Scholarship)* [1618]
Johnnie L. Cochran, Jr./MWH Scholarships *(Undergraduate/Scholarship)* [4894]
Alice Yuriko Endo Memorial Scholarships *(Undergraduate/Scholarship)* [4016]
The Future Colleagues Scholarships *(Undergraduate/Scholarship)* [4895]
John Gardner Fellowships *(Undergraduate/Fellowship)* [7087]
Land-Use Planning Scholarships *(Graduate/Scholarship)* [4896]
Lewis-Clark State College Governor's Cup Scholarships *(Undergraduate/Scholarship)* [4195]
Willie T. Loud - CH2M Hill Scholarships *(Undergraduate/Scholarship)* [4897]
Walter Moran Farmer Scholarships

(Undergraduate/Scholarship) [7385]
NFBPA/CDM Scholarships *(Undergraduate/Scholarship)* [4899]
Rotary Public Safety Scholarship Fund *(Undergraduate/Scholarship)* [3075]
Donald A. Strauss Scholarships *(Undergraduate/Scholarship)* [7088]
Sheila Tarr-Smith Memorial Scholarships *(Undergraduate/Scholarship)* [5864]
Harry S. Truman Scholarships *(Postgraduate/Scholarship)* [6930]
UAA College of Business & Public Policy Scholarships *(Graduate, Undergraduate/Scholarship)* [7047]
UAA Pignalberi Public Policy Scholarships *(Graduate/Scholarship)* [7070]
Judith Warner Memorial Scholarships *(Undergraduate/Scholarship)* [5867]
Webster Society Scholarships *(Undergraduate/Scholarship)* [7388]

Publishing

WNBA Eastman Grants *(Professional Development/Grant)* [7504]

Quality assurance and control

Ellis R. Ott Scholarships *(Graduate, Undergraduate/Scholarship)* [1037]

Radio and television

American Radio Relay League Louisiana Memorial Scholarships *(Undergraduate/Scholarship)* [815]
American Radio Relay League Scholarships Honoring Barry Goldwater, K7UGA *(Undergraduate/Scholarship)* [816]
Earl I. Anderson Scholarships *(Undergraduate/Scholarship)* [817]
ARRL Foundation General Fund Scholarships *(Undergraduate/Scholarship)* [818]
ARRLF Mississippi Scholarships *(Undergraduate/Scholarship)* [819]
Richard W. Bendicksen Memorial Scholarships *(Undergraduate/Scholarship)* [820]
William Bennett W7PHO Memorial Scholarships *(Undergraduate/Scholarship)* [821]
Henry Broughton, K2AE Memorial Scholarships *(Undergraduate/Scholarship)* [822]
Mary Lou Brown Scholarships *(Undergraduate/Scholarship)* [823]
John Cannon Memorial Scholarships *(Undergraduate/Scholarship)* [4626]
L.B. Cebik, W4RNL, and Jean Cebik, N4TZP, Memorial Scholarships *(Undergraduate/Scholarship)* [824]
Central Arizona DX Association Scholarships *(Undergraduate/Scholarship)* [825]
Challenge Met Scholarships *(Undergraduate/Scholarship)* [826]
Chicago FM Club Scholarships *(Undergraduate/Scholarship)* [827]
Tom and Judith Comstock Scholarships *(Undergraduate/Scholarship)* [828]
Irvine W. Cook WA0CGS Scholarships *(Undergraduate/Scholarship)* [829]
Charles Clarke Cordle Memorial Scholarships *(Undergraduate/Scholarship)* [830]
Albuquerque ARC/Toby Cross Scholarships *(Undergraduate/Scholarship)* [831]
Dayton Amateur Radio Association Scholarships *(Undergraduate/Scholarship)* [832]
Charles N. Fisher Memorial Scholarships *(Undergraduate/Scholarship)* [833]
Allison E. Fisher Scholarships *(Undergraduate/Scholarship)* [2984]
William R. Goldfarb Memorial Scholarships *(Undergraduate/Scholarship)* [834]
Paul and Helen L. Grauer Scholarships *(Undergraduate/Scholarship)* [835]
K2TEO Martin J. Green, Sr. Memorial Scholarships *(Undergraduate/Scholarship)* [836]
Perry F. Hadlock Memorial Scholarships *(Undergraduate/Scholarship)* [837]
Albert H. Hix, W8AH Memorial Scholarships *(Undergraduate/Scholarship)* [838]
Seth Horen, K1LOM Memorial Scholarships *(Undergraduate/Scholarship)* [839]
IRARC Memorial Joseph P. Rubino WA4MMD Scholarships *(Undergraduate/Scholarship)* [840]
Dr. James L. Lawson Memorial Scholarships *(Undergraduate/Scholarship)* [841]
MANAA Media Scholarships *(Graduate, Undergraduate/Scholarship)* [4439]
Fred R. McDaniel Memorial Scholarships *(Undergraduate/Scholarship)* [842]
Edmond A. Metzger Scholarships *(Undergraduate/Scholarship)* [843]
David W. Misek, N8NPX Memorial Scholarships *(Undergraduate/Scholarship)* [844]
Muddy Waters Scholarships *(Undergraduate/Scholarship)* [1768]
NCDXF Scholarships *(Undergraduate/Scholarship)* [845]
New England FEMARA Scholarships *(Undergraduate/Scholarship)* [846]
Ray, NORP and Katie, WOKTE Pautz Scholarships *(Undergraduate/Scholarship)* [847]
Peoria Area Amateur Radio Club Scholarships *(Undergraduate/Scholarship)* [848]
PHD ARA Scholarships *(Undergraduate/Scholarship)* [849]
Thomas W. Porter, W8KYZ Scholarships Honoring Michael Daugherty, W8LSE *(Undergraduate/Scholarship)* [850]
QCWA Memorial Scholarships *(Undergraduate/Scholarship)* [5888]
Donald Riebhoff Memorial Scholarships *(Undergraduate/Scholarship)* [851]
Bill Salerno, W2ONV, Memorial Scholarships *(Undergraduate/Scholarship)* [852]
Eugene Gene Sallee, W4YFR Memorial Scholarships *(Undergraduate/Scholarship)* [853]
Scholarships of the Morris Radio Club of New Jersey *(Undergraduate/Scholarship)* [854]
Six Meter Club of Chicago Scholarships *(Undergraduate/Scholarship)* [855]
Zachary Taylor Stevens Memorial Scholarships *(Undergraduate/Scholarship)* [856]
Carole J. Streeter, KB9JBR Scholarships *(Undergraduate/Scholarship)* [857]
Norman E. Strohmeier, W2VRS Memorial Scholarships *(Undergraduate/Scholarship)* [858]
Gary Wagner, K3OMI Scholarships *(Undergraduate/Scholarship)* [859]
Francis Walton Memorial Scholarships *(Undergraduate/Scholarship)* [860]
L. Phil Wicker Scholarships *(Undergraduate/Scholarship)* [861]
Yankee Clipper Contest Club, Inc. Youth Scholarships *(Undergraduate/Scholarship)* [862]
Yasme Foundation Scholarships *(Undergraduate/Scholarship)* [863]

Radiology

American Roentgen Ray Society Scholarships *(Professional Development/Scholarship)* [906]
Anna Ames Clinical Excellence Student Grants *(Undergraduate/Grant)* [1854]
Jerman-Cahoon Student Scholarship Program *(Undergraduate/Scholarship)* [1040]
Stacy Kaiser Memorial Funds *(Undergraduate/Scholarship)* [6843]
Lewis-Clark State College Presidential Technical Out-of-State Scholarships *(Undergraduate/Scholarship)* [4199]
Ruth McMillan Student Grants *(Undergraduate/Grant)* [1855]
Monster Medical Imaging Educators Scholarship Program *(Postdoctorate/Scholarship)* [1041]
Royce-Osborn Minority Scholarship Program *(Undergraduate/Scholarship)* [1042]
Siemens Clinical Advancement Scholarship Program *(Postgraduate/Scholarship)* [1043]
Society for Pediatric Radiology Research Fellows *(Graduate, Professional Development/Fellowship)* [6535]
Society for Pediatric Radiology Seed Grants *(Graduate, Professional Development/Grant)* [6536]
Superior District Legislative Mentoring Student Grants *(Undergraduate/Grant)* [1856]
Superior District Legislative Mentoring Student Grants RT to DC *(Undergraduate/Grant)* [1857]
Varian Radiation Therapy Scholarship Program *(Postdoctorate/Scholarship)* [1044]

Reading

Jeanne S. Chall Research Fellowships *(Doctorate, Graduate/Grant)* [3888]
Elva Knight Research Grants *(All/Grant)* [3889]
Helen M. Robinson Grants *(Doctorate/Grant)* [3890]
Nila Banton Smith Research Dissemination Support Grants *(All/Grant)* [3891]
Steven A. Stahl Research Grants *(Graduate/Grant)* [3892]

Real estate

Appraisal Institute Education Trust Scholarships *(Graduate, Undergraduate/Scholarship)* [1189]
George M. Brooker Collegiate Scholarships for Minorities *(Graduate, Postgraduate, Undergraduate/Scholarship)* [3748]
Connecticut Mortgage Bankers Scholarships-Social Affairs Committee *(Undergraduate/Scholarship)* [3439]
The Rick Crane Group Real Estate Scholarships Fund *(Undergraduate/Scholarship)* [4173]
Donald M. Furbush Scholarships *(Professional Development/Scholarship)* [3749]
Kenneth M. Good Graduate Students Fellowship Program *(Undergraduate/Fellowship)* [7295]
IREM Foundation Minority Outreach Scholarships *(Professional Development/Scholarship)* [3750]
Michigan Association of Realtors Scholarship Trust *(Undergraduate/Scholarship)* [4474]
Pension Real Estate Association Scholarships *(Undergraduate/Scholarship)* [5568]
Paul H. Rittle Sr. Memorial Scholarships *(Professional Development/Scholarship)* [3751]

Rehabilitation, Physical/Psychological

Patricia Pownder Conolly Memorial Scholarships *(Undergraduate/Scholarship)* [4462]
Linda Lyons Memorial Scholarship Fund *(Undergraduate/Scholarship)* [4464]

Religion

Ambrose-Ramsey Trust Scholarships *(Undergraduate/Scholarship)* [5464]
Martha and Robert Atherton Ministerial Scholarships *(Graduate, Master's/Scholarship)* [6947]
Lewis B. Barber Memorial Scholarships *(Undergraduate/Scholarship)* [6641]
Olympia Brown and Max Kapp Awards *(Graduate/Scholarship)* [6948]
Bujea Memorial Scholarships *(Undergraduate/Scholarship)* [911]
David Eaton Scholarships *(Graduate, Master's/Scholarship)* [6951]
Dorris W. Frey Memorial Scholarships *(Undergraduate/Scholarship)* [6654]
Magoichi & Shizuko Kato Memorial Scholarships *(Graduate/Scholarship)* [4018]
Molly McKay Scholarships *(Undergraduate/Scholarship)* [7178]
Leonard M. Perryman Communications Scholarships for Ethnic Minority Students *(Undergraduate/Scholarship)* [6965]
David Pohl Scholarships *(Graduate, Master's/Scholarship)* [6952]
Roy H. Pollack Scholarships *(Graduate, Master's/Scholarship)* [6953]
David W. Self Scholarships *(Undergraduate/Scholarship)* [6967]
John M. and Mary A. Shanley Memorial Scholarships *(Undergraduate/Scholarship)* [6673]
Richard S. Smith Scholarships *(Undergraduate/Scholarship)* [6968]
Rev. Chuck and Nancy Thomas Scholarships *(Graduate, Master's/Scholarship)* [6958]

Von Ogden Vogt Scholarships *(Graduate, Master's/Scholarship)* [6959]

Remote sensing

Robert N. Colwell Memorial Fellowships *(Doctorate, Graduate/Fellowship)* [1026]
William A. Fisher Memorial Scholarships *(Graduate/Scholarship)* [1027]
Leica Geosystems Internships *(Graduate/Internship)* [1029]
Ta Liang Memorial Awards *(Graduate/Grant)* [1030]
Francis H. Moffitt Memorial Scholarships *(Graduate, Undergraduate/Scholarship)* [1031]

Resource management

Alaska Support Industry Alliance Scholarships *(Undergraduate/Scholarship)* [4341]

Risk management

Gongaware Scholarships College of Business *(Undergraduate/Scholarship)* [3700]
Thompson Scholarship for Women in Safety *(Graduate/Scholarship)* [1072]

Secretarial sciences

Diane Basilone-Engle Memorial Scholarships *(Undergraduate/Scholarship)* [1889]

Science

AAAS Science and Technology Policy Fellowships *(Postdoctorate/Fellowship)* [317]
Academic Promise Scholarships *(Undergraduate/Scholarship)* [3697]
AeA Scholarships *(Undergraduate/Scholarship)* [6162]
AFCEA Math and Science Teachers Scholarships *(Graduate/Scholarship)* [1239]
African American Network - Carolinas Scholarship Fund *(Undergraduate/Scholarship)* [3037]
Janet and Horace Allen Scholarship *(Undergraduate/Scholarship)* [147]
American Association of Family and Consumer Sciences Scholarships *(Undergraduate/Scholarship)* [347]
Hettie M. Anthony Fellowships *(Postdoctorate/Fellowship)* [4051]
Mike Ardaw Scholarships *(Undergraduate/Scholarship)* [4345]
ASBC Foundation Graduate Scholarships *(Doctorate, Graduate/Scholarship)* [922]
Elizabeth and Sherman Asche Memorial Scholarship Fund *(Graduate, Undergraduate/Scholarship)* [1356]
ASMS Research Awards *(Professional Development/Grant)* [993]
Astronaut Scholarship Foundation Scholarships *(Undergraduate/Scholarship)* [1527]
B&W Y-12 Scholarship Fund *(Undergraduate/Scholarship)* [2806]
Bill & Nell Biggs Scholarships *(Undergraduate/Scholarship)* [4348]
Blow Molding Division Memorial Scholarships *(Graduate, Undergraduate/Scholarship)* [6547]
Rev. Andrew L. Bouwhuis Memorial Scholarship Program *(Graduate/Scholarship)* [2073]
Henry Broughton, K2AE Memorial Scholarships *(Undergraduate/Scholarship)* [822]
Catching the Dream Scholarship *(Graduate, Undergraduate/Scholarship)* [632]
Channabasappa Memorial Scholarships *(Graduate, Professional Development/Scholarship)* [3837]
Charline Chilson Scholarships *(Undergraduate/Scholarship)* [2684]
Congressional Science Fellowships *(Postdoctorate/Fellowship)* [1006]
Robert E. Cramer Scholarships *(Graduate, Undergraduate/Scholarship)* [6548]
Critical Language Scholarships for Intensive Summer Institutes *(Graduate, Undergraduate/Scholarship)* [892]
Robert G. Dailey Scholarships *(Graduate, Undergraduate/Scholarship)* [6549]
Delta Gamma Scholarships *(Undergraduate/Scholarship)* [2675]
Development Fund for Black Students in Science and Technology Scholarship *(Undergraduate/Scholarship)* [2707]
Lt. Col. Romeo and Josephine Bass Ferretti Scholarships *(Undergraduate/Scholarship)* [51]
Dr. Mary Finegold Scholarships *(Undergraduate/Scholarship)* [6389]
Reuben H. Fleet Memorial Scholarships *(Undergraduate/Scholarship)* [6189]
Fleming/Blaszcak Scholarships *(Graduate, Undergraduate/Scholarship)* [6550]
The Ginny Frankenthaler Memorial Scholarship *(Undergraduate/Scholarship)* [6629]
Friends of Loutit District Library Scholarships Fund *(Undergraduate/Scholarship)* [3280]
The Gates Millennium Scholars *(Undergraduate/Scholarship)* [3590]
Eloise Gerry Fellowships *(Graduate, Postdoctorate/Fellowship)* [6339]
GET Ready for Math and Science Conditional Scholarships *(Four Year College, Two Year College, Undergraduate/Scholarship)* [7365]
Harold Giles Scholarships *(Graduate, Undergraduate/Scholarship)* [6551]
Benjamin A. Gilman International Scholarship *(Undergraduate/Scholarship)* [7031]
Dr. Robert H. Goddard Memorial Scholarships *(Graduate, Undergraduate/Scholarship)* [5085]
William R. Goldfarb Memorial Scholarships *(Undergraduate/Scholarship)* [834]
Barry M. Goldwater Scholarships *(Undergraduate/Scholarship)* [7256]
GREAT MINDS Collegiate Scholarship Program *(Undergraduate/Scholarship)* [236]
Gulf Coast Hurricane Scholarships *(Graduate, Undergraduate/Scholarship)* [6552]
Guntley-Lorimer Science and Arts Scholarships *(Undergraduate/Scholarship)* [1733]
Hertz Foundation's Graduate Fellowships *(Doctorate/Fellowship)* [4705]
Hinman-Jensen Endowed Scholarships *(Undergraduate/Scholarship)* [4184]
Hispanic College Fund Scholarship Programs *(Undergraduate/Scholarship)* [3583]
Jane Hood Memorial Fund *(Undergraduate/Scholarship)* [2959]
IDA Fellowship Award *(Professional Development/Fellowship)* [3838]
Injection Molding Division Scholarships *(Graduate, Undergraduate/Scholarship)* [6553]
Jamaica National Building Society Scholarships *(Undergraduate/Scholarship)* [4001]
Nancy Lorraine Jensen Memorial Scholarships *(Undergraduate/Scholarship)* [6603]
Lakselaget Foundation Scholarships *(Graduate, Undergraduate/Scholarship)* [4107]
Erwin Lew Memorial Scholarships *(Graduate, Undergraduate/Scholarship)* [6554]
Carie and George Lyter Scholarship Fund *(Undergraduate/Scholarship)* [3110]
James I. MacKenzie Memorial Scholarships *(Graduate, Undergraduate/Scholarship)* [6555]
Pat and John MacTavish Scholarship Fund *(Undergraduate/Scholarship)* [3293]
Masonic-Range Science Scholarships *(Undergraduate/Scholarship)* [6578]
MESBEC Scholarships *(Undergraduate/Scholarship)* [2067]
Nell I. Mondy Fellowships *(Graduate, Postdoctorate/Fellowship)* [6340]
Robert E. and Judy More Scholarship Fund *(Undergraduate/Scholarship)* [2967]
John H. Moss Scholarships *(Undergraduate/Scholarship)* [7230]
National Co-op Scholarship Program *(Undergraduate/Scholarship)* [4809]
National Security Technologies Engineering and Science Scholarships *(Undergraduate/Scholarship)* [5843]
Ted and Ruth Neward Scholarships *(Graduate, Undergraduate/Scholarship)* [6556]
Virginia Nicklas Scholarships *(Undergraduate/Scholarship)* [2658]
Stuart L. Noderer Memorial Scholarships *(Undergraduate/Scholarship)* [6211]
Maureen E. Nolan-Cahill Memorial Scholarships *(Undergraduate/Scholarship)* [4374]
Vessa Notchev Fellowships *(Graduate, Postdoctorate/Fellowship)* [6341]
Robert Noyce Scholarship Program *(Undergraduate/Scholarship)* [5565]
Noyce Scholarships for Secondary Math and Science Education *(Undergraduate/Scholarship)* [3711]
Omicron Nu Research Fellowships *(Postdoctorate/Fellowship)* [4054]
Pennsylvania Library Association Scholarships for MLS Students *(Undergraduate/Scholarship)* [5559]
Phi Theta Kappa Scholarships *(Undergraduate/Scholarship)* [3712]
Plastics Pioneers Association Scholarships *(Graduate, Undergraduate/Scholarship)* [6557]
Polymer Modifiers and Additives Division Scholarships *(Graduate, Undergraduate/Scholarship)* [6558]
RBC Royal Bank Scholarships for Undergraduates *(Undergraduate/Scholarship)* [6068]
Rechsteiner Family Scholarship Fund *(Undergraduate/Scholarship)* [2971]
Leo S. Rowe Pan American Fund *(Undergraduate/Loan)* [5404]
Charles A. Ryskamp Research Fellowships *(Doctorate/Fellowship)* [511]
SDF Community College Transfer Scholarships for Math and Science *(Undergraduate/Scholarship)* [6229]
Sigma Delta Epsilon Fellowships *(Graduate, Postdoctorate/Fellowship)* [6342]
Society of Plastics Engineers General Scholarships *(Graduate, Undergraduate/Scholarship)* [6559]
Society of Plastics Engineers Pittsburgh Scholarships *(Graduate, Undergraduate/Scholarship)* [6560]
Sons of Norway Foundation Scholarships to Oslo International School *(Undergraduate/Scholarship)* [6604]
StraightForward Media's Science Scholarships *(Undergraduate/Scholarship)* [6805]
Anil and Neema Thakrar Family Fund *(Undergraduate/Scholarship)* [3122]
Thermoforming Scholarships *(Graduate, Undergraduate/Scholarship)* [6561]
Thermoplastic Materials and Foams Division Scholarships *(Graduate, Undergraduate/Scholarship)* [6562]
Thermoplastics Elastomers Special Interest Group Scholarships *(Graduate, Undergraduate/Scholarship)* [6563]
UAA Jack & Martha Roderick Scholarships *(Graduate, Undergraduate/Scholarship)* [7057]
UAA Quanterra Scholarships *(Undergraduate/Scholarship)* [7071]
Vinyl Plastics Division Scholarships *(Graduate, Undergraduate/Scholarship)* [6564]
Washington University Law School Chancellor's Graduate Fellowships *(Graduate/Fellowship)* [7386]
William S. Wilson Memorial Scholarships *(Undergraduate/Scholarship)* [4389]
Ross A. Wilson Science Scholarships *(Undergraduate/Scholarship)* [6888]
Woodcock Family Education Scholarship Program *(Undergraduate/Scholarship)* [196]
Yasme Foundation Scholarships *(Undergraduate/Scholarship)* [863]

Science technologies

AAAS Mass Media Science and Engineering Fellowships *(Graduate, Postgraduate, Undergraduate/Fellowship)* [316]
AAAS Science and Technology Policy Fellowships *(Postdoctorate/Fellowship)* [317]
Graduate Fellowships in Alternatives in Scientific Research *(Doctorate, Graduate/Fellowship)* [3854]
The Homeland Security Graduate Fellowships *(Graduate/Fellowship)* [6985]
The Homeland Security Undergraduate Scholarships *(Undergraduate/Scholarship)* [6986]
Lewis-Clark State College/American Chemical Soci-

ety Scholars Program
(Undergraduate/Scholarship) [4192]
Scholarships for Technology Students
(Postgraduate/Scholarship) [1945]
UAA Mark A. Beltz Scholarships (Graduate, Undergraduate/Scholarship) [7063]

Scottish studies (See also: British studies)

Clan Ross Foundation Scholarships
(Undergraduate/Scholarship) [2245]

Sculpture

Alex J. Ettl Grants (Professional Development/Grant) [5037]
National Sculpture Society Scholarships
(Undergraduate/Scholarship) [5038]
UAA Ken Gray Endowment Scholarships
(Undergraduate/Scholarship) [7059]

Sexuality

James J. Harvey Dissertation Fellowships
(Doctorate/Fellowship) [6111]
Society for the Scientific Study of Sexuality Student Research Grants (Undergraduate/Grant) [6587]

Sleep and sleep disorders

NSF Pickwick Postdoctoral Research Fellowships
(Postdoctorate/Fellowship) [5042]

Social sciences

ACLS Frederick Burkhardt Fellowships (Professional Development/Fellowship) [299]
Lorraine Allison Scholarships
(Postgraduate/Scholarship) [1199]
American Society of Comparative Law TransCoop Programs (All/Fellowship) [937]
Association for the Social Scientific Study of Jewry Travel Grant (Graduate/Grant) [1495]
Behavioral Sciences Post-Doctoral Fellowships
(Postdoctorate/Fellowship) [2867]
Beinecke Brothers Memorial Scholarships
(Undergraduate/Scholarship) [7085]
Canada Graduate Scholarships Program
(Graduate/Scholarship) [6418]
Critical Language Scholarships for Intensive Summer Institutes (Graduate, Undergraduate/Scholarship) [892]
Dissertation Proposal Development Fellowships
(Doctorate/Fellowship) [6415]
Fellowships in the Humanities and Social Sciences in Turkey (Postdoctorate/Fellowship) [894]
Fuchs-Harden Educational Scholarships Fund
(Undergraduate/Scholarship) [3375]
Harry Frank Guggenheim Fellowships
(Doctorate/Fellowship) [3385]
Harry Frank Guggenheim Foundation Grants
(All/Grant) [3386]
Conrad N. Hilton Scholarships
(Undergraduate/Scholarship) [2841]
Lois Hole Humanities and Social Sciences Scholarship (Undergraduate/Scholarship) [158]
Jacob K. Javits Fellowships (Doctorate, Master's/Fellowship) [4707]
Korean Studies Dissertation Workshop Funds
(Graduate/Grant) [6416]
Law and Social Science Dissertation Fellowship and Mentoring Program (Doctorate, Graduate/Fellowship) [434]
Henry Luce Foundation Dissertation Fellowships in American Art (Doctorate/Fellowship) [509]
Major Collaborative Research Initiatives Grants
(Graduate/Grant) [6419]
Clara Mayo Grants (Graduate/Grant) [6575]
Andrew W. Mellon Dissertation Completion Fellowships (Doctorate/Fellowship) [510]
Mellon Fellowships (Doctorate, Graduate/Fellowship) [2550]
NAFA International Dissertation Research Fellowships (Graduate/Fellowship) [4709]
National Endowment for the Humanities Advanced Fellowship for Research in Turkey
(Postdoctorate/Fellowship) [900]
National Institute of Health Undergraduate Scholarship Program (Undergraduate/Scholarship) [4949]
Persian Language Study in Tehran (Doctorate, Graduate/Fellowship) [663]
Post-Doctoral Summer Travel-Research Grants
(Doctorate/Grant) [3756]
Short-term senior fellowships in Iranian Studies
(Doctorate, Graduate/Fellowship) [665]
Social Sciences and Humanities Research Council of Canada Standard Research Grants (Doctorate, Graduate/Grant) [6420]
SSHRC Doctoral Fellowships Program
(Doctorate/Fellowship, Scholarship) [6421]
John Streiff Memorial Scholarships
(Undergraduate/Scholarship) [4218]
Summer Language Study Grants in Turkey
(Graduate/Grant) [3758]
Summer Research Diversity Fellowships in Law and Social Science (Undergraduate/Fellowship) [435]
Summer Research Grants in Turkey
(Graduate/Grant) [3759]
Trudeau Foundation Doctoral Scholarships
(Doctorate/Scholarship) [6928]
UAA Michael Baring-Gould Memorial Scholarships
(Graduate, Undergraduate/Scholarship) [7065]
Washington University Law School Chancellor's Graduate Fellowships (Graduate/Fellowship) [7386]

Social work

Emma and Meloid Algood Tuition Scholarships
(Undergraduate/Scholarship) [4664]
Associates in Behavioral Health Scholarships
(Graduate/Scholarship) [5752]
Dr. Joyce Beckett Scholarships
(Undergraduate/Scholarship) [4665]
Mildred Cater Bradham Social Work Fellowships
(Graduate/Fellowship) [7553]
Selena Danette Brown Book Scholarships
(Undergraduate/Scholarship) [4666]
Patricia Pownder Conolly Memorial Scholarships
(Undergraduate/Scholarship) [4462]
Douglas-Coldwell Foundation Scholarships in Social Affairs (Graduate/Scholarship) [2729]
Family and Children's Services of Lebanon County Fund (Undergraduate/Scholarship) [3098]
Randy Green Memorial Scholarship Fund (High School/Scholarship) [2598]
Guynn Family Foundation Book Scholarships
(Undergraduate/Scholarship) [4667]
International Scholarship Program for Community Service (Other/Scholarship) [4460]
Jewish Federation Academic Scholarships (Graduate, Undergraduate/Scholarship) [4029]
Maude Keisling/Cumberland County Extension Homemakers Scholarships
(Undergraduate/Scholarship) [2425]
Linda Lyons Memorial Scholarship Fund
(Undergraduate/Scholarship) [4464]
Joseph McCulley Educational Scholarships (Graduate, Undergraduate/Scholarship) [7229]
Pi Gamma Mu Scholarships (Graduate/Scholarship) [5691]
Portuguese American Police Association Scholarships (Undergraduate/Scholarship) [5740]
Social Work Scholarships (Graduate, Undergraduate/Scholarship) [5778]
Taylor Statten Memorial Fellowships
(Graduate/Scholarship) [7233]
Transgender Scholarships and Education Legacy Fund (Undergraduate/Scholarship) [6142]
Tropicana Community Services - Robert K. Brown Scholarships (Undergraduate/Scholarship) [1743]
Philip F. Vineberg Travelling Fellowship in the Humanities (Graduate/Scholarship) [4432]
Emanuel Weiner Scholarship
(Postgraduate/Scholarship) [3563]
Cenie Jomo Williams Tuition Scholarships
(Undergraduate/Scholarship) [4668]

Sociology (See also: Aggression and violence)

Patricia Pownder Conolly Memorial Scholarships
(Undergraduate/Scholarship) [4462]
Douglas-Coldwell Foundation Scholarships in Social Affairs (Graduate/Scholarship) [2729]
Garikian Scholarship Fund
(Undergraduate/Scholarship) [1279]
Linda Lyons Memorial Scholarship Fund
(Undergraduate/Scholarship) [4464]
NASSS Graduate Minority Scholarships
(Graduate/Scholarship) [5228]
Pi Gamma Mu Scholarships (Graduate/Scholarship) [5691]
UAA Eveline Schuster Memorial Award/Scholarships
(Graduate, Undergraduate/Scholarship) [7053]
UAA Michael Baring-Gould Memorial Scholarships
(Graduate, Undergraduate/Scholarship) [7065]
Minoru Yasui Memorial Scholarship
(Graduate/Scholarship) [4022]

Soil science

Dr. Karl C. Ivarson Scholarships
(Postgraduate/Scholarship) [36]

Spanish studies (See also: Area and ethnic studies)

Jane Salanky-Onzik Scholarship Fund
(Undergraduate/Scholarship) [2974]

Speech, Debate, and Forensics

Gongoro Nakamura Memorial Scholarships
(Undergraduate/Scholarship) [4020]

Speech and language pathology/audiology

AMBUCS Scholarships for Therapists Program
(Graduate, Undergraduate/Scholarship) [258]
Fred Berg Awards (All/Award/Prize) [2828]
Educational Audiology Association Doctoral Scholarships (Doctorate/Scholarship) [2829]
Dwight A. Hamilton Scottish Rite Foundation of Colorado Graduate Scholarships
(Graduate/Scholarship) [6284]
Houston/Nancy Holliman Scholarships
(Undergraduate/Scholarship) [2690]
Noel D. Matkin Awards
(Undergraduate/Award/Prize) [2830]
Helen Woodruff Nolop Scholarship in Audiology and Allied Fields (Graduate/Scholarship) [2696]
Research Grants in Speech Science
(Doctorate/Grant) [1106]
Student Research Grants in Audiology
(Doctorate/Grant) [1107]
Student Research Grants in Early Childhood Language Development (Doctorate/Grant) [1108]

Sports studies

Athletic Excellence Scholarships
(Undergraduate/Scholarship) [5753]
Bernice Barabash Sports Scholarship
(Undergraduate/Scholarship) [3972]
BCA Ethnic Minority Postgraduate Scholarships for Careers in Athletics (Undergraduate/Scholarship) [1748]
Walter Byers Postgraduate Scholarships
(Postgraduate/Scholarship) [4802]
Ethnic Minority and Women's Enhancement Postgraduate Scholarships (Graduate/Scholarship) [4803]
Georgia Hilton Academic Scholarships
(Undergraduate/Scholarship) [6074]

John McLendon Memorial Minority Postgraduate Scholarships *(Postdoctorate/Scholarship)* [4691]

Sports writing

Freedom Forum-NCAA Sports-Journalism Scholarships *(Undergraduate/Scholarship)* [4804]
Chuck Pezzano Scholarships *(Undergraduate/Scholarship)* [1770]

Statistics

AAUW Legal Advocacy Fund Selected Professions Fellowships *(Doctorate, Graduate/Fellowship)* [7]
ASA/NSF/BLS Fellowships *(Graduate/Fellowship)* [1112]
Avista Corporation Minds in Motion Scholarships *(Undergraduate/Scholarship)* [4163]
Edward C. Bryant Scholarships Trust Fund *(Graduate/Fellowship)* [1113]
Jorge Espejal Contreras Memorial Scholarships *(Graduate, Undergraduate/Scholarship)* [3804]
Gertrude M. Cox Scholarships *(Doctorate, Graduate/Fellowship)* [1114]
Ellis R. Ott Scholarships *(Graduate, Undergraduate/Scholarship)* [1037]
Wilks Memorial Awards *(Undergraduate/Award/Prize)* [1115]

Substance abuse

ASA Minority Fellowships Program *(Doctorate, Master's/Fellowship)* [1094]

Suicide

AFSP - Distinguished Investigator Grants *(Postgraduate/Grant)* [587]
AFSP Postdoctoral Research Fellowships *(Postgraduate/Fellowship)* [588]
AFSP Standard Research Grants *(Postgraduate/Grant)* [589]
AFSP Young Investigator Grants *(Postgraduate/Grant)* [590]
American Foundation for Suicide and Prevention Pilot Grants *(Postgraduate/Grant)* [591]
Eleanor Benett Scholarships *(All/Scholarship)* [6815]

Surgery

AAST/ACS/NIGMS Scholarships *(Professional Development/Scholarship)* [407]
AAST/KCI Research Grants *(All/Grant)* [408]
AAST Medical Student Scholarships *(All/Scholarship)* [409]
American Association for Hand Surgery Annual Research Awards *(Professional Development/Award/Prize)* [349]
APSNA Educational Scholarships *(Professional Development/Scholarship)* [763]
AST National Honor Society Student Scholarships *(Graduate/Scholarship)* [1499]
Ivan Braga Scholarships *(Undergraduate/Scholarship)* [6308]
Career Mobility Scholarship Awards *(Doctorate, Undergraduate/Scholarship)* [16]
Daland Fellowships in Clinical Investigation *(Doctorate/Fellowship)* [767]
Thomson Delmar Learning Surgical Technology Scholarships *(Graduate/Scholarship)* [1500]
Foundation for Surgical Technology Advanced Education/Medical Mission Scholarships *(Graduate/Scholarship)* [1501]
Foundation for Surgical Technology Scholarships *(Graduate/Scholarship)* [1502]
Hemostasis and Resuscitation Research Scholarships *(All/Scholarship)* [410]
Local Wound Haemostatics and Hemorrhage Control Scholarships *(All/Scholarship)* [411]
SUS Foundation Junior Faculty Grants *(Graduate/Grant)* [6589]
SUS - Wyeth Clinical Scholar Award *(Graduate/Award/Prize)* [6590]

Swedish studies

Lilly Lorenzen Scholarships *(Undergraduate/Scholarship)* [1119]
Malmberg Fellowships *(Undergraduate/Fellowship)* [1120]
Malmberg Scholarships *(Undergraduate/Scholarship)* [1121]

Systems engineering

ISA Aerospace Industries Division - William H. Atkinson Scholarships *(Graduate, Undergraduate/Scholarship)* [3940]
Norman E. Huston Scholarships *(Graduate, Undergraduate/Scholarship)* [3941]
ISA Educational Foundation Scholarships *(Graduate, Undergraduate/Scholarship)* [3942]
ISA Executive Board Scholarships *(Graduate, Undergraduate/Scholarship)* [3943]
ISA Section and District Scholarships - Birmingham *(Graduate, Undergraduate/Scholarship)* [3944]
ISA Section and District Scholarships - Houston *(Graduate, Undergraduate/Scholarship)* [3945]
ISA Section and District Scholarships - Lehigh Valley *(Graduate, Undergraduate/Scholarship)* [3946]
ISA Section and District Scholarships - New Jersey *(Graduate, Undergraduate/Scholarship)* [3947]
ISA Section and District Scholarships - Niagara Frontier *(Graduate, Undergraduate/Scholarship)* [3948]
ISA Section and District Scholarships - Northern California *(Graduate, Undergraduate/Scholarship)* [3949]
ISA Section and District Scholarships - Richmond (Hopewell) *(Graduate, Undergraduate/Scholarship)* [3950]
ISA Section and District Scholarships - Savannah River *(Graduate, Undergraduate/Scholarship)* [3951]
ISA Section and District Scholarships - Southwestern Wyoming *(Graduate, Undergraduate/Scholarship)* [3952]
ISA Section and District Scholarships - Texas, Louisiana and Mississippi *(Graduate, Undergraduate/Scholarship)* [3953]
ISA Section and District Scholarships - Wilmington *(Graduate, Undergraduate/Scholarship)* [3954]
ISA Technical Division Scholarships - Analysis Division *(Graduate, Undergraduate/Scholarship)* [3955]
ISA Technical Division Scholarships - Chemical and Petroleum Industries Division *(Graduate, Undergraduate/Scholarship)* [3956]
ISA Technical Division Scholarships - Computer Technology Division *(Graduate, Undergraduate/Scholarship)* [3957]
ISA Technical Division Scholarships - Food and Pharmaceutical Industries Division *(Graduate, Undergraduate/Scholarship)* [3958]
ISA Technical Division Scholarships - Power Industry Division *(Graduate, Undergraduate/Scholarship)* [3959]
ISA Technical Division Scholarships - Process Measurement and Control Division *(Graduate, Undergraduate/Scholarship)* [3960]
ISA Technical Division Scholarships - Pulp and Paper Industry Division *(Graduate, Undergraduate/Scholarship)* [3961]
ISA Technical Division Scholarships - Test Measurement Division *(Graduate, Undergraduate/Scholarship)* [3962]
ISA Technical Division Scholarships - Water and Wastewater Industries Division *(Graduate, Undergraduate/Scholarship)* [3963]
Bob and Mary Ives Scholarships *(Graduate, Undergraduate/Scholarship)* [3964]

Taxonomy

Charlie Fleming Education Fund Scholarships *(Undergraduate/Scholarship)* [5106]

Teaching

AMS Teacher Education Scholarships *(Undergraduate/Scholarship)* [718]
Quincy Brown Memorial Scholarships *(Undergraduate/Scholarship)* [5923]
Jennifer Coulter Memorial Scholarships *(Undergraduate/Scholarship)* [5474]
Patricia Ann Hughes Eastaugh Memorial Teaching Scholarships *(Undergraduate/Scholarship)* [4355]
Ford Foundation Predoctoral Fellowships for Minorities *(Doctorate/Fellowship)* [4703]
Jonathan Hastings Foster Scholarships *(Undergraduate/Scholarship)* [6190]
Future Teachers Conditional Scholarships and Loan Repayment *(Professional Development, Undergraduate/Loan)* [7364]
Ida L. Hartenberg Charitable Scholarships *(Undergraduate/Scholarship)* [3456]
Hartford County Retired Teachers Association Scholarships *(Undergraduate/Scholarship)* [3457]
Illinois Future Teacher Corps Scholarships *(Undergraduate/Scholarship)* [3663]
Johnson and Wales University Scholarships *(Undergraduate/Scholarship)* [4039]
KHEAA Teacher Scholarships *(Undergraduate/Scholarship)* [1704]
Doreen Legg Memorial Scholarships *(Undergraduate/Scholarship)* [5955]
Minority Teachers of Illinois Scholarships *(Undergraduate/Scholarship)* [3670]
Pierce County Retired Teachers Scholarships *(Undergraduate/Scholarship)* [5694]
John M. and Mary A. Shanley Memorial Scholarships *(Undergraduate/Scholarship)* [6673]
StraightForward Media's Teacher Scholarships *(Undergraduate/Scholarship)* [6806]
John I. and Madeleine R. Taeni Scholarships *(Undergraduate/Scholarship)* [6678]
Transgender Scholarships and Education Legacy Fund *(Undergraduate/Scholarship)* [6142]
University of Hawaii at Manoa Graduate Assistantship Awards *(Graduate/Award/Prize)* [7096]
Edwyna Wheadon Postgraduate Training Scholarship Fund *(Professional Development/Scholarship)* [4827]

Technical communications

Alaska Aerospace Development Corporation Scholarships *(Undergraduate/Scholarship)* [4338]
Youth Scholarships *(Undergraduate/Scholarship)* [6528]

Technology

Accenture American Indian Scholarship Program *(Graduate, Undergraduate/Scholarship)* [640]
AFFIRM University Scholarships *(Undergraduate/Scholarship)* [1414]
Bank of America Junior Achievement Scholarship Fund *(Undergraduate/Scholarship)* [3040]
Arthur and Gladys Cervenka Scholarships *(Undergraduate/Scholarship)* [6472]
Chapter - 6 Fairfield County Scholarships *(Undergraduate/Scholarship)* [6474]
CN Scholarships for Women *(Postgraduate/Scholarship)* [6433]
Development Fund for Black Students in Science and Technology Scholarship *(Undergraduate/Scholarship)* [2707]
William P. Elrod Memorial Scholarships *(Undergraduate/Scholarship)* [6853]
Lt. Col. Romeo and Josephine Bass Ferretti Scholarships *(Undergraduate/Scholarship)* [51]
GREAT MINDS Collegiate Scholarship Program *(Undergraduate/Scholarship)* [236]
Perry F. Hadlock Memorial Scholarships *(Undergraduate/Scholarship)* [837]
Helm Family Scholarships *(Undergraduate/Scholarship)* [6192]
Henry Ford Academy Scholarships *(Undergraduate/Scholarship)* [6492]
Hinman-Jensen Endowed Scholarships *(Undergraduate/Scholarship)* [4184]
Jamaica National Building Society Scholarships *(Undergraduate/Scholarship)* [4001]

Johnson and Wales University Scholarships (Undergraduate/Scholarship) [4039]
Lucile B. Kaufman Women's Scholarships (Undergraduate/Scholarship) [6493]
Laser Technology, Engineering and Applications Scholarships (Graduate, Undergraduate/Scholarship) [6697]
Litherland/FTE Scholarships (Undergraduate/Scholarship) [3911]
Litherland/FTE Scholarships (Undergraduate/Scholarship) [3912]
Maley/FTE Teacher Scholarships (Graduate/Scholarship) [3913]
Giuliano Mazzetti Scholarships (Undergraduate/Scholarship) [6497]
Dr. Ezra Nesbeth Scholarships (Undergraduate/Scholarship) [4002]
Robert Noyce Scholarship Program (Undergraduate/Scholarship) [5565]
Rachael Patterson Memorial Scholarships (Undergraduate/Scholarship) [6846]
PSAI Scholarship Funds (Undergraduate/Scholarship) [5735]
Wendell Scott Awards (Graduate, Undergraduate/Scholarship) [3570]
SME Ford PAS Scholarships (Undergraduate/Scholarship) [6504]
Eben Tisdale Fellowships (Graduate, Undergraduate/Fellowship) [3148]
TSA Teach Technology Scholarships (Undergraduate/Scholarship) [6854]
Joseph A. Vasta Memorial Scholarships (Undergraduate/Scholarship) [2924]
Myrtle and Earl Walker Scholarships (Undergraduate/Scholarship) [6505]
William E. Weisel Scholarships (Undergraduate/Scholarship) [6507]
Lisa Winkler Memorial Scholarships (Undergraduate/Scholarship) [1415]

Telecommunications systems

The Access Intelligence Scholarships (Graduate, Undergraduate/Scholarship) [6580]
APS/ASU Scholarships (Undergraduate/Scholarship) [5697]
Jim Bourque Scholarships (Postgraduate/Scholarship) [1200]
Dickey Rural Networks College Scholarship Program (Undergraduate/Scholarship) [2709]
Richard Gregory Freeland, II Educational Scholarships (High School/Scholarship) [1762]
Future Leader in Radiocommunications Scholarships (Postgraduate/Scholarship) [5893]
NABTP Collegian (Undergraduate/Scholarship) [4670]
The A.W. Perigard Fund (Graduate, Undergraduate/Scholarship) [6581]
The PSSC Legacy Fund (Graduate, Undergraduate/Scholarship) [6582]
Snodgrass Scholarships (Undergraduate/Scholarship) [4384]
The SSPI Mid-Atlantic Chapter Scholarships (Graduate, Undergraduate/Scholarship) [6583]
The SSPI Northeast Chapter Scholarships (Graduate, Undergraduate/Scholarship) [6584]
The SSPI Southern California Scholarships (Graduate, Undergraduate/Scholarship) [6585]

Testing, educational/psychological

AERA-ETS Fellowship Program in Measurement (Postdoctorate/Fellowship) [544]
ASNT Fellowship Awards (Graduate/Fellowship) [1022]
Robert B. Oliver ASNT Scholarships (Undergraduate/Scholarship) [1023]

Textile science

California Association of Family and Consumer Sciences (CAFCS)-San Diego Chapter Scholarships (Graduate, Undergraduate/Scholarship) [6177]
S. Penny Chappell Scholarships (Undergraduate/Scholarship) [5658]
Charles H. Stone Scholarships (Undergraduate/Scholarship) [413]
Sutherland/Purdy Scholarships (Undergraduate/Scholarship) [5682]

Theater arts

Margaret M. Alkek Scholarship (Undergraduate/Scholarship) [2637]
American Society for Theatre Research Dissertation Research Fellowships (Doctorate/Fellowship) [1076]
Artistic Scholarship Awards (Undergraduate/Scholarship) [1598]
ASTR Research Fellowships (All/Grant) [1077]
Charly Baker and Health Merriwether Memorial Scholarships (Undergraduate/Scholarship) [5755]
Leighton M. Ballew Directing Scholarships (Undergraduate/Scholarship) [6631]
Diane Basilone-Engle Memorial Scholarships (Undergraduate/Scholarship) [1889]
David Beltran Memorial Scholarships (Undergraduate/Scholarship) [5919]
William R. Durham/Theater Scholarship (Undergraduate/Scholarship) [2463]
S. Randolph Edmonds Young Scholars Competition (Graduate, Undergraduate/Scholarship) [1753]
Henry and Janet Guareillo Scholarship Fund (Undergraduate/Scholarship) [3103]
Polly Holliday Scholarships (Undergraduate/Scholarship) [6632]
Indiana State Alumni Association Creative and Performing Arts Award (Undergraduate/Scholarship) [3701]
Patricia Van Kirk Scholarships (Undergraduate/Scholarship) [5768]
Montana Broadcasters Association Directors' Scholarships (Undergraduate/Scholarship) [4571]
Orange County Centennial Arts Scholarships (Undergraduate/Scholarship) [5363]
Palo Verde High School Faculty Follies Scholarships (Undergraduate/Scholarship) [5847]
Robert Porterfield Graduate Scholarships (Graduate/Scholarship) [6633]
Stephen Schwartz Musical Theatre Scholarships (Undergraduate/Scholarship) [3625]
Anne Shaw Fellowships (Graduate/Fellowship) [6879]
Marian A. Smith Scholarships (Graduate/Scholarship) [6634]
Southeastern Theatre Conference Secondary School Scholarships (Undergraduate/Scholarship) [6635]
William E. Wilson Scholarships (Graduate/Scholarship) [6636]
Gwen Yarnell Theatre Scholarships (Undergraduate/Scholarship) [2934]

Theology (See also: Religion)

Rev. and Mrs. A.K. Jizmejian Educational Fund (Undergraduate/Scholarship) [1286]

Toxicology

Clinical Toxicology Fellowships (Doctorate/Fellowship) [389]
School of Pharmacy Continuing Student Scholarships (Undergraduate/Scholarship) [7269]
University of Wisconsin-Madison Pharmacy New Student Scholarships (Undergraduate/Scholarship) [7280]

Transportation

ABA Academic Merit Scholarships (Undergraduate/Scholarship) [445]
ABA Diversity Scholarships (Undergraduate/Scholarship) [446]
ABA Members Scholarships (All ABA Member Companies) (Undergraduate/Scholarship) [448]
Academic Scholarship Program A (Undergraduate/Scholarship) [4843]
Academic Scholarship Program B (Undergraduate/Scholarship) [4844]
Air Traffic Control Association Full-time Employee Student Scholarships (Other/Scholarship) [62]
Air Traffic Control Association Non-employee Student Scholarships (Undergraduate/Scholarship) [63]
Sharon D. Banks Undergraduate Memorial Scholarships (Undergraduate/Scholarship) [7508]
Bison Transport Scholarships (Undergraduate/Scholarship) [5341]
Continuing Education Awards (All/Scholarship) [4734]
CTP Scholarship Program (Professional Development/Scholarship) [5024]
Ginger and Fred Deines Canada Scholarships (Undergraduate/Scholarship) [6917]
Ginger and Fred Deines Mexico Scholarships (Undergraduate/Scholarship) [6918]
Delta Nu Alpha Foundation Scholarships (Undergraduate/Scholarship) [2677]
Gabe A. Hartl Scholarships (Undergraduate/Scholarship) [64]
Hooper Memorial Scholarships (Undergraduate/Scholarship) [6919]
Anne Koby Legacy Scholarships (Undergraduate/Scholarship) [7509]
Denny Lydic Scholarships (Undergraduate/Scholarship) [6920]
Marathon Oil Corporation College Scholarship Program (Graduate, Undergraduate/Scholarship) [3600]
Helen M. Overly Memorial Scholarships (Undergraduate/Scholarship) [7510]
Peter L. Picknelly Honorary Scholarships (Undergraduate/Scholarship) [449]
Frank J. Richter Scholarships (Graduate, Undergraduate/Scholarship) [395]
SC and R Foundation Grant Program (Undergraduate/Grant) [6686]
SC and R Foundation Scholarships (Undergraduate/Scholarship) [6687]
E.J. Sierleja Memorial Fellowships (Graduate/Fellowship) [3739]
Snowmobile Association of Massachusetts Scholarships (Undergraduate/Scholarship) [6413]
TAC Foundation-3M Canada Company (Postgraduate, Undergraduate/Scholarship) [6898]
TAC Foundation-Albert M. Stevens Scholarships (Postgraduate/Scholarship) [6899]
TAC Foundation-Armtec Scholarships (Undergraduate/Scholarship) [6900]
TAC Foundation-BA Group Scholarships (Postgraduate, Undergraduate/Scholarship) [6901]
TAC Foundation-Cement Association of Canada Scholarships (Postgraduate, Undergraduate/Scholarship) [6902]
TAC Foundation-Delcan Corporation Scholarships (Postgraduate, Undergraduate/Scholarship) [6903]
TAC Foundation-Dillon Consulting Scholarships (Undergraduate/Scholarship) [6904]
TAC Foundation-EBA Engineering Consultants Ltd. Scholarships (Postgraduate, Undergraduate/Scholarship) [6905]
TAC Foundation-IBI Group Scholarships (Postgraduate, Undergraduate/Scholarship) [6906]
TAC Foundation-iTRANS Consulting Scholarships (Postgraduate/Scholarship) [6907]
TAC Foundation-McCormick Rankin Corporation Scholarships (Undergraduate/Scholarship) [6908]
TAC Foundation-MMM Group Limited Scholarships (Postgraduate, Undergraduate/Scholarship) [6909]
TAC Foundation-Municipalities Scholarships (Postgraduate, Undergraduate/Scholarship) [6910]
TAC Foundation-Provinces and Territories Scholarships (Postgraduate, Undergraduate/Scholarship) [6911]
TAC Foundation Scholarships (Postgraduate, Undergraduate/Scholarship) [6912]
TAC Foundation-Stantec Consulting Scholarships (Postgraduate/Scholarship) [6913]
TAC Foundation-UMA Engineering Ltd. Scholarships (Undergraduate/Scholarship) [6914]
TAC Foundation-Waterloo Alumni Scholarships (Postgraduate/Scholarship) [6915]
Texas Transportation Scholarships (Undergraduate/Scholarship) [6921]

Alice Glaisyer Warfield Scholarships (Undergraduate/Scholarship) [6922]

Travel and tourism

ABA Academic Merit Scholarships (Undergraduate/Scholarship) [445]
ABA Diversity Scholarships (Undergraduate/Scholarship) [446]
ABA Members Scholarships (All ABA Member Companies) (Undergraduate/Scholarship) [448]
Alaska Airlines Scholarships (Undergraduate/Scholarship) [1079]
Alaska Visitors Association/Gomar Scholarships (Undergraduate/Scholarship) [4342]
American Express Travel Scholarships (Undergraduate/Scholarship) [1080]
American Society of Travel Agents AVIS Scholarships (Graduate, Professional Development, Undergraduate/Scholarship) [1081]
Applied Hospitality Degree Scholarships (Undergraduate/Scholarship) [1975]
Arizona Chapter Gold Scholarships (Undergraduate/Scholarship) [1082]
Canadian Hospitality Foundation College Entrance Scholarships (Undergraduate/Scholarship) [1976]
Canadian Hospitality Foundation University Entrance Scholarships (Undergraduate/Scholarship) [1977]
Sue and Ken Dyer Foundation Travel Scholarship Award (Undergraduate/Scholarship) [3096]
GLP Program Scholarships (Other/Scholarship) [4784]
David J. Hallissey Memorial Scholarships (Undergraduate/Scholarship) [1083]
Healy Scholarships (Undergraduate/Scholarship) [1084]
Barbara and Nicole Heicox Foreign Travel and Study Scholarships Fund (Undergraduate/Scholarship) [3284]
Holland America Line-Westours Research Grants (Undergraduate/Grant) [1085]
Independent Studies Program Scholarships (Other/Scholarship) [4785]
Peter Meyer Memorial Scholarships (Undergraduate/Scholarship) [7398]
Mike Kabo Global Scholarships (Other/Scholarship) [4786]
Orange County Tourism Council Scholarships (Undergraduate/Scholarship) [5365]
Peter L. Picknelly Honorary Scholarships (Undergraduate/Scholarship) [449]
Pleasant Hawaiian Holidays Scholarships (Undergraduate/Scholarship) [1086]
Stan and Leone Pollard Scholarships (Undergraduate/Scholarship) [1087]
George Reinke Scholarships (Undergraduate/Scholarship) [1088]
Ollie Rosenberg Scholarship Travel Fund (Undergraduate/Scholarship) [3118]
South Carolina Tourism and Hospitality Educational Foundation Scholarships (Undergraduate/Scholarship) [3618]
Nancy Stewart Scholarships (Undergraduate/Scholarship) [1089]
United States Tour Operators Association Scholarships (Undergraduate/Scholarship) [7019]
West Virginia Educational Foundation Hospitality Business Alliance Scholarships (Undergraduate/Scholarship) [7399]
West Virginia Hospitality and Travel Association General Scholarships (Undergraduate/Scholarship) [7400]
Youth for Understanding Scholarships (Undergraduate/Scholarship) [7549]

Turfgrass management

Nu-Gro Corporation Turfgrass Scholarships (Graduate) (Graduate, Postgraduate/Scholarship) [6075]
Nu-Gro Corporation Turfgrass Scholarships (Undergraduate) (Undergraduate/Scholarship) [6076]
Ratcliffe Hicks School of Agriculture Heritage Scholarships (Undergraduate/Scholarship) [3492]

Turkish studies

Institute of Turkish Studies Dissertation Writing Grants (Doctorate/Grant) [3753]
Institute of Turkish Studies Sabbatical Research Grants (Professional Development/Grant) [3754]
Post-Doctoral Summer Travel-Research Grants (Doctorate/Grant) [3756]
Research Grants in Comparative Studies of Modern Turkey (Graduate, Postdoctorate/Grant) [3757]
Summer Language Study Grants in Turkey (Graduate/Grant) [3758]
Summer Research Grants in Turkey (Graduate/Grant) [3759]

Ukrainian studies

Leo J. Krysa Family Undergraduate Scholarships (Undergraduate/Scholarship) [1982]
Ukrainian Canadian Professional and Business Club Scholarships in Education (Undergraduate/Scholarship) [1983]

United States studies

AAS-American Historical Print Collectors Society Fellowships (Doctorate/Fellowship) [294]
The Christoph Daniel Ebeling Fellowships (Doctorate/Fellowship) [302]
Hench Post-Dissertation Fellowships (Postdoctorate/Fellowship) [303]
Institute-NEH Postdoctoral Fellowships (Doctorate, Professional Development/Fellowship) [5338]
Marshall-Baruch Fellowships (Doctorate/Fellowship) [4318]
Institute Andrew W. Mellon Postdoctoral Research Fellowships (Professional Development/Fellowship) [5339]
National Academies Postdoctoral Fellowships (Postdoctorate/Fellowship) [4620]
The Reese Fellowships (Doctorate/Fellowship) [307]
Savatori Fellowships (Graduate/Fellowship) [3773]
United States Capitol Historical Society Fellowships (Graduate/Fellowship) [6983]

Urban affairs/design/planning

Charles Abrams Scholarship Program (Graduate/Scholarship) [775]
APA Planning Fellowships (Graduate/Fellowship) [776]
Robert A. Catlin/David W. Long Memorial Scholarships (Graduate/Scholarship) [777]
CIGNA Healthcare Graduate Scholarships (Graduate/Scholarship) [4892]
CIGNA Healthcare Undergraduate Scholarships (Undergraduate/Scholarship) [4893]
Economic Development Division Graduate Scholarships (Graduate/Scholarship) [778]
Environment, Natural Resource and Energy (ENRE) Division Fellowships (Graduate/Scholarship) [779]
Jewish Federation Academic Scholarships (Graduate, Undergraduate/Scholarship) [4029]
McKinley Financial Scholarships (Graduate, Undergraduate/Scholarship) [4898]
Judith McManus Price Scholarships (Graduate, Undergraduate/Scholarship) [780]

Urology

AUA Foundation/Astellas Rising Star in Urology Research Awards (Postdoctorate/Fellowship) [1126]
AUA Foundation Bridge Awards (Postgraduate/Fellowship) [1127]
AUA Foundation M.D./Ph.D. Fellowships (Postdoctorate, Postgraduate/Fellowship) [1128]
AUA Foundation M.D. Post-resident Fellowships (Postgraduate/Fellowship) [1129]
AUA Foundation - NIDDK/NCI Surgeon-Scientist Awards (Postgraduate/Fellowship) [1130]
AUA Foundation Ph.D. Post-Doctoral Fellowships (Postdoctorate/Fellowship) [1131]

Vacuum science and technology

IUVSTA Welch Scholarships (Professional Development/Scholarship) [1581]

Veterinary science and medicine

AABP Amstutz Scholarships (Undergraduate/Scholarship) [326]
AABP Bovine Veterinary Student Recognition Award (Undergraduate/Scholarship) [327]
AABP Education Grants (Undergraduate/Grant) [328]
AABP Research Assistantship (Doctorate/Scholarship) [329]
AABP Student Externship Program (Undergraduate/Scholarship) [330]
AAEP/ALSIC Scholarships (Undergraduate/Scholarship) [344]
AAEP Foundation Research Fellowships (Doctorate/Scholarship) [345]
American Quarter Horse Foundation Scholarships (Undergraduate/Scholarship) [811]
Association for Women Veterinarians Foundation Scholarships Program (Graduate/Scholarship) [1523]
Auburn University College of Veterinary Medicine Scholarships (Undergraduate/Scholarship) [113]
Diane Basilone-Engle Memorial Scholarships (Undergraduate/Scholarship) [1889]
CDC Foundation Scholarships (Undergraduate/Scholarship) [2075]
DAAD Study Scholarship Awards (Graduate/Scholarship) [3223]
Keith Gilmore Foundation - Postgraduate Scholarships (Postgraduate/Scholarship) [3241]
Keith Gilmore Foundation - Undergraduate Scholarships (Undergraduate/Scholarship) [3242]
Dr. M.G. "Doc" Headley Scholarships (Undergraduate/Scholarship) [6778]
Dr. Roger E. Meisner Veterinary Medicine Educational Scholarship Fund (Undergraduate/Scholarship) [5257]
NCF Fort Dodge Animal Health Legacy Scholarships for Veterinary Students (Undergraduate/Scholarship) [4792]
North Dakota Veterinary Medical Association Scholarships (Undergraduate/Scholarship) [5258]
Laurie Page-Peck Scholarships Fund (Undergraduate/Scholarship) [1525]
Stark County Dairy Promoters Scholarships (Undergraduate/Scholarship) [6755]
E.L. Stubbs Research Grants (Graduate/Grant) [4507]
Dr. William "Tim" Whalen Memorial Scholarship (Undergraduate/Scholarship) [5259]
Saul T. Wilson, Jr. Scholarships (Graduate, Undergraduate/Scholarship) [7300]

Video

UFVA Carole Fielding Student Grants (Graduate, Undergraduate/Grant) [7091]

Vietnamese studies

Gamewarden Scholarship program (High School, Undergraduate/Scholarship) [3156]
James Elliott Williams Scholarship Fund (Undergraduate/Scholarship) [5537]

Visual arts

Artistic Scholarship Awards (Undergraduate/Scholarship) [1598]
William E. Barto Scholarships (Undergraduate/Scholarship) [2772]
Bill Bendiner and Doug Morgenson Scholarships (Undergraduate/Scholarship) [5757]
Sally Cole Visual Arts Scholarship Fund (Undergraduate/Scholarship) [3054]

Constant Memorial Scholarship for Aquidneck Island Resident *(Undergraduate/Scholarship)* [6036]
Inez Demonet Scholarships *(Graduate/Scholarship)* [7316]
Jane Hood Memorial Fund *(Undergraduate/Scholarship)* [2959]
Patricia Van Kirk Scholarships *(Undergraduate/Scholarship)* [5768]
Manzer-Keener-Wefler Scholarships *(Undergraduate/Scholarship)* [6739]
Jack D. Motteler Scholarships *(Undergraduate/Scholarship)* [5771]
Orange County Centennial Arts Scholarships *(Undergraduate/Scholarship)* [5363]
Pride Foundation Scholarships *(Undergraduate/Scholarship)* [6134]
RBC Royal Bank Scholarships for Undergraduates *(Undergraduate/Scholarship)* [6068]
Ric Ulrich and Chuck Pischke Scholarships *(Undergraduate/Scholarship)* [5782]
Vesalius Trust Student Scholarships *(Undergraduate/Scholarship)* [7317]

Visual impairment

William and Dorothy Ferrell Scholarship Program *(Undergraduate/Scholarship)* [1390]

Viticulture

American Society for Enology and Viticulture Scholarships *(Undergraduate/Scholarship)* [958]

Waste management

Environmental Research and Education Foundation Scholarships *(Postdoctorate/Scholarship)* [2865]

Water resources

ACWA Water Law and Policy Scholarships *(Graduate/Scholarship)* [1375]
Association of California Water Agencies Scholarships *(Undergraduate/Scholarship)* [1376]
Thomas R. Camp Scholarships *(Graduate/Scholarship)* [1142]
Canadian Water Resources Association Scholarships *(All/Scholarship)* [2047]
Channabasappa Memorial Scholarships *(Graduate, Professional Development/Scholarship)* [3837]
Holly A. Cornell Scholarships *(Graduate/Scholarship)* [1143]
Richard A. Herbert Memorial Scholarships *(Undergraduate/Scholarship)* [1138]
Clair A. Hill Scholarships *(Undergraduate/Scholarship)* [1377]
IDA Fellowship Award *(Professional Development/Fellowship)* [3838]
Larson Aquatic Research Support *(Graduate/Scholarship)* [1144]
Ken Thomson Scholarships *(Undergraduate/Scholarship)* [2048]
Abel Wolman Fellowships *(Doctorate/Fellowship)* [1145]

Water supply industry

Len Assante Scholarship Fund *(Undergraduate/Scholarship)* [4915]
Thomas R. Camp Scholarships *(Graduate/Scholarship)* [1142]
Holly A. Cornell Scholarships *(Graduate/Scholarship)* [1143]
Larson Aquatic Research Support *(Graduate/Scholarship)* [1144]
Michigan Stormwater-Floodplain Association Scholarships *(Undergraduate/Scholarship)* [4492]
Abel Wolman Fellowships *(Doctorate/Fellowship)* [1145]

Welding

Howard E. and Wilma J. Adkins Scholarships *(Undergraduate/Scholarship)* [1149]
American Welding Society District Scholarships *(Undergraduate/Scholarship)* [1150]
American Welding Society International Scholarships *(Undergraduate/Scholarship)* [1151]
American Welding Society National Scholarships *(Undergraduate/Scholarship)* [1152]
American Welding Society Past Presidents Scholarships *(Undergraduate/Scholarship)* [1153]
American Welding Society Research Fellowships *(Postgraduate/Scholarship)* [1154]
Arsham Amirikian Engineering Scholarships *(Undergraduate/Scholarship)* [1155]
Jerry Baker Scholarships *(Undergraduate/Scholarship)* [1156]
Jack R. Barckhoff Welding Management Scholarships *(Undergraduate/Scholarship)* [1157]
Edward J. Brady Memorial Scholarships *(Undergraduate/Scholarship)* [1158]
William A. and Ann M. Brothers Scholarships *(Undergraduate/Scholarship)* [1159]
Donald F. Hastings Scholarships *(Undergraduate/Scholarship)* [1160]
Donald and Shirley Hastings Scholarships *(Undergraduate/Scholarship)* [1161]
William B. Howell Scholarships *(Undergraduate/Scholarship)* [1162]
Hypertherm International HyTech Leadership Scholarships *(Postgraduate/Scholarship)* [1163]
ITW Welding Companies Scholarships *(Undergraduate/Scholarship)* [1164]
Terry Jarvis Memorial Scholarships *(Undergraduate/Scholarship)* [1165]
LCSC Welding Club Scholarships *(Undergraduate/Scholarship)* [4190]
John C. Lincoln Memorial Scholarships *(Undergraduate/Scholarship)* [1166]
Miller Electric International WorldSkills Competition Scholarships *(Undergraduate/Scholarship)* [1167]
Robert L. Peaslee-Detroit Brazing and Soldiering Division Scholarships *(Undergraduate/Scholarship)* [1168]
Ronald C. and Joyce Pierce Scholarships *(Undergraduate/Scholarship)* [1169]
Praxair International Scholarships *(Undergraduate/Scholarship)* [1170]
Resistance Welder Manufacturers' Association Scholarships *(Undergraduate/Scholarship)* [1171]
Jerry Robinson Inweld Corporation Scholarships *(Undergraduate/Scholarship)* [1172]
James A. Turner, Jr. Memorial Scholarships *(Undergraduate/Scholarship)* [1173]
Armos and Marilyn Winsand-Detroit Section Named Scholarships *(Undergraduate/Scholarship)* [1174]

Western European studies

Western Civilization Fellowships *(Graduate/Fellowship)* [3775]

Wildlife conservation, management, and science

Alaska Support Industry Alliance Scholarships *(Undergraduate/Scholarship)* [4341]
Lyle Carlson Wildlife Management Scholarships *(Undergraduate/Scholarship)* [4353]
Charles Dobbins FTA Scholarships *(Undergraduate/Scholarship)* [3154]
Ben Meadows Natural Resource Scholarships - Academic Achievement Scholarships *(Undergraduate/Scholarship)* [1620]
Ben Meadows Natural Resource Scholarships - Leadership Scholarships *(Undergraduate/Scholarship)* [1621]
Dennis Raveling Scholarships *(Undergraduate/Scholarship)* [1862]
Dr. Orrin J. Rongstad Wildlife Management Scholarships *(Undergraduate/Scholarship)* [4380]
Russian/Central Asian Student Scholarships *(Undergraduate/Scholarship)* [4381]

Women's studies

American Association of University Women American Fellowships *(All/Fellowship)* [422]
American Association of University Women Career Development Grants *(Postdoctorate/Grant)* [423]
American Association of University Women Engineering Dissertation Awards *(Professional Development/Award/Prize)* [424]
American Association of University Women Master's and First Professional Awards *(Professional Development/Award/Prize)* [426]
Tara Lynne Arnold Scholarships *(Undergraduate/Scholarship)* [6768]
City of Toronto Women's Studies Scholarships *(Graduate, Undergraduate/Scholarship)* [7220]
Rita Mae Kelly Awards *(All/Award/Prize)* [6294]
Student Research Grants *(Undergraduate/Grant)* [2083]

Writing

AAS Fellowships for Creative and Performing Artists and Writers *(All/Fellowship)* [296]
Association for College And University Clubs Scholarships *(Other/Scholarship)* [1383]
Velma Shotwell Griffin Memorial Scholarship Fund *(Undergraduate/Scholarship)* [6724]
Bodie McDowell Scholarships *(Graduate, Undergraduate/Scholarship)* [5430]
McNamara Family Creative Arts Project Grants *(Graduate, Undergraduate/Grant)* [3601]
Jim Poore Memorial Scholarship *(Undergraduate/Scholarship)* [3648]

Zoology

Margaret Dowell-Gravatt, M.D. Scholarship *(Undergraduate/Scholarship)* [1625]
Dennis Raveling Scholarships *(Undergraduate/Scholarship)* [1862]

Legal Residence Index

This index lists awards that are restricted by the applicant's residence of legal record. Award citations are arranged alphabetically by country and subarranged by region, state or province. Each citation is followed by the study level and award type, which appear in parentheses. The numbers following the parenthetical information indicate book entry numbers for awards, not page numbers.

UNITED STATES

4th Infantry Division Association Scholarships *(Four Year College, Postgraduate, Two Year College/Scholarship)* [4613]
92109 Community Fund-Mark and Karla Stuart Family Scholarships *(Undergraduate/Scholarship)* [6161]
The AAA (American Automobile Association) Five Diamond Hospitality Scholarships *(Undergraduate/Scholarship)* [608]
AAAA Scholarship Program *(Undergraduate/Scholarship)* [1299]
AAACN Scholarships *(Undergraduate/Scholarship)* [320]
AAAS Mass Media Science and Engineering Fellowships *(Graduate, Postgraduate, Undergraduate/Fellowship)* [316]
AAAS Science and Technology Policy Fellowships *(Postdoctorate/Fellowship)* [317]
AABA Read Carlock Memorial Scholarship Fund *(Professional Development/Scholarship)* [1206]
AABP Amstutz Scholarships *(Undergraduate/Scholarship)* [326]
AABP Bovine Veterinary Student Recognition Award *(Undergraduate/Scholarship)* [327]
AABP Education Grants *(Undergraduate/Grant)* [328]
AABP Research Assistantship *(Doctorate/Scholarship)* [329]
AABP Student Externship Program *(Undergraduate/Scholarship)* [330]
AACE International Competitive Scholarships *(Undergraduate/Scholarship)* [1350]
AACN Excellence in Academics Nursing Scholarships *(Undergraduate/Scholarship)* [334]
AACN Minority Nurse Faculty Scholarships *(Graduate/Scholarship)* [335]
AACOM Scholar in Residence Program *(Graduate, Undergraduate/Scholarship)* [339]
AACT Undergraduate Scholarships *(Undergraduate/Scholarship)* [5711]
AAEP/ALSIC Scholarships *(Undergraduate/Scholarship)* [344]
AAEP Foundation Research Fellowships *(Doctorate/Scholarship)* [345]
AAG IGIF Graduate Research Awards *(Graduate, Undergraduate/Scholarship)* [1352]
AAG IGIF Student Travel Grants *(Graduate, Undergraduate/Grant)* [1353]
AAGS Graduate Fellowship Award *(Undergraduate/Fellowship)* [481]
AAGS Joseph F. Dracup Scholarship Award *(Undergraduate/Scholarship)* [482]
AAIB Scholarships *(Undergraduate/Scholarship)* [355]
AAJ Trial Advocacy Scholarships *(Undergraduate/Scholarship)* [357]
AAJA/CNN Scholar Program *(Graduate, Undergraduate/Scholarship)* [1328]
AAJA/COX Foundation Scholarships *(Graduate, Undergraduate/Scholarship)* [1329]
AAJA/S.I. Newhouse Foundation Scholarships *(Graduate, Undergraduate/Scholarship)* [1330]
AALL Scholarships for Continuing Education Classes *(Postgraduate/Scholarship)* [362]
AALL Scholarships for Library School Graduates Seeking a Non-Law Degree *(Postgraduate/Scholarship)* [363]
AALL & Thomson West - George A. Strait Minority Scholarship Endowment *(Postgraduate/Scholarship)* [364]
AANS Medical Student Summer Research Fellowships (MSSRF) *(Undergraduate/Fellowship)* [370]
AAOHN Academic Study Scholarships *(Graduate, Undergraduate/Scholarship)* [378]
AAOHN Continuing Education Scholarships *(Professional Development/Scholarship)* [379]
AAS-American Historical Print Collectors Society Fellowships *(Doctorate/Fellowship)* [294]
AAS-American Society for Eighteenth Century Studies Fellowships *(Postdoctorate/Fellowship)* [295]
AAS CIAC Small Grants *(Graduate, Other/Grant)* [1370]
AAS Fellowships for Creative and Performing Artists and Writers *(All/Fellowship)* [296]
AAS Korean Studies Scholarship Program *(Doctorate, Graduate/Scholarship)* [1371]
AAS National Endowment for the Humanities Long-Term Fellowships *(Postdoctorate/Fellowship)* [297]
AAS-Northeast Modern Language Association Fellowships *(All/Fellowship)* [298]
AAST/ACS/NIGMS Scholarships *(Professional Development/Scholarship)* [407]
AAST/KCI Research Grants *(All/Grant)* [408]
AAST Medical Student Scholarships *(All/Scholarship)* [409]
AATA Anniversary Scholarships *(Graduate/Scholarship)* [312]
AAUW Legal Advocacy Fund American Fellowships *(Doctorate/Fellowship)* [4]
AAUW Legal Advocacy Fund Career Development Grants *(Professional Development/Grant)* [5]
AAUW Legal Advocacy Fund International Fellowships *(Doctorate, Graduate/Fellowship)* [6]
AAUW Legal Advocacy Fund Selected Professions Fellowships *(Doctorate, Graduate/Fellowship)* [7]
ABA Academic Merit Scholarships *(Undergraduate/Scholarship)* [445]
ABA Diversity Scholarships *(Undergraduate/Scholarship)* [446]
ABA Legal Opportunity Scholarship Funds *(Undergraduate/Scholarship)* [3582]
ABA Legal Scholarships *(Graduate/Scholarship)* [382]
ABA Members Scholarships (ABA Bus and Tour Operators Only) *(Undergraduate/Scholarship)* [447]
ABA Members Scholarships (All ABA Member Companies) *(Undergraduate/Scholarship)* [448]
ABA Scholarships *(Undergraduate/Scholarship)* [437]
Anthony Abbene Scholarships *(Undergraduate/Scholarship)* [3635]
Clifford V. Abbott Memorial Scholarships *(Undergraduate/Scholarship)* [6766]
Abbott Scholarships *(Undergraduate/Scholarship)* [6822]
ABC-Clio Research Grants *(Graduate/Grant)* [6514]
Alejandro "Alex" Abecia Reaching High Scholarships *(Undergraduate/Scholarship)* [2259]
Jack Abelson Scholarships *(Graduate/Scholarship)* [3171]
Abercrombie and Fitch Global Diversity Scholar Awards *(High School/Scholarship)* [5066]
Ruth Abernathy Presidential Scholarships *(Graduate, Undergraduate/Scholarship)* [351]
ABF Doctoral Fellowships *(Doctorate, Graduate/Fellowship)* [433]
ABFSE National Scholarship Program *(Undergraduate/Scholarship)* [441]
Kyutaro & Yasuo Abiko Memorial Scholarships *(Undergraduate/Scholarship)* [4015]
Mandel & Lauretta Abrahamer Scholarships *(Undergraduate/Scholarship)* [6767]
Evelyn Abrams Memorial Scholarships *(Undergraduate/Scholarship)* [5797]
Charles Abrams Scholarship Program *(Graduate/Scholarship)* [775]
The Frederick B. Abramson Public Interest Fellowships Award *(All/Fellowship)* [12]
Academic Promise Scholarships *(Undergraduate/Scholarship)* [3697]
Academic Scholarship Program A *(Undergraduate/Scholarship)* [4843]
Academic Scholarship Program B *(Undergraduate/Scholarship)* [4844]
L'Academie de Cuisine Culinary Arts Scholarships *(All, Professional Development/Scholarship)* [2568]
Accenture American Indian Scholarship Program *(Graduate, Undergraduate/Scholarship)* [640]
The Access Intelligence Scholarships *(Graduate, Undergraduate/Scholarship)* [6580]
ACE K-12 Scholarships Program *(High School/Scholarship)* [234]
ACHE/American Legion Auxiliary Scholarships *(Undergraduate/Scholarship)* [98]
ACHE/American Legion Scholarships *(Undergraduate/Scholarship)* [99]
ACHE Junior and Community College Athletic Scholarships *(Undergraduate/Scholarship)* [100]
ACHE Junior and Community College Performing Arts Scholarships *(Undergraduate/Scholarship)* [101]
ACHE Two-Year College Academic Scholarships *(Two Year College, Undergraduate/Scholarship)* [104]
Renee Achter Scholarship Program *(Postgraduate/Scholarship)* [726]
Ken and Pat Ackerman Family Scholarship Fund *(Undergraduate/Scholarship)* [2938]
Wayne D. Ackerman Family Scholarship Fund *(Undergraduate/Scholarship)* [6707]
Naida Ackley Scholarship Program *(Postgraduate/Scholarship)* [727]
ACLS Frederick Burkhardt Fellowships *(Professional Development/Fellowship)* [299]
ACMPE Scholarship Fund Program *(Graduate, Undergraduate/Scholarship)* [22]
ACNM Foundation, Inc. Fellowship for Graduate Education *(Doctorate, Postdoctorate/Fellowship)* [469]
ACNP Nurse Practitioner Student Scholarship Awards *(Undergraduate/Scholarship)* [473]
ACRES Scholarships *(Postgraduate, Professional*

Development/Scholarship) [513]
ACS/ASA Health Policy and Management Scholarships *(Professional Development/Scholarship)* [1117]
ACS/NREF-AANS Faculty Career Development Award *(Professional Development/Award/Prize)* [371]
ACSM Fellowship Scholarships *(Undergraduate/Scholarship)* [483]
Larry Acterman Public Education Awards *(Undergraduate/Scholarship)* [5355]
Actuarial Scholarships for Minority Students *(Undergraduate/Scholarship)* [383]
ACUA Scholarships *(Graduate, Undergraduate/Scholarship)* [1381]
ACWA Water Law and Policy Scholarships *(Graduate/Scholarship)* [1375]
Nancy Ashley Adams/Ashley Adams Koetje Scholarships *(Undergraduate/Scholarship)* [2635]
Adams Family Scholarships *(Undergraduate/Scholarship)* [2636]
Ruth D. Adams Fund *(Undergraduate/Scholarship)* [2939]
Mamie Adams Memorial Awards *(Undergraduate/Scholarship)* [4161]
The Clarke B. Adams Memorial Foundation Lapeer County Community Foundation Fund *(Undergraduate/Scholarship)* [4138]
Lt. Holly Adams Memorial Scholarship *(Undergraduate/Scholarship)* [2404]
Ed Adams Memorial Scholarships *(Professional Development/Scholarship)* [6030]
Ruth Adams Memorial Scholarships *(Undergraduate/Scholarship)* [5903]
Frederick G. Adams Scholarships *(Undergraduate/Scholarship)* [3411]
Henry Adams Scholarships *(Undergraduate/Scholarship)* [962]
Carl Joseph Adelhardt Memorial Scholarships *(Undergraduate/Scholarship)* [3167]
Adelson Family Scholarships *(Undergraduate/Scholarship)* [5798]
Adelson Scholarships *(Undergraduate/Scholarship)* [5799]
ADGEF Scholarships *(All/Scholarship)* [246]
Howard E. and Wilma J. Adkins Scholarships *(Undergraduate/Scholarship)* [1149]
Chris Nance Adler Scholarship Fund *(High School/Scholarship)* [2260]
Adolescent Literacy Predoctoral Fellowships *(Doctorate/Fellowship)* [4623]
Herb Adrian Memorial Scholarship Fund *(Undergraduate/Scholarship)* [3036]
Adults Students in Scholastic Transition (ASIST) *(All/Scholarship)* [2894]
Advanced Cardiovascular Surgery Fellowships *(Graduate, Postdoctorate/Fellowship)* [415]
Advertising Production Club Scholarship Awards *(Graduate, Undergraduate/Scholarship)* [28]
AE Flight Training Scholarships *(Professional Development/Scholarship)* [5206]
AE Jet Type Rating Scholarships *(Professional Development/Scholarship)* [5207]
AE Technical Training Scholarships *(Professional Development/Scholarship)* [5208]
AeA Scholarships *(Undergraduate/Scholarship)* [6162]
AERA-AIR Fellows Program *(Postdoctorate/Fellowship)* [543]
AERA-ETS Fellowship Program in Measurement *(Postdoctorate/Fellowship)* [544]
AERA Minority Fellowship Program in Education Research *(Postdoctorate/Fellowship)* [545]
AFCEA Distance Learning/Online Scholarships *(Undergraduate/Scholarship)* [1236]
AFCEA Fellowships *(Doctorate, Graduate/Fellowship)* [1237]
AFCEA General John A. Wickham Scholarships *(Undergraduate/Scholarship)* [1238]
AFCEA Math and Science Teachers Scholarships *(Graduate/Scholarship)* [1239]
AFCEA Scholarship for Working Professionals *(Graduate/Scholarship)* [1240]
AFFIRM University Scholarships *(Undergraduate/Scholarship)* [1414]
Affirmative Action Mini Grant and Student Scholarships *(All/Grant)* [14]
Affirmative Action Scholarships *(Graduate/Scholarship)* [6680]
AFIA Scholarships *(Undergraduate/Scholarship)* [573]
AFPPA Student Scholarships *(Undergraduate/Scholarship)* [1412]
AFROTC Scholarships *(Undergraduate/Scholarship)* [46]
AFSA Chapter 155 Division 1 Scholarships - Category 1 *(Undergraduate/Scholarship)* [56]
AFSA Chapter 155 Division 1 Scholarships - Category 2 *(Undergraduate/Scholarship)* [57]
AFSA Chapter 155 Division 1 Scholarships - Category 3 *(Undergraduate/Scholarship)* [58]
AFSA Scholarship Program *(Undergraduate/Scholarship)* [54]
AFSP - Distinguished Investigator Grants *(Postgraduate/Grant)* [587]
AFSP Postdoctoral Research Fellowships *(Postgraduate/Fellowship)* [588]
AFSP Standard Research Grants *(Postgraduate/Grant)* [589]
AFSP Young Investigator Grants *(Postgraduate/Grant)* [590]
After-the-Fires Scholarships *(Undergraduate/Scholarship)* [6163]
AfterCollege/AACN Nursing Scholarships *(Graduate, Undergraduate/Scholarship)* [336]
AGBU Scholarships *(Graduate/Loan)* [1255]
AGC Foundation Outstanding Educator Awards *(Professional Development/Award/Prize)* [1344]
AGC New York State Chapter Scholarship Program *(Undergraduate/Scholarship)* [1427]
Agriculture Future of America Community Scholarships *(Undergraduate/Scholarship)* [39]
Agriculture Future of America Scholarship Program *(Undergraduate/Scholarship)* [40]
Patty Ahearn Victoria Elementary Scholarships *(Undergraduate/Scholarship)* [5904]
Ahepa Buckeye Scholarship Awards *(Undergraduate/Scholarship)* [42]
Ahepa District No. 1 Scholarship Program *(Graduate, Undergraduate/Scholarship)* [44]
AHNS-ACS Career Development Awards *(Professional Development/Grant)* [599]
AHNS Pilot Research Grants *(Professional Development/Grant)* [600]
AHNS Young Investigator Awards *(Professional Development/Grant)* [601]
AIA and the Global Automotive Aftermarket Symposium Scholarships *(Undergraduate/Scholarship)* [1569]
AIAA Foundation Scholarship Program *(Undergraduate/Scholarship)* [646]
AIAS/AIA Trust Scholarships for Emerging Professionals *(Postgraduate/Scholarship)* [648]
AIBS Junior Fellowships *(Doctorate/Fellowship)* [652]
AIBS Senior Fellowships *(Doctorate, Postdoctorate/Fellowship)* [653]
AIChE/Donald F. and Mildred Topp Othmer National Scholarship Awards *(Undergraduate/Scholarship)* [655]
AICPA Scholarships for Graduate Accounting Students *(Postgraduate/Scholarship)* [4641]
AICPA Scholarships for Minority Accounting Students *(Undergraduate/Scholarship)* [4642]
AIDS Awareness Scholarships *(Undergraduate/Scholarship)* [6093]
AIGC Fellowship for Graduates *(Graduate/Fellowship)* [641]
AIMS Long-term Research Grants *(Postdoctorate/Grant)* [667]
AIMS Short-term Research Grants *(Postdoctorate/Grant)* [668]
Air Force Association Excellence Scholarships *(Undergraduate/Scholarship)* [47]
Air Force Association/Grantham Scholarships *(Undergraduate/Scholarship)* [48]
Air Force Association Spouse Scholarships *(Undergraduate/Scholarship)* [49]
Air Force ROTC Enhanced HBCU Scholarships *(Undergraduate/Scholarship)* [6972]
Air Products and Chemicals, Inc. Scholarships *(Undergraduate/Scholarship)* [1429]
Air Traffic Control Association Full-time Employee Student Scholarships *(Other/Scholarship)* [62]
Air Traffic Control Association Non-employee Student Scholarships *(Undergraduate/Scholarship)* [63]
Aircraft Owners and Pilots Association Scholarships *(Undergraduate/Scholarship)* [66]
Airports Council International-North America Scholarship *(Graduate, Undergraduate/Scholarship)* [94]
AISC/Carolina Steel Scholarships *(Undergraduate/Scholarship)* [676]
AISC/Fred R. Havens Fellowships *(Graduate, Undergraduate/Fellowship)* [677]
AISC/Great Lakes Fabricators and Erectors Association Fellowships *(Graduate/Fellowship)* [678]
AISC/Rocky Mountain Steel Construction Association Fellowships *(Graduate/Fellowship)* [679]
AISC/Southern Association of Steel Fabricators Fellowships *(Graduate/Fellowship)* [680]
AISC/Southern Association of Steel Fabricators Scholarships *(Undergraduate/Scholarship)* [681]
AISC/Structural Steel Education Council Fellowships *(Graduate/Fellowship)* [682]
AISC/US Steel Fellowships *(Graduate/Fellowship)* [683]
AIST Baltimore Chapter Scholarships *(Undergraduate/Scholarship)* [1438]
AIST Detroit Chapter Scholarships *(Undergraduate/Scholarship)* [1439]
AIST Northwest Chapter Scholarships *(Undergraduate/Scholarship)* [1440]
AIST Ronald E. Lincoln Memorial Scholarships *(Undergraduate/Scholarship)* [1441]
AIST San Francisco Chapter Scholarships *(Undergraduate/Scholarship)* [1442]
AIST William E. Schwabe Memorial Scholarships *(Undergraduate/Scholarship)* [1443]
AIST Willy Korf Memorial Fund *(Undergraduate/Scholarship)* [1444]
Diane Blicksilver Aja Memorial Scholarship Program *(Postgraduate/Scholarship)* [728]
AJL Convention Travel Grants *(All/Grant)* [1459]
AJL Scholarship Program *(Undergraduate/Scholarship)* [1460]
Akao Scholarships for QFD *(Undergraduate/Scholarship)* [5886]
Akron Bar Association Foundation Scholarships *(Undergraduate/Scholarship)* [96]
Al Muammar Scholarships for Journalism *(Undergraduate/Scholarship)* [1191]
Alabama Horse Council Scholarships *(Undergraduate/Scholarship)* [111]
Alabama Power Scholarships *(Undergraduate/Scholarship)* [5275]
Alabama Scholarships for Dependents of Blind Parents *(Undergraduate/Scholarship)* [107]
Alabama Student Assistance Programs *(Undergraduate/Scholarship)* [108]
Alabama Student Grant Programs *(Undergraduate/Grant)* [109]
Alaska Airlines Scholarships *(Undergraduate/Scholarship)* [1079]
Alaska Community Foundation Sven E. & Lorraine Eriksson Scholarships *(Undergraduate/Scholarship)* [7029]
Alaska Kidney Foundation-ASN Research Grants *(Doctorate/Grant)* [1017]
Bruce and Betty Alberts Endowed Scholarships in Physiology *(Undergraduate/Scholarship)* [4282]
ALD Graduate Fellowships *(Undergraduate/Fellowship)* [4634]
Owen F. Aldis Scholarship Fund *(Graduate/Scholarship)* [3904]
Anne L. Alexander and Blaise Robert Alexander Memorial Scholarships *(Undergraduate/Scholarship)* [2940]
Floyd S. Alford Jr. Scholarships *(Undergraduate/Scholarship)* [7141]
Horatio Alger Ak-Sar-Ben Scholarships *(Undergraduate/Scholarship)* [198]
Horatio Alger Alabama Scholarships *(Undergraduate/Scholarship)* [199]
Horatio Alger California and California Orange

County Scholarships *(Undergraduate/Scholarship)* [200]
Horatio Alger Delaware Scholarships *(Undergraduate/Scholarship)* [201]
Horatio Alger District of Columbia, Maryland, and Virginia Scholarships *(Undergraduate/Scholarship)* [202]
Horatio Alger Florida Scholarships *(Undergraduate/Scholarship)* [203]
Horatio Alger Franklin Scholarships *(Undergraduate/Scholarship)* [204]
Horatio Alger Georgia Scholarships *(Undergraduate/Scholarship)* [205]
Horatio Alger Idaho University Scholarships *(Undergraduate/Scholarship)* [206]
Horatio Alger Illinois Scholarships *(Undergraduate/Scholarship)* [207]
Horatio Alger Indiana Scholarships *(Undergraduate/Scholarship)* [208]
Horatio Alger Iowa Scholarships *(Undergraduate/Scholarship)* [209]
Horatio Alger Kentucky Scholarships *(Undergraduate/Scholarship)* [210]
Horatio Alger Lola and Duane Hagadone Idaho Scholarships *(Undergraduate/Scholarship)* [211]
Horatio Alger Louisiana Scholarships *(Undergraduate/Scholarship)* [212]
Horatio Alger Minnesota Scholarships *(Undergraduate/Scholarship)* [213]
Horatio Alger Mississippi Scholarships *(Undergraduate/Scholarship)* [214]
Horatio Alger Missouri Scholarships *(Undergraduate/Scholarship)* [215]
Horatio Alger Montana Scholarships *(Undergraduate/Scholarship)* [216]
Horatio Alger National Scholarships *(Undergraduate/Scholarship)* [217]
Horatio Alger New Jersey Scholarships *(Undergraduate/Scholarship)* [218]
Horatio Alger New York Scholarships *(Undergraduate/Scholarship)* [219]
Horatio Alger North Dakota Scholarships *(Undergraduate/Scholarship)* [220]
Horatio Alger Oregon Scholarships *(Undergraduate/Scholarship)* [221]
Horatio Alger Pennsylvania Scholarships *(Undergraduate/Scholarship)* [222]
Horatio Alger South Dakota Scholarships *(Undergraduate/Scholarship)* [223]
Horatio Alger Texas - Fort Worth Scholarships *(Undergraduate/Scholarship)* [224]
Horatio Alger Texas Scholarships *(Undergraduate/Scholarship)* [225]
Horatio Alger Utah Scholarships *(Undergraduate/Scholarship)* [226]
Horatio Alger Washington Scholarships *(Undergraduate/Scholarship)* [227]
Horatio Alger Wyoming Scholarships *(Undergraduate/Scholarship)* [228]
Emma and Meloid Algood Tuition Scholarships *(Undergraduate/Scholarship)* [4664]
Margaret M. Alkek Scholarship *(Undergraduate/Scholarship)* [2637]
All-American Vector Marketing Scholarship Program *(Undergraduate/Scholarship)* [7311]
Paul Shearman Allen and Associate Scholarships *(Undergraduate/Scholarship)* [7003]
Robinson G. Allen Athletic Memorial Scholarships *(Undergraduate/Scholarship)* [5905]
Peggy Allen Community Newspaper Internships *(Undergraduate/Internship)* [7142]
Allen (Dan) Memorial Scholarships *(Undergraduate/Scholarship)* [6095]
William A. Allen Memorial Metal Shop/Auto Body Scholarships *(Undergraduate/Scholarship)* [5906]
Julie Allen World Classroom Scholarships *(Undergraduate/Scholarship)* [6164]
Alliance for Academic Achievement Program Scholarships *(Undergraduate/Scholarship)* [3412]
Alliance of Black Culinarians Scholarships *(Undergraduate/Scholarship)* [5800]
Alliance Francaise of Hartford Harpin/Rohinsky Scholarships *(Undergraduate/Scholarship)* [3413]
Robert W. Allington Fellowships *(Doctorate, Postdoctorate/Fellowship)* [2106]
Dorothy G. Allsop Scholarships *(Undergraduate/Scholarship)* [4721]
ALOA Scholarship Foundation *(Undergraduate/Scholarship)* [1346]
Tillie B. Alperin Scholarships *(Undergraduate/Scholarship)* [7109]
Harvey and Laura Alpert Scholarship Award *(Undergraduate/Scholarship)* [3845]
ALPFA Scholarship Programs *(Postgraduate, Undergraduate/Scholarship)* [1492]
Alpha Chi Sigma Scholarship Award *(Graduate, Undergraduate/Award/Prize)* [244]
Alpha Eta Scholarships *(Undergraduate/Scholarship)* [2638]
Alpha Kappa Alpha - Educational Advancement Foundation Financial Need-Based Scholarships *(Graduate, Undergraduate/Scholarship)* [248]
Alpha Kappa Alpha - Educational Advancement Foundation Merit Scholarships *(Graduate, Undergraduate/Scholarship)* [249]
Alpha Mu Tau Undergraduate Scholarships *(Undergraduate/Scholarship)* [931]
Alpha Rho Leadership Scholarships *(Undergraduate/Scholarship)* [2639]
Justin Scot Alston Memorial Scholarships *(Undergraduate/Scholarship)* [3636]
Phillip Alston Scholarships *(Undergraduate/Scholarship)* [7143]
Robert E. Altenhofen Memorial Scholarships *(Graduate, Undergraduate/Scholarship)* [1025]
AMA/Charles H. Grant Scholarships *(Undergraduate/Scholarship)* [18]
AMA Foundation Minority Scholars Award *(Undergraduate/Scholarship)* [712]
AMA Foundation Physicians of Tomorrow Scholarships *(Undergraduate/Scholarship)* [713]
AMACESP Student Scholarships *(Undergraduate/Scholarship)* [92]
AMBUCS Scholarships for Therapists Program *(Graduate, Undergraduate/Scholarship)* [258]
Lou Amen Legacy Scholarship *(Undergraduate/Scholarship)* [1819]
America Responds Memorial Scholarships *(Undergraduate/Scholarship)* [1046]
American Academy of Periodontology Educator Scholarships *(Postdoctorate/Scholarship)* [283]
American Academy of Periodontology Foundation Education Fellowships *(Postdoctorate/Fellowship)* [284]
American Academy of Periodontology Teaching Fellowships *(Postdoctorate/Fellowship)* [285]
American Advertising Federation-Cleveland College Scholarships *(Undergraduate/Scholarship)* [291]
American Advertising Federation-Cleveland High School Scholarships *(Undergraduate/Scholarship)* [292]
American Association of Blacks in Energy Scholarships *(Undergraduate/Scholarship)* [324]
American Association of Critical-Care Nurses BSN Scholarships *(Undergraduate/Scholarship)* [341]
American Association of Critical-Care Nurses Graduate Scholarships *(Doctorate, Graduate/Scholarship)* [342]
American Association of Family and Consumer Sciences Scholarships *(Undergraduate/Scholarship)* [347]
American Association for Hand Surgery Annual Research Awards *(Professional Development/Award/Prize)* [349]
American Association of Law Libraries Library School Scholarships *(Postgraduate/Scholarship)* [365]
American Association of Plastic Surgeons Academic Scholars Program *(Graduate/Grant)* [387]
American Association of State Troopers Scholarship Foundation First Scholarships *(Undergraduate/Scholarship)* [400]
American Association of State Troopers Scholarship Foundation Second Scholarships *(Undergraduate/Scholarship)* [401]
American Association of Stratigraphic Palynologists Student Scholarships *(Graduate/Scholarship)* [404]
American Association for Thoracic Surgery Clinical Fellowships *(Graduate/Fellowship)* [416]
American Association of University Women American Fellowships *(All/Fellowship)* [422]
American Association of University Women Career Development Grants *(Postdoctorate/Grant)* [423]
American Association of University Women Engineering Dissertation Awards *(Professional Development/Award/Prize)* [424]
American Association of University Women Master's and First Professional Awards *(Professional Development/Award/Prize)* [426]
American Astronomical Society Small Research Grants *(Doctorate/Grant)* [428]
American Business Women's Association Sarasota Chapter Scholarships *(Undergraduate/Scholarship)* [2503]
American College of Radiation Oncology Resident Scholarships *(Graduate/Scholarship)* [475]
American Composites Manufacturers Association Scholarships *(Undergraduate/Scholarship)* [477]
American Composites Manufacturers Association Western Chapter Scholarships *(Undergraduate/Scholarship)* [478]
American Conifer Society Scholarships *(Undergraduate/Scholarship)* [493]
American Council of Engineering Companies of Illinois Scholarships *(Doctorate, Graduate, Undergraduate/Scholarship)* [497]
American Council of Independent Laboratories Scholarships *(Undergraduate/Scholarship)* [506]
American Council of Learned Societies Fellowships *(Postdoctorate/Fellowship)* [508]
American Counsel Association Scholarships *(Undergraduate/Scholarship)* [515]
American Criminal Justice Association Scholarships *(Undergraduate/Scholarship)* [519]
American Culinary Federation Chair's Scholarship Grants *(All/Scholarship)* [521]
American Culinary Federation Educational Scholarship Grants *(All/Scholarship)* [522]
American Dental Association Dental Assisting Scholarship Program *(Undergraduate/Scholarship)* [535]
American Dental Association Dental Hygiene Scholarship Program *(Undergraduate/Scholarship)* [536]
American Dental Association Dental Laboratory Technology Scholarship Program *(Undergraduate/Scholarship)* [537]
American Dental Association Dental Student Scholarship *(Undergraduate/Scholarship)* [538]
American Dental Association Minority Dental Student Scholarships *(Undergraduate/Scholarship)* [539]
American Division Veterans Association Scholarships *(Undergraduate/Scholarship)* [541]
American Dream Scholarship Program *(Undergraduate/Scholarship)* [6155]
American Express Professional Development Scholarships *(Professional Development/Scholarship)* [609]
The American Express Scholarship Competition *(Undergraduate/Scholarship)* [610]
American Express Travel Scholarships *(Undergraduate/Scholarship)* [1080]
American Federation of Police and Concerned Citizen Scholarships *(Undergraduate/Scholarship)* [547]
American Fire Sprinkler Association Scholarships *(Undergraduate/Scholarship)* [3414]
American Floral Endowment Scholarships *(Undergraduate/Scholarship)* [549]
American Foreign Service Association Scholarship Fund *(Undergraduate/Scholarship)* [575]
American Foundation for Pharmaceutical Education Gateway Research Scholarships *(Professional Development/Scholarship)* [577]
American Foundation for Pharmaceutical Education Pre-Doctoral Fellowships in the Pharmaceutical Sciences *(Doctorate/Fellowship)* [578]
American Foundation for Pharmaceutical Education Pre-Doctoral Fellowships in the Pharmaceutical Sciences *(Doctorate/Fellowship)* [579]
American Foundation for Suicide and Prevention Pilot Grants *(Postgraduate/Grant)* [591]
American GI Forum of San Jose Scholarships *(Undergraduate/Scholarship)* [595]
American Guild of Organists, Canton Chapter Charitable Fund *(Undergraduate/Scholarship)* [6708]
American History Scholarships *(Undergraduate/Scholarship)* [5062]

American Indian Endowed Scholarships *(Graduate, Undergraduate/Scholarship)* [7363]
American Institute of Baking Scholarships *(Undergraduate/Scholarship)* [650]
American Institute for Paralegal Studies Alumni Achievement Scholarships *(Undergraduate/Scholarship)* [670]
American Institute for Paralegal Studies Alumni Competitive Scholarships *(Undergraduate/Scholarship)* [671]
American Institute for Paralegal Studies Merit Scholarships *(Undergraduate/Scholarship)* [672]
American Kidney Fund's Patient Scholarship Program *(Other/Scholarship)* [690]
American Lebanese Engineering Society Scholarship Program *(Other/Scholarship)* [692]
American Legion Eagle Scout of the Year Scholarships *(High School/Scholarship)* [4850]
The American Legion Legacy Scholarships *(Undergraduate/Scholarship)* [694]
The American Legion National High School Oratorical Scholarships Contest *(Undergraduate/Scholarship)* [695]
American Liver Foundation Liver Scholar Awards *(Doctorate/Award/Prize)* [703]
American Liver Foundation Special Research Initiatives *(Doctorate/Award/Prize)* [704]
American Marketing Association-Connecticut Chapter, Anna C. Klune Memorial Scholarships *(Graduate/Scholarship)* [3415]
American Nuclear Society Incoming Freshman Scholarships *(High School/Scholarship)* [723]
American Nuclear Society Nevada Section Scholarships *(Undergraduate/Scholarship)* [5801]
American Nuclear Society Undergraduates Scholarships *(Undergraduate/Scholarship)* [724]
American Paint Horse Foundation Scholarships *(Undergraduate/Scholarship)* [755]
American Physical Society Undergraduate Scholarships *(Undergraduate/Scholarship)* [773]
American Political Science Association Federal Executives Fellowships *(Professional Development/Fellowship)* [782]
American Political Science Association Journalists Fellowships *(Professional Development/Fellowship)* [783]
American Political Science Association/MCI Scholarships *(Postdoctorate/Scholarship)* [784]
American Political Science Association Political Scientists Fellowships *(All/Fellowship)* [785]
American Quarter Horse Foundation Scholarships *(Undergraduate/Scholarship)* [811]
American Radio Relay League Louisiana Memorial Scholarships *(Undergraduate/Scholarship)* [815]
American Radio Relay League Scholarships Honoring Barry Goldwater, K7UGA *(Undergraduate/Scholarship)* [816]
American Rental Association Foundation Scholarships *(Undergraduate/Scholarship)* [888]
American Roentgen Ray Society Scholarships *(Professional Development/Scholarship)* [906]
American Savings Foundation Scholarships *(Undergraduate/Scholarship)* [3416]
American Society of Comparative Law TransCoop Programs *(All/Fellowship)* [937]
American Society for Enology and Viticulture Scholarships *(Undergraduate/Scholarship)* [958]
American Society of Heating, Refrigerating, and Air-Conditioning Memorial Scholarships *(Undergraduate/Scholarship)* [963]
American Society of Heating, Refrigerating, and Air-Conditioning Undergraduate Scholarships *(Undergraduate/Scholarship)* [964]
American Society for Horticultural Science Student Travel Grants *(Graduate, Undergraduate/Grant)* [972]
American Society of Landscape Architects Council of Fellow Scholarships *(Undergraduate/Scholarship)* [979]
American Society for Microbiology International Fellowships for Africa *(Postdoctorate/Fellowship)* [1001]
American Society for Microbiology International Fellowships for Asia *(Postdoctorate/Fellowship)* [1002]
American Society for Microbiology International Fellowships for Latin America *(Postdoctorate/Fellowship)* [1003]
American Society for Microbiology Undergraduate Research Fellowships *(Undergraduate/Fellowship)* [1004]
American Society of Military Comptrollers National Scholarship Program *(Undergraduate/Scholarship)* [1011]
American Society of Mining and Reclamation Memorial Scholarships *(Undergraduate/Scholarship)* [1013]
American Society for Theatre Research Dissertation Research Fellowships *(Doctorate/Fellowship)* [1076]
American Society of Travel Agents AVIS Scholarships *(Graduate, Professional Development, Undergraduate/Scholarship)* [1081]
American Sokol Merit Awards *(Undergraduate/Scholarship)* [1096]
American Speech Language Hearing Foundation Clinical Research Grants *(Doctorate/Grant)* [1098]
American Speech Language Hearing Foundation Endowed Scholarships *(Postdoctorate/Scholarship)* [1099]
American Speech Language Hearing Foundation General Scholarships *(Postgraduate/Scholarship)* [1100]
American Speech Language Hearing Foundation Scholarships for International Students *(Graduate/Scholarship)* [1101]
American Speech Language Hearing Foundation Scholarships for Students with Disability *(All/Scholarship)* [1102]
American Standard Scholarships *(Undergraduate/Scholarship)* [5700]
American Turkish Society Arif Mardin Music Fellowships *(Professional Development/Fellowship)* [6936]
American Water Ski Educational Foundation Scholarships *(Undergraduate/Scholarship)* [1140]
American Watercolor Society Scholarship Program for Art Teachers *(Professional Development/Scholarship)* [1147]
American Welding Society District Scholarships *(Undergraduate/Scholarship)* [1150]
American Welding Society International Scholarships *(Undergraduate/Scholarship)* [1151]
American Welding Society National Scholarships *(Undergraduate/Scholarship)* [1152]
American Welding Society Past Presidents Scholarships *(Undergraduate/Scholarship)* [1153]
American Welding Society Research Fellowships *(Postgraduate/Scholarship)* [1154]
Americans for Informed Democracy Global Scholar Tuition *(Undergraduate/Scholarship)* [1176]
Anna Ames Clinical Excellence Student Grants *(Undergraduate/Grant)* [1854]
Amherst College Connecticut Alumni Scholarships *(Undergraduate/Scholarship)* [3417]
Arsham Amirikian Engineering Scholarships *(Undergraduate/Scholarship)* [1155]
AMS Teacher Education Scholarships *(Undergraduate/Scholarship)* [718]
ISPE/M.E. Amstutz Memorial Award *(Undergraduate/Scholarship)* [3658]
The AMTF Graduate Scholarships *(Graduate/Scholarship)* [932]
AMVETS National Scholarships - Entering College Freshmen *(Undergraduate/Scholarship)* [1133]
AMVETS National Scholarships - For Veterans *(Undergraduate/Scholarship)* [1134]
AMVETS National Scholarships - JROTC *(Undergraduate/Scholarship)* [1135]
Anaheim Police Survivors and Scholarship Fund *(Undergraduate/Scholarship)* [1178]
ANCA Scholarships *(Graduate, Undergraduate/Scholarship)* [1301]
Anchor Plastics Scholarships *(Graduate, Undergraduate/Scholarship)* [5634]
Anchor Scholarship Foundation *(Undergraduate/Scholarship)* [6826]
William G. Anderson, DO, Minority Scholarship *(Undergraduate/Scholarship)* [749]
The Anderson Group Summer Institute Scholarships *(Other/Scholarship)* [1180]
Judge Isaac Anderson, Jr. Scholarships *(Undergraduate/Scholarship)* [6640]
Charles Lee Anderson Memorial Scholarship *(Undergraduate/Scholarship)* [2455]
Wilbur H. Anderson Memorial Scholarships *(Undergraduate/Scholarship)* [1182]
Earl I. Anderson Scholarships *(Undergraduate/Scholarship)* [817]
Jane E. Anderson Scholarships *(Undergraduate/Scholarship)* [2640]
Kathy D. and Stephen J. Anderson Scholarships *(Undergraduate/Scholarship)* [2405]
Michael P. Anderson Scholarships in Space Science *(Undergraduate/Scholarship)* [5050]
Warren M. Anderson Scholarships *(Undergraduate/Scholarship)* [3698]
Margaret J. Andrew Memorial Scholarships *(Undergraduate/Scholarship)* [6344]
Cindy Andrews Educational Scholarships *(Undergraduate/Scholarship)* [5907]
William H. Andrews/HAWS Scholarships *(Undergraduate/Scholarship)* [7419]
Richard E. Andrews Memorial Scholarships *(Undergraduate/Scholarship)* [438]
John D. Anello Sr. and Albert A. Silverman Memorial Scholarships *(Undergraduate/Scholarship)* [2237]
Angus Foundation Scholarships *(Undergraduate/Scholarship)* [4967]
Anheuser-Busch International Scholarships *(Graduate, Undergraduate/Scholarship)* [5635]
Anheuser-Busch NAPABA Law Foundation Presidential Scholarships *(Undergraduate/Scholarship)* [4646]
Jack Anson Fellowships *(Graduate/Fellowship)* [5220]
Hettie M. Anthony Fellowships *(Postdoctorate/Fellowship)* [4051]
Anxiety Disorders Association of America Career Development Travel Awards *(Professional Development/Award/Prize)* [1184]
Anxiety Disorders Association of America Junior Faculty Research Grants *(Professional Development/Grant)* [1185]
AOA Research Fellowships *(Doctorate/Fellowship)* [33]
AOA Research Grants *(Graduate/Grant)* [34]
AOFAS Research Grants Program *(Graduate/Grant)* [746]
AORN Foundation Scholarship Program *(Undergraduate/Scholarship)* [1477]
AOSA Research Grants *(All/Grant)* [739]
AOSA Research Partnership Grants *(All/Grant)* [740]
APA Minority Fellowships Program *(Postdoctorate/Fellowship)* [1334]
APA Planning Fellowships *(Graduate/Fellowship)* [776]
APACVS Scholarships *(Professional Development/Scholarship)* [1479]
APAGS-CLGBTC Grant Program *(Graduate/Grant)* [795]
APAGS' Committee on Ethic Minority Affairs (CEMA) Grant Program *(Graduate/Grant)* [796]
APALA Scholarship Program *(Doctorate, Graduate/Scholarship)* [1336]
APC High School Scholarships *(Undergraduate/Scholarship)* [29]
APC Tuition-Assist Scholarship Awards *(Graduate, Undergraduate/Scholarship)* [30]
APDA Postdoctoral Fellowships *(Professional Development/Fellowship)* [757]
APDA Research Grants *(Professional Development/Grant)* [758]
APDA Summer Fellowships *(Doctorate/Fellowship)* [759]
APIASF Scholarships *(Undergraduate/Scholarship)* [1340]
Apple Scholars *(Undergraduate/Scholarship)* [6096]
APPMA's Jules Schwimmer Scholarship Program *(Undergraduate/Scholarship)* [765]
Appraisal Institute Education Trust Scholarships *(Graduate, Undergraduate/Scholarship)* [1189]
APS/ASU Scholarships *(Undergraduate/Scholarship)* [5697]
APS/Maricopa County Community Colleges Scholarships *(Undergraduate/Scholarship)* [5698]
APS Scholarships for Minority Undergraduate Phys-

ics Majors *(Undergraduate/Scholarship)* [5051]
APS Student Grants *(Graduate, Undergraduate/Grant)* [1481]
APSAIL's Ralph Silverman Memorial Scholarships *(Undergraduate/Scholarship)* [1542]
APSNA Educational Scholarships *(Professional Development/Scholarship)* [763]
APT US&C Scholarships *(All/Scholarship)* [1483]
APWA Engineering Scholarships *(Undergraduate/Scholarship)* [806]
Aquatics Booster Club Scholarships *(Undergraduate/Scholarship)* [5908]
ARA Scholarship Awards *(Undergraduate/Scholarship)* [1575]
Frank G. Araujo Memorial Scholarships *(Undergraduate/Scholarship)* [5909]
Fred Archibald Communications Internships *(Undergraduate/Internship)* [6568]
AREMA Committee Scholarships 18 - Light Density & Short Line Railways *(Undergraduate/Scholarship)* [865]
AREMA Committee Scholarships 24 - Education and Training *(Undergraduate/Scholarship)* [866]
AREMA Committee Scholarships 33 - Electric Energy Utilization *(Undergraduate/Scholarship)* [867]
AREMA Presidential Spouse Scholarships *(Undergraduate/Scholarship)* [868]
AREMA Scholarships *(Undergraduate/Scholarship)* [869]
AREMA Staff Scholarships *(Undergraduate/Scholarship)* [870]
Arent Fox Diversity Scholarships *(Undergraduate/Scholarship)* [1202]
A.R.F.O.R.A. Undergraduate Scholarships for Women *(Undergraduate/Scholarship)* [909]
William Argo Scholarships *(Undergraduate/Scholarship)* [3172]
Arizona Chapter Gold Scholarships *(Undergraduate/Scholarship)* [1082]
Arizona Christian School Tuition Organization Scholarships *(Undergraduate/Scholarship)* [1214]
Arizona Nurses Foundation Scholarships *(Graduate, Undergraduate/Scholarship)* [1221]
Arizona Parks and Recreation Educational Scholarship Program *(Graduate, Undergraduate/Scholarship)* [1223]
Rick Arkans Eagle Scout Scholarships *(High School/Scholarship)* [4851]
Arkansas Nursing Foundation - Dorothea Funk Scholarships *(Professional Development/Scholarship)* [1230]
Arkansas Nursing Foundation - Mary Gray Scholarships *(Professional Development/Scholarship)* [1231]
Connie "Chelo" Armendariz Memorial Scholarships *(Undergraduate/Scholarship)* [5910]
Armenian American Citizen's League Scholarships *(Undergraduate/Scholarship)* [1266]
Armenian American Medical Association Scholarships *(Undergraduate/Scholarship)* [1267]
Armenian American Pharmacists' Association Scholarships *(Doctorate, Graduate/Scholarship)* [1268]
Armenian General Athletic Union Scholarships *(Undergraduate/Scholarship)* [1269]
Armenian Professional Society Scholarship Fund *(Graduate/Scholarship)* [1257]
Armenian Relief Society Scholarships *(Graduate, Undergraduate/Scholarship)* [1270]
Armenian Scholarship Foundation Scholarships *(Graduate, Undergraduate/Scholarship)* [1262]
Louis Armstrong Scholarships *(High School/Scholarship)* [939]
Marvin Arnold and Irene Jaquetta Heye Scholarships *(Undergraduate/Scholarship)* [6165]
Paul Arnold Memorial Scholarships *(Undergraduate/Scholarship)* [5750]
Tara Lynne Arnold Scholarships *(Undergraduate/Scholarship)* [6768]
Judge Sidney M. Aronovitz Memorial Scholarships *(High School/Scholarship)* [2594]
Merle Aronson Point Scholarships *(Graduate, Undergraduate/Scholarship)* [5714]
A.R.O.Y. Stanitz Scholarships *(Undergraduate/Scholarship)* [910]
ARREOLA/CBSPM Scholarships *(Undergraduate/Scholarship)* [6166]
ARRL Foundation General Fund Scholarships *(Undergraduate/Scholarship)* [818]
ARRLF Mississippi Scholarships *(Undergraduate/Scholarship)* [819]
ARS Undergraduate Scholarships *(Four Year College, Two Year College, Undergraduate/Scholarship)* [1259]
Art Institute of Colorado Scholarships *(Undergraduate/Scholarship)* [1310]
Art Institute's Best Teen Chef in America Culinary Scholarships *(Undergraduate/Scholarship)* [1311]
ARTC Glenn Moon Scholarships *(Undergraduate/Scholarship)* [3418]
Artistic Scholarship Awards *(Undergraduate/Scholarship)* [1598]
David Arver Memorial Scholarships *(Undergraduate/Scholarship)* [67]
Dutch and Ginger Arver Scholarships *(Undergraduate/Scholarship)* [68]
Chester Arzell and Helen Miller Montgomery Scholarships *(Undergraduate/Scholarship)* [7420]
ASA Minority Fellowships Program *(Doctorate, Master's/Fellowship)* [1094]
ASA/NSF/BLS Fellowships *(Graduate/Fellowship)* [1112]
ASBA College Scholarship Program *(Undergraduate/Scholarship)* [918]
ASBC Foundation Graduate Scholarships *(Doctorate, Graduate/Scholarship)* [922]
ASBC Foundation Undergraduate Scholarships *(Undergraduate/Scholarship)* [923]
ASBPE Young Leaders Scholarships *(All, Professional Development/Scholarship)* [925]
ASCEND/ING Scholarships *(Undergraduate/Scholarship)* [4643]
Elizabeth and Sherman Asche Memorial Scholarship Fund *(Graduate, Undergraduate/Scholarship)* [1356]
ASDSO Undergraduate Scholarships *(Undergraduate/Scholarship)* [1497]
Officer Brian A. Aselton Memorial Scholarships *(Undergraduate/Scholarship)* [3419]
ASET Educational Seminars, Courses and Program Scholarships *(All, Professional Development/Scholarship)* [953]
ASET Student Education Grants *(All/Grant)* [954]
ASG Scholar Awards *(Professional Development/Scholarship)* [960]
William and Lucille Ash Scholarships *(Undergraduate/Scholarship)* [6167]
ASHA Scholarships *(Graduate, Undergraduate/Scholarship)* [915]
ASHA Student Research Grants *(Graduate, Undergraduate/Scholarship)* [916]
ASHFA Scholarships for Minority Students *(Postgraduate/Scholarship)* [1103]
ASHS Industry Division Student Travel Grants *(Graduate, Undergraduate/Grant)* [973]
ASHS Scholars Awards *(Undergraduate/Scholarship)* [974]
Asian American Lawyers Associations of Massachusetts Scholarships *(Undergraduate/Scholarship)* [1332]
Asian American Scholarships *(Undergraduate/Scholarship)* [7004]
Asian/Pacific Gays and Friends Scholarships *(Undergraduate/Scholarship)* [6097]
Asian and Pacific Islander Queers Sisters Scholarships *(Undergraduate/Scholarship)* [5751]
ASIL Helton Fellowship Program *(All/Fellowship)* [977]
ASIS Foundation Chapter Matching Scholarships *(Undergraduate/Scholarship)* [1342]
ASLA Council of Fellows Scholarships *(Undergraduate/Scholarship)* [4118]
ASM/CCID Program in Infectious Disease and Public Health Microbiology *(Postdoctorate/Fellowship)* [1005]
ASMS Research Awards *(Professional Development/Grant)* [993]
ASNE Scholarships *(Graduate, Undergraduate/Scholarship)* [1015]
ASNT Fellow Awards *(Postdoctorate/Fellowship)* [1021]
ASNT Fellowship Awards *(Graduate/Fellowship)* [1022]
Myron Asplin Foundation Scholarships *(Undergraduate/Scholarship)* [3687]
ASPPB Larry J. Bass Jr., PhD. Memorial Scholarship Awards *(Graduate, Undergraduate/Grant)* [797]
Len Assante Scholarship Fund *(Undergraduate/Scholarship)* [4915]
Michael M. Assarian Scholarships *(Undergraduate/Scholarship)* [1271]
ASSE Construction Safety Scholarships *(Undergraduate/Scholarship)* [1047]
ASSE Diversity Committee Scholarships *(Graduate, Undergraduate/Scholarship)* [1048]
Darrell and Palchie Asselin Scholarships *(Undergraduate/Scholarship)* [2771]
Associated General Contractors of Connecticut Scholarships *(Undergraduate/Scholarship)* [2531]
Associated Women for Pepperdine (AWP) Scholarships *(Undergraduate/Scholarship)* [5572]
Associates in Behavioral Health Scholarships *(Graduate/Scholarship)* [5752]
Association for the Advancement of Baltic Studies Dissertation Grants for Graduate Students *(Doctorate/Grant)* [1348]
Association on American Indian Affairs Emergency Aid Scholarship *(Undergraduate/Scholarship)* [630]
Association of American Indian Physicians Scholarships *(Graduate, Undergraduate/Scholarship)* [1360]
Association for College And University Clubs Scholarships *(Other/Scholarship)* [1383]
Association for Compensatory Educators of Texas Paraprofessionals Scholarships *(Undergraduate/Scholarship)* [1385]
Association for Compensatory Educators of Texas Scholarships *(Undergraduate/Scholarship)* [1386]
Association of Desk and Derrick Clubs Education Trust Scholarships *(Undergraduate/Scholarship)* [1388]
Association of Electronic Journalists President's Scholarships *(Undergraduate/Scholarship)* [1392]
Association of Energy Engineers Foundation Scholarship Program *(Graduate, Undergraduate/Scholarship)* [1407]
Association of Flight Attendants Scholarship Fund *(Undergraduate/Scholarship)* [1419]
Association for Preservation Technology International Student Scholarships *(All/Scholarship)* [1518]
Association of Rehabilitation Nurses Scholarship Program *(Undergraduate/Scholarship)* [1485]
Association for the Social Scientific Study of Jewry Travel Grant *(Graduate/Grant)* [1495]
Association for Women in Sports Media Internship Program *(Graduate, Undergraduate/Internship)* [1521]
Association for Women Veterinarians Foundation Scholarships Program *(Graduate/Scholarship)* [1523]
AST National Honor Society Student Scholarships *(Graduate/Scholarship)* [1499]
ASTR Research Fellowships *(All/Grant)* [1077]
Astronaut Scholarship Foundation Scholarships *(Undergraduate/Scholarship)* [1527]
ASWA 2-Year College Scholarships *(Undergraduate/Scholarship)* [1091]
ASWA Undergraduate Scholarships *(Undergraduate/Scholarship)* [1092]
Martha and Robert Atherton Ministerial Scholarships *(Graduate, Master's/Scholarship)* [6947]
Athletic Equipment Managers Association College Scholarships *(Undergraduate/Scholarship)* [1531]
Athletic Excellence Scholarships *(Undergraduate/Scholarship)* [5753]
ISA Aerospace Industries Division - William H. Atkinson Scholarships *(Graduate, Undergraduate/Scholarship)* [3940]
Atlanta Alumnae Achievement Scholarships *(Undergraduate/Scholarship)* [2641]
Atlantic Salmon Federation Olin Fellowships *(All/Fellowship)* [1536]
Attorney-CPA Foundation Scholarships *(Undergraduate/Scholarship)* [322]
AUA Foundation/Astellas Rising Star in Urology Research Awards *(Postdoctorate/Fellowship)* [1126]

AUA Foundation Bridge Awards (Postgraduate/Fellowship) [1127]
AUA Foundation M.D./Ph.D. Fellowships (Postdoctorate, Postgraduate/Fellowship) [1128]
AUA Foundation M.D. Post-resident Fellowships (Postgraduate/Fellowship) [1129]
AUA Foundation - NIDDK/NCI Surgeon-Scientist Awards (Postgraduate/Fellowship) [1130]
AUA Foundation Ph.D. Post-Doctoral Fellowships (Postdoctorate/Fellowship) [1131]
Aubespin Scholarships (Undergraduate/Scholarship) [495]
Auburn Animal Science Department Graduate Student Scholarships (Graduate/Scholarship) [112]
Auburn University College of Veterinary Medicine Scholarships (Undergraduate/Scholarship) [113]
Audio Engineering Society Educational Foundation Scholarships (Undergraduate/Grant) [1538]
Frank H. Ault Scholarships (Undergraduate/Scholarship) [6168]
Automotive Technician Scholarship Program (Undergraduate/Scholarship) [4334]
Automotive Women's Alliance Foundation Scholarships (Undergraduate/Scholarship) [1577]
Auxiliary Undergraduate Scholarships (Undergraduate/Scholarship) [995]
Delores A. Auzenne Fellowship (Postgraduate/Fellowship) [2995]
Larry H. Averill Memorial Scholarships (Undergraduate/Scholarship) [1549]
AVI Scholarships (Undergraduate/Scholarship) [1543]
Aviation Distributors and Manufacturers Association Scholarship Fund (All/Scholarship) [1579]
John L. Avila Memorial Scholarships (Professional Development/Scholarship) [4260]
Avista Corporation Minds in Motion Scholarships (Undergraduate/Scholarship) [4163]
AWG Maria Luisa Crawford Field Camp Scholarships (Undergraduate/Scholarship) [1508]
AWG Minority Scholarships (Undergraduate/Scholarship) [1509]
AWIS College Scholarships (Undergraduate/Scholarship) [1519]
Susan Ayers Memorial Scholarships (Undergraduate/Scholarship) [5802]
William Stone Ayres Scholarships (Undergraduate/Scholarship) [2732]
John M. Azarian Memorial Armenian Youth Scholarships Fund (Undergraduate/Scholarship) [1272]
B-Brave McMahon/Stratton Scholarship Fund (Undergraduate/Scholarship) [2941]
Tom Babcox Memorial Scholarships (All/Scholarship) [1544]
BACUS Scholarships (Graduate, Undergraduate/Scholarship) [6695]
Leo Baeck Fellowships Program (Doctorate, Postdoctorate/Fellowship) [2079]
Leo Baeck Institute - DAAD Fellowship (Doctorate/Fellowship) [3222]
BAEO Children's Scholarship Fund (High School/Scholarship) [1721]
Baha'i Faith Scholarships for Racial Harmony (Undergraduate/Scholarship) [5911]
The Bailey Family Foundation College Scholarship Program (Undergraduate/Scholarship) [1586]
The Bailey Family Foundation High School Scholarship Program (Undergraduate/Scholarship) [1587]
Lincoln C. Bailey Memorial Scholarship Fund (Undergraduate/Scholarship) [3900]
Bambey Bailey Scholarships (Undergraduate/Scholarship) [2391]
Barbara Bailey Scholarships (Undergraduate/Scholarship) [5754]
Don Bailey Scholarships (Undergraduate/Scholarship) [4913]
Sandra Sebrell Bailey Scholarships (Undergraduate/Scholarship) [2683]
Marian Wood Baird Scholarships (Undergraduate/Scholarship) [7302]
Michael Baker Corporation Scholarship Program (Undergraduate/Scholarship) [1430]
Howard Baker Foundation Scholarships (Undergraduate/Scholarship) [1589]
Charly Baker and Health Merriwether Memorial Scholarships (Undergraduate/Scholarship) [5755]
Frances Warren Baker Memorial Scholarships (Undergraduate/Scholarship) [6345]
Richard L. Baker Memorial Scholarships (Undergraduate/Scholarship) [6769]
Robby Baker Memorial Scholarships (Undergraduate/Scholarship) [189]
Jerry Baker Scholarships (Undergraduate/Scholarship) [1156]
Bernt Balchen, Jr. Hardingfele Scholarships (All, Professional Development/Scholarship) [3399]
Malcolm Baldridge Scholarships (Undergraduate/Scholarship) [3420]
Donald A. Baldwin Sr. Business Aviation Management Scholarships (Undergraduate/Scholarship) [4770]
Balestreri/Cutino Scholarships (Undergraduate/Scholarship) [523]
Lloyd G. Balfour Fellowships (Graduate/Fellowship) [5221]
Ball Horticultural Company Scholarships (Undergraduate/Scholarship) [550]
Vic and Margaret Ball Student Intern Scholarships (Undergraduate/Internship) [551]
Ballantyne Resident Research Grants (Professional Development/Grant) [602]
Ballard Family Foundation Scholarships (Undergraduate/Scholarship) [6169]
G. Thomas Balsbaugh Memorial Scholarship Fund (Undergraduate/Scholarship) [3090]
B&W Y-12 Scholarship Fund (Undergraduate/Scholarship) [2806]
Bank of America Junior Achievement Scholarship Fund (Undergraduate/Scholarship) [3040]
Brenda S. Bank Educational Workshop Scholarships (Undergraduate/Scholarship) [6447]
Dr. Johnella Banks Memorial Scholarships (Undergraduate/Scholarship) [1750]
Harvey Washington Banks Scholarships in Astronomy (Undergraduate/Scholarship) [5052]
Sharon D. Banks Undergraduate Memorial Scholarships (Undergraduate/Scholarship) [7508]
Banner Bank Business Scholarships (Undergraduate/Scholarship) [4164]
Donald W. Banner Corporate Intern Scholarships (Undergraduate/Scholarship) [3769]
Donald W. Banner Diversity Scholarship for Law Students (Undergraduate/Scholarship) [1594]
Bernice Barabash Sports Scholarship (Undergraduate/Scholarship) [3972]
Barakat Trust and Barakat Foundation Scholarships (Graduate/Scholarship) [1192]
Leslie Baranowski Scholarships for Professional Excellence (All/Scholarship) [3721]
Lewis B. Barber Memorial Scholarships (Undergraduate/Scholarship) [6641]
Barbri Scholarships for Bar Preparation (Undergraduate/Scholarship) [3578]
Jack R. Barckhoff Welding Management Scholarships (Undergraduate/Scholarship) [1157]
Janice K. Barden Aviation Scholarships (Undergraduate/Scholarship) [4771]
Gina L. Barnhart Memorial Scholarship Fund (Undergraduate/Scholarship) [2942]
Robbie Baron Memorial Scholarships (Undergraduate/Scholarship) [3091]
Laura Beckley Barsotti Memorial Scholarships (Undergraduate/Scholarship) [3637]
Leon and Talin Barsoumian Scholarships (Graduate, Undergraduate/Scholarship) [1263]
Barta-Lehman Musical Scholarships (Undergraduate/Scholarship) [6170]
Avery Bayle Barth Scholarships (Undergraduate/Scholarship) [2642]
William E. Barto Scholarships (Undergraduate/Scholarship) [2772]
Elsa Barton Educational Scholarships Fund (Undergraduate/Scholarship) [791]
Basic Midwifery Student Scholarship Program (Undergraduate/Scholarship) [470]
Basic Research Fellowships (Postdoctorate/Fellowship) [443]
Diane Basilone-Engle Memorial Scholarships (Undergraduate/Scholarship) [1889]
Bat Conservation International Student Research Scholarships (Undergraduate/Scholarship) [1601]
William H. Bates Oxford Cup Scholarships (Graduate, Undergraduate/Scholarship) [1641]
Jim Batten Community Newspaper Internships (Undergraduate/Internship) [7144]
Hazel Reed Baumeister Scholarship Program (Undergraduate/Scholarship) [6385]
Jeannette Bautista Memorial Scholarships (Undergraduate/Scholarship) [5803]
Bob Baxter Scholarships (Undergraduate/Scholarship) [5017]
Timothy Baylink Good Fellowship Awards (Undergraduate/Scholarship) [5912]
John Bayliss Broadcast Foundation Internship Programs (Undergraduate/Internship) [1603]
BCA Ethnic Minority Postgraduate Scholarships for Careers in Athletics (Undergraduate/Scholarship) [1748]
BCCC Foundation Scholarships (Undergraduate/Scholarship) [1591]
BCEN Undergraduate Scholarships (Undergraduate/Scholarship) [2850]
James Beard Foundation/Art Institute of Colorado Scholarships (Undergraduate/Scholarship) [1312]
Catherine H. Beattie Fellowships (Graduate/Fellowship) [2089]
Beau Gunn Redlands Baseball For Youth Scholarships (Undergraduate/Scholarship) [5913]
Michael Beaudry Scholarships (Graduate/Scholarship) [3173]
Sally Beauty Scholarships for High School Graduates (Undergraduate/Scholarship) [4822]
Beaver Medical Clinic-Glen Adams Scholarship Awards (Undergraduate/Scholarship) [5914]
Beaver Medical Clinic-H.E.A.R.T. Scholarship Awards (Undergraduate/Scholarship) [5915]
Beaver Medical Clinic-Premed Scholarship Awards (Undergraduate/Scholarship) [5916]
Don C. Beaver Memorial Scholarship (Undergraduate/Scholarship) [1820]
BECA Foundation-CUSM Scholarships (Undergraduate/Scholarship) [1610]
BECA Foundation General Scholarships Fund (Undergraduate/Scholarship) [1611]
Bechtel Group Foundation Scholarship for Safety & Health (Undergraduate/Scholarship) [1049]
Stephen D. Bechtel Oxford Cup Scholarships (Graduate, Undergraduate/Scholarship) [1642]
Stan Beck Fellowships (Undergraduate/Fellowship) [2861]
Dennis J. Beck Memorial Scholarship (Undergraduate/Scholarship) [3973]
Beck-Pfann Memorial Scholarships (Undergraduate/Scholarship) [5573]
Garvin L. Beck Scholarships (Undergraduate/Scholarship) [5917]
Dr. Joyce Beckett Scholarships (Undergraduate/Scholarship) [4665]
Beef Industry Scholarships (Undergraduate/Scholarship) [4788]
Raymond and Donald Beeler Memorial Scholarships (Undergraduate/Scholarship) [5918]
Notah Begay III Scholarship Program (Undergraduate/Scholarship) [190]
Beginning Freshmen Awards (Undergraduate/Scholarship) [4056]
Behavioral Sciences Post-Doctoral Fellowships (Postdoctorate/Fellowship) [2867]
Behavioral Sciences Student Fellowships (Graduate, Undergraduate/Fellowship) [2868]
Norbert J. Beihoff Scholarships (Undergraduate/Scholarship) [2238]
Beinecke Brothers Memorial Scholarships (Undergraduate/Scholarship) [7085]
N.S. Beinstock Fellowships (Undergraduate/Fellowship) [1393]
Belfer-Aptman Dissertation Research Awards (Doctorate/Grant) [4456]
March and Ruti Bell Foundation Scholarships (Undergraduate/Scholarship) [1618]
John Bell and Lawrence Thornton Scholarship Fund (Undergraduate/Scholarship) [3421]
Ray and Mary Bell Memorial Scholarships (Undergraduate/Scholarship) [6171]
Alfred D. Bell Travel Grants (All/Grant) [3030]
Harry A. Bell Travel Grants (All/Grant) [2569]
Bellevue PFLAG Scholarships (Undergraduate/Scholarship) [5756]

Belmont University Commercial Music Scholarships (Undergraduate/Scholarship) [2406]
David Beltran Memorial Scholarships (Undergraduate/Scholarship) [5919]
Samuel Flagg Bemis Research Grants (Doctorate, Graduate/Grant) [6452]
Benchwarmers of Redlands-Jess Mercado Football Scholarships (Undergraduate/Scholarship) [5920]
Reckitt Benckiser Student Scholarships (Graduate/Scholarship) [4729]
Richard W. Bendicksen Memorial Scholarships (Undergraduate/Scholarship) [820]
Bill Bendiner and Doug Morgenson Scholarships (Undergraduate/Scholarship) [5757]
Benedict Fellowships (Graduate/Fellowship) [238]
Eleanor Benett Scholarships (All/Scholarship) [6815]
Mary Elizabeth Lockwood Beneventi MBA Scholarships (Graduate/Scholarship) [3422]
Dr. Francis Anthony Beneventi Medical Scholarships (Undergraduate/Scholarship) [3423]
Benign Essential Blepharospasm Research Foundation Research Grant (Postdoctorate/Grant) [1623]
Bertram W. Bennett Memorial Scholarships (Graduate, Undergraduate/Scholarship) [1643]
Casey Bennett Scholarships (Undergraduate/Scholarship) [2926]
Pete and Ellen Bensley Memorial Scholarship Fund (Undergraduate/Scholarship) [3041]
Elizabeth Benson Scholarship Awards (Undergraduate/Scholarship) [6018]
Linn Benton Scholarships (Undergraduate/Scholarship) [5398]
Lester G. Benz Memorial Scholarships for College Journalism Study (Other/Scholarship) [5890]
Fred Berg Awards (All/Award/Prize) [2828]
Charlotte V. Bergen Scholarships (Undergraduate/Scholarship) [940]
Bergman Scholarships (Undergraduate/Scholarship) [5249]
ARRS/Leonard Berlin Scholarships in Medical Professionalism (Professional Development/Scholarship) [907]
Richard L. Bernardi Memorial Scholarship (Undergraduate/Scholarship) [2456]
Stuart L. Bernath Dissertation Grants (Doctorate/Grant) [6453]
Myrna F. Bernath Fellowships (Doctorate, Graduate/Fellowship) [6454]
Peggy Bernheim Memorial Scholarships (Undergraduate/Scholarship) [1792]
Donald H. Bernstein/John B. Talbert, Jr. Scholarship Fund (Undergraduate/Scholarship) [3042]
The Bernsten International Scholarships in Surveying Technology (Undergraduate/Scholarship) [484]
James R. and Geraldine F. Bertelsen Scholarships (Undergraduate/Scholarship) [6172]
Beta Gamma Memorial Scholarship Fund (Undergraduate/Scholarship) [2643]
Beta Nu/Caryl Cordis D'hondt Scholarships (Undergraduate/Scholarship) [6346]
Beta Omega Scholarships (Undergraduate/Scholarship) [6347]
Beta Sigma Phi-VCT Scholarships (Undergraduate/Scholarship) [6306]
Beta Sigma Scholarships (Undergraduate/Scholarship) [6348]
Bethune-Cookman University Excelsior Scholarships (Undergraduate/Scholarship) [1690]
Bethune-Cookman University Presidential Scholarships (Undergraduate/Scholarship) [1691]
Betsy Plank/PRSSA Scholarships (Undergraduate/Scholarship) [5874]
Harold Bettinger Scholarships (Undergraduate/Scholarship) [552]
Leonard Bettinger Scholarships (Undergraduate/Scholarship) [553]
Beverly Estate Scholarships (Undergraduate/Scholarship) [2733]
Beverly Willis Architecture Foundation Dissertation Fellowships (Doctorate/Fellowship) [6426]
BIA Higher Education Grants (Undergraduate/Grant) [1208]
BIE-Loan for Service for Graduates (Graduate/Loan) [642]
BIGALA (Bisexual Gay and Lesbian Alliance) Scholarships (Undergraduate/Scholarship) [6098]
Frank and Ruth Bila Scholarships (Undergraduate/Scholarship) [5356]
James Bilder Scholarships (Undergraduate/Scholarship) [6642]
Barry Bingham Sr. Fellowships (Professional Development/Fellowship) [4819]
Biocom Scholarships (Undergraduate/Scholarship) [6173]
BioQuip Scholarships (Undergraduate/Scholarship) [2862]
BioRx/Hemophilia of North Carolina Educational Scholarships (Undergraduate/Scholarship) [5006]
Birmingham-Southern College Eagle Scout Scholarships (Undergraduate/Scholarship) [4852]
BISA's Scholarship Assistance Program (Undergraduate/Scholarship) [1759]
BISA's Scholarships Assistance Program (High School/Scholarship) [1761]
Bisexual Foundation Scholarships (Graduate/Scholarship) [6572]
Bishop State Community College Scholarships (Undergraduate/Scholarship) [4907]
Lebbeus F. Bissell Scholarships (Undergraduate/Scholarship) [3424]
Black Data Processing Associates Scholarships (High School/Scholarship) [1606]
Black Student Fund (High School/Scholarship) [1722]
Black Women Lawyers Association of Los Angeles Scholarships (Undergraduate/Scholarship) [1757]
Reid Blackburn Scholarships (Undergraduate/Scholarship) [5018]
William T. Blackwell Scholarship Fund (Undergraduate/Scholarship) [4951]
Beatrice K. Blair Scholarships (Undergraduate/Scholarship) [1764]
Margaret Blanchard Dissertation Support Fund (Postgraduate/Grant) [7146]
Joan Blend Scholarship Fund (Undergraduate/Scholarship) [6709]
M. Hildred Blewett Scholarships (Postdoctorate/Scholarship) [6431]
Ellin Bloch and Pierre Ritchie Honorary Scholarships (Doctorate, Graduate/Grant) [798]
Bloch-Selinger Education Fund (Undergraduate/Scholarship) [2943]
F.A. and Charlotte Blount Scholarships (Undergraduate/Scholarship) [7421]
Blow Molding Division Memorial Scholarships (Graduate, Undergraduate/Scholarship) [6547]
Blues Ambassador Scholarships (Undergraduate/Scholarship) [5804]
Jordan ABDO/Michael Bluett Memorial Scholarships (Undergraduate/Scholarship) [6643]
Harry and Edith Blunt Scholarships (Undergraduate/Scholarship) [457]
David and Camille Boatwright Endowed Scholarships (Undergraduate/Scholarship) [5574]
Sandra Bobbitt Continuing Education Scholarships (Undergraduate/Scholarship) [1474]
Edith and Arnold N. Bodtker Grant (All/Grant) [2613]
Boeing Business Scholarships (Undergraduate/Scholarship) [3250]
Boeing Company Scholarships (Undergraduate/Scholarship) [6307]
Boeing Engineering Scholarships (Undergraduate/Scholarship) [3251]
Hagop Bogigian Scholarship Fund (Undergraduate/Scholarship) [1273]
Frances P. Bolton Fellowships (Doctorate/Fellowship) [5456]
Dorothy M. Bolyard Memorial Scholarships (Undergraduate/Scholarship) [6174]
BOMA/NY Scholarships (Undergraduate/Scholarship) [1802]
Carol Bond College Scholarships (Undergraduate/Scholarship) [5230]
Carol Bond Environmental Educator Scholarships (Professional Development/Scholarship) [5231]
Carol Bond University Scholarships (Undergraduate/Scholarship) [5232]
Barbara Bonnema Memorial Scholarships (Undergraduate/Scholarship) [5921]
Ellis J. Bonner Scholarships (Doctorate, Graduate, Undergraduate/Scholarship) [4715]
Scott Bonners Memorial Scholarships (Undergraduate/Scholarship) [1890]
Admiral Mike Boorda Scholarship Program (Undergraduate/Scholarship) [5146]
T. Frank Booth Memorial Scholarship Fund (Undergraduate/Scholarship) [3043]
Diane Booth Memorial Scholarships (Undergraduate/Scholarship) [2944]
Tom Boots Memorial Scholarships (Undergraduate/Scholarship) [5159]
David L. Boren Undergraduate Scholarships (Graduate, Undergraduate/Scholarship) [1424]
Maria Borrero Scholarships (Undergraduate/Scholarship) [3425]
Tom Bost Scholarships (Undergraduate/Scholarship) [7147]
Stephen Botein Fellowships (Doctorate/Fellowship) [300]
Dr. George T. Bottomley Scholarships (Undergraduate/Scholarship) [4414]
Miranda Bouldin General Scholarships (Undergraduate/Scholarship) [4255]
Bound to Stay Bound Books (BTSB) Scholarships (Graduate/Scholarship) [1464]
Rev. Andrew L. Bouwhuis Memorial Scholarship Program (Graduate/Scholarship) [2073]
Emma L. Bowen Foundation Scholarships for Minority Interests in Media work/study Program (Undergraduate/Scholarship) [7333]
William R. Bowen Scholarship (Undergraduate/Scholarship) [2368]
Billy Bowling Memorial Scholarships (Undergraduate/Scholarship) [5276]
Boy Scouts of America General Scholarships (Undergraduate/Scholarship) [3426]
Boy Scouts of America Troop 3 Scholarships - Art Till/Nathan E. Smith Memorial Scholarships (Undergraduate/Scholarship) [5922]
Elizabeth W. Boyce Scholarships (Undergraduate/Scholarship) [2239]
Dody Boyd Scholarships (Undergraduate/Scholarship) [2408]
Verna Curry Boyer Scholarships (Undergraduate/Scholarship) [6770]
Mildred Cater Bradham Social Work Fellowships (Graduate/Fellowship) [7553]
Carol June Bradley Awards (All/Grant) [4596]
Charles Bradley Memorial Scholarships (Undergraduate/Scholarship) [3403]
Donald Franklin Bradley Memorial Scholarships (Undergraduate/Scholarship) [5805]
Ed Bradley Scholarships (Undergraduate/Scholarship) [1394]
Edward J. Brady Memorial Scholarships (Undergraduate/Scholarship) [1158]
W. Philip Braender and Nancy Coleman Braender Scholarships (Undergraduate/Scholarship) [3427]
Ivan Braga Scholarships (Undergraduate/Scholarship) [6308]
Susan Brager Occupational Education Scholarships (Undergraduate/Scholarship) [5806]
William E. "Buck" Bragunier Scholarships (Undergraduate/Scholarship) [1241]
George and Mary Brammer Scholarships (Undergraduate/Scholarship) [2734]
The Helen and Edward Brancati Teacher Development Scholarships (Professional Development/Scholarship) [2054]
Breakthrough to Nursing Scholarships (Undergraduate/Scholarship) [3129]
Ann Marie Bredefeld Scholarships (Undergraduate/Scholarship) [5575]
The Lela Breitbart Memorial Scholarship Fund (All/Scholarship) [6881]
Lee Brennan Memorial Scholarships (Undergraduate/Scholarship) [5357]
Breslauer Family Scholarships (Undergraduate/Scholarship) [6175]
Estelle Shohet Brettman Fellowship (Postdoctorate/Fellowship) [3821]
Hilda E. Bretzlaff Foundation Scholarships (Undergraduate/Grant) [1777]
Rick Brewer Scholarships (Undergraduate/Scholarship) [7148]
Mary Ann Brichta Scholarships (Undergraduate/Scholarship) [7249]
James Bridenbaugh Memorial Scholarship

(Undergraduate/Scholarship) [554]
Lloyd Bridges Scholarships *(Graduate/Scholarship)* [2077]
Donald J. Bristow Memorial Scholarship Program *(Graduate, Undergraduate/Scholarship)* [4655]
Broadcast News Management Fellowships *(Undergraduate/Scholarship)* [1395]
Margaret Martin Brock Scholarships in Law *(Undergraduate/Scholarship)* [5576]
Louise A. Broderick San Diego County Scholarships *(Undergraduate/Scholarship)* [6176]
Ross P. Broesamle Educational Scholarships Fund *(Undergraduate/Scholarship)* [4139]
John G. Brokaw Scholarships *(Undergraduate/Scholarship)* [5138]
Shirley J. Brooke Endowed Scholarships *(Undergraduate/Scholarship)* [5578]
George M. Brooker Collegiate Scholarships for Minorities *(Graduate, Postgraduate, Undergraduate/Scholarship)* [3748]
Seth R. and Corrine H. Brooks Memorial Scholarships *(Graduate, Undergraduate/Scholarship)* [1644]
Carl E. Brooks Scholarships *(Undergraduate/Scholarship)* [6644]
Dorothy B. Brothers Executive Scholarship Program *(High School/Scholarship)* [7492]
William A. and Ann M. Brothers Scholarships *(Undergraduate/Scholarship)* [1159]
The Allen E. Broussard Scholarships *(Undergraduate/Scholarship)* [431]
Selena Danette Brown Book Scholarships *(Undergraduate/Scholarship)* [4666]
Brown and Caldwell Minority Scholarships *(Undergraduate/Scholarship)* [7334]
Diana Brown Endowed Scholarships *(Undergraduate/Scholarship)* [4165]
Marjorie M. Brown Fellowships Program *(Postdoctorate/Fellowship)* [4052]
Brown Foundation Academic Scholarships *(Undergraduate/Scholarship)* [1796]
Brown Foundation College Scholarship *(Undergraduate/Scholarship)* [631]
The John Carter Brown Library Long-Term Fellowships *(All/Fellowship)* [2061]
The John Carter Brown Library Short-Term Fellowships *(Doctorate, Postdoctorate/Fellowship)* [2062]
Olympia Brown and Max Kapp Awards *(Graduate/Scholarship)* [6948]
Quincy Brown Memorial Scholarships *(Undergraduate/Scholarship)* [5923]
Jesse Brown Memorial Youth Scholarship Program *(Undergraduate/Scholarship)* [2722]
JoAhn Brown-Nash Memorial Scholarships *(Undergraduate/Scholarship)* [2409]
Edward M. Brown Oxford Cup Memorial Scholarships *(Graduate, Undergraduate/Scholarship)* [1645]
Ron Brown Scholars Program *(High School/Scholarship)* [1798]
Jack H. Brown Scholarship *(Undergraduate/Scholarship)* [1821]
Mary L. Brown Scholarships *(Undergraduate/Scholarship)* [3929]
Charles S. Brown Scholarships in Physics *(Graduate, Undergraduate/Scholarship)* [5053]
Warren K. Brown Scholarships *(Undergraduate/Scholarship)* [1050]
Robert Browning Scholarships *(Undergraduate/Scholarship)* [5758]
Sheriff W. Bruce Umpleby Law Enforcement Scholarship Fund *(Undergraduate/Scholarship)* [6710]
Gregory Brunk Scholarships *(Undergraduate/Scholarship)* [2735]
The Robert W. Brunsman Memorial Scholarships *(Graduate, Undergraduate/Scholarship)* [3875]
Bernard and Mary Brusin Scholarships *(Undergraduate/Scholarship)* [2773]
Edward C. Bryant Scholarships Trust Fund *(Graduate/Fellowship)* [1113]
Patricia Buchanan Memorial Scholarships *(Undergraduate/Scholarship)* [7250]
LT.G. Douglas D. Buchholz Memorial Scholarships *(Undergraduate/Scholarship)* [1242]
John and Elisabeth Buck Endowed Scholarships *(Undergraduate/Scholarship)* [4283]
Buder Scholarship for American Indian Law Students *(Undergraduate/Scholarship)* [7384]
Gary L. Buffington Memorial Scholarships *(Undergraduate/Scholarship)* [3717]
Builders Association of Northeast Indiana (BANI) Scholarships *(Undergraduate/Scholarship)* [6771]
Bujea Memorial Scholarships *(Undergraduate/Scholarship)* [911]
William T. Burbage Family Memorial Scholarship *(Undergraduate/Scholarship)* [2369]
C. Lalor Burdick Scholarships *(Undergraduate/Scholarship)* [4284]
George M. Burditt Scholarships *(Undergraduate/Scholarship)* [1421]
Adam S. Burford Memorial Scholarships *(Graduate, Undergraduate/Scholarship)* [1646]
Max M. Burger Endowed Scholarships in Embryology *(Undergraduate/Scholarship)* [4285]
Dorothy and Dick Burgess Scholarship *(Undergraduate/Scholarship)* [3974]
Eleanor McWilliams Burke Fund *(Undergraduate/Scholarship)* [2945]
Ethel Beard Burstein Scholarship Program *(Postgraduate/Scholarship)* [729]
Kathy Bush Memorial Scholarships *(Undergraduate/Scholarship)* [5924]
Business and Transactional Law Center Scholarships *(Undergraduate/Scholarship)* [7347]
Lindsay Buster Memorial Scholarship *(Undergraduate/Scholarship)* [2457]
Nellie Love Butcher Scholarships *(Undergraduate/Scholarship)* [3428]
Walter Byers Postgraduate Scholarships *(Postgraduate/Scholarship)* [4802]
Donald C. and Doris K. Byers Scholarships *(Undergraduate/Scholarship)* [2736]
Joe Bynum/Raymond James Investment Services Technical Excellence Scholarships Fund *(Undergraduate/Scholarship)* [2346]
byourself Scholarship Fund *(Undergraduate/Scholarship)* [2504]
Robert C. Byrd Honors Scholarships *(Undergraduate/Scholarship)* [3662]
Dr. F. Ross Byrd Scholarships *(Graduate/Scholarship)* [7379]
Thad Byrne Memorial Scholarships *(Graduate, Undergraduate/Scholarship)* [1647]
George J. Bysiewicz Scholarship Fund *(Undergraduate/Scholarship)* [2392]
C200 Scholar Awards *(All/Scholarship)* [2337]
Cabrillo Clubs of California Scholarships *(Undergraduate/Scholarship)* [5737]
Dr. Aurelio M. Caccomo Family Foundation Memorial Scholarships *(Undergraduate/Scholarship)* [1136]
Cadmus Communications Corporation Graphics Scholarship Endowment Fund *(Undergraduate/Scholarship)* [3044]
Gordon Cain Fellowships in Technology, Policy, and Entrepreneurship *(Doctorate, Postdoctorate/Fellowship)* [2107]
Cal State San Macros Alumna Scholarships *(Undergraduate/Scholarship)* [1859]
Tese Caldarelli Memorial Scholarships *(Undergraduate/Scholarship)* [4672]
J.E. Caldwell Centennial Scholarships *(Undergraduate/Scholarship)* [5063]
Calhoun County Auduburn University Scholarships *(Undergraduate/Scholarship)* [2347]
Calhoun Scholarships *(Undergraduate/Scholarship)* [1810]
Hermoine Grant Calhoun Scholarships *(Undergraduate/Scholarship)* [4875]
California Association of Family and Consumer Sciences (CAFCS)-San Diego Chapter Scholarships *(Graduate, Undergraduate/Scholarship)* [6177]
California Association of Private Postsecondary Schools Scholarships *(Undergraduate/Scholarship)* [1814]
California Bar Foundation Diversity Scholarships *(Undergraduate/Scholarship)* [1325]
California Bar Law Foundation Scholarships *(Undergraduate/Scholarship)* [1326]
California Community Service Scholarships *(Undergraduate/Scholarship)* [4985]
California Community Service Scholarships - Bay Area *(Undergraduate/Scholarship)* [4986]
The California Endowment and AACN Minority Nurse Faculty Scholarships *(Graduate/Scholarship)* [337]
California Landscape Contractors Association Scholarships *(Undergraduate/Scholarship)* [1839]
California Scottish Rite Foundation Scholarships *(Undergraduate/Scholarship)* [1852]
California Shopping Cart Retrieval Corporation Inc. Scholarships *(Undergraduate/Scholarship)* [1822]
Calista Scholarships *(Undergraduate/Scholarship)* [1864]
Harry D. Callahan Educational Trust *(Undergraduate/Scholarship)* [6711]
Jodi Callahan Memorial Scholarships *(Undergraduate/Scholarship)* [50]
Calvin Alumni Association-Black Alumni Chapter Scholarships *(Undergraduate/Scholarship)* [1867]
Calvin Alumni Association British Columbia Scholarships *(Undergraduate/Scholarship)* [1868]
Calvin Alumni Association Colorado Chapter Scholarships *(Undergraduate/Scholarship)* [1870]
Calvin Alumni Association-Washington, D.C. Scholarships *(Undergraduate/Scholarship)* [1885]
Camden County College Employee Memorial Scholarships *(Undergraduate/Scholarship)* [1891]
Camden County College Foundation Scholarships *(Undergraduate/Scholarship)* [1892]
Camden County Retired Educators Association Scholarships *(Undergraduate/Scholarship)* [1893]
Stuart Cameron and Margaret McLeod Memorial Scholarships (SCMS) *(Graduate, Undergraduate/Scholarship/Forgivable Loan)* [3744]
Wesley C. Cameron Scholarships *(Undergraduate/Scholarship)* [5139]
Lois Campbell Scholarship Award *(Undergraduate/Scholarship)* [3846]
Robert G. Campbell Scholarships *(Undergraduate/Scholarship)* [5925]
Canada Millennium Scholarship Foundation Millennium Bursary Award *(Undergraduate/Award/Prize)* [1910]
Canada Study Grant for the Accommodation of Students with Permanent Disabilities *(Undergraduate/Grant)* [4156]
Cancer Survivors' Fund Scholarships *(Undergraduate/Scholarship)* [2052]
Therese A. Cannon Educational Scholarships *(Professional Development/Scholarship)* [3884]
John Cannon Memorial Scholarships *(Undergraduate/Scholarship)* [4626]
Agustin Cano Memorial Scholarships *(Undergraduate/Scholarship)* [5807]
John Caoile Memorial Scholarships *(Undergraduate/Scholarship)* [5808]
Cape Fear Community College Merit Scholarships *(Undergraduate/Scholarship)* [2057]
Rhea Sourifman Caplin Memorial Scholarships *(Undergraduate/Scholarship)* [3429]
Cardiac Sonographer Education Development Grants *(Professional Development, Undergraduate/Grant)* [950]
Career Advancement Scholarships *(Undergraduate/Scholarship)* [1806]
Career Colleges Scholarships *(Undergraduate/Scholarship)* [3672]
Career Mobility Scholarship Awards *(Doctorate, Undergraduate/Scholarship)* [16]
Career Mobility Scholarships *(Graduate, Undergraduate/Scholarship)* [3130]
Beth Carew Memorial Scholarships *(Undergraduate/Scholarship)* [5007]
John Carew Memorial Scholarships *(Undergraduate/Scholarship)* [555]
Glen and Babs Carlson Endowed Scholarships *(Undergraduate/Scholarship)* [4166]
Walta Wilkinson Carmichael Scholarships *(Undergraduate/Scholarship)* [6349]
Joe Carnes Scholarship *(Undergraduate/Scholarship)* [2458]
Carolina's Gay & Lesbian Scholarships *(Undergraduate/Scholarship)* [6099]
Carolinas-Virginias Retail Hardware Scholarship Fund *(Undergraduate/Scholarship)* [3048]
Jeffrey Carollo Music Scholarships

(Undergraduate/Scholarship) [5177]
Walter & Elsie Carr Endowed Scholarships (Undergraduate/Scholarship) [4167]
Commander James Carr Forensic Science Scholarships (Undergraduate/Scholarship) [252]
Willis H. Carrier Scholarships (Undergraduate/Scholarship) [965]
Rosalynn Carter Fellowships (Professional Development/Fellowship) [4820]
Deloris Carter Hampton Scholarships (Undergraduate/Scholarship) [5759]
Leigh Carter Scholarships (Undergraduate/Scholarship) [2411]
Cartwright Scholarships Program (Undergraduate/Scholarship) [618]
Casabella Family Memorial Scholarships (Undergraduate/Scholarship) [3430]
Case-Swayne Company Scholarships (Undergraduate/Scholarship) [5358]
Casey Family Scholars Scholarships (Undergraduate/Scholarship) [5415]
Elton Casey Scholarships (Undergraduate/Scholarship) [7149]
George H. and Anna Casper Fund (Undergraduate/Scholarship) [6712]
Thomas D. and Karen Cassady Scholarships (Graduate, Undergraduate/Scholarship) [1648]
May Cassioppi Scholarship (Undergraduate/Scholarship) [2459]
Catching the Dream Scholarship (Graduate, Undergraduate/Scholarship) [632]
Caterpillar Scholars Award (Undergraduate/Scholarship) [6471]
Caterpillar Scholarships in Diesel Mechanics (Undergraduate/Scholarship) [4168]
Catholic Biblical Association of America Scholarships (Undergraduate/Scholarship) [2071]
Catholic Healthcare Partners Scholarships (Undergraduate/Scholarship) [7525]
The Robert A Catlin/David W. Long Memorial Scholarship (Undergraduate/Scholarship) [2996]
Robert A. Catlin/David W. Long Memorial Scholarships (Graduate/Scholarship) [777]
Marshall Cavendish Scholarships (Graduate/Scholarship) [699]
Christine Kerr Cawthorne Scholarships (Undergraduate/Scholarship) [6350]
CCFA Career Development Awards (Doctorate, Graduate/Grant) [2559]
CCFA Research Fellowship Awards (Doctorate, Graduate/Fellowship) [2560]
CCFA Student Research Fellowship Awards (Graduate, Undergraduate/Grant) [2561]
CCSD School Counselors' Scholarships (Undergraduate/Scholarship) [5809]
CCU Alumni Endowed Scholarships (Undergraduate/Scholarship) [2304]
CD-HCF Chair's Scholarships (Professional Development/Scholarship) [2536]
CDC Foundation Scholarships (Undergraduate/Scholarship) [2075]
L.B. Cebik, W4RNL, and Jean Cebik, N4TZP, Memorial Scholarships (Undergraduate/Scholarship) [824]
Cedarcrest Farms Scholarships (Undergraduate/Scholarship) [687]
Cemanahuac Educational Community Scholarships (Other/Scholarship) [5263]
Delmar Cengage Learning-NAAE Upper Division Scholarships (Undergraduate/Scholarship) [4653]
Center for Congressional and Presidential Studies (CPPS) Endowment (Graduate, Undergraduate/Scholarship) [1123]
Center for Women in Government and Civil Society Fellowships (Postgraduate/Fellowship) [2091]
Central Indiana ASSE Scholarships (Graduate, Undergraduate/Scholarship) [1051]
CentraState Associated Auxiliaries Scholarships (Undergraduate/Scholarship) [2099]
CentraState Band Aid Open Committee Scholarships (Undergraduate/Scholarship) [2100]
CentraState Healthcare Foundation Health Professional Scholarships (Undergraduate/Scholarship) [2101]
CEPS-Tyco Scholarships (Undergraduate/Scholarship) [7137]
Certified Landscape Technician Scholarships (Undergraduate/Scholarship) [5242]
Certified Municipal Clerk Scholarships (CMC) (Professional Development/Scholarship) [3872]
Certified Neuroscience Registered Nurse (CNRN) Recertification Grants Program (Professional Development/Grant) [374]
Arthur and Gladys Cervenka Scholarships (Undergraduate/Scholarship) [6472]
CEW Scholarships (All/Scholarship) [2081]
CFERP Masters Fellowships (Graduate/Fellowship) [2343]
CFI Sid Solow Scholarships (Graduate/Scholarship) [1467]
CFIDS Association of America NP Student Scholarships (Graduate/Scholarship) [263]
Rick Chace Foundation Scholarships (Graduate/Scholarship) [1468]
Chaine des Rotisseurs Scholarships (Undergraduate/Scholarship) [524]
Emily Chaison Gold Award Scholarships (Undergraduate/Scholarship) [3431]
Jeanne S. Chall Research Fellowships (Doctorate, Graduate/Grant) [3888]
Challenge Met Scholarships (Undergraduate/Scholarship) [826]
Chambersburg/Fannett-Metal School District Scholarship Fund (Undergraduate/Scholarship) [3092]
Change Your World Scholarships (Undergraduate/Scholarship) [6819]
Channabasappa Memorial Scholarships (Graduate, Professional Development/Scholarship) [3837]
Harry H. and Floy B. Chapin Scholarship (Undergraduate/Scholarship) [2460]
Oscar Chapman Memorial Scholarships (Graduate, Undergraduate/Scholarship) [1649]
S. Penny Chappell Scholarships (Undergraduate/Scholarship) [5658]
Chapter 4 - Lawrence A. Wacker Memorial Awards (Undergraduate/Scholarship) [6473]
Chapter - 6 Fairfield County Scholarships (Undergraduate/Scholarship) [6474]
Chapter 31 - Peoria Endowed Scholarships (Undergraduate/Scholarship) [6477]
Chapter 52 - Wichita Scholarships (Graduate, Undergraduate/Scholarship) [6478]
Chapter 56 - Fort Wayne Scholarships (Graduate, Undergraduate/Scholarship) [6479]
Chapter 67 - Phoenix Scholarships (Undergraduate/Scholarship) [6482]
Chapter One - Detroit Founding Chapter Scholarships (Graduate, Undergraduate/Scholarship) [6486]
Abram and Sylvia Chasens Teaching and Research Fellowships (Postdoctorate/Fellowship) [286]
Chautauqua Scholarship Program (All/Scholarship) [3882]
Cesar E. Chavez Scholarships (Undergraduate/Scholarship) [5926]
Cheerful Giver Scholarships (Undergraduate/Scholarship) [6178]
Cherry Lane Foundation/Music Alive! Scholarships (Undergraduate/Scholarship) [941]
Cheyenne High School Faculty Memorial Scholarships (Undergraduate/Scholarship) [5810]
CHF Travel Grants (All/Grant) [2108]
Chi Chapter Undergraduate Scholarships (Undergraduate/Scholarship) [2644]
Chi Phi Educational Trust (Undergraduate/Scholarship) [2117]
Chicago Division Scholarships (Undergraduate/Scholarship) [4513]
Chicago FM Club Scholarships (Undergraduate/Scholarship) [827]
Child of Alumni Book Voucher Awards (Undergraduate/Scholarship) [3699]
Child and Family Advocacy Fellowships (Undergraduate/Scholarship) [7348]
Julia Child Memorial Scholarships (Undergraduate/Scholarship) [525]
Kevin Child Scholarships (Undergraduate/Scholarship) [4917]
Childbirth Educator Program Scholarships (Other/Scholarship) [4114]
John and Ruth Childe Scholarships (Undergraduate/Scholarship) [6645]
Children of Unitarian Universalist Ministers College Scholarships (Undergraduate/Scholarship) [6949]
Charline Chilson Scholarships (Undergraduate/Scholarship) [2684]
Vincent Chin Memorial Fund Scholarships (Graduate/Scholarship) [455]
Chinese American Medical Society Summer Research Outreach Programs (Undergraduate/Grant) [2135]
Choose Your Future Scholarships (Undergraduate/Scholarship) [2413]
Chopin Foundation of the United States Scholarships (Undergraduate/Scholarship) [2139]
George Choy Memorial/Gay Asian Pacific Alliance (GAPA) Scholarships (Undergraduate/Scholarship) [6100]
Andrew G. Chressanthis Memorial Scholarships (Undergraduate/Scholarship) [3527]
Chretien International Research Grants (Doctorate, Professional Development/Grant) [429]
Christian Pharmacist Fellowship International Scholarships (Professional Development/Fellowship) [2143]
Christmas Tree Chapter Scholarship Awards (Undergraduate/Scholarship) [5378]
Chrysalis Scholarships (Graduate/Grant) [1510]
Chrysler Technical Scholarships Fund (Undergraduate/Scholarship) [2633]
Church Family Scholarships (Undergraduate/Scholarship) [4169]
Edward D. Churchill Research Scholarships (Professional Development/Scholarship) [417]
The Churchill Scholarships (Postgraduate/Scholarship) [2147]
CIA Undergraduate Scholarships (Undergraduate/Scholarship) [1425]
CIGNA Healthcare Graduate Scholarships (Graduate/Scholarship) [4892]
CIGNA Healthcare Undergraduate Scholarships (Undergraduate/Scholarship) [4893]
Cincinnati High School Scholarships (High School/Scholarship) [2149]
Nate Mack/Cindi Turner Scholarships (Undergraduate/Scholarship) [5811]
Carlos Enrique Cisneros Point Scholarships (Graduate, Undergraduate/Scholarship) [5716]
Citi Foundation Scholarships Program (Undergraduate/Scholarship) [619]
City of Sanibel Employee Dependent Scholarships (Undergraduate/Scholarship) [6646]
Civitan Shropshire Scholarships (Undergraduate/Scholarship) [2243]
Clackamas Chapter Scholarship Awards (Undergraduate/Scholarship) [5379]
CLAGS Fellowships (Graduate/Fellowship) [2085]
Clan Ross Foundation Scholarships (Undergraduate/Scholarship) [2245]
Cecil Earl Clapp, Sr. Memorial Scholarships (Undergraduate/Scholarship) [5277]
Michelle Clark Fellowships (Undergraduate/Fellowship) [1396]
Ann E. Clark Foundation Scholarships (Undergraduate/Scholarship) [5140]
Clark High School Academy of Finance Scholarships (Undergraduate/Scholarship) [5812]
Clark High School Alumni Leadership Circle Scholarships (Undergraduate/Scholarship) [5813]
Clark High School Teacher Education Academy Scholarships (Undergraduate/Scholarship) [5814]
Howard A. Clark Horticulture Scholarships (Undergraduate/Scholarship) [2414]
Robert A. Clark Memorial Educational Scholarships (Other/Scholarship) [5074]
Fisher Clark Memorial Endowed Scholarships (Undergraduate/Scholarship) [4170]
Athalie Clarke Endowed Scholarships (Undergraduate/Scholarship) [5579]
Lucy and Charles W.E. Clarke Scholarships (Undergraduate/Scholarship) [996]
CLASS Fund Irrigation Scholarship Program (Graduate, Undergraduate/Scholarship) [4119]
CLASS Fund Landscape Architecture Scholarship Program (Graduate, Undergraduate/Scholarship) [4120]
Class Fund Ornamental Horticulture Scholarship Program (Undergraduate/Scholarship) [980]

CLASS Fund University Scholarship Program *(Graduate, Undergraduate/Scholarship)* [4121]
Class Nobel Academic Scholarships for Members *(High School/Scholarship)* [5067]
Classic Wines of California Scholarships *(Undergraduate/Scholarship)* [1823]
Brian Dane Cleary Memorial Scholarships *(Undergraduate/Scholarship)* [5580]
Lula Faye Clegg Memorial Scholarship Fund *(Undergraduate/Scholarship)* [3052]
Cleveland Alumni Association Scholarships *(Graduate, Undergraduate/Scholarship)* [1650]
Geraldine Clewell Fellowships - Doctoral Student *(Graduate/Fellowship)* [5659]
Geraldine Clewell Fellowships - Masteral *(Graduate/Fellowship)* [5660]
Geraldine Clewell Scholarships - Undergraduate *(Undergraduate/Scholarship)* [5661]
David H. Clift Scholarships *(Graduate/Scholarship)* [700]
Bryan Cline Memorial Soccer Scholarship Program *(Undergraduate/Scholarship)* [191]
Clinical Pharmacy Post-Pharm.D. Fellowships in the Biomedical Research Sciences *(Postdoctorate/Fellowship)* [580]
Clinical Research Training Fellowships *(Other/Fellowship)* [260]
Clinical Toxicology Fellowships *(Doctorate/Fellowship)* [389]
Clinician Scientist Development Awards *(Postgraduate/Fellowship)* [5532]
Irene Culver Cllins and Louis Franklin Collins Scholarship *(Undergraduate/Scholarship)* [2370]
Closs/Parnitzke/Clarke Scholarships *(Undergraduate/Scholarship)* [5662]
L. Robert Clough Memorial Scholarships *(Graduate, Undergraduate/Scholarship)* [1651]
Club Managers Association of America (CMAA) Research Grants *(All/Grant)* [2250]
The Club at Morningside Scholarships *(Undergraduate/Scholarship)* [6179]
CMAA Student Conference Travel Grants *(All/Grant)* [2251]
CNA Foundation Scholarships *(Graduate, Undergraduate/Scholarship)* [1052]
Co Dental Hygiene Scholarships *(Undergraduate/Scholarship)* [6309]
The Helena B. Cobb Annual Scholarships *(Undergraduate/Scholarship)* [7501]
The Helena B. Cobb Four-Year Higher Education Grants *(Undergraduate/Scholarship)* [7502]
J.C. and Rheba Cobb Memorial Scholarships *(Undergraduate/Scholarship)* [4811]
Gordon W. and Agnes P. Cobb Scholarships *(Undergraduate/Scholarship)* [2808]
Coca-Cola First Generation Scholarships *(Undergraduate/Scholarship)* [620]
Coca-Cola Scholars Foundation Four-Year Award for Seniors *(Undergraduate/Scholarship)* [2296]
Johnnie L. Cochran, Jr./MWH Scholarships *(Undergraduate/Scholarship)* [4894]
Frank M. Coda Scholarships *(Undergraduate/Scholarship)* [966]
CODY Foundation Fund *(Undergraduate/Scholarship)* [3093]
Coeur d'Alene Alumni Scholarships *(Undergraduate/Scholarship)* [4171]
Claude T. Coffman Memorial Scholarships *(Undergraduate/Scholarship)* [7110]
Donald O. Coffman Scholarships *(Undergraduate/Scholarship)* [5760]
Ruth M. Cogan Scholarship Fund *(Undergraduate/Scholarship)* [6713]
COHEAO Scholarships *(Undergraduate/Scholarship)* [2257]
Paul I. and Elena H. Cohen Scholarships *(Graduate, Undergraduate/Scholarship)* [871]
Ardis Cohoon Scholarships *(Undergraduate/Scholarship)* [7150]
Jack Kent Coke Graduate Scholarships *(Graduate/Scholarship)* [7086]
Cole Family Scholarships *(Undergraduate/Scholarship)* [5761]
Arthur H. Cole Grants in Aid *(Doctorate/Grant)* [2818]
Frank Cole Memorial Emergency NP Student Scholarships *(Graduate/Scholarship)* [264]
Paul Cole Scholarships *(Undergraduate/Scholarship)* [6522]
Dennis Coleman Choral Conducting Scholarships *(Undergraduate/Scholarship)* [5762]
College of Agriculture and Natural Resources Scholarships *(Undergraduate/Scholarship)* [3432]
The College Club of Hartford Scholarships *(Undergraduate/Scholarship)* [3433]
College Education Loan Scholarships For U.S. Resident Students *(Undergraduate/Loan)* [3779]
College of Marin Gay and Lesbian Student Scholarships *(Undergraduate/Scholarship)* [6101]
College Scholarship Awards *(Undergraduate/Scholarship)* [1614]
College and Trade/Technical School Scholarships *(Undergraduate/Scholarship)* [2898]
Jennet Colliflower Nursing Scholarships *(Undergraduate/Scholarship)* [2595]
Capt. Winifred Quick Collins Scholarships *(Undergraduate/Scholarship)* [5141]
Elmer and Rosa Lee Collins Scholarships *(Undergraduate/Scholarship)* [7426]
Lloyd E. and Rachel S. Collins Scholarships *(Undergraduate/Scholarship)* [7427]
Colorado PROSTART/Art Institute of Colorado Art Scholarships for High School Seniors *(Undergraduate/Scholarship)* [1313]
Colorado Springs Pikes Peak Region School District Young Peoples Art Show Scholarships *(Undergraduate/Scholarship)* [1314]
ColorMasters Scholarships *(Undergraduate/Scholarship)* [3174]
Columbian Lawyers Association of Westchester County Scholarships *(Undergraduate/Scholarship)* [2331]
Columbus Citizens Foundation High School Scholarships *(High School/Scholarship)* [2335]
Robert N. Colwell Memorial Fellowships *(Doctorate, Graduate/Fellowship)* [1026]
Committee 12 - Rail Transit Scholarships *(Undergraduate/Scholarship)* [872]
Committee 27 - Maintenance-of-Way Work Equipment Scholarships *(Undergraduate/Scholarship)* [873]
Commonwealth "Good Citizen" Scholarships *(Undergraduate/Scholarship)* [1431]
Communal Studies Association Research Fellowships *(Graduate/Grant)* [2339]
Communications Workers of America Scholarships *(Undergraduate/Scholarship)* [2341]
Community-based Natural Resource Management Assistantships *(All/Internship)* [2344]
The Community Foundation DBI Scholarships *(Undergraduate/Scholarship)* [2415]
Community Foundation of the Fox River Valley Scholarships *(Undergraduate/Scholarship)* [2389]
Community Foundation of Sarasota County Adult Learner Scholarships *(Undergraduate/Scholarship)* [2505]
Community Foundation Scholarships *(Undergraduate/Scholarship)* [2461]
The Community Foundation Student Education Loans *(Undergraduate/Loan)* [2416]
Compassionate Care Scholarships *(Undergraduate/Scholarship)* [5763]
Tom and Judith Comstock Scholarships *(Undergraduate/Scholarship)* [828]
Maridell Braham Condon Scholarships *(Undergraduate/Scholarship)* [6351]
Conference of State Bank Supervisors Graduate School Scholarships *(Graduate/Award/Prize)* [2527]
Congressional Research Awards *(Graduate/Award/Prize)* [2719]
Congressional Scholarships Award *(Undergraduate/Scholarship)* [3147]
Congressional Science Fellowships *(Postdoctorate/Fellowship)* [1006]
Alan H. Conklin Business Aviation Management Scholarships *(Undergraduate/Scholarship)* [4772]
Connecticut Association of Latinos in Higher Education Scholarships *(Undergraduate/Scholarship)* [3434]
Connecticut Association of Women Police Scholarships *(Undergraduate/Scholarship)* [3435]
Connecticut Building Congress Scholarships *(Undergraduate/Scholarship)* [3436]
Connecticut Capitol Scholarship Program *(Undergraduate/Scholarship)* [3437]
Connecticut League of Nursing Scholarships *(Undergraduate/Scholarship)* [3438]
Connecticut Mortgage Bankers Scholarships-Social Affairs Committee *(Undergraduate/Scholarship)* [3439]
Connecticut Nurserymen's Foundation Scholarships *(Undergraduate/Scholarship)* [3440]
Mary Adeline Conner Professional Development Scholarships *(Graduate/Scholarship)* [6681]
James F. Connolly LexisNexis Academic & Library Solutions Scholarships *(Postgraduate/Scholarship)* [366]
Louis M. Connor Jr. Scholarships *(Undergraduate/Scholarship)* [7151]
Patricia Pownder Conolly Memorial Scholarships *(Undergraduate/Scholarship)* [4462]
Construction Trades Scholarships *(Undergraduate/Scholarship)* [4749]
Contemporary Club Scholarships *(Undergraduate/Scholarship)* [5927]
The Continental Group Scholarship Fund *(High School/Scholarship)* [2596]
Continuing Education Awards *(Graduate/Grant)* [4441]
Continuing Education Awards *(All/Scholarship)* [4734]
Jorge Espejal Contreras Memorial Scholarships *(Graduate, Undergraduate/Scholarship)* [3804]
Convergence Assistantship Grants *(Undergraduate/Grant)* [3394]
James & Maryetta Cook Scholarships *(Undergraduate/Scholarship)* [1894]
Irvine W. Cook WA0CGS Scholarships *(Undergraduate/Scholarship)* [829]
Cooley's Anemia Foundation Research Fellowships *(Doctorate/Fellowship)* [2539]
Madison and Edith Cooper Scholarships *(Undergraduate/Scholarship)* [6180]
Milton E. Cooper/Young AFCEAN Graduate Scholarships *(Graduate/Scholarship)* [1243]
Cope Middle School PTSA Scholarships *(Undergraduate/Scholarship)* [5928]
Rob Copeland Memorial Scholarships *(Undergraduate/Scholarship)* [4172]
Copper and Brass Service Center Inc. Scholarship Program *(Undergraduate/Scholarship)* [2541]
Corbett-Porter Building Bridges Scholarships *(Undergraduate/Scholarship)* [5815]
Hazel Corbin/Childbirth Connection Grant for Evidence-based Midwifery Care *(Professional Development/Award/Prize)* [471]
Charles Clarke Cordle Memorial Scholarships *(Undergraduate/Scholarship)* [830]
Bill Cormack Scholarships *(Undergraduate/Scholarship)* [6862]
The Frank Cormier Scholarships *(Undergraduate/Scholarship)* [7409]
Cornaro Scholarships for Graduate Studies *(Graduate/Scholarship)* [4042]
D.C. Cornelius Memorial Scholarships *(Undergraduate/Scholarship)* [7428]
Holly A. Cornell Scholarships *(Graduate/Scholarship)* [1143]
Corporate Aviation Management Scholarships *(Professional Development/Scholarship)* [4773]
Correctional Education Association Scholarships *(Graduate, Undergraduate/Scholarship)* [2546]
NSS Sara Corrie Memorial Grants *(All/Grant)* [5087]
Tom Cory Memorial Scholarships *(Undergraduate/Scholarship)* [1197]
Richard Cossette/Gale Memorial Scholarships *(All/Scholarship)* [1545]
Cost-of-Books Relief Scholarships *(Undergraduate/Scholarship)* [1860]
James Costello Memorial Scholarships *(Undergraduate/Scholarship)* [3920]
John Costello Memorial Scholarships *(Undergraduate/Scholarship)* [2532]
Cotner Family Scholarships *(Undergraduate/Scholarship)* [2948]
George C. Cotzias, MD Memorial Fellowships *(Professional Development/Fellowship)* [760]

Council on Social Work Education Minority Fellowship Programs *(Postdoctorate/Fellowship)* [2553]
Council on Social Work Education Scholars Program *(Postdoctorate/Scholarship)* [2554]
Soozie Courter Sharing a Brighter Tomorrow Hemophilia Scholarship Program *(Graduate, Undergraduate/Scholarship)* [4918]
COUSE-Gram Scholarships *(Undergraduate/Scholarship)* [6647]
Richard P. Covert, Ph.D./FHIMSS Scholarships for Management Systems *(Other/Scholarship)* [3516]
The Joe E. Covington Award for Research on Bar Admissions Testing *(Doctorate/Award/Prize)* [4817]
Reuben R. Cowles Youth Awards *(Undergraduate/Award/Prize)* [688]
Gertrude M. Cox Scholarships *(Doctorate, Graduate/Fellowship)* [1114]
CPCU Laman Educational Foundation Scholarships *(Professional Development/Scholarship)* [3761]
Crafton Elementary School PTA Scholarships *(Undergraduate/Scholarship)* [5929]
Crafton Hills College Foundation Scholarships *(Undergraduate/Scholarship)* [5930]
Margaret T. Craig Community Service Scholarship *(Undergraduate/Scholarship)* [2462]
Crain Educational Grants Program *(Undergraduate/Scholarship)* [6386]
Robert E. Cramer Scholarships *(Graduate, Undergraduate/Scholarship)* [6548]
Cranberry Institute NP Student Scholarships *(Graduate/Scholarship)* [265]
The Rick Crane Group Real Estate Scholarships Fund *(Undergraduate/Scholarship)* [4173]
Mike Crapo Math and Science Scholarship Fund *(Undergraduate/Scholarship)* [3644]
Meredith P. Crawford Fellowship in I/O Psychology *(Undergraduate/Fellowship)* [3627]
Crawford Scholarships *(Undergraduate/Scholarship)* [6181]
L.D. "Crow" Crawford Scholarships *(Undergraduate/Scholarship)* [7001]
Creative Glass Center of America Fellowships *(All/Fellowship)* [2557]
Critical Language Scholarships for Intensive Summer Institutes *(Graduate, Undergraduate/Scholarship)* [892]
Crohn's and Colitis Foundation of America Senior Research Awards *(Doctorate, Graduate/Grant)* [2562]
Cromwell Fellowships *(Undergraduate/Fellowship)* [991]
Kathryn M. Cronin Scholarships *(Undergraduate/Scholarship)* [7152]
Albuquerque ARC/Toby Cross Scholarships *(Undergraduate/Scholarship)* [831]
R.G Crossno Memorial Scholarships *(Undergraduate/Scholarship)* [2810]
CRS Scholarships *(Undergraduate/Scholarship)* [2145]
Lydia Cruz and Sandra Maria Ramos Scholarships *(Undergraduate/Scholarship)* [2681]
The Crystal Green Blood Assurance Scholarships *(Undergraduate/Scholarship)* [1766]
CSA Fraternal Life Scholarships *(Undergraduate/Scholarship)* [2564]
CSX Scholarships *(Undergraduate/Scholarship)* [874]
CTP Scholarship Program *(Professional Development/Scholarship)* [5024]
Cuisinart Culinary Study Scholarships *(All, Professional Development/Scholarship)* [2570]
John P. Culhane Memorial Scholarships *(Undergraduate/Scholarship)* [125]
Culinary and Hospitality Foundation of San Benito County Scholarships *(Undergraduate/Scholarship)* [2566]
The Culinary Trust's Memorial Journalism Scholarships *(Professional Development/Grant)* [2571]
Linda Cullen Memorial Scholarships *(High School/Scholarship)* [526]
Murtha Cullina Scholarships *(Undergraduate/Scholarship)* [2393]
Brian Cummins Memorial Scholarships *(Undergraduate/Scholarship)* [3441]
John J. Cunningham Memorial Scholarships *(Undergraduate/Scholarship)* [875]
Curry Award for Girls and Young Women *(Undergraduate/Scholarship)* [6387]
Nancy Curry Scholarships *(Postgraduate/Scholarship)* [6256]
Michael D. Curtin Renaissance Student Memorial Scholarships *(Undergraduate/Scholarship)* [2811]
The Jennifer Curtis Byler Scholarships *(Undergraduate/Scholarship)* [5095]
Don and Barbara Curtis Excellence Fund for Extracurricular Student Activities *(Undergraduate/Grant)* [7153]
Dewey Lee Curtis Scholarship Fund *(Doctorate, Graduate/Scholarship)* [2631]
CVS/All Kids Can Scholars Program *(Undergraduate/Scholarship)* [1540]
Cystic Fibrosis Cholestatic Liver Disease Liver Scholarships *(Doctorate/Award/Prize)* [705]
Cystic Fibrosis Foundation Scholarships *(Undergraduate/Scholarship)* [2585]
DAAD Study Scholarship Awards *(Graduate/Scholarship)* [3223]
DAAD Undergraduate Scholarship Program *(Undergraduate/Scholarship)* [3224]
Daddy Longlegs Scholarships *(Undergraduate/Scholarship)* [6182]
Daggy Youth/Student Scholarships *(Professional Development/Scholarship)* [3915]
Daiichi Sankyo Inc. NP Student Scholarships *(Graduate/Scholarship)* [266]
Robert G. Dailey Scholarships *(Graduate, Undergraduate/Scholarship)* [6549]
Daimler Chrysler Scholarships Award *(Undergraduate/Scholarship)* [3565]
Daland Fellowships in Clinical Investigation *(Doctorate/Fellowship)* [767]
Angela D. Dales Merit Scholarship Program *(Undergraduate/Loan)* [1187]
The John L. Dales Scholarship Fund *(Undergraduate/Scholarship)* [6288]
Dallas Hispanic Bar Association Scholarships *(Undergraduate/Scholarship)* [2611]
Serena D. Dalton Scholarships *(Undergraduate/Scholarship)* [7429]
Marvin E. Daly Memorial Scholarships *(Undergraduate/Scholarship)* [5278]
June Danby and Pat Pearse Education Scholarship *(Undergraduate/Scholarship)* [3975]
Dance Education Scholarship Program *(High School/Scholarship)* [6244]
D&A Florida Scholarships *(Undergraduate/Scholarship)* [6648]
The Dangermond Fellowships *(Postgraduate/Fellowship)* [981]
Robin M. Daniels Memorial Scholarships *(Undergraduate/Scholarship)* [5816]
Arthur H. Daniels Scholarships *(Undergraduate/Scholarship)* [5931]
Danville Education Association Scholarship Fund *(Undergraduate/Scholarship)* [2949]
Danville High School Class of 1963 Scholarship Fund *(Undergraduate/Scholarship)* [2950]
Danville Rotary Scholarships *(Undergraduate/Scholarship)* [2951]
Darden Restaurants Scholarships *(Undergraduate/Scholarship)* [7005]
Hugh and Hazel Darling Dean Scholarships *(Undergraduate/Scholarship)* [5581]
Darling Foundation Endowed School of Law Scholarships *(Undergraduate/Scholarship)* [5582]
Darrel Hess Community College Geography Scholarships *(Undergraduate/Scholarship)* [1354]
Datatel Angelfire Scholarships *(Graduate, Undergraduate/Scholarship)* [2615]
Datatel Scholarships *(Graduate, Undergraduate/Scholarship)* [2616]
Daughters of the American Revolution American Indian Scholarships *(Undergraduate/Scholarship)* [633]
The Dave Family "Humor Studies" Scholarships *(Undergraduate/Scholarship)* [1364]
David Rose Scholarships *(Undergraduate/Scholarship)* [942]
Davis Educational Scholarship Fund *(Undergraduate/Scholarship)* [2506]
Kenneth and Kathleen Davis Endowed Scholarships *(Undergraduate/Scholarship)* [4175]
Davis Family Scholarships *(Undergraduate/Scholarship)* [6183]
The William H. Davis, Jr. Scholarship Fund *(Undergraduate/Scholarship)* [2399]
Davis Memorial Foundation Scholarship Award Program *(Graduate, Undergraduate/Scholarship)* [2621]
Dwight F. Davis Memorial Scholarships *(Undergraduate/Scholarship)* [7303]
Johnny Davis Memorial Scholarships *(Undergraduate/Scholarship)* [69]
Arlene Davis Scholarships *(Undergraduate/Scholarship)* [2685]
Fran Morgenstern Davis Scholarships *(Undergraduate/Scholarship)* [943]
James Davis Scholarships *(Undergraduate/Internship)* [7154]
James H. Davis Scholarships *(Undergraduate/Scholarship)* [3012]
Rebecca Davis Scholarships *(Professional Development/Scholarship)* [2619]
Davis Wright Tremaine 1L Diversity Scholarships *(Undergraduate/Scholarship)* [2623]
William W. Dawson Memorial Scholarships *(Graduate, Undergraduate/Scholarship)* [1652]
Colonel Richard M. Dawson Scholarships *(Undergraduate/Scholarship)* [2417]
Brian M. Day Scholarships *(Undergraduate/Scholarship)* [5764]
Dayton Amateur Radio Association Scholarships *(Undergraduate/Scholarship)* [832]
DCH Freehold Toyota Scholarships *(Undergraduate/Scholarship)* [2102]
Edilia and Francois Auguste de Montequin Fellowships *(Doctorate/Scholarship)* [6427]
Elsie De Wolfe Point Scholarships *(Graduate, Undergraduate/Scholarship)* [5717]
Deaf Queer Youth Scholarships *(Undergraduate/Scholarship)* [6102]
Deafness Research Foundation Research Grants *(Doctorate/Grant)* [2625]
Alphonso Deal Scholarship Awards *(Undergraduate/Scholarship)* [4766]
Dean Prim Scholarships *(Undergraduate/Scholarship)* [7430]
Death Valley '49ers Scholarships *(Undergraduate/Scholarship)* [2627]
DeBakey International Society Fellowship Awards *(Professional Development/Award/Prize)* [2629]
Don Debolt Franchising Scholarship Program *(Undergraduate/Scholarship)* [3856]
Walter M. Decker Point Scholarships *(Graduate, Undergraduate/Scholarship)* [5718]
DEED Student Research Grant/Internships *(Graduate, Undergraduate/Grant)* [804]
Anthony R. Dees Educational Workshop Scholarships *(Undergraduate/Scholarship)* [6448]
Deets-Laine Geriatric NP Student Scholarships *(Doctorate, Graduate/Scholarship)* [267]
Jane Delano Society Scholarships *(Undergraduate/Scholarship)* [886]
Jan DiMartino Delany Memorial Scholarship Fund *(Undergraduate/Scholarship)* [3094]
Antonia Dellas Memorial Scholarship *(Undergraduate/Scholarship)* [3976]
Alexander A. DelleCese Memorial Scholarships *(Undergraduate/Scholarship)* [1793]
Martha Delman and Milton Arthur Krug Endowed Scholarships *(Undergraduate/Scholarship)* [5583]
Thomson Delmar Learning Surgical Technology Scholarships *(Graduate/Scholarship)* [1500]
Vine Deloria Jr. Memorial Scholarships *(Graduate/Scholarship)* [621]
Eric Delson Memorial Scholarships *(Graduate, High School, Undergraduate/Scholarship)* [4919]
Delta Chi Alumnae Memorial Scholarships *(Undergraduate/Scholarship)* [6352]
Delta Daily Food (Canada) Inc. Scholarships *(Undergraduate/Scholarship)* [3847]
Delta Faucet Scholarships *(Undergraduate/Scholarship)* [5701]
Delta Gamma Scholarships *(Undergraduate/Scholarship)* [2675]
Delta Iota Alumni Scholarships *(Undergraduate/Scholarship)* [6404]

Delta Nu Alpha Foundation Scholarships (Undergraduate/Scholarship) [2677]
Delta Phi Epsilon Educational Foundation Scholarships (Undergraduate/Scholarship) [2679]
Delta Sigma Theta Hartford Alumnae Scholarships (Undergraduate/Scholarship) [3442]
Delta Tau Chapter Scholarships (Graduate, Undergraduate/Scholarship) [1653]
Delta/VPPPA Safety, Health and Environmental Scholarships (Undergraduate/Scholarship) [7338]
Delta Zeta Undergraduate Scholarships (Undergraduate/Scholarship) [2686]
C. Rodney Demarest Memorial Scholarships (Undergraduate/Scholarship) [3443]
DEMCO New Leaders Travel Grants (All/Grant) [5871]
Christopher Demetris Scholarships (Undergraduate/Scholarship) [3528]
Inez Demonet Scholarships (Graduate/Scholarship) [7316]
Ruth DeMoss Scholarships (Undergraduate/Scholarship) [6184]
Dennis Foltz Scholarships (Graduate/Scholarship) [3175]
Albert W. Dent Graduate Student Scholarships (Undergraduate/Scholarship) [466]
Michael Denton Scholarships (Undergraduate/Scholarship) [5279]
John Denver Music Scholarships (Undergraduate/Scholarship) [944]
Denver Public School Art Award/Scholarships for High School Seniors (Undergraduate/Scholarship) [1315]
Denver Scholarship Foundation Scholarships (Undergraduate/Scholarship) [2705]
ROP - Dr. Linda Denver Scholarships (Undergraduate/Scholarship) [5932]
Tommy Depaola Scholarship Award (Undergraduate/Scholarship) [3848]
Dick Depaolis Memorial Scholarships (Undergraduate/Scholarship) [2512]
Dependents of Deceased Service Members Scholarship Program (Undergraduate/Scholarship) [5147]
Depression and ADHD Fellowships (Professional Development/Fellowship) [4078]
DEPS Graduate Scholarship Program (Graduate/Scholarship) [2715]
Karekin DerAvedision Memorial Endowment Fund (Undergraduate/Scholarship) [1276]
Derivative Duo Scholarships (Undergraduate/Scholarship) [5765]
Herman H. Derksen Scholarships (Undergraduate/Scholarship) [6185]
Pat Dermargosian Memorial Scholarships (Undergraduate/Scholarship) [5933]
Descendant Scholarships (Undergraduate/Scholarship) [2606]
Detroit Tigers Willie Horton Scholarships (Undergraduate/Scholarship) [2514]
Development Fund for Black Students in Science and Technology Scholarship (Undergraduate/Scholarship) [2707]
Albert and Jane Dewey Scholarships (Undergraduate/Scholarship) [3444]
Edward D. Di Loreto-Odell S. McConnell Scholarships (Undergraduate/Scholarship) [5584]
Julio C. Diaz Memorial Scholarship Fund (Undergraduate/Scholarship) [6714]
Jean Dearth Dickerscheid Fellowships (Graduate/Fellowship) [5663]
Dickey Rural Networks College Scholarship Program (Undergraduate/Scholarship) [2709]
Bill Dickey Scholarship Association Scholarships (Undergraduate/Scholarship) [2711]
Harold Dieckmann Draper, Sr. Scholarships (Undergraduate/Scholarship) [1550]
Rob Digiacomo Scholarship Fund (Undergraduate/Scholarship) [6715]
Carol DiMaiti Scholarship Awards (Undergraduate/Scholarship) [4328]
Gretchen Dimico Memorial Scholarships (Undergraduate/Scholarship) [4176]
Raymond DiPaglia Endowment Scholarships (Undergraduate/Scholarship) [2737]
Disabled War Veterans Scholarships (Undergraduate/Scholarship) [1244]
Dissertation Proposal Development Fellowships (Doctorate/Fellowship) [6415]
Distinguished Flying Cross Society Scholarship (Undergraduate/Scholarship) [2724]
LaRue A. Ditmore Music Scholarships (Undergraduate/Scholarship) [7481]
Diversity Dissertation Scholarships (Doctorate/Fellowship) [799]
Diversity Executive Leadership Program Scholarships (Professional Development/Scholarship) [920]
Robert A. and Barbara Divine Graduate Student Travel Grants (Graduate/Grant) [6455]
Peggy Dixon Two-Year Scholarships (Undergraduate/Scholarship) [6541]
Charles Dobbins FTA Scholarships (Undergraduate/Scholarship) [3154]
Doctoral and Postdoctoral Fellowships (Doctorate, Postgraduate/Fellowship) [3233]
F. Atlee Dodge Maintenance Scholarships (Undergraduate/Scholarship) [126]
Robert Winchester Dodson Scholarships (Undergraduate/Scholarship) [7155]
Hans H. and Margaret B. Doe Scholarships (Graduate, Undergraduate/Scholarship) [6186]
Emmett J. Doerr Memorial Distinguished Scout Scholarships (High School/Scholarship) [4853]
Dofflemyer Scholarships (Undergraduate/Scholarship) [4854]
Dokmo Family Scholarships (Undergraduate/Scholarship) [6187]
Dolphin Scholarships (Undergraduate/Scholarship) [2726]
Scott Dominguez - Craters of the Moon Chapter Scholarships (Graduate, Undergraduate/Scholarship) [1053]
Marian Jones Donaldson Scholarship Fund (Undergraduate/Scholarship) [2952]
Harvey N. Dondero Communication and Journalism Excellence Scholarships (Undergraduate/Scholarship) [5817]
Harry A. Donn Scholarships (Undergraduate/Scholarship) [3445]
Mickey Donnelly Memorial Scholarships (Undergraduate/Scholarship) [5818]
Jim Doogan Memorial Scholarships (Undergraduate/Scholarship) [7075]
Joseph M. Dorgan Scholarships (Undergraduate/Scholarship) [2739]
Dorizas Memorial Scholarships (Undergraduate/Scholarship) [3529]
Pauly D'Orlando Memorial Art Scholarships (Graduate, Undergraduate/Scholarship) [6950]
Dosatron International Inc. Scholarships (Undergraduate/Scholarship) [557]
Eric Dostie Memorial College Scholarships (Four Year College, Two Year College, Undergraduate/Scholarship) [4920]
Father Connie Dougherty Scholarships (Undergraduate/Scholarship) [2507]
Sergeant Douglas and Charlotte DeHorse Scholarships (Undergraduate/Scholarship) [2066]
Douglas County Art Awards Scholarship for High School Seniors (Undergraduate/Scholarship) [1316]
Harold K. Douhhit Regional Scholarships (Undergraduate/Scholarship) [5322]
Margaret Dowell-Gravatt, M.D. Scholarship (Undergraduate/Scholarship) [1625]
Nettie Dracup Memorial Scholarships (Undergraduate/Scholarship) [485]
Drake University Law School Law Opportunity Scholarships - Disadvantage (Undergraduate/Scholarship) [2740]
Drake University Law School Law Opportunity Scholarships - Diversity (Undergraduate/Scholarship) [2741]
Drake University Law School Public Service Scholarships (Undergraduate/Scholarship) [2742]
The "Drawn to Art" Fellowships (Doctorate/Fellowship) [301]
Cleveland Drennon, Jr. Memorial Scholarships (Undergraduate/Scholarship) [7111]
Wilma Sackett Dressel Scholarships (Undergraduate/Scholarship) [6353]
Margaret Drew Alpha Fellowships (Graduate/Fellowship) [5664]
Louis Dreyfus Warner-Chappell City College Scholarships (Undergraduate/Scholarship) [945]
DRI Law Student Diversity Scholarships (Undergraduate/Scholarship) [1755]
Drinkwater Family Scholarships (Undergraduate/Scholarship) [6188]
Lillian Cooper Droke Memorial Scholarships (Undergraduate/Scholarship) [4463]
Richard Drukker Memorial Scholarships (Undergraduate/Scholarship) [5180]
Drum Major Institute Scholars (Undergraduate/Scholarship) [6332]
Sergeant Major Douglas R. Drum Memorial Scholarship Fund (Undergraduate/Scholarship) [716]
Martin Duberman Fellowships (Professional Development/Fellowship) [2086]
Lee Dubin Scholarship Fund (Undergraduate/Scholarship) [6103]
Charles Dubose Scholarships (Undergraduate/Scholarship) [3446]
John W. Duckett Jr., AFUD Pediatric Research Scholarships (Undergraduate/Scholarship) [6538]
Deborah Gandee Dudding Memorial Scholarships (Undergraduate/Scholarship) [5479]
Edward J. Dulis Scholarships (Undergraduate/Scholarship) [4397]
Duluth Building and Construction Trades Council Scholarships (Undergraduate/Scholarship) [2774]
Duluth Central HS Alumni Scholarships (Undergraduate/Scholarship) [2775]
Dunbar Heritage Scholarships (Undergraduate/Scholarship) [6650]
Duncan Aviation Scholarships (Undergraduate/Scholarship) [70]
John Holt Duncan Memorial Scholarships (Graduate, Undergraduate/Scholarship) [1654]
Wade and Marcelene Duncan Scholarships (Undergraduate/Scholarship) [7431]
Ed Dunkelblau Scholarships (All/Scholarship) [1365]
Travis Dunning Memorial Scholarships (Undergraduate/Scholarship) [5819]
Bus and Mary Ellen Durant Timberline High School Endowed Scholarships (Undergraduate/Scholarship) [4177]
William R. Durham/Theater Scholarship (Undergraduate/Scholarship) [2463]
Durning Sisters Scholarships (Graduate/Scholarship) [2645]
Joe Durso Memorial Scholarships (Undergraduate/Scholarship) [4569]
Roger C. Duvoisin, MD Research Grants (Professional Development/Grant) [761]
Sue and Ken Dyer Foundation Travel Scholarship Award (Undergraduate/Scholarship) [3096]
Dystonia Medical Research Foundation Fellowships (Postdoctorate/Fellowship) [2800]
Eagles Fly for Leukemia Scholarships (Undergraduate/Scholarship) [2127]
Amelia Earhart Fellowship Program (Postdoctorate/Fellowship) [7563]
Amelia Earhart Memorial Academic Scholarships (Undergraduate/Scholarship) [5209]
Early Childhood Development Scholarships (Undergraduate/Scholarship) [1701]
Robert E. Early Memorial Scholarships (Undergraduate/Scholarship) [2743]
Earthquake Engineering Research Institute/Fema Graduate Fellowships (Graduate/Scholarship) [2804]
Bob East Scholarships (Undergraduate/Scholarship) [5019]
East Tennessee Foundation Scholarships (Undergraduate/Scholarship) [7112]
Eastern Orthodox Scouting Scholarships (High School/Scholarship) [4855]
Eastern Shore Builder's Association Scholarships (Undergraduate/Scholarship) [2371]
David Eaton Scholarships (Graduate, Master's/Scholarship) [6951]
The Christoph Daniel Ebeling Fellowships (Doctorate/Fellowship) [302]
Ellen Eberhardt Memorial Scholarships (Undergraduate/Scholarship) [6772]
ECA Alumni Small Grants Program (Professional

Development/Grant) [3894]
John E. Echlin Memorial Scholarships (Undergraduate/Scholarship) [1551]
Economic Development Division Graduate Scholarships (Graduate/Scholarship) [778]
Sidney M. Edelstein Fellowships (Doctorate, Postdoctorate/Fellowship) [2109]
Edgecliff Alumni Awards (Undergraduate/Scholarship) [7526]
Edgecliff McAuley Art Scholarships (Undergraduate/Scholarship) [7527]
Edgecliff McAuley Music Scholarships (Undergraduate/Scholarship) [7528]
Vivian Edmonds Scholarships (Undergraduate/Scholarship) [7156]
S. Randolph Edmonds Young Scholars Competition (Graduate, Undergraduate/Scholarship) [1753]
Melanie and Todd Edmonson Memorial Scholarship (Undergraduate/Scholarship) [2348]
Edon Farmers Cooperative Scholarships (Undergraduate/Scholarship) [2826]
Education is Power Scholarships (Undergraduate/Scholarship) [4921]
Education Resource Center (ERC) Scholarships (Undergraduate/Scholarship) [6399]
Educational Administration Scholarships Award (Postgraduate/Scholarship) [397]
Educational Audiology Association Doctoral Scholarships (Doctorate/Scholarship) [2829]
Educational Enrichment Awards (Undergraduate/Scholarship) [1209]
Educational Leadership Foundation Grants (Undergraduate/Grant) [2300]
Educational Opportunity Fund (Undergraduate/Scholarship) [3097]
Educational Portal of the Americas Graduate Scholarships (Postgraduate/Scholarship) [2838]
Educational Portal of the Americas Undergraduate Scholarships (Undergraduate/Scholarship) [2839]
Educational and Professional Achievement Scholarships (Undergraduate/Scholarship) [451]
Palo Verde High School - Barbara Edwards Memorial Scholarships (Undergraduate/Scholarship) [5820]
Jimmy Edwards Scholarships (Undergraduate/Scholarship) [2419]
John and Alice Egan Multi-Year Mentioning Scholarships (Undergraduate/Scholarship) [2607]
Bill Egan Scholarship Program (Undergraduate/Scholarship) [5380]
The eGullet Society for Culinary Arts and Letters Brian and Thelma Moore Memorial Culinary Journalist Independent Study Scholarships (Professional Development/Grant) [2572]
The eGullet Society for Culinary Arts and Letters Culinary Journalist Independent Study Scholarships (Professional Development/Grant) [2573]
The eGullet Society for Culinary Arts and Letters Matthew X. Hassett Memorial Culinary Arts Scholarships (All, Professional Development/Scholarship) [2574]
The eGullet Society for Culinary Arts and Letters Professional Chef Independent Study Scholarships (Other, Professional Development/Grant) [2575]
Christine H. Eide Memorial Scholarships (Graduate, Undergraduate/Scholarship) [4242]
Eight and Forty Lung and Respiratory Disease Nursing Scholarships (Professional Development/Scholarship) [696]
Einhorn New Investigator Awards (Undergraduate/Award/Prize) [6466]
Farouk El-Baz Student Research Grants (Doctorate, Graduate, Undergraduate/Grant) [3209]
ELA Foundation Scholarships (Graduate/Scholarship) [1297]
George & Isabelle Elanjian Scholarships (Undergraduate/Scholarship) [1277]
W. Eldridge and Emily Lowe Scholarships (Undergraduate/Scholarship) [6405]
Electric Cooperative Pioneer Trust Fund Scholarships (Undergraduate/Scholarship) [2744]
Electronic Document Systems Foundation Scholarships (Undergraduate/Scholarship) [2846]
Electronics Division Lewis C. Hoffman Scholarships (Undergraduate/Scholarship) [453]
Herman E. Elgar Memorial Scholarships (Undergraduate/Scholarship) [2745]
Todd Elias Memorial Scholarships (Graduate, Undergraduate/Scholarship) [1655]
Elks National Foundation Scholarships (Undergraduate/Scholarship) [2848]
Dr. Robert Elliott Memorial Scholarships (Undergraduate/Scholarship) [4415]
Pauline Elliott Scholarships (Undergraduate/Scholarship) [4416]
Robert A. Ellis Scholarships in Physics (Undergraduate/Scholarship) [5054]
Robertson Lola Ellis Scholarships (Undergraduate/Scholarship) [4286]
William P. Elrod Memorial Scholarships (Undergraduate/Scholarship) [6853]
Emerald Empire Chapter Scholarship Awards (Undergraduate/Scholarship) [5381]
Emergency Medicine Physician Scholarships for Health Information Management Program (Undergraduate/Scholarship) [6716]
Emergency Medicine Physicians Scholarship Fund for Non-Physician Employee Dependents (Undergraduate/Scholarship) [6717]
Emergency Nurses Association Undergraduate Scholarships (Undergraduate/Scholarship) [2851]
Emerging Leaders Scholarships (Undergraduate/Scholarship) [1841]
Emerging Teacher-Leaders in Elementary School Mathematics Grants for Grades K-5 Teachers (Professional Development/Grant) [4829]
EMLF Law Student Scholarships (Undergraduate/Scholarship) [2855]
Emmanuel Bible College Scholarships (Undergraduate/Scholarship) [1278]
Employee Education Scholarships (Other/Scholarship) [4946]
ENA Foundation Advanced Practice Scholarships (Undergraduate/Scholarship) [2852]
Priscilla Maxwell Endicott Scholarships (Undergraduate/Scholarship) [3447]
Alice Yuriko Endo Memorial Scholarships (Undergraduate/Scholarship) [4016]
Endowment Fund for Education Grants (Undergraduate/Grant) [1707]
Endowment Fund for Education (Loan) (Undergraduate/Loan) [1708]
Endowment Fund for Education (Loan/Grants for Equipment) (Undergraduate/Grant) [1709]
Endowment Fund for Education (Loans/Grants for Educational Materials) (Undergraduate/Grant) [1710]
The Eneslow Pedorthic Institute Scholarships (Undergraduate/Scholarship) [5545]
Vice Admiral Donald D. Engen Scholarships (Undergraduate/Scholarship) [5132]
Engineering Diversity Affairs Scholarships (All/Scholarship) [7252]
Engineers for Tomorrow Scholarships Program (Undergraduate/Scholarship) [4563]
Don English Memorial Scholarships (Undergraduate/Scholarship) [5821]
Harold E. Ennes Scholarships (Professional Development/Scholarship) [6526]
Enterprise Rent-A-Car Scholarships (Graduate, Undergraduate/Scholarship) [5636]
Lindsay M. Entz Memorial Scholarships (Undergraduate/Scholarship) [2953]
Environment, Natural Resource and Energy (ENRE) Division Fellowships (Graduate/Scholarship) [779]
Environmental Research and Education Foundation Scholarships (Postdoctorate/Scholarship) [2865]
Epicurean Charitable Foundation Scholarships (Undergraduate/Scholarship) [5822]
Epilepsy Foundation Post-doctoral Research Fellowships (Postdoctorate, Professional Development/Grant) [2869]
Epilepsy Foundation Pre-doctoral Research Training Fellowships (Graduate/Grant) [2870]
Epilepsy Foundation Research Grants (All/Grant) [2871]
Epilepsy Foundation Research and Training Fellowships for Clinicians (Doctorate, Professional Development/Grant) [2872]
Epsilon Epsilon Scholarships (Undergraduate/Scholarship) [6354]
Epsilon Tau Pi's Soaring Eagle Scholarships (Undergraduate/Scholarship) [4856]
Epsilon Tau Scholarships (Undergraduate/Scholarship) [6355]
Dena Epstein Award for Archival and Library Research in American Music (All/Grant) [4597]
Alan R. Epstein "Reach for the Stars" Scholarships (Undergraduate/Scholarship) [2597]
Equal Access to Justice Scholarships (Undergraduate/Scholarship) [4752]
Equal Justice Works Fellowship Program (Graduate, Undergraduate/Fellowship) [2882]
eQuality Scholarships (Undergraduate/Scholarship) [6104]
Robert C. Erb Sr. Scholarships (Undergraduate/Scholarship) [4417]
Harriet Erich Graduate Fellowships (Graduate/Scholarship) [2646]
Kenan Erim Fellowships for Research at Ancient Aphrodisiacs (Postdoctorate/Fellowship) [893]
Ernest Hemingway Research Grants (Professional Development/Grant) [3538]
The Eleonor A. Ernest Scholarship (Undergraduate/Scholarship) [3977]
Melissa Eleonor Ernest Scholarship (Undergraduate/Scholarship) [3978]
Robert P. Ernest Scholarship (Undergraduate/Scholarship) [3979]
Kevin Ernst Memorial Scholarship Fund (Undergraduate/Scholarship) [3275]
Ernst and Young/Ascend Leadership Scholarship Program (Undergraduate/Scholarship) [4644]
Ahmet Ertegun Memorial Scholarships (Graduate, Undergraduate/Scholarship) [6937]
ESA Foundation Computer and Video Game Scholarship Program (Undergraduate/Scholarship) [2859]
Boomer Esiason Foundation Scholarship Program (All/Scholarship) [2587]
Charles A. Esser Memorial Scholarships (Graduate/Scholarship) [1217]
NSPF Ray B. Essick Scholarship Awards (Other/Scholarship) [5102]
R. Wayne Estes Endowed Scholarships (Undergraduate/Scholarship) [5585]
Larry L. Etherton Scholarships (Graduate, Undergraduate/Scholarship) [876]
Ethnic Minority and Women's Enhancement Postgraduate Scholarships (Graduate/Scholarship) [4803]
Alex J. Ettl Grants (Professional Development/Grant) [5037]
Brad Evans Memorial Scholarships (Undergraduate/Scholarship) [5359]
Lee S. Evans/National Housing Endowment Scholarship (Graduate, Undergraduate/Scholarship) [4941]
Evans and Petree Law Firm Scholarships (Undergraduate/Scholarship) [7113]
Ruth Murphy Evans Scholarship (Undergraduate/Scholarship) [3373]
Evans Scholarships (Undergraduate/Scholarship) [4554]
Chuck Evans Scholarships (Undergraduate/Scholarship) [7405]
Evening Mesquite Club Scholarships (Undergraduate/Scholarship) [5823]
Evjue Foundation, Inc./Capital Times Scholarships (Undergraduate/Scholarship) [7253]
David E. Ewald Journalism Scholarships (Undergraduate/Scholarship) [4774]
Excel Staffing Companies Scholarships for Excellence in Continuing Education (Undergraduate/Scholarship) [192]
Executive Women International Fellows Program (Graduate/Fellowship) [2895]
Executive Women International Scholarship Program (EWISP) (High School/Scholarship) [2896]
Exercise For Life Athletic Scholarships Program (Undergraduate/Scholarship) [2588]
Exploratory Travel and Data Grants (Doctorate/Grant) [2819]
Exxon Mobil Aviation and the Avitats International Operators Scholarships (All/Scholarship) [4775]
Eye On Jewels Scholarships (Undergraduate/Scholarship) [3176]

The William C. Ezell Fellowships (Postgraduate/Fellowship) [276]
FACS Graduate Fellowships (Graduate/Fellowship) [4747]
FACT Graduating Senior Scholarship Program (Undergraduate/Scholarship) [2920]
Faculty Doctoral Scholarships (Doctorate/Scholarship) [2853]
Faculty Research Visit Grant (Doctorate/Grant) [3225]
Faegre & Benson Diversity Scholarships (Undergraduate/Scholarship) [2900]
FAIC Latin American and Caribbean Scholars Program (Professional Development/Scholarship) [660]
Fairbanks Chapter Legacy Scholarships (Undergraduate/Scholarship) [7076]
D.J. Fairgrave Education Trust (Undergraduate/Scholarship) [2746]
AIST Benjamin F. Fairless Scholarships (AIME) (Undergraduate/Scholarship) [1445]
Falcon Achievement Scholarships (Undergraduate/Scholarship) [5731]
Fall Fellowships in Korean Studies (Professional Development/Fellowship) [4082]
James Mackenzie Fallows Scholarships Honoring Gertrude Baccus (Undergraduate/Scholarship) [5934]
Families of Freedom Scholarship Fund - America Scholarships (Undergraduate/Scholarship) [2902]
William M. Fanning Maintenance Scholarships (Undergraduate/Scholarship) [4776]
Farella Braun Martel LLP Diversity Scholarships (Undergraduate/Scholarship) [2904]
Senior Chef Frank Farello Scholarships (Professional Development/Scholarship) [527]
John S.W. Fargher Scholarships (Graduate/Scholarship) [3730]
Judge McIntyre Faries Scholarships (Undergraduate/Scholarship) [5586]
Farmers State Bank Scholarships (Undergraduate/Scholarship) [6773]
Farmers Union Marketing and Processing Foundation Stanley Moore Scholarships (Undergraduate/Scholarship) [5250]
Farmington UNICO Scholarships (Undergraduate/Scholarship) [3448]
W.D. Farr Scholarships (Graduate/Scholarship) [4789]
David Edward Farson Scholarships (Undergraduate/Scholarship) [5480]
Anne M. Fassett Scholarships (Undergraduate/Scholarship) [6651]
Miklos Faust International Travel Awards (Postdoctorate/Fellowship) [975]
FCBA Foundation Scholarships (Undergraduate/Scholarship) [2909]
Fecon Scholarships (Undergraduate/Scholarship) [3001]
Federal Employee Education and Assistance Fund Scholarships (Other/Scholarship) [2913]
Federalsburg Rotary Club Scholarships (Undergraduate/Scholarship) [2372]
Federated Insurance Scholarships (Graduate, Undergraduate/Scholarship) [5637]
Adrienne Zoe Fedok Art and Music Scholarships (Undergraduate/Scholarship) [3099]
FEEA Scholarship Program (Other/Scholarship) [2914]
Nolan W. Feeser Scholarship Fund (Undergraduate/Scholarship) [2954]
Symee Ruth Feinburg Memorial Scholarships (Undergraduate/Scholarship) [3449]
Edward R. and Hazel N. Felber Scholarships (Undergraduate/Scholarship) [7254]
Harold E. Fellows Scholarships (All/Scholarship) [1784]
Fellowships in Aerospace History (Doctorate/Fellowship) [605]
Fellowships in the Humanities and Social Sciences in Turkey (Postdoctorate/Fellowship) [894]
Fellowships for Intensive Advanced Turkish Language Study in Turkey (Undergraduate/Fellowship) [895]
Reese Felts Scholarships (Undergraduate/Scholarship) [7157]
Jennica Ferguson Memorial Scholarships (Undergraduate/Scholarship) [4876]
Dr. Joan W. Fernandez Point Scholarships (Graduate, Undergraduate/Scholarship) [5719]
William and Dorothy Ferrell Scholarship Program (Undergraduate/Scholarship) [1390]
Lt. Col. Romeo and Josephine Bass Ferretti Scholarships (Undergraduate/Scholarship) [51]
FHSMAI Scholarship Program (Graduate/Scholarship) [3127]
FICE Scholarships (Undergraduate/Scholarship) [3002]
Field Aviation Co., Inc. Scholarships (Undergraduate/Scholarship) [71]
UFVA Carole Fielding Student Grants (Graduate, Undergraduate/Grant) [7091]
Beth K. Fields Scholarships (Undergraduate/Scholarship) [7100]
Film Arts Foundation Development Grants (All/Grant) [2928]
Herb Fincher Memorial Scholarship (Undergraduate/Scholarship) [2373]
Fine Arts and Music Scholarships (Undergraduate/Scholarship) [2420]
Dr. Mary Finegold Scholarships (Undergraduate/Scholarship) [6389]
Gordy Fink Memorial Scholarships (Undergraduate/Scholarship) [5824]
Helen R. Finley-Loescher Scholarships (Undergraduate/Scholarship) [2464]
Finnegan, Henderson, Farabow, Garrett & Dunner, LLP Diversity Scholarships (Undergraduate/Scholarship) [2936]
Dayton E. Finnigan Scholarship (Undergraduate/Scholarship) [3374]
First Church of Christ in Wethersfield - Metcalf Scholarships (Undergraduate/Scholarship) [3450]
First Friday Breakfast Club Scholarships (Undergraduate/Scholarship) [6105]
First in My Family Scholarship Program (Undergraduate/Scholarship) [6156]
First Security Foundation Business Scholarships (Undergraduate/Scholarship) [4178]
Fisher Healthcare Educational Scholarships (Other/Scholarship) [5075]
Charles N. Fisher Memorial Scholarships (Undergraduate/Scholarship) [833]
William A. Fisher Memorial Scholarships (Graduate/Scholarship) [1027]
Arthur and Juna Fisher Memorial Track Scholarships (Undergraduate/Scholarship) [5935]
Jack B. Fisher Scholarship Fund (Undergraduate/Scholarship) [6718]
Allison E. Fisher Scholarships (Undergraduate/Scholarship) [2984]
Ameel J. Fisher Scholarships (Undergraduate/Scholarship) [7158]
Fitzgerald Fellowships (Undergraduate/Fellowship) [2672]
Fitzgerald Health Education Associates NP Student Scholarships (Graduate/Scholarship) [268]
Carol C. Fitzgerald Scholarship Program (Professional Development/Scholarship) [2911]
Fitzgerald Scholarships (Undergraduate/Scholarship) [2673]
Gloria Flaherty Scholarships (Graduate/Scholarship) [3248]
Scott A. Flahive Memorial Scholarship Fund (Undergraduate/Scholarship) [3277]
Reuben H. Fleet Memorial Scholarships (Undergraduate/Scholarship) [6189]
Fleming/Blaszcak Scholarships (Graduate, Undergraduate/Scholarship) [6550]
Charlie Fleming Education Fund Scholarships (Undergraduate/Scholarship) [5106]
Laura M. Fleming Scholarship Fund (Undergraduate/Scholarship) [3058]
FLEOA Foundation Scholarship Program (Undergraduate/Scholarship) [2916]
Flexible Packaging Academic Scholarships & Summer Internship Program (Undergraduate/Internship) [2988]
Flight Attendants/Flight Technician Scholarships (Undergraduate/Scholarship) [4777]
Grant H. Flint International Scholarships - Category I (Undergraduate/Scholarship) [6596]
Grant H. Flint International Scholarships - Category II (Undergraduate/Scholarship) [6597]
Flora English Creative Writing Scholarships (Undergraduate/Scholarship) [5825]
Florida Association District of Nursing Administration Scholarships (Undergraduate/Scholarship) [2990]
Florida Atlantic Planning Society Graduate Fellowships for Academic Excellence (Postgraduate/Fellowship) [2997]
Florida Automotive Industry Scholarships (Undergraduate/Scholarship) [1546]
Florida Engineering Society Junior College Scholarships (Undergraduate/Scholarship) [3003]
Florida Engineering Society University Scholarships (Undergraduate/Scholarship) [3004]
Florida Fertilizer and Agrichemical Association Scholarships (Undergraduate/Scholarship) [3010]
Florida Nurses Association Scholarships (Professional Development/Scholarship) [3014]
Florida Outdoor Writers Association Scholarships (Undergraduate/Scholarship) [3016]
John Flynn Memorial Scholarship (Undergraduate/Scholarship) [2465]
Paul B. & Aline Flynn Scholarships (Undergraduate/Scholarship) [6652]
FMA-FEEA Scholarship Program (Undergraduate/Scholarship) [2918]
FMA Foundation Scholarships (Undergraduate/Scholarship) [3022]
Alice J. Foit Scholarships (Undergraduate/Scholarship) [6719]
Frank Fong Scholarships (Undergraduate/Scholarship) [6423]
Food Engineering Scholarships (Postdoctorate, Postgraduate/Scholarship) [3024]
Ford Foundation Diversity Fellowships (Doctorate/Fellowship) [4618]
Ford Foundation Predoctoral Fellowships for Minorities (Doctorate/Fellowship) [4703]
Ford Motor Company Scholarship Program (Undergraduate/Scholarship) [3589]
Anne Ford Scholarships (Undergraduate/Scholarship) [4796]
Fordham Fellowships (Undergraduate/Fellowship) [3027]
Fordham Scholarships (Doctorate/Scholarship) [3028]
George Foreman Tribute to Lyndon B. Johnson Scholarships (Undergraduate/Scholarship) [1397]
Nancy B. Forest and L. Michael Honaker Master's Scholarships for Research (Doctorate, Graduate/Scholarship) [800]
Leland Stanford Forrest Scholarships (Undergraduate/Scholarship) [2747]
Forsyth County Nursing Scholarships (Undergraduate/Scholarship) [7433]
Genevieve Forthun Scholarships (Undergraduate/Scholarship) [5665]
Forward Face Scholarships (Professional Development/Scholarship) [3033]
Barbara Palo Foster Memorial Scholarships (Undergraduate/Scholarship) [2128]
Jonathan Hastings Foster Scholarships (Undergraduate/Scholarship) [6190]
Foundation of American Institute for Conservation Lecture Grants (Professional Development/Grant) [661]
Foundation for the Carolinas Rotary Scholarship Fund (Undergraduate/Scholarship) [3059]
Foundation of the Federal Bar Association Public Service Scholarships (Undergraduate/Scholarship) [3125]
The Foundation of the National Student Nurses' Association Scholarships (Graduate, Undergraduate/Scholarship) [5100]
Foundation Scholarships (Undergraduate/Scholarship) [4064]
Foundation for Surgical Technology Advanced Education/Medical Mission Scholarships (Graduate/Scholarship) [1501]
Foundation for Surgical Technology Scholarships (Graduate/Scholarship) [1502]
Founders Circle Professional Scholarships (Professional Development/Scholarship) [3762]
Jacob and Lewis Fox Scholarships (Undergraduate/Scholarship) [3451]

Paris Fracasso Production Floriculture Scholarships *(Undergraduate/Scholarship)* [558]
Louise J. Franchini Rockford Police Department Scholarships *(Undergraduate/Scholarship)* [2466]
Franchise Law Diversity Scholarship Awards *(Undergraduate/Scholarship)* [3857]
Joe Francis Haircare Scholarships *(Undergraduate/Scholarship)* [3141]
Joey and Florence Franco Legacy Scholarship *(Undergraduate/Scholarship)* [1824]
Mayme and Herb Frank Scholarship Program *(Graduate, Undergraduate/Scholarship)* [1323]
Michael W. and Jean D. Franke Family Foundation Scholarships *(Graduate, Undergraduate/Scholarship)* [877]
Mary Weiking Franken Scholarships *(Undergraduate/Scholarship)* [5666]
The Ginny Frankenthaler Memorial Scholarship *(Undergraduate/Scholarship)* [6629]
John Hope Franklin Dissertation Fellowships *(Doctorate/Fellowship)* [768]
Franklin Elementary School PTA Scholarships *(Undergraduate/Scholarship)* [5936]
Denise Franklin Journalism Scholarships *(Undergraduate/Scholarship)* [7434]
Franklin Research Grants *(Doctorate/Grant)* [769]
Joseph Frasca Excellence in Aviation Scholarships *(Undergraduate/Scholarship)* [7081]
Fraser Family Scholarships *(Undergraduate/Scholarship)* [5826]
Carlyle Fraser/Wilton Looney Scholarships *(Undergraduate/Scholarship)* [1552]
Freedom Alliance Scholarships *(Undergraduate/Scholarship)* [3143]
Freedom Forum-NCAA Sports-Journalism Scholarships *(Undergraduate/Scholarship)* [4804]
Richard Gregory Freeland, II Educational Scholarships *(High School/Scholarship)* [1762]
Belknap Freeman Carnegie Mellon Scholarships *(Undergraduate/Scholarship)* [878]
Kevin Freeman Travel Grants *(Graduate, Professional Development/Grant)* [4598]
The French Culinary Institute Classic Pastry Arts Scholarships *(All, Professional Development/Scholarship)* [2576]
The French Culinary Institute Culinary Arts Scholarships *(All, Professional Development/Scholarship)* [2577]
The French Culinary Institute's Food and Technology Scholarships - Magic Potions Transglutaminase *(Professional Development/Scholarship)* [2578]
French Embassy Scholarships *(Other/Scholarship)* [5264]
Ruth M. French Graduate Scholarships *(Doctorate, Graduate/Scholarship)* [933]
Dorris W. Frey Memorial Scholarships *(Undergraduate/Scholarship)* [6654]
Carleton A. Friday Memorial Scholarships *(Undergraduate/Scholarship)* [4522]
Dale E. Fridell Memorial Scholarships *(Undergraduate/Scholarship)* [6793]
A.E. Robert Friedman Scholarships *(Postgraduate, Undergraduate/Scholarship)* [5445]
Phil Friel Scholarships *(Undergraduate/Scholarship)* [4418]
Friends and Family of Jennifer Balber Scholarships *(Undergraduate/Scholarship)* [5937]
Friends of Loutit District Library Scholarships Fund *(Undergraduate/Scholarship)* [3280]
Friends of Mary Automotive Scholarships *(Undergraduate/Scholarship)* [6312]
Friends of Megan Bolton Memorial Fund *(Undergraduate/Scholarship)* [3100]
Friendship Scholarship Fund *(Undergraduate/Scholarship)* [3101]
Froberg-Suess JD/MBA Scholarships *(Undergraduate/Scholarship)* [5587]
Dean A. Froehlich Endowed Scholarships *(Undergraduate/Scholarship)* [4179]
Fruits and Vegetable Industries Scholarships *(Undergraduate/Scholarship)* [4489]
Marian Johnson Frutiger Scholarships *(Undergraduate/Scholarship)* [6356]
Fuchs-Harden Educational Scholarships Fund *(Undergraduate/Scholarship)* [3375]
Gerard Swartz Fudge Memorial Scholarships *(Undergraduate/Scholarship)* [3638]
Fulbright New Century Scholars Program *(Professional Development/Scholarship)* [1714]
Don and Eileen Fulton Nursing Scholarships *(Undergraduate/Scholarship)* [6774]
Daniel G. and Helen I. Fultz Scholarship Fund *(Undergraduate/Scholarship)* [2955]
Donald M. Furbush Scholarships *(Professional Development/Scholarship)* [3749]
The Future Colleagues Scholarships *(Undergraduate/Scholarship)* [4895]
Future Leaders of Manufacturing Scholarships *(Graduate, Undergraduate/Scholarship)* [6488]
Future Teachers Conditional Scholarships and Loan Repayment *(Professional Development, Undergraduate/Loan)* [7364]
Mearl K. Gable II Memorial Grants *(Professional Development/Grant)* [3395]
Gaddy Student Scholarships *(Undergraduate/Scholarship)* [7435]
Gadsden State/McClellan Campus Nursing Scholarships Award *(Undergraduate/Scholarship)* [2349]
Gaebe Eagle Scout Awards *(Undergraduate/Scholarship)* [4857]
Gail Burns-Smith "Dare to Dream" Fund *(Undergraduate/Scholarship)* [3452]
Farley Moody Galbraith Scholarship Fund *(Undergraduate/Scholarship)* [2350]
Thomas W. Gallagher Scholarship Fund *(Undergraduate/Scholarship)* [6720]
Louise Bales Gallagher Scholarships *(Undergraduate/Scholarship)* [2647]
Whitney Laine Gallahar Memorial Scholarship Fund *(Undergraduate/Scholarship)* [2351]
Gamewarden Scholarship program *(High School, Undergraduate/Scholarship)* [3156]
Gamma Iota Scholarships - Gamma Tau *(Undergraduate/Scholarship)* [6357]
Gamma Iota Scholarships - Kappa Eta *(Undergraduate/Scholarship)* [6358]
Gamma Iota Scholarships - Zeta Kappa *(Undergraduate/Scholarship)* [6359]
Gamma Iota Scholarships - Zeta Nu *(Undergraduate/Scholarship)* [6360]
Veronica Gantt Memorial Scholarships *(Undergraduate/Scholarship)* [5827]
GAP, Inc. Scholarships Award *(Undergraduate/Scholarship)* [3566]
GAPA Scholarships *(Undergraduate/Scholarship)* [3165]
Michael and Gina Garcia Rail Engineering Scholarships *(Undergraduate/Scholarship)* [879]
William R. Gard Memorial Scholarships *(Undergraduate/Scholarship)* [4608]
Garden Club Council of Winston-Salem and Forsyth County Council *(Undergraduate/Scholarship)* [7436]
Garden State Rotary Club of Cherry Hill Scholarships *(Undergraduate/Scholarship)* [1895]
Jewels Gardiner Scholarships *(Undergraduate/Scholarship)* [1848]
John Gardner Fellowships *(Undergraduate/Fellowship)* [7087]
Gardner Foundation INS Education Scholarship *(All/Scholarship)* [3722]
Victoria M. Gardner Scholarships *(Undergraduate/Scholarship)* [7159]
Eugene Garfield Doctoral Dissertation Fellowships *(Doctorate, Graduate/Fellowship)* [1636]
Peter M. Gargano Scholarship Fund *(Undergraduate/Scholarship)* [2776]
Garikian Scholarship Fund *(Undergraduate/Scholarship)* [1279]
Garmin Scholarships *(Undergraduate/Scholarship)* [72]
Gerald Garner Memorial Scholarships *(Undergraduate/Scholarship)* [5588]
Gail Garner R.I.S.E. Memorial Scholarships *(Undergraduate/Scholarship)* [5938]
Eileen J. Garrett Scholarships *(Undergraduate/Scholarship)* [5457]
Marcus Garvey Scholarships *(Undergraduate/Scholarship)* [3453]
Kays Gary Scholarships *(Undergraduate/Scholarship)* [7160]
Gaston Scholarships *(Undergraduate/Scholarship)* [239]
Gates Cambridge Scholarships *(Doctorate, Postgraduate/Scholarship)* [4704]
The Gates Millennium Scholars *(Undergraduate/Scholarship)* [3590]
William H. Gates Public Service Law Scholarships *(Undergraduate/Scholarship)* [3163]
Stephen Gates Scholarships *(Undergraduate/Scholarship)* [7161]
Raffin Gathercole Scholarships *(Undergraduate/Scholarship)* [3168]
David A. and Pamela A. Gault Charitable Fund *(Undergraduate/Scholarship)* [6721]
James L. Gavin Memorial Scholarships *(Graduate, Undergraduate/Scholarship)* [1656]
A.R.F.O.R.A. Martha Gavrila Scholarships for Women *(Graduate/Scholarship)* [912]
Gay, Lesbian, Bisexual, Transgender Alumni Council Scholarships *(Undergraduate/Scholarship)* [7255]
Gay and Lesbian Business Association of Santa Barbara Scholarships *(Undergraduate/Scholarship)* [6106]
Lowell Gaylor Memorial Scholarships *(Undergraduate/Scholarship)* [73]
Florence S. Gaynor Scholarships *(Doctorate, Graduate, Undergraduate/Scholarship)* [4716]
GCA Awards in Tropical Botany *(Doctorate/Award/Prize)* [3158]
GE Healthcare Management Scholarship Program *(Postgraduate/Scholarship)* [1039]
GED Jump Start Scholarships *(Other/Scholarship)* [6257]
Lawrence Gelfand - Armin Rappaport Fellowships *(Doctorate, Graduate/Grant)* [6456]
Irma Gelhausen Scholarship Fund *(Undergraduate/Scholarship)* [4140]
Elaine Gelman Scholarship Award *(Undergraduate/Scholarship)* [4730]
Gen III Scholarships *(Undergraduate/Scholarship)* [2822]
The Gene and John Athletic Scholarships *(Undergraduate/Scholarship)* [6789]
General Falcon Scholarships *(Undergraduate/Scholarship)* [5732]
General Mills Foundation Scholarships *(Undergraduate/Scholarship)* [622]
General Scholarship Awards *(Undergraduate/Scholarship)* [1599]
Geological Society of America Graduate Student Research Grants *(Doctorate, Graduate/Grant)* [3210]
Gerber Fellowships in Pediatric Nutrition *(Undergraduate/Fellowship)* [4987]
Gerber Foundation Merit Scholarships *(Undergraduate/Scholarship)* [3219]
Burton L. Gerber Scholarships *(Graduate, Undergraduate/Scholarship)* [1657]
Doris Y. and John J. Gerber Scholarships *(Undergraduate/Scholarship)* [7380]
Daniel Gerber, Sr. Medallion Scholarships *(Undergraduate/Scholarship)* [3220]
Walter Gerboth Awards *(All/Grant)* [4599]
German Studies Research Grant *(Undergraduate/Grant)* [3226]
Eloise Gerry Fellowships *(Graduate, Postdoctorate/Fellowship)* [6339]
GET Ready for Math and Science Conditional Scholarships *(Four Year College, Two Year College, Undergraduate/Scholarship)* [7365]
Mary Ghezzi Nursing Scholarships *(Undergraduate/Scholarship)* [6842]
GHI Fellowships at the Horner Library *(Doctorate/Fellowship)* [3234]
GIA Endowment Scholarships - Distance Education *(Graduate/Scholarship)* [3177]
GIA Endowment Scholarships - On Campus *(Graduate/Scholarship)* [3178]
GIA Endowment Scholarships - School of Business *(Undergraduate/Scholarship)* [3179]
Joy Gibson Scholarships *(Undergraduate/Scholarship)* [7162]
L.C. Gifford Distinguished Journalism Scholarships *(Undergraduate/Scholarship)* [7163]
Dr. Virginia Gilbert Memorial Scholarships *(Undergraduate/Scholarship)* [5828]

Margaret S. Gilbert Scholarship Fund *(Undergraduate/Scholarship)* [6722]
Terry M. Giles Honor Scholarships *(Undergraduate/Scholarship)* [5589]
Harold Giles Scholarships *(Graduate, Undergraduate/Scholarship)* [6551]
William Harrison Gill Education Fund *(Undergraduate/Scholarship)* [1627]
Gill Foundation Scholarships (Colorado) *(Undergraduate/Scholarship)* [6107]
Midwest Chapter Scholarships - Jack Gill *(Undergraduate/Scholarship)* [1446]
Benjamin A. Gilman International Scholarship *(Undergraduate/Scholarship)* [7031]
Leo Gilmartin Scholarships *(High School/Scholarship)* [5708]
Susan Kay Munson Gilmore Memorial Scholarship *(Undergraduate/Scholarship)* [2467]
Lawrence Ginocchio Aviation Scholarships *(Undergraduate/Scholarship)* [4778]
Nick Giorgione Hope for Hearts Scholarships *(Undergraduate/Scholarship)* [5829]
Alex Gissler Memorial Scholarships *(Undergraduate/Scholarship)* [4419]
Jane R. Glaser Scholarships *(Undergraduate/Scholarship)* [1124]
John Glaser Scholarships *(Undergraduate/Scholarship)* [2298]
Elizabeth Glaser Scientist Award *(Other/Award/Prize)* [5539]
Ann and Brad Glassco Scholarships *(Undergraduate/Scholarship)* [5939]
Glazing Industry Scholarships *(Undergraduate/Scholarship)* [5830]
Gleaner Life Insurance Scholarship Foundation *(Undergraduate/Scholarship)* [3244]
Jane S. Glenn Memorial Endowed Scholarships *(Undergraduate/Scholarship)* [6046]
Globe-Trotters Chapter Scholarships *(Undergraduate/Scholarship)* [1447]
Bud Glover Memorial Scholarships *(Undergraduate/Scholarship)* [74]
GLP Program Scholarships *(Other/Scholarship)* [4784]
Ray Glynn Scholarships *(Undergraduate/Scholarship)* [3180]
Irene Carlson Gnaedinger Memorial Scholarships *(Undergraduate/Scholarship)* [4180]
Dr. Robert H. Goddard Memorial Scholarships *(Graduate, Undergraduate/Scholarship)* [5085]
Max Godwin Endowed Scholarships *(Undergraduate/Scholarship)* [6871]
John Goerlich Memorial Scholarships *(Undergraduate/Scholarship)* [1553]
Goethe-Institut AATG Scholarships *(Other/Scholarship)* [5265]
Gogos Scholarships *(Undergraduate/Scholarship)* [2302]
Gold Key Scholarships *(Undergraduate/Scholarship)* [4065]
Daniel B. Goldberg Scholarships *(Other/Scholarship)* [3264]
Golden Key International Honour Society New Graduate Member Scholarships *(Undergraduate/Scholarship)* [3252]
Golden Key International Honour Society Study Abroad Scholarships *(Undergraduate/Scholarship)* [3253]
Golden Key International Honour Society Undergraduate Research Grants *(Undergraduate/Grant)* [3254]
Golden Key Math Scholarships *(Undergraduate/Scholarship)* [3255]
William R. Goldfarb Memorial Scholarships *(Undergraduate/Scholarship)* [834]
Dr. Guido Goldman Fellowships *(Doctorate, Postdoctorate/Fellowship)* [503]
Goldmann Scholarships Fund *(Undergraduate/Scholarship)* [3645]
Barry M. Goldwater Scholarships *(Undergraduate/Scholarship)* [7256]
Joshua Gomes Memorial Scholarship Fund *(Graduate, Undergraduate/Scholarship)* [4922]
Gongaware Scholarships College of Business *(Undergraduate/Scholarship)* [3700]
Millie Gonzalez Memorial Scholarships *(Undergraduate/Scholarship)* [4923]
Kenneth M. Good Graduate Students Fellowship Program *(Undergraduate/Fellowship)* [7295]
Goodman and Company, LLP Annual Scholarships *(Undergraduate/Scholarship)* [3262]
David B. Goodstein Point Scholarships *(Graduate, Undergraduate/Scholarship)* [5720]
James L. and Genevieve H. Goodwin Scholarships *(Undergraduate/Scholarship)* [3454]
Richard Goolsby Scholarship Fund *(Undergraduate/Scholarship)* [3060]
L. Gordon, Jr. and June D. Pfefferkorn Scholarships *(Undergraduate/Scholarship)* [7439]
Thomas Boston Gordon Memorial Scholarships *(Graduate, Undergraduate/Scholarship)* [1658]
Robert W. Gore Fellowships in Materials Innovation *(Doctorate, Postdoctorate/Fellowship)* [2110]
Richard C. Gorecki Scholarships *(Undergraduate/Scholarship)* [5733]
Nettie and Jesse Gorov Scholarship *(Undergraduate/Scholarship)* [2468]
Carl W. Gottschalk Research Scholar Grants *(Doctorate/Grant)* [1018]
Norma Gotwalt Scholarship Fund *(Undergraduate/Scholarship)* [3102]
Wilford Hayes Gowen Scholarships *(Undergraduate/Scholarship)* [7115]
Graduate Dissertation Fellowships *(Doctorate/Fellowship)* [2820]
Graduate Education Loan Scholarships *(Graduate/Loan)* [3780]
Graduate Fellowships in Alternatives in Scientific Research *(Doctorate, Graduate/Fellowship)* [3854]
Graduate Student Travel Grants *(Graduate, Professional Development/Grant)* [6437]
Rachel Graham Memorial Scholarships *(Undergraduate/Scholarship)* [5940]
Jim Graham Scholarships *(Undergraduate/Scholarship)* [5245]
Nicholas J. Grant Scholarships *(Undergraduate/Scholarship)* [4398]
Lucile Cheever Graubart/Lambda Scholarships *(Undergraduate/Scholarship)* [6361]
Paul and Helen L. Grauer Scholarships *(Undergraduate/Scholarship)* [835]
Thomas B. Grave and Elizabeth F. Grave Scholarships *(Undergraduate/Scholarship)* [4287]
Caswell Grave Scholarships *(Undergraduate/Scholarship)* [4288]
Great Falls Broadcasters Association Scholarships *(Undergraduate/Scholarship)* [4570]
Great Lakes Commission Sea Grant Fellowships *(Graduate/Scholarship)* [3364]
GREAT MINDS Collegiate Scholarship Program *(Undergraduate/Scholarship)* [236]
Greater Baton Rouge Chapter - Don Jones Excellence in Safety Scholarships *(Undergraduate/Scholarship)* [1056]
Frank L. Greathouse Government Accounting Scholarships *(Other/Scholarship)* [3265]
Philip F. Greco Memorial Scholarships *(Undergraduate/Scholarship)* [4272]
Green Hill Yacht and Country Club Scholarships *(Undergraduate/Scholarship)* [2374]
Green Knight Economic Development Corporation (GKEDC) Scholarships *(Undergraduate/Scholarship)* [3381]
Randy Green Memorial Scholarship Fund *(High School/Scholarship)* [2598]
James H. and Shirley L. Green Scholarship Fund *(Undergraduate/Scholarship)* [6723]
William G. and Mayme J. Green Scholarships *(Undergraduate/Scholarship)* [3455]
K2TEO Martin J. Green, Sr. Memorial Scholarships *(Undergraduate/Scholarship)* [836]
Helen R. Greenamyer Memorial Scholarships *(Undergraduate/Scholarship)* [6775]
Robert D. Greenberg Scholarships *(Professional Development/Scholarship)* [6527]
Curt Greene Memorial Scholarships *(Undergraduate/Scholarship)* [3405]
Guy P. Greenwald Jr. Endowed Scholarships *(Undergraduate/Scholarship)* [5590]
Francis Harris Gresham Scholarships *(Undergraduate/Scholarship)* [6657]
Lily H. Gridley Memorial Scholarships *(Undergraduate/Scholarship)* [7482]
Griffin Foundation Scholarships *(Undergraduate/Scholarship)* [3383]
Velma Shotwell Griffin Memorial Scholarship Fund *(Undergraduate/Scholarship)* [6724]
Griffith College Scholarships for NSHSS Members *(High School/Scholarship)* [5068]
Griffith Foundation Scholarships *(Undergraduate/Scholarship)* [902]
Russ Griffith Memorial Scholarships *(Graduate, Undergraduate/Scholarship)* [2617]
Homajean Grisham Memorial Scholarships *(Undergraduate/Scholarship)* [5280]
Enid Hall Griswold Memorial Scholarships *(Undergraduate/Scholarship)* [5064]
Grow your Own @Your Library Institutional Scholarships *(Graduate, Professional Development/Scholarship)* [5872]
Elizabeth M. Gruber Scholarships *(Graduate/Scholarship)* [2687]
Jack & Mary Lou Gruber Scholarships *(Undergraduate/Scholarship)* [4181]
Gruwell Scholarships *(Undergraduate/Scholarship)* [2375]
Henry and Janet Guareillo Scholarship Fund *(Undergraduate/Scholarship)* [3103]
Leonor R. Guerrero Memorial Scholarships *(Undergraduate/Scholarship)* [4689]
Harry Frank Guggenheim Foundation Grants *(All/Grant)* [3386]
Community Bank - Lee Guggisberg Foundation Memorial Scholarships *(Undergraduate/Scholarship)* [5941]
Bobette Bibo Gugliotta Memorial Scholarships for Creative Writing *(Undergraduate/Scholarship)* [6390]
Guide Dogs for the Blind Dorothea and Roland Bohde Leadership Scholarships *(Postgraduate/Scholarship)* [4877]
Jimmy Guild Memorial Scholarships *(Undergraduate/Scholarship)* [4182]
GuildScholar Awards *(Undergraduate/Scholarship)* [4027]
Guin-Stanford Scholarships *(Professional Development/Scholarship)* [2352]
Calouste Gulbenkian Foundation Scholarships *(Graduate, Undergraduate/Scholarship)* [1281]
Gulf Coast Hurricane Scholarships *(Graduate, Undergraduate/Scholarship)* [6552]
Gulf Coast Past President's Scholarships *(Undergraduate/Scholarship)* [1057]
Larry Gulley Scholarships *(Undergraduate/Scholarship)* [6449]
Tim and Tom Gullikson Foundation Scholarships *(Undergraduate/Scholarship)* [2129]
Warren and Rosalie Gummow Endowed Scholarships *(Undergraduate/Scholarship)* [5591]
Connie and Robert T. Gunter Scholarships *(Undergraduate/Scholarship)* [6489]
Patricia S. Gustafson '56 Memorial Scholarships *(Undergraduate/Scholarship)* [2777]
George Gustafson HSE Memorial Scholarships *(Graduate, Undergraduate/Scholarship)* [1058]
Guynn Family Foundation Book Scholarships *(Undergraduate/Scholarship)* [4667]
Guzkowski Family Scholarships *(Undergraduate/Scholarship)* [5942]
John C. Haas Fellowships in the History of Chemical Industries *(Doctorate, Postdoctorate/Fellowship)* [2111]
Gene Haas Foundation Manufacturing Technology Scholarships *(Undergraduate/Scholarship)* [6490]
Ed Haas Memorial Scholarships *(Undergraduate/Scholarship)* [6776]
Wesley R. Habley NACADA Summer Institute Scholarships *(Professional Development/Scholarship)* [4615]
Louise Wallace Hackney Fellowship for the Study of Chinese Art *(Doctorate/Fellowship)* [744]
HACU/Wal-Mart Achievers Scholarships *(Undergraduate/Scholarship)* [3567]
Jaye Haddad Memorial Fund *(Undergraduate/Scholarship)* [6110]
Perry F. Hadlock Memorial Scholarships *(Undergraduate/Scholarship)* [837]
Joseph E. Hagan Memorial Scholarships

(Undergraduate/Scholarship) [3150]
Charles V. Hagler Scholarships (Undergraduate/Scholarship) [1554]
Sophia Hagopian Memorial Fund (Undergraduate/Scholarship) [1282]
Leslie Jane Hahn Memorial Scholarships (Undergraduate/Scholarship) [6191]
The Richard D. Hailey AAJ Law Student Scholarships (Undergraduate/Scholarship) [358]
Marion H. Halfacre Scholarships (Graduate/Scholarship) [3181]
Hall of Achievement Scholarships (Undergraduate/Scholarship) [1825]
Joyce C. Hall College Scholarships (Undergraduate/Scholarship) [5570]
Anna E. Hall Memorial Scholarships (Undergraduate/Scholarship) [5625]
Chappie Hall Scholarship Program (Graduate, Postgraduate, Undergraduate/Scholarship) [2]
David J. Hallissey Memorial Scholarships (Undergraduate/Scholarship) [1083]
Dwight A. Hamilton Scottish Rite Foundation of Colorado Graduate Scholarships (Graduate/Scholarship) [6284]
Richard A. Hammill Scholarships Fund (Undergraduate/Scholarship) [708]
Jay Hammond Memorial Scholarships (Undergraduate/Scholarship) [7077]
Tommie J. Hamner Scholarships (Undergraduate/Scholarship) [5667]
Adam Hampton Memorial Scholarship Fund (Undergraduate/Scholarship) [2956]
Morris Hanauer Scholarships (Undergraduate/Scholarship) [3182]
Hancock Family Snow Hill High School Scholarships (Undergraduate/Scholarship) [2376]
Robert Hancock Memorial Scholarship Award (Undergraduate/Scholarship) [4499]
H. Pauline Hand Memorial Scholarships (Undergraduate/Scholarship) [6777]
Ilse and George Hanfmann Fellowships (Doctorate/Fellowship) [897]
John M. Haniak Scholarships (Undergraduate/Scholarship) [4399]
Byron Hanke Fellowships (Undergraduate/Fellowship) [3088]
Hanover-Horton High School Youth of Promise Scholarships (Undergraduate/Scholarship) [3980]
Zenon C.R. Hansen Leadership Scholarships (Undergraduate/Scholarship) [4859]
Martha and Oliver Hansen Memorial Scholarship (Undergraduate/Scholarship) [3981]
Zenon C.R. Hansen Memorial Scholarships (Undergraduate/Scholarship) [1555]
Penelope Hanshaw Scholarships (Graduate, Undergraduate/Scholarship) [1511]
Cleam T. Hanson Scholarship Fund (Undergraduate/Scholarship) [4564]
Duane Hanson Scholarships (Undergraduate/Scholarship) [967]
Charles Henry Hardin Memorial Scholarships (Graduate, Undergraduate/Scholarship) [1659]
Chris Harding Scholarships (Undergraduate/Scholarship) [880]
Bob and Dawn Hardy Automotive Scholarship (Undergraduate/Scholarship) [3982]
Bryce Harlow Fellowship Program (Undergraduate/Fellowship) [3401]
Matt Harmon Memorial Scholarships (Undergraduate/Scholarship) [6658]
Harness Tracks of America Scholarship Fund (Undergraduate/Scholarship) [3407]
Walter and Lucille Harper Scholarship (Undergraduate/Scholarship) [4066]
Marcia S. Harris Legacy Fund Scholarships (Undergraduate/Scholarship) [4322]
Leon Harris/Les Nichols Memorial Scholarships to Spartan College of Aeronautics & Technology (Undergraduate/Scholarship) [75]
William H. Harris Memorial Scholarships (Graduate, Undergraduate/Scholarship) [5638]
Frank and Charlene Harris Scholarships (Undergraduate/Scholarship) [2422]
Peg Hart Harrison Memorial Scholarships (Undergraduate/Scholarship) [2648]
Evelyn W. Harrison Point Scholarships (Graduate, Undergraduate/Scholarship) [5721]
Lullelia W. Harrison Scholarships in Counseling (Graduate, Undergraduate/Scholarship) [7554]
Claude B. Hart Memorial Scholarships (Undergraduate/Scholarship) [7440]
Carroll Hart Scholarships (Graduate/Scholarship) [6450]
Ida L. Hartenberg Charitable Scholarships (Undergraduate/Scholarship) [3456]
Mollie Harter Memorial Fund (Undergraduate/Scholarship) [2958]
Karen Harter Recruitment Scholarship Grant (Undergraduate/Scholarship) [2469]
Karen Harter Recruitment Scholarship Grant (Undergraduate/Scholarship) [2470]
Hartford County Retired Teachers Association Scholarships (Undergraduate/Scholarship) [3457]
Hartford Foundation College Scholarship Program (Undergraduate/Scholarship) [3458]
Hartford Foundation for Public Giving Occupational Therapy Scholarships (Undergraduate/Scholarship) [3459]
Hartford Grammar School Scholarships (Undergraduate/Scholarship) [3460]
Hartford Jazz Society Scholarships (Undergraduate/Scholarship) [3461]
Hartford Whalers Booster Club Scholarships (Undergraduate/Scholarship) [3462]
Gabe A. Hartl Scholarships (Undergraduate/Scholarship) [64]
William T. Hartzell Memorial Scholarships (Undergraduate/Scholarship) [5943]
James J. Harvey Dissertation Fellowships (Doctorate/Fellowship) [6111]
Donald F. Hastings Scholarships (Undergraduate/Scholarship) [1160]
Donald and Shirley Hastings Scholarships (Undergraduate/Scholarship) [1161]
Gretchen Hauff Memorial Scholarships (Undergraduate/Scholarship) [5831]
Charles Hauser Scholarships (Undergraduate/Scholarship) [7164]
Lex and Scott Hawkins Endowed Scholarships (Undergraduate/Scholarship) [2748]
Don C. Hawkins Memorial Scholarships (Undergraduate/Scholarship) [76]
Thomas T. Hayashi Memorial Scholarships (Graduate, Undergraduate/Scholarship) [4017]
R. Garn Haycock Memorial Scholarships (Undergraduate/Scholarship) [5944]
Edward and Cora Hayes Scholarships (Undergraduate/Scholarship) [2749]
The Erika A. Hayes Scholarships (Undergraduate/Scholarship) [4323]
Dick and Pat Hazel Minority Scholarships (Professional Development/Scholarship) [2377]
HBO Point Scholarships (Graduate, Undergraduate/Scholarship) [5722]
HDR Engineering, Inc. Scholarship for Diversity in Engineering (Undergraduate/Scholarship) [1432]
HDSA Research Fellowships (Postdoctorate/Fellowship) [3631]
HDSA Research Grants (Other/Grant) [3632]
Edith Head Scholarships (Undergraduate/Scholarship) [2688]
Dr. M.G. "Doc" Headley Scholarships (Undergraduate/Scholarship) [6778]
Health and Aging Policy Fellows (Professional Development/Fellowship) [786]
Health Sciences Scholarship Program (Undergraduate/Scholarship) [7402]
Health Sciences Student Fellowships (Doctorate, Graduate/Fellowship) [2873]
Healthcare Information Management Systems Scholarships (Other/Scholarship) [3517]
Healy Scholarships (Undergraduate/Scholarship) [1084]
Richard F. Heaney Memorial Scholarship Fund (Graduate, Undergraduate/Scholarship) [3817]
Annamae Heaps Law Scholarships (Undergraduate/Scholarship) [2750]
Erin Kumelos Heard Memorial Scholarships (Undergraduate/Scholarship) [2649]
William Randolph Hearst Educational Endowments (Undergraduate/Scholarship) [4289]
Hebrew Ladies Sheltering Home Scholarships (Undergraduate/Scholarship) [3463]
Dr. James H. Heckaman Memorial Scholarship Fund (Undergraduate/Scholarship) [6725]
Professor Ulla Hedner Scholarships (Undergraduate/Scholarship) [4924]
Howell Heflin Memorial Scholarships (Undergraduate/Scholarship) [5281]
Lavonne Heghinian Scholarships (Undergraduate/Scholarship) [2689]
Dale O. Heimberger CRNA Memorial Scholarship Fund (Graduate/Scholarship) [6726]
Helicopter Foundation International Commercial Helicopter Rating Scholarships (All/Scholarship) [3520]
Helicopter Foundation International Maintenance Technician Certificate Scholarships (Professional Development/Scholarship) [3521]
Hellenic University Club of Philadelphia Founders Scholarships (Undergraduate/Scholarship) [3530]
Joan Heller-Diane Bernard Fellowships (Graduate, Undergraduate/Fellowship) [2087]
Helm Family Scholarships (Undergraduate/Scholarship) [6192]
Ronald, Randall and Roger Helman Scholarships (Graduate, Undergraduate/Scholarship) [1660]
PPQ William F. Helms Student Scholarships (Undergraduate/Scholarship) [7299]
Clinton J. Helton Manufacturing Scholarships (Undergraduate/Scholarship) [6491]
Jeanne H. Hemmingway Scholarships (Undergraduate/Scholarship) [2778]
Hemophilia Federation of America Educational Scholarships (Undergraduate/Scholarship) [3542]
Hemophilia Health Services Memorial Scholarship Program (Graduate, Undergraduate/Scholarship) [4925]
Hemostasis and Resuscitation Research Scholarships (All/Scholarship) [410]
Hench Post-Dissertation Fellowships (Postdoctorate/Fellowship) [303]
Henderson Memorial Endowed Scholarships (Undergraduate/Scholarship) [4183]
Edith H. Henderson Scholarships (Undergraduate/Scholarship) [982]
Doris Hendren Memorial Scholarships (Undergraduate/Scholarship) [6193]
Marjorie M. Hendricks Environmental Education Scholarships Fund (Undergraduate/Scholarship) [3285]
Henigson Human Rights Fellowships (Undergraduate/Fellowship) [3504]
Henry Ford Academy Scholarships (Undergraduate/Scholarship) [6492]
Richard A. Herbert Memorial Scholarships (Undergraduate/Scholarship) [1138]
Hereditary Disease Foundation Research Grants (Postdoctorate/Grant) [3550]
Herbert Herff Presidential Law Scholarships (Undergraduate/Scholarship) [7116]
Alia Herrera Memorial Scholarships (Undergraduate/Scholarship) [359]
Isabel M. Herson Scholarships in Education (Graduate, Undergraduate/Scholarship) [7555]
Hertz Foundation's Graduate Fellowships (Doctorate/Fellowship) [4705]
Peter Hess Scholarships (Undergraduate/Scholarship) [3183]
June Hester Memorial Scholarships (Undergraduate/Scholarship) [5282]
Nicholas S. Hetos, DDS, Memorial Graduate Scholarships (Graduate/Scholarship) [3531]
HGA and Dendel Scholarships (Undergraduate/Scholarship) [3396]
Mark and Michelle Hiepler Endowed Scholarships (Undergraduate/Scholarship) [5592]
Regina Higdon Scholarships (Undergraduate/Scholarship) [2423]
High School Councilors Scholarships (Undergraduate/Scholarship) [3673]
Highway Worker Memorial Scholarship Program (Undergraduate/Scholarship) [904]
Doris E. Higley Memorial Scholarships (Undergraduate/Scholarship) [3464]
Hilb, Rogal and Hobbs Scholarships (Undergraduate/Scholarship) [7328]
Wayne Hildebrant Police Scholarships Fund

(Undergraduate/Scholarship) [4141]
Douglas W. Hill, Jr. Memorial Scholarships (Graduate, Undergraduate/Scholarship) [1661]
John A. Hill Memorial Scholarships (Graduate, Undergraduate/Scholarship) [1662]
Gus and Henrietta Hill Scholarships (Graduate/Scholarship) [2779]
Judge Delmas C. Hill Scholarships (Undergraduate/Scholarship) [7349]
Ryan Hill Thoracoesophageal Fellowships (Graduate/Fellowship) [418]
Cecilia Hillman Scholarships (Undergraduate/Scholarship) [3465]
Conrad N. Hilton Scholarships (Undergraduate/Scholarship) [2841]
Hilton Tribal College Diversity Scholarships (Undergraduate/Scholarship) [623]
D. Glenn Hilts Scholarships Program (Graduate, Undergraduate/Scholarship) [1493]
Lucy Hilty Research Grants (All/Grant) [813]
Brooke Hindle Postdoctoral Fellowships (Postdoctorate/Fellowship) [6461]
Jim & Nancy Hinkle Travel Grants (Postdoctorate/Grant) [3539]
Hinman-Jensen Endowed Scholarships (Undergraduate/Scholarship) [4184]
William A. Hipp Scholarships (All/Scholarship) [4336]
Ernest and Charlotte Hirst Family Scholarships (Undergraduate/Scholarship) [3466]
Hispanic Association of Colleges and Universities Scholarships (Undergraduate/Scholarship) [3568]
Hispanic Association on Corporate Responsibility Scholarship Program (Undergraduate/Scholarship) [3573]
Hispanic College Fund Scholarship Programs (Undergraduate/Scholarship) [3583]
Hispanic Lawyers Association of Illinois Public Interest Fellowships (Undergraduate/Scholarship) [3579]
Hispanic Scholarship Fund (HSF) College Scholarship Program (Graduate, Undergraduate/Scholarship) [3591]
Hispanic Serving Institution Scholarships (Undergraduate/Scholarship) [6973]
Historically Black College or University Scholarships (Undergraduate/Scholarship) [6974]
Albert H. Hix, W8AH Memorial Scholarships (Undergraduate/Scholarship) [838]
HLS/MLA Professional Development Grants (Doctorate/Grant) [4442]
HNBF Princeton Review Duard Bradshaw Memorial Scholarships (Undergraduate/Scholarship) [3584]
James E. Hoff, S.J. Scholars (Undergraduate/Scholarship) [7529]
John Hoffbauer Memorial Scholarships (Undergraduate/Scholarship) [2780]
Henry Hoffman Memorial Scholarship Fund (Undergraduate/Scholarship) [4695]
Robert and Elaine Hoffman Memorial Scholarships (Undergraduate/Scholarship) [7117]
Michael J. Hogan Fellowships (Graduate/Fellowship) [6457]
The Thelma S. Hoge Memorial Scholarship Fund (Undergraduate/Scholarship) [2400]
Raymond T. Hoge Scholarship Fund (Undergraduate/Scholarship) [6727]
Michael J. Hoggard Memorial Scholarships (Undergraduate/Scholarship) [5832]
R.W. "Bob" Holden Scholarships (Undergraduate/Scholarship) [3508]
John Holden Vocational Scholarships (Undergraduate/Scholarship) [559]
Holland America Line-Westours Research Grants (Undergraduate/Grant) [1085]
Cleve Holloway Memorial Scholarship Fund (Undergraduate/Scholarship) [2353]
Martin Holmason Memorial Scholarship Awards (Undergraduate/Scholarship) [5382]
Robert Holmes Scholarships (Undergraduate/Scholarship) [2515]
W. Stull Holt Dissertation Fellowships (Doctorate, Graduate/Grant) [6458]
Caroline Holt Nursing Scholarships (Undergraduate/Scholarship) [3467]
Holy Name Of Jesus Parish Scholarships (Undergraduate/Scholarship) [5945]
Home Depot Scholarships (Undergraduate/Scholarship) [7006]
The Homeland Security Graduate Fellowships (Graduate/Fellowship) [6985]
The Homeland Security Undergraduate Scholarships (Undergraduate/Scholarship) [6986]
Honeywell Avionics Scholarships (Undergraduate/Scholarship) [77]
Jane Hood Memorial Fund (Undergraduate/Scholarship) [2959]
Kathryn Hookanson Law Fellowships (Undergraduate/Scholarship) [7118]
Hooper Memorial Scholarships (Undergraduate/Scholarship) [6919]
Hopi Education Awards (All/Award/Prize) [1210]
Minnie Hopkins Memorial Scholarship Fund of Lathrop/Compton School (Undergraduate/Scholarship) [6728]
Sam J. Hord Memorial Scholarships (Undergraduate/Scholarship) [6625]
Seth Horen, K1LOM Memorial Scholarships (Undergraduate/Scholarship) [839]
Hormel Foods Charitable Trust Scholarships (Undergraduate/Scholarship) [3615]
Edward L. Horne, Jr. Scholarships (All/Scholarship) [5406]
Judge and Mrs. Robert D. Horowitz Legal Scholarship Fund (Graduate/Scholarship) [6729]
HOSA Scholarships (Undergraduate/Scholarship) [5108]
Hospitality Food Service Scholarships (Undergraduate/Scholarship) [5168]
John C. "Jack" Hough Memorial Law Scholarships (Undergraduate/Scholarship) [7119]
Max and Julia Houghton Duluth Central Scholarships (Undergraduate/Scholarship) [2781]
Houston Alumnae Undergraduate Tri Delta Scholarships (Undergraduate/Scholarship) [2651]
Houston/Nancy Holliman Scholarships (Undergraduate/Scholarship) [2690]
Paul Green Houston Scholarships (Undergraduate/Scholarship) [7165]
Sarah Jane Houston Scholarships (Undergraduate/Scholarship) [2691]
Houtan Scholarships (Graduate/Scholarship) [3623]
Hirair and Anna Hovnanian Foundation Presidential Scholarships (Undergraduate/Scholarship) [1284]
Hirair and Anna Hovnanian Foundation Scholarships (Undergraduate/Scholarship) [1285]
NORDAM Dee Howard/Etienne Fage Scholarships (Undergraduate/Scholarship) [4779]
William B. Howell Scholarships (Undergraduate/Scholarship) [1162]
Christopher Hoy/ERT Scholarships (Graduate/Scholarship) [701]
Carol Hoy Scholarship fund (Undergraduate/Scholarship) [3106]
HRP Global Human Rights Fellowships (Graduate/Fellowship) [3505]
HSBC-North America Scholarship Program (Undergraduate/Scholarship) [3592]
HSF/Atrisco Heritage Foundation Scholarship Program (Graduate, Undergraduate/Scholarship) [3593]
HSF/Citi Fellows Program (Undergraduate/Scholarship) [3594]
HSF/General Motors Scholarship Program (Undergraduate/Scholarship) [3595]
HSF/Hewlett Packard (HP) Diversity in Education Scholarship Program (Undergraduate/Scholarship) [3596]
HSF/IDT Hope High School Scholarship Program (Undergraduate/Scholarship) [3597]
HSF/Nissan Community College Transfer Scholarship Program (Undergraduate/Scholarship) [3598]
HSF/Wal-Mart Stores Inc. Scholarship Program (Graduate, Undergraduate/Scholarship) [3599]
Albert W. and Mildred Hubbard Scholarships (Undergraduate/Scholarship) [6194]
Amber Huber Memorial Scholarship (Undergraduate/Scholarship) [2471]
Huenefeld/Denton Scholarships (Undergraduate/Scholarship) [2692]
Dale Hughes, Jr. Memorial Scholarships (Undergraduate/Scholarship) [6779]
Roger K. Hughes Legacy Scholarship (Undergraduate/Scholarship) [1826]
Howard Hughes Medical Institute Predoctoral Fellowships (Graduate/Fellowship) [4706]
Paul A. Hughes Memorial Scholarship (Undergraduate/Scholarship) [1827]
Human Ecology Continuing Undergraduate Student Scholarships (Undergraduate/Scholarship) [7257]
Humane Studies Fellowships (Graduate/Fellowship) [3728]
Humanism in Medicine Scholarships (Undergraduate/Scholarship) [6811]
Kevin Hummer Point Scholarships (Graduate, Undergraduate/Scholarship) [5723]
Cecil C. Humphreys Law Fellowships (Undergraduate/Scholarship) [7120]
Dr. Richard M. Hunt Fellowships (Doctorate, Postdoctorate/Fellowship) [504]
Michael A. Hunter Memorial Scholarships (Undergraduate/Scholarship) [2130]
Clay Huntington Sports Communications Scholarships (Undergraduate/Scholarship) [3376]
James F. Hurley III Bicentennial Merit Scholarships (Undergraduate/Scholarship) [7166]
Doc Hurley Scholarships (Undergraduate/Scholarship) [3468]
Zora Neale Hurston Scholarships (Graduate/Scholarship) [7556]
Norman E. Huston Scholarships (Graduate, Undergraduate/Scholarship) [3941]
Dr. James L. Hutchinson and Evelyn Ribbs Hutchinson Medical School Scholarship Fund (Undergraduate/Scholarship) [6391]
Fred Hutchison Travel Scholarships (Undergraduate/Scholarship) [7167]
The Hyatt Hotels Fund For Minority Lodging Management Students (Undergraduate/Scholarship) [611]
Mike Hylton and Ron Niederman Memorial Scholarships (Undergraduate/Scholarship) [4926]
The Steve Hymans Extended Stay Scholarship Program (Undergraduate/Scholarship) [612]
Hypertherm International HyTech Leadership Scholarships (Postgraduate/Scholarship) [1163]
IADR David B. Scott Fellowships (Undergraduate/Fellowship) [3790]
IADR John Clarkson Fellowships (Postdoctorate/Fellowship) [3791]
IADR John Gray Fellowships (Professional Development/Fellowship) [3792]
IADR Norton Ross Fellowships (Professional Development/Fellowship) [3793]
IAESTE United States Scholarships (Undergraduate/Scholarship) [1435]
IAHCSMM - Purdue University Scholarship Awards (Professional Development/Scholarship) [3801]
IALD Scholarship Programs (Graduate, Undergraduate/Scholarship) [3809]
Ice Skating Institute of America Education Foundation (Undergraduate/Scholarship) [3642]
IDA Fellowship Award (Professional Development/Fellowship) [3838]
Idaho Attorney General Scholarships (Undergraduate/Scholarship) [4186]
Idaho Nursery and Landscape Association Scholarships (Undergraduate/Scholarship) [3652]
Idaho Nursing Scholarships (Undergraduate/Scholarship) [3646]
Idaho Society of CPA's Scholarships (Undergraduate/Scholarship) [3647]
David Iden Memorial Safety Scholarships (Undergraduate/Scholarship) [1059]
IEHA Education Foundation Scholarship Awards (Undergraduate/Scholarship) [3842]
IFDA Educational Foundation (Undergraduate/Scholarship) [3859]
IFDA Part-time Student Scholarships (Undergraduate/Scholarship) [3860]
IFSEA Worthy Goal Scholarships (Four Year College, Two Year College/Scholarship) [3850]
IIE Council of Fellows Undergraduate Scholarships (Undergraduate/Scholarship) [3733]
Illinois Association of Chamber of Commerce Executives Scholarships (Postdoctorate/Scholarship) [3654]
Illinois Future Teacher Corps Scholarships

(Undergraduate/Scholarship) [3663]
Illinois Landscape Contractors Association Scholarships (Undergraduate/Scholarship) [3656]
Illinois Special Education Teacher Tuition Waiver Scholarships (Undergraduate/Scholarship) [3664]
Illinois Student Assistance Commission Merit Recognition Scholarships (Undergraduate/Scholarship) [3666]
Illinois Student Assistance Commission Nurse Educator Scholarships (Undergraduate/Scholarship) [3667]
Illinois Student Assistance Commission Nursing Education Scholarships (Undergraduate/Scholarship) [3668]
Illuminator Educational Foundation Scholarships (Undergraduate/Scholarship) [1828]
IMA FAR Doctoral Student Grant Program (Doctorate/Grant) [3745]
IMA Memorial Education Fund Scholarships (MEF) (Graduate, Undergraduate/Scholarship/Forgivable Loan) [3746]
Imagine America Online Scholarships (Undergraduate/Scholarship) [3674]
Imagine America Scholarships (Undergraduate/Scholarship) [3675]
Elmer S. Imes Scholarships in Physics (Undergraduate/Scholarship) [5055]
John L. Imhoff Scholarships (Graduate, Undergraduate/Scholarship) [3734]
Imogene Ward Nursing Scholarships (Undergraduate/Scholarship) [2991]
Imperial Sovereign Court of Tacoma Scholarships (Professional Development/Scholarship) [5766]
Independent Studies Program Scholarships (Other/Scholarship) [4785]
Indian Health Service Scholarship Program (Undergraduate/Scholarship) [634]
Indiana Library Federation AIME Scholarships (Undergraduate/Scholarship) [3693]
Indiana State Alumni Association Creative and Performing Arts Award (Undergraduate/Scholarship) [3701]
Indiana State Alumni Association Dean's Scholarships (Undergraduate/Scholarship) [3702]
Indiana State Alumni Association Incentive Scholarships (Undergraduate/Scholarship) [3703]
Indiana State Alumni Association President's Academic Excellence Scholarships (Undergraduate/Scholarship) [3704]
Indiana State Alumni Association President's Scholarships (Undergraduate/Scholarship) [3705]
Indiana State Alumni Association Transfer Student Scholarships (Undergraduate/Scholarship) [3707]
Indiana Top Scholar Award (Undergraduate/Scholarship) [3708]
Individual Advanced Research Opportunities Program (IARO) For Master's Student (Graduate/Grant) [3895]
Individual Advanced Research Opportunities Program (IARO) For Pre-doctoral Students (Postgraduate/Grant) [3896]
Individual Advanced Research Opportunities Program (IARO) For Professionals (Professional Development/Grant) [3897]
Individual Advanced Research Opportunities Program (IARO) for Postdoctoral Scholars (Postdoctorate/Grant) [3898]
Individual-Investigator Grants Program (Postdoctorate/Grant) [5011]
Terrance Ingraham Pediatric Optometry Residency Award (Graduate/Award/Prize) [277]
Jennifer Ingrum Scholarships (Undergraduate/Scholarship) [2424]
INIA Scholarship Program (All/Scholarship) [3880]
Injection Molding Division Scholarships (Graduate, Undergraduate/Scholarship) [6553]
Inland Northwest Business Alliance (INBA) Scholarships (Undergraduate/Scholarship) [5767]
Institute of Food Technologists Graduate Scholarships (Graduate/Scholarship) [3724]
Institute of Food Technologists Junior/Senior Scholarships (Undergraduate/Scholarship) [3725]
Institute of Food Technologists Sophomore Scholarships (Undergraduate/Scholarship) [3726]
Institute-NEH Postdoctoral Fellowships (Doctorate, Professional Development/Fellowship) [5338]
Institute for Scientific Information (ISI) Scholarships (Doctorate, Graduate/Scholarship) [6682]
Institute of Turkish Studies Dissertation Writing Grants (Doctorate/Grant) [3753]
Institute of Turkish Studies Sabbatical Research Grants (Professional Development/Grant) [3754]
Institute of Turkish Studies Undergraduate Study Grants (Undergraduate/Grant) [3755]
Institutional Grants: Educational and Research Projects (All/Grant) [7336]
Insurance Scholarship Foundation of America College Scholarships (Undergraduate/Scholarship) [3763]
Insurance Scholarship Foundation of America Professional Scholarships (Professional Development/Scholarship) [3764]
Insurance Women of Portland Scholarships (Graduate/Scholarship) [3767]
Integra Foundation NNF Research Grants Award (Professional Development/Grant) [375]
Inter American Press Association Scholarships (Undergraduate/Scholarship) [3771]
Intergraph Scholarships (Graduate/Scholarship) [1028]
Intermediaries and Reinsurance Underwriters Association Scholarships (Undergraduate/Internship) [3777]
International Association of Black Actuaries Scholarships (Undergraduate/Scholarship) [3786]
International Association of Emergency Managers Scholarships (Undergraduate/Scholarship) [3796]
International Association of Foundation Drilling Scholarships for Civil Engineering Students (Postgraduate/Scholarship) [3798]
International Association of Foundation Drilling Scholarships for Part-time Civil Engineering Graduate School Students (Postgraduate/Scholarship) [3799]
International Dairy-Deli-Bakery Association Undergraduate Scholarships (Graduate, Undergraduate/Scholarship) [3835]
International Doctoral Scholarships for Studies Specializing in Jewish Fields (Doctorate/Scholarship) [4458]
International Door Association Scholarship Awards (Undergraduate/Scholarship) [3840]
International Fellowships in Jewish Studies (Professional Development/Fellowship) [4459]
International Foodservice Editorial Council Scholarships (Graduate, Undergraduate/Scholarship) [3852]
International Graduate Student Awards (Graduate/Scholarship) [26]
International Management Council (IMC) Scholarships (Undergraduate/Scholarship) [2472]
International Order of the King's Daughters and Sons North American Indian Scholarship Program (Undergraduate/Scholarship) [635]
International Peace Scholarships (Undergraduate/Scholarship) [5684]
International Scholar Awards (Postdoctorate/Award/Prize) [5540]
International Scholarship Program for Community Service (Other/Scholarship) [4460]
International Society for Humor Studies Graduate Student Awards (GSA) (Graduate/Award/Prize) [3906]
International Society for Humor Studies Scholarly Contribution Awards (SCA) (Graduate/Award/Prize) [3907]
Internships in International Civil Society Law (Undergraduate/Internship) [3824]
InternXchange (Undergraduate/Internship) [3228]
Interracial Scholarship Fund of Greater Hartford (Undergraduate/Scholarship) [3469]
Iowa Division Scholarships (All/Scholarship) [4514]
Iowa Journalism Institute Scholarships (Undergraduate/Scholarship) [3935]
Iowa Library Association Foundation Scholarships (Graduate/Scholarship) [3931]
IPSA Student Recognition Awards (Undergraduate/Scholarship) [3688]
Iranian American Bar Association Scholarships (Undergraduate/Scholarship) [3938]
The Iranian-American Scholarship Fund (Undergraduate/Scholarship) [4953]
Iranian Artist Scholarships (Undergraduate/Scholarship) [4954]
Iranian Association of Boston's IAB Scholarships (Undergraduate/Scholarship) [4955]
Iranian Federated Women's Club Scholarships (Undergraduate/Scholarship) [4956]
IRARC Memorial Joseph P. Rubino WA4MMD Scholarships (Undergraduate/Scholarship) [840]
IREM Foundation Minority Outreach Scholarships (Professional Development/Scholarship) [3750]
Greg Irons Student Scholarships (Undergraduate/Scholarship) [2782]
Harriet Irsay Scholarships (Graduate, Undergraduate/Scholarship) [674]
IRTS Foundation Summer Fellowship Program (Graduate, Undergraduate/Fellowship) [3886]
ISA Educational Foundation Scholarships (Graduate, Undergraduate/Scholarship) [3942]
ISA Executive Board Scholarships (Graduate, Undergraduate/Scholarship) [3943]
ISA Section and District Scholarships - Birmingham (Graduate, Undergraduate/Scholarship) [3944]
ISA Section and District Scholarships - Houston (Graduate, Undergraduate/Scholarship) [3945]
ISA Section and District Scholarships - Lehigh Valley (Graduate, Undergraduate/Scholarship) [3946]
ISA Section and District Scholarships - New Jersey (Graduate, Undergraduate/Scholarship) [3947]
ISA Section and District Scholarships - Niagara Frontier (Graduate, Undergraduate/Scholarship) [3948]
ISA Section and District Scholarships - Northern California (Graduate, Undergraduate/Scholarship) [3949]
ISA Section and District Scholarships - Richmond (Hopewell) (Graduate, Undergraduate/Scholarship) [3950]
ISA Section and District Scholarships - Savannah River (Graduate, Undergraduate/Scholarship) [3951]
ISA Section and District Scholarships - Southwestern Wyoming (Graduate, Undergraduate/Scholarship) [3952]
ISA Section and District Scholarships - Texas, Louisiana and Mississippi (Graduate, Undergraduate/Scholarship) [3953]
ISA Section and District Scholarships - Wilmington (Graduate, Undergraduate/Scholarship) [3954]
ISA Technical Division Scholarships - Analysis Division (Graduate, Undergraduate/Scholarship) [3955]
ISA Technical Division Scholarships - Chemical and Petroleum Industries Division (Graduate, Undergraduate/Scholarship) [3956]
ISA Technical Division Scholarships - Computer Technology Division (Graduate, Undergraduate/Scholarship) [3957]
ISA Technical Division Scholarships - Food and Pharmaceutical Industries Division (Graduate, Undergraduate/Scholarship) [3958]
ISA Technical Division Scholarships - Power Industry Division (Graduate, Undergraduate/Scholarship) [3959]
ISA Technical Division Scholarships - Process Measurement and Control Division (Graduate, Undergraduate/Scholarship) [3960]
ISA Technical Division Scholarships - Pulp and Paper Industry Division (Graduate, Undergraduate/Scholarship) [3961]
ISA Technical Division Scholarships - Test Measurement Division (Graduate, Undergraduate/Scholarship) [3962]
ISA Technical Division Scholarships - Water and Wastewater Industries Division (Graduate, Undergraduate/Scholarship) [3963]
Martha Isabell Memorial Scholarships (Undergraduate/Scholarship) [5283]
The ISASI Rudolf Kapustin Memorial Scholarships (Undergraduate/Scholarship) [3902]
Hazel D. Isbell Fellowships (Graduate/Fellowship) [2652]
Broughton Isom Memorial Scholarships (Undergraduate/Scholarship) [5284]
ISOPE Offshore Mechanics Scholarships for Outstanding Students (Graduate/Scholarship) [3909]
ISPE Advantage Award/Foundation Scholarships

(Undergraduate/Scholarship) [3659]
Italian Language Scholarships (Undergraduate/Scholarship) [5372]
ITNS Research Grants (Professional Development/Grant) [3918]
ITW Welding Companies Scholarships (Undergraduate/Scholarship) [1164]
IUVSTA Welch Scholarships (Professional Development/Scholarship) [1581]
Bob and Mary Ives Scholarships (Graduate, Undergraduate/Scholarship) [3964]
IWFA Scholarships (Graduate/Scholarship) [3925]
J and K Foundation Scholarships (Undergraduate/Scholarship) [3470]
Virginia C. Jack and Ralph L. Jack Scholarships (Undergraduate/Scholarship) [6730]
Jackman Scholarships (Undergraduate/Scholarship) [5668]
The Jackson Club Scholarships (Undergraduate/Scholarship) [2783]
Jackson High School Alumni Scholarship Fund (Undergraduate/Scholarship) [6731]
Gene Jackson Scholarships (Undergraduate/Scholarship) [7169]
Sylvia E. Jackson Scholarships (Undergraduate/Scholarship) [6780]
Ruth K. Jacobs Memorial Scholarship Fund (Graduate, Undergraduate/Scholarship) [2141]
Eric L. Jacobson Memorial Scholarships (Undergraduate/Scholarship) [5946]
Karl A. Jacobson Scholarships (Undergraduate/Scholarship) [1060]
Peter Lars Jacobson Scholarships (Undergraduate/Scholarship) [7170]
Cory Jam Awards (Undergraduate/Scholarship) [2784]
Jamail/Long Challenge Grant Scholarships (Graduate, Undergraduate/Scholarship) [3576]
Frederick George James Memorial Scholarships (Undergraduate/Scholarship) [6195]
The J. Franklin Jameson Fellowship in American History (Doctorate/Fellowship) [606]
The Dawn Janisse Scholarships (Undergraduate/Scholarship) [5546]
Japan Foundation, New York Doctoral Fellowship Program (Doctorate/Fellowship) [4009]
Japan Foundation, New York Research Fellowship Program (Undergraduate/Fellowship) [4010]
Japan Foundation, New York Short-Term Fellowship Program (Doctorate/Fellowship) [4011]
Carl and Lucille Jarrett Scholarship Fund (Graduate, Undergraduate/Scholarship) [2961]
Terry Jarvis Memorial Scholarships (Undergraduate/Scholarship) [1165]
Jacob K. Javits Fellowships (Doctorate, Master's/Fellowship) [4707]
JD/MBA Scholarships (Undergraduate/Scholarship) [5593]
Sister Rita Jeanne Scholarships (Undergraduate/Scholarship) [4033]
Jefferson County Art Awards Scholarship for High school Seniors (Undergraduate/Scholarship) [1317]
Elise Reed Jenkins Memorial Scholarships - Gamma Lambda (Undergraduate/Scholarship) [6362]
Elise Reed Jenkins Memorial Scholarships - Gamma Psi (Undergraduate/Scholarship) [6363]
Martha Combs Jenkins Scholarships (Undergraduate/Scholarship) [5669]
Ruth E. Jenkins Scholarships (Undergraduate/Scholarship) [6196]
Gaynold Jensen Education Stipends (Postdoctorate, Professional Development/Scholarship) [2537]
Walter J. Jensen Fellowships (Professional Development/Fellowship) [5622]
Nancy Lorraine Jensen Memorial Scholarships (Undergraduate/Scholarship) [6603]
Mike Jensen R.I.S.E. Memorial Scholarships (Undergraduate/Scholarship) [5947]
Stanley "Doc" Jensen Scholarships (High School/Scholarship) [528]
Jerman-Cahoon Student Scholarship Program (Undergraduate/Scholarship) [1040]
Kenneth Jernigan Scholarships (Undergraduate/Scholarship) [4878]
James Jesinski Scholarships (Undergraduate/Scholarship) [7258]
Jewish Caucus Scholarships (Undergraduate/Scholarship) [5123]
The Jhaveri Scholarships (Graduate/Scholarship) [3184]
Brian Jimenez Memorial Scholarships (Undergraduate/Scholarship) [5948]
Rev. and Mrs. A.K. Jizmejian Educational Fund (Undergraduate/Scholarship) [1286]
JLTLA Scholarships (Undergraduate/Scholarship) [6942]
JMA Architecture Studios Scholarships (Undergraduate/Scholarship) [5833]
Oliver Joel and Ellen Pell Denny Healthcare Scholarship Fund (Undergraduate/Scholarship) [7441]
John Bayliss Broadcast Foundation Scholarships (Undergraduate/Scholarship) [1604]
Alvin H. Johnson AMS Dissertation Fellowships (Undergraduate/Fellowship) [720]
The Robert Wood Johnson Health Policy Fellowship Program (All/Fellowship) [787]
Joseph C. Johnson Memorial Grants (Undergraduate/Scholarship) [927]
Fred Johnson Memorial Scholarships (Graduate/Scholarship) [4790]
Gregory D. Johnson Memorial Scholarships (Graduate, Undergraduate/Scholarship) [4971]
Jimmy Johnson Memorial Scholarships (Undergraduate/Scholarship) [7442]
Dr. Bill Johnson Scholarships (Undergraduate/Scholarship) [6313]
Stella B. Johnson Scholarships (Undergraduate/Scholarship) [7443]
Julian C. Johnston Memorial Scholarships (Undergraduate/Scholarship) [6064]
Napoleon A. Jones, III Memorial Scholarships (Undergraduate/Scholarship) [6197]
Edward H. Jones Scholarships (Undergraduate/Scholarship) [2753]
Alice Newell Joslyn Medical Fund (Undergraduate/Scholarship) [1612]
Journyx Scholarships (Graduate, Undergraduate/Scholarship) [4035]
JSR Foundation Endowed School of Law Scholarships (Undergraduate/Scholarship) [5594]
Clem Judd Jr. Memorial Scholarships (Undergraduate/Scholarship) [3509]
George E. Judd Scholarships (Undergraduate/Scholarship) [6660]
Woodrow Judkins Endowed Scholarships (Undergraduate/Scholarship) [5595]
Junior Achievement of East Central Ohio, Inc. Scholarship Fund (Undergraduate/Scholarship) [6732]
Junior Firefighter Scholarships (Undergraduate/Scholarship) [5121]
Junior Women of the Contemporary Club Scholarships (Undergraduate/Scholarship) [5949]
George W. Juno Memorial Scholarships (Graduate/Scholarship) [3185]
Just Out Scholarship Fund (Undergraduate/Scholarship) [2885]
Justicia En Diversidad Scholarships (Undergraduate/Scholarship) [3585]
Juvenile Arthritis Scholarships (Undergraduate/Scholarship) [3471]
K-12 Edu-Grants (High School/Grant) [4927]
Kade-Heideking Fellowships (Doctorate/Fellowship) [3235]
David A. Kaiser Memorial Scholarship Fund (Undergraduate/Scholarship) [6733]
Kaiser Permanente Northwest Pride Scholarships (Undergraduate/Scholarship) [2886]
Benjamin Kaminer Endowed Scholarships in Physiology (Undergraduate/Scholarship) [4290]
Robert Kammerling Scholarships (Graduate/Scholarship) [3186]
Martin S. Kane Memorial Community Service Award Scholarships (Undergraduate/Scholarship) [2378]
Kansas City Division Scholarships (All/Scholarship) [4515]
Walter Kapala Scholarships (Undergraduate/Scholarship) [3472]
Don Kaplan Legacy Scholarship (Undergraduate/Scholarship) [1829]
Kaplan Scholarships (Undergraduate/Scholarship) [3580]
Kaplan Test Prep and Admission Scholarships for NSHSS Members (High School/Scholarship) [5069]
Steve Kaplan TV and Film Studies Scholarships (Professional Development/Scholarship) [946]
Kappa Chapter Centennial Scholarships (Undergraduate/Scholarship) [2653]
Kappa Delta Phi Scholarship Program (Postgraduate/Scholarship) [730]
Kappa Kappa Gamma Graduate Scholarships (Graduate/Scholarship) [4044]
Kappa Kappa Gamma Undergraduate Scholarships (Undergraduate/Scholarship) [4045]
Kappa Omicron Nu Honor Society Scholars Program Grants (Undergraduate/Grant) [4053]
Kappa Omicron Nu National Alumni Fellowships (Graduate/Fellowship) [4047]
Kappa Omicron Nu Undergraduate Scholarships (Undergraduate/Scholarship) [4048]
Kappa Zeta Scholarships (Undergraduate/Scholarship) [6364]
KASF Chair Scholarships (Graduate, Undergraduate/Scholarship) [4085]
KASF Designated Scholarships (Graduate, Undergraduate/Scholarship) [4086]
KASF General Scholarships (Graduate, Undergraduate/Scholarship) [4087]
Ken Kashiwara Scholarships (Undergraduate/Scholarship) [1398]
Magoichi & Shizuko Kato Memorial Scholarships (Graduate/Scholarship) [4018]
Peter Kaufman Memorial Scholarships (Undergraduate/Scholarship) [6112]
Lucile B. Kaufman Women's Scholarships (Undergraduate/Scholarship) [6493]
N.G. Kaul Memorial Scholarships (Postdoctorate/Scholarship) [5197]
William and Beatrice Kavanaugh Scholarship (Undergraduate/Scholarship) [3983]
Kawano Family Scholarships (Undergraduate/Scholarship) [6198]
E. Wayne Kay Co-op Scholarships (Undergraduate/Scholarship) [6494]
E. Wayne Kay Community College Scholarships (Undergraduate/Scholarship) [6495]
E. Wayne Kay High School Scholarships (Undergraduate/Scholarship) [6496]
Kazanjian Scholarships (Undergraduate/Scholarship) [3187]
Norair M. Kebabjian Memorial Scholarships (Undergraduate/Scholarship) [1264]
Doc Keen Memorial Scholarships (Undergraduate/Scholarship) [6661]
Kegler Brown Minority Merit Scholarships (Undergraduate/Scholarship) [4062]
Annette and Ernest Keith Scholarships (Undergraduate/Scholarship) [5950]
John W. Kelley Memorial Scholarships (Undergraduate/Scholarship) [6781]
Kellogg Company Career Scholarships (Undergraduate/Scholarship) [4067]
W.K. Kellogg Foundation Doctoral Fellowships in Health Policy (Professional Development/Fellowship) [4988]
Rita Mae Kelly Awards (All/Award/Prize) [6294]
Kendall College Bachelor of Arts in Culinary Arts Scholarships (Undergraduate/Scholarship) [2579]
Willmoore H. Kendall Scholarships (Postgraduate/Scholarship) [2252]
Raymond A. Kent-Navy V-12/ROTC (Undergraduate/Scholarship) [7101]
Kentucky Educational Excellence Scholarships (Graduate, Undergraduate/Scholarship) [1702]
Kentucky Paralegal Association Student Scholarships (Undergraduate/Scholarship) [4072]
Richard Kern Scholarships (Undergraduate/Scholarship) [3188]
Kerr Foundation Scholarships (Undergraduate/Scholarship) [5329]
Kerrigan Scholarships (Undergraduate/Scholarship) [5596]
Dr. Leizon and Barbara Kessel Scholarships (Undergraduate/Scholarship) [3473]
Ashley E. Ketcher Memorial Scholarships

(Undergraduate/Scholarship) [2473]
Key Memories Scholarships
(Undergraduate/Scholarship) [3151]
Luella Akins Key Scholarships
(Undergraduate/Scholarship) [2654]
KFC Colonel's Scholars Program
(Undergraduate/Scholarship) [4070]
Debbie Khalil Memorial Scholarships *(Graduate, Undergraduate/Scholarship)* [5639]
Louise Nader Khourey/Kappa Delta Pi Scholarships
(Undergraduate/Scholarship) [6734]
Bill Kidder Fund Awards
(Undergraduate/Scholarship) [6113]
Julia Kiene Fellowship in Electrical Energy
(Graduate/Fellowship) [7494]
Kilbuck Family Native American Scholarship
(Undergraduate/Scholarship) [1629]
Bernard Kilgore Memorial Scholarships
(Undergraduate/Scholarship) [5181]
Killam Fellowships Program
(Undergraduate/Fellowship) [7033]
Kimberly Elementary School PTA Scholarships
(Undergraduate/Scholarship) [5951]
James N. Kincanon Scholarships
(Undergraduate/Scholarship) [6047]
Dr. Martin Luther King & Coretta Scott King Student Leadership Scholarships
(Undergraduate/Scholarship) [1896]
Arthur M. and Berdena King Eagle Scout Scholarships *(High School/Scholarship)* [4860]
Kit C. King Graduate Scholarships
(Postgraduate/Scholarship) [5020]
Martin Luther King Law Scholarships
(Undergraduate/Scholarship) [2754]
Steven G. King Play Environments Scholarships
(Undergraduate/Scholarship) [4123]
Forest A. King Scholarships
(Undergraduate/Scholarship) [2755]
Jessica King Scholarships
(Undergraduate/Scholarship) [1436]
Don King Student Fellowships
(Undergraduate/Fellowship) [3633]
Kingsbury Elementary School PTA Scholarships
(Undergraduate/Scholarship) [5952]
Treva C. Kintner Scholarships
(Undergraduate/Scholarship) [5670]
Edyie G. Kirby Nursing Scholarships Award
(Undergraduate/Scholarship) [2354]
Patricia Van Kirk Scholarships
(Undergraduate/Scholarship) [5768]
James P. Kirkgasser Memorial Scholarships *(Graduate, Undergraduate/Scholarship)* [1663]
Isabel Mayer Kirkpatrick Scholarships
(Undergraduate/Scholarship) [6662]
Kiwanis Club of Escondido Scholarships I
(Undergraduate/Scholarship) [6199]
Kiwanis Club of Escondido Scholarships II
(Undergraduate/Scholarship) [6200]
Margie Klein "Paper Plate" Scholarships
(All/Scholarship) [1366]
Gerda and Kurt Klein Scholarships *(High School/Scholarship)* [3621]
Klingenstein Fellowships in the Neurosciences
(Doctorate, Professional Development/Fellowship) [4076]
Arthur Klorfein Scholarships and Fellowship Funds
(Undergraduate/Scholarship) [4291]
Joseph H. Klupenger Scholarship Awards
(Undergraduate/Scholarship) [5383]
Bryan L. Knapp Point Scholarships *(Graduate, Undergraduate/Scholarship)* [5724]
John S. Knight Fellowships *(Professional Development/Fellowship)* [6705]
Elva Knight Research Grants *(All/Grant)* [3889]
Knights of Pythias Scholarships
(Undergraduate/Scholarship) [5834]
Knights of Vartan, Fresno Lodge No. 9 Scholarships
(Undergraduate/Scholarship) [1287]
Knox-Hume Scholarships
(Undergraduate/Scholarship) [2426]
John Reily Knox Memorial Scholarships *(Graduate, Undergraduate/Scholarship)* [1664]
Glenn Knudsvig Memorial Scholarships *(Graduate, Undergraduate/Scholarship)* [460]
Ina Knutsen Scholarships
(Undergraduate/Scholarship) [6314]
Anne Koby Legacy Scholarships
(Undergraduate/Scholarship) [7509]
Koch Scholarships *(Undergraduate/Scholarship)* [7350]
Kodak Fellowships in Film Preservation
(Graduate/Scholarship) [1469]
Senator Carl O. Koella, Jr. Memorial Scholarships
(Undergraduate/Scholarship) [2427]
Christopher J. Kohlmeier Scholarships
(Undergraduate/Scholarship) [5953]
James P. Kohn Memorial Scholarships
(Graduate/Scholarship) [1061]
Susan G. Komen Breast Cancer Foundation College Scholarship Awards
(Undergraduate/Award/Prize) [4080]
John W. Koons, Sr. Memorial Scholarships
(Undergraduate/Scholarship) [1556]
Herman P. Kopplemann Scholarships
(Undergraduate/Scholarship) [3474]
Korean Language Study Awards
(Graduate/Scholarship) [4083]
Korean Studies Dissertation Workshop Funds
(Graduate/Grant) [6416]
Kosciuszko Foundation Graduate Study and Research in Poland Scholarships
(Graduate/Scholarship) [4089]
Kosciuszko Foundation Tuition Scholarships
(Undergraduate/Scholarship) [4090]
Kosciuszko Foundation Year Abroad Scholarships
(Undergraduate/Scholarship) [4091]
Carl A. Kountz Engineering Scholarships
(Undergraduate/Scholarship) [4109]
KPMG Foundation Minority Accounting Doctoral Scholarships *(Postdoctorate/Scholarship)* [4097]
Eve Kraft Education and College Scholarships
(Undergraduate/Scholarship) [7304]
Norman Kramer Scholarship Award
(Undergraduate/Scholarship) [4500]
Melvin Kranzberg Dissertation Fellowships
(Doctorate/Fellowship) [6462]
Samuel C. Kraus, Jr. Memorial Scholarships
(Undergraduate/Scholarship) [5096]
Sharon Kreikemeier Memorial Scholarships
(Undergraduate/Scholarship) [5160]
Robert Krembil Scholarships of Merit
(Postgraduate/Scholarship) [2082]
Kress Conservation Fellowships
(Graduate/Fellowship) [4099]
Kress Curatorial Fellowships *(Doctorate/Fellowship)* [4100]
Kress Fellowships in Art History at Foreign Institutions *(Doctorate/Fellowship)* [4101]
Samuel H. Kress Foundation Dissertation Fellowships *(Doctorate/Fellowship)* [6428]
Kress Pre-Doctoral Fellowships in the History of Art and Archeology in Turkey
(Postdoctorate/Fellowship) [898]
Kress Travel Fellowships in the History of Art
(Doctorate/Fellowship) [4102]
Krist-Reavley Minority Scholarships
(Undergraduate/Scholarship) [5597]
Carl A. Kroch Oxford Cup Memorial Scholarships
(Graduate, Undergraduate/Scholarship) [1665]
David A. Kronick Travelling Fellowships
(Doctorate/Fellowship) [4443]
Eugene S. Kropf Scholarships
(Undergraduate/Scholarship) [7082]
Melvin Kruger Endowed Scholarship Program
(Undergraduate/Scholarship) [5034]
Samuel Krugliak Legal Scholarship Fund
(Graduate/Scholarship) [6735]
Ken Krum/Bud Kouts Memorial Scholarships
(Undergraduate/Scholarship) [1557]
Judith Keller Marx Krumholz Scholarships
(Undergraduate/Scholarship) [6201]
Kuchler-Killian Memorial Scholarships
(Undergraduate/Scholarship) [4879]
Heloise Werthan Kuhn Scholarships
(Undergraduate/Scholarship) [2429]
Kumin Scholars Program
(Undergraduate/Scholarship) [6392]
Kris M. Kunze Memorial Scholarships
(Undergraduate/Scholarship) [486]
Charles Kuralt Fellowships in International Broadcasting *(Postgraduate/Scholarship)* [7172]
Chris Kurzweil Scholarships
(Undergraduate/Scholarship) [2516]
Sam S. Kuwahara Memorial Scholarships
(Undergraduate/Scholarship) [4019]
Julia Kwan Endowed Scholarships
(Graduate/Scholarship) [5598]
L-3 Avionics Systems Scholarships
(Undergraduate/Scholarship) [78]
La Unidad Latina Foundation Scholarships *(Graduate, Undergraduate/Scholarship)* [3586]
La Voz Latina Scholarships
(Undergraduate/Scholarship) [2474]
Gretchen Laatsch Scholarships
(Undergraduate/Scholarship) [1379]
LAF/Class Fund AILA/YAMAGAMI/Hope Fellowships
(Postgraduate/Fellowship) [983]
Ken LaFountaine First Nations Scholarships
(Undergraduate/Scholarship) [6315]
Ron LaFreniere Business Scholarships
(Undergraduate/Scholarship) [6316]
The Lagrant Foundation - Graduate Students Scholarships *(Graduate/Scholarship)* [4104]
The Lagrant Foundation - Undergraduate Students Scholarship *(Undergraduate/Scholarship)* [4105]
Ray and Kathy LaHood Scholarships for the Study of American Government
(Undergraduate/Scholarship) [2720]
Casey Laine Armed Forces Scholarships *(High School/Scholarship)* [2279]
Lake Dollars for Scholars Endowment Fund
(Undergraduate/Scholarship) [6736]
Lakselaget Foundation Scholarships *(Graduate, Undergraduate/Scholarship)* [4107]
Lam Research Corporation Core Value and Performance Scholarships for Interns
(Undergraduate/Scholarship) [4110]
Lam Research Corporation Core Values Scholarships *(Undergraduate/Scholarship)* [4111]
Lam Research Corporation - San Jose State University Scholarships *(Undergraduate/Scholarship)* [4112]
Lamar University College of Engineering Scholarships *(Undergraduate/Scholarship)* [4861]
Lambda Alumni (UCLA Lesbian & Gay Alumni Association) Scholarships Program
(Undergraduate/Scholarship) [6114]
Frank S. Land Scholarships
(Undergraduate/Scholarship) [2702]
Landscape Forms Design for People Scholarships
(Undergraduate/Scholarship) [4124]
Otho E. Lane Memorial Scholarships *(Graduate, Undergraduate/Scholarship)* [1666]
Susan Lang Scholarship Program
(Postgraduate/Scholarship) [731]
Lapeer County Medical Scholarships Fund
(Undergraduate/Scholarship) [4142]
The Otis and Florence Lapham Memorial Scholarship *(Undergraduate/Scholarship)* [3984]
Christian Larew Memorial Scholarships
(Graduate/Scholarship) [4236]
Peter and Jody Larkin Legacy Scholarship
(Undergraduate/Scholarship) [1830]
Joseph C. Larson Entrepreneurial Scholarships
(Undergraduate/Scholarship) [6202]
Las Limas Community Scholarships
(Undergraduate/Scholarship) [6782]
Las Vegas Chinatown Scholarships
(Undergraduate/Scholarship) [5835]
Las Vegas Elks Scholarships
(Undergraduate/Scholarship) [5836]
Las Vegas Elks Scholarships for the Physically Challenged *(Undergraduate/Scholarship)* [5837]
Laser Technology, Engineering and Applications Scholarships *(Graduate, Undergraduate/Scholarship)* [6697]
Daniel Lasky Scholarship Fund
(Undergraduate/Scholarship) [4998]
Jay and Deborah Last Fellowships
(Doctorate/Fellowship) [304]
Robert J. Lavidge Nonprofit Marketing Research Scholarships *(Professional Development/Scholarship)* [709]
Law Enforcement Memorial Scholarship Fund
(Undergraduate/Scholarship) [3066]
Law and Social Science Dissertation Fellowship and Mentoring Program *(Doctorate, Graduate/Fellowship)* [434]

Dr. James L. Lawson Memorial Scholarships *(Undergraduate/Scholarship)* [841]
Verne Lawyer Scholarships *(Undergraduate/Scholarship)* [2756]
Jonathan Lax Scholarship Fund for Gay Men *(Undergraduate/Scholarship)* [6115]
Lazarian Graduate Scholarships *(Graduate/Scholarship)* [1260]
Lazarus Foundation Scholarships *(Undergraduate/Scholarship)* [3475]
Richard J. Lazzara Fellowships in Advanced Implant Surgery *(Postdoctorate/Fellowship)* [287]
LCSC Welding Club Scholarships *(Undergraduate/Scholarship)* [4190]
Betsy B. and Garold A. Leach Scholarship for Museum Studies *(Undergraduate/Scholarship)* [2693]
Leaders at Work Scholarship in Textiles and Apparel *(Undergraduate/Scholarship)* [5109]
Leadership Development Scholarships *(Professional Development/Scholarship)* [380]
League of Attorneys' Wives Scholarships *(Undergraduate/Scholarship)* [2757]
LEAGUE Foundation Scholarships *(Undergraduate/Scholarship)* [6116]
Learn German in Germany *(Doctorate/Grant)* [3229]
William C. Leary Memorial Emergency Services Scholarships *(Undergraduate/Scholarship)* [6844]
Patrick Ledden Honorary Scholarships *(Undergraduate/Scholarship)* [6203]
Albert J. and Mae Lee Memorial Scholarships *(Undergraduate/Scholarship)* [5599]
Ken Lee Memorial Scholarships *(Undergraduate/Scholarship)* [6204]
Bruce Lee Scholarships *(Undergraduate/Scholarship)* [7007]
Harold Leeming Memorial Scholarships *(Undergraduate/Scholarship)* [5954]
LeePapa and Associates Scholarship for Travel *(Graduate, Undergraduate/Scholarship)* [7008]
The Leesfield/AAJ Law Student Scholarships *(Undergraduate/Scholarship)* [360]
Judge William B. Leffler Scholarships *(Undergraduate/Scholarship)* [7121]
The Legacy Fellowships *(Doctorate/Fellowship)* [305]
Legacy Scholarship Program *(Undergraduate/Scholarship)* [6867]
Legal Research Service Scholarships *(Undergraduate/Scholarship)* [2758]
Legal Scholarship for Law Students *(Undergraduate/Scholarship)* [5440]
Legal Scholarship for Non-Tenured Law Professors *(All/Scholarship)* [5441]
Legal Scholarship for Tenured Law Professors *(All/Scholarship)* [5442]
Doreen Legg Memorial Scholarships *(Undergraduate/Scholarship)* [5955]
Jay C. and B. Nadine Leggett Charitable Scholarship Fund *(Undergraduate/Scholarship)* [6737]
Legislative Incentive for Future Excellence (LIFE) Scholarships *(Undergraduate/Scholarship)* [232]
Herbert Lehman Education Scholarships *(Undergraduate/Scholarship)* [7345]
Lehman Family Scholarships *(Undergraduate/Scholarship)* [6205]
Leiber and Stoller Music Scholarships *(Undergraduate/Scholarship)* [947]
Leica Geosystems Internships *(Graduate/Internship)* [1029]
Imelda and Ralph LeMar Scholarship Program *(Undergraduate/Scholarship)* [2517]
The Lemon Grove Education Foundation Scholarships *(Undergraduate/Scholarship)* [6206]
Stan Lencki Scholarships *(Undergraduate/Scholarship)* [4420]
Craig Lensch Memorial Scholarships *(Undergraduate/Scholarship)* [1794]
Franklin A. Lentesty Scholarships *(Undergraduate/Scholarship)* [5285]
V.A. Leonard Scholarships *(Graduate, Undergraduate/Scholarship)* [253]
Leopold Education Project Scholarships *(Undergraduate/Scholarship)* [2475]
Irwin S. Lerner Student Scholarships *(Undergraduate/Scholarship)* [5076]
The Irving Leuchter Memorial Scholarships *(All/Scholarship)* [5202]
Gerald J. Levandoski Memorial Scholarship Fund *(Undergraduate/Scholarship)* [2962]
Myra Levick Scholarships *(Graduate/Scholarship)* [313]
Harold A. Levin Scholarships *(Undergraduate/Scholarship)* [2240]
Jack A. and Louise S. Levine Memorial Scholarships *(Undergraduate/Scholarship)* [5956]
Herbert Levy Memorial Endowment Fund Scholarships *(Undergraduate/Scholarship)* [6542]
Erwin Lew Memorial Scholarships *(Graduate, Undergraduate/Scholarship)* [6554]
Lewis-Clark Coin Club Endowed Scholarships *(Undergraduate/Scholarship)* [4191]
Lewis and Clark Fund for Exploration and Field Research *(Doctorate/Grant)* [770]
Lewis-Clark State College/American Chemical Society Scholars Program *(Undergraduate/Scholarship)* [4192]
Lewis-Clark State College Non-Traditional Student Scholarships *(Undergraduate/Scholarship)* [4197]
Lewis-Clark State College Presidential Out-of-State Scholarships *(Undergraduate/Scholarship)* [4198]
Lewis-Clark State College Presidential Technical Out-of-State Scholarships *(Undergraduate/Scholarship)* [4199]
Lewis-Clark State College Transfer Scholarships *(Undergraduate/Scholarship)* [4201]
George T. Lewis, Jr. Academic Scholarship Fund *(Undergraduate/Scholarship)* [3067]
Frederick D. Lewis Jr. Scholarships *(Undergraduate/Scholarship)* [2759]
S. Evelyn Lewis Memorial Scholarships in Medical Health Sciences *(Graduate, Undergraduate/Scholarship)* [7557]
Jonathan D. Lewis Point Scholarships *(Graduate, Undergraduate/Scholarship)* [5725]
Lewiston Service League Memorial Scholarships *(Undergraduate/Scholarship)* [4203]
Lexington Alumni Scholarships *(Undergraduate/Scholarship)* [4224]
Lexington Community Foundation Annual Scholarships *(Undergraduate/Scholarship)* [4225]
Lexington Community Foundation/CCC Scholarships *(Undergraduate/Scholarship)* [4226]
Lexington Teacher Appreciation Scholarships *(Professional Development/Scholarship)* [4227]
George C. Liacouras Memorial Scholarships *(Undergraduate/Scholarship)* [3532]
Ta Liang Memorial Awards *(Graduate/Grant)* [1030]
Liberace Scholarship Fund *(Undergraduate/Scholarship)* [4234]
Liberty Mutual Scholarships *(Undergraduate/Scholarship)* [1062]
Richard T. Liddicoat Scholarships *(Graduate/Scholarship)* [3189]
LIFE Lessons Scholarships Program *(Undergraduate/Scholarship)* [4240]
Frank R. Lillie Fellowships and Scholarships *(Undergraduate/Scholarship)* [4292]
Lilly Fellow Scholarships *(Undergraduate/Fellowship)* [3709]
Lily Scholarships in Religion for Journalists *(Professional Development/Scholarship)* [6021]
Esther Lim Memorial Scholarships *(Undergraduate/Scholarship)* [2136]
Lim, Ruger and Kim Scholarships *(Undergraduate/Scholarship)* [4647]
LIN Television Corporation Minority Scholarships and Training Program *(Undergraduate/Scholarship)* [4247]
John C. Lincoln Memorial Scholarships *(Undergraduate/Scholarship)* [1166]
Donald A. B. Lindberg Research Fellowships *(Doctorate, Graduate/Fellowship)* [4444]
Lindenwood University Scouting Scholarships *(Undergraduate/Scholarship)* [4862]
Johny Lineberry Memorial Scholarships *(Undergraduate/Scholarship)* [7445]
David Linton Memorial Scholarships *(Graduate, Undergraduate/Scholarship)* [1667]
F. Maynard Lipe Scholarship Award *(Postdoctorate/Award/Prize)* [464]
Listerhill Credit Union Scholarships *(Undergraduate/Scholarship)* [5286]
LIT Scholarships *(Graduate, Undergraduate/Scholarship)* [4116]
LITA and LSSI Minority Scholarships *(Graduate/Scholarship)* [4237]
LITA/OCLC Minority Scholarships *(Graduate/Scholarship)* [4238]
Litherland/FTE Scholarships *(Undergraduate/Scholarship)* [3911]
Litherland/FTE Scholarships *(Undergraduate/Scholarship)* [3912]
Lucius Littauer Foundation Travel Grants *(All/Grant)* [1461]
Ruth Liu Memorial Scholarships *(Undergraduate/Scholarship)* [2137]
Live Out Loud Annual Scholarships *(Undergraduate/Scholarship)* [6118]
E.C. Lloyd and J.C.U. Johnson Scholarships Fund *(Undergraduate/Scholarship)* [2355]
Loan Forgiveness Scholarships *(Undergraduate/Scholarship)* [6689]
Virgil K. Lobring Scholarships *(Undergraduate/Scholarship)* [2518]
Local Wound Haemostatics and Hemorrhage Control Scholarships *(All/Scholarship)* [411]
Leon I. Lock and Barbara R. Lock Scholarship Fund *(Undergraduate/Scholarship)* [3109]
Lockheed Martin IT Scholarships *(Undergraduate/Scholarship)* [1245]
William J. Locklin Scholarships *(Undergraduate/Scholarship)* [984]
Lodging Management Program (LMP) Scholarships *(Undergraduate/Scholarship)* [613]
Audrey Loftus Memorial Scholarships *(Undergraduate/Scholarship)* [7078]
Stephen Logan Memorial Scholarships *(Undergraduate/Scholarship)* [3169]
Lone Star GIA Associate and Alumni Scholarships *(Undergraduate/Scholarship)* [3190]
Long-Term Postdoctoral Fellowships for Biomedical and Behavioral Research in Japan *(Professional Development/Fellowship)* [1715]
Audre Lord Scholarships *(Graduate, Undergraduate/Scholarship)* [6119]
Lilly Lorenzen Scholarships *(Undergraduate/Scholarship)* [1119]
Barbara Lotze Scholarships for Future Teachers *(Undergraduate/Scholarship)* [385]
Willie T. Loud - CH2M Hill Scholarships *(Undergraduate/Scholarship)* [4897]
First Lieutenant Scott McClean Love Memorial Scholarship - Children of Soldiers *(Undergraduate/Scholarship)* [1303]
First Lieutenant Scott McClean Love Memorial Scholarship - Spouses of Soldiers *(Undergraduate/Scholarship)* [1304]
D.J. Lovell Scholarships *(Graduate, Undergraduate/Scholarship)* [6698]
The Lowell H. and Dorothy Loving Undergraduate Scholarships *(Undergraduate/Scholarship)* [487]
Gertie S. Lowe Nursing Scholarships Award *(Undergraduate/Scholarship)* [2356]
H.B. Paul Lowenberg Lions Scholarships *(Undergraduate/Scholarship)* [3476]
Horace G. Lozier Memorial Scholarships *(Graduate, Undergraduate/Scholarship)* [1668]
Henry Luce Foundation Dissertation Fellowships in American Art *(Doctorate/Fellowship)* [509]
James R. Lucey Scholarships *(Graduate/Scholarship)* [3191]
Elsa Ludeke Graduate Scholarships *(Graduate/Scholarship)* [2694]
David F. Ludovici Scholarships *(Undergraduate/Scholarship)* [3005]
Lugonia Alumni/Harrison Lightfoot Scholarships *(Undergraduate/Scholarship)* [5957]
LULAC GE Scholarships *(Undergraduate/Scholarship)* [4151]
LULAC GM Scholarships *(Graduate, High School, Undergraduate/Award/Prize)* [4152]
LULAC National Scholarship Fund *(Graduate, High School, Undergraduate/Scholarship)* [4153]
Luso-American Education Foundation C-1 General Scholarships *(Undergraduate/Scholarship)* [4261]
Luso-American Education Foundation G-1 Grants *(Professional Development/Grant)* [4262]

Luso-American Education Foundation G-2 Grants *(Professional Development/Grant)* [4263]
Luso-American Fraternal Federation B-2 Scholarships *(Postgraduate/Scholarship)* [4265]
Luso-American Fraternal Federation B-3 Scholarships *(All/Scholarship)* [4266]
Luso-American Fraternal Federation B-4 Scholarships *(All/Scholarship)* [4267]
Norval Neil Luxon Prize for Scholarship to a Junior Scholarships *(Undergraduate/Scholarship)* [7173]
Denny Lydic Scholarships *(Undergraduate/Scholarship)* [6920]
Melissa A. Lyles Memorial Scholarships *(Undergraduate/Scholarship)* [5838]
The C. Lyons Fellowship Program *(All/Fellowship)* [4980]
Linda Lyons Memorial Scholarship Fund *(Undergraduate/Scholarship)* [4464]
Carie and George Lyter Scholarship Fund *(Undergraduate/Scholarship)* [3110]
John Mabry Forestry Scholarships *(Undergraduate/Award/Prize)* [5895]
MAC Emeritus Scholarships for First-Time Meeting Attendees *(All, Professional Development/Scholarship)* [4509]
Dr. Mac Scholarships *(Undergraduate/Scholarship)* [2431]
Bill MacAloney Legacy Scholarship *(Undergraduate/Scholarship)* [1831]
MACC Scholarships *(Professional Development/Scholarship)* [4466]
Irene and Daisy MacGregor Memorial Scholarships *(Graduate/Scholarship)* [3477]
Mach 1 Air Services Scholarships *(Graduate, Undergraduate/Scholarship)* [5640]
Irene Mack Scholarships *(Undergraduate/Scholarship)* [3192]
James Mackenzie Fallows Scholarship Honoring William Cunningham *(Undergraduate/Scholarship)* [5958]
James I. MacKenzie Memorial Scholarships *(Graduate, Undergraduate/Scholarship)* [6555]
Mackey-Byars Scholarships for Communication Excellence *(Undergraduate/Scholarship)* [7174]
Carol E. Macpherson Memorial Scholarship and Alumnae Society Scholarships *(Graduate, Undergraduate/Scholarship)* [7133]
MacPherson Scholarships *(Undergraduate/Scholarship)* [5360]
Andrew Macrina Scholarships *(High School/Scholarship)* [529]
Eileen C. Maddex Fellowships *(Graduate/Fellowship)* [4049]
Dave Madeiros Scholarship Program - Continued Education *(Four Year College, Two Year College/Scholarship)* [4928]
Dave Madeiros Scholarship Program - Creative Arts *(Other/Grant)* [4929]
Lawrence Madeiros Scholarships *(Undergraduate/Scholarship)* [4930]
Gordon and Delores Madson Scholarships *(Undergraduate/Scholarship)* [2760]
Jay Magazine Memorial Fund (JMMF) College Scholarships *(Undergraduate/Scholarship)* [4454]
Dr. Edward May Magruder Medical Scholarships *(Other/Scholarship)* [458]
Sonia S. Maguire Outstanding Scholastic Achievement Awards *(Graduate, Undergraduate/Scholarship)* [6828]
Lillian Grace Mahan Scholarship Fund *(Undergraduate/Scholarship)* [6738]
Rick Mahoney Scholarships *(Undergraduate/Scholarship)* [4421]
Mary Main Memorial Scholarships *(Undergraduate/Scholarship)* [3478]
Maintenance Technical Reward and Career Scholarships *(Undergraduate/Scholarship)* [4780]
MALDEF Law School Scholarships *(Undergraduate/Scholarship)* [3587]
MALDEF Law School Scholarships *(Undergraduate/Scholarship)* [4470]
Maley/FTE Teacher Scholarships *(Graduate/Scholarship)* [3913]
Mallet Nursing Scholarships *(Undergraduate/Scholarship)* [6317]
Malmberg Fellowships *(Undergraduate/Fellowship)* [1120]
Malmberg Scholarships *(Undergraduate/Scholarship)* [1121]
David C. Maloney Scholarship Program *(Undergraduate/Scholarship)* [4996]
Dr. Julianne Malveaux Scholarships *(Undergraduate/Scholarship)* [4722]
Malyon-Smith Scholarships *(Graduate/Scholarship)* [6573]
Lyle Mamer Fellowships *(Graduate/Fellowship)* [7495]
MANAA Media Scholarships *(Graduate, Undergraduate/Scholarship)* [4439]
Manchester Scholarship Foundation Scholarships *(Undergraduate/Scholarship)* [3479]
Horace Mann Insurance Scholarships *(High School/Scholarship)* [5336]
Raleigh Mann Scholarships *(Undergraduate/Scholarship)* [7175]
Vincent Manson Scholarships *(Graduate/Scholarship)* [3193]
Paul Mansur Scholarships *(Undergraduate/Scholarship)* [3869]
Manzer-Keener-Wefler Scholarships *(Undergraduate/Scholarship)* [6739]
Marathon Oil Corporation College Scholarship Program *(Graduate, Undergraduate/Scholarship)* [3600]
Harold and Inge Marcus Scholarships *(Undergraduate/Scholarship)* [3735]
The Eric Marder Scholarships *(Undergraduate/Scholarship)* [3678]
Aurella Varallo Mariani Scholarship Program *(Undergraduate/Scholarship)* [4610]
Marine Biological Laboratory Pioneers Fund *(Undergraduate/Scholarship)* [4293]
Marine Corps Engineer Association Assistance Fund *(Graduate, High School, Undergraduate/Scholarship)* [4306]
Marine Corps League National Scholarships *(Undergraduate/Scholarship)* [4308]
Marine Technology Society ROV Scholarships *(Undergraduate/Scholarship)* [4310]
Marine Technology Society Scholarships for Graduate and Undergraduate Students *(Undergraduate/Scholarship)* [4311]
Marine Technology Society Student Scholarships for Graduating High School Seniors *(Undergraduate/Scholarship)* [4312]
Marine Technology Society Student Scholarships for Two-year Technical, Engineering and Community College Students *(Undergraduate/Scholarship)* [4313]
Dr. Frank and Florence Marino Scholarships *(Undergraduate/Scholarship)* [3480]
Mariposa Elementary School PTA Scholarships *(Undergraduate/Scholarship)* [5959]
Howard T. Markey Memorial Scholarships *(Undergraduate/Scholarship)* [2906]
Markey Scholarships *(Undergraduate/Scholarship)* [4673]
Ed Markham International Scholarships *(Undergraduate/Scholarship)* [560]
Markley Family Scholarship Fund *(Undergraduate/Scholarship)* [6740]
Markowski-Leach Scholarships Fund *(Graduate, Undergraduate/Scholarship)* [6120]
Kaia Lynn Markwalter Endowed Scholarships *(Undergraduate/Scholarship)* [4204]
Marliave Scholarship Fund *(Undergraduate/Scholarship)* [1409]
Marmot Leadership Scholarships *(Postgraduate, Professional Development, Undergraduate/Scholarship)* [5432]
Abraham Lincoln Marovitz Public Interest Law Scholarships *(Undergraduate/Scholarship)* [2119]
Carl J. Marrara Memorial Scholarship Fund *(Undergraduate/Scholarship)* [2963]
Marsh College Scholarships *(Undergraduate/Scholarship)* [3765]
Barry H. Marshal Scholarships *(Undergraduate/Scholarship)* [6121]
Marshall-Baruch Fellowships *(Doctorate/Fellowship)* [4318]
Samuel Taylor Marshall Memorial Scholarships *(Graduate, Undergraduate/Scholarship)* [1669]
Ray and Gertrude Marshall Scholarships *(Undergraduate/Scholarship)* [530]
Ron Marshall Scholarships *(Undergraduate/Scholarship)* [889]
Sarah Shinn Marshall Scholarships *(Undergraduate/Scholarship)* [2655]
Lockheed Martin Graduate Scholarships *(Graduate/Scholarship)* [1246]
Edna Martin Scholarships *(Undergraduate/Scholarship)* [2432]
Martin Sisters Scholarships *(Undergraduate/Scholarship)* [2656]
John S. Martinez and Family Scholarships Fund *(Undergraduate/Scholarship)* [2394]
Corporal Joseph Martinez U.S. Army Memorial Scholarships *(Undergraduate/Scholarship)* [5839]
Michael Marucci Memorial Scholarships *(Undergraduate/Scholarship)* [4880]
Michael L. Marx and Donald K. Marshall Scholarships *(Undergraduate/Scholarship)* [6122]
Maryland Hospitality Education Foundation Co-Branded Scholarships *(Undergraduate/Scholarship)* [4324]
The Maschhoffs Inc. Pork Production Scholarships *(Undergraduate/Scholarship)* [4972]
Masonic-Range Science Scholarships *(Undergraduate/Scholarship)* [6578]
Massachusetts Federation of Polish Women's Clubs Scholarships *(Undergraduate/Scholarship)* [4092]
Massachusetts General Hospital Summer Scholars Program *(Undergraduate/Fellowship)* [419]
S.O. Mast Founder's Scholarships *(Undergraduate/Scholarship)* [4294]
The Master Gardeners of Pierce County Scholarships *(Undergraduate/Scholarship)* [3377]
Master Municipal Clerks Academy Scholarships *(Professional Development/Scholarship)* [3873]
Matching Scholarships Program *(Undergraduate/Scholarship)* [2608]
Material Handling Institute of America Scholarships *(Graduate, Undergraduate/Scholarship)* [4395]
Materials Information Society National Merit Scholarships *(Undergraduate/Scholarship)* [4400]
Noel D. Matkin Awards *(Undergraduate/Award/Prize)* [2830]
Rene Matos Memorial Scholarships *(Undergraduate/Scholarship)* [4937]
The Renardo A. Matteucci Scholarship Fund *(Undergraduate/Scholarship)* [2401]
Greg Matthews Memorial Scholarships *(Undergraduate/Scholarship)* [5600]
Randall Matthis for Environmental Studies Scholarships *(Graduate, Undergraduate/Scholarship)* [1226]
Katherine Portnoy Mattleson Scholarships *(Undergraduate/Scholarship)* [3481]
Antonio Mattos Memorial Scholarships *(Undergraduate/Scholarship)* [4268]
Aaron Matusek Memorial Scholarships *(Undergraduate/Scholarship)* [5840]
Donald Mauer Scholarships *(Undergraduate/Scholarship)* [7176]
Armistead Maupin Creative Writing Scholarship Fund *(Undergraduate/Scholarship)* [2887]
Maxwell Graduate Scholarships in Medical Journalism *(Postgraduate/Scholarship)* [7177]
Juliann and Joseph Maxwell Scholarships *(Undergraduate/Scholarship)* [2433]
Juliann King Maxwell Scholarships for Students in White County, Arkansas *(Undergraduate/Scholarship)* [2434]
Howard Mayer Brown Fellowships *(Postdoctorate/Fellowship)* [721]
John E. Mayfield ABLE Scholarships *(Undergraduate/Scholarship)* [2435]
Clara Mayo Grants *(Graduate/Grant)* [6575]
Charles D. Mayo Student Scholarships *(Undergraduate/Scholarship)* [3861]
Giuliano Mazzetti Scholarships *(Undergraduate/Scholarship)* [6497]
Bill McAdam Scholarships *(Undergraduate/Scholarship)* [5008]
Walter Samuel McAfee Scholarships in Space Physics *(Undergraduate/Scholarship)* [5056]
Durwood McAlister Scholarships

(Undergraduate/Scholarship) [3214]
McBurney Disability Scholarships (Undergraduate/Scholarship) [7262]
MCCA Lloyd M. Johnson, Jr. Scholarships (Undergraduate/Scholarship) [4558]
Bill McCarthy Scout Scholarship Fund (Undergraduate/Scholarship) [6741]
Brian McCartney Scholarships (Undergraduate/Scholarship) [4472]
Russell C. McCaughan, DO, Education Scholarships (Undergraduate/Scholarship) [750]
McClatchy Scholarships (Undergraduate/Scholarship) [6616]
McColl Family Fellowships (Professional Development/Fellowship) [593]
Anne O'Hare McCormick Scholarship Fund (Undergraduate/Scholarship) [5204]
Dr. Cladwell McCoy, Jr. Memorial Scholarships (Undergraduate/Scholarship) [3482]
McDaniel College Eagle Scout Scholarships (Undergraduate/Scholarship) [4863]
Fred R. McDaniel Memorial Scholarships (Undergraduate/Scholarship) [842]
Ronald McDonald House Charities of Las Vegas Scholarships (Undergraduate/Scholarship) [5841]
J. McDonald and Judy Williams School of Law Scholarships (Undergraduate/Scholarship) [5601]
Larry McDonald Scholarships (Undergraduate/Scholarship) [2888]
Michele L. McDonald Scholarships (Undergraduate/Scholarship) [2832]
McDonald's USA National Employee Scholarship Program (Undergraduate/Scholarship) [4412]
Bodie McDowell Scholarships (Graduate, Undergraduate/Scholarship) [5430]
McFarffels Scholarships (Undergraduate/Scholarship) [5769]
Foster G. McGaw Graduate Student Scholarships (Undergraduate/Scholarship) [467]
Nancy B. Woolridge McGee Graduate Fellowships (Graduate/Fellowship) [7558]
Lucile E. McGee Scholarship (Undergraduate/Scholarship) [3985]
Lee Kimche McGrath Worldwide Fellowships (Professional Development/Fellowship) [1490]
Janice McGraw Memorial Scholarship Program (Postgraduate/Scholarship) [732]
Brouwer D. McIntyre Memorial Scholarships (Undergraduate/Scholarship) [1558]
Molly McKay Scholarships (Undergraduate/Scholarship) [7178]
McKelvey Foundation Entrepreneurial Scholarships (Undergraduate/Scholarship) [4434]
McKelvey Scholarships (Undergraduate/Scholarship) [4435]
Robert V. McKenna Scholarships (Undergraduate/Scholarship) [3369]
McKesson Scholarships (Undergraduate/Scholarship) [3131]
John J. McKetta Undergraduate Scholarships (Undergraduate/Scholarship) [656]
Arthur Patch McKinlay Scholarships (Graduate, Undergraduate/Scholarship) [461]
McKinley Elementary School PTA Scholarships (Undergraduate/Scholarship) [5960]
McKinley Financial Scholarships (Graduate, Undergraduate/Scholarship) [4898]
John L. and Eleanore I. Mckinley Scholarships (Undergraduate/Scholarship) [2695]
Elizabeth McKissick Memorial Scholarships (Undergraduate/Scholarship) [4205]
H.H. McKnight Memorial Scholarships (Undergraduate/Scholarship) [7122]
C.A. "Pete" McKnight Scholarships (Undergraduate/Scholarship) [7179]
Jacinta McKoy Memorial Scholarships (Undergraduate/Scholarship) [5770]
McLean Scholarships (Undergraduate/Scholarship) [1433]
John McLendon Memorial Minority Postgraduate Scholarships (Postdoctorate/Scholarship) [4691]
Charles McMahon Memorial Construction Management/Engineering Scholarship Awards (Undergraduate/Scholarship) [1320]
David McMeans Memorial Scholarships (Undergraduate/Scholarship) [5287]
Anneka McMillan Creative Arts Scholarships (Undergraduate/Scholarship) [6207]
Ruth McMillan Student Grants (Undergraduate/Grant) [1855]
Ronald E. McNair Scholarships in Space and Optical Physics (Undergraduate/Scholarship) [5057]
McNamara Family Creative Arts Project Grants (Graduate, Undergraduate/Grant) [3601]
McNeil Dissertation Fellowships (All/Fellowship) [7467]
Joan Reagin McNeill Scholarships - Alpha Theta (Undergraduate/Scholarship) [6365]
Joan Reagin McNeill Scholarships - Theta Phi (Undergraduate/Scholarship) [6366]
MDA Development Grants (Doctorate/Grant) [4593]
MDA Research Grants (Doctorate/Grant) [4594]
Mead Leadership Fellows Program (Professional Development/Fellowship) [5266]
David Meador Student Scholarships (Undergraduate/Scholarship) [5169]
Ben Meadows Natural Resource Scholarships - Academic Achievement Scholarships (Undergraduate/Scholarship) [1620]
Ben Meadows Natural Resource Scholarships - Leadership Scholarships (Undergraduate/Scholarship) [1621]
Jerry Medforth Nursing Scholarships Award (Undergraduate/Scholarship) [2357]
Medical Student Summer Research Scholarships (Undergraduate/Scholarship) [261]
Medical Students Loan Program (Undergraduate/Loan) [7403]
Medicus Student Exchange (Graduate, Undergraduate/Scholarship) [6829]
Augustine and Sandra Medina Memorial Scholarships (Undergraduate/Scholarship) [5961]
Medina Scholarships for Hispanics in Safety (Graduate, Undergraduate/Scholarship) [1063]
Edward Heywood Megson Scholarships (Undergraduate/Scholarship) [7180]
Karl Mehlmann Scholarships (Undergraduate/Scholarship) [2306]
Dr. Roger E. Meisner Veterinary Medicine Educational Scholarship Fund (Undergraduate/Scholarship) [5257]
Frederic G. Melcher Scholarships (Graduate/Scholarship) [1465]
Andrew W. Mellon Dissertation Completion Fellowships (Doctorate/Fellowship) [510]
Mellon Fellowships (Doctorate, Graduate/Fellowship) [2550]
Institute Andrew W. Mellon Postdoctoral Research Fellowships (Professional Development/Fellowship) [5339]
Mentoring Travel Grants for Women (Postdoctorate/Scholarship) [1515]
Merck Undergraduate Science Research Scholarships (Undergraduate/Scholarship) [318]
John Merrick Law Scholarships (Undergraduate/Scholarship) [5602]
Steven Craig Merrill Memorial Scholarships (Graduate, Undergraduate/Scholarship) [1670]
William J. Merriman American Council on Exercise Educational Scholarships (Undergraduate/Scholarship) [500]
VISTAKON George Mertz and Sheldon Wechsler Residency Awards (All/Award/Prize) [278]
MESBEC Scholarships (Undergraduate/Scholarship) [2067]
Scott Mesh Honorary Scholarships for Research in Psychology (Graduate/Fellowship) [801]
Christopher Mesi Music Scholarships (Undergraduate/Scholarship) [2064]
Mesothelioma Memorial Scholarships (Undergraduate/Scholarship) [6794]
Messenger-Anderson Journalism Scholarships and Internships Program (Undergraduate/Scholarship) [6123]
Ruth Messmer Memorial Scholarships (Undergraduate/Scholarship) [6665]
Sanders J. Mestel Legal Scholarship Fund (Undergraduate/Scholarship) [6742]
Harry Mestel Memorial Accounting Scholarship Fund (Undergraduate/Scholarship) [6743]
Edmond A. Metzger Scholarships (Undergraduate/Scholarship) [843]
Mexican American Grocers Association Scholarships (Undergraduate/Scholarship) [4468]
Peter Meyer Memorial Scholarships (Undergraduate/Scholarship) [7398]
MGFA Student Fellowships (Undergraduate/Fellowship) [4601]
MHS Health Career Scholarships (Undergraduate/Scholarship) [4450]
Michael Jewelers Foundation Scholarships for Athletes (Undergraduate/Scholarship) [3483]
Michaels Jewelers Foundation General Scholarships (Undergraduate/Scholarship) [3484]
Michigan Association of Realtors Scholarship Trust (Undergraduate/Scholarship) [4474]
Michigan Council of Women in Technology College Scholarship Program (Graduate, Undergraduate/Scholarship) [4476]
Michigan Council of Women in Technology High School Scholarships Program (Undergraduate/Scholarship) [4477]
Michigan Education Association Scholarships (Undergraduate/Scholarship) [4479]
Michigan League for Nursing Scholarships (Undergraduate/Scholarship) [4481]
Michigan Nursery and Landscape Association Scholarships (Undergraduate/Scholarship) [4483]
Michigan Society of Professional Engineers Scholarships (Undergraduate/Scholarship) [4487]
Michigan Stormwater-Floodplain Association Scholarships (Undergraduate/Scholarship) [4492]
Michigan Sugar Company Hotel Restaurant/Resort Management Scholarships (Undergraduate/Scholarship) [4496]
Michigan Tech Alumni Scholarships (Undergraduate/Scholarship) [881]
John G. and Betty J. Mick Scholarship Fund (Undergraduate/Scholarship) [6744]
Microbiology Undergraduate Research Fellowships (Undergraduate/Fellowship) [1007]
Microbiology Undergraduate Teaching Fellowships (Undergraduate/Fellowship) [1008]
Mid-Continent Instrument Scholarships (Undergraduate/Scholarship) [79]
Beth Middleton Memorial Scholarships (Undergraduate/Scholarship) [5110]
Midwest Chapter Scholarships - Betty McKern (Undergraduate/Scholarship) [1448]
Midwest Chapter Scholarships - Don Nelson (Undergraduate/Scholarship) [1449]
Midwest Chapter Scholarships - Engineering (Undergraduate/Scholarship) [1450]
Midwest Chapter Scholarships - Mel Nickel (Undergraduate/Scholarship) [1451]
Midwest Chapter Scholarships - Non-Engineering (Undergraduate/Scholarship) [1452]
Midwest Chapter Scholarships - Western States Award (Undergraduate/Scholarship) [1453]
Albert and Eloise Midyette Memorial Scholarship Fund (Undergraduate/Scholarship) [3068]
Keith Miffioli Scholarship (Undergraduate/Scholarship) [2476]
Migrant Health Scholarships (Professional Development/Scholarship) [4794]
Mihaly Russin Scholarship Awards (Graduate/Scholarship) [6087]
Mike Kabo Global Scholarships (Other/Scholarship) [4786]
Mikimoto Scholarships (Graduate/Scholarship) [3194]
Mary Ann Mikulic Scholarships (Undergraduate/Scholarship) [1486]
Milan Getting Scholarships (Undergraduate/Scholarship) [6594]
Milbank Diversity Scholarships (Undergraduate/Scholarship) [4525]
Eunice Miles Scholarships (Undergraduate/Scholarship) [3195]
Military Intelligence Corps Association Scholarships (Undergraduate/Scholarship) [4527]
Military Order of the Perpetual Heart Foundation Scholarships (Undergraduate/Scholarship) [4206]
Millennium Charter Academy College Scholarships (Undergraduate/Scholarship) [7447]
Mark Miller Award (Graduate, Undergraduate/Scholarship) [4656]
Miller Electric International WorldSkills Competition

Scholarships (Undergraduate/Scholarship) [1167]
Robbie Miller Memorial Scholarships (Undergraduate/Scholarship) [4207]
Raymond W. Miller, PE and Alice E. Miller Scholarships (Undergraduate/Scholarship) [3006]
Raymond W. Miller, PE Scholarships (Undergraduate/Scholarship) [3007]
Fizz and Dutch Miller Scholarship Fund (Undergraduate/Scholarship) [6745]
Glenn Miller Scholarships (Undergraduate/Scholarship) [4535]
Quincy Sharpe Mills Scholarships (Undergraduate/Scholarship) [7181]
Mined Land Reclamation Educational Grant Program (Undergraduate/Grant) [4745]
Mary Minglen Scholarship Program (Postgraduate/Scholarship) [733]
Minneapolis Camp Scholarships (Undergraduate/Scholarship) [4541]
Minnesota Association County Probation Officers Scholarships (Undergraduate/Scholarship) [4544]
Minnesota Association of Public Accountant Scholarships (Undergraduate/Scholarship) [4546]
Minnesota Association of Township Scholarships (Undergraduate/Scholarship) [4548]
Minnesota Division Scholarships (Undergraduate/Scholarship) [4516]
Minnesota GLBT Educational Fund (Undergraduate/Scholarship) [6125]
Minnesota Power Community Involvement Scholarships (Undergraduate/Scholarship) [2785]
Minnesota State Archery Association Scholarship Program (Undergraduate/Scholarship) [4556]
Jacque I. Minnotte Health Reporting Fellowships (Undergraduate/Fellowship) [1399]
Minorities in Government Finance Scholarships (Graduate, Undergraduate/Scholarship) [3266]
Minority Medical Student Fellowships in HIV Psychiatry (Undergraduate/Fellowship) [793]
Minority Pharmacy Faculty New Investigator Grants (Professional Development/Grant) [581]
Minority Scholarship Awards for College Students (Undergraduate/Scholarship) [657]
Minority Scholarship Awards for Incoming College Freshmen (Undergraduate/Scholarship) [658]
Minority Student Gateway to Research Scholarships (Professional Development/Scholarship) [582]
Minority Teachers of Illinois Scholarships (Undergraduate/Scholarship) [3670]
MiraCosta College Two-Year Colleges Scholarships (Undergraduate/Scholarship) [4560]
The Aristotle Mirones Scholarships (Undergraduate/Scholarship) [5547]
David W. Misek, N8NPX Memorial Scholarships (Undergraduate/Scholarship) [844]
Joseph and Catherine Missigman Memorial Nursing Scholarships (Undergraduate/Scholarship) [2965]
Missigman Scholarship Fund (Undergraduate/Scholarship) [2966]
Mission Bay Hospital Auxiliary Scholarships (Undergraduate/Scholarship) [6208]
Joshua Esch Mitchell Aviation Scholarships (Undergraduate/Scholarship) [3342]
N.W. Mitchell-Piedmont Federal Savings and Loans Endowed Scholarships (Undergraduate/Scholarship) [7448]
George J. Mitchell Postgraduate Scholarships (Postgraduate/Scholarship) [4708]
Dorothy Mitchell Scholarships (Undergraduate/Scholarship) [5962]
George J. Mitchell Scholarships (Undergraduate/Scholarship) [6999]
Robert L. & Hilda Treasure Mitchell Scholarships (Undergraduate/Scholarship) [3343]
Sam Mizrahi Memorial Scholarships (Undergraduate/Scholarship) [3111]
MJSA Education Foundation Scholarship Fund (Undergraduate/Scholarship) [4278]
MJSA Educational Foundation Jewelry Scholarships (Undergraduate/Scholarship) [6039]
MKC Scholarships (Undergraduate/Scholarship) [6209]
MLA/NLM Spectrum Scholarship Program (Graduate/Scholarship) [4445]
MLA Research, Development, and Demonstration Project Grants (Graduate/Grant) [4446]
MLA Scholarships for Minority Students (Graduate/Scholarship) [4447]
MOAA American Patriot Scholarships (Undergraduate/Scholarship) [4529]
MOAA Base/Post Scholarships (Undergraduate/Scholarship) [4530]
Modern Woodmen of America Scholarships (Undergraduate/Scholarship) [2786]
Ralph Modjeski Scholarships (Graduate, Undergraduate/Scholarship) [5729]
Francis H. Moffitt Memorial Scholarships (Graduate, Undergraduate/Scholarship) [1031]
Donald and Idabelle Mohr Scholarships (Undergraduate/Scholarship) [2241]
Antoinette M. Molinari Memorial Scholarships (Doctorate/Scholarship) [279]
Momeni Foundation Scholarships (Undergraduate/Scholarship) [4957]
Nell I. Mondy Fellowships (Graduate, Postdoctorate/Fellowship) [6340]
Ed Monk Scholarships (Professional Development/Scholarship) [2093]
Monsanto Company Agriculture Scholarships (Undergraduate/Scholarship) [4567]
Monster Medical Imaging Educators Scholarship Program (Postdoctorate/Scholarship) [1041]
Montana Broadcasters Association Directors' Scholarships (Undergraduate/Scholarship) [4571]
Montana Broadcasters Association Engineers' Scholarships (Undergraduate/Scholarship) [4572]
Cary Moore Memorial Scholarship Fund (Undergraduate/Scholarship) [2519]
Moore Middle School PTA Scholarships (Undergraduate/Scholarship) [5963]
Stanley Moore Scholarships (Undergraduate/Scholarship) [5251]
Willie Hobbs Moore Scholarships (Undergraduate/Scholarship) [5058]
Walter Moran Farmer Scholarships (Undergraduate/Scholarship) [7385]
Jim Moran Scholarships (Undergraduate/Scholarship) [1559]
Jake S. More Scholarships (Undergraduate/Scholarship) [2761]
Thomas More Scholarships (Undergraduate/Scholarship) [3260]
Lt. Colonel Robert G. Moreland Vocational/Technical Fund (Undergraduate/Scholarship) [6746]
Herbie Morici Memorial Scholarships (Undergraduate/Scholarship) [1843]
Alexander Morisey Scholarships (Undergraduate/Scholarship) [7183]
Leo F. Moro Baseball Memorial Scholarships (Undergraduate/Scholarship) [3112]
Frank Morrell Endowed Memorial Scholarships (Undergraduate/Scholarship) [4295]
Morris County Psychological Association Scholarships (Undergraduate/Scholarship) [4574]
Morris Newspaper Corp. Scholarships (Undergraduate/Scholarship) [3215]
Edith Cantor Morrison Memorial Scholarships (Graduate, Undergraduate/Scholarship) [1671]
Harry L. Morrison Scholarships (Undergraduate/Scholarship) [5059]
Dorothy Morrison Undergraduate Scholarships (Undergraduate/Scholarship) [934]
Mortar Board National Foundation Fellowships (Postdoctorate/Fellowship) [4578]
Dwight Mosley Scholarships (Undergraduate/Scholarship) [7305]
Mossmiller Student Intern Scholarships Program (Undergraduate/Internship) [561]
Archie Motley Memorial Scholarships for Minority Students (Graduate/Scholarship) [4511]
John R. Mott Scholarships (Undergraduate/Scholarship) [4580]
Jack D. Motteler Scholarships (Undergraduate/Scholarship) [5771]
Mt. Hood Chapter Scholarship Awards (Undergraduate/Scholarship) [5384]
Mountain Memorial Scholarships (Undergraduate/Scholarship) [4296]
MPAEA Memorial Scholarships (Graduate/Scholarship) [4582]
MPAEA Professional Development Scholarships (All/Scholarship) [4583]
MPAEA State Association Professional Development Grants (Other/Grant) [4584]
MPAEA Student Scholarships (Other/Scholarship) [4585]
MPI CRV Continuing Education Scholarships (Professional Development/Scholarship) [4452]
MPower Scholarships (Graduate, Undergraduate/Scholarship) [5641]
MSPT Sports Medicine Scholarships (Undergraduate/Scholarship) [5842]
Ruth Mu-Lan and James S.C. Chao Scholarship (Undergraduate/Scholarship) [7009]
Muddy Waters Scholarships (Undergraduate/Scholarship) [1768]
Brittany Mueller Memorial Scholarships (High School/Scholarship) [5161]
Ryan Mullaly Second Chance Fund Scholarships (Undergraduate/Scholarship) [4587]
Gary B. Multanen/CM Magazine Scholarships (All/Scholarship) [479]
Muncy Rotary Club Scholarship Fund (Undergraduate/Scholarship) [2968]
Muncy Scholars Award Fund (Undergraduate/Award/Prize) [2969]
Marvin Mundel Memorial Scholarships (Undergraduate/Scholarship) [3736]
Harry Munoz Memorial Scholarships (Undergraduate/Scholarship) [5964]
Rick Munoz Memorial Scholarships (Undergraduate/Scholarship) [5965]
Carolyn Murray Memorial Scholarships (Undergraduate/Scholarship) [1897]
Muscle Shoals Kiwanis/Wal-Mart Scholarships (Undergraduate/Scholarship) [5288]
Sam A. Myar, Jr. Law Scholarships (Undergraduate/Scholarship) [7123]
Myasthenia Gravis Foundation of America Nursing Fellowships (Undergraduate/Fellowship) [4602]
Myasthenia Gravis Foundation of America Post-Doctoral Fellowships (Postdoctorate/Fellowship) [4603]
Clarence and Josephine Myers Scholarships (Graduate, Undergraduate/Scholarship) [6498]
Mary Fran Myers Scholarships (All/Grant) [5130]
NABA Corporate Scholarship Program (Graduate, Undergraduate/Scholarship) [4657]
NABA National Scholarship Program (Graduate, Undergraduate/Scholarship) [4658]
NABTP Collegian (Undergraduate/Scholarship) [4670]
NACA East Coast Graduate Student Scholarships (Postdoctorate/Scholarship) [4674]
NACA East Coast Higher Education Research Scholarships (Postgraduate/Scholarship) [4675]
NACA East Coast Undergraduate Scholarships for Student Leaders (Undergraduate/Scholarship) [4676]
NACA Foundation Graduate Student Scholarships (Postdoctorate/Scholarship) [4677]
NACA Regional Council Student Leadership Scholarships (Undergraduate/Scholarship) [4678]
NACA Southeast Student Leadership Scholarships (Undergraduate/Scholarship) [4679]
NACADA Scholarships (Doctorate, Graduate/Scholarship) [4616]
NACBS Dissertation Year Fellowships (Postdoctorate/Fellowship) [5217]
NACBS-Huntington Library Fellowships (Postdoctorate/Fellowship) [5218]
NACCED Annual John C. Murphy Scholarships (Graduate, Undergraduate/Scholarship) [4697]
NAFA International Dissertation Research Fellowships (Graduate/Fellowship) [4709]
NAFEO Internship Program (Undergraduate/Internship) [4699]
Jack Nagasaka Memorial Scholarships (Undergraduate/Scholarship) [5966]
Gongoro Nakamura Memorial Scholarships (Undergraduate/Scholarship) [4020]
IADR Toshio Nakao Fellowships (Professional Development/Fellowship) [3794]
NANBPWC National Scholarships (Undergraduate/Scholarship) [4723]
NANBPWC Woman of Substance Scholarships (Undergraduate/Scholarship) [4724]
Robyn Nance Memorial Scholarships

(Undergraduate/Scholarship) [5967]
NAPABA Law Foundation Scholarships (Undergraduate/Scholarship) [4648]
NAPNAP McNeil Annual Scholarships (Undergraduate/Scholarship) [4731]
NAPNAP McNeil Rural and Underserved Scholarships (Undergraduate/Scholarship) [4732]
NARFE-FEEA Scholarship Awards Program (Undergraduate/Scholarship) [4628]
NARRP Student Conference Scholarships (Graduate, Undergraduate/Scholarship) [4736]
NASA Aeronautics Scholarship Undergraduate Program (Undergraduate/Scholarship) [956]
NASCOE Scholarships (Other/Scholarship) [4701]
NASE Future Entrepreneur Scholarships (Undergraduate/Scholarship) [4740]
Kermit B. Nash Academic Scholarships (Undergraduate/Scholarship) [6327]
Archie Hartwell Nash Memorial Scholarships (Undergraduate/Scholarship) [2440]
Mike Nash Memorial Scholarships (Undergraduate/Scholarship) [7319]
Nashville Unit Scholarships (Undergraduate/Scholarship) [3544]
NASIG Conference Student Grants (Postdoctorate/Grant) [5225]
The NASSCO Jeffrey D. Ralston Memorial Scholarships (Undergraduate/Scholarship) [4743]
NASSLEO Scholarships (Undergraduate/Scholarship) [4738]
NASSS Graduate Minority Scholarships (Graduate/Scholarship) [5228]
National AAHAM Scholarships (Undergraduate/Scholarship) [353]
The National Academies Dissertation Fellowships (Doctorate/Fellowship) [4619]
National Academies Postdoctoral Fellowships (Postdoctorate/Fellowship) [4620]
The National Academies Predoctoral Fellowships (Doctorate/Fellowship) [4621]
National Air Filtration Association Scholarship Fund (Undergraduate/Scholarship) [4630]
National Alliance of Preservation Commission Student Scholarships (Undergraduate/Scholarship) [4632]
National American Arab Nurses Association Scholarships (Undergraduate/Scholarship) [4637]
National Association for Armenian Studies and Research Scholarships (Undergraduate/Scholarship) [1289]
National Association of Campus Activities Multicultural Scholarship Programs (Undergraduate/Scholarship) [4680]
National Association of Campus Activities Scholarships for Student Leaders (Undergraduate/Scholarship) [4681]
National Association of Conservation District Employees Scholarships (Undergraduate/Scholarship) [4693]
National Association of Fellowships Advisors Graduate Scholar Awards (Postgraduate, Professional Development/Fellowship) [4710]
National Association of Financial Aid and Administrators Nursing Scholarships (Undergraduate/Scholarship) [4712]
National Association of Financial Aid and Administrators Scholarships for Disadvantaged Students (Undergraduate/Scholarship) [4713]
National Association of Pastoral Musicians Academic Scholarships (Graduate, Undergraduate/Scholarship) [4726]
National Association for the Self-Employed Scholarships (Undergraduate/Scholarship) [4741]
National Ataxia Foundation Research Fellowships (Postdoctorate/Fellowship) [4754]
National Ataxia Foundation Research Grants (Postdoctorate/Fellowship) [4755]
National Beta Club Scholarships (Undergraduate/Scholarship) [4757]
National Black Coalition of Federal Aviation Employees Scholarship (Other/Scholarship) [4759]
National Black Nurses Association Scholarships (Undergraduate/Scholarship) [4764]
The National Board Technical Scholarships (Other/Scholarship) [4768]
National Candy Technologist Scholarship Program (Undergraduate/Scholarship) [332]
National Co-op Scholarship Program (Undergraduate/Scholarship) [4809]
National Coal Transportation Association At Large Scholarships (Undergraduate/Scholarship) [4800]
National College Scholarship Award (Undergraduate/Scholarship) [3970]
National Collegiate Athletic Association Postgraduate Scholarships (Postgraduate/Scholarship) [4805]
National Collegiate Cancer Foundation Scholarships (Undergraduate/Scholarship) [4807]
National Community Pharmacists Association Internship Programs (Undergraduate/Internship) [4812]
National Community Pharmacists Association Presidential Scholarships (Undergraduate/Scholarship) [4813]
National Costumers Association Scholarships (Undergraduate/Scholarship) [4824]
National Court Reporters Association Student Intern Scholarships (Undergraduate/Scholarship) [4835]
National Dairy Herd Improvement Association Scholarship Program (Undergraduate/Scholarship) [4839]
National Dental Hygienists' Association Scholarships (Undergraduate/Scholarship) [4846]
National Endowment for the Humanities Advanced Fellowship for Research in Turkey (Postdoctorate/Fellowship) [900]
National Environmental Health Association Scholarship Fund (Graduate, Undergraduate/Scholarship) [4873]
National Federation of the Blind Educator of Tomorrow Award (Undergraduate/Scholarship) [4881]
National Greenhouse Manufacturers Association Scholarships (Undergraduate/Scholarship) [562]
National Heartburn Alliance NP Student Scholarships (Graduate/Scholarship) [269]
National Honor Roll Scholarships (Undergraduate/Scholarship) [1808]
National Huguenot Society Scholarships (Undergraduate/Scholarship) [4944]
National Institute of Health Undergraduate Scholarship Program (Undergraduate/Scholarship) [4949]
National Iranian American Council Fellowships (Graduate, Undergraduate/Fellowship) [4958]
National Italian American Bar Association Scholarships (Postgraduate/Scholarship) [4960]
National Judges Association Scholarships (Professional Development/Scholarship) [4965]
National Junior Horticultural Association Alumni Scholarships (Undergraduate/Scholarship) [4969]
National Junior Swine Association Outstanding Member Scholarships (Graduate/Scholarship) [4973]
National Kindergarten Alliance Graduate Scholarships (Graduate/Scholarship) [4978]
National Lesbian and Gay Journalists Association (NLGJA) Scholarships (Undergraduate/Scholarship) [6126]
National Medical Fellowships Need-Based Scholarships (Undergraduate/Scholarship) [4989]
National Organization of Italian-American Women Scholarships (All/Scholarship) [5000]
National Osteoporosis Foundation Research Grants (Doctorate, Graduate/Grant) [5004]
National Pathfinder Scholarships (Graduate, Undergraduate/Scholarship) [4889]
National Poultry and Food Distributors Association Scholarships (Undergraduate/Scholarship) [5013]
National Preservation Institute Scholarships (Other/Scholarship) [5015]
National Recreation and Park Association Diversity Scholarships (Undergraduate/Scholarship) [5028]
National Recycling Coalition Congress Scholarships (Undergraduate/Scholarship) [5030]
National Sculpture Society Scholarships (Undergraduate/Scholarship) [5038]
National Security Education Program Fellowships (Undergraduate/Fellowship) [7093]
National Security Technologies Engineering and Science Scholarships (Undergraduate/Scholarship) [5843]
National Slovak Society of the USA Scholarships (Undergraduate/Scholarship) [5044]
National Slovak Society of the USA Senior Scholarships (Undergraduate/Scholarship) [5045]
National Society of Accountants Scholarship Program (Undergraduate/Scholarship) [5047]
National Stroke Association Research Fellowships in Cerebrovascular Disease (Doctorate/Fellowship) [5098]
National Technical Honor Society Scholarships (Undergraduate/Scholarship) [5111]
National Women's Studies Association Lesbian Scholarships (Doctorate, Graduate/Scholarship) [5124]
Native American Charter High Schools After-the-Fires Scholarships (Undergraduate/Scholarship) [6210]
Native American Education Grants (Graduate, Undergraduate/Grant) [636]
Native American Leadership Education (NALE) Scholarships (Postdoctorate, Undergraduate/Scholarship) [2068]
Native Hawaiian Scholarships (Undergraduate/Scholarship) [3510]
Naval Reserve Association Scholarships (Undergraduate/Scholarship) [5136]
Navy, Army or Air Force ROTC Scholarship Program (Undergraduate/Scholarship) [2609]
NAWIC Founders Undergraduate Scholarships (Undergraduate/Scholarship) [4750]
The Nazareth Scholarships (Undergraduate/Scholarship) [5151]
NBMBAA Graduate Scholarship Programs (Graduate/Scholarship) [4761]
NBMBAA PhD Fellowship Programs (Doctorate/Fellowship) [4762]
N.C. Psychoanalytic Foundation Journalism Scholarships (Postgraduate/Scholarship) [7184]
NCBWL Scholarships (High School/Scholarship) [4611]
NCDXF Scholarships (Undergraduate/Scholarship) [845]
NCF Fort Dodge Animal Health Legacy Scholarships for Undergraduate Students (Undergraduate/Scholarship) [4791]
NCF Fort Dodge Animal Health Legacy Scholarships for Veterinary Students (Undergraduate/Scholarship) [4792]
NCOA Scholarships (Undergraduate/Scholarship) [5211]
NCTE Research Foundation Grants (Professional Development/Grant) [4826]
NDEOA Scholarships (Undergraduate/Scholarship) [4848]
H.N. Neal Memorial Scholarships (Undergraduate/Scholarship) [1898]
Nebraska Grain Sorghum Producers Association Scholarships (Undergraduate/Scholarship) [5157]
Nebraska Hospital Association Tuition Aid and Scholarships (Undergraduate/Scholarship) [5164]
Douglas J. Neeley Memorial Scholarships (Graduate, Undergraduate/Scholarship) [1672]
NEF Scholarships for Leadership (Doctorate/Scholarship) [5311]
Paul and Ruth Neidhold Business Scholarship (Undergraduate/Scholarship) [2477]
Edward J. Nell Memorial Scholarships in Journalism (Undergraduate/Scholarship) [5891]
Dave Nelsen Scholarships (Undergraduate/Scholarship) [4719]
Charles I. Nelson Endowed Scholarships (Undergraduate/Scholarship) [5603]
Bill Nelson Scholarship Endowment (Undergraduate/Scholarship) [5428]
Hubert A. Nelson Scholarships (Undergraduate/Scholarship) [2787]
NEMRA Educational Scholarship Foundation (Undergraduate/Scholarship) [4871]
Amelia and Emanuel Nessell Scholarships (Undergraduate/Scholarship) [2788]
Reverend John S. Nettled Scholarship (Undergraduate/Scholarship) [2358]
Networks Scholarships College of Business (Undergraduate/Scholarship) [3710]
Nevada Black Police Association Scholarships (Undergraduate/Scholarship) [5844]
Nevada Parent Teacher Association Scholarships (Undergraduate/Scholarship) [5845]
Roy G. Neville Fellowships (Doctorate,

Postdoctorate/Fellowship) [2112]
New Century Scholars Doctoral Scholarships (Postdoctorate/Scholarship) [1104]
New Century Scholars Research Grants (Doctorate/Grant) [1105]
New England Culinary Institute Scholarships (All/Scholarship) [2581]
New England FEMARA Scholarships (Undergraduate/Scholarship) [846]
New Hampshire Snowmobile Association Scholarships (Undergraduate/Scholarship) [5173]
New Jersey Psychological Association Scholarships for Minority Graduate Students (Postgraduate/Scholarship) [5184]
New Mexico Association for Bilingual Education Scholarships (Undergraduate/Scholarship) [5187]
New Mexico Manufactured Housing Association Scholarship Program (Undergraduate/Scholarship) [193]
New Opportunities Through Retraining Scholarship Fund (Undergraduate/Scholarship) [5361]
New Professional Reporter Grants (Professional Development/Grant) [4836]
New York Financial Writers' Associations Scholarships (Graduate, Undergraduate/Scholarship) [5189]
The New York Times College Scholarships (Undergraduate/Scholarship) [5195]
New York Water Environment Association Scholarships (Undergraduate/Scholarship) [5198]
Ted and Ruth Neward Scholarships (Graduate, Undergraduate/Scholarship) [6556]
Newcomer Supply Student Scholarships (Undergraduate/Scholarship) [5077]
Edsel Newman Scholarship (Undergraduate/Scholarship) [4228]
Newman University Scouting Scholarships (Undergraduate/Scholarship) [4864]
Alwin B. Newton Scholarships (Undergraduate/Scholarship) [968]
NFBPA/CDM Scholarships (Undergraduate/Scholarship) [4899]
NFDA Professional Women's Conference Scholarships (Undergraduate/Scholarship) [3152]
NFID Advanced Vaccinology Course Travel Grants (Postdoctorate/Grant) [4904]
NFPA/PACE Scholarships (Professional Development/Scholarship) [4886]
NFPA and Thomson West Scholarships (Undergraduate/Scholarship) [4887]
NFPA Youth Scholarships (Undergraduate/Scholarship) [4902]
NGPA Education Fund Scholarships (Undergraduate/Scholarship) [4911]
NHPGA Apprentice Scholarships (Undergraduate/Scholarship) [4422]
NHS National Scholarships (Undergraduate/Scholarship) [4939]
NIAF Scholarships - General Category I (Undergraduate/Scholarship) [4962]
NIAF Scholarships - General Category II (Undergraduate/Scholarship) [4963]
Donald E. Nichols Scholarships (Undergraduate/Scholarship) [969]
Gunnar Nicholson Endowed Scholarships (Undergraduate/Scholarship) [5604]
Herbert W. Nickens Medical Student Scholarships (Undergraduate/Scholarship) [1362]
Virginia Nicklas Scholarships (Undergraduate/Scholarship) [2658]
George A. Nielsen Public Investor Scholarships (Graduate, Undergraduate/Scholarship) [3267]
Mike Niemeyer Memorial Football Scholarships (Undergraduate/Scholarship) [5968]
Eric Niemitalo Scholarships in Earth and Environmental Science (Undergraduate/Scholarship) [6318]
Helen W. Nies Scholarships (Undergraduate/Scholarship) [2907]
The Nightingale Scholarships Award (Undergraduate/Scholarship) [2359]
Evelyn S. Nish Scholarships (Undergraduate/Scholarship) [6367]
Anderson Niskanen Scholarships (Undergraduate/Scholarship) [2789]
Nissan North America, Inc. Scholarships (Undergraduate/Scholarship) [624]
NJSA Visionary Leader Scholarships (Graduate/Scholarship) [4974]
NLBRA/Wrangler Academic Scholarships (Undergraduate/Scholarship) [4982]
NMIA Scholarship Program (Undergraduate/Scholarship) [4991]
NNF Scholarships Program (Graduate, Undergraduate/Scholarship) [376]
Leonard Noble Educational Scholarships (Other/Scholarship) [5078]
NOBLE Fellowship Program (All/Fellowship) [4993]
NOBLE Southern California Chapter Scholarship Program (Undergraduate/Scholarship) [4994]
Stuart L. Noderer Memorial Scholarships (Undergraduate/Scholarship) [6211]
George H. Nofer Scholarships for Law and Public Policy (Doctorate, Graduate/Scholarship) [1615]
Nolle Scholarships (Undergraduate/Scholarship) [240]
Helen Woodruff Nolop Scholarship in Audiology and Allied Fields (Graduate/Scholarship) [2696]
Nor' Easters Scholarships - Four-year Program (Undergraduate/Scholarship) [5214]
Nor' Easters Scholarships - Two-year Program (Undergraduate/Scholarship) [5215]
Norall Scholarships Trust (Undergraduate/Scholarship) [4229]
Arthur L. Norberg Travel Grants (All/Grant) [1583]
Norfolk Southern Foundation Scholarships (Undergraduate/Scholarship) [882]
Norfolk Southern Scholarships (Undergraduate/Scholarship) [7329]
Norkus Charitable Foundation Scholarships (Undergraduate/Scholarship) [2103]
Norm Manly - YMTA Maritime Educational Scholarships (Undergraduate/Scholarship) [7547]
North Carolina Association of Health Care Recruiters Scholarships (Undergraduate/Scholarship) [5234]
North Carolina Commercial Flower Growers Association Floriculture Scholarships (Undergraduate/Scholarship) [5236]
North Carolina Nursery and Landscape Association Horticulture Scholarships (Undergraduate/Scholarship) [5243]
North Carolina Vending Association Academic Scholarships (Undergraduate/Scholarship) [5247]
North Central (Region 9) Scholarships (Undergraduate/Scholarship) [6499]
North Dakota Division Scholarships (Undergraduate/Scholarship) [4517]
North Dakota Farmers Union Agricultural Studies Scholarships (Undergraduate/Scholarship) [5252]
North Dakota Farmers Union Co-op House Scholarships (Undergraduate/Scholarship) [5253]
North Dakota Farmers Union Scholarships (Undergraduate/Scholarship) [5254]
North Dakota Veterinary Medical Association Scholarships (Undergraduate/Scholarship) [5258]
North Florida Chapter Safety Education Scholarships (Graduate, Undergraduate/Scholarship) [1064]
North Las Vegas Firefighters - William J. Harnedy Memorial Scholarships (Undergraduate/Scholarship) [5846]
North Mecklenburg Teachers' Memorial Scholarships (Undergraduate/Scholarship) [3071]
North Ottawa Hospital Auxiliary Scholarships Fund (Undergraduate/Scholarship) [3295]
Michelle North Scholarships for Safety (Professional Development/Scholarship) [3522]
North Texas GIA Alumni Association Scholarships (Undergraduate/Scholarship) [3196]
Northampton County Medical Society Alliance Scholarships (Undergraduate/Scholarship) [5261]
NorthCoast Medical Scholarship Program (Postgraduate/Scholarship) [734]
Northeastern Illinois Chapter Scholarships (Graduate, Undergraduate/Scholarship) [1065]
Northeastern Ohio Chapter Scholarships - Alfred B. Glossbrenner and John Klusch Scholarships (Undergraduate/Scholarship) [1454]
Northern Arizona Native-American Foundation Scholarships (Undergraduate/Scholarship) [5269]
Northern California Chapter of HIMSS Scholarships (Other/Scholarship) [3518]
Northern Virginia Alumnae Chapter Scholarships (Undergraduate/Scholarship) [2659]
Eugene Northrup Scholarships (Undergraduate/Scholarship) [4208]
Northwest Community Center Scholarships (Undergraduate/Scholarship) [2478]
Northwest-Shoals Community College Academic Scholarships (Undergraduate/Scholarship) [5289]
Northwest-Shoals Community College Applied Technology Scholarships (Undergraduate/Scholarship) [5290]
Northwest-Shoals Community College Athletic Scholarships (Undergraduate/Scholarship) [5291]
Northwest-Shoals Community College Bank Independent Scholarships (Undergraduate/Scholarship) [5292]
Northwest-Shoals Community College Fine Arts Scholarships - Art (Undergraduate/Scholarship) [5293]
Northwest-Shoals Community College Fine Arts Scholarships - Drama (Undergraduate/Scholarship) [5294]
Northwest-Shoals Community College Fine Arts Scholarships - Music (Undergraduate/Scholarship) [5295]
Northwest-Shoals Community College High School Academic Scholarships (Undergraduate/Scholarship) [5296]
Northwest-Shoals Community College Independent Computer Scholarships (Undergraduate/Scholarship) [5297]
Northwest-Shoals Community College Student Activities Scholarships (Undergraduate/Scholarship) [5298]
Northwestern Mutual Financial Network Scholarships (Graduate, Undergraduate/Scholarship) [5642]
Vessa Notchev Fellowships (Graduate, Postdoctorate/Fellowship) [6341]
Notre Dame Club of Canton Scholarships (Undergraduate/Scholarship) [6747]
Novartis Pharmaceutical Corporation NP Student Scholarships (Graduate/Scholarship) [270]
Novo Nordisk NP Doctoral Education Scholarships (Doctorate/Scholarship) [271]
Mike and Flo Novovesky Scholarships (Undergraduate/Scholarship) [563]
Robert Noyce Scholarship Program (Undergraduate/Scholarship) [5565]
Noyce Scholarships for Secondary Math and Science Education (Undergraduate/Scholarship) [3711]
NPELRA Foundation Scholarships (Graduate/Scholarship) [5309]
NPM Program Scholarships (Undergraduate/Scholarship) [4727]
NSA Scholarship Program (Undergraduate/Scholarship) [5040]
NSF Pickwick Postdoctoral Research Fellowships (Postdoctorate/Fellowship) [5042]
NSHSS Academic Paper Awards (High School/Scholarship) [5070]
NSHSS National Scholar Awards (High School/Scholarship) [5071]
NSPF Board of Directors' Scholarship Awards (Other/Scholarship) [5103]
NSPF Scholarship Awards (Other/Scholarship) [5104]
NSPS Board of Governors Scholarships (Undergraduate/Scholarship) [489]
The NSPS Scholarships (Undergraduate/Scholarship) [490]
NSS Conservation Grants (All/Grant) [5088]
NSS Education Grants (All/Grant) [5089]
NSSA/NSCA Collegiate Scholarships (Undergraduate/Scholarship) [5093]
Nurseries Foundation Scholarship Awards (Undergraduate/Scholarship) [5385]
Nurseries Memorial Scholarship Awards (Graduate/Scholarship) [5386]
Nursing Scholarship Program (Undergraduate/Scholarship) [3512]
NW-SCC/American Cancer Society College Scholarships (Undergraduate/Scholarship) [5299]
NW-SCC American Legion Scholarships -

Florence/Lauderdale Post No. 11 *(Undergraduate/Scholarship)* [5300]
NWF's Women for Sustainable Development (WSD) Scholarships *(Undergraduate/Scholarship)* [6333]
NWSA Distinguished Fellowships *(All/Fellowship)* [5125]
NWSA Graduate Scholarships *(Graduate/Scholarship)* [5126]
NWSA Graduate Scholarships in Lesbian Studies *(Doctorate, Graduate/Fellowship)* [6127]
NYNEX Diversity Scholarship Awards *(Undergraduate/Scholarship)* [6128]
OBAP Fellowships - Airline Transport (ATP) *(Professional Development/Fellowship)* [5407]
OBAP Fellowships - Commercial *(Professional Development/Fellowship)* [5408]
OBAP Fellowships - Instructor rating (CFI/CFII/MEI) *(Professional Development/Fellowship)* [5409]
OBAP Fellowships - Multi-Engine *(Professional Development/Fellowship)* [5410]
OBAP General Scholarships *(All/Scholarship)* [5411]
Obrzut Ling Scholarships *(Undergraduate/Scholarship)* [5772]
Katharine H. Obye Scholarship Award *(Undergraduate/Scholarship)* [2479]
OCA Scholarships *(Undergraduate/Scholarship)* [5413]
Occupational Physicians Scholarship Fund *(Undergraduate/Scholarship)* [5313]
John O'Connor Memorial Scholarship Fund *(Undergraduate/Scholarship)* [5114]
Odd Fellows Lodge No. 8 Endowed Scholarships *(Undergraduate/Scholarship)* [4209]
Captain Jennifer Shafer Odom Memorial Scholarships - Children of Soldiers *(Undergraduate/Scholarship)* [1305]
Captain Jennifer Shafer Odom Memorial Scholarships - Spouses of Soldiers *(Undergraduate/Scholarship)* [1306]
Office Depot Scholarships *(Undergraduate/Scholarship)* [3569]
Ohio Association of Broadcaster's Kids Scholarships *(Undergraduate/Scholarship)* [5317]
Ohio Newspaper Association Minority Scholarships *(Undergraduate/Scholarship)* [5323]
Ohio Newspaper Association University Journalism Scholarships *(Undergraduate/Scholarship)* [5324]
Ohio Newspaper Association Women's Scholarships *(Undergraduate/Scholarship)* [5325]
Ohio Valley Chapter Scholarships *(Undergraduate/Scholarship)* [1455]
Ohio War Orphan Scholarships *(Undergraduate/Scholarship)* [7531]
Lawrence "Bud" Ohlman Memorial Scholarships *(Undergraduate/Scholarship)* [564]
O'Jays Scholarship Fund *(Undergraduate/Scholarship)* [6748]
OKAIDE Scholarships *(Undergraduate/Scholarship)* [5327]
Oklahoma City University Merit Scholarships *(Undergraduate/Scholarship)* [5330]
The Oklahoma State University at Okmulgee Scholarships *(Undergraduate/Scholarship)* [5548]
Robert B. Oliver ASNT Scholarships *(Undergraduate/Scholarship)* [1023]
Roy C. and Dorothy Jean Olson Memorial Scholarships *(Undergraduate/Scholarship)* [3876]
Olympia Tumwater Foundation Traditional Scholarships *(Undergraduate/Scholarship)* [5333]
Olympia Tumwater Foundation Transitional (non-traditional) Scholarships *(Undergraduate/Scholarship)* [5334]
O'Meara Foundation Scholarships *(Undergraduate/Scholarship)* [3485]
Omicron Nu Research Fellowships *(Postdoctorate/Fellowship)* [4054]
Eloise Pitts O'More Scholarships *(Undergraduate/Scholarship)* [2442]
Open Society Fellowships *(Professional Development/Fellowship)* [5347]
Opera Foundation Scholarships *(Professional Development/Scholarship)* [5349]
Operation Homefront Scholarships *(Undergraduate/Scholarship)* [5351]
Sheldon Oppenheim Memorial Scholarships *(Undergraduate/Scholarship)* [6129]
Frank Oppenheimer Scholarship Program *(Postgraduate/Scholarship)* [735]
Dwight D. Opperman Scholarships *(Undergraduate/Scholarship)* [2762]
Optimist Club Of Redlands - Ralph Maloof Scholarships *(Undergraduate/Scholarship)* [5969]
Optimist Club of Redlands - Virginia Elliott Scholarships *(Undergraduate/Scholarship)* [5970]
OPWA Educational Scholarships *(Undergraduate/Scholarship)* [5315]
Orange County Centennial Academic Scholarships *(Undergraduate/Scholarship)* [5362]
Orange County Centennial Arts Scholarships *(Undergraduate/Scholarship)* [5363]
Orange County Centennial Certification Scholarships *(Undergraduate/Scholarship)* [5364]
Orange County Tourism Council Scholarships *(Undergraduate/Scholarship)* [5365]
Order Sons of Italy Foundation General Scholarships *(Graduate, Undergraduate/Scholarship)* [5373]
Oregon Association of Nurseries Scholarship Program *(Undergraduate/Scholarship)* [5387]
Oregon Farm Bureau Memorial Scholarships *(Undergraduate/Scholarship)* [5393]
Oregon Logging Conference Scholarships *(Undergraduate/Scholarship)* [4210]
Doris Orenstein Memorial Convention Travel Grants *(All/Grant)* [1462]
Organization of American States Academic Scholarships *(Undergraduate/Scholarship)* [5400]
Organization of American States AOS-Placed Scholarships *(Undergraduate/Scholarship)* [5401]
Organization of American States Graduate Scholarships *(Undergraduate/Scholarship)* [5402]
Organization of American States Self-Placed Scholarships *(Undergraduate/Scholarship)* [5403]
The Deborah Orin-Eilbeck Scholarships *(Graduate/Scholarship)* [7410]
Orthopedic Foot and Ankle Fellowships *(Graduate/Fellowship)* [747]
The Kenneth J. Osborn Memorial Scholarships *(Undergraduate/Scholarship)* [1032]
Margaret E. Oser Scholarships for Women *(Undergraduate/Scholarship)* [5366]
OSU Gay, Lesbian, Bisexual and Transgender Alumni Society (PFLAG Scholarships) *(Undergraduate/Scholarship)* [6130]
OTA Research Grants *(Graduate/Grant)* [5417]
Ellis R. Ott Scholarships *(Graduate, Undergraduate/Scholarship)* [1037]
Ottawa Police 150th Anniversary Scholarships *(Undergraduate/Scholarship)* [1772]
Outstanding Undergraduate Scholarships (SOAR) *(Undergraduate/Scholarship)* [7106]
Outward Bound Leadership Scholarships for Educators *(Professional Development/Scholarship)* [5433]
Outward Bound Wilderness Leadership Awards *(High School, Professional Development/Award/Prize)* [5434]
Helen M. Overly Memorial Scholarships *(Undergraduate/Scholarship)* [7510]
Charles and Melva T. Owen Memorial Scholarships *(Undergraduate/Scholarship)* [4882]
Owner-Operator Independent Drivers Association Scholarships *(Undergraduate/Scholarship)* [5436]
Ozarks Division Scholarships *(Undergraduate/Scholarship)* [4518]
The Pac-10 Postgraduate Scholarships *(Graduate/Scholarship)* [5438]
PACE/Columbian Lawyers Association of Westchester County Endowed Scholarships *(Undergraduate/Scholarship)* [2332]
Pacific Legal Foundation Faculty Grants *(All/Grant)* [5443]
The Arthur J. Packard Memorial Scholarship Competition *(Undergraduate/Scholarship)* [614]
Dr. Nicholas Padis Memorial Graduate Scholarships *(Graduate/Scholarship)* [3533]
Laurie Page-Peck Scholarships Fund *(Undergraduate/Scholarship)* [1525]
Raymond E. Page Scholarships *(Undergraduate/Scholarship)* [985]
AFCEA General Emmett Paige Scholarships *(Undergraduate/Scholarship)* [1247]
Paleontological Society Student Research Grants *(Graduate, Undergraduate/Grant)* [405]
E. William Palmer Memorial Scholarships *(Graduate, Undergraduate/Scholarship)* [1673]
Dorothy D. Palmer Scholarship for the Study of Optimal Aging in Women *(Postdoctorate/Scholarship)* [5185]
Palo Verde High School Faculty Follies Scholarships *(Undergraduate/Scholarship)* [5847]
PAMA Foundation Scholarship Program *(Graduate, Undergraduate/Scholarship)* [5789]
The PanHellenic Scholarships *(Undergraduate/Scholarship)* [3525]
Panther Cafe Scholarships *(Undergraduate/Scholarship)* [5848]
Katharine Pantzer Senior Fellowships in the British Book Trades *(Professional Development/Fellowship)* [1696]
Paper Stock Industries Chapter of ISRI Scholarship Program *(Undergraduate/Scholarship)* [5452]
Paper Stock Industries/RRF Scholarships *(Undergraduate/Scholarship)* [5450]
Parapsycological Association Research Endowment *(All/Grant)* [5454]
Pardee Community Building Scholarships *(Undergraduate/Scholarship)* [5849]
Parents Scholarships *(Undergraduate/Scholarship)* [3676]
Joseph M. Parish Memorial Grants *(Undergraduate/Scholarship)* [928]
William Park Woodside Founder's Scholarships *(Undergraduate/Scholarship)* [4401]
Cissy McDaniel Parker Scholarships *(Undergraduate/Scholarship)* [2660]
E.U. Parker Scholarships *(Undergraduate/Scholarship)* [4883]
Parking Industry Institute Scholarship Program *(Undergraduate/Scholarship)* [5009]
Fitzroy and Mildred Parkinson Memorial Scholarships *(Undergraduate/Scholarship)* [3486]
Sylvia Parkinson Scholarships *(Undergraduate/Scholarship)* [3487]
PARMA Scholarships *(Undergraduate/Scholarship)* [5795]
The Paros-Digiquartz Scholarships *(Undergraduate/Scholarship)* [4314]
Elizabeth M. and Winchell M. Parson Scholarships *(Doctorate/Scholarship)* [997]
Partnership for Pediatric Epilepsy Research *(Doctorate/Grant)* [2874]
Patient Advocate Foundations Scholarships *(Undergraduate/Scholarship)* [5535]
James H. Patrenos Memorial Scholarships *(Undergraduate/Scholarship)* [6406]
Gail Patrick Charitable Trust Scholarships *(Undergraduate/Scholarship)* [2697]
Alice Conger Patterson Scholarships *(Undergraduate/Scholarship)* [7450]
Walter S. Patterson Scholarships *(All/Scholarship)* [1785]
Paul and Inger Friend 4-H Scholarships *(Undergraduate/Scholarship)* [6783]
Courtland Paul Scholarships *(Undergraduate/Scholarship)* [4125]
Ray, NORP and Katie, WOKTE Pautz Scholarships *(Undergraduate/Scholarship)* [847]
Kenyon T. Payne Outstanding Student Awards *(Undergraduate/Award/Prize)* [4501]
PB Rail Engineering Scholarships *(Undergraduate/Scholarship)* [883]
PCH Architects/Steven J. Lehnhof Memorial Architectural Scholarships *(Undergraduate/Scholarship)* [5971]
PDC Scholarships *(Undergraduate/Scholarship)* [1066]
PDF International Research Grants Program *(Postdoctorate/Grant)* [5533]
Chuck Peacock Memorial Scholarships *(Undergraduate/Scholarship)* [81]
Charles S. Pearce Scholarships *(Undergraduate/Prize, Scholarship)* [7264]
Minnie Pearl Scholarship Program *(Undergraduate/Scholarship)* [2802]
Pearman Family Scholarships *(Undergraduate/Scholarship)* [6212]
Robert L. Peaslee-Detroit Brazing and Soldiering

Division Scholarships (Undergraduate/Scholarship) [1168]
Laura Ann Peck Memorial Endowed Scholarships (Undergraduate/Scholarship) [4211]
Pediatric Endocrinology Nursing Society Academic Education Scholarships (Undergraduate/Scholarship) [5542]
Pediatric Endocrinology Nursing Society Continuing Education Scholarships (Undergraduate/Scholarship) [5543]
Peierls Rising Star Scholarship Program (Undergraduate/Scholarship) [3602]
Pellegrini Scholarships (Graduate, Undergraduate/Scholarship) [6830]
Margaret Pemberton Scholarships (Undergraduate/Scholarship) [1751]
Dorothy E. Hofmann Pembroke Scholarships (Undergraduate/Scholarship) [3488]
Robert B. and Dorothy Pence Scholarships (Undergraduate/Scholarship) [6667]
Penn-Bird Family Memorial Scholarships (Undergraduate/Scholarship) [5850]
Penndelphia Scholarships Foundation (Undergraduate/Scholarship) [5553]
Pennsylvania Association of Arson Investigators Scholarships (Undergraduate/Scholarship) [5555]
Pennsylvania Heartland Unit Scholarships (Undergraduate/Scholarship) [3545]
Pennsylvania Society of Professional Engineers Scholarships (Undergraduate/Scholarship) [5561]
Pension Real Estate Association Scholarships (Undergraduate/Scholarship) [5568]
PEO Educational Loan Funds (Graduate, Undergraduate/Loan) [5685]
Pepperdine University Armenian Student Scholarships (Undergraduate/Scholarship) [5605]
Pepperdine University Dean's Scholarships (Doctorate, Graduate/Scholarship) [5606]
Pepperdine University Diversity Scholarships (Doctorate, Graduate/Scholarship) [5607]
Pepperdine University Faculty Scholarships (Doctorate, Graduate/Scholarship) [5608]
Pepsi Escribe tu Futuro Scholarships (Undergraduate/Scholarship) [4154]
Pepsi Scholarships (Undergraduate/Scholarship) [615]
Pepsico Scholarships (Undergraduate/Scholarship) [7010]
Joe Perdue Scholarships (Undergraduate/Scholarship) [2253]
Joaquin Pereira Memorial Scholarships (Undergraduate/Scholarship) [4269]
Rudy Perez Songwriting Scholarships (Undergraduate/Scholarship) [948]
Peridian International, Inc./Rae L. Price, FASLA Scholarships (Undergraduate/Scholarship) [4126]
The A.W. Perigard Fund (Graduate, Undergraduate/Scholarship) [6581]
Sanky Perlowin Memorial Scholarships (Undergraduate/Scholarship) [2713]
Zoe Gore Perrin Scholarships (Undergraduate/Scholarship) [2661]
Eleanor Perry Memorial Endowed Scholarships (Undergraduate/Scholarship) [4212]
Chet and Jannett Perry Scholarships (Undergraduate/Scholarship) [6668]
Perry Township School Memorial Scholarship Fund (Undergraduate/Scholarship) [6749]
Jim Perry Vocational Scholarships (Undergraduate/Scholarship) [565]
Leonard M. Perryman Communications Scholarships for Ethnic Minority Students (Undergraduate/Scholarship) [6965]
Persian Language Study in Tehran (Doctorate, Graduate/Fellowship) [663]
Dr. Connell Persico Scholarships (Undergraduate/Scholarship) [6131]
Kate B. and Hall J. Peterson Fellowships (Doctorate/Fellowship) [306]
Lizette Peterson Homer Injury Prevention Grant Awards (Professional Development, Undergraduate/Grant) [6532]
Charles E. Peterson Research Senior Fellowships (Professional Development/Fellowship) [1529]
Steve Petix Journalism Scholarship (Undergraduate/Scholarship) [6213]
William H. and Lena M. Petree Scholarships (Undergraduate/Scholarship) [7451]
Silvio and Eugenio Petrini Grants (Professional Development/Grant) [3397]
Petroleum Packaging Council Scholarships (Undergraduate/Scholarship) [5620]
Jerome S. Petz, S.J., Scholarships (Undergraduate/Scholarship) [2763]
Chuck Pezzano Scholarships (Undergraduate/Scholarship) [1770]
Pfafftown Jaycees/Lynn Canada Memorial Scholarships (Undergraduate/Scholarship) [7452]
Dr. Harry V. Pfautz Memorial Scholarship Fund (Undergraduate/Scholarship) [3114]
Ruth Cook Pfautz Memorial Scholarship Fund (Undergraduate/Scholarship) [3115]
Pfizer Inc. 2007 NP Student Scholarships (Graduate/Scholarship) [272]
Pfizer Inc. Endowed Scholarships (Undergraduate/Scholarship) [4297]
Pfizer Minority Medical Journalism Scholarships (Postgraduate/Scholarship) [7185]
PFLAG/HATCH Youth Scholarship Foundation (Undergraduate/Scholarship) [6132]
Carl H. Pforzheimer, Jr., Research Grants (Graduate/Grant) [4057]
PGSF-GATF Scholarships (Graduate, Undergraduate/Scholarship) [31]
Pharmacy Faculty Fellowships in Community Pharmacy Practice (Postdoctorate/Fellowship) [583]
Pharmacy Faculty Fellowships in Geriatric Pharmacy/Geriatric Pharmaceutical Science (Postdoctorate/Fellowship) [584]
Pharmacy Faculty New Investigator Grants Program (Doctorate/Grant) [585]
Pharmacy Student Scholarship Program (Postdoctorate/Scholarship) [4687]
Pharmavite LLC NP Doctoral Education Scholarships (Doctorate/Scholarship) [273]
Marshall Phelps Athletic Memorial Scholarships (Undergraduate/Scholarship) [5972]
Phi Kappa Phi Emerging Scholar Awards (Undergraduate/Award/Prize) [5628]
Phi Kappa Phi Fellowships (Other/Fellowship) [5629]
Phi Kappa Sigma Need-Based Scholarships (Undergraduate/Scholarship) [5631]
Phi Kappa Sigma Participation-Based Scholarships (Undergraduate/Scholarship) [5632]
Phi Sigma Epsilon Innovation Scholarships (Graduate, Undergraduate/Scholarship) [5643]
Phi Sigma Epsilon Past National President Scholarships (Graduate, Undergraduate/Scholarship) [5644]
Phi Theta Kappa Scholarships (Undergraduate/Scholarship) [3712]
Phi Upsilon Omicron Candle Fellowships (Graduate/Fellowship) [5671]
Phi Upsilon Omicron Challenge Scholarships (Undergraduate/Scholarship) [5672]
Phi Upsilon Omicron Diamond Anniversary Fellowships (Graduate/Fellowship) [5673]
Phi Upsilon Omicron Founders Fellowships (Graduate/Fellowship) [5674]
Phi Upsilon Omicron Golden Anniversary Scholarships (Undergraduate/Scholarship) [5675]
Phi Upsilon Omicron Past Presidents Scholarships (Undergraduate/Scholarship) [5676]
Phi Upsilon Omicron Presidents Research Fellowships (Graduate/Fellowship) [5677]
Philip Morris USA Scholarships (Undergraduate/Scholarship) [7011]
Walter T. Philippy Scholarships (Undergraduate/Scholarship) [4423]
Phillip Morris USA Scholarships (Undergraduate/Scholarship) [7330]
Jamie Phillips Endowed Scholarships (Undergraduate/Scholarship) [5609]
Phillips Fund Grant for Native American Research (Graduate/Grant) [771]
Margaret E. Phillips Scholarships (Undergraduate/Scholarship) [7243]
William Philpott Scholarships (All/Scholarship) [1712]
Ed Phinney Commemorative Scholarships (Graduate, Undergraduate/Scholarship) [462]
Howard and Mildred Phoenix Scholarships (Undergraduate/Scholarship) [5973]
Pi Gamma Mu Scholarships (Graduate/Scholarship) [5691]
Mary Pickford Scholarships (Graduate/Scholarship) [1470]
Peter L. Picknelly Honorary Scholarships (Undergraduate/Scholarship) [449]
Pierce College Foundation Coca-Cola Scholarships (Undergraduate/Scholarship) [5693]
Pierce County Retired Teachers Scholarships (Undergraduate/Scholarship) [5694]
Ronald C. and Joyce Pierce Scholarships (Undergraduate/Scholarship) [1169]
Nicholas J. Piergrossi Scholarships (Undergraduate/Scholarship) [3489]
William Pigott Memorial Scholarship (Undergraduate/Scholarship) [2480]
David Pilon Scholarships for Training in Professional Psychology (Doctorate, Graduate/Scholarship) [802]
Pioneer Hi-Bred International Graduate Student Fellowships (Graduate/Fellowship) [2863]
Stephen D. Pisinski Memorial Scholarships (Undergraduate/Scholarship) [5875]
Christopher Pitkin Memorial Scholarships (Undergraduate/Scholarship) [4931]
Day Pitney LLP Scholarships (Undergraduate/Scholarship) [3490]
Peter George Pitsakis Memorial Scholarships (Undergraduate/Scholarship) [3534]
Pitsenbarger Awards (Undergraduate/Scholarship) [52]
Robert Pittman Scholarships (Undergraduate/Scholarship) [7186]
Pittsburg State University Distinguished Graduate Scholarships (Undergraduate/Scholarship) [7351]
Al Plamann Legacy Scholarship (Undergraduate/Scholarship) [1832]
Plane and Pilot Magazine/Garmin Scholarships (Undergraduate/Scholarship) [82]
TFC Edward A. Plank, Jr. Memorial Scholarship (Undergraduate/Scholarship) [2379]
Plastics Pioneers Association Scholarships (Graduate, Undergraduate/Scholarship) [6557]
Pleasant Hawaiian Holidays Scholarships (Undergraduate/Scholarship) [1086]
Plenum Scholarships (Doctorate/Scholarship) [6683]
Plumbing-Heating-Cooling Contractors Association Educational Foundation Massachusetts Auxiliary Scholarships (Undergraduate/Scholarship) [5702]
Plumbing-Heating-Cooling Contractors Association Educational Foundation Need-Based Scholarships (Undergraduate/Scholarship) [5703]
Plumbing-Heating-Cooling Contractors Association Educational Foundation Scholarships (Undergraduate/Scholarship) [5704]
PLUS Foundation Financial Aid Grants (Undergraduate/Scholarship) [5709]
PMCA Graduate Fellowships at Pennsylvania State University (Graduate/Fellowship) [5712]
David Pohl Scholarships (Graduate, Master's/Scholarship) [6952]
Point Foundation Scholarships (Graduate, Postgraduate, Undergraduate/Scholarship) [6133]
Daniel H. Pokorny Memorial Scholarship Awards (Undergraduate/Scholarship) [6019]
Donald and Susie Polden Dean's Scholarships (Undergraduate/Scholarship) [7124]
Police Explorer Scholarships Program (Undergraduate/Scholarship) [3018]
Polish American Club of North Jersey Scholarships (Undergraduate/Scholarship) [4093]
Polish National Alliance of Brooklyn, USA Scholarships (Undergraduate/Scholarship) [4094]
Political Leadership Scholarships (Undergraduate/Scholarship) [5773]
Roy H. Pollack Scholarships (Graduate, Master's/Scholarship) [6953]
Pollard-Bailey Scholarships (Undergraduate/Scholarship) [6214]
Stan and Leone Pollard Scholarships (Undergraduate/Scholarship) [1087]
David J. Pollini Scholarships (Undergraduate/Scholarship) [4424]
The Sidney M. Pols Scholarships

(Undergraduate/Scholarship) [5549]
Polsinelli Diversity Scholarships *(Undergraduate/Scholarship)* [7352]
Harold F. Polston Scholarships *(Undergraduate/Scholarship)* [1067]
Polymer Modifiers and Additives Division Scholarships *(Graduate, Undergraduate/Scholarship)* [6558]
Ken and Pam Pong Scholarships *(Undergraduate/Scholarship)* [7012]
Buster Pool Memorial Scholarships *(Undergraduate/Scholarship)* [2443]
Jim Poore Memorial Scholarship *(Undergraduate/Scholarship)* [3648]
Pope Scholarships Award *(Undergraduate/Scholarship)* [4425]
Port with No Borders Scholarships *(Undergraduate/Scholarship)* [6215]
Gail Porterfield Memorial Scholarships *(Undergraduate/Scholarship)* [5974]
Portland Area Business Association Scholarships *(Undergraduate/Scholarship)* [2890]
Portuguese-American Scholarship Foundation *(Undergraduate/Scholarship)* [5738]
Post 4137 Veterans Foundation Scholarships *(Undergraduate/Scholarship)* [5695]
Post-Doctoral or Sabbatical Fellowships *(Doctorate/Fellowship)* [4158]
Post-Doctoral Summer Travel-Research Grants *(Doctorate/Grant)* [3756]
Postdoctoral Research Fellowships *(Doctorate/Award/Prize)* [706]
Terry Linda Potter Scholarship Fund *(Undergraduate/Scholarship)* [3298]
Barbara Potter Scholarships *(All/Scholarship)* [741]
Erwin Potts Scholarships *(Undergraduate/Scholarship)* [7187]
George V. Powell Diversity Scholarships *(Undergraduate/Scholarship)* [4130]
Gerald Powell Scholarship *(Undergraduate/Scholarship)* [2360]
The Power to Continue Learning Scholarships *(Undergraduate/Scholarship)* [5975]
Powers-Knapp Scholarships *(Undergraduate/Scholarship)* [7266]
Master Sergeant Neal E. Powers Memorial Scholarships *(Undergraduate/Scholarship)* [59]
Practising Law Institute Law Student Scholarships *(Undergraduate/Scholarship)* [5742]
Lou and Carole Prato Sports Reporting Scholarships *(Undergraduate/Scholarship)* [1400]
Praxair International Scholarships *(Undergraduate/Scholarship)* [1170]
Presbyterian Association of Musicians Scholarships *(Other/Scholarship)* [5744]
Presidents Scholarships *(Undergraduate/Scholarship)* [3737]
Charles C. Price Fellowships in Polymer History *(Doctorate, Postdoctorate/Fellowship)* [2113]
Judith McManus Price Scholarships *(Graduate, Undergraduate/Scholarship)* [780]
Rae L. Price Scholarships *(Undergraduate/Scholarship)* [986]
William H. Price Scholarships *(Graduate, Undergraduate/Scholarship)* [6699]
Pride Foundation Regional Scholarships *(Undergraduate/Scholarship)* [5774]
Pride Foundation Scholarships *(Undergraduate/Scholarship)* [6134]
Eric Primavera Memorial Scholarships *(Undergraduate/Scholarship)* [3008]
Josef Princ Memorial Scholarships *(Undergraduate/Scholarship)* [5851]
R.M. Princ Scholarships *(Undergraduate/Scholarship)* [5852]
Private High School Awards *(Undergraduate/Award/Prize)* [1211]
Miguel Pro Scholarships *(Undergraduate/Scholarship)* [7532]
Procida Tile Importers Scholarships *(Undergraduate/Scholarship)* [5853]
Procter and Gamble Complex PE Scholars Grant *(Undergraduate/Award/Prize)* [751]
Producers Academy Scholarships *(All/Scholarship)* [2543]
Progress Lane Scholarships *(Undergraduate/Scholarship)* [2380]
Progressive Dairy Producers Award *(All/Grant)* [4841]
Project Red Flag Academic Scholarships for Women with Bleeding Disorders *(Undergraduate/Scholarship)* [4932]
Prospective Secondary Teacher Course Work Scholarships *(Postgraduate/Scholarship)* [4830]
Prostart National Certificate of Achievement Scholarships *(Undergraduate/Scholarship)* [3617]
Providence Alaska Medical Center Auxiliary Scholarships *(Undergraduate/Scholarship)* [7035]
ProWorld Study Abroad Scholarships *(Undergraduate/Scholarship)* [3256]
Peter DeWitt Pruden and Phyliss Harrill Pruden Scholarships *(Undergraduate/Scholarship)* [7188]
Neil Pruitt, Sr. Memorial Scholarships *(Undergraduate/Scholarship)* [4814]
Pryor Graduate Fellowships *(Graduate/Fellowship)* [241]
Cheryl White Pryor Memorial Scholarships *(Undergraduate/Scholarship)* [2662]
PSAI Scholarship Funds *(Undergraduate/Scholarship)* [5735]
The PSSC Legacy Fund *(Graduate, Undergraduate/Scholarship)* [6582]
Public Agency Training Council Criminal Justice Scholarships *(Undergraduate/Scholarship)* [254]
Public Education Foundation Opportunity Scholarships *(Undergraduate/Scholarship)* [5854]
Public Employee Retirement Research and Administration Scholarships *(Graduate/Scholarship)* [3268]
Public Interest Scholarships *(Undergraduate/Scholarship)* [1816]
Duane V. Puerde Memorial Scholarship *(Undergraduate/Scholarship)* [2381]
Puerto Rican Bar Association Scholarships *(Undergraduate/Scholarship)* [5884]
Puget Sound Chapter Scholarships *(Undergraduate/Scholarship)* [1512]
Puget Sound LGBT Leadership Scholarships Fund *(Undergraduate/Scholarship)* [6135]
Eugene C. Pulliam Fellowships for Editorial Writing *(All/Fellowship)* [6337]
Pulliam/Kilgore Freedom of Information Internships *(Undergraduate/Internship)* [6569]
John Purfield Endowed Scholarships *(Undergraduate/Scholarship)* [5610]
Elizabeth Pusey Scholarship *(Undergraduate/Scholarship)* [2382]
The Henley Putnam University Scholarships *(Professional Development/Scholarship)* [3805]
Davis Putter Scholarships Fund *(Undergraduate/Scholarship)* [6136]
QCWA Memorial Scholarships *(Undergraduate/Scholarship)* [5888]
Qualcomm San Diego Science, Technology, Engineering and Mathematics Scholarships *(Undergraduate/Scholarship)* [6216]
Quality Initiative Grant-in-Aid *(Doctorate, Graduate/Grant)* [951]
Michael J. Quill Scholarships *(Undergraduate/Scholarship)* [6896]
Salvatore E. Quinci Foundation Scholarships *(Undergraduate/Scholarship)* [4933]
Bob Quincy Scholarships *(Undergraduate/Scholarship)* [7189]
RA Consulting Service Maria Riley Scholarships *(Graduate, Undergraduate/Scholarship)* [4900]
Dr. J. Glenn Radcliffe Memorial Scholarships *(Undergraduate/Scholarship)* [6784]
Dr. Sidney Rafal Memorial Scholarships *(Undergraduate/Scholarship)* [3491]
Rain Bird Intelligent Use of Water Scholarships *(Undergraduate/Scholarship)* [4127]
Rain Bird Scholarships *(Undergraduate/Scholarship)* [987]
Rainwater Family Scholarships *(Undergraduate/Scholarship)* [4983]
Tom D. Ralls Memorial Scholarships *(Professional Development/Scholarship)* [3020]
Rama Scholarships for the American Dream *(Graduate, Undergraduate/Scholarship)* [616]
Raul Ramirez Memorial Scholarships *(Undergraduate/Scholarship)* [5976]
Michael A. Ramnes Professional Scholarships *(Professional Development/Scholarship)* [1224]
Rancho Bernardo/Smith Scholarships *(Undergraduate/Scholarship)* [6217]
Herbert W. Rand Fellowships and Scholarships *(Undergraduate/Scholarship)* [4298]
Newell S. Rand Jr. Memorial Scholarships *(Undergraduate/Scholarship)* [5460]
Helen F. "Jerri" Rand Memorial Scholarships *(Undergraduate/Scholarship)* [2509]
Jeannette Rankin Scholarships *(Undergraduate/Scholarship)* [5897]
General John Paul Ratay Educational Grants *(Undergraduate/Grant)* [4531]
Ratcliffe Hicks School of Agriculture Heritage Scholarships *(Undergraduate/Scholarship)* [3492]
V. Duane Rath Graduate Research Fellowships *(Doctorate, Graduate, Postdoctorate/Fellowship)* [3025]
Dr. Mark Rathke Family Scholarships *(Undergraduate/Scholarship)* [2790]
James K. Rathmell Jr. Scholarships *(Undergraduate/Scholarship)* [566]
Ratner and Sugarmon Scholarships *(Undergraduate/Scholarship)* [7125]
Carol A. Ratza Memorial Scholarships *(Undergraduate/Scholarship)* [3365]
Dennis Raveling Scholarships *(Undergraduate/Scholarship)* [1862]
Lenny Ravich "Shalom" Scholarships *(All/Scholarship)* [1367]
Rawley Silver Award for Excellence *(Graduate/Scholarship)* [314]
Mary C. Rawlins Scholarships *(Undergraduate/Scholarship)* [3493]
Raytheon Scholarship Program *(Undergraduate/Scholarship)* [5899]
Ronald Reagan College Leaders Scholarship Program *(Undergraduate/Scholarship)* [5687]
Rechsteiner Family Scholarship Fund *(Undergraduate/Scholarship)* [2971]
Redlands Area Interfaith Council Scholarships *(Undergraduate/Scholarship)* [5977]
Redlands Community Scholarship Foundation Scholarships *(Undergraduate/Scholarship)* [5978]
Redlands Council PTA - Dorathy Jolley Memorial Scholarships *(Undergraduate/Scholarship)* [5979]
Redlands Footlighters, Inc. - Merle and Peggy Williams Scholarships *(Undergraduate/Scholarship)* [5980]
Redlands High School Academic Decathalon Scholarships *(Undergraduate/Scholarship)* [5981]
Redlands High School Boy's Varsity Volleyball Scholarships *(Undergraduate/Scholarship)* [5982]
Redlands High School Class of 1957 *(Undergraduate/Scholarship)* [5983]
Redlands High School Drama Boosters Award *(Undergraduate/Scholarship)* [5984]
Redlands High School Girls' Volleyball Boosters Scholarship Awards *(Undergraduate/Scholarship)* [5985]
Redlands High School Mock Trial Scholarships *(Undergraduate/Scholarship)* [5986]
Redlands High School-PTSA Scholarships *(Undergraduate/Scholarship)* [5987]
Redlands High School Soccer Boosters Scholarship Awards *(Undergraduate/Scholarship)* [5988]
Redlands High School Softball Booster Scholarship Awards *(Undergraduate/Scholarship)* [5989]
Redlands High School Speech Boosters Scholarship Awards *(Undergraduate/Scholarship)* [5990]
Redlands High School Spiritleaders Scholarships *(Undergraduate/Scholarship)* [5991]
Redlands High School Terrier Band Boosters Club Scholarships *(Undergraduate/Scholarship)* [5992]
Redlands High School Vocal Music Boosters Scholarship Awards *(Undergraduate/Scholarship)* [5993]
Redlands Morning Kiwanis Club Foundation Scholarships *(Undergraduate/Scholarship)* [5994]
Redlands Noon Kiwanis Club Foundation Scholarships *(Undergraduate/Scholarship)* [5995]
Redlands Noon Kiwanis Club - Martin and Dorothy Munz Scholarships *(Undergraduate/Scholarship)* [5996]
Redlands Rotary Club - Donald C. Anderson Scholarships *(Undergraduate/Scholarship)* [5997]
Redlands Rotary Club - Ernest L. Cronemeyer Me-

morial Scholarships *(Undergraduate/Scholarship)* [5998]
Redlands Rotary Club Foundation Discretionary Scholarships *(Undergraduate/Scholarship)* [5999]
Redlands Teachers Association Scholarships *(Undergraduate/Scholarship)* [6000]
Sarah Rebecca Reed Scholarships *(Graduate/Scholarship)* [1637]
Vern W. Reeder Memorial Scholarships *(Undergraduate/Scholarship)* [3574]
The Reese Fellowships *(Doctorate/Fellowship)* [307]
Bob Reeve Professional Aviation Management Scholarships *(Undergraduate/Scholarship)* [127]
REFORMA Scholarship Program *(Graduate/Scholarship)* [6016]
Marjorie Usher Regan Scholarships *(Undergraduate/Scholarship)* [7190]
Mark A. Reid Memorial Scholarship Grant *(Undergraduate/Scholarship)* [2481]
Ida and May Reilly Graduate Scholarships *(Doctorate, Graduate/Scholarship)* [935]
Henry J. Reilly Memorial Scholarships - For Freshmen in College *(Undergraduate/Scholarship)* [6023]
Henry J. Reilly Memorial Scholarships - For Graduating High School Seniors *(Undergraduate/Scholarship)* [6024]
Henry J. Reilly Memorial Scholarships - For Sophomores and Juniors in College *(Undergraduate/Scholarship)* [6025]
Henry J. Reilly Memorial Scholarships - Graduate Program *(Graduate, Professional Development/Scholarship)* [6026]
George Reinke Scholarships *(Undergraduate/Scholarship)* [1088]
The Remington Club Scholarships *(Undergraduate/Scholarship)* [6218]
REMSA Scholarships *(Undergraduate/Scholarship)* [884]
Betty Rendel Scholarships *(Undergraduate/Scholarship)* [4890]
Don Renschler Scholarships *(Graduate/Scholarship)* [5775]
Bertha and Byron L. Reppert Scholarship Fund *(Undergraduate/Scholarship)* [3116]
Republic Services Environmental Studies Scholarships *(Undergraduate/Scholarship)* [5855]
Research Fellowships in Iranian Studies (Resident Director-Tehran) *(Doctorate, Graduate/Fellowship)* [664]
Research Grants in Comparative Studies of Modern Turkey *(Graduate, Postdoctorate/Grant)* [3757]
Research Grants in Speech Science *(Doctorate/Grant)* [1106]
Reserve Officers Training Corps (ROTC) Scholarships *(Undergraduate/Scholarship)* [7267]
Resistance Welder Manufacturers' Association Scholarships *(Undergraduate/Scholarship)* [1171]
Retail Chapter Scholarship Awards *(Undergraduate/Scholarship)* [5388]
Retired League Postmasters Scholarship Program *(Undergraduate/Scholarship)* [6032]
Dr. Felix H. Reyler Memorial Scholarships *(Undergraduate/Scholarship)* [2599]
Nike Reynolds Journalism Scholarships *(Undergraduate/Scholarship)* [1401]
Janet Reynoldson Memorial Scholarships *(Undergraduate/Scholarship)* [2764]
Lori Rhett Memorial Scholarships *(Undergraduate/Scholarship)* [4682]
John J. and Elizabeth Rhodes Scholarships *(Graduate, Undergraduate/Scholarship)* [1674]
Rice-Cullimore Scholarships *(Graduate/Scholarship)* [998]
Haynes Rice Scholarships *(Doctorate, Graduate, Undergraduate/Scholarship)* [4717]
Ben C. Rich Memorial Scholarships *(Graduate, Undergraduate/Scholarship)* [1675]
Barbara Hagan Richards Scholarships *(Undergraduate/Scholarship)* [2444]
James Edward "Bill" Richards Scholarships *(Undergraduate/Scholarship)* [2445]
Philip Guy Richardson Memorial Scholarship *(Undergraduate/Scholarship)* [3986]
Frank J. Richter Scholarships *(Graduate, Undergraduate/Scholarship)* [395]
Howard B. Rickard Scholarships *(Undergraduate/Scholarship)* [4884]
Jasper Ridge Restoration Fellowships Jasper Ridge Biological Preserve *(Graduate, Postdoctorate/Fellowship)* [2816]
Donald Riebhoff Memorial Scholarships *(Undergraduate/Scholarship)* [851]
Rieser Fellowships *(Undergraduate/Fellowship)* [1804]
Ameen Rihani Scholarship Program *(Undergraduate/Scholarship)* [1193]
Susan E. Riley Scholarships *(Undergraduate/Scholarship)* [2663]
Fauneil J. Rinn Scholarships *(Undergraduate/Scholarship)* [6394]
Marsh Risk Consulting Scholarships *(Undergraduate/Scholarship)* [1069]
Paul H. Rittle Sr. Memorial Scholarships *(Professional Development/Scholarship)* [3751]
Jean Wiggin Roach Scholarships *(Undergraduate/Scholarship)* [2664]
Clifford Roberts Graduate Fellowships *(Doctorate/Fellowship)* [2842]
Eugene L. Roberts Jr. Prize *(Undergraduate/Prize)* [7191]
Liz Roberts Memorial Scholarships *(Undergraduate/Scholarship)* [6001]
George A. Roberts Scholarships *(Undergraduate/Scholarship)* [4402]
David G. Robinson Arts Scholarships *(Undergraduate/Scholarship)* [6670]
Isador M. Robinson Endowment Scholarships *(Undergraduate/Scholarship)* [2765]
Jackie Robinson Foundation Minority Scholarship *(Undergraduate/Scholarship)* [637]
Helen M. Robinson Grants *(Doctorate/Grant)* [3890]
Jerry Robinson Inweld Corporation Scholarships *(Undergraduate/Scholarship)* [1172]
Claude Robinson Scholarships *(Undergraduate/Scholarship)* [4975]
Jackie Robinson Scholarships *(Undergraduate/Scholarship)* [6049]
Nell Bryant Robinson Scholarships *(Undergraduate/Scholarship)* [5678]
August M. Rocco Scholarship Fund *(Undergraduate/Scholarship)* [6750]
Rockford Area Habitat for Humanity College Scholarships *(Undergraduate/Scholarship)* [2482]
Rockford Chapter Daughters of the American Revolution Memorial Scholarships *(Undergraduate/Scholarship)* [2483]
Rockin' Christmas Fund Scholarships *(Undergraduate/Scholarship)* [6671]
Rockwell Collins Scholarships *(Undergraduate/Scholarship)* [83]
Rocky Mountain Coal Mining Institute Engineering/Geology Scholarships *(Undergraduate/Scholarship)* [6051]
Rocky Mountain Coal Mining Institute Technical Scholarships *(Undergraduate/Scholarship)* [6052]
Rocky Mountain Research Fellowships *(Graduate/Fellowship)* [6056]
R.O.E.A. Dumitru Golea Goldy-Gemu Scholarships *(Undergraduate/Scholarship)* [913]
ROFY Scholarships *(Undergraduate/Scholarship)* [5901]
Kimberly Marie Rogers Memorial Scholarship Fund *(Undergraduate/Scholarship)* [2972]
Joseph Wood Rogers Memorial Scholarships *(Undergraduate/Scholarship)* [6319]
Kenneth Rogers Memorial Scholarships *(Undergraduate/Scholarship)* [4213]
Mary Stuart Rogers Scholarships *(Undergraduate/Scholarship)* [7415]
Richard C. Rolfs Scholarships *(Undergraduate/Scholarship)* [5776]
Mary Louise Roller Panhellenic Scholarships *(Undergraduate/Scholarship)* [5223]
Ronald McDonald House Charities African American Future Achievers Scholarships *(Undergraduate/Scholarship)* [4407]
Ronald McDonald House Charities of Hispanic Heritage *(Undergraduate/Scholarship)* [4408]
Ronald McDonald House Charities Scholarships *(Undergraduate/Scholarship)* [4409]
Ronald McDonald House Charities Scholarships in Asia *(Undergraduate/Scholarship)* [4410]
Charles and Ruth Ronin Memorial Scholarships *(Undergraduate/Scholarship)* [6002]
Dorothy Worden Ronken Scholarships *(Graduate/Scholarship)* [2698]
Roofing Industry Alliance for Progress Scholarships *(Graduate, Undergraduate/Scholarship)* [6058]
Roofing Industry Scholarships *(Graduate, Undergraduate/Scholarship)* [5035]
Alice W. Rooke Scholarships *(Undergraduate/Scholarship)* [3494]
Roothbert Fund Scholarships *(Undergraduate/Scholarship)* [6060]
ROP - Ambassadors Scholarships *(Undergraduate/Scholarship)* [6003]
ROP - Rob Bruce Memorial Scholarships *(Undergraduate/Scholarship)* [6004]
Barnes W. Rose, Jr. and Eva Rose Nichol Scholarship Fund *(Undergraduate/Scholarship)* [194]
Florence C. Rose and S. Meryl Rose Scholarships *(Undergraduate/Scholarship)* [4299]
Dr. Wayne F. Rose Scholarship Fund *(Undergraduate/Scholarship)* [2973]
Ollie Rosenberg Educational Trust *(Undergraduate/Scholarship)* [3117]
Rosenberg-Ibarra Scholarships *(Undergraduate/Scholarship)* [5777]
Ollie Rosenberg Scholarship Travel Fund *(Undergraduate/Scholarship)* [3118]
Mandell and Lester Rosenblatt and Robert N. Herbert Undergraduate Scholarships *(Undergraduate/Scholarship)* [6519]
Rosenthal Bar Exam Scholarships *(Undergraduate/Scholarship)* [1817]
Jean and Tom Rosenthal Scholarship Program *(Undergraduate/Scholarship)* [2520]
Marty Rosness Student Scholarships *(Undergraduate/Scholarship)* [1204]
Bettsy Ross Educational Fund *(All, Professional Development/Scholarship)* [5212]
Ross-Fahey Scholarships *(Postgraduate/Scholarship)* [4683]
Dorothy M. Ross Memorial Scholarships *(Undergraduate/Scholarship)* [1560]
Ross Trust Graduate Student Scholarships *(Graduate/Scholarship)* [517]
The Rotary Club of Cape Coral Goldcoast Scholarships Fund *(Undergraduate/Scholarship)* [2055]
The Rotary Club of Rancho Bernardo Sunrise Abraxas Student Scholarships *(Undergraduate/Scholarship)* [6219]
The Rotary Foundation Ambassadorial Scholarships *(Undergraduate/Scholarship)* [6062]
Bernard Rotberg Memorial Scholarships *(Undergraduate/Scholarship)* [4031]
Edward S. Roth Manufacturing Engineering Scholarships *(Graduate, Undergraduate/Scholarship)* [6500]
Isaac Roth Newspaper Carrier Scholarships Program *(Undergraduate/Scholarship)* [5182]
Marjorie Roy Rothermel Scholarship *(Graduate/Scholarship)* [999]
Routh Student Research Grants *(Undergraduate/Grant)* [6533]
Rowling, Dold and Associates LLP Scholarships *(Undergraduate/Scholarship)* [2833]
Royal Palm Audobon Society Environmental Fellowships *(Postgraduate/Fellowship)* [2998]
Royce-Osborn Minority Scholarship Program *(Undergraduate/Scholarship)* [1042]
RPA Scholarships *(Undergraduate/Scholarship)* [6028]
RSDSA Research Grants *(Postdoctorate, Professional Development/Grant)* [6014]
The RTKL Traveling Fellowships *(Undergraduate/Fellowship)* [310]
Rubber Division American Chemical Society Scholarships *(Undergraduate/Scholarship)* [6079]
Mike Ruben Scholarships *(Undergraduate/Scholarship)* [5517]
Rubinstein Family Scholarships *(Undergraduate/Scholarship)* [6220]
William Rucker Greenwood Scholarships *(Graduate, Undergraduate/Scholarship)* [1513]
Lawrence E. & Mabel Jackson Rudberg Scholarships *(Undergraduate/Scholarship)* [2791]

Joe Rudd Scholarships (Undergraduate/Scholarship) [6054]
Matthew A. Runci, MJSA Scholarships (Undergraduate/Scholarship) [3197]
Anna M. Rundguist Memorial Scholarship (Undergraduate/Scholarship) [3378]
Damon Runyon Cancer Research Foundation Fellowships (Postdoctorate/Fellowship) [6081]
Damon Runyon Clinical Investigator Awards (Postdoctorate/Fellowship) [6082]
Damon Runyon-Rachleff Innovation Awards (Postdoctorate/Fellowship) [6083]
Ruppert Educational Grant Program (Undergraduate/Scholarship) [6395]
Rural Telephone Company Scholarships (Undergraduate/Scholarship) [6085]
Hermann G. Rusch Scholarships (Professional Development/Scholarship) [531]
Norman K. Russell Scholarships (Graduate/Scholarship) [5002]
Michael A. Russo Memorial Scholarships (Undergraduate/Scholarship) [6005]
The Anthony C. Russo Scholarships (Graduate/Scholarship) [5026]
Lucile Rust Scholarships (Undergraduate/Scholarship) [5679]
Michael Clarkson Ryan Memorial Scholarships (Graduate, Undergraduate/Scholarship) [1676]
Deborah Jean Rydberg Memorial Scholarship (Undergraduate/Scholarship) [2484]
Jeanne Graves Ryland Scholarships (Undergraduate/Scholarship) [2665]
Charles A. Ryskamp Research Fellowships (Doctorate/Fellowship) [511]
Sacks For CF Scholarships (All/Scholarship) [2589]
Julie Anne Sadlier Memorial Scholarships (Undergraduate/Scholarship) [2666]
Ruth Sager Scholarships (Undergraduate/Scholarship) [4300]
SAH Study Tour Fellowships (Doctorate/Fellowship) [6429]
Virginia Hartford Saharov Memorial Scholarships (Undergraduate/Scholarship) [2667]
Saint Andrews Scholarships (Undergraduate/Scholarship) [6150]
St. James Armenian Church Memorial Scholarships (Undergraduate/Scholarship) [1290]
St. Louis Division Scholarships (Undergraduate/Scholarship) [4519]
St. Stephen A.M.E. Allison E. Fisher Book Awards (Undergraduate/Scholarship) [2985]
Saint Vincent College Eagle Scout Scholarships (Undergraduate/Scholarship) [4865]
Saints Cyril and Methodius Scholarships (Undergraduate/Scholarship) [6088]
SAJA Journalism Scholarships (Undergraduate/Scholarship) [6608]
Casey Sakir Point Scholarships (Graduate, Undergraduate/Scholarship) [5726]
Joseph and Amelia Saks Scholarship Fund (Undergraduate/Scholarship) [2361]
Sakura Finetek Student Scholarships (Undergraduate/Scholarship) [5079]
Jane Salanky-Onzik Scholarship Fund (Undergraduate/Scholarship) [2974]
Bill Salerno, W2ONV, Memorial Scholarships (Undergraduate/Scholarship) [852]
Sales and Marketing Executives International Scholarships (Graduate, Undergraduate/Scholarship) [5645]
The Sallie Mae 911 Education Fund (Undergraduate/Scholarship) [6157]
Marie V. Saltwick Scholarships (Undergraduate/Scholarship) [2792]
Henry Salvatori Scholarships (Undergraduate/Scholarship) [5374]
Samalot - Sebastian Scholarship Fund (High School/Scholarship) [2600]
The Walter Samek III Memorial Scholarship Fund (Undergraduate/Scholarship) [2402]
Margaret Jerome Sampson Scholarships (Undergraduate/Scholarship) [5680]
Samsung American Legion Scholarships (Undergraduate/Scholarship) [697]
San Diego City College Study Abroad Scholarships (Undergraduate/Scholarship) [6221]
The San Diego Foundation Community Scholarship II (Undergraduate/Scholarship) [6222]
The San Diego Foundation Community Scholarships I (Undergraduate/Scholarship) [6223]
San Diego National Bank Scholarships (Undergraduate/Scholarship) [6224]
San Diego Pathways to College Scholarships (Undergraduate/Scholarship) [6225]
San Diego Regional Aviation Association Scholarships (Undergraduate/Scholarship) [6226]
San Pasqual Academy Scholarships (Undergraduate/Scholarship) [6227]
Barbara Sanchez Scholarships (Undergraduate/Scholarship) [6443]
Sand Hill Scholars Program (Undergraduate/Scholarship) [6397]
Bill Sanderson Aviation Maintenance Technician Scholarship (Professional Development/Scholarship) [3523]
SAPA Scholarships (Undergraduate/Scholarship) [6408]
Bert Saperstein Communication Scholarships (Undergraduate/Scholarship) [6246]
Saratoga County Bar Association Law Student Scholarships (All/Scholarship) [6248]
Frank Sarli Memorial Scholarships (Undergraduate/Scholarship) [4837]
Saskatchewan Trucking Association Scholarships (Undergraduate/Scholarship) [6250]
Roger C. Sathre Memorial Scholarship Fund (Undergraduate/Scholarship) [3649]
Malini E. Sathyadev Memorial Scholarships (Undergraduate/Scholarship) [6228]
Satter Human Rights Fellowships (Graduate/Fellowship) [3506]
Curtis M. Saulsbury Scholarship Fund (Undergraduate/Scholarship) [2395]
Savatori Fellowships (Graduate/Fellowship) [3773]
Save Mart Legacy Scholarships (Undergraduate/Scholarship) [1833]
John A. Savoy Scholarship Fund (Undergraduate/Scholarship) [2975]
Savvy Student Traveler Grant Program (Undergraduate/Grant) [752]
SAWE Scholarships (Undergraduate/Scholarship) [6424]
Mark Dauglas Sawyer Memorial Scholarship (High School/Scholarship) [2362]
Bill Sawyer Memorial Scholarships (Undergraduate/Scholarship) [4214]
SBA Four-Year Scholarships Program (Undergraduate/Scholarship) [6702]
SBA One-Year Scholarships Program (Undergraduate/Scholarship) [6703]
SC and R Foundation Grant Program (Undergraduate/Grant) [6686]
SC and R Foundation Scholarships (Undergraduate/Scholarship) [6687]
Leslie and Mary Ella Scales Memorial Scholarship (Undergraduate/Scholarship) [2363]
Edith Scandlyn/Sammie Lynn Scandlyn Puett Memorial Scholarships (Undergraduate/Scholarship) [2668]
SCDAA Post-Doctoral Research Fellowships (Doctorate/Fellowship) [6328]
Mary Turnbull Schacht Memorial Scholarships (Undergraduate/Scholarship) [6368]
David W. Schacht Native American Student Scholarship (Undergraduate/Scholarship) [1630]
Schaible Health Care Services Scholarships (Undergraduate/Scholarship) [6847]
Abe Schecter Graduate Scholarships (Postgraduate/Scholarship) [1402]
Scheduler and Dispatchers Scholarships (Professional Development/Scholarship) [4781]
William C. Scheetz Family Scholarships (Graduate, Undergraduate/Scholarship) [1677]
Robert C. and Margaret A. Schikora Scholarships (Undergraduate/Scholarship) [6672]
Esther Schlundt Memorial Scholarships (Undergraduate/Scholarship) [3694]
Julie Schmid Research Scholarships (All/Scholarship) [1475]
Ronald L. Schmied Scholarships (Professional Development, Undergraduate/Grant) [3388]
Prof. George Schneider, Jr. Manufacturing Technology Education Scholarships (Undergraduate/Scholarship) [6501]
Richard J. Schnell Memorial Scholarship (Postdoctorate/Scholarship) [2485]
Lillian P. Schoephoerster Scholarships (Undergraduate/Scholarship) [5681]
Scholarship Challenge Flight (Undergraduate/Scholarship) [3409]
Scholarship Foundation of Santa Barbara Art Scholarship Program (High School/Scholarship) [6252]
Scholarship for Junior PHS Commissioned Officers (Undergraduate/Scholarship) [5689]
Scholarships of the Arts (Graduate, Undergraduate/Scholarship) [2590]
Scholarships for Disadvantaged Students (Undergraduate/Scholarship) [3513]
Scholarships for Leadership Training and Coaching (Professional Development/Scholarship) [2717]
Scholarships for Lutheran College Students (Undergraduate/Scholarship) [1687]
Scholarships for Lutheran Nursing Students (Undergraduate/Scholarship) [1688]
Scholarships of the Morris Radio Club of New Jersey (Undergraduate/Scholarship) [854]
The Dr. William M. Scholl College of Podiatric Medicine Scholarships (Undergraduate/Scholarship) [5550]
The Schonstedt Scholarships in Surveying (Undergraduate/Scholarship) [491]
School Age Financial Aid Program (Undergraduate/Scholarship) [1616]
School In-Service Training Grants for Grades 6-8 Teachers (Graduate/Grant) [4831]
School In-Service Training Grants for Grades 9-12 Teachers (Graduate/Grant) [4832]
School In-Service Training Grants for Grades K-5 Teachers (Graduate/Grant) [4833]
School of Pharmacy Continuing Student Scholarships (Undergraduate/Scholarship) [7269]
Schoolsfirst Federal Credit Union Scholarships (Undergraduate/Scholarship) [6006]
Susan P. Schroeder Memorial Scholarships (Undergraduate/Scholarship) [4215]
Alice Schulman Simmons Scholarships for UU Women (Undergraduate/Scholarship) [6954]
Richard E. Schultes Research Awards (Graduate/Grant) [6439]
Al Schuman Ecolab Undergraduate Entrepreneurial Scholarships (Undergraduate/Scholarship) [5032]
Schwan's Food Service Scholarships (Undergraduate/Scholarship) [6258]
Stephen Schwartz Musical Theatre Scholarships (Undergraduate/Scholarship) [3625]
Fritz Schwartz Serials Education Scholarships (Other/Scholarship) [5226]
Scleroderma Foundation Established Investigator Grants (Doctorate/Grant) [6279]
Scleroderma Foundation New Investigator Grants (Doctorate/Grant) [6280]
Wendell Scott Awards (Graduate, Undergraduate/Scholarship) [3570]
Carl A. Scott Book Scholarships (Undergraduate/Scholarship) [2555]
Roy Scrivner Research Grants (Graduate, Postdoctorate/Grant) [6137]
SCSPA Scholarships (Undergraduate/Scholarship) [6617]
SCSPA Yearbook Scholarships (Undergraduate/Scholarship) [6618]
Bonnie Sorenson Scudder Scholarship (Undergraduate/Scholarship) [2486]
SDF Community College Transfer Scholarships for Math and Science (Undergraduate/Scholarship) [6229]
Seaspace Scholarships (Postgraduate, Undergraduate/Scholarship) [6292]
Fred A. Seaton Memorial Scholarships (Graduate, Undergraduate/Scholarship) [1678]
Seattle Chapter ASWA Scholarships (All/Scholarship) [2834]
Seed Companies Scholarships (Undergraduate/Scholarship) [567]
Elisabeth Seegmiller Recruitment Scholarship Grant (Undergraduate/Scholarship) [2487]
Aaron Seesan Memorial Scholarship Fund (Graduate/Scholarship) [6751]

D.R. Segal Memorial Scholarships for Journalistic Excellence *(Undergraduate/Scholarship)* [5367]
Deedee Segel - Hartford Courant Internships *(Undergraduate/Internship)* [3495]
Detective Cheryl Seiden Memorial Scholarships *(Undergraduate/Scholarship)* [255]
The John and Marion Selby Engineering Scholarship *(Undergraduate/Scholarship)* [3987]
D. Mitchell Self Memorial Scholarships *(Undergraduate/Scholarship)* [5301]
David W. Self Scholarships *(Undergraduate/Scholarship)* [6967]
G. Helner Sell Research and Training Grants *(Professional Development/Grant)* [1110]
Walter and Rita Selvy Scholarships *(Undergraduate/Scholarship)* [2766]
Tadeusz Sendzimir Scholarships *(Undergraduate/Scholarship)* [3496]
Senior Memorial Scholarships *(Undergraduate/Scholarship)* [2488]
William "Buddy" Sentner Scholarship Awards *(Undergraduate/Scholarship)* [391]
Felix R. Sepulveda Memorial Scholarships - Northside Booster Club *(Undergraduate/Scholarship)* [6007]
Serbian Bar Association of America Scholarships *(Undergraduate/Scholarship)* [6296]
Captain Anthony D. Sesow Scholarships *(Undergraduate/Scholarship)* [5133]
Frank B. Sessa Scholarships for Continuing Professional Education *(Professional Development/Scholarship)* [1638]
Seton Hall Law School's Merit Scholarship Program *(Undergraduate/Scholarship)* [6298]
Hubert K. Seymour Scholarships *(Undergraduate/Scholarship)* [5255]
Barbara A. Shacochis Scholarships *(Undergraduate/Scholarship)* [5611]
Elizabeth Shafer Memorial Scholarships *(Undergraduate/Scholarship)* [5856]
SHAFR Dissertation Completion Fellowships *(Doctorate/Fellowship)* [6459]
Shamberg Scholarships *(Undergraduate/Scholarship)* [7353]
William Shannon American Council on Exercise Certification Scholarships *(Professional Development, Undergraduate/Scholarship)* [501]
William H. Shannon Fellowships *(Professional Development/Fellowship)* [3916]
Commander Dan F. Shanower Scholarships *(Undergraduate/Scholarship)* [5134]
W.L. Shattuck Scholarship *(Undergraduate/Scholarship)* [3650]
Benjamin G. Shatz Scholarships *(Undergraduate/Scholarship)* [5612]
Anne Shaw Fellowships *(Graduate/Fellowship)* [6879]
Regina B. Shearn Scholarships *(Graduate, Undergraduate/Scholarship)* [256]
Dezna C. Sheehan Memorial Educational Scholarships *(Other/Scholarship)* [5080]
Jim Sheerin Scholarships *(Undergraduate/Scholarship)* [4426]
Nettie and Edward Shelah Scholarships *(Undergraduate/Scholarship)* [6785]
Shell Incentive Scholarships Fund *(Undergraduate/Scholarship)* [6302]
Shell Process Technology Scholarships *(Undergraduate/Scholarship)* [6303]
Shell Technical Scholarships *(Undergraduate/Scholarship)* [6304]
Bruce Shelton Scholarships *(Undergraduate/Scholarship)* [7455]
Matthew Shepard Scholarships *(Undergraduate/Scholarship)* [6138]
Bill and Ann Sheperd Legal Scholarships Fund *(Undergraduate/Scholarship)* [2892]
Joseph Henry Shepherd Scholarships *(Undergraduate/Scholarship)* [7126]
Robert P. Sheppard Leadership Awards *(High School/Scholarship)* [5072]
Shervin Tehranchi Wrestling Scholarships *(Undergraduate/Scholarship)* [6008]
Marion A. And Ruth Sherwood Family Fund Education Scholarships *(Undergraduate/Scholarship)* [3307]
Shields-Gillespie Scholarships *(All/Scholarship)* [742]
Drs. Poh Shien and Judy Young Scholarships *(Undergraduate/Scholarship)* [7013]
Milton L. Shifman Endowed Scholarships *(Undergraduate/Scholarship)* [4301]
The Shincho Graduate Fellowships for Study in Japan *(Graduate/Fellowship)* [4060]
Ethel Shinn Alumni-Vocational Scholarships *(Undergraduate/Scholarship)* [4216]
Jason Shipley Memorial Scholarships *(Undergraduate/Scholarship)* [4976]
Shoals Home Builders Association Scholarships *(Undergraduate/Scholarship)* [5302]
Misty and Sally Shoop Scholarships *(Graduate, Undergraduate/Scholarship)* [1679]
Shoreline Community College Academic Excellence Scholarships for Graduating High School Seniors *(Undergraduate/Scholarship)* [6320]
Shoreline Community College Academic Improvement Scholarships for Graduating High School Seniors *(Undergraduate/Scholarship)* [6321]
Shoreline Community College Continuing Students Scholarships *(Undergraduate/Scholarship)* [6322]
Shoreline Community College Part-Time Students Scholarships *(Undergraduate/Scholarship)* [6323]
Short-term senior fellowships in Iranian Studies *(Doctorate, Graduate/Fellowship)* [665]
SHOT-NASA Fellowships *(Doctorate, Postdoctorate/Fellowship)* [6463]
Tom Shown Scholarships *(Undergraduate/Scholarship)* [7456]
Ralph W. Shrader Diversity Scholarships *(Graduate/Scholarship)* [1248]
SHRM Certification Scholarships - Individual *(Graduate/Scholarship)* [6444]
SHRM Foundation Regional Academic Scholarships *(Graduate, Undergraduate/Scholarship)* [6445]
Phil Shykes Memorial Scholarships *(Undergraduate/Scholarship)* [2793]
Mary Isabel Sibley Fellowships *(Doctorate/Fellowship)* [5623]
Don and Madalyn Sickafoose Educational Trust *(Undergraduate/Scholarship)* [6752]
Norman Siegel Research Scholar Grants *(Doctorate/Grant)* [1019]
Jeff Siegel Scholarships *(Undergraduate/Scholarship)* [5191]
Siemens Clinical Advancement Scholarship Program *(Postgraduate/Scholarship)* [1043]
Siemens Teacher Scholarships *(Graduate, Undergraduate/Scholarship)* [6330]
E.J. Sierleja Memorial Fellowships *(Graduate/Fellowship)* [3739]
Sig Memorial Scholarships *(Undergraduate/Scholarship)* [19]
Sigma Delta Epsilon Fellowships *(Graduate, Postdoctorate/Fellowship)* [6342]
Sigma Diagnostics Student Scholarships *(Undergraduate/Scholarship)* [5081]
Sigma Kappa Foundation Alumnae Continuing Education Scholarships *(Undergraduate/Scholarship)* [6369]
Sigma Kappa Foundation Alzheimer's/Gerontology Scholarships *(Undergraduate/Scholarship)* [6370]
Sigma Kappa Foundation Founders' Scholarships *(Undergraduate/Scholarship)* [6371]
Sigma Kappa Foundation Gerontology Scholarships *(Undergraduate/Scholarship)* [6372]
Sigma Pi Sigma Undergraduate Research Awards *(Undergraduate/Grant)* [6543]
Silver Nugget Family Scholarships *(Undergraduate/Scholarship)* [5857]
Silver Nugget Gaming Ambassadors Scholarships *(Undergraduate/Scholarship)* [5858]
S.H. Silver Scholarships *(Graduate/Scholarship)* [3198]
Meyer and Dorothy Silverman Scholarships *(Undergraduate/Scholarship)* [2446]
Stuart Silverman Scholarships *(Undergraduate/Scholarship)* [5613]
Harvey L. Simmons Memorial Scholarships *(Undergraduate/Scholarship)* [6230]
Williard B. Simmons Sr. Memorial Scholarships *(Undergraduate/Scholarship)* [4815]
Hazel Simms Nursing Scholarship *(Professional Development/Scholarship)* [4143]
Simon Youth Foundation Community Scholarships *(Undergraduate/Scholarship)* [6400]
Simonton Windows Scholarship Fund *(Undergraduate/Scholarship)* [5521]
DW Simpson Actuarial Science Scholarship Program *(Undergraduate/Scholarship)* [6402]
Bro. Dr. Frank T. Simpson *(Undergraduate/Scholarship)* [3497]
John R. Simpson Memorial Scholarships *(Graduate, Undergraduate/Scholarship)* [1680]
Carole Simpson Scholarships *(Undergraduate/Scholarship)* [1403]
Aaron B. Singleton Memorial Scholarships *(Undergraduate/Scholarship)* [5303]
Helen J. Sioussat/Fay Wells Scholarships *(All/Scholarship)* [1786]
Wiggsy Sivertsen Scholarships *(Undergraduate/Scholarship)* [6139]
Rajadi Sjarif Memorial Scholarships *(Undergraduate/Scholarship)* [6009]
R. Skeeles Memorial Scholarship Fund *(Undergraduate/Scholarship)* [6753]
Francelene Skinner Memorial Scholarship *(Undergraduate/Scholarship)* [4230]
SLA Scholarships *(Graduate/Scholarship)* [6684]
Allogan Slagle Memorial Scholarships *(Graduate/Scholarship)* [1357]
Sledge Fellowships *(Graduate/Fellowship)* [242]
Sloan Northwood Heavy-Duty Scholarships *(Undergraduate/Scholarship)* [1547]
Thomas J. Slocum Memorial Scholarships to Westwood College of Aviation Technology *(Undergraduate/Scholarship)* [84]
The Aaron and Rita Slom Scholarships *(Undergraduate/Scholarship)* [6892]
SMACNA College of Fellows Scholarships *(Undergraduate/Scholarship)* [6300]
Small Cash Grants *(Undergraduate/Scholarship)* [929]
Small Station Training Scholarships *(Professional Development/Scholarship)* [2544]
SME Coal and Energy Division Scholarships *(Undergraduate/Scholarship)* [6516]
SME Directors Scholarships *(Undergraduate/Scholarship)* [6502]
SME Education Foundation Family Scholarships *(Undergraduate/Scholarship)* [6503]
SME Environmental Division Scholarships *(Undergraduate/Scholarship)* [6517]
SME Ford PAS Scholarships *(Undergraduate/Scholarship)* [6504]
SMFM/AAOGF Scholarship Award *(Graduate/Scholarship)* [6512]
Smiley Elementary School PTA - Beverly Roberts Memorial Scholarships *(Undergraduate/Scholarship)* [6010]
Gladys Ann Smith Greater Los Angeles Women's Council Scholarships *(Undergraduate/Scholarship)* [5142]
Charles Smith Memorial Scholarship Awards *(Undergraduate/Scholarship)* [1321]
Drew Smith Memorial Scholarship *(Undergraduate/Scholarship)* [2384]
Tacy Ana Smith Memorial Scholarship Fund *(Undergraduate/Scholarship)* [3076]
Colonel Nate Smith Memorial Scholarships *(Graduate, Undergraduate/Scholarship)* [4437]
James George Smith Memorial Scholarships *(Graduate, Undergraduate/Scholarship)* [1681]
Nila Banton Smith Research Dissemination Support Grants *(All/Grant)* [3891]
Smith-Reynolds Founder Fellowships *(Graduate/Fellowship)* [3540]
The Eileen J. Smith, R.N. Memorial Scholarship *(Undergraduate/Scholarship)* [3988]
Brian Smith Scholarship *(Undergraduate/Scholarship)* [1773]
Esther M. Smith Scholarship *(Undergraduate/Scholarship)* [2385]
Ralph and Josephine Smith Scholarship Fund *(Undergraduate/Scholarship)* [2976]
Helen J. and Harold Gilman Smith Scholarship *(Graduate, Undergraduate/Scholarship)* [1631]
A.O. Smith Scholarships *(Undergraduate/Scholarship)* [5705]

Joseph Sumner Smith Scholarships *(All/Scholarship)* [6955]
Richard S. Smith Scholarships *(Undergraduate/Scholarship)* [6968]
Drue Smith/Society of Professional Journalists Scholarships *(Undergraduate/Scholarship)* [2447]
Smith's Personal Best Scholarships *(Undergraduate/Scholarship)* [5859]
Gladys Snauble Scholarships *(Undergraduate/Scholarship)* [3348]
SNF Professional Growth Scholarships *(Graduate, Undergraduate/Scholarship)* [6259]
SNMTS Bachelor's Degree Completion Scholarships *(Undergraduate/Scholarship)* [6523]
SNMTS Clinical Advancement Scholarships *(Other/Scholarship)* [6524]
Helen D. Snow Memorial Scholarships *(Undergraduate/Scholarship)* [5626]
Ray Snow Memorial Scholarships *(Undergraduate/Scholarship)* [4947]
A.C. Snow Scholarships *(Undergraduate/Scholarship)* [7192]
Snowmobile Association of Massachusetts Scholarships *(Undergraduate/Scholarship)* [6413]
Stuart H. Snyder Memorial Scholarships *(Undergraduate/Scholarship)* [1561]
Social Work Scholarships *(Graduate, Undergraduate/Scholarship)* [5778]
Society of Automotive Analyst Scholarships *(Undergraduate/Scholarship)* [1562]
Society of Exploration Geophysicists Foundation Scholarships *(Graduate, Undergraduate/Scholarship)* [6441]
Society of Louisiana Certified Public Accountants Scholarships *(Undergraduate/Scholarship)* [6468]
Society of Marine Port Engineers Scholarship Loans *(Undergraduate/Scholarship/Forgivable Loan)* [6510]
Society of Naval Architects and Marine Engineers Undergraduate Scholarships *(Undergraduate/Scholarship)* [6520]
Society of Pediatric Nurses Educational Scholarship *(Graduate, Professional Development/Scholarship)* [6530]
Society for Pediatric Radiology Research Fellows *(Graduate, Professional Development/Fellowship)* [6535]
Society for Pediatric Radiology Seed Grants *(Graduate, Professional Development/Grant)* [6536]
Society for Pediatric Urology Research Grant Program *(Undergraduate/Grant)* [6539]
Society of Plastics Engineers General Scholarships *(Graduate, Undergraduate/Scholarship)* [6559]
Society of Plastics Engineers Pittsburgh Scholarships *(Graduate, Undergraduate/Scholarship)* [6560]
Society for the Scientific Study of Sexuality Student Research Grants *(Undergraduate/Grant)* [6587]
Society of Women Engineers Scholarships *(Undergraduate/Scholarship)* [6592]
Dale and Betty George Sola Scholarships *(Undergraduate/Scholarship)* [2794]
Dr. Kiyoshi Sonoda Memorial Scholarships *(Graduate/Scholarship)* [4021]
Sons of Norway Foundation Scholarships to Oslo International School *(Undergraduate/Scholarship)* [6604]
Sony Pictures Scholarships *(Graduate/Scholarship)* [1471]
Soroptimist International of Chambersburg Scholarship Fund *(Undergraduate/Scholarship)* [3120]
Soroptimist International of Redlands Scholarships *(Undergraduate/Scholarship)* [6011]
South Carolina Association for Financial Professionals Certified Treasury Professional Scholarships *(Professional Development/Scholarship)* [6610]
South Carolina Tourism and Hospitality Educational Foundation Scholarships *(Undergraduate/Scholarship)* [3618]
South Carolina Undergraduate Scholarships *(Undergraduate/Scholarship)* [3619]
South Central Power Scholarships *(Undergraduate/Scholarship)* [6620]
South Coast Area High School Senior Honors Scholarship Program *(High School/Scholarship)* [6253]
South Dakota Division Scholarships *(Undergraduate/Scholarship)* [4520]
South Jersey Golf Association Scholarships *(Undergraduate/Scholarship)* [6623]
South Kentucky RECC High School Senior Scholarships *(Undergraduate/Scholarship)* [6626]
South Texas Unit Scholarships *(Undergraduate/Scholarship)* [3546]
Anna Doris Southall Nursing Scholarships *(Undergraduate/Scholarship)* [6848]
Southeast Aerospace Inc. Scholarships *(Undergraduate/Scholarship)* [85]
Southeast Member Chapter Scholarships *(Undergraduate/Scholarship)* [1457]
Southern Nevada Sports Hall of Fame Athletic Scholarships *(Undergraduate/Scholarship)* [5860]
Southern Scholarship Foundation Scholarships *(Undergraduate/Scholarship)* [6638]
Southwest Chapter Roy Kinslow Scholarships *(Undergraduate/Scholarship)* [1070]
Sovereign Nations Scholarship Fund *(Undergraduate/Scholarship)* [625]
Master Sergeant William Sowers Memorial Scholarships *(Undergraduate/Scholarship)* [60]
Willard and Spackman Scholarship Program *(Postgraduate/Scholarship)* [736]
Kathy Spadoni Memorial Scholarships *(Undergraduate/Scholarship)* [5779]
Amy E. Spain Memorial Scholarships *(Undergraduate/Scholarship)* [7127]
Spanish Embassy Scholarships *(Graduate, Other/Scholarship)* [5267]
Nathan Sparks Memorial Scholarship *(Undergraduate/Scholarship)* [2364]
Spartan Scholarship Awards *(Undergraduate/Scholarship)* [3843]
Spartan Staff Scholarships *(Undergraduate/Scholarship)* [5861]
Special Law School Scholarships *(Undergraduate/Scholarship)* [5614]
Specialty Equipment Market Association Scholarships *(Undergraduate/Scholarship)* [6690]
Specialty Nursing Scholarships *(Undergraduate/Scholarship)* [3132]
Faith Speckhard Scholarships *(Undergraduate/Scholarship)* [3989]
Spencer Foundation Research Grants *(All/Grant)* [6693]
Spice Box Grants *(Professional Development/Grant)* [532]
Patrick Spielman Memorial Scholarship Program *(Undergraduate/Scholarship)* [6290]
Spirit of Allison Graduation Award *(High School/Award/Prize)* [2986]
The Spirit Square Center for Arts and Education Scholarship Fund *(Undergraduate/Scholarship)* [3077]
SPOOM Research Grants *(Graduate/Grant)* [6566]
Sporty's Pilot Shop/Cincinnati Avionics Scholarships *(Undergraduate/Scholarship)* [86]
Spouse Tuition Aids Program *(Graduate, Undergraduate/Scholarship)* [5148]
SPPSI Grants-In-Aid Program *(Graduate, Postdoctorate/Grant)* [6576]
James F. and Donna Springfield Scholarships *(Undergraduate/Scholarship)* [7128]
SPS Future Teacher Scholarships *(Undergraduate/Scholarship)* [6544]
SPS Leadership Scholarships *(Undergraduate/Scholarship)* [6545]
SPSmedical CS Scholarships *(Other/Scholarship)* [3802]
SRF Post-doctoral Fellowships *(Postdoctorate/Fellowship)* [6282]
SSC-Building Environmental Campus Community (BECC) Fellowships *(Undergraduate/Scholarship)* [6334]
SSF Research Grants *(Doctorate/Grant)* [6410]
SSF Student Fellowships *(Graduate, Undergraduate/Fellowship)* [6411]
The SSPI Mid-Atlantic Chapter Scholarships *(Graduate, Undergraduate/Scholarship)* [6583]
The SSPI Northeast Chapter Scholarships *(Graduate, Undergraduate/Scholarship)* [6584]
The SSPI Southern California Scholarships *(Graduate, Undergraduate/Scholarship)* [6585]
Ernest and Charlene Stachowiak Memorial Scholarship *(Undergraduate/Scholarship)* [2489]
Matt Stager Memorial Scholarship Fund *(Undergraduate/Scholarship)* [7390]
Steven A. Stahl Research Grants *(Graduate/Grant)* [3892]
The Standard Scholarships *(Graduate, Undergraduate/Scholarship)* [5646]
Marion Barr Stanfield Art Scholarships *(Graduate, Undergraduate/Scholarship)* [6956]
Otto M. Stanfield Law Scholarships *(Graduate/Scholarship)* [6957]
H.T. and Terrell Stanford Scholarship *(Undergraduate/Scholarship)* [2365]
Morgan Stanley Tribal Scholars Program *(Undergraduate/Scholarship)* [626]
Stark County Bar Association Fund *(Undergraduate/Scholarship)* [6754]
Stark County Dairy Promoters Scholarships *(Undergraduate/Scholarship)* [6755]
Starr Foundation Graduate Fellowship in Asian Studies *(Graduate/Grant)* [7094]
Matt Stauffer Memorial Scholarships *(Undergraduate/Scholarship)* [2131]
The Mabel Keaton Staupers National Scholarship Award *(Doctorate, Graduate, Undergraduate/Scholarship)* [2115]
The Stanley H. Stearman Awards *(Undergraduate/Scholarship)* [5048]
Robert P. Stearns/SCS Engineers Awards *(Graduate/Scholarship)* [6598]
Gwen Stefani After-the-Fires Scholarships *(Undergraduate/Scholarship)* [6231]
Peter T. Steinwedell Scholarships *(Undergraduate/Scholarship)* [3498]
Elin J. Stene/Xi Scholarships *(Undergraduate/Scholarship)* [6374]
Step Up Scholarships *(Undergraduate/Scholarship)* [6232]
H. Hiram Stephenson Oxford Cup Scholarships *(Graduate, Undergraduate/Scholarship)* [1682]
Hugh E. Stephenson Oxford Cup Scholarships *(Graduate, Undergraduate/Scholarship)* [1683]
Elizabeth Coulter Stephenson Scholarships *(Undergraduate/Scholarship)* [2699]
Richie Stevenson Scholarships *(Undergraduate/Scholarship)* [2448]
Nancy Stewart Scholarships *(Undergraduate/Scholarship)* [1089]
Dr. Gunnar B. Stickler Scholarships *(Undergraduate/Scholarship)* [6787]
Still Photographer Scholarships *(Undergraduate/Scholarship)* [5021]
Walter W. Stillman Scholarships *(Undergraduate/Scholarship)* [1563]
Ralph W. Stone Graduate Fellowships *(Graduate/Grant)* [5090]
James E. Stoner Memorial Scholarships *(Undergraduate/Scholarship)* [1417]
Stop Hunger Scholarships *(Undergraduate/Scholarship)* [398]
Martin L. Stout Scholarships *(Undergraduate/Scholarship)* [1410]
StraightForward Media's Art School Scholarships *(Undergraduate/Scholarship)* [6795]
StraightForward Media's Business School Scholarships *(Undergraduate/Scholarship)* [6796]
StraightForward Media's Engineering Scholarships *(Undergraduate/Scholarship)* [6797]
StraightForward Media's Law Enforcement Scholarships *(Professional Development, Undergraduate/Scholarship)* [6798]
StraightForward Media's Law School Scholarships *(Undergraduate/Scholarship)* [6799]
StraightForward Media's Liberal Arts Scholarships *(Undergraduate/Scholarship)* [6800]
StraightForward Media's Media and Communications Scholarships *(Undergraduate/Scholarship)* [6801]
StraightForward Media's Medical Professions Scholarships *(Undergraduate/Scholarship)* [6802]
StraightForward Media's Minority Scholarships *(Undergraduate/Scholarship)* [6803]
StraightForward Media's Nursing School Scholar-

ships *(Undergraduate/Scholarship)* [6804]
StraightForward Media's Science Scholarships *(Undergraduate/Scholarship)* [6805]
StraightForward Media's Teacher Scholarships *(Undergraduate/Scholarship)* [6806]
StraightForward Media's Vocational-Technical School Scholarships *(Undergraduate/Scholarship)* [6807]
Bonnie Strangio Education Scholarships *(Graduate, Undergraduate/Scholarship)* [2591]
Donald A. Strauss Scholarships *(Undergraduate/Scholarship)* [7088]
Carole J. Streeter, KB9JBR Scholarships *(Undergraduate/Scholarship)* [857]
John Streiff Memorial Scholarships *(Undergraduate/Scholarship)* [4218]
Stanley W. Strew Educational Fund Scholarship *(Undergraduate/Scholarship)* [1812]
Striving for Success Scholarships *(Undergraduate/Scholarship)* [5862]
Fraser Stryker Diversity Scholarship Program *(Undergraduate/Scholarship)* [5166]
Fraser Stryker Diversity Scholarships *(Undergraduate/Scholarship)* [6809]
E.L. Stubbs Research Grants *(Graduate/Grant)* [4507]
Student Media Group Scholarships *(Graduate, Undergraduate/Scholarship)* [5647]
Student Osteopathic Medical Student Fellowships and Research *(Undergraduate/Fellowship)* [6812]
Student Research Grants *(Undergraduate/Grant)* [2083]
Student Research Grants in Audiology *(Doctorate/Grant)* [1107]
Student Research Grants in Early Childhood Language Development *(Doctorate/Grant)* [1108]
Student Travel Grants *(Graduate, Undergraduate/Grant)* [6700]
Study Scholarships for Artists or Musicians *(Graduate/Scholarship)* [3230]
Marco Polo Stufano Garden Conservancy Fellowships *(Professional Development/Fellowship)* [3161]
Stultz Scholarships *(Undergraduate/Scholarship)* [7457]
Horace W. Stunkard Scholarships *(Undergraduate/Scholarship)* [4302]
Anne Sturrock Nursing Scholarships *(Undergraduate/Scholarship)* [6675]
Leo Suarez Journalism Scholarships *(Undergraduate/Scholarship)* [2601]
Subic Bay-Cubi Point 1 Scholarships *(Undergraduate/Scholarship)* [5143]
John A. Sullivan Scholarships *(Undergraduate/Scholarship)* [2795]
Phil Sullivan Scholarships *(Undergraduate/Scholarship)* [5780]
VPPPA William Sullivan Scholarships *(Graduate, Undergraduate/Scholarship)* [7339]
William A. Sullivan Scholarships *(Undergraduate/Scholarship)* [5144]
Summer Intern Scholarships in Cardiothoracic Surgery *(Undergraduate/Scholarship)* [420]
Summer Language Study Grants in Turkey *(Graduate/Grant)* [3758]
Summer Research Diversity Fellowships in Law and Social Science *(Undergraduate/Fellowship)* [435]
Summer Research Grants in Turkey *(Graduate/Grant)* [3759]
Hatton W. Sumners Scholarships *(Undergraduate/Scholarship)* [5331]
Sun Country Amateur Golf Association Scholarships *(Undergraduate/Scholarship)* [6817]
Superior District Legislative Mentoring Student Grants *(Undergraduate/Grant)* [1856]
Superior District Legislative Mentoring Student Grants RT to DC *(Undergraduate/Grant)* [1857]
Surety Industry Scholarship Program for Minority Students *(Undergraduate/Scholarship)* [6824]
Surgeon Scientist Career Development Awards *(Professional Development/Grant)* [603]
Survival Scholarship Program *(Undergraduate/Scholarship)* [7514]
SUS Foundation Junior Faculty Grants *(Graduate/Grant)* [6589]
SUS - Wyeth Clinical Scholar Award *(Graduate/Award/Prize)* [6590]
Sussman-Miller Educational Assistance Award Program *(Undergraduate/Scholarship)* [195]
Sutherland/Purdy Scholarships *(Undergraduate/Scholarship)* [5682]
Michael Bendix Sutton Foundation *(Undergraduate/Scholarship)* [4934]
SUVCW Scholarships *(Undergraduate/Scholarship)* [6606]
Margaret Svec Scholarships *(Undergraduate/Scholarship)* [6324]
Lorraine E. Swain Scholarships *(Undergraduate/Scholarship)* [6375]
Swede Swanson Memorial Scholarships *(Undergraduate/Scholarship)* [5162]
Daniel Swarovski and Company Scholarships *(Graduate/Scholarship)* [3199]
Jeffery Tyler Sweitzer Wrestling Memorial Scholarship Fund *(Undergraduate/Scholarship)* [6756]
Timothy S. Sweterlitsch Memorial Scholarship Fund *(Undergraduate/Scholarship)* [6757]
SWFL Deputy Sheriffs Association Fund Scholarships *(Undergraduate/Scholarship)* [6676]
SWFL Professional Golfers Association Scholarships *(Undergraduate/Scholarship)* [6677]
Swivel Media Scholarships *(Graduate, Undergraduate/Scholarship)* [5648]
Sycamore Scholar Awards *(Undergraduate/Scholarship)* [3713]
Harry Taback 9/11 Memorial Scholarships *(Undergraduate/Scholarship)* [1071]
Hazaros Tabakoglu Scholarship Fund *(Undergraduate/Scholarship)* [1291]
The Tabat Scholarship Fund *(Graduate/Scholarship)* [2922]
The Tacoma Athletic Commission Scholarships *(Undergraduate/Scholarship)* [3379]
Tagged for Greatness Scholarships *(Undergraduate/Scholarship)* [116]
Tailhook Educational Foundation Scholarships Program *(Undergraduate/Scholarship)* [6836]
Taiwanese American Community Scholarships *(Undergraduate/Scholarship)* [6838]
Kei Takemoto Memorial Scholarships *(Undergraduate/Scholarship)* [87]
Tall Awareness Scholarships *(Undergraduate/Scholarship)* [5863]
Tall Clubs International Student Scholarships *(Undergraduate/Scholarship)* [6840]
Tanana Valley Campus Culinary Arts Scholarships *(Undergraduate/Scholarship)* [6849]
Alexander M. Tanger Scholarships *(All/Scholarship)* [1787]
Hal Tanner Jr. Scholarships *(Undergraduate/Scholarship)* [7193]
Lee Tarbox Memorial Scholarships *(Undergraduate/Scholarship)* [88]
Targeted Research Initiative for Health Outcomes *(Doctorate/Grant)* [2875]
Targeted Research Initiative for Mood Disorders *(Doctorate/Grant)* [2876]
Targeted Research Initiative for Seniors *(Doctorate/Grant)* [2877]
Sheila Tarr-Smith Memorial Scholarships *(Undergraduate/Scholarship)* [5864]
Bud and Linda Tarrson Fellowships *(Postdoctorate/Fellowship)* [288]
Tarrson Regeneration Scholarships *(Postdoctorate/Scholarship)* [289]
Charles T. and Judith A. Tart Student Incentive Awards *(Graduate, Postdoctorate, Undergraduate/Grant)* [5458]
Jack Tate/ThinkCOLLEGE Scholarship Fund *(Undergraduate/Scholarship)* [3079]
Jordan B. Tatter Scholarships *(Undergraduate/Scholarship)* [4490]
Taylor/Blakeslee University Fellowships *(Undergraduate/Fellowship)* [2548]
Charles "Buck" and Dora Taylor Endowed Law Scholarships *(Undergraduate/Scholarship)* [2767]
Ryan "Munchie" Taylor Memorial Scholarships *(Undergraduate/Scholarship)* [4270]
Tom Taylor Memorial Scholarships to Spartan College of Aeronautics and Technology *(Undergraduate/Scholarship)* [89]
TCA-BAACBH Scholarships *(Undergraduate/Scholarship)* [6938]
TCA Turkish American Scholarships *(Undergraduate/Scholarship)* [6939]
TCA-UMD Scholarships *(Undergraduate/Scholarship)* [6940]
TCATA College Scholarship Program *(Undergraduate/Scholarship)* [6875]
TDC Scholarship Program *(Graduate, Undergraduate/Scholarship)* [4659]
TEACH Scholarships *(Undergraduate/Scholarship)* [5865]
Team DC Student-Athlete Scholarships *(Undergraduate/Scholarship)* [6140]
Marvin H. and Kathleen G. Teget Leadership Scholarships *(Undergraduate/Scholarship)* [6813]
Paul Tejada Memorial Scholarship *(Undergraduate/Scholarship)* [3990]
Telamon Scholarships *(Undergraduate/Scholarship)* [7014]
Telecommunications Association of Michigan Scholarship Fund *(Undergraduate/Scholarship)* [6856]
Television News Scholarships *(Undergraduate/Scholarship)* [5022]
Telford Scholarships *(Undergraduate/Scholarship)* [20]
Telluride Association Summer Program Scholarships *(High School/Scholarship)* [6858]
Tennessee Bar Foundation IOLTA Law School Scholarships *(Undergraduate/Scholarship)* [7129]
Charles L. Terrell/New Haven Savings Bank Scholarship Fund *(Undergraduate/Scholarship)* [2396]
Texas Music Educators Association Past-Presidents Memorial Scholarships *(Undergraduate/Scholarship)* [6863]
Texas Mutual Scholarship Program *(Undergraduate/Scholarship)* [6865]
Texas Society of Professional Engineers Scholarships *(Undergraduate/Scholarship)* [6869]
Texas State Technical College Scholarships *(Undergraduate/Scholarship)* [90]
Texas Telephone Association Foundation Scholarships *(Undergraduate/Scholarship)* [6873]
Texas Transportation Scholarships *(Undergraduate/Scholarship)* [6921]
Jim and Pat Thacker Sports Communication Internships *(Undergraduate/Internship)* [7194]
ThanksUSA Scholarships *(Undergraduate/Scholarship)* [6877]
The Rodney Thaxton Justice Fund *(Undergraduate/Scholarship)* [2602]
Dr. Peter A. Theodos Memorial Graduate Scholarships *(Graduate/Scholarship)* [3535]
Thermo Scientific Educational Scholarships *(Other/Scholarship)* [5082]
Thermoforming Scholarships *(Graduate, Undergraduate/Scholarship)* [6561]
Thermoplastic Materials and Foams Division Scholarships *(Graduate, Undergraduate/Scholarship)* [6562]
Thermoplastics Elastomers Special Interest Group Scholarships *(Graduate, Undergraduate/Scholarship)* [6563]
Theta/Caryl Cordis D'hondt Scholarships *(Undergraduate/Scholarship)* [6376]
Theta Tau Scholarships *(Undergraduate/Scholarship)* [6377]
Douglas Dockery Thomas Fellowships *(Graduate/Fellowship)* [4128]
E.D. Thomas Post Doctoral Fellowships *(Postdoctorate/Fellowship)* [3145]
Ralph and Valerie Thomas Scholarship Program *(Graduate, Undergraduate/Scholarship)* [4660]
Barber Owen Thomas Scholarships *(Undergraduate/Scholarship)* [6378]
Elizabeth Thomas Scholarships *(Undergraduate/Scholarship)* [6325]
Rev. Chuck and Nancy Thomas Scholarships *(Graduate, Master's/Scholarship)* [6958]
Honorable Raymond Thompson Endowed Scholarships *(Undergraduate/Scholarship)* [5615]
Barbara and Howard Thompson Scholarship *(Undergraduate/Scholarship)* [3991]
Thompson Scholarship for Women in Safety *(Graduate/Scholarship)* [1072]
Thomson Scientific/MLA Doctoral Fellowships *(Doctorate/Fellowship)* [4448]

Thornberg/Havens Scholarships *(Undergraduate/Scholarship)* [2700]
Thrivent Financial Scholarships *(Graduate, Undergraduate/Scholarship)* [5649]
Thyssen-Heideking Fellowships *(Postdoctorate/Fellowship)* [3236]
Raymond A. Tice Scholarships I *(Undergraduate/Scholarship)* [6233]
Raymond A. Tice Scholarships II *(Undergraduate/Scholarship)* [6234]
Tidewater Builders Association Scholarships *(Undergraduate/Scholarship)* [6890]
Jack E. Tillson Scholarships *(Graduate/Scholarship)* [3932]
Time Warner Point Scholarships *(Graduate, Undergraduate/Scholarship)* [5727]
Time Warner Tribal Scholars Program *(Undergraduate/Scholarship)* [627]
Mark P. Tiner Education Scholarships *(Undergraduate/Scholarship)* [5368]
Eben Tisdale Fellowships *(Graduate, Undergraduate/Fellowship)* [3148]
TLMI Scholarships - Four-Year Colleges *(Undergraduate/Scholarship)* [6833]
TLMI Scholarships - Two-Year Colleges *(Undergraduate/Scholarship)* [6834]
TMCF Scholarships *(Undergraduate/Scholarship)* [4316]
Star and Barry Tobias Scholarships *(Undergraduate/Scholarship)* [2104]
Mario J. Tocco Hydrocephalus Foundation Scholarships *(Undergraduate/Scholarship)* [3639]
Richard Cecil Todd and Clauda Pennock Todd Tripod Scholarships *(Graduate, Undergraduate/Scholarship)* [5655]
Michael W. Toennis Scholarships *(Graduate, Undergraduate/Scholarship)* [1684]
The Adelle and Erwin Tomash Fellowships *(Doctorate/Fellowship)* [1584]
John Tomasovic, Sr. Scholarships *(Undergraduate/Scholarship)* [568]
Tomato Fest Scholarship Grants *(Undergraduate/Scholarship)* [533]
Travis C. Tomlin Memorial Scholarship Program *(Graduate, Undergraduate/Scholarship)* [4661]
Touchstone Special Achievement Scholarships *(Undergraduate/Scholarship)* [6621]
Judith A. Towle Environmental Studies Fund *(Undergraduate/Fellowship)* [3966]
Town and County Club Scholarships *(Undergraduate/Scholarship)* [3499]
Toyota Community Scholars *(Undergraduate/Scholarship)* [6894]
Toyota High School Scholarship Program *(Undergraduate/Scholarship)* [3603]
The Joyce Tracy Fellowships *(Doctorate/Fellowship)* [308]
Traditional Student Scholarships *(Undergraduate/Scholarship)* [2510]
TRALA Scholarships Program *(Undergraduate/Scholarship)* [6924]
Reuben Trane Scholarships *(Undergraduate/Scholarship)* [970]
Transfer Engineering Student Awards *(Undergraduate/Scholarship)* [4058]
Transgender Scholarships and Education Legacy Fund *(Undergraduate/Scholarship)* [6142]
Traub-Dicker Rainbow Scholarships *(Undergraduate/Scholarship)* [6790]
Travel Grants for Women Researchers *(Postdoctorate/Scholarship)* [1516]
Trelut Family Legacy Scholarships *(Undergraduate/Scholarship)* [1834]
Tribal Business Management Program (TBM) Scholarships *(Undergraduate/Scholarship)* [2069]
Trillion Diamond Company Scholarships *(Undergraduate/Scholarship)* [3200]
Thomas and Glenna Trimble Endowed Scholarships *(Undergraduate/Scholarship)* [5616]
Tim Triner Letter Carriers Scholarship Fund *(Undergraduate/Scholarship)* [6758]
J.P. Madeline Trinkaus Endowed Scholarships in Embryology *(Undergraduate/Scholarship)* [4303]
Vincent Trotter Health Care Scholarships *(Undergraduate/Scholarship)* [6235]
Charlie Trotters's Culinary Education Foundation Culinary Study Scholarships *(All, Professional Development/Scholarship)* [2582]
Jo Anne J. Trow Scholarships *(Undergraduate/Scholarship)* [4635]
Troy University Rodeo Team Scholarships *(Graduate/Scholarship)* [117]
Truckload Carriers Association Scholarships *(Undergraduate/Scholarship)* [6926]
True North Land Surveying Scholarships *(Undergraduate/Scholarship)* [5781]
Harry S. Truman Scholarships *(Postgraduate/Scholarship)* [6930]
Truss Plate Institute Scholarships *(Doctorate/Scholarship)* [6932]
Trustee, Schawe, Presidential and Honor Scholarships *(Undergraduate/Scholarship)* [7533]
Trustee Scholarships *(Undergraduate/Scholarship)* [4068]
Trustees College Scholarships *(Undergraduate/Scholarship)* [4273]
Trustees Law School Scholarships *(Undergraduate/Scholarship)* [4274]
TRW Foundation Scholarships *(Undergraduate/Scholarship)* [1564]
TSA Teach Technology Scholarships *(Undergraduate/Scholarship)* [6854]
Norman J. Tschantz/Walter C. Deuble Scholarships *(Undergraduate/Scholarship)* [6759]
Tsutako Curo Scholarships *(Undergraduate/Scholarship)* [5866]
Tucker Family Scholarships *(Undergraduate/Scholarship)* [7195]
Barry Tuckwell Scholarships *(All/Scholarship)* [3870]
Richard R. Tufenkian Memorial Scholarships *(Undergraduate/Scholarship)* [1253]
Edward Tuinier Memorial Scholarships *(Undergraduate/Scholarship)* [569]
Tunxis Community College Foundation Scholarships *(Undergraduate/Scholarship)* [3500]
Turf and Ornamental Communicators Association Scholarship Program *(Undergraduate/Scholarship)* [6934]
Jeff Turner-Forsyth Audubon Society Scholarships *(Undergraduate/Scholarship)* [7458]
James A. Turner, Jr. Memorial Scholarships *(Undergraduate/Scholarship)* [1173]
Mark and Vera Turner Memorial Scholarship *(Undergraduate/Scholarship)* [4231]
Emmett H. Turner Scholarships *(Undergraduate/Scholarship)* [2450]
Ira G. Turpin Scholar Fund *(Undergraduate/Scholarship)* [6760]
Tuscumbia Kiwanis Scholarships *(Undergraduate/Scholarship)* [5304]
Vice Adm. Jerry O. Tuttle, USN (Ret.) and Mrs. Barbara A. Tuttle Science and Technology Scholarships *(Undergraduate/Scholarship)* [1249]
TU@UT HSF College Scholarship Program *(Undergraduate/Scholarship)* [3604]
TWO Scholarship Program *(Undergraduate/Scholarship)* [6851]
Two Year/Community Broadcast Education Association Scholarships Award *(All/Scholarship)* [1788]
TYLENOL Scholarships *(Undergraduate/Scholarship)* [4561]
UAF Alumni Association Scholarships *(Undergraduate/Scholarship)* [7079]
UCB, Inc. NP Student Scholarships *(Graduate/Scholarship)* [274]
The UCSD Black Alumni Scholarship for Arts and Humanities *(Undergraduate/Scholarship)* [6236]
The UCSD Black Alumni Scholarships for Engineering, Mathematics and Science *(Undergraduate/Scholarship)* [6237]
Udall Scholarships *(Undergraduate/Scholarship)* [7089]
Morris K. Udall Scholarships *(Undergraduate/Scholarship)* [6945]
UFCW Scholarships *(Undergraduate/Scholarship)* [6963]
UJFC and Council of St. Paul Annual Scholarships *(All/Scholarship)* [4542]
Sandy Ulm Scholarships *(Undergraduate/Scholarship)* [2993]
Ric Ulrich and Chuck Pischke Scholarships *(Undergraduate/Scholarship)* [5782]
Undergraduate and Medical/Graduate General Scholarship and Loan Program *(Graduate/Scholarship)* [6254]
UNH Alumni Association Legacy Scholarships *(Undergraduate/Scholarship)* [7138]
UNH Parent's Association Endowment Scholarship Fund *(Undergraduate/Scholarship)* [7139]
Union Plus Scholarship Program *(Undergraduate/Scholarship)* [3922]
United Engineering Foundation Grants *(All/Grant)* [6961]
United Parcel Service Scholarship for Female Students *(Undergraduate/Scholarship)* [3740]
United Parcel Service Scholarship for Minority Students *(Undergraduate/Scholarship)* [3741]
United South and Eastern Tribes Scholarship Fund *(Undergraduate/Scholarship)* [6970]
U.S. Air Force ROTC Enhanced HSI Scholarship *(Undergraduate/Scholarship)* [6975]
U.S. Air Force ROTC Express Scholarships *(Undergraduate/Scholarship)* [6976]
U.S. Air Force ROTC High School Scholarships *(Undergraduate/Scholarship)* [6977]
U.S. Air Force ROTC In-College Scholarships *(Undergraduate/Scholarship)* [6978]
U.S. Aircraft Insurance Group Professional Development Program Scholarships *(Undergraduate/Scholarship)* [4782]
U.S. Bates Scholarship Program *(Undergraduate/Scholarship)* [3923]
U.S. BIA Indian Higher Education Grants *(Undergraduate/Grant)* [638]
United States Capitol Historical Society Fellowships *(Graduate/Fellowship)* [6983]
United States Geospatial Intelligence Foundation Graduate Scholarships *(Postgraduate/Scholarship)* [6988]
United States Geospatial Intelligence Foundation High School Scholarships *(Undergraduate/Scholarship)* [6989]
United States Geospatial Intelligence Foundation Undergraduate Scholarships *(Undergraduate/Scholarship)* [6990]
United States Golf Association Fellowship Program *(All/Fellowship)* [6992]
United States Golf Association Scholarship Program *(Undergraduate/Scholarship)* [6993]
U.S. Pan Asian American Chamber of Commerce CBS Scholarships *(Undergraduate/Scholarship)* [7015]
U.S. Pan Asian American Chamber of Commerce McDonald's Scholarships *(Undergraduate/Scholarship)* [7016]
U.S. Pan Asian American Chamber of Commerce UPS Scholarships *(Undergraduate/Scholarship)* [7017]
United States Tour Operators Association Scholarships *(Undergraduate/Scholarship)* [7019]
United Teachers Los Angeles Stonewall Scholarship Fund *(Undergraduate/Scholarship)* [6143]
Universal Studios Preservation Scholarships *(Graduate/Scholarship)* [1472]
Universal Underwriters Scholarships *(Undergraduate/Scholarship)* [1565]
University of Alaska Scholars Program *(Undergraduate/Scholarship)* [4388]
University Alliance HSF/UGA College Scholarship Program *(Undergraduate/Scholarship)* [3605]
University of California LGBT Alumni (UCGALA) scholarships *(Undergraduate/Scholarship)* [6144]
University of Hawaii at Manoa East-West Center Graduate Fellowships *(Graduate, Postdoctorate/Fellowship)* [7095]
University of Hawaii at Manoa Graduate Assistantship Awards *(Graduate/Award/Prize)* [7096]
University of Hawaii at Manoa Graduate Student Organization Travel Funds *(Graduate/Grant)* [7097]
University of Hawaii at Manoa Japan Travel Bureau Scholarships *(Graduate, Undergraduate/Scholarship)* [7098]
University of Minnesota Women Student Travel Grants *(Graduate, Undergraduate/Grant)* [7134]
University of Oregon Dean's Scholarships *(Undergraduate/Scholarship)* [7203]
University of Oregon Diversity-Building Scholarships

(Graduate, Undergraduate/Scholarship) [7204]
University of Oregon General University Scholarships (Undergraduate/Scholarship) [7205]
University of Phoenix First Chance Scholarship Fund (Undergraduate/Scholarship) [7297]
University of Phoenix Touchdown Mondays Scholarship Program (All/Scholarship) [2592]
University Summer Course Grants (Undergraduate/Grant) [3231]
University of West Alabama Rodeo Team Scholarships (Graduate/Scholarship) [118]
University of Wisconsin-Madison African American Alumni Scholarships (Undergraduate/Scholarship) [7271]
University of Wisconsin-Madison American Indian Alumni Scholarships (Undergraduate/Scholarship) [7272]
University of Wisconsin-Madison/CALS Continuing Student Scholarships (Undergraduate/Scholarship) [7273]
University of Wisconsin-Madison/CALS Minority Scholarships (Undergraduate/Scholarship) [7274]
University of Wisconsin-Madison Chancellor's Scholarships (Undergraduate/Scholarship) [7275]
University of Wisconsin-Madison Hispanic/Latino Alumni Scholarships (Undergraduate/Scholarship) [7276]
University of Wisconsin-Madison Music Scholarships (Undergraduate/Scholarship) [7278]
University of Wisconsin-Madison National Merit Scholarships (Undergraduate/Scholarship) [7279]
University of Wisconsin-Madison Pharmacy New Student Scholarships (Undergraduate/Scholarship) [7280]
University of Wisconsin-Madison Single Parent and Adult Scholarships (Undergraduate/Scholarship) [7281]
Unmet Need Scholarships (Undergraduate/Scholarship) [6158]
Samuel Upchurch Memorial Scholarships (Undergraduate/Scholarship) [119]
UPE/ACM Scholarship Awards (Graduate, Undergraduate/Award/Prize) [7288]
UPE Scholarship Awards (Graduate, Undergraduate/Award/Prize) [7289]
UPS Diversity Scholarships (Undergraduate/Scholarship) [1073]
The Urban Scholarships Fund (Undergraduate/Scholarship) [6860]
USA Freestyle Martial Arts Scholarships (Undergraduate/Scholarship) [6238]
USAWOASF/Grantham University On-Line Scholarships (Graduate, Undergraduate/Scholarship) [6980]
USAWOASF Regular Scholarships (Undergraduate/Scholarship) [6981]
USHJA Athletic Scholarships (Undergraduate/Scholarship) [6995]
USHJA General Scholarships (Undergraduate/Scholarship) [6996]
USHJA Postgraduate Scholarships (Postgraduate/Scholarship) [6997]
USS Tennessee Scholarship Fund (Undergraduate/Scholarship) [5149]
USTA Tennis and Education Foundation College Education Scholarships (Undergraduate/Scholarship) [7306]
USTA Tennis and Education Foundation College Textbook Scholarships (Undergraduate/Scholarship) [7307]
Utility Workers Union of America Scholarship Program (Undergraduate/Scholarship) [7309]
John D. Utterback Undergraduate Scholarships (Undergraduate/Scholarship) [230]
Valley Alliance of Mentors for Opportunities and Scholarship (VAMOS) Program (Undergraduate/Scholarship) [3606]
Valpak Scholarships (Graduate, Undergraduate/Scholarship) [5650]
Valuing Diversity PhD Scholarships (Doctorate/Scholarship) [710]
Hurad Van Der Bedrosian Memorial Scholarships (Graduate/Scholarship) [1294]
Adolph Van Pelt Special Fund for Indians Scholarships (Undergraduate/Scholarship) [1358]
William P. Van Wagenen Fellowships (Undergraduate/Fellowship) [372]
Jacob VanNamen-Vans Marketing Scholarships (Undergraduate/Scholarship) [570]
Varian Radiation Therapy Scholarship Program (Postdoctorate/Scholarship) [1044]
Joseph A. Vasta Memorial Scholarships (Undergraduate/Scholarship) [2924]
Vector Marketing Canadian Scholarship Awards (Undergraduate/Scholarship) [7312]
Vector Marketing Scholarships (Graduate, Undergraduate/Scholarship) [5651]
Ventana Medical Systems In Situ Hybridization Awards (Other/Award/Prize) [5083]
Ventura County Medical Association Alliance Scholarships (Undergraduate/Scholarship) [7314]
Veolia ES Waste-to-Energy/Terrence L. Guest Memorial Awards (Graduate/Scholarship) [6599]
Verizon Scholarship Program (Undergraduate/Scholarship) [3607]
Chester M. Vernon Memorial Eagle Scout Scholarships (High School/Scholarship) [4867]
Dimitri J. Ververelli Memorial Scholarships (Undergraduate/Scholarship) [3536]
Vesalius Trust Student Scholarships (Undergraduate/Scholarship) [7317]
Lari Ann Vest Memorial Scholarships (Undergraduate/Scholarship) [809]
Veterans of Enduring Freedom (Afghanistan) and Iraqi Freedom Scholarships (Undergraduate/Scholarship) [1250]
Veterans of Foreign Wars Scout of the Year (High School/Scholarship) [4868]
Zelda Walling Vicha Memorial Scholarships (Undergraduate/Scholarship) [1035]
Vilas Equity Scholarships (Undergraduate/Scholarship) [7282]
William F. Vilas Scholarships (Undergraduate/Scholarship) [7283]
Vincennes University Scholarships (Undergraduate/Scholarship) [4909]
Vinyl Plastics Division Scholarships (Graduate, Undergraduate/Scholarship) [6564]
Violin Society of America Scholarships (Undergraduate/Scholarship) [7326]
VISTAKON Research Grants (All/Grant) [280]
Gupton A. Vogt Oxford Cup Memorial Scholarships (Graduate, Undergraduate/Scholarship) [1685]
Von Ogden Vogt Scholarships (Graduate, Master's/Scholarship) [6959]
Irma E. Voigt Memorial Scholarships (Undergraduate/Scholarship) [6379]
The Sibyl Jennings Vorheis Memorial Scholarship Program (Undergraduate/Scholarship) [3081]
Abe Voron Scholarships (All/Scholarship) [1789]
VPPPA June Brothers Scholarships (Graduate, Undergraduate/Scholarship) [7340]
VPPPA Stephen Brown Scholarships (Graduate, Undergraduate/Scholarship) [7341]
VSP Research Grants (All/Grant) [281]
Wachovia Scholarship Awards (Undergraduate/Scholarship) [3571]
Bruce Wade Memorial Scholarships for Lesbian, Gay and Bisexual (Undergraduate/Scholarship) [6145]
Robert R. Wade Scholarship (Undergraduate/Scholarship) [4232]
Mercedes Laurie Wade Scholarships (Undergraduate/Scholarship) [1901]
WAEPA Scholarship Program (Undergraduate/Scholarship) [7520]
Jack H. Wagner Scholarships (Undergraduate/Scholarship) [4505]
Selma A. Waksman Endowed Scholarships in Microbial Diversity (Undergraduate/Scholarship) [4304]
Jane C. Waldbaum Archaeological Field School Scholarships (Undergraduate/Scholarship) [1195]
Margaret E. Waldron Scholarship Fund (Undergraduate/Scholarship) [2977]
Sue Walicki Nursing Scholarship (Undergraduate/Scholarship) [3992]
Gary Walker Memorial Scholarships (Professional Development/Scholarship) [3788]
Arthur BC Walker Scholarships (Undergraduate/Scholarship) [5060]
Myrtle and Earl Walker Scholarships (Undergraduate/Scholarship) [6505]
Wall-Mart Stores, Inc. Fellowships - Graduate (Undergraduate/Scholarship) [643]
WALPA Lake Scholarships (Graduate, Undergraduate/Scholarship) [7382]
Alice Glaisyer Warfield Scholarships (Undergraduate/Scholarship) [6922]
Judith Warner Memorial Scholarships (Undergraduate/Scholarship) [5867]
Rachel Warner Memorial Scholarships (Graduate, Undergraduate/Scholarship) [4935]
James L. Warner Scholarships (Undergraduate/Scholarship) [5369]
Earl Warren Civil Rights Training Scholarships (Graduate/Scholarship) [4605]
John R. and Joan F. Warren Scholarship Fund (Undergraduate/Scholarship) [6761]
Earl Warren Shearman and Sterling Scholarships (Graduate/Scholarship) [4606]
Washington College Bound Scholarships (Undergraduate/Scholarship) [7366]
Washington County Farm Bureau Scholarships (Undergraduate/Scholarship) [5394]
Washington Group International Safety Scholarships (Undergraduate/Scholarship) [1074]
Washington Higher Education Coordinating Board Educational Opportunity Grants (Undergraduate/Grant) [7367]
Washington Higher Education Coordinating Board Health Professional Scholarships (Undergraduate/Scholarship) [7368]
Washington Higher Education Coordinating Board State Need Grants (Undergraduate/Grant) [7369]
Washington Metropolitan Scholarships (Undergraduate/Scholarship) [7374]
Washington Reciprocity Out-of-State Scholarships (Undergraduate/Scholarship) [4220]
Washington University Law School Chancellor's Graduate Fellowships (Graduate/Fellowship) [7386]
Washington University Law School Olin Fellowships for Women (Graduate/Fellowship) [7387]
Vincent T. Wasilewski Scholarships (All/Scholarship) [1790]
John J. Wasmuth Postdoctoral Fellowships (Postdoctorate/Fellowship) [3551]
Stand Watie Scholarships (Undergraduate/Scholarship) [6601]
Robert D. Watkins Graduate Research Fellowships (Postdoctorate/Fellowship) [1009]
Watson-Brown Scholarships (Undergraduate/Scholarship) [7392]
Thomas S. Watson, Jr. Memorial Scholarships (Graduate, Undergraduate/Scholarship) [4662]
Watsontown Volunteer Fire Company Scholarships (Undergraduate/Scholarship) [1902]
The Wax Company Scholarships (Undergraduate/Scholarship) [121]
Wayne County Bank Scholarships (Undergraduate/Scholarship) [5305]
Kurt Wayne Scholarships (Graduate/Scholarship) [3201]
Richard M. Weaver Fellowships (Graduate/Fellowship) [3774]
Faye and Rendell Webb Scholarships (High School, Undergraduate/Scholarship) [2292]
Allen and Loureena Weber Scholarships (Undergraduate/Scholarship) [6506]
Lester and Eleanor Webster Charitable Trust Fund (Undergraduate/Scholarship) [6762]
Jerome P. Webster Fellowships (Professional Development/Fellowship) [3927]
Webster Society Scholarships (Undergraduate/Scholarship) [7388]
Kenneth G. Weckel Scholarships (Undergraduate/Scholarship) [4523]
Frank L. Weil Memorial Eagle Scout Scholarships (Undergraduate/Scholarship) [4869]
Edith Weingarten Scholarship Program (Postgraduate/Scholarship) [737]
The Bee Winkler Weinstein Scholarship Fund (All/Scholarship) [6791]
William E. Weisel Scholarships (Undergraduate/Scholarship) [6507]
Weissbuch Family Scholarships (Undergraduate/Scholarship) [6239]

Edward Kent Welch Memorial Scholarships *(Undergraduate/Scholarship)* [7461]
Welch Scholars Grants *(Undergraduate/Grant)* [753]
Sue Marsh Weller Memorial Scholarships *(Graduate, Postgraduate, Undergraduate/Scholarship)* [3695]
Dorothy Wellnitz Canadian Scholarships *(Undergraduate/Scholarship)* [890]
Wells Fargo American Indian Scholarship for Graduates *(Graduate/Scholarship)* [644]
Wells Fargo Scholarship Program *(Graduate, Undergraduate/Scholarship)* [3608]
Wells Fargo Scholarships *(Undergraduate/Scholarship)* [5783]
Teri Wenglein-Callender Undergraduate Scholarships *(Undergraduate/Scholarship)* [2669]
Francis X. Weninger Scholarships *(Undergraduate/Scholarship)* [7534]
Lucille and Charles A. Wert Scholarships *(Undergraduate/Scholarship)* [4403]
West Indian Migrant Farm Workers Memorial Scholarships *(Undergraduate/Scholarship)* [3501]
West Virginia Hospitality and Travel Association General Scholarships *(Undergraduate/Scholarship)* [7400]
West Virginia PTA Scholarships *(Undergraduate/Scholarship)* [7396]
Redlands Evening Lions Club - Barbara Westen Scholarships *(Undergraduate/Scholarship)* [6012]
Western Civilization Fellowships *(Graduate/Fellowship)* [3775]
Western Governors University Scholarship Program *(Undergraduate/Scholarship)* [3609]
Western Michigan Greenhouse Association Scholarships *(Undergraduate/Scholarship)* [571]
Western Reserve Herb Society Scholarships *(Undergraduate/Scholarship)* [3547]
Robert B. Westover Scholarships *(Undergraduate/Scholarship)* [3202]
Frederick K. Weyerhaeuser Forest History Fellowships *(Graduate/Fellowship)* [3031]
Dr. William "Tim" Whalen Memorial Scholarship *(Undergraduate/Scholarship)* [5259]
J. Irving Whalley Memorial Scholarships *(Undergraduate/Scholarship)* [1566]
Whan Memorial Scholarships *(Graduate, Undergraduate/Scholarship)* [5652]
Edwyna Wheadon Postgraduate Training Scholarship Fund *(Professional Development/Scholarship)* [4827]
Haemer Wheatcraft Scholarships *(Undergraduate/Scholarship)* [2768]
Seitlin Franklin E. Wheeler Scholarship Fund *(Undergraduate/Scholarship)* [2604]
Paul A. Whelan Aviation Scholarships *(Undergraduate/Scholarship)* [7083]
Whidbey Island Giving Circle Scholarships *(Undergraduate/Scholarship)* [5784]
Brian J. White Endowed Law Scholarships *(Undergraduate/Scholarship)* [5617]
Howard A. White Endowed Scholarships *(Undergraduate/Scholarship)* [5618]
White House Fellows *(Professional Development/Fellowship)* [5748]
Mary Kean White Memorial Scholarship Fund *(Undergraduate/Scholarship)* [6763]
White Rose Scholarships *(Undergraduate/Scholarship)* [6146]
Bradford White Scholarships *(Undergraduate/Scholarship)* [5706]
Herbert W. Whiteman, Jr. Scholarships *(Graduate, Undergraduate/Scholarship)* [7293]
Robert B. and Sophia Whiteside Scholarships *(Undergraduate/Scholarship)* [2796]
Ann Cook Whitman Scholarships for Perry High School *(Undergraduate/Scholarship)* [2843]
Ann Cook Whitman Washington, DC Scholarships *(Undergraduate/Scholarship)* [2844]
Donna Axum Whitworth Scholarships *(Undergraduate/Scholarship)* [2670]
Louise Wachter Wichman Scholarship Fund *(Undergraduate/Scholarship)* [3314]
Alice Hersey Wick Scholarships *(Undergraduate/Scholarship)* [6380]
Tom Wicker Scholarships *(Undergraduate/Scholarship)* [7197]
Wicomico High School Class of '55 Scholarships *(Undergraduate/Scholarship)* [2386]
Ethyl and Armin Wiebke Memorial Scholarships *(Undergraduate/Scholarship)* [7483]
Barbara Wiedner and Dorothy Vandercook Memorial Peace Scholarships *(Undergraduate/Scholarship)* [3360]
Edwin F. Wiegand Science and Technology Scholarships *(Undergraduate/Scholarship)* [5868]
The WIFLE Scholarship Fund *(Graduate, Postdoctorate, Undergraduate/Scholarship)* [7477]
Fred C. Wikoff, Jr. Scholarship Fund *(Undergraduate/Scholarship)* [3083]
Teddy Wilburn Scholarships *(Undergraduate/Scholarship)* [2451]
WildBird/Clements Memorial Scholarships *(Undergraduate/Scholarship)* [439]
Wiley Publishing Inc. Scholarships *(Undergraduate/Scholarship)* [5112]
Wilks Memorial Awards *(Undergraduate/Award/Prize)* [1115]
Andrea Will Memorial Scholarships *(Undergraduate/Scholarship)* [6381]
Willa Beach-Porter Music Scholarships *(Undergraduate/Scholarship)* [2097]
Willamette Chapter Scholarship Awards *(Undergraduate/Scholarship)* [5389]
Willamette Valley AG Association Scholarships *(Undergraduate/Scholarship)* [5395]
M. William and Frances J. Tilghman Scholarship *(Undergraduate/Scholarship)* [2387]
William Goldberg Diamond Corp. Scholarships *(Undergraduate/Scholarship)* [3203]
Williams Foundation Scholarships *(Undergraduate/Scholarship)* [5869]
Sidney B. Williams, Jr. Scholarships *(Undergraduate/Scholarship)* [685]
Rodney Williams Legacy Scholarships *(Undergraduate/Grant)* [7107]
James Elliott Williams Scholarship Fund *(Undergraduate/Scholarship)* [5537]
CSM Virgil R. Williams Scholarships *(Undergraduate/Scholarship)* [2857]
Elizabeth T. Williams Scholarships *(Undergraduate/Scholarship)* [7462]
Leon Williams Scholarships *(Undergraduate/Scholarship)* [6240]
Maxine Williams Scholarships *(Postdoctorate/Scholarship)* [368]
Randy Williams Scholarships *(Undergraduate/Scholarship)* [6241]
Cenie Jomo Williams Tuition Scholarships *(Undergraduate/Scholarship)* [4668]
Edwin H. and Louise N. Williamson Endowed Scholarships *(Undergraduate/Scholarship)* [7463]
Mary Katherine "Kathy" Williamson Scholarship Fund *(Undergraduate/Scholarship)* [2366]
Williamsport-Lycoming Community Foundation - Benjamin Franklin Scholarships *(Undergraduate/Scholarship)* [2980]
Gary S. Wilmer RAMI Music Scholarship *(Undergraduate/Scholarship)* [2490]
Larry Wilson for Environmental Studies Scholarships *(Graduate, Undergraduate/Scholarship)* [1227]
Pete Wilson Graduate Scholarships *(Postgraduate/Scholarship)* [1404]
Pete Wilson Journalism Scholarships *(Undergraduate/Scholarship)* [1405]
Saul T. Wilson, Jr. Scholarships *(Graduate, Undergraduate/Scholarship)* [7300]
Bob Wilson Legacy Scholarship *(Undergraduate/Scholarship)* [1835]
The Arthur N. Wilson, MD, Scholarships *(Undergraduate/Scholarship)* [714]
John Charles Wilson Scholarships *(Undergraduate/Scholarship)* [3784]
Larry Wilson Scholarships for Undergraduate Civil Engineering Students *(Undergraduate/Scholarship)* [1228]
Harriet Barnhart Wimmer Scholarships *(Undergraduate/Scholarship)* [988]
Lisa Winkler Memorial Scholarships *(Undergraduate/Scholarship)* [1415]
Winston-Salem Foundation Scholarships *(Undergraduate/Scholarship)* [7464]
Winston Scholarships *(Graduate, Undergraduate/Scholarship)* [6260]
Marine Corps Sgt. Jeannette L. Winters Memorial Scholarships *(Undergraduate/Scholarship)* [1251]
Winterthur Research Fellowships *(All/Fellowship)* [7468]
WINUP Member Scholarships *(Professional Development/Scholarship)* [7496]
Wisconsin Broadcasters Association Scholarships *(Undergraduate/Scholarship)* [7472]
Wisconsin-Madison Journalism Scholarships *(Undergraduate/Scholarship)* [7285]
Wisconsin-Madison Music Clinic Scholarships *(Undergraduate/Scholarship)* [7286]
Wisconsin Region Student Leadership Scholarships *(Undergraduate/Scholarship)* [4684]
Witt Mares Scholarships *(Undergraduate/Scholarship)* [7331]
WKIX Alumni Association Scholarships *(Undergraduate/Scholarship)* [7198]
WMA Memorial Scholarships *(Undergraduate/Scholarship)* [7484]
WNBA Eastman Grants *(Professional Development/Grant)* [7504]
WOCN Accredited Nursing Education Scholarships *(Graduate, Undergraduate/Scholarship)* [7522]
WOCN Advanced Education Scholarships *(Doctorate, Graduate, Undergraduate/Scholarship)* [7523]
Woksape Oyate: "Wisdom of the People" Distinguished Scholars Award *(Undergraduate/Scholarship)* [628]
Paul R. Wolf Memorial Scholarships *(Graduate/Scholarship)* [1033]
Milton Wolf Scholarships *(Undergraduate/Scholarship)* [3204]
Wolf Trap Foundation Scholarship Program for Performing Arts Teachers *(Professional Development/Scholarship)* [7474]
The Wolf Trap Internship Program *(Graduate, Professional Development, Undergraduate/Internship)* [7475]
Deborah Partridge Wolfe International Fellowships *(Graduate, Undergraduate/Fellowship)* [7559]
Charles H. and Ethel E. Wolfe Scholarships *(Undergraduate/Scholarship)* [5370]
Tim Wolfred Scholarships *(Undergraduate/Scholarship)* [6147]
Eleanor M. Wolfson Memorial Scholarship Fund *(Undergraduate/Scholarship)* [2981]
Wendy Y. Wolfson Memorial Scholarship Fund *(Undergraduate/Scholarship)* [2982]
Abel Wolman Fellowships *(Doctorate/Fellowship)* [1145]
Lee Womack Scholarships Fund *(Undergraduate/Scholarship)* [4565]
Woman In Rural Electrification Scholarships *(Undergraduate/Scholarship)* [6627]
Woman's Club of Grand Haven Scholarships Fund *(Undergraduate/Scholarship)* [3315]
Women In Defense HORIZONS Scholarships *(Graduate, Undergraduate/Scholarship)* [7479]
Women In Need Scholarships *(Undergraduate/Scholarship)* [2835]
Women In Transition Scholarships *(Undergraduate/Scholarship)* [2836]
Women of Today's Manufacturing Scholarships *(Undergraduate/Scholarship)* [2491]
Women's Army Corps Veterans Association Scholarships *(Undergraduate/Scholarship)* [7486]
Women's Independence Scholarship Programs *(Undergraduate/Scholarship)* [6820]
Women's Jewelry Association Member Grants *(All/Grant)* [7498]
Women's Jewelry Association Scholarships *(Undergraduate/Scholarship)* [7499]
Women's Leadership in Agriculture Scholarship Program *(Undergraduate/Scholarship)* [5320]
Women's Overseas and Service League Scholarships for Women *(Undergraduate/Scholarship)* [7506]
Carolyn Wones Recruitment Scholarships Grant *(Undergraduate/Scholarship)* [2492]
Charles Fred Wonson Scholarships *(Undergraduate/Scholarship)* [7244]
Dr. Harold S. Wood Award for Excellence *(Undergraduate/Award/Prize)* [3207]

Wood County Bar Association Memorial Scholarships *(Undergraduate/Scholarship)* [5530]
Rolla F. Wood Graduate Scholarships *(Graduate/Scholarship)* [5656]
Ed Wood Memorial Scholarship Awards *(Undergraduate/Scholarship)* [5390]
Woodcock Family Education Scholarship Program *(Undergraduate/Scholarship)* [196]
Betsy B. Woodward Scholarships *(Undergraduate/Scholarship)* [1422]
Blance E. Woolls Scholarships *(Graduate/Scholarship)* [1639]
Patty Wooten Scholarships *(Undergraduate/Scholarship)* [1368]
John W. Work III Memorial Foundation Scholarships *(Undergraduate/Scholarship)* [2453]
Working for Farmers' Success Scholarships *(Undergraduate/Scholarship)* [7516]
The Working Press Internships *(Undergraduate/Internship)* [6570]
Workshop, Inc. and Stark MRDD Fostering Diversity Through Special Needs Scholarship Fund *(Undergraduate/Scholarship)* [6764]
World Book Graduate Scholarships in Library and Information Science *(Graduate/Scholarship)* [1987]
James and Colin Lee Wozumi Scholarships *(Undergraduate/Scholarship)* [5785]
Jean Wright-Elson Scholarships *(Graduate, Undergraduate/Scholarship)* [6242]
Writers of Passage Scholarship Program *(Undergraduate/Prize)* [6159]
WTVD Endowment Scholarships *(Undergraduate/Scholarship)* [7199]
WYCUP Scholarships *(Professional Development/Scholarship)* [7518]
Margaret Wyeth Scholarship *(Undergraduate/Scholarship)* [2493]
Wyoming Art Symposium Scholarships *(Undergraduate/Scholarship)* [1318]
St. Francis Xavier Scholarships *(Undergraduate/Scholarship)* [7535]
Xavier Service Fellowships *(Undergraduate/Fellowship)* [7536]
Xavier University Chancellor Scholarships *(Undergraduate/Scholarship)* [7537]
Xavier University Departmental Scholarships *(Undergraduate/Scholarship)* [7538]
Xavier University Honors Bachelor of Arts Scholarships *(Undergraduate/Scholarship)* [7539]
Xavier University Legacy Scholarships *(Undergraduate/Scholarship)* [7540]
Xavier University ROTC Scholarships - Air Force ROTC *(Undergraduate/Scholarship)* [7541]
Xavier University ROTC Scholarships - Army ROTC *(Undergraduate/Scholarship)* [7542]
Xavier University Williams Scholarships *(Undergraduate/Scholarship)* [7543]
Xilinx Scholarships *(Graduate, Undergraduate/Scholarship)* [5653]
The Xtra Depth University Scholarships *(Undergraduate/Scholarship)* [5551]
M.H. Yager Memorial Scholarships *(Undergraduate/Scholarship)* [1567]
Yamhill County Farm Bureau Scholarships *(Undergraduate/Scholarship)* [5396]
William J. Yankee Memorial Scholarships *(Undergraduate/Scholarship)* [789]
Gwen Yarnell Theatre Scholarships *(Undergraduate/Scholarship)* [2934]
Yasme Foundation Scholarships *(Undergraduate/Scholarship)* [863]
Minoru Yasui Memorial Scholarship *(Graduate/Scholarship)* [4022]
Marilyn Yetso Memorial Scholarships *(Undergraduate/Scholarship)* [2132]
Vera Yip Memorial Scholarships *(Undergraduate/Scholarship)* [2133]
YMA Fashion Scholarships *(Undergraduate/Scholarship)* [7545]
York Rite Grand Chapter Royal Arch Masons Scholarships *(Undergraduate/Scholarship)* [2703]
Gary Yoshimura Scholarships *(Undergraduate/Scholarship)* [5876]
Jack and Edna May Yost Scholarship Fund *(Undergraduate/Scholarship)* [3123]
You Go Girl! Scholarships *(Undergraduate/Scholarship)* [5786]
Alma H. Young Emerging Scholar Award *(Doctorate/Scholarship)* [7291]
Young Investigator Grants *(Undergraduate/Grant)* [5091]
Young People For (YP4) Scholarships *(Undergraduate/Fellowship)* [6335]
Donnell B. Young Scholarships *(Undergraduate/Scholarship)* [4074]
Elmer Cooke Young - Taylor Young Scholarships *(Undergraduate/Scholarship)* [3502]
Youth Partners Accessing Capital (P.A.C.) *(Graduate, Undergraduate/Scholarship)* [250]
The Youth Scholarship Program *(Undergraduate/Scholarship)* [2095]
Youth Scholarships *(Undergraduate/Scholarship)* [6528]
Youth for Understanding Scholarships *(Undergraduate/Scholarship)* [7549]
Diane Yu Loan Repayment Assistance Program *(Undergraduate/Loan)* [4649]
Zagunis Student Leader Scholarships *(Undergraduate/Scholarship)* [4685]
Lisa Zaken Award For Excellence *(Graduate, Undergraduate/Award/Prize)* [3742]
Dr. Marie E. Zakrzewski Medical Scholarships *(Undergraduate/Scholarship)* [4095]
Zale Corporation Scholarships *(Undergraduate/Scholarship)* [3205]
Michael A. Zamperini/W. Clay Burchell Scholarships *(Undergraduate/Scholarship)* [6148]
Zarley, McKee, Thomte, Voorhees, Sease Law Scholarships *(Undergraduate/Scholarship)* [2769]
Urashi Zen Scholarships *(Undergraduate/Scholarship)* [5787]
Harry and Angel Zerigian Scholarships *(Undergraduate/Scholarship)* [1295]
Zeta Chapter Memorial Scholarships Award *(Undergraduate/Scholarship)* [2494]
Zeta Phi Beta Sorority General Graduate Scholarships *(Graduate, Postdoctorate/Scholarship)* [7560]
Zeta Phi Beta Sorority General Undergraduate Scholarships *(Undergraduate/Scholarship)* [7561]
Blanche Raper Zimmerman Scholarships *(Professional Development/Scholarship)* [7465]
Zimmermann Scholarships *(Graduate/Scholarship)* [6831]
A.R. Zipf Fellowships *(Graduate/Fellowship)* [2551]
Morris and Rebecca Ziskind Memorial Scholarships *(Undergraduate/Scholarship)* [3640]
Ruth and Sherman Zudekoff Scholarships *(Undergraduate/Scholarship)* [2397]
Leo Zupin Memorial Scholarship Fund *(Undergraduate/Scholarship)* [3317]
Francis Sylvia Zverina Scholarship *(Undergraduate/Scholarship)* [3548]
Zwilling, J.A. Henckels Culinary Arts Scholarships *(All, Professional Development/Scholarship)* [2583]

UNITED STATES (BY REGION)

Midwestern states

Midwest Chapter Scholarships - Jack Gill *(Undergraduate/Scholarship)* [1446]
MAC Emeritus Scholarships for First-Time Meeting Attendees *(All, Professional Development/Scholarship)* [4509]
MAC Louisa Bowen Memorial Scholarships for Graduate Students in Archival Administration *(Graduate/Scholarship)* [4510]
Midwest Chapter Scholarships - Betty McKern *(Undergraduate/Scholarship)* [1448]
Midwest Chapter Scholarships - Don Nelson *(Undergraduate/Scholarship)* [1449]
Midwest Chapter Scholarships - Engineering *(Undergraduate/Scholarship)* [1450]
Midwest Chapter Scholarships - Mel Nickel *(Undergraduate/Scholarship)* [1451]
Midwest Chapter Scholarships - Non-Engineering *(Undergraduate/Scholarship)* [1452]
Midwest Chapter Scholarships - Western States Award *(Undergraduate/Scholarship)* [1453]
Archie Motley Memorial Scholarships for Minority Students *(Graduate/Scholarship)* [4511]

New England states

Dvora Brodie Scholarships *(Other/Scholarship)* [3515]

Northeastern states

Elizabeth M. and Winchell M. Parson Scholarships *(Doctorate/Scholarship)* [997]
The SSPI Northeast Chapter Scholarships *(Graduate, Undergraduate/Scholarship)* [6584]
Walter W. Stillman Scholarships *(Undergraduate/Scholarship)* [1563]

Northwestern states

AIST Northwest Chapter Scholarships *(Undergraduate/Scholarship)* [1440]
William Bennett W7PHO Memorial Scholarships *(Undergraduate/Scholarship)* [821]
Earl Deadman Memorial Scholarships *(Undergraduate/Scholarship)* [556]
Gold Country Section & Region II Scholarships *(Graduate, Undergraduate/Scholarship)* [1055]

Southeastern states

Leighton M. Ballew Directing Scholarships *(Undergraduate/Scholarship)* [6631]
Polly Holliday Scholarships *(Undergraduate/Scholarship)* [6632]
Robert Porterfield Graduate Scholarships *(Graduate/Scholarship)* [6633]
Marian A. Smith Scholarships *(Graduate/Scholarship)* [6634]
Southeast Member Chapter Scholarships *(Undergraduate/Scholarship)* [1457]
Southeastern Theatre Conference Secondary School Scholarships *(Undergraduate/Scholarship)* [6635]
William E. Wilson Scholarships *(Graduate/Scholarship)* [6636]

Southern states

The SSPI Southern California Scholarships *(Graduate, Undergraduate/Scholarship)* [6585]

Southwestern states

AISC/Structural Steel Education Council Fellowships *(Graduate/Fellowship)* [682]
Rocky Mountain Coal Mining Institute Engineering/Geology Scholarships *(Undergraduate/Scholarship)* [6051]
Rocky Mountain Coal Mining Institute Technical Scholarships *(Undergraduate/Scholarship)* [6052]

UNITED STATES (BY STATE)

Alabama

ACHE/American Legion Auxiliary Scholarships *(Undergraduate/Scholarship)* [98]
ACHE/American Legion Scholarships *(Undergraduate/Scholarship)* [99]
ACHE Junior and Community College Athletic Scholarships *(Undergraduate/Scholarship)* [100]
ACHE Junior and Community College Performing Arts Scholarships *(Undergraduate/Scholarship)* [101]
ACHE Police Officers and Firefighters Survivors' Educational Assistance Programs *(Undergraduate/Scholarship)* [102]
ACHE Senior Adult Scholarships *(Two Year College, Undergraduate/Scholarship)* [103]
Alabama Gi Dependents Educational Benefit Programs *(Undergraduate/Scholarship)* [105]
Alabama National Guard Educational Assistance Programs *(Undergraduate/Scholarship)* [106]

Alabama Scholarships for Dependents of Blind Parents *(Undergraduate/Scholarship)* [107]
Alabama Student Assistance Programs *(Undergraduate/Scholarship)* [108]
Alabama Student Grant Programs *(Undergraduate/Grant)* [109]
Horatio Alger Alabama Scholarships *(Undergraduate/Scholarship)* [199]
Howard Baker Foundation Scholarships *(Undergraduate/Scholarship)* [1589]
Johnston Cabaniss Scholarships *(Undergraduate/Scholarship)* [123]
Charles Clarke Cordle Memorial Scholarships *(Undergraduate/Scholarship)* [830]
Cecil Lane Family Scholarships *(Undergraduate/Scholarship)* [114]
NW-SCC/American Cancer Society College Scholarships *(Undergraduate/Scholarship)* [5299]
Ina E. Powell Memorial Scholarships *(Undergraduate/Scholarship)* [115]
Ed Wadsworth Memorial Scholarships *(Undergraduate/Scholarship)* [120]
Mary Katherine "Kathy" Williamson Scholarship Fund *(Undergraduate/Scholarship)* [2366]

Alaska

Alaska Aerospace Development Corporation Scholarships *(Undergraduate/Scholarship)* [4338]
Alaska Community Foundation Sven E. & Lorraine Eriksson Scholarships *(Undergraduate/Scholarship)* [7029]
Alaska Native Medical Center Auxiliary Scholarships *(Undergraduate/Scholarship)* [4339]
Alaska Press Club Scholarships *(Undergraduate/Scholarship)* [4340]
Alaska Support Industry Alliance Scholarships *(Undergraduate/Scholarship)* [4341]
Alaska Visitors Association/Gomar Scholarships *(Undergraduate/Scholarship)* [4342]
Alaska Yukon Pioneer Memorial Scholarships *(Undergraduate/Scholarship)* [4343]
Amos Joe Alter ASCE Section Alaska Section Scholarships *(Undergraduate/Scholarship)* [4344]
APC Scholarships *(Undergraduate/Scholarship)* [131]
Mike Ardaw Scholarships *(Undergraduate/Scholarship)* [4345]
Lawrence Bayer Business Administration Scholarships *(Undergraduate/Scholarship)* [4346]
Charles E. Behlke Engineering Memorial Scholarships *(Undergraduate/Scholarship)* [4347]
Bill & Nell Biggs Scholarships *(Undergraduate/Scholarship)* [4348]
Bolick Foreign Student Scholarships *(Undergraduate/Scholarship)* [4349]
Mary Lou Brown Scholarships *(Undergraduate/Scholarship)* [823]
Charles E. Bunnell Scholarships *(Undergraduate/Scholarship)* [4351]
Loyal D. Burkett Memorial Scholarships *(Undergraduate/Scholarship)* [4352]
Lyle Carlson Wildlife Management Scholarships *(Undergraduate/Scholarship)* [4353]
Chugach Gem & Mineral Society Scholarships *(Undergraduate/Scholarship)* [7030]
Mable B. Crawford Memorial Scholarships *(Undergraduate/Scholarship)* [4354]
Patricia Ann Hughes Eastaugh Memorial Teaching Scholarships *(Undergraduate/Scholarship)* [4355]
Excellence in Geographic Information Systems Scholarships *(Undergraduate/Scholarship)* [4356]
Lydia Fohn-Hansen/Lola Hill Memorial Scholarships *(Undergraduate/Scholarship)* [4357]
Johnny and Sarah Frank Scholarships *(Undergraduate/Scholarship)* [4358]
Ray Glynn Scholarships *(Undergraduate/Scholarship)* [3180]
Charles F. Gould Endowment Scholarships *(Undergraduate/Scholarship)* [4359]
Patty Hamilton Early Childhood Development Scholarships *(Undergraduate/Scholarship)* [4360]
Lenore & George Hedla Accounting Scholarships *(Undergraduate/Scholarship)* [7032]
John B. Henderson Scholarships *(Undergraduate/Scholarship)* [4361]
Donald Wills Jacobs Scholarships *(Undergraduate/Scholarship)* [4362]
Stacy Kaiser Memorial Funds *(Undergraduate/Scholarship)* [6843]
Iver & Cora Knapstad Scholarships *(Undergraduate/Scholarship)* [4363]
Robert Wade Korn Endowed Scholarships *(Undergraduate/Scholarship)* [4364]
Arlene Kuhner Memorial Scholarships *(Undergraduate/Scholarship)* [7034]
Austin E. Lathrop Scholarships *(Undergraduate/Scholarship)* [4365]
Franklin M. Leach Scholarships *(Undergraduate/Scholarship)* [4366]
Ruth Lister Scholarships *(Undergraduate/Scholarship)* [6845]
Mat-Su Health Foundation Scholarships *(Undergraduate/Scholarship)* [4367]
Matanuska-Susitna College Regent's Scholarships *(Undergraduate/Scholarship)* [4368]
Dave McCloud Aviation Memorial Scholarships *(Undergraduate/Scholarship)* [4369]
The Cady McDonnell Memorial Scholarships *(Undergraduate/Scholarship)* [488]
Richard Mellon Endowment Scholarships *(Undergraduate/Scholarship)* [4370]
Andrew Nerland Endowment Scholarships *(Undergraduate/Scholarship)* [4373]
Maureen E. Nolan-Cahill Memorial Scholarships *(Undergraduate/Scholarship)* [4374]
Nordic Ski Association of Anchorage Scholarships *(Undergraduate/Scholarship)* [129]
Don & Jan O'Dowd/SWAA Scholarships *(Undergraduate/Scholarship)* [4375]
Alvin G. Ott Fish and Wildlife Scholarships *(Undergraduate/Scholarship)* [4376]
Rachael Patterson Memorial Scholarships *(Undergraduate/Scholarship)* [6846]
Point Lay Memorial Scholarships *(Undergraduate/Scholarship)* [4377]
A.D. 'Al' Robertson Memorial Scholarships *(Undergraduate/Scholarship)* [4378]
Pat and Cliff Rogers Nursing Scholarships *(Undergraduate/Scholarship)* [4379]
Dr. Orrin J. Rongstad Wildlife Management Scholarships *(Undergraduate/Scholarship)* [4380]
Clair Shirey Scholarships *(Undergraduate/Scholarship)* [4382]
Ward Sims Memorial Scholarships *(Undergraduate/Scholarship)* [4383]
Lillian Smith Scholarship for Teaching Students *(Graduate, Undergraduate/Scholarship)* [7036]
Snodgrass Scholarships *(Undergraduate/Scholarship)* [4384]
Sourdough Reunion Memorial Scholarships *(Undergraduate/Scholarship)* [4385]
Sheri Stears Education Scholarships *(Undergraduate/Scholarship)* [7037]
Sturgulewski Family Scholarships *(Graduate, Undergraduate/Scholarship)* [7038]
Togiak Village Scholarships *(Undergraduate/Scholarship)* [4386]
UAA Accounting Club Scholarships *(Undergraduate/Scholarship)* [7039]
UAA Alaska Kidney Foundation Scholarships *(Graduate, Undergraduate/Scholarship)* [7040]
UAA Alumni Association Scholarships *(Undergraduate/Scholarship)* [7041]
UAA Anchorage Daily News Minority Journalism Scholarships *(Undergraduate/Scholarship)* [7042]
UAA April Relyea Scholarships *(Graduate, Undergraduate/Scholarship)* [7043]
UAA Ardell French Memorial Scholarships *(Undergraduate/Scholarship)* [7044]
UAA Brown Schoenheit Memorial Scholarships *(Undergraduate/Scholarship)* [7045]
UAA Chris L. Kleinke Scholarships *(Graduate, Undergraduate/Scholarship)* [7046]
UAA College of Business & Public Policy Scholarships *(Graduate, Undergraduate/Scholarship)* [7047]
UAA Diane Olsen Memorial Scholarships *(Undergraduate/Scholarship)* [7048]
UAA Dr. Jon Baker Memorial Scholarships *(Graduate, Undergraduate/Scholarship)* [7049]
UAA Edward Rollin Clinton Memorial for Music *(Undergraduate/Scholarship)* [7050]
UAA Elaine Atwood Scholarships *(Undergraduate/Scholarship)* [7051]
UAA Emi Chance Memorial Scholarships *(Undergraduate/Scholarship)* [7052]
UAA Eveline Schuster Memorial Award/Scholarships *(Graduate, Undergraduate/Scholarship)* [7053]
UAA Friends of the Performing Arts Scholarships *(Undergraduate/Scholarship)* [7054]
UAA GCI, Inc. Scholarships *(Undergraduate/Scholarship)* [7055]
UAA Governor William A. Egan Scholarships *(Undergraduate/Scholarship)* [7056]
UAA Jack & Martha Roderick Scholarships *(Graduate, Undergraduate/Scholarship)* [7057]
UAA Jan & Glenn Fredericks Scholarships *(Graduate, Undergraduate/Scholarship)* [7058]
UAA Ken Gray Endowment Scholarships *(Undergraduate/Scholarship)* [7059]
UAA Kimura Scholarship Fund (Photography Scholarships) *(Undergraduate/Scholarship)* [7060]
UAA Kimura Scholarship Funds (Illustration Scholarships) *(Undergraduate/Scholarship)* [7061]
UAA Kris Knudson Memorial Scholarships *(Graduate, Undergraduate/Scholarship)* [7062]
UAA Mark A. Beltz Scholarships *(Graduate, Undergraduate/Scholarship)* [7063]
UAA Melissa J. Wolf Scholarships *(Undergraduate/Scholarship)* [7064]
UAA Michael Baring-Gould Memorial Scholarships *(Graduate, Undergraduate/Scholarship)* [7065]
UAA Michael D. Ford Memorial Scholarships *(Graduate, Undergraduate/Scholarship)* [7066]
UAA Muriel Hannah Scholarships in Art *(Undergraduate/Scholarship)* [7067]
UAA Pat Brakke Political Science Scholarships *(Undergraduate/Scholarship)* [7068]
UAA Paul G. Landis Scholarships *(Undergraduate/Scholarship)* [7069]
UAA Pignalberi Public Policy Scholarships *(Graduate/Scholarship)* [7070]
UAA Quanterra Scholarships *(Undergraduate/Scholarship)* [7071]
UAA RRANN Program Scholarships *(Undergraduate/Scholarship)* [7072]
UAA Wells Fargo Career Scholarships *(Graduate/Scholarship)* [7073]
Umialik Scholarships *(Undergraduate/Scholarship)* [4387]
University of Alaska Scholars Program *(Undergraduate/Scholarship)* [4388]
William S. Wilson Memorial Scholarships *(Undergraduate/Scholarship)* [4389]
Guy A. Woodings Scholarships *(Undergraduate/Scholarship)* [4390]
Ralph Yetka Memorial Scholarships *(Undergraduate/Scholarship)* [4391]
Joan C. Yoder Memorial Nursing Scholarships *(Undergraduate/Scholarship)* [4392]
Yukon Delta Fisheries Development Association Scholarships *(Undergraduate/Scholarship)* [4393]

Arizona

Marvin A. Andrews Scholarships/Internships *(Graduate/Scholarship)* [1216]
APS/ASU Scholarships *(Undergraduate/Scholarship)* [5697]
APS/Maricopa County Community Colleges Scholarships *(Undergraduate/Scholarship)* [5698]
Arizona Nursery Association Scholarships *(Undergraduate/Scholarship)* [1219]
Walt Bartram Memorial Education Awards (Region 12 and Chapter 119) *(Undergraduate/Scholarship)* [6470]

Calvin Alumni Association Arizona Central Chapter Scholarships *(Undergraduate/Scholarship)* [1866]
Central Arizona DX Association Scholarships *(Undergraduate/Scholarship)* [825]
Charles N. Fisher Memorial Scholarships *(Undergraduate/Scholarship)* [833]
HSBC-North America Scholarship Program *(Undergraduate/Scholarship)* [3592]
Stephen T. Marchello Scholarships *(Undergraduate/Scholarship)* [4280]
The Cady McDonnell Memorial Scholarships *(Undergraduate/Scholarship)* [488]
Prescott Fine Arts Association Scholarship Program *(Undergraduate/Scholarship)* [5746]
William C. Ray, CIH, CSP Arizona Scholarships *(Graduate, Undergraduate/Scholarship)* [1068]
John J. and Elizabeth Rhodes Scholarships *(Graduate, Undergraduate/Scholarship)* [1674]
Rocky Mountain Coal Mining Institute Engineering/Geology Scholarships *(Undergraduate/Scholarship)* [6051]
Rocky Mountain Coal Mining Institute Technical Scholarships *(Undergraduate/Scholarship)* [6052]
Tribal Priority Scholarships *(Undergraduate/Scholarship)* [1212]

Arkansas

Arkansas Public Health Association Scholarships *(Undergraduate/Scholarship)* [1233]
Arkansas Society of Professional Sanitarians Scholarships *(Undergraduate/Scholarship)* [1234]
Arkansas State University Mountain Home Scholarships *(Undergraduate/Scholarship)* [4906]
Lone Star GIA Associate and Alumni Scholarships *(Undergraduate/Scholarship)* [3190]
Randall Matthis for Environmental Studies Scholarships *(Graduate, Undergraduate/Scholarship)* [1226]
Fred R. McDaniel Memorial Scholarships *(Undergraduate/Scholarship)* [842]
NW-SCC/American Cancer Society College Scholarships *(Undergraduate/Scholarship)* [5299]
Hatton W. Sumners Scholarships *(Undergraduate/Scholarship)* [5331]
Larry Wilson for Environmental Studies Scholarships *(Graduate, Undergraduate/Scholarship)* [1227]
Larry Wilson Scholarships for Undergraduate Civil Engineering Students *(Undergraduate/Scholarship)* [1228]

California

92109 Community Fund-Mark and Karla Stuart Family Scholarships *(Undergraduate/Scholarship)* [6161]
Above and Beyond Scholarships *(Graduate/Scholarship)* [1846]
AeA Scholarships *(Undergraduate/Scholarship)* [6162]
After-the-Fires Scholarships *(Undergraduate/Scholarship)* [6163]
AISC/Structural Steel Education Council Fellowships *(Graduate/Fellowship)* [682]
AIST San Francisco Chapter Scholarships *(Undergraduate/Scholarship)* [1442]
Horatio Alger California and California Orange County Scholarships *(Undergraduate/Scholarship)* [200]
Julie Allen World Classroom Scholarships *(Undergraduate/Scholarship)* [6164]
Armenian American Citizen's League Scholarships *(Undergraduate/Scholarship)* [1266]
Marvin Arnold and Irene Jaquetta Heye Scholarships *(Undergraduate/Scholarship)* [6165]
ARREOLA/CBSPM Scholarships *(Undergraduate/Scholarship)* [6166]
William and Lucille Ash Scholarships *(Undergraduate/Scholarship)* [6167]
Asian/Pacific Bar Association of Sacramento Law Foundation Scholarships *(Undergraduate/Scholarship)* [1338]
Association of California Water Agencies Scholarships *(Undergraduate/Scholarship)* [1376]
Association for Women in Architecture Scholarships *(Undergraduate/Scholarship)* [1506]
Frank H. Ault Scholarships *(Undergraduate/Scholarship)* [6168]
Ballard Family Foundation Scholarships *(Undergraduate/Scholarship)* [6169]
Barta-Lehman Musical Scholarships *(Undergraduate/Scholarship)* [6170]
Walt Bartram Memorial Education Awards (Region 12 and Chapter 119) *(Undergraduate/Scholarship)* [6470]
Bay Area Minority Law Student Scholarships *(Graduate, Undergraduate/Scholarship)* [1596]
Beacon of Hope Scholarships *(Undergraduate/Scholarship)* [1608]
Ray and Mary Bell Memorial Scholarships *(Undergraduate/Scholarship)* [6171]
James R. and Geraldine F. Bertelsen Scholarships *(Undergraduate/Scholarship)* [6172]
Biocom Scholarships *(Undergraduate/Scholarship)* [6173]
Norman Blachford Point Scholarships *(Graduate, Undergraduate/Scholarship)* [5715]
John Blanchard Memorial Scholarships *(Graduate/Scholarship)* [1847]
Dorothy M. Bolyard Memorial Scholarships *(Undergraduate/Scholarship)* [6174]
Breslauer Family Scholarships *(Undergraduate/Scholarship)* [6175]
Louise A. Broderick San Diego County Scholarships *(Undergraduate/Scholarship)* [6176]
California Association of Family and Consumer Sciences (CAFCS)-San Diego Chapter Scholarships *(Graduate, Undergraduate/Scholarship)* [6177]
California Association of Private Postsecondary Schools Scholarships *(Undergraduate/Scholarship)* [1814]
California Community Service Scholarships *(Undergraduate/Scholarship)* [4985]
California Community Service Scholarships - Bay Area *(Undergraduate/Scholarship)* [4986]
The California Endowment and AACN Minority Nurse Faculty Scholarships *(Graduate/Scholarship)* [337]
California Groundwater Association Scholarships *(Undergraduate/Scholarship)* [1837]
California Scottish Rite Foundation Scholarships *(Undergraduate/Scholarship)* [1852]
Calvin Alumni Association Southern California Chapter Scholarships *(Undergraduate/Scholarship)* [1883]
Cheerful Giver Scholarships *(Undergraduate/Scholarship)* [6178]
Chicana Latina Scholarship Fund *(Graduate, Undergraduate/Scholarship)* [2121]
The Club at Morningside Scholarships *(Undergraduate/Scholarship)* [6179]
Madison and Edith Cooper Scholarships *(Undergraduate/Scholarship)* [6180]
Crawford Scholarships *(Undergraduate/Scholarship)* [6181]
Culinary and Hospitality Foundation of San Benito County Scholarships *(Undergraduate/Scholarship)* [2566]
Curry Award for Girls and Young Women *(Undergraduate/Scholarship)* [6387]
Daddy Longlegs Scholarships *(Undergraduate/Scholarship)* [6182]
Davis Family Scholarships *(Undergraduate/Scholarship)* [6183]
Death Valley '49ers Scholarships *(Undergraduate/Scholarship)* [2627]
Ruth DeMoss Scholarships *(Undergraduate/Scholarship)* [6184]
Herman H. Derksen Scholarships *(Undergraduate/Scholarship)* [6185]
Hans H. and Margaret B. Doe Scholarships *(Graduate, Undergraduate/Scholarship)* [6186]
Dokmo Family Scholarships *(Undergraduate/Scholarship)* [6187]
Drinkwater Family Scholarships *(Undergraduate/Scholarship)* [6188]
Eustace-Kwan Family Foundation Scholarships *(Undergraduate/Scholarship)* [6388]
Film Arts Foundation Development Grants *(All/Grant)* [2928]
Charles N. Fisher Memorial Scholarships *(Undergraduate/Scholarship)* [833]
Reuben H. Fleet Memorial Scholarships *(Undergraduate/Scholarship)* [6189]
Jonathan Hastings Foster Scholarships *(Undergraduate/Scholarship)* [6190]
Bobby Griffith Memorial Scholarships *(Undergraduate/Scholarship)* [6109]
Leslie Jane Hahn Memorial Scholarships *(Undergraduate/Scholarship)* [6191]
Helm Family Scholarships *(Undergraduate/Scholarship)* [6192]
Melvin Henderson-Rubio Scholarships *(Undergraduate/Scholarship)* [7414]
Doris Hendren Memorial Scholarships *(Undergraduate/Scholarship)* [6193]
Clair A. Hill Scholarships *(Undergraduate/Scholarship)* [1377]
HSBC-North America Scholarship Program *(Undergraduate/Scholarship)* [3592]
HSF/Citi Fellows Program *(Undergraduate/Scholarship)* [3594]
HSF/Nissan Community College Transfer Scholarship Program *(Undergraduate/Scholarship)* [3598]
Albert W. and Mildred Hubbard Scholarships *(Undergraduate/Scholarship)* [6194]
Frederick George James Memorial Scholarships *(Undergraduate/Scholarship)* [6195]
Ruth E. Jenkins Scholarships *(Undergraduate/Scholarship)* [6196]
Napoleon A. Jones, III Memorial Scholarships *(Undergraduate/Scholarship)* [6197]
Kawano Family Scholarships *(Undergraduate/Scholarship)* [6198]
Kiwanis Club of Escondido Scholarships I *(Undergraduate/Scholarship)* [6199]
Kiwanis Club of Escondido Scholarships II *(Undergraduate/Scholarship)* [6200]
Judith Keller Marx Krumholz Scholarships *(Undergraduate/Scholarship)* [6201]
Joseph C. Larson Entrepreneurial Scholarships *(Undergraduate/Scholarship)* [6202]
Patrick Ledden Honorary Scholarships *(Undergraduate/Scholarship)* [6203]
Rebecca Lee, M.D. Scholarships *(Undergraduate/Scholarship)* [1373]
Ken Lee Memorial Scholarships *(Undergraduate/Scholarship)* [6204]
Lehman Family Scholarships *(Undergraduate/Scholarship)* [6205]
The Lemon Grove Education Foundation Scholarships *(Undergraduate/Scholarship)* [6206]
Library Media Teacher Scholarships *(Graduate/Scholarship)* [1849]
Luso-American Education Foundation C-1 General Scholarships *(Undergraduate/Scholarship)* [4261]
Luso-American Education Foundation G-1 Grants *(Professional Development/Grant)* [4262]
Luso-American Education Foundation G-2 Grants *(Professional Development/Grant)* [4263]
Luso-American Education Foundation G-3 Grants *(Postgraduate/Grant)* [4264]
Stephen T. Marchello Scholarships *(Undergraduate/Scholarship)* [4280]
Antonio Mattos Memorial Scholarships *(Undergraduate/Scholarship)* [4268]
The Cady McDonnell Memorial Scholarships *(Undergraduate/Scholarship)* [488]
Anneka McMillan Creative Arts Scholarships *(Undergraduate/Scholarship)* [6207]
Medical Staff Scholarships *(Undergraduate/Scholarship)* [7371]
Harvey Milk/Tom Homann Gay and Lesbian Student Scholarships *(Undergraduate/Scholarship)* [6124]
Mission Bay Hospital Auxiliary Scholarships *(Undergraduate/Scholarship)* [6208]
MKC Scholarships *(Undergraduate/Scholarship)* [6209]
Native American Charter High Schools After-the-

Fires Scholarships *(Undergraduate/Scholarship)* [6210]
NOBLE Southern California Chapter Scholarship Program *(Undergraduate/Scholarship)* [4994]
Stuart L. Noderer Memorial Scholarships *(Undergraduate/Scholarship)* [6211]
OCAEOP Community Service Scholarship Program *(Undergraduate/Scholarship)* [5353]
Orange County Centennial Academic Scholarships *(Undergraduate/Scholarship)* [5362]
Orange County Centennial Arts Scholarships *(Undergraduate/Scholarship)* [5363]
Orange County Centennial Certification Scholarships *(Undergraduate/Scholarship)* [5364]
Pearman Family Scholarships *(Undergraduate/Scholarship)* [6212]
Steve Petix Journalism Scholarship *(Undergraduate/Scholarship)* [6213]
Pollard-Bailey Scholarships *(Undergraduate/Scholarship)* [6214]
Port with No Borders Scholarships *(Undergraduate/Scholarship)* [6215]
Qualcomm San Diego Science, Technology, Engineering and Mathematics Scholarships *(Undergraduate/Scholarship)* [6216]
Rambus Scholarship Fund *(Undergraduate/Scholarship)* [6393]
Rancho Bernardo/Smith Scholarships *(Undergraduate/Scholarship)* [6217]
The Remington Club Scholarships *(Undergraduate/Scholarship)* [6218]
The Rotary Club of Rancho Bernardo Sunrise Abraxas Student Scholarships *(Undergraduate/Scholarship)* [6219]
Rubinstein Family Scholarships *(Undergraduate/Scholarship)* [6220]
San Diego City College Study Abroad Scholarships *(Undergraduate/Scholarship)* [6221]
The San Diego Foundation Community Scholarship II *(Undergraduate/Scholarship)* [6222]
The San Diego Foundation Community Scholarships I *(Undergraduate/Scholarship)* [6223]
San Diego National Bank Scholarships *(Undergraduate/Scholarship)* [6224]
San Diego Pathways to College Scholarships *(Undergraduate/Scholarship)* [6225]
San Diego Regional Aviation Association Scholarships *(Undergraduate/Scholarship)* [6226]
San Pasqual Academy Scholarships *(Undergraduate/Scholarship)* [6227]
Leo and Trinidad Sanchez Scholarships *(Undergraduate/Scholarship)* [6396]
Malini E. Sathyadev Memorial Scholarships *(Undergraduate/Scholarship)* [6228]
School Library Paraprofessional Scholarships *(Graduate/Scholarship)* [1850]
SDF Community College Transfer Scholarships for Math and Science *(Undergraduate/Scholarship)* [6229]
Service League Volunteer Scholarships *(Undergraduate/Scholarship)* [7372]
Harvey L. Simmons Memorial Scholarships *(Undergraduate/Scholarship)* [6230]
Gladys Ann Smith Greater Los Angeles Women's Council Scholarships *(Undergraduate/Scholarship)* [5142]
The SSPI Southern California Scholarships *(Graduate, Undergraduate/Scholarship)* [6585]
Gwen Stefani After-the-Fires Scholarships *(Undergraduate/Scholarship)* [6231]
Step Up Scholarships *(Undergraduate/Scholarship)* [6232]
William A. Sullivan Scholarships *(Undergraduate/Scholarship)* [5144]
Ryan "Munchie" Taylor Memorial Scholarships *(Undergraduate/Scholarship)* [4270]
Raymond A. Tice Scholarships I *(Undergraduate/Scholarship)* [6233]
Raymond A. Tice Scholarships II *(Undergraduate/Scholarship)* [6234]
Joseph Towner Fund for Gay and Lesbian Families *(Undergraduate/Scholarship)* [6141]
Vincent Trotter Health Care Scholarships *(Undergraduate/Scholarship)* [6235]
The UCSD Black Alumni Scholarship for Arts and Humanities *(Undergraduate/Scholarship)* [6236]
The UCSD Black Alumni Scholarships for Engineering, Mathematics and Science *(Undergraduate/Scholarship)* [6237]
USA Freestyle Martial Arts Scholarships *(Undergraduate/Scholarship)* [6238]
Verizon Scholarship Program *(Undergraduate/Scholarship)* [3607]
Weissbuch Family Scholarships *(Undergraduate/Scholarship)* [6239]
Leon Williams Scholarships *(Undergraduate/Scholarship)* [6240]
Randy Williams Scholarships *(Undergraduate/Scholarship)* [6241]
Milton Wolf Scholarships *(Undergraduate/Scholarship)* [3204]
Jean Wright-Elson Scholarships *(Graduate, Undergraduate/Scholarship)* [6242]
YMA Fashion Scholarships *(Undergraduate/Scholarship)* [7545]
Youth Leadership Scholarships *(Undergraduate/Scholarship)* [1844]

Colorado

ACE K-12 Scholarships Program *(High School/Scholarship)* [234]
Roy Anderson Memorial Scholarships *(Graduate, Undergraduate/Scholarship)* [2308]
Banner Health System - McKee Medical Center, Loveland: Nightingale Scholarships *(Graduate, Undergraduate/Scholarship)* [2309]
Banner Health System - North Colorado Medical Center, Greeley: Nightingale Scholarships *(Graduate, Undergraduate/Scholarship)* [2310]
Marcy and Bruce Benson: Nightingale Scholarships *(Graduate, Undergraduate/Scholarship)* [2311]
Colorado Nurses Association: Nightingale Scholarships *(Graduate, Undergraduate/Scholarship)* [2312]
Colorado Nurses Association: Virginia Paulson Memorial Scholarships *(Graduate, Undergraduate/Scholarship)* [2313]
Colorado Nurses Foundation Nightingale Scholarships *(Graduate, Undergraduate/Scholarship)* [2314]
Colorado Organization of Nursing Leaders Scholarships *(Graduate, Undergraduate/Scholarship)* [2315]
Arthur L. Davis Publishing Agency Scholarships *(Graduate, Undergraduate/Scholarship)* [2316]
Red and Lola Fehr: Nightingale Scholarships *(Graduate, Undergraduate/Scholarship)* [2317]
Amy and Horace Hagedorn Trust: Nightingale Scholarships *(Graduate, Undergraduate/Scholarship)* [2318]
Dwight A. Hamilton Scottish Rite Foundation of Colorado Graduate Scholarships *(Graduate/Scholarship)* [6284]
Johnson and Johnson: Nightingale Scholarships *(Graduate, Undergraduate/Scholarship)* [2319]
Kaiser Permanente: Nightingale Scholarships *(Graduate, Undergraduate/Scholarship)* [2320]
Latin American Educational Foundation Scholarships *(Undergraduate/Scholarship)* [4145]
Stephen T. Marchello Scholarships *(Undergraduate/Scholarship)* [4280]
The Cady McDonnell Memorial Scholarships *(Undergraduate/Scholarship)* [488]
Metropolitan State College of Denver, President's Office: Nightingale Scholarships *(Graduate, Undergraduate/Scholarship)* [2321]
H.M. Muffly Memorial Scholarships *(Graduate, Undergraduate/Scholarship)* [2322]
Peierls Rising Star Scholarship Program *(Undergraduate/Scholarship)* [3602]
Poudre Valley Health System, Fort Collins: Nightingale Scholarships *(Graduate, Undergraduate/Scholarship)* [2323]
Rocky Mountain Coal Mining Institute Engineering/Geology Scholarships *(Undergraduate/Scholarship)* [6051]
Rocky Mountain Coal Mining Institute Technical Scholarships *(Undergraduate/Scholarship)* [6052]
Rocky Mountain Region of Wound Ostomy Continence Nurses Society Scholarships *(Graduate, Undergraduate/Scholarship)* [2324]
Rose Medical Center, Denver: Nightingale Scholarships *(Graduate, Undergraduate/Scholarship)* [2325]
SACHS Foundation Graduate Scholarships *(Graduate/Scholarship)* [6090]
SACHS Foundation Undergraduate Scholarships for Colorado Black Students *(High School/Scholarship)* [6091]
St. Anthony's Hospitals, Denver: Nightingale Scholarships *(Graduate, Undergraduate/Scholarship)* [2326]
St. Mary's Hospital and Medical Center, Grand Junction: Nightingale Scholarships *(Graduate, Undergraduate/Scholarship)* [2327]
Seedworks Fund: Nightingale Scholarships *(Graduate, Undergraduate/Scholarship)* [2328]
Patty Walter Memorial Scholarships *(Graduate, Undergraduate/Scholarship)* [2329]

Connecticut

Frederick G. Adams Scholarships *(Undergraduate/Scholarship)* [3411]
Alliance for Academic Achievement Program Scholarships *(Undergraduate/Scholarship)* [3412]
Alliance Francaise of Hartford Harpin/Rohinsky Scholarships *(Undergraduate/Scholarship)* [3413]
Dorothy G. Allsop Scholarships *(Undergraduate/Scholarship)* [4721]
American Fire Sprinkler Association Scholarships *(Undergraduate/Scholarship)* [3414]
American Marketing Association-Connecticut Chapter, Anna C. Klune Memorial Scholarships *(Graduate/Scholarship)* [3415]
American Savings Foundation Scholarships *(Undergraduate/Scholarship)* [3416]
Amherst College Connecticut Alumni Scholarships *(Undergraduate/Scholarship)* [3417]
Officer Brian A. Aselton Memorial Scholarships *(Undergraduate/Scholarship)* [3419]
Malcolm Baldridge Scholarships *(Undergraduate/Scholarship)* [3420]
John Bell and Lawrence Thornton Scholarship Fund *(Undergraduate/Scholarship)* [3421]
W. Philip Braender and Nancy Coleman Braender Scholarships *(Undergraduate/Scholarship)* [3427]
Rhea Sourifman Caplin Memorial Scholarships *(Undergraduate/Scholarship)* [3429]
Cemanahuac Educational Community Scholarships *(Other/Scholarship)* [5263]
Emily Chaison Gold Award Scholarships *(Undergraduate/Scholarship)* [3431]
The College Club of Hartford Scholarships *(Undergraduate/Scholarship)* [3433]
Columbus Citizens Foundation College Scholarships *(Undergraduate/Scholarship)* [2334]
Connecticut Association of Land Surveyors Memorial Scholarships *(Undergraduate/Scholarship)* [2529]
Connecticut Association of Latinos in Higher Education Scholarships *(Undergraduate/Scholarship)* [3434]
Connecticut Association of Women Police Scholarships *(Undergraduate/Scholarship)* [3435]
Connecticut Building Congress Scholarships *(Undergraduate/Scholarship)* [3436]
Connecticut Capitol Scholarship Program *(Undergraduate/Scholarship)* [3437]
Connecticut League of Nursing Scholarships *(Undergraduate/Scholarship)* [3438]
Connecticut Mortgage Bankers Scholarships-Social Affairs Committee *(Undergraduate/Scholarship)* [3439]
Connecticut Nurserymen's Foundation Scholarships *(Undergraduate/Scholarship)* [3440]
C. Rodney Demarest Memorial Scholarships *(Undergraduate/Scholarship)* [3443]
Albert and Jane Dewey Scholarships *(Undergraduate/Scholarship)* [3444]
Harry A. Donn Scholarships *(Undergraduate/Scholarship)* [3445]

Charles Dubose Scholarships (Undergraduate/Scholarship) [3446]
Priscilla Maxwell Endicott Scholarships (Undergraduate/Scholarship) [3447]
Farmington UNICO Scholarships (Undergraduate/Scholarship) [3448]
Symee Ruth Feinburg Memorial Scholarships (Undergraduate/Scholarship) [3449]
French Embassy Scholarships (Other/Scholarship) [5264]
Gail Burns-Smith "Dare to Dream" Fund (Undergraduate/Scholarship) [3452]
GLSEN Connecticut Chapter Scholarships (Undergraduate/Scholarship) [6108]
Goethe-Institut AATG Scholarships (Other/Scholarship) [5265]
James L. and Genevieve H. Goodwin Scholarships (Undergraduate/Scholarship) [3454]
Ida L. Hartenberg Charitable Scholarships (Undergraduate/Scholarship) [3456]
Hartford County Retired Teachers Association Scholarships (Undergraduate/Scholarship) [3457]
Hartford Foundation College Scholarship Program (Undergraduate/Scholarship) [3458]
Hartford Jazz Society Scholarships (Undergraduate/Scholarship) [3461]
Hartford Whalers Booster Club Scholarships (Undergraduate/Scholarship) [3462]
Hebrew Ladies Sheltering Home Scholarships (Undergraduate/Scholarship) [3463]
Doris E. Higley Memorial Scholarships (Undergraduate/Scholarship) [3464]
Cecilia Hillman Scholarships (Undergraduate/Scholarship) [3465]
Ernest and Charlotte Hirst Family Scholarships (Undergraduate/Scholarship) [3466]
Interracial Scholarship Fund of Greater Hartford (Undergraduate/Scholarship) [3469]
J and K Foundation Scholarships (Undergraduate/Scholarship) [3470]
Dr. Leizon and Barbara Kessel Scholarships (Undergraduate/Scholarship) [3473]
Herman P. Kopplemann Scholarships (Undergraduate/Scholarship) [3474]
Dr. James L. Lawson Memorial Scholarships (Undergraduate/Scholarship) [841]
Lighthouse International Scholarships - College-bound Awards (High School/Scholarship) [4243]
Lighthouse International Scholarships - Graduate Awards (Graduate/Scholarship) [4244]
Lighthouse International Scholarships - Undergraduate Awards (Undergraduate/Scholarship) [4245]
H.B. Paul Lowenberg Lions Scholarships (Undergraduate/Scholarship) [3476]
Mary Main Memorial Scholarships (Undergraduate/Scholarship) [3478]
Manchester Scholarship Foundation Scholarships (Undergraduate/Scholarship) [3479]
Michael Jewelers Foundation Scholarships for Athletes (Undergraduate/Scholarship) [3483]
New England FEMARA Scholarships (Undergraduate/Scholarship) [846]
New York Women in Communications, Inc. Foundation Scholarships (Graduate, Undergraduate/Scholarship) [5200]
O'Meara Foundation Scholarships (Undergraduate/Scholarship) [3485]
Orange County Tourism Council Scholarships (Undergraduate/Scholarship) [5365]
Sylvia Parkinson Scholarships (Undergraduate/Scholarship) [3487]
Dorothy E. Hofmann Pembroke Scholarships (Undergraduate/Scholarship) [3488]
Nicholas J. Piergrossi Scholarships (Undergraduate/Scholarship) [3489]
Mary C. Rawlins Scholarships (Undergraduate/Scholarship) [3493]
Tadeusz Sendzimir Scholarships (Undergraduate/Scholarship) [3496]
Spanish Embassy Scholarships (Graduate, Other/Scholarship) [5267]
The SSPI Northeast Chapter Scholarships (Graduate, Undergraduate/Scholarship) [6584]
Town and County Club Scholarships (Undergraduate/Scholarship) [3499]
Trillion Diamond Company Scholarships (Undergraduate/Scholarship) [3200]
Yankee Clipper Contest Club, Inc. Youth Scholarships (Undergraduate/Scholarship) [862]

Delaware

Horatio Alger Delaware Scholarships (Undergraduate/Scholarship) [201]
Cemanahuac Educational Community Scholarships (Other/Scholarship) [5263]
Chrysler Technical Scholarships Fund (Undergraduate/Scholarship) [2633]
Columbus Citizens Foundation College Scholarships (Undergraduate/Scholarship) [2334]
French Embassy Scholarships (Other/Scholarship) [5264]
Gen III Scholarships (Undergraduate/Scholarship) [2822]
German Society Scholarships (Undergraduate/Scholarship) [3238]
Goethe-Institut AATG Scholarships (Other/Scholarship) [5265]
Gruwell Scholarships (Undergraduate/Scholarship) [2375]
Lighthouse International Scholarships - College-bound Awards (High School/Scholarship) [4243]
Lighthouse International Scholarships - Graduate Awards (Graduate/Scholarship) [4244]
Lighthouse International Scholarships - Undergraduate Awards (Undergraduate/Scholarship) [4245]
Drew Smith Memorial Scholarship (Undergraduate/Scholarship) [2384]
Spanish Embassy Scholarships (Graduate, Other/Scholarship) [5267]
The SSPI Mid-Atlantic Chapter Scholarships (Graduate, Undergraduate/Scholarship) [6583]
The SSPI Northeast Chapter Scholarships (Graduate, Undergraduate/Scholarship) [6584]

District of Columbia

The Frederick B. Abramson Memorial Foundation Scholarships (Undergraduate/Scholarship) [11]
Horatio Alger District of Columbia, Maryland, and Virginia Scholarships (Undergraduate/Scholarship) [202]
Black Student Fund (High School/Scholarship) [1722]
Cemanahuac Educational Community Scholarships (Other/Scholarship) [5263]
Columbus Citizens Foundation College Scholarships (Undergraduate/Scholarship) [2334]
D.C. Opportunity Scholarship Program (Undergraduate/Scholarship) [7376]
Richard Gregory Freeland, II Educational Scholarships (High School/Scholarship) [1762]
French Embassy Scholarships (Other/Scholarship) [5264]
Goethe-Institut AATG Scholarships (Other/Scholarship) [5265]
HSBC-North America Scholarship Program (Undergraduate/Scholarship) [3592]
Dwight P. Jacobus Scholarships (Undergraduate/Scholarship) [1488]
Lighthouse International Scholarships - College-bound Awards (High School/Scholarship) [4243]
Lighthouse International Scholarships - Graduate Awards (Graduate/Scholarship) [4244]
Lighthouse International Scholarships - Undergraduate Awards (Undergraduate/Scholarship) [4245]
Spanish Embassy Scholarships (Graduate, Other/Scholarship) [5267]
Spring Internship in International NGO Law (Undergraduate/Internship) [3825]
The SSPI Mid-Atlantic Chapter Scholarships (Graduate, Undergraduate/Scholarship) [6583]
Verizon Scholarship Program (Undergraduate/Scholarship) [3607]
Washington Scholarship Fund Signature Scholarships Program (Undergraduate/Scholarship) [7377]

Florida

Horatio Alger Florida Scholarships (Undergraduate/Scholarship) [203]
Earl I. Anderson Scholarships (Undergraduate/Scholarship) [817]
Lewis B. Barber Memorial Scholarships (Undergraduate/Scholarship) [6641]
Cesar A. Calas/FES Miami Chapter Scholarships (Undergraduate/Scholarship) [3000]
Calvin Alumni Association Florida-Gulf Coast Scholarships (Undergraduate/Scholarship) [1871]
Calvin Alumni Association-South Florida Scholarships (Undergraduate/Scholarship) [1879]
Calvin Alumni Association-South Florida Sophomore Scholarships (Undergraduate/Scholarship) [1880]
Doctors IRA & UDAYA Nursing Scholarships (Undergraduate/Scholarship) [6649]
Florida Engineering Society Junior College Scholarships (Undergraduate/Scholarship) [3003]
Florida Engineering Society University Scholarships (Undergraduate/Scholarship) [3004]
Charles and Margaret Foster Scholarships (Undergraduate/Scholarship) [6653]
James Franklin and Dorothy J. Warnell Scholarship Fund (Undergraduate/Scholarship) [2508]
American Association of University Women-Mary Sue Gottcent Memorial Scholarships (Undergraduate/Scholarship) [6655]
William L. Graddy Law School Scholarships (Undergraduate/Scholarship) [6656]
Ronald, Randall and Roger Helman Scholarships (Graduate, Undergraduate/Scholarship) [1660]
HSBC-North America Scholarship Program (Undergraduate/Scholarship) [3592]
HSF/Citi Fellows Program (Undergraduate/Scholarship) [3594]
IAAP Wings Chapter Scholarships (Undergraduate/Scholarship) [3782]
IRARC Memorial Joseph P. Rubino WA4MMD Scholarships (Undergraduate/Scholarship) [840]
V.J. Johnson Memorial Scholarships (Undergraduate/Scholarship) [402]
Chip Johnson Scholarships (Undergraduate/Scholarship) [6659]
Michael Kidger Memorial Scholarships in Optical Design (Graduate/Scholarship) [6696]
Robert A. Kleckner Scholarships (Undergraduate/Scholarship) [6663]
Otho E. Lane Memorial Scholarships (Graduate, Undergraduate/Scholarship) [1666]
Lighthouse International Scholarships - College-bound Awards (High School/Scholarship) [4243]
Lighthouse International Scholarships - Graduate Awards (Graduate/Scholarship) [4244]
Lighthouse International Scholarships - Undergraduate Awards (Undergraduate/Scholarship) [4245]
Love of Bonita Empowerment Scholarships (Undergraduate/Scholarship) [6664]
Robert V. McKenna Scholarships (Undergraduate/Scholarship) [3369]
Judge William J. Nelson Scholarships (Undergraduate/Scholarship) [6666]
Faye Lynn Roberts Educational Scholarships (Undergraduate/Scholarship) [6669]
The Rotary Club of Cape Coral Goldcoast Scholarships Fund (Undergraduate/Scholarship) [2055]
John M. and Mary A. Shanley Memorial Scholarships (Undergraduate/Scholarship) [6673]
Southwest Florida Community Foundation College Assistance Scholarships (Undergraduate/Scholarship) [6674]
John I. and Madeleine R. Taeni Scholarships (Undergraduate/Scholarship) [6678]
Jacki Tuckfield Memorial Graduate Business Scholarship Fund (Undergraduate/Scholarship) [2603]
Verizon Scholarship Program (Undergraduate/Scholarship) [3607]

Ted C. Wilson Memorial Scholarships *(Undergraduate/Scholarship)* [5791]
YMA Fashion Scholarships *(Undergraduate/Scholarship)* [7545]

Georgia

Horatio Alger Georgia Scholarships *(Undergraduate/Scholarship)* [205]
Charles Clarke Cordle Memorial Scholarships *(Undergraduate/Scholarship)* [830]
Larry Dean Davis Scholarships Program *(Undergraduate/Scholarship)* [1775]
Forsyth County United Way Scholarships *(Undergraduate/Scholarship)* [4133]
Georgia Chapter of ASSE Annual Scholarships *(Undergraduate/Scholarship)* [1054]
Georgia Engineering Foundation Scholarships *(Undergraduate/Scholarship)* [3212]
HSF/Nissan Community College Transfer Scholarship Program *(Undergraduate/Scholarship)* [3598]
Lighthouse International Scholarships - College-bound Awards *(High School/Scholarship)* [4243]
Lighthouse International Scholarships - Graduate Awards *(Graduate/Scholarship)* [4244]
Lighthouse International Scholarships - Undergraduate Awards *(Undergraduate/Scholarship)* [4245]
Edna A. Noblin Dawsonville Lions Club Scholarships *(Undergraduate/Scholarship)* [4136]
William C. Rogers Scholarships *(Undergraduate/Scholarship)* [3216]
Eugene Gene Sallee, W4YFR Memorial Scholarships *(Undergraduate/Scholarship)* [853]
Kirk Sutlive Scholarships *(Undergraduate/Scholarship)* [3217]
University Alliance HSF/UGA College Scholarship Program *(Undergraduate/Scholarship)* [3605]
Watson-Brown Scholarships *(Undergraduate/Scholarship)* [7392]
Ted C. Wilson Memorial Scholarships *(Undergraduate/Scholarship)* [5791]
YMA Fashion Scholarships *(Undergraduate/Scholarship)* [7545]

Hawaii

Hawaii Chapter/David T. Woolsey Scholarships *(Graduate, Undergraduate/Scholarship)* [4122]
R.W. "Bob" Holden Scholarships *(Undergraduate/Scholarship)* [3508]
Clem Judd Jr. Memorial Scholarships *(Undergraduate/Scholarship)* [3509]
The Cady McDonnell Memorial Scholarships *(Undergraduate/Scholarship)* [488]
Native Hawaiian Scholarships *(Undergraduate/Scholarship)* [3510]
David T. Woolsey Scholarships *(Undergraduate/Scholarship)* [989]

Idaho

The "21" Endowed Scholarships *(Undergraduate/Scholarship)* [4160]
Horatio Alger Idaho University Scholarships *(Undergraduate/Scholarship)* [206]
Horatio Alger Lola and Duane Hagadone Idaho Scholarships *(Undergraduate/Scholarship)* [211]
American Legion Boys/Girls State Scholarships *(Undergraduate/Scholarship)* [4162]
Mary Lou Brown Scholarships *(Undergraduate/Scholarship)* [823]
Laura Moore Cunningham Foundation General Scholarships *(Undergraduate/Scholarship)* [4174]
Ray Glynn Scholarships *(Undergraduate/Scholarship)* [3180]
Frank and Gladys Hopkins Endowed Scholarships *(Undergraduate/Scholarship)* [4185]
Idaho Promise Category B Scholarships *(Undergraduate/Scholarship)* [4187]
Idaho Society of CPA's Scholarships *(Undergraduate/Scholarship)* [3647]
Inland Northwest Business Alliance (INBA) Scholarships *(Undergraduate/Scholarship)* [5767]
Margaret G. Johnson and Marge J. Stout Scholarships *(Undergraduate/Scholarship)* [4188]
Lewiston Clarkston Kiwanis Club Scholarships *(Undergraduate/Scholarship)* [4189]
Lewis-Clark State College Foundation Scholars Scholarships *(Undergraduate/Scholarship)* [4193]
Lewis-Clark State College Freshman Scholarships *(Undergraduate/Scholarship)* [4194]
Lewis-Clark State College Governor's Cup Scholarships *(Undergraduate/Scholarship)* [4195]
Lewis-Clark State College/Idaho Society of CPAs Scholarships Fund *(Undergraduate/Scholarship)* [4196]
Lewis-Clark State College Provost Scholarships *(Undergraduate/Scholarship)* [4200]
Lewis-Clark State College Valley Scholarships *(Undergraduate/Scholarship)* [4202]
The Cady McDonnell Memorial Scholarships *(Undergraduate/Scholarship)* [488]
Roger C. Sathre Memorial Scholarship Fund *(Undergraduate/Scholarship)* [3649]
State of Idaho Scholarships Category A *(Undergraduate/Scholarship)* [4217]
Tschudy Family Scholarships *(Undergraduate/Scholarship)* [4219]

Illinois

Adoptive Families Today Commemorative Scholarships *(Undergraduate/Scholarship)* [24]
Horatio Alger Illinois Scholarships *(Undergraduate/Scholarship)* [207]
Allied Health Care Professional Scholarships *(Undergraduate/Scholarship)* [3661]
Earl I. Anderson Scholarships *(Undergraduate/Scholarship)* [817]
Robert C. Byrd Honors Scholarships *(Undergraduate/Scholarship)* [3662]
Calvin Alumni Association-Illinois Scholarships *(Undergraduate/Scholarship)* [1872]
Chapter 23 - Quad Cities Iowa/Illinois Scholarships *(Undergraduate/Scholarship)* [6476]
Chicago FM Club Scholarships *(Undergraduate/Scholarship)* [827]
Community Foundation of the Fox River Valley Scholarships *(Undergraduate/Scholarship)* [2389]
Community Foundation Scholarships *(Undergraduate/Scholarship)* [2461]
Margaret T. Craig Community Service Scholarship *(Undergraduate/Scholarship)* [2462]
Felicia De Bow Memorial Scholarships *(All/Scholarship)* [5447]
William R. Durham/Theater Scholarship *(Undergraduate/Scholarship)* [2463]
Louise J. Franchini Rockford Police Department Scholarships *(Undergraduate/Scholarship)* [2466]
HSBC-North America Scholarship Program *(Undergraduate/Scholarship)* [3592]
HSF/Nissan Community College Transfer Scholarship Program *(Undergraduate/Scholarship)* [3598]
Illinois Future Teacher Corps Scholarships *(Undergraduate/Scholarship)* [3663]
Illinois Landscape Contractors Association Scholarships *(Undergraduate/Scholarship)* [3656]
Illinois Special Education Teacher Tuition Waiver Scholarships *(Undergraduate/Scholarship)* [3664]
Illinois Student Assistance Commission Medical Student Scholarships *(Graduate/Scholarship)* [3665]
Illinois Student Assistance Commission Merit Recognition Scholarships *(Undergraduate/Scholarship)* [3666]
Illinois Student Assistance Commission Nurse Educator Scholarships *(Undergraduate/Scholarship)* [3667]
Illinois Student Assistance Commission Nursing Education Scholarships *(Undergraduate/Scholarship)* [3668]
Illinois Student Assistance Commission Podiatric Scholarship Program *(Undergraduate/Scholarship)* [3669]
International Management Council (IMC) Scholarships *(Undergraduate/Scholarship)* [2472]
Jewish Federation Academic Scholarships *(Graduate, Undergraduate/Scholarship)* [4029]
La Voz Latina Scholarships *(Undergraduate/Scholarship)* [2474]
Susan Lang Scholarship Program *(Postgraduate/Scholarship)* [731]
MAC Louisa Bowen Memorial Scholarships for Graduate Students in Archival Administration *(Graduate/Scholarship)* [4510]
Edmond A. Metzger Scholarships *(Undergraduate/Scholarship)* [843]
Minority Teachers of Illinois Scholarships *(Undergraduate/Scholarship)* [3670]
Muddy Waters Scholarships *(Undergraduate/Scholarship)* [1768]
Daniel Murphy Scholarships *(High School/Scholarship)* [4591]
Northwest Community Center Scholarships *(Undergraduate/Scholarship)* [2478]
Palos Fine Arts Association Scholarships *(Undergraduate/Scholarship)* [5448]
Peoria Area Amateur Radio Club Scholarships *(Undergraduate/Scholarship)* [848]
Rockford Area Habitat for Humanity College Scholarships *(Undergraduate/Scholarship)* [2482]
Rockford Chapter Daughters of the American Revolution Memorial Scholarships *(Undergraduate/Scholarship)* [2483]
Carl Sandburg College Scholarships *(Undergraduate/Scholarship)* [4908]
Six Meter Club of Chicago Scholarships *(Undergraduate/Scholarship)* [855]
Ernest and Charlene Stachowiak Memorial Scholarship *(Undergraduate/Scholarship)* [2489]
Charlie Trotters's Culinary Education Foundation Culinary Study Scholarships *(All, Professional Development/Scholarship)* [2582]
Francis Walton Memorial Scholarships *(Undergraduate/Scholarship)* [860]
Women of Today's Manufacturing Scholarships *(Undergraduate/Scholarship)* [2491]
Margaret Wyeth Scholarship *(Undergraduate/Scholarship)* [2493]

Indiana

Mandel & Lauretta Abrahamer Scholarships *(Undergraduate/Scholarship)* [6767]
Horatio Alger Indiana Scholarships *(Undergraduate/Scholarship)* [208]
Earl I. Anderson Scholarships *(Undergraduate/Scholarship)* [817]
Richard L. Baker Memorial Scholarships *(Undergraduate/Scholarship)* [6769]
Builders Association of Northeast Indiana (BANI) Scholarships *(Undergraduate/Scholarship)* [6771]
Chicago FM Club Scholarships *(Undergraduate/Scholarship)* [827]
Ellen Eberhardt Memorial Scholarships *(Undergraduate/Scholarship)* [6772]
Farmers State Bank Scholarships *(Undergraduate/Scholarship)* [6773]
Granger Business Association College Scholarships *(Undergraduate/Scholarship)* [3362]
Katherine M. Grosscup Scholarships *(Graduate, Undergraduate/Scholarship)* [3159]
Ed Haas Memorial Scholarships *(Undergraduate/Scholarship)* [6776]
H. Pauline Hand Memorial Scholarships *(Undergraduate/Scholarship)* [6777]
Dale Hughes, Jr. Memorial Scholarships *(Undergraduate/Scholarship)* [6779]
Indiana Alumni Scholarships *(Undergraduate/Scholarship)* [7530]
Indiana Broadcasters Association for College Scholarship Program *(Undergraduate/Scholarship)* [3690]
Indiana Broadcasters Association High School Scholarship Program *(Undergraduate/Scholarship)* [3691]
Indiana State Alumni Association Rural Health Scholarships *(Undergraduate/Scholarship)* [3706]

Sylvia E. Jackson Scholarships (Undergraduate/Scholarship) [6780]
Jewish Federation Academic Scholarships (Graduate, Undergraduate/Scholarship) [4029]
John W. Kelley Memorial Scholarships (Undergraduate/Scholarship) [6781]
Las Limas Community Scholarships (Undergraduate/Scholarship) [6782]
MAC Louisa Bowen Memorial Scholarships for Graduate Students in Archival Administration (Graduate/Scholarship) [4510]
Edmond A. Metzger Scholarships (Undergraduate/Scholarship) [843]
Anthony Munoz Scholarships (Undergraduate/Scholarship) [4589]
NW-SCC/American Cancer Society College Scholarships (Undergraduate/Scholarship) [5299]
Dr. J. Glenn Radcliffe Memorial Scholarships (Undergraduate/Scholarship) [6784]
Frederick Rakestraw Law Scholarships (Undergraduate/Scholarship) [5271]
University of Louisville Eagle Scout Scholarships (Undergraduate/Scholarship) [4866]
Francis Walton Memorial Scholarships (Undergraduate/Scholarship) [860]

Iowa

Horatio Alger Ak-Sar-Ben Scholarships (Undergraduate/Scholarship) [198]
Horatio Alger Iowa Scholarships (Undergraduate/Scholarship) [209]
Chapter 23 - Quad Cities Iowa/Illinois Scholarships (Undergraduate/Scholarship) [6476]
Grace O. Doane Scholarships (Undergraduate/Scholarship) [2738]
Paul and Helen L. Grauer Scholarships (Undergraduate/Scholarship) [835]
John M. Helmick Law Scholarships (Undergraduate/Scholarship) [2751]
Herbert Hoover Uncommon Student Awards (Undergraduate/Scholarship) [3613]
INF Scholarships (Undergraduate/Scholarship) [3934]
James P. Irish Scholarships (Undergraduate/Scholarship) [2752]
MAC Louisa Bowen Memorial Scholarships for Graduate Students in Archival Administration (Graduate/Scholarship) [4510]
James B. Morris Scholarships (Undergraduate/Scholarship) [4576]
Ray, NORP and Katie, WOKTE Pautz Scholarships (Undergraduate/Scholarship) [847]
PHD ARA Scholarships (Undergraduate/Scholarship) [849]
Carter Pitts Scholarships (Undergraduate/Scholarship) [3936]

Kansas

Irvine W. Cook WA0CGS Scholarships (Undergraduate/Scholarship) [829]
Paul and Helen L. Grauer Scholarships (Undergraduate/Scholarship) [835]
MAC Louisa Bowen Memorial Scholarships for Graduate Students in Archival Administration (Graduate/Scholarship) [4510]
Ray, NORP and Katie, WOKTE Pautz Scholarships (Undergraduate/Scholarship) [847]
PHD ARA Scholarships (Undergraduate/Scholarship) [849]
John J. and Elizabeth Rhodes Scholarships (Graduate, Undergraduate/Scholarship) [1674]
Hatton W. Sumners Scholarships (Undergraduate/Scholarship) [5331]
J.L. Weigand, Jr. Legal Education Trust Scholarships (Undergraduate/Scholarship) [7354]

Kentucky

Horatio Alger Kentucky Scholarships (Undergraduate/Scholarship) [210]
Early Childhood Development Scholarships (Undergraduate/Scholarship) [1701]
Katherine M. Grosscup Scholarships (Graduate, Undergraduate/Scholarship) [3159]
Kentucky Alumni Club Scholarships - Capital Region Alumni Club (Undergraduate/Scholarship) [7102]
Kentucky Alumni Club Scholarships - Central Kentucky Alumni Club (Undergraduate/Scholarship) [7103]
Kentucky Alumni Club Scholarships - Lake Cumberland Alumni Club (Undergraduate/Scholarship) [7104]
Kentucky Alumni Club Scholarships - Northern Kentucky Alumni Club (Undergraduate/Scholarship) [7105]
Kentucky Educational Excellence Scholarships (Graduate, Undergraduate/Scholarship) [1702]
Kentucky Tuition Grants (Undergraduate/Grant) [1703]
KHEAA Teacher Scholarships (Undergraduate/Scholarship) [1704]
MAC Louisa Bowen Memorial Scholarships for Graduate Students in Archival Administration (Graduate/Scholarship) [4510]
Anthony Munoz Scholarships (Undergraduate/Scholarship) [4589]
NW-SCC/American Cancer Society College Scholarships (Undergraduate/Scholarship) [5299]
South Kentucky RECC High School Senior Scholarships (Undergraduate/Scholarship) [6626]
University of Louisville Eagle Scout Scholarships (Undergraduate/Scholarship) [4866]
Woman In Rural Electrification Scholarships (Undergraduate/Scholarship) [6627]
Wyatt, Tarrant and Combs, LLP Scholarships (Undergraduate/Scholarship) [7131]
Mary Jo Young Scholarships (Undergraduate/Scholarship) [1705]

Louisiana

Horatio Alger Louisiana Scholarships (Undergraduate/Scholarship) [212]
American Radio Relay League Louisiana Memorial Scholarships (Undergraduate/Scholarship) [815]
Frank L. Dautriel Memorial Scholarships (Graduate) (Graduate/Scholarship) [4257]
Frank L. Dautriel Memorial Scholarships (Undergraduate) (Undergraduate/Scholarship) [4258]
Lone Star GIA Associate and Alumni Scholarships (Undergraduate/Scholarship) [3190]
Fred R. McDaniel Memorial Scholarships (Undergraduate/Scholarship) [842]
NW-SCC/American Cancer Society College Scholarships (Undergraduate/Scholarship) [5299]
Hatton W. Sumners Scholarships (Undergraduate/Scholarship) [5331]

Maine

Cemanahuac Educational Community Scholarships (Other/Scholarship) [5263]
Clinical Laboratory Management Association High School Senior Scholarships (High School/Scholarship) [2247]
Clinical Laboratory Management Association Undergraduate Scholarships (Undergraduate/Scholarship) [2248]
Columbus Citizens Foundation College Scholarships (Undergraduate/Scholarship) [2334]
French Embassy Scholarships (Other/Scholarship) [5264]
Goethe-Institut AATG Scholarships (Other/Scholarship) [5265]
Dr. James L. Lawson Memorial Scholarships (Undergraduate/Scholarship) [841]
Lighthouse International Scholarships - College-bound Awards (High School/Scholarship) [4243]
Lighthouse International Scholarships - Graduate Awards (Graduate/Scholarship) [4244]
Lighthouse International Scholarships - Undergraduate Awards (Undergraduate/Scholarship) [4245]
New England FEMARA Scholarships (Undergraduate/Scholarship) [846]
Spanish Embassy Scholarships (Graduate, Other/Scholarship) [5267]
Lawrence Alan Spiegel Remembrance Scholarships (Undergraduate/Scholarship) [3611]
The SSPI Northeast Chapter Scholarships (Graduate, Undergraduate/Scholarship) [6584]
Verizon Scholarship Program (Undergraduate/Scholarship) [3607]
Yankee Clipper Contest Club, Inc. Youth Scholarships (Undergraduate/Scholarship) [862]

Maryland

Horatio Alger District of Columbia, Maryland, and Virginia Scholarships (Undergraduate/Scholarship) [202]
BCCC Foundation Workforce Scholarships (Undergraduate/Scholarship) [1592]
Leticia B. Carter Scholarships (All/Scholarship) [4321]
Cemanahuac Educational Community Scholarships (Other/Scholarship) [5263]
Columbus Citizens Foundation College Scholarships (Undergraduate/Scholarship) [2334]
Richard Gregory Freeland, II Educational Scholarships (High School/Scholarship) [1762]
French Embassy Scholarships (Other/Scholarship) [5264]
Goethe-Institut AATG Scholarships (Other/Scholarship) [5265]
Hancock Family Snow Hill High School Scholarships (Undergraduate/Scholarship) [2376]
Dick and Pat Hazel Minority Scholarships (Professional Development/Scholarship) [2377]
Dwight P. Jacobus Scholarships (Undergraduate/Scholarship) [1488]
Land-Use Planning Scholarships (Graduate/Scholarship) [4896]
Lighthouse International Scholarships - College-bound Awards (High School/Scholarship) [4243]
Lighthouse International Scholarships - Graduate Awards (Graduate/Scholarship) [4244]
Lighthouse International Scholarships - Undergraduate Awards (Undergraduate/Scholarship) [4245]
Duane V. Puerde Memorial Scholarship (Undergraduate/Scholarship) [2381]
Lana K. Rinehart Scholarship (Undergraduate/Scholarship) [2383]
Drew Smith Memorial Scholarship (Undergraduate/Scholarship) [2384]
Spanish Embassy Scholarships (Graduate, Other/Scholarship) [5267]
The SSPI Mid-Atlantic Chapter Scholarships (Graduate, Undergraduate/Scholarship) [6583]
The SSPI Northeast Chapter Scholarships (Graduate, Undergraduate/Scholarship) [6584]
Gary Wagner, K3OMI Scholarships (Undergraduate/Scholarship) [859]

Massachusetts

Cemanahuac Educational Community Scholarships (Other/Scholarship) [5263]
Sgt. Michael F. Cherven Memorial Scholarships (Undergraduate/Scholarship) [4330]
Columbus Citizens Foundation College Scholarships (Undergraduate/Scholarship) [2334]
Community Foundation of Western Massachusetts Community Scholarship Program (Undergraduate/Scholarship) [2523]
Early Childhood Educators Scholarship Program (Undergraduate/Scholarship) [4332]
French Embassy Scholarships (Other/Scholarship) [5264]
Goethe-Institut AATG Scholarships (Other/Scholarship) [5265]
Hai Guin Scholarships Association (Undergraduate/Scholarship) [1280]
Lighthouse International Scholarships - College-bound Awards (High School/Scholarship) [4243]
Lighthouse International Scholarships - Graduate Awards (Graduate/Scholarship) [4244]
Lighthouse International Scholarships - Undergraduate Awards (Undergraduate/Scholarship) [4245]

MALSE Scholarships *(Undergraduate/Scholarship)* [4326]
Massachusetts Federation of Polish Women's Clubs Scholarships *(Undergraduate/Scholarship)* [4092]
Plumbing-Heating-Cooling Contractors Association Educational Foundation Massachusetts Auxiliary Scholarships *(Undergraduate/Scholarship)* [5702]
Portuguese American Police Association Scholarships *(Undergraduate/Scholarship)* [5740]
Spanish Embassy Scholarships *(Graduate, Other/Scholarship)* [5267]
The SSPI Northeast Chapter Scholarships *(Graduate, Undergraduate/Scholarship)* [6584]
Verizon Scholarship Program *(Undergraduate/Scholarship)* [3607]
Worcester District Medical Society Scholarship Fund *(Undergraduate/Scholarship)* [7512]
Yankee Clipper Contest Club, Inc. Youth Scholarships *(Undergraduate/Scholarship)* [862]
Dr. Marie E. Zakrzewski Medical Scholarships *(Undergraduate/Scholarship)* [4095]

Michigan

Altrusa International of Grand Rapids Scholarships *(Undergraduate/Scholarship)* [3319]
Earl I. Anderson Scholarships *(Undergraduate/Scholarship)* [817]
Dr. Noyes L. Avery, Jr. & Ann E. Avery Scholarships *(Undergraduate/Scholarship)* [3320]
Bernice Barabash Sports Scholarship *(Undergraduate/Scholarship)* [3972]
Charles A. Bassett Endowed Memorial Scholarship Fund *(Undergraduate/Scholarship)* [3270]
Birmingham Student Scholarship Fund Association *(Undergraduate/Scholarship)* [1717]
Geraldine Geistert Boss Scholarships *(Undergraduate/Scholarship)* [3321]
Phil Brimhall Memorial Scholarships *(Undergraduate/Scholarship)* [4494]
James W. Jr.and Jane T. Brown Scholarship Fund *(Undergraduate/Scholarship)* [3271]
Calvin Alumni Association California- Bay Area Scholarships *(Undergraduate/Scholarship)* [1869]
Calvin Alumni Association-Iowa/Pella Scholarships *(Undergraduate/Scholarship)* [1873]
Calvin Alumni Association-Maryland/Baltimore Scholarships *(Undergraduate/Scholarship)* [1874]
Calvin Alumni Association-Michigan Lakeshore Scholarships *(Undergraduate/Scholarship)* [1875]
Calvin Alumni Association-Michigan, Lansing Scholarships *(Undergraduate/Scholarship)* [1876]
Calvin Alumni Association-New York, Rochester Scholarships *(Undergraduate/Scholarship)* [1878]
Calvin Alumni Association-Southeast Michigan Scholarships *(Undergraduate/Scholarship)* [1881]
Calvin Alumni Association-Southwest Michigan, Kalamazoo Scholarships *(Undergraduate/Scholarship)* [1884]
Calvin Alumni Association-Washington, Lynden Scholarships *(Undergraduate/Scholarship)* [1886]
Orrie & Dorothy Cassada Scholarships *(Undergraduate/Scholarship)* [3322]
Chapter 198 - Downriver Detroit Scholarships *(Graduate, Undergraduate/Scholarship)* [6484]
Chapter 311 - Tri City Scholarships *(Undergraduate/Scholarship)* [6485]
Geri Coccodrilli Culinary Scholarship Fund *(Undergraduate/Scholarship)* [3272]
Thomas D. Coffield Scholarships *(Undergraduate/Scholarship)* [3324]
Paul Collins Scholarships *(Undergraduate/Scholarship)* [3325]
Dake Community Manufacturing Scholarships *(Undergraduate/Scholarship)* [3273]
Antenore C. "Buth" Davanzo Scholarships *(Undergraduate/Scholarship)* [4503]
Achille & Irene Despres, William & Andre Scholarships *(Undergraduate/Scholarship)* [3326]
Detroit Economic Club Scholarships *(Undergraduate/Scholarship)* [2513]
Chapter 116 - Kalamazoo - Roscoe Douglas Scholarships *(Undergraduate/Scholarship)* [6487]
E.V. Erickson Field of Interest Education Scholarships Fund *(Undergraduate/Scholarship)* [3274]
Melissa Eleonor Ernest Scholarship *(Undergraduate/Scholarship)* [3978]
Bertha M. Fase Memorial Scholarship Fund *(Undergraduate/Scholarship)* [3276]
Virginia Valk Fehsenfeld Scholarships *(Undergraduate/Scholarship)* [3327]
Albert Flegenheimer Memorial Scholarships *(Undergraduate/Scholarship)* [4495]
Floto-Peel Family Scholarships Fund *(Undergraduate/Scholarship)* [3278]
John and Victory E. Frantz Scholarship Fund *(Undergraduate/Scholarship)* [3279]
Melbourne & Alice E. Frontjes Scholarships *(Undergraduate/Scholarship)* [3328]
Carolyn Gallmeyer Scholarships *(Undergraduate/Scholarship)* [3329]
Mathilda & Carolyn Gallmeyer Scholarships *(Undergraduate/Scholarship)* [3330]
Gautier Family Scholarships Fund *(Undergraduate/Scholarship)* [3281]
Tim Gifford Scholarship Fund *(Undergraduate/Scholarship)* [3282]
Grand Haven Offshore Challenge Scholarships Fund *(Undergraduate/Scholarship)* [3283]
Grand Rapids Scholarship Association *(Undergraduate/Scholarship)* [3331]
Katherine M. Grosscup Scholarships *(Graduate, Undergraduate/Scholarship)* [3159]
Guy D. & Mary Edith Halladay Graduate Scholarships *(Undergraduate/Scholarship)* [3332]
Guy D. & Mary Edith Halladay Music Scholarships *(Graduate, Undergraduate/Scholarship)* [3333]
Harry and Lucille Brown Scholarships *(Undergraduate/Scholarship)* [3334]
Barbara and Nicole Heicox Foreign Travel and Study Scholarships Fund *(Undergraduate/Scholarship)* [3284]
Ronald, Randall and Roger Helman Scholarships *(Graduate, Undergraduate/Scholarship)* [1660]
John P. Hennessy Scholarships *(Undergraduate/Scholarship)* [4504]
Michael Herman Memorial Scholarship Fund *(Undergraduate/Scholarship)* [3286]
Hierholzer-Fojtik Scholarship Fund *(Undergraduate/Scholarship)* [3287]
Wayne Hildebrant Police Scholarships Fund *(Undergraduate/Scholarship)* [4141]
Douglas W. Hill, Jr. Memorial Scholarships *(Graduate, Undergraduate/Scholarship)* [1661]
Hoffman Family Scholarships Fund *(Undergraduate/Scholarship)* [3288]
Donald & Florence Hunting Scholarships *(Undergraduate/Scholarship)* [3335]
Jack Family Scholarships *(Undergraduate/Scholarship)* [3336]
Camilla C. Johnson Scholarships *(Undergraduate/Scholarship)* [3337]
Kellogg Company Career Scholarships *(Undergraduate/Scholarship)* [4067]
Seth Koehler Central High School Scholarship Fund *(Undergraduate/Scholarship)* [3289]
Lavina Laible Scholarships *(Undergraduate/Scholarship)* [3338]
Paul J. Laninga Memorial Scholarship Fund *(Undergraduate/Scholarship)* [3290]
Stephen Lankester Scholarships *(Undergraduate/Scholarship)* [3339]
Lapeer County Medical Scholarships Fund *(Undergraduate/Scholarship)* [4142]
Rick and Beverly Lattin Education Scholarships Fund *(Undergraduate/Scholarship)* [3291]
Jack W. Leatherman Family Scholarship Fund *(Undergraduate/Scholarship)* [3292]
Shepard L. & Mabel C. Lepard Scholarships *(Undergraduate/Scholarship)* [3340]
MAC Louisa Bowen Memorial Scholarships for Graduate Students in Archival Administration *(Graduate/Scholarship)* [4510]
Pat and John MacTavish Scholarship Fund *(Undergraduate/Scholarship)* [3293]
John T. & Frances Maghielse Scholarships *(Undergraduate/Scholarship)* [3341]
Michigan Council of Women in Technology College Scholarship Program *(Graduate, Undergraduate/Scholarship)* [4476]
Michigan Nurses Foundation Scholarships *(Undergraduate/Scholarship)* [4485]
Michigan Sugar Queen Scholarships *(Undergraduate/Scholarship)* [4497]
Kyle Moreland Memorial Endowment Scholarships Fund *(Undergraduate/Scholarship)* [3294]
NANBPWC Woman of Substance Scholarships *(Undergraduate/Scholarship)* [4724]
R.D. Neuman Memorial Scholarships *(Undergraduate/Scholarship)* [5273]
Peggy (Kommer) Novosad Scholarships *(Graduate, Postgraduate/Scholarship)* [3344]
Patricia & Armen Oumedian Scholarships *(Undergraduate/Scholarship)* [3345]
Marvin R. and Pearl E. Patterson Family Scholarships Fund *(Undergraduate/Scholarship)* [3296]
P.E.O. Chapter Scholarship Fund *(Undergraduate/Scholarship)* [3297]
Jacob L. Reinecke Memorial Scholarship Fund *(Undergraduate/Scholarship)* [3299]
Daniel L. Reiss Memorial Scholarship Fund *(Undergraduate/Scholarship)* [3300]
Harold and Eleonor Ringelberg Scholarship Fund *(Undergraduate/Scholarship)* [3301]
Josephine Ringold Scholarships *(Undergraduate/Scholarship)* [3346]
Charles and Eleonor Rycenga Education Scholarships Fund *(Undergraduate/Scholarship)* [3302]
Millicent M. Schaffner Endowed Memorial Scholarship *(Undergraduate/Scholarship)* [3303]
David and Ginny Schultz Family Scholarship Fund *(Undergraduate/Scholarship)* [3304]
Jeptha Wade Schureman Scholarship Program *(Undergraduate/Scholarship)* [2521]
David and Sharon Seaver Family Scholarship Fund *(Undergraduate/Scholarship)* [3305]
Margery J. Seeger Scholarships *(Undergraduate/Scholarship)* [3347]
Ken and Sandy Sharkey Family Scholarship Fund *(Undergraduate/Scholarship)* [3306]
Marion A. and Ruth K. Sherwood Family Fund Engineering Scholarships *(Undergraduate/Scholarship)* [3308]
Miller G. Sherwood Family Scholarship Fund *(Undergraduate/Scholarship)* [3309]
Sigma Kappa Foundation Michigan Scholarships *(Undergraduate/Scholarship)* [6373]
Christine Soper Scholarships *(Undergraduate/Scholarship)* [3349]
Dr. William E. & Norma Sprague Scholarships *(Undergraduate/Scholarship)* [3350]
Zachary Taylor Stevens Memorial Scholarships *(Undergraduate/Scholarship)* [856]
Edward P. Suchecki Family Scholarship Fund *(Undergraduate/Scholarship)* [3310]
Henry D. and Ruth G. Swartz Family Scholarship Fund *(Undergraduate/Scholarship)* [3311]
Dorothy B. & Charles E. Thomas Scholarships *(Undergraduate/Scholarship)* [3351]
Dorothy J. Thurston Graduate Scholarships *(Undergraduate/Scholarship)* [3352]
Mildred E. Troske Music Scholarships *(Undergraduate/Scholarship)* [3353]
TRW Foundation Scholarships *(Undergraduate/Scholarship)* [1564]
H. Wayne Van Agtmael Cosmetology Scholarship Fund *(Undergraduate/Scholarship)* [3312]
Keith C. Vanderhyde Scholarships *(Undergraduate/Scholarship)* [3354]
Jacob R. & Mary M. VanLoo & Lenore K. VanLoo Scholarships *(Undergraduate/Scholarship)* [3355]
Sue Walicki Nursing Scholarship *(Undergraduate/Scholarship)* [3992]
Warner Norcross & Judd LLP Law School Studies Scholarships *(Undergraduate/Scholarship)* [7343]
Donald M. Wells Scholarships

(Undergraduate/Scholarship) [3356]
West Michigan Nursery and Landscape Association Scholarships Fund
(Undergraduate/Scholarship) [3313]
Western Michigan Society of Health-System Pharmacists Scholarships (All/Scholarship) [7407]
Elmo Wierenga Alumni Scholarships
(Undergraduate/Scholarship) [3357]
Armos and Marilyn Winsand-Detroit Section Named Scholarships
(Undergraduate/Scholarship) [1174]
Audrey L. Wright Scholarships
(Undergraduate/Scholarship) [3358]
Zenko Family Scholarship Fund
(Undergraduate/Scholarship) [3316]

Minnesota

Horatio Alger Minnesota Scholarships
(Undergraduate/Scholarship) [213]
Bascom Hill Society Scholarships
(Undergraduate/Scholarship) [7248]
Gunnar Isberg Student Scholarships
(Undergraduate/Scholarship) [4550]
The Jackson Club Scholarships
(Undergraduate/Scholarship) [2783]
Lakselaget Foundation Scholarships (Graduate, Undergraduate/Scholarship) [4107]
Lawton Minority Retention Grants
(Undergraduate/Scholarship) [7261]
Lilly Lorenzen Scholarships
(Undergraduate/Scholarship) [1119]
MAC Louisa Bowen Memorial Scholarships for Graduate Students in Archival Administration
(Graduate/Scholarship) [4510]
Minneapolis Camp Scholarships
(Undergraduate/Scholarship) [4541]
Minnesota Association of Public Accountant Scholarships (Undergraduate/Scholarship) [4546]
Minnesota GLBT Educational Fund
(Undergraduate/Scholarship) [6125]
Minnesota Health Information Management Association Scholarships
(Undergraduate/Scholarship) [4552]
Minnesota Power Community Involvement Scholarships (Undergraduate/Scholarship) [2785]
Dale and Betty George Sola Scholarships
(Undergraduate/Scholarship) [2794]
UJFC and Council of St. Paul Annual Scholarships (All/Scholarship) [4542]
Upper Midwest Human Rights Fellowship Program (Professional Development/Fellowship) [7135]

Mississippi

Horatio Alger Mississippi Scholarships
(Undergraduate/Scholarship) [214]
ARRLF Mississippi Scholarships
(Undergraduate/Scholarship) [819]
Beacon of Hope Scholarships
(Undergraduate/Scholarship) [1608]
Gold Award/Eagle Scout Scholarships
(Undergraduate/Scholarship) [4858]
HSF/Nissan Community College Transfer Scholarship Program (Undergraduate/Scholarship) [3598]
Fred R. McDaniel Memorial Scholarships
(Undergraduate/Scholarship) [842]
NW-SCC/American Cancer Society College Scholarships (Undergraduate/Scholarship) [5299]

Missouri

Horatio Alger Missouri Scholarships
(Undergraduate/Scholarship) [215]
Chapter 17 - St. Louis Scholarships
(Undergraduate/Scholarship) [6475]
Paul and Helen L. Grauer Scholarships
(Undergraduate/Scholarship) [835]
Samuel C. Kraus, Jr. Memorial Scholarships
(Undergraduate/Scholarship) [5096]
John Allen Love Scholarships (Graduate, Undergraduate/Scholarship) [7242]
Ray, NORP and Katie, WOKTE Pautz Scholarships (Undergraduate/Scholarship) [847]
PHD ARA Scholarships
(Undergraduate/Scholarship) [849]
Hatton W. Sumners Scholarships
(Undergraduate/Scholarship) [5331]
YMA Fashion Scholarships
(Undergraduate/Scholarship) [7545]

Montana

Horatio Alger Montana Scholarships
(Undergraduate/Scholarship) [216]
Mary Lou Brown Scholarships
(Undergraduate/Scholarship) [823]
Ray Glynn Scholarships
(Undergraduate/Scholarship) [3180]
Inland Northwest Business Alliance (INBA) Scholarships (Undergraduate/Scholarship) [5767]
Stephen T. Marchello Scholarships
(Undergraduate/Scholarship) [4280]
The Cady McDonnell Memorial Scholarships
(Undergraduate/Scholarship) [488]
Rocky Mountain Coal Mining Institute Engineering/Geology Scholarships
(Undergraduate/Scholarship) [6051]
Rocky Mountain Coal Mining Institute Technical Scholarships (Undergraduate/Scholarship) [6052]
Upper Midwest Human Rights Fellowship Program (Professional Development/Fellowship) [7135]

Nebraska

Horatio Alger Ak-Sar-Ben Scholarships
(Undergraduate/Scholarship) [198]
Susan Thompson Buffett Foundation Scholarships
(Undergraduate/Scholarship) [1800]
Todd Elias Memorial Scholarships (Graduate, Undergraduate/Scholarship) [1655]
Paul and Helen L. Grauer Scholarships
(Undergraduate/Scholarship) [835]
MAC Louisa Bowen Memorial Scholarships for Graduate Students in Archival Administration
(Graduate/Scholarship) [4510]
Nebraska Association of Legal Assistants Student Scholarships (Undergraduate/Scholarship) [5153]
Nebraska Farm Bureau Young Farmers and Ranchers Greater Horizon Scholarships
(Undergraduate/Scholarship) [5155]
Ray, NORP and Katie, WOKTE Pautz Scholarships (Undergraduate/Scholarship) [847]
PHD ARA Scholarships
(Undergraduate/Scholarship) [849]
Fraser Stryker Diversity Scholarship Program
(Undergraduate/Scholarship) [5166]
Hatton W. Sumners Scholarships
(Undergraduate/Scholarship) [5331]

Nevada

AISC/Structural Steel Education Council Fellowships (Graduate/Fellowship) [682]
Aaron Edward Arnoldsen Memorial Scholarships
(Undergraduate/Scholarship) [1308]
Fraser Family Scholarships
(Undergraduate/Scholarship) [5826]
HSBC-North America Scholarship Program
(Undergraduate/Scholarship) [3592]
Michael Koizumi APWA Scholarships
(Undergraduate/Scholarship) [808]
Las Vegas Elks Scholarships
(Undergraduate/Scholarship) [5836]
Las Vegas Elks Scholarships for the Physically Challenged (Undergraduate/Scholarship) [5837]
The Cady McDonnell Memorial Scholarships
(Undergraduate/Scholarship) [488]

New Hampshire

Cemanahuac Educational Community Scholarships (Other/Scholarship) [5263]
Columbus Citizens Foundation College Scholarships (Undergraduate/Scholarship) [2334]
French Embassy Scholarships (Other/Scholarship) [5264]
Goethe-Institut AATG Scholarships
(Other/Scholarship) [5265]
Dr. James L. Lawson Memorial Scholarships
(Undergraduate/Scholarship) [841]
Lighthouse International Scholarships - College-bound Awards (High School/Scholarship) [4243]
Lighthouse International Scholarships - Graduate Awards (Graduate/Scholarship) [4244]
Lighthouse International Scholarships - Undergraduate Awards (Undergraduate/Scholarship) [4245]
Rick Mahoney Scholarships
(Undergraduate/Scholarship) [4421]
The Medallion Fund Scholarships
(Undergraduate/Scholarship) [5171]
New England FEMARA Scholarships
(Undergraduate/Scholarship) [846]
Spanish Embassy Scholarships (Graduate, Other/Scholarship) [5267]
The SSPI Northeast Chapter Scholarships
(Graduate, Undergraduate/Scholarship) [6584]
Yankee Clipper Contest Club, Inc. Youth Scholarships (Undergraduate/Scholarship) [862]

New Jersey

Horatio Alger New Jersey Scholarships
(Undergraduate/Scholarship) [218]
Armen H. Bululian Scholarships
(Undergraduate/Scholarship) [1274]
Calvin Alumni Association-New Jersey Scholarships (Undergraduate/Scholarship) [1877]
Cemanahuac Educational Community Scholarships (Other/Scholarship) [5263]
CentraState Associated Auxiliaries Scholarships
(Undergraduate/Scholarship) [2099]
Columbus Citizens Foundation College Scholarships (Undergraduate/Scholarship) [2334]
Constantinople Armenian Relief Society (C.A.R.S.) Scholarships (Undergraduate/Scholarship) [1275]
French Embassy Scholarships (Other/Scholarship) [5264]
Gallo Blue Chip Scholarships
(Undergraduate/Scholarship) [3404]
Goethe-Institut AATG Scholarships
(Other/Scholarship) [5265]
HSBC-North America Scholarship Program
(Undergraduate/Scholarship) [3592]
HSF/Nissan Community College Transfer Scholarship Program (Undergraduate/Scholarship) [3598]
Lighthouse International Scholarships - College-bound Awards (High School/Scholarship) [4243]
Lighthouse International Scholarships - Graduate Awards (Graduate/Scholarship) [4244]
Lighthouse International Scholarships - Undergraduate Awards (Undergraduate/Scholarship) [4245]
New Jersey Association of Osteopathic Physicians and Surgeons Scholarships
(Undergraduate/Scholarship) [5175]
New York Women in Communications, Inc. Foundation Scholarships (Graduate, Undergraduate/Scholarship) [5200]
Jerrothia Allenfonzo Riggs & Anna & Dorothy Mae Barnes Scholarships
(Undergraduate/Scholarship) [1899]
Spanish Embassy Scholarships (Graduate, Other/Scholarship) [5267]
The SSPI Northeast Chapter Scholarships
(Graduate, Undergraduate/Scholarship) [6584]
Star-Ledger Scholarships for the Performing Arts
(Undergraduate/Scholarship) [5178]
Walter W. Stillman Scholarships
(Undergraduate/Scholarship) [1563]
Madlyn D. Thompson Memorial Scholarships
(Undergraduate/Scholarship) [1900]
Trillion Diamond Company Scholarships
(Undergraduate/Scholarship) [3200]

Verizon Scholarship Program (Undergraduate/Scholarship) [3607]

New Mexico

Albuquerque Lesbian and Gay Chamber of Commerce Scholarships (Undergraduate/Scholarship) [6094]
Walt Bartram Memorial Education Awards (Region 12 and Chapter 119) (Undergraduate/Scholarship) [6470]
Chapter 93 - Albuquerque Scholarships (Undergraduate/Scholarship) [6483]
Albuquerque ARC/Toby Cross Scholarships (Undergraduate/Scholarship) [831]
Excel Staffing Companies Scholarships for Excellence in Continuing Education (Undergraduate/Scholarship) [192]
Lesbians for Change Scholarships (Undergraduate/Scholarship) [6117]
Lone Star GIA Associate and Alumni Scholarships (Undergraduate/Scholarship) [3190]
Fred R. McDaniel Memorial Scholarships (Undergraduate/Scholarship) [842]
The Cady McDonnell Memorial Scholarships (Undergraduate/Scholarship) [488]
New Mexico Manufactured Housing Association Scholarship Program (Undergraduate/Scholarship) [193]
Rocky Mountain Coal Mining Institute Engineering/Geology Scholarships (Undergraduate/Scholarship) [6051]
Rocky Mountain Coal Mining Institute Technical Scholarships (Undergraduate/Scholarship) [6052]
Hatton W. Sumners Scholarships (Undergraduate/Scholarship) [5331]

New York

Advertising Production Club Scholarship Awards (Graduate, Undergraduate/Scholarship) [28]
Horatio Alger New York Scholarships (Undergraduate/Scholarship) [219]
APC Tuition-Assist Scholarship Awards (Graduate, Undergraduate/Scholarship) [30]
Henry Broughton, K2AE Memorial Scholarships (Undergraduate/Scholarship) [822]
Calvin Alumni Association-New Jersey Scholarships (Undergraduate/Scholarship) [1877]
Cemanahuac Educational Community Scholarships (Other/Scholarship) [5263]
Columbian Lawyers Association of Westchester County Scholarships (Undergraduate/Scholarship) [2331]
Columbus Citizens Foundation College Scholarships (Undergraduate/Scholarship) [2334]
Constantinople Armenian Relief Society (C.A.R.S.) Scholarships (Undergraduate/Scholarship) [1275]
French Embassy Scholarships (Other/Scholarship) [5264]
Gallo Blue Chip Scholarships (Undergraduate/Scholarship) [3404]
Joseph H. Gellert/Dutchess County Bar Association Scholarships (Undergraduate/Scholarship) [2798]
Goethe-Institut AATG Scholarships (Other/Scholarship) [5265]
HSBC-North America Scholarship Program (Undergraduate/Scholarship) [3592]
HSF/Citi Fellows Program (Undergraduate/Scholarship) [3594]
HSF/Nissan Community College Transfer Scholarship Program (Undergraduate/Scholarship) [3598]
JFEW/UJA-Federation Rose Biller Scholarships (Undergraduate/Scholarship) [4024]
Bryan L. Knapp Point Scholarships (Graduate, Undergraduate/Scholarship) [5724]
Dr. James L. Lawson Memorial Scholarships (Undergraduate/Scholarship) [841]
Lighthouse International Scholarships - College-bound Awards (High School/Scholarship) [4243]
Lighthouse International Scholarships - Graduate Awards (Graduate/Scholarship) [4244]
Lighthouse International Scholarships - Undergraduate Awards (Undergraduate/Scholarship) [4245]
Barry H. Marshal Scholarships (Undergraduate/Scholarship) [6121]
New York State Association of Agricultural Fairs Scholarships (Undergraduate/Scholarship) [5193]
New York Women in Communications, Inc. Foundation Scholarships (Graduate, Undergraduate/Scholarship) [5200]
PGSF-GATF Scholarships (Graduate, Undergraduate/Scholarship) [31]
Saint Andrews Scholarships (Undergraduate/Scholarship) [6150]
Saratoga County Bar Association Law Student Scholarships (All/Scholarship) [6248]
Scholarships for Emigres in the Health Sciences (Undergraduate/Scholarship) [4025]
Spanish Embassy Scholarships (Graduate, Other/Scholarship) [5267]
The SSPI Northeast Chapter Scholarships (Graduate, Undergraduate/Scholarship) [6584]
Norman E. Strohmeier, W2VRS Memorial Scholarships (Undergraduate/Scholarship) [858]
Trillion Diamond Company Scholarships (Undergraduate/Scholarship) [3200]
Verizon Scholarship Program (Undergraduate/Scholarship) [3607]
Albert E. Wischmeyer Memorial Scholarships (Undergraduate/Scholarship) [6508]
Yankee Clipper Contest Club, Inc. Youth Scholarships (Undergraduate/Scholarship) [862]
YMA Fashion Scholarships (Undergraduate/Scholarship) [7545]

North Carolina

Henry S. and Carolyn Adams Scholarship Fund (Undergraduate/Scholarship) [3035]
African American Network - Carolinas Scholarship Fund (Undergraduate/Scholarship) [3037]
William Tasse Alexander Scholarship Fund (Undergraduate/Scholarship) [3038]
Andersen Nontraditional Scholarship for Women's Education and Retraining (Undergraduate/Scholarship) [3039]
BellSouth Business Internship Awards (Postgraduate/Internship) [7145]
Pete and Ellen Bensley Memorial Scholarship Fund (Undergraduate/Scholarship) [3041]
Sam L. Booke, Sr. Scholarships (Undergraduate/Scholarship) [7422]
Tien Bui Memorial Scholarships (Undergraduate/Scholarship) [7423]
Wes Burton Memorial Scholarships (Undergraduate/Scholarship) [7424]
Kasie Ford Capling Memorial Scholarship Endowment Fund (Undergraduate/Scholarship) [3045]
Julian E. Carnes Scholarship Fund (Undergraduate/Scholarship) [3046]
Carolina Panthers Scholarship Fund (Graduate/Scholarship) [3047]
Carolina's Gay & Lesbian Scholarships (Undergraduate/Scholarship) [6099]
Charlotte Housing Authority Scholarship Fund (CHASF) (Undergraduate/Scholarship) [3049]
Charlotte-Mecklenburg Schools Scholarship Incentive Program (Undergraduate/Scholarship) [3050]
Children's Scholarship Fund of Charlotte (High School/Scholarship) [3051]
Andrew Blake Clark Memorial Scholarships (Undergraduate/Scholarship) [7425]
Cole Foundation Undergraduate Scholarship Program (Undergraduate/Scholarship) [3053]
Sally Cole Visual Arts Scholarship Fund (Undergraduate/Scholarship) [3054]
Crowder Scholarship Fund (Undergraduate/Scholarship) [3056]
Serena D. Dalton Scholarships (Undergraduate/Scholarship) [7429]
The E.R. and Lilian B. Dimmette Scholarship Fund (Undergraduate/Scholarship) [3057]
Virginia Elizabeth and Alma Vane Taylor Student Nurse Scholarships (Undergraduate/Scholarship) [7432]
Jack Ervin EDI Scholarships (Professional Development/Scholarship) [5238]
Forsyth County Nursing Scholarships (Undergraduate/Scholarship) [7433]
John L. Gilmer Educational Grants (Undergraduate/Scholarship) [7437]
John L. Gilmer Merit Based Scholarships (Undergraduate/Scholarship) [7438]
L. Gordon, Jr. and June D. Pfefferkorn Scholarships (Undergraduate/Scholarship) [7439]
Governor James E. Holshouser Professional Development Scholarships (Professional Development/Scholarship) [5239]
Edward Jackson International Scholarships (Undergraduate/Scholarship) [7168]
Oliver Joel and Ellen Pell Denny Healthcare Scholarship Fund (Undergraduate/Scholarship) [7441]
Jimmy Johnson Memorial Scholarships (Undergraduate/Scholarship) [7442]
James V. Johnson Scholarship Fund (Undergraduate/Scholarship) [3063]
Stella B. Johnson Scholarships (Undergraduate/Scholarship) [7443]
Annabel Lambeth Jones Scholarship Fund (Undergraduate/Scholarship) [3064]
Glenn Keever Scholarships (Undergraduate/Scholarship) [7171]
Mary and Millard Kiker Scholarship Fund (Undergraduate/Scholarship) [3065]
Douglas Gray Kinel Scholarships (Undergraduate/Scholarship) [7444]
Lighthouse International Scholarships - College-bound Awards (High School/Scholarship) [4243]
Lighthouse International Scholarships - Graduate Awards (Graduate/Scholarship) [4244]
Lighthouse International Scholarships - Undergraduate Awards (Undergraduate/Scholarship) [4245]
L.D. and Elsie Long Memorial Scholarships (Undergraduate/Scholarship) [7446]
Janice McGraw Memorial Scholarship Program (Postgraduate/Scholarship) [732]
Carolina Panthers Players Sam Mills Memorial Scholarship Fund (Undergraduate/Scholarship) [3069]
Minority Presence Grant Program for Doctoral Study (Undergraduate/Grant) [7182]
North Carolina League for Nursing Academic Scholarship Fund (Graduate/Scholarship) [3070]
Orthopaedic Specialists Nursing Scholarships (Undergraduate/Scholarship) [7449]
Ted H. Ousley Scholarship Fund (Undergraduate/Scholarship) [3072]
William H. and Lena M. Petree Scholarships (Undergraduate/Scholarship) [7451]
Pfafftown Jaycees/Lynn Canada Memorial Scholarships (Undergraduate/Scholarship) [7452]
John S. and Jacqueline P. Rider Scholarships (Undergraduate/Scholarship) [7453]
Ben Robinette Scholarship Endowment Fund (Undergraduate/Scholarship) [3074]
Rotary Public Safety Scholarship Fund (Undergraduate/Scholarship) [3075]
Ray and Pearly Sams Scholarships (Undergraduate/Scholarship) [7454]
Tom Shown Scholarships (Undergraduate/Scholarship) [7456]
The Dan Stewart Scholarships (Professional Development/Scholarship) [5240]
Mary Stewart and William T. Covington, Jr. Scholarship Fund (Undergraduate/Scholarship) [3078]
Charles H. Stone Scholarships (Undergraduate/Scholarship) [413]
Stultz Scholarships (Undergraduate/Scholarship) [7457]
Turner Family Scholarship Fund (Undergraduate/Scholarship) [3080]
Jeff Turner-Forsyth Audubon Society Scholarships (Undergraduate/Scholarship) [7458]
Nell and Spencer Waggoner Scholarships (Undergraduate/Scholarship) [7459]
Gary Wagner, K3OMI Scholarships (Undergraduate/Scholarship) [859]
Laramie Walden Memorial Fund

(Undergraduate/Scholarship) [3082]
Art and Dannie Weber Scholarships *(Undergraduate/Scholarship)* [7460]
David Julian Wichard Scholarships *(Undergraduate/Scholarship)* [7196]
L. Phil Wicker Scholarships *(Undergraduate/Scholarship)* [861]
The Wilmore Scholarship Fund *(Undergraduate/Scholarship)* [3084]
Ted C. Wilson Memorial Scholarships *(Undergraduate/Scholarship)* [5791]
Mary and Elliot Wood Foundation Graduate Scholarship Fund *(Graduate/Scholarship)* [3085]
Mary and Elliot Wood Foundation Undergraduate Scholarship Fund *(Undergraduate/Scholarship)* [3086]
YMA Fashion Scholarships *(Undergraduate/Scholarship)* [7545]

North Dakota

Horatio Alger North Dakota Scholarships *(Undergraduate/Scholarship)* [220]
MAC Louisa Bowen Memorial Scholarships for Graduate Students in Archival Administration *(Graduate/Scholarship)* [4510]
North Dakota Veterinary Medical Association Scholarships *(Undergraduate/Scholarship)* [5258]
Rocky Mountain Coal Mining Institute Engineering/Geology Scholarships *(Undergraduate/Scholarship)* [6051]
Rocky Mountain Coal Mining Institute Technical Scholarships *(Undergraduate/Scholarship)* [6052]
Upper Midwest Human Rights Fellowship Program *(Professional Development/Fellowship)* [7135]
Dr. William "Tim" Whalen Memorial Scholarship *(Undergraduate/Scholarship)* [5259]

Ohio

American Advertising Federation-Cleveland College Scholarships *(Undergraduate/Scholarship)* [291]
American Guild of Organists, Canton Chapter Charitable Fund *(Undergraduate/Scholarship)* [6708]
Harry D. Callahan Educational Trust *(Undergraduate/Scholarship)* [6711]
George H. and Anna Casper Fund *(Undergraduate/Scholarship)* [6712]
Cincinnati Scholarship Foundation CFT/ACPSOP Scholarships *(Undergraduate/Scholarship)* [2150]
Dave Couch Memorial Scholarships *(Undergraduate/Scholarship)* [5473]
CSF Ach Family Scholarships *(Undergraduate/Scholarship)* [2151]
CSF Barr Foundation Scholarships *(Undergraduate/Scholarship)* [2152]
CSF Barrett Family Scholarships *(Undergraduate/Scholarship)* [2153]
CSF Bigg's/Curtis Breeden Scholarships *(Undergraduate/Scholarship)* [2154]
CSF Bob and Linda Kohlhepp Scholarships *(Undergraduate/Scholarship)* [2155]
CSF Borden Inc. Scholarships *(Undergraduate/Scholarship)* [2156]
CSF Carl H. Linder Family Scholarships *(Undergraduate/Scholarship)* [2157]
CSF Castellini Foundation Scholarships *(Undergraduate/Scholarship)* [2158]
CSF Charles and Claire Phillips Scholarships *(Undergraduate/Scholarship)* [2159]
CSF Charlotte R. Schmidlapp Scholarships *(Undergraduate/Scholarship)* [2160]
CSF Christopher Todd Grant Memorial Scholarships *(Undergraduate/Scholarship)* [2161]
CSF Cincinnati Bell Scholarships *(Undergraduate/Scholarship)* [2162]
CSF Cincinnati Financial Corporation Scholarships *(Undergraduate/Scholarship)* [2163]
CSF Cincinnati Milacron Scholarships *(Undergraduate/Scholarship)* [2164]
CSF Corwin Nixon Scholarships *(Undergraduate/Scholarship)* [2165]
CSF Crosset Family Scholarships *(Undergraduate/Scholarship)* [2166]
CSF Dater Foundation Scholarships *(Undergraduate/Scholarship)* [2167]
CSF David J. Joseph Company Scholarships *(Undergraduate/Scholarship)* [2168]
CSF Dee Wacksman Memorial Scholarships *(Undergraduate/Scholarship)* [2169]
CSF Duke Energy Scholarships *(Undergraduate/Scholarship)* [2170]
CSF Dwight Hibbard Scholarships *(Undergraduate/Scholarship)* [2171]
CSF Ella Wilson Johnson Scholarships *(Undergraduate/Scholarship)* [2172]
CSF Estelle Davis Memorial Scholarships *(Undergraduate/Scholarship)* [2173]
CSF Eugene Carroll Scholarships *(Undergraduate/Scholarship)* [2174]
CSF E.W. Scripps Scholarships *(Undergraduate/Scholarship)* [2175]
CSF Farmer Family Foundation Scholarships *(Undergraduate/Scholarship)* [2176]
CSF Fifth Third Bank Combined Scholarships *(Undergraduate/Scholarship)* [2177]
CSF Fletemeyer Family Scholarships *(Undergraduate/Scholarship)* [2178]
CSF Florette B. Hoffheimer Scholarships *(Undergraduate/Scholarship)* [2179]
CSF Frank Foster Skillman Scholarships *(Undergraduate/Scholarship)* [2180]
CSF Gardner Foundation Scholarships *(Undergraduate/Scholarship)* [2181]
CSF G.E. Aircraft Engines Scholarships *(Undergraduate/Scholarship)* [2182]
CSF George and Amy Polley Scholarships *(Undergraduate/Scholarship)* [2183]
CSF Goldman, Sachs and Company Scholarships *(Undergraduate/Scholarship)* [2184]
CSF Greater Cincinnati Scholarships Association *(Undergraduate/Scholarship)* [2185]
CSF H.C. Schott Foundation Scholarships *(Undergraduate/Scholarship)* [2186]
CSF HCRTA/Glen O. and Wyllabeth Wise Scholarships *(Undergraduate/Scholarship)* [2187]
CSF Heidelberg Distributing Co. Scholarships *(Undergraduate/Scholarship)* [2188]
CSF Heinz Pet Products Scholarships *(Undergraduate/Scholarship)* [2189]
CSF Helen Steiner Rice Scholarships *(Undergraduate/Scholarship)* [2190]
CSF Johnny Bench Scholarships *(Undergraduate/Scholarship)* [2191]
CSF Joseph S. Stern, Jr. Scholarships *(Undergraduate/Scholarship)* [2192]
CSF Judge Benjamin Schwartz Scholarships *(Undergraduate/Scholarship)* [2193]
CSF Juilfs Foundation Scholarships *(Undergraduate/Scholarship)* [2194]
CSF Kroger Cincinnati/Dayton Scholarships *(Undergraduate/Scholarship)* [2195]
CSF L and T Woolfolk Memorial Scholarships *(Undergraduate/Scholarship)* [2196]
CSF Lazarus/Federated Scholarships *(Undergraduate/Scholarship)* [2197]
CSF L.B. Zapoleon Scholarships *(Undergraduate/Scholarship)* [2198]
CSF Lowe Simpson Scholarships *(Undergraduate/Scholarship)* [2199]
CSF Lyle and Arlene Everingham Scholarships *(Undergraduate/Scholarship)* [2200]
CSF Lyle Everingham Scholarships *(Undergraduate/Scholarship)* [2201]
CSF M and E Brown Scholarships *(Undergraduate/Scholarship)* [2202]
CSF M. Kantor and Brothers Scholarships *(Undergraduate/Scholarship)* [2203]
CSF Martha W. Tanner Memorial Scholarships *(Undergraduate/Scholarship)* [2204]
CSF Marvin Rammelsberg Memorial Scholarships *(Undergraduate/Scholarship)* [2205]
CSF Mary Roberts Scholarships *(Undergraduate/Scholarship)* [2206]
CSF McCall Educational Scholarships *(Undergraduate/Scholarship)* [2207]
CSF Michael Bany Memorial Scholarships *(Undergraduate/Scholarship)* [2208]
CSF Midland Company Scholarships *(Undergraduate/Scholarship)* [2209]
CSF Nelson Schwab Jr. Family Scholarships *(Undergraduate/Scholarship)* [2210]
CSF Nethercott Family Scholarships *(Undergraduate/Scholarship)* [2211]
CSF Ohio National Foundation Scholarships *(Undergraduate/Scholarship)* [2212]
CSF Pepper Family Scholarships *(Undergraduate/Scholarship)* [2213]
CSF Pichler Family Scholarships *(Undergraduate/Scholarship)* [2214]
CSF PNC Bank Scholarships *(Undergraduate/Scholarship)* [2215]
CSF Priscilla Gamble Scholarships *(Undergraduate/Scholarship)* [2216]
CSF Procter and Gamble Scholarships *(Undergraduate/Scholarship)* [2217]
CSF Raymond and Augusta Klink Scholarships *(Undergraduate/Scholarship)* [2218]
CSF Richard Heekin Scholarships *(Undergraduate/Scholarship)* [2219]
CSF Robert H. Reakirt Foundation Scholarships *(Undergraduate/Scholarship)* [2220]
CSF Roger and Joyce Howe Family Scholarships *(Undergraduate/Scholarship)* [2221]
CSF S. David Shor Scholarships *(Undergraduate/Scholarship)* [2222]
CSF SC Johnson, A Family Company Scholarships *(Undergraduate/Scholarship)* [2223]
CSF Scripps Headliners Scholarships *(Undergraduate/Scholarship)* [2224]
CSF Semple Foundation Scholarships *(Undergraduate/Scholarship)* [2225]
CSF Thomas J. Emery Memorial Scholarships *(Undergraduate/Scholarship)* [2226]
CSF T.L. Conlan Memorial Scholarships *(Undergraduate/Scholarship)* [2227]
CSF Union Central 135th Anniversary Scholarships *(Undergraduate/Scholarship)* [2228]
CSF U.S. Bank N.A. Scholarships *(Undergraduate/Scholarship)* [2229]
CSF Walter and Marilyn Bartlett Scholarships *(Undergraduate/Scholarship)* [2230]
CSF Western-Southern Foundation Scholarships *(Undergraduate/Scholarship)* [2231]
CSF William A. Friedlander Scholarships *(Undergraduate/Scholarship)* [2232]
CSF Wm. J. Rielly/MCURC Scholarships *(Undergraduate/Scholarship)* [2233]
CSF Woodward Trustees Scholarships *(Undergraduate/Scholarship)* [2234]
CSF Wynne Family Memorial Scholarships *(Undergraduate/Scholarship)* [2235]
Rob Digiacomo Scholarship Fund *(Undergraduate/Scholarship)* [6715]
Fine Arts Association Minority Scholarships *(Undergraduate/Scholarship)* [2932]
Fine Arts Association United Way Scholarships *(Undergraduate/Scholarship)* [2933]
Alice J. Foit Scholarships *(Undergraduate/Scholarship)* [6719]
David A. and Pamela A. Gault Charitable Fund *(Undergraduate/Scholarship)* [6721]
Laverne L. Gibson Memorial Scholarships *(Undergraduate/Scholarship)* [5483]
Katherine M. Grosscup Scholarships *(Graduate, Undergraduate/Scholarship)* [3159]
International Door Association Scholarship Awards *(Undergraduate/Scholarship)* [3840]
Virginia C. Jack and Ralph L. Jack Scholarships *(Undergraduate/Scholarship)* [6730]
Samuel Krugliak Legal Scholarship Fund *(Graduate/Scholarship)* [6735]
Lake Dollars for Scholars Endowment Fund *(Undergraduate/Scholarship)* [6736]
Marvin Lewis Scholarships *(Undergraduate/Scholarship)* [4222]
MAC Louisa Bowen Memorial Scholarships for Graduate Students in Archival Administration *(Graduate/Scholarship)* [4510]
Lillian Grace Mahan Scholarship Fund *(Undergraduate/Scholarship)* [6738]
Sanders J. Mestel Legal Scholarship Fund

(Undergraduate/Scholarship) [6742]
Fizz and Dutch Miller Scholarship Fund (Undergraduate/Scholarship) [6745]
David W. Misek, N8NPX Memorial Scholarships (Undergraduate/Scholarship) [844]
Lt. Colonel Robert G. Moreland Vocational/Technical Fund (Undergraduate/Scholarship) [6746]
Anthony Munoz Scholarships (Undergraduate/Scholarship) [4589]
Ohio Association of Broadcasters Scholarships (Undergraduate/Scholarship) [5318]
Ohio Valley Chapter Scholarships (Undergraduate/Scholarship) [1455]
O'Jays Scholarship Fund (Undergraduate/Scholarship) [6748]
Perry Township School Memorial Scholarship Fund (Undergraduate/Scholarship) [6749]
Thomas W. Porter, W8KYZ Scholarships Honoring Michael Daugherty, W8LSE (Undergraduate/Scholarship) [850]
Thomas Warren Roberts Scholarships (Undergraduate/Scholarship) [5513]
St. Joseph's Hospital School of Nursing Alumnae Scholarships (Undergraduate/Scholarship) [5518]
Stephen Schwartz Musical Theatre Scholarships (Undergraduate/Scholarship) [3625]
Don and Madalyn Sickafoose Educational Trust (Undergraduate/Scholarship) [6752]
South Central Power Scholarships (Undergraduate/Scholarship) [6620]
Stark County Dairy Promoters Scholarships (Undergraduate/Scholarship) [6755]
Zachary Taylor Stevens Memorial Scholarships (Undergraduate/Scholarship) [856]
Jeffery Tyler Sweitzer Wrestling Memorial Scholarship Fund (Undergraduate/Scholarship) [6756]
John R. and Joan F. Warren Scholarship Fund (Undergraduate/Scholarship) [6761]
Lester and Eleanor Webster Charitable Trust Fund (Undergraduate/Scholarship) [6762]
Western Reserve Herb Society Scholarships (Undergraduate/Scholarship) [3547]
Whitaker-Minard Memorial Scholarships (Undergraduate/Scholarship) [5528]
Glenn Wilson Broadcast Journalism Scholarships (Undergraduate/Scholarship) [5529]
Workshop, Inc. and Stark MRDD Fostering Diversity Through Special Needs Scholarship Fund (Undergraduate/Scholarship) [6764]

Oklahoma

Tom and Judith Comstock Scholarships (Undergraduate/Scholarship) [828]
Lone Star GIA Associate and Alumni Scholarships (Undergraduate/Scholarship) [3190]
Fred R. McDaniel Memorial Scholarships (Undergraduate/Scholarship) [842]
OKAIDE Scholarships (Undergraduate/Scholarship) [5327]
Hatton W. Sumners Scholarships (Undergraduate/Scholarship) [5331]

Oregon

Horatio Alger Oregon Scholarships (Undergraduate/Scholarship) [221]
Mary Lou Brown Scholarships (Undergraduate/Scholarship) [823]
Chapter 63 - Portland James E. Morrow Scholarships (Graduate, Undergraduate/Scholarship) [6480]
Chapter 63 - Portland Uncle Bud Smith Scholarships (Graduate, Undergraduate/Scholarship) [6481]
Clackamas County Farm Bureau Scholarships (Undergraduate/Scholarship) [5392]
Ray Glynn Scholarships (Undergraduate/Scholarship) [3180]
Gregori Jakovina Endowment Scholarships (Undergraduate/Scholarship) [2884]
The Cady McDonnell Memorial Scholarships (Undergraduate/Scholarship) [488]
Orchard-Hoyman Fund for GLBT Student Scholarships (Undergraduate/Scholarship) [2889]
Oregon Association of Broadcasters Scholarships (Undergraduate/Scholarship) [5376]
Oregon Community Credit Union Scholarships (Undergraduate/Scholarship) [7201]
Pride of the Rose Scholarships Fund (Undergraduate/Scholarship) [2891]
Robert W. and Bernice Ingalls Staton Scholarships (Undergraduate/Scholarship) [7202]
University of Oregon Presidential Scholarships (Undergraduate/Scholarship) [7206]

Pennsylvania

Horatio Alger Franklin Scholarships (Undergraduate/Scholarship) [204]
Horatio Alger Pennsylvania Scholarships (Undergraduate/Scholarship) [222]
Allegheny County Medical Society (ACMS) Medical Student Scholarship (Undergraduate/Scholarship) [3134]
Alliance Medical Education Scholarship Fund (AMES) (Undergraduate/Scholarship) [3135]
Joe Q. Bryant American Council on Exercise Educational Scholarships (Undergraduate/Scholarship) [499]
Ethel Beard Burstein Scholarship Program (Postgraduate/Scholarship) [729]
Joseph R. Calder, Jr., MD Scholarship Fund (Undergraduate/Scholarship) [2946]
Cemanahuac Educational Community Scholarships (Other/Scholarship) [5263]
Warren E. "Whitey" Cole American Society of Highway Engineers Scholarships (Undergraduate/Scholarship) [2947]
Columbus Citizens Foundation College Scholarships (Undergraduate/Scholarship) [2334]
Malcolm U. Dantzler Scholarships (Professional Development/Scholarship) [6613]
Lou Drane Fund (Undergraduate/Scholarship) [3095]
Wayne G. Failor Scholarships (High School/Scholarship) [5563]
Family and Children's Services of Lebanon County Fund (Undergraduate/Scholarship) [3098]
Howard Fox Memorial Law Scholarship (Undergraduate/Scholarship) [1634]
French Embassy Scholarships (Other/Scholarship) [5264]
Gen III Scholarships (Undergraduate/Scholarship) [2822]
Goethe-Institut AATG Scholarships (Other/Scholarship) [5265]
Greater Philadelphia Law Library Association Scholarships (Undergraduate/Scholarship) [3371]
Green Knight Economic Development Corporation (GKEDC) Scholarships (Undergraduate/Scholarship) [3381]
Katherine M. Grosscup Scholarships (Graduate, Undergraduate/Scholarship) [3159]
Scott A. Gunder, MD, DCMS Presidential Scholarships (Undergraduate/Scholarship) [3136]
Morton Harrison Scholarship Fund (Undergraduate/Scholarship) [2957]
Gordon B. and Josephine Hewlet Memorial Fund (Undergraduate/Scholarship) [3104]
Roberta L. Houpt Scholarship Fund (Undergraduate/Scholarship) [3105]
James Hughes Memorial Scholarship Fund (Undergraduate/Scholarship) [5564]
ISCALC International Scholarship Fund (Undergraduate/Scholarship) [2960]
Erin L. Jenkins Memorial Scholarship Fund (Undergraduate/Scholarship) [3107]
Ken and Romaine Kauffman Scholarship Fund (Undergraduate/Scholarship) [3108]
Lighthouse International Scholarships - College-bound Awards (High School/Scholarship) [4243]
Lighthouse International Scholarships - Graduate Awards (Graduate/Scholarship) [4244]
Lighthouse International Scholarships - Undergraduate Awards (Undergraduate/Scholarship) [4245]
Lycoming County Medical Society (LCMS) Scholarships (Undergraduate/Scholarship) [3137]
Walter A. and Nan C. McCloskey Memorial Scholarships (Undergraduate/Scholarship) [2964]
Montgomery County Medical Society (MCMS) Scholarships (Undergraduate/Scholarship) [3138]
Robert E. and Judy More Scholarship Fund (Undergraduate/Scholarship) [2967]
Albert and Alice Nacinovich Music Scholarships (Undergraduate/Scholarship) [2970]
New York Women in Communications, Inc. Foundation Scholarships (Graduate, Undergraduate/Scholarship) [5200]
Northampton County Medical Society Alliance Scholarships (Undergraduate/Scholarship) [5261]
Pathways to Success Scholarships (Undergraduate/Scholarship) [3113]
Pennsylvania Heartland Unit Scholarships (Undergraduate/Scholarship) [3545]
Pennsylvania Land Surveyors Foundation Scholarships (Undergraduate/Scholarship) [5557]
Pennsylvania Library Association Scholarships for MLS Students (Undergraduate/Scholarship) [5559]
William C. Scheetz Family Scholarships (Graduate, Undergraduate/Scholarship) [1677]
Myrtle Siegfried, MD and Michael Vigilante, MD Scholarships (Undergraduate/Scholarship) [3139]
John R. Simpson Memorial Scholarships (Graduate, Undergraduate/Scholarship) [1680]
J. Ward Sleichter and Frances F. Sleichter Memorial Scholarship Fund (Undergraduate/Scholarship) [3119]
South Carolina Public Health Association Scholarships (Undergraduate/Scholarship) [6614]
Spanish Embassy Scholarships (Graduate, Other/Scholarship) [5267]
The SSPI Northeast Chapter Scholarships (Graduate, Undergraduate/Scholarship) [6584]
Minnie Patton Stayman Scholarships (Undergraduate/Scholarship) [5566]
Joseph L. and Vivian E. Steele Music Scholarship Fund (Undergraduate/Scholarship) [3121]
Anil and Neema Thakrar Family Fund (Undergraduate/Scholarship) [3122]
Verizon Scholarship Program (Undergraduate/Scholarship) [3607]
Monica M. Weaver Memorial Fund (Undergraduate/Scholarship) [2978]
John G. Williams Scholarships Fund (Undergraduate/Scholarship) [7417]
Williamsport High School Class of 1970 Scholarship Fund (Undergraduate/Scholarship) [2979]
Yankee Clipper Contest Club, Inc. Youth Scholarships (Undergraduate/Scholarship) [862]

Rhode Island

Bach Organ and Keyboard Music Scholarships (Undergraduate/Scholarship) [6034]
Cemanahuac Educational Community Scholarships (Other/Scholarship) [5263]
Antonio Cirino Memorial Art Education Fellowships (Undergraduate/Fellowship) [6035]
Columbus Citizens Foundation College Scholarships (Undergraduate/Scholarship) [2334]
Constant Memorial Scholarship for Aquidneck Island Resident (Undergraduate/Scholarship) [6036]
Edward Leon Duhamel Freemasons Scholarships (Undergraduate/Scholarship) [6037]
French Embassy Scholarships (Other/Scholarship) [5264]
GFWC Women's Club of South County Scholarships (Undergraduate/Scholarship) [6038]
Goethe-Institut AATG Scholarships (Other/Scholarship) [5265]
Dr. James L. Lawson Memorial Scholarships (Undergraduate/Scholarship) [841]
Lighthouse International Scholarships - College-bound Awards (High School/Scholarship) [4243]
Lighthouse International Scholarships - Graduate Awards (Graduate/Scholarship) [4244]
Lighthouse International Scholarships - Under-

graduate Awards (Undergraduate/Scholarship) [4245]
New England FEMARA Scholarships (Undergraduate/Scholarship) [846]
Rhode Island Association of Former Legislators Scholarships (Undergraduate/Scholarship) [6040]
Rhode Island Commission on Women/Freda H. Goldman Education Awards (Undergraduate/Award/Prize) [6041]
Lily and Catello Sorrentino Memorial Scholarships (Undergraduate/Scholarship) [6042]
Spanish Embassy Scholarships (Graduate, Other/Scholarship) [5267]
The SSPI Northeast Chapter Scholarships (Graduate, Undergraduate/Scholarship) [6584]
Bruce and Marjorie Sundlun Scholarships (Undergraduate/Scholarship) [6043]
Marilyn Graboys Wool Scholarships (Undergraduate/Scholarship) [6044]
Yankee Clipper Contest Club, Inc. Youth Scholarships (Undergraduate/Scholarship) [862]

South Carolina

African American Network - Carolinas Scholarship Fund (Undergraduate/Scholarship) [3037]
Andersen Nontraditional Scholarship for Women's Education and Retraining (Undergraduate/Scholarship) [3039]
Julian E. Carnes Scholarship Fund (Undergraduate/Scholarship) [3046]
Carolina Panthers Scholarship Fund (Graduate/Scholarship) [3047]
Carolina's Gay & Lesbian Scholarships (Undergraduate/Scholarship) [6099]
Judy Crocker Memorial Scholarship Fund (Undergraduate/Scholarship) [3055]
Howard B. Higgins South Carolina Dental Scholarships (Undergraduate/Scholarship) [3061]
Wilbert L. and Zora F. Holmes Scholarship Endowment Fund (Undergraduate/Scholarship) [3062]
Legislative Incentive for Future Excellence (LIFE) Scholarships (Undergraduate/Scholarship) [232]
Lighthouse International Scholarships - College-bound Awards (High School/Scholarship) [4243]
Lighthouse International Scholarships - Graduate Awards (Graduate/Scholarship) [4244]
Lighthouse International Scholarships - Undergraduate Awards (Undergraduate/Scholarship) [4245]
Carolina Panthers Players Sam Mills Memorial Scholarship Fund (Undergraduate/Scholarship) [3069]
Henry DeWitt Plyler Scholarship Fund (Undergraduate/Scholarship) [3073]
South Carolina Association for Financial Professionals College Education Scholarships (Undergraduate/Scholarship) [6611]
Charles H. Stone Scholarships (Undergraduate/Scholarship) [413]
Watson-Brown Scholarships (Undergraduate/Scholarship) [7392]
L. Phil Wicker Scholarships (Undergraduate/Scholarship) [861]
Ted C. Wilson Memorial Scholarships (Undergraduate/Scholarship) [5791]

South Dakota

Horatio Alger South Dakota Scholarships (Undergraduate/Scholarship) [223]
L. Robert Clough Memorial Scholarships (Graduate, Undergraduate/Scholarship) [1651]
MAC Louisa Bowen Memorial Scholarships for Graduate Students in Archival Administration (Graduate/Scholarship) [4510]
Upper Midwest Human Rights Fellowship Program (Professional Development/Fellowship) [7135]

Tennessee

George Oliver Benton Memorial Scholarships (Undergraduate/Scholarship) [2407]
Ruby A. Brown Memorial Scholarships (Undergraduate/Scholarship) [2807]
William and Clara Bryan Scholarships (Undergraduate/Scholarship) [2410]
Cheatham County Scholarships (Undergraduate/Scholarship) [2412]
Steven L. Coffey Memorial Scholarships (Undergraduate/Scholarship) [2809]
B.J. Dean Scholarships (Undergraduate/Scholarship) [2418]
Federal Court Bench and Bar Scholarships (Undergraduate/Scholarship) [7114]
Pauline LaFon Gore Scholarships (Undergraduate/Scholarship) [2421]
HSF/Nissan Community College Transfer Scholarship Program (Undergraduate/Scholarship) [3598]
Maude Keisling/Cumberland County Extension Homemakers Scholarships (Undergraduate/Scholarship) [2425]
Michael B. Kruse Scholarships (Undergraduate/Scholarship) [2428]
Diane G. Lowe and John Gomez, IV Scholarships (Undergraduate/Scholarship) [2430]
Aurella Varallo Mariani Scholarship Program (Undergraduate/Scholarship) [4610]
John E. Mayfield Scholarships for Cheatham County Central High School (Undergraduate/Scholarship) [2436]
John E. Mayfield Scholarships for Harpeth High School (Undergraduate/Scholarship) [2437]
John E. Mayfield Scholarships Pleasant View Christian School (Undergraduate/Scholarship) [2438]
John E. Mayfield Scholarships for Sycamore High School (Undergraduate/Scholarship) [2439]
Nashville Unit Scholarships (Undergraduate/Scholarship) [3544]
Jerry Newson Scholarships (Undergraduate/Scholarship) [2441]
NW-SCC/American Cancer Society College Scholarships (Undergraduate/Scholarship) [5299]
Tennessee Board of Regents Law Scholarships (Undergraduate/Scholarship) [7130]
Tennessee Trucking Association Scholarships (Undergraduate/Scholarship) [2449]
Gary Wagner, K3OMI Scholarships (Undergraduate/Scholarship) [859]
The Woman's Club of Nashville Scholarships (Undergraduate/Scholarship) [2452]
Wyatt, Tarrant and Combs, LLP Scholarships (Undergraduate/Scholarship) [7131]

Texas

Horatio Alger Texas - Fort Worth Scholarships (Undergraduate/Scholarship) [224]
Horatio Alger Texas Scholarships (Undergraduate/Scholarship) [225]
Allen - Marty Allen Scholarships (High School, Undergraduate/Scholarship) [2261]
BAFTX Early Starters Awards (Undergraduate/Scholarship) [1779]
BAFTX Graduate Awards (Undergraduate/Scholarship) [1780]
BAFTX Junior Achievers Awards (Undergraduate/Scholarship) [1781]
BAFTX Undergraduate Awards (Undergraduate/Scholarship) [1782]
Zachary Barriger Memorial Scholarships (High School/Scholarship) [2262]
O.J. Beck, Jr. Memorial Scholarships (Undergraduate/Scholarship) [2263]
Beecroft Family Scholarships (High School/Scholarship) [2264]
Reverend E.F. Bennett Scholarships (High School/Scholarship) [2265]
Mary E. Bivins Foundation Religious Scholarship Program (Graduate, Undergraduate/Scholarship) [1719]
Marion Luna Brem/Pat McNeil Teen Parent Scholarships (Undergraduate/Scholarship) [2266]
Kae and Kay Brockermeyer Endowed Scholarships (Undergraduate/Scholarship) [5577]
Cecil E. Burney Scholarships (High School, Undergraduate/Scholarship) [2267]
C.C.H.R.M.A. Scholarships (High School, Undergraduate/Scholarship) [2268]
Tom and Judith Comstock Scholarships (Undergraduate/Scholarship) [828]
Justin Forrest Cox "Beat the Odds" Memorial Scholarships (Undergraduate/Scholarship) [2269]
D.C. and Virginia Brown Scholarships (High School, Undergraduate/Scholarship) [2270]
B.J. Dean Scholarships (Undergraduate/Scholarship) [2418]
Derek Lee Dean Soccer Scholarships (High School/Scholarship) [2271]
Cindy P. Dennis Scholarship Fund (Undergraduate/Scholarship) [2534]
Doraine Pursuit of Educational Excellence Scholarships (High School/Scholarship) [2272]
Jay Downes Memorial Scholarships (High School/Scholarship) [2273]
John R. Eidson Jr., Scholarships (Undergraduate/Scholarship) [2274]
Barney Flynn Memorial Scholarships (High School/Scholarship) [2275]
Food for Thought Scholarships (High School/Scholarship) [2276]
Melissa Guerra Scholarships (Undergraduate/Scholarship) [2277]
George and Mary Josephine Hamman Foundation Scholarships (High School/Scholarship) [3392]
Manuel Hernandez, Jr. Foundation Scholarships (High School/Scholarship) [2278]
Houston Alumnae Chapter Graduate Fellowships (Graduate/Fellowship) [2650]
HSF/Citi Fellows Program (Undergraduate/Scholarship) [3594]
HSF/Nissan Community College Transfer Scholarship Program (Undergraduate/Scholarship) [3598]
JLTLA Scholarships (Undergraduate/Scholarship) [6942]
Sue Kay Lay Memorial Scholarships (High School/Scholarship) [2280]
Danny T. Le Memorial Scholarships (High School, Undergraduate/Scholarship) [7321]
Lone Star GIA Associate and Alumni Scholarships (Undergraduate/Scholarship) [3190]
Fred R. McDaniel Memorial Scholarships (Undergraduate/Scholarship) [842]
McKinney Sisters Undergraduate Scholarships (Undergraduate/Scholarship) [2657]
Brian and Colleen Miller Scholarships (High School/Scholarship) [2281]
Le Hoang Nguyen (LHN) College Scholarships (High School/Scholarship) [7322]
The Thuy Nguyen Scholarships (High School/Scholarship) [7323]
North Texas GIA Alumni Association Scholarships (Undergraduate/Scholarship) [3196]
Peierls Rising Star Scholarship Program (Undergraduate/Scholarship) [3602]
Puedo Scholarships - Joseph Huerta (High School/Scholarship) [2282]
J.J. Rains Memorial Scholarships (High School/Scholarship) [2283]
W.B. Ray HS Class of '56 Averill Johnson Scholarships (High School/Scholarship) [2284]
Rocky Mountain Coal Mining Institute Engineering/Geology Scholarships (Undergraduate/Scholarship) [6051]
Rocky Mountain Coal Mining Institute Technical Scholarships (Undergraduate/Scholarship) [6052]
Rotary Club of Corpus Christi Scholarships (High School/Scholarship) [2285]
Seaman Family Scholarships (High School/Scholarship) [2286]
Judge Terry Shamsie Scholarships (High School/Scholarship) [2287]
Herman J. Smith Scholarships (Undergraduate/Scholarship) [4942]
South Texas Lighthouse for the Blind Scholarships (Undergraduate/Scholarship) [2288]
South Texas Unit Scholarships (Undergraduate/Scholarship) [3546]
Jim Springer Memorial Scholarships (Undergraduate/Scholarship) [2289]

Stewart Title Firefighters Scholarships *(High School, Undergraduate/Scholarship)* [2290]
Hatton W. Sumners Scholarships *(Undergraduate/Scholarship)* [5331]
Talbert Family Memorial Accounting Scholarships *(Undergraduate/Scholarship)* [2291]
Vera Tran Memorial Scholarships *(Undergraduate/Scholarship)* [7324]
Valley Alliance of Mentors for Opportunities and Scholarship (VAMOS) Program *(Undergraduate/Scholarship)* [3606]
Verizon Scholarship Program *(Undergraduate/Scholarship)* [3607]
Wheelchair Success Foundation Scholarships *(Undergraduate/Scholarship)* [2293]
Dr. Dana Williams Scholarships *(High School, Undergraduate/Scholarship)* [2294]
YMA Fashion Scholarships *(Undergraduate/Scholarship)* [7545]

Utah

Horatio Alger Utah Scholarships *(Undergraduate/Scholarship)* [226]
The Cady McDonnell Memorial Scholarships *(Undergraduate/Scholarship)* [488]
Rocky Mountain Coal Mining Institute Engineering/Geology Scholarships *(Undergraduate/Scholarship)* [6051]
Rocky Mountain Coal Mining Institute Technical Scholarships *(Undergraduate/Scholarship)* [6052]

Vermont

Cemanahuac Educational Community Scholarships *(Other/Scholarship)* [5263]
Columbus Citizens Foundation College Scholarships *(Undergraduate/Scholarship)* [2334]
French Embassy Scholarships *(Other/Scholarship)* [5264]
Goethe-Institut AATG Scholarships *(Other/Scholarship)* [5265]
Dr. James L. Lawson Memorial Scholarships *(Undergraduate/Scholarship)* [841]
Lighthouse International Scholarships - College-bound Awards *(High School/Scholarship)* [4243]
Lighthouse International Scholarships - Graduate Awards *(Graduate/Scholarship)* [4244]
Lighthouse International Scholarships - Undergraduate Awards *(Undergraduate/Scholarship)* [4245]
New England FEMARA Scholarships *(Undergraduate/Scholarship)* [846]
Spanish Embassy Scholarships *(Graduate, Other/Scholarship)* [5267]
The SSPI Northeast Chapter Scholarships *(Graduate, Undergraduate/Scholarship)* [6584]
Yankee Clipper Contest Club, Inc. Youth Scholarships *(Undergraduate/Scholarship)* [862]

Virginia

Horatio Alger District of Columbia, Maryland, and Virginia Scholarships *(Undergraduate/Scholarship)* [202]
Bayly-Tiffany Scholarships *(Undergraduate/Scholarship)* [7239]
Cemanahuac Educational Community Scholarships *(Other/Scholarship)* [5263]
V. Thomas Forehand, Jr. Scholarships *(Undergraduate/Scholarship)* [7240]
Richard Gregory Freeland, II Educational Scholarships *(High School/Scholarship)* [1762]
French Embassy Scholarships *(Other/Scholarship)* [5264]
Friends of Coal Scholarships *(Undergraduate/Scholarship)* [7394]
Jane S. Glenn Memorial Endowed Scholarships *(Undergraduate/Scholarship)* [6046]
Goethe-Institut AATG Scholarships *(Other/Scholarship)* [5265]
HSBC-North America Scholarship Program *(Undergraduate/Scholarship)* [3592]
Kaprielian Memorial Scholarships *(Undergraduate/Scholarship)* [7241]
James N. Kincanon Scholarships *(Undergraduate/Scholarship)* [6047]
Lighthouse International Scholarships - College-bound Awards *(High School/Scholarship)* [4243]
Lighthouse International Scholarships - Graduate Awards *(Graduate/Scholarship)* [4244]
Lighthouse International Scholarships - Undergraduate Awards *(Undergraduate/Scholarship)* [4245]
Marshall Undergraduate Scholars Programs *(Undergraduate/Award/Prize)* [4319]
Steven Craig Merrill Memorial Scholarships *(Graduate, Undergraduate/Scholarship)* [1670]
Annie B. Rose Educational Scholarships *(Undergraduate/Scholarship)* [4651]
Drew Smith Memorial Scholarship *(Undergraduate/Scholarship)* [2384]
Spanish Embassy Scholarships *(Graduate, Other/Scholarship)* [5267]
The SSPI Mid-Atlantic Chapter Scholarships *(Graduate, Undergraduate/Scholarship)* [6583]
The SSPI Northeast Chapter Scholarships *(Graduate, Undergraduate/Scholarship)* [6584]
Charles H. Stone Scholarships *(Undergraduate/Scholarship)* [413]
Tidewater Builders Association Scholarships *(Undergraduate/Scholarship)* [6890]
Verizon Scholarship Program *(Undergraduate/Scholarship)* [3607]
Gary Wagner, K3OMI Scholarships *(Undergraduate/Scholarship)* [859]
L. Phil Wicker Scholarships *(Undergraduate/Scholarship)* [861]
Ted C. Wilson Memorial Scholarships *(Undergraduate/Scholarship)* [5791]

Washington

Horatio Alger Washington Scholarships *(Undergraduate/Scholarship)* [227]
American Indian Endowed Scholarships *(Graduate, Undergraduate/Scholarship)* [7363]
Wilbur H. Anderson Memorial Scholarships *(Undergraduate/Scholarship)* [1182]
Mary Lou Brown Scholarships *(Undergraduate/Scholarship)* [823]
Calvin Alumni Association-Washington-Seattle/Tacoma Scholarships *(Undergraduate/Scholarship)* [1887]
Chapter 63 - Portland James E. Morrow Scholarships *(Graduate, Undergraduate/Scholarship)* [6480]
Chapter 63 - Portland Uncle Bud Smith Scholarships *(Graduate, Undergraduate/Scholarship)* [6481]
Dr. Princeton L. Co Emergency Fund for Dental Hygiene Scholarships *(Undergraduate/Scholarship)* [6310]
Cole Family Scholarships *(Undergraduate/Scholarship)* [5761]
Derivative Duo Scholarships *(Undergraduate/Scholarship)* [5765]
Carli Edwards Memorial Scholarships *(Undergraduate/Scholarship)* [6311]
Richard Gregory Freeland, II Educational Scholarships *(High School/Scholarship)* [1762]
Fuchs-Harden Educational Scholarships Fund *(Undergraduate/Scholarship)* [3375]
Future Teachers Conditional Scholarships and Loan Repayment *(Professional Development, Undergraduate/Loan)* [7364]
GET Ready for Math and Science Conditional Scholarships *(Four Year College, Two Year College, Undergraduate/Scholarship)* [7365]
Ray Glynn Scholarships *(Undergraduate/Scholarship)* [3180]
Greater Seattle Business Association Scholarships *(Undergraduate/Scholarship)* [3367]
Imperial Sovereign Court of Tacoma Scholarships *(Professional Development/Scholarship)* [5766]
Inland Northwest Business Alliance (INBA) Scholarships *(Undergraduate/Scholarship)* [5767]
Gregori Jakovina Endowment Scholarships *(Undergraduate/Scholarship)* [2884]
Edmund F. Maxwell Scholarships *(Undergraduate/Scholarship)* [4405]
The Cady McDonnell Memorial Scholarships *(Undergraduate/Scholarship)* [488]
Mill Creek Business Association Scholarships *(Undergraduate/Scholarship)* [4533]
Olympia Tumwater Foundation Traditional Scholarships *(Undergraduate/Scholarship)* [5333]
Olympia Tumwater Foundation Transitional (non-traditional) Scholarships *(Undergraduate/Scholarship)* [5334]
Pride of the Rose Scholarships Fund *(Undergraduate/Scholarship)* [2891]
Don Renschler Scholarships *(Graduate/Scholarship)* [5775]
Richard C. Rolfs Scholarships *(Undergraduate/Scholarship)* [5776]
WALPA Lake Scholarships *(Graduate, Undergraduate/Scholarship)* [7382]
Washington Higher Education Coordinating Board Educational Opportunity Grants *(Undergraduate/Grant)* [7367]
Washington Higher Education Coordinating Board State Need Grants *(Undergraduate/Grant)* [7369]
Whidbey Island Giving Circle Scholarships *(Undergraduate/Scholarship)* [5784]

West Virginia

Bob Adkins Memorial Scholarships *(Undergraduate/Scholarship)* [5462]
Martin K. Alsup Scholarships *(Undergraduate/Scholarship)* [5463]
Ambrose-Ramsey Trust Scholarships *(Undergraduate/Scholarship)* [5464]
Joe Barbarow Memorial Scholarships *(Undergraduate/Scholarship)* [5465]
Lewis and Gurry Batten Scholarships *(Undergraduate/Scholarship)* [5466]
William (Billbo) Boston Scholarships *(Undergraduate/Scholarship)* [5467]
Chester H. Bruce Memorial Scholarships *(Undergraduate/Scholarship)* [5468]
Bryce-Lietzke Martin Scholarships *(Undergraduate/Scholarship)* [5469]
Adam S. Burford Memorial Scholarships *(Graduate, Undergraduate/Scholarship)* [1646]
Freda Burge Scholarships *(Undergraduate/Scholarship)* [5470]
Cemanahuac Educational Community Scholarships *(Other/Scholarship)* [5263]
George H. Clinton Scholarship Fund *(Undergraduate/Scholarship)* [5471]
Dwight O. Conner and Ellen Conner Lepp Scholarships *(Undergraduate/Scholarship)* [5472]
Jennifer Coulter Memorial Scholarships *(Undergraduate/Scholarship)* [5474]
Cindy Curry Memorial Scholarships *(Undergraduate/Scholarship)* [5475]
Kenneth D. and Katherine D. Davis Scholarships *(Undergraduate/Scholarship)* [5476]
Lawrence E. Davis Scholarships *(Undergraduate/Scholarship)* [5477]
Doddridge County Promise Scholarships *(Undergraduate/Scholarship)* [5478]
Fostering Hope Scholarship Fund *(Undergraduate/Scholarship)* [5481]
French Embassy Scholarships *(Other/Scholarship)* [5264]
William E. "Bill" Gallagher Scholarships *(Undergraduate/Scholarship)* [5482]
Laverne L. Gibson Memorial Scholarships *(Undergraduate/Scholarship)* [5483]
Shane Gilbert Memorial Scholarships *(Undergraduate/Scholarship)* [5484]
Goethe-Institut AATG Scholarships *(Other/Scholarship)* [5265]
S. William & Martha R. Golf Educational Scholarships *(Undergraduate/Scholarship)* [5485]
Russ Grant Memorial Scholarship for Tennis *(Undergraduate/Scholarship)* [5486]
Katherine M. Grosscup Scholarships *(Graduate, Undergraduate/Scholarship)* [3159]
Sarah Gwisdalla Memorial Scholarships *(Undergraduate/Scholarship)* [5487]
Nathaniel Hafer Memorial Scholarships *(Undergraduate/Scholarship)* [5488]
Clayburn and Garnet R. Hanna Scholarships

(Undergraduate/Scholarship) [5489]
H.G. Hardbarger Science and Mathematics Awards (Undergraduate/Scholarship) [5490]
Ruth Harris Memorial Scholarships (Undergraduate/Scholarship) [5491]
Harrisville Lions Club Scholarships (Undergraduate/Scholarship) [5492]
Harry C. Hartleben III. Scholarships (Undergraduate/Scholarship) [5493]
Gail Hartshorn Scholarships (Undergraduate/Scholarship) [5494]
Gregory Lynn Haught Citizenship Awards (Undergraduate/Award/Prize) [5495]
Dorcas Edmonson Haught Scholarships (Undergraduate/Scholarship) [5496]
Ella Beren Hersch Scholarships (Undergraduate/Scholarship) [5497]
Albert H. Hix, W8AH Memorial Scholarships (Undergraduate/Scholarship) [838]
Holly Jackson-Wuller Memorial Scholarships (Undergraduate/Scholarship) [5498]
K.A.S.A Memorial Scholarships (Undergraduate/Scholarship) [5499]
Dr. Charles Kelly Memorial Scholarships (Undergraduate/Scholarship) [5500]
Judge Oliver Kessel Memorial Scholarship-Ripley Rotary (Undergraduate/Scholarship) [5501]
Rhonda Knopp Memorial Scholarships (Undergraduate/Scholarship) [5502]
Harold Knopp Scholarships (Undergraduate/Scholarship) [5503]
Langfitt-Ambrose Trust Fund (Undergraduate/Scholarship) [5504]
Lighthouse International Scholarships - College-bound Awards (High School/Scholarship) [4243]
Lighthouse International Scholarships - Graduate Awards (Graduate/Scholarship) [4244]
Lighthouse International Scholarships - Undergraduate Awards (Undergraduate/Scholarship) [4245]
Megan Nicole Longwell Scholarships (Undergraduate/Scholarship) [5505]
Dudley Mullins/Cabot Corporation Scholarships (Undergraduate/Scholarship) [5506]
Pennsboro Alumni Scholarship Fund (Undergraduate/Scholarship) [5507]
Pepsi Wood County Technical/Caperton Center Scholarship Fund (Undergraduate/Scholarship) [5508]
William R. Pfalzgraf Scholarships (Undergraduate/Scholarship) [5509]
Herschel Pifer Memorial Scholarships (Undergraduate/Scholarship) [5510]
Thomas W. Porter, W8KYZ Scholarships Honoring Michael Daugherty, W8LSE (Undergraduate/Scholarship) [850]
William Reaser Scholarships (Undergraduate/Scholarship) [5511]
James H. Roberts Athletic Scholarships (Undergraduate/Scholarship) [5512]
James Robinson Memorial Scholarships (Undergraduate/Scholarship) [5514]
Carl M. Rose Memorial Scholarship Fund (Undergraduate/Scholarship) [5515]
S. Byrl Ross Memorial Scholarship Fund (Undergraduate/Scholarship) [5516]
St. Joseph's Hospital School of Nursing Alumnae Scholarships (Undergraduate/Scholarship) [5518]
Everett Oscar Shimp Memorial Scholarships (Undergraduate/Scholarship) [5519]
Pat Shimp Memorial Scholarships (Undergraduate/Scholarship) [5520]
Bill Six Memorial Scholarship Fund (Undergraduate/Scholarship) [5522]
Mary K. Smith Rector Scholarships (Undergraduate/Scholarship) [5523]
Spanish Embassy Scholarships (Graduate, Other/Scholarship) [5267]
The SSPI Mid-Atlantic Chapter Scholarships (Graduate, Undergraduate/Scholarship) [6583]
Zachary Taylor Stevens Memorial Scholarships (Undergraduate/Scholarship) [856]
Charles H. Stone Scholarships (Undergraduate/Scholarship) [413]
C.R. Thomas Scholarships (Undergraduate/Scholarship) [5524]
Charles A. Townsend Scholarships (Undergraduate/Scholarship) [5525]
Gary Wagner, K3OMI Scholarships (Undergraduate/Scholarship) [859]
Wayne-Meador-Elliott Scholarships (Undergraduate/Scholarship) [5526]
West Virginia Educational Foundation Hospitality Business Alliance Scholarships (Undergraduate/Scholarship) [7399]
West Virginia Nurses Association District No. 3 Scholarships (Undergraduate/Scholarship) [5527]
Whitaker-Minard Memorial Scholarships (Undergraduate/Scholarship) [5528]
L. Phil Wicker Scholarships (Undergraduate/Scholarship) [861]
Glenn Wilson Broadcast Journalism Scholarships (Undergraduate/Scholarship) [5529]

Wisconsin

Victor Albright Scholarships-Dane County (Undergraduate/Scholarship) [7246]
Victor Albright Scholarships (Undergraduate/Scholarship) [7247]
Bascom Hill Society Scholarships (Undergraduate/Scholarship) [7248]
Calvin Alumni Association-Southeastern Wisconsin Scholarships (Undergraduate/Scholarship) [1882]
Chicago FM Club Scholarships (Undergraduate/Scholarship) [827]
Engineering Departmental Scholarships (Undergraduate/Scholarship) [7251]
Kemper K. Knapp Scholarships (Undergraduate/Scholarship) [7259]
George Koeppel and Roland W. Zinns Scholarships (Undergraduate/Scholarship) [7260]
Lawton Minority Retention Grants (Undergraduate/Scholarship) [7261]
MAC Louisa Bowen Memorial Scholarships for Graduate Students in Archival Administration (Graduate/Scholarship) [4510]
E.H. Marth Food and Environmental Scholarships (Undergraduate/Scholarship) [7470]
Edmond A. Metzger Scholarships (Undergraduate/Scholarship) [843]
John P. and Tashia F. Morgridge Scholarships (Undergraduate/Scholarship) [7263]
Pi Lambda Theta Scholarships (Undergraduate/Scholarship) [7265]
School of Education Scholarships for Students from Underrepresented Groups (Undergraduate/Scholarship) [7268]
University of Wisconsin-Madison Academic Excellence Scholarships (Undergraduate/Scholarship) [7270]
University of Wisconsin-Madison Minority Teacher Loans (Professional Development, Undergraduate/Loan, Scholarship) [7277]
Upper Midwest Human Rights Fellowship Program (Professional Development/Fellowship) [7135]
Francis Walton Memorial Scholarships (Undergraduate/Scholarship) [860]
Wisconsin High School Scholarships (Undergraduate/Scholarship) [7284]

Wyoming

Horatio Alger Wyoming Scholarships (Undergraduate/Scholarship) [228]
The Cady McDonnell Memorial Scholarships (Undergraduate/Scholarship) [488]
Rocky Mountain Coal Mining Institute Engineering/Geology Scholarships (Undergraduate/Scholarship) [6051]
Rocky Mountain Coal Mining Institute Technical Scholarships (Undergraduate/Scholarship) [6052]

CANADA

AABP Amstutz Scholarships (Undergraduate/Scholarship) [326]
AANS Medical Student Summer Research Fellowships (MSSRF) (Undergraduate/Fellowship) [370]
Dr. Anderson Abbott Awards (Undergraduate/Scholarship) [7208]
Jack Ackroyd Scholarships (Professional Development/Scholarship) [1925]
ACS/NREF-AANS Faculty Career Development Award (Professional Development/Award/Prize) [371]
AHNS Pilot Research Grants (Professional Development/Grant) [600]
Airports Council International-North America Scholarship (Graduate, Undergraduate/Scholarship) [94]
Al Mercury Scholarships (Undergraduate/Scholarship) [7209]
Alaska Airlines Scholarships (Undergraduate/Scholarship) [1079]
Alberta Agricultural Economics Association Scholarships (Graduate/Scholarship) [137]
Alberta Agricultural Economics Association Undergraduate Scholarships (Undergraduate/Scholarship) [138]
Alberta Award for the Study of Canadian Human Rights and Multiculturalism (Doctorate, Graduate/Award/Prize) [145]
Alberta Centennial Premier's Scholarships - Alberta (Undergraduate/Scholarship) [146]
Alberta Press Council Scholarships (Undergraduate/Scholarship) [187]
Alberta Ukrainian Centennial Commemorative Scholarships (Undergraduate/Scholarship) [7356]
Hon. Lincoln Alexander Scholarships (Undergraduate/Scholarship) [1724]
Stephanie Ali Memorial Scholarships (Undergraduate/Scholarship) [7210]
Jim Allard Broadcast Journalism Scholarships (Undergraduate/Scholarship) [1921]
Janet and Horace Allen Scholarship (Undergraduate/Scholarship) [147]
Lorraine Allison Scholarships (Postgraduate/Scholarship) [1199]
AMEC Aboriginal Undergraduate Scholarships (Undergraduate/Scholarship) [1947]
AMEC Masters Scholarships (Graduate/Scholarship) [1948]
American College of Radiation Oncology Resident Scholarships (Graduate/Scholarship) [475]
American Express Travel Scholarships (Undergraduate/Scholarship) [1080]
American Society of Comparative Law TransCoop Programs (All/Fellowship) [937]
American Standard Scholarships (Undergraduate/Scholarship) [5700]
American Welding Society International Scholarships (Undergraduate/Scholarship) [1151]
Bernard Amtmann Fellowships (Postgraduate/Grant) [1698]
APALA Scholarship Program (Doctorate, Graduate/Scholarship) [1336]
Aplastic, Anemia and Myelosdysplasia Scholarships (Graduate/Scholarship) [1991]
Applied Hospitality Degree Scholarships (Undergraduate/Scholarship) [1975]
Architects Association of PEI Scholarships (Undergraduate/Scholarship) [2496]
Arizona Chapter Gold Scholarships (Undergraduate/Scholarship) [1082]
Art Graduate Scholarships (Graduate/Scholarship) [148]
Arts for Career Development Scholarships (Professional Development/Internship) [149]
Association of Desk and Derrick Clubs Education Trust Scholarships (Undergraduate/Scholarship) [1388]
Association of Universities and Colleges of Canada Public Scholarships (Undergraduate/Scholarship) [1504]
Association for Women Veterinarians Foundation Scholarships Program (Graduate/Scholarship) [1523]
Astra Zeneca RURAL Scholarships (Doctorate/Scholarship) [1992]
Martha and Robert Atherton Ministerial Scholarships (Graduate, Master's/Scholarship) [6947]
Atlantic Provinces Library Association Memorial

Awards *(Professional Development/Scholarship)* [1533]
Atlantic Salmon Federation Olin Fellowships *(All/Fellowship)* [1536]
Joan Auld Scholarships *(Undergraduate/Scholarship)* [2497]
Jerry Baker Scholarships *(Undergraduate/Scholarship)* [1156]
Ballantyne Resident Research Grants *(Professional Development/Grant)* [602]
Helen Bassett Commemorative Scholarships *(Undergraduate/Scholarship)* [5128]
Baxter Corporation Canadian Research Awards in Anesthesia *(Professional Development/Award/Prize)* [1912]
BBM Canada Scholarships *(Undergraduate/Scholarship)* [1922]
Suzanne Beauregard Scholarships *(Undergraduate/Scholarship)* [6070]
Stan Beck Fellowships *(Undergraduate/Fellowship)* [2861]
Ann Beckingham Scholarships *(Doctorate/Scholarship)* [1993]
Dade Behring Student Scholarship Awards *(Postgraduate/Scholarship)* [2040]
Beverlee Bell Scholarships in Human Rights and Democracy *(Graduate/Scholarship)* [2728]
Louise Bennett-Coverley Scholarships *(Undergraduate/Scholarship)* [1725]
Dr. Noorali & Sabiya Bharwani Endowment *(Undergraduate/Scholarship)* [1693]
Hussein Jina Bharwani Memorial Endowment *(Undergraduate/Scholarship)* [1694]
J.P. Bickell Mining Scholarships *(Undergraduate/Scholarship)* [7211]
BioQuip Scholarships *(Undergraduate/Scholarship)* [2862]
Birks Family Foundation Scholarships *(Undergraduate/Scholarship)* [1994]
Bison Transport Scholarships *(Undergraduate/Scholarship)* [5341]
Black Canadian Scholarships *(Undergraduate/Scholarship)* [5419]
M. Hildred Blewett Scholarships *(Postdoctorate/Scholarship)* [6431]
Lawrence Bloomberg Entrance Awards *(Postgraduate/Award/Prize)* [6262]
BMO Financial Group Scholarships *(Undergraduate/Scholarship)* [1726]
Therese and David Bohbot Scholarship *(Undergraduate/Scholarship)* [3553]
Steve Bonk Scholarships *(Postgraduate/Scholarship)* [2050]
Lorne and Ruby Bonnell Scholarships *(Undergraduate/Scholarship)* [2498]
Anne-Marie Bonner Scholarships *(Undergraduate/Scholarship)* [3994]
Bound to Stay Bound Books (BTSB) Scholarships *(Graduate/Scholarship)* [1464]
Jim Bourque Scholarships *(Postgraduate/Scholarship)* [1200]
Eugene Boyko Scholarships *(Undergraduate/Scholarship)* [140]
Marlene Brand Memorial Scholarship *(Undergraduate/Scholarship)* [3554]
Louis J. Brody Q.C. Entrance Scholarships *(Postgraduate/Scholarship)* [6263]
Peter F. Bronfman Entrance Awards *(Postgraduate/Award/Prize)* [6264]
Peter F. Bronfman Scholarships of Merit *(Postgraduate/Scholarship)* [6265]
Randall Brown and Associates Awards *(Postgraduate/Award/Prize)* [1962]
Brown Dental Scholarships *(Undergraduate/Scholarship)* [3995]
Olympia Brown and Max Kapp Awards *(Graduate/Scholarship)* [6948]
Bernic and Gordon Brown Scholarship *(All/Scholarship)* [3555]
Bujea Memorial Scholarships *(Undergraduate/Scholarship)* [911]
Sam Bull Memorial Scholarships *(Undergraduate/Scholarship)* [142]
Leon C. Bynoe Memorial Scholarships *(Undergraduate/Scholarship)* [7212]
CAG Donald Menzies Bursary Awards *(Postgraduate/Award/Prize)* [1927]
CAG Margery Boyce Bursary Awards *(Postgraduate/Award/Prize)* [1928]
CALL/ACBD Education Reserve Fund Grants *(Graduate/Grant)* [1930]
Cameco Corporation Scholarships in the Geological Sciences - Continuing Students *(Undergraduate/Scholarship)* [1904]
Cameco Corporation Scholarships in the Geological Sciences - Entering Students *(Undergraduate/Scholarship)* [1905]
Cameco Northern Scholarships - Technical Institute *(Undergraduate/Scholarship)* [1906]
Cameco Northern Scholarships - University *(Undergraduate/Scholarship)* [1907]
Theodore R. Campbell Scholarship *(Undergraduate/Scholarship)* [150]
Canada Graduate Scholarships Program *(Graduate/Scholarship)* [6418]
Canada Millennium Bursary *(Undergraduate/Scholarship)* [151]
Canadian Aboriginal Science and Technology Society Scholarships *(Undergraduate/Scholarship)* [2042]
Canadian Anesthesiologists' Society Research Awards *(Professional Development/Award/Prize)* [1913]
Canadian Association of Law Libraries CALL Research Grants *(Graduate/Grant)* [1931]
Canadian Federation of University Women Etobicoke Bursary *(Graduate, Undergraduate/Scholarship)* [7213]
Canadian Hard of Hearing Association Scholarships *(Undergraduate/Scholarship)* [1968]
Canadian Hospitality Foundation College Entrance Scholarships *(Undergraduate/Scholarship)* [1976]
Canadian Hospitality Foundation University Entrance Scholarships *(Undergraduate/Scholarship)* [1977]
Canadian Macedonian Federation Scholarships *(Undergraduate/Scholarship)* [7214]
Canadian Nurses Foundation - Baxter Corporation Scholarships *(Graduate/Scholarship)* [1995]
Canadian Nurses Foundation Northern Scholarships *(Undergraduate/Scholarship)* [1996]
Canadian Nurses Foundation Scholarships *(Undergraduate/Scholarship)* [1997]
Canadian Occupational Therapy Foundation Graduate Scholarships *(Graduate/Scholarship)* [2017]
Canadian Occupational Therapy Foundation Invacare Master's Scholarships *(Graduate/Scholarship)* [2018]
Canadian Parking Association Scholarships *(Undergraduate/Scholarship)* [2027]
Canadian Sanitation Supply Association Scholarships *(Undergraduate/Scholarship)* [2029]
Canadian Seniors Golf Association Scholarships *(Undergraduate/Scholarship)* [6071]
Canadian Society of Petroleum Geologists Regional Graduate Scholarships *(Doctorate, Graduate/Scholarship)* [2043]
Canadian Society of Petroleum Geologists Regional Undergraduate Scholarships *(Undergraduate/Scholarship)* [2044]
Canadian Water Resources Association Scholarships *(All/Scholarship)* [2047]
Thelma Cardwell Scholarships *(Graduate/Scholarship)* [2019]
Carmangay Home and School Association Scholarships *(Undergraduate/Scholarship)* [152]
Herb Carnegie Scholarships *(Undergraduate/Scholarship)* [1727]
Robert C. Carson Memorial Bursary *(Undergraduate/Scholarship)* [153]
CAS/GE Healthcare Canada Inc. Research Awards *(Professional Development/Award/Prize)* [1914]
CAS/Vitaid-LMA Residents' Research Grant Competition *(Professional Development/Award/Prize)* [1915]
Fraser Milner Casgrain LLP Scholarships *(Undergraduate/Scholarship)* [1728]
Caterpillar Scholars Award *(Undergraduate/Scholarship)* [6471]
Marshall Cavendish Scholarships *(Graduate/Scholarship)* [699]
CAWEE International Student Fellowships *(Postgraduate/Fellowship)* [6266]
CEMF Claudette MacKay-Lassonde Scholarships *(Postdoctorate/Scholarship)* [6432]
CEMF Undergraduate Engineering Scholarships *(Undergraduate/Scholarship)* [1949]
CFIG National Scholarships *(Undergraduate/Scholarship)* [1954]
Mary Anne Chambers Scholarships *(Undergraduate/Scholarship)* [3996]
Chapter 4 - Lawrence A. Wacker Memorial Awards *(Undergraduate/Scholarship)* [6473]
Chapter - 6 Fairfield County Scholarships *(Undergraduate/Scholarship)* [6474]
Hadar J. Chemtob Scholarship *(Undergraduate/Scholarship)* [3556]
Childhood Cancer Foundation Candlelighters Canada Scholarships *(All/Scholarship)* [2125]
Childhood Cancer Foundation Scholarships *(Undergraduate/Scholarship)* [2123]
Chinese-Canadian History and Culture Fellowships *(Graduate/Fellowship)* [7215]
Patricia Smith Christensen Scholarships *(Postdoctorate/Scholarship)* [6383]
CHS - Bursary Program Scholarships *(Undergraduate/Scholarship)* [1970]
CHS - Mature Student Bursary Program Scholarships *(Professional Development/Scholarship)* [1971]
CHS Scholarships *(Undergraduate/Scholarship)* [1972]
CIBC Scholarships *(Undergraduate/Scholarship)* [1729]
CIP Fellow's Travel Scholarships *(Postgraduate/Scholarship)* [1980]
City of Toronto Graduate Scholarships for Women in Mathematics *(Graduate/Scholarship)* [7216]
City of Toronto Queen Elizabeth II Sesquicentennial Scholarships in Community Health Nursing (Graduate) *(Graduate/Scholarship)* [7217]
City of Toronto Queen Elizabeth II Sesquicentennial Scholarships in Community Health Nursing (Undergraduate) *(Undergraduate/Scholarship)* [7218]
City of Toronto Scholarships for Aboriginal Students *(Graduate, Undergraduate/Scholarship)* [7219]
City of Toronto Women's Studies Scholarships *(Graduate, Undergraduate/Scholarship)* [7220]
CLA/ACB Dafoe Scholarships *(Graduate/Scholarship)* [1985]
David H. Clift Scholarships *(Graduate/Scholarship)* [700]
CN Scholarships for Women *(Postgraduate/Scholarship)* [6433]
Marshall A. Cohen Entrance Awards *(Postgraduate/Award/Prize)* [6267]
Dr. Mark Cohen Scholarship *(Undergraduate/Scholarship)* [3557]
Erma Collins Scholarships *(Undergraduate/Scholarship)* [1730]
Connor/Spafford Scholarships *(Undergraduate/Scholarship)* [6072]
Continuing Education Awards *(Graduate/Grant)* [4441]
Copnick/Hilliard Scholarships *(Professional Development/Scholarship)* [2024]
Gertrude M. Cox Scholarships *(Doctorate, Graduate/Fellowship)* [1114]
CSEG Scholarship Trust Fund *(Postgraduate/Scholarship)* [2038]
Culinary (1-Year Program) Scholarships *(Undergraduate/Scholarship)* [1978]
DAAD Study Scholarship Awards *(Graduate/Scholarship)* [3223]
DAAD Undergraduate Scholarship Program *(Undergraduate/Scholarship)* [3224]
Laurence Decore Awards for Student Leadership *(Undergraduate/Scholarship)* [154]
Ginger and Fred Deines Canada Scholarships *(Undergraduate/Scholarship)* [6917]
Delta Faucet Scholarships *(Undergraduate/Scholarship)* [5701]
Albert W. Dent Graduate Student Scholarships *(Undergraduate/Scholarship)* [466]
Helen L. Dewar Scholarships *(Undergraduate/Scholarship)* [6883]
Dr. Allan A. Dixon Memorial Scholarships *(Postgraduate/Scholarship)* [2034]

Douglas-Coldwell Foundation Scholarships in Social Affairs *(Graduate/Scholarship)* [2729]
Tommy Douglas Scholarships *(Undergraduate/Scholarship)* [5116]
Mary Ellen Driscoll Scholarships *(Undergraduate/Scholarship)* [6073]
Joshua Dyke Family Scholarships *(Undergraduate/Scholarship)* [6884]
Earl and Countess of Wessex - World Championships in Athletics Scholarships *(Undergraduate/Scholarship)* [155]
David Eaton Scholarships *(Graduate, Master's/Scholarship)* [6951]
Edmonton Epilepsy Continuing Education Scholarships *(Undergraduate/Scholarship)* [2824]
Erb Group Companies Service to Community Scholarships *(Undergraduate/Scholarship)* [5342]
Extendicare Scholarships *(Graduate/Scholarship)* [1998]
Faculty Research Visit Grant *(Doctorate/Grant)* [3225]
Fellowships for Full-time Studies in French *(Undergraduate/Fellowship)* [156]
Fellowships in the Humanities and Social Sciences in Turkey *(Postdoctorate/Fellowship)* [894]
Fire Safety Awards *(Postgraduate/Award/Prize)* [1963]
Food Engineering Scholarships *(Postdoctorate, Postgraduate/Scholarship)* [3024]
Foresters Scholarships *(Undergraduate/Scholarship)* [3682]
Foundation for the Advancement of Aboriginal Youth Bursary Program *(Undergraduate/Scholarship)* [1939]
Foundation for the Advancement of Aboriginal Youth Scholarships *(Undergraduate/Scholarship)* [1940]
Terry Fox Memorial Scholarships *(Undergraduate/Scholarship)* [5117]
Future Leader in Radiocommunications Scholarships *(Postgraduate/Scholarship)* [5893]
Harry Gairey Scholarships *(Undergraduate/Scholarship)* [1731]
Marcus Mosiah Garvey Scholarships *(Undergraduate/Scholarship)* [3997]
Geological Society of America Graduate Student Research Grants *(Doctorate, Graduate/Grant)* [3210]
Keith Gilmore Foundation - Diploma Scholarships *(Professional Development/Scholarship)* [3240]
Keith Gilmore Foundation - Postgraduate Scholarships *(Postgraduate/Scholarship)* [3241]
Keith Gilmore Foundation - Undergraduate Scholarships *(Undergraduate/Scholarship)* [3242]
Helen Glass Scholarships *(Doctorate/Scholarship)* [1999]
Daniel B. Goldberg Scholarships *(Other/Scholarship)* [3264]
Goodfellow Professional Development Fund *(Professional Development/Scholarship)* [4250]
J.O. Goodman Scholarship Awards *(Undergraduate/Scholarship)* [5343]
Baxter Corporation - Jean Goodwill Scholarships *(Postgraduate/Scholarship)* [9]
Lucille May Gopie Scholarships *(Undergraduate/Scholarship)* [1732]
Graduate Student Scholarship *(Graduate/Scholarship)* [157]
Graduate Student Scholarships *(Postgraduate/Scholarship)* [3833]
Frank L. Greathouse Government Accounting Scholarships *(Other/Scholarship)* [3265]
Reginald K. Groome Memorial Scholarships *(Postgraduate/Scholarship)* [6286]
Guntley-Lorimer Science and Arts Scholarships *(Undergraduate/Scholarship)* [1733]
David J. Hallissey Memorial Scholarships *(Undergraduate/Scholarship)* [1083]
Hamilton Industrial Environmental Association Bursaries-Mohawk College *(Undergraduate/Scholarship)* [3390]
Al Hamilton Scholarships *(Undergraduate/Scholarship)* [1734]
Ruth Hancock Scholarships *(Undergraduate/Scholarship)* [1923]
Phyllis P. Harris Scholarships *(Postgraduate/Award/Prize)* [1956]
Healy Scholarships *(Undergraduate/Scholarship)* [1084]
Richard F. Heaney Memorial Scholarship Fund *(Graduate, Undergraduate/Scholarship)* [3817]
Dr. Stan Heaps Memorial Scholarships *(Undergraduate/Scholarship)* [3719]
Elizabeth Heath Post-Secondary Awards *(Undergraduate/Scholarship)* [5422]
Mary Jane Hendrie Memorial Scholarships *(Graduate, Undergraduate/Scholarship)* [7221]
Hewlett-Packard Undergraduate Scholarships *(Undergraduate/Scholarship)* [1950]
HGA and Dendel Scholarships *(Undergraduate/Scholarship)* [3396]
Judy Hill Scholarships *(Undergraduate/Scholarship)* [2000]
Georgia Hilton Academic Scholarships *(Undergraduate/Scholarship)* [6074]
D. Glenn Hilts Scholarships Program *(Graduate, Undergraduate/Scholarship)* [1493]
Hispanic Serving Institution Scholarships *(Undergraduate/Scholarship)* [6973]
C.V. Hoar Scholarship Awards *(Undergraduate/Scholarship)* [5344]
Hoffman-Laroche Scholarships *(Graduate/Scholarship)* [2001]
Irving J. Hoffman Memorial Scholarships *(Undergraduate/Scholarship)* [7222]
Lois Hole Humanities and Social Sciences Scholarship *(Undergraduate/Scholarship)* [158]
Holland America Line-Westours Research Grants *(Undergraduate/Grant)* [1085]
Hosinec Family Scholarships *(Graduate, Undergraduate/Scholarship)* [7223]
Goldwin Howland Scholarships *(Graduate/Scholarship)* [2020]
Christopher Hoy/ERT Scholarships *(Graduate/Scholarship)* [701]
William Peyton Hubbard Scholarships *(Undergraduate/Scholarship)* [1735]
Steven Huesing Scholarships *(Undergraduate/Scholarship)* [2255]
Humber College Institute of Technology and Advanced Learning Scholarships *(Undergraduate/Scholarship)* [3998]
John Peter Humphrey Student Fellowships *(Graduate/Fellowship)* [1942]
I Have a Dream Scholarships *(Undergraduate/Scholarship)* [3999]
IBA Law Student Scholarships Foundation *(Undergraduate/Scholarship)* [3715]
IBM Canada Undergraduate Scholarships *(Undergraduate/Scholarship)* [1951]
IIE Council of Fellows Undergraduate Scholarships *(Undergraduate/Scholarship)* [3733]
In-course Scholarships - Chinese Dance Workshop Scholarships *(Undergraduate/Scholarship)* [7224]
Informatics Circle of Research Excellence Scholarships *(Doctorate, Graduate/Scholarship)* [159]
Barbara Ingram, Janet W. McCarthy and W.J.P. Jack Robertson Memorial Scholarships *(Undergraduate/Scholarship)* [5424]
International Association of Black Actuaries Scholarships *(Undergraduate/Scholarship)* [3786]
International Association of Foundation Drilling Scholarships for Civil Engineering Students *(Postgraduate/Scholarship)* [3798]
International Association of Foundation Drilling Scholarships for Part-time Civil Engineering Graduate School Students *(Postgraduate/Scholarship)* [3799]
International Association of Law Libraries Scholarship Program *(Professional Development/Scholarship)* [3807]
International Education Awards - Ukraine *(Undergraduate/Scholarship)* [160]
International Grenfell Association Bursary *(Undergraduate/Scholarship)* [3863]
International Grenfell Association Secondary/High School Scholarships *(Undergraduate/Scholarship)* [3864]
International Grenfell Association University/College Scholarships *(Undergraduate/Scholarship)* [3865]
International Municipal Lawyers Association Canadian Scholarships *(Professional Development/Scholarship)* [3878]
International Sanitary Supply Association Foundation Scholarships *(High School/Scholarship)* [2030]
Dr. Karl C. Ivarson Scholarships *(Postgraduate/Scholarship)* [36]
Jamaica Day Basil Duncan Memorial Scholarships *(Undergraduate/Scholarship)* [4000]
Jamaica National Building Society Scholarships *(Undergraduate/Scholarship)* [4001]
Terry Jarvis Memorial Scholarships *(Undergraduate/Scholarship)* [1165]
JAUW Fellowship Awards *(Postgraduate/Fellowship)* [1960]
Right Hon. Michaelle Jean Scholarships *(Undergraduate/Scholarship)* [1736]
Harry Jerome Scholarships *(Undergraduate/Scholarship)* [1737]
Johnson & Johnson Scholarships *(Undergraduate/Scholarship)* [2002]
Kalmen Kaplansky Scholarships in Economic and Social Rights *(Graduate/Scholarship)* [2730]
Lucile B. Kaufman Women's Scholarships *(Undergraduate/Scholarship)* [6493]
E. Wayne Kay Community College Scholarships *(Undergraduate/Scholarship)* [6495]
Dorothy Kergin Scholarships *(Doctorate/Scholarship)* [2003]
Khaki University and Y.M.C.A. Memorial Scholarships *(Undergraduate/Scholarship)* [7225]
Helen and George Kilik Scholarship *(Undergraduate/Scholarship)* [161]
Killam Fellowships Program *(Undergraduate/Fellowship)* [7033]
Mackenzie King Open Scholarships *(Graduate/Scholarship)* [4428]
Mackenzie King Travelling Scholarships *(Graduate/Scholarship)* [4429]
Anna and John Kolesay Memorial Scholarship *(Undergraduate/Scholarship)* [162]
Bernie Kom Memorial Awards *(Postgraduate/Award/Prize)* [6268]
Korean Studies Dissertation Workshop Funds *(Graduate/Grant)* [6416]
Kress Pre-Doctoral Fellowships in the History of Art and Archeology in Turkey *(Postdoctorate/Fellowship)* [898]
David A. Kronick Travelling Fellowships *(Doctorate/Fellowship)* [4443]
Leo J. Krysa Family Undergraduate Scholarships *(Undergraduate/Scholarship)* [1982]
Leila Klinger Kurtzman Mamorial Scholarship Fund *(Undergraduate/Scholarship)* [3558]
Allen T. Lambert Scholarships *(Postgraduate/Scholarship)* [6269]
John and Lois Lamont Graduate Scholarships *(Postgraduate/Award/Prize)* [1957]
James D. Lang Memorial Scholarships *(Graduate/Scholarship)* [1932]
Jason Lang Scholarship *(Undergraduate/Scholarship)* [163]
Language Teacher Bursary Program Awards *(Professional Development/Award/Prize)* [164]
Languages In Teacher Education Scholarships *(Professional Development/Scholarship)* [165]
Karen E. Latt Memorial Scholarship *(Undergraduate/Scholarship)* [3559]
Kenneth Laundy Entrance Scholarships *(Postgraduate/Scholarship)* [6270]
Law Foundation of British Columbia Graduate Fellowships *(Undergraduate/Fellowship)* [4147]
Le Cordon Bleu Ottawa Culinary Arts Institute Basic Cuisine Certificate Scholarships *(All, Professional Development/Scholarship)* [2580]
The Leaders of Tomorrow Scholarships *(Undergraduate/Scholarship)* [2813]
Leber Rubes Inc. Awards *(Postgraduate/Award/Prize)* [1964]
Carol Anne Letheren Entrance Awards *(Postgraduate/Award/Prize)* [6271]
Irene Brand Lieberman Scholarship *(Postgraduate/Scholarship)* [3560]
Tecla Lin & Nelia Laroza Memorial Scholarships *(Undergraduate/Scholarship)* [2004]
Donald A. B. Lindberg Research Fellowships *(Doctorate, Graduate/Fellowship)* [4444]
LITA and LSSI Minority Scholarships

(Graduate/Scholarship) [4237]
LITA/OCLC Minority Scholarships *(Graduate/Scholarship)* [4238]
Ian Lithgow Memorial Awards *(Postgraduate/Award/Prize)* [6272]
Lo Family Scholarships *(Undergraduate/Scholarship)* [7226]
Sir James Lougheed Awards of Distinction *(Doctorate, Graduate/Award/Prize)* [166]
Gertrude and Edith Lowidt and Mary Catherine Preiss Memorial Bursaries in Nutritional Sciences *(Undergraduate/Scholarship)* [7227]
John Macara, Barrister of Goderich, Scholarships *(Undergraduate/Scholarship)* [7228]
Major Collaborative Research Initiatives Grants *(Graduate/Grant)* [6419]
Marathon Pulp Inc. Education Achievement Scholarships *(Undergraduate/Scholarship)* [6885]
Dick Martin Scholarships *(Postgraduate/Scholarship)* [1943]
Eleanor Martin Scholarships *(Graduate/Scholarship)* [2005]
Beverly Mascoll Scholarships *(Undergraduate/Scholarship)* [1738]
Val Mason Scholarships *(Postgraduate/Scholarship)* [2036]
Hans McCorriston Motive Power Machinist Grant Programs *(Postgraduate/Scholarship)* [1570]
Joseph McCulley Educational Scholarships *(Graduate, Undergraduate/Scholarship)* [7229]
Foster G. McGaw Graduate Student Scholarships *(Undergraduate/Scholarship)* [467]
McGill University Alma Mater Student Travel Grants *(Graduate/Grant)* [4430]
McGill University Scholarships for Research Trips to Europe *(Graduate/Scholarship)* [4431]
Louise McKinney Post-secondary Scholarship *(Undergraduate/Scholarship)* [167]
James H. McLaughlin Scholarships *(Undergraduate/Scholarship)* [5222]
John Alexander McLean Scholarships *(Undergraduate/Scholarship)* [6886]
Douglas McRorie Memorial Scholarships *(Doctorate, Graduate/Scholarship)* [37]
Medical Student Summer Research Scholarships *(Undergraduate/Scholarship)* [261]
Dr. Ernest and Minnie Mehl Scholarship *(Undergraduate/Scholarship)* [168]
Frederic G. Melcher Scholarships *(Graduate/Scholarship)* [1465]
Meloche-Monnex Scholarships *(Doctorate/Scholarship)* [2006]
Bernard Michel Scholarships *(Undergraduate/Scholarship)* [1908]
Military Nurses Association Scholarships *(Graduate/Scholarship)* [2007]
Millennium Alberta Rural Incentive Bursary Award *(Undergraduate/Award/Prize)* [169]
Mineralogical Association of Canada Scholarships *(Postgraduate/Scholarship)* [4539]
Minerva Scholarships *(Undergraduate/Scholarship)* [1739]
Minorities in Government Finance Scholarships *(Graduate, Undergraduate/Scholarship)* [3266]
MLA Research, Development, and Demonstration Project Grants *(Graduate/Grant)* [4446]
MLA Scholarships for Minority Students *(Graduate/Scholarship)* [4447]
Thomas More Scholarships *(Undergraduate/Scholarship)* [3260]
Dr. Henry Morgentaler Future Choice Scholarships *(Postgraduate/Award/Prize)* [1958]
John H. Moss Scholarships *(Undergraduate/Scholarship)* [7230]
Marvin Mundel Memorial Scholarships *(Undergraduate/Scholarship)* [3736]
Margaret Munro Scholarships *(Undergraduate/Scholarship)* [2008]
Helen Mussallem Scholarships *(Graduate/Scholarship)* [2009]
Myasthenia Gravis Foundation of America Post-Doctoral Fellowships *(Postdoctorate/Fellowship)* [4603]
NACBS Dissertation Year Fellowships *(Postdoctorate/Fellowship)* [5217]
NACBS-Huntington Library Fellowships *(Postdoctorate/Fellowship)* [5218]
Irwin Allen Nadal Entrance Awards *(Postgraduate/Award/Prize)* [6273]
Miles Spencer Nadal Entrance Awards *(Postgraduate/Award/Prize)* [6274]
Nadine International Inc. Awards *(Postgraduate/Award/Prize)* [1965]
National Geophysics Scholarships *(Postgraduate/Scholarship)* [7488]
National Scholarships *(Postgraduate/Scholarship)* [7489]
National Society of Accountants Scholarship Program *(Undergraduate/Scholarship)* [5047]
Dr. Ezra Nesbeth Scholarships *(Undergraduate/Scholarship)* [4002]
New Brunswick Nurses Association Scholarships *(Graduate/Scholarship)* [2010]
Frank Newman Leadership Awards *(Undergraduate/Scholarship)* [1916]
Norman Nicholson Scholarships *(Undergraduate/Scholarship)* [1937]
Sharon Nield Memorial Scholarships *(Undergraduate/Scholarship)* [2011]
George A. Nielsen Public Investor Scholarships *(Graduate, Undergraduate/Scholarship)* [3267]
Charles S. Noble Scholarships for Study at Harvard *(Undergraduate/Scholarship)* [170]
Norfolk Southern Foundation Scholarships *(Undergraduate/Scholarship)* [882]
Nortel Institute Undergraduate Scholarships *(Undergraduate/Scholarship)* [7231]
Northern Alberta Development Council Bursary Award *(Undergraduate/Award/Prize)* [171]
Northern Alberta Development Council Bursary for Medical Students *(Undergraduate/Award/Prize)* [172]
Northern Alberta Development Council Bursary Partnership Program *(Undergraduate/Award/Prize)* [173]
Northern Alberta Development Council Bursary for Pharmacy Students *(Undergraduate/Scholarship)* [174]
Northern Student Supplement *(Undergraduate/Award/Prize)* [175]
Nova Scotia Salmon Association Scholarships *(All/Scholarship)* [5307]
Novo Nordisk Canada-CAS Research Awards *(Professional Development/Award/Prize)* [1917]
NSERC Canada Graduate Scholarships *(Graduate, Postdoctorate/Scholarship)* [6434]
NSERC Postgraduate Scholarships *(Graduate, Postdoctorate/Scholarship)* [6435]
Nu-Gro Corporation Turfgrass Scholarships (Graduate) *(Graduate, Postgraduate/Scholarship)* [6075]
Nu-Gro Corporation Turfgrass Scholarships (Undergraduate) *(Undergraduate/Scholarship)* [6076]
Ontario Hockey Association War Memorial Scholarships *(Undergraduate/Scholarship)* [7232]
Orin Carver Scholarships *(Undergraduate/Scholarship)* [2499]
OTA Education Foundation Scholarships *(Undergraduate/Scholarship)* [5345]
Senator Norman Paterson Fellowship Scholarships *(Doctorate/Scholarship)* [2012]
Arthur Paulin Automotive Aftermarket Scholarship Awards *(Postgraduate/Scholarship)* [1571]
Mary Pelmutter Scholarships *(Postgraduate/Award/Prize)* [2022]
Persons Case Scholarships *(Undergraduate/Scholarship)* [176]
Phillips Scholarships *(Undergraduate/Scholarship)* [2500]
Pleasant Hawaiian Holidays Scholarships *(Undergraduate/Scholarship)* [1086]
Plumbing-Heating-Cooling Contractors Association Educational Foundation Need-Based Scholarships *(Undergraduate/Scholarship)* [5703]
Plumbing-Heating-Cooling Contractors Association Educational Foundation Scholarships *(Undergraduate/Scholarship)* [5704]
David Pohl Scholarships *(Graduate, Master's/Scholarship)* [6952]
Roy H. Pollack Scholarships *(Graduate, Master's/Scholarship)* [6953]
Stan and Leone Pollard Scholarships *(Undergraduate/Scholarship)* [1087]
J.R. (Joe) Power National Scholarships *(Postgraduate/Scholarship)* [5878]
Prairie Baseball Academy Scholarships *(Undergraduate/Scholarship)* [177]
Gerald Pratley Awards *(Doctorate, Graduate/Award/Prize)* [2930]
Diana M. Priestly Memorial Scholarships *(Undergraduate/Scholarship)* [1933]
Prince Edward Island Law Student Scholarships *(Undergraduate/Scholarship)* [4149]
Professional Institute of the Public Service of Canada Expanded Scholarships *(Undergraduate/Scholarship)* [5793]
Provincial and Regional 4-H Scholarships *(Undergraduate/Scholarship)* [134]
ProWorld Study Abroad Scholarships *(Undergraduate/Scholarship)* [3256]
PSAC - Coughlin National Scholarships *(Postgraduate/Scholarship)* [5879]
PSAC - Groulx National Scholarships *(Postgraduate/Scholarship)* [5880]
PSAC National Scholarships *(Postgraduate/Scholarship)* [5881]
PSAC Regional Scholarships *(Postgraduate/Scholarship)* [5882]
Public Employee Retirement Research and Administration Scholarships *(Graduate/Scholarship)* [3268]
Queen Elizabeth II Graduate Scholarship Program *(Doctorate, Graduate/Scholarship)* [178]
RBC Financial Group Scholarships *(Graduate/Scholarship)* [1740]
RBC Royal Bank Scholarships for First Year Medical & Dental Students *(Undergraduate/Scholarship)* [6066]
RBC Royal Bank Scholarships for New Canadians *(Undergraduate/Scholarship)* [6067]
RBC Royal Bank Scholarships for Undergraduates *(Undergraduate/Scholarship)* [6068]
Registered Apprenticeship Program (RAP) Scholarships *(Undergraduate/Scholarship)* [179]
George Reinke Scholarships *(Undergraduate/Scholarship)* [1088]
Marion Roberts Memorial Scholarships *(Postgraduate/Scholarship)* [1572]
R.O.E.A. Dumitru Golea Goldy-Gemu Scholarships *(Undergraduate/Scholarship)* [913]
Geraldine Ruth Rogers Scholarships *(Undergraduate/Scholarship)* [6887]
Mandell and Lester Rosenblatt and Robert N. Herbert Undergraduate Scholarships *(Undergraduate/Scholarship)* [6519]
Robin Rousseau Memorial Mountain Achievement Scholarship *(Undergraduate/Scholarship)* [180]
Glen Ruby Memorial Scholarships *(Undergraduate/Scholarship)* [2045]
Rutherford Scholars *(Undergraduate/Scholarship)* [181]
Alexander Rutherford Scholarships for High School Achievement *(Undergraduate/Scholarship)* [182]
Ryerson Scholarships *(Undergraduate/Scholarship)* [4003]
Saint Paul University Excellence Scholarships *(Undergraduate/Scholarship)* [6152]
Saint Paul University Financial Aid Brasseries *(Undergraduate/Scholarship)* [6153]
AIST David H. Samson Scholarships *(Undergraduate/Scholarship)* [1456]
Sanofi Pasteur Scholarships *(Graduate/Scholarship)* [2013]
Dr. Oskar and Sally Schickler Scholarship *(Undergraduate/Scholarship)* [3561]
Scholarship Award of The Aliant Pioneer Volunteers *(Postgraduate/Scholarship)* [1989]
Scholarships for Aboriginal Canadians *(Undergraduate/Scholarship)* [5118]
Scholarships for Technology Students *(Postgraduate/Scholarship)* [1945]
Scholarships for Visible Minorities *(Undergraduate/Scholarship)* [5119]
School Age Financial Aid Program *(Undergraduate/Scholarship)* [1616]
Tanna H. Schulich MBA Entrance Scholarships *(Postgraduate/Scholarship)* [6275]
Fritz Schwartz Serials Education Scholarships *(Other/Scholarship)* [5226]

Scotiabank Scholarships *(Graduate/Scholarship)* [1741]
SEMA Memorial Scholarships *(Graduate/Scholarship)* [1573]
Dr. Robert Norman Shaw Scholarship *(Undergraduate/Scholarship)* [183]
Dr. Robert and Anna Shaw Scholarships *(Undergraduate/Scholarship)* [184]
David S. Sheridan Canadian Research Awards *(Professional Development/Award/Prize)* [1918]
Sigma Theta Tau International Scholarships *(Doctorate/Scholarship)* [2014]
Julia Viola Simms Science Scholarships *(Postgraduate/Scholarship)* [1742]
SME Education Foundation Family Scholarships *(Undergraduate/Scholarship)* [6503]
Eva Smith Bursary *(Undergraduate/Scholarship)* [4004]
A.O. Smith Scholarships *(Undergraduate/Scholarship)* [5705]
Smiths Medical Canada Ltd. Research Awards *(Professional Development/Award/Prize)* [1919]
Social Sciences and Humanities Research Council of Canada Standard Research Grants *(Doctorate, Graduate/Grant)* [6420]
Society of Naval Architects and Marine Engineers Undergraduate Scholarships *(Undergraduate/Scholarship)* [6520]
Carin Alma E. Somers Scholarship Trust *(Undergraduate/Scholarship)* [1534]
SSHRC Doctoral Fellowships Program *(Doctorate/Fellowship, Scholarship)* [6421]
Peter Stainsby Awards *(Postgraduate/Award/Prize)* [1973]
The Stanley H. Stearman Awards *(Undergraduate/Scholarship)* [5048]
Harry Steele Entrance Awards *(Postgraduate/Award/Prize)* [6276]
Mireille and Murray Steinberg Scholarship *(Postgraduate/Scholarship)* [3562]
Ralph Steinhauer Awards of Distinction *(Doctorate, Graduate/Award/Prize)* [185]
Marlene Streit Golf Scholarships *(Undergraduate/Scholarship)* [6077]
Study Scholarships for Artists or Musicians *(Graduate/Scholarship)* [3230]
Summerside-Natick Hockey Scholarships *(Undergraduate/Scholarship)* [2501]
Sun Life Financial Peer Support Scholarships *(Professional Development/Scholarship)* [2025]
TAC Foundation-3M Canada Company *(Postgraduate, Undergraduate/Scholarship)* [6898]
TAC Foundation-Albert M. Stevens Scholarships *(Postgraduate/Scholarship)* [6899]
TAC Foundation-Armtec Scholarships *(Undergraduate/Scholarship)* [6900]
TAC Foundation-BA Group Scholarships *(Postgraduate, Undergraduate/Scholarship)* [6901]
TAC Foundation-Cement Association of Canada Scholarships *(Postgraduate, Undergraduate/Scholarship)* [6902]
TAC Foundation-Delcan Corporation Scholarships *(Postgraduate, Undergraduate/Scholarship)* [6903]
TAC Foundation-Dillon Consulting Scholarships *(Undergraduate/Scholarship)* [6904]
TAC Foundation-EBA Engineering Consultants Ltd. Scholarships *(Postgraduate, Undergraduate/Scholarship)* [6905]
TAC Foundation-IBI Group Scholarships *(Postgraduate, Undergraduate/Scholarship)* [6906]
TAC Foundation-iTRANS Consulting Scholarships *(Postgraduate/Scholarship)* [6907]
TAC Foundation-McCormick Rankin Corporation Scholarships *(Undergraduate/Scholarship)* [6908]
TAC Foundation-MMM Group Limited Scholarships *(Postgraduate, Undergraduate/Scholarship)* [6909]
TAC Foundation-Municipalities Scholarships *(Postgraduate, Undergraduate/Scholarship)* [6910]
TAC Foundation-Provinces and Territories Scholarships *(Postgraduate, Undergraduate/Scholarship)* [6911]
TAC Foundation Scholarships *(Postgraduate, Undergraduate/Scholarship)* [6912]
TAC Foundation-Stantec Consulting Scholarships *(Postgraduate/Scholarship)* [6913]
TAC Foundation-UMA Engineering Ltd. Scholarships *(Undergraduate/Scholarship)* [6914]
TAC Foundation-Waterloo Alumni Scholarships *(Postgraduate/Scholarship)* [6915]
Taylor Statten Memorial Fellowships *(Graduate/Scholarship)* [7233]
Barbara Thomas Bursary *(Undergraduate/Scholarship)* [4005]
Rev. Chuck and Nancy Thomas Scholarships *(Graduate, Master's/Scholarship)* [6958]
Miller Thomson Foundation Scholarships *(Undergraduate/Scholarship)* [4537]
Ken Thomson Scholarships *(Undergraduate/Scholarship)* [2048]
Thomson Scientific/MLA Doctoral Fellowships *(Doctorate/Fellowship)* [4448]
Evald Torokvei Foundation Scholarships *(Graduate/Scholarship)* [7234]
Marie Tremaine Fellowships *(Postgraduate/Grant)* [1699]
Tropicana Community Services - Robert K. Brown Scholarships *(Undergraduate/Scholarship)* [1743]
Trudeau Foundation Doctoral Scholarships *(Doctorate/Scholarship)* [6928]
Sam Tughan Scholarships *(Undergraduate/Scholarship)* [2031]
Ukrainian Canadian Professional and Business Club Scholarships in Education *(Undergraduate/Scholarship)* [1983]
Underwriters' Laboratories of Canada Awards *(Postgraduate/Award/Prize)* [1966]
United Parcel Service Scholarship for Female Students *(Undergraduate/Scholarship)* [3740]
United Parcel Service Scholarship for Minority Students *(Undergraduate/Scholarship)* [3741]
University Summer Course Grants *(Undergraduate/Grant)* [3231]
University of Toronto Accenture Scholarships *(Undergraduate/Scholarship)* [7235]
University of Toronto SAC Undergraduate Grants *(Undergraduate/Grant)* [7236]
Urban Financial Services Coalition Scholarships *(Undergraduate/Scholarship)* [1744]
Vale Inco Limited Masters Scholarships *(Graduate/Scholarship)* [1952]
John Vanderlee Scholarships *(Undergraduate/Scholarship)* [2015]
Philip F. Vineberg Travelling Fellowship in the Humanities *(Graduate/Scholarship)* [4432]
The Viscount Bennett Fellowships *(Graduate/Fellowship)* [1935]
Von Ogden Vogt Scholarships *(Graduate, Master's/Scholarship)* [6959]
Frank M. Waddell Scholarships *(Graduate, Undergraduate/Scholarship)* [7237]
Jane C. Waldbaum Archaeological Field School Scholarships *(Undergraduate/Scholarship)* [1195]
War Memorial Doctoral Scholarships *(Postgraduate/Scholarship)* [4798]
Jerome P. Webster Fellowships *(Professional Development/Fellowship)* [3927]
Emanuel Weiner Scholarship *(Postgraduate/Scholarship)* [3563]
Bradford White Scholarships *(Undergraduate/Scholarship)* [5706]
Portia White Scholarships *(Undergraduate/Scholarship)* [1745]
Dwight Whylie Scholarships *(Undergraduate/Scholarship)* [1746]
Wilkinson & Company LLP Secondary School Scholarships *(Undergraduate/Scholarship)* [7412]
H.W. Wilson Scholarships *(Graduate/Scholarship)* [1986]
Ross A. Wilson Science Scholarships *(Undergraduate/Scholarship)* [6888]
Abel Wolman Fellowships *(Doctorate/Fellowship)* [1145]
Wood Bursary Awards *(Postgraduate/Award/Prize)* [7490]
Geofrey H. Wood Scholarships *(Undergraduate/Scholarship)* [2032]
World Book Graduate Scholarships in Library and Information Science *(Graduate/Scholarship)* [1987]
York Graduate Scholarships *(Graduate/Scholarship)* [6277]
York Regional Police Scholarships *(Undergraduate/Scholarship)* [4006]
Youth Affairs Committee Rising Star Scholarships *(Undergraduate/Scholarship)* [4007]
Yukon Law Foundation Scholarships *(Undergraduate/Scholarship)* [7551]

CANADA (BY PROVINCE)

Alberta

Alberta Centennial Premier's Scholarships - Alberta *(Undergraduate/Scholarship)* [146]
Alberta Press Council Scholarships *(Undergraduate/Scholarship)* [187]
Janet and Horace Allen Scholarship *(Undergraduate/Scholarship)* [147]
Art Graduate Scholarships *(Graduate/Scholarship)* [148]
Arts for Career Development Scholarships *(Professional Development/Internship)* [149]
Eugene Boyko Scholarships *(Undergraduate/Scholarship)* [140]
Sam Bull Memorial Scholarships *(Undergraduate/Scholarship)* [142]
Theodore R. Campbell Scholarship *(Undergraduate/Scholarship)* [150]
Canada Millennium Bursary *(Undergraduate/Scholarship)* [151]
Carmangay Home and School Association Scholarships *(Undergraduate/Scholarship)* [152]
Robert C. Carson Memorial Bursary *(Undergraduate/Scholarship)* [153]
Laurence Decore Awards for Student Leadership *(Undergraduate/Scholarship)* [154]
Earl and Countess of Wessex - World Championships in Athletics Scholarships *(Undergraduate/Scholarship)* [155]
Fellowships for Full-time Studies in French *(Undergraduate/Fellowship)* [156]
Senator James Gladstone Memorial Scholarships *(Undergraduate/Scholarship)* [143]
Goodfellow Nursing Scholarships *(Undergraduate/Scholarship)* [4249]
Grande Prairie 4-H District Scholarships *(Undergraduate/Scholarship)* [133]
Helen and George Kilik Scholarship *(Undergraduate/Scholarship)* [161]
Anna and John Kolesay Memorial Scholarship *(Undergraduate/Scholarship)* [162]
Language Teacher Bursary Program Awards *(Professional Development/Award/Prize)* [164]
Languages In Teacher Education Scholarships *(Professional Development/Scholarship)* [165]
Sir James Lougheed Awards of Distinction *(Doctorate, Graduate/Award/Prize)* [166]
Louise McKinney Post-secondary Scholarship *(Undergraduate/Scholarship)* [167]
Millennium Alberta Rural Incentive Bursary Award *(Undergraduate/Award/Prize)* [169]
Charles S. Noble Scholarships for Study at Harvard *(Undergraduate/Scholarship)* [170]
Northern Alberta Development Council Bursary Award *(Undergraduate/Award/Prize)* [171]
Northern Alberta Development Council Bursary for Medical Students *(Undergraduate/Award/Prize)* [172]
Northern Alberta Development Council Bursary Partnership Program *(Undergraduate/Award/Prize)* [173]
Northern Alberta Development Council Bursary for Pharmacy Students *(Undergraduate/Scholarship)* [174]
Northern Student Supplement *(Undergraduate/Award/Prize)* [175]
Persons Case Scholarships *(Undergraduate/Scholarship)* [176]
George Phillips Scholarships *(Undergraduate/Scholarship)* [4251]
Prairie Baseball Academy Scholarships *(Undergraduate/Scholarship)* [177]
Pat Redden Memorial Scholarships *(Undergraduate/Scholarship)* [4252]
Registered Apprenticeship Program (RAP) Scholarships *(Undergraduate/Scholarship)* [179]
Robin Rousseau Memorial Mountain Achievement

Scholarship *(Undergraduate/Scholarship)* [180]
Alexander Rutherford Scholarships for High School Achievement *(Undergraduate/Scholarship)* [182]
Servus Credit Union 4-H Scholarships *(Undergraduate/Scholarship)* [135]
Dr. Robert Norman Shaw Scholarship *(Undergraduate/Scholarship)* [183]
Dr. Robert and Anna Shaw Scholarships *(Undergraduate/Scholarship)* [184]
Ken Stanley Memorial Scholarships *(Undergraduate/Scholarship)* [4253]
Ralph Steinhauer Awards of Distinction *(Doctorate, Graduate/Award/Prize)* [185]
TAC Foundation-EBA Engineering Consultants Ltd. Scholarships *(Postgraduate, Undergraduate/Scholarship)* [6905]

British Columbia

Law Foundation of British Columbia Graduate Fellowships *(Undergraduate/Fellowship)* [4147]
TAC Foundation-EBA Engineering Consultants Ltd. Scholarships *(Postgraduate, Undergraduate/Scholarship)* [6905]

Manitoba

Helen Glass Scholarships *(Doctorate/Scholarship)* [1999]
TAC Foundation-EBA Engineering Consultants Ltd. Scholarships *(Postgraduate, Undergraduate/Scholarship)* [6905]

New Brunswick

Mary Ellen Driscoll Scholarships *(Undergraduate/Scholarship)* [6073]
New Brunswick Nurses Association Scholarships *(Graduate/Scholarship)* [2010]

Newfoundland and Labrador

Jim Hierlihy Memorial Scholarships *(Undergraduate/Scholarship)* [2879]
Mature Student Scholarships *(Undergraduate/Scholarship)* [2880]

Nova Scotia

Scholarship Award of The Aliant Pioneer Volunteers *(Postgraduate/Scholarship)* [1989]

Ontario

George Joseph Cooper Awards *(Undergraduate/Scholarship)* [5420]
Lord Dundonald Chapter (IODE) Scholarships *(Undergraduate/Scholarship)* [5421]
Elizabeth Heath Technical, Trades Training and Development Awards *(Undergraduate/Scholarship)* [5423]
Kildonan Education Awards *(Undergraduate/Scholarship)* [5425]
Jack Meadows Memorial Awards *(Undergraduate/Scholarship)* [5426]
Nortel Institute Undergraduate Scholarships *(Undergraduate/Scholarship)* [7231]
Beatrice Drinnan Spence Scholarships *(Undergraduate/Scholarship)* [2814]

Prince Edward Island

Joan Auld Scholarships *(Undergraduate/Scholarship)* [2497]
Phillips Scholarships *(Undergraduate/Scholarship)* [2500]
Scholarship Award of The Aliant Pioneer Volunteers *(Postgraduate/Scholarship)* [1989]

Quebec

Marlene Brand Memorial Scholarship *(Undergraduate/Scholarship)* [3554]
Bernic and Gordon Brown Scholarship *(All/Scholarship)* [3555]
Mireille and Murray Steinberg Scholarship *(Postgraduate/Scholarship)* [3562]

Saskatchewan

Cameco Northern Scholarships - Technical Institute *(Undergraduate/Scholarship)* [1906]
Cameco Northern Scholarships - University *(Undergraduate/Scholarship)* [1907]
TAC Foundation-EBA Engineering Consultants Ltd. Scholarships *(Postgraduate, Undergraduate/Scholarship)* [6905]

INTERNATIONAL

Jane Beattie Memorial Scholarships *(All/Scholarship)* [6465]
IOIA Andrew Rutherford Scholarships *(Professional Development/Scholarship)* [3684]
IOIA Organic Community Initiative Scholarship *(Other/Scholarship)* [3685]
University of Maryland International Student Scholarships *(Undergraduate/Scholarship)* [7023]

INTERNATIONAL (BY REGION)

Asia

University of Hawaii at Manoa East-West Center Graduate Fellowships *(Graduate, Postdoctorate/Fellowship)* [7095]

Caribbean

Caribbean Hotel Association Academic Scholarships *(Undergraduate/Scholarship)* [2059]

Europe

Monte R. Mitchell Global Scholarships *(Undergraduate/Scholarship)* [80]

Latin America

Fellowships to Promote Research on the Legal Framework for Civil Society in Latin America, Africa and Asia *(All/Fellowship)* [3823]
Leo S. Rowe Pan American Fund *(Undergraduate/Loan)* [5404]

North America

AAPA Research Scholarships *(Undergraduate/Award/Prize)* [393]
Robert E. Dougherty Scholarships *(Undergraduate/Scholarship)* [2525]
Independent Lubricant Manufacturers Association Scholarships *(Undergraduate/Scholarship)* [3680]
J. Merrill Knapp Research Fellowships *(Undergraduate/Fellowship)* [597]

INTERNATIONAL (BY COUNTRY)

American Samoa

Al Schuman Ecolab Undergraduate Entrepreneurial Scholarships *(Undergraduate/Scholarship)* [5032]

Australia

ProWorld Study Abroad Scholarships *(Undergraduate/Scholarship)* [3256]

British Virgin Islands

Judith A. Towle Environmental Studies Fund *(Undergraduate/Fellowship)* [3966]

Bulgaria

Mellon Post-Doctoral Fellowships in Turkey for East European Scholars *(Doctorate/Fellowship)* [899]

Czech Republic

Mellon Post-Doctoral Fellowships in Turkey for East European Scholars *(Doctorate/Fellowship)* [899]

Denmark

Edith and Arnold N. Bodtker Grant *(All/Grant)* [2613]

Estonia

Mellon Post-Doctoral Fellowships in Turkey for East European Scholars *(Doctorate/Fellowship)* [899]

Federated States of Micronesia

APIASF Scholarships *(Undergraduate/Scholarship)* [1340]

Germany

American Society of Comparative Law TransCoop Programs *(All/Fellowship)* [937]

Ghana

GANA Scholarship Program *(Undergraduate/Scholarship)* [3258]

Greenland

Fritz Schwartz Serials Education Scholarships *(Other/Scholarship)* [5226]

Guam

Al Schuman Ecolab Undergraduate Entrepreneurial Scholarships *(Undergraduate/Scholarship)* [5032]

Hungary

Dr. Elemer and Eva Kiss Scholarships Fund *(Undergraduate/Scholarship)* [3629]
Mellon Post-Doctoral Fellowships in Turkey for East European Scholars *(Doctorate/Fellowship)* [899]

Kazakhstan

Russian/Central Asian Student Scholarships *(Undergraduate/Scholarship)* [4381]

Kirgizstan

Russian/Central Asian Student Scholarships *(Undergraduate/Scholarship)* [4381]

Latvia

Mellon Post-Doctoral Fellowships in Turkey for East European Scholars *(Doctorate/Fellowship)* [899]

Lebanon

American Lebanese Engineering Society Scholarship Program *(Other/Scholarship)* [692]

Lithuania

Mellon Post-Doctoral Fellowships in Turkey for East European Scholars *(Doctorate/Fellowship)* [899]

Marshall Islands

APIASF Scholarships

(Undergraduate/Scholarship) [1340]

Mexico

Stan Beck Fellowships (Undergraduate/Fellowship) [2861]
BioQuip Scholarships (Undergraduate/Scholarship) [2862]
Ginger and Fred Deines Mexico Scholarships (Undergraduate/Scholarship) [6918]
Fleming/Blaszcak Scholarships (Graduate, Undergraduate/Scholarship) [6550]
Geological Society of America Graduate Student Research Grants (Doctorate, Graduate/Grant) [3210]
IIE Council of Fellows Undergraduate Scholarships (Undergraduate/Scholarship) [3733]
Marvin Mundel Memorial Scholarships (Undergraduate/Scholarship) [3736]
Ronald L. Schmied Scholarships (Professional Development, Undergraduate/Grant) [3388]
Fritz Schwartz Serials Education Scholarships (Other/Scholarship) [5226]
United Parcel Service Scholarship for Female Students (Undergraduate/Scholarship) [3740]
United Parcel Service Scholarship for Minority Students (Undergraduate/Scholarship) [3741]
Abel Wolman Fellowships (Doctorate/Fellowship) [1145]

Nepal

Hugh and Helen Wood Nepales Scholarship (Undergraduate/Scholarship) [1632]

Northern Mariana Islands

APIASF Scholarships (Undergraduate/Scholarship) [1340]

Palau

APIASF Scholarships (Undergraduate/Scholarship) [1340]

People's Republic of China

Lucy Hsu Ho Scholarship (Undergraduate/Scholarship) [1628]

Poland

Mellon Post-Doctoral Fellowships in Turkey for East European Scholars (Doctorate/Fellowship) [899]

Portugal

Al Schuman Ecolab Undergraduate Entrepreneurial Scholarships (Undergraduate/Scholarship) [5032]

Romania

Mellon Post-Doctoral Fellowships in Turkey for East European Scholars (Doctorate/Fellowship) [899]

Russia

Russian/Central Asian Student Scholarships (Undergraduate/Scholarship) [4381]

Slovakia

Mellon Post-Doctoral Fellowships in Turkey for East European Scholars (Doctorate/Fellowship) [899]

St. Kitts and Nevis

Judith A. Towle Environmental Studies Fund (Undergraduate/Fellowship) [3966]

Taiwan

Joel R. Friend Scholarship (Undergraduate/Scholarship) [1626]

Thailand

Joel R. Friend Scholarship (Undergraduate/Scholarship) [1626]

Turkey

Getty Research Exchange Fellowship Program for Cultural Heritage Preservation (Doctorate/Fellowship) [896]

Turkmenistan

Russian/Central Asian Student Scholarships (Undergraduate/Scholarship) [4381]

Ukraine

Alberta Ukrainian Centennial Commemorative Scholarships (Undergraduate/Scholarship) [7356]
Canada-Ukraine Parliamentary Program (CUPP) Internship Scholarships (Undergraduate/Scholarship) [7357]
Chopivsky Fellowships (Undergraduate/Scholarship) [7358]
Eugene & Elinor Kotur Scholarship Trust Fund (Undergraduate/Scholarship) [7359]
The Ivan Shandor Memorial Ukrainian American Bar Association Scholarships (Undergraduate/Scholarship) [7360]
USA/USA-Ukramerazha Scholarships (Undergraduate/Scholarship) [7024]
Marusia Yaworska Entrance Scholarships (Undergraduate/Scholarship) [7361]

United Republic of Tanzania

Godparents for Tanzania Scholarships (Undergraduate/Scholarship) [3246]

Uzbekistan

Russian/Central Asian Student Scholarships (Undergraduate/Scholarship) [4381]

Virgin Islands of the United States

Al Schuman Ecolab Undergraduate Entrepreneurial Scholarships (Undergraduate/Scholarship) [5032]

Place of Study Index

This index lists awards that carry restrictions on where study may take place. Award citations are arranged alphabetically under the following geographic headings: United States, United States (by region), United States (by state), Canada, Canada (by province), International, International (by region), and International (by country). Each citation is followed by the study level and award type, which appear in parentheses. Numbers following the parenthetical information indicate book entry numbers for particular awards, not page numbers.

UNITED STATES

Place of Study Index

ciation Scholarships *(Undergraduate/Internship)* [3777]
International Association of Black Actuaries Scholarships *(Undergraduate/Scholarship)* [3786]
International Association of Emergency Managers Scholarships *(Undergraduate/Scholarship)* [3796]
International Association of Foundation Drilling Scholarships for Civil Engineering Students *(Postgraduate/Scholarship)* [3798]
International Association of Foundation Drilling Scholarships for Part-time Civil Engineering Graduate School Students *(Postgraduate/Scholarship)* [3799]
International Dairy-Deli-Bakery Association Undergraduate Scholarships *(Graduate, Undergraduate/Scholarship)* [3835]
International Doctoral Scholarships for Studies Specializing in Jewish Fields *(Doctorate/Scholarship)* [4458]
International Door Association Scholarship Awards *(Undergraduate/Scholarship)* [3840]
International Fellowships in Jewish Studies *(Professional Development/Fellowship)* [4459]
International Foodservice Editorial Council Scholarships *(Graduate, Undergraduate/Scholarship)* [3852]
International Graduate Student Awards *(Graduate/Scholarship)* [26]
International Management Council (IMC) Scholarships *(Undergraduate/Scholarship)* [2472]
International Order of the King's Daughters and Sons North American Indian Scholarship Program *(Undergraduate/Scholarship)* [635]
International Peace Scholarships *(Undergraduate/Scholarship)* [5684]
International Scholar Awards *(Postdoctorate/Award/Prize)* [5540]
International Scholarship Program for Community Service *(Other/Scholarship)* [4460]
International Society for Humor Studies Graduate Student Awards (GSA) *(Graduate/Award/Prize)* [3906]
International Society for Humor Studies Scholarly Contribution Awards (SCA) *(Graduate/Award/Prize)* [3907]
Internships in International Civil Society Law *(Undergraduate/Internship)* [3824]
InternXchange *(Undergraduate/Internship)* [3228]
Interracial Scholarship Fund of Greater Hartford *(Undergraduate/Scholarship)* [3469]
IOIA Andrew Rutherford Scholarships *(Professional Development/Scholarship)* [3684]
IOIA Organic Community Initiative Scholarship *(Other/Scholarship)* [3685]
Iowa Division Scholarships *(All/Scholarship)* [4514]
IPSA Student Recognition Awards *(Undergraduate/Scholarship)* [3688]
Iranian American Bar Association Scholarships *(Undergraduate/Scholarship)* [3938]
The Iranian-American Scholarship Fund *(Undergraduate/Scholarship)* [4953]
Iranian Artist Scholarships *(Undergraduate/Scholarship)* [4954]
Iranian Federated Women's Club Scholarships *(Undergraduate/Scholarship)* [4956]
IRARC Memorial Joseph P. Rubino WA4MMD Scholarships *(Undergraduate/Scholarship)* [840]
IREM Foundation Minority Outreach Scholarships *(Professional Development/Scholarship)* [3750]
Greg Irons Student Scholarships *(Undergraduate/Scholarship)* [2782]
Harriet Irsay Scholarships *(Graduate, Undergraduate/Scholarship)* [674]
IRTS Foundation Summer Fellowship Program *(Graduate, Undergraduate/Fellowship)* [3886]
ISA Educational Foundation Scholarships *(Graduate, Undergraduate/Scholarship)* [3942]
ISA Executive Board Scholarships *(Graduate, Undergraduate/Scholarship)* [3943]
ISA Section and District Scholarships - Birmingham *(Graduate, Undergraduate/Scholarship)* [3944]
ISA Section and District Scholarships - Houston *(Graduate, Undergraduate/Scholarship)* [3945]
ISA Section and District Scholarships - Lehigh Valley *(Graduate, Undergraduate/Scholarship)* [3946]
ISA Section and District Scholarships - New Jersey *(Graduate, Undergraduate/Scholarship)* [3947]
ISA Section and District Scholarships - Niagara Frontier *(Graduate, Undergraduate/Scholarship)* [3948]
ISA Section and District Scholarships - Northern California *(Graduate, Undergraduate/Scholarship)* [3949]
ISA Section and District Scholarships - Richmond (Hopewell) *(Graduate, Undergraduate/Scholarship)* [3950]
ISA Section and District Scholarships - Savannah River *(Graduate, Undergraduate/Scholarship)* [3951]
ISA Section and District Scholarships - Southwestern Wyoming *(Graduate, Undergraduate/Scholarship)* [3952]
ISA Section and District Scholarships - Texas, Louisiana and Mississippi *(Graduate, Undergraduate/Scholarship)* [3953]
ISA Section and District Scholarships - Wilmington *(Graduate, Undergraduate/Scholarship)* [3954]
ISA Technical Division Scholarships - Analysis Division *(Graduate, Undergraduate/Scholarship)* [3955]
ISA Technical Division Scholarships - Chemical and Petroleum Industries Division *(Graduate, Undergraduate/Scholarship)* [3956]
ISA Technical Division Scholarships - Computer Technology Division *(Graduate, Undergraduate/Scholarship)* [3957]
ISA Technical Division Scholarships - Food and Pharmaceutical Industries Division *(Graduate, Undergraduate/Scholarship)* [3958]
ISA Technical Division Scholarships - Power Industry Division *(Graduate, Undergraduate/Scholarship)* [3959]
ISA Technical Division Scholarships - Process Measurement and Control Division *(Graduate, Undergraduate/Scholarship)* [3960]
ISA Technical Division Scholarships - Pulp and Paper Industry Division *(Graduate, Undergraduate/Scholarship)* [3961]
ISA Technical Division Scholarships - Test Measurement Division *(Graduate, Undergraduate/Scholarship)* [3962]
ISA Technical Division Scholarships - Water and Wastewater Industries Division *(Graduate, Undergraduate/Scholarship)* [3963]
The ISASI Rudolf Kapustin Memorial Scholarships *(Undergraduate/Scholarship)* [3902]
Hazel D. Isbell Fellowships *(Graduate/Fellowship)* [2652]
ISCALC International Scholarship Fund *(Undergraduate/Scholarship)* [2960]
ISOPE Offshore Mechanics Scholarships for Outstanding Students *(Graduate/Scholarship)* [3909]
Italian Language Scholarships *(Undergraduate/Scholarship)* [5372]
ITNS Research Grants *(Professional Development/Grant)* [3918]
ITW Welding Companies Scholarships *(Undergraduate/Scholarship)* [1164]
IUVSTA Welch Scholarships *(Professional Development/Scholarship)* [1581]
Bob and Mary Ives Scholarships *(Graduate, Undergraduate/Scholarship)* [3964]
IWFA Scholarships *(Graduate/Scholarship)* [3925]
J and K Foundation Scholarships *(Undergraduate/Scholarship)* [3470]
Virginia C. Jack and Ralph L. Jack Scholarships *(Undergraduate/Scholarship)* [6730]
Jackman Scholarships *(Undergraduate/Scholarship)* [5668]
The Jackson Club Scholarships *(Undergraduate/Scholarship)* [2783]
Jackson High School Alumni Scholarship Fund *(Undergraduate/Scholarship)* [6731]
Edward Jackson International Scholarships *(Undergraduate/Scholarship)* [7168]
Gene Jackson Scholarships *(Undergraduate/Scholarship)* [7169]
Sylvia E. Jackson Scholarships *(Undergraduate/Scholarship)* [6780]
Ruth K. Jacobs Memorial Scholarship Fund *(Graduate, Undergraduate/Scholarship)* [2141]
Eric L. Jacobson Memorial Scholarships *(Undergraduate/Scholarship)* [5946]
Karl A. Jacobson Scholarships *(Undergraduate/Scholarship)* [1060]
Peter Lars Jacobson Scholarships *(Undergraduate/Scholarship)* [7170]
Dwight P. Jacobus Scholarships *(Undergraduate/Scholarship)* [1488]
Gregori Jakovina Endowment Scholarships *(Undergraduate/Scholarship)* [2884]
Cory Jam Awards *(Undergraduate/Scholarship)* [2784]
Frederick George James Memorial Scholarships *(Undergraduate/Scholarship)* [6195]
The J. Franklin Jameson Fellowship in American History *(Doctorate/Fellowship)* [606]
The Dawn Janisse Scholarships *(Undergraduate/Scholarship)* [5546]
Carl and Lucille Jarrett Scholarship Fund *(Graduate, Undergraduate/Scholarship)* [2961]
Terry Jarvis Memorial Scholarships *(Undergraduate/Scholarship)* [1165]
Jacob K. Javits Fellowships *(Doctorate, Master's/Fellowship)* [4707]
Sister Rita Jeanne Scholarships *(Undergraduate/Scholarship)* [4033]
Jefferson County Art Awards Scholarship for High school Seniors *(Undergraduate/Scholarship)* [1317]
Erin L. Jenkins Memorial Scholarship Fund *(Undergraduate/Scholarship)* [3107]
Elise Reed Jenkins Memorial Scholarships - Gamma Lambda *(Undergraduate/Scholarship)* [6362]
Elise Reed Jenkins Memorial Scholarships - Gamma Psi *(Undergraduate/Scholarship)* [6363]
Martha Combs Jenkins Scholarships *(Undergraduate/Scholarship)* [5669]
Ruth E. Jenkins Scholarships *(Undergraduate/Scholarship)* [6196]
Gaynold Jensen Education Stipends *(Postdoctorate, Professional Development/Scholarship)* [2537]
Walter J. Jensen Fellowships *(Professional Development/Fellowship)* [5622]
Nancy Lorraine Jensen Memorial Scholarships *(Undergraduate/Scholarship)* [6603]
Mike Jensen R.I.S.E. Memorial Scholarships *(Undergraduate/Scholarship)* [5947]
Stanley "Doc" Jensen Scholarships *(High School/Scholarship)* [528]
Jerman-Cahoon Student Scholarship Program *(Undergraduate/Scholarship)* [1040]
Kenneth Jernigan Scholarships *(Undergraduate/Scholarship)* [4878]
James Jesinski Scholarships *(Undergraduate/Scholarship)* [7258]
Jewish Caucus Scholarships *(Undergraduate/Scholarship)* [5123]
The Jhaveri Scholarships *(Graduate/Scholarship)* [3184]
Brian Jimenez Memorial Scholarships *(Undergraduate/Scholarship)* [5948]
Rev. and Mrs. A.K. Jizmejian Educational Fund *(Undergraduate/Scholarship)* [1286]
JMA Architecture Studios Scholarships *(Undergraduate/Scholarship)* [5833]
John Bayliss Broadcast Foundation Scholarships *(Undergraduate/Scholarship)* [1604]
Alvin H. Johnson AMS Dissertation Fellowships *(Undergraduate/Fellowship)* [720]
The Robert Wood Johnson Health Policy Fellowship Program *(All/Fellowship)* [787]
Joseph C. Johnson Memorial Grants *(Undergraduate/Scholarship)* [927]
Fred Johnson Memorial Scholarships *(Graduate/Scholarship)* [4790]
Gregory D. Johnson Memorial Scholarships *(Graduate, Undergraduate/Scholarship)* [4971]
V.J. Johnson Memorial Scholarships *(Undergraduate/Scholarship)* [402]
Stella B. Johnson Scholarships *(Undergraduate/Scholarship)* [7443]
Julian C. Johnston Memorial Scholarships *(Undergraduate/Scholarship)* [6064]
Napoleon A. Jones, III Memorial Scholarships *(Undergraduate/Scholarship)* [6197]
Edward H. Jones Scholarships

Robert Noyce Scholarship Program *(Undergraduate/Scholarship)* [5565]
NPELRA Foundation Scholarships *(Graduate/Scholarship)* [5309]
NPM Program Scholarships *(Undergraduate/Scholarship)* [4727]
NSA Scholarship Program *(Undergraduate/Scholarship)* [5040]
NSF Pickwick Postdoctoral Research Fellowships *(Postdoctorate/Fellowship)* [5042]
NSHSS Academic Paper Awards *(High School/Scholarship)* [5070]
NSHSS National Scholar Awards *(High School/Scholarship)* [5071]
NSPF Board of Directors' Scholarship Awards *(Other/Scholarship)* [5103]
NSPF Scholarship Awards *(Other/Scholarship)* [5104]
NSPS Board of Governors Scholarships *(Undergraduate/Scholarship)* [489]
The NSPS Scholarships *(Undergraduate/Scholarship)* [490]
NSS Conservation Grants *(All/Grant)* [5088]
NSS Education Grants *(All/Grant)* [5089]
NSSA/NSCA Collegiate Scholarships *(Undergraduate/Scholarship)* [5093]
Nurseries Foundation Scholarship Awards *(Undergraduate/Scholarship)* [5385]
Nurseries Memorial Scholarship Awards *(Graduate/Scholarship)* [5386]
Nursing Scholarship Program *(Undergraduate/Scholarship)* [3512]
NW-SCC/American Cancer Society College Scholarships *(Undergraduate/Scholarship)* [5299]
NW-SCC American Legion Scholarships - Florence/Lauderdale Post No. 11 *(Undergraduate/Scholarship)* [5300]
NWF's Women for Sustainable Development (WSD) Scholarships *(Undergraduate/Scholarship)* [6333]
NWSA Distinguished Fellowships *(All/Fellowship)* [5125]
NWSA Graduate Scholarships *(Graduate/Scholarship)* [5126]
NWSA Graduate Scholarships in Lesbian Studies *(Doctorate, Graduate/Fellowship)* [6127]
NYNEX Diversity Scholarship Awards *(Undergraduate/Scholarship)* [6128]
OBAP Fellowships - Airline Transport (ATP) *(Professional Development/Fellowship)* [5407]
OBAP Fellowships - Commercial *(Professional Development/Fellowship)* [5408]
OBAP Fellowships - Instructor rating (CFI/CFII/MEI) *(Professional Development/Fellowship)* [5409]
OBAP Fellowships - Multi-Engine *(Professional Development/Fellowship)* [5410]
OBAP General Scholarships *(All/Scholarship)* [5411]
Obrzut Ling Scholarships *(Undergraduate/Scholarship)* [5772]
Katharine H. Obye Scholarship Award *(Undergraduate/Scholarship)* [2479]
OCA Scholarships *(Undergraduate/Scholarship)* [5413]
OCAEOP Community Service Scholarship Program *(Undergraduate/Scholarship)* [5353]
Occupational Physicians Scholarship Fund *(Undergraduate/Scholarship)* [5313]
John O'Connor Memorial Scholarship Fund *(Undergraduate/Scholarship)* [5114]
Captain Jennifer Shafer Odom Memorial Scholarships - Children of Soldiers *(Undergraduate/Scholarship)* [1305]
Captain Jennifer Shafer Odom Memorial Scholarships - Spouses of Soldiers *(Undergraduate/Scholarship)* [1306]
Office Depot Scholarships *(Undergraduate/Scholarship)* [3569]
Ohio Association of Broadcaster's Kids Scholarships *(Undergraduate/Scholarship)* [5317]
Ohio Association of Broadcasters Scholarships *(Undergraduate/Scholarship)* [5318]
Ohio Valley Chapter Scholarships *(Undergraduate/Scholarship)* [1455]
Ohio War Orphan Scholarships *(Undergraduate/Scholarship)* [7531]
Lawrence "Bud" Ohlman Memorial Scholarships *(Undergraduate/Scholarship)* [564]
O'Jays Scholarship Fund *(Undergraduate/Scholarship)* [6748]
OKAIDE Scholarships *(Undergraduate/Scholarship)* [5327]
Oklahoma City University Merit Scholarships *(Undergraduate/Scholarship)* [5330]
Robert B. Oliver ASNT Scholarships *(Undergraduate/Scholarship)* [1023]
Roy C. and Dorothy Jean Olson Memorial Scholarships *(Undergraduate/Scholarship)* [3876]
Olympia Tumwater Foundation Traditional Scholarships *(Undergraduate/Scholarship)* [5333]
Olympia Tumwater Foundation Transitional (non-traditional) Scholarships *(Undergraduate/Scholarship)* [5334]
O'Meara Foundation Scholarships *(Undergraduate/Scholarship)* [3485]
Omicron Nu Research Fellowships *(Postdoctorate/Fellowship)* [4054]
Open Society Fellowships *(Professional Development/Fellowship)* [5347]
Opera Foundation Scholarships *(Professional Development/Scholarship)* [5349]
Operation Homefront Scholarships *(Undergraduate/Scholarship)* [5351]
Sheldon Oppenheim Memorial Scholarships *(Undergraduate/Scholarship)* [6129]
Frank Oppenheimer Scholarship Program *(Postgraduate/Scholarship)* [735]
Optimist Club Of Redlands - Ralph Maloof Scholarships *(Undergraduate/Scholarship)* [5969]
Optimist Club of Redlands - Virginia Elliott Scholarships *(Undergraduate/Scholarship)* [5970]
OPWA Educational Scholarships *(Undergraduate/Scholarship)* [5315]
Orange County Centennial Academic Scholarships *(Undergraduate/Scholarship)* [5362]
Orange County Centennial Arts Scholarships *(Undergraduate/Scholarship)* [5363]
Orange County Centennial Certification Scholarships *(Undergraduate/Scholarship)* [5364]
Orange County Tourism Council Scholarships *(Undergraduate/Scholarship)* [5365]
Orchard-Hoyman Fund for GLBT Student Scholarships *(Undergraduate/Scholarship)* [2889]
Order Sons of Italy Foundation General Scholarships *(Graduate, Undergraduate/Scholarship)* [5373]
Oregon Association of Nurseries Scholarship Program *(Undergraduate/Scholarship)* [5387]
Oregon Farm Bureau Memorial Scholarships *(Undergraduate/Scholarship)* [5393]
Oregon Logging Conference Scholarships *(Undergraduate/Scholarship)* [4210]
Doris Orenstein Memorial Convention Travel Grants *(All/Grant)* [1462]
Organization of American States Academic Scholarships *(Undergraduate/Scholarship)* [5400]
Organization of American States AOS-Placed Scholarships *(Undergraduate/Scholarship)* [5401]
Organization of American States Graduate Scholarships *(Undergraduate/Scholarship)* [5402]
Organization of American States Self-Placed Scholarships *(Undergraduate/Scholarship)* [5403]
The Deborah Orin-Eilbeck Scholarships *(Graduate/Scholarship)* [7410]
Orthopedic Foot and Ankle Fellowships *(Graduate/Fellowship)* [747]
The Kenneth J. Osborn Memorial Scholarships *(Undergraduate/Scholarship)* [1032]
Margaret E. Oser Scholarships for Women *(Undergraduate/Scholarship)* [5366]
OSU Gay, Lesbian, Bisexual and Transgender Alumni Society (PFLAG Scholarships) *(Undergraduate/Scholarship)* [6130]
OTA Research Grants *(Graduate/Grant)* [5417]
Ellis R. Ott Scholarships *(Graduate, Undergraduate/Scholarship)* [1037]
Ottawa Police 150th Anniversary Scholarships *(Undergraduate/Scholarship)* [1772]
Ted H. Ousley Scholarship Fund *(Undergraduate/Scholarship)* [3072]
Outstanding Undergraduate Scholarships (SOAR) *(Undergraduate/Scholarship)* [7106]
Outward Bound Leadership Scholarships for Educators *(Professional Development/Scholarship)* [5433]
Outward Bound Wilderness Leadership Awards *(High School, Professional Development/Award/Prize)* [5434]
Helen M. Overly Memorial Scholarships *(Undergraduate/Scholarship)* [7510]
Charles and Melva T. Owen Memorial Scholarships *(Undergraduate/Scholarship)* [4882]
Owner-Operator Independent Drivers Association Scholarships *(Undergraduate/Scholarship)* [5436]
Ozarks Division Scholarships *(Undergraduate/Scholarship)* [4518]
The Pac-10 Postgraduate Scholarships *(Graduate/Scholarship)* [5438]
PACE/Columbian Lawyers Association of Westchester County Endowed Scholarships *(Undergraduate/Scholarship)* [2332]
Pacific Legal Foundation Faculty Grants *(All/Grant)* [5443]
The Arthur J. Packard Memorial Scholarship Competition *(Undergraduate/Scholarship)* [614]
Dr. Nicholas Padis Memorial Graduate Scholarships *(Graduate/Scholarship)* [3533]
Laurie Page-Peck Scholarships Fund *(Undergraduate/Scholarship)* [1525]
Raymond E. Page Scholarships *(Undergraduate/Scholarship)* [985]
AFCEA General Emmett Paige Scholarships *(Undergraduate/Scholarship)* [1247]
Paleontological Society Student Research Grants *(Graduate, Undergraduate/Grant)* [405]
E. William Palmer Memorial Scholarships *(Graduate, Undergraduate/Scholarship)* [1673]
PAMA Foundation Scholarship Program *(Graduate, Undergraduate/Scholarship)* [5789]
The PanHellenic Scholarships *(Undergraduate/Scholarship)* [3525]
Katharine Pantzer Senior Fellowships in the British Book Trades *(Professional Development/Fellowship)* [1696]
Paper Stock Industries Chapter of ISRI Scholarship Program *(Undergraduate/Scholarship)* [5452]
Paper Stock Industries/RRF Scholarships *(Undergraduate/Scholarship)* [5450]
Parapsycological Association Research Endowment *(All/Grant)* [5454]
Parents Scholarships *(Undergraduate/Scholarship)* [3676]
Joseph M. Parish Memorial Grants *(Undergraduate/Scholarship)* [928]
William Park Woodside Founder's Scholarships *(Undergraduate/Scholarship)* [4401]
Cissy McDaniel Parker Scholarships *(Undergraduate/Scholarship)* [2660]
E.U. Parker Scholarships *(Undergraduate/Scholarship)* [4883]
Parking Industry Institute Scholarship Program *(Undergraduate/Scholarship)* [5009]
Fitzroy and Mildred Parkinson Memorial Scholarships *(Undergraduate/Scholarship)* [3486]
Sylvia Parkinson Scholarships *(Undergraduate/Scholarship)* [3487]
PARMA Scholarships *(Undergraduate/Scholarship)* [5795]
The Paros-Digiquartz Scholarships *(Undergraduate/Scholarship)* [4314]
Elizabeth M. and Winchell M. Parson Scholarships *(Doctorate/Scholarship)* [997]
Partnership for Pediatric Epilepsy Research *(Doctorate/Grant)* [2874]
Pathways to Success Scholarships *(Undergraduate/Scholarship)* [3113]
Patient Advocate Foundations Scholarships *(Undergraduate/Scholarship)* [5535]
James H. Patrenos Memorial Scholarships *(Undergraduate/Scholarship)* [6406]
Gail Patrick Charitable Trust Scholarships *(Undergraduate/Scholarship)* [2697]
Marvin R. and Pearl E. Patterson Family Scholarships Fund *(Undergraduate/Scholarship)* [3296]
Walter S. Patterson Scholarships *(All/Scholarship)* [1785]
Paul and Inger Friend 4-H Scholarships *(Undergraduate/Scholarship)* [6783]
Courtland Paul Scholarships

UNITED STATES (BY REGION)

New England states

Northeastern states

Southeastern states

UNITED STATES (BY STATE)

Alabama

Alaska

Arizona

Arkansas

California

Brad Evans Memorial Scholarships *(Undergraduate/Scholarship)* [5359]
Farella Braun Martel LLP Diversity Scholarships *(Undergraduate/Scholarship)* [2904]
Judge McIntyre Faries Scholarships *(Undergraduate/Scholarship)* [5586]
Dr. Mary Finegold Scholarships *(Undergraduate/Scholarship)* [6389]
Reuben H. Fleet Memorial Scholarships *(Undergraduate/Scholarship)* [6189]
Jonathan Hastings Foster Scholarships *(Undergraduate/Scholarship)* [6190]
GAPA Scholarships *(Undergraduate/Scholarship)* [3165]
John Gardner Fellowships *(Undergraduate/Fellowship)* [7087]
Garikian Scholarship Fund *(Undergraduate/Scholarship)* [1279]
Gerald Garner Memorial Scholarships *(Undergraduate/Scholarship)* [5588]
Lucile Cheever Graubart/Lambda Scholarships *(Undergraduate/Scholarship)* [6361]
Guy P. Greenwald Jr. Endowed Scholarships *(Undergraduate/Scholarship)* [5590]
Bobette Bibo Gugliotta Memorial Scholarships for Creative Writing *(Undergraduate/Scholarship)* [6390]
Warren and Rosalie Gummow Endowed Scholarships *(Undergraduate/Scholarship)* [5591]
Jaye Haddad Memorial Fund *(Undergraduate/Scholarship)* [6110]
Sophia Hagopian Memorial Fund *(Undergraduate/Scholarship)* [1282]
James J. Harvey Dissertation Fellowships *(Doctorate/Fellowship)* [6111]
Helm Family Scholarships *(Undergraduate/Scholarship)* [6192]
Clair A. Hill Scholarships *(Undergraduate/Scholarship)* [1377]
JD/MBA Scholarships *(Undergraduate/Scholarship)* [5593]
JSR Foundation Endowed School of Law Scholarships *(Undergraduate/Scholarship)* [5594]
Woodrow Judkins Endowed Scholarships *(Undergraduate/Scholarship)* [5595]
Steve Kaplan TV and Film Studies Scholarships *(Professional Development/Scholarship)* [946]
Annette and Ernest Keith Scholarships *(Undergraduate/Scholarship)* [5950]
Knights of Vartan, Fresno Lodge No. 9 Scholarships *(Undergraduate/Scholarship)* [1287]
Judith Keller Marx Krumholz Scholarships *(Undergraduate/Scholarship)* [6201]
Julia Kwan Endowed Scholarships *(Graduate/Scholarship)* [5598]
Lambda Alumni (UCLA Lesbian & Gay Alumni Association) Scholarships Program *(Undergraduate/Scholarship)* [6114]
Patrick Ledden Honorary Scholarships *(Undergraduate/Scholarship)* [6203]
Rebecca Lee, M.D. Scholarships *(Undergraduate/Scholarship)* [1373]
Albert J. and Mae Lee Memorial Scholarships *(Undergraduate/Scholarship)* [5599]
Mangasar M. Mangasarian Scholarship Fund *(Graduate/Scholarship)* [1288]
Markowski-Leach Scholarships Fund *(Graduate, Undergraduate/Scholarship)* [6120]
Michael L. Marx and Donald K. Marshall Scholarships *(Undergraduate/Scholarship)* [6122]
Greg Matthews Memorial Scholarships *(Undergraduate/Scholarship)* [5600]
J. McDonald and Judy Williams School of Law Scholarships *(Undergraduate/Scholarship)* [5601]
Charles McMahon Memorial Construction Management/Engineering Scholarship Awards *(Undergraduate/Scholarship)* [1320]
Ruth McMillan Student Grants *(Undergraduate/Grant)* [1855]
John Merrick Law Scholarships *(Undergraduate/Scholarship)* [5602]
Herbie Morici Memorial Scholarships *(Undergraduate/Scholarship)* [1843]
Native American Charter High Schools After-the-Fires Scholarships *(Undergraduate/Scholarship)* [6210]
Charles I. Nelson Endowed Scholarships *(Undergraduate/Scholarship)* [5603]
Gunnar Nicholson Endowed Scholarships *(Undergraduate/Scholarship)* [5604]
Northern California Chapter of HIMSS Scholarships *(Other/Scholarship)* [3518]
Margaret E. Oser Scholarships for Women *(Undergraduate/Scholarship)* [5366]
Pepperdine University Armenian Student Scholarships *(Undergraduate/Scholarship)* [5605]
Pepperdine University Dean's Scholarships *(Doctorate, Graduate/Scholarship)* [5606]
Pepperdine University Diversity Scholarships *(Doctorate, Graduate/Scholarship)* [5607]
Pepperdine University Faculty Scholarships *(Doctorate, Graduate/Scholarship)* [5608]
Peridian International, Inc./Rae L. Price, FASLA Scholarships *(Undergraduate/Scholarship)* [4126]
Jamie Phillips Endowed Scholarships *(Undergraduate/Scholarship)* [5609]
Pollard-Bailey Scholarships *(Undergraduate/Scholarship)* [6214]
Public Interest Scholarships *(Undergraduate/Scholarship)* [1816]
John Purfield Endowed Scholarships *(Undergraduate/Scholarship)* [5610]
Qualcomm San Diego Science, Technology, Engineering and Mathematics Scholarships *(Undergraduate/Scholarship)* [6216]
Rambus Scholarship Fund *(Undergraduate/Scholarship)* [6393]
Rancho Bernardo/Smith Scholarships *(Undergraduate/Scholarship)* [6217]
Redlands High School Vocal Music Boosters Scholarship Awards *(Undergraduate/Scholarship)* [5993]
Fauneil J. Rinn Scholarships *(Undergraduate/Scholarship)* [6394]
Rosenthal Bar Exam Scholarships *(Undergraduate/Scholarship)* [1817]
Edward S. Roth Manufacturing Engineering Scholarships *(Graduate, Undergraduate/Scholarship)* [6500]
Ruppert Educational Grant Program *(Undergraduate/Scholarship)* [6395]
San Diego City College Study Abroad Scholarships *(Undergraduate/Scholarship)* [6221]
The San Diego Foundation Community Scholarship II *(Undergraduate/Scholarship)* [6222]
San Diego National Bank Scholarships *(Undergraduate/Scholarship)* [6224]
San Diego Pathways to College Scholarships *(Undergraduate/Scholarship)* [6225]
Leo and Trinidad Sanchez Scholarships *(Undergraduate/Scholarship)* [6396]
Sand Hill Scholars Program *(Undergraduate/Scholarship)* [6397]
Mary Turnbull Schacht Memorial Scholarships *(Undergraduate/Scholarship)* [6368]
Al Schuman Ecolab Undergraduate Entrepreneurial Scholarships *(Undergraduate/Scholarship)* [5032]
D.R. Segal Memorial Scholarships for Journalistic Excellence *(Undergraduate/Scholarship)* [5367]
Barbara A. Shacochis Scholarships *(Undergraduate/Scholarship)* [5611]
Stuart Silverman Scholarships *(Undergraduate/Scholarship)* [5613]
Wiggsy Sivertsen Scholarships *(Undergraduate/Scholarship)* [6139]
Charles Smith Memorial Scholarship Awards *(Undergraduate/Scholarship)* [1321]
Special Law School Scholarships *(Undergraduate/Scholarship)* [5614]
Superior District Legislative Mentoring Student Grants *(Undergraduate/Grant)* [1856]
Superior District Legislative Mentoring Student Grants RT to DC *(Undergraduate/Grant)* [1857]
Honorable Raymond Thompson Endowed Scholarships *(Undergraduate/Scholarship)* [5615]
Raymond A. Tice Scholarships I *(Undergraduate/Scholarship)* [6233]
Raymond A. Tice Scholarships II *(Undergraduate/Scholarship)* [6234]
Aram Torossian Memorial Scholarships *(Undergraduate/Scholarship)* [1292]
Thomas and Glenna Trimble Endowed Scholarships *(Undergraduate/Scholarship)* [5616]
The UCSD Black Alumni Scholarship for Arts and Humanities *(Undergraduate/Scholarship)* [6236]
The UCSD Black Alumni Scholarships for Engineering, Mathematics and Science *(Undergraduate/Scholarship)* [6237]
U.S. Air Force ROTC Enhanced HSI Scholarship *(Undergraduate/Scholarship)* [6975]
United Teachers Los Angeles Stonewall Scholarship Fund *(Undergraduate/Scholarship)* [6143]
Ventura County Medical Association Alliance Scholarships *(Undergraduate/Scholarship)* [7314]
James L. Warner Scholarships *(Undergraduate/Scholarship)* [5369]
Howard A. White Endowed Scholarships *(Undergraduate/Scholarship)* [5618]
Tim Wolfred Scholarships *(Undergraduate/Scholarship)* [6147]
Xavier University Williams Scholarships *(Undergraduate/Scholarship)* [7543]
Michael A. Zamperini/W. Clay Burchell Scholarships *(Undergraduate/Scholarship)* [6148]

Colorado

AISC/Rocky Mountain Steel Construction Association Fellowships *(Graduate/Fellowship)* [679]
Roy Anderson Memorial Scholarships *(Graduate, Undergraduate/Scholarship)* [2308]
Banner Health System - McKee Medical Center, Loveland: Nightingale Scholarships *(Graduate, Undergraduate/Scholarship)* [2309]
Banner Health System - North Colorado Medical Center, Greeley: Nightingale Scholarships *(Graduate, Undergraduate/Scholarship)* [2310]
Marcy and Bruce Benson: Nightingale Scholarships *(Graduate, Undergraduate/Scholarship)* [2311]
CCU Alumni Endowed Scholarships *(Undergraduate/Scholarship)* [2304]
Colorado Nurses Association: Nightingale Scholarships *(Graduate, Undergraduate/Scholarship)* [2312]
Colorado Nurses Association: Virginia Paulson Memorial Scholarships *(Graduate, Undergraduate/Scholarship)* [2313]
Colorado Nurses Foundation Nightingale Scholarships *(Graduate, Undergraduate/Scholarship)* [2314]
Colorado Organization of Nursing Leaders Scholarships *(Graduate, Undergraduate/Scholarship)* [2315]
Arthur L. Davis Publishing Agency Scholarships *(Graduate, Undergraduate/Scholarship)* [2316]
John Denver Music Scholarships *(Undergraduate/Scholarship)* [944]
Red and Lola Fehr: Nightingale Scholarships *(Graduate, Undergraduate/Scholarship)* [2317]
Gill Foundation Scholarships (Colorado) *(Undergraduate/Scholarship)* [6107]
Amy and Horace Hagedorn Trust: Nightingale Scholarships *(Graduate, Undergraduate/Scholarship)* [2318]
Dwight A. Hamilton Scottish Rite Foundation of Colorado Graduate Scholarships *(Graduate/Scholarship)* [6284]
Clinton J. Helton Manufacturing Scholarships *(Undergraduate/Scholarship)* [6491]
Johnson and Johnson: Nightingale Scholarships *(Graduate, Undergraduate/Scholarship)* [2319]
Kaiser Permanente: Nightingale Scholarships *(Graduate, Undergraduate/Scholarship)* [2320]
Metropolitan State College of Denver, President's Office: Nightingale Scholarships *(Graduate, Undergraduate/Scholarship)* [2321]
H.M. Muffly Memorial Scholarships *(Graduate, Undergraduate/Scholarship)* [2322]
Poudre Valley Health System, Fort Collins: Nightingale Scholarships *(Graduate, Undergraduate/Scholarship)* [2323]
Rocky Mountain Region of Wound Ostomy Conti-

nence Nurses Society Scholarships *(Graduate, Undergraduate/Scholarship)* [2324]
Rose Medical Center, Denver: Nightingale Scholarships *(Graduate, Undergraduate/Scholarship)* [2325]
St. Anthony's Hospitals, Denver: Nightingale Scholarships *(Graduate, Undergraduate/Scholarship)* [2326]
St. Mary's Hospital and Medical Center, Grand Junction: Nightingale Scholarships *(Graduate, Undergraduate/Scholarship)* [2327]
Seedworks Fund: Nightingale Scholarships *(Graduate, Undergraduate/Scholarship)* [2328]
Thomas J. Slocum Memorial Scholarships to Westwood College of Aviation Technology *(Undergraduate/Scholarship)* [84]
Lorraine E. Swain Scholarships *(Undergraduate/Scholarship)* [6375]
Patty Walter Memorial Scholarships *(Graduate, Undergraduate/Scholarship)* [2329]

Connecticut

Frederick G. Adams Scholarships *(Undergraduate/Scholarship)* [3411]
Alliance for Academic Achievement Program Scholarships *(Undergraduate/Scholarship)* [3412]
Alliance Francaise of Hartford Harpin/Rohinsky Scholarships *(Undergraduate/Scholarship)* [3413]
Armenian American Pharmacists' Association Scholarships *(Doctorate, Graduate/Scholarship)* [1268]
ARTC Glenn Moon Scholarships *(Undergraduate/Scholarship)* [3418]
Malcolm Baldridge Scholarships *(Undergraduate/Scholarship)* [3420]
W. Philip Braender and Nancy Coleman Braender Scholarships *(Undergraduate/Scholarship)* [3427]
George J. Bysiewicz Scholarship Fund *(Undergraduate/Scholarship)* [2392]
Chopivsky Fellowships *(Undergraduate/Scholarship)* [7358]
College of Agriculture and Natural Resources Scholarships *(Undergraduate/Scholarship)* [3432]
The College Club of Hartford Scholarships *(Undergraduate/Scholarship)* [3433]
Connecticut League of Nursing Scholarships *(Undergraduate/Scholarship)* [3438]
Connecticut Mortgage Bankers Scholarships-Social Affairs Committee *(Undergraduate/Scholarship)* [3439]
B.J. Dean Scholarships *(Undergraduate/Scholarship)* [2418]
C. Rodney Demarest Memorial Scholarships *(Undergraduate/Scholarship)* [3443]
Harry A. Donn Scholarships *(Undergraduate/Scholarship)* [3445]
Symee Ruth Feinburg Memorial Scholarships *(Undergraduate/Scholarship)* [3449]
Gail Burns-Smith "Dare to Dream" Fund *(Undergraduate/Scholarship)* [3452]
Ida L. Hartenberg Charitable Scholarships *(Undergraduate/Scholarship)* [3456]
Hartford County Retired Teachers Association Scholarships *(Undergraduate/Scholarship)* [3457]
Hartford Foundation College Scholarship Program *(Undergraduate/Scholarship)* [3458]
Doris E. Higley Memorial Scholarships *(Undergraduate/Scholarship)* [3464]
Doc Hurley Scholarships *(Undergraduate/Scholarship)* [3468]
Interracial Scholarship Fund of Greater Hartford *(Undergraduate/Scholarship)* [3469]
Iranian Association of Boston's IAB Scholarships *(Undergraduate/Scholarship)* [4955]
Herman P. Kopplemann Scholarships *(Undergraduate/Scholarship)* [3474]
Lazarus Foundation Scholarships *(Undergraduate/Scholarship)* [3475]
Mary Main Memorial Scholarships *(Undergraduate/Scholarship)* [3478]
Dr. Frank and Florence Marino Scholarships *(Undergraduate/Scholarship)* [3480]
Dr. Cladwell McCoy, Jr. Memorial Scholarships *(Undergraduate/Scholarship)* [3482]
Michaels Jewelers Foundation General Scholarships *(Undergraduate/Scholarship)* [3484]
Sylvia Parkinson Scholarships *(Undergraduate/Scholarship)* [3487]
Dorothy E. Hofmann Pembroke Scholarships *(Undergraduate/Scholarship)* [3488]
Nicholas J. Piergrossi Scholarships *(Undergraduate/Scholarship)* [3489]
Dr. Sidney Rafal Memorial Scholarships *(Undergraduate/Scholarship)* [3491]
Ratcliffe Hicks School of Agriculture Heritage Scholarships *(Undergraduate/Scholarship)* [3492]
Bro. Dr. Frank T. Simpson *(Undergraduate/Scholarship)* [3497]
Peter T. Steinwedell Scholarships *(Undergraduate/Scholarship)* [3498]
Town and County Club Scholarships *(Undergraduate/Scholarship)* [3499]
Tunxis Community College Foundation Scholarships *(Undergraduate/Scholarship)* [3500]
Eleanor M. Wolfson Memorial Scholarship Fund *(Undergraduate/Scholarship)* [2981]
Wendy Y. Wolfson Memorial Scholarship Fund *(Undergraduate/Scholarship)* [2982]

Delaware

AISC/US Steel Fellowships *(Graduate/Fellowship)* [683]

District of Columbia

Carlos Enrique Cisneros Point Scholarships *(Graduate, Undergraduate/Scholarship)* [5716]
Congressional Scholarships Award *(Undergraduate/Scholarship)* [3147]
D.C. Opportunity Scholarship Program *(Undergraduate/Scholarship)* [7376]
FCBA Foundation Scholarships *(Undergraduate/Scholarship)* [2909]
Norfolk Southern Foundation Scholarships *(Undergraduate/Scholarship)* [882]
The Ivan Shandor Memorial Ukrainian American Bar Association Scholarships *(Undergraduate/Scholarship)* [7360]
Washington Scholarship Fund Signature Scholarships Program *(Undergraduate/Scholarship)* [7377]

Florida

AISC/Southern Association of Steel Fabricators Fellowships *(Graduate/Fellowship)* [680]
AISC/Southern Association of Steel Fabricators Scholarships *(Undergraduate/Scholarship)* [681]
Judge Sidney M. Aronovitz Memorial Scholarships *(High School/Scholarship)* [2594]
Beta Gamma Memorial Scholarship Fund *(Undergraduate/Scholarship)* [2643]
byourself Scholarship Fund *(Undergraduate/Scholarship)* [2504]
Calvin Alumni Association Florida-Gulf Coast Scholarships *(Undergraduate/Scholarship)* [1871]
Jennet Colliflower Nursing Scholarships *(Undergraduate/Scholarship)* [2595]
D&A Florida Scholarships *(Undergraduate/Scholarship)* [6648]
James H. Davis Scholarships *(Undergraduate/Scholarship)* [3012]
Doctors IRA & UDAYA Nursing Scholarships *(Undergraduate/Scholarship)* [6649]
Anne M. Fassett Scholarships *(Undergraduate/Scholarship)* [6651]
Fecon Scholarships *(Undergraduate/Scholarship)* [3001]
Florida Engineering Society Junior College Scholarships *(Undergraduate/Scholarship)* [3003]
Florida Engineering Society University Scholarships *(Undergraduate/Scholarship)* [3004]
Florida Fertilizer and Agrichemical Association Scholarships *(Undergraduate/Scholarship)* [3010]
Florida Outdoor Writers Association Scholarships *(Undergraduate/Scholarship)* [3016]
Charles and Margaret Foster Scholarships *(Undergraduate/Scholarship)* [6653]
Randy Green Memorial Scholarship Fund *(High School/Scholarship)* [2598]
Imogene Ward Nursing Scholarships *(Undergraduate/Scholarship)* [2991]
Chip Johnson Scholarships *(Undergraduate/Scholarship)* [6659]
Michael Kidger Memorial Scholarships in Optical Design *(Graduate/Scholarship)* [6696]
David F. Ludovici Scholarships *(Undergraduate/Scholarship)* [3005]
Robert V. McKenna Scholarships *(Undergraduate/Scholarship)* [3369]
Raymond W. Miller, PE and Alice E. Miller Scholarships *(Undergraduate/Scholarship)* [3006]
Raymond W. Miller, PE Scholarships *(Undergraduate/Scholarship)* [3007]
Judge William J. Nelson Scholarships *(Undergraduate/Scholarship)* [6666]
Eric Primavera Memorial Scholarships *(Undergraduate/Scholarship)* [3008]
Helen F. "Jerri" Rand Memorial Scholarships *(Undergraduate/Scholarship)* [2509]
Dr. Felix H. Reyler Memorial Scholarships *(Undergraduate/Scholarship)* [2599]
Edward S. Roth Manufacturing Engineering Scholarships *(Graduate, Undergraduate/Scholarship)* [6500]
Al Schuman Ecolab Undergraduate Entrepreneurial Scholarships *(Undergraduate/Scholarship)* [5032]
Southern Scholarship Foundation Scholarships *(Undergraduate/Scholarship)* [6638]
Leo Suarez Journalism Scholarships *(Undergraduate/Scholarship)* [2601]
Jacki Tuckfield Memorial Graduate Business Scholarship Fund *(Undergraduate/Scholarship)* [2603]
Ted C. Wilson Memorial Scholarships *(Undergraduate/Scholarship)* [5791]

Georgia

AISC/Southern Association of Steel Fabricators Fellowships *(Graduate/Fellowship)* [680]
AISC/Southern Association of Steel Fabricators Scholarships *(Undergraduate/Scholarship)* [681]
Brenda S. Bank Educational Workshop Scholarships *(Undergraduate/Scholarship)* [6447]
Kenneth H. Breeden Scholarships *(Undergraduate/Scholarship)* [4132]
Charles Clarke Cordle Memorial Scholarships *(Undergraduate/Scholarship)* [830]
Anthony R. Dees Educational Workshop Scholarships *(Undergraduate/Scholarship)* [6448]
Forsyth County United Way Scholarships *(Undergraduate/Scholarship)* [4133]
Georgia Engineering Foundation Scholarships *(Undergraduate/Scholarship)* [3212]
Larry Gulley Scholarships *(Undergraduate/Scholarship)* [6449]
Richard A. Hammill Scholarships Fund *(Undergraduate/Scholarship)* [708]
Carroll Hart Scholarships *(Graduate/Scholarship)* [6450]
Lanier Merit Scholarships *(Undergraduate/Scholarship)* [4134]
Lanier Need-Based Scholarships *(Undergraduate/Scholarship)* [4135]
Durwood McAlister Scholarships *(Undergraduate/Scholarship)* [3214]
Edna A. Noblin Dawsonville Lions Club Scholarships *(Undergraduate/Scholarship)* [4136]
William C. Rogers Scholarships *(Undergraduate/Scholarship)* [3216]
Kirk Sutlive Scholarships *(Undergraduate/Scholarship)* [3217]

Ted C. Wilson Memorial Scholarships (Undergraduate/Scholarship) [5791]

Hawaii

AISC/US Steel Fellowships (Graduate/Fellowship) [683]
University of Hawaii at Manoa East-West Center Graduate Fellowships (Graduate, Postdoctorate/Fellowship) [7095]

Idaho

The "21" Endowed Scholarships (Undergraduate/Scholarship) [4160]
Mamie Adams Memorial Awards (Undergraduate/Scholarship) [4161]
Horatio Alger Idaho University Scholarships (Undergraduate/Scholarship) [206]
Horatio Alger Lola and Duane Hagadone Idaho Scholarships (Undergraduate/Scholarship) [211]
American Legion Boys/Girls State Scholarships (Undergraduate/Scholarship) [4162]
Avista Corporation Minds in Motion Scholarships (Undergraduate/Scholarship) [4163]
Banner Bank Business Scholarships (Undergraduate/Scholarship) [4164]
Diana Brown Endowed Scholarships (Undergraduate/Scholarship) [4165]
Glen and Babs Carlson Endowed Scholarships (Undergraduate/Scholarship) [4166]
Walter & Elsie Carr Endowed Scholarships (Undergraduate/Scholarship) [4167]
Caterpillar Scholarships in Diesel Mechanics (Undergraduate/Scholarship) [4168]
Church Family Scholarships (Undergraduate/Scholarship) [4169]
Fisher Clark Memorial Endowed Scholarships (Undergraduate/Scholarship) [4170]
Coeur d'Alene Alumni Scholarships (Undergraduate/Scholarship) [4171]
Rob Copeland Memorial Scholarships (Undergraduate/Scholarship) [4172]
The Rick Crane Group Real Estate Scholarships Fund (Undergraduate/Scholarship) [4173]
Mike Crapo Math and Science Scholarship Fund (Undergraduate/Scholarship) [3644]
Laura Moore Cunningham Foundation General Scholarships (Undergraduate/Scholarship) [4174]
Kenneth and Kathleen Davis Endowed Scholarships (Undergraduate/Scholarship) [4175]
Gretchen Dimico Memorial Scholarships (Undergraduate/Scholarship) [4176]
Bus and Mary Ellen Durant Timberline High School Endowed Scholarships (Undergraduate/Scholarship) [4177]
First Security Foundation Business Scholarships (Undergraduate/Scholarship) [4178]
Dean A. Froehlich Endowed Scholarships (Undergraduate/Scholarship) [4179]
Irene Carlson Gnaedinger Memorial Scholarships (Undergraduate/Scholarship) [4180]
Goldmann Scholarships Fund (Undergraduate/Scholarship) [3645]
Jack & Mary Lou Gruber Scholarships (Undergraduate/Scholarship) [4181]
Jimmy Guild Memorial Scholarships (Undergraduate/Scholarship) [4182]
Henderson Memorial Endowed Scholarships (Undergraduate/Scholarship) [4183]
Hinman-Jensen Endowed Scholarships (Undergraduate/Scholarship) [4184]
Frank and Gladys Hopkins Endowed Scholarships (Undergraduate/Scholarship) [4185]
Idaho Attorney General Scholarships (Undergraduate/Scholarship) [4186]
Idaho Nursery and Landscape Association Scholarships (Undergraduate/Scholarship) [3652]
Idaho Nursing Scholarships (Undergraduate/Scholarship) [3646]
Idaho Promise Category B Scholarships (Undergraduate/Scholarship) [4187]
Idaho Society of CPA's Scholarships (Undergraduate/Scholarship) [3647]
Margaret G. Johnson and Marge J. Stout Scholarships (Undergraduate/Scholarship) [4188]
Lewiston Clarkston Kiwanis Club Scholarships (Undergraduate/Scholarship) [4189]
LCSC Welding Club Scholarships (Undergraduate/Scholarship) [4190]
Lewis-Clark Coin Club Endowed Scholarships (Undergraduate/Scholarship) [4191]
Lewis-Clark State College/American Chemical Society Scholars Program (Undergraduate/Scholarship) [4192]
Lewis-Clark State College Foundation Scholars Scholarships (Undergraduate/Scholarship) [4193]
Lewis-Clark State College Freshman Scholarships (Undergraduate/Scholarship) [4194]
Lewis-Clark State College Governor's Cup Scholarships (Undergraduate/Scholarship) [4195]
Lewis-Clark State College/Idaho Society of CPAs Scholarships Fund (Undergraduate/Scholarship) [4196]
Lewis-Clark State College Non-Traditional Student Scholarships (Undergraduate/Scholarship) [4197]
Lewis-Clark State College Presidential Out-of-State Scholarships (Undergraduate/Scholarship) [4198]
Lewis-Clark State College Presidential Technical Out-of-State Scholarships (Undergraduate/Scholarship) [4199]
Lewis-Clark State College Provost Scholarships (Undergraduate/Scholarship) [4200]
Lewis-Clark State College Transfer Scholarships (Undergraduate/Scholarship) [4201]
Lewis-Clark State College Valley Scholarships (Undergraduate/Scholarship) [4202]
Lewiston Service League Memorial Scholarships (Undergraduate/Scholarship) [4203]
Kaia Lynn Markwalter Endowed Scholarships (Undergraduate/Scholarship) [4204]
Armistead Maupin Creative Writing Scholarship Fund (Undergraduate/Scholarship) [2887]
Elizabeth McKissick Memorial Scholarships (Undergraduate/Scholarship) [4205]
Military Order of the Perpetual Heart Foundation Scholarships (Undergraduate/Scholarship) [4206]
Robbie Miller Memorial Scholarships (Undergraduate/Scholarship) [4207]
Eugene Northrup Scholarships (Undergraduate/Scholarship) [4208]
Odd Fellows Lodge No. 8 Endowed Scholarships (Undergraduate/Scholarship) [4209]
Laura Ann Peck Memorial Endowed Scholarships (Undergraduate/Scholarship) [4211]
Eleanor Perry Memorial Endowed Scholarships (Undergraduate/Scholarship) [4212]
Kenneth Rogers Memorial Scholarships (Undergraduate/Scholarship) [4213]
Rosenberg-Ibarra Scholarships (Undergraduate/Scholarship) [5777]
Roger C. Sathre Memorial Scholarship Fund (Undergraduate/Scholarship) [3649]
Bill Sawyer Memorial Scholarships (Undergraduate/Scholarship) [4214]
Susan P. Schroeder Memorial Scholarships (Undergraduate/Scholarship) [4215]
Ethel Shinn Alumni-Vocational Scholarships (Undergraduate/Scholarship) [4216]
State of Idaho Scholarships Category A (Undergraduate/Scholarship) [4217]
John Streiff Memorial Scholarships (Undergraduate/Scholarship) [4218]
Tschudy Family Scholarships (Undergraduate/Scholarship) [4219]
WALPA Lake Scholarships (Graduate, Undergraduate/Scholarship) [7382]
Washington Reciprocity Out-of-State Scholarships (Undergraduate/Scholarship) [4220]

Illinois

Horatio Alger Louisiana Scholarships (Undergraduate/Scholarship) [212]
Allied Health Care Professional Scholarships (Undergraduate/Scholarship) [3661]
American Council of Engineering Companies of Illinois Scholarships (Doctorate, Graduate, Undergraduate/Scholarship) [497]
Richard L. Bernardi Memorial Scholarship (Undergraduate/Scholarship) [2456]
Beta Nu/Caryl Cordis D'hondt Scholarships (Undergraduate/Scholarship) [6346]
Calvin Alumni Association-Illinois Scholarships (Undergraduate/Scholarship) [1872]
Chapter 31 - Peoria Endowed Scholarships (Undergraduate/Scholarship) [6477]
Paul I. and Elena H. Cohen Scholarships (Graduate, Undergraduate/Scholarship) [871]
Felicia De Bow Memorial Scholarships (All/Scholarship) [5447]
Larry L. Etherton Scholarships (Graduate, Undergraduate/Scholarship) [876]
Michael W. and Jean D. Franke Family Foundation Scholarships (Graduate, Undergraduate/Scholarship) [877]
Karen Harter Recruitment Scholarship Grant (Undergraduate/Scholarship) [2469]
Karen Harter Recruitment Scholarship Grant (Undergraduate/Scholarship) [2470]
Illinois Future Teacher Corps Scholarships (Undergraduate/Scholarship) [3663]
Illinois Landscape Contractors Association Scholarships (Undergraduate/Scholarship) [3656]
Illinois Special Education Teacher Tuition Waiver Scholarships (Undergraduate/Scholarship) [3664]
Illinois Student Assistance Commission Medical Student Scholarships (Graduate/Scholarship) [3665]
Illinois Student Assistance Commission Merit Recognition Scholarships (Undergraduate/Scholarship) [3666]
Illinois Student Assistance Commission Nurse Educator Scholarships (Undergraduate/Scholarship) [3667]
Illinois Student Assistance Commission Nursing Education Scholarships (Undergraduate/Scholarship) [3668]
Illinois Student Assistance Commission Podiatric Scholarship Program (Undergraduate/Scholarship) [3669]
Iowa Journalism Institute Scholarships (Undergraduate/Scholarship) [3935]
ISPE Advantage Award/Foundation Scholarships (Undergraduate/Scholarship) [3659]
Jewish Federation Academic Scholarships (Graduate, Undergraduate/Scholarship) [4029]
Kendall College Bachelor of Arts in Culinary Arts Scholarships (Undergraduate/Scholarship) [2579]
Ray and Kathy LaHood Scholarships for the Study of American Government (Undergraduate/Scholarship) [2720]
Abraham Lincoln Marovitz Public Interest Law Scholarships (Undergraduate/Scholarship) [2119]
Edmond A. Metzger Scholarships (Undergraduate/Scholarship) [843]
Minority Teachers of Illinois Scholarships (Undergraduate/Scholarship) [3670]
Palos Fine Arts Association Scholarships (Undergraduate/Scholarship) [5448]
Edward S. Roth Manufacturing Engineering Scholarships (Graduate, Undergraduate/Scholarship) [6500]
The Dr. William M. Scholl College of Podiatric Medicine Scholarships (Undergraduate/Scholarship) [5550]
Al Schuman Ecolab Undergraduate Entrepreneurial Scholarships (Undergraduate/Scholarship) [5032]
Elisabeth Seegmiller Recruitment Scholarship Grant (Undergraduate/Scholarship) [2487]
Andrea Will Memorial Scholarships (Undergraduate/Scholarship) [6381]

Indiana

Academic Promise Scholarships (Undergraduate/Scholarship) [3697]
Warren M. Anderson Scholarships (Undergraduate/Scholarship) [3698]

Warren K. Brown Scholarships (Undergraduate/Scholarship) [1050]
Chapter 56 - Fort Wayne Scholarships (Graduate, Undergraduate/Scholarship) [6479]
Child of Alumni Book Voucher Awards (Undergraduate/Scholarship) [3699]
Gongaware Scholarships College of Business (Undergraduate/Scholarship) [3700]
Indiana Broadcasters Association for College Scholarship Program (Undergraduate/Scholarship) [3690]
Indiana Broadcasters Association High School Scholarship Program (Undergraduate/Scholarship) [3691]
Indiana State Alumni Association Creative and Performing Arts Award (Undergraduate/Scholarship) [3701]
Indiana State Alumni Association Dean's Scholarships (Undergraduate/Scholarship) [3702]
Indiana State Alumni Association Incentive Scholarships (Undergraduate/Scholarship) [3703]
Indiana State Alumni Association President's Academic Excellence Scholarships (Undergraduate/Scholarship) [3704]
Indiana State Alumni Association President's Scholarships (Undergraduate/Scholarship) [3705]
Indiana State Alumni Association Transfer Student Scholarships (Undergraduate/Scholarship) [3707]
Indiana Top Scholar Award (Undergraduate/Scholarship) [3708]
Edmond A. Metzger Scholarships (Undergraduate/Scholarship) [843]
Clarence and Josephine Myers Scholarships (Graduate, Undergraduate/Scholarship) [6498]
Networks Scholarships College of Business (Undergraduate/Scholarship) [3710]
Notre Dame Club of Canton Scholarships (Undergraduate/Scholarship) [6747]
Noyce Scholarships for Secondary Math and Science Education (Undergraduate/Scholarship) [3711]
Phi Theta Kappa Scholarships (Undergraduate/Scholarship) [3712]
August M. Rocco Scholarship Fund (Undergraduate/Scholarship) [6750]
Esther Schlundt Memorial Scholarships (Undergraduate/Scholarship) [3694]
Nettie and Edward Shelah Scholarships (Undergraduate/Scholarship) [6785]
Sycamore Scholar Awards (Undergraduate/Scholarship) [3713]
Barber Owen Thomas Scholarships (Undergraduate/Scholarship) [6378]

Iowa

AISC/US Steel Fellowships (Graduate/Fellowship) [683]
William Stone Ayres Scholarships (Undergraduate/Scholarship) [2732]
Beverly Estate Scholarships (Undergraduate/Scholarship) [2733]
George and Mary Brammer Scholarships (Undergraduate/Scholarship) [2734]
Gregory Brunk Scholarships (Undergraduate/Scholarship) [2735]
Raymond DiPaglia Endowment Scholarships (Undergraduate/Scholarship) [2737]
Herman E. Elgar Memorial Scholarships (Undergraduate/Scholarship) [2745]
D.J. Fairgrave Education Trust (Undergraduate/Scholarship) [2746]
Leland Stanford Forrest Scholarships (Undergraduate/Scholarship) [2747]
Edward and Cora Hayes Scholarships (Undergraduate/Scholarship) [2749]
Annamae Heaps Law Scholarships (Undergraduate/Scholarship) [2750]
John M. Helmick Law Scholarships (Undergraduate/Scholarship) [2751]
Herbert Hoover Uncommon Student Awards (Undergraduate/Scholarship) [3613]
INF Scholarships (Undergraduate/Scholarship) [3934]
Iowa Journalism Institute Scholarships (Undergraduate/Scholarship) [3935]
Iowa Library Association Foundation Scholarships (Graduate/Scholarship) [3931]
James P. Irish Scholarships (Undergraduate/Scholarship) [2752]
Forest A. King Scholarships (Undergraduate/Scholarship) [2755]
Verne Lawyer Scholarships (Undergraduate/Scholarship) [2756]
Frederick D. Lewis Jr. Scholarships (Undergraduate/Scholarship) [2759]
Gordon and Delores Madson Scholarships (Undergraduate/Scholarship) [2760]
Jake S. More Scholarships (Undergraduate/Scholarship) [2761]
North Central (Region 9) Scholarships (Undergraduate/Scholarship) [6499]
Dwight D. Opperman Scholarships (Undergraduate/Scholarship) [2762]
Jerome S. Petz, S.J., Scholarships (Undergraduate/Scholarship) [2763]
Carter Pitts Scholarships (Undergraduate/Scholarship) [3936]
Janet Reynoldson Memorial Scholarships (Undergraduate/Scholarship) [2764]
Isador M. Robinson Endowment Scholarships (Undergraduate/Scholarship) [2765]
Walter and Rita Selvy Scholarships (Undergraduate/Scholarship) [2766]
Matthew Shepard Scholarships (Undergraduate/Scholarship) [6138]
Jack E. Tillson Scholarships (Graduate/Scholarship) [3932]
Haemer Wheatcraft Scholarships (Undergraduate/Scholarship) [2768]

Kansas

AISC/Fred R. Havens Fellowships (Graduate, Undergraduate/Fellowship) [677]
Business and Transactional Law Center Scholarships (Undergraduate/Scholarship) [7347]
Chapter 52 - Wichita Scholarships (Graduate, Undergraduate/Scholarship) [6478]
Child and Family Advocacy Fellowships (Undergraduate/Scholarship) [7348]
Judge Delmas C. Hill Scholarships (Undergraduate/Scholarship) [7349]
Koch Scholarships (Undergraduate/Scholarship) [7350]
Pittsburg State University Distinguished Graduate Scholarships (Undergraduate/Scholarship) [7351]
Polsinelli Diversity Scholarships (Undergraduate/Scholarship) [7352]
Shamberg Scholarships (Undergraduate/Scholarship) [7353]
Hatton W. Sumners Scholarships (Undergraduate/Scholarship) [5331]
Theta/Caryl Cordis D'hondt Scholarships (Undergraduate/Scholarship) [6376]
Theta Tau Scholarships (Undergraduate/Scholarship) [6377]
J.L. Weigand, Jr. Legal Education Trust Scholarships (Undergraduate/Scholarship) [7354]

Kentucky

AISC/Southern Association of Steel Fabricators Fellowships (Graduate/Fellowship) [680]
AISC/Southern Association of Steel Fabricators Scholarships (Undergraduate/Scholarship) [681]
Warren K. Brown Scholarships (Undergraduate/Scholarship) [1050]
Early Childhood Development Scholarships (Undergraduate/Scholarship) [1701]
Beth K. Fields Scholarships (Undergraduate/Scholarship) [7100]
Kentucky Educational Excellence Scholarships (Graduate, Undergraduate/Scholarship) [1702]
Kentucky Paralegal Association Student Scholarships (Undergraduate/Scholarship) [4072]
Kentucky Tuition Grants (Undergraduate/Grant) [1703]
KHEAA Teacher Scholarships (Undergraduate/Scholarship) [1704]
Joan Reagin McNeill Scholarships - Alpha Theta (Undergraduate/Scholarship) [6365]
Joan Reagin McNeill Scholarships - Theta Phi (Undergraduate/Scholarship) [6366]
USHJA Athletic Scholarships (Undergraduate/Scholarship) [6995]
Allen and Loureena Weber Scholarships (Undergraduate/Scholarship) [6506]
Mary Jo Young Scholarships (Undergraduate/Scholarship) [1705]

Louisiana

AISC/Southern Association of Steel Fabricators Fellowships (Graduate/Fellowship) [680]
AISC/Southern Association of Steel Fabricators Scholarships (Undergraduate/Scholarship) [681]
Horatio Alger Louisiana Scholarships (Undergraduate/Scholarship) [212]
American Radio Relay League Louisiana Memorial Scholarships (Undergraduate/Scholarship) [815]
Greater Baton Rouge Chapter - Don Jones Excellence in Safety Scholarships (Undergraduate/Scholarship) [1056]
Society of Louisiana Certified Public Accountants Scholarships (Undergraduate/Scholarship) [6468]

Maine

Iranian Association of Boston's IAB Scholarships (Undergraduate/Scholarship) [4955]

Maryland

AISC/US Steel Fellowships (Graduate/Fellowship) [683]
Irene Culver Cllins and Louis Franklin Collins Scholarship (Undergraduate/Scholarship) [2370]
The Frank Cormier Scholarships (Undergraduate/Scholarship) [7409]
Eastern Shore Builder's Association Scholarships (Undergraduate/Scholarship) [2371]
Land-Use Planning Scholarships (Graduate/Scholarship) [4896]
Lana K. Rinehart Scholarship (Undergraduate/Scholarship) [2383]
Spirit of Allison Graduation Award (High School/Award/Prize) [2986]
Charles A. Townsend Scholarships (Undergraduate/Scholarship) [5525]
University of Maryland International Student Scholarships (Undergraduate/Scholarship) [7023]
Gary Wagner, K3OMI Scholarships (Undergraduate/Scholarship) [859]

Massachusetts

Charles Abrams Scholarship Program (Graduate/Scholarship) [775]
AISC/Fred R. Havens Fellowships (Graduate, Undergraduate/Fellowship) [677]
Armenian American Pharmacists' Association Scholarships (Doctorate, Graduate/Scholarship) [1268]
Asian American Lawyers Associations of Massachusetts Scholarships (Undergraduate/Scholarship) [1332]
Bambey Bailey Scholarships (Undergraduate/Scholarship) [2391]
Hagop Bogigian Scholarship Fund (Undergraduate/Scholarship) [1273]
Tim Gifford Scholarship Fund (Undergraduate/Scholarship) [3282]
Hai Guin Scholarships Association (Undergraduate/Scholarship) [1280]
Henigson Human Rights Fellowships (Undergraduate/Fellowship) [3504]
HRP Global Human Rights Fellowships (Graduate/Fellowship) [3505]
Iranian Association of Boston's IAB Scholarships (Undergraduate/Scholarship) [4955]
Leiber and Stoller Music Scholarships (Undergraduate/Scholarship) [947]

Michigan

Minnesota

(Undergraduate/Scholarship) [6125]
Minnesota Health Information Management Association Scholarships
(Undergraduate/Scholarship) [4552]
Hubert A. Nelson Scholarships
(Undergraduate/Scholarship) [2787]
Anderson Niskanen Scholarships
(Undergraduate/Scholarship) [2789]
North Central (Region 9) Scholarships
(Undergraduate/Scholarship) [6499]
Edward S. Roth Manufacturing Engineering Scholarships (Graduate, Undergraduate/Scholarship) [6500]
University of Minnesota Women Student Travel Grants (Graduate, Undergraduate/Grant) [7134]

Mississippi

AISC/Southern Association of Steel Fabricators Fellowships (Graduate/Fellowship) [680]
AISC/Southern Association of Steel Fabricators Scholarships (Undergraduate/Scholarship) [681]

Missouri

AISC/Fred R. Havens Fellowships (Graduate, Undergraduate/Fellowship) [677]
Chapter 52 - Wichita Scholarships (Graduate, Undergraduate/Scholarship) [6478]
Hatton W. Sumners Scholarships
(Undergraduate/Scholarship) [5331]
Washington University Law School Olin Fellowships for Women (Graduate/Fellowship) [7387]

Montana

Horatio Alger Montana Scholarships
(Undergraduate/Scholarship) [216]
Great Falls Broadcasters Association Scholarships
(Undergraduate/Scholarship) [4570]

Nebraska

AISC/US Steel Fellowships (Graduate/Fellowship) [683]
Artistic Scholarship Awards
(Undergraduate/Scholarship) [1598]
Beta Omega Scholarships
(Undergraduate/Scholarship) [6347]
Tom Boots Memorial Scholarships
(Undergraduate/Scholarship) [5159]
Susan Thompson Buffett Foundation Scholarships
(Undergraduate/Scholarship) [1800]
General Scholarship Awards
(Undergraduate/Scholarship) [1599]
Sharon Kreikemeier Memorial Scholarships
(Undergraduate/Scholarship) [5160]
Brittany Mueller Memorial Scholarships (High School/Scholarship) [5161]
North Central (Region 9) Scholarships
(Undergraduate/Scholarship) [6499]
Swede Swanson Memorial Scholarships
(Undergraduate/Scholarship) [5162]
Mark and Vera Turner Memorial Scholarship
(Undergraduate/Scholarship) [4231]
Robert R. Wade Scholarship
(Undergraduate/Scholarship) [4232]

Nevada

AISC/Structural Steel Education Council Fellowships (Graduate/Fellowship) [682]
Aaron Edward Arnoldsen Memorial Scholarships
(Undergraduate/Scholarship) [1308]
Donald Franklin Bradley Memorial Scholarships
(Undergraduate/Scholarship) [5805]
Susan Brager Occupational Education Scholarships (Undergraduate/Scholarship) [5806]
John Caoile Memorial Scholarships
(Undergraduate/Scholarship) [5808]
Cheyenne High School Faculty Memorial Scholarships (Undergraduate/Scholarship) [5810]
Robin M. Daniels Memorial Scholarships
(Undergraduate/Scholarship) [5816]
Mickey Donnelly Memorial Scholarships
(Undergraduate/Scholarship) [5818]
Palo Verde High School - Barbara Edwards Memorial Scholarships
(Undergraduate/Scholarship) [5820]
Evening Mesquite Club Scholarships
(Undergraduate/Scholarship) [5823]
Gordy Fink Memorial Scholarships
(Undergraduate/Scholarship) [5824]
Veronica Gantt Memorial Scholarships
(Undergraduate/Scholarship) [5827]
Dr. Virginia Gilbert Memorial Scholarships
(Undergraduate/Scholarship) [5828]
Las Vegas Chinatown Scholarships
(Undergraduate/Scholarship) [5835]
Aaron Matusek Memorial Scholarships
(Undergraduate/Scholarship) [5840]
Ronald McDonald House Charities of Las Vegas Scholarships (Undergraduate/Scholarship) [5841]
North Las Vegas Firefighters - William J. Harnedy Memorial Scholarships
(Undergraduate/Scholarship) [5846]
Palo Verde High School Faculty Follies Scholarships (Undergraduate/Scholarship) [5847]
Panther Cafe Scholarships
(Undergraduate/Scholarship) [5848]
Pardee Community Building Scholarships
(Undergraduate/Scholarship) [5849]
Procida Tile Importers Scholarships
(Undergraduate/Scholarship) [5853]
Public Education Foundation Opportunity Scholarships (Undergraduate/Scholarship) [5854]
Silver Nugget Gaming Ambassadors Scholarships
(Undergraduate/Scholarship) [5858]
Striving for Success Scholarships
(Undergraduate/Scholarship) [5862]
Sheila Tarr-Smith Memorial Scholarships
(Undergraduate/Scholarship) [5864]
Judith Warner Memorial Scholarships
(Undergraduate/Scholarship) [5867]
Edwin F. Wiegand Science and Technology Scholarships (Undergraduate/Scholarship) [5868]

New Hampshire

Dr. George T. Bottomley Scholarships
(Undergraduate/Scholarship) [4414]
CEPS-Tyco Scholarships
(Undergraduate/Scholarship) [7137]
Dr. Robert Elliott Memorial Scholarships
(Undergraduate/Scholarship) [4415]
Pauline Elliott Scholarships
(Undergraduate/Scholarship) [4416]
Robert C. Erb Sr. Scholarships
(Undergraduate/Scholarship) [4417]
Phil Friel Scholarships
(Undergraduate/Scholarship) [4418]
Alex Gissler Memorial Scholarships
(Undergraduate/Scholarship) [4419]
Iranian Association of Boston's IAB Scholarships
(Undergraduate/Scholarship) [4955]
Bill Kidder Fund Awards
(Undergraduate/Scholarship) [6113]
Stan Lencki Scholarships
(Undergraduate/Scholarship) [4420]
Rick Mahoney Scholarships
(Undergraduate/Scholarship) [4421]
NHPGA Apprentice Scholarships
(Undergraduate/Scholarship) [4422]
Walter T. Philippy Scholarships
(Undergraduate/Scholarship) [4423]
David J. Pollini Scholarships
(Undergraduate/Scholarship) [4424]
Pope Scholarships Award
(Undergraduate/Scholarship) [4425]
Jim Sheerin Scholarships
(Undergraduate/Scholarship) [4426]
UNH Alumni Association Legacy Scholarships
(Undergraduate/Scholarship) [7138]

New Jersey

Jeffrey Carollo Music Scholarships
(Undergraduate/Scholarship) [5177]
CentraState Band Aid Open Committee Scholarships (Undergraduate/Scholarship) [2100]
Constantinople Armenian Relief Society (C.A.R.S.) Scholarships (Undergraduate/Scholarship) [1275]
DCH Freehold Toyota Scholarships
(Undergraduate/Scholarship) [2102]
Hirair and Anna Hovnanian Foundation Scholarships (Undergraduate/Scholarship) [1285]
New Jersey Psychological Association Scholarships for Minority Graduate Students
(Postgraduate/Scholarship) [5184]
Norkus Charitable Foundation Scholarships
(Undergraduate/Scholarship) [2103]
Dorothy D. Palmer Scholarship for the Study of Optimal Aging in Women
(Postdoctorate/Scholarship) [5185]
Seton Hall Law School's Merit Scholarship Program (Undergraduate/Scholarship) [6298]
Star-Ledger Scholarships for the Performing Arts
(Undergraduate/Scholarship) [5178]
Star and Barry Tobias Scholarships
(Undergraduate/Scholarship) [2104]

New Mexico

Albuquerque Lesbian and Gay Chamber of Commerce Scholarships
(Undergraduate/Scholarship) [6094]
Walt Bartram Memorial Education Awards (Region 12 and Chapter 119)
(Undergraduate/Scholarship) [6470]
Chapter 93 - Albuquerque Scholarships
(Undergraduate/Scholarship) [6483]
General Mills Foundation Scholarships
(Undergraduate/Scholarship) [622]
New Mexico Association for Bilingual Education Scholarships (Undergraduate/Scholarship) [5187]
Charles A. Townsend Scholarships
(Undergraduate/Scholarship) [5525]
U.S. Air Force ROTC Enhanced HSI Scholarship
(Undergraduate/Scholarship) [6975]

New York

Charles Abrams Scholarship Program
(Graduate/Scholarship) [775]
Advertising Production Club Scholarship Awards
(Graduate, Undergraduate/Scholarship) [28]
Constantinople Armenian Relief Society (C.A.R.S.) Scholarships (Undergraduate/Scholarship) [1275]
Fran Morgenstern Davis Scholarships
(Undergraduate/Scholarship) [943]
Louis Dreyfus Warner-Chappell City College Scholarships (Undergraduate/Scholarship) [945]
The Eneslow Pedorthic Institute Scholarships
(Undergraduate/Scholarship) [5545]
Ahmet Ertegun Memorial Scholarships (Graduate, Undergraduate/Scholarship) [6937]
Perry F. Hadlock Memorial Scholarships
(Undergraduate/Scholarship) [837]
JFEW/UJA-Federation Rose Biller Scholarships
(Undergraduate/Scholarship) [4024]
Bryan L. Knapp Point Scholarships (Graduate, Undergraduate/Scholarship) [5724]
McKelvey Scholarships
(Undergraduate/Scholarship) [4435]
William J. Merriman American Council on Exercise Educational Scholarships
(Undergraduate/Scholarship) [500]
New York Financial Writers' Associations Scholarships (Graduate, Undergraduate/Scholarship) [5189]
New York State Association of Agricultural Fairs Scholarships (Undergraduate/Scholarship) [5193]
The New York Times College Scholarships
(Undergraduate/Scholarship) [5195]
Saint Andrews Scholarships
(Undergraduate/Scholarship) [6150]
Scholarships for Emigres in the Health Sciences
(Undergraduate/Scholarship) [4025]
Al Schuman Ecolab Undergraduate Entrepreneurial Scholarships (Undergraduate/Scholarship) [5032]

Albert E. Wischmeyer Memorial Scholarships *(Undergraduate/Scholarship)* [6508]

North Carolina

Herb Adrian Memorial Scholarship Fund *(Undergraduate/Scholarship)* [3036]
African American Network - Carolinas Scholarship Fund *(Undergraduate/Scholarship)* [3037]
Air Force ROTC Enhanced HBCU Scholarships *(Undergraduate/Scholarship)* [6972]
AISC/Carolina Steel Scholarships *(Undergraduate/Scholarship)* [676]
Andersen Nontraditional Scholarship for Women's Education and Retraining *(Undergraduate/Scholarship)* [3039]
Carol Bond College Scholarships *(Undergraduate/Scholarship)* [5230]
Carol Bond Environmental Educator Scholarships *(Professional Development/Scholarship)* [5231]
Carol Bond University Scholarships *(Undergraduate/Scholarship)* [5232]
Sam L. Booke, Sr. Scholarships *(Undergraduate/Scholarship)* [7422]
T. Frank Booth Memorial Scholarship Fund *(Undergraduate/Scholarship)* [3043]
Cadmus Communications Corporation Graphics Scholarship Endowment Fund *(Undergraduate/Scholarship)* [3044]
Julian E. Carnes Scholarship Fund *(Undergraduate/Scholarship)* [3046]
Carolina Panthers Scholarship Fund *(Graduate/Scholarship)* [3047]
Carolina's Gay & Lesbian Scholarships *(Undergraduate/Scholarship)* [6099]
Elton Casey Scholarships *(Undergraduate/Scholarship)* [7149]
Children's Scholarship Fund of Charlotte *(High School/Scholarship)* [3051]
Lula Faye Clegg Memorial Scholarship Fund *(Undergraduate/Scholarship)* [3052]
Don and Barbara Curtis Excellence Fund for Extracurricular Student Activities *(Undergraduate/Grant)* [7153]
Virginia Elizabeth and Alma Vane Taylor Student Nurse Scholarships *(Undergraduate/Scholarship)* [7432]
Jack Ervin EDI Scholarships *(Professional Development/Scholarship)* [5238]
L.C. Gifford Distinguished Journalism Scholarships *(Undergraduate/Scholarship)* [7163]
L. Gordon, Jr. and June D. Pfefferkorn Scholarships *(Undergraduate/Scholarship)* [7439]
Governor James E. Holshouser Professional Development Scholarships *(Professional Development/Scholarship)* [5239]
Oliver Joel and Ellen Pell Denny Healthcare Scholarship Fund *(Undergraduate/Scholarship)* [7441]
Jimmy Johnson Memorial Scholarships *(Undergraduate/Scholarship)* [7442]
James V. Johnson Scholarship Fund *(Undergraduate/Scholarship)* [3063]
Annabel Lambeth Jones Scholarship Fund *(Undergraduate/Scholarship)* [3064]
Kappa Zeta Scholarships *(Undergraduate/Scholarship)* [6364]
Law Enforcement Memorial Scholarship Fund *(Undergraduate/Scholarship)* [3066]
L.D. and Elsie Long Memorial Scholarships *(Undergraduate/Scholarship)* [7446]
Norval Neil Luxon Prize for Scholarship to a Junior Scholarships *(Undergraduate/Scholarship)* [7173]
Carolina Panthers Players Sam Mills Memorial Scholarship Fund *(Undergraduate/Scholarship)* [3069]
Minority Presence Grant Program for Doctoral Study *(Undergraduate/Grant)* [7182]
N.W. Mitchell-Piedmont Federal Savings and Loans Endowed Scholarships *(Undergraduate/Scholarship)* [7448]
North Carolina Association of Health Care Recruiters Scholarships *(Undergraduate/Scholarship)* [5234]
North Carolina Nursery and Landscape Association Horticulture Scholarships *(Undergraduate/Scholarship)* [5243]
Orthopaedic Specialists Nursing Scholarships *(Undergraduate/Scholarship)* [7449]
Alice Conger Patterson Scholarships *(Undergraduate/Scholarship)* [7450]
Peter DeWitt Pruden and Phyliss Harrill Pruden Scholarships *(Undergraduate/Scholarship)* [7188]
John S. and Jacqueline P. Rider Scholarships *(Undergraduate/Scholarship)* [7453]
Ben Robinette Scholarship Endowment Fund *(Undergraduate/Scholarship)* [3074]
Ray and Pearly Sams Scholarships *(Undergraduate/Scholarship)* [7454]
William Shannon American Council on Exercise Certification Scholarships *(Professional Development, Undergraduate/Scholarship)* [501]
Bruce Shelton Scholarships *(Undergraduate/Scholarship)* [7455]
Tom Shown Scholarships *(Undergraduate/Scholarship)* [7456]
Tacy Ana Smith Memorial Scholarship Fund *(Undergraduate/Scholarship)* [3076]
The Dan Stewart Scholarships *(Professional Development/Scholarship)* [5240]
Charles H. Stone Scholarships *(Undergraduate/Scholarship)* [413]
Jack Tate/ThinkCOLLEGE Scholarship Fund *(Undergraduate/Scholarship)* [3079]
Turner Family Scholarship Fund *(Undergraduate/Scholarship)* [3080]
Gary Wagner, K3OMI Scholarships *(Undergraduate/Scholarship)* [859]
Edward Kent Welch Memorial Scholarships *(Undergraduate/Scholarship)* [7461]
Frederick K. Weyerhaeuser Forest History Fellowships *(Graduate/Fellowship)* [3031]
Elizabeth T. Williams Scholarships *(Undergraduate/Scholarship)* [7462]
Edwin H. and Louise N. Williamson Endowed Scholarships *(Undergraduate/Scholarship)* [7463]
Ted C. Wilson Memorial Scholarships *(Undergraduate/Scholarship)* [5791]

North Dakota

North Central (Region 9) Scholarships *(Undergraduate/Scholarship)* [6499]
North Dakota Farmers Union Co-op House Scholarships *(Undergraduate/Scholarship)* [5253]

Ohio

AISC/US Steel Fellowships *(Graduate/Fellowship)* [683]
American Advertising Federation-Cleveland College Scholarships *(Undergraduate/Scholarship)* [291]
American Advertising Federation-Cleveland High School Scholarships *(Undergraduate/Scholarship)* [292]
Jack R. Barckhoff Welding Management Scholarships *(Undergraduate/Scholarship)* [1157]
William (Billbo) Boston Scholarships *(Undergraduate/Scholarship)* [5467]
Catholic Healthcare Partners Scholarships *(Undergraduate/Scholarship)* [7525]
Ruth M. Cogan Scholarship Fund *(Undergraduate/Scholarship)* [6713]
Lawrence E. Davis Scholarships *(Undergraduate/Scholarship)* [5477]
Harold K. Douhhit Regional Scholarships *(Undergraduate/Scholarship)* [5322]
Epsilon Tau Pi's Soaring Eagle Scholarships *(Undergraduate/Scholarship)* [4856]
Dorcas Edmonson Haught Scholarships *(Undergraduate/Scholarship)* [5496]
Dale O. Heimberger CRNA Memorial Scholarship Fund *(Graduate/Scholarship)* [6726]
Manzer-Keener-Wefler Scholarships *(Undergraduate/Scholarship)* [6739]
Markley Family Scholarship Fund *(Undergraduate/Scholarship)* [6740]
Harry Mestel Memorial Accounting Scholarship Fund *(Undergraduate/Scholarship)* [6743]
John G. and Betty J. Mick Scholarship Fund *(Undergraduate/Scholarship)* [6744]
Lt. Colonel Robert G. Moreland Vocational/Technical Fund *(Undergraduate/Scholarship)* [6746]
Ohio Newspaper Association Minority Scholarships *(Undergraduate/Scholarship)* [5323]
Ohio Newspaper Association University Journalism Scholarships *(Undergraduate/Scholarship)* [5324]
Ohio Newspaper Association Women's Scholarships *(Undergraduate/Scholarship)* [5325]
Edward S. Roth Manufacturing Engineering Scholarships *(Graduate, Undergraduate/Scholarship)* [6500]
Stephen Schwartz Musical Theatre Scholarships *(Undergraduate/Scholarship)* [3625]
Dr. William E. & Norma Sprague Scholarships *(Undergraduate/Scholarship)* [3350]
Ira G. Turpin Scholar Fund *(Undergraduate/Scholarship)* [6760]
Irma E. Voigt Memorial Scholarships *(Undergraduate/Scholarship)* [6379]
Lester and Eleanor Webster Charitable Trust Fund *(Undergraduate/Scholarship)* [6762]
Xavier University ROTC Scholarships - Army ROTC *(Undergraduate/Scholarship)* [7542]

Oklahoma

Chapter 52 - Wichita Scholarships *(Graduate, Undergraduate/Scholarship)* [6478]
Leon Harris/Les Nichols Memorial Scholarships to Spartan College of Aeronautics & Technology *(Undergraduate/Scholarship)* [75]
OKAIDE Scholarships *(Undergraduate/Scholarship)* [5327]
The Oklahoma State University at Okmulgee Scholarships *(Undergraduate/Scholarship)* [5548]
Southwest Chapter Roy Kinslow Scholarships *(Undergraduate/Scholarship)* [1070]
Hatton W. Sumners Scholarships *(Undergraduate/Scholarship)* [5331]
Tom Taylor Memorial Scholarships to Spartan College of Aeronautics and Technology *(Undergraduate/Scholarship)* [89]

Oregon

Clackamas County Farm Bureau Scholarships *(Undergraduate/Scholarship)* [5392]
Emerald Empire Chapter Scholarship Awards *(Undergraduate/Scholarship)* [5381]
Insurance Women of Portland Scholarships *(Graduate/Scholarship)* [3767]
Kilbuck Family Native American Scholarship *(Undergraduate/Scholarship)* [1629]
Armistead Maupin Creative Writing Scholarship Fund *(Undergraduate/Scholarship)* [2887]
Oregon Association of Broadcasters Scholarships *(Undergraduate/Scholarship)* [5376]
Oregon Community Credit Union Scholarships *(Undergraduate/Scholarship)* [7201]
Robert W. and Bernice Ingalls Staton Scholarships *(Undergraduate/Scholarship)* [7202]
University of Oregon Diversity-Building Scholarships *(Graduate, Undergraduate/Scholarship)* [7204]
Willamette Valley AG Association Scholarships *(Undergraduate/Scholarship)* [5395]
Ed Wood Memorial Scholarship Awards *(Undergraduate/Scholarship)* [5390]
Yamhill County Farm Bureau Scholarships *(Undergraduate/Scholarship)* [5396]

Pennsylvania

Charles Abrams Scholarship Program *(Graduate/Scholarship)* [775]
Air Products and Chemicals, Inc. Scholarships *(Undergraduate/Scholarship)* [1429]
Allegheny County Medical Society (ACMS) Medical Student Scholarship *(Undergraduate/Scholarship)* [3134]
Alliance Medical Education Scholarship Fund

(AMES) *(Undergraduate/Scholarship)* [3135]
B-Brave McMahon/Stratton Scholarship Fund *(Undergraduate/Scholarship)* [2941]
Michael Baker Corporation Scholarship Program *(Undergraduate/Scholarship)* [1430]
Joe Q. Bryant American Council on Exercise Educational Scholarships *(Undergraduate/Scholarship)* [499]
Warren E. "Whitey" Cole American Society of Highway Engineers Scholarships *(Undergraduate/Scholarship)* [2947]
Malcolm U. Dantzler Scholarships *(Professional Development/Scholarship)* [6613]
Danville Education Association Scholarship Fund *(Undergraduate/Scholarship)* [2949]
The William H. Davis, Jr. Scholarship Fund *(Undergraduate/Scholarship)* [2399]
Sue and Ken Dyer Foundation Travel Scholarship Award *(Undergraduate/Scholarship)* [3096]
Wayne G. Failor Scholarships *(High School/Scholarship)* [5563]
Nolan W. Feeser Scholarship Fund *(Undergraduate/Scholarship)* [2954]
Belknap Freeman Carnegie Mellon Scholarships *(Undergraduate/Scholarship)* [878]
Daniel G. and Helen I. Fultz Scholarship Fund *(Undergraduate/Scholarship)* [2955]
Norma Gotwalt Scholarship Fund *(Undergraduate/Scholarship)* [3102]
Scott A. Gunder, MD, DCMS Presidential Scholarships *(Undergraduate/Scholarship)* [3136]
HDR Engineering, Inc. Scholarship for Diversity in Engineering *(Undergraduate/Scholarship)* [1432]
Alia Herrera Memorial Scholarships *(Undergraduate/Scholarship)* [359]
Conrad N. Hilton Scholarships *(Undergraduate/Scholarship)* [2841]
Hirair and Anna Hovnanian Foundation Presidential Scholarships *(Undergraduate/Scholarship)* [1284]
James Hughes Memorial Scholarship Fund *(Undergraduate/Scholarship)* [5564]
George C. Liacouras Memorial Scholarships *(Undergraduate/Scholarship)* [3532]
Leon I. Lock and Barbara R. Lock Scholarship Fund *(Undergraduate/Scholarship)* [3109]
Carl J. Marrara Memorial Scholarship Fund *(Undergraduate/Scholarship)* [2963]
Barry H. Marshal Scholarships *(Undergraduate/Scholarship)* [6121]
Walter A. and Nan C. McCloskey Memorial Scholarships *(Undergraduate/Scholarship)* [2964]
McKelvey Scholarships *(Undergraduate/Scholarship)* [4435]
McLean Scholarships *(Undergraduate/Scholarship)* [1433]
Joseph and Catherine Missigman Memorial Nursing Scholarships *(Undergraduate/Scholarship)* [2965]
Missigman Scholarship Fund *(Undergraduate/Scholarship)* [2966]
Robert E. and Judy More Scholarship Fund *(Undergraduate/Scholarship)* [2967]
Pennsylvania Society of Professional Engineers Scholarships *(Undergraduate/Scholarship)* [5561]
PMCA Graduate Fellowships at Pennsylvania State University *(Graduate/Fellowship)* [5712]
Ollie Rosenberg Educational Trust *(Undergraduate/Scholarship)* [3117]
Jane Salanky-Onzik Scholarship Fund *(Undergraduate/Scholarship)* [2974]
South Carolina Public Health Association Scholarships *(Undergraduate/Scholarship)* [6614]
Minnie Patton Stayman Scholarships *(Undergraduate/Scholarship)* [5566]
Anil and Neema Thakrar Family Fund *(Undergraduate/Scholarship)* [3122]
John R. and Joan F. Warren Scholarship Fund *(Undergraduate/Scholarship)* [6761]
Williamsport-Lycoming Community Foundation - Benjamin Franklin Scholarships *(Undergraduate/Scholarship)* [2980]

Rhode Island

Armenian American Pharmacists' Association Scholarships *(Doctorate, Graduate/Scholarship)* [1268]
Iranian Association of Boston's IAB Scholarships *(Undergraduate/Scholarship)* [4955]
Johnson and Wales University Scholarships *(Undergraduate/Scholarship)* [4039]
Al Schuman Ecolab Undergraduate Entrepreneurial Scholarships *(Undergraduate/Scholarship)* [5032]
Lily and Catello Sorrentino Memorial Scholarships *(Undergraduate/Scholarship)* [6042]
Bruce and Marjorie Sundlun Scholarships *(Undergraduate/Scholarship)* [6043]

South Carolina

African American Network - Carolinas Scholarship Fund *(Undergraduate/Scholarship)* [3037]
AISC/Carolina Steel Scholarships *(Undergraduate/Scholarship)* [676]
Andersen Nontraditional Scholarship for Women's Education and Retraining *(Undergraduate/Scholarship)* [3039]
Julian E. Carnes Scholarship Fund *(Undergraduate/Scholarship)* [3046]
Carolina Panthers Scholarship Fund *(Graduate/Scholarship)* [3047]
Judy Crocker Memorial Scholarship Fund *(Undergraduate/Scholarship)* [3055]
Howard B. Higgins South Carolina Dental Scholarships *(Undergraduate/Scholarship)* [3061]
Albert and Eloise Midyette Memorial Scholarship Fund *(Undergraduate/Scholarship)* [3068]
Carolina Panthers Players Sam Mills Memorial Scholarship Fund *(Undergraduate/Scholarship)* [3069]
Henry DeWitt Plyler Scholarship Fund *(Undergraduate/Scholarship)* [3073]
SCSPA Scholarships *(Undergraduate/Scholarship)* [6617]
SCSPA Yearbook Scholarships *(Undergraduate/Scholarship)* [6618]
South Carolina Association for Financial Professionals College Education Scholarships *(Undergraduate/Scholarship)* [6611]
South Carolina Undergraduate Scholarships *(Undergraduate/Scholarship)* [3619]
Ted C. Wilson Memorial Scholarships *(Undergraduate/Scholarship)* [5791]

South Dakota

North Central (Region 9) Scholarships *(Undergraduate/Scholarship)* [6499]
South Dakota Division Scholarships *(Undergraduate/Scholarship)* [4520]

Tennessee

Air Force ROTC Enhanced HBCU Scholarships *(Undergraduate/Scholarship)* [6972]
AISC/Southern Association of Steel Fabricators Fellowships *(Graduate/Fellowship)* [680]
AISC/Southern Association of Steel Fabricators Scholarships *(Undergraduate/Scholarship)* [681]
B&W Y-12 Scholarship Fund *(Undergraduate/Scholarship)* [2806]
Belmont University Commercial Music Scholarships *(Undergraduate/Scholarship)* [2406]
George Oliver Benton Memorial Scholarships *(Undergraduate/Scholarship)* [2407]
JoAhn Brown-Nash Memorial Scholarships *(Undergraduate/Scholarship)* [2409]
Steven L. Coffey Memorial Scholarships *(Undergraduate/Scholarship)* [2809]
Claude T. Coffman Memorial Scholarships *(Undergraduate/Scholarship)* [7110]
Cleveland Drennon, Jr. Memorial Scholarships *(Undergraduate/Scholarship)* [7111]
Federal Court Bench and Bar Scholarships *(Undergraduate/Scholarship)* [7114]
Pauline LaFon Gore Scholarships *(Undergraduate/Scholarship)* [2421]
Herbert Herff Presidential Law Scholarships *(Undergraduate/Scholarship)* [7116]
Regina Higdon Scholarships *(Undergraduate/Scholarship)* [2423]
Robert and Elaine Hoffman Memorial Scholarships *(Undergraduate/Scholarship)* [7117]
Kathryn Hookanson Law Fellowships *(Undergraduate/Scholarship)* [7118]
Cecil C. Humphreys Law Fellowships *(Undergraduate/Scholarship)* [7120]
Michael B. Kruse Scholarships *(Undergraduate/Scholarship)* [2428]
Judge William B. Leffler Scholarships *(Undergraduate/Scholarship)* [7121]
Dr. Mac Scholarships *(Undergraduate/Scholarship)* [2431]
Joan Reagin McNeill Scholarships - Alpha Theta *(Undergraduate/Scholarship)* [6365]
Joan Reagin McNeill Scholarships - Theta Phi *(Undergraduate/Scholarship)* [6366]
Sam A. Myar, Jr. Law Scholarships *(Undergraduate/Scholarship)* [7123]
Archie Hartwell Nash Memorial Scholarships *(Undergraduate/Scholarship)* [2440]
NCBWL Scholarships *(High School/Scholarship)* [4611]
Eloise Pitts O'More Scholarships *(Undergraduate/Scholarship)* [2442]
Donald and Susie Polden Dean's Scholarships *(Undergraduate/Scholarship)* [7124]
Peter DeWitt Pruden and Phyliss Harrill Pruden Scholarships *(Undergraduate/Scholarship)* [7188]
Ratner and Sugarmon Scholarships *(Undergraduate/Scholarship)* [7125]
Barbara Hagan Richards Scholarships *(Undergraduate/Scholarship)* [2444]
Joseph Henry Shepherd Scholarships *(Undergraduate/Scholarship)* [7126]
Amy E. Spain Memorial Scholarships *(Undergraduate/Scholarship)* [7127]
James F. and Donna Springfield Scholarships *(Undergraduate/Scholarship)* [7128]
Tennessee Bar Foundation IOLTA Law School Scholarships *(Undergraduate/Scholarship)* [7129]
Emmett H. Turner Scholarships *(Undergraduate/Scholarship)* [2450]
Gary Wagner, K3OMI Scholarships *(Undergraduate/Scholarship)* [859]
Teddy Wilburn Scholarships *(Undergraduate/Scholarship)* [2451]

Texas

AISC/US Steel Fellowships *(Graduate/Fellowship)* [683]
BAFTX Early Starters Awards *(Undergraduate/Scholarship)* [1779]
BAFTX Graduate Awards *(Undergraduate/Scholarship)* [1780]
BAFTX Junior Achievers Awards *(Undergraduate/Scholarship)* [1781]
BAFTX Undergraduate Awards *(Undergraduate/Scholarship)* [1782]
Zachary Barriger Memorial Scholarships *(High School/Scholarship)* [2262]
O.J. Beck, Jr. Memorial Scholarships *(Undergraduate/Scholarship)* [2263]
Beecroft Family Scholarships *(High School/Scholarship)* [2264]
Reverend E.F. Bennett Scholarships *(High School/Scholarship)* [2265]
Marion Luna Brem/Pat McNeil Teen Parent Scholarships *(Undergraduate/Scholarship)* [2266]
C.C.H.R.M.A. Scholarships *(High School, Undergraduate/Scholarship)* [2268]
Bill Cormack Scholarships *(Undergraduate/Scholarship)* [6862]
Dallas Hispanic Bar Association Scholarships *(Undergraduate/Scholarship)* [2611]
DeBakey International Society Fellowship Awards *(Professional Development/Award/Prize)* [2629]
Educational and Professional Achievement Schol-

arships *(Undergraduate/Scholarship)* [451]
John R. Eidson Jr., Scholarships *(Undergraduate/Scholarship)* [2274]
George Foreman Tribute to Lyndon B. Johnson Scholarships *(Undergraduate/Scholarship)* [1397]
Gamma Iota Scholarships - Gamma Tau *(Undergraduate/Scholarship)* [6357]
Gamma Iota Scholarships - Kappa Eta *(Undergraduate/Scholarship)* [6358]
Gamma Iota Scholarships - Zeta Kappa *(Undergraduate/Scholarship)* [6359]
Gamma Iota Scholarships - Zeta Nu *(Undergraduate/Scholarship)* [6360]
Max Godwin Endowed Scholarships *(Undergraduate/Scholarship)* [6871]
Melissa Guerra Scholarships *(Undergraduate/Scholarship)* [2277]
George and Mary Josephine Hamman Foundation Scholarships *(High School/Scholarship)* [3392]
Hispanic Association of Colleges and Universities Scholarships *(Undergraduate/Scholarship)* [3568]
Jamail/Long Challenge Grant Scholarships *(Graduate, Undergraduate/Scholarship)* [3576]
JLTLA Scholarships *(Undergraduate/Scholarship)* [6942]
Sue Kay Lay Memorial Scholarships *(High School/Scholarship)* [2280]
Danny T. Le Memorial Scholarships *(High School, Undergraduate/Scholarship)* [7321]
Le Hoang Nguyen (LHN) College Scholarships *(High School/Scholarship)* [7322]
The Thuy Nguyen Scholarships *(High School/Scholarship)* [7323]
PFLAG/HATCH Youth Scholarship Foundation *(Undergraduate/Scholarship)* [6132]
Rotary Club of Corpus Christi Scholarships *(High School/Scholarship)* [2285]
Edward S. Roth Manufacturing Engineering Scholarships *(Graduate, Undergraduate/Scholarship)* [6500]
Seaman Family Scholarships *(High School/Scholarship)* [2286]
Judge Terry Shamsie Scholarships *(High School/Scholarship)* [2287]
Herman J. Smith Scholarships *(Undergraduate/Scholarship)* [4942]
South Texas Unit Scholarships *(Undergraduate/Scholarship)* [3546]
Hatton W. Sumners Scholarships *(Undergraduate/Scholarship)* [5331]
Talbert Family Memorial Accounting Scholarships *(Undergraduate/Scholarship)* [2291]
Texas Music Educators Association Past-Presidents Memorial Scholarships *(Undergraduate/Scholarship)* [6863]
Texas Telephone Association Foundation Scholarships *(Undergraduate/Scholarship)* [6873]
Vera Tran Memorial Scholarships *(Undergraduate/Scholarship)* [7324]
TU@UT HSF College Scholarship Program *(Undergraduate/Scholarship)* [3604]
U.S. Air Force ROTC Enhanced HSI Scholarship *(Undergraduate/Scholarship)* [6975]
Faye and Rendell Webb Scholarships *(High School, Undergraduate/Scholarship)* [2292]
Wheelchair Success Foundation Scholarships *(Undergraduate/Scholarship)* [2293]

Utah

Edward S. Roth Manufacturing Engineering Scholarships *(Graduate, Undergraduate/Scholarship)* [6500]

Vermont

Iranian Association of Boston's IAB Scholarships *(Undergraduate/Scholarship)* [4955]

Virginia

AISC/Carolina Steel Scholarships *(Undergraduate/Scholarship)* [676]
Bayly-Tiffany Scholarships *(Undergraduate/Scholarship)* [7239]
V. Thomas Forehand, Jr. Scholarships *(Undergraduate/Scholarship)* [7240]
Jane S. Glenn Memorial Endowed Scholarships *(Undergraduate/Scholarship)* [6046]
Goodman and Company, LLP Annual Scholarships *(Undergraduate/Scholarship)* [3262]
Hilb, Rogal and Hobbs Scholarships *(Undergraduate/Scholarship)* [7328]
Kaprielian Memorial Scholarships *(Undergraduate/Scholarship)* [7241]
John Allen Love Scholarships *(Graduate, Undergraduate/Scholarship)* [7242]
Norfolk Southern Scholarships *(Undergraduate/Scholarship)* [7329]
Phillip Morris USA Scholarships *(Undergraduate/Scholarship)* [7330]
Margaret E. Phillips Scholarships *(Undergraduate/Scholarship)* [7243]
Peter DeWitt Pruden and Phyliss Harrill Pruden Scholarships *(Undergraduate/Scholarship)* [7188]
Gary Wagner, K3OMI Scholarships *(Undergraduate/Scholarship)* [859]
West Virginia PTA Scholarships *(Undergraduate/Scholarship)* [7396]
Ted C. Wilson Memorial Scholarships *(Undergraduate/Scholarship)* [5791]
Witt Mares Scholarships *(Undergraduate/Scholarship)* [7331]

Washington

Air Force ROTC Enhanced HBCU Scholarships *(Undergraduate/Scholarship)* [6972]
Louis Armstrong Scholarships *(High School/Scholarship)* [939]
Barbara Bailey Scholarships *(Undergraduate/Scholarship)* [5754]
Beta Sigma Phi-VCT Scholarships *(Undergraduate/Scholarship)* [6306]
Boeing Company Scholarships *(Undergraduate/Scholarship)* [6307]
Ivan Braga Scholarships *(Undergraduate/Scholarship)* [6308]
Nellie Love Butcher Scholarships *(Undergraduate/Scholarship)* [3428]
Co Dental Hygiene Scholarships *(Undergraduate/Scholarship)* [6309]
Dr. Princeton L. Co Emergency Fund for Dental Hygiene Scholarships *(Undergraduate/Scholarship)* [6310]
Carli Edwards Memorial Scholarships *(Undergraduate/Scholarship)* [6311]
Ruth Murphy Evans Scholarship *(Undergraduate/Scholarship)* [3373]
Dayton E. Finnigan Scholarship *(Undergraduate/Scholarship)* [3374]
Friends of Mary Automotive Scholarships *(Undergraduate/Scholarship)* [6312]
William H. Gates Public Service Law Scholarships *(Undergraduate/Scholarship)* [3163]
Margaret S. Gilbert Scholarship Fund *(Undergraduate/Scholarship)* [6722]
Dr. Bill Johnson Scholarships *(Undergraduate/Scholarship)* [6313]
Ina Knutsen Scholarships *(Undergraduate/Scholarship)* [6314]
Ken LaFountaine First Nations Scholarships *(Undergraduate/Scholarship)* [6315]
Ron LaFreniere Business Scholarships *(Undergraduate/Scholarship)* [6316]
Mallet Nursing Scholarships *(Undergraduate/Scholarship)* [6317]
Armistead Maupin Creative Writing Scholarship Fund *(Undergraduate/Scholarship)* [2887]
Mill Creek Business Association Scholarships *(Undergraduate/Scholarship)* [4533]
Eric Niemitalo Scholarships in Earth and Environmental Science *(Undergraduate/Scholarship)* [6318]
Olympia Tumwater Foundation Traditional Scholarships *(Undergraduate/Scholarship)* [5333]
Olympia Tumwater Foundation Transitional (non-traditional) Scholarships *(Undergraduate/Scholarship)* [5334]
Pierce College Foundation Coca-Cola Scholarships *(Undergraduate/Scholarship)* [5693]
Puget Sound Chapter Scholarships *(Undergraduate/Scholarship)* [1512]
Joseph Wood Rogers Memorial Scholarships *(Undergraduate/Scholarship)* [6319]
Richard C. Rolfs Scholarships *(Undergraduate/Scholarship)* [5776]
Seattle Chapter ASWA Scholarships *(All/Scholarship)* [2834]
Shoreline Community College Academic Excellence Scholarships for Graduating High School Seniors *(Undergraduate/Scholarship)* [6320]
Shoreline Community College Academic Improvement Scholarships for Graduating High School Seniors *(Undergraduate/Scholarship)* [6321]
Shoreline Community College Continuing Students Scholarships *(Undergraduate/Scholarship)* [6322]
Shoreline Community College Part-Time Students Scholarships *(Undergraduate/Scholarship)* [6323]
Margaret Svec Scholarships *(Undergraduate/Scholarship)* [6324]
Team DC Student-Athlete Scholarships *(Undergraduate/Scholarship)* [6140]
Elizabeth Thomas Scholarships *(Undergraduate/Scholarship)* [6325]
WALPA Lake Scholarships *(Graduate, Undergraduate/Scholarship)* [7382]

West Virginia

Bob Adkins Memorial Scholarships *(Undergraduate/Scholarship)* [5462]
William (Billbo) Boston Scholarships *(Undergraduate/Scholarship)* [5467]
Freda Burge Scholarships *(Undergraduate/Scholarship)* [5470]
Cindy Curry Memorial Scholarships *(Undergraduate/Scholarship)* [5475]
Lawrence E. Davis Scholarships *(Undergraduate/Scholarship)* [5477]
David Edward Farson Scholarships *(Undergraduate/Scholarship)* [5480]
William E. "Bill" Gallagher Scholarships *(Undergraduate/Scholarship)* [5482]
Health Sciences Scholarship Program *(Undergraduate/Scholarship)* [7402]
Albert H. Hix, W8AH Memorial Scholarships *(Undergraduate/Scholarship)* [838]
Holly Jackson-Wuller Memorial Scholarships *(Undergraduate/Scholarship)* [5498]
K.A.S.A Memorial Scholarships *(Undergraduate/Scholarship)* [5499]
Dr. Charles Kelly Memorial Scholarships *(Undergraduate/Scholarship)* [5500]
McKelvey Scholarships *(Undergraduate/Scholarship)* [4435]
Medical Students Loan Program *(Undergraduate/Loan)* [7403]
James H. Roberts Athletic Scholarships *(Undergraduate/Scholarship)* [5512]
James Robinson Memorial Scholarships *(Undergraduate/Scholarship)* [5514]
Mary K. Smith Rector Scholarships *(Undergraduate/Scholarship)* [5523]
Gary Wagner, K3OMI Scholarships *(Undergraduate/Scholarship)* [859]

Wisconsin

AISC/US Steel Fellowships *(Graduate/Fellowship)* [683]
Victor Albright Scholarships-Dane County *(Undergraduate/Scholarship)* [7246]
Victor Albright Scholarships *(Undergraduate/Scholarship)* [7247]
John D. Anello Sr. and Albert A. Silverman Memorial Scholarships *(Undergraduate/Scholarship)* [2237]
Mary Ann Brichta Scholarships *(Undergraduate/Scholarship)* [7249]
Patricia Buchanan Memorial Scholarships *(Undergraduate/Scholarship)* [7250]
Duluth Central HS Alumni Scholarships *(Undergraduate/Scholarship)* [2775]

Engineering Departmental Scholarships *(Undergraduate/Scholarship)* [7251]
Engineering Diversity Affairs Scholarships *(All/Scholarship)* [7252]
Carleton A. Friday Memorial Scholarships *(Undergraduate/Scholarship)* [4522]
Human Ecology Continuing Undergraduate Student Scholarships *(Undergraduate/Scholarship)* [7257]
Iowa Journalism Institute Scholarships *(Undergraduate/Scholarship)* [3935]
Kemper K. Knapp Scholarships *(Undergraduate/Scholarship)* [7259]
George Koeppel and Roland W. Zinns Scholarships *(Undergraduate/Scholarship)* [7260]
Harold A. Levin Scholarships *(Undergraduate/Scholarship)* [2240]
McBurney Disability Scholarships *(Undergraduate/Scholarship)* [7262]
Edmond A. Metzger Scholarships *(Undergraduate/Scholarship)* [843]
John P. and Tashia F. Morgridge Scholarships *(Undergraduate/Scholarship)* [7263]
Hubert A. Nelson Scholarships *(Undergraduate/Scholarship)* [2787]
North Central (Region 9) Scholarships *(Undergraduate/Scholarship)* [6499]
Pi Lambda Theta Scholarships *(Undergraduate/Scholarship)* [7265]
Powers-Knapp Scholarships *(Undergraduate/Scholarship)* [7266]
School of Education Scholarships for Students from Underrepresented Groups *(Undergraduate/Scholarship)* [7268]
School of Pharmacy Continuing Student Scholarships *(Undergraduate/Scholarship)* [7269]
John A. Sullivan Scholarships *(Undergraduate/Scholarship)* [2795]
University of Wisconsin-Madison Academic Excellence Scholarships *(Undergraduate/Scholarship)* [7270]
University of Wisconsin-Madison African American Alumni Scholarships *(Undergraduate/Scholarship)* [7271]
University of Wisconsin-Madison American Indian Alumni Scholarships *(Undergraduate/Scholarship)* [7272]
University of Wisconsin-Madison/CALS Continuing Student Scholarships *(Undergraduate/Scholarship)* [7273]
University of Wisconsin-Madison/CALS Minority Scholarships *(Undergraduate/Scholarship)* [7274]
University of Wisconsin-Madison Minority Teacher Loans *(Professional Development, Undergraduate/Loan, Scholarship)* [7277]
University of Wisconsin-Madison Music Scholarships *(Undergraduate/Scholarship)* [7278]
University of Wisconsin-Madison National Merit Scholarships *(Undergraduate/Scholarship)* [7279]
University of Wisconsin-Madison Pharmacy New Student Scholarships *(Undergraduate/Scholarship)* [7280]
Vilas Equity Scholarships *(Undergraduate/Scholarship)* [7282]
William F. Vilas Scholarships *(Undergraduate/Scholarship)* [7283]
Kenneth G. Weckel Scholarships *(Undergraduate/Scholarship)* [4523]
Wisconsin Broadcasters Association Scholarships *(Undergraduate/Scholarship)* [7472]
Wisconsin High School Scholarships *(Undergraduate/Scholarship)* [7284]
Wisconsin-Madison Journalism Scholarships *(Undergraduate/Scholarship)* [7285]
Wisconsin-Madison Music Clinic Scholarships *(Undergraduate/Scholarship)* [7286]
Wisconsin Region Student Leadership Scholarships *(Undergraduate/Scholarship)* [4684]

Wyoming

AISC/Rocky Mountain Steel Construction Association Fellowships *(Graduate/Fellowship)* [679]

CANADA

AABP Amstutz Scholarships *(Undergraduate/Scholarship)* [326]
AABP Student Externship Program *(Undergraduate/Scholarship)* [330]
AANS Medical Student Summer Research Fellowships (MSSRF) *(Undergraduate/Fellowship)* [370]
AAS Korean Studies Scholarship Program *(Doctorate, Graduate/Scholarship)* [1371]
Jack Ackroyd Scholarships *(Professional Development/Scholarship)* [1925]
ACS/NREF-AANS Faculty Career Development Award *(Professional Development/Award/Prize)* [371]
AIA and the Global Automotive Aftermarket Symposium Scholarships *(Undergraduate/Scholarship)* [1569]
Airports Council International-North America Scholarship *(Graduate, Undergraduate/Scholarship)* [94]
Al Mercury Scholarships *(Undergraduate/Scholarship)* [7209]
Alberta Agricultural Economics Association Scholarships *(Graduate/Scholarship)* [137]
Alberta Agricultural Economics Association Undergraduate Scholarships *(Undergraduate/Scholarship)* [138]
Alberta Award for the Study of Canadian Human Rights and Multiculturalism *(Doctorate, Graduate/Award/Prize)* [145]
Alberta Centennial Premier's Scholarships - Alberta *(Undergraduate/Scholarship)* [146]
Alberta Press Council Scholarships *(Undergraduate/Scholarship)* [187]
Hon. Lincoln Alexander Scholarships *(Undergraduate/Scholarship)* [1724]
Jim Allard Broadcast Journalism Scholarships *(Undergraduate/Scholarship)* [1921]
Janet and Horace Allen Scholarship *(Undergraduate/Scholarship)* [147]
Lorraine Allison Scholarships *(Postgraduate/Scholarship)* [1199]
AMEC Aboriginal Undergraduate Scholarships *(Undergraduate/Scholarship)* [1947]
AMEC Masters Scholarships *(Graduate/Scholarship)* [1948]
American College of Radiation Oncology Resident Scholarships *(Graduate/Scholarship)* [475]
Bernard Amtmann Fellowships *(Postgraduate/Grant)* [1698]
Aplastic, Anemia and Myelosdysplasia Scholarships *(Graduate/Scholarship)* [1991]
Applied Hospitality Degree Scholarships *(Undergraduate/Scholarship)* [1975]
Architects Association of PEI Scholarships *(Undergraduate/Scholarship)* [2496]
Art Graduate Scholarships *(Graduate/Scholarship)* [148]
Arts for Career Development Scholarships *(Professional Development/Internship)* [149]
Association of Universities and Colleges of Canada Public Scholarships *(Undergraduate/Scholarship)* [1504]
Association for Women Veterinarians Foundation Scholarships Program *(Graduate/Scholarship)* [1523]
Astra Zeneca RURAL Scholarships *(Doctorate/Scholarship)* [1992]
Atlantic Provinces Library Association Memorial Awards *(Professional Development/Scholarship)* [1533]
Atlantic Salmon Federation Olin Fellowships *(All/Fellowship)* [1536]
Joan Auld Scholarships *(Undergraduate/Scholarship)* [2497]
Jerry Baker Scholarships *(Undergraduate/Scholarship)* [1156]
Helen Bassett Commemorative Scholarships *(Undergraduate/Scholarship)* [5128]
Baxter Corporation Canadian Research Awards in Anesthesia *(Professional Development/Award/Prize)* [1912]
BBM Canada Scholarships *(Undergraduate/Scholarship)* [1922]
Suzanne Beauregard Scholarships *(Undergraduate/Scholarship)* [6070]
Stan Beck Fellowships *(Undergraduate/Fellowship)* [2861]
Ann Beckingham Scholarships *(Doctorate/Scholarship)* [1993]
Dade Behring Student Scholarship Awards *(Postgraduate/Scholarship)* [2040]
Beverlee Bell Scholarships in Human Rights and Democracy *(Graduate/Scholarship)* [2728]
Louise Bennett-Coverley Scholarships *(Undergraduate/Scholarship)* [1725]
Dr. Noorali & Sabiya Bharwani Endowment *(Undergraduate/Scholarship)* [1693]
Hussein Jina Bharwani Memorial Endowment *(Undergraduate/Scholarship)* [1694]
BioQuip Scholarships *(Undergraduate/Scholarship)* [2862]
Birks Family Foundation Scholarships *(Undergraduate/Scholarship)* [1994]
Bison Transport Scholarships *(Undergraduate/Scholarship)* [5341]
M. Hildred Blewett Scholarships *(Postdoctorate/Scholarship)* [6431]
Lawrence Bloomberg Entrance Awards *(Postgraduate/Award/Prize)* [6262]
BMO Financial Group Scholarships *(Undergraduate/Scholarship)* [1726]
Therese and David Bohbot Scholarship *(Undergraduate/Scholarship)* [3553]
Steve Bonk Scholarships *(Postgraduate/Scholarship)* [2050]
Lorne and Ruby Bonnell Scholarships *(Undergraduate/Scholarship)* [2498]
Jim Bourque Scholarships *(Postgraduate/Scholarship)* [1200]
Eugene Boyko Scholarships *(Undergraduate/Scholarship)* [140]
Marlene Brand Memorial Scholarship *(Undergraduate/Scholarship)* [3554]
Louis J. Brody Q.C. Entrance Scholarships *(Postgraduate/Scholarship)* [6263]
Peter F. Bronfman Entrance Awards *(Postgraduate/Award/Prize)* [6264]
Peter F. Bronfman Scholarships of Merit *(Postgraduate/Scholarship)* [6265]
William A. and Ann M. Brothers Scholarships *(Undergraduate/Scholarship)* [1159]
Randall Brown and Associates Awards *(Postgraduate/Award/Prize)* [1962]
Bernic and Gordon Brown Scholarship *(All/Scholarship)* [3555]
Bujea Memorial Scholarships *(Undergraduate/Scholarship)* [911]
Sam Bull Memorial Scholarships *(Undergraduate/Scholarship)* [142]
CAG Donald Menzies Bursary Awards *(Postgraduate/Award/Prize)* [1927]
CAG Margery Boyce Bursary Awards *(Postgraduate/Award/Prize)* [1928]
CALL/ACBD Education Reserve Fund Grants *(Graduate/Grant)* [1930]
Cameco Corporation Scholarships in the Geological Sciences - Continuing Students *(Undergraduate/Scholarship)* [1904]
Cameco Corporation Scholarships in the Geological Sciences - Entering Students *(Undergraduate/Scholarship)* [1905]
Cameco Northern Scholarships - Technical Institute *(Undergraduate/Scholarship)* [1906]
Cameco Northern Scholarships - University *(Undergraduate/Scholarship)* [1907]
Thomas R. Camp Scholarships *(Graduate/Scholarship)* [1142]
Theodore R. Campbell Scholarship *(Undergraduate/Scholarship)* [150]
Canada Graduate Scholarships Program *(Graduate/Scholarship)* [6418]
Canada Millennium Bursary *(Undergraduate/Scholarship)* [151]
Canada-Ukraine Parliamentary Program (CUPP) Internship Scholarships *(Undergraduate/Scholarship)* [7357]
Canadian Aboriginal Science and Technology Society Scholarships *(Undergraduate/Scholarship)* [2042]
Canadian Anesthesiologists' Society Research

Steven Huesing Scholarships *(Undergraduate/Scholarship)* [2255]
John Peter Humphrey Student Fellowships *(Graduate/Fellowship)* [1942]
IBA Law Student Scholarships Foundation *(Undergraduate/Scholarship)* [3715]
IBM Canada Undergraduate Scholarships *(Undergraduate/Scholarship)* [1951]
IIE Council of Fellows Undergraduate Scholarships *(Undergraduate/Scholarship)* [3733]
In-course Scholarships - Chinese Dance Workshop Scholarships *(Undergraduate/Scholarship)* [7224]
Informatics Circle of Research Excellence Scholarships *(Doctorate, Graduate/Scholarship)* [159]
Intensive Language Course Grants *(Doctorate/Grant)* [3227]
International Association of Foundation Drilling Scholarships for Civil Engineering Students *(Postgraduate/Scholarship)* [3798]
International Association of Foundation Drilling Scholarships for Part-time Civil Engineering Graduate School Students *(Postgraduate/Scholarship)* [3799]
International Association of Law Libraries Scholarship Program *(Professional Development/Scholarship)* [3807]
International Education Awards - Ukraine *(Undergraduate/Scholarship)* [160]
International Grenfell Association Bursary *(Undergraduate/Scholarship)* [3863]
International Grenfell Association Secondary/High School Scholarships *(Undergraduate/Scholarship)* [3864]
International Grenfell Association University/College Scholarships *(Undergraduate/Scholarship)* [3865]
International Municipal Lawyers Association Canadian Scholarships *(Professional Development/Scholarship)* [3878]
International Sanitary Supply Association Foundation Scholarships *(High School/Scholarship)* [2030]
Dr. Karl C. Ivarson Scholarships *(Postgraduate/Scholarship)* [36]
Terry Jarvis Memorial Scholarships *(Undergraduate/Scholarship)* [1165]
JAUW Fellowship Awards *(Postgraduate/Fellowship)* [1960]
Right Hon. Michaelle Jean Scholarships *(Undergraduate/Scholarship)* [1736]
Harry Jerome Scholarships *(Undergraduate/Scholarship)* [1737]
Johnson & Johnson Scholarships *(Undergraduate/Scholarship)* [2002]
Kalmen Kaplansky Scholarships in Economic and Social Rights *(Graduate/Scholarship)* [2730]
Lucile B. Kaufman Women's Scholarships *(Undergraduate/Scholarship)* [6493]
E. Wayne Kay Co-op Scholarships *(Undergraduate/Scholarship)* [6494]
E. Wayne Kay Community College Scholarships *(Undergraduate/Scholarship)* [6495]
Dorothy Kergin Scholarships *(Doctorate/Scholarship)* [2003]
Khaki University and Y.M.C.A. Memorial Scholarships *(Undergraduate/Scholarship)* [7225]
Kildonan Education Awards *(Undergraduate/Scholarship)* [5425]
Helen and George Kilik Scholarship *(Undergraduate/Scholarship)* [161]
Killam Fellowships Program *(Undergraduate/Fellowship)* [7033]
Mackenzie King Open Scholarships *(Graduate/Scholarship)* [4428]
Anna and John Kolesay Memorial Scholarship *(Undergraduate/Scholarship)* [162]
Bernie Kom Memorial Awards *(Postgraduate/Award/Prize)* [6268]
Korean Studies Dissertation Workshop Funds *(Graduate/Grant)* [6416]
Kress Pre-Doctoral Fellowships in the History of Art and Archeology in Turkey *(Postdoctorate/Fellowship)* [898]
Leo J. Krysa Family Undergraduate Scholarships *(Undergraduate/Scholarship)* [1982]
Leila Klinger Kurtzman Mamorial Scholarship Fund *(Undergraduate/Scholarship)* [3558]
Allen T. Lambert Scholarships *(Postgraduate/Scholarship)* [6269]
John and Lois Lamont Graduate Scholarships *(Postgraduate/Award/Prize)* [1957]
James D. Lang Memorial Scholarships *(Graduate/Scholarship)* [1932]
Jason Lang Scholarship *(Undergraduate/Scholarship)* [163]
Language Teacher Bursary Program Awards *(Professional Development/Award/Prize)* [164]
Languages In Teacher Education Scholarships *(Professional Development/Scholarship)* [165]
Larson Aquatic Research Support *(Graduate/Scholarship)* [1144]
Karen E. Latt Memorial Scholarship *(Undergraduate/Scholarship)* [3559]
Kenneth Laundy Entrance Scholarships *(Postgraduate/Scholarship)* [6270]
Law Foundation of British Columbia Graduate Fellowships *(Undergraduate/Fellowship)* [4147]
Le Cordon Bleu Ottawa Culinary Arts Institute Basic Cuisine Certificate Scholarships *(All, Professional Development/Scholarship)* [2580]
The Leaders of Tomorrow Scholarships *(Undergraduate/Scholarship)* [2813]
Leber Rubes Inc. Awards *(Postgraduate/Award/Prize)* [1964]
Carol Anne Letheren Entrance Awards *(Postgraduate/Award/Prize)* [6271]
Irene Brand Lieberman Scholarship *(Postgraduate/Scholarship)* [3560]
Tecla Lin & Nelia Laroza Memorial Scholarships *(Undergraduate/Scholarship)* [2004]
Ian Lithgow Memorial Awards *(Postgraduate/Award/Prize)* [6272]
Lo Family Scholarships *(Undergraduate/Scholarship)* [7226]
Sir James Lougheed Awards of Distinction *(Doctorate, Graduate/Award/Prize)* [166]
Gertrude and Edith Lowidt and Mary Catherine Preiss Memorial Bursaries in Nutritional Sciences *(Undergraduate/Scholarship)* [7227]
John Macara, Barrister of Goderich, Scholarships *(Undergraduate/Scholarship)* [7228]
Major Collaborative Research Initiatives Grants *(Graduate/Grant)* [6419]
Marathon Pulp Inc. Education Achievement Scholarships *(Undergraduate/Scholarship)* [6885]
Dick Martin Scholarships *(Postgraduate/Scholarship)* [1943]
Eleanor Martin Scholarships *(Graduate/Scholarship)* [2005]
Beverly Mascoll Scholarships *(Undergraduate/Scholarship)* [1738]
Val Mason Scholarships *(Postgraduate/Scholarship)* [2036]
Mature Student Scholarships *(Undergraduate/Scholarship)* [2880]
Giuliano Mazzetti Scholarships *(Undergraduate/Scholarship)* [6497]
Hans McCorriston Motive Power Machinist Grant Programs *(Postgraduate/Scholarship)* [1570]
Joseph McCulley Educational Scholarships *(Graduate, Undergraduate/Scholarship)* [7229]
McGill University Alma Mater Student Travel Grants *(Graduate/Grant)* [4430]
McGill University Scholarships for Research Trips to Europe *(Graduate/Scholarship)* [4431]
John J. McKetta Undergraduate Scholarships *(Undergraduate/Scholarship)* [656]
Louise McKinney Post-secondary Scholarship *(Undergraduate/Scholarship)* [167]
James H. McLaughlin Scholarships *(Undergraduate/Scholarship)* [5222]
Douglas McRorie Memorial Scholarships *(Doctorate, Graduate/Scholarship)* [37]
Jack Meadows Memorial Awards *(Undergraduate/Scholarship)* [5426]
Medical Student Summer Research Scholarships *(Undergraduate/Scholarship)* [261]
Dr. Ernest and Minnie Mehl Scholarship *(Undergraduate/Scholarship)* [168]
Meloche-Monnex Scholarships *(Doctorate/Scholarship)* [2006]
Bernard Michel Scholarships *(Undergraduate/Scholarship)* [1908]
Military Nurses Association Scholarships *(Graduate/Scholarship)* [2007]
Millennium Alberta Rural Incentive Bursary Award *(Undergraduate/Award/Prize)* [169]
Mineralogical Association of Canada Scholarships *(Postgraduate/Scholarship)* [4539]
Minerva Scholarships *(Undergraduate/Scholarship)* [1739]
Thomas More Scholarships *(Undergraduate/Scholarship)* [3260]
Dr. Henry Morgentaler Future Choice Scholarships *(Postgraduate/Award/Prize)* [1958]
John H. Moss Scholarships *(Undergraduate/Scholarship)* [7230]
Marvin Mundel Memorial Scholarships *(Undergraduate/Scholarship)* [3736]
Margaret Munro Scholarships *(Undergraduate/Scholarship)* [2008]
Helen Mussallem Scholarships *(Graduate/Scholarship)* [2009]
Myasthenia Gravis Foundation of America Post-Doctoral Fellowships *(Postdoctorate/Fellowship)* [4603]
NAAMA Scholarships *(Undergraduate/Scholarship)* [4639]
NACBS Dissertation Year Fellowships *(Postdoctorate/Fellowship)* [5217]
NACBS-Huntington Library Fellowships *(Postdoctorate/Fellowship)* [5218]
Irwin Allen Nadal Entrance Awards *(Postgraduate/Award/Prize)* [6273]
Miles Spencer Nadal Entrance Awards *(Postgraduate/Award/Prize)* [6274]
Nadine International Inc. Awards *(Postgraduate/Award/Prize)* [1965]
The National Board Technical Scholarships *(Other/Scholarship)* [4768]
National Geophysics Scholarships *(Postgraduate/Scholarship)* [7488]
National Scholarships *(Postgraduate/Scholarship)* [7489]
National Society of Accountants Scholarship Program *(Undergraduate/Scholarship)* [5047]
NAWIC Founders Undergraduate Scholarships *(Undergraduate/Scholarship)* [4750]
Dr. Ezra Nesbeth Scholarships *(Undergraduate/Scholarship)* [4002]
New Brunswick Nurses Association Scholarships *(Graduate/Scholarship)* [2010]
Frank Newman Leadership Awards *(Undergraduate/Scholarship)* [1916]
Norman Nicholson Scholarships *(Undergraduate/Scholarship)* [1937]
Sharon Nield Memorial Scholarships *(Undergraduate/Scholarship)* [2011]
Norfolk Southern Foundation Scholarships *(Undergraduate/Scholarship)* [882]
Nortel Institute Undergraduate Scholarships *(Undergraduate/Scholarship)* [7231]
Northern Alberta Development Council Bursary Award *(Undergraduate/Award/Prize)* [171]
Northern Alberta Development Council Bursary for Medical Students *(Undergraduate/Award/Prize)* [172]
Northern Alberta Development Council Bursary Partnership Program *(Undergraduate/Award/Prize)* [173]
Northern Alberta Development Council Bursary for Pharmacy Students *(Undergraduate/Scholarship)* [174]
Northern Student Supplement *(Undergraduate/Award/Prize)* [175]
Nova Scotia Salmon Association Scholarships *(All/Scholarship)* [5307]
Novo Nordisk Canada-CAS Research Awards *(Professional Development/Award/Prize)* [1917]
NSERC Canada Graduate Scholarships *(Graduate, Postdoctorate/Scholarship)* [6434]
NSERC Postgraduate Scholarships *(Graduate, Postdoctorate/Scholarship)* [6435]
NSF Pickwick Postdoctoral Research Fellowships *(Postdoctorate/Fellowship)* [5042]
Nu-Gro Corporation Turfgrass Scholarships (Graduate) *(Graduate, Postgraduate/Scholarship)* [6075]
Nu-Gro Corporation Turfgrass Scholarships (Undergraduate) *(Undergraduate/Scholarship)* [6076]

(Undergraduate/Scholarship) [2032]
World Book Graduate Scholarships in Library and Information Science (Graduate/Scholarship) [1987]
Marusia Yaworska Entrance Scholarships (Undergraduate/Scholarship) [7361]
York Graduate Scholarships (Graduate/Scholarship) [6277]
Yukon Law Foundation Scholarships (Undergraduate/Scholarship) [7551]

CANADA (BY PROVINCE)

Alberta

Alberta Award for the Study of Canadian Human Rights and Multiculturalism (Doctorate, Graduate/Award/Prize) [145]
Alberta Press Council Scholarships (Undergraduate/Scholarship) [187]
Alberta Ukrainian Centennial Commemorative Scholarships (Undergraduate/Scholarship) [7356]
Eugene Boyko Scholarships (Undergraduate/Scholarship) [140]
Robert C. Carson Memorial Bursary (Undergraduate/Scholarship) [153]
Laurence Decore Awards for Student Leadership (Undergraduate/Scholarship) [154]
Graduate Student Scholarship (Graduate/Scholarship) [157]
Grande Prairie 4-H District Scholarships (Undergraduate/Scholarship) [133]
Informatics Circle of Research Excellence Scholarships (Doctorate, Graduate/Scholarship) [159]
Jason Lang Scholarship (Undergraduate/Scholarship) [163]
Queen Elizabeth II Graduate Scholarship Program (Doctorate, Graduate/Scholarship) [178]
Servus Credit Union 4-H Scholarships (Undergraduate/Scholarship) [135]
Ralph Steinhauer Awards of Distinction (Doctorate, Graduate/Award/Prize) [185]

Ontario

Dr. Anderson Abbott Awards (Undergraduate/Scholarship) [7208]
Stephanie Ali Memorial Scholarships (Undergraduate/Scholarship) [7210]
J.P. Bickell Mining Scholarships (Undergraduate/Scholarship) [7211]
Black Canadian Scholarships (Undergraduate/Scholarship) [5419]
Anne-Marie Bonner Scholarships (Undergraduate/Scholarship) [3994]
Brown Dental Scholarships (Undergraduate/Scholarship) [3995]
Leon C. Bynoe Memorial Scholarships (Undergraduate/Scholarship) [7212]
Mary Anne Chambers Scholarships (Undergraduate/Scholarship) [3996]
Chinese-Canadian History and Culture Fellowships (Graduate/Fellowship) [7215]
Marcus Mosiah Garvey Scholarships (Undergraduate/Scholarship) [3997]
J.O. Goodman Scholarship Awards (Undergraduate/Scholarship) [5343]
Elizabeth Heath Technical, Trades Training and Development Awards (Undergraduate/Scholarship) [5423]
C.V. Hoar Scholarship Awards (Undergraduate/Scholarship) [5344]
Humber College Institute of Technology and Advanced Learning Scholarships (Undergraduate/Scholarship) [3998]
I Have a Dream Scholarships (Undergraduate/Scholarship) [3999]
Barbara Ingram, Janet W. McCarthy and W.J.P. Jack Robertson Memorial Scholarships (Undergraduate/Scholarship) [5424]
Jamaica Day Basil Duncan Memorial Scholarships (Undergraduate/Scholarship) [4000]
Jamaica National Building Society Scholarships (Undergraduate/Scholarship) [4001]
John Alexander McLean Scholarships (Undergraduate/Scholarship) [6886]
Norfolk Southern Foundation Scholarships (Undergraduate/Scholarship) [882]
OTA Education Foundation Scholarships (Undergraduate/Scholarship) [5345]
Ryerson Scholarships (Undergraduate/Scholarship) [4003]
Eva Smith Bursary (Undergraduate/Scholarship) [4004]
Brian Smith Scholarship (Undergraduate/Scholarship) [1773]
Barbara Thomas Bursary (Undergraduate/Scholarship) [4005]
University of Toronto Accenture Scholarships (Undergraduate/Scholarship) [7235]
York Regional Police Scholarships (Undergraduate/Scholarship) [4006]
Youth Affairs Committee Rising Star Scholarships (Undergraduate/Scholarship) [4007]

Prince Edward Island

Orin Carver Scholarships (Undergraduate/Scholarship) [2499]

Quebec

Marlene Brand Memorial Scholarship (Undergraduate/Scholarship) [3554]
Bernic and Gordon Brown Scholarship (All/Scholarship) [3555]
Dr. Mark Cohen Scholarship (Undergraduate/Scholarship) [3557]
Mireille and Murray Steinberg Scholarship (Postgraduate/Scholarship) [3562]

Saskatchewan

Cameco Northern Scholarships - Technical Institute (Undergraduate/Scholarship) [1906]
Bernard Michel Scholarships (Undergraduate/Scholarship) [1908]

INTERNATIONAL

S. Randolph Edmonds Young Scholars Competition (Graduate, Undergraduate/Scholarship) [1753]
Barbara and Nicole Heicox Foreign Travel and Study Scholarships Fund (Undergraduate/Scholarship) [3284]
James K. Rathmell Jr. Scholarships (Undergraduate/Scholarship) [566]
The RTKL Traveling Fellowships (Undergraduate/Fellowship) [310]

INTERNATIONAL (BY REGION)

Africa

AIMS Long-term Research Grants (Postdoctorate/Grant) [667]
AIMS Short-term Research Grants (Postdoctorate/Grant) [668]

Caribbean

AABP Student Externship Program (Undergraduate/Scholarship) [330]
Caribbean Hotel Association Academic Scholarships (Undergraduate/Scholarship) [2059]

Europe

Individual Advanced Research Opportunities Program (IARO) For Master's Student (Graduate/Grant) [3895]
Individual Advanced Research Opportunities Program (IARO) For Pre-doctoral Students (Postgraduate/Grant) [3896]
Individual Advanced Research Opportunities Program (IARO) For Professionals (Professional Development/Grant) [3897]
Individual Advanced Research Opportunities Program (IARO) for Postdoctoral Scholars (Postdoctorate/Grant) [3898]
Monte R. Mitchell Global Scholarships (Undergraduate/Scholarship) [80]

Latin America

Fellowships to Promote Research on the Legal Framework for Civil Society in Latin America, Africa and Asia (All/Fellowship) [3823]

Middle East

Research Fellowships in Iranian Studies (Resident Director-Tehran) (Doctorate, Graduate/Fellowship) [664]

North America

AAPA Research Scholarships (Undergraduate/Award/Prize) [393]
Kenneth M. Good Graduate Students Fellowship Program (Undergraduate/Fellowship) [7295]
Independent Lubricant Manufacturers Association Scholarships (Undergraduate/Scholarship) [3680]
J. Merrill Knapp Research Fellowships (Undergraduate/Fellowship) [597]
National Candy Technologist Scholarship Program (Undergraduate/Scholarship) [332]

U.S. Territories

Academic Promise Scholarships (Undergraduate/Scholarship) [3697]
ACHE/American Legion Auxiliary Scholarships (Undergraduate/Scholarship) [98]
ACHE/American Legion Scholarships (Undergraduate/Scholarship) [99]
ACHE Junior and Community College Athletic Scholarships (Undergraduate/Scholarship) [100]
ACHE Junior and Community College Performing Arts Scholarships (Undergraduate/Scholarship) [101]
ACHE Police Officers and Firefighters Survivors' Educational Assistance Programs (Undergraduate/Scholarship) [102]
ACHE Senior Adult Scholarships (Two Year College, Undergraduate/Scholarship) [103]
ACHE Two-Year College Academic Scholarships (Two Year College, Undergraduate/Scholarship) [104]
AISC/Carolina Steel Scholarships (Undergraduate/Scholarship) [676]
AISC/Fred R. Havens Fellowships (Graduate, Undergraduate/Fellowship) [677]
AISC/Great Lakes Fabricators and Erectors Association Fellowships (Graduate/Fellowship) [678]
AISC/Rocky Mountain Steel Construction Association Fellowships (Graduate/Fellowship) [679]
AISC/Southern Association of Steel Fabricators Fellowships (Graduate/Fellowship) [680]
AISC/Southern Association of Steel Fabricators Scholarships (Undergraduate/Scholarship) [681]
AISC/US Steel Fellowships (Graduate/Fellowship) [683]
AIST William E. Schwabe Memorial Scholarships (Undergraduate/Scholarship) [1443]
Alabama Gi Dependents Educational Benefit Programs (Undergraduate/Scholarship) [105]
Alabama Scholarships for Dependents of Blind Parents (Undergraduate/Scholarship) [107]
Alabama Student Assistance Programs (Undergraduate/Scholarship) [108]
Alabama Student Grant Programs (Undergraduate/Grant) [109]
American Indian Endowed Scholarships (Graduate, Undergraduate/Scholarship) [7363]
Warren M. Anderson Scholarships (Undergraduate/Scholarship) [3698]
Association of Desk and Derrick Clubs Education Trust Scholarships (Undergraduate/Scholarship) [1388]
Myrna F. Bernath Fellowships (Doctorate, Graduate/Fellowship) [6454]
Birmingham-Southern College Eagle Scout Scholarships (Undergraduate/Scholarship) [4852]
Career Advancement Scholarships

(Undergraduate/Scholarship) [1806]
Child of Alumni Book Voucher Awards *(Undergraduate/Scholarship)* [3699]
The Frank Cormier Scholarships *(Undergraduate/Scholarship)* [7409]
Dofflemyer Scholarships *(Undergraduate/Scholarship)* [4854]
Jim Doogan Memorial Scholarships *(Undergraduate/Scholarship)* [7075]
The Eneslow Pedorthic Institute Scholarships *(Undergraduate/Scholarship)* [5545]
Epsilon Tau Pi's Soaring Eagle Scholarships *(Undergraduate/Scholarship)* [4856]
John S.W. Fargher Scholarships *(Graduate/Scholarship)* [3730]
Gaebe Eagle Scout Awards *(Undergraduate/Scholarship)* [4857]
Dwight D. Gardner Scholarships *(Undergraduate/Scholarship)* [3731]
German Society Scholarships *(Undergraduate/Scholarship)* [3238]
GET Ready for Math and Science Conditional Scholarships *(Four Year College, Two Year College, Undergraduate/Scholarship)* [7365]
Gilbreth Memorial Fellowships *(Graduate/Scholarship)* [3732]
Gold Award/Eagle Scout Scholarships *(Undergraduate/Scholarship)* [4858]
Gongaware Scholarships College of Business *(Undergraduate/Scholarship)* [3700]
Jay Hammond Memorial Scholarships *(Undergraduate/Scholarship)* [7077]
Zenon C.R. Hansen Leadership Scholarships *(Undergraduate/Scholarship)* [4859]
Clinton J. Helton Manufacturing Scholarships *(Undergraduate/Scholarship)* [6491]
Indiana State Alumni Association Creative and Performing Arts Award *(Undergraduate/Scholarship)* [3701]
Indiana State Alumni Association Dean's Scholarships *(Undergraduate/Scholarship)* [3702]
Indiana State Alumni Association President's Academic Excellence Scholarships *(Undergraduate/Scholarship)* [3704]
Indiana State Alumni Association President's Scholarships *(Undergraduate/Scholarship)* [3705]
Indiana State Alumni Association Rural Health Scholarships *(Undergraduate/Scholarship)* [3706]
Indiana Top Scholar Award *(Undergraduate/Scholarship)* [3708]
Klingenstein Fellowships in the Neurosciences *(Doctorate, Professional Development/Fellowship)* [4076]
Lamar University College of Engineering Scholarships *(Undergraduate/Scholarship)* [4861]
Lindenwood University Scouting Scholarships *(Undergraduate/Scholarship)* [4862]
Lodging Management Program (LMP) Scholarships *(Undergraduate/Scholarship)* [613]
Audrey Loftus Memorial Scholarships *(Undergraduate/Scholarship)* [7078]
Marmot Leadership Scholarships *(Postgraduate, Professional Development, Undergraduate/Scholarship)* [5432]
Giuliano Mazzetti Scholarships *(Undergraduate/Scholarship)* [6497]
McDaniel College Eagle Scout Scholarships *(Undergraduate/Scholarship)* [4863]
McNamara Family Creative Arts Project Grants *(Graduate, Undergraduate/Grant)* [3601]
MESBEC Scholarships *(Undergraduate/Scholarship)* [2067]
The Aristotle Mirones Scholarships *(Undergraduate/Scholarship)* [5547]
Native American Leadership Education (NALE) Scholarships *(Postdoctorate, Undergraduate/Scholarship)* [2068]
Networks Scholarships College of Business *(Undergraduate/Scholarship)* [3710]
Newman University Scouting Scholarships *(Undergraduate/Scholarship)* [4864]
Novo Nordisk NP Doctoral Education Scholarships *(Doctorate/Scholarship)* [271]
The Oklahoma State University at Okmulgee Scholarships *(Undergraduate/Scholarship)* [5548]
The Deborah Orin-Eilbeck Scholarships *(Graduate/Scholarship)* [7410]
Outward Bound Leadership Scholarships for Educators *(Professional Development/Scholarship)* [5433]
Elizabeth M. and Winchell M. Parson Scholarships *(Doctorate/Scholarship)* [997]
Pharmavite LLC NP Doctoral Education Scholarships *(Doctorate/Scholarship)* [273]
Phi Theta Kappa Scholarships *(Undergraduate/Scholarship)* [3712]
Phillips Fund Grant for Native American Research *(Graduate/Grant)* [771]
The Sidney M. Pols Scholarships *(Undergraduate/Scholarship)* [5549]
A.O. Putnam Memorial Scholarships *(Undergraduate/Scholarship)* [3738]
Research Grants in Comparative Studies of Modern Turkey *(Graduate, Postdoctorate/Grant)* [3757]
Rocky Mountain Coal Mining Institute Engineering/Geology Scholarships *(Undergraduate/Scholarship)* [6051]
Rocky Mountain Coal Mining Institute Technical Scholarships *(Undergraduate/Scholarship)* [6052]
Saint Vincent College Eagle Scout Scholarships *(Undergraduate/Scholarship)* [4865]
The Dr. William M. Scholl College of Podiatric Medicine Scholarships *(Undergraduate/Scholarship)* [5550]
Alice Schulman Simmons Scholarships for UU Women *(Undergraduate/Scholarship)* [6954]
SME Directors Scholarships *(Undergraduate/Scholarship)* [6502]
SME Ford PAS Scholarships *(Undergraduate/Scholarship)* [6504]
Joseph Sumner Smith Scholarships *(All/Scholarship)* [6955]
Sycamore Scholar Awards *(Undergraduate/Scholarship)* [3713]
Tribal Business Management Program (TBM) Scholarships *(Undergraduate/Scholarship)* [2069]
Harry S. Truman Scholarships *(Postgraduate/Scholarship)* [6930]
UAF Alumni Association Scholarships *(Undergraduate/Scholarship)* [7079]
University of Louisville Eagle Scout Scholarships *(Undergraduate/Scholarship)* [4866]
University of Phoenix Touchdown Mondays Scholarship Program *(All/Scholarship)* [2592]
Washington Higher Education Coordinating Board Educational Opportunity Grants *(Undergraduate/Grant)* [7367]
The Wolf Trap Internship Program *(Graduate, Professional Development, Undergraduate/Internship)* [7475]
Women's Jewelry Association Member Grants *(All/Grant)* [7498]
Women's Jewelry Association Scholarships *(Undergraduate/Scholarship)* [7499]
The Xtra Depth University Scholarships *(Undergraduate/Scholarship)* [5551]

INTERNATIONAL (BY COUNTRY)

Austria

Barbara Potter Scholarships *(All/Scholarship)* [741]

Bangladesh

AIBS Junior Fellowships *(Doctorate/Fellowship)* [652]
AIBS Senior Fellowships *(Doctorate, Postdoctorate/Fellowship)* [653]

British Virgin Islands

Judith A. Towle Environmental Studies Fund *(Undergraduate/Fellowship)* [3966]

Denmark

Edith and Arnold N. Bodtker Grant *(All/Grant)* [2613]

Federated States of Micronesia

APIASF Scholarships *(Undergraduate/Scholarship)* [1340]

France

French Embassy Scholarships *(Other/Scholarship)* [5264]
NFID Advanced Vaccinology Course Travel Grants *(Postdoctorate/Grant)* [4904]

Germany

DAAD Study Scholarship Awards *(Graduate/Scholarship)* [3223]
DAAD Undergraduate Scholarship Program *(Undergraduate/Scholarship)* [3224]
The Christoph Daniel Ebeling Fellowships *(Doctorate/Fellowship)* [302]
European College of Liberal Arts (ECLA) Scholarships *(Undergraduate/Scholarship)* [7022]
Faculty Research Visit Grant *(Doctorate/Grant)* [3225]
Goethe-Institut AATG Scholarships *(Other/Scholarship)* [5265]
Intensive Language Course Grants *(Doctorate/Grant)* [3227]
Learn German in Germany *(Doctorate/Grant)* [3229]
Study Scholarships for Artists or Musicians *(Graduate/Scholarship)* [3230]
University Summer Course Grants *(Undergraduate/Grant)* [3231]

Guam

APIASF Scholarships *(Undergraduate/Scholarship)* [1340]
Thomas R. Camp Scholarships *(Graduate/Scholarship)* [1142]
Hispanic Scholarship Fund (HSF) College Scholarship Program *(Graduate, Undergraduate/Scholarship)* [3591]
HSBC-North America Scholarship Program *(Undergraduate/Scholarship)* [3592]
HSF/Atrisco Heritage Foundation Scholarship Program *(Graduate, Undergraduate/Scholarship)* [3593]
HSF/General Motors Scholarship Program *(Undergraduate/Scholarship)* [3595]
Larson Aquatic Research Support *(Graduate/Scholarship)* [1144]

Israel

Sidney M. Edelstein Fellowships *(Doctorate, Postdoctorate/Fellowship)* [2109]
Jane R. Glaser Scholarships *(Undergraduate/Scholarship)* [1124]
Ollie Rosenberg Scholarship Travel Fund *(Undergraduate/Scholarship)* [3118]

Japan

Japan Foundation, New York Doctoral Fellowship Program *(Doctorate/Fellowship)* [4009]
Japan Foundation, New York Research Fellowship Program *(Undergraduate/Fellowship)* [4010]
Japan Foundation, New York Short-Term Fellowship Program *(Doctorate/Fellowship)* [4011]
Long-Term Postdoctoral Fellowships for Biomedi-

cal and Behavioral Research in Japan *(Professional Development/Fellowship)* [1715]

Marshall Islands

APIASF Scholarships *(Undergraduate/Scholarship)* [1340]

Mexico

Stan Beck Fellowships *(Undergraduate/Fellowship)* [2861]
BioQuip Scholarships *(Undergraduate/Scholarship)* [2862]
Thomas R. Camp Scholarships *(Graduate/Scholarship)* [1142]
Ginger and Fred Deines Mexico Scholarships *(Undergraduate/Scholarship)* [6918]
Dwight D. Gardner Scholarships *(Undergraduate/Scholarship)* [3731]
Geological Society of America Graduate Student Research Grants *(Doctorate, Graduate/Grant)* [3210]
Gilbreth Memorial Fellowships *(Graduate/Scholarship)* [3732]
IIE Council of Fellows Undergraduate Scholarships *(Undergraduate/Scholarship)* [3733]
Larson Aquatic Research Support *(Graduate/Scholarship)* [1144]
John J. McKetta Undergraduate Scholarships *(Undergraduate/Scholarship)* [656]
Marvin Mundel Memorial Scholarships *(Undergraduate/Scholarship)* [3736]
NWF's Women for Sustainable Development (WSD) Scholarships *(Undergraduate/Scholarship)* [6333]
A.O. Putnam Memorial Scholarships *(Undergraduate/Scholarship)* [3738]
Ronald L. Schmied Scholarships *(Professional Development, Undergraduate/Grant)* [3388]
United Parcel Service Scholarship for Female Students *(Undergraduate/Scholarship)* [3740]
United Parcel Service Scholarship for Minority Students *(Undergraduate/Scholarship)* [3741]
Abel Wolman Fellowships *(Doctorate/Fellowship)* [1145]

Northern Mariana Islands

APIASF Scholarships *(Undergraduate/Scholarship)* [1340]

Norway

Sons of Norway Foundation Scholarships to Oslo International School *(Undergraduate/Scholarship)* [6604]

Palau

APIASF Scholarships *(Undergraduate/Scholarship)* [1340]

Poland

Tadeusz Sendzimir Scholarships *(Undergraduate/Scholarship)* [3496]

Puerto Rico

Thomas R. Camp Scholarships *(Graduate/Scholarship)* [1142]
Hispanic Scholarship Fund (HSF) College Scholarship Program *(Graduate, Undergraduate/Scholarship)* [3591]
HSBC-North America Scholarship Program *(Undergraduate/Scholarship)* [3592]
HSF/Atrisco Heritage Foundation Scholarship Program *(Graduate, Undergraduate/Scholarship)* [3593]
HSF/General Motors Scholarship Program *(Undergraduate/Scholarship)* [3595]
Larson Aquatic Research Support *(Graduate/Scholarship)* [1144]
McNamara Family Creative Arts Project Grants *(Graduate, Undergraduate/Grant)* [3601]

Spain

Spanish Embassy Scholarships *(Graduate, Other/Scholarship)* [5267]

St. Kitts and Nevis

Judith A. Towle Environmental Studies Fund *(Undergraduate/Fellowship)* [3966]

Sweden

Lilly Lorenzen Scholarships *(Undergraduate/Scholarship)* [1119]
Malmberg Fellowships *(Undergraduate/Fellowship)* [1120]
Malmberg Scholarships *(Undergraduate/Scholarship)* [1121]

Turkey

Institute of Turkish Studies Sabbatical Research Grants *(Professional Development/Grant)* [3754]
Institute of Turkish Studies Undergraduate Study Grants *(Undergraduate/Grant)* [3755]
Post-Doctoral Summer Travel-Research Grants *(Doctorate/Grant)* [3756]
Summer Language Study Grants in Turkey *(Graduate/Grant)* [3758]
Summer Research Grants in Turkey *(Graduate/Grant)* [3759]

Ukraine

Alberta Ukrainian Centennial Commemorative Scholarships *(Undergraduate/Scholarship)* [7356]
Mychajlo Dmytrenko Fine Arts Foundation Scholarships *(Undergraduate/Scholarship)* [7021]

United Kingdom

Mackenzie King Travelling Scholarships *(Graduate/Scholarship)* [4429]
USA/USA-Ukramerazha Scholarships *(Undergraduate/Scholarship)* [7024]

United Republic of Tanzania

Godparents for Tanzania Scholarships *(Undergraduate/Scholarship)* [3246]

Virgin Islands of the United States

Hispanic Scholarship Fund (HSF) College Scholarship Program *(Graduate, Undergraduate/Scholarship)* [3591]
HSBC-North America Scholarship Program *(Undergraduate/Scholarship)* [3592]
HSF/Atrisco Heritage Foundation Scholarship Program *(Graduate, Undergraduate/Scholarship)* [3593]
HSF/General Motors Scholarship Program *(Undergraduate/Scholarship)* [3595]
McNamara Family Creative Arts Project Grants *(Graduate, Undergraduate/Grant)* [3601]

Special Recipient Index

This index arranges awards according to qualifying factors related to membership or affiliation. Awards are listed under all appropriate headings. Each citation is followed by the study level and award type, which appear in parentheses. Numbers following the parenthetical information indicate the book entry number for particular awards, not page numbers.

African American

AALL & Thomson West - George A. Strait Minority Scholarship Endowment *(Postgraduate/Scholarship)* [364]
Actuarial Scholarships for Minority Students *(Undergraduate/Scholarship)* [383]
Affirmative Action Mini Grant and Student Scholarships *(All/Grant)* [14]
Affirmative Action Scholarships *(Graduate/Scholarship)* [6680]
African American Network - Carolinas Scholarship Fund *(Undergraduate/Scholarship)* [3037]
AICPA Scholarships for Graduate Accounting Students *(Postgraduate/Scholarship)* [4641]
AICPA Scholarships for Minority Accounting Students *(Undergraduate/Scholarship)* [4642]
Air Products and Chemicals, Inc. Scholarships *(Undergraduate/Scholarship)* [1429]
Emma and Meloid Algood Tuition Scholarships *(Undergraduate/Scholarship)* [4664]
Dorothy G. Allsop Scholarships *(Undergraduate/Scholarship)* [4721]
AMA Foundation Minority Scholars Award *(Undergraduate/Scholarship)* [712]
American Dream Scholarship Program *(Undergraduate/Scholarship)* [6155]
American Foundation for Pharmaceutical Education Pre-Doctoral Fellowships in the Pharmaceutical Sciences *(Doctorate/Fellowship)* [578]
APA Planning Fellowships *(Graduate/Fellowship)* [776]
APS Scholarships for Minority Undergraduate Physics Majors *(Undergraduate/Scholarship)* [5051]
AWG Minority Scholarships *(Undergraduate/Scholarship)* [1509]
Michael Baker Corporation Scholarship Program *(Undergraduate/Scholarship)* [1430]
Ballard Family Foundation Scholarships *(Undergraduate/Scholarship)* [6169]
Beacon of Hope Scholarships *(Undergraduate/Scholarship)* [1608]
Dr. Joyce Beckett Scholarships *(Undergraduate/Scholarship)* [4665]
Black Student Fund *(High School/Scholarship)* [1722]
Emma L. Bowen Foundation Scholarships for Minority Interests in Media work/study Program *(Undergraduate/Scholarship)* [7333]
Selena Danette Brown Book Scholarships *(Undergraduate/Scholarship)* [4666]
California Community Service Scholarships *(Undergraduate/Scholarship)* [4985]
California Community Service Scholarships - Bay Area *(Undergraduate/Scholarship)* [4986]
The Robert A Catlin/David W. Long Memorial Scholarship *(Undergraduate/Scholarship)* [2996]
Robert A. Catlin/David W. Long Memorial Scholarships *(Graduate/Scholarship)* [777]
Cherry Lane Foundation/Music Alive! Scholarships *(Undergraduate/Scholarship)* [941]
CIGNA Healthcare Graduate Scholarships *(Graduate/Scholarship)* [4892]
CIGNA Healthcare Undergraduate Scholarships *(Undergraduate/Scholarship)* [4893]
Johnnie L. Cochran, Jr./MWH Scholarships *(Undergraduate/Scholarship)* [4894]
Delta Sigma Theta Hartford Alumnae Scholarships *(Undergraduate/Scholarship)* [3442]
Ruth DeMoss Scholarships *(Undergraduate/Scholarship)* [6184]
Development Fund for Black Students in Science and Technology Scholarship *(Undergraduate/Scholarship)* [2707]
Joseph M. Dorgan Scholarships *(Undergraduate/Scholarship)* [2739]
DRI Law Student Diversity Scholarships *(Undergraduate/Scholarship)* [1755]
Dunbar Heritage Scholarships *(Undergraduate/Scholarship)* [6650]
Evans and Petree Law Firm Scholarships *(Undergraduate/Scholarship)* [7113]
Franchise Law Diversity Scholarship Awards *(Undergraduate/Scholarship)* [3857]
John Hope Franklin Dissertation Fellowships *(Doctorate/Fellowship)* [768]
Richard Gregory Freeland, II Educational Scholarships *(High School/Scholarship)* [1762]
Fuchs-Harden Educational Scholarships Fund *(Undergraduate/Scholarship)* [3375]
The Future Colleagues Scholarships *(Undergraduate/Scholarship)* [4895]
The Gates Millennium Scholars *(Undergraduate/Scholarship)* [3590]
Gerber Fellowships in Pediatric Nutrition *(Undergraduate/Fellowship)* [4987]
Guynn Family Foundation Book Scholarships *(Undergraduate/Scholarship)* [4667]
The Richard D. Hailey AAJ Law Student Scholarships *(Undergraduate/Scholarship)* [358]
HDR Engineering, Inc. Scholarship for Diversity in Engineering *(Undergraduate/Scholarship)* [1432]
HSF/Hewlett Packard (HP) Diversity in Education Scholarship Program *(Undergraduate/Scholarship)* [3596]
The Hyatt Hotels Fund For Minority Lodging Management Students *(Undergraduate/Scholarship)* [611]
Ruth E. Jenkins Scholarships *(Undergraduate/Scholarship)* [6196]
W.K. Kellogg Foundation Doctoral Fellowships in Health Policy *(Professional Development/Fellowship)* [4988]
Martin Luther King Law Scholarships *(Undergraduate/Scholarship)* [2754]
KPMG Foundation Minority Accounting Doctoral Scholarships *(Postdoctorate/Scholarship)* [4097]
Land-Use Planning Scholarships *(Graduate/Scholarship)* [4896]
Lewis-Clark State College/American Chemical Society Scholars Program *(Undergraduate/Scholarship)* [4192]
LITA and LSSI Minority Scholarships *(Graduate/Scholarship)* [4237]
LITA/OCLC Minority Scholarships *(Graduate/Scholarship)* [4238]
Audre Lord Scholarships *(Graduate, Undergraduate/Scholarship)* [6119]
Willie T. Loud - CH2M Hill Scholarships *(Undergraduate/Scholarship)* [4897]
Dr. Julianne Malveaux Scholarships *(Undergraduate/Scholarship)* [4722]
Marathon Oil Corporation College Scholarship Program *(Graduate, Undergraduate/Scholarship)* [3600]
McKinley Financial Scholarships *(Graduate, Undergraduate/Scholarship)* [4898]
Minorities in Government Finance Scholarships *(Graduate, Undergraduate/Scholarship)* [3266]
Minority Pharmacy Faculty New Investigator Grants *(Professional Development/Grant)* [581]
Minority Student Gateway to Research Scholarships *(Professional Development/Scholarship)* [582]
Minority Teachers of Illinois Scholarships *(Undergraduate/Scholarship)* [3670]
MLA/NLM Spectrum Scholarship Program *(Graduate/Scholarship)* [4445]
MLA Scholarships for Minority Students *(Graduate/Scholarship)* [4447]
Archie Motley Memorial Scholarships for Minority Students *(Graduate/Scholarship)* [4511]
NANBPWC National Scholarships *(Undergraduate/Scholarship)* [4723]
NANBPWC Woman of Substance Scholarships *(Undergraduate/Scholarship)* [4724]
National Association of Campus Activities Multicultural Scholarship Programs *(Undergraduate/Scholarship)* [4680]
National College Scholarship Award *(Undergraduate/Scholarship)* [3970]
National Dental Hygienists' Association Scholarships *(Undergraduate/Scholarship)* [4846]
National Medical Fellowships Need-Based Scholarships *(Undergraduate/Scholarship)* [4989]
Nevada Black Police Association Scholarships *(Undergraduate/Scholarship)* [5844]
NFBPA/CDM Scholarships *(Undergraduate/Scholarship)* [4899]
Ohio Newspaper Association Minority Scholarships *(Undergraduate/Scholarship)* [5323]
Pearman Family Scholarships *(Undergraduate/Scholarship)* [6212]
Judith McManus Price Scholarships *(Graduate, Undergraduate/Scholarship)* [780]
RA Consulting Service Maria Riley Scholarships *(Graduate, Undergraduate/Scholarship)* [4900]
Jerrothia Allenfonzo Riggs & Anna & Dorothy Mae Barnes Scholarships *(Undergraduate/Scholarship)* [1899]
Ronald McDonald House Charities African American Future Achievers Scholarships *(Undergraduate/Scholarship)* [4407]
SACHS Foundation Undergraduate Scholarships for Colorado Black Students *(High School/Scholarship)* [6091]
Carl A. Scott Book Scholarships *(Undergraduate/Scholarship)* [2555]
Faith Speckhard Scholarships *(Undergraduate/Scholarship)* [3989]
Fraser Stryker Diversity Scholarship Program *(Undergraduate/Scholarship)* [5166]
Fraser Stryker Diversity Scholarships *(Undergraduate/Scholarship)* [6809]

Jacki Tuckfield Memorial Graduate Business Scholarship Fund *(Undergraduate/Scholarship)* [2603]
The UCSD Black Alumni Scholarship for Arts and Humanities *(Undergraduate/Scholarship)* [6236]
The UCSD Black Alumni Scholarships for Engineering, Mathematics and Science *(Undergraduate/Scholarship)* [6237]
University of Wisconsin-Madison African American Alumni Scholarships *(Undergraduate/Scholarship)* [7271]
Valuing Diversity PhD Scholarships *(Doctorate/Scholarship)* [710]
Earl Warren Shearman and Sterling Scholarships *(Graduate/Scholarship)* [4606]
Washington Metropolitan Scholarships *(Undergraduate/Scholarship)* [7374]
Francis X. Weninger Scholarships *(Undergraduate/Scholarship)* [7534]
Ann Cook Whitman Washington, DC Scholarships *(Undergraduate/Scholarship)* [2844]
Leon Williams Scholarships *(Undergraduate/Scholarship)* [6240]
Cenie Jomo Williams Tuition Scholarships *(Undergraduate/Scholarship)* [4668]
Hugh and Helen Wood Nepales Scholarship *(Undergraduate/Scholarship)* [1632]
Writers of Passage Scholarship Program *(Undergraduate/Prize)* [6159]

Asian American

AALL & Thomson West - George A. Strait Minority Scholarship Endowment *(Postgraduate/Scholarship)* [364]
Kyutaro & Yasuo Abiko Memorial Scholarships *(Undergraduate/Scholarship)* [4015]
Affirmative Action Mini Grant and Student Scholarships *(All/Grant)* [14]
Affirmative Action Scholarships *(Graduate/Scholarship)* [6680]
AICPA Scholarships for Graduate Accounting Students *(Postgraduate/Scholarship)* [4641]
AICPA Scholarships for Minority Accounting Students *(Undergraduate/Scholarship)* [4642]
Air Products and Chemicals, Inc. Scholarships *(Undergraduate/Scholarship)* [1429]
Paul Shearman Allen and Associate Scholarships *(Undergraduate/Scholarship)* [7003]
Anheuser-Busch NAPABA Law Foundation Presidential Scholarships *(Undergraduate/Scholarship)* [4646]
APALA Scholarship Program *(Doctorate, Graduate/Scholarship)* [1336]
APIASF Scholarships *(Undergraduate/Scholarship)* [1340]
Asian American Lawyers Associations of Massachusetts Scholarships *(Undergraduate/Scholarship)* [1332]
Asian American Scholarships *(Undergraduate/Scholarship)* [7004]
Asian/Pacific Gays and Friends Scholarships *(Undergraduate/Scholarship)* [6097]
Michael Baker Corporation Scholarship Program *(Undergraduate/Scholarship)* [1430]
Emma L. Bowen Foundation Scholarships for Minority Interests in Media work/study Program *(Undergraduate/Scholarship)* [7333]
George Choy Memorial/Gay Asian Pacific Alliance (GAPA) Scholarships *(Undergraduate/Scholarship)* [6100]
Darden Restaurants Scholarships *(Undergraduate/Scholarship)* [7005]
DRI Law Student Diversity Scholarships *(Undergraduate/Scholarship)* [1755]
Alice Yuriko Endo Memorial Scholarships *(Undergraduate/Scholarship)* [4016]
Franchise Law Diversity Scholarship Awards *(Undergraduate/Scholarship)* [3857]
The Gates Millennium Scholars *(Undergraduate/Scholarship)* [3590]
The Richard D. Hailey AAJ Law Student Scholarships *(Undergraduate/Scholarship)* [358]
Thomas T. Hayashi Memorial Scholarships *(Graduate, Undergraduate/Scholarship)* [4017]
HDR Engineering, Inc. Scholarship for Diversity in Engineering *(Undergraduate/Scholarship)* [1432]
Home Depot Scholarships *(Undergraduate/Scholarship)* [7006]
Magoichi & Shizuko Kato Memorial Scholarships *(Graduate/Scholarship)* [4018]
W.K. Kellogg Foundation Doctoral Fellowships in Health Policy *(Professional Development/Fellowship)* [4988]
Sam S. Kuwahara Memorial Scholarships *(Undergraduate/Scholarship)* [4019]
Danny T. Le Memorial Scholarships *(High School, Undergraduate/Scholarship)* [7321]
Bruce Lee Scholarships *(Undergraduate/Scholarship)* [7007]
LeePapa and Associates Scholarship for Travel *(Graduate, Undergraduate/Scholarship)* [7008]
Herbert Lehman Education Scholarships *(Undergraduate/Scholarship)* [7345]
LITA and LSSI Minority Scholarships *(Graduate/Scholarship)* [4237]
LITA/OCLC Minority Scholarships *(Graduate/Scholarship)* [4238]
Marathon Oil Corporation College Scholarship Program *(Graduate, Undergraduate/Scholarship)* [3600]
Minorities in Government Finance Scholarships *(Graduate, Undergraduate/Scholarship)* [3266]
Minority Teachers of Illinois Scholarships *(Undergraduate/Scholarship)* [3670]
MLA/NLM Spectrum Scholarship Program *(Graduate/Scholarship)* [4445]
MLA Scholarships for Minority Students *(Graduate/Scholarship)* [4447]
Archie Motley Memorial Scholarships for Minority Students *(Graduate/Scholarship)* [4511]
Ruth Mu-Lan and James S.C. Chao Scholarship *(Undergraduate/Scholarship)* [7009]
Gongoro Nakamura Memorial Scholarships *(Undergraduate/Scholarship)* [4020]
National Association of Campus Activities Multicultural Scholarship Programs *(Undergraduate/Scholarship)* [4680]
Le Hoang Nguyen (LHN) College Scholarships *(High School/Scholarship)* [7322]
The Thuy Nguyen Scholarships *(High School/Scholarship)* [7323]
Ohio Newspaper Association Minority Scholarships *(Undergraduate/Scholarship)* [5323]
Pepsico Scholarships *(Undergraduate/Scholarship)* [7010]
Philip Morris USA Scholarships *(Undergraduate/Scholarship)* [7011]
Ken and Pam Pong Scholarships *(Undergraduate/Scholarship)* [7012]
Ronald McDonald House Charities Scholarships in Asia *(Undergraduate/Scholarship)* [4410]
Drs. Poh Shien and Judy Young Scholarships *(Undergraduate/Scholarship)* [7013]
Dr. Kiyoshi Sonoda Memorial Scholarships *(Graduate/Scholarship)* [4021]
Fraser Stryker Diversity Scholarship Program *(Undergraduate/Scholarship)* [5166]
Fraser Stryker Diversity Scholarships *(Undergraduate/Scholarship)* [6809]
Taiwanese American Community Scholarships *(Undergraduate/Scholarship)* [6838]
Telamon Scholarships *(Undergraduate/Scholarship)* [7014]
Vera Tran Memorial Scholarships *(Undergraduate/Scholarship)* [7324]
U.S. Pan Asian American Chamber of Commerce CBS Scholarships *(Undergraduate/Scholarship)* [7015]
U.S. Pan Asian American Chamber of Commerce McDonald's Scholarships *(Undergraduate/Scholarship)* [7016]
U.S. Pan Asian American Chamber of Commerce UPS Scholarships *(Undergraduate/Scholarship)* [7017]
Minoru Yasui Memorial Scholarship *(Graduate/Scholarship)* [4022]

Association

4th Infantry Division Association Scholarships *(Four Year College, Postgraduate, Two Year College/Scholarship)* [4613]
AAAA Scholarship Program *(Undergraduate/Scholarship)* [1299]
AAACN Scholarships *(Undergraduate/Scholarship)* [320]
AABA Read Carlock Memorial Scholarship Fund *(Professional Development/Scholarship)* [1206]
AABP Bovine Veterinary Student Recognition Award *(Undergraduate/Scholarship)* [327]
AABP Education Grants *(Undergraduate/Grant)* [328]
AABP Research Assistantship *(Doctorate/Scholarship)* [329]
AAGS Graduate Fellowship Award *(Undergraduate/Fellowship)* [481]
AAGS Joseph F. Dracup Scholarship Award *(Undergraduate/Scholarship)* [482]
AAJ Trial Advocacy Scholarships *(Undergraduate/Scholarship)* [357]
AALL Scholarships for Continuing Education Classes *(Postgraduate/Scholarship)* [362]
AALL Scholarships for Library School Graduates Seeking a Non-Law Degree *(Postgraduate/Scholarship)* [363]
AAPA Research Scholarships *(Undergraduate/Award/Prize)* [393]
AAS-American Historical Print Collectors Society Fellowships *(Doctorate/Fellowship)* [294]
AAS-American Society for Eighteenth Century Studies Fellowships *(Postdoctorate/Fellowship)* [295]
AAS Fellowships for Creative and Performing Artists and Writers *(All/Fellowship)* [296]
AAS National Endowment for the Humanities Long-Term Fellowships *(Postdoctorate/Fellowship)* [297]
AAS-Northeast Modern Language Association Fellowships *(All/Fellowship)* [298]
AATA Anniversary Scholarships *(Graduate/Scholarship)* [312]
AAUW Legal Advocacy Fund Career Development Grants *(Professional Development/Grant)* [5]
ABA Academic Merit Scholarships *(Undergraduate/Scholarship)* [445]
ABA Members Scholarships (ABA Bus and Tour Operators Only) *(Undergraduate/Scholarship)* [447]
ABA Members Scholarships (All ABA Member Companies) *(Undergraduate/Scholarship)* [448]
ABA Scholarships *(Undergraduate/Scholarship)* [437]
Abbott Scholarships *(Undergraduate/Scholarship)* [6822]
ABC-Clio Research Grants *(Graduate/Grant)* [6514]
Abercrombie and Fitch Global Diversity Scholar Awards *(High School/Scholarship)* [5066]
Ruth Abernathy Presidential Scholarships *(Graduate, Undergraduate/Scholarship)* [351]
Academic Scholarship Program A *(Undergraduate/Scholarship)* [4843]
Academic Scholarship Program B *(Undergraduate/Scholarship)* [4844]
The Access Intelligence Scholarships *(Graduate, Undergraduate/Scholarship)* [6580]
Renee Achter Scholarship Program *(Postgraduate/Scholarship)* [726]
Naida Ackley Scholarship Program *(Postgraduate/Scholarship)* [727]
Jack Ackroyd Scholarships *(Professional Development/Scholarship)* [1925]
ACLS Frederick Burkhardt Fellowships *(Professional Development/Fellowship)* [299]
ACNM Foundation, Inc. Fellowship for Graduate Education *(Doctorate, Postdoctorate/Fellowship)* [469]
ACNP Nurse Practitioner Student Scholarship Awards *(Undergraduate/Scholarship)* [473]
ACS/ASA Health Policy and Management Scholarships *(Professional Development/Scholarship)* [1117]
ACSM Fellowship Scholarships *(Undergraduate/Scholarship)* [483]
Ed Adams Memorial Scholarships *(Professional Development/Scholarship)* [6030]
Advertising Production Club Scholarship Awards

(Graduate, Undergraduate/Scholarship) [28]
AE Flight Training Scholarships (Professional Development/Scholarship) [5206]
AE Jet Type Rating Scholarships (Professional Development/Scholarship) [5207]
AE Technical Training Scholarships (Professional Development/Scholarship) [5208]
AFIA Scholarships (Undergraduate/Scholarship) [573]
AFROTC Scholarships (Undergraduate/Scholarship) [46]
AFSA Chapter 155 Division 1 Scholarships - Category 1 (Undergraduate/Scholarship) [56]
AFSA Chapter 155 Division 1 Scholarships - Category 2 (Undergraduate/Scholarship) [57]
AFSA Chapter 155 Division 1 Scholarships - Category 3 (Undergraduate/Scholarship) [58]
AFSA Scholarship Program (Undergraduate/Scholarship) [54]
AGC Foundation Outstanding Educator Awards (Professional Development/Award/Prize) [1344]
AGC New York State Chapter Scholarship Program (Undergraduate/Scholarship) [1427]
Ahepa Buckeye Scholarship Awards (Undergraduate/Scholarship) [42]
AHNS-ACS Career Development Awards (Professional Development/Grant) [599]
AHNS Young Investigator Awards (Professional Development/Grant) [601]
AIA and the Global Automotive Aftermarket Symposium Scholarships (Undergraduate/Scholarship) [1569]
AIChE/Donald F. and Mildred Topp Othmer National Scholarship Awards (Undergraduate/Scholarship) [655]
AIMS Long-term Research Grants (Postdoctorate/Grant) [667]
AIMS Short-term Research Grants (Postdoctorate/Grant) [668]
Air Force Association/Grantham Scholarships (Undergraduate/Scholarship) [48]
Air Force Association Spouse Scholarships (Undergraduate/Scholarship) [49]
Air Traffic Control Association Full-time Employee Student Scholarships (Other/Scholarship) [62]
Air Traffic Control Association Non-employee Student Scholarships (Undergraduate/Scholarship) [63]
AISC/Carolina Steel Scholarships (Undergraduate/Scholarship) [676]
AISC/Fred R. Havens Fellowships (Graduate, Undergraduate/Fellowship) [677]
AISC/Great Lakes Fabricators and Erectors Association Fellowships (Graduate/Fellowship) [678]
AISC/Rocky Mountain Steel Construction Association Fellowships (Graduate/Fellowship) [679]
AISC/Southern Association of Steel Fabricators Fellowships (Graduate/Fellowship) [680]
AISC/Southern Association of Steel Fabricators Scholarships (Undergraduate/Scholarship) [681]
AISC/Structural Steel Education Council Fellowships (Graduate/Fellowship) [682]
AISC/US Steel Fellowships (Graduate/Fellowship) [683]
AIST Baltimore Chapter Scholarships (Undergraduate/Scholarship) [1438]
AIST Detroit Chapter Scholarships (Undergraduate/Scholarship) [1439]
AIST Northwest Chapter Scholarships (Undergraduate/Scholarship) [1440]
AIST Ronald E. Lincoln Memorial Scholarships (Undergraduate/Scholarship) [1441]
AIST San Francisco Chapter Scholarships (Undergraduate/Scholarship) [1442]
AIST William E. Schwabe Memorial Scholarships (Undergraduate/Scholarship) [1443]
AIST Willy Korf Memorial Fund (Undergraduate/Scholarship) [1444]
Diane Blicksilver Aja Memorial Scholarship Program (Postgraduate/Scholarship) [728]
AJL Convention Travel Grants (All/Grant) [1459]
Alabama Horse Council Scholarships (Undergraduate/Scholarship) [111]
Alaska Kidney Foundation-ASN Research Grants (Doctorate/Grant) [1017]
Alberta Ukrainian Centennial Commemorative Scholarships (Undergraduate/Scholarship) [7356]
ALOA Scholarship Foundation (Undergraduate/Scholarship) [1346]
Robert E. Altenhofen Memorial Scholarships (Graduate, Undergraduate/Scholarship) [1025]
AMA/Charles H. Grant Scholarships (Undergraduate/Scholarship) [18]
American Academy of Periodontology Educator Scholarships (Postdoctorate/Scholarship) [283]
American Academy of Periodontology Foundation Education Fellowships (Postdoctorate/Fellowship) [284]
American Association of Critical-Care Nurses BSN Scholarships (Undergraduate/Scholarship) [341]
American Association of Critical-Care Nurses Graduate Scholarships (Doctorate, Graduate/Scholarship) [342]
American Association for Hand Surgery Annual Research Awards (Professional Development/Award/Prize) [349]
American Association of State Troopers Scholarship Foundation First Scholarships (Undergraduate/Scholarship) [400]
American Association of State Troopers Scholarship Foundation Second Scholarships (Undergraduate/Scholarship) [401]
American Association of University Women American Fellowships (All/Fellowship) [422]
American Association of University Women Career Development Grants (Postdoctorate/Grant) [423]
American College of Radiation Oncology Resident Scholarships (Graduate/Scholarship) [475]
American Composites Manufacturers Association Western Chapter Scholarships (Undergraduate/Scholarship) [478]
American Conifer Society Scholarships (Undergraduate/Scholarship) [493]
American Criminal Justice Association Scholarships (Undergraduate/Scholarship) [519]
American Culinary Federation Chair's Scholarship Grants (All/Scholarship) [521]
American Culinary Federation Educational Scholarship Grants (All/Scholarship) [522]
American Division Veterans Association Scholarships (Undergraduate/Scholarship) [541]
The American Express Scholarship Competition (Undergraduate/Scholarship) [610]
American Legion Eagle Scout of the Year Scholarships (High School/Scholarship) [4850]
American Paint Horse Foundation Scholarships (Undergraduate/Scholarship) [755]
American Society for Microbiology International Fellowships for Africa (Postdoctorate/Fellowship) [1001]
American Society for Microbiology International Fellowships for Asia (Postdoctorate/Fellowship) [1002]
American Society for Microbiology International Fellowships for Latin America (Postdoctorate/Fellowship) [1003]
American Society for Microbiology Undergraduate Research Fellowships (Undergraduate/Fellowship) [1004]
American Society of Military Comptrollers National Scholarship Program (Undergraduate/Scholarship) [1011]
American Sokol Merit Awards (Undergraduate/Scholarship) [1096]
American Water Ski Educational Foundation Scholarships (Undergraduate/Scholarship) [1140]
Anna Ames Clinical Excellence Student Grants (Undergraduate/Grant) [1854]
AMS Teacher Education Scholarships (Undergraduate/Scholarship) [718]
Bernard Amtmann Fellowships (Postgraduate/Grant) [1698]
Anaheim Police Survivors and Scholarship Fund (Undergraduate/Scholarship) [1178]
ANCA Scholarships (Graduate, Undergraduate/Scholarship) [1301]
The Anderson Group Summer Institute Scholarships (Other/Scholarship) [1180]
Richard E. Andrews Memorial Scholarships (Undergraduate/Scholarship) [438]
Angus Foundation Scholarships (Undergraduate/Scholarship) [4967]
AOA Research Grants (Graduate/Grant) [34]
AOFAS Research Grants Program (Graduate/Grant) [746]
AOSA Research Grants (All/Grant) [739]
AOSA Research Partnership Grants (All/Grant) [740]
APACVS Scholarships (Professional Development/Scholarship) [1479]
APAGS-CLGBTC Grant Program (Graduate/Grant) [795]
APAGS' Committee on Ethic Minority Affairs (CEMA) Grant Program (Graduate/Grant) [796]
APC High School Scholarships (Undergraduate/Scholarship) [29]
APC Tuition-Assist Scholarship Awards (Graduate, Undergraduate/Scholarship) [30]
APPMA's Jules Schwimmer Scholarship Program (Undergraduate/Scholarship) [765]
APS Student Grants (Graduate, Undergraduate/Grant) [1481]
APSNA Educational Scholarships (Professional Development/Scholarship) [763]
APT US&C Scholarships (All/Scholarship) [1483]
ARA Scholarship Awards (Undergraduate/Scholarship) [1575]
A.R.F.O.R.A. Undergraduate Scholarships for Women (Undergraduate/Scholarship) [909]
A.R.O.Y. Stanitz Scholarships (Undergraduate/Scholarship) [910]
ASBA College Scholarship Program (Undergraduate/Scholarship) [918]
ASBC Foundation Graduate Scholarships (Doctorate, Graduate/Scholarship) [922]
ASBC Foundation Undergraduate Scholarships (Undergraduate/Scholarship) [923]
ASET Educational Seminars, Courses and Program Scholarships (All, Professional Development/Scholarship) [953]
ASHA Student Research Grants (Graduate, Undergraduate/Scholarship) [916]
ASNE Scholarships (Graduate, Undergraduate/Scholarship) [1015]
ASNT Fellow Awards (Postdoctorate/Fellowship) [1021]
Myron Asplin Foundation Scholarships (Undergraduate/Scholarship) [3687]
ASPPB Larry J. Bass Jr., PhD. Memorial Scholarship Awards (Graduate, Undergraduate/Grant) [797]
Association of Desk and Derrick Clubs Education Trust Scholarships (Undergraduate/Scholarship) [1388]
Association of Flight Attendants Scholarship Fund (Undergraduate/Scholarship) [1419]
Association of Rehabilitation Nurses Scholarship Program (Undergraduate/Scholarship) [1485]
Association for the Social Scientific Study of Jewry Travel Grant (Graduate/Grant) [1495]
AST National Honor Society Student Scholarships (Graduate/Scholarship) [1499]
ASTR Research Fellowships (All/Grant) [1077]
AUA Foundation Bridge Awards (Postgraduate/Fellowship) [1127]
AUA Foundation M.D./Ph.D. Fellowships (Postdoctorate, Postgraduate/Fellowship) [1128]
AUA Foundation M.D. Post-resident Fellowships (Postgraduate/Fellowship) [1129]
AUA Foundation - NIDDK/NCI Surgeon-Scientist Awards (Postgraduate/Fellowship) [1130]
AUA Foundation Ph.D. Post-Doctoral Fellowships (Postdoctorate/Fellowship) [1131]
John L. Avila Memorial Scholarships (Professional Development/Scholarship) [4260]
BACUS Scholarships (Graduate, Undergraduate/Scholarship) [6695]
Lincoln C. Bailey Memorial Scholarship Fund (Undergraduate/Scholarship) [3900]
Sandra Sebrell Bailey Scholarships (Undergraduate/Scholarship) [2683]
Balestreri/Cutino Scholarships (Undergraduate/Scholarship) [523]
Brenda S. Bank Educational Workshop Scholarships (Undergraduate/Scholarship) [6447]

Special Recipient Index

Leslie Baranowski Scholarships for Professional Excellence *(All/Scholarship)* [3721]
Barbri Scholarships for Bar Preparation *(Undergraduate/Scholarship)* [3578]
Walt Bartram Memorial Education Awards (Region 12 and Chapter 119) *(Undergraduate/Scholarship)* [6470]
Basic Midwifery Student Scholarship Program *(Undergraduate/Scholarship)* [470]
Baxter Corporation Canadian Research Awards in Anesthesia *(Professional Development/Award/Prize)* [1912]
BCEN Undergraduate Scholarships *(Undergraduate/Scholarship)* [2850]
Dade Behring Student Scholarship Awards *(Postgraduate/Scholarship)* [2040]
Reckitt Benckiser Student Scholarships *(Graduate/Scholarship)* [4729]
Eleanor Benett Scholarships *(All/Scholarship)* [6815]
Elizabeth Benson Scholarship Awards *(Undergraduate/Scholarship)* [6018]
Fred Berg Awards *(All/Award/Prize)* [2828]
ARRS/Leonard Berlin Scholarships in Medical Professionalism *(Professional Development/Scholarship)* [907]
The Bernsten International Scholarships in Surveying Technology *(Undergraduate/Scholarship)* [484]
Betsy Plank/PRSSA Scholarships *(Undergraduate/Scholarship)* [5874]
Black Data Processing Associates Scholarships *(High School/Scholarship)* [1606]
William T. Blackwell Scholarship Fund *(Undergraduate/Scholarship)* [4951]
Beatrice K. Blair Scholarships *(Undergraduate/Scholarship)* [1764]
John Blanchard Memorial Scholarships *(Graduate/Scholarship)* [1847]
Ellin Bloch and Pierre Ritchie Honorary Scholarships *(Doctorate, Graduate/Grant)* [798]
Harry and Edith Blunt Scholarships *(Undergraduate/Scholarship)* [457]
Sandra Bobbitt Continuing Education Scholarships *(Undergraduate/Scholarship)* [1474]
Edith and Arnold N. Bodtker Grant *(All/Grant)* [2613]
Boeing Business Scholarships *(Undergraduate/Scholarship)* [3250]
Boeing Engineering Scholarships *(Undergraduate/Scholarship)* [3251]
Frances P. Bolton Fellowships *(Doctorate/Fellowship)* [5456]
BOMA/NY Scholarships *(Undergraduate/Scholarship)* [1802]
Ellis J. Bonner Scholarships *(Doctorate, Graduate, Undergraduate/Scholarship)* [4715]
Stephen Botein Fellowships *(Doctorate/Fellowship)* [300]
Bound to Stay Bound Books (BTSB) Scholarships *(Graduate/Scholarship)* [1464]
W. Scott Boyd Group Grants *(All/Grant)* [3813]
Donald J. Bristow Memorial Scholarship Program *(Graduate, Undergraduate/Scholarship)* [4655]
Dvora Brodie Scholarships *(Other/Scholarship)* [3515]
John G. Brokaw Scholarships *(Undergraduate/Scholarship)* [5138]
Selena Danette Brown Book Scholarships *(Undergraduate/Scholarship)* [4666]
The Robert W. Brunsman Memorial Scholarships *(Graduate, Undergraduate/Scholarship)* [3875]
Bujea Memorial Scholarships *(Undergraduate/Scholarship)* [911]
Ethel Beard Burstein Scholarship Program *(Postgraduate/Scholarship)* [729]
CAG Donald Menzies Bursary Awards *(Postgraduate/Award/Prize)* [1927]
CAG Margery Boyce Bursary Awards *(Postgraduate/Award/Prize)* [1928]
CALL/ACBD Education Reserve Fund Grants *(Graduate/Grant)* [1930]
Stuart Cameron and Margaret McLeod Memorial Scholarships (SCMS) *(Graduate, Undergraduate/Scholarship/Forgivable Loan)* [3744]
Wesley C. Cameron Scholarships *(Undergraduate/Scholarship)* [5139]
Canada-Ukraine Parliamentary Program (CUPP) Internship Scholarships *(Undergraduate/Scholarship)* [7357]
Canadian Anesthesiologists' Society Research Awards *(Professional Development/Award/Prize)* [1913]
Canadian Association of Law Libraries CALL Research Grants *(Graduate/Grant)* [1931]
Canadian Macedonian Federation Scholarships *(Undergraduate/Scholarship)* [7214]
Canadian Parking Association Scholarships *(Undergraduate/Scholarship)* [2027]
Canadian Water Resources Association Scholarships *(All/Scholarship)* [2047]
Therese A. Cannon Educational Scholarships *(Professional Development/Scholarship)* [3884]
Career Mobility Scholarship Awards *(Doctorate, Undergraduate/Scholarship)* [16]
Carolinas-Virginias Retail Hardware Scholarship Fund *(Undergraduate/Scholarship)* [3048]
CAS/GE Healthcare Canada Inc. Research Awards *(Professional Development/Award/Prize)* [1914]
CAS/Vitaid-LMA Residents' Research Grant Competition *(Professional Development/Award/Prize)* [1915]
Local 827 Peter J. Casey Scholarships *(Undergraduate/Scholarship)* [3819]
CD-HCF Chair's Scholarships *(Professional Development/Scholarship)* [2536]
Delmar Cengage Learning-NAAE Upper Division Scholarships *(Undergraduate/Scholarship)* [4653]
CFIDS Association of America NP Student Scholarships *(Graduate/Scholarship)* [263]
Chaine des Rotisseurs Scholarships *(Undergraduate/Scholarship)* [524]
Jeanne S. Chall Research Fellowships *(Doctorate, Graduate/Grant)* [3888]
Logan S. Chambers Individual Scholarships *(Professional Development/Scholarship)* [3814]
Chapter 4 - Lawrence A. Wacker Memorial Awards *(Undergraduate/Scholarship)* [6473]
Chapter 31 - Peoria Endowed Scholarships *(Undergraduate/Scholarship)* [6477]
Chapter 63 - Portland James E. Morrow Scholarships *(Graduate, Undergraduate/Scholarship)* [6480]
Chapter 63 - Portland Uncle Bud Smith Scholarships *(Graduate, Undergraduate/Scholarship)* [6481]
Chapter 93 - Albuquerque Scholarships *(Undergraduate/Scholarship)* [6483]
Chapter 198 - Downriver Detroit Scholarships *(Graduate, Undergraduate/Scholarship)* [6484]
Sgt. Michael F. Cherven Memorial Scholarships *(Undergraduate/Scholarship)* [4330]
Julia Child Memorial Scholarships *(Undergraduate/Scholarship)* [525]
Childbirth Educator Program Scholarships *(Other/Scholarship)* [4114]
Chopivsky Fellowships *(Undergraduate/Scholarship)* [7358]
Christian Pharmacist Fellowship International Scholarships *(Professional Development/Fellowship)* [2143]
CIP Fellow's Travel Scholarships *(Postgraduate/Scholarship)* [1980]
City of Sanibel Employee Dependent Scholarships *(Undergraduate/Scholarship)* [6646]
Clan Ross Foundation Scholarships *(Undergraduate/Scholarship)* [2245]
Ann E. Clark Foundation Scholarships *(Undergraduate/Scholarship)* [5140]
Lucy and Charles W.E. Clarke Scholarships *(Undergraduate/Scholarship)* [996]
Class Nobel Academic Scholarships for Members *(High School/Scholarship)* [5067]
CMAA Student Conference Travel Grants *(All/Grant)* [2251]
The Helena B. Cobb Annual Scholarships *(Undergraduate/Scholarship)* [7501]
The Helena B. Cobb Four-Year Higher Education Grants *(Undergraduate/Scholarship)* [7502]
Arthur H. Cole Grants in Aid *(Doctorate/Grant)* [2818]
Frank Cole Memorial Emergency NP Student Scholarships *(Graduate/Scholarship)* [264]
Capt. Winifred Quick Collins Scholarships *(Undergraduate/Scholarship)* [5141]
Communal Studies Association Research Fellowships *(Graduate/Grant)* [2339]
Congressional Science Fellowships *(Postdoctorate/Fellowship)* [1006]
Mary Adeline Conner Professional Development Scholarships *(Graduate/Scholarship)* [6681]
The Continental Group Scholarship Fund *(High School/Scholarship)* [2596]
Continuing Education Awards *(Graduate/Grant)* [4441]
Continuing Education Awards *(All/Scholarship)* [4734]
Jorge Espejal Contreras Memorial Scholarships *(Graduate, Undergraduate/Scholarship)* [3804]
Milton E. Cooper/Young AFCEAN Graduate Scholarships *(Graduate/Scholarship)* [1243]
Copper and Brass Service Center Inc. Scholarship Program *(Undergraduate/Scholarship)* [2541]
Correctional Education Association Scholarships *(Graduate, Undergraduate/Scholarship)* [2546]
NSS Sara Corrie Memorial Grants *(All/Grant)* [5087]
Richard P. Covert, Ph.D./FHIMSS Scholarships for Management Systems *(Other/Scholarship)* [3516]
Cranberry Institute NP Student Scholarships *(Graduate/Scholarship)* [265]
L.D. "Crow" Crawford Scholarships *(Undergraduate/Scholarship)* [7001]
CSA Fraternal Life Scholarships *(Undergraduate/Scholarship)* [2564]
CTP Scholarship Program *(Professional Development/Scholarship)* [5024]
Linda Cullen Memorial Scholarships *(High School/Scholarship)* [526]
Nancy Curry Scholarships *(Postgraduate/Scholarship)* [6256]
The Jennifer Curtis Byler Scholarships *(Undergraduate/Scholarship)* [5095]
DAAD Study Scholarship Awards *(Graduate/Scholarship)* [3223]
Daiichi Sankyo Inc. NP Student Scholarships *(Graduate/Scholarship)* [266]
The John L. Dales Scholarship Fund *(Undergraduate/Scholarship)* [6288]
Malcolm U. Dantzler Scholarships *(Professional Development/Scholarship)* [6613]
Antenore C. "Buth" Davanzo Scholarships *(Undergraduate/Scholarship)* [4503]
The Dave Family "Humor Studies" Scholarships *(Undergraduate/Scholarship)* [1364]
Davis Memorial Foundation Scholarship Award Program *(Graduate, Undergraduate/Scholarship)* [2621]
Edilia and Francois Auguste de Montequin Fellowships *(Doctorate/Scholarship)* [6427]
Anthony R. Dees Educational Workshop Scholarships *(Undergraduate/Scholarship)* [6448]
Deets-Laine Geriatric NP Student Scholarships *(Doctorate, Graduate/Scholarship)* [267]
Delta Gamma Scholarships *(Undergraduate/Scholarship)* [2675]
Delta/VPPPA Safety, Health and Environmental Scholarships *(Undergraduate/Scholarship)* [7338]
DEMCO New Leaders Travel Grants *(All/Grant)* [5871]
Albert W. Dent Graduate Student Scholarships *(Undergraduate/Scholarship)* [466]
Dependents of Deceased Service Members Scholarship Program *(Undergraduate/Scholarship)* [5147]
Descendant Scholarships *(Undergraduate/Scholarship)* [2606]
Distinguished Flying Cross Society Scholarship *(Undergraduate/Scholarship)* [2724]
Diversity Dissertation Scholarships *(Doctorate/Fellowship)* [799]
Diversity Executive Leadership Program Scholar-

ships *(Professional Development/Scholarship)* [920]
Robert A. and Barbara Divine Graduate Student Travel Grants *(Graduate/Grant)* [6455]
Dr. Allan A. Dixon Memorial Scholarships *(Postgraduate/Scholarship)* [2034]
Peggy Dixon Two-Year Scholarships *(Undergraduate/Scholarship)* [6541]
Charles Dobbins FTA Scholarships *(Undergraduate/Scholarship)* [3154]
Chapter 116 - Kalamazoo - Roscoe Douglas Scholarships *(Undergraduate/Scholarship)* [6487]
Tommy Douglas Scholarships *(Undergraduate/Scholarship)* [5116]
Nettie Dracup Memorial Scholarships *(Undergraduate/Scholarship)* [485]
The "Drawn to Art" Fellowships *(Doctorate/Fellowship)* [301]
Amelia Earhart Memorial Academic Scholarships *(Undergraduate/Scholarship)* [5209]
The Christoph Daniel Ebeling Fellowships *(Doctorate/Fellowship)* [302]
Educational Audiology Association Doctoral Scholarships *(Doctorate/Scholarship)* [2829]
Farouk El-Baz Student Research Grants *(Doctorate, Graduate, Undergraduate/Grant)* [3209]
Emergency Nurses Association Undergraduate Scholarships *(Undergraduate/Scholarship)* [2851]
Emerging Teacher-Leaders in Elementary School Mathematics Grants for Grades K-5 Teachers *(Professional Development/Grant)* [4829]
Employee Education Scholarships *(Other/Scholarship)* [4946]
ENA Foundation Advanced Practice Scholarships *(Undergraduate/Scholarship)* [2852]
Vice Admiral Donald D. Engen Scholarships *(Undergraduate/Scholarship)* [5132]
Harold E. Ennes Scholarships *(Professional Development/Scholarship)* [6526]
Jack Ervin EDI Scholarships *(Professional Development/Scholarship)* [5238]
NSPF Ray B. Essick Scholarship Awards *(Other/Scholarship)* [5102]
Alex J. Ettl Grants *(Professional Development/Grant)* [5037]
Executive Women International Fellows Program *(Graduate/Fellowship)* [2895]
Exploratory Travel and Data Grants *(Doctorate/Grant)* [2819]
Faculty Doctoral Scholarships *(Doctorate/Scholarship)* [2853]
AIST Benjamin F. Fairless Scholarships (AIME) *(Undergraduate/Scholarship)* [1445]
Families of Freedom Scholarship Fund - America Scholarships *(Undergraduate/Scholarship)* [2902]
Senior Chef Frank Farello Scholarships *(Professional Development/Scholarship)* [527]
John S.W. Fargher Scholarships *(Graduate/Scholarship)* [3730]
Harold E. Fellows Scholarships *(All/Scholarship)* [1784]
Film Arts Foundation Development Grants *(All/Grant)* [2928]
William A. Fisher Memorial Scholarships *(Graduate/Scholarship)* [1027]
Fitzgerald Health Education Associates NP Student Scholarships *(Graduate/Scholarship)* [268]
Carol C. Fitzgerald Scholarship Program *(Professional Development/Scholarship)* [2911]
Charlie Fleming Education Fund Scholarships *(Undergraduate/Scholarship)* [5106]
Laura M. Fleming Scholarship Fund *(Undergraduate/Scholarship)* [3058]
FLEOA Foundation Scholarship Program *(Undergraduate/Scholarship)* [2916]
Flexible Packaging Academic Scholarships & Summer Internship Program *(Undergraduate/Internship)* [2988]
Grant H. Flint International Scholarships - Category II *(Undergraduate/Scholarship)* [6597]
FMA Foundation Scholarships *(Undergraduate/Scholarship)* [3022]
Frank Fong Scholarships *(Undergraduate/Scholarship)* [6423]
Food Engineering Scholarships *(Postdoctorate, Postgraduate/Scholarship)* [3024]
Nancy B. Forest and L. Michael Honaker Master's Scholarships for Research *(Doctorate, Graduate/Scholarship)* [800]
Foresters Scholarships *(Undergraduate/Scholarship)* [3682]
Foundation for Surgical Technology Advanced Education/Medical Mission Scholarships *(Graduate/Scholarship)* [1501]
Terry Fox Memorial Scholarships *(Undergraduate/Scholarship)* [5117]
Freedom Alliance Scholarships *(Undergraduate/Scholarship)* [3143]
Kevin Freeman Travel Grants *(Graduate, Professional Development/Grant)* [4598]
A.E. Robert Friedman Scholarships *(Postgraduate, Undergraduate/Scholarship)* [5445]
Future Leaders of Manufacturing Scholarships *(Graduate, Undergraduate/Scholarship)* [6488]
Mearl K. Gable II Memorial Grants *(Professional Development/Grant)* [3395]
Gamewarden Scholarship program *(High School, Undergraduate/Scholarship)* [3156]
William R. Gard Memorial Scholarships *(Undergraduate/Scholarship)* [4608]
Gardner Foundation INS Education Scholarship *(All/Scholarship)* [3722]
Dwight D. Gardner Scholarships *(Undergraduate/Scholarship)* [3731]
Peter M. Gargano Scholarship Fund *(Undergraduate/Scholarship)* [2776]
Eileen J. Garrett Scholarships *(Undergraduate/Scholarship)* [5457]
A.R.F.O.R.A. Martha Gavrila Scholarships for Women *(Graduate/Scholarship)* [912]
Florence S. Gaynor Scholarships *(Doctorate, Graduate, Undergraduate/Scholarship)* [4716]
GED Jump Start Scholarships *(Other/Scholarship)* [6257]
Geological Society of America Graduate Student Research Grants *(Doctorate, Graduate/Grant)* [3210]
Walter Gerboth Awards *(All/Grant)* [4599]
Gilbreth Memorial Fellowships *(Graduate/Scholarship)* [3732]
Midwest Chapter Scholarships - Jack Gill *(Undergraduate/Scholarship)* [1446]
Leo Gilmartin Scholarships *(High School/Scholarship)* [5708]
John Glaser Scholarships *(Undergraduate/Scholarship)* [2298]
Globe-Trotters Chapter Scholarships *(Undergraduate/Scholarship)* [1447]
GLP Program Scholarships *(Other/Scholarship)* [4784]
Golden Key International Honour Society New Graduate Member Scholarships *(Undergraduate/Scholarship)* [3252]
Golden Key International Honour Society Study Abroad Scholarships *(Undergraduate/Scholarship)* [3253]
Golden Key International Honour Society Undergraduate Research Grants *(Undergraduate/Grant)* [3254]
Golden Key Math Scholarships *(Undergraduate/Scholarship)* [3255]
Goodfellow Professional Development Fund *(Professional Development/Scholarship)* [4250]
Carl W. Gottschalk Research Scholar Grants *(Doctorate/Grant)* [1018]
Graduate Dissertation Fellowships *(Doctorate/Fellowship)* [2820]
Graduate Student Travel Grants *(Graduate, Professional Development/Grant)* [6437]
Grande Prairie 4-H District Scholarships *(Undergraduate/Scholarship)* [133]
Robert D. Greenberg Scholarships *(Professional Development/Scholarship)* [6527]
Griffith College Scholarships for NSHSS Members *(High School/Scholarship)* [5068]
Reginald K. Groome Memorial Scholarships *(Postgraduate/Scholarship)* [6286]
Larry Gulley Scholarships *(Undergraduate/Scholarship)* [6449]
Scott A. Gunder, MD, DCMS Presidential Scholarships *(Undergraduate/Scholarship)* [3136]
Wesley R. Habley NACADA Summer Institute Scholarships *(Professional Development/Scholarship)* [4615]
The Richard D. Hailey AAJ Law Student Scholarships *(Undergraduate/Scholarship)* [358]
Joyce C. Hall College Scholarships *(Undergraduate/Scholarship)* [5570]
Chappie Hall Scholarship Program *(Graduate, Postgraduate, Undergraduate/Scholarship)* [2]
Carroll Hart Scholarships *(Graduate/Scholarship)* [6450]
Gabe A. Hartl Scholarships *(Undergraduate/Scholarship)* [64]
Healthcare Information Management Systems Scholarships *(Other/Scholarship)* [3517]
Hench Post-Dissertation Fellowships *(Postdoctorate/Fellowship)* [303]
John P. Hennessy Scholarships *(Undergraduate/Scholarship)* [4504]
Alia Herrera Memorial Scholarships *(Undergraduate/Scholarship)* [359]
Peter Hess Scholarships *(Undergraduate/Scholarship)* [3183]
Jim Hierlihy Memorial Scholarships *(Undergraduate/Scholarship)* [2879]
Jim & Nancy Hinkle Travel Grants *(Postdoctorate/Grant)* [3539]
William A. Hipp Scholarships *(All/Scholarship)* [4336]
Hispanic Association of Colleges and Universities Scholarships *(Undergraduate/Scholarship)* [3568]
Hispanic Association on Corporate Responsibility Scholarship Program *(Undergraduate/Scholarship)* [3573]
Hispanic Lawyers Association of Illinois Public Interest Fellowships *(Undergraduate/Scholarship)* [3579]
HLS/MLA Professional Development Grants *(Doctorate/Grant)* [4442]
Henry Hoffman Memorial Scholarship Fund *(Undergraduate/Scholarship)* [4695]
Governor James E. Holshouser Professional Development Scholarships *(Professional Development/Scholarship)* [5239]
Sam J. Hord Memorial Scholarships *(Undergraduate/Scholarship)* [6625]
Edward L. Horne, Jr. Scholarships *(All/Scholarship)* [5406]
HOSA Scholarships *(Undergraduate/Scholarship)* [5108]
Houston Alumnae Undergraduate Tri Delta Scholarships *(Undergraduate/Scholarship)* [2651]
C.D. Howard Scholarships *(Undergraduate/Scholarship)* [3827]
IADR David B. Scott Fellowships *(Undergraduate/Fellowship)* [3790]
IADR John Clarkson Fellowships *(Postdoctorate/Fellowship)* [3791]
IADR John Gray Fellowships *(Professional Development/Fellowship)* [3792]
IADR Norton Ross Fellowships *(Professional Development/Fellowship)* [3793]
IAESTE United States Scholarships *(Undergraduate/Scholarship)* [1435]
Ice Skating Institute of America Education Foundation *(Undergraduate/Scholarship)* [3642]
IDA Fellowship Award *(Professional Development/Fellowship)* [3838]
IEHA Education Foundation Scholarship Awards *(Undergraduate/Scholarship)* [3842]
IMA Memorial Education Fund Scholarships (MEF) *(Graduate, Undergraduate/Scholarship/Forgivable Loan)* [3746]
INIA Scholarship Program *(All/Scholarship)* [3880]
Institute for Scientific Information (ISI) Scholarships *(Doctorate, Graduate/Scholarship)* [6682]
Intergraph Scholarships *(Graduate/Scholarship)* [1028]
International Association of Emergency Managers Scholarships *(Undergraduate/Scholarship)* [3796]
International Code Council Foundation General

Scholarship Fund *(Undergraduate/Scholarship)* [3828]
International Door Association Scholarship Awards *(Undergraduate/Scholarship)* [3840]
International Harvester Collectors Scholarships *(Undergraduate/Scholarship)* [3867]
IOIA Andrew Rutherford Scholarships *(Professional Development/Scholarship)* [3684]
IOIA Organic Community Initiative Scholarship *(Other/Scholarship)* [3685]
IPSA Student Recognition Awards *(Undergraduate/Scholarship)* [3688]
Iranian Association of Boston's IAB Scholarships *(Undergraduate/Scholarship)* [4955]
The ISASI Rudolf Kapustin Memorial Scholarships *(Undergraduate/Scholarship)* [3902]
ISPE Advantage Award/Foundation Scholarships *(Undergraduate/Scholarship)* [3659]
ITNS Research Grants *(Professional Development/Grant)* [3918]
Dr. Karl C. Ivarson Scholarships *(Postgraduate/Scholarship)* [36]
Freddy L. Jacobs Scholarships *(Undergraduate/Scholarship)* [3815]
Frederick George James Memorial Scholarships *(Undergraduate/Scholarship)* [6195]
JAUW Fellowship Awards *(Postgraduate/Fellowship)* [1960]
Sister Rita Jeanne Scholarships *(Undergraduate/Scholarship)* [4033]
Elise Reed Jenkins Memorial Scholarships - Gamma Lambda *(Undergraduate/Scholarship)* [6362]
Gaynold Jensen Education Stipends *(Postdoctorate, Professional Development/Scholarship)* [2537]
Walter J. Jensen Fellowships *(Professional Development/Fellowship)* [5622]
Nancy Lorraine Jensen Memorial Scholarships *(Undergraduate/Scholarship)* [6603]
Stanley "Doc" Jensen Scholarships *(High School/Scholarship)* [528]
Joseph C. Johnson Memorial Grants *(Undergraduate/Scholarship)* [927]
Gregory D. Johnson Memorial Scholarships *(Graduate, Undergraduate/Scholarship)* [4971]
V.J. Johnson Memorial Scholarships *(Undergraduate/Scholarship)* [402]
Kaplan Scholarships *(Undergraduate/Scholarship)* [3580]
Kaplan Test Prep and Admission Scholarships for NSHSS Members *(High School/Scholarship)* [5069]
Kappa Delta Phi Scholarship Program *(Postgraduate/Scholarship)* [730]
Doc Keen Memorial Scholarships *(Undergraduate/Scholarship)* [6661]
Willmoore H. Kendall Scholarships *(Postgraduate/Scholarship)* [2252]
Michael Kidger Memorial Scholarships in Optical Design *(Graduate/Scholarship)* [6696]
Julia Kiene Fellowship in Electrical Energy *(Graduate/Fellowship)* [7494]
Margie Klein "Paper Plate" Scholarships *(All/Scholarship)* [1366]
Elva Knight Research Grants *(All/Grant)* [3889]
Eugene & Elinor Kotur Scholarship Trust Fund *(Undergraduate/Scholarship)* [7359]
David A. Kronick Travelling Fellowships *(Doctorate/Fellowship)* [4443]
Kris M. Kunze Memorial Scholarships *(Undergraduate/Scholarship)* [486]
Frank S. Land Scholarships *(Undergraduate/Scholarship)* [2702]
Cecil Lane Family Scholarships *(Undergraduate/Scholarship)* [114]
James D. Lang Memorial Scholarships *(Graduate/Scholarship)* [1932]
Susan Lang Scholarship Program *(Postgraduate/Scholarship)* [731]
Laser Technology, Engineering and Applications Scholarships *(Graduate, Undergraduate/Scholarship)* [6697]
Daniel Lasky Scholarship Fund *(Undergraduate/Scholarship)* [4998]
Jay and Deborah Last Fellowships *(Doctorate/Fellowship)* [304]
Leaders at Work Scholarship in Textiles and Apparel *(Undergraduate/Scholarship)* [5109]
The Leesfield/AAJ Law Student Scholarships *(Undergraduate/Scholarship)* [360]
The Legacy Fellowships *(Doctorate/Fellowship)* [305]
Legal Research Service Scholarships *(Undergraduate/Scholarship)* [2758]
Leica Geosystems Internships *(Graduate/Internship)* [1029]
Myra Levick Scholarships *(Graduate/Scholarship)* [313]
Herbert Levy Memorial Endowment Fund Scholarships *(Undergraduate/Scholarship)* [6542]
Ta Liang Memorial Awards *(Graduate/Grant)* [1030]
Library Media Teacher Scholarships *(Graduate/Scholarship)* [1849]
LIT Scholarships *(Graduate, Undergraduate/Scholarship)* [4116]
Litherland/FTE Scholarships *(Undergraduate/Scholarship)* [3912]
Lucius Littauer Foundation Travel Grants *(All/Grant)* [1461]
D.J. Lovell Scholarships *(Graduate, Undergraduate/Scholarship)* [6698]
The Lowell H. and Dorothy Loving Undergraduate Scholarships *(Undergraduate/Scholarship)* [487]
Luso-American Fraternal Federation B-2 Scholarships *(Postgraduate/Scholarship)* [4265]
Luso-American Fraternal Federation B-3 Scholarships *(All/Scholarship)* [4266]
Luso-American Fraternal Federation B-4 Scholarships *(All/Scholarship)* [4267]
The C. Lyons Fellowship Program *(All/Fellowship)* [4980]
Carol E. Macpherson Memorial Scholarship and Alumnae Society Scholarships *(Graduate, Undergraduate/Scholarship)* [7133]
Andrew Macrina Scholarships *(High School/Scholarship)* [529]
Dr. Edward May Magruder Medical Scholarships *(Other/Scholarship)* [458]
Maley/FTE Teacher Scholarships *(Graduate/Scholarship)* [3913]
David C. Maloney Scholarship Program *(Undergraduate/Scholarship)* [4996]
Lyle Mamer Fellowships *(Graduate/Fellowship)* [7495]
Harold and Inge Marcus Scholarships *(Undergraduate/Scholarship)* [3735]
Ray and Gertrude Marshall Scholarships *(Undergraduate/Scholarship)* [530]
The Maschhoffs Inc. Pork Production Scholarships *(Undergraduate/Scholarship)* [4972]
Val Mason Scholarships *(Postgraduate/Scholarship)* [2036]
Noel D. Matkin Awards *(Undergraduate/Award/Prize)* [2830]
Antonio Mattos Memorial Scholarships *(Undergraduate/Scholarship)* [4268]
Mature Student Scholarships *(Undergraduate/Scholarship)* [2880]
Clara Mayo Grants *(Graduate/Grant)* [6575]
Hans McCorriston Motive Power Machinist Grant Programs *(Postgraduate/Scholarship)* [1570]
The Cady McDonnell Memorial Scholarships *(Undergraduate/Scholarship)* [488]
Foster G. McGaw Graduate Student Scholarships *(Undergraduate/Scholarship)* [467]
McGill University Alma Mater Student Travel Grants *(Graduate/Grant)* [4430]
Janice McGraw Memorial Scholarship Program *(Postgraduate/Scholarship)* [732]
John J. McKetta Undergraduate Scholarships *(Undergraduate/Scholarship)* [656]
Arthur Patch McKinlay Scholarships *(Graduate, Undergraduate/Scholarship)* [461]
McKinney Sisters Undergraduate Scholarships *(Undergraduate/Scholarship)* [2657]
Ruth McMillan Student Grants *(Undergraduate/Grant)* [1855]
MDA Development Grants *(Doctorate/Grant)* [4593]
MDA Research Grants *(Doctorate/Grant)* [4594]
Frederic G. Melcher Scholarships *(Graduate/Scholarship)* [1465]
Scott Mesh Honorary Scholarships for Research in Psychology *(Graduate/Fellowship)* [801]
Edmond A. Metzger Scholarships *(Undergraduate/Scholarship)* [843]
Beth Middleton Memorial Scholarships *(Undergraduate/Scholarship)* [5110]
Midwest Chapter Scholarships - Betty McKern *(Undergraduate/Scholarship)* [1448]
Midwest Chapter Scholarships - Don Nelson *(Undergraduate/Scholarship)* [1449]
Midwest Chapter Scholarships - Engineering *(Undergraduate/Scholarship)* [1450]
Midwest Chapter Scholarships - Mel Nickel *(Undergraduate/Scholarship)* [1451]
Midwest Chapter Scholarships - Non-Engineering *(Undergraduate/Scholarship)* [1452]
Midwest Chapter Scholarships - Western States Award *(Undergraduate/Scholarship)* [1453]
Mike Kabo Global Scholarships *(Other/Scholarship)* [4786]
Milan Getting Scholarships *(Undergraduate/Scholarship)* [6594]
Military Intelligence Corps Association Scholarships *(Undergraduate/Scholarship)* [4527]
Mark Miller Award *(Graduate, Undergraduate/Scholarship)* [4656]
Mary Minglen Scholarship Program *(Postgraduate/Scholarship)* [733]
Minority Scholarship Awards for College Students *(Undergraduate/Scholarship)* [657]
MLA Research, Development, and Demonstration Project Grants *(Graduate/Grant)* [4446]
MPAEA Professional Development Scholarships *(All/Scholarship)* [4583]
MPI CRV Continuing Education Scholarships *(Professional Development/Scholarship)* [4452]
Marvin Mundel Memorial Scholarships *(Undergraduate/Scholarship)* [3736]
Clarence and Josephine Myers Scholarships *(Graduate, Undergraduate/Scholarship)* [6498]
NABA Corporate Scholarship Program *(Graduate, Undergraduate/Scholarship)* [4657]
NABA National Scholarship Program *(Graduate, Undergraduate/Scholarship)* [4658]
NACADA Scholarships *(Doctorate, Graduate/Scholarship)* [4616]
IADR Toshio Nakao Fellowships *(Professional Development/Fellowship)* [3794]
NARFE-FEEA Scholarship Awards Program *(Undergraduate/Scholarship)* [4628]
NASE Future Entrepreneur Scholarships *(Undergraduate/Scholarship)* [4740]
The NASSCO Jeffrey D. Ralston Memorial Scholarships *(Undergraduate/Scholarship)* [4743]
National AAHAM Scholarships *(Undergraduate/Scholarship)* [353]
National Air Filtration Association Scholarship Fund *(Undergraduate/Scholarship)* [4630]
National Association for the Self-Employed Scholarships *(Undergraduate/Scholarship)* [4741]
National Black Coalition of Federal Aviation Employees Scholarship *(Other/Scholarship)* [4759]
National Black Nurses Association Scholarships *(Undergraduate/Scholarship)* [4764]
National Coal Transportation Association At Large Scholarships *(Undergraduate/Scholarship)* [4800]
National Court Reporters Association Student Intern Scholarships *(Undergraduate/Scholarship)* [4835]
National Dairy Herd Improvement Association Scholarship Program *(Undergraduate/Scholarship)* [4839]
National Dental Hygienists' Association Scholarships *(Undergraduate/Scholarship)* [4846]
National Heartburn Alliance NP Student Scholarships *(Graduate/Scholarship)* [269]
National Honor Roll Scholarships *(Undergraduate/Scholarship)* [1808]
National Huguenot Society Scholarships *(Undergraduate/Scholarship)* [4944]
National Italian American Bar Association Scholarships *(Postgraduate/Scholarship)* [4960]
National Junior Swine Association Outstanding

Member Scholarships *(Graduate/Scholarship)* [4973]
National Kindergarten Alliance Graduate Scholarships *(Graduate/Scholarship)* [4978]
National Recreation and Park Association Diversity Scholarships *(Undergraduate/Scholarship)* [5028]
National Slovak Society of the USA Scholarships *(Undergraduate/Scholarship)* [5044]
National Slovak Society of the USA Senior Scholarships *(Undergraduate/Scholarship)* [5045]
National Technical Honor Society Scholarships *(Undergraduate/Scholarship)* [5111]
Naval Reserve Association Scholarships *(Undergraduate/Scholarship)* [5136]
NBMBAA Graduate Scholarship Programs *(Graduate/Scholarship)* [4761]
NCOA Scholarships *(Undergraduate/Scholarship)* [5211]
NCTE Research Foundation Grants *(Professional Development/Grant)* [4826]
NDEOA Scholarships *(Undergraduate/Scholarship)* [4848]
J.W. "Bill" Neese Scholarships *(Undergraduate/Scholarship)* [3829]
NEMRA Educational Scholarship Foundation *(Undergraduate/Scholarship)* [4871]
New Hampshire Snowmobile Association Scholarships *(Undergraduate/Scholarship)* [5173]
New Professional Reporter Grants *(Professional Development/Grant)* [4836]
Frank Newman Leadership Awards *(Undergraduate/Scholarship)* [1916]
NFPA/PACE Scholarships *(Professional Development/Scholarship)* [4886]
NFPA Youth Scholarships *(Undergraduate/Scholarship)* [4902]
NHS National Scholarships *(Undergraduate/Scholarship)* [4939]
Norman Nicholson Scholarships *(Undergraduate/Scholarship)* [1937]
Herbert W. Nickens Medical Student Scholarships *(Undergraduate/Scholarship)* [1362]
NJSA Visionary Leader Scholarships *(Graduate/Scholarship)* [4974]
NLBRA/Wrangler Academic Scholarships *(Undergraduate/Scholarship)* [4982]
NMIA Scholarship Program *(Undergraduate/Scholarship)* [4991]
NOBLE Fellowship Program *(All/Fellowship)* [4993]
Nor' Easters Scholarships - Four-year Program *(Undergraduate/Scholarship)* [5214]
Nor' Easters Scholarships - Two-year Program *(Undergraduate/Scholarship)* [5215]
Nordic Ski Association of Anchorage Scholarships *(Undergraduate/Scholarship)* [129]
North Central (Region 9) Scholarships *(Undergraduate/Scholarship)* [6499]
NorthCoast Medical Scholarship Program *(Postgraduate/Scholarship)* [734]
Northeastern Ohio Chapter Scholarships - Alfred B. Glossbrenner and John Klusch Scholarships *(Undergraduate/Scholarship)* [1454]
Northern California Chapter of HIMSS Scholarships *(Other/Scholarship)* [3518]
Northern Virginia Alumnae Chapter Scholarships *(Undergraduate/Scholarship)* [2659]
Novartis Pharmaceutical Corporation NP Student Scholarships *(Graduate/Scholarship)* [270]
Novo Nordisk Canada-CAS Research Awards *(Professional Development/Award/Prize)* [1917]
Novo Nordisk NP Doctoral Education Scholarships *(Doctorate/Scholarship)* [271]
NPM Program Scholarships *(Undergraduate/Scholarship)* [4727]
NSA Scholarship Program *(Undergraduate/Scholarship)* [5040]
NSHSS Academic Paper Awards *(High School/Scholarship)* [5070]
NSHSS National Scholar Awards *(High School/Scholarship)* [5071]
NSPF Board of Directors' Scholarship Awards *(Other/Scholarship)* [5103]
NSPF Scholarship Awards *(Other/Scholarship)* [5104]
NSPS Board of Governors Scholarships *(Undergraduate/Scholarship)* [489]
The NSPS Scholarships *(Undergraduate/Scholarship)* [490]
NSSA/NSCA Collegiate Scholarships *(Undergraduate/Scholarship)* [5093]
NW-SCC American Legion Scholarships - Florence/Lauderdale Post No. 11 *(Undergraduate/Scholarship)* [5300]
NWSA Distinguished Fellowships *(All/Fellowship)* [5125]
NWSA Graduate Scholarships *(Graduate/Scholarship)* [5126]
OBAP Fellowships - Airline Transport (ATP) *(Professional Development/Fellowship)* [5407]
OBAP Fellowships - Commercial *(Professional Development/Fellowship)* [5408]
OBAP Fellowships - Instructor rating (CFI/CFII/MEI) *(Professional Development/Fellowship)* [5409]
OBAP Fellowships - Multi-Engine *(Professional Development/Fellowship)* [5410]
OBAP General Scholarships *(All/Scholarship)* [5411]
John O'Connor Memorial Scholarship Fund *(Undergraduate/Scholarship)* [5114]
Ohio Valley Chapter Scholarships *(Undergraduate/Scholarship)* [1455]
Roy C. and Dorothy Jean Olson Memorial Scholarships *(Undergraduate/Scholarship)* [3876]
Charlie O'Meilia Scholarships *(Undergraduate/Scholarship)* [3830]
Frank Oppenheimer Scholarship Program *(Postgraduate/Scholarship)* [735]
OPWA Educational Scholarships *(Undergraduate/Scholarship)* [5315]
Doris Orenstein Memorial Convention Travel Grants *(All/Grant)* [1462]
Owner-Operator Independent Drivers Association Scholarships *(Undergraduate/Scholarship)* [5436]
Paleontological Society Student Research Grants *(Graduate, Undergraduate/Grant)* [405]
Panther Cafe Scholarships *(Undergraduate/Scholarship)* [5848]
Paper Stock Industries Chapter of ISRI Scholarship Program *(Undergraduate/Scholarship)* [5452]
Joseph M. Parish Memorial Grants *(Undergraduate/Scholarship)* [928]
Parking Industry Institute Scholarship Program *(Undergraduate/Scholarship)* [5009]
Walter S. Patterson Scholarships *(All/Scholarship)* [1785]
Arthur Paulin Automotive Aftermarket Scholarship Awards *(Postgraduate/Scholarship)* [1571]
Ray, NORP and Katie, WOKTE Pautz Scholarships *(Undergraduate/Scholarship)* [847]
Pediatric Endocrinology Nursing Society Academic Education Scholarships *(Undergraduate/Scholarship)* [5542]
Pediatric Endocrinology Nursing Society Continuing Education Scholarships *(Undergraduate/Scholarship)* [5543]
Pennsylvania Association of Arson Investigators Scholarships *(Undergraduate/Scholarship)* [5555]
Joaquin Pereira Memorial Scholarships *(Undergraduate/Scholarship)* [4269]
The A.W. Perigard Fund *(Graduate, Undergraduate/Scholarship)* [6581]
Sanky Perlowin Memorial Scholarships *(Undergraduate/Scholarship)* [2713]
Kate B. and Hall J. Peterson Fellowships *(Doctorate/Fellowship)* [306]
Silvio and Eugenio Petrini Grants *(Professional Development/Grant)* [3397]
Petroleum Packaging Council Scholarships *(Undergraduate/Scholarship)* [5620]
Pfizer Inc. 2007 NP Student Scholarships *(Graduate/Scholarship)* [272]
PGSF-GATF Scholarships *(Graduate, Undergraduate/Scholarship)* [31]
Pharmavite LLC NP Doctoral Education Scholarships *(Doctorate/Scholarship)* [273]
Ed Phinney Commemorative Scholarships *(Graduate, Undergraduate/Scholarship)* [462]
Peter L. Picknelly Honorary Scholarships *(Undergraduate/Scholarship)* [449]
David Pilon Scholarships for Training in Professional Psychology *(Doctorate, Graduate/Scholarship)* [802]
Stephen D. Pisinski Memorial Scholarships *(Undergraduate/Scholarship)* [5875]
Christopher Pitkin Memorial Scholarships *(Undergraduate/Scholarship)* [4931]
Pitsenbarger Awards *(Undergraduate/Scholarship)* [52]
Plenum Scholarships *(Doctorate/Scholarship)* [6683]
PLUS Foundation Financial Aid Grants *(Undergraduate/Scholarship)* [5709]
Daniel H. Pokorny Memorial Scholarship Awards *(Undergraduate/Scholarship)* [6019]
Polish American Club of North Jersey Scholarships *(Undergraduate/Scholarship)* [4093]
Polish National Alliance of Brooklyn, USA Scholarships *(Undergraduate/Scholarship)* [4094]
Barbara Potter Scholarships *(All/Scholarship)* [741]
Ina E. Powell Memorial Scholarships *(Undergraduate/Scholarship)* [115]
J.R. (Joe) Power National Scholarships *(Postgraduate/Scholarship)* [5878]
Master Sergeant Neal E. Powers Memorial Scholarships *(Undergraduate/Scholarship)* [59]
Presbyterian Association of Musicians Scholarships *(Other/Scholarship)* [5744]
Presidents Scholarships *(Undergraduate/Scholarship)* [3737]
William H. Price Scholarships *(Graduate, Undergraduate/Scholarship)* [6699]
Professional Institute of the Public Service of Canada Expanded Scholarships *(Undergraduate/Scholarship)* [5793]
ProWorld Study Abroad Scholarships *(Undergraduate/Scholarship)* [3256]
PSAC - Coughlin National Scholarships *(Postgraduate/Scholarship)* [5879]
PSAC - Groulx National Scholarships *(Postgraduate/Scholarship)* [5880]
PSAC National Scholarships *(Postgraduate/Scholarship)* [5881]
PSAC Regional Scholarships *(Postgraduate/Scholarship)* [5882]
PSAI Scholarship Funds *(Undergraduate/Scholarship)* [5735]
The PSSC Legacy Fund *(Graduate, Undergraduate/Scholarship)* [6582]
A.O. Putnam Memorial Scholarships *(Undergraduate/Scholarship)* [3738]
The Henley Putnam University Scholarships *(Professional Development/Scholarship)* [3805]
Quality Initiative Grant-in-Aid *(Doctorate, Graduate/Grant)* [951]
Michael J. Quill Scholarships *(Undergraduate/Scholarship)* [6896]
Rainwater Family Scholarships *(Undergraduate/Scholarship)* [4983]
Tom D. Ralls Memorial Scholarships *(Professional Development/Scholarship)* [3020]
Lenny Ravich "Shalom" Scholarships *(All/Scholarship)* [1367]
Rawley Silver Award for Excellence *(Graduate/Scholarship)* [314]
The Reese Fellowships *(Doctorate/Fellowship)* [307]
Henry J. Reilly Memorial Scholarships - For Freshmen in College *(Undergraduate/Scholarship)* [6023]
Henry J. Reilly Memorial Scholarships - For Graduating High School Seniors *(Undergraduate/Scholarship)* [6024]
Henry J. Reilly Memorial Scholarships - For Sophomores and Juniors in College *(Undergraduate/Scholarship)* [6025]
Henry J. Reilly Memorial Scholarships - Graduate Program *(Graduate, Professional Development/Scholarship)* [6026]
Retired League Postmasters Scholarship Program *(Undergraduate/Scholarship)* [6032]
Haynes Rice Scholarships *(Doctorate, Graduate,*

Undergraduate/Scholarship) [4717]
Donald Riebhoff Memorial Scholarships (Undergraduate/Scholarship) [851]
Marion Roberts Memorial Scholarships (Postgraduate/Scholarship) [1572]
Helen M. Robinson Grants (Doctorate/Grant) [3890]
Claude Robinson Scholarships (Undergraduate/Scholarship) [4975]
R.O.E.A. Dumitru Golea Goldy-Gemu Scholarships (Undergraduate/Scholarship) [913]
Roofing Industry Alliance for Progress Scholarships (Graduate, Undergraduate/Scholarship) [6058]
Roofing Industry Scholarships (Graduate, Undergraduate/Scholarship) [5035]
Bettsy Ross Educational Fund (All, Professional Development/Scholarship) [5212]
Routh Student Research Grants (Undergraduate/Grant) [6533]
RPA Scholarships (Undergraduate/Scholarship) [6028]
The RTKL Traveling Fellowships (Undergraduate/Fellowship) [310]
Hermann G. Rusch Scholarships (Professional Development/Scholarship) [531]
The Anthony C. Russo Scholarships (Graduate/Scholarship) [5026]
SAH Study Tour Fellowships (Doctorate/Fellowship) [6429]
AIST David H. Samson Scholarships (Undergraduate/Scholarship) [1456]
Barbara Sanchez Scholarships (Undergraduate/Scholarship) [6443]
Frank Sarli Memorial Scholarships (Undergraduate/Scholarship) [4837]
Saskatchewan Trucking Association Scholarships (Undergraduate/Scholarship) [6250]
Savatori Fellowships (Graduate/Fellowship) [3773]
SAWE Scholarships (Undergraduate/Scholarship) [6424]
SC and R Foundation Grant Program (Undergraduate/Grant) [6686]
SC and R Foundation Scholarships (Undergraduate/Scholarship) [6687]
Scholarships for Aboriginal Canadians (Undergraduate/Scholarship) [5118]
Scholarships for Leadership Training and Coaching (Professional Development/Scholarship) [2717]
Scholarships for Technology Students (Postgraduate/Scholarship) [1945]
Scholarships for Visible Minorities (Undergraduate/Scholarship) [5119]
The Schonstedt Scholarships in Surveying (Undergraduate/Scholarship) [491]
School In-Service Training Grants for Grades 6-8 Teachers (Graduate/Grant) [4831]
School In-Service Training Grants for Grades 9-12 Teachers (Graduate/Grant) [4832]
School In-Service Training Grants for Grades K-5 Teachers (Graduate/Grant) [4833]
School Library Paraprofessional Scholarships (Graduate/Scholarship) [1850]
Alice Schulman Simmons Scholarships for UU Women (Undergraduate/Scholarship) [6954]
Richard E. Schultes Research Awards (Graduate/Grant) [6439]
Schwan's Food Service Scholarships (Undergraduate/Scholarship) [6258]
G. Helner Sell Research and Training Grants (Professional Development/Grant) [1110]
SEMA Memorial Scholarships (Graduate/Scholarship) [1573]
William "Buddy" Sentner Scholarship Awards (Undergraduate/Scholarship) [391]
Servus Credit Union 4-H Scholarships (Undergraduate/Scholarship) [135]
Captain Anthony D. Sesow Scholarships (Undergraduate/Scholarship) [5133]
SHAFR Dissertation Completion Fellowships (Doctorate/Fellowship) [6459]
William H. Shannon Fellowships (Professional Development/Fellowship) [3916]
Commander Dan F. Shanower Scholarships (Undergraduate/Scholarship) [5134]
Anne Shaw Fellowships (Graduate/Fellowship) [6879]
Robert P. Sheppard Leadership Awards (High School/Scholarship) [5072]
David S. Sheridan Canadian Research Awards (Professional Development/Award/Prize) [1918]
Shields-Gillespie Scholarships (All/Scholarship) [742]
Jason Shipley Memorial Scholarships (Undergraduate/Scholarship) [4976]
Mary Isabel Sibley Fellowships (Doctorate/Fellowship) [5623]
Norman Siegel Research Scholar Grants (Doctorate/Grant) [1019]
Jeff Siegel Scholarships (Undergraduate/Scholarship) [5191]
Sig Memorial Scholarships (Undergraduate/Scholarship) [19]
Sigma Pi Sigma Undergraduate Research Awards (Undergraduate/Grant) [6543]
Silver Nugget Family Scholarships (Undergraduate/Scholarship) [5857]
Helen J. Sioussat/Fay Wells Scholarships (All/Scholarship) [1786]
Small Cash Grants (Undergraduate/Scholarship) [929]
SME Coal and Energy Division Scholarships (Undergraduate/Scholarship) [6516]
SME Education Foundation Family Scholarships (Undergraduate/Scholarship) [6503]
SME Environmental Division Scholarships (Undergraduate/Scholarship) [6517]
SMFM/AAOGF Scholarship Award (Graduate/Scholarship) [6512]
Gladys Ann Smith Greater Los Angeles Women's Council Scholarships (Undergraduate/Scholarship) [5142]
Nila Banton Smith Research Dissemination Support Grants (All/Grant) [3891]
Smiths Medical Canada Ltd. Research Awards (Professional Development/Award/Prize) [1919]
SNF Professional Growth Scholarships (Graduate, Undergraduate/Scholarship) [6259]
SNMTS Bachelor's Degree Completion Scholarships (Undergraduate/Scholarship) [6523]
SNMTS Clinical Advancement Scholarships (Other/Scholarship) [6524]
Ray Snow Memorial Scholarships (Undergraduate/Scholarship) [4947]
Society of Marine Port Engineers Scholarship Loans (Undergraduate/Scholarship/Forgivable Loan) [6510]
Society of Pediatric Nurses Educational Scholarship (Graduate, Professional Development/Scholarship) [6530]
Society for Pediatric Radiology Research Fellows (Graduate, Professional Development/Fellowship) [6535]
Society for Pediatric Radiology Seed Grants (Graduate, Professional Development/Grant) [6536]
Sons of Norway Foundation Scholarships to Oslo International School (Undergraduate/Scholarship) [6604]
South Carolina Public Health Association Scholarships (Undergraduate/Scholarship) [6614]
Southeast Member Chapter Scholarships (Undergraduate/Scholarship) [1457]
Master Sergeant William Sowers Memorial Scholarships (Undergraduate/Scholarship) [60]
Willard and Spackman Scholarship Program (Postgraduate/Scholarship) [736]
Spartan Scholarship Awards (Undergraduate/Scholarship) [3843]
Spice Box Grants (Professional Development/Grant) [532]
SPOOM Research Grants (Graduate/Grant) [6566]
Spouse Tuition Aids Program (Graduate, Undergraduate/Scholarship) [5148]
SPPSI Grants-In-Aid Program (Graduate, Postdoctorate/Grant) [6576]
SPS Future Teacher Scholarships (Undergraduate/Scholarship) [6544]
SPS Leadership Scholarships (Undergraduate/Scholarship) [6545]
The SSPI Mid-Atlantic Chapter Scholarships (Graduate, Undergraduate/Scholarship) [6583]
The SSPI Northeast Chapter Scholarships (Graduate, Undergraduate/Scholarship) [6584]
The SSPI Southern California Scholarships (Graduate, Undergraduate/Scholarship) [6585]
Steven A. Stahl Research Grants (Graduate/Grant) [3892]
The Stanley H. Stearman Awards (Undergraduate/Scholarship) [5048]
Robert P. Stearns/SCS Engineers Awards (Graduate/Scholarship) [6598]
Elizabeth Coulter Stephenson Scholarships (Undergraduate/Scholarship) [2699]
The Dan Stewart Scholarships (Professional Development/Scholarship) [5240]
Ralph W. Stone Graduate Fellowships (Graduate/Grant) [5090]
James E. Stoner Memorial Scholarships (Undergraduate/Scholarship) [1417]
E.L. Stubbs Research Grants (Graduate/Grant) [4507]
Student Travel Grants (Graduate, Undergraduate/Grant) [6700]
Study Scholarships for Artists or Musicians (Graduate/Scholarship) [3230]
Subic Bay-Cubi Point 1 Scholarships (Undergraduate/Scholarship) [5143]
VPPPA William Sullivan Scholarships (Graduate, Undergraduate/Scholarship) [7339]
William A. Sullivan Scholarships (Undergraduate/Scholarship) [5144]
Summer Intern Scholarships in Cardiothoracic Surgery (Undergraduate/Scholarship) [420]
Superior District Legislative Mentoring Student Grants (Undergraduate/Grant) [1856]
Superior District Legislative Mentoring Student Grants RT to DC (Undergraduate/Grant) [1857]
SUS Foundation Junior Faculty Grants (Graduate/Grant) [6589]
SWFL Deputy Sheriffs Association Fund Scholarships (Undergraduate/Scholarship) [6676]
Tagged for Greatness Scholarships (Undergraduate/Scholarship) [116]
Tailhook Educational Foundation Scholarships Program (Undergraduate/Scholarship) [6836]
Alexander M. Tanger Scholarships (All/Scholarship) [1787]
William J. Tangye Scholarships (Undergraduate/Scholarship) [3831]
Ryan "Munchie" Taylor Memorial Scholarships (Undergraduate/Scholarship) [4270]
TCATA College Scholarship Program (Undergraduate/Scholarship) [6875]
TDC Scholarship Program (Graduate, Undergraduate/Scholarship) [4659]
Telford Scholarships (Undergraduate/Scholarship) [20]
Ralph and Valerie Thomas Scholarship Program (Graduate, Undergraduate/Scholarship) [4660]
Thomson Scientific/MLA Doctoral Fellowships (Doctorate/Fellowship) [4448]
Tomato Fest Scholarship Grants (Undergraduate/Scholarship) [533]
Travis C. Tomlin Memorial Scholarship Program (Graduate, Undergraduate/Scholarship) [4661]
The Joyce Tracy Fellowships (Doctorate/Fellowship) [308]
TRALA Scholarships Program (Undergraduate/Scholarship) [6924]
Marie Tremaine Fellowships (Postgraduate/Grant) [1699]
Troy University Rodeo Team Scholarships (Graduate/Scholarship) [117]
Two Year/Community Broadcast Education Association Scholarships Award (All/Scholarship) [1788]
UAA Governor William A. Egan Scholarships (Undergraduate/Scholarship) [7056]
UAF Alumni Association Scholarships (Undergraduate/Scholarship) [7079]
UCB, Inc. NP Student Scholarships (Graduate/Scholarship) [274]
UFCW Scholarships (Undergraduate/Scholarship) [6963]
Union Plus Scholarship Program

(Undergraduate/Scholarship) [3922]
United Parcel Service Scholarship for Female Students *(Undergraduate/Scholarship)* [3740]
U.S. Bates Scholarship Program *(Undergraduate/Scholarship)* [3923]
United States Tour Operators Association Scholarships *(Undergraduate/Scholarship)* [7019]
University of Minnesota Women Student Travel Grants *(Graduate, Undergraduate/Grant)* [7134]
University of West Alabama Rodeo Team Scholarships *(Graduate/Scholarship)* [118]
Samuel Upchurch Memorial Scholarships *(Undergraduate/Scholarship)* [119]
USAWOASF/Grantham University On-Line Scholarships *(Graduate, Undergraduate/Scholarship)* [6980]
USAWOASF Regular Scholarships *(Undergraduate/Scholarship)* [6981]
USS Tennessee Scholarship Fund *(Undergraduate/Scholarship)* [5149]
John D. Utterback Undergraduate Scholarships *(Undergraduate/Scholarship)* [230]
Veolia ES Waste-to-Energy/Terrence L. Guest Memorial Awards *(Graduate/Scholarship)* [6599]
Irma E. Voigt Memorial Scholarships *(Undergraduate/Scholarship)* [6379]
Abe Voron Scholarships *(All/Scholarship)* [1789]
VPPPA June Brothers Scholarships *(Graduate, Undergraduate/Scholarship)* [7340]
VPPPA Stephen Brown Scholarships *(Graduate, Undergraduate/Scholarship)* [7341]
Ed Wadsworth Memorial Scholarships *(Undergraduate/Scholarship)* [120]
Jack H. Wagner Scholarships *(Undergraduate/Scholarship)* [4505]
Vincent T. Wasilewski Scholarships *(All/Scholarship)* [1790]
Stand Watie Scholarships *(Undergraduate/Scholarship)* [6601]
Robert D. Watkins Graduate Research Fellowships *(Postdoctorate/Fellowship)* [1009]
Thomas S. Watson, Jr. Memorial Scholarships *(Graduate, Undergraduate/Scholarship)* [4662]
The Wax Company Scholarships *(Undergraduate/Scholarship)* [121]
Richard M. Weaver Fellowships *(Graduate/Fellowship)* [3774]
Edith Weingarten Scholarship Program *(Postgraduate/Scholarship)* [737]
Western Civilization Fellowships *(Graduate/Fellowship)* [3775]
Robert B. Westover Scholarships *(Undergraduate/Scholarship)* [3202]
WildBird/Clements Memorial Scholarships *(Undergraduate/Scholarship)* [439]
Wiley Publishing Inc. Scholarships *(Undergraduate/Scholarship)* [5112]
Rodney Williams Legacy Scholarships *(Undergraduate/Grant)* [7107]
James Elliott Williams Scholarship Fund *(Undergraduate/Scholarship)* [5537]
CSM Virgil R. Williams Scholarships *(Undergraduate/Scholarship)* [2857]
Cenie Jomo Williams Tuition Scholarships *(Undergraduate/Scholarship)* [4668]
Winston Scholarships *(Graduate, Undergraduate/Scholarship)* [6260]
WINUP Member Scholarships *(Professional Development/Scholarship)* [7496]
WOCN Advanced Education Scholarships *(Doctorate, Graduate, Undergraduate/Scholarship)* [7523]
Paul R. Wolf Memorial Scholarships *(Graduate/Scholarship)* [1033]
Women's Jewelry Association Member Grants *(All/Grant)* [7498]
Dr. Harold S. Wood Award for Excellence *(Undergraduate/Award/Prize)* [3207]
Patty Wooten Scholarships *(Undergraduate/Scholarship)* [1368]
Marusia Yaworska Entrance Scholarships *(Undergraduate/Scholarship)* [7361]
York Rite Grand Chapter Royal Arch Masons Scholarships *(Undergraduate/Scholarship)* [2703]
Gary Yoshimura Scholarships *(Undergraduate/Scholarship)* [5876]
Young Investigator Grants *(Undergraduate/Grant)* [5091]
Lisa Zaken Award For Excellence *(Graduate, Undergraduate/Award/Prize)* [3742]

Disabled

Alabama Scholarships for Dependents of Blind Parents *(Undergraduate/Scholarship)* [107]
American Speech Language Hearing Foundation Scholarships for Students with Disability *(All/Scholarship)* [1102]
Elsa Barton Educational Scholarships Fund *(Undergraduate/Scholarship)* [791]
Hermoine Grant Calhoun Scholarships *(Undergraduate/Scholarship)* [4875]
Canadian Hard of Hearing Association Scholarships *(Undergraduate/Scholarship)* [1968]
John and Ruth Childe Scholarships *(Undergraduate/Scholarship)* [6645]
Copnick/Hilliard Scholarships *(Professional Development/Scholarship)* [2024]
CRS Scholarships *(Undergraduate/Scholarship)* [2145]
Deaf Queer Youth Scholarships *(Undergraduate/Scholarship)* [6102]
C. Rodney Demarest Memorial Scholarships *(Undergraduate/Scholarship)* [3443]
Disabled War Veterans Scholarships *(Undergraduate/Scholarship)* [1244]
Diversity Executive Leadership Program Scholarships *(Professional Development/Scholarship)* [920]
Edmonton Epilepsy Continuing Education Scholarships *(Undergraduate/Scholarship)* [2824]
Christine H. Eide Memorial Scholarships *(Graduate, Undergraduate/Scholarship)* [4242]
ELA Foundation Scholarships *(Graduate/Scholarship)* [1297]
Families of Freedom Scholarship Fund - America Scholarships *(Undergraduate/Scholarship)* [2902]
Anne M. Fassett Scholarships *(Undergraduate/Scholarship)* [6651]
Jennica Ferguson Memorial Scholarships *(Undergraduate/Scholarship)* [4876]
William and Dorothy Ferrell Scholarship Program *(Undergraduate/Scholarship)* [1390]
Terry Fox Memorial Scholarships *(Undergraduate/Scholarship)* [5117]
Guide Dogs for the Blind Dorothea and Roland Bohde Leadership Scholarships *(Postgraduate/Scholarship)* [4877]
GuildScholar Awards *(Undergraduate/Scholarship)* [4027]
Highway Worker Memorial Scholarship Program *(Undergraduate/Scholarship)* [904]
Doris E. Higley Memorial Scholarships *(Undergraduate/Scholarship)* [3464]
Kenneth Jernigan Scholarships *(Undergraduate/Scholarship)* [4878]
Kuchler-Killian Memorial Scholarships *(Undergraduate/Scholarship)* [4879]
Las Vegas Elks Scholarships for the Physically Challenged *(Undergraduate/Scholarship)* [5837]
The Leaders of Tomorrow Scholarships *(Undergraduate/Scholarship)* [2813]
Lighthouse International Scholarships - College-bound Awards *(High School/Scholarship)* [4243]
Lighthouse International Scholarships - Graduate Awards *(Graduate/Scholarship)* [4244]
Lighthouse International Scholarships - Undergraduate Awards *(Undergraduate/Scholarship)* [4245]
Mary Main Memorial Scholarships *(Undergraduate/Scholarship)* [3478]
Michael Marucci Memorial Scholarships *(Undergraduate/Scholarship)* [4880]
McBurney Disability Scholarships *(Undergraduate/Scholarship)* [7262]
Brian McCartney Scholarships *(Undergraduate/Scholarship)* [4472]
National Federation of the Blind Educator of Tomorrow Award *(Undergraduate/Scholarship)* [4881]
Charles and Melva T. Owen Memorial Scholarships *(Undergraduate/Scholarship)* [4882]
E.U. Parker Scholarships *(Undergraduate/Scholarship)* [4883]
Minnie Pearl Scholarship Program *(Undergraduate/Scholarship)* [2802]
Phillips Scholarships *(Undergraduate/Scholarship)* [2500]
Betty Rendel Scholarships *(Undergraduate/Scholarship)* [4890]
Howard B. Rickard Scholarships *(Undergraduate/Scholarship)* [4884]
SBA Four-Year Scholarships Program *(Undergraduate/Scholarship)* [6702]
SBA One-Year Scholarships Program *(Undergraduate/Scholarship)* [6703]
School Age Financial Aid Program *(Undergraduate/Scholarship)* [1616]
Esther M. Smith Scholarship *(Undergraduate/Scholarship)* [2385]
Beatrice Drinnan Spence Scholarships *(Undergraduate/Scholarship)* [2814]
Dr. Gunnar B. Stickler Scholarships *(Undergraduate/Scholarship)* [6787]
Sun Life Financial Peer Support Scholarships *(Professional Development/Scholarship)* [2025]
Wheelchair Success Foundation Scholarships *(Undergraduate/Scholarship)* [2293]

Employer

Donald H. Bernstein/John B. Talbert, Jr. Scholarship Fund *(Undergraduate/Scholarship)* [3042]
Crowder Scholarship Fund *(Undergraduate/Scholarship)* [3056]
Leo Gilmartin Scholarships *(High School/Scholarship)* [5708]
Henry Hoffman Memorial Scholarship Fund *(Undergraduate/Scholarship)* [4695]
Horace Mann Insurance Scholarships *(High School/Scholarship)* [5336]
National Association of Conservation District Employees Scholarships *(Undergraduate/Scholarship)* [4693]
Ohio Association of Broadcaster's Kids Scholarships *(Undergraduate/Scholarship)* [5317]
Paper Stock Industries/RRF Scholarships *(Undergraduate/Scholarship)* [5450]
PARMA Scholarships *(Undergraduate/Scholarship)* [5795]
PLUS Foundation Financial Aid Grants *(Undergraduate/Scholarship)* [5709]
Raytheon Scholarship Program *(Undergraduate/Scholarship)* [5899]
Rotary Public Safety Scholarship Fund *(Undergraduate/Scholarship)* [3075]
SACHS Foundation Undergraduate Scholarships for Colorado Black Students *(High School/Scholarship)* [6091]
Saskatchewan Trucking Association Scholarships *(Undergraduate/Scholarship)* [6250]
South Texas Lighthouse for the Blind Scholarships *(Undergraduate/Scholarship)* [2288]
Matt Stager Memorial Scholarship Fund *(Undergraduate/Scholarship)* [7390]
Texas Mutual Scholarship Program *(Undergraduate/Scholarship)* [6865]
Turner Family Scholarship Fund *(Undergraduate/Scholarship)* [3080]
Fred C. Wikoff, Jr. Scholarship Fund *(Undergraduate/Scholarship)* [3083]

Ethnic

Accenture American Indian Scholarship Program *(Graduate, Undergraduate/Scholarship)* [640]
AGBU Scholarships *(Graduate/Loan)* [1255]
AIGC Fellowship for Graduates *(Graduate/Fellowship)* [641]
Al Muammar Scholarships for Journalism *(Undergraduate/Scholarship)* [1191]
American Lebanese Engineering Society Scholarship Program *(Other/Scholarship)* [692]
American Physical Society Undergraduate Scholarships *(Undergraduate/Scholarship)* [773]
Armenian American Citizen's League Scholarships

(Undergraduate/Scholarship) [1266]
Armenian American Medical Association Scholarships (Undergraduate/Scholarship) [1267]
Armenian American Pharmacists' Association Scholarships (Doctorate, Graduate/Scholarship) [1268]
Armenian General Athletic Union Scholarships (Undergraduate/Scholarship) [1269]
Armenian Relief Society Scholarships (Graduate, Undergraduate/Scholarship) [1270]
Armenian Scholarship Foundation Scholarships (Graduate, Undergraduate/Scholarship) [1262]
ARS Undergraduate Scholarships (Four Year College, Two Year College, Undergraduate/Scholarship) [1259]
Michael M. Assarian Scholarships (Undergraduate/Scholarship) [1271]
Association of American Indian Physicians Scholarships (Graduate, Undergraduate/Scholarship) [1360]
John M. Azarian Memorial Armenian Youth Scholarships Fund (Undergraduate/Scholarship) [1272]
BCA Ethnic Minority Postgraduate Scholarships for Careers in Athletics (Undergraduate/Scholarship) [1748]
Beginning Freshmen Awards (Undergraduate/Scholarship) [4056]
BIE-Loan for Service for Graduates (Graduate/Loan) [642]
Hagop Bogigian Scholarship Fund (Undergraduate/Scholarship) [1273]
Donald J. Bristow Memorial Scholarship Program (Graduate, Undergraduate/Scholarship) [4655]
Armen H. Bululian Scholarships (Undergraduate/Scholarship) [1274]
Leon C. Bynoe Memorial Scholarships (Undergraduate/Scholarship) [7212]
California Community Service Scholarships (Undergraduate/Scholarship) [4985]
California Community Service Scholarships - Bay Area (Undergraduate/Scholarship) [4986]
Andrew G. Chressanthis Memorial Scholarships (Undergraduate/Scholarship) [3527]
Citi Foundation Scholarships Program (Undergraduate/Scholarship) [619]
Coca-Cola First Generation Scholarships (Undergraduate/Scholarship) [620]
Columbian Lawyers Association of Westchester County Scholarships (Undergraduate/Scholarship) [2331]
Constantinople Armenian Relief Society (C.A.R.S.) Scholarships (Undergraduate/Scholarship) [1275]
Christopher Demetris Scholarships (Undergraduate/Scholarship) [3528]
Karekin DerAvedision Memorial Endowment Fund (Undergraduate/Scholarship) [1276]
Doctoral and Postdoctoral Fellowships (Doctorate, Postgraduate/Fellowship) [3233]
Dorizas Memorial Scholarships (Undergraduate/Scholarship) [3529]
Robert E. Dougherty Scholarships (Undergraduate/Scholarship) [2525]
Margaret Dowell-Gravatt, M.D. Scholarship (Undergraduate/Scholarship) [1625]
George & Isabelle Elanjian Scholarships (Undergraduate/Scholarship) [1277]
Emmanuel Bible College Scholarships (Undergraduate/Scholarship) [1278]
GAPA Scholarships (Undergraduate/Scholarship) [3165]
Garikian Scholarship Fund (Undergraduate/Scholarship) [1279]
General Mills Foundation Scholarships (Undergraduate/Scholarship) [622]
Gerber Fellowships in Pediatric Nutrition (Undergraduate/Fellowship) [4987]
Hai Guin Scholarships Association (Undergraduate/Scholarship) [1280]
Calouste Gulbenkian Foundation Scholarships (Graduate, Undergraduate/Scholarship) [1281]
Sophia Hagopian Memorial Fund (Undergraduate/Scholarship) [1282]
Hellenic University Club of Philadelphia Founders Scholarships (Undergraduate/Scholarship) [3530]
Nicholas S. Hetos, DDS, Memorial Graduate Scholarships (Graduate/Scholarship) [3531]
Hilton Tribal College Diversity Scholarships (Undergraduate/Scholarship) [623]
Lucy Hsu Ho Scholarship (Undergraduate/Scholarship) [1628]
Kaspar Hovannisian Memorial Scholarships (Graduate/Scholarship) [1283]
Hirair and Anna Hovnanian Foundation Presidential Scholarships (Undergraduate/Scholarship) [1284]
Hirair and Anna Hovnanian Foundation Scholarships (Undergraduate/Scholarship) [1285]
Iranian Artist Scholarships (Undergraduate/Scholarship) [4954]
Japanese American Bar Association Scholarships (Undergraduate/Scholarship) [4013]
Rev. and Mrs. A.K. Jizmejian Educational Fund (Undergraduate/Scholarship) [1286]
Kade-Heideking Fellowships (Doctorate/Fellowship) [3235]
KASF Chair Scholarships (Graduate, Undergraduate/Scholarship) [4085]
KASF Designated Scholarships (Graduate, Undergraduate/Scholarship) [4086]
KASF General Scholarships (Graduate, Undergraduate/Scholarship) [4087]
Norair M. Kebabjian Memorial Scholarships (Undergraduate/Scholarship) [1264]
Dr. Elemer and Eva Kiss Scholarships Fund (Undergraduate/Scholarship) [3629]
Knights of Vartan, Fresno Lodge No. 9 Scholarships (Undergraduate/Scholarship) [1287]
Krist-Reavley Minority Scholarships (Undergraduate/Scholarship) [5597]
Lazarian Graduate Scholarships (Graduate/Scholarship) [1260]
George C. Liacouras Memorial Scholarships (Undergraduate/Scholarship) [3532]
Mangasar M. Mangasarian Scholarship Fund (Graduate/Scholarship) [1288]
Mark Miller Award (Graduate, Undergraduate/Scholarship) [4656]
Ralph Modjeski Scholarships (Graduate, Undergraduate/Scholarship) [5729]
Dwight Mosley Scholarships (Undergraduate/Scholarship) [7305]
NAAMA Scholarships (Undergraduate/Scholarship) [4639]
NABA Corporate Scholarship Program (Graduate, Undergraduate/Scholarship) [4657]
NABA National Scholarship Program (Graduate, Undergraduate/Scholarship) [4658]
NASSS Graduate Minority Scholarships (Graduate/Scholarship) [5228]
National Association for Armenian Studies and Research Scholarships (Undergraduate/Scholarship) [1289]
National Medical Fellowships Need-Based Scholarships (Undergraduate/Scholarship) [4989]
National Recreation and Park Association Diversity Scholarships (Undergraduate/Scholarship) [5028]
NIAF Scholarships - General Category I (Undergraduate/Scholarship) [4962]
Nissan North America, Inc. Scholarships (Undergraduate/Scholarship) [624]
PACE/Columbian Lawyers Association of Westchester County Endowed Scholarships (Undergraduate/Scholarship) [2332]
Dr. Nicholas Padis Memorial Graduate Scholarships (Graduate/Scholarship) [3533]
Pepperdine University Armenian Student Scholarships (Undergraduate/Scholarship) [5605]
Peter George Pitsakis Memorial Scholarships (Undergraduate/Scholarship) [3534]
Ameen Rihani Scholarship Program (Undergraduate/Scholarship) [1193]
Jackie Robinson Foundation Minority Scholarship (Undergraduate/Scholarship) [637]
St. James Armenian Church Memorial Scholarships (Undergraduate/Scholarship) [1290]
SAJA Journalism Scholarships (Undergraduate/Scholarship) [6608]
Scholarships for Aboriginal Canadians (Undergraduate/Scholarship) [5118]
Tadeusz Sendzimir Scholarships (Undergraduate/Scholarship) [3496]
Sovereign Nations Scholarship Fund (Undergraduate/Scholarship) [625]
Morgan Stanley Tribal Scholars Program (Undergraduate/Scholarship) [626]
Summer Research Diversity Fellowships in Law and Social Science (Undergraduate/Fellowship) [435]
Hazaros Tabakoglu Scholarship Fund (Undergraduate/Scholarship) [1291]
TDC Scholarship Program (Graduate, Undergraduate/Scholarship) [4659]
Dr. Peter A. Theodos Memorial Graduate Scholarships (Graduate/Scholarship) [3535]
Ralph and Valerie Thomas Scholarship Program (Graduate, Undergraduate/Scholarship) [4660]
Time Warner Tribal Scholars Program (Undergraduate/Scholarship) [627]
Travis C. Tomlin Memorial Scholarship Program (Graduate, Undergraduate/Scholarship) [4661]
Aram Torossian Memorial Scholarships (Undergraduate/Scholarship) [1292]
Transfer Engineering Student Awards (Undergraduate/Scholarship) [4058]
Richard R. Tufenkian Memorial Scholarships (Undergraduate/Scholarship) [1253]
Morris K. Udall Scholarships (Undergraduate/Scholarship) [6945]
Union of Marash Armenian Scholarships (Graduate, Undergraduate/Scholarship) [1293]
University of Wisconsin-Madison American Indian Alumni Scholarships (Undergraduate/Scholarship) [7272]
UPS Diversity Scholarships (Undergraduate/Scholarship) [1073]
Hurad Van Der Bedrosian Memorial Scholarships (Graduate/Scholarship) [1294]
Dimitri J. Ververelli Memorial Scholarships (Undergraduate/Scholarship) [3536]
Warner Norcross & Judd LLP Law School Studies Scholarships (Undergraduate/Scholarship) [7343]
Thomas S. Watson, Jr. Memorial Scholarships (Graduate, Undergraduate/Scholarship) [4662]
Wells Fargo American Indian Scholarship for Graduates (Graduate/Scholarship) [644]
Harry and Angel Zerigian Scholarships (Undergraduate/Scholarship) [1295]

Female

AAUW Legal Advocacy Fund American Fellowships (Doctorate/Fellowship) [4]
AAUW Legal Advocacy Fund Career Development Grants (Professional Development/Grant) [5]
AAUW Legal Advocacy Fund International Fellowships (Doctorate, Graduate/Fellowship) [6]
AAUW Legal Advocacy Fund Selected Professions Fellowships (Doctorate, Graduate/Fellowship) [7]
Evelyn Abrams Memorial Scholarships (Undergraduate/Scholarship) [5797]
Ruth Adams Memorial Scholarships (Undergraduate/Scholarship) [5903]
Air Products and Chemicals, Inc. Scholarships (Undergraduate/Scholarship) [1429]
AMEC Aboriginal Undergraduate Scholarships (Undergraduate/Scholarship) [1947]
AMEC Masters Scholarships (Graduate/Scholarship) [1948]
American Association of University Women International Fellowships (All/Fellowship) [425]
American Business Women's Association Sarasota Chapter Scholarships (Undergraduate/Scholarship) [2503]
AREMA Presidential Spouse Scholarships (Undergraduate/Scholarship) [868]
A.R.F.O.R.A. Undergraduate Scholarships for Women (Undergraduate/Scholarship) [909]
Associated Women for Pepperdine (AWP) Scholarships (Undergraduate/Scholarship) [5572]
AWG Maria Luisa Crawford Field Camp Scholarships (Undergraduate/Scholarship) [1508]

AWG Minority Scholarships *(Undergraduate/Scholarship)* [1509]
AWIS College Scholarships *(Undergraduate/Scholarship)* [1519]
Sandra Sebrell Bailey Scholarships *(Undergraduate/Scholarship)* [2683]
Michael Baker Corporation Scholarship Program *(Undergraduate/Scholarship)* [1430]
Sharon D. Banks Undergraduate Memorial Scholarships *(Undergraduate/Scholarship)* [7508]
Helen Bassett Commemorative Scholarships *(Undergraduate/Scholarship)* [5128]
Myrna F. Bernath Fellowships *(Doctorate, Graduate/Fellowship)* [6454]
Lawrence Bloomberg Entrance Awards *(Postgraduate/Award/Prize)* [6262]
The Lela Breitbart Memorial Scholarship Fund *(All/Scholarship)* [6881]
Louis J. Brody Q.C. Entrance Scholarships *(Postgraduate/Scholarship)* [6263]
Peter F. Bronfman Entrance Awards *(Postgraduate/Award/Prize)* [6264]
Peter F. Bronfman Scholarships of Merit *(Postgraduate/Scholarship)* [6265]
Shirley J. Brooke Endowed Scholarships *(Undergraduate/Scholarship)* [5578]
Dorothy B. Brothers Executive Scholarship Program *(High School/Scholarship)* [7492]
JoAhn Brown-Nash Memorial Scholarships *(Undergraduate/Scholarship)* [2409]
C200 Scholar Awards *(All/Scholarship)* [2337]
Canadian Federation of University Women Etobicoke Bursary *(Graduate, Undergraduate/Scholarship)* [7213]
Career Advancement Scholarships *(Undergraduate/Scholarship)* [1806]
CAWEE International Student Fellowships *(Postgraduate/Fellowship)* [6266]
CEMF Undergraduate Engineering Scholarships *(Undergraduate/Scholarship)* [1949]
Chicana Latina Scholarship Fund *(Graduate, Undergraduate/Scholarship)* [2121]
Chrysalis Scholarships *(Graduate/Grant)* [1510]
City of Toronto Graduate Scholarships for Women in Mathematics *(Graduate/Scholarship)* [7216]
Michelle Clark Fellowships *(Undergraduate/Fellowship)* [1396]
Fisher Clark Memorial Endowed Scholarships *(Undergraduate/Scholarship)* [4170]
Marshall A. Cohen Entrance Awards *(Postgraduate/Award/Prize)* [6267]
Holly A. Cornell Scholarships *(Graduate/Scholarship)* [1143]
Gertrude M. Cox Scholarships *(Doctorate, Graduate/Fellowship)* [1114]
Lydia Cruz and Sandra Maria Ramos Scholarships *(Undergraduate/Scholarship)* [2681]
Curry Award for Girls and Young Women *(Undergraduate/Scholarship)* [6387]
Felicia De Bow Memorial Scholarships *(All/Scholarship)* [5447]
B.J. Dean Scholarships *(Undergraduate/Scholarship)* [2418]
Delta Sigma Theta Hartford Alumnae Scholarships *(Undergraduate/Scholarship)* [3442]
Margaret Dowell-Gravatt, M.D. Scholarship *(Undergraduate/Scholarship)* [1625]
DRI Law Student Diversity Scholarships *(Undergraduate/Scholarship)* [1755]
Mary Ellen Driscoll Scholarships *(Undergraduate/Scholarship)* [6073]
Amelia Earhart Fellowship Program *(Postdoctorate/Fellowship)* [7563]
David Eaton Scholarships *(Graduate, Master's/Scholarship)* [6951]
ELA Foundation Scholarships *(Graduate/Scholarship)* [1297]
Engineering Diversity Affairs Scholarships *(All/Scholarship)* [7252]
Evening Mesquite Club Scholarships *(Undergraduate/Scholarship)* [5823]
Dr. Joan W. Fernandez Point Scholarships *(Graduate, Undergraduate/Scholarship)* [5719]
Friends of Mary Automotive Scholarships *(Undergraduate/Scholarship)* [6312]
A.R.F.O.R.A. Martha Gavrila Scholarships for Women *(Graduate/Scholarship)* [912]
Eloise Gerry Fellowships *(Graduate, Postdoctorate/Fellowship)* [6339]
GFWC Women's Club of South County Scholarships *(Undergraduate/Scholarship)* [6038]
American Association of University Women-Mary Sue Gottcent Memorial Scholarships *(Undergraduate/Scholarship)* [6655]
GREAT MINDS Collegiate Scholarship Program *(Undergraduate/Scholarship)* [236]
Patricia S. Gustafson '56 Memorial Scholarships *(Undergraduate/Scholarship)* [2777]
Leslie Jane Hahn Memorial Scholarships *(Undergraduate/Scholarship)* [6191]
Penelope Hanshaw Scholarships *(Graduate, Undergraduate/Scholarship)* [1511]
Ruth Harris Memorial Scholarships *(Undergraduate/Scholarship)* [5491]
Karen Harter Recruitment Scholarship Grant *(Undergraduate/Scholarship)* [2469]
Karen Harter Recruitment Scholarship Grant *(Undergraduate/Scholarship)* [2470]
Gretchen Hauff Memorial Scholarships *(Undergraduate/Scholarship)* [5831]
HDR Engineering, Inc. Scholarship for Diversity in Engineering *(Undergraduate/Scholarship)* [1432]
Hewlett-Packard Undergraduate Scholarships *(Undergraduate/Scholarship)* [1950]
Amber Huber Memorial Scholarship *(Undergraduate/Scholarship)* [2471]
IAWP International Recognition and Scholarship Award *(Professional Development/Scholarship)* [3811]
IBM Canada Undergraduate Scholarships *(Undergraduate/Scholarship)* [1951]
International Peace Scholarships *(Undergraduate/Scholarship)* [5684]
Nancy Lorraine Jensen Memorial Scholarships *(Undergraduate/Scholarship)* [6603]
JFEW/UJA-Federation Rose Biller Scholarships *(Undergraduate/Scholarship)* [4024]
Lucile B. Kaufman Women's Scholarships *(Undergraduate/Scholarship)* [6493]
Martin Luther King Law Scholarships *(Undergraduate/Scholarship)* [2754]
Anne Koby Legacy Scholarships *(Undergraduate/Scholarship)* [7509]
Bernie Kom Memorial Awards *(Postgraduate/Award/Prize)* [6268]
Robert Krembil Scholarships of Merit *(Postgraduate/Scholarship)* [2082]
Lakselaget Foundation Scholarships *(Graduate, Undergraduate/Scholarship)* [4107]
Allen T. Lambert Scholarships *(Postgraduate/Scholarship)* [6269]
Kenneth Laundy Entrance Scholarships *(Postgraduate/Scholarship)* [6270]
League of Attorneys' Wives Scholarships *(Undergraduate/Scholarship)* [2757]
Carol Anne Letheren Entrance Awards *(Postgraduate/Award/Prize)* [6271]
S. Evelyn Lewis Memorial Scholarships in Medical Health Sciences *(Graduate, Undergraduate/Scholarship)* [7557]
Ian Lithgow Memorial Awards *(Postgraduate/Award/Prize)* [6272]
Carol E. Macpherson Memorial Scholarship and Alumnae Society Scholarships *(Graduate, Undergraduate/Scholarship)* [7133]
Aurella Varallo Mariani Scholarship Program *(Undergraduate/Scholarship)* [4610]
Massachusetts Federation of Polish Women's Clubs Scholarships *(Undergraduate/Scholarship)* [4092]
Michele L. McDonald Scholarships *(Undergraduate/Scholarship)* [2832]
The Cady McDonnell Memorial Scholarships *(Undergraduate/Scholarship)* [488]
Mentoring Travel Grants for Women *(Postdoctorate/Scholarship)* [1515]
Michigan Council of Women in Technology High School Scholarships Program *(Undergraduate/Scholarship)* [4477]
Midwest Chapter Scholarships - Betty McKern *(Undergraduate/Scholarship)* [1448]
Nell I. Mondy Fellowships *(Graduate, Postdoctorate/Fellowship)* [6340]
Brittany Mueller Memorial Scholarships *(High School/Scholarship)* [5161]
Irwin Allen Nadal Entrance Awards *(Postgraduate/Award/Prize)* [6273]
Miles Spencer Nadal Entrance Awards *(Postgraduate/Award/Prize)* [6274]
NCBWL Scholarships *(High School/Scholarship)* [4611]
Helen W. Nies Scholarships *(Undergraduate/Scholarship)* [2907]
Helen Woodruff Nolop Scholarship in Audiology and Allied Fields *(Graduate/Scholarship)* [2696]
Vessa Notchev Fellowships *(Graduate, Postdoctorate/Fellowship)* [6341]
NWF's Women for Sustainable Development (WSD) Scholarships *(Undergraduate/Scholarship)* [6333]
Katharine H. Obye Scholarship Award *(Undergraduate/Scholarship)* [2479]
Optimist Club of Redlands - Virginia Elliott Scholarships *(Undergraduate/Scholarship)* [5970]
Margaret E. Oser Scholarships for Women *(Undergraduate/Scholarship)* [5366]
Helen M. Overly Memorial Scholarships *(Undergraduate/Scholarship)* [7510]
Alice Conger Patterson Scholarships *(Undergraduate/Scholarship)* [7450]
Dorothy E. Hofmann Pembroke Scholarships *(Undergraduate/Scholarship)* [3488]
P.E.O. Chapter Scholarship Fund *(Undergraduate/Scholarship)* [3297]
Gail Porterfield Memorial Scholarships *(Undergraduate/Scholarship)* [5974]
Ina E. Powell Memorial Scholarships *(Undergraduate/Scholarship)* [115]
The Power to Continue Learning Scholarships *(Undergraduate/Scholarship)* [5975]
Judith McManus Price Scholarships *(Graduate, Undergraduate/Scholarship)* [780]
R.M. Princ Scholarships *(Undergraduate/Scholarship)* [5852]
Project Red Flag Academic Scholarships for Women with Bleeding Disorders *(Undergraduate/Scholarship)* [4932]
Puget Sound Chapter Scholarships *(Undergraduate/Scholarship)* [1512]
Jeannette Rankin Scholarships *(Undergraduate/Scholarship)* [5897]
Marjorie Usher Regan Scholarships *(Undergraduate/Scholarship)* [7190]
Rhode Island Commission on Women/Freda H. Goldman Education Awards *(Undergraduate/Award/Prize)* [6041]
Jerrothia Allenfonzo Riggs & Anna & Dorothy Mae Barnes Scholarships *(Undergraduate/Scholarship)* [1899]
Fauneil J. Rinn Scholarships *(Undergraduate/Scholarship)* [6394]
Faye Lynn Roberts Educational Scholarships *(Undergraduate/Scholarship)* [6669]
Mary Louise Roller Panhellenic Scholarships *(Undergraduate/Scholarship)* [5223]
Rowling, Dold and Associates LLP Scholarships *(Undergraduate/Scholarship)* [2833]
William Rucker Greenwood Scholarships *(Graduate, Undergraduate/Scholarship)* [1513]
Deborah Jean Rydberg Memorial Scholarship *(Undergraduate/Scholarship)* [2484]
Ruth Sager Scholarships *(Undergraduate/Scholarship)* [4300]
Scholarships for Emigres in the Health Sciences *(Undergraduate/Scholarship)* [4025]
Tanna H. Schulich MBA Entrance Scholarships *(Postgraduate/Scholarship)* [6275]
Alice Schulman Simmons Scholarships for UU Women *(Undergraduate/Scholarship)* [6954]
Bonnie Sorenson Scudder Scholarship *(Undergraduate/Scholarship)* [2486]
Seattle Chapter ASWA Scholarships *(All/Scholarship)* [2834]
Elisabeth Seegmiller Recruitment Scholarship Grant *(Undergraduate/Scholarship)* [2487]
Mary Isabel Sibley Fellowships *(Doctorate/Fellowship)* [5623]
Sigma Delta Epsilon Fellowships *(Graduate,*

Postdoctorate/Fellowship) [6342]
Julia Viola Simms Science Scholarships *(Postgraduate/Scholarship)* [1742]
Society of Women Engineers Scholarships *(Undergraduate/Scholarship)* [6592]
Southern Nevada Sports Hall of Fame Athletic Scholarships *(Undergraduate/Scholarship)* [5860]
The SSPI Southern California Scholarships *(Graduate, Undergraduate/Scholarship)* [6585]
Harry Steele Entrance Awards *(Postgraduate/Award/Prize)* [6276]
Marlene Streit Golf Scholarships *(Undergraduate/Scholarship)* [6077]
Madlyn D. Thompson Memorial Scholarships *(Undergraduate/Scholarship)* [1900]
Thompson Scholarship for Women in Safety *(Graduate/Scholarship)* [1072]
Town and County Club Scholarships *(Undergraduate/Scholarship)* [3499]
Travel Grants for Women Researchers *(Postdoctorate/Scholarship)* [1516]
Tsutako Curo Scholarships *(Undergraduate/Scholarship)* [5866]
United Parcel Service Scholarship for Female Students *(Undergraduate/Scholarship)* [3740]
Vale Inco Limited Masters Scholarships *(Graduate/Scholarship)* [1952]
Irma E. Voigt Memorial Scholarships *(Undergraduate/Scholarship)* [6379]
Mercedes Laurie Wade Scholarships *(Undergraduate/Scholarship)* [1901]
Washington University Law School Olin Fellowships for Women *(Graduate/Fellowship)* [7387]
The WIFLE Scholarship Fund *(Graduate, Postdoctorate, Undergraduate/Scholarship)* [7477]
Harriet Barnhart Wimmer Scholarships *(Undergraduate/Scholarship)* [988]
Woman's Club of Grand Haven Scholarships Fund *(Undergraduate/Scholarship)* [3315]
The Woman's Club of Nashville Scholarships *(Undergraduate/Scholarship)* [2452]
Women In Defense HORIZONS Scholarships *(Graduate, Undergraduate/Scholarship)* [7479]
Women In Need Scholarships *(Undergraduate/Scholarship)* [2835]
Women In Transition Scholarships *(Undergraduate/Scholarship)* [2836]
Women's Jewelry Association Member Grants *(All/Grant)* [7498]
Women's Leadership in Agriculture Scholarship Program *(Undergraduate/Scholarship)* [5320]
Women's Overseas and Service League Scholarships for Women *(Undergraduate/Scholarship)* [7506]
Carolyn Wones Recruitment Scholarships Grant *(Undergraduate/Scholarship)* [2492]
Marilyn Graboys Wool Scholarships *(Undergraduate/Scholarship)* [6044]
Dr. Marie E. Zakrzewski Medical Scholarships *(Undergraduate/Scholarship)* [4095]
Zeta Chapter Memorial Scholarships Award *(Undergraduate/Scholarship)* [2494]
Zeta Phi Beta Sorority General Graduate Scholarships *(Graduate, Postdoctorate/Scholarship)* [7560]

Fraternal

Nancy Ashley Adams/Ashley Adams Koetje Scholarships *(Undergraduate/Scholarship)* [2635]
Adams Family Scholarships *(Undergraduate/Scholarship)* [2636]
ADGEF Scholarships *(All/Scholarship)* [246]
ALD Graduate Fellowships *(Undergraduate/Fellowship)* [4634]
Margaret M. Alkek Scholarship *(Undergraduate/Scholarship)* [2637]
Alpha Chi Sigma Scholarship Award *(Graduate, Undergraduate/Award/Prize)* [244]
Alpha Eta Scholarships *(Undergraduate/Scholarship)* [2638]
Alpha Kappa Alpha - Educational Advancement Foundation Financial Need-Based Scholarships *(Graduate, Undergraduate/Scholarship)* [248]
Alpha Kappa Alpha - Educational Advancement Foundation Merit Scholarships *(Graduate, Undergraduate/Scholarship)* [249]
Alpha Rho Leadership Scholarships *(Undergraduate/Scholarship)* [2639]
Anchor Plastics Scholarships *(Graduate, Undergraduate/Scholarship)* [5634]
Jane E. Anderson Scholarships *(Undergraduate/Scholarship)* [2640]
Margaret J. Andrew Memorial Scholarships *(Undergraduate/Scholarship)* [6344]
Anheuser-Busch International Scholarships *(Graduate, Undergraduate/Scholarship)* [5635]
Jack Anson Fellowships *(Graduate/Fellowship)* [5220]
Atlanta Alumnae Achievement Scholarships *(Undergraduate/Scholarship)* [2641]
Frances Warren Baker Memorial Scholarships *(Undergraduate/Scholarship)* [6345]
Lloyd G. Balfour Fellowships *(Graduate/Fellowship)* [5221]
Avery Bayle Barth Scholarships *(Undergraduate/Scholarship)* [2642]
William H. Bates Oxford Cup Scholarships *(Graduate, Undergraduate/Scholarship)* [1641]
Stephen D. Bechtel Oxford Cup Scholarships *(Graduate, Undergraduate/Scholarship)* [1642]
Bertram W. Bennett Memorial Scholarships *(Graduate, Undergraduate/Scholarship)* [1643]
Beta Gamma Memorial Scholarship Fund *(Undergraduate/Scholarship)* [2643]
Beta Nu/Caryl Cordis D'hondt Scholarships *(Undergraduate/Scholarship)* [6346]
Beta Omega Scholarships *(Undergraduate/Scholarship)* [6347]
Beta Sigma Scholarships *(Undergraduate/Scholarship)* [6348]
Mildred Cater Bradham Social Work Fellowships *(Graduate/Fellowship)* [7553]
Seth R. and Corrine H. Brooks Memorial Scholarships *(Graduate, Undergraduate/Scholarship)* [1644]
Edward M. Brown Oxford Cup Memorial Scholarships *(Graduate, Undergraduate/Scholarship)* [1645]
Adam S. Burford Memorial Scholarships *(Graduate, Undergraduate/Scholarship)* [1646]
Thad Byrne Memorial Scholarships *(Graduate, Undergraduate/Scholarship)* [1647]
Walta Wilkinson Carmichael Scholarships *(Undergraduate/Scholarship)* [6349]
Commander James Carr Forensic Science Scholarships *(Undergraduate/Scholarship)* [252]
Thomas D. and Karen Cassady Scholarships *(Graduate, Undergraduate/Scholarship)* [1648]
Christine Kerr Cawthorne Scholarships *(Undergraduate/Scholarship)* [6350]
Oscar Chapman Memorial Scholarships *(Graduate, Undergraduate/Scholarship)* [1649]
S. Penny Chappell Scholarships *(Undergraduate/Scholarship)* [5658]
Chi Chapter Undergraduate Scholarships *(Undergraduate/Scholarship)* [2644]
Chi Phi Educational Trust *(Undergraduate/Scholarship)* [2117]
Charline Chilson Scholarships *(Undergraduate/Scholarship)* [2684]
Patricia Smith Christensen Scholarships *(Postdoctorate/Scholarship)* [6383]
Clan Ross Foundation Scholarships *(Undergraduate/Scholarship)* [2245]
Cleveland Alumni Association Scholarships *(Graduate, Undergraduate/Scholarship)* [1650]
Geraldine Clewell Fellowships - Doctoral Student *(Graduate/Fellowship)* [5659]
Geraldine Clewell Fellowships - Masteral *(Graduate/Fellowship)* [5660]
Geraldine Clewell Scholarships - Undergraduate *(Undergraduate/Scholarship)* [5661]
Closs/Parnitzke/Clarke Scholarships *(Undergraduate/Scholarship)* [5662]
L. Robert Clough Memorial Scholarships *(Graduate, Undergraduate/Scholarship)* [1651]
Maridell Braham Condon Scholarships *(Undergraduate/Scholarship)* [6351]
Cornaro Scholarships for Graduate Studies *(Graduate/Scholarship)* [4042]
CSA Fraternal Life Scholarships *(Undergraduate/Scholarship)* [2564]
Arlene Davis Scholarships *(Undergraduate/Scholarship)* [2685]
William W. Dawson Memorial Scholarships *(Graduate, Undergraduate/Scholarship)* [1652]
Delta Chi Alumnae Memorial Scholarships *(Undergraduate/Scholarship)* [6352]
Delta Nu Alpha Foundation Scholarships *(Undergraduate/Scholarship)* [2677]
Delta Phi Epsilon Educational Foundation Scholarships *(Undergraduate/Scholarship)* [2679]
Delta Tau Chapter Scholarships *(Graduate, Undergraduate/Scholarship)* [1653]
Delta Zeta Undergraduate Scholarships *(Undergraduate/Scholarship)* [2686]
Jean Dearth Dickerscheid Fellowships *(Graduate/Fellowship)* [5663]
Wilma Sackett Dressel Scholarships *(Undergraduate/Scholarship)* [6353]
Margaret Drew Alpha Fellowships *(Graduate/Fellowship)* [5664]
John Holt Duncan Memorial Scholarships *(Graduate, Undergraduate/Scholarship)* [1654]
Durning Sisters Scholarships *(Graduate/Scholarship)* [2645]
Todd Elias Memorial Scholarships *(Graduate, Undergraduate/Scholarship)* [1655]
Enterprise Rent-A-Car Scholarships *(Graduate, Undergraduate/Scholarship)* [5636]
Epsilon Epsilon Scholarships *(Undergraduate/Scholarship)* [6354]
Epsilon Tau Scholarships *(Undergraduate/Scholarship)* [6355]
Harriet Erich Graduate Fellowships *(Graduate/Scholarship)* [2646]
Falcon Achievement Scholarships *(Undergraduate/Scholarship)* [5731]
Federated Insurance Scholarships *(Graduate, Undergraduate/Scholarship)* [5637]
Fitzgerald Fellowships *(Undergraduate/Fellowship)* [2672]
Fitzgerald Scholarships *(Undergraduate/Scholarship)* [2673]
Foresters Scholarships *(Undergraduate/Scholarship)* [3682]
Genevieve Forthun Scholarships *(Undergraduate/Scholarship)* [5665]
Mary Weiking Franken Scholarships *(Undergraduate/Scholarship)* [5666]
Marian Johnson Frutiger Scholarships *(Undergraduate/Scholarship)* [6356]
Louise Bales Gallagher Scholarships *(Undergraduate/Scholarship)* [2647]
Gamma Iota Scholarships - Gamma Tau *(Undergraduate/Scholarship)* [6357]
Gamma Iota Scholarships - Kappa Eta *(Undergraduate/Scholarship)* [6358]
Gamma Iota Scholarships - Zeta Kappa *(Undergraduate/Scholarship)* [6359]
Gamma Iota Scholarships - Zeta Nu *(Undergraduate/Scholarship)* [6360]
James L. Gavin Memorial Scholarships *(Graduate, Undergraduate/Scholarship)* [1656]
General Falcon Scholarships *(Undergraduate/Scholarship)* [5732]
Burton L. Gerber Scholarships *(Graduate, Undergraduate/Scholarship)* [1657]
Thomas Boston Gordon Memorial Scholarships *(Graduate, Undergraduate/Scholarship)* [1658]
Richard C. Gorecki Scholarships *(Undergraduate/Scholarship)* [5733]
Lucile Cheever Graubart/Lambda Scholarships *(Undergraduate/Scholarship)* [6361]
Elizabeth M. Gruber Scholarships *(Graduate/Scholarship)* [2687]
Anna E. Hall Memorial Scholarships *(Undergraduate/Scholarship)* [5625]
Tommie J. Hamner Scholarships *(Undergraduate/Scholarship)* [5667]
Charles Henry Hardin Memorial Scholarships *(Graduate, Undergraduate/Scholarship)* [1659]
William H. Harris Memorial Scholarships *(Graduate, Undergraduate/Scholarship)* [5638]
Peg Hart Harrison Memorial Scholarships *(Undergraduate/Scholarship)* [2648]

Edith Head Scholarships (Undergraduate/Scholarship) [2688]
Erin Kumelos Heard Memorial Scholarships (Undergraduate/Scholarship) [2649]
Lavonne Heghinian Scholarships (Undergraduate/Scholarship) [2689]
Ronald, Randall and Roger Helman Scholarships (Graduate, Undergraduate/Scholarship) [1660]
Douglas W. Hill, Jr. Memorial Scholarships (Graduate, Undergraduate/Scholarship) [1661]
John A. Hill Memorial Scholarships (Graduate, Undergraduate/Scholarship) [1662]
Houston Alumnae Chapter Graduate Fellowships (Graduate/Fellowship) [2650]
Houston/Nancy Holliman Scholarships (Undergraduate/Scholarship) [2690]
Sarah Jane Houston Scholarships (Undergraduate/Scholarship) [2691]
Huenefeld/Denton Scholarships (Undergraduate/Scholarship) [2692]
Hazel D. Isbell Fellowships (Graduate/Fellowship) [2652]
Jackman Scholarships (Undergraduate/Scholarship) [5668]
Elise Reed Jenkins Memorial Scholarships - Gamma Psi (Undergraduate/Scholarship) [6363]
Martha Combs Jenkins Scholarships (Undergraduate/Scholarship) [5669]
Kappa Chapter Centennial Scholarships (Undergraduate/Scholarship) [2653]
Kappa Kappa Gamma Graduate Scholarships (Graduate/Scholarship) [4044]
Kappa Kappa Gamma Undergraduate Scholarships (Undergraduate/Scholarship) [4045]
Kappa Omicron Nu Honor Society Scholars Program Grants (Undergraduate/Grant) [4053]
Kappa Omicron Nu National Alumni Fellowships (Graduate/Fellowship) [4047]
Kappa Omicron Nu Undergraduate Scholarships (Undergraduate/Scholarship) [4048]
Kappa Zeta Scholarships (Undergraduate/Scholarship) [6364]
Luella Akins Key Scholarships (Undergraduate/Scholarship) [2654]
Debbie Khalil Memorial Scholarships (Graduate, Undergraduate/Scholarship) [5639]
Treva C. Kintner Scholarships (Undergraduate/Scholarship) [5670]
James P. Kirkgasser Memorial Scholarships (Graduate, Undergraduate/Scholarship) [1663]
John Reily Knox Memorial Scholarships (Graduate, Undergraduate/Scholarship) [1664]
Carl A. Kroch Oxford Cup Memorial Scholarships (Graduate, Undergraduate/Scholarship) [1665]
Otho E. Lane Memorial Scholarships (Graduate, Undergraduate/Scholarship) [1666]
Betsy B. and Garold A. Leach Scholarship for Museum Studies (Undergraduate/Scholarship) [2693]
V.A. Leonard Scholarships (Graduate, Undergraduate/Scholarship) [253]
David Linton Memorial Scholarships (Graduate, Undergraduate/Scholarship) [1667]
Horace G. Lozier Memorial Scholarships (Graduate, Undergraduate/Scholarship) [1668]
Elsa Ludeke Graduate Scholarships (Graduate/Scholarship) [2694]
Mach 1 Air Services Scholarships (Graduate, Undergraduate/Scholarship) [5640]
Eileen C. Maddex Fellowships (Graduate/Fellowship) [4049]
Samuel Taylor Marshall Memorial Scholarships (Graduate, Undergraduate/Scholarship) [1669]
Sarah Shinn Marshall Scholarships (Undergraduate/Scholarship) [2655]
Martin Sisters Scholarships (Undergraduate/Scholarship) [2656]
Nancy B. Woolridge McGee Graduate Fellowships (Graduate/Fellowship) [7558]
John L. and Eleanore I. Mckinley Scholarships (Undergraduate/Scholarship) [2695]
James H. McLaughlin Scholarships (Undergraduate/Scholarship) [5222]
Joan Reagin McNeill Scholarships - Alpha Theta (Undergraduate/Scholarship) [6365]
Joan Reagin McNeill Scholarships - Theta Phi (Undergraduate/Scholarship) [6366]
Steven Craig Merrill Memorial Scholarships (Graduate, Undergraduate/Scholarship) [1670]
Mihaly Russin Scholarship Awards (Graduate/Scholarship) [6087]
Edith Cantor Morrison Memorial Scholarships (Graduate, Undergraduate/Scholarship) [1671]
MPower Scholarships (Graduate, Undergraduate/Scholarship) [5641]
Douglas J. Neeley Memorial Scholarships (Graduate, Undergraduate/Scholarship) [1672]
Virginia Nicklas Scholarships (Undergraduate/Scholarship) [2658]
Evelyn S. Nish Scholarships (Undergraduate/Scholarship) [6367]
Northwestern Mutual Financial Network Scholarships (Graduate, Undergraduate/Scholarship) [5642]
E. William Palmer Memorial Scholarships (Graduate, Undergraduate/Scholarship) [1673]
Cissy McDaniel Parker Scholarships (Undergraduate/Scholarship) [2660]
Gail Patrick Charitable Trust Scholarships (Undergraduate/Scholarship) [2697]
Zoe Gore Perrin Scholarships (Undergraduate/Scholarship) [2661]
Phi Kappa Phi Fellowships (Other/Fellowship) [5629]
Phi Kappa Sigma Need-Based Scholarships (Undergraduate/Scholarship) [5631]
Phi Kappa Sigma Participation-Based Scholarships (Undergraduate/Scholarship) [5632]
Phi Sigma Epsilon Innovation Scholarships (Graduate, Undergraduate/Scholarship) [5643]
Phi Sigma Epsilon Past National President Scholarships (Graduate, Undergraduate/Scholarship) [5644]
Phi Upsilon Omicron Candle Fellowships (Graduate/Fellowship) [5671]
Phi Upsilon Omicron Challenge Scholarships (Undergraduate/Scholarship) [5672]
Phi Upsilon Omicron Diamond Anniversary Fellowships (Graduate/Fellowship) [5673]
Phi Upsilon Omicron Founders Fellowships (Graduate/Fellowship) [5674]
Phi Upsilon Omicron Golden Anniversary Scholarships (Undergraduate/Scholarship) [5675]
Phi Upsilon Omicron Past Presidents Scholarships (Undergraduate/Scholarship) [5676]
Phi Upsilon Omicron Presidents Research Fellowships (Graduate/Fellowship) [5677]
Pi Gamma Mu Scholarships (Graduate/Scholarship) [5691]
Pryor Graduate Fellowships (Graduate/Fellowship) [241]
Cheryl White Pryor Memorial Scholarships (Undergraduate/Scholarship) [2662]
Public Agency Training Council Criminal Justice Scholarships (Undergraduate/Scholarship) [254]
John J. and Elizabeth Rhodes Scholarships (Graduate, Undergraduate/Scholarship) [1674]
Ben C. Rich Memorial Scholarships (Graduate, Undergraduate/Scholarship) [1675]
Susan E. Riley Scholarships (Undergraduate/Scholarship) [2663]
Jean Wiggin Roach Scholarships (Undergraduate/Scholarship) [2664]
Nell Bryant Robinson Scholarships (Undergraduate/Scholarship) [5678]
Mary Louise Roller Panhellenic Scholarships (Undergraduate/Scholarship) [5223]
Dorothy Worden Ronken Scholarships (Graduate/Scholarship) [2698]
Lucile Rust Scholarships (Undergraduate/Scholarship) [5679]
Michael Clarkson Ryan Memorial Scholarships (Graduate, Undergraduate/Scholarship) [1676]
Jeanne Graves Ryland Scholarships (Undergraduate/Scholarship) [2665]
Julie Anne Sadlier Memorial Scholarships (Undergraduate/Scholarship) [2666]
Virginia Hartford Saharov Memorial Scholarships (Undergraduate/Scholarship) [2667]
Saints Cyril and Methodius Scholarships (Undergraduate/Scholarship) [6088]
Sales and Marketing Executives International Scholarships (Graduate, Undergraduate/Scholarship) [5645]
Margaret Jerome Sampson Scholarships (Undergraduate/Scholarship) [5680]
Edith Scandlyn/Sammie Lynn Scandlyn Puett Memorial Scholarships (Undergraduate/Scholarship) [2668]
Mary Turnbull Schacht Memorial Scholarships (Undergraduate/Scholarship) [6368]
William C. Scheetz Family Scholarships (Graduate, Undergraduate/Scholarship) [1677]
Lillian P. Schoephoerster Scholarships (Undergraduate/Scholarship) [5681]
Fred A. Seaton Memorial Scholarships (Graduate, Undergraduate/Scholarship) [1678]
Detective Cheryl Seiden Memorial Scholarships (Undergraduate/Scholarship) [255]
Regina B. Shearn Scholarships (Graduate, Undergraduate/Scholarship) [256]
Misty and Sally Shoop Scholarships (Graduate, Undergraduate/Scholarship) [1679]
Sigma Kappa Foundation Alumnae Continuing Education Scholarships (Undergraduate/Scholarship) [6369]
Sigma Kappa Foundation Founders' Scholarships (Undergraduate/Scholarship) [6371]
Sigma Kappa Foundation Gerontology Scholarships (Undergraduate/Scholarship) [6372]
Sigma Kappa Foundation Michigan Scholarships (Undergraduate/Scholarship) [6373]
John R. Simpson Memorial Scholarships (Graduate, Undergraduate/Scholarship) [1680]
James George Smith Memorial Scholarships (Graduate, Undergraduate/Scholarship) [1681]
Helen D. Snow Memorial Scholarships (Undergraduate/Scholarship) [5626]
The Standard Scholarships (Graduate, Undergraduate/Scholarship) [5646]
The Mabel Keaton Staupers National Scholarship Award (Doctorate, Graduate, Undergraduate/Scholarship) [2115]
Elin J. Stene/Xi Scholarships (Undergraduate/Scholarship) [6374]
H. Hiram Stephenson Oxford Cup Scholarships (Graduate, Undergraduate/Scholarship) [1682]
Hugh E. Stephenson Oxford Cup Scholarships (Graduate, Undergraduate/Scholarship) [1683]
Student Media Group Scholarships (Graduate, Undergraduate/Scholarship) [5647]
Sutherland/Purdy Scholarships (Undergraduate/Scholarship) [5682]
Lorraine E. Swain Scholarships (Undergraduate/Scholarship) [6375]
Swivel Media Scholarships (Graduate, Undergraduate/Scholarship) [5648]
Theta/Caryl Cordis D'hondt Scholarships (Undergraduate/Scholarship) [6376]
Theta Tau Scholarships (Undergraduate/Scholarship) [6377]
Barber Owen Thomas Scholarships (Undergraduate/Scholarship) [6378]
Thornberg/Havens Scholarships (Undergraduate/Scholarship) [2700]
Thrivent Financial Scholarships (Graduate, Undergraduate/Scholarship) [5649]
Richard Cecil Todd and Clauda Pennock Todd Tripod Scholarships (Graduate, Undergraduate/Scholarship) [5655]
Michael W. Toennis Scholarships (Graduate, Undergraduate/Scholarship) [1684]
Jo Anne J. Trow Scholarships (Undergraduate/Scholarship) [4635]
UPE/ACM Scholarship Awards (Graduate, Undergraduate/Award/Prize) [7288]
UPE Scholarship Awards (Graduate, Undergraduate/Award/Prize) [7289]
Valpak Scholarships (Graduate, Undergraduate/Scholarship) [5650]
Vector Marketing Scholarships (Graduate, Undergraduate/Scholarship) [5651]
Gupton A. Vogt Oxford Cup Memorial Scholarships (Graduate, Undergraduate/Scholarship) [1685]
Teri Wenglein-Callender Undergraduate Scholarships (Undergraduate/Scholarship) [2669]
Whan Memorial Scholarships (Graduate,

Undergraduate/Scholarship) [5652]
Donna Axum Whitworth Scholarships *(Undergraduate/Scholarship)* [2670]
Alice Hersey Wick Scholarships *(Undergraduate/Scholarship)* [6380]
Andrea Will Memorial Scholarships *(Undergraduate/Scholarship)* [6381]
Rolla F. Wood Graduate Scholarships *(Graduate/Scholarship)* [5656]
Xilinx Scholarships *(Graduate, Undergraduate/Scholarship)* [5653]
Donnell B. Young Scholarships *(Undergraduate/Scholarship)* [4074]
Youth Partners Accessing Capital (P.A.C.) *(Graduate, Undergraduate/Scholarship)* [250]

Hispanic American

AACN Minority Nurse Faculty Scholarships *(Graduate/Scholarship)* [335]
AALL & Thomson West - George A. Strait Minority Scholarship Endowment *(Postgraduate/Scholarship)* [364]
ABA Legal Opportunity Scholarship Funds *(Undergraduate/Scholarship)* [3582]
Affirmative Action Mini Grant and Student Scholarships *(All/Grant)* [14]
Affirmative Action Scholarships *(Graduate/Scholarship)* [6680]
AICPA Scholarships for Graduate Accounting Students *(Postgraduate/Scholarship)* [4641]
AICPA Scholarships for Minority Accounting Students *(Undergraduate/Scholarship)* [4642]
Air Products and Chemicals, Inc. Scholarships *(Undergraduate/Scholarship)* [1429]
ALPFA Scholarship Programs *(Postgraduate, Undergraduate/Scholarship)* [1492]
AMA Foundation Minority Scholars Award *(Undergraduate/Scholarship)* [712]
American Society for Microbiology International Fellowships for Latin America *(Postdoctorate/Fellowship)* [1003]
APA Planning Fellowships *(Graduate/Fellowship)* [776]
APS Scholarships for Minority Undergraduate Physics Majors *(Undergraduate/Scholarship)* [5051]
Frank G. Araujo Memorial Scholarships *(Undergraduate/Scholarship)* [5909]
Artistic Scholarship Awards *(Undergraduate/Scholarship)* [1598]
AWG Minority Scholarships *(Undergraduate/Scholarship)* [1509]
Michael Baker Corporation Scholarship Program *(Undergraduate/Scholarship)* [1430]
Barbri Scholarships for Bar Preparation *(Undergraduate/Scholarship)* [3578]
BECA Foundation-CUSM Scholarships *(Undergraduate/Scholarship)* [1610]
Maria Borrero Scholarships *(Undergraduate/Scholarship)* [3425]
Emma L. Bowen Foundation Scholarships for Minority Interests in Media work/study Program *(Undergraduate/Scholarship)* [7333]
California Community Service Scholarships *(Undergraduate/Scholarship)* [4985]
California Community Service Scholarships - Bay Area *(Undergraduate/Scholarship)* [4986]
The California Endowment and AACN Minority Nurse Faculty Scholarships *(Graduate/Scholarship)* [337]
Connecticut Association of Latinos in Higher Education Scholarships *(Undergraduate/Scholarship)* [3434]
Lydia Cruz and Sandra Maria Ramos Scholarships *(Undergraduate/Scholarship)* [2681]
Daimler Chrysler Scholarships Award *(Undergraduate/Scholarship)* [3565]
Dallas Hispanic Bar Association Scholarships *(Undergraduate/Scholarship)* [2611]
Davis Family Scholarships *(Undergraduate/Scholarship)* [6183]
Ruth DeMoss Scholarships *(Undergraduate/Scholarship)* [6184]
DRI Law Student Diversity Scholarships *(Undergraduate/Scholarship)* [1755]
FAIC Latin American and Caribbean Scholars Program *(Professional Development/Scholarship)* [660]
First in My Family Scholarship Program *(Undergraduate/Scholarship)* [6156]
Ford Motor Company Scholarship Program *(Undergraduate/Scholarship)* [3589]
Foundation of American Institute for Conservation Lecture Grants *(Professional Development/Grant)* [661]
Franchise Law Diversity Scholarship Awards *(Undergraduate/Scholarship)* [3857]
John Hope Franklin Dissertation Fellowships *(Doctorate/Fellowship)* [768]
GAP, Inc. Scholarships Award *(Undergraduate/Scholarship)* [3566]
The Gates Millennium Scholars *(Undergraduate/Scholarship)* [3590]
General Scholarship Awards *(Undergraduate/Scholarship)* [1599]
Gerber Fellowships in Pediatric Nutrition *(Undergraduate/Fellowship)* [4987]
Leonor R. Guerrero Memorial Scholarships *(Undergraduate/Scholarship)* [4689]
HACU/Wal-Mart Achievers Scholarships *(Undergraduate/Scholarship)* [3567]
The Richard D. Hailey AAJ Law Student Scholarships *(Undergraduate/Scholarship)* [358]
HDR Engineering, Inc. Scholarship for Diversity in Engineering *(Undergraduate/Scholarship)* [1432]
Hispanic Association of Colleges and Universities Scholarships *(Undergraduate/Scholarship)* [3568]
Hispanic College Fund Scholarship Programs *(Undergraduate/Scholarship)* [3583]
Hispanic Lawyers Association of Illinois Public Interest Fellowships *(Undergraduate/Scholarship)* [3579]
Hispanic Scholarship Fund (HSF) College Scholarship Program *(Graduate, Undergraduate/Scholarship)* [3591]
HNBF Princeton Review Duard Bradshaw Memorial Scholarships *(Undergraduate/Scholarship)* [3584]
HSBC-North America Scholarship Program *(Undergraduate/Scholarship)* [3592]
HSF/Atrisco Heritage Foundation Scholarship Program *(Graduate, Undergraduate/Scholarship)* [3593]
HSF/Citi Fellows Program *(Undergraduate/Scholarship)* [3594]
HSF/General Motors Scholarship Program *(Undergraduate/Scholarship)* [3595]
HSF/Hewlett Packard (HP) Diversity in Education Scholarship Program *(Undergraduate/Scholarship)* [3596]
HSF/IDT Hope High School Scholarship Program *(Undergraduate/Scholarship)* [3597]
HSF/Nissan Community College Transfer Scholarship Program *(Undergraduate/Scholarship)* [3598]
HSF/Wal-Mart Stores Inc. Scholarship Program *(Graduate, Undergraduate/Scholarship)* [3599]
The Hyatt Hotels Fund For Minority Lodging Management Students *(Undergraduate/Scholarship)* [611]
Justicia En Diversidad Scholarships *(Undergraduate/Scholarship)* [3585]
Kaplan Scholarships *(Undergraduate/Scholarship)* [3580]
W.K. Kellogg Foundation Doctoral Fellowships in Health Policy *(Professional Development/Fellowship)* [4988]
KPMG Foundation Minority Accounting Doctoral Scholarships *(Postdoctorate/Scholarship)* [4097]
La Unidad Latina Foundation Scholarships *(Graduate, Undergraduate/Scholarship)* [3586]
La Voz Latina Scholarships *(Undergraduate/Scholarship)* [2474]
Latin American Educational Foundation Scholarships *(Undergraduate/Scholarship)* [4145]
Lewis-Clark State College/American Chemical Society Scholars Program *(Undergraduate/Scholarship)* [4192]
LITA and LSSI Minority Scholarships *(Graduate/Scholarship)* [4237]
LITA/OCLC Minority Scholarships *(Graduate/Scholarship)* [4238]
LULAC GM Scholarships *(Graduate, High School, Undergraduate/Award/Prize)* [4152]
LULAC National Scholarship Fund *(Graduate, High School, Undergraduate/Scholarship)* [4153]
MALDEF Law School Scholarships *(Undergraduate/Scholarship)* [3587]
Marathon Oil Corporation College Scholarship Program *(Graduate, Undergraduate/Scholarship)* [3600]
McNamara Family Creative Arts Project Grants *(Graduate, Undergraduate/Grant)* [3601]
Medina Scholarships for Hispanics in Safety *(Graduate, Undergraduate/Scholarship)* [1063]
Minority Teachers of Illinois Scholarships *(Undergraduate/Scholarship)* [3670]
MLA/NLM Spectrum Scholarship Program *(Graduate/Scholarship)* [4445]
MLA Scholarships for Minority Students *(Graduate/Scholarship)* [4447]
Archie Motley Memorial Scholarships for Minority Students *(Graduate/Scholarship)* [4511]
National Association of Campus Activities Multicultural Scholarship Programs *(Undergraduate/Scholarship)* [4680]
National Medical Fellowships Need-Based Scholarships *(Undergraduate/Scholarship)* [4989]
National Organization of Italian-American Women Scholarships *(All/Scholarship)* [5000]
Ohio Newspaper Association Minority Scholarships *(Undergraduate/Scholarship)* [5323]
Peierls Rising Star Scholarship Program *(Undergraduate/Scholarship)* [3602]
Judith McManus Price Scholarships *(Graduate, Undergraduate/Scholarship)* [780]
Miguel Pro Scholarships *(Undergraduate/Scholarship)* [7532]
Puerto Rican Bar Association Scholarships *(Undergraduate/Scholarship)* [5884]
Ronald McDonald House Charities of Hispanic Heritage *(Undergraduate/Scholarship)* [4408]
Leo and Trinidad Sanchez Scholarships *(Undergraduate/Scholarship)* [6396]
Wendell Scott Awards *(Graduate, Undergraduate/Scholarship)* [3570]
Fraser Stryker Diversity Scholarship Program *(Undergraduate/Scholarship)* [5166]
Fraser Stryker Diversity Scholarships *(Undergraduate/Scholarship)* [6809]
Toyota High School Scholarship Program *(Undergraduate/Scholarship)* [3603]
TU@UT HSF College Scholarship Program *(Undergraduate/Scholarship)* [3604]
University Alliance HSF/UGA College Scholarship Program *(Undergraduate/Scholarship)* [3605]
University of Wisconsin-Madison Hispanic/Latino Alumni Scholarships *(Undergraduate/Scholarship)* [7276]
Valley Alliance of Mentors for Opportunities and Scholarship (VAMOS) Program *(Undergraduate/Scholarship)* [3606]
Valuing Diversity PhD Scholarships *(Doctorate/Scholarship)* [710]
Verizon Scholarship Program *(Undergraduate/Scholarship)* [3607]
Wachovia Scholarship Awards *(Undergraduate/Scholarship)* [3571]
Wells Fargo Scholarship Program *(Graduate, Undergraduate/Scholarship)* [3608]
Western Governors University Scholarship Program *(Undergraduate/Scholarship)* [3609]
Writers of Passage Scholarship Program *(Undergraduate/Prize)* [6159]

Male

American Legion Eagle Scout of the Year Scholarships *(High School/Scholarship)* [4850]
Rick Arkans Eagle Scout Scholarships *(High School/Scholarship)* [4851]
Asian/Pacific Gays and Friends Scholarships *(Undergraduate/Scholarship)* [6097]
Birmingham-Southern College Eagle Scout Scholarships *(Undergraduate/Scholarship)* [4852]
Cartwright Scholarships Program

(Undergraduate/Scholarship) [618]
Emmett J. Doerr Memorial Distinguished Scout Scholarships *(High School/Scholarship)* [4853]
Dofflemyer Scholarships *(Undergraduate/Scholarship)* [4854]
Epsilon Tau Pi's Soaring Eagle Scholarships *(Undergraduate/Scholarship)* [4856]
Gaebe Eagle Scout Awards *(Undergraduate/Scholarship)* [4857]
Zenon C.R. Hansen Leadership Scholarships *(Undergraduate/Scholarship)* [4859]
Brian Jimenez Memorial Scholarships *(Undergraduate/Scholarship)* [5948]
Arthur M. and Berdena King Eagle Scout Scholarships *(High School/Scholarship)* [4860]
Lindenwood University Scouting Scholarships *(Undergraduate/Scholarship)* [4862]
Bill McCarthy Scout Scholarship Fund *(Undergraduate/Scholarship)* [6741]
H.N. Neal Memorial Scholarships *(Undergraduate/Scholarship)* [1898]
Optimist Club Of Redlands - Ralph Maloof Scholarships *(Undergraduate/Scholarship)* [5969]
Josef Princ Memorial Scholarships *(Undergraduate/Scholarship)* [5851]
Redlands High School Boy's Varsity Volleyball Scholarships *(Undergraduate/Scholarship)* [5982]
Saint Vincent College Eagle Scout Scholarships *(Undergraduate/Scholarship)* [4865]
Sons of Norway Foundation Scholarships to Oslo International School *(Undergraduate/Scholarship)* [6604]
Swede Swanson Memorial Scholarships *(Undergraduate/Scholarship)* [5162]
Jeffery Tyler Sweitzer Wrestling Memorial Scholarship Fund *(Undergraduate/Scholarship)* [6756]
University of Louisville Eagle Scout Scholarships *(Undergraduate/Scholarship)* [4866]
John Vanderlee Scholarships *(Undergraduate/Scholarship)* [2015]
Chester M. Vernon Memorial Eagle Scout Scholarships *(High School/Scholarship)* [4867]
Veterans of Foreign Wars Scout of the Year *(High School/Scholarship)* [4868]
Frank L. Weil Memorial Eagle Scout Scholarships *(Undergraduate/Scholarship)* [4869]
American Legion Eagle Scout of the Year Scholarships *(High School/Scholarship)* [4850]
Rick Arkans Eagle Scout Scholarships *(High School/Scholarship)* [4851]
Birmingham-Southern College Eagle Scout Scholarships *(Undergraduate/Scholarship)* [4852]
Emmett J. Doerr Memorial Distinguished Scout Scholarships *(High School/Scholarship)* [4853]
Dofflemyer Scholarships *(Undergraduate/Scholarship)* [4854]
Epsilon Tau Pi's Soaring Eagle Scholarships *(Undergraduate/Scholarship)* [4856]
Gaebe Eagle Scout Awards *(Undergraduate/Scholarship)* [4857]
Zenon C.R. Hansen Leadership Scholarships *(Undergraduate/Scholarship)* [4859]
Brian Jimenez Memorial Scholarships *(Undergraduate/Scholarship)* [5948]
Arthur M. and Berdena King Eagle Scout Scholarships *(High School/Scholarship)* [4860]
Lindenwood University Scouting Scholarships *(Undergraduate/Scholarship)* [4862]
Bill McCarthy Scout Scholarship Fund *(Undergraduate/Scholarship)* [6741]
H.N. Neal Memorial Scholarships *(Undergraduate/Scholarship)* [1898]
Optimist Club Of Redlands - Ralph Maloof Scholarships *(Undergraduate/Scholarship)* [5969]
Josef Princ Memorial Scholarships *(Undergraduate/Scholarship)* [5851]
Redlands High School Boy's Varsity Volleyball Scholarships *(Undergraduate/Scholarship)* [5982]
Saint Vincent College Eagle Scout Scholarships *(Undergraduate/Scholarship)* [4865]
Swede Swanson Memorial Scholarships *(Undergraduate/Scholarship)* [5162]
Jeffery Tyler Sweitzer Wrestling Memorial Scholarship Fund *(Undergraduate/Scholarship)* [6756]
University of Louisville Eagle Scout Scholarships *(Undergraduate/Scholarship)* [4866]
John Vanderlee Scholarships *(Undergraduate/Scholarship)* [2015]
Chester M. Vernon Memorial Eagle Scout Scholarships *(High School/Scholarship)* [4867]
Veterans of Foreign Wars Scout of the Year *(High School/Scholarship)* [4868]
Frank L. Weil Memorial Eagle Scout Scholarships *(Undergraduate/Scholarship)* [4869]

Military

AAAA Scholarship Program *(Undergraduate/Scholarship)* [1299]
ACHE/American Legion Auxiliary Scholarships *(Undergraduate/Scholarship)* [98]
ACHE/American Legion Scholarships *(Undergraduate/Scholarship)* [99]
Alabama Gi Dependents Educational Benefit Programs *(Undergraduate/Scholarship)* [105]
Alabama National Guard Educational Assistance Programs *(Undergraduate/Scholarship)* [106]
The American Legion Legacy Scholarships *(Undergraduate/Scholarship)* [694]
Anchor Scholarship Foundation *(Undergraduate/Scholarship)* [6826]
LT.G. Douglas D. Buchholz Memorial Scholarships *(Undergraduate/Scholarship)* [1242]
Dr. Aurelio M. Caccomo Family Foundation Memorial Scholarships *(Undergraduate/Scholarship)* [1136]
Datatel Angelfire Scholarships *(Graduate, Undergraduate/Scholarship)* [2615]
LaRue A. Ditmore Music Scholarships *(Undergraduate/Scholarship)* [7481]
Dolphin Scholarships *(Undergraduate/Scholarship)* [2726]
Sergeant Major Douglas R. Drum Memorial Scholarship Fund *(Undergraduate/Scholarship)* [716]
FEEA Scholarship Program *(Other/Scholarship)* [2914]
Lily H. Gridley Memorial Scholarships *(Undergraduate/Scholarship)* [7482]
Khaki University and Y.M.C.A. Memorial Scholarships *(Undergraduate/Scholarship)* [7225]
First Lieutenant Scott McClean Love Memorial Scholarship - Children of Soldiers *(Undergraduate/Scholarship)* [1303]
First Lieutenant Scott McClean Love Memorial Scholarship - Spouses of Soldiers *(Undergraduate/Scholarship)* [1304]
Marine Corps Engineer Association Assistance Fund *(Graduate, High School, Undergraduate/Scholarship)* [4306]
Marine Corps League National Scholarships *(Undergraduate/Scholarship)* [4308]
Military Order of the Perpetual Heart Foundation Scholarships *(Undergraduate/Scholarship)* [4206]
MOAA American Patriot Scholarships *(Undergraduate/Scholarship)* [4529]
MOAA Base/Post Scholarships *(Undergraduate/Scholarship)* [4530]
Captain Jennifer Shafer Odom Memorial Scholarships - Children of Soldiers *(Undergraduate/Scholarship)* [1305]
Captain Jennifer Shafer Odom Memorial Scholarships - Spouses of Soldiers *(Undergraduate/Scholarship)* [1306]
Ohio War Orphan Scholarships *(Undergraduate/Scholarship)* [7531]
Ontario Hockey Association War Memorial Scholarships *(Undergraduate/Scholarship)* [7232]
General John Paul Ratay Educational Grants *(Undergraduate/Grant)* [4531]
Samsung American Legion Scholarships *(Undergraduate/Scholarship)* [697]
ThanksUSA Scholarships *(Undergraduate/Scholarship)* [6877]
Veterans of Enduring Freedom (Afghanistan) and Iraqi Freedom Scholarships *(Undergraduate/Scholarship)* [1250]
Ethyl and Armin Wiebke Memorial Scholarships *(Undergraduate/Scholarship)* [7483]
WMA Memorial Scholarships *(Undergraduate/Scholarship)* [7484]
Women's Army Corps Veterans Association Scholarships *(Undergraduate/Scholarship)* [7486]
Women's Overseas and Service League Scholarships for Women *(Undergraduate/Scholarship)* [7506]

Minority

AACN Minority Nurse Faculty Scholarships *(Graduate/Scholarship)* [335]
Dr. Anderson Abbott Awards *(Undergraduate/Scholarship)* [7208]
AERA Minority Fellowship Program in Education Research *(Postdoctorate/Fellowship)* [545]
Affirmative Action Scholarships *(Graduate/Scholarship)* [6680]
Alliance of Black Culinarians Scholarships *(Undergraduate/Scholarship)* [5800]
American Association of Blacks in Energy Scholarships *(Undergraduate/Scholarship)* [324]
American Dental Association Minority Dental Student Scholarships *(Undergraduate/Scholarship)* [539]
William G. Anderson, DO, Minority Scholarship *(Undergraduate/Scholarship)* [749]
Judge Sidney M. Aronovitz Memorial Scholarships *(High School/Scholarship)* [2594]
ASA Minority Fellowships Program *(Doctorate, Master's/Fellowship)* [1094]
ASHFA Scholarships for Minority Students *(Postgraduate/Scholarship)* [1103]
Howard Baker Foundation Scholarships *(Undergraduate/Scholarship)* [1589]
Bay Area Minority Law Student Scholarships *(Graduate, Undergraduate/Scholarship)* [1596]
BCA Ethnic Minority Postgraduate Scholarships for Careers in Athletics *(Undergraduate/Scholarship)* [1748]
Dennis J. Beck Memorial Scholarship *(Undergraduate/Scholarship)* [3973]
Mary Ann Brichta Scholarships *(Undergraduate/Scholarship)* [7249]
George M. Brooker Collegiate Scholarships for Minorities *(Graduate, Postgraduate, Undergraduate/Scholarship)* [3748]
Brown and Caldwell Minority Scholarships *(Undergraduate/Scholarship)* [7334]
Brown Foundation Academic Scholarships *(Undergraduate/Scholarship)* [1796]
Patricia Buchanan Memorial Scholarships *(Undergraduate/Scholarship)* [7250]
The California Endowment and AACN Minority Nurse Faculty Scholarships *(Graduate/Scholarship)* [337]
Holly A. Cornell Scholarships *(Graduate/Scholarship)* [1143]
Council on Social Work Education Minority Fellowship Programs *(Postdoctorate/Fellowship)* [2553]
Albert and Jane Dewey Scholarships *(Undergraduate/Scholarship)* [3444]
Diversity Executive Leadership Program Scholarships *(Professional Development/Scholarship)* [920]
DRI Law Student Diversity Scholarships *(Undergraduate/Scholarship)* [1755]
Engineering Diversity Affairs Scholarships *(All/Scholarship)* [7252]
Ethnic Minority and Women's Enhancement Postgraduate Scholarships *(Graduate/Scholarship)* [4803]
Fine Arts Association Minority Scholarships *(Undergraduate/Scholarship)* [2932]
Ford Foundation Predoctoral Fellowships for Minorities *(Doctorate/Fellowship)* [4703]
Dick and Pat Hazel Minority Scholarships *(Professional Development/Scholarship)* [2377]
IREM Foundation Minority Outreach Scholarships *(Professional Development/Scholarship)* [3750]
JLTLA Texas Bar Review Scholarships *(Undergraduate/Scholarship)* [6943]
Kegler Brown Minority Merit Scholarships *(Undergraduate/Scholarship)* [4062]
Lawton Minority Retention Grants *(Undergraduate/Scholarship)* [7261]

Special Recipient Index

LIN Television Corporation Minority Scholarships and Training Program (Undergraduate/Scholarship) [4247]
MCCA Lloyd M. Johnson, Jr. Scholarships (Undergraduate/Scholarship) [4558]
McClatchy Scholarships (Undergraduate/Scholarship) [6616]
John McLendon Memorial Minority Postgraduate Scholarships (Postdoctorate/Scholarship) [4691]
Minority Medical Student Fellowships in HIV Psychiatry (Undergraduate/Fellowship) [793]
Minority Scholarship Awards for Incoming College Freshmen (Undergraduate/Scholarship) [658]
John P. and Tashia F. Morgridge Scholarships (Undergraduate/Scholarship) [7263]
NASSS Graduate Minority Scholarships (Graduate/Scholarship) [5228]
National Association of Campus Activities Multicultural Scholarship Programs (Undergraduate/Scholarship) [4680]
National Co-op Scholarship Program (Undergraduate/Scholarship) [4809]
National Recreation and Park Association Diversity Scholarships (Undergraduate/Scholarship) [5028]
NBMBAA PhD Fellowship Programs (Doctorate/Fellowship) [4762]
New Jersey Psychological Association Scholarships for Minority Graduate Students (Postgraduate/Scholarship) [5184]
Ohio Newspaper Association Minority Scholarships (Undergraduate/Scholarship) [5323]
Pfizer Minority Medical Journalism Scholarships (Postgraduate/Scholarship) [7185]
Polsinelli Diversity Scholarships (Undergraduate/Scholarship) [7352]
Powers-Knapp Scholarships (Undergraduate/Scholarship) [7266]
Jackie Robinson Foundation Minority Scholarship (Undergraduate/Scholarship) [637]
Jackie Robinson Scholarships (Undergraduate/Scholarship) [6049]
Edward S. Roth Manufacturing Engineering Scholarships (Graduate, Undergraduate/Scholarship) [6500]
Rowling, Dold and Associates LLP Scholarships (Undergraduate/Scholarship) [2833]
Royce-Osborn Minority Scholarship Program (Undergraduate/Scholarship) [1042]
William Rucker Greenwood Scholarships (Graduate, Undergraduate/Scholarship) [1513]
Scholarships for Visible Minorities (Undergraduate/Scholarship) [5119]
School of Education Scholarships for Students from Underrepresented Groups (Undergraduate/Scholarship) [7268]
StraightForward Media's Minority Scholarships (Undergraduate/Scholarship) [6803]
Surety Industry Scholarship Program for Minority Students (Undergraduate/Scholarship) [6824]
United Parcel Service Scholarship for Minority Students (Undergraduate/Scholarship) [3741]
University of Wisconsin-Madison/CALS Minority Scholarships (Undergraduate/Scholarship) [7274]
University of Wisconsin-Madison Chancellor's Scholarships (Undergraduate/Scholarship) [7275]
University of Wisconsin-Madison Minority Teacher Loans (Professional Development, Undergraduate/Loan, Scholarship) [7277]
Lari Ann Vest Memorial Scholarships (Undergraduate/Scholarship) [809]
Herbert W. Whiteman, Jr. Scholarships (Graduate, Undergraduate/Scholarship) [7293]

Native American

AALL & Thomson West - George A. Strait Minority Scholarship Endowment (Postgraduate/Scholarship) [364]
Affirmative Action Mini Grant and Student Scholarships (All/Grant) [14]
AICPA Scholarships for Graduate Accounting Students (Postgraduate/Scholarship) [4641]
AICPA Scholarships for Minority Accounting Students (Undergraduate/Scholarship) [4642]
Air Products and Chemicals, Inc. Scholarships (Undergraduate/Scholarship) [1429]
Alaska Native Medical Center Auxiliary Scholarships (Undergraduate/Scholarship) [4339]
AMA Foundation Minority Scholars Award (Undergraduate/Scholarship) [712]
APA Planning Fellowships (Graduate/Fellowship) [776]
APS Scholarships for Minority Undergraduate Physics Majors (Undergraduate/Scholarship) [5051]
Association on American Indian Affairs Emergency Aid Scholarship (Undergraduate/Scholarship) [630]
AWG Minority Scholarships (Undergraduate/Scholarship) [1509]
Michael Baker Corporation Scholarship Program (Undergraduate/Scholarship) [1430]
Notah Begay III Scholarship Program (Undergraduate/Scholarship) [190]
Emma L. Bowen Foundation Scholarships for Minority Interests in Media work/study Program (Undergraduate/Scholarship) [7333]
Buder Scholarship for American Indian Law Students (Undergraduate/Scholarship) [7384]
Sam Bull Memorial Scholarships (Undergraduate/Scholarship) [142]
California Community Service Scholarships (Undergraduate/Scholarship) [4985]
California Community Service Scholarships - Bay Area (Undergraduate/Scholarship) [4986]
Cartwright Scholarships Program (Undergraduate/Scholarship) [618]
Catching the Dream Scholarship (Graduate, Undergraduate/Scholarship) [632]
Daughters of the American Revolution American Indian Scholarships (Undergraduate/Scholarship) [633]
Vine Deloria Jr. Memorial Scholarships (Graduate/Scholarship) [621]
Ruth DeMoss Scholarships (Undergraduate/Scholarship) [6184]
Sergeant Douglas and Charlotte DeHorse Scholarships (Undergraduate/Scholarship) [2066]
DRI Law Student Diversity Scholarships (Undergraduate/Scholarship) [1755]
Franchise Law Diversity Scholarship Awards (Undergraduate/Scholarship) [3857]
John Hope Franklin Dissertation Fellowships (Doctorate/Fellowship) [768]
Marcus Garvey Scholarships (Undergraduate/Scholarship) [3453]
The Gates Millennium Scholars (Undergraduate/Scholarship) [3590]
Gerber Fellowships in Pediatric Nutrition (Undergraduate/Fellowship) [4987]
William Harrison Gill Education Fund (Undergraduate/Scholarship) [1627]
Senator James Gladstone Memorial Scholarships (Undergraduate/Scholarship) [143]
Graduate Education Loan Scholarships (Graduate/Loan) [3780]
The Richard D. Hailey AAJ Law Student Scholarships (Undergraduate/Scholarship) [358]
HDR Engineering, Inc. Scholarship for Diversity in Engineering (Undergraduate/Scholarship) [1432]
HSF/Hewlett Packard (HP) Diversity in Education Scholarship Program (Undergraduate/Scholarship) [3596]
Indian Health Service Scholarship Program (Undergraduate/Scholarship) [634]
International Order of the King's Daughters and Sons North American Indian Scholarship Program (Undergraduate/Scholarship) [635]
W.K. Kellogg Foundation Doctoral Fellowships in Health Policy (Professional Development/Fellowship) [4988]
Kilbuck Family Native American Scholarship (Undergraduate/Scholarship) [1629]
KPMG Foundation Minority Accounting Doctoral Scholarships (Postdoctorate/Scholarship) [4097]
Lewis-Clark State College/American Chemical Society Scholars Program (Undergraduate/Scholarship) [4192]
LITA and LSSI Minority Scholarships (Graduate/Scholarship) [4237]
LITA/OCLC Minority Scholarships (Graduate/Scholarship) [4238]
Marathon Oil Corporation College Scholarship Program (Graduate, Undergraduate/Scholarship) [3600]
MESBEC Scholarships (Undergraduate/Scholarship) [2067]
Minorities in Government Finance Scholarships (Graduate, Undergraduate/Scholarship) [3266]
Minority Teachers of Illinois Scholarships (Undergraduate/Scholarship) [3670]
MLA/NLM Spectrum Scholarship Program (Graduate/Scholarship) [4445]
MLA Scholarships for Minority Students (Graduate/Scholarship) [4447]
Archie Motley Memorial Scholarships for Minority Students (Graduate/Scholarship) [4511]
National Association of Campus Activities Multicultural Scholarship Programs (Undergraduate/Scholarship) [4680]
National Medical Fellowships Need-Based Scholarships (Undergraduate/Scholarship) [4989]
Native American Charter High Schools After-the-Fires Scholarships (Undergraduate/Scholarship) [6210]
Native American Education Grants (Graduate, Undergraduate/Grant) [636]
Native American Leadership Education (NALE) Scholarships (Postdoctorate, Undergraduate/Scholarship) [2068]
Ohio Newspaper Association Minority Scholarships (Undergraduate/Scholarship) [5323]
Fitzroy and Mildred Parkinson Memorial Scholarships (Undergraduate/Scholarship) [3486]
Phillips Fund Grant for Native American Research (Graduate/Grant) [771]
Judith McManus Price Scholarships (Graduate, Undergraduate/Scholarship) [780]
David W. Schacht Native American Student Scholarship (Undergraduate/Scholarship) [1630]
Carl A. Scott Book Scholarships (Undergraduate/Scholarship) [2555]
Helen J. and Harold Gilman Smith Scholarship (Graduate, Undergraduate/Scholarship) [1631]
Fraser Stryker Diversity Scholarship Program (Undergraduate/Scholarship) [5166]
Fraser Stryker Diversity Scholarships (Undergraduate/Scholarship) [6809]
Tribal Business Management Program (TBM) Scholarships (Undergraduate/Scholarship) [2069]
Tribal Priority Scholarships (Undergraduate/Scholarship) [1212]
Udall Scholarships (Undergraduate/Scholarship) [7089]
United South and Eastern Tribes Scholarship Fund (Undergraduate/Scholarship) [6970]
U.S. BIA Indian Higher Education Grants (Undergraduate/Grant) [638]
Valuing Diversity PhD Scholarships (Doctorate/Scholarship) [710]
West Indian Migrant Farm Workers Memorial Scholarships (Undergraduate/Scholarship) [3501]
Western Michigan Society of Health-System Pharmacists Scholarships (All/Scholarship) [7407]
Woksape Oyate: "Wisdom of the People" Distinguished Scholars Award (Undergraduate/Scholarship) [628]

Other

APS Scholarships for Minority Undergraduate Physics Majors (Undergraduate/Scholarship) [5051]
Beginning Freshmen Awards (Undergraduate/Scholarship) [4056]
MLA/NLM Spectrum Scholarship Program (Graduate/Scholarship) [4445]
MLA Scholarships for Minority Students (Graduate/Scholarship) [4447]

Transfer Engineering Student Awards *(Undergraduate/Scholarship)* [4058]

Religion

Stephanie Ali Memorial Scholarships *(Undergraduate/Scholarship)* [7210]
Rick Arkans Eagle Scout Scholarships *(High School/Scholarship)* [4851]
Associated Women for Pepperdine (AWP) Scholarships *(Undergraduate/Scholarship)* [5572]
Martha and Robert Atherton Ministerial Scholarships *(Graduate, Master's/Scholarship)* [6947]
James R. and Geraldine F. Bertelsen Scholarships *(Undergraduate/Scholarship)* [6172]
Mary E. Bivins Foundation Religious Scholarship Program *(Graduate, Undergraduate/Scholarship)* [1719]
Olympia Brown and Max Kapp Awards *(Graduate/Scholarship)* [6948]
Catholic Biblical Association of America Scholarships *(Undergraduate/Scholarship)* [2071]
Chautauqua Scholarship Program *(All/Scholarship)* [3882]
Children of Unitarian Universalist Ministers College Scholarships *(Undergraduate/Scholarship)* [6949]
The Helena B. Cobb Annual Scholarships *(Undergraduate/Scholarship)* [7501]
The Helena B. Cobb Four-Year Higher Education Grants *(Undergraduate/Scholarship)* [7502]
College Education Loan Scholarships For U.S. Resident Students *(Undergraduate/Loan)* [3779]
Emmett J. Doerr Memorial Distinguished Scout Scholarships *(High School/Scholarship)* [4853]
Pauly D'Orlando Memorial Art Scholarships *(Graduate, Undergraduate/Scholarship)* [6950]
Eastern Orthodox Scouting Scholarships *(High School/Scholarship)* [4855]
David Eaton Scholarships *(Graduate, Master's/Scholarship)* [6951]
Emmanuel Bible College Scholarships *(Undergraduate/Scholarship)* [1278]
Dorris W. Frey Memorial Scholarships *(Undergraduate/Scholarship)* [6654]
Jewish Federation Academic Scholarships *(Graduate, Undergraduate/Scholarship)* [4029]
Rev. and Mrs. A.K. Jizmejian Educational Fund *(Undergraduate/Scholarship)* [1286]
Lily Scholarships in Religion for Journalists *(Professional Development/Scholarship)* [6021]
MACC Scholarships *(Professional Development/Scholarship)* [4466]
David Pohl Scholarships *(Graduate, Master's/Scholarship)* [6952]
Roy H. Pollack Scholarships *(Graduate, Master's/Scholarship)* [6953]
St. James Armenian Church Memorial Scholarships *(Undergraduate/Scholarship)* [1290]
Scholarships for Lutheran College Students *(Undergraduate/Scholarship)* [1687]
Scholarships for Lutheran Nursing Students *(Undergraduate/Scholarship)* [1688]
David W. Self Scholarships *(Undergraduate/Scholarship)* [6967]
Joseph Sumner Smith Scholarships *(All/Scholarship)* [6955]
Richard S. Smith Scholarships *(Undergraduate/Scholarship)* [6968]
Marion Barr Stanfield Art Scholarships *(Graduate, Undergraduate/Scholarship)* [6956]
Otto M. Stanfield Law Scholarships *(Graduate/Scholarship)* [6957]
Anne Sturrock Nursing Scholarships *(Undergraduate/Scholarship)* [6675]
Rev. Chuck and Nancy Thomas Scholarships *(Graduate, Master's/Scholarship)* [6958]
Thomas and Glenna Trimble Endowed Scholarships *(Undergraduate/Scholarship)* [5616]
Chester M. Vernon Memorial Eagle Scout Scholarships *(High School/Scholarship)* [4867]
Von Ogden Vogt Scholarships *(Graduate, Master's/Scholarship)* [6959]
Frank L. Weil Memorial Eagle Scout Scholarships *(Undergraduate/Scholarship)* [4869]
Brian J. White Endowed Law Scholarships *(Undergraduate/Scholarship)* [5617]

Union

Tommy Douglas Scholarships *(Undergraduate/Scholarship)* [5116]
Duluth Building and Construction Trades Council Scholarships *(Undergraduate/Scholarship)* [2774]
Farmers Union Marketing and Processing Foundation Stanley Moore Scholarships *(Undergraduate/Scholarship)* [5250]
Raymond A. Kent-Navy V-12/ROTC *(Undergraduate/Scholarship)* [7101]
Stanley Moore Scholarships *(Undergraduate/Scholarship)* [5251]
North Dakota Farmers Union Co-op House Scholarships *(Undergraduate/Scholarship)* [5253]
Hubert K. Seymour Scholarships *(Undergraduate/Scholarship)* [5255]
SUVCW Scholarships *(Undergraduate/Scholarship)* [6606]
Utility Workers Union of America Scholarship Program *(Undergraduate/Scholarship)* [7309]

Veteran

AMVETS National Scholarships - Entering College Freshmen *(Undergraduate/Scholarship)* [1133]
AMVETS National Scholarships - For Veterans *(Undergraduate/Scholarship)* [1134]
AMVETS National Scholarships - JROTC *(Undergraduate/Scholarship)* [1135]
Dr. Aurelio M. Caccomo Family Foundation Memorial Scholarships *(Undergraduate/Scholarship)* [1136]
Disabled War Veterans Scholarships *(Undergraduate/Scholarship)* [1244]
Sergeant Douglas and Charlotte DeHorse Scholarships *(Undergraduate/Scholarship)* [2066]
Forsyth County Nursing Scholarships *(Undergraduate/Scholarship)* [7433]
H.H. McKnight Memorial Scholarships *(Undergraduate/Scholarship)* [7122]
Mike Nash Memorial Scholarships *(Undergraduate/Scholarship)* [7319]
Post 4137 Veterans Foundation Scholarships *(Undergraduate/Scholarship)* [5695]
Bernard Rotberg Memorial Scholarships *(Undergraduate/Scholarship)* [4031]
SUVCW Scholarships *(Undergraduate/Scholarship)* [6606]
Veterans of Enduring Freedom (Afghanistan) and Iraqi Freedom Scholarships *(Undergraduate/Scholarship)* [1250]

Sponsor and Scholarship Index

This index lists, in a single alphabetic sequence, all of the administering and sponsoring organizations and awards covered in the "Sponsors and Their Scholarships" section. Also included are co-sponsoring organizations and organization acronyms. The numbers that follow citations indicate the book entry numbers for particular organizations and awards, not page numbers. Book entry numbers for administering organizations appear in boldface type.

4th Infantry Division Association Scholarships [4613]
The "21" Endowed Scholarships [4160]
101st Airborne Division Association **[1]**
92109 Community Fund-Mark and Karla Stuart Family Scholarships [6161]
The AAA (American Automobile Association) Five Diamond Hospitality Scholarships [608]
AAAA Scholarship Program [1299]
AAACN Scholarships [320]
AAAS Mass Media Science and Engineering Fellowships [316]
AAAS Science and Technology Policy Fellowships [317]
AABA Read Carlock Memorial Scholarship Fund [1206]
AABP Amstutz Scholarships [326]
AABP Bovine Veterinary Student Recognition Award [327]
AABP Education Grants [328]
AABP Research Assistantship [329]
AABP Student Externship Program [330]
AACE International Competitive Scholarships [1350]
AACN Excellence in Academics Nursing Scholarships [334]
AACN Minority Nurse Faculty Scholarships [335]
AACOM Scholar in Residence Program [339]
AACT Undergraduate Scholarships [5711]
AAEP/ALSIC Scholarships [344]
AAEP Foundation Research Fellowships [345]
AAG IGIF Graduate Research Awards [1352]
AAG IGIF Student Travel Grants [1353]
AAGS Graduate Fellowship Award [481]
AAGS Joseph F. Dracup Scholarship Award [482]
AAIB Scholarships [355]
AAJ Trial Advocacy Scholarships [357]
AAJA/CNN Scholar Program [1328]
AAJA/COX Foundation Scholarships [1329]
AAJA/S.I. Newhouse Foundation Scholarships [1330]
AALL Scholarships for Continuing Education Classes [362]
AALL Scholarships for Library School Graduates Seeking a Non-Law Degree [363]
AALL & Thomson West - George A. Strait Minority Scholarship Endowment [364]
AANS Medical Student Summer Research Fellowships (MSSRF) [370]
AAOHN Academic Study Scholarships [378]
AAOHN Continuing Education Scholarships [379]
AAPA Research Scholarships [393]
AAS-American Historical Print Collectors Society Fellowships [294]
AAS-American Society for Eighteenth Century Studies Fellowships [295]
AAS CIAC Small Grants [1370]
AAS Fellowships for Creative and Performing Artists and Writers [296]
AAS Korean Studies Scholarship Program [1371]
AAS National Endowment for the Humanities Long-Term Fellowships [297]
AAS-Northeast Modern Language Association Fellowships [298]
AAST/ACS/NIGMS Scholarships [407]
AAST/KCI Research Grants [408]
AAST Medical Student Scholarships [409]
AATA Anniversary Scholarships [312]
AAUW Legal Advocacy Fund **[3]**
AAUW Legal Advocacy Fund American Fellowships [4]
AAUW Legal Advocacy Fund Career Development Grants [5]
AAUW Legal Advocacy Fund International Fellowships [6]
AAUW Legal Advocacy Fund Selected Professions Fellowships [7]
ABA Academic Merit Scholarships [445]
ABA Diversity Scholarships [446]
ABA Legal Opportunity Scholarship Funds [3582]
ABA Legal Scholarships [382]
ABA Members Scholarships (ABA Bus and Tour Operators Only) [447]
ABA Members Scholarships (All ABA Member Companies) [448]
ABA Scholarships [437]
Abbene Scholarships; Anthony [3635]
Abbott Awards; Dr. Anderson [7208]
Abbott Memorial Scholarships; Clifford V. [6766]
Abbott Scholarships [6822]
ABC-Clio Research Grants [6514]
Abecia Reaching High Scholarships; Alejandro "Alex" [2259]
Abelson Scholarships; Jack [3171]
Abercrombie and Fitch Global Diversity Scholar Awards [5066]
Abernathy Presidential Scholarships; Ruth [351]
ABF Doctoral Fellowships [433]
ABFSE National Scholarship Program [441]
Abiko Memorial Scholarships; Kyutaro & Yasuo [4015]
Aboriginal Nurse Association of Canada **[8]**
Above and Beyond Scholarships [1846]
Abrahamer Scholarships; Mandel & Lauretta [6767]
Abrams Memorial Scholarships; Evelyn [5797]
Abrams Scholarship Program; Charles [775]
Abramson Memorial Foundation; The Frederick B. **[10]**
Abramson Memorial Foundation Scholarships; The Frederick B. [11]
Abramson Public Interest Fellowships Award; The Frederick B. [12]
Academic Promise Scholarships [3697]
Academic Scholarship Program A [4843]
Academic Scholarship Program B [4844]
L'Academie de Cuisine Culinary Arts Scholarships [2568]
Academy of Criminal Justice Science **[13]**
Academy of Medical-Surgical Nurses **[15]**
Academy of Model Aeronautics **[17]**
Accenture American Indian Scholarship Program [640]
The Access Intelligence Scholarships [6580]
ACE K-12 Scholarships Program [234]
ACHE/American Legion Auxiliary Scholarships [98]
ACHE/American Legion Scholarships [99]
ACHE Junior and Community College Athletic Scholarships [100]
ACHE Junior and Community College Performing Arts Scholarships [101]
ACHE Police Officers and Firefighters Survivors' Educational Assistance Programs [102]
ACHE Senior Adult Scholarships [103]
ACHE Two-Year College Academic Scholarships [104]
Achter Scholarship Program; Renee [726]
Ackerman Family Scholarship Fund; Ken and Pat [2938]
Ackerman Family Scholarship Fund; Wayne D. [6707]
Ackley Scholarship Program; Naida [727]
Ackroyd Scholarships; Jack [1925]
ACLS Frederick Burkhardt Fellowships [299]
ACMPE Scholarship Fund **[21]**
ACMPE Scholarship Fund Program [22]
ACNM Foundation, Inc. Fellowship for Graduate Education [469]
ACNP Nurse Practitioner Student Scholarship Awards [473]
ACRES Scholarships [513]
ACS/ASA Health Policy and Management Scholarships [1117]
ACS/NREF-AANS Faculty Career Development Award [371]
ACSM Fellowship Scholarships [483]
Acterman Public Education Awards; Larry [5355]
Actuarial Scholarships for Minority Students [383]
ACUA Scholarships [1381]
ACWA Water Law and Policy Scholarships [1375]
Adams/Ashley Adams Koetje Scholarships; Nancy Ashley [2635]
Adams Family Scholarships [2636]
Adams Fund; Ruth D. [2939]
Adams Memorial Awards; Mamie [4161]
Adams Memorial Foundation Lapeer County Community Foundation Fund; The Clarke B. [4138]
Adams Memorial Scholarship; Lt. Holly [2404]
Adams Memorial Scholarships; Ed [6030]
Adams Memorial Scholarships; Ruth [5903]
Adams Scholarship Fund; Henry S. and Carolyn [3035]
Adams Scholarships; Frederick G. [3411]
Adams Scholarships; Henry [962]
Adelhardt Memorial Scholarships; Carl Joseph [3167]
Adelson Family Scholarships [5798]
Adelson Scholarships [5799]
ADGEF Scholarships [246]
Adkins Memorial Scholarships; Bob [5462]
Adkins Scholarships; Howard E. and Wilma J. [1149]
Adler Scholarship Fund; Chris Nance [2260]
Adolescent Literacy Predoctoral Fellowships [4623]
Adoptive Families Today **[23]**
Adoptive Families Today Commemorative Scholarships [24]
Adrian Memorial Scholarship Fund; Herb [3036]
Adult Higher Education Alliance **[25]**
Adults Students in Scholastic Transition (ASIST) [2894]
Advanced Cardiovascular Surgery Fellowships [415]
Advertising Production Club of New York **[27]**
Advertising Production Club Scholarship Awards [28]
Advocates for the American Osteopathic Association **[32]**
AE Flight Training Scholarships [5206]

AE Jet Type Rating Scholarships [5207]
AE Technical Training Scholarships [5208]
AeA Scholarships [6162]
AERA-AIR Fellows Program [543]
AERA-ETS Fellowship Program in Measurement [544]
AERA Minority Fellowship Program in Education Research [545]
AFCEA Distance Learning/Online Scholarships [1236]
AFCEA Fellowships [1237]
AFCEA General John A. Wickham Scholarships [1238]
AFCEA Math and Science Teachers Scholarships [1239]
AFCEA Scholarship for Working Professionals [1240]
AFFIRM University Scholarships [1414]
Affirmative Action Mini Grant and Student Scholarships [14]
Affirmative Action Scholarships [6680]
AFIA Scholarships [573]
AFPPA Student Scholarships [1412]
African American Network - Carolinas Scholarship Fund [3037]
AFROTC Scholarships [46]
AFSA Chapter 155 Division 1 Scholarships - Category 1 [56]
AFSA Chapter 155 Division 1 Scholarships - Category 2 [57]
AFSA Chapter 155 Division 1 Scholarships - Category 3 [58]
AFSA Scholarship Program [54]
AFSP - Distinguished Investigator Grants [587]
AFSP Postdoctoral Research Fellowships [588]
AFSP Standard Research Grants [589]
AFSP Young Investigator Grants [590]
After-the-Fires Scholarships [6163]
AfterCollege/AACN Nursing Scholarships [336]
AGBU Scholarships [1255]
AGC Foundation Outstanding Educator Awards [1344]
AGC New York State Chapter Scholarship Program [1427]
Agricultural Institute of Canada **[35]**
Agriculture Future of America **[38]**
Agriculture Future of America Community Scholarships [39]
Agriculture Future of America Scholarship Program [40]
Ahearn Victoria Elementary Scholarships; Patty [5904]
Ahepa Buckeye Scholarship Awards [42]
Ahepa Buckeye Scholarship Foundation **[41]**
Ahepa District No. 1 Scholarship Foundation **[43]**
Ahepa District No. 1 Scholarship Program [44]
AHNS-ACS Career Development Awards [599]
AHNS Pilot Research Grants [600]
AHNS Young Investigator Awards [601]
AIA and the Global Automotive Aftermarket Symposium Scholarships [1569]
AIAA Foundation Scholarship Program [646]
AIAS/AIA Trust Scholarships for Emerging Professionals [648]
AIBS Junior Fellowships [652]
AIBS Senior Fellowships [653]
AIChE/Donald F. and Mildred Topp Othmer National Scholarship Awards [655]
AICPA Scholarships for Graduate Accounting Students [4641]
AICPA Scholarships for Minority Accounting Students [4642]
AIDS Awareness Scholarships [6093]
AIGC Fellowship for Graduates [641]
AIMS Long-term Research Grants [667]
AIMS Short-term Research Grants [668]
Air Force Association **[45]**
Air Force Association Excellence Scholarships [47]
Air Force Association/Grantham Scholarships [48]
Air Force Association Spouse Scholarships [49]
Air Force ROTC Enhanced HBCU Scholarships [6972]
Air Force Sergeants Association **[53]**
Air Force Sergeants Association-Chapter 155 **[55]**
Air Products and Chemicals, Inc. Scholarships [1429]
Air Traffic Control Association **[61]**
Air Traffic Control Association Full-time Employee Student Scholarships [62]
Air Traffic Control Association Non-employee Student Scholarships [63]
Aircraft Electronics Association **[65]**
Aircraft Owners and Pilots Association Scholarships [66]
Airport Minority Advisory Council Educational and Scholarship Program **[91]**
Airports Council International-North America **[93]**
Airports Council International-North America Scholarship [94]
AISC/Carolina Steel Scholarships [676]
AISC/Fred R. Havens Fellowships [677]
AISC/Great Lakes Fabricators and Erectors Association Fellowships [678]
AISC/Rocky Mountain Steel Construction Association Fellowships [679]
AISC/Southern Association of Steel Fabricators Fellowships [680]
AISC/Southern Association of Steel Fabricators Scholarships [681]
AISC/Structural Steel Education Council Fellowships [682]
AISC/US Steel Fellowships [683]
AIST Baltimore Chapter Scholarships [1438]
AIST Detroit Chapter Scholarships [1439]
AIST Northwest Chapter Scholarships [1440]
AIST Ronald E. Lincoln Memorial Scholarships [1441]
AIST San Francisco Chapter Scholarships [1442]
AIST William E. Schwabe Memorial Scholarships [1443]
AIST Willy Korf Memorial Fund [1444]
Aja Memorial Scholarship Program; Diane Blicksilver [728]
AJL Convention Travel Grants [1459]
AJL Scholarship Program [1460]
Akao Scholarships for QFD [5886]
Akron Bar Association Foundation **[95]**
Akron Bar Association Foundation Scholarships [96]
Al Mercury Scholarships [7209]
Al Muammar Scholarships for Journalism [1191]
Alabama Commission on Higher Education **[97]**
Alabama Gi Dependents Educational Benefit Programs [105]
Alabama Horse Council **[110]**
Alabama Horse Council Scholarships [111]
Alabama Law Foundation **[122]**
Alabama National Guard Educational Assistance Programs [106]
Alabama Power Scholarships [5275]
Alabama Scholarships for Dependents of Blind Parents [107]
Alabama Student Assistance Programs [108]
Alabama Student Grant Programs [109]
Alaska Aerospace Development Corporation Scholarships [4338]
Alaska Airlines Scholarships [1079]
Alaska Airmen Association **[124]**
Alaska Community Foundation **[128]**
Alaska Community Foundation Sven E. & Lorraine Eriksson Scholarships [7029]
Alaska Kidney Foundation-ASN Research Grants [1017]
Alaska Native Medical Center Auxiliary Scholarships [4339]
Alaska Press Club Scholarships [4340]
Alaska Pulp Scholarship Foundation **[130]**
Alaska Support Industry Alliance Scholarships [4341]
Alaska Visitors Association/Gomar Scholarships [4342]
Alaska Yukon Pioneer Memorial Scholarships [4343]
Alberta 4-H **[132]**
Alberta Agricultural Economics Association **[136]**
Alberta Agricultural Economics Association Scholarships [137]
Alberta Agricultural Economics Association Undergraduate Scholarships [138]
Alberta Award for the Study of Canadian Human Rights and Multiculturalism [145]
Alberta Barley Commission **[139]**
Alberta Centennial Premier's Scholarships - Alberta [146]
Alberta Indian Investment Corporation **[141]**
Alberta Learning Information Service - Alberta Scholarship Program **[144]**
Alberta Press Council **[186]**
Alberta Press Council Scholarships [187]
Alberta Ukrainian Centennial Commemorative Scholarships [7356]
Alberts Endowed Scholarships in Physiology; Bruce and Betty [4282]
Albright Scholarships-Dane County; Victor [7246]
Albright Scholarships; Victor [7247]
Albuquerque Community Foundation **[188]**
Albuquerque Lesbian and Gay Chamber of Commerce Scholarships [6094]
ALD Graduate Fellowships [4634]
Aldis Scholarship Fund; Owen F. [3904]
Alexander and Blaise Robert Alexander Memorial Scholarships; Anne L. [2940]
Alexander Scholarship Fund; William Tasse [3038]
Alexander Scholarships; Hon. Lincoln [1724]
Alford Jr. Scholarships; Floyd S. [7141]
Alger Ak-Sar-Ben Scholarships; Horatio [198]
Alger Alabama Scholarships; Horatio [199]
Alger Association; Horatio **[197]**
Alger California and California Orange County Scholarships; Horatio [200]
Alger Delaware Scholarships; Horatio [201]
Alger District of Columbia, Maryland, and Virginia Scholarships; Horatio [202]
Alger Florida Scholarships; Horatio [203]
Alger Franklin Scholarships; Horatio [204]
Alger Georgia Scholarships; Horatio [205]
Alger Idaho University Scholarships; Horatio [206]
Alger Illinois Scholarships; Horatio [207]
Alger Indiana Scholarships; Horatio [208]
Alger Iowa Scholarships; Horatio [209]
Alger Kentucky Scholarships; Horatio [210]
Alger Lola and Duane Hagadone Idaho Scholarships; Horatio [211]
Alger Louisiana Scholarships; Horatio [212]
Alger Minnesota Scholarships; Horatio [213]
Alger Mississippi Scholarships; Horatio [214]
Alger Missouri Scholarships; Horatio [215]
Alger Montana Scholarships; Horatio [216]
Alger National Scholarships; Horatio [217]
Alger New Jersey Scholarships; Horatio [218]
Alger New York Scholarships; Horatio [219]
Alger North Dakota Scholarships; Horatio [220]
Alger Oregon Scholarships; Horatio [221]
Alger Pennsylvania Scholarships; Horatio [222]
Alger South Dakota Scholarships; Horatio [223]
Alger Texas - Fort Worth Scholarships; Horatio [224]
Alger Texas Scholarships; Horatio [225]
Alger Utah Scholarships; Horatio [226]
Alger Washington Scholarships; Horatio [227]
Alger Wyoming Scholarships; Horatio [228]
Algood Tuition Scholarships; Emma and Meloid [4664]
Ali Memorial Scholarships; Stephanie [7210]
Alkek Scholarship; Margaret M. [2637]
All-American Vector Marketing Scholarship Program [7311]
All Star Association **[229]**
Allard Broadcast Journalism Scholarships; Jim [1921]
Allegheny County Medical Society (ACMS) Medical Student Scholarship [3134]
Allen and Associate Scholarships; Paul Shearman [7003]
Allen Athletic Memorial Scholarships; Robinson G. [5905]
Allen Community Newspaper Internships; Peggy [7142]
Allen (Dan) Memorial Scholarships [6095]
Allen Memorial Metal Shop/Auto Body Scholarships; William A. [5906]
Allen Scholarship; Janet and Horace [147]
Allen Scholarships; Allen - Marty [2261]
Allen University **[231]**
Allen World Classroom Scholarships; Julie [6164]
Alliance for Academic Achievement Program Scholarships [3412]
Alliance of Black Culinarians Scholarships [5800]
Alliance for Choice in Education **[233]**
Alliance Francaise of Hartford Harpin/Rohinsky Scholarships [3413]

Sponsor and Scholarship Index

American Handel Society **[596]**
American Head and Neck Society **[598]**
American Historical Association **[604]**
American History Scholarships [5062]
American Hotel and Lodging Educational Foundation **[607]**
American Indian College Fund **[617]**
American Indian Education Foundation **[629]**
American Indian Endowed Scholarships [7363]
American Indian Graduate Center Scholars (AIGCS) **[639]**
American Institute of Aeronautics and Astronautics Foundation **[645]**
American Institute of Architecture Students **[647]**
American Institute of Baking **[649]**
American Institute of Baking Scholarships [650]
American Institute of Bangladesh Studies **[651]**
American Institute of Chemical Engineers **[654]**
American Institute for Conservation of the Historic and Artistic Works **[659]**
American Institute of Iranian Studies **[662]**
American Institute for Maghrib Studies **[666]**
American Institute for Paralegal Studies **[669]**
American Institute for Paralegal Studies Alumni Achievement Scholarships [670]
American Institute for Paralegal Studies Alumni Competitive Scholarships [671]
American Institute for Paralegal Studies Merit Scholarships [672]
American Institute of Polish Culture **[673]**
American Institute of Steel Construction **[675]**
American Intellectual Property Law Education Foundation **[684]**
American Jersey Cattle Association **[686]**
American Kidney Fund **[689]**
American Kidney Fund's Patient Scholarship Program [690]
American Lebanese Engineering Society **[691]**
American Lebanese Engineering Society Scholarship Program [692]
The American Legion **[693]**
American Legion Boys/Girls State Scholarships [4162]
American Legion Eagle Scout of the Year Scholarships [4850]
The American Legion Legacy Scholarships [694]
The American Legion National High School Oratorical Scholarships Contest [695]
American Library Association **[698]**
American Liver Foundation **[702]**
American Liver Foundation Liver Scholar Awards [703]
American Liver Foundation Special Research Initiatives [704]
American Marketing Association-Connecticut Chapter, Anna C. Klune Memorial Scholarships [3415]
American Marketing Association Foundation **[707]**
American Medical Association **[711]**
American Military Retirees Association **[715]**
American Montessori Society **[717]**
American Musicological Society **[719]**
American Nuclear Society **[722]**
American Nuclear Society Incoming Freshman Scholarships [723]
American Nuclear Society Nevada Section Scholarships [5801]
American Nuclear Society Undergraduates Scholarships [724]
American Occupational Therapy Foundation **[725]**
American Orff-Schulwerk Association **[738]**
American Oriental Society **[743]**
American Orthopedic Foot and Ankle Society **[745]**
American Osteopathic Foundation **[748]**
American Paint Horse Foundation **[754]**
American Paint Horse Foundation Scholarships [755]
American Parkinson Disease Association **[756]**
American Pediatric Surgical Nurses Association **[762]**
American Pet Products Manufacturers Association **[764]**
American Philosophical Society **[766]**
American Physical Society **[772]**
American Physical Society Undergraduate Scholarships [773]
American Planning Association **[774]**
American Political Science Association **[781]**
American Political Science Association Federal Executives Fellowships [782]
American Political Science Association Journalists Fellowships [783]
American Political Science Association/MCI Scholarships [784]
American Political Science Association Political Scientists Fellowships [785]
American Polygraph Association **[788]**
American Psychiatric Association Alliance **[790]**
American Psychiatric Publishing Inc. **[792]**
American Psychological Association of Graduate Students **[794]**
American Public Power Association **[803]**
American Public Works Association **[805]**
American Public Works Association-Nevada **[807]**
American Quarter Horse Foundation Scholarships [811]
American Quarter Horse Youth Association **[810]**
American Quilt Study Group **[812]**
American Radio Relay League (ARRL) Foundation **[814]**
American Radio Relay League Louisiana Memorial Scholarships [815]
American Radio Relay League Scholarships Honoring Barry Goldwater, K7UGA [816]
American Railway Engineering and Maintenance-of-Way Association **[864]**
American Red Cross **[885]**
American Rental Association Foundation **[887]**
American Rental Association Foundation Scholarships [888]
American Research Institute in Turkey **[891]**
American Risk and Insurance Association **[901]**
American Road and Transportation Builders Association **[903]**
American Roentgen Ray Society **[905]**
American Roentgen Ray Society Scholarships [906]
American Romanian Orthodox Youth **[908]**
American Savings Foundation Scholarships [3416]
American School Health Association **[914]**
American Small Businesses Association **[917]**
American Society of Association Executives **[919]**
American Society of Brewing Chemists **[921]**
American Society of Business Publication Editors **[924]**
American Society of Certified Engineering Technicians **[926]**
American Society for Clinical Laboratory Science **[930]**
American Society of Comparative Law **[936]**
American Society of Comparative Law TransCoop Programs [937]
American Society of Composers, Authors and Publishers (ASCAP) Foundation **[938]**
American Society of Echocardiography **[949]**
American Society of Electroneurodiagnostic Technologists **[952]**
American Society for Engineering Education **[955]**
American Society for Enology and Viticulture **[957]**
American Society for Enology and Viticulture Scholarships [958]
American Society of Genealogists **[959]**
American Society of Heating, Refrigerating and Air-Conditioning Engineers **[961]**
American Society of Heating, Refrigerating, and Air-Conditioning Memorial Scholarships [963]
American Society of Heating, Refrigerating, and Air-Conditioning Undergraduate Scholarships [964]
American Society for Horticultural Science **[971]**
American Society for Horticultural Science Student Travel Grants [972]
American Society of International Law **[976]**
American Society of Landscape Architects **[978]**
American Society of Landscape Architects Council of Fellow Scholarships [979]
American Society for Legal History **[990]**
American Society for Mass Spectrometry **[992]**
American Society of Mechanical Engineers **[994]**
American Society for Microbiology **[1000]**
American Society for Microbiology International Fellowships for Africa [1001]
American Society for Microbiology International Fellowships for Asia [1002]
American Society for Microbiology International Fellowships for Latin America [1003]
American Society for Microbiology Undergraduate Research Fellowships [1004]
American Society of Military Comptrollers **[1010]**
American Society of Military Comptrollers National Scholarship Program [1011]
American Society of Mining and Reclamation **[1012]**
American Society of Mining and Reclamation Memorial Scholarships [1013]
American Society of Naval Engineers **[1014]**
American Society of Nephrology **[1016]**
American Society for Nondestructive Testing **[1020]**
American Society for Photogrammetry and Remote Sensing **[1024]**
American Society of Podiatric Medical Assistants **[1034]**
American Society for Quality - Statistic Division **[1036]**
American Society of Radiologic Technologists **[1038]**
American Society of Safety Engineers **[1045]**
American Society for Theatre Research **[1075]**
American Society for Theatre Research Dissertation Research Fellowships [1076]
American Society of Travel Agents **[1078]**
American Society of Travel Agents AVIS Scholarships [1081]
American Society of Women Accountants **[1090]**
American Sociological Association **[1093]**
American Sokol **[1095]**
American Sokol Merit Awards [1096]
American Speech Language Hearing Foundation **[1097]**
American Speech Language Hearing Foundation Clinical Research Grants [1098]
American Speech Language Hearing Foundation Endowed Scholarships [1099]
American Speech Language Hearing Foundation General Scholarships [1100]
American Speech Language Hearing Foundation Scholarships for International Students [1101]
American Speech Language Hearing Foundation Scholarships for Students with Disability [1102]
American Spinal Injury Association **[1109]**
American Standard Scholarships [5700]
American Statistical Association **[1111]**
American Surgical Association **[1116]**
American Swedish Institute **[1118]**
American Turkish Society Arif Mardin Music Fellowships [6936]
American University - School of Public Affairs **[1122]**
American Urological Association Foundation **[1125]**
American Veterans **[1132]**
American Water Resources Association **[1137]**
American Water Ski Educational Foundation **[1139]**
American Water Ski Educational Foundation Scholarships [1140]
American Water Works Association **[1141]**
American Watercolor Society **[1146]**
American Watercolor Society Scholarship Program for Art Teachers [1147]
American Welding Society **[1148]**
American Welding Society District Scholarships [1150]
American Welding Society International Scholarships [1151]
American Welding Society National Scholarships [1152]
American Welding Society Past Presidents Scholarships [1153]
American Welding Society Research Fellowships [1154]
Americans for Informed Democracy **[1175]**
Americans for Informed Democracy Global Scholar Tuition [1176]
Ames Clinical Excellence Student Grants; Anna [1854]
Amherst College Connecticut Alumni Scholarships [3417]
Amirikian Engineering Scholarships; Arsham [1155]
AMS Teacher Education Scholarships [718]
Amstutz Memorial Award; ISPE/M.E. [3658]
The AMTF Graduate Scholarships [932]
Amtmann Fellowships; Bernard [1698]
AMVETS National Scholarships - Entering College Freshmen [1133]

AMVETS National Scholarships - For Veterans [1134]
AMVETS National Scholarships - JROTC [1135]
Anaheim Police Association **[1177]**
Anaheim Police Survivors and Scholarship Fund [1178]
ANCA Scholarships [1301]
Anchor Plastics Scholarships [5634]
Anchor Scholarship Foundation [6826]
Andersen Nontraditional Scholarship for Women's Education and Retraining [3039]
Anderson, DO, Minority Scholarship; William G. [749]
The Anderson Group Summer Institute **[1179]**
The Anderson Group Summer Institute Scholarships [1180]
Anderson, Jr. Scholarships; Judge Isaac [6640]
Anderson Memorial Scholarship; Charles Lee [2455]
Anderson Memorial Scholarship Foundation, Inc.; Wilbur H. **[1181]**
Anderson Memorial Scholarships; Roy [2308]
Anderson Memorial Scholarships; Wilbur H. [1182]
Anderson Scholarships; Earl I. [817]
Anderson Scholarships; Jane E. [2640]
Anderson Scholarships; Kathy D. and Stephen J. [2405]
Anderson Scholarships in Space Science; Michael P. [5050]
Anderson Scholarships; Warren M. [3698]
Andrew Memorial Scholarships; Margaret J. [6344]
Andrews Educational Scholarships; Cindy [5907]
Andrews/HAWS Scholarships; William H. [7419]
Andrews Memorial Scholarships; Richard E. [438]
Andrews Scholarships/Internships; Marvin A. [1216]
Anello Sr. and Albert A. Silverman Memorial Scholarships; John D. [2237]
Angus Foundation Scholarships [4967]
Anheuser-Busch International Scholarships [5635]
Anheuser-Busch NAPABA Law Foundation Presidential Scholarships [4646]
Anson Fellowships; Jack [5220]
Anthony Fellowships; Hettie M. [4051]
Anxiety Disorders Association of America **[1183]**
Anxiety Disorders Association of America Career Development Travel Awards [1184]
Anxiety Disorders Association of America Junior Faculty Research Grants [1185]
AOA Research Fellowships [33]
AOA Research Grants [34]
AOFAS Research Grants Program [746]
AORN Foundation Scholarship Program [1477]
AOSA Research Grants [739]
AOSA Research Partnership Grants [740]
APA Minority Fellowships Program [1334]
APA Planning Fellowships [776]
APACVS Scholarships [1479]
APAGS-CLGBTC Grant Program [795]
APAGS' Committee on Ethic Minority Affairs (CEMA) Grant Program [796]
APALA Scholarship Program [1336]
APC High School Scholarships [29]
APC Scholarships [131]
APC Tuition-Assist Scholarship Awards [30]
APDA Postdoctoral Fellowships [757]
APDA Research Grants [758]
APDA Summer Fellowships [759]
APIASF Scholarships [1340]
Aplastic, Anemia and Myelosdysplasia Scholarships [1991]
Appalachian School of Law **[1186]**
Apple Scholars [6096]
Applicant Name [6410, 6411]
Applied Hospitality Degree Scholarships [1975]
APPMA's Jules Schwimmer Scholarship Program [765]
Appraisal Institute Education Trust **[1188]**
Appraisal Institute Education Trust Scholarships [1189]
APS/ASU Scholarships [5697]
APS/Maricopa County Community Colleges Scholarships [5698]
APS Scholarships for Minority Undergraduate Physics Majors [5051]
APS Student Grants [1481]
APSAIL's Ralph Silverman Memorial Scholarships [1542]
APSNA Educational Scholarships [763]
APT US&C Scholarships [1483]
APWA Engineering Scholarships [806]
Aquatics Booster Club Scholarships [5908]
ARA Scholarship Awards [1575]
Arab American Institute **[1190]**
Araujo Memorial Scholarships; Frank G. [5909]
Archaeological Institute of America **[1194]**
Archibald Communications Internships; Fred [6568]
Architects Association of PEI Scholarships [2496]
Architectural Precast Association **[1196]**
Arctic Institute of North America **[1198]**
Ardaw Scholarships; Mike [4345]
AREMA Committee Scholarships 18 - Light Density & Short Line Railways [865]
AREMA Committee Scholarships 24 - Education and Training [866]
AREMA Committee Scholarships 33 - Electric Energy Utilization [867]
AREMA Presidential Spouse Scholarships [868]
AREMA Scholarships [869]
AREMA Staff Scholarships [870]
Arent Fox Diversity Scholarships [1202]
Arent Fox LLP **[1201]**
A.R.F.O.R.A. Undergraduate Scholarships for Women [909]
Argo Scholarships; William [3172]
Arizona Airport Association **[1203]**
Arizona Artist Blacksmith Association **[1205]**
Arizona Association of Student Financial Aid Administrators **[1207]**
Arizona Chapter Gold Scholarships [1082]
Arizona Christian School Tuition Organization **[1213]**
Arizona Christian School Tuition Organization Scholarships [1214]
Arizona City County Management Association **[1215]**
Arizona Nursery Association **[1218]**
Arizona Nursery Association Scholarships [1219]
Arizona Nurses Association **[1220]**
Arizona Nurses Foundation Scholarships [1221]
Arizona Parks and Recreation Association **[1222]**
Arizona Parks and Recreation Educational Scholarship Program [1223]
Arkans Eagle Scout Scholarships; Rick [4851]
Arkansas Environmental Federation **[1225]**
Arkansas Nurses Association **[1229]**
Arkansas Nursing Foundation - Dorothea Funk Scholarships [1230]
Arkansas Nursing Foundation - Mary Gray Scholarships [1231]
Arkansas Public Health Association **[1232]**
Arkansas Public Health Association Scholarships [1233]
Arkansas Society of Professional Sanitarians Scholarships [1234]
Arkansas State University Mountain Home Scholarships [4906]
Armed Forces Communications and Electronics Association **[1235]**
Armendariz Memorial Scholarships; Connie "Chelo" [5910]
Armenian American Citizen's League Scholarships [1266]
Armenian American Medical Association Scholarships [1267]
Armenian American Pharmacists' Association Scholarships [1268]
Armenian Educational Foundation **[1252]**
Armenian General Athletic Union Scholarships [1269]
Armenian General Benevolent Union **[1254]**
Armenian Professional Society **[1256]**
Armenian Professional Society Scholarship Fund [1257]
Armenian Relief Society - Eastern United States **[1258]**
Armenian Relief Society Scholarships [1270]
Armenian Scholarship Foundation **[1261]**
Armenian Scholarship Foundation Scholarships [1262]
Armenian Students' Association of America **[1265]**
Armstrong Foundation; Ethel Louise **[1296]**
Armstrong Scholarships; Louis [939]
Army Aviation Association of America **[1298]**
Army Nurse Corps Association **[1300]**
Army Scholarship Foundation **[1302]**
Arnold and Irene Jaquetta Heye Scholarships; Marvin [6165]
Arnold Memorial Scholarships; Paul [5750]
Arnold Scholarships; Tara Lynne [6768]
Arnoldsen Memorial Scholarship Fund; Aaron **[1307]**
Arnoldsen Memorial Scholarships; Aaron Edward [1308]
Aronovitz Memorial Scholarships; Judge Sidney M. [2594]
Aronson Point Scholarships; Merle [5714]
A.R.O.Y. Stanitz Scholarships [910]
ARREOLA/CBSPM Scholarships [6166]
ARRL Foundation General Fund Scholarships [818]
ARRLF Mississippi Scholarships [819]
ARS Undergraduate Scholarships [1259]
Art Graduate Scholarships [148]
Art Institute of Colorado **[1309]**
Art Institute of Colorado Scholarships [1310]
Art Institute's Best Teen Chef in America Culinary Scholarships [1311]
ARTC Glenn Moon Scholarships [3418]
Artistic Scholarship Awards [1598]
Arts for Career Development Scholarships [149]
Arver Memorial Scholarships; David [67]
Arver Scholarships; Dutch and Ginger [68]
Arzell and Helen Miller Montgomery Scholarships; Chester [7420]
ASA Minority Fellowships Program [1094]
ASA/NSF/BLS Fellowships [1112]
ASBA College Scholarship Program [918]
ASBC Foundation Graduate Scholarships [922]
ASBC Foundation Undergraduate Scholarships [923]
ASBPE Young Leaders Scholarships [925]
ASCE San Diego Section **[1319]**
ASCEND/ING Scholarships [4643]
Asche Memorial Scholarship Fund; Elizabeth and Sherman [1356]
ASDSO Undergraduate Scholarships [1497]
Aselton Memorial Scholarships; Officer Brian A. [3419]
ASET Educational Seminars, Courses and Program Scholarships [953]
ASET Student Education Grants [954]
ASG Scholar Awards [960]
Ash Scholarships; William and Lucille [6167]
ASHA Scholarships [915]
ASHA Student Research Grants [916]
Ashburn Institute **[1322]**
ASHFA Scholarships for Minority Students [1103]
ASHS Industry Division Student Travel Grants [973]
ASHS Scholars Awards [974]
Asian American Bar Association **[1324]**
Asian American Journalists Association **[1327]**
Asian American Lawyers Association of Massachusetts **[1331]**
Asian American Lawyers Associations of Massachusetts Scholarships [1332]
Asian American Psychological Association **[1333]**
Asian American Scholarships [7004]
Asian Pacific American Librarians Association **[1335]**
Asian/Pacific Bar Association of Sacramento **[1337]**
Asian/Pacific Bar Association of Sacramento Law Foundation Scholarships [1338]
Asian/Pacific Gays and Friends Scholarships [6097]
Asian and Pacific Islander American Scholarship Fund **[1339]**
Asian and Pacific Islander Queers Sisters Scholarships [5751]
ASIL Helton Fellowship Program [977]
ASIS Foundation Chapter Matching Scholarships [1342]
ASIS International **[1341]**
ASLA Council of Fellows Scholarships [4118]
ASM/CCID Program in Infectious Disease and Public Health Microbiology [1005]
ASMS Research Awards [993]
ASNE Scholarships [1015]
ASNT Fellow Awards [1021]
ASNT Fellowship Awards [1022]
Asplin Foundation Scholarships; Myron [3687]

ASPPB Larry J. Bass Jr., PhD. Memorial Scholarship Awards [797]
Assante Scholarship Fund; Len [4915]
Assarian Scholarships; Michael M. [1271]
ASSE Construction Safety Scholarships [1047]
ASSE Diversity Committee Scholarships [1048]
Asselin Scholarships; Darrell and Palchie [2771]
Associated General Contractors of America **[1343]**
Associated General Contractors of Connecticut Scholarships [2531]
Associated Locksmiths of America **[1345]**
Associated Women for Pepperdine (AWP) Scholarships [5572]
Associates in Behavioral Health Scholarships [5752]
Association for the Advancement of Baltic Studies **[1347]**
Association for the Advancement of Baltic Studies Dissertation Grants for Graduate Students [1348]
Association for the Advancement of Cost Engineering **[1349]**
Association of American Geographers **[1351]**
Association on American Indian Affairs **[1355]**
Association on American Indian Affairs Emergency Aid Scholarship [630]
Association of American Indian Physicians **[1359]**
Association of American Indian Physicians Scholarships [1360]
Association of American Medical Colleges **[1361]**
Association for Applied and Therapeutic Humor **[1363]**
Association for Asian Studies **[1369]**
Association of Black Women Physicians **[1372]**
Association of California Water Agencies **[1374]**
Association of California Water Agencies Scholarships [1376]
Association for College And University Clubs Scholarships [1383]
Association of College Unions International **[1378]**
Association of College and University Auditors **[1380]**
Association for College and University Clubs **[1382]**
Association for Compensatory Educators of Texas **[1384]**
Association for Compensatory Educators of Texas Paraprofessionals Scholarships [1385]
Association for Compensatory Educators of Texas Scholarships [1386]
Association of Desk and Derrick Clubs **[1387]**
Association of Desk and Derrick Clubs Education Trust Scholarships [1388]
Association for Education and Rehabilitation of the Blind and Visually Impaired **[1389]**
Association of Electronic Journalists **[1391]**
Association of Electronic Journalists President's Scholarships [1392]
Association of Energy Engineers Foundation **[1406]**
Association of Energy Engineers Foundation Scholarship Program [1407]
Association of Environmental and Engineering Geologists **[1408]**
Association of Family Practice Physician Assistants **[1411]**
Association for Federal Information Resources Management **[1413]**
Association for Financial Technology **[1416]**
Association of Flight Attendants **[1418]**
Association of Flight Attendants Scholarship Fund [1419]
Association of Food and Drug Officials **[1420]**
Association of Former Intelligence Officers **[1423]**
Association General Contractors of America, New York State Chapter **[1426]**
Association of Independent Colleges and Universities of Pennsylvania **[1428]**
Association for International Training **[1434]**
Association for Iron and Steel Technology **[1437]**
Association of Jewish Libraries **[1458]**
Association for Library Service to Children **[1463]**
Association of Moving Image Archivists **[1466]**
Association of Occupational Health Professionals in Healthcare **[1473]**
Association of PeriOperative Registered Nurses **[1476]**
Association of Physician Assistants in Cardiovascular Surgery **[1478]**
Association for Preservation Technology International Student Scholarships [1518]
Association for Psychological Science **[1480]**
Association of Public Treasurers of the United States and Canada **[1482]**
Association of Rehabilitation Nurses **[1484]**
Association of Rehabilitation Nurses Scholarship Program [1485]
Association of School Business Officials of Maryland and the District of Columbia **[1487]**
Association of Science-Technology Centers **[1489]**
Association of Seventh-Day Adventist Librarians **[1491]**
Association for the Social Scientific Study of Jewry **[1494]**
Association for the Social Scientific Study of Jewry Travel Grant [1495]
Association of State Dam Safety Officials **[1496]**
Association of Surgical Technologists **[1498]**
Association of Universities and Colleges of Canada **[1503]**
Association of Universities and Colleges of Canada Public Scholarships [1504]
Association for Women in Architecture **[1505]**
Association for Women in Architecture Scholarships [1506]
Association for Women Geoscientists **[1507]**
Association for Women in Mathematics **[1514]**
Association for Women in Science **[1517]**
Association for Women in Sports Media **[1520]**
Association for Women in Sports Media Internship Program [1521]
Association for Women Veterinarians **[1522]**
Association for Women Veterinarians Foundation Scholarships Program [1523]
Association of Zoo Veterinary Technicians (AZVT) **[1524]**
AST National Honor Society Student Scholarships [1499]
ASTR Research Fellowships [1077]
Astra Zeneca RURAL Scholarships [1992]
Astronaut Scholarship Foundation **[1526]**
Astronaut Scholarship Foundation Scholarships [1527]
ASWA 2-Year College Scholarships [1091]
ASWA Undergraduate Scholarships [1092]
Athenaeum of Philadelphia **[1528]**
Atherton Ministerial Scholarships; Martha and Robert [6947]
Athletic Equipment Managers Association **[1530]**
Athletic Equipment Managers Association College Scholarships [1531]
Athletic Excellence Scholarships [5753]
Atkinson Scholarships; ISA Aerospace Industries Division - William H. [3940]
Atlanta Alumnae Achievement Scholarships [2641]
Atlantic Provinces Library Association **[1532]**
Atlantic Provinces Library Association Memorial Awards [1533]
Atlantic Salmon Federation **[1535]**
Atlantic Salmon Federation Olin Fellowships [1536]
Attorney-CPA Foundation Scholarships [322]
AUA Foundation/Astellas Rising Star in Urology Research Awards [1126]
AUA Foundation Bridge Awards [1127]
AUA Foundation M.D./Ph.D. Fellowships [1128]
AUA Foundation M.D. Post-resident Fellowships [1129]
AUA Foundation - NIDDK/NCI Surgeon-Scientist Awards [1130]
AUA Foundation Ph.D. Post-Doctoral Fellowships [1131]
Aubespin Scholarships [495]
Auburn Animal Science Department Graduate Student Scholarships [112]
Auburn University College of Veterinary Medicine Scholarships [113]
Audio Engineering Society **[1537]**
Audio Engineering Society Educational Foundation Scholarships [1538]
Auld Scholarships; Joan [2497]
Ault Scholarships; Frank H. [6168]
Autism Society of America **[1539]**
Automotive Aftermarket Industry Association **[1541]**
Automotive Hall of Fame **[1548]**
Automotive Industries Association of Canada **[1568]**
Automotive Recyclers Association **[1574]**
Automotive Technician Scholarship Program [4334]
Automotive Women's Alliance Foundation **[1576]**
Automotive Women's Alliance Foundation Scholarships [1577]
Auxiliary Undergraduate Scholarships [995]
Auzenne Fellowship; Delores A. [2995]
Averill Memorial Scholarships; Larry H. [1549]
Avery, Jr. & Ann E. Avery Scholarships; Dr. Noyes L. [3320]
AVI Scholarships [1543]
Aviation Distributors and Manufacturers Association **[1578]**
Aviation Distributors and Manufacturers Association Scholarship Fund [1579]
Avila Memorial Scholarships; John L. [4260]
Avista Corporation Minds in Motion Scholarships [4163]
AVS Science and Technology Society **[1580]**
AWG Maria Luisa Crawford Field Camp Scholarships [1508]
AWG Minority Scholarships [1509]
AWIS College Scholarships [1519]
Ayers Memorial Scholarships; Susan [5802]
Ayres Scholarships; William Stone [2732]
Azarian Memorial Armenian Youth Scholarships Fund; John M. [1272]
B-Brave McMahon/Stratton Scholarship Fund [2941]
Babbage Institute; Charles **[1582]**
Babcox Memorial Scholarships; Tom [1544]
Bach Organ and Keyboard Music Scholarships [6034]
BACUS Scholarships [6695]
Baeck Fellowships Program; Leo [2079]
Baeck Institute - DAAD Fellowship; Leo [3222]
BAEO Children's Scholarship Fund [1721]
BAFTX Early Starters Awards [1779]
BAFTX Graduate Awards [1780]
BAFTX Junior Achievers Awards [1781]
BAFTX Undergraduate Awards [1782]
Baha'i Faith Scholarships for Racial Harmony [5911]
The Bailey Family Foundation **[1585]**
The Bailey Family Foundation College Scholarship Program [1586]
The Bailey Family Foundation High School Scholarship Program [1587]
Bailey Memorial Scholarship Fund; Lincoln C. [3900]
Bailey Scholarships; Bambey [2391]
Bailey Scholarships; Barbara [5754]
Bailey Scholarships; Don [4913]
Bailey Scholarships; Sandra Sebrell [2683]
Baird Scholarships; Marian Wood [7302]
Baker Corporation Scholarship Program; Michael [1430]
Baker Foundation; Howard **[1588]**
Baker Foundation Scholarships; Howard [1589]
Baker and Health Merriwether Memorial Scholarships; Charly [5755]
Baker Memorial Scholarships; Frances Warren [6345]
Baker Memorial Scholarships; Richard L. [6769]
Baker Memorial Scholarships; Robby [189]
Baker Scholarships; Jerry [1156]
Balchen, Jr. Hardingfele Scholarships; Bernt [3399]
Baldridge Scholarships; Malcolm [3420]
Baldwin Sr. Business Aviation Management Scholarships; Donald A. [4770]
Balestreri/Cutino Scholarships [523]
Balfour Fellowships; Lloyd G. [5221]
Ball Horticultural Company Scholarships [550]
Ball Student Intern Scholarships; Vic and Margaret [551]
Ballantyne Resident Research Grants [602]
Ballard Family Foundation Scholarships [6169]
Ballew Directing Scholarships; Leighton M. [6631]
Balsbaugh Memorial Scholarship Fund; G. Thomas [3090]
Baltimore City College **[1590]**
B&W Y-12 Scholarship Fund [2806]
Bank of America Junior Achievement Scholarship Fund [3040]
Bank Educational Workshop Scholarships; Brenda S. [6447]
Banks Memorial Scholarships; Dr. Johnella [1750]
Banks Scholarships in Astronomy; Harvey Washington [5052]

Banks Undergraduate Memorial Scholarships; Sharon D. [7508]
Banner Bank Business Scholarships [4164]
Banner Corporate Intern Scholarships; Donald W. [3769]
Banner Diversity Scholarship for Law Students; Donald W. [1594]
Banner Health System - McKee Medical Center, Loveland: Nightingale Scholarships [2309]
Banner Health System - North Colorado Medical Center, Greeley: Nightingale Scholarships [2310]
Banner & Witcoff, Ltd. **[1593]**
Bar Association of San Francisco **[1595]**
Barabash Sports Scholarship; Bernice [3972]
Barakat Trust and Barakat Foundation Scholarships [1192]
Baranowski Scholarships for Professional Excellence; Leslie [3721]
Barbarow Memorial Scholarships; Joe [5465]
Barber Memorial Scholarships; Lewis B. [6641]
Barbri Scholarships for Bar Preparation [3578]
Barckhoff Welding Management Scholarships; Jack R. [1157]
Barden Aviation Scholarships; Janice K. [4771]
Barnhart Memorial Scholarship Fund; Gina L. [2942]
Baron Memorial Scholarships; Robbie [3091]
Barrientos Scholarship Foundation **[1597]**
Barriger Memorial Scholarships; Zachary [2262]
Barsotti Memorial Scholarships; Laura Beckley [3637]
Barsoumian Scholarships; Leon and Talin [1263]
Barta-Lehman Musical Scholarships [6170]
Barth Scholarships; Avery Bayle [2642]
Barto Scholarships; William E. [2772]
Barton Educational Scholarships Fund; Elsa [791]
Bartram Memorial Education Awards (Region 12 and Chapter 119); Walt [6470]
Bascom Hill Society Scholarships [7248]
Basic Midwifery Student Scholarship Program [470]
Basic Research Fellowships [443]
Basilone-Engle Memorial Scholarships; Diane [1889]
Bassett Commemorative Scholarships; Helen [5128]
Bassett Endowed Memorial Scholarship Fund; Charles A. [3270]
Bat Conservation International **[1600]**
Bat Conservation International Student Research Scholarships [1601]
Bates Oxford Cup Scholarships; William H. [1641]
Batten Community Newspaper Internships; Jim [7144]
Batten Scholarships; Lewis and Gurry [5466]
Baumeister Scholarship Program; Hazel Reed [6385]
Bautista Memorial Scholarships; Jeannette [5803]
Baxter Corporation Canadian Research Awards in Anesthesia [1912]
Baxter Scholarships; Bob [5017]
Bay Area Minority Law Student Scholarships [1596]
Bayer Business Administration Scholarships; Lawrence [4346]
Baylink Good Fellowship Awards; Timothy [5912]
Bayliss Broadcast Foundation Internship Programs; John [1603]
Bayliss Broadcast Foundation; John **[1602]**
Bayly-Tiffany Scholarships [7239]
BBM Canada Scholarships [1922]
BCA Ethnic Minority Postgraduate Scholarships for Careers in Athletics [1748]
BCCC Foundation Scholarships [1591]
BCCC Foundation Workforce Scholarships [1592]
BCEN Undergraduate Scholarships [2850]
BDPA Education Technology Foundation **[1605]**
Beacon of Hope Scholarship Foundation **[1607]**
Beacon of Hope Scholarships [1608]
Beard Foundation/Art Institute of Colorado Scholarships; James [1312]
Beattie Fellowships; Catherine H. [2089]
Beattie Memorial Scholarships; Jane [6465]
Beau Gunn Redlands Baseball For Youth Scholarships [5913]
Beaudry Scholarships; Michael [3173]
Beauregard Scholarships; Suzanne [6070]
Beauty Scholarships for High School Graduates; Sally [4822]
Beaver Medical Clinic-Glen Adams Scholarship Awards [5914]
Beaver Medical Clinic-H.E.A.R.T. Scholarship Awards [5915]
Beaver Medical Clinic-Premed Scholarship Awards [5916]
Beaver Memorial Scholarship; Don C. [1820]
BECA Foundation **[1609]**
BECA Foundation-CUSM Scholarships [1610]
BECA Foundation General Scholarships Fund [1611]
Bechtel Group Foundation Scholarship for Safety & Health [1049]
Bechtel Oxford Cup Scholarships; Stephen D. [1642]
Beck Fellowships; Stan [2861]
Beck, Jr. Memorial Scholarships; O.J. [2263]
Beck Memorial Scholarship; Dennis J. [3973]
Beck-Pfann Memorial Scholarships [5573]
Beck Scholarships; Garvin L. [5917]
Beckett Scholarships; Dr. Joyce [4665]
Beckingham Scholarships; Ann [1993]
Beecroft Family Scholarships [2264]
Beef Industry Scholarships [4788]
Beeler Memorial Scholarships; Raymond and Donald [5918]
Begay III Scholarship Program; Notah [190]
Beginning Freshmen Awards [4056]
Behavioral Sciences Post-Doctoral Fellowships [2867]
Behavioral Sciences Student Fellowships [2868]
Behlke Engineering Memorial Scholarships; Charles E. [4347]
Behring Student Scholarship Awards; Dade [2040]
Beihoff Scholarships; Norbert J. [2238]
Beinecke Brothers Memorial Scholarships [7085]
Beinstock Fellowships; N.S. [1393]
Belfer-Aptman Dissertation Research Awards [4456]
Bell Association for the Deaf and Hard of Hearing; Alexander Graham **[1613]**
Bell Foundation; March and Ruti **[1617]**
Bell Foundation Scholarships; March and Ruti [1618]
Bell and Lawrence Thornton Scholarship Fund; John [3421]
Bell Memorial Scholarships; Ray and Mary [6171]
Bell Scholarships in Human Rights and Democracy; Beverlee [2728]
Bell Travel Grants; Alfred D. [3030]
Bell Travel Grants; Harry A. [2569]
Bellevue PFLAG Scholarships [5756]
BellSouth Business Internship Awards [7145]
Belmont University Commercial Music Scholarships [2406]
Beltran Memorial Scholarships; David [5919]
Bemis Research Grants; Samuel Flagg [6452]
Ben Meadows **[1619]**
Benchwarmers of Redlands-Jess Mercado Football Scholarships [5920]
Benckiser Student Scholarships; Reckitt [4729]
Bendicksen Memorial Scholarships; Richard W. [820]
Bendiner and Doug Morgenson Scholarships; Bill [5757]
Benedict Fellowships [238]
Benett Scholarships; Eleanor [6815]
Beneventi MBA Scholarships; Mary Elizabeth Lockwood [3422]
Beneventi Medical Scholarships; Dr. Francis Anthony [3423]
Benign Essential Blepharospasm Research Foundation **[1622]**
Benign Essential Blepharospasm Research Foundation Research Grant [1623]
Bennett-Coverley Scholarships; Louise [1725]
Bennett Memorial Scholarships; Bertram W. [1643]
Bennett Scholarships; Casey [2926]
Bennett Scholarships; Reverend E.F. [2265]
Bennett W7PHO Memorial Scholarships; William [821]
Bensley Memorial Scholarship Fund; Pete and Ellen [3041]
Benson: Nightingale Scholarships; Marcy and Bruce [2311]
Benson Scholarship Awards; Elizabeth [6018]
Benton County Foundation **[1624]**
Benton Memorial Scholarships; George Oliver [2407]
Benton Scholarships; Linn [5398]
Benz Memorial Scholarships for College Journalism Study; Lester G. [5890]
Berg Awards; Fred [2828]
Bergen Scholarships; Charlotte V. [940]
Bergman Scholarships [5249]
Berks County Bar Foundation **[1633]**
Berlin Scholarships in Medical Professionalism; ARRS/Leonard [907]
Bernardi Memorial Scholarship; Richard L. [2456]
Bernath Dissertation Grants; Stuart L. [6453]
Bernath Fellowships; Myrna F. [6454]
Bernheim Memorial Scholarships; Peggy [1792]
Bernstein/John B. Talbert, Jr. Scholarship Fund; Donald H. [3042]
The Bernsten International Scholarships in Surveying Technology [484]
Bertelsen Scholarships; James R. and Geraldine F. [6172]
Beta Gamma Memorial Scholarship Fund [2643]
Beta Nu/Caryl Cordis D'hondt Scholarships [6346]
Beta Omega Scholarships [6347]
Beta Phi Mu **[1635]**
Beta Sigma Phi-VCT Scholarships [6306]
Beta Sigma Scholarships [6348]
Beta Theta Pi **[1640]**
Bethesda Lutheran Homes and Services **[1686]**
Bethune-Cookman University **[1689]**
Bethune-Cookman University Excelsior Scholarships [1690]
Bethune-Cookman University Presidential Scholarships [1691]
Betsy Plank/PRSSA Scholarships [5874]
Bettinger Scholarships; Harold [552]
Bettinger Scholarships; Leonard [553]
Beverly Estate Scholarships [2733]
Beverly Willis Architecture Foundation Dissertation Fellowships [6426]
Bharwani Endowment; Dr. Noorali & Sabiya [1693]
Bharwani Memorial Endowment; Hussein Jina [1694]
Bharwani Professional Corporation; Noorali **[1692]**
BIA Higher Education Grants [1208]
Bibliographical Society of America **[1695]**
Bibliographical Society of Canada **[1697]**
Bickell Mining Scholarships; J.P. [7211]
BIE-Loan for Service for Graduates [642]
Big Sandy Community and Technical College **[1700]**
BIGALA (Bisexual Gay and Lesbian Alliance) Scholarships [6098]
Biggs Scholarships; Bill & Nell [4348]
Bila Scholarships; Frank and Ruth [5356]
Bilder Scholarships; James [6642]
Bingham Sr. Fellowships; Barry [4819]
Biocom Scholarships [6173]
BioCommunications Association **[1706]**
Biomagnetic Therapy Association **[1711]**
Biophysical Society **[1713]**
BioQuip Scholarships [2862]
BioRx/Hemophilia of North Carolina Educational Scholarships [5006]
Birks Family Foundation Scholarships [1994]
Birmingham Public School **[1716]**
Birmingham-Southern College Eagle Scout Scholarships [4852]
Birmingham Student Scholarship Fund Association [1717]
BISA's Scholarship Assistance Program [1759]
BISA's Scholarships Assistance Program [1761]
Bisexual Foundation Scholarships [6572]
Bishop State Community College Scholarships [4907]
Bison Transport Scholarships [5341]
Bissell Scholarships; Lebbeus F. [3424]
Bivins Foundation; Mary E. **[1718]**
Bivins Foundation Religious Scholarship Program; Mary E. [1719]
Blachford Point Scholarships; Norman [5715]
Black Alliance for Educational Options **[1720]**
Black Business and Professional Association **[1723]**
Black Canadian Scholarships [5419]
Black Coaches and Administrators **[1747]**
Black Data Processing Associates Scholarships [1606]

Cabrillo Clubs of California Scholarships [5737]
Caccomo Family Foundation Memorial Scholarships; Dr. Aurelio M. [1136]
Cadmus Communications Corporation Graphics Scholarship Endowment Fund [3044]
CAG Donald Menzies Bursary Awards [1927]
CAG Margery Boyce Bursary Awards [1928]
Cain Fellowships in Technology, Policy, and Entrepreneurship; Gordon [2107]
Cal State San Macros Alumna Scholarships [1859]
Calas/FES Miami Chapter Scholarships; Cesar A. [3000]
Caldarelli Memorial Scholarships; Tese [4672]
Calder, Jr., MD Scholarship Fund; Joseph R. [2946]
Caldwell Centennial Scholarships; J.E. [5063]
Calhoun Community College **[1809]**
Calhoun County Audubum University Scholarships [2347]
Calhoun Scholarships [1810]
Calhoun Scholarships; Hermoine Grant [4875]
California Association of Family and Consumer Sciences (CAFCS)-San Diego Chapter Scholarships [6177]
California Association of Pest Control Advisers **[1811]**
California Association of Private Postsecondary Schools **[1813]**
California Association of Private Postsecondary Schools Scholarships [1814]
California Bar Association **[1815]**
California Bar Foundation Diversity Scholarships [1325]
California Bar Law Foundation Scholarships [1326]
California Community Service Scholarships [4985]
California Community Service Scholarships - Bay Area [4986]
The California Endowment and AACN Minority Nurse Faculty Scholarships [337]
California Grocers Association **[1818]**
California Groundwater Association **[1836]**
California Groundwater Association Scholarships [1837]
California Landscape Contractors Association **[1838]**
California Landscape Contractors Association Scholarships [1839]
California Library Association **[1840]**
California Police Youth Charities **[1842]**
California School Library Association **[1845]**
California Scottish Rite Foundation **[1851]**
California Scottish Rite Foundation Scholarships [1852]
California Shopping Cart Retrieval Corporation Inc. Scholarships [1822]
California Society of Radiologic Technologists **[1853]**
California State University San Macros Alumni Association **[1858]**
California Waterfowl Association **[1861]**
Calista Corporation **[1863]**
Calista Scholarships [1864]
CALL/ACBD Education Reserve Fund Grants [1930]
Callahan Educational Trust; Harry D. [6711]
Callahan Memorial Scholarships; Jodi [50]
Calvin Alumni Association **[1865]**
Calvin Alumni Association Arizona Central Chapter Scholarships [1866]
Calvin Alumni Association-Black Alumni Chapter Scholarships [1867]
Calvin Alumni Association British Columbia Scholarships [1868]
Calvin Alumni Association California- Bay Area Scholarships [1869]
Calvin Alumni Association Colorado Chapter Scholarships [1870]
Calvin Alumni Association Florida-Gulf Coast Scholarships [1871]
Calvin Alumni Association-Illinois Scholarships [1872]
Calvin Alumni Association-Iowa/Pella Scholarships [1873]
Calvin Alumni Association-Maryland/Baltimore Scholarships [1874]
Calvin Alumni Association-Michigan Lakeshore Scholarships [1875]
Calvin Alumni Association-Michigan, Lansing Scholarships [1876]
Calvin Alumni Association-New Jersey Scholarships [1877]
Calvin Alumni Association-New York, Rochester Scholarships [1878]
Calvin Alumni Association-South Florida Scholarships [1879]
Calvin Alumni Association-South Florida Sophomore Scholarships [1880]
Calvin Alumni Association-Southeast Michigan Scholarships [1881]
Calvin Alumni Association-Southeastern Wisconsin Scholarships [1882]
Calvin Alumni Association Southern California Chapter Scholarships [1883]
Calvin Alumni Association-Southwest Michigan, Kalamazoo Scholarships [1884]
Calvin Alumni Association-Washington, D.C. Scholarships [1885]
Calvin Alumni Association-Washington, Lynden Scholarships [1886]
Calvin Alumni Association-Washington-Seattle/Tacoma Scholarships [1887]
Camden County College **[1888]**
Camden County College Employee Memorial Scholarships [1891]
Camden County College Foundation Scholarships [1892]
Camden County Retired Educators Association Scholarships [1893]
Cameco Corporation **[1903]**
Cameco Corporation Scholarships in the Geological Sciences - Continuing Students [1904]
Cameco Corporation Scholarships in the Geological Sciences - Entering Students [1905]
Cameco Northern Scholarships - Technical Institute [1906]
Cameco Northern Scholarships - University [1907]
Cameron and Margaret McLeod Memorial Scholarships (SCMS); Stuart [3744]
Cameron Scholarships; Wesley C. [5139]
Camp Scholarships; Thomas R. [1142]
Campbell Scholarship Award; Lois [3846]
Campbell Scholarship; Theodore R. [150]
Campbell Scholarships; Robert G. [5925]
Canada Graduate Scholarships Program [6418]
Canada Millennium Bursary [151]
Canada Millennium Scholarship Foundation **[1909]**
Canada Millennium Scholarship Foundation Millennium Bursary Award [1910]
Canada Study Grant for the Accommodation of Students with Permanent Disabilities [4156]
Canada-Ukraine Parliamentary Program (CUPP) Internship Scholarships [7357]
Canadian Aboriginal Science and Technology Society Scholarships [2042]
Canadian Anesthesiologists' Society **[1911]**
Canadian Anesthesiologists' Society Research Awards [1913]
Canadian Association of Broadcasters **[1920]**
Canadian Association of Chiefs of Police **[1924]**
Canadian Association on Gerontology **[1926]**
Canadian Association of Law Libraries **[1929]**
Canadian Association of Law Libraries CALL Research Grants [1931]
Canadian Bar Association **[1934]**
Canadian Cartographic Association **[1936]**
Canadian Council for Aboriginal Business **[1938]**
Canadian Council on International Law **[1941]**
Canadian Council of Technicians and Technologists **[1944]**
Canadian Engineering Memorial Foundation **[1946]**
Canadian Federation of Independent Grocers **[1953]**
Canadian Federation for Sexual Health **[1955]**
Canadian Federation of University Women **[1959]**
Canadian Federation of University Women Etobicoke Bursary [7213]
Canadian Fire Safety Association **[1961]**
Canadian Hard of Hearing Association **[1967]**
Canadian Hard of Hearing Association Scholarships [1968]
Canadian Hemophilia Society **[1969]**
Canadian Hospitality Foundation **[1974]**
Canadian Hospitality Foundation College Entrance Scholarships [1976]
Canadian Hospitality Foundation University Entrance Scholarships [1977]
Canadian Institute of Planners **[1979]**
Canadian Institute of Ukrainian Studies **[1981]**
Canadian Library Association **[1984]**
Canadian Macedonian Federation Scholarships [7214]
Canadian National Institute for the Blind **[1988]**
Canadian Nurses Foundation **[1990]**
Canadian Nurses Foundation - Baxter Corporation Scholarships [1995]
Canadian Nurses Foundation Northern Scholarships [1996]
Canadian Nurses Foundation Scholarships [1997]
Canadian Occupational Therapy Foundation **[2016]**
Canadian Occupational Therapy Foundation Graduate Scholarships [2017]
Canadian Occupational Therapy Foundation Invacare Master's Scholarships [2018]
Canadian Organic Growers **[2021]**
Canadian Paraplegic Association **[2023]**
Canadian Parking Association **[2026]**
Canadian Parking Association Scholarships [2027]
Canadian Sanitation Supply Association **[2028]**
Canadian Sanitation Supply Association Scholarships [2029]
Canadian Seniors Golf Association Scholarships [6071]
Canadian Simmental Association **[2033]**
Canadian Society of Club Managers **[2035]**
Canadian Society of Exploration Geophysicists **[2037]**
Canadian Society for Medical Laboratory Science **[2039]**
Canadian Society of Petroleum Geologists **[2041]**
Canadian Society of Petroleum Geologists Regional Graduate Scholarships [2043]
Canadian Society of Petroleum Geologists Regional Undergraduate Scholarships [2044]
Canadian Water Resources Association **[2046]**
Canadian Water Resources Association Scholarships [2047]
Canadian Water and Wastewater Association **[2049]**
Cancer Survivors Fund **[2051]**
Cancer Survivors' Fund Scholarships [2052]
Cannon Educational Scholarships; Therese A. [3884]
Cannon Memorial Scholarships; John [4626]
Cano Memorial Scholarships; Agustin [5807]
Caoile Memorial Scholarships; John [5808]
Cape Coral Community Foundation **[2053]**
Cape Fear Community College Foundation **[2056]**
Cape Fear Community College Merit Scholarships [2057]
Caplin Memorial Scholarships; Rhea Sourifman [3429]
Capling Memorial Scholarship Endowment Fund; Kasie Ford [3045]
Cardiac Sonographer Education Development Grants [950]
Cardwell Scholarships; Thelma [2019]
Career Advancement Scholarships [1806]
Career Colleges Scholarships [3672]
Career Mobility Scholarship Awards [16]
Career Mobility Scholarships [3130]
Carew Memorial Scholarships; Beth [5007]
Carew Memorial Scholarships; John [555]
Caribbean Hotel Association **[2058]**
Caribbean Hotel Association Academic Scholarships [2059]
Carlson Endowed Scholarships; Glen and Babs [4166]
Carlson Wildlife Management Scholarships; Lyle [4353]
Carmangay Home and School Association Scholarships [152]
Carmichael Scholarships; Walta Wilkinson [6349]
Carnegie Scholarships; Herb [1727]
Carnes Scholarship Fund; Julian E. [3046]
Carnes Scholarship; Joe [2458]
Carolina Panthers Scholarship Fund [3047]
Carolina's Gay & Lesbian Scholarships [6099]
Carolinas-Virginias Retail Hardware Scholarship Fund [3048]

Sponsor and Scholarship Index

Carollo Music Scholarships; Jeffrey [5177]
Carr Endowed Scholarships; Walter & Elsie [4167]
Carr Forensic Science Scholarships; Commander James [252]
Carrier Scholarships; Willis H. [965]
Carson Memorial Bursary; Robert C. [153]
Carter Brown Library; The John **[2060]**
Carter Fellowships; Rosalynn [4820]
Carter Hampton Scholarships; Deloris [5759]
Carter Scholarships; Leigh [2411]
Carter Scholarships; Leticia B. [4321]
Cartwright Scholarships Program [618]
CAS/GE Healthcare Canada Inc. Research Awards [1914]
CAS/Vitaid-LMA Residents' Research Grant Competition [1915]
Casabella Family Memorial Scholarships [3430]
Cascade Blues Association **[2063]**
Case-Swayne Company Scholarships [5358]
Casey Family Scholars Scholarships [5415]
Casey Scholarships; Elton [7149]
Casey Scholarships; Local 827 Peter J. [3819]
Casgrain LLP Scholarships; Fraser Milner [1728]
Casper Fund; George H. and Anna [6712]
Cassada Scholarships; Orrie & Dorothy [3322]
Cassady Scholarships; Thomas D. and Karen [1648]
Cassioppi Scholarship; May [2459]
Catching the Dream **[2065]**
Catching the Dream Scholarship [632]
Caterpillar Scholars Award [6471]
Caterpillar Scholarships in Diesel Mechanics [4168]
Catholic Biblical Association of America **[2070]**
Catholic Biblical Association of America Scholarships [2071]
Catholic Healthcare Partners Scholarships [7525]
Catholic Library Association **[2072]**
Catlin/David W. Long Memorial Scholarship; The Robert A [2996]
Catlin/David W. Long Memorial Scholarships; Robert A. [777]
Cavendish Scholarships; Marshall [699]
CAWEE International Student Fellowships [6266]
Cawthorne Scholarships; Christine Kerr [6350]
Cayvan String Instrument Scholarships; Llewellyn L. [3323]
CCFA Career Development Awards [2559]
CCFA Research Fellowship Awards [2560]
CCFA Student Research Fellowship Awards [2561]
C.C.H.R.M.A. Scholarships [2268]
CCSD School Counselors' Scholarships [5809]
CCU Alumni Endowed Scholarships [2304]
CD-HCF Chair's Scholarships [2536]
GDC Foundation **[2074]**
CDC Foundation Scholarships [2075]
Cebik, W4RNL, and Jean Cebik, N4TZP, Memorial Scholarships; L.B. [824]
CEDAM International **[2076]**
Cedarcrest Farms Scholarships [687]
Cemanahuac Educational Community Scholarships [5263]
CEMF Claudette MacKay-Lassonde Scholarships [6432]
CEMF Undergraduate Engineering Scholarships [1949]
Cengage Learning-NAAE Upper Division Scholarships; Delmar [4653]
Center for Austrian Studies **[2078]**
Center for Congressional and Presidential Studies (CPPS) Endowment [1123]
Center for the Education of Women **[2080]**
Center for Lesbian and Gay Studies **[2084]**
Center for Plant Conservation **[2088]**
Center for Women in Government and Civil Society **[2090]**
Center for Women in Government and Civil Society Fellowships [2091]
Center for Wooden Boats **[2092]**
Central Arizona DX Association Scholarships [825]
Central Indiana ASSE Scholarships [1051]
Central Ohio Diabetes Association **[2094]**
Central Texas Bluegrass Association **[2096]**
CentraState Associated Auxiliaries Scholarships [2099]
CentraState Band Aid Open Committee Scholarships [2100]
CentraState Healthcare Foundation **[2098]**
CentraState Healthcare Foundation Health Professional Scholarships [2101]
CEPS-Tyco Scholarships [7137]
Certified Landscape Technician Scholarships [5242]
Certified Municipal Clerk Scholarships (CMC) [3872]
Certified Neuroscience Registered Nurse (CNRN) Recertification Grants Program [374]
Cervenka Scholarships; Arthur and Gladys [6472]
CEW Scholarships [2081]
CFERP Masters Fellowships [2343]
CFI Sid Solow Scholarships [1467]
CFIDS Association of America NP Student Scholarships [263]
CFIG National Scholarships [1954]
Chace Foundation Scholarships; Rick [1468]
Chaine des Rotisseurs Scholarships [524]
Chaison Gold Award Scholarships; Emily [3431]
Chall Research Fellowships; Jeanne S. [3888]
Challenge Met Scholarships [826]
Chambers Individual Scholarships; Logan S. [3814]
Chambers Scholarships; Mary Anne [3996]
Chambersburg/Fannett-Metal School District Scholarship Fund [3092]
Change Your World Scholarships [6819]
Channabasappa Memorial Scholarships [3837]
Chapin Scholarship; Harry H. and Floy B. [2460]
Chapman Memorial Scholarships; Oscar [1649]
Chappell Scholarships; S. Penny [5658]
Chapter 4 - Lawrence A. Wacker Memorial Awards [6473]
Chapter - 6 Fairfield County Scholarships [6474]
Chapter 17 - St. Louis Scholarships [6475]
Chapter 23 - Quad Cities Iowa/Illinois Scholarships [6476]
Chapter 31 - Peoria Endowed Scholarships [6477]
Chapter 52 - Wichita Scholarships [6478]
Chapter 56 - Fort Wayne Scholarships [6479]
Chapter 63 - Portland James E. Morrow Scholarships [6480]
Chapter 63 - Portland Uncle Bud Smith Scholarships [6481]
Chapter 67 - Phoenix Scholarships [6482]
Chapter 93 - Albuquerque Scholarships [6483]
Chapter 198 - Downriver Detroit Scholarships [6484]
Chapter 311 - Tri City Scholarships [6485]
Chapter One - Detroit Founding Chapter Scholarships [6486]
Charlotte Housing Authority Scholarship Fund (CHASF) [3049]
Charlotte-Mecklenburg Schools Scholarship Incentive Program [3050]
Chasens Teaching and Research Fellowships; Abram and Sylvia [286]
Chautauqua Scholarship Program [3882]
Chavez Scholarships; Cesar E. [5926]
Cheatham County Scholarships [2412]
Cheerful Giver Scholarships [6178]
Chemical Heritage Foundation **[2105]**
Chemtob Scholarship; Hadar J. [3556]
Cherry Lane Foundation/Music Alive! Scholarships [941]
Cherven Memorial Scholarships; Sgt. Michael F. [4330]
Cheyenne High School Faculty Memorial Scholarships [5810]
CHF Travel Grants [2108]
Chi Chapter Undergraduate Scholarships [2644]
Chi Eta Phi Sorority **[2114]**
Chi Phi Educational Trust [2117]
Chi Phi Fraternity **[2116]**
Chicago Bar Foundation **[2118]**
Chicago Division Scholarships [4513]
Chicago FM Club Scholarships [827]
Chicana/Latina Foundation **[2120]**
Chicana Latina Scholarship Fund [2121]
Child of Alumni Book Voucher Awards [3699]
Child and Family Advocacy Fellowships [7348]
Child Memorial Scholarships; Julia [525]
Child Scholarships; Kevin [4917]
Childbirth Educator Program Scholarships [4114]
Childe Scholarships; John and Ruth [6645]
Childhood Cancer Foundation **[2122]**
Childhood Cancer Foundation Candlelighters Canada **[2124]**
Childhood Cancer Foundation Candlelighters Canada Scholarships [2125]
Childhood Cancer Foundation Scholarships [2123]
Children of Unitarian Universalist Ministers College Scholarships [6949]
Children's Hospital of Philadelphia **[2126]**
Children's Scholarship Fund of Charlotte [3051]
Chilson Scholarships; Charline [2684]
Chin Memorial Fund Scholarships; Vincent [455]
Chinese American Medical Society **[2134]**
Chinese American Medical Society Summer Research Outreach Programs [2135]
Chinese-Canadian History and Culture Fellowships [7215]
Choose Your Future Scholarships [2413]
Chopin Foundation of the United States **[2138]**
Chopin Foundation of the United States Scholarships [2139]
Chopivsky Fellowships [7358]
Choristers Guild **[2140]**
Choy Memorial/Gay Asian Pacific Alliance (GAPA) Scholarships; George [6100]
Chressanthis Memorial Scholarships; Andrew G. [3527]
Chretien International Research Grants [429]
Christensen Scholarships; Patricia Smith [6383]
Christian Pharmacist Fellowship International Scholarships [2143]
Christian Pharmacists Fellowship International **[2142]**
Christian Record Services **[2144]**
Christmas Tree Chapter Scholarship Awards [5378]
Chrysalis Scholarships [1510]
Chrysler Technical Scholarships Fund [2633]
CHS - Bursary Program Scholarships [1970]
CHS - Mature Student Bursary Program Scholarships [1971]
CHS Scholarships [1972]
Chugach Gem & Mineral Society Scholarships [7030]
Church Family Scholarships [4169]
Churchill Foundation; Winston **[2146]**
Churchill Research Scholarships; Edward D. [417]
The Churchill Scholarships [2147]
CIA Undergraduate Scholarships [1425]
CIBC Scholarships [1729]
CIGNA Healthcare Graduate Scholarships [4892]
CIGNA Healthcare Undergraduate Scholarships [4893]
Cincinnati High School Scholarships [2149]
Cincinnati Scholarship Foundation **[2148]**
Cincinnati Scholarship Foundation CFT/ACPSOP Scholarships [2150]
/Cindi Turner Scholarships; Nate Mack [5811]
CIP Fellow's Travel Scholarships [1980]
Cirino Memorial Art Education Fellowships; Antonio [6035]
Cisneros Point Scholarships; Carlos Enrique [5716]
Citi Foundation Scholarships Program [619]
City of Sanibel Employee Dependent Scholarships [6646]
City of Toronto Graduate Scholarships for Women in Mathematics [7216]
City of Toronto Queen Elizabeth II Sesquicentennial Scholarships in Community Health Nursing (Graduate) [7217]
City of Toronto Queen Elizabeth II Sesquicentennial Scholarships in Community Health Nursing (Undergraduate) [7218]
City of Toronto Scholarships for Aboriginal Students [7219]
City of Toronto Women's Studies Scholarships [7220]
Civic Music Association of Milwaukee **[2236]**
Civitan International **[2242]**
Civitan Shropshire Scholarships [2243]
CLA/ACB Dafoe Scholarships [1985]
Clackamas Chapter Scholarship Awards [5379]
Clackamas County Farm Bureau Scholarships [5392]
CLAGS Fellowships [2085]
Clan Ross Association of the United States **[2244]**
Clan Ross Foundation Scholarships [2245]
Clapp, Sr. Memorial Scholarships; Cecil Earl [5277]
Clark Fellowships; Michelle [1396]
Clark Foundation Scholarships; Ann E. [5140]

Copper and Brass Service Center Inc. Scholarship Program [2541]
Corbett-Porter Building Bridges Scholarships [5815]
Corbin/Childbirth Connection Grant for Evidence-based Midwifery Care; Hazel [471]
Cordle Memorial Scholarships; Charles Clarke [830]
Cormack Scholarships; Bill [6862]
Cormier Scholarships; The Frank [7409]
Cornaro Scholarships for Graduate Studies [4042]
Cornelius Memorial Scholarships; D.C. [7428]
Cornell Scholarships; Holly A. [1143]
Corporate Aviation Management Scholarships [4773]
Corporation for Public Broadcasting **[2542]**
Correctional Education Association **[2545]**
Correctional Education Association Scholarships [2546]
Corrie Memorial Grants; NSS Sara [5087]
Cory Memorial Scholarships; Tom [1197]
Cossette/Gale Memorial Scholarships; Richard [1545]
Cost-of-Books Relief Scholarships [1860]
Costello Memorial Scholarships; James [3920]
Costello Memorial Scholarships; John [2532]
Cotner Family Scholarships [2948]
Cotzias, MD Memorial Fellowships; George C. [760]
Couch Memorial Scholarships; Dave [5473]
Coulter Memorial Scholarships; Jennifer [5474]
Council for the Advancement of Science Writing **[2547]**
Council on Library and Information Resources **[2549]**
Council on Social Work Education **[2552]**
Council on Social Work Education Minority Fellowship Programs [2553]
Council on Social Work Education Scholars Program [2554]
Courter Sharing a Brighter Tomorrow Hemophilia Scholarship Program; Soozie [4918]
COUSE-Gram Scholarships [6647]
Covert, Ph.D./FHIMSS Scholarships for Management Systems; Richard P. [3516]
Covington Award for Research on Bar Admissions Testing; The Joe E. [4817]
Cowles Youth Awards; Reuben R. [688]
Cox "Beat the Odds" Memorial Scholarships; Justin Forrest [2269]
Cox Scholarships; Gertrude M. [1114]
CPCU Laman Educational Foundation Scholarships [3761]
Crafton Elementary School PTA Scholarships [5929]
Crafton Hills College Foundation Scholarships [5930]
Craig Community Service Scholarship; Margaret T. [2462]
Crain Educational Grants Program [6386]
Cramer Scholarships; Robert E. [6548]
Cranberry Institute NP Student Scholarships [265]
Crane Group Real Estate Scholarships Fund; The Rick [4173]
Crapo Math and Science Scholarship Fund; Mike [3644]
Crawford Fellowship in I/O Psychology; Meredith P. [3627]
Crawford Memorial Scholarships; Mable B. [4354]
Crawford Scholarships [6181]
Crawford Scholarships; L.D. "Crow" [7001]
Creative Glass Center of America **[2556]**
Creative Glass Center of America Fellowships [2557]
Critical Language Scholarships for Intensive Summer Institutes [892]
Crocker Memorial Scholarship Fund; Judy [3055]
Crohn's and Colitis Foundation of America **[2558]**
Crohn's and Colitis Foundation of America Senior Research Awards [2562]
Cromwell Fellowships [991]
Cronin Scholarships; Kathryn M. [7152]
Cross Scholarships; Albuquerque ARC/Toby [831]
Crossno Memorial Scholarships; R.G [2810]
Crowder Scholarship Fund [3056]
CRS Scholarships [2145]
Cruz and Sandra Maria Ramos Scholarships; Lydia [2681]
The Crystal Green Blood Assurance Scholarships [1766]
CSA Fraternal Life **[2563]**
CSA Fraternal Life Scholarships [2564]
CSEG Scholarship Trust Fund [2038]
CSF Ach Family Scholarships [2151]
CSF Barr Foundation Scholarships [2152]
CSF Barrett Family Scholarships [2153]
CSF Bigg's/Curtis Breeden Scholarships [2154]
CSF Bob and Linda Kohlhepp Scholarships [2155]
CSF Borden Inc. Scholarships [2156]
CSF Carl H. Linder Family Scholarships [2157]
CSF Castellini Foundation Scholarships [2158]
CSF Charles and Claire Phillips Scholarships [2159]
CSF Charlotte R. Schmidlapp Scholarships [2160]
CSF Christopher Todd Grant Memorial Scholarships [2161]
CSF Cincinnati Bell Scholarships [2162]
CSF Cincinnati Financial Corporation Scholarships [2163]
CSF Cincinnati Milacron Scholarships [2164]
CSF Corwin Nixon Scholarships [2165]
CSF Crosset Family Scholarships [2166]
CSF Dater Foundation Scholarships [2167]
CSF David J. Joseph Company Scholarships [2168]
CSF Dee Wacksman Memorial Scholarships [2169]
CSF Duke Energy Scholarships [2170]
CSF Dwight Hibbard Scholarships [2171]
CSF Ella Wilson Johnson Scholarships [2172]
CSF Estelle Davis Memorial Scholarships [2173]
CSF Eugene Carroll Scholarships [2174]
CSF E.W. Scripps Scholarships [2175]
CSF Farmer Family Foundation Scholarships [2176]
CSF Fifth Third Bank Combined Scholarships [2177]
CSF Fletemeyer Family Scholarships [2178]
CSF Florette B. Hoffheimer Scholarships [2179]
CSF Frank Foster Skillman Scholarships [2180]
CSF Gardner Foundation Scholarships [2181]
CSF G.E. Aircraft Engines Scholarships [2182]
CSF George and Amy Polley Scholarships [2183]
CSF Goldman, Sachs and Company Scholarships [2184]
CSF Greater Cincinnati Scholarships Association [2185]
CSF H.C. Schott Foundation Scholarships [2186]
CSF HCRTA/Glen O. and Wyllabeth Wise Scholarships [2187]
CSF Heidelberg Distributing Co. Scholarships [2188]
CSF Heinz Pet Products Scholarships [2189]
CSF Helen Steiner Rice Scholarships [2190]
CSF Johnny Bench Scholarships [2191]
CSF Joseph S. Stern, Jr. Scholarships [2192]
CSF Judge Benjamin Schwartz Scholarships [2193]
CSF Juilfs Foundation Scholarships [2194]
CSF Kroger Cincinnati/Dayton Scholarships [2195]
CSF L and T Woolfolk Memorial Scholarships [2196]
CSF Lazarus/Federated Scholarships [2197]
CSF L.B. Zapoleon Scholarships [2198]
CSF Lowe Simpson Scholarships [2199]
CSF Lyle and Arlene Everingham Scholarships [2200]
CSF Lyle Everingham Scholarships [2201]
CSF M and E Brown Scholarships [2202]
CSF M. Kantor and Brothers Scholarships [2203]
CSF Martha W. Tanner Memorial Scholarships [2204]
CSF Marvin Rammelsberg Memorial Scholarships [2205]
CSF Mary Roberts Scholarships [2206]
CSF McCall Educational Scholarships [2207]
CSF Michael Bany Memorial Scholarships [2208]
CSF Midland Company Scholarships [2209]
CSF Nelson Schwab Jr. Family Scholarships [2210]
CSF Nethercott Family Scholarships [2211]
CSF Ohio National Foundation Scholarships [2212]
CSF Pepper Family Scholarships [2213]
CSF Pichler Family Scholarships [2214]
CSF PNC Bank Scholarships [2215]
CSF Priscilla Gamble Scholarships [2216]
CSF Procter and Gamble Scholarships [2217]
CSF Raymond and Augusta Klink Scholarships [2218]
CSF Richard Heekin Scholarships [2219]
CSF Robert H. Reakirt Foundation Scholarships [2220]
CSF Roger and Joyce Howe Family Scholarships [2221]
CSF S. David Shor Scholarships [2222]
CSF SC Johnson, A Family Company Scholarships [2223]
CSF Scripps Headliners Scholarships [2224]
CSF Semple Foundation Scholarships [2225]
CSF Thomas J. Emery Memorial Scholarships [2226]
CSF T.L. Conlan Memorial Scholarships [2227]
CSF Union Central 135th Anniversary Scholarships [2228]
CSF U.S. Bank N.A. Scholarships [2229]
CSF Walter and Marilyn Bartlett Scholarships [2230]
CSF Western-Southern Foundation Scholarships [2231]
CSF William A. Friedlander Scholarships [2232]
CSF Wm. J. Rielly/MCURC Scholarships [2233]
CSF Woodward Trustees Scholarships [2234]
CSF Wynne Family Memorial Scholarships [2235]
CSX Scholarships [874]
CTP Scholarship Program [5024]
Cuisinart Culinary Study Scholarships [2570]
Culhane Memorial Scholarships; John P. [125]
Culinary (1-Year Program) Scholarships [1978]
Culinary and Hospitality Foundation of San Benito County **[2565]**
Culinary and Hospitality Foundation of San Benito County Scholarships [2566]
The Culinary Trust **[2567]**
The Culinary Trust's Memorial Journalism Scholarships [2571]
Cullen Memorial Scholarships; Linda [526]
Cullina Scholarships; Murtha [2393]
Cummins Memorial Scholarships; Brian [3441]
Cunningham Foundation General Scholarships; Laura Moore [4174]
Cunningham Memorial Scholarships; John J. [875]
Curry Award for Girls and Young Women [6387]
Curry Memorial Scholarships; Cindy [5475]
Curry Scholarships; Nancy [6256]
Curtin Renaissance Student Memorial Scholarships; Michael D. [2811]
Curtis Byler Scholarships; The Jennifer [5095]
Curtis Excellence Fund for Extracurricular Student Activities; Don and Barbara [7153]
Curtis Scholarship Fund; Dewey Lee [2631]
CVS/All Kids Can Scholars Program [1540]
Cystic Fibrosis Cholestatic Liver Disease Liver Scholarships [705]
Cystic Fibrosis Foundation **[2584]**
Cystic Fibrosis Foundation Scholarships [2585]
Cystic Fibrosis Worldwide **[2586]**
DAAD Study Scholarship Awards [3223]
DAAD Undergraduate Scholarship Program [3224]
Daddy Longlegs Scholarships [6182]
Dade Community Foundation, Inc. **[2593]**
Daedalian Foundation **[2605]**
Daggy Youth/Student Scholarships [3915]
Daiichi Sankyo Inc. NP Student Scholarships [266]
Dailey Scholarships; Robert G. [6549]
Daimler Chrysler Scholarships Award [3565]
Dake Community Manufacturing Scholarships [3273]
Daland Fellowships in Clinical Investigation [767]
Dales Merit Scholarship Program; Angela D. [1187]
Dales Scholarship Fund; The John L. [6288]
Dallas Hispanic Bar Association **[2610]**
Dallas Hispanic Bar Association Scholarships [2611]
Dalton Scholarships; Serena D. [7429]
Daly Memorial Scholarships; Marvin E. [5278]
Danby and Pat Pearse Education Scholarship; June [3975]
Dance Education Scholarship Program [6244]
D&A Florida Scholarships [6648]
The Dangermond Fellowships [981]
Daniels Memorial Scholarships; Robin M. [5816]
Daniels Scholarships; Arthur H. [5931]
Danish America Heritage Society **[2612]**
Dantzler Scholarships; Malcolm U. [6613]
Danville Education Association Scholarship Fund [2949]
Danville High School Class of 1963 Scholarship Fund [2950]
Danville Rotary Scholarships [2951]
Darden Restaurants Scholarships [7005]
Darling Dean Scholarships; Hugh and Hazel [5581]

Darling Foundation Endowed School of Law Scholarships [5582]
Darrel Hess Community College Geography Scholarships [1354]
Datatel **[2614]**
Datatel Angelfire Scholarships [2615]
Datatel Scholarships [2616]
Daughters of the American Revolution American Indian Scholarships [633]
Dautriel Memorial Scholarships (Graduate); Frank L. [4257]
Dautriel Memorial Scholarships (Undergraduate); Frank L. [4258]
Davanzo Scholarships; Antenore C. "Buth" [4503]
The Dave Family "Humor Studies" Scholarships [1364]
David Rose Scholarships [942]
Davis Dance Company; Rebecca **[2618]**
Davis Educational Scholarship Fund [2506]
Davis Endowed Scholarships; Kenneth and Kathleen [4175]
Davis Family Scholarships [6183]
Davis, Jr. Scholarship Fund; The William H. [2399]
Davis Memorial Foundation **[2620]**
Davis Memorial Foundation Scholarship Award Program [2621]
Davis Memorial Scholarships; Dwight F. [7303]
Davis Memorial Scholarships; Johnny [69]
Davis Publishing Agency Scholarships; Arthur L. [2316]
Davis Scholarships; Arlene [2685]
Davis Scholarships; Fran Morgenstern [943]
Davis Scholarships; James [7154]
Davis Scholarships; James H. [3012]
Davis Scholarships; Kenneth D. and Katherine D. [5476]
Davis Scholarships; Lawrence E. [5477]
Davis Scholarships Program; Larry Dean [1775]
Davis Scholarships; Rebecca [2619]
Davis Wright Tremaine 1L Diversity Scholarships [2623]
Davis Wright Tremaine LLP **[2622]**
Dawson Memorial Scholarships; William W. [1652]
Dawson Scholarships; Colonel Richard M. [2417]
Day Scholarships; Brian M. [5764]
Dayton Amateur Radio Association Scholarships [832]
D.C. Opportunity Scholarship Program [7376]
D.C. and Virginia Brown Scholarships [2270]
DCH Freehold Toyota Scholarships [2102]
De Bow Memorial Scholarships; Felicia [5447]
de Montequin Fellowships; Edilia and Francois Auguste [6427]
De Wolfe Point Scholarships; Elsie [5717]
Deadman Memorial Scholarships; Earl [556]
Deaf Queer Youth Scholarships [6102]
Deafness Research Foundation **[2624]**
Deafness Research Foundation Research Grants [2625]
Deal Scholarship Awards; Alphonso [4766]
Dean Prim Scholarships [7430]
Dean Scholarships; B.J. [2418]
Dean Soccer Scholarships; Derek Lee [2271]
Death Valley '49ers **[2626]**
Death Valley '49ers Scholarships [2627]
DeBakey International Society Fellowship Awards [2629]
DeBakey International Surgical Society; Michael E. **[2628]**
Debolt Franchising Scholarship Program; Don [3856]
Decker Point Scholarships; Walter M. [5718]
Decorative Arts Trust **[2630]**
Decore Awards for Student Leadership; Laurence [154]
DEED Student Research Grant/Internships [804]
Dees Educational Workshop Scholarships; Anthony R. [6448]
Deets-Laine Geriatric NP Student Scholarships [267]
Deines Canada Scholarships; Ginger and Fred [6917]
Deines Mexico Scholarships; Ginger and Fred [6918]
Delano Society Scholarships; Jane [886]
Delany Memorial Scholarship Fund; Jan DiMartino [3094]
Delaware Community Foundation **[2632]**
Dellas Memorial Scholarship; Antonia [3976]
DelleCese Memorial Scholarships; Alexander A. [1793]
Delman and Milton Arthur Krug Endowed Scholarships; Martha [5583]
Delmar Learning Surgical Technology Scholarships; Thomson [1500]
Deloria Jr. Memorial Scholarships; Vine [621]
Delson Memorial Scholarships; Eric [4919]
Delta Chi Alumnae Memorial Scholarships [6352]
Delta Daily Food (Canada) Inc. Scholarships [3847]
Delta Delta Delta **[2634]**
Delta Epsilon Sigma **[2671]**
Delta Faucet Scholarships [5701]
Delta Gamma **[2674]**
Delta Gamma Scholarships [2675]
Delta Iota Alumni Scholarships [6404]
Delta Nu Alpha Foundation Scholarships [2677]
Delta Nu Alpha Transportation Fraternity **[2676]**
Delta Phi Epsilon **[2678]**
Delta Phi Epsilon Educational Foundation Scholarships [2679]
Delta Sigma Theta Hartford Alumnae Scholarships [3442]
Delta Tau Chapter Scholarships [1653]
Delta Tau Lambda Sorority **[2680]**
Delta/VPPPA Safety, Health and Environmental Scholarships [7338]
Delta Zeta Sorority **[2682]**
Delta Zeta Undergraduate Scholarships [2686]
Demarest Memorial Scholarships; C. Rodney [3443]
DEMCO New Leaders Travel Grants [5871]
Demetris Scholarships; Christopher [3528]
DeMolay International **[2701]**
Demonet Scholarships; Inez [7316]
DeMoss Scholarships; Ruth [6184]
Dennis Foltz Scholarships [3175]
Dennis Scholarship Fund; Cindy P. [2534]
Dent Graduate Student Scholarships; Albert W. [466]
Denton Scholarships; Michael [5279]
Denver Music Scholarships; John [944]
Denver Public School Art Award/Scholarships for High School Seniors [1315]
Denver Scholarship Foundation **[2704]**
Denver Scholarship Foundation Scholarships [2705]
Denver Scholarships; ROP - Dr. Linda [5932]
Depaola Scholarship Award; Tommy [3848]
Depaolis Memorial Scholarships; Dick [2512]
Dependents of Deceased Service Members Scholarship Program [5147]
Depression and ADHD Fellowships [4078]
DEPS Graduate Scholarship Program [2715]
DerAvedision Memorial Endowment Fund; Karekin [1276]
Derivative Duo Scholarships [5765]
Derksen Scholarships; Herman H. [6185]
Dermargosian Memorial Scholarships; Pat [5933]
Descendant Scholarships [2606]
Despres, William & Andre Scholarships; Achille & Irene [3326]
Detroit Economic Club Scholarships [2513]
Detroit Tigers Willie Horton Scholarships [2514]
Development Fund for Black Students in Science and Technology **[2706]**
Development Fund for Black Students in Science and Technology Scholarship [2707]
Dewar Scholarships; Helen L. [6883]
Dewey Scholarships; Albert and Jane [3444]
Di Loreto-Odell S. McConnell Scholarships; Edward D. [5584]
Diaz Memorial Scholarship Fund; Julio C. [6714]
Dickerscheid Fellowships; Jean Dearth [5663]
Dickey Rural Networks **[2708]**
Dickey Rural Networks College Scholarship Program [2709]
Dickey Scholarship Association; Bill **[2710]**
Dickey Scholarship Association Scholarships; Bill [2711]
Dieckmann Draper, Sr. Scholarships; Harold [1550]
Digiacomo Scholarship Fund; Rob [6715]
DiMaiti Scholarship Awards; Carol [4328]
Dimico Memorial Scholarships; Gretchen [4176]
Dimmette Scholarship Fund; The E.R. and Lilian B. [3057]
DiPaglia Endowment Scholarships; Raymond [2737]
Direct Marketing Fundraisers Association **[2712]**
Directed Energy Professional Society **[2714]**
Directors of Health Promotion and Education **[2716]**
Dirksen Cogressional Center **[2718]**
Disabled American Veterans **[2721]**
Disabled War Veterans Scholarships [1244]
Disney Company Foundation Scholarships; Walt [4037]
Dissertation Proposal Development Fellowships [6415]
Distinguished Flying Cross Society **[2723]**
Distinguished Flying Cross Society Scholarship [2724]
Ditmore Music Scholarships; LaRue A. [7481]
Diversity Dissertation Scholarships [799]
Diversity Executive Leadership Program Scholarships [920]
Divine Graduate Student Travel Grants; Robert A. and Barbara [6455]
Dixon Memorial Scholarships; Dr. Allan A. [2034]
Dixon Two-Year Scholarships; Peggy [6541]
Dmytrenko Fine Arts Foundation Scholarships; Mychajlo [7021]
Doane Scholarships; Grace O. [2738]
Dobbins FTA Scholarships; Charles [3154]
Doctoral and Postdoctoral Fellowships [3233]
Doctors IRA & UDAYA Nursing Scholarships [6649]
Doddridge County Promise Scholarships [5478]
Dodge Maintenance Scholarships; F. Atlee [126]
Dodson Scholarships; Robert Winchester [7155]
Doe Scholarships; Hans H. and Margaret B. [6186]
Doerr Memorial Distinguished Scout Scholarships; Emmett J. [4853]
Dofflemyer Scholarships [4854]
Dokmo Family Scholarships [6187]
Dolphin Scholarship Foundation **[2725]**
Dolphin Scholarships [2726]
Dominguez - Craters of the Moon Chapter Scholarships; Scott [1053]
Donaldson Scholarship Fund; Marian Jones [2952]
Dondero Communication and Journalism Excellence Scholarships; Harvey N. [5817]
Donn Scholarships; Harry A. [3445]
Donnelly Memorial Scholarships; Mickey [5818]
Doogan Memorial Scholarships; Jim [7075]
Doraine Pursuit of Educational Excellence Scholarships [2272]
Dorgan Scholarships; Joseph M. [2739]
Dorizas Memorial Scholarships [3529]
D'Orlando Memorial Art Scholarships; Pauly [6950]
Dosatron International Inc. Scholarships [557]
Dostie Memorial College Scholarships; Eric [4920]
Dougherty Scholarships; Father Connie [2507]
Dougherty Scholarships; Robert E. [2525]
Douglas and Charlotte DeHorse Scholarships; Sergeant [2066]
Douglas-Coldwell Foundation **[2727]**
Douglas-Coldwell Foundation Scholarships in Social Affairs [2729]
Douglas County Art Awards Scholarship for High School Seniors [1316]
Douglas Scholarships; Chapter 116 - Kalamazoo - Roscoe [6487]
Douglas Scholarships; Tommy [5116]
Douhhit Regional Scholarships; Harold K. [5322]
Dowell-Gravatt, M.D. Scholarship; Margaret [1625]
Downes Memorial Scholarships; Jay [2273]
Dracup Memorial Scholarships; Nettie [485]
Drake University Law School **[2731]**
Drake University Law School Law Opportunity Scholarships - Disadvantage [2740]
Drake University Law School Law Opportunity Scholarships - Diversity [2741]
Drake University Law School Public Service Scholarships [2742]
Drane Fund; Lou [3095]
The "Drawn to Art" Fellowships [301]
Drennon, Jr. Memorial Scholarships; Cleveland [7111]
Dressel Scholarships; Wilma Sackett [6353]
Drew Alpha Fellowships; Margaret [5664]
Dreyfus Warner-Chappell City College Scholarships; Louis [945]

DRI Law Student Diversity Scholarships [1755]
Drinkwater Family Scholarships [6188]
Driscoll Scholarships; Mary Ellen [6073]
Droke Memorial Scholarships; Lillian Cooper [4463]
Drukker Memorial Scholarships; Richard [5180]
Drum Major Institute Scholars [6332]
Drum Memorial Scholarship Fund; Sergeant Major Douglas R. [716]
Duberman Fellowships; Martin [2086]
Dubin Scholarship Fund; Lee [6103]
Dubose Scholarships; Charles [3446]
Duckett Jr., AFUD Pediatric Research Scholarships; John W. [6538]
Dudding Memorial Scholarships; Deborah Gandee [5479]
Duhamel Freemasons Scholarships; Edward Leon [6037]
Dulis Scholarships; Edward J. [4397]
Duluth Building and Construction Trades Council Scholarships [2774]
Duluth Central HS Alumni Scholarships [2775]
Duluth Superior Area Community Foundation **[2770]**
Dunbar Heritage Scholarships [6650]
Duncan Aviation Scholarships [70]
Duncan Memorial Scholarships; John Holt [1654]
Duncan Scholarships; Wade and Marcelene [7431]
Dundonald Chapter (IODE) Scholarships; Lord [5421]
Dunkelblau Scholarships; Ed [1365]
Dunning Memorial Scholarships; Travis [5819]
Durant Timberline High School Endowed Scholarships; Bus and Mary Ellen [4177]
Durham/Theater Scholarship; William R. [2463]
Durning Sisters Scholarships [2645]
Durso Memorial Scholarships; Joe [4569]
Dutchess County Bar Association **[2797]**
Duvoisin, MD Research Grants; Roger C. [761]
Dyer Foundation Travel Scholarship Award; Sue and Ken [3096]
Dyke Family Scholarships; Joshua [6884]
Dystonia Medical Research Foundation **[2799]**
Dystonia Medical Research Foundation Fellowships [2800]
Eagles Fly for Leukemia Scholarships [2127]
Ear Foundation **[2801]**
Earhart Fellowship Program; Amelia [7563]
Earhart Memorial Academic Scholarships; Amelia [5209]
Earl and Countess of Wessex - World Championships in Athletics Scholarships [155]
Early Childhood Development Scholarships [1701]
Early Childhood Educators Scholarship Program [4332]
Early Memorial Scholarships; Robert E. [2743]
Earthquake Engineering Research Institute **[2803]**
Earthquake Engineering Research Institute/Fema Graduate Fellowships [2804]
East Scholarships; Bob [5019]
East Tennessee Foundation **[2805]**
East Tennessee Foundation Scholarships [7112]
Eastaugh Memorial Teaching Scholarships; Patricia Ann Hughes [4355]
Easter Seals Ontario **[2812]**
Eastern Orthodox Scouting Scholarships [4855]
Eastern Shore Builder's Association Scholarships [2371]
Eaton Scholarships; David [6951]
Ebeling Fellowships; The Christoph Daniel [302]
Eberhardt Memorial Scholarships; Ellen [6772]
ECA Alumni Small Grants Program [3894]
Echlin Memorial Scholarships; John E. [1551]
Ecological Society of America **[2815]**
Economic Development Division Graduate Scholarships [778]
Economic History Association **[2817]**
Edelstein Fellowships; Sidney M. [2109]
Edgecliff Alumni Awards [7526]
Edgecliff McAuley Art Scholarships [7527]
Edgecliff McAuley Music Scholarships [7528]
EDiS Company **[2821]**
Edmonds Scholarships; Vivian [7156]
Edmonds Young Scholars Competition; S. Randolph [1753]
Edmonson Memorial Scholarship; Melanie and Todd [2348]
Edmonton Epilepsy Association **[2823]**
Edmonton Epilepsy Continuing Education Scholarships [2824]
Edon Farmers Cooperative Association **[2825]**
Edon Farmers Cooperative Scholarships [2826]
Education is Power Scholarships [4921]
Education Resource Center (ERC) Scholarships [6399]
Educational Administration Scholarships Award [397]
Educational Audiology Association **[2827]**
Educational Audiology Association Doctoral Scholarships [2829]
Educational Enrichment Awards [1209]
Educational Foundation for Women in Accounting **[2831]**
Educational Leadership Foundation Grants [2300]
Educational Opportunity Fund [3097]
Educational Portal of the Americas **[2837]**
Educational Portal of the Americas Graduate Scholarships [2838]
Educational Portal of the Americas Undergraduate Scholarships [2839]
Educational and Professional Achievement Scholarships [451]
Edwards Memorial Scholarships; Carli [6311]
Edwards Memorial Scholarships; Palo Verde High School - Barbara [5820]
Edwards Scholarships; Jimmy [2419]
Egan Multi-Year Mentioning Scholarships; John and Alice [2607]
Egan Scholarship Program; Bill [5380]
The eGullet Society for Culinary Arts and Letters Brian and Thelma Moore Memorial Culinary Journalist Independent Study Scholarships [2572]
The eGullet Society for Culinary Arts and Letters Culinary Journalist Independent Study Scholarships [2573]
The eGullet Society for Culinary Arts and Letters Matthew X. Hassett Memorial Culinary Arts Scholarships [2574]
The eGullet Society for Culinary Arts and Letters Professional Chef Independent Study Scholarships [2575]
Eide Memorial Scholarships; Christine H. [4242]
Eidson Jr., Scholarships; John R. [2274]
Eight and Forty Lung and Respiratory Disease Nursing Scholarships [696]
Einhorn New Investigator Awards [6466]
Eisenhower Institute **[2840]**
El-Baz Student Research Grants; Farouk [3209]
ELA Foundation Scholarships [1297]
Elanjian Scholarships; George & Isabelle [1277]
Eldridge and Emily Lowe Scholarships; W. [6405]
Electric Cooperative Pioneer Trust Fund Scholarships [2744]
Electronic Document Systems Foundation **[2845]**
Electronic Document Systems Foundation Scholarships [2846]
Electronics Division Lewis C. Hoffman Scholarships [453]
Elgar Memorial Scholarships; Herman E. [2745]
Elias Memorial Scholarships; Todd [1655]
Elizabeth and Alma Vane Taylor Student Nurse Scholarships; Virginia [7432]
Elks National Foundation **[2847]**
Elks National Foundation Scholarships [2848]
Elliott Memorial Scholarships; Dr. Robert [4415]
Elliott Scholarships; Pauline [4416]
Ellis Scholarships in Physics; Robert A. [5054]
Ellis Scholarships; Robertson Lola [4286]
Elrod Memorial Scholarships; William P. [6853]
Emerald Empire Chapter Scholarship Awards [5381]
Emergency Medicine Physician Scholarships for Health Information Management Program [6716]
Emergency Medicine Physicians Scholarship Fund for Non-Physician Employee Dependents [6717]
Emergency Nurses Association **[2849]**
Emergency Nurses Association Undergraduate Scholarships [2851]
Emerging Leaders Scholarships [1841]
Emerging Teacher-Leaders in Elementary School Mathematics Grants for Grades K-5 Teachers [4829]
EMLF Law Student Scholarships [2855]
Emmanuel Bible College Scholarships [1278]
Employee Education Scholarships [4946]
ENA Foundation Advanced Practice Scholarships [2852]
Endicott Scholarships; Priscilla Maxwell [3447]
Endo Memorial Scholarships; Alice Yuriko [4016]
Endowment Fund for Education Grants [1707]
Endowment Fund for Education (Loan) [1708]
Endowment Fund for Education (Loan/Grants for Equipment) [1709]
Endowment Fund for Education (Loans/Grants for Educational Materials) [1710]
Energy and Mineral Law Foundation **[2854]**
The Eneslow Pedorthic Institute Scholarships [5545]
Engen Scholarships; Vice Admiral Donald D. [5132]
Engineering Departmental Scholarships [7251]
Engineering Diversity Affairs Scholarships [7252]
Engineers for Tomorrow Scholarships Program [4563]
English Memorial Scholarships; Don [5821]
Enlisted Association of National Guard of the United States **[2856]**
Ennes Scholarships; Harold E. [6526]
Enterprise Rent-A-Car Scholarships [5636]
Entertainment Software Association **[2858]**
Entomological Society of America **[2860]**
Entz Memorial Scholarships; Lindsay M. [2953]
Environment, Natural Resource and Energy (ENRE) Division Fellowships [779]
Environmental Research and Education Foundation **[2864]**
Environmental Research and Education Foundation Scholarships [2865]
Epicurean Charitable Foundation Scholarships [5822]
Epilepsy Foundation **[2866]**
Epilepsy Foundation Post-doctoral Research Fellowships [2869]
Epilepsy Foundation Pre-doctoral Research Training Fellowships [2870]
Epilepsy Foundation Research Grants [2871]
Epilepsy Foundation Research and Training Fellowships for Clinicians [2872]
Epilepsy Newfoundland and Labrador **[2878]**
Epsilon Epsilon Scholarships [6354]
Epsilon Tau Pi's Soaring Eagle Scholarships [4856]
Epsilon Tau Scholarships [6355]
Epstein Award for Archival and Library Research in American Music; Dena [4597]
Epstein "Reach for the Stars" Scholarships; Alan R. [2597]
Equal Access to Justice Scholarships [4752]
Equal Justice Works **[2881]**
Equal Justice Works Fellowship Program [2882]
eQuality Scholarships [6104]
Equity Foundation **[2883]**
Erb Group Companies Service to Community Scholarships [5342]
Erb Sr. Scholarships; Robert C. [4417]
Erich Graduate Fellowships; Harriet [2646]
Erickson Field of Interest Education Scholarships Fund; E.V. [3274]
Erim Fellowships for Research at Ancient Aphrodisiacs; Kenan [893]
Ernest Hemingway Research Grants [3538]
Ernest Scholarship; The Eleonor A. [3977]
Ernest Scholarship; Melissa Eleonor [3978]
Ernest Scholarship; Robert P. [3979]
Ernst Memorial Scholarship Fund; Kevin [3275]
Ernst and Young/Ascend Leadership Scholarship Program [4644]
Ertegun Memorial Scholarships; Ahmet [6937]
Ervin EDI Scholarships; Jack [5238]
ESA Foundation Computer and Video Game Scholarship Program [2859]
Esiason Foundation Scholarship Program; Boomer [2587]
Esser Memorial Scholarships; Charles A. [1217]
Essick Scholarship Awards; NSPF Ray B. [5102]
Estes Endowed Scholarships; R. Wayne [5585]
Etherton Scholarships; Larry L. [876]
Ethnic Minority and Women's Enhancement Postgraduate Scholarships [4803]
Ettl Grants; Alex J. [5037]
European College of Liberal Arts (ECLA) Scholarships [7022]
Eustace-Kwan Family Foundation Scholarships [6388]

Evans Memorial Scholarships; Brad [5359]
Evans/National Housing Endowment Scholarship; Lee S. [4941]
Evans and Petree Law Firm Scholarships [7113]
Evans Scholarship; Ruth Murphy [3373]
Evans Scholarships [4554]
Evans Scholarships; Chuck [7405]
Evening Mesquite Club Scholarships [5823]
Evjue Foundation, Inc./Capital Times Scholarships [7253]
Ewald Journalism Scholarships; David E. [4774]
Excel Staffing Companies Scholarships for Excellence in Continuing Education [192]
Excellence in Geographic Information Systems Scholarships [4356]
Executive Women International **[2893]**
Executive Women International Fellows Program [2895]
Executive Women International Scholarship Program (EWISP) [2896]
Exercise For Life Athletic Scholarships Program [2588]
Exploratory Travel and Data Grants [2819]
Extendicare Scholarships [1998]
Exxon Mobil Aviation and the Avitats International Operators Scholarships [4775]
Eye On Jewels Scholarships [3176]
Ezell Fellowships; The William C. [276]
Fabricators and Manufacturers Association Foundation **[2897]**
FACS Graduate Fellowships [4747]
FACT Graduating Senior Scholarship Program [2920]
Faculty Doctoral Scholarships [2853]
Faculty Research Visit Grant [3225]
Faegre & Benson Diversity Scholarships [2900]
Faegre & Benson LLP **[2899]**
FAIC Latin American and Caribbean Scholars Program [660]
Failor Scholarships; Wayne G. [5563]
Fairbanks Chapter Legacy Scholarships [7076]
Fairgrave Education Trust; D.J. [2746]
Fairless Scholarships (AIME); AIST Benjamin F. [1445]
Falcon Achievement Scholarships [5731]
Fall Fellowships in Korean Studies [4082]
Fallows Scholarships Honoring Gertrude Baccus; James Mackenzie [5934]
Families of Freedom Scholarship Fund **[2901]**
Families of Freedom Scholarship Fund - America Scholarships [2902]
Family and Children's Services of Lebanon County Fund [3098]
Fanning Maintenance Scholarships; William M. [4776]
Farella Braun Martel LLP **[2903]**
Farella Braun Martel LLP Diversity Scholarships [2904]
Farello Scholarships; Senior Chef Frank [527]
Fargher Scholarships; John S.W. [3730]
Faries Scholarships; Judge McIntyre [5586]
Farmers State Bank Scholarships [6773]
Farmers Union Marketing and Processing Foundation Stanley Moore Scholarships [5250]
Farmington UNICO Scholarships [3448]
Farr Scholarships; W.D. [4789]
Farson Scholarships; David Edward [5480]
Fase Memorial Scholarship Fund; Bertha M. [3276]
Fassett Scholarships; Anne M. [6651]
Faust International Travel Awards; Miklos [975]
FCBA Foundation Scholarships [2909]
Fecon Scholarships [3001]
Federal Circuit Bar Association **[2905]**
Federal Communication Bar Association Foundation **[2908]**
Federal Court Bench and Bar Scholarships [7114]
Federal Court Clerks Association **[2910]**
Federal Employee Education and Assistance Fund **[2912]**
Federal Employee Education and Assistance Fund Scholarships [2913]
Federal Law Enforcement Officers Association **[2915]**
Federal Managers Association **[2917]**
Federalsburg Rotary Club Scholarships [2372]
Federated Insurance Scholarships [5637]
Federation of American Consumers and Travelers **[2919]**
Federation of Diocesan Liturgical Commissions **[2921]**
Federation of Societies for Coatings Technology **[2923]**
Fedok Art and Music Scholarships; Adrienne Zoe [3099]
FEEA Scholarship Program [2914]
Feeser Scholarship Fund; Nolan W. [2954]
Fehr: Nightingale Scholarships; Red and Lola [2317]
Fehsenfeld Scholarships; Virginia Valk [3327]
FEI Company **[2925]**
Feinburg Memorial Scholarships; Symee Ruth [3449]
Felber Scholarships; Edward R. and Hazel N. [7254]
Fellows Scholarships; Harold E. [1784]
Fellowships in Aerospace History [605]
Fellowships for Full-time Studies in French [156]
Fellowships in the Humanities and Social Sciences in Turkey [894]
Fellowships for Intensive Advanced Turkish Language Study in Turkey [895]
Fellowships to Promote Research on the Legal Framework for Civil Society in Latin America, Africa and Asia [3823]
Felts Scholarships; Reese [7157]
Ferguson Memorial Scholarships; Jennica [4876]
Fernandez Point Scholarships; Dr. Joan W. [5719]
Ferrell Scholarship Program; William and Dorothy [1390]
Ferretti Scholarships; Lt. Col. Romeo and Josephine Bass [51]
FHSMAI Scholarship Program [3127]
FICE Scholarships [3002]
Field Aviation Co., Inc. Scholarships [71]
Fielding Student Grants; UFVA Carole [7091]
Fields Scholarships; Beth K. [7100]
Film Arts Foundation **[2927]**
Film Arts Foundation Development Grants [2928]
Film Studies Association of Canada **[2929]**
Fincher Memorial Scholarship; Herb [2373]
Fine Arts Association **[2931]**
Fine Arts Association Minority Scholarships [2932]
Fine Arts Association United Way Scholarships [2933]
Fine Arts and Music Scholarships [2420]
Finegold Scholarships; Dr. Mary [6389]
Fink Memorial Scholarships; Gordy [5824]
Finley-Loescher Scholarships; Helen R. [2464]
Finnegan, Henderson, Farabow, Garrett & Dunner LLP **[2935]**
Finnegan, Henderson, Farabow, Garrett & Dunner, LLP Diversity Scholarships [2936]
Finnigan Scholarship; Dayton E. [3374]
Fire Safety Awards [1963]
First Church of Christ in Wethersfield - Metcalf Scholarships [3450]
First Community Foundation of Pennsylvania, Williamsport-Lycoming **[2937]**
First Friday Breakfast Club Scholarships [6105]
First in My Family Scholarship Program [6156]
First Security Foundation Business Scholarships [4178]
Fisher Healthcare Educational Scholarships [5075]
Fisher Memorial Fund; Allison E. **[2983]**
Fisher Memorial Scholarships; Charles N. [833]
Fisher Memorial Scholarships; William A. [1027]
Fisher Memorial Track Scholarships; Arthur and Juna [5935]
Fisher Scholarship Fund; Jack B. [6718]
Fisher Scholarships; Allison E. [2984]
Fisher Scholarships; Ameel J. [7158]
Fitzgerald Fellowships [2672]
Fitzgerald Health Education Associates NP Student Scholarships [268]
Fitzgerald Scholarship Program; Carol C. [2911]
Fitzgerald Scholarships [2673]
Flaherty Scholarships; Gloria [3248]
Flahive Memorial Scholarship Fund; Scott A. [3277]
Fleet Memorial Scholarships; Reuben H. [6189]
Flegenheimer Memorial Scholarships; Albert [4495]
Fleming/Blaszcak Scholarships [6550]
Fleming Education Fund Scholarships; Charlie [5106]
Fleming Scholarship Fund; Laura M. [3058]
FLEOA Foundation Scholarship Program [2916]
Flexible Packaging Academic Scholarships & Summer Internship Program [2988]
The Flexible Packaging Association **[2987]**
Flight Attendants/Flight Technician Scholarships [4777]
Flint International Scholarships - Category I; Grant H. [6596]
Flint International Scholarships - Category II; Grant H. [6597]
Flora English Creative Writing Scholarships [5825]
Florida Association Directors of Nursing Administration **[2989]**
Florida Association District of Nursing Administration Scholarships [2990]
Florida Association for Media in Education **[2992]**
Florida Atlantic Planning Society **[2994]**
Florida Atlantic Planning Society Graduate Fellowships for Academic Excellence [2997]
Florida Automotive Industry Scholarships [1546]
Florida Engineering Society **[2999]**
Florida Engineering Society Junior College Scholarships [3003]
Florida Engineering Society University Scholarships [3004]
Florida Fertilizer and Agrichemical Association **[3009]**
Florida Fertilizer and Agrichemical Association Scholarships [3010]
Florida Nursery, Growers, and Landscape Association **[3011]**
Florida Nurses Association **[3013]**
Florida Nurses Association Scholarships [3014]
Florida Outdoor Writers Association **[3015]**
Florida Outdoor Writers Association Scholarships [3016]
Florida Police Chiefs Association **[3017]**
Floto-Peel Family Scholarships Fund [3278]
Fluid Power Distributor Association **[3019]**
Flynn Memorial Scholarship; John [2465]
Flynn Memorial Scholarships; Barney [2275]
Flynn Scholarships; Paul B. & Aline [6652]
FMA-FEEA Scholarship Program [2918]
FMA Foundation **[3021]**
FMA Foundation Scholarships [3022]
Fohn-Hansen/Lola Hill Memorial Scholarships; Lydia [4357]
Foit Scholarships; Alice J. [6719]
Fong Scholarships; Frank [6423]
Food Engineering Scholarships [3024]
Food Processing Suppliers Association **[3023]**
Food for Thought Scholarships [2276]
Ford Foundation Diversity Fellowships [4618]
Ford Foundation Predoctoral Fellowships for Minorities [4703]
Ford Motor Company Scholarship Program [3589]
Ford Scholarships; Anne [4796]
Fordham Fellowships [3027]
Fordham Scholarships [3028]
Fordman Foundation; Thomas B. **[3026]**
Forehand, Jr. Scholarships; V. Thomas [7240]
Foreman Tribute to Lyndon B. Johnson Scholarships; George [1397]
Forest History Society **[3029]**
Forest and L. Michael Honaker Master's Scholarships for Research; Nancy B. [800]
Foresters Scholarships [3682]
Forrest Scholarships; Leland Stanford [2747]
Forsyth County Nursing Scholarships [7433]
Forsyth County United Way Scholarships [4133]
Forthun Scholarships; Genevieve [5665]
Forward Face **[3032]**
Forward Face Scholarships [3033]
Foster Memorial Scholarships; Barbara Palo [2128]
Foster Scholarships; Charles and Margaret [6653]
Foster Scholarships; Jonathan Hastings [6190]
Fostering Hope Scholarship Fund [5481]
Foundation for the Advancement of Aboriginal Youth Bursary Program [1939]
Foundation for the Advancement of Aboriginal Youth Scholarships [1940]
Foundation of American Institute for Conservation Lecture Grants [661]
Foundation for the Carolinas **[3034]**

Foundation for the Carolinas Rotary Scholarship Fund [3059]
Foundation for Community Association Research **[3087]**
Foundation for Enhancing Communities **[3089]**
Foundation of the Federal Bar Association **[3124]**
Foundation of the Federal Bar Association Public Service Scholarships [3125]
Foundation of the Hospitality Sales and Marketing Association International **[3126]**
Foundation of the National Student Nurses Association **[3128]**
The Foundation of the National Student Nurses' Association Scholarships [5100]
Foundation of the Pennsylvania Medical Society **[3133]**
Foundation Scholarships [4064]
Foundation for Surgical Technology Advanced Education/Medical Mission Scholarships [1501]
Foundation for Surgical Technology Scholarships [1502]
Founders Circle Professional Scholarships [3762]
Fox Memorial Law Scholarship; Howard [1634]
Fox Memorial Scholarships; Terry [5117]
Fox Scholarships; Jacob and Lewis [3451]
Fracasso Production Floriculture Scholarships; Paris [558]
Franchini Rockford Police Department Scholarships; Louise J. [2466]
Franchise Law Diversity Scholarship Awards [3857]
Francis Haircare Scholarship Foundation; Joe **[3140]**
Francis Haircare Scholarships; Joe [3141]
Franco Legacy Scholarship; Joey and Florence [1824]
Francomano Scholarships; Joe [4038]
Frank Scholarship Program; Mayme and Herb [1323]
Frank Scholarships; Johnny and Sarah [4358]
Franke Family Foundation Scholarships; Michael W. and Jean D. [877]
Franken Scholarships; Mary Weiking [5666]
Frankenthaler Memorial Scholarship; The Ginny [6629]
Franklin Dissertation Fellowships; John Hope [768]
Franklin and Dorothy J. Warnell Scholarship Fund; James [2508]
Franklin Elementary School PTA Scholarships [5936]
Franklin Journalism Scholarships; Denise [7434]
Franklin Research Grants [769]
Frantz Scholarship Fund; John and Victory E. [3279]
Frasca Excellence in Aviation Scholarships; Joseph [7081]
Fraser Family Scholarships [5826]
Fraser/Wilton Looney Scholarships; Carlyle [1552]
Freedom Alliance **[3142]**
Freedom Alliance Scholarships [3143]
Freedom Forum-NCAA Sports-Journalism Scholarships [4804]
Freeland, II Educational Scholarships; Richard Gregory [1762]
Freeman Carnegie Mellon Scholarships; Belknap [878]
Freeman Travel Grants; Kevin [4598]
The French Culinary Institute Classic Pastry Arts Scholarships [2576]
The French Culinary Institute Culinary Arts Scholarships [2577]
The French Culinary Institute's Food and Technology Scholarships - Magic Potions Transglutaminase [2578]
French Embassy Scholarships [5264]
French Graduate Scholarships; Ruth M. [933]
Frey Memorial Scholarships; Dorris W. [6654]
Friday Memorial Scholarships; Carleton A. [4522]
Fridell Memorial Scholarships; Dale E. [6793]
Friedman Scholarships; A.E. Robert [5445]
Friel Scholarships; Phil [4418]
Friend Scholarship; Joel R. [1626]
Friends of Coal Scholarships [7394]
Friends and Family of Jennifer Balber Scholarships [5937]
Friends of the Jose Carreras International Leukemia Foundation **[3144]**
Friends of Loutit District Library Scholarships Fund [3280]
Friends of Mary Automotive Scholarships [6312]
Friends of Megan Bolton Memorial Fund [3100]
Friendship Scholarship Fund [3101]
Froberg-Suess JD/MBA Scholarships [5587]
Froehlich Endowed Scholarships; Dean A. [4179]
Frontjes Scholarships; Melbourne & Alice E. [3328]
Fruits and Vegetable Industries Scholarships [4489]
Frutiger Scholarships; Marian Johnson [6356]
Fuchs-Harden Educational Scholarships Fund [3375]
Fudge Memorial Scholarships; Gerard Swartz [3638]
Fulbright New Century Scholars Program [1714]
Fulton Nursing Scholarships; Don and Eileen [6774]
Fultz Scholarship Fund; Daniel G. and Helen I. [2955]
The Fund for American Studies **[3146]**
Funeral Service Foundation **[3149]**
Fur Takers of America **[3153]**
Furbush Scholarships; Donald M. [3749]
The Future Colleagues Scholarships [4895]
Future Leader in Radiocommunications Scholarships [5893]
Future Leaders of Manufacturing Scholarships [6488]
Future Teachers Conditional Scholarships and Loan Repayment [7364]
Gable II Memorial Grants; Mearl K. [3395]
Gaddy Student Scholarships [7435]
Gadsden State/McClellan Campus Nursing Scholarships Award [2349]
Gaebe Eagle Scout Awards [4857]
Gail Burns-Smith "Dare to Dream" Fund [3452]
Gairey Scholarships; Harry [1731]
Galbraith Scholarship Fund; Farley Moody [2350]
Gallagher Scholarship Fund; Thomas W. [6720]
Gallagher Scholarships; Louise Bales [2647]
Gallagher Scholarships; William E. "Bill" [5482]
Gallahar Memorial Scholarship Fund; Whitney Laine [2351]
Gallmeyer Scholarships; Carolyn [3329]
Gallmeyer Scholarships; Mathilda & Carolyn [3330]
Gallo Blue Chip Scholarships [3404]
Gamewarden Scholarship program [3156]
Gamewarden of Vietnam Association **[3155]**
Gamma Iota Scholarships - Gamma Tau [6357]
Gamma Iota Scholarships - Kappa Eta [6358]
Gamma Iota Scholarships - Zeta Kappa [6359]
Gamma Iota Scholarships - Zeta Nu [6360]
GANA Scholarship Program [3258]
Gantt Memorial Scholarships; Veronica [5827]
GAP, Inc. Scholarships Award [3566]
GAPA Scholarships [3165]
Garcia Rail Engineering Scholarships; Michael and Gina [879]
Gard Memorial Scholarships; William R. [4608]
Garden Club of America **[3157]**
Garden Club Council of Winston-Salem and Forsyth County Council [7436]
Garden Conservancy **[3160]**
Garden State Rotary Club of Cherry Hill Scholarships [1895]
Gardiner Scholarships; Jewels [1848]
Gardner Fellowships; John [7087]
Gardner Foundation INS Education Scholarship [3722]
Gardner Scholarships; Dwight D. [3731]
Gardner Scholarships; Victoria M. [7159]
Garfield Doctoral Dissertation Fellowships; Eugene [1636]
Gargano Scholarship Fund; Peter M. [2776]
Garikian Scholarship Fund [1279]
Garmin Scholarships [72]
Garner Memorial Scholarships; Gerald [5588]
Garner R.I.S.E. Memorial Scholarships; Gail [5938]
Garrett Scholarships; Eileen J. [5457]
Garvey Scholarships; Marcus [3453]
Garvey Scholarships; Marcus Mosiah [3997]
Gary Scholarships; Kays [7160]
Gaston Scholarships [239]
Gates Cambridge Scholarships [4704]
Gates Foundation; Bill and Melinda **[3162]**
The Gates Millennium Scholars [3590]
Gates Public Service Law Scholarships; William H. [3163]
Gates Scholarships; Stephen [7161]
Gathercole Scholarships; Raffin [3168]
Gault Charitable Fund; David A. and Pamela A. [6721]
Gautier Family Scholarships Fund [3281]
Gavin Memorial Scholarships; James L. [1656]
Gavrila Scholarships for Women; A.R.F.O.R.A. Martha [912]
Gay Asian Pacific Alliance **[3164]**
Gay, Lesbian, Bisexual, Transgender Alumni Council Scholarships [7255]
Gay and Lesbian Business Association of Santa Barbara **[3166]**
Gay and Lesbian Business Association of Santa Barbara Scholarships [6106]
Gaylor Memorial Scholarships; Lowell [73]
Gaynor Scholarships; Florence S. [4716]
GCA Awards in Tropical Botany [3158]
GE Healthcare Management Scholarship Program [1039]
GED Jump Start Scholarships [6257]
Gelfand - Armin Rappaport Fellowships; Lawrence [6456]
Gelhausen Scholarship Fund; Irma [4140]
Gellert/Dutchess County Bar Association Scholarships; Joseph H. [2798]
Gelman Scholarship Award; Elaine [4730]
Gemological Institute of America **[3170]**
Gen III Scholarships [2822]
The Gene and John Athletic Scholarships [6789]
General Aviation Manufacturers Association **[3206]**
General Falcon Scholarships [5732]
General Mills Foundation Scholarships [622]
General Scholarship Awards [1599]
Geological Society of America **[3208]**
Geological Society of America Graduate Student Research Grants [3210]
Georgia Chapter of ASSE Annual Scholarships [1054]
Georgia Engineering Foundation **[3211]**
Georgia Engineering Foundation Scholarships [3212]
Georgia Press Educational Foundation **[3213]**
Gerber Fellowships in Pediatric Nutrition [4987]
Gerber Foundation **[3218]**
Gerber Foundation Merit Scholarships [3219]
Gerber Scholarships; Burton L. [1657]
Gerber Scholarships; Doris Y. and John J. [7380]
Gerber, Sr. Medallion Scholarships; Daniel [3220]
Gerboth Awards; Walter [4599]
German Academic Exchange Service **[3221]**
German Historical Institute **[3232]**
The German Society of Pennsylvania **[3237]**
German Society Scholarships [3238]
German Studies Research Grant [3226]
Gerry Fellowships; Eloise [6339]
GET Ready for Math and Science Conditional Scholarships [7365]
Getty Research Exchange Fellowship Program for Cultural Heritage Preservation [896]
GFWC Women's Club of South County Scholarships [6038]
Ghezzi Nursing Scholarships; Mary [6842]
GHI Fellowships at the Horner Library [3234]
GIA Endowment Scholarships - Distance Education [3177]
GIA Endowment Scholarships - On Campus [3178]
GIA Endowment Scholarships - School of Business [3179]
Gibson Memorial Scholarships; Laverne L. [5483]
Gibson Scholarships; Joy [7162]
Gifford Distinguished Journalism Scholarships; L.C. [7163]
Gifford Scholarship Fund; Tim [3282]
Gilbert Memorial Scholarships; Dr. Virginia [5828]
Gilbert Memorial Scholarships; Shane [5484]
Gilbert Scholarship Fund; Margaret S. [6722]
Gilbreth Memorial Fellowships [3732]
Giles Honor Scholarships; Terry M. [5589]
Giles Scholarships; Harold [6551]
Gill Education Fund; William Harrison [1627]
Gill Foundation Scholarships (Colorado) [6107]
Gill; Midwest Chapter Scholarships - Jack [1446]

Gilman International Scholarship; Benjamin A. [7031]
Gilmartin Scholarships; Leo [5708]
Gilmer Educational Grants; John L. [7437]
Gilmer Merit Based Scholarships; John L. [7438]
Gilmore Foundation - Diploma Scholarships; Keith [3240]
Gilmore Foundation; Keith **[3239]**
Gilmore Foundation - Postgraduate Scholarships; Keith [3241]
Gilmore Foundation - Undergraduate Scholarships; Keith [3242]
Gilmore Memorial Scholarship; Susan Kay Munson [2467]
Ginocchio Aviation Scholarships; Lawrence [4778]
Giorgione Hope for Hearts Scholarships; Nick [5829]
Gissler Memorial Scholarships; Alex [4419]
Gladstone Memorial Scholarships; Senator James [143]
Glaser Scholarships; Jane R. [1124]
Glaser Scholarships; John [2298]
Glaser Scientist Award; Elizabeth [5539]
Glass Scholarships; Helen [1999]
Glassco Scholarships; Ann and Brad [5939]
Glazing Industry Scholarships [5830]
Gleaner Life Insurance Association **[3243]**
Gleaner Life Insurance Scholarship Foundation [3244]
Glenn Memorial Endowed Scholarships; Jane S. [6046]
Globe-Trotters Chapter Scholarships [1447]
Glover Memorial Scholarships; Bud [74]
GLP Program Scholarships [4784]
GLSEN Connecticut Chapter Scholarships [6108]
Glynn Scholarships; Ray [3180]
Gnaedinger Memorial Scholarships; Irene Carlson [4180]
Goddard Memorial Scholarships; Dr. Robert H. [5085]
Godparents for Tanzania **[3245]**
Godparents for Tanzania Scholarships [3246]
Godwin Endowed Scholarships; Max [6871]
Goerlich Memorial Scholarships; John [1553]
Goethe-Institut AATG Scholarships [5265]
Goethe Society of North America **[3247]**
Gogos Scholarships [2302]
Gold Award/Eagle Scout Scholarships [4858]
Gold Country Section & Region II Scholarships [1055]
Gold Key Scholarships [4065]
Goldberg Scholarships; Daniel B. [3264]
Golden Key International Honour Society **[3249]**
Golden Key International Honour Society New Graduate Member Scholarships [3252]
Golden Key International Honour Society Study Abroad Scholarships [3253]
Golden Key International Honour Society Undergraduate Research Grants [3254]
Golden Key Math Scholarships [3255]
Goldfarb Memorial Scholarships; William R. [834]
Goldman Fellowships; Dr. Guido [503]
Goldmann Scholarships Fund [3645]
Goldwater Scholarships; Barry M. [7256]
Golf Educational Scholarships; S. William & Martha R. [5485]
Gomes Memorial Scholarship Fund; Joshua [4922]
Gongaware Scholarships College of Business [3700]
Gonja Association of North America **[3257]**
Gonzaga University School of Law **[3259]**
Gonzalez Memorial Scholarships; Millie [4923]
Good Graduate Students Fellowship Program; Kenneth M. [7295]
Goodfellow Nursing Scholarships [4249]
Goodfellow Professional Development Fund [4250]
Goodman and Company, LLP **[3261]**
Goodman and Company, LLP Annual Scholarships [3262]
Goodman Scholarship Awards; J.O. [5343]
Goodstein Point Scholarships; David B. [5720]
Goodwill Scholarships; Baxter Corporation - Jean [9]
Goodwin Scholarships; James L. and Genevieve H. [3454]
Goolsby Scholarship Fund; Richard [3060]
Gopie Scholarships; Lucille May [1732]
Gordon, Jr. and June D. Pfefferkorn Scholarships; L. [7439]
Gordon Memorial Scholarships; Thomas Boston [1658]
Gore Fellowships in Materials Innovation; Robert W. [2110]
Gore Scholarships; Pauline LaFon [2421]
Gorecki Scholarships; Richard C. [5733]
Gorov Scholarship; Nettie and Jesse [2468]
Gottcent Memorial Scholarships; American Association of University Women-Mary Sue [6655]
Gottschalk Research Scholar Grants; Carl W. [1018]
Gotwalt Scholarship Fund; Norma [3102]
Gould Endowment Scholarships; Charles F. [4359]
Government Finance Officers Association of United States and Canada **[3263]**
Gowen Scholarships; Wilford Hayes [7115]
Graddy Law School Scholarships; William L. [6656]
Graduate Dissertation Fellowships [2820]
Graduate Education Loan Scholarships [3780]
Graduate Fellowships in Alternatives in Scientific Research [3854]
Graduate Student Scholarship [157]
Graduate Student Scholarships [3833]
Graduate Student Travel Grants [6437]
Graham Memorial Scholarships; Rachel [5940]
Graham Scholarships; Jim [5245]
Grand Haven Area Community Foundation **[3269]**
Grand Haven Offshore Challenge Scholarships Fund [3283]
Grand Rapids Community Foundation **[3318]**
Grand Rapids Scholarship Association [3331]
Grande Prairie 4-H District Scholarships [133]
Grandmothers for Peace International **[3359]**
Granger Business Association **[3361]**
Granger Business Association College Scholarships [3362]
Grant Memorial Scholarship for Tennis; Russ [5486]
Grant Scholarships; Nicholas J. [4398]
Graubart/Lambda Scholarships; Lucile Cheever [6361]
Grauer Scholarships; Paul and Helen L. [835]
Grave and Elizabeth F. Grave Scholarships; Thomas B. [4287]
Grave Scholarships; Caswell [4288]
Great Falls Broadcasters Association Scholarships [4570]
Great Lakes Commission **[3363]**
Great Lakes Commission Sea Grant Fellowships [3364]
GREAT MINDS Collegiate Scholarship Program [236]
Great Seattle Business Association **[3366]**
Greater Baton Rouge Chapter - Don Jones Excellence in Safety Scholarships [1056]
Greater Dayton IT Alliance **[3368]**
Greater Philadelphia Law Library Association **[3370]**
Greater Philadelphia Law Library Association Scholarships [3371]
Greater Seattle Business Association Scholarships [3367]
The Greater Tacoma Community Foundation **[3372]**
Greathouse Government Accounting Scholarships; Frank L. [3265]
Greco Memorial Scholarships; Philip F. [4272]
Green Hill Yacht and Country Club Scholarships [2374]
Green Knight Economic Development Corporation **[3380]**
Green Knight Economic Development Corporation (GKEDC) Scholarships [3381]
Green Memorial Scholarship Fund; Randy [2598]
Green Scholarship Fund; James H. and Shirley L. [6723]
Green Scholarships; William G. and Mayme J. [3455]
Green, Sr. Memorial Scholarships; K2TEO Martin J. [836]
Greenamyer Memorial Scholarships; Helen R. [6775]
Greenberg Scholarships; Robert D. [6527]
Greene Memorial Scholarships; Curt [3405]
Greenwald Jr. Endowed Scholarships; Guy P. [5590]
Gresham Scholarships; Francis Harris [6657]
Gridley Memorial Scholarships; Lily H. [7482]
Griffin Foundation **[3382]**
Griffin Foundation Scholarships [3383]
Griffin Memorial Scholarship Fund; Velma Shotwell [6724]
Griffith College Scholarships for NSHSS Members [5068]
Griffith Foundation Scholarships [902]
Griffith Memorial Scholarships; Bobby [6109]
Griffith Memorial Scholarships; Russ [2617]
Grisham Memorial Scholarships; Homajean [5280]
Griswold Memorial Scholarships; Enid Hall [5064]
Groome Memorial Scholarships; Reginald K. [6286]
Grosscup Scholarships; Katherine M. [3159]
Grow your Own @Your Library Institutional Scholarships [5872]
Gruber Scholarships; Elizabeth M. [2687]
Gruber Scholarships; Jack & Mary Lou [4181]
Gruwell Scholarships [2375]
Guareillo Scholarship Fund; Henry and Janet [3103]
Guerra Scholarships; Melissa [2277]
Guerrero Memorial Scholarships; Leonor R. [4689]
Guggenheim Fellowships; Harry Frank [3385]
Guggenheim Foundation Grants; Harry Frank [3386]
Guggenheim Foundation; Harry Frank **[3384]**
Guggisberg Foundation Memorial Scholarships; Community Bank - Lee [5941]
Gugliotta Memorial Scholarships for Creative Writing; Bobette Bibo [6390]
Guide Dogs for the Blind Dorothea and Roland Bohde Leadership Scholarships [4877]
Guild Memorial Scholarships; Jimmy [4182]
GuildScholar Awards [4027]
Guin Scholarships Association; Hai [1280]
Guin-Stanford Scholarships [2352]
Gulbenkian Foundation Scholarships; Calouste [1281]
Gulf and Caribbean Fisheries Institute **[3387]**
Gulf Coast Hurricane Scholarships [6552]
Gulf Coast Past President's Scholarships [1057]
Gulley Scholarships; Larry [6449]
Gullikson Foundation Scholarships; Tim and Tom [2129]
Gummow Endowed Scholarships; Warren and Rosalie [5591]
Gunder, MD, DCMS Presidential Scholarships; Scott A. [3136]
Gunter Scholarships; Connie and Robert T. [6489]
Guntley-Lorimer Science and Arts Scholarships [1733]
Gustafson '56 Memorial Scholarships; Patricia S. [2777]
Gustafson HSE Memorial Scholarships; George [1058]
Guynn Family Foundation Book Scholarships [4667]
Guzkowski Family Scholarships; [5942]
Gwisdalla Memorial Scholarships; Sarah [5487]
Haas Fellowships in the History of Chemical Industries; John C. [2111]
Haas Foundation Manufacturing Technology Scholarships; Gene [6490]
Haas Memorial Scholarships; Ed [6776]
Habley NACADA Summer Institute Scholarships; Wesley R. [4615]
Hackney Fellowship for the Study of Chinese Art; Louise Wallace [744]
HACU/Wal-Mart Achievers Scholarships [3567]
Haddad Memorial Fund; Jaye [6110]
Hadlock Memorial Scholarships; Perry F. [837]
Hafer Memorial Scholarships; Nathaniel [5488]
Hagan Memorial Scholarships; Joseph E. [3150]
Hagedorn Trust: Nightingale Scholarships; Amy and Horace [2318]
Hagler Scholarships; Charles V. [1554]
Hagopian Memorial Fund; Sophia [1282]
Hahn Memorial Scholarships; Leslie Jane [6191]
Hailey AAJ Law Student Scholarships; The Richard D. [358]
Halfacre Scholarships; Marion H. [3181]
Hall of Achievement Scholarships [1825]
Hall College Scholarships; Joyce C. [5570]
Hall Memorial Scholarships; Anna E. [5625]
Hall Scholarship Program; Chappie [2]
Halladay Graduate Scholarships; Guy D. & Mary Edith [3332]
Halladay Music Scholarships; Guy D. & Mary Edith [3333]

Hallissey Memorial Scholarships; David J. [1083]
Hamilton Early Childhood Development Scholarships; Patty [4360]
Hamilton Industrial Environmental Association **[3389]**
Hamilton Industrial Environmental Association Bursaries-Mohawk College [3390]
Hamilton Scholarships; Al [1734]
Hamilton Scottish Rite Foundation of Colorado Graduate Scholarships; Dwight A. [6284]
Hamman Foundation; George and Mary Josephine **[3391]**
Hamman Foundation Scholarships; George and Mary Josephine [3392]
Hammill Scholarships Fund; Richard A. [708]
Hammond Memorial Scholarships; Jay [7077]
Hamner Scholarships; Tommie J. [5667]
Hampton Memorial Scholarship Fund; Adam [2956]
Hanauer Scholarships; Morris [3182]
Hancock Family Snow Hill High School Scholarships [2376]
Hancock Memorial Scholarship Award; Robert [4499]
Hancock Scholarships; Ruth [1923]
Hand Memorial Scholarships; H. Pauline [6777]
Handweavers Guild of America **[3393]**
Hanfmann Fellowships; Ilse and George [897]
Haniak Scholarships; John M. [4399]
Hanke Fellowships; Byron [3088]
Hanna Scholarships; Clayburn and Garnet R. [5489]
Hanover-Horton High School Youth of Promise Scholarships [3980]
Hansen Leadership Scholarships; Zenon C.R. [4859]
Hansen Memorial Scholarship; Martha and Oliver [3981]
Hansen Memorial Scholarships; Zenon C.R. [1555]
Hanshaw Scholarships; Penelope [1511]
Hanson Scholarship Fund; Cleam T. [4564]
Hanson Scholarships; Duane [967]
Hardanger Fiddle Association of America **[3398]**
Hardbarger Science and Mathematics Awards; H.G. [5490]
Hardin Memorial Scholarships; Charles Henry [1659]
Harding Scholarships; Chris [880]
Hardy Automotive Scholarship; Bob and Dawn [3982]
Harlow Fellowship Program; Bryce [3401]
Harlow Foundation; Bryce **[3400]**
Harmon Memorial Scholarships; Matt [6658]
Harness Horse Youth Foundation **[3402]**
Harness Tracks of America **[3406]**
Harness Tracks of America Scholarship Fund [3407]
Harper Scholarship; Walter and Lucille [4066]
Harris Legacy Fund Scholarships; Marcia S. [4322]
Harris/Les Nichols Memorial Scholarships to Spartan College of Aeronautics & Technology; Leon [75]
Harris Memorial Scholarships; Ruth [5491]
Harris Memorial Scholarships; William H. [5638]
Harris Scholarships; Frank and Charlene [2422]
Harris Scholarships; Phyllis P. [1956]
Harrison Memorial Scholarships; Peg Hart [2648]
Harrison Point Scholarships; Evelyn W. [5721]
Harrison Scholarship Fund; Morton [2957]
Harrison Scholarships in Counseling; Lullelia W. [7554]
Harrisville Lions Club Scholarships [5492]
Harry and Lucille Brown Scholarships [3334]
Hart Memorial Scholarships; Claude B. [7440]
Hart Scholarships; Carroll [6450]
Hartenberg Charitable Scholarships; Ida L. [3456]
Harter Memorial Fund; Mollie [2958]
Harter Recruitment Scholarship Grant; Karen [2469, 2470]
Hartfield Coalition **[3408]**
Hartford County Retired Teachers Association Scholarships [3457]
Hartford Foundation College Scholarship Program [3458]
Hartford Foundation for Public Giving **[3410]**
Hartford Foundation for Public Giving Occupational Therapy Scholarships [3459]
Hartford Grammar School Scholarships [3460]
Hartford Jazz Society Scholarships [3461]
Hartford Whalers Booster Club Scholarships [3462]
Hartl Scholarships; Gabe A. [64]
Hartleben III. Scholarships; Harry C. [5493]
Hartshorn Scholarships; Gail [5494]
Hartzell Memorial Scholarships; William T. [5943]
Harvard Law School **[3503]**
Harvey Dissertation Fellowships; James J. [6111]
Hastings Scholarships; Donald F. [1160]
Hastings Scholarships; Donald and Shirley [1161]
Hauff Memorial Scholarships; Gretchen [5831]
Haught Citizenship Awards; Gregory Lynn [5495]
Haught Scholarships; Dorcas Edmonson [5496]
Hauser Scholarships; Charles [7164]
Hawaii Chapter/David T. Woolsey Scholarships [4122]
Hawaii Hotel and Lodging Association **[3507]**
Hawkins Endowed Scholarships; Lex and Scott [2748]
Hawkins Memorial Scholarships; Don C. [76]
Hayashi Memorial Scholarships; Thomas T. [4017]
Haycock Memorial Scholarships; R. Garn [5944]
Hayes Scholarships; Edward and Cora [2749]
Hayes Scholarships; The Erika A. [4323]
Hazel Minority Scholarships; Dick and Pat [2377]
HBO Point Scholarships [5722]
HDR Engineering, Inc. Scholarship for Diversity in Engineering [1432]
HDSA Research Fellowships [3631]
HDSA Research Grants [3632]
Head Scholarships; Edith [2688]
Headley Scholarships; Dr. M.G. "Doc" [6778]
Health and Aging Policy Fellows [786]
Health Resources and Services Administration - Bureau of Health Professions **[3511]**
Health Sciences Scholarship Program [7402]
Health Sciences Student Fellowships [2873]
Healthcare Information Management Systems Scholarships [3517]
Healthcare Information and Management Systems Society **[3514]**
Healy Scholarships [1084]
Heaney Memorial Scholarship Fund; Richard F. [3817]
Heaps Law Scholarships; Annamae [2750]
Heaps Memorial Scholarships; Dr. Stan [3719]
Heard Memorial Scholarships; Erin Kumelos [2649]
Hearst Educational Endowments; William Randolph [4289]
Heath Post-Secondary Awards; Elizabeth [5422]
Heath Technical, Trades Training and Development Awards; Elizabeth [5423]
Hebrew Ladies Sheltering Home Scholarships [3463]
Heckaman Memorial Scholarship Fund; Dr. James H. [6725]
Hedla Accounting Scholarships; Lenore & George [7032]
Hedner Scholarships; Professor Ulla [4924]
Heflin Memorial Scholarships; Howell [5281]
Heghinian Scholarships; Lavonne [2689]
Heicox Foreign Travel and Study Scholarships Fund; Barbara and Nicole [3284]
Heimberger CRNA Memorial Scholarship Fund; Dale O. [6726]
Helicopter Foundation International **[3519]**
Helicopter Foundation International Commercial Helicopter Rating Scholarships [3520]
Helicopter Foundation International Maintenance Technician Certificate Scholarships [3521]
Hellenic News of America **[3524]**
Hellenic University Club of Philadelphia **[3526]**
Hellenic University Club of Philadelphia Founders Scholarships [3530]
Heller-Diane Bernard Fellowships; Joan [2087]
Helm Family Scholarships [6192]
Helman Scholarships; Ronald, Randall and Roger [1660]
Helmick Law Scholarships; John M. [2751]
Helms Student Scholarships; PPQ William F. [7299]
Helton Manufacturing Scholarships; Clinton J. [6491]
Hemingway Foundation and Society **[3537]**
Hemmingway Scholarships; Jeanne H. [2778]
Hemophilia Federation of America **[3541]**
Hemophilia Federation of America Educational Scholarships [3542]
Hemophilia Health Services Memorial Scholarship Program [4925]
Hemostasis and Resuscitation Research Scholarships [410]
Hench Post-Dissertation Fellowships [303]
Henderson Memorial Endowed Scholarships [4183]
Henderson-Rubio Scholarships; Melvin [7414]
Henderson Scholarships; Edith H. [982]
Henderson Scholarships; John B. [4361]
Hendren Memorial Scholarships; Doris [6193]
Hendricks Environmental Education Scholarships Fund; Marjorie M. [3285]
Hendrie Memorial Scholarships; Mary Jane [7221]
Henigson Human Rights Fellowships; [3504]
Hennessy Scholarships; John P. [4504]
Henry Ford Academy Scholarships [6492]
The Herb Society of America **[3543]**
Herbert Memorial Scholarships; Richard A. [1138]
Hereditary Disease Foundation **[3549]**
Hereditary Disease Foundation Research Grants [3550]
Herff Presidential Law Scholarships; Herbert [7116]
Herman Memorial Scholarship Fund; Michael [3286]
Hernandez, Jr. Foundation Scholarships; Manuel [2278]
Herrera Memorial Scholarships; Alia [359]
Hersch Scholarships; Ella Beren [5497]
Herson Scholarships in Education; Isabel M. [7555]
Hertz Foundation's Graduate Fellowships [4705]
Hess Scholarships; Peter [3183]
Hester Memorial Scholarships; June [5282]
Hetos, DDS, Memorial Graduate Scholarships; Nicholas S. [3531]
Hewlet Memorial Fund; Gordon B. and Josephine [3104]
Hewlett-Packard Undergraduate Scholarships [1950]
HGA and Dendel Scholarships [3396]
Hiepler Endowed Scholarships; Mark and Michelle [5592]
Hierholzer-Fojtik Scholarship Fund [3287]
Hierlihy Memorial Scholarships; Jim [2879]
Higdon Scholarships; Regina [2423]
Higgins South Carolina Dental Scholarships; Howard B. [3061]
High School Councilors Scholarships [3673]
Highway Worker Memorial Scholarship Program [904]
Higley Memorial Scholarships; Doris E. [3464]
Hilb, Rogal and Hobbs Scholarships [7328]
Hildebrant Police Scholarships Fund; Wayne [4141]
Hill, Jr. Memorial Scholarships; Douglas W. [1661]
Hill Memorial Scholarships; John A. [1662]
Hill Scholarships; Clair A. [1377]
Hill Scholarships; Gus and Henrietta [2779]
Hill Scholarships; Judge Delmas C. [7349]
Hill Scholarships; Judy [2000]
Hill Thoracoesophageal Fellowships; Ryan [418]
Hillel Montreal **[3552]**
Hillman Scholarships; Cecilia [3465]
Hilton Academic Scholarships; Georgia [6074]
Hilton Scholarships; Conrad N. [2841]
Hilton Tribal College Diversity Scholarships [623]
Hilts Scholarships Program; D. Glenn [1493]
Hilty Research Grants; Lucy [813]
Hindle Postdoctoral Fellowships; Brooke [6461]
Hinkle Travel Grants; Jim & Nancy [3539]
Hinman-Jensen Endowed Scholarships [4184]
Hipp Scholarships; William A. [4336]
Hirst Family Scholarships; Ernest and Charlotte [3466]
Hispanic Association of Colleges and Universities **[3564]**
Hispanic Association of Colleges and Universities Scholarships [3568]
Hispanic Association on Corporate Responsibility **[3572]**
Hispanic Association on Corporate Responsibility Scholarship Program [3573]
Hispanic College Fund Scholarship Programs [3583]
Hispanic Faculty Staff Association **[3575]**
Hispanic Lawyers Association of Illinois **[3577]**
Hispanic Lawyers Association of Illinois Public Interest Fellowships [3579]
Hispanic National Bar Association **[3581]**
Hispanic Scholarship Fund **[3588]**

Hispanic Scholarship Fund (HSF) College Scholarship Program [3591]
Hispanic Serving Institution Scholarships [6973]
Historically Black College or University Scholarships [6974]
Hix, W8AH Memorial Scholarships; Albert H. [838]
HLS/MLA Professional Development Grants [4442]
HNBF Princeton Review Duard Bradshaw Memorial Scholarships [3584]
Ho Scholarship; Lucy Hsu [1628]
Hoar Scholarship Awards; C.V. [5344]
Hoff, S.J. Scholars; James E. [7529]
Hoffbauer Memorial Scholarships; John [2780]
Hoffman Family Scholarships Fund [3288]
Hoffman-Laroche Scholarships [2001]
Hoffman Memorial Scholarship Fund; Henry [4695]
Hoffman Memorial Scholarships; Irving J. [7222]
Hoffman Memorial Scholarships; Robert and Elaine [7117]
Hogan Fellowships; Michael J. [6457]
Hoge Memorial Scholarship Fund; The Thelma S. [2400]
Hoge Scholarship Fund; Raymond T. [6727]
Hoggard Memorial Scholarships; Michael J. [5832]
Holden Scholarships; R.W. "Bob" [3508]
Holden Vocational Scholarships; John [559]
Hole Humanities and Social Sciences Scholarship; Lois [158]
Holland America Line-Westours Research Grants [1085]
Holliday Scholarships; Polly [6632]
Holloway Memorial Scholarship Fund; Cleve [2353]
Holmason Memorial Scholarship Awards; Martin [5382]
Holmes Scholarship Endowment Fund; Wilbert L. and Zora F. [3062]
Holmes Scholarships; Robert [2515]
Holocaust and Human Rights Center of Maine **[3610]**
Holshouser Professional Development Scholarships; Governor James E. [5239]
Holt Dissertation Fellowships; W. Stull [6458]
Holt Nursing Scholarships; Caroline [3467]
Holy Name Of Jesus Parish Scholarships [5945]
Home Depot Scholarships [7006]
The Homeland Security Graduate Fellowships [6985]
The Homeland Security Undergraduate Scholarships [6986]
Honeywell Avionics Scholarships [77]
Hood Memorial Fund; Jane [2959]
Hookanson Law Fellowships; Kathryn [7118]
Hooper Memorial Scholarships [6919]
Hoover Presidential Library Association; Herbert **[3612]**
Hoover Uncommon Student Awards; Herbert [3613]
Hopi Education Awards [1210]
Hopkins Endowed Scholarships; Frank and Gladys [4185]
Hopkins Memorial Scholarship Fund of Lathrop/Compton School; Minnie [6728]
Hord Memorial Scholarships; Sam J. [6625]
Horen, K1LOM Memorial Scholarships; Seth [839]
Hormel Foods Charitable Trust Scholarships [3615]
Hormel Foods Corporation **[3614]**
Horne, Jr. Scholarships; Edward L. [5406]
Horowitz Legal Scholarship Fund; Judge and Mrs. Robert D. [6729]
HOSA Scholarships [5108]
Hosinec Family Scholarships [7223]
Hospitality Association of South Carolina **[3616]**
Hospitality Food Service Scholarships [5168]
Hough Memorial Law Scholarships; John C. "Jack" [7119]
Houghton Duluth Central Scholarships; Max and Julia [2781]
Houghton Mifflin Company **[3620]**
Houpt Scholarship Fund; Roberta L. [3105]
Houston Alumnae Chapter Graduate Fellowships [2650]
Houston Alumnae Undergraduate Tri Delta Scholarships [2651]
Houston/Nancy Holliman Scholarships [2690]
Houston Scholarships; Paul Green [7165]
Houston Scholarships; Sarah Jane [2691]
Houtan Scholarship Foundation **[3622]**
Houtan Scholarships [3623]
Hovannisian Memorial Scholarships; Kaspar [1283]
Hovnanian Foundation Presidential Scholarships; Hirair and Anna [1284]
Hovnanian Foundation Scholarships; Hirair and Anna [1285]
Howard/Etienne Fage Scholarships; NORDAM Dee [4779]
Howard Scholarships; C.D. [3827]
Howell Scholarships; William B. [1162]
Howland Scholarships; Goldwin [2020]
Hoy/ERT Scholarships; Christopher [701]
Hoy Scholarship fund; Carol [3106]
HRP Global Human Rights Fellowships [3505]
HSBC-North America Scholarship Program [3592]
HSF/Atrisco Heritage Foundation Scholarship Program [3593]
HSF/Citi Fellows Program [3594]
HSF/General Motors Scholarship Program [3595]
HSF/Hewlett Packard (HP) Diversity in Education Scholarship Program [3596]
HSF/IDT Hope High School Scholarship Program [3597]
HSF/Nissan Community College Transfer Scholarship Program [3598]
HSF/Wal-Mart Stores Inc. Scholarship Program [3599]
Hubbard Scholarships; Albert W. and Mildred [6194]
Hubbard Scholarships; William Peyton [1735]
Huber Memorial Scholarship; Amber [2471]
Huenefeld/Denton Scholarships [2692]
Huesing Scholarships; Steven [2255]
Hughes, Jr. Memorial Scholarships; Dale [6779]
Hughes Legacy Scholarship; Roger K. [1826]
Hughes Medical Institute Predoctoral Fellowships; Howard [4706]
Hughes Memorial Scholarship Fund; James [5564]
Hughes Memorial Scholarship; Paul A. [1827]
Human Ecology Continuing Undergraduate Student Scholarships [7257]
Human Race Theatre Company **[3624]**
Human Resources Research Management **[3626]**
Humane Studies Fellowships [3728]
Humanism in Medicine Scholarships [6811]
Humber College Institute of Technology and Advanced Learning Scholarships [3998]
Hummer Point Scholarships; Kevin [5723]
Humphrey Student Fellowships; John Peter [1942]
Humphreys Law Fellowships; Cecil C. [7120]
Hungarian American Coalition **[3628]**
Hunt Fellowships; Dr. Richard M. [504]
Hunter Memorial Scholarships; Michael A. [2130]
Hunting Scholarships; Donald & Florence [3335]
Huntington Sports Communications Scholarships; Clay [3376]
Huntington's Disease Society of America **[3630]**
Hurley III Bicentennial Merit Scholarships; James F. [7166]
Hurley Scholarships; Doc [3468]
Hurston Scholarships; Zora Neale [7556]
Huston Scholarships; Norman E. [3941]
Hutchinson and Evelyn Ribbs Hutchinson Medical School Scholarship Fund; Dr. James L. [6391]
Hutchison Travel Scholarships; Fred [7167]
The Hyatt Hotels Fund For Minority Lodging Management Students [611]
Hydrocephalus Association **[3634]**
Hylton and Ron Niederman Memorial Scholarships; Mike [4926]
Hymans Extended Stay Scholarship Program; The Steve [612]
Hypertherm International HyTech Leadership Scholarships [1163]
I Have a Dream Scholarships [3999]
IAAP Wings Chapter Scholarships [3782]
IADR David B. Scott Fellowships [3790]
IADR John Clarkson Fellowships [3791]
IADR John Gray Fellowships [3792]
IADR Norton Ross Fellowships [3793]
IAESTE United States Scholarships [1435]
IAHCSMM - Purdue University Scholarship Awards [3801]
IALD Scholarship Programs [3809]
IAWP International Recognition and Scholarship Award [3811]
IBA Law Student Scholarships Foundation [3715]
IBM Canada Undergraduate Scholarships [1951]
Ice Skating Institute of America **[3641]**
Ice Skating Institute of America Education Foundation [3642]
IDA Fellowship Award [3838]
Idaho Attorney General Scholarships [4186]
Idaho Community Foundation **[3643]**
Idaho Nursery and Landscape Association **[3651]**
Idaho Nursery and Landscape Association Scholarships [3652]
Idaho Nursing Scholarships [3646]
Idaho Promise Category B Scholarships [4187]
Idaho Society of CPA's Scholarships [3647]
Iden Memorial Safety Scholarships; David [1059]
IEHA Education Foundation Scholarship Awards [3842]
IFDA Educational Foundation [3859]
IFDA Part-time Student Scholarships [3860]
IFSEA Worthy Goal Scholarships [3850]
IIE Council of Fellows Undergraduate Scholarships [3733]
Illinois Association of Chamber of Commerce Executives **[3653]**
Illinois Association of Chamber of Commerce Executives Scholarships [3654]
Illinois Future Teacher Corps Scholarships [3663]
Illinois Landscape Contractors Association **[3655]**
Illinois Landscape Contractors Association Scholarships [3656]
Illinois Society of Professional Engineers **[3657]**
Illinois Special Education Teacher Tuition Waiver Scholarships [3664]
Illinois Student Assistance Commission **[3660]**
Illinois Student Assistance Commission Medical Student Scholarships [3665]
Illinois Student Assistance Commission Merit Recognition Scholarships [3666]
Illinois Student Assistance Commission Nurse Educator Scholarships [3667]
Illinois Student Assistance Commission Nursing Education Scholarships [3668]
Illinois Student Assistance Commission Podiatric Scholarship Program [3669]
Illuminator Educational Foundation Scholarships [1828]
IMA FAR Doctoral Student Grant Program [3745]
IMA Memorial Education Fund Scholarships (MEF) [3746]
Imagine America Foundation **[3671]**
Imagine America Online Scholarships [3674]
Imagine America Scholarships [3675]
Imes Scholarships in Physics; Elmer S. [5055]
Imhoff Scholarships; John L. [3734]
Immune Deficiency Foundation **[3677]**
Imogene Ward Nursing Scholarships [2991]
Imperial Sovereign Court of Tacoma Scholarships [5766]
In-course Scholarships - Chinese Dance Workshop Scholarships [7224]
Independent Lubricant Manufacturers Association **[3679]**
Independent Lubricant Manufacturers Association Scholarships [3680]
Independent Order of Foresters **[3681]**
Independent Organic Inspectors Association **[3683]**
Independent Professional Seed Association **[3686]**
Independent Studies Program Scholarships [4785]
Indian Health Service Scholarship Program [634]
Indiana Alumni Scholarships [7530]
Indiana Broadcasters Association **[3689]**
Indiana Broadcasters Association for College Scholarship Program [3690]
Indiana Broadcasters Association High School Scholarship Program [3691]
Indiana Library Federation **[3692]**
Indiana Library Federation AIME Scholarships [3693]
Indiana State Alumni Association **[3696]**
Indiana State Alumni Association Creative and Performing Arts Award [3701]
Indiana State Alumni Association Dean's Scholarships [3702]
Indiana State Alumni Association Incentive Scholarships [3703]
Indiana State Alumni Association President's Academic Excellence Scholarships [3704]

Indiana State Alumni Association President's Scholarships [3705]
Indiana State Alumni Association Rural Health Scholarships [3706]
Indiana State Alumni Association Transfer Student Scholarships [3707]
Indiana Top Scholar Award [3708]
Indigenous Bar Association **[3714]**
Individual Advanced Research Opportunities Program (IARO) For Master's Student [3895]
Individual Advanced Research Opportunities Program (IARO) For Pre-doctoral Students [3896]
Individual Advanced Research Opportunities Program (IARO) For Professionals [3897]
Individual Advanced Research Opportunities Program (IARO) for Postdoctoral Scholars [3898]
Individual-Investigator Grants Program [5011]
Industrial Supply Association **[3716]**
INF Scholarships [3934]
Informatics Circle of Research Excellence Scholarships [159]
Information Technology Industry Alliance of Nova Scotia **[3718]**
Infusion Nurses Society **[3720]**
Ingraham Pediatric Optometry Residency Award; Terrance [277]
Ingram, Janet W. McCarthy and W.J.P. Jack Robertson Memorial Scholarships; Barbara [5424]
Ingrum Scholarships; Jennifer [2424]
INIA Scholarship Program [3880]
Injection Molding Division Scholarships [6553]
Inland Northwest Business Alliance (INBA) Scholarships [5767]
Institute of Food Technologists **[3723]**
Institute of Food Technologists Graduate Scholarships [3724]
Institute of Food Technologists Junior/Senior Scholarships [3725]
Institute of Food Technologists Sophomore Scholarships [3726]
Institute for Humane Studies **[3727]**
Institute of Industrial Engineers **[3729]**
Institute of Management Accountants **[3743]**
Institute-NEH Postdoctoral Fellowships [5338]
Institute of Real Estate Management **[3747]**
Institute for Scientific Information (ISI) Scholarships [6682]
Institute of Turkish Studies **[3752]**
Institute of Turkish Studies Dissertation Writing Grants [3753]
Institute of Turkish Studies Sabbatical Research Grants [3754]
Institute of Turkish Studies Undergraduate Study Grants [3755]
Institutional Grants: Educational and Research Projects [7336]
Insurance Scholarship Foundation of America **[3760]**
Insurance Scholarship Foundation of America College Scholarships [3763]
Insurance Scholarship Foundation of America Professional Scholarships [3764]
Insurance Women of Portland **[3766]**
Insurance Women of Portland Scholarships [3767]
Integra Foundation NNF Research Grants Award [375]
Intellectual Property Owners Association **[3768]**
Intensive Language Course Grants [3227]
Inter American Press Association **[3770]**
Inter American Press Association Scholarships [3771]
Intercollegiate Studies Institute **[3772]**
Intergraph Scholarships [1028]
Intermediaries and Reinsurance Underwriters Association **[3776]**
Intermediaries and Reinsurance Underwriters Association Scholarships [3777]
International Alumni Association of Shri Mahavir Jain Vidyalaya **[3778]**
International Association of Administrative Professionals **[3781]**
International Association of Arson Investigators **[3783]**
International Association of Black Actuaries **[3785]**
International Association of Black Actuaries Scholarships [3786]
International Association of Defense Counsel **[3787]**
International Association for Dental Research **[3789]**
International Association of Emergency Managers **[3795]**
International Association of Emergency Managers Scholarships [3796]
International Association of Foundation Drilling **[3797]**
International Association of Foundation Drilling Scholarships for Civil Engineering Students [3798]
International Association of Foundation Drilling Scholarships for Part-time Civil Engineering Graduate School Students [3799]
International Association of Healthcare Central Service Materiel Management **[3800]**
International Association of Law Enforcement Intelligence Analysts **[3803]**
International Association of Law Libraries **[3806]**
International Association of Law Libraries Scholarship Program [3807]
International Association of Lighting Designers **[3808]**
International Association of Women Police **[3810]**
International Association of Workforce Professionals **[3812]**
International Beverage Packing Association **[3816]**
International Brotherhood of Electrical Workers **[3818]**
International Catacomb Society **[3820]**
International Center for Not-for-Profit Law **[3822]**
International Code Council Foundation **[3826]**
International Code Council Foundation General Scholarship Fund [3828]
International Council for Canadian Studies **[3832]**
International Dairy-Deli-Bakery Association **[3834]**
International Dairy-Deli-Bakery Association Undergraduate Scholarships [3835]
International Desalination Association **[3836]**
International Doctoral Scholarships for Studies Specializing in Jewish Fields [4458]
International Door Association **[3839]**
International Door Association Scholarship Awards [3840]
International Education Awards - Ukraine [160]
International Executive House Keepers Association **[3841]**
International Fellowships in Jewish Studies [4459]
International Flight Services Association **[3844]**
International Food Service Executives Association **[3849]**
International Foodservice Editorial Council **[3851]**
International Foodservice Editorial Council Scholarships [3852]
International Foundation for Ethical Research **[3853]**
International Franchise Association **[3855]**
International Furnishings and Design Association **[3858]**
International Graduate Student Awards [26]
International Grenfell Association **[3862]**
International Grenfell Association Bursary [3863]
International Grenfell Association Secondary/High School Scholarships [3864]
International Grenfell Association University/College Scholarships [3865]
International Harvester Collectors **[3866]**
International Harvester Collectors Scholarships [3867]
International Horn Society **[3868]**
International Institute for Municipal Clerks **[3871]**
International Management Council (IMC) Scholarships [2472]
International Military Community Executives Association **[3874]**
International Municipal Lawyers Association **[3877]**
International Municipal Lawyers Association Canadian Scholarships [3878]
International Narcotics Interdiction Association **[3879]**
International Order of the King's Daughters and Sons **[3881]**
International Order of the King's Daughters and Sons North American Indian Scholarship Program [635]
International Paralegal Management Association **[3883]**
International Peace Scholarships [5684]
International Radio and Television Society Foundation **[3885]**
International Reading Association **[3887]**
International Research and Exchanges Board **[3893]**
International Safety Equipment Association **[3899]**
International Sanitary Supply Association Foundation Scholarships [2030]
International Scholar Awards [5540]
International Scholarship Program for Community Service [4460]
International Society of Air Safety Investigators **[3901]**
International Society for Human Ethology **[3903]**
International Society for Humor Studies **[3905]**
International Society for Humor Studies Graduate Student Awards (GSA) [3906]
International Society for Humor Studies Scholarly Contribution Awards (SCA) [3907]
International Society of Offshore and Polar Engineers **[3908]**
International Technology Education Association **[3910]**
International Thomas Merton Society **[3914]**
International Transplant Nurses Society **[3917]**
International Transportation Management Association **[3919]**
International Union of Bricklayers and Allied Craftworkers **[3921]**
International Women's Fishing Association **[3924]**
Internships in International Civil Society Law [3824]
InternXchange [3228]
Interplast **[3926]**
Interracial Scholarship Fund of Greater Hartford [3469]
IOIA Andrew Rutherford Scholarships [3684]
IOIA Organic Community Initiative Scholarship [3685]
Iowa Court Reporters Association **[3928]**
Iowa Division Scholarships [4514]
Iowa Journalism Institute Scholarships [3935]
Iowa Library Association **[3930]**
Iowa Library Association Foundation Scholarships [3931]
Iowa Newspaper Association **[3933]**
IPSA Student Recognition Awards [3688]
Iranian American Bar Association **[3937]**
Iranian American Bar Association Scholarships [3938]
The Iranian-American Scholarship Fund [4953]
Iranian Artist Scholarships [4954]
Iranian Association of Boston's IAB Scholarships [4955]
Iranian Federated Women's Club Scholarships [4956]
IRARC Memorial Joseph P. Rubino WA4MMD Scholarships [840]
IREM Foundation Minority Outreach Scholarships [3750]
Irish Scholarships; James P. [2752]
Irons Student Scholarships; Greg [2782]
Irsay Scholarships; Harriet [674]
IRTS Foundation Summer Fellowship Program [3886]
ISA Educational Foundation Scholarships [3942]
ISA Executive Board Scholarships [3943]
ISA (Instrumentation, Systems, and Automation) **[3939]**
ISA Section and District Scholarships - Birmingham [3944]
ISA Section and District Scholarships - Houston [3945]
ISA Section and District Scholarships - Lehigh Valley [3946]
ISA Section and District Scholarships - New Jersey [3947]
ISA Section and District Scholarships - Niagara Frontier [3948]
ISA Section and District Scholarships - Northern California [3949]
ISA Section and District Scholarships - Richmond (Hopewell) [3950]
ISA Section and District Scholarships - Savannah River [3951]
ISA Section and District Scholarships - Southwestern Wyoming [3952]

ISA Section and District Scholarships - Texas, Louisiana and Mississippi [3953]
ISA Section and District Scholarships - Wilmington [3954]
ISA Technical Division Scholarships - Analysis Division [3955]
ISA Technical Division Scholarships - Chemical and Petroleum Industries Division [3956]
ISA Technical Division Scholarships - Computer Technology Division [3957]
ISA Technical Division Scholarships - Food and Pharmaceutical Industries Division [3958]
ISA Technical Division Scholarships - Power Industry Division [3959]
ISA Technical Division Scholarships - Process Measurement and Control Division [3960]
ISA Technical Division Scholarships - Pulp and Paper Industry Division [3961]
ISA Technical Division Scholarships - Test Measurement Division [3962]
ISA Technical Division Scholarships - Water and Wastewater Industries Division [3963]
Isabell Memorial Scholarships; Martha [5283]
The ISASI Rudolf Kapustin Memorial Scholarships [3902]
Isbell Fellowships; Hazel D. [2652]
Isberg Student Scholarships; Gunnar [4550]
ISCALC International Scholarship Fund [2960]
Island Resources Foundation **[3965]**
Isom Memorial Scholarships; Broughton [5284]
ISOPE Offshore Mechanics Scholarships for Outstanding Students [3909]
ISPE Advantage Award/Foundation Scholarships [3659]
Italian American Lawyers Association **[3967]**
Italian American Lawyers Association Annual Scholarships [3968]
Italian Language Scholarships [5372]
ITNS Research Grants [3918]
ITW Welding Companies Scholarships [1164]
IUVSTA Welch Scholarships [1581]
Ivarson Scholarships; Dr. Karl C. [36]
Ives Scholarships; Bob and Mary [3964]
IWFA Scholarships [3925]
J and K Foundation Scholarships [3470]
Jack Family Scholarships [3336]
Jack and Jill of America Foundation **[3969]**
Jack and Ralph L. Jack Scholarships; Virginia C. [6730]
Jackman Scholarships [5668]
The Jackson Club Scholarships [2783]
Jackson County Community Foundation **[3971]**
Jackson High School Alumni Scholarship Fund [6731]
Jackson International Scholarships; Edward [7168]
Jackson Scholarships; Gene [7169]
Jackson Scholarships; Sylvia E. [6780]
Jackson-Wuller Memorial Scholarships; Holly [5498]
Jacobs Memorial Scholarship Fund; Ruth K. [2141]
Jacobs Scholarships; Donald Wills [4362]
Jacobs Scholarships; Freddy L. [3815]
Jacobson Memorial Scholarships; Eric L. [5946]
Jacobson Scholarships; Karl A. [1060]
Jacobson Scholarships; Peter Lars [7170]
Jacobus Scholarships; Dwight P. [1488]
Jakovina Endowment Scholarships; Gregori [2884]
Jam Awards; Cory [2784]
Jamaica Day Basil Duncan Memorial Scholarships [4000]
Jamaica National Building Society Scholarships [4001]
Jamaican Canadian Association **[3993]**
Jamail/Long Challenge Grant Scholarships [3576]
James Memorial Scholarships; Frederick George [6195]
Jameson Fellowship in American History; The J. Franklin [606]
Janisse Scholarships; The Dawn [5546]
Japan Foundation, New York **[4008]**
Japan Foundation, New York Doctoral Fellowship Program [4009]
Japan Foundation, New York Research Fellowship Program [4010]
Japan Foundation, New York Short-Term Fellowship Program [4011]
Japanese American Bar Association **[4012]**
Japanese American Bar Association Scholarships [4013]
Japanese American Citizens League **[4014]**
Jarrett Scholarship Fund; Carl and Lucille [2961]
Jarvis Memorial Scholarships; Terry [1165]
JAUW Fellowship Awards [1960]
Javits Fellowships; Jacob K. [4707]
JD/MBA Scholarships [5593]
Jean Scholarships; Right Hon. Michaelle [1736]
Jeanne Scholarships; Sister Rita [4033]
Jefferson County Art Awards Scholarship for High school Seniors [1317]
Jenkins Memorial Scholarship Fund; Erin L. [3107]
Jenkins Memorial Scholarships - Gamma Lambda; Elise Reed [6362]
Jenkins Memorial Scholarships - Gamma Psi; Elise Reed [6363]
Jenkins Scholarships; Martha Combs [5669]
Jenkins Scholarships; Ruth E. [6196]
Jensen Education Stipends; Gaynold [2537]
Jensen Fellowships; Walter J. [5622]
Jensen Memorial Scholarships; Nancy Lorraine [6603]
Jensen R.I.S.E. Memorial Scholarships; Mike [5947]
Jensen Scholarships; Stanley "Doc" [528]
Jerman-Cahoon Student Scholarship Program [1040]
Jernigan Scholarships; Kenneth [4878]
Jerome Scholarships; Harry [1737]
Jesinski Scholarships; James [7258]
Jewish Caucus Scholarships [5123]
Jewish Federation Academic Scholarships [4029]
Jewish Foundation for Education of Women **[4023]**
Jewish Guild for the Blind **[4026]**
Jewish Vocational Service **[4028]**
Jewish War Veterans of the United States of America **[4030]**
JFEW/UJA-Federation Rose Biller Scholarships [4024]
The Jhaveri Scholarships [3184]
Jimenez Memorial Scholarships; Brian [5948]
Jizmejian Educational Fund; Rev. and Mrs. A.K. [1286]
JLTLA Scholarships [6942]
JLTLA Texas Bar Review Scholarships [6943]
JMA Architecture Studios Scholarships [5833]
Joel and Ellen Pell Denny Healthcare Scholarship Fund; Oliver [7441]
John Bayliss Broadcast Foundation Scholarships [1604]
Johnson AMS Dissertation Fellowships; Alvin H. [720]
Johnson Health Policy Fellowship Program; The Robert Wood [787]
Johnson and Johnson: Nightingale Scholarships [2319]
Johnson & Johnson Scholarships [2002]
Johnson and Marge J. Stout Scholarships; Margaret G. [4188]
Johnson Memorial Grants; Joseph C. [927]
Johnson Memorial Scholarships; Fred [4790]
Johnson Memorial Scholarships; Gregory D. [4971]
Johnson Memorial Scholarships; Jimmy [7442]
Johnson Memorial Scholarships; V.J. [402]
Johnson Scholarship Fund; James V. [3063]
Johnson Scholarships; Camilla C. [3337]
Johnson Scholarships; Chip [6659]
Johnson Scholarships; Dr. Bill [6313]
Johnson Scholarships; Stella B. [7443]
Johnson and Wales University Scholarships [4039]
Johnston Memorial Scholarships; Julian C. [6064]
Jones, III Memorial Scholarships; Napoleon A. [6197]
Jones Scholarship Fund; Annabel Lambeth [3064]
Jones Scholarships; Edward H. [2753]
Joslyn Medical Fund; Alice Newell [1612]
Journalism Education Association **[4032]**
Journyx **[4034]**
Journyx Scholarships [4035]
JSR Foundation Endowed School of Law Scholarships [5594]
Judd Jr. Memorial Scholarships; Clem [3509]
Judd Scholarships; George E. [6660]
Judkins Endowed Scholarships; Woodrow [5595]
Junior Achievement **[4036]**
Junior Achievement of East Central Ohio, Inc. Scholarship Fund [6732]
Junior Firefighter Scholarships [5121]
Junior Women of the Contemporary Club Scholarships [5949]
Juno Memorial Scholarships; George W. [3185]
Just Out Scholarship Fund [2885]
Justicia En Diversidad Scholarships [3585]
Juvenile Arthritis Scholarships [3471]
K-12 Edu-Grants [4927]
Kade-Heideking Fellowships [3235]
Kaiser Memorial Funds; Stacy [6843]
Kaiser Memorial Scholarship Fund; David A. [6733]
Kaiser Permanente: Nightingale Scholarships [2320]
Kaiser Permanente Northwest Pride Scholarships [2886]
Kaminer Endowed Scholarships in Physiology; Benjamin [4290]
Kammerling Scholarships; Robert [3186]
Kane Memorial Community Service Award Scholarships; Martin S. [2378]
Kansas City Division Scholarships [4515]
Kapala Scholarships; Walter [3472]
Kaplan Legacy Scholarship; Don [1829]
Kaplan Scholarships [3580]
Kaplan Test Prep and Admission Scholarships for NSHSS Members [5069]
Kaplan TV and Film Studies Scholarships; Steve [946]
Kaplansky Scholarships in Economic and Social Rights; Kalmen [2730]
Kappa Chapter Centennial Scholarships [2653]
Kappa Delta Phi Scholarship Program [730]
Kappa Gamma Pi **[4041]**
Kappa Kappa Gamma **[4043]**
Kappa Kappa Gamma Graduate Scholarships [4044]
Kappa Kappa Gamma Undergraduate Scholarships [4045]
Kappa Omicron Nu **[4046]**
Kappa Omicron Nu Honor Society **[4050]**
Kappa Omicron Nu Honor Society Scholars Program Grants [4053]
Kappa Omicron Nu National Alumni Fellowships [4047]
Kappa Omicron Nu Undergraduate Scholarships [4048]
Kappa Zeta Scholarships [6364]
Kaprielian Memorial Scholarships [7241]
K.A.S.A Memorial Scholarships [5499]
KASF Chair Scholarships [4085]
KASF Designated Scholarships [4086]
KASF General Scholarships [4087]
Kashiwara Scholarships; Ken [1398]
Kato Memorial Scholarships; Magoichi & Shizuko [4018]
Kauffman Scholarship Fund; Ken and Romaine [3108]
Kaufman Memorial Scholarships; Peter [6112]
Kaufman Women's Scholarships; Lucile B. [6493]
Kaul Memorial Scholarships; N.G. [5197]
Kavanaugh Scholarship; William and Beatrice [3983]
Kawano Family Scholarships [6198]
Kay Co-op Scholarships; E. Wayne [6494]
Kay Community College Scholarships; E. Wayne [6495]
Kay High School Scholarships; E. Wayne [6496]
Kazanjian Scholarships [3187]
Keats-Shelley Association of America **[4055]**
Kebabjian Memorial Scholarships; Norair M. [1264]
Keen Memorial Scholarships; Doc [6661]
Keene Center of Japanese Culture; Donald **[4059]**
Keever Scholarships; Glenn [7171]
Kegler, Brown, Hill and Ritter **[4061]**
Kegler Brown Minority Merit Scholarships [4062]
Keisling/Cumberland County Extension Homemakers Scholarships; Maude [2425]
Keith Scholarships; Annette and Ernest [5950]
Kelley Memorial Scholarships; John W. [6781]
Kellogg Community College Foundation **[4063]**
Kellogg Company Career Scholarships [4067]
Kellogg Foundation Doctoral Fellowships in Health Policy; W.K. [4988]
Kelly Awards; Rita Mae [6294]
Kelly Memorial Scholarships; Dr. Charles [5500]

Lattin Education Scholarships Fund; Rick and Beverly [3291]
Laundy Entrance Scholarships; Kenneth [6270]
Lavidge Nonprofit Marketing Research Scholarships; Robert J. [709]
Law Enforcement Memorial Scholarship Fund [3066]
Law Foundation of British Columbia **[4146]**
Law Foundation of British Columbia Graduate Fellowships [4147]
Law and Social Science Dissertation Fellowship and Mentoring Program [434]
Law Society of Prince Edward Island **[4148]**
Lawson Memorial Scholarships; Dr. James L. [841]
Lawton Minority Retention Grants [7261]
Lawyer Scholarships; Verne [2756]
Lax Scholarship Fund for Gay Men; Jonathan [6115]
Lay Memorial Scholarships; Sue Kay [2280]
Lazarian Graduate Scholarships [1260]
Lazarus Foundation Scholarships [3475]
Lazzara Fellowships in Advanced Implant Surgery; Richard J. [287]
LCSC Welding Club Scholarships [4190]
Le Cordon Bleu Ottawa Culinary Arts Institute Basic Cuisine Certificate Scholarships [2580]
Le Memorial Scholarships; Danny T. [7321]
Leach Scholarship for Museum Studies; Betsy B. and Garold A. [2693]
Leach Scholarships; Franklin M. [4366]
The Leaders of Tomorrow Scholarships [2813]
Leaders at Work Scholarship in Textiles and Apparel [5109]
Leadership Development Scholarships [380]
League of Attorneys' Wives Scholarships [2757]
LEAGUE Foundation Scholarships [6116]
League of Latin American Citizens **[4150]**
Learn German in Germany [3229]
Learning Disabilities Association of Ottawa-Carleton **[4155]**
Leary Memorial Emergency Services Scholarships; William C. [6844]
Leatherman Family Scholarship Fund; Jack W. [3292]
Leber Rubes Inc. Awards [1964]
Ledden Honorary Scholarships; Patrick [6203]
Lee, M.D. Scholarships; Rebecca [1373]
Lee Memorial Scholarships; Albert J. and Mae [5599]
Lee Memorial Scholarships; Ken [6204]
Lee Scholarships; Bruce [7007]
Leeming Memorial Scholarships; Harold [5954]
LeePapa and Associates Scholarship for Travel [7008]
The Leesfield/AAJ Law Student Scholarships [360]
Leffler Scholarships; Judge William B. [7121]
The Legacy Fellowships [305]
Legacy Scholarship Program [6867]
Legal Research Service Scholarships [2758]
Legal Scholarship for Law Students [5440]
Legal Scholarship for Non-Tenured Law Professors [5441]
Legal Scholarship for Tenured Law Professors [5442]
Legg Memorial Scholarships; Doreen [5955]
Leggett Charitable Scholarship Fund; Jay C. and B. Nadine [6737]
Legislative Incentive for Future Excellence (LIFE) Scholarships [232]
Lehman Education Scholarships; Herbert [7345]
Lehman Family Scholarships [6205]
Leiber and Stoller Music Scholarships [947]
Leica Geosystems Internships [1029]
LeMar Scholarship Program; Imelda and Ralph [2517]
The Lemon Grove Education Foundation Scholarships [6206]
Lencki Scholarships; Stan [4420]
Lensch Memorial Scholarships; Craig [1794]
Lentesty Scholarships; Franklin A. [5285]
Lentz Peace Research Association **[4157]**
Leonard Scholarships; V.A. [253]
Leopold Education Project Scholarships [2475]
Lepard Scholarships; Shepard L. & Mabel C. [3340]
Lerner Student Scholarships; Irwin S. [5076]
Lesbians for Change Scholarships [6117]
Letheren Entrance Awards; Carol Anne [6271]
Leuchter Memorial Scholarships; The Irving [5202]
Levandoski Memorial Scholarship Fund; Gerald J. [2962]
Levick Scholarships; Myra [313]
Levin Scholarships; Harold A. [2240]
Levine Memorial Scholarships; Jack A. and Louise S. [5956]
Levy Memorial Endowment Fund Scholarships; Herbert [6542]
Lew Memorial Scholarships; Erwin [6554]
Lewis-Clark Coin Club Endowed Scholarships [4191]
Lewis and Clark Fund for Exploration and Field Research [770]
Lewis-Clark State College **[4159]**
Lewis-Clark State College/American Chemical Society Scholars Program [4192]
Lewis-Clark State College Foundation Scholars Scholarships [4193]
Lewis-Clark State College Freshman Scholarships [4194]
Lewis-Clark State College Governor's Cup Scholarships [4195]
Lewis-Clark State College/Idaho Society of CPAs Scholarships Fund [4196]
Lewis-Clark State College Non-Traditional Student Scholarships [4197]
Lewis-Clark State College Presidential Out-of-State Scholarships [4198]
Lewis-Clark State College Presidential Technical Out-of-State Scholarships [4199]
Lewis-Clark State College Provost Scholarships [4200]
Lewis-Clark State College Transfer Scholarships [4201]
Lewis-Clark State College Valley Scholarships [4202]
Lewis Community Fund; Marvin **[4221]**
Lewis, Jr. Academic Scholarship Fund; George T. [3067]
Lewis Jr. Scholarships; Frederick D. [2759]
Lewis Memorial Scholarships in Medical Health Sciences; S. Evelyn [7557]
Lewis Point Scholarships; Jonathan D. [5725]
Lewis Scholarships; Marvin [4222]
Lewiston Service League Memorial Scholarships [4203]
Lexington Alumni Scholarships [4224]
Lexington Community Foundation **[4223]**
Lexington Community Foundation Annual Scholarships [4225]
Lexington Community Foundation/CCC Scholarships [4226]
Lexington Teacher Appreciation Scholarships [4227]
Liacouras Memorial Scholarships; George C. [3532]
Liang Memorial Awards; Ta [1030]
The Liberace Museum and Foundation **[4233]**
Liberace Scholarship Fund [4234]
Liberty Mutual Scholarships [1062]
Library and Information Technology Association **[4235]**
Library Media Teacher Scholarships [1849]
Liddicoat Scholarships; Richard T. [3189]
Lieberman Scholarship; Irene Brand [3560]
Life and Health Insurance Foundation for Education **[4239]**
LIFE Lessons Scholarships Program [4240]
Lighthouse International **[4241]**
Lighthouse International Scholarships - College-bound Awards [4243]
Lighthouse International Scholarships - Graduate Awards [4244]
Lighthouse International Scholarships - Undergraduate Awards [4245]
Lillie Fellowships and Scholarships; Frank R. [4292]
Lilly Fellow Scholarships [3709]
Lily Scholarships in Religion for Journalists [6021]
Lim Memorial Scholarships; Esther [2136]
Lim, Ruger and Kim Scholarships [4647]
Lin & Nelia Laroza Memorial Scholarships; Tecla [2004]
LIN Television Corporation **[4246]**
LIN Television Corporation Minority Scholarships and Training Program [4247]
Lincoln Memorial Scholarships; John C. [1166]
Lindberg Research Fellowships; Donald A. B. [4444]
Lindenwood University Scouting Scholarships [4862]
Lineberry Memorial Scholarships; Johny [7445]
Linton Memorial Scholarships; David [1667]
Lipe Scholarship Award; F. Maynard [464]
Lister Scholarships; Ruth [6845]
Listerhill Credit Union Scholarships [5286]
LIT Scholarships [4116]
LITA and LSSI Minority Scholarships [4237]
LITA/OCLC Minority Scholarships [4238]
Litherland/FTE Scholarships [3911, 3912]
Lithgow Memorial Awards; Ian [6272]
Littauer Foundation Travel Grants; Lucius [1461]
Liu Memorial Scholarships; Ruth [2137]
Live Out Loud Annual Scholarships [6118]
Lloyd and J.C.U. Johnson Scholarships Fund; E.C. [2355]
Lloydminster Region Health Foundation **[4248]**
Lo Family Scholarships [7226]
Loan Forgiveness Scholarships [6689]
Lobring Scholarships; Virgil K. [2518]
Local Wound Haemostatics and Hemorrhage Control Scholarships [411]
Lock and Barbara R. Lock Scholarship Fund; Leon I. [3109]
Lockheed Martin IT Scholarships [1245]
Locklin Scholarships; William J. [984]
Lodging Management Program (LMP) Scholarships [613]
Loftus Memorial Scholarships; Audrey [7078]
Logan Memorial Scholarships; Stephen [3169]
LogiCore Corporation **[4254]**
Lone Star GIA Associate and Alumni Scholarships [3190]
Long Memorial Scholarships; L.D. and Elsie [7446]
Long-Term Postdoctoral Fellowships for Biomedical and Behavioral Research in Japan [1715]
Longwell Scholarships; Megan Nicole [5505]
Lord Scholarships; Audre [6119]
Lorenzen Scholarships; Lilly [1119]
Lotze Scholarships for Future Teachers; Barbara [385]
Loud - CH2M Hill Scholarships; Willie T. [4897]
Lougheed Awards of Distinction; Sir James [166]
Louisiana Environmental Health Association **[4256]**
Love of Bonita Empowerment Scholarships [6664]
Love Memorial Scholarship - Children of Soldiers; First Lieutenant Scott McClean [1303]
Love Memorial Scholarship - Spouses of Soldiers; First Lieutenant Scott McClean [1304]
Love Scholarships; John Allen [7242]
Lovell Scholarships; D.J. [6698]
Loving Undergraduate Scholarships; The Lowell H. and Dorothy [487]
Lowe and John Gomez, IV Scholarships; Diane G. [2430]
Lowe Nursing Scholarships Award; Gertie S. [2356]
Lowenberg Lions Scholarships; H.B. Paul [3476]
Lowidt and Mary Catherine Preiss Memorial Bursaries in Nutritional Sciences; Gertrude and Edith [7227]
Lozier Memorial Scholarships; Horace G. [1668]
Luce Foundation Dissertation Fellowships in American Art; Henry [509]
Lucey Scholarships; James R. [3191]
Ludeke Graduate Scholarships; Elsa [2694]
Ludovici Scholarships; David F. [3005]
Lugonia Alumni/Harrison Lightfoot Scholarships [5957]
LULAC GE Scholarships [4151]
LULAC GM Scholarships [4152]
LULAC National Scholarship Fund [4153]
Luso-American Education Foundation **[4259]**
Luso-American Education Foundation C-1 General Scholarships [4261]
Luso-American Education Foundation G-1 Grants [4262]
Luso-American Education Foundation G-2 Grants [4263]
Luso-American Education Foundation G-3 Grants [4264]
Luso-American Fraternal Federation B-2 Scholarships [4265]
Luso-American Fraternal Federation B-3 Scholarships [4266]
Luso-American Fraternal Federation B-4 Scholarships [4267]

McDonough Golf Scholarship Foundation; Richard D. **[4413]**
McDowell Scholarships; Bodie [5430]
McFarffels Scholarships [5769]
McGaw Graduate Student Scholarships; Foster G. [467]
McGee Graduate Fellowships; Nancy B. Woolridge [7558]
McGee Scholarship; Lucile E. [3985]
McGill University **[4427]**
McGill University Alma Mater Student Travel Grants [4430]
McGill University Scholarships for Research Trips to Europe [4431]
McGrath Worldwide Fellowships; Lee Kimche [1490]
McGraw Memorial Scholarship Program; Janice [732]
McIntyre Memorial Scholarships; Brouwer D. [1558]
McKay Scholarships; Molly [7178]
McKelvey Foundation **[4433]**
McKelvey Foundation Entrepreneurial Scholarships [4434]
McKelvey Scholarships [4435]
McKenna Scholarships; Robert V. [3369]
McKesson Scholarships [3131]
McKetta Undergraduate Scholarships; John J. [656]
McKinlay Scholarships; Arthur Patch [461]
McKinley Elementary School PTA Scholarships [5960]
McKinley Financial Scholarships [4898]
Mckinley Scholarships; John L. and Eleanore I. [2695]
McKinney Post-secondary Scholarship; Louise [167]
McKinney Sisters Undergraduate Scholarships [2657]
McKissick Memorial Scholarships; Elizabeth [4205]
McKnight Memorial Scholarships; H.H. [7122]
McKnight Scholarships; C.A. "Pete" [7179]
McKoy Memorial Scholarships; Jacinta [5770]
McLaughlin Scholarships; James H. [5222]
McLean Scholarships [1433]
McLean Scholarships; John Alexander [6886]
McLendon Memorial Minority Postgraduate Scholarships; John [4691]
McMahon Memorial Construction Management/Engineering Scholarship Awards; Charles [1320]
McMeans Memorial Scholarships; David [5287]
McMillan Creative Arts Scholarships; Anneka [6207]
McMillan Student Grants; Ruth [1855]
McNair Scholarships in Space and Optical Physics; Ronald E. [5057]
McNamara Family Creative Arts Project Grants [3601]
McNeil Dissertation Fellowships [7467]
McNeill Scholarships - Alpha Theta; Joan Reagin [6365]
McNeill Scholarships - Theta Phi; Joan Reagin [6366]
MCRD Museum Historical Society **[4436]**
McRorie Memorial Scholarships; Douglas [37]
MDA Development Grants [4593]
MDA Research Grants [4594]
Mead Leadership Fellows Program [5266]
Meador Student Scholarships; David [5169]
Meadows Memorial Awards; Jack [5426]
Meadows Natural Resource Scholarships - Academic Achievement Scholarships; Ben [1620]
Meadows Natural Resource Scholarships - Leadership Scholarships; Ben [1621]
The Medallion Fund Scholarships [5171]
Medforth Nursing Scholarships Award; Jerry [2357]
Media Action Network for Asian Americans **[4438]**
Medical Library Association **[4440]**
Medical Staff Scholarships [7371]
Medical Student Summer Research Scholarships [261]
Medical Students Loan Program [7403]
MediCorp Health System **[4449]**
Medicus Student Exchange [6829]
Medina Memorial Scholarships; Augustine and Sandra [5961]
Medina Scholarships for Hispanics in Safety [1063]
Meeting Professionals International-Connecticut River Valley Chapter **[4451]**
Meeting Professionals International-Greater New York Chapter **[4453]**
Megson Scholarships; Edward Heywood [7180]
Mehl Scholarship; Dr. Ernest and Minnie [168]
Mehlmann Scholarships; Karl [2306]
Meisner Veterinary Medicine Educational Scholarship Fund; Dr. Roger E. [5257]
Melcher Scholarships; Frederic G. [1465]
The Melissa Institute **[4455]**
Mellon Dissertation Completion Fellowships; Andrew W. [510]
Mellon Endowment Scholarships; Richard [4370]
Mellon Fellowships [2550]
Mellon Post-Doctoral Fellowships in Turkey for East European Scholars [899]
Mellon Postdoctoral Research Fellowships; Institute Andrew W. [5339]
Meloche-Monnex Scholarships [2006]
Memorial Foundation for Jewish Culture **[4457]**
Menezes Scholarships; Joseph C. [4276]
Mental Health Association of Tarrant County **[4461]**
Mentoring Travel Grants for Women [1515]
Merck Undergraduate Science Research Scholarships [318]
Merrick Law Scholarships; John [5602]
Merrill Memorial Scholarships; Steven Craig [1670]
Merriman American Council on Exercise Educational Scholarships; William J. [500]
Mertz and Sheldon Wechsler Residency Awards; VISTAKON George [278]
MESBEC Scholarships [2067]
Mesh Honorary Scholarships for Research in Psychology; Scott [801]
Mesi Music Scholarships; Christopher [2064]
Mesothelioma Memorial Scholarships [6794]
Messenger-Anderson Journalism Scholarships and Internships Program [6123]
Messmer Memorial Scholarships; Ruth [6665]
Mestel Legal Scholarship Fund; Sanders J. [6742]
Mestel Memorial Accounting Scholarship Fund; Harry [6743]
Metropolitan State College of Denver, President's Office: Nightingale Scholarships [2321]
Metzger Scholarships; Edmond A. [843]
Mexican American Cultural Center **[4465]**
Mexican American Grocers Association **[4467]**
Mexican American Grocers Association Scholarships [4468]
Mexican American Legal Defense and Educational Fund **[4469]**
Meyer Memorial Scholarships; Peter [7398]
MGFA Student Fellowships [4601]
MHS Health Career Scholarships [4450]
Michael Jewelers Foundation Scholarships for Athletes [3483]
Michaels Jewelers Foundation General Scholarships [3484]
Michel Scholarships; Bernard [1908]
Michigan Association for Deaf and Hard Hearing **[4471]**
Michigan Association of Realtors **[4473]**
Michigan Association of Realtors Scholarship Trust [4474]
Michigan Council of Women in Technology **[4475]**
Michigan Council of Women in Technology College Scholarship Program [4476]
Michigan Council of Women in Technology High School Scholarships Program [4477]
Michigan Education Association **[4478]**
Michigan Education Association Scholarships [4479]
Michigan League for Nursing **[4480]**
Michigan League for Nursing Scholarships [4481]
Michigan Nursery and Landscape Association **[4482]**
Michigan Nursery and Landscape Association Scholarships [4483]
Michigan Nurses Foundation **[4484]**
Michigan Nurses Foundation Scholarships [4485]
Michigan Society of Professional Engineers **[4486]**
Michigan Society of Professional Engineers Scholarships [4487]
Michigan State Horticultural Society **[4488]**
Michigan Stormwater-Floodplain Association **[4491]**
Michigan Stormwater-Floodplain Association Scholarships [4492]
Michigan Sugar Company **[4493]**
Michigan Sugar Company Hotel Restaurant/Resort Management Scholarships [4496]
Michigan Sugar Queen Scholarships [4497]
Michigan Tech Alumni Scholarships [881]
Michigan Turfgrass Foundation **[4498]**
Michigan Water Environment Association **[4502]**
Mick Scholarship Fund; John G. and Betty J. [6744]
Microbiology Undergraduate Research Fellowships [1007]
Microbiology Undergraduate Teaching Fellowships [1008]
Mid-Atlantic States Association of Avian Veterinarians **[4506]**
Mid-Continent Instrument Scholarships [79]
Middleton Memorial Scholarships; Beth [5110]
Midwest Archives Conference **[4508]**
Midwest Chapter Scholarships - Betty McKern [1448]
Midwest Chapter Scholarships - Don Nelson [1449]
Midwest Chapter Scholarships - Engineering [1450]
Midwest Chapter Scholarships - Mel Nickel [1451]
Midwest Chapter Scholarships - Non-Engineering [1452]
Midwest Chapter Scholarships - Western States Award [1453]
Midwest Dairy Association **[4512]**
Midwest Food Processors Association **[4521]**
Midyette Memorial Scholarship Fund; Albert and Eloise [3068]
Miffioli Scholarship; Keith [2476]
Migrant Health Scholarships [4794]
Mihaly Russin Scholarship Awards [6087]
Mike Kabo Global Scholarships [4786]
Mikimoto Scholarships [3194]
Mikulic Scholarships; Mary Ann [1486]
Milan Getting Scholarships [6594]
Milbank Diversity Scholarships [4525]
Milbank, Tweed, Hadley & McCloy LLP **[4524]**
Miles Scholarships; Eunice [3195]
Military Intelligence Corps Association **[4526]**
Military Intelligence Corps Association Scholarships [4527]
Military Nurses Association Scholarships [2007]
Military Officers Association of America **[4528]**
Military Order of the Perpetual Heart Foundation Scholarships [4206]
Milk/Tom Homann Gay and Lesbian Student Scholarships; Harvey [6124]
Mill Creek Business Association **[4532]**
Mill Creek Business Association Scholarships [4533]
Millennium Alberta Rural Incentive Bursary Award [169]
Millennium Charter Academy College Scholarships [7447]
Miller Award; Mark [4656]
Miller Birthplace Society; Glenn **[4534]**
Miller Electric International WorldSkills Competition Scholarships [1167]
Miller Memorial Scholarships; Robbie [4207]
Miller, PE and Alice E. Miller Scholarships; Raymond W. [3006]
Miller, PE Scholarships; Raymond W. [3007]
Miller Scholarship Fund; Fizz and Dutch [6745]
Miller Scholarships; Brian and Colleen [2281]
Miller Scholarships; Glenn [4535]
Miller Thomson LLP **[4536]**
Mills Memorial Scholarship Fund; Carolina Panthers Players Sam [3069]
Mills Scholarships; Quincy Sharpe [7181]
Mined Land Reclamation Educational Grant Program [4745]
Mineralogical Association of Canada **[4538]**
Mineralogical Association of Canada Scholarships [4539]
Minerva Scholarships [1739]
Minglen Scholarship Program; Mary [733]
Minneapolis Camp Scholarships [4541]
Minneapolis Jewish Federation **[4540]**
Minnesota Association County Probation Officers **[4543]**
Minnesota Association County Probation Officers Scholarships [4544]
Minnesota Association of Public Accountant Scholarships [4546]
Minnesota Association of Public Accountants **[4545]**
Minnesota Association of Township **[4547]**

National Active and Retired Federal Employees Association **[4627]**
National Air Filtration Association **[4629]**
National Air Filtration Association Scholarship Fund [4630]
National Alliance of Preservation Commission **[4631]**
National Alliance of Preservation Commission Student Scholarships [4632]
National Alpha Lambda Delta **[4633]**
National American Arab Nurses Association **[4636]**
National American Arab Nurses Association Scholarships [4637]
National Arab American Medical Association **[4638]**
National Asian American Society of Accountants **[4640]**
National Asian Pacific American Bar Association **[4645]**
National Association for the Advancement of Colored People **[4650]**
National Association of Agricultural Educators **[4652]**
National Association for Armenian Studies and Research Scholarships [1289]
National Association of Black Accountants **[4654]**
National Association of Black Social Workers **[4663]**
National Association of Black Telecommunications Professionals **[4669]**
National Association of Campus Activities **[4671]**
National Association of Campus Activities Multicultural Scholarship Programs [4680]
National Association of Campus Activities Scholarships for Student Leaders [4681]
National Association of Chain Drug Stores Foundation **[4686]**
National Association for Chicana and Chicano Studies **[4688]**
National Association of Collegiate Directors of Athletics **[4690]**
National Association of Conservation District Employees **[4692]**
National Association of Conservation District Employees Scholarships [4693]
National Association of Container Distributors **[4694]**
National Association for County Community and Economic Development **[4696]**
National Association for Equal Opportunity in Higher Education **[4698]**
National Association of Farm Service Agency County Office Employees **[4700]**
National Association of Fellowships Advisors **[4702]**
National Association of Fellowships Advisors Graduate Scholar Awards [4710]
National Association of Financial Aid and Administrators **[4711]**
National Association of Financial Aid and Administrators Nursing Scholarships [4712]
National Association of Financial Aid and Administrators Scholarships for Disadvantaged Students [4713]
National Association of Health Services Executives **[4714]**
National Association of Heating Service Managers **[4718]**
National Association of Negro Business and Professional Women's Clubs **[4720]**
National Association of Pastoral Musicians **[4725]**
National Association of Pastoral Musicians Academic Scholarships [4726]
National Association of Pediatric Nurse Practitioners **[4728]**
National Association for Pupil Transportation **[4733]**
National Association of Recreation Resource Planners **[4735]**
National Association of School Safety and Law Enforcement Officers **[4737]**
National Association for the Self-Employed **[4739]**
National Association for the Self-Employed Scholarships [4741]
National Association of Sewer Service Companies **[4742]**
National Association of State Land Reclamationists **[4744]**
National Association of Teacher Educators for Family and Consumer Sciences **[4746]**
National Association of Women in Construction **[4748]**
National Association of Women Judges **[4751]**
National Ataxia Foundation **[4753]**
National Ataxia Foundation Research Fellowships [4754]
National Ataxia Foundation Research Grants [4755]
National Beta Club **[4756]**
National Beta Club Scholarships [4757]
National Black Coalition of Federal Aviation Employees **[4758]**
National Black Coalition of Federal Aviation Employees Scholarship [4759]
National Black MBA Association **[4760]**
National Black Nurses Association **[4763]**
National Black Nurses Association Scholarships [4764]
National Black Police Association **[4765]**
National Board of Boiler and Pressure Vessel Inspectors **[4767]**
The National Board Technical Scholarships [4768]
National Business Aviation Association **[4769]**
National Business Travel Association **[4783]**
National Candy Technologist Scholarship Program [332]
National Cattlemen's Foundation **[4787]**
National Center for Farmworker Health **[4793]**
National Center for Learning Disabilities **[4795]**
National Chapter of Canada IODE **[4797]**
National Co-op Scholarship Program [4809]
National Coal Transportation Association **[4799]**
National Coal Transportation Association At Large Scholarships [4800]
National College Scholarship Award [3970]
National Collegiate Athletic Association **[4801]**
National Collegiate Athletic Association Postgraduate Scholarships [4805]
National Collegiate Cancer Foundation **[4806]**
National Collegiate Cancer Foundation Scholarships [4807]
National Commission for Cooperative Education **[4808]**
National Community Pharmacists Association **[4810]**
National Community Pharmacists Association Internship Programs [4812]
National Community Pharmacists Association Presidential Scholarships [4813]
National Conference of Bar Examiners **[4816]**
National Conference of Editorial Writers **[4818]**
National Cosmetology Association **[4821]**
National Costumers Association **[4823]**
National Costumers Association Scholarships [4824]
National Council of Teachers of English **[4825]**
National Council of Teachers of Mathematics **[4828]**
National Court Reporters Association **[4834]**
National Court Reporters Association Student Intern Scholarships [4835]
National Dairy Herd Improvement Association **[4838]**
National Dairy Herd Improvement Association Scholarship Program [4839]
National Dairy Shrine **[4840]**
National Defense Transportation Association **[4842]**
National Dental Hygienists' Association **[4845]**
National Dental Hygienists' Association Scholarships [4846]
National Drug Enforcement Officers Association **[4847]**
National Eagle Scout Association **[4849]**
National Electrical Manufacturers Representatives Association **[4870]**
National Endowment for the Humanities Advanced Fellowship for Research in Turkey [900]
National Environmental Health Association **[4872]**
National Environmental Health Association Scholarship Fund [4873]
National Federation of the Blind **[4874]**
National Federation of the Blind Educator of Tomorrow Award [4881]
National Federation of Paralegal Associations **[4885]**
National Federation of Republican Women **[4888]**
National Forum for Black Public Administrators **[4891]**
National Foster Parent Association **[4901]**
National Foundation for Infectious Diseases **[4903]**
National Funeral Directors and Morticians Association **[4905]**
National Gay Pilots Association **[4910]**
National Geophysics Scholarships [7488]
National Government Publishing Association **[4912]**
National Greenhouse Manufacturers Association Scholarships [562]
National Ground Water Association **[4914]**
National Heartburn Alliance NP Student Scholarships [269]
National Hemophilia Foundation **[4916]**
National Hispanic Coalition of Federal Aviation Employees **[4936]**
National Honor Roll Scholarships [1808]
National Honor Society **[4938]**
National Housing Endowment **[4940]**
National Huguenot Society **[4943]**
National Huguenot Society Scholarships [4944]
National Industrial Belting Association **[4945]**
National Institute of Health **[4948]**
National Institute of Health Undergraduate Scholarship Program [4949]
National Investment Company Service Association **[4950]**
National Iranian American Council **[4952]**
National Iranian American Council Fellowships [4958]
National Italian American Bar Association **[4959]**
National Italian American Bar Association Scholarships [4960]
National Italian American Foundation **[4961]**
National Judges Association **[4964]**
National Judges Association Scholarships [4965]
National Junior Angus Association **[4966]**
National Junior Horticultural Association **[4968]**
National Junior Horticultural Association Alumni Scholarships [4969]
National Junior Swine Association **[4970]**
National Junior Swine Association Outstanding Member Scholarships [4973]
National Kindergarten Alliance **[4977]**
National Kindergarten Alliance Graduate Scholarships [4978]
National Legal Aid and Defender Association **[4979]**
National Lesbian and Gay Journalists Association (NLGJA) Scholarships [6126]
National Little Britches Rodeo Association **[4981]**
National Medical Fellowships **[4984]**
National Medical Fellowships Need-Based Scholarships [4989]
National Military Intelligence Association **[4990]**
National Organization of Black Law Enforcement Executives **[4992]**
National Organization for Human Services **[4995]**
National Organization of Industrial Trade Unions **[4997]**
National Organization of Italian-American Women **[4999]**
National Organization of Italian-American Women Scholarships [5000]
National Orientation Directors Association **[5001]**
National Osteoporosis Foundation **[5003]**
National Osteoporosis Foundation Research Grants [5004]
National Parking Association **[5005]**
National Parkinson Foundation **[5010]**
National Pathfinder Scholarships [4889]
National Poultry and Food Distributors Association **[5012]**
National Poultry and Food Distributors Association Scholarships [5013]
National Preservation Institute **[5014]**
National Preservation Institute Scholarships [5015]
National Press Photographers Association **[5016]**
National Private Truck Council **[5023]**
National Public Employer Labor Relations Association **[5025]**
National Recreation and Park Association **[5027]**
National Recreation and Park Association Diversity Scholarships [5028]
National Recycling Coalition **[5029]**
National Recycling Coalition Congress Scholarships [5030]
National Restaurant Association Educational Foundation **[5031]**
National Roofing Contractors Association **[5033]**

ciation Floriculture Scholarships [5236]
North Carolina Economic Developers Association **[5237]**
North Carolina League for Nursing Academic Scholarship Fund [3070]
North Carolina Nursery and Landscape Association **[5241]**
North Carolina Nursery and Landscape Association Horticulture Scholarships [5243]
North Carolina Simmental Association **[5244]**
North Carolina Vending Association **[5246]**
North Carolina Vending Association Academic Scholarships [5247]
North Central (Region 9) Scholarships [6499]
North Dakota Division Scholarships [4517]
North Dakota Farmers Union **[5248]**
North Dakota Farmers Union Agricultural Studies Scholarships [5252]
North Dakota Farmers Union Co-op House Scholarships [5253]
North Dakota Farmers Union Scholarships [5254]
North Dakota Veterinary Medical Association **[5256]**
North Dakota Veterinary Medical Association Scholarships [5258]
North Florida Chapter Safety Education Scholarships [1064]
North Las Vegas Firefighters - William J. Harnedy Memorial Scholarships [5846]
North Mecklenburg Teachers' Memorial Scholarships [3071]
North Ottawa Hospital Auxiliary Scholarships Fund [3295]
North Scholarships for Safety; Michelle [3522]
North Texas GIA Alumni Association Scholarships [3196]
Northampton County Medical Society Alliance **[5260]**
Northampton County Medical Society Alliance Scholarships [5261]
NorthCoast Medical Scholarship Program [734]
Northeast Conference on The Teaching of Foreign Languages **[5262]**
Northeastern Illinois Chapter Scholarships [1065]
Northeastern Ohio Chapter Scholarships - Alfred B. Glossbrenner and John Klusch Scholarships [1454]
Northern Alberta Development Council Bursary Award [171]
Northern Alberta Development Council Bursary for Medical Students [172]
Northern Alberta Development Council Bursary Partnership Program [173]
Northern Alberta Development Council Bursary for Pharmacy Students [174]
Northern Arizona Native-American Foundation **[5268]**
Northern Arizona Native-American Foundation Scholarships [5269]
Northern California Chapter of HIMSS Scholarships [3518]
Northern Indiana Community Foundation **[5270]**
Northern Student Supplement [175]
Northern Virginia Alumnae Chapter Scholarships [2659]
Northrup Scholarships; Eugene [4208]
Northwest Community Center Scholarships [2478]
Northwest Michigan Home Builders Association **[5272]**
Northwest-Shoals Community College **[5274]**
Northwest-Shoals Community College Academic Scholarships [5289]
Northwest-Shoals Community College Applied Technology Scholarships [5290]
Northwest-Shoals Community College Athletic Scholarships [5291]
Northwest-Shoals Community College Bank Independent Scholarships [5292]
Northwest-Shoals Community College Fine Arts Scholarships - Art [5293]
Northwest-Shoals Community College Fine Arts Scholarships - Drama [5294]
Northwest-Shoals Community College Fine Arts Scholarships - Music [5295]
Northwest-Shoals Community College High School Academic Scholarships [5296]
Northwest-Shoals Community College Independent Computer Scholarships [5297]
Northwest-Shoals Community College Student Activities Scholarships [5298]
Northwestern Mutual Financial Network Scholarships [5642]
Notchev Fellowships; Vessa [6341]
Notre Dame Club of Canton Scholarships [6747]
Nova Scotia Salmon Association **[5306]**
Nova Scotia Salmon Association Scholarships [5307]
Novartis Pharmaceutical Corporation NP Student Scholarships [270]
Novo Nordisk Canada-CAS Research Awards [1917]
Novo Nordisk NP Doctoral Education Scholarships [271]
Novosad Scholarships; Peggy (Kommer) [3344]
Novovesky Scholarships; Mike and Flo [563]
Noyce Scholarship Program; Robert [5565]
Noyce Scholarships for Secondary Math and Science Education [3711]
NPELRA Foundation **[5308]**
NPELRA Foundation Scholarships [5309]
NPM Program Scholarships [4727]
NSA Scholarship Program [5040]
NSERC Canada Graduate Scholarships [6434]
NSERC Postgraduate Scholarships [6435]
NSF Pickwick Postdoctoral Research Fellowships [5042]
NSHSS Academic Paper Awards [5070]
NSHSS National Scholar Awards [5071]
NSPF Board of Directors' Scholarship Awards [5103]
NSPF Scholarship Awards [5104]
NSPS Board of Governors Scholarships [489]
The NSPS Scholarships [490]
NSS Conservation Grants [5088]
NSS Education Grants [5089]
NSSA/NSCA Collegiate Scholarships [5093]
Nu-Gro Corporation Turfgrass Scholarships (Graduate) [6075]
Nu-Gro Corporation Turfgrass Scholarships (Undergraduate) [6076]
Nurseries Foundation Scholarship Awards [5385]
Nurseries Memorial Scholarship Awards [5386]
Nurses Educational Fund **[5310]**
Nursing Scholarship Program [3512]
NW-SCC/American Cancer Society College Scholarships [5299]
NW-SCC American Legion Scholarships - Florence/Lauderdale Post No. 11 [5300]
NWF's Women for Sustainable Development (WSD) Scholarships [6333]
NWSA Distinguished Fellowships [5125]
NWSA Graduate Scholarships [5126]
NWSA Graduate Scholarships in Lesbian Studies [6127]
NYNEX Diversity Scholarship Awards [6128]
OBAP Fellowships - Airline Transport (ATP) [5407]
OBAP Fellowships - Commercial [5408]
OBAP Fellowships - Instructor rating (CFI/CFII/MEI) [5409]
OBAP Fellowships - Multi-Engine [5410]
OBAP General Scholarships [5411]
Obrzut Ling Scholarships [5772]
Obye Scholarship Award; Katharine H. [2479]
OCA Scholarships [5413]
OCAEOP Community Service Scholarship Program [5353]
Occupational Physicians Scholarship Fund **[5312,** 5313]
O'Connor Memorial Scholarship Fund; John [5114]
Odd Fellows Lodge No. 8 Endowed Scholarships [4209]
Odom Memorial Scholarships - Children of Soldiers; Captain Jennifer Shafer [1305]
Odom Memorial Scholarships - Spouses of Soldiers; Captain Jennifer Shafer [1306]
O'Dowd/SWAA Scholarships; Don & Jan [4375]
Office Depot Scholarships [3569]
Office Products Wholesaler Association **[5314]**
Ohio Association of Broadcasters **[5316]**
Ohio Association of Broadcaster's Kids Scholarships [5317]
Ohio Association of Broadcasters Scholarships [5318]
Ohio Farm Bureau Federation **[5319]**
Ohio Newspaper Association **[5321]**
Ohio Newspaper Association Minority Scholarships [5323]
Ohio Newspaper Association University Journalism Scholarships [5324]
Ohio Newspaper Association Women's Scholarships [5325]
Ohio Valley Chapter Scholarships [1455]
Ohio War Orphan Scholarships [7531]
Ohlman Memorial Scholarships; Lawrence "Bud" [564]
O'Jays Scholarship Fund [6748]
OKAIDE Scholarships [5327]
Oklahoma Association for the Improvement of Developmental Education **[5326]**
Oklahoma City University Merit Scholarships [5330]
Oklahoma City University School of Law **[5328]**
The Oklahoma State University at Okmulgee Scholarships [5548]
Oliver ASNT Scholarships; Robert B. [1023]
Olson Memorial Scholarships; Roy C. and Dorothy Jean [3876]
Olympia Tumwater Foundation **[5332]**
Olympia Tumwater Foundation Traditional Scholarships [5333]
Olympia Tumwater Foundation Transitional (non-traditional) Scholarships [5334]
Omaha Education Association **[5335]**
O'Meara Foundation Scholarships [3485]
O'Meilia Scholarships; Charlie [3830]
Omicron Nu Research Fellowships [4054]
Omohundro Institute of Early American History and Culture **[5337]**
O'More Scholarships; Eloise Pitts [2442]
one of whom should be from the principal (Dean/Chair) of the institution where the applicant is employed [3794]
Ontario Hockey Association War Memorial Scholarships [7232]
Ontario Trucking Association **[5340]**
Open Society Fellowships [5347]
Open Society Institute **[5346]**
Opera Foundation **[5348]**
Opera Foundation Scholarships [5349]
Operation Homefront **[5350]**
Operation Homefront Scholarships [5351]
Oppenheim Memorial Scholarships; Sheldon [6129]
Oppenheimer Scholarship Program; Frank [735]
Opperman Scholarships; Dwight D. [2762]
Optimist Club Of Redlands - Ralph Maloof Scholarships [5969]
Optimist Club of Redlands - Virginia Elliott Scholarships [5970]
OPWA Educational Scholarships [5315]
Orange County Association of Educational Office Professionals **[5352]**
Orange County Centennial Academic Scholarships [5362]
Orange County Centennial Arts Scholarships [5363]
Orange County Centennial Certification Scholarships [5364]
Orange County Community Foundation **[5354]**
Orange County Tourism Council Scholarships [5365]
Orchard-Hoyman Fund for GLBT Student Scholarships [2889]
Order Sons of Italy in America **[5371]**
Order Sons of Italy Foundation General Scholarships [5373]
Oregon Association of Broadcasters **[5375]**
Oregon Association of Broadcasters Scholarships [5376]
Oregon Association of Nurseries **[5377]**
Oregon Association of Nurseries Scholarship Program [5387]
Oregon Community Credit Union Scholarships [7201]
Oregon Farm Bureau **[5391]**
Oregon Farm Bureau Memorial Scholarships [5393]
Oregon Logging Conference Scholarships [4210]
Oregon Medical Association **[5397]**
Orenstein Memorial Convention Travel Grants; Doris [1462]
Organization of American States **[5399]**
Organization of American States Academic Scholarships [5400]

Quill and Scroll Society **[5889]**
Quinci Foundation Scholarships; Salvatore E. [4933]
Quincy Scholarships; Bob [7189]
RA Consulting Service Maria Riley Scholarships [4900]
Radcliffe Memorial Scholarships; Dr. J. Glenn [6784]
Radio Advisory Board of Canada **[5892]**
Rafal Memorial Scholarships; Dr. Sidney [3491]
Railway Tie Association **[5894]**
Rain Bird Intelligent Use of Water Scholarships [4127]
Rain Bird Scholarships [987]
Rains Memorial Scholarships; J.J. [2283]
Rainwater Family Scholarships [4983]
Rakestraw Law Scholarships; Frederick [5271]
Ralls Memorial Scholarships; Tom D. [3020]
Rama Scholarships for the American Dream [616]
Rambus Scholarship Fund [6393]
Ramirez Memorial Scholarships; Raul [5976]
Ramnes Professional Scholarships; Michael A. [1224]
Rancho Bernardo/Smith Scholarships [6217]
Rand Fellowships and Scholarships; Herbert W. [4298]
Rand Jr. Memorial Scholarships; Newell S. [5460]
Rand Memorial Scholarships; Helen F. "Jerri" [2509]
Randolph Peace Scholar Dissertation Program; The Jennings [7026]
Rankin Foundation; Jeannette **[5896]**
Rankin Scholarships; Jeannette [5897]
Ratay Educational Grants; General John Paul [4531]
Ratcliffe Hicks School of Agriculture Heritage Scholarships [3492]
Rath Graduate Research Fellowships; V. Duane [3025]
Rathke Family Scholarships; Dr. Mark [2790]
Rathmell Jr. Scholarships; James K. [566]
Ratner and Sugarmon Scholarships [7125]
Ratza Memorial Scholarships; Carol A. [3365]
Raveling Scholarships; Dennis [1862]
Ravich "Shalom" Scholarships; Lenny [1367]
Rawley Silver Award for Excellence [314]
Rawlins Scholarships; Mary C. [3493]
Ray, CIH, CSP Arizona Scholarships; William C. [1068]
Ray HS Class of '56 Averill Johnson Scholarships; W.B. [2284]
Raytheon Company **[5898]**
Raytheon Scholarship Program [5899]
RBC Financial Group Scholarships [1740]
RBC Royal Bank Scholarships for First Year Medical & Dental Students [6066]
RBC Royal Bank Scholarships for New Canadians [6067]
RBC Royal Bank Scholarships for Undergraduates [6068]
Reach Out for Youth with Ileitis and Colitis **[5900]**
Reagan College Leaders Scholarship Program; Ronald [5687]
Reaser Scholarships; William [5511]
Rechsteiner Family Scholarship Fund [2971]
Redden Memorial Scholarships; Pat [4252]
Redlands Area Interfaith Council Scholarships [5977]
Redlands Community Scholarship Foundation **[5902]**
Redlands Community Scholarship Foundation Scholarships [5978]
Redlands Council PTA - Dorothy Jolley Memorial Scholarships [5979]
Redlands Footlighters, Inc. - Merle and Peggy Williams Scholarships [5980]
Redlands High School Academic Decathalon Scholarships [5981]
Redlands High School Boy's Varsity Volleyball Scholarships [5982]
Redlands High School Class of 1957 [5983]
Redlands High School Drama Boosters Award [5984]
Redlands High School Girls' Volleyball Boosters Scholarship Awards [5985]
Redlands High School Mock Trial Scholarships [5986]
Redlands High School-PTSA Scholarships [5987]
Redlands High School Soccer Boosters Scholarship Awards [5988]
Redlands High School Softball Booster Scholarship Awards [5989]
Redlands High School Speech Boosters Scholarship Awards [5990]
Redlands High School Spiritleaders Scholarships [5991]
Redlands High School Terrier Band Boosters Club Scholarships [5992]
Redlands High School Vocal Music Boosters Scholarship Awards [5993]
Redlands Morning Kiwanis Club Foundation Scholarships [5994]
Redlands Noon Kiwanis Club Foundation Scholarships [5995]
Redlands Noon Kiwanis Club - Martin and Dorothy Munz Scholarships [5996]
Redlands Rotary Club - Donald C. Anderson Scholarships [5997]
Redlands Rotary Club - Ernest L. Cronemeyer Memorial Scholarships [5998]
Redlands Rotary Club Foundation Discretionary Scholarships [5999]
Redlands Teachers Association Scholarships [6000]
Reed Scholarships; Sarah Rebecca [1637]
Reeder Memorial Scholarships; Vern W. [3574]
The Reese Fellowships [307]
Reeve Professional Aviation Management Scholarships; Bob [127]
Reflex Sympathetic Dystrophy Syndrome Association of America **[6013]**
REFORMA: National Association to Promote Library and Information Services **[6015]**
REFORMA Scholarship Program [6016]
Regan Scholarships; Marjorie Usher [7190]
Registered Apprenticeship Program (RAP) Scholarships [179]
Registry of Interpreters for the Deaf **[6017]**
Reid Memorial Scholarship Grant; Mark A. [2481]
Reilly Graduate Scholarships; Ida and May [935]
Reilly Memorial Scholarships - For Freshmen in College; Henry J. [6023]
Reilly Memorial Scholarships - For Graduating High School Seniors; Henry J. [6024]
Reilly Memorial Scholarships - For Sophomores and Juniors in College; Henry J. [6025]
Reilly Memorial Scholarships - Graduate Program; Henry J. [6026]
Reinecke Memorial Scholarship Fund; Jacob L. [3299]
Reinke Scholarships; George [1088]
Reiss Memorial Scholarship Fund; Daniel L. [3300]
Religion Newswriters Association **[6020]**
The Remington Club Scholarships [6218]
REMSA Scholarships [884]
Rendel Scholarships; Betty [4890]
Renschler Scholarships; Don [5775]
Reppert Scholarship Fund; Bertha and Byron L. [3116]
Republic Services Environmental Studies Scholarships [5855]
Research Fellowships in Iranian Studies (Resident Director-Tehran) [664]
Research Grants in Comparative Studies of Modern Turkey [3757]
Research Grants in Speech Science [1106]
Reserve Officers Association of the United States **[6022]**
Reserve Officers Training Corps (ROTC) Scholarships [7267]
Resistance Welder Manufacturers' Association Scholarships [1171]
Retail Chapter Scholarship Awards [5388]
Retail Packaging Association **[6027]**
Retail Print Music Dealers Association **[6029]**
Retired League Postmasters of the National League of Postmasters **[6031]**
Retired League Postmasters Scholarship Program [6032]
Reyler Memorial Scholarships; Dr. Felix H. [2599]
Reynolds Journalism Scholarships; Nike [1401]
Reynoldson Memorial Scholarships; Janet [2764]
Rhett Memorial Scholarships; Lori [4682]
Rhode Island Association of Former Legislators Scholarships [6040]
Rhode Island Commission on Women/Freda H. Goldman Education Awards [6041]
Rhode Island Foundation **[6033]**
Rhodes Scholarships; John J. and Elizabeth [1674]
Rice-Cullimore Scholarships [998]
Rice Scholarships; Haynes [4717]
Rich Memorial Scholarships; Ben C. [1675]
Richards Scholarships; Barbara Hagan [2444]
Richards Scholarships; James Edward "Bill" [2445]
Richardson Memorial Scholarship; Philip Guy [3986]
Richter Scholarships; Frank J. [395]
Rickard Scholarships; Howard B. [4884]
Rider Scholarships; John S. and Jacqueline P. [7453]
Ridge Restoration Fellowships Jasper Ridge Biological Preserve; Jasper [2816]
Riebhoff Memorial Scholarships; Donald [851]
Rieser Fellowships [1804]
Riggs & Anna & Dorothy Mae Barnes Scholarships; Jerrothia Allenfonzo [1899]
Rihani Scholarship Program; Ameen [1193]
Riley Scholarships; Susan E. [2663]
Rinehart Scholarship; Lana K. [2383]
Ringelberg Scholarship Fund; Harold and Eleonor [3301]
Ringold Scholarships; Josephine [3346]
Rinn Scholarships; Fauneil J. [6394]
Risk Consulting Scholarships; Marsh [1069]
Rittle Sr. Memorial Scholarships; Paul H. [3751]
Roach Scholarships; Jean Wiggin [2664]
Roanoke Bar Association **[6045]**
Roberts Athletic Scholarships; James H. [5512]
Roberts Educational Scholarships; Faye Lynn [6669]
Roberts Graduate Fellowships; Clifford [2842]
Roberts Jr. Prize; Eugene L. [7191]
Roberts Memorial Scholarships; Liz [6001]
Roberts Memorial Scholarships; Marion [1572]
Roberts Scholarships; George A. [4402]
Roberts Scholarships; Thomas Warren [5513]
Robertson Memorial Scholarships; A.D. 'Al' [4378]
Robinette Scholarship Endowment Fund; Ben [3074]
Robinson Arts Scholarships; David G. [6670]
Robinson Endowment Scholarships; Isador M. [2765]
Robinson Foundation; Jackie **[6048]**
Robinson Foundation Minority Scholarship; Jackie [637]
Robinson Grants; Helen M. [3890]
Robinson Inweld Corporation Scholarships; Jerry [1172]
Robinson Memorial Scholarships; James [5514]
Robinson Scholarships; Claude [4975]
Robinson Scholarships; Jackie [6049]
Robinson Scholarships; Nell Bryant [5678]
Rocco Scholarship Fund; August M. [6750]
Rockford Area Habitat for Humanity College Scholarships [2482]
Rockford Chapter Daughters of the American Revolution Memorial Scholarships [2483]
Rockin' Christmas Fund Scholarships [6671]
Rockwell Collins Scholarships [83]
Rocky Mountain Coal Mining Institute **[6050]**
Rocky Mountain Coal Mining Institute Engineering/Geology Scholarships [6051]
Rocky Mountain Coal Mining Institute Technical Scholarships [6052]
Rocky Mountain Mineral Law Foundation **[6053]**
Rocky Mountain Nature Association **[6055]**
Rocky Mountain Region of Wound Ostomy Continence Nurses Society Scholarships [2324]
Rocky Mountain Research Fellowships [6056]
R.O.E.A. Dumitru Golea Goldy-Gemu Scholarships [913]
ROFY Scholarships [5901]
Rogers Memorial Scholarship Fund; Kimberly Marie [2972]
Rogers Memorial Scholarships; Joseph Wood [6319]
Rogers Memorial Scholarships; Kenneth [4213]
Rogers Nursing Scholarships; Pat and Cliff [4379]
Rogers Scholarships; Geraldine Ruth [6887]
Rogers Scholarships; Mary Stuart [7415]
Rogers Scholarships; William C. [3216]
Rolfs Scholarships; Richard C. [5776]
Roller Panhellenic Scholarships; Mary Louise [5223]

Ronald McDonald House Charities African American Future Achievers Scholarships [4407]
Ronald McDonald House Charities of Hispanic Heritage [4408]
Ronald McDonald House Charities Scholarships [4409]
Ronald McDonald House Charities Scholarships in Asia [4410]
Rongstad Wildlife Management Scholarships; Dr. Orrin J. [4380]
Ronin Memorial Scholarships; Charles and Ruth [6002]
Ronken Scholarships; Dorothy Worden [2698]
Roofing Industry Alliance for Progress **[6057]**
Roofing Industry Alliance for Progress Scholarships [6058]
Roofing Industry Scholarships [5035]
Rooke Scholarships; Alice W. [3494]
Roothbert Fund **[6059]**
Roothbert Fund Scholarships [6060]
ROP - Ambassadors Scholarships [6003]
ROP - Rob Bruce Memorial Scholarships [6004]
Rose Educational Scholarships; Annie B. [4651]
Rose, Jr. and Eva Rose Nichol Scholarship Fund; Barnes W. [194]
Rose Medical Center, Denver: Nightingale Scholarships [2325]
Rose Memorial Scholarship Fund; Carl M. [5515]
Rose and S. Meryl Rose Scholarships; Florence C. [4299]
Rose Scholarship Fund; Dr. Wayne F. [2973]
Rosenberg Educational Trust; Ollie [3117]
Rosenberg-Ibarra Scholarships [5777]
Rosenberg Scholarship Travel Fund; Ollie [3118]
Rosenblatt and Robert N. Herbert Undergraduate Scholarships; Mandell and Lester [6519]
Rosenthal Bar Exam Scholarships [1817]
Rosenthal Scholarship Program; Jean and Tom [2520]
Rosness Student Scholarships; Marty [1204]
Ross Educational Fund; Bettsy [5212]
Ross-Fahey Scholarships [4683]
Ross Memorial Scholarship Fund; S. Byrl [5516]
Ross Memorial Scholarships; Dorothy M. [1560]
Ross Trust Graduate Student Scholarships [517]
The Rotary Club of Cape Coral Goldcoast Scholarships Fund [2055]
Rotary Club of Corpus Christi Scholarships [2285]
The Rotary Club of Rancho Bernardo Sunrise Abraxas Student Scholarships [6219]
The Rotary Foundation **[6061]**
The Rotary Foundation Ambassadorial Scholarships [6062]
Rotary Public Safety Scholarship Fund [3075]
Rotberg Memorial Scholarships; Bernard [4031]
Roth Manufacturing Engineering Scholarships; Edward S. [6500]
Roth Newspaper Carrier Scholarships Program; Isaac [5182]
Rothermel Scholarship; Marjorie Roy [999]
Rousseau Memorial Mountain Achievement Scholarship; Robin [180]
Routh Student Research Grants [6533]
Rowan Business Alliance **[6063]**
Rowe Pan American Fund; Leo S. [5404]
Rowling, Dold and Associates LLP Scholarships [2833]
Royal Bank of Canada **[6065]**
Royal Canadian Golf Association **[6069]**
Royal Palm Audobon Society Environmental Fellowships [2998]
Royce-Osborn Minority Scholarship Program [1042]
RPA Scholarships [6028]
RSDSA Research Grants [6014]
The RTKL Traveling Fellowships [310]
Rubber Division American Chemical Society **[6078]**
Rubber Division American Chemical Society Scholarships [6079]
Ruben Scholarships; Mike [5517]
Rubinstein Family Scholarships [6220]
Ruby Memorial Scholarships; Glen [2045]
Rucker Greenwood Scholarships; William [1513]
Rudberg Scholarships; Lawrence E. & Mabel Jackson [2791]
Rudd Scholarships; Joe [6054]
Runci, MJSA Scholarships; Matthew A. [3197]
Rundguist Memorial Scholarship; Anna M. [3378]
Runyon Cancer Research Foundation; Damon **[6080]**
Runyon Cancer Research Foundation Fellowships; Damon [6081]
Runyon Clinical Investigator Awards; Damon [6082]
Runyon-Rachleff Innovation Awards; Damon [6083]
Ruppert Educational Grant Program [6395]
Rural Telephone Company **[6084]**
Rural Telephone Company Scholarships [6085]
Rusch Scholarships; Hermann G. [531]
Russell Scholarships; Norman K. [5002]
Russian Brotherhood Organization of the USA **[6086]**
Russian/Central Asian Student Scholarships [4381]
Russo Memorial Scholarships; Michael A. [6005]
Russo Scholarships; The Anthony C. [5026]
Rust Scholarships; Lucile [5679]
Rutherford Scholars [181]
Rutherford Scholarships for High School Achievement; Alexander [182]
Ryan Memorial Scholarships; Michael Clarkson [1676]
Rycenga Education Scholarships Fund; Charles and Eleonor [3302]
Rydberg Memorial Scholarship; Deborah Jean [2484]
Ryerson Scholarships [4003]
Ryland Scholarships; Jeanne Graves [2665]
Ryskamp Research Fellowships; Charles A. [511]
SACHS Foundation **[6089]**
SACHS Foundation Graduate Scholarships [6090]
SACHS Foundation Undergraduate Scholarships for Colorado Black Students [6091]
Sacks For CF Scholarships [2589]
Sadlier Memorial Scholarships; Julie Anne [2666]
Safe Schools Coalition **[6092]**
Sager Scholarships; Ruth [4300]
SAH Study Tour Fellowships [6429]
Saharov Memorial Scholarships; Virginia Hartford [2667]
Saint Andrews Scholarships [6150]
Saint Andrew's Society of the State of New York **[6149]**
St. Anthony's Hospitals, Denver: Nightingale Scholarships [2326]
St. James Armenian Church Memorial Scholarships [1290]
St. Joseph's Hospital School of Nursing Alumnae Scholarships [5518]
St. Louis Division Scholarships [4519]
St. Mary's Hospital and Medical Center, Grand Junction: Nightingale Scholarships [2327]
Saint Paul University Canada **[6151]**
Saint Paul University Excellence Scholarships [6152]
Saint Paul University Financial Aid Brasseries [6153]
St. Stephen A.M.E. Allison E. Fisher Book Awards [2985]
Saint Vincent College Eagle Scout Scholarships [4865]
Saints Cyril and Methodius Scholarships [6088]
SAJA Journalism Scholarships [6608]
Sakir Point Scholarships; Casey [5726]
Saks Scholarship Fund; Joseph and Amelia [2361]
Sakura Finetek Student Scholarships [5079]
Salanky-Onzik Scholarship Fund; Jane [2974]
Salerno, W2ONV, Memorial Scholarships; Bill [852]
Sales and Marketing Executives International Scholarships [5645]
Sallee, W4YFR Memorial Scholarships; Eugene Gene [853]
The Sallie Mae 911 Education Fund [6157]
Sallie Mae Fund **[6154]**
Saltwick Scholarships; Marie V. [2792]
Salvatori Scholarships; Henry [5374]
Samalot - Sebastian Scholarship Fund [2600]
Samek III Memorial Scholarship Fund; The Walter [2402]
Sampson Scholarships; Margaret Jerome [5680]
Sams Scholarships; Ray and Pearly [7454]
Samson Scholarships; AIST David H. [1456]
Samsung American Legion Scholarships [697]
San Diego City College Study Abroad Scholarships [6221]
The San Diego Foundation **[6160]**
The San Diego Foundation Community Scholarship II [6222]
The San Diego Foundation Community Scholarships I [6223]
San Diego National Bank Scholarships [6224]
San Diego Pathways to College Scholarships [6225]
San Diego Regional Aviation Association Scholarships [6226]
San Pasqual Academy Scholarships [6227]
Sanchez Scholarships; Barbara [6443]
Sanchez Scholarships; Leo and Trinidad [6396]
Sand Hill Scholars Program [6397]
Sandburg College Scholarships; Carl [4908]
Sanderson Aviation Maintenance Technician Scholarship; Bill [3523]
Sanofi Pasteur Scholarships [2013]
Santa Barbara Dance Alliance **[6243]**
SAPA Scholarships [6408]
Saperstein Communication Scholarships; Bert [6246]
Saperstein Communications Scholarship Fund; Bert **[6245]**
Saratoga County Bar Association **[6247]**
Saratoga County Bar Association Law Student Scholarships [6248]
Sarli Memorial Scholarships; Frank [4837]
Saskatchewan Trucking Association **[6249]**
Saskatchewan Trucking Association Scholarships [6250]
Sathre Memorial Scholarship Fund; Roger C. [3649]
Sathyadev Memorial Scholarships; Malini E. [6228]
Satter Human Rights Fellowships; [3506]
Saulsbury Scholarship Fund; Curtis M. [2395]
Savatori Fellowships [3773]
Save Mart Legacy Scholarships [1833]
Savoy Scholarship Fund; John A. [2975]
Savvy Student Traveler Grant Program [752]
SAWE Scholarships [6424]
Sawyer Memorial Scholarship; Mark Dauglas [2362]
Sawyer Memorial Scholarships; Bill [4214]
SBA Four-Year Scholarships Program [6702]
SBA One-Year Scholarships Program [6703]
SC and R Foundation Grant Program [6686]
SC and R Foundation Scholarships [6687]
Scales Memorial Scholarship; Leslie and Mary Ella [2363]
Scandlyn/Sammie Lynn Scandlyn Puett Memorial Scholarships; Edith [2668]
SCDAA Post-Doctoral Research Fellowships [6328]
Schacht Memorial Scholarships; Mary Turnbull [6368]
Schacht Native American Student Scholarship; David W. [1630]
Schaffner Endowed Memorial Scholarship; Millicent M. [3303]
Schaible Health Care Services Scholarships [6847]
Schecter Graduate Scholarships; Abe [1402]
Scheduler and Dispatchers Scholarships [4781]
Scheetz Family Scholarships; William C. [1677]
Schickler Scholarship; Dr. Oskar and Sally [3561]
Schikora Scholarships; Robert C. and Margaret A. [6672]
Schlundt Memorial Scholarships; Esther [3694]
Schmid Research Scholarships; Julie [1475]
Schmied Scholarships; Ronald L. [3388]
Schneider, Jr. Manufacturing Technology Education Scholarships; Prof. George [6501]
Schnell Memorial Scholarship; Richard J. [2485]
Schoephoerster Scholarships; Lillian P. [5681]
Scholarship Award of The Aliant Pioneer Volunteers [1989]
Scholarship Challenge Flight [3409]
Scholarship Foundation of Santa Barbara **[6251]**
Scholarship Foundation of Santa Barbara Art Scholarship Program [6252]
Scholarship for Junior PHS Commissioned Officers [5689]
Scholarships for Aboriginal Canadians [5118]
Scholarships of the Arts [2590]
Scholarships for Disadvantaged Students [3513]
Scholarships for Emigres in the Health Sciences [4025]
Scholarships for Leadership Training and Coaching [2717]
Scholarships for Lutheran College Students [1687]

Scholarships for Lutheran Nursing Students [1688]
Scholarships of the Morris Radio Club of New Jersey [854]
Scholarships for Technology Students [1945]
Scholarships for Visible Minorities [5119]
Scholl College of Podiatric Medicine Scholarships; The Dr. William M. [5550]
The Schonstedt Scholarships in Surveying [491]
School Age Financial Aid Program [1616]
School of Education Scholarships for Students from Underrepresented Groups [7268]
School In-Service Training Grants for Grades 6-8 Teachers [4831]
School In-Service Training Grants for Grades 9-12 Teachers [4832]
School In-Service Training Grants for Grades K-5 Teachers [4833]
School Library Paraprofessional Scholarships [1850]
School Nutrition Association **[6255]**
School of Pharmacy Continuing Student Scholarships [7269]
Schoolsfirst Federal Credit Union Scholarships [6006]
Schroeder Memorial Scholarships; Susan P. [4215]
Schulich MBA Entrance Scholarships; Tanna H. [6275]
Schulich School of Business **[6261]**
Schulman Simmons Scholarships for UU Women; Alice [6954]
Schultes Research Awards; Richard E. [6439]
Schultz Family Scholarship Fund; David and Ginny [3304]
Schuman Ecolab Undergraduate Entrepreneurial Scholarships; Al [5032]
Schureman Scholarship Program; Jeptha Wade [2521]
Schwan's Food Service Scholarships [6258]
Schwartz Musical Theatre Scholarships; Stephen [3625]
Schwartz Serials Education Scholarships; Fritz [5226]
Scleroderma Foundation **[6278]**
Scleroderma Foundation Established Investigator Grants [6279]
Scleroderma Foundation New Investigator Grants [6280]
Scleroderma Research Foundation **[6281]**
Scotiabank Scholarships [1741]
Scott Awards; Wendell [3570]
Scott Book Scholarships; Carl A. [2555]
Scottish Rite Foundation of Colorado **[6283]**
Scouts Canada **[6285]**
Screen Actors Guild **[6287]**
Scrivner Research Grants; Roy [6137]
Scrollsaw Association of the World **[6289]**
SCSPA Scholarships [6617]
SCSPA Yearbook Scholarships [6618]
Scudder Scholarship; Bonnie Sorenson [2486]
SDF Community College Transfer Scholarships for Math and Science [6229]
Seaman Family Scholarships [2286]
Seaspace Incorporation **[6291]**
Seaspace Scholarships [6292]
Seaton Memorial Scholarships; Fred A. [1678]
Seattle Chapter ASWA Scholarships [2834]
Seaver Family Scholarship Fund; David and Sharon [3305]
Section for Women in Public Administration **[6293]**
Seed Companies Scholarships [567]
Seedworks Fund: Nightingale Scholarships [2328]
Seeger Scholarships; Margery J. [3347]
Seegmiller Recruitment Scholarship Grant; Elisabeth [2487]
Seesan Memorial Scholarship Fund; Aaron [6751]
Segal Memorial Scholarships for Journalistic Excellence; D.R. [5367]
Segel - Hartford Courant Internships; Deedee [3495]
Seiden Memorial Scholarships; Detective Cheryl [255]
Selby Engineering Scholarship; The John and Marion [3987]
Self Memorial Scholarships; D. Mitchell [5301]
Self Scholarships; David W. [6967]
Sell Research and Training Grants; G. Helner [1110]
Selvy Scholarships; Walter and Rita [2766]
SEMA Memorial Scholarships [1573]
Sendzimir Scholarships; Tadeusz [3496]
Senior Memorial Scholarships [2488]
Sentner Scholarship Awards; William "Buddy" [391]
Sepulveda Memorial Scholarships - Northside Booster Club; Felix R. [6007]
Serbian Bar Association of America **[6295]**
Serbian Bar Association of America Scholarships [6296]
Service League Volunteer Scholarships [7372]
Servus Credit Union 4-H Scholarships [135]
Sesow Scholarships; Captain Anthony D. [5133]
Sessa Scholarships for Continuing Professional Education; Frank B. [1638]
Seton Hall Law School's Merit Scholarship Program [6298]
Seton Hall University School of Law **[6297]**
Seymour Scholarships; Hubert K. [5255]
Shacochis Scholarships; Barbara A. [5611]
Shafer Memorial Scholarships; Elizabeth [5856]
SHAFR Dissertation Completion Fellowships [6459]
Shamberg Scholarships [7353]
Shamsie Scholarships; Judge Terry [2287]
Shandor Memorial Ukrainian American Bar Association Scholarships; The Ivan [7360]
Shanley Memorial Scholarships; John M. and Mary A. [6673]
Shannon American Council on Exercise Certification Scholarships; William [501]
Shannon Fellowships; William H. [3916]
Shanower Scholarships; Commander Dan F. [5134]
Sharkey Family Scholarship Fund; Ken and Sandy [3306]
Shattuck Scholarship; W.L. [3650]
Shatz Scholarships; Benjamin G. [5612]
Shaw Fellowships; Anne [6879]
Shaw Scholarship; Dr. Robert Norman [183]
Shaw Scholarships; Dr. Robert and Anna [184]
Shearn Scholarships; Regina B. [256]
Sheehan Memorial Educational Scholarships; Dezna C. [5080]
Sheerin Scholarships; Jim [4426]
Sheet Metal And Air Conditioning Contractors' National Association **[6299]**
Shelah Scholarships; Nettie and Edward [6785]
Shell Incentive Scholarships Fund [6302]
Shell Oil Company **[6301]**
Shell Process Technology Scholarships [6303]
Shell Technical Scholarships [6304]
Shelton Scholarships; Bruce [7455]
Shepard Scholarships; Matthew [6138]
Sheperd Legal Scholarships Fund; Bill and Ann [2892]
Shepherd Scholarships; Joseph Henry [7126]
Sheppard Leadership Awards; Robert P. [5072]
Sheridan Canadian Research Awards; David S. [1918]
Shervin Tehranchi Wrestling Scholarships [6008]
Sherwood Family Fund Education Scholarships; Marion A. And Ruth [3307]
Sherwood Family Fund Engineering Scholarships; Marion A. and Ruth K. [3308]
Sherwood Family Scholarship Fund; Miller G. [3309]
Shields-Gillespie Scholarships [742]
Shien and Judy Young Scholarships; Drs. Poh [7013]
Shifman Endowed Scholarships; Milton L. [4301]
Shimp Memorial Scholarships; Everett Oscar [5519]
Shimp Memorial Scholarships; Pat [5520]
The Shincho Graduate Fellowships for Study in Japan [4060]
Shinn Alumni-Vocational Scholarships; Ethel [4216]
Shipley Memorial Scholarships; Jason [4976]
Shirey Scholarships; Clair [4382]
Shoals Home Builders Association Scholarships [5302]
Shoop Scholarships; Misty and Sally [1679]
Shoreline Community College Academic Excellence Scholarships for Graduating High School Seniors [6320]
Shoreline Community College Academic Improvement Scholarships for Graduating High School Seniors [6321]
Shoreline Community College Continuing Students Scholarships [6322]
Shoreline Community College Foundation **[6305]**
Shoreline Community College Part-Time Students Scholarships [6323]
Short-term senior fellowships in Iranian Studies [665]
SHOT-NASA Fellowships [6463]
Shown Scholarships; Tom [7456]
Shrader Diversity Scholarships; Ralph W. [1248]
SHRM Certification Scholarships - Individual [6444]
SHRM Foundation Regional Academic Scholarships [6445]
Shykes Memorial Scholarships; Phil [2793]
Sibley Fellowships; Mary Isabel [5623]
Sickafoose Educational Trust; Don and Madalyn [6752]
Sickle Cell Disease Association of America **[6326]**
Siegel Research Scholar Grants; Norman [1019]
Siegel Scholarships; Jeff [5191]
Siegfried, MD and Michael Vigilante, MD Scholarships; Myrtle [3139]
Siemens Clinical Advancement Scholarship Program [1043]
Siemens Foundation **[6329]**
Siemens Teacher Scholarships [6330]
Sierleja Memorial Fellowships; E.J. [3739]
Sierra Student Coalition **[6331]**
Sig Memorial Scholarships [19]
Sigma Delta Chi Foundation **[6336]**
Sigma Delta Epsilon Fellowships [6342]
Sigma Delta Epsilon, Graduate Women in Science **[6338]**
Sigma Diagnostics Student Scholarships [5081]
Sigma Kappa Foundation **[6343]**
Sigma Kappa Foundation Alumnae Continuing Education Scholarships [6369]
Sigma Kappa Foundation Alzheimer's/Gerontology Scholarships [6370]
Sigma Kappa Foundation Founders' Scholarships [6371]
Sigma Kappa Foundation Gerontology Scholarships [6372]
Sigma Kappa Foundation Michigan Scholarships [6373]
Sigma Pi Sigma Undergraduate Research Awards [6543]
Sigma Theta Tau International Honor Society of Nursing **[6382]**
Sigma Theta Tau International Scholarships [2014]
Silicon Valley Community Foundation **[6384]**
Silver Nugget Family Scholarships [5857]
Silver Nugget Gaming Ambassadors Scholarships [5858]
Silver Scholarships; S.H. [3198]
Silverman Scholarships; Meyer and Dorothy [2446]
Silverman Scholarships; Stuart [5613]
Simmons Memorial Scholarships; Harvey L. [6230]
Simmons Sr. Memorial Scholarships; Williard B. [4815]
Simms Nursing Scholarship; Hazel [4143]
Simms Science Scholarships; Julia Viola [1742]
Simon Youth Foundation **[6398]**
Simon Youth Foundation Community Scholarships [6400]
Simonton Windows Scholarship Fund [5521]
Simpson Actuarial Science Scholarship Program; DW [6402]
Simpson; Bro. Dr. Frank T. [3497]
Simpson Global Actuarial Recruitment; DW **[6401]**
Simpson Memorial Scholarships; John R. [1680]
Simpson Scholarships; Carole [1403]
Sims Memorial Scholarships; Ward [4383]
SINFONIA Educational Foundation **[6403]**
Singleton Memorial Scholarships; Aaron B. [5303]
Sino-American Pharmaceutical Professionals Association **[6407]**
Sioussat/Fay Wells Scholarships; Helen J. [1786]
Sivertsen Scholarships; Wiggsy [6139]
Six Memorial Scholarship Fund; Bill [5522]
Six Meter Club of Chicago Scholarships [855]
Sjarif Memorial Scholarships; Rajadi [6009]
Sjogrens Syndrome Foundation **[6409]**
Skeeles Memorial Scholarship Fund; R. [6753]
Skinner Memorial Scholarship; Francelene [4230]
SLA Scholarships [6684]
Slagle Memorial Scholarships; Allogan [1357]
Sledge Fellowships [242]
Sleichter and Frances F. Sleichter Memorial Schol-

arship Fund; J. Ward [3119]
Sloan Northwood Heavy-Duty Scholarships [1547]
Slocum Memorial Scholarships to Westwood College of Aviation Technology; Thomas J. [84]
Slom Scholarships; The Aaron and Rita [6892]
SMACNA College of Fellows Scholarships [6300]
Small Cash Grants [929]
Small Station Training Scholarships [2544]
SME Coal and Energy Division Scholarships [6516]
SME Directors Scholarships [6502]
SME Education Foundation Family Scholarships [6503]
SME Environmental Division Scholarships [6517]
SME Ford PAS Scholarships [6504]
SMFM/AAOGF Scholarship Award [6512]
Smiley Elementary School PTA - Beverly Roberts Memorial Scholarships [6010]
Smith Bursary; Eva [4004]
Smith Greater Los Angeles Women's Council Scholarships; Gladys Ann [5142]
Smith Memorial Scholarship Awards; Charles [1321]
Smith Memorial Scholarship; Drew [2384]
Smith Memorial Scholarship Fund; Tacy Ana [3076]
Smith Memorial Scholarships; Colonel Nate [4437]
Smith Memorial Scholarships; James George [1681]
Smith Rector Scholarships; Mary K. [5523]
Smith Research Dissemination Support Grants; Nila Banton [3891]
Smith-Reynolds Founder Fellowships [3540]
Smith, R.N. Memorial Scholarship; The Eileen J. [3988]
Smith Scholarship; Brian [1773]
Smith Scholarship; Esther M. [2385]
Smith Scholarship Fund; Ralph and Josephine [2976]
Smith Scholarship; Helen J. and Harold Gilman [1631]
Smith Scholarship for Teaching Students; Lillian [7036]
Smith Scholarships; A.O. [5705]
Smith Scholarships; Herman J. [4942]
Smith Scholarships; Joseph Sumner [6955]
Smith Scholarships; Marian A. [6634]
Smith Scholarships; Richard S. [6968]
Smith/Society of Professional Journalists Scholarships; Drue [2447]
Smiths Medical Canada Ltd. Research Awards [1919]
Smith's Personal Best Scholarships [5859]
Snauble Scholarships; Gladys [3348]
SNF Professional Growth Scholarships [6259]
SNMTS Bachelor's Degree Completion Scholarships [6523]
SNMTS Clinical Advancement Scholarships [6524]
Snodgrass Scholarships [4384]
Snow Memorial Scholarships; Helen D. [5626]
Snow Memorial Scholarships; Ray [4947]
Snow Scholarships; A.C. [7192]
Snowmobile Association of Massachusetts **[6412]**
Snowmobile Association of Massachusetts Scholarships [6413]
Snyder Memorial Scholarships; Stuart H. [1561]
Social Science Research Council **[6414]**
Social Sciences and Humanities Research Council of Canada **[6417]**
Social Sciences and Humanities Research Council of Canada Standard Research Grants [6420]
Social Work Scholarships [5778]
Society of Allied Weight Engineers **[6422]**
Society of Architectural Historians **[6425]**
Society of Automotive Analyst Scholarships [1562]
Society for Canadian Women in Science and Technology **[6430]**
Society of Dance History Scholars **[6436]**
Society for Economic Botany **[6438]**
Society of Exploration Geophysicists **[6440]**
Society of Exploration Geophysicists Foundation Scholarships [6441]
Society For Human Resource Management **[6442]**
Society of Georgia Archivists **[6446]**
Society for Historians of American Foreign Relations **[6451]**
Society for the History of Technology **[6460]**
Society for Judgment and Decision Making **[6464]**
Society of Louisiana Certified Public Accountants **[6467]**
Society of Louisiana Certified Public Accountants Scholarships [6468]
Society of Manufacturing Engineers Education Foundation **[6469]**
Society of Marine Port Engineers **[6509]**
Society of Marine Port Engineers Scholarship Loans [6510]
Society for the Maternal-Fetal Medicine **[6511]**
Society for Military History **[6513]**
Society for Mining, Metallurgy and Exploration **[6515]**
Society of Naval Architects and Marine Engineers **[6518]**
Society of Naval Architects and Marine Engineers Undergraduate Scholarships [6520]
Society of Nuclear Medicine **[6521]**
Society Of Broadcast Engineers **[6525]**
Society of Pediatric Nurses **[6529]**
Society of Pediatric Nurses Educational Scholarship [6530]
Society of Pediatric Psychology **[6531]**
Society for Pediatric Radiology **[6534]**
Society for Pediatric Radiology Research Fellows [6535]
Society for Pediatric Radiology Seed Grants [6536]
Society for Pediatric Urology **[6537]**
Society for Pediatric Urology Research Grant Program [6539]
Society of Physics Students **[6540]**
Society of Plastics Engineers **[6546]**
Society of Plastics Engineers General Scholarships [6559]
Society of Plastics Engineers Pittsburgh Scholarships [6560]
Society for the Preservation of Old Mills **[6565]**
Society of Professional Journalists **[6567]**
Society for the Psychological Study of Lesbian, Gay and Bisexual Issues **[6571]**
Society for the Psychological Study for Social Issues **[6574]**
Society for Range Management **[6577]**
Society of Satellite Professionals International **[6579]**
Society for the Scientific Study of Sexuality **[6586]**
Society for the Scientific Study of Sexuality Student Research Grants [6587]
Society of University of Surgeons **[6588]**
Society of Women Engineers **[6591]**
Society of Women Engineers Scholarships [6592]
Sokol USA **[6593]**
Sola Scholarships; Dale and Betty George [2794]
Solid Waste Association of North America **[6595]**
Somers Scholarship Trust; Carin Alma E. [1534]
Sonoda Memorial Scholarships; Dr. Kiyoshi [4021]
Sons of Confederate Veterans **[6600]**
Sons of Norway Foundation **[6602]**
Sons of Norway Foundation Scholarships to Oslo International School [6604]
Sons of Union Veterans of the Civil War **[6605]**
Sony Pictures Scholarships [1471]
Soper Scholarships; Christine [3349]
Soroptimist International of Chambersburg Scholarship Fund [3120]
Soroptimist International of Redlands Scholarships [6011]
Sorrentino Memorial Scholarships; Lily and Catello [6042]
Sourdough Reunion Memorial Scholarships [4385]
South Asian Journalists Association **[6607]**
South Carolina Association for Financial Professionals **[6609]**
South Carolina Association for Financial Professionals Certified Treasury Professional Scholarships [6610]
South Carolina Association for Financial Professionals College Education Scholarships [6611]
South Carolina Public Health Association **[6612]**
South Carolina Public Health Association Scholarships [6614]
South Carolina Scholastic Press Association **[6615]**
South Carolina Tourism and Hospitality Educational Foundation Scholarships [3618]
South Carolina Undergraduate Scholarships [3619]
South Central Power Company **[6619]**
South Central Power Scholarships [6620]
South Coast Area High School Senior Honors Scholarship Program [6253]
South Dakota Division Scholarships [4520]
South Jersey Golf Association **[6622]**
South Jersey Golf Association Scholarships [6623]
South Kentucky RECC High School Senior Scholarships [6626]
South Kentucky Rural Electric Cooperative Corporation **[6624]**
South Texas Lighthouse for the Blind Scholarships [2288]
South Texas Unit Scholarships [3546]
Southall Nursing Scholarships; Anna Doris [6848]
Southeast Aerospace Inc. Scholarships [85]
Southeast Member Chapter Scholarships [1457]
Southeastern Library Association **[6628]**
Southeastern Theatre Conference **[6630]**
Southeastern Theatre Conference Secondary School Scholarships [6635]
Southern Nevada Sports Hall of Fame Athletic Scholarships [5860]
Southern Scholarship Foundation **[6637]**
Southern Scholarship Foundation Scholarships [6638]
Southwest Chapter Roy Kinslow Scholarships [1070]
Southwest Florida Community Foundation **[6639]**
Southwest Florida Community Foundation College Assistance Scholarships [6674]
Sovereign Nations Scholarship Fund [625]
Sowers Memorial Scholarships; Master Sergeant William [60]
Spackman Scholarship Program; Willard and [736]
Spadoni Memorial Scholarships; Kathy [5779]
Spain Memorial Scholarships; Amy E. [7127]
Spanish Embassy Scholarships [5267]
Sparks Memorial Scholarship; Nathan [2364]
Spartan Scholarship Awards [3843]
Spartan Staff Scholarships [5861]
Special Law School Scholarships [5614]
Special Libraries Association **[6679]**
Specialized Carriers and Rigging Association **[6685]**
Specialty Equipment Market Association **[6688]**
Specialty Equipment Market Association Scholarships [6690]
Specialty Nursing Scholarships [3132]
Speckhard Scholarships; Faith [3989]
Spence Scholarships; Beatrice Drinnan [2814]
Spencer Foundation **[6691]**
Spencer Foundation Dissertation Fellowship Program [6692]
Spencer Foundation Research Grants [6693]
Spice Box Grants [532]
SPIE (The International Society for Optical Engineering) **[6694]**
Spiegel Remembrance Scholarships; Lawrence Alan [3611]
Spielman Memorial Scholarship Program; Patrick [6290]
Spina Bifida Association of America **[6701]**
Spirit of Allison Graduation Award [2986]
The Spirit Square Center for Arts and Education Scholarship Fund [3077]
SPOOM Research Grants [6566]
Sporty's Pilot Shop/Cincinnati Avionics Scholarships [86]
Spouse Tuition Aids Program [5148]
SPPSI Grants-In-Aid Program [6576]
Sprague Scholarships; Dr. William E. & Norma [3350]
Spring Internship in International NGO Law [3825]
Springer Memorial Scholarships; Jim [2289]
Springfield Scholarships; James F. and Donna [7128]
SPS Future Teacher Scholarships [6544]
SPS Leadership Scholarships [6545]
SPSmedical CS Scholarships [3802]
SRF Post-doctoral Fellowships [6282]
SSC-Building Environmental Campus Community (BECC) Fellowships [6334]
SSF Research Grants [6410]
SSF Student Fellowships [6411]
SSHRC Doctoral Fellowships Program [6421]
The SSPI Mid-Atlantic Chapter Scholarships [6583]
The SSPI Northeast Chapter Scholarships [6584]
The SSPI Southern California Scholarships [6585]

Stachowiak Memorial Scholarship; Ernest and Charlene [2489]
Stager Memorial Scholarship Fund; Matt [7390]
Stahl Research Grants; Steven A. [3892]
Stainsby Awards; Peter [1973]
The Standard Scholarships [5646]
Stanfield Art Scholarships; Marion Barr [6956]
Stanfield Law Scholarships; Otto M. [6957]
Stanford Scholarship; H.T. and Terrell [2365]
Stanford University Knight Fellowships **[6704]**
Stanley Memorial Scholarships; Ken [4253]
Stanley Tribal Scholars Program; Morgan [626]
Star-Ledger Scholarships for the Performing Arts [5178]
Stark Community Foundation **[6706]**
Stark County Bar Association Fund [6754]
Stark County Dairy Promoters Scholarships [6755]
Starr Foundation Graduate Fellowship in Asian Studies [7094]
State of Idaho Scholarships Category A [4217]
Staton Scholarships; Robert W. and Bernice Ingalls [7202]
Stauffer Memorial Scholarships; Matt [2131]
Staupers National Scholarship Award; The Mabel Keaton [2115]
Stayman Scholarships; Minnie Patton [5566]
Stearman Awards; The Stanley H. [5048]
Stearns/SCS Engineers Awards; Robert P. [6598]
Stears Education Scholarships; Sheri [7037]
Steele Entrance Awards; Harry [6276]
Steele Music Scholarship Fund; Joseph L. and Vivian E. [3121]
Stefani After-the-Fires Scholarships; Gwen [6231]
Steinberg Scholarship; Mireille and Murray [3562]
Steinhauer Awards of Distinction; Ralph [185]
Steinwedell Scholarships; Peter T. [3498]
Stene/Xi Scholarships; Elin J. [6374]
Step Up Scholarships [6232]
Stephenson Oxford Cup Scholarships; H. Hiram [1682]
Stephenson Oxford Cup Scholarships; Hugh E. [1683]
Stephenson Scholarships; Elizabeth Coulter [2699]
Steuben County Community Foundation **[6765]**
Stevens Memorial Scholarships; Zachary Taylor [856]
Stevenson Scholarships; Richie [2448]
Stewart Scholarships; The Dan [5240]
Stewart Scholarships; Nancy [1089]
Stewart Title Firefighters Scholarships [2290]
Stewart and William T. Covington, Jr. Scholarship Fund; Mary [3078]
Stickler Involved People **[6786]**
Stickler Scholarships; Dr. Gunnar B. [6787]
Still Photographer Scholarships [5021]
Stillman Scholarships; Walter W. [1563]
Stone Graduate Fellowships; Ralph W. [5090]
Stone Scholarships; Charles H. [413]
Stoner Memorial Scholarships; James E. [1417]
Stonewall Community Foundation **[6788]**
Stop Hunger Scholarships [398]
Stout Scholarships; Martin L. [1410]
StraightForward Media **[6792]**
StraightForward Media's Art School Scholarships [6795]
StraightForward Media's Business School Scholarships [6796]
StraightForward Media's Engineering Scholarships [6797]
StraightForward Media's Law Enforcement Scholarships [6798]
StraightForward Media's Law School Scholarships [6799]
StraightForward Media's Liberal Arts Scholarships [6800]
StraightForward Media's Media and Communications Scholarships [6801]
StraightForward Media's Medical Professions Scholarships [6802]
StraightForward Media's Minority Scholarships [6803]
StraightForward Media's Nursing School Scholarships [6804]
StraightForward Media's Science Scholarships [6805]
StraightForward Media's Teacher Scholarships [6806]
StraightForward Media's Vocational-Technical School Scholarships [6807]
Strangio Education Scholarships; Bonnie [2591]
Strauss Scholarships; Donald A. [7088]
Streeter, KB9JBR Scholarships; Carole J. [857]
Streiff Memorial Scholarships; John [4218]
Streit Golf Scholarships; Marlene [6077]
Strew Educational Fund Scholarship; Stanley W. [1812]
Striving for Success Scholarships [5862]
Strohmeier, W2VRS Memorial Scholarships; Norman E. [858]
Stryker Diversity Scholarship Program; Fraser [5166]
Stryker Diversity Scholarships; Fraser [6809]
Stryker; Fraser **[6808]**
Stubbs Research Grants; E.L. [4507]
Student Media Group Scholarships [5647]
Student Osteopathic Medical Association **[6810]**
Student Osteopathic Medical Student Fellowships and Research [6812]
Student Research Grants [2083]
Student Research Grants in Audiology [1107]
Student Research Grants in Early Childhood Language Development [1108]
Student Travel Grants [6700]
Study Scholarships for Artists or Musicians [3230]
Stufano Garden Conservancy Fellowships; Marco Polo [3161]
Stultz Scholarships [7457]
Stunkard Scholarships; Horace W. [4302]
Sturgulewski Family Scholarships [7038]
Sturrock Nursing Scholarships; Anne [6675]
Suarez Journalism Scholarships; Leo [2601]
Subic Bay-Cubi Point 1 Scholarships [5143]
Suchecki Family Scholarship Fund; Edward P. [3310]
Suicide Prevention Action Network USA **[6814]**
Sullivan Scholarships; John A. [2795]
Sullivan Scholarships; Phil [5780]
Sullivan Scholarships; VPPPA William [7339]
Sullivan Scholarships; William A. [5144]
Summer Intern Scholarships in Cardiothoracic Surgery [420]
Summer Language Study Grants in Turkey [3758]
Summer Research Diversity Fellowships in Law and Social Science [435]
Summer Research Grants in Turkey [3759]
Summerside-Natick Hockey Scholarships [2501]
Sumners Scholarships; Hatton W. [5331]
Sun Country Amateur Golf Association **[6816]**
Sun Country Amateur Golf Association Scholarships [6817]
Sun Life Financial Peer Support Scholarships [2025]
Sundlun Scholarships; Bruce and Marjorie [6043]
Sunshine Lady Foundation **[6818]**
Superior District Legislative Mentoring Student Grants [1856]
Superior District Legislative Mentoring Student Grants RT to DC [1857]
Supreme Council, Ancient Accepted Scottish Rite of Free-Masonry **[6821]**
Surety and Fidelity Association of America **[6823]**
Surety Industry Scholarship Program for Minority Students [6824]
Surface Officer Spouses **[6825]**
Surgeon Scientist Career Development Awards [603]
Survival Scholarship Program [7514]
SUS Foundation Junior Faculty Grants [6589]
SUS - Wyeth Clinical Scholar Award [6590]
Sussman-Miller Educational Assistance Award Program [195]
Sutherland/Purdy Scholarships [5682]
Sutlive Scholarships; Kirk [3217]
Sutton Foundation; Michael Bendix [4934]
SUVCW Scholarships [6606]
Svec Scholarships; Margaret [6324]
Swain Scholarships; Lorraine E. [6375]
Swanson Memorial Scholarships; Swede [5162]
Swarovski and Company Scholarships; Daniel [3199]
Swartz Family Scholarship Fund; Henry D. and Ruth G. [3311]
Sweeny Scholarships; Hugh B. [4040]
Sweitzer Wrestling Memorial Scholarship Fund; Jeffery Tyler [6756]
Sweterlitsch Memorial Scholarship Fund; Timothy S. [6757]
SWFL Deputy Sheriffs Association Fund Scholarships [6676]
SWFL Professional Golfers Association Scholarships [6677]
Swiss Benevolent Society of New York **[6827]**
Swivel Media Scholarships [5648]
Sycamore Scholar Awards [3713]
Taback 9/11 Memorial Scholarships; Harry [1071]
Tabakoglu Scholarship Fund; Hazaros [1291]
The Tabat Scholarship Fund [2922]
TAC Foundation-3M Canada Company [6898]
TAC Foundation-Albert M. Stevens Scholarships [6899]
TAC Foundation-Armtec Scholarships [6900]
TAC Foundation-BA Group Scholarships [6901]
TAC Foundation-Cement Association of Canada Scholarships [6902]
TAC Foundation-Delcan Corporation Scholarships [6903]
TAC Foundation-Dillon Consulting Scholarships [6904]
TAC Foundation-EBA Engineering Consultants Ltd. Scholarships [6905]
TAC Foundation-IBI Group Scholarships [6906]
TAC Foundation-iTRANS Consulting Scholarships [6907]
TAC Foundation-McCormick Rankin Corporation Scholarships [6908]
TAC Foundation-MMM Group Limited Scholarships [6909]
TAC Foundation-Municipalities Scholarships [6910]
TAC Foundation-Provinces and Territories Scholarships [6911]
TAC Foundation Scholarships [6912]
TAC Foundation-Stantec Consulting Scholarships [6913]
TAC Foundation-UMA Engineering Ltd. Scholarships [6914]
TAC Foundation-Waterloo Alumni Scholarships [6915]
The Tacoma Athletic Commission Scholarships [3379]
Taeni Scholarships; John I. and Madeleine R. [6678]
Tag and Label Manufacturers Institute **[6832]**
Tagged for Greatness Scholarships [116]
Tailhook Association **[6835]**
Tailhook Educational Foundation Scholarships Program [6836]
Taiwanese American Citizens League **[6837]**
Taiwanese American Community Scholarships [6838]
Takemoto Memorial Scholarships; Kei [87]
Talbert Family Memorial Accounting Scholarships [2291]
Tall Awareness Scholarships [5863]
Tall Clubs International **[6839]**
Tall Clubs International Student Scholarships [6840]
Tanana Valley Campus **[6841]**
Tanana Valley Campus Culinary Arts Scholarships [6849]
Tanger Scholarships; Alexander M. [1787]
Tangye Scholarships; William J. [3831]
Tanner Jr. Scholarships; Hal [7193]
Tarbox Memorial Scholarships; Lee [88]
Targeted Research Initiative for Health Outcomes [2875]
Targeted Research Initiative for Mood Disorders [2876]
Targeted Research Initiative for Seniors [2877]
Tarr-Smith Memorial Scholarships; Sheila [5864]
Tarrson Fellowships; Bud and Linda [288]
Tarrson Regeneration Scholarships [289]
Tart Student Incentive Awards; Charles T. and Judith A. [5458]
Tate/ThinkCOLLEGE Scholarship Fund; Jack [3079]
Tatter Scholarships; Jordan B. [4490]
Taylor/Blakeslee University Fellowships [2548]
Taylor Endowed Law Scholarships; Charles "Buck" and Dora [2767]
Taylor Memorial Scholarships; Ryan "Munchie" [4270]

Taylor Memorial Scholarships to Spartan College of Aeronautics and Technology; Tom [89]
Taylor Statten Memorial Fellowships [7233]
TCA-BAACBH Scholarships [6938]
TCA Turkish American Scholarships [6939]
TCA-UMD Scholarships [6940]
TCATA College Scholarship Program [6875]
TDC Scholarship Program [4659]
TEACH Scholarships [5865]
Team DC Student-Athlete Scholarships [6140]
Technical Women's Organization **[6850]**
Technology Student Association **[6852]**
Teget Leadership Scholarships; Marvin H. and Kathleen G. [6813]
Tejada Memorial Scholarship; Paul [3990]
Telamon Scholarships [7014]
Telecommunications Association of Michigan **[6855]**
Telecommunications Association of Michigan Scholarship Fund [6856]
Television News Scholarships [5022]
Telford Scholarships [20]
Telluride Association **[6857]**
Telluride Association Summer Program Scholarships [6858]
Tennessee Bar Foundation IOLTA Law School Scholarships [7129]
Tennessee Board of Regents Law Scholarships [7130]
Tennessee Trucking Association Scholarships [2449]
Terrell/New Haven Savings Bank Scholarship Fund; Charles L. [2396]
Texas Association of Developing Colleges **[6859]**
Texas Music Educators Association **[6861]**
Texas Music Educators Association Past-Presidents Memorial Scholarships [6863]
Texas Mutual Insurance Company **[6864]**
Texas Mutual Scholarship Program [6865]
Texas Scottish Rite Hospital for Children **[6866]**
Texas Society of Professional Engineers **[6868]**
Texas Society of Professional Engineers Scholarships [6869]
Texas State Technical College Scholarships [90]
Texas State University - San Marcos Development Foundation **[6870]**
Texas Telephone Association **[6872]**
Texas Telephone Association Foundation Scholarships [6873]
Texas Transportation Scholarships [6921]
Textile Care Allied Trades Association **[6874]**
Thacker Sports Communication Internships; Jim and Pat [7194]
Thakrar Family Fund; Anil and Neema [3122]
ThanksUSA **[6876]**
ThanksUSA Scholarships [6877]
Thaxton Justice Fund; The Rodney [2602]
Theatre for Young Audiences/USA **[6878]**
Theodos Memorial Graduate Scholarships; Dr. Peter A. [3535]
Thermo Scientific Educational Scholarships [5082]
Thermoforming Scholarships [6561]
Thermoplastic Materials and Foams Division Scholarships [6562]
Thermoplastics Elastomers Special Interest Group Scholarships [6563]
Theta/Caryl Cordis D'hondt Scholarships [6376]
Theta Tau Scholarships [6377]
Third Wave Foundation **[6880]**
Thomas Bursary; Barbara [4005]
Thomas Fellowships; Douglas Dockery [4128]
Thomas Post Doctoral Fellowships; E.D. [3145]
Thomas Scholarship Program; Ralph and Valerie [4660]
Thomas Scholarships; Barber Owen [6378]
Thomas Scholarships; C.R. [5524]
Thomas Scholarships; Dorothy B. & Charles E. [3351]
Thomas Scholarships; Elizabeth [6325]
Thomas Scholarships; Rev. Chuck and Nancy [6958]
Thompson Endowed Scholarships; Honorable Raymond [5615]
Thompson Memorial Scholarships; Madlyn D. [1900]
Thompson Scholarship; Barbara and Howard [3991]
Thompson Scholarship for Women in Safety [1072]
Thomson Foundation Scholarships; Miller [4537]
Thomson Scholarships; Ken [2048]
Thomson Scientific/MLA Doctoral Fellowships [4448]
Thornberg/Havens Scholarships [2700]
Thrivent Financial Scholarships [5649]
Thunder Bay Community Foundation **[6882]**
Thurston Graduate Scholarships; Dorothy J. [3352]
Thyssen-Heideking Fellowships [3236]
Tice Scholarships I; Raymond A. [6233]
Tice Scholarships II; Raymond A. [6234]
Tidewater Builders Association **[6889]**
Tidewater Builders Association Scholarships [6890]
Tillson Scholarships; Jack E. [3932]
Time Warner Point Scholarships [5727]
Time Warner Tribal Scholars Program [627]
Tiner Education Scholarships; Mark P. [5368]
Tisdale Fellowships; Eben [3148]
TLMI Scholarships - Four-Year Colleges [6833]
TLMI Scholarships - Two-Year Colleges [6834]
TMCF Scholarships [4316]
Tobias Scholarships; Star and Barry [2104]
Tocco Hydrocephalus Foundation Scholarships; Mario J. [3639]
Todd and Clauda Pennock Todd Tripod Scholarships; Richard Cecil [5655]
Toennis Scholarships; Michael W. [1684]
Togiak Village Scholarships [4386]
Tomash Fellowships; The Adelle and Erwin [1584]
Tomasovic, Sr. Scholarships; John [568]
Tomato Fest Scholarship Grants [533]
Tomlin Memorial Scholarship Program; Travis C. [4661]
Torokvei Foundation Scholarships; Evald [7234]
Torossian Memorial Scholarships; Aram [1292]
Touchstone Special Achievement Scholarships [6621]
Touro Synagogue Foundation **[6891]**
Towle Environmental Studies Fund; Judith A. [3966]
Town and County Club Scholarships [3499]
Towner Fund for Gay and Lesbian Families; Joseph [6141]
Townsend Scholarships; Charles A. [5525]
Toyota Community Scholars [6894]
Toyota High School Scholarship Program [3603]
Toyota Motor Sales **[6893]**
Tracy Fellowships; The Joyce [308]
Traditional Student Scholarships [2510]
TRALA Scholarships Program [6924]
Tran Memorial Scholarships; Vera [7324]
Trane Scholarships; Reuben [970]
Transfer Engineering Student Awards [4058]
Transgender Scholarships and Education Legacy Fund [6142]
Transport Workers Union of America **[6895]**
Transportation Association of Canada **[6897]**
Transportation Clubs International **[6916]**
Traub-Dicker Rainbow Scholarships [6790]
Travel Grants for Women Researchers [1516]
Trelut Family Legacy Scholarships [1834]
Tremaine Fellowships; Marie [1699]
Tribal Business Management Program (TBM) Scholarships [2069]
Tribal Priority Scholarships [1212]
Trillion Diamond Company Scholarships [3200]
Trimble Endowed Scholarships; Thomas and Glenna [5616]
Triner Letter Carriers Scholarship Fund; Tim [6758]
Trinkaus Endowed Scholarships in Embryology; J.P. Madeline [4303]
Tropicana Community Services - Robert K. Brown Scholarships [1743]
Troske Music Scholarships; Mildred E. [3353]
Trotter Health Care Scholarships; Vincent [6235]
Trotters's Culinary Education Foundation Culinary Study Scholarships; Charlie [2582]
Trow Scholarships; Jo Anne J. [4635]
Troy University Rodeo Team Scholarships [117]
Truck Renting and Leasing Association **[6923]**
Truckload Carriers Association **[6925]**
Truckload Carriers Association Scholarships [6926]
Trudeau Foundation Doctoral Scholarships [6928]
Trudeau Foundation; Pierre Elliott **[6927]**
True North Land Surveying Scholarships [5781]
Truman Scholarship Foundation; The Harry S. **[6929]**
Truman Scholarships; Harry S. [6930]
Truss Plate Institute **[6931]**
Truss Plate Institute Scholarships [6932]
Trustee, Schawe, Presidential and Honor Scholarships [7533]
Trustee Scholarships [4068]
Trustees College Scholarships [4273]
Trustees Law School Scholarships [4274]
TRW Foundation Scholarships [1564]
TSA Teach Technology Scholarships [6854]
Tschantz/Walter C. Deuble Scholarships; Norman J. [6759]
Tschudy Family Scholarships [4219]
Tsutako Curo Scholarships [5866]
Tucker Family Scholarships [7195]
Tuckfield Memorial Graduate Business Scholarship Fund; Jacki [2603]
Tuckwell Scholarships; Barry [3870]
Tufenkian Memorial Scholarships; Richard R. [1253]
Tughan Scholarships; Sam [2031]
Tuinier Memorial Scholarships; Edward [569]
Tunxis Community College Foundation Scholarships [3500]
Turf and Ornamental Communicators Association **[6933]**
Turf and Ornamental Communicators Association Scholarship Program [6934]
Turkish Coalition of America **[6935]**
Turner Family Scholarship Fund [3080]
Turner-Forsyth Audubon Society Scholarships; Jeff [7458]
Turner, Jr. Memorial Scholarships; James A. [1173]
Turner Legal Association; J.L. **[6941]**
Turner Memorial Scholarship; Mark and Vera [4231]
Turner Scholarships; Emmett H. [2450]
Turpin Scholar Fund; Ira G. [6760]
Tuscumbia Kiwanis Scholarships [5304]
Tuttle, USN (Ret.) and Mrs. Barbara A. Tuttle Science and Technology Scholarships; Vice Adm. Jerry O. [1249]
TU@UT HSF College Scholarship Program [3604]
TWO Scholarship Program [6851]
Two Year/Community Broadcast Education Association Scholarships Award [1788]
TYLENOL Scholarships [4561]
UAA Accounting Club Scholarships [7039]
UAA Alaska Kidney Foundation Scholarships [7040]
UAA Alumni Association Scholarships [7041]
UAA Anchorage Daily News Minority Journalism Scholarships [7042]
UAA April Relyea Scholarships [7043]
UAA Ardell French Memorial Scholarships [7044]
UAA Brown Schoenheit Memorial Scholarships [7045]
UAA Chris L. Kleinke Scholarships [7046]
UAA College of Business & Public Policy Scholarships [7047]
UAA Diane Olsen Memorial Scholarships [7048]
UAA Dr. Jon Baker Memorial Scholarships [7049]
UAA Edward Rollin Clinton Memorial for Music [7050]
UAA Elaine Atwood Scholarships [7051]
UAA Emi Chance Memorial Scholarships [7052]
UAA Eveline Schuster Memorial Award/Scholarships [7053]
UAA Friends of the Performing Arts Scholarships [7054]
UAA GCI, Inc. Scholarships [7055]
UAA Governor William A. Egan Scholarships [7056]
UAA Jack & Martha Roderick Scholarships [7057]
UAA Jan & Glenn Fredericks Scholarships [7058]
UAA Ken Gray Endowment Scholarships [7059]
UAA Kimura Scholarship Fund (Photography Scholarships) [7060]
UAA Kimura Scholarship Funds (Illustration Scholarships) [7061]
UAA Kris Knudson Memorial Scholarships [7062]
UAA Mark A. Beltz Scholarships [7063]
UAA Melissa J. Wolf Scholarships [7064]
UAA Michael Baring-Gould Memorial Scholarships [7065]
UAA Michael D. Ford Memorial Scholarships [7066]
UAA Muriel Hannah Scholarships in Art [7067]
UAA Pat Brakke Political Science Scholarships [7068]
UAA Paul G. Landis Scholarships [7069]
UAA Pignalberi Public Policy Scholarships [7070]
UAA Quanterra Scholarships [7071]
UAA RRANN Program Scholarships [7072]

Vineberg Travelling Fellowship in the Humanities; Philip F. [4432]
Vinyl Plastics Division Scholarships [6564]
Violin Society of America **[7325]**
Violin Society of America Scholarships [7326]
Virginia Foundation for Independent Colleges **[7327]**
Virginia Tech Multicultural Programs and Services **[7332]**
The Viscount Bennett Fellowships [1935]
VISTAKON Research Grants [280]
Vogt Oxford Cup Memorial Scholarships; Gupton A. [1685]
Vogt Scholarships; Von Ogden [6959]
The Voice Foundation **[7335]**
Voigt Memorial Scholarships; Irma E. [6379]
Voluntary Protection Programs Participants' Association **[7337]**
Vorheis Memorial Scholarship Program; The Sibyl Jennings [3081]
Voron Scholarships; Abe [1789]
VPPPA June Brothers Scholarships [7340]
VPPPA Stephen Brown Scholarships [7341]
VSP Research Grants [281]
Wachovia Scholarship Awards [3571]
Waddell Scholarships; Frank M. [7237]
Wade Memorial Scholarships for Lesbian, Gay and Bisexual; Bruce [6145]
Wade Scholarship; Robert R. [4232]
Wade Scholarships; Mercedes Laurie [1901]
Wadsworth Memorial Scholarships; Ed [120]
WAEPA Scholarship Program [7520]
Waggoner Scholarships; Nell and Spencer [7459]
Wagner, K3OMI Scholarships; Gary [859]
Wagner Scholarships; Jack H. [4505]
Waksman Endowed Scholarships in Microbial Diversity; Selma A. [4304]
Waldbaum Archaeological Field School Scholarships; Jane C. [1195]
Walden Memorial Fund; Laramie [3082]
Waldron Scholarship Fund; Margaret E. [2977]
Walicki Nursing Scholarship; Sue [3992]
Walker Memorial Scholarships; Gary [3788]
Walker Scholarships; Arthur BC [5060]
Walker Scholarships; Myrtle and Earl [6505]
Wall-Mart Stores, Inc. Fellowships - Graduate [643]
WALPA Lake Scholarships [7382]
Walter Memorial Scholarships; Patty [2329]
Walton Memorial Scholarships; Francis [860]
War Memorial Doctoral Scholarships [4798]
Warfield Scholarships; Alice Glaisyer [6922]
Warner Memorial Scholarships; Judith [5867]
Warner Memorial Scholarships; Rachel [4935]
Warner Norcross & Judd LLP **[7342]**
Warner Norcross & Judd LLP Law School Studies Scholarships [7343]
Warner Scholarships; James L. [5369]
Warren Civil Rights Training Scholarships; Earl [4605]
Warren Legal Training Program; Earl **[7344]**
Warren Scholarship Fund; John R. and Joan F. [6761]
Warren Shearman and Sterling Scholarships; Earl [4606]
Washburn University School of Law **[7346]**
Washington College Bound Scholarships [7366]
Washington County Farm Bureau Scholarships [5394]
The Washington Group **[7355]**
Washington Group International Safety Scholarships [1074]
Washington Higher Education Coordinating Board **[7362]**
Washington Higher Education Coordinating Board Educational Opportunity Grants [7367]
Washington Higher Education Coordinating Board Health Professional Scholarships [7368]
Washington Higher Education Coordinating Board State Need Grants [7369]
Washington Hospital Health Care System **[7370]**
Washington Metropolitan Scholars **[7373]**
Washington Metropolitan Scholarships [7374]
Washington Reciprocity Out-of-State Scholarships [4220]
Washington Scholarship Fund **[7375]**
Washington Scholarship Fund Signature Scholarships Program [7377]
Washington State Business Education Association **[7378]**
Washington State Lake Protection Association **[7381]**
Washington University Law School **[7383]**
Washington University Law School Chancellor's Graduate Fellowships [7386]
Washington University Law School Olin Fellowships for Women [7387]
Wasilewski Scholarships; Vincent T. [1790]
Wasmuth Postdoctoral Fellowships; John J. [3551]
Water and Sewer Distributors of America **[7389]**
Watie Scholarships; Stand [6601]
Watkins Graduate Research Fellowships; Robert D. [1009]
Watson-Brown Foundation **[7391]**
Watson-Brown Scholarships [7392]
Watson, Jr. Memorial Scholarships; Thomas S. [4662]
Watsontown Volunteer Fire Company Scholarships [1902]
The Wax Company Scholarships [121]
Wayne County Bank Scholarships [5305]
Wayne-Meador-Elliott Scholarships [5526]
Wayne Scholarships; Kurt [3201]
Weaver Fellowships; Richard M. [3774]
Weaver Memorial Fund; Monica M. [2978]
Webb Scholarships; Faye and Rendell [2292]
Weber Scholarships; Allen and Loureena [6506]
Weber Scholarships; Art and Dannie [7460]
Webster Charitable Trust Fund; Lester and Eleanor [6762]
Webster Fellowships; Jerome P. [3927]
Webster Society Scholarships [7388]
Weckel Scholarships; Kenneth G. [4523]
Weigand, Jr. Legal Education Trust Scholarships; J.L. [7354]
Weil Memorial Eagle Scout Scholarships; Frank L. [4869]
Weiner Scholarship; Emanuel [3563]
Weingarten Scholarship Program; Edith [737]
Weinstein Scholarship Fund; The Bee Winkler [6791]
Weisel Scholarships; William E. [6507]
Weissbuch Family Scholarships [6239]
Welch Memorial Scholarships; Edward Kent [7461]
Welch Scholars Grants [753]
Weller Memorial Scholarships; Sue Marsh [3695]
Wellnitz Canadian Scholarships; Dorothy [890]
Wells Fargo American Indian Scholarship for Graduates [644]
Wells Fargo Scholarship Program [3608]
Wells Fargo Scholarships [5783]
Wells Scholarships; Donald M. [3356]
Wenglein-Callender Undergraduate Scholarships; Teri [2669]
Weninger Scholarships; Francis X. [7534]
Wert Scholarships; Lucille and Charles A. [4403]
West Indian Migrant Farm Workers Memorial Scholarships [3501]
West Michigan Nursery and Landscape Association Scholarships Fund [3313]
West Virginia Coal Association **[7393]**
West Virginia Congress of Parents and Teachers **[7395]**
West Virginia Educational Foundation Hospitality Business Alliance Scholarships [7399]
West Virginia Hospitality and Travel Association **[7397]**
West Virginia Hospitality and Travel Association General Scholarships [7400]
West Virginia Nurses Association District No. 3 Scholarships [5527]
West Virginia PTA Scholarships [7396]
West Virginia Rural Health Education Partnerships **[7401]**
Westen Scholarships; Redlands Evening Lions Club - Barbara [6012]
Western Civilization Fellowships [3775]
Western Golf Association **[7404]**
Western Governors University Scholarship Program [3609]
Western Michigan Greenhouse Association Scholarships [571]
Western Michigan Society of Health-System Pharmacists **[7406]**
Western Michigan Society of Health-System Pharmacists Scholarships [7407]
Western Reserve Herb Society Scholarships [3547]
Westover Scholarships; Robert B. [3202]
Weyerhaeuser Forest History Fellowships; Frederick K. [3031]
Whalen Memorial Scholarship; Dr. William "Tim" [5259]
Whalley Memorial Scholarships; J. Irving [1566]
Whan Memorial Scholarships [5652]
Wheadon Postgraduate Training Scholarship Fund; Edwyna [4827]
Wheatcraft Scholarships; Haemer [2768]
Wheelchair Success Foundation Scholarships [2293]
Wheeler Scholarship Fund; Seitlin Franklin E. [2604]
Whelan Aviation Scholarships; Paul A. [7083]
Whidbey Island Giving Circle Scholarships [5784]
Whitaker-Minard Memorial Scholarships [5528]
White Endowed Law Scholarships; Brian J. [5617]
White Endowed Scholarships; Howard A. [5618]
White House Correspondents' Association **[7408]**
White House Fellows [5748]
White Memorial Scholarship Fund; Mary Kean [6763]
White Rose Scholarships [6146]
White Scholarships; Bradford [5706]
White Scholarships; Portia [1745]
Whiteman, Jr. Scholarships; Herbert W. [7293]
Whiteside Scholarships; Robert B. and Sophia [2796]
Whitman Scholarships for Perry High School; Ann Cook [2843]
Whitman Washington, DC Scholarships; Ann Cook [2844]
Whitworth Scholarships; Donna Axum [2670]
Whylie Scholarships; Dwight [1746]
Wichard Scholarships; David Julian [7196]
Wichman Scholarship Fund; Louise Wachter [3314]
Wick Scholarships; Alice Hersey [6380]
Wicker Scholarships; L. Phil [861]
Wicker Scholarships; Tom [7197]
Wicomico High School Class of '55 Scholarships [2386]
Wiebke Memorial Scholarships; Ethyl and Armin [7483]
Wiedner and Dorothy Vandercook Memorial Peace Scholarships; Barbara [3360]
Wiegand Science and Technology Scholarships; Edwin F. [5868]
Wierenga Alumni Scholarships; Elmo [3357]
The WIFLE Scholarship Fund [7477]
Wikoff, Jr. Scholarship Fund; Fred C. [3083]
Wilburn Scholarships; Teddy [2451]
WildBird/Clements Memorial Scholarships [439]
Wiley Publishing Inc. Scholarships [5112]
Wilkinson & Company LLP **[7411]**
Wilkinson & Company LLP Secondary School Scholarships [7412]
Wilks Memorial Awards [1115]
Will Memorial Scholarships; Andrea [6381]
Willa Beach-Porter Music Scholarships [2097]
Willamette Chapter Scholarship Awards [5389]
Willamette University **[7413]**
Willamette Valley AG Association Scholarships [5395]
William and Frances J. Tilghman Scholarship; M. [2387]
William Goldberg Diamond Corp. Scholarships [3203]
Williams Foundation; John G. **[7416]**
Williams Foundation Scholarships [5869]
Williams, Jr. Scholarships; Sidney B. [685]
Williams Legacy Scholarships; Rodney [7107]
Williams Scholarship Fund; James Elliott [5537]
Williams Scholarships; CSM Virgil R. [2857]
Williams Scholarships; Dr. Dana [2294]
Williams Scholarships; Elizabeth T. [7462]
Williams Scholarships Fund; John G. [7417]
Williams Scholarships; Leon [6240]
Williams Scholarships; Maxine [368]
Williams Scholarships; Randy [6241]
Williams Tuition Scholarships; Cenie Jomo [4668]
Williamson Endowed Scholarships; Edwin H. and Louise N. [7463]

Williamson Scholarship Fund; Mary Katherine "Kathy" [2366]
Williamsport High School Class of 1970 Scholarship Fund [2979]
Williamsport-Lycoming Community Foundation - Benjamin Franklin Scholarships [2980]
Wilmer RAMI Music Scholarship; Gary S. [2490]
The Wilmore Scholarship Fund [3084]
Wilson Broadcast Journalism Scholarships; Glenn [5529]
Wilson for Environmental Studies Scholarships; Larry [1227]
Wilson Graduate Scholarships; Pete [1404]
Wilson Journalism Scholarships; Pete [1405]
Wilson, Jr. Scholarships; Saul T. [7300]
Wilson Legacy Scholarship; Bob [1835]
Wilson, MD, Scholarships; The Arthur N. [714]
Wilson Memorial Scholarships; Ted C. [5791]
Wilson Memorial Scholarships; William S. [4389]
Wilson Scholarships; H.W. [1986]
Wilson Scholarships; John Charles [3784]
Wilson Scholarships for Undergraduate Civil Engineering Students; Larry [1228]
Wilson Scholarships; William E. [6636]
Wilson Science Scholarships; Ross A. [6888]
Wimmer Scholarships; Harriet Barnhart [988]
Winkler Memorial Scholarships; Lisa [1415]
Winsand-Detroit Section Named Scholarships; Armos and Marilyn [1174]
Winston-Salem Foundation **[7418]**
Winston-Salem Foundation Scholarships [7464]
Winston Scholarships [6260]
Winters Memorial Scholarships; Marine Corps Sgt. Jeannette L. [1251]
Winterthur Museum and Country Estate **[7466]**
Winterthur Research Fellowships [7468]
WINUP Member Scholarships [7496]
Wischmeyer Memorial Scholarships; Albert E. [6508]
Wisconsin Association for Food Protection **[7469]**
Wisconsin Broadcasters Association **[7471]**
Wisconsin Broadcasters Association Scholarships [7472]
Wisconsin High School Scholarships [7284]
Wisconsin-Madison Journalism Scholarships [7285]
Wisconsin-Madison Music Clinic Scholarships [7286]
Wisconsin Region Student Leadership Scholarships [4684]
Witt Mares Scholarships [7331]
WKIX Alumni Association Scholarships [7198]
WMA Memorial Scholarships [7484]
WNBA Eastman Grants [7504]
WOCN Accredited Nursing Education Scholarships [7522]
WOCN Advanced Education Scholarships [7523]
Woksape Oyate: "Wisdom of the People" Distinguished Scholars Award [628]
Wolf Memorial Scholarships; Paul R. [1033]
Wolf Scholarships; Milton [3204]
Wolf Trap Foundation for the Performing Arts **[7473]**
Wolf Trap Foundation Scholarship Program for Performing Arts Teachers [7474]
The Wolf Trap Internship Program [7475]
Wolfe International Fellowships; Deborah Partridge [7559]
Wolfe Scholarships; Charles H. and Ethel E. [5370]
Wolfred Scholarships; Tim [6147]
Wolfson Memorial Scholarship Fund; Eleanor M. [2981]
Wolfson Memorial Scholarship Fund; Wendy Y. [2982]
Wolman Fellowships; Abel [1145]
Womack Scholarships Fund; Lee [4565]
Woman In Rural Electrification Scholarships [6627]
Woman's Club of Grand Haven Scholarships Fund [3315]
The Woman's Club of Nashville Scholarships [2452]
Women in Federal Law Enforcement **[7476]**
Women In Defense **[7478]**
Women In Defense HORIZONS Scholarships [7479]
Women In Need Scholarships [2835]
Women In Transition Scholarships [2836]
Women Marines Association **[7480]**
Women of Today's Manufacturing Scholarships [2491]
Women's Army Corps Veterans Association **[7485]**
Women's Army Corps Veterans Association Scholarships [7486]
Women's Association of the Mining Industry of Canada Foundation **[7487]**
Women's Business Enterprise National Council **[7491]**
Women's Independence Scholarship Programs [6820]
Women's International Network of Utility Professionals **[7493]**
Women's Jewelry Association **[7497]**
Women's Jewelry Association Member Grants [7498]
Women's Jewelry Association Scholarships [7499]
Women's Leadership in Agriculture Scholarship Program [5320]
Women's Missionary Council of the Christian Methodist Episcopal Church **[7500]**
Women's National Book Association **[7503]**
Women's Overseas and Service League **[7505]**
Women's Overseas and Service League Scholarships for Women [7506]
Women's Transportation Seminar **[7507]**
Wones Recruitment Scholarships Grant; Carolyn [2492]
Wonson Scholarships; Charles Fred [7244]
Wood Award for Excellence; Dr. Harold S. [3207]
Wood Bursary Awards [7490]
Wood County Bar Association Memorial Scholarships [5530]
Wood Foundation Graduate Scholarship Fund; Mary and Elliot [3085]
Wood Foundation Undergraduate Scholarship Fund; Mary and Elliot [3086]
Wood Graduate Scholarships; Rolla F. [5656]
Wood Memorial Scholarship Awards; Ed [5390]
Wood Nepales Scholarship; Hugh and Helen [1632]
Wood Scholarships; Geofrey H. [2032]
Woodcock Family Education Scholarship Program [196]
Woodings Scholarships; Guy A. [4390]
Woodward Scholarships; Betsy B. [1422]
Wool Scholarships; Marilyn Graboys [6044]
Woolls Scholarships; Blance E. [1639]
Woolsey Scholarships; David T. [989]
Wooten Scholarships; Patty [1368]
Worcester District Medical Society **[7511]**
Worcester District Medical Society Scholarship Fund [7512]
Work III Memorial Foundation Scholarships; John W. [2453]
Working Against Cancer **[7513]**
Working for Farmers' Success **[7515]**
Working for Farmers' Success Scholarships [7516]
The Working Press Internships [6570]
Workshop, Inc. and Stark MRDD Fostering Diversity Through Special Needs Scholarship Fund [6764]
World Book Graduate Scholarships in Library and Information Science [1987]
World Council of Credit Unions **[7517]**
Worldwide Assurance for Employees of Public Agencies **[7519]**
Wound, Ostomy and Continence Nurses Society **[7521]**
Wozumi Scholarships; James and Colin Lee [5785]
Wright-Elson Scholarships; Jean [6242]
Wright Scholarships; Audrey L. [3358]
Writers of Passage Scholarship Program [6159]
WTVD Endowment Scholarships [7199]
Wyatt, Tarrant and Combs, LLP Scholarships [7131]
WYCUP Scholarships [7518]
Wyeth Scholarship; Margaret [2493]
Wyoming Art Symposium Scholarships [1318]
Xavier Scholarships; St. Francis [7535]
Xavier Service Fellowships [7536]
Xavier University **[7524]**
Xavier University Chancellor Scholarships [7537]
Xavier University Departmental Scholarships [7538]
Xavier University Honors Bachelor of Arts Scholarships [7539]
Xavier University Legacy Scholarships [7540]
Xavier University ROTC Scholarships - Air Force ROTC [7541]
Xavier University ROTC Scholarships - Army ROTC [7542]
Xavier University Williams Scholarships [7543]
Xilinx Scholarships [5653]
The Xtra Depth University Scholarships [5551]
Yager Memorial Scholarships; M.H. [1567]
Yamhill County Farm Bureau Scholarships [5396]
Yankee Clipper Contest Club, Inc. Youth Scholarships [862]
Yankee Memorial Scholarships; William J. [789]
Yarnell Theatre Scholarships; Gwen [2934]
Yasme Foundation Scholarships [863]
Yasui Memorial Scholarship; Minoru [4022]
Yaworska Entrance Scholarships; Marusia [7361]
Yetka Memorial Scholarships; Ralph [4391]
Yetso Memorial Scholarships; Marilyn [2132]
Yip Memorial Scholarships; Vera [2133]
YMA Fashion Scholarships [7545]
Yoder Memorial Nursing Scholarships; Joan C. [4392]
York Graduate Scholarships [6277]
York Regional Police Scholarships [4006]
York Rite Grand Chapter Royal Arch Masons Scholarships [2703]
Yoshimura Scholarships; Gary [5876]
Yost Scholarship Fund; Jack and Edna May [3123]
You Go Girl! Scholarships [5786]
Young Emerging Scholar Award; Alma H. [7291]
Young Investigator Grants [5091]
Young Menswear Association **[7544]**
Young People For (YP4) Scholarships [6335]
Young Scholarships; Donnell B. [4074]
Young Scholarships; Mary Jo [1705]
Young - Taylor Young Scholarships; Elmer Cooke [3502]
Youth Affairs Committee Rising Star Scholarships [4007]
Youth Leadership Scholarships [1844]
Youth Maritime Training Association **[7546]**
Youth Partners Accessing Capital (P.A.C.) [250]
The Youth Scholarship Program [2095]
Youth Scholarships [6528]
Youth for Understanding **[7548]**
Youth for Understanding Scholarships [7549]
Yu Loan Repayment Assistance Program; Diane [4649]
Yukon Delta Fisheries Development Association Scholarships [4393]
Yukon Law Foundation **[7550]**
Yukon Law Foundation Scholarships [7551]
Zagunis Student Leader Scholarships [4685]
Zaken Award For Excellence; Lisa [3742]
Zakrzewski Medical Scholarships; Dr. Marie E. [4095]
Zale Corporation Scholarships [3205]
Zamperini/W. Clay Burchell Scholarships; Michael A. [6148]
Zarley, McKee, Thomte, Voorhees, Sease Law Scholarships [2769]
Zen Scholarships; Urashi [5787]
Zenko Family Scholarship Fund [3316]
Zerigian Scholarships; Harry and Angel [1295]
Zeta Chapter Memorial Scholarships Award [2494]
Zeta Phi Beta Sorority **[7552]**
Zeta Phi Beta Sorority General Graduate Scholarships [7560]
Zeta Phi Beta Sorority General Undergraduate Scholarships [7561]
Zimmerman Scholarships; Blanche Raper [7465]
Zimmermann Scholarships [6831]
Zipf Fellowships; A.R. [2551]
Ziskind Memorial Scholarships; Morris and Rebecca [3640]
Zonta Club of Hilo **[7562]**
Zudekoff Scholarships; Ruth and Sherman [2397]
Zupin Memorial Scholarship Fund; Leo [3317]
Zverina Scholarship; Francis Sylvia [3548]
Zwilling, J.A. Henckels Culinary Arts Scholarships [2583]

IUPUI
UNIVERSITY LIBRARY
755 W. MICHIGAN ST
INDIANAPOLIS, IN 46202-5195

University Library of Columbus
4555 Central Avenue LC 1600
Columbus, IN 47203-1892